AFRICA
South of the Sahara
1995

AFRICA South of the Sahara 1995

TWENTY-FOURTH EDITION

EUROPA PUBLICATIONS LIMITED

Twenty-Fourth Edition 1995

18 Bedford Square, London, WC1B 3JN, England

Australia and New Zealand
James Bennett (Collaroy) Pty Ltd, 4 Collaroy Street,
Collaroy, NSW 2097, Australia

Japan
Maruzen Co Ltd, POB 5050, Tokyo International 100-31

ISBN 0-946653-97-6
ISSN 0065-3896

Library of Congress Catalog Card Number 78-112271

Printed in England by
Staples Printers Rochester Limited
Rochester, Kent

Bound by
Hartnolls Ltd
Bodmin, Cornwall

FOREWORD

This twenty-fourth edition of AFRICA SOUTH OF THE SAHARA encompasses the widening panorama of economic, social and political change throughout the 52 states comprising the sub-Saharan region. During the period covered by this edition, the descent of tragedy in Rwanda, together with the long awaited transition to democracy in South Africa, have provided the focal points of world interest in the affairs of Africa. However, manifestations of change and unrest have been widely apparent throughout the continent, with civil and political upheaval dominating the affairs of Liberia, Somalia, Angola, Mozambique and Sudan. Nigeria faces a major crisis of democracy, while many other countries of the region experience domestic disquiet and economic uncertainty.

These events and their background are comprehensively narrated, analysed and placed in a wider regional and international context by a panel of specialist authors and commentators. All statistical and directory material in the new edition has been extensively updated, revised and expanded, and a calendar of the key political events of 1993–94 provides a convenient reference guide to the year's main developments. Extensive coverage of international organizations and research bodies active in Africa is included, together with detailed background information on the continent's major agricultural and mineral commodities.

The Editor is once again grateful to all the contributors for their articles and advice and to the numerous governments and organizations which have returned questionnaires and provided statistical and other information.

October 1994

ACKNOWLEDGEMENTS

The editors gratefully acknowledge the interest and co-operation of all the contributors to this volume, and of many national statistical and information offices in Africa and embassies and high commissions in London, Brussels, Paris and Africa, whose valued assistance in updating the material contained in AFRICA SOUTH OF THE SAHARA is greatly appreciated.

We acknowledge particular indebtedness for permission to reproduce material from the following publications: the United Nations' *Demographic Yearbook, Statistical Yearbook* and *Industrial Statistics Yearbook;* the Food and Agriculture Organization of the United Nations' *Production Yearbook, Yearbook of Fishery Statistics* and *Yearbook of Forest Products;* and *The Military Balance 1993–94*, published by the International Institute for Strategic Studies, 23 Tavistock Street, London, WC2E 7NQ, England. We acknowledge *La Zone Franc et l'Afrique* (Ediafric, Paris) and the *La Zone Franc* as the sources of some of our information on budgets in francophone Africa.

The articles on St Helena, Ascension, Tristan da Cunha and Seychelles make use of material from *A Year Book of the Commonwealth,* with the kind permission of the Controller of Her Majesty's Stationery Office.

EXPLANATORY NOTE ON THE DIRECTORY SECTION

The Directory section of each chapter is arranged under the following headings, where they apply:

THE CONSTITUTION

THE GOVERNMENT
- HEAD OF STATE
- CABINET/COUNCIL OF MINISTERS/
- POLITICAL BUREAU OF PARTY
- MINISTRY ADDRESSES

LEGISLATURE

POLITICAL ORGANIZATIONS

DIPLOMATIC REPRESENTATION

JUDICIAL SYSTEM

RELIGION

THE PRESS

PUBLISHERS

RADIO AND TELEVISION

FINANCE
- CENTRAL BANK
- STATE BANKS
- DEVELOPMENT BANKS
- COMMERCIAL BANKS
- FOREIGN BANKS
- STOCK EXCHANGE
- INSURANCE

TRADE AND INDUSTRY
- PUBLIC CORPORATIONS
- CHAMBERS OF COMMERCE AND INDUSTRY
- COMMERCIAL AND INDUSTRIAL ORGANIZATIONS
- EMPLOYERS' ORGANIZATIONS
- MAJOR INDUSTRIAL COMPANIES
- TRADE UNIONS
- CO-OPERATIVES

TRANSPORT
- RAILWAYS
- ROADS
- SHIPPING
- CIVIL AVIATION

TOURISM

DEFENCE

EDUCATION

CONTENTS

CONTENTS

CONTENTS

CONTENTS

CONTENTS

THE CONTRIBUTORS

J. A. Allan. Professor of Geography, School of Oriental and African Studies, University of London.

Kojo S. Amanor. Writer specializing in developing countries.

L. Berry. Former Professor of Geography, University of Dar es Salaam.

E. A. Boateng. Environmental consultant and educationalist.

Sir Mervyn Brown. Former British Ambassador in Madagascar. Member, Académie Malgache.

Richard Brown. School of African and Asian Studies, University of Sussex at Brighton.

Michael Chapman. Assistant Editor—Africa, Economist Intelligence Unit, London.

Christopher Clapham. Professor of Politics and International Relations, University of Lancaster.

W. G. Clarence-Smith. Reader in the Economic History of Asia and Africa, School of Oriental and African Studies, University of London.

John I. Clarke. Professor of Geography, University of Durham.

Pierre Englebert. Political Economy and Public Policy Program, University of Southern California.

Soule M. Funna. Former Director, Economic Policy Unit, Ministry of Finance, Government of Sierra Leone.

Patrick Gilkes. Writer on Africa and the Third World for the BBC External Services.

Pierre Gourou. Professor of Geography, Université Libre de Bruxelles and Collège de France, Paris.

R. J. Harrison Church. Emeritus Professor of Geography, London School of Economics.

David Hilling. Senior Lecturer in Geography, Royal Holloway and Bedford New College, University of London.

Edith Hodgkinson. Writer specializing in the economies of developing countries.

Diana Hubbard. Writer specializing in the financial and economic affairs of francophone African countries.

Arnold Hughes. Director, Centre of West African Studies, University of Birmingham.

A. MacGregor Hutcheson. Lecturer in Geography, Aberdeen College of Education.

Leo Katzen. Former Senior Lecturer in Economics, University of Leicester.

George Kay. Head of the Department of Geography and Recreation Studies, North Staffordshire Polytechnic.

B. W. Langlands. Late Professor of Geography, Makerere University College, Kampala.

Bernard Lanne. Specialist on Chad and Editor-in-Chief of *La Documentation française*, Paris.

G. C. Last. Former Adviser, Ethiopian Ministry of Education and Fine Arts.

Richard Levin. Senior Lecturer, Department of Sociology, University of the Witwatersrand, Johannesburg.

I. M. Lewis. Professor of Anthropology, London School of Economics and Political Science.

Janet E. Lewis. School of Languages and European Studies, University of Wolverhampton.

John Lonsdale. Lecturer and Director of Studies in History, Trinity College, University of Cambridge.

Akin L. Mabogunje. Former Professor of Geography, University of Ibadan.

T. C. McCaskie. Lecturer in the Social History of West Africa in the Twentieth Century, Centre of West African Studies, University of Birmingham.

Graham Matthews. Lecturer in Economics, University of Swaziland.

François Misser. Writer specializing in the business and economic affairs of developing countries.

Peter K. Mitchell. Honorary Senior Research Fellow, Centre of West African Studies, University of Birmingham.

W. T. W. Morgan. Senior Lecturer, Department of Geography, University of Durham.

J. D. Omer-Cooper. Professor of History, University of Otago.

René Pélissier. Author specializing in contemporary Spanish-speaking and Portuguese-speaking Africa.

James Pickett. Director, David Livingstone Institute of Overseas Development Studies, University of Strathclyde.

David Pool. Lecturer in Government, University of Manchester.

Shamlal Puri. Managing Editor of *Newslink Africa*, London.

Alan Rake. Managing Editor of *African Business* and *New African* magazines, London.

Filip Reyntjens. Professor of Law and Politics, Universities of Antwerp and Leuven.

Andrew D. Roberts. Professor of the History of Africa, School of Oriental and African Studies, University of London.

Christopher Saunders. Associate Professor and Head of the Department of History, University of Capetown.

Gerhard Seibert. Researcher, Centre for Non-Western Studies, University of Leiden.

Adele Simmons. President, Hampshire College, Amherst, Massachusetts.

Patrick Smith. Editor of *Africa Confidential* magazine, London.

Miles Smith-Morris. Writer specializing in developing countries.

THE CONTRIBUTORS

Donald L. Sparks. Associate Professor of Economics, The Citadel, Charleston, South Carolina.

Richard Synge. Editor of *Africa Analysis*, London.

Virginia Thompson. Writer specializing in francophone Africa.

Linda Van Buren. Editor of *African Business* and *New African Yearbook*, London.

Jacques Vanderlinden. Former Professor of Law, Université Libre de Bruxelles.

Richard Walker. Writer specializing in African countries.

Gavin Williams. Fellow and Tutor in Politics and Sociology, St Peter's College, University of Oxford.

Geoffrey J. Williams. Former Professor of Geography, University of Zambia.

John A. Wiseman. Department of Politics, University of Newcastle.

Peter Woodward. Department of Politics, University of Reading.

ABBREVIATIONS

Acad.	Academician; Academy
ACP	African, Caribbean and Pacific (States)
ADB	African Development Bank
ADF	African Development Fund
Adm.	Admiral
Admin.	Administration; Administrative; Administrator
AEF	Afrique équatoriale française
AG	Aktiengesellschaft (limited company)
a.i.	ad interim
AIDS	Acquired Immunodeficiency Syndrome
Alt.	Alternate
AM	Amplitude Modulation
Apdo	Apartado (Post Box)
approx.	approximately
Apt	Apartment
Ass.	Assembly
Asscn	Association
Assoc.	Associate
Asst	Assistant
Aug.	August
auth.	authorized
Avda	Avenida (Avenue)
Ave	Avenue
Bd	Board
b/d	barrels per day
Bldg(s)	Building(s)
Blvd	Boulevard
BP	Boîte Postale (Post Box)
Br	Brother
br.(s)	branch(es)
Brig.	Brigadier
C	Centigrade
c.	circa
cap.	capital
Capt.	Captain
CAR	Central African Republic
Cdre	Commodore
Cen.	Central
CEO	Chief Executive Officer
cf.	confer (compare)
CFA	Communauté financière africaine; Coopération financière en Afrique centrale
Ch.	Chapter
Chair.	Chairman/woman
Cie	Compagnie
c.i.f.	cost, insurance and freight
C-in-C	Commander-in-Chief
circ.	circulation
CIS	Commonwealth of Independent States
cm	centimetre(s)
cnr	corner
c/o	care of
Co	Company; County
Col	Colonel
Comm.	Commission
Commdr	Commander
Commdt	Commandant
Commr	Commissioner
Conf.	Conference
Confed.	Confederation
Corpn	Corporation
CP	Caixa Postal, Case Postale (Post Box); Cape Province
Cpl	Corporal
Cttee	Committee
cu	cubic
cwt	hundredweight
d	died
Dec.	December
Del.	Delegate
Dep.	Deputy
dep.	deposits
Dept	Department
Devt	Development
Dir	Director
Div.	Division(al)
Dr	Doctor
dwt	dead weight tons
E	East; Eastern
EAC	East African Community
EC	European Community
ECA	Economic Commission for Africa (UN)
ECOWAS	Economic Community of West African States
ECU	European Currency Unit(s)
Ed.(s)	Editor(s)
EDF	European Development Fund
edn	edition
EEZ	Exclusive Economic Zone
e.g.	exempli gratia (for example)
Eng.	Engineer; Engineering
EPZ	Export Processing Zone
est.	established; estimate; estimated
etc.	etcetera
EU	European Union
excl.	excluding
Exec.	Executive
exhbn(s)	exhibition(s)
f.	founded
FAC	Fonds d'aide et coopération
FAO	Food and Agriculture Organization
f.a.s.	free alongside
Feb.	February
Fed.	Federal; Federation
FG	Guinea Franc
FIDES	Fonds d'investissement et de développement économique et social
fl.	floruit (flourished)
Flt	Flight
FMG	Malagasy Franc
fmr(ly)	former(ly)
f.o.b.	free on board
Fr	Father
Fr.	Franc(s)
Fri.	Friday
ft	foot (feet)
g	gram(s)
GATT	General Agreement on Tariffs and Trade
GDP	Gross Domestic Product
Gen.	General
GNP	Gross National Product
Gov.	Governor
Govt	Government
GPO	General Post Office
grt	gross registered ton(s)
GWh	gigawatt hour(s)
ha	hectare(s)
HE	His (or Her) Excellency; His Eminence
HIV	Human Immunodeficiency Virus
hl	hectolitre(s)
HM	His (or Her) Majesty
Hon.	Honorary
HQ	Headquarters
HRH	His (or Her) Royal Highness
ibid.	ibidem (from the same source)
IBRD	International Bank for Reconstruction and Development (World Bank)
ID	Islamic Dinar(s)
IDA	International Development Association
i.e.	id est (that is to say)
ILO	International Labour Organisation
IMF	International Monetary Fund
in	inch (inches)
Inc	Incorporated
incl.	include, including
Ind.	Independent
Ing.	Engineer
Insp.	Inspector

ABBREVIATIONS

Inst.	Institute
Int.	International
Is	Islands
ISIC	International Standard Industrial Classification
Jan.	January
Jr	Junior
Jt	Joint
K	Kwacha (Malawi and Zambia currencies)
kg	kilogramme(s)
km	kilometre(s)
kW	kilowatt(s)
kWh	kilowatt hour(s)
lb	pound(s)
Lda	Limitada (limited company)
Le.	Leone (Sierra Leone currency)
Legis.	Legislative
Lt	Lieutenant
Ltd	Limited
m	metre(s)
m.	million
Maj.	Major
Man.	Manager; Managing
Me	Maître
mem.	member
Mfg	Manufacturing
mfr(s)	manufacturer(s)
mg	milligram(s)
Mgr	Monseigneur, Monsignor
Mil.	Military
mm	millimetre(s)
Mme	Madame
Mon.	Monday
MP	Member of Parliament
MSS	manuscripts
Mt	Mount
MW	megawatt(s); medium wave
MWh	megawatt hour(s)
N	North; Northern
₦	Naira (Nigerian currency)
NA	National Association (banking)
n.a.	not available
Nat.	National
NCO	Non-Commissioned Officer
n.e.s.	not elsewhere specified
No.	number
Nov.	November
nr	near
nrt	net registered ton(s)
OAU	Organization of African Unity
OCAM	Organisation commune africaine et mauricienne
Oct.	October
OECD	Organisation for Economic Co-operation and Development
OIC	Organization of the Islamic Conference
OMVS	Organisation pour la mise en valeur du fleuve Sénégal
OPEC	Organization of the Petroleum Exporting Countries
Org.(s)	Organization(s)
oz	ounce(s)
p.	page
p.a.	per annum
Parl.	Parliament(ary)
PB	Private Bag
Perm.	Permanent
PLC	Public Limited Company
PMB	Private Mail Bag
PO	Post Office
POB	Post Office Box
Pres.	President
Prin.	Principal
Prof.	Professor
Propr	Proprietor
Prov.	Province; Provincial
Pt	Point
Pte	Private
Pty	Proprietary
Pvt	Private
p.u.	paid up
publ.(s)	published; publication(s)
Publr	Publisher
q.v.	quod vide (to which refer)
R	Rand (South African currency)
Rd	Road
regd	registered
Rep.	Representative
Repub.	Republic
reorg.	reorganized
res	reserves
retd	retired
Rev.	Reverend
Rm	Room
RN	Royal Navy
Rs	Rupee(s) (Mauritius currency)
Rt	Right
S	South; Southern
SA	Société Anonyme, Sociedad Anónima (limited company); South Africa
SADC	Southern African Development Community
SADCC	Southern African Development Co-ordination Conference
SARL	Sociedade Anônima de Responsabilidade Limitada (limited company)
Sat.	Saturday
SDR	Special Drawing Right(s)
Sec.	Secretary
Secr.	Secretariat
Sept.	September
Sgt	Sergeant
SITC	Standard International Trade Classification
Soc.	Society
SpA	Società per Azioni (limited company)
Sq.	Square
sq	square (in measurements)
SR	Seychelles Rupee(s)
Sr	Senior
St	Street; Saint, San, Santo
Sta	Santa
Ste	Sainte
Stn	Station
Sun.	Sunday
Supt	Superintendent
tech.	technical, technology
trans.	translator, translated
Treas.	Treasurer
TV	Television
UA	Unit(s) of Account
UDEAC	Union douanière et économique de l'Afrique centrale
UEE	Unidade Económica Estatal
UK	United Kingdom
ul.	ulitsa (street)
UM	ouguiya (Mauritania currency)
UN	United Nations
UNCTAD	United Nations Conference on Trade and Development
UNDP	United Nations Development Programme
UNESCO	United Nations Educational, Scientific and Cultural Organization
UNHCR	United Nations High Commissioner for Refugees
UNIDO	United Nations Industrial Development Organization
Univ.	University
US(A)	United States (of America)
USSR	Union of Soviet Socialist Republics
viz.	videlicet (namely)
Vol.(s)	Volume(s)
W	West; Western
WHO	World Health Organization
yr(s)	year(s)

POLITICAL EVENTS IN AFRICA SOUTH OF THE SAHARA, 1993–94

1993

AUGUST

4 Formal peace accord signed in Arusha, Tanzania, between President Habyarimana of Rwanda and the rebel Front patriotique rwandais.

6 Kenyan opposition MPs call for UN intervention to halt inter-ethnic conflict.

8 Mali government reshuffled.

9 Francisque Ravony elected as prime minister of Madagascar.

13 The president of Zanzibar, Salmin Amour, announces the withdrawal of Zanzibar from the Organization of the Islamic Conference.

16 South Africa agrees to cede Walvis Bay enclave to Namibia.

State of emergency lifted in The Congo.

18 Paul Bérenger dismissed from the Mauritius cabinet, precipitating a split in the Mouvement Militant Mauricien.

23 The national assembly in Tanzania endorses proposals for a constitutional revision and the provision of a separate legislature for mainland Tanganyika.

25 Gen. Gnassingbe Eyadéma re-elected president of Togo.

26 Gen. Ibrahim Babangida resigned as head of state in Nigeria.

27 An interim federal executive council, headed by Chief Ernest Shonekan, installed in Nigeria.

New council of ministers appointed in Madagascar.

Legislative elections held in the Central African Republic.

SEPTEMBER

3 Burkina Faso government reshuffled.

Benin government reshuffled.

6–7 Meeting of the Intergovernmental Authority on Drought and Development (IGADD) forms committee comprising the presidents of Eritrea, Ethiopia, Kenya and Uganda to seek a negotiated settlement between the government of Sudan and the insurgent Sudan People's Liberation Army.

11 Malawi government reshuffled.

18 First round of legislative elections in Swaziland.

19 Ange-Félix Patassé elected president of the Central African Republic.

23 South African parliament establishes a multi-racial Transitional Executive Council.

25 Jean-Luc Mandaba appointed prime minister of the Central African Republic.

30 President Mobutu of Zaire and principal opposition groups agree on the adoption of a constitutional text for a transitional period.

OCTOBER

1 Transitional legislative assembly established in Liberia.

Abdoulaye Wade, leader of the opposition Parti democratique sénégalais, charged with associates in connection with the murder in May 1993 of the vice-president of the constitutional court of Senegal.

3 and 6 Partial second round of legislative elections repeated in The Congo.

5 Ministerial appointments in Madagascar.

UN Assistance Mission to Rwanda (UNAMIR) created by Resolution 872 of the UN Security Council.

7 Foundation of the 'Freedom Alliance' in South Africa.

11 Second round of legislative elections in Swaziland.

13 Transitional presidential council formed in Malawi.

16 Revolutionary Command Council in Sudan succeeded by a civilian government, also led by President al-Bashir.

21–25 Coup attempt in Burundi, in which several prominent politicians, including President Ndadaye, are killed by insurgent forces.

28 Resignation of Fidèle Moungar as prime minister of Chad.

30 Coalition government formed in Central African Republic.

NOVEMBER

2 Mauritius government coalition reshuffled following withdrawal of support by the Mouvement Militant Mauricien.

4 James Mbilini Dlamini appointed prime minister of Swaziland.

6 Delwa Kassire Koumakoye elected by legislative vote as prime minister of Chad.

9 Mauritania government reshuffled.

10 New council of ministers appointed in Swaziland.

13 New transitional government appointed in Chad.

17 Chief Ernest Shonekan resigns as head of state in Nigeria, and is succeeded by Gen. Sani Abacha.

18 Existing organs of state are dissolved in Nigeria. State governors are replaced with military administrators.

Multi-party negotiating forum in South Africa endorses the interim constitution.

Government reshuffle in Comoros.

21 Legislative elections held in Equatorial Guinea.

24 A new federal executive council, together with a provisional ruling council, are established in Nigeria.

26 The head of state of Sierra Leone, Capt. Valentine Strasser, announces a two-year programme for transition to civilian government.

30 Kenya, Uganda and Tanzania sign as East African Co-operation Treaty.

DECEMBER

5 Re-election of President Omar Bongo of Gabon.

7 Inauguration of the Transitional Executive Council in South Africa.

Death of President Houphouët-Boigny of Côte d'Ivoire. Henri Konan-Bédié succeeds to the presidency.

9 Alassane Ouattara resigns as prime minister of Côte d'Ivoire.

11 Daniel Kablan Duncan appointed prime minister of Côte d'Ivoire.

12 and
20 Legislative elections in Comoros.
15 New government appointed in Côté d'Ivoire.
19 Lansana Conté elected president of Guinea.
22 New government formed in Equatorial Guinea.
South African parliament ratifies the interim constitution.

1994

JANUARY

2 Mohamed Abdou Madi appointed prime minister of Comoros.
4 New council of ministers appointed in Comoros.
5 Juvénal Habyarimana invested as president of Rwanda for a 22-month transitional period.
11 Zambia cabinet reshuffled.
Army mutiny in Lesotho.
13 Cyprien Ntaryamira elected president of Burundi by the national assembly.
14 President Mobutu of Zaire announces the dissolution of the legislature and the government of national salvation, led by Faustin Birindwa.
18 Reorganization of transitional government of Chad.
Burkina Faso government reshuffled.

FEBRUARY

1 Army mutiny ends in Lesotho.
2 Abdoulaye Sekou Sow resigns as prime minister of Mali.
4 Ibrahim Boubacar Keita appointed prime minster of Mali.
5 Cyprien Ntaryamira takes office as president of Burundi.
6 New government appointed in Mali.
6 and
20 Legislative elections in Togo.
7 Anatole Kanyenkiko appointed prime minister of Burundi.
10–17 The Eritrean People's Liberation Front is reorganized as a political organization, the People's Front for Democracy and Justice.
11 New council of ministers appointed in Burundi.
25 Col Bilal Saloum, leader of the Mouvement populaire de l'Azaouad, assassinated in Mali.

MARCH

1 South Africa cedes Walvis Bay to Namibia.
4 Cape Verde government reshuffled.
Eritrea government reshuffled.
7 Council of state, under chairmanship of David Kpomakpor, takes office in Liberia.
11 Reorganization of council of ministers in Ghana.
14 Angola government reshuffled.
16 Youssouf Ouédraogo resigns as prime minister of Burkina Faso.
Alleged attempt to assassinate the president of Comoros.
20 Roch Marc Christian Kaboré appointed prime minister of Burkina Faso.
22 New government appointed in Burkina Faso.
25 New council of ministers formed in Gabon.
28 Elections held to constituent assembly in Uganda.
31 Deadline for withdrawal of US and other Western military contingents from Somalia.

APRIL

4 Chad legislature extends transitional period by one year.
6 Rwandan presidential aircraft shot down over Kigali airport, killing President Habyarimana and all passengers, including President Ntaryamira of Burundi and two Burundian cabinet ministers. The prime minister of Rwanda, Agathe Uwilingiyimana, is among the first victims of a brutal campaign of retributive violence unleashed by the presidential guard against political opponents of Habyarimana. Violence swiftly escalates and is manipulated by sections of the armed forces and pro-Hutu groups to provoke widespread massacres of the Tutsi.
8 Théodore Sindikubwabo, the speaker of the national legislature, announces that he has assumed the interim presidency of Rwanda. A new prime minister, Jean Kambanda, and a council of ministers is appointed.
Sylvestre Ntibantunganya, speaker of the national assembly of Burundi, is confirmed as interim president for a three-month period.
A further transitional constitution act is approved by the Zaire legislature, defining the institutions of government for a 15-month period.
10 Legislation is approved in Sudan establishing an independent commission to supervise a constitutional referendum.
14 Assassination of Solmetsi Baholo, deputy prime minister of Lesotho.
15–22 Elections for one-third of the seats in the Mauritania senate.
21 Inkatha Freedom Party agrees to participate in South African elections.
23 Edem Kodjo appointed prime minister of Togo.
26–29 Legislative elections in South Africa.
27 Reintegration into South Africa of the 'independent homelands'.

MAY

9 National Assembly elects Nelson Mandela as president of South Africa
10 Nelson Mandela takes office as president of South Africa.
11 New government takes office in South Africa.
12 Cabinet of Liberian national transitional government takes office.
16 Government of Mali reshuffled.
UN Security Council agrees to an expansion of UN forces in Rwanda.
17 Transitional government of Chad is reorganized.
18 Draft declaration of principles for future negotiations between the government of Sudan and the Sudan People's Liberation Army is announced by the IGADD committee.
19 Presidential and legislative elections in Malawi.
21 Council of ministers in Ghana is reorganized.
22 Bakili Muluzi takes office as president of Malawi.
24 New government appointed in Malawi.
25 New government appointed in Togo.
31 Completion of the withdrawal of Libyan troops from the Aozou region of Chad.
UNOSOM II mandate in Somalia extended for a further four months.

JUNE

1 South Africa re-enters the Commonwealth.
4 Major opposition parties form United Democratic

Alliance in Kenya.

5 Elections to constituent assembly in Ethiopia.

11 Coronation in Uganda of the king of Bunyoro.

11–12 Peace agreement signed between government of Djibouti and the insurgent Front pour la restauration de l'unité et de la démocratie.

14 Kengo Wa Dondo elected prime minister of Zaire by the transitional legislature.

20 Arrest in Sudan of former prime minister Sadiq al-Mahdi, on charges of conspiracy.

23 Commencement of French military intervention in Rwanda.

JULY

1 UN commission of inquiry established to investigate acts of genocide in Rwanda.

2 Government of São Tomé and Príncipe dismissed by the president.

3 Presidential and legislative elections in Guinea-Bissau.

4 Evaristo Carvalho appointed prime minister of São Tomé and Príncipe.

French troops declare a humanitarian 'safe haven' for refugees in south-west Rwanda.

6 Transitional government takes office in Zaire.

8 New government appointed in São Tomé and Príncipe.

11 Mandate of interim president Ntibantunganya of Burundi is extended for a further three-month period.

16 The final government stronghold of Gisenyi is captured by the Front patriotique rwandais in Rwanda. An estimated 1m. flee to the border town of Goma, in Zaire. A further 1m.-2m. displaced Rwandans seek refuge in the French-protected zone in south-west Rwanda.

19 Pasteur Bizimungu is installed as president of Rwanda by the Front patriotique rwandais. A multi-party 'government of national unity' is formed, with Faustin Twagiramungu as prime minister.

21 Cabinet reshuffle in Cameroon.

22 President Jawara of The Gambia overthrown by military coup.

26 Lt Yaya Jammeh declares himself head of state of The Gambia.

28 Armed Forces Provisional Ruling Council appoints new government in The Gambia.

LATE INFORMATION

BENIN (p. 170)

Government Change
(October 1994)

Minister of Transport and Public Works: (vacant).

BURUNDI (p. 219)

Government Changes
(September 1994)

On 30 September 1994 SYLVESTRE NTIBANTUNGANYA, the incumbent interim president, was appointed president of the republic by broad political consensus, and was subsequently confirmed in the post by the national assembly. Ntibantunganya took office on 1 October 1994. On 3 October ANATOLE KANYENKIKO was reappointed prime minister, and was expected to announce the composition of a new multi-party council of ministers before mid-October.

NIGER (p. 696)

Government Changes
(October 1994)

Minister of National Defence: ABDOU LABO.

Minister of Administrative Reform and Decentralization: OUSMANE OUMAROU.

Minister of Foreign Affairs and Co-operation: ABDOURAHMANE HAMA.

Minister of Justice and Keeper of the Seals: AMADOU TAHIROU.

Minister of Finance and Planning: MOHAMED MOUDI.

Minister of Commerce, Transport and Tourism: MAHAMANE KOULOU.

Minister of Secondary and Higher Education and Research: DJIBO GARBA.

Minister of Civil Service, Labour and Employment: ISSOUFOU MAYAKI.

Minister of Communication, Culture, Youth and Sports and Government Spokesman: ABDOU HAMANI.

Minister of Equipment, Housing and Territorial Administration: AMADOU MAMANE LAOUALI.

Minister of Industry, Cottage Industry, Small and Medium Enterprises: AICHATOU DJIBO BEN WAHAB.

Minister of Water Supply and Environment: SOUMANA BILLO.

Minister of Mines and Energy: OUSMANE BOUREIMA.

Minister of Public Health: ISSAKA LABO.

Minister of Agriculture and Animal Husbandry: ABDOULAYE BANKOULA.

Minister of Social Development, Population and Women's Promotion: MARIAMA MAILLELE.

Secretary of State for Communication: SOULEYMANE KANE.

Secretary of State for Planning: GABRIEL MARTIN.

Secretary of State for National Education: MOHAMED AITOK.

Secretary of State for Transport and Tourism: MAHAMANE ZAKOU AOUTA.

Secretary of State for Decentralization: GOUKOUNI MAHAMANE ZENE.

PART ONE
Background to the Continent

AFRICA IN RETROSPECT AND PROSPECT

GAVIN WILLIAMS

NATIONALISM AND DEVELOPMENT

The period from the Second World War to the present in Africa has been dominated by two related themes: political nationalism and economic development. African nationalists sought state power as a means of transferring control of political office and economic resources from foreigners to Africans. The state would take responsibility for bringing 'development' to Africa. Nationalists appealed to international organizations to help bring an end to colonial rule and racist regimes, and looked to international agencies and the governments of industrial societies to fund development projects. The African state was central to achieving the goals of nationalism and development. It was the object of the struggle for power. It became the key instrument in the continuing battle to maintain power.

In February 1990, President de Klerk released Nelson Mandela and lifted the ban on the African National Congress of South Africa (ANC), the first African nationalist movement in sub-Saharan Africa. This opened the way to negotiate to end the white monopoly of political power. The independence of Eritrea from Ethiopia in 1993 and the election of Nelson Mandela as president of South Africa in April 1994 marked the culmination of the African struggle for national independence, with only the status of Western Sahara still unresolved. However, throughout Africa, it remained clear that the hopes invested in national independence and economic development had not been realized. The post-war era of nationalism and development was drawing to an ignominious close.

By the outset of the 1990s, most African states were bankrupt. Their economic policies were in the hands of the International Monetary Fund (IMF) and the World Bank. African rulers, whether drawn from civilian politicians or military officers, had lost moral credibility as a result of arbitrary and corrupt government, the exclusion of significant class, regional and ethnic groups from access to political decisions, and increasing economic and personal insecurity. One-party states and military governments, of a whole range of ideological postures, were confronted with popular demands for free elections and multi-party governments. In some countries these demands were met by the defeat of the ruling party in elections. In others, the ruling party was able to maintain itself in power by winning elections. In South Africa, the new government is the product of an elaborate exercise in power-sharing. In several instances, ruling cliques, and the armed groups associated with them, or in Angola an armed opposition, have refused to concede power to the claimants to democratic authority. In a number of places, governments have been unable to maintain their own authority and political order. Civil wars, exacerbated by external interventions, have left many people dead, in exile, or exposed to famine. As at the end of the colonial period, democratic elections have provided a mechanism for deciding who is to inherit power. They have not always been able to proceed, nor have their results always been acceptable to those excluded from office. Political uncertainty has all too often encouraged people to resort to political violence.

The end of superpower rivalries led to peace negotiations, and sometimes agreements, but the divisive and destructive results of foreign military interventions, and of the flow of arms to African clients, continued. African governments fear the loss of funds as Western attention turns to the reconstruction of east and central Europe. As post-war international rivalries have dissolved, the USA and its allies have retreated from their vision of a 'new world order'. In Africa, as elsewhere, the 1990s are a period of transitions in political arrangements, economic strategies and international relations, but it is not clear what forms and directions the transitions will take.

NATIONALISTS, POLITICIANS AND SOLDIERS

'Seek ye first the political kingdom' advised Kwame Nkrumah. During and after the Second World War, African nationalists were able to gain widespread support from a broad coalition of groups for their demands for equal rights for all and an end to colonial and white settler rule. Workers, particularly dockers, railwaymen and miners, went on strike for a living wage to match war-time and post-war price increases. Rural people variously evaded and resisted the forced cultivation of cotton, and the imposition of conservationist policies of agricultural improvement, and demanded access to more land and better prices for their crops. Traders and consumers resented the scarcity of imported goods and the monopolistic practices of foreign firms. The small 'middle classes', themselves a product of mission education and the expansion of the colonial economy, sought access to political office, state and private employment, and commercial opportunities from which Europeans, and Asians, had excluded them (Hodgkin).

African nationalists combined petitions with direct action, and in some cases armed resistance and guerrilla warfare, to persuade colonial powers and settler regimes to negotiate a transfer of power. Nationalist governments, Afrikaner as well as African, looked to the state to give them control over the allocation of resources and to promote 'development'. Hence the attraction to the commercial, as well as the bureaucratic, middle classes of 'socialism' in its 'African', 'Marxist-Leninist' and other variants, and the tendency to extend state activity and intervention in the economy, often far beyond its fiscal and administrative capacities.

At independence, ruling parties took control of state office and the distribution of patronage. Their opponents usually had to choose between joining the ruling alliance or risking suppression. Governments sought to curb the capacities of trade unions for independent action and, in some cases, incorporated trade unions into the ruling parties. In a number of countries, including Ghana, Zambia and, in the 1970s, Nigeria, governments strengthened the funding and organization of central trade union federations with the aim of controlling industrial unrest. Co-opted trade union leaders lost credibility among their members. When trade unions were unable, or unwilling, to prevent strikes, governments promoted divisions among them, undermined their funding and arrested their leaders. Strategies of incorporation and of exclusion and suppression both proved to be of limited use in controlling workers (Akwetey).

In a number of countries—e.g. Sudan, Congo (now Zaire), Dahomey (now Benin), Nigeria and Uganda—rival parties proved unable to settle regional conflicts and resolve their own rivalries within an agreed constitutional framework. Party competition gave way to military governments. African governments were confronted by wars of secession in Southern Sudan, which still continue, in Eastern Nigeria ('Biafra'), and in Katanga (now Shaba, Zaire). Wars have also been fought to liberate countries from repressive regimes in Uganda (twice), in Ethiopia, in Liberia and in Rwanda. They have intensified violent conflicts and led to massacres of civilians. In Uganda and Ethiopia the victors have re-established political order. On the African continent, parties have thus far been able to contend consistently for national elections by the whole adult population since independence only in Botswana, The Gambia and Zimbabwe.

In a number of countries, ruling parties formed one-party states. They claimed legitimacy from their leadership of the national struggle and the needs to overcome ethnic and regional divisions and to unite the people in pursuit of 'development' and even 'socialism'. During the 1960s, a series of one-party regimes, in, for example, Congo-Brazzaville (now The Congo), Upper Volta (Burkina Faso), Ghana and Mali, were replaced by military governments, in some cases after general strikes and popular risings, and usually to popular acclaim. It appeared that the one-party state was a transitional form of government between colonial and military rule.

Military rulers typically claim to act in the name of the whole nation against the corruption and sectionalism of politicians. They deny any political ambitions of their own and generally promise to restore constitutional government. However, armies usually act in the interests of all or a part of the armed forces. Military interventions inherently tend to create further political instability. Coups divide armies along lines of rank and generation, and/or political and regional affiliations. Military governments take on the problems which their civilian predecessors failed to solve; they are divided by the political and ethnic conflicts of the rest of society, or come to be associated with particular regions or factions. They seek support by favouring specific regional or religious interests to the exclusion of others. Army officers are as susceptible as politicians to the temptations of office and even more likely to resort to authoritarian measures to deal with opposition. Coups set precedents for further coups, whether against military regimes or their civilian successors. Between 1965 and 1979, military governments in Dahomey (thrice), Ghana (twice), and Nigeria (once) held elections and returned power to civilian politicians. Their various successors stayed in office for between one and four years before a new group of soldiers removed them.

By contrast, one-party governments survived the initial wave of military coups and provided in several countries a stable form of government for nearly three decades after independence. They included places with high rates of economic growth, such as Kenya, Malawi, Cameroon and Côte d'Ivoire, and also Tanzania and Zambia with records of stagnation and decline. These governments were usually headed by a founder of the nationalist party and in several cases of a venerable age. They successfully combined centralized, bureaucratic direction of policy and administration with a regional distribution of patronage (Allen).

Government policies were decided and implemented by ministers and civil servants, under presidential authority. In both Kenya and Tanzania, policies were administered by powerful regional or provincial commissioners, acting either in the name of the government (Kenya) or the party (Tanzania); by comparison, central ministries were relatively weak. African governments had recreated the administrative forms of colonial rule. Local institutions were redefined as instruments of the 'development' policies of central governments. In Kenya and Côte d'Ivoire, each group was given some access to political offices and state resources, but larger shares were reserved to the areas from which the president came. In Tanzania, Kenya and Zambia, several candidates were allowed to compete for each parliamentary seat. These elections turned on local rivalries and the ability of candidates to secure resources for their constituents. Presidential nominations were not contested and parliaments had little chance even to discuss government policies.

In the Sahelian countries, governments came into conflict with nomadic peoples, as French military administrators had done before them. In Chad this led to a series of civil wars, which involved French and Libyan troops and an unsuccessful Nigerian attempt to mediate. In Eritrea and Western Sahara, nationalist movements claimed independence for territories colonized by Italy and Spain and taken over by Ethiopia and Morocco.

The 1974 coup in Lisbon opened the way for armed liberation movements to take power in Portugal's colonies and to convert themselves into 'Marxist-Leninist' parties committed to 'socialist construction'. Emperor Haile Selassie of Ethiopia was deposed the same year and replaced by a radical junta, the Dergue, which repressed its rivals in a savage conflict, and established a centralized form of military socialism under the slogan of 'Ethiopia First'. The regime continued to reject Eritrean claims to independence and the demands of Tigrayans and other nationalities for autonomy. Cuban troops and Soviet arms were instrumental in enabling the Movimento Popular de Libertação de Angola (MPLA) to retain power and repel a South African invasion; they enabled the Dergue to defeat a Somali attack on Ethiopia in 1977–78 and to sustain their war in Eritrea and within Ethiopia itself. The USA viewed the increased Cuban and Soviet involvement in Africa with disquiet, and armed and financed regimes and political movements opposed to those aligned with the Eastern bloc.

In Congo-Brazzaville, Somalia, Dahomey, Ghana and Upper Volta, radical officers took power with a programme of populist policies. In some cases, socialism was no more than official rhetoric. In others, it gave way to pragmatic choices. In Somalia, President Siad Barre switched his international allegiances when the Soviet government supported the Ethiopians against him. Confronted by extreme economic crises, the Ghanaian, and also the Ugandan governments, proved to be apt pupils of World Bank structural adjustment policies.

The independence of Portugal's colonies shifted southwards the 'front line' between independent and white-ruled countries. Guerrilla war and international pressures forced the illegal white regime in Southern Rhodesia into negotiations which culminated in the emergence of independent Zimbabwe in 1980. In South Africa, the Botha government sought to devise a strategy to reform apartheid while retaining the substance of white control of power and using its military resources to exclude the ANC and its allies from the political process. To this end, it created three racially-based parliamentary chambers, and took measures to relegate the African population to 'Bantustans' and to urban councils. Repressive reforms and rising fiscal burdens on the African townships provoked popular resistance. The South African regime effected the assassinations of opponents both inside and outside its borders, bombed and invaded its neighbours, and escalated its war of occupation in Namibia and repression at home. Mozambique signed the Nkomati Accord with South Africa in 1984, without, however, securing an end to South African support for the terrorist war waged against it by the Resistência Nacional Moçambicana (Renamo). US-Soviet negotiations led to South African and Cuban withdrawal from Angola and Namibian independence. In South Africa itself, President de Klerk recognized that 'reform' had to be negotiated with the ANC.

A CONTINENT IN CRISIS?

Since the severe droughts in the Sahel and the Horn of Africa in the early 1970s, Africa has been presented as a continent in crisis, ravaged by problems of famines, wars, corrupt and repressive governments, and now by an AIDS pandemic; phenomena which have indeed been all too common. These dramatic and selective images of parts of the continent have stood in for Africa as a whole. 'Disaster tourism' (de Waal) portrays Africans as victims, unable to cope with the problems which beset them and thus in need of emergency aid and famine relief. 'Development discourse' (Ferguson) describes African countries as backward, subsistence economies, in need of 'modernization and monetization' and therefore provided with 'development aid'.

World Bank analyses have hitherto identified two main sources for these problems. One is the combination of excessive government intervention in the economy with inadequate administrative capacities (overlooking the World Bank's own part in encouraging and funding such activities). The second is the rapid and sustained growth in population over the last three decades, which is held responsible for desertification and environmental degradation, and for inadequate food supplies and rising food imports. The solution is to reduce the birth rate and promote the adoption of yield-enhancing agricultural technologies. Neither argument nor evidence seems to be necessary to support the self-evident association of more people, less land, lower productivity and less food for everyone.

African countries are characterized by great differences in climate, soils and vegetation. The extensive arid and semi-arid regions which cover large parts of Africa, although containing a far smaller proportion of the continent's total population, have been subject to considerable climatic variations, over successive years and for much longer periods. Broadly, rainfall was generally much higher in the years between 1930 and 1960 than in the preceding, and the subsequent, decades. Recent years show no signs of sustained recovery from the poor rains of the 1970s and 1980s, and in 1992-93, southern Africa was confronted by a drought of unprecedented severity.

There is little reason to attribute these trends to African farming and livestock practices. Changes in the west African climate have been linked to surface temperatures in the Atlantic, and severe droughts in southern Africa appear to be associated with the Pacific current, 'El Niño'. Global climatic changes will affect African countries, but in what ways it is hard to predict. Models of changes in the earth's climate, e.g. of global warming, are still speculative; they cannot specify the impact of the interactions of the elements which affect the different regions of the world.

Confronted by droughts, African pastoralists and farmers have adopted a variety of responses: changing their farming practices and grazing patterns; selling livestock and other assets, in some cases land, and exploring alternative sources of food and income; seeking assistance from kin, friends and patrons; migrating to other rural areas and to towns. De Waal observes that the people of Darfur, western Sudan, when confronted by famine, were not primarily concerned to ward off starvation, but instead 'to preserve the basis of an acceptable future way of life, which involves not only material well-being but social cohesion.' These strategies involve severe costs; wealthy and powerful people are better able to sustain them, sometimes even to exploit them, than the poor and vulnerable. However, rural people continue to show great 'resilience' (Mortimore) in finding ways to cope with ecological uncertainty and sustained drought.

African farmers have combined numerous strategies in response to changing economic opportunities, competing demands on male and female labour, and ecological risks: adoption of high-value crops, such as tea, coffee or cocoa; substitution of less for more labour-intensive crops, such as cassava for yams; adopting more intensive forms of land use; multicropping crops with complementary ecological and labour requirements; or combining different forms of land use. Attempts by colonial and national governments and international agencies to improve African farming methods have had a few successes and many failures.

After independence, land reforms in Kenya protected the land values of departing settlers and enabled governments to allocate land to African smallholders. The World Bank has proposed an ambitious target for a similar redistribution programme in South Africa. Successful policies may need to be more sensitive to varied local circumstances than these plans appear to be if they are not to become another expensive exercise in resettlement.

The distribution of people in relation to land resources varies considerably within, and between African countries. Migration relaxes the pressures on land use in some areas, and allows others to be opened up for cultivation. In semi-arid regions, conservationary methods of cultivation tend to be labour-intensive. Appropriation of land for settler agriculture confined Africans to 'native reserves', intensifying demands on land for cultivation, grazing and residence and leading to severe erosion of soils. Demands on land for commercial ranches, large farms and irrigation schemes, have excluded pastoralists from access to seasonal grazing resources; competition for land has sometimes brought farmers into conflict with pastoralists on whom they previously relied for animal manures. In several countries, large farms have used machinery in environmentally destructive ways to clear land to grow food crops for urban markets, moving on to new investments when they exhausted the soils. Smallholders tend to make more intensive use of land and to be able to sustain larger populations than large farms.

The impact of AIDS in Africa was initially greatest around the road and lake transport routes of central Africa. In the most vulnerable districts of Uganda, the number of deaths attributed to AIDS rose steadily for a time and then increased very rapidly. As yet, male mortality has been higher than female, but HIV infection seems to be greater for women than men in Uganda. Families and communities have responded to the spread of AIDS by adapting existing strategies of coping with disease and mortality wihin the limited resources available to them (Barnett and Blaikie). The epidemiology of AIDS in Africa, and the nature of the disease itself, are still poorly understood.

Rural, as well as urban people in Africa have been vulnerable to the impact of changes in climate, endemic and epidemic diseases, and changing economic conditions. They have proved their capacity to find ways of responding to familiar and unfamiliar challenges, to the extent that their resources and the constraints imposed by government actions, wars, and national and international economic changes have allowed them to do so.

FROM DEVELOPMENT TO STRUCTURAL ADJUSTMENT

In 1895 the British politician Joseph Chamberlain proclaimed the 'dual mandate', to 'develop' the 'estates' of the tropics to the mutual benefit of the native populations and the imperial power. In 1945, the post-war Labour government took up the challenge. Peasant producers of cocoa, coffee and vegetable oils were taxed through state monopoly marketing boards to contribute surplus funds to the costs of reconstructing the British economy. Across southern, central, and east Africa, agricultural officers imposed methods of cultivation, the 'second colonial occupation' (Low and Lonsdale), which did little to protect the soil and much to promote rural nationalism.

Whereas colonial development had focused on agriculture, independent governments identified development with industrial growth and the expansion of formal education. They sought to finance it from the foreign exchange and tax revenues derived from agricultural and mineral exports, supplemented by transfers of foreign 'aid' and investments. Fabian economists argued that marketing board revenues could be used to fund investments in infrastructure and industry to reduce dependence on agricultural and mineral exports. Most governments encouraged foreign and local investment in industry through protective tariffs, tax rebates, and high exchange rates. Several governments sought to take control of strategic industries and partially or wholly nationalized mines, as in Zambia, production, as in Nigeria and banks, as in Tanzania, and invested in industry themselves. This may have hastened a tendency for local capitalist entrepreneurs to expand their share of commercial activities; it enabled governments to decide who would have access to the opportunities to acquire shares and contracts.

Secondary industry expanded rapidly in South Africa under the stimuli of the 1933 increase in the price of gold and subsequently by the Second World War, and by the creation of the state-owned electricity, steel and oil-from-coal industries. After 1948 the National Party supported Afrikaner commercial and industrial interests and funded white education—setting precedents for other nationalist regimes in Africa. The share of capital owned by South African firms continued to expand, although net foreign investment increased until the 1980s. Divestment of shares by foreign firms accentuated a continuing trend. Even in South Africa, where manufacturing exceeds production by mining and agriculture combined and its share of output has continued to grow, industry has continued to import far more in the way of machinery and other inputs than it exports. Economic expansion generated by industrial growth thus places renewed strain on the balance of payments. Investment was sustained by foreign borrowing in the 1970s. Falling gold and other export revenues, rising interest rates and capital exports trapped South Africa in a debt crisis in 1985, forcing the government to devalue the rand and declare a moratorium on debt repayments. The South African case exemplifies the contradictions of import-substituting industrialization confronted by countries throughout the continent.

Ironically, import-substitution replaced the import of finished with intermediate goods and with raw materials. The growth of industry therefore depended upon the sustained expansion of earnings from agriculture and mining or, temporarily, on foreign borrowing. Foreign firms invested in consumer goods industries to maintain or secure their access to African markets in which, in most African countries, the demand for goods depends ultimately on earnings from agriculture.

Several countries were able to expand their agricultural exports rapidly after independence, thus increasing their import capacity and expanding demand for industrial production. Availability of forest land for cocoa cultivation and cheap migrant labour allowed Côte d'Ivoire to repeat the expansion of cocoa production which Ghana and Nigeria had seen earlier in the century, and to replace them as the world's leading cocoa producer. In Kenya, smallholders gained access to land and were free to grow coffee and tea which had largely been reserved to settler farmers before independence. In Zimbabwe communal area farmers with access to sufficient land sharply increased their share of maize and cotton output in the 1980s. In all these countries, large farms and plantations still account for a substantial share of total output and benefit disproportionately from government subsidies. By the 1980s, the expansion of export markets for most Ivorian and Kenyan crops had reached their limits, and prices were falling. They could no longer sustain their levels of imports of industrial inputs and consumer goods, even less service the debts they had contracted in their earlier periods of prosperity.

Peasant production stagnated or even declined in countries, notably Ghana and Uganda, as well as Nigeria, which had developed a prosperous peasant economy in the colonial period. The marketing boards provided a boon to politicians, who used them to finance development spending, political campaigns and private business activities. Political competition turned on the ability to dispose of government revenues and intensified the struggle to monopolize political offices. Governments sought to maintain their revenues from marketing boards in a falling market and kept the official exchange rates of their currencies at unrealistic levels, which penalized export producers and lowered the cost of food and other imports. The eventual outcome was a collapse of export earnings, scarcity of imports, and pervasive resort to smuggling and corruption.

In Nigeria, export earnings and tax revenues from petroleum increased sharply after the civil war, as the levels of production increased and prices rose in 1973. This income more than replaced agricultural revenues and export earnings and paid for numerous infrastructural, industrial and agricultural contracts. Federal and state governments increased spending beyond their incomes and contracted debts they could not meet, especially when the price of oil fell in the 1980s. These policies enriched foreign and local contractors, sometimes with little benefit for the population. Agricultural exports declined sharply, to zero in the case of groundnuts and palm oil, of which Nigeria had been the world's largest producer in 1965.

Some countries, such as Mali, Tanzania and Zambia, tried to bring the marketing of food and essential consumer goods under state control and keep down the prices to consumers. This disrupted trade between rural areas, created local trading monopolies for those protected by state officials, encouraged the smuggling of food to neighbouring countries, discouraged local food production, increased the budget deficits, and left governments to depend on imports to meet their obligations to feed the cities.

Between 1972–74 countries in the Sahel and east Africa were confronted with a severe drought followed by the sharp rise in the price of oil in 1973. The leading mineral and agricultural exporters were able to borrow from banks, at high and variable interest rates, others resorted to food aid and loans from governments and international agencies. Food aid and food imports increased rapidly in 1974, and again in the 1980s. Over one-half the record level of aid in 1984–85 was to the war-stricken countries of Ethiopia, Sudan, Somalia, Mozambique and Angola; another 19% to five Sahelian countries. Cereal imports to Egypt and the Maghreb were much larger than for the whole of sub-Saharan Africa and rising faster.

Manufacturing output increased rapidly in the first decade after independence in most African countries, albeit from a low base. However, declining access to the means to import machinery and materials led to a fall in the use of manufacturing capacity, rising unit costs and lay-offs of workers. The share of manufacturing in production fell in most countries in the 1980s. Similarly, education and health spending increased significantly after independence. Child mortality continued to diminish and life expectancy and literacy to rise. However, these gains are threatened by declining import capacity and falling government revenues and may even have been reversed in some countries, in addition to those torn apart by wars.

Many African governments sought to limit inflation by maintaining the exchange rate of the national currency and controlling access to foreign exchange and imports. This encouraged demand for imports, while restricting supply. Currency controls restricted legal trade among African countries, while creating lucrative opportunities for smuggling. Foreign exchange and import permits became licences to print money. Access to goods at the official exchange rate depended on one's political and geographical distance from the loci of power.

Foreign firms responded to political uncertainties and the problems of converting profits into 'hard' currencies by shifting away from direct investment in mining, plantations and industries into the provision of goods and managerial and financial services, paid for directly and in 'hard' currencies, often funded by development agencies or guaranteed by their own governments. The World Bank increased its lending to Africa in the 1970s, particularly for agricultural development projects. These loans funded interventionist policies, paid for fertilizer imports and contributed to the debts of African governments without making any significant impact on crop production.

In the 1980s interest rates increased, debts fell due, and export earnings decreased. By the end of the decade, the cost of debt-servicing rose, on average to almost one-half of export earnings; only about one-quarter actually went to amortize debts, leading to an increase in the totals outstanding. The World Bank and the IMF addressed the problem by arranging rescheduling of debts and making structural adjustment loans. These loans, and the continued creditworthiness of most African governments, were conditional on the adoption of a standardized range of policies, encompassing reductions in government spending and subsidies, liberal foreign trade policies and domestic marketing, privatization of state corporations and, most crucially, currency devaluation.

These policies defined the terms on which governments would be allowed not to repay their debts. Fiscal policies and development strategies in most African countries came to depend upon the approval of the World Bank and the IMF. They have taken over Joseph Chamberlain's mandate to develop the undeveloped economies in Africa, and other continents, in the interests of the 'less developed countries' and the global, capitalist economy.

THE CONTRADICTIONS OF STRUCTURAL ADJUSTMENT

In Africa, as in Eastern Europe, strategies of economic reform preceded the movement towards political democracy. The critical element in most structural adjustment programmes (SAP) was radical devaluation of the exchange rate. This was resisted by most governments both because it would sharply raise the cost of imported goods, and because it would deprive them of the capacity to allocate foreign exchange and imported goods.

Devaluation is designed to encourage agricultural production by raising the price of exports and of imported food. Those who were enriched by access to state resources under a previous regime are financially well placed to take advantage of economic liberalization. If government spending and the money supply are not stringently controlled, the demand to exchange the national currency for foreign exchange will either lead to further devaluations, or to a renewed discrepancy between the exchange rates in official and parallel markets. Consequently, rising prices cannot be compensated for by raising wages and government spending. Unless other items of government expenditure, such as the army budget, are reduced instead, government spending on education and health will be cut. The burden of SAP will therefore fall most heavily on wage and salary earners, who cannot pass the effects of rising prices on to others, and on students and other consumers of public services. In the absence of effective instruments and policies for taxing high incomes and for recovering, usually from abroad, gains from illicit activities, there is no alternative. In conditions of increasing unemployment and rising inflation, trade unions have generally been ineffective in protecting their members' living standards and found it hard to protect jobs, but they have asserted their independence from governments and contributed in different ways to the struggle for more democratic forms of government.

The effects of SAP on economic activities and distribution of incomes depend upon the mechanisms adopted to implement them. Initially, fixed exchange rates were replaced with foreign exchange auctions open to banks. The result, in Ghana and Nigeria for example, was a proliferation of banks. The Ghana Cocoa Board tended to raise cedi prices of cocoa by less than the extent of the devaluation, thus raising revenues and limiting demand. After the marketing boards were abolished in Nigeria, traders bought cocoa for a time at prices well exceeding world market levels as a convenient method of exporting currency. Unpopular increases in the naira price of petrol were insufficient to narrow the difference between Nigerian and cross-border prices, leading to extensive smuggling, massive hoarding in anticipation of further price rises, and severe fuel shortages in sub-Saharan Africa's leading petroleum producer. Although liberalization has closed some avenues of corrupt enrichment, it has been accompanied by new techniques of appropriating public resources for private use.

SAP seem to have encouraged official agricultural exports and allowed a modest improvement in the use of industrial capacity. Further expansion has been constrained by the suppression of consumer demand and the high cost of imported materials. In the longer term, a net inflow of foreign exchange is needed if SAP are to generate sustained economic expansion without high inflation and further devaluations. SAP have been accompanied by declining export prices, and net financial outflows to service debts, including payments to the IMF and the World Bank, without reducing total debt.

SAP have been associated with declining living standards for urban people, blatant inequalities in incomes, and intense competition for access to the limited resources available. Many people have turned to evangelical religious movements, Christian and Islamic, to try to find a new moral and social order. Christian and Muslim evangelists have drawn on substantial funds from US and Middle Eastern sources. The repressive military regime in Sudan gained political support, ideological justification and foreign funding from Islamic fundamentalists. Religious revivalism has offered alternative ways to salvation, and, in Nigeria, contributed to communal conflicts.

TOWARDS MULTI-PARTY DEMOCRACY?

In the late 1980s, authoritarian governments, whether civilian or military, firmly capitalist or of 'socialist orientation' were clearly unable to resolve the economic crisis and political conflicts which confronted them. The contraction of resources at their disposal lead those in power to appropriate ever larger shares. This narrowed their capacity to co-opt élites and maintain a measure of public acceptance. They lacked the credibility to persuade workers and others to accept the stringent requirements of SAP. Broad opposition coalitions, such as the Movement for Multi-party Democracy in Zambia and the Forum for the Restoration of Democracy (FORD) in Kenya, emerged, variously drawing support from dissatisfied regional élites, excluded politicians or army officers, businessmen seeking fairer access to state resources, trade unions, professionals and students. Some governments tried to preserve their power by managing political reforms; others resisted changes. Some form of democratic elections have been held or scheduled in almost all African countries.

President Senghor of Senegal opened the way in 1974, when he licensed two opposition parties. The ruling party retained control of political patronage, the electoral machinery and the security services, thus tolerating opposition while maintaining power. In Nigeria, the Second Republic sought to regulate competition for the spoils of office by replacing the Westminster model with a regulated variant on the US presidential system. The National Party of Nigeria (NPN) divided its opponents and exploited its control of the electoral rules and procedures to determine the outcome of the 1983 election, thereby discrediting the political system and opening the way to further periods of military rule. The Buhari government sought to save Nigeria by initiating a 'War Against Indiscipline' and fiscal stringency. The Babangida regime adopted an SAP and decreed that only two political parties would be permitted to contend for office within a presidential system on the US model.

Babangida repeatedly changed the rules governing the recognition of parties and eligibility to stand for office. The result was a presidential contest in 1993 between two parties enriched by public and private funds, both of which had originally supported the defunct NPN. In the event, the military regime annulled the results of the election: Chief Abiola, who was widely regarded as having won, was insufficiently compliant to the wishes of the Military. Gen. Abacha replaced both Babangida and his caretaker successor, Chief Shonekan, and proceeded to co-opt many leading politicians with government appointments and the promise of a national constitutional conference. Abacha's economic programme, which represented in part a return to the strategies of the Buhari regime, appeared unsustainable in the face of the country's inadequate export earnings, and in mid-1994 had not succeeded in quelling widespread internal opposition.

In early 1991 opposition parties triumphed in multi-party elections in the island states of Cape Verde and São Tomé and Príncipe.

In Benin a series of strikes led to the calling of a national conference, which elected its own prime minister, Nicéphore Soglo, and cleared the way to legislative and presidential elections. Soglo became president, 12 parties were elected to the 64-member legislature. The pattern of national conferences, representing a multiplicity of aspiring parties and other interests, was repeated in Chad, The Congo, Gabon, Madagascar, Niger, Togo and Zaire, as well as in South Africa. The Benin example persuaded the regimes in Burkina Faso, Burundi and Cameroon to accept multi-party elections, but to resist a national conference. By contrast, President Houphouët-Boigny responded to protests in Côte d'Ivoire in 1990 by calling multi-party elections which he won, offering other regimes a precedent for retaining power through elections. In Gabon the ruling party maintained control of the national assembly in multi-party elections in 1990: in 1993 the president secured re-election with 51% of the vote.

In Zaire Mobutu and his supporters in the army resisted the claims of the national conference to appoint a prime minister, and installed its own candidate, subsequently ignoring agreements to share power with the opposition. Mobutu's manipulation of ethnic interests to divide the opposition led to the forcible expulsion from Shaba and North Kivu of people originating from other provinces. Similarly in Togo, President Eyadéma, with military support, initially refused to accept the national conference's nominee as prime minister. His intransigence was maintained in his refusal to concede the prime ministership to the leader of the main opposition group, following his own party's defeat in the 1994 elections. In Zambia, President Kaunda reluctantly conceded demands for an end to one-party rule and was defeated in the 1991 elections by a trade union leader, Frederick Chiluba, with broad national support. In Malawi, the electorate voted for democracy in a referendum held in 1993; President Banda was defeated in the ensuing election in 1994. The Tanzanian government agreed to hold multi-party elections in 1995. In Kenya, foreign creditors insisted that President Moi agree to multi-party elections when it became clear that authoritarian rule could no longer ensure political stability. He responded by unleashing violent communal attacks, thus proving that multi-party politics would lead to tribal conflict. Meanwhile, FORD began to divide into rival regional and political camps, each asserting its claim to the presidency, thereby allowing Moi to win the presidential and parliamentary elections at the end of 1992. Uganda held elections in 1994 without the benefit of political parties. The Swazi monarchy continued in 1993 to hold legislative elections without parties.

In Zimbabwe, Zimbabwe African National Union-Patriotic Front (ZANU-PF) won the 1980 and 1985 elections overwhelmingly in the Shona areas but coercion and patronage were not sufficient to defeat the Zimbabwe African People's Union (ZAPU) electorally in Matabeleland. Mugabe incorporated ZAPU into the ruling party and proposed to set up a one-party state in 1989. He withdrew this proposal in the face of foreign disapproval and opposition from within his own party and was able to eclipse a disparate opposition alliance in the 1990 elections. In Namibia, the South West African People's Organisation of Nambia (SWAPO) consolidated its victory in the 1989 independence elections in the 1992 regional polls; two opposition parties retained control of regional strongholds.

In Ghana, Flight-Lt Rawlings used the state machinery in the 1992 elections to defeat opposition parties whose support was limited to particular regions. A divided opposition could not prevent President Compaoré being re-elected in Burkina Faso in 1992. Biya in Cameroon, having won with a questionable three-way election with 40% of the vote in 1992, offered a 'constitutional debate'. This divided the opposition and highlighted the unresolved problems of the relations between the anglophone and francophone provinces.

Military interventions opened the way to the election of civilian governments in Mali in 1992 and Niger. In Niger a nine-party alliance united to elect President Ousmane in 1993 against the military candidate of the previous ruling party. Both governments had to confront rebellions in the Saharan regions. The transitional government in Chad has been unable to prevent armed conflicts by its own forces and rival militias, and the government is confronted by a southern rebellion, demanding a share of power in a federal state. In Lesotho the Basotho Congress Party was able to win an election in 1993 but was soon faced by unrest within the army. The government elected in Congo in 1992 has been confronted by continued armed clashes between rival political factions. In Sierra Leone, a coup by junior officers in 1992 has not led to democratic elections or ended the abuse of power and armed rebellion.

The overthrow of the Doe regime in Liberia in 1990, and of the Barre government in Somalia in 1991 led to violent contests for power between rival militias and the dispatch of external forces to restore order. The Nigerian-led forces installed an interim government in Liberia. Rival factions agreed to replace it with a transitional council in 1993, and quarrelled over cabinet posts without giving up their arms. The US marines opened routes for delivering food aid in parts of Somalia but failed to remove the leaders of clan militias. In Angola, the anti-government União Nacional para a Independência Total de Angola (UNITA) refused to accept electoral defeat by the ruling MPLA and resorted again to war. Remano agreed to peace negotiations with the government in Mozambique leading to an election in late 1994.

In Burundi, the Tutsi military leadership assassinated the elected Hutu president in 1993, provoking extensive political and ethnic violence. The military failed to regain power for themselves but could constrain the elected government from exercising it. In Rwanda, a peace agreement between the Hutu government and the insurgent Rwanda Liberation Front ended in 1994 with the death of the president in a plane crash, followed by massacres of political opponents and Tutsi generally by Hutu militia, which have left hundreds of thousands dead and enormous numbers of refugees fleeing to neighbouring countries. In Rwanda, as in Nigeria in 1966, and subsequently in Burundi, Kenya, Zaire and South Africa, political leaders have been able to ignite the flames of political violence when particular groups fear that their own security and access to local resources are threatened by changes in national politics.

In South Africa, successive rounds of political negotiations were constrained by the determination of the National Party to find a constitutional mechanism to ensure its continued share in future political arrangements and by the threats and use of force by those who feared exclusion from power to obstruct changes which did not accommodate their demands. The constitution provided for voters to choose parties whose leaders nominated candidates for national and regional lists. The ANC predictably won the election, securing overwhelming support from African voters in most provinces. The majority of white, Indian and urban Coloured voters preferred the National Party, who won the election in the Western Cape. The Inkatha Freedom Party entered the lists at the last moment and were rewarded by an agreement to accept their claim to an electoral majority in Natal/Kwazulu. A settlement by the national parties took precedence over electoral procedures to secure an acceptable outcome. This brought political violence in Natal under control but sets a dubious precedent for future elections.

Elite and popular opposition to exclusion from opportunities and economic deprivation has been articulated through demands for multi-party democracy. The opening of political competition has brought a plethora of parties into the arena, usually lacking distinctive policies, and seeking only a chance to vie for power. National conferences and multi-party elections have provided a means for transferring power to elected rulers; they have also been used to maintain regimes in power or to broker power-sharing agreements. In a few countries they have allowed the contest for power to be decided peacefully. In many cases, opposition parties have, with more or less justification, denounced the re-election of incumbent rulers as fraudulent. In others, they have lead to confrontations between military rulers and democratic challengers, and to ethnic violence or even a renewal of civil war. New, and old, ruling parties have had to live with other parties but have not necessarily accepted the legitimacy of opposition. Already there are signs of popular scepticism of a new round of government by politicians. Politics continues to turn on the capture and uses of state power which does not provide a sufficient foundation for democratic societies.

BIBLIOGRAPHY

Akwetey, E. *Stockholm Studies in Politics*, Stockholm University, 1994.

Allen, C. et al. 'Restructuring an authoritarian state: the limits of democratic renewal in Benin', in *Review of African Political Economy,* No. 54, 1992.

Allen, C. and Williams, G. (Eds). *Sociology of Developing Societies: Sub-Saharan Africa.* London, Macmillan, 1982.

Barnett, T. and Blaikie, P. *AIDS in Africa: Its Present and Future Impact.* London, Belhaven, 1992.

Bates, R. H. *Markets and States in Tropical Africa: The Political Basis of Agricultural Policies.* Berkeley, University of California Press, 1981.

Bauer, P. T. *West African Trade.* Cambridge University Press, 1954.

De Waal, A. *Famine that Kills: Darfur, Sudan 1984–1985.* Oxford, Clarendon Press, 1989.

Ferguson, J. *The Anti-politics Machine: 'Development', Depoliticization and Bureaucratic Power in Lesotho.* Cambridge University Press, 1990.

First, R. *The Barrel of a Gun.* London, Allen Lane, 1970.

Heyer, J., Roberts, P. and Williams, G. (Eds). *Rural Development in Tropical Africa.* London, Macmillan, 1981.

Hodgkin, T. L. *Nationalism in Colonial Africa.* London, Muller, 1956.

Low, D. A. and Lonsdale, J. M. 'Introduction: Towards the New Order', in Low, D. A. and Smith, A. (Eds) *Oxford History of East Africa,* Vol. 3. Oxford University Press, 1976.

Marshall, R. 'Power in the Name of Jesus', in *Review Of African Political Economy* No. 52, 1991.

Mortimore, M. *Adapting to Drought: Farmers, Famines and Desertification in West Africa.* Cambridge University Press, 1989.

Raikes, P. *Modernising Hunger: Famine, Food Surplus and Farm Policy in the EEC and Africa.* London, James Currey, 1988.

Richards, P. *Indigenous Agricultural Revolution.* London, Hutchinson, 1985.

Sandbrook, R. and Cohen R. *The Development of an African Working Class: Studies in Class Formation and Action.* London, Longman, 1975.

Williams, G. 'Modernising Malthus': the World Bank, population control and the African environment', in *South African Sociological Review*, 1992.

'Structural adjustment: why it is necessary and why it doesn't work', in *Review of African Political Economy*, No. 60, 1994.

ECONOMIC TRENDS IN AFRICA SOUTH OF THE SAHARA, 1994

DONALD L. SPARKS

The economies of sub-Saharan Africa are diverse, yet share many common characteristics. This diversity is to be expected from the scale of its population and the varying size of its economies. The region's population may now total 550m. people. South Africa and Nigeria

The 51 states in the region range significantly in population size. That of Nigeria, the largest, 885m. at the 1991 census, while 10 other countries of the region each contain less than 1m. people; Seychelles, the smallest, has a population of less than 70,000. Some countries are more intensively urbanized than others. Zambia's urban population, for example, represents 50% of the country's total, while in Burundi it is only 6%. Climate and topography vary from desert to rain forest to mountains to plains. Income per head ranges from Mozambique's US$80 to Gabon's $3,330. Educational levels also vary greatly; for example, 54% of all students of secondary school age are enrolled in schools in Mauritius, followed by 52% in Zimbabwe, while for Rwanda the proportion is only 2%, (just behind Tanzania's 4%). Mauritius has a literacy rate of about 80%, while Mozambique's is 33%. Some sub-Saharan countries like South Africa, Zaire and Zimbabwe are relatively well-endowed with natural resources, while others, such as Niger and Somalia, have few such assets. Sub-Saharan Africa contains the world's largest reserves of a number of strategic minerals, including gold, platinum, cobalt and chromium.

It is accordingly difficult to draw general conclusions about the continent's economic performance as a whole during any given year. Nevertheless, some general points and comparisons can be made. The region's overall economic growth rate during the past two decades has been dismal. While sub-Saharan Africa has recorded a 3.4% average annual GDP growth rate in gross domestic product (GDP) since 1961, this is just slightly above the rate of population growth. During 1965–75 regional GDP grew by 2.6% in GDP in per caput terms, but then stagnated. Taking inflation into account, the region's real GDP per caput actually fell by an annual rate of 2.2% from 1980–90. None the less, sub-Saharan Africa has achieved a small measure of economic growth since the late 1980s, owing both to policies implemented by African governments themselves, and also to events outside their direct control. In 1992 and 1993 Africa's economic performance continued slowly to improve slightly. The region's GDP advanced by 2.7% in real terms in 1992, according to the International Monetary Fund (IMF). In terms of GDP per caput, however, the region did not record significant gains. According to estimates by the World Bank, the region's GDP will increase by 3.3% annually between 1990–2000, but given a population increase projected at 3.2% annually this will result in a growth rate per caput of only 0.1%.

By virtually any economic or social indicator, sub-Saharan Africa performs less well than any other developing region. In fact, in many ways sub-Saharan Africa has found itself retreating economically while other developing areas of the world are advancing strongly. For example, at independence in 1957, Ghana was more prosperous than the Republic of Korea, and in 1965 Indonesia's economic output was about the same as Nigeria's. By 1993 Indonesia's output was three times greater than that of Nigeria, while the Republic of Korea's economy was six times larger than Ghana's.

Sub-Saharan Africa contains about 11% of the total population of the world's developing countries, while at the same time representing about 16% of the developing world's poor. For example, of the four major developing groups (sub-Saharan Africa, East Asia, South Asia and Latin America), Africa South of the Sahara has the lowest GDP per caput growth rate (which was negative during most of the 1980s), the lowest life expectancy (51 years), the lowest primary school enrolment rate (just over one-half of total eligible school-age children), the smallest number of children immunized against childhood diseases (just under one-half), the lowest daily caloric intake, and the highest percentage of people living just under the international poverty line (by the year 2000, it is estimated, about 43% will be existing on incomes of less than US$350 per year). The region also has the developing world's highest population growth rate (3.2%) and the highest rate of infant mortality (196 children out of every 1,000 die before reaching the age of five years). Of the 7.0m. infant deaths annually world-wide, 5.0m. occur in sub-Saharan Africa.

Despite the limited improvements achieved during the late 1980s and early 1990s, almost every sub-Saharan economy declined in virtually every measurable way during the past three decades. By 1994, per caput GDP was about 15% below its level a decade earlier, and per caput income down by over one-fifth. In some of the continent's least developed countries (LDC), such as Chad and Niger, the fall has been perhaps 30% or more. The poorer countries of Africa were even poorer in 1994 than they were at their independence in the 1960s. While some states in East Asia have twice doubled their incomes, 19 nations in sub-Saharan Africa are now poorer than a generation ago. For example, Africa's GDP per caput declined during the 1980s, while that of East Asian and South Asian countries grew by 6.3% and 2.9% respectively. Africa has lost the ability to feed itself: in 1974 it imported 3.9m. metric tons of cereals, but by 1989 it had to import 7.4m. tons, almost double the 1974 level. Food aid also increased during that period, from 0.9m. tons to 4.8m. tons of cereals. Currently, about one-quarter of African population does not obtain the necessary average daily intake of calories required to sustain a healthy life. Efforts by the UN and the USA in late 1992 and early 1993 helped to meet the immediate food shortages in Somalia, but many other countries such as Liberia, Mozambique, Somalia, Sudan and Ethiopia faced critical food shortages in 1994.

The factors underlying Africa's parlous economic condition can be broadly categorized either as 'external' or 'internal'. The major external factors include adverse movements in the terms of trade and declines in foreign aid and foreign investment. The internal factors include poor soils, widely fluctuating and harsh climates, poor human and physical infrastructure, rapid urbanization and population growth, and inappropriate public policies. Unfortunately, African governments have but limited control over many of these factors, particularly the external ones.

EXTERNAL CAUSES OF ECONOMIC DECLINE

The pillars of Africa's external relationship with the Western industrialized countries are trade, aid and investment, and the declines of all three have added to the continent's poor economic performance during the past 15 years.

Trade

One of the most serious of these external factors is Africa's worsening terms of trade, with declining traditional exports, both in price and quantities, and increasing imports, also in both price and volume. According to the latest data from the IMF, in 1992 more than 50% of sub-Saharan Africa's exports went to the Western industrialized countries. In the same year, Africa bought about 80% of its imports from these countries. The region operated a positive trade balance during 1990–92, with a surplus estimated at $7,200m. in 1992. This surplus, however, was attributable mainly to sales of petroleum, without which there would have been negative trade balances in each of these years.

African countries typically produce one or two major agricultural or mineral commodities for export to the industrialized countries in the West. Primary products account for about 80% of the region's export revenues, about the same level as during the 1960s. Poor export performances, combined with the range of problems dealt with below, have resulted in larger deficits in most African countries' current balance-of-payments accounts. The average current account deficit rose from about 4% of GDP in the 1970s to almost 8% of GDP in the 1980s. The current account deficit improved in 1990 by about US$2,500m., compared with 1989. Africa's petroleum-exporting countries were severely affected by the decline in international prices for crude petroleum and by diminished world-wide demand.

Price levels for the region's primary exports have been uneven. Prices for many agricultural commodities (including cotton and sugar) rose during the period 1986–90, but prices for many others (coffee, cocoa and tobacco) have remained steady or fallen. Except for some petroleum producers, the 'terms of trade' for most African states continued to worsen between 1970–81. They stabilized somewhat in the late 1980s, and by 1988 stood at about 60% of the 1970–73 level. Importantly, the poorest group of countries are the least able to withstand the side effects of a worsening terms of trade. According to the Global Coalition for Africa, revenues from Uganda's coffee exports fell by about 50% between 1985–90, despite a rise in volume terms. Between 1970–84, the region's world market share of coffee, cotton and cocoa fell by 13%, 29% and 33% respectively.

The purchasing power of the region's exports has fallen by 24% since 1985, due primarily to the decline in world petroleum prices. The steep decline in Africa's export revenues was due more to falls in volume than to relative prices. between 1970–85 Africa's share of the world market for primary (non-petroleum) exports fell from 7% to 4% of the total. Maintenance of Africa's 7% market share would have added US$10,000m. to its overall export income. Sub-Saharan Africa's share of total world exports declined to 1.4% by 1994.

The import policies of the Western industrialized countries have played a major, and often negative, role in Africa's export performance. The industrialized market economies are Africa's major trade partners, and the trend is towards increasing trade relations with these countries. Notwithstanding the benefits of the third Lomé Convention, protectionism and restrictive agricultural practices, especially in the European Community and (to a lesser extent) the USA, have resulted in an over-supply of some agricultural commodities, and thus dampened world-wide demand and weakened world prices. Tariff and non-tariff barriers to trade by the Western industrialized countries have discouraged value-added or semi-processed agricultural imports from African states.

According to figures published by the General Agreement on Tariffs and Trade (GATT), trade among African states is low; in 1990, regional trade accounted for only about 6% (US$4,400m.) of Africa's export volume. Equally significant was that virtually no growth was recorded during the period 1984–90. Most African states produce similar products for export, generally primary agricultural or mineral products, and, as most of the value added is carried out in Western industrialized countries, there is little African demand for these products. African states themselves often discourage trade by their strongly inward-orientated, import-substitution development strategies, including over-valued exchange rates and protectionist trade policies. Their transport infrastructure is geared for export to Western Europe, Japan and North America, rather than to nearby countries. In southern Africa, for example, only 4% of the export trade of the 10-member Southern African Development Community (SADC) is transacted between SADC members.

African states have tried various methods of improving their trade performance, and of developing overall regional economic co-operation. There have been several attempts to form free trade areas or customs unions. Several have failed and have been abandoned, such as the colonially-imposed Central African Federation, of Zambia, Zimbabwe and Malawi, and the East African Community, comprising Kenya, Tanzania and Uganda. Two somewhat more recent groupings, with perhaps better long-term prospects of success, are the SADC and the Economic Community of West African States (ECOWAS). ECOWAS has as its eventual goal the removal of barriers to trade, employment and movement between its 16 member states, as well as the rationalization of currency and financial payments among its members (see Regional Organizations). This membership is drawn from francophone as well as anglophone states, with as much economic diversity as Nigeria and Togo. Because of the political and economic disparity of its members, it is likely to be many years before any of the above objectives are fully met. The SADC was established initially as the Southern African Development Co-ordination Conference (SADCC) to provide a counter to South Africa's economic hegemony over the region. The SADCC did not at first seek to achieve an economic association or customs union, but to act instead as a sort of sub-regional planning centre to ensure rational development planning. Its reconstitution in 1992 as the SADC placed binding obligations on member countries with the aim of promoting economic integration towards a fully developed common market. However, each of its members continues to depend, to varying degrees, on South Africa's trade and transportation infrastructure.

The Franc Zone was established in 1948 and comprises, together with France, 13 former French colonies and Equatorial Guinea, a former Spanish colony (see Regional Organizations—The Franc Zone). It operated with general success by providing a solid base of support for the members' financial and economic policies before encountering difficulties in the late 1980s. Each of the Zone's members are small states, none with a population exceeding 12m., and most are poor. A few, such as Cameroon, Congo and Gabon, are heavily reliant on petroleum export revenues. The French government guarantees the convertibility of the CFA franc, and this system automatically finances members' budgetary deficits, which aggregated at US$15m. in 1986 but had increased to $928m. by 1990.

During the early 1990s the French franc appreciated and thus made the CFA countries' exports relatively less competitive on world markets (as the value of the CFA franc also increased, its exports became more expensive). In addition, the Zone's terms of trade declined by about 45% due primarily to a fall in world commodity prices (coffee, cocoa and petroleum in particular). In consequence of these factors, the Zone's attractiveness to potential foreign investment declined and the outflow of capital from the CFA bloc increased. According to a study by the World Bank, the appreciation of the CFA franc against other currencies between 1986–91, with its adverse impact on trade competitiveness, had reduced the CFA countries' output by 0.2% per year, while GDP in comparable countries outside the Franc Zone had achieved average growth of 4.5% annually during that period. After prolonged pressure from the IMF and France to remedy the situation, in January 1994 the CFA central banks devalued the CFA franc by an effective 100%, to French francs 1.00 = CFA francs 100 from the rate of French francs 1.00 = CFA 50, which had operated since 1948. (The Comoros franc, which is also aligned with the CFA franc and French franc exchange rate, was devalued by 33.3%.) The decision forestalled individual member countries from unilaterally devaluing, and also set the stage for potential closer links for a common market in the region. Following the exchange rate realignment, each country introduced individual changes in fiscal, wages and structural adjustments. It was hoped that the realignment would lead to increases in agricultural output and exports, and also suppress inflation, as member governments are restricted in the growth of their respective money supplies. It should be noted, however, that in the short term the economic interests of the urban sector will be damaged by the devaluation, as prices increase for imported goods and services. Indeed, in February 1994 thousands of disgruntled Senegalese massed in the streets of their capital, Dakar when the prices of imported rice, sugar and cooking oil doubled following the devaluation. Immediately following the devaluation, the

IMF announced it would assist 11 of the 14 eligible member countries under its Enhanced Strucural Adjustment Facility (ESAF) by providing financing on concessionary terms. Debt-relief assistance was also forthcoming from France.

Foreign Debt and Investment

Two of the most obvious manifestations of external difficulties are foreign debt and the difficulty of attracting outside investment. In 1960 the region's external debt amounted to less than US$3,000m., and the average debt-service ratio was only 2% of exports. During the 1970s and 1980s the debt increased rapidly, from $6,000m. in 1970 to $90,000m. in 1980 to $290,000m. in 1992. Total external debt as a percentage of total exports of goods and services increased from 96% of exports in 1980 to 362% in 1989. Although the region's debt represents only 20% of the developing world's total, and not large by Latin American standards, it is nevertheless 1.15 times greater than the region's GDP and 3.7 times greater than the foreign exchange it annually earns from exports. Of the 17 most highly indebted countries listed by the World Bank in 1989, only two, Côte d'Ivoire and Nigeria, were in sub-Saharan Africa. As measured on a country-by-country basis, the relative amounts of debt give rise to concern. For example, Mozambique's total external debt as a percentage of its exports of goods and services was 1,573% in 1991. Tanzania's was 1,070% and Somalia's was 2,576%. Between 1980–88 the region's debt-service payments increased from 18% of export earnings to about 26%. In 1989, sub-Saharan Africa's debt-service obligations amounted to 22.1% of export revenues. For the poorest countries the debt-service obligation ratio increased to 49% in 1987. In several countries, such as Burundi, Madagascar and Uganda, the debt-service obligation ratio reached about 50%. More importantly, these actual debt-service payments do not reflect the debt reschedulings of the past few years. During the past decade, some 25 countries in the region rescheduled their official and private debt with their creditors over 100 times; even so, by 1991 the arrears on interest obligations have been estimated at more than $14,000m., against only $1,000m. in 1980.

Foreign official creditors wrote off about US$10,000m. of loans during 1990–91. These creditor nations generally converted loans to grants. The World Bank has estimated that if all the proposed debt forgiveness plans were implemented, the total debt would be reduced by perhaps $6,000m., or 8% of the total. Indeed, Africa spends four times more on debt-servicing than on the provision of health services. Without debt relief, some countries are now paying more than their exports bring in. Indeed, by the mid-1980s and continuing through the early 1990s, as much in debt-service payments was leaving Africa as foreign aid was entering. Nevertheless, according to a recent assessment of the World Bank, African debtors and their creditors have made, 'surprisingly rapid progress' in dealing with the debt issue. African states owe 65% of their total external debt to foreign governments and multilateral development agencies such as the World Bank. This should make debt relief easier than in Latin America and Eastern Europe, where private banks are more deeply involved. During 1973–80, private debt in the sub-Saharan region increased annually by an average of 24.9%, and by 16.9% in the period 1980–85. By 1988, the region's total private debt had increased by only 5.3%. In 1992 Africa owed over $70,000m. to private creditors.

Africa's ability to service its debts has been hampered by severe falls in foreign exchange earnings. Additionally, after nearly two decades of annual increases in net foreign financial flows (including concessionary economic assistance), during the mid-1980s these flows had levelled off and actually begun to decline. These general decreases in financial intakes from all sources are the result of fewer and smaller private-sector foreign direct investments and commercial bank lending, as well as from decreased levels of 'aid' (in real terms) from traditional Western and multilateral donors. Official development assistance (ODA) continues to decline, even from traditionally generous donors. For example, Sweden reduced its ODA by 10% in 1992. Even though gross ODA to the region increased from US$16,100m. in 1990 to $21,100m. in 1991, net total economic assistance, which averaged about $8,000m. annually during the years 1980–85 and reached a record $21,700m. in 1989, declined sharply, to $11,700m. in 1991. Significantly, members of the OECD provided only 0.3% of their GDP in the form of ODA in 1991, as compared with 0.5% in 1982. However, major bilateral creditors have reduced or written off certain categories of debt, with cancellations totalling $12,000m. by 1991.

International banks have been hesitant about increasing their loan commitments in Africa. Of the total US$22,500m. flow of net resources to sub-Saharan countries in 1980, about $13,000m. came as aid from official sources, with about $9,500m. provided privately, mainly by banks. By 1989 the total net flow had declined to about $21,000m., of which only $3,000m. was attributable to private sources. None the less, sub-Saharan Africa received about four times the per caput official development assistance than does the remainder of the developing world. Aid per caput in the region was approximately $32 (and 8% of GDP) per caput, compared to $9 per caput (and 2% of GDP) for the other developing regions.

At only US$1,600m. in 1993, sub-Saharan Africa was the recipient of less than 1% of world-wide direct foreign investment. Of that total, about half now goes to Nigeria, and another $190m. to other petroleum-producing countries. The level of foreign investment has been decreasing during the past decade. In 1980 the region's share of total global inward investment was 4.5%, but that proportion had declined to 0.7% by 1991. Africa's share of developing countries' inward investment declined from 7.5% of the total in the early 1980s to about 5.5% by the early 1990s. Foreign investment has diminished for a number of reasons. The region has yet to broaden its investment base beyond energy and mining, which remain the prime attractions. And, while foreign investors are attracted by the region's vast raw materials and low-wage economies, they are fearful of internal political volatility and the uncertainty of obtaining the enforcement of contracts. These considerations, combined with the deteriorating human and physical infrastructure, have virtually extinguished investor confidence.

INTERNAL CAUSES OF ECONOMIC DECLINE

Africa faces a number of 'internal' economic problems which, in the view of many analysts, outweigh the 'external' factors discussed above. Indeed, the World Bank's 1989 study on sub-Saharan Africa's quest for sustainable growth suggested that 'underlying the litany of Africa's problems is a crisis of governance'.

Physical Infrastructure and the Structure of the Economies

Physical infrastructure has generally deteriorated since the achievement of independence in the early and mid-1960s. Such essential services as roads, railways, ports and communications have been neglected, particularly in rural areas. Millions of US dollars worth of investment in transportation will be required if Africa is to take advantage of any improvement in agricultural output performances. Additional resources will also be needed if Africa's industrial sectors are to grow. African industry has expanded during the past generation, from about 25% of the continent's GDP in 1965 to over 30% by 1987. However, this contribution to GDP is lower than the LDC average. Manufacturing has not increased, because of low capacity utilization, limited trained manpower at all levels, small domestic markets, inappropriate technology and poor plant design. Further, manufactured exports accounted for less of the total merchandise exports for Africa in 1987 than they did 25 years previously.

The structure of sub-Saharan Africa's economies has not changed dramatically since the time of independence. In 1965, agriculture accounted for 39% of GDP, and industry 19%. By 1980 agriculture had declined to 27%, with industry at 34%. African goals of rapid industrialization, however, did not materialize. Manufacturing advanced rapidly in the early 1960s, but then slowed to about the same average growth rate as GDP. While petroleum production expanded more swiftly, only a few states—Angola, Cameroon, Congo, Gabon and Nigeria—benefited. By the early 1990s manufacturing represented only 11% of the region's economic productivity (against 9% in 1965). Mining, petroleum, and other industries constituted another 17%, while farming accounted for 33% and services 40%.

While few sub-Saharan countries have experienced rates of inflation on the scale witnessed in some parts of Latin America, the region's average inflation rate has been increasing in recent years, reaching an annual average of 16.7% between 1975–89. During the 1980s, the rate of inflation was generally lower in countries belonging to the Franc Zone. The sub-Saharan region has seen its overall rates of inflation decline from 22.1% in 1989 to 13.8% in 1990, according to the IMF.

Many African countries' currencies appreciated in exchange rate terms during the mid-1970s. While inflation raised domestic prices, local currencies were not devalued to compensate. Thus, currencies became overvalued, meaning that their purchasing power was stronger for goods from abroad than at home, leading to increased demand for imports. Further, their exports became increasingly uncompetitive in price. As their currencies became overvalued, and in short supply, many African governments had to limit or ration foreign exchange. This in turn led to 'parallel' or 'black' markets for foreign currencies. Foreign exchange overvaluation was a product of inflation, which in turn was caused at least partially by escalations of government budget deficits. In addition, export and import tariff revenue provides a significant portion of African government revenues, as there is little personal or corporate taxation. As trade declines, so does government revenue, thus exacerbating budget deficits.

Governance, Social Factors and Natural Environment

Social and political stability are generally associated with higher economic growth rates. More than half of sub-Saharan Africa's countries have been caught up in civil wars, uprisings, mass migrations and famine. Ethnic conflicts and civil wars continued in 1994 in Angola, Sudan, Liberia, Rwanda, Burundi, Mozambique and Somalia. According to the World Bank, between 1965–85 the more unstable countries' average annual GDP per caput growth was 0.5%, while the region's 11 most politically stable countries achieved an average rate of 1.4%. Also, many stable governments have been openly hostile toward the business community, be it foreign or domestic. For example, Ghana has made it illegal to carry out 'any act with intent to sabotage the economy.' This law has been interpreted with great flexibility, and some local entrepreneurs have actually been executed for merely making profits. After independence, most African countries expanded the size of their civil service more rapidly than their economic growth justified. This expansion was designed to provide employment, and to the extent this reduced growth in the private sector, civil servants received lower and lower real wages. Governments became bloated and corrupt. For many, the need for better governance became critical.

Until relatively recently, most African governments did not view rapid population growth as a matter for concern. During the past decade, however, a succession of countries have realized that their resources cannot service such growth. Some countries of Africa have the highest rates of population growth in the world: for example, Kenya's and Côte d'Ivoire's 3.8% annual rate of natural increase is the developing world's highest. The region's projected annual growth rate of 3.2% for the years 1980–2000 compares with 2.9% for the period 1973–84. Sub-Saharan Africa's population has been forecast to reach 750m. by the year 2000. Although some demographers predict that the region's population will reach 1,000m. in 20 years' time, some medical researchers into the AIDS pandemic believe that the rate of population growth could advance by only 1% annually, while others have suggested an actual decline by the year 2010. By 1988 about three-quarters of all African countries had family planning programmes, and some have set targets for population growth. Fertility appears to be declining in the small number of states that have established family planning services. Stemming rapid population growth in Africa is difficult because of social as well as economic factors. Most Africans live in rural areas on farms, and require large numbers of helpers. The cheapest way of obtaining such assistance is for a farmer to have more children. Because the infant mortality rate is so high (owing to poor health and nutrition), rural couples tend to want, and have, more babies. Additionally, African countries do not have organized old-age support schemes, and children are often viewed as potential providers of support for the elderly. Modern contraceptive methods, according to a recent study by the World Bank, are used by only 6% of couples in sub-Saharan Africa, as against 30% in India and 70% in China.

Rapid urbanization has also caused stresses in many African economies. Africa is still very largely rural and agricultural—some 75% of all Africans live outside cities and towns. Nevertheless, during the past generation, urbanization has increased at an alarming pace. More than 42% of all urban-dwelling sub-Saharan Africans now reside in cities of more than 500,000 population, compared with only 8% in 1960. In fact, there were only two cities in the region with populations exceeding 500,000 in 1960. If recent trends should continue, Africa will have 60 cities with populations of more than 1m. by the year 2000, as against 19 such cities at present. Unemployment and under-employment are rampant in every major city of Africa. The population growth has put additional pressure on good agricultural and grazing lands, and on fuelwood. About 80% of the region's energy needs are supplied by fuelwood gathered by rural dwellers. In addition, population pressures add to deforestation, soil degredation and declines in agricultural output.

African states face significant problems in the provision of health services and education. Although both have improved since the mid-1960s, their levels remain the lowest in the world. Health care is unevenly distributed throughout most African countries, with most of the care centred in urban areas. With declining export receipts and general budget austerity, many African countries have been compelled to decrease their budgetary provisions for health. This has resulted in, for example, diminished levels of immunization. Only about 10% of Africa's population has access to clean, piped water, and some 80% of illness in Africa's least-developed countries can be associated with inadequate water supplies or poor sanitation.

The World Health Organization (WHO) has estimated that during the 1990s about 9m. adults in sub-Saharan Africa will develop AIDS, in addition to the 1.2m. who have already died from the disease. By the turn of the century nearly 30m. adults and 10m. children will have been infected with HIV (the virus widely believed to be the causative factor in AIDS), about 90% of the world's total. More than 10m. cases of HIV infection are expected in 1994. AIDS in Africa generally affects adults (20–45 year old age group) in their most economically productive years and in Africa the educated, urban élite have been hardest hit. In fact, infection rates in urban areas are about double those of rural areas. AIDS is now the leading cause of adult death in Africa. In Uganda about 10% of the population is thought to be infected by HIV, and the Zambian ministry of health has estimated that nearly 20% of women of child-bearing age in Zambia are infected. By the year 2000 there will probably be over 10m. orphans in Africa, and this will result in major stresses on the individual governments' ability to provide housing, health care and education. Given the size of the pandemic in several central and eastern African states, it is reasonable to expect that AIDS will curtail GDP growth in several countries during the next decade. Additionally, tuberculosis has seen dramatic increases in the recent past, claiming more than 1.3m. deaths during the 1980s. This increase has been linked to the growing AIDS incidence, as about 50% of tuberculosis patients are HIV-infected.

After initial improvements following independence, education is also declining in many sub-Saharan African countries. There has been a direct link between education and growth. Between 1960–80, the African countries which had higher percentages of children enrolled in primary school also had higher economic growth rates. Shortly after independence, most countries initiated programmes aiming at universal primary education. By 1980 some countries had achieved this goal. Nevertheless, according to UNESCO, enrollment ratios for primary education declined during 1980–83 in 12 African countries. For sub-Saharan Africa, an estimated 76% of primary school-aged children were enrolled in primary schools in the early 1990s, up from 37% in 1965, but still poor in comparison with all developing countries (91%) or Western industrial countries (almost 100%). Here again, many governments have found education to be a service for which budgetary allocations may be cut back during times of fiscal crisis. African governments' emphasis on higher education at the expense of primary education has also been a negative factor for economic development. For example, average expenditures on secondary-school students per caput is some 40 times that of expeditures on primary school students as compared with a ratio of 1:16 in the Western industrialized countries. Additionally, because courses and textbooks were generally 'imported' directly from the former European colonial powers, much of the education has been inappropriate to the rural settings where most of the students live and will eventually work.

Africa's environment has been under intense pressure especially during the past two decades. With the increases in population discussed earlier, over-cultivation and overgrazing have turned huge areas into virtual wastelands. The United Nations Environment Programme (UNEP) estimates that an area twice the size of India is under threat of desertification. The region annually losses about 2.7m. ha of woodland. In 1983 the FAO estimated that Africa's 700m. ha of undisturbed forest were being cleared at the rate of 3.7m. ha per year. Civil wars have also contributed to environmental degredation. In the late 1980s and early 1990s wars have had devastating effects on the environment in famine such countries as Chad, Sudan, Somalia, Mozambique and Angola. In addition, the region's 5m. displaced persons have fled not only repressive political conditions, but degraded environments incapable of supporting them economically.

Many government leaders in the past suggested that the achievement of economic growth was inconsistent with environmental protection, and that African development could only advance at the expense of its environment. It has only been in the past few years that the two goals have been recognized as not mutually exclusive. Indeed, it is now generally accepted that sustained economic growth will be impossible without adequate environmental protection. Specifically, many nations, such as Kenya, Tanzania and South Africa will increasingly depend on tourism based on wildlife and undisturbed natural habitats. In the late 1980s Lesotho, Madagascar and Mauritius became the first three African countries to develop national environmental action plans (NEAP). These NEAP are intended to create a framework for the better integration of environmental concerns into a country's economic development. By 1994 25 African states had begun the NEAP process, with support from a number of UN and bilateral donors. Loss of bio-diversity is also a serious problem as many of Africa's plant and animal numbers have been lost for ever. The long-term success of agriculture, the region's most important economic sector, ultimately will depend on the wise use of the environment.

Agriculture and Famine

Unquestionably the leading factor behind the drastic declines in African economies has been the general neglect of agriculture. Agriculture accounts for about one-third of GDP for the continent as a whole, two-thirds of employment and 40% of export value. For virtually all African economies, the major agricultural exports consist of one or perhaps two or three primary products (cash crops such as coffee, tea, sugar, sisal, etc.) whose prices fluctuate widely from year to year on the world market. For 44 sub-Saharan African countries, their three leading agricultural exports comprise some 82% of their agricultural exports. As suggested by the World Bank, 'if agriculture is in trouble, Africa is in trouble.' And agriculture has been in trouble for the past 25 years. As discussed above, many governments have pursued economic policies that were designed to keep urban wages and living conditions high and farm prices low by maintaining the value of currencies at unrealistic rates of exchange. This is understandable and obvious; political power in Africa rests in the city, not in the village. Sometimes this was a conscious policy, at other times it was more a policy of rural neglect, and on many occasions such policies were supported by the international development community.

On average, agricultural growth was slower during 1970–90 (when it rose by 1.4% annually, about one-half the rate of population growth) than in the 1960s, when it advanced at an annual rate of 2.7%. The decline in basic food production means that available food per caput has also fallen. The World Bank has estimated that food production will have to rise by 4.0% annually between 1992–2000 to meet this growing demand. In many countries the agricultural sector is the largest source of employment (albeit, much of that is at subsistence level), and provides a high percentage of exports and foreign exchange earnings.

About 40% of Africa's population suffer from chronic food insecurity because there is either not enough food locally, or they cannot afford enough food. Other Africans suffer from transitory food insecurity due to fluctuations in prices and production levels resulting from natural climatic difficulties and civil wars. A smaller number, although several million, suffer from, or are at immediate risk of famine.

Parastatal Organizations

Central to the understanding of direct state involvement in many African economies is the role of parastatal organizations. These organizations' influence and involvement in many African countries have been of particular concern in overall economic policy debates. After independence, most newly-formed African governments had three fundamental choices about how to develop and manage their economies, and how specifically to encourage industrialization in the broadest sense. They could (i) nationalize existing entities; (ii) try to attract private investment from abroad by offering favourable investment incentives (tax 'holidays', for example); or (iii) invest heavily in public enterprises. Most governments used combinations of all three, but virtually every national administration south of the Sahara opted for heavy parastatal involvement. At independence, the majority of new states had few other options open to them. By and large there was little African participation in the modern sector, and almost none in the industrial sectors.

Most of the early parastatal organizations operated in natural monopoly areas: large infrastructural projects (highways, railways and dams) and social service entities (schools, hospitals and clinics). Government soon moved into areas that had previously been dominated by the private sector (or, at least, traditionally dominated by the colonial sector in most 'mixed' economies). There is actually little precise data on the size of the public sector in the region. Public enterprises account for as much as 70% of GDP in Malawi and 58% in Tanzania. The share of parastatal bodies in employment was as high as 60% of the total in Mozambique in the late 1980s, and accounted for more than one-third of employment in many other countries. In several countries, including Kenya, Mozambique, Nigeria, Tanzania, Zambia and others, parastatal organizations accounted for more than 10% of GDP. In the 1980s Ghana, Mozambique, Nigeria and Tanzania each operated more than 300 parastatal bodies. This expanded use of parastatal bodies ideally complemented a range of domestic economic development philosophies, such as 'scientific socialism', 'humanism', 'ujamaa' or whichever term the particular African government applied to its own mode of economic planning. During this period, many governments had justifiable concerns that the private sector could not, or would not, help to improve living conditions for the poorest citizens. Most analysts have generally considered parastatal organizations to have failed, at least in terms of economic efficiency criteria.

PRESSURES FOR ECONOMIC POLICY REFORM

African governments have been coming under increasing pressure from a variety of sources to 'liberalize' their public economic policies. During the 1970s and early 1980s, the most direct pressure came from the IMF. It insisted on 'conditionality' for its support; that is, the IMF required specific policy changes, sometimes termed 'structural adjustments', usually in the area of exchange rates (i.e. devaluation), and reductions in government spending before a new loan agreement could be signed. By 1990 32 African countries had launched structural adjustment operations or had borrowed from the IMF to support reform policies. Additional pressures have come from the World Bank and the US Agency for International Development (USAID). Specifically, the 1981 World Bank study proposed four major and basic policy changes which it felt were critical: namely (i) the correction of overvalued exchange rates; (ii) the improvement of price incentives for exports and agriculture; (iii) the protection of industry in a more uniform and less direct way; and (iv) the reduction of direct governmental controls. Other pressures have originated and grown internally, as more people have become increasingly dissatisfied with their declining standard of living and the poor economic performance in their own countries.

On the grounds of poor performance, African governments are currently scaling down their involvement in parastatal organizations. The growth of parastatal companies expanded more slowly in the 1980s and early 1990s than in the 1970s. Although the number of parastatal bodies remained fairly constant during the years 1980–86 at about 3,000, more than 12 countries have reduced the number of public enterprises. In 1987 alone, according to the World Bank, nearly 100 parastatal organizations were scheduled for privatization. Numerous African countries are either reforming the institutional structures of parastatal bodies, or providing them both with greater operating autonomy, or, in some cases, disbanding them entirely. None the less, by the early 1990s less than one-fifth of parastatal companies still extant had been transferred to private-sector ownership, and few of these had operated in key economic sectors, such as mining, public utilities and telecommunications. In 1991 Ghana sold 21 state companies, but the country's state privatization agency reported that 11 of these were brought back into public ownership by 1992. The bulk of privatization has taken place in just five states: Ghana, Guinea, Mozambique, Nigeria and Senegal.

CURRENT OUTLOOK

Evidence provided by the World Bank suggests that economic reforms have in general led to improved economic performance. In 1994 the World Bank studied 29 countries in sub-Saharan Africa which had undertaken adjustment strategies in the 1980s. The study concluded that no African country has firmly established, in the broadest sense, a sound macro-economic policy. However, the report found that the six countries—Ghana, Tanzania, The Gambia, Burkina Faso, Nigeria and Zimbabwe—which have made the most improvement in macro-economic policies between 1981–91 also performed best in economic terms. And, while these six countries had substantially improved policies, nine others achieved modest improvements, while 11 countries actually evidenced actual deterioration. For the six most successful states, their median rate of GDP per caput growth between 1987–91 was 0.4%, and although low, it did represent a turnaround from the 1% annual declines during the early and mid-1980s. In contrast, the other 21 countries saw median GDP per caput growth fall by 2.1%. The six best-performing countries achieved a median increase in export growth of 8%, while those 11 with ineffective policy reforms sustained an export decline of 0.7%. The best-performing countries saw their industrial growth accelerate by 6%, compared with 1.7% for the least successful 11 countries. Agricultural output advanced more quickly (by 2%) in the countries which had substantially reduced their taxation of export crops, while agricultural production declined by 1.6% in countries which taxed their farmers more. The countries which devalued their currencies also increased their GDP per caput growth by an average of 2.3%, while those countries with appreciating foreign exchange rates experienced growth rate declines of an average 1.7%.

The World Bank report concluded by suggesting that 'In African countries that have undertaken some reforms and achieved increase in growth, the majority of the poor are probably better off and almost certainly no worse off. As consumers, both the urban and the rural poor tend to be hurt by rising food prices. But adjustment measures have seldom had a major impact on food prices in either the open market or the parallel market, which supplies most of the poor.' While there is some area of disagreement with this evaluation, most observers believe there is little doubt that the numerous SAP have played an important part in arresting the region's sharp economic decline of the 1980s. During 1988–90 countries engaged in the World Bank-led Special Programme of Assistance (SPA), which generally comprised structural adjustment programmes. Economic growth in these 20 countries increased from an annual rate of 1% at the start of the 1980s to about 4% by 1992. Most importantly, this growth exceeded population growth rate, while growth in those countries not engaged in the SPA programmes was approximately one-half that of those pursuing SPA, as well as below population growth rates.

A new breed of leader is emerging in sub-Saharan Africa. In countries as diverse as Uganda, Namibia, Ghana, and Eritrea, leaders are developing their own brand of reform. This reform must include better public management and good governance. If African governments implement their plans for economic liberalism, encompassing generally higher agricultural producer prices, revised and realistic foreign exchange rates, together with other publicly unpopular policy measures, they will require increased outside support. By the early 1990s, economic assistance to the region was being increasingly made dependent upon economic reform, and by 1989 the 16 major donor countries of the OECD had reallocated most of their economic assistance to countries implementing reform programmes. Additionally, the major multilateral donors were also reallocating their resources on this basis. The OAU and the UN have launched a number of major initiatives supporting Africa's economic development. The African Priority Programme for Economic Recovery (AAPER) was adopted by the OAU in 1985, followed by the United Nations Program of Action for African Economic Recovery and Development 1986–1990 (UN–PAAERD) and the latest, the African Alternative Framework to Structural Adjustment Programs for Socio-economic Recovery and Transformation (AAF–SAP) which was proposed by the Economic Commission for Africa in 1989 in Addis Ababa. This latter programme was designed to counter the effects of IMF and World Bank structural adjustment programmes. The US$128,000m. African Development Programme, endorsed by the UN in 1986 (under the UN–PAAERD) and the new IMF facilities have been moves in the right direction. Nevertheless, net external flows to Africa have declined by two-fifths in US dollar terms during the past five years.

It is ironic that many of the development policies that the international donor community is now criticizing are those that they had formerly supported, especially during the 1960s, when import substitution was actively promoted. The region now employs perhaps 100,000 expatriate economic advisers at an annual cost to donors and African governments of about US$4,000m. In addition, most of these economies are small and fragile, and need some form of government protection. Large parastatal organizations continue to wield considerable power, and liberalization ultimately means competition.

Developments in South Africa will have profound and generally positive economic impacts on southern Africa and the entire region. In 1994 South Africa made a peaceful transition to majority rule. There is no doubt that South African-inspired or supported wars and destabilizations during the 1980s cost the southern African sub-region in direct economic costs and indirectly with opportunity costs. The region will reap a significant 'peace dividend' in the form of reduced military expenditures, more reliable transportation and transportation alternatives, increased trade and commerce, domestic and international investor confidence, increased government revenues, increased employment and general economic growth. Such a dividend should boost sub-regional GDP by as much as 1%–1.5% annually above the World Bank-projected growth of perhaps 2.5%–3.0%. The entire region might also rightly expect to benefit from South Africa's advanced training, research and technology. For example, South Africa has more university-level agricultural and technical facilities than the other SADC countries combined. The sharing of research and institution of training schemes between South Africa and its neighbours will be inhibited, however, by South Africa's own shortages in certain skills. Second, as expectations in South Africa rise, it will need all of its skills to facilitate domestic economic growth.

South Africa's return to the full economic community of nations will no doubt bring significant benefits to its neighbours. Paradoxically, those with the weakest ties will probably be helped most, and those with the closest ties today will probably gain least. The potential gainers include Mozambique and Angola, and probably Malawi and Tanzania. South Africa and Angola have, for example, been meeting since 1990 to negotiate terms for South Africa to purchase and refine Angolan oil. There will probably be very little change for Namibia, Botswana, Lesotho or Swaziland. Their ties are so strong and extensive that it will take years to lessen them, even if there is sufficient economic rationale to do so. Except in the area of trade diversion–being able to buy from the most competitive producer in cost terms (and possibly by import-substitution) there will be little gain for these states. Zimbabwe will also probably gain little, and may indeed prove less competitive than South Africa. Moreover, it should be stressed that South Africa under majority rule will have few incentives to be unduly beneficent towards its smaller neighbours and will no doubt pursue economic policies designed to enhance its own prosperity. In a wider context, however, there can be little doubt that recent political developments in South Africa will exercise generally positive effects on neighbouring states.

Africa is a resilient continent. It has withstood drastic changes during the past three centuries and especially during the past three decades. It has moved from colonial domination to independence in less than two generations. Recent history elsewhere, particularly in Asia, suggests that the unacceptable economic deterioration of the past 20 years can be reversed. As sub-Saharan Africa moves towards the year 2000 its governments have begun to realize that while many economic problems were inherited, responsibility must be taken for problems that are soluble. Rather than being hostile to foreign entrepreneurs, most African governments are now actively seeking foreign business involvement. By 1994 most African governments were giving the appearance of reform, and acknowledging the parallel between political pluralism and economic development. The combination of liberalized economic policies, together with more political openness could signal the beginning of sub-Saharan Africa's transformation towards economic recovery and sustained long-term development. The road ahead is uncertain, however, and the vital question is posed by the extent of African countries' true commitment to genuine reform.

EUROPEAN COLONIAL RULE IN AFRICA

RICHARD BROWN

The colonial era in Africa began with the continent's hectic partition by the European powers in the final quarter of the 19th century. It ended in circumstances of equal haste less than a century later, leaving the present states of Africa as its political legacy. However, Europe had been in direct contact with sub-Saharan Africa from the mid-15th century, following the Portuguese maritime explorations. Commercial contacts gradually became dominated by the massive and destructive trade in slaves carried on by the Portuguese, Dutch, French, British and others. In all, some 14m. Africans are estimated to have been transported to the Caribbean and the Americas or to have lost their lives as a result of the trade. Colonizing efforts were few before the 19th century, but Portugal maintained a token presence in the areas that much later were extended to become Angola and Mozambique, while the Dutch initiated European settlement from Cape Town in 1652. Elsewhere the prolonged trade contacts generated only scattered European footholds along the African coasts.

Britain was the leading trafficker in slaves in the 18th century, but after 1807, when British subjects were prohibited from further participation in the slave trade, a new era began. The subsequent campaign against the slave trade of other nations; the search for new trade products such as palm oil; the onset of geographical exploration; the outburst of Christian missionary zeal; improved communications (the telegraph and steam ships); growing knowledge of tropical medicine; and Europe's new industrial might all combined to make Africa increasingly vulnerable to European colonial encroachment. The discovery of diamonds in southern Africa in 1867 and the opening of the Suez canal two years later further focused attention on the continent. Even before the main scramble for colonies began in the 1870s, Britain and France had been steadily increasing their commercial and political involvement in Africa.

Britain developed a settlement at Freetown, (Sierra Leone) as a base for freed slaves from 1808, and subsequently engaged in a series of conflicts with inland Ashanti from its outposts on the Gold Coast (Ghana), while steadily increasing its influence in the Niger delta region, in Zanzibar, and in southern Africa. In mid-century Gen. Louis Faidherbe began France's expansion into the West African interior along the River Senegal from its long-held trading settlements at the river's mouth. Simultaneously, the interests of both countries grew in Madagascar, but it was France that later annexed the island (1896). During this period of colonial expansion, France extended its penetration of West Africa from existing bases in the interior as well as from enclaves on the coast. It created, too, a second colonial fiefdom in Equatorial Africa, with its administrative base in Libreville, on the Gabon coast. The result of this strategy was the emergence of two large federations of colonies: the AOF (Afrique occidentale française, 1895) eventually included Senegal, Upper Volta (Burkina Faso), Soudan (Mali), Dahomey (Benin), Guinea, Niger, Mauritania, and Côte d'Ivoire; the AEF (Afrique equatoriale française, 1908) comprised Gabon, Middle Congo, Oubangui Chari (Central African Republic), and Chad. Meanwhile, in West Africa, Britain extended its foothold on the Gambian coast into a protectorate, enlarged its territorial holdings in Sierra Leone, created the Gold Coast Colony (1874, later conquering Ashanti and adding territory to the north as the scramble proceeded), and sanctioned the advance of the Royal Niger Co into the heavily populated region that subsequently, as Nigeria, became Britain's most important African colony.

The quest for colonies gained momentum as other European powers entered the field. The first of these was Belgium, whose ambitious monarch, Leopold II, created the International Association for the Exploration and Civilization of Central Africa (1876) as the means of establishing and administering a vast personal empire in the Congo basin, which was ironically named the Congo Free State. The king's infamous regime of exploitation led to international outrage and eventually, in 1908, to the transfer of the territory to the Belgian state. Another late participant in the drive to colonize Africa was Germany, which had newly emerged as a major industrial power. In 1884 its chancellor, Bismarck, declared German protectorates over Togoland, Kamerun and South West Africa (Namibia). Bismarck then moved swiftly to organize the Berlin West Africa Conference (1884–85) which created a generally agreed framework for colonial expansion so as to avert any major conflict among the European powers. Shortly afterwards Bismarck added German East Africa (Tanganyika, the mainland of modern Tanzania) to Germany's list of colonial possessions. (After the German defeat in the First World War, the administration of these territories passed to the victors as League of Nations mandates. South Africa obtained Namibia, Tanganyika was awarded to Britain, and Ruanda-Urundi to Belgium, while Kamerun and Togoland were each partitioned between Britain and France.)

Although Britain, as the leading European economic power, would have preferred to adhere to its traditionally gradual method of empire-building, it nevertheless emerged from the scramble as the dominant colonial power, both in terms of territory and population. Apart from its West African possessions, Britain acquired substantial holdings in eastern and southern Africa. The largest of these was the Sudan, a consequence of Britain's involvement in Egypt and the importance attached to the Suez canal. Egypt had been employing British soldier-administrators in its efforts to gain control of the Sudan, but in 1881 a Muslim cleric proclaimed himself the mahdi (supreme spiritual leader) and declared a *jihad* (holy war). In 1885, the mahdi's forces captured Khartoum, killing Gen. Gordon and causing outrage in Britain. Eventually the mahdist state was destoyed by a huge Anglo-Egyptian army led by Gen. Kitchener in 1898, just in time to forestall a parallel French expedition at Fashoda. The Sudan officially became an Anglo-Egyptian condominium, but was in effect administered as a British colony which became highly valued for its cotton production. Fertile Uganda, supposedly a key to control of the Nile valley, had been made a protectorate in 1894, and neighbouring Kenya was added by Britain the following year in order to secure access to the sea. The offshore island of Zanzibar, long a focus of British interest and commercially important as an exporter of cloves, was formally declared a protectorate in 1890. Further to the south, missionaries played an important part in the British acquisition of the land-locked Nyasaland protectorate (Malawi) in 1891.

In the extreme south, Britain had obtained the Cape Colony by treaty at the end of the Napoleonic Wars (1814), and soon found itself in conflict both with its white settlers of mainly Dutch origin (Afrikaners, or Boers), as well as with the area's many indigenous kingdoms and chieftaincies. In 1843 the British coastal colony of Natal was founded, principally as a means of containing the Afrikaners in the interior, where they established the Orange Free State and Transvaal republics. Fatefully, these developments coincided with the discovery of immense reserves of diamonds (1867) and gold (1886). The ensuing upheavals and an insatiable demand for 'cheap native labour', brought about the final conquest of the African peoples (most notably in the Zulu War, 1879). Acting on Britain's behalf, the mining magnate Cecil Rhodes organized from the Cape the further northward conquest and occupation of Southern Rhodesia (Zimbabwe) and Northern Rhodesia (Zambia), beginning in 1890: earlier Rhodes had been instrumental in Britain's acquisition of Bechuanaland (Botswana) as a protectorate, to safeguard the land route from the Cape into the interior, which had been threatened by German activity in South West Africa. Britain also obtained Basutoland (Lesotho) and the Swaziland protectorate. However, British claims to paramountcy throughout southern Africa were challenged by the two Afrikaner republics in the Boer War (1899–1902). Britain overcame the republics only with great difficulty, and then left the Afrikaners, who formed the main element of the privileged white minority, in political control of a newly-fashioned Union of South Africa which was then granted virtual independence (1910). Known as the high commission territories, Botswana, Lesotho and Swaziland, however, remained under British rule. Subsequent South Africa's ambitions to incorporate them were thwarted, and they eventually proceeded to independence in the 1960s.

Despite its economic backwardness in relation to the other European powers, Portugal obtained a major share of the colonial division of southern Africa. British diplomatic support helped Portugal to secure the vast colonies of Angola (including Portuguese Congo, later known as Cabinda) and Mozambique: in West Africa Portugal had long been in control of mainland (Portuguese) Guinea (now Guinea-Bissau), the Cape Verde archipelago and the islands of São Tomé and Príncipe. Spain, meanwhile, acquired the islands of Fernando Póo (Bioko) and Annobón (Pagalu), together with the mainland enclave of Río Muni, which now form the republic of Equatorial Guinea.

Some African polities themselves participated in the scramble: the kingdoms of Buganda and Ethiopia both seized opportunities to expand. Indeed, Ethiopia successfully defended itself against Italian aggression by winning a famous victory at the battle of Adowa (1896). Italy had to content itself with Eritrea and the major part of Somalia, until Mussolini's armies overran Ethiopia in 1935 (Italian occupation was ended by an Anglo-Ethiopian military expedition in 1941). Eritrea, however, was not to emerge as an independent state until 1993. Liberia, an American-inspired republic founded in 1847 and politically dominated by descendants of former slaves, remained nominally independent throughout the colonial era, but in practice became an economic dependency of US rubber-growing interests.

COLONIAL RULE

There was much resistance to the European intrusion by many of the Islamized as well as the indigenous cultures of West Africa. There were also major rebellions against the Germans in South West Africa and Tanganyika, and against the British in Zimbabwe; however, divisions within and between African ethnic groups, superior European weaponry and the widespread use of African troops enabled the colonial powers generally to secure control of their territorial acquisitions without great difficulty (although military operations continued in some areas until the 1920s). Boundaries were, in the main, effectively settled by 1900 or soon afterwards. Most colonies enclosed a varied assortment of societies, but many African groupings found themselves divided by the new frontiers (the Somali, for example, were split among British, French, Italian and Ethiopian administrations). Although in the long run colonialism did much to undermine previous patterns of life, its administrative policies and the development of written languages (mainly by missionaries) fostered ethnic identity, helping to replace pre-colonial cultural and political fluidity by modern tribalism. African reactions to colonialism also contributed to the growing sense of ethnic self-awareness. At the same time, members of the Western-educated indigenous élites were also exploring alternative identities based on the colonial territory (nationalism) or, indeed, on the broader concept of Pan-Africanism.

As military control gave way to civil administration, economic issues came to the fore. In the early decades of colonial rule a considerable amount of railway construction was carried out, and there was a marked development of the export-orientated economy. Colonial taxation was an important stimulus to peasant production and to wage-labour, but in the early period all colonies conscripted labour by force. In the more primitive and undeveloped colonies, (as in the Portuguese territories) coercion persisted into the 1960s. In much of West Africa and parts of East Africa, export production remained mainly in indigenous hands. Elsewhere concessionary companies (as in the Congo and AEF) or white settlers (as in South Africa and Southern Rhodesia) were the major agricultural producers. White settlers, whose interests were almost invariably given priority, were also a significant force in Kenya, and in many other colonies such as Northern Rhodesia, the Belgian Congo, Angola, Mozambique, Kamerun and Côte d'Ivoire. Mining was a dominant force in a number of areas. In South Africa, it provided the main impetus to the development of a strong industrial base by the late 1930s. Southern Rhodesia followed a similar pattern, although on a smaller scale. The important copper mines of the Katanga region of the Belgian Congo (Zaire) were later (1920s) joined by those of Northern Rhodesia. Tin in Nigeria, gold in the Gold Coast, and, later, diamonds and uranium in Namibia augmented the primary agricultural exports of these territories. Overall, the growth of a money economy did most to change African life as different areas developed new production, supplied labour, stagnated, or developed the towns which were essential to the conduct of trade and, in the late colonial period, to the growth of manufacturing in some areas additional to that already established in South Africa.

Where settlers monopolized land and resources, colonialism tended to bear harshly on traditional African life. Elsewhere, however, the direct European impact was more muted. The very small number of European colonial officials in non-settler colonies necessitated reliance on African intermediaries to sustain rule. Such administrations had to limit their interventions in African life and rely on traditional and created chiefs to carry out day-to-day administration (although often in arbitrary and non-traditional ways); but military power was never far away in the event of any breakdown in control. By the 1920s air power could be used to transport troops quickly to suppress uprisings. The British, in particular, favoured the policy of 'indirect rule', bolstering traditional authorities as subordinate allies, but often with new powers and resources unavailable to their predecessors. Britain's colonial doctrine emphasized the separateness of its colonies from the imperial power and theoretically envisaged eventual political independence. Some degree of freedom of expression was allowed (many African newspapers flourished in British West Africa), and a limited political outlet for a circumscribed few was eventually provided through the establishment of legislative councils. In contrast, the French doctrine of assimilation theoretically envisaged Africans as citizens of a greater France, but little was done to make this a reality until after the Second World War. These contrasting British and French principles were not without influence on policy, for example in the educational sphere, and they also helped to shape the later patterns of decolonization and post-colonial relationships. Whatever the theory, all colonial regimes were deeply influenced by the racist outlook which had taken hold of the European mind in the 19th century and in practice treated their colonial subjects as inferior beings.

Racial discrimination was deeply resented by the Western-educated élites. In coastal west Africa and in South Africa the existence of these élites actually pre-dated the scramble, and soon lawyers, clergy, teachers and merchants founded moderate protest associations, such as the Aborigines' Protection Society (1897) in the Gold Coast and the Native National Congress (1912), later the African National Congress, in South Africa. By the 1920s clerks and traders in Tanganyika were able to form an African Association on a territory-wide basis. In other social strata, religious associations were often the chief vehicles for African assertion. These could be traditional, Christian, Islamic or syncretic in inspiration, and often aroused mass enthusiasm to the concern of the colonial authorities. Occasionally there were violent clashes. In 1915, the Rev. John Chilembwe led an armed uprising protesting at the recruitment of Africans for service in the First World War and at conditions for tenants on European-owned estates in Nyasaland. Worker protest appeared early in towns, and on the railways and mines. Rural protest was often about taxation (as in the

1929 riots by women in Eastern Nigeria) or commodity prices (as in the Gold Coast cocoa boycotts of the 1930s). Yet, whatever the level of discontent, prior to the Second World War the colonial grip remained unshaken.

Any complacency about the underlying state of colonial Africa had, however, already been shattered by the world economic depression beginning in 1929–30. The effects of the collapse of prices were so severe that the major European powers, Britain, France, and Belgium, began to perceive the need to provide development funds and to improve social welfare and education in their colonies if Africa's ability to export tropical products and to import finished goods was to be sustained. These ideas, however, only began to make themselves strongly felt after the Second World War, when they were to add to the ferment of change then gathering force throughout the continent.

DECOLONIZATION

Events inside and outside Africa interacted to produce the surge towards independence after 1945. The Second World War itself provided the immediate context. The war greatly weakened the colonial powers, and brought to the fore the USA, which opposed European colonial control of Africa. African troops were enrolled to fight in Asia and the Mediterranean, returning with a deep resentment at post-war conditions and the continuing colonial subordination. The victory over fascism and the enunciation of the Atlantic Charter also encouraged thoughts of liberation within the continent. Economic change intensified as both the war and its aftermath stimulated demand, and there was a surge of African migration to the towns. Economic and social grievances multiplied, especially in relation to the inadequacy of urban facilities and lack of educational opportunities. Among peasant farmers, prices, marketing arrangements and new levels of bureaucratic interference aroused intense resentment. Because of labour migration, links between town and country were close, and provided opportunities to newly militant nationalist parties in the more developed colonies such as Ghana and Côte d'Ivoire to put pressure on the colonial authorities. For the democratic European powers, the increasing African discontent raised both the moral and material costs of maintaining colonial rule. In any case, with the exception of Portugal, political control was no longer regarded as essential to the safeguarding of economic interests, particularly as capitalism was becoming increasingly internationalized and the concept of possessing colonies was beginning to appear outmoded.

In French Africa, the Second World War helped directly to set in train events which were ultimately to lead to independence. Following the German defeat of France in 1940, the AEF repudiated the Vichy government and declared its support for the 'Free French' under Gen. De Gaulle. The Brazzaville Conference convened by De Gaulle in 1944 spoke in general terms of a new deal for Africans, while the new French constitution adopted in 1946 provided for direct African elections to the French national assembly. Political parties established themselves throughout francophone Africa, although their demands were for fuller rights of citizenship within the French state rather than for independence. Attempts by the French government to thwart African political progress altogether were unsuccessful. The 1956 *loi cadre* (enabling law) introduced universal suffrage, but to the dismay of many nationalist politicians the franchise was applied individually to the separate states of the two federations, so that the structures of the AOF and AEF were allowed to wither away. In 1958, De Gaulle, still attempting to salvage something of the greater France concept, organized a referendum in which only Guinea voted for full independence. By 1960, however, the remaining AOF and AEF territories had insisted upon receiving *de jure* independence, even if, despite outward appearances, they remained tied economically and militarily to France.

The events which ended the French empire in sub-Saharan Africa were hastened by concurrent developments in neighbouring British colonies, especially the Gold Coast. With no settler communities to placate, decolonization in British West Africa proceeded relatively smoothly, although much more rapidly than had been contemplated. Popular grievances gave a new edge to the political demands of the now sizeable educated middle classes, and Britain's cautious post-war moves towards granting internal self-government were soon perceived as inadequate even by the British themselves. When police fired on an ex-serviceman's peaceful demonstration in Accra (Gold Coast) in 1948, the resulting unrest, strikes and rural agitation led to major policy changes. Sensing the new mood, the militant nationalist, Kwame Nkrumah, formed the Convention People's Party (CPP) in 1949 with the slogan 'self-government now'. Its populist appeal enabled it in 1951 to overcome the more moderate United Gold Coast Convention party (of which Nkrumah had earlier been general secretary) in an election based on a new and more democratic constitution. Although in jail for sedition, Nkrumah was released and invited to become head of an independent government. This dramatic development, followed by the grant of independence in 1957 as Ghana (whose boundaries also took in the former mandated territory of British Togoland), had repercussions throughout black Africa. (In fact, the Sudan had achieved independence in the previous year, when the Anglo-Egyptian condominium was brought to an end, but this had attracted little outside attention). Nkrumah sought, with some success, to intensify African revolutionary sentiment still further by organizing an African Peoples' Conference in Accra in 1958. Nigeria's progress towards independence, meanwhile, was complicated by its enormous size and colonially imposed regional structure. Rival regional and ethnic nationalisms competed, and no one party could achieve the degree of overall dominance enjoyed by the CPP in the Gold Coast. None the less a federal Nigeria became independent in 1960, followed by Sierra Leone (1961) and The Gambia (1965).

Belgium initially remained aloof from the movement towards decolonization. It appeared to believe that its relatively advanced provision for social welfare and the rapid post-war economic growth in the Belgian Congo would enable it to avoid making political concessions and to maintain the authoritarian style of government which had characterized its administration of the territory since it took over from the Belgian king. The Belgian Congo, however, could not be insulated—any more than any other part of Africa—from the anti-colonial influences at work throughout the continent. From 1955 onwards nationalist feeling spread rapidly, despite the difficulties in building effective national parties in such a huge country. Urban riots in 1959 led to a precipitate reversal in Belgian policy: at the Brussels Round Table Conference in January 1960 it was abruptly decided that independence was to follow in only six months. Not surprisingly, the disintegration of political unity and order in the country speedily followed the termination of Belgian administration. Belgian rule in the mandated territory of Ruanda-Urundi ended in 1962, and was followed by its division into the separate countries of Rwanda and Burundi.

Meanwhile, in eastern and southern Africa, Britain was also encountering difficulties in implementing decolonization. In Uganda, where its authority rested to a large extent on an alliance with the kingdom of Buganda, British policies had tended to stratify existing ethnic divisions. The deeply ingrained internal problems which preceded independence in 1962 continued to plague Uganda for more than two decades. In contrast, however, the nationalist movement led by Julius Nyerere in Tanganyika was exceptionally united, and there was little friction prior to independence in 1961. Three years later Tanganyika united with Zanzibar (independence, 1963) as Tanzania. In Kenya, as in other colonies with significant settler minorities, the process of decolonization was troubled. In the post-war period, the settlers of Kenya sought political domination and obstructed emergent African nationalism as much as they could. African frustrations, particularly about access to land among the Kikuyu, and growing unrest among the urban poor, led in 1952 to the declaration of a state of emergency and the violent revolt the British knew as Mau Mau. This was fiercely suppressed, but only with the help of troops from Britain, a factor which helped finally to destroy the settlers' political credibility. Kenya eventually achieved independence in 1963 under the leadership of the veteran nationalist, Jomo Kenyatta. Vilified by the settlers in the 1950s as a personification of evil, Kenyatta as head of government in fact strove to protect the economic role of the settler population and to maintain cordial relations with Britain.

Settler interests were more obstructive further to the south. The whites of Southern Rhodesia had obtained internal self-government as early as 1923, but in 1953 the colony was allowed by Britain to become the dominant partner in a federation with Northern Rhodesia and Nyasaland. There were bitter clashes with African nationalists in the two northern territories, and the federation eventually collapsed in 1963 when Britain had to concede that its policy of decolonization could only effectively apply to the two northern territories whose governments it still controlled. In 1964, Nyasaland became independent as Malawi and Northern Rhodesia as Zambia. When Britain then refused white-minority rule independence to Southern Rhodesia, its settler dominated government, led by Ian Smith, unilaterally declared independence (1965). This was resisted by Britain and condemned by the United Nations, but an ineffectual campaign of economic sanctions was defeated by support for the Smith regime by neighbouring South Africa and Portugal. African nationalists eventually succeeded in organizing the guerrilla war which in the 1970s paved the way for a negotiated settlement. With Robert Mugabe as its leader, the country became independent as Zimbabwe (1980), a development which owed much to the collapse of Portuguese rule in Africa after 1974.

During the lengthy dictatorship of Dr Salazar, Portugal regarded its African colonial possessions as inalienable, and in 1951 they were declared to be overseas provinces. However, intense political repression failed to prevent the emergence of armed resistance movements in Angola (1961), Guinea-Bissau (1963) and Mozambique (1964). Most successfully in Guinea-Bissau under the leadership of Amílcar Cabral, these guerrilla movements succeeded in mobilizing rural support. Eventually, in 1974, following the military overthrow of the Portuguese regime, progress towards internal democratization was accompanied by a determination to implement an accelerated policy of decolonization. In Angola, where the divided nationalist movement provided opportunities for external intervention on opposite sides by South African and Cuban forces, independence proved difficult to consolidate. Mozambique also suffered greatly from South Africa's policy of destabilizing its newly-independent neighbours.

During this period South Africa was itself conducting a colonial war in South West Africa (Namibia), which it continued to occupy in defiance of the United Nations after it had terminated the mandate in 1966. The war against the South West African People's Organisation of Namibia continued until a negotiated settlement finally led to independence in 1990, effectively concluding the colonial era in Africa.

DATES OF INDEPENDENCE OF AFRICAN COUNTRIES

IN CHRONOLOGICAL ORDER OF INDEPENDENCE—POST-WAR

Libya	24 Dec.	1951
Sudan	1 Jan.	1956
Morocco	2 March	1956
Tunisia	20 March	1956
Ghana	6 March	1957
Guinea	2 Oct.	1958
Cameroon	1 Jan.	1960
Togo	27 April	1960
Mali	20 June	1960
Senegal	20 June	1960
Madagascar	26 June	1960
Zaire (as the Congo)	30 June	1960
Somalia	1 July	1960
Benin (as Dahomey)	1 Aug.	1960
Niger	3 Aug.	1960
Burkina Faso (as Upper Volta)	5 Aug.	1960
Côte d'Ivoire	7 Aug.	1960
Chad	11 Aug.	1960
The Central African Republic	13 Aug.	1960
The Congo (People's Republic)	15 Aug.	1960
Gabon	17 Aug.	1960
Nigeria	1 Oct.	1960
Mauritania	28 Nov.	1960
Sierra Leone	27 April	1961
Tanzania (as Tanganyika)	9 Dec.	1961
Rwanda	1 July	1962
Burundi	1 July	1962
Algeria	3 July	1962
Uganda	9 Oct.	1962
Zanzibar (now part of Tanzania)	10 Dec.	1963
Kenya	12 Dec.	1963
Malawi	6 July	1964
Zambia	24 Oct.	1964
The Gambia	18 Feb.	1965
Botswana	30 Sept.	1966
Lesotho	4 Oct.	1966
Mauritius	12 March	1968
Swaziland	6 Sept.	1968
Equatorial Guinea	12 Oct.	1968
Guinea-Bissau	10 Sept.	1974
Mozambique	25 June	1975
Cape Verde	5 July	1975
The Comoros	*6 July	1975
São Tomé and Príncipe	12 July	1975
Angola	11 Nov.	1975
Seychelles	29 June	1976
Djibouti	27 June	1977
Zimbabwe	18 April	1980
Namibia	21 March	1990
Eritrea	24 May	1993

* Date of unilateral declaration of independence, recognized by France (in respect of three of the four islands) in December 1975.

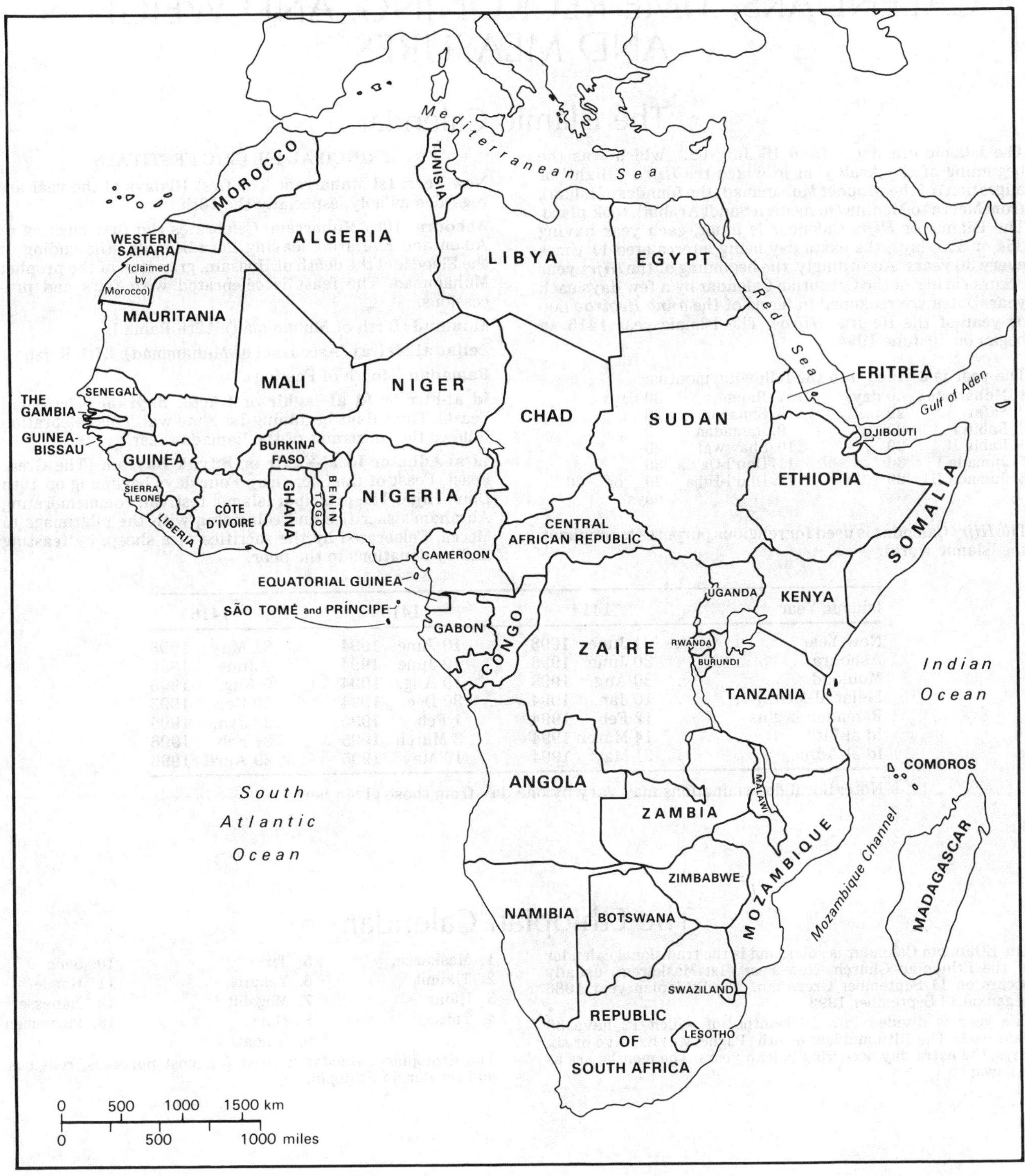

Outline Political Map of Contemporary Africa

CALENDARS, TIME RECKONING, AND WEIGHTS AND MEASURES

The Islamic Calendar

The Islamic era dates from 16 July 622, which was the beginning of the Arab year in which the *Hijra* ('flight' or migration) of the prophet Muhammad (the founder of Islam), from Mecca to Medina (in modern Saudi Arabia), took place. The Islamic or *Hijri* Calendar is lunar, each year having 354 or 355 days, the extra day being intercalated 11 times every 30 years. Accordingly, the beginning of the *Hijri* year occurs earlier in the Gregorian Calendar by a few days each year. Dates are reckoned in terms of the *anno Hegirae* (AH) or year of the Hegira (*Hijra*). The Islamic year 1415 AH began on 10 June 1994.

The year is divided into the following months:

1. Muharram	30 days	7. Rajab	30 days
2. Safar	29 „	8. Shaaban	29 „
3. Rabia I	30 „	9. Ramadan	30 „
4. Rabia II	29 „	10. Shawwal	29 „
5. Jumada I	30 „	11. Dhu'l-Qa'da	30 „
6. Jumada II	29 „	12. Dhu'l-Hijja	29 or 30 days

The *Hijri* Calendar is used for religious purposes throughout the Islamic world.

PRINCIPAL ISLAMIC FESTIVALS

New Year: 1st Muharram. The first 10 days of the year are regarded as holy, especially the 10th.

Ashoura: 10th Muharram. Celebrates the first meeting of Adam and Eve after leaving Paradise, also the ending of the Flood and the death of Hussain, grandson of the prophet Muhammad. The feast is celebrated with fairs and processions.

Mouloud (Birth of Muhammad): 12th Rabia I.

Leilat al-Meiraj (Ascension of Muhammad): 27th Rajab.

Ramadan (Month of Fasting).

Id al-Fitr or **Id al-Saghir** or **Küçük Bayram** (The Small Feast): Three days beginning 1st Shawwal. This celebration follows the constraint of the Ramadan fast.

Id al-Adha or **Id al-Kabir** or **Büyük Bayram** (The Great Feast, Feast of the Sacrifice): Four days beginning on 10th Dhu'l-Hijja. The principal Islamic festival, commemorating Abraham's sacrifice and coinciding with the pilgrimage to Mecca. Celebrated by the sacrifice of a sheep, by feasting and by donations to the poor.

Islamic Year	1414	1415	1416
New Year	21 June 1993	10 June 1994	31 May 1995
Ashoura	30 June 1993	19 June 1994	9 June 1995
Mouloud	30 Aug. 1993	19 Aug. 1994	9 Aug. 1995
Leilat al-Meiraj	10 Jan. 1994	30 Dec. 1994	20 Dec. 1995
Ramadan begins	12 Feb. 1994	1 Feb. 1995	22 Jan. 1996
Id al-Fitr	14 March 1994	3 March 1995	21 Feb. 1996
Id al-Adha	21 May 1994	10 May 1995	29 April 1996

Note: Local determinations may vary by one day from those given here.

The Ethiopian Calendar

The Ethiopian Calendar is solar, and is the traditional calendar of the Ethiopian Church. New Year (1st Maskarem) usually occurs on 11 September Gregorian. The Ethiopian year 1986 began on 11 September 1993.

The year is divided into 13 months, of which 12 have 30 days each. The 13th and last month (Paguemen) has five or six days, the extra day occurring in leap years. The months are as follows:

1. Maskarem
2. Tikimit
3. Hidar
4. Tahsas
5. Tir
6. Yekatit
7. Megabit
8. Maiza
9. Ginbat
10. Sene
11. Hamle
12. Nahasse
13. Paguemen

The Ethiopian Calendar is used for most purposes, religious and secular, in Ethiopia.

Standard Time

One hour behind GMT	Greenwich Mean Time (GMT)	One hour ahead of GMT	Two hours ahead of GMT	Three hours ahead of GMT	Four hours ahead of GMT
Cape Verde	Ascension	Algeria	Botswana	Comoros	Mauritius
	Burkina Faso	Angola	Burundi	Djibouti	Réunion
	Côte d'Ivoire	Benin	Egypt*	Eritrea	Seychelles
	The Gambia	Cameroon	Lesotho	Ethiopia	
	Ghana	Central African Republic	Malawi	Kenya	
	Guinea	Chad	Mozambique	Madagascar	
	Guine-Bissau	Congo	Namibia	Mayotte	
	Liberia	Equatorial Guinea	Rwanda	Somalia	
	Mali	Gabon	South Africa	Tanzania	
	Mauritania	Libya	Sudan	Uganda	
	Morocco	Niger	Swaziland		
	St Helena	Nigeria	Zambia		
	São Tomé and Príncipe	Tunisia	Zimbabwe		
	Senegal	Zaire			
	Sierra Leone				
	Togo				
	Tristan da Cunha				

* Egypt observes summer time, the only country in Africa to do so.

Weights and Measures

Principal weights and units of measurement in common use as alternatives to the imperial and metric systems

WEIGHT

Unit	Country	Metric equivalent	Imperial equivalent
Frazila	Tanzania (Zanzibar)	15.87 kg	35 lb
Kantar	Sudan	44.928 kg	99.05 lb
Metir or Netir	Ethiopia	453.59 grams	1 lb
Pound (Dutch)	South Africa	494 grams	1.09 lb
Wakiah	Tanzania (Zanzibar)	280 grams	9.88 oz

LENGTH

Unit	Country	Metric equivalent	Imperial equivalent
Busa	Sudan	2.54 cm	1 in
Cubito	Somalia	55.88 cm	22 in
Foot (Cape)	South Africa	31.5 cm	12.4 in
Foot (French)	Mauritius	32.5 cm	12.8 in
Kadam or Qadam	Sudan	30.48 cm	12 in
Pouce	Mauritius	2.54 cm	1 in
Senzer	Ethiopia	23.114 cm	9.1 in

CAPACITY

Unit	Country	Metric equivalent	Imperial equivalent
Ardabb or Ardeb	Sudan	198.024 litres	45.36 gallons
Bali	South Africa	46 litres	10.119 gallons
Cabaho	Ethiopia	5.91 litres	1.3 gallons
Corde	Mauritius	3.584 cu m	128 cu ft
Gantang	South Africa	9.2 litres	2.024 gallons
Kadah	Sudan	2.063 litres	3.63 pints
Keila	Sudan	16.502 litres	3.63 gallons
Kuma	Ethiopia	5 litres	1.1 gallons
Messe	Ethiopia	1.477 litres	2.6 pints
Mud or Muid	South Africa	109.1 litres	24 gallons
Ratel	Sudan	0.568 litre	1 pint

AREA

Unit	Country	Metric equivalent	Imperial equivalent
Are	Mauritius	0.01 ha	0.0247 acre
Darat or Dural	Somalia	8,000 sq m	1.98 acres
Feddan	Sudan	4,201 sq m	1.038 acres
Gasha	Ethiopia	40 ha	99 acres
Morgen	South Africa	0.857 ha	2.117 acres

Metric to Imperial Conversions

Metric units	Imperial units	To convert Metric into Imperial units, multiply by:	To convert Imperial into Metric units, multiply by:
Weight			
Gram	Ounce (Avoirdupois)	0.035274	28.3495
Kilogram (kg)	Pound (lb)	2.204623	0.453952
Metric ton	Short ton (2,000 lb)	1.102311	0.907185
	Long ton (2,240 lb)	0.984207	1.016047
	(The short ton is in general use in the USA, while the long ton is normally used in the United Kingdom and in some other countries in the Commonwealth.)		
Length			
Centimetre (cm)	Inch (in)	0.3937008	2.54
Metre (m)	Yard (=3 feet)	1.09361	0.9144
Kilometre (km)	Mile	0.62137	1.609344
Volume			
Cubic metre (cu m)	Cubic foot	35.315	0.028317
	Cubic yard	1.30795	0.764555
Capacity			
Litre	Gallon (=8 pints)	0.219969	4.54609
	Gallon (US)	0.264172	3.78541
Area			
Square metre (sq m)	Square yard	1.19599	0.836127
Hectare (ha)	Acre	2.47105	0.404686
Square kilometre (sq km)	Square mile	0.386102	2.589988

MAJOR COMMODITIES OF AFRICA

Note: For each of the commodities in this section, there are generally two statistical tables: one relating to recent levels of production, and one indicating recent trends in prices. Each production table shows estimates of output for the world and for Africa (including northern Africa, a region not covered by this volume). In addition, the table lists the main African producing countries and, for comparison, the leading producers from outside the continent. In most cases, the table referring to prices provides indexes of export prices, calculated in US dollars. The index for each commodity is based on specific price quotations for representative grades of that commodity in countries that are major traders (excluding countries of eastern Europe and the former USSR).

Aluminium and Bauxite

Aluminium is the most abundant metallic element in the earth's crust, comprising about 8% of the total. However, it is much less widely used than steel, despite having about the same strength and only half the weight. Aluminium has important applications as a metal because of its lightness, ease of fabrication and other desirable properties. Other products of alumina (aluminium oxide) are also important industrial minerals for use as refractories, abrasives, glass manufacture, other ceramic products, catalysts and absorbers. Alumina hydrates are also used for the production of aluminium chemicals, fire retardant in carpet backing, industrial fillers in plastics and related products.

The major markets for aluminium are in building and construction, transportation, consumer durables, electrical machinery and equipment, and the packaging industry, which in the early 1990s accounted for about 22% of all aluminium use. Although the production of aluminium is energy-intensive, its light weight results in a net saving, particularly in the transportation industry. About one-quarter of aluminium output is consumed in the manufacture of transport equipment, particularly road motor vehicles and components, where the metal is increasingly being used as a substitute for steel. In the early 1990s steel substitution accounted for about 16% of world aluminium consumption, and it has been forecast that aluminium demand by the motor vehicle industry alone could more than double, to exceed 5.7m. tons in 2010, from around 2.4m. tons in 1990. Aluminium is of great value to the aerospace industry for its weight-saving characteristics and its low cost relative to alternative materials. Aluminium-lithium alloys command considerable potential for use in this sector, although the traditional dominance of aluminium in the aerospace sector was under challenge in the early 1990s from 'composites' such as carbon-epoxy, a fusion of carbon fibres and hardened resins, whose lightness and durability can exceed that of many aluminium alloys.

The world aluminium industry is dominated by seven Western producers—Alcan (Canada), Alcoa, Alumax, Reynolds, Kaiser (all USA), Pechiney (France) and Alusuisse (Switzerland). However, their level of dominance has been lessened in recent years by a major geographical shift in the location of alumina and aluminium production to areas where cheap power is available, such as Australia, Brazil, Norway, Canada and Venezuela. The Gulf states of Bahrain, Dubai and Qatar, and also Saudi Arabia, with the advantage of low energy costs, have entered the world aluminium market and are expected to become substantial producers during the 1990s, if plans for the expansion of existing capacity and the construction of new smelters are implemented. By contrast, the seven major 'integrated' producers have so far been able to retain their dominance in the markets for semi-finished and finished aluminium products.

Bauxite is the principal aluminium ore, but nepheline syenite, kaolin, shale, anorthosite and alunite are all potential alternative sources of alumina, although not currently economic to process. The developing countries, with 70% of known bauxite reserves, supply 45% of the ore required. The industry is structured in three stages: bauxite mining, alumina refining and smelting. While the high degree of 'vertical integration' (i.e. the control of successive stages of production) in the industry means that the movement of a significant proportion of trade in bauxite and alumina is in the form of intra-company transfers, and the increasing tendency to site alumina refineries on or near to bauxite deposits has resulted in a shrinking bauxite trade, there is a growing free market in alumina, catering for the needs of the increasing number of independent (i.e. non-integrated) smelters.

The alumina is separated from the ore by modifications to the Bayer process. After mining, bauxite is fed to process directly if mine-run material is adequate (as in Jamaica) or is crushed and beneficiated. Where the 'as-mined' ore presents handling problems, or weight reduction is desirable, it may be dried prior to shipment.

At the alumina plant the ore is slurried with spent-liquor directly, if the soft Caribbean type is used, or, in the case of other types, it is ball-milled to reduce it to a size which will facilitate the extraction of the alumina. The bauxite slurry is then digested with caustic soda to extract the alumina from the ore while leaving the impurities as an insoluble residue. The digest conditions depend on the aluminium minerals in the ore and the impurities. The liquor, with the dissolved alumina, is then separated from the insoluble impurities by combinations of sedimentation, decantation and filtration and the residue washed to minimize the soda losses. The clarified liquor is concentrated and the alumina precipitated by seeding with hydrate. The precipitated alumina is then filtered, washed and calcined to produce alumina. The ratio of bauxite to alumina is approximately 1.95:1.

The smelting of the aluminium is generally by electrolysis in molten cryolite. Because of the high consumption of electricity by the smelting process, alumina is usually smelted in areas where low-cost electricity is available. However, most of the electricity now used in primary smelting in the Western world is generated by hydroelectricity—a renewable energy source.

The recycling of aluminium is economically (as well as environmentally) desirable, as the process uses only 5% of the electricity required to produce a similar quantity of primary aluminium. Aluminium that has been recycled from scrap currently accounts for about 40% of the total aluminium supply in the USA, and for about 30% of Western European consumption. With the added impetus of environmental concerns, considerable growth world-wide in the recycling of used beverage cans (UBC) has been forecast for the 1990s.

Excluding the People's Republic of China, the Democratic People's Republic of Korea, the USSR and the former communist countries of eastern Europe, total world output of primary aluminium in 1992 was estimated at 15m. metric tons, of which African producers accounted for about 610,000 tons. The USA usually accounts for about one-third of total aluminium consumption (excluding communist and former communist countries). However, its role as a producer has declined. The USA accounted for 27% of Western world output of aluminium in 1992, compared with 49% in 1961. US smelters have ceased to produce a surplus of ingots, and the country increasingly produces as much as it requires for fabrication and purchases the remainder from lower-cost producers elsewhere.

Guinea possesses more than one-quarter of the world's known bauxite reserves, and is the world's largest exporter of bauxite, ranking second only to Australia in terms of ore production. Guinean bauxite ore, which is of very high grade, is domestically processed into alumina, and some Guinean alumina is exported to Cameroon for refining. Cameroon has extensive bauxite deposits, estimated at some 1,200m. metric tons, but these have yet to be exploited. Ghana's bauxite reserves are estimated at 780m. tons. Although the country lacks an alumina refinery, it has Africa's largest aluminium smelter, located at Tema and owned by the US-based Kaiser and Reynolds interests, which processes imported alumina. Sierra Leone has estimated bauxite reserves of 100m. metric tons. Production from the Mokanji deposits, in the Southern province, began in 1964. Egypt and South Africa also possess primary aluminium smelters. In Nigeria an aluminium smelter with a projected capacity of 180,000 tons per year was to enter production in 1995. Plans for a 250,000 tons-per-year smelter project in Mozambique were announced by Kaiser in 1992, and in the same year the South African aluminium producer Alusaf announced that it was proceeding with plans to construct the largest smelter ever to be built in the Western world, with an annual capacity of 466,000 tons. In November 1993 the company stated that the smelter would enter production in June 1995 and was targeted to reach full-capacity output in mid-1996, by which time Alusaf expected a recovery in the world market for aluminium.

Although world demand for aluminium has been advancing by an average of 3% annually since the late 1980s, industrial recession began, in 1990, to create conditions of over-supply. Despite the implementation of capacity reductions at an annual rate of 10% by the major Western producers, stock levels began to accumulate by about 1.8m. tons per year. The supply problem was exacerbated by a rapid rise, beginning in 1991, of exports by the USSR and its successor states, which had begun to accumulate substantial stocks of aluminium as a consequence of the collapse of the Soviet arms industry. The wish of these countries to obtain

Production of Bauxite (crude ore, '000 metric tons)

	1990	1991
World total	109,333	104,719
Africa	19,357	18,753
Leading African producers		
Ghana	381	400
Guinea*	17,524	17,054
Sierra Leone	1,445	1,288
Leading non-African producers		
Australia†	39,983	41,831
Brazil	9,876	10,414
China, People's Repub.	3,655	2,600
Hungary	2,559	2,013
India	4,984	4,738
Jamaica‡	10,965	11,610
Suriname	3,267	3,136
USSR (former) §	4,200	n.a.
Yugoslavia, Socialist Fed. Repub.	2,953	2,700

* Source: *World Metal Statistics.*
† Twelve months ending 30 June of year stated.
‡ Dried equivalent of crude ore.
§ Estimates by the US Bureau of Mines.

foreign exchange to restructure their economies led to a rapid acceleration in low-cost exports of high-grade aluminium to Western markets. These sales, which had averaged 200,000 tons per year in the late 1980s, had advanced to 1.2m. tons in 1992, causing considerable dislocation of the market and involving the major Western producers in heavy financial losses. Producing members of the European Community (EC, now the European Union—EU, which had reduced their smelter capacity by 25% since mid-1991, were particularly severely affected, and in August 1993 the EC imposed quota arrangements, under which aluminium imports from the former USSR were to be cut by 50% for an initial three-month period while efforts were made to negotiate an agreement that would reduce the flow of low-price imports and achieve a reduction in aluminium stocks (by then estimated to total 4.5m. tons world-wide).

These negotiations, which involved the EC, the USA, Canada, Norway, Australia and Russia (but in which the minor producers, Brazil, the Gulf states, Venezuela and Ukraine were not invited to take part), began in October 1993, but initially made little progress, and in the following month the market price of high-grade aluminium ingots fell to an 11-year 'low'. The resumption of negotiations in December again failed to achieve a voluntary reduction in output by the producers, largely as a result of Russia's reluctance to curtail its production. Following further meetings in January 1994, however, a plan was agreed under which Russia was to 'restructure' its aluminium industry and reduce its output by 500,000 tons annually. In March the major Western producers agreed to cut back their production by about 10%, to 1.2m. tons annually, for a two-year period. Additionally, Russia was to receive US $2,000m. in cash and loans. The agreement provided for participants to monitor world aluminium supplies and prices on a regular basis. In March the EU quota was terminated. By July 1994 the world price had recovered by about 50% on the November 1993 level, although stocks remained at a high level.

Export Price Index for Aluminium (base: 1980 = 100)

	Average	Highest month(s)	Lowest month(s)
1985	72		
1990	93		
1991	74	86 (Jan.-March)	63 (Dec.)
1992	72	76 (April)	66 (Nov.)
1993	66	69 (Jan., Feb., July)	60 (Nov.)

In July 1993 the price of high-grade aluminium (minimum purity 99.7%) on the London Metal Exchange (LME) reached US $1,240.5 (£821) per metric ton, but in November the price declined to $ 1,023.5 (£691) per ton, its lowest level for about eight years. In July 1994 the London price of aluminium advanced to $ 1,529.5 (£981) per ton, the highest quotation for more than three years. The recovery occurred despite a steady accumulation in LME stocks of aluminium, which rose to a series of record levels over the period, increasing from 1,899,375 tons at mid-1993 to 2,661,525 tons in June 1994.

In 1974 seven major bauxite-producing countries —Australia, Guinea, Guyana, Jamaica, Sierra Leone, Suriname and Yugoslavia — formed the International Bauxite Association (IBA), with its headquarters in Kingston, Jamaica, to promote the orderly development of the industry and to safeguard producers' interests. The IBA member states, now numbering eight (with the participation of Ghana and Indonesia), controlled, until Australia withdrew from the Association in 1991, about 85% of the world's known bauxite reserves and bauxite production, and accounted for 54% of alumina production but only 18% of primary aluminium output. The IBA share would be increased by the participation of Brazil, which has delayed its accession to membership, possibly owing to its economic problems. The IBA operates a system of recommended prices for bauxite and alumina.

Almost all the producers of primary aluminium outside communist or former communist countries are members of the International Primary Aluminium Institute (IPAI), based in London. The IPAI's membership comprises some 40 companies which, among them, operate 118 primary aluminium smelters, representing substantially all of the Western countries' production of primary aluminium. In April 1993 the International Aluminium Committee was formed to represent most of the aluminium smelters in the former USSR.

Cassava (Manioc, Tapioca, Yuca) (*Manihot esculenta*)

Cassava is a perennial woody shrub, up to 5 m in height, which is cultivated mainly for its enlarged starch-rich roots, although the young shoots and leaves of the plant are also edible. A native of South and Central America, cassava is now one of the most important food plants in all parts of the tropics (except at the highest altitudes), having a wide range of adaptation for rainfall (500–8,000 mm per year). Cassava is also well adapted to low-fertility soils, and grows where other crops will not. It is produced mainly on marginal agricultural land, with virtually no input of fertilizers, fungicides or insecticides. The varieties of the plant fall into two broad groups, bitter and sweet cassava, formerly classed as two separate species, *M. utilissima* and *M. dulcis* or *aipi*. The roots of the sweet variety are usually boiled and then eaten. The roots of the bitter variety are either soaked, pounded and fermented to make a paste (such as 'fufu' in west Africa), or given an additional roasting to produce 'gari'. They can also be made into flour and starch, or dried and pelletized as animal feed.

Cassava, which was introduced to Africa from South America in the 16th century, is the most productive source of carbohydrates and produces more calories per unit of land than any cereal crop. Although the nutrient content of the roots consists almost entirely of starch, the leaves are high in vitamins, minerals and protein and, processed as meal or eaten as a fresh vegetable ('saka saka'), provide a useful source of nutrition in many parts of Africa, especially in Zaire, the Congo basin, Sierra Leone, Malawi, Mozambique, Tanzania and Uganda. A plot of cassava may be left unattended in the ground for two years after maturity without deterioration of the roots, and the plant is resistant to prolonged drought, so the crop is valued as a famine reserve. The roots are highly perishable after harvest and, if not consumed immediately, must be processed (flour, starch, pellets, etc.).

While the area under cassava has expanded considerably in recent years, there is increasing concern that the rapid expansion of cassava root planting may threaten the fertility of the soil and subsequently other crops. Under cropping systems where no fertilizer is used, cassava is the last crop in the succession because of its particular adaptability to infertile soils and its high nutrient use-efficiency in

Production of Cassava ('000 metric tons)

	1991	1992
World total	151,668*	152,218*
Africa	69,940*	70,444*
Leading African producers		
Angola	1,850*	1,885*
Benin	1,046	932
Burundi	584	597
Cameroon	1,230*	1,230*
Central African Repub.	575†	606†
Congo	780*	790*
Côte d'Ivoire	1,465	1,350*
Ghana	3,600†	4,000†
Guinea	658	660*
Kenya	761	770*
Madagascar	2,307	2,320
Mozambique	3,690	3,239†
Nigeria	20,339†	20,000*
Tanzania	6,266	7,111
Togo	511	480
Uganda	3,599	3,780
Zaire	18,227	18,300*
Leading non-African producers		
Brazil	24,531	22,652
India	5,111	5,200*
Indonesia	15,594	16,318
Thailand	19,705	21,130†

* FAO estimate. † Unofficial figure.

yield terms (although there is now evidence to suggest that cassava yields increase with the use of fertilizer). With the exception of potassium, cassava produces more dry matter with fewer nutrients than most other food crops. Soil fertility is not threatened by cassava itself, but rather by the cultivation systems which employ it without fertilizer use.

As a staple source of carbohydrates in the tropics, cassava is an essential part of the diet of about 300m. people. It is cultivated on about 8m. ha in Africa and provides more than one-half of the caloric requirements of about 200m. people in the continent. Although the area in Africa planted to cassava amounts to considerably more than one-half of the world total, Africa's output accounts for less than 47% of world production. Most of the African crop is produced by subsistence farmers and traded domestically; only a small amount enters world trade.

Since the early 1970s African cassava production has been seriously undermined by mealybug infestation. Indigenous to South America, the mealybug (*Phenacoccus manihoti*) encountered few natural enemies in Africa, and by 1990 had infected all African cassava-growing areas, with the exceptions of Uganda and Madagascar. In 1981 the parasitic wasp *Epidinocarsis lopezi* was introduced into Nigeria from Paraguay to attack the mealybug, and by 1990 *E. lopezi* was established in 25 African countries. The green spider mite, also a threat to cassava cultivation, is also being combated by the introduction of a natural enemy, the phytoseiid mite. African cassava is also vulnerable to African cassava leaf mosaic disease, which deprives the plant of chlorophyll and results in low yields.

In recent years there has been interest in the utilization of cassava as an industrial raw material as well as a food crop. Cassava has the potential to become a basic energy source for ethyl alcohol (ethanol), a substitute for petroleum. 'Alcogas' (a blend of cassava alcohol and petrol) can be mixed with petrol to provide motor fuel, while the high-protein residue from its production can be used for animal feed. The possibility of utilizing cassava leaves and stems (which represent about 50% of the plant and are normally discarded) as cattle-feed concentrates has also been receiving scientific attention.

During 1993 the average monthly import price of hard cassava pellets at the port of Rotterdam, in the Netherlands, declined from US $160 per metric ton in January to $130 per ton in July.

Export Price Index for Cassava (base: 1980 = 100)

	Average	Highest month(s)	Lowest month(s)
1985	52		
1990	78		
1991	81	90 (Jan.)	76 (May)
1992	83	86 (Aug., Nov., Dec.)	80 (April)
1993	86	89 (Sept.)	85 (Jan.-April, June, July)

Chromium

Chromite is the name applied both to the mineral and to the ore containing that mineral. Chromite is the only ore from which chromium is obtained, and the terms chromite ore, chromium ore and chrome ore are used interchangeably. Chromite is used by the metallurgical, chemical and refractory industries. About 80% of total demand for chromite is from the metallurgical industry, 13% from the chemical industry and 8% from the refractory industry. For the metallurgical industry, chromite ore is smelted in an electric furnace and then marketed in the form of ferrochromium. Within the metallurgical industry the major use of chromium is as an essential alloying element in stainless steel, which is valued for its toughness and resistance to most forms of corrosion. Chromium chemicals are used for wood preservation, dyeing, and tanning. Chrome plating is popular. Chromite is used as a refractory mineral.

Production of Chromium Ore ('000 metric tons, gross weight)

	1991	1992
World total	13,445	10,896
Africa	5,747	3,994
African producers		
Madagascar	63	63
South Africa	5,110	3,361
Sudan	10	10
Zimbabwe	564	560
Leading non-African producers		
Albania	800	150
Brazil	340	340
Finland	458	480
India	995	1,000
Iran	90	100
Kazakhstan	n.a.	3,600
Philippines	184	132
Turkey	870	850
USSR (former)	3,800	—

Source: US Bureau of Mines.

World reserves of chromite ore are estimated to total about 1,400m. metric tons. Approximately 70% of known reserves are in South Africa, and 10% each in Zimbabwe and Kazakhstan. South Africa and Kazakhstan each produce about one-third of world chromite ore supplies. South Africa, accounting for 20%–30% of the market, is the world's largest ferrochrome producer. Zimbabwe accounts for about 6% of world ferrochromium requirements. South African charge-grade, high-carbon ferrochromium (which has a chromium content of 52%–55%) has been replacing the more expensive high- and low-carbon ferrochromium (which have a chromium content of 60%–70%) since the development, during the years 1965–75, of the Argon Oxygen Decarbonizing Process, which permits the widespread use of less costly charge-grade, high-carbon ferrochromium.

Strong demand for ferrochromium in the late 1980s generated an expansion of South African capacity. The potentially damaging effects of international boycotts and trade bans, and of civil disturbances, on South Africa's ferrochrome industry led, in the 1980s, to the development of new production capacity, generally close to ore deposits, in Brazil, Finland, Greece, India, Sweden and Turkey. Conditions of under-supply in the late 1980s stimulated capacity additions and expansions in South Africa. Zimbabwe's higher-cost mining operations also became more competitive, and output began to rise.

Pressure on ferrochromium supplies arose from strong demand for stainless steel in the USA, Japan and Western Europe, and in 1989 and early 1990 plans for new ferrochromium plants and expansions of existing capacity were in progress. During 1989 a downward trend in US production of stainless steel permitted the rebuilding of depleted ferrochromium stocks, while an increase in supplies (resulting from the expansions in productive capacity) led to a decline in ferrochromium prices. Ferrochromium production capacity increased by an estimated 300,000 tons (equivalent to 7% of world capacity) in 1989, and by a further 300,000 tons in 1990. Despite strong demand for ferrochromium from stainless steel producers, excess production capacity led to a decline in prices, which had reached record levels in 1988. World ferrochromium production capacity was reduced in 1990 and 1991 by delays in the inauguration of new furnaces and the temporary closure of some furnace plants.

During 1992 major producers of ferrochromium continued to operate at levels substantially below full capacity. European markets for chromium and ferrochromium had been destabilized by a sharp rise in imports of the metals from Kazakhstan. This influx and the sharp decline in demand for stainless steel by the successor states of the USSR, particularly Russia, left substantial quantities of ferrochromium available to world markets. The market imbalance persisted in 1993–94, while major Western producers of ferrochromium continued to operate at levels substantially below full capacity.

Export Price Index for Chrome Ore (base: 1980 = 100)

	Average	Highest month(s)	Lowest month(s)
1985	93		
1990	144		
1991	120	123 (March-July)	116 (Sept.-Dec.)
1992	108	116 (Jan.-June)	99 (July-Dec.)
1993	99	*	*

* The monthly index remained constant at 99 from January to December.

Clove (*Eugenia caryophyllus*)

This tropical tree, native to Indonesia, is a small evergreen, up to 14 m high, and cloves are its dried, unopened flower-buds. These buds are picked by hand and dried in the sun to be used as spices. The trees are planted from seed, come into bearing after eight or nine years and normally live for about 60 years. Cloves are a cyclical crop, however, and trees produce at their peak only once in every four years. Clove oil, produced by distillation of cloves, flower stalks and leaves, is used in perfumes and toiletries. The chief constituent of clove oil is eugenol, which is used as a dental anaesthetic.

In the 19th century cloves were transplanted from Mauritius to the island of Zanzibar (now an autonomous part of Tanzania), where they became the principal cash crop. Formerly the world's largest exporter of cloves, Zanzibar now ranks only fourth. Clove is a notoriously volatile crop and harvests tend to proceed in a three-year cycle of good, medium and poor years. The level of marketed production has also been affected by low producer prices (despite annual increases since 1979), smuggling and tree disease. Since the early 1980s, however, thousands of tons of Zanzibari cloves have remained unsold, owing to a surplus of supplies on the world market. In 1989 these stocks were estimated at about 8,000 tons. Harvested cloves are purchased by the state clove board. Zanzibar's principal customers for cloves are Singapore, the Netherlands, India and Thailand.

Since the early 1980s, when Indonesia ceased to be a clove importer, the volume and value of shipments from Madagascar have been subject to wide fluctuations, and cloves have been replaced by vanilla as the island's second most profitable export. With Zanzibar, Madagascar formerly produced most of the cloves entering world trade. However, Indonesia, which requires 30,000–35,000 tons of cloves per year to satisfy its kretek (clove) cigarette industry, has become self-sufficient in clove production and now accounts for about 60% of total world production, which reached 60,000 tons in 1991/92.

Since the early 1980s the world market, which is estimated at just over 10,000 tons per year (excluding Indonesia's requirements), has been heavily oversupplied, and prices have fallen steadily, reaching an all-time low of US $1,800 per ton in 1989. In 1991 the Indonesian government, which holds substantial stocks of cloves, established a state monopoly in an attempt to stabilize the clove trade.

Cobalt

Cobalt is usually mined as a by-product of another metal; in the case of African cobalt, this is principally copper, although cobalt is also produced from nickel-copper-cobalt ores in Botswana and Zimbabwe and from platinum ores in South Africa. It is rarely mined as the primary product of an ore, and is found in very weak concentration, generally 0.1%–0.5%. The ore must be crushed and ground after mining and subjected to a flotation process to obtain the concentrate. About 35% of cobalt production is used in the metallic form as superalloys (in turbine engines), hardfacing and stellite. Approximately 34% is applied to chemical uses in such industries as glass manufacture, paints and inks and, increasingly, as catalysts in the processing of oil and petroleum feed stocks and synthetic materials. A further 10% is used in the manufacture of ceramics, 11% in magnetic alloys and 10% in the fabrication of hard metals. Sales agencies in the USA, Europe and the Far East market the major part of African production. Zaire, the world's leading cobalt producer with an estimated 65% of known cobalt reserves, has the highest grade of the metal, with up to six tons of cobalt produced with every 100 tons of copper. The mining, marketing and export of Zairean cobalt are controlled by a state monopoly, La Générale des carrières et des mines (GÉCAMINES). Since 1990, however, Zaire's cobalt output has been adversely affected by internal unrest.

Since the early 1980s Zambia has promoted the expansion of its cobalt production in an attempt to offset declines in the country's copper output. In the early 1990s three mining companies in South Africa were producing cobalt metal as a by-product of platinum production. In 1992 the Ugandan government signed an agreement with European interests for a project to extract cobalt, at an estimated rate of 1,000 tons per year, from waste dumps at the Kilembe copper mine. Construction of an extraction plant was proceeding in 1994.

Traditional cobalt-mining may be challenged during the next 20 years by the wide-scale retrieval of manganese nodules from the world's seabeds. It is estimated that the cobalt content of each nodule is about 0.25%, although nodules recovered from the Pacific Ocean in 1983 had a cobalt content of 2.5%. Ferromanganese crusts, containing extractable cobalt, have been identified at relatively shallow depths within the USA's exclusive economic zones, which extend 370 km (200 nautical miles) into US coastal waters.

On the free market, the price of high-grade cobalt (minimum purity 99.8%) stood at more than US $14 per lb in early June 1993, but declined to $11.175 in November. Following reports of unrest in Zaire, the price of cobalt rose sharply in January 1994, reaching $22.75 per lb. The cobalt price eased to $21.00 per lb in February, but the upward trend later resumed, with the price reaching $27.00 in April. It retreated to $22.20 per lb in August.

The Cobalt Development Institute, founded in 1982, comprises almost 40 members, including consumers, processors, merchants and the eight leading producers, including Zaire and Zambia.

Production of Cobalt Ore (cobalt content, metric tons)

	1991	1992*
World total	26,803	21,924
Africa	17,832	13,655
African producers		
Botswana	208	200
Morocco	325	300
South Africa	300*	350
Zaire	9,900	5,700
Zambia	6,994	7,000
Zimbabwe	105	105
Non-African producers		
Australia	1,200	1,350
Canada	2,171	2,219
Cuba	1,600	1,500
New Caledonia	800	800
Russia	n.a.	1,700
USSR (former)	2,200	—

* Estimates.
Source: US Bureau of Mines.

Cocoa (*Theobroma cacao*)

This tree, up to 14 m tall, originated in the tropical forests of Central and South America. The first known cocoa plantations were in southern Mexico around AD 600. Cocoa first came to Europe in the 16th century. The Spanish and Portuguese introduced cocoa into Africa — on the islands of Fernando Póo (now Bioko), in Equatorial Guinea, and São Tomé and Príncipe — at the beginning of the 19th century. At the end of the century the tree was established on the African mainland, first in Ghana and then in other west African countries.

Cocoa is now widely grown in the tropics, usually at altitudes less than 300 m above sea-level, where it needs a fairly high rainfall and good soil. The cocoa tree has a much shallower tap root than, for example, the coffee bush, making cocoa more vulnerable to dry weather. Cocoa trees can take up to four years from planting before producing sufficient fruit for harvesting. They may live to 80 years or more, although the fully productive period is usually about 20 years. The tree is highly vulnerable to pests and diseases, and it is also very sensitive to climatic changes. Its fruit is a large pod, about 15–25 cm in length, which at maturity is yellow in some varieties and red in others. The ripe pods are cut from the tree, where they grow directly out of the trunk and branches. When opened, cocoa pods disclose a mass of seeds (beans) surrounded by white mucilage. After harvesting, the beans and mucilage are scooped out and fermented. Fermentation lasts several days, allowing the flavour to develop. The mature fermented beans, dull red in colour, are then dried, ready to be bagged as raw cocoa which may be further processed or exported.

Cultivated cocoa trees may be broadly divided into three groups. All west African cocoas belong to the Amazonian Forastero group, which now provides more than 80% of world cocoa production. It includes the Amelonado variety, suitable for chocolate manufacturing, grown in Ghana, Côte d'Ivoire and Nigeria. Criollo cocoa is not widely grown and is used only for luxury confectionary. The third group is Trinitario, which accounts for about 15% of world output and grows mainly in Central America and the northern regions of South America.

Cocoa processing takes place mainly in importing countries, although processing industries were established in west Africa during the 1960s and processed products now account for a significant part of the value of their cocoa exports. The processes include shelling, roasting and grinding the beans. Almost half of each bean after shelling consists of a fat called cocoa butter. In the manufacture of cocoa powder for use as a beverage, this fat is largely removed. Cocoa is a mildly stimulating drink, because of its caffeine content, and — unlike coffee and tea — is highly nutritional.

The most important use of cocoa is in the manufacture of chocolate, of which it is the main ingredient. About 90% of all cocoa produced is used in chocolate making, for which extra cocoa butter is added, as well as other substances such as sugar — and milk in the case of milk chocolate. Proposals that were announced in December 1993 by the consumer countries of the European Union, permitting the increasing use of substances other than cocoa butter in the manufacture of chocolate products, have been perceived as potentially damaging to the world cocoa trade.

After coffee and sugar, cocoa is the most important agricultural export commodity in international trade. Recorded world exports (including re-exports) of cocoa beans, which totalled 1,856,450 tons in the 12 months ending 30 September 1991, declined to 1,793,600 tons in 1991/92. In 1992/93, however, export volume was estimated to have recovered to 1,835,550 tons, of which African countries provided 1,093,640 tons. The world's leading exporters of cocoa beans in 1992/93 were Côte d'Ivoire (626,944 tons), Ghana (230,406 tons), Indonesia (213,545 tons), Malaysia (121,312 tons), Nigeria (115,000 tons), Singapore (108,448 tons, all re-exports), Brazil (92,355 tons), and Cameroon (89,271 tons).

The principal importers of cocoa are developed countries with market economies, which account for about 80% of cocoa imports from developing countries. Recorded world imports of cocoa beans in 1992/93 were 1,913,890 tons. The principal importing countries in that year were the USA (with 394,931 tons, representing 20.6% of the total), the Netherlands (318,000 tons) and Germany (313,581 tons).

Production of Cocoa Beans
('000 metric tons, year ending 30 September)

	1991/92	1992/93*
World total	2,266	2,358
Africa	1,242	1,266
Leading African producers		
Cameroon	105	90
Côte d'Ivoire	747	697
Equatorial Guinea	4	6
Ghana	243	312
Nigeria	110	135
Sierra Leone	8	3
Togo	8	6
Leading non-African producers		
Brazil	290	295
Colombia	50	50
Dominican Repub.	48	51
Ecuador	85	70
Indonesia	180	245
Malaysia	220	225
Mexico	45	50
Papua New Guinea	41	39

* Estimates.

Source: International Cocoa Organization.

Since the mid-1960s, when it accounted for more than one-third of world production, Ghana's share of the world market has fallen to less than 14%, owing to the neglect of the industry and to the official policy of maintaining prices payable to producers at uneconomic levels. The decline has been exacerbated by the smuggling of cocoa to neighbouring countries, where higher prices are obtainable. In recent years, however, Ghana has sought to revive cocoa production through programmes of replanting, insect spraying, storage and transport improvement. In 1992 cocoa was overtaken by gold as Ghana's main export commodity. From July 1993 the Ghana Cocoa Board (COCOBOD) was deprived of its monopoly, and three trading companies were licensed to purchase cocoa direct from farmers. However, COCOBOD retained exclusive control over Ghanaian cocoa exports. Among the smaller African producers, cocoa exports are a significant component of the economies of Cameroon, Equatorial Guinea and Togo. Although cocoa remains Nigeria's main export crop, its significance to the economy has been overtaken by petroleum.

World prices for cocoa are highly sensitive to changes in supply and demand, making its market position volatile. Negotiations to secure international agreement on stabilizing the cocoa industry began in 1956. Full-scale cocoa conferences, under United Nations auspices, were held in 1963, 1966 and 1967, but all proved abortive. A major difficulty was the failure to agree on a fixed minimum price. In 1972 the fourth UN Cocoa Conference took place in Geneva and resulted in the first International Cocoa Agreement (ICCA), adopted by 52 countries, although the USA, the world's principal cocoa importer, did not sign. The ICCA took formal effect in October 1973. It operated for three quota years and provided for an export quota system for producing countries, a fixed price range for cocoa beans and a buffer stock to support the agreed prices. In accordance with the ICCA, the International Cocoa Organization (ICCO), based in London, was established in 1973. In 1994 its members comprised 13 exporting countries, accounting for about three-quarters of world production and exports, excluding re-exports, of cocoa beans, and 14 importing countries, accounting for about 55% of world imports of cocoa beans. The USA, the world's leading importer of cocoa, is not a member. Nor is Indonesia, whose production and exports of cocoa has expanded rapidly in recent years. The governing body of the ICCO is the International Cocoa Council (ICC), established to supervise implementation of the ICCA.

A second ICCA operated during 1979–81. It was followed by an extended agreement, which was in force in 1981–87. A fourth ICCA took effect in 1987. (For detailed information on these agreements, see *Africa South of the Sahara 1991*.) During the period of these ICCA, the effective operation of cocoa price stabilization mechanisms was frequently impeded by a number of factors, principally by crop and stock surpluses, which continued to overshadow the cocoa market in the early 1990s. In addition, the achievement of ICCA objectives was affected by the divergent views of producers and consumers, led by Côte d'Ivoire, on one side, and by the USA, on the other, as to appropriate minimum price levels. Disagreements also developed over the allocation of members' export quotas and the conduct of price support measures by means of the buffer stock (which ceased to operate during 1983–88), and subsequently over the disposal of unspent buffer stock funds. The effectiveness of financial operations under the fourth ICCA was severely curtailed by the accumulation of arrears of individual members' levy payments, notably by Côte d'Ivoire and Brazil. The fourth ICCA was extended for a two-year period from October 1990, although the suspension of the economic clauses relating to cocoa price support operations rendered the agreement ineffective in terms of exerting any influence over cocoa market prices.

Preliminary discussions on a fifth ICCA, again held under UN auspices, ended without agreement in May 1992, when consumer members, while agreeing to extend the fourth ICCA for a further year (until October 1993), refused to accept producers' proposals for the creation of an export quota system as a means of stabilizing prices, on the grounds that such arrangements would not impose sufficient limits on total production to restore equilibrium between demand and supply. Additionally, no agreement was reached on the disposition of cocoa buffer stocks, then totalling 240,000 tons. At a further meeting of the ICCO, held in July, delegates again failed to reach an accord on these issues. Negotiations were renewed in November, and again in February–March 1993, when it was decided to abandon efforts to formulate arrangements under which prices would be stabilized by means of a stock-withholding scheme. At a further negotiating conference in July, however, terms were finally agreed for a new ICCA, to take effect from October, subject to its ratification by at least five exporting countries (accounting for at least 80% of total world exports) and by importing countries (representing at least 60% of total imports). Unlike previous commodity agreements sponsored by the UN, the fifth ICCA aimed to achieve stable prices by regulating supplies and promoting consumption, rather than through the operation of buffer stocks and export quotas.

Following a delay in its formal ratification, the fifth ICCA, operating until September 1998, entered into effect in February 1994. Under the new agreement, buffer stocks totalling 233,000 that had accrued from the previous ICCA were to be released on the market at the rate of 51,000 tons annually over a maximum period of 4½ years, beginning in the 1993/94 crop season. The market impact of these sales, however, was offset by forecasts of a production shortfall of 110,000 tons in 1993/94, while expectations of cocoa output falling short of demand by about 209,000 tons in 1994/95 assisted the maintenance of a firm tone in market prices. In June 1994, however, disagreements arose among ICCA signatories on operating rules for the production and consumption committees. Further negotiations to define their functions were to take place in September.

Export Price Index for Cocoa (base: 1980 = 100)

	Average	Highest month(s)	Lowest month(s)
1985	86		
1990	49		
1991	44	50 (Dec.)	37 (July)
1992	43	48 (Jan.)	39 (June)
1993	43	51 (Dec.)	39 (March, June)

As the above table indicates, international prices for cocoa have generally been very low in recent years. In 1992 the average of the ICCO's daily prices (based on selected quotations from the London and New York markets) was US $1,099.5 per metric ton (49.9 US cents per lb), its lowest level since 1972. The annual average was slightly higher in 1993, at $1,117 per ton. In that year the monthly average ranged from $975 per ton in March to $1,355 in December. On the London Commodity Exchange the price of cocoa for short-term delivery increased from £637 ($983) per ton in May 1993 to £1,003.5 in November, but it later retreated. In April 1994 the London cocoa quotation (for May delivery) fell to £825.5 per ton, but in July, following forecasts that the global production deficit would rise, the price reached £1,093.5 ($1,694), its highest level, in terms of sterling, for more than six years.

The Cocoa Producers' Alliance (COPAL), whose 13 members number among them seven African countries and include all the major producers except Indonesia, was formed in 1962 with the aim of preventing excessive price fluctuations by regulating the supply of cocoa. Members of COPAL account for about 82% of world cocoa production, with African members providing about 53%. COPAL has acted in concert with successive ICCA, and in October 1993 announced that its members were to reduce their total production by 370,000 tons over a five-year period from 1993/94. COPAL's headquarters is in Lagos, Nigeria.

The principal centres for cocoa-trading in the industrialized countries are the London Cocoa Terminal Market, in the United Kingdom, and the New York Coffee, Sugar and Cocoa Exchange, in the USA.

Coffee (*Coffea*)

This is an evergreen shrub or small tree, generally 5 m–10 m in height, indigenous to Asia and tropical Africa. Wild trees grow to 10 m but the cultivated shrubs are pruned to much lower heights. The dried seeds (beans) are roasted, ground and brewed in hot water to provide the most popular of the world's non-alcoholic beverages. Coffee is drunk in every country in the world and its consumers comprise an estimated one-third of the world's population. Although it has little nutrient value, coffee acts as a mild stimulant, owing to the presence of caffeine, an alkaloid also present in tea and cocoa.

There are about 40 species of *Coffea*, most of which grow wild in the eastern hemisphere. The species of economic importance are *C. arabica* (native to Ethiopia), which accounts for about 70%–75% of world production, and *C. canephora* (the source of robusta coffee), which accounts for all but 1% of the remainder. Arabica coffee is more aromatic but robusta, as the name implies, is a stronger plant. Coffee grows in the tropical belt, between 20°N and 20°S, and from sea-level to as much as 2,000 m above. The optimum growing conditions are found at 1,250–1,500 m above sea-level, with an average temperature of around 17°C and an average annual rainfall of 1,000–1,750 mm. Trees begin bearing fruit three to five years after planting, depending upon the variety, and give their maximum yield (up to 5 kg of fruit per year) from the sixth to the 15th year. Few shrubs remain profitable beyond 30 years.

Arabica coffee trees are grown mostly in the American tropics and supply the largest quantity and the best quality of coffee beans. In Africa and Asia arabica coffee is vulnerable in lowland areas to a serious leaf disease and consequently cultivation has been concentrated on highland areas. Some highland arabicas, such as those grown in Kenya, have a high reputation for quality.

The robusta coffee tree, grown mainly in east and west Africa, has larger leaves than arabica but the beans are generally smaller and of lower quality and price. However, robusta coffee has a higher yield than arabica as the trees are more resistant to disease. Robusta is also more suitable for the production of soluble ('instant') coffee. About 75% of African coffee is of the robusta variety. Soluble coffee accounts for more than one-fifth of world coffee consumption.

Each coffee berry, green at first but red when ripe, usually contains two beans (white in arabica, light brown in robusta) which are the commercial product of the plant. To produce the best quality arabica beans — known in the trade as 'mild' coffee — the berries are opened by a pulping machine and the beans fermented briefly in water before being dried and hulled into green coffee. Much of the crop is exported in green form. Robusta beans are generally prepared by dry-hulling. Roasting and grinding are usually undertaken in the importing countries, for economic reasons and because roasted beans rapidly lose their freshness when exposed to air.

Apart from beans, coffee produces a few minor by-products. When the coffee beans have been removed from the fruit, what remains is a wet mass of pulp and, at a later stage, the dry material of the 'hull' or fibrous sleeve that protects the beans. Coffee pulp is used as cattle feed, the fermented pulp makes a good fertilizer and coffee bean oil is an ingredient in soaps, paints and polishes.

Production of Green Coffee Beans ('000 metric tons)

	1991	1992
World total	6,128*	5,783*
Africa	1,201*	1,059*
Leading African producers		
Burundi	34	34
Cameroon	115	76
Côte d'Ivoire	199	125
Ethiopia	210†	216†
Guinea	30	30*
Kenya	86	85
Madagascar	85	87
Rwanda	39†	28†
Tanzania	46	56
Uganda	147	121
Zaire	102†	98†
Leading non-African producers		
Brazil‡	1,520	1,293
Colombia	971	1,050
Costa Rica	158	168
Ecuador	139	138
El Salvador	138	149
Guatemala	207	205
Honduras	102	135
India	170	180
Indonesia	419	421
Mexico	334	207†
Philippines	133	128

* FAO estimate.

† Unofficial figure.

‡ Data that were officially reported in terms of dry cherries have been converted into clean coffee at 50%.

More than one-half of the world's coffee is produced on smallholdings of less than 5 ha. In most producing countries, and especially in Africa, coffee is almost entirely an export crop, with little domestic consumption. Green coffee accounts for some 96% of all the coffee that is exported, with soluble and roasted coffee comprising the balance. Tariffs on green/raw coffee are usually low or non-existent. The USA is the largest single importer, although its volume of coffee purchases was overtaken in 1975 by the combined imports of the (then) nine countries of the European Community (EC, later the European Union). In 1991 the 12 countries of the EC together accounted for 45.4% of world imports of coffee, while the USA absorbed 21.1%.

After petroleum, coffee is the major raw material in world trade, and the single most valuable agricultural export of the tropics. Africa (with 18.3% of world output in 1992) ranks second to Latin America (64.7%) as a coffee-producing region, although production in Asian countries has expanded in recent years, accounting in 1992 for 16.2% of world coffee production, compared with 11.5% in the period 1979–81.

In every year since 1970, except in 1974, 1984, 1991 and 1992, Côte d'Ivoire has been Africa's leading coffee producer, although since 1980 cocoa has outstripped coffee as its most important export crop. It has been estimated that about one-half of Côte d'Ivoire's population depend for their livelihood on coffee, grown mostly on small plantations. However, by the early 1990s, more than three-quarters of the coffee trees in Côte d'Ivoire had passed their most productive age. Government plans provide for extensive replanting: the total area under coffee cultivation is projected to increase by 270,000 ha to 1.3m. ha by the year 2000.

The African countries which are most dependent on coffee as a source of foreign exchange are Burundi and Uganda. Coffee sales generally account for 70%–85% of Burundi's total export revenue, and in 1991 the proportion was 81%. In Uganda coffee provided 99.2% of exports in 1981, and 91% in 1990; over the period 1977–85 its average annual contribution was more than 94%. Ethiopia is a significant regional producer, exceeding Côte d'Ivoire in output in 1991 and 1992, but, with high domestic consumption and widespread smuggling, official exports accounted for only about one-quarter of total production in the early 1990s. None the less, coffee accounted for 61.6% of Ethiopia's total export earnings in 1991. Among other African countries where coffee is a major export are Cameroon, the Central African Republic, Kenya, Madagascar, Tanzania and Zaire. Angola was formerly the world's leading exporter of robusta coffee, but production since 1975 has been severely disrupted by civil conflict. Plans have been proceeding since 1991 for the transfer to private-sector ownership of the country's major plantations, but the eventual rehabilitation of Angola's coffee industry, following the political and military settlement pending in 1994, is expected to span many years.

Effective international attempts to stabilize coffee prices began in 1959, when a number of producing countries made a short-term agreement to fix export quotas. After three such agreements, a five-year International Coffee Agreement (ICA), covering both producers and consumers, and introducing a quota system, was signed in 1962. This led to the establishment in 1963 of the International Coffee Organization (ICO), with its headquarters in London. The ICO comprises 71 members (51 exporting countries, accounting for 99% of world supplies, and 20 importing countries, accounting, until the withdrawal of the USA in 1993, for over 80% of world imports). Subsequent ICA were negotiated in 1976 and 1983 (extended to 1994, see below), but the system of export quotas to stabilize prices was eventually abandoned in July 1989 (for detailed information on these agreements, see *Africa South of the Sahara 1991*.) During each successive ICA, contention arose over the allocation of members' export quotas, the operation of price support mechanisms, and, most importantly, illicit sales by some members of surplus stocks to non-members of the ICO (notably to the USSR and to countries in Eastern Europe and the Middle East). These 'leaks' of low-price coffee, often at less than one-half of the official ICA rate, also found their way to consumer members of the ICO through free ports, depressing the general market price and making it more difficult for exporters to fulfil their quotas. In the late 1980s such sales were estimated to approximate as much as one-quarter of total production by ICO members.

The issue of coffee export quotas became further complicated in the 1980s, as consumer tastes in the main importing market, the USA, and, to a lesser extent, in the EC moved away from the robustas exported by Brazil and the main African producers and in favour of the milder arabica coffees grown in Central America. Disagreements over a new system of quota allocations, taking account of coffee by variety, had the effect of undermining efforts in 1989 to preserve the economic provisions of the ICA, pending the negotiation of a new agreement. The ensuing deadlock between consumers and producers, as well as among the producers themselves, led in July to the collapse of the quota system and the suspension of the economic provisions of the ICA. The administrative clauses of the agreement, however, continued to operate and were subsequently extended until October 1993, pending an eventual settlement of the quota issue and the entering into force of a successor ICA.

With the abandonment of the ICA quotas, coffee prices fell sharply in world markets, and were further depressed by a substantial accumulation of coffee stocks held by consumers; in mid-1992 these totalled about 20m. bags (each of 60 kg). By mid-1992, it was estimated, the value of world coffee trade had fallen to US $7,000m. annually, compared with more than $18,000m. in 1986. The response by some Latin American producers was to seek to revive prices by imposing temporary suspensions of exports; this strategy, however, merely increased losses of coffee revenue. By early 1992 there was general agreement among the ICO exporting members that the export quota mechanism should be revived; however, disagreements persisted over the allocation of quotas. In June the ICO met in London to seek agreement on transitional measures to revive the coffee market, ahead of fuller negotiations to formulate a new ICA (to take effect from 1 October). No substantive progress was made, although a 20-nation working group was formed to study means of reintroducing export controls in the next ICA. It was also proposed that the new agreement should implement coffee-export controls to all destinations, including countries that are not signatories to an ICA. It was hoped that both consuming and producing countries would agree on a successor ICA containing provisions for a target stabilization price for coffee, an equitable distribution of export quotas among the producers, and mechanisms to be used for its adjustment. Subsequent negotiations, in December 1992 and January–February 1993, ended in deadlock, although both producers and consumers agreed that any new ICA should be based on a universal quota system. In April, following further meetings of the ICO in London, it was announced that efforts to achieve a new Agreement had finally collapsed. In the following month Brazil and Colombia, the two largest coffee producers, inaugurated a joint plan to limit their annual coffee exports to 17m. and 13m. bags respectively, while Central American producers agreed to withhold 15% of their coffee production in the 1993/94 crop year. During that period, world shipments of coffee declined to 76.3m. bags from 77.8m. bags in 1991/92. Brazil, the leading exporter, shipped 17.6m. bags in 1992/93, down from 21.2m. bags in 1991/92. Coffee exports by Colombia declined from 15.5.m. bags to 14.5m. bags, and those by Mexico from 3.3m. bags to 2.4m. bags. Increased exports were recorded by Côte d'Ivoire (4.9m. bags in 1992/93, compared with 3.9m. bags in 1991/92), and higher shipments were also reported by Indonesia (4.4m. bags in 1991/92 to 5.5m. bags in 1992/93), Guatemala (3.3m. bags to 3.7m.), El Salvador (2.2m. bags to 3.0m.) and Costa Rica (2.3m. bags to 2.6m.). Although world consumption of coffee exceeded these levels of production, prices were severely depressed by surpluses of coffee stocks totalling 62m. bags, with an additional 21m. bags held in reserve by consumer companies. Prices, in real terms, stood at historic 'lows'.

In July 1993 the Latin American producers announced that the formation of an Association of Coffee Producing Countries (ACPC), with headquarters in Brasília, to implement an export-withholding scheme. In the following month the Inter-African Coffee Organization (IACO, see below), whose 24 members include Côte d'Ivoire, Kenya and Uganda, announced that it would join the Latin American producers in a new plan to withhold 20% of output whenever market prices fell below an agreed limit. With the participation of Asian producers, an expanded, 40-member ACPC was formally established in August. Its member countries represent about two-thirds of African production and approximately 80% of coffee output world-wide.

The ACPC withholding scheme came into operation in October 1993 and gradually generated improved prices; by April 1994 market quotations for all grades and origins of coffee had achieved their highest levels since 1989. In June and July 1994 coffee prices escalated sharply, following reports that as much as 50% of the 1995/96 Brazilian crop had been damaged by frosts. In July 1994 both Brazil and Colombia announced a temporary suspension of coffee exports.

The market operations of the ACPC were initially endorsed by the ICO, whose members agreed in June 1993 to a further extension of the ICA, to September 1994. However, the influence of the ICO, from which the USA withdrew in October 1993, was increasingly perceived as having been eclipsed by the ACPC. In June 1994 the ICO called a meeting of members for October to discuss the possibility of a resumption of quota arrangements, which the ICO has continued to view as the most effective means of preventing sharp fluctuations in market prices.

Export Price Index for Coffee (base: 1980 = 100)

	Average	Highest month(s)	Lowest month(s)
1985	81		
1990	46		
1991	42	46 (March, April)	38 (Dec.)
1992	33	40 (Dec.)	28 (Aug.)
1993	38	44 (Sept.)	31 (April)

As indicated in the table above, international prices for coffee beans have generally been at very low levels in recent years, even in nominal terms (i.e. without taking inflation into account). On the London Commodity Exchange (LCE) the price of raw robusta coffee for short-term delivery fell in May 1992 to US $652.5 (£365) per metric ton, its lowest level, in terms of dollars, for more than 22 years. By December the London coffee price had recovered to $1,057.5 per ton (for delivery in January 1993). The LCE quotation eased to $837 (£542) per ton in January 1993, and remained within this range until August, when a sharp increase began. The coffee price advanced in September to $1,371 (£885) per ton, its highest level for the year. Thereafter, the coffee market moved within narrow limits until March 1994, when the London quotation per ton rose from $1,198.5 (£801.5) to $1,352 (£906). In April a further surge in prices began, and in May coffee was traded in London at more than $2,000 per ton for the first time since 1989. In late June 1994 there were reports from Brazil that frost had damaged the potential coffee harvest for future seasons, and the LCE quotation exceeded $3,000 per ton. In July, after further reports of frost damage to Brazilian coffee plantations, the London price reached $3,975 (£2,538) per ton, its highest level for more than eight years.

The IACO was formed in 1960, with its headquarters at Abidjan in Côte d'Ivoire. In 1994 the IACO represented 24 producer countries, all of which were also members of the ICO. The aim of the IACO is to study common problems and to encourage the harmonization of production.

Copper

The ores containing copper are mainly copper sulphide or copper oxide. They are mined both underground and by open-cast or surface mining. After break-up of the ore body by explosives, the lumps of ore are crushed, ground and mixed with reagents and water in the case of sulphide ores, and then subjected to a flotation process by which copper-rich minerals are extracted. The resulting concentrate, which contains about 30% copper, is then dried, smelted and cast into anode copper, which is further refined to about 99.98% purity by electrolysis (chemical decomposition by electrical action). The cathodes are then cast into convenient shapes for working or are sold as such. Oxide ores, less important than sulphides, are treated in ways rather similar to the solvent extraction process described below.

Two alternative processes of copper extraction, both now in operation in Zambia, have been developed in recent years. The first of these techniques, and as yet of minor importance in the industry, is known as 'Torco' (treatment of refractory copper ores) and is used for extracting copper from silicate ores which were previously not treatable.

The second, and relatively low-cost, technique is the solvent extraction process. This is suited to the treatment of very low-grade oxidized ores and is currently being used on both new ores and waste dumps that have accumulated over previous years from conventional copper working. The copper in the ore or waste material is dissolved in acid and mixed with a special organic-containing chemical reagent which selectively extracts the copper. After allowing the two layers to separate, the layer containing the copper is separated from the acid leach solution and the copper extracted from it.

Copper is ductile, resists corrosion and is an excellent conductor of heat and electricity. Its industrial uses are mainly in the electrical industry (about 60% of copper is made into wire for use in power cables, telecommunications, domestic and industrial wiring) and the building, engineering and chemical industries. In the latter industry it is principally in alloy form. The bronzes and brasses are typical copper alloys used for both industrial and decorative purposes. There are, however, substitutes for copper in almost all of its industrial uses, and in recent years aluminium has presented an increasing challenge in the electrical and transport industries.

The current world reserve base of copper has been estimated by the US Bureau of Mines at 590m. metric tons. Reserves located within Zaire and Zambia jointly account for about 11% of the total.

Copper production is the mainstay of Zambia's economy, and copper sales normally account for about 85% of Zambia's export earnings. Mining operations are conducted by the Zambia Consolidated Copper Mines (ZCCM), and production is marketed exclusively by the state-owned Metal Marketing Corporation (MEMACO). Before being overtaken by Canada in 1983, Zambia ranked second only to Chile among the world's copper exporters. Zambian copper exports are virtually all in refined but unwrought form. About 43% of its sales are to EU countries. Production of refined copper in Zambia entered a gradual decline in the mid-1980s; dwindling ore grades, high extraction costs, transport problems, shortages of foreign exchange, equipment and skilled labour, lack of maintenance and labour unrest combined to make the copper industry seem an unstable basis for the Zambian economy. However, following the country's change of government in 1991, a number of remedial measures, including the proposed transfer of ZCCM to private-sector ownership, have been announced. A range of reforms within ZCCM have been carried out, and higher production targets for copper have been set. Plans are also proceeding for the expansion of productive capacity and a wide-ranging programme of exploration and modernization.

The Zairean copper industry has become increasingly vulnerable to competition from other producers, such as Chile, which have been establishing new open-cast, low-cost mines. Increasing emphasis has been placed on efforts to increase refined production capacity, and in the late 1980s about one-half of Zaire's copper exports were in the form of refined copper leach cathodes and blister copper. The export proportion of copper concentrates was expected to fall substantially during the 1990s. About 70% of Zairean copper exports are to EC countries. The mining and marketing of copper in Zaire is the responsibility of the state-owned minerals enterprise, La Générale des Carrières et des Mines (GÉCAMINES), which in 1990 completed a large-scale five-year investment plan to improve copper-mining equipment and related infrastructure. As a result of continuing unrest in Zaire, however, the company's copper output, which had been more than 500,000 tons per year in the mid-1980s, declined to about 290,000 tons in 1991 and to an estimated 147,000 tons in 1992. Production in 1993 was forecast at less than 50,000 tons. The uncertainty of supplies from Zaire was an important factor in maintaining a generally firm tone in world copper prices during 1993 and early 1994.

Production of Copper Ore (copper content, '000 metric tons)

	1990	1991
World total	8,961.9	8,192.8
Africa	1,234.9	919.0
Leading African producers		
Namibia*	32.5	30.0
South Africa	178.7	192.9
Zaire	355.5	250.0
Zambia	621.6	400.0
Leading non-African producers		
Canada*	793.8	797.6
Chile	1,616.3	1,855.1
Kazakhstan†	n.a.	350.0
Peru	318.0	399.1
Poland	369.6	381.7
Russia†	n.a.	375.0
USSR (former)‡	900.0	—
USA§	1,587.7	1,631.1

* Data from *World Metal Statistics*.
† Estimate by US Bureau of Mines.
‡ Estimates by Metallgesellschaft AG (Frankfurt am Main, Germany).
§ Copper content calculated as recoverable.

South Africa is the continent's other main producer, although in the 1980s copper output began to be affected by declining grades of ore, leading to mine closures and a reduction in the level of operations to about 75% of capacity. Although as yet a minor producer, Namibia derived more than 10% of its total export revenue from copper in the late 1980s. Mining operations there are conducted by a South African-owned company, the Tsumeb Corporation Ltd (TCL), which controls four mines. The mine at Tsumeb itself is expected to close in 1995, when the TCL copper smelter will need replacement ore. However, in 1992 another South African company announced plans to develop a new copper mine in Namibia, which was to ensure that production levels would be maintained at the Tsumeb smelter complex after 1995. In Botswana copper and nickel are mined at Selebi-Phikwe, and high-grade copper ore deposits have also been identified in the Ghanzi area. The exploitation of low-grade deposits at Akjoujt, in Mauritania, ceased in 1978, but a subsequent investment programme, initiated by Arab interests, was expected to reactivate operations in the early 1990s, with the eventual production of gold, as a by-product. Uganda possesses a copper ore reserve base estimated to be in the range of 4m.–5m. tons, although the mines, at Kilembe, have remained closed since 1980.

The major copper-importing countries are the countries of the European Union, Japan and the USA. At the close of the 1980s, demand for copper was not being satisfied in full by current production levels, which were being affected by industrial and political unrest in some of the non-African producing countries, notably Chile, with the consequence that levels of copper stocks were declining. Production surpluses, reflecting lower levels of industrial activity in the main importing countries, began to appear in the early 1990s.

There is no international agreement between producers and consumers governing the stabilization of supplies and prices, and most of the world's supply of primary and secondary copper is traded on the London Metal Exchange or the New York Commodity Exchange.

Export Price Index for Copper (base: 1980 = 100)

	Average	Highest month(s)	Lowest month(s)
1985	64		
1990	123		
1991	107	113 (April)	101 (June, Dec.)
1992	104	115 (July, Aug.)	98 (Jan.)
1993	87	103 (Jan.)	74 (Nov.)

On the London Metal Exchange (LME) the price of Grade 'A' copper (minimum purity 99.95%) per metric ton declined from £1,563.5 (US $2,219) in February 1993 to £1,108.5 (US $1,746) in May. From 1 July 1993 the LME replaced sterling by US dollars as the basis for pricing its copper contract. In September the London copper quotation increased to $2,011.5 (£1,304) per ton, but in October, with LME stocks of copper at a 15-year 'high', the price slumped to $1,596 (£1,079), its lowest level, in terms of US currency, for about six years. The copper price subsequently revived, with the LME quotation exceeding $1,800 per ton by the end of the year. The market remained buoyant in January 1994, although, during that month, copper stocks in LME warehouses reached 617,800 tons, their highest level since February 1978. However, stocks were quickly reduced, and the London copper price moved above $2,000 per ton in May 1994. It continued to rise, reaching $2,533.5 (£1,635) per ton in July. Concurrently, LME stocks of the metal declined to less than 340,000 tons.

The Intergovernmental Council of Copper Exporting Countries (CIPEC), comprising Zaire, Zambia, Chile and Peru (controlling about 70% of world copper exports but less than 50% of world output), operated as a policy co-ordinating body during 1967–92. In June 1992 the International Copper Study Group (ICSG), initially comprising 18 producing and importing countries accounting for about 61% of world trade in copper, was formed to compile and publish statistical information. The ICSG does not participate in trade or exercise any form of intervention in the market.

Cotton *(Gossypium)*

This is the name given to the hairs which grow on the epidermis of the seed of the plant genus *Gossypium*. The initial development of the cotton fibres takes place within a closed pod, called a boll, which, after a period of growth lasting about 50 days (depending upon climatic conditions), opens to reveal the familiar white tufts of cotton hair. After the seed cotton has been picked, the cotton fibre, or lint, has to be separated from the seeds by means of a mechanical process, known as ginning. Depending upon the variety and growing conditions, it takes about 3 metric tons of seed cotton to produce one ton of raw cotton fibre. After ginning, a fuzz of very short cotton hairs remains on the seed. These are called linters and may be removed and used in the manufacture of paper, cellulose-based chemicals, explosives, etc.

About one-half of the cotton produced in the world is used in the manufacture of clothing, about one-third is used for household textiles, and the remainder for numerous

Production of Cotton Lint ('000 metric tons, excluding linters)

	1991	1992
World total	20,678*	18,052*
Africa	1,383*	1,263*
Leading African producers		
Benin	75	69
Burkina Faso	77†	71†
Cameroon	47†	45†
Chad	68	50
Côte d'Ivoire	115	88
Egypt	291	357
Mali	115	114
Nigeria	60†	63†
South Africa	49	20
Sudan	92†	87†
Tanzania	85†	73
Zimbabwe	72	21†
Leading non-African producers		
Brazil	675†	651†
China, People's Repub.	5,675	4,508
India	1,672	1,982
Pakistan	2,181	1,540
Turkey	537	574
USSR (former)	2,427	2,007†
USA	3,835	3,531

* FAO estimate.
† Unofficial figure.

industrial products (tarpaulins, rubber reinforcement, abrasive backings, filters, high-quality papers, etc.).

The official cotton 'season' (for trade purposes) runs from 1 August to 31 July of the following year. Quantities are measured in both metric tons and bales; for statistical purposes, one bale of cotton is 226.8 kg (500 lb) gross or 217.7 kg (480 lb) net.

The price of a particular type of cotton depends upon its availability relative to demand and upon characteristics related to yarn quality and suitability for processing. These include fibre length, fineness, cleanliness, strength and colour. The most important of these is length. Generally speaking, the length of the fibre determines the quality of the yarn produced from it, with the longer fibres being preferred for the finer, stronger and more expensive yarns. Five lengths are recognized: short staple (less than 21 mm); medium staple (21–25 mm); medium-long staple (26–28 mm); long staple (28–33 mm); and extra-long staple (over 34 mm).

Cotton is the world's leading textile fibre. However, over the period 1960–75, as the use of synthetics grew, cotton's share in the world's total consumption of fibre declined from 68% to about 50%, despite an overall increase in cotton consumption of about 2% each year. Cotton's share later stabilized, and since the mid-1970s it has remained close to 50% of the world market. In certain areas, notably the major consumer markets of Western Europe and Japan, cotton has significantly improved its competitive position in recent years.

The area devoted to cotton cultivation has been 31m. – 35m. ha since the 1950s, accounting for about 4% of world cropped area. During the mid-1980s, however, world cotton consumption failed to keep pace with the growth in production, and the resultant surpluses led to a fall in prices, which had serious consequences for the many African countries that rely on cotton sales for a major portion of their export earnings. The leading exporters are the USA, successor states of the former USSR (of which Uzbekistan is the major cotton-producing area) and Pakistan, while the major cotton-importing countries are Russia, Japan, Indonesia, the Republic of Korea, Thailand, Italy, Taiwan, Brazil, Turkey and Germany. China, although one of the largest producing countries, is also a net importer of cotton.

Cotton is a major source of income and employment for many developing countries, both as a primary product and, increasingly, through sales of yarn, fabrics and finished goods. Cotton is the principal commercial crop, in terms of foreign exchange earnings, in Benin, Burkina Faso, Chad, Egypt, Mali, Mozambique, Sudan and Togo, and is second in importance in Angola, the Central African Republic, Senegal, Tanzania, Uganda and Zimbabwe. Other African countries in which cotton is a significant source of foreign exchange, compared with other agricultural commodities, include Cameroon, Côte d'Ivoire, The Gambia, Madagascar, Malawi, Swaziland and Zambia. The cultivation of cotton is also of some economic importance in Nigeria and Uganda.

For many years Sudan was the largest cotton producer in Africa south of the Sahara. The industry has, however, been beset by problems since the 1980s, not only on account of the surplus of cotton supplies on the world market, but also as a result of domestic difficulties resulting from climatic factors, an inflexible, government-dictated marketing policy and crop infestation by white-fly. Although cotton production, classification and marketing were reorganized in the late 1980s, and in 1990 special foreign exchange incentives were offered to producers, levels of output had yet to recover in the early 1990s.

International prices for cotton lint are subject to considerable fluctuation on world markets, and reflect, among other factors, levels of surplus stocks. In reaction to sharp declines in world cotton output during the early 1990s (following plant disease and pest infestation in China and Pakistan), in 1993/94 world cotton prices exceeded the averages of recent years. Although co-operation in cotton affairs has a long history, there have been no international agreements governing the cotton trade. Proposals in recent years to link producers and consumers in price stabilization arrangements have been opposed by the USA (the world's largest cotton exporter), and by Japan and the EU. The International Cotton Advisory Committee (ICAC), an intergovernmental body, established in 1939, with its headquarters in Washington, DC, publishes statistical and economic information and provides a forum for consultation and discussion among its 46 members.

Export Price Index for Cotton Lint (base: 1980 = 100)

	Average	Highest month(s)	Lowest month(s)
1985	75		
1990	93		
1991	88	103 (May)	70 (Dec.)
1992	68	75 (July)	64 (Oct.)
1993	65	70 (March, April)	59 (Oct.)

The index recovered to 73 in January 1994, and to 77 in February. The average import price of Memphis cotton lint from the USA at the port of Liverpool, in the United Kingdom, declined from US$1,792 per metric ton in 1991 to $1,378 per ton in 1992. The monthly average slumped from $2,189 per ton in May 1991 to $1,318 in March 1992. It recovered to $1,572 per ton in July 1992, but retreated to $1,281 in October. The average price of US cotton rose to $1,464 per ton in March and April 1993, but was reduced to $1,257 in September.

Diamonds

The primary source of diamonds is a rock known as kimberlite, occurring in volcanic pipes which may vary in area from a few to more than 100 ha and volcanic fissures which are considerably smaller. Among the indicator minerals for kimberlite are chrome diopside, pyrope garnet, ilmenite and zircon. Few kimberlites contain diamonds and, in ore which does, the ratio of diamond to waste is about one part per 20m. There are four methods of diamond mining, of which open-cast mining is the commonest; diamonds are recovered also by underground, alluvial and offshore mining. The diamond is separated from its ore by careful crushing and gravity concentration which maximizes the diamond's high specific gravity in a process called dense media separation. Stones are of two categories: gem qualities (used for jewellery), which are superior in terms of colour or quality; and industrial quality, about one-half of the total by weight, which are used for high-precision machining or crushed into an abrasive powder called boart.

The size of diamonds and other precious stones is measured in carats. One metric carat is equal to 0.2 gram, so one ounce avoirdupois equals 141.75 carats.

Africa is the major producing region for natural diamonds, although Australia joined the ranks of the major producers in 1983, and the Argyle diamond mine, in Western Australia, is the world's largest producing mine and main source of industrial diamonds. Output is predominantly of industrial grade diamonds, with some lower-quality gem diamonds and a few pink diamonds. In 1993 Australian diamond output represented more than 40% of world production by volume.

Diamonds are Botswana's principal source of export earnings, normally accounting for about 80% of export receipts and 30%–35% of government revenues. Diamond production began in 1971, initially at the Orapa mine, which covers an area of 113 ha and is the world's second largest, after the Mwadui field in Tanzania. In 1977 extraction began from a nearby mine at Letlhakane, and in 1982 a major new mine at Jwaneng entered production. All current diamond mining operations are conducted by the Debswana Diamond Co (Pty), which is owned equally by the Botswana government and De Beers.

About 90% of Zaire's production, from Eastern Kasai, is industrial diamonds, of which Zaire was the world's principal producer until 1986, when it was overtaken by the Argyle mine in Australia. In 1993 Zaire's combined output of industrial and gem diamonds exceeded that of Botswana; its official production figures, moreover, exclude diamonds illicitly mined and marketed (some of which are smuggled out of the country and eventually acquired by dealers in Antwerp, Belgium).

About 98% of Namibian diamonds are of gem quality, although recovery costs are high. Until 1993, when the government of Namibia granted marine exploration concessions to a new privately-financed venture, the Namibian Minerals Corpn (NAMCO), Consolidated Diamond Mining (CDM), a subsidiary of the De Beers group, held exclusive rights to diamond exploration and mining in Namibia. Following independence in March 1990, the government was expected to acquire a substantial minority shareholding in CDM. In 1990 diamond mining commenced at Auchas, and a second mine, at Elizabeth Bay, began in 1991. Operations at the Oranjemund open-cast mine are not expected to remain economic after the year 2000, and the exploitation of an 'offshore' diamond field, extending 300 m from the coast, is proceeding. In 1993 'offshore' recoveries of gem-quality stones accounted for more than 27.5% of Namibia's diamond output.

Production of Uncut Diamonds
(gem and industrial stones, million metric carats)

	1992	1993
Leading African producers		
Angola	2.7	1.0
Botswana	15.9	14.7
Central African Repub.	0.4	0.4
Ghana	0.5	0.7
Guinea	0.1	0.4
Namibia	1.6	1.1
Sierra Leone	0.6	0.4
South Africa	10.0	9.8
Zaire	15.0	17.0
Producers in other areas		
Australia	40.0	41.0
South America	2.6	2.9
USSR (former)	11.3	11.5
Other	0.4	0.5
World total	101.0	100.9

Source: Central Selling Organisation.

Angola's diamond production exceeded 2m. carats in 1973 but subsequently fell sharply, as a result of the civil war. Annual production recovered in the late 1980s to about 1m.–1.2m. carats, about 90% of which were of gem quality, and which were worth approximately US $180m. annually. However, official exports of Angolan diamonds declined from 1,245,000 carats in 1990 to 955,000 carats in 1991. At the end of 1992 official diamond production in Angola was again interrupted by civil disorder, following a controversial election. There is considerable potential for diamond production in Angola: the country is known to possess large reserves of diamondiferous deposits, which occur in both kimberlite and alluvial formations. In 1990 the Empresa Nacional de Diamantes de Angola (ENDIAMA, the state-controlled diamond enterprise) resumed its marketing association with the De Beers group (see below), from which it had withdrawn in 1985. Under the new arrangements (covering a five-year period from 1991), ENDIAMA was to market the entire production from Cuango, accounting for about 80% of Angola's diamond output, through the London-based Central Selling Organisation (see below). As part of the agreement, De Beers was to assist ENDIAMA with prospecting and mining operations. However, illicit prospecting and trading continued in Angola, and an estimated $500m.-worth of diamonds were smuggled out of the country in 1992.

The Mwadui diamond pipe in Tanzania is the world's largest, covering an area of 146 ha. Tanzania's diamond output was 838,000 carats in 1971, but production later declined, owing to deterioration in diamond grades, technical engineering problems and difficulties in maintaining the mines. By the late 1980s, annual production had fallen to about 150,000 carats. New prospecting agreements were signed in 1993 by the Tanzania government and the De Beers operating subsidiary managing the Mwadui mine, and also with Canadian interests, which obtained mining leases and exploration licences covering almost 9,000 sq km.

South African diamond production, which is conducted at five mine locations, has been in decline since 1987. A sixth mine, Venetia (discovered in 1980 and opened in 1992), is expected by the mid-1990s to become South Africa's largest producing diamond mine. Small-scale marine mining is conducted off the west coast by independent operators.

In Sierra Leone the diamond industry is faced by the dual problems of inefficient management and widespread illicit digging and smuggling. Legal exports of diamonds have declined steadily since 1970, and in 1988 were estimated at only 32,000 carats, compared with 2m. carats in 1970. In neighbouring Liberia, diamond exports have recently averaged about 200,000 carats per year, but much of this total has been attributed to stones smuggled from adjoining countries and attracted to Liberia by its currency link with the US dollar. The civil war that began in late 1989 has effectively halted the country's diamond trade, and has also affected production in neighbouring Sierra Leone. In the Central African Republic diamonds are found in alluvial deposits, mainly in the west of the country. Here, too, there is widespread evasion of export duties, with as much as 60% of total diamond production being smuggled out of the country. In Côte d'Ivoire small-scale mining is practised by private companies. Figures for the country's diamond production range from 20,000 carats per year (legal exports) to 250,000 carats annually (including illicit production). The diamond sector in Ghana, which has been in decline since the 1960s, was estimated in 1993 still to contain reserves sufficient for 15 years, and the exploitation of these alluvial deposits was to be placed under De Beers' management. Among the smaller-scale African producers of diamonds are Lesotho and Swaziland. In 1994 Zimbabwe began to emerge as a potentially significant regional producer; exploration applications covering about one-third of the country's land area were pending, and a processing plant, commissioned in January, had by March produced approximately 70,000 carats from the country's first operating mine, River Ranch, near Beitbridge.

Considerable exploration interest has been focused since 1992 on the Northwest Territories of Canada, where De Beers, through its Canadian subsidiary Monopros, leads a consortium of mining enterprises conducting geological investigations in kimberlite pipes over a 25,900 sq km (10,000 sq mile) claim area. In December 1992 it was reported that the world's largest diamond-bearing rock formation had been identified in Arkansas, USA.

In 1930 the major diamond producers formed The Diamond Corporation to act as the single channel through which most of the world's rough diamond production would be sold. To stabilize the market, the corporation puts surplus output into reserve, to be sold at a time when conditions are favourable. The corporation is now one of a group of companies, centred in London, known as the Central Selling Organisation (CSO). The CSO contracts to sell on behalf of producers and handles about 80% of world production. Almost all Africa's diamonds, although not those of Ghana and Guinea, are marketed through the CSO, which has about 160 direct clients. The CSO markets the rough diamond production of De Beers Consolidated Mines Ltd. The De Beers group had an output of 25.7m. carats in 1991 and 26.6m. carats in 1992. A reorganization of De Beers interests, undertaken in 1990, placed the CSO, together with the group's diamond stocks and other non-South African based interests, under the control of a new Swiss-domiciled corporation, De Beers Centenary AG.

In 1990 De Beers Centenary entered into an arrangement with Glavalmazzoloto (the diamond monopoly operated by the former USSR), under which 95% of rough diamonds destined for export were to be purchased and marketed by the CSO. This agreement, which operates until mid-1995, has been continued by the successor Russian diamond corporation, Rosalmazzoloto. In 1992 De Beers negotiated an agreement with the Russian Autonomous Republic of Sakha (Yakutia), which occupies a large part of Siberia and accounts for virtually all Russian diamond output, to market the proportion of its diamond production (currently 20%) not procured by the central diamond authority. In January

1993 the functions of this authority were transferred to an independent body, Diamonds of Russia-Sakha. It was announced in March that plans were being prepared for the creation of an exchange in Moscow for the internal marketing of rough diamonds. In December 1993 the Russian government denied allegations by De Beers that it was selling uncut diamonds on the Antwerp market (see below) in violation of the marketing agreement.

Rough diamonds, of which there are currently more than 5,000 categories, are sold by the CSO in mixed packages 10 times each year at regular sales, known as 'sights', in London, Johannesburg and Lucerne, Switzerland. Gems account for about 20% of total sales by weight, but, it is estimated, over 90% by value. After being sold by the CSO, gem diamonds are sent to be cut and polished in preparation for jewellery manufacture. The leading cutting centres are in Antwerp, Bombay, New York and Tel Aviv, which in 1993 opened an exchange for 'raw', or uncut, diamonds, with the intention of lessening the dependence of Israeli cutters on allocations from the CSO and purchases from the small, independent diamond exchange in Antwerp. The principal markets for diamond jewellery are the USA and Japan (which account for about 60% of world consumption).

The CSO provides a guaranteed market to producers and has successfully followed a policy of stockpiling diamonds during times of recession in order to stabilize prices (which are never reduced). At the end of 1993 the value of the stockpile stood at about US$4,120m., an increase of $350m. in 12 months.

Diamond prices (quoted in US dollars) were increased by 15.5% in March 1989, by 5.5% in March 1990 and by 1.5% in February 1993 (mainly in respect of stones of 0.75 carat and above). As there are so many varieties of diamond, the CSO price increases represent averages only. There are wide discrepancies in price, depending on such factors as rarity, colour and quality. In 1991 the CSO achieved a sales turnover of US$3,927m. This declined to $3,417m. in 1992, representing a six-year 'low'. Sales volume recovered sharply, however, in 1993, totalling $4,366m., an increase of 27.8%. This recovery was, in part, attributable to reductions in producers' quotas during 1993. Sales continued to advance during the first six months of 1994, representing, at about $2.580m., a rise of 42% on the total for the corresponding period in 1993.

Synthetic diamonds for industrial use have been produced since the mid-1950s by a number of companies, including De Beers, using a method which simulates the intense heat present in the geological formation of diamonds. These stones, which are always very small, account for the major proportion of all abrasive diamonds, and are used for a wide variety of industrial applications.

Gold

Gold minerals are commonly found in quartz and may occur in alluvial deposits, or in rich thin underground veins. In South Africa gold occurs in sheets of low-grade ore (reefs) which may be at great depths below ground level. Gold is associated with silver, which is its commonest by-product. Uranium oxide is another valuable by-product, particularly in the case of South Africa. Depending upon its associations, gold is separated by cyaniding, or concentrated and smelted.

Gold, silver and platinum are customarily measured in troy weight. A troy pound (now obsolete) contains 12 ounces, each of 480 grains. One troy oz is equal to 31.1 grams (1 kg = 32.15 troy oz), compared with the avoirdupois oz of 28.3 grams.

In modern times the principal function of gold has been as bullion in reserve for bank notes issued. Since the early 1970s, however, the USA has actively sought to 'demonetize' gold and so make it simply another commodity. This view was later adopted by the IMF, which has attempted to end the position that gold occupied for many years in the international monetary system (see below).

Gold was discovered near Johannesburg, South Africa, in 1884, and its exploitation formed the basis of the country's subsequent economic prosperity. For many years, South Africa has been the world's leading gold producer, accounting in 1993 for 32.8% of world gold output outside the former Eastern bloc and for more than 85% of that mined in Africa. Since the mid-1980s, however, the South African gold industry has been adversely affected by the rising costs of extracting generally declining grades of ore from ageing and increasingly marginal (low-return) mines. Additionally, the level of world gold prices has not been sufficiently high to stimulate the active exploration and development of new mines. The share of gold in South Africa's export revenue has accordingly declined in recent years, and in 1989, for the first time, the commercial profitability of South African gold production was exceeded by profits from mining activities other than gold.

The relative decline of South Africa's position in world gold markets has been accompanied by the prospect of substantial increases in output as new capacity comes into production in Australia, Brazil, Canada, Indonesia, Papua New Guinea and the USA. Following the dissolution of the USSR, the successor republics, notably Russia (which accounted for about two-thirds of Soviet output) and Uzbekistan (which contains what is reputedly the world's largest open-cast gold-mine), were expected to assume a significant role in international gold trading during the 1990s. Despite adverse short-term factors, (which have included shortages of mining equipment, transport difficulties and sharp rises in the cost of electric power), proposals outlined by the Russian government in 1993 to abolish the state monopoly on gold purchases, and other measures to liberalize the market and attract foreign investment, were likely to have a significant future impact on international markets. Foreign participation in the development of gold deposits in Uzbekistan, Kazakhstan and Kyrgyzstan was under way in 1994. The People's Republic of China, with about 500 operating gold-mines, is increasing its output of gold.

Ghana, formerly a significant African producer of gold, has, since 1990, been reversing a long period of decline. Output doubled during 1990-92, and increased by almost 25% in 1993 as a result of the continuing rehabilitation of the country's gold industry. Ashanti Goldfields, which operates one of the world's largest gold-mines (with 18m. oz of proven reserves), was reopened to private-sector investment in early 1994. Its output has been targeted to reach 1m. oz annually by 1996. Gold was overtaken in 1980 by tobacco as Zimbabwe's major source of foreign exchange; other minor African producers include Ethiopia, Burkina Faso, Guinea, Sudan, Tanzania, Zaire, Côte d'Ivoire and Namibia. Gold production in Mali is expected to increase substantially after 1997, when the exploitation of a deposit under development at Sadiola, with a potential capacity of 11 tons per year, is due to begin.

The supply of gold to the non-communist world, after allowing for central bank transactions and not including scrap, declined from 2,508 metric tons in 1989 to 2,383 tons in 1990, representing the first net decline in gold supplies to Western markets since 1983. The reduction reflected both an increase in the use of gold scrap and a low level of Western mine production. In 1991, when an estimated 2,413 tons of gold entered the market, the rate of increase in Western supplies of gold was influenced by a sharp fall, to 230 tons from 388 tons in 1990, in gold sales by the Eastern bloc, which has formed a significant component of international gold trading. In 1992, when the supply of gold to Western countries advanced to 2,820 tons, a further fall in Eastern bloc sales (to only 65 tons), was more than offset by an increase in net official sales (from 28 tons in 1991 to 626 tons) and an expansion in mine production.

Total world demand for gold, including the former USSR and China, rose from 3,114 tons in 1991 to 3,570 tons in 1992. Demand in 1993 was 3,538 tons, reflecting a decline in requirements for jewellery fabrication, which accounted for 75.4% (2,693 tons) in 1992 and 70.7% (2,501 tons) in 1993. The remainder of industrial demand was absorbed mainly by medals, dentistry and the electronics industry. Of total gold fabrication in 1993 (2,987 tons), the principal consuming countries were Italy (15.1%), India (9.5%), the USA (7.8%) and Japan (7.3%).

Production of Gold Ore (metric tons, gold content)

	1992	1993
World total*	2,237.3	2,281.1
Africa	712.0	728.2
Leading African producers		
Ghana	33.3	41.4
South Africa	614.1	619.5
Tanzania	5.0	7.0
Zaire	7.0	6.7
Zimbabwe	20.3	21.4
Leading non-African producers		
Australia	243.5	247.2
Brazil	76.5	75.7
Canada	160.4	150.9
Chile	39.3	39.5
China, People's Repub.*	118.0	127.0
Colombia	29.9	26.4
Indonesia	40.4	46.3
Korea, Dem. People's Repub.*	17.0	15.0
Papua New Guinea	71.2	61.8
Peru	18.0	23.5
Philippines	27.2	28.0
USSR (former)*	237.0	244.0
USA	329.1	336.0

* Estimates.

Source: Gold Fields Mineral Services Ltd.

The fabrication of official coins is another important use of gold bullion, although the demand for these coins has declined since the mid-1980s. South African 'krugerrand' coins, containing exactly 1 troy oz of pure (24-carat) gold, were first issued in 1970 and held about 70% of the world market for gold bullion coins until 1985, when international sales virtually ceased, owing to the prohibition of krugerrand imports (during 1986–90) by Japan, the European Community and the USA. A number of other countries, notably Australia, Canada, Austria and the USA entered the gold coin market and subsequently benefited from the krugerrand's decline.

As a portable real asset which is easily convertible into cash, gold is widely esteemed as a store of value. Another distinguishing feature of gold is that new production in any one year is very small in relation to existing stocks. Much of the world's gold is in private bullion stocks, held for investment purposes, or is hoarded as a 'hedge' against inflation. Private investment stocks of gold throughout the world are estimated at 15,000–20,000 tons, the bulk of it held in France and India.

During the 19th century gold was increasingly adopted as a monetary standard, with prices set by governments. In 1919 the Bank of England allowed some South African gold to be traded in London 'at the best price obtainable'. The market was suspended in 1925–31, when sterling returned to a limited form of the gold standard, and again between 1939–54. In 1934 the official price of gold was fixed at US $35 per troy oz, and, by international agreement, all transactions in gold had to take place within narrow margins around that price. In 1960 the official gold price came under pressure from market demand. As a result, an international gold 'pool' was established in 1961 at the initiative of the USA. This 'pool' was originally a consortium of leading central banks with the object of restraining the London price of gold in case of excessive demand. It later widened into an arrangement by which eight central banks agreed that all purchases and sales of gold should be handled by the Bank of England. However, growing private demand for gold continued to exert pressure on the official price and the gold 'pool' was ended in 1968, in favour of a two-tier price system. Central banks continued to operate the official price of $35 per troy ounce, but private markets were permitted to deal freely in gold. However, the free market price did not rise significantly above the official price.

In August 1971 the US government announced that it would cease dealing freely in gold to maintain exchange rates for the dollar within previously agreed margins. This 'floating' of the dollar against other major currencies continued until December, when it was agreed to raise the official gold price to $38 per oz. Gold prices on the free market rose to $70 per oz in August 1972. In February 1973 the US dollar was devalued by a further 10%, the official gold price rising to $42.22 per oz. Thereafter the free market price rose even higher, reaching $127 per oz in June 1973. In November it was announced that the two-tier system would be terminated, and from 1974 governments were permitted to value their official gold stocks at market prices.

In 1969 the IMF introduced a new unit for international monetary dealings, the special drawing right (SDR), with a value of US $1.00, and the first allocation of SDRs was made on 1 January 1971. The SDR was linked to gold at an exchange rate of SDR 35 per troy oz. When the US dollar was devalued in December 1971 the SDR retained its gold value and a new parity with the US dollar was established. A further adjustment was made following the second dollar devaluation, in February 1973, and in July 1974 the direct link between the SDR and the US dollar was ended and the SDR was valued in terms of a weighted 'basket' of national currencies. At the same time the official gold price of SDR 35 per troy oz was retained as the IMF's basis for valuing official reserves. The SDR's average value in 1993 was $1.3963. At 30 June 1994 the exchange rate was SDR 1 = $1.4484.

In 1976 the membership of the IMF agreed on proposals for far-reaching changes in the international monetary system. These reforms, which were implemented on a gradual basis during 1977–81, included a reduction in the role of gold in the international system and the abolition of the official price of gold. (For detailed information on these arrangements, see *Africa South of the Sahara 1991*). A principal objective of the IMF plan was achieved in April 1978, when central banks were able to buy and sell gold at market prices. The physical quantity of reserve gold held by the IMF and member countries' central banks as national reserves has subsequently fallen. The USA still maintains the largest national stock of gold, although the volume of its reserves has been substantially reduced in recent years. At the end of 1949 US gold reserves were 701.8m. oz, but since the beginning of the 1980s, the level has been in the range of 261.7m.–264.6m. oz. At the end of 1993 the total gold reserves held by members of the IMF, excluding countries not reporting (principally the successor states of the USSR), amounted to 911.6 m. oz, of which the USA had 261.8 m. oz (28.7%).

The unit of dealing in international gold markets is the 'good delivery' gold bar, weighing about 400 oz (12.5 kg). The principal centres for gold trading are London, Hong Kong and Zürich, Switzerland. The dominant markets for gold 'futures' (buying and selling for future delivery) are the Commodity Exchange in New York (COMEX) and the Tokyo Commodity Exchange (Tocom).

Gold Prices on the London Bullion Market
(afternoon 'fixes', US $ per troy oz)

	Average	Highest month(s)	Lowest month(s)
1980	612.7		
1985	317.2		
1990	383.6		
1991	362.3	403.0 (16 Jan.)	344.3 (13 Sept.)
1992	344.0	359.6 (28 July)	330.4 (10 Nov.)
1993	359.8	405.6 (2 Aug.)	326.1 (10 March)

A small group of dealers meet twice on each working day (morning and afternoon) to 'fix' the price of gold in the London Bullion Market, and the table above is based on the second of these daily 'fixes'. During any trading day, however, prices may fluctuate above or below these levels. In each of the five years 1988–92 the London price of gold bullion was lower at the year's end than at the beginning. In March 1993 the price fell to US $326.1 (equivalent to £227.6 sterling) per troy oz, its lowest level, in terms of US currency, since January 1986. However, from April 1993 there was a strong recovery in the bullion market, owing partly to speculative activity, and in late July and early

August the London price exceeded $400 per oz. The gold price declined to $344 (£222) per oz in September, but ended the year at $390.75 (£264.1). The advance continued in January 1994, with the London price of gold reaching $396.5 (£266.8) per oz. In late February and early March the price eased to around $375 per oz, but in late March it moved above $390. Another decline ensued, with the gold price falling in April to less than $370 per oz, although in June the metal was traded at more than $390 again. The London quotation was reduced to $378 per oz in August.

Groundnut (Peanut, Monkey Nut, Earth Nut) *(Arachis hypogaea)*

This is not a true nut, although the underground pod, which contains the kernels, forms a more or less dry shell at maturity. The plant is a low-growing annual herb introduced from South America, and resembles the indigenous African Bambarra groundnut, which it now outnumbers.

Each groundnut pod contains between two and four kernels, enclosed in a reddish skin. The kernels are highly nutritious because of their high content both of protein (about 30%) and oil (40%–50%). In tropical countries the crop is grown partly for domestic consumption and partly for export. Whole nuts of selected large dessert types, with the skin removed, are eaten raw or roasted. Peanut butter is made by removing the skin and germ and grinding the roasted nuts. The most important commercial use of groundnuts is the extraction of oil. Groundnut oil is used as a cooking and salad oil, as an ingredient in margarine, and, in the case of lower-quality oil, in soap manufacture. The oil is faced with strong competition from soybean, cottonseed and sunflower oils — all produced in the USA. In the late 1980s groundnut oil was the fifth most important of soft edible oils in terms of production, although its position in terms of exports was ninth, accounting for only 1.5% of total world exports of food oils.

Production of Groundnuts (in shell; '000 metric tons)

	1991	1992
World total	23,421*	24,172*
Africa	4,484*	4,432*
Leading African producers		
Benin	74	74
Burkina Faso	99	110*
Cameroon	100†	100†
Central African Repub.	60	43†
Chad	97	147
Côte d'Ivoire	135	140
Ethiopia	53*	54*
The Gambia	84	55
Ghana	67†	100†
Guinea	78	104
Malawi	57†	23†
Mali	143†	135†
Mozambique	115*	80*
Niger	46	57
Nigeria	1,219	1,214†
Senegal	724	578
South Africa	110	114†
Sudan	179†	315
Tanzania	70*	65*
Uganda	144	147
Zaire	435	435*
Zimbabwe	107	34
Leading non-African producers		
Argentina	444	364†
China, People's Repub.	6,303	5,953
India	7,065	8,600†
Indonesia	1,056†	1,037†
Myanmar	472	466
USA	2,235	1,943
Viet Nam	235	227

* FAO estimate. † Unofficial figure.

An oilcake, used in animal feeding, is manufactured from the groundnut residue left after oil extraction. However, trade in this groundnut meal is limited by health laws in some countries, as groundnuts can be contaminated by a mould which generates toxic and carcinogenic metabolites, the most common and most dangerous of which is aflatoxin B_1. The European Community (now the European Union) has banned imports of oilcake and meal for use as animal feed which contain more than 0.03 mg of aflatoxin per kg. The meal can be treated with ammonia, which both eliminates the aflatoxin and enriches the cake. Groundnut shells, which are usually incinerated or simply discarded as waste, are suitable for conversion into a low-cost organic fertilizer, and such production has been undertaken since the early 1970s. Although three times as much groundnut-based fertilizer per ha is required, the chemical alternatives are 20 times as expensive.

About 80% of the world's groundnut output comes from developing countries. Groundnuts are the most important of Africa's oil seeds and form the chief export crop of The Gambia and Senegal, which in the late 1980s was the world's leading groundnut exporter. Except when affected by drought, South Africa and Sudan are also important exporters. Niger and Mali, formerly significant exporters, have ceased to feature in the international groundnut trade, largely as a consequence of the Sahel drought. Groundnut harvests in southern Africa, notably in Mozambique, South Africa and Zimbabwe, were also affected by drought during the second half of the 1980s. African groundnut exports have been declining since the late 1970s, and most African countries grow the nut as a subsistence, particularly storage, crop. Senegal's groundnut production suffered from persistent drought, and also from marketing problems, in the early 1980s; however, subsequent output was substantially aided by government incentives to producers. These measures included the establishment of a groundnut price guarantee fund, which also had the unwelcome effect of attracting smuggled groundnut supplies from the neighbouring state of The Gambia.

Export Price Index for Groundnuts (base: 1980 = 100)

	Average	Highest month(s)	Lowest month(s)
1985	70		
1990	102		
1991	99	101 (Feb.)	96 (Nov., Dec.)
1992	97	98 (Dec.)	95 (March)
1993	97	98 (Jan., Feb., May–Aug.)	96 (March, Oct.)

Export Price Index for Groundnut Oil (base: 1980 = 100)

	Average	Highest month(s)	Lowest month(s)
1985	107		
1990	113		
1991	105	121 (Feb.)	72 (Dec.)
1992	72	78 (June)	66 (Sept., Oct.)
1993	87	109 (Dec.)	71 (March)

The index of export prices for groundnut oil advanced to 117 in January 1994, and to 119 in February. In recent years, as the tables above make clear, these prices have fluctuated much more than those for groundnuts. The average import price of groundnut oil at the port of Rotterdam, in the Netherlands, declined from US $893 per metric ton in 1991 to $609 per ton in 1992. On a monthly basis, the average price of groundnut oil per ton was reduced from $1,031 in February 1991 to $561 in September 1992, although it recovered to $858 in August 1993.

The African Groundnut Council, founded in 1964 with headquarters in Lagos, advises its member producing countries (The Gambia, Mali, Niger, Nigeria, Senegal, Sudan) on marketing policies and, for this purpose, has a sales promotion office in Geneva, Switzerland. Western Europe, particularly France, is the largest market for African groundnuts. The market for edible groundnuts is particularly sensitive to the level of production in the USA, which provides about one-half of world import requirements.

Iron Ore

The chief economic iron-ore minerals are magnetite and haematite. Most iron ore is processed after mining to improve its chemical and physical characteristics and is often agglomerated by pelletizing or sintering. The transformation of the ore into pig-iron is achieved through reduction by coke in blast furnaces; the proportion of ore to pig-iron yielded is usually about 1.5 or 1.6:1. Pig-iron is used to make cast iron and wrought iron products, but most of it is converted into steel by removing most of the carbon content. Particular grades of steel (e.g. stainless) are made by the addition of ferro-alloys such as chromium, nickel and manganese.

Iron is, after aluminium, the second most abundant metallic element in the earth's crust, and its ore volume production is far greater than that of any other metal. Some ores contain 70% iron, while a grade of only 25% is commercially exploitable in certain areas. As the basic feedstock for the production of steel, iron ore is a major raw material in the world economy and in international trade. Because mining the ore usually involves substantial long-term investment, about 60% of trade is conducted under long-term contracts, and the mine investments are financed with some financial participation from consumers.

Iron ore is widely distributed throughout Africa, with several countries having substantial reserves of high-grade deposits (60%–68% iron). One of the world's largest unexploited iron ore deposits (an estimated 850m. metric tons, with a metal content of 64.5%) has been located in north-east Gabon, and there are future prospects for the exploitation of ore reserves in Côte d'Ivoire and Senegal. Identified reserves in Guinea include some 350m. tons of iron ore (66.7% iron) at Mt Nimba, near the border with Liberia. The two governments have developed a joint scheme to exploit the deposits for transhipment through Liberia. Ore shipments by rail through Liberia were intended to commence in 1990, but this intention has been thwarted by the civil conflict which has caused widespread dislocation of the Liberian economy. The project, which was still pending in 1994, envisaged an annual mine output of 12m. tons. The exploitation of iron ore deposits, estimated at 200m. tons, has been proceeding since 1986 in Nigeria. In 1980 Zambia discovered a deposit estimated at 20m. tons of ore (50% iron) in the west of the country, which it plans to exploit. Tanzania has sought external financing for the exploitation of ore reserves at Liganga as part of a proposed coal and steel complex, but implementation of the scheme has been delayed by cost considerations.

The continent's leading producer of iron ore is South Africa. The industry is dominated by the Iron and Steel Corporation of South Africa (ISCOR), which operates 10 ore mines and four steel mills. Formerly state-owned, ISCOR was transferred to private-sector control in 1989. South African iron ore exports, particularly to Japan, have been an important source of foreign revenue since the late 1980s, despite declining world demand for steel. Among the African producers, the country most dependent on the mineral as a source of foreign exchange is Mauritania, which has large deposits of high-grade ore (65%) in the Kédia region, near Zouérate. The Guelbs region, about 40 km to the north of Kédia, contains reserves of workable ores, estimated at 5,000m.–6,000m. tons. Although the metal content of Guelbs' ore, at 37%, is lower than at Kédia, enrichment processes are expected to produce an iron content of 67%, making it the richest in Mauritania. The first phase of the project, an enrichment plant, was opened in 1984, with a projected production target of 15m. tons per year by the mid-1990s, when the Kédia deposits are expected to be depleted. The second phase, involving a new mine at Oum Arwagen and another ore-enrichment plant, is scheduled to begin in the mid-1990s, with initial output forecast at 6m. tons per year. Preparations have also been proceeding for the exploitation of deposits at M'Haoudat, which are estimated to contain recoverable reserves of 100m. tons, and which, at a proposed production rate of 5.6m. tons annually, were expected to prove more economic, albeit more short-lived, than the Guelbs deposits.

Production of Iron Ore (iron content, '000 metric tons)

	1990	1991
World total	589,836	477,551
Africa	32,490	33,739
Leading African producers		
Algeria	1,589	1,270
Egypt	1,202	1,072
Liberia	2,490	n.a.
Mauritania	7,250	n.a.
South Africa	18,962	18,119
Leading non-African producers		
Australia†	83,281	69,553
Brazil	103,200	103,000
Canada‡	23,724	21,631
China, People's Repub.	86,080	60,000
India	35,564	36,790
Sweden	12,382*	13,046
USSR (former)	133,578	n.a.
USA§	34,942*	35,801
Venezuela	13,034	13,187

* Estimated production.

† Twelve months ending 30 June of year stated.

‡ Shipments.

§ Including the metal content of by-product ore.

In the late 1980s Liberia was the largest exporter of iron ore in Africa, followed by South Africa and Mauritania. It was hoped that the project for the joint exploitation of iron ore deposits in Guinea (see above) would compensate for the expected exhaustion of Liberia's own iron reserves in the late 1990s. Liberia's largest iron ore producer, the Liberian-American-Swedish Minerals Co (LAMCO), which is jointly-controlled by government and private interests, expects to be able to sustain mine production at Yekepa, in Buchanan County, until 2006. In common with other sectors of the economy, LAMCO's mining activities have been severely disrupted since 1990 as a consequence of the Liberian civil war. Iron ore mining in Angola has also been beset by civil conflict, and ceased entirely in 1975–84. At present, output is stockpiled and the resumption of export trade in the ore depends on the eventual rehabilitation of the 520-km rail link between the mines at Cassinga and the coast. At Falémé in eastern Senegal there exist deposits of 330m. tons of high-grade ore (60% iron) and an estimated 115m. tons of lower-grade ore. However, the depressed world iron and steel market has impeded their exploitation. The Marampa mine in Sierra Leone has been inactive since the mid-1980s, although plans exist for the eventual resumption of operations to extract its ore deposits, which have an iron content of 69%.

Since the early 1970s world trade in iron ore has regularly exceeded 200m. metric tons (iron content) per year. In the early 1990s the leading exporting countries were Brazil, Australia, the republics of the former USSR, Canada and India. The principal importers are Japan and the countries of the European Union (formerly the European Community—EC). World iron ore reference prices are decided annually at a series of meetings between producers and purchasers (the steel industry accounts for about 95% of all iron ore consumption). The USA and the republics of the former USSR, although major steel-producing countries, rely on domestic ore production and take little part in the price negotiations. It is generally accepted that, because of its diversity in form and quality, iron ore is ill-suited to price stabilization through an international buffer stock arrangement, although the UN Conference on Trade and Development (UNCTAD) has, for some years, been considering proposals to improve market information by compiling statistics on iron ore production and trade, and to establish a more permanent forum for the discussion of the industry's problems. Efforts by 36 steel-exporting countries, led by the EC and the USA, to negotiate a Multilateral Steel Arrangement (MSA), aimed at the eventual elimination of trade barriers and subsidies, were suspended in 1992.

The index of export prices for iron ore declined to 115 in January 1994, and to 111 in February. The two leading exporters of the mineral in 1990–92 were Brazil and Australia. In 1992 exports of iron ore and concentrates

Export Price Index for Iron Ore (base: 1980 = 100)

	Average	Highest month(s)	Lowest month(s)
1985	84		
1990	124		
1991	129	141 (Feb.)	125 (April, Aug.)
1992	127	132 (Jan.)	122 (June)
1993	122	131 (Jan.)	115 (July)

(excluding agglomerates) by these two countries were valued at about US $20 per metric ton.

The Association of Iron Ore Exporting Countries (known by its French initials as APEF) was established in 1975 to promote close co-operation among members, to safeguard their interests as iron ore exporters, to ensure the orderly growth of international trade in iron ore and to secure 'fair and remunerative' returns from its exploitation, processing and marketing. In 1993 the APEF, with its secretariat in Geneva, had nine members, including Algeria, Liberia, Mauritania and Sierra Leone.

Maize (Indian Corn, Mealies) (*Zea mays*)

Maize is one of the world's three principal cereal crops, with wheat and rice. Originally from America, maize has been dispersed to many parts of the world. The principal varieties are dent maize (which has large, soft, flat grains) and flint maize (which has round, hard grains). Dent maize is the predominant type world-wide but flint maize is widely grown in southern Africa. Maize may be white or yellow (there is little nutritional difference), but the former is preferred for human consumption in Africa. Maize is an annual crop, planted from seed, and matures within three to five months. It requires a warm climate and ample water supplies during the growing season.

Maize is an important foodstuff in regions such as sub-Saharan Africa and the tropical zones of Latin America, where the climate precludes the extensive cultivation of other cereals. It is, however, inferior in nutritive value to wheat, being especially deficient in lysine, and tends to be replaced by wheat in diets, when the opportunity arises. In

Production of Maize ('000 metric tons)

	1992	1993*
World total†	529,800	459,680
Africa	33,600	37,100
Leading African producers		
Angola	370	350
Benin	400	400
Cameroon	430	450
Côte d'Ivoire	430	500
Egypt	4,500	4,800
Ethiopia	1,630	1,700
Ghana	580	800
Kenya	2,650	2,200
Malawi	1,860	1,900
Morocco	220	300
Mozambique	130	350
Nigeria	1,650	1,950
Somalia	100	250
South Africa	9,430	12,500
Tanzania	2,200	1,700
Uganda	600	600
Zaire	920	850
Zambia	1,620	1,250
Zimbabwe	2,020	2,350
Leading non-African producers		
Argentina	10,900	10,300
Brazil	28,800	27,500
China, People's Repub.	95,400	100,000
France	14,900	15,100
Mexico	17,000	16,800
USSR (former)	6,700	8,600
USA	240,900	161,100

* Provisional.

† Includes Southern Hemisphere crops seeded in the year shown, but harvested in the following calendar year.

Source: International Wheat Council.

many African countries, the grain is ground into a meal, mixed with water, and boiled to produce a gruel or porridge. In other areas it is made into (unleavened) corn bread or breakfast cereals. Maize is also the source of an oil, which is used in cooking.

The high starch content of maize makes it highly suitable for animal feed, which is its main use in North America, Europe, Russia and other areas of the former USSR, and Japan. Feed use is also becoming important in some developing countries, particularly in the Far East and North Africa. Maize has a variety of industrial uses, including the preparation of ethyl alcohol (ethanol), which may be added to petrol to produce a blended motor fuel. Maize is also a source of dextrose and fructose, which can be used as artificial sweeteners, many times as sweet as sugar. The amounts of maize used for these purposes depend, critically, on its price to the users relative to that of petroleum, sugar and other potential raw materials. Maize cobs, previously regarded as a waste product, may be used as feedstock to produce various chemicals (e.g. acetic acid and formic acid).

Apart from Egypt, most maize in Africa is grown south of the Sahara. Annual output there is estimated to average about 27m. tons, although it can exceed 30m. tons in good years. Records of maize output are, however, extremely unreliable because, as a subsistance crop, very little is marketed in many African countries. Maize is not grown under irrigation in most of sub-Saharan Africa, as scarce water supplies are reserved instead for higher-value export crops. Yields are therefore low. In most countries, commercial farming is hindered by the lack of foreign exchange to buy essential equipment, as well as transport difficulties which make marketing expensive and uncertain.

The region's main producer is South Africa, where, however, output is periodically affected by drought. A particularly severe drought, which began in late 1991, reduced the crop to only 3m. tons in that year. Production recovered to normal levels of around 9m. tons in 1992 and, following good rains, the 1993 crop reached a record of more than 12m. tons. Zimbabwe, too, is vulnerable to drought, but good crops in the late 1980s led to acute storage problems, and official prices paid to producers of maize were reduced, in an attempt to limit the surpluses. In Kenya successful efforts to increase exports in the 1980s kept stock levels under control, but drought conditions in 1993, compounded by civil unrest in country areas, resulted in a severe shortfall of food maize in early 1994. The progressive elimination of fertilizer subsidies by the Nigerian government has prevented improved seed varieties, introduced there, from achieving their full potential.

One of the most notable differences between maize production in developed and developing countries is in yields. In the USA, the pre-eminent world producer, the continual development of new hybrids and the availability of adequate fertilizer and water supplies have resulted in a substantial increase in yields, interrupted only by the occasional years of drought. In good years yields exceed 8 tons per ha. South Africa, Kenya and Zimbabwe usually achieve yields of at least 2 tons per ha, but in much of west and central Africa yields of 1 ton are normal. Although hybrid forms of maize suited to African conditions are being developed, their adoption is hindered in many countries by low producer prices, inefficient marketing arrangements, and, above all, the inability of producers to obtain regular supplies of fertilizers at economic prices.

World trade in maize reached a record 73m. tons in 1989/90 (July–June), but fell to less than 60m. tons per year in 1990/91 and 1991/92, largely because of a fall in purchases by the former USSR. The African drought raised world imports to 63m. tons in 1992/93, but these fell back to 58m. tons in 1993/94. The pre-eminent world exporter is the USA, which in some years accounts for two-thirds of the total. Its sales totalled 44m. tons in 1992/93, but reduced supplies diminished the export volume to 35m. tons in 1993/94. The People's Republic of China, now the second largest exporter, sold over 11m. tons in world markets in 1993/94. Argentina, formerly a major exporter, accounted for barely 3m. tons annually in the late 1980s, although liberalization of its marketing system has since led to a recovery, to around 5m. tons. South Africa, too, was a considerable maize exporter in the 1970s, and was of particular importance to neighbouring food-deficit countries as a source of white maize (which comprises about one-half its crop). When exports became unprofitable in the 1980s, the government encouraged some farmers to substitute other crops. After the 1992 drought South Africa itself required imports of more than 4m. tons to maintain its supplies of food and feed. The record 1993 crop, however, generated a surplus of around 4m. tons. White maize exports were made to Kenya and other destinations in sub-Saharan Africa, although it proved difficult for South African exports of yellow maize to compete with abundunt low-priced supplies from China.

The world's principal maize importer is Japan, which regularly purchases about 16m. tons annually. Rapidly increasing livestock production in the countries of the Pacific basin, notably the Republic of Korea and Taiwan, have generated substantial imports of maize in recent years. In the 1980s, the USSR was a major market, but the livestock industry in the successor republics of the USSR declined sharply in the early 1990s, greatly reducing feed needs. Imports of maize dwindled from 18m. tons in 1989/90 to only 5m. tons in 1993/94.

Maize imports by sub-Saharan Africa vary from around 1m. tons annually in years of good crops to far higher amounts after droughts. In 1992/93, for example, these imports exceeded 8m. tons, most of which entered through South African ports, either for that country's own use or for onward transport overland to neighbouring countries.

Export Price Index for Maize (base: 1980 = 100)

	Average	Highest month(s)	Lowest month(s)
1985	57		
1990	92		
1991	113	119 (Feb.)	108 (June, July)
1992	117	130 (June)	96 (Nov.)
1993	85	95 (Jan.)	64 (Nov.)

The average export price of US No. 2 Yellow corn (f.o.b. Gulf ports) was US $107 per metric ton in 1991 and $104 per ton in 1992. On a monthly basis, the average price of this maize increased from $104 per ton in June and July 1991 to $117 in March 1992. The price was reduced to $93 per ton in June 1993, but recovered to $106 in October.

During the late 1980s world maize consumption exceeded production, leading to the liquidation of most of the burdensome 'carry-over' stocks which had been accumulated by the USA. The latter declined from 124m. tons at end-August 1987 to only 28m. tons in 1992. Following the latter year's record crop, US stocks doubled, to 57m. tons, in 1993, only to fall again to 21m. tons in 1994. Despite these large fluctuations in supplies in the principal exporting country, prices moved within a comparatively narrow range, and were held down in 1993/94 by depressed import demand, the abundance of supplies from China and the continued availability of low-priced feed wheat from several exporting countries.

Manganese

This metal is obtained from various ores containing such minerals as hausmannite, manganite and pyrolusite. The ore is usually washed or hand-sorted and then smelted to make ferromanganese (80% manganese), in which form it is chiefly used to alloy into steel, manganese steel being particularly hard and tough. Almost 95% of manganese produced is thus used in the manufacture of steel, which, on average, consumes about 6 kg of manganese per metric ton of steel. Electrolytic manganese is used to make stainless steel and in the aluminium industry. Minor uses of manganese as oxides are in dry-cell batteries, paints and varnishes, and in ceramics and glass making.

World reserves of manganese in 1992 were estimated by the US Bureau of Mines at 800m. metric tons of manganese content, of which 370m. tons are in South Africa and 300m. tons in the republics of the former USSR. These two areas account for more than 80% of the world's identified resources. Africa's second major producer, Gabon, has estimated reserves of 52m. tons. In April 1994 it was announced that substantial deposits of manganese had been identified in Bulgaria.

Until overtaken by Gabon in 1990, South Africa was, during the late 1980s, the world's leading exporter of manganese ore, exporting almost three-fifths of its mine output. Where possible, South Africa's policy has been to maximize export revenues by shipping as much as possible in processed ferro-alloy form. Export volumes of ferromanganese have generally followed steel production trends, and reached a record of almost 390,000 tons in 1988. South African exports of silicomanganese more than doubled during the 1980s, reaching a record 250,000 tons in 1987. The expansion by Gabon of its manganese exports was stimulated by the opening, in 1988, of a new mineral port at Owendo. Shipments of ore by rail through the Congo to the port of Pointe-Noire, however, were suspended following a dispute in 1991.

Ghana, the other principal African producer, benefited in the late 1980s from government measures to revive manganese operations, assisted by loan finance from the World Bank. In 1991 a mine project was initiated that would make Burkina Faso a minor regional producer. These reserves, located at Tambao, 400 km north-west of Ouagadougou, and estimated at 19m. tons, contain an average ore content of 50% manganese. Production began in May 1993 and was targeted to reach 140,000 tons annually by 1995. Zaire, once a significant source of manganese exports, has mined only on a sporadic basis since 1980. The exploitation of manganese deposits in Angola has been interrupted by two decades of civil war.

Extensive accumulations of manganese in marine environments have been identified. The characteristic occurrences are as nodules on deep ocean floors and as crusts on seamounts at shallower depths. Both forms are oxidic and are often termed 'ferromanganese' because they generally contain iron and manganese. The main commercial interest in both types of deposit derives from the copper, nickel and cobalt contents also present, which represent large resources of these metals. Attention was focused initially on nodules, of which the Pacific Ocean encompasses the areas with the densest coverage and highest concentration of potentially economic metals. However, the exploitation of nodules has, to date, been impeded by legal, technical and economic factors.

The index of export prices for manganese ore remained at 135 in January and February 1994. The leading importers of manganese ores and concentrates in 1992 were Japan, France and Norway. In the case of Norway, the average import cost of these minerals (including manganiferous iron ores) declined from US $143 per metric ton in 1991 to $132 per ton in 1992.

Production of Manganese Ore
(manganese content, '000 metric tons)

	1991	1992*
World total	7,273	6,701
Africa	2,268	1,933
African producers		
Gabon†	748	718
Ghana†	120	107
Morocco†	31	31
South Africa†	1,369	1,077
Leading non-African producers		
Australia	701	570
Brazil†	760	684
China, People's Repub.†	680	700
India†	525	525
USSR (former)†	2,150	2,050

* Preliminary.
† Gross weight reported; metal content estimated.
Source: US Bureau of Mines.

Export Price Index for Manganese Ore (base: 1980 = 100)

	Average	Highest month(s)	Lowest month(s)
1985	85		
1990	243		
1991	245	*	*
1992	231	245 (Jan.–July)	212 (Aug.–Dec.)
1993	164	212 (Jan.–April)	135 (June–Dec.)

* The monthly index remained constant at 245 from January to December.

Most of the Western bloc countries' manganese ore output is sold by means of annual contracts between producers and their customers, the manufacturers of steel and ferro-alloys.

Millet and Sorghum

Millet and sorghum are often grouped together in economic analyses of world cereals, not because they are a particularly closely related species—in fact they are quite dissimilar—but because in many developing countries they are both little-traded subsistence crops. Figures for the production of the individual grains should be treated only as broad estimates in most cases. Data cover only crops harvested for grain.

Data on millet relate mainly to the following: cat-tail millet (*Pennisetum glaucum* or *typhoides*), also known as bulrush millet, pearl millet or, in India and Pakistan, as 'bajra'; finger millet (*Eleusine coracana*), known in India as 'ragi'; common or bread millet (*Panicum miliaceum*), also called 'proso'; foxtail millet (*Setaria italica*), or Italian millet; and barnyard millet (*Echinochloa crusgalli*), also often called Japanese millet.

Production of Millet and Sorghum ('000 metric tons)
M = Millet; S = Sorghum.

	1991	1992*
World total†: M	25,420	27,600
World total†: S	52,860	65,200
Africa: M	8,600	8,560
Africa: S	13,640	14,140
Leading African producers		
Burkina Faso: M	600	550
Burkina Faso: S	1,000	950
Chad: M	250	250
Chad: S	300	300
Egypt: S	620	630
Ethiopia: S	900	1,000
Mali: M	750	800
Mali: S	550	550
Niger: M	1,400	1,400
Niger: S	400	400
Nigeria: M	2,700	2,600
Nigeria: S	3,500	3,800
Senegal: M	590	600
South Africa: S	100	100
Sudan: M	310	350
Sudan: S	2,940	3,000
Tanzania: M	300	300
Tanzania: S	700	700
Uganda: M	500	500
Uganda: S	350	350
Zimbabwe: M	250	300
Leading non-African producers		
Argentina: S	2,640	2,800
Australia: S	1,060	1,300
China, People's Repub.: M	4,000	4,000
China, People's Repub.: S	4,900	5,100
India: M	8,300	10,600
India: S	8,400	12,300
Mexico: S	2,600	2,200
USSR (former): M	3,180	3,180
USA: S	14,860	27,460

* Provisional.

† Includes Southern Hemisphere crops seeded in the year shown, but harvested in the following year.

Source: International Wheat Council.

Sorghum statistics refer mainly to the several varieties of *Sorghum vulgare*, known by various names, such as great millet, Guinea corn, kafir or kafircorn (*caffrorum*), milo (in the USA and Argentina), feterita, durra, jowar, sorgo or maicillo. Other species included in the table are Sudan grass (*S. sudanense*) and Columbus grass or sorgo negro (*S. almum*). The use of grain sorghum hybrids has resulted in a considerable increase in yields in recent years.

Millet and sorghum are cultivated particularly in semi-arid areas where there is too little rainfall to sustain maize and the temperature is too high for wheat. These two cereals constitute the staple diet of people over large areas of Africa, the People's Republic of China (PRC) and parts of the former USSR. They are usually consumed as porridge or unleavened bread. Both grains have good nutritive properties, but are less palatable than wheat, and tend to be replaced by the latter when circumstances permit. In many African countries sorghum is used to make beer. Sorghum is also produced and used in certain countries in the western hemisphere (particularly Argentina, Mexico and the USA), where it is used mainly as an animal feed, although the high tannin content of some varieties lowers their feeding value.

World production of both sorghum and millet has been in decline for many years, as farmers have preferred to cultivate more profitable and higher-yielding crops. Because sorghum is more drought-resistant than most cereals, it tends to be grown in marginal areas, or to be substituted at short notice for maize in dry years. Production is therefore very variable. The output of millet in Africa averages about 8m. tons per year. Mali, Niger and Nigeria are important producers, but most countries south of the Sahara grow at least some of the grain.

For one variety of sorghum from the USA, Milo No. 2 Yellow, the average export price (f.o.b. Gulf ports) was US $106 per metric ton in 1991 and $105 per ton in 1992. On a monthly basis, the average price per ton of the cereal declined from $121 in March 1992 to $91 in October, although it recovered to $96 in December. The price declined to $90 per ton in June 1993, but reached $101 in July.

World trade in sorghum averages about 9m. tons per year, but reached 10m. tons in 1992/93 (July–June). The principal exporters are the USA (which usually accounts for two-thirds of the total), Argentina and the PRC. South Africa and Sudan are occasional exporters. Problems of transport limit the potential for sorghum exports by other sub-Saharan countries. Japan is the main importer, accounting for over one-third of the world market, and certain other countries, including Israel and Venezuela, are regular importers. Mexico buys sorghum in large quantities when its price is competitive with maize. Its occasional large purchases, together with those of the former USSR, tend to make the world market for sorghum unpredictable. Except in periods of shortage in sorghum supplies, its price is usually at a discount compared with maize. The West and Central African Sorghum Research Institute, with headquarters in Bamako, Mali, links 17 regional producing countries in conducting research and co-ordinating the expansion of sorghum cultivation. Very little millet enters world trade and there are no regular export price quotations.

Oil Palm (*Elaeis guineensis*)

This tree is native to west Africa and grows wild in tropical forests along the coast of that region. The entire fruit is of use commercially; palm oil is made from its pulp, and palm kernel oil from the seed. Palm oil is a versatile product and, because of its very low acid content (4%–5%), it is almost all used in food. It is used in margarine and other edible fats; as a 'shortener' for pastry and biscuits; as an ingredient in ice cream and chocolate; and in the manufacture of soaps and detergents. Palm kernel oil, which is similar to coconut oil, is also used for making soaps and fats. The sap from the stems of the tree produces palm wine, an intoxicating beverage.

Palm oil can be produced virtually through the year once the palms have reached oil-bearing age, which takes about five years. The palms continue to bear oil for 30 years or more and the yield far exceeds that of any other oil plant, with 1 ha of oil palms producing as much oil as 6 ha of groundnuts or 10–12 ha of soybeans. However, it is an intensive crop, needing considerable investment and skilled labour.

During the 1980s palm oil accounted for more than 15% of world production of vegetable oils (second only to soybean oil), owing mainly to a substantial expansion in Malaysian production. In 1989 palm oil accounted for 14.5% of world vegetable oil output, compared with 22% for soybean oil and about 11% each for sunflower and rapeseed oils. In export terms, Africa has, since 1980, accounted for less than 3% of world trade in palm oil. The increase in output of palm oil has posed a challenge to the soybean industry, particularly in the USA, which has, since the mid-1970s, been reducing its imports of palm oil. In 1988, in response to health reports that both palm and coconut oils tended to raise levels of cholesterol (a substance believed to promote arteriosclerosis in the body), several leading US food processors announced that they were to discontinue their use. These reports, however, have been vigorously challenged by palm oil producers.

Production of Palm Kernels ('000 metric tons)

	1991	1992
World total	3,581*	3,822*
Africa	718*	746*
Leading African producers		
Cameroon	53†	53†
Côte d'Ivoire	37	41
Ghana	31†	34*
Guinea	40*	40*
Nigeria	369†	385†
Sierra Leone	30	35*
Zaire	75*	76*
Leading non-African producers		
Brazil‡	225†	240*
Colombia	53	56
Indonesia§	551†	643†
Malaysia	1,786	1,874
Papua New Guinea	50†	57†
Thailand	53	51

* FAO estimate. † Unofficial figure.
‡ Figures relate to babassu kernels.
§ Production on estates only.

Production of Palm Oil ('000 metric tons)

	1991	1992
World total	11,938*	12,839*
Africa	1,792*	1,876*
Leading African producers		
Angola	40*	40*
Benin	39*	39*
Cameroon	130	120*
Côte d'Ivoire	228	261
Ghana	90†	100†
Guinea	40*	40
Nigeria	900*	940
Sierra Leone	51	60*
Zaire	182*	183*
Leading non-African producers		
Colombia	291	304
Indonesia‡	2,658	3,162
Malaysia	6,141	6,373
Papua New Guinea	180†	206†
Thailand	234†	270†

* FAO estimate. † Unofficial figure.
‡ Production on estates only.

In Africa a large proportion of oil palms still grow in wild groves and the bulk of oil production is for local consumption. Nigeria was the world's leading producer of palm oil until overtaken by Malaysia in 1971. The loss of Nigeria's market dominance was, in part, a result of civil war and the authorities' neglect to replace old, unproductive trees. Since the early 1980s, however, measures have been taken to revive palm oil output and to enhance the efficiency and capacity of associated mills and refineries. Foreign investment has been encouraged, as has the transfer of inefficiently managed state-owned plantations to private-sector ownership. A ban on palm oil imports, in force since 1986, was partially relaxed in 1990, however, as domestic output (of which an estimated 70% came from smallholder producers) was able to satisfy only two-thirds of a forecast annual demand of 900,000 tons.

In Benin, where the oil palm has traditionally been a staple crop of the national economy, oil palm plantations and natural palm groves cover more than 450,000 ha. Côte d'Ivoire is now Africa's principal palm oil exporter and the fourth largest in the world, behind Malaysia (by far the largest, accounting for about 80% of all palm oil trade), Indonesia and Singapore. However, more than one-half of Côte d'Ivoire's palms were planted in 1965–70 and have passed their peak of productivity. Management and financial difficulties, as well as declining world prices for palm oil, have resulted in a scaling-down of the replanting programme, and plans to increase processing capacity have been postponed. Other African producers, notably Liberia and Ghana, also lack sufficient refinery capacity to service their palm oil output. Plans were proceeding in 1993, however, for the construction by Malaysian producers of a palm oil refinery in Tanzania to process Malaysian crude palm oil. The plant, located in Dar es Salaam, would initially produce 30,000 tons of edible oils annually.

Internationally, palm oil is faced with sustained competition from the other major edible lauric oils — soybean, rapeseed and sunflower oils — and these markets are subject to a complex and changing interaction of production, stocks and trade. In the longer term, prospects for palm oil exporters (particularly the higher-cost producers in sub-Saharan Africa) do not appear favourable. Technological advances in oil palm cultivation, particularly in the introduction of laboratory-produced higher-yielding varieties (HYVs), may also militate against the smaller-scale producer, as, for economic and technical reasons, many HYVs can be produced only on large estates, exposing smallholder cultivators to increasingly intense price pressure.

Export Price Index for Palm Oil (base: 1980 = 100)

	Average	Highest month(s)	Lowest month(s)
1985	86		
1990	49		
1991	58	64 (Dec.)	53 (June)
1992	67	71 (Nov.)	65 (Jan., Feb., July, Aug.)
1993	65	73 (Feb.)	57 (Oct.)

The index of export prices for palm oil recovered to 70 in December 1993. The average import price of Indonesian palm oil at European ports on the North Sea increased from US $339 per metric ton in 1991 to $394 per ton in 1992. On a monthly basis, the average price eased from $404 per ton in June 1992 to $381 in July. It advanced to $426 per ton in February 1993, but slumped to $332 in October.

Petroleum

Crude oils, from which petroleum fuel is derived, consist essentially of a wide range of hydrocarbon molecules which are separated by distillation in the refining process. Refined oil is treated in different ways to make the different varieties of fuel. More than four-fifths of total world oil supplies are used as fuel for the production of energy in the form of power or heating.

Petroleum is the leading raw material in world trade. The world's 'published proven' reserves of petroleum and natural gas liquids at 31 December 1993 were estimated to total 137,815m. metric tons, equivalent to about 1,006,000m. barrels (1 metric ton is equivalent to approximately 7.3 barrels, each of 42 US gallons or 34.97 imperial gallons, i.e. 159 litres). Of this, about 8,488m. tons (6.2%) were in Africa.

Nigeria's first petroleum discovery was made in the Niger delta region in 1956, and exports began in 1958. Production

Production of Crude Petroleum
(estimates, '000 metric tons, including natural gas liquids)

	1992	1993*
World total	3,110,317	3,079,351
Africa	317,835	310,668
Leading African producers		
Algeria	38,446	37,350
Angola	26,356	25,803
Cameroon	6,978	6,435
Congo	9,003	9,988
Egypt	46,113	47,446
Gabon	14,940	14,776
Libya	74,351	68,082
Nigeria	94,720	94,411
Tunisia	5,353	4,977
Leading non-African producers		
Canada	97,391	102,718
China, People's Repub.†	141,566	144,014
Indonesia	76,456	75,356
Iran	181,272	172,059
Kuwait‡	52,315	93,274
Mexico	155,206	154,976
Norway	106,535	114,455
Russia	397,837	340,600
Saudi Arabia‡	413,714	406,476
United Arab Emirates	113,794	109,271
United Kingdom	94,147	98,247
USA	412,628	402,845
Venezuela	115,237	116,119

* Preliminary. † Including oil from shale and coal.
‡ Including share of production in the Neutral Zone (also known as the Partitioned Zone), divided equally between Kuwait and Saudi Arabia.

Source: The Institute of Petroleum.

and exports increased steadily until output was disrupted by the outbreak of civil war in 1967. After the end of hostilities, in 1970, Nigeria's oil production greatly increased and it became the country's major industry. Since Libya restricted output in 1973, Nigeria has been Africa's leading petroleum-producing country. Being of low sulphur content and high quality, its petroleum is much in demand on the European market. Nigeria's proven reserves were estimated to be 2,452m. tons at 31 December 1993. A five-year investment programme, initiated in 1991, aimed to increase petroleum output capacity from 1.95m.–2m. barrels per day (b/d) to 2.5m. b/d by 1995. Proven reserves are targeted to reach 2,739m. tons by the mid-1990s. A member of the Organization of the Petroleum Exporting Countries (OPEC, see below), Nigeria accounted for 7.7% of total OPEC production of 1,230m. tons in 1993. The state petroleum enterprise, the Nigerian National Petroleum Corpn (NNPC), operates refinery facilities at Kaduna, Warri, Port Harcourt and Alesa Eleme. In 1992 their total annual capacity was 21.6m. metric tons, although Nigeria occasionally has recourse to imports of refined petroleum products in order to satisfy its domestic requirements. Petroleum sales dominate Nigeria's earnings of foreign exchange, providing about 90% of the total and accounting for approximately 80% of federal government revenue. However, considerable revenue is lost to the Nigerian government through illegal exports of oil to neighbouring countries, in the form of petrol, kerosene, diesel oil and fuel oil.

Angola's first petroleum discovery was made in 1955 near Luanda. However, the Cabinda province has a major offshore deposit, in production since 1968, which now forms the basis of Angola's oil industry. Production from Cabinda was briefly disrupted by the country's civil war, but has proceeded uninterruptedly since 1977, and output has increased steadily since 1982. In the early 1990s Angola relied on exports of crude petroleum for more than 90% of foreign earnings and for about 40% of government revenue. In 1993 Angola's proven oil reserves were assessed at 205m. tons; however, with a number of oilfields currently under development, prospects exist for a considerable expansion in the petroleum sector, given an eventual settlement of the civil conflict. Most of Angola's oil output is exported in crude form, although there are long-term plans to expand the capacity of Angola's sole refinery, at Luanda, from 1.6m. to 2m. tons annually.

The Congo, with proven recoverable reserves estimated at 114m. tons in 1993, entered onshore petroleum production in 1957. Subsequent expansion, however, has been in operations off shore, where significant new deposits, discovered in 1992, were expected to add 2m. tons annually to the Congo's petroleum output from 1996. A petroleum refinery at Pointe-Noire also processes some Angolan production. In neighbouring Gabon exploitation of petroleum deposits began in 1956, and, as in the Congo, was increased as offshore fields came into production. In the late 1980s petroleum and petroleum products provided almost 71% of export revenue. Gabon's estimated proven reserves stood at 100m. tons in 1993. A member of OPEC, Gabon's output accounted for only 1.2% of the organization's 1993 total. In 1992 its annual refinery capacity was 1.2m. tons.

In the early 1990s Cameroon was virtually self-sufficient in oil and petroleum products. New exploration and development projects, however, were not being actively pursued, and it has been forecast that the country's proven reserves (estimated at 55m. tons in 1993) could be exhausted by the end of the decade. Cameroon's annual refinery capacity was 2.1m. tons in 1992. Zaire entered offshore petroleum production in 1975, operating from oilfields near the Atlantic coast and at the mouth of the River Zaire. These deposits became substantially depleted during the 1980s (Zaire's total proven reserves fell from 13.2m. tons in 1989 to 7.6m. tons in 1990). The level of proven reserves was substantially replenished during 1991, however, raising estimates to 25.6m. tons for each of the subsequent two years. Although Zaire has a refinery capacity of 847,000 tons per year, its exceptionally heavy-grade petroleum cannot be processed locally and Zaire therefore cannot consume its own output. In June 1992 the Zaire government took control of the assets of US and European oil companies. Côte d'Ivoire, with estimated proven reserves of 7m. tons in 1993, and Benin, whose proven reserves were estimated at 2.7m. tons in that year, are among the other smaller sub-Saharan offshore producers, which were joined in 1992 by Equatorial Guinea. Deposits of an estimated 52m.–58m. tons of petroleum have been identified off the coast of Senegal, but the development of these reserves (which are overwhelmingly of heavy oil) is not economically feasible at present. Chad, with total petroleum deposits estimated to exceed 70m. tons, has revived plans for their exploitation, which had been interrupted by prolonged internal unrest. In early 1994 negotiations were proceeding for the construction of an oil export pipeline, through Cameroon, to the Atlantic coast, following the identification of two substantial oilfields in Southern Chad. Commercial deposits of petroleum in Southern Sudan also remain unexploited, pending the resolution of internal unrest.

Among other African countries where petroleum reserves are known or believed to exist, but which do not yet produce, are Mozambique, Swaziland and Madagascar. Exploration has also taken place in Ethiopia, Eritrea, Namibia, Kenya and South Africa.

OPEC was formed in 1960 to maintain prices in the producing countries. Nigeria joined OPEC in 1971 and Gabon became a full member in 1975. The two other African members are Algeria and Libya.

The four African members of OPEC formed the African Petroleum Producers' Association (APPA) in 1986. Angola, Benin, Cameroon, Congo, Côte d'Ivoire, Egypt and Zaire subsequently joined the association, in which Tunisia has observer status. Apart from promoting co-operation among regional producers, the APPA, which is based in Lagos, co-operates with OPEC in stabilizing oil prices.

The two leading western European producers and exporters of crude petroleum are Norway and the United Kingdom. In 1992 Norway's petroleum exports had an average value of US $144 per metric ton, and those of the United Kingdom $145 per ton. The comparable averages in the previous year were, respectively, $151 and $150 per

Export Price Index for Crude Petroleum (base: 1980 = 100)

	Average	Highest month(s)	Lowest month(s)
1985	91		
1990	68		
1991	55	63 (Jan.)	51 (Feb., March, Dec.)
1992	53	57 (June)	50 (Jan., March, Dec.)
1993	47	52 (March, April)	37 (Dec.)

ton. Prices per barrel averaged about $20 in 1992, but declined to only about $14 in late 1993.

Platinum

This is one of a group of six related metals, also including palladium, rhodium, ruthenium, iridium and osmium. In nature, platinum is usually associated with the sulphides of iron, copper and nickel. Depending on the relative concentration of the platinum-group metals (PGM) and copper and nickel in the deposit, platinum is either the major product or a by-product of base metal production. PGM are highly resistant to corrosion, and do not oxidize in air. They are also extremely malleable and have a high melting point, giving them a wide range of industrial uses.

Although widely employed in the petroleum refining and petrochemical sectors, the principal industrial use for platinum is in catalytic converters in motor vehicles (which reduce pollution from exhaust emissions), accounting for more than one-third of total platinum consumption by Western countries (an estimated 35%, or 1,415,000 troy ounces, in 1993). The USA, Canada, Japan, Australia, Taiwan, the Republic of Korea, the European Community (EC, now the European Union) and certain Latin American countries have implemented legislation to neutralize vehicle exhaust gases, and this necessitates the fitting of catalytic converters, using platinum, rhodium and palladium, to vehicles. In 1989 the EC Council of (Environment) Ministers decided to oblige vehicle manufacturers within the Community to fit three-way catalytic converters as compulsory features in passenger cars with an engine capacity of less than 1,400 cc, effective for all new models from mid-1992 and for all new cars from January 1993. It was predicted that the new measures would reduce emissions of exhaust gases by 60%–70%. The EC Commission subsequently extended similar anti-pollution requirements to larger cars, and to heavy trucks, with effect from 1995. The resultant increase in demand for automotive emission control catalysts (autocatalysts) is expected to generate a rising trend in the consumption of platinum and rhodium during the early 1990s. Also of considerable potential significance to platinum demand has been the development of fuel cells incorporating platinum catalysts which produce pollution-free electricity from a controlled chemical reaction between oxygen and hydrogen. The only by-products of this reaction are carbon dioxide and water, so that the fuel cell avoids environmental damage, in contrast to the disposal of radioactive waste products from nuclear plants and the production of sulphur and nitrogen oxides at coal- and oil-fired power stations. The use of these cells in power generation, assuming that their operating costs would approximate those of conventional electricity-generating plant, could substantially increase world demand for platinum and palladium.

Alloyed platinum is very heavy and hard. Platinum's white colour makes it popular for jewellery, which accounts for the other principal source of consumption (39.9%, or 1,610,000 oz, in 1993). Japan is the world's main consumer of platinum, and its jewellery industry absorbed a record 1,350,000 oz in 1993. Industrial and other miscellaneous applications accounted for the balance of platinum consumption; these uses include platinum for minting coins and small bars purchased as an investment, petroleum refining, production of nitric acid, glass manufacture, electrical applications and dentistry. Reflecting the world-wide economic recession, international demand for platinum in 1993 totalled 4,040,000 oz, a decline of 3% from the 1992 level. Supplies entering the market in 1993 rose to 4,380,000 oz from 3,820,000 oz in 1992. This increase in supplies resulted from a higher level of production in South Africa, reflecting mine capacity expansions carried out in recent years. In addition, an increased intake of supplies from North America and Colombia offset a decline in sales by Russia.

The US Bureau of Mines has estimated world reserves of platinum-group metals to be approximately 2,000m. oz. Production is dominated by South Africa, which accounts for more than three-quarters of supplies to the international market. It produced 3.36m. oz in 1993. Russia, the second largest producer, supplied 680,000 oz. An agreement that was signed in 1991 by the USSR and the South African Chamber of Mines, under which the USSR was to receive technical assistance for the development of its platinum industry, has subsequently been enlarged and extended with the Russian government. Russian production levels were, however, being adversely affected in 1993 by deterioration in plant and equipment, resulting from a lack of funds for essential maintenance. Sales of platinum from the former USSR in 1992 were 750,000 oz, compared with 1,100,000 oz in 1991. Canada is the third largest producer, its platinum being a by-product of its nickel production. Minor producers include the USA, Australia, Finland and Colombia. Zimbabwe, the only other African platinum producer, is developing several new mine projects. Elsewhere in Africa, there are known or probable deposits of platinum in Ethiopia, Kenya and Sierra Leone.

Whereas platinum-group metals are produced in Canada and Russia as by-products of copper and/or nickel production, platinum-group metals in South Africa are produced as the primary products, with nickel and copper as by-products. Another fundamental difference between the platinum deposits in South Africa and those in Russia and Canada is the ratio of platinum to palladium. In South Africa the percentage of platinum contained in the platinum-group metals has, to date, exceeded that of palladium, although the ratio is expected to favour palladium in new mines being brought into production in the early 1990s (see below). In Russia, Canada and the USA there is a higher proportion of palladium than platinum.

South African production capacity was substantially increased in 1993, following the completion of a number of expansion projects which had been under development since the mid-1980s. However, the level of world platinum prices, together with rises in production costs, have made it unlikely that the total increase in annual capacity (originally targeted at 1.56m. oz) will exceed 1.1m. oz after all existing projects have entered full operation in 1994 and 1995. Together with the current surplus in world supplies, cost factors led to the delay or cancellation in 1993 of several expansion projects and to the closure of unprofitable operations. Similar considerations have also affected producers in North America, and have, in the short term, eclipsed the possibility of any significant western participation in the rehabilitation of Russian platinum production.

In September 1993 the London price of platinum declined to US $351.5 (equivalent to £227 sterling) per troy oz, but in December it recovered to $393.5 (£266) per oz. In early January 1994 the platinum price reached $398 (£269) per oz, but later in the month it was reduced to $378.5 (£253). The London quotation exceeded $400 per oz in February, and reached $418 (£282) at the end of March. Following another decline, the price of platinum advanced in July to $427.5 (£279) per oz, its highest level, in terms of US currency, since late 1990.

Prices for Platinum
(London Platinum and Palladium Market, US$ per troy oz)

	Average	Highest month(s)	Lowest month(s)
1990	471.7		
1991	376.2	424.3 (Jan.)	330.0 (Dec.)
1992	359.9	392.1 (July)	330.8 (Jan.)
1993	374.1	419.0 (Aug.)	339.8 (March)

Rice (*Oryza*)

In Africa and Asia, unmilled rice is referred to as paddy, although 'rough' rice is the common appellation in the West. After removal of the outer husk, it is called brown rice. After the grain is milled to varying degrees to remove the bran layers, it is called milled rice. Since rice loses 30%–40% of its weight in the milling process, most rice is traded in the milled form to save shipping expenses.

There are two cultivated species of rice, *Oryza sativa* and *O. glaberrima*. *O. sativa* is widely grown in the world, though it originated in tropical Asia, while the cultivation of *O. glaberrima* is limited to the high rainfall zone of west Africa. In Africa rice is grown mainly as a subsistence crop. Methods of cultivation differ from region to region and yields tend to be low by world standards. Rice is a staple food in several African countries, including Madagascar, Tanzania and some west coast countries.

Production of Paddy Rice ('000 metric tons)

	1991	1992
World total	517,761*	526,360*
Africa	13,539*	13,858*
Leading African producers		
Côte d'Ivoire	687	710
Egypt	3,448	3,910
Guinea	688	501
Madagascar	2,342	2,450
Mali	454	405
Nigeria	3,185†	3,453†
Sierra Leone	411†	420†
Tanzania	625	371
Zaire	365	365*
Leading non-African producers		
Bangladesh	27,241	27,033†
China, People's Repub.	183,813	186,222
India	110,591	108,011†
Indonesia	44,688	47,700†
Thailand	20,400	19,935
Viet Nam	19,622	21,590

* FAO estimate. † Unofficial figure.

World rice production is dominated by the Asian region (which produces more than 90% of the world's total), and expanded rapidly in the 1980s. African rice production accounts for only about 2.5% of total world output. As the bulk of rice production is consumed mainly in the producing countries, international trade accounts for less than 5% of world output. The market is subject to great volatility and fluctuating prices. Less than 1% of the African rice crop enters international trade and more than 90% of African rice exports come from Egypt. Africa, especially in recent years, has been a substantial net importer of rice, although the volume growth in imports has been held in check by the impact of higher world rice prices on the depleted foreign exchange reserves of many African importing countries. The major African importers include Côte d'Ivoire, Nigeria, Guinea, Sierra Leone, Senegal and Madagascar, which ranks as the world's largest rice consumer per caput. Africa, and especially west African countries (where rice is a staple food of 40% of the population), imports large quantities of rice from Thailand and the USA, two major world exporters. The volume of rice imports by west African states rose by more than 5% annually during 1980-92, with consumption exceeding 9.5m. tons in the latter year. Because rice is a relatively new crop to the region, suitable high-yielding varieties (HYV) have yet to be propagated. The development of HYV is among the activities of the 17-member West Africa Rice Development Association (WARDA), formed by the producing countries in 1970. Based in Bouaké, Côte d'Ivoire, WARDA maintains regional research stations in Côte d'Ivoire, Senegal and Sierra Leone, from which it conducts scientific research on crop improvement and provides technical assistance, with the aim of advancing the region towards eventual self-sufficiency in rice production.

Export Price Index for Rice (base: 1980 = 100)

	Average	Highest month(s)	Lowest month(s)
1985	66		
1990	74		
1991	79	82 (March, June)	75 (Jan.)
1992	75	78 (Jan.-April)	71 (Dec.)
1993	72	110 (Dec.)	61 (May, June)

The index of export prices for rice advanced to 111 in January 1994. The average export price of Thai white rice (f.o.b. Bangkok) declined from US $302 per metric ton in 1991 to $278 per ton in 1992. On a monthly basis, the highest average price per ton in 1992 was $293 in July. The monthly average fell to only $200 per ton in May 1993, but increased to $277 in October.

Sisal *(Agave sisalana)*

Sisal, which is not indigenous to Africa, was introduced to Tanganyika (now mainland Tanzania) from Mexico at the end of the 19th century. The leaf tissue of this plant yields hard, flexible fibres which are suitable for making rope and twine, cord matting, padding and upholstery. Sisal accounts for two-thirds of world production of hard fibres, and about three-quarters of sisal consumption is for agricultural twine. World output of sisal and other hard fibres has generally declined in recent years, owing to competition from nylons and petroleum-based synthetics (in particular, polypropylene harvest twine, which is stronger than sisal and less labour-intensive to produce), although the intensity of the competition and the success of hard fibres depend on fluctuations in the price of petroleum.

In 1970 Tanzania, whose sisal is generally regarded as being of the best quality, was overtaken as the world's leading producer by Brazil. The nationalization of more than one-half of Tanzania's sisal estates in 1976, together with low prices, inefficient management and lack of equipment and spare parts, contributed to the decline of the Tanzanian crop. During the 1980s, however, the government sought to revive the industry by returning some state-owned estates to private or co-operative ownership. In 1992 the government announced that it was to return all its estates to the private sector. However, despite the introduction of a replanting programme aimed at doubling production by the mid-1990s, prospects have been overshadowed by the longer-term outlook for sisal (according to FAO projections, world demand has been falling at a rate of 7% per year). Efforts are being made, however, to create new uses in such products as specialized papers and surgical bandages. With the decline of the Tanzanian sisal sector, Kenya has emerged as Brazil's main rival, although it exports only fibre, as it has no processing industry.

Although sisal producers operate a quota system, in an attempt to improve the pricing structure of the crop, the average price of sisal has been in general decline since 1981, as relatively stable prices for petroleum have allowed polypropylene to regain its competitiveness.

Production of Sisal ('000 metric tons)

	1991	1992
World total	416*	364*
Africa	104*	89*
Leading African producers		
Kenya	39	34
Madagascar	20	19
Tanzania	36	24†
Leading non-African producers		
Brazil	234	204
Mexico	36	30†

* FAO estimate. † Unofficial figure.

The index of export prices for sisal remained at 86 in January and February 1994. Two main grades of sisal are exported to Europe from eastern Africa. The average import

Export Price Index for Sisal (base: 1980 = 100)

	Average	Highest month(s)	Lowest month(s)
1985	74		
1990	89		
1991	84	90 (Jan.-March)	70 (Nov., Dec.)
1992	64	70 (Jan.-March)	58 (Nov.)
1993	78	86 (Aug.-Dec.)	60 (Jan.)

price of the less expensive grade at European ports declined from US $639 per metric ton in 1991 to $479 per ton in 1992. On a monthly basis, the lowest average price per ton in 1992 was $438 in October (compared with more than $700 in the early months of 1991). The monthly average recovered to $628 per ton in June 1993.

Sugar

Sugar is a sweet crystalline substance, which may be derived from the juices of various plants. Chemically, the basis of sugar is sucrose, one of a group of soluble carbohydrates which are important dietary sources of energy. It can be obtained from trees, including the maple and certain palms, but virtually all manufactured sugar comes from two plants, sugar beet (*Beta vulgaris*) and sugar cane, a giant perennial grass of the genus *Saccharum*.

Sugar cane, found in tropical areas, grows to a height of up to 5 m. The plant is native to Polynesia, but its distribution is now widespread. It is not necessary to plant cane every season as, if the root of the plant is left in the ground, it will grow again in the following year. This practice, known as 'ratooning', may be continued for as long as three years, when yields begin to decline. Cane is ready for cutting 12–24 months after planting, depending on local conditions. Much of the world's sugar cane is still cut by hand, but rising costs are hastening the change-over to mechanical harvesting. The cane is cut as close as possible to the ground, and the top leaves, which may be used as cattle fodder, are removed.

After cutting, the cane is loaded by hand or by machine into trucks or trailers and towed directly to a factory for processing. Sugar cane deteriorates quickly after it has been cut and should be processed as quickly as possible. At the factory the cane passes first through shredding knives or crushing rollers, which break up the hard rind and expose the inner fibre, and then to squeezing rollers, where the crushed cane is subjected to high pressure and sprayed with water. The resulting juice is heated and lime is added for clarification and the removal of impurities. The clean juice is then concentrated in evaporators. This thickened juice is next boiled in steam-heated vacuum pans until a mixture or 'massecuite' of sugar crystals and 'mother syrup' is produced. The massecuite is then spun in centrifugal machines to separate the sugar crystals (raw cane sugar) from the residual syrup (cane molasses).

The production of beet sugar follows the same process, except that the juice is extracted by osmotic diffusion. Its manufacture produces white sugar crystals which do not require further refining. In most producing countries, it is consumed domestically, although the EU, which accounts for about 15% of total world sugar production, is a net exporter of white refined sugar. Beet sugar accounts for more than one-third of world production. Production data for sugar cane and sugar beet cover generally all crops harvested, except crops grown explicitly for feed. The third table covers the production of raw sugar by the centrifugal process. In the early 1990s global output of non-centrifugal sugar (i.e. produced from sugar cane which has not undergone centrifugation) was about 12m.-13m. tons per year.

Most of the raw cane sugar produced in the world is sent to refineries outside the country of origin, unless the sugar is for local consumption. Cuba, Thailand, Brazil and India are among the few cane-producers that export part of their output as refined sugar. The refining process further purifies the sugar crystals and eventually results in finished products of various grades, such as granulated, icing or castor sugar. The ratio of refined to raw sugar is usually about 0.9:1.

Production of Sugar Cane ('000 metric tons)

	1991	1992
World total	1,090,328*	1,102,630*
Africa	75,117*	66,997*
Leading African producers		
Côte d'Ivoire	1,600*	1,600*
Egypt	11,624	11,700*
Ethiopia	1,530*	1,620*
Kenya	4,580*	4,430*
Madagascar	1,950	1,900
Malawi	1,800*	1,950*
Mauritius	5,621	6,400*
Réunion	2,010	1,973
South Africa‡	20,078	14,788
Sudan	4,500	4,600*
Swaziland	3,900*	3,700*
Zimbabwe	3,236	300*
Leading non-African producers		
Brazil	260,888	271,432
China, People's Repub.	67,898	73,011
Cuba	71,000*	58,000*
India	241,046	249,256
Mexico	38,387	39,955
Pakistan	35,989	38,865
Thailand	47,480	34,860

* FAO estimate. † Unofficial figure.
‡ Cane crushed for sugar.

As well as providing sugar, quantities of cane are grown in some countries for seed, feed, fresh consumption, the manufacture of alcohol and other uses. Molasses may be used as cattle feed or fermented to produce alcoholic beverages for human consumption, such as rum, a distilled spirit manufactured in Caribbean countries. Sugar cane juice may be used to produce ethyl alcohol (ethanol). This chemical can be mixed with petroleum derivatives to produce fuel for motor vehicles. The steep rise in the price of petroleum after 1973 made the large-scale conversion of sugar cane into alcohol economically attractive (particularly to developing nations), especially as sugar, unlike petroleum, is a renewable source of energy. Several countries developed alcohol production by this means in order to reduce petroleum imports and to support cane growers. The blended fuel used in cars is known as 'gasohol', 'alcogas' or 'green petrol'. The pioneer in this field was Brazil, which established the largest 'gasohol' production programme in the world. By the late 1980s ethanol accounted for about one-half of the fuel consumption of Brazilian motorists. In Africa, 'gasohol' plants have been planned or established in Kenya, Malawi, South Africa, Tanzania and Zambia.

After the milling of sugar, the cane has dry fibrous remnants known as bagasse, which is usually burned as fuel in sugar mills but can be pulped and used for making fibreboard, particle board and most grades of paper. As the costs of imported wood pulp have risen, cane-growing regions have turned increasingly to the manufacture of paper from bagasse. A paper mill based on this process has been established in South Africa. In view of rising energy costs, some countries (such as Mauritius) are encouraging the use of bagasse as fuel for electricity production to save on foreign exchange from imports of oil. Another by-product, cachaza (which had formerly been discarded), is now being exploited as an animal feed.

In recent years sugar has encountered increased competition from other sweeteners, including maize-based products, such as isoglucose (a form of high-fructose corn syrup or HFCS), and chemical additives, such as saccharine, aspartame and xylitol. Consumption of HFCS in the USA was equivalent to about 42% of the country's sugar consumption in the late 1980s, while in Japan and the Republic of Korea HFCS accounted for 19% and 25%, respectively, of domestic sweetener use. Aspartame (APM) was the most widely used high-intensity artificial sweetener in the late 1980s, although its market dominance was expected to be challenged during the 1990s by sucralose, which is about 600 times as sweet as sugar (compared with 200–300 times for

Production of Sugar Beets ('000 metric tons)

	1991	1992
World total	283,588*	279,460*
Africa	4,352	3,789
Leading African producer		
Morocco	3,036	2,754
Leading non-African producers		
France	29,528	31,675
Germany	25,926	27,150
USSR (former)	65,912	59,772†
USA	25,585	26,243

* FAO estimate. † Unofficial figure.

other intense sweeteners) and is more resistant to chemical deterioration than aspartame. In the late 1980s research was being conducted in the USA to formulate means of synthesizing thaumatin, a substance derived from the fruit of a west African plant, *Thaumatoccus daniellii*, which is several thousand times as sweet as sugar. If, as is widely predicted, thaumatin can be commercially produced by the year 2000, it could obtain a substantial share of the markets for both sugar and artificial sweeteners.

South Africa, whose sugar industry is widely regarded as one of the world's most efficient, is the principal producer and exporter of sugar in sub-Saharan Africa. The other leading exporters are Mauritius, Swaziland, Zimbabwe and Réunion.

Sugar is the staple product in the economies of Mauritius and Réunion, although output depends on climatic conditions. Both islands are in the Indian Ocean and subject to cyclones. In Mauritius, despite the fact that an estimated 90% (84,400 ha) of cultivated land is devoted to sugar production, the significance of sugar sales to the economy has been declining in recent years, although in the early 1990s it accounted for about 30% of the island's export revenue. In Réunion almost one-half of the island's 63,050 ha of cultivable land is planted with sugar cane, and sales of sugar provided more than 68% of export income in 1992.

The Mozambique sugar industry, formerly the country's primary source of foreign exchange, is experiencing the effects of many years of disruption and neglect. Plans to rehabilitate production were pending in 1994, but any significant progress must await the resolution of the country's internal guerrilla conflict. Sugar is Malawi's third most important export commodity (after tobacco and tea), providing 6.1% of export earnings (excluding re-exports) in 1991.

In Sudan one of the world's largest single sugar projects was inaugurated in 1981 at Kenana, south of Khartoum. The Kenana Sugar Co (in which the Sudan government has a 50% share), comprising an estate and processing facilities, has been instrumental in the elimination of sugar import costs, which were, until the mid-1980s, Sudan's single largest import item after petroleum. Swaziland is continental Africa's second largest sugar exporter. The majority of the country's sales of sugar are to countries of the European Union (EU, formerly the European Community — EC), under the terms of quota agreements. Sugar cane grows wild throughout Nigeria, although the country's sugar industry remains largely undeveloped. However, six sugar complexes are planned, and it is hoped that self-sufficiency in sugar will be achieved by the year 2000.

The first International Sugar Agreement (ISA) was negotiated in 1958, and its economic provisions operated until 1961. A second ISA did not come into operation until 1969. It included quota arrangements and associated provisions for regulating the price of sugar traded on the open market, and established the International Sugar Organization (ISO) to administer the agreement. However, the USA and the six original members of the EC did not participate in the ISA, and, following its expiry in 1974, it was replaced by a purely administrative interim agreement, which remained operational until the finalization of a third ISA, which took

Production of Centrifugal Sugar (raw value, '000 metric tons)

	1991	1992
World total	112,198*	117,431*
Africa	7,961*	7,228*
Leading African producers		
Côte d'Ivoire	168†	167†
Egypt	1,064†	1,077†
Ethiopia	155†	163†
Kenya	464	402†
Malawi	191	211†
Mauritius	629	643
Morocco	498	461
Réunion	215	246†
South Africa	2,289	1,869
Sudan	471†	513†
Swaziland	517	495†
Zimbabwe	346†	9†
Leading non-African producers		
Australia	3,195†	4,260†
Brazil	9,348†	9,986†
China (incl. Taiwan)	9,078†	8,750†
Cuba	7,623†	7,000†
France	4,423	4,735
Germany	4,224	4,373
India	12,940	14,575†
Mexico	3,365†	3,574†
Thailand	4,055	5,106†
USSR (former)	6,638	6,801
USA	6,495	7,057

* FAO estimate. † Unofficial figure.

effect in 1978. The new agreement's implementation was supervised by an International Sugar Council (ISC), which was empowered to establish price ranges for sugar-trading and to operate a system of quotas and special sugar stocks. Owing to the reluctance of the USA and EC countries (which were not a party to the agreement) to accept export controls, the ISO ultimately lost most of its power to regulate the market, and since 1984 the activities of the organization have been restricted to recording statistics and providing a forum for discussion between producers and consumers. Subsequent ISA, without effective regulatory powers, have been in operation since 1985. (For detailed information on the successive agreements, see *Africa South of the Sahara 1991*.)

Special arrangements for exports of African sugar exist in the successive Lomé Conventions, in operation since 1975, between the EU and a group of African, Caribbean and Pacific (ACP) countries, whereby a special Protocol on sugar, forming part of each Convention, requires the EU to import specified quantities of raw sugar annually from ACP countries.

In tandem with world output of cane and beet sugars, stock levels are an important factor in determining the prices at which sugar is traded internationally. These stocks, which were at relatively low levels in the late 1980s, increased significantly in the 1990/91 trading year (September–August), and in May 1991 the world surplus of raw sugar (production less consumption) for that year was forecast by the ISO at 3.69m. metric tons. The scale of the surplus, which was partly a result of disruptions caused by the Gulf War to demand in the Middle East (normally a major sugar-consuming area), was intensified by substantially increased production in Mexico and the Far East. Additionally, the output of beet sugar was forecast to continue rising, as a result of substantial producers' subsidies within the EC. World sugar stocks again increased in 1991/92, but in August 1993 they were forecast to decline by more than 1.8m. tons in 1992/93, following estimates of lower output from Australia, Brazil, Cuba, South Africa and Thailand. Consumption, which totalled 112.2m. tons worldwide in 1992/93, was forecast in May 1994 to reach 113.9m. tons in 1993/94, resulting in a supply deficit of almost 4.4m. tons.

Most of the world's sugar output is traded at fixed prices under long-term agreements. On the free market, however, sugar prices often fluctuate with extreme volatility.

Export Price Index for Sugar (base: 1980 = 100)

	Average	Highest month(s)	Lowest month(s)
1985	15		
1990	45		
1991	33	38 (July)	28 (May)
1992	33	38 (June, July)	29 (Feb.)
1993	37	43 (May)	30 (Jan.)

In February 1992 the import price of raw cane sugar on the London market was only US $193.0 (equivalent to £107.9 sterling) per metric ton, its lowest level, in terms of US currency, since November 1987. The London price of sugar advanced to $324.9 (£211.9) per ton in May 1993, following predictions of a world sugar deficit in 1992/93. Concurrently, sugar prices in New York were at their highest levels for three years. The London sugar price declined to $237.2 (£157.9) per ton in August 1993, but recovered to $312.7 (£203.1) in June 1994.

The Group of Latin American and Caribbean Sugar Exporting Countries (GEPLACEA), with a membership of 22 Latin American and Caribbean countries, together with the Philippines, and representing about 66% of world cane production and 45% of sugar exports, complements the activities of the ISO (comprising 25 countries in 1993) as a forum for co-operation and research. At the end of 1992 the USA withdrew from the ISO, following a disagreement over the formulation of members' financial contributions. The USA had previously provided about 9% of the ISO's annual budget.

Tea (*Camellia sinensis*)

Tea is a beverage made by infusing in boiling water the dried young leaves and unopened leaf-buds of the tea plant, an evergreen shrub or small tree. Black and green tea are the most common finished products. The former accounts for the bulk of the world's supply and is associated with machine manufacture and, generally, the plantation system, which guarantees an adequate supply of leaf to the factory. The latter, produced mainly in China and Japan, is grown mostly on smallholdings, and much of it is consumed locally. There are two main varieties of tea, the China and the Assam, although hybrids may be obtained, such as Darjeeling. Wherever possible, data on production and trade relate to made tea, i.e. dry, manufactured tea. Where figures have been reported in terms of green (unmanufactured) leaf, appropriate allowances have been made to convert the reported amounts to the approximate equivalent weight of made tea.

Total recorded tea exports by producing countries achieved successive records in each of the years 1983 – 90. World exports (excluding transactions between former Soviet republics) were 1,132,000 tons in 1990, but declined to an estimated 1,070,000 tons in 1991, and to 1,013,000 tons in 1992, before recovering to an estimated 1,111,000 tons in 1993. India (the world's largest consumer) and Sri Lanka have traditionally been the two leading tea exporters, with roughly equal sales, but the quantity which they jointly supply has remained fairly stable (350,000 – 425,000 tons per year in 1977–93), so their share of the world tea trade has been declining. During the 1960s these two countries together exported more than two-thirds of all the tea sold by producing countries, but in 1993 the proportion was 34.9%. Since 1986, India and Sri Lanka have vied for position as the leading tea exporter. In 1989, however, the People's Republic of China (whose sales include a large proportion of green tea) became the second-largest exporter, ahead of Sri Lanka. Nevertheless, in each year since 1990 Sri Lanka has ranked as the main exporting country, and in 1993 China's tea exports were estimated to have exceeded those of India. Exports of tea by African producers have accounted for about one-quarter of world trade since 1990, reaching a record 280,991 tons in 1993.

One of the fastest-growing exporters is Kenya, which ranked fourth in the world during 1975–92. In 1993 Kenya's exports reached a record 188,390 tons, establishing it as the world's third-largest tea supplier, and the source of 67% of the African export total. In 1989 a total of 84,400 ha in Kenya were planted with tea, of which almost 57,000 ha represented smallholder operations. Kenya is expanding its tea exports, as India conserves supplies to satisfy rising domestic consumption. Kenya has replaced India as the United Kingdom's principal supplier, and now provides about 55% of British tea imports. Kenya's tea sales provide about one-quarter of its total export receipts, making tea the country's most valuable export crop after coffee.

Production of Made Tea ('000 metric tons)

	1992	1993
World total	2,404.6*	2,588.8*
Africa	294.4*	339.6*
Leading African producers		
Kenya	188.1	211.2
Malawi	28.1	39.5
Rwanda	13.6	9.5*
South Africa	9.7	10.8
Tanzania	18.4	23.2
Uganda	9.4	11.8
Zimbabwe	7.8	14.1
Leading non-African producers		
China, People's Repub.[1]	559.8	570.0*
India[2]	703.9*	758.1*
Indonesia[3]	145.7	153.0*
Japan[4]	92.1	90.0*
Sri Lanka	178.9	233.3
Turkey	156.3	150.0*
USSR (former)[5]	55.0*	70.0*

* Provisional.

[1] Mainly green tea (338,302 tons in 1992; about 380,000 tons in 1993).

[2] Including a small quantity of green tea (about 6,500 tons in 1992; about 6,000 tons in 1993).

[3] Including green tea (about 35,000 tons in 1992; about 38,000 tons in 1993).

[4] All green tea.

[5] Including green tea (about 11,000 tons in 1992; about 14,000 tons in 1993).

Source: International Tea Committee, *Supplement to Annual Bulletin of Statistics 1993*.

Prior to the Amin regime and the nationalization of tea plantations in 1972, neighbouring Uganda was second only to Kenya among African producers. Uganda's tea exports were negligible by the early 1980s, but, following agreements between tea companies and the subsequent Ugandan governments, exports were resumed. In 1993 Uganda's exports of tea were 10,056 tons, the highest annual total since 1977. Uganda's role in east African tea production has been eclipsed by Tanzania, whose level of exports during the 1980s followed an uneven course, within the range of 10,000–15,000 tons annually. Exports in 1992, however, approached 18,000 tons, advancing to 19,387 tons in 1993. Malawi is, after Kenya, Africa's second largest producer and exporter. Its exports in 1993 were estimated at 34,000 tons, accounting for 12.1% of all African exports. Zimbabwe was Africa's fifth largest exporter of tea in 1993, exporting an estimated 9,000 tons in that year (compared with 12,768 tons in 1989, when it ranked third among African tea-exporters). Tea is a significant component of exports from Burundi and Rwanda: these sales were estimated at 5,760 and 7,000 tons, respectively, in 1993.

For many years the United Kingdom was the largest single importer of tea. However, the country's consumption of tea per person, which amounted to 4.55 kg in 1958, has declined in recent years, averaging 2.52 kg in 1990, 2.63 kg in 1991 and 2.54kg in 1992. A similar trend has been observed in other developed countries, while consumption and imports have expanded significantly in the developing countries (notably Middle East countries) and, particularly, in the USSR, which in 1990 accounted for 21.5% of world imports, having overtaken the United Kingdom in 1989 as the world's principal tea importer. This trend was interrupted in 1991 and 1992, however, by a fall in Middle Eastern (particularly

Iraqi) imports, as a result of the Gulf War, and by a decline in the USSR's tea imports, necessitated by the internal economic problems of the USSR and its successor states. Although Middle Eastern demand remained depressed in 1993, purchases by the former USSR (excluding inter-republican trade) were estimated to have recovered to 160,200 tons from 75,900 tons in 1992, increasing its share of world imports from 7.7% to 15.1%.

Export Price Index for Tea (base: 1980 = 100)

	Average	Highest month(s)	Lowest month(s)
1985	112		
1990	127		
1991	128	139 (Jan.)	115 (July)
1992	150	169 (Dec.)	123 (Feb.)
1993	200	227 (Oct.)	168 (Feb.)

Much of the tea traded internationally is sold by auction, first in the exporting country and then again in the importing country. At the weekly London auctions five categories of tea are offered for sale: 'low medium' (based on a medium Malawi tea), 'medium' (based on a medium Assam and Kenyan tea), 'good medium' (representing an above-average East African tea), 'good' (referring to teas of above-average standard) and (since April 1994) 'best available'. The average price of all grades of tea sold at London auctions increased from £1,047 sterling per metric ton in 1991 to £1,130 per ton in 1992. During 1992 the monthly average ranged from £916 per ton in February to £1,494 in December. It advanced to £1,564 per ton in January 1993, but declined to £1,100 in June. Based on country of origin, the highest-priced tea at London auctions during 1989–92 was that from Rwanda, which realized an average of £1,393 per ton in the latter year. In 1992 the price of 'medium' tea increased from £860 per ton in February to £1,600 in December. The quotation rose to £1,650 per ton in January 1993, but fell to £1,000 in June. Medium tea was traded at £1,250 per ton in October, but the price eased to £1,020 in November and ended the year at £1,140. The London price of this grade was reduced to £1,030 per ton in January 1994, but reached £1,250 in late February and again in June and July.

An International Tea Agreement (ITA), signed in 1933 by the governments of India, Ceylon (now Sri Lanka) and the Netherlands East Indies (now Indonesia), established the International Tea Committee (ITC), based in London, as an administrative body. Although ITA operations ceased after 1955, the ITC has continued to function as a statistical and information centre. In 1993 there were six producer/exporter members (the tea boards or associations of Kenya, Malawi, India, Indonesia, Bangladesh and Sri Lanka), four associate members (including tea-producers' associations from Zimbabwe and the former Soviet republic of Georgia, which accounted for more than 90% of the USSR's tea output in 1990), four consumer members and five other members.

In 1969 the FAO Consultative Committee on Tea was formed and an exporters' group, meeting under this committee's auspices, set export quotas in an attempt to stabilize tea prices. These quotas have applied since 1970 but are generally regarded as too liberal to have any significant effect on prices. The perishability of tea makes the effective operation of a buffer stock very difficult, while African countries are opposed to quota arrangements and are committed to the maximum expansion of tea cultivation. India, while not favouring the revival of a formal ITA to regulate supplies and prices, has advocated greater co-operation between producers to regulate the market. The International Tea Promotion Association (ITPA), founded in 1979 and based in Nairobi, Kenya, comprises eight countries (excluding, however, India and Sri Lanka), accounting for about 35% of the world's exports of black tea.

Tin

The world's main tin deposits occur in the equatorial zones of Asia and Africa, in central South America and in Australia. Cassiterite is the only economically important tin-bearing mineral, and it is generally associated with tungsten, silver and tantalum minerals. There is a clear association of cassiterite with igneous rocks of granitic composition, and 'primary' cassiterite deposits occur as disseminations, or in veins and fissures in or around granites. If the primary deposits are eroded, by rivers for instance, cassiterite may be concentrated and deposited in 'secondary' sedimentary deposits. These secondary deposits comprise the bulk of the world's tin reserves. The ore is treated, generally by gravity method or flotation, to produce concentrates prior to smelting.

Tin owes its special place in industry to its unique combination of properties: low melting point, the ability to form alloys with most other metals, resistance to corrosion, non-toxicity and good appearance. Its main uses are in tinplate (about 40% of world tin consumption), in alloys (tin-lead solder, bronze, brass, pewter, bearing and type metal), and in chemical compounds (in paints, plastics, medicines, coatings and as fungicides and insecticides).

The output of tin concentrates from Nigeria, formerly Africa's main producer, has been in decline since the late 1960s, and Zaire's production has also fallen. Depressed conditions in the world tin market led, in 1990–91, to the suspension of open-cast tin mining in Namibia, formerly a significant regional producer. In 1991 Africa accounted for only 2.8% of world output of tin concentrates; in 1992 the proportion was 2.5%.

Over the period 1956–85, much of the world's tin production and trade was covered by successive international agreements, administered by the International Tin Council (ITC), based in London. The main object of each successive International Tin Agreement (ITA), of which there were six, was to stabilize prices within an agreed range by using a buffer stock to regulate the supply of tin. (For detailed information on the last of these agreements, see *Africa South of the Sahara 1991*.) The buffer stock was financed by producing countries, with voluntary contributions by some consuming countries. 'Floor' and 'ceiling' prices were fixed, and market operations conducted by a buffer stock manager who intervened, as necessary, to maintain prices within these agreed limits. For added protection, the ITA provided for the imposition of export controls if the 'floor' price was being threatened. The ITA was effectively terminated in October 1985, when the ITC's buffer stock manager informed the London Metal Exchange (LME) that he no longer had the funds with which to support the tin market. The factors underlying the collapse of the ITA included its limited membership (Bolivia and the USA, leading producing and consuming countries, were not signatories) and the accumulation of tin stocks which resulted from the widespread circumvention of producers' quota limits. The LME

Production of Tin Concentrates (tin content, metric tons)

	1991	1992
World total	180,199	172,855
Africa	5,028	4,277
Leading African producers		
Burundi	50*	50*
Morocco	200	200*
Niger	19	40
Nigeria	230	230
Rwanda	1,050	900*
South Africa	1,042	600
Zaire	1,600*	1,500*
Zimbabwe	797	716
Leading non-African producers		
Bolivia	16,830	16,516
Brazil	29,500	21,700
China, People's Repub.	39,000*	45,000*
Indonesia	22,163	25,794
Malaysia	20,710	14,339
Thailand	10,122	11,484
USSR (former)	12,000*	10,000*

* Estimated production.

Source: *International Tin Statistics*.

responded by suspending trading in tin, leaving the ITC owing more than £500m. to some 36 banks, tin smelters and metals traders. The crisis was eventually resolved in March 1990, when a financial settlement of £182.5m. was agreed between the ITC and its creditors. The ITC was itself dissolved in July.

These events lent new significance to the activities of the Association of Tin Producing Countries (ATPC), founded in 1983 by Malaysia, Indonesia and Thailand and later joined by Bolivia, Nigeria, Australia and Zaire. Members of the ATPC account for about 45% of world production. The ATPC, which was intended to operate as a complement to the ITC and not in competition with it, introduced export quotas for tin for the year from 1 March 1987. Brazil and the People's Republic of China agreed to co-operate with the ATPC in implementing these supply restrictions, which have been renegotiated to cover succeeding years, with the aim of raising prices and reducing the level of surplus stocks. The ATPC membership has also taken stringent measures to control smuggling. Brazil and China (jointly accounting for almost 40% of world tin production) both have observer status at the ATPC (it was announced in October 1993 that China was to become a full member) and have undertaken to comply with the export quota system, for which the ATPC has no formal powers of enforcement. The ATPC members' quota was fixed at 95,849 tons for 1991, and was reduced to 87,091 tons for 1992. However, the substantial level of world tin stocks (which stood at at 38,200 tons at end-1992), combined with depressed demand, led to mine closures and production cuts, with the result that members' exports in 1991 were below quota entitlements. The continuing depletion of stock levels led to a forecast by the ATPC, in May 1992, that export quotas would be removed in 1994 if these disposals continued at their current rate. The ATPC had previously set a target level of 20,000 tons, representing six weeks of world tin consumption. Projections that world demand for tin would remain at about 160,000 tons annually, together with continued optimism about the rate of stock disposals, led the ATPC to increase its 1993 export quota to 89,700 tons. The persistence, however, of high levels of tin exports by China (estimated to have totalled 30,000 tons in 1993), together with sales of surplus defence stocks of tin by the US government, necessitated a reduction of the quota to 78,000 tons for 1994. In late 1993 prices had fallen to a 20-year 'low' and world tin stocks were estimated at 38,000-40,000 tons, owing partly to the non-observance of quota limits by Brazil and China, as well as to increased production by non-ATPC members.

The success, after 1985, of the ATPC in restoring orderly conditions in tin trading (partly by the voluntary quotas and partly by working towards the reduction of tin stockpiles) unofficially established it as the effective successor to the ITC as the international co-ordinating body for tin interests. The International Tin Study Group (ITSG), comprising 36 producing and consuming countries, was established by the ATPC in 1989 to assume the informational functions of the ITC. In 1991 the secretariat of the United Nations Conference on Trade and Development (UNCTAD) assumed responsibility for the publication of statistical information on the international tin market.

Export Price Index for Tin (base: 1980 = 100)

	Average	Highest month(s)	Lowest month(s)
1985	68		
1990	42		
1991	33	34 (Jan., May-Aug.)	33 (Feb.-April, Sept.-Dec.)
1992	36	42 (July)	33 (Jan.)
1993	31	35 (Jan., Feb.)	27 (Sept.)

Although transactions in tin contracts were resumed on the LME in 1989, the Kuala Lumpur Commodity Exchange (KLCE), in Malaysia, has now become the main centre for international trading in the metal. In January 1993 the price of tin (ex-works) on the KLCE reached 15.28 Malaysian ringgits (RM) per kg, equivalent to £3,828 sterling (or US $5,892) per metric ton. From March, however, the Malaysian tin market gradually eased, and in May a sharp decline began. In September the KLCE price slumped to only RM 10.78 per kg, equivalent to £2,756 (or $4,233) per ton. Measured in terms of US currency, international prices for tin were at their lowest level for 20 years, without taking inflation into account. In October the Malaysian tin price recovered to RM 12.71 per kg (£3,376 or $4,990 per ton), but in November it declined to RM 11.60 per kg (£3,056 or $4,545 per ton). At the end of the year, following a sharp fall in the ringgit's value, tin traded on the KLCE at 12.39 per kg (£3,120 or $4,608 per ton). The rise in tin prices continued in the early weeks of 1994, and in February the Malaysian quotation reached RM 15.15 per kg (£3,684 or $5,449 per ton). In early March the metal's price eased to RM 14.00 per kg (£3,449 or $5,146 per ton), but later in the month it rose to RM 15.01 per kg (£3,715 or $5,515 per ton). The KLCE price was reduced in August to RM 13.00 per kg (£3,265 or $5,053 per ton).

Tobacco (*Nicotiana tabacum*)

Tobacco originated in South America and was used in rituals and ceremonials or as a medicine; it was smoked and chewed for centuries before its introduction into Europe. The generic name *Nicotiana* denotes the presence of the alkaloid nicotine in its leaves. The most important species in commercial tobacco cultivation is *N. tabacum.* Another species, *N. rustica,* is widely grown, but on a smaller scale, to yield cured leaf for snuff or simple cigarettes and cigars.

Commercially grown tobacco (from *N. tabacum*) can be divided into four major types — flue-cured, air-cured (including burley, cigar, light and dark), fire-cured and sun-cured (including oriental) — depending on the procedures used to dry or 'cure' the leaves. Each system imparts specific chemical and smoking characteristics to the cured leaf, although these may also be affected by other factors, such as the type of soil on which the crop is grown, the type and quantity of fertilizer applied to the crop, the cultivar used, the spacing of the crop in the field and the number of leaves left at topping (the removal of the terminal growing point). Each type is used, separately or in combination, in specific products (e.g. flue-cured in Virginia cigarettes). All types are grown in Africa.

As in other major producing areas, local research organizations in Africa have developed new cultivars with specific desirable chemical characteristics, disease-resistance properties and improved yields. The most important tobacco research centres are in Zimbabwe, Malawi and South Africa.

Production of Tobacco Leaves (farm sales weight, '000 metric tons)

	1991	1992
World total	7,462*	8,017*
Africa	427*	477*
Leading African producers		
Kenya	10†	9*
Malawi	113	127
Morocco	7†	7*
Nigeria	9*	9*
South Africa	30	36
Tanzania	17	17
Zimbabwe	179	211†
Leading non-African producers		
Brazil	414	577
China, People's Repub.	3,031	3,158†
Greece	162	187
India	559	579
Italy	193†	185†
Turkey	241	320
USSR (former)	223†	233†
USA	755	764

* FAO estimate. † Unofficial figure.

In Zimbabwe, Malawi, South Africa and, to a lesser extent, in Zambia and Tanzania, tobacco is grown mainly as a direct-labour crop on large farms, some capable of producing as much as 250 metric tons of cured leaf per year. In other parts of Africa, however, tobacco is a small farmers' crop, with each farmer cultivating, on average, 1 or 2 ha of tobacco as well as essential food crops and, usually, other cash crops. Emphasis has been placed on improving yields by the selection of cultivars, by the increased use of fertilizers, by the elimination or reduction of crop loss (through the use of crop chemicals) and by reducing hand-labour requirements through the mechanization of land-preparation and the use of crop chemicals. Where small farmers are responsible for producing the crop, harvesting remains a manual operation, as the area under tobacco and their limited financial means preclude the adoption of mechanical harvesting devices (now commonly used in the USA and Canada). In Zimbabwe, however, small manually-operated units are in use.

The principal type of tobacco that African farmers cultivate is flue-cured, and production within Africa is dominated by Malawi and Zimbabwe. The tobacco sector normally accounts for about 47% of Zimbabwe's total agricultural earnings and is a significant source of foreign exchange. Zimbabwean tobacco is highly regarded for its quality and flavour, and its relatively low tar content has helped to extend its range of customers, particularly in Europe. Depressed conditions in international tobacco markets in the early 1990s were, however, encouraging some Zimbabwean growers to switch to cotton cultivation.

During 1987–90 Malawi obtained 65% of its export revenue from the sale of its tobacco, principally the flue-cured, fire-cured and burley varieties. Malawi is the only significant African producer of burley tobacco, which accounts for about 15% of world exports. Production is limited to commercial estates, but in 1991 the government stated that it was proceeding with plans to extend its cultivation to smallholders, in order to promote a more equitable distribution of agricultural incomes. Demand for burley tobacco has been stimulated by increased manufacturers' emphasis on low-tar cigarettes. The production of burley tobacco in Zimbabwe is being expanded.

Tanzania contributes a small but significant quantity of flue-cured tobacco to the world market. South African production is increasing and quality is improving, particularly in one area, and attracting overseas interest. Tobacco production in Nigeria is fairly static, and its flue-cured crop is entirely reserved for local consumption. Kenya has greatly increased its output of flue-cured leaf since commencing tobacco exports in 1984, and tobacco cultivation has recently been increasing in importance in Uganda, as part of a government programme to offset declining earnings from coffee. There are small but increasingly important exports of flue-cured tobacco from Sierra Leone and Zimbabwe. In the case of the sun- and air-cured types of tobacco, Nigeria, Malawi and South Africa account for the African crop. Modest quantities of oriental tobacco are cultivated in Malawi and South Africa.

Export Price Index for Tobacco (base: 1980 = 100)

	Average	Highest month(s)	Lowest month(s)
1985	129		
1990	125		
1991	131	135 (Oct.)	128 (Aug.)
1992	132	136 (Sept.-Dec.)	130 (Jan.-Aug.)
1993	128	142 (Feb.)	119 (May-July)

The index of export prices for tobacco recovered to 136 in December 1993, and remained at that level in January and February 1994. In the USA the average tobacco price received by farmers was US $3,902 per metric ton in 1991 and $3,918 per ton in 1992. The monthly average was reduced from $4,233 per ton in February 1992 to $3,450 in July. It increased to $4,409 per ton in February 1993, but declined to $3,472 in April.

The International Tobacco Growers' Association (ITGA), formed in 1984 by growers' groups in Argentina, Brazil, Canada, Malawi, the USA and Zimbabwe, now extends to 17 countries, collectively producing more than 80% of the world's internationally traded tobacco. The ITGA provides a forum for the exchange of information among tobacco producers, and publishes data on tobacco production.

Uranium

Uranium occurs in a variety of ores, often in association with other minerals such as gold, phosphate and copper, and may be mined by open-cast, underground or *in situ* leach methods, depending on the circumstances. The concentration of uranium that is needed to form an economic mineral deposit varies widely, depending upon its geological setting and physical location. Average ore grades at operating uranium mines vary from 0.03% U to as high as 10% U, but are most frequently less than 1% U. South Africa, which accounts for about 15% of the world's uranium reserves, produces uranium concentrates as a by-product of gold mining and copper mining, and possesses uranium conversion and enrichment facilities. Both copper mining and the exploitation of phosphates by wet (phosphoric acid-yielding) processes offer a more widespread potential for by-product uranium production. Uranium is chiefly used as a fuel in nuclear reactors for the production of electricity. In 1992 nuclear power plants generated approximately 17% of the world's electricity. Enriched uranium is used as fuel in most nuclear power stations and in the manufacture of nuclear weapons. In the latter, however, the abandonment of East–West confrontation and the prospect of significant nuclear disarmament is likely to reverse the process, with the release of substantial quantities of uranium. In 1993 a report by the OECD's Nuclear Energy Agency and the International Atomic Energy Agency estimated that probable economic reserves of uranium (excluding those in the former Eastern bloc countries and the People's Republic of China) totalled 2.1m. tons.

Because of uranium's strategic military value, there was intense prospecting activity in the 1940s and 1950s, but the market was later depressed as government purchase programmes ceased. Uranium demand fell in the late 1960s and early 1970s, until industrialized countries responded to the 1973–74 petroleum crisis by intensifying their civil nuclear power programmes. Anticipated strong demand for rapidly expanding nuclear power further improved the uranium market until the early 1980s, when lower than expected growth in electricity consumption forced nuclear power programmes to be restricted, leaving both producers and consumers with high levels of accumulated stocks requiring liquidation. A number of mining operations were also scaled down or closed. The market was further depressed in the late 1980s, in the aftermath of the accident in 1986 at the Chernobyl nuclear plant in Ukraine (then part of the USSR), and these factors continued to dominate market conditions in early 1994. Following the scaling-down of its civil and military nuclear power programmes, the USSR began in 1990 to export substantial quantities of low-priced uranium. This factor, together with reduced world demand, has resulted in the close-down of a number of uranium mining operations in Canada, France, the USA and in several of the former Eastern bloc countries. It has been forecast, however, that uranium demand will revive rapidly after the mid-1990s, with the expected increase in world nuclear electricity generating capacity. This has been forecast to grow at an annual compound rate of about 1.5% during the period 1993–2000. Annual world demand will, according to projections by the Uranium Institute, rise to 64,000 tons by the year 2000, from 56,450 tons in 1993.

Canada has, in recent years, become the world's leading producer of uranium, and is expected to retain its position into the 21st century. South Africa has Africa's largest identified uranium resources (currently estimated at 241,000 metric tons), followed by Niger (with ore reserves of about 166,000 tons), Namibia (97,000 tons) and Gabon (15,000 tons). Uranium production has been an important component of the South African mining industry since uranium extraction began in 1951, with production reaching a record 6,146 tons in 1980. Production has subsequently declined sharply, and South Africa has been supplanted by Niger as the continent's main producer. In 1993 Niger ranked

Production of Uranium (uranium content of ores, metric tons)

	1992	1993
World total	35,197	32,532
Africa	6,873	6,855
African producers		
Gabon	540	556
Namibia	1,692	1,665
Niger	2,965	2,914
South Africa	1,676	1,720
Leading non-African producers		
Australia	2,335	2,268
Canada	9,385	9,173
France	2,122	1,708
Kazakhstan	2,700	2,700
Russia	2,640	2,399
Uzbekistan	2,680	2,600

Source: Uranium Institute.

as the world's second-largest producer, and fourth-largest exporter, of uranium. Deliveries of ore from the world's largest open-pit uranium mine, at Rössing in Namibia, began in 1976. Output exceeded its planned level in 1980, but subsequently declined, owing to a reduction in demand and increased competition from low-cost producers. The removal of sanctions against Namibian uranium, following that country's independence from South Africa in 1990, coincided with a decline in world demand, which led to the restructuring of operations and a reduction in the work-force during 1991.

Uranium ore reserves were first identified in Gabon in 1956 and their exploitation began in 1958. During 1956–81 exploration efforts led to the discovery of several deposits: at Mounana (1956), Mikouloungou (1965), Boyindzi (1967), Oklo (1968), Okélobondo (1974) and Bagombé (1980). The deposits at Bagombé and Mikouloungou have yet to be exploited. Known reserves are sufficient for 50 years' output at current production rates. Uranium exploitation and development is handled by a consortium which is controlled mainly by French interests, but with a 25% participation by the government of Gabon. Since 1958 a total of 24,000 tons of uranium has been produced and delivered to customers. Since 1989 the level of production has declined, owing to a reduction in the volume sold. Measures to increase productivity and competitiveness have included a 54% reduction in the work-force, compared with 1989 levels.

Uranium exploration in Niger started in the 1950s, around the Aïr mountains near Agadez, with production commencing at the Arlit mine in 1971. Niger also has a uranium mine at Akouta, where production commenced in 1978, and there are several other sites awaiting development. France purchases most of Niger's uranium production, with the remainder taken by German, Japanese and Spanish customers. Like Namibia, Niger has recently been compelled to restructure and streamline its uranium operations to take account of lower levels of world demand.

Uranium has also been found in Algeria, Botswana, the Central African Republic, Chad, Egypt, Guinea, Madagascar, Mali, Mauritania, Morocco, Nigeria, Somalia, Tanzania, Togo, Zaire and Zambia. However, under current economic conditions, it is unlikely that any of these deposits will be exploited in the immediate future.

The European market price for uranium oxide reached US $8.75 per lb in October 1992, but was reduced to $8.00 per lb in November and to $7.90 in December. Market conditions remained depressed in 1993, with the price moving steadily downward to $7.00 per lb in July. It fell to $6.90 per lb in August and was maintained at that level for the remainder of the year. The price of uranium oxide was adjusted to $7.00 per lb in January 1994, and to $7.10 in July.

The Uranium Institute — the International Industrial Association for Energy from Nuclear Fuel — comprises mining companies, electricity utilities and nuclear fuel processors and traders from 20 countries in Europe, North America, Asia, Africa and Australia. Founded in 1975 to promote the use of uranium for peaceful purposes, the Institute organizes meetings, conducts research, and disseminates information on uranium production and the nuclear fuel industry.

Wheat (*Triticum*)

The most common species of wheat (*T. vulgare*) includes hard, semi-hard and soft varieties which have different milling characteristics but which, in general, are suitable for bread-making. Another species, *T. durum*, is grown mainly in semi-arid areas, including north Africa and the Mediterranean. This wheat is very hard and is suitable for the manufacture of semolina. In north Africa, in addition to being used for making local bread, semolina is the basic ingredient of pasta and couscous. A third species, spelt (*T. spelta*), is also included in production figures for wheat. It is grown in very small quantities in parts of Europe and is used as animal feed.

Although a most adaptable crop, wheat does not thrive in hot and humid climates. Most of Africa is, therefore, climatically unsuitable, and the continent's wheat production is mainly concentrated in a narrow strip along the Mediterranean coast from Morocco to Tunisia, in the Nile valley, and in parts of South Africa. Zimbabwe, Kenya, Ethiopia and Sudan also grow limited quantities, but many countries in west Africa produce virtually no wheat. In contrast with some developing countries of Asia, the potential of improved wheat varieties has yet to be realized in much of Africa, especially south of the Sahara. One reason is the undeveloped state of the transport systems in many countries, which hinders both the distribution of production inputs (e.g. seeds and fertilizers) and the marketing of farmers' surplus produce. Until recently, many governments have also been unwilling to pay sufficiently attractive producer prices for wheat.

Wheat production in sub-Saharan Africa averages about 4m. tons annually, South Africa itself accounting for almost two-thirds of the total. Production there is rain-fed, and levels of output are highly variable. Large crops in the 1980s caused financial loss to the Wheat Board, as the surpluses had to be exported against subsidized competition on world markets. The policy of self-sufficiency in wheat production was modified, and marginal land has been taken out of production. In some other wheat-producing countries (e.g. Tanzania and Zimbabwe) the crop is grown mainly on large commercial farms, and, with the benefit of irrigation, usually yields well. Efforts to produce wheat in tropical countries, such as Nigeria and Zaire, have not as yet been successful.

In the long term, world wheat production has been increasing at an average rate of more than 3% per year, but there are wide year-to-year fluctuations, owing to variations in weather conditions in the main producing areas, especially the occurrence of drought, and to the production policies adopted by some exporting countries to regulate output and to keep their stock levels under control. World consumption, which, in the long term, has been growing at a similar rate to production, fluctuates much less from year to year. Nearly 70% of total consumption is directly used as human food, while about 20%, on average, is used for animal feed, mainly in developed countries and the former USSR, but increasingly in developing countries. Feed use increases when wheat prices are low in comparison with those of coarse grains, such as maize. Wheat is believed to be the principal food of more than 40% of the world's population. It was not until recently an important constituent of diets in many countries of sub-Saharan Africa, but in the 1980s wheat consumption increased rapidly in most African countries, often as a consequence of urbanization. The rate of increase appears to have eased in the 1990s, for reasons that may include improved domestic food supplies, together with the difficulty that African countries encounter in financing more commercial wheat imports. As sub-Saharan Africa (unlike North Africa, for example) is not regarded by the major wheat-exporting countries as a theatre for competition, wheat exports to that region are generally not heavily subsidized, although significant amounts are regularly provided as food aid.

There is more international trade in wheat than in any other cereal. The principal exporters are the USA (which accounts for about one-third of the total), the EC, Canada, Australia and Argentina. Developed countries were formerly the main markets, but the role of developing countries as importers has been steadily increasing, accounting for more than three-quarters (70m. tons) of world imports in 1993/94. Africa's imports have recently averaged about 20m. tons per year. The major African markets are in the north (Algeria, Egypt and Morocco). Sub-Saharan Africa accounts for around 5m. tons annually, but for larger quantities in drought years, especially when white maize is not available on world markets. In 1993/94 the region imported more than 7m. tons, including about 1m. tons of flour.

Since 1949 nearly all world trade in wheat has been conducted under the auspices of successive international agreements, administered by the International Wheat Council (IWC) in London. The early agreements involved regulatory price controls and supply and purchase obligations, but such provisions became inoperable in more competitive market conditions, and were abandoned in 1972. The IWC subsequently concentrated on providing detailed market assessments to its members and encouraging them to confer on matters of mutual concern. Under a new Wheat Trade Convention, which entered into force in 1986, the IWC obtained a wider mandate, allowing it to consider developments in markets for coarse grains as well as wheat, while also reinforcing international co-operation among members, especially for the benefit of developing country members. This Convention has a membership of 48 countries, including most of the major grain-exporting and importing nations. African members include Algeria, Côte d'Ivoire, Egypt, Mauritius, Morocco, South Africa and Tunisia.

The 1986 Food Aid Convention was brought into force in July 1986 as one of the instruments of the new International Wheat Agreement. Donor members of the Convention pledge to supply minimum annual quantities of food aid to developing countries in the form of wheat and other grains suitable for human consumption. The obligations are basically quantitative, ensuring that the volume of aid is not reduced in times of very short supplies and rising grain prices. In recent seasons, upwards of 10m. tons of food aid has been provided annually under the Convention, of which 2m.–3m. tons (not all in the form of wheat) was directed to sub-Saharan Africa. The Food Aid Committee, which administers the Convention, is a focal point of international co-operation in food aid matters.

Production of Wheat ('000 metric tons)

	1992	1993*
World total	560,600	555,500
Africa	13,500	13,450
Leading African producers		
Algeria	1,750	1,350
Egypt	4,800	5,000
Ethiopia	900	900
Kenya	200	150
Libya	150	130
Morocco	1,560	1,530
South Africa	1,320	1,960
Sudan	900	600
Tunisia	1,580	1,410
Zimbabwe	80	200
Leading non-African producers		
Australia	16,200	18,000
Canada	29,870	27,820
China, People's Repub.	100,500	105,000
France	32,500	29,420
Germany	15,540	15,780
India	55,700	56,760
Turkey	17,300	17,000
USSR (former)	89,600	81,700
USA	66,920	65,370

* Provisional.

Source: International Wheat Council.

In the case of one widely-traded variety of wheat from the USA, Hard Winter No.2, the average export price (f.o.b. Gulf ports) increased from US $129 per metric ton in 1991 to $151 per ton in 1992. On a monthly basis, the average price of this cereal was reduced from $177 per ton in February 1992 to $130 in August. It recovered to $156 per ton in January 1993, but fell to $124 in June.

Export Price Index for Wheat (base: 1980 = 100)

	Average	Highest month(s)	Lowest month(s)
1985	81		
1990	82		
1991	72	87 (Dec.)	63 (Jan.)
1992	83	96 (Feb.)	71 (Aug.)
1993	81	92 (Dec.)	75 (June)

ACKNOWLEDGEMENTS

We gratefully acknowledge the assistance of the following organizations in the preparation of this section:

African Groundnut Council
Association of Iron Ore Exporting Countries
British-American Tobacco Co
Bureau of Mines, US Department of the Interior
Central Selling Organisation
Centro Internacional de Agricultura Tropical
Cobalt Information Centre
Copper Development Association
Cotton Research Corporation
De Beers
Food and Agricultural Organization of the UN
Gill & Duffus Group PLC
Gold Fields Mineral Services Ltd
Institute of Petroleum
Intergovernmental Council of Copper Exporting Countries
International Bauxite Association
International Cocoa Organization
International Coffee Organization
International Cotton Advisory Committee
International Institute for Cotton
International Iron and Steel Institute
International Monetary Fund
International Primary Aluminium Institute
International Rice Research Institute
International Sugar Organization
International Tea Committee
International Wheat Council
Johnson Matthey PLC
Malaysian Oil Palm Growers' Council
United Nations Conference on Trade and Development
US Department of Energy
Uranium Institute
World Bureau of Metal Statistics

Sources for Agricultural Production Tables (unless otherwise indicated): FAO, *Production Yearbook 1992* (Rome 1993); FAO, *Quarterly Bulletin of Statistics*, issues to November 1993.

Source for Mineral Production Tables (unless otherwise indicated): UN, *Industrial Statistics Yearbook*.

Source for Export Price Indexes: UN, *Monthly Bulletin of Statistics*, issues to June 1994.

RESEARCH INSTITUTES

ASSOCIATIONS AND INSTITUTIONS STUDYING AFRICA

See also Regional Organizations in Part II

ARGENTINA

Instituto de Filosophia, Seccion de Estudios Interdisciplinario de Asia y Africa: 25 de Mayo 221, 4° piso, 1002 Buenos Aires; tel. (1) 334-7512; fax (1) 343-2733; f. 1982; multidisciplinary seminars and lectures; Dir Prof. MARÍA ELENA VELA; publ. *Temas de Africa y Asia* (2 a year).

Nigeria House: Florida 142, 1337 Buenos Aires; tel. (1) 326-5543; f. 1963; library specializing in Nigerian material and general information on Africa; Dir EMILIA MARÍA SANNAZZARI.

AUSTRALIA

Australian Institute of International Affairs: 32 Thesiger Court, Deakin, ACT 2600; tel. (06) 2822133; fax (6) 2852334; f. 1933; 1,800 mems; brs in all States; Pres. R. H. SEARBY; publs include *Australian Journal of International Affairs* (2 a year).

Indian Ocean Centre for Peace Studies: University of Western Australia, Nedlands, WA 6009; tel. (9) 3803993; fax (9) 3801074; Exec. Dir Assoc. Prof. KENNETH MCPHERSON; publ. *Indian Ocean Review* (quarterly).

AUSTRIA

Afro-Asisatisches Institut in Wien (Afro-Asian Institute in Vienna): 1090 Vienna, Türkenstrasse 3; tel. (1) 3105145; f. 1959; cultural and other exchanges between Austria and African and Asian countries; economic and social research; lectures, seminars; Pres. Bishop FLORIAN KUNTNER; Gen. Sec. Dr NICOLAI WOCHINZ.

Österreichische Forschungsstiftung für Entwicklungshilfe (Austrian Foundation for Development Research): 1090 Vienna, Berggasse 7; tel. (1) 3174010; fax 3174015; f. 1967; documentation and information on development aid and developing countries, particularly in relation to Austria; library of 21,000 vols and 250 periodicals; publs *Ausgewählte neue Literatur zur Entwicklungspolitik* (2 a year), *Österreichische Entwicklungspolitik* (annually).

Österreichische Gesellschaft fur Aussenpolitik und Internationale Beziehungen (Austrian Society for Foreign Policy and International Relations): 1010 Vienna, Hofburg/Schweizerhof; tel. (1) 5354627; f. 1958; lectures, discussions; 360 mems; Pres. Dr HANS HAUMER; publ. *Österreichisches Jahrbuch für Internationale Politik* (annually).

Österreichisches Institut für Entwicklungshilfe und technische Zusammenarbeit mit den Entwicklungsländern (Austrian Institute for Development Aid and Technical Co-operation with the Developing Countries): 1010 Vienna, Wipplingerstrasse 35; tel. (1) 426504; f. 1963; projects for management training; Pres Dr HANS INGLER, ERICH HOFSTETTER.

BELGIUM

Académie royale des sciences d'outre-mer/Koninklijke Academie voor Overzeese Wetenschappen: 1 rue Defacqz, Boîte 3, 1050 Brussels; tel. (2) 5380211; fax (2) 5392353; f. 1928; the promotion of scientific knowledge of overseas areas, especially those with special development problems; 88 mems, 75 assoc. mems, 71 corresp. mems; Perm. Exec. Sec. Prof. J.-J. SYMOENS.

Bibliothèque africaine: 65 rue Belliard, 1040 Brussels; tel. (2) 2382511; f. 1885; library of 400,000 vols; large collections in the fields of African history, ethnography, economics, politics; Dir Mlle FR. PEEMANS.

Centre international de formation et de recherche en population et développement en association avec les Nations Unies (CIDEP): 1/17 place Montesquieu, 1348 Louvain-La-Neuve; tel. (32) 10474542; fax (32) 10472997; f. 1986; research and training in population and development issues; Nat. Dir H. GERARD; Int. Dir M. MAZOUZ; publs *La Lettre du CIDEP* (quarterly), *Les Cahiers du CIDEP* (irregular).

College voor de Ontwikkelingslanden–Institute of Development Policy and Management: University of Antwerp–RUCA, Middelheimlaan 1, 2020 Antwerp; tel. (3) 2180660; fax (3) 2180666; f. 1920; library and documentation centre; Pres. Prof. C. VAN HERBRUGGEN; publs research reports and papers (irregular).

Fondation pour favoriser les recherches scientifiques en Afrique: 1 rue Defacqz, BP 5, 1050 Brussels; tel. (2) 2693905; f. 1969 to conduct scientific research in Africa with special reference to environmental management and conservation; Dir Dr A. G. ROBYNS; publs *Exploration des Parcs nationaux, Etudes du Continent africain.*

Institut Africain/Afrika Instituut: Centre d'étude et de documentation africaines/Afrika Studie– en Dokumentatiecentrum, 65 rue Belliard, 1040 Brussels; tel. (2) 2307562; fax (2) 2307605; f. 1970; research and documentation on African social and economic problems, with special reference to Burundi, Rwanda and Zaire; Dir G. DE VILLERS; publ. *Cahiers Africains–Afrika Studies* (6 a year).

Institut d'études du développement: Université catholique de Louvain, Dépt des sciences de la population et du développement, 3 place Montesquieu, 1348 Louvain-La-Neuve; tel. (32) 473935; fax (010) 472997; f. 1961; Pres. F. DEBUYST.

Institut royal des relations internationales: 65 rue de Belliard, 4e étage, 1040 Brussels; tel. (2) 2302230; fax (2) 2305230; f. 1947; research in international relations, economics, law and politics; archives and library of 15,000 vols and 600 periodicals; Dir-Gen. TONY HOLLANTS-VAN LOOCKE; Exec. Dir Mme M. T. BOCKSTAELE; publs *Studia Diplomatica* (bi-monthly), *Internationale Spectator* (monthly).

Koninklijk Museum voor Midden-Afrika/Musée royal de l'Afrique centrale: Leuvensesteenweg 13, 3080 Tervuren; tel. (2) 7695211; fax (2) 7670242; f. 1897; collections of prehistory, ethnography, nature arts and crafts; geology, mineralogy, palaeontology; zoology (entomology, ornithology, mammals, reptiles, etc.); history; economics; library of 90,000 vols and 4,500 periodicals; Dir D. THYS VAN DEN AUDENAERDE; publs include *Annales du Musée royal de l'Afrique centrale.*

Société belge d'etudes géographiques (Belgian Society for Geographical Studies): de Croylaan 42, 3001 Heverlee (Leuven); tel. (16) 286611; f. 1931; centralizes and co-ordinates geographical research in Belgium; 395 mems; Pres. Y. VERHASSELT; Sec. H. VAN DER HAEGEN; publ. *Bulletin* (2 a year).

Union royale belge pour les pays d'outre-mer: 22 rue de Stassart, 1050 Brussels; tel. (2) 5111693; f. 1912; fed. of 29 asscns; Chair. PIERRE ANDRES; Gen. Sec. OSCAR LIBOTTE.

BRAZIL

Centro de Estudos Africanos (African Studies Centre): University of São Paulo, CP 8105, 05508-900 São Paulo SP; tel. (11) 2109416; telex 80902; fax (11) 2116281; f. 1969; co-ordinating unit for all depts with African interests; specialist studies in sociology, international relations and literature concerning Africa; library; Dir Prof. FERNANDO A. A. MOURÃO; publ. *África* (annually).

Centro de Estudos Afro-Asiáticos—CEAA (Afro-Asian Studies Centre): Conjunto Universitário Candido Mendes, Rua da Assembléia 10, Conjunto 501, 20011 Rio de Janeiro

RJ; tel. (21) 2213536; f. 1973; instruction and seminars; library; Dir CANDIDO MENDES; publ. *Estudos Afro-Asiáticos*.

Centro de Estudos Afro-Orientais—CEAO (Afro-Oriental Studies Centre): Federal University of Bahia, CP 1163, 40145 Salvador BA; tel. (71) 2450120; f. 1959; African and Afro-Brazilian studies; library; Dir Dr JULIO SANTANA BRAGA; publs include *Afro-Ásia* (irregular).

Centro de Estudos e Pesquisas de Cultura Yorubana (Yoruba Culture Study and Research Centre): CP 40099, CEP 20272, Rio de Janeiro RJ; tel. (21) 2930649; instruction in Yoruba language and religion; Dir Prof. FERNANDES PORTUGAL; publs include occasional papers.

Núcleo de Estudos Afro-Asiáticos Afro-Asian Studies Unit): State University of Londrina, CP 6001, 86051 Londrina PR; tel. (432) 275151; f. 1986; seminars and lectures; Dir Prof. EDUARDO JUDAS BARROS; publ. *África Asia* (annually).

Núcleo Ibérico, Latino-Americano e Luso-Africano—NILALA (Iberian, Latin American and Luso-African Unit): University of Ijuí, Rua São Francisco 501, 98700 Ijuí RGS; f. 1984; lectures; Dir Prof. MARÍA LUIZA DE CARVALHO ARMANDO; publ. *Cadernos Luso-Africanos* (irregular).

BULGARIA

Institute for International Relations and Socialist Integration: '7 Noemvri' 1, 1040 Sofia; tel. (2) 523075; f. 1976; attached to the Presidium of the Bulgarian Acad. of Sciences; Dir Prof. N. CAREVSKI; publs *Afrikano-Aziatski Problemi, Meždunarodni Otnošenija*.

CANADA

Canadian Association of African Studies: c/o Roger Riendeau, Innis College, University of Toronto, 2 Sussex Ave, Toronto, ON M5S 2G8; f. 1971; publs *Canadian Journal of African Studies* (English and French), *CAAS Newsletter* (English and French).

Canadian Council for International Co-operation: 1 Nicholas St, Suite 300, Ottawa, ON K1N 7B7; tel. (613) 241-7007; fax (613) 241-5302; f. 1968; fed. of 120 voluntary orgs promoting global development; Pres. JACQUES CHAMPAGNE; Exec. Dir BETTY PLEWES; publs include monthly newsletter.

Centre for African Studies: Dalhousie University, Halifax, NS B3H 4H6; tel. (902) 494-3814; telex 019-21863; fax (902) 494-2319; f. 1975; Dir Dr JANE L. PARPART (acting); publs include *Dalhousie African Studies* series, *Dalhousie African Working Papers* series, *Briefing Papers on the African Crisis*.

Centre for Developing-Area Studies: McGill University, 3715 rue Peel, Montréal, PQ H3A 1X1; tel. (514) 398-3507; telex 052-168510; fax (514) 398-8432; publs include *LABOUR, Capital and Society* (English and French—2 a year), discussion papers.

Institute for International Development and Co-operation: c/o University of Ottawa, 550 Cumberland Ave, Ottawa, ON K1N 6N5; tel. (613) 564-5773; fax (613) 564-9518; f. 1968; Dir Dr GEORGES HENAULT; publs include *Proceedings of International Conferences* (French and English, annually), *Selective Bibliographies* (French and English, annually), *Canadian Journal of Development Studies* (English and French, bi-annually).

International Development Research Centre: POB 8500, Ottawa, ON K1G 3H9; tel. (613) 236-6163; telex 053-3753; fax (613) 238-7230; f. 1970 by the govt to support research projects designed to meet the basic needs of developing countries and to address problems associated with poverty; regional offices in Kenya, Senegal, Egypt, Singapore, Uruguay, India and South Africa; Pres. Dr KEITH A. BEZANSON; publs include *The IDRC Reports* (French, Spanish and English—quarterly).

Lester Pearson Institute for International Development: 1321 Edward St, Halifax, NS B3H 3H5; tel. (902) 494-2038; telex 019-21863; fax (902) 494-1216; f. 1985; admin. dept. of Dalhousie Univ. responsible for univ.'s externally-funded int. devt. activities; also promotes academic research and conducts seminars; publs include *PearsonNews* (bi-monthly), *Pearson Notes* (quarterly).

CHILE

Instituto Chileno-Zaireno de Cultura (Chilean-Zairean Cultural Institute): Casilla 144, Correo 10, Las Condes, Santiago; tel. (2) 2201464; f. 1981; affiliated inst. of the Univ. of Chile; holds seminars and exhbns and promotes cultural and academic exchanges with Zaire; Dir Ing. GONZALO BELTRÁN.

PEOPLE'S REPUBLIC OF CHINA

Centre for International Studies: 22 Xianmen Dajie, POB 7411, Beijing; f. 1982; conducts research on international relations and problems; organizes academic exchanges; Gen. Dir Prof. HUAN XING.

West Asian and African Studies Institute: Chinese Academy of Social Sciences, 5 Jianguomen Nei Da Jie 5 Hao, Beijing; f. 1980; Dir. GE JIE.

CZECH REPUBLIC

Ústav mezinárodních vztahů (Institute of International Relations): Prague 1, Nerudova 3; tel. (2) 24511253; fax (2) 24511257; f. 1970; Dir Prof. JIŘÍ VALENTA; Scientific Sec. Dr PETER KAŇKA; publs include *International Relations* (quarterly).

DENMARK

Center for Udviklingsforskning (Centre for Development Research): Gammel Kongeveg 5, 1610 Copenhagen V; tel. 33251200; fax 33258110; f. 1969 to promote and undertake research in the economic, social and political problems of developing countries; library of 30,000 vols; Dir Prof. KNUD ERIK SVENDSEN; publs include *Den ny Verden* (quarterly), *CDR Library Papers* (irregular), *CDR Research Reports* (in English, irregular), *CDR Working Papers* (in English, irregular).

Udenrigspolitiske Selskab (Foreign Policy Society): Amaliegade 40A, 1256 Copenhagen K; tel. 148886; f. 1946; studies, debates, courses and conferences on international affairs; Dir KLAUS CARSTEN PEDERSEN; publs *Udenrigs, Udenrigspolitiske Skrifter*.

EGYPT

African Association: 5 Ahmet Hishmat St, 11561 Zamalik, Cairo; tel. (2) 3407658; Sec.-Gen. MOHAMED FOUAD EL BEDEWY.

Society for Coptic Archaeology: 222 Sharia Ramses, Cairo; tel. (2) 824252; f. 1934; 360 mems; library of c. 14,500 vols; Pres. WASSIF BOUTROS GHALI; Sec.-Gen. Dr A. KHATER; publs include *Bulletin* (annually), monographs.

FRANCE

Académie des sciences d'outre-mer: 15 rue La-pérouse, 75116 Paris; tel. 47208793; fax 47208972; f. 1922; 255 mems, of which 275 mems are attached to sections on geography, politics and administration, law, economics and sociology, science and medicine, education; library of 45,000 vols and 2,500 periodicals; Perm. Sec. GILBERT MANGIN; publs include *Mondes et Cultures* (quarterly).

Association d'études et d'informations politiques internationales: 86 blvd Haussmann, 75008 Paris; f. 1949; Dir G. ALBERTINI; publs include *Les Informations politiques et sociales* (weekly), *Est & Ouest* (fortnightly).

Centre d'études politiques et juridiques du tiers monde–UFR 07: Université de Paris I, 12 place du Panthéon, 75231 Paris Cedex 05; tel. 46349756; fax 44070833; f. 1965; Dir Prof. JEAN-PIERRE QUÉNEUDEC.

Centre d'études et de recherches sur le développement international (CERDI): Faculté des sciences economiques, Université de Clermont-Ferrand, 65 blvd Gergovia, 63000 Clermont-Ferrand; tel. 73431200; fax 73431228.

Centre de recherches africaines: 9 rue Malher, 75181 Paris Cedex 04; tel. 42783322; fax 40299887; an inst. of the Universities of Paris I, III, V; Dir JEAN BOULEGUE.

Centre des hautes études sur l'Afrique et l'Asie modernes: 13 rue du Four, 75006 Paris; tel. 444138180; fax

40510358; f. 1936; an affiliated inst. of Fondation nationale des sciences politiques; Dir PH. DECRAENE; publs *L'Afrique et L'Asie modernes* (quarterly), *Publications du CHEAM* (irregular), *Notes africaines, asiatiques et caraïbes* (irregular).

Ecole libre de hautes études internationales: 4 place St-Germain-des-Près, 75006 Paris; tel. 2226806; f. 1924; Dir PASCAL CHAIGNEAU.

Institut français de recherche scientifique pour le développement en coopération (ORSTOM): 213 rue La Fayette, 75480 Paris Cedex 10; tel. 48037777; telex 214627; fax 48030829; f. 1943, reorg. 1982; self-financing; centres, missions and rep. offices in Burkina Faso, Cameroon, the Central African Republic, Chad, the Congo, Côte d'Ivoire, Gabon, Madagascar, Mali, Niger, Senegal and Togo; Pres. MICHEL LEVALLOIS; Dir GÉRARD WINTER; scientific publs.

Institut français des relations internationales: 6 rue Ferrus, 75683 Paris; tel. 40789100; telex 201680; fax 45651514; f. 1979; 900 mems; library of 30,000 vols; Chair. MAURICE FAURE; Dir THIERRY DE MONTBRIAL; publs include *Politique etrangère* (quarterly), *Lettre d'Information* (bi-monthly), *Ramses* (annually).

Musée de l'Homme: Palais de Chaillot, place du Trocadéro, 75116 Paris; tel. 44057272; f. 1878; library of 250,000 vols (c. 30,000 on Africa) and 5,000 periodicals; ethnography, physical anthropology, prehistory; also a research and education centre; Dirs Profs BERNARD DUPAIGNE (Ethnology), ANDRÉ LANGANEY (Anthropology), HENRY DE LUMLEY (Prehistory).

Société des africanistes (CSSF): Musée de l'Homme, Palais de Chaillot, 75116 Paris; tel. 47277255; f. 1931; 350 mems; Pres. MARC PIAULT; publ. *Journal des Africanistes.*

Société française d'histoire d'outre-mer: 9 rue Robert de Flers, 75015 Paris; tel. 40584873 (Mon. afternoons); f. 1913; Pres. CHARLES-ROBERT AGERON; Sec.-Gen. ROGER PASQUIER; publs include *Revue française d'histoire d'outre-mer* (quarterly).

GERMANY

Centre of African Studies: Leipzig University, 7010 Leipzig, Augustusplatz 9; tel. (41) 7193281; telex 51350; fax (41) 209325; Dir Dr ANNE-SOPHIE ARNOLD.

Deutsche Gesellschaft für Auswärtige Politik eV (German Society for Foreign Affairs): 53113 Bonn, Adenauerallee 131; tel. (228) 26750; fax (228) 2675173; f. 1955; promotes research on problems of international politics; library of 48,000 vols; 1,500 mems; Pres. Dr WERNER LAMBY; Exec. Vice-Pres. REINHARD SCHLAGINTWEIT; Dir Research Inst. Prof. Dr KARL KAISER; publs *Europa-Archiv—Zeitschrift für internationale Politik* (fortnightly), *Die Internationale Politik* (annually).

IFO–Institut für Wirtschaftsforschung (IFO–Institute for Economic Research): Dept of Development Studies, 81679 Munich, Poschingerstrasse 5, POB 860460; tel. (89) 92240; telex 522269; fax (89) 9224462; f. 1949; library of 80,000 vols; Head of Dept Dr S. SCHÖNHERR; publs include *Afrika-Studien, IFO-Studien zur Entwicklungsforschung, Forschungsberichte der Abteilung Entwicklungsländer.*

Informationsstelle Südliches Afrika eV (Information Centre on Southern Africa): 53227 Bonn 3, Königswintererstrasse 116; tel. (228) 464369; fax (228) 468177; f. 1971; research, documentation, and information on southern Africa; publs include *Informationsdienst Südliches Africa* (6 a year).

Institut für Afrika-Kunde (Institute of African Affairs): 20354 Hamburg, Neuer Jungfernstieg 21; tel. (40) 3562523; fax (40) 3562547; f. 1963; research, documentation, information; library of 47,000 vols and 500 periodicals; Dir Dr ROLF HOFMEIER; publs include *Hamburg African Studies, Hamburger Beiträge zur Afrika-Kunde, Arbeiten aus dem Institut für Afrika-Kunde, Afrika Spectrum, Aktueller Informationsdienst Afrika.*

HUNGARY

Magyar Tudományos Akadémia Világgazdasági Kutató Intézete (Institute for World Economics of the Hungarian Academy of Sciences): 1124 Budapest, Kálló esperes u. 15; tel. (1) 1668433; telex 227713; fax (1) 1620661; f. 1965; library of 70,000 vols; Dir Prof. ANDRÁS INOTAI; publs *Studies on Developing Countries* (irregular, in English), *Trends in World Economy* (irregular, in English), working papers (irregular, in English).

INDIA

Centre for Development Studies: Prasanthnagar Rd, Ulloor, Thiruvananthapuram 695011; tel. (471) 448881; telex 425227; fax (471) 447137; f. 1971; instruction and research in disciplines relevant to development; library of 102,000 vols.

Centre for West Asian and African Studies: School of International Studies, Jawaharlal Nehru University, New Delhi (11) 110067; tel. 667676, ext. 359; telex 73167; Prof. and Chair. Dr VIJAY GUPTA.

Centre of East African Studies: University of Bombay, Vidyanagari (Kalina) Campus, Santacruz (East), Bombay 400098; tel. (22) 6113091; Dir Dr ANKUSH B. SAWANT (acting).

Department of African Studies: University of Delhi, Delhi (11) 110007; tel. 7257725; Head of Dept Prof. K. MATHEWS; publ. *Indian Journal of African Studies.*

Indian Centre for Africa: Indian Council for Cultural Relations, Azad Bhavan, Indraprastha Estate, New Delhi (11) 110002; tel. 3319226; telex 3161860; fax 3712639; f. 1987; publ. *Africa Quarterly.*

Indian Council of World Affairs: Sapru House, Barakhamba Rd, New Delhi 110001; tel. (11) 3317246; f. 1943; independent institution for the study of Indian and international questions; library of 123,000 vols, 624 periodicals, 2.3m. press clippings and 12,580 microfilms and microfiches; 1,500 mems; Pres. HARCHARAN SINGH JOSH; publs include *Foreign Affairs Reports* (monthly), *India Quarterly.*

ISRAEL

Harry S. Truman Research Institute for the Advancement of Peace: The Hebrew University of Jerusalem, Mt Scopus, Jerusalem 91905; tel. (2) 882300; telex 26458; fax (2) 828076; f. 1966; conducts a broad range of research relating to non-Western and developing countries; Chair. Prof. MOSHE MA'OZ; Exec. Dir Dr EDY KAUFMAN.

Institute of Asian and African Studies: The Hebrew University of Jerusalem, Mt Scopus, Jerusalem 91905; tel. (2) 883516; telex 26458; fax (2) 322545; provides degree and postgraduate courses, covering history, social sciences and languages; Chair. of Inst. Prof. ARYEH LEVIN.

International Institute for Labour, Development and Co-operative Studies (ILDEC)—Histadrut: 7 Neharde'a St, POB 16201, Tel-Aviv 64235; tel. (3) 522-9195; telex 361480; fax (3) 522-2714; f. 1958 to train leadership for trade unions, co-operatives, community orgs, women's and youth groups, etc. in developing countries; library of 17,600 vols and pamphlets; Chair. Prof. SHIMON SHETREET; Dir and Prin. Dr YEHUDAH PAZ.

The Israel Oriental Society: The Hebrew University, Mt Scopus, Jerusalem; f. 1949; arranges lectures and symposia on contemporary Middle Eastern, Asian and African affairs; Pres. T. KOLLEK; publs include *Hamizrah Hehadash* The New East (Hebrew, quarterly), *Asian and African Studies* (3 a year).

Shiloah Institute for Middle Eastern and African Studies: Ramat-Aviv, Tel-Aviv 69978; tel. (3) 6409100; telex 342171; fax (3) 6415802; f. 1959; an attached inst. of the Moshe Dayan Center for Middle Eastern and African Studies; Dir Dr ASHER SUSSER; publs include *Current Contents of Periodicals on the Middle East* (6 a year), *Middle East Contemporary Survey* (annually).

ITALY

The Bologna Center, Paul H. Nitze School of Advanced International Studies, The Johns Hopkins University: Via Belmeloro 11, 40126 Bologna; tel. (51) 232185; telex 511339; fax (51) 228505; f. 1955; graduate studies in international affairs; Dir STEPHEN LOW; publs include occasional papers series.

Istituto Italo-Africano: Via Ulisse Aldrovandi 16, 00197 Rome; tel. (6) 3221258; telex 620386; fax (6) 3225348; f. 1906; Pres. Prof. TULLIA CARETTONI; Sec.-Gen. Ambassador PASQUALE A. BALDOCCI; publ. *Africa* (quarterly).

Istituto per gli Studi di Politica Internazionale: Palazzo Clerici, Via Clerici 5, 20121 Milan; tel. (2) 878266; fax (2) 8692055; f. 1933 for the promotion of the study of international relations; conducts research, documentation and training; Man. Dir Dr ENZO MARIA CALABRESE; publs *Relazioni Internazionali* (quarterly), *Quaderni-Papers* (10 a year).

JAPAN

Ajia Keizai Kenkyusho (Institute of Developing Economies): 42 Ichigaya-Hommura-cho, Shinjuku-ku, Tokyo 162; tel. (3) 3353-4231; telex 32473; fax (3) 3226-8475; f. 1958; library; 257 mems; Chair. YOTARO IIDA; Pres. KATSUHISA YAMADA; publs include *Ajia Keizai* (Japanese, monthly), *The Developing Economies* (English, quarterly).

Institute for the Study of Languages and Cultures of Asia and Africa: Tokyo University of Foreign Studies, 4-51-21 Nishigahara, Kita-ku, Tokyo 114; tel. (3) 3917-6111; fax (3) 3910-0613; f. 1964; library of 100,000 vols; Dir Prof. KOJI KAMIOKA; publs *Newsletter* (3 a year), *Journal of Asian and African Studies* (2 a year).

Nihon Afurika Gakkai (Japan Asscn for African Studies): c/o Dogura and Co Ltd, 1–8 Koyama Nishihanaikecho, Kita-ku, Kyoto 603; promotes multi-disciplinary African studies; Pres. K. SUWA; publs *Afurika Kenkyu/Journal of African Studies* (2 a year), *Kaiho* (annually).

Nihon Kokusai Mondai Kenkyusho (Japan Inst. of International Affairs): 3F Toranomon, Mitsui Bldg, 3-8-1 Kasumigaseki, Chiyoda ku, Tokyo 100; tel. (3) 3503-7261; telex 02223469; fax (3) 3595 1755; f. 1959; Chair. YOSHIZANE IWASA; Pres. NOBUO MATSUNAGA; publs include *Kokusai Mondai* (International Affairs, monthly), *Japan Review of International Affairs* (quarterly).

REPUBLIC OF KOREA

Institute of African Studies: Hankuk University of Foreign Studies, 270 Ly Moondong, Seoul 130-080; tel. (2) 961-4161; fax (2) 960-7898; Dir Dr WON-TAK PARK.

MEXICO

Asociación Latinoamericana de Estudios Afro-Asiáticos (Latin American Asscn for Afro-Asian Studies): El Colegio de México, Camino al Ajusco 20, Pedregal Sta Teresa, CP 10740, Mexico DF; tel. (5) 645-4954; telex 1777585; fax (5) 645-0464; f. 1976; promotes African and Asian studies in Latin America; 400 mems; Sec.-Gen. Prof. JORGE SILVA CASTILLO; publ. proceedings.

Centro de Estudios de Africa y Asia–CEAA (Centre for Asian and African Studies): El Colegio de México, Camino al Ajusco 20, Tlalpan, 01000, Mexico DF; tel. (5) 645-4954; telex 1777585; fax (5) 645-0464; f. 1964; postgraduate studies and research; library; Dir Prof. FLORA BOTTON; publs include *Estudios de Asia y Africa* (quarterly).

THE NETHERLANDS

Afrika Instituut: 181 Bezuidenhoutseweg, POB 10, 2501 CA, The Hague; tel. (70) 344-1544; telex 32306; fax (70) 385-3531; f. 1946; an information bureau, contact address and documentation centre for businessmen in African countries and in the Netherlands; Chair. Jonkheer F. J. C. MOLLERUS; Sec. Mrs H. D. VAN DE POLDER.

Afrika-Studiecentrum: POB 9555, 2300 RB, Leiden; tel. (71) 273372; fax (71) 273344; f. 1947 to promote study of Africa, especially in the social sciences; encourages the co-operation of all Netherlands institutions engaged in the study of Africa; Chair. Prof. Dr PETER GESCHIERE; Dir Dr STEPHEN ELLIS; publs include *African Studies Abstracts* (quarterly).

Institute of Social Studies: POB 29776, 2502 LT, The Hague; tel. (70) 4260460; telex 31491; fax (70) 4260799; f. 1952; post-graduate instruction, research and consultancy in development studies; Rector Prof. G. LYCKLAMA À NIJEHOLT; publs *Development and Change* (quarterly), working papers, occasional papers.

NORWAY

Norsk Utenrikspolitisk Institutt (Norwegian Institute of International Affairs): Grønlandsleiret 25, POB 8159 Dep, 0033 Oslo 1; tel. (2) 22177050; fax (2) 22177015; f. 1959; information and research in international relations; Pres. ODDMUND GRAHAM; Dir OLAV F. KNUDSEN; publs include *Forum for Development Studies, Internasjonal Politikk* (quarterly), *NUPI Notat* and *NUPI Rapport* (research reports), *Norwegian Foreign Policy Studies.*

PAKISTAN

Pakistan Institute of International Affairs: Aiwan-e-Sadar Rd, POB 1447, Karachi 74200; tel. (21) 5682891; f. 1947 to study international affairs and to promote the study of international politics, economics and law; over 600 mems; library of c. 25,600 vols; Admin. Dr MASUMA HASAN; Sec. Dr SYED ADIL HUSAIN; publs include *Pakistan Horizon* (quarterly).

POLAND

Departament Badań Strategicznych-PISM MSZ (Dept of Strategic Research-PISM, Ministry of Foreign Affairs): 00-950 Warsaw, Warecka 1A; tel. (22) 263021; fax (22) 263026; f. 1947; library of 125,000 vols; Dir Dr HENRYK SZLAJFER; publs include *Sprawy Międzynarodowe* (quarterly, in Polish and English), *Zbiór Dokumentów* (quarterly, in Polish, French, English and German), occasional papers (in English).

Institute of Developing Countries, University of Warsaw: 00-324 Warsaw, ul. Karowa 20; tel. (22) 263071, Ext. 237; fax (22) 267520; undergraduate and postgraduate studies; inter-disciplinary research on developing countries; Dir Prof. JERZY MAKOWSKI; publs include *Africana Bulletin* (irregular, in French and English), *Afryka, Azja, Ameryka Łacińska* (irregular).

PORTUGAL

Amílcar Cabral Information and Documentation Centre: Rua Pinheiro Chagas, 77-2 E, 1000 Lisbon; tel. (1) 3528718; fax (1) 3534009.

Centro de Estudos Africanos (African Studies Centre): University of Coimbra, Instituto de Antropologia, Rua Arco da Traição, 3049 Coimbra; tel. (39) 29051; fax (39) 23491; f. 1982; seminars and lectures; Dir Prof. M. L. RODRIGUES DE AREIA; publ. *Publicações do Centro de Estudos Africanos.*

Centro de Estudos Sobre África e do Desenvolvimento (Study Centre on Africa and Development): Instituto Superior de Economía, Rua Miguel Lupi 20, 1200 Lisbon; tel. (1) 607099; fax (1) 3974153; conducts research and holds seminars; publs occasional papers.

Instituto de Estudos Africanos (Institute of African Studies): Faculty of Letters, University of Lisbon, Cidade Universitária, 1669 Lisbon; literary studies and documentation centre; Dirs Prof. MANUEL FERREIRA, Prof. MANUEL VIEGAS GUERREIRO.

Instituto de Investigação Científica Tropical (Institute for Tropical Scientific Research): Ministério do Planeamento e da Administração do Território, Rua da Junqueira 86-1°, 1300 Lisbon; f. 1883; tel. (1) 3645071; telex 66932; fax (1) 3631460; development, research and documentation centre, dealing mainly with lusophone African countries; Pres. J. CRUZ E SILVA; publs include monographs, serials and maps.

RUSSIA

Institute for African Studies: attached to the Dept of Economics, Academy of Sciences, ul. Alexeya Tolstogo 30/I, 103001 Moscow; tel. (095) 2902752; Chair. AN. A. GROMYKO.

Scientific Council on Problems of Africa: Section of Social Sciences of Academy of Sciences, ul. Alexeya Tolstogo 30/I, 103001 Moscow; tel. (095) 2902752; Chair. AN. A. GROMYKO.

SAUDI ARABIA

King Faisal Centre for Research and Islamic Studies: POB 5149, Riyadh 11543; tel. (1) 4652255; telex 205470; f. 1983; advances research and studies into Islamic civilization; provides grants for research and organizes symposia, lectures and conferences on Islamic matters; library of over 30,000 vols and periodicals; Dir-Gen. Dr ZEID AL-HUSAIN; publ. *Newsletter*.

SOUTH AFRICA

Africa Institute: Soms Bldg, cnr Hamilton and Belvedere Sts, Arcadia, POB 630, Pretoria 0001; tel. (12) 328-6970; fax (12) 323-8153; f. 1960; undertakes research and collects and disseminates information on all aspects of continental Africa; Dir Dr DENIS VENTER; publs include *Bulletin* (monthly), *Africa Insight* (quarterly).

African Studies Institute: University of the Witwatersrand, 1 Jan Smuts Ave, Private Bag 3, Wits 2050, Johannesburg; tel. (11) 716-2414; telex 427125; fax (11) 716-8030; f. 1973; Dir Prof. CHARLES VAN ONSELEN.

Institute for the Study of Man in Africa (ISMA): Room 2B10, University of the Witwatersrand Medical School, York Rd, Parktown, Johannesburg 2193; tel. (11) 647-2203; fax (11) 643-4318; f. 1960 to perpetuate the work of the late Prof. Raymond A. Dart on the study of man in Africa, past and present; serves as a centre of anthropological and related field work; publs include the Raymond Dart series and occasional papers.

South African Institute of Race Relations: POB 31044, Braamfontein 2017; tel. (11) 403-3600; fax (11) 403-3671; f. 1929; research, education, publishing; library; 4,313 mems, 250 affiliated bodies; Pres. HELEN SUZMAN; Dir J. KANE-BERMAN; publs *Race Relations News* (monthly), *Fast Facts* (monthly), *A Survey of Race Relations in South Africa* (annually).

University of Cape Town Centre for African Studies: Rondebosch 7700; tel. (21) 650-2308; telex 57222085; fax (21) 650-3274; f. 1976; funded by the Harry Oppenheimer Inst. for African Studies; promotes study and research and collects source material; Dir (vacant); publs include *Social Dynamics* (bi-annually).

SPAIN

Centre d'Estudis Africans: Travessera de Gracia 100, Pral. 1, 08012 Barcelona; tel. (3) 4153192; f. 1988; instruction and research; Pres. ALFRED BOSCH.

Centro de Información y Documentación Africanas–CIDAF: Gaztambide 31, 28015 Madrid; tel. (1) 5441818; f. 1979; seminars and lectures; specialized library of 13,000 vols and periodicals; Dir Fr JOSÉ MARÍA SARASOLA CELAYA; Chief Librarian F. D. SEGURA GOMEZ; publs include *Noticias de Africa* (monthly), *Cuadernos CIDAF*.

Colegio Mayor Universitario Nuestra Señora de Africa: Avda Ramiro de Maeztu s/n, Ciudad Universitaria, 28040 Madrid; tel. (1) 5540104; fax (1) 5540401; f. 1964; attached inst. of the Complutense Univ. of Madrid and the Spanish Ministry of Foreign Affairs; linguistic studies and cultural activities; Dir OLEGARIO NEGRÍN.

Dirección de Programas de Cooperación con Iberoamérica, Asia y Africa: Vice-Rectorado de Relaciones Internacionales, Universidad de Alcalá de Henares, Plaza de Dan Diego, s/n, 28801 Alcalá de Henares (Madrid); tel. (1) 8854087; fax (1) 8854130; f. 1989; promotes and co-ordinates co-operation with African universities; organizes seminars, lectures and courses; Vice-Rector Dr LUIS BELTRÁN.

Mundo Negro: Arturo Soria 101; 28043 Madrid; tel. (1) 4152412; fax (1) 5192550; f. 1960; holds lectures; library and museum; Dir Fr ANTONIO VILLARINO RODRÍGUEZ; publ. *Mundo Negro* (monthly).

SWEDEN

Institutet för Internationell Ekonomi (Institute for International Economic Studies): Universitetsvägen 10A, 106 91 Stockholm; tel. (8) 162000; telex 8105199; fax (8) 165886; f. 1962; attached to Stockholm University; Dir ASSAR LINDBECK.

Nordiska Afrikainstitutet (Scandinavian Institute of African Studies): POB 1703, 751 47 Uppsala; tel. (18) 155480; telex 8195077; fax (18) 695629; f. 1962; documentation and research centre for current African affairs, library, publication work, lectures and seminars; library of 38,000 vols and 900 periodicals; Dir L. WOHLGEMUTH; publs include *Africana*, seminar proceedings, research reports, discussion papers, annual report.

Utrikespolitiska Institutet (Swedish Institute of International Affairs): Lilla Nygatan 23, POB 1253, 111 82 Stockholm; tel. (8) 234060; fax (8) 201049; f. 1938; promotes studies of international affairs; library of c. 20,000 vols and 400 periodicals; Pres. Ambassador LEIF LEIFLAND; Dir Dr RUTGER LINDAHL; publs include *Världspolitikens Dagsfrågor*, *Världens Fakta*, *Internationella Studier*, *Länder i fickformat*, *Yearbook*, conference papers, research reports (in English).

SWITZERLAND

Institut universitaire d'études du développement: 24 rue Rothschild, 1211 Geneva 21; tel. (22) 7315940; telex 412584; fax (22) 7384416; f. 1961; a centre of higher education and research into development problems of Africa, Latin America and Asia; conducts courses, seminars and practical work; Dir JEAN-LUC MAURER; publs include *Nouveaux*, *Cahiers de l'IUED*, *Annuaire Suisse-Tiers Monde*, *Itinéraires*.

Institut universitaire de hautes études internationales: 132 rue de Lausanne, 1211 Geneva 21; tel. (21) 7311730; fax (21) 7384306; f. 1927; a research and teaching institution studying international judicial, historical, political and economic questions; Dir Dr A. SWOBODA.

Schweizerisches Institut für Auslandforschung: Wiesenstrasse 9, 8008 Zürich; tel. (1) 2573113; fax (1) 3820285; Dir Prof. Dr DIETER RULOFF; publ. *Sozialwissenschaftliche Studien* (annually).

UNITED KINGDOM

African Studies Association of the United Kingdom: School of African and Oriental Studies, Thornhaugh St, Russell Sq., London, WC1H 0XG; tel. (71) 323-6253; f. 1963 to advance academic studies relating to Africa by providing facilities for the interchange of information and ideas; holds inter-disciplinary conferences and symposia; 350 mems; Hon. Pres. Prof. CHRISTOPHER CLAPHAM; Hon. Sec. Dr N. NELSON.

African Studies Unit: University of Leeds, Leeds, West Yorkshire, LS2 9JT; tel. (532) 335069; a liaison unit for all depts with African interests.

Catholic Institute for International Relations (CIIR): Unit 3, Canonbury Yard, 190A New North Rd, London, N1 7BJ; tel. (71) 354-0883; fax (71) 359-0017; f. 1940; information and analysis of socio-economic, political, church and human rights issues in the developing countries; Gen. Sec. IAN LINDEN; publs include specialized studies on southern Africa and EU development policy.

Centre for Southern African Studies: University of York, Heslington, York, North Yorkshire, YO1 5DD; tel. (904) 433670; telex 57933; fax (904) 433433; f. 1972; postgraduate inter-disciplinary studies; Dir LANDEG WHITE.

Centre of African Studies: Free School Lane, Cambridge, CB2 3QR; tel. (223) 334396; telex 81240; fax (223) 334748; attached inst. of the Univ. of Cambridge; Dir Dr KEITH HART.

Centre of African Studies: University of Edinburgh, Adam Ferguson Bldg, George Sq., Edinburgh, EH8 9LL, Scotland; tel. (31) 650-3878; telex 727442; fax (31) 650-6535; f. 1962; postgraduate studies; Dir Prof. KENNETH KING; publs include occasional paper series.

Centre of West African Studies: University of Birmingham, Edgbaston, Birmingham, B15 2TT; tel. (21) 414-5128; Dir ARNOLD HUGHES.

Development and Project Planning Centre: University of Bradford, Bradford, West Yorkshire, BD7 1DP; tel. (274) 383955; telex 51309; fax (274) 385280; f. 1969 to carry out postgraduate teaching, professional training, research and consultancy in project planning and management and macroeconomic policy and planning; an attached inst. of the Univ. of Bradford; Head of Centre JOHN CUSWORTH; publs include monographs and discussion papers.

Institute of Development Studies at the University of Sussex: Brighton, East Sussex, BN1 9RE; tel. (273) 606261; telex 877997; fax (273) 621202; Dir J. TOYE.

International African Institute (IAI): School of Oriental and African Studies, Thornhaugh St, London, WC1H 0XG; tel. (71) 323-6035; fax (71) 323-6118; f. 1926 to promote the study of African peoples, their languages, cultures and social life in their traditional and modern settings; holds seminars and conducts projects; Chair. Prof. WILLIAM A. SHACK; Dir Prof. DAVID PARKIN; publs include *Africa* (quarterly), *Africa Bibliography* (annually), monograph series.

International Institute for Environment and Development (IIED): 3 Endsleigh St, London, WC1H 0DD; tel. (71) 388-2117; telex 261681; fax (71) 388-2826; f. 1971; to promote the sound management and sustainable use of natural resources; conducts research into drylands, forestry and land use, human settlements, sustainable agriculture, environmental economics, climate change and institutional co-operation; publications unit from offices in London and Buenos Aires; Exec. Dir RICHARD SANDBROOK.

Overseas Development Institute (ODI): Regent's College, Inner Circle, Regent's Park, London, NW1 4NS; tel. (71) 487-7413; telex 94082191; fax (71) 487-7590; f. 1960 as a research centre and forum for the discussion of development issues and problems; publishes its research findings in books and working papers; Chair. Sir PETER LESLIE; Dir Dr JOHN HOWELL; publs include *Development Policy Review* (quarterly).

Royal African Society: School of Oriental and African Studies, Thornhaugh St, Russell Sq., London, WC1H 0XG; tel. (71) 323-6253; f. 1901; 800 mems; Pres. Prof. KENNETH ROBINSON; Sec. Mrs M. L. ALLAN; publ. *African Affairs* (quarterly).

Royal Institute of International Affairs: Chatham House, 10 St James's Sq., London, SW1Y 4LE; tel. (71) 957-5700; fax (71) 957-5710; f. 1920 to study international issues; c. 3,000 mems; Chair. Lord TUGENDHAT; Dir Prof. LAURENCE MARTIN; Dir of Studies Prof. JACK SPENCE; affiliated insts in Canada, Australia, NZ, India, Singapore, Nigeria, Trinidad and Tobago, Guyana, Sri Lanka and the USA; publs include *International Affairs* (quarterly), *The World Today* (monthly), *Chatham House Papers, Annual Report, discussion papers.*

School of African and Asian Studies: University of Sussex, Falmer, Brighton, East Sussex, BN1 9QN; tel. (273) 606755; fax (273) 623572; Dean Dr D. R. ROBINSON.

School of Oriental and African Studies: Thornhaugh St, Russell Sq., London, WC1H 0XG; tel. (71) 637-2388; telex 262433; fax (71) 436-3844; f. 1916; a school of the Univ. of London; Dir M. D. MCWILLIAM; Sec. F. DABELL; 200 teachers, including 37 professors; 2,200 students; publs *The Bulletin, Calendar, Annual Report, Journal of African Law, African Languages and Cultures.*

School of Oriental and African Studies Library: Thornhaugh St, Russell Sq., London, WC1H 0XG; tel. (71) 637-2388; telex 291829; fax (71) 436-3844; f. 1916; 750,000 vols and pamphlets; 5,100 current periodicals, 50,000 maps, 6,300 microforms, 2,800 MSS and private papers collections, extensive missionary archives, all covering Asian and African languages, literatures, philosophy, religions, history, law, cultural anthropology, art and archaeology, social sciences, geography and music; Librarian MARY AUCKLAND.

UNITED STATES OF AMERICA

Africa Fund: 198 Broadway, New York, NY 10038; tel. (212) 962-1210; f. 1966; conducts research and issues publs on southern Africa; provides health and educational aid to developing African countries; Chair. Bd of Trustees TILDEN J. LE MELLE; Exec. Sec. JENNIFER DAVIS.

Africa News Service: POB 3851, Durham, NC 27702; tel. (919) 286-0747; fax (919) 286-2614; f. 1973; researches and supplies broadcast and print media with information on African politics, economics and culture, international issues and US policy affecting Africa; library of 5,000 vols and newspaper archives; Pres. REED KRAMER; Exec. Editor TAMI HULTMAN; publs include *Africa News* (24 a year).

Africa Watch: 485 Fifth Ave, 3rd Floor, New York, NY 10017; tel. (212) 972-8400; fax (212) 972-0905; also office in Washington, DC.

African-American Institute: 833 UN Plaza, New York, NY 10017; tel. (212) 949-5666; telex 666565; fax (212) 682-6174; f. 1953; organizes training programmes and offers devt assistance; maintains reps in 21 African countries; also sponsors confs and seminars; Pres. VIVIAN DERRYCK; publ. *Africa Report* (6 a year).

African-American Labor Center: 1400 K St, NW, Rm 700, Washington, DC 20005; tel. (202) 789-1020; publ. *AALC Reporter*.

African and Afro-American Studies Center: University of Texas, Jester Center A232A, Austin, TX 78705; tel. (512) 471-1784; fax (512) 471-1798; f. 1969; Dir Prof. SHEILA S. WALKER; publs working papers and reprint series (irregular).

African Development Foundation: 1400 Eye St, NW, 10th Floor, Washington, DC 20005; tel. (202) 673-3916; telex 6711367; fax (202) 673-3810; an independent agency of the US federal govt; Pres. GREGORY ROBESON SMITH.

African Studies and Research Program: Dept of African Studies, Howard University, Washington, DC 20059; tel. (202) 806-7115; fax (202) 806-4425; f. 1959; Chair. Dr SULAYMAN S. NYANG; publs include monographs and occasional papers.

African Studies Association of the US: Credit Union Bldg, Emory University, Atlanta, GA 30322; tel. (404) 329-6410; fax (404) 329-6433; f. 1957; 2,600 mems; conducts research; collects and publishes information on Africa; Pres. Prof. EDWARD A. ALPERS; Exec. Dir Dr EDNA G. BAY; publs *African Studies Review, Issue, ASA News.*

African Studies Center: Boston University, 270 Bay State Rd, Boston, MA 02215; tel. (617) 353-3673; fax (617) 353-4975; f. 1953; research and teaching on archaeology, African languages, anthropology, economics, history, geography and political science of Africa; library of 125,000 vols and document titles, 1,000 periodicals and an extensive collection of non-current newspapers and periodicals; Dir Dr JAMES MCCANN; publs include *International Journal of African Historical Studies* (3 a year), working papers, discussion papers.

African Studies Center: 100 International Center, Michigan State University, East Lansing, MI 48824-1035; tel. (517) 353-1700; fax (517) 432-1209; f. 1960; Dir Dr DAVID WILEY; offers instruction in 25 African languages; Library of over 200,000 vols; publs include *African Rural and Urban Studies* (quarterly), *Northeast African Studies* (3 a year).

African Studies Program: Ohio University, 56 East Union St, Athens, OH 45701; tel. (614) 593-1834; telex 2392992; fax (614) 593-1837; African politics, education, economics, geography, anthropology, languages, literature, philosophy and history; Dir Prof. WILLIAM STEPHEN HOWARD.

African Studies Program: University of Wisconsin, 1454 Van Hise Hall, 1220 Linden Drive, Madison, WI 53706; tel. (608) 262-2380; telex 265452; fax (608) 262-6998; study courses; library of over 100,000 vols; Chair. Prof. HERB LEWIS; publs include *News and Notes* (bi-annually), occasional papers and African texts and grammars.

Africare: 440 R St, NW, Washington, DC 20001; tel. (202) 462-3614; telex 64239; f. 1971; aims to improve basic health services, water resource devt and food production in rural Africa; maintains African resource information centre and personnel data bank available to orgs interested in Africa; 2,300 mems; library of c. 3,300 vols; Exec. Dir C. PAYNE LUCAS; publs include *Newsletter* (2 a year).

American Committee on Africa: 198 Broadway, Rm 401, New York, NY 10038; tel. (212) 962-1210; publ. *ACOA Action News.*

Association of African Studies Programs: 236 Grange Bldg, Penn State University, University Park, PA 16802; tel. (814) 238-0997; mems represent more than 40 centres of African studies at US colleges and univs; publ. *Newsletter* (2 a year).

Berkeley/Stanford Joint Center for African Studies: 356 Stephens Hall 2314, University of California, Berkeley, CA 94720-2314; tel. (510) 642-8338; telex 3667114; fax (510) 643-5045; f. 1979; African languages, society, culture, foreign policy and social and behavioural sciences; holds research conferences; offers jt degree in African studies for students enrolled in professional schools; Co-Chair. ROBERT PRICE, RICHARD ROBERTS; Assoc. Dir MARTHA E. SAAVEERA.

Brookings Institution: 1775 Massachusetts Ave, NW, Washington, DC 20036; tel. (202) 797-6000; fax (202) 797-6004; f. 1916; research, education, and publishing in economics, govt and foreign policy; organizes conferences and seminars; library of c. 95,000 vols; Pres. BRUCE K. MACLAURY; publs include *The Brookings Review* (quarterly), *National Newsletter* (quarterly), *Brookings Papers on Economic Activity* (3 a year), *Directory of Scholars* (annually), *Annual Report.*

Center for African Studies: 427 Grinter Hall, University of Florida, Gainesville, FL 32611; tel. (904) 392-2183; telex 568757; fax (904) 392-9605; encourages research projects and sponsors lectures, exhbns and conferences; library of 50,000 vols, 500 periodical titles, 40,000 maps; Dir Dr PETER R. SCHMIDT.

Center for African Studies: University of Illinois at Urbana-Champaign, 210 International Studies Bldg, 910 South Fifth St, Urbana, IL 61820; tel. (303) 871-2164.

Center for International Studies: Massachusetts Institute of Technology, Bldg E38, Room 648, Cambridge, MA 02139; tel. (617) 253-8093; telex 921473; f. 1951; Dir Dr KENNETH OYE.

Center for Research on Economic Development: University of Michigan, 340 Lorch Hall, Ann Arbor, MI 48109-1220; tel. (313) 764-9490; telex 4320815; fax (313) 747-2743; f. 1961; devt research projects and training programmes; Dir Dr MARK GERSOVITZ; publs include *CREDITS* (newsletter) and research reports.

Center of International Studies: Princeton University, Princeton, NJ 08544-1022; tel. (609) 258-4851; Dir Prof. JOHN WATERBURY.

Council on Foreign Relations, Inc: 58 East 68th St, New York, NY 10021; tel. (212) 734-0400; fax (212) 861-1789; f. 1921; 3,010 mems; library of 5,000 vols, 221 periodicals, clippings files and data bases; Pres. LESLIE H. GELB; publs include *Foreign Affairs* (quarterly).

Council on Regional Studies: 218 Palmer Hall, Princeton University, Princeton, NJ 08544; tel. (609) 258-4720; f. 1961; Dir GILBERT ROZMAN.

Institute of African Affairs: Duquesne University, 600 Forbes Ave, Pittsburgh, PA 15282; tel. (412) 434-6000; fax (412) 434-5146; f. 1957; research into uncommon languages of sub-Saharan Africa; library of 9,000 vols; Dir Rev. JOSEPH L. VARGA; publ. *African Reprint Series.*

Institute of African Studies: Columbia University School of International and Public Affairs, 420 West 118th St, New York, NY 10027; tel. (212) 854-4633; fax (212) 864-4847; Dir GEORGE C. BOND.

James S. Coleman African Studies Center: University of California, Los Angeles, CA 90024-1310; tel. (310) 825-3686; fax (310) 206-3555; f. 1959; centre for co-ordination of and research on Africa in the social sciences, the arts, humanities, the sciences and public health; and for multidisciplinary graduate training in African studies; Dir Dr EDMOND KELLER; publs include *African Arts* (quarterly), *Studies in African Linguistics* (quarterly), *Ufahamu: Journal of the African Activists Association* (3 a year), *African Studies Centre Newsletter* (2 a year).

Library of International Relations: Chicago-Kent College of Law, Illinois Institute of Technology, 565 West Adams St, Chicago, IL 60661; tel. (312) 906-5622; fax (312) 906-5685; f. 1932; financed by voluntary contributions; stimulates interest and research in international problems; conducts seminars and offers special services to businesses and academic institutions; library of 500,000 items; Pres. HOKEN SEKI; Dir MICKIE A. VOGES.

Program of African and Asian Languages: Northwestern University, 1859 Sheridan Rd, Evanston, IL 60208-2209; tel. (708) 491-5288 fax (708) 467-1097; f. 1973; languages offered include Amharic, Arabic and Swahili; Dir RICHARD LEPINE.

Program of African Studies: Northwestern University, 620 Library Place, Evanston, IL 60208; tel. (708) 491-7323; fax (708) 491-3739; f. 1948; supported by various foundation and govt grants for research in Africa and the USA, as well as by university; awards undergraduate and graduate certificates of African studies and sponsors fellowship awards for African students; Asst Dir Prof. AKBAR VIRMANI; publs include *PAS Newsletter, Passages Journal,* conference proceedings.

School of Advanced International Studies: Johns Hopkins University, 1740 Massachusetts Ave, NW, Washington, DC 20036-1983; tel. (202) 663-5600; fax (202) 663-5683; Dean PAUL WOLFOWITZ; Dir of African Studies I. WILLIAM ZARTMAN; publ. *SAIS Studies on Africa.*

Stanford Center for African Studies: Stanford University, Encina Hall, Rm 200, Stanford, CA 94305-6055; tel. (415) 723-0295; publ. *Stanford-UC Berkeley Joint Center for African Studies Newsletter.*

TransAfrica: 1744 R St, NW, Washington, DC 20009-2410; tel. (202) 797-2301; fax (202) 797-2382; Exec. Dir RANDALL ROBINSON; publs *TransAfrica Forum Journal, TransAfrica Issue Brief, TransAfrica Newsletter.*

Universities Field Staff International: 737 Spring Mill Lane, Indianapolis, IN 46260; tel. (317) 283-9873; f. 1951; research, conferences and seminars on contemporary international affairs; Exec. Dir AARON MILLER; publs include *Field Staff Reports* (18 a year).

Woodrow Wilson School of Public and International Affairs: Princeton University, Princeton, NJ 08544; tel. (609) 258-4836; fax (609) 258-2809; Dean (vacant).

SELECT BIBLIOGRAPHY (PERIODICALS)

Actividade Economica de Angola. Instituto Nacional de Estatistica, Avda Ho Chi Minh, CP 1215, Luanda, Angola; tel. and fax (2) 330420; f. 1936; Dir Mario Alberto Adauta de Sousa; 3 a year.

Africa. Istituto Italo-Africano, via Ulisse Aldrovandi 16, 00197 Rome, Italy; tel. (6) 3216712; fax (6) 3225348; f. 1946; Dir Prof. Gianluigi Rossi; quarterly.

Africa. Edinburgh University Press, 22 George Sq., Edinburgh, EH8 9LF, Scotland; tel. (31) 650-4218; telex 727442; fax (31) 662-0053; Editor Dr Murray Last; quarterly; also annual bibliography.

Africa Analysis. Ludgate House, Suite 71, 107-111 Fleet St, London, EC4A 2AB, England; tel. (71) 353-1117; fax (71) 353-1516; f. 1986; Editors Ahmed Rajab, Richard Synge; fortnightly.

Africa Confidential. 73 Farringdon Rd, London, EC1M 3JB, England; tel. (71) 831-3511; fax (71) 831-6778; f. 1960; political news and analysis; Editor Patrick Smith; fortnightly.

Africa Contemporary Record. Africana Publishing Co, Holmes & Meier Publishers, Inc, 160 Broadway, East Bldg, New York, NY 10038, USA; tel. (212) 374-0100; fax (212) 374-1313; annual documents, country surveys, special essays, indices.

Africa Development. Council for the Development of Economic and Social Research in Africa (CODESRIA), BP 3304, Dakar, Senegal; tel. 259822; fax 241289; f. 1976; in French and English; Editor Tade Akin Aina; quarterly.

Africa Economic Digest. 26–32 Whistler St, London, N5 1NH, England; tel. (71) 359-5335; telex 262505; fax (71) 359-9173; f. 1980; Publr and Man. Editor Shamusideen Abiola; fortnightly.

Africa Education Bulletin. UNESCO Regional Centre for Educational Information and Research, POB 2739, Accra, Ghana; f. 1963; irregular.

Africa Energy and Mining. 10 rue de Sentier, 75002 Paris, France; tel. (1) 45081480; fax (1) 45085983; f. 1983; Man. Editor Antoine Glaser; fortnightly.

Africa Forum. POB 1374, London, SW9 8ET, England; tel. (71) 737-7177; fax (71) 738-3641; f. 1991; Editor-in-Chief Ad'Obe Obe; quarterly.

Africa Health. Vine House, Fair Green, Reach, Cambridge, CB5 0JD, England; tel. (638) 743633; fax (638) 743966; f. 1978; Editor Paul Chinnock; 6 a year.

Africa Insider. Matthews Associates, POB 53398, Temple Heights Station, Washington, DC 20009, USA; tel. (301) 897-3242; f. 1984; Editor Dan Matthews; fortnightly.

Africa Insight. Africa Institute, POB 630, 0001 Pretoria, South Africa; tel. (12) 328-6970; fax (12) 323-8153; f. 1971; Editor Madeline Lass; quarterly.

Africa International. 21 rue Jean-Pierre Timbaud, 75011 Paris, France; tel. (1) 47003585; telex 216054; fax (1) 47007057; f. 1958; political, economic and social development in francophone Africa; Editor Marie-Roger Biloa; monthly.

Africa Investment Monitor. POB 25683, Washington, DC 20007, USA; tel. (202) 338-4440; fax (202) 338-4440; Editor-in-Chief Richard M. Synge; 24 a year.

Africa Letter. Business International, SA, 18 chemin des Verneys, 1297 Founex, Switzerland; tel. (22) 7761134; fax (22) 7765897; business, economics and finance; Editor Graham Hatton; 10 a year.

Africa Museum. Africa-Museum Tervuren, Leuvensesteenweg 13, 3080 Tervuren, Belgium; tel. (2) 7695211; fax (2) 7670242; f. 1993; ethnology, history and archaeology of Africa; quarterly.

Africa News. Africa News Service, Inc, POB 3851, Durham, NC 27702, USA; tel. (919) 286-0747; fax (919) 286-2614; f. 1973; Man. Editor Reed Kramer; twice monthly (by computer only).

Africa Quarterly. Indian Council for Cultural Relations, Azad Bhavan, Indraprastha Estate, New Delhi 110002, India; tel. (11) 3319309; telex 3161860; fax (11) 3712639; Editor A. R. Basu.

Africa Recovery. DPI, Rm S-391, United Nations, New York, NY 10017, USA; tel. (212) 963-6857; fax (212) 963-4556; Editor-in-Chief Salim Lone; in English and French; quarterly.

Africa Report. African-American Institute, 833 UN Plaza, New York, NY 10017, USA; tel. (212) 949-5666; telex 666565; fax (212) 682-6421; political and economic analyses, with attention to current US Africa policy; Editor Margaret A. Novicki; every 2 months.

Africa Research Bulletin. Africa Research Ltd, c/o Blackwell Publishers, 108 Cowley Rd, Oxford, OX4 1JF, England; tel. (865) 791100; fax (865) 791347; f. 1964; bulletins on political and economic topics; monthly.

Africa Review. Walden Publishing Ltd, 2 Market St, Saffron Walden, Essex, CB10 1HZ, England; tel. (799) 521150; telex 817197; fax (799) 524805; f. 1977; Editor Howard Hill; annually.

Africa Today. Africa Today Associates, Graduate School of International Studies, University of Denver, Denver, CO 80208, USA; tel. (303) 871-3678; fax (303) 871-2456; f. 1954; Editor Jendayi Frazer; quarterly.

Africa 2000. Centro Cultural Hispano-Guineano, Apdo 180, Malabo, Equatorial Guinea; tel. 2720; f. 1985; Equato-Guinean social and cultural review; Spanish; Editor Donato Ndongo-Bidyogo; quarterly.

African Administrative Studies. Centre africain de formation et de recherche administratives pour le développement (CAFRAD), BP 310, Tangier, Morocco; tel. (9) 942632; telex 33664; fax (9) 941415; English, French and Arabic; 2 a year.

African Affairs. Royal African Society, School of African and Oriental Studies, Thornhaugh St, Russell Sq., London, WC1H 0XB, England; tel. (71) 323-6253; f. 1901; social sciences and history; Editors David Killingray, Peter Woodward; quarterly.

African Arts. James S. Coleman African Studies Center, University of California, Los Angeles, CA 90024-1310, USA; tel. (310) 825-1218; fax (310) 206-3555; Editors Donald J. Cosentino, Doran H. Ross; quarterly.

African Book Publishing Record. Hans Zell Publishers, 11 Richmond Rd, POB 56, Oxford, OX1 2SJ, England; tel. (865) 511428; fax (865) 311534; f. 1975; bibliographic listings, book reviews, information on book trade activities in Africa; Editor Hans M. Zell; quarterly.

African Business. 7 Coldbath Sq., London, EC1R 4LQ, England; tel. (71) 713-7711; telex 8811757; fax (71) 713-7970; f. 1966; economics, business, commerce and finance; Editor Linda Van Buren; monthly.

African Concord. 26–32 Whistler St, London, N5 1NH, England; tel. (71) 359-5335; telex 262505; fax (71) 359-9173; African and international current affairs; Nigerian and international edns; Editor Soji Omotunde; weekly.

African Farmer. Hunger Project Global Office, 15 East 26th St, New York, NY 10010, USA; tel. (212) 532-4255; fax (212) 532-9785; Editor-in-Chief Ernest Harsch; quarterly.

African Farming and Food Processing. Alain Charles Publishing Ltd, 27 Wilfred St, London, SW1E 6PR, England; tel. (71) 834-7676; fax (71) 973-0076; Editor Jonquil L. Phelan; 6 a year.

African Journal of Agricultural Sciences. Association for the Advancement of Agricultural Sciences in Africa, POB 30087 MA, Addis Ababa, Ethiopia; f. 1971; in English and French; 2 a year.

African Peoples Review. 34–36 Crown St, Reading, Berks, RG1 2SE, England; tel. (734) 391010; fax (734) 594442; f. 1992; reviews of publications and creative arts; Editor Herbert Ekwe-Ekwe; quarterly.

African Publishing Review. POB 4209, Harare, Zimbabwe; tel. (4) 729904; fax (4) 729905; Editors Lesley Humphrey, Jenny Waddington; 6 a year.

African Recorder. A-126 Niti Bagh, POB 595, New Delhi 110049, India; tel. 665405; f. 1962; news digest; Editor A. K. B. Menon; fortnightly.

The African Review. Dept of Political Science and Public Administration, University of Dar es Salaam, POB 35042, Dar es Salaam, Tanzania; tel. (51) 43130; telex 41327; fax (51) 49052; f. 1971; 2 a year.

African Review of Business and Technology. Alain Charles Publishing Ltd, 27 Wilfred St, London, SW1E 6PR, England; tel. (71) 834-7676; fax (71) 973-0076; Editor Jonquil L. Phelan; monthly.

African Studies. Witwatersrand University Press, PO Wits, 2050 Johannesburg, South Africa; tel. (11) 484-5907; fax (11) 484-5971; f. 1921; social and cultural studies of southern Africa; Editor D. James; 2 a year.

African Studies Review. African Studies Association, Emory University, Credit Union Bldg, Atlanta, GA 30322, USA; tel. (404) 329-6410; Editor Mark DeLancey; 3 a year.

African Textiles. Alain Charles Publishing Co, 27 Wilfred St, London, SW1E 6PR, England; tel. (71) 834-7676; telex 297165; fax (71) 973-0076; Editor Zsa Tebbit; 6 a year.

Africana Bulletin. Institute of Developing Countries, Faculty of Geography and Regional Studies, University of Warsaw, Krakowskie Przedmieścle 26/28, 00-325 Warsaw 64, Poland; tel. (22) 269871; telex 815439; f. 1964; articles in English or French; Editor Prof. Dr Bogodar Winid; irregular.

Africana Marburgensia. Universität Marburg, c/o Seminar für Religionsgeschichte, 3550 Marburg, Am Plan 3, Germany; f. 1968; religion, law, economics; in English, French and German; Editors Hans-Jürgen Greschat, Hans-H. Münkner; 2 a year.

Africana Research Bulletin. Institute of African Studies, POB 87, Fourah Bay College, Freetown, Sierra Leone; f. 1971; Editor Arthur Abraham; 2 a year.

Afrika Spectrum. Institut für Afrika-Kunde, 20354 Hamburg, Neuer Jungfernstieg 21, Germany; tel. (40) 3562523; fax (40) 3562547; mostly in German, but with contributions and summaries in English and French; 3 a year.

Afrika und Übersee, Sprachen–Kulturen. c/o Dietrich Reimer Verlag, 12203 Berlin, Unter den Eichen 57, Germany; tel. (30) 8314081; fax (30) 8316323; f. 1910; African linguistics and cultures; in German, English and French; Editors E. Dammann, L. Gerhardt, E. Kähler-Meyer, H. Meyer-Bahlburg, J. Zwernemann, L. S. Uhlig; 2 a year.

Afrique Agriculture. 6 rue du Dr Solomon, 60119 Henonville, France; tel. 44498387; fax 44498242; f. 1975; Editor Alain Zolty; monthly.

Afrique Contemporaine. La Documentation française, 29–31 quai Voltaire, 75340 Paris Cedex 07, France; tel. 40157000; telex 204826; fax 40157230; f. 1962; political, economic and sociological studies; Editor-in-Chief Michel Gaud; quarterly.

Afrique Médicale. BP 1826, Dakar, Senegal; f. 1960; tel. (221) 234880; telex 1300; fax (221) 225630; f. 1960; medical review; Editors Joel Decupper, Prof. Paul Correa; monthly.

Afro-Asian Economic Review. Afro-Asian Organization for Economic Co-operation, Chamber of Commerce Bldg, Mindan El Falaki, Special PO Bag, Cairo, Egypt; monthly.

Afryka, Azja, Ameryka Łacińska. Institute of Developing Countries, Faculty of Geography and Regional Studies, University of Warsaw, Krakowskie Przedmieście 26/28, 00-325, Warsaw 64, Poland; tel. (22) 200381; f. 1974; in Polish; English and French summaries; Editor Prof. Władysław Kubiak; irregular.

Aktueller Informationsdienst Afrika. Spiegel der afrikanischen Presse, Institut für Afrika-Kunde, 20354 Hamburg, Neuer Jungfernstieg 21, Germany; tel. (40) 3562523; fax (40) 3562547; press digest from African publs; English, French and Portuguese; fortnightly.

Asian and African Studies. Israel Oriental Society, The Gustav Heinemann Institute of Middle Eastern Studies, University of Haifa, Haifa 31999, Israel; tel. (9724) 240654; fax (9724) 342104; f. 1965; Editors Gabriel R. Warburg, Gad G. Gilbar; 3 a year.

Botswana Notes and Records. The Botswana Society, POB 71, Gaborone, Botswana; tel. (267) 351500; fax 359321; f. 1969; annually.

Bulletin de Madagascar. Direction de la presse et des publications, Ministère de l'Information, BP 271, Antananarivo, Madagascar; f. 1960; economic, social, cultural, linguistic studies; Editorial Dir Jeannot Feno; every 2 months.

Bulletin of the International Committee on Urgent Anthropological and Ethnological Research. International Committee on Urgent Anthropological and Ethnological Research, International Union of Anthropological and Ethnological Sciences, c/o Institut für Völkerkunde, Universitätsstrasse 7, 1010 Vienna, Austria; tel. 40103/2849; f. 1958; Editor Dr Anna Hohenwart-Gerlachstein; annually.

Bulletin of the School of Oriental and African Studies. School of Oriental and African Studies, Thornhaugh St, Russell Sq., London, WC1H 0XG, England; tel. (071) 637-2388; telex 291829; fax (071) 436-3844; f. 1917; 3 a year.

Bulletin of Sudanese Studies. Institute of African and Asian Studies, University of Khartoum, POB 321, Khartoum, Sudan; tel. 75820; telex 22738; in Arabic; Editor Dr Medani Mohamed Ahmed; 2 a year.

CAFRAD News. Centre africain de formation et de recherche administratives pour le développement, (CAFRAD), BP 310, Tangier, Morocco; tel. (9) 942632; fax (9) 941415; English, French and Arabic; 2 a year.

Cahiers d'Etudes Africaines. Ecole des hautes études en sciences sociales, 54 blvd Raspail, 75006 Paris, France; tel. 49542469; fax 49542692; f. 1960; Editor J.-L. Amselle; bilingual; quarterly.

Canadian Journal of African Studies. Canadian Association of African Studies, c/o Barry Riddell, Dept of Geography, Queen's University, Kingston, ON K7L 2W3, Canada; tel. (613) 545-6037; fax (613) 545-6122; Editors Barry Riddell, (vacant); 3 a year.

Communications Africa. Alain Charles Publishing Ltd, 27 Wilfred St, London, SW1E 6PR, England; tel. (071) 834-7676; fax (071) 973-0076; f. 1991; telecommunications, broadcasting and information technology; in French and English; 6 a year.

The Courier ACP–EU. Commission of the European Communities, 200 rue de la Loi, 1049 Brussels, Belgium; tel. (2) 2993012; telex 21877; fax 2993002; affairs of the African, Caribbean and Pacific countries and the European Union; English and French edns; Editor Dominique David; 6 a year.

CSIS Africa Notes. Center for Strategic and International Studies, 1800 K St, NW, Suite 400, Washington, DC 20006, USA; tel. (202) 775-3219; telex 8229583; fax (202) 775-3199; f. 1982; political, economic and policy analysis; Editor Helen Kitchen; 12 a year and occasional supplements.

Development Policy Review. Overseas Development Institute, Regent's College, Inner Circle, Regent's Park, London, NW1 4NS, England; tel. (071) 487-7413; telex 94082191; fax (071) 487-7590; f. 1982; Editor Sheila Page; quarterly.

Development and Socio-Economic Progress. Afro-Asian People's Solidarity Organization, 89 Abdel Aziz Al-Saoud St, Manial El-Roda, Cairo, Egypt; tel. (2) 845495; English, Arabic and French edns; Editor-in-Chief Nouri Abdel Razzak; quarterly.

Dokumentationsdienst Afrika. Ausgewählte neuere Literatur, Deutsches Übersee-Institut, Übersee-Dokumentation, Referat Afrika (AFDOK), 20354 Hamburg, Neuer Jungfernstieg 21, Germany; tel. (40) 3562598; fax (40) 3562547; current bibliography; quarterly.

East Africa Journal. East African Institute of Social and Cultural Affairs, POB 30492, Uniafric Bldg, Koinange St, Nairobi, Kenya; monthly.

East African Studies. Makerere Institute of Social Research, Makerere University, POB 16022, Kampala, Uganda; irregular.

Economic and Financial Review. Central Bank of Nigeria, PMB 12194, Tinubu Sq., Lagos, Nigeria; tel. (1) 660100; telex 22565; f. 1963; analysis of the economy and finances of Nigeria; quarterly.

Economic Bulletin of Ghana. Economic Society of Ghana, POB 57, Legon, Accra, Ghana; tel. (1) 775381; Editors Dr Charles D. Jebuni, Dr K. N. Afful; quarterly.

English Studies in Africa. c/o Dept of English, University of the Witwatersrand, 1 Jan Smuts Ave, PO Wits, 2050 Johannesburg, South Africa; tel. (11) 716-2832; fax (11) 716-3000; f. 1959; journal of the humanities; Editor Prof. G. I. Hughes; bi-annually.

Europe Outremer. 178 quai L. Blériot, 75016 Paris, France; tel. 46477844; f. 1923; economic and political material on francophone Africa; Dir Robert Taton; monthly.

Genève-Afrique. Institut universitaire d'études du développement, 24 rue Rothschild, CP 136, 1211 Geneva 21, Switzerland; tel. (22) 7315940; fax (22) 7384416; Editor Dr Laurent Monnier; 2 a year.

Géopolitique africaine. 12 rue du 4 septembre, 75002 Paris, France; fax 45556295; f. 1986; Editor Jean Marc Kelflèche; quarterly.

Heritage of Zimbabwe. History Society of Zimbabwe, POB CY35, Causeway, Zimbabwe; f. 1956; history of Zimbabwe and adjoining territories; Editor Michael J. Kimberley; annually.

Indian Ocean Newsletter. 10 rue du Sentier, 75002 Paris, France; tel. 45081480; fax 45085983; f. 1981; French and English edns; Editor-in-chief Francis Soler; 48 a year.

Informationsdienst Südliches Afrika. Informationsstelle Südliches Afrika eV, 53227 Bonn, Königswintererstrasse 116, Germany; tel. (228) 464369; fax (228) 468177; politics, economics, social and military affairs of southern Africa and German relations with the area; 6 a year.

International Journal of African Historical Studies. African Studies Center, Boston University, 270 Bay State Rd, Boston, MA 02215, USA; tel. (617) 353-7306; fax (617) 353-4975; f. 1968; Editor Norman R. Bennett; 3 a year.

Jeune Afrique. JAPRESS, 57 bis d'Auteuil, 75016 Paris, France; tel. 44301960; telex 651105; fax 45200822; f. 1960; Editor-in-Chief Béchir ben Yahmed; weekly.

Journal of African Economies. St Cross Bldg, Manor Rd, University of Oxford, Oxford OX1 3UL, England; tel. (865) 56767; telex 837330; fax (865) 267773; f. 1992; Man. Editors Paul Collier, J. W. Gunning, Benno Ndulu, Ademola Oyejide; 3 a year.

Journal des Africanistes. Société des Africanistes, Musée de l'Homme, Palais de Chaillot, 75116 Paris, France; tel. 47277255; f. 1931; some articles in English; 2 a year.

Journal of African History. School of Oriental and African Studies, Thornhaugh St, Russell Sq., London, WC1H 0XG, England; tel. (71) 637-2388; telex 291829; fax (71) 436-3844; f. 1960; Editors David Anderson, Robin Law, Joseph Miller, Phyllis Martin; 3 a year.

Journal of African Studies. African Studies Center, 6265 Bunche Hall, UCLA, 405 Hilgard Ave, Los Angeles, CA 90024, USA; tel. (213) 825-4601; Editor Prof. Boniface I. Obichere; publ. by Heldref Publications, 4000 Albemarle St, NW, Washington, DC 20016, USA; quarterly.

Journal of Asian and African Studies. Dept of Sociology, Vari Hall 2106, York University, 4700 Keele St, Downsview, ON M3J 1P3, Canada; tel. (416) 441-6343; publ. by E. J. Brill, Plantijnstraat 2, 2321 JC, Leiden, Netherlands; Editor K. Ishwaran.

Journal of Development Studies. Frank Cass and Co Ltd, Newbury House, 890-900 Eastern Ave, Newbury Park, Ilford, Essex IG2 7HH, England; tel. (81) 599-8866; fax (81) 599-0984; f. 1964; Editors Christopher Colclough, Colin Kirkpatrick, Mick Moore, David Wall; quarterly.

Journal of Ethiopian Studies. Institute of Ethiopian Studies, Addis Ababa University, POB 1176, Addis Ababa, Ethiopia; telex 21205; fax (1) 552688; f. 1963; social and cultural anthropology, literature, history, linguistics, political science, economics; Editors Bahru Zewde, Taddesse Beyene, Taddesse Tamrat; Man. Editor Taye Assefa; 2 a year.

Journal of Imperial and Commonwealth History. Frank Cass and Co Ltd, Newbury House, 890-900 Eastern Ave, Newbury Park, Ilford, Essex, IG2 7HH, England; tel. (81) 599-8866; fax (81) 599-0984; f. 1972; Editors A. J. Stockwell, Peter Burroughs; 3 a year.

Journal of Modern African Studies. Cambridge University Press, The Edinburgh Bldg, Shaftesbury Rd, Cambridge CB2 2RU, England; tel. (223) 312393; fax (223) 315052; politics and economics; Editor Dr David Kimble; quarterly.

Journal of Peasant Studies. Frank Cass and Co Ltd, Newbury House, 890-900 Eastern Ave, Newbury Park, Ilford, Essex, IG2 7HH, England; tel. (81) 530-4226; fax (81) 530-7795; f. 1973; Editors Terry Byres, Henry Bernstein, Tom Brass; quarterly.

Journal of Racial Affairs. South African Bureau for Racial Affairs, POB 2768, Pretoria, South Africa; tel. (12) 3430284; f. 1948; in Afrikaans and English; Editor D. J. Viljoen; quarterly.

Journal of Religion in Africa. Dept of Theology and Religious Studies, University of Leeds, Leeds, West Yorkshire, LS2 9JT, England; tel. (532) 333640; telex 556473; fax (532) 333654; f. 1967; Editor Adrian Hastings; quarterly.

Journal of Southern African Studies. c/o Colin Stoneman, Centre for Southern African Studies, University of York, Heslington, York, North Yorkshire YO1 5DD, England; tel. (0904) 433698; telex 57933; fax (0904) 433433; f. 1974; Editors Saul Dubow, Liz Gunner, Debby Potts; publ. by Oxford University Press; quarterly.

Leeds African Studies Bulletin. African Studies Unit, The University, Leeds, West Yorkshire, LS2 9JT, England; tel. (532) 335069; 2 a year.

La Lettre d'Afrique Expansion. 17 rue d'Uzès, 75002 Paris, France; tel. 40133381; fax 40419495; f. 1984; business affairs; Editor Michel Levron; weekly.

La Lettre du Continent. 10 rue de Sentier, 75002 Paris, France; tel. 45081480; fax 45085983; f. 1985; Man. Editor Antoine Glaser; fortnightly.

Marchés Tropicaux et Mediterranéens. 190 blvd Haussmann, 75008 Paris, France; tel. 45631155; telex 641544; fax 42890872; f. 1945; current affairs, mainly economics; Editor François Gaulme; weekly.

New African. 7 Coldbath Sq., London, EC1R 4LQ, England; tel. (71) 713-7711; telex 8811757; fax (71) 713-7970; f. 1977; politics and general interest; Editor Alan Rake; monthly.

Newslink Africa. 7-11 Kensington High St, London, W8 5NP, England; tel. (71) 411-3111; telex 268141; fax (71) 938-4168; business and development issues; Editor Shamlal Puri; weekly.

Nigeria Newsletter. Frank Cass and Co Ltd, Newbury House, 890-900 Eastern Ave, Newbury Park, Ilford, Essex, IG2 7HH, England; tel. (81) 599-8866; telex 897719; fax (81) 599-0984; Editor Averill McGarvey; fortnightly.

Nigrizia. Vicolo Pozzo 1, 37129 Verona, Italy; tel. (45) 596238; fax (45) 8031455; fax (45) 8001737; f. 1883; Editors Efrem Tresoldi, Giuseppe Cavallini; monthly.

Notes Africaines. Institut fondamental d'Afrique noire, Université de Dakar, BP 206, Dakar, Senegal; quarterly.

Nouvelles du CAFRAD. Centre africain de Formation et de Recherche administratives pour le Développement (CAFRAD), BP 310, Tangier, Morocco; tel. (9) 942632; telex 33664; fax (9) 941415; Arabic, English, French; monthly.

Odu. A Journal of West African Studies, New Series (1968–). Obafemi Awolowo University Press, PMB 004, OAU Post Office, Ile-Ife, Nigeria; tel. (36) 230284; Editor Biodun Adediran; 2 a year.

Opportunity Africa. Westoning House Ltd, 55 St John St, London, EC1M 4AN, England; tel. (71) 336-7212; fax (71) 336-7211; f. 1994; Editor Margaret Park; Quarterly.

Optima. POB 61587, 2107 Marshalltown, South Africa; tel. (11) 638-5125; telex 487167; fax (11) 638-3771; f. 1951; political, economic, social, cultural and scientific aspects of African development; circulated mainly to shareholders of Anglo-American Corpn of South Africa, De Beers Consolidated Mines and to educational institutions; Editor Mark Irvine; 2 a year.

Peuples Noirs–Peuples Africains. 82 ave de la Porte-des-Champs, 76000 Rouen, France; tel. 35893197; f. 1978; 6 a year.

Politique Africaine. Editions Karthala, 22–24 blvd Arago, 75013 Paris, France; tel. 43311559; fax 45352705; f. 1981; political science and international relations; Editor-in-Chief Alain Ricard; quarterly.

Race Relations Survey. South African Institute of Race Relations, POB 31044, Braamfontein 2017, South Africa; tel. (11) 403-3600; fax (11) 403-3671; Dir J. S. Kane-Berman; annually.

Recherches Africaines. Direction de la Recherche Scientifique et Technique, Secrétariat d'Etat à la Recherche Scientifique, BP 561, Conakry, Guinea; quarterly.

Recueil Penant. Les Editions d'Iéna, 17 rue Thiers, 78110 Le Vésinet, France; tel. 39763993; f. 1981; review of law in African countries; Sec.-Gen. Martin Kirsch; quarterly.

Research in African Literatures. University of Indiana Press, 601 North Morton, Bloomington, IN 47404, USA; tel. (812) 855-9449; fax (812) 855-7931; literary features and reviews, research reports; Editor Richard Bjornson; quarterly.

Research Review. Institute of African Studies, POB 73, University of Ghana, Legon, Ghana; tel. (21) 775512; telex 2556; 3 a year.

Review of African Political Economy. Regency House, 75–77 St Mary's Rd, Sheffield, South Yorkshire, S2 4AN, England; tel. (742) 752671; fax (742) 738214; f. 1974; Man. Editor Jan Burgess; quarterly.

Revue Française d'Etudes Politiques Africaines. Société Africaine d'Edition, BP 1877, Dakar, Senegal; f. 1966; political; Editors Pierre Biarnès, Philippe Decraene; monthly.

Sierra Leone Studies. Dept of Modern History, Fourah Bay College, Freetown, Sierra Leone; 2 a year.

SIMNOW. SIM International Media Dept, 10 Huntingdale Blvd, Scarborough, ON M1W 2S5, Canada; tel. (416) 497-2424; fax (416) 497-2444; f. 1958; edns also publ. in Australia, NZ, Southern Africa, Singapore, Switzerland and UK; French, German, Italian and Chinese edns; Editorial Dir David W. Fuller; quarterly.

Southern Africa Business Intelligence. Financial Times Newsletters, 126 Jermyn St, London, SW1Y 4UJ, England; tel. (71) 411-4414; telex 296926; fax (71) 411-4415; f. 1992; Editor Dennis Kiley; fortnightly.

Southern Africa Exclusive. Ludgate House, Suite 71, 107-111 Fleet St, London, EC4A 2AB, England; tel. (71) 353-1117; fax (71) 353-1516; f. 1992; Editor Terry Bell; monthly.

Southern Africa Monthly Regional Bulletin. POB 724, London, N16 5RZ, England; tel. (71) 359-2328; fax (71) 359-2443; f. 1992; Publr David Coetzee.

Southern Africa Report. POB 261579, Excom 2023, South Africa; tel. (11) 646-8790; fax (11) 646-2596; f. 1983; current affairs and financial newsletter; Publr and Editor Raymond Louw; 50 a year.

SouthScan. POB 724, London, N16 5RZ, England; tel. (71) 359-2328; fax (71) 359-2443; f. 1986; political and economic affairs in southern Africa; Publr David Coetzee; weekly.

Sudan Notes and Records. POB 555, Khartoum, Sudan; f. 1918; academic articles and scientific data relating to Sudan; Editor Yusuf Fadl Hasan; annually.

Tanzania Notes and Records. Tanzania Society, National Museum, POB 511, Dar es Salaam, Tanzania; tel. (51) 44311; f. 1936; annually.

Third World Quarterly. 188 Copse Hill, London, SW20 0SP, England; tel. (81) 947-1043; telex 9312131582; fax (81) 947-1043; Editor Shahid Qadir.

Third World Resources. 464 19th St, Oakland, CA 94612-2297, USA; tel. (510) 835-4692; fax (510) 835-3017; f. 1984; Editors Tom Fenton, Mary Heffron; quarterly.

Uganda Journal. Uganda Society, POB 4980, Kampala, Uganda; tel. (41) 244061; history, literature, local ethnology, science and education; Editor Prof. W. B. Banage.

Vostok (Oriens). Afro-Aziatskiye Obtchestva: Istoria i Sovremenost, 30/1 ul. Spiridonovka, 103001, Moscow; Rossiyskaya Akad. Nauk, Institut Vostokovedeniya, Institut Afriki, 2026650 Moscow, Russia; tel. (95) 92900531; f. 1955; Editor-in-Chief Dr L. B. Alaev; Man. Editor V. A. Tyurin; bi-monthly.

Washington Report on Africa. 1413 K St, NW, Suite 1400, Washington, DC 20005, USA; tel. (202) 371-0555; telex 281409; fax (202) 408-9369; Editor Rick Sherman; fortnightly.

West Africa. West Africa Publishing Co Ltd, 43–45 Coldharbour Lane, London, SE5 9NR, England; tel. (71) 737-2946; telex 892420; fax (71) 978-8334; f. 1917; Editor-in-Chief Kaye Whiteman; weekly.

Zambia Museums Journal. c/o Dr Francis Musonda, The Lusaka National Museum, POB 50491, Lusaka, Zambia; tel. (1) 320991; fax (1) 223788; f. 1970; Editor Dr Francis Musonda; irregular.

ZAST. c/o Dr Christian Neugebauer, 1100 Vienna, Postfach 3, Austria; tel. and fax (1) 0222-5264387; 2 a year.

PART TWO

Regional Organizations

THE UNITED NATIONS IN AFRICA

Address: United Nations Plaza, New York, NY 10017, USA.

Telephone: (212) 963-1234; **fax:** (212) 758-2718.

The United Nations (UN) was founded on 24 October 1945. The organization aims to maintain international peace and security, and to develop international co-operation in economic, social, cultural and humanitarian problems. The principal organs of the UN are the General Assembly, the Security Council, the Economic and Social Council (ECOSOC), the International Court of Justice and the Secretariat. The General Assembly, which meets for three months each year, comprises representatives of all UN member states. The Security Council investigates disputes between member countries, and may recommend ways and means of peaceful settlement: it comprises five permanent members (the People's Republic of China, France, Russia, the United Kingdom and the USA) and 10 other members elected by the General Assembly for a two-year period. The Economic and Social Council comprises representatives of 54 member states, elected by the General Assembly for a three-year period: it promotes co-operation on economic, social, cultural and humanitarian matters, acting as a central policy-making body and co-ordinating the activities of the UN's specialized agencies. The International Court of Justice comprises 15 judges of different nationalities, elected for nine-year terms by the General Assembly and the Security Council: it adjudicates in legal disputes between UN member states.

Secretary-General of the United Nations: Dr BOUTROS BOUTROS-GHALI (Egypt) (1992–96).

MEMBER STATES IN AFRICA SOUTH OF THE SAHARA

(with assessments for percentage contributions to UN budget for 1992–94, and year of admission)

Angola	0.01	1976
Benin	0.01	1960
Botswana	0.01	1966
Burkina Faso	0.01	1960
Burundi	0.01	1962
Cameroon	0.01	1960
Cape Verde	0.01	1975
Central African Republic	0.01	1960
Chad	0.01	1960
Comoros	0.01	1975
Congo	0.01	1960
Côte d'Ivoire	0.02	1960
Djibouti	0.01	1977
Equatorial Guinea	0.01	1968
Eritrea	n.a.	1993
Ethiopia	0.01	1945
Gabon	0.02	1960
The Gambia	0.01	1965
Ghana	0.01	1957
Guinea	0.01	1958
Guinea-Bissau	0.01	1974
Kenya	0.01	1963
Lesotho	0.01	1966
Liberia	0.01	1945
Madagascar	0.01	1960
Malawi	0.01	1964
Mali	0.01	1960
Mauritania	0.01	1961
Mauritius	0.01	1968
Mozambique	0.01	1975
Namibia	0.01	1990
Niger	0.01	1960
Nigeria	0.20	1960
Rwanda	0.01	1962
São Tomé and Príncipe	0.01	1975
Senegal	0.01	1960
Seychelles	0.01	1976
Sierra Leone	0.01	1961
Somalia	0.01	1960
South Africa	0.45	1945
Sudan	0.01	1956
Swaziland	0.01	1968
Tanzania	0.01	1961
Togo	0.01	1960
Uganda	0.01	1962
Zaire	0.01	1960
Zambia	0.01	1964
Zimbabwe	0.01	1980

AFRICAN PERMANENT MISSIONS TO THE UNITED NATIONS

(with Permanent Representatives — June 1994)

Angola: 125 East 73rd St, New York, NY 10021; tel. (212) 861-5656; fax (212) 861-9295; AFONSO VAN DÚNEM (MBINDA).

Benin: 4 East 73rd St, New York, NY 10021; tel. (212) 249-6014; fax (212) 734-4735; RENÉ VALÉRY MONGBE.

Botswana: 103 East 37th St, New York, NY 10016; tel. (212) 889-2277; fax (212) 725-5061; LEGWAILA JOSEPH LEGWAILA.

Burkina Faso: 115 East 73rd St, New York, NY 10021; tel. (212) 288-7515; GAËTAN RIMWANGUIYA OUEDRAOGO.

Burundi: 336 East 45th St, 12th Floor, New York, NY 10017; tel. (212) 687-1180; fax (212) 687-1197; THÉRENCE SINUNGURUZA.

Cameroon: 22 East 73rd St, New York, NY 10021; tel. (212) 794-2295; fax (212) 249-0533; PASCAL BILOA TANG.

Cape Verde: 27 East 69th St, New York, NY 10021; tel. (212) 472-0333; fax (212) 794-1398; (vacant).

Central African Republic: 386 Park Ave South, Room 1614, New York, NY 10016; tel. (212) 689-6195; JEAN-PIERRE SOHAHONG-KOMBET.

Chad: 211 East 43rd St, Suite 1703, New York, NY 10017; tel. (212) 986-0980; fax (212) 818-9583; LAOUMAYE MEKONYO KOUMBAIRIA.

Comoros: 336 East 45th St, 2nd Floor, New York, NY 10017; tel. (212) 972-8010; fax (212) 983-4712; (vacant).

Congo: 14 East 65th St, New York, NY 10021; tel. (212) 744-7840; fax (212) 744-7975; DANIEL ABIBI.

Côte d'Ivoire: 46 East 74th St, New York, NY 10021; tel. (212) 717-5555; fax (212) 717-4492; JEAN-MARIE KACOU GERVAIS.

Djibouti: 866 United Nations Plaza, Suite 4011, New York, NY 10017; tel. (212) 753-3163; fax (212) 223-1276; ROBLE OLHAYE.

Equatorial Guinea: 57 Magnolia Ave, Mount Vernon, NY 10553; tel. (914) 667-6913; fax (914) 667-6838; DÁMASO-OBIANG NDONG.

Eritrea: 211 East 43rd St, Suite 2203, New York, NY 10017; tel. (212) 687-3390; fax (212) 687-3138; (vacant).

Ethiopia: 866 United Nations Plaza, Room 560, New York, NY 10017; tel. (212) 421-1830; fax (212) 754-0360; Dr MULUGETA ETEFFA.

Gabon: 18 East 41st St, 6th Floor, New York, NY 10017; tel. (212) 686-9720; fax (212) 689-5769; DENIS DANGUE REWAKA.

The Gambia: 820 Second Ave, 9th Floor, New York, NY 10017; tel. (212) 949-6640; fax (212) 808-4975; OUSMAN AHMADU SALLAH.

Ghana: 19 East 47th St, New York, NY 10017; tel. (212) 832-1300; fax (212) 751-6743; GEORGE O. LAMPTEY.

Guinea: 140 East 39th St, New York, NY 10016; tel. (212) 687-8115; fax (212) 687-8248; LANSANA KOUYATE.

Guinea-Bissau: 211 East 43rd St, Room 604, New York, NY 10017; tel. (212) 661-3977; fax (212) 983-2794; BOUBACAR TOURE.

Kenya: 866 United Nations Plaza, Room 486, New York, NY 10017; tel. (212) 421-4740; fax (212) 486-1985; FRANCIS K. MUTHAURA.

Lesotho: 204 East 39th St, New York, NY 10016; tel. (212) 661-1690; fax (212) 682-4388; MONYANE P. PHOOFOLO.

Liberia: 820 Second Ave, 4th Floor, New York, NY 10017; tel. (212) 687-1033; fax (212) 687-1035; WILLIAM BULL.

Madagascar: 801 Second Ave, Suite 404, New York, NY 10017; tel. (212) 986-9491; fax (212) 986-6271; (vacant).

Malawi: 600 Third Ave, 30th Floor, New York, NY 10016; tel. (212) 949-0180; fax (212) 599-5021; NGELESI M. MWAUNGULU.

Mali: 111 East 69th St, New York, NY 10021; tel. (212) 737-4150; fax (212) 472-3778; NOUHOUM SAMASSEKOU.

Mauritania: 211 East 43rd St, Suite 2000, New York, NY 10017; tel. (212) 986-7963; fax (212) 986-8419; MOHAMEDOU OULD MOHAMED MAHMOUD.

Mauritius: 211 East 43rd St, 15th Floor, New York, NY 10017; tel. (212) 949-0190; fax (212) 697-3829; SATTEEANUND PEERTHUM.

Mozambique: 70 East 79th St, New York, NY 10021; tel. (212) 517-4550; fax (212) 734-3083; PEDRO COMISSARIO AFONSO.

Namibia: 135 East 36th St, New York, NY 10016; tel. (212) 685-2003; fax (212) 685-1561; Dr TUNGURA HUARAKA.

Niger: 417 East 50th St, New York, NY 10022; tel. (212) 421-3260; fax (212) 753-6931; ADAMOU SEYDOU.

Nigeria: 828 Second Ave, New York, NY 10017; tel. (212) 953-9130; fax (212) 697-1970; Prof. IBRAHIM AGOOLA GAMBARI.

Rwanda: 124 East 39th St, New York, NY 10016; tel. (212) 696-0644; fax (212) 689-3304; JEAN DAMASCÈNE BIZIMANA.

São Tomé and Príncipe: 122 East 42nd St, Suite 1604, New York, NY 10017; tel. (212) 697-4211; fax (212) 687-8389; JOAQUIM RAFAEL BRANCO.

Senegal: 238 East 68th St, New York, NY 10021; tel. (212) 517-9030; fax (212) 737-7461; KÉBA BIRANE CISSE.

Seychelles: 820 Second Ave, Room 900F, New York, NY 10017; tel. (212) 687-9766; fax (212) 922-9177; MARC MICHAEL MARENGO.

Sierra Leone: 245 East 49th St, New York, NY 10017; tel. (212) 688-1656; fax (212) 688-4924; ALIMAMY PALLO BANGURA.

Somalia: 425 East 61st St, Suite 703, New York, NY 10021; tel. (212) 688-9140; fax (212) 759-0651; (vacant).

South Africa: 333 East 38th St, 9th Floor, New York, NY 10016; tel. (212) 213-5583; fax (212) 692-2498; VERNON R. W. STEWARD.

Sudan: 733 Third Ave, 9th Floor, New York, NY 10017; tel. (212) 573-6033; fax (212) 573-6160; ALI MOHAMED OSMAN YASSIN.

Swaziland: 866 United Nations Plaza, Suite 420, New York, NY 10017; tel. (212) 371-8910; Dr TIMOTHY L. L. DLAMINI.

Tanzania: 205 East 42nd St, 13th Floor, New York, NY 10017; tel. (212) 972-9160; fax (212) 682-5232; ANTHONY B. NYAKYI.

Togo: 112 East 40th St, New York, NY 10016; tel. (212) 490-3455; fax (212) 983-6684; SOUMI-BIOVA PENNANEACH.

Uganda: 336 East 45th St, New York, NY 10017; tel. (212) 949-0110; fax (212) 687-4517; Prof. PEREZI KARUKUBIRO-KAMUNANWIRE.

Zaire: 767 Third Ave, 25th Floor, New York, NY 10017; tel. (212) 754-1966; fax (212) 754-1970; (vacant).

Zambia: 237 East 52nd St, New York, NY 10022; tel. (212) 758-1110; fax (212) 758-1319; OTEMA S. MUSUKA.

Zimbabwe: 128 East 56th St, New York, NY 10022; tel. (212) 980-9511; fax (212) 755-4188; SIMBARASHE SIMBANENDUKU MUMBENGEGWI.

Observers

Asian-African Legal Consultative Committee: 404 East 66th St, Apt 12C, New York, NY 10021; tel. (212) 734-7608; K. BHAGWAT-SINGH.

Commonwealth Secretariat: 820 Second Ave, Suite 800A, New York, NY 10017; tel. (212) 599-6190; fax (212) 972-3970.

International Committee of the Red Cross: 780 Third Ave, Suite 2802, New York, NY 10017; tel. (212) 371-0770; fax (212) 838-5397; PETER KÜNG.

Organization of African Unity: 346 East 50th St, New York, NY 10022; tel. (212) 319-5490; fax (212) 319-7135; IBRAHIMA SY.

Organization of the Islamic Conference: 130 East 40th St, 5th Floor, New York, NY 10016; tel. (212) 883-0140; fax (212) 883-0143.

The African, Caribbean and Pacific Group of States and the African Development Bank (q.v.) have standing invitations to participate in the work of the General Assembly, but do not maintain permanent offices in New York.

GENERAL ASSEMBLY BODIES CONCERNED WITH AFRICA SOUTH OF THE SAHARA

Advisory Committee on the UN Educational and Training Programme for Southern Africa: f. 1968; 13 mems.

Committee of Trustees of the United Nations Trust Fund for South Africa: f. 1965; five mems, nominated by the Assembly President.

Economic Commission for Africa—ECA

Address: Africa Hall, POB 3005, Addis Ababa, Ethiopia.

Telephone: (1) 517200; **telex:** 21029; **fax:** (1) 514416.

The UN Economic Commission for Africa was founded in 1958 by a resolution of ECOSOC to initiate and take part in measures for facilitating Africa's economic development.

MEMBERS*

Algeria	Ethiopia	Niger
Angola	Gabon	Nigeria
Benin	The Gambia	Rwanda
Botswana	Ghana	São Tomé and Príncipe
Burkina Faso	Guinea	Senegal
Burundi	Guinea-Bissau	Seychelles
Cameroon	Kenya	Sierra Leone
Cape Verde	Lesotho	Somalia
Central African Republic	Liberia	Sudan
Chad	Libya	Swaziland
Comoros	Madagascar	Tanzania
Congo	Malawi	Togo
Côte d'Ivoire	Mali	Tunisia
Djibouti	Mauritania	Uganda
Egypt	Mauritius	Zaire
Equatorial Guinea	Morocco	Zambia
Eritrea	Mozambique	Zimbabwe
	Namibia	

* South Africa's membership was suspended in 1965; however, following its readmission to the UN General Assembly in June 1994 South Africa was expected to reassume its membership of ECA.

Organization

(June 1994)

COMMISSION

The Commission may only act with the agreement of the government of the country concerned. It is also empowered to make recommendations on any matter within its competence directly to the government of the member or associate member concerned, to governments admitted in a consultative capacity, and to the UN Specialized Agencies. The Commission is required to submit for prior consideration by ECOSOC any of its proposals for actions that would be likely to have important effects on the international economy.

CONFERENCE OF MINISTERS

The Conference, which meets annually, is attended by ministers responsible for economic or financial affairs, planning and development of governments of member states, and is the main deliberative body of the Commission. A Technical Preparatory Committee of the Whole, representing all member states, was established in 1979 to deal with matters submitted for the consideration of the Conference.

The Commission's responsibility to promote concerted action for the economic and social development of Africa is vested primarily in the Conference, which considers matters of general policy and the priorities to be assigned to the Commission's programmes, considers inter-African and international economic policy, and makes recommendations to member states in connection with such matters. It reviews the course of programmes being implemented in the preceding year and examines and approves the programmes proposed for the next.

OTHER POLICY-MAKING BODIES

Conference of African Ministers of Economic Planning and Development.

Conference of African Ministers of Finance.

Conference of African Ministers of Industry.

Conference of African Ministers of Social Affairs.

Conference of African Ministers of Trade.

Conference of African Ministers of Transport, Communications and Planning.

Conference of Ministers of Finance.

Conference of Ministers Responsible for Human Resources Planning, Development and Utilization.

Councils of Ministers of the MULPOCs (see below).

SECRETARIAT

The Secretariat provides the services necessary for the meeting of the Conference of Ministers and the meetings of the Commission's subsidiary bodies, carries out the resolutions and implements the programmes adopted there.

The headquarters of the Secretariat is in Addis Ababa, Ethiopia. It comprises an Executive Direction and Management office and 10 Divisions.

Executive Direction and Management:

African Training and Research Centre for Women
Economic Co-operation Office

Information Service
Office of the Secretary of the Commission
Pan-African Documentation and Information Service (PADIS)
Policy and Programme Co-ordination
Technical Assistance Co-ordination and Operations Office

Divisions:
Administration and Conference Services
Industry and Human Settlements
Joint ECA/FAO Food and Agriculture
Natural Resources
Population
Public Administration, Human Resources and Social Development
Socio-Economic Research and Planning
Statistics
Trade and Development Finance
Transport, Communications and Tourism

Executive Secretary: LAYASHI YAKER (Algeria).

Subsidiary Bodies

Conference of Ministers of African Least-Developed Countries.

Follow-up Committee on Industrialization in Africa.

Intergovernmental Committee of Experts of African Least-Developed Countries.

Intergovernmental Committee of Experts for Science and Technology Development.

Intergovernmental Regional Committee on Human Settlements and Environment.

Joint Conference of African Planners, Statisticians and Demographers.

Regional Operational Centres

Multinational Programming and Operational Centres (MULPOC) act as 'field agents' for the implementation of regional development programmes. The Centres are located in Yaoundé, Cameroon (serving central Africa), Gisenyi, Rwanda (Great Lakes Community), Lusaka, Zambia (east and southern Africa), Niamey, Niger (west Africa) and Tangier, Morocco (north Africa). Each centre holds regular ministerial meetings.

African Institute for Economic Development and Planning: POB 3186, Addis Ababa, Ethiopia; tel. (1) 22577; Dir JEGGAN C. SENGHOR.

Activities

The Commission's activities are designed to encourage sustainable socio-economic development in Africa and to increase economic co-operation among African countries and between Africa and other parts of the world. The Secretariat is guided in its efforts by major regional strategies including the Abuja Treaty establishing the African Economic Community signed under the aegis of the Organization of African Unity and the UN New Agenda for the Development for Africa covering the period 1991–2000.

AGRICULTURE

During 1991–92 ECA's activities in the agricultural sector were intended to achieve three principal objectives: the alleviation of poverty, the attainment of food self-sufficiency and the promotion of food security. To these ends ECA provided support in the areas of development of livestock; inter-state co-operation; reduction or prevention of food losses; monitoring and evaluation of agricultural and rural development projects; conservation, expansion and rational utilization of natural resources, particularly land and forests; and preparation of related technical publications or reports.

ENERGY

In 1991–92 the ECA, under its Energy Programme, provided assistance to member states in the development of indigenous energy resources and the formulation of energy policies to extricate member states from continued energy crises. Studies were carried out on strengthening the institutional arrangements for management in the energy sector in Zambia and Zimbabwe; on increasing the efficiency in the utilization of energy in Burundi, Rwanda and Zaire; on maximizing revenue from petroleum operations; and on new and renewable sources of energy and the technologies needed to harness them. The ECA's Secretariat supports the African Regional Centre for Solar Energy (Bujumbura, Burundi). Together with the World Bank, the ECA organized a training workshop on energy policy and the environment for senior African officials involved in energy planning and management.

ENVIRONMENT AND DEVELOPMENT

During 1991–92 reports were compiled on the development, implementation and sound management of environmental programmes at national, sub-regional and regional levels. ECA members adopted a common African position for the UN Conference on Environment and Development, held in June 1992.

INDUSTRY

Following the failure to implement many of the proposals under the UN Industrial Development Decade for Africa (IDDA, 1980–90) and the UN Programme of Action for African Economic Recovery and Development (1986–90), a second IDDA was adopted by the Conference of African Ministers of Industry in July 1991. The main objectives of the second IDDA include the consolidation and rehabilitation of existing industries, the expansion of new investments, and the promotion of small-scale industries and technological capabilities. Various technical publications were to be produced, including a directory of project profiles in the field of entrepreneurship in small-scale industries.

ECA is organizing a global conference for the promotion of investment in Africa, scheduled to be held in November 1994.

INFORMATION

The Pan-African Documentation and Information Service (PADIS) was established in 1980. The main objectives of PADIS are: to provide access to numerical and other information on African social, economic, scientific and technological development issues; to assist African countries in their efforts to develop national information handling capabilities through advisory services and training; to establish a data communication network to facilitate the timely use of information on development; and to design sound technical specifications, norms and standards to minimize technical barriers in the exchange of information.

INTERNATIONAL TRADE AND FINANCE

ECA assists African countries in expanding trade among themselves and with other regions of the world and in promoting financial and monetary co-operation. ECA attempts to ensure that African countries should participate effectively in current international negotiations. To this end, assistance has been provided to member states in negotiations under UNCTAD and GATT; in the annual conferences of the IMF and the World Bank; in negotiations with the EC; and in meetings related to economic co-operation among developing countries. Studies have been prepared on problems and prospects likely to arise for the African region from the implementation of the Common Fund for Commodities and the Generalized System of Trade Preferences (both supervised by UNCTAD); the impacts of exchange-rate fluctuations on the economies of African countries; and on long-term implications of different debt arrangements for African economies. ECA assists individual member states by undertaking studies on domestic trade, expansion of inter-African trade, transnational corporations, integration of women in trade and development, and strengthening the capacities of state-trading organizations. ECA promotes co-operation between developing countries, and the expansion of African trade with overseas countries.

The expansion of trade within Africa is constrained by the low level of industrial production, and by the strong emphasis on commodity trade. ECA encourages the diversification of production and the expansion of domestic trade structures, within regional economic groupings. ECA helps to organize regional and 'All-Africa' trade fairs.

In early 1992 ECA, in co-ordination with the OAU and the African Development Bank (q.v.), embarked on a series of meetings with western governments and financial institutions in an attempt to persuade them to cancel, partially or completely, debts owed by African countries, and to encourage them to invest in the region.

NATURAL RESOURCES

The Fourth Regional Conference on the Development and Utilization of Mineral Resources in Africa, held in March 1991, adopted an action plan that included the formulation of national mineral exploitation policies; and the promotion of the gemstone industry, small-scale mining and the iron and steel industry. ECA continues to provide support to the Southern African Mineral Resources Development Centre in Dar-es-Salaam, Tanzania, and the Central African Mineral Development Centre in Brazzaville, Congo, which provide advisory and laboratory services to their respective member states.

ECA sponsors the two leading institutions in the field of cartography and remote-sensing. The Regional Centre for Services in Surveying, Mapping and Remote-Sensing is based in Nairobi, Kenya; it is currently establishing a satellite receiving station for processing remotely-sensed data for use by member states. The Regional Centre for Training in Aerospace Surveys, base in Ile Ife, Nigeria, provides training in cartography and remote-sensing. The Eighth Regional Cartographic Conference for Africa was scheduled to be held in early 1993.

ECA assists member states in the assessment and use of water resources and the development of river and lake basins common to more than one country. The annual information bulletin on water resources in Africa, *Maji,* disseminates technical information to African governments, and inter-governmental and non-governmental organizations. In the field of marine affairs, ECA provides advisory services to member states on the opportunities and challenges provided by the UN Convention on the Law of the Sea. A guide to African policy-makers and negotiators on legal arrangements for joint ventures among developed and developing countries for the exploration and exploitation of non-living resources of the sea was published in 1991.

POLICY AND PROGRAMME CO-ORDINATION

Policy and programme co-ordination is one of the tasks of the Executive Direction and Management office. The office provides guidance in the formulation of policies towards the achievement of Africa's development objectives to the policy-making organs of the UN and OAU. It contributes to the work of the General Assembly and other specialized agencies by providing an African perspective in the preparation of development strategies.

POPULATION

ECA assists its member states in (i) population data collection and data processing, which is carried out by the Statistics Division of the Commission (q.v.); (ii) analysis of demographic data obtained from censuses or surveys: this assistance is given by the Population Division; (iii) training demographers at the Regional Institute for Population Studies (RIPS) in Accra (Ghana) and at the Institut de formation et de recherche démographiques (IFORD) in Yaoundé (Cameroon); (iv) formulation of population policies and integrating population variables in development planning, through advisory missions and through the organization of national seminars on population and development; and (v) dissemination of information through its *Newsletter, Demographic Handbook for Africa,* the *African Population Studies* series and other publications. The Sixth Joint Conference of African Planners, Statisticians and Demographers was held in 1990; the Third African Population Conference was held in Dakar, Senegal, in December 1992, in order to prepare for the International Conference on Population and Development in September 1994.

PUBLIC ADMINISTRATION, HUMAN RESOURCES AND SOCIAL DEVELOPMENT

The Division aims to assist governments, public corporations, universities and the private sector in improving their financial management; strengthening policy-making and analytical capacities; adopting measures to redress skill shortages; enhance human resources development and utilization; and promote social development through programmes focusing on youth, people with disabilities and the elderly. The Division conducts training workshops, seminars and conferences at national, sub-regional and regional levels for ministers, public administrators, senior policy-makers as well as for private and non-governmental organizations.

SCIENCE AND TECHNOLOGY

The Commission's activities in the field of science and technology focus on three areas: the development of policies and institutions; the training and effective utilization of the workforce; and the promotion of regional and inter-regional co-operation. In 1991–92 ECA's Secretariat completed a review of science and technology policy institutions; provided advisory services to a number of countries on strengthening their science and technology structures; and provided technical support to the African Regional Centre for Technology and the African Regional Organization for Standardization.

SOCIO-ECONOMIC RESEARCH AND PLANNING

Monitoring economic and social trends in the African region and studying the development problems concerning it are among the fundamental tasks of the Commission. Every year the Commission publishes the *Survey of Economic and Social Conditions in Africa* and the *Economic Report on Africa.*

The Commission gives assistance to governments in general economic analysis, in fiscal, financial and monetary issues and in planning. The ECA's work on economic planning has been recently broadened, in order to give more emphasis to macro-economic management in a mixed economy approach: a project is being undertaken to develop short-term forecasting and policy models to support economic management. The Commission has also started a major study on the informal sector in African countries. Special assistance is given to least-developed, land-locked and island countries which have a much lower income level than other countries and which are faced with heavier constraints than others. Studies are also undertaken to assist longer-term planning.

The Conference of African Planners, Statisticians and Demographers is held every two years and provides an opportunity for African governments to exchange views and experiences, and to keep abreast of new policy approaches.

In 1989 ECA published a report entitled *African Alternative Framework to Structural Adjustment Programmes for Socio-Economic Recovery and Transformation,* which argued that programmes of strict economic reform, as imposed by the International Monetary Fund and the World Bank, had not resulted in sustained economic growth in Africa over the past decade. In July 1991 ECA proposed a series of measures which countries might adopt, in a more flexible approach to long-term development. These proposals were subsequently published under the title *Selected Policy Instruments* and included multiple exchange rates (as opposed to generalized currency devaluation), differential interest rates and subsidies to agricultural producers.

STATISTICS

The Statistics Division of ECA, which comprises two sections (Statistical Development and Economic Statistics) promotes the development and co-ordination of national statistical services in the region and the improvement and comparability of statistical data. It prepares documents to assist in the improvement of statistical methodology and undertakes the collection, evaluation and dissemination of statistical information. A plan of action for statistical development in Africa in the 1990s has been drawn up and a Co-ordinating Committee on African Statistical Development (CASD) has been established. ECA's work in the field of statistics has been concentrated in five main areas: the African Household Survey Capability Programme, which aims to assist in the collection and analysis of demographic, social and economic data on households; the Statistical Training Programme for Africa, which aims to make the region self-sufficient in statistical personnel at all levels; the Technical Support Services, which provides technical advisory services for population censuses, demographic surveys and civil registration; the National Accounts Capability Programme, which aims at improving economic statistics generally by building up a capability in each country for the collection, processing and analysis of economic data; and the ECA-Regional Statistical Data Base, part of PADIS (see above), which provides on-line statistical information to users.

TRANSPORT AND COMMUNICATIONS

The ECA was appointed lead agency for the second United Nations Transport and Communications Decade in Africa (UNTACDA II), comprising the period 1991–2000. The principal aim of UNTACDA II is the establishment of an efficient integrated transport and communications system in Africa, to facilitate national and international traffic. The specific objectives of the programme include: (i) the removal of physical and non-physical barriers to intra-African trade and travel, and improvement in the road transport sector; (ii) improvement in the efficiency and financial viability of railways; (iii) development of Africa's shipping capacity and improvement in the performance of Africa's ports; (iv) development of integrated transport systems for each lake and river basin; (v) improvement of integration of all modes of transport in order to carry cargo in one chain of transport smoothly; (vi) integration of African airlines, and restructuring of civil aviation and airport management authorities; (vii) improvement in the quality and availability of transport in urban areas; (viii) development of integrated regional telecommunications networks; (ix) development of broadcasting services, with the aim of supporting socio-economic development; and (x) expansion of Africa's postal network.

In May 1991 the Conference of African Ministers of Transport, Communications and Planning approved a programme which comprised 669 projects, of which 478 were in the transport and

191 were in the telecommunications sector. The projects were submitted by 43 African countries, four sub-regional organizations and eight specialized institutions.

BUDGET

ECA's proposed programme budget for the two years 1992–93 was US $143.9m.

PUBLICATIONS

ECA Annual Report.
Africa Index (3 a year).
African Compendium on Environmental Statistics (irregular).
African Directory of Demographers (irregular).
African Population Newsletter (2 a year).
African Population Studies Series (irregular).
African Socio-Economic Indicators (annually).
African Statistical Yearbook.
African Trade Bulletin (2 a year).
Bulletin of ECA-sponsored Institutions (irregular).
Demographic Handbook for Africa (irregular).
Devindex Africa (quarterly).
Directory of African Statisticians (every 2 years).
ECA Environment Newsletter (3 a year).
Flash on Trade Opportunities (quarterly).
Focus on African Industry (2 a year).
Foreign Trade Statistics for Africa series.
Direction of Trade (quarterly).
Summary Table (annually).
Maji Water Resources Bulletin (annually).
PADIS Newsletter (quarterly).
Report of the Executive Secretary (every 2 years).
Rural Progress (2 a year).
Statistical Newsletter (2 a year).
Survey on Economic and Social Conditions in Africa (annually).

United Nations Development Programme—UNDP

Address: One United Nations Plaza, New York, NY 10017, USA.
Telephone: (212) 906-5000; **fax:** (212) 826-2057.
The Programme was established in 1965 by the UN General Assembly to help the developing countries to increase the wealth-producing capabilities of their natural and human resources.

Organization

(June 1994)

UNDP is responsible to the UN General Assembly, to which it reports through the UN Economic and Social Council.

EXECUTIVE BOARD

In January 1994 the Governing Council of UNDP and the UN Population Fund (UNFPA, of which UNDP is the governing body) was replaced by an Executive Board, as agreed by the UN General Assembly. The Board is responsible for providing intergovernmental support to and supervision of the activities of UNDP and UNFPA. It comprises 36 members: eight from Africa, seven from Asia, four from eastern Europe, five from Latin America and the Caribbean and 12 from western Europe and other countries.

President: MOHAMMAD HAMID ANSARI (India).

SECRETARIAT

Administrator: JAMES GUSTAVE (GUS) SPETH (USA).

REGIONAL BUREAUX

Headed by assistant administrators, the regional bureaux share the responsibility for implementing the programme with the Administrator's office. Within certain limitations, large-scale projects may be approved and funding allocated by the Administrator, and smaller-scale projects by the Resident Representatives, based in 129 countries.

The four regional bureaux, all at the Secretariat in New York, cover: Africa; Asia and the Pacific; the Arab states and Europe; and Latin America and the Caribbean; there is also a Division for Global and Interregional Programmes.

Assistant Administrator and Director, Regional Bureau for Africa: ELLEN JOHNSON-SIRLEAF (Liberia).

FIELD OFFICES

In almost every country receiving UNDP assistance there is a Country Office, headed by the UNDP Resident Representative, who advises the Government on formulating the country programme, sees that field activities are carried out, and acts as the leader of the UN team of experts working in the country. Resident Representatives are normally designated as co-ordinators for all UN operational development activities; the field offices function as the primary presence of the UN in most developing countries.

OFFICES OF UNDP REPRESENTATIVES IN AFRICA SOUTH OF THE SAHARA

Angola: Rua Major Kanhangulo 197, CP 910, Luanda; tel. (2) 334986; fax (2) 335609.

Benin: Lot 3, Zone Residentielle, BP 506, Cotonou; tel. 31-30-45; fax 31-57-86.

Botswana: Barclays House, Khama Crescent, POB 54, Gaborone; tel. 351680; fax 356093.

Burkina Faso: Immeuble SONAR, Quartier Ex-Koulouba, Secteur 4, 01 BP 575, Ouagadougou 01; tel. (3) 30-67-65; fax (3) 31-04-70.

Burundi: 3 rue du Marché, BP 1490, Bujumbura; tel. (2) 26619; fax (2) 225850.

Cameroon: Immeuble Stamatiades, ave Indépendence, BP 836, Yaoundé; tel. 22-17-79; fax 22-43-69.

Cape Verde: Casa Moeda, Rua Unidade Guiné-Cabo Verde, CP 62, Praia; tel. 61-57-40; fax 61-43-70.

Central African Republic: ave de l'Indépendance, BP 872, Bangui; tel. 61-12-07; fax 61-17-32.

Chad: PNUD, ave Colonel D'Ornano, BP 906, N'Djamena; tel. 51-41-00; fax 51-63-30.

Comoros: route du Bord de Mer, BP 648, Moroni; tel. 73-29-90; fax 73-28-93.

Congo: ave du Maréchal Foch, BP 465, Brazzaville; tel. 83-59-53; fax 83-39-87.

Côte d'Ivoire: angle rue Gourgas et ave Marchand, Abidjan-Plateau, 01 BP 1747, Abidjan 01; tel. 21-29-95; fax 21-13-67.

Djibouti: blvd Marchal Joffre Plâteau du Serpent, BP 2001, Djibouti; tel. 351361; fax 350587.

Equatorial Guinea: CP 399, Esquina Calle de Kenia con Calle Rey Boncoro, Malabo; tel. 3269; fax (871) 1505363.

Eritrea: Andinet St, Airport Rd, POB 5366, Asmara; tel. 181143; fax 1507653.

Ethiopia: Africa Hall, Old ECA Bldg, 7th Floor, Menelik II Ave, POB 5580, Addis Ababa; tel. (1) 511025; fax (1) 514599.

Gabon: Immeuble Africa No 1, Boulevard Triomphal Omar Bongo entre Ministère des Affaires Etrangères et Hypermarché Mbolo, BP 2183, Libreville; tel. 74-52-35; fax 74-34-99.

The Gambia: ave Ann Marie Javouhey, POB 553, Banjul; tel. (2) 28722; fax (2) 28921.

Ghana: Ring Rd Dual Carriage, near Police HQ, POB 1423, Accra; tel. 777831; fax (871) 773899.

Guinea: Immeuble Union, ave de la République, BP 222, Conakry; tel. 41-36-22; fax 41-24-85.

Guinea-Bissau: Rua Justino Lopes, 72 A/B, POB 1011, Bissau; tel. 201368; fax (874) 1504342.

Kenya: Kenyata International Conference Centre (20th/25th Floors), Harambee Ave, POB 30218, Nairobi; tel. (2) 213749; fax (2) 331897.

Lesotho: Corner Hilton and Nightingale Rds, POB 301, Maseru 100; tel. 313944; fax 310042.

Liberia: Daher Apt, UN Drive, Mamba Point, POB 10-0274, Monrovia 10; tel. 224603; fax 225771.

Madagascar: Rue Rainitovo, Antsahavola, BP 1348, Antananarivo 101; tel. (2) 21907; fax (2) 33315.

Malawi: Plot No 7, Area 40, POB 30135, Lilongwe 3; tel. 782278; fax 783637.

Mali: Immeuble Me Hamaciré N'Douré, Badalabougou-Est, BP 120, Bamako; tel. 23-06-17; fax 22-62-98.

Mauritania: Lot K, Lots No. 159–161, BP 620, Nouakchott; tel. 256900; fax 252616.

Mauritius: Anglo-Mauritius House, Intendance St, POB 253, Port Louis; tel. 208-8691; fax 208-4871.

Mozambique: Avda Kenneth Kaunda, 921/931, POB 4595, Maputo; tel. 491475; fax 491691.

Namibia: Sanlam Centre, 154 Independence St, Private Bag 13329, Windhoek 9000; tel. (61) 229083; fax (61) 229084.

Niger: Maison de l'Afrique, BP 11207, Niamey; tel. 72-34-90; fax 72-36-30.

Nigeria: 11 Oyinkan Abayomi Drive, Ikoyi, POB 2075, Lagos; tel. 269-1722; fax 269-1746.

Rwanda: ave de l'Armée 12, BP 445, Kigali; tel. 75541; fax 76263.

São Tomé and Príncipe: CP 109, Avda das Naçoes Unidas, São Tomé; tel. 22562; fax 22198.

Seychelles: covered by office in Mauritius.

Senegal: Immeuble Faycal, 19 rue Parchappe, BP 154, Dakar; tel. 23-60-12; fax 23-55-00.

Sierra Leone: United Nations House, 43 Siaka Stevens St, POB 1011, Freetown; tel. (22) 225346; fax (871) 151-3121.

Somalia: covered by office in Kenya.

Sudan: House No 7, Block 5, R.F.E., Gama'a Ave, POB 913, Khartoum; tel. (11) 83755; fax (873) 151-6741.

Swaziland: SRIC Bldg, Gilfillan St, Mbabane; tel. 42305; fax 45341.

Tanzania: Matasalamat Mansions, 2nd Floor, Zanaki St, POB 9182, Dar es Salaam; tel. (51) 46716; fax (51) 46718.

Togo: 40 ave des Nations Unies, 1ère étage, BP 911, Lomé; tel. 21-20-22; fax 21-16-41.

Uganda: UN House, 15 Clement Hill Rd, POB 7184, Kampala; tel. (41) 245290; fax (41) 244801.

Zaire: Immeuble Royal, blvd du 30 juin, BP 7248, Kinshasa; tel. (12) 33431; fax (871) 1503261.

Zambia: Plot No. 11867, Alick Nkhata Ave, Longacres, POB 31966, Lusaka; tel. (1) 262258; fax (1) 253805.

Zimbabwe: Takura House, 67-169 Union Ave, POB 4775, Harare; tel. (4) 792687; fax (2) 798695.

Activities

As the world's largest source of grant technical assistance in developing countries, UNDP works with more than 150 governments and 40 international agencies for faster economic growth and better standards of living throughout the world. Agriculture (including forestry and fisheries) is a major component of UNDP activities, accounting for about 16% of core project expenditure in 1992. Most of the work is undertaken in the field by the various United Nations agencies, or by the government of the country concerned.

Assistance is mostly non-monetary, comprising the provision of experts' services, consultancies, equipment, and fellowships for advanced study abroad. In 1992 nearly one-half of spending on projects was for the services of experts, 17% was for subcontracts, 15% was for equipment, 11% was for training, and the remainder was for other costs, such as maintenance of equipment. Most UNDP projects incorporate training for local workers. Developing countries themselves provide 50% or more of the total project costs in terms of personnel, facilities, equipment and supplies.

UNDP concentrates on building national capacity in six specific areas (as defined by the Governing Council in 1990): eradication of poverty through 'grass-roots' participation in development; environmental protection; management development (under the Management Development Programme) technical co-operation among developing countries; transfer of technology; and the promotion of women in development (under the Division for women and Development).

Countries receiving UNDP assistance are allocated an indicative planning figure (IPF) for a five-year period. The IPF represents the approximate total value of funding that a country can expect to receive, based on a formula taking per caput gross national product (GNP), population size and other criteria into account. In partnership with UNDP's Country Offices, governments calculate their technical assistance requirements on the basis of this formula. Activities covering more than one region are developed by UNDP's Division for Global and Interregional Projects, in consultation with the relevant national and regional institutions. These activities include the promotion of international agricultural research, the improvement of drinking water supply and sanitation, and addressing the economic consequences of HIV/AIDS, while promoting measures to prevent its spread.

From 1990 UNDP published an annual *Human Development Report* and adopted an overall approach to its work, described as 'sustainable human development'. The objective of this approach was to put the focus of UNDP's work on people and to measure the effectiveness of programmes by their capacity to promote individual well-being and choice (in terms of health, education and purchasing power). UNDP also introduced the Human Development Index, which ranked countries in terms of human development, using three key indicators: life expectancy, adult literacy and basic income required for a decent standard of living.

In 1991 the Global Environment Facility (GEF), which is managed jointly by UNDP, the World Bank and the UN Environment Programme, became operational. The GEF supports projects in developing countries aimed at protecting the environment, where UNDP is responsible for technical assistance and training. UNDP administers the Small Grants Programme of the GEF, which finances non-governmental and community initiatives. Also in 1991 UNDP established a panel of experts, the Environmental and Natural Resources Group, which was to monitor the environmental implications of the Programme's work; and the Sustainable Development Network (SDN) designed to facilitate the exchange of information on environmental protection between developing countries. At the UN Conference on Environment and Development, held in Rio de Janeiro, Brazil, in June 1992, UNDP initiated 'Capacity 21', a programme to support developing countries in preparing and implementing sustainable development policies.

During 1992, UNDP made available the services of 21,989 national and international experts world-wide, and awarded 10,366 fellowships for nationals of developing countries to study abroad. In that year UNDP estimated expenditure on projects in Africa amounted to US $339m., or about 33% of total project expenditure.

New projects approved for countries in sub-Saharan Africa during the first half of 1994 included: in Chad, expert and technical assistance for national education and employment programmes (UNDP contribution US $7.6m.); in Eritrea, economic and financial structural reforms ($3.2m.); in Guinea, support for rural development and local land management programmes ($2.9m.); in Mozambique, technical support for the electoral process ($0.3m.); in Nigeria, agricultural development for small-scale farmers and rural enterprises ($11.8m.), support for education and training in the health sector ($4.6m.), improvements to the national statistical and information systems ($4.9m.), and encouragement for the participation of women in development ($7.2m.); in Somalia, support for national reconstruction and rehabilitation ($2.6m.); and in Tanzania, assistance to the national income generation programme ($14.4m.). In 1992–93 UNDP, along with other UN and non-governmental agencies, provided emergency assistance in Liberia and Somalia.

In early 1993 the UNDP Regional Bureau for Africa published a book entitled *Rethinking Technical Co-operation: Reforms for Capacity Building in Africa,* which contained proposals for increasing the effectiveness of training given to indigenous people by foreign experts.

UNDP supports the Africa Project Development Facility (APDF) which is administered by the International Finance Corporation (q.v.), and which aims to encourage private investment in the region. By 31 December 1992 the APDF had helped to raise US $166m. in investment for 130 projects since the Facility's establishment in 1986.

FINANCE

UNDP is financed by the voluntary contributions of members of the United Nations and the Programme's participating agencies. Voluntary contributions pledged for 1992 amounted to US $1,514m. (of which $294m. was cost-sharing by recipient governments). In 1992 total core project expenditure amounted to $1,027m. The number of new projects approved in that year was 972, bringing the total of ongoing projects to 5,736.

In UNDP's 1992–96 programme cycle 55% of the resources available was to be devoted to 45 of the world's poorest countries, most of which are in Africa.

PUBLICATIONS

Annual Report.

Update (every 2 weeks).

Human Development Report (annually).

World Development (every 2 months).

Co-operation South (2 a year).

Associated Funds and Programmes

UNDP is the central funding, planning and co-ordinating body for technical co-operation within the UN. Associated funds and programmes, financed separately by means of voluntary contributions, provide specific services through the UNDP network. Total expenditure on these funds and programmes amounted to an estimated US $137.6m. in 1992 (53% of which was accounted for by Africa).

UNITED NATIONS CAPITAL DEVELOPMENT FUND—UNCDF

The Fund was established in 1966 and became fully operational in 1974. It assists developing countries by supplementing existing sources of capital assistance by means of grants and loans on concessionary terms. Rapid assistance is available to governments for small-scale projects directly and immediately benefiting the low-income groups who have not benefited from earlier development efforts. Assistance may be given to any of the member states of the UN system, and is not necessarily limited to specific projects. The Fund is mainly used for the benefit of the least-developed countries. During 1991 UNCDF was engaged in 251 projects which were estimated to cost US $438m. In 1992 UNCDF approved new projects costing a total of $50m.

Examples of projects financed by UNCDF include: creation of 'revolving funds' for village co-operatives to obtain supplies of seeds and fertilizers; credit for low-cost housing or small businesses; provision of facilities for irrigation, drinking-water and food storage; construction of roads, schools and health centres; and reafforestation of land.

Executive-Secretary: JULES FRIPPIAT (Belgium).

UNITED NATIONS DEVELOPMENT FUND FOR WOMEN—UNIFEM

UNIFEM became an associated fund of UNDP in 1985. Its purpose is to provide direct financial and technical support to enable low-income women in developing countries to increase earnings, gain access to labour-saving technologies and otherwise improve the quality of their lives. It also funds activities that include women in decision-making related to mainstream development projects. UNIFEM collaborates with other UN organizations, governments and non-government organizations to promote women's issues in the planning and implementation of projects. Pledges for 1992 totalled US $10.5m.

Director: (acting) MARJORIE THORPE (Trinidad and Tobago).

UNITED NATIONS FUND FOR SCIENCE AND TECHNOLOGY FOR DEVELOPMENT—UNFSTD

UNFSTD was established in 1982 to help developing countries acquire the capacity to formulate science and technology policies linked to their development goals. Advisory services and the exchange of information are its principal activities. Included among these is a 'Transfer of Knowledge through Expatriate Nationals' programme, whereby expatriates volunteer to return to their countries of origin for short-term consultancy assignments. By the end of 1992 more than 3,600 professionals had undertaken such assignments in 33 developing countries. A Technology Rights Bank enables small businesses in developing countries to acquire technical expertise from their counterparts in Europe and North America. Income is obtained from contributions, cost-sharing and sub-trust funds.

Director: SHIGEAKI TOMITA (Japan).

UNITED NATIONS REVOLVING FUND FOR NATURAL RESOURCES EXPLORATION—UNRFNRE

UNRFNRE was established in 1974 to provide risk capital to finance exploration for natural resources (particularly minerals) in developing countries, and, when discoveries are made, to help to attract investment. The revolving character of the Fund, which distinguishes it from most other UN technical co-operation programmes, lies in the undertaking of contributing governments to make replenishment contributions to the Fund when the projects it finances lead to commercial production. Contributions pledged to the Fund amounted to US $3.3m. for 1992.

Director: SHIGEAKI TOMITA (Japan).

UNITED NATIONS SUDANO-SAHELIAN OFFICE—UNSO

Established in 1973, UNSO assists 22 countries across the Sudano-Sahelian belt of Africa in combating drought and desertification. By 1992 UNSO had been involved in more than 130 projects concerned with the sustainable management of natural resources. In that year 14 new projects were approved. Ongoing activities included the provision of tree seedlings, and land rehabilitation. Special emphasis is given to strengthening the environmental planning and management capacities of national institutions.

UN Sahelian Regional Office: 14 ave Dimdolobsom, BP 366, Ouagadougou, Burkina Faso; tel. 306355; telex 5262; fax 310581.

Director: PETER BRANNER.

UNITED NATIONS VOLUNTEERS—UNV

The United Nations Volunteers is an important source of middle-level skills for the UN development system, supplied at modest cost, particularly in the least-developed countries. Volunteers expand the scope of UNDP project activities by supplementing the work of international and host-country experts and by extending the influence of projects to local community levels. One of the most important parts of UNV's work is the support of technical co-operation within and among the developing countries by encouraging volunteers from the countries themselves and by forming regional exchange teams made up of such volunteers. UNV is also engaged in a variety of activities to increase youth participation in development and to promote the involvement of domestic development services.

In 1992 3,300 volunteers from both developed and developing nations served in 119 countries.

Executive Co-ordinator: BRENDA MCSWEENEY.

United Nations High Commissioner for Refugees—UNHCR

Address: Case postale 2500, 1211 Geneva 2 dépôt, Switzerland.

Telephone: (22) 7398111; **telex:** 415740; **fax:** (22) 7319546.

The Office of the High Commissioner was established in 1951 to provide international protection for refugees and to seek durable solutions to their problems.

Organization

(June 1994)

HIGH COMMISSIONER

The High Commissioner is elected by the United Nations General Assembly on the nomination of the Secretary-General, and is responsible to the General Assembly and to the UN Economic and Social Council (ECOSOC).

High Commissioner: SADAKO OGATA (Japan).

Deputy High Commissioner: GERALD WALZER.

EXECUTIVE COMMITTEE

The Executive Committee of the High Commissioner's Programme, established by ECOSOC, gives the High Commissioner policy directives in respect of material assistance programmes and advice in the field of international protection. It meets once a year in Geneva. It includes representatives of 46 states, both members and non-members of the UN.

ADMINISTRATION

Headquarters includes the High Commissioner's Office, the Division of International Protection, and five Regional Bureaux (Africa; Asia and Oceania; Europe; the Americas; South-West Asia, the Middle East and North Africa). In 1993 the High Commissioner had some 193 field offices.

Activities

The competence of the High Commissioner extends to any person who, owing to well-founded fear of being persecuted for reasons of race, religion, nationality or political opinion, is outside the country of his or her nationality and is unable or, owing to such fear or for reasons other than personal convenience, remains unwilling to accept the protection of that country; or who, not having a nationality and being outside the country of former habitual residence, is unable or, owing to such fear or for reasons other than personal convenience, is unwilling to return to it. Refugees meeting these criteria are entitled to the protection of the Office of the High Commissioner irrespective of their geographical location. Refugees who are assisted by other United Nations agencies, or who have the same rights or obligations as nationals of their country of residence, are outside the mandate of UNHCR.

INTERNATIONAL PROTECTION

As laid down in the Statute of the Office, one of the two primary functions of UNHCR is to extend international protection to refugees. In the exercise of this function UNHCR seeks to ensure that refugees and asylum-seekers are protected against *refoulement* (forcible return), that they receive asylum, and that they are treated according to internationally recognized standards of treatment. UNHCR pursues these objectives by a variety of means which include promoting the conclusion and ratification by states of international conventions for the protection of refugees, particularly the 1951 UN Convention relating to the Status of Refugees, extended by a Protocol adopted in 1967 (a total of 121 states had acceded to either or both of these instruments by mid-1993). The Convention defines the rights and duties of refugees and contains provisions dealing with a variety of matters which affect their day-to-day lives. UNHCR has also continued to encourage further accessions to the 1969 OAU Convention Governing the Specific Aspects of Refugee Problems in Africa. UNHCR has given close attention to the problem of military attacks against refugee camps and settlements in southern Africa and elsewhere, in the hope of formulating a set of internationally recognized principles to ensure the safety of refugees.

MATERIAL ASSISTANCE TO REFUGEES

Emergency relief is provided to refugees when food supplies, medical aid or other forms of assistance are required on a large scale at short notice. Other members of the UN system, as well as inter-governmental and non-governmental organizations, co-operate closely with UNHCR in this field.

Even in the more stable refugee circumstances, UNHCR is often called upon to provide material assistance beyond the initial emergency phase, while permanent solutions are being sought. This assistance can take various forms, including the provision of food, shelter, medical care and essential supplies. Also often covered are basic services, including education and counselling.

As far as possible, assistance is geared towards the identification and implementation of durable solutions to refugee problems—this being the second statutory responsibility of UNHCR. Such solutions generally take one of three forms: voluntary repatriation, local integration or resettlement in another country. Where voluntary repatriation is feasible, the Office assists refugees to overcome obstacles preventing their return to their country of origin. This may be done through negotiations with governments involved, or by providing funds for the physical movement of refugees or for the rehabilitation of returnees once back in their own country.

When voluntary repatriation is not feasible, efforts are made to assist refugees to integrate locally and to become self-supporting in their countries of asylum. The majority of refugees in Africa, and some of those in Asia, are assisted through local settlement in agriculture. Loans and vocational training are also offered to assist refugees to find alternative employment or educational opportunities. Special refugee counselling services identify employment opportunities or facilitate the establishment of small-scale enterprises. The provision of housing is an important form of assistance enabling refugees to re-establish outside the camps. In Africa, the consolidation of refugee settlements frequently requires close co-operation between UNHCR and other members of the UN system which provide development assistance to the areas affected. In cases where resettlement through emigration is the only viable solution, UNHCR negotiates with governments in an endeavour to obtain suitable resettlement opportunities, to encourage liberalization of admission criteria and to draw up special immigration schemes.

In 1993 there were more than 6m. refugees in Africa (including North Africa), and an estimated 15m. internally displaced people. During the early 1990s UNHCR provided assistance to refugee populations in many parts of the continent, where civil conflict, violations of human rights, drought, famine or environmental degradation had forced people to flee their countries.

The Horn of Africa, afflicted in recent years by famine, separatist violence and ethnic conflict, has experienced large-scale population movements. In early 1991 some 150,000 Somalis fled to Ethiopia, while later in the year more than 100,000 fled renewed violence in the south of the country into Kenya. By the end of 1992 there were estimated to be 400,000 Somalis in Kenya. UNHCR initiated a repatriation programme for Somali refugees, which included assistance with reconstruction projects and a cross-border operation conducted from Kenya to provide food to returnees and displaced persons. In late 1993 UNHCR appealed for funds to improve security at camps in Kenya where many female Somali refugees had been raped, as well as to provide medical and counselling services for the victims.

By mid-1991 some 175,000 Ethiopians had arrived in Sudan following the overthrow of the Ethiopian Government in May. UNHCR provided care and maintenance to the refugees and assisted over 200,000 Sudanese who had been forced to return from Ethiopia, by means of 'Operation Life-line Sudan'. An estimated 600,000 Eritreans took refuge in Sudan as a result of separatist conflicts: following Eritrea's accession to independence in May 1993 UNHCR initiated a repatriation programme in co-operation with the new Government. By the end of 1993 Sudan still hosted a total of 745,000 refugees, although there were 350,000 Sudanese refugees in Zaire, Ethiopia, Kenya and Uganda owing to continuing civil unrest and the threat of famine.

In West Africa the refugee population increased by one-third during 1992 and the first half of 1993, with the addition of new refugees fleeing Togo, Liberia and Senegal. Between February and August 1993 more than 300,000 people fled abuses of human rights in Togo, crossing the borders into Benin and Ghana. With the majority of Togolese being accommodated by individuals in the host countries, UNHCR aimed to strengthen these countries' infrastructures. In May 1993 UNHCR issued an appeal for US $10m. for the Togolese refugees, but by mid-July only US $4.3m. had been pledged. In accordance with a peace agreement, signed in July 1993, UNHCR is responsible for the repatriation of 700,000 Liberian refugees who had fled to Guinea, Côte d'Ivoire and Sierra Leone during the civil conflict. The voluntary repatriation programme was to include substantial assistance to rebuild Liberia's infrastructure; UNHCR also began to provide emergency relief to displaced persons within the country.

In February 1992 the Dar-es-Salaam Declaration was signed, under the terms of which UNHCR and the Organization of African Unity were to devise a Plan of Action aimed at finding a durable solution to the long-term problem of the estimated 590,000 Rwandan refugees in Burundi, Tanzania, Uganda and Zaire. In late 1993 some 600,000 Burundis crossed the border to Rwanda and Tanzania, following a military coup in October, although many had returned by early 1994. By May 1994 an estimated 860,000 people from Burundi and Rwanda had fled to neighbouring countries, following a resurgence of ethnic violence in both countries, including 250,000 Rwandans who entered Tanzania in a 24-hour period in late April in the most rapid mass exodus ever witnessed by UNHCR. In May, UNHCR began an immediate operation to airlift emergency supplies to the refugees and issued an appeal for US $57m. to provide aid over an initial three-month period.

In January 1993 there were estimated to be 1.7m. Mozambican refugees in the neighbouring countries of Malawi (which, alone hosted some 1m. of the refugees), Tanzania, Zambia, Zimbabwe, Botswana and South Africa. UNHCR was the principal agency responsible for the channelling of food aid to these people. In March 1993 UNHCR announced that it was about to undertake an operation to repatriate the Mozambican refugees, following the signing of a peace agreement in October 1992. This was to take three years and was to be UNHCR's largest-ever undertaking in Africa with an estimated cost of US $203m., much of which was to be used to rehabilitate the country's infrastructure. By mid-1994 UNHCR had assisted more than 800,000 refugees to return to Mozambique.

In September 1991 South Africa signed an agreement with UNHCR on the voluntary repatriation of an estimated 40,000 refugees and political exiles around the world. Under the agreement, the South African Government granted an amnesty to all returnees charged with political offences. By late April 1992 more than 3,100 of the 7,170 people who had applied to return to South Africa under the programme had been repatriated, with UNHCR having downwardly revised its estimate of the number of South African refugees and exiles to about 14,000. In March 1994 UNHCR inaugurated a US $1.2m. project to train exiles returning to South Africa in specialized and vocational skills. In September 1993 UNHCR and South Africa signed an agreement allowing UNHCR to protect and assist all refugees in that country. UNHCR was to gain access for the first time to the estimated 300,000 Mozambican refugees living in South Africa.

REFUGEES OF CONCERN TO UNHCR IN AFRICA SOUTH OF THE SAHARA* (31 December 1993, to the nearest 100)

Country of asylum	Registered refugees
Angola	10,900
Benin	156,200
Burundi	271,900
Cameroon	44,000
Central African Republic	44,100
Congo	13,600
Côte d'Ivoire	251,700
Djibouti	34,100
Ethiopia	247,600
Ghana	150,100
Guinea	577,200
Guinea-Bissau	15,700
Kenya	301,600
Liberia	150,200
Malawi	713,600
Mali	15,200
Mauritania	46,700
Rwanda	300,000
Senegal	73,000
Sierra Leone	15,800
South Africa	250,000
Sudan	745,200
Swaziland	45,500
Tanzania	564,500
Uganda	286,500
Zaire	486,800
Zambia	141,100
Zimbabwe	237,100

* Figures are provided mostly by governments, based on their own records and methods of estimation; in certain instances they include persons in 'refuge-like' situations (e.g. those displaced within their own country). Countries with fewer than 10,000 refugees are not listed.

FINANCE

UNHCR administrative expenditure is financed under the United Nations regular budget, under which it was allocated US $20.5m. for 1993. General Programmes of material assistance are financed from voluntary contributions made by governments, and also from non-governmental sources. In addition, UNHCR undertakes a number of Special Programmes, as requested by the UN General Assembly, the Secretary-General of the UN or a member state, to assist returnees and, in some cases, displaced persons. Total contributions in 1993 were estimated to amount to more than $1,000m. In 1993 UNHCR expenditure for assistance in Africa south of the Sahara amounted to $332.3m. (about 25% of total expenditure world-wide).

UNHCR Expenditure (US $ million)

Source	1992	1993	1994* projections
UN Regular Budget	21.2	20.5	21.0
Voluntary funds:			
General Programmes	382.1	392.4	418.5
Special Programmes	689.3	914.6	399.2
Total	1,092.6	1,327.7	838.7

* Projected figures.

PUBLICATIONS

Refugees (quarterly, in English, French, German, Italian, Japanese and Spanish).

UNHCR Handbook for Emergencies.

Refugee Abstracts.

Food and Agriculture Organization—FAO

Address: Viale delle Terme di Caracalla, 00100 Rome, Italy.

Telephone: (6) 52251; **telex:** 625852; **fax:** (6) 5225-5155.

FAO, the first specialized agency of the UN to be founded after World War II, was established in Québec, Canada, in October 1945. The Organization combats malnutrition and hunger, and serves as a co-ordinating agency for development programmes in the whole range of food and agriculture, including forestry and fisheries. It helps developing countries to promote educational and training facilities and the creation of appropriate institutions.

Organization

(June 1994)

CONFERENCE

The governing body is the FAO Conference of member nations. It meets every two years, formulates policy, determines the Organization's programme and budget on a biennial basis, and elects new members. It also elects the Director-General of the Secretariat and the Independent Chairman of the Council. Every second year, FAO also holds conferences in each of its five regions (the Near East, Asia and the Pacific, Africa, Latin America and the Caribbean, and Europe).

COUNCIL

The FAO Council is composed of representatives of 49 member nations, elected by the Conference for staggered three-year terms. It is the interim governing body of FAO between sessions of the Conference. The most important standing Committees of the Council are: the Finance and Programme Committees, the Committee on Commodity Problems, the Committee on Fisheries, the Committee on Agriculture and the Committee on Forestry.

SECRETARIAT

The total number of staff at FAO headquarters in December 1992 was 3,147, while staff in field, regional and country offices numbered 2,717; there were also 66 associate experts at headquarters and 206 in field, regional and country offices. Work is supervised by the following Departments: Administration and Finance; General Affairs and Information; Economic and Social Policy; Agriculture; Forestry; Fisheries; and Development.

Director-General: JACQUES DIOUF (Senegal).

REGIONAL OFFICE

Regional Office for Africa: UN Agency Bldg, North Maxwell Rd, POB 1628, Accra, Ghana; tel. 666851; telex 2139; fax 668427; Regional Rep. R. T. N'DAW.

Activities

FAO aims to raise levels of nutrition and standards of living, by improving the production and distribution of food and other commodities derived from farms, fisheries and forests. Under FAO's medium-term plan for 1992–97 its work covers five basic areas: advising governments on policy and planning; training and technical assistance; promotion of sustainable development; enhancing the economic status of women; and promotion of economic and technical co-operation among developing countries.

AGRICULTURE

In 1986 FAO adopted a Plan of Action for African Agriculture. The plan suggested changes in agricultural policies to give greater priority to food production by concentrating on measures to conserve the environment; by providing small-scale producers with the inputs and access to credit needed for increased production; and by improving incentives (for example with more favourable pricing policies), together with the development of the institutions and infrastructure required to support increased production.

FAO's Field Programme provides training and technical assistance to enable small farmers to increase production, by a number of methods, including improved seeds and fertilizer use, soil conservation and reforestation, better water resource management techniques, upgrading storage facilities, and improvements in processing and marketing. FAO promotes the production of under-exploited traditional food crops, such as cassava, yams, breadfruit, sweet potato and plantains and was involved in the preparation of programmes to promote these crops in nine African countries which began in 1987. During the 1980s FAO developed 'wheatless bread', which can be made using cassava, sorghum or millet flour, and is intended to reduce dependence on imports of wheat. Governments are advised on the conservation of genetic resources, on improving the supply of seeds and on crop protection: animal and plant gene banks are maintained. The Seed Exchange and Information Centre, based in Rome, helps to locate and distribute seed samples for trial and evaluation in developing countries. In 1992 20,000 samples were dispatched to meet about 300 requests from more than 100 developing countries. The Centre also supplies emergency shipments of seed: in 1992 a large quantity of cereal and vegetable seed was sent to farmers in Somalia and Ethiopia. During 1992–93 FAO's activities in Africa included programmes to increase cashew nut production in Tanzania, milk production in Uganda, onion production in Côte d'Ivoire, seed production in the Sahelian region, and to develop market garden produce in the West African region.

Plant protection, weed control, and animal health programmes form an important part of FAO's work as farming methods become more intensive, and pests more resistant to control methods. In 1985 the FAO Conference approved an International Code of Conduct on the Distribution and Use of Pesticides and in 1989 the Conference adopted an additional clause concerning 'Prior Informed Consent', whereby international shipments of newly banned or restricted pesticides should not proceed without the agreement of importing countries. Under the clause FAO aims to inform governments about the hazards of toxic chemicals and to encourage them to take proper measures to curb trade in highly toxic agrochemicals, while keeping the pesticides industry informed of control actions. In accordance with its efforts to reduce over-reliance on pesticides and to encourage the use of biological control methods and natural predators to avert pests, FAO is introducing its Integrated Pest Management (IPM), which began in Asia in 1988, to Africa. In 1992 FAO helped to train agricultural experts and rural workers in Sudan to apply IPM principles to cotton and rotational food crops. FAO's Joint Division with the International Atomic Energy Agency (IAEA), tests controlled-release formulas of pesticides and herbicides that can limit the amount of agrochemicals needed to protect crops. The Joint FAO-IAEA Division is engaged in exploring biotechnologies and in developing non-toxic fertilizers (especially those that are locally available) and improved strains of food crops (especially from indigenous varieties). In animal production and health, the Joint Division has developed progesterone-measuring and disease-diagnostic kits, thousands of which are delivered to developing countries every year. In 1991 FAO and the Kenyan Government planned a five-year programme to control a plague of cypress aphids in eastern and southern Africa. In 1986 FAO set up the Emergency Centre for Locust Operations (ECLO) to counter the threat to much of Africa posed by enormous numbers of five separate species of grasshoppers and locusts. In 1988 FAO gave support to an emergency programme to destroy the insects in their main breeding areas in Chad, Mali and Niger. ECLO was reactivated in September 1992 following outbreaks of the 'migratory locust' in Madagascar and in countries on either side of the Red Sea, and co-ordinated a prompt international response to combat the pest.

FAO's work on soil conservation includes erosion control and the reclamation of degraded land. In 1993 FAO was involved in a successful project to control soil erosion in Burundi, by means of building mounds and planting trees, shrubs and grasses. FAO also assists in developing water resources and irrigation.

FISHERIES

FAO's Fisheries Department consists of a multi-disciplinary body of experts who are involved in every aspect of fisheries development from coastal surveys, improved production, processing and storage, to the compilation of statistics, development of computer databases, improvement of fishing gear, institution building and training. In 1991 FAO was investigating the use of selected fishing gear to reduce the incidental catch of non-target fish species, and is currently drafting an International Code of Conduct for responsible fishing. Other fisheries initiatives in the early 1990s included support for aquaculture, protection and restocking of endangered species, and programmes aimed at supporting women in the fisheries communities of developing countries. In 1992 FAO completed trials into the viability of fish culture development in rice paddy fields in Madagascar. The trials showed that many African countries could follow the Asian example of combining fish and rice production. In late 1993 FAO's Aquaculture for Local Community Development Program (ALCOM), which assists the 10 member countries of the Southern African Development Community (SADC–q.v.), was funding a project to restock some 200 dams in Zimbabwe. ALCOM was also co-operating with the Zimbabwe Government to develop community management of fisheries.

FORESTRY

In collaboration with UNDP, the World Bank and the World Resources Unit, FAO has devised the Tropical Forestry Action Programme (TFAP). The Programme aims to improve the lives of rural people, to increase food production, to intensify forestry activities and to establish interdisciplinary national and regional programmes that both safeguard the forest and make rational use of its resources. Another primary concern of the Forestry Department is the critical fuel wood situation in many developing countries. In 1990 FAO estimated that by 2000 more than one-half of the population of the developing world will face fuel wood shortages and will be caught in a cycle of deforestation, fuel wood scarcity, poverty and malnutrition. In 1992 FAO helped to establish and develop National Tree Seed Centres in Sahal countries to improve the genetic resources of forests.

PROCESSING AND MARKETING

An estimated 20% of all food harvested is lost before it can be consumed. FAO helps reduce immediate post-harvest losses, with the introduction of improved processing methods and storage systems. It also advises on the distribution and marketing of agricultural produce and on the selection and preparation of foods for optimum nutrition. A new Centre for Agricultural Marketing Training in Eastern and Southern Africa has been established with FAO assistance in Harare, Zimbabwe, to serve Kenya, Malawi, Tanzania and Zimbabwe. By early 1993 some 200 government and university staff had participated in 14 workshops and produced training materials on marketing, for use in universities and other institutions.

ENVIRONMENT

In April 1991 a Conference on Agriculture and the Environment was held in the Netherlands, organized jointly by FAO and the Netherlands Government. The alleviation of poverty was identified as being a major prerequisite for sustainable agricultural production. At the UN Conference on Environment and Development, held in Rio de Janeiro in June 1992, FAO played a leading role in drafting several sections, notably the chapters on combating deforestation, desertification and drought, on sustainable mountain development, sustainable agriculture and rural development and oceans and marine resources, all of which have long been integral parts of FAO programmes.

NUTRITION

In December 1992 an International Conference on Nutrition was held in Rome, administered jointly by FAO and WHO. The Conference approved a World Declaration on nutrition and a Plan of Action, with the aim of eliminating hunger and reducing levels of malnutrition by incorporating nutritional objectives into national development policies and governmental programmes.

FOOD SECURITY

FAO's food security policy aims to encourage the production of adequate food supplies, to maximize stability in the flow of supplies, and to ensure access on the part of those who need them. The Global Information and Early Warning System (GIEWS) monitors the world food situation and identifies countries threatened by shortages to guide potential donors. In early 1992 the GIEWS warned of impending famine in southern Africa, owing to prolonged drought and crop devastation, which enabled the UN and SADC to issue an appeal for international assistance. An environmental monitoring system, ARTEMIS (Africa Real-Time Environmental Monitoring Information System), installed in 1988, processes data from orbiting and stationary satellites to provide continuous monitoring of rainfall and vegetation conditions across Africa, the Near East and south-west Asia. FAO established the Regional Early Warning System for Food Security in Southern Africa in 1991, which comprises early warning units in each of the member states of SADC, co-ordinated by an office in Harare. However, the System, which requires local monitoring of conditions, was undermined by problems of corruption, lack of adequate funds to collect and process data and a failure to distribute food aid. By mid-1993 Mali was the only country that had benefited from increased food aid on the basis of a recommendation of an early warning unit. In March and April 1993 FAO/WFP undertook food supply assessment missions in many parts of southern Africa.

FAO INVESTMENT CENTRE

The Investment Centre was established in 1964 to help countries prepare viable investment projects that would attract external financing. By the end of 1992 it had assisted 916 investment projects, which were expected to generate US $46,900m. of agricultural investment in more than 100 countries. Each year the Centre undertakes about 200 missions under its own responsibility, and participates in about 50 missions led by co-operating financial institutions.

EMERGENCY RELIEF

The Office for Special Relief Operations (OSRO) was established in 1973, in response to the disastrous drought in the Sahel in that year. In 1975 the office was expanded to handle such emergencies globally. As well as providing emergency aid, OSRO aims to rehabilitate agricultural production following disasters. During 1988–89 OSRO conducted 43 relief operations following natural disasters in 26 African countries, at a cost of US $6.7m. Jointly with the United Nations, FAO is responsible for the World Food Programme (q.v.) which provides emergency food supplies, and food aid in support of development projects.

INFORMATION AND RESEARCH

FAO issues regular statistical reports, commodity studies, and technical manuals in local languages (see list of publications below).

General and specialized computer data bases co-ordinated by FAO contain information on every area of food and agriculture; the Current Agricultural Research Information System (CARIS), for example, enables over 70 countries to exchange information on current research; other systems provide information on agricultural sciences and technology (AGRIS), plant genetics (PGRIS), commodities (ICS), fisheries (ASFIS, GLOBEFISH and FISHDAB) and forest resources (FORIS). FAO's Research and Technology Development Division helps to co-ordinate members' research. Missions to review and plan agricultural research are sent to member countries. In 1993 FAO awarded priority to its computerized network of Geographic Information Systems (GIS) which assess land and water resources with information on regional climate and population.

FAO REGIONAL COMMISSIONS

African Commission on Agricultural Statistics: c/o FAO Regional Office for Africa, POB 1628, Accra, Ghana; f. 1961 to advise member countries on the development and standardization of food and agricultural statistics. Mems: 37 states.

African Forestry and Wildlife Commission: Via delle Terme di Caracalla, 00100 Rome, Italy; f. 1959 to advise on the formulation of forest policy and to review and co-ordinate its implementation on a regional level; to exchange information and advise on technical problems. Mems: 42 states.

Commission on African Animal Trypanosomiasis: Via delle Terme di Caracalla, 00100 Rome, Italy; f. 1979 to develop and implement programmes to combat this disease. Mems: 39 states.

Joint FAO/WHO/OAU Regional Food and Nutrition Commission for Africa: c/o FAO Regional Office for Africa, POB 1628, Accra, Ghana; f. 1962 to provide liaison in matters pertaining to food and nutrition, and to review food and nutrition problems in Africa. Mems: 43 states.

FINANCE

FAO's Regular Programme, which is financed by contributions from member governments, covers the cost of the FAO's Secretariat, its Technical Co-operation Programme and part of the cost of several special action programmes. The working budget proposed for the two years 1994–95 amounted to US $752.7m. Much of FAO's Field Programme of technical assistance is funded from extra-budgetary sources. The single largest contributor is the United Nations Development Programme (UNDP), which in 1992 accounted for $136.2m., or 40% of Field Programme expenditure. Equally important are the trust funds that come mainly from donor countries and international financing institutions. In 1991 they totalled $164.3m., or 49% of Field Programme expenditure. FAO's contribution under its Technical Co-operation programme (TCP, FAO's regular budgetary funds for the Field Programme) was $36.1m.

WORLD FOOD PROGRAMME—WFP

Address: Via Cristoforo Colombo 426, 00145 Rome, Italy.

Telephone: (6) 522821; **telex:** 626675; **fax:** (6) 5127400.

WFP is a joint UN-FAO effort to stimulate economic and social development through food aid and to provide emergency relief. It became operational in 1963.

WFP provides food aid, primarily to low-income, food-deficit countries to support economic and social development projects. Food is supplied, for example, as an incentive in labour-intensive projects which provide employment and strengthen self-help capacity. WFP supports activities to boost agricultural production, to rehabilitate and improve local infrastructure, particularly transport systems, and to encourage education, training and health programmes. One of the criteria for WFP aid to projects is that the recipient country can continue them after the aid has ceased. Priority is given to vulnerable groups such as pregnant women and children. Some WFP projects are intended to alleviate the effects of structural adjustment programmes (particularly programmes which involve reductions in public expenditure and in subsidies for basic foods). In 1992 the largest proportion of WFP development assistance, amounting to US $143.7m. in food aid, was allocated to Africa south of the Sahara.

In the early 1990s there was a substantial shift in the balance between emergency and development assistance provided by WFP, owing to the growing needs of victims of drought and other natural disasters, refugees and displaced persons. WFP provides food supplies mainly from the International Emergency Food Reserve, which it manages. In 1993 WFP issued emergency assistance to Liberian refugees in Côte d'Ivoire, Guinea and Sierra Leone, Mauritanian refugees in Senegal, and other victims of civil conflict in Angola, Sudan, Somalia, Ethiopia and Mozambique. In November 1993 WFP conducted a large-scale regional emergency relief operation for people fleeing ethnic conflict in Burundi, and in May 1994 organized emergency provisions for Rwandan refugees in Tanzania and Zaire. In November 1993 WFP approved a US $80m. plan, which was to be operational from January 1994 to mid-1995, to assist refugees from Mozambique returning to their country. In early 1992 WFP initiated its largest-ever preventive operation in order to provide food aid to some 18m. people threatened with famine in drought-stricken southern Africa. By mid-1993 food commodities had been successfully distributed to the affected countries, due to effective regional co-operation and use of the local infrastructure, although WFP continued to provide emergency food aid to Lesotho. Persistant drought in eastern Africa in 1993 necessitated a WFP emergency programme to assist some 500,000 people in Eritrea, and was expected to cause serious food shortages in 1994.

WFP Executive Director: CATHERINE A. BERTINI (USA).

FAO PUBLICATIONS

FAO Annual Review.

Quarterly Bulletin of Statistics.

Food Outlook (monthly).

Production Yearbook (in English, French and Spanish).

Yearbook of Fishery Statistics (in English, French and Spanish).

Yearbook of Forest Products (in English, French and Spanish).

Trade Yearbook.

Fertilizer Yearbook.

Commodity Review and Outlook (annually).

Animal Health Yearbook.

The State of Food and Agriculture (annually).

Technical Co-operation Among Developing Countries Newsletter (in English only).

Plant Protection Bulletin.

Ceres (every 2 months).

Unasylva (quarterly).

Environment and Energy Bulletin.

Commodity reviews; studies; manuals.

International Bank for Reconstruction and Development—IBRD—and International Development Association—IDA (World Bank)

Address: 1818 H St, NW, Washington, DC 20433, USA.

Telephone: (202) 477-1234; **telex:** 248423; **fax:** (202) 477-6391.

The IBRD was established on 27 December 1945. Initially it was concerned with post-war reconstruction in Europe; since then its aim has been to assist the economic development of member nations by making loans where private capital is not available on reasonable terms to finance productive investments. Loans are made either direct to governments, or to private enterprises with the guarantee of their governments. The IBRD has three affiliates, the International Development Association (IDA) the International Finance Corporation (IFC, q.v.) and the Multilateral Investment Guarantee Agency (MIGA, q.v.). The 'World Bank', as it is commonly known, comprises the IBRD and IDA. Only members of the International Monetary Fund (IMF, q.v.) may be considered for membership in the Bank. Subscriptions to the capital stock of the Bank are based on each member's quota in the IMF, which is designed to reflect the country's relative economic strength. Voting rights are related to shareholdings.

Organization

(June 1994)

Officers and staff of the IBRD serve concurrently as officers and staff in the International Development Association (IDA). The World Bank has offices in New York, Paris, London and Tokyo; regional missions in Nairobi (for eastern Africa), Abidjan (for western Africa), Bangkok and Latvia; and resident missions in 55 countries.

BOARD OF GOVERNORS

The Board of Governors consists of one Governor appointed by each member nation. Typically, a Governor is the country's finance minister, central bank governor, or a minister or an official of comparable rank. The Board normally meets once a year.

EXECUTIVE DIRECTORS

The general operations of the World Bank are conducted by a Board of 24 Executive Directors. Five Directors are appointed by the five members having the largest number of shares of capital stock, and the rest are elected by the Governors representing the other members. The President of the Bank is Chairman of the Board.

OFFICERS

President and Chairman of Executive Directors: LEWIS T. PRESTON (USA).

Vice-President, Africa Regional Office: EDWARD V. K. JAYCOX.

REGIONAL OFFICES

Regional Mission in Eastern Africa: POB 30577, View Park Towers, Monrovia St, Nairobi, Kenya; Chief F. STEPHEN O'BRIEN.

Regional Mission in Western Africa: BP 1850, cnr Booker Washington and Jacques AKA Sts, Abidjan 01, Côte d'Ivoire; tel. 44-32-44; telex 28132; fax 44-16-87; Chief ROBERT A. CALDERISI.

Activities

FINANCIAL OPERATIONS

The World Bank has traditionally financed capital infrastructure projects (e.g. in communications and energy). In the early 1990s the World Bank's primary objectives were economic adjustment and the achievement of sustainable economic growth, the reduction of poverty, and the protection of the environment. In the context of stimulating economic growth the Bank promotes both private-sector development and human resource development. The Bank's efforts to reduce poverty comprise two main elements: the compiling of country-specific assessments and the formulation of country-specific strategies to ensure that the Bank's own projects support and complement the programmes of the country concerned.

IBRD loans are usually for a period of 20 years or less. Loans are made to governments, or must be guaranteed by the government concerned. IDA assistance is aimed at the poorer developing countries (i.e. those with a per capita GNP of less than US $765 in 1991 dollars), and in 1992 all but five countries of sub-Saharan Africa were eligible to receive it. Under IDA lending conditions, credits can be extended to countries whose balance of payments could not sustain the burden of repayment required for IBRD loans. Terms are more favourable than those provided by the IBRD; credits are for a period of 35–40 years, with a 'grace' period of 10 years, and no interest charges.

The IBRD's capital is derived from members' subscriptions to capital shares, the calculation of which is based on their quotas in the International Monetary Fund (q.v.). In April 1988 the Board of Governors approved an increase of about 80% in the IBRD's authorized capital, to US $171,000m. At 30 June 1993 the total subscribed capital of the IBRD was US $165,589m., of which the paid-in portion was 6.5%; the remainder is subject to call if required. Most of the IBRD's lendable funds come from its borrowing in world capital markets, and also from its retained earnings and the flow of repayments on its loans. Bank loans carry a variable interest rate, rather than a rate fixed at the time of borrowing.

IDA's total resources, consisting of members' subscriptions and supplementary resources (additional subscriptions and contributions) amounted to US $80,886m. at 30 June 1993. Resources are replenished periodically by contributions from the more affluent member countries. In December 1992 34 donor countries agreed on a tenth replenishment of SDR 13,000m. (see IMF for explanation of SDR), roughly equivalent to $18,000m., for the period July 1993 to June 1996.

During the year ending 30 June 1993 75 operations were approved for Africa south of the Sahara amounting to US $2,817.3m. (11.9% of World Bank assistance in that year), of which $47.0m. was in IBRD loans and $2,770.3m. was in IDA credits.

In July 1985 a Special Facility for sub-Saharan Africa became effective for a three-year period, with funds of US $1,250m., to finance structural adjustment, sectoral reform programmes and rehabilitation. A 'Special Programme of Assistance' (SPA) for sub-Saharan Africa, available from 1988, increased concessional lending to heavily-indebted and impoverished African countries. At 31 December 1992, under the second phase of the SPA (1991-93), assistance amounting to $5,300m. had been allocated to eligible countries i.e. those implementing a policy adjustment programme with a debt-service ration of more than 30%. In 1991 the African Capacity Building Foundation was established by the World Bank, the African Development Bank and UNDP, with the aim of encouraging indigenous research and managerial capabilities, by supporting or creating institutions for training, research and analysis.

From 1987 the World Bank accorded greater importance to the protection of the environment and in 1989/90 systematic 'screening' of all new projects was introduced, in order to assess their environmental impact. The World Bank administers the Global Environment Facility (GEF), which was established in 1990, in conjunction with UNDP and UNEP. The aim of the GEF, which became operational in 1991 for an initial three-year period,was to assist developing countries in implementing policies that benefit the global environment. In March 1994 87 countries participating in the Facility agreed to restructure and replenish the GEF for a further three-year period from mid-1994. Funds amounting to US $2,000m. were to be made available by 26 donor countries which would enable the GEF to act as the financial mechanism for the conventions on climate changes and biological diversity that were signed at the UN Conference on Environment and Development in June 1992.

Over half the population in sub-Saharan Africa are estimated to be living in poverty. The Bank's poverty reduction strategy for Africa involves projects that aim to alleviate the adverse effects of structural adjustment programmes; that assist governments to assess and monitor poverty; and that increase food security.

TECHNICAL ASSISTANCE

The provision of technical assistance to member countries is a major component of Bank activities. The economic, sector and project analysis undertaken by the Bank in the normal course of its operations is the vehicle for considerable technical assistance. In addition, project loans and credits may include funds designated specifically for feasibility studies, resource surveys, management or planning advice, and training.

ECONOMIC RESEARCH AND STUDIES

The World Bank's research, carried out by its own research staff, is intended to provide a source of policy advice to members, and to encourage the development of indigenous research. The principal areas of research in 1992/93 included: alleviation of poverty; human resource development; the environment and natural resources; macroeconomic issues and management (including structural adjustment, debt, trade, finance, reform of the public sector and development of the private sector); and infrastructure and urban development research. The Bank chairs the Consultative Group for International Agricultural Research (CGIAR), which was formed in 1971 to raise financial support for research on improving crops and animal production in developing countries. The Group supports 18 research centres.

CO-OPERATION WITH OTHER ORGANIZATIONS

The World Bank co-operates closely with other UN bodies through consultations, meetings, and joint activities, particularly in response to the economic crisis in Africa south of the Sahara, where co-operation with UNDP and WHO is especially important. It collaborates with the IMF in implementing economic adjustment programmes in developing countries. The Bank holds regular consultations with the European Community and OECD on development issues, and the Bank-NGO Committee provides an annual forum for discussion with non-governmental organizations (NGO). The Bank chairs meetings of donor governments and organizations for the co-ordination of aid to particular countries. The Bank also conducts co-financing and aid co-ordination projects with official aid agencies, export credit institutions and commercial banks.

PUBLICATIONS

World Bank Catalog of Publications.
World Bank News (weekly).
World Bank Annual Report.
World Development Report (annually).
The World Bank and the Environment (annually).
Global Economic Prospects and Developing Countries (annually).
World Bank Economic Review (3 a year).
World Bank Research Observer (2 a year).
Research News (quarterly).
World Bank Atlas (annually).
Abstracts of Current Studies: The World Bank Research Program (annually).
Annual Review of Project Performance Results.
Staff Working Papers.
World Tables (annually).

WORLD BANK OPERATIONS IN AFRICA SOUTH OF THE SAHARA

IBRD Loans Approved, 1 July 1992–30 June 1993 (US $ million)

Country	Purpose	Amount
Gabon	Forestry and environment	22.5
Mauritius	Education development	20.0
Seychelles	Environment and transport	4.5

Note: Joint IBRD/IDA operations are counted only once, as IBRD operations. When more than one loan is made for a single project, they are counted only once.

IDA Credits Approved, 1 July 1992–30 June 1993 (US $ million)

Country	Purpose	Amount
Angola	Health	19.9
	Transport recovery	41.0
	Financial institutions' modernization	21.0
Benin	Rural savings and loan co-operative rehabilitation	3.8
Burkina Faso	Water supply engineering	4.2
	Private sector assistance	7.0
	Food security and nutrition	7.5
Burundi	Social action	10.4
	Agribusiness promotion	3.1
Cape Verde	Transport and infrastructure	12.5
Chad	Transport sector	37.0
	Education	19.3
Côte d'Ivoire	Human resources management	6.7
	Economic management	17.0
Equatorial Guinea	Petroleum technical assistance	2.4
Ethiopia	Structural adjustment	250.0
	Recovery and rehabilitation (Eritrea)	25.0
	Road rehabilitation	96.0
The Gambia	Agricultural services	12.3
Ghana	Primary school development	65.1
	Private enterprise and export development	41.0
	Urban transport	76.2
	National power supply	80.0
	Private investment and sustained development promotion	6.5*
	National livestock services	22.5
	Tertiary education	45.0
	Environmental resource management	18.1
Guinea	Structural adjustment	0.1*
	Post and telecommunications technical assistance	14.6
	Power	50.0
	Agricultural export promotion	20.8
Guinea-Bissau	Social sector	8.8
Kenya	Emergency drought recovery	20.0
	Education sector adjustment	52.1*
	Agricultural sector management	19.4
	Privatization technical assistance	23.3
Madagascar	Financial institutions development	6.3
	Food security and nutrition	21.3
	Rural finance technical assistance	3.7
	Public sector adjustment	1.4*
Malawi	Rural financial services	25.0
	Agricultural services	45.8
	Entrepreneurship development and drought recovery	5.9*
Mali	Private sector assistance	12.0
Mauritania	Construction capacity and employment	12.0
	Public enterprise sector adjustment	2.2*
Mozambique	Local government reform and engineering	23.2
	Food security capacity	6.3
	Rural rehabilitation	20.0
	Maputo Corridor revitalization project	9.3
	Human resources development	48.6
	Public sector and legal institutions development	15.5
Nigeria	Drainage and sanitation	63.0
	Roads (two credits)	153.0
	Development communication	8.0
	Economic management technical assistance	20.0
Rwanda	Energy sector rehabilitation	26.0
Senegal	Human resources development	40.0
Sierra Leone	Infrastructure rehabilitation	26.0
	Reconstruction import	0.3*
	Road rehabilitation and maintenance	45.0
	Public sector management support	10.0
Tanzania	Public sector reform	34.9
	Power	200.0
	Telecommunciations	74.5
	Financial sector adjustment	11.3*
	Financial and legal management improvements	20.0
Uganda	Financial sector adjustment	100.0
	Primary education and teacher development	52.6
	Structural adjustment	1.4*
	Agricultural research and training	25.0
	Agricultural extension	15.8
	Economic and financial management	29.0
Zambia	Privatization and industrial reform (two credits)	120.9*
	Transport engineering and technical assistance	8.5
	Education rehabilitation	32.0
	Agricultural marketing and processing infrastructure	33.0
Zimbabwe	Structural adjustment	125.0
	Sexually-transmitted infections prevention and care	64.5
Total		2,770.3

* Supplements to existing operations.
Source: *World Bank Annual Report 1993.*

International Finance Corporation—IFC

Address: 1850 I St, NW, Washington, DC 20433, USA.

Telephone: (202) 473-7711; **telex:** 248423; **fax:** (202) 676-0365.

IFC was founded in 1956 as an affiliate of the World Bank to encourage the growth of productive private enterprise in its member countries, particularly in the less-developed areas.

Organization

(June 1994)

IFC is a separate legal entity in the World Bank Group. Executive Directors of the World Bank also serve as Directors of IFC. The President of the World Bank is, ex officio, Chairman of the IFC Board of Directors, which has appointed him President of IFC. Subject to his overall supervision, the day-to-day operations of IFC are conducted by its staff under the direction of the Executive Vice-President.

PRINCIPAL OFFICERS

President: LEWIS T. PRESTON (USA).

Executive Vice-President: JANNIK LINDBAEK (Norway).

REGIONAL MISSIONS

Central Africa: rue Flatteurs, BP 4616, Douala, Cameroon; tel. 42-80-33; fax 42-80-14; Regional Rep. (vacant).

Eastern Africa: PO Box 30577, View Park Towers, Monrovia St, Nairobi, Kenya; tel. (02) 224726; fax (02) 213925; Regional Rep. GUY C. ANTOINE.

Southern Africa: CABS Centre, Jason Moyo Ave, POB 2960, Harare, Zimbabwe; tel. (04) 794860; fax (04) 708659; Regional Rep. THOMAS MILTON.

West Africa: BP 1850, cnr Booker Washington and Jacques Aka Cocody Sts, Abidjan 01, Côte d'Ivoire; tel. 44-32-44; telex 28132; fax 44-44-83; Regional Rep. WOLFGANG BERTELSMEIER.

Activities

The IFC's activities are guided by three major principles:

(i) The catalytic principle. IFC should seek above all to be a catalyst in helping private investors and markets to make good investments.

(ii) The business principle. IFC should function like a business in partnership with the private sector and take the same commercial risks, so that its funds, although backed by public sources, are transferred under market disciplines.

(iii) The principle of the special contribution. IFC should participate in an investment only when it makes a special contribution that supplements or complements the role of market operators.

From 1989/90 onwards, IFC adopted a 'rolling' three-year planning process, with annual updating of objectives for the next three years. Emphasis was placed on closer co-operation with the World Bank, particularly in the following areas: development of the financial sector in member countries; privatization of public enterprises; encouraging private investment; and conducting research and policy studies. IFC's agenda for the 1990s, as discussed by the Board of Directors in 1990/91, was to involve an expansion of its direct resource mobilization operations and the creation of other mobilizing activities. In June 1991 the Board of Directors approved an increase in authorized capital, by US $1,000m., to $2,300m. This was expected to allow IFC to expand its project-financing at a rate of 11%–12% annually through the 1990s.

The World Bank is the principal source of borrowed funds, but IFC also borrows from private capital markets. At 30 June 1993 paid-in capital was US $1,423m. In that financial year total investments approved amounted to $3,936m. for 185 projects, compared with $3,226m. for 167 projects in the previous year. Of the total approved, $2,133m. was for IFC's own account, while $1,803m. was used in loan syndications and underwriting of securities issues and investment funds. About 22% of financing was for countries with a per caput annual income of less than $400.

In fiscal 1993 IFC approved 45 projects (including those under the African Enterprise Fund—see below) in 18 countries in sub-Saharan Africa. These included projects concerned with textile manufacturing in Swaziland; natural gas facilities in Nigeria; flower farming in Kenya and Uganda; coal production in Zimbabwe; bauxite mining in Sierra Leone; development of a petroleum industry in Côte d'Ivoire; poultry farming in Ghana; and hotels in Cape Verde, Guinea, Nigeria, Tanzania and Zimbabwe.

In April 1989 IFC (with UNDP and the African Development Bank) initiated the African Management Services Company (AMSCo): its aim is to help find qualified senior executives from around the world to work with African companies, assist in the training of local managers, and provide supporting services. At the end of 1992 AMSCo was providing management services to 24 companies in 12 countries. The IFC's Africa Enterprise Fund (AEF) provides financial assistance to small and medium-sized enterprises: in 1992/93 IFC approved total financing through the AEF of US $11m. for 20 small projects in 13 countries.

The Foreign Investment Advisory Service is operated jointly by IFC and MIGA (q.v.), and provides advice to governments on attracting foreign investment.

AFRICA PROJECT DEVELOPMENT FACILITY (APDF)

APDF was established by IFC, UNDP and the African Development Bank (ADB) in 1986, to provide technical assistance to entrepreneurs in sub-Saharan Africa, with IFC as the executing agency. The Facility advises entrepreneurs seeking to start businesses or expand existing ones, and helps them identify and prepare viable projects. APDF does not finance projects, but assists entrepreneurs in obtaining debt and equity financing and identifying business partners, both foreign and domestic. Typically, projects assisted by APDF are small, with costs ranging from US $500,000 to $5m. APDF is funded by IFC, UNDP, the ADB and 15 industrialized countries. In addition Brazil, India and Israel make technical experts available to APDF for short-term assignments. During the year to 31 December 1992 APDF assisted the finding of 30 projects. Since its foundation APDF has helped to raise $166m. for over 130 projects, which are estimated to have created 13,000 jobs and estimated annual foreign exchange earnings of $124m.

Headquarters: 1850 I St, NW, Washington, DC 20433, USA; tel. (202) 473-0508; fax (202) 676-0387; Co-ordinator MACODOU N'DAW.

Eastern Africa: International House, 6th Floor, Mama Ngina St, PO Box 46534, Nairobi, Kenya; tel. (2) 217370; fax (2) 339121; Regional Man. JOHN JAMES.

Southern Africa: Southampton House, 5th Floor, 68-70 Union Ave, Box UA 400, Harare, Zimbabwe; tel. (4) 730967; fax (4) 730959; Regional Man. JOHN J. THOMPSON.

West Africa: Immeuble CCIA, 17th Floor, 01 BP 8669, Abidjan 01, Côte d'Ivoire; tel. 21-96-97; fax 21-61-51; Regional Man. ROBERT SHAKOTKO.

Multilateral Investment Guarantee Agency—MIGA

Address: 1818 H Street, NW, Washington, DC 20433, USA.

Telephone: (202) 477-1234; **telex:** 248423; **fax:** (202) 477-6391.

MIGA was founded in 1988 as an affiliate of the World Bank, to encourage the flow of investments for productive purposes among its member countries, especially developing countries, through the mitigation of non-commercial barriers to investment (especially political risk).

MEMBERS

By mid-1993 MIGA had 107 member countries. Membership is open to all countries that are members of the World Bank.

Organization

(June 1994)

MIGA is legally and financially separate from the World Bank. It is supervised by a Board of Directors.

President: LEWIS T. PRESTON (USA).

Executive Vice-President: AKIRA IIDA (Japan).

Activities

The convention establishing MIGA took effect in April 1988. Authorized capital was US $1,082m. By mid-1993 subscribed capital amounted to $948m.

MIGA's purpose is to guarantee eligible investments against losses resulting from non-commercial risks, under four main categories:

transfer risk resulting from host government restrictions on currency conversion and transfer;

risk of loss resulting from legislative or administrative actions of the host government;

repudiation by the host government of contracts with investors in cases in which the investor has no access to a competent forum;

the risk of armed conflict and civil unrest.

Before guaranteeing any investment, MIGA must ensure that it is commercially viable, contributes to the development process and is not harmful to the environment.

MIGA also provides policy and advisory services to promote foreign investment in developing countries. Jointly with IFC, MIGA operates the Foreign Investment Advisory Service (FIAS), which advises governments on their legislation and policies relating to foreign investment.

During the year ending 30 June 1993 MIGA issued 27 investment insurance contracts. The contracts had a combined maximum coverage of US $374m., and the amount of direct investment associated with the contracts totalled approximately $1,900m. In the financial year ending mid-1993 MIGA issued guarantees for a cobalt-extraction project in Uganda, a foreign bank in Tanzania and a gold mine in Ghana.

International Fund for Agricultural Development—IFAD

Address: Via del Serafico 107, 00142 Rome, Italy.

Telephone: (6) 54591; **telex:** 620330; **fax:** (6) 5043463.

Following a decision by the 1974 UN World Food Conference, IFAD was established in 1976 to fund rural development programmes specifically aimed at the poorest of the world's people. It began operations in January 1978.

Organization

(June 1994)

GOVERNING COUNCIL

Each member state is represented in the Governing Council by a Governor and an Alternate. There are three categories of members: industrialized countries (OECD members) forming Category I; petroleum-exporting developing countries (OPEC members) forming Category II; and recipient developing countries (Category III). Categories I and II *shall* contribute to the resources of the Fund while Category III *may* do so.

EXECUTIVE BOARD

The Board consists of 18 members and 17 alternates, elected by the Governing Council, one third by each category of membership. Members serve for three years. The Executive Board is responsible for the conduct and general operation of IFAD and approves loans and grants for projects; it holds three regular sessions each year.

The total number of votes in the Governing Council and the Executive Board is 1,800, distributed equally between the three categories of membership. Thus two-thirds of the votes lie with the developing countries (Categories II and III) which will therefore have a major influence on the investment decisions of the Fund. At the same time two-thirds of the votes are held by donor countries (Categories I and II).

President and Chairman of Executive Board: FAWZI HAMAD AL-SULTAN (Kuwait).

Vice-President: DONALD S. BROWN.

Activities

The Fund's objective is to mobilize additional resources to be made available on concessional terms for agricultural development in developing member states. IFAD provides financing primarily for projects and programmes specifically designed to introduce, expand or improve food production systems and to strengthen related policies, services and institutions within the framework of national priorities and strategies. In allocating resources IFAD is guided by: the need to increase food production in the poorest food-deficit countries; the potential for increasing food production in other developing countries; and the importance of improving the nutritional level of the poorest people in developing countries and the conditions of their lives. All projects focus on those who often do not benefit from other development programmes: small farmers, artisanal fishermen, nomadic pastoralists, women, and the rural landless.

PROJECTS IN AFRICA SOUTH OF THE SAHARA APPROVED IN 1992

Country	Loan amount (US $m.)
Gambia	3.6
Guinea	14.1
Mauritania	10.9
Mauritania	1.6
Nigeria	9.6
Rwanda	9.5
Senegal	8.2
Sierra Leone	14.7
Sudan	12.0
Uganda	10.0
Total	94.2

IFAD is empowered to make both grants and loans. Under its Agreement, grants are limited to 5% of the resources committed in any one financial year. There are three kinds of loan: highly concessional loans, which carry no interest but have an annual service charge of 1% and a maturity period of 50 years, including a grace period of 10 years; intermediate term loans, which have an annual interest rate of 4% and a maturity period of 20 years, including a grace period of five years; and ordinary term loans which have an interest rate of 8% and a maturity period of 15–18 years, including a grace period of three years. To avoid duplication of work, the administration of loans, for the purpose of disbursements and supervision of project implementation, is entrusted to competent international financial institutions, with the Fund retaining an active interest.

IFAD's development projects usually include a number of components, such as infrastructure (e.g. improvement of water supplies, small-scale irrigation and road construction); input supply (e.g. improved seeds, fertilizers and pesticides); institutional support (e.g. research, training and extension services); and producer incentives (e.g. pricing and marketing improvements). IFAD also attempts to enable the landless to acquire income-generating assets: by increasing the provision of credit for the rural poor, it seeks to free them from dependence on the unorganized and exploitative capital market and to generate productive activities.

From the late 1980s, increased emphasis was given to environmental conservation, in an effort to alleviate poverty that results from the deterioration of natural resources. In addition to promoting small-scale irrigation (which has proved more economically and ecologically viable than large-scale systems), projects include low-cost anti-erosion measures, land improvement, soil conservation, agro-forestry systems, improved management of arid rangeland, and safe biological control of pests.

In 1986 IFAD inaugurated a Special Programme for sub-Saharan African Countries Affected by Drought and Desertification (SPA) in response to the critical failure of agricultural and economic systems during a severe drought in the region in the mid-1980s. The SPA aimed to improve sustainable food-crop production through soil and water conservation (with emphasis on traditional techniques), small-scale irrigation and local forestry development. The SPA is funded separately from IFAD's regular programme by the Special Resources for sub-Saharan Africa (SRS). During 1986–92 the SPA funded 32 projects in 22 African countries, committing a total of US $300.8m. in grants and loans. A second phase of the programme (SPA II) became effective in January 1993, with the wider objective of developing local infrastructure and agricultural enterprise. The list of countries eligible for assistance increased from 22 under SPA I to 27 under SPA II.

During 1992 IFAD approved 10 projects in Africa (excluding Somalia), involving loans of US $94.2m. The total amount approved represented some 29% of IFAD's total loans for that year.

FINANCE

IFAD is financed by contributions from OECD and OPEC member states. IFAD's proposed administrative budget for 1993 was US $61.2m., including $6.3m. for the Special Programme for Africa. Agreed funds for loans and grants to be allocated during the year amounted to $425m., including $84m. for the SPA.

International Monetary Fund—IMF

Address: 700 19th St, NW, Washington, DC 20431, USA.

Telephone: (202) 623-7430; **telex:** 440040; **fax:** (202) 623-6772.

The IMF was established at the same time as the World Bank (IBRD) in 1945.

Organization

(July 1994)

BOARD OF GOVERNORS

The highest authority of the Fund is exercised by the Board of Governors, on which each member country is represented by a Governor and an Alternate Governor. The Board normally meets annually, and an Interim Committee meets twice a year. The voting power of each country is related to its quota in the Fund.

BOARD OF EXECUTIVE DIRECTORS

The 24-member Board of Executive Directors is responsible for the day-to-day operations of the Fund. The USA, the United Kingdom, Germany, France and Japan each appoint one Executive Director, while 16 of the remainder are elected by groups of member countries sharing similar interests; there is also one Executive Director each from the People's Republic of China, Russia and Saudi Arabia.

OFFICERS

Managing Director: MICHEL CAMDESSUS (France).

Deputy Managing Directors: RICHARD D. ERB (USA), (from 1 September 1994) STANLEY FISCHER (USA); ALASSANE D. OUATTARA (Côte d'Ivoire); PRABHAKAR R. NARVEKAR (India).

Director, African Department: MAMOUDOU TOURÉ (Senegal).

Activities

The purposes of the IMF, as defined in the Articles of Agreement, are:

(i) To promote international monetary co-operation through a permanent institution which provides the machinery for consultation and collaboration on monetary problems;

(ii) To facilitate the expansion and balanced growth of international trade, and to contribute thereby to the promotion and maintenance of high levels of employment and real income and to the development of members' productive resources;

(iii) To promote exchange stability, to maintain orderly exchange arrangements among members, and to avoid competitive exchange depreciation;

(iv) To assist in the establishment of a multilateral system of payments in respect of current transactions between members and in the elimination of foreign exchange restrictions which hamper the growth of trade;

(v) To give confidence to members by making the general resources of the Fund temporarily available to them, under adequate safeguards, thus providing them with the opportunity to correct maladjustments in their balance of payments, without resorting to measures destructive of national or international prosperity; and

(vi) In accordance with the above, to shorten the duration of and lessen the degree of disequilibrium in the international balances of payments of members.

In joining the Fund, each country agrees to co-operate with the above objectives, and the Fund monitors members' compliance by holding an annual consultation with each country, in order to survey the country's exchange rate policies and determine its need for assistance.

RESOURCES

Members' subscriptions form the basic resource of the IMF. They are supplemented by borrowing. Under the General Arrangements to Borrow (GAB), established in 1962, the 'Group of Ten' industrialized nations (Belgium, Canada, France, Germany, Italy, Japan, the Netherlands, Sweden, the United Kingdom and the USA) and Switzerland (which became a member of the IMF in 1992, but which had been a full participant in the GAB from 1984) undertake to lend the Fund up to SDR 17,000m. in their own currencies, so as to help fulfill the balance-of-payments requirements of any member of the group, or to meet requests to the Fund from countries with balance-of-payments problems that could threaten the stability of the international monetary system.

MEMBERSHIP AND QUOTAS IN AFRICA SOUTH OF THE SAHARA (million SDR)*

Country	October 1993
Angola	207.3
Benin	45.3
Botswana	36.6
Burkina Faso	44.2
Burundi	57.2
Cameroon	135.1
Cape Verde	7.0
Central African Republic	41.2
Chad	41.3
Comoros	6.5
Congo	57.9
Côte d'Ivoire	238.2
Djibouti	11.5
Equatorial Guinea	24.3
Ethiopia	98.3
Gabon	110.3
The Gambia	22.9
Ghana	274.0
Guinea	78.7
Guinea-Bissau	10.5
Kenya	199.4
Lesotho	23.9
Liberia†	(96.2) 71.3
Madagascar	90.4
Malawi	50.9
Mali	68.9
Mauritania	47.5
Mauritius	73.3
Mozambique	84.0
Namibia	99.6
Niger	48.3
Nigeria	1,281.6
Rwanda	59.5
São Tomé and Príncipe	5.5
Senegal	118.9
Seychelles	6.0
Sierra Leone†	(77.2) 57.9
Somalia†	(60.9) 44.2
South Africa	1,365.4
Sudan†	(233.1) 169.7
Swaziland	36.5
Tanzania	146.9
Togo	54.3
Uganda	133.9
Zaire†	(394.8) 291.0
Zambia†	(363.5) 270.3
Zimbabwe	261.3

* The Special Drawing Right (SDR) was introduced in 1970 as a substitute for gold in international payments, and is intended eventually to become the principal reserve asset in the international monetary system. Its value (which was US $1.44837 at 30 June 1994 and averaged $1.39633 in 1993) is based on the currencies of the five largest exporting countries. Each member is assigned a quota related to its national income, monetary reserves, trade balance and other economic indicators; the quota approximately determines a member's voting power and the amount of foreign exchange it may purchase from the Fund. A member's subscription is equal to its quota. Under the Ninth General Review of quotas, which was completed in June 1990, an increase of about 50% in total quotas (from SDR 90,035m. to SDR 135,200m.) was authorized. The increase entered into effect in November 1992; with additional contributions from countries that joined the IMF subsequent to June 1990, by October 1993 total quotas amounted to SDR 144,606.2m.

† As of 13 October 1993, these members had not yet paid for their quota increases under the Ninth General Review. The quotas listed are those determined under the Eighth General Review, and the figures in parentheses are the proposed Ninth Review quotas.

DRAWING ARRANGEMENTS

Exchange transactions within the Fund take the form of members' purchases (i.e. drawings) from the Fund of the currencies of other members for the equivalent amounts of their own currencies. Fund resources are available to eligible members on an essentially short-term and revolving basis to provide members with temporary assistance to contribute to the solution of their payments problems. Before making a purchase, a member must show that its balance of payments or reserve position make the purchase necessary. Apart from this requirement, reserve tranche purchases (i.e. purchases that do not bring the Fund's holdings of the member's currency to a level above its quota) are permitted unconditionally.

PURCHASES OF CURRENCIES AND SPECIAL DRAWING RIGHTS FROM THE IMF BY MEMBERS IN AFRICA SOUTH OF THE SAHARA

1 May 1992–30 April 1993		1 May 1993–30 April 1994	
Member	Total purchases (million SDR)	Member	Total purchases (million SDR)
Zimbabwe	31.3	Cameroon	21.9
		Central African Republic	10.7
		Chad	10.3
		Gabon	5.5
		Niger	1.1
		Senegal	30.9

With further purchases, however, the Fund's policy of 'conditionality' means that a member requesting assistance must agree to adjust its economic policies, as stipulated by the IMF. All requests other than for use of the reserve tranche are examined by the Executive Board to determine whether the proposed use would be consistent with the Fund's policies, and a member must discuss its proposed adjustment programme (including fiscal, monetary, exchange and trade policies) with IMF staff. Purchases outside the reserve tranche are made in four credit tranches, each equivalent to 25% of the member's quota; a member must reverse the transaction by repurchasing its own currency (with SDR or currencies specified by the Fund) within a specified time. A credit tranche purchase is usually made under a 'stand-by arrangement' with the Fund, or under the extended Fund facility. A stand-by arrangement is normally of one or two years' duration, and the amount is made available in instalments, subject to the member's observance of 'performance criteria'; repurchases must be made within three-and-a-quarter to five years. An extended arrangement is normally of three years' duration, and the member must submit detailed economic programmes and progress reports for each year; repurchases must be made within four-and-a-half to 10 years. A member whose payments imbalance is large in relation to its quota may make use of temporary facilities established by the Fund using borrowed resources, namely the 'enlarged access policy' established in 1981, which helps to finance stand-by and extended arrangements for such a member, up to a limit of between 90% and 110% of the member's quota annually.

In addition, there are special-purpose arrangements, all of which are subject to the member's co-operation with the Fund to find an appropriate solution to its difficulties. The buffer stock financing facility (BSFF, established in 1969) enables members to pay their contributions to the buffer stocks which are intended to stabilize primary commodity markets. Members may draw up to 45% of their quota for this purpose. In August 1988 the Fund established the compensatory and contingency financing facility (CCFF), which replaced and expanded the former compensatory financing facility, established in 1963. The CCFF provides compensation to members whose export earnings are reduced owing to circumstances beyond their control, or who are affected by excess costs of cereal imports. Contingency financing is provided to help members maintain their efforts at economic adjustment even when affected by a sharp increase in interest rates or other externally-derived difficulties. Under the BSFF and CCFF repurchases are made within three-and-a-quarter to five years.

The structural adjustment facility (SAF, established in 1986) supports medium-term macroeconomic adjustment and structural reforms in low-income developing countries on concessionary terms. SAF loans carry an interest rate of 0.5%, repayable within 10 years, including a five-and-a-half-year grace period, and the recipient must agree to a three-year structural adjustment programme to restore sustainable economic growth. Of the 61 countries eligible for SAF loans, 34 are in sub-Saharan Africa.

The enhanced structural adjustment facility (ESAF, which was established in 1987) provides assistance on a similar basis to the SAF except that maximum access is set at 190% (255% in exceptional circumstances) of the member's quota (compared with 70% under the SAF). Originally 34 African countries were eligible for ESAF loans; in April 1992 Angola, Côte d'Ivoire, Nigeria and Zimbabwe were granted eligibility for the first time.

NEW SAF AND ESAF ARRANGEMENTS AGREED FOR COUNTRIES IN AFRICA SOUTH OF THE SAHARA

1 May 1992–30 April 1993

Country	Loan (million SDR)
Benin	47.0 (ESAF)
Burkina Faso	48.6 (ESAF)
Equatorial Guinea	12.9 (ESAF)
Ethiopia	49.4 (SAF)
Mali	61.0 (ESAF)
Mauritania	33.9 (ESAF)
Zimbabwe	200.6 (ESAF)

1 May 1993–30 April 1994

Country	Loan (million SDR)
Côte d'Ivoire	333.5 (ESAF)
Kenya	45.2 (ESAF)
Sierra Leone	88.8 (ESAF) 27.0 (SAF)

By 30 April 1993 total commitments approved under SAF and ESAF arrangements amounted to SDR 4,600m., while total disbursements in the financial year 1992/93 amounted to SDR 600m.

In December 1993 the Executive Board approved a new ESAF to replace the facility which had been due to expire in November. The commitment period of the existing ESAF was extended, until its successor became operational in February 1994, to ensure continuity of lending. The terms and conditions of the new facility remain the same as those of the original ESAF, but the list of countries eligible for assistance was enlarged by six, of which Cameroon was the only African country, to 78. By mid-April 43 IMF member countries had committed funds to the renewed ESAF amounting to SDR 1,373m. in subsidies and SDR 4,501.4m. in loan contributions.

TECHNICAL ASSISTANCE

Technical assistance is provided by special missions or resident representatives who advise members on every aspect of economic management. The Central Banking Department and the Fiscal Affairs Department are particularly involved in technical assistance. The IMF Institute, founded in 1964, trains officials from member countries in financial analysis and policy, balance-of-payments methodology and public finance: it also gives assistance to national and regional training centres.

PUBLICATIONS

Annual Report.

International Financial Statistics (monthly and annually).

Balance of Payments Statistics (monthly and annually).

Government Finance Statistics Yearbook.

Direction of Trade Statistics (monthly and annually).

IMF Survey (2 a month).

Finance and Development (quarterly, issued jointly with the World Bank).

Staff Studies for the World Economic Outlook (annually).

World Economic Outlook (2 a year).

Export Credits: Development and Prospects (annually).

International Capital Markets (annually).

Primary Commodities: Market Developments and Outlook (annually).

Occasional papers, books and pamphlets.

United Nations Educational, Scientific and Cultural Organization—UNESCO

Address: 7 place de Fontenoy, 75352 Paris, France.

Telephone: (1) 45-68-10-00; **telex:** 204461; **fax:** (1) 45-67-16-90.

UNESCO was established in 1946 'for the purpose of advancing, through the educational, scientific and cultural relations of the peoples of the world, the objectives of international peace and the common welfare of mankind'.

Organization

(June 1994)

GENERAL CONFERENCE

The supreme governing body of the Organization, the Conference meets in ordinary session once in two years and is composed of representatives of the member states.

EXECUTIVE BOARD

The Board, comprising 51 members, prepares the programme to be submitted to the Conference and supervises its execution; it meets twice or sometimes three times a year.

SECRETARIAT

Director-General: FEDERICO MAYOR ZARAGOZA (Spain).

Director of the Executive Office: DANIEL JANICOT (France).

REGIONAL OFFICES

Regional Office for Education in Africa: BP 3311, Dakar, Senegal; tel. 23-50-82; telex 410; fax 23-83-93; Dir PIUS OBANYA (acting).

Regional Office for Science and Technology for Africa: POB 30592, Nairobi, Kenya; tel. (2) 621234; telex 22275; fax (2) 215991; Dir Prof. P. B. VITTA.

Activities

UNESCO's activities, which take three main forms as outlined below, are funded through a regular budget provided by member states and also through other sources, particularly UNDP. UNESCO co-operates with many other UN agencies and international non-governmental organizations.

International Intellectual Co-operation: UNESCO assists the interchange of experience, knowledge and ideas through a world network of specialists. Apart from the work of its professional staff, UNESCO co-operates regularly with the national associations and international federations of scientists, artists, writers and educators, some of which it helped to establish. UNESCO convenes conferences and meetings, and co-ordinates international scientific efforts; it helps to standardize procedures of documentation and provides clearing house services; it offers fellowships; and it publishes a wide range of specialized works, including source books and works of reference. UNESCO promotes various international agreements, including the International Copyright Convention and the World Cultural and Natural Heritage Convention, which member states are invited to accept.

Operational Assistance: UNESCO has established missions which advise governments, particularly in the developing member countries, in the planning of projects; and it appoints experts to assist in carrying them out. The projects are concerned with the teaching of functional literacy to workers in development undertakings; teacher training; establishing of libraries and documentation centres; provision of training for journalists, radio, television and film workers; improvement of scientific and technical education; training of planners in cultural development; and the international exchange of persons and information.

Promotion of Peace: UNESCO organizes various research efforts on racial problems, and is particularly concerned with prevention of discrimination in education and improving access for women to education. It also promotes studies and research on conflicts and peace, violence and obstacles to disarmament, and the role of international law and organizations in building peace. It is stressed that human rights, peace and disarmament cannot be dealt with separately, as the observance of human rights is a prerequisite to peace and vice versa.

In November 1992 UNESCO announced the establishment of a 21-member panel, composed mainly of academics and writers with experience in government, to draw up guidelines for the agency's activities in the coming decade.

EDUCATION

UNESCO's most important activities, as stipulated in its programme for 1990–95, are in the sphere of education, particularly the spread of literacy, adult education, and teacher-training, and the encouragement of universal primary education, partly through assistance for the construction of primary schools. It places special emphasis on the attainment of education by women and people with disabilities and on literacy as an integral part of rural development. Each year UNESCO sends expert missions to member states on request to advise on all matters concerning education, and provides fellowships and travel grants, with priority given to the rural regions of developing member countries. Assistance is given for the education of refugees in Africa. The International Institute for Educational Planning and the International Bureau of Education undertake training, research and the exchange of information on aspects of education.

In 1991 UNESCO initiated a project for developing the management skills of senior administrators of African universities.

UNESCO was given responsibility for organizing International Literacy Year (1990), which was proclaimed by the UN as a means of initiating a plan of action for the spread of literacy (based on regional literacy programmes that had been established by UNESCO over the past decade in Africa, Latin America and the Caribbean, the Arab states and Asia and the Pacific). The principal aims of the International Literacy Year were to increase action by governments to eliminate illiteracy among women and disadvantaged groups; and to increase public awareness of the extent and implications of illiteracy.

In March 1990 UNESCO, with other UN agencies, sponsored the World Conference on Education for All. In 1991 it organized a conference of African ministers of education to discuss the development of education in the 1990s. In early 1992 UNESCO and the Commonwealth (q.v.) initiated a joint project to improve the managerial skills of head teachers of primary schools in 19 anglophone African countries.

NATURAL SCIENCES AND TECHNOLOGY

At the international level, UNESCO has established various forms of intergovernmental co-operation concerned with the environmental sciences and research on natural resources. Examples of these are the Man and Biosphere Programme (MAB) which by late 1992 had undertaken over 1,000 projects in 100 countries involving local people in solving practical problems of environmental resource management in diverse bioclimatic and geographical situations around the world, where research, conservation and training in environmental resource management are undertaken; the International Geological Correlation Programme (IGCP), run jointly with the International Union of Geological Sciences; the International Hydrological Programme (IHP), dealing with the scientific aspects of water resources assessment and management; and the Intergovernmental Oceanographic Commission which promotes scientific investigation into the nature and resources of the oceans through the concerted action of its member states. The Intergovernmental Informatics Programme encourages co-operation between developed and developing countries in computer sciences.

At the regional and sub-regional level, UNESCO promotes co-operation and research on science and technology, particularly concerning their application to the development process in Africa, by organizing meetings, communicating with research institutions, and establishing or strengthening co-operative networks; the African Network of Scientific and Technological Institutions, for example, was launched in 1980 at UNESCO's Nairobi Regional Office. In February 1994 UNESCO launched the International Fund for the Technological Development of Africa, which was to be managed jointly by UNESCO and the African scientific community.

At the national level, UNESCO assists member states, upon request, in policy-making and planning in the field of science and technology generally, and by organizing training and research programmes in basic sciences, engineering sciences and environmental sciences, particularly work relevant to development, such as projects concerning the use of small-scale energy sources for rural and dispersed populations.

SOCIAL SCIENCES

UNESCO's activities in the field of the social and human sciences aim to promote teaching and research in these disciplines and to encourage their application to a number of prioritized issues by the Organization including education, development, urbanization, population, youth, human rights, democracy and peace. The social sciences constitute a link between UNESCO's two main functions: international intellectual co-operation leading to reflection on major problems, and action to solve these problems. For example, studies are conducted to elucidate the complex relations between demographic changes and socio-cultural transformation on a global scale. Co-operation with the United Nations Population Fund has led to a technical assistance programme which benefits developing countries in the areas of population education and communications. Other examples of research activities include the ways in which societies react to climatic and environmental change, and changes affecting women and families.

UNESCO's social and human sciences programme gives high priority to the problems of young people who are the first victims of unemployment, economic and social inequalities and the widening gap between developing and industrialized countries. Under the project 'Youth Shaping the Future', an International Youth Clearing House and Information Service is to be established in order to increase and consolidate the information available on the situation of young people in society, and to heighten awareness of their needs, aspirations and potential among public and private decision-makers. UNESCO's programme also focuses on the educational and cultural dimensions of physical education and sport and their capacity to preserve and improve health. An activity specifically aimed at young people is education designed to prevent the spread of AIDS.

The programme helps countries in defining national strategies for the development of human resources and in strengthening research and training capabilities in order better to anticipate social, economic and cultural changes and their impact on development. The social and human sciences programme also focuses on the promotion and protection of human rights and democracy through education, information and documentation and research, particularly those rights related to UNESCO's areas of competence, i.e. education, science, culture and communication. The struggle against all forms of discrimination is a central part of the programme. It disseminates scientific information aimed at combating racial prejudice, works to improve the status of women and their access to education, and promotes equality between men and women.

CULTURE

UNESCO's cultural heritage programme is in three parts: activities designed to foster the world-wide application of three international conventions that aim to protect and conserve cultural property; international safeguarding campaigns to help member states to conserve and restore monuments and sites (in 1992 there were 24 such campaigns in progress); and the training of museum managers and conservationists and promotion of public awareness of the cultural heritage.

UNESCO encourages the translation and publication of literary works, publishes albums of art, and produces records, audiovisual programmes and travelling art exhibitions. It supports the development of book publishing and distribution and the training of editors and managers in publishing. UNESCO is active in preparing and encouraging the enforcement of international legislation on copyright. An eight-volume *General History of Africa*, with versions in French and Arabic, prepared under the aegis of UNESCO, was published in 1993.

The regional centres for the training of archivists (Dakar, Senegal and Accra, Ghana) and for the training of museum technicians (Jos, Nigeria) have been assisted by UNESCO. In Kinshasa, Zaire, UNESCO collaborates with the Centre for the Co-ordination of Social Science Research and Documentation in Africa south of the Sahara (CERDAS). A 10-year programme for the collection and safeguarding of humanity's non-material heritage (oral traditions, music, dance, medicine etc.) was begun in 1988.

UNESCO's World Heritage Programme, launched in 1978, aims to protect historic sites and natural landmarks of outstanding universal significance, in accordance with the UNESCO Convention Concerning the Protection of the World Cultural and Natural Heritage, by providing financial aid for restoration, technical assistance, training and management planning. Designated sites in Africa include the Dja nature reserve in Cameroon, the island of Gorée (a former point of departure for the slave trade) off the coast of Senegal, the Ngorongoro Conservation Area and Kilimanjaro national park in Tanzania and the Virunga 1National Park in Zaire.

UNESCO's Decade for Cultural Development began in 1990. In December 1992 UNESCO established the World Commission on Culture and Development to strengthen links between culture and development and prepare a report on the issue.

COMMUNICATION

UNESCO has helped to set up information agencies on the continent, to create rural newspapers and to train journalists and other personnel. Under the International Programme for the Development of Communication, launched in 1981, UNESCO supports the Pan-African News Agency based in Senegal (q.v.) and the West African News Agencies Development Project, founded in 1984 and based in Cotonou, Benin, which assists in establishing national news agencies and training editors and technicians. In May 1991 UNESCO co-sponsored a seminar in Windhoek, Namibia, on promoting an independent and pluralistic African press.

FINANCE

UNESCO's Regular Programme budget for the two years 1992–93 was US $444.7m., with extra-budgetary resources estimated at $274.9m.

PUBLICATIONS

(mostly in English, French and Spanish editions; Arabic, Chinese and Russian versions are also available in many cases)

UNESCO Statistical Yearbook.

UNESCO Courier (monthly, in 36 languages).

UNESCO Sources (monthly).

Copyright Bulletin (quarterly).

Museum (quarterly).

Impact of Science on Society (quarterly).

International Social Science Journal (quarterly).

Nature and Resources (quarterly review of the Man and Biosphere programme, the International Hydrological Programme and the International Geological Correlation Programme).

Prospects (quarterly review on education).

Books, statistics, scientific maps and atlases.

World Health Organization—WHO

Address: ave Appia, 1211 Geneva 27, Switzerland.

Telephone: (22) 7912111; **telex:** 415416; **fax:** (22) 7910746.

WHO was established in 1948 as the central agency directing international health work. Of its many activities, the most important single aspect is technical co-operation with national health administrations, particularly in the developing countries.

Organization

(June 1994)

WORLD HEALTH ASSEMBLY

The Assembly meets annually in Geneva; it is responsible for policy making, and the biennial programme and budget; it appoints the Director-General, admits new members and reviews budget contributions.

EXECUTIVE BOARD

The Board is composed of 31 health experts designated by, but not representing, their governments; they serve for three years, and the World Health Assembly elects 10 or 11 member states each year to the Board. It meets at least twice a year to review the Director-General's programme, which it forwards to the Assembly with any recommendations that seem necessary. It advises on questions referred to it by the Assembly and is responsible for putting into effect the decisions and policies of the Assembly. It is also empowered to take emergency measures in case of epidemics or disasters.

SECRETARIAT

Director-General: Dr HIROSHI NAKAJIMA (Japan).

Deputy Director-General: Dr MOHAMED ABDELMOUMÈNE (Algeria).

Assistant Directors-General: Dr HU CHING-LI (People's Republic of China), Dr JEAN-PAUL JARDEL (France), Dr RALPH H. HENDERSON (USA), Dr NIKOLAI P. NAPALKOV (Russia), DENIS G. AITKEN (UK), Dr FERNANDO ANTEZANA ARANIBAR (Bolivia).

Regional Office in Africa: BP 6, Brazzaville, Congo; tel. 83-91-11; telex 5217; fax 83-94-00; Dir Prof. GOTTLIEB LOBE MONEKOSSO.

Sub-regional offices were established in Bamako, Mali and Harare, Zimbabwe, in 1985.

Activities

WHO's objective is stated in the constitution as 'the attainment by all peoples of the highest possible level of health'.

It acts as the central authority directing international health work, and establishes relations with professional groups and government health authorities on that basis.

It supports, on request from member states, programmes to prevent and control health problems, control or eradicate disease, train health workers best suited to local needs and strengthen national health systems. Aid is provided in emergencies and natural disasters.

A global programme of collaborative research and exchange of scientific information is carried out in co-operation with about 1,000 leading national institutions. Particular stress is laid on the widespread communicable diseases of the tropics, and the countries directly concerned are assisted in developing their research capabilities.

It keeps diseases and other health problems under constant surveillance, formulates health regulations for international travel, and sets standards for the quality control of drugs, vaccines and other substances affecting health.

It collects and disseminates health data and carries out statistical analyses and comparative studies in such diseases as cancer, heart disease and mental illness.

It promotes improved environmental conditions, including housing, sanitation and working conditions. All available information on effects on human health of the pollutants in the environment is critically reviewed and published.

Co-operation among scientists and professional groups is encouraged, and WHO may propose international conventions and agreements. It assists in developing an informed public opinion on matters of health.

Strengthening of the national health services has been one of WHO's primary tasks in Africa south of the Sahara. Integrated health systems are being developed to provide services related to medical care, rehabilitation, family health, communicable disease control, environmental health, health education, and health statistics. By providing educators and fellowships and by organizing training courses, support is given to national programmes aimed at preparing health workers best suited to local needs and resources. Specialists and advisory services are provided to assist in planning the health sector, which in most African countries forms an integral part of the overall plan for socio-economic development.

WHO promotes national, regional and global strategies for the attainment of the main target of member states: 'Health for all by the year 2000', or the attainment by all citizens of the world of a level of health that will permit them to lead a socially and economically productive life. In May 1981 the World Health Assembly adopted a Global Strategy in support of this aim. Primary health care was considered to be the key to 'Health for all', with the following as minimum requirements:

(i) safe water in the home or within 15 minutes' walking distance, and adequate sanitary facilities in the home or immediate vicinity;

(ii) immunization against diphtheria, pertussis, tetanus, poliomyelitis, measles and tuberculosis;

(iii) local health care, including availability of at least 20 essential drugs, within one hour's travel; and

(iv) trained personnel to attend childbirth, and to care for pregnant mothers and children up to at least one year old.

DISEASE PREVENTION AND CONTROL

One of WHO's major achievements was the eradication of smallpox, which, following a massive international campaign of vaccination and surveillance, begun in 1958 and intensified in 1967, was declared to have been achieved in 1977. In 1988 the World Health Assembly declared its commitment to the similar eradication of poliomyelitis by the year 2000; and in 1990 the Assembly resolved to eliminate iodine deficiency disorders (causing mental handicap) by 2000.

The objective of providing immunization for all children by 1990 was adopted by the World Health Assembly in 1977. Six diseases (measles, whooping cough, tetanus, poliomyelitis, tuberculosis and diphtheria) that killed or maimed some 10m. children annually became the target of the Expanded Programme on Immunization (EPI) in which WHO, UNICEF and many other organizations collaborated. In 1990 more than 100m. children in the developing world under the age of one had been successfully vaccinated against the targeted diseases. This achieved the EPI's objective of a rate of vaccination of 80%, which compared with a rate of vaccination of 20% in 1980, saving the lives of about 3m. children every year. Some 74 governments and more than 400 voluntary organizations were involved in the EPI. The ultimate aim of the EPI is to achieve universal childhood immunization; to eradicate poliomyelitis and cases of tetanus in infants aged one month or younger; and to reduce dramatically the incidence of measles and deaths caused by it.

In September 1991 WHO launched the Children's Vaccine Initiative (CVI), jointly sponsored by the Rockefeller Foundation, UNDP, UNICEF, and the World Bank, which aims to facilitate the development and provision of children's vaccines. The CVI has as its ultimate goal the development of a single oral immunization shortly after birth that will protect against all major childhood diseases. WHO's Division of Diarrhoeal and Acute Respiratory Disease Control encourages national programmes aimed at reducing childhood deaths as a result of diarrhoea, particularly through the use of oral rehydration therapy, and preventive measures. The Division is also seeking to reduce deaths from pneumonia in infants through the use of a simple case-management strategy involving the recognition of danger signs and treatment with an appropriate antibiotic. In keeping with the priority given by WHO to integrated disease control, an integrated approach to management to the sick child is being developed by the Division in collaboration with other relevant WHO programmes and with UNICEF.

The Division of Integrated Control of Tropical Diseases provides member states with technical support to assist in the implementation of disease control. The programme focuses on six major groups of tropical diseases: malaria, leprosy, schistosomiasis and other trematode (fluke) infections, filariasis (onchocerciasis and the lymphatic filariases), leishmaniasis, African and American trupanosomiasis and dracunculiasis (Guinea worm disease). The Division formulates control strategies for global, regional or sub-regional application. Direct technical support is given in the design and implementation of programmes by means of visiting countries and training programmes. Special attention is given to the adoption of realistic sustainable control programmes and to the integration of such programmes in the health services and the social and economic sectors of member countries. WHO efforts to eradicate dracunculiasis aimed to interrupt transmission of the parasite in all affected areas by the end of 1995. In May 1994 the onchocerciasis control programme, initiated in 1974 and operational in 11 west African countries, was nearing completion and responsibility for protecting against the disease was to be passed onto the countries concerned. WHO's Special Programme for Research and Training in Tropical Diseases, sponsored jointly by WHO, UNDP and the World Bank, was established in 1975, and comprises a world-wide network of about 5,000 scientists working on the development of vaccines, new drugs, diagnostic kits, preventive measures, and applied field research on practical community issues affecting the target diseases. The programme aims to strengthen research institutions in developing countries, and to encourage participation by scientists from the countries most affected by tropical diseases. A Ministerial Conference on Malaria, organized by WHO in October 1992, adopted a global strategy specifying requirements for effective control of the disease, which kills about 2.5m. people every year, with 90% of the deaths occurring in tropical Africa.

WHO's Global Programme on AIDS (Acquired Immunodeficiency Syndrome) began in 1987. By December 1993, WHO had received reports of over 850,000 cases of AIDS, and estimated the true number of cases to be about 3m. The cumulative number of adults and children infected with the human immunodeficiency virus (HIV), which causes AIDS, was estimated at15m., of which 10m. were in sub-Saharan Africa, with the majority in central and eastern Africa. The aims of WHO's Global Programme are to prevent HIV transmission, to care for people with HIV or AIDS, and to co-ordinate national and international efforts against AIDS. In March 1988 WHO formed an alliance with UNDP, aiming to expand the campaign against AIDS by using UNDP's already existing network of resident representatives and development programmes. WHO supports national AIDS control plans, which (in the absence of a vaccine) stress education and information as vital in stopping the spread of HIV. Programmes also include funds for training health personnel; improving facilities for testing and protecting blood supplies; epidemiological surveillance; and establishing or expanding laboratory facilities for diagnosing AIDS and treatment facilities for AIDS patients. WHO's Global Programme on AIDS was to receive US $180m. for the period 1994–95, the largest amount allocated to a single programme within WHO. The Global Commission on AIDS, comprising biomedical and social scientists and other experts, is the advisory body to the WHO's Global Programme on AIDS.

WHO's Programme for the Promotion of Environmental Health undertakes a wide range of initiatives to tackle the increasing threats to health and well-being from a changing environment, especially in relation to air pollution, control of monitoring of water quality, sanitation, protection against radiation, management of hazardous waste, chemical safety and housing hygiene. The major part of WHO's technical co-operation in environmental health in developing countries is concerned with community water supply and sanitation. In sub-Saharan Africa, where conditions are considered to be the worst in the world, WHO estimated that 53% of people in the region, in 1990, were lacking safe drinking water, and 69% were living without adequate sanitation. In March 1994 WHO called for an international partnership between national and international organizations involved in water and sanitation programmes in sub-Saharan countries, where the poor conditions contribute to the problems of endemic malnutrition and diarrhoeal diseases. The Programme also gives prominence to the assessment of health risks from chemical, physical and biological agents. To contribute to the solution of environmental health problems associated with the rapid urbanization of cities in the developing world, the Programme was promoting globally in the early 1990s the Healthy City approach that had been initiated in Europe.

WHO's Tobacco or Health Programme aims to reduce the use of tobacco, which is estimated to be responsible for more than 3m. deaths annually (through lung cancer, heart disease, chronic bronchitis and other effects). The Programme aims to educate tobacco-users and to prevent young people from adopting the habit.

'Inter-Health', a programme to combat non-communicable diseases (such as those arising from an unhealthy diet) was initiated in 1990, with the particular aim of preventing an increase in the incidence of such diseases in developing countries.

FOOD AND NUTRITION

WHO's nutrition programme identifies and supports those countries with high levels of malnutrition in all its forms, including dietary deficiency of protein and energy, and deficiencies of iron, vitamin A and iodine. With FAO and UNICEF, WHO operates a programme of surveillance of food and nutrition. In December 1992 an International Conference on Nutrition, co-sponsored by FAO and WHO, was held in Rome. It was attended by ministers of agriculture and health from over 150 countries and adopted a World Declaration on Nutrition and a Plan of Action designed to make the fight against malnutrition a development priority. Following the Conference WHO identified 81 countries that required immediate support in drawing up their national plans of action on nutrition. By May 1993 WHO had provided financial assistance for implementation of nutrition programmes in 17 of the world's poorest countries, including 13 in Africa.

Together with UNICEF and several bilateral development agencies, WHO is implementing a strategy of promoting breast-feeding. The strategy emphasizes the central importance of health-care routines in breast-feeding, particularly in maternity wards and hospitals; appropriate weaning practices, using nourishing local foods; relevant information, education and training; the social status of women and its impact on infant-feeding; and the appropriate marketing and distribution of breast-milk substitutes, including measures that countries have adopted to give effect to the International Code of Marketing of Breast-milk Substitutes.

DRUGS

The WHO Action Programme on Essential Drugs aims to prevent the inappropriate and excessive prescription of drugs and to ensure the availability of a selected number of safe and effective drugs and vaccines of acceptable quality and at low cost, in support of primary health care. WHO maintains and regularly revises a Model List of Essential Drugs, which is complemented by information on the prescription of medications. WHO's Division of Drug Policies and Management provides information on international standards for the manufacture of pharmaceutical products in international trade, and advises national health agencies on the safety and efficacy of drugs. WHO is also active in monitoring drug abuse and in developing effective approaches to the management of health problems resulting from drug abuse.

WHO's Programme on Traditional Medicine encourages the incorporation of traditional health practices that have been evaluated as safe and effective into primary health care systems.

EMERGENCY RELIEF

Through its Division of Emergency and Humanitarian Action, WHO acts as the 'health arm' of disaster relief undertaken by the UN system. It works in close co-operation with the UNHCR, UNDP, the UN's Department of Humanitarian Affairs/UNDRO and UNICEF. Its emergency preparedness activities include co-ordination, policy making and planning, awareness-building, technical advice, training, publication of standards and guidelines, and research on emergency preparedness issues. Its emergency relief activities include an emergency response fund, emergency drugs and supplies, stockpiles and technical emergency assessment missions. The Division's objective is to build the capacity of disaster-vulnerable member states to reduce the adverse health consequences of disasters. In mid-1993 WHO was providing emergency health-care assistance in the Horn of Africa and in southern African states. In May 1994 WHO provided emergency health supplies to assist refugees fleeing ethnic conflict in Rwanda. As soon as the conflicting parties could guarantee safe conduct for relief workers, WHO expected to conduct a mission to evaluate health and emergency needs in the country and mobilize the necessary personnel and supplies.

FINANCE

WHO's regular budget is provided by assessment of member states and associate members. An additional fund for specific projects is provided by voluntary contributions from members and other sources. Funds are received from the UN Development Programme for particular projects and from UNFPA for population programmes. A budget of US $734.9m. was approved for 1992–93. Of this amount 18.7% was allocated to Africa. Extra-budgetary funds were expected to amount to $926.6m. during this period. For the period 1994–95 the regular working budget was to amount to $822.1m., while extra-budgetary contributions were expected to total nearly $1,000m.

PUBLICATIONS

Full catalogue of publications supplied free on request.

World Health (6 a year in English, French, Russian and Spanish; quarterly in Arabic and Farsi).

Environmental Health Criteria.

Bulletin of WHO (6 a year).

Weekly Epidemiological Record.

World Health Statistics Quarterly.

World Health Statistics Annual.

International Digest of Health Legislation (quarterly).

Reports on the World Health Situation: (approximately every 6 years) the latest report covers the period 1985–90.

World Health Forum (quarterly, in Arabic, Chinese, English, French, Russian and Spanish).

WHO Drug Information (quarterly).

Other UN Organizations active in Africa

OFFICE OF THE UNITED NATIONS DISASTER RELIEF CO-ORDINATOR—UNDRO

Address: Department of Humanitarian Affairs, Palais des Nations, 1211 Geneva 10, Switzerland.

Telephone: (22) 9171234; **telex:** 414242; **fax:** (22) 9170023.

UNDRO was established in 1972 to mobilize and co-ordinate international emergency relief to disaster-stricken areas, and to co-operate in promoting disaster preparedness and prevention. In 1992 UNDRO became part of the newly-established United Nations Department of Humanitarian Affairs.

UNITED NATIONS CENTRE FOR HUMAN SETTLEMENTS—UNCHS (Habitat)

Address: POB 30030, Nairobi, Kenya.

Telephone: (2) 520600; **telex:** 22996; **fax:** (2) 226473.

The Centre was established in 1978 to service the inter-governmental Commission on Human Settlements, and to serve as a focus for human settlements activities in the UN system.

UNITED NATIONS CHILDREN'S FUND—UNICEF

Address: 3 United Nations Plaza, New York, NY 10017, USA.

Telephone: (212) 326-7000; **telex:** 7607848; **fax:** (212) 888-7465.

UNICEF was established in 1946 by the UN General Assembly as the UN International Children's Emergency Fund, to meet the emergency needs of children in post-war Europe and China. In 1950 its mandate was changed to emphasize programmes giving long-term benefits to children everywhere, particularly those in developing countries who are in the greatest need.

Regional Office for Central and West Africa: BP 443, Abidjan 04, Côte d'Ivoire; tel. 213131; telex 23340.

Regional Office for Eastern and Southern Africa: POB 44145, Nairobi, Kenya; tel. (2) 520671; telex 25130.

UNITED NATIONS CONFERENCE ON TRADE AND DEVELOPMENT—UNCTAD

Address: Palais des Nations, 1211 Geneva 10, Switzerland.

Telephone: (22) 9071234; **telex:** 412962; **fax:** (22) 9070057.

UNCTAD was established in 1964. Its role is to promote international trade, particularly that of developing countries, with a view to accelerating economic development. It is the principal instrument of the UN General Assembly for deliberation and negotiation in the field of international trade and related issues of international economic co-operation, including commodity agreements.

UNITED NATIONS ENVIRONMENT PROGRAMME—UNEP

Address: POB 30552, Nairobi, Kenya.

Telephone: (2) 230800; **telex:** 22068; **fax:** (2) 226890.

UNEP was established in 1972 to encourage international co-operation in matters relating to the human environment.

UNITED NATIONS POPULATION FUND—UNFPA

Address: 220 East 42nd St, New York, NY 10017, USA.

Telephone: (212) 297-5000; **telex:** 422031; **fax:** (212) 370-0201.

Created in 1967 as the Trust Fund for Population Activities, the UN Fund for Population Activities (UNFPA) was established as a Fund of the UN General Assembly in 1972 and was made a subsidiary organ of the UN General Assembly in 1979, with the UNDP Governing Council designated as its governing body. In 1987 UNFPA's name was changed to the United Nations Population Fund (retaining the same acronym).

UN Specialized Agencies

GENERAL AGREEMENT ON TARIFFS AND TRADE—GATT

Address: Centre William Rappard, 154 rue de Lausanne, 1211 Geneva 21, Switzerland.

Telephone: (22) 7395007; **telex:** 412324; **fax:** (22) 7395458.

GATT was established in 1948 as a multilateral treaty aiming to liberalize world trade and place it on a secure basis. Contracting parties conduct negotiations on specific trade problems affecting individual commodities or countries, and also major multilateral trade negotiations.

INTERNATIONAL ATOMIC ENERGY AGENCY—IAEA

Address: POB 100, Wagramerstrasse 5, 1400 Vienna, Austria.

Telephone: (1) 2360; **telex:** 1-12645; **fax:** (1) 234564.

The Agency was founded in 1957 with the aim of enlarging the contribution of atomic energy to peace, health and prosperity throughout the world, through technical co-operation (assisting research on and practical application of atomic energy for peaceful uses) and safeguards (ensuring that materials and services provided by the Agency are not used for any military purpose).

INTERNATIONAL CIVIL AVIATION ORGANIZATION—ICAO

Address: 1000 ouest, rue Sherbrooke, Montréal, PQ H3A 2R2, Canada.

Telephone: (514) 285-8219; **telex:** 05-24513; **fax:** (514) 288-4772.

ICAO was founded in 1947 to develop the techniques of international air navigation and to help in the planning and improvement of international air transport. It is based on the Convention on International Civil Aviation, signed in Chicago, 1944.

Regional Office for Western and Central Africa: BP 2356, Dakar, Senegal; tel. 23-54-52; telex 61348; fax 23-69-26.

Regional Office for Eastern and Southern Africa: POB 46294, Nairobi, Kenya; tel. 333930; telex 25295; fax 520199.

INTERNATIONAL LABOUR ORGANISATION—ILO

Address: 4 route des Morillons, 1211 Geneva 22, Switzerland.

Telephone: (22) 7996111; **telex:** 415647; **fax:** (22) 7988685.

ILO was founded in 1919 to work for social justice as a basis for lasting peace. It carries out this mandate by promoting decent living standards, satisfactory conditions of work and pay and adequate employment opportunities. Methods of action include the creation of international labour standards; the provision of technical co-operation services; and research and publications on social and labour matters.

Regional Office for Africa: 01 BP 3960, Abidjan 01, Côte d'Ivoire; tel. 32-27-16.

INTERNATIONAL MARITIME ORGANIZATION—IMO

Address: 4 Albert Embankment, London, SE1 7SR, England.

Telephone: (71) 735-7611; **telex:** 23588; **fax:** (71) 587-3210.

The Inter-Governmental Maritime Consultative Organization (IMCO) began operations in 1959, as a specialized agency of the UN to facilitate co-operation among governments on technical matters affecting international shipping. Its main functions are the achievement of safe and efficient navigation, and the control of pollution caused by ships and craft operating in the marine environment. IMCO became IMO in 1982.

INTERNATIONAL TELECOMMUNICATION UNION—ITU

Address: Place des Nations, 1211 Geneva 20, Switzerland.

Telephone: (22) 7305111; **telex:** 421000; **fax:** (22) 7337256.

Founded in 1865, ITU became a specialized agency of the UN in 1947. It acts to encourage world co-operation in the use of telecommunication, to promote technical development and to harmonize national policies in the field.

UNITED NATIONS INDUSTRIAL DEVELOPMENT ORGANIZATION—UNIDO

Address: POB 300, 1400 Vienna, Austria.

Telephone: (1) 211310; **telex:** 135612; **fax:** (1) 232156.

UNIDO began operations in 1967, following a resolution of the UN General Assembly, to assist in the industrialization of the developing countries through direct assistance and mobilization of national and international resources.

UNIVERSAL POSTAL UNION—UPU

Address: Case postale, 3000 Berne 15, Switzerland.

Telephone: (31) 3503111; **telex:** 912761; **fax:** (31) 3503110.

The General Postal Union was founded by the Treaty of Berne (1874), begining operations in July 1875. Three years later its name was changed to the Universal Postal Union. In 1948 UPU became a specialized agency of the UN. It aims to develop and unify the international postal service, to study problems and to provide training.

WORLD INTELLECTUAL PROPERTY ORGANIZATION—WIPO

Address: 34 chemin des Colombettes, 1211 Geneva 20, Switzerland.

Telephone: (022) 7309111; **telex:** 412912; **fax:** (022) 7335428.

WIPO was established in 1970. It became a specialized agency of the UN in 1974. WIPO aims to promote the protection of intellectual property (e.g. industrial and technical patents and literary copyrights) throughout the world through co-operation among states and, where appropriate, with other international organizations. It also centralizes the administration of the Unions which deal with legal and technical aspects of intellectual property. Each Union is founded on a multilateral treaty.

WORLD METEOROLOGICAL ORGANIZATION—WMO

Address: CP 2300, 41 ave Giuseppe Motta, 1211 Geneva 2, Switzerland.

Telephone: (22) 7308111; **telex:** 414199; **fax:** (22) 7342326.

WMO started its activities in 1951, aiming to improve the exchange of weather information and its applications.

Regional Office for Africa: BP 605, Bujumbura, Burundi; tel. (2) 25237; telex 5027; fax (2) 22990.

United Nations Information Centres

Burkina Faso: rue de la Gare 218, Secteur no 3, BP 135, Ouagadougou; tel. (3) 306076; telex 5302; fax (3) 311322. (Also covers Chad, Mali and Niger.)

Burundi: ave de la Poste 117, place de l'Indépendance, BP 2160, Bujumbura; tel. (2) 25018; telex 5078; fax (2) 25850.

Cameroon: Immeuble Kamden, rue Joseph Clère, BP 836, Yaoundé; tel. 22-50-43; telex 978-8304; fax 23-51-73. (Also covers the Central African Republic and Gabon.)

Congo: ave Foch, Case ORTF 15, BNP 13210, Brazzaville; tel. 835090; telex 5399; fax 836140.

Ethiopia: Africa Hall, POB 3001, Addis Ababa; tel. (1) 517200; telex 976-21029; fax (1) 514416.

Ghana: Roman Ridge Ambassadorial Estate, Extension Area, Plot N78, Accra; tel. 666851; telex 0942452; fax 665578. (Also covers Sierra Leone.)

Kenya: POB 34135, United Nations Office, Gigiri, Nairobi; tel. (2) 333930; telex 963-22447; fax (2) 2520711. (Also covers Seychelles and Uganda.)

Lesotho: POB 301, cnr Kingsway and Hilton Rd, opposite Sanlam Centre, Maseru 100; tel. 312496; telex 342; fax 310042.

Liberia: POB 274, Liberian Bank for Development and Investment Bldg, Tubman Blvd, Monrovia; tel. 262345; telex 4334.

Madagascar: 22 rue Rainitovo, Antasahavola, BP 1348, Antananarivo; tel. (2) 24115; telex 983-22345.

Namibia: Sanlan Centre, 154 Independence St, Windhoek; fax (61) 229220.

Nigeria: 17 Kingsway Rd, POB 1068, Ikoyi, Lagos; tel. (01) 680221; telex 22857; fax (01) 681324.

Senegal: 12 ave Roume, BP 154, Dakar; tel. 233070; telex 51450; fax 222679. (Also covers Cape Verde, Côte d'Ivoire, The Gambia, Guinea, Guinea-Bissau and Mauritania.)

Sudan: United Nations Compound, University Ave, POB 1992, Khartoum; tel. (11) 77816; telex 970214. (Also covers Somalia.)

Tanzania: Matasalamat Bldg, 1st Floor, Samora Machel Ave, POB 9224, Dar es Salaam; tel. (51) 25374; telex 975-41284; fax (51) 36836.

Togo: 107 blvd de 13 janvier, BP 911, Lomé; tel. 212306; telex 986-5261; fax 211641. (Also covers Benin.)

Zaire: Bâtiment Deuxième République, blvd du 30 juin, BP 7248, Kinshasa; tel. (12) 30400 ext. 67; telex 21164.

Zambia: POB 32905, Lusaka; tel. (1) 228487; telex 45930; fax (1) 222958. (Also covers Botswana, Malawi and Swaziland.)

Zimbabwe: Dolphin House, 123 Moffat St, POB 4408, Harare; tel. (4) 79-15-21; telex 22601; fax (4) 700873.

AFRICAN DEVELOPMENT BANK—ADB

Address: 01 BP 1387, Abidjan 01, Côte d'Ivoire.

Telephone: 20-44-44; **telex:** 23717; **fax:** 22-78-39.

Established in August 1963, the Bank began operations in July 1966.

AFRICAN MEMBERS

Algeria	Gabon	Nigeria
Angola	The Gambia	Rwanda
Benin	Ghana	São Tomé and Príncipe
Botswana	Guinea	Senegal
Burkina Faso	Guinea-Bissau	Seychelles
Burundi	Kenya	Sierra Leone
Cameroon	Lesotho	Somalia
Cape Verde	Liberia	Sudan
Central African Republic	Libya	Swaziland
Chad	Madagascar	Tanzania
Comoros	Malawi	Togo
Congo	Mali	Tunisia
Côte d'Ivoire	Mauritania	Uganda
Djibouti	Mauritius	Zaire
Egypt	Morocco	Zambia
Equatorial Guinea	Mozambique	Zimbabwe
Ethiopia	Namibia	
	Niger	

There are also 25 non-African members.

Organization

(June 1994)

BOARD OF GOVERNORS

The highest policy-making body of the Bank. Each member country nominates one Governor, usually its Minister of Finance and Economic Affairs, and an alternate Governor. The Board meets once a year. It elects the Board of Directors and the President.

BOARD OF DIRECTORS

The Board consists of 18 members (of whom six are non-African and hold 33.33% of the voting power), elected by the Board of Governors for a term of three years; it is responsible for the general operations of the Bank. It holds ordinary meetings twice a month.

OFFICERS

The President is responsible for the organization and the day-to-day operations of the Bank under guidance of the Board of Directors. The President is elected for a five-year term and serves as the Chairman of the Board of Directors. He is assisted by five Vice-Presidents, elected for a three-year term by the Board of Directors on his recommendation.

The Bank's activities are divided into three sections (for eastern, western and central Africa) and there is a separate department for disbursements. There are regional offices in Cameroon, Ethiopia, Guinea, Kenya, Morocco, Nigeria and Zimbabwe.

Executive President and Chairman of Board of Directors: Babacar N'Diaye (Senegal).

Secretary-General: Hedi Meliane.

FINANCIAL STRUCTURE

The Bank uses a unit of account (BUA) which is equivalent to one United States dollar before the devaluation of 1971. In 1992 the value of BUA was US $1.37500. The unit of account of the African Development Fund (see below) is known as the FUA and in 1992 had a value of $1.26645. In July 1993 the Fund decided to align the value of the FUA to that of the BUA, with effect from 1 January 1993.

The capital stock of the Bank was at first exclusively open for subscription by African countries, with each member's subscription consisting of an equal number of paid-up and callable shares. In 1978, however, the Governors agreed to open the capital stock of the Bank to subscription by non-regional states on the basis of nine principles aimed at maintaining the African character of the institution. The decision was finally ratified in May 1982, and the participation of non-regional countries became effective on 30 December. It was agreed that African members should still hold two-thirds of the share capital, that all loan operations should be restricted to African members, and that the Bank's President should always be an African national. In 1992 the ADB's authorized capital was US $22,275. At the end of 1992 subscribed capital was $21,017.3m. (of which the paid-up portion was $2,523.3m.).

Activities

The ADB Group of development financing institutions comprises the African Development Fund (ADF) and the Nigeria Trust Fund (NTF), which provide concessionary loans, and the African Development Bank itself.

At the end of 1992 total loan and grant approvals by the ADB Group since the beginning of its operations amounted to US $25,325m. and increased to $27,843m. at the end of 1993. In 1992 the group approved loans and grants amounting to $2,993m., compared with $3,447m. in 1991. Disbursement of loans and grants during 1992 increased to $2,164m. from $2,127m. in 1991. Public utilities received the largest proportion of group loans (21.6%), while multi-sector activities (including structural adjustment loans) received 19.4%, social projects 18%, agriculture 16.8%, transport 13.7%, and industry 10.5%.

The ADB contributed funds for the establishment in 1986 of the Africa Project Development Facility, which assists the private sector in Africa by providing advisory services and finance for entrepreneurs: it is managed by the International Finance Corporation (IFC—q.v.). In 1989 the ADB, in co-ordination with IFC and UNDP, created the African Management Services Company (AMSCo) which provides management support and training to private companies in Africa.

The Bank also provides technical assistance to regional member countries in the form of experts' services, pre-investment feasibility studies, and staff training; much of this assistance is financed through bilateral aid funds contributed by non-African member states. In 1990 the ADB established the African Business Round Table (ABR), which is composed of the chief executives of Africa's leading corporations. The ABR aims to strengthen Africa's private sector, promote intra-African trade and investment, and attract foreign investment to Africa. The ABR is chaired by the ADB's Executive President and held its third annual meeting in Abidjan in March 1993. In early 1992 plans to create a 'round table' of African and US business executives in order to encourage US investment in Africa were announced by the ADB. The new group, which was established in Côte d'Ivoire later in that year, would also help to channel technical assistance to newly established African firms.

In 1990 a Memorandum of Understanding for the Reinforcement of Co-operation between the Organization of African Unity (OAU—q.v.), the UN's Economic Commission for Africa (q.v.) and the ADB was signed by the three organizations. The ADB is actively involved in the development of the Pan-African Economic Community (PAEC), the creation of which was agreed by member states of the OAU in 1991, and which was to be fully effective by 2025. In 1992 the Bank was involved in the drafting of protocols to the treaty establishing the PAEC.

The ADB co-ordinated preparations for the establishment of an African Export Import Bank (Afreximbank), which became operational in December 1993 with the remit to increase the volume of African exports and to expand intra-African trade. The Bank's authorized capital amounted to US $750m., and by May 1994 almost $500m. had been subscribed by the ADB itself, African governments and central banks, African and non-African financial institutions and private investors. The new bank was to promote African trade by financing exporters and importers directly and indirectly through trade finance institutions such as commercial banks. The Afreximbank has its headquarters in Cairo, Egypt, with a southern African branch in Harare, Zimbabwe.

AFRICAN DEVELOPMENT BANK (ADB)

The Bank makes loans at a variable annual interest rate (7.5% in 1990), plus commission and commitment fees of 1% each. Loan approvals amounted to $1,868m. for 36 loans in 1992, compared with $2,254m. for 41 loans in 1991.

AFRICAN DEVELOPMENT FUND (ADF)

The Fund commenced operations in 1973. It grants interest-free loans to African countries for projects with repayment over 50 years (including a 10-year grace period) and with a service charge of 0.75% per annum. Grants for project feasibility studies are made to the poorest countries.

In 1987 donor countries agreed on a fifth replenishment of the Fund's resources, amounting to $2,800m. for 1988–90. In future 85% of available resources was to be reserved for the poorest countries (those with annual GDP per caput of less than $510, at 1985 prices). Commitments approved by the ADF in 1992 amounted to $1,099m. for 106 operations, compared with $1,158m. for 122 operations in 1991. In that year a sixth replenishment of the Fund's resources amounting to $3,340m. was approved for 1991–93. In May 1993 the Bank's Board of Directors proposed an increase of 50% for the seventh replenishment of the Fund's resources. However, in May 1994, donor countries withheld funds to replenish the Fund until the ADB imposes greater restrictions on its lending policies and reduces its administrative costs.

NIGERIA TRUST FUND (NTF)

The Agreement establishing the Nigeria Trust Fund was signed in February 1976 by the Bank and the Government of Nigeria. The Fund is administered by the Bank and its loans are granted for up to 25 years, including grace periods of up to five years, and carry 0.75% commitment charges and 4% interest charges. The loans are intended to provide financing for projects in co-operation with other lending institutions. In early 1992 a diversification of the activities of the Fund (which had hitherto focused on project financing) was announced. The Fund was to establish a data-base providing information on African and international financial institutions able to finance African trade, with the aim of promoting the private sector and trade between African countries.

In 1992 lending amounted to $26.6m. for four loans, compared with $34.3m. for four loans in 1991.

Summary of Bank Group Activities (US $ million)

	1991	1992	Cumulative total*
ADB loans			
Amount approved	2,254.41	1,867.78	15,735.23
Disbursements	1,473.89	1,460.02	8,347.64
ADF loans and grants			
Amount approved	1,157.94	1,099.01	9,307.10
Disbursements	641.33	688.03	4,394.87
NTF loans			
Amount approved	34.33	26.61	282.61
Disbursements	12.05	16.09	178.51
Group total			
Amount approved	3,446.68	2,933.40	25,324.94
Disbursements	2,127.27	2,164.14	12,921.02

* Since the initial operations of the three institutions (1967 for ADB, 1974 for ADF and 1976 for NTF).

Bank Group Loan and Grant Approvals by Region, 1991–92 (US $ million)

Country	1991	%	1992	%
Central Africa	391.56	11.36	307.29	10.27
Angola	94.43		56.41	
Burundi	24.37		34.60	
Cameroon	136.62		61.44	
Central African Republic	23.72		12.66	
Chad	34.78		—	
Congo	—		—	
Equatorial Guinea	2.12		12.66	
Gabon	34.33		128.75	
Rwanda	27.67		0.76	
São Tomé & Príncipe	4.73		—	
Zaire	8.80		—	
Multinational	—		—	
East Africa	362.96	10.53	351.73	11.75
Comoros	11.20		1.43	
Djibouti	20.50		16.64	
Ethiopia	15.41		276.56	
Kenya	107.16		6.33	
Madagascar	27.47		35.31	
Mauritius	37.11		—	
Seychelles	24.17		—	
Somalia	—		—	
Uganda	119.93		15.45	
North Africa	944.06	27.39	1,120.55	37.43
Algeria	70.21		257.74	
Egypt	143.04		152.81	
Mauritania	34.74		12.66	
Morocco	378.92		332.64	
Sudan	7.53		45.28	
Tunisia	309.62		319.41	
Southern Africa	499.47	14.49	520.12	17.37
Botswana	41.61		—	
Lesotho	1.11		92.22	
Malawi	81.22		25.63	
Mozambique	29.00		150.96	
Namibia	0.90		18.17	
Swaziland	9.28		70.83	
Tanzania	52.72		124.94	
Zambia	58.59		35.84	
Zimbabwe	187.04		1.52	
Multinational	38.01		—	
West Africa	1,237.96	35.92	689.35	23.03
Benin	36.76		21.40	
Burkina Faso	69.55		14.56	
Cape Verde	28.78		—	
Côte d'Ivoire	105.03		220.84	
Gambia	3.95		17.54	
Ghana	69.12		4.20	
Guinea	76.73		16.98	
Guinea-Bissau	2.11		—	
Mali	51.41		36.76	
Niger	—		—	
Nigeria	522.05		278.45	
Senegal	185.87		17.63	
Sierra Leone	38.27		32.93	
Togo	44.16		15.83	
Multinational	4.16		12.22	
Multiregional	10.68	0.31	4.37	0.15
Total	3,446.68	100.00	2,993.40	100.00

ASSOCIATED INSTITUTIONS

The ADB actively participated in the establishment of four associated institutions:

Africa Reinsurance Corporation—Africa-Re: Reinsurance House, 46 Marina, PMB 12765, Lagos, Nigeria; tel. (1) 66-52-82; telex 22647; f. 1977; started operations in 1978; its purpose is to foster the development of the insurance and reinsurance industry in Africa and to promote the growth of national and regional underwriting capacities. Africa-Re has an authorized capital of US $30m., of which the ADB holds 10%; paid-up capital was $9.7m. in June 1991. There are nine directors, one appointed by the Bank. Mems: 40 countries and the ADB. Sec.-Gen. Bakary Kamara.

Association of African Development Finance Institutions—AADFI: c/o ADB, 01 BP 1387, Abidjan 01, Côte d'Ivoire; tel. 20-44-44; telex 23717; f. 1975; aims to promote co-operation among the development banks of the region in matters relating to development ideas, project design and financing. Mems: 81 institutions in 53 African and non-African countries. Sec.-Gen. J. A. Hammond (acting)

Shelter-Afrique (Société pour l'habitat et le logement territorial en Afrique): Mamlaka Rd, POB 41479, Nairobi, Kenya; tel. (2) 722305; telex 25355; fax (2) 722024; f. 1982 to finance housing in ADB member countries. Share capital is US $300m., held by 28 African countries, the ADB, Africa-Re and the Commonwealth Development Corporation. Sec.-Gen. Dr T. Ramdin.

Société internationale financière pour les investissements et le développement en Afrique—SIFIDA: 22 rue François-Perréard, BP 310, 1225 Chêne-Bourg/Génève, Switzerland; tel. (22) 3486000; telex 418647; fax (22) 3482161; f. 1970; holding company which aims to promote the establishment and growth of productive enterprises in Africa. It finances industrial projects, organizes syndicated loans, project identification and development, and export finance. Its shareholders include the ADB, IFC and about 130 financial, industrial and commercial institutions in North America, the Caribbean, Europe, Asia and Australia; authorized share capital US $50m., subscribed capital $21.1m. Chair. Derek C. Pey; Man. Dir Philippe Séchaud. Publ. *African Banking Directory* (annually).

PUBLICATIONS

Annual Report.

ADB Today (every 2 months).

African Development Report.

African Development Review.
Basic Information (annually).
Economic Research Papers.
Quarterly Operational Summary.
Statistical Handbook (annually).
Summaries of operations in each member country and various background documents.

THE COMMONWEALTH

Address: Marlborough House, Pall Mall, London, SW1Y 5HX, England.

Telephone: (71) 839-3411; **telex:** 27678; **fax:** (71) 930-0827.

The Commonwealth is a voluntary association of 51 independent states, comprising nearly one-quarter of the world's population. It includes the United Kingdom and most of its former dependencies, and former dependencies of Australia and New Zealand (themselves Commonwealth countries). All Commonwealth countries accept Queen Elizabeth II as the symbol of the free association of the independent member nations and as such the Head of the Commonwealth.

MEMBERS IN AFRICA SOUTH OF THE SAHARA

Botswana	Mauritius	Swaziland
The Gambia	Namibia	Tanzania
Ghana	Nigeria	Uganda
Kenya	Seychelles	Zambia
Lesotho	Sierra Leone	Zimbabwe
Malawi	South Africa	

Dependencies

British Indian Ocean Territory
St Helena
  Ascension
  Tristan da Cunha

Organization

(June 1994)

The Commonwealth is not a federation: there is no central government nor are there any rigid contractual obligations such as bind members of the United Nations.

The Commonwealth has no written constitution but its members subscribe to the ideals of the Declaration of Commonwealth Principles (see below) unanimously approved by a meeting of heads of government in Singapore in 1971. Members also approved the 1977 statement on apartheid in sport (the Gleneagles Agreement); the 1979 Lusaka Declaration on Racism and Racial Prejudice (see below); the 1981 Melbourne Declaration on relations between developed and developing countries; the 1983 New Delhi Statement on Economic Action; the 1983 Goa Declaration on International Security; the 1985 Nassau Declaration on World Order; the Commonwealth Accord on Southern Africa (1985); the 1987 Vancouver Declaration on World Trade; the Okanagan Statement and Programme of Action on Southern Africa (1987); the Langkawi Declaration on the Environment (1989); the Kuala Lumpur Statement on Southern Africa (1989); the Harare Commonwealth Declaration (1991) (see below); the Ottawa Declaration on Women and Structural Adjustment (1991); and the Limassol Statement on the Uruguay Round of multilateral trade negotiations (1993).

MEETINGS OF HEADS OF GOVERNMENT

Meetings are private and informal and operate not by voting but by consensus. The emphasis is on consultation and exchange of views for co-operation. A communiqué is issued at the end of every meeting. Meetings are held every two years in different capitals in the Commonwealth. The 1993 meeting was held in Cyprus in October, and the 1995 meeting was to be held in New Zealand.

OTHER CONSULTATIONS

Meetings at ministerial and official level are also held regularly. Since 1959 finance ministers have met in a Commonwealth country in the week prior to the annual meetings of the IMF and the World Bank. Meetings on education, legal, women's and youth affairs are held at ministerial level every three years. Ministers of health hold annual meetings, with major meetings every three years, and ministers of agriculture meet every two years. Ministers of trade, labour and employment, industry, science and the environment also hold periodic meetings.

Senior officials—cabinet secretaries, permanent secretaries to heads of government and others—meet regularly in the year between meetings of heads of government to provide continuity and to exchange views on various developments.

COMMONWEALTH SECRETARIAT

The Secretariat, established by Commonwealth heads of government in 1965, operates as an international organization at the service of all Commonwealth countries. It organizes consultations between governments and runs programmes of co-operation. Meetings of heads of government, ministers and senior officials decide these programmes and provide overall direction.

The Secretariat is headed by a secretary-general (elected by heads of government), assisted by three deputy secretaries-general. One deputy is responsible for political affairs, one for economic and social affairs, and one for development co-operation (including the Commonwealth Fund for Technical Co-operation—see below). In 1993 the Secretariat was restructured in accordance with priorities for action by the Commonwealth set out in the Harare Commonwealth Declaration. As a result, the existing 17 Divisions were replaced from 1 July 1993 by 13 Divisions in the fields of political affairs; legal and constitutional affairs; information and public affairs; administration; economic affairs; human resource development; women's and youth affairs; science and technology; economic and legal advisory services; export and industrial development; management and training services; general technical assistance services; and strategic planning and evaluation.

Secretary-General: Chief E. CHUKWUEMEKA (EMEKA) ANYAOKU (Nigeria).

Deputy Secretary-General (Political): Sir ANTHONY SIAGURU (Papua New Guinea).

Deputy Secretary-General (Economic and Social): Sir HUMPHREY MAUD (UK).

Deputy Secretary-General (Development Co-operation): EWAN (NICK) HARE (Canada).

BUDGET

The Secretariat's budget for 1992/93 was 8,981,530, and the budget for 1993/94 was £9,141,160. Member governments meet the cost of the Secretariat through subscriptions on a scale related to income and population, similar to the scale for contributions to the United Nations.

Activities

INTERNATIONAL AFFAIRS

In 1977 Commonwealth heads of government reached an agreement on discouraging sporting links with South Africa, The Gleneagles Agreement on Sporting Contacts with South Africa, which was designed to express their abhorrence of that country's policy of apartheid. At their 1979 meeting in Lusaka, Zambia, the heads of government endorsed a nine-point plan to direct Zimbabwe-Rhodesia towards internationally recognized independence. The leaders also issued the Lusaka Declaration on Racism and Racial Prejudice as a formal expression of their abhorrence of all forms of racist policy.

In October 1985 heads of government, meeting at Nassau, Bahamas, issued the Nassau Declaration on World Order, reaffirming Commonwealth commitment to the United Nations, to international co-operation for development and to the eventual elimination of nuclear weapons. The same meeting issued the Commonwealth Accord on Southern Africa, calling on the South African authorities to dismantle apartheid and open dialogue with a view to establishing a representative government. The meeting also established a Commonwealth 'Eminent Persons Group'. It visited South Africa in February and March 1986 and attempted unsuccessfully to establish a dialogue between the South African Government and opposition leaders. In August the heads of government of seven Commonwealth countries (Australia, the Bahamas, Canada, India, the

United Kingdom, Zambia and Zimbabwe) met to consider the Group's report, and (with the exception of the United Kingdom) agreed to adopt a series of measures to exert economic pressure on the South African Government, and to encourage other countries to adopt such measures. These included bans on the following: air links with South Africa; government assistance to investment in, and trade with, South Africa; government contracts with majority-owned South African companies; promotion of tourist visits to South Africa; new bank loans to South Africa; imports of uranium, coal, iron and steel from South Africa.

In October 1987 heads of government, meeting at Vancouver, Canada, issued the Okanagan Statement and Programme of Action on Southern Africa, to strengthen the Commonwealth effort to end apartheid in South Africa. They also established the Commonwealth Committee of Foreign Ministers on Southern Africa, comprising the ministers of foreign affairs of Australia, Canada, Guyana, India, Nigeria, Tanzania, Zambia and Zimbabwe (and, subsequently, of Malaysia). The Committee was to provide impetus and guidance in furtherance of the objectives of the Statement. The Vancouver meeting also issued the Vancouver Declaration on World Trade, condemning protectionism and reaffirming the leaders' commitment to work for a durable and just world trading system. They pledged to work to strengthen the General Agreement on Tariffs and Trade (GATT), and gave their support to the Uruguay Round of multilateral trade negotiations (begun in 1986).

In October 1989 heads of government, meeting in Kuala Lumpur, Malaysia, issued the Langkawi Declaration on the Environment, a 16-point joint programme of action to combat environmental degradation and ensure sustainable development.

In October 1991 heads of government, meeting in Harare, Zimbabwe, issued the Harare Commonwealth Declaration, in which they reaffirmed their commitment to the Commonwealth Principles declared in 1971, and stressed the need to promote sustainable development and the alleviation of poverty. The Declaration placed emphasis on the promotion of democracy and respect for human rights and resolved to strengthen the Commonwealth's capacity to assist countries in entrenching democratic practices. The meeting also welcomed the political reforms introduced by the South African Government and urged all South African political parties to commence negotiations on a new constitution as soon as possible. The meeting endorsed measures on the phased removal of sanctions against South Africa. 'People-to-people' sanctions (including consular and visa restrictions, cultural and scientific boycotts and restrictions on tourism promotion) were removed immediately, with economic sanctions to remain in place until a constitution for a new democratic, non-racial state had been agreed. The sports boycott would continue to be repealed on a sport-by-sport basis, as each sport in South Africa became integrated and non-racial. The embargo on the supply of armaments would remain in place until a post-apartheid, democratic regime had been firmly established in South Africa. At the request of the heads of government in Harare, the Commonwealth Secretary-General went to South Africa in November and held discussions with the Government and the major political parties. He offered the Commonwealth's assistance in the multi-party negotiations on the future of South Africa which were to begin in late December. An invitation to the Commonwealth to send a mission to the conference was duly issued, and in late December a group of six eminent Commonwealth citizens was dispatched to observe the negotiations and to assist the process where possible. In mid-October 1992, in a fresh attempt to assist the South African peace process, a Commonwealth team of 18 observers was sent to monitor political violence in the country. A second phase of the Commonwealth Mission to South Africa (COMSA) began in February 1993, comprising 10 observers from nine countries with backgrounds in policing, the law, politics and public life. COMSA issued a report in May in which it urged a concerted effort to build a culture of political tolerance in South Africa. In a report on its third phase, issued in December 1993, COMSA appealed strongly to all political parties to participate in the transitional arrangements leading to democratic elections.

In October 1993 the Commonwealth heads of government, meeting in Limassol, Cyprus, agreed that a democratic and non-racial South Africa would be invited to join the organization; a Commonwealth team of 60 experts was to monitor the South African elections, to be held in April 1994, constituting the largest operation ever undertaken by the Commonwealth. The heads of government endorsed the removal of all economic sanctions against South Africa, but agreed to retain the arms embargo until a post-apartheid, democratic government had been established. The summit meeting's communiqué urged a speedy withdrawal from Cyprus of all Turkish forces and settlers: this was the first time that the Commonwealth had taken sides so explicitly in the dispute over Cyprus. As an expression of the Commonwealth's collective support for the Uruguay Round of negotiations under GATT, the heads of government established a five-nation task force, which, in November, met with representatives of the Governments of France, Belgium, Germany, Switzerland, the United Kingdom, the USA and Japan to emphasize the importance of a successful and balanced conclusion to the Round.

Political Affairs Division: assists consultation among member governments on international and Commonwealth matters of common interest. In association with host governments, it organizes the meetings of heads of government and senior officials. The Division services committees and special groups set up by heads of government dealing with political matters. The Secretariat has observer status at the United Nations, and the Division manages an office in New York to enable small states, which would otherwise be unable to afford facilities there, to maintain a presence at the United Nations. The Division monitors political developments in the Commonwealth and international progress in such matters as disarmament, the concerns of small states, dismantling of apartheid and the Law of the Sea. It also undertakes research on matters of common interest to member governments, and reports back to them. The Division is involved in diplomatic training and consular co-operation.

The Division is responsible for election monitoring, conducted by the Commonwealth. In 1990–94 it serviced observer missions sent to monitor parliamentary, presidential or other general elections in Malaysia, Bangladesh, Zambia, Seychelles, Guyana, Ghana, Kenya, Lesotho, Pakistan, South Africa and Malawi, at the request of their governments. The Division also undertook preparatory missions in connection with these elections. The mission to South Africa (the Commonwealth Observer Group to South Africa—COGSA), deployed in April 1994, constituted the largest ever monitoring undertaking by the Commonwealth. COGSA numbered some 160 members, including COMSA observers and experts providing technical advice.

LAW

Legal and Constitutional Affairs Division: services the meetings of law ministers and attorneys-general. It operates a Commonwealth unit to help to counter commercial crime, administers a training programme for legislative draftsmen, and assists co-operation and exchange of information on law reform, taxation policy, extradition, the reciprocal enforcement of judgments, the Commonwealth Scheme for Mutual Assistance in Criminal Matters, the scheme for the Transfer of Convicted Offenders within the Commonwealth, and other legal matters. It liaises with the Commonwealth Magistrates' Association, the Commonwealth Legal Education Association, the Commonwealth Lawyers' Association, the Commonwealth Association of Legislative Counsel, and with other international organizations. It also provides in-house legal advice for the Secretariat, and helps to prepare the triennial Commonwealth Law Conference for the practising profession. An annual 'colloquium' of chief justices is also held. The quarterly *Commonwealth Law Bulletin* reports on legal developments in and beyond the Commonwealth.

The Division also includes a unit for the promotion of human rights in the Commonwealth.

ECONOMIC CO-OPERATION

Economic Affairs Division: organizes and services the regular meetings of Commonwealth ministers of finance, and periodic meetings of ministers of labour and employment, and assists in servicing the biennial meetings of heads of government. It engages in research and analysis on economic issues of interest to member governments; organizes seminars and conferences of government officials and experts; and publishes regular bulletins on international development policies, capital markets, regional co-operation and on basic statistics of small countries. The Division initiated a major programme of technical assistance to enable developing Commonwealth countries to participate in the Uruguay Round of multilateral trade negotiations. The Division also services groups of experts on economic affairs commissioned by governments. Such groups have reported on, among other things, protectionism; obstacles to the North-South negotiating process; reform of the international financial and trading system; the debt crisis; management of technological change; the special needs of small states; the impact of change on the development process; environmental issues; women and structural adjustment; and youth unemployment. The Division co-ordinates the Secretariat's environmental work. The Division undertook preparatory work for the establishment of a Commonwealth Equity Fund, initiated in September 1990, to allow developing member countries to improve their access to private institutional investment, and promoted a Caribbean Investment

Fund. The Division is supporting the establishment of a Commonwealth Privatisation Fund (CPF), which was to invest in newly privatized companies on a commercial basis. The CPF was expected to become operational in late 1994.

The restructured Division, while maintaining its focus on international and macroeconomic concerns, is giving more attention than previously to microeconomic and national issues.

HUMAN RESOURCES

Human Resource Development Division: consists of two departments concerned with education and health. The Division co-operates with member countries in devising strategies for human resource development; in 1993 it published a report on this subject entitled 'Foundation for the Future'.

The **Education Department** arranges specialist seminars and co-operative projects and commissions studies in areas identified by ministers of education, whose three-yearly meetings it also services. Its present areas of emphasis include improving the quality of basic education, facilitating Commonwealth student mobility and co-operation at tertiary level to strengthen higher education, and assisting ministers of education during conditions of austerity.

The **Health Department,** guided by the meetings of Commonwealth health ministers, assists governments to strengthen their health services. It supports the work of regional health organizations, undertakes studies and provides advisory services at the request of governments.

Management and Training Services Division: provides awards, arranges training attachments and study visits. Applicants must be nominated by their governments. In 1992/93 4,400 trainees were supported, of which the majority were at middle management and technician level. Most training is provided in developing countries. The Division administers the Langkawi awards for the study of environmental subjects, funded by Canada. A new programme of training in administration and technical services, to enable black South Africans to occupy positions in public administration and business in a non-racial South Africa, was devised in 1991. The Division provided assistance for the establishment of a Commonwealth Local Government Forum, launched in March 1994, which was to promote local democracy and participatory government by providing a network for national local government associations.

Women's and Youth Affairs Division: consists of the Women's Affairs Department and the Youth Affairs Department.

The **Women's Affairs Department** seeks to enhance women's participation in and benefits from development through training, policy analysis, research, and consultancies on issues such as employment and income, women and the environment, and violence against women.

The Youth Affairs Department administers the Commonwealth Youth Programme, funded through separate contributions from governments, which seeks to promote the involvement of young people in the economic and social development of their countries. It provides policy advice for governments and operates regional training programmes for youth workers and policy-makers through its centres in Africa, Asia, the Caribbean and the Pacific. It conducts a Youth Study Fellowship scheme, a Youth Project Fund, a Youth Exchange Programme (in the Caribbean), and a Youth Service Awards Scheme, holds conferences and seminars, carries out research and disseminates information.

SCIENCE

Science and Technology Division: provides the secretariat of the Commonwealth Science Council of 36 governments; organizes regional and global programmes to enhance the scientific and technological capabilities of member countries, through co-operative research, training and the exchange of information. Work is carried out in the areas of energy, water and mineral resources, biological resources, environmental planning, agriculture, industrial support, and science management and organization. The Division administers the Commonwealth Consultative Group on Technology Management, which was established in 1990.

TECHNICAL CO-OPERATION

Commonwealth Fund for Technical Co-operation (CFTC): financed by voluntary subscriptions from all member governments, funds the development co-operation activities of the Secretariat. Among these activities the Secretariat provides technical assistance to developing Commonwealth countries, including consultancy and advisory services, assigns experts to work in member countries, and finances specialized training. The CFTC also supports human resource development. CFTC expenditure during the year ending 30 June 1993 was £22.5m. and was estimated to be £23.1m. for 1993/94. The number of experts on long-term assignments in 1992/93 averaged some 225, with about 400 experts on assignments of less than six months' duration.

General Technical Assistance Division: supplies experts and consultants and commissions specialist studies. Each year it provides governments with experts in (for example) economics, telecommunications, computers, transport and agriculture.

Economic and Legal Advisory Services Division: is an in-house consultancy providing governments with assistance (including financial, legal and policy advice) in negotiations on natural resources and other investment projects, maritime boundary delimitation, macroeconomic policies and debt management.

Export and Industrial Development Division: assists governments in the development and implementation of industrial projects; assistance includes investment planning and project design, entrepreneurial development, transfer of technology, advice on environmental protection, and upgrading enterprises. It also assists governments to improve foreign exchange earnings through identification and exploration of export markets, using trade promotion events such as export business intensification programmes, buyer-seller meetings, integrated marketing programmes and contact promotion programmes. The Division includes an agricultural development unit.

The Secretariat also includes an Administration Division, a Strategic Planning and Evaluation Unit, and an Information and Public Affairs Division, which produces information publications, and radio and television programmes, about Commonwealth co-operation and consultation activities.

SELECTED PUBLICATIONS

Commonwealth Currents (every 2 months).
Commonwealth Declarations 1971–91.
Commonwealth Education News.
The Commonwealth Factbook.
Commonwealth Organisations (directory).
The Commonwealth Today (revised every 2 years).
In Common (quarterly newsletter of the Youth Programme).
International Development Policies (quarterly).
Link In (quarterly newsletter of the Women and Development Programme).
Notes on the Commonwealth (series of reference leaflets).
Report of the Commonwealth Secretary-General (every 2 years).
The Commonwealth Yearbook.
Numerous reports, studies and papers (catalogue available).

Commonwealth Organizations

(In the United Kingdom, unless otherwise stated)

AGRICULTURE AND FORESTRY

CAB INTERNATIONAL (CABI): Wallingford, Oxon, OX10 8DE; tel. (491) 832111; telex 847964; fax (491) 833508; f. 1929; formerly Commonwealth Agricultural Bureaux; consists of four institutes, five specialist information divisions and a development services unit, under the control of an executive council comprising representatives from member countries which contribute to its funds. CABI aims to improve human welfare through the generation, dissemination and application of scientific knowledge in support of sustainable development. It places particular emphasis on agriculture, forestry, human health and the management of natural resources, with priority given to the needs of developing countries.

Each institute and information division is concerned with its own particular branch of agricultural science and acts as an effective clearing house for the collection, collation and dissemination of information of value to research workers. The information, compiled from world-wide literature, is published in 26 main journals, 21 specialist journals and several serial publications. Annotated bibliographies provide information on specific topics, and review articles, books, maps and monographs are also issued. The CAB ABSTRACTS database is available on CD-Rom, as well as being accessible online through the following retrieval services: DIALOG (USA), BRS (USA), CAN/OLE (Canada), ESA-IRS (Italy), DIMDI (Germany), DATASTAR and STN (Japan); many organizations provide SDI services from CABI tapes.

In addition, Institutes of Entomology, Mycology and Parasitology provide identification and taxonomic services and the

Institute of Biological Control undertakes field work in biological control throughout the world. There are regional offices in Malaysia and Trinidad and Tobago. Dir-Gen. D. LAING.

International Institute of Biological Control: Silwood Park, Buckhurst Rd, Ascot, Berks, SL5 7TA; tel. (334) 872999; telex 93121-02255; fax (334) 875007; f. 1927 as the Farnham House Laboratory of the Imperial Institute of Entomology; transferred to Canada 1940 and to Trinidad 1962; since 1983 its main research and administrative centre has been in the United Kingdom, with field stations in Kenya, Malaysia, Pakistan, Switzerland and Trinidad; its purpose is the biological control of injurious insects and noxious weeds, and the collection and distribution throughout the world of beneficial organisms with which to attack the pests. Dir Dr J. K. WAAGE. Publs *Natural Enemy Databank, Biocontrol News and Information* (quarterly).

International Institute of Entomology: 56 Queen's Gate, London, SW7 5JR; tel. (71) 584-0067; telex 93121-02251; fax (71) 581-1676; f. 1913 for the collection, co-ordination and dissemination of all information concerning injurious and useful insects and other arthropods; undertakes identifications; organizes international training courses and workshops on applied taxonomy of insects and mites. Dir Prof. TEEWYN JONES. Publs *Bulletin of Entomological Research* (quarterly), *Distribution Maps of Pests* (18 a year), bibliographies and monographs.

International Institute of Parasitology: 395A Hatfield Rd, St Albans, Herts, AL4 0XU; tel. (727) 833151; telex 93121-02254; fax (727) 868721; f. 1929; conducts taxonomic and applied research on helminths (parasitic worms), particularly those of economic and medical importance, and on plant parasitic nematodes; provides advisory services and training. Dir W. HOMINICK.

International Mycological Institute: Bakeham Lane, Englefield Green, Egham, Surrey, TW20 9TY; tel. (784) 470111; telex 93121-02252; fax (784) 470909; f. 1920 for the collection and dissemination of information on the fungal, bacterial, virus and physiological disorders of plants; on fungal diseases of man and animals; and on the taxonomy of fungi; undertakes identifications of micro-fungi and plant pathogenic bacteria from all over the world; incorporates major collection of fungus cultures and a biodeterioration and industrial services centre; consultancy services, especially in industrial mycology, food spoilage by fungi, bacteria and yeasts, and surveys of plant diseases; holds training courses in the UK and in other countries. Dir Prof. D. L. HAWKSWORTH. Publs *Distribution Maps of Plant Diseases* (42 a year), *Index of Fungi* (2 a year), *Mycological Papers* (irregular), *Phytopathological Papers* (irregular), *Descriptions of Fungi and Bacteria* (4 sets a year), *Bibliography of Systematic Mycology* (2 a year), *Systema Ascomycetum* (2 a year), books on mycology and plant pathology.

Commonwealth Forestry Association: c/o Oxford Forestry Institute, South Parks Rd, Oxford, OX1 3RB; tel. (865) 275072; fax (865) 275074; f. 1921; produces, collects and circulates information relating to temperate, sub-tropical and tropical forestry and the commercial utilization of forest products and provides a means of communications in the Commonwealth and other interested countries. Mems: 1,700. Chair. P. J. WOOD. Publs *Commonwealth Forestry Review* (quarterly), *Commonwealth Forestry Handbook*.

Standing Committee on Commonwealth Forestry: Forestry Commission, 231 Corstorphine Rd, Edinburgh, EH12 7AT; tel. (31) 334-0303; telex 727879; fax (31) 334-0442; f. 1923 to provide continuity between Conferences, and to provide a forum for discussion on any forestry matters of common interest to member governments which may be brought to the Committee's notice by any member country or organization; mems about 50. 1993 Conference: Kuala Lumpur, Malaysia. Sec. (vacant). Publs *Newsletter*.

COMMONWEALTH STUDIES

Institute of Commonwealth Studies: 28 Russell Sq., London, WC1B 5DS; tel. (71) 580-5876; fax (71) 255-2160; f. 1949 to promote advanced study of the Commonwealth; provides a library and meeting place for postgraduate students and academic staff engaged in research in this field; offers postgraduate teaching. Incorporates the Sir Robert Menzies Centre for Australian Studies. Dir Prof. JAMES MANOR; Publs *Annual Report, Commonwealth Papers* (series), *Collected Seminar Papers, Newsletter, Theses in Progress in Commonwealth Studies.*

COMMUNICATIONS

Commonwealth Telecommunications Bureau: Clareville House, 26–27 Oxendon St, London, SW1Y 4EL; tel. (71) 930-5516; telex 27328; fax (71) 930-4248; f. 1967 to enhance the development of telecommunications in Commonwealth countries and contribute to the communications infrastructure required for economic and social development. Gen. Sec. GRAHAM H. CUNNOLD.

EDUCATION AND CULTURE

Association of Commonwealth Universities: John Foster House, 36 Gordon Sq., London, WC1H 0PF; tel. (71) 387-8572; fax (71) 387-2655; f. 1913; holds major meetings of Commonwealth universities and their executive heads; publishes factual information about Commonwealth universities and access to them; acts as a general information centre and provides an appointments service; hosts a management consultancy service; supplies secretariats for the Commonwealth Scholarship Commission in the United Kingdom and the Marshall Aid Commemoration Commission; administers various other fellowship and scholarship programmes. Mems: 432 universities in 32 Commonwealth countries or regions. Sec. Gen. Dr A. CHRISTODOULOU. Publs include *The Association of Commonwealth Universities: What it is and what it does* (annually), *Commonwealth Universities Yearbook, Checklist of University Institutions in the Commonwealth, ACU Bulletin of Current Documentation, Report of the Council of the ACU* (annually), *Quinquennial Report of the Secretary General to the Commonwealth Universities Congress, Awards for University Teachers and Research Workers, Awards for Postgraduate Study at Commonwealth Universities, Awards for First Degree Study at Commonwealth Universities, Awards for University Administrators and Librarians, Who's Who of Commonwealth University Vice-Chancellors, Presidents and Rectors, Appointments in Commonwealth Universities,* Student Information Papers (study abroad series).

Commonwealth Association of Science, Technology and Mathematics Educators—CASTME: c/o Fellowships and Training Programme, HRDG, Commonwealth Secretariat, Marlborough House, Pall Mall, London, SW1Y 5HX; tel. (71) 839-3411; telex 27678; f. 1974; special emphasis is given to the social significance of education in these subjects. Organizes an Awards Scheme to promote effective teaching and learning in these subjects, and biennial regional seminars. Pres. Dr MAURICE GOLDSMITH; Hon. Sec. Prof. S. T. BAJAH. Publ. *CASTME Journal* (quarterly).

Commonwealth Council for Educational Administration: c/o Faculty of Education, Nursing and Professional Studies, University of New England, Armidale, NSW 2351, Australia; tel. (67) 732543; telex 166050; fax (67) 733363; f. 1970; aims to foster quality in professional development and links among educational administrators; holds national and regional conferences, as well as visits and seminars. Mems: 30 affiliated groups representing 6,000 persons. Pres. Dr BILL MULFORD; Exec. Dir Dr BERNADETTE TAYLOR. Publs *Newsletter* (2 a year), *International Directions in Education, Studies in Educational Administration* (2 a year), *Directory of Courses*.

Commonwealth Institute: Kensington High St, London, W8 6NQ; tel. (71) 603-4535; fax (71) 602-7374; f. 1893 as the Imperial Institute; the centre for Commonwealth education and culture in the UK, the Institute provides educational facilities, including workshops, seminars, conferences and a programme for schools; houses a permanent exhibition designed to express Commonwealth countries in visual terms, and a picture library and multi-media resource centre; organizes visual arts exhibitions and performances of drama, dance and music. Dir-Gen. STEPHEN COX.

Commonwealth Institute Northern Regional Centre: Salts Mill, Victoria Rd, Shipley, Bradford, West Yorkshire, BD18 3LB; tel. (274) 530251; fax (274) 530253; facilities include an exhibition space, educational resources and an information service.

Commonwealth Institute, Scotland: 8 Rutland Sq., Edinburgh, EH1 2AS, Scotland; tel. (31) 229-6668; fax (31) 229-6041; Dir C. G. CARROL.

Commonwealth Music Association: Sebastian St, London EC1V 0JD; tel. (71) 253-0437; f. 1990 to promote inter-cultural understanding in the field of music, and to encourage exchanges between musicians, music educators and promotors within the Commonwealth. Convenor Dr AKIN EUBA.

League for the Exchange of Commonwealth Teachers: 7 Lion Yard, Tremadoc Rd, London, SW4 7NQ; tel. (71) 498-1101; fax (71) 720-5403; f. 1901; promotes educational exchanges for a period of one year between teachers in Australia, the Bahamas, Barbados, Bermuda, Canada, Guyana, India, Jamaica, Kenya, New Zealand, Pakistan and Trinidad and Tobago. Dir PATRICIA SWAIN. Publ. *Annual Report*.

HEALTH

Commonwealth Medical Association: BMA House, Tavistock Sq., London, WC1H 9JP; tel. (71) 383-6095; fax (71) 383-6195; f. 1962 for the exchange of information; provision of technical co-operation and advice; formulation and maintenance of a code of ethics; provision of continuing medical education; development and promotion of health education programmes; and liaison with WHO and the UN on health issues; meetings of its Council are held every three years. Mems: medical associations in Commonwealth countries. Dir MARIANNE HASLEGRAVE; Sec. Dr J. D. J. HAVARD. Publ. *Common Health* (quarterly bulletin).

Commonwealth Pharmaceutical Association: 1 Lambeth High St, London, SE1 7JN; tel. (71) 735-9141; telex 93121-131542; fax (71) 735-7629; f. 1970 to promote the interests of pharmaceutical sciences and the profession of pharmacy in the Commonwealth; to maintain high professional standards, encourage links between members and the creation of national associations; and to facilitate the dissemination of information. Holds conferences (every four years) and regional meetings. Mems: 38 pharmaceutical associations. Sec. RAYMOND DICKINSON. Publ. *Quarterly Newsletter*.

Commonwealth Society for the Deaf: Dilke House, Malet St, London, WC1E 7JA; tel. (71) 631-5311; promotes the health, education and general welfare of the deaf in developing Commonwealth countries; encourages and assists the development of educational facilities, the training of teachers of the deaf, and the provision of support for parents of deaf children; organizes visits by volunteer specialists to work for 2–3 weeks with local communities; provides audiological equipment and encourages the establishment of maintenance services for such equipment; conducts research into the causes and prevention of deafness. Admin. Sec. Miss E. LUBIENSKA. Publs *Annual Report, Research Report*.

Sight Savers (Royal Commonwealth Society for the Blind): Grosvenor Hall, Bolnore Rd, Haywards Heath, Sussex, RH16 4BX; tel. (444) 412424; telex 87167; fax (444) 415866; f. 1950 to prevent blindness and to promote the education, employment and welfare of blind people in the developing world; operates through governments and non-governmental organizations to contribute to the development of national and regional programmes; gives high priority to training local staff; Chair. DAVID THOMPSON; Dir A. W. JOHNS. Publs *Annual Report, Horizons* (newsletter).

INFORMATION AND THE MEDIA

Commonwealth Broadcasting Association: Broadcasting House, London, W1A 1AA; tel. (71) 927-5151; telex 265781; fax (71) 927-5152; f. 1945; general conferences are held every two years. Mems: 58 national public service broadcasting organizations in 51 Commonwealth countries. Pres. MOHAMMED IBRAHIM; Sec.-Gen. STUART REVILL. Publs *COMBROAD* (quarterly), *CBA Handbook* (updated every 2 years).

Commonwealth Institute: see under Education.

Commonwealth Journalists Association: Suite 41, 4th Floor, 8–14 St Pancras Way, London, NW1 0QG; tel. (71) 383-0009; fax (71) 383-7576; f. 1978 to promote co-operation between journalists in Commonwealth countries, organize training facilities and conferences, and foster understanding among Commonwealth peoples. Pres. RAY EKPU; Exec. Dir LAWRIE BREEN.

Commonwealth Press Union (Association of Commonwealth Newspapers, News Agencies and Periodicals): Studio House, 184 Fleet St, London, EC4A 2DU; tel. (71) 242-1056; fax (71) 831-4923; f. 1950 (succeeding the Empire Press Union, f. 1909) to promote the welfare of the Commonwealth press by defending its freedom and providing training for journalists; organizes biennial conferences. Mems: about 500 newspapers, news agencies, periodicals in 30 countries. Pres. Sir GORDON BRUNTON; Dir ROBIN MACKICHAN. Publs *CPU News, Annual Report*.

LAW

Commonwealth Lawyers' Association: c/o The Law Society, 50 Chancery Lane, London, WC2A 1SX; tel. (71) 242-1222; telex 261203; fax (71) 831-0057; f. 1983 (fmrly the Commonwealth Legal Bureau); seeks to maintain and promote the rule of law throughout the Commonwealth, by ensuring that the people of the Commonwealth are served by an independent and efficient legal profession; upholds professional standards and promotes the availability of legal services; assists in organizing the triennial Commonwealth law conferences. Pres. P. D. K. FRASER; Exec. Sec. HAMISH C. ADAMSON. Publs. *The Commonwealth Lawyer*.

Commonwealth Legal Advisory Service: c/o British Institute of International and Comparative Law, Charles Clore House, 17 Russell Sq., London, WC1B 5DR; tel. (71) 636-5802; fax (71) 323-2016; financed by the British Institute and by contributions from Commonwealth governments; provides research facilities for Commonwealth governments and non-governmental organizations. Dir ROGER ROSE.

Commonwealth Legal Education Association: Legal Division, Commonwealth Secretariat, Marlborough House, Pall Mall, London, SW1Y 5HX; tel. (71) 839-3411; f. 1971; to promote contacts and exchanges; to provide information. Hon. Sec. JEREMY POPE. Publs *Commonwealth Legal Education Newsletter, List of Schools of Law in the Commonwealth* (every 2 years), *Compendium of Post-Graduate Law Courses in the Commonwealth*.

Commonwealth Magistrates' and Judges' Association: 10 Duke St, London, W1M 5AA; tel. (71) 487-2886; fax (71) 487-4386; f. 1970 to advance the administration of the law by promoting the independence of the judiciary, to further education in law and crime prevention and to disseminate information; conferences and study tours; corporate membership for associations of the judiciary or courts of limited jurisdiction; associate membership for individuals. Pres. SANDRA OXNER; Sec. Dr J. S. BUCHANAN. Publ. *Commonwealth Judicial Journal* (2 a year).

PARLIAMENTARY AFFAIRS

Commonwealth Parliamentary Association: 7 Millbank, London, SW1P 3JA; tel. (71) 799-1460; telex 911569; fax (71) 222-6073; f. 1911 to promote understanding and co-operation between Commonwealth parliamentarians; organization: Executive Committee of 28 Members of Parliament responsible to annual General Assembly; 122 branches throughout the Commonwealth; holds annual Commonwealth Parliamentary Conferences and seminars, and also regional conferences and seminars; Sec.-Gen. ARTHUR DONAHOE. Publ. *The Parliamentarian* (quarterly).

PROFESSIONAL AND INDUSTRIAL RELATIONS

Commonwealth Association of Architects: 66 Portland Place, London, W1N 4AD; tel. (71) 636-8276; fax (71) 255-1541; f. 1964; an association of 34 societies of architects in various Commonwealth countries. Objects: to facilitate the reciprocal recognition of professional qualifications; to provide a clearing house for information on architectural practice, and to encourage collaboration. Plenary conferences every three years; regional conferences are also held. Exec. Dir GEORGE WILSON. Publs *Handbook, Objectives and Procedures: CAA Schools Visiting Boards, Architectural Education in the Commonwealth* (annotated bibliography of research), *List of Recognised Schools of Architecture, CAA News* (2 a year).

Commonwealth Foundation: Marlborough House, Pall Mall, London, SW1Y 5HY; tel. (71) 930-3783; fax (71) 839-8157; f. 1966 to administer a fund to promote closer professional co-operation within the Commonwealth (reconstituted as an international organization 1983). The Foundation is an autonomous body assisting professionals and staff of voluntary organizations from Commonwealth countries to visit other Commonwealth countries to attend conferences and undertake advisory and study visits and training attachments. Also supports Commonwealth professional associations and professional centres; administers short-term fellowship schemes. Funds are provided by 44 Commonwealth governments: in 1992/93 £1.9m. was available for grant-making. Chair. Sir RICHARD LUCE (United Kingdom); Dir Dr HUMAYUN KHAN (Pakistan).

Commonwealth Trade Union Council: c/o TUC, Congress House, 23–28 Great Russell St, London, WC1B 3LS; tel. (71) 631-0728; telex 266006; fax (71) 436-0301; f. 1979 to promote the interests of workers in the Commonwealth and encourage the development of trades unions in developing countries of the Commonwealth; provides assistance for training. Dir PATRICK QUINN (UK). Publs *CTUC Update* (quarterly), *Annual Report*.

SCIENCE AND TECHNOLOGY

Commonwealth Engineers' Council: c/o Institution of Civil Engineers, 1–7 Great George St, London, SW1P 3AA; tel. (71) 222-7722; fax (71) 222-7500; f. 1946; the Conference meets every two years to provide an opportunity for officers of engineering institutions of Commonwealth countries to exchange views on collaboration; there is a standing committee on engineering education and training; organizes seminars on related topics. Sec. J. C. MCKENZIE.

Commonwealth Geological Surveys Consultative Group: c/o Commonwealth Science Council, CSC Earth Sciences Programme, Marlborough House, Pall Mall, London, SW1Y 5HX; tel. (71) 839-3411; telex 27678; fax (71) 930-0827; f. 1948 (as the Commonwealth Committee on Mineral Resources and Geology) to promote collaboration in geological, geochemical, geophysical and remote sensing techniques and the exchange of information. Geological Programme Officer Dr SIYAN MALOMO; Publ. *Earth Sciences Newsletter.*

SPORT

Commonwealth Games Federation: Walkden House, 3–10 Melton St, London, NW1 2EB; tel. (71) 383-5596; fax (71) 383-5506; the Games were first held in 1930 and are now held every four years; participation is limited to amateur teams representing the member countries of the Commonwealth; held in Auckland, New Zealand, in 1990 and to be held in Victoria, Canada, in 1994 and in Kuala Lumpur, Malaysia, in 1998. Mems: 66 affiliated bodies. Chair. A. O. DE SALES; Hon. Sec. DAVID DIXON.

YOUTH

Commonwealth Youth Exchange Council: 7 Lion Yard, Tremadoc Rd, London, SW4 7NQ; tel. (71) 498-6151; fax (71) 720-5403; f. 1970; promotes contact between groups of young people of the United Kingdom and other Commonwealth countries by means of educational exchange visits, provides information for organizers and allocates grants; 193 member organizations. Dir V. S. G. CRAGGS. Publs *Contact* (handbook), *Exchange* (newsletter).

Duke of Edinburgh's Award International Association: 19 St James's Square, London, SW1Y 4JG; tel. (71) 839-7888; telex 919885; fax (71) 839-5546; f. 1956; offers a programme of leisure activities for young people, comprising service, expeditions, sport and skills, operating in 58 countries (not confined to the Commonwealth). International Sec.-Gen. PAUL ARENGO-JONES. Publs *Award World* (3 a year), handbooks and guides.

MISCELLANEOUS

British Commonwealth Ex-Services League: 48 Pall Mall, London, SW1Y 5JG; tel. (71) 973-0633, ext. 263; links the ex-service organizations in the Commonwealth, assists ex-servicemen of the Crown and their dependants who are resident abroad; holds triennial conferences. Sec.-Gen. Brig. M. J. DOYLE. Publ. *Triennial Report.*

Commonwealth Countries League: 14 Thistleworth Close, Isleworth, Middx, TW7 4QQ; tel. (81) 568-9868; f. 1925 to secure equal opportunities and status between men and women in the Commonwealth, and the social and political education of women, to act as a link between Commonwealth women's organizations, and to promote and finance secondary education of disadvantaged girls of high ability in their own countries, through the CCL Educational Fund; holds meetings with speakers and an annual Conference, organizes the annual Commonwealth Fair for fund-raising; individual mems and affiliated socs in the Commonwealth. Sec.-Gen. SHEILA O'REILLY. Publ. *CCL Newsletter* (3 a year).

Commonwealth Trust: Commonwealth House, 18 Northumberland Ave, London WC2N 5BJ; tel. (71) 930-6733; fax (71) 930-9705; f. 1989; administers the activities of the Royal Commonwealth Society and is linked to the Victoria League for Commonwealth Friendship (q.v.), which together have more than 100 trusts, leagues and branches world-wide; acts as the Commonwealth liaison unit for the United Kingdom. Pres. HRH Princess MARGARET, Countess of Snowdon; Chair. Sir OLIVER FORSTER; Dir-Gen. Sir DAVID THORNE. Publ. *Commonwealth Trust News* (3 a year).

Commonwealth War Graves Commission: 2 Marlow Rd, Maidenhead, Berks, SL6 7DX; tel. (628) 34221; telex 847526; fax (628) 771208; f. 1917 (as Imperial War Graves Commission); provides for the marking and permanent care of the graves of members of the Commonwealth Forces who died during the wars of 1914–18 and 1939–45; maintains over 1m. graves in 141 countries and commemorates by name on memorials more than 760,000 who have no known grave or who were cremated. Mems: Australia, Canada, India, New Zealand, South Africa, United Kingdom. Pres. HRH The Duke of KENT; Dir-Gen. D. KENNEDY.

Joint Commonwealth Societies' Council: c/o Commonwealth Trust, Commonwealth House, 18 Northumberland Ave, London, WC2N 5BJ; tel. (71) 930-6733; fax (71) 930-9705; f. 1947; provides a forum for the exchange of information regarding activities of member organizations which promote understanding among countries of the Commonwealth; co-ordinates the distribution of the Commonwealth Day message by Queen Elizabeth; mems: 16 unofficial Commonwealth organizations and four official bodies. Chair. Sir DONALD TEBBIT; Sec. JENNY GROVES.

Royal Commonwealth Society: 18 Northumberland Ave, London, WC2N 5BJ; tel. (71) 930-6733; fax (71) 930-9705; f. 1868; to promote internationally understanding of the Commonwealth and its people; information service; library housed by Cambridge University Library; administered through the Commonwealth Trust. Grand Pres. HRH the Duchess of York; Chair. Sir OLIVER FORSTER; Sec.-Gen. Sir DAVID THORNE. Publs *Annual Report.*

Royal Over-Seas League: Over-Seas House, Park Place, St James's St, London, SW1A 1LR; tel. (71) 408-0214; telex 268995; fax (71) 499-6738; f. 1910 to promote friendship and understanding in the Commonwealth; club houses in London and Edinburgh; membership is open to all British subjects and Commonwealth citizens. Chair. PETER MCENTEE; Dir-Gen. ROBERT F. NEWELL. Publ. *Overseas* (quarterly).

Victoria League for Commonwealth Friendship: 55 Leinster Square, London W2 4PU; tel. (71) 243-2633; fax (71) 229-2994; f. 1901; aims to further personal friendship among Commonwealth peoples; and to assist and provide accommodation for visitors and students in Commonwealth countries; has branches elsewhere in the UK and abroad. Pres. HRH Princess MARGARET, Countess of Snowdon; Chair. Capt. CHRISTOPHER KNIGHT; Gen. Sec. ANNA G. KELLER. Publ. *Annual Report.*

Declaration of Commonwealth Principles

Agreed by the Commonwealth Heads of Government Meeting at Singapore, 22 January 1971.

The Commonwealth of Nations is a voluntary association of independent sovereign states, each responsible for its own policies, consulting and co-operating in the common interests of their peoples and in the promotion of international understanding and world peace.

Members of the Commonwealth come from territories in the six continents and five oceans, include peoples of different races, languages and religions, and display every stage of economic development from poor developing nations to wealthy industrialized nations. They encompass a rich variety of cultures, traditions and institutions.

Membership of the Commonwealth is compatible with the freedom of member-governments to be non-aligned or to belong to any other grouping, association or alliance. Within this diversity all members of the Commonwealth hold certain principles in common. It is by pursuing these principles that the Commonwealth can continue to influence international society for the benefit of mankind.

We believe that international peace and order are essential to the security and prosperity of mankind; we therefore support the United Nations and seek to strengthen its influence for peace in the world, and its efforts to remove the causes of tension between nations.

We believe in the liberty of the individual, in equal rights for all citizens regardless of race, colour, creed or political belief, and in their inalienable right to participate by means of free and democratic political processes in framing the society in which they live. We therefore strive to promote in each of our countries those representative institutions and guarantees for personal freedom under the law that are our common heritage.

We recognize racial prejudice as a dangerous sickness threatening the healthy development of the human race and racial discrimination as an unmitigated evil of society. Each of us will vigorously combat this evil within our own nation.

No country will afford to regimes which practise racial discrimination assistance which in its own judgment directly contributes to the pursuit or consolidation of this evil policy. We oppose all forms of colonial domination and racial oppression and are committed to the principles of human dignity and equality.

We will therefore use all our efforts to foster human equality and dignity everywhere, and to further the principles of self-determination and non-racialism.

We believe that the wide disparities in wealth now existing between different sections of mankind are too great to be tolerated. They also create world tensions. Our aim is their progressive removal. We therefore seek to use our efforts to overcome poverty, ignorance and disease, in raising standards of life and achieving a more equitable international society.

To this end our aim is to achieve the freest possible flow of international trade on terms fair and equitable to all, taking into account the special requirements of the developing countries, and to encourage the flow of adequate resources, including governmental and private resources, to the developing countries, bearing in mind the importance of doing this in a true spirit of partnership and of establishing for this purpose in the developing countries conditions which are conducive to sustained investment and growth.

We believe that international co-operation is essential to remove the causes of war, promote tolerance, combat injustice, and secure development among the peoples of the world. We are convinced that the Commonwealth is one of the most fruitful associations for these purposes.

In pursuing these principles the members of the Commonwealth believe that they can provide a constructive example of the multi-national approach which is vital to peace and progress in the modern world. The association is based on consultation, discussion and co-operation.

In rejecting coercion as an instrument of policy they recognize that the security of each member state from external aggression is a matter of concern to all members. It provides many channels for continuing exchanges of knowledge and views on professional, cultural, economic, legal and political issues among member states.

These relationships we intend to foster and extend, for we believe that our multi-national association can expand human understanding and understanding among nations, assist in the elimination of discrimination based on differences of race, colour or creed, maintain and strengthen personal liberty, contribute to the enrichment of life for all, and provide a powerful influence for peace among nations.

The Lusaka Declaration on Racism and Racial Prejudice

The Declaration, adopted by Heads of Government in 1979, includes the following statements:

United in our desire to rid the world of the evils of racism and racial prejudice, we proclaim our faith in the inherent dignity and worth of the human person and declare that:

(i) the peoples of the Commonwealth have the right to live freely in dignity and equality, without any distinction or exclusion based on race, colour, sex, descent, or national or ethnic origin;

(ii) while everyone is free to retain diversity in his or her culture and lifestyle this diversity does not justify the perpetuation of racial prejudice or racially discriminatory practices;

(iii) everyone has the right to equality before the law and equal justice under the law; and

(iv) everyone has the right to effective remedies and protection against any form of discrimination based on the grounds of race, colour, sex, descent, or national or ethnic origin.

We reject as inhuman and intolerable all policies designed to perpetuate apartheid, racial segregation or other policies based on theories that racial groups are or may be inherently superior or inferior.

We reaffirm that it is the duty of all the peoples of the Commonwealth to work together for the total eradication of the infamous policy of apartheid which is internationally recognized as a crime against the conscience and dignity of mankind and the very existence of which is an affront to humanity.

We agree that everyone has the right to protection against acts of incitement to racial hatred and discrimination, whether committed by individuals, groups or other organizations. . . .

Inspired by the principles of freedom and equality which characterise our association, we accept the solemn duty of working together to eliminate racism and racial prejudice. This duty involves the acceptance of the principle that positive measures may be required to advance the elimination of racism, including assistance to those struggling to rid themselves and their environment of the practice.

Being aware that legislation alone cannot eliminate racism and racial prejudice, we endorse the need to initiate public information and education policies designed to promote understanding, tolerance, respect and friendship among peoples and racial groups. . . .

We note that racism and racial prejudice, wherever they occur, are significant factors contributing to tension between nations and thus inhibit peaceful progress and development. We believe that the goal of the eradication of racism stands as a critical priority for governments of the Commonwealth committed as they are to the promotion of the ideals of peaceful and happy lives for their people.

Harare Commonwealth Declaration

The following are the major points of the Declaration adopted by Heads of Government at the meeting held in Harare, Zimbabwe, in 1991:

Having reaffirmed the principles to which the Commonwealth is committed, and reviewed the problems and challenges which the world, and the Commonwealth as part of it, face, we pledge the Commonwealth and our countries to work with renewed vigour, concentrating especially in the following areas: the protection and promotion of the fundamental political values of the Commonwealth; equality for women, so that they may exercise their full and equal rights; provision of universal access to education for the population of our countries; continuing action to bring about the end of apartheid and the establishment of a free, democratic, non-racial and prosperous South Africa; the promotion of sustainable development and the alleviation of poverty in the countries of the Commonwealth; extending the benefits of development within a framework of respect for human rights; the protection of the environment through respect for the principles of sustainable development which we enunicated at Langkawi; action to combat drug trafficking and abuse and communicable diseases; help for small Commonwealth states in tackling their particular economic and security problems; and support of the United Nations and other international institutions in the world's search for peace, disarmament and effective arms control; and in the promotion of international consensus on major global political, economic and social issues.

To give weight and effectiveness to our commitments we intend to focus and improve Commonwealth co-operation in these areas. This would include strengthening the capacity of the Commonwealth to respond to requests from members for assistance in entrenching the practices of democracy, accountable administration and the rule of law.

In reaffirming the principles of the Commonwealth and in committing ourselves to pursue them in policy and action in response to the challenges of the 1990s, in areas where we believe that the Commonwealth has a distinctive contribution to offer, we the Heads of Government express our determination to renew and enhance the value and importance of the Commonwealth as an institution which can and should strengthen and enrich the lives not only of its own members and their peoples but also of the wider community of peoples of which they are a part.

ECONOMIC COMMUNITY OF WEST AFRICAN STATES—ECOWAS

Address: Secretariat Bldg, Asokoro, Abuja, Nigeria.

Telephone: (9) 5231858.

The Treaty of Lagos, establishing ECOWAS, was signed in May 1975 by 15 states, with the object of promoting trade, co-operation and self-reliance in West Africa. Outstanding protocols bringing certain key features of the Treaty into effect were ratified in November 1976. Cape Verde joined in 1977. A revised ECOWAS treaty, designed to accelerate economic integration and to increase political co-operation, was drafted in 1991–92, and was signed in July 1993 (see below).

MEMBERS

Benin	Guinea	Niger
Burkina Faso	Guinea-Bissau	Nigeria
Cape Verde	Liberia	Senegal
Côte d'Ivoire	Mali	Sierra Leone
The Gambia	Mauritania	Togo
Ghana		

Organization

(June 1994)

CONFERENCE OF HEADS OF STATE AND GOVERNMENT

The Conference, the highest authority of ECOWAS, meets once a year. The Chairman is drawn from the member states in turn.

COUNCIL OF MINISTERS

The Council consists of two representatives from each country; a chairman is drawn from each country in turn. It meets twice a year, and is responsible for the running of the Community.

TRIBUNAL

The treaty provides for a Community Tribunal, whose composition and competence are determined by the Authority of Heads of State and Government; it interprets the provisions of the treaty and settles disputes between member states that are referred to it.

EXECUTIVE SECRETARIAT

The Executive Secretary is elected for a four-year term, which may be renewed once only.

Executive Secretary: EDOUARD E. BENJAMIN (Guinea).

SPECIALIZED COMMISSIONS

There are six commissions:

(i) Trade, Customs, Immigration, Monetary and Payments;
(ii) Industry, Agriculture and Natural Resources;
(iii) Transport, Communications and Energy;
(iv) Social and Cultural Affairs;
(v) Administration and finance;
(vi) Information.

ECOWAS FUND FOR CO-OPERATION, COMPENSATION AND DEVELOPMENT

Address: BP 2704, ave du 24 Janvier, Lomé, Togo.

Telephone: 216864; **telex:** 218389; **fax:** 218389.

The Fund is administered by a Board of Directors. The chief executive of the Fund is the Managing Director, who holds office for a renewable term of four years. There is a staff of 50. The authorized capital of the Fund was raised from US $90m. to $360m. in 1986. In 1988 agreements were reached with the African Development Bank and the Islamic Development Bank on the co-financing of projects and joint training of staff, and it was agreed that the Fund should be opened to non-regional participants.

Managing Director: SAMUEL KYE APEA (Ghana).

Activities

ECOWAS aims to promote co-operation and development in economic, social and cultural activity, particularly in the fields for which specialized commissions (see above) are appointed, to raise the standard of living of the people of the member countries, increase and maintain economic stability, improve relations among member countries and contribute to the progress and development of Africa.

The treaty provides for compensation for states whose import duties are reduced through trade liberalization and contains a clause permitting safeguard measures in favour of any country affected by economic disturbances through the application of the treaty.

The treaty also contains a commitment to abolish all obstacles to the free movement of people, services and capital, and to promote: harmonization of agricultural policies; common projects in marketing, research and the agriculturally based industries; joint development of economic and industrial policies and elimination of disparities in levels of development; and common monetary policies.

Lack of success in many of ECOWAS' aims has been attributed to the existence of numerous other intergovernmental organizations in the region (such as the francophone CEAO and the Mano River Union, q.v.), and to member governments' lack of commitment, shown by their reluctance to implement policies at the national level, their failure to provide the agreed financial resources (arrears in contributions were reported to total US $28m. at mid-1992), and the absence of national links with the Secretariat.

The ECOWAS summit conference that was convened in July 1991 in Abuja, Nigeria, issued a 'declaration of political principles' in which member states reaffirmed their commitment to refrain from aggression against one another (see below). Member states also pledged to respect 'human rights and fundamental freedoms', and to promote political pluralism and democratic processes in their countries.

At the ECOWAS summit meeting in July 1992 a minimum programme of action for the implementation of Community agreements on the free movement of goods and people (see below) was approved. This programme aimed to remove non-tariff barriers and included the simplification of customs and transit procedures and a reduction in the number of control posts on international roads.

A revised treaty for the Community was drawn up by an ECOWAS Committee of Eminent Persons in 1991–92, and was signed at the ECOWAS summit conference that took place in Cotonou, Benin, in July 1993. The treaty, which was to extend economic and political co-operation among member states, designates the achievement of a common market and a single currency as economic objectives, while in the political sphere it envisages the establishment of a West African parliament, an economic and social council and an ECOWAS court of justice to replace the existing Tribunal and enforce Community decisions. The treaty also formally assigned the Community with the responsibility of preventing and settling regional conflicts. By mid-1994 the treaty still had to be ratified by each member state.

TRADE AND MONETARY UNION

Elimination of tariffs and other obstructions to trade among member states, and the establishment of a common external tariff, were planned over a transitional period of 15 years. At the 1978 Conference of Heads of State and Government it was decided that from 28 May 1979 no member state might increase its customs tariff on goods from another member. This was regarded as the first step towards the abolition of customs duties within the Community. During the first two years import duties on intra-community trade were to be maintained, and then eliminated in phases over the next eight years. Quotas and other restrictions of equivalent effect were to be abolished in the first 10 years. In the remaining five years all differences between external customs tariffs were to be abolished.

The 1980 Conference of Heads of State and Government decided to establish a free trade area for unprocessed agricultural products and handicrafts from May 1981. Tariffs on industrial products made by specified community enterprises were also to be abolished from that date, but implementation was delayed by difficulties in defining the enterprises. From 1 January 1990 tariffs were lifted from 25 listed items manufactured in ECOWAS member states: by mid-1991 the number had increased to 90. Over the ensuing decade, tariffs on other industrial products were to be eliminated as follows: the 'most-developed' countries of ECOWAS (Côte d'Ivoire, Ghana, Nigeria and Senegal) were to abolish tariffs on 'priority' products within four years and on 'non-priority' products within six years; the second group (Benin, Guinea, Liberia, Sierra Leone and Togo) were to abolish tariffs on 'priority' products within six years, and on 'non-priority' products within eight years; and the 'least-developed' members (Burkina Faso, Cape Verde, The Gambia, Guinea-Bissau, Mali, Mauritania and Niger) were to abolish tariffs on 'priority' products within eight years and on 'non-priority' products within 10 years.

In 1990 the Conference of Heads of State and Government agreed to adopt measures that would create a single monetary zone and remove barriers to trade in goods that originated in the Community. By early 1992 ECOWAS had set up a study group to examine the feasibility of introducing a single currency in the region by the agreed date. ECOWAS regards monetary union as necessary to encourage investment in the region, since it would greatly facilitate capital transactions with foreign countries. In September 1992 it was announced that the West African Clearing House (q.v.) was to become the West African Monetary Agency and was to be responsible for administering an ECOWAS exchange rate system (EERS) and for establishing the single monetary zone. A credit guarantee scheme and travellers' cheque system were to be established in association with the EERS. The new agency was expected to be established in late 1994.

ECOWAS planned to spend about US $12.6m. (the majority of its budget) on the promotion of free trade among its member states in 1993. In December 1992 ECOWAS ministers agreed on the institutionalization of an ECOWAS trade fair, with the first one to be held in Dakar, Senegal in May/June 1995.

TRAVEL, TRANSPORT AND COMMUNICATIONS

At the 1979 Conference of Heads of State a Protocol was signed relating to free circulation of the region's citizens and to rights of residence and establishment of commercial enterprises. The first provision (the right of entry without a visa) came into force in 1980, following ratification by eight members. The second provision, allowing unlimited rights of residence, was signed in 1986 (although Nigeria indicated that unskilled workers and certain categories of professionals would not be allowed to stay for an indefinite period) and came into force in 1989. The third provision, concerning the right to establish a commercial enterprise in another member state was signed in 1990, but remained to enter into force in July 1992.

The Conference also adopted a programme for the improvement and extension of the internal and interstate telecommunications network, 'Intelcom', estimated to cost US $60m. The first and second phases of the programme, comprising the construction of microwave telephone, telex and television links between Ghana and Burkina Faso, Benin and Burkina Faso, Nigeria and Niger, and Mali and Côte d'Ivoire, were completed in October 1988.

A programme for the development of an integrated regional road network was adopted by the 1980 Conference. Under the programme two major trans-regional roads were to be completed: the Trans-Coastal Highway, linking Lagos, Nigeria, with Nouackchott, Mauritania (4,767 km); and the Trans-Sahelian Highway, linking Dakar, Senegal with N'Djamena, Chad (4,633 km). By mid-1993 about 88% of the trans-coastal route was complete, and about 78% of the trans-Sahelian route. A network of interconnecting roads, linking land-locked countries to the coast was also planned; however, by mid-1992 projects had only been identified, but not started.

ECONOMIC AND INDUSTRIAL DEVELOPMENT

In November 1984 ECOWAS heads of state and government approved the establishment of a private regional investment bank, to be known as Ecobank Transnational Inc. The bank, which was based in Lomé, Togo, opened in March 1988. ECOWAS has a 10% share in the bank. By mid-1990 Ecobank affiliates had been opened in Benin, Côte d'Ivoire, Ghana, Nigeria and Togo.

The West African Industrial Forum, sponsored by ECOWAS, is held every two years to promote regional industrial investment. The Secretariat is formulating a West African Industrial Master Plan. The first phase involved the compilation of an inventory of industrial enterprises, while the second phase was to comprise study of important industrial sub-sectors, prior to the drawing up of the Master Plan.

DEFENCE

At the third Conference of Heads of State and Government a protocol of non-aggression was signed. Thirteen members signed a protocol on mutual defence assistance at the 1981 Conference. In 1990 a Standing Mediation Committee was formed to mediate in disputes between member states. In July ECOWAS ministers attempted to mediate in civil conflict in Liberia, and in August they sent an ECOWAS Monitoring Group (ECOMOG—initially comprising about 4,000 troops from The Gambia, Ghana, Guinea, Nigeria and Sierra Leone, later increased in number to 8,000, and joined in 1991 by troops from Mali and Senegal) to Liberia, to try to bring about a cease-fire between the rival factions there, to restore public order, and to establish an interim government, until elections could be held. In September 1990 ECOMOG failed to prevent the capture and killing of the Liberian President, Samuel Doe, by rebel forces, and fighting between rival groups continued. In November a temporary cease-fire was agreed by the protagonists in Liberia, and an interim president was installed by ECOMOG. Following the signature of a new cease-fire agreement in February 1991, a national conference, organized by ECOWAS in March, established a temporary government, pending elections to be held in early 1992. In June 1991 ECOWAS established a five-member committee to co-ordinate the peace negotiations. In September, at a meeting in Yamoussoukro, Côte d'Ivoire, held under the aegis of the five-nation committee, two of the rival factions in Liberia agreed to encamp their troops in designated areas and to disarm under ECOMOG supervision. At a further meeting, held in late October, it was agreed that the disarmament process would be effected within a 60-day period, to be followed by the repatriation and rehabilitation of Liberian refugees. During the period preceding the proposed elections (due to take place in May 1992), ECOMOG would occupy Liberian air and sea ports, and would create a 'buffer zone' along the country's border with Sierra Leone. By September 1992, however, ECOMOG had been unable either to effect the disarmament of two of the principal military factions, the National Patriotic Front of Liberia (NPFL) and the United Liberation Movement of Liberia for Democracy (ULIMO), or to occupy positions in substantial areas of the country, as a result of resistance on the part of the NPFL. The proposed elections were consequently postponed indefinitely. In October ECOMOG began offensive action against NPFL positions, with a campaign of aerial bombardment. Hostilities between the two sides continued into 1993 (see chapter on Liberia). In November 1992 ECOWAS imposed sanctions on the NPFL's territory, comprising a land, sea and air blockade, in response to the Front's refusal to comply with the Yamoussoukro accord of October 1991. In April 1993 ECOMOG announced that the disarmament of ULIMO had been completed, amid widespread accusations that ECOMOG had supported ULIMO against the NPFL, and was no longer a neutral force. In mid-July the principal parties to the conflict signed a new peace agreement in Geneva, under the auspices of the UN, the OAU and ECOWAS. An ECOWAS-brokered cease-fire agreement was signed in Cotonou, Benin, at the end of July, and came into effect on 1 August. This agreement expanded on that drawn up in Geneva by specifying that a neutral transitional government was to be formed, and that there was to be a disarming of troops prior to the holding of fair and free elections, scheduled to take place in February 1994. In September 1993 a 300-member UN observer mission (UNOMIL) was established in Liberia to work alongside ECOMOG, which was to be expanded in accordance with the cease-fire agreement, in monitoring the disarmament process, as well as to verify the impartiality of ECOMOG. In that month ECOMOG consisted of some 12,000 troops from six African countries; Nigeria alone contributed about three-quarters of the personnel. In January 1994 contingents from Tanzania and Uganda were deployed in the country facilitated by a Trust Fund established by the UN. In March a transitional executive council was installed (elections now were to be conducted in September), however, continued fighting prevented ECOMOG conducting its principal functions of disarming and demobilizing the conflicting parties. By late April only some 2,500 combatants had been demobilized of an estimated target of 60,000.

RURAL WATER RESOURCES

The ECOWAS programme for the development of village and pastoral water resources involves the creation of 3,200 water points throughout the region: 200 water points per member state. During the first phase of the programme (1992–96) attention was to be concentrated on the needs of the 10 member states most seriously affected or threatened by drought and desertification (Burkina Faso, Cape Verde, Guinea, Guinea Bissau, Mali, Mauritania, Niger, Nigeria, Senegal and Togo). By mid-1992 preparatory missions had been conducted in all of these member states. The first phase of the programme was exepected to cost US $40.7m., with international donors to provide the necessary resources.

AGRICULTURE AND FISHING

An Agricultural Development Strategy was adopted in 1982, aiming at sub-regional self-sufficiency by the year 2000. The strategy included plans for selecting seeds and cattle species, and called for solidarity among member states during international commodity negotiations. Seven seed selection and multiplication centres and eight livestock-breeding centres were designated in 1984. In 1988 it was announced that ECOWAS was to establish a cattle-ranch in southern Mali, over an area of 18,000 ha, to breed cattle for distribution in the ECOWAS region. A tsetse-fly control programme was also undertaken.

In February 1993 ECOWAS signed an agreement with the EC concerning an EC grant of US $9.6m. to help with the development of the fishing industry in the ECOWAS region over a five-year period.

SOCIAL PROGRAMME

Four organizations have been established within ECOWAS by the Executive Secretariat: the Organization of Trade Unions of West Africa, which held its first meeting in 1984; the West African Youth Association; the West African Universities' Association; and the West Africa Women's Association (whose statutes were approved by a meeting of ministers of social affairs in May 1987). Regional sports competitions are held annually. The West African Health Organization (q.v.) was formed in 1989 by ECOWAS member states.

INFORMATION AND MEDIA

In March 1990 ECOWAS ministers of information formulated a policy on the dissemination of information about ECOWAS throughout the region and the appraisal of attitudes of its population towards the Community. The ministers established a new information commission. In November 1991 ECOWAS organized a conference on press communication and African integration. The conference's recommendations included the creation of an ECOWAS press card, judicial safeguards to protect journalists, training programmes for journalists and the establishment of a regional documentation centre and data bank.

FINANCE

ECOWAS is financed by contributions from member states, although there is a poor record of punctual payment of dues, which has hampered the work of the Secretariat. Under the revised treaty, ECOWAS was to receive revenue from a community tax, based on the total value of imports from member countries.

In March 1993 a budget of 4,135m. francs CFA (roughly US $14.9m.) for the 1993 financial year was approved.

EUROPEAN UNION—THE LOMÉ CONVENTION

The European Union (EU) as a whole provides emergency aid for developing and other non-EC countries. In 1992 ECU 43m. was granted in emergency humanitarian assistance to six African countries, with Somalia receiving the largest share (ECU 35m.). However, the principal means of co-operation between the Community and developing countries is the Lomé Convention, concluded by the EU and African, Caribbean and Pacific (ACP) countries.

The First Lomé Convention (Lomé I), which came into force on 1 April 1976, replaced the Yaoundé Conventions and the Arusha Agreement, and was designed to provide a new framework of co-operation, taking into account the varying needs of developing countries. Lomé II was concluded at Lomé, Togo, in October 1979, and came into force on 1 January 1981. Lomé III was signed in December 1984, and came into force on 1 March 1985 (trade provisions) and 1 May 1986 (aid). The Fourth Lomé Convention was signed in December 1989: its trade provisions entered into force on 1 March 1990, and the remainder followed in September 1991. In mid-1994 70 ACP states were parties to the Convention.

SIGNATORY STATES

The European Union

Belgium; Denmark; France; Germany; Greece; Ireland; Italy; Luxembourg; Netherlands; Portugal; Spain; United Kingdom.

African states adhering to the Convention

Angola; Benin; Botswana; Burkina Faso; Burundi; Cameroon; Cape Verde; Central African Republic; Chad; Comoros; Congo; Côte d'Ivoire; Djibouti; Equatorial Guinea; Eritrea; Ethiopia; Gabon; The Gambia; Ghana; Guinea; Guinea-Bissau; Kenya; Lesotho; Liberia; Madagascar; Malawi; Mali; Mauritania; Mauritius; Mozambique; Namibia; Niger; Nigeria; Rwanda; São Tomé and Príncipe; Senegal; Seychelles; Sierra Leone; Somalia; Sudan; Swaziland; Tanzania; Togo; Uganda; Zaire; Zambia; Zimbabwe. There are also 15 Caribbean and eight Pacific signatories.

Organization

ACP–EU INSTITUTIONS

Council of Ministers: one minister from each signatory state; one co-chairman from each of the two groups; meets annually.

Committee of Ambassadors: one ambassador from each signatory state; chairmanship alternates between the two groups; meets at least every six months.

Joint Assembly: EU and ACP are equally represented; attended by delegates from each of the 70 ACP countries and an equal number of members of the European Parliament; one co-chairman from each group; meets twice a year.

Centre for the Development of Industry: 28 rue de l'Industrie, 1040 Brussels, Belgium; tel. (2) 513-41-00; telex 61427; fax (2) 511-75-93; f. 1977 to encourage investment in the ACP states by providing contacts and advice, holding promotion meetings, and helping to finance feasibility studies; Dir PAUL FRIX.

Technical Centre for Agricultural and Rural Co-operation: Postbus 380, 6700 AJ Wageningen, Netherlands; tel. (8380) 60400; telex 30169; fax (8380) 31052; f. 1983 to provide ACP states with better access to information, research, training and innovations in agricultural development and extension; Dir DANIEL ASSOUMOU MBA.

ACP INSTITUTIONS

ACP Council of Ministers.

ACP Committee of Ambassadors.

ACP Secretariat: ACP House, 451 ave Georges Henri, 1200 Brussels, Belgium; tel. (2) 733-96-00; telex 26558; fax (2) 735-55-73; Sec.-Gen. Dr GHEBRAY BERHANE.

Activities

Under the first Lomé Convention (Lomé I), the Community committed 3,052.4m. European Currency Units (ECU) for aid and investment in developing countries, through the European Development Fund (EDF) and the European Investment Bank (EIB). Provision was made for over 99% of ACP (mainly agricultural) exports to enter the EC market duty free, while certain products which compete directly with Community agriculture, such as sugar, were given preferential treatment but not free access. The Stabex (Stabilization of Export Earnings) scheme was designed to help developing countries to withstand fluctuations in the price of their agricultural products, by paying compensation for reduced export earnings.

The second Lomé Convention (January 1981–February 1985) envisaged Community expenditure of ECU 5,530m.; it extended some of the provisions of Lomé I, and introduced new fields of co-operation. One of the most important innovations was a scheme, Sysmin, similar to Stabex, to safeguard exports of minerals.

Negotiations for a third Convention began in October 1983, with delegations from Angola and Mozambique (at that time not ACP states) participating. Lomé III provided a total of ECU 8,500m. (about US $6,000m. at 30 January 1985) in assistance to the ACP states over the five years from March 1985, representing little or no increase, in real terms, over the amount provided by Lomé II.

In January 1986 agreement was reached with the SADCC (now the SADC, q.v.) on financing for projects in southern Africa, amounting to ECU 110m. over the next four to five years.

The fourth Lomé Convention covers the 10-year period 1990–99. The financial protocol for 1990–95 made commitments of ECU 12,000m. (US $13,700m.), of which ECU 10,800m. was from the EDF (including ECU 1,500m. for Stabex and ECU

480m. for Sysmin) and ECU 1,200m. from the EIB. Under the fourth Convention the obligation of most of the ACP states to contribute to the replenishment of Stabex resources, including the repayment of transfers made under the first three Conventions, was removed. In addition, special loans made to ACP member countries were to be cancelled, except in the case of profit-oriented businesses. Other innovations included the provision of assistance for structural adjustment programmes, measures to avoid increasing the recipient countries' indebtedness (e.g. by providing Stabex and Sysmin assistance in the form of grants, rather than loans), and increased support for the private sector, environmental protection, and control of growth in population.

To offset losses in export earnings sustained by ACP countries in 1992, 32 states were entitled in 1993 to receive a total of 60 transfers under the Stabex system, amounting to ECU 848m., however, this was reduced by ECU 84m., in accordance with the Convention, owing to lack of resources.

In late June 1993 the European Community (EC, as the EU was previously entitled) introduced a regime concerning the import of bananas into the Community, which was designed to protect the banana industries of ACP countries (mostly in the Caribbean), which were threatened by cheaper bananas produced by countries in Latin America. The new regime, which was opposed by the low-cost producing countries and by Germany (the largest EU consumer of bananas), placed a quota of 2m. metric tons of bananas imported from Latin America, which would incur a uniform duty of 20%, while imports above this level were to be subject to a tariff of ECU 850 per ton. In February 1994 a dispute panel of the General Agreement on Tariffs and Trade (GATT) upheld a complaint brought by five Latin American countries that the EU import regime, which reserved 30% of its market for production of member states and ACP countries, was in contravention of free trade. An agreement was subsequently reached in March under which the EU increased the quota for Latin American banana imports to 2.1m. tons from October 1994 and 2.2m. tons in 1995.

In early September 1993 the Community announced plans to revise and strengthen its relations with the ACP countries under the Lomé Convention. The revision of the agreement was intended to establish 'more open, equitable and transparent relations among the signatories'. Amendment of the Convention was to be guided by three objectives: the promotion of democracy, the rule of law and good governance in ACP countries; open dialogue, avoiding paternalistic or colonial attitudes; and the simplification of the Convention's mechanisms. In May 1994 ministers from the EU member states and ACP countries met for a mid-term review of the Lomé IV Convention, at which the Community reiterated its intention to maintain the Convention as an aid instrument but to adapt it in response to international trade developments, particularly the successful conclusion of the Uruguay Round of GATT negotiations.

COMMITMENTS MADE UNDER THE LOMÉ CONVENTION (ECU million)

	1992	1993*
Trade promotion	40.8	81.8
Cultural and social development	209.5	334.3
Education and training	73.5	88.6
Water engineering, urban infrastructure and housing	54.4	129.2
Health	81.6	116.6
Economic infrastructure (transport and communications)	310.1	165.6
Development of production	811.7	816.9
Rural production	209.9	225.8
Industrialization	149.9	142.3
Campaigns on specific themes[1]	451.8	448.8
Exceptional aid, Stabex	497.3	138.1
Rehabilitation	9.8	−0.7
Disasters	58.9	110.1
Stabex	397.0	2.5
AIDS	0.3	–
Refugees and returnees	31.3	25.6
Other[2]	187.1	62.9
Total	2,056.5	1,599.7

* Provisional figures.

[1] Including desertification and drought, disasters, major endemic and epidemic diseases, hygiene and basic health, endemic cattle diseases, energy-saving research, sectoral imports programme and long-term schemes.

[2] Including information and documentation, seminars, programmes and general technical co-operation, general studies, multisectoral programmes, delegations, administrative and financial costs, improvements to public buildings, project-linked multisectoral technical cooperation (all projects).

Source: Commission of the EC, *General Report* (1993).

THE FRANC ZONE

Address: Direction Générale des Services Etrangers (Service de la Zone Franc), Banque de France, 39 rue Croix-des-Petits-Champs, BP 140-01, Paris Cedex 01, France.

Telephone: (1) 42-92-31-26; **telex:** 220932; **fax:** (1) 42-92-39-88.

MEMBERS

Benin	Equatorial Guinea
Burkina Faso	French Republic*
Cameroon	Gabon
Central African Republic	Mali
Chad	Niger
Comoros	Senegal
Congo	Togo
Côte d'Ivoire	

* Metropolitan France, Mayotte, St Pierre and Miquelon and the Overseas Departments and Territories.

The Franc Zone embraces all those countries and groups of countries whose currencies are linked with the French franc at a fixed rate of exchange and who agree to hold their reserves mainly in the form of French francs and to effect their exchange on the Paris market. Each of these countries or groups of countries has its own central issuing bank and its currency is freely convertible into French francs. This monetary union is based on agreements concluded between France and each country or group of countries.

Apart from Guinea and Mauritania, all of the countries that formerly comprised French West and Equatorial Africa are members of the Franc Zone. The former West and Equatorial African territories are still grouped within the currency areas that existed before independence, each group having its own currency issued by a central bank.

A number of states left the Franc Zone during the period 1958–73: Guinea, Tunisia, Morocco, Algeria, Mauritania and Madagascar.

The Comoros, formerly a French Overseas Territory, did not join the Franc Zone on achieving independence in 1975. However, francs CFA were used as the currency of the new state and the Institut d'émission des Comores continued to function as a Franc Zone organization. In 1976 the Comoros formally assumed membership. In July 1981 the Banque centrale des Comores replaced the Institut d'émission des Comores, establishing its own currency, the Comoros franc.

Equatorial Guinea, a former Spanish colony, joined the Franc Zone in January 1985.

During the late 1980s and early 1990s the economies of the African Franc Zone countries were adversely affected by increasing foreign debt and by a decline in the prices paid for their principal export commodities. The French Government, however, refused to devalue the franc CFA, as recommended by the IMF. In 1990 the Franc Zone governments agreed to develop economic union, with integrated public finances and common commercial legislation. In 1991 ministers of the Franc Zone approved the creation of a regional body responsible for compiling statistics and economic studies, which was to be called 'Afristat'. In April 1992, at a meeting of Franc Zone ministers, a treaty was signed on the insurance industry whereby a regulatory body for the industry was to be established: the Conférence Intrafricaine des Marchés d'Assurances. Under the treaty, which was to be effective from 31 December 1992, a council of Franc Zone ministers responsible for the insurance industry was also to be established with its secretariat in Libreville, Gabon. It was agreed that a further council of ministers was to be created with the task of monitoring the social security systems in Franc Zone countries. A programme drawn up by Franc Zone finance ministers concerning the harmonization of commercial legislation in member states was approved by the Franco-African summit in October; ministers of finance and justice were requested to make implementation of the programme a priority. A treaty to align corporate and investment regulations was signed by 11 member countries at the annual meeting with France in October 1993. Devaluations of the franc CFA and the Comoros franc were agreed in January 1994 (see below).

EXCHANGE REGULATIONS

Currencies of the Franc Zone are freely convertible into the French franc at a fixed rate, through 'operations accounts' established by agreements concluded between the French Treasury and the individual issuing banks. It is backed fully by the French Treasury, which also provides the issuing banks with overdraft facilities.

The monetary reserves of the CFA countries are normally held in French francs in the French Treasury. However, the Banque centrale des états de l'Afrique de l'ouest (BCEAO) and the Banque des états de l'Afrique centrale (BEAC) are authorized to hold up to 35% of their foreign exchange holdings in currencies other than the franc. Exchange is effected on the Paris market. Part of the reserves earned by richer members can be used to offset the deficits incurred by poorer countries.

Regulations drawn up in 1967 provided for the free convertibility of currency with that of countries outside the Franc Zone. Restrictions were removed on the import and export of CFA banknotes, although some capital transfers are subject to approval by the governments concerned.

When the French Government instituted exchange control to protect the French franc in May 1968, other Franc Zone countries were obliged to take similar action in order to maintain free convertibility within the Franc Zone. The franc CFA was devalued following devaluation of the French franc in August 1969. Since March 1973 the French authorities have ceased to maintain the franc⁸US dollar rate within previously agreed margins, and, as a result, the value of the franc CFA has fluctuated on foreign exchange markets in line with the French franc.

In August 1993, as a result of the financial turmoil regarding the European exchange rate mechanism and the continuing weakness of the French franc, the BCEAO and the BEAC decided to suspend repurchasing of francs CFA outside the Franc Zone. Effectively this signified the withdrawal of guaranteed convertibility of the franc CFA with the French franc. In January 1994 the franc CFA was devalued by 50%, and the Comoros franc by 33.3%.

CURRENCIES OF THE FRANC ZONE

French franc (= 100 centimes): used in Metropolitan France, in the Overseas Departments of Guadeloupe, French Guiana, Martinique, Réunion, and in the Overseas Collectivités Territoriales of Mayotte and St Pierre and Miquelon.

1 franc CFA=1 French centime. CFA stands for Communauté financière africaine in the West African area and for Coopération financière en Afrique centrale in the Central African area. Used in the monetary areas of West and Central Africa respectively.

1 Comoros franc=1.333 French centimes. Used in the Comoros, where it replaced the franc CFA in 1981.

1 franc CFP=5.5 French centimes. CFP stands for Comptoirs français du Pacifique. Used in New Caledonia, French Polynesia and the Wallis and Futuna Islands.

WEST AFRICA

Union monétaire ouest-africaine—UMOA (West African Monetary Union): established by Treaty of November 1973, entered into force 1974; comprises Benin, Burkina Faso, Côte d'Ivoire, Mali, Niger, Senegal (all parts of former French West Africa) and Togo; in 1990 the UMOA Banking Commission was established, which is responsible for supervising the activities of banks and financial institutions in the region, with the authority to prohibit the operation of a banking institution. UMOA was expected to be transformed into UEMOA (see below) as part of the process of greater economic integration in the region.

Union Economique et monétaire ouest-africaine—UEMOA: f. 1994, it is expected to replace the Communauté économique de l'Afrique de l'ouest–CEAO (see p.xxx). Chair. BLAISE CAMPAORE.

Banque centrale des états de l'Afrique de l'ouest—BCEAO: ave Abdoulaye Fadiga, BP 3108, Dakar, Senegal; tel. 23-16-15; telex 21815; fax 23-93-35; f. 1962 by Benin, Burkina Faso, Côte d'Ivoire, Mali, Niger, Senegal and Togo (in co-operation with France) in order to manage the franc CFA; central bank of issue for the members of UMOA; cap. and res 379,881m. francs CFA (Sept. 1992). Gov. CHARLES KONAN BANNY (Côte d'Ivoire); Sec.-Gen. for monetary policy OUMAROU SIDIKOU; Sec.-Gen. for general administration MARCEL KODJO (Togo). Publs *Annual Report, Notes d'Information et Statistiques* (monthly).

Banque ouest-africaine de développement—BOAD: 68 ave de la Libération, BP 1172, Lomé, Togo; tel. 21-42-44; telex 5289; fax 21-52-67; f. 1973 by heads of member states of UMOA, to promote the balanced development of member states and the economic integration of West Africa; cap. (authorized) 140,000m. francs CFA, (subscribed) 121,700m. francs CFA (Aug. 1991). Mems: Benin, Burkina Faso, Côte d'Ivoire, Mali, Niger, Senegal, Togo. Chair. ABOU BAKAR BABA-MOUSSA; Vice-Chair. ALPHA TOURE. Publ. *Rapport Annuel, BOAD-INFO* (every 3 months).

CENTRAL AFRICA

Union douanière et économique de l'Afrique centrale—UDEAC (Customs and Economic Union of Central Africa): BP 969, Bangui, Central African Republic; tel. 61-09-22; telex 5254; f. 1966 by the Brazzaville Treaty of 1964 (revised in 1974); forms customs union, with free trade between members and a common external tariff for imports from other countries. UDEAC has a common code for investment policy and a Solidarity Fund to counteract regional disparities of wealth and economic development. In December 1988 a meeting of heads of state of the Franc Zone countries urged the immediate implementation of the following schemes by UDEAC: a common market in meat; joint production of pharmaceuticals; a training school for telecommunications engineers; joint agricultural research centres; tax harmonization; and the construction of new roads that would link the Central African Republic and Gabon to the Trans-African Highway (Lagos–Mombasa). In May 1993 UDEAC announced that it was soon to establish a maritime transport company, to operate between West and Central Africa, in order to encourage traffic between the two regions. Budget (1990) 1,331m. francs CFA. Mems: Cameroon, Central African Republic, Chad, Congo, Equatorial Guinea, Gabon. Sec.-Gen. THOMAS DAKAYI KAMGA (Cameroon). Publs *Annuaire du Commerce Extérieur de l'UDEAC, Bulletin des Statistiques Générales* (quarterly).

At a summit meeting in December 1981, UDEAC leaders agreed in principle to form an economic community of Central African states (Communauté économique des états d'Afrique centrale—CEEAC), to include UDEAC members and Burundi, Rwanda, São Tomé and Príncipe and Zaire. CEEAC (q.v.) began operations in 1985.

In March 1994 UDEAC leaders signed a treaty establishing the Communauté économique et monétaire en Afrique centrale (CEMAC), which was to promote the process of sub-regional integration within the framework of an economic union and a monetary union.

Banque de développement des états de l'Afrique centrale (BDEAC): place du Gouvernement, BP 1177, Brazzaville, Congo; tel. 83-02-12; telex 5306; fax 83-02-66; f. 1976; cap. p.u. 57,250m. francs CFA (June 1993); shareholders: Cameroon, Central African Republic, Chad, Congo, Gabon, Equatorial Guinea, African Development Bank, BEAC, France, Germany and Kuwait; Chair. IBNI OUMAR MAHAMAT SALEH; Dir-Gen. JEAN-MARIE MBIOKA.

Banque des états de l'Afrique centrale (BEAC): ave Mgr François Xavier Vogt, BP 1917, Yaoundé, Cameroon; tel. 23-40-30; telex 8343; fax 23-33-29; f. 1973 as the central bank of issue of Cameroon, the Central African Republic, Chad, Congo, Equatorial Guinea and Gabon; cap. 40,000m. francs CFA, res 163,500m. francs CFA (Jan. 1993). Gov. JEAN-FÉLIX MAMALEPOT; Vice-Gov. JEAN-EDOUARD SATHOUD (Congo). Publs *Rapport annuel, Etudes et statistiques* (monthly).

CENTRAL ISSUING BANKS

Banque centrale des Comores: BP 405, Moroni, Comoros; tel. 73-10-02; telex 213231; f. 1981; Dir-Gen. MOHAMED HALIFA.

Banque centrale des états de l'Afrique de l'ouest: see above.

Banque des états de l'Afrique centrale: see above.

Banque de France: 1 rue de la Vrillière, Paris, France; f. 1800; issuing authority for Metropolitan France; Gov. JEAN-CLAUDE TRICHET; Dep. Govs HERVÉ HANNOUN, DENIS FERMAN.

Institut d'émission des départements d'outre-mer: Cité du Retiro, 35/37 rue Boissy d'Anglas, 75379 Paris Cedex 08, France; tel. (1) 40-06-41-41; issuing authority for the French Overseas Departments and the French Overseas Collectivité Territoriale of St Pierre and Miquelon; Pres. DENIS FERMAN; Dir-Gen. PHILIPPE JURGENSEN; Dir. OLIVIER BEUGNOT.

Institut d'émission d'outre-mer: Cité du Retiro, 35/37 rue Boissy d'Anglas, 75379 Paris Cedex 08, France; tel. (1) 40-06-41-41; issuing authority for the French Overseas Territories and the French Overseas Collectivité Territoriale of Mayotte; Pres. DENIS FERMAN; Dir-Gen. PHILIPPE JURGENSEN; Dir. OLIVIER BEUGNOT.

FRENCH ECONOMIC AID

France's ties with the African Franc Zone countries involve not only monetary arrangements, but also include comprehensive French assistance in the forms of budget support, foreign aid, technical assistance and subsidies on commodity exports.

Official French financial aid and technical assistance to developing countries is administered by the following agencies:

Caisse française de développement—CFD (fmrly the Caisse centrale de coopération économique—CCCE): Cité du Retiro, 35/37 rue Boissy d'Anglas, 75379 Paris Cedex 08, France; tel. (1) 40-06-31-31; telex 212632; f. 1941. French development bank which lends money to member states and former member states of the Franc Zone and several other states, and executes the financial operations of the FAC. Financial aid to Franc Zone countries disbursed in 1991 totalled 9,153m. French francs; following the devaluation of the franc CFA in January 1994 the French Government cleared all debt arrears owed by member states to the CFD. In early 1994 the CFD made available funds totalling 2,420m. francs CFA to assist the establishment of CEMAC (see above); Dir-Gen. PHILIPPE JURGENSEN.

Fonds d'aide et de coopération—FAC: 20 rue Monsieur, 75007 Paris, France; tel. (1) 47831010; fax (1) 43064163; in 1959 FAC took over from FIDES (Fonds d'investissement pour le développement économique et social) the administration of subsidies and loans from the French Government to the former French African states. FAC is administered by the Ministry of Co-operation and Development, which allocates budgetary funds to it.

ISLAMIC DEVELOPMENT BANK

Address: POB 5925, Jeddah 21432, Saudi Arabia.

Telephone: (2) 6361400; **telex:** 601137; **fax:** (2) 6366871.

An international financial institution established following a conference of finance ministers of member countries of the Organization of the Islamic Conference (q.v.), held in Jeddah in December 1973. Its aim is to encourage the economic development and social progress of member countries and of Muslim communities in non-member countries, in accordance with the principles of the Islamic Shari'a (sacred law). The Bank formally opened in October 1975.

MEMBERS

There are 46 members (see table of subscriptions below). Turkmenistan was admitted as a member in June 1992, and Azerbaijan in July.

Organization

(June 1994)

BOARD OF GOVERNORS

Each member country is represented by a governor, usually its Finance Minister, and an alternate. The Board of Governors is the supreme authority of the Bank, and meets annually.

BOARD OF EXECUTIVE DIRECTORS

The Board consists of 11 members, five of whom are appointed by the five largest subscribers to the capital stock of the Bank; the remaining six are elected by Governors representing the other subscribers. Members of the Board of Executive Directors are elected for three-year terms. The Board is responsible for the direction of the general operations of the Bank.

President of the Bank and Chairman of the Board of Executive Directors: OSSAMA JAAFAR FAQIH (Saudi Arabia).

Bank Secretary: Dr MOHAMED BEN SEDDIQ.

FINANCIAL STRUCTURE

In July 1992 the Board of Governors decided to increase the authorized capital of the Bank from 2,028.74m. to 6,000m. Islamic Dinars (to be divided into 600,000 shares, having a value of 10,000 Islamic Dinars each). The Islamic Dinar (ID) is the Bank's unit of account and is equivalent to the value of one Special Drawing Right of the IMF (SDR 1 = US $1.40360 at 30 June 1993).

In July 1992 subscribed capital was raised from ID 2,028.74m. to ID 4,000m.; in the Islamic year 1413 (1 July 1992–20 June 1993) paid-up capital and reserves amounted to ID 2,293.5m.

SUBSCRIPTIONS (million Islamic Dinars, as at 30 June 1993)

Afghanistan	5.00	Maldives	2.50
Algeria	124.32	Mali	4.92
Azerbaijan	2.50	Mauritania	4.92
Bahrain	7.00	Morocco	24.81
Bangladesh	49.29	Niger	12.41
Benin	4.92	Oman	13.78
Brunei	12.41	Pakistan	124.26
Burkina Faso	12.41	Palestine Liberation Organization	9.85
Cameroon	12.41	Qatar	49.23
Chad	4.92	Saudi Arabia	997.17
Comoros	2.50	Senegal	12.42
Djibouti	2.50	Sierra Leone	2.50
Egypt	49.23	Somalia	2.50
Gabon	14.77	Sudan	19.69
The Gambia	2.50	Syria	5.00
Guinea	12.41	Tunisia	9.85
Guinea-Bissau	2.50	Turkey	315.47
Indonesia	124.26	Uganda	12.41
Iran	349.97	United Arab Emirates	283.03
Iraq	13.05	Yemen	24.81
Jordan	19.89	**Total**	3,654.29
Kuwait	496.64		
Lebanon	2.50		
Libya	315.30		
Malaysia	79.56		

Activities

The Bank adheres to the Islamic principle forbidding usury, and does not grant loans or credits for interest. Instead, its methods of financing are: provision of interest-free loans (with a service fee), mainly for infrastructural projects which are expected to have a marked impact on long-term socio-economic development; provision of technical assistance (e.g. for feasibility studies); equity participation in industrial and agricultural projects; leasing operations, involving the leasing of equipment such as ships, and instalment sale financing; and profit-sharing operations. Funds not immediately needed for projects are used for foreign trade financing, particularly for importing commodities to be used in development (i.e. raw materials and intermediate industrial goods, rather than consumer goods); priority is given to the import of goods from other member countries (see table). A longer-term trade financing scheme was introduced in 1987/88. In addition, the Special Assistance Account provides emergency aid and other assistance, with particular emphasis on education in Islamic communities in non-member countries.

By 20 June 1993 the Bank had approved a total of ID 2,408.81m. for project financing and technical assistance, a total of ID 7,008.25m. for foreign trade financing, and ID 346.41 for special assistance operations. During the Islamic year 1413, from 1 July 1992 to 20 June 1993, the Bank approved a total of ID 658.90m. for 155 operations, compared with ID 713.01m. for 158 operations in the previous year. Of financing approved in the year to 20 June 1993, about 62% was for foreign trade financing.

The Bank approved 15 interest-free loans in the year ending 20 June 1993, amounting to ID 74.72m. (compared with 13 loans, totalling ID 63.75m., in the previous year). These loans supported the following projects: rural electrification and road construction in Bangladesh; an agricultural college in Benin; land development in Chad and Guinea; a general hospital in Indonesia; telecommunications in Lebanon; the International

Islamic University in Malaysia; livestock development in Mali; agricultural development in Mauritania; a technical institute and village support in Pakistan; construction of dykes in Senegal; road construction in Sudan; and sewerage in Tunisia.

The Bank approved 11 technical assistance operations for 7 countries in the form of grants during the year, amounting to ID 6.58m.

Twenty member countries are among the world's least-developed countries (as designated by the United Nations). During the year 63% of loan financing was directed to these countries.

Import trade financing approved during the year amounted to ID 380.54 for 68 operations in 12 member countries: of this amount 29.7% was for imports of intermediate industrial goods, 26.6% for crude petroleum, 10.6% for cotton, 9.7% for vegetable oil and 7.5% for fertilizers.

Under the Bank's Special Assistance Account, 23 operations were approved during the year, amounting to ID 11.37m., providing assistance primarily in the education and health sectors; 15 of the operations were for Muslim communities in non-member countries. The Bank's scholarships programme sponsored 420 students from 27 countries during the year to 20 June 1993. The Bank also undertakes the distribution of meat sacrificed by Muslim pilgrims: during the year to July 1991 meat from 410,566 head of sheep, 2,262 head of cows and 8,912 head of camel was distributed to the needy in 23 member countries.

Disbursements during the year ending 20 June 1993 totalled ID 386.65m. (compared with ID 410.96m. in the previous year). Of this total ID 96.79m. was for project financing and technical assistance, and ID 273.30m. was for foreign trade financing, while ID 16.56m. was provided for special operations.

In January 1990 the Bank launched its Unit Investment Fund in order to mobilize additional resources. The initial issue of the Fund was US $100m., with a minimum subscription of $100,000. By 20 June 1993 18 institutions, mainly in GCC countries, had subscribed to the Fund. The Fund finances mainly private-sector industrial projects in middle-income countries; by 20 June 1993 a total of US $171.81m. had been approved in financing for 18 projects in nine countries.

Operations approved, Islamic year 1413 (1 July 1992–20 June 1993)

Type of operation	Number of operations	Total amount (million Islamic Dinars)
Ordinary operations	50	236.10
Loan	15	74.72
Equity	8	20.92
Leasing	2	14.80
Lines of finance	2	8.60
Instalment sales	12	110.47
Technical assistance	11	6.58
Project financing	39	229.52
Foreign trade financing	82	411.43
Operations financed from the Special Assistance Account	23	11.37
Total	155	658.90

Project financing and technical assistance by sector, 1 July 1992–20 June 1993

Sector	Amount (million Islamic Dinars)	%
Agriculture and agro-industry	52.62	22.3
Industry and mining	38.32	16.2
Transport and communications	39.86	16.9
Utilities	51.88	22.0
Social services	23.60	10.0
Other	29.81	12.6
Total	236.10	100.0

RESEARCH AND TRAINING INSTITUTE

Islamic Research and Training Institute: POB 9201, Jeddah 21413, Saudi Arabia; tel. (2) 6361400; telex 601137; fax (2) 6378927; f. 1982 for research enabling economic, financial and banking activities to conform to Islamic law, and to provide training for staff involved in development activities in the Bank's member countries. During the Islamic year 1 July 1992–20 June 1993 the Institute conducted 12 research studies on economic, financial and general development issues relevant to the Bank's member states. The Institute also organized seminars and workshops, and held training courses aimed at furthering the expertise of government and financial officials in Islamic developing countries. Dir Dr ABDELHAMID EL-GHAZALI.

PUBLICATION

Annual Report.

ORGANIZATION OF AFRICAN UNITY—OAU

Address: POB 3243, Addis Ababa, Ethiopia.

Telephone: (1) 517700; **telex:** 21046; **fax:** (1) 513036.

The Organization was founded in 1963 to promote unity and solidarity among African states.

FORMATION

There were various attempts at establishing an inter-African organization before the OAU Charter was drawn up. In November 1958 Ghana and Guinea (later joined by Mali) drafted a Charter which was to form the basis of a Union of African States. In January 1961 a conference was held at Casablanca, attended by the heads of state of Ghana, Guinea, Mali, Morocco, and representatives of Libya and of the provisional government of the Algerian Republic (GPRA). Tunisia, Nigeria, Liberia and Togo declined the invitation to attend. An African Charter was adopted and it was decided to set up an African Military Command and an African Common Market.

Between October 1960 and March 1961 three conferences were held by French-speaking African countries, at Abidjan, Brazzaville and Yaoundé. None of the 12 countries which attended these meetings had been present at the Casablanca Conference. These conferences led eventually to the signing in September 1961, at Tananarive, of a charter establishing the Union africaine et malgache, later the Organisation commune africaine et mauricienne (OCAM).

In May 1961 a conference was held at Monrovia, Liberia, attended by the heads of state or representatives of 19 countries: Cameroon, Central African Republic, Chad, Congo Republic (ex-French), Côte d'Ivoire, Dahomey, Ethiopia, Gabon, Liberia, Madagascar, Mauritania, Niger, Nigeria, Senegal, Sierra Leone, Somalia, Togo, Tunisia and Upper Volta. They met again (with the exception of Tunisia and with the addition of the ex-Belgian Congo Republic) in January 1962 at Lagos, Nigeria, and set up a permanent secretariat and a standing committee of finance ministers, and accepted a draft charter for an Organization of Inter-African and Malagasy States.

It was the Conference of Addis Ababa, held in 1963, which finally brought together African states despite the regional, political and linguistic differences which divided them. The foreign ministers of 32 African states attended the Preparatory Meeting held in May: Algeria, Burundi, Cameroon, Central African Republic, Chad, Congo (Brazzaville) (now the Congo), Congo (Léopoldville) (now Zaire), Côte d'Ivoire, Dahomey (now Benin), Ethiopia, Gabon, Ghana, Guinea, Liberia, Libya, Madagascar, Mali, Mauritania, Morocco, Niger, Nigeria, Rwanda, Senegal, Sierra Leone, Somalia, Sudan, Tanganyika (now Tanzania), Togo, Tunisia, Uganda, the United Arab Republic (Egypt) and Upper Volta (now Burkina Faso).

The topics discussed by the meeting were: (i) creation of the Organization of African States; (ii) co-operation among African states in the following fields: economic and social; education, culture and science; collective defence; (iii) decolonization; (iv) apartheid and racial discrimination; (v) effects of economic grouping on the economic development of Africa; (vi) disarmament; (vii) creation of a Permanent Conciliation Commission; and (viii) Africa and the United Nations.

The Heads of State Conference which opened on 23 May drew up the Charter of the Organization of African Unity, which was then signed by the heads of 30 states on 25 May 1963. The Charter was essentially functional and reflected a compromise between the concept of a loose association of states favoured by the Monrovia Group and the federal idea supported by the Casablanca Group, and in particular by Ghana.

SUMMARY OF OAU CHARTER

Article I. Establishment of the Organization of African Unity. The Organization to include continental African states, Madagascar, and other islands surrounding Africa.

Article II. Aims of the OAU:

1. To promote unity and solidarity among African states.
2. To intensify and co-ordinate efforts to improve living standards in Africa.
3. To defend sovereignty, territorial integrity and independence of African states.
4. To eradicate all forms of colonialism from Africa.
5. To promote international co-operation in keeping with the Charter of the United Nations.

Article III. Member states adhere to the principles of sovereignty, non-interference in internal affairs of member states, respect for territorial integrity, peaceful settlement of disputes, condemnation of political subversion, dedication to the emancipation of dependent African territories, and international non-alignment.

Article IV. Each independent sovereign African state shall be entitled to become a member of the Organization.

Article V. All member states shall have equal rights and duties.

Article VI. All member states shall observe scrupulously the principles laid down in Article III.

Article VII. Establishment of the Assembly of Heads of State and Government, the Council of Ministers, the General Secretariat, and the Commission of Mediation, Conciliation and Arbitration.

Articles VIII–XI. The Assembly of Heads of State and Government co-ordinates policies and reviews the structure of the Organization.

Articles XII–XV. The Council of Ministers shall prepare conferences of the Assembly, and co-ordinate inter-African co-operation. All resolutions shall be by simple majority.

Articles XVI–XVIII. The General Secretariat. The Administrative Secretary-General and his staff shall not seek or receive instructions from any government or other authority external to the Organization. They are international officials responsible only to the Organization.

Article XIX. Commission of Mediation, Conciliation and Arbitration. A separate protocol concerning the composition and nature of this Commission shall be regarded as an integral part of the Charter.

Articles XX–XXII. Specialized Commissions shall be established, composed of Ministers or other officials designated by Member Governments. Their regulations shall be laid down by the Council of Ministers.

Article XXIII. The Budget shall be prepared by the Secretary-General and approved by the Council of Ministers. Contributions shall be in accordance with the scale of assessment of the United Nations. No Member shall pay more than 20% of the total yearly amount.

Article XXIV. Texts of the Charter in African languages, English and French shall be equally authentic. Instruments of ratification shall be deposited with the Government of Ethiopia.

Article XXV. The Charter shall come into force on receipt by the Government of Ethiopia of the instruments of ratification of two-thirds of the signatory states.

Article XXVI. The Charter shall be registered with the Secretariat of the United Nations.

Article XXVII. Questions of interpretation shall be settled by a two-thirds majority vote in the Assembly of Heads of State and Government.

Article XXVIII. Admission of new independent African states to the Organization shall be decided by a simple majority of the Member States.

Articles XXIX–XXXIII. The working languages of the Organization shall be African languages, English, French, Arabic and Portuguese. The Secretary-General may accept gifts and bequests to the Organization, subject to the approval of the Council of Ministers. The Council of Ministers shall establish privileges and immunities to be accorded to the personnel of the Secretariat in the territories of Member States. A State wishing to withdraw from the Organization must give a year's written notice to the Secretariat. The Charter may only be amended after consideration by all Member States and by a two-thirds majority vote of the Assembly of Heads of State and Government. Such amendments will come into force one year after submission.

MEMBERS*

Algeria
Angola
Benin
Botswana
Burkina Faso
Burundi
Cameroon
Cape Verde
Central African Republic
Chad
The Comoros
Congo
Côte d'Ivoire
Djibouti
Egypt
Equatorial Guinea
Eritrea
Ethiopia
Gabon
The Gambia
Ghana
Guinea
Guinea-Bissau
Kenya
Lesotho
Liberia
Libya
Madagascar
Malawi
Mali
Mauritania
Mauritius
Mozambique
Namibia
Niger
Nigeria
Rwanda
São Tomé and Príncipe
Senegal
Seychelles
Sierra Leone
Somalia
South Africa
Sudan
Swaziland
Tanzania
Togo
Tunisia
Uganda
Zaire
Zambia
Zimbabwe

* The Sahrawi Arab Democratic Republic (Western Sahara) was admitted to the OAU in February 1982, following recognition by 26 of the 50 members, but its membership was disputed by Morocco and other states which claimed that a two-thirds majority was needed to admit a state whose existence was in question. Morocco withdrew from the OAU with effect from November 1985.

Organization

(June 1994)

ASSEMBLY OF HEADS OF STATE

The Assembly of Heads of State and Government meets annually to co-ordinate policies of African states. Resolutions are passed by a two-thirds majority, procedural matters by a simple majority. A chairman is elected at each meeting from among the members, to hold office for one year.

Chairman (1994/95): ZINE AL-ABIDINE BEN ALI (Tunisia).

COUNCIL OF MINISTERS

Consists of ministers of foreign affairs and others and meets twice a year, with provision for extraordinary sessions. Each session elects its own Chairman. Prepares meetings of, and is responsible to, the Assembly of Heads of State.

GENERAL SECRETARIAT

The permanent headquarters of the organization. It carries out functions assigned to it in the Charter of the OAU and by other agreements and treaties made between member states. Departments: Political; Finance; Education, Science, Culture and Social Affairs; Economic Development and Co-operation; Administration and Conferences. The Secretary-General is elected for a four-year term by the Assembly of Heads of State.

Secretary-General: SALIM AHMED SALIM (Tanzania).

ARBITRATION COMMISSION

Commission of Mediation, Conciliation and Arbitration: Addis Ababa; f. 1964; consists of 21 members elected by the Assembly of Heads of State for a five-year term; no state may have more than one member; has a Bureau consisting of a President and two Vice-Presidents, who shall not be eligible for re-election. Its task is to hear and settle disputes between member states by peaceful means.

SPECIALIZED COMMISSIONS

There are specialized commissions for economic, social, transport and communications affairs; education, science, culture and health; defence; human rights; and labour.

BUDGET

Member states contribute in accordance with their United Nations assessment. No member state is assessed for an amount exceeding 20% of the yearly regular budget of the Organization. In February 1994 the Organization's first biennial budget was approved by the Council of Ministers. The budget for 1994-96 was US $59.66m. At 31 December 1993 total outstanding contributions amounted to $69m, while only $3.93m. of the $24.76m. 1993/94 budget had been received.

Principal Events, 1982–94

1982

Feb. An OAU committee on Chad established a timetable for ceasefire, negotiations, a provisional constitution and elections in Chad, and announced that the OAU peace-keeping force's mandate would cease at the end of June. The committee on Western Sahara empowered Pres. Moi of Kenya to conduct negotiations for a ceasefire between Morocco and the Polisario Front. At a meeting of ministers of foreign affairs, the admission of a representative of the SADR led to a walk-out by 19 countries.

Aug. The 19th Assembly of Heads of State, due to be held in Tripoli, Libya, failed to achieve a quorum when 19 states boycotted the meeting owing to the dispute over the admission of the SADR. A five-member committee was set up to try to convene another summit before the end of the year.

Nov. A second attempt to hold the 19th Assembly of Heads of State in Tripoli was abandoned after a dispute over the representation of Chad: the Libyan leader, Col Gaddafi, and others opposed the presence of Pres. Hissène Habré in favour of the former Pres. Goukouni Oueddei, leading to a boycott by representatives of 14 moderate states.

1983

June The 19th Assembly of Heads of State met in Addis Ababa: SADR representatives agreed not to attend, in order to avoid a boycott of the meeting by their opponents. The Assembly again called for a referendum in Western Sahara and for direct negotiations between Morocco and the SADR.

1984

Jan. The OAU-sponsored talks between the rival factions in Chad, held in Addis Ababa, broke down without result, chiefly owing to the refusal of Pres. Habré to attend.

Nov. Nigeria became the 30th OAU member to recognize the Sahrawi Arab Democratic Republic. A delegation from the SADR was admitted to the 20th Assembly, held in Addis Ababa, and Morocco immediately announced its resignation from the OAU (to take effect after one year); only Zaire supported Morocco by withdrawing from the meeting. The Assembly concentrated on economic matters, discussing Africa's balance-of-payments problems, debts and the drought affecting many countries. An emergency fund was set up to combat the effects of drought.

1985

July The 21st Assembly of Heads of State was held in Addis Ababa. It resulted in the Addis Ababa Declaration, in which member countries reiterated their commitment to the Lagos Plan of Action on the establishment of an African common market by 2000 (adopted in 1980) and approved a priority programme for the next five years, emphasizing the rehabilitation of African agriculture through greater public investment. The meeting also expressed concern at Africa's heavy external debt: it proposed the convening of a special conference of creditors and borrowers to seek a solution to the problem, and an increase in concessional financial resources.

1986

July The 22nd Assembly of Heads of State called for comprehensive economic sanctions against South Africa, and strongly criticized the governments of the United Kingdom and the USA for opposing sanctions. Among other resolutions the Assembly condemned outside interference in Angola; called upon France to return the island of Mayotte to the Comoros; and resolved to continue efforts (led by the OAU Chairman) to bring about reconciliation in Chad. A council of 'wise men', comprising former African heads of state, was established to mediate, when necessary, in disputes between member countries.

1987

Feb. The OAU Chairman, President Sassou-Nguessou of the Congo, undertook a tour of Europe to discuss the possibility of a negotiated settlement in Chad; the political situation in South Africa; and African debt.

July The Assembly of Heads of State reiterated its demands that Western countries should impose economic sanctions on South Africa. It renewed the mandate of the special OAU committee which had been attempting to resolve the dispute between Chad and Libya. It also discussed the spread of the disease AIDS in Africa; and approved the establishment of an African Commission on Human and People's Rights (see below), now that the African Charter on Human and People's Rights (approved in 1981) had been ratified by a majority of member states.

Nov. A summit meeting on the subject of Africa's external debt (now estimated to total US $200,000m.) was held in Addis Ababa (but was attended by only 10 heads of state and government). The meeting issued a statement requesting the conversion of past bilateral loans into grants, a 10-year suspension of debt-service payments, reduction of interest rates and the lengthening of debt-maturity periods. It asked that creditors should observe the principle that debt-servicing should not exceed a 'reasonable and bearable' percentage of the debtor country's export earnings. A 'contact group' was established to enlist support for an international conference on African debt.

1988

May The Assembly of Heads of State recognized that no conference on debt was likely to be held in 1988, owing to the reluctance of creditors to participate. It condemned the links with South Africa still maintained by some African countries, and protested at the recently-reported unauthorized disposal of toxic waste in Africa by industrial companies from outside the continent.

Aug. The OAU organized an international conference in Oslo, Norway, on refugees and displaced persons in southern Africa.

1989

Jan. A meeting on apartheid, organized by the OAU, resulted in the formation of the African Anti-Apartheid Committee (see below).

May The OAU Chairman, President Traoré of Mali, undertook a mission of mediation between the governments of Mauritania and Senegal, following ethnic conflict between the citizens of the two countries.

July The Assembly of Heads of State discussed the Namibian independence process, and urged that the UN should ensure that the forthcoming elections there would be fairly conducted. They again requested that an international conference on Africa's debts should be held.

Sept.–Dec. The newly-elected OAU Chairman, Hosni Mubarak, and the newly-appointed OAU Secretary-General, Salim Ahmed Salim, attempted to mediate in the dispute between Mauritania and Senegal. In November a mediation committee, comprising representatives of six countries, visited Mauritania and Senegal.

1990

March A monitoring group was formed by the OAU to report on events in South Africa. The OAU urged the international community to continue imposing economic sanctions on South Africa.

July The Assembly of Heads of State reviewed the implications for Africa of recent socio-economic and political changes in Eastern Europe, and of the European Community's progress towards monetary and political union.

1991

Feb. A draft treaty on the creation of an African Economic Community was adopted unanimously by the Council of Ministers.

June The Assembly of Heads of State signed the treaty on the creation of the African Economic Community. The treaty was to enter into force after ratification by two-thirds of OAU member states. The Community was to be established by 2025, beginning with a five-year stage during which measures would be taken to strengthen existing economic groupings. The meeting also established a committee of heads of state to assist national reconciliation in Ethiopia; and gave a mandate to the OAU Secretary-General to undertake a mission to assist in restoring political stability in Somalia.

1992

Feb.–March The OAU was involved, together with the UN and the Organization of the Islamic Conference (OIC, q.v.), in mediation between the warring factions in Mogadishu, Somalia. The OAU subsequently continued to assist in efforts to achieve a peace settlement in Somalia.

May An OAU mission was dispatched to South Africa to monitor the continued violence in that country.

June–July Proposals were advanced at the Assembly of the Heads of State, held in Dakar, Senegal, for a mechanism to be established within the OAU for 'conflict management, prevention and resolution'. These proposals were accepted in principle, but operational details were to be elaborated at a later stage.

Oct. The Ad Hoc Committee on Southern Africa met in Gaborone, Botswana, to discuss a report compiled by a team of OAU experts on practical steps to be taken towards the democratization of South Africa. Plans to send a mission to monitor the Mozambican peace accord were announced.

Nov. An International Conference on Assistance to African Children, which was organized by the OAU with assistance from UNICEF, was held in Dakar, Senegal. The Conference aimed to focus awareness on the plight of many of Africa's children and to encourage African countries to honour commitments made at the UN World Summit for Children in 1991, whereby governments were to allocate greater resources to programmes benefiting children. An OAU-UNICEF study, presented at the Conference, also recommended that a greater proportion of bilateral aid be directed at helping children.

1993

Feb. A session of the Council of Ministers discussed the OAU's serious financial crisis, of which outstanding contributions amounting to US $70m. were a major factor. The meeting agreed to allocate $250,000 to the creation of a conflict prevention bureau, and a further $250,000 for the purposes of monitoring elections.

May A Pan-African Conference on Reparations for the suffering caused by colonialism in Africa, organized by the OAU together with the Nigerian Government, was held in Abuja. The Conference appealed to those countries which had benefited from the colonization of Africa and the use of Africans as slaves (particularly European countries and the USA) to make reparations to Africans and their descendants, either in the form of capital transfers, or cancellation of debt.

June Eritrea was admitted as the 52nd member of the OAU. In his first address to the Organization (at the 29th Assembly), the Eritrean President, Issaias Afewerki, strongly criticized the OAU's failure to achieve many of its declared aims. The Assembly resolved to establish a mechanism for conflict prevention and resolution. The mechanism's primary objective was to be anticipation and prevention of conflict. In cases where conflicts had already occurred, the OAU was to undertake peace-making and peace-building activities, including the deployment of civilian or military monitoring missions. However, in the case of a conflict seriously degenerating, assistance would be sought from the United Nations.

July A seminar on the African Economic Community was held in Addis Ababa, Ethiopia, concerned with the popularization of the treaty establishing the Community. Lack of resources emerged as one of the main barriers to the actual creation of the Community.

Sept. The OAU announced the immediate removal of economic sanctions against South Africa, following the approval by that country's parliament of a bill to establish a transitional executive council prior to the democratic elections, scheduled to be conducted in April 1994.

Oct. A planned OAU mission to mediate in the dispute over a presidential election in Angola was postponed, following consultations with the Angolan authorities. The OAU Secretary-General condemned an attempted military coup in Burundi, in which the President and six Cabinet ministers were killed, and the subsequent civil unrest.

Nov. A summit conference of African ministers of foreign affairs, conducted in Addis Ababa, resolved to establish an OAU protection and observation mission to Burundi, consisting of 180 military personnel and 20 civilians, and appealed for international financial and material support to assist the mission. The conference approved the principles for the establishment of a mechanism for conflict prevention, management and resolution. The conference suggested that 5% of the OAU budget, but not less than US $1m., be allocated for an OAU Peace Fund to finance the mechanism, and that $0.5m. be made available for 1993.

Dec. A meeting of 11 African Heads of State approved the establishment of the Peace Fund and called for contributions from the international community. A draft statement for the mechanism for conflict prevention, management and resolution, issued by the OAU Secretary-General, expressed support for the efforts to resolve the conflict in Somalia and emphasized the need to promote national reconciliation.

1994

Feb. The Council of Ministers, at its 59th ordinary session, reaffirmed its support for the results of elections in Burundi, that were conducted in 1993, and approved the establishment of an OAU mission to promote dialogue and national reconciliation in that country. The Council condemned anti-government forces for the escalation of violence in Angola.

April The OAU mission to South Africa participated as observers of the electoral process. An OAU delegation visited Nigeria and Cameroon to investigate the border dispute between the two countries.

May South Africa was admitted as the 53rd member of the OAU.

June Consultations with each of the conflicting parties in Rwanda were conducted by the OAU. The Assembly of Heads of State, meeting in Tunis, approved a code of conduct for inter-African relations, in order to strengthen political consultation and co-operation for the promotion of security and stability in the region. Nine countries were nominated to serve on the OAU Bureau of Conflict Resolution, the central committee of its conflict mechanism, which was to implement an early-warning system for identifying potential conflicts and introduce measures to manage and resolve conflicts.

Specialized Agencies

African Anti-Apartheid Committee: Brazzaville, Congo; f. 1989; aims to link anti-apartheid movements within and outside Africa, and to co-ordinate anti-apartheid strategy. Chair. DANIEL ABIBI (Congo).

African Bureau for Educational Sciences: 29 ave de la Justice, BP 1764, Kinshasa I, Zaire; tel. (12) 22006; telex 21166; f. 1973 to conduct educational research. Publs *Bulletin d'Information* (quarterly), *Revue africaine des sciences de l'éducation* (2 a year), *Répertoire africain des institutions de recherche* (annually).

African Civil Aviation Commission—AFCAC: 15 blvd de la République, BP 2356, Dakar, Senegal; tel. 23-20-30; telex 61182; fax 23-26-61; f. 1969 to encourage co-operation in all civil aviation activities; promotes co-ordination and better utilization and development of African air transport systems and the standardization of aircraft, flight equipment and training programmes for pilots and mechanics; organizes working groups and seminars, and compiles statistics. Pres. VASSIRIKI SAVANE (Côte d'Ivoire); Sec. J. R. RAZAFY.

African Commission on Human and People's Rights: Kairaba Ave, POB 673, Banjul, The Gambia; tel. 96042; telex 2346; f. 1987; meets twice a year for two weeks in March and October; the October session is always held in Banjul, The Gambia, and the March session may be held in any other African country.

The Commission comprises 11 members, elected by the OAU's Assembly of Heads of State and Government: one from each sub-region of Africa. Its mandate is to monitor compliance with the African Charter on Human and People's Rights (ratified in 1986), and it investigates claims of human rights abuses perpetrated by governments that have ratified the Charter. Claims may be brought by other African governments, the victims themselves, or by a third party. Sec. Prof. MUTSINZI NGABISHEMA.

Co-ordinating Committee for the Liberation of Africa: POB 1767, Dar es Salaam, Tanzania; tel. (51) 277711; telex 41031; fax (51) 20029; f. 1963; to provide financial and military aid to nationalist movements in dependent countries; regional offices in Luanda, Angola, Lusaka, Zambia and Maputo, Mozambique. Exec. Sec. Brig. HASHIM MBITA (Tanzania).

International Scientific Council for Trypanosomiasis Research and Control: Joint Secretariat, OAU/STRC, PM Bag 2359, Lagos, Nigeria; tel. (1) 633289; telex 22199; fax (1) 2636093; f. 1949 to review the work on tsetse and trypanosomiasis problems carried out by organizations and workers concerned in laboratories and in the field; to stimulate further research and discussion and to promote co-ordination between research workers and organizations in the different countries in Africa, and to provide a regular opportunity for the discussion of particular problems and for the exposition of new experiments and discoveries.

Organization of African Trade Union Unity—OATUU: POB M386, Accra, Ghana; tel. 772574; telex 2673; fax 772621; f. 1973 as a single continental trade union organization, independent of international trade union organizations; has affiliates from all African trade unions. Congress, composed of four delegates from all affiliated trade union centres, meets at least every four years as supreme policy-making body; General Council, composed of one representative from all affiliated trade unions, meets annually to implement Congress decisions and to approve annual budget. Mems: trade union movements in 52 independent African countries. Sec.-Gen. HASSAN SUNMONU (Nigeria). Publ. *Voice of African Workers*.

Pan-African News Agency—PANA: BP 4056, Dakar, Senegal; tel. 25-61-20; telex 21647; regional headquarters in Khartoum, Sudan; Lusaka, Zambia; Kinshasa, Zaire; Lagos, Nigeria; Tripoli, Libya; began operations in May 1983; receives information from national news agencies and circulates news in English and French. Co-ordinator-Gen. BABACAR FALL (Senegal). Publ. *PANA Review*.

Pan-African Postal Union—PAPU: POB 6026, Arusha, Tanzania; tel. (57) 8603; telex 42096; fax (57) 8606; f. 1980 to extend members' co-operation in the improvement of postal services. Sec.-Gen. GEZAHEGN GEBREWOLD (Ethiopia).

Scientific, Technical and Research Commission—OAU/STRC: Nigerian Ports Authority Bldg, PMB 2359, Marina, Lagos, Nigeria; tel. (1) 633289; telex 22199; f. 1965 to succeed the Commission for Technical Co-operation in Africa (f. 1954). Supervises the Inter-African Bureau for Animal Resources (Nairobi, Kenya), the Inter-African Bureau for Soils (Lagos, Nigeria) and the Inter-African Phytosanitary Commission (Yaoundé, Cameroon) and several joint research projects (see also International Scientific Council for Trypanosomiasis Research and Control, above); a centre for Fertilizer Development was to be established in 1988. The Commission provides training in agricultural management, and conducts pest control programmes.

Special Health Fund for Africa: c/o WHO Regional Office for Africa, Brazzaville, POB 6, Congo; f. 1990 to finance health activities, in co-operation with the World Health Organization.

Supreme Council for Sports in Africa: BP 1363, Yaoundé, Cameroon; tel. 22-27-11; telex 8295. Sec.-Gen. DR AWOTURE ELEYAE (Nigeria).

Union of African Railways: BP 687, Kinshasa, Zaire; tel. (12) 23861; telex 21258; f. 1972 to standardize, expand, co-ordinate and improve members' railway services; the ultimate aim is to link all systems; main organs: General Assembly, Executive Board, General Secretariat, five technical cttees. Mems in 30 African countries. Pres. TOM MMARI; Sec.-Gen. ROBERT GEBE NKANA (Malawi).

ORGANIZATION OF THE ISLAMIC CONFERENCE—OIC

Address: Kilo 6, Mecca Rd, POB 178, Jeddah 21411, Saudi Arabia.

Telephone: (2) 680-0800; **telex:** 601366; **fax:** (2) 687-3568.

The Organization was formally established in May 1971, when its Secretariat became operational, following a summit meeting of Muslim heads of state at Rabat, Morocco, in September 1969, and the Islamic Foreign Ministers' Conference in Jeddah in March 1970, and in Karachi, Pakistan, in December 1970.

MEMBERS

Afghanistan	Indonesia	Qatar
Albania	Iran	Saudi Arabia
Algeria	Iraq	Senegal
Azerbaijan	Jordan	Sierra Leone
Bahrain	Kuwait	Somalia
Bangladesh	Kyrgyzstan	Sudan
Benin	Lebanon	Syria
Brunei	Libya	Tajikistan
Burkina Faso	Malaysia	Tunisia
Cameroon	Maldives	Turkey
Chad	Mali	Turkmenistan
The Comoros	Mauritania	Uganda
Djibouti	Morocco	United Arab Emirates
Egypt	Niger	Yemen
Gabon	Nigeria	Zanzibar
The Gambia	Oman	
Guinea	Pakistan	
Guinea-Bissau	Palestine	

Note: Observer status has been granted to the Muslim community of the 'Turkish Federated State of Cyprus' (which declared independence as the 'Turkish Republic of Northern Cyprus' in November 1983). Mozambique also has observer status. Azerbaijan was admitted as a member in 1991, Turkmenistan in June 1992, and Albania, Kyrgyzstan, Tajikistan and Zanzibar (which forms part of Tanzania) were granted membership of the Conference in December 1992.

Organization

(June 1994)

SUMMIT CONFERENCES

The supreme body of the Organization is the Conference of Heads of State, which met in 1969 at Rabat, Morocco, in 1974 at Lahore, Pakistan, and in January 1981 at Mecca, Saudi Arabia, when it was decided that summit conferences would be held every three years in future. Fifth Conference: Kuwait, January 1987; sixth Conference: Dakar, Senegal, December 1991. The next Conference was to be held in Saudi Arabia.

CONFERENCE OF MINISTERS OF FOREIGN AFFAIRS

Conferences take place annually, to consider the means for implementing the general policy of the Organization, although they may also be convened for extraordinary sessions.

SECRETARIAT

The executive organ of the Organization, headed by a Secretary-General (who is elected by the Conference of Ministers of Foreign Affairs for a non-renewable four-year term) and four Assistant Secretaries-General (similarly appointed).

Secretary-General: Dr HAMID ALGABID (Niger).

At the summit conference in January 1981 it was decided that an International Islamic Court of Justice should be established to adjudicate in disputes between Muslim countries. Experts met in January 1983 to draw up a constitution for the court, but by 1994 it was not yet in operation.

SPECIALIZED COMMITTEES

Al-Quds Committee: f. 1975 to implement the resolutions of the Islamic Conference on the status of Jerusalem (Al-Quds); it meets at the level of foreign ministers; Chair. King HASSAN II of Morocco.

Standing Committee for Economic and Commercial Co-operation (COMCEC): f. 1981; Chair. SÜLEYMAN DEMIREL (Pres. of Turkey).

Standing Committee for Information and Cultural Affairs (COMIAC): f. 1981; Chair. ABDOU DIOUF (Pres. of Senegal).

Standing Committee for Scientific and Technological Co-operation (COMSTECH): f. 1981; Chair. FAROOQ A. LEGHARI (Pres. of Pakistan).

Islamic Commission for Economic, Cultural and Social Affairs: f. 1976.

Permanent Finance Committee.

Other committees comprise the Committee for Southern Africa, the Committee of Islamic Solidarity with the Peoples of the Sahel, the Six-Member Committee on the Situation of Muslims in the Philippines, the Six-Member Committee on Palestine, the ad-hoc Committee on Afghanistan, and the OIC contact group on Bosnia and Herzegovina.

Activities

The Organization's aims, as proclaimed in the Charter that was adopted in 1972, are:

(i) To promote Islamic solidarity among member states;

(ii) To consolidate co-operation among member states in the economic, social, cultural, scientific and other vital fields, and to arrange consultations among member states belonging to international organizations;

(iii) To endeavour to eliminate racial segregation and discrimination and to eradicate colonialism in all its forms;

(iv) To take necessary measures to support international peace and security founded on justice;

(v) To co-ordinate all efforts for the safeguard of the Holy Places and support of the struggle of the people of Palestine, and help them to regain their rights and liberate their land;

(vi) To strengthen the struggle of all Muslim people with a view to safeguarding their dignity, independence and national rights; and

(vii) To create a suitable atmosphere for the promotion of co-operation and understanding among member states and other countries.

The first summit conference of Islamic leaders (representing 24 states) took place in 1969 following the burning of the Al Aqsa Mosque in Jerusalem. At this conference it was decided that Islamic governments should 'consult together with a view to promoting close co-operation and mutual assistance in the economic, scientific, cultural and spiritual fields, inspired by the immortal teachings of Islam'. Thereafter the foreign ministers of the countries concerned met annually, and adopted the Charter of the Organization of the Islamic Conference in 1972.

At the second Islamic summit conference (Lahore, Pakistan, 1974), the Islamic Solidarity Fund was established, together with a committee of representatives which later evolved into the Islamic Commission for Economic, Cultural and Social Affairs. Subsequently, numerous other subsidiary bodies have been set up (see below).

ECONOMIC CO-OPERATION

A general agreement for economic, technical and commercial co-operation came into force in 1981, providing for the establishment of joint investment projects and trade co-ordination. This was followed by an agreement on promotion, protection and guarantee of investments among member states. A plan of action to strengthen economic co-operation was adopted at the third Islamic summit conference in 1981, aiming to promote collective self-reliance and the development of joint ventures in all sectors. In May 1993 the OIC committee for economic and commercial co-operation, meeting in Istanbul, agreed to review and update the 1981 plan of action.

A meeting of ministers of industry was held in February 1982, and agreed to promote industrial co-operation, including joint ventures in agricultural machinery, engineering and other basic industries.

In December 1988 it was announced that a committee of experts, established by the OIC, was to draw up a 10-year programme of assistance to developing countries (mainly in Africa) in science and technology.

CULTURAL CO-OPERATION

The Organization supports education in Muslim communities throughout the world, and, through the Islamic Solidarity Fund, has helped to establish Islamic universities in Niger, Uganda, Bangladesh and Malaysia. It organizes seminars on various aspects of Islam, and encourages dialogue with the other monotheistic religions. Support is given to publications on Islam both in Muslim and Western countries.

In March 1989 the Conference of Ministers of Foreign Affairs denounced as an apostate the author of the controversial novel *The Satanic Verses* (Salman Rushdie), demanded the withdrawal of the book from circulation, and urged member states to boycott publishing houses that refused to comply.

HUMANITARIAN ASSISTANCE

Assistance is given to Muslim communities affected by wars and natural disasters, in co-operation with UN organizations, particularly UNHCR. The countries of the Sahel region (Burkina Faso, Cape Verde, Chad, The Gambia, Guinea, Guinea-Bissau, Mali, Mauritania, Niger and Senegal) receive particular attention as victims of drought. In April 1993 member states pledged US $80m. in emergency assistance for Muslims affected by the war in Bosnia and Herzegovina.

POLITICAL CO-OPERATION

The Organization is also active at a political level. From the beginning it called for vacation of Arab territories by Israel, recognition of the rights of Palestinians and of the Palestine Liberation Organization as their sole legitimate representative, and the restoration of Jerusalem to Arab rule. The 1981 summit conference called for a *jihad* (holy war—though not necessarily in a military sense) 'for the liberation of Jerusalem and the occupied territories'; this was to include an Islamic economic boycott of Israel.

In January 1980 an extraordinary conference of ministers of foreign affairs demanded the immediate and unconditional withdrawal of Soviet troops from Afghanistan and suspended Afghanistan's membership of the organization. The conference adopted a resolution condemning armed aggression against Somalia and denouncing the presence of military forces of the USSR and some of its allies in the Horn of Africa.

In 1982 Islamic ministers of foreign affairs decided to establish Islamic offices for boycotting Israel and for military co-operation with the Palestine Liberation Organization. The 1984 summit conference agreed to reinstate Egypt (suspended following the peace treaty signed with Israel in 1979) as a member of the Organization, although the resolution was opposed by seven states.

The fifth summit conference, held in January 1987, discussed the continuing Iran–Iraq war, and agreed that the Islamic Peace Committee should attempt to prevent the sale of military equipment to the parties in the conflict. The conference also discussed the conflicts in Chad and Lebanon, and requested the holding of a United Nations conference to define international terrorism, as opposed to legitimate fighting for freedom. The conference also approved proposals for joint development of modern technology, and for improving scientific and technical skills in the less-developed Islamic countries.

In March 1989 ministers of foreign affairs agreed to readmit Afghanistan, as represented by the 'interim government' formed by the *mujahidin* ('holy warriors'), following the withdrawal of Soviet troops from Afghanistan.

In August 1990 a majority of ministers of foreign affairs condemned Iraq's recent invasion of Kuwait, and demanded the withdrawal of Iraqi forces. In August 1991 the Conference of Ministers of Foreign Affairs obstructed Iraq's attempt to propose a resolution demanding the repeal of economic sanctions against the country. The sixth summit conference, held in Senegal in December 1991, reflected the divisions in the Arab world that resulted from Iraq's invasion of Kuwait and the ensuing war. Twelve heads of state did not attend, sending representatives, reportedly to register protest at the presence of Jordan and the PLO at the conference, both of which had given support to Iraq. Disagreement also arose between the PLO and the majority of other OIC member states when it was proposed to cease the OIC's support for the PLO's *jihad* in the Arab territories occupied by Israel. The proposal, which was adopted, represented an attempt to further the Middle East peace negotiations currently being sponsored by the USA.

In late August 1992 the UN General Assembly approved a non-binding resolution, introduced by the OIC, that requested the UN Security Council to take increased action, including the use of force, in order to defend the non-Serbian population of Bosnia and Herzegovina (some 43% of Bosnians being Muslims) from Serbian aggression, and to restore its 'territorial integrity'. The OIC Conference of Ministers of Foreign Affairs, which was held in Jeddah, Saudi Arabia, in early December, demanded anew that the UN Security Council take all necessary measures against Serbia and Montenegro, including military intervention, in accordance with Article 42 of the UN Charter, in order to protect the Bosnian Muslims. In early February 1993 the OIC appealed to the Security Council to remove the embargo on armaments to Bosnia and Herzegovina with regard to the Bosnian Muslims, to allow them to defend themselves from the

Bosnian Serbs, who were far better armed. At the Conference of Ministers of Foreign Affairs, held in Karachi, Pakistan, in late April 1993, a co-ordination group on action to help the Bosnian Muslims was created, composed of representatives from Egypt, Iran, Malaysia, Saudi Arabia, Senegal and Turkey.

A report by an OIC fact-finding mission investigating allegations of repression of the largely Muslim population of the Indian state of Jammu and Kashmir by the Indian armed forces was presented to the 1993 Conference. The Conference urged member states to take the necessary measures to persuade India to cease the 'massive human rights violations' in Jammu and Kashmir and to allow the Indian Kashmiris to 'exercise their inalienable right to self-determination'. A second OIC fact-finding mission was to be dispatched to Kashmir. The Conference also condemned the destruction of a historic mosque in India by extremist Hindus; 'Israeli acts of terrorism, suppression, killing and deportation', directed at Palestinians; and Armenian offensive action against Azerbaijan.

A special ministerial meeting on Bosnia and Herzegovina was held in mid-July 1993, at which seven OIC countries committed themselves to sending troops to serve in the UN Protection Force in the former Yugoslavia (UNPROFOR), to assist the United Nations in providing adequate protection and relief to the victims of war in Bosnia and Herzegovina. More than 17,000 troops were to be made available, with the OIC demanding that member states should be represented at the highest level in UNPROFOR's command structure. (The UN subsequently decided that 5,000 troops from three Islamic countries—Malaysia, Pakistan and Tunisia—should be dispatched to Bosnia and Herzegovina before the end of the year.) The meeting also decided to dispatch immediately a ministerial mission to persuade influential governments to support the OIC's demands for the removal of the arms embargo on Bosnian Muslims and athe convening of a restructured international conference to bring about a political solution to the conflict.

SUBSIDIARY ORGANS

Al-Quds Fund: c/o OIC, Kilo 6, Mecca Rd, POB 178, Jeddah 21411, Saudi Arabia; f. 1976 to support the struggle of the Palestinian people in Jerusalem.

International Commission for the Preservation of Islamic Cultural Heritage: POB 24, 80692 Beşiktaş, Istanbul, Turkey; tel. (212) 2605988; telex 26484; fax (212) 2584365; f. 1982. Chair. Prince Faisal bin Fahd bin Abdul Aziz (Saudi Arabia).

Islamic Centre for the Development of Trade: Complexe Commerciale des Habous, ave des FAR, BP 13545, Casablanca, Morocco; tel. (2) 314974; telex 46296; fax (2) 310110; f. 1983 to encourage regular commercial contacts, harmonize policies and promote investments among OIC members. Dir Badre Eddine Allali. Publs *Tijaris: International and Inter-Islamic Trade Magazine, Inter-Islamic Trade Report* (annual).

Islamic Centre for Technical and Vocational Training and Research: KB Bazar, Joydebpur, Gazipur Dist., Dhaka, Bangladesh; tel. (2) 892366; telex 642739; fax (2) 892396; f. 1981 to provide skilled technicians and instructors in mechanical, electrical, electronic and chemical technology, and to conduct research; capacity of 65 staff and 650 students. Dir Prof. A. M. Patwari. Publs News Bulletin (quarterly), reports, human resources development series.

Islamic Foundation for Science, Technology and Development—IFSTAD: POB 9833, Jeddah 21423, Saudi Arabia; tel. (2) 632-2273; telex 604081; fax (2) 632-2274; f. 1981 to promote co-operation in science and technology within the Islamic world. Dir-Gen. Dr Arafat R. Altamemi.

Islamic Jurisprudence Academy: Jeddah, Saudi Arabia; f. 1982. Sec.-Gen. Sheikh Mohamed Habib Belkhojah.

Islamic Solidarity Fund: c/o OIC Secretariat, POB 178, Jeddah, Saudi Arabia; f. 1974 to meet the needs of Islamic communities by providing emergency aid and the wherewithal to build mosques, Islamic centres, hospitals, schools and universities. Chair. Sheikh Nasir Abdullah bin Hamdan; Exec. Dir Abdullah Hersi.

Research Centre for Islamic History, Art and Culture: POB 24, Beşiktaş 80692, Istanbul, Turkey; tel. (212) 2605988; telex 26484; fax (212) 2584365; f. 1979; library of 40,000 vols. Dir-Gen. Prof. Dr Ekmeleddin İhsanoğlu. Publ. *Newsletter* (3 a year).

Statistical, Economic and Social Research and Training Centre for the Islamic Countries: Attar Sok. 4, GOP, Ankara, Turkey; tel. (4) 1286105; telex 43163; f. 1978. Dir Dr Şadi Cindoruk.

SPECIALIZED INSTITUTIONS

International Islamic News Agency (IINA): King Khalid Palace, Madinah Rd, POB 5054, Jeddah, Saudi Arabia; tel. (2) 665-8561; telex 601090; fax (2) 665-9358; f. 1972. Dir-Gen. Abdulwahab Kashif.

Islamic Development Bank: POB 5925, Jeddah 21432, Saudi Arabia; tel. (2) 6361400; telex 601137; fax (2) 6366871; f. 1975; promotes the economic and social development of OIC member countries and Muslim communities in non-member countries; provides assistance in the form of loans and grants for technical aid, in accordance with the principles of the Islamic Shari'a (sacred law). Pres. and Chair. Ossama Jaafar Faqih (Saudi Arabia).

Islamic Educational, Scientific and Cultural Organization (ISESCO): BP 755, 16 bis Charia Omar Ben Khattab, Agdal, Rabat, Morocco; tel. (7) 772433; telex 32645; fax (7) 777425; f. 1982. Dir-Gen. Dr Abdulaziz bin Othman al-Twaijri. Publs *ISESCO Bulletin* (quarterly), *Islam Today* (2 a year), *ISESCO Triennial.*

Islamic States Broadcasting Organization (ISBO): POB 6351, Jeddah 21442, Saudi Arabia; tel. (2) 6721121. Sec.-Gen. Hussein al-Askary.

OTHER INSTITUTIONS

Islamic Research and Training Institute: POB 9201, Jeddah 21413, Saudi Arabia; tel. (2) 636-1400; telex 601137; fax (2) 637-8927; f. 1982 for research enabling economic, financial and banking activities to conform to Islamic law, and to provide training for staff involved in development activities in member countries.

AFFILIATED INSTITUTIONS

International Association of Islamic Banks: 47 Aruba St, Heliopolis Houria'a, POB 2828, Cairo, Egypt; mems: 28 banks and other financial institutions in 11 Islamic countries. Sec.-Gen. Samir A. Sheikh.

Islamic Cement Association: Posta Kutsu 2, 06582 Bankanhiklar, Ankara, Turkey; f. 1984; aims to encourage co-operation in the production of cement.

Islamic Chamber of Commerce, Industry and Commodity Exchange: POB 3831, Karachi, Pakistan; tel. (21) 530535; telex 25533; fax (21) 532656; f. 1979 to promote trade and industry among member states; comprises national chambers or federations of chambers of commerce and industry. Sec.-Gen. Ageel Ahmad al-Jassim.

Islamic Committee for the International Crescent: Benghazi, Libya; f. 1979 to attempt to alleviate the suffering caused by natural disasters and war. Sec.-Gen. Dr Ahmad Abdallah Cherif.

Islamic Shipowners'Association: POB 14900, Jeddah 21434, Saudi Arabia; tel. (2) 6653379; telex 607303; fax (2) 6604920; f. 1981 to promote co-operation among maritime companies in Islamic countries. Sec.-Gen. Abdullatif A. Sultan.

Organization of Islamic Capitals and Cities: POB 13621, Jeddah 21414, Saudi Arabia; tel. (2) 6657516; telex 606562; fax (2) 6657516; f. 1978 to develop co-operation among the Islamic capitals and to preserve their character and heritage. Sec.-Gen. Abdulqadir Hamzak Koshak.

Sports Federation of Islamic Solidarity: POB 5844, Riyadh, Saudi Arabia; telex 404760; fax (1) 4013216; f. 1981. Sec.-Gen. Dr Saleh Gazdar.

SOUTHERN AFRICAN DEVELOPMENT COMMUNITY—SADC

Address: SADC Building, Private Bag 0095, Gaborone, Botswana.

Telephone: 351863; **telex:** 2555; **fax:** 372848.

The first Southern African Development Co-ordination Conference (SADCC) was held at Arusha, Tanzania, in July 1979, to harmonize development plans and to reduce the region's economic dependence on South Africa. On 17 August 1992 the 10 member countries of the SADCC signed a treaty establishing the Southern African Development Community (SADC) which replaced the SADCC. The treaty places binding obligations on member countries with the aim of promoting economic integration towards a fully developed common market. A tribunal was to be established to arbitrate in the case of disputes between member states arising from the treaty. By September 1993 all of the member states had ratified the treaty; it came into effect on 5 October.

MEMBERS

Angola	Mozambique	Zambia
Botswana	Namibia	Zimbabwe
Lesotho	Swaziland	
Malawi	Tanzania	

TREATY ESTABLISHING THE SADC

The Treaty declares the following aims:

(i) deeper economic co-operation and integration, on the basis of balance, equality and mutual benefit, providing for cross-border investment and trade, and freer movement of factors of production, goods and services across national boundaries;

(ii) common economic, political and social values and systems, enhancing enterprise competitiveness, democracy and good governance, respect for the rule of law and human rights, popular participation, and the alleviation of poverty; and

(iii) strengthened regional solidarity, peace and security, in order for the people of the region to live and work in harmony.

Organization

(June 1994)

SUMMIT MEETING

The meeting is held annually and is attended by Heads of State and Government or their representatives. It is the supreme policy-making organ of the SADC.

COUNCIL OF MINISTERS

Representatives of SADC member countries at ministerial level meet at least twice a year; in addition, special meetings are held to co-ordinate regional policy in a particular field by, for example, ministers of energy and ministers of transport.

CONFERENCES ON CO-OPERATION

A conference with the SADC's 'international co-operating partners' (donor governments and international agencies) is held annually to review progress in the various sectors of the SADC programme and to present new projects requiring assistance.

SECRETARIAT

Executive Secretary: Kaire Mbuende (Namibia).

SECTORAL CO-ORDINATION OFFICES

Agricultural Research, Animal Disease Control and Livestock Production: Ministry of Agriculture, Private Bag 0032, Gaborone, Botswana; tel. 350581; telex 2543; fax 356027.

Culture and Information: Ministry of Information, Avda Francisco Orlando Magumbwe 750, Maputo, Mozambique; tel. (1) 493423; telex 6821; fax (1) 493427.

Energy Sector Technical and Administrative Unit: CP 172, Luanda, Angola; tel. 23382; telex 3170.

Economic Affairs: Ministry of Finance and Development Planning, Private Bag 008, Gaborone, Botswana; tel. 350292; telex 2401; fax 356086.

Food Security Technical and Administrative Unit: 88 Rezende St, POB 4046, Harare, Zimbabwe; tel. (4) 736053; telex 22440; fax (4) 704363.

Human Resources Development: Dept of Economic Planning and Statistics, POB 602, Mbabane, Swaziland; tel. 46344; telex 3020; fax 46407.

Inland Fisheries, Wildlife and Forestry: Ministry of Forestry and Natural Resources, Private Bag 350, Lilongwe 3, Malawi; tel. 782600; telex 44465; fax 782537.

Marine Fisheries and Resources: Private Bag 13355, Windhoek, Namibia; tel. (61) 3963187; fax (61) 224566.

Mining: Ministry of Mines, POB 31969, Lusaka, Zambia; tel. (1) 251719; telex 40539; fax (1) 252095.

SADC Environment and Land Management Sector Co-ordination Unit: Ministry of Agriculture, Co-operatives and Marketing, POB 24, Maseru 100, Lesotho; tel. 322158; telex 4414; fax 310190; f. 1985; Dir B. Leleka.

SADC Press Trust: Katanga House, 19 Selous Ave, POB 6290, Harare, Zimbabwe; tel. (4) 738891; telex 6367; Editor-in-Chief Dominic C. Mulaisho.

Southern African Centre for Co-operation in Agricultural Research (SACCAR): Private Bag 00108, Gaborone, Botswana; tel. 373847; telex 2752; fax 375204; Dir Dr M. L. Kyomo.

Southern Africa Transport and Communications Commission (SATCC): CP 2677, Maputo, Mozambique; tel. (1) 420246; telex 6606; fax (1) 420213; Dir P. M. Mangoaela.

Tourism: Ministry of Tourism, Sports and Culture, POB 52, Maseru 100, Lesotho; tel. 323034; telex 4228; fax 310194.

Trade and Industrial Co-ordination Division: Ministry of Industries and Trade, POB 9503, Dar es Salaam, Tanzania; tel. (51) 31457; telex 41686; (51) 46919.

Activities

In July 1979 the first Southern African Development Co-ordination Conference was attended by delegations from Angola, Botswana, Mozambique, Tanzania and Zambia, with representatives from donor governments and international agencies; the group was later joined by Lesotho, Malawi, Swaziland and Zimbabwe, and Namibia became a member in 1990.

In April 1980 a regional economic summit conference was held in Lusaka, Zambia, and the Lusaka Declaration, a statement of strategy entitled 'Southern Africa: Towards Economic Liberation', was approved, together with a programme of action allotting specific studies and tasks to member governments (see list of co-ordinating offices, above). The members aimed to reduce their dependence on South Africa for rail and air links and port facilities, imports of raw materials and manufactured goods, and the supply of electric power. In 1985, however, an SADCC report noted that since 1980 the region had become still more dependent on South Africa for its trade outlets, and the 1986 summit meeting, although it recommended the adoption of economic sanctions against South Africa, failed to establish a timetable for doing so.

At the donors' conference held in January 1990, the World Bank announced that it was to provide $4,000m. for SADCC member states over the next five years. In July 1993 it was reported that US $4,284m. of the $8,748m. required for SADC projects had been secured.

In January 1992 a meeting of the SADCC Council of Ministers approved proposals to transform the organization into a fully integrated economic community and in mid-August the treaty establishing the SADC (see above) was signed.

A possible merger between the SADC and the Preferential Trade Area for Eastern and Southern Africa (PTA, q.v.), which consists of all the members of the SADC apart from Botswana and has similar aims of enhancing economic co-operation was rejected by the SADC's Executive Secretary in January 1993. He denied that the two organizations were duplicating each other's work, as had been suggested.

TRANSPORT AND COMMUNICATIONS

At the SADCC's inception transport was seen as the most important area to be developed, on the grounds that, as the

Lusaka Declaration noted. Without the establishment of an adequate regional transport and communications system, other areas of co-operation become impractical'. Priority was to be given to the improvement of road and railway services into Mozambique, so that the landlocked countries of the region could transport their goods through Mozambican ports instead of South African ones. The successful distribution of emergency supplies in 1992/93 following a severe drought in the region (see below) was reliant on improvements made to the region's infrastructure in recent years. The facilities of 12 ports in Southern Africa, including South Africa, were used to import some 11.5m. metric tons of drought-related commodities, and the SADC co-ordinated six transport corridors to ensure unobstructed movement of food and supplies.

Rehabilitation of the railway between Malawi and Beira on the coast of Mozambique was under way in 1982, while work on the line from Malawi to the port of Nacala in Mozambique began in 1983. In 1984 a 12-year project for the rehabilitation of the main railway line in Botswana, from Gaborone to the Zimbabwe border, was initiated. In early 1988 plans were announced for the second phase of the rehabilitation of the Limpopo railway, running from Zimbabwe to Maputo, Mozambique. In February 1989 donors agreed to provide $90m. for the first phase of a rehabilitation scheme for the Benguela railway, which terminates at the port of Lobito in Angola. A 10-year project to develop the railway system in Zambia was initiated in 1990.

In 1991 completion of projects improving port facilities at Beira, Mozambique, were reported, which increased the capacity of SADC's ports by 9%. Work on the port facilities at Beira, Nacala and Maputo (in Mozambique), Dar es Salaam (Tanzania) and Lobito and Luanda (Angola) was continuing in 1993. In early 1994 a port training institute in Mozambique was reported to have been completed and become operational. The rehabilitation of port schools in Angola and Tanzania was underway. There are plans for the rehabilitation and upgrading of roads throughout the region. Major projects include the improvement of the trans-Caprivi highway in Namibia; rehabilitation of the roads connecting Zambia with Zaire, and Botswana with Zambia, Zimbabwe and Namibia; strengthening the road network in Lesotho; and road safety programmes for all SADC countries. A training programme for top and middle management in the transport sector was to commence in 1995. Civil aviation projects include a new airport at Maseru, Lesotho, completed in 1985, and improvements of major airports in Angola, Mozambique, Swaziland, Zambia and Zimbabwe, together with studies on the joint use of maintenance facilities, on regional airworthiness certification and aviation legislation, and on navigational aids. Work on a satellite earth station in Swaziland had been completed by 1984, while two more, in Angola and Zimbabwe, were being constructed. Projects are undertaken in telecommunications and postal services, and there is a SADC Post Office Expedited Mail Service.

At July 1993 the transport and communications programme consisted of 208 projects amounting to US $6,874m., of which only $3,238m. had been secured.

In January 1991 it was announced that a special programme was to be undertaken for the rehabilitation of essential transport facilities in Angola.

FOOD, AGRICULTURE AND NATURAL RESOURCES

The food, agriculture and natural resources sector covers six sub-sectors: agricultural research and training; inland fisheries, forestry and wildlife; marine fisheries and resources; food security; livestock production and animal disease control; and environment and land management. At July 1993 funding required for 120 projects in this sector was US $899m., of which $363m. had been secured. The sector's principle objectives are regional food security, agricultural development and natural resource development. In 1989 a regional food programme (including price incentives for farmers and the construction of strategic storage facilities) was established. The Southern African Centre for Co-operation in Agricultural Research (SACCAR), in Gaborone, Botswana, began operations in 1985. It co-ordinates national research systems and operates a small research grants programme. In mid-1993 SACCAR had implemented nine programmes, including its initial programmes of sorghum and millet improvement, grain legume improvement, and land and water management. In 1992–93 five research grants were awarded to SADC scientists.

The sector aims to promote inland and marine fisheries as an important, sustainable source of animal protein. Marine fisheries are also considered to be a potential source of income of foreign exchange. In May 1993 the first formal meeting of SADC ministers of marine fisheries convened in Namibia, and it was agreed to hold annual meetings. The development of fresh water fisheries is focused on aquaculture projects, and their integration into rural community activities. The environment and land management sub-sector is concerned with sustainability as an essential quality of development. Following the severe drought in the region in 1991/92 (see below) the need for water resources development has become a priority. The sector also undertakes projects for the conservation and sustainable development of forestry and wildlife, the control of animal diseases and the improvement of livestock production.

In early 1992 the SADC's Regional Early Warning System, which aims to anticipate food shortages, issued a report warning of imminent famine in southern Africa, as a result of the worst drought in the region for 50 years. In April the SADCC signed a co-operation agreement with South Africa on the import of grain into the drought-stricken region, this being the first occasion on which the SADCC had co-operated with that country. In the same month an SADCC ministerial meeting decided that a Regional Drought Task Force should be established, comprising officials and ministers responsible for transport and agriculture, to co-ordinate a relief programme. In addition, a logistics advisory unit was established, in co-operation with the UN's World Food Programme, to provide logistical information for the planning and transport of emergency supplies. In June an international conference on the drought emergency in Southern Africa was held in Geneva, at which the SADCC and the United Nations issued a joint appeal for assistance. A total of US $571m., of the $854m. requested, was pledged by donor countries at the conference, and by November about 80% of the requested food aid had been received, although only 41% of the requested non-food aid, such as water, health care, agricultural resources, had been provided. A joint SADC/UN Monitoring Group was established at the UN Department of Humanitarian Affairs in Geneva, in order to co-ordinate the dissemination of updated information on the food situation in Southern Africa to relevant UN agencies and the SADC itself. As a result of the drought crisis experience, SADC member states have agreed to inform the food security sector of their food and non-food requirements on a regular basis, in order to assess the needs of the region as a whole. A regional food reserve project was also to be developed.

ENERGY

The energy programme consists of 76 projects, with total funding requirements of US $875m., as at July 1993, when $648m. had been secured. The main areas of work comprised: joint petroleum exploration, training programmes for the petroleum sector and studies for strategic fuel storage facilities; promotion of the use of coal; development of hydroelectric power, the co-ordination of SADC generation and transmission capacities and the linking of national electricity grids (principally Zimbabwe-Mozambique and energy audits to assess efficiency at industrial plants); new and renewable sources of energy, including pilot projects in solar energy; assessment of the environmental and socio-economic impact of wood-fuel scarcity and relevant education programmes; and energy conservation.

TRADE, INDUSTRY AND MINING

In the industry and trade sector 13 projects were being planned in July 1993, at a total cost of $12m., of which $2m. had been secured.

In 1986 it was announced that, as well as attempting to improve the region's physical infrastructure, the SADCC would also place more emphasis on increasing the production of goods and on stimulating intra-regional trade, which accounted for only about 5% of the members' total external trade. The annual co-operation conference that took place in February 1987 was attended by about 120 representatives of private-sector businesses, and it was hoped that this would stimulate private investment in the region. In March 1989, following a meeting of national business organizations, it was announced that an SADCC regional investment council was to be established, with the aim of identifying and promoting opportunities for investment in the member states. An SADC trade directory was completed in 1991/92. In August 1993 the trade advisory department urged member states to establish export-processing zones in order to stimulate local economies. The sector has initiated programmes aimed at encouraging industrial investment and strengthening industrial and trade support services. The standardization and quality assurance programme provides direct assistance to enterprises, including consultancy and training in export packaging.

In July 1993 29 planned mining projects required financing of $20m., of which $7m. had been secured. Projects currently being undertaken include the study of the shared use of mineral processing facilities; the establishment of a regional seismic network and data centre; small-scale mining; diamond exploration; the establishment of a mining sector industrial training and development advisory unit; the exploration of the Kalahari sands; and the establishment of a SADC central data bank for mining equipment and spares. In January 1992 a new five-year strategy for the promotion of mining in the region was approved. Investment in mining was to be encouraged by means of financial incentives.

HUMAN RESOURCES DEVELOPMENT

The SADC helps to supply the region's requirements in skilled manpower by providing training in the following categories: high-level managerial personnel; agricultural managers; high- and medium-level technicians; artisans; and instructors. The sector also operates the SADC's scholarship and training awards programme. In July 1993 the funding required for 22 human resource development projects was US $52.5m., of which $21m. had been secured.

CULTURE AND INFORMATION

A new culture and information sector was established in 1990, and is co-ordinated by Mozambique. In late November 1991 an SADCC conference on cultural co-operation was held in Arusha, Tanzania, at which strategies in this field were discussed. Following the ratification of the new treaty establishing the Community the sector was expected to emphasize regional socio-cultural development as part of the process of greater integration. Public education initiatives have commenced to encourage the involvement of people in the process of regional integration and development, as well as to promote democratic and human rights' values. A four-year programme entitled the SADC Festival on Arts and Culture was expected to commence activities in 1994. At July 1993 funding required for four projects in this sector amounted to US $12m. of which $2m. had been secured.

TOURISM

The sector's current programme is to promote tourism within the context of national and regional socio-economic development objectives. It comprises four components: tourism product development; tourism marketing and research; tourism services; and human resources development and training. The SADC has promoted tourism for the region at trade fairs in Europe, and has initiated a project to provide a range of promotional material. By September 1993 a project to design a standard grading classification system for tourist accommodation in the region was completed, with the assistance of the World Tourism Organization, and the Council approved its implementation. The sector also aims to assess the needs of intra-regional tourism, to achieve standardization of tourism statistics in the region and to introduce training schemes, facilities and workshops for people involved in the tourism industry. At July 1993 the sector consisted of eight projects which required funding of US $4.5m., of which $2.5m. had been secured.

FINANCE

SADC PROJECT FINANCING BY SECTOR (July 1993)

Sector	Number of projects	Total cost (US $ million)	Funding secured (US $ million)*
Culture and information	4	11.6	2.4
Energy	76	874.8	648.0
Agricultural research and training	15	120.3	72.9
Inland fisheries, forestry and wildlife	40	248.8	104.0
Food security	30	194.2	71.7
Livestock production and animal disease control	17	122.9	82.5
Environment and land management	12	80.1	31.3
Marine fisheries and resources	6	132.6	0.2
Industry and trade	13	12.0	1.8
Human resources development	22	52.5	21.2
Mining	29	20.1	7.1
Tourism	8	4.5	2.5
Transport and communications	208	6,874.1	3,238.1
Total	480	8,748.3	4,283.8

* Includes both local and foreign resources.

PUBLICATIONS

SACCAR Newsletter.

SADC Annual Report.

SADC Energy Bulletin.

SKILLS.

SPLASH.

OTHER REGIONAL ORGANIZATIONS

These organizations are arranged under the following categories:

Agriculture, Forestry and Fisheries	Government and Politics	Religion
Aid, Development and Economic Co-operation	Labour and Employers' Organizations	Science and Technology
Arts and Culture	Law	Social Sciences and Humanistic Studies
Education	Medicine and Public Health	Trade and Industry
Finance and Economic Research	Press, Radio and Telecommunications	Transport and Tourism

AGRICULTURE, FORESTRY AND FISHERIES

African Feed Resources Research Network—AFRNET: c/o International Livestock Centre for Africa, POB 46847, Nairobi, Kenya; tel. (2) 632013; fax (2) 25774; f. 1991 by merger of three African livestock fodder research networks; aims to assist farmers in finding effective ways to feed their livestock; Co-ordinator Dr John Ndikumama.

African Oil Palm Development Association—AFOPDA: 15 BP 341, Abidjan 15, Côte d'Ivoire; tel. 251518; f. 1985; seeks to increase production of and investment in palm oil. Mems: Benin, Cameroon, Côte d'Ivoire, Ghana, Guinea, Nigeria, Togo, Zaire. Exec. Sec. Baudelaire Sourou.

African Timber Organization: BP 1077, Libreville, Gabon; tel. 732928; telex 5620; fax 734030; f. 1976 to enable mems to study and co-ordinate ways of ensuring the optimum utilization and conservation of their forests. Mems: Angola, Cameroon, Central African Republic, Congo, Côte d'Ivoire, Equatorial Guinea, Gabon, Ghana, Liberia, Nigeria, São Tomé and Príncipe, Tanzania, Zaire. Sec.-Gen. Mohammed Lawal Garba. Publs *ATO-Information* (every 2 months), *Annual Report*.

Association for the Advancement of Agricultural Science in Africa—AAASA: POB 30087, Addis Ababa, Ethiopia; tel. (1) 44-35-36; f. 1968 to promote the development and application of agricultural sciences and the exchange of ideas; to encourage Africans to enter training; holds several seminars each year in different African countries. Mems: individual agricultural scientists, research insts, orgs in the agricultural sciences in Africa. Sec.-Gen. Prof. M. El-Fouly (acting). Publs *Journal* (2 a year), *Newsletter* (quarterly).

Desert Locust Control Organization for Eastern Africa: POB 30023, Nairobi, Kenya; tel. (2) 501704; telex 25510; fax (2) 505137; f. 1962 to promote most effective control of desert locust in the region and to carry out research into the locust's environment and behaviour; conducts pesticides residue analysis; assists member states in the monitoring and extermination of other migratory pests such as the quelea-quelea (grain-eating birds), the army worm and the tsetse fly; bases at Asmara and Dire Dawa (Ethiopia), Mogadishu and Hargeisa (Somalia), Nairobi (Kenya), Khartoum (Sudan), Arusha (Tanzania) and Djibouti. Mems: Djibouti, Ethiopia, Kenya, Somalia, Sudan, Tanzania and Uganda. Dir-Gen. Prof. Hosea Y. Kayumbo. Publs *Desert Locust Situation Reports* (monthly), *Annual Report*.

International Institute of Tropical Agriculture—IITA: Oyo Rd, PMB 5320, Ibadan, Nigeria; tel. (22) 400300; telex 31417; fax (22) 1772276; f. 1967; principal financing arranged by the Consultative Group on International Agricultural Research (CGIAR), an informal group of donor countries, development banks, foundations and agencies, co-ordinated by the World Bank. The three main research programmes comprise crop improvement (chiefly cassava, maize, plantain/banana, yam and soybean), plant health management, and resource and crop management. The international co-operation programme comprises large-scale research projects with national programmes and a training programme for scientists and technicians in tropical agriculture. The information services programme produces publications on research results and has a library of 75,000 vols and data-base of 95,500 records; it also maintains six agro-ecological research stations. Dir-Gen. Dr Lukas Brader. Publs *Annual Report, IITA Research*.

International Laboratory for Research on Animal Diseases—ILRAD: POB 30709, Nairobi, Kenya; tel. (2) 630743; telex 22040; fax (2) 631499; f. 1973; conducts laboratory and field research on improved immunological and other controls of animal trypanosomiasis and theileriosis; training programme for scientists and technicians; specialized science library. Dir Dr A. R. Gray. Publs *Annual Report, Annual Scientific Report, ILRAD Report* (quarterly).

International Livestock Centre for Africa—ILCA: POB 5689, Addis Ababa, Ethiopia; tel. (1) 613215; telex 21207; fax (1) 611892; f. 1974; an international research centre supported by and financed largely through the Consultative Group on International Agricultural Research; a multidisciplinary research, information and training institute concerned with livestock and agricultural production, animal traction, feed resources, tolerance of disease, and livestock policy; collaborates with national and international research programmes; research sites in Ethiopia, Kenya, Mali, Niger and Nigeria. Dir-Gen. Dr Hank Fitzhugh. Publs *ILCA Newsletter, Annual Report*, Monographs.

International Red Locust Control Organization for Central and Southern Africa: POB 240252, Ndola, Zambia; tel. (2) 615684; telex 30072; fax (2) 614285; f. 1971; controls locusts in eastern, central and southern Africa, and assists in the control of African army-worm and quelea-quelea. Mems: nine countries. Dir E. K. Byaruhanga. Publs *Annual Report, Monthly Report* and scientific reports.

International Tobacco Growers' Association: POB 125, East Grinstead, West Sussex RH18 5FA, England; tel. (342) 823549; telex 957718; fax (342) 825502; f. 1984 to provide a forum for the exchange of information of concern to tobacco producers and to provide information relating to tobacco production; members collectively produce more than 80% of the world's internationally traded tobacco. Mems: 17 countries. Chair. Henry Ntaba (Malawi); Chief Exec. David Walder (United Kingdom).

International Tropical Timber Organization—ITTO: International Organizations Center, 5th Floor, Pacifico-Yokohama, 1-1-1, Minato-Mirai, Nishi-ku, Yokohama 220, Japan; tel. (45) 223-1110; telex 3822480; fax (45) 223-1111; f. 1985 under the International Tropical Timber Agreement 1983; aims to promote the conservation of tropical forest resources through sustainable management; conducts research and development in marketing and economics, and reforestation and forest management; and provides a forum for consultation and co-operation between producers and consumers, as well as non-governmental organizations; facilitates progress towards the 'Year 2000' objective (all trade in tropical timber to be derived from sustainably managed resources by the year 2000). Mems: 52 producing and consuming countries. Exec. Dir Freezailah bin Che Yeom (Malaysia).

Joint Organization for Control of Desert Locust and Bird Pests (Organisation commune de lutte antiacridienne et de lutte antiaviaire—OCLALAV): Route des Pères Maristes, BP 1066, Dakar, Senegal; f. 1965 to eradicate the desert locust and grain-eating birds, in particular the quelea-quelea, and to sponsor related research projects. Mems: Benin, Burkina Faso, Cameroon, Chad, Côte d'Ivoire, The Gambia, Mali, Mauritania, Niger, Senegal. Dir-Gen. Abdullahi Ould Soueid Ahmed. Publ. *Bulletin* (monthly).

West Africa Rice Development Association: 01 BP 2551, Bouaké 01, Côte d'Ivoire; tel. 63-45-14; telex 69138; fax 63-47-14; f. 1970; undertakes research to improve rice production in West Africa; maintains research stations in Côte d'Ivoire, Nigeria, Sierra Leone and Senegal; provides training and consulting services; revenue (31 Dec. 1992) US $9.9m., of which member states contributed $0.2m., expenditure $8.1m. Mems: Benin, Burkina Faso, Cameroon, Chad, Côte d'Ivoire, The Gambia, Ghana, Guinea, Guinea-Bissau, Liberia, Mali, Mauritania, Niger, Nigeria, Senegal, Sierra Leone, Togo. Dir-Gen. Eugene Terry (Sierra Leone). Publ. *Annual Report*.

AID, DEVELOPMENT AND ECONOMIC CO-OPERATION

African Capacity Building Foundation: POB 1562, Harare, Zimbabwe; tel. (4) 702931; fax (4) 702915; f. 1991 by the World Bank, UNDP and the African Development Bank and bilateral donors; provides assistance to African countries to strengthen local skills and institutions in public policy analysis and development management; a fund of US $100m. was to be provided over the first four years of operations. Mems: 12 countries. Exec. Sec. PIERRE-CLAVER DAMIBA.

African Organization of Cartography and Remote Sensing: BP 3, 16040 Hussein Dey, Algiers, Algeria; tel. (2) 77-79-34; telex 65474; fax (2) 77-79-34; f. 1988 by amalgamation of African Association of Cartography and African Council for Remote Sensing; aims to encourage the development of cartography and of remote-sensing by satellites; organizes confs and other meetings, promotes establishment of training institutions; four regional training centres (in Burkina Faso, Kenya, Nigeria and Tunisia). Mems: principal cartographic services in 29 countries. Sec.-Gen. Dr MOHAMED BOUALGA.

Afro-Asian Rural Reconstruction Organization—AARRO: Plot No. 2, State Guest Houses Complex, Near telephone exchange Chanakyapuri, New Delhi 110021, India; tel. (11) 600475; telex 72326; fax (11) 672045; f. 1962 to act as a catalyst for co-operative restructuring of rural life in Africa and Asia and to explore, collectively, opportunities for co-ordination of efforts to promote welfare and eradicate malnutrition, disease, illiteracy and poverty amongst rural people. Activities include collaborative research on development issues; training; assistance in forming organizations of farmers and other rural people; the exchange of information; international conferences and seminars; and awarding 100 individual training fellowships at nine insts in Egypt, India, Japan, the Repub. of Korea, Malaysia and Taiwan. Mems: 11 African, 12 Asian, and one African assoc. Sec.-Gen. AHMED ABDELWAHED KHALIL. Publs *Annual Report, Rural Reconstruction* (2 a year), *AARRO Newsletter* (4 a year), conference and committee reports.

Agence de coopération culturelle et technique: 13 quai André Citroën, 75015 Paris, France; tel. (1) 44-37-33-00; telex 201916; fax (1) 45-79-14-98; f. 1970 to exchange knowledge of the cultures of French-speaking countries, to provide tech. assistance and to assist relations between mem. countries; tech. and financial assistance has been given to projects in every mem. country, mainly to aid rural people. Mems: 37 countries, mainly African; Assoc. Mems: Egypt, Guinea-Bissau, Mauritania, Morocco, Saint Lucia; participants: Canadian Provinces of Québec and New Brunswick. Sec.-Gen. JEAN-LOUIS ROY (Canada). Publ. *Lettre de la Francophonie* (monthly).

Arab Bank for Economic Development in Africa (Banque arabe pour le développement économique en Afrique—BADEA): Sayed Abdar-Rahman el-Mahdi Ave, POB 2640, Khartoum, Sudan; tel. 73646; telex 22248; fax 70600; f. 1973 by Arab League; provides loans and grants to sub-Saharan African countries to finance development projects; paid-up cap. US $1,045.8m. (Dec. 1992); in 1992 the Bank approved loans and grants totalling $74.0m. Subscribing countries: all countries of Arab League, except Djibouti, Somalia and Yemen; recipient countries: all countries of Organization of African Unity (q.v.), except those belonging to the Arab League. Chair. AHMAD ABDALLAH AL-AKEIL (Saudi Arabia); Dir.-Gen. AHMAD AL-HARTI AL-OUARDI (Morocco). Publs *Annual Report, Co-operation for Development*, Studies on Afro-Arab co-operation.

Centre africain de formation et de recherche administratives pour le développement—CAFRAD (African Training and Research Centre in Administration for Development): ave Mohamed V, BP 310, Tangier, Morocco; tel. 942632; telex 33664; fax 941415; f. 1964 by agreement between Morocco and UNESCO; undertakes research into administrative problems in Africa, documentation of results, provision of a consultative service for govts and orgs; holds frequent seminars; aided by national and international orgs. Mems: 27 African countries. Pres. AZIZ HASBI; Dir-Gen. MAMADOU THIAM. Publs include *Cahiers Africains d'Administration Publique* (2 a year), *African Administrative Studies* (2 a year), *CAFRAD News* (2 a year, in English, French and Arabic), *Collection: Etudes et Documents, Répertoire des Consultants*.

Centre on Integrated Rural Development for Africa—CIRDAfrica: POB 6115, Arusha, Tanzania; tel. (51) 2576; telex 42053; fax (51) 8532; f. 1979 (operational 1982) to promote integrated rural development through a network of national institutions; to improve the production, income and living conditions of small-scale farmers and other rural groups; to provide technical support; and to foster the exchange of ideas and experience; financed by member states and donor agencies; serious arrears in contributions by mems were reported in 1987. Mems: 17 African countries. Dir Dr ABDELMONEIM M. ELSHEIKH. Publ. *Rural Africa* (2 a year).

Club du Sahel (Club of the Sahel): c/o OECD, 2 rue André Pascal, 75775 Paris, France; tel. (1) 45-24-82-00; telex 640048; fax (1) 45-24-90-31; f. 1976; an informal forum of donor countries and member states of the Permanent Inter-State Committee on Drought Control in the Sahel—CILSS (q.v.), for promoting the co-ordination of long-term policies and programmes in key development sectors affecting food production and drought control in the nine mem. countries of the CILSS; formed by the CILSS in assocn with the OECD. The Club collects information, conducts studies and helps to mobilize resources for the development of the Sahel region in agriculture, livestock, cereals pricing policy, ecology, forestry and village water supplies.

Club of Dakar: 76B rue Lecourbe, 75015 Paris, France; tel. (1) 42-67-16-00; f. 1974; an informal international forum for dialogue and development research, particularly concerned with Africa. Mems: 200 administrators, industrial executives, scientists and bankers from many industrialized and developing countries. Pres. AMADOU SEYDOU; Dir E. GUILLON.

Communauté économique de l'Afrique de l'ouest—CEAO (West African Economic Community): rue Agostino Neto, 01 BP 643 Ouagadougou 01, Burkina Faso; tel. (3) 30-61-87; telex 5212; f. 1974; within the community non-manufactured, crude goods are exempt from import taxes, and industrial products may benefit from a preferential system (introduced in 1976) whereby import duties are replaced by a Regional Co-operation Tax. In 1984 policies were adopted on the harmonization of tariffs for imports from outside the community, and rates of taxation for nationals of member states. The CEAO undertakes joint projects aimed at improving member states' infrastructures, (especially improvement of rural water supplies) which are financed by external donors. In March 1994 CEAO heads of state meeting in Ouagadougou, Burkina Faso, agreed to dissolve the community. Mems: Benin, Burkina Faso, Côte d'Ivoire, Mali, Mauritania, Niger, Senegal. Sec.-Gen. MAMADOU HAIDARA (Mali). Publs *Rapport annuel, Integration africaine* (2 a year).

Union économique et monétaire ouest-africaine—UEMOA (West African Economic and Monetary Union): f. 1994, as eventual successor to CEAO. Chair. BLAISE CAMPAORE.

Fonds de Solidarité et d'Intervention pour le Développement—FOSIDEC (Solidarity and Intervention Fund): BP 643, Ouagadougou, Burkina Faso; tel. (3) 33-47-94; telex 5342; f. 1977 to contribute to regional equilibrium by granting and guaranteeing loans, financing studies and granting subsidies. The Fund's initial capital was 5,000m. francs CFA. By June 1985 the Fund's total interventions amounted to 26,267.6m. francs CFA. Dir.-Gen. AMADOU SY.

Communauté Economique des Etats de l'Afrique Centrale—CEEAC: BP 2112, Libreville, Gabon; f. 1983; operational since 1985; aims to promote co-operation between member states by abolishing trade restrictions, establishing a common external customs tariff, linking commercial banks, and setting up a development fund, over a period of 12 years; budget (1991) US $4m. Membership comprises the states belonging to UDEAC (q.v.) and five others: Burundi, Cameroon, Central African Republic, Chad, Congo, Equatorial Guinea, Gabon, Rwanda, São Tomé and Príncipe and Zaire; Angola has observer status. Pres. MELCHIOR NDADAYE (Burundi); Sec.-Gen. KASASA MUTATI CHINYATA (Zaire).

Conseil de l'Entente (Entente Council): 01 BP 3734, Abidjan 01, Côte d'Ivoire; tel. 33-28-35; telex 23558; fax 33-11-49; f. 1959; aims to promote economic development in the region. The Council's Mutual Aid and Loan Guarantee Fund (Fonds d'Entraide et de Garantie des Emprunts) finances development projects, including agricultural projects, vocational training centres, research into new sources of energy and building of hotels to encourage tourism. Fund budget (1992): 1,746m. francs CFA. Mems: Benin, Burkina Faso, Côte d'Ivoire, Niger, Togo. Administrative Sec. of Fund PAUL KAYA. Publs *Entente africaine* (quarterly), *Rapport d'activité* (annually).

Communauté économique du bétail et de la viande du Conseil de l'Entente (Livestock and Meat Economic Community of the Entente Council): BP 638, Ouagadougou, Burkina Faso; f. 1970 to promote the production, processing and marketing of livestock and meat; negotiates between members and with third countries on tech. and financial co-operation and co-ordinated legislation; attempts to co-ordinate measures to combat drought and cattle disease. Budget (1987): 105.4m. francs CFA. Mems: states belonging to the Conseil de l'Entente. Sec. Dr ALOUA MOUSSA.

Eastern and Southern African Mineral Resources Development Centre: POB 1250, Dodoma, Tanzania; tel. (61) 20364; telex 53324; f. 1975, sponsored by the ECA (q.v.); provides advisory and consultancy services in exploration geology, geophysics, geochemistry, mining and mineral processing. Mems: 18 countries. Dir J. E. N. KAGULE-MAGAMBO.

Economic Community of the Great Lakes Countries (Communauté économique des pays des Grands Lacs—CEPGL): POB 58, Gisenyi, Rwanda; tel. 40228; telex 602; fax 40785; f. 1976; main organs: annual conf. of heads of state, council of ministers, perm. exec. secr., consultative comm., Security Commission, three Specialized Tech. Commissions. There are three specialized agencies: the Banque de Développement des Etats des Grands Lacs (BDEGL, BP 3355, Goma, Zaire); the Organisation de la CEPGL pour l'Energie (BP 1912, Bujumbura, Burundi); the Institut de Recherche Agronomique et Zoologique (BP 91, Gitega, Burundi); and four joint enterprises, producing electric power, glass bottles, cement and hoes. A five-year plan (1987–91) was adopted in 1986, requiring financing of about US $3.87m. for agricultural, industrial and energy projects. Mems: Burundi, Rwanda, Zaire. Exec. Sec. ANTOINE NOUWAYO. Publs *Grands Lacs* (quarterly review), *Journal* (annually).

Gambia River Basin Development Organization (Organisation pour la mise en valeur du fleuve Gambie—OMVG): BP 2353, 13 passage Le Blanc, Dakar, Senegal; tel. 22-31-59; telex 51487; fax 22-59-26; f. 1978 by Senegal and The Gambia; Guinea joined in 1981 and Guinea-Bissau in 1983. Plans include the construction of a bridge over the River Gambia, feasibility studies began in 1993; a study on an agricultural development of the Kayanga/Geba and Koliba/Corubal river basins commenced in 1993; studies on the integration of investments in electric energy production and transmission within the OMVG member states and a hydraulic plan of the River Gambia are to commence soon; maintains documentation centre. Administrative budget (1993): 116.3m. francs CFA. Exec. Sec. MAMADOU NASSIROU DIALLO.

Indian Ocean Commission—IOC: Q4, ave Sir Guy Forget, BP 7, Quatre Bornes, Mauritius; tel. 425-9564; telex 5273; fax 425-1209; f. 1982 to promote regional co-operation, particularly in economic devt; prin. projects under way in the early 1990s (at a cost of 11.6m. francs CFA) comprised tuna-fishing and regional tourism development and the protection and management of environmental resources, reinforcement of meteorological services; with assistance principally from the European Community; tariff reduction is also envisaged. Perm. tech. cttees cover: tuna-fishing; regional industrial co-operation; regional commerce; tourism; environment; maritime transport; handicrafts; sports. The IOC organizes an annual regional trade fair (1994: Madagascar). Mems: Comoros, France (representing the French Overseas Department of Réunion), Madagascar, Mauritius and Seychelles. Sec.-Gen. J. BONNELAME. Publ. *Guide Import/Export*.

Inter-African Committee for Hydraulic Studies (Comité interafricain d'études hydrauliques—CIEH): 01 BP 369, Ouagadougou, Burkina Faso; tel. (3) 30-71-12; telex 5277; fax (3) 36-24-41; f. 1960 to ensure co-operation in hydrology, hydrogeology, climatology, urban sanitation and other water sciences; co-ordination of research and other projects. Mems: 14 African countries. Sec.-Gen. AMADOU CISSÉ. Publs scientific and technical research studies, *Bulletin de liaison technique* (quarterly).

Intergovernmental Authority on Drought and Development—IGADD: BP 2653, Djibouti; tel. 354050; telex 5978; fax 356994; f. 1986 by six drought-affected states to co-ordinate measures to combat the effects of drought and desertification; programmes of action include food security, desertification control, environmental protection, agricultural research, water resources management, fisheries, early warning and remote-sensing for food security and manpower devt. Mems: Djibouti, Ethiopia, Eritrea, Kenya, Somalia, Sudan, Uganda. Exec. Sec. Dr DAVID STEPHEN MUDUULI (Uganda). Publs *IGADD News* (2 a year), *Annual Report, Food Situation Report* (quarterly), *Agromet Bulletin* (quarterly).

Lake Chad Basin Commission: BP 727, N'Djamena, Chad; tel. 51-41-45; telex 5251; fax 51-41-37; f. 1964 to encourage co-operation in developing the Lake Chad region and to attract financial and technical assistance; work programmes emphasize anti-desertification measures; protection and sound environmental management of Lake Chad; improvements in roads, railways and communications links between mem. countries; co-ordination of nat. development projects; and activities concerned with crops, livestock and forestry. Mems: Cameroon, Central African Republic, Chad, Niger, Nigeria. Exec. Sec. ABUBAKAR B. JAURO.

Liptako-Gourma Integrated Development Authority (Autorité de développement intégré de la région du Liptako-Gourma): BP 619, ave M. Thevenond, Ouagadougou, Burkina Faso; tel. (3) 30-61-48; telex 5247; f. 1972; scope of activities includes water infrastructure, telecommunications and construction of roads and railways; in 1986 undertook study on development of water resources in the basin of the Niger river (for hydroelectricity and irrigation). Budget (1988) 161.4m. francs CFA. Mems: Burkina Faso, Mali, Niger. Sec.-Gen. SILIMANE GANOU (Niger).

Mano River Union: Mail Bag 133, Freetown, Sierra Leone; tel. (22) 226883; f. 1973 to establish a customs and economic union between mem. states, in order to accelerate development by means of integration. A common external tariff was instituted in April 1977; intra-union free trade was officially introduced on 1 May 1981, as the first stage in progress towards a customs union. An industrial development unit was set up in 1980 to identify projects and encourage investment. Construction of the Monrovia-Freetown–Monrovia highway was partially completed by 1991, and other road projects were also being undertaken in 1991. Feasibility studies for a hydroelectric scheme were completed in 1983. Joint institutes have been set up to provide training in posts and telecommunications, forestry, and maritime activities. A joint airline, Air Mano, was established in 1989, and was expected to become operational in 1990. Decisions are taken at meetings of a joint ministerial council. Mems: Guinea, Liberia, Sierra Leone. Sec.-Gen. Dr ABDOULAYE DIALLO (Guinea).

Niger Basin Authority (Autorité du bassin du Niger): BP 729, Niamey, Niger; tel. 723102; f. 1964 (as River Niger Commission; name changed 1980) to harmonize national programmes concerned with the River Niger Basin and to execute an integrated development plan; activities comprise: statistics; navigation regulation; hydrological forecasting; environmental control; infrastructure and agro-pastoral development; and arranging assistance for these projects. Mems: Benin, Burkina Faso, Cameroon, Chad, Côte d'Ivoire, Guinea, Mali, Niger, Nigeria. Exec. Sec. OTHMAN MUSTAPHA (Nigeria). Publs *Bulletin, Bibliographical Index*.

Organization for the Development of the Senegal River (Organisation pour la mise en valeur du fleuve Sénégal—OMVS): 46 rue Carnot, BP 3152, Dakar, Senegal; tel. 22-36-79; telex 51670; fax 23-47-62; f. 1972 to use the Senegal river for hydroelectricity, irrigation and navigation. The Djama dam in Senegal (completed in 1986) provides a barrage to prevent salt water from moving upstream, and the Manantali dam in Mali (completed in 1988) is intended to provide a reservoir for irrigation of about 400,000 ha of land and (eventually) for production of hydroelectricity and provision of year-round navigation for ocean-going vessels. In 1991 an agreement was signed whereby a company, l'Agence de gestion pour les ouvrages communs (AGOC), was formed; the member states were to hold 75% of the capital and private shareholders 25%. Mems: Mali, Mauritania, Senegal; the admission of Guinea was approved in principle by heads of state of the mem. countries in 1987. High Commr BABA OULD SIDI ABDALLAH; Sec.-Gen. K. DEMBELE.

Organization for the Management and Development of the Kagera River Basin (Organisation pour l'aménagement et le développement du bassin de la rivière Kagera): BP 297, Kigali, Rwanda; tel. (7) 84665; telex 0909 22567; fax (7) 82172; f. 1978; envisages jt devt and management of resources, incl. the construction of a 61.5-MW hydroelectric dam at Rusumo Falls, on the Rwanda-Tanzania border, a 2,000-km railway network between the four mem. countries; road construction (914 km); agricultural projects; river transport; and a polytechnic inst. Budget (1992): US $2m. Mems: Burundi, Rwanda, Tanzania, Uganda. Exec. Sec. JEAN-BOSCO BALINDA.

Pan-African Institute for Development—PAID: BP 4056, Douala, Cameroon; tel. 421061; telex 6048; fax 424335; f. 1964 to train rural development officers from Africa (44 countries in 1992), chiefly at an intermediate level but also some higher specialists, in devt questions; emphasis in education is given to: involvement of local populations in development; women in devt; promotion of small- and medium-scale enterprises; implementation of regional projects for training development staff; preparation of projects for regional co-operation; applied research, consultation and project support. Four regional insts in Africa, two anglophone (BP 133, Buéa, Cameroon; POB 80448, Kabwe, Zambia), two francophone (BP 4078, Douala, Cameroon; BP 1756, Ouagadougou, Burkina Faso). Sec.-Gen. Prof. A. C. MONDJANAGNI. Publs *Newsletter* (3 a year), *PAID Report* (2 a year).

Permanent Inter-State Committee on Drought Control in the Sahel (Comité permanent inter-états de lutte contre la sécheresse dans le Sahel—CILSS): BP 7049, Ouagadougou, Burkina Faso; tel. (3) 306758; telex 5263; fax (3) 306757; f. 1973; works in co-operation with UN Sudano-Sahelian Office (UNSO, q.v.); aims to combat the effects of chronic drought in the Sahel region, where the deficit in grain production was estimated at 1.7m. metric tons for 1988, by improving irrigation and food production, halting deforestation and creating food reserves. Budget (1994): 318.5m. francs CFA. Mems: Burkina Faso, Cape Verde, Chad, The Gambia, Guinea-Bissau, Mali, Mauritania, Niger, Senegal. Exec. Sec. CISSE MARIAM K. SIDIBE.

Regional Centre for Services in Surveying, Mapping and Remote Sensing: POB 18118, Nairobi, Kenya; tel. (2) 803320; telex 25285; fax (2) 802767; f. 1975 to provide services in the professional techniques of map-making and the application of satellite and remote sensing data in resource analysis and devt planning; undertakes training and research and provides advisory services to African govts. Mems: 13 signatory and 9 non-signatory states. Dir-Gen. ASFAW FANTA.

Regional Centre for Training in Aerospace Surveys (RECTAS): PMB 5545, Ile-Ife, Nigeria; tel. (36) 230050; telex 34262; fax (36) 230481; f. 1972 to provide training, research and advisory services in aerial surveying; administered by the ECA (q.v.). Mems: Benin, Burkina Faso, Cameroon, Ghana, Mali, Niger, Nigeria, Senegal. Dir J. A. OGUNLAMI. Publ. *RECTAS Newsletter* (annually).

United Nations African Institute for Economic Development and Planning (institut africain de développement économique et de planification—IDEP): BP 3186, Dakar, Senegal; tel. 23-10-20; telex 51579; fax 21-21-85; f. 1963 by ECA (q.v.) to train economic development planners, conduct research and provide advisory services; has library of books, journals and documents. Dir Dr JEGGAN C. SENGHOR.

ARTS AND CULTURE

African Cultural Institute (Institut culturel africain): BP 01, 13 ave du Président Bourguiba, Dakar, Senegal; tel. 24-78-82; telex 61334; f. 1971 to promote scientific and cultural development; established (1976) the Centre régional d'action culturelle, Lomé, Togo, (1977) the Centre Inter-Etats pour la promotion de l'artisanat et du tourisme culturel, Abomey, Benin, and (1978) the Centre régional de recherche et de documentation pour le développement culturel, Dakar, Senegal. Annual budget: 850m. francs CFA. Mems: 18 African states. Dir-Gen. MESSANVI KOKOU KEKEH. Publ. *ICA-Information* (quarterly).

Afro-Asian Writers' Association: 'Al Ahram', Al Gala's St, Cairo, Egypt; tel. (2) 5747011; telex 20185; fax (2) 5747023; f. 1958. Mems: writers' orgs in 51 countries. Sec.-Gen. LOTFI EL-KHOLY. Publs *Lotus Magazine of Afro-Asian Writings* (quarterly in English, French and Arabic), *Afro-Asian Literature Series* (in English, French and Arabic).

Organization for Museums, Monuments and Sites in Africa: c/o Dr J. M. Essomba, University of Yaoundé I, Faculty of Arts, Lettres and Humanities, BP 755, Yaoundé, Cameroon; f. 1975; aims to foster the collection, study and conservation of the natural and cultural heritage of Africa; co-operation between mem. countries through seminars, workshops, confs, etc., exchange of personnel, training facilities. Mems from 30 countries. Pres. Dr J. M. ESSOMBA (Cameroon); Sec.-Gen. KWASI MYLES.

Pan-African Writers' Association-PAWA: POB C450, Cantonments, Accra, Ghana; f. 1989; awards the African Prize for Literature; in 1993 launched a US $10m. fund to encourage the development of African writers. Sec.-Gen. ATUKWEI OKAI (Ghana).

Society of African Culture (Société africaine de culture): 25 bis rue des Ecoles, 75005 Paris, France; tel. (1) 43-54-15-88; telex 200891; f. 1956 to create unity and friendship among black scholars in Africa, the Caribbean, Europe and America for the encouragement of their own cultures. Mems: from 45 countries. Pres. AIMÉ CÉSAIRE; Sec.-Gen. CHRISTIANE YANDÉ DIOP. Publ. *Présence Africaine* (quarterly).

EDUCATION

African Association for Literacy and Adult Education: POB 50768, Finance House, 6th Floor, Loita St, Nairobi, Kenya; tel. (2) 222391; telex 22096; fax (2) 340849; f. 1984, combining the fmr African Adult Education Asscn and the AFROLIT Society (both f. 1968); aims to promote adult education and literacy in Africa, to study the problems involved, and to allow the exchange of information; programmes are developed and implemented by 'networks' of educators; holds assembly every three years. Mems: 21 national education associations and 85 institutions. Chair. Dr ANTHONY SETSABI (Lesotho); Sec.-Gen. PAUL WANGOOLA (Uganda). Publs. *The Spider Newsletter* (quarterly, French and English), *Regional Conference Report* (every 3 years), *Journal* (2 a year).

Association of African Universities (Association des universités africaines): POB 5744, Accra North, Ghana; tel. 774495; telex 2284; fax 774821; f. 1967 to promote exchanges, contacts and co-operation between African university institutions; to study and make known educational needs in Africa, and to co-ordinate arrangements to meet these needs, to collect, classify and disseminate information on high education and research, particularly in Africa. Mems: 115 universities in 39 African countries. Pres. Prof. GEORGE BENNEH (Ghana); Sec.-Gen. Prof. DONALD E. U. EKONG (Nigeria). Publs include *Newsletter* (3 a year), *Handbook of African Universities* (every 2 years).

International Association for the Development of Documentation, Libraries and Archives in Africa: BP 375, Dakar, Senegal; tel. 24-09-54; f. 1957 to organize and develop documentation and archives in all African countries. Sec.-Gen. ZACHEUS SUNDAY ALI (Nigeria); Perm. Sec. EMMANUEL K. W. DADZIE (Togo).

International Congress of African Studies: c/o Institute of African and Asian Studies, University of Khartoum, POB 321, Khartoum, Sudan; tel. (11) 75100; f. 1962 to encourage co-operation and research in African studies; Congress convened every five years, most recently in Khartoum, Sudan, in 1990. Sec.-Gen. Prof. SAYYID H. HURREIZ (Sudan). Publ. *Proceedings*.

West African Examinations Council—WEAC (Conseil des examens de l'Afrique orientale): Examination loop, POB 125, Accra, Ghana; tel. 22-15-11; telex 2204; f. 1952; administers prescribed examinations in mem. countries; aims to harmonize examinations procedures and standards. Mems: The Gambia, Ghana, Liberia, Nigeria, Sierra Leone; Chair. Dr EMMANUEL EVANS-ANFOM; Registrar S. A. ESEZOBOR.

FINANCE AND ECONOMIC RESEARCH

African Centre for Monetary Studies: 15 blvd F. Roosevelt, BP 1791, Dakar, Senegal; tel. 23-38-21; telex 61256; fax 23-77-60; f. 1978 as an organ of the Association of African Central Banks (AACB, see below) as a result of a decision by the OAU Heads of State and Government; aims to promote better understanding of banking and monetary matters; to study monetary problems of African countries and the effect on them of international monetary devts; seeks to enable African countries to co-ordinate strategies in international monetary affairs. Mems: all mems of AACB. Dir. JEAN-MARIE GANKOU. Publs *Financial Journal* (2 a year), *Annual Report*.

African Insurance Organization: BP 5860, Douala, Cameroon; tel. 432655; telex 5504; fax 432008; f. 1972 to promote the expansion of the insurance and reinsurance industry in Africa, and to increase regional co-operation; has established African insurance 'pools' for aviation, petroleum and fire risks; holds annual conference, and arranges meetings for reinsurers, brokers, consultants and supervisory authorities in Africa; has created the African Insurance Educators' Agency, the Association of African Insurance Brokers and the Association of African Insurance Supervisory Authorities. Mems: insurers, reinsurers, brokers and supervisory authorities in 42 African countries. Sec.-Gen. Y. ASEFFA.

Association of African Central Banks—AACB: 15 blvd F. Roosevelt, BP 1791, Dakar, Senegal; tel. 23-38-21; telex 61256; fax 23-77-60; f. 1968 to promote co-operation among member central banks in monetary and banking policy, and to provide a forum for views and information on matters of interest to monetary and financial stability on the African continent. Mems: 36 African central banks, representing 47 countries. Chair. SABER MOHAMED HASSAN (Sudan).

East African Development Bank: 4 Nile Ave, POB 7128, Kampala, Uganda; tel. (41) 230021; telex 61074; fax (41) 259763; f. 1967 by the fmr East African Community, to promote development within Kenya, Tanzania and Uganda which each hold 25.78% of the equity capital; in 1991 the Bank approved two loans amounting to SDR 1.5m., and disbursed funds totalling SDR 10.9m. paid-up cap. SDR 25.4m. (1991). Dir-Gen. F. R. TIBEITA (acting).

Union africaine des banques pour le développement: BP 2045, Cotonou, Benin; tel. 30-15-00; telex 5024; fax 30-02-84; f. 1962 to promote devt through exchanges, training and co-operation by regional banks. Mems: National or central banks of 12 countries. Exec. Sec. KOUANVI TIGOUE (Togo).

West African Bankers' Association: 22 Wilberforce St, PMB 1012, Freetown, Sierra Leone; fax 229024; f. 1981; aims to strengthen links between banks in West Africa, to enable exchange of information, and to contribute to regional economic devt; holds annual general assembly. Mems: 135 commercial banks. Publ. *West African Banking Almanac*.

West African Clearing House—WACH: PMB 218, Freetown, Sierra Leone; tel. (22) 224485; telex 3368; fax (22) 223943; f. 1975, began operating in 1976; administers payments among its 10 mem. central banks in order to promote the use of local currencies for sub-regional trade and monetary co-operation, thus effecting savings in mems' foreign reserves. Mems: Banque centrale des états de l'Afrique de l'ouest (serving Benin, Burkina Faso, Côte d'Ivoire, Mali, Niger, Senegal and Togo: see under Franc Zone) and the central banks of Cape Verde, The Gambia, Ghana, Guinea, Guinea-Bissau, Liberia, Mauritania, Nigeria and Sierra Leone. Exec. Sec. CHEIKH S. B. DIAO (Mauritania). Publ. *Annual Report*.

GOVERNMENT AND POLITICS

African Association for Public Administration and Management: POB 48677, Nairobi, Kenya; tel. (2) 52-19-44; fax (2) 52-

18-45; f. 1971 to provide senior officials with opportunities for exchanging ideas and experience, to promote the study of professional techniques and encourage research in particular African administrative problems. Mems: 500 individual and 50 corporate. Pres. WILLIAM N. WAMALWA; Sec.-Gen. Prof. A. D. YAHAYA. Publs include *Newsletter* (quarterly), annual seminar reports.

Afro-Asian Peoples' Solidarity Organization—AAPSO: 89 Abdel Aziz Al-Saoud St, 11559-61 Manial El-Roda, Cairo, Egypt; tel. (2) 3636081; telex 92627; fax (2) 3637361; f. 1957; acts among and for the peoples of Africa and Asia in their struggle for genuine independence, sovereignty, socio-economic development, peace and disarmament; sixth congress held in 1984 (the first since 1972). Mems: 82 nat. cttees from African and Asian countries, and 10 European orgs as assoc. mems. Pres. Dr MORAD GHALEB; Sec.-Gen. NOURI ABDEL RAZZAK (Iraq). Publ. *Development and Socio-Economic Progress* (quarterly).

Association of African Tax Administrators: POB 13255, Yaounde, Cameroon; tel. 224157; fax 224151; f. 1980 to promote co-operation among African countries in the fields of taxation policy, legislation and administration. Mems: 20 states. Pres. GEORGE CHIPUMBU.

Inter-African Socialists and Democrats: 6 rue al-Waquidi 1004, al-Menzah IV, Tunis, Tunisia; tel. (1) 231-138; telex 15415; f. 1981 as Inter-African Socialists; name changed 1988. Chair. ABDOU DIOUF (Senegal); Sec.-Gen. SADOK FAYALA (Tunisia).

Pan-African Youth Movement: 19 rue Debbih Cherif, BP 72, Didouch Morad, 16000 Algiers, Algeria; tel. and fax (2) 71-64-71; telex 61244; f. 1962; promotes participation of African youth in socio-economic and political development; organizes confs, seminars and festivals. Mems: over 50 orgs and independence movements in African countries. Sec.-Gen. HAMADOUN IBRAHIM ISSEBERE. Publ. *MPJ News* (quarterly).

Union of African Parliaments: BP 1381, Abidjan 01, Côte d'Ivoire; tel. 213757; telex 22338; fax 222087; f. 1976; holds annual conf. Mems: 28 states. Pres. HABIB BOULARES (Tunisia); Sec.-Gen. HENRI ADOU SESS.

LABOUR AND EMPLOYERS' ORGANIZATIONS

International Confederation of Free Trade Unions—African Regional Organization (ICFTU—AFRO): POB 67273, Nairobi, Kenya; f. 1957. Mems: 3.3m. workers in 27 African countries; Regional Sec. ANDREW KAILEMBO (Tanzania).

Pan-African Employers' Federation: c/o Federation of Kenya Employers, POB 48311, Nairobi, Kenya; tel. (2) 721929; telex 22642; fax (2) 721990; f. 1986 to link African employers' orgs, and to represent them at the UN, the International Labour Organisation and the OAU. Pres. HEDI JILIANI (Tunisia); Sec.-Gen. TOM DIJU OWUOR (Kenya).

LAW

African Bar Association: POB 3451, 29 La Tebu St, East Cantonments, Accra, Ghana; f. 1971; aims to uphold the rule of law, to maintain the independence of the judiciary, and to improve legal services. Pres. CHARLES IDEHEN (Nigeria).

African Society of International and Comparative Law: Kairaba Ave, Private Bag 520, Banjul, The Gambia; tel. 390462; fax 390461; f. 1986; promotes public education on law and civil liberties; aims to provide a legal aid and advice system in each African country, and to allow the exchange of information on civil liberties in Africa; seeks to promote the Rule of Law by the publication of legal materials and organization of conferences. Pres. MOHAMMED BEDJAOUI; Sec. EMILE YAKPO. Publs *African Journal of International and Comparative Law* (quarterly in French and English), *Proceedings of the Annual Conferences of the African Society of International and Comparative Law* (annually in French and English), *Review of the African Commission on Human and People's Rights* (biennially in French and English).

Asian-African Legal Consultative Committee: 27 Ring Rd, Lajpat Nagar IV, New Delhi 110024, India; tel. (11) 6414265; fax (11) 6451344; f. 1956 to consider legal problems referred to it by mem. countries and to be a forum for Afro-Asian co-operation in international law and economic relations; provides background material for confs, prepares standard/model contract forms suited to the needs of the region; promotes arbitration as a means of settling international commercial disputes; trains officers of mem. states; has perm. UN observer status. Mems: 44 states. Pres. CHUSEI YAMADA (Japan); Sec.-Gen. TANG CHENGYAN (China).

Inter-African Union of Lawyers: 12 rue du Prince Moulay Abdullah, Casablanca, Morocco; tel. 271017; fax 204686; f. 1980; holds congress every three years. Pres. ABDELAZIZ BENZAKOUR (Morocco); Sec.-Gen. FRANÇOIS XAVIER AGONDJO-OKAWE (Gabon). Publ. *L'avocat africain* (2 a year).

MEDICINE AND PUBLIC HEALTH

International Federation of Red Cross and Red Crescent Societies—IFRC: 17 Chemin des Crêts, Petit-Saconnex, Case Postale 372, 1211 Geneva 19, Switzerland; tel. (22) 7304222; telex 412133; fax (22) 7330395; f. 1919 to prevent and alleviate human suffering, and to promote humanitarian activities by national Red Cross and Red Crescent societies; conducts relief operations for refugees and victims of disasters, co-ordinates relief supplies and assists in disaster prevention; Pres. Dr MARIO VILLARROEL LANDER (Venezuela); Sec.-Gen. GEORGE WEBBER (Canada); Treas.-Gen. BENGT BERGMAN (Sweden). Publs *Annual Review*, *Red Cross Red Crescent* (quarterly), *Weekly News*, *Transfusion International* (quarterly).

Organization for Co-ordination and Co-operation in the Struggle against Endemic Diseases (Organisation de coordination et de coopération pour la lutte contre les grandes endémies—OCCGE): 01 BP 153, Bobo-Dioulasso 01, Burkina Faso; tel. 970101; telex 8260; fax 970099; f. 1960; conducts research, provides training and maintains a documentation centre and computer information system; merger with anglophone West African Health Community to form West African Health Organization (q.v.) announced in 1990. Mems: Govts of Benin, Burkina Faso, Côte d'Ivoire, Mali, Mauritania, Niger, Senegal, Togo; assoc. mem.: France. Sec.-Gen. Dr YOUSSOUF KANE. Publs *OCCGE Info*, *Rapport annuel*. Centres of the OCCGE are:

Centre de recherches sur les méningites et les schistosomiases: BP 10887, Niamey, Niger; tel. 75-20-45; telex 5534; fax 75-28-04; f. 1979.

Centre Muraz: 01 BP 153, Bobo-Dioulasso 01, Burkina Faso; tel. 98-28-75; telex 8260; fax 98-02-60; multi-discipline medical research centre with special interest in biology and epidemiology of tropical diseases and training of health workers. Dir Prof. JEAN-PAUL CHIRON.

Institut Marchoux: BP 251, Bamako, Mali; tel. 22-51-31; telex 1200; fax 22-28-45; f. 1935; staff of seven doctors; research on leprosy, epidemiology, training. Dir Dr PIERRE BOBIN.

Institut d'ophtalmologie tropicale africaine—IOTA: BP 248, Bamako, Mali; tel. 22-34-21; fax 22-51-86; f. 1952; undertakes training, research and specialized care in ophthalmology. Dir Dr SERGE RESNIKOFF.

Institut Pierre Richet: 01 BP 1500, 01 Bouaké, Côte d'Ivoire; tel. 63-37-46; fax 63-27-38; research on malaria, trypanosomiasis and onchocerciasis; Dir Dr FRANÇOIS RIVIÈRE.

Office de recherches sur l'alimentation et la nutrition africaine—ORANA: BP 2098, Dakar, Senegal; tel. 22-58-92; f. 1956. Dir Dr A. M. NDIAYE.

Offices are also based in Cotonou, Benin (entomology), Lomé, Togo (nutrition), Nouakchott, Mauritania (tuberculosis) and Bafoulabé, Mali (leprosy).

Organization for Co-ordination of the Control of Endemic Diseases in Central Africa (Organisation de coordination pour la lutte contre les endémies en Afrique centrale—OCEAC): BP 288, Yaoundé, Cameroon; tel. 23-22-32; telex 8411; fax 23-00-61; f. 1965 to standardize methods of fighting endemic diseases, to co-ordinate national action, and to negotiate programmes of assistance on a regional scale. Mems: Cameroon, Central African Republic, Chad, Congo, Equatorial Guinea, Gabon. Pres. J. R. PENDY BOUYIKI (Cameroon); Sec.-Gen. Dr BILONGO MANENE. Publs *Rapport Final des Conférences Techniques* (every 2 years), *Rapport annuel*, *Bulletin de liaison et de documentation* (quarterly), *EPI-Notes OCEAC* (quarterly).

West African Health Community: PMB 2023, Yaba, Lagos, Nigeria; tel. and fax (1) 862324; telex 27896; fax 862324; f. 1972 to promote higher medical and allied professional education, disseminate tech. health information, establish special agencies and programmes and collaborate with other medical orgs in mem. states and in third countries; Ministers of Health meet annually. Three specialized agencies have been set up: the West African Postgraduate Medical College, the West African Pharmaceutical Federation and the West African College of Nursing. Mems: The Gambia, Ghana, Liberia, Nigeria and Sierra Leone; in 1990 it was announced that the West African Health Community was to be amalgamated with the francophone Organization for Co-ordination and Co-operation in the Fight against Endemic Diseases (q.v.) to form the West African Health Organization, covering all the mem. states of ECOWAS (subject to ratification by member states). Exec. Dir Dr KABBA T. JOINER. Publ. *West African Journal of Medicine*, *West African Journal of Nursing*, *West African Pharmacy Journal*.

PRESS, RADIO AND TELECOMMUNICATIONS

African Postal and Telecommunications Union: ave Patrice Lumumba, BP 44, Brazzaville, Congo; tel. 832778; telex 5212; f. 1961 to improve postal and telecommunication services between mem. administrations; consists of three Commissions: Post and Financial Services, Telecommunications, Administrative and Budget Affairs. Mems: Benin, Burkina Faso, Central African Republic, Chad, Congo, Côte d'Ivoire, Mali, Mauritania, Niger, Rwanda, Senegal, Togo. Sec.-Gen. MAHMOUDOU SAMOURA.

Regional African Satellite Communications System—RASCOM: c/o International Telecommunication Union, Place des Nations, 1211 Geneva 20, Switzerland; tel. (22) 7305111; telex 421000; fax (22) 7337256; f. 1992; aims to put Africa's first satellite into space within five years. Mems: 42 countries.

Union of National Radio and Television Organizations of Africa—URTNA (Union des radiodiffusions et télévisions nationales d'Afrique): BP 3237, 101 rue Carnot, Dakar, Senegal; tel. 21-59-70; telex 650; fax 22-51-13; f. 1962; co-ordinates radio and television services, including monitoring and frequency allocation, the exchange of information and coverage of national and international events, among African countries; maintains programme exchange centre (Nairobi, Kenya), tech. centre (Bamako, Mali) and a centre for rural radio studies (Ouagadougou, Burkina Faso); AFRO-VISION co-ordinating centre for the exchange of television news in Algiers, Algeria. Budget (1993): US $1.8m. There are 49 active, two supplementary active and nine assoc. mem. orgs. Sec.-Gen. EFOE ADODO MENSAH (Togo). Publs *URTNA Review* (2 a year in English and French).

West African Journalists' Association: 135 rue Carnot, BP 4130 Dakar, Senegal; tel. 223625; f. 1986; defends journalists and the freedom of the press, and promotes links between journalists' associations. Mems: journalists' asscns in the mem. states of ECOWAS. Pres. MUHAMED SANI ZORRO (Nigeria); Sec.-Gen. MADEMBA N'DIAYE (Senegal).

RELIGION

All Africa Conference of Churches: POB 14205, Waiyaki Way, Nairobi, Kenya; tel. (2) 441483; telex 22175; fax (2) 443241; f. 1958; an organ of fellowship and co-operation among Protestant, Orthodox and independent Churches and Christian Councils in Africa; last assembly Harare, Zimbabwe, 1992. Mems: 147 churches and associated councils in 39 African countries. Pres. Most Rev. DESMOND TUTU (South Africa); Gen. Sec. Rev. JOSÉ CHIPENDA (Angola). Publs *The African Challenge book series, ACLA News, Tam Tam.*

World Council of Churches: BP 2100, 150 route de Ferney, 1211 Geneva 2, Switzerland; tel. (22) 7916111; telex 415730; fax (22) 7910361; f. 1948 to promote co-operation between Christian churches; carries out varied programmes related to Christian unity, mission, international affairs, development, inter-church aid, refugees, education, youth and women. The programme to combat racism (PCR) is responsible for working out WCC policies and programmes on combating racism; giving expression to solidarity with the racially oppressed; assisting churches in education for racial justice; studying the causes and effects of all forms of racism, especially white racism; organizing action-orientated research; and operating the Special Fund to Combat Racism for movements of the racially oppressed. Gen. Sec. Rev. Dr KONRAD RAISER (Germany). Publs *One World* (monthly), *Ecumenical Review* (quarterly), *International Review of Mission* (quarterly).

SCIENCE AND TECHNOLOGY

African Regional Centre for Technology: Ave Cheikh Anta Diop, BP 2435, Dakar, Senegal; tel. 25-77-12; telex 61282; fax 25-77-13; f. 1980 to encourage the development of indigenous tech. and to improve the terms of access to imported tech.; assists the establishment of nat. centres. Dir Dr B. J. OLUFEAGBA. Publs include *African Technodevelopment, Alert Africa, Infomet.*

Association for the Taxonomic Study of the Tropical African Flora: Dept of Plant Taxonomy, Wageningen Agricultural Univ., POB 8010, 6700 ED Wageningen, Netherlands; tel. (8370) 82170; fax (8370) 84917; f. 1950 to facilitate co-operation and liaison between botanists engaged in the study of the flora of tropical Africa; maintains a library. Mems: about 800 botanists in 63 countries. Sec.-Gen. Prof. L. J. G. VAN DER MAESEN. Publs *AETFAT Bulletin* (annually), *Proceedings.*

Association of African Geological Surveys (Association des services géologiques africains): c/o CIFEG, ave de Concyr, BP 6517, Orléans Cedex 2, France; tel. 38-64-36-57; fax 38-64-34-72; f. 1929. Aims: synthesis of the geological knowledge of Africa and neighbouring countries; encouragement of research in geological and allied sciences for the benefit of Africa; dissemination of scientific knowledge; maintains Pan-African Network for a Geological Information System (PANGIS); affiliated to the International Union of Geological Sciences. Mems: about 60 (official geological surveys, public and private orgs). Pres. G. O. KESSE (Ghana); Sec.-Gen. M. BENSAÏD (Morocco).

Institute for Natural Resources in Africa (INRA): c/o University of Ghana, POB 25, Legon, Nr Accra; f. 1986 as a research and training centre of the United Nations University (Tokyo, Japan); moved to Ghana in 1993; aims at human resource development and institutional capacity building through co-ordination with African universities and associated research institutes in advanced research, training and dissemination of knowledge and information on the conservation and management of Africa's natural resources and their rational utilization for sustainable development; became operational in 1990 with an initial programme co-ordinated from Nairobi, Kenya. INRA has a mineral resources unit at the University of Zambia in Lusaka.

Pan-African Union of Science and Technology: POB 2339, Brazzaville, Congo; tel. 832265; telex 5511; fax 832185; f. 1987 to promote the use of science and tech. in furthering the devt of Africa; membership is open to any scientific or technological institution or asscn in Africa. Pres. Prof. EDWARD AYENSU (Ghana); Sec.-Gen. Prof. LÉVY MAKANY.

SOCIAL SCIENCES AND HUMANISTIC STUDIES

African Centre for Applied Research and Training in Social Development—ACARTSOD: Africa Centre, Wahda Quarter, Zawia Rd, POB 80606, Tripoli, Libya; tel. (21) 833640; fax (21) 832357; f. 1977 under the jt auspices of the ECA and OAU to promote and co-ordinate applied research and training in social devt, and to assist in formulating nat. devt strategies. Exec. Dir Dr MOHAMMED EL-MUSTAPHA KABBAJ.

African Social and Environmental Studies Programme: Box 44777, Nairobi, Kenya; tel. (2) 747960; fax (2) 747960; f. 1968; develops and disseminates educational material on social studies, environmental studies, primary health care and child survival. Mems: 17 African countries. Chair. Prof. WILLIAM SEMTEZA KAJUBI; Exec. Dir Dr PETER MUYANDA MUTEBI. Publs *African Social Studies Forum* (2 a year), teaching guides.

Association of Social Work Education in Africa: Addis Ababa University, POB 1176, Addis Ababa, Ethiopia; tel. 126827; f. 1971 to promote teaching and research in social development, to improve standards of institutions in this field, to exchange information and experience. Mems: schools of social work, community development training centres, other institutions and centres; 55 training institutions and 150 social work educators in 33 African countries; 22 non-African assoc. mems in Europe and North America. Sec.-Gen. Dr SEYOUM G. SELASSIE. Publ. *Journal for Social Work Education in Africa.*

Council for the Development of Social Science Research in Africa—CODESRIA: BP 3304, Ave Cheikh Anta Diop, Angle Canal IV, Dakar, Senegal; tel. 25-98-22; telex 61339; fax 24-12-89; f. 1973; promotes research, provides confs, working groups and information services. Mems: research institutes and university faculties in African countries. Exec. Sec. THANDIKA MKANDAWIRE. Publs *Africa Development/Afrique et Développement* (quarterly), *CODESRIA Bulletin* (quarterly), *Index of African Social Science Periodical Articles* (annually).

Third World Forum: 39 Dokki St, POB 43, Orman, Cairo, Egypt; f. 1973 to link social scientists and others from the developing countries, to discuss alternative development policies and encourage research. Regional offices in Mexico, Senegal and Sri Lanka. Mems: individuals in more than 50 countries. Chair. ISMAIL-SABRI ABDALLA. Publ. *TWF Newsletter.*

TRADE AND INDUSTRY

African Groundnut Council: Trade Fair Complex, Badagry Expressway Km 15, POB 3025, Lagos, Nigeria; tel. (1) 880982; telex 21366; fax (1) 880982; f. 1964 to advise producing countries on marketing policies; administers compensation fund. Mems: The Gambia, Mali, Niger, Nigeria, Senegal, Sudan. Chair. E. T. IBANGA (Nigeria); Exec. Sec. Alhaji MOUR MAMADOU SAMB (Senegal). Publs *Groundnut Review, Newsletter* (French and English).

African Petroleum Producers' Association: POB 1097, Brazzaville, Congo; tel. 836438; telex 5552; fax 836799; f. 1986 by African petroleum-producing countries to reinforce co-operation among regional producers and to stabilize prices; council of ministers responsible for the hydrocarbons sector of each country takes place twice a year. Mems: Algeria, Angola, Benin, Cameroon, Congo, Côte d'Ivoire, Egypt, Gabon, Libya, Nigeria, Zaire. Pres. BELKACEM NABI (Algeria). Publ. *Technical Bulletin* (quarterly).

African Regional Industrial Property Organization—ARIPO: POB 4228, Harare, Zimbabwe; tel. 794338; telex 24063; fax 794840; f. 1976 to promote devt and harmonization of laws concerning industrial property. Mems: Botswana, The Gambia, Ghana, Kenya, Lesotho, Malawi, Sierra Leone, Somalia, Sudan, Swaziland, Tanzania, Uganda, Zambia and Zimbabwe. Dir.-Gen. ANDERSON R. ZIKONDA.

African Regional Organization for Standardization: POB 57363, Nairobi, Kenya; tel. (2) 224561; telex 22097; fax (2) 218792; f. 1977 to promote standardization, quality control, certification and metrology in the continent, to formulate regional standards to promote the exchange of information on standards, technical regulations and related subjects and to co-ordinate participation in international standardization activities. Mems: 24 states. Sec.-Gen. ZAWDU FELLEKE. Publs *News Bulletin* (2 a year).

Association of African Trade Promotion Organizations —AATPO: Pavillon International, BP 23, Tangier, Morocco; tel. 41687; telex 33695; f. 1974 under the auspices of the ECA and OAU to encourage regular trade contact between African states and to assist in the harmonization of their commercial policies in order to promote intra-African trade. Mems: 26 states. Sec.-Gen. Dr ROLAND EKOTOME UBOGU. Publs include *FLASH: African Trade* (monthly), *Directory of Trade Promotion Institutions in Africa, Directory of State Trading Organizations, Directory of Exporters and Importers of Food Products in Africa, Calendar of Major Trade Events in Africa, African Trade Perspective* (on individual countries).

Association of Coffee Producing Countries: c/o Brazilian Embassy, 32 Green St, London W1Y 4AT, England; tel. (71) 499-0877; fax (71) 493-4790; f. 1993; aims to co-ordinate policies of coffee production and to co-ordinate the efforts of producer countries to secure a stable situation in the world coffee market. Mems: 28 African, Asian and Latin American countries. Pres. RUBENS BARBOSA; Sec.-Gen. ROBÉRIO OLIVEIRA SILVA.

Cocoa Producers' Alliance: POB 1718, Western House, 8–10 Broad St, Lagos, Nigeria; tel. (1) 2635506; telex 28288; fax (1) 2635684; f. 1962 to exchange scientific and technical information; to discuss problems of mutual concern to producers; to ensure adequate supplies at remunerative prices; to promote consumption. Mem. states: Brazil, Cameroon, Côte d'Ivoire, Dominican Republic, Ecuador, Gabon, Ghana, Malaysia, Mexico, Nigeria, São Tomé and Príncipe, Togo, and Trinidad and Tobago. Sec.-Gen. DJEUMO SILAS KAMGA.

Federation of African Chambers of Commerce: c/o ECA, POB 3001, Addis Ababa, Ethiopia; tel. (1) 517200; telex 21029; fax (1) 514416; f. 1983. Dir Dr B. W. MUTHAUKA.

Inter-African Coffee Organization—IACO: BP V210, Abidjan, Côte d'Ivoire; tel. 21-61-31; telex 22406; f. 1960 to adopt a united policy on the marketing of coffee. General Assembly meets annually; Board of Dirs holds quarterly meetings to direct policy; the financial contribution of mem. countries is based on the volume of their exports; mem. countries account for about 97% of African coffee exports. Mems: Angola, Benin, Burundi, Cameroon, Central African Republic, Congo, Côte d'Ivoire, Equatorial Guinea, Ethiopia, Gabon, Ghana, Guinea, Kenya, Liberia, Madagascar, Malawi, Nigeria, Rwanda, Sierra Leone, Tanzania, Togo, Uganda, Zaire, Zambia and Zimbabwe. Pres. R. H. KAIJUKA (Côte d'Ivoire); Sec.-Gen. AREGA WORKU (Ethiopia). Publs *African Coffee* (quarterly), *Directory of African Exporters* (every 2 years).

International Cocoa Organization—ICCO: 22 Berners St, London, W1P 3DB, England; tel. (71) 637-3211; telex 28173; fax (71) 631-0114; f. 1973 under the first International Cocoa Agreement, 1972 (renewed in 1975, 1980, 1986 and the fifth ICA entered into force in Feb. 1994). ICCO supervises the implementation of the agreement, and provides member governments with conference facilities and up-to-date information on the world cocoa economy and the operation of the agreement. Mems: 13 exporting countries which account for over 85% of world cocoa exports, and 15 importing countries which account for about 55% of world cocoa imports. (The USA is not a member.) Chair. H. STREICHERT (Germany); Exec. Dir EDOUARD KOUAMÉ (Côte d'Ivoire); Buffer Stock Manager J. PLAMBECK (Germany). Publs *Quarterly Bulletin of Cocoa Statistics, Annual Report, The World Cocoa Directory, Cocoa Newsletter*, studies on the world cocoa economy.

International Coffee Organization: 22 Berners St, London, W1P 4DD, England; tel. (71) 580-8591; telex 267659; fax (71) 580-6129; f. 1963 under the International Coffee Agreement, 1962, which was renegotiated in 1968, 1976, 1983 and 1994; aims to achieve a reasonable balance between supply and demand on a basis which will assure adequate supplies at fair prices to consumers and expanding markets at remunerative prices to producers; system of export quotas, to stabilize prices, was abandoned in July 1989. Mems: 42 exporting countries accounting for over 95% of world coffee exports, and 17 importing countries accounting for approximately 60% of world imports. Chair. of Council (1993/94) SIMEON ONCHERE (Kenya); Exec. Dir CELSIUS A. LODDER (Brazil).

International Tea Promotion Association: POB 20064, Tea Board of Kenya, Nairobi, Kenya; tel. (2) 220241; telex 987-22190; fax (2) 331650; f. 1979. Mems: eight countries (Bangladesh, Indonesia, Kenya, Malawi, Mauritius, Mozambique, Tanzania, and Uganda), accounting for about 35% of world exports of black tea. Chair. GEORGE M. KIMANI; Liaison Officer NGOIMA WA MWAURA. Publ. *International Tea Journal* (2 a year).

Organization of the Petroleum Exporting Countries—OPEC: 1020 Vienna, Obere Donaustrasse 93, Austria; tel. (222) 21-11-20; telex 134474; fax (222) 26-43-20; f. 1960 to unify and co-ordinate members' petroleum policies and to safeguard their interests generally: holds regular confs of mem. countries to set prices and production levels; conducts research in energy studies, economics and finance; provides data services and news agency covering petroleum and energy issues. Mems: Algeria, Gabon, Indonesia, Iran, Iraq, Kuwait, Libya, Nigeria, Qatar, Saudi Arabia, United Arab Emirates, Venezuela. Pres. ABDULLAH BIN HAMAD AL-ATTIYAR (Qatar). Publs *OPEC Bulletin* (monthly), *OPEC Review* (quarterly), *Annual Report, Annual Statistical Bulletin.*

OPEC Fund for International Development: POB 995, 1011 Vienna, Austria; tel. (222) 51-56-40; telex 1-31734; fax (222) 513-92-38; f. 1976 by mem. countries of OPEC, to provide financial co-operation and assistance for developing countries; in 1992 commitments amounted to US $125.7m., of which c. 46% was for Africa south of the Sahara. Dir-Gen. Y. SEYYID ABDULAI (Nigeria). Publs *Annual Report, OPEC Fund Newsletter* (3 a year).

Preferential Trade Area for Eastern and Southern Africa—PTA: Lottie House, Cairo Rd, POB 30051, Lusaka, Zambia; tel. (1) 229725; telex 40127; fax (1) 225107; f. 1981 with the aim of improving commercial and economic co-operation in the region and transforming the structure of production of national economies in the region; promotes regional trade and the creation of institutional mechanisms, including monetary arrangements, for facilitating trade; supports inter-country co-operation in the rationalization of existing national excess capacity and high-cost industries, and the development of basic and strategic industries; promotes co-operation in agricultural development and improvement of transport links, and the development of technical and professional skills. In Nov. 1993 the PTA mem. states signed a treaty transforming the PTA into the Common Market for Eastern and Southern Africa (COMESA). COMESA will have the following aims: a full free trade area by 2000; a customs union with a common external tariff 10 years after COMESA comes into force; free movement of capital and finance; a payments union and freedom of movement of people. In addition, COMESA will have a reserve fund with an initial capital of UAPTA 100m. to support the activities of the Clearing House which is now an autonomous body, an Investment Fund to be subscribed by international investors and a fund for Women in Business. In order to facilitate integration in Eastern and Southern Africa, the following have been established: the Road Customs Declaration Document (RCTD), the Regional Customs Bond Guarantee Scheme, the Trade Information Network (TINET) which will be tranformed into COMNET, the Automated System of Customs Data (ASYCUDA), the Clearing House, the UAPTA TC, the PTA Bank, the PTA Federation of Chambers of Commerce and Industry (PTA-FCCI), the PTA Association of Commercial Banks, the Federation of National Association of Women in Business (FEMCOM), the Third Party Motor Vehicle Insurance Scheme (Yellow Card), the Re-insurance Co (ZEPRE), the PTA Leather and Leather Products Institute (LLPI). Mergers are proposed with other organizations such as the SADC (q.v.). Mems: Angola, Burundi, the Comoros, Djibouti, Egypt, Eritrea, Ethiopia, Kenya, Lesotho, Madagascar, Malawi, Mauritius, Mozambique, Namibia, Rwanda, Seychelles, Somalia, Sudan, Swaziland, Tanzania, Uganda, Zambia, Zimbabwe. Sec.-Gen. Dr BINGU WA MUTHARIKA (Malawi). Publs *PTA Trade Information Newsletter* (monthly); *Official Trade and Investment Journal of the PTA.*

Eastern and Southern African Trade and Development Bank (PTA Bank): BP 1750, Bujumbura, Burundi; tel. (22) 5432; telex 5142; fax (22) 4983; f. 1986; finances PTA projects and trade-related activities, and manages PTA travellers' cheques.

Southern African Customs Union: no permanent headquarters; f. 1969; provides common pool of customs, excise and sales duties, according to the relative volume of trade and production in each country; goods are traded within the union free of duty and quotas, subject to certain protective measures for less developed members; the South African rand is legal tender in Lesotho and Swaziland. The Customs Union Commission meets annually in each of the members' capital cities in turn. Mems: Botswana, Lesotho, Namibia, South Africa, Swaziland.

Union of Producers, Conveyors and Distributors of Electric Power in Africa—UPDEA: 01 BP 1345, Abidjan 01, Côte d'Ivoire; tel. 32-64-33; telex 23483; fax 33-12-10; f. 1970 to study technical matters and to promote efficient development of enterprises in this sector; runs training school in Côte d'Ivoire. Mems: 22 national electricity authorities in Africa. Sec.-Gen. LIONEL KELLER. Publs *AFRIQUELEC* (periodical), technical papers.

TRANSPORT AND TOURISM

African Airlines Association: POB 20116, Nairobi, Kenya; tel. (2) 502645; fax (2) 502504; f. 1968 to give African air companies expert advice in tech., financial, juridical and market matters; to improve communications in Africa; to represent African airlines; and to develop manpower resources; published first continent-wide timetable in 1988. Mems: 35 nat. carriers. Pres. E. OLEKAMBAINEI (Tanzania); Sec.-Gen. Capt. MOHAMMED AHMED (Ethiopia).

Agency for the Safety of Air Navigation in Africa and Madagascar—ASECNA (Agence pour la sécurité de la navigation aérienne en Afrique et Madagascar): BP 8132, Dakar, Senegal; tel. 20-10-80; telex 31519; fax 20-06-00; f. 1959; organizes air-traffic communications in mem. states; co-ordinates meteorological forecasts; provides training for air-traffic controllers, meteorologists and airport fire-fighters. ASECNA is under the authority of a cttee comprising Ministers of Civil Aviation of member states. Mems: Benin, Burkina Faso, Cameroon, Central African Republic, Chad, Congo, Côte d'Ivoire, France, Gabon, Madagascar, Mali, Mauritania, Niger, Senegal, Togo. Dir-Gen. MAURICE RAJAOFETRA (Madagascar).

INDEX OF REGIONAL ORGANIZATIONS

(Main references only)

R

S

T

U

V

W

Z

PART THREE

Country Surveys

ANGOLA

Physical and Social Geography

RENÉ PÉLISSIER

PHYSICAL FEATURES

The Republic of Angola, covering an area of 1,246,700 sq km (481,354 sq miles), is the largest Portuguese-speaking state in Africa. It is composed of 18 provinces, one of which, Cabinda, is separated from the others by the oceanic outlet of Zaire and the River Congo. On its landward side Cabinda is surrounded by Zaire and the Republic of the Congo. Greater Angola is bordered to the north and east by Zaire, to the east by Zambia and to the south by Namibia. Excluding Cabinda, Angola extends 1,277 km from the northern to the southern border, and 1,236 km from the mouth of the Cunene river to the Zambian border.

Two-thirds of Angola is a plateau. The average elevation is 1,050–1,350 m above sea-level, with higher ranges and massifs reaching above 2,000 m. The highest point of Angola is Mt Moco (2,620 m) in the Huambo province. Through the central part of the inland plateau runs the watershed of Angola's rivers. The coastal plain on the Atlantic is separated from this plateau by a sub-plateau zone which varies in breadth from about 160 km in the north to about 25–40 km in the centre and south. The Namib desert occupies the coastal plain at a considerable height above Namibe. Towards the Cuango (Kwango) basin, in Zaire, a sedimentary hollow forms the Cassange depression, in which cotton is cultivated. The north-western section of the Angolan plateau has jungle-covered mountains which are suitable for the cultivation of coffee. The Mayombe range in Cabinda is covered by equatorial jungle.

Except for the Cuanza (Kwanza) river, which is navigable up to Dondo (193 km upstream), Angolan rivers do not provide easy access to the interior from the coast. On the other hand, they are harnessed for the production of electricity and for irrigation. The main rivers are, above the Cuanza, the Chiloango (Cabinda), the Congo, the M'bridge, the Loge, the Dange and the Bengo. The Cassai (Kasai), Cuilo (Kwilu) and Cuango rivers are known more for their importance to Zaire than for their upper reaches in Angola, although many tributaries of the Kasai intersect the Angolan plateau, exposing rich diamond fields in the Lunda provinces.

Angola has a tropical climate, locally tempered by altitude. The Benguela current, along the coast, influences and reduces rainfall in that part of the country which is arid or semi-arid. The interior uplands in the Bié, Huambo and Huíla provinces enjoy an equable climate. On the other hand, along the Cuanza river, in the north-west and north-east, and in the eastern and southern provinces, high temperatures and heavy seasonal rainfall discouraged European colonization wherever there were no economic incentives, such as coffee in the Congo provinces of Zaire and Uíge, and diamonds in Lunda.

POPULATION

Angola is an underpopulated country, with only 5,646,166 inhabitants enumerated at the 1970 census, when the population density was 4.5 persons per sq km. By mid-1992, when the population was officially estimated at 10,609,000, the density had risen to 8.5 persons per sq km. Angola is overwhelmingly rural and has considerable ethnic diversity, although all indigenous groups, of which the Ovimbundu (1.7m. in 1960) and Mbundu (1m.) are the largest, are of Bantu stock. An important characteristic of the population is its youth, as 45% are under 15 years old and only 5% are over 60. The average life expectancy at birth is about 45 years. In 1985–92 Angola's population increased at an average annual rate of 2.9%.

Since the onset of civil strife in the mid-1970s, Angola has experienced considerable economic dislocation, accompanied by a widespread regrouping of African populations, brought about by insecurity and massacres. There has also been general movement from cities to rural areas. In the late 1980s less than 25% of the population were believed to be residing in urban centres of more than 2,000 inhabitants. The population is predominantly engaged in food-crop farming and, in the south, in cattle-raising. Only in areas where coffee, cotton and maize are cultivated are Africans engaged to any extent in commercial agriculture. Some 70% of the economically active population are believed to be engaged in the farming and cattle-raising sectors. Since the mid-1980s, government-controlled towns and villages have, over large parts of the country, co-existed with regroupings of guerrilla-controlled populations sheltered in shifting villages: this has applied mostly to the south-east, east and north-east. Serious food shortages and periods of famine have periodically beset central and southern Angola during the years of post-independence strife. The war has also created problems of 'internal' refugees (estimated to number up to 650,000 people), while in the late 1980s it was estimated that more than 500,000 Angolans had fled to neighbouring countries.

The population of the capital, Luanda (which was 480,613 at the 1970 census), was estimated to have risen to 1.3m. by 1986. Outside the capital, most urban centres are operating at a reduced level, some having been partially destroyed or looted. Benguela and Lobito (the outlet of the Benguela railway, which has been effectively out of operation since 1975) have felt the impact of war, and Lobito harbour is still suffering from the disruption of traffic with Zaire and Zambia. Progress with the rehabilitation of the Lobito corridor, which will benefit both cities, still awaits the cessation of civil unrest. Huambo, formerly an important centre for rail traffic to the eastern regions, and to Zaire and Zambia, and for road traffic to Luanda and Namibia, should again become a focal point of economic activity. Other centres, such as Namibe, Lubango, Kuito and Luena, have also suffered from the war and local disorder. The city of Cabinda has benefited from the exploitation of offshore petroleum resources, while pioneer towns such as Menongue and Saurimo may eventually assume new importance as regional centres.

Recent History

MILES SMITH-MORRIS

Based on an earlier article by W. G. CLARENCE-SMITH

INDEPENDENCE AND CIVIL WAR

In Angola, uniquely among the former Portuguese-ruled African territories, the colonial power was not confronted by a unified nationalist movement. Instead, there were three rival groups: the Movimento Popular de Libertação de Angola (MPLA), founded in 1956; the União das Populações de Angola/Frente Nacional de Libertação de Angola (UPA/FNLA), founded in 1962; and the União Nacional para a Independência Total de Angola (UNITA), founded in 1966. This fragmentation was attributable to ethnic divisions, rivalries among the leading figures, and genuine ideological differences. All three groups engaged in armed activity, mainly in areas bordering Zambia and Zaire: the MPLA was probably the most effective, partly because of an increase in support from the Organization of African Unity (OAU) from 1967 onwards. The nationalists' success was reduced by conflicts within and between the movements, despite the OAU's efforts at reconciliation. The three groups vied for external support, both from governments and from non-governmental organizations. The major Western powers supported the Portuguese, while the USSR and its allies were the principal sponsors of the MPLA.

Following a military coup in Portugal in April 1974, the new Portuguese government, under Gen. António Spínola, did not favour rapid decolonization. Within Angola, intermittent fighting occurred between nationalists and the Portuguese armed forces, while violent random attacks were also made on Africans by extremist right-wing Portuguese settlers. In September a new Portuguese government, under Gen. Francisco da Costa Gomes, expressed its determination to end the fighting and to grant rapid independence to the African territories, overriding the interests of the white settlers.

In 1974 the MPLA, the least cohesive of the three nationalist movements, agreed upon a formal internal structure, appointing Dr Agostinho Neto as president, with Daniel Chipenda and Mário Pinto de Andrade as vice-presidents. Later in the year, pacts were made between the FNLA and UNITA, and between the MPLA and UNITA, and in January 1975 the three groups, meeting in Kenya, agreed to form a common political programme. In the same month agreement was reached with the Portuguese government, establishing the date of Angola's independence as 11 November 1975: until then Angola would be governed by a transitional administration, comprising representatives of the three independence movements and a Portuguese high commissioner. A constituent assembly was to be elected, comprising only candidates who had been endorsed by the three movements.

During the first half of 1975 fighting broke out on several occasions between the MPLA and the FNLA, despite their January agreements. Another co-operation pact, adopted by the three movements in Kenya in June (meeting under the chairmanship of President Kenyatta), proved to be equally unsuccessful. In July the MPLA expelled the FNLA from the Angolan capital, Luanda, and UNITA also became fully involved in the fighting. By October the MPLA controlled 12 of the country's 16 provincial capitals. Considerable financial and military aid was received by the MPLA from the USSR and its allies, and by the FNLA and UNITA from the USA and other Western countries. In October South African forces entered Angola, in support of UNITA and the FNLA, and in November Cuban troops arrived to assist the MPLA. Independence was declared on 11 November, as originally planned, by the MPLA in Luanda, by UNITA in Huambo, and by the FNLA in Carmona and Ambriz. In January 1976 the MPLA decisively defeated the FNLA, and at the end of the month South African forces withdrew. In February the MPLA captured the main UNITA town of Huambo, and on the same day the OAU recognized Angola as a member state. Cuban forces remained in the country.

Despite its military successes, the MPLA government was confronted by considerable difficulties: Angola's infrastructure had been damaged by war, most of the Portuguese population (who had dominated the modern sector of the economy) had fled abroad, and there were large numbers of refugees requiring support. Neto's administration refused to contemplate sharing power with the FNLA and UNITA, and during 1976 it acted to quell its opponents both within and outside the MPLA. In that year Nito Alves, the minister of the interior, and his supporters expressed resentment against the disproportionate number of white and *mestiço* (mixed-race) members at the senior levels of the party. In late 1976 Alves' post was abolished, and in May 1977 he was removed from the MPLA central committee. This precipitated an attempt by rebellious army units to seize power: the coup was quickly suppressed, and there ensued a purge of the country's mass organizations (the trade union federation, and women's and young people's organizations), the provincial administrations, and the armed forces. In December the Neto leadership formulated a rigorous Marxist-Leninist course for the MPLA, changing its name to the MPLA—Partido do Trabalho (Party of Labour) (MPLA—PT). In December 1978 Neto's power was further reinforced by a reorganization of the government (abolishing the posts of the prime minister and the three deputy prime ministers) and of the party structure.

Following the death of President Neto in September 1979, the party effected a smooth transfer of power to José Eduardo dos Santos, hitherto the minister of planning, and reiterated its commitment to the policies that had been formulated under Neto's leadership. In 1980 there were further changes in the political structure, which confirmed the MPLA—PT's greater sense of self-confidence. The central committee had decided in 1976 that elections could be held only when MPLA structures were sufficiently strong, and by 1980 it was felt that they were. In August the central committee initiated a series of constitutional changes, to create a people's assembly and a number of provincial assemblies. These bodies were elected through an electoral college system, and the candidates at every level were vetted by the MPLA—PT or the mass organizations. A new people's assembly was inaugurated in November.

The process of internal political consolidation after 1976 went in tandem with a foreign policy that was designed to weaken external support for the enemies of the MPLA and to secure for Angola the benefits of friendly relations with other states, including commercial and other agreements which would help in Angola's development. The cornerstone of Angolan foreign policy was a close relationship with the Eastern bloc countries, especially Cuba, the USSR and, to some extent, the German Democratic Republic. A treaty of friendship and co-operation was signed with the USSR in 1976 and ratified by both countries in the following year. Nevertheless, the Angolan leaders vigorously denied that their country was a Soviet client state, and actively pursued other diplomatic initiatives. In relation to Angola's immediate neighbours, this policy was most successful with Zambia, which recognized the Angolan republic in April 1976 and, at the government's request, expelled UNITA forces operating from Zambian soil at the end of that year. Relations with Zaire, which Angola eagerly sought to improve, remained difficult and, despite an attempt at conciliation (the Brazzaville agreement) in 1976, deteriorated considerably during 1977 and 1978, as a result of two incursions from Angola into the Shaba province of Zaire by forces of the Zairean anti-government Front National pour la Libération du Congo. In addition, President Neto had, in 1977, claimed knowledge of a plot to invade Angola ('Operation Cobra'), in which Zaire was said to be implicated. Whatever the involvement of some Western interests in plots against Angola, one effect of the Second Shaba Crisis (during which French and Belgian troops were flown to Zaire) was Western insistence that Zaire should improve its relations with Angola. This duly took place in July 1978, and the *rapprochement* brought its greatest benefit to Angola in October 1979, when President Mobutu ordered the deportation from Zaire of the leaders of anti-MPLA—PT groups.

Relations with Portugal were strained immediately after independence, and diplomatic links were not formalized until September 1976. These relations were not particularly cordial until a meeting between President Neto and President Eanes of Portugal in June 1978 resolved most of the outstanding differences between the two countries. The United Kingdom opened an embassy in Angola in 1977. Full diplomatic relations were established with France and the Federal Republic of Germany in 1979, and in the same year Angola introduced legislation offering attractive incentives to foreign companies to invest in the country's economy. The most significant example of successful co-operation between Angola and Western multinational corporations is to be found in the petroleum industry, whose contributions to Angola's balance of payments and to government revenue have been of crucial importance.

CONFLICT WITH SOUTH AFRICA AND THE RESURGENCE OF UNITA

By early 1981, although it was still confronted by grave economic problems, the Angolan government could look back on some success and look forward with some optimism. However, from this point onwards, national life came to be increasingly dominated by the damaging effects of Angola's undeclared war with South Africa.

The roots of this conflict lay in South Africa's refusal to concede independence to Namibia and in its unremitting campaign against the South West Africa People's Organisation of Namibia (SWAPO), the principal nationalist group conducting an armed struggle against South African rule in the territory. From 1978 onwards, South African troops made periodic incursions into Angolan territory, and from 1981 these attacks intensified and were directed as much against Angolan as against SWAPO targets. The most notable escalation was 'Operation Protea' in August 1981, in which several thousand South African troops advanced at least 120 km into Angola. These attacks were augmented by the activities of UNITA, which assumed a more prominent military role, expanding its operations in eastern Angola while the government deployed its main forces in the west against 'Operation Protea'. Throughout 1982 and 1983, South Africa and UNITA together intensified their activities in Angola, with the South Africans occupying large sections of Cunene province, while UNITA launched attacks on a wide variety of targets, and on several occasions captured foreign nationals. In August 1983 there was a further escalation in the conflict when a large UNITA force captured the strategic town of Cangamba, in Moxico province, with the aid of intense aerial bombardment by the South African air force. This type of operation was increasingly difficult to justify as a 'hot-pursuit' action against SWAPO, and was clearly aimed at destabilizing the dos Santos government. UNITA continued to conduct operations throughout 1984.

The Angolan government struggled to meet these challenges with new foreign and domestic policy initiatives. While maintaining good relations with its Eastern bloc allies, it continued to diversify its international contacts, establishing relations with the People's Republic of China in 1983, and moving towards a relationship with the European Community (EC). The petroleum industry, the country's economic mainstay, continued to prosper. At least 50% of the government's revenue from the petroleum sector was used for expenditure on defence and security, including the purchase of increasingly sophisticated military equipment and the training of Angolans to operate it. In July 1983 regional military councils were established in all areas affected by the fighting, concentrating all state power in the hands of military men directly responsible to the president. Counter-attacks against UNITA by the government forces, the Forças Armadas Populares de Libertação de Angola (FAPLA), had some success in 1982 and 1983.

For reasons which remain conjectural, South Africa abruptly changed course in January 1984, and proposed to withdraw its troops in exchange for Angola's restraining the activities of SWAPO guerrillas. By the terms of this proposal, formulated in February as the Lusaka Accord, South Africa was to withdraw from Angola, Angola was to control the activities of SWAPO and the whole agreement was conditional on South Africa's proceeding towards Namibian independence in accordance with the UN Security Council's Resolution 435. As these developments ran almost concurrently with the Nkomati Accord between South Africa and Mozambique, they engendered considerable confidence in certain circles when perhaps scepticism would have been more appropriate: as stipulated by the Lusaka Accord, South Africa officially withdrew its troops from Angola in April 1985, only to have a unit of its special forces captured in the following month while engaged in operations against oil installations in Cabinda. 'Hot-pursuit' operations into Angola were resumed in June 1985, after which South Africa periodically deployed troops in Angola until August 1988 (see below).

Despite differences within each of the governments of the USA, South Africa and Angola on the appropriate course of action to follow, the position of the three main protagonists became clearer in the period following the Lusaka Accord. In US policy-making circles the view that the Angolan government must be weakened sufficiently in order to force the withdrawal of the Cubans clearly came to prevail over the view that Angola's legitimate security needs were better served by a resolution of the Namibian issue. Protracted negotiations, usually involving the USA as well as Angola and South Africa, collapsed because of a failure to agree on the question of 'linkage', i.e. the withdrawal of the Cubans as a *quid pro quo* for South African withdrawal from Angola and the creation of an independent Namibia.

From the mid-1980s, Angolan relations with the USA deteriorated, largely as a result of the reverse in US policy towards UNITA. In July 1985 the US congress repealed legislation which had prohibited US military support for UNITA since 1976. In September 1985, as a result of the military situation, a South African delegation visited Washington to seek US aid for UNITA. This was followed in January 1986 by a visit to the USA by UNITA's leader, Dr Jonas Savimbi. His reception there was comparable to that for a head of state, and included well-publicized meetings with President Reagan and leading members of the administration who openly expressed their support for UNITA. The US congress subsequently agreed to provide UNITA with armaments, and these began to arrive in Angola during the second half of the year. In April President dos Santos had complained to the UN secretary-general of the US government's escalating support for UNITA, and requested the UN to terminate the role of the USA as primary mediator in negotiations over Namibia. In August, however, the Angolan government approached the US government, with a view to improving relations. The Reagan administration was not receptive to these overtures, and in October the US congress approved legislation prohibiting the purchase of Angolan petroleum and petroleum products by the US department of defense. Savimbi attempted to improve UNITA's international standing in October, when he accepted an invitation by centrist and right-wing members to visit the European parliament. However, his trip was largely unsuccessful; the European parliament refused to grant him official recognition and proceeded to condemn US support for UNITA and to propose the imposition of compulsory and comprehensive sanctions against South Africa. In March 1987 UNITA continued to seek international recognition in a move which some observers believe to have been prompted by the US

Central Intelligence Agency: UNITA offered to allow non-military traffic to operate on the Benguela railway, which had been effectively closed since 1975, owing to persistent sabotage by the rebels. In April 1987 Angola, Zaire, Zambia and Zimbabwe discussed the possible reopening of the railway line, which provides the shortest west coast route from Zambia and Zaire. However, UNITA's sincerity with regard to ceasing its sabotage activities became questionable in June, when it launched an attack on the railway.

By mid-1987 it was apparent that South African security forces were becoming increasingly active inside Angola and Namibia, and in October South Africa confirmed, for the first time, that it was maintaining a 'limited presence' inside Angola. In the following month South Africa confirmed that it was providing military support to UNITA, and announced that it had engaged in direct action against Soviet and Cuban forces. UNITA, however, denied that South Africa was providing military reinforcements to the rebels. South Africa's intensification of aggression against Angola was widely condemned, and in late November the UN Security Council demanded the unconditional withdrawal of South African troops from Angola within two weeks. Having eventually agreed to comply with this demand, South Africa nevertheless remained militarily active in Angola in the first half of 1988 (see below).

In April 1987 Angola and the USA resumed talks aimed at achieving a negotiated settlement over Namibia and Angola, and the Angolan government made considerable efforts to secure diplomatic recognition from the USA, in spite of the announcement by the US administration, in June, of its intentions to continue to provide covert military aid to UNITA in both 1987 and 1988. In July 1987 it was reported that the Namibia talks had failed to produce agreement, but talks were resumed in September. Angola's readiness to establish good relations with the USA was reflected in the change in the direction of the government's economic policy, indicated in August by President dos Santos' announcement that Angola was applying for membership of the International Monetary Fund (IMF). In the following month the president made visits to several European capitals, including Paris and Lisbon, aimed at securing economic and, in some cases, military aid, and at obtaining support for Angola's proposed membership of the IMF. The visit to Lisbon was particularly significant, in that it was the first visit by an Angolan president to Portugal since Angola gained independence in 1975.

Negotiations relating to a regional peace agreement were resumed in January 1988 between the USA and Angola, without success. In March, when it appeared that, in spite of a sharp escalation in the armed conflict in late 1987 and early 1988, a deadlock had again been reached between the two sides, renewed attempts to settle the guerrilla war by means of negotiation were made by the parties involved. In that month, representatives of Angola, Cuba and the USA held a meeting in Luanda, at which Angola and Cuba presented a peace plan, which included a new proposal for the evacuation of Cuban forces from southern Angola. The Angolan government also indicated that it was prepared to be flexible regarding the timetable for this evacuation. However, South Africa received these peace proposals without enthusiasm, on the grounds that their provisions were too vague. Discussions were also held in March between the South African government and UNITA, and between the USA and the USSR.

TOWARDS A REGIONAL ACCORD

One of the main obstacles to progress towards a regional peace settlement was South Africa's reluctance to commit itself to a comprehensive withdrawal from Angola and to the implementation of an independence settlement for Namibia. Nevertheless, in May 1988 Cuba and Angola held 'exploratory talks' with South Africa in London, with the USA as mediator. At talks between Angola and South Africa, held nine days later, modest progress was reportedly made towards reaching a compromise. Later in May, at a meeting in Lisbon, the USA and the USSR discussed an outline peace plan for Angola, involving the withdrawal of both the Cuban and South African troops from Angola within one year. During a summit meeting between the USSR and the USA, held in Moscow in late May and early June, a target date of 29 September 1988 was set for reaching a settlement on the Angolan and Namibian conflicts. However, South Africa indicated that it regarded this deadline as unrealistic. At this time, the security situation worsened considerably; it was suggested by observers that UNITA and South Africa were intensifying their offensive in order to precipitate a peace agreement by Angola. Cuba, meanwhile, was reported to have increased its military forces from 35,000 to 50,000 troops. UNITA, which was excluded from the London meeting and subsequent consultations, initiated a diplomatic campaign in major Western capitals to advance its terms for an Angolan settlement. Discussions between representatives of the governments of Angola, Cuba, South Africa and the USA, held in July, resulted in a mutually agreed 'statement of principle', encompassing a programme that the US negotiator described as 'containing the essential elements of a peaceful settlement in south-western Africa'. Its provisions included the termination of US support for UNITA, South African assent to independence for Namibia on terms and conditions acceptable to the UN, and the simultaneous withdrawal of Cuban and South African troops from Angola. No timetable, however, was agreed for the start of the proposed withdrawals.

In early August 1988 discussions in Geneva resulted in an agreement on a 'sequence of steps' towards a regional peace settlement, whereby a cease-fire was to commence on 8 August, pending the withdrawal of all South African troops from Angola by 1 September, and the agreement, by that date, of a timetable for the evacuation of all Cuban forces from Angola; the implementation of the UN Security Council's Resolution 435 for Namibian independence was to commence on 1 November. However, although the cease-fire was observed and it was reported that all South African troops had duly departed by the end of August, agreement on a timetable for the Cuban withdrawal was not concluded. As a result, implementation of the Namibian independence process was postponed. Following further negotiations on an exact schedule for the Cuban withdrawal, an agreement in principle was eventually reached in Geneva in mid-November, although the signing of a formal protocol was delayed until mid-December, owing to South African dissatisfaction over verification procedures for the Cuban troop departures.

On 22 December 1988 the participants in the negotiations met in New York, where a bilateral agreement was signed by Angola and Cuba, and a tripartite accord by Angola, Cuba and South Africa: under these agreements, 1 April 1989 was designated as the implementation date for the Namibian independence process, which was to culminate in elections to a constituent assembly from 1 November 1989, and Cuba undertook to complete a phased withdrawal of its estimated 50,000 troops from Angola by July 1991. Angola, Cuba and South Africa were to establish a joint commission, in which the USA and the USSR would be present as observers. All prisoners of war were to be exchanged, and the signatories of the tripartite accord were to refrain from supporting forces intent on undermining each other's governments. The latter clause necessitated both the curtailment of South African aid to UNITA and the departure from Angola of an estimated 6,000 members of the African National Congress of South Africa (ANC). In accordance with the agreements, the UN Security Council authorized the creation of a UN Angola Verification Mission (UNAVEM) to monitor the redeployment and withdrawal of Cuban troops. UNAVEM, comprising 60 military observers from 10 countries, commenced operations in January 1989. Its mandate was for a period of 31 months.

Following the signing of the New York accords, the new Bush administration reassured UNITA of continued US support. The Angolan government remained intransigent towards appeals by UNITA for a cease-fire, but in early February 1989 it offered a 12-month amnesty to members of the rebel organization, reaffirming the regime's aim of re-assimilating defectors from UNITA into society. However,

UNITA, restating its own aim of negotiating a settlement with the government which would lay the foundations for a multi-party democracy in Angola, reacted to the government's amnesty by launching a major offensive against FAPLA targets. This was abandoned shortly afterwards, owing to the intercession of President Houphouet-Boigny of Côte d'Ivoire. In the following month, both the government and UNITA showed a new willingness to end the civil war, and in early March President dos Santos announced that he was ready to attend a regional 'summit' conference to advance a resolution of the conflict. Shortly afterwards, Dr Savimbi announced that UNITA would honour a unilateral moratorium on offensive military operations until mid-July, during which time he hoped that African leaders would mediate an internal settlement. In addition, Savimbi offered to exclude himself from any peace negotiations, in order that this might make them more palatable to the dos Santos government. In mid-May eight African heads of state attended a conference in Luanda, at which President dos Santos presented a peace plan. He did not appear to have altered his terms for a peaceful solution to the Angolan civil war, demanding the cessation of US aid to UNITA and offering rebels reintegration into society.

In June 1989, however, President dos Santos and Dr Savimbi both agreed to attend a further conference, held at Gbadolite, in Zaire, under the auspices of President Mobutu, at which 18 African leaders were present. Dos Santos (who had earlier released 700 UNITA prisoners as a gesture of goodwill) consented to hold direct negotiations with Savimbi, as a result of which a cease-fire was signed between UNITA and the Angolan government, with effect from midnight on 23 June. It was decided that the Zairean, Gabonese and Congolese presidents would oversee a commission responsible for monitoring the implementation of the peace agreement. The full terms of the accord were not, however, made public at that time, and it subsequently became apparent that these were interpreted differently by each party: claims by the Angolan government that Savimbi had agreed to go into temporary exile and that members of UNITA were to be absorbed into existing Angolan institutions and to respect the existing constitution were strongly denied by the rebels. Within one week each side had accused the other of violating the cease-fire. In late August Savimbi announced a resumption of hostilities: he was reported to have been angered by his exclusion from a meeting of the OAU's Special Committee on Peace in Angola during that month, and by criticism of him at that meeting by President Kaunda of Zambia.

In September 1989, after boycotting a conference of eight African heads of state at Kinshasa, Zaire, at which the Gbadolite accord had been redrafted, Savimbi announced a series of counter-proposals, envisaging the creation of an African peace-keeping force to supervise a renewed cease-fire, and the commencement of direct negotiations between UNITA and the government, with the objective of agreeing a settlement which could lay the foundation of a multi-party democracy in Angola. In early October, following a meeting with US President Bush, Savimbi agreed to resume peace talks with the Angolan government, with President Mobutu of Zaire acting as mediator: the US government announced during that month, however, that it would continue to support UNITA until 'national reconciliation' was achieved. Tentative indirect talks between Savimbi and the government, mediated by Mobutu, took place in mid-October. In late December President dos Santos proposed an eight-point peace plan which envisaged some political reform but did not compromise on the issue of a one-party state; the plan was rejected by UNITA. In mid-January 1990 Cuba temporarily suspended its troop withdrawal, following an attack by UNITA forces which resulted in the deaths of four Cuban soldiers. In early February a summit of four African heads of state took place in Zaire; although he had been invited, President dos Santos did not attend the meeting. During that month fighting intensified between FAPLA and UNITA forces in the Mavinga region of southern Angola, a UNITA stronghold. In early March UNITA, admitting that the government troops had made substantial advances, announced that it would accept an immediate cease-fire on condition that FAPLA forces withdraw from Mavinga.

THE ESTORIL PEACE AGREEMENT

In early April 1990, following a further summit meeting of four African heads of state, held in São Tomé and Príncipe and this time including the Angolan president, dos Santos reaffirmed his commitment to achieving a peace settlement. Shortly afterwards, UNITA agreed to respect an immediate cease-fire and requested direct talks with the government, abandoning its demand for the withdrawal of FAPLA troops from Mavinga. The government agreed to restart negotiations, and exploratory talks between representatives of UNITA and the government were held in Portugal later in that month, under the supervision of the Portuguese minister of foreign affairs. Six further rounds of negotiations took place before May 1991 (see below). In May 1990 the government announced that it was withdrawing its forces from Mavinga, and in the following month FAPLA troops were withdrawn from south-eastern Angola, as a 'gesture of goodwill'.

The government and UNITA both made significant political concessions during 1990. In early May UNITA announced that it would recognize dos Santos as Angola's head of state, and in October the rebel organization announced its acceptance of the MPLA—PT government as an interim administration, pending elections. During an historic meeting of the central committee of the MPLA—PT in late June and early July, it was decided that the country would 'evolve towards a multi-party political system', thus conceding one of UNITA's principal demands. In late October the MPLA's central committee proposed a general programme of reforms, including the replacement of the party's official Marxist-Leninist ideology with a commitment to 'democratic socialism', the introduction of a market economy, the legalization of political parties (after which UNITA would be recognized as a legitimate political force), the transformation of the army from a party to a state institution, a revision of the constitution and the holding of multi-party elections in 1994, following a population census. The decisions of the central committee were formally approved by the party's third congress in December. However, the government and UNITA continued to disagree over the timing of elections and the status of UNITA pending the elections. UNITA insisted on immediate political recognition as a precondition for a cease-fire, and elections by the end of 1991.

In March 1991 the national people's assembly approved legislation permitting the formation of political parties. On 1 May, as a result of the rounds of talks which commenced in April 1990, the government and UNITA concluded a peace agreement in Estoril, Portugal. The agreement provided for a cease-fire from midnight on 15 May, to be monitored by a joint political and military committee, comprising representatives from the MPLA—PT, UNITA, the UN, Portugal, the USA and the USSR. Immediately following the cease-fire, aid from abroad to the government and UNITA would cease, and a new national army was to be established, composed of equal numbers of FAPLA and UNITA soldiers. Free and democratic elections were to be held by the end of 1992. In early May 1991 the government approved legislation giving all exiles one year in which to return to Angola. The cease-fire took effect, according to plan, on 15 May, despite an intensification of FAPLA and UNITA activities prior to that date. On 31 May the government and UNITA signed a formal agreement in Lisbon, ratifying the Estoril peace agreement. The joint political and military committee met for the first time in June.

Following the legalization of opposition parties in March 1991, numerous groupings emerged, attracting widespread public support. Among the most influential of these were the Associação Cívica Angolana, which was expected to deflect votes from the MPLA—PT (which had attracted much public protest following the implementation of economic austerity measures in late 1990 and early 1991), and the Fórum Democrático Angolano, which was expected to compete with UNITA for support. In early 1991 UNITA began the process of becoming a legally recognized political movement. Legislation approved by the national people's assembly in May stipulated that political parties must enjoy support in at least 14 of Angola's 18 provinces, in order to discourage the emergence of ethnically-based political movements. This measure operated to the disadvantage of the Frente de Libertação do Enclave de Cabinda (FLEC), a movement which advocates the secession of Cabinda province from Angola.

The USA and the USSR were both influential in bringing about the Estoril peace agreement. In September 1990 both powers joined the negotiations between UNITA and the government. In the following month the US congress agreed to provide UNITA with assistance worth US $60m. in 1991, but voted to suspend aid to the rebel organization if the government respected a cease-fire and promised to hold multi-party elections within two years of the cease-fire. However, in mid-June 1991, following the conclusion of the Estoril peace agreement (in which these conditions were fulfilled) in May, the US congress agreed to continue supplying aid to UNITA, at a reduced level of $20m.

In July 1991 President dos Santos carried out a cabinet reshuffle, in which the post of prime minister, which had been abolished in 1977, was given to a former minister of planning, Fernando José França Van-Dúnem.

Implementation of the peace accord was subject to considerable delay in its initial stages. In September 1991 UNITA briefly withdrew from participation in the joint political and military commission, demanding that the government proceed more rapidly with the confinement of its forces to assembly points and with agreeing on an electoral timetable. UNITA agreed to return to the commission following a meeting between Savimbi and the US vice-president, Dan Quayle. At the end of September Savimbi returned to Luanda for the first time since the civil war began in 1975; UNITA headquarters were transferred to the capital from Jamba in October.

In November 1991 dos Santos announced a provisional date for general elections. Voting was to take place in the second half of September, subject to consultations with political parties and to the extension of state administration to areas still under UNITA control. The arrangements were also contingent on the confinement of all UNITA forces to assembly points by mid-December. A step towards the creation of a unified national army was taken in January 1992, with the appointment of Gen. João de Matos, commander of FAPLA's ground forces, and Gen. Ahilo Camalata Numa, commander of UNITA's northern front, as supreme commanders of the armed forces.

In January 1992, on the recommendation of the joint political and military commission, a monitoring task group was established to expedite the implementation of the peace accord. The creation of the group, which was to include members of the government, UNITA and UNAVEM, followed growing concern over the reported decline in the number of government and UNITA troops in confinement areas and the reoccupation of territory by UNITA forces; troops from both armies, abandoning confinement areas, were believed to be responsible for rising levels of criminal activity. Concern about the security situation was heightened in the same month by the murder of four British tourists near a UNITA base in Huíla province.

Representatives of the government and 26 political parties met in Luanda in the second half of January 1992 to discuss the transition to multi-party democracy; the government rejected demands to convene a national conference to formulate the transition arrangements. UNITA declined to attend the meeting, but in February it held talks with the government, at which agreement was reached on various points of electoral procedure. It was agreed that the elections would be organized on the basis of proportional representation, with the president elected for a five-year term, renewable for three terms. The legislative assembly would be elected for a four-year term. On 2 April dos Santos announced that the elections would be held on 29 and 30 September. Two days after this announcement, the people's assembly adopted electoral legislation providing for an assembly of 223 members (90 to be elected in 18 provincial constituencies and the remainder from national lists). Provision was also made for the creation of a national electoral council to supervise the elections. The members of the council were appointed in early May.

Evidence of serious divisions within UNITA became apparent in early March 1992, with the announcement that two leading members, Gen. Miguel N'Zau Puna (the movement's spokesman for internal affairs) and Gen. Tony da Costa Fernandes (the spokesman for foreign affairs), had resigned. Both men were from Cabinda and were stated by UNITA to have resigned because of differences over the future of the petroleum-producing enclave, whose secession from Angola they were alleged to support. In February the two men had secretly left Angola for Paris, France, from where they issued statements denouncing Savimbi as a dictator and claiming that he was maintaining a clandestine force of some 2,000 troops near the Namibian border. They further accused Savimbi of ordering the killing in 1991 of Tito Chingunji and Wilson dos Santos, UNITA's former representatives in the USA and Portugal respectively. Requested by the US administration to provide an explanation, Savimbi claimed that Puna had been responsible for the killings, which had taken place at UNITA's Jamba headquarters while he had been absent. It was widely forecast that the defection of Puna and Fernandes, founder members of UNITA but not members of the Ovimbundu ethnic group which formed the majority of its supporters, could prove to be damaging to UNITA's electoral prospects. Puna and Fernandes subsequently returned to Angola and formed a 'Democratic Breakaway Tendency' to attract disaffected elements of UNITA.

The demobilization of FAPLA and UNITA forces began on 31 March 1992 and was to be completed by the end of July. According to the joint military and political commission, by the end of March 94% of UNITA's forces and 64% of those of FAPLA had gathered at the assembly points. There were reports, however, that both sides planned to keep some forces in reserve, and there were fears that the demobilization process, and the creation of a unified national army, would fall behind schedule.

The Partido Renovador, regarded as the third largest of the 30 or more political parties that had been formed since the introduction of a multi-party system, held its first congress in late April 1992, and immediately afterwards divided into two factions. The party's former honorary president, Joaquim Pinto de Andrade, and his supporters resigned from the party, alleging that the election of the party president, Luís dos Passos, and a new party executive during the congress had been the result of electoral malpractice. The MPLA—PT held an extraordinary congress in early May to prepare for the forthcoming elections. The 600 delegates voted to enlarge the membership of the central committee from 140 to 193, to allow the inclusion of prominent dissidents who had returned to the party. Among those who were readmitted to the party at the congress was Daniel Chipenda, a leading figure in the struggle for independence, who had left the MPLA in 1975, in protest at its alliance with the USSR, and had lived in exile until 1986. A meeting of the new central committee elected Chipenda to the political bureau. During the congress the delegates voted to remove the suffix 'Partido do Trabalho' from the party's official name.

Dos Santos, Savimbi, Chipenda and the president of the FNLA, Holden Roberto, were among 12 candidates who had registered by the end of July 1992 for the presidential election. Chipenda, who was proposed by the National Democratic Party of Angola (PNDA), had earlier resigned as the election organizer of the MPLA. Despite concerns about delays in voter registration, some 4.8m. Angolans had been registered to vote in the elections by the deadline on 10 August (following a 10-day extension).

In August 1992 the legislature approved a revision of the constitution, removing the remnants of the country's former Marxist ideology, and deleting the worlds 'People's' and 'Popular' from the constitution and from the names of official institutions. The name of the country was changed from the People's Republic of Angola to the Republic of Angola.

On 27 September 1992 FAPLA and the UNITA forces were formally disbanded, and the new national army, the Forças Armadas de Angola (FAA), was officially established. However, the process of training and incorporating FAPLA and UNITA troops into the new 50,000-strong national army had been hindered by delays in the demobilization programme. By 28 September fewer than 10,000 soldiers were ready to be inducted into the FAA. Tens of thousands of government troops were reported to be awaiting demobilization or to have abandoned confinement areas, owing to poor conditions and non-payment of wages. Military observers reported that only a small percentage of UNITA soldiers had been demobilized, and that UNITA retained a heavily-armed and disciplined force. UNITA had deliberately slowed the process of demobilizing its soldiers, in protest at the formation of a new government paramilitary unit, the 'emergency police', recruited from the MPLA's own special forces.

Increased tension and outbreaks of violence in the period preceding the general election seriously threatened to disrupt the electoral process. Nevertheless, presidential and legislative elections took place, as scheduled, on 29–30 September 1992. Some 800 foreign observers, one-half of them provided by the UN, monitored the voting at nearly 6,000 polling stations. Despite fears of violence or intimidation, the level of participation was high, averaging almost 90% of the electorate, although a low turnout was reported from Cabinda, where FLEC had urged its supporters to boycott the elections. International observers reported that the conduct of the elections had been free and fair, but, when preliminary results indicated that the MPLA had obtained a majority of seats in the new national assembly, Savimbi accused the government of electoral fraud and demanded the suspension of the official announcement of the election results, pending an inquiry into the alleged electoral irregularities. On 5 October UNITA withdrew from the FAA. Heavy fighting between UNITA supporters and police broke out in Luanda on 11 October, and similar incidents were reported in Malanje, Huambo and Huíla provinces.

According to the official election results, published on 17 October 1992, dos Santos received 49.57% of the total votes cast in the presidential election, just short of the 50% required to avoid a second round against Savimbi, who secured 40.07% of the votes. However, the MPLA had achieved a clear majority in the legislative elections, winning 129 of the 220 seats in the national assembly, compared with UNITA's 70. Ten other parties won between one and six seats each. Three seats reserved for Angolans abroad were not filled, by mutual agreement among the parties. UNITA's share of the total vote was 34.1%, compared with the MPLA's 53.7%.

Savimbi, who had withdrawn to the UNITA-dominated province of Huambo, had agreed to participate in a second round of presidential elections on the condition that it be conducted by the UN, while the government insisted that the election should not take place until UNITA had conformed to the rules of the Estoril peace agreement by transferring its troops to assembly points and by returning to the FAA.

REASSERTION OF CIVIL STRIFE

Following the announcement of the official election results, however, violence erupted between MPLA and UNITA supporters in various cities, including Luanda and Huambo, as UNITA launched a new offensive. By the end of October 1992 hostilities had spread throughout Angola, with the majority of UNITA's demobilized soldiers returning to arms. Serious fighting took place in Luanda and the central and southern towns of Benguela, Huambo, Lobito and Lubango in the first week of November, despite UN attempts to arrange a cease-fire. Several senior UNITA officials, including Elias Salupeto Pena (the senior UNITA representative on the joint military and political commission) and Jeremias Chitunda (vice-president of UNITA), were reported to be among some 1,000 people killed in the renewed conflict. Reports that South Africa and Zaire had been providing logistical support to UNITA led to a deterioration in relations with these states.

On 6 November 1992 the UN under-secretary-general for peace-keeping operations, Marrack Goulding, arrived in Angola. Following discussions with Goulding and the UN special representative, Margaret Anstee, on 17 November, Savimbi announced that he would abide by the election results, although he maintained that the ballot had been fraudulent, and stated that he would participate in the second round of presidential elections, expected to take palce in December 1992 or January 1993. Despite assurances that it would attend, UNITA was absent from multi-party talks convened by the government on 21 November. The national assembly convened on 26 November, without the 70 elected UNITA delegates, who claimed that to convene the assembly in the absence of an elected president was illegal. Fernando José França van-Dúnem, a former prime minister, was elected president of the assembly. On the following day, dos Santos appointed Marcolino José Carlos Moco, the secretary-general of the MPLA, as prime minister. Savimbi, meanwhile, continued to engage in negotiations with the government and the UN while his forces remained on the offensive outside the capital. On 27 November, after direct talks between dos Santos and Savimbi, the two leaders issued a declaration reaffirming their commitment to the Estoril peace accords, and committing themselves to the implementation of a cease-fire and a continuing UN presence in Angola. Shortly afterwards, UNITA launched an offensive in the north, capturing Uíge and an air base at Negage. By the end of November UNITA was reported to be in control of about two-thirds of the country.

The composition of a council of ministers was announced on 2 December 1992. The majority of the posts were asigned to members of the MPLA, with four smaller parties also represented. One full and four deputy ministerial posts (including that of deputy defence minister) were allocated to UNITA, along with the positions of armed forces deputy chief of the general staff and chief of army general staff. The names of their appointees were announced by UNITA and accepted by Moco, although he stipulated that their appointment would be dependent upon the full implementation of the peace accords. Relations with South Africa deteriorated further with the announcement by the South African government that it was withdrawing its diplomatic representation from Luanda; earlier the Angolan government had announced that it had detained the crew of a South African aircraft that had made an emergency landing on Angolan soil, an incident which it cited as further evidence of South African support for UNITA.

International pressure on the warring parties to reach a negotiated solution continued with the visit of the US deputy assistant secretary of state for African affairs, Jeffrey Davidow, in the second half of December 1992 for meetings with both leaders. As a result of the talks, UNITA withdrew its forces from Uíge and Negage, but fighting nevertheless intensified in late December, as the government launched an offensive. The offensive had some success, driving UNITA out of most major towns, but with heavy casualties reported, particularly in southern Angola. A fierce battle began for control of Huambo in the central highlands, the country's second largest city and traditionally a UNITA stronghold. In mid-January 1993 UNITA claimed to have captured the petroleum producing centre of Soyo, on the Zaire border. UNITA appeared, however, to have been deterred from attacking the petroleum installations of the Cabinda enclave, many of them operated by US companies, by a direct warning from the US representative in Angola, Edmund De Jarnette.

From late January 1993 diplomatic efforts to end the hostilities centred on peace talks convened by the UN in Addis Ababa, Ethiopia, with Portugal, Russia and the USA attending as observers. A first round began on 27 January, with discussions reported to be focusing on four issues: the establishment of a cease-fire; the implementation of the Estoril peace accord; the definition of the UN's role in a cease-fire and the second round of the presidential elections;

and the release of prisoners. A second round of talks, due to begin on 7 February, was repeatedly delayed by the failure of the UNITA delegation to attend and was finally cancelled on 1 March, amid sharp criticism of UNITA by the observers. Meanwhile, evidence of fragmentation in the senior ranks of UNITA was reflected by the decision, on 6 February, by six UNITA generals in custody in Luanda to rejoin the FAA, and by the decision, on 18 February, by 10 UNITA deputies, also in custody in Luanda, to take their seats in the national assembly.

In early March 1993 the government confirmed that it had withdrawn its remaining forces from Huambo, after a two-month siege in which some 10,000 people were thought to have died. In a speech broadcast on 9 March Savimbi issued a call to arms to his supporters and listed the terms for returning to the peace talks, which included a change of venue and the replacement of Margaret Anstee as the UN's representative. His demands were rejected by both the government and the UN. On 12 March the UN security council adopted a resolution condemning UNITA's violations of the peace accords and requesting the UN secretary-general, Dr Boutros Boutros-Ghali, to arrange a meeting between the combatants. The government claimed military successes during March, recapturing Soyo and M'banza-Congo, in the north, and Caxito, north-east of Luanda, and repelling a UNITA assault on Cubal, west of Huambo. Meanwhile, UNITA besieged the government garrison in the central city of Kuito, capital of Bié province. Peace talks resumed, under UN auspices, in Abidjan, Côte d'Ivoire, on 12 April, but, despite some signs of progress on the issue of power-sharing, were hampered by UNITA's intransigence in its demand for the deployment of a UN peace-keeping force to precede negotiation of a formal cease-fire. By early May most issues appeared to have been resolved, except UNITA's refusal to comply with the government's demand that it withdraw from areas that its forces had occupied since the elections. After an adjournment while both delegations returned to Angola for consultations, the talks resumed on 14 May, with the government delegation announcing that it accepted the entire 47-point memorandum of understanding that had been drafted during the negotiations. UNITA, however, continued to raise objections, refusing to withdraw from captured territory until government troops had been confined to barracks and UN peace-keeping forces deployed. The talks were finally suspended indefinitely on 21 May.

UNITA's actions appeared by this stage to have lost it the sympathy of even its former supporters. In May 1993 South Africa reopened its representative office in Luanda (closed since November 1992), with the South African government promising to suppress any assistance being provided to Savimbi from private sources in South Africa. However, South Africa did not grant full recognition to the Angolan government, stating that this would occur only when a 'fully representative' administration was in power. UNITA's refusal to sign the Abidjan agreement proved to be a deciding factor for the USA, UNITA's principal source of support during the Reagan and Bush administrations. On 19 May 1993 President Clinton announced that the USA was to recognize the Angolan government. With diplomatic efforts becalmed, hostilities intensified. In late May UNITA recaptured the petroleum centre of Soyo, although production from the offshore fields appeared to be continuing uninterrupted. Meanwhile, Zambia announced that it was stationing troops on its north-western border with Angola, to counter any threat of attack by UNITA.

In June 1993, in a move reflecting a further improvement in their diplomatic relations, Angola and South Africa agreed to upgrade their diplomatic missions in Luanda and Pretoria to embassies. In the same month a US embassy was opened in Luanda, and a Malian diplomat, Alioune Blondin Beye, was appointed to replace Margaret Anstee as UN secretary general's special representative in Angola. Prior to relinquishing the post, Anstee made an urgent appeal for humanitarian aid at a conference in Geneva, Switzerland. Donor countries were informed that in excess of $227m. would be required to help some 2m. people suffering the direct and indirect consequences of the civil war. On 15 July the UN Security Council extended the mandate of the UN Angola Verification Mission (UNAVEM II) for a further two months and warned that an embargo would be enforced against UNITA unless an effective cease-fire had been established by 15 September.

Fighting intensified during August 1993 with the government forces launching a major bombing campaign against the UNITA stronghold of Huambo, and UNITA intensifying its attacks on the besieged city of Kuito. On 9 August, in recognition of the government's 'legitimate right of self-defence', the United Kingdom ended its arms embargo against the Angolan government (which had been in force since independence in 1975). Later in the month the government signed an agreement with the World Food Programme, providing for a six-month emergency food operation, which was intended to reach almost 2m. people.

On 14 September 1993 UNITA announced that it would implement a unilateral cease-fire, to begin on 20 September, thus prompting the UN Security Council to delay its deadline for imposing an embargo against UNITA until 25 September. However, despite UNITA's claims that it was observing the cease-fire, diplomatic sources reported an intensification of UNITA activity beyond the UN deadline. Consequently, on 26 September the UN imposed an arms and petroleum embargo against UNITA. Observers calculated, however, that clandestine supplies of arms and petroleum from Zaire, in addition to UNITA's existing stockpiles of arms, would ensure that the rebels' military capacity would be sustained for some years, despite the embargo. Further UN sanctions, including the expulsion of UNITA representatives from foreign capitals and the freezing of the rebels' assets abroad, were to be imposed on 1 November should UNITA fail to cease hostilities.

Optimism about a resumption of the peace talks increased in October 1993 after apparent concessions by UNITA in discussions with the UN and the three international observers of the peace process, Portugal, Russia and the USA. UNITA announced that it was prepared to accept the results of the September 1992 elections, although still declaring them to have been 'fraudulent', and accepted the validity of the May 1991 peace accord, but added that the agreement needed revision. UNITA also agreed to co-operate with the UN and to maintain the cease-fire declared on 20 September. After talks between the UN, UNITA and the observers in Lusaka, Zambia in late October there were suggestions that direct talks between the rebels and the government were imminent. On 1 November, Beye informed the UN Security Council that UNITA had agreed to withdraw its forces to UN-monitored confinement areas. In response the UN agreed to delay the imposition of further sanctions against UNITA until 15 December, provided the rebels comply with their undertakings.

Direct talks between UNITA and the government resumed in Lusaka on 16 November 1993. The talks, which had been adjourned in May, were to be conducted, at Beye's insistence and despite objections from UNITA, in conformity with the provisions of the May 1991 peace accords. Following three days of discussions a five-point agenda for the talks was agreed: a cease-fire, the mandate of UNAVEM II, the police, the armed forces, and national reconciliation. By 10 December agreement had reportedly been reached on issues concerning the demobilization and confinement of UNITA troops, the surrender of UNITA weapons to the UN, and the integration of UNITA generals into the FAA. On 13 December UNITA temporarily withdrew from the talks, alleging that a premeditated attempt had been made by the government to assassinate Savimbi. A UN enquiry found nothing to support the allegations and UNITA subsequently agreed to resume talks. On 15 December the UN Security Council extended the mandate of UNAVEM II for a further three months and agreed to a further postponement of additional sanctions against UNITA.

The Lusaka talks resumed on 6 January 1994, focusing on issues concerning the police force. On 30 January an agreement was announced on the formation of a national police force of 26,700 members, of which UNITA was to provide 5,500, to be formed under UN supervision. The force would be open to legal challenge in court and detention without trial would be outlawed. Talks continued during February, concentrating on the issue of national reconciliation, culminating in the signing of a document on 17 February enshrining five fundamental principles and urging Angolans to 'forgive and forget all the wrongs resulting from the conflict'. Acceptance of the September 1992 election results by both sides was also reaffirmed.

The resignation of the minister of finance, Emmanuel Moreira Carneiro, prompted a wider reorganization of the cabinet in mid-March 1994, including the appointment of Alvaro Craveiro as the new finance minister. In addition a new ministry, of economic planning, was created, and José Pedro de Morais was appointed as minister in charge of the new portfolio. On 16 March the UN Security Council extended the mandate of UNAVEM II until 31 May. Progress at the Lusaka peace talks slowed as discussions moved on to the issue of the participation of UNITA in central and local government. Negotiations on the distribution of cabinet posts appeared to have reached an impasse in mid-March, after the government offered UNITA the ministerial posts of health, tourism, commerce and construction materials, plus the governorships of Cuando-Cubango, Uíge and Lunda Sul, in response to UNITA demands for the key portfolios of defence, the interior and finance. UNITA was believed to be seeking the governorships of Benguela, Huambo, Bengo and Cuanza Norte and the public works portfolio in place of that of construction materials. With the government refusing to amend its offer and the talks deadlocked, Beye announced at the end of March that negotiations would instead move on to discuss the conclusion of the electoral process: the second round of presidential elections between dos Santos and Savimbi. On 20 April it was announced that agreement had been reached on four principles to ensure the free and fair conduct of the second-round elections. These concerned the reinstatement of the state administration throughout the country, guarantees of security, freedom of expression, and the resumption of air and ground communications nationwide to ensure free movement of people and goods. The UN was to be responsible for monitoring and declaring whether the conditions for conducting the elections had been met. It was agreed, in late April, that once the UN had made this declaration, the national assembly would select a date for the election. It was also agreed that a timetable for the implementation of the conditions would be formulated in early May.

On 5 May 1994 agreement was officially confirmed regarding the provisions for the second round of presidential elections, although some related issues remained to be discussed, including the role of the independent observers. Further talks, concerning the issues of UNITA's representation in the cabinet and the status of Savimbi, reached an impasse in May. The talks took place against a background of intensified hostilities, particularly in Kuito and Malanje. On 31 May the UN Security Council extended the mandate of UNAVEM II until 30 June, when it said it would reconsider the role of the UN if a peace accord had not been reached. The Security Council emphasized that its decision would take into account the extent to which the two sides demonstrated their political will to achieve a lasting peace. On 8 June UNITA responded by announcing that it had accepted the government's offer of four ministries, seven vice-ministries, three provincial governorships, seven deputy provincial governorships, six embassies, 30 municipal, 35 vice-municipal and 75 communal administrative posts. UNITA subsequently claimed that it had made one amendment to the list, requesting the governorship of Huambo. However, the government immediately responded that the offer was not negotiable, and that UNITA had accepted only the number of posts offered, not the specific portfolios. On 13 June agreement was reached on the extension of the state administration throughout the entire national territory.

Economy

W. G. CLARENCE-SMITH

Revised for this edition by MILES SMITH-MORRIS

INTRODUCTION

Prior to independence in 1975, Angola enjoyed a high-output economy, with a rapidly expanding manufacturing sector, near self-sufficiency in agriculture, with crop surpluses for export, and abundant natural resources, such as petroleum and iron ore. The petroleum sector continues to prosper, but almost all other sectors of the economy are operating at a fraction of pre-independence levels. The civil war that began in 1975, and still remained unresolved in mid-1994, disrupted output, made transport and distribution increasingly difficult and led to the displacement of a large part of the population. Resources have been diverted towards defence; in the late 1980s defence spending absorbed as much as 48% of the government's total budget expenditure.

Assessments of output are uncertain, although, according to estimates by the UN, Angola's gross domestic product (GDP) increased, in real terms, by an average of 1.4% per year in 1975–80, by 3.1% per year in 1980–85, and by 7.4% in 1985–91. These figures should be regarded with great caution, however, and it must be remembered that the economy has experienced severe disruption since 1975. Petroleum has become the mainstay of the economy, accounting for more than 90% of export earnings in 1990. Mining, of which petroleum is by far the largest component, provided 57.6% of GDP in 1990. It is estimated, however, that some 70% of the economically active population are dependent on the depressed agricultural sector.

Following independence, the government implemented economic policies based on its Marxist-Leninist ideology. During 1987, however, President dos Santos announced that the government intended to implement major reforms of the economy, aimed at reducing reliance on the state sector, and increasing productivity, purchasing power and consumption levels. In August 1987 dos Santos announced that Angola would seek membership of the International Monetary Fund (IMF) in order to take advantage of Western financial assistance for a programme of economic reform. This economic and financial restructuring programme, the Saneamento Económico e Financeiro (SEF), was instituted on 1 January 1988. The main elements included: a restructuring of state enterprises, allowing for much greater managerial and financial autonomy; redeployment of civil servants to more productive enterprises; improvements in the supply and distribution systems; and more price incentives for smaller enterprises. External financial support is needed for the success of the programme, and the government is actively encouraging joint ventures between foreign and Angolan enterprises. In 1988 the government introduced a new law relating to foreign investment, offering tax concessions and permitting the repatriation of profits. Angola was admitted to the IMF in September 1989, thus enhancing prospects for a rescheduling of payments on Angola's external debt, which was estimated at US $9,645m. at the end of 1992, with debt-service payments for that year of $642m. The largest creditor is the former Soviet Union, owed some $4,000m. for military purchases. In September 1990 the kwanza was replaced, at par, by a new kwanza. With effect from October 1990, the new kwanza was devalued by more than 50%, with the exchange rate adjusted to US $1 = 60 new kwanza.

Despite intense popular opposition to this measure, a further devaluation was implemented in March 1991. In late October the central committee of the ruling MPLA—PT proposed the introduction of a market economy. In April 1991 the government announced that 100 companies which were nationalized after independence would be returned to their original owners, and that some state-owned enterprises, including the national airline and the state diamond company, Empresa Nacional de Diamantes de Angola (ENDIAMA), would sell as much as 49% of their equity to the private sector.

A programme of radical economic reforms was announced in November 1991, as part of the government's commitment to move towards a market economy. The measures included: a 33.3% devaluation of the currency, bringing the exchange rate of US $1 = 90 new kwanza; reductions in personal income and consumer taxes; the abolition of price 'ceilings' on all except a few basic commodities; salary increases for public-sector workers, to compensate for the withdrawal of ration cards, and a national minimum wage of 12,000 kwanza per month. A further 50% devaluation, with the exchange rate adjusted to US $1 = 180 new kwanza, was announced in December, followed by a devaluation of 67% (to US $1 = 550 new kwanza) in April 1992. A severe devaluation of the currency, to US $1 = 7,000 new kwanza, was announced on 1 February 1993. This measure, which brought the official exchange rate closer to the 'black market' rate of approximately 10,000 new kwanza per dollar, was poorly received by the legislature and the local business community. In late February the minister of finance, Salomão Xirimbimbi, and Sebastião Labrador, the governor of the central bank, were dismissed, on the grounds that they had exceeded their authority in authorizing the devaluation. In mid-April the exchange rate was adjusted to US $1 = 4,000 new kwanza.

The state budget for 1993, envisaging expenditure of 1,300,000m. new kwanza, was announced in early April and included subsidies of some 150,000m. new kwanza for a fund to assist in mitigating the effects of sharply rising unemployment. A tripling of the budgetary deficit in the previous year, due to unplanned (largely military) spending, had contributed to a rise in inflation to an annual rate of some 500%. In conjunction with the budget statement, the government announced an emergency programme to combat inflation and the effects of devaluation, including measures to control prices and the award of increases in salaries for civil servants.

In October 1993 the new kwanza was devalued by 39.5% in an effort to narrow the difference between the official rate and the free market rate. The devaluation established an exchange rate of US $1 = 6,500 new kwanza, compared with a free market rate of US $1 = 50,000 new kwanza. A series of devaluations of the currency followed, taking the official rate to US $1 = 35,000 new kwanza at the end of March 1994, when it compared with a free market rate of US $1 = 135,000 new kwanza. In April the government introduced a new method of fixing exchange rates through agreement between the central bank and the commercial banks, with the effect that the currency underwent an effective devaluation, decreasing to US $1 = 68,297 in that month. The new policy provided for an end to the system of multiple exchange rates, with the fixed rate and the free market rate expected to converge by mid-1994.

The state budget for 1994 was announced in mid-March 1994. The main feature of the budget, which totalled the equivalent of US $1,700m., was a policy to guarantee the prices of basic commodities, although defence remained the sector with the largest allocation of funds. GDP growth of 2.5% was envisaged for 1994, with inflation targeted to decline by December to an annual rate of 260%, from 1,840% registered in December 1993.

MAJOR CROPS

Only about 3% of Angola's total area is cultivated as arable or permanent crop land. Reliable statistics have not yet revealed the true magnitude of the deterioration of modern agriculture caused by the departure of Portuguese settlers in 1974–75. The main cash crop is coffee. Prior to independence, annual production of green coffee was more than 200,000 metric tons, with the USA as the main export customer. In the mid-1970s Angola was the second largest African coffee producer and the world's main supplier of *robusta* coffee, cultivated mainly in the Uíge, Cuanza Norte, Cuanza Sul and Luanda provinces. Coffee was cultivated on a variety of Portuguese plantations (*fazendas*), ranging from substantial commercial holdings, employing thousands of labourers, down to family plantations with only a score of workers, where the owner combined agriculture with minor trade with local Africans. However, the subsequent departure of the Portuguese, neglect of the plantations (which were nationalized following independence), drought, insufficient transport, excessive bureaucracy and the continuing armed conflict have all contributed to the decline, reducing production to about one-fiftieth of pre-independence levels. Output was estimated at about 5,000 tons in 1992. The impact of the decline in agricultural production has been aggravated by reductions in world prices for *robusta* coffee, owing to the collapse of the International Coffee Organization's export quota systems, by increasing competition from Asian producers of *robusta* and by a shift in Western consumer demand to *arabica* varieties. Export earnings from coffee fell from $80m. in 1984 to an estimated $5m. in 1990. In recent years the main buyers of Angolan coffee have been Algeria, the former German Democratic Republic, Portugal, Spain and the former USSR. In 1983 the government established the Empresa de Rebenefício e Exportação do Café de Angola (CAFANGOL), a state-controlled coffee-processing and trading organization. Plans to sell all 33 state-owned coffee plantations were announced in August 1991. Foreign investment in the plantations would be welcomed, but overall foreign ownership was to be limited to 30% or 40%; the British-based Lonrho company and a Portuguese group, Espírito Santo, were among those bidding for the plantations.

Sisal exports reached 66,719 tons in 1974, when Angola was Africa's second most important producer. Production has since fallen sharply; according to FAO estimates, output amounted to only 1,000 tons per year during the period 1987–92. Exports have declined to very low levels, estimated at about 200 tons per year in 1985 and 1986. In the intervening years the crop was adversely affected by a slump in world prices and by the transition from private ownership to state enterprise. The main producing regions were the Benguela plateau, Huíla, Cuanza Norte and Malanje provinces. Maize formerly ranked fifth or sixth among Angola's agricultural exports, with a harvest of 700,000 tons in 1973. However, by 1975 the country's output of cereals was declining, and from that year Angola has been a recipient of food aid. Maize output was reduced to some 300,000 tons in 1980, and had fallen further, to an estimated 250,000 tons, in 1985. Output increased to 300,000 tons in 1987, falling to 180,000 tons in 1990, before rising again, to 299,000 tons in 1991, and to an estimated 369,000 tons in 1992.

Cotton was formerly one of the most promising products of Angola, and was both a concessionary and an African cultivation. At independence, the main areas of cultivation were the Baixa de Cassange, in the Malanje province, and the region east of Luanda. Organized planters in the Cuanza Sul province were responsible for a large increase in mechanized production, and an increasing part of production was processed in Angola by three textile mills. The breakdown of activities in most European-owned plantations reduced production of seed (unginned) cotton from 104,000 tons in 1974 to an estimated 33,000 tons annually during the 1980s, according to the FAO. Advisers from the USSR were unable to revive this activity and, for the first time in Angola's history, cotton was imported in 1983.

Prior to independence, sugar production was controlled by three Portuguese companies, and output of raw sugar was about 85,000 tons per year. Following independence, the main sugar cane plantations were reorganized as workers' co-operatives, with Cuban management and assistance. Production of raw sugar subsequently declined sharply, and nearly all sugar for domestic consumption is imported. The withdrawal of Cuban personnel by mid-1991 was expected to lead to further deterioration in the sector.

Cassava is the main Angolan crop in terms of volume produced, and is the staple food of the majority of the population. Production was an estimated 1.885m. tons in 1992, and most of the crop is consumed domestically, with no transaction above the local market level. The cultivation of bananas is being increased in the lower reaches of the rivers north of Luanda and of the Cuvo river. Estimated output was 280,000 tons in 1992.

OTHER CROPS

Exports of palm oil totalled 4,410 tons in 1973. From the 1980s onwards estimated annual production was 12,000 tons of palm kernels and 40,000 tons of palm oil. Tobacco grows well on the formerly white-owned farms in the central and southern provinces of Benguela, Huíla and Namibe. Other commodities (such as rice, millet, sorghum, beans, tropical and temperate fruit, cocoa and groundnuts) are testimony to the agricultural potential of Angola, provided that investment capital and expertise can be deployed for this sector.

Because of its large area and variety of climate, Angola is one of the most promising agricultural countries of southern Africa. However, owing to civil unrest, transport problems, the lack of proper marketing facilities and incentives, and drought, shortages have been prevalent and famine has been a frequent occurrence. By early 1984 malnutrition affected some 15% of Luanda's population, and physical survival had become the prime objective of more than 50% of Angola's rural population. By early 1991 it was estimated that food shortages threatened 1.8m. people. In recent years less than one-half of the country's cereal requirements have been produced locally, and high levels of cereal imports have been required. According to the UN Special Relief Programme for Angola, the cereal deficit for 1990 was 565,000 tons. Some 236,000 tons of cereals were not covered by commercial imports, and were therefore required as food aid. The resumption of the civil war in late 1992 represented a considerable reverse to efforts to effect a recovery in agricultural production. By February 1993 the UN World Food Programme (WFP) was warning that as many as 3m. people were threatened with hunger and disease, with harvests in many areas destroyed or disrupted by the hostilities. In April the WFP appealed for 350,000 tons of emergency food supplies for nearly 2m. Angolans. Those in need of assistance included 344,000 people displaced from their homes, 122,000 former refugees who had returned from Zambia and Zaire, and 256,000 affected by drought in the south-western provinces of Huíla, Cunene and Namibe.

LIVESTOCK, FORESTRY AND FISHERIES

Livestock raising is concentrated in southern and central Angola, owing to the prevalence of the tsetse fly and the poor quality of the natural pastures in the north of the country. Some two-thirds of all cattle are found in Huíla province alone. The modern ranching sector, established by the Portuguese, was nationalized following independence, and has subsequently been adversely affected by civil war and drought. Meat shortages are prevalent in all cities, and imports of meat are indispensable. In 1973 Angola had only about 4.4m. head of cattle, 2m. goats, 1.4m. pigs and 350,000 sheep. In 1992 cattle numbers were estimated by the FAO at 3.2m., pigs at 810,000, sheep at 250,000 and goats at 1.55m. (These figures appear to be inflated: the full extent of damage to the livestock industry in the civil war may not have been taken into account.)

Angola possesses important forestry resources, especially in the Cabinda, Moxico, Luanda and Kwanza-Norte provinces. Cabinda, in particular, has some valuable indigenous species, such as African sandalwood, rosewood and ebony. Softwood plantations of eucalyptus and cypress are used for fuel and grow along the Benguela railway and near Benguela, where they are used for wood pulp and paper manufacture. Exports of timber however, ceased at independence. As in other sectors, output of logs fell sharply after independence, from over 550,000 cu m in 1973 to 39,750 cu m in 1981. Although this activity is especially sensitive to guerrilla actions, output of logs recovered to 116,000 cu m in 1984, and to 134,000 cu m in 1985. However, production was estimated at only 66,000 cu m in 1991.

Fisheries are mainly in and off Namibe, Tombua and Benguela. However, of a total of 263 Angolan trawlers in 1981, only 87 were operational, owing to lack of maintenance. In that year the government formed a fisheries enterprise, in an attempt to restore the industry, and Angola was granted a loan of $10m. from the Arab Bank for Economic Development in Africa (BADEA) for the rehabilitation of fishing facilities. A further grant of ECU 6.76m. was made to the fishing sector by the EC in 1984. Foreign trawlers operate off the coast and have significantly depleted the fish reserves in Angolan waters. In February 1988 the USSR agreed to strengthen co-operation in the fisheries sector, with the possibility of the establishment of a joint fisheries venture and the construction of a fishing port in Namibe province. The total catch declined from an annual average of 450,000 tons in the early 1970s to 191,000 tons in 1985. According to FAO figures, the total catch had declined to 75,100 tons by 1991.

MINERALS

Angola is believed to be one of the richest countries in mineral reserves of southern Africa. Two minerals, petroleum and diamonds, are of paramount importance to the Angolan economy, and Angola is the second largest exporter of hydrocarbons in sub-Saharan Africa, after Nigeria.

Angola's kimberlite pipes are believed to rank among the world's five richest deposits of embedded diamonds, and it has been forecast that revenue from diamond sales, assuming a cessation of guerrilla warfare, could increase ninefold by the mid-1990s. Since 1986, full control of this sector has been exercised by the state enterprise, ENDIAMA, which instigated a new national diamond policy, whereby mining was to be divided into blocks, to be exploited under production-sharing agreements with foreign concessionaires. In October 1986 ENDIAMA signed an agreement with Roan Selection Trust International to operate at Kafunfo in the Cuango province. Output was 2.4m. carats in 1974, falling to about 300,000 carats in 1976, following independence. Production rose to about 699,000 carats in 1979, and to 1.5m. carats in 1980, but declined to an estimated 900,000 carats in 1985, owing to guerrilla attacks and smuggling. In 1986, when the industry was reorganized (see above), output declined further, to only 200,000 carats (less than 0.3% of total world output of uncut diamonds). Output is estimated to have recovered sharply, to nearly 1m. carats in 1988 and to 1.3m. carats in 1989, although falling to 1.1m. carats in 1990 and to 961,000 carats in 1991. In 1992 output was estimated to have risen to 2.7m. carats, but in 1993 production fell back to around 1m. carats. Sales of diamonds declined from $221m. in 1981 to $15m. in 1986, but increased to $100m. in 1987, to an estimated $180m. in 1988, and to about $230m. per year in 1989 and 1990, before falling to $178m. in 1991. However, figures of diamond output are deceptive, since a significant proportion (perhaps one-half) of the real production has been mined and smuggled by UNITA, whose leader, Dr Jonas Savimbi, admits that his movement has derived a significant share of its resources from the diamond-producing area, which remained partially under his control during the civil war. The fall in official sales in 1991 was accompanied by evidence of a sharp rise in illicit sales. In mid-1992 the director-general of ENDIAMA, Noé Baltazar, revealed that illegal excavation and smuggling were depriving the government of $200m.–$300m. per year in revenue. Following the resumption of the civil war in late 1992, diamond mining areas again came under UNITA control. Nevertheless, official sales for that year were estimated at 1.2m. carats, valued at $250m. However, losses incurred by ENDIAMA due to illegal excavation and smuggling in the first half of 1993 alone were reported to have reached $ 300m.

In December 1987 Angola and the USSR signed a co-operation agreement, covering the mining of diamonds and quartz. De Beers Consolidated Mines lost exclusive marketing rights over ENDIAMA diamonds in 1985; however, in May 1989 ENDIAMA and De Beers signed a 'declaration of intent' to enter into co-operation in diamond prospecting, mining and marketing, and in 1991 an agreement was signed to market all production from the Cuango area through De Beers' Central Selling Organisation. De Beers also agreed to lend $50m. to finance exploration for further diamond reserves. Further investment by De Beers in evaluating kimberlite deposits was announced in 1992. In January 1990 ENDIAMA granted a two-year concession to Portuguese interests to conduct diamond exploration over a 700 sq km area in north-east Angola. In April 1991 the government announced that ENDIAMA was to sell as much as 49% of its equity to the private sector.

The petroleum industry is the sole economic mainstay of the government, with petroleum extraction, refining and distribution constituting Angola's most important economic activity. Hydrocarbons generally accounted for more than 90% of total exports during the 1980s. The petroleum sector accounts for more than 50% of state revenues and for about 30% of GDP. Total proven recoverable reserves of crude petroleum were estimated at 1,818m. barrels in 1991. Petroleum production was largely protected from the effects of the civil war by Cuban troops.

In 1955 a Belgian-owned company, Petrofina, discovered petroleum in the Kwanza valley. A petroleum company, Fina Petróleos de Angola (PETRANGOL), was subsequently established, under the joint ownership of the Angola government and Petrofina interests. PETRANGOL constructed a refinery in the suburbs of Luanda. The greatest impetus to expansion came from the Cabinda Gulf Oil Co (Cabgoc), which discovered petroleum offshore at Cabinda in 1966. In 1976 a national oil company, the Sociedade Nacional de Combustíveis de Angola (SONANGOL), was established to manage all fuel production and distribution. In 1978 SONANGOL was authorized to acquire a 51% interest in all oil companies operating in Angola, although the management of operations was to remain under the control of foreign companies. In the late 1970s the government initiated a campaign to attract foreign oil companies. In 1978–79 SONANGOL divided the Angolan coast, excluding Cabinda, into 13 exploration blocks, which were leased to foreign companies under production-sharing agreements. Although Cabgoc's Cabinda offshore fields (which are operated by the US Chevron Corporation) remain the core of the Angolan petroleum industry (accounting for about two-thirds of total output), production is buoyant at other concessions, held by Agip, Elf Aquitaine, Conoco and Texaco. In addition SONANGOL itself operates a production block in association with Petrobrás Internacional (BRASPETRO) of Brazil and Petrofina. In 1992 Elf took a 10% interest in Cabgoc, reducing SONANGOL's share to 41%, with Chevron holding 39.2% and Agip 9.8%. Onshore, Petrofina remains the operator. SONANGOL has taken a 51% interest in Petrofina's original Kwanza valley operations, including the Luanda refinery, whose capacity meets most domestic requirements. SONANGOL also has a 51% interest in a new onshore venture by Petrofina in the River Congo estuary area, in which Texaco holds a 16.33% share. Onshore production in 1991 was estimated at 30,000 barrels per day (b/d); however, production is stagnant and likely to decline soon, especially in the older Kwanza valley area, where it is estimated that 85% of recoverable petroleum has already been extracted. Petrofina is conducting further exploration work, but onshore activities were particularly vulnerable to UNITA attacks during the civil war. Despite the uncertain security situation in the Cabinda enclave, exploration licences for three onshore blocks were awarded in October 1992. The principal operators for the three concessions, Cabinda North, Central and South, were to be Occidental of the USA, British Petroleum and Petrofina respectively.

Output of petroleum expanded rapidly during the 1980s, reflecting continued investment in the sector. It was estimated that total investment in Angola by oil companies for the period 1987–90 would reach $2,050m. Total Angolan production averaged 155,000 b/d in late 1982, rising to about 285,000 b/d in 1986, to 358,000 b/d, in 1987 and to 450,000 b/d in 1988 and 1989. Output rose to 475,000 b/d in 1990, 491,000 b/d in 1991, and 549,000 b/d in 1992. Production declined to 505,000 b/d in 1993 but was projected to increase to 524,000 b/d in 1994. Petroleum production appeared to be relatively unaffected by the resumption of hostilities in late 1992, despite the loss of 25,000 b/d following the seizure by UNITA of the northern town of Soyo in early 1993. The onshore petroleum installations at Soyo were severely damaged in the fighting but the main installations in Cabinda escaped attack by UNITA or the regional separatist organization, FLEC. The major portion of the petroleum is exported to the USA in its crude form, although Angola refines about 30,000 b/d and exports lubricating oil, bunkering oils and heavy fuels. Plans to build a new petroleum refinery were announced in August 1992, but depended on obtaining as much as $2,000m. to finance the project. In October 1986 the US congress banned the purchase by the defense department of petroleum or petroleum products from Angolan sources. This measure (which can be waived if in the US 'national interest') has not made a significant impact on US oil operations in Angola.

Angola's export earnings from petroleum increased after 1982, following the rise in production, and reached $1,191m. in 1985. With the sharp fall in the price of petroleum, export earnings declined to $1,140m. in the following year, but recovered to $2,100m. in 1987, $2,250m. in 1988, $2,700m. in 1989 and—helped by increased production and a period of higher prices, due to the Gulf crisis—an estimated $3,580m. in 1990. As Angola is not a member of OPEC, the country is not constrained by production quotas, enabling it to stabilize the value of its petroleum exports during the late 1980s, when world prices remained depressed, by increasing output.

Iron mining began in 1956 and production averaged 700,000–800,000 tons annually in the 1960s from mines in the Huambo and Bié provinces. However, the Cassinga mines in the Huíla province, which have proven reserves of more than 1,000m. tons of high-grade haematite, were the decisive factor in increasing production. A railway spur was built to link the mines with the Namibe–Menongue railway, and a new harbour built to the north of Namibe. Annual ore output was about 6m. tons (60%–65% iron) in the early 1970s. However, in 1975 the Cassinga mines were partially destroyed in the fighting, and they have remained out of operation. All Angolan iron ore production was halted during 1975–84. Rehabilitation work on the Cassinga North mine was completed in 1986, but the depressed world market for iron ore and continuing insecurity, caused by the armed conflict, have since delayed reopening. At present, Angola holds considerable ore production stockpiles, which await the eventual rehabilitation of rail links to the coast. In 1981 a state-owned iron company, the Empresa Nacional de Ferro de Angola (FERRANGOL), was created.

Other minerals abound. Reserves of copper have been identified in the Uíge province, and other deposits are known to exist in the Namibe, Huíla and Moxico provinces. Important deposits of feldspar have been found in the southern province of Huíla. Manganese ore was mined in the Malanje province, with 4,682 tons exported in 1973. Unexploited reserves of phosphate rock exist in the Zaire and Cabinda provinces, and deposits of uranium have been found along the border with Namibia. In 1991 a new secretariat of geology and mines was established to co-ordinate mining activity and to formulate mineral policy in preparation for the restoration of civil order, when plans to stimulate private investment in the sector can be implemented.

POWER

Angola's power potential exceeds its needs. Most of Angola's energy output is of hydroelectric origin, and there is an impressive dam on the Cuanza at Cambambe, constructed and operated by a Brazilian company, which produced 370.7m. kWh in 1972, and whose generating capacity stood at 450MW in 1989. Luanda's industries are the main beneficiaries of Cambambe power. A 520-MW power station is being constructed at Kapunda, on the Cuanza river, with assistance from Brazilian and former Soviet contractors. The $1,230m. project, described by the World Bank as the key to Angola's post-war reconstruction, would increase the country's generating capacity by almost 100%. The first two Russian-built turbines were scheduled to be installed in 1993, but in early 1992 the project's future appeared to be in some doubt, pending agreement on the repayment of Angola's military debt to the former Soviet Union. An attack on the dam site by UNITA in November 1992 was reported to have caused damage amounting to $40m., delaying completion by as much as one year. Further south, Lobito and Benguela were provided with electricity by two privately-owned dams, the Lomaum and the Biópio, both on the Catumbela river. Production exceeded 206m. kWh in 1973. Destruction of the Lomaum dam reportedly reduced the power resources of Lobito and Benguela. In late 1987 it was announced that a Portuguese banking consortium was providing $11m. towards the first stage of a scheme to rehabilitate the Lomaum dam, and earlier in the year the Portuguese government granted a credit of $140m. towards the scheme. Still further south, the Matala dam serves Lubango, Namibe and Cassinga. However, this project is only a very small part of the grandiose Angolan-Namibian scheme for damming the Cunene river, thus providing Namibia, which is deficient in power and water, with cheap electricity and a permanent water supply. The Gove dam, in the Huambo course of the Cunene river, was completed with South African capital. The construction of a major power station at the Ruacaná Falls, where the Cunene river reaches the Namibian border, has been impeded by the military and political instability in the region, although the first stage became operational in 1977. The potential annual output of the scheme is provisionally assessed at 1,000m. kWh. At a meeting in southern Angola in October 1991 between President dos Santos and Namibia's President Sam Nujoma, the two leaders agreed to pursue feasibility studies for construction of a hydro-electric dam on the Cunene, although its location remained to be decided.

INDUSTRY

Angola's industrial activity is centred on construction materials, petroleum refining, food processing, textiles, equipment for the petroleum industry, steel, chemicals, electrical goods and vehicle assembly. Output from Angola's industrial sector has dwindled to a fraction of pre-independence levels. Following the withdrawal of Portuguese owners, many enterprises were brought under state control and ownership, and by the mid-1980s about 80% of the industrial workforce was employed in state-owned companies. Under the SEF, introduced in January 1988 (see above), legislation was to be reformed, granting state enterprises autonomous control of management. The continuing civil unrest, shortages of raw materials, unreliability of power supplies and disruption of the transport infrastructure have all since contributed to the sharp reduction in industrial output. Official figures showed manufacturing output in 1985 to be only 54% of its 1973 level, and the sector suffered more in the ensuing three years, when a decline in earnings from petroleum exports, caused by the sharp fall in the price of petroleum, reduced the supply of foreign exchange needed for industrial raw materials and imports of capital goods. However, the allocation of foreign exchange for this purpose was more than doubled in 1990.

Angola's manufacturing sector has considerable potential, in view of the country's abundance of raw materials, such as petroleum and iron ore. During 1962–70, manufacturing output expanded at an average rate of 19% per year. The food-processing, brewing and tobacco industries were the most developed. The textile industry flourished after the ban on the creation of industries competing against metropolitan manufacturers was repealed in 1966. Cotton is the principal fibre used, and in 1973 textile industries occupied second place in Angola. In 1979 French industrialists built a new textile complex at Lobito, with a capacity of 16m. metres of cloth per year, and a second is planned in Luanda, with a capacity of 18m. metres per year. In 1987 production of textile fabrics was equivalent to only one-third of its 1973 level. A steel plant, built in Luanda in 1972–73, was reopened in 1984. Production of steel bars was 6,589 metric tons in 1986, compared with 26,572 tons in 1973.

Most branches of the manufacturing sector continued to contract during the 1980s. However, there are a few exceptions to the general depressed state of the sector. A yard for the construction of oil equipment was built at Ambriz in 1984/85. In mid-1987 a loan was approved by the African Development Bank for the construction of three pharmaceutical plants, and construction work on one of these commenced in February 1989. In September 1987 the government signed a contract with a Dutch company for the import and assembly of trucks at a plant in Luanda. In 1988 the existing foreign investment code (introduced in 1979) was replaced by a new code, which aimed to increase the rights of foreign companies regarding operation, transfer of profits, taxation, etc., while, in return, foreign investors were expected to expand transfer of technical and managerial skills to Angolan industrial personnel. Under the new code, however, many sectors remained barred to foreign investment: these include the postal and tele-communications industries, the news media, air transport and shipping, defence and security and state banking. The approval in April 1994 of a US export credit guarantee protocol, under which US investors were to be insured against political upheaval and have access to loans, was expected to encourage increased investment by the USA. In mid-1994 the government introduced proposals to parliament for new regulations regarding foreign investment and privatization aimed at attracting foreign capital, increasing private investment in national economic activity and reducing state participation.

After independence, the building trade came to a standstill, except for the reconstruction of some of the 130 bridges destroyed in the conflict (by 1978 more than 60 had been rebuilt). Major housing programmes have been initiated in large cities. Acute shortages of building materials have limited construction, for the most part, to shanty buildings, resulting in unzoned urban growth. However, the construction sector has been helped by the rehabilitation of the main cement works, operated by the Empresa de Cimento de Angola (CIMANGOLA), in Luanda, and the sector is expected to benefit greatly from the Kapanda dam project. Output of cement was estimated at 390,000 metric tons in 1986. In late 1992 CIMANGOLA was due for transfer to private ownership, pending a return to relative peace. Production targets were likely to be raised from 450,000 to 500,000 metric tons per year, following the purchase by a Scandinavian group comprising Industry AB Euroc of Sweden and Aker A/S of Norway.

TRANSPORT AND TRADE

Angola's colonial administration made a considerable effort to improve the communications network. In 1974 there were 8,317 km of tarred roads in a total road network of 72,323 km. In 1973 there were 127,271 passenger cars, 26,221 lorries and 20,029 motor cycles in use. However, most lorries and cars were taken back to Portugal by their owners, and others were destroyed or left without spare parts. It is now theoretically possible to drive on tarred roads from Quimbele (Uíge province) to the Namibian border, and from Luanda to Lumbala (Moxico province), close to the Zambian frontier. Bus transportation was fairly developed following independence, carrying some 22.4m. passengers in 1978, but has since suffered from shortages of imported spare parts. Since 1983, guerrilla warfare has dramatically curtailed most road transportation.

Railways serve a dual purpose, to open the interior and to provide export channels for Zambia and the land-locked Zairean province of Shaba, which export large volumes of minerals. Hence, all railway lines run towards the coast. The Luanda railway, chiefly for local goods traffic and passengers, was the only line functioning with a degree of regularity during the late 1980s, albeit at a low level of activity, transporting only 63,000 metric tons of freight in 1985. The Namibe railway, in the south, was assuming a new importance as a carrier of iron ore from Cassinga before the security situation resulted in the closure of the mines. This railway transported 196,000 tons of freight in 1985. The Benguela railway was of international importance and was the strategic outlet for exports of copper and zinc from Zaire and Zambia, bypassing South Africa and providing the most direct link to the west coast. However, UNITA guerrilla attacks caused the suspension of all cross-border traffic after 1975. In April 1987 a declaration of intent to restore these services was signed by the governments of Angola, Zambia and Zaire. The domestic Lobito–Huambo section of the railway has been maintained in operation, although at a reduced level; it transported 262,000 tons of freight along the coastal tracks during 1985. The Amboim railway was of local importance, but is not currently operational. The volume of freight handled on Angolan railways was 9,272,883 tons in 1973, but the annual total had declined to 443,200 tons by 1990.

Internal air transport is well developed, with a network of good airports and rural landing strips, and has become the only moderately safe means of transportation, owing to the insecurity on road and rail routes: 198,667 passengers were carried by air in 1973, with the total increasing to 927,000 in 1985, but falling to 456,000 in 1991. Angola's main harbours are Lobito, Luanda and Namibe. Cabinda has become the principal loading port, with 7,552,652 tons (mostly petroleum) handled in 1973. In 1985 Lobito handled 522,000 tons of cargo, compared with 2.5m. tons in 1973; Luanda handled more than 942,000 tons in 1985, compared with 2.3m. tons in 1973. Namibe's traffic declined from 6,379,000 tons in 1973 to 171,000 tons in 1985. As the country exports very little except petroleum, unloaded goods account for about 85% of traffic south of Cabinda. Passenger traffic is now almost negligible. A state-owned shipping company has commenced operation, with Cuban-trained crews.

In 1988 an emergency programme was launched to rehabilitate the transport infrastructure. Under the programme, which was to cost a total of $340m., $142m. was allocated to the rehabilitation of roads and $121m. to the rehabilitation of the Luanda and Namibe railways. The programme was also to include work on the ports of Luanda and Namibe, and on Saurino and Luena airports. In February 1992 a Portuguese consortium, led by the state railway authority (Caminhos de Ferro de Portugal), signed an $11.5m. agreement to repair port and railway installations that had been damaged during the civil war. The work was expected to last two years.

In January 1989 international donors pledged most of the $94m. required to finance the first phase of a 10-year programme initiated by the Southern African Development Co-ordination Conference (SADCC) for the development of the Lobito corridor: the programme was to include the rehabilitation of the ports of Lobito and Benguela, while the rehabilitation of the Benguela railway (see above) was also to come under its auspices. An emergency plan to restore services on the Benguela railway between Lobito and Kuito was announced, following the May 1991 ceasefire between the government and UNITA. Estimated to cost $17m., the project aimed to restore full services to Kuito by 1995. Discussions were to be held with the World Bank in late 1992 on rehabilitation of the line from Kuito to the Zaire border, following the completion of a new study of the Lobito corridor.

Angola's trade balance during the last years of the Portuguese presence was traditionally positive. In 1974 the country exported goods to the value of 30,996m. escudos and imported 15,836m. escudos' worth. Portugal was the chief supplier of Angolan imports, providing products worth 3,481m. escudos. In 1974 the USA was the main market for Angolan exports, buying goods valued at 11,772m. escudos, compared with Portugal's 8,419m. escudos.

It is estimated that more than one-half of the country's food requirements are now imported, and Angola survives as a result of external purchases and assistance, mostly from the socialist countries, Western Europe and the UN organizations. The principal exported commodities in 1990 were: crude and refined petroleum and oil products $3,581m. (92.2%); diamonds $242m. (6.2%). In 1991 the value of exports was $3,354m., and the value of imports was $1,600m., leaving a trade surplus of $1,754m. There was a deficit of $680m. on the current account of the balance of payments in 1991. In 1989 the USA remained Angola's principal customer (taking about 60% of total exports), followed by the Benelux countries (13%) and the Bahamas (8%). The main sources of imports in that year were Portugal (24%), France (13%), Brazil (9%) and the USA (7%). Economic relations with Portugal have developed renewed momentum since the conclusion of the Estoril peace agreement. In February 1992 Portugal agreed to lend $325m. to enable Angola to import Portuguese goods. At the same time, it was agreed that Portugal would increase its purchases of petroleum from Angola to 20,000 b/d in 1992, from 13,000 b/d in the previous year, and that four Portuguese banks were to open branches in Angola.

Angola's inclusion in the African, Caribbean and Pacific group of signatories of the third and fourth Lomé Conventions should, in addition to making more EC funds available, increase both the range and volume of its trading operations. Angola participates fully in the Southern African Development Community (SADC, successor to the SADCC), and has special responsibility for the co-ordination of energy development and conservation.

Statistical Survey

Source (unless otherwise stated): Instituto Nacional de Estatística, Luanda.

Area and Population

AREA, POPULATION AND DENSITY

Area (sq km)	1,246,700*
Population (census results)	
30 December 1960	4,480,719
15 December 1970	
Males	2,943,974
Females	2,702,192
Total	5,646,166
Population (official estimates at mid-year)	
1990	10,020,000
1991	10,303,000
1992	10,609,000
Density (per sq km) at mid-1992	8.5

* 481,354 sq miles.

DISTRIBUTION OF POPULATION BY DISTRICT (1991, provisional estimates)

	Area (sq km)	Population	Density (per sq km)
Cabinda	7,270	163,000	22.4
Zaire	40,130	192,000	4.8
Uíge	58,698	837,000	14.3
Luanda	2,418	1,629,000	673.7
Cuanza-Norte	24,110	378,000	15.7
Cuanza-Sul	55,660	651,000	11.7
Malanje	87,246	892,000	10.2
Lunda-Norte	102,783	292,000	2.8
Lunda-Sul	56,985	155,000	2.7
Benguela	31,788	644,000	20.3
Huambo	34,274	1,524,000	44.5
Bié	70,314	1,125,000	16.0
Moxico	223,023	316,000	1.4
Cuando-Cubango	199,049	130,000	0.7
Namibe	58,137	115,000	2.0
Huíla	75,002	869,000	11.6
Bengo	31,371	166,000	5.3
Cunene	88,342	232,000	2.6
Total	1,246,600	10,310,000	8.3

PRINCIPAL TOWNS (population at 1970 census)

Luanda (capital)	480,613*	Benguela	40,996
Huambo (Nova Lisboa)	61,885	Lubango (Sá da Bandeira)	31,674
Lobito	59,258	Malanje	31,559

* 1982 estimate: 1,200,000.

Source: Direcção dos Serviços de Estatística, Luanda.

BIRTHS AND DEATHS (UN estimates, annual averages)

	1975–80	1980–85	1985–90
Birth rate (per 1,000)	49.8	50.8	51.3
Death rate (per 1,000)	24.4	22.8	21.3

Expectation of life (UN estimates, years at birth, 1985–90): 44.0 (males 42.4; females 45.6).

Source: UN, *World Population Prospects: The 1992 Revision.*

ECONOMICALLY ACTIVE POPULATION ('000 persons, 1991)

	Males	Females	Total
Agriculture	1,518	1,374	2,892
Industries	405	33	438
Services	644	192	836
Total	2,567	1,599	4,166

Source: UN Economic Commission for Africa, *African Statistical Yearbook.*

Mid-1992 (estimates in '000): Agriculture, etc. 2,619; Total (incl. others) 3,798. Source: FAO, *Production Yearbook.*

Agriculture

PRINCIPAL CROPS ('000 metric tons)

	1990	1991	1992
Wheat	3	3	3
Rice (paddy)*	18	18	18
Maize	180	299	369†
Millet and sorghum	63	67	75†
Potatoes	34	36	40
Sweet potatoes*	170	170	170
Cassava (Manioc)*	1,900	1,850	1,885
Dry beans	33	36	36
Groundnuts (in shell)	14	15	18
Sunflower seed*	10	10	10
Cottonseed*	22	22	22
Cotton (lint)*	11	11	11
Palm kernels*	12	12	12
Palm oil*	40	40	40
Vegetables	244	245	235
Citrus fruit*	80	80	80
Pineapples*	35	35	35
Bananas*	280	280	280
Sugar cane*	270	335	320
Coffee (green)	4	5	5
Tobacco	4†	4†	3*
Sisal	1†	1*	1*

* FAO estimate(s). † Unofficial estimate.

Source: FAO, *Production Yearbook.*

LIVESTOCK ('000 head, year ending September)

	1990	1991	1992
Cattle	3,100*	3,150	3,200
Pigs	800	805	810
Sheep	240	240	250
Goats	1,500	1,500	1,550

* FAO estimate.

Poultry (FAO estimates, million): 6 in 1990; 6 in 1991; 6 in 1992.

Source: FAO, *Production Yearbook.*

LIVESTOCK PRODUCTS (FAO estimates, '000 metric tons)

	1990	1991	1992
Beef and veal	56	57	57
Goats' meat	4	4	4
Pig meat	18	18	19
Poultry meat	7	7	7
Other meat	7	7	7
Cows' milk	148	148	148
Butter and ghee	0.8	0.8	0.8
Cheese	2.5	2.5	2.5
Hen eggs	3.9	3.9	3.9
Cattle hides	8.8	9.0	9.0

Honey: 15,000 metric tons per year (FAO estimate).

Source: FAO, *Production Yearbook*.

Forestry

ROUNDWOOD REMOVALS
('000 cubic metres, excluding bark)

	1989	1990	1991
Sawlogs, veneer logs and logs for sleepers	70	66	66*
Other industrial wood*	820	843	866
Fuel wood*	5,388	5,539	5,661
Total	6,278	6,448	6,593

* FAO estimate(s).

Source: FAO, *Yearbook of Forest Products*.

SAWNWOOD PRODUCTION ('000 cubic metres, incl. railway sleepers)

	1989	1990	1991
Total	5	5	5*

* FAO estimate.

Source: FAO, *Yearbook of Forest Products*.

Fishing

('000 metric tons, live weight)

	1989	1990	1991
Freshwater fishes*	8.0	8.0	7.0
Cunene horse mackerel	59.6	64.9	34.6
Sardinellas	19.9	11.9	18.1
Other marine fishes (incl. unspecified)	23.3	22.0	14.6
Total fish	110.9	106.8	74.2
Crustaceans and molluscs	0.3	0.1	0.9
Total catch	111.1	106.9	75.1

* Assumed to be unchanged between 1973 and 1990.

Source: FAO, *Yearbook of Fishery Statistics*.

Mining

('000 metric tons, unless otherwise indicated)

	1989	1990	1991
Crude petroleum	22,642	23,553	24,731
Natural gas (petajoules)	7	7	7
Salt (unrefined)*	70	70	70
Diamonds ('000 carats)*:			
Industrial	80†	85	85
Gem	1,165	1,215	1,215
Gypsum (crude)*	57	57	57

* Data from the US Bureau of Mines.

† Estimate.

Source: UN, *Industrial Statistics Yearbook*.

Industry

SELECTED PRODUCTS
('000 metric tons, unless otherwise indicated)

	1989	1990	1991
Raw sugar*	25	25	32
Cigarettes (million)†	2,400‡	2,400	2,400
Jet fuels	155	157	155
Motor spirit	105	108	105
Distillate fuel oils	320	323	325
Residual fuel oils	650	653	655
Cement§	1,000	1,000	998
Crude steel§	10‡	10‡	10
Electric energy (million kWh)	1,820	1,840	1,840

* FAO figures.

† Data from the US Department of Agriculture.

‡ Estimate(s).

§ Data from the US Bureau of Mines.

Source: UN, *Industrial Statistics Yearbook*.

Finance

CURRENCY AND EXCHANGE RATES

Monetary Units

100 lwei (LW) = 1 new kwanza (NKZ).

Sterling and Dollar Equivalents (31 March 1994)

£1 sterling = 51,961 new kwanza;
US $1 = 35,000 new kwanza;
100,000 new kwanza = £1.925 = $2.857.

Exchange Rate

An official exchange rate of US $1 = 29.62 kwanza was introduced in 1976 and remained in force until September 1990. In that month the kwanza was replaced, at par, by the new kwanza. At the same time, it was announced that the currency was to be devalued by more than 50%, with the exchange rate adjusted to US $1 = 60 new kwanza, with effect from 1 October 1990. This rate remained in force until 18 November 1991, when a basic rate of US $1 = 90 new kwanza was established. The currency underwent further devaluation, by 50% in December 1991, and by more than 67% on 15 April 1992, when a basic rate of US $1 = 550 new kwanza was established. In February 1993 the currency was again devalued, when a basic rate of US $1 = 7,000 new kwanza was established. In April 1993 this was adjusted to US $1 = 4,000 new kwanza, and in October to US $1 = 6,500 new kwanza, a devaluation of 38.5%. Following a series of four devaluations in February and March 1994, a rate of US $1 = 35,000 new kwanza was established in late March. In April 1994 the introduction of a new method of setting exchange rates resulted in an effective devaluation, to US $1 = 68,297 new kwanza, and provided for an end to the system of multiple exchange rates, with the fixed rate and the free market rate expected to converge by mid-1994.

BUDGET (million kwanza)

Revenue	1988	1989	1990*
Government revenue	73,173	74,135	76,700
Taxes	45,293	57,748	62,929
Dividends	6,236	6,230	3,260
Other	21,644	10,157	10,511
Loans	22,413	45,704	55,768
Total	95,586	119,839	132,468

* Provisional estimates.

Expenditure	1988	1989	1990*
Economic development	16,740	17,758	16,475
Social services	20,063	24,836	29,592
Defence and security	43,961	58,267	52,391
Administration	11,232	13,782	18,064
Other	3,590	5,196	15,946
Total	95,586	119,839	132,468

* Provisional estimates.

NATIONAL ACCOUNTS

Composition of the Gross National Product (US $ million)

	1987	1988	1989
Gross domestic product (GDP) at factor cost	6,482	6,877	7,682
Indirect taxes	94	95	117
Less Subsidies	189	122	93
GDP in purchasers' values	6,386	6,850	7,706
Net factor income from abroad	−402	−938	−1,079
Gross national product	5,984	5,912	6,627

Gross Domestic Product by Economic Activity
(estimates, million kwanza at factor cost)

	1988	1989	1990
Agriculture, forestry and fishing	28,681	28,474	27,736
Mining	148,305	149,390	155,481
Petroleum refining	2,903	3,250	3,196
Other manufacturing industries	5,499	5,944	5,516
Other energy	633	666	585
Construction	5,792	5,803	5,861
Transport and communications	6,447	6,543	6,642
Trade	11,622	12,203	11,959
Financial services	2,665	2,335	2,206
Other services	45,398	47,918	50,713
Total	257,944	262,527	269,894

BALANCE OF PAYMENTS (US $ million)

	1989	1990	1991
Merchandise exports f.o.b.	3,013	3,884	3,354
Merchandise imports f.o.b.	−1,273	−1,578	−1,600
Trade balance	1,740	2,306	1,754
Exports of services	131	108	113
Imports of services	−1,143	−1,425	−1,477
Other income (net)	−744	−765	−1,000
Unrequited transfers (net)	−4	−77	−70
Current balance	−20	147	−680
Direct investment (net)	200	−335	300
Other long-term capital (net)	−356	−273	−1,262
Short-term capital (net)	−753	—	—
Net errors and omissions	923	462	1,627
Overall balance	−6	1	−15

Source: World Bank, *Trends In Developing Economies.*

External Trade

SELECTED COMMODITIES

Imports (million kwanza)	1983	1984	1985
Animal products	1,315	1,226	1,084
Vegetable products	2,158	3,099	2,284
Fats and oils	946	1,006	1,196
Food and beverages	2,400	1,949	1,892
Mineral products	317	130	127
Industrial chemical products	1,859	1,419	1,702
Plastic materials	431	704	454
Paper products	376	380	411
Textiles	1,612	1,816	1,451
Footwear and headgear	207	265	218
Base metals	1,985	3,730	2,385
Electrical equipment	3,296	2,879	2,571
Transport equipment	2,762	2,240	3,123
Masonry products	132	137	132
Optical instruments	230	192	271
Total (incl. others)	20,197	21,370	19,694

Total Imports (million kwanza): 18,691 in 1986; 13,372 in 1987; 29,845 in 1988; 34,392 in 1989. Source: UN, *Monthly Bulletin of Statistics.*

Exports (US $ million)	1988	1989	1990*
Crude petroleum	2,179	2,657	3,525
Refined petroleum products	91	70	56
Natural gas	19	13	26
Diamonds	183	229	242
Coffee	18	12	5
Total (incl. others)	2,520	3,013	3,883

* Estimates.

Total Exports (million kwanza): 277,801 in 1991. Source: UN, *Monthly Bulletin of Statistics.*

SELECTED TRADING PARTNERS (million kwanza)

Imports	1983	1984	1985
Argentina	n.a.	780	848
Brazil	1,639	1,611	2,116
France	2,449	2,080	2,208
Germany, Fed. Repub.	1,023	1,347	1,519
Italy	861	1,022	725
Netherlands	1,633	1,520	1,424
Portugal	3,282	3,027	2,607
Sweden	688	511	1,090
United Kingdom	955	785	968
USA	1,462	3,300	1,406
Total (incl. others)	20,197	21,370	19,694

Exports	1983	1984	1985
Belgium and Luxembourg	897	802	1,016
Brazil	4,899	3,539	4,194
German Dem. Repub.	1,079	1,446	950
Netherlands	5,650	4,724	2,417
Portugal	255	700	2,144
Spain	4,432	5,234	7,873
United Kingdom	5,674	9,868	6,937
USA	26,090	23,667	29,077
Total (incl. others)	54,501	60,823	66,968

1986 (million kwanza): Total exports 38,973 (incl. USA 14,941). Source: UN Economic Commission for Africa, *African Statistical Yearbook.*

Transport

GOODS TRANSPORT ('000 metric tons)

	1988	1989	1990
Road	1,056.7	690.1	867.3
Railway	580.9	510.3	443.2
Water	780.8	608.6	812.1
Air	24.6	10.5	28.3
Total	2,443.0	1,819.5	2,150.9

Sources: Instituto Nacional de Estatística; Ministério de Transporte e Comunicações.

PASSENGER TRANSPORT ('000 journeys)

	1988	1989	1990
Road	12,699.2	32,658.7	48,796.1
Railway	6,659.7	6,951.2	6,455.8
Water	151.8	163.2	223.8
Air	608.9	618.4	615.9
Total	20,119.6	40,391.5	56,091.6

Sources: Instituto Nacional de Estatística; Ministério de Transporte e Comunicações, Luanda.

INTERNATIONAL SEA-BORNE SHIPPING
(estimated freight traffic, '000 metric tons)

	1989	1990	1991
Goods loaded	19,980	21,102	23,288
Goods unloaded	1,235	1,242	1,261

Source: UN Economic Commission for Africa, *African Statistical Yearbook*.

CIVIL AVIATION (traffic on scheduled services)

	1989	1990	1991
Kilometres flown (million)	14	10	10
Passengers carried ('000)	510	452	456
Passenger-km (million)	822	1,189	1,241
Freight ton-km (million)	52	40	42

Source: UN, *Statistical Yearbook*.

Communications Media

	1989	1990	1991
Radio receivers ('000 in use)	n.a.	n.a.	270
Television receivers ('000 in use)	55	57	59
Telephones ('000 in use)*	45	45	45

Book production: 47 titles (books 35, pamphlets 12) and 419,000 copies (books 338,000, pamphlets 81,000) in 1985; 14 titles (all books) and 130,000 copies in 1986.

Daily newspapers: 4 (estimated circulation 103,000) in 1986; 4 (estimated circulation 85,000) in 1988; 4 (estimated circulation 115,000) in 1990.

*UN estimates.

Source: mainly UNESCO, *Statistical Yearbook*.

Education

(1989/90)

	Teachers	Pupils
Pre-primary	32,157 (Pre-primary and Primary combined)	141,882
Primary		1,038,126
Secondary:		
general	5,138	148,837
teacher training	280*	7,688
vocational	286	6,216
Higher	383	6,048

* Figure for school year 1987/88.

Source: Ministério da Educação, Luanda.

Directory

The Constitution

The MPLA regime adopted an independence constitution for Angola in November 1975. It was amended in October 1976, September 1980, March 1991, and April and August 1992. The main provisions of the Constitution, as amended, are summarized below:

BASIC PRINCIPLES

The Republic of Angola shall be a sovereign and independent state whose prime objective shall be to build a free and democratic society of peace, justice and social progress. It shall be a democratic state based on the rule of law, founded on national unity, the dignity of human beings, pluralism of expression and political organization, respecting and guaranteeing the basic rights and freedoms of persons, whether as individuals or as members of organized social groups. Sovereignty shall be vested in the people, which shall exercise political power through periodic universal suffrage.

The Republic of Angola shall be a unitary and indivisible state. Economic, social and cultural solidarity shall be promoted between all the Republic's regions for the common development of the entire nation and the elimination of regionalism and tribalism.

Religion

The Republic shall be a secular state and there shall be complete separation of the State and religious institutions. All religions shall be respected.

The Economy

The economic system shall be based on the coexistence of diverse forms of property—public, private, mixed, co-operative and family—and all shall enjoy equal protection. The State shall protect foreign investment and foreign property, in accordance with the law. The fiscal system shall aim to satisfy the economic, social and administrative needs of the State and to ensure a fair distribution of income and wealth. Taxes may be created and abolished only by law, which shall determine applicability, rates, tax benefits and guarantees for taxpayers.

Education

The Republic shall vigorously combat illiteracy and obscurantism and shall promote the development of education and of a true national culture.

FUNDAMENTAL RIGHTS AND DUTIES

The State shall respect and protect the human person and human dignity. All citizens shall be equal before the law. They shall be subject to the same duties, without any distinction based on colour, race, ethnic group, sex, place of birth, religion, level of education, or economic or social status.

All citizens aged 18 years and over, other than those legally deprived of political and civil rights, shall have the right and duty to take an active part in public life, to vote and be elected to any state organ, and to discharge their mandates with full dedication to the cause of the Angolan nation. The law shall establish limitations in respect of non-political allegiance of soldiers on active service, judges and police forces, as well as the electoral incapacity of soldiers on active service and police forces.

Freedom of expression, of assembly, of demonstration, of association and of all other forms of expression shall be guaranteed. Groupings whose aims or activities are contrary to the constitutional order and penal laws, or that, even indirectly, pursue political objectives through organizations of a military, paramilitary or militarized nature shall be forbidden. Every citizen has the right to a defence if accused of a crime. Individual freedoms are guaranteed. Freedom of conscience and belief shall be inviolable. Work shall be the right and duty of all citizens. The State shall promote measures necessary to ensure the right of citizens to medical and health care, as well as assistance in childhood, motherhood, disability, old age, etc. It shall also promote access to education, culture and sports for all citizens.

STATE ORGANS

President of the Republic

The President of the Republic shall be the Head of State, Head of Government and Commander-in-Chief of the Angolan armed forces. The President of the Republic shall be elected directly by a secret universal ballot and shall have the following powers:

- to appoint and dismiss the Prime Minister, Ministers and other government officials determined by law;
- to appoint the judges of the Supreme Court;
- to preside over the Council of Ministers;
- to declare war and make peace, following authorization by the National Assembly;
- to sign, promulgate and publish the laws of the National Assembly, government decrees and statutory decrees;
- to preside over the National Defence Council;
- to decree a state of siege or state of emergency;
- to announce the holding of general elections;
- to issue pardons and commute sentences;
- to perform all other duties provided for in the Constitution.

National Assembly

The National Assembly is the supreme state legislative body, to which the Government is responsible. The National Assembly shall be composed of 223 deputies, elected for a term of four years. The National Assembly shall convene in ordinary session twice yearly and in special session on the initiative of the President of the National Assembly, the Standing Commission of the National Assembly or of no less than one-third of its deputies. The Standing Commission shall be the organ of the National Assembly that represents and assumes its powers between sessions.

Government

The Government shall comprise the President of the Republic, the ministers and the secretaries of state, and other members whom the law shall indicate, and shall have the following functions:

- to organize and direct the implementation of state domestic and foreign policy, in accordance with decision of the National Assembly and its Standing Commission;
- to ensure national defence, the maintenance of internal order and security, and the protection of the rights of citizens;
- to prepare the draft National Plan and General State Budget for approval by the National Assembly, and to organize, direct and control their execution;

The Council of Ministers shall be answerable to the National Assembly. In the exercise of its powers, the Council of Ministers shall issue decrees and resolutions.

Judiciary

The organization, composition and competence of the courts shall be established by law. Judges shall be independent in the discharge of their functions.

Local State Organs

The organs of state power at provincial level shall be the Provincial Assemblies and their executive bodies. The Provincial Assemblies shall work in close co-operation with social organizations and rely on the initiative and broad participation of citizens. The Provincial Assemblies shall elect commissions of deputies to perform permanent or specific tasks. The executive organs of Provincial Assemblies shall be the Provincial Governments, which shall be led by the Provincial Governors. The Provincial Governors shall be answerable to the President of the Republic, the Council of Ministers and the Provincial Assemblies.

National Defence

The State shall ensure national defence. The National Defence Council shall be presided over by the President of the Republic, and its composition shall be determined by law. The Angolan armed forces, as a state institution, shall be permanent, regular and non-partisan. Defence of the country shall be the right and the highest indeclinable duty of every citizen. Military service shall be compulsory. The forms in which it is fulfilled shall be defined by the law.

FINAL AND TRANSITIONAL PROVISIONS

Laws and regulations in force in the Republic of Angola shall be applicable unless amended or repealed, provided that they do not conflict with the letter and the spirit of the present law. The National Assembly and the assemblies at local level shall continue to function until the investiture of new deputies, following the holding of a general election.

Note: In May 1991 the MPLA—PT and UNITA signed an agreement providing for legislative and presidential elections to be held by the end of 1992. The elections took place on 29–30 September 1992. However, following the resumption of hostilities between UNITA and government forces after the elections, UNITA refused to attend the inauguration of the National Assembly. A second round of presidential elections was placed in abeyance, pending a resolution of the prevailing hostilities.

The Government

HEAD OF STATE

President: JOSÉ EDUARDO DOS SANTOS (assumed office 21 September 1979).

COUNCIL OF MINISTERS
(August 1994)

All ministers and secretaries of state are members of the Movimento Popular de Libertação de Angola (MPLA) unless otherwise indicated.

Prime Minister: Dr MARCOLINO JOSÉ CARLOS MOCO.

Minister of Defence: Col-Gen. PEDRO MARIA TONHA.

Minister of the Interior: ANDRÉ PITRA.

Minister of Foreign Affairs: Dr VENANCIO DA SILVA MOURA.

Minister of Territorial Administration: JOSÉ ANÍBAL LOPES ROCHA.

Minister of Finance: ALVARO CRAVEIRO.

Minister of Economic Planning: JOSÉ PEDRO DE MORAIS.

Minister of Petroleum: ALBINA FARIA DE ASSIS PEREIRA AFRICANO.

Minister of Industry: Dr ISALINO MANUEL MENDES.

Minister of Agriculture and Rural Development: ISAAC FRANCISCO MARIA DOS ANJOS.

Minister of Fisheries: MARIA DE FÁTIMA MONTEIRO JARDIM.

Minister of Geology and Mines: JOSÉ DOMINGOS ANTÓNIO DIAS.

Minister of Public Works and Urbanization: Dr MATEUS MORAIS DE BRITO JÚNIOR.

Minister of Transport and Communications: ANDRÉ LUÍS BRANDÃO.

Minister of Trade and Tourism: JOÃO CELESTINO DIAS.

Minister of Health: Dr MARTINHO SANCHES EPALANGA.

Minister of Education: Dr JOÃO MANUEL BERNARDO.

Minister of Assistance and Social Reintegration: ALBINO MALUNGO.

Minister of Culture: (vacant)*.

Minister of Youth and Sports: JOSÉ DA ROCHA SARDINHA DE CASTRO.

Minister of Justice: Dr PAULO CHIPILICA (Fórum Democrático Angolano).

Minister of Public Administration, Employment and Social Security: Dr ANTÓNIO DOMINGOS PITRA COSTA NETO.

Minister of Information: Dr PEDRO HENDRIK VAAL NETO.

Minister in the President's Office in charge of Civic Affairs: JOSÉ MATEUS PEIXOTO.

Secretary of the Council of Ministers: DR CARLOS MARIA FEIJO.

* In mid-December 1992 the União Nacional para a Independência Total de Angola (UNITA), which had been requested by the Prime Minister to nominate a Minister of Culture, appointed VITORINO DOMINGOS HOSSI as its representative in the Council of Ministers. However, with the escalation in hostilities in the following weeks, and with the appointment of UNITA officials to the Council of Ministers dependent on the implementation of the Estoril peace agreement (concluded in May 1991), the post remained vacant.

SECRETARIES OF STATE

(August 1994)

Secretary of State for Co-operation: JOHNNY EDUARDO PINNOCK.

Secretary of State for Coffee: GILBERTO BUTA LUTUKUTA.

Secretary of State for the Environment: DR MANUEL DAVID MENDES (PAJOCA).

Secretary of State for Energy and Waters: JOÃO MOREIRA PINTO SARAIVA.

Secretary of State for the Promotion and Development of Women: DR JOANA LIMA RAMOS BAPTISTA CRISTIANO.

Secretary of State for Housing: DR MIGUEL CORREIA.

Secretary of State for Planning: JOSÉ PEDRO DE MORAIS.

MINISTRIES

Office of the President: Luanda; telex 3072.

Ministry of Agriculture and Rural Development: Avda Norton de Matos 2, Luanda; telex 3322.

Ministry of Defence: Rua Silva Carvalho ex Quartel General, Luanda; telex 3138.

Ministry of Economic Planning: Luanda.

Ministry of Education: Avda Comandante Jika, CP 1281, Luanda; tel. 321592; telex 4121; fax 321592.

Ministry of Finance: Avda 4 de Fevereiro, Luanda; tel. 344628; telex 3363.

Ministry of Fisheries: Avda 4 de Fevereiro 25, Predio Atlantico, Luanda; tel. 392782; telex 3273.

Ministry of Foreign Affairs: Avda Comandante Jika, Luanda; telex 3127.

Ministry of Health: Rua Diogo Cão, Luanda.

Ministry of Information: Luanda.

Ministry of the Interior: Avda 4 de Fevereiro, Luanda.

Ministry of Justice: Largo do Palácio, Luanda.

Ministry of Petroleum: Avda 4 de Fevereiro 105, CP 1279, Luanda; tel. 337448; telex 3300.

Ministry of Public Administration, Employment and Social Security: Largo do Palácio, Luanda.

Ministry of Territorial Administration: Luanda.

Ministry of Trade and Tourism: Largo Kinaxixi 14, Luanda; tel. 344525; telex 3282.

Ministry of Transport and Communications: Avda 4 de Fevereiro 42, CP 1250-C, Luanda; tel. 370061; telex 3108.

PROVINCIAL GOVERNORS*

Bengo: ANTÓNIO DANIEL VENTURA DE AZEVEDO.

Benguela: PAULO TEIXEIRA JORGE.

Bié: LUÍS PAULINO DOS SANTOS.

Cabinda: AUGUSTO DA SILVA TOMÁS.

Cuando-Cubango: Col DOMINGOS HUNGO (SKS).

Cuanza-Norte: MANUEL PEDRO PACAVIRA.

Cuanza-Sul: FRANCISCO JOSÉ RAMOS DA CRUZ.

Cunene: PEDRO MUTINDE.

Huambo: GRACIANO MANDE.

Huíla: DUMILDE DAS CHAGAS SIMÕES RANGEL.

Luanda: JUSTINO JOSÉ FERNANDES.

Lunda Norte: JOSÉ MANUEL SALUCOMBO.

Lunda Sul: GONÇALVES MANUEL MANVUMBRA.

Malanje: FLAVIO FERNANDES.

Moxico: JOÃO ERNESTO DOS SANTOS (LIBERDADE).

Namibe: JOAQUIM DA SILVA MATIAS.

Uíge: (vacant)

Zaire: ZEFERINO ESTEVÃO JULIANA.

*All Governors are ex-officio members of the Government.

President and Legislature*

PRESIDENT

Presidential Election, 29 and 30 September 1992

	Votes	% of votes
JOSÉ EDUARDO DOS SANTOS (MPLA)	1,953,335	49.57
DR JONAS MALHEIRO SAVIMBI (UNITA)	1,579,298	40.07
ANTÓNIO ALBERTO NETO (PDA)	85,249	2.16
HOLDEN ROBERTO (FNLA)	83,135	2.11
HONORATO LANDO (PDLA)	75,789	1.92
LUÍS DOS PASSOS (PRD)	59,121	1.47
BENGUI PEDRO JOÃO (PSD)	38,243	0.97
SIMÃO CACETE (FPD)	26,385	0.67
DANIEL JÚLIO CHIPENDA (Independent)	20,646	0.52
ANÁLIA DE VICTÓRIA PEREIRA (PLD)	11,475	0.29
RUI DE VICTÓRIA PEREIRA (PRA)	9,208	0.23
Total	3,940,884	100.00

NATIONAL ASSEMBLY

President: FERNANDO JOSÉ FRANÇA VAN-DÚNEM.

Legislative Election, 29 and 30 September 1992

	Votes	% of votes	Seats
MPLA	2,124,126	53.74	129
UNITA	1,347,636	34.10	70
FNLA	94,742	2.40	5
PLD	94,269	2.39	3
PRS	89,875	2.27	6
PRD	35,293	0.89	1
AD Coalition	34,166	0.86	1
PSD	33,088	0.84	1
PAJOCA	13,924	0.35	1
FDA	12,038	0.30	1
PDP—ANA	10,620	0.27	1
PNDA	10,281	0.26	1
CNDA	10,237	0.26	—
PSDA	19,217	0.26	—
PAI	9,007	0.23	—
PDLA	8,025	0.20	—
PDA	8,014	0.20	—
PRA	6,719	0.17	—
Total	3,952,277	100.00	220

Note: According to the Constitution, the total number of seats in the National Assembly is 223. On the decision of the National Electoral Council, however, elections to fill three seats reserved for Angolans abroad were abandoned.

* Under the terms of the electoral law, a second round of presidential elections was required to take place in order to determine which of the two leading candidates from the first round would be elected. However, a resumption of hostilities between UNITA and government forces prevented a second round of presidential elections from taking place. The electoral process was to resume only when the provisions of the Estoril peace agreement, concluded in May 1991, had been satisfied.

Political Organizations

Aliança Democrática de Angola: Leader SIMBA DA COSTA.

Angolan Alliance and Hamista Party (PADHA).

Angolan Democratic Coalition (AD Coalition): Pres. EVIDOR QUIELA (acting).

Angolan Democratic Confederation: f. 1994; Chair. GASPAR NETO.

Angolan Democratic Unification (UDA)*: Leader EDUARDO MILTON SIVI.

Angolan Reformers' Party (PRA): Leader RUI DE VICTÓRIA PEREIRA.

Angolan Social Democratic Party (PSDA): Leader ANDRÉ MILTON KILANDAMOKO.

Associação Cívica Angolana (ACA): f. 1990; Leader JOAQUIM PINTO DE ANDRADE.

Christian Democratic Convention (CDC): Leader GASPAR NETO.

Democratic Civilian Opposition: f. 1994; opposition alliance comprising 14 parties including:

Angolan National Democratic Convention (CNDA)*: Leader PAULINO PINTO JOÃO.

Democratic Party for the Progress of the National Angolan Alliance (PDP—ANA)*: Leader MFUFUMPINGA NLANDU VICTOR.

Frente Nacional de Libertação de Angola (FNLA)*: f. 1962; Pres. HOLDEN ROBERTO.

Frente para a Democracia (FPD)*: Leader NELSO PESTANA; Sec.-Gen. FILOMENO VIEIRA LOPES.

Liberal Democratic Party of Angola (PDLA)*: Leader HONORATO LANDO.

Movimento de Defesa dos Interesses de Angola—Partido de Consciência Nacional*: Leader ISIDORO KLALA.

National Ecological Party of Angola (PNEA)*: Leader SUKAWA DIZIZEKO RICARDO.

National Union for Democracy (UND)*: Leader SEBASTIÃO ROGERIO SUZAMA.

Partido Angolano Liberal (PAL): Leader MANUEL FRANCISCO LULO (acting).

Partido Renovador Social (PRS): Leader ANTÓNIO JOÃO MUACHICUNGO.

Partido Social Democrata de Angola (PSDA): Leader ANDRÉ KILANDONOCO.

Party of Solidarity and the Conscience of Angola (PSCA): Leader FERNANDO DOMBASSI QUIESSE.

Democratic Liberal Party (PLD): Leader ANÁLIA DE VICTÓRIA PEREIRA.

Fórum Democrático Angolano (FDA): Leader JORGE REBELO PINTO CHICOTI.

Frente de Libertação do Enclave de Cabinda (FLEC): f. 1963; comprises several factions seeking the secession of Cabinda province; Pres. HENRIQUE TIAHO N'ZITA.

Movimento Amplo para a Democracia: Leader FRANCISCO VIANA.

Movimento Popular de Libertação de Angola (MPLA) (People's Movement for the Liberation of Angola): Luanda; telex 3369; f. 1956; in 1961–74, as MPLA, conducted guerrilla operations against Portuguese rule; governing party since 1975; known as Movimento Popular de Libertação de Angola—Partido do Trabalho (MPLA—PT) (People's Movement for the Liberation of Angola—Workers' Party) 1977–92; in Dec. 1990 replaced Marxist-Leninist ideology with commitment to 'democratic socialism'; Chair. JOSÉ EDUARDO DOS SANTOS; Sec.-Gen. LOPO FORTUNATO FERREIRA DO NASCIMENTO.

Movimento de Unidade Democrática para a Reconstrução (Mudar)*: Leader MANUEL DOS SANTOS LIMA.

National Democratic Party of Angola (PNDA)*: Leader GERALDO PEREIRA JOÃO DA SILVA.

National Union for the Light of Democracy and Development of Angola (UNLDDA): Pres. MIGUEL MUENDO; Sec.-Gen. DOMINGOS CHIZELA.

Partido de Aliança de Juventude, Operários e Camponêses de Angola (PAJOCA) (Angolan Youth, Workers and Peasants' Alliance Party): Leader MIGUEL JOÃO SEBASTIÃO.

Partido Angolano Independente (PAI): Leader ADRIANO PARREIRA.

Partido Democrático Angolano (PDA): Leader ANTÓNIO ALBERTO NETO.

Partido para a Aliança Popular: Leader CAMPOS NETO.

Partido Renovador Democrático (PRD)*: Leader LUÍS DOS PASSOS.

Partido Social Democrata (PSD)*: Leader BENGUI PEDRO JOÃO.

Peaceful Democratic Party of Angola (PDPA)*: Leader ANTÓNIO KUNZOLAKO.

Unangola: Leader ANDRÉ FRANCO DE SOUSA.

União Nacional para a Independência Total de Angola (UNITA): f. 1966 to secure independence from Portugal; later received Portuguese support to oppose the MPLA; UNITA and the FNLA conducted guerrilla campaign against the MPLA Govt with aid from some Western nations, 1975–76; supported by South Africa until 1984 and in 1987–88; has received US aid since 1986; support drawn mainly from Ovimbundu ethnic group; operates mainly in central and southern Angola, with an est. strength of 28,000 'regular' soldiers and 37,000 militia; Pres. Dr JONAS MALHEIRO SAVIMBI; Sec.-Gen. ALICERCES MANGO.

Vofangola: Leader LOMBY ZUENDOKI.

* Member of National Opposition Council (CNO).

Diplomatic Representation

EMBASSIES IN ANGOLA

Algeria: Luanda; Ambassador: HANAFI OUSSEDIK.

Belgium: CP 1203, Luanda; tel. 336437; telex 3356; Ambassador: GUIDO VANSINA.

Brazil: CP 5428, Luanda; tel. 343275; telex 3365; Ambassador: PAULO DYRCEU PINHEIRO.

Bulgaria: Luanda; telex 3375; Ambassador: BOYAN MIHAYLOV.

Cape Verde: Luanda; telex 3247; Ambassador: JOSÉ LUÍS JESUS.

China, People's Republic: Luanda; Ambassador: ZHANG BAOSHENG.

Congo: Luanda; Ambassador: ANATOLE KHONDO.

Côte d'Ivoire: Rua Karl Marx 43, Luanda; Ambassador: JEAN-MARIE KACOU GERVAIS.

Cuba: Luanda; telex 3236; Ambassador: NARCISCO MARTÍN MORA.

Czech Republic: Rua Amílcar Cabral 5, CP 2691, Luanda; tel. 334456.

Egypt: Luanda; telex 3380; Ambassador: ANWAR DAKROURY.

France: Luanda; Ambassador: JACQUES GASSEAU.

Gabon: Avda 4 de Fevereiro 95, Luanda; tel. 372614; telex 3263; Ambassador: RAPHAËL NKASSA-NZOGHO.

Germany: CP 1295, Luanda; tel. 334516; telex 3372; Ambassador: HANS HELMUT FREUNDT.

Ghana: Rua Vereador Castelo Branco 5, CP 1012, Luanda; telex 3331; Ambassador: Dr KELI NORDOR.

Guinea: Luanda; telex 3177.

Holy See: Rua Luther King 123, CP 1030, Luanda (Apostolic Delegation); tel. 336289; fax 332378; Apostolic Delegate: Most Rev. FÉLIX DEL BLANCO PRIETO, Titular Archbishop of Vannida.

Hungary: Rua Cdte Stona 226-228, Luanda; tel. 32313; telex 3084; fax 322448; Ambassador: Dr GÁBOR TÓTH.

India: Prédio Dos Armazens Carrapas 81, 1°, D, 6040, Luanda; tel. 345398; telex 3233; fax 342061; Ambassador: BALDEV RAJ GHULIANI.

Italy: Luanda; tel. 393533; telex 3265; Ambassador: FRANCESCO LANATA.

Korea, Democratic People's Republic: Luanda; Ambassador: KANG SUN YONG.

Mozambique: Luanda; tel. 330811; Ambassador: M. SALESSIO.

Netherlands: CP 3624, Luanda; telex 3051; Ambassador: CORNELIS DE SROOT.

Nigeria: CP 479, Luanda; tel. 340084; telex 3014; Ambassador: GABRIEL SAM AKUMAFOR.

Poland: CP 1340, Luanda; telex 3222; Ambassador: JAN BOJKO.

Portugal: Rua Karl Marx 50, CP 1346, Luanda; tel. 333027; telex 3370; Ambassador: JOÃO ROCHA PÁRIS.

Romania: Rua 5 de Outubro 68, Luanda; tel. 336757; telex 3022; Ambassador: MARIN ILIESCU.

Russia: CP 3141, Luanda; tel. 345028; Ambassador: YURI KAPRALOV.

São Tomé and Príncipe: Luanda; Ambassador: ARIOSTO CASTELO DAVID.

Slovakia: Rua Amílcar Cabral 5, CP 2691, Luanda; tel. 334456.

South Africa: Rua Manuel Fernandes Caldeira, 6B, Luanda; tel. 397391; fax 396788; Chargé d'affaires: ROGER BALLARD-TREMEER.

Spain: CP 3061, Luanda; tel. 391187; telex 2621; fax 391188; Ambassador: JOSÉ LUIS ROSELLÓ SERRA.

Sweden: Luanda; telex 3126; Ambassador: ANDERS MÖLLANDER.

Switzerland: CP 3163, Luanda; tel. 338314; telex 3172; Chargé d'affaires: GIAMBATTISTA MONDADA.

United Kingdom: Rua Diogo Cão 4, CP 1244, Luanda; tel. 392991; telex 3130; fax 333331; Ambassador: A. RICHARD THOMAS.

USA: Prédio BPA, 11° andar, Luanda; tel. 392498; Ambassador: EDMUND T. DEJARNETTE.

Viet Nam: Luanda; telex 3226; Ambassador: NGUYEN HUY LOI.

Yugoslavia: Luanda; telex 3234; Ambassador: PAVLE ŽIVKOVIĆ.

Zaire: Luanda; Ambassador: MONDINDE DEDE TALENGO.

Zambia: CP 1496, Luanda; tel. 331145; telex 3439; Ambassador: BONIFACE ZULU.

Zimbabwe: Edif. Secil, 11th Floor, Avda 4 de Fevereiro 42, CP 428, Luanda; tel. 332338; telex 3275; fax 332339; Ambassador: NEVILLE NDONDO.

Judicial System

There is a Supreme Court and Court of Appeal in Luanda. There are also civil, criminal and military courts.

Chief Justice of the Supreme Court: JOÃO FELIZARDO.

Religion

Much of the population follows traditional African beliefs, although a majority profess to be Christians, mainly Roman Catholics.

CHRISTIANITY

Conselho Angolano de Igrejas Evangélicas (Angolan Council of Evangelical Churches): Rua Amílcar Cabral 182, 1° andar, CP 1659, Luanda; tel. 330415; telex 3255; f. 1977; 12 mem. churches; two assoc. mems; two observers; Pres. Rev. EMILIO J. M. DE CARVALHO; Gen. Sec. Rev. AUGUSTO CHIPESSE.

Protestant Churches

Evangelical Congregational Church in Angola (Igreja Evangélica Congregacional em Angola: CP 551, Huambo; tel. 3087; 100,000 mems; Gen. Sec. Rev. JÚLIO FRANCISCO.

Evangelical Pentecostal Church of Angola (Missão Evangélica Pentecostal de Angola): CP 219, Porto Amboim; 13,600 mems; Sec. Rev. JOSÉ DOMINGOS CAETANO.

United Evangelical Church of Angola (Igreja Evangélica Unida de Angola): CP 122, Uíge; 11,000 mems; Gen. Sec. Rev. A. L. DOMINGOS.

Other active denominations include the African Apostolic Church, the Church of Apostolic Faith in Angola, the Church of Our Lord Jesus Christ in the World, the Evangelical Baptist Church, the Evangelical Church in Angola, the Evangelical Church of the Apostles of Jerusalem, the Evangelical Reformed Church of Angola, the Kimbanguist Church in Angola and the United Methodist Church.

The Roman Catholic Church

Angola comprises three archdioceses and 12 dioceses. At 31 December 1992 an estimated 47.7% of the total population were adherents.

Bishops' Conference: Conferência Episcopal de Angola e São Tomé, CP 3579, Luanda; tel. 343686; fax 345504; f. 1967; Pres. Cardinal ALEXANDRE DO NASCIMENTO, Archbishop of Luanda.

Archbishop of Huambo: Most Rev. FRANCISCO VITI, Arcebispado, CP 10, Huambo; tel. 2371.

Archbishop of Luanda: Cardinal ALEXANDRE DO NASCIMENTO, Arcebispado, CP 87, 1230C, Luanda; tel. 334640; fax 334433.

Archbishop of Lubango: Most Rev. MANUEL FRANKLIN DA COSTA, Arcebispado, CP 231, Lubango; tel. 20405.

The Press

The press was nationalized in 1976.

DAILIES

Diário da República: CP 1306, Luanda; official govt bulletin.

O Jornal de Angola: CP 1312, Luanda; tel. 331623; telex 3341; f. 1923; Dir-Gen. ADELINO MARQUES DE ALMEIDA; mornings and Sun.; circ. 41,000.

Newspapers are also published in several regional towns.

PERIODICALS

Angola Norte: Malanje; weekly.

A Célula: Luanda; political journal of MPLA; monthly.

Correio da Semana: CP 1312, Luanda; f. 1992; weekly tabloid; owned by O Jornal de Angola; Editor-in-Chief MANUEL DIONISIO.

Jornal de Benguela: CP 17, Benguela; 2 a week.

Lavra & Oficina: CP 2767-C, Luanda; tel. 322155; f. 1975; journal of the Union of Angolan Writers; monthly; circ. 5,000.

Militar: Luanda; f. 1993; Editor-in-Chief CARMO NETO.

Noticia: Calçada G. Ferreira, Luanda; weekly.

Novembro: CP 3947, Luanda; tel. 331660; monthly; Dir ROBERTO DE ALMEIDA.

O Planalto: CP 96, Huambo; 2 a week.

A Voz do Trabalhador: Avda 4 de Fevereiro 210, CP 28, Luanda; telex 3387; journal of União Nacional de Trabalhadores Angolanos (National Union of Angolan Workers); monthly.

NEWS AGENCIES

ANGOP: Rua Rei Katiavala 120, Luanda; tel. 334595; telex 4162; Dir-Gen. and Editor-in-Chief AVELINO MIGUEL.

Foreign Bureaux

Agence France-Presse (AFP): Prédio Mutamba, CP 2357, Luanda; tel. 334939; telex 3334; Bureau Chief MANUELA TEIXEIRA.

Allgemeiner Deutscher Nachrichtendienst (ADN) (Germany): CP 3193, Luanda; telex 3323; Correspondent GUDRUN GROSS.

Informatsionnoye Telegrafnoye Agentstvo Rossii—Telegrafnoye Agentstvo Suverennykh Stran (ITAR—TASS) (Russia): Rua Marechal Tito 75, Luanda; telex 3244; Correspondent NIKOLAI SEMYONOV.

Inter Press Service (IPS) (Italy): Rua Alberto Lemos 34, CP 3593, Luanda; tel. 338724; telex 3304; Correspondent JUAN PEZZUTO.

Prensa Latina (Cuba): Rua D. Miguel de Melo 92-2, Luanda; tel. 336804; telex 3253; Chief Correspondent LUÍS MANUEL SÁEZ.

Rossiyskoye Informatsionnoye Agentstvo—Novosti (RIA—Novosti) (Russia): Luanda; Chief Officer VLADISLAV Z. KOMAROV.

Xinhua (New China) News Agency (People's Republic of China): Rua Karl Marx 57-3, andar E, Bairro das Ingombotas, Zona 4, Luanda; tel. 332415; telex 4054; Correspondent ZHAO XIAOZHONG.

Publishers

Empresa Distribuidora Livreira (EDIL), UEE: Rua da Missão 107, CP 1245, Luanda; tel. 334034.

Neográfica, SARL: CP 6518, Luanda; publ. *Novembro*.

Nova Editorial Angolana, SARL: CP 1225, Luanda; f. 1935; general and educational; Man. Dir POMBO FERNANDES.

Offsetográfica Gráfica Industrial Lda: CP 911, Benguela; tel. 32568; f. 1966; Man. FERNANDO MARTINS.

Government Publishing House

Imprensa Nacional, UEE: CP 1306, Luanda; f. 1845; Gen. Man. Dr ANTÓNIO DUARTE DE ALMEIDA E CARMO.

Radio and Television

In 1991 there were an estimated 270,000 radio receivers and 59,000 television receivers in use.

RADIO

Rádio Nacional de Angola: Rua Comandante Jika, CP 1329, Luanda; tel. 321558; telex 3066; fax 324647; broadcasts in Portuguese, English, French, Spanish and vernacular languages (Chokwe, Kikongo, Kimbundu, Kwanyama, Fiote, Ngangela, Luvale, Songu, Umbundu); Dir-Gen. AGOSTINHO V. LOPES.

TELEVISION

Televisão Popular de Angola (TPA): Rua Ho Chi Minh, CP 2604, Luanda; tel. 320025; telex 3238; fax 391091; f. 1975; state-controlled; Man. Dir CARLOS CUNHA.

Finance

(cap. = capital; dep. = deposits; res = reserves; m. = million; brs = branches; amounts in old kwanza)

BANKING

All banks were nationalized in 1975.

Central Bank

Banco Nacional de Angola: Avda 4 de Fevereiro 151, CP 1243, Luanda; tel. 399141; telex 3005; fax 390579; f. 1976 to replace Banco de Angola; bank of issue; cap. and res 7,657m.; dep. 111,975m. (1983); Gov. GENEROSO HERMENEGILDO GASPAR DE ALMEIDA; Vice-Govs AMÍLCAR SANTOS AZEVEDO DA SILVA, JOÃO BAPTISTA MADEIRA TORRES; 9 brs and 46 agencies.

Commercial Banks

Banco de Crédito Comercial e Industrial: CP 1395, Luanda.

Banco de Poupança e Crédito (BPC): Largo Saydi Mingas, CP 1343, Luanda; tel. 339158; telex 4149; fax 393790; cap. 10,100m. (Dec. 1992); Chair. AMILCAR S. AZEVEDO SILVA; brs throughout Angola.

Development Bank

Banco de Comércio e Indústria: Avda 4 de Fevereiro 86, CP 1395, Luanda; tel. 333684; telex 2009; fax 333823; f. 1991; provides loans to businesses in all sectors; cap. 1,000m., dep. 424,591.3m. (1992); Chair. PEDRO MAIANGALA PUNA; 2 brs.

Foreign Banks

Banco Espírito Santo e Comercial de Lisboa: 5-3°, Rua Cirilo da Conceição Silva, CP 1471, Luanda; tel. 392287; telex 3400; fax 391484; Rep. JOSE RIBEIRO DA SILVA.

Banco de Fomento e Exterior SA: Edifício BPC, 7° andar, Rua Dr Alfredo Trony, Luanda; Man. TERESA MATEUS.

Banco Totta e Açores SA: Avda 4 de Fevereiro 99, CP 1231, Luanda; tel. 332729; telex 2015; fax 333233; Gen. Man. EDUARDO BARBIERI FIGUEIREDO.

Banque Paribas (France): Edificio BPC, 18° andar, Rua Dr Alfredo Trony, CP 1385, Luanda; tel. 391890; telex 4068; fax 392339; Rep. ALVA GONÇALVES.

INSURANCE

Empresa Nacional de Seguros e Resseguros de Angola (ENSA), UEE: Avda 4 de Fevereiro 93, CP 5778, Luanda; tel. 332991; telex 3087.

Trade and Industry

SUPERVISORY BODY

National Supplies Commission: Luanda; f. 1977 to combat sabotage and negligence.

CHAMBER OF COMMERCE

Associação Comercial de Luanda: Edifício Palácio de Comércio, 1° andar, CP 1275, Luanda; tel. 322453.

STATE TRADING ORGANIZATIONS

Angomédica, UEE: Rua Dr Américo Boavida 85/87, CP 2698, Luanda; tel. 332945; telex 4195; f. 1981 to import pharmaceutical goods; Gen. Dir Dr A. PITRA.

Direcção dos Serviços de Comércio (Dept of Trade): Largo Diogo Cão, CP 1337, Luanda; f. 1970; brs throughout Angola.

Epmel, UEE: Rua Karl Marx 35–37, Luanda; tel. 330943; industrial agricultural machinery.

Exportang, UEE: Rua dos Enganos 1A, CP 1000, Luanda; tel. 332363; telex 3318; co-ordinates exports.

Importang, UEE: Calçada do Município 10, CP 1003, Luanda; tel. 337994; telex 3169; f. 1977; co-ordinates majority of imports; Dir-Gen. SIMÃO DIOGO DA CRUZ.

Maquimport, UEE: Rua Rainha Ginga 152, CP 2975, Luanda; tel. 339044; telex 4175; f. 1981 to import office equipment.

Mecanang, UEE: Rua dos Enganos, 1°–7° andar, CP 1347, Luanda; tel. 390644; telex 4021; f. 1981 to import agricultural and construction machinery, tools and spare parts.

STATE INDUSTRIAL ENTERPRISES

Companhia do Açúcar de Angola: 77 Rua Direita, Luanda; production of sugar.

Companhia Geral dos Algodões de Angola (COTONANG): Avda da Boavista, Luanda; production of cotton textiles.

Empresa Abastecimento Técnico Material (EMATEC), UEE: Largo Rainha Ginga 3, CP 2952, Luanda; tel. 338891; telex 3349; technical and material suppliers to the Ministry of Defence.

Empresa Açucareira Centro (OSUKA), UEE: Estrada Principal do Lobito, CP 37, Catumbela; tel. 24681; telex 08268; sugar industry.

Empresa Açucareira Norte (ACUNOR), UEE: Rua Robert Shilds, CP 225, Caxito, Bengo; tel. 71720; sugar production.

Empresa Angolana de Embalagens (METANGOL), UEE: Rua Estrada do Cacuaco, CP 151, Luanda; tel. 370680; production of non-specified metal goods.

Empresa de Cimento de Angola (CIMANGOLA), UEE: Avda 4 de Fevereiro 42, Luanda; tel. 371190; telex 3142; f. 1954; 69% state-owned; cement production; exports to several African countries.

Empresa de Construção de Edificações (CONSTROI), UEE: Rua Alexandre Peres, CP 2566, Luanda; tel. 333930; telex 3165; construction.

Empresa de Pesca de Angola (PESCANGOLA), UEE: Luanda; f. 1981; state fishing enterprise, responsible to Ministry of Fisheries.

Empresa de Rebenefício e Exportação do Café de Angola (CAFANGOL), UEE: Avda 4 de Fevereiro 107, CP 342, Luanda; tel. 337916; telex 3011; f. 1983; national coffee-processing and trade organization.

Empresa de Tecidos de Angola (TEXTANG), UEE: Rua N'gola Kiluanji-Kazenga, CP 5404, Luanda; tel. 381134; telex 4062; production of textiles.

Empresa Nacional de Cimento (ENCIME), UEE: CP 157, Lobito; tel. 2325; cement production.

Empresa Nacional de Comercialização e Distribuição de Produtos Agrícolas (ENCODIPA): Luanda; central marketing agency for agricultural produce; numerous brs throughout Angola.

Empresa Nacional de Construções Eléctricas (ENCEL), UEE: Rua Comandante Che Guevara 185/7, Luanda; tel. 391630; fax 331411; f. 1982; electric energy.

Empresa Nacional de Diamantes de Angola (ENDIAMA), UEE: Rua Rainha Ginga 74, 3° andar, Luanda; tel. 392336; telex 3046; fax 391586; f. 1981 as the sole diamond-mining concession; commenced operations 1986; Dir-Gen. NOÉ BALTAZAR.

Empresa Nacional de Electricidade (ENE), UEE: Edifício Geominas, 6°–7° andar, CP 772, Luanda; tel. 323568; telex 3170; fax 323382; f. 1980; production and distribution of electricity; Dir-Gen. Eng. LUIS FILIPE DA SILVA.

Empresa Nacional de Ferro de Angola (FERRANGOL): Rua João de Barros 26, CP 2692, Luanda; tel. 373800; iron production; Dir ARMANDO DE SOUSA (MACHADINHO).

Empresa Nacional de Manutenção (MANUTECNICA), UEE: Rua 7A Avda do Cazenga 10L, CP 3508, Luanda; tel. 383646; assembly of machines and specialized equipment for industry.

Empresa Publica de Telecomunicações (EPTEL), UEE: Rua I Congresso 26, CP 625, Luanda; tel. 392285; telex 3012; fax 391688; international telecommunications.

Empresa Texteis de Angola (ENTEX), UEE: Avda Comandante Kima Kienda, CP 5720, Luanda; tel. 336182; telex 3086; weaving and tissue finishing.

Fina Petróleos de Angola SARL: CP 1320, Luanda; tel. 336855; telex 3246; fax 391031; f. 1957; petroleum production, refining and exploration; operates Luanda petroleum refinery, Petrangol, with capacity of 35,000 b/d; also operates Quinfuquena terminal; Man. Dir J. R. MULS.

Siderurgia Nacional, UEE: CP Zona Industrial do Forel das Lagostas, Luanda; tel. 373028; telex 3178; f. 1963, nationalized 1980; steelworks and rolling mill plant.

Sociedade Nacional de Combustíveis de Angola (SONANGOL): Rua I Congresso do MPLA, CP 1318, Luanda; tel. 331690; telex 3148; f. 1976 for exploration, production and refining of crude petroleum, and marketing and distribution of petroleum products; sole concessionary in Angola, supervises on- and offshore operations of foreign petroleum cos; holds majority interest in jt ventures with Cabinda Gulf Oil Co (Cabgoc), Fina Petróleos de Angola and Texaco Petróleos de Angola; Dir-Gen. JOAQUIM DAVID.

Sociedade Unificada de Tabacos de Angola, Lda (SUT): Rua Deolinda Rodrigues 530/537, CP 1263, Luanda; tel. 360180; telex 3237; fax 360170; f. 1919; tobacco products; Gen. Man. A. CAMPOS.

MAJOR INDUSTRIAL COMPANY

Cabinda Gulf Oil Co (Cabgoc): CP 2950, Luanda; tel. 392646; telex 3167; wholly-owned subsidiary of Chevron Corpn (USA): undertakes exploration and production of petroleum in Cabinda province, in asscn with SONANGOL, which holds a 51% interest in these jt ventures; Man. Dir R. K. CONNON.

TRADE UNION

União Nacional de Trabalhadores Angolanos (UNTA) (National Union of Angolan Workers): Avda 4 de Fevereiro 210, CP 28, Luanda; telex 3387; f. 1960; Sec.-Gen. PASCOAL LUVUALU; 600,000 mems.

Transport

In 1988 a US $340m. emergency programme was launched to rehabilitate the transport infrastructure, which was severely disrupted by the civil war.

RAILWAYS

The total length of track operated was 2,952 km in 1987. There are plans to extend the Namibe line beyond Menongue and to construct north–south rail links. Under the emergency transport programme that was initiated in 1988, US $121m. was allocated to the rehabilitation of the Namibe (Moçamêdes) and Luanda railways.

Caminhos de Ferro de Angola: Avda 4 de Fevereiro 42, CP 1250-C, Luanda; tel. 339794; telex 3224; fax 339976; national network operating four fmrly independent systems; Nat. Dir R. M. DA CONCEIÇÃO JUNIOR.

Amboim Railway: Porto Amboim; f. 1945; 123 track-km; Dir A. GUIA.

Benguela Railway (Companhia do Caminho de Ferro de Benguela): Rua Praça 11 Novembro 3, CP 32, Lobito; tel. 22645; telex 2922; fax 22865; f. 1903; owned 90% by Tank Consolidated Investments (a subsidiary of Société Générale de Belgique), 10% by Govt of Angola; line carrying passenger and freight traffic from the port of Lobito across Angola, via Huambo and Luena, to the Zaire border, where it connects with the Société Nationale des Chemins de Fer Zaïrois system, which, in turn, links with Zambia Railways, thus providing the shortest west coast route for central African trade; 1,394 track-km; guerrilla operations by UNITA suspended all international traffic from 1975, with only irregular services from Lobito to Huambo being maintained; a declaration of intent to reopen the cross-border lines was signed in April 1987 by Angola, Zambia and Zaire, and the rehabilitation of the railway was a priority of a 10-year programme, planned by the SADCC, to develop the 'Lobito corridor'; plans to restore full services between Lobito and Cuito by 1995, at an estimated cost of US $17m., were initiated following the signing of the cease-fire agreement between the Govt and UNITA in May 1991; following the resumption of hostilities in October 1992, however, rehabilitation work was suspended; Dir-Gen. LUKOKI SEBASTIÃO.

Luanda Railway (Empresa de Caminho de Ferro de Luanda, UEE): CP 1250C, Luanda; tel. 370061; telex 3108; f. 1886; serves an iron, cotton and sisal-producing region between Luanda and Malanje; 505 track-km; Man. A. ALVARO AGANTE.

Namibe Railway: CP 130, Lubango; f. 1905; main line from Namibe to Menongue, via Lubango; br. lines to Chibia and iron ore mines at Cassinga; 899 track-km; Gen. Man. J. SALVADOR.

ROADS

In 1992 Angola had 72,626 km of roads, of which 7,701 km were main roads and 15,825 km were secondary roads. About 25% of roads were paved. Rehabilitation of roads was to receive US $142m. under the emergency transport programme initiated in 1988.

SHIPPING

The main harbours are at Lobito, Luanda and Namibe; the commercial port of Porto Amboim, in Cuanza-Sul province, has been closed for repairs since July 1984. The expansion of port facilities in Cabinda was planned. In May 1983 a regular shipping service began to operate between Luanda and Maputo (Mozambique). Under the emergency transport programme launched in 1988, refurbishment work was to be undertaken on the ports of Luanda and Namibe. The first phase of a 10-year SADCC programme to develop the Lobito corridor, for which funds were pledged in January 1989, was to include the rehabilitation of the ports of Lobito and Benguela.

Angonave—Linhas Marítimas de Angola, UEE: Rua Serqueira 31, CP 5953, Luanda; tel. 330144; telex 3313; national shipping line; Dir-Gen. FRANCISCO VENÂNCIO.

Cabotang-Cabotagem Nacional Angolana, UEE: Avda 4 de Fevereiro 83A, Luanda; tel. 373133; telex 3007; operates off the coasts of Angola and Mozambique; Dir-Gen. JOÃO OCTAVIO VAN-DÚNEM.

Empresa Portuaria do Lobito, UEE: Avda da Independência, CP 16, Lobito; tel. 2710; telex 8233; long-distance sea transport.

Empresa Portuaria de Moçâmedes—Namibe, UEE: Rua Pedro Benje 10A and 10C, CP 49, Namibe; tel. 60643; long-distance sea transport; Dir HUMBERTO DE ATAIDE DIAS.

Linhas Marítimas de Angola, UEE: Rua Serqueira 31, CP 5953, Luanda; tel. 30144; telex 3313.

Secil Marítima SARL, UEE: Avda 4 de Fevereiro 42, 1° andar, CP 5910, Luanda; tel. 335230; telex 3060.

CIVIL AVIATION

TAAG—Linhas Aéreas de Angola: Rua da Missão 123, CP 79, Luanda; tel. 336510; telex 3285; fax 392229; f. 1939; internal scheduled passenger and cargo services, and services from Luanda to destinations within Africa and to Europe, South America and the Caribbean; Pres. JULIO SAMPAIO; Gen. Dir ABEL LOPES.

Transafrik International: Rua Joaquim Kapango, CP 2839, Luanda; tel. 351723; fax 393397; f. 1986; operates contract cargo services mainly within Africa; Man. Dir ERICH KOCH.

Tourism

National Tourist Agency: Palácio de Vidro, CP 1240, Luanda; tel. 372750.

Defence

In December 1990 the governing party, the Movimento Popular de Libertação de Angola—Partido do Trabalho (MPLA—PT), agreed to terminate its direct link with the armed forces. In accordance with the peace agreement concluded by the government and the União Nacional para a Independência Total de Angola (UNITA) in May 1991 (see Recent History), a new 50,000-strong national army, the Forças Armadas de Angola (FAA), was to be established, comprising equal numbers of government forces, the Forças Armadas Populares de Libertação de Angola (FAPLA), and UNITA soldiers. The formation of the FAA was to coincide with the holding of a general election in late September 1992. Pending the general election, a cease-fire between FAPLA and UNITA forces, which commenced in mid-May 1991, was monitored by a joint political and military commission, comprising representatives of the MPLA—PT, UNITA, the UN, Portugal, the USA and the USSR. This commission was to oversee the withdrawal of FAPLA and UNITA forces to specific confinement areas, to await demobilization. Although not all troops had entered the confinement areas, demobilization began in late March 1992. Military advisers from Portugal, France and the United Kingdom were to assist with the formation of the new national army. However, the demobilization process and the formation of the FAA fell behind schedule and were only partially completed by the end of September and the holding of the general election. Following the election, UNITA withdrew its troops from the FAA, alleging electoral fraud on the part of the MPLA.

In June 1993 the FAA had an estimated total strength of 45,000: army 35,000, navy 4,000 and air force 6,000. In addition there was a paramilitary force numbering an estimated 20,000. UNITA forces totalled an estimated 40,000.

Defence Expenditure: Budgeted at 52,391m. kwanza for 1990.

Chief of General Staff of the Armed Forces: Gen. JOÃO BAPTISTA DE MATOS.

Education

Education is officially compulsory for eight years, between seven and 15 years of age, and is provided free of charge by the government. Primary education begins at the age of six and lasts for four years. Secondary education, beginning at the age of 10, lasts for up to seven years, comprising a first cycle of four years and a second of three years. As a proportion of the school-age population, the total enrolment at primary and secondary schools was 45% in 1990. Enrolment at primary schools stood at 1,038,126 in 1989/90, and that at secondary schools (including students receiving vocational instruction and teacher training) totalled 148,837. There is one university, at Luanda, with 5,736 students in 1986/87. In 1991 the government approved legislation permitting the foundation of private educational establishments.

At independence the adult illiteracy rate was over 85%, and Angola's independent economic development continues to be hampered by the widespread lack of basic skills. A national literacy campaign was launched in 1976, since when almost 1m. adults have received instruction in reading, writing and basic arithmetic. The average rate of adult illiteracy in 1990 was estimated by UNESCO to be 58.3% (males 71.5%, females 44.4%).

Bibliography

Bhagavan, M.R. *Angola's Political Economy: 1975–1985*. Uppsala, Scandinavian Institute of African Studies, 1986.

Bridgland, F. *Jonas Savimbi: A Key to Africa*. Edinburgh, Mainstream, 1986.

Cohen, R. (Ed.) *African Islands and Enclaves*. London, Sage Publications, 1983.

Davidson, B. *In the Eye of the Storm: Angola's People*. London, Longman, 1972.

Ekwe-Ekwe, H. *Conflict and Intervention in Africa: Nigeria, Angola and Zaire*. London, Macmillan, 1990.

Estermann, C. *Ethnographie du sud-ouest de l'Angola* (2 vols). Paris, Académie des Sciences d'Outre-mer, 1984.

Heimer, F.-W. *The Decolonisation Conflict in Angola 1974–1976*. Geneva, Institut Universitaire de Hautes Etudes, 1979.

Henderson, L.W. *Angola: Five Centuries of Conflict*. Ithaca, NY, Cornell University Press, 1979.

Herrick, A. B., et al. *Area Handbook for Angola*. Washington, DC, 1967.

Hodges, T. *Angola to the 1990s: The Potential for Recovery*. London, Economist Intelligence Unit, 1987.

Instituto Superior de Ciências Sociais e Política Ultramarina (ISCSPU). *Angola*. Lisbon, 1964.

Klinghoffer, A. J. *The Angolan War*. Boulder, CO, Westview Press.

Konczacki, Z. A., Parpart, J. L., and Shaw, T. M. (Eds). *Studies in the Economic History of Southern Africa*. Vol. I. London, Cass, 1990.

Martin, P. M. *Historical Dictionary of Angola*. London, 1980.

Menendez del Valle, E. *Angola, imperialismo y guerra civil*. Madrid, Akal, 1976.

Mozambique, Angola and Guiné Information Centre (MAGIC). *State Papers and Party Proceedings* (series). London, 1978, 1979 and 1980.

Pélissier, R. *Explorar. Voyages en Angola*. Orgeval, Editions Pélissier, 1980.

Africana. Bibliographies sur l'Afrique luso-hispanophone (1800–1980). Orgeval, Editions Pélissier, 1982.

Somerville, K. *Angola*. London, Frances Pinter, 1986.

Wheeler, D. L., and Pélissier, R. *Angola*. London, Greenwood Press, 1978.

Wolfers, M., and Bergerol, J. *Angola in the Front Line*. London, Zed Press, 1983.

World Bank. *Angola: An Introductory Economic Review*. Washington, DC, International Bank for Reconstruction and Development, 1990.

BENIN

Physical and Social Geography

R. J. HARRISON CHURCH

The Republic of Benin, bordered on the west by Nigeria, on the east by Togo and to the north by Burkina Faso and Niger, covers an area of 112,622 sq km (43,484 sq miles). From a coastline of some 100 km on the Gulf of Guinea, the republic extends inland about 650 km to the Niger river. Provisional census results indicated a population of 4,855,349 at February 1992, giving an average population density of 43.1 inhabitants per sq km. The population of Cotonou, the political capital and major port, was officially estimated at 350,000 in 1989. Porto-Novo, the official capital, had an estimated population of 144,000 in 1981.

The coast is a straight sand-bar, pounded by heavy surf on the seaward side and backed by one or more lagoons and former shorelines on the landward side. Rivers flow into these lagoons, Lakes Ahémé and Nokoué being estuaries of two rivers whose seaward exits are obstructed by the sand-bar. A lagoon waterway is navigable for barges to Lagos, in Nigeria.

North of Lake Nokoué the Ouémé river has a wide marshy delta, with considerable agricultural potential. Elsewhere the lagoons are backed northward by the Terre de Barre, a fertile and intensively farmed region of clay soils. North again is the seasonally flooded Lama swamp. Beyond are areas comparable with the Terre de Barre, and the realm of the pre-colonial kingdom of Dahomey.

Most of the rest of the country is underlain by Pre-Cambrian rocks, with occasional bare domes, laterite cappings on level surfaces, and poor soils. In the north-west are the Atacora mountains whose soils, though less poor, are much eroded. On the northern borders are Primary and other sandstones, extremely infertile and short of water.

Deposits of iron, chrome, rutile and phosphates occur in the north of the country, although none are economically exploitable. The small Sémé oilfield, offshore from Cotonou, came into production in 1982. Limestone, marble and also small quantities of gold are mined.

Southern Benin has an equatorial climate, most typical along the coast, though with a low rainfall of some 1,300 mm. Away from the coast the dry months increase until a tropical climate prevails over the northern half of the country. There a dry season alternates with a wet one, the latter being of seven months in the centre and four months in the north; the rainfall nevertheless averages 1,300 mm per year.

In colonial days the Fon and Yoruba of the south enjoyed educational advantages and were prominent in administration throughout French West Africa. After independence many were expelled to Benin, where there is great unemployment or underemployment of literates. The northern peoples, such as the Somba and Bariba, are less Westernized.

Recent History

PIERRE ENGLEBERT

Benin (then known as Dahomey) was formerly part of French West Africa. It became a self-governing republic within the French Community in December 1958 and an independent state on 1 August 1960. In the decade following independence, political life in the republic was extremely unstable, as regionally-based interests contended for power. Hubert Maga, a northerner, became the republic's first president following elections held in December 1960, but in October 1963 he was deposed by an army *coup d'état*, led by Col (later Gen.) Christophe Soglo. In January 1964 Soglo installed a coalition government led by Sourou-Migan Apithy, a south-easterner who had been vice-president under Maga, with Justin Ahomadegbé, who represented the interests of the south-western region, as prime minister. Intense opposition from the north, however, led to a series of political crises which resulted in army intervention and the return to power of Soglo in December 1965. A further military coup in December 1967 brought Lt-Col Alphonse Alley to power as head of state. During 1967–70 three successive army-supported regimes sought unsuccessfully to resolve regional rivalries, and in May 1970 power was transferred by the army to a civilian triumvirate comprising Ahomadegbé, Apithy and Maga.

KEREKOU TAKES POWER

In October 1972 a junta, led by Maj. (later Brig.-Gen.) Mathieu Kerekou, seized power. Kerekou established a ruling military council, containing equal numbers of army officers from each of the three main regions, and introduced Marxism-Leninism as the national ideology. In December 1975 the country was renamed the People's Republic of Benin. Meanwhile, banking, insurance and important industrial sectors were nationalized. Beginning in 1975, Kerekou endeavoured to reform Benin's organs of state. A new ruling party, the Parti de la révolution populaire du Bénin (PRPB), was formed. A *loi fondamentale*, adopted in August 1977, defined the structure of government. The regime was 'civilianized' in November 1979, when a single list of PRPB candidates for a new Assemblée nationale revolutionnaire (ANR) was overwhelmingly endorsed by the electorate. Kerekou was himself unanimously elected president of the republic by the ANR in February 1980.

During the 1980s the government began to replace its socialist philosophy with a more pragmatic approach to the country's economic needs. Western private investment was encouraged, and, beginning in 1982, the government undertook a reform of the country's largely corrupt and inefficient parastatal companies (see Economy). Meanwhile, in 1981 the release from house arrest of Maga, Apithy and Ahomadegbé, who had been detained in the aftermath of the October 1972 coup, was generally interpreted as a sign of political liberalization.

At the same time, Kerekou asserted his personal authority over the various rival factions within the ruling élite, demoting or removing during 1982 several extreme leftist government ministers. The consolidation process continued in 1984, with the election of a new ANR. Candidates who had been proposed at public meetings were subjected to a selection process, based by the PRPB on complex socio-professional quotas within which there was undoubtedly further selection by region and ethnic background. The final list was then endorsed in June by the electorate, whose choice was limited to accepting or rejecting the entire list. In the event, it was approved by 97.96% of voters. In late July the ANR re-elected Kerekou to the presidency for an extended five-year term. In the following month Kerekou granted an amnesty for most political prisoners (notably excluding those implicated in a raid on Cotonou by mercenaries in January 1977), indicating that the regime felt largely secure from the ambitions of old-guard politicians and Kerekou associates alike.

The economic and relative political liberalization of the early 1980s was accompanied by a reorientation of Benin's foreign policy at the expense of the Eastern bloc, relations with which had been fostered in the early years of the Kerekou regime but whose aid contributions had declined considerably. Conversely, relations with France, Benin's principal trading partner and supplier of development aid, improved following the election of François Mitterrand to the French presidency in 1981.

ECONOMIC PROBLEMS AND INTERNAL UNREST

In an attempt to reduce smuggling, Nigeria closed its border with Benin in April 1984, bringing recession to Benin in 1985 and causing a sharp deterioration in relations between the two countries. The reopening of the frontier in March 1986 brought few benefits, in view of the prevailing depressed economic climate.

The announcement, in April 1985, that graduates could no longer be guaranteed jobs by the state led to student unrest, to which the government reacted by closing the national university and by arresting alleged communist students. In June the ministers of secondary and higher education and of culture, youth and sports were dismissed, leaving the powerful Fon people without high-level representation.

During 1986 the worsening economic crisis caused Benin to move increasingly towards the Western bloc and the IMF. In October Kerekou made a series of visits to Western European countries, where he sought increased aid and the rescheduling of Benin's external debts. France had by now replaced the USSR as the principal supplier of military equipment, while also remaining predominant in other forms of co-operation. Similarly, in late 1986 Kerekou sent one of his closest advisers to visit some of the more conservative African countries, including Côte d'Ivoire, Cameroon and Gabon, to seek financial support. Civil servants' salaries were subsequently paid for the first time in three months.

In 1986 Kerekou ordered the release of 50 of those implicated in the 1985 student riots, claiming that there were then no political prisoners left in Benin (an assertion disputed by the human rights organization, Amnesty International). In March 1987 a demonstration by students was dispersed by police, and the PRPB made a public statement of its intention to suppress any 'subversive elements' within the university. Economic problems, meanwhile, exacerbated social tensions and ethnic rivalries. Kerekou's confidence in the continuance of his regime resulted from a much-strengthened internal security network.

Kerekou, who resigned from the army in January 1987 to become a civilian head of state, reshuffled the government in the following month, in an apparent attempt to restore equilibrium in both north-south and military-civilian representation. However, ensuing tensions between Kerekou's civilian government and the army culminated in an attempted *coup d'état* in March 1988. More than 150 army members were arrested in connection with the plot, which had been instigated by three disaffected southerners, including the chief of staff of the paramilitary forces. The incident was widely believed to reflect the army's dissatisfaction with widespread corruption within the government, and its opposition to the establishment of a state security court. A further attempt to overthrow the government occurred in June, while Kerekou was attending a regional conference in neighbouring Togo. In February 1989 two of those arrested in connection with this coup attempt were sentenced to 20 years' imprisonment, and two further defendants received lesser sentences. Allegations by the defendants that Libyan interests had been involved in the coup attempt exacerbated tensions between the two countries. In May 1988 the USA had accused Benin of allowing Libyan agents to use its territory as a base for terrorist activities. Anxious to secure financial aid from the West, the Kerekou government ordered the closure of a Libyan-controlled import-export company, and expelled the head of the Libyan diplomatic mission in Cotonou.

'CIVILIAN COUP'

A period of repression in the aftermath of the coup attempts, in conjunction with popular dissatisfaction at the government's austerity measures (imposed in co-operation with the IMF), served only to engender an atmosphere of increased social tension and instability that was to precipitate the disintegration of the Kerekou regime. In January 1989 public-sector employees, including civil servants and schoolteachers, went on strike in Cotonou and Porto Novo, in protest against protracted delays in the payment of salaries, while students boycotted classes in support of their demands for the disbursement of grants and scholarships. Adding to the mood of discontent were revelations of corruption within the government and in the banking sector, together with allegations that the government had agreed to accept shipments of hazardous waste from Western countries.

Elections to the ANR took place in June 1989, at which a single list of 206 candidates was approved by 89.6% of the votes cast; malpractice was alleged by Kerekou's opponents. In early August the ANR re-elected Kerekou to the presidency for a further five-year term. Government changes followed: the new administration comprised relatively fewer military officers and PRPB members, while several independent ministers were known proponents of multi-party democracy.

In August 1989 the government agreed to a partial payment of the salaries owed to public-sector employees. In the same month an amnesty was announced for some 200 dissidents; among those pardoned was Dr Emile-Derlin Zinsou, who had been installed as president by the military in July 1968, only to be deposed in December 1969, and who was now leading an opposition movement based in Paris. Fifty of those who had been detained in the aftermath of the 1985 student unrest were released in April 1989.

Although academic staff and students agreed to resume classes in October 1989, persistent social and political difficulties continued to undermine Kerekou's authority. Also in October, the Union nationale des syndicats des travailleurs du Bénin (UNSTB), the sole officially recognized trade union, announced that it was to sever its links with the PRPB. By December the government's failure to pay the salaries of public-sector employees caused further disruption, and in response to demands made by the Beninois population and by the country's external creditors (notably France), the Kerekou government announced that Marxism-Leninism would no longer be the official ideology of the state. A national conference was promised for early 1990, at which the drafting of a new constitution would be initiated. Benin's external creditors subsequently agreed to fund a partial repayment of outstanding salaries.

The national conference of the 'active forces of the nation', which was convened in Cotonou in February 1990, was attended by 488 delegates representing more than 50 political organizations (including the PRPB and opposition movements, which, while still officially banned, had become increasingly active in the light of Kerekou's proposals for reform). The conference declared itself sovereign and voted to abolish the 1977 *loi fondamentale*: decisions taken by the delegates were to provide the basis of a new constitution. The ANR was to be dissolved, and its functions were to be assumed by an interim Haut conseil de la République (HCR, a 27-member body which was to include the principal opposition leaders), pending elections, by universal suffrage, to a new legislature. The president of the republic was similarly to be elected by universal suffrage, for a five-year term, renewable only once. The conference also designated a former official of the World Bank, Nicéphore Soglo, as

Benin's prime minister. Kerekou, who reluctantly agreed to the decisions, relinquished the defence portfolio to Soglo, and accepted the conference's resolution to change the country's name to the Republic of Benin. In early March 1990 an amnesty was announced for all dissidents, and a human rights commission was established. In the same month the HCR was inaugurated, while Soglo appointed a 15-member civilian government (to act as a transitional authority until the 1991 elections); of the members of the previous administration, only Kerekou remained in office. The Soglo government announced that financial commitments to public-sector employees and students would be discharged in full.

In May 1990 the prefects of Benin's six provinces, all of whom were military officers, were replaced by civilians. In the following month the transitional government undertook an extensive restructuring of the armed forces, as a result of which responsibility for several services (including the police and the customs authorities) was transferred to civilian control, and the people's militia was disbanded (the dissolution of the presidential guard was announced in April 1991). Also in May 1990 a new party, the Union des forces du progrès (UFP), was formed to replace the PRPB. In August legislation was promulgated to permit the registration of political parties. Independent journals flourished, following the relaxation of restrictions on the press.

Benin thus became the first sub-Saharan African country to experience a 'civilian coup': a single-party regime, dominated by the armed forces, that had assumed power following a *coup d'état*, was obliged by popular coercion to accept a return to multi-party democracy.

Soglo's transitional government made attempts to alleviate Benin's chronic economic difficulties. It was announced that corrupt officials would be prosecuted and deprived of embezzled gains, and measures to restructure the state sector were intensified. However, some popular dissatisfaction at the inability of the Soglo administration to bring about immediate economic relief was apparent, notably among students, who boycotted classes on several occasions during the year that followed the appointment of the transitional government.

The draft constitution was published in May 1990, and, after some delay, was submitted to a national referendum on 2 December. Voters were asked to choose between two versions of the constitution, one of which incorporated a clause stipulating upper and lower age-limits for presidential candidates (thereby automatically disqualifying ex-presidents Ahomadegbé, Maga and Zinsou). It was reported that 95.8% of those who voted gave their assent to one or other of the versions, with 79.7% of voters endorsing the document in full.

Of the 34 political parties that had been accorded official status by early 1991, as many as 24 participated in the general election that took place on 17 February. While no party or group of parties won an overall majority of the 64 seats in the Assemblée nationale a pro-Soglo alliance (comprising the Union démocratique des forces du progrès, the Mouvement pour la démocratie et le progrès social and the Union pour la liberté et le développement) secured the greatest number of seats (12) in the new legislature. The UFP failed to win any seats in the assembly.

A total of 13 candidates, including Kerekou and Soglo, contested the first round of the presidential election on 10 March 1991. The distribution of votes between the two leading candidates largely reflected ethnic divisions: Soglo, who secured 36.16% of the total, received his greatest support in the south of the country, while Kerekou, who was reported to have enjoyed the support of more than 80% of voters in the north, received 27.33% of the overall vote. Soglo and Kerekou proceeded to a second round of voting, which was conducted on 24 March amid allegations of electoral malpractice and violence involving supporters of the rival candidates. Despite continuing support for Kerekou in the north, Soglo was elected president, securing 67.73% of the total votes cast. In late March, immediately prior to its dissolution, the HCR granted Kerekou immunity from any legal proceedings connected with actions committed since the coup of October 1972.

THE SOGLO PRESIDENCY

Soglo was inaugurated as president on 4 April 1991. Minor cabinet changes were implemented shortly afterwards, a result of which Soglo relinquished the defence portfolio to his brother-in-law, Désiré Vieyra, who was designated minister of state. In July Adrien Houngbédji (the leader of the Parti du renouveau démocratique, who had also contested the presidency earlier in the year) was elected speaker of the Assemblée nationale; Soglo had been known to favour a different candidate. In a wider reorganization of the government, also in July, Vieyra was promoted to the rank of senior minister, secretary-general at the office of the president of the republic; three former ministers left the government, and eight of the council of ministers' 20 portfolios were allocated to little-known technocrats (who were reported to be members of parties that had supported Soglo's presidential candidature).

In November 1991, following attempts by the military in Togo to frustrate the transition to multi-party civilian rule, President Soglo (apparently fearing that army hard-liners in Benin might attempt to undermine the country's own civilian institutions) allowed France temporarily to deploy 300 troops in Benin. Although opposition deputies criticized Soglo's co-operation with France in this matter, his policy won considerable public support, and there were popular demonstrations in Cotonou, appealing to France to intervene to protect Togo's interim government.

By the end of 1991 three broad groupings of delegates had emerged within the Assemblée nationale: the 'pro-Soglo' Nouvelle République, the 'moderate' Démocratie et solidarité, and the 'opposition' Convergence. During the early part of 1992, in an apparent assertion of the legislature's independence from the executive, deputies opposed the (previously agreed) sale to a French company of the state-owned brewery, and delayed ratification of budget proposals for the forthcoming financial year.

Following his inauguration as President, Soglo furthered the attempts to address the economic problems that had been initiated under his transitional administration, and several former close associates of Kerekou were charged with financial corruption. None the less, labour unrest persisted in the second half of 1991, as civil servants again withdrew their labour, expressing frustration that salary arrears which had been accumulated in the final years of the Kerekou regime remained unpaid and demanding that future salary increases be indexed to the rate of inflation. A demonstration in Cotonou, involving some 5,000 striking civil sevants, was reported in May 1992, in support of demands for wage increases and for access to the state-owned media. Moreover, the university had been closed in March, following renewed unrest involving students who were demanding the payment of grant arrears, together with the dismissal of students' representatives and of the recently-appointed university chancellor. Subsequent revelations that members of the Assemblée nationale were to receive substantial pay rises, which would increase deputies' remuneration to 40 times the national minimum wage, prompted widespread popular criticism, and the government was obliged to postpone the increases.

In May 1992 soldiers were arrested in suspicious circumstances near the presidential palace in Cotonou, suspected of trying to prepare a coup. Among those detained was Capt. Pascal Tawes, a former deputy commander of Kerekou's presidential guard. However, Tawes (with some of his associates) subsequently escaped from custody, and in August he gained control of the Kaba army base, near the northern town of Natitingou. However, the rebels failed to win support from other northern garrisons and the rebellion collapsed when the government dispatched élite paratroops to recover Kaba (although it was reported that local officials had already negotiated a peaceful end to the mutiny). One rebel was killed, and about 45 mutineers were detained, although Tawes himself evaded arrest.

Coalition Alliances

Meanwhile, the president's position had been strengthened by the formation, in June 1992, of a pro-Soglo majority group of deputies in the Assemblée nationale. The new coalition, Le Renouveau, initially comprising 34 deputies from 10 political parties, included former members of Nouvelle République, together with defectors from Démocratie et solidarité (which remained the principal bloc opposing Soglo) and Convergence.

In September 1992 Mohamed Cissé, a former minister of state who had until mid-1989 been spiritual adviser to President Kerekou, was fined and sentenced to 10 years' imprisonment, after having been found guilty of defrauding some 3,500m. francs CFA from Beninois state banks. Lesser fines and custodial sentences were imposed on nine other defendants. None the less, economic difficulties continued to undermine domestic harmony, and in October 1992 the president of the Assemblée nationale, in his speech at the opening of the new parliamentary session, was severely critical of the government's political and economic programme.

Despite the existence of legislation guaranteeing press freedom, libel proceedings were instigated during 1992 and 1993 against several journalists who had criticized Soglo and his associates. None the less, Soglo sought to consolidate popular support for his administration, and appeared particularly anxious to develop contacts in the north. He also displayed a conciliatory attitude towards practitioners of voodoo religious rites, which had been discouraged under the Kerekou regime. Social unrest persisted in Cotonou, however; government proposals for a 10% reduction in civil servants' salaries (in accordance with the economic adjustment programme) provoked a three-day strike in February 1993, and during February and March university students staged a boycott of classes, in support of demands for the equitable distribution of financial grants.

In March 1993 more than 100 prisoners escaped from detention in the south-western town of Ouidah. Among them were several soldiers who were suspected of involvement in the previous year's alleged coup plot. The dismissal, shortly afterwards, of the armed forces chief of staff and of other senior members of the security forces prompted the resignation of the government minister responsible for defence, Florentin Feliho, who protested that Soglo had acted unconstitutionally by making new appointments without consulting him. Later in the same month Soglo declared an amnesty for 23 people who had been detained in connection with the violence that had followed the 1991 presidential election.

The installation of the organs of state envisaged in the 1991 constitution continued with the inauguration of a constitutional court in June 1993, and of an economic and social council in May 1994. In September 1993 Soglo announced a reorganization of the government. Désiré Vieyra (as minister of state, in charge of national defence) remained the most senior cabinet member. Among the seven new appointees was Robert Dossou (who had briefly been a 'reformist' government minister under Kerekou in 1989) as minister of foreign affairs and co-operation. Members of the Assemblée nationale, who believed that Soglo had acted discourteously in leaving Benin for a private visit to Europe without first having presented the new government list to parliament, delayed the official publication of the cabinet changes for several days. In the following month 15 members of Le Renouveau, including the group's chairman, withdrew from the pro-Soglo coalition, alleging that the president was consistently excluding the legislature from the decision-making process. With Le Renouveau reduced in size to 19 members, Soglo lost his majority support in parliament.

Social unrest emerged following the devaluation, in January 1994, of the CFA franc (see Economy). Although the government adopted emergency measures in an attempt to offset the adverse effects of the devaluation, trade unions immediately demanded 30% salary increases. In late January the deployment of security forces to disperse an unauthorized demonstration by union activists was denounced by workers' and human rights organizations as 'undemocratic', and prompted union leaders to withdraw contacts with the authorities; a 3,000 strong demonstration proceeded at the beginning of February, in support of the unions' demands. In February and March gatherings of students, to protest against new restrictions on the allocation of scholarships and to demand that the value of grants be doubled, were ended by force. Workers' organizations (excluding the UNSTB) organized a three-day general strike in early March, and a five-day strike later in the same month, causing widespread disruption. At the beginning of May the government announced salary increases of 10% for all state employees, as well as the reintroduction of housing allowances (abolished in 1986) and an end to the eight-year 'freeze' on promotions within the civil service.

In early May 1994 Pierre Nevi was appointed to succeed Yves Yehouessi as minister of justice and legislation. Yehouessi had been named by Soglo as president of the supreme court; however, his appointment was subsequently rejected by the constitutional court, since the five-year mandate of the incumbent president, as specified under the constitution, had not yet expired.

Numerous political parties and alliances were formed during 1993–94, potentially the most influential opposition alliance being the Convention nationale des forces du changement, formed by some 25 organizations in February 1993. In July Soglo, who had previously asserted his political neutrality, made public his membership of the Parti de la renaissance du Bénin (PRB), an organization formed by his wife in the previous year. President Soglo was appointed leader of the PRB in July 1994.

REGIONAL AFFAIRS

Benin's regional relations were, for much of the 1980s, dominated by frontier tensions with Nigeria. Relations began to improve in mid-1987, following a visit to Benin by President Babangida. A series of meetings of representatives of the two countries was inaugurated in May 1988. Since April 1989 the major purpose of these sessions has been to discuss the demarcation of the frontier and trans-border co-operation. Measures aimed at curbing smuggling have also been introduced.

Benin's international standing was enhanced following the 'civilian coup'. Beginning in 1990 Soglo and his ministers travelled extensively abroad, in an attempt to foster harmonious trading and diplomatic relations with external creditors. In mid-1991, while receiving medical treatment in France, President Soglo held discussions with President Mitterrand and with other French government officials. In early 1992 the French authorities announced that, in view of the recent political changes in their homeland, Beninois nationals could no longer be accorded refugee status in France. During subsequent visits to France, Soglo maintained cordial contacts with French government officials. In the course of his numerous official visits, both within the region and overseas, Soglo has repeatedly appealed to Western donors to provide financial support for those African countries undergoing the transition to political pluralism.

Soglo assumed a role as a regional mediator when, in his capacity as chairman (for 1992/93 and 1993/94) of the conference of heads of government of the Economic Community of West African States, he participated in attempts to resolve the crises in Liberia and Togo. An agreement providing for a resolution of the conflict and for the installation of transitional authorities in Liberia was signed in Cotonou in July 1993. In April 1994 it became known that the Beninois ambassador to Côte d'Ivoire had been dismissed, following his alleged involvement in the forging of a letter, purportedly signed by Soglo, that was unduly favourable to the interests of the National Patriotic Front of Liberia. An escalation of the crisis in Togo, from early 1993, prompted thousands of Togolese nationals to cross into Benin: at mid-1993 there were an estimated 100,000 Togolese refugees in Benin. Relations between Benin and Togo deteriorated in March of that year, following a meeting in Benin of Togolese opposition representatives; in January 1994, however, the Beninois authorities prohibited further meetings of the Togolese opposition in Benin.

Economy

EDITH HODGKINSON

The dominant characteristics of the economy of Benin are its dualism and its dependence on Nigeria. There is an official, documented sector covering government and relatively modern industry and agriculture, and an unofficial, largely unrecorded sector consisting of basic food production and cross-border trade with Nigeria. Changes in the rate of economic growth are largely determined by trends in Nigeria. Overall economic growth has been slow, with the annual increase in Benin's gross domestic product (GDP) averaging only 2.0%, in real terms, in 1980–90. During this period the performance of the Beninois economy fluctuated fairly widely. Beginning in 1985 Benin suffered a period of economic depression, caused by the closure of the border with Nigeria (which was in force between April 1984 and March 1986), by the continuing economic recession in Nigeria and by the decline in international prices for Benin's major export commodities, cotton and petroleum, while the strengthening of the CFA franc in relation to the US dollar reduced the proceeds from these commodities in local currency terms. GDP declined in both 1986 and 1987 (by 3.4% and 2.0%, respectively). Subsequent years saw fluctuation between modest recovery (of 0.8% in 1988 and 2.6% in 1990) and further decline (0.7% in 1989), with the result that the ambitious target of average growth of 7% per year, to double GDP by 1990, that was envisaged in the country's 1981–90 Development Plan, was far from being achieved.

The more modest aim of the structural adjustment programme for 1989–92, that was agreed with the IMF in 1989, was average annual GDP growth of 3% over that period. As indicated above, the target was just missed in 1990, although GDP easily attained the target in both 1991 and 1992, with growth of 4.7% and 4.0%, respectively. In 1992, according to estimates by the World Bank, Benin's gross national product (GNP) was US $2,058m., equivalent to $410 per head.

The improvement in economic performance in 1991 and 1992 owed much to good harvests; also of significance, however, was the complete reversal in economic policy in 1990–91 under the new regime (see Recent History), which aimed to enhance the role of the private sector and to reduce government participation in production. Bolstered by the significant rescheduling of debt that was agreed by bilateral official creditors in December 1991 (see below) and an Enhanced Structural Adjustment Facility at the IMF for the period 1993–95, the Soglo administration hopes to set Benin on the path to sustainable economic growth, with a target of annual GDP growth of 4% during this period. This objective was apparently easily met in the first year of the programme, with GDP growth estimated at 4.5% in 1993. Moreover, the domestic political acceptability of the programme of reform was improved by the IMF's agreement to redundancy payments for civil servants and parastatal workers, as well as the rehabilitation of the social infrastructure.

However, the context for the programme was fundamentally modified by the devaluation, by 50%, of the CFA franc in January 1994. This will be seen to have had severe short-term costs, in the form of a sudden increase in the rate of inflation which the government was not fully able to counter by the imposition of price controls, and a consequent decline in consumers' purchasing power. In the longer term, none the less, it is envisaged that the devaluation will have had positive effects—by stimulating export growth (since producers of export goods, in particular agricultural commodities, will suddently command more in local currency terms) and by stimulating demand for local products, notably foodstuffs. With increased inflows of foreign aid promised to allow the maintenance of imports that are essential for the economy's expansion, and to allow some scope for temporary price subsidies to ease the impact of devaluation on consumers, GDP growth was expected to remain on target in 1994, while in the medium term the prospect is of stronger, sustained growth.

POPULATION AND EMPLOYMENT

Despite its relative lack of urbanization in previous decades, Benin has for some time had a high standard of education; the existence of a large élite—for whom employment cannot easily be found in an underdeveloped, slowly-growing economy—was at the root of Benin's unstable political situation in the years after independence. Another contributory factor, again exacerbated by the unsatisfactory economic situation, is the rift between three clearly-defined regions: Parakou and the north, Abomey and the centre-south, and the narrow coastal zone around Cotonou (the main port) and Porto-Novo (the official capital). Almost three-quarters of the country's inhabitants reside in the southern regions, giving a population density there of more than 120 per sq km—one of the highest in western Africa. Recent years have seen a pronounced movement to the towns. About 40% of the inhabitants are urban, and the population of Cotonou, officially estimated at some 350,000 in 1989, was thought to exceed 400,000 in the early 1990s. While agriculture, livestock and fishing engaged an estimated 70% of the workforce in 1980, the public sector has also been a significant source of employment, accounting for about one-half of wage and salary earners. This proportion can be expected to decline as the government's 'privatization' and fiscal stabilization programmes proceed. According to provisional census figures, the population totalled 4,855,349 in February 1992.

AGRICULTURE

The economy is dependent on the agricultural sector, which accounts for about two-fifths of GDP and occupies some two-thirds of the working population. Output of the major food crops has been rising strongly since the drought of 1981–83, reflecting both improved climatic conditions and a transfer of emphasis from cash crops to the cultivation of staple foods. Production levels since 1987/88 have been 50%–100% higher than 1983/84 figures. In 1992/93 output of cassava was 1,040,800 metric tons, yams 1,124,900, maize 459,500 and millet and sorghum 110,300. Benin is therefore self-sufficient in staple foods, and there is a growing export trade to Nigeria, mainly through informal channels.

In the past the major cash crop was oil palm, which remains the principal tree crop. Output of palm products, which was formerly based on natural plantations covering 400,000 ha, benefited in the 1970s from intensive cultivation on some 30,000 ha of industrial plantations, partly financed by France's Fonds d'aide et de coopération and by the European Development Fund (EDF). Production of palm kernels was estimated at 70,000 tons in 1976, and palm oil at more than 23,000 tons. However, output has since fallen, owing to low producer prices with marketed production of palm kernels declining to an average of only about 3,000 tons per year by the early 1990s, while output of palm oil was last recorded in 1987/88, at 12,500 tons. In both cases the figures for marketed production were distorted by the incidence of smuggling from Nigeria (in order to secure payment in the 'hard currency' CFA franc, rather than in the devalued naira).

The most valuable commercial crop is cotton, the production of which expanded rapidly in the mid- and late 1980s, and which now constitutes by far the most important export commodity. Benin's annual output of unginned (seed) cotton increased from 9,000 tons in 1966/67 to 50,000 tons in 1972/73, as cultivation was established in the northern areas, supported by funds from the World Bank. Output declined in subsequent years, to an annual average of around

14,000 tons in the late 1970s and early 1980s. The overall decline in cotton production was partly the result of the departure of a French cotton company and partly the result of poor marketing organization and smuggling to neighbouring countries, because of low producer prices locally. However, with new investment in this sector, including a project assisted by the International Development Association (IDA) in Zou province, output tripled between 1983/84 and 1986/87, reaching 131,262 tons in the latter year. Output was almost halved in the following year, owing to a reduction in the official price paid to producers of this crop (reflecting the fall in international prices), but resumed its expansion in subsequent years, reaching 161,594 tons in 1992/93 and an estimated 200,000 tons in 1993/94 (attributable to an increase in the area under cultivation).

Other cash crops include coffee, production of which reached 2,880 tons in 1974/75, but which has more recently fluctuated widely below 1,000 tons, and cocoa, output of which was more than 6,000 tons in 1983/84, but which was recorded at only 54 tons in 1985/86, recovering to 1,045 tons by 1988/89. These fluctuations reflect the fact that most of the recorded production is normally not from Benin but originates in Nigeria. Production of cash crops has been declining because official purchase prices have not kept up with the rise in the cost of living, and so farmers have tended to switch to subsistence food crops, or to sell their output outside official channels, on the local 'black market' or across the border in Nigeria. This situation will be corrected to the extent that the government passes on to producers the doubling in export prices in local currency, as a consequence of the devaluation of the CFA franc. In early 1994 the government gave assurances that producer prices would be increased.

Exploitation of timber resources (mainly for fuel) is still limited, though rising, with annual roundwood removals increasing from 2.05m. cu m in 1970 to an estimated 5.4m. cu m in 1992. A reafforestation programme, which was inaugurated in 1985 to counter desertification, is concentrating on fast-growing species around populated areas. Livestock farming is practised in its traditional form in the north. In 1992 cattle herds were estimated by the FAO to number 1m., there were some 2.0m. sheep and goats, while an estimated 750,000 pigs were kept, mainly in the south. The EDF has provided finance to develop animal husbandry, including a cattle-farming project in Borgou province in the south. Food supply is also supplemented by fishing (according to the FAO, the total annual catch has, in recent years, averaged a little more than 40,000 tons). The more advanced sector of fishing should grow rapidly as new investment comes into effect: two deep-sea fishing boats have been bought for the national fishing company. Meanwhile, the traditional sector is in decline, owing to salination of the lagoons from the development of the port of Cotonou.

MINING AND POWER

Although phosphates, chromium, rutile and iron ore have been located in the north, the only minerals so far exploited are limestone, marble, gold (at an artisanal level) and petroleum. Production of petroleum in Benin began in the Sémé oilfield, offshore from Cotonou, in late 1982, with initial output averaging 4,000 barrels per day (b/d). Production rose to 8,000 b/d in 1984 and 10,000 b/d in 1985, with the entry into operation of a third well and of water-injection facilities. This output exceeded Benin's domestic requirements. Development, which is estimated to have cost $120m., was largely financed by Norway, with the IDA contributing $8m. Further development began in 1984, including the drilling of five new wells and the evaluation of reserves of natural gas, at a total cost of $45m., partly financed by credits from the IDA ($18m.) and the European Investment Bank ($14m.). In 1985, however, the service and development contract was transferred from Saga Petroleum of Norway to a Swiss-based company, Pan Ocean, which undertook to raise output to 25,000 b/d. However, the project was unsuccessful; the contract was cancelled a year later, and the IDA and the European Investment Bank suspended loan finance. Production fell to 5,400 b/d in 1986 and increased to 6,200 b/d in 1987, but totalled only 3,000 b/d by mid-1988, when Ashland Exploration of the USA signed a service contract to manage the field for two years. Following remedial work, output recovered to an average of 4,500 b/d in 1988, but declined again, to 2,600 b/d by 1991. An enhanced recovery programme was then implemented, involving the deepening of three existing wells and the drilling of a further three, supported by funds from the IDA. Output increased to 3,000 b/d in 1992, and was expected to have remained at this level during 1993. The cancellation by Norway of debt totalling more than $40m. also enhanced the viability of operations.

Consumption of electricity (162.9m. kWh in 1989) was formerly almost wholly met by energy from the Akosombo hydroelectric dam in Ghana. At the beginning of 1988, however, operations began at the 62-MW hydroelectric installation on the frontier with Togo at Nangbeto, on the River Mono. This will eventually produce 150,000 kWh and thus substantially reduce Benin's reliance on imported energy. The scheme was aided by a number of foreign agencies, including the African Development Fund, the IDA, and the Kuwaiti Fund for African Economic Development, as well as France and Canada. A second dam is under construction downstream, at Adjarala, with the aim of achieving self-sufficiency in power for both Benin and Togo. Total domestic electricity generation was 5m. kWh in 1991.

MANUFACTURING

Manufacturing activity is still small-scale and, apart from the construction materials industry, is confined to the processing of primary products for export (cotton ginning, oil palm processing), or import substitution of simple consumer goods. The sector accounted for about 9% of GDP in 1991. Oil palm processing capacity, of 215,000 metric tons, is currently grossly under-utilized, but it is planned to revitalize this sector with French assistance. Conversely, cotton ginning capacity (at 78,000 tons) was inadequate during much of the 1980s; however, two additional ginning plants came into operation in 1990, increasing capacity to 120,000 tons, and construction of a further installation is planned, as part of a modernization of the Société nationale pour la promotion agricole. In 1975 the textile complex at Parakou began production, aiming primarily at the export market. Capacity is 3,000 tons, but output in 1977 was only 850 tons. A rehabilitation programme is now under way at the installation, with aid from the West African Development Bank (BOAD). Capacity is scheduled to reach 3.5m. metres of fabric and 1,254 tons of finished garments. Two joint ventures with Nigeria, planned during the 1970s, have come into operation but have proved unprofitable. The cement plant at Onigbolo began production in 1982. Plans to sell one-half of the scheduled annual output of 600,000 tons to Nigeria have yet to materialize, because of the downturn in its economy and the overcapacity that has developed in cement production in west Africa. The plant had attained a production level of only 85,000 tons per year by 1985, and the first deliveries to Nigeria were not made until mid-1988. Meanwhile, the other joint venture with Nigeria, a sugar complex at Savé, with an annual capacity of 45,000 tons, operated only intermittently following its commissioning in 1983. Production reached 7,000 tons in 1985/86, from 4,400 ha planted: it was hoped to extend cultivation to the targeted area of 5,200 ha in the 1986/87 season. However, with world sugar prices still much lower than the project's production costs, the complex remained unprofitable. Plans for a petroleum refinery, earlier postponed, have been revived, and there have been discussions with US interests concerning a proposed venture costing $900m. A private US investor has established a wire and steel mill (a similar plant is in operation in Togo) with capacity of 14,000 tons. It is hoped that output will serve both domestic and regional markets. Following President Kerekou's accession to power in 1972, there was an increasing emphasis on state participation in industry, exemplified by the nationalization of a number of private enterprises. However, the worsening in budget finances, as the economy contracted, forced the government to reconsider the desirability of maintaining the parastatal organizations (which cover a wide range of services as well as products). Through the 'privatization', rehabilitation or liquidation of these organizations, the number of parastatals was reduced from a high point of 120 to only about 40 at the time of the Soglo administration's accession to power. The process was continued, but slowed from 1993, when it became increasingly difficult to attract offers at acceptable prices for the 20 enterprises remaining to be sold.

TRANSPORT INFRASTRUCTURE

The country's transport infrastructure is comparatively good. Most internal transportation uses the country's road network, which extends over some 6,070 km (of which about 1,200 km are paved). A number of major road construction schemes, including the upgrading of the 222-km Dassa–Parakou link of the Cotonou–Niger highway, have been implemented, with financial support from the European Community (now European Union—EU), BOAD, the African Development Bank and the Arab Bank for Economic Development in Africa. Feeder roads are also being built for the marketing of agricultural products. Benin's foreign earnings benefit from the transit trade from Niger via the 579-km Benin–Niger railway; in 1987 the network handled 444,000 tons, of which approximately three-quarters was for Niger. A joint authority with Niger planned to construct an extension from Parakou to Niamey, and 164,000m. francs CFA was reserved for this purpose under the 1981–90 Development Plan; however, the project has been postponed, in view of the country's economic circumstances and strained budget resources, and the project's implementation is now only a remote possibility. France provided the funding for a 5,100m. francs CFA programme, implemented in 1987–91, for the rehabilitation of rolling stock and the overhaul of 440 km of track between Cotonou and Parakou, as well as the restructuring of the rail company's finances. The port of Cotonou has a capacity of 2m. metric tons of merchandise. Of the 1,482,350 tons handled at the port in 1991, some 438,738 tons was in transit. During the 1980s there had been a general decline in the volume handled, since congestion had eased at Nigerian ports and some transit trade from Burkina Faso and Nigeria had been transferred to Lomé, in Togo. However, the political upheaval in Togo since 1991 has resulted in the transfer to Benin of a significant part of its import-export activity, and Cotonou port handled 1,734,875 tons in 1992 (of which 383,806 tons was in transit) and was operating close to capacity in early 1993. A rehabilitation programme for the port, projected to cost 3,300m. francs CFA, has received pledges of aid from multilateral and French agencies. Among infrastructural projects currently planned is the construction of a 425-km road from Savalou (in the centre of the country) to Djougou (in the north-east), which would improve communications with Burkina Faso and Mali, and the reconstruction of the Parakou–Djougou–Natitingou road, as the first stage of the Benin–Burkina Faso–Togo highway. External finance has been obtained for these projects.

FINANCE

Budget spending rose sharply during the early 1980s, more than doubling between 1979–83, but eased noticeably in subsequent years, in response to the impact on revenues of economic recession in Nigeria and of the temporary closure of the border (customs duties account for the greater part of budgetary revenue), in conjunction with the decline in international prices for commodities and the mismanagement of parastatal organizations. In view of the continued rise in the budget deficit, which reached 7.3% of GDP (after grants equivalent to 2.5% of GDP) in 1986, a wide-ranging austerity programme was implemented in 1987, with the aim of reducing current expenditure. Public enterprises were transferred to private ownership, liquidated or rehabilitated, and public-sector salaries were initially 'frozen' (in 1987) and subsequently reduced (in 1988). Consequently, the budget deficit narrowed to 5.2% of GDP (after grants) in 1988: in that year the deficit was 46,500m. francs CFA (before grants), on total expenditure of 105,700m. francs CFA. Further retrenchment was projected for 1989, with reductions both in personnel and salaries in the civil service, together with measures to accelerate the collection of taxes. However, the political turmoil of late 1989 and early 1990 meant that revenue from taxation virtually ceased, and it was the accumulation of salary arrears that precipitated the downfall of the Kerekou regime. The budget deficit surged to 10.4% of GDP in 1989. The transitional government which assumed power in March 1990 adopted a more comprehensive approach to fiscal stabilization, and the deficit was reduced to 7.9% of GDP in 1991. However, the trend was reversed in 1992, when the ratio increased to the equivalent of 9.7% of GDP. The Soglo administration's aim was to reduce the deficit to 6.7% in 1993 and, still further, to 5% of GDP by 1975. This is to be achieved principally by means of the transfer to private ownership of further parastatal organizations, reductions in expenditure on salaries in the public sector (by cutting the number of civil servants by 8,000–10,000, or as many as 20% of the total, by 1995), and the broadening of the tax base. In support of the programme, the government of France donated 2,500m. francs CFA to assist in the payment of salary arrears, and pledged 6,500m. francs CFA in budgetary support for 1991 and 1992. The debt-relief that was agreed in December 1991 was also of benefit, by reducing government outgoings in interest on foreign aid. According to Soglo, the 1993 deficit target was broadly achieved (the ratio being 6.9% of GDP). This would appear to reflect an improvement in revenue arising from the displacement of port trade from Togo to Benin, along with a reduction in government expenditure.

Benin's fiscal difficulties were compounded by the breakdown of the banking system in 1988, when the state-owned Banque Commerciale du Bénin (the country's sole commercial bank, created in 1974 following the nationalization of all banks) collapsed as a result of protracted mismanagement and corruption. In 1989 the Banque Béninoise de Développement was obliged to close, and the Caisse Nationale de Crédit Agricole was finally wound up in 1990. This left the state with a debt of 57,000m. francs CFA to the regional central bank, the Banque centrale des états de l'Afrique de l'ouest. An important component of the structural adjustment programme that was adopted in 1989 is the rehabilitation of the banking system, with the aid of a loan of 5,000m. francs CFA from France. The state's monopoly over the sector has thus been ended; four new, foreign-owned banks have been established, and Crédit Lyonnais of France opened a subsidiary in Cotonou in 1993.

FOREIGN TRADE AND PAYMENTS

Benin has traditionally maintained a very substantial external trade deficit, with import spending usually more than twice the level of export receipts. In 1981 the trade deficit was estimated at 55,000m. francs CFA, on exports of 65,000m. francs CFA (as shown in balance-of-payments statistics). Customs returns indicate an export total that is only a small fraction of the payments figure—some 13,000m. francs CFA in 1980, compared with 47,000m.—because they do not include the substantial volume of unrecorded exports to Nigeria. In recent years export earnings have been adversely affected by the recession in Nigeria, and by the closure of the border between the two countries during 1984–86, as well as by the impact of drought upon palm products, cocoa and coffee in 1981–83, and the decline in international cotton prices in 1986 and 1987 (cotton now accounts for about two-thirds of export earnings). Exports declined sharply in 1989, to $178m.—less than one half of the 1988 level of $379m.—as political unrest paralysed the economy. The decline had been almost fully reversed by 1992, when exports reached $369m., as the economy recovered under the new administration. However, the gap between exports and imports remained massive, since the resumption in economic growth prompted an increase in the level of imports, and the trade deficit widened from $132m. in 1988 to $183m. in 1992. This trend is expected to have been reversed in 1994, as the realignment of the currency depresses imports and stimulates exports, although the deficit will remain substantial.

The deficit on foreign trade is partly met by remittances from Beninois overseas (equivalent to around one-half of export earnings) and, more significantly, by aid inflows. Disbursements of development aid by non-communist countries and agencies, which averaged some $84m. per year in the early 1980s, increased in the second half of that decade, to reach $285m. in 1990, boosted by French aid for the programme for the restructuring of the banking sector. This level was largely maintained in 1991 and 1992, with aid, averaging $290m. per year, equivalent to more than 80% of annual export earnings. In the 1970s loans from governments and multilateral agencies accounted for the major part of the external public debt ($158.4m. out of $192.2m. at the end of 1979), as Benin's radical economic policies tended to deter foreign private capital. Commercial borrowing then increased sharply in the early 1980s, to finance the oil development programme, and at the end of 1987 42% of the long-term debt was owed to private creditors. The situation was reversed again as a result of the 1989 debt-relief agreement (see below), and at the end of 1992 virtually all of Benin's medium- and long-term debt was owed to official creditors (multilateral and bilateral), with 81% on concessionary terms.

Reflecting the high concessionary element in official flows of aid, service payments on the external public debt in 1979 amounted to only 5.1% of total earnings from exports of goods and services in that year. The rise in borrowing from private sources, at much higher interest rates, caused debt-servicing payments to rise more than 10-fold by 1986, when they reached $62m. (equivalent to 13.6% of export earnings in that year). However, this represented only half the debt-servicing payments that were due in 1986, and arrears on interest continued to accrue during the following two years, to total $88m. (on the long-term debt) by the end of 1988. Arrears on repayments were also accumulating (this is reflected in the 'exceptional financing' element of Benin's balance-of-payments figures, which increased from $31.6m. in 1985 to $102.4m. in 1988), and had reached $321m. by the end of 1988. Benin was one of the 22 sub-Saharan African countries identified by the World Bank as 'debt-distressed' (those countries whose debt-service ratio would exceed 30% in 1988–90 on the basis of existing commitments), and therefore became eligible for new debt assistance schemes at the IMF. However, access to such assistance was dependent upon Benin's compliance with a structural adjustment programme agreed with, and monitored by, that body. In June 1989 the IMF approved a three-year (1989–92) structural adjustment facility of SDR 21.9m. in support of such a programme. The 'Paris Club' of Western creditor governments thereupon agreed to the rescheduling, on concessionary terms, of debt amounting to $193m. in principal and interest due to July 1990. Additionally, Benin's debt to the US government was cancelled in December 1989, and, more significantly, debts to France valued at $81m. were cancelled in November 1990. Benin's burden of debt, while still considerable, was thus eased during 1989, when debt-servicing payments declined to $26m. (representing 7.7% of the value of exports of goods and services), while arrears on interest payments were reduced to $23m. Further debt-relief was accorded in December 1991, when the 'Paris Club', recognizing the efforts of the new government to resolve the country's public-financing difficulties, undertook to reduce the debt-service burden by one-half. Creditors would either cancel 30% of outstanding debt, rescheduling the balance over 23 years (including six years' grace), or reduce interest rates so as to halve the net payments. Repayment of official development aid was to be extended over 'a very long period'. Debt-servicing payments in 1992 (when the total external debt was $1,367m.), were thus reduced to 4.4% of export earnings. There was a similar rescheduling of official debt (entailing the cancellation of one-half of the debt principal) in June 1993. Such concessions, which affect only one-quarter of the total debt, do not solve Benin's debt problem, but do relieve pressure on government finances at a time when the economic adjustment programme would otherwise have even greater consequences for employment and income within the country.

Immediately upon the devaluation of the CFA franc, in January 1994, the burden on the Beninois economy of servicing foreign debt (the value of which had doubled in local currency terms) was greatly increased. Supplementary assistance was therefore arranged (for the entire Franc Zone in Africa) by the IMF, the World Bank and the EU, and France accorded debt waivers. In the case of Benin, 600m. French francs (then equivalent to $109m.) was cancelled with immediate effect, and further reductions were expected.

Statistical Survey

Source (unless otherwise stated): Institut National de la Statistique et de l'Analyse Economique, BP 323, Cotonou; tel. 31-40-81.

Area and Population

AREA, POPULATION AND DENSITY

Area (sq km)	112,622*
Population (census results)	
20–30 March 1979	
Males	1,596,939
Females	1,734,271
Total	3,331,210
February 1992	4,855,349†
Density (per sq km) 1992 census	43.1

* 43,484 sq miles.
† Provisional.

ETHNIC GROUPS

1979 census (percentages): Fon 39.2; Yoruba 11.9; Adja 11.0; Bariba 8.5; Houeda 8.5; Peulh 5.6; Djougou 3.0; Dendi 2.1; Non-Africans 6.5; Others 1.2; Unknown 2.4.

POPULATION BY PROVINCE (1979 census)

Atakora	479,604
Atlantique	686,258
Borgou	490,669
Mono	477,378
Ouémé	626,868
Zou	570,433
Total	3,331,210

PRINCIPAL TOWNS
(estimated population at 1 July 1981)

Cotonou 383,250; Porto-Novo (capital) 144,000.
(estimate, 1989) Cotonou 350,000.

BIRTHS AND DEATHS (UN estimates, annual averages)

	1975–80	1980–85	1985–90
Birth rate (per 1,000)	49.4	49.3	49.1
Death rate (per 1,000)	23.1	21.2	19.4

Expectation of life (UN estimates, years at birth, 1985–90: 45.5 (males 43.9; females 47.1).

Source: UN, *World Population Prospects: The 1992 Revision.*

ECONOMICALLY ACTIVE POPULATION
(ILO estimates, '000 persons at mid-1980)

	Males	Females	Total
Agriculture, etc.	598	648	1,246
Industry	91	28	118
Services	218	193	410
Total	906	869	1,775

Source: ILO, *Economically Active Population Estimates and Projections, 1950–2025.*

Mid-1992 (estimates in '000): Agriculture, etc. 1,350; Total 2,268 (Source: FAO, *Production Yearbook*).

Agriculture

PRINCIPAL CROPS ('000 metric tons)

	1990	1991	1992
Rice (paddy)	11	10	9
Maize	410	431	399
Millet	22	27	25
Sorghum	99	115	104
Sweet potatoes	33	32	28
Cassava (Manioc)	937	1,046	932
Yams	1,046	1,178	1,177
Taro (Coco yam)	3	3	2*
Dry beans	48	55	50
Groundnuts (in shell)	64	74	70
Cottonseed	82	95	100*
Cotton (lint)	59	76	65†
Coconuts*	20	20	20
Palm kernels*	9.0	9.0	9.0
Tomatoes	68	72	71
Chillies and peppers (green)	13	12	12
Oranges*	12	12	12
Mangoes*	12	12	12
Bananas*	13	13	13
Pineapples*	3	3	3

* FAO estimate(s). † Unofficial figure.

Source: FAO, *Production Yearbook.*

LIVESTOCK ('000 head, year ending September)

	1990	1991	1992
Horses*	6	6	6
Asses*	1	1	1
Cattle	961	981	1,000*
Pigs	714	730*	750*
Sheep	869	893	920*
Goats	1,017	1,041	1,120†

Poultry (million)*: 25 in 1990; 25 in 1991; 25 in 1992.

* FAO estimate(s). † Unofficial figure.

Source: FAO, *Production Yearbook.*

LIVESTOCK PRODUCTS (FAO estimates, '000 metric tons)

	1990	1991	1992
Beef and veal	14	14	14
Mutton and lamb	3	3	3
Goats' meat	3	3	3
Pig meat	8	8	8
Poultry meat	30	30	30
Other meat	6	7	7
Cows' milk	16	16	16
Goats' milk	5	5	5
Hen eggs	18.0	18.0	18.0

Source: FAO, *Production Yearbook.*

Forestry

ROUNDWOOD REMOVALS
('000 cubic metres, excluding bark)

	1990	1991*	1992*
Sawlogs, veneer logs and logs for sleepers	40	60	50
Other industrial wood*	231	238	246
Fuel wood*	4,767	4,915	5,075
Total	5,038	5,213	5,371

* FAO estimates.

Source: FAO, *Yearbook of Forest Products.*

SAWNWOOD PRODUCTION ('000 cubic metres, including railway sleepers)

	1990	1991	1992
Total	14*	27	24

* FAO estimate.

Source: FAO, *Yearbook of Forest Products.*

Fishing

('000 metric tons, live weight)

	1989	1990*	1991*
Cichlids	9.2	9.0	8.8
Black catfishes	1.2	1.2	1.2
Torpedo-shaped catfishes	2.1	2.1	2.1
Other freshwater fishes	9.2	9.3	9.1
Groupers and seabasses	1.8	1.8	1.8
Threadfins and tasselfishes	1.2	1.2	1.2
Sardinellas	1.8	1.8	1.9
Bonga shad	2.5	2.5	2.4
Other marine fishes	4.9	4.8	4.9
Total fish	34.0	33.8	33.3
Freshwater crustaceans	4.1	4.1	4.0
Marine crustaceans	3.8	3.8	3.7
Total catch	41.9	41.7	41.0

* FAO estimates.

Source: FAO, *Yearbook of Fishery Statistics.*

Mining

(Provisional or estimated figures, '000 metric tons)

	1989	1990	1991
Crude petroleum	285	291	295

Source: UN, *Industrial Statistics Yearbook*.

Industry

SELECTED PRODUCTS
('000 metric tons, unless otherwise indicated)

	1989	1990	1991
Palm oil and palm kernel oil*	40	40	40
Salted, dried or smoked fish*	2.1	2.1	n.a.
Cement†	250	272	272
Electric energy (million kWh)	5	5	5

* Estimates by the FAO.
† Data from the US Bureau of Mines.
Source: UN, *Industrial Statistics Yearbook*.

Finance

CURRENCY AND EXCHANGE RATES

Monetary Units

100 centimes = 1 franc de la Communauté financière africaine (CFA).

French Franc, Sterling and Dollar Equivalents (31 March 1994)

1 French franc = 100 francs CFA;
£1 sterling = 846.40 francs CFA;
US $1 = 570.14 francs CFA;
1,000 francs CFA = £1.181 = $1.754.

Average Exchange Rate (francs CFA per US $)

1991 282.11
1992 264.69
1993 283.16

Note: An exchange rate of 1 French franc = 50 francs CFA, established in 1948, remained in force until January 1994, when the CFA franc was devalued by 50%, with the exchange rate adjusted to 1 French franc = 100 francs CFA.

BUDGET (estimates, million francs CFA)

Revenue*	1988†	1989‡	1990‡
Fiscal receipts	42,943	37,179	39,694
Taxes on income and profits	10,140	6,030	8,508
Taxes on goods and services	4,825	4,314	4,427
Taxes on international trade and transactions	21,010	24,417	20,434
Other current receipts	8,961	10,870	10,733
Capital receipts	25	17	47
Aid, grants and subsidies	—	14,700	12,334
Total	51,929	62,766	62,808

Expenditure	1988†	1989‡	1990‡
General public services	8,212	6,295	11,017
Defence	11,039	9,125	8,937
Public order and security	1,376	1,105	1,093
Education	15,701	16,116	14,839
Health	3,304	2,531	5,427
Social security and welfare	574	4,987	6,484
Housing and community services	—	—	332
Other community and social services	655	711	2,499
Economic services	4,918	6,075	25,039
Agriculture, forestry and fishing	3,289	3,286	10,119
Mining, manufacturing and construction	—	277	133
Electricity and other energy resources	—	—	4,955
Transport and communications	1,332	2,255	7,292
Other economic services	297	258	2,540
Debt-servicing	600	17,248	32,343
Other purposes	7,358	39,452	7,793
Total	53,737	103,646	115,803

* Revenue excludes borrowing from abroad: 12,500 million francs CFA in 1989; 14,218 million francs CFA in 1990.
† Administrative budget.
‡ Consolidated budget.
Source: Banque centrale des états de l'Afrique de l'ouest.

1991 (administrative budget estimates, million francs CFA): Revenue 61,500; Expenditure 109,400.
1992 (consolidated budget estimates, million francs CFA): Revenue 136,500; Expenditure 203,800.
1993 (consolidated budget estimates, million francs CFA): Budget balanced at 234,240.

Investment Budget (estimates, million francs CFA): 54,100 in 1988; 54,848 in 1989; 52,000 in 1990; 59,300 in 1992; 78,130 in 1993.

CENTRAL BANK RESERVES (US $ million at 31 December)

	1991	1992	1993
Gold*	3.9	3.8	4.1
IMF special drawing rights	0.2	—	0.1
Reserve position in IMF	2.9	2.8	2.9
Foreign exchange	188.5	242.4	241.0
Total	195.5	249.0	248.1

* Valued at market-related prices.
Source: IMF, *International Financial Statistics*.

MONEY SUPPLY ('000 million francs CFA at 31 December)

	1991	1992	1993
Currency outside banks	46.48	51.73	26.56
Demand deposit at deposit money banks	67.35	72.89	84.59
Checking deposits at post office	1.48	1.94	—
Total money (incl. others)	116.66	128.21	111.74

Source: IMF, *International Financial Statistics*.

COST OF LIVING (estimates, Consumer Price Index; base: 1985 = 100)

	1989	1990	1991
All items	73	86	89

Source: UN Economic Commission for Africa, *African Statistical Yearbook*.

NATIONAL ACCOUNTS

Composition of the Gross National Product
(million francs CFA at current prices)

	1987	1988	1989
Gross domestic product (GDP) at factor cost	430,800	451,080	465,735
Indirect taxes, *less* subsidies	38,754	31,354	21,790
GDP in purchasers' values	469,554	482,434	487,525
Net factor income from abroad	−8,600	−10,000	−12,300
Gross national product	460,954	472,434	475,225

Source: UN, *National Accounts Statistics.*

Expenditure on the Gross Domestic Product
('000 million francs CFA at current prices)

	1989	1990	1991
Government final consumption expenditure	62.3	66.1	64.3
Private final consumption expenditure	390.1	404.1	442.2
Increase in stocks	−3.1	4.0	5.0
Gross fixed capital formation	59.7	67.4	72.6
Total domestic expenditure	509.0	541.6	584.1
Exports of goods and services	87.6	102.3	118.0
Less Imports of goods and services	117.4	141.6	166.6
GDP in purchasers' values	479.2	502.3	535.5

Gross Domestic Product by Economic Activity
('000 million francs CFA at current prices)

	1989	1990	1991
Agriculture, livestock-rearing, hunting, forestry and fishing	181.4	181.2	199.0
Industry and handicrafts	42.0	44.3	45.1
Water and electricity	5.3	5.6	5.0
Construction	13.9	16.6	17.6
Trade and hotels	74.8	83.7	89.3
Transport and communications	36.6	38.2	40.3
Banking, insurance and other services	57.0	59.6	64.0
Public administration	50.2	52.3	50.6
GDP at factor cost	461.2	481.5	510.9
Indirect taxes, *less* subsidies	18.0	20.8	24.4
GDP in purchasers' values	479.2	502.3	535.5

Source: Banque centrale des états de l'Afrique de l'ouest.

BALANCE OF PAYMENTS (US $ million)

	1990	1991	1992
Merchandise exports f.o.b.	287.2	329.0	369.1
Merchandise imports f.o.b.	−427.9	−482.4	−551.6
Trade balance	−140.7	−153.5	−182.5
Exports of services	114.6	122.6	141.7
Imports of services	−135.2	−138.6	−157.2
Other income (net)	−38.9	−30.8	−63.1
Private unrequited transfers (net)	86.3	87.9	99.0
Official unrequited transfers (net)	112.4	101.7	133.0
Current balance	−1.5	−10.6	−29.1
Capital (net)	45.6	52.8	−45.2
Net errors and omissions	−34.2	19.7	0.5
Overall balance	10.0	61.8	−73.8

Source: IMF, *International Financial Statistics.*

External Trade

Source: Banque centrale des états de l'Afrique de l'ouest.

PRINCIPAL COMMODITIES (million francs CFA)

Imports c.i.f.	1987	1988	1989
Food products of animal origin	2,469	2,856	2,040
Cereals	17,954	15,825	6,808
Processed foodstuffs	3,291	3,222	2,195
Beverages and tobacco	7,971	4,643	4,688
Fuel products	7,675	13,343	10,113
Refined petroleum products	4,299	9,355	5,795
Other raw materials	4,061	4,745	2,998
Non-electrical machinery	5,120	5,478	3,486
Electrical machinery	3,789	4,239	2,251
Road transport equipment	5,202	3,454	3,812
Chemicals	5,925	7,726	4,710
Miscellaneous manufactured articles	40,375	27,048	20,326
Cotton yarn and fabrics	10,973	14,988	11,160
Total (incl. others)	104,980	97,257	66,132

Exports f.o.b.	1987	1988	1989
Processed foodstuffs	1,068	276	121
Palm products	1,421	1,663	1,468
Fuels	9,429	6,388	6,636
Cottonseed	1,164	717	1,119
Cotton (ginned)	17,903	7,725	18,681
Machinery and transport equipment	408	1,278	613
Miscellaneous manufactured articles	598	1,337	1,378
Cotton yarn and fabrics	359	189	1,008
Total (incl. others)	34,266	20,995	31,090

PRINCIPAL TRADING PARTNERS (million francs CFA)

Imports	1987	1988	1989
Belgium and Luxembourg	2,002	1,345	856
Brazil	798	1,066	481
China, People's Republic	4,253	3,667	2,498
Côte d'Ivoire	2,481	4,487	3,814
Czechoslovakia	809	1,240	1,401
France	18,493	18,786	12,357
German Democratic Republic	226	1,183	165
Germany, Federal Republic	3,924	2,739	2,507
Ghana	3,449	4,245	4,390
Ireland	188	66	1,526
Italy	3,707	2,198	8
Japan	5,894	2,265	1,806
Netherlands	7,427	5,223	5,895
Nigeria	1,851	4,296	3,181
Senegal	1,013	1,517	692
Spain	1,372	1,138	801
Thailand	14,766	11,649	3,958
Togo	1,375	2,688	2,359
USSR	526	2,352	181
United Kingdom	4,897	4,012	2,902
USA	4,124	5,117	4,804
Total (incl. others)	104,980	97,257	66,132

Exports	1987	1988	1989
Belgium and Luxembourg	364	131	551
China, People's Republic	1,983	36	3,581
France	1,298	1,536	453
Germany, Federal Republic	1,044	356	278
Italy	4,742	443	1,785
Morocco	298	105	668
Netherlands	480	159	720
Niger	207	315	460
Nigeria	2,505	2,692	1,928
Portugal	7,189	2,889	3,800
Spain	864	289	367
Switzerland	260	337	368
Taiwan	1,910	—	878
Togo	212	1,048	684
United Kingdom	1,080	991	469
USA	5,742	6,328	6,636
Total (incl. others)	34,266	20,995	31,090

Transport

RAILWAYS (traffic)

	1990	1991	1992
Passenger-km (million)	97.2	63.4	62.1
Freight ton-km (million)	148.3	162.5	238.0

Source: Banque centrale des états de l'Afrique de l'ouest.

ROAD TRAFFIC (estimates, '000 motor vehicles in use)

	1989	1990	1991
Passenger cars	27	27	27
Commercial vehicles	14	15	15

Source: UN Economic Commission for Africa, *African Statistical Yearbook*.

INTERNATIONAL SEA-BORNE SHIPPING (freight traffic at Cotonou, including goods in transit, '000 metric tons)

	1990	1991	1992
Goods loaded	124.1	145.8	246.3
Goods unloaded	995.0	1,336.6	1,488.6

Source: Banque centrale des états de l'Afrique de l'ouest.

CIVIL AVIATION (traffic on scheduled services)*

	1989	1990	1991
Kilometres flown (million)	2	2	2
Passengers carried ('000)	74	76	64
Passenger-km (million)	224	232	203
Freight ton-km (million)	18	18	16

* Including an apportionment of the traffic of Air Afrique.

Source: UN, *Statistical Yearbook*.

Tourism

	1988	1989	1990
Tourist arrivals ('000)	45	43	50
Tourist receipts (US $ million)	40	41	47

Source: UN, *Statistical Yearbook*.

Communications Media

	1989	1990	1991
Radio receivers ('000 in use)	400	415	428
Television receivers ('000 in use)	20	23	24
Telephones ('000 in use)*	25	26	27
Daily newspapers			
Number	n.a.	1	n.a.
Average circulation ('000 copies)	n.a.	12	n.a.

* Estimates.

Sources: UNESCO, *Statistical Yearbook*; UN Economic Commission for Africa, *African Statistical Yearbook*.

Education

(1988/89)

	Institutions	Teachers	Students		
			Males	Females	Total
Pre-primary	306	650	7,290	5,998	13,288
Primary	2,840	14,067	311,683	158,583	470,266
Secondary					
General	150	2,726	61,981	24,381	86,362
Vocational	42	279	3,402	2,098	5,500
Higher	16	880	7,575	1,293	8,868

Source: Ministère de l'Education Nationale, Cotonou.

1991/92: *Pre-primary* 527 teachers, 13,433 students; *Primary* (public education only) 2,952 institutions, 505,970 students; *General secondary* (public education only) 2,178 teachers, 76,672 students (males 55,309; females 21,363).

Higher (1990/91): 956 teachers, 10,873 students.

Source: UNESCO: *Statistical Yearbook*.

Directory

The Constitution

A new Constitution was approved in a national referendum on 2 December 1990.

The Constitution of the Republic of Benin guarantees the basic rights and freedoms of citizens. The functions of the principal organs of state are delineated therein.

The President of the Republic is directly elected, by universal adult suffrage, for a period of five years, renewable only once. The executive is responsible to the legislature—the Assemblée nationale—which is elected, also by direct universal suffrage, for a period of four years.

The Constitution upholds the principle of an independent judiciary, and provides for the creation of a Constitutional Council, an Economic and Social Council and a broadcasting authority, all of which are intended to counterbalance executive authority.

The Government

HEAD OF STATE

President: NICÉPHORE SOGLO (took office 4 April 1991).

COUNCIL OF MINISTERS
(August 1994)

President: NICÉPHORE SOGLO.

Minister of State, in charge of National Defence: DÉSIRÉ VIEYRA.

Minister of Foreign Affairs and Co-operation: ROBERT DOSSOU.

Minister of the Interior, Security and Territorial Administration: ALABI ANTOINE GBEGAN.

Minister of Finance: PAUL DOSSOU.

Keeper of the Seals and Minister of Justice and Legislation: PIERRE NEVI.

Minister of Planning and Economic Reorganization: ROBERT TAGNON.

Minister of National Education: KARIM DRAMANE.

Minister of Rural Development: MAMA ADAMOU N'DIAYE.

Minister in charge of Relations with the National Assembly and Spokesperson for the Government: THÉODORE HOLO.

Minister of Culture and Communications: MARIUS FRANCISCO.

Minister of Labour, Employment and Social Welfare: KAPOUE KOUMOURADE OSSEINI.

Minister of Public Works and Transport: LAZARE KPATOKPA.

Minister of the Civil Service and Administrative Reform: TIMOTHÉE ADAHUI.

Minister of Industry and Small and Medium-sized Enterprises: RIGOBERT LADIKPO.

Minister of the Environment, Housing and Town Planning: ROGER J. AHOYO.

Minister of Public Health: VÉRONIQUE LAWSON.

Minister of Energy, Mines and Water Resources: AURÉLIEN HOUESSOU.

Minister of Trade and Tourism: YACOUMO KPATASHI.

Minister of Youth and Sports: ALASSANI IDRISS.

MINISTRIES

Office of the President: BP 1288, Cotonou; tel. 30-02-28; telex 5222.

Ministry of the Civil Service and Administrative Reform: BP 907, Cotonou; tel. 31-26-18.

Ministry of Culture and Communications: BP 120, Cotonou; tel. 31-59-31; telex 5266.

Ministry of Energy, Mines and Water Resources: BP 363, Cotonou; tel. 31-45-20; fax 31-08-90.

Ministry of the Environment, Housing and Town Planning: BP 01-3621, Cotonou; tel. 31-21-00.

Ministry of Finance: BP 302, Cotonou; tel. 30-10-20.

Ministry of Foreign Affairs and Co-operation: BP 318, Cotonou; tel. 30-04-00; telex 5200.

Ministry of Industry and Small and Medium-sized Enterprises: BP 363, Cotonou; tel. 30-16-46; telex 5252.

Ministry of the Interior, Security and Territorial Administration: BP 925, Cotonou; tel. 30-10-06; telex 5065.

Ministry of Justice and Legislation: BP 967, Cotonou; tel. 31-31-46.

Ministry of Labour, Employment and Social Welfare: BP 907, Cotonou; tel. 31-31-12.

Ministry of National Defence: BP 2493, Cotonou; tel. 30-08-90.

Ministry of National Education: BP 348, Cotonou; tel. 30-06-81.

Ministry of Planning and Economic Reorganization: BP 342, Cotonou; tel. 30-05-41; telex 5118.

Ministry of Public Health: BP 882, Cotonou; tel. 33-08-70.

Ministry of Public Works and Transport: BP 372, Cotonou; tel. 31-31-06; telex 5004.

Ministry of Rural Development: BP 06-438, Cotonou; tel. 33-09-05.

Ministry of Trade and Tourism: BP 2037, Cotonou; tel. 31-54-02; telex 5040; fax 31-52-58.

Ministry of Youth and Sports: BP 03-2103, Cotonou; tel. 31-46-00; telex 5036.

Office of the Minister in charge of Relations with the National Assembly and Spokesperson for the Government: BP 04-1379, Cotonou; tel. 30-08-13.

President and Legislature

PRESIDENT

Presidential Election, First Ballot, 10 March 1991

Candidates	Votes	%
NICÉPHORE SOGLO	420,088	36.16
MATHIEU KEREKOU	317,345	27.33
ALBERT TÉVOÉDJRÉ	165,454	14.24
BRUNO AMOUSSOU	66,063	5.69
ADRIEN HOUNGBÉDJI	53,219	4.58
MOÏSE MENSAH	40,037	3.45
SÉVÉRIN ADJOVI	30,794	2.65
BERTIN BORNA	18,679	1.61
IDELPHONSE LEMON	11,559	0.99
ASSANI FASSASSI	10,402	0.90
GATIEN HOUNGBÉDJI	10,313	0.89
ROBERT DOSSOU	9,757	0.84
THOMAS GOUDOU	8,071	0.69
Total	1,161,781	100.00

Second Ballot, 24 March 1991

Candidates	%
NICÉPHORE SOGLO	67.73
MATHIEU KEREKOU	32.27
Total	100.00

ASSEMBLÉE NATIONALE

Speaker: ADRIEN HOUNGBÉDJI.

General election, 17 February 1991

	Seats
UDFP/MDPS/ULD	12
PNDD/PRD	9
PSD/UNSP	8
RND	7
MNDD/MSUP/UDRN	6
NCC	6
UDS	5
RDL-Vivoten	4
ASD/BSD	3
ADP/UDRS	2
UNDP	1
URP/PNT	1
Total	64

In total, 51.6% of the electorate voted in the general election; 1,024,485 votes were valid (96.3% of the votes cast).

Advisory Councils

Cour Constitutionnelle: Cotonou; f. 1993; seven mems (four appointed by the Assemblée nationale, three by the President of the Republic); advises on the constitutionality of all legislation: Pres. ELYZABETH KAYISSAN POGNON.

Conseil Economique et Social (ECOSOC): Cotonou; f. 1994; 30 mems, representing the executive, legislature and 'all sections of the nation'; competent to advise on proposed economic and social legislation, as well as to recommend economic and social reforms.

Political Organizations

The registration of opposition parties was legalized in August 1990. Of the 34 parties that held official status at the February 1991 general election, the following secured seats in the legislature:

The **Alliance pour la démocratie et le progrès (ADP):** Leader ADEKPEDJOU S. AKINDES; the **Alliance pour la social-démocratie (ASD):** Leader ROBERT DOSSOU; the **Bloc pour la social-démocratie (BSD):** Leader MICHEL MAGNIDÉ; the **Mouvement pour la démocratie et le progrès social (MDPS):** Leader JOSEPH MARCELLIN DEGBÉ; the **Mouvement national pour la démocratie et le développement (MNDD):** Leader BERTIN BORNA; the **Mouvement pour la solidarité, l'union et le progrès (MSUP):** Leader ADEBO ADENIYI DJAMIOU; **Notre cause commune (NCC):** Leader ALBERT TÉVOÉDJRÉ; the **Parti national pour la démocratie et le développement (PNDD):** Leader JOSEPH COPIERY; the **Parti national du travail (PNT):** Leader INOUSSA BELLO; the **Parti du renouveau démocratique (PRD):** Leader ADRIEN HOUNGBÉDJI; the **Parti social-démocrate (PSD):** Leader BRUNO AMOUSSOU; the **Rassemblement des démocrates libéraux pour la reconstruction nationale (RDL-Vivoten):** Leader SÉVÉRIN ADJOVI; the **Rassemblement national pour la démocratie (RND):** Leader JOSEPH ADJIGNON KÉKÉ; the **Union pour la démocratie et la reconstruction nationale (UDRN):** Leader AZARIA FAKORÉDÉ; the **Union pour la démocratie et la solidarité nationale (UDS):** Leader ADAMOU N'DIAYE MAMA; the **Union démocratique des forces du progrès (UDFP):** Leader TIMOTHÉE ADANLIN; the **Union démocratique pour le renouveau social (UDRS):** Leader DENI AMOUSSOU-YÉYÉ; the **Union pour la liberté et le développement (ULD):** Leader MARIUS FRANCISCO; the **Union nationale pour la démocratie et le progrès (UNDP):** Leader Dr EMILE DERLIN ZINSOU; the **Union nationale pour la solidarité et le progrès (UNSP):** Leader EUSTACHE SARRE; and the **Union républicaine du peuple (URP):** Leader MICHEL BAMENOU TOKO.

The **Union des forces du progrès (UFP)**, led by MACHIOUDI DISSOU and established in May 1990 as the successor to the former ruling Parti de la révolution populaire du Bénin, failed to win seats in the legislature. Numerous other parties have been created since 1991, including the **Parti de la renaissance du Bénin**, led by President NICÉPHORE SOGLO.

The **Parti communiste du Bénin** (successor to the banned Parti communiste dahoméen), led by PASCAL FATONDJI, obtained legal status in 1993.

Diplomatic Representation

EMBASSIES IN BENIN

Chad: BP 080359, Cotonou; tel. 33-08-51; Chargé d'affaires a.i.: DARKOU AHMAT KALABASSOU.

China, People's Republic: BP 196, Cotonou; tel. 30-12-92; Ambassador: ZHAO HUIMIN.

Cuba: BP 948, Cotonou; tel. 31-52-97; telex 5277; Ambassador: EVANGELIO MONTERO HERNÁNDEZ.

Egypt: BP 1215, Cotonou; tel. 30-08-42; telex 5274; Ambassador: FAYEZ SALEH BICTACHE.

France: route de l'Aviation, BP 966, Cotonou; tel. 30-08-24; telex 5209; Ambassador: JEAN-PAUL TAÏX.

Germany: 7 route Inter-Etats, BP 504, Cotonou; tel. 31-29-67; telex 5224; Ambassador: ULRICH HOCHSCHILDT.

Ghana: Les Cocotiers, BP 488, Cotonou; tel. 30-07-46; Ambassador: CHRISTIAN T. K. QUARSHIE.

Korea, Democratic People's Republic: BP 317, Cotonou; tel. 30-10-97; Ambassador: PAIK HEUNG.

Libya: Les Cocotiers, BP 405, Cotonou; tel. 30-04-52; telex 5254; People's Bureau Representative: SANOUSSI AWAD ABDALLAH.

Niger: derrière Hôtel de la Plage, BP 352, Cotonou; tel. 31-56-65; Chargé d'affaires a.i.: SOUMANA AMINATA.

Nigeria: blvd de France Marina, BP 2019, Cotonou; tel. 30-11-42; telex 5247; Chargé d'affaires a.i.: EBENEZER A. ADIGUN.

Russia: BP 2013, Cotonou; tel. 31-28-34; telex 9725008; fax 31-28-35; Ambassador: YURI TCHEPIK.

USA: rue Caporal Anani Bernard, BP 2012, Cotonou; tel. 30-17-92; fax 30-19-74; Ambassador: RUTH A. DAVIS.

Zaire: BP 130, Cotonou; Ambassador: TATU LONGWA.

Judicial System

The Constitution of December 1990 establishes the judiciary as an organ of state whose authority may counterbalance that of the executive and of the legislature. There is provision for a Constitutional Court (see Advisory Councils, above), a High Court of Justice and a Supreme Court.

President of the Supreme Court: FRÉDÉRIC NOUTAI HOUNDETON.

Religion

Some 65% of the population hold animist beliefs; about 20% are Christians (mainly Roman Catholics) and 15% Muslims. Religious and spiritual cults, which were discouraged under the Kerekou regime, re-emerged as a prominent force in Beninois society during the early 1990s.

CHRISTIANITY

The Roman Catholic Church

Benin comprises one archdiocese and five dioceses. At 31 December 1992 there were an estimated 1,136,688 Roman Catholics (about 21.4% of the population), mainly in the south of the country.

Bishops' Conference: Conférence Episcopale du Bénin, Archevêché, BP 491, Cotonou; tel. 30-01-45; fax 30-07-07; Pres. Rt Rev. LUCIEN MONSI-AGBOKA, Bishop of Abomey.

Archbishop of Cotonou: Most Rev. ISIDORE DE SOUZA, Archevêché, BP 491, Cotonou; tel. 30-01-45; fax 30-07-07.

Protestant Church

There are 257 Protestant mission centres, with a personnel of about 120.

Eglise protestante méthodiste en République du Bénin: 54 ave Sékou Touré, Carré 206, BP 34, Cotonou; tel. 31-25-20; f. 1843; 62,000 mems (1985); Pres. Rev. Dr MOÏSE SAGBOHAN; Sec. Rev. SAMUEL J. DOSSOU.

The Press

In 1994 more than 50 newspapers and magazines were being published in Benin.

La Croix du Bénin: BP 105, Cotonou; tel. 32-11-19; f. 1946; fortnightly; Roman Catholic; Dir BARTHÉLEMY CAKPO ASSOGBA.

FLASH-HEBDO: BP 120, Cotonou; tel. 30-18-57; weekly; Dir PASCAL ADISSODA.

Le Forum de la Semaine: BP 04-0391, Cotonou; tel. 30-03-40; weekly; Dir BRUNO SODEHOU.

La Gazette du Golfe: Carré 961 'J' Etoile Rouge, BP 03-1624, Cotonou; tel. 31-35-58; telex 5053; fax 30-01-99; f. 1987; weekly; Dir ISMAËL Y. SOUMANOU; Editor KARIM OKANLA; circ. national edn 18,000, international edn 15,000.

Initiatives: BP 2093, Cotonou; tel. 31-44-47; six a year; Dir THÉOPHILE CAPO-CHICHI.

Journal Officiel de la République du Bénin: BP 59, Porto-Novo; tel. 21-39-77; f. 1890; official govt bulletin; fortnightly; Dir AFIZE D. ADAMON.

La Lumière de l'Islam: BP 08-0430, Cotonou; tel. 31-34-59; fortnightly; Dir MOHAMED BACHIR SOUMANOU.

Le Matin: Cotonou; f. 1994; daily; Dir SAID SAHNOUN.

La Nation: BP 1210, Cotonou; tel. 30-08-75; f. 1990 to replace *Ehuzu* as official newspaper; daily; Dir AKUETE ASSCOI.

L'Observateur: Cotonou; fortnightly; Dir FRANÇOIS COMLAN.

Le Patriote: BP 2093, Cotonou; tel. 31-44-47; monthly; Dir CALIXTE DA SILVA.

Le Pays: BP 06-2170, Cotonou; tel. 33-10-09; fortnightly; Dir ENOCK YAKA.

La Récade: BP 08-0086, Cotonou; tel. 33-11-15; monthly; Dir TITOMAS MEGNASSAN.

La Sentinelle: BP 34, Cotonou; tel. 31-25-20; monthly; Dir MICHÉE D. AHOUANDJINOU.

Le Soleil: Cotonou; tel. 30-14-90; fortnightly; Dir EDGARD KAHO.

Tam-Tam-Express: BP 2302, Cotonou; tel. and fax 30-12-05; f. 1988; fortnightly; Dir DENIS HODONOU; circ. 15,000.

L'Union: BP 04-1416, Cotonou; tel. 31-55-05; fortnightly; Dir PAUL HERVÉ D'ALMEIDA.

NEWS AGENCIES

Agence Bénin-Presse (ABP): BP 72, Cotonou; tel. 31-26-55; telex 5221; f. 1961; national news agency; section of the Ministry of Culture and Communications; Dir BONIFACE AGUEH.

Foreign Bureaux

Agence France-Presse (AFP): BP 06-1382, Cotonou; tel. 33-24-02; Correspondent VIRGILE C. AHISSOU.

Reuters (UK): Cotonou; tel. 33-16-33; Correspondent ALI IDRISSOU TOURÉ.

Publishers

Imprimerie Industrielle Nouvelle Presse: Cotonou; tel. 33-10-09; telex 1110.

Government Publishing House

Office National d'Edition, de Presse et d'Imprimerie (ONEPI): BP 1210, Cotonou; tel. 30-08-75; f. 1975; Dir-Gen. BONI ZIMÉ MAKO.

Radio and Television

In 1991, according to UNESCO, there were an estimated 428,000 radio receivers and 24,000 television receivers in use.

Office de Radiodiffusion et de Télévision du Bénin: BP 366, Cotonou; tel. 30-10-96; telex 5132; state-owned; radio programmes broadcast from Cotonou and Parakou in French, English and 18 local languages; TV transmissions 25 hours weekly; Dir-Gen. NICOLAS BENON; Dir of Radio EMILE DÉSIRÉ OLOGODOU; Dir of TV MICHÈLE BADAROU.

Finance

(cap. = capital; res = reserves; m. = million; br. = branch; amounts in francs CFA)

BANKING

Central Bank

Banque Centrale des Etats de l'Afrique de l'Ouest (BCEAO): ave d'Ornano, Zone Portuaire, BP 325, Cotonou; tel. 31-24-66; telex 5211; fax 31-24-65; headquarters in Dakar, Senegal; f. 1955; bank of issue for the seven states of the Union monétaire ouest-africaine (UMOA), comprising Benin, Burkina Faso, Côte d'Ivoire, Mali, Niger, Senegal and Togo; cap. and res 379,881m. (Sept. 1992); Gov. CHARLES KONAN BANNY; Dir in Benin PAULIN COSSI; br. at Parakou.

Commercial Banks

Bank of Africa–Bénin: blvd Jean-Paul II, BP 08-0879, Cotonou; tel. 31-32-28; telex 5079; fax 31-31-71; f. 1990; 58% owned by private Beninois interests, 24% by African Financial Holding; cap. 1,500m. (Sept. 1993; Pres. FRANÇOIS TANKPINOU; Man. Dir PAUL DERREUMAUX.

Banque Internationale du Bénin (BIBE): ave Pape Jean-Paul II, BP 03-2098, Cotonou; tel. 31-55-49; telex 5075; fax 31-27-07; f. 1989; 70% owned by Nigerian commercial banks and private investors, 30% by private Beninois interests; cap. 1,000m. (Sept. 1992); Pres. Chief JOSEPH OLADELI SANUSI; Man. Dir OLADÉLÉ ADEBOLU.

Crédit Lyonnais Bénin: carrefour des 3 Banques, route Inter-Etats, BP 2020, Cotonou; tel. 31-24-24; telex 5151; fax 31-51-77; f. 1992, operations commenced 1993; wholly-owned subsidiary of Crédit Lyonnais, SA (France); cap. 1,000m.; Pres. DANIEL CHOQUART; Man. Dir MARC BRUAND.

Ecobank–Bénin SA: rue du Gouverneur Bayol, BP 1280, Cotonou; tel. 31-40-23; telex 5394; fax 31-33-85; f. 1989; 70% owned by Ecobank Transnational Inc (operating in asscn with ECOWAS), 30% by private Beninois interests; cap. 1,500m. (Sept. 1993); Pres. MAHENTA BIRIMA FALL; Man. Dir RIZWAN HAIDER; 2 brs.

Financial Bank: Immeuble Adjibi, rue du Commandant Decoeur, BP 2700, Cotonou; tel. 31-31-00; telex 5280; fax 31-31-02; f. 1988; 99% owned by Financial BC (Switzerland); cap. 1,000m. (Sept. 1992); Pres. CHARLES BAYSSET; Dir-Gen. JACKY VASSEUR; 3 brs.

Financial Institution

Caisse Autonome d'Amortissement du Bénin: BP 59, Cotonou; tel. 31-42-61; telex 5289; manages state funds; Man. Dir OKE-TOKUN GAFARIOU.

INSURANCE

Société Nationale d'Assurances et de Réassurance (SONAR): Lot 11, Les Cocotiers, BP 2030, Cotonou; tel. 30-16-49; telex 5231; fax 30-09-84; f. 1974; state-owned; cap. 300m.; Pres. ANTOINE URSULE CAKPO; Man. Dir INOUSSA BOUKARI-YABARA.

Trade and Industry

DEVELOPMENT ORGANIZATIONS

Caisse Française de Développement (CFD): blvd JEAN-PAUL II, BP 38, Cotonou; tel. 31-35-80; telex 5082; fax 31-20-18; f. 1992 to succeed the Caisse Centrale de Coopération Economique; Dir HENRI PHILIPPE DE CLERCQ.

Mission de Coopération et d'Action Culturelle (Mission Française d'Aide et de Coopération): BP 476, Cotonou; tel. 30-08-24; telex 5209; centre for administering bilateral aid from France according to the co-operation agreement of Feb. 1975; Dir BERNARD HADJADJ.

STATE MARKETING BOARDS AND ENTERPRISES

Office National du Bois (ONAB): BP 1238, Cotonou; tel. 33-16-32; telex 5160; f. 1983; forest development and management, manufacture and marketing of wood products; cap. 300m. francs CFA; transfer of industrial activities to private ownership pending in 1994; Man. Dir GABRIEL LOKOUN.

Société Béninoise d'Electricité et d'Eau (SBEE): BP 123, Cotonou; tel. 31-21-45; telex 5213; fax 31-50-28; f. 1973; cap. 3,000m. francs CFA; state-owned; produces and distributes electricity and water; Man. Dir PHILIPPE HOUNKPATIN.

Société des Ciments d'Onigbolo (SCO): Onigbolo; f. 1975; cap. 6,000m. francs CFA; 51% state-owned, 43% owned by Govt of Nigeria; produces and markets cement; Pres. JUSTIN GNIDEHOU; Man. Dir NESTOR ROKO.

Société Nationale de Commercialisation des Produits Pétroliers (SONACOP): ave d'Ornano, BP 245, Cotonou; tel. 31-22-90; telex 5245; f. 1974; cap. 1,500m. francs CFA; state-owned; imports and distributes petroleum products; Pres. PATRICE NADJO; Man. Dir EDMOND-PIERRE AMOUSSOU.

Société Nationale pour l'Industrie des Corps Gras (SONICOG): BP 312, Cotonou; tel. 33-07-01; telex 5205; fax 33-15-20; f. 1962; cap. 2,555m. francs CFA; state-owned; processes sheanuts (karité nuts), palm kernels and cottonseed; Man. Dir JOSEPH GABIN DOSSOU.

Société Nationale pour la Promotion Agricole (SONAPRA): BP 933, Cotonou; tel. 33-08-20; telex 5248; fax 33-19-48; f. 1983; cap. 500m. francs CFA; state-owned; manages five cotton-ginning plants and one fertilizer plant; distributes fertilizers and markets agricultural products; Pres. IMOROU SALLEY; Man. Dir MICHEL DASSI.

CHAMBER OF COMMERCE

Chambre de Commerce, d'Agriculture et d'Industrie de la République du Bénin (CCIB): ave du Général de Gaulle, BP 31, Cotonou; tel. 31-32-99; Pres. RAFFET LOKO; Sec.-Gen. N. A. VIADENOU.

EMPLOYERS' ORGANIZATIONS

Association des Syndicats du Bénin (ASYNBA): Cotonou; Pres. PIERRE FOURN.

Conseil Nationale des Chargeurs du Bénin (CNCB): carré no 114, Zone Industrielle d'Akpakpa PK3, BP 06-2528, Cotonou; tel. 33-13-71; telex 5023; fax 33-18-49; Pres. FIDELIA AZODOGBEHOU.

Groupement Interprofessionnel des Entreprises du Bénin (GIBA): BP 6, Cotonou; Pres. A. JEUKENS.

Syndicat des Commerçants Importateurs et Exportateurs du Bénin: BP 6, Cotonou; Pres. M. BENCHIMOL.

Syndicat Interprofessionnel des Entreprises Industrielles du Bénin: Cotonou; Pres. M. DOUCET.

Syndicat National des Commerçants et Industriels Africains du Bénin (SYNACIB): BP 367, Cotonou; Pres. URBAIN DA SILVA.

Syndicat des Transporteurs Routiers du Bénin: Cotonou; Pres. PASCAL ZENON.

MAJOR INDUSTRIAL COMPANIES

The following are among the largest companies in terms of either capital investment or employment.

CFAO Bénin: ave Pierre Delorme, BP 7, Cotonou; tel. 31-34-61; fax 31-34-63; f. 1973; cap. 963.4m. francs CFA; import-export co, mfrs of bicycles and mopeds; Pres. and Man. Dir EMMANUEL KOUTON.

Communauté Electrique de Bénin (CEB): BP 385, Cotonou; see under Togo.

Complexe Textile du Bénin SA (COTEB): BP 231, Parakou; tel. 61-09-49; fax 61-11-99; production of textiles and garments; Dir-Gen. D. LENAERTS.

Grands Moulins du Bénin (GMB): Zone Industrielle d'Akpakpa, BP 949, Cotonou; tel. 33-08-17; telex 5267; f. 1971; cap. 438m. francs CFA; Lebanese shareholders hold majority interest; wheat-milling; Man. Dir GILBERT CHAGOURY-RAMEZ.

Société Béninoise de Brasserie (SOBEBRA): route de Porto-Novo, BP 135, Cotonou; tel. 33-10-61; telex 5275; fax 33-01-48; f. 1957, nationalized 1975–91 (as Société Nationale de Boissons); cap. 3,200m. francs CFA; production and marketing of beer, soft drinks and ice; Pres. BARNABÉ BIDOUZO; Man. Dir ANDRÉ FONTANA.

Société Béninoise de Sidérurgie (SBS): Cotonou; f. 1989; operates a wire and steel mill; Chair. JOHN MOORE.

Société Béninoise des Tabacs et Allumettes du Bénin (SOBETA): BP 07, Ouidah; tel. 34-13-04; fax 34-13-23; f. 1984 as Manufacture de Cigarettes et d'Allumettes de Ouidah owned by Rothmans International PLC (UK); mfrs of tobacco products and matches; Pres. SÉFOU FAGBOHOUN; Man. Dir ERIC PACITTI.

Société Béninoise des Textiles (SOBETEX): BP 208, Cotonou; tel. 33-09-16; telex 5239; f. 1968; cap. 500m. francs CFA; 49% state-owned; bleaching, printing and dyeing of imported fabrics; Pres. FRANÇOIS VRINAT; Man. Dir ALBERT CHAMBOST.

Société Sucrière de Savé (SSR): BP 7093, Savé; f. 1975; cap. 7,500m. francs CFA; 49% state-owned, 46% owned by Govt of Nigeria; transfer to private ownership was scheduled for 1993; operates of an agro-industrial sugar complex at Savé; Man. Dir CYPRIEN SOUWIN AHOUANSOU.

TRADE UNIONS

Confédération Générale du Travail (CGT): Leader: PASCAL TODJENOU.

Confédération des Syndicats Autonomes du Bénin (CSAB): Cotonou; First Sec. ALBERT GOUGAN.

Syndicat National de l'Enseignement Supérieur (SNES): Cotonou; withdrew from UNSTB in Aug. 1989; Sec.-Gen. LÉOPOLD DOSSOU.

Union Nationale des Syndicats des Travailleurs du Bénin (UNSTB): BP 69, Cotonou; tel. 31-56-13; telex 5200; f. 1974 as the sole officially-recognized trade union, incorporating all pre-existing trade union organizations; severed links with the then ruling party in Oct. 1989; Sec.-Gen. AMIDOU LAWANI.

Other autonomous labour organizations participating in industrial action in early 1994 included the **Collectif des Syndicats Indépendants**, the **Confédération Générale des Travailleurs du Bénin** and the **Confédération des Syndicats des Travailleurs du Bénin**.

Transport

RAILWAYS

In 1987 the network handled 444,000 metric tons of goods. Plans for a 650-km extension, linking Parakou to Niamey (Niger), via Gaya, were postponed in the late 1980s, owing to lack of finance.

Organisation Commune Bénin-Niger des Chemins de Fer et des Transports (OCBN): BP 16, Cotonou; tel. 31-33-80; telex 5210; fax 31-41-50; f. 1959; 50% owned by Govt of Benin, 50% by Govt of Niger; total of 579 track-km; main line runs for 438 km from Cotonou to Parakou in the interior; br. line runs westward via Ouidah to Sègboroué (34 km); also line of 107 km from Cotonou via Porto-Novo to Pobè near the Nigerian border; Man. Dir ISAAC ENIDÉ KILANYOSSI.

ROADS

In 1992 there were 6,070 km of classified roads, of which 3,440 km were main roads. About 20% of the network was paved. The reconstruction of the road linking Parakou with Djougou and Natitingou, with financial aid from multilateral agencies, was to begin in 1991. The road is the first phase of a highway that is intended ultimately to link Benin with Burkina Faso and Togo.

Compagnie de Transit et de Consignation du Bénin (CTCB Express): route de l'Aéroport, BP 7079, Cotonou; f. 1986; Pres. SOULÉMAN KOURA ZOUMAROU.

SHIPPING

The main port is at Cotonou. In 1992 the port handled 1,734,875 metric tons of goods, of which 383,806 tons was in transit. The port's capacity is 2m. tons per year. Development of a terminal at Cotonou, capable of landing 6,500 containers, began in 1994.

Port Autonome de Cotonou: BP 927, Cotonou; tel. 31-28-90; telex 5004; fax 31-28-91; f. 1965; state-owned; Man. Dir ISSA BADAROU SOULÉ.

Association pour Défendre les Intérêts du Port Autonome de Cotonou (AIPC): Cotonou; f. 1993 to promote port activities; Pres. ISSA BADAROU SOULÉ.

Association des Professionnels Agréés en Douanes du Bénin (APRAD): BP 2141, Cotonou; tel. 31-55-05; telex 5355; Chair. GATIEN HOUNGBÉDJI.

Cie Béninoise de Navigation Maritime (COBENAM): BP 2032, Cotonou; tel. 31-27-96; telex 5225; f. 1974; 51% state-owned, 49% by Govt of Algeria; Pres. ABDER KADER ALLAL; Man. Dir PIERRE MEVI.

Delmas—Bénin: route du Collège de l'Union, BP 213, Cotonou; tel. 33-11-78; telex 5308; fax 33-16-78; f. 1986; Pres. ANTOINE HORVATH; Dir ALEXIS AHOUANSOU.

Société Béninoise des Manutentions Portuaires (SOBEMAP): place des Martyrs, BP 35, Cotonou; tel. 31-39-83; telex 5135; state-owned; Pres. GEORGES SEKLOKA; Man. Dir THÉODORE AHOUMÉNOU AHOUASSOU.

CIVIL AVIATION

The international airport at Cotonou has a 2.4-km runway, and there are secondary airports at Parakou, Natitingou, Kandi and Abomey.

Air Afrique: ave du Gouverneur Ballot, BP 200, Cotonou; tel. 31-21-07; fax 31-53-41; see under Côte d'Ivoire; Dir in Benin JOSEPH KANZA.

Bénin Inter-Régional: Cotonou; f. 1991 as a jt venture by private Beninois interests and Aeroflot (then the state airline of the USSR); operates domestic and regional flights.

Tourism

Benin's national parks and game reserves are its principal tourist attractions. About 50,000 tourists visited Benin in 1990.

Conseil National du Tourisme: Cotonou; f. 1993.

Defence

A major restructuring of the armed forces took place in 1990. At the time of the reorganization, according to official figures, the army numbered 3,800, the air force 350, the navy 200 (officially reduced to about 150 by June 1993) and the gendarmerie 2,000. However, it was later revealed that the number of armed forces personnel in fact totalled some 12,000. France was expected to support plans for a reduction in the size of the Beninois armed forces (initially by 800 men) during the early 1990s.

Defence Expenditure: Estimated at 7,200m. francs CFA in 1992.

Chief of Staff: Col SÉRAPHIN NOUKPO.

Education

Primary education, which is officially compulsory, begins at six years of age and lasts for six years. Secondary education, beginning at 12 years of age, lasts for up to seven years, comprising a first cycle of four years and a second of three years. In 1989 only 45% of children in the relevant age-group were enrolled at primary schools (60% of boys; 31% of girls); primary enrolment in 1991 was equivalent to 66% of children in the appropriate age-group. Enrolment at secondary schools in 1991 was equivalent to only 12% (17% of boys; 7% of girls). The University of Benin was founded at Cotonou in 1970; there were some 13,000 students registered in 1993/94. In 1990, according to UNESCO estimates, the average rate of adult illiteracy was 76.6% (males 68.3%; females 84.4%).

Consolidated budget estimates for 1990 allocated 14,839m. francs CFA to the education sector (12.8% of central government expenditure).

Bibliography

Allen, C., Radu, M. S., and Somerville, K., (Eds). *Benin, The Congo, Burkina Faso: Economics, Politics and Society.* New York and London, Pinter Publishers, Marxist Regimes Series, 1989.

Cornevin, R. *La République populaire du Bénin, des Origines dahoméennes à nos jours.* Paris, Académie des Sciences d'Outre-mer, 1984.

Le Dahomey. Paris, Presses universitaires de France, 1965.

Histoire du Dahomey. Paris, Berger-Levrault, 1962; new edn as *Histoire du Bénin.* Paris, Maisonneuve et Larose.

Decalo, S. *Historical Dictionary of Dahomey.* Metuchen, NJ, Scarecrow Press, 1975; new edn as *Historical Dictionary of Benin*, 1988.

Dunn, J. (Ed.). *West African States: Failure and Promise.* Cambridge University Press, 1978.

Garcia, L. *Le royaume du Dahomé face à la pénétration coloniale.* Paris, Editions Karthala, 1988.

Harrison Church, R. J. *West Africa.* 8th Edn, London, Longman, 1979.

Journaux, A., Pélissier, P., and Parisse, R. *Géographie du Dahomey.* Caen, Imprimerie Ozanne, 1962.

Lusignan, G. de. *French-Speaking Africa since Independence.* London, Pall Mall, 1969.

Manning, P. *Slavery, Colonialism and Economic Growth in Dahomey, 1640–1960.* Cambridge, Cambridge University Press, 1982.

Medeiros, F. de. *Peuples du golfe du Bénin (Aja-Ewé).* Paris, Editions Karthala, 1984.

Rimmer, D. *The Economies of West Africa.* London, Weidenfeld and Nicolson, 1984.

BOTSWANA

Physical and Social Geography

A. MACGREGOR HUTCHESON

PHYSICAL FEATURES

The Republic of Botswana is a land-locked country, bordered by Namibia to the west and north, by the latter's Caprivi Strip to the north, by Zimbabwe to the north-east, and by South Africa to the south and south-east. Botswana occupies 582,000 sq km (224,711 sq miles) of the downwarped Kalahari Basin of the great southern African plateau, which has here an average altitude of 900 m above sea-level. Gentle undulations to flat surfaces, consisting of Kalahari sands overlying Archean rocks, are characteristic of most of the country but the east is more hilly and broken. Most of southern Botswana is without surface drainage and, apart from the bordering Limpopo and Chobe rivers, the rest of the country's drainage is interior and does not reach the sea. Flowing into the north-west from the Angolan highlands, the perennial Okavango river is Botswana's major system. The Okavango drains into a depression in the plateau, 145 km from the border, to form the Okavango swamps and the ephemeral Lake Ngami. From this vast marsh covering 16,000 sq km there is a seasonal flow of water eastwards along the Botletle river 260 km to Lake Xau and thence into the Makarakari salt pan. Most of the water brought into Botswana by the Okavango is lost through evaporation and transpiration in the swamps.

The Kalahari Desert dominates southern and western Botswana. From the near-desert conditions of the extreme south-west with an average annual rainfall around 130 mm, there is a gradual increase in precipitation towards the north (635 mm) and east (380–500 mm). There is an associated transition in the natural vegetation from the sparse thornveld of the Kalahari Desert to the dry woodland savannah of the north and east, and the infertile sands give way eastwards to better soils developed on granitic and sedimentary rocks.

POPULATION AND RESOURCES

The eastern strip, the best-endowed and most developed region of Botswana, possesses about 80% of the population, which was enumerated at 1,326,796 by the census of August 1991. Seven of the eight Batswana tribes, and most of the Europeans and Asians, are concentrated in the east. A substantial number of Batswana (the figure is unrecorded but estimated to be at least 50,000) are employed in South Africa, many of them (more than 20,000 in 1987) in mining. The absence of these workers helps to ease pressure on resources and contributes to the country's income through deferred pay and remittances sent home to their families. However, as a result of the rapid population growth, and since a large proportion of the population is less than 15 years of age, there is a pressing need for improvements in agricultural productivity and in other sectors of the economy to provide work for the growing number of young people who are entering the labour market.

Shortage of water, resulting from the low annual rainfall and aggravated by considerable fluctuations in the monthly distribution and total seasonal rainfall, is the main hindrance to the development of Botswana's natural resources, although a number of projects have improved water supply to the main centres of economic activity. Limitations imposed by rainfall make much of the country more suitable for the rearing of livestock, especially cattle, but it has been estimated that in eastern Botswana 4.45m. ha are suitable for cultivation, of which only about 10% is actually cultivated. Although in the east the irrigation potential is limited, the Okavango-Chobe swamps offer substantial scope for irrigation (as much as an estimated 600,000 ha).

In recent years Botswana's economic base has been considerably widened. Exploitable deposits of diamonds, gold, uranium, copper, nickel, coal, manganese, asbestos, common salt, potash, soda ash and sodium sulphate have been proved (some are already being mined) and the search for further minerals is continuing. In particular, the major developments of diamond mining at Orapa, Letlhakane and Jwaneng, and copper-nickel mining focused on Selebi-Phikwe, with their attendant infrastructural improvements, are helping to diversify the predominantly agricultural economy.

Recent History

RICHARD BROWN

The political history of Botswana (known as Bechuanaland until its independence in 1966) has been influenced by three main factors: the country's geographical position, adjoining the formerly white-ruled South Africa, Namibia and Zimbabwe; the absence of a significant African nationalist movement before independence; and the strong allegiances between the eight main tribal groups.

In 1885 the British government declared Bechuanaland a protectorate, at the request of local rulers who wished to deter encroachment by Boers from the Transvaal. The British assumed that Bechuanaland would eventually be absorbed into the Union of South Africa, but this was resolutely opposed by the indigenous population, particularly after the introduction of apartheid by South Africa in 1948. In 1950 the British administration approved the formation of a joint advisory council, and elections to a legislative council took place in 1961: Bechuanaland's 3,200 white inhabitants were represented by 10 elected members, while a further 10 were indirectly elected to represent the 317,000 Africans.

In 1960 the Bechuanaland People's Party (BPP) was founded, maintaining close links with the African National Congress of South Africa (ANC). The BPP soon split into two factions, which later became the Botswana Independence Party (BIP) and the more important Botswana People's Party (BPP). In 1961 Seretse (later Sir Seretse) Khama, the former heir to the chieftainship of the important Bamangwato tribe (who had been forced to renounce the chieftainship in 1956, by pressure from the British, South African and Southern Rhodesian governments, after he had married a white woman), gained a seat on the legislative council, and was also appointed to the territory's executive council.

In 1962 Khama formed the Bechuanaland Democratic Party (BDP), securing the support of 10 of the African members of the legislative council. Many whites also gave their support to the BDP, in preference to the more militant BPP. In the territory's first direct election, held in March 1965 (in accordance with a pre-independence constitution which granted internal self-government), the BDP won 28 of the 31 seats in a new legislative assembly, chosen by universal adult suffrage. Khama duly became prime minister. Independence was achieved on 30 September 1966, when Bechuanaland became the Republic of Botswana, with Khama as president.

During the years following independence, the BDP (restyled the Botswana Democratic Party) encountered electoral challenges from the BPP (particularly in the towns) and from a new party of Marxist orientation, the Botswana National Front (BNF), both of which won small numbers of parliamentary seats in the 1969, 1974 and 1979 general elections. The BDP nevertheless remained by far the most strongly represented party in the legislature. Khama's government significantly reduced the powers of the tribal chiefs, including their traditional rights to allocate land and to control mineral concessions.

Following the unilateral declaration of independence by Rhodesia (now Zimbabwe) in 1965, President Khama denounced the illegal regime; however, he was unable to enforce strict economic sanctions against Rhodesia, owing to Botswana's dependence on the Rhodesian-owned railways for its economic survival. During the 1970s Botswana, with the other 'front-line' states (Angola, Mozambique, Tanzania and Zambia), declared support for the nationalist Patriotic Front in Rhodesia, and allowed sanctuary and passage for nationalist guerrillas, although they were not permitted to establish military bases in Botswana. Zimbabwe's achievement of independence in April 1980 brought considerable economic benefits to Botswana. Botswana was a founder member of the Southern African Development Co-ordination Conference (SADCC), which first met in 1979, with the aim of encouraging regional development and reducing members' economic dependence on South Africa. (The SADCC was superseded by the Southern African Development Community—SADC—in 1992.)

BOTSWANA UNDER MASIRE

Internal Developments

On his death in 1980, Sir Seretse Khama was succeeded by Dr Quett Masire (later Sir Ketumile Masire), a founder of the BDP and hitherto the vice-president, who was elected by secret ballot in the national assembly on 18 July 1980 and subsequently confirmed as president by the legislature. Masire, who had served for several years as minister of finance and development planning, had played a pivotal role in the country's economic development.

Masire's presidency was renewed in September 1984, when, in a general election to the national assembly, the BDP again won a decisive victory, originally gaining 29 of the 34 elective seats in an enlarged chamber. The 1984 election was contested by the six registered political parties, and 78% of the electorate voted. The BNF originally won four of the elective seats; the party's leader, Kenneth Koma, initially failed to gain a seat, losing to the vice-president, Peter Mmusi, by a narrow margin. However, this result was challenged by the BNF, and was subsequently ruled null and void by the high court in October, following the discovery of an unopened ballot box. Mmusi had to relinquish the vice-presidency, but retained his other post as minister of finance and development planning. His position in the cabinet appeared to be in jeopardy after he was defeated by Koma in a re-contest, held in December. However, following the resignation of an MP during that month, Mmusi was appointed to the vacant seat and was subsequently reinstated as vice-president.

Although the BDP's success in the parliamentary elections consolidated its position, some discontent among the population at the country's high level of unemployment was reflected in the outcome of the local government elections (held on the same day as the parliamentary elections), in which the BDP lost control of all the town councils except that of Selebi-Phikwe. The BDP's strength was also undermined by the defection, in November 1985, of two prominent party members to the opposition BNF.

Tension between the BDP and the BNF continued to grow in early 1987. In May some members of the BDP alleged that youthful elements within the BNF were being trained in insurgency techniques by Libya and the USSR. The government, however, dissociated itself from these allegations. In September 1987 a referendum was held on constitutional amendments concerning the electoral system; a large majority reportedly voted in favour of endorsing the reforms, although the BNF boycotted the referendum.

At parliamentary elections held in October 1989, the BDP strengthened its position by winning 31 of the 34 elective seats, receiving 65% of all votes cast. The BNF, weakened by internal disagreements earlier in the year, won only three seats, although it obtained 27% of the total votes. As in 1984, the BNF challenged the results in a number of constituencies. The BPP lost its only seat, and four other parties also failed to secure representation. In October the new national assembly elected Masire for a third term as president. He subsequently threatened that his government would take action against workers involved in illegal strikes, as a measure to suppress widespread unrest among bank employees, mineworkers and primary school teachers.

In 1990 the BNF and the BPP formed an opposition alliance, agreeing to nominate a single candidate in each constituency at future elections. However, the BNF candidate failed to win a by-election at Mochudi in June (caused by a high court ruling upholding BNF charges of irregularities at the 1989 elections). The subsequent assertion by some BNF leaders that the party had become a national liberation movement disrupted the harmony of the opposition coalition. Despite the high court ruling on the Mochudi election result, the president later accused the opposition parties of bringing Botswana's democratic system into disrepute by persistently challenging election results. In November 1991 the government dismissed some 12,000 striking workers from public-sector unions, who had been campaigning for wage increases. In early March 1992 the vice-president, Peter Mmusi, and the minister of agriculture, Daniel Kwelagobe, resigned, having been implicated by a commission of inquiry in a corruption scandal involving the illegal transfer of land. Festus Mogae, the minister of finance and development planning, was appointed vice-president and also allocated the portfolio of local government and lands; a new minister of agriculture was appointed at the same time. In June Mmusi and Kwelagobe were suspended from the central committee of the BDP, but were re-elected at the party's congress in July 1993. As leaders of one of the two main factions into which the BDP was increasingly divided, Mmusi and Kwelagobe opposed the government's economic liberalization policy, as well as seeking to overturn the findings of the commission on illegal land dealings. A corruption scandal involving the Botswana Housing Corporation in 1993 led to the resignation of two other government ministers. The government's reputation was also undermined by the revelation that seven ministers were among the debtors of the troubled National Development Bank (which was being restructured in 1994). Uncertainty about the future leadership of the BDP (President Masire is 69 years of age) and the president's silence on this matter added to the divisions within the ruling party during the period leading to general elections due to take place in 1994.

Meanwhile, the opposition BNF's demands, made in May 1993, for the appointment of an independent electoral commission and for the reduction of the voting age (to 18 years) were rejected by the government. In spite of this, the BNF abandoned its threat to boycott elections and sought, instead, to mobilize popular support on the issues of government corruption and the recession in Botswana's economy. In late 1993, however, the low numbers registering to vote suggested a growing disillusionment with the political process in Botswana.

External Relations

During the 1980s, relations with South Africa remained strained, and Botswana was not immune to South Africa's general destabilizing pressures on its black-ruled neighbours. Revelations in mid-1980 that the South African armed forces had been recruiting Basarwa (Bushmen) from Botswana to serve in Namibia against guerrillas of the South West Africa People's Organisation of Namibia (SWAPO) caused alarm, and President Masire promised that the government would conduct an investigation. During 1981 tensions developed with South Africa over the supply of Soviet military equipment for the Botswana Defence Force (BDF). Masire defended the purchases on financial grounds and reiterated Botswana's adherence to its policy of non-alignment, stating that the instructors who accompanied the weapons had all left the country. By expanding the capabilities of the BDF, Botswana sought to achieve a more extensive and effective surveillance of its borders, thereby preventing insurgents from crossing into South Africa, and so removing any South African excuse for making punitive raids into Botswana. At the same time, it remained Botswana's policy to accommodate South African refugees, while not allowing them to use the country as a base for attacks on South Africa.

Several incidents, including, in April 1982, an exchange of fire over the border between Botswana and South African troops, kept the two countries' relationship uneasy. In May 1984 Masire accused South Africa of attempting to coerce Botswana into signing a non-aggression pact similar to that negotiated by the Pretoria government with Lesotho. The president claimed that South Africa had hinted that, if Botswana refused to sign, it might position troops along the frontier between the two countries and cause disruptions of cross-border traffic. However, in late February 1985 South Africa reportedly abandoned its insistence that Botswana sign a formal joint security pact. Relations deteriorated once again in June, following a raid on alleged ANC bases in Gaborone by South African forces, in which at least 15 people were killed. Representatives of the two countries met in September 1985 to discuss demands by Botswana for compensation from South Africa for the June raid. Although Botswana's demands were supported by the UN, South Africa was reluctant to pay compensation.

In early 1986 the United Kingdom and the USA pledged military aid to help Botswana to deter South African attacks and terrorist infiltration. In February Botswana's government reiterated its undertaking that the country was not to be used as a base for attacks by terrorists, and in March the government expelled ANC representatives. The improvement in relations was short-lived, for in May 1986, in conjunction with attacks on Zambia and Zimbabwe, South African troops launched land and air attacks on targets near Gaborone, causing one death. South Africa again claimed that its action was aimed at ANC bases. Although Botswana fully sympathized with the renewed international condemnation of apartheid, the vulnerability of the country's position, both geographically and economically, prevented the government from committing itself to the imposition of economic sanctions against South Africa, which was recommended by the SADCC in August.

With the approach of the South African general election in May 1987, tension increased as South Africa warned Botswana and other 'front-line' states that it would launch attacks against them in order to pre-empt disruption of the election by the ANC. Such an attack was alleged to have taken place in April, when four people were killed in a bomb explosion in Gaborone. In March 1988 South Africa openly admitted responsibility for a commando raid on a house in Gaborone, in which four alleged members of the ANC were killed. In June President Masire announced the capture of two members of a South African defence force unit which had allegedly opened fire on Botswana security forces while engaged in a commando raid. South Africa claimed that the unit had been on an intelligence mission. The captured South African commandos were subsequently tried and sentenced to 10 years' imprisonment. South African armed intrusions continued in the subsequent months, and in March 1989 nine South Africans were expelled from Botswana for 'security reasons'. The Botswana government maintained its strong denials of South African allegations that Botswana permitted ANC guerrillas to use Botswana as an infiltration route into South Africa. The relaxation of the political climate within South Africa in 1990, however, led to an improvement in relations between the two countries.

In late 1986 tension arose between the authorities of the South African 'homeland' of Bophuthatswana and the Botswana government, when Bophuthatswana announced that all Botswana train crews would be required to obtain visas to travel through its territory; in April 1987, however, the 'homeland' agreed to abandon these visa requirements.

Relations between Botswana and Zimbabwe (whose ideologies are far apart) have been correct rather than friendly. Although Masire made an official visit to Harare in 1982, tension subsequently increased as a large number of former guerrillas of the Zimbabwe African People's Union (ZAPU), supporters of Joshua Nkomo (viewed as insurgents by the Zimbabwe government), crossed the border and entered refugee camps. A sharp deterioration in Botswana-Zimbabwe relations occurred in March 1983, when, with serious unrest in Zimbabwe's Matabeleland province, Nkomo fled to Botswana. Zimbabwe had already claimed that Botswana was providing a base for pro-Nkomo insurgents. To the considerable relief of the Botswana government, Nkomo left for London after only a few days in the country.

The issue of Zimbabwean refugees in Botswana persistently beset relations between the two countries throughout the 1980s. In 1983 allegations that armed dissidents from Zimbabwe were being sheltered among the 3,000–4,000 Zimbabwean refugees encamped in Botswana led the Botswana government to agree to impose stricter controls on the refugees. In May 1983 Botswana and Zimbabwe established full diplomatic relations. In August Robert Mugabe, the prime minister (later president) of Zimbabwe, visited Botswana for discussions, and it was announced that a joint trade agreement was being drafted. However, the recurrence of incidents on the Botswana–Zimbabwe border between members of the BDF and armed men wearing Zimbabwean military uniforms created further tension, and led to security talks between the two countries in late 1983. In July 1984 Zimbabwe claimed that Botswana had repatriated more than 1,200 Zimbabwean refugees, including more than 300 alleged guerrillas, and relations between the two countries appeared to improve later that year. The first meeting of the Botswana–Zimbabwe joint commission for co-operation was held in October 1984. Following the July 1985 general election in Zimbabwe, a new influx of refugees threatened to disrupt relations once again. In May 1988, however, President Masire expressed confidence that the remaining Zimbabwean exiles would return to their country voluntarily as a result of an apparent improvement in the political climate in Zimbabwe. Nevertheless, in April 1989 there were still some 600 Zimbabweans in Botswana. At the end of that month the Botswana government announced that refugee status for Zimbabwean nationals in the country was to be revoked, and by September almost all Zimbabwean refugees were reported to have left Botswana.

Following the achievement of independence by Namibia in March 1990, presidential visits were exchanged by Botswana and Namibia and steps were taken to ensure bilateral co-operation. However, in 1992 a border dispute developed between the two countries regarding their rival territorial claims over a small island in the Chobe river. Further tension was created by the building of the huge Molepolole airbase, due to be completed in 1995. (The scale and expense of this project also arouse controversy within Botswana itself.)

Botswana is a member of the OAU, the UN and the Commonwealth. It is also a non-aligned nation and its principled stands over issues such as apartheid, coupled with general moderation of approach, have given Botswana an effective voice in many international deliberations. In mid-1993 several hundred Botswana troops were deployed in UN operations.

Economy

RICHARD BROWN

At independence in 1966, Botswana was one of the 20 poorest countries in the world, with minimal infrastructural development and a predominantly subsistence economy. Government revenues were critically dependent on foreign aid and the remittances of the Batswana males employed in South Africa. Dominated by a few large-scale, predominantly expatriate, farmers, the commercial livestock sector was the largest contributor to gross domestic product (GDP) and export earnings. During the 1980s, however, Botswana's economic performance exceeded that of all other non-petroleum producing countries in Africa. GDP rose, in real terms, by an annual average of 11.3% in 1980–90, giving Botswana one of the world's highest growth rates. This exceptional record was partly due to the rapid expansion of the beef industry, but the predominant cause was the discovery and development of valuable mineral resources, especially diamonds. Apart from transforming the export base, the development of the mining sector has also helped to stimulate and finance the development of the infrastructure, the manufacturing sector and the social services. By 1993 Botswana had become an 'upper middle income' country under World Bank definitions.

The rise in the mineral sector is reflected in alteration to the economic structure after 1966. The contribution of agriculture to GDP fell dramatically, exacerbated by prolonged periods of drought during 1981–87, from almost 40% of the total at independence to 5% in early 1994. The contribution of mining increased from 0% to 51% during the same period, and growth in manufacturing, transport and communications, financial and social services sectors was also impressive, if less dramatic. A similar situation has prevailed in exports, with beef sales falling from over 90% of merchandise earnings in 1966 to 4% in 1991. Visible export earnings from diamonds rose from 0% to 80% of the total during the same period. When combined with exports of copper-nickel matte, minerals accounted for about 87% of total export earnings in 1991.

Growth based on such narrow foundations is vulnerable and difficult to sustain in the long term. The sixth National Development Plan (1985–91) was predicated on a substantial diminution in growth rates, to an average of 4.8% per year, through a stabilization of diamond and beef output and the lack of alternative means to sustain high growth levels, particularly in the mining sector. However, higher than anticipated diamond production and price levels rendered the projections for the Plan too pessimistic, with real average annual growth rates of about 10% in both 1985/86 and 1986/87. In 1987/88 and 1988/89 growth in GDP slowed to an average annual rate of about 8.7%, and over the period 1989/90–1991/92 an average annual growth rate, in real terms, of 6.6% was recorded. Nevertheless, it is of concern that growth in GDP during the late 1980s and early 1990s was also greatly assisted by a rapid increase in government expenditure, which cannot be sustained indefinitely. The government plans to encourage the short-term development of the manufacturing and tourism sectors in order to combat lower diamond and beef sales and to stimulate future growth. The seventh National Development Plan (1991–97) aimed to increase earnings from the mining sector sufficiently to support a doubling of government expenditure, and envisaged an expanded role for the private sector in economic development. In early 1993 the Plan's targets were reviewed and scaled down, the shortage of skilled manpower being identified as the major constraint on faster progress. Botswana's economic performance was adversely affected during the early 1990s by the international recession, and real growth in GDP, provisionally estimated at only 1.8% in 1993, has dropped below the rate of population growth for the first time since independence. The recovery in the diamond market late in that year is expected to restore the situation by 1995/96.

AGRICULTURE

Despite recent rapid urbanization, an estimated 62.1% of the labour force were engaged in agriculture in 1991. Composed partly of semi-desert and partly of a savannah area with highly erratic rainfall and relatively poor soils, Botswana is more suited to grazing than to arable production. There have been some recent attempts to compensate for this through development of the country's irrigation potential, but agriculture remains dominated by the livestock sector generally, and the cattle industry in particular, which is the main activity of rural Botswana, and which contributes over 80% of agricultural GDP.

The national herd increased dramatically after independence, from 1.4m. head in 1965 to a peak of almost 3m. in 1981, stimulated by improved beef export prices, the expansion of available grazing through drilling of new boreholes, and the establishment of effective disease control, based on a system of cordon fences and vaccination, which has kept the country free of foot-and-mouth disease since 1981. The cordon system has opened up the lucrative European market, which offers preferential terms to Lomé Convention signatories able to satisfy the stringent disease-control criteria, but it has also involved the government in international controversy over the impact on wildlife. The criticism has been intensified by the fact that the economic benefit of beef exports has largely accrued to the 5% of households who are estimated to own more than one-half of the national herd, with about 20% of the total held by the country's 360 large-scale commercial farms. Approximately 50% of rural households neither own nor have access to cattle.

The recurrence of drought from 1981 until 1986/87 had a severe impact on cattle numbers, reducing the national herd by an estimated 25%, to 2.3m. The ending of the drought in the 1987/88 rainy season enabled the replenishment of stocks to an estimated 2.7m. head in 1990. An exceptionally severe drought in 1991/92, however, reduced the national herd drastically. For the beef industry, the recurrent drought has caused a decline in cattle weight, and the Botswana Meat Commission (BMC) has been able to fulfil no more than 70% of its annual EC quota of 18,910 metric tons of beef since 1985. Nevertheless, Europe remains its single most important market, taking more than 50% of total exports. Although previously profitable, the BMC made a loss in 1990/91. In 1991/92 the severe drought conditions resulted in an increased number of cattle slaughtered and a corresponding improvement in the BMC's profitability. It has excess slaughtering capacity, following the opening in 1989 of a new abattoir in Francistown, which complements the commission's existing facilities at Lobatse and Maun.

In contrast to cattle, sheep and goat numbers withstood the 1981–87 drought reasonably well. After an initial decline from an estimated 628,000 head in 1978 to 621,000 in 1981, they were estimated to total 2.4m. by 1991. They remain predominantly a subsistence sector resource, and the main commercial development outside beef has been in urban poultry. It was hoped during the 1985–91 Development Plan to improve the availability of eggs and chickens in rural areas, and also to improve local production of milk and fish. At present, more than 70% of domestic milk requirements have to be imported in the form of milk powder, and it is estimated that fish production is only 15% of the potential annual catch.

In the arable sector, as in beef, commercial farmers provide a disproportionate amount of crop production: official figures indicate that just 100 commercial farms account for

37% of total output of sorghum, maize, millet, beans and pulses. Of the 85% of small-scale farms producing crops, almost one-third are less than 3 ha, and only 6.8% over the 10 ha minimum necessary for household self-sufficiency, even in years of reasonable rains. As a result, two-thirds of rural households are reported to depend for as much as 40% of their income on members employed in the formal, predominantly commercial, agricultural sector. In 1992 a commission of inquiry revealed widespread corruption in the sale and distribution of land.

As a result of the 1991/92 drought (the worst this century), the total area planted with food crops was reduced by 70%–80%; even prior to this, however, the government had abandoned its former aim of achieving national self-sufficiency in cereals. In accordance with the seventh National Development Plan, shortfalls in cereal production are to be offset by imports, and efforts are to be made to improve household incomes, in order to reduce reliance on subsidies.

In the mid-1980s land under irrigation totalled only 1,000 ha, the majority consisting of privately-owned farms producing primarily cotton, citrus fruits and tobacco. Botswana is considered to have substantial irrigated potential, however, particularly in the Okavango Delta and Chobe areas. In view of the unique and fragile nature of the Okavango, especially, there are also significant possible environmental risks in realizing this potential, which have been the subject of considerable study in recent years. Some experimental plots, utilizing flood-recession irrigation, have been initiated at Molapo, on the eastern fringe of the Okavango. Pending the final outcome of environmental studies on the project, it is planned to proceed with a scheme, costing P180m., to develop 5,000–10,000 ha of high-yielding crops by improving water- and crop-management systems. Other projects are being studied under the government's 'accelerated water resource development programme'.

MINERALS AND MINING

Botswana is now Africa's third largest mineral producer by value, but it was not until after independence in 1966 that the country was found to have abundant reserves of diamonds, coal, copper-nickel, soda ash, potash and sodium sulphate. Substantial deposits of salts and plutonium, as well as smaller reserves of gold, silver and a variety of industrial minerals, were also identified.

Large-scale mineral exploitation began in 1971, when the Orapa diamond mine began production, and Botswana now has a relatively diverse mining sector, with three major diamond mines, coal and copper-nickel mines, as well as small-scale mining of gold, industrial minerals and semi-precious stones. The diamond mines are owned and operated by the Debswana Diamond Co (Pty), a joint venture owned equally by the Botswana government and De Beers Consolidated Mines of South Africa. De Beers began diamond exploration in 1955, but it was not until 1967 that the 106-ha Orapa kimberlite pipe, the world's second largest, was discovered. Mining at Orapa, which commenced in 1971, was followed in 1977 by the inauguration of production at the adjacent Letlhakane pipe, and in 1982 a major new mine at Jwaneng, 125 km west of Gaborone, was brought into production. In 1993 the combined output of Debswana's diamond-mining operations totalled 14.7m. carats, compared with 15.9m. carats in 1992 and 16.5m. carats in 1991. Although all current mining operations are conducted by Debswana, another company, Challenger Mining International (CMI), has, through its operating subsidiary, Kalahari Resources, carried out an extensive ground survey over an area of 25,000 sq km and believes that it has identified four kimberlite pipes under the desert sands. The group holds 27 diamond-prospecting licences in Botswana.

Since the mid-1980s, the diamond industry has continued to strengthen its role as the mainstay of Botswana's vigorous economic performance. In 1987 earnings from the export of diamonds more than doubled, although this increase was attributable to two exceptional factors: a 10% increase in the diamond price in October, and the sale in that year by Debswana of its stockpile to De Beers. The sale, valued at some US $600m., formed part of an agreement giving Debswana a 5.27% shareholding in De Beers. For the government, this meant an effective 2.6% interest, entitling it to appoint two directors both to the main De Beers board and to that of its London-based Diamond Trading Co subsidiary, in reflection of Botswana's increasing importance in production by the group. In 1987 Debswana accounted for 58% of total output by the De Beers group, compared with 55% in 1986. For the Botswana government, the agreement was not only a long-term investment, but also a means of gaining access to decision-making on the diamond market. In 1988 and 1989 diamonds accounted for around 75% of Botswana's total export revenues; in 1990 and 1991 the proportion slightly exceeded 80%, accounting for more than 50% of government spending. During the early 1990s the government encouraged the development of two diamond-cutting and -polishing ventures. The diamond industry is Botswana's largest private-sector employer, with more than 6,000 workers on Debswana's wage list in 1993.

Production of copper-nickel matte at Selebi-Phikwe began in 1974, and output rose steadily, reaching around 50,000 tons per year by the late 1980s. However, the value of sales of matte per ton declined consistently during the 1980s, owing to depressed international prices for nickel and copper. This created profound financial problems for the operating company, BCL, and the shareholders in its parent group, Botswana Roan Selection Trust (BRST), in which the Botswana government holds 15%, with Anglo American Corpn of South Africa and Amax Corpn of the USA holding the remainder. To offset these problems, a series of financial restructurings and debt-reschedulings was undertaken, while the resurgence of prices for base metals after mid-1987 led to a considerable improvement in BCL's financial position. This has been advantageous to the economy as a whole: the company is the country's largest private-sector employer, with a work-force of 5,000, and an important source of foreign exchange, accounting for up to 10% of Botswana's total export earnings. The improvement in prices also enabled two new copper-nickel mines to be brought into production. In July 1988 BCL announced plans to bring the high-grade Selebi North mine into production, to replace deteriorating ore bodies at its other two mines. Work on the project started in early 1989, with a view to reaching full capacity of about 1,500 tons of ore per day by mid-1990. The other copper-nickel mine (at Selkirk, east of Francistown) was brought into production at the end of 1988 by a consortium of Swiss and British investors. At full capacity, output is expected to reach 60,000 tons of high-grade ore per year; BCL is to undertake refining of the output on a toll basis. There are plans to develop the adjacent, and larger, Phoenix deposit. Depressed prices for copper and nickel in the early 1990s, however, exacerbated the financial problems of the industry and reduced its export earnings in 1991/92 to an estimated $102m., less than 6% of Botswana's total export revenue.

Plans to exploit Botswana's coal reserves have been restricted by the low level of international prices. Some 17,000m. tons of steam coal suitable for power-plant use have been identified in the east, and coal is extracted at the Moropule colliery, whose output rose from 579,400 tons in 1987 to 901,500 tons in 1992. Most of the coal is for electricity generation to service the mining industry and the new soda ash plant. The government is also encouraging domestic coal use, in order to conserve fuel wood.

Following independence, there were several attempts to exploit brine deposits at Sua Pan, in central Botswana, by establishing a soda ash/salt plant (soda ash is used by the glass-, paper-, steel- and detergent-making industries). In 1986 private South African interests began talks with British Petroleum to acquire its subsidiary, Soda Ash Botswana, with Botswana government participation in a project to build a plant at Makgadikgadi, with forecast annual output of some 300,000 tons of soda ash and 650,000 tons of salt. Agreement to undertake the project was completed in 1988, and production began, on schedule, in early 1991. However, output of 62,000 tons of soda ash in 1991 was considerably below expectations, owing to continuing technical problems.

Subsequently, the lack of demand and competition in the South African market have restricted output to about 60% of capacity, an amount well below profitable operation.

Botswana's dependence on South African support to implement the soda ash project has raised domestic and regional concern that the government is increasing the country's vulnerability to political pressure. Similar concerns have surrounded exploration work on plutonium deposits being carried out in the south by two South African firms, Gold Fields of South Africa (GFSA) and Southern Prospecting. GFSA holds three prospecting licences, through its Gold Fields of Botswana subsidiary, for a 3,000 sq km concession north of the Molopo river and adjacent to its existing concession in South Africa's Bushveld igneous complex, which contains substantial reserves of platinum and chromium. Botswana's reserves, however, are thought to be of lower grade and far less substantial, and in 1992 platinum exploration in the Molopo area was suspended.

For many years, gold has been mined, on a small scale, in Botswana. In 1987 a joint venture, Shashe Mines, was formed between the government, a Canadian company and a US company, to conduct exploration work on gold deposits at Map Nora, near Francistown, and exploitation of the mineral commenced in 1989. Botswana's total output of gold reached 67 kg in 1989, but had dropped back to only 20 kg two years later.

MANUFACTURING AND CONSTRUCTION

Although manufacturing contributed only 4% of GDP in 1991 and has been constrained by a small domestic market, limited export outlets, weak infrastructure, import dependence and shortage of skilled manpower, it has emerged since the late 1970s as one of Botswana's most dynamic economic sectors. Manufacturing GDP increased by an annual average of 7.5% over the period 1980–91. Formal employment in manufacturing increased from 4,400 in August 1978 to 26,000 in March 1991. This expansion did much to reduce the parastatal BMC's domination of the sector, with its share of industrial employment declining from 36% to 18% over the period 1979–84. It also represented a considerable diversification of Botswana's manufacturing base, with textiles, beverages, chemicals, paper, metals, plastics and electrical products experiencing the highest rates of expansion. The sector's strong performance was attributable to a number of government policies, based on a financial assistance programme (FAP), inaugurated in 1982, which provides a wide range of subsidies to potential entrepreneurs, particularly in the small-scale sector, and a highly attractive foreign investment code. The government's current diversification programme also places a priority on the country's need to develop the manufacturing sector.

The parastatal Botswana Development Corporation (BDC) has been a major promoter of industrial development, identifying projects and potential joint-venture partners, and establishing industrial sites for smaller firms to rent. BDC's interests include brewing, sugar packaging, furniture and clothing manufacturing, tourism, milling and concrete products. In 1984 BDC established the Setshaba Investment Trust Co as a vehicle for offering shares in its subsidiaries to the public. Since 1986, Botswana's strong foreign exchange position has proved an increasing attraction for foreign companies, mainly from South Africa. In addition, the UK's Lonrho and Metal Box, and Heinz and Colgate Palmolive of the USA, have made investments since the beginning of 1988. The government is currently promoting textile production as part of its diversification programme, partly because Botswana has a less skilled work-force than South Africa, the dominant industrial power in the region.

The construction sector developed rapidly during the 1980s, particularly from 1988 (in 1988/89 it registered growth of 30%). In the early 1990s, however, growth in the sector slowed, reflecting both the general downturn in economic performance and the management crisis at the Botswana Housing Corporation (see Recent History).

ENERGY AND WATER DEVELOPMENT

Respectively rapid economic and population growth have resulted in a rapid expansion in demand for energy and water. Shortfalls in supply have been offset by imports from South Africa, although these were sufficient to satisfy only 8.5% of total demand in 1987/88. The principal consumers of energy are urban areas, including industrial consumers, and the mines. Botswana Power Corporation (BPC) has been implementing a continuing programme of capacity expansion, of which the major project has been the Moropule power station. Using coal mined at Moropule, the station is the focus of a new national grid system linking the existing northern and southern networks, based on Selebi-Phikwe and Gaborone power stations. The first phase of the power station, comprising three 30-MW units, was commissioned in 1987, and work on a fourth 30-MW unit was completed in 1989. Units five and six have been planned for the early 1990s, and as many as 14 units could be operational by the year 2000, if demand increases as predicted. It is expected that additional supplies of electricity will continue to be imported from South Africa, to cover demand surges and to ensure alternative sources in the event of problems at Moropule. In accordance with this objective, a project to link Botswana into the Zambian and Zimbabwean grids was completed in 1991. Apart from the further work at Moropule, the main short-term focus of the electricity programme will be the extension of the rural catchment area of the national grid, with the aim of conserving fuelwood and reducing oil demand. Although oil imports have not imposed as heavy a burden on foreign exchange as in many other African countries, they account for some 10% of the cost of total imports: the mining industry is the major consumer.

Botswana's vast coal reserves and the substantial surplus power generated in neighbouring countries has made it relatively easy to satisfy the rising energy demand, when compared with the problem of the increasing domestic and livestock requirements for water. The country has minimal surface water supplies outside the remote Okavango and Chobe areas, and 80% of national demand is met from groundwater sources, with livestock the largest single user, consuming about one-third, followed by mining, urban areas and rural areas and villages. Although not fully assessed, groundwater supplies are not expected to exceed 4,000m. cu m per year, and intense competition for water resources has emerged in the main urban-mining areas in the east, leading to the postponement of plans for the development of industrial sites, particularly in Gaborone. The situation has been exacerbated by recurrent drought. Aid from overseas is currently being used to develop water resources within Botswana and the South African 'homeland' of Bophuthatswana. In addition, an 'accelerated water resource development programme' commenced in 1989: this was to provide more dams, in an attempt to fulfil the projected requirements of the 1990s. A project to provide water for the southern Okavango region was suspended in early 1991, following pressure from international environmentalists.

FOREIGN TRADE AND BALANCE OF PAYMENTS

Diamonds have been Botswana's principal export (accounting for as much as 80% of total earnings and for 30%–35% of government revenue) since the mid-1970s, when they replaced beef, which, from having been the country's sole export at independence, now accounts for about 4% of export earnings. Other exports are copper-nickel matte (which contributed 5.9% of export earnings in 1992) and textiles. The four main categories of imports in 1992 were food, beverages and tobacco (19.8%), vehicles and transport equipment (18.1%), machinery and electrical goods (17.3%) and chemical and rubber products (8.2%). Europe provides the largest export market (87% in 1992) and the Southern African Customs Union (SACU) the main source of imports (85%). A persistent deficit on the merchandise trade account was replaced by a small trade surplus, of P27m., in 1983. With the recovery of world diamond prices in 1985, the surplus rapidly escalated, reaching

P459m. in 1986. In 1987 it surged by almost 170%, to P1,230.5m., reflecting the effect of the sale of Debswana's diamond stockpile to De Beers (see above). In 1988 the surplus declined to P1,088m., but, with the distorting effect of the stockpile sale removed, the trend was still one of steady improvement. In 1989 a surplus of P1,450m. was recorded. Although export earnings declined in 1992 due to recession in many purchaser countries, the merchandise trade account remained in surplus, according to preliminary figures.

Botswana operates an open economy, with combined import and export values exceeding GDP, making both the domestic economy and external account vulnerable to fluctuations in the terms of trade and exchange rates. The government has operated a flexible, trade-orientated exchange rate policy since the pula was established in 1976 as the national currency. It was initially tied to the US dollar exchange rates, but the appreciation of the South African rand against the dollar forced several revaluations in the following four years, in order to contain import costs and domestic inflation. In June 1980 the pula was linked to a trade-weighted 'basket' of currencies, in order to minimize such disruptions. However, after 1982 the relationship between the US dollar and the South African rand began to reverse, while the pula strengthened in relation to the rand as the annual rate of domestic inflation fell from 12.7% in 1982 to 5.5%, considerably below the South African rate, at the end of 1984. The result was a series of trade-orientated devaluations between 1982 and 1985. Domestic inflation rose to 10% in 1985, and, according to official figures, has since steadily increased, averaging 11.6% per year in 1988–92; however, unofficial estimates indicate that it is appreciably higher. The pula was devalued in 1991.

Apart from maintaining trade competitiveness, the exchange rate adjustments have also ameliorated the effect on the balance of payments of the steady deterioration in the country's terms of trade. Since 1976 Botswana has generally enjoyed a secure balance-of-payments position, with the current account in surplus in every year since 1982. Net transfers, including Botswana's share of revenue from SACU, and capital inflows of private investment and foreign aid more than offset the continuing deficit on both the invisible and overall trade account. During the 1980s the healthy balance-of-payments position was assured by the expansion of export earnings, particularly from diamonds, which, apart from pushing the trade account into surplus, underpinned a rapid growth in the overall surplus. This reached P942m. in 1987, a record created by the sale of the Debswana stockpile. Over the subsequent four years the estimated annual surplus on the current account of the balance of payments averaged P366m.

The most obvious effect of Botswana's strong balance-of-payments position has been the increase in official reserves of foreign exchange. These were sufficient to cover 5.5 months of imports in 1980. At the end of 1993, the reserves stood at just over P10,000m., or 34 months' cover. The government views the high level of reserves as essential to sustain Botswana's future economic development as diamond earnings level out, with no single source of export revenue to replace them. The rapid escalation in reserves after 1985 was paralleled, however, by growing criticism of the Botswana government's concern with long-term financial security. According to the critics, the government's conservative fiscal policies were depressing productive investment, particularly by the private sector, and were subsequently hindering job-creation.

Botswana's balance-of-payments situation has also been helped by its low debt burden. The total external public debt was US $550m. at the end of 1992. In that year the cost of debt-servicing was equivalent to 4.5% of the total value of exports of goods and services.

GOVERNMENT FINANCE

At independence about one-half of Botswana's public expenditure was financed directly by the government of the United Kingdom. This extreme level of reliance on external support was altered by Botswana's accession to SACU in 1969, and the country had become financially independent of the UK by 1972/73. From 1977/78 until 1982/83 customs revenue constituted the principal component of government income, but since then this source has been overtaken by mineral revenue, which now accounts for about 50% of the total, compared with about 15% for customs revenue. Since the unexpected fall in diamond revenues in 1981/82, the government has adopted a generally cautious approach to expenditure, which has been reflected in a succession of budget surpluses. The financial surplus that was generated by the sale of the Debswana stockpile led the government, in December 1987, to adopt a more positively expansionary approach, based on increases in public spending. Additional recurrent and development expenditure was approved, but the government continued to exercise caution, warning that any levelling out of revenues from the diamond industry would quickly lead to the return of an overall deficit, as had happened in 1981/82. Although deficits were anticipated in 1992/93 and 1993/94, the 1994 budget statement (February) indicated surpluses of P881m. and P431m. in recurrent and development expenditure respectively. The 1994/95 budget is expected to balance, but with an increased proportion being allocated to recurrent expenditure, especially for educational reform. Changes to income tax and foreign exchange controls were announced with the aim of increasing both international competitiveness and foreign investment.

EMPLOYMENT AND WAGES

Botswana's population growth rate accelerated significantly during the 1980s, from 3.1% per year in 1981 to an estimated 3.5% per year by 1994. As a result, the total population increased from 941,027 at the census of August 1981 to 1,326,796 at the August 1991 census. Current projections indicate a total of 1.8m. in 2000. As a result of the high growth rate, the net addition to the labour force of people aged 15–64 years has been in the region of 20,000 per year, many of them joining the 53% of the working-age population who were estimated in 1985/86 to be unemployed or in school. Only around 20% of the labour force are employed in the formal sector, while about 10% are self-employed. The strong economic growth rates since 1979 have led to a significant expansion in job-creation, with formal-sector employment rising from 65,500 in 1978 to 100,600 in 1983, and to 223,000 in 1991, amounting to an annual average growth rate of more than 10%. The main sectors in which employment has increased are manufacturing, finance and business services, construction, transport and communications and social services. From the beginning of 1988 government employment expanded significantly. By early 1994 the civil service wage bill represented more than one-third of recurrent spending. Despite the rate of economic growth exceeding that of population growth, formal-sector employment in terms of absolute numbers was unable to absorb the increase in the labour force during the early 1980s. This situation was exacerbated by a decline in the number of Batswana working abroad from a peak of 25,500 in 1976 to 18,800 in 1983. During the late 1980s the increase in employment opportunities began to exceed the growth rate of the labour force, causing unemployment to fall temporarily. Nevertheless, an estimated 30%–35% of the labour force were unemployed in mid-1993. By early 1993 the number of Batswana employed in South African mines had fallen to less than 14,000.

Job creation has become a major political issue and the main priority in government planning. Another priority is to increase the country's pool of trained labour. In 1993 the government was considering the adoption of a strategy to stimulate employment by promoting small-scale and informal-sector enterprises.

Statistical Survey

Source (unless otherwise stated): Central Statistics Office, Private Bag 0024, Gaborone; tel. 352200; fax 352201.

Area and Population

AREA, POPULATION AND DENSITY

Area (sq km)	582,000*
Population (census results)	
31 August 1971	574,094†
12–26 August 1981	941,027‡
14–23 August 1991	
Males	634,400
Females	692,396
Total	1,326,796
Population (official estimate at 19 August)	
1992	1,373,000
Density (per sq km) at August 1992	2.4

* 224,711 sq miles.
† Excluding 10,550 nomads and 10,861 non-citizens.
‡ Excluding 42,069 citizens absent from the country during enumeration.

POPULATION BY CENSUS DISTRICT
(August 1991 preliminary census results)

Barolong	18,365	Lobatse	25,992
Central	395,564	Ngamiland	94,322
Chobe	14,186	Ngwaketse	129,474
Francistown	65,026	North-East	43,361
Gaborone	133,791	Orapa	8,853
Ghanzi	24,695	Palapye	17,131
Jwaneng	11,199	Selibe-Phikwe	39,769
Kgalagadi	30,873	South-East	31,101
Kgatleng	57,168	Sowa	2,220
Kweneng	169,835	Tlokweng	12,366

PRINCIPAL TOWNS (August 1988 estimates)

Gaborone (capital)	110,973	Kanye	26,300
Francistown	49,396	Mahalapye	26,239
Selebi-Phikwe	46,490	Lobatse	25,689
Molepolole	29,212	Maun	18,470
Serowe	28,267	Ramotswa	17,961
Mochudi	26,320		

August 1990 (estimates): Gaborone 129,535; Francistown 56,021; Selibe-Phikwe 52,560; Lobatse 27,928.

BIRTHS AND DEATHS
(UN estimates, annual averages)

	1975–80	1980–85	1985–90
Birth rate (per 1,000)	52.8	46.8	40.6
Death rate (per 1,000)	15.5	14.2	11.2

Expectation of life (UN estimates, years at birth, 1985–90): 58.5 (males 55.5; females 61.5).

Source: UN, *World Population Prospects: The 1992 Revision.*

ECONOMICALLY ACTIVE POPULATION
(persons aged 12 years and over, 1991 census*)

	Males	Females	Total
Agriculture, hunting, forestry and fishing	72,781	27,665	100,446
Mining and quarrying	12,520	767	13,287
Manufacturing	13,298	13,337	26,635
Electricity, gas and water	5,644	781	6,425
Construction	49,500	7,501	57,001
Trade, restaurants and hotels	13,588	20,734	34,322
Transport, storage and communications	8,304	1,790	10,094
Financing, insurance, real estate and business services	8,758	4,634	13,392
Community, social and personal services	45,802	57,243	103,045
Activities not adequately defined	10,786	6,384	17,170
Total employed	240,981	140,836	381,817
Unemployed	32,134	29,504	61,638
Total labour force	273,115	170,340	443,455

* Excluding members of the armed forces.

Source: ILO, *Year Book of Labour Statistics.*

CIVILIAN EMPLOYMENT
(formal sector only; March each year)

	1990	1991*	1992*
Agriculture	6,500	6,700	6,100
Mining and quarrying	7,800	7,800	7,600
Manufacturing	23,300	26,000	25,500
Electricity and water	2,100	2,500	2,600
Construction	29,300	33,800	33,800
Trade, restaurants and hotels	35,700	41,000	40,900
Transport and communications	8,100	9,100	10,200
Finance and business services	13,200	16,100	17,600
Community, social and personal services	72,500	79,600	83,200
Total	198,500	222,800	227,500
Males	n.a.	146,700	145,600
Females	n.a.	76,100	81,900

* Source: ILO, *Year Book of Labour Statistics.*

Note: The number of Batswana employed in South African mines was 13,516 in 1990.

Agriculture

PRINCIPAL CROPS ('000 metric tons)

	1990	1991	1992
Wheat	1	2†	1†
Maize	8	4	3
Millet	2	1	1†
Sorghum	43	38	11
Roots and tubers*	7	7	8
Pulses*	14	14	12
Cottonseed*	2	2	2
Cotton (lint)*	1	1	1
Vegetables*	16	16	16
Fruit*	11	11	11

* FAO estimates. † Unofficial figure.

Source: FAO, *Production Yearbook.*

LIVESTOCK ('000 head, year ending September)

	1990	1991*	1992*
Cattle	2,696	2,500	2,500
Horses	34	34	34
Asses	152*	153	153
Sheep	317	320	325
Goats	2,092	2,090	2,090
Pigs	16	16	16

Chickens (million): 2 in 1990; 2* in 1991; 2* in 1992.

* FAO estimate(s).

Source: FAO, *Production Yearbook*.

LIVESTOCK PRODUCTS (FAO estimates, '000 metric tons)

	1990	1991	1992
Beef and veal	38	32	31
Goats' meat	6	6	6
Other meat	9	8	9
Cows' milk	105	105	94
Goats' milk	3	3	3
Cheese	1.3	1.3	1.5
Butter and ghee	1.5	1.5	1.5
Hen eggs	0.8	0.8	0.8
Cattle hides	4.9	4.0	4.2

Source: FAO, *Production Yearbook*.

Forestry

ROUNDWOOD REMOVALS
(FAO estimates, '000 cubic metres)

	1989	1990	1991
Industrial wood	83	86	89
Fuel wood	1,256	1,303	1,351
Total	1,339	1,389	1,440

Source: FAO, *Yearbook of Forest Products*.

Fishing

	1989	1990	1991
Total catch (metric tons)	1,900	1,900*	1,900*

* FAO estimate.

Source: FAO, *Yearbook of Fishery Statistics*.

Mining

(metric tons, unless otherwise indicated)

	1990	1991	1992
Coal	794,041	783,873	901,452
Copper ore*	20,612	20,576	20,413
Nickel ore*	19,022	19,294	18,873
Cobalt ore*	205	212	208
Gold ore (kilograms)*	46	n.a.	n.a.
Diamonds ('000 carats)	17,351	16,506	15,978
Soda ash	—	56,683	123,593
Salt	—	2,600	50,000

* Figures refer to the metal content of ores.

Sources: Bank of Botswana, Gaborone, and UN, *Industrial Statistics Yearbook*.

Industry

SELECTED PRODUCTS

	1988	1989	1990
Beer ('000 hectolitres)	1,002	1,076	1,214
Soft drinks ('000 hectolitres)	190	222	283
Electric energy (million kWh)	1,058	1,804	1,814

Source: UN, *Industrial Statistics Yearbook*.

Finance

CURRENCY AND EXCHANGE RATES

Monetary Units
100 thebe = 1 pula (P).

Sterling and Dollar Equivalents (31 March 1994)
£1 sterling = 3.808 pula;
US $1 = 2.565 pula;
100 pula = £26.26 = $38.99.

Average Exchange Rate (US $ per pula)
1991 0.4957
1992 0.4689
1993 0.4134

RECURRENT BUDGET ('000 pula, year ending 31 March)

Revenue	1988/89	1989/90*	1990/91*
Taxation	1,989,040	2,194,940	2,810,550
Mineral revenues	1,508,060	1,550,900	2,056,830
Customs pool revenues	292,590	374,000	480,000
Non-mineral income tax	164,760	240,800	240,800
Other current revenue	450,230	407,230	446,190
Interest	94,120	52,250	53,610
Other property income	321,060	327,430	359,830
Fees, charges, etc.	35,050	27,550	32,750
Sales of fixed assets and land	7,090	2,040	6,390
Total (incl. others)	2,446,360	2,604,210	3,263,130

* Estimates.

Expenditure	1988/89	1989/90	1990/91*
Office of the President	115,539	154,555	177,656
Finance and development planning	50,416	91,877	59,747
Labour and home affairs	20,815	24,691	30,535
Agriculture	64,970	79,227	89,112
Education	182,809	236,051	264,850
Commerce and industry	9,867	14,812	18,457
Local government and lands	137,337	181,261	214,754
Works and communications	125,764	166,364	199,294
Mineral resources and water affairs	22,470	29,573	35,204
Health	53,319	63,176	74,581
External affairs	11,192	15,114	13,997
Public debt interest	104,349	90,977	129,888
Total (incl. others)	933,754	1,191,657	1,357,149

* Estimates.

INTERNATIONAL RESERVES (US $ million at 31 December)

	1990	1991	1992
IMF special drawing rights	30.87	34.47	30.88
Reserve position in IMF	23.00	19.24	20.34
Foreign exchange	3,331.46	3,718.66	3,793.42
Total	3,385.34	3,772.37	3,844.64

Source: IMF, *International Financial Statistics*.

MONEY SUPPLY (million pula at 31 December)

	1990	1991	1992
Currency outside banks	143.7	158.1	163.0
Demand deposits at commercial banks	442.4	455.5	444.0
Total money	586.1	613.6	607.0

Source: IMF, *International Financial Statistics.*

COST OF LIVING (Consumer Price Index; base: 1981 = 100)

	1990	1991	1992
Food	244.2	273.2	324.2
Clothing	284.0	317.0	384.2
All items (incl. others)	234.4	262.0	304.4

Source: ILO, *Year Book of Labour Statistics.*

NATIONAL ACCOUNTS
(million pula, year ending 30 June)

National Income and Product (at current prices)

	1984/85	1985/86	1986/87
Compensation of employees	602.2	700.7	849.6
Operating surplus	793.0	1,084.9	1,312.3
Domestic factor incomes	1,395.2	1,785.6	2,161.9
Consumption of fixed capital	278.4	349.8	432.4
Gross domestic product (GDP) at factor cost	1,673.6	2,135.4	2,594.3
Indirect taxes	155.4	292.2	226.2
Less Subsidies	0.4	7.0	10.7
GDP in purchasers' values	1,828.6	2,420.6	2,809.8
Factor income received from abroad	118.0	173.0	225.8
Less Factor income paid abroad	313.2	495.8	477.9
Gross national product	1,633.4	2,097.8	2,557.7
Less Consumption of fixed capital	278.4	349.8	432.4
National income in market prices	1,355.0	1,748.0	2,125.3
Other current transfers from abroad	26.4	141.5	123.2
Less Other current transfers paid abroad	5.0	68.5	78.6
National disposable income	**1,376.4**	**1,821.0**	**2,169.9**

Source: UN, *National Accounts Statistics.*

Expenditure on the Gross Domestic Product
(at current prices)

	1986/87	1987/88	1988/89
Government final consumption expenditure	722.6	1,052.3	1,208.2
Private final consumption expenditure	987.4	1,116.0	1,236.5
Increase in stocks	18.6	−804.3	56.1
Gross fixed capital formation	669.9	1,081.8	2,232.0
Total domestic expenditure	2,398.5	2,445.8	4,732.8
Exports of goods and services	1,838.8	3,119.0	3,706.0
Less Imports of goods and services	1,427.5	1,769.2	2,966.8
GDP in purchasers' values	2,809.8	3,795.6	5,472.0
GDP at constant 1984/85 prices	2,140.6	2,467.5	2,791.2

Source: IMF, *International Financial Statistics.*

Gross Domestic Product by Economic Activity
(at constant 1985/86 prices)

	1989/90	1990/91	1991/92
Agriculture, hunting, forestry and fishing	209.9	215.6	219.9
Mining and quarrying	1,425.6	1,521.1	1,550.0
Manufacturing	173.2	184.6	196.5
Water and electricity	84.2	91.3	96.5
Construction	188.2	202.2	211.2
Trade, restaurants and hotels	513.8	558.0	642.5
Transport	117.9	136.3	150.1
Finance, insurance and business services	193.4	209.6	217.8
Government services	659.3	756.2	839.1
Social and personal services	103.2	110.4	116.4
Sub-total	3,668.7	3,985.1	4,240.0
Less Imputed bank service charge	71.9	69.9	72.1
GDP in purchasers' values	3,596.8	3,915.2	4,167.9

Source: Bank of Botswana, Gaborone.

BALANCE OF PAYMENTS (US $ million)

	1988	1989	1990
Merchandise exports f.o.b.	1,468.9	1,819.7	1,753.2
Merchandise imports f.o.b.	−986.9	−1,185.2	−1,606.2
Trade balance	482.0	634.6	147.0
Exports of services	110.3	110.5	134.1
Imports of services	−219.1	−213.0	−268.1
Other income received	220.1	244.8	363.2
Other income paid	−572.8	−498.5	−514.0
Private unrequited transfers (net)	−17.5	−30.6	−40.8
Official unrequited transfers (net)	184.6	250.5	316.2
Current balance	187.6	498.3	137.5
Direct investment (net)	39.9	42.2	38.2
Other capital (net)	−65.2	70.8	153.3
Net errors and omissions	220.0	−34.8	−21.7
Overall balance	382.3	576.5	307.2

Source: IMF, *International Financial Statistics.*

External Trade

PRINCIPAL COMMODITIES ('000 pula)

Imports c.i.f.	1988*	1989*	1990†
Food, beverages and tobacco	302,510	293,635	367,115
Fuel	134,775	146,859	183,609
Chemicals and rubber	184,201	241,334	301,726
Wood and paper	93,830	122,936	153,700
Textiles and footwear	180,736	217,692	272,168
Metal and metal products	177,732	325,569	407,039
Machinery and electrical goods	403,045	695,452	869,482
Vehicles and transport equipment	418,598	424,249	530,413
Other commodities	288,020	353,491	441,948
Total	2,183,447	2,821,217	3,527,200

Exports f.o.b.	1988*	1989*	1990†
Meat and meat products	116,638	147,058	130,863
Diamonds	1,979,162	2,886,560	2,664,917
Copper-nickel matte	370,936	496,041	287,626
Textiles	60,261	66,584	75,029
Hides and skins	4,570	—	—
Other commodities	138,229	230,970	163,799
Total	2,669,796	3,827,213	3,322,233

* Provisional figures. † Estimates.

PRINCIPAL TRADING PARTNERS ('000 pula)

Imports	1986	1987	1988†
SACU*	1,021,532	1,250,954	1,690,437
Other Africa	101,161	121,674	153,305
United Kingdom	32,836	36,248	133,538
Other Europe	82,147	106,182	90,463
USA	37,805	29,703	49,999
Others	55,798	27,696	65,705
Total	1,331,279	1,572,457	2,183,447

Exports	1986	1987	1988
SACU*	91,066	110,658	144,766
Other Africa	97,047	128,286	215,553
United Kingdom	59,632	30,560	30,578
Other Europe	1,353,588	2,381,592	2,263,242
USA	3,688	4,371	7,134
Others	8,409	8,336	8,522
Total	1,613,430	2,663,802	2,669,796

* Southern African Customs Union, of which Botswana is a member; also including Lesotho, Namibia, South Africa and Swaziland.

† Provisional figures.

Transport

RAILWAYS

	1986	1987	1988
Passenger journeys	507,730	439,680	441,931
Freight (net ton-km)	1,236,853	1,141,455	772,620

ROAD TRAFFIC (vehicles registered at 31 December)

	1989	1990	1991
Total	63,643	74,399	77,942

Source: Bank of Botswana, Gaborone.

CIVIL AVIATION (traffic on scheduled services)

	1989	1990	1991
Kilometres flown (million)	3	3	4
Passengers carried ('000)	82	101	102
Passenger-km (million)	50	63	73

Source: UN, *Statistical Yearbook*.

Tourism

FOREIGN TOURIST ARRIVALS (incl. same-day visitors)

Country of origin	1989	1990	1991
South Africa and Namibia	309,747	363,840	419,785
United Kingdom and Ireland	25,735	35,973	34,710
Zambia	25,241	26,454	28,205
Zimbabwe	249,283	338,264	334,688
Total (incl. others)	691,041	844,295	899,005

Source: Bank of Botswana, Gaborone.

Communications Media

Radio receivers ('000 in use): 155 in 1991.
Television receivers ('000 in use): 21 in 1991.
Book production (1987): 289 titles (books 134; pamphlets 155).
Daily newspaper (1990): 1 title (estimated circulation 18,000 copies).

Telephones in use: 34,000 in 1988; 41,000 in 1989; 48,000 in 1990.

Sources: UNESCO, *Statistical Yearbook*; Central Statistics Office, Gaborone; UN, *Statistical Yearbook*.

Education

(1994)

	Institutions	Teachers	Students
Primary	781	9,552	301,370
Secondary	199	5,190	99,560
Brigades*	32	227	2,128
Teacher training	6	290	2,354
Technical education	7	339	5,088
University	1	475	4,533

* Semi-autonomous units providing craft and practical training.

Source: Ministry of Education, Gaborone.

Directory

The Constitution

The Constitution of the Republic of Botswana took effect at independence on 30 September 1966.

EXECUTIVE

President

Executive power lies with the President of Botswana, who is also Commander-in-Chief of the armed forces. Election for the office of President is linked with the election of members of the National Assembly. Presidential candidates must be over 30 years of age and receive at least 1,000 nominations. If there is more than one candidate for the Presidency, each candidate for office in the Assembly must declare support for a presidential candidate. The candidate for President who commands the votes of more than one-half of the elected members of the Assembly will be declared President. If the Presidency falls vacant the members of the National Assembly will themselves elect a new President. The President, who is an ex officio member of the National Assembly, holds office for the duration of Parliament. The President chooses four members of the National Assembly.

Cabinet

There is also a Vice-President, whose office is ministerial. The Vice-President is appointed by the President and deputizes in the absence of the President. The Cabinet consists of the President, the Vice-President and 14 other Ministers, including four Assistant Ministers, appointed by the President. The Cabinet is responsible to the National Assembly.

LEGISLATURE

Legislative power is vested in Parliament, consisting of the President and the National Assembly, acting after consultation in certain cases with the House of Chiefs. The President may withhold assent to a Bill passed by the National Assembly. If the same Bill is again presented after six months, the President is required to assent to it or to dissolve Parliament within 21 days.

House of Chiefs

The House of Chiefs comprises the Chiefs of the eight principal tribes of Botswana as ex officio members, four members elected by sub-chiefs from their own number, and three members elected by the other 12 members of the House. Bills and motions relating to chieftaincy matters and alterations of the Constitution must be referred to the House, which may also deliberate and make representations on any matter.

National Assembly

The National Assembly consists of the Speaker, the Attorney-General, who does not have a vote, 30 members elected by universal adult suffrage and four specially elected members chosen by the President. The life of the Assembly is five years.

The Constitution contains a code of human rights, enforceable by the High Court.

The Government

HEAD OF STATE

President: Sir KETUMILE MASIRE (took office as Acting President 29 June 1980; elected President 18 July 1980; re-elected 10 September 1984 and 7 October 1989).

CABINET
(August 1994)

President: Sir KETUMILE MASIRE.

Vice-President and Minister of Finance and Development Planning: FESTUS G. MOGAE.

Minister of Health: B. K. TEMANE.

Minister of Agriculture: KEBATHLAMANG MORAKE.

Minister of External Affairs: Dr GAOSITWE CHIEPE.

Minister of Mineral Resources and Water Affairs: ARCHIE MOGWE.

Minister of Commerce and Industry: PONATSHENGO KEDIKILWE.

Minister of Local Government, Lands and Housing: C. J. BUTALE.

Minister of Works, Transport and Communications: D. N. MAGAN.

Minister of Presidential Affairs and Public Administration: Lt-Gen. MOMPATI MERAFE.

Minister of Education: RAY MOLOMO.

Minister of Labour and Home Affairs: PATRICK BALOPI.

There are, in addition, four assistant ministers.

MINISTRIES

Office of the President: Private Bag 001, Gaborone; tel. 350800; telex 2414.

Ministry of Agriculture: Private Bag 003, Gaborone; tel. 350581; telex 2543; fax 356027.

Ministry of Commerce and Industry: Private Bag 004, Gaborone; tel. 3601200; telex 2674; fax 371539.

Ministry of Education: Private Bag 005, Gaborone; tel. 3600400; fax 3600458.

Ministry of External Affairs: Private Bag 00368, Gaborone; tel. 356056.

Ministry of Finance and Development Planning: Private Bag 008, Gaborone; tel. 350100; telex 2401; fax 356086.

Ministry of Health: Private Bag 0038, Gaborone; tel. 352000; telex 2959.

Ministry of Labour and Home Affairs: Private Bag 002, Gaborone; tel. 3601000.

Ministry of Local Government, Lands and Housing: Private Bag 006, Gaborone; tel. 354100.

Ministry of Mineral Resources and Water Affairs: Private Bag 0018, Gaborone; tel. 352454; telex 2503; fax 372738.

Ministry of Works, Transport and Communications: Private Bag 007, Gaborone; tel. 358500; telex 2743; fax 358500.

Legislature

NATIONAL ASSEMBLY

Speaker: M. P. K. MWAKO.

General Election, 7 October 1989

Party	Votes	%	Seats
Botswana Democratic Party	157,824	65.0	31*
Botswana National Front	67,317	27.7	3
Botswana People's Party	9,699	4.0	—
Botswana Independence Party	4,393	1.8	—
Botswana Progressive Union	2,186	0.9	—
Botswana Freedom Party	1,363	0.6	—
Total	242,782	100.0	34†

* Of the 31 members of the BDP in the National Assembly, four were specially elected by the President.

† There are two additional members of the Assembly: the Speaker and the Attorney-General. The President is an ex officio member.

HOUSE OF CHIEFS

The House has a total of 15 members.

Chairman: Chief SEEPAPITSO IV.

Political Organizations

Botswana Democratic Party (BDP): Gaborone; f. 1962; Pres. Sir KETUMILE JONI MASIRE; Chair. (vacant); Sec.-Gen. (vacant).

Botswana Freedom Party (BFP): f. 1989; Pres. LEACH TLHOMELANG.

Botswana Independence Party (BIP): POB 3, Maun; f. 1962; Pres. MOTSAMAI K. MPHO; Sec.-Gen. EMMANUEL R. MOKOBI.

Botswana Labour Party: f. 1989; Pres. LENYELETSE KOMA.

Botswana People's Progressive Front (BPPF): f. 1991; an alliance comprising:

Botswana National Front (BNF): POB 42, Mahalapye; f. 1967; Pres. Dr KENNETH KOMA; Sec.-Gen. JAMES PILANE.

Botswana People's Party (BPP): POB 159, Francistown; f. 1960; Pres. Dr KNIGHT MARIPE; Chair. KENNETH MKHWA; Sec.-Gen. MATLHOMOLA MODISE.

Botswana Progressive Union (BPU): POB 10229, Francistown; f. 1982; Pres. G. G. BAGWASI; Sec.-Gen. R. K. MONYATSIWA.

Diplomatic Representation

EMBASSIES AND HIGH COMMISSIONS IN BOTSWANA

Angola: Private Bag 111, Phala Crescent, Gaborone; tel. 300204; telex 2361; fax 375089; Ambassador: PEDRO F. MAVUNZA.

China, People's Republic: POB 1031, Gaborone; tel. 352209; telex 2428; fax 300156; Ambassador: WANG YIHAO.

Germany: POB 315, Gaborone; tel. 353143; telex 2225; fax 353038; Ambassador: HERMANN F. KRÖGER.

India: Private Bag 249, Gaborone; tel. 372676; telex 2622; fax 374636; High Commissioner: SATYABRATA PAL.

Libya: POB 180, Gaborone; tel. 352481; telex 2501; Ambassador: TAHER ETTOUMI.

Nigeria: POB 274, Gaborone; tel. 313561; telex 2415; fax 313738; High Commissioner: ALABA OGUNSANWO.

Poland: Private Bag 00209, Gaborone; tel. 352501; Chargé d'affaires: Dr JAN RUDKOWSKI.

Russia: POB 81, Gaborone; tel. 353389; telex 2595; Ambassador: (vacant).

Sweden: Private Bag 0017, Gaborone; tel. 353912; telex 2421; fax 353942; Ambassador: RASMUS RASMUSSON.

United Kingdom: Private Bag 0023, Gaborone; tel. 352841; fax 356105; High Commissioner: JOHN C. EDWARDS.

USA: POB 90, Gaborone; tel. 353982; telex 2554; fax 356947; Ambassador: HOWARD F. JETER.

Zambia: POB 362, Gaborone; tel. 351951; telex 2416; fax 353952; High Commissioner: KASONDE P. KASUTO.

Zimbabwe: POB 1232, Gaborone; tel. 314495; telex 2701; High Commissioner: Dr N. G. G. MAKURA.

Judicial System

There is a High Court at Lobatse and a branch at Francistown, and Magistrates' Courts in each district. Appeals lie to the Court of Appeal of Botswana.

High Court: Private Bag 1, Lobatse; tel. 330607; telex 2758; fax 332317.

Chief Justice: MOLELEKI D. MOKAMA.

President of the Court of Appeal: A. N. E. AMMISSAH.

Justices of Appeal: T. A. AGUDA, G. BIZOS, W. H. R. SCHREINER, D. R. DOYLE.

Puisne Judges: I. R. ABOADYE, K. J. GYEKE-DAKO.

Registrar and Master of the High Court: K. YOGANATHAS.

Chief Magistrates: G. RWELENGA, F. B. SWANNIKER.

Senior Magistrates: K. OBENG, Y. D. PETKAR, K. B. MOESI, E. T. GALAFOROWE, I. M. I. NGITAMI, V. JEGASOTHY, N. Z. BOPA, S. N. NTOMIWA.

Attorney-General: PHANDU SKELEMANI.

Religion

The majority of the population hold animist beliefs; an estimated 30% are thought to be Christians. There are Islamic mosques in Gaborone and Lobatse. The Bahá'í Faith is also represented.

CHRISTIANITY

Lekgotla la Sekeresete la Botswana (Botswana Christian Council): POB 355, Gaborone; tel. 351981; f. 1966; comprises 25 churches and organizations; Pres. Rev. JOSEPH MATSHENG; Gen. Sec. CHURCHILL M. GAPE.

The Anglican Communion

Anglicans are adherents of the Church of the Province of Central Africa, comprising 10 dioceses and covering Botswana, Malawi, Zambia and Zimbabwe. The Province was inaugurated in 1955, and the diocese of Botswana was formed in 1972.

Archbishop of the Province of Central Africa and Bishop of Botswana: Most Rev. WALTER PAUL KHOTSO MAKHULU, POB 769, Gaborone; fax 313015.

Protestant Churches

African Methodist Episcopal Church: POB 141, Lobatse; Rev. L. M. MBULAWA.

Evangelical Lutheran Church in Botswana: POB 1976, Gaborone; tel. 352227; fax 313966; Bishop Rev. PHILIP ROBINSON; 16,305 mems.

Evangelical Lutheran Church in Southern Africa (Botswana Diocese): POB 400, Gaborone; tel. 353976; Bishop Rev. M. NTUPING.

Methodist Church in Botswana: POB 260, Gaborone; Dist. Supt Rev. Z. S. M. MOSAI.

Seventh-day Adventists: POB 20975, Gaborone; tel. 373264.

United Congregational Church of Southern Africa: POB 1263, Gaborone; tel. 352491; Synod status since 1980; Chair. Rev. L. T. S. MATLHABAPHIRI (acting); Sec. Rev. J. D. JONES; 15,000 mems.

Other denominations active in Botswana include the Church of God in Christ, the Dutch Reformed Church and the United Methodist Church.

The Roman Catholic Church

Botswana comprises a single diocese. The metropolitan see is Bloemfontein, South Africa. The church was established in Botswana in 1928, and had an estimated 49,226 adherents in the country at 31 December 1991. The Bishop participates in the Southern African Catholic Bishops' Conference, currently based in Pretoria, South Africa.

Bishop of Gaborone: Rt Rev. BONIFACE TSHOSA SETLALEKGOSI, POB 218, Bishop's House, Gaborone; tel. 312958; fax 356970.

The Press

DAILY NEWSPAPER

Dikgang tsa Gompieno (Botswana Daily News): Private Bag 0060, Gaborone; tel. 352541; telex 2409; f. 1964; publ. by Dept of Information and Broadcasting; Setswana and English; Mon.–Fri.; Editor L. LESHAGA; circ. 40,000.

PERIODICALS

Agrinews: Private Bag 003, Gaborone; f. 1971; monthly; technical journal on agriculture and rural development; circ. 6,000.

Botswana Advertiser: POB 130, 5647 Nakedi Rd, Broadhurst, Gaborone; tel. 312844; telex 2351; weekly.

The Botswana Gazette: POB 1605, Gaborone; tel. 312833; fax 312774; weekly; circ. 16,000.

Botswana Guardian: POB 1641, Gaborone; tel. 314937; telex 2692; fax 374381; f. 1982; weekly; Editor JOEL SEBONEGO; circ. 16,500.

Government Gazette: Private Bag 0081, Gaborone; tel. 314441; telex 2414.

Kutlwano: Private Bag 0060, Gaborone; tel. 352541; telex 2409; monthly; Setswana and English; publ. by Dept of Information and Broadcasting; circ. 24,000.

The Midweek Sun: Private Bag 00153, Gaborone; tel. 352085; fax 374381; weekly; circ. 12,096.

Mmegi/The Reporter: Private Bag BR50, Gaborone; tel. 374784; fax 314311; f. 1984; weekly; Setswana and English; publ. by Mmegi Publishing Trust; circ. 15,000.

Northern Advertiser: POB 402, Francistown; tel. 212265; fax 213769; f. 1985; weekly; advertisements, local interest, sport; Editor GRACE FISH; circ. 5,500.

The Sun: POB 40063, Gaborone; tel. 372852; fax 374558.

The Zebra's Voice: Private Bag 00114, Gaborone; f. 1982; quarterly; cultural magazine; publ. by the National Museum, Monuments and Art Gallery; circ. 4,000.

NEWS AGENCIES

Botswana Press Agency (BOPA): Private Bag 0060, Gaborone; tel. 313601; telex 2284; f. 1981.

Foreign Bureaux

Inter Press Service (IPS) (Italy): POB 1605, Gaborone; tel. 312833; telex 2631.

Xinhua (New China) News Agency (People's Republic of China): POB 1031, Plot 5379, President's Drive, Gaborone; tel. 353434; telex 2428; Correspondent CHEN GUOWEI.

Publishers

A.C. Braby (Botswana) (Pty) Ltd: POB 1549, Gaborone; tel. 371444; fax 373462; telephone directories.

Department of Information and Broadcasting: Private Bag 0060, Gaborone; tel. 352541; telex 2409; fax 357138; publs include *Dikgang tsa Gompieno* and *Kutlwano*.

Heinemann Educational Boleswa (Pty) Ltd: Plot 10223, Mokolwane Rd, Gaborone; tel. 372305; fax 371832.

Longman Botswana (Pty) Ltd: POB 1083, Gaborone; tel. 313969; fax 374682; f. 1981; educational; Gen. Man. K. RAKHUDU.

Macmillan Botswana Publishing Co (Pty) Ltd: POB 1155, Gaborone; tel. 314379; telex 2841; fax 374326.

Magnum Press (Pty) Ltd: Private Bag 40063, Gaborone; tel. 372852; fax 374558.

Printing and Publishing Co (Botswana) (Pty) Ltd: POB 130, 5647 Nakedi Rd, Broadhurst, Gaborone; tel. 312844; telex 2351; publr of *Botswana Advertiser*.

Government Publishing House

Department of Government Printing and Publishing Services: Private Bag 0081, Gaborone; tel. 314441; telex 2414.

Radio and Television

There were an estimated 150,000 radio receivers and 20,000 television receivers in use in 1990.

RADIO

Radio Botswana: Private Bag 0060, Gaborone; tel. 352541; telex 2633; broadcasts in Setswana and English; f. 1965; Dir TED MAKGEKGENENE.

Radio Botswana II: Private Bag 0060, Gaborone; tel. 352541; telex 2409; f. 1992; commercial radio network.

TELEVISION

TV Association of Botswana: Gaborone; relays SABC-TV and BOP-TV programmes from South Africa; plans for a national TV service are under consideration.

Finance

(cap. = capital; res = reserves; dep. = deposits; m. = million; brs = branches; amounts in pula)

BANKING

Central Bank

Bank of Botswana: POB 712, Khama Crescent, Gaborone; tel. 351911; telex 2448; fax 372984; f. 1975; bank of issue; cap. and res 1,351.0m., dep. 6,218.1m., (Dec. 1992); Gov. H. C. L. HERMANS; Dir of Operations LINA MOHOHLO.

Commercial Banks

Barclays Bank of Botswana Ltd: POB 478, Barclays House, Khama Crescent, Gaborone; tel. 352041; telex 2417; fax 313672; f. 1975; 74.9% owned by Barclays Bank PLC, London; cap. and res 94.2m., dep. 907.6m. (Dec. 1992); Chair. B. GAOLATHE; Man. Dir C. MIDDLETON; 17 brs.

First National Bank of Botswana: POB 1552, Plot 8844, Khama Crescent, Gaborone; tel. 374370; telex 2520; fax 374369; f. 1991; subsidiary of First National Bank of Southern Africa, Johannesburg (South Africa); Man. Dir D. G. PRICE; 5 brs.

Stanbic Bank Botswana Ltd: Private Bag 00168, Travaglini House, Old Lobatse Rd, Gaborone; tel. 301600; telex 2562; fax 300171; subsidiary of Australia and New Zealand Banking Group Ltd; Chair. G. C. BELL; Gen. Man. Dir D. J. BROWN.

Standard Chartered Bank Botswana Ltd: POB 496, Standard House, 5th Floor, The Mall, Gaborone; tel. 353111; telex 2422; fax 372933; f. 1975 as Standard Bank Botswana Ltd, present name adopted 1984; wholly-owned subsidiary of Standard Chartered Bank Africa PLC, London; cap. and res 46.5m., dep. 3,989.9m. (Dec. 1990); Chair. P. L. STEENKAMP; Man. Dir C. J. MALLARD; 15 brs.

Zimbank Botswana Ltd: Private Bag B052, Zimbank House, The Mall, Gaborone; tel. 312622; telex 2985; fax 312596; f. 1990; wholly-owned subsidiary of Zimbabwe Banking Corpn.; cap. and res 7.0m., dep. 54.8m. (Sept. 1991); Chair. S. BIYAM; Man. Dir A. O'DWYER; 2 brs.

Other Banks

Botswana Co-operative Bank Ltd: POB 40106, Co-operative Bank House, Broadhurst Mall, Gaborone; tel. 371398; fax 352396; f. 1974; cap. and res 300,000, loans 5.9m. (1987); central source of credit for registered co-operative societies; Chair. P. L. SIELE; Gen. Man. Dr HARRY TLALE.

Botswana Savings Bank: POB 1150, Gaborone; tel. 312555; telex 2401; fax 352608; Chair. F. MODISE.

National Development Bank: POB 225, Development House, The Mall, Gaborone; tel. 352801; telex 2553; fax 374446; f. 1964; cap. and res 5.7m., dep. 45.8m. (March 1990); priority given to agricultural credit for Botswana farmers, and co-operative credit and loans for local business ventures; Chair. F. MODISE; Gen. Man. E. W. JOHWA; 6 brs.

STOCK EXCHANGE

Botswana Share Market: Barclays House, Khama Crescent, Gaborone; tel. 357900; fax 357901; f. 1989; CEO W. J. PICKEN.

INSURANCE

Associated Insurance Brokers of Botswana (Pty) Ltd: POB 624, Standard House, Gaborone; tel. 351481; fax 314608; f. 1982.

Botswana Co-operative Insurance Co Ltd: POB 199, Gaborone; tel. 313654; fax 313654.

Botswana Eagle Insurance Co Ltd: POB 1221, 501 Botsalano House, Gaborone; tel. 352897; telex 2259; fax 353395.

Botswana Insurance Co (Pty) Ltd: POB 336, BIC House, Gaborone; tel. 351791; telex 2359; fax 313290; Gen. Man. P. B. SUMMER.

Sedgwick James Insurance Brokers (Pty) Ltd: POB 103, Plot 730, The Mall, Botswana Rd, Gaborone; tel. 314241; fax 373120.

Tshireletso Insurance Brokers: POB 1967, Gaborone; tel. 357064; telex 2916; fax 371558.

Trade and Industry

PUBLIC CORPORATIONS

Botswana Housing Corporation: POB 412, Gaborone; tel. 353341; telex 2729; fax 352070; provides housing for central govt and local authority needs and assists with private-sector housing schemes; Chair. Z. P. PITSO; Gen. Man. (vacant); 900 employees.

Botswana Meat Commission (BMC): Private Bag 4, Lobatse; tel. 330321; telex 2420; fax 330530; f. 1966; slaughter of livestock, exports of hides and skins, carcasses, frozen and chilled boneless beef; operates tannery and beef products cannery; Exec. Chair. Dr MARTIN M. MANNATHOKO.

Botswana Power Corporation: POB 48, Motlakase House, Macheng Way, Gaborone; tel. 352211; telex 2431; fax 373563; operates power stations at Selebi-Phikwe and Moropule, with capacity of 65 MW and 132 MW respectively; Chair. the Dep. Perm. Sec., Ministry of Mineral Resources and Water Affairs; CEO K. SITHOLE.

Botswana Telecommunications Corporation: POB 700, Gaborone; tel. 358000; f. 1980; CEO M. T. CURRY.

Water Utilities Corporation: Private Bag 00276, Gaborone; tel. 352521; telex 2545; fax 373852; f. 1970; public water supply undertaking for principal townships; Chair. the Perm. Sec., Ministry of Mineral Resources and Water Affairs; CEO P. GRIFFITH.

CHAMBER OF COMMERCE

Botswana National Chamber of Commerce and Industry: POB 20344, Gaborone; tel. 52677.

MARKETING BOARD

Botswana Agricultural Marketing Board: Private Bag 0053, 1227 Haile Selassie Rd, Gaborone; tel. 351341; telex 2530; fax 352926; Chair. the Perm. Sec., Ministry of Agriculture; Gen. Man. S. B. TAUKOBONG.

DEVELOPMENT ORGANIZATIONS

Botswana Development Corporation Ltd: Private Bag 160, Madirelo House, Mmanaka Rd, Gaborone; tel. 351811; telex 2251; fax 373539; Chair. G. J. STONEHAM; Man. Dir M. O. MOLEFANE.

Botswana Livestock Development Corporation (Pty) Ltd: POB 455, Gaborone; tel. 351949; fax 357251; f.1977; Chair. M. M. MANNATHOKO; Gen. Man. S. M. R. BURNETT.

Department of Trade and Investment Promotion (TIPA), Ministry of Commerce and Industry: Private Bag 00367 Gaborone; tel. 351790; telex 2674; fax 305375; promotes industrial and commercial investment, diversification and expansion, offers consultancy, liaison and information services; participates in int. trade fairs and trade and investment missions; Dir D. TSHEKO.

Financial Services Co of Botswana (Pty) Ltd: POB 1129, Finance House, Khama Crescent, Gaborone; tel. 351363; telex 2207; fax 357815; f. 1974; hire purchase, mortgages, industrial leasing and debt factoring; Chair. M. E. HOPKINS; Man. Dir R. A. PAWSON.

Integrated Field Services: Private Bag 004, Ministry of Commerce and Industry, Gaborone; tel. 353024; telex 2674; fax 371539; promotes industrialization and rural development; Dir B. T. TIBONE.

EMPLOYERS' ASSOCIATION

Botswana Confederation of Commerce, Industry and Manpower: POB 432, Botsalano House, Gaborone; f. 1971; Chair. GEORGE KGOROBA; Sec.-Gen. MODIRI J. MBAAKANYI; 600 affiliated mems.

MAJOR INDUSTRIAL COMPANIES

The following are among the leading companies in Botswana in terms of capital investment and employment.

Botswana RST Ltd (Botrest): POB 3, Selebi-Phikwe; tel. 810211; telex 2219; fax 810441; f. 1967 as Botswana Roan Selection Trust Ltd; holding co with 85% shareholding in copper-nickel producers, BCL Ltd; Chair. S. M. JOHNSON; Man. Dir M. A. FOREMAN.

Debswana Co (Pty) Ltd (Diamond): Botsalano House, The Mall, POB 329, Gaborone; tel. 351131; telex 2410; fax 352941; sole diamond-mining interest in Botswana; owned equally by De Beers Consolidated Mines Ltd and the Botswana govt; CEO BALEDZI GAOLATHE.

TRADE UNIONS

Botswana Federation of Trade Unions: POB 440, Gaborone; tel. 357978; f. 1977; Gen. Sec. RONALD DUST BAIPIDI.

Affiliated Unions

Air Botswana Employees' Union: POB 92, Gaborone; Gen. Sec. DANIEL MOTSUMI.

Barclays Management Staff Union: POB 478, Gaborone; Gen. Sec. Tefo Lionjanga.

B.C.L. Senior Staff Union: POB 383, Selebi-Phikwe; Gen. Sec. Kabelo Matthews.

Botswana Agricultural Marketing Board Workers' Union: Private Bag 0053, Gaborone; Gen. Sec. M. E. Semathane.

Botswana Bank Employees' Union: POB 111, Gaborone; Gen. Sec. Keolopile Gaborone.

Botswana Beverages and Allied Workers' Union: POB 41358, Gaborone; Gen. Sec. S. Senwelo.

Botswana Brigade Teachers' Union: Private Bag 007, Molepolole; Gen. Sec. Sadike Kgokong.

Botswana Commercial and General Workers' Union: POB 62, Gaborone; Gen. Sec. Kediretse Mpetang.

Botswana Construction Workers' Union: POB 1508, Gaborone; Gen. Sec. Joshua Kesiilwe.

Botswana Diamond Sorters-Valuators' Union: POB 1186, Gaborone; Gen. Sec. Felix T. Lesetedi.

Botswana Housing Corporation Staff Union: POB 412, Gaborone; Gen. Sec. Gorata Dingalo.

Botswana Meat Industry Workers' Union: POB 181, Lobatse; Gen. Sec. Johnson Bojosi.

Botswana Mining Workers' Union: POB 14, Gaborone; Gen. Sec. Balekamang S. Ganasiane.

Botswana Postal Services Workers' Union: POB 87, Gaborone; Gen. Sec. Aaron Mosweu.

Botswana Power Corporation Workers' Union: Private Bag 0053, Gaborone; Gen. Sec. Molefe Modise.

Botswana Railways and Artisan Employees' Union: POB 1486, Gaborone; Gen. Sec. Patrick Magowe.

Botswana Railways Senior Staff Union: POB 582, Mahalapye; Gen. Sec. Lentswe Letsweletse.

Botswana Railways Workers' Union: POB 181, Gaborone; Gen. Sec. Ernest T. G. Mohutsiwa.

Botswana Telecommunications Employees' Union: POB 2032, Gaborone; Gen. Sec. Sedibana Robert.

Botswana Vaccine Institute Staff Union: Private Bag 0031, Gaborone; Gen. Sec. Elliot Modise.

Central Bank Union: POB 712, Gaborone; Gen. Sec. Godfrey Ngidi.

National Development Bank Employees' Union: POB 225, Gaborone; Sec.-Gen. Matshediso Fologang.

National Amalgamated Local and Central Government, Parastatal, Statutory Body and Manual Workers' Union: POB 374, Gaborone; Gen. Sec. Dickson Kelatlhegetswe.

Non-Academic Staff Union: Private Bag 0022, Gaborone; Gen. Sec. Isaac Thothe.

CO-OPERATIVES

Department of Co-operative Development: POB 86, Gaborone; f. 1964; promotes marketing and supply, consumer, dairy, horticultural and fisheries co-operatives, thrift and loan societies, credit societies, a co-operative union and a co-operative bank.

Botswana Co-operative Union: Gaborone; telex 2298; f. 1970; Dir Aaron Ramosako.

Transport

RAILWAYS

In 1992 there were 888 km of 1,067-mm-gauge track within Botswana, including three branches serving the Selebi-Phikwe mining complex (56 km), the Morupule colliery (16 km) and the Sua Pan soda ash deposits (175 km). The entire main railway line in Botswana is to be rehabilitated under an SADC project, estimated to cost US $114m. The 960-km railway line from Mafikeng, South Africa, to Bulawayo, Zimbabwe, passes through Botswana.

Botswana Railways: Private Bag 00125, Moapare Rd, Gaborone; tel. 373185; telex 2980; fax 312305; Chair. A. V. Lionjanga; Gen. Man. C. M. Khosla.

ROADS

In 1991 there were some 13,500 km of roads, of which about 2,500 km were bituminized (including a main road from Gaborone, via Francistown, to Kazungula, where the borders of Botswana, Namibia, Zambia and Zimbabwe meet). The Government aims to construct several main roads and to extend the networks of both feeder and rural roads serving the remoter areas. The construction of a 340-km road between Nata and Maun was under way. Construction of a trans-Kalahari road from Jwaneng to the port of Walvis Bay on the Namibian coast (which remained under South African jurisdiction following Namibia's independence in 1990) commenced in 1990 and was expected to be completed in 1996. There is a car-ferry service from Kazungula across the Zambezi river into Zambia.

CIVIL AVIATION

The main international airport is at Gaborone. A second major airport, at Kasane in the Chobe area of northern Botswana, opened in 1992. There are airfields at Francistown, Maun and at other population centres, and there are numerous airstrips throughout the country. Scheduled services of Air Botswana are supplemented by an active charter and business sector. In addition, most regional airlines operate services to Gaborone. Botswana assumed control of its airspace from South Africa in 1992.

Air Botswana: POB 92, Head Office Bldg, Sir Seretse Khama Airport, Gaborone; tel. 352812; telex 2413; fax 374802; f. 1972; govt-owned; domestic services and regional services to most countries in eastern and southern Africa; Chair. A. V. Lionjanga; Gen. Man. Capt. Brian L. R. Pocock.

Tourism

There are five game reserves and three national parks, including Chobe, near Victoria Falls, on the Zambia-Zimbabwe border. Efforts to expand the tourist industry include plans for the construction of new hotels and the rehabilitation of existing hotel facilities. In 1991 an estimated 899,005 tourists visited Botswana, and earnings from tourism amounted to US $65m.

Department of Wildlife and National Parks: POB 131, Gaborone; tel. 371405; Dir. G. Seeletso.

Tourism Development Unit, Ministry of Commerce and Industry: Private Bag 004, Gaborone; tel. 353024; telex 2674; fax 371539; f. 1973 to promote tourism in Botswana; Dir Tutu Tsiang.

Defence

Military service is voluntary. Botswana established a permanent defence force in 1977. In June 1993 the army's total strength was over 6,000; there was also an air force of over 100. In addition, there was a paramilitary police force of 1,000.

Defence Expenditure: Budgeted at P243.5m. in 1989/90.

Defence Force Commander: Lt-Gen. Mompati Merafe.

Education

Education is not compulsory, although the government has an obligation to provide universal access to 10 years of basic education. Primary education, which is provided free of charge, begins at seven years of age and lasts for up to seven years. Secondary education, beginning at the age of 14, lasts for a further five years, comprising a first cycle of two years and a second of three years. As a proportion of the school-age population, the total enrolment at primary and secondary schools increased from 52% in 1975 to 83% in 1991. Botswana continues to rely heavily on expatriate secondary school teachers.

In 1990 enrolment at primary schools included 91% of children in the relevant age-group (boys 88%; girls 93%), while secondary schools were attended by only 36% of children in the relevant age-group (boys 33%; girls 39%). In 1994 there were 301,370 pupils in primary schools, 99,560 secondary students, 5,088 technical students, and 4,533 students at the University of Botswana. In addition, there were 2,128 students in Brigades, which are semi-autonomous community-based units providing craft and practical training. There were also 2,354 students enrolled at teacher-training colleges.

Adult illiteracy averaged 59% (males 63%; females 56%) in 1971, but, according to estimates by UNESCO, the rate had declined to 26.4% (males 16.3%; females 34.9%) by 1990. A National Literacy Programme was initiated in 1980, and 9,473 people were enrolled under the programme in 1991. Education was allocated 22% of recurrent expenditure in the 1994/95 budget, and was to receive some 10% of total projected expenditure under the National Development Plan for 1991–97.

Bibliography

Benson, M. *Tshekedi Khama*. London, Faber and Faber, 1960.

Botswana Society. *Settlement in Botswana*. London, Heinemann Educational, 1982.

Colclough, C., and McCarthy, S. *The Political Economy of Botswana: A Study of Growth and Distribution*. Oxford, Oxford University Press, 1980.

Hailey, Lord. *The Republic of South Africa and the High Commission Territories*. London, Oxford University Press, 1963.

Halpern, J. *South Africa's Hostages. Basutoland, Bechuanaland and Swaziland*. Harmondsworth, Penguin Books, 1965.

Harvey, C. (Ed.). *Papers on the Economy of Botswana*. London, Heinemann Educational, 1981.

Harvey, C., and Lewis, S. R. *Policy Choice and Development Performance in Botswana*. Basingstoke, Macmillan, 1990.

Hayward, M. F. *Elections in Independent Africa*. Boulder, Colo, Westview Press, 1987.

Jones, D. *Aid and Development in Southern Africa*. London, Croom Helm/Overseas Development Institute, 1977.

Konczacki, Z. A., Parpart, J. L., and Shaw, T. M. (Eds). *Studies in the Economic History of Southern Africa*. Vol. I. London, Cass, 1990.

Lipton, M. *Employment and Labour Use in Botswana*. Gaborone, Botswana Government Printer, 1978.

Oommen, M. A., et al. *Botswana Economy since Independence*. New Delhi, Tata/McGraw-Hill, 1983.

Parsons, N., and Crowder, M. (Eds). *Monarch of All I Survey: Bechuanaland Diaries of Sir Charles Rey, 1929–37*. London, James Currey (for Botswana Society), 1988.

Picard, L. A. (Ed.). *The Evolution of Modern Botswana*. London, Rex Collings, 1988.

Schapera, I., et al. *Ethnographic Survey of Africa: The Tswana*. London, International African Institute, 1953.

Selwyn, P. *Industries in the Southern African Periphery: a Study of Industrial Development in Botswana, Lesotho and Swaziland*. London, Croom Helm/Institute of Development Studies, 1976.

Sillery, A. *Botswana, A Short Political History*. London, Methuen, 1974.

Thomas, E. M. *The Harmless People*. London, Secker and Warburg, 1959.

BURKINA FASO

Physical and Social Geography

R. J. HARRISON CHURCH

Like Niger and Mali, Burkina Faso (formerly the Republic of Upper Volta) is a land-locked state of west Africa and is situated north of Côte d'Ivoire, Ghana and Togo. Burkina has an area of 274,200 sq km (105,870 sq miles). The December 1985 census recorded a total population of 7,964,705, giving an average density of 29 inhabitants per sq km. According to official estimates, the population had risen to 9,490,000 at mid-1992. In recent years there has been large-scale emigration to neighbouring Côte d'Ivoire and Ghana by people seeking work on farms, in industries and the service trades, although economic difficulties in these host countries have prompted the return of large numbers of migrant workers to Burkina. The main ethnic groups are the Bobo in the south-west, and the Mossi and Gourma in the north and east respectively. Along the northern border are the semi-nomadic Fulani, who are also present in the east of the country.

Towards the south-western border with Mali there are Primary sandstones, terminating eastward in the Banfora escarpment. As in Guinea, Mali and Ghana, where there are also great expanses of these rocks, their residual soils are poor and water percolates deeply within them. Although most of the rest of the country is underlain by granite, gneisses and schists, there is much loose sand or bare laterite; consequently, there are extensive infertile areas. Moreover, annual rainfall is only some 635–1,145 mm, and comes in a rainy season of at the most five months. Water is scarce except by the rivers or in the Gourma swampy area; by the former the simulium fly, whose bite leads to blindness, can still occur despite extensive eradication projects, while in the latter the tsetse, a fly which can cause sleeping sickness in man and beast, is found. Given the grim physical environment, the density of population in the north-central Mossi area is remarkable. The area is, in fact, one of the oldest indigenous kingdoms of west Africa, dating back to the 11th century. Islam first penetrated the area during the 14th–16th centuries. At the end of the 18th century it was adopted by some local rulers, notably the moro naba of the Mossi, but traditional religious practices among the population remained strong. Islam's expansion was facilitated by the circumstances of French rule but more than one half of the population retain their traditional beliefs.

Burkina Faso is believed to contain considerable mineral resources, although only gold, manganese, marble and antimony are currently exploited. Deposits of silver, nickel, zinc, lead, phosphates and vanadium have also been identified.

Recent History

PIERRE ENGLEBERT

Burkina Faso (then known as Upper Volta) became a self-governing republic within the French community in December 1958. Full independence followed on 5 August 1960, when a government was formed by the Union démocratique voltaïque (UDV). Maurice Yaméogo, the leader of the UDV, became the first president of the new republic. Support for the UDV was centred on the Mossi, the country's dominant ethnic group, constituting about 50% of the population.

Yaméogo's administration was autocratic in style. Opposition parties were declared illegal, while popular support for the government receded as the country's economic condition worsened. Following a prolonged period of economic crisis and social unrest, Yaméogo was deposed in an army coup in January 1966. The new head of state, Lt-Col Sangoulé Lamizana, suspended the constitution and introduced austerity measures which led to improved economic conditions.

In December 1970 the military regime assented to the formation of an elected civilian administration under the prime ministership of Gérard Ouédraogo, the president of the UDV. Several new parties entered the political arena, notably the Mouvement de libération nationale (MLN), an urban-supported radical group led by Prof. Joseph Ki-Zerbo, and the Parti du regroupement africain, led by Dr Dongolo Traoré, with a predominantly rural base. These groups were later joined by the Mouvement national pour le renouveau, a short-lived national unity movement formed by President Lamizana, and the Union nationale pour la défense de la démocratie (UNDD), a party favouring the interests of ex-president Yaméogo and led by his son, Herman. The UDV, meanwhile, began to experience factional strain, while Ki-Zerbo's MLN allied itself with other elements to form the Union progressiste voltaïque (UPV).

For much of the 1970s, Upper Volta was ravaged by the Sahelian drought, which disrupted the economy and brought a large part of the rural population to the brink of starvation. In the mid-1970s a long-standing border dispute between Upper Volta and Mali suddenly erupted when Malian troops were sent in to occupy the disputed area, the 'Agacher strip', which is believed to contain significant mineral deposits. Mediation by the Organization of African Unity (OAU) failed effectively to address this problem, which was to create strained relations for more than a decade.

In 1977 President Lamizana promulgated a new constitution, under which presidential and legislative elections were held in May 1978. A mainly civilian government, in which the UDV predominated, took office. All political parties except the UDV, the UNDD and the UPV were suppressed.

ARMY REGIMES, 1980–83

In November 1980, following a period of renewed economic difficulty and popular unrest, President Lamizana was overthrown in a bloodless military coup led by Col Saye Zerbo, who formed a Comité militaire de redressement pour le progrès national (CMRPN) to govern Upper Volta. The

CMRPN suspended the 1977 constitution and proscribed political parties.

Although the trade unions initially supported the coup, they soon became discontented with the ban on political activities. Conflict between government and unions came closer when, in May 1981, Zerbo announced that priority was to be given to the rural sector, and emphasized the need for restraint by urban workers. Relations deteriorated steadily, and in November, following criticisms of its policies by trade unions, the CMRPN withdrew the right to strike. Tensions remained when the right to strike was restored in February 1982. At the same time, serious rifts began to appear in the CMRPN, and the resignation, in April, of Capt. Thomas Sankara (a populist with increasing support) from the information ministry was perceived to be indicative of dissatisfaction in some quarters of the military.

Ouédraogo and the CSP

On 7 November 1982 a group of NCOs seized power and issued a statement accusing Zerbo of corruption, suppression of liberties and arrests of workers and students. A Conseil provisoire du salut du peuple (CPSP) was formed of NCOs and officers up to the rank of major, with Surgeon-Maj. Jean-Baptiste Ouédraogo as chairman, head of state and minister of defence. The chief of staff of the army, Col Gabriel Somé, remained in his post, and some of Zerbo's ministers were retained in the new government which was formed in late November, at which time the CPSP was given permanent status as the Conseil du salut du peuple (CSP). Although Sankara was rumoured to have been involved in the coup, his formal inclusion in the regime was not confirmed until January 1983, when he was appointed prime minister.

The CSP adopted a radical stance in favour of the unions and the right to strike. Ouédraogo also repeatedly promised that there would be a return to civilian rule in 1984, and that a major restructuring of the armed forces would take place.

By mid-1983, however, it had become apparent that Ouédraogo was presiding over an increasingly divided government, as the compromise between traditionalists in the army (led by Somé) and the radicals (led by Sankara) degenerated into open conflict. The catalyst for a split was a visit to Upper Volta in early May by the Libyan leader, Col Qaddafi, at Sankara's invitation. A few days after Qaddafi's departure, Ouédraogo ordered the arrest of Sankara and his radical colleagues in the CSP, and the Libyan chargé d'affaires was expelled. Sankara was accused of 'dangerously threatening national unity'.

Sankara's Coup

Members of Sankara's commando unit in Pô, near the Ghana border, immediately rebelled against Sankara's arrest, which they interpreted as having been masterminded by Somé (who was now in charge of national defence) and influenced by France (whose presidential adviser on African affairs happened to be in Ouagadougou when Sankara was arrested). The Pô commandos, led by Capt. Blaise Compaoré, took control of the town and refused orders from the capital. Ouédraogo wavered in the face of this crisis, and twice released Sankara to negotiate with the Pô rebels. Ouédraogo was unwilling to accede to the rebels' demand for Somé's dismissal, but Sankara was freed unconditionally in June 1983. However, the Pô mutiny spread, and in August Sankara deposed Ouédraogo in a military coup. There were skirmishes involving the opposing factions in the days that followed, during which Somé was killed.

On taking power, Sankara installed a Conseil national de la révolution (CNR) and formed a new government, with himself as head of state and Compaoré as minister of state to the presidency. The CNR, composed of junior officers and NCOs, proceeded to effect wide-ranging measures, with the support of left-wing civilians grouped in the previously underground Ligue patriotique pour le développement (LIPAD).

REVOLUTION AND REFORM, 1983–87

Sankara encouraged the establishment of Comités pour la défense de la révolution (CDR) throughout the country, and purged the army of 'reactionary' elements. In its first months in power the CNR reorganized the administrative regions of the country, deprived the country's traditional chiefs of their privileges and influence, and installed revolutionary 'people's tribunals' to hold trials of former public officials charged with political crimes and embezzlement.

The new tribunals began work in January 1984. The first politician to be tried was ex-president Lamizana, who was acquitted on charges of misusing official funds. However, several former ministers were subsequently imprisoned, after having been found guilty of embezzlement; other former government officials were fined, and some were acquitted. In April ex-president Zerbo was jailed for 15 years (seven of them suspended) and ordered to make financial restitution. In June Gérard Ouédraogo was sentenced to 10 years' imprisonment, with six years suspended, for embezzlement; however, both were released in 1986.

By March 1984 there was growing opposition to the new regime, principally from teachers, who staged a strike in protest against the arrest of three of their leaders. Internal discord was also burgeoning, as LIPAD's attempts to gain full control of the CNR met with resistance from other elements. A prominent LIPAD member was dismissed from the government in May, and in June seven army officers, who had been accused of plotting a coup, were executed, while others received sentences of hard labour, ranging from 15 years to life.

Relations with France became strained as a result of these events, and the French Socialist Party was accused of providing support to Joseph Ki-Zerbo, who had resumed political activities in exile. It was some months before quiet diplomacy could restore some calm to the two countries' usually close relationship. However, Western governments encouraged Sankara's efforts to distance his regime from both Libya and the USSR.

To symbolize the political changes that were taking place, and as an expression of 'decolonization', Sankara changed the name of the country to Burkina Faso ('Land of the Incorruptible Men') in August 1984. Later in the month Sankara dismissed his entire government, as a prelude to a complete break with LIPAD. Sankara's closest advisers remained Compaoré, as minister of state, Maj. Jean-Baptiste Boukary Lingani, as minister of defence, and Capt. Henri Zongo, who became minister of economic promotion. In October several LIPAD members were arrested, and 19 junior army officers and lower-ranking military personnel were dismissed, accused of 'subversive attitudes'. In January 1985 the general secretary of the Confédération syndicale burkinabè and a prominent member of LIPAD, Soumane Touré, was detained, and several trade union leaders were removed from office.

The momentum for change was maintained by a thorough reform of the judicial and education systems. Sankara's revolution was now generally seen to be less identified with Marxist forces, and as seeking to accommodate a wider cross-section of society. The extended role of the CDR in imposing government policy and organizing local affairs helped to consolidate Sankara's power. Opposition to economic austerity measures was mild, and there was no evidence of major political dissent at this time. Sankara's growing confidence in his own authority was manifested during 1986 with the release from detention of all his significant political opponents.

The long-standing disagreement between Burkina and Mali over the demarcation of their borders along the Agacher strip erupted into six days of armed conflict in late December 1985. Fifty people were estimated to have died in the conflict, during which Mali, with its superior forces and armaments, inflicted considerable damage inside Burkinabè territory. Members of the Accord de non-agression et d'assistance en matière de défense (ANAD), the defence grouping of the Communauté économique de l'Afrique de l'ouest, negotiated a cease-fire, and in January 1986, following successful efforts by ANAD peace-keeping forces,

Sankara and President Traoré of Mali agreed to a reconciliation. Both countries subsequently withdrew their troops from the disputed area, and in June ambassadors were exchanged for the first time in 12 years. In December the International Court of Justice, to which the dispute had been referred in 1983, ruled that the territory be divided equally between the two countries, with Burkina gaining sovereignty over the eastern district of Beli.

Sankara established close relations with Ghana's head of state, Flight-Lt Jerry Rawlings, in both military and political spheres, and arrangements were discussed for an eventual union of the two countries. However, other neighbouring states, particularly Togo and Côte d'Ivoire, opposed such an alliance, and Togo accused Burkina and Ghana of acting to promote a coup attempt in Lomé in September 1986.

The Fall of Sankara

During 1987 divisions between Sankara and the other military leaders of the CNR, Compaoré, Boukary Lingani and Zongo, became increasingly evident. In particular, Compaoré opposed Sankara's attitude to the trade unions, which was exemplified, in May, by the renewed imprisonment of Soumane Touré. Divisions were equally apparent between the semi-official political organizations participating in the CNR: the Union des luttes communistes reconstruite (ULCR), which continued to support Sankara; the Groupe communiste burkinabè (GCB); and the Union des communistes burkinabè (UCB), which was closely associated with Compaoré. A split in the ULCR undermined Sankara's principal base of civilian support, and forced him to dismiss two of the three ULCR ministers in a government reshuffle in August. In an attempt to prevent his further marginalization within the CNR, Sankara proposed that a single party be formed to embrace all existing political organizations, a suggestion which was vehemently opposed by his former allies. Dissensions became apparently irreconcilable, and on 15 October a commando unit loyal to Compaoré opened fire on Sankara, killing him and 13 of his associates. Sankara was denounced as a traitor and a renegade, and it was stated that the CNR was to be replaced by a Front populaire (FP). Compaoré, as chairman of the FP, was to be head of state.

Sankara's death was widely mourned, both by the inhabitants of Burkina and by the country's allies. Students boycotted classes in Ouagadougou, and there was a brief rebellion at the Koudougou army garrison. Many of Sankara's close associates, including former ministers and members of his family, were arrested, and a campaign of denigration against Sankara and his widow was instigated by the FP.

THE FRONT POPULAIRE

While the FP pledged a continuation of the CNR's revolutionary process, a new phase, to be known as 'rectification', was announced. This concept embraced both an elimination of Sankara loyalists and attempts to foster private enterprise, as well as the instigation of negotiations with the IMF and the World Bank. The CDR were abolished in March 1988 and replaced by Comités révolutionnaires (CR); however, attempts at recruitment to these attracted little popular interest.

By mid-1988, as civilian opposition to the new regime appeared to recede, the FP allowed Sankara's widow to seek asylum in Gabon and released several of those arrested in the aftermath of the coup. However, military factionalism persisted, and in December seven army officers were executed, after having been convicted of the murder of the officer who had defeated the Koudougou mutiny in October 1987; in January 1989 it was reported that five further Sankara loyalists had been executed.

In April 1989 the formation was announced of a new political group, the Organisation pour la démocratie populaire/Mouvement du travail (ODP/MT). The UCB and a breakaway faction of the Union des luttes communistes (ULC) declared their loyalty to the ODP/MT, which was to be led by the former leader of the UCB, Clément Oumarou Ouédraogo. In the same month the secretary-general of the GCB, Jean-Marc Palm, and the leader of the ULC, Alain Zougba (both of whom had refused to sanction the affiliation of their organizations to the ODP/MT), were dismissed from the government, while Clément Oumarou Ouédraogo was appointed to the newly-created position of minister-delegate to the co-ordinating committee of the FP.

The process of 'rectification' assumed more radical implications in September 1989, when Zongo and Boukary Lingani were summarily executed, together with two others, following the alleged discovery of a plot to overthrow Compaoré. The only remaining 'orthodox' elements of the 1983 revolution were thus eliminated, following a trial that showed little evidence of their guilt. Compaoré subsequently assumed the popular defence and security portfolio (previously held by Boukary Lingani), in a reallocation of ministerial portfolios that coincided with a reorganization of the executive committee of the FP. None the less, the continuing 'revolutionary' dogma of the ODP/MT, in contrast with Compaoré's increasingly moderate orientation, remained a potential source of instability within the FP. In late December 1989 it was announced that a further coup plot had been foiled. About 30 people (both army personnel and civilians) were detained; that no executions took place was probably attributable to impending visits to Burkina by Pope John Paul II and a French government minister.

The first congress of the FP was convened in March 1990 and attended by representatives of seven political organizations. Delegates appointed a commission to draft a new constitution that would define a process of 'democratization'. Meanwhile, the congress approved a reorganization of the executive committee of the FP that included the appointment to that body of Herman Yaméogo, who was regarded as a political 'moderate'. (Three months later, however, Yaméogo and his supporters were expelled from the FP.)

In April 1990 Compaoré reaffirmed his authority over the ODP/MT when Clément Oumarou Ouédraogo, accused of having deviated from the organization's political doctrine, was dismissed from its leadership and subsequently removed from ministerial office. Compaoré's more moderate supporter, Roch Marc Christian Kaboré, assumed both the leadership of the ODP/MT and the post of secretary for political affairs within the FP's executive committee. Kaboré was promoted to the rank of minister of state in September.

The constitutional commission, which began work in May 1990, was not given plenary powers, suggesting that the FP intended to exercise close supervision over the process of democratization. In the event, however, the first draft of the constitution, published in October, provided for a multiparty political system in what was designated the fourth republic. Among the main provisions of the final document was a clause denying legitimacy to any regime that might take power as the result of a *coup d'état*. The division of powers between the executive, legislative and judicial organs of state was defined, and provision was made for presidential and legislative elections to take place by universal adult suffrage. The seven-year mandate of the head of state would be renewable only once, while elections to the Assemblée des députés populaires (ADP) would be held every five years. It was envisaged that a second, consultative chamber, to be composed of the 'active forces of the nation', would eventually be established.

The draft constitution was submitted for approval in a national referendum on 2 June 1991: it was reported that 93% of those who voted (about 49% of the electorate) endorsed the document. The constitution took effect on 11 June, whereupon the functions of a restructured FP were separated from the organs of state. Meanwhile, political movements flourished. In March 1991 a congress of the ODP/MT adopted Compaoré as the party's official candidate to contest the forthcoming presidential election, and at the same time replaced its Marxist-Leninist ideology with a commitment to policies of free enterprise. (Similarly, in the same month the GCB was renamed the Mouvement pour la démocratie sociale.) In April an official amnesty was proclaimed for the alleged perpetrators of the December 1989 coup attempt; the rehabilitation was announced, in May 1991, of Maurice Yaméogo, and an appeal was made to political exiles to return to Burkina. In June plans were announced for the construction of a memorial honouring Thomas Sankara, and in August Compaoré declared an amnesty for all political crimes committed since independence.

THE FOURTH REPUBLIC

Following the adoption of the new constitution, the council of ministers was dissolved, and a transitional government was appointed in mid-June 1991. Compaoré remained head of state on an 'interim' basis, pending the presidential election. The most senior member of the new administration was Kaboré (as minister of state, in charge of the co-ordination of government action), and its composition was notable for the appointment of a civilian, Lassane Ouangraoua, as minister of popular defence and security. Many political parties criticized the dominant role of the ODP/MT, and several nominated government members declined to accept their appointments. Tensions between Compaoré and opposition leaders had emerged earlier in the month, when 13 parties had withdrawn from a 'round-table' conference that had been convened to discuss the implementation of the constitution and the organization of the forthcoming elections: the boycotting parties protested that the conference was merely consultative, rather than sovereign, and demanded that a national conference be held to discuss the political reform process. A new transitional government, appointed in late July, included three opposition leaders (among them Herman Yaméogo, himself a presidential contender, who, following his expulsion from the FP, had formed the Alliance pour la démocratie et la fédération—ADF) and several other opposition supporters.

Compaoré's refusal to accede to opposition demands that a sovereign national conference be convened in advance of the presidential and legislative elections caused considerable disquiet among opposition groups in the second half of 1991. In August Yaméogo and two other ADF members resigned their government posts, in protest against proposed electoral procedures. In the following month opposition parties established an 'umbrella' organization, the Coordination des forces démocratiques (CFD), to which about 20 political organizations had affiliated by the end of the year. The CFD appealed to Compaoré to call a national conference by a given date in late September: the deadline passed, and the seven opposition members duly resigned from the transitional government. Attempts to reach a compromise failed, and in mid-October five CFD representatives who had previously declared their intention to contest the presidency withdrew their candidatures.

Compaoré, who had resigned his army commission in order to contest the presidency as a civilian, was thus the sole candidate in the presidential election, which took place, as scheduled, on 1 December 1991, despite demands from Burkinabè human rights and religious leaders that the poll be postponed. Accordingly, Compaoré was elected, having secured the support of 90.4% of those who voted. However, an appeal by the CFD for a boycott of the poll was widely heeded, with an abstention rate of 74.7% being recorded. Some disturbances were reported at the time of the election, most notably in the south-western town of Bobo-Dioulasso.

Following the election President Compaoré appealed for national reconciliation. Shortly afterwards, however, Clément Oumarou Ouédraogo was assassinated while leaving a CFD meeting. Attacks on other CFD leaders were also reported. Although the government and the ODP/MT condemned the attacks, opposition leaders accused the Compaoré adminstration of seeking to eliminate those who held evidence of its misdeeds. Two days after Ouédraogo's death the government announced the indefinite postponement of the legislative elections. (The CFD had for some weeks been advocating a boycott of the elections to the ADP, and by mid-November 1991 only 11 organizations—of some 60 authorized political parties—had registered their intention to present candidates.)

In mid-December 1991, in an apparent attempt to restore a national consensus, Compaoré proposed a 'national reconciliation forum', embracing diverse political and social groups, to discuss the democratic process, human rights and development issues. Compaoré was sworn in as president of the fourth republic on 24 December, and in the following month he rehabilitated some 4,000 people who had been punished for political or trade union activity since 1983. The agenda of the reconciliation forum (which was convened in February 1992 and attended by some 380 delegates) was, however, restricted by Compaoré, and the conference was suspended within two weeks. In late February, none the less, the government was reorganized to include Herman Yaméogo and three other opposition members. In March it was announced that legislative elections would take place on 24 May.

In all, 27 parties contested the elections to the ADP. Although international observers declared that the poll had been conducted in a 'satisfactory' manner, Compaoré's opponents alleged widespread malpractice. The ODP/MT won 78 of the new legislature's 107 seats; Pierre Tapsoba's Convention nationale des patriotes progressistes—Parti social-démocrate (CNPP—PSD) obtained 12 seats, while Herman Yaméogo's ADF secured four seats. An abstention rate of 64.8% was recorded. The ADP was inaugurated on 15 June 1992. On the following day Compaoré appointed a young economist, Youssouf Ouédraogo, to be the country's new prime minister. Ouédraogo's council of ministers, the composition of which was announced shortly afterwards, included representatives of seven political organizations, although the ODP/MT, which was allocated 13 government posts, retained control of most strategic ministries. Herman Yaméogo remained in the government as minister of state without portfolio, and Kaboré was named as minister of state, with responsibility for finance and planning.

In December 1992 the government, trade unions and representatives of the private sector began a series of negotiations, with a view to defining a 'social charter'. During late 1992 and the early months of 1993, none the less, there was a resurgence of social tensions, partially linked to the government's adoption of austerity measures (in the context of its structural adjustment programme—see Economy). Unrest at the University of Ouagadougou, where students had begun a boycott of classes in late 1992, continued in January 1993 with campus and street demonstrations to protest against proposed reductions in grant levels and to demand the payment of scholarship arrears. About 15 students were injured in clashes with security forces outside government buildings in Ouagadougou. The government established a commission of inquiry, and later announced that most grant arrears had been paid, although students renewed their boycott of classes in early February, in continuing protest against the planned reductions (in some cases by more than 45%) in the value of grants.

The government's austerity programme also prompted some labour unrest, although the Burkinabè trade union movement was generally seen to lack cohesion—an attempt by the Confédération générale du travail burkinabè (CGTB) to organize a three-day strike in March 1993, in protest against the provisions of the new budget, had little success. A 'freeze' in public-sector salaries, in force since 1987, was ended in January 1993; however, workers' representatives judged a new salary structure to be unfavourable in real terms. In April the CGTB withdrew from the 'social charter' negotiations, protesting at the government's tardiness in addressing workers' grievances. Meeting in Ouagadougou in March–May 1993, the ADP approved proposals for the establishment of a consultative assembly, as provided for in the 1991 constitution: the Chambre des représentants was to comprise 120 members, nominated for a three-year term. The ODP/MT's predominance in the legislature was enhanced following a split in the CNPP—PSD in May 1993, as a result of which six of the party's parliamentary members joined Joseph Ki-Zerbo's newly-formed Parti pour la démocratie et le progrès.

Youssouf Ouédraogo reorganized the government in September 1993, reducing the number of ministers from 29 to 25. Kaboré was redesignated minister of state, with responsibility for relations with the organs of state. Two of the CNPP—PSD's three ministers left the government. The death of Maurice Yaméogo was announced later in the month. A further government reshuffle in January 1994 included the appointment of new ministers of defence and of justice.

Following the devaluation of the CFA franc, in January 1994, the government introduced emergency measures, including controls on the prices of essential commodities and tax adjustments, in an attempt to offset the immediate adverse effects of the currency's depreciation. However, workers' representatives denounced such measures as insufficient, and began a campaign for compensatory salary increases of 40%–50%. Negotiations between the government and trade unions failed to reach a compromise, and in mid-March Youssouf Ouédraogo resigned from the government. Kaboré was named as his successor, and a new, 23-member council of ministers, again dominated by the ODP/MT and its associates, was appointed shortly afterwards. It was generally believed that the primary function of Kaboré's administration, which included a new minister of the economy, finance and planning (Zéphirin Diabiré—hitherto minister of industry, trade and mines) and in which Herman Yaméogo was designated minister of state, with responsibility for African integration and solidarity, would be to endorse Compaoré's desire to enforce austerity measures necessitated by the devaluation and the structural adjustment programme. None the less, a meeting between Kaboré and union leaders in early April, at which the government offered salary increases of 6%–10%, as well as other concessions designed to mitigate the effects of the ending of price controls, failed to prevent a three-day general strike by members of the CGTB which began the following day.

FOREIGN RELATIONS

The *coup d'état* of October 1987 had a generally favourable effect on Burkina's external relations. Relations with Ghana, which had been particularly close under Sankara, underwent considerable strain, and the coup was condemned by the Congo and Gabon, while Côte d'Ivoire and Togo expressed their support for the new regime. Libya has maintained close links, and relations with France are generally cordial. In December 1988 Compaoré attended the Franco-African summit, held in Morocco (the first occasion on which the country had been represented since 1983); subsequent meetings of this bloc have also been attended.

Following the escalation of the civil conflict in Liberia after early 1990, Burkina's relations with some members of the Economic Community of West African States (ECOWAS) deteriorated as a result of the Compaoré government's open support for Charles Taylor's rebel National Patriotic Front of Liberia (NPFL) and the FP's initial refusal to participate in the ECOWAS military monitoring group (ECOMOG) that was sent to Liberia in mid-1990. Allegations that the government of Burkina was aiding the NPFL were renewed in 1991, when in May a Burkinabè-chartered vessel was intercepted by ECOMOG forces outside the Liberian port of Buchanan: the ship was apparently transporting rubber from NPFL-controlled plantations, allegedly to Libya, where it was to be exchanged for a shipment of arms. Shortly afterwards two Burkinabè soldiers were captured in Sierra Leone, where they were said to have been aiding NPFL troops. In September Compaoré admitted that some 700 Burkinabè troops had been assisting the NPFL in Liberia. However, Compaoré's assertion that his country's involvement in Liberia had ended contrasted with reports in late 1991 that a pro-NPFL mercenary force, comprising Liberian, Burkinabè, Ivorian and Guinean nationals, was being trained at the Pô military base, and with accusations made by the Liberian interim president, Dr Amos Sawyer, that Burkina and Côte d'Ivoire were providing the NPFL with arms and training facilities. In November 1992 the US government recalled its ambassador to Burkina, and announced that the recently-appointed Burkinabè ambassador to Washington would not be welcome in the USA, owing to Burkina's alleged role in transporting arms from Libya to the NPFL. Shortly afterwards, however, Compaoré expressed willingness to contribute a military contingent to the ECOWAS force, on condition that ECOMOG's role be confined to that of a neutral peace-keeping body.

From 1990 the conflict between Tuareg rebels and government forces in Mali and Niger promoted some 7,000 refugees from those countries to enter Burkina: at mid-1994 many were sheltering in a camp administered by the office of the UN High Commissioner for Refugees (UNHCR) to the north of Djibo, near the border with Mali. During the second half of 1992 Compaoré and the president of Mali, Alpha Oumar Konaré, met twice to discuss the Tuareg issue, including allegations that rebels were using Burkinabè territory as a base for attacks on Malian government forces. Sporadic attacks in northern Burkina during late 1993 and the first half of 1994 were attributed to dissident Tuaregs. Negotiations between the government of Niger and Tuareg leaders took place in Ouagadougou in February 1994, and in June the heads of state of Burkina, Mali and Niger met with Col Qaddafi in Libya, where regional security issues were discussed. In late July a meeting in Mali of the ministers responsible for territorial administration in Burkina and Mali, together with a UNHCR regional representative, resulted in an agreement regarding the repatriation of refugees from Burkina to Mali. Compaoré also hosted negotiations between the Togolese government and opposition in Ouagadougou in mid-1993; a Burkinabè military contingent was dispatched to Togo, and Burkina also contributed to an international diplomatic mission charged with overseeing the presidential election in that country in August. Burkina also agreed, in December, to contribute troops to the small OAU protection force in Burundi, as part of efforts to restore order following the assassination, in October, of President Melchior Ndadaye.

Compaoré's first official visit to France, in June 1993, was widely interpreted as a recognition by the French authorities of his legitmacy following the installation of elected organs of state; he made a further visit in April 1994, during which co-operation issues were discussed with President Mitterrand and the prime minister, Edouard Balladur. Diplomatic relations with Israel (severed in 1973) were re-established in October 1993, and, following the restoration of links with Taiwan (also suspended in 1973) in February 1994, the Taiwan government formally announced a comprehensive programme of assistance. The People's Republic of China terminated relations with Burkina shortly afterwards. Diplomatic relations were established with South Africa in May 1994.

Economy

RICHARD SYNGE

Based on an earlier article by EDITH HODGKINSON

A land-locked country in the savannah lands of the west African Sahel, Burkina Faso is continually challenged in its efforts to ensure the survival of its agricultural and pastoral economy, and has only limited prospects for modernization, whether through industrialization or the expansion of the country's external trade. The population (estimated at 9.5m. in mid-1992) is largely rural, depending on traditional farming methods for subsistence and receiving modest earnings from the sale of cash crops, fruit, vegetables, livestock or firewood. The climate is arid, with a short rainy season between mid-May and mid-September. The rivers are mostly seasonal, and supplies of water can run low during the long dry season.

Burkina is highly dependent on the maintenance of good economic and political relations with its six neighbours. Large numbers of Burkinabè work in Côte d'Ivoire, some seasonally and some permanently. There is also seasonal migration to Ghana. Such migrations reinforce Burkina's commercial contacts with its southern neighbours, where many consumer goods are purchased for resale in Burkina, and these links form a possible basis for more substantial intra-regional trade and integration in the future. Workers' remittances also contribute substantially to the national balance of payments. While Burkina's balance of merchandise trade shows a large deficit (amounting to 100,200m. francs CFA in 1992), overall balance-of-payments deficits are partially, or even entirely, offset by aid flows.

Manufacturing activity is restricted to small units, established principally in Bobo-Dioulasso and, to a lesser extent, in Ouagadougou. Import-substitution activities such as brewing, flour milling, motorcycle assembly and battery production are oriented towards the domestic market alone. The processing of local produce includes cotton ginning, textile manufacture, leather tanning, sugar refining, and the processing of fruit and vegetables. Apart from cotton ginning, the industrial sector makes little contribution to exports. Small-scale artisanal production includes leather, cloth, wood and metal products for the regional and tourist markets. The informal sector is active and plays an important role in expanding the industrial framework and in creating jobs. The country's mineral resources are only beginning to be exploited on a significant scale, and it remains to be demonstrated what contribution a comprehensive development of the mining sector can make towards Burkina's foreign exchange earnings. Gold has been mined in small quantities for centuries; although activities at the only modern gold mine, at Poura, have encountered difficulties, substantial concessions are being awarded for further exploration. Trial exports of manganese and zinc were under way in 1993–94.

The rate of growth in gross national product (GNP) per head in 1985–92 was only 0.9% per year, partly on account of poor weather in some years, and partly because of a decline in remittances from migrant workers. Burkina's persistent poverty is exemplified by the fact that GNP per caput in 1992 was only US $290, lower than in any year during the 1980s. Since 1991 the government has been implementing a structural adjustment programme, supported by the IMF, the World Bank and other donors. The devaluation, by 50%, of the CFA franc in January 1994 is certain to have a major impact on the performance of Burkina's economy in future, stimulating earnings from exports but also increasing the costs of the transport and communications on which the country depends for both exports and imports. Several industrial enterprises are threatened with closure if exposed to full competition from imported goods. The devaluation will, however, reinforce Burkina's trading relations with its immediate neighbours, as traders and industrialists look for the cheapest sources of supply.

Reversing the trend towards nationalization that was advocated by the Sankara regime, in 1992 the Compaoré government inaugurated a privatization and divestiture programme, in an apparent indication of its willingness to promote the private sector. Although the programme has attracted some interest from domestic and foreign private investors, the response has been restricted to a few companies. The domestic private sector is itself limited in size and influence—having had little opportunity to develop in a small and previously state-controlled environment—while foreign investors have in general been reluctant to locate in African members of the franc zone, at least while the CFA franc remained overvalued. Burkina, none the less, wishes to be regarded as more attractive to foreign investment than other countries in the region. Its best prospects for modernization and economic growth lie in the development of the mining sector, small-scale, resource-based manufacturing, increased exports of horticultural products to Europe and in a modest expansion of the tourism industry.

AGRICULTURE

Agriculture and livestock—which in 1990 accounted for an estimated 44% of Burkina's gross domestic product (GDP), and which employs about 85% of the labour force—is largely at subsistence level. In those years when conditions are favourable, the country rebuilds its food stocks to last through periods of unfavourable climatic conditions, when severe shortages have been experienced. In 1992/93 production of millet and sorghum was 2,075,600 metric tons, while that of maize was 341,300 tons and rice 46,700 tons. Some improvements in productivity have been brought about by development programmes, but the scope for expansion is limited by generally unfavourable climatic conditions, inadequate water supplies and poor soils. Subsistence farming is estimated to take up 90% of the cultivated area, or almost 5m. ha. There are plans to develop rice cultivation, to meet local demand. A project is being implemented at Bagre, on the Nankabe (formerly White Volta) river, providing irrigation for 5,000 ha on which 32,000 tons of paddy rice are to be produced, together with 15,000 tons of maize and 7,500 tons of vegetables.

In the past, cash crops were the surplus of subsistence cultivation, mainly shea-nuts (karité nuts) at almost 70,000 tons per year, and sesame seeds, which ranged from 4,000 to 6,500 tons per year in the mid-1980s. In recent years, however, there has been considerable government investment in cotton, groundnuts, sugar, cashew nuts and market gardening, with financial aid from, among others, the European Development Fund. The most important cash crop is cotton, output of which more than doubled in the decade to 1985. After a low point of 145,898 tons in 1988/89, production of cottonseed recovered to 189,543 tons in 1990/91, but declined to 161,524 tons in 1992/93. One-third of the country's farmers are now believed to be engaged in cotton production. Mainly because of the greater profitability of cotton cultivation, production of groundnuts has tended to decline, while the area devoted to the cultivation of subsistence grains has come under pressure. Output of cane sugar, which began in 1974/75, has recently averaged in excess of 40,000 tons (refined) annually.

To achieve its aim of self-sufficiency in basic foods, the Sankara government (1983–87) nationalized land, doubled the agricultural sector's share of budget spending (to 40%) and raised all producer prices. Emphasis was placed on small-scale projects, implemented by village co-operatives. This policy has been broadly maintained under the Compaoré government. The leading self-help project is in the Sourou valley, where local labour has been used to build a dam and canal, to irrigate 15,700 ha of land worked in smallholder plots (cereals and vegetables) and state-run land for the development of cash crops (sugar, cotton and oilseeds). The second phase, currently under way, includes the construction of a barrage and the irrigation of a further 40,000 ha.

In 1991 the livestock sector (including livestock and livestock products, hides and skins) accounted for 14.1% of the country's export earnings—significantly less than its contribution in earlier years (although much of the production and trade is unrecorded). Stock-rearing is practised by the semi-nomadic Fulani in the thinly populated area of the north and east, although a large-scale programme is redeveloping livestock production in the west of the country. A west African regional development project, supported by the FAO, for those areas affected by trypanosomiasis (usually 'sleeping-sickness'), includes Burkina Faso. In 1992 there were some 4.1m. cattle, 5.4m. sheep and 6.9m. goats. The small fish catch (about 7,600 tons per year) is consumed locally. Timber production is insignificant, despite the large area under forest (almost one-quarter of the total); however, foreign agencies are now funding timber development projects in the Kompienga and Bagre dam regions.

MINING AND POWER

Efforts are now in progress to exploit Burkina's mineral resources, which include gold, manganese, zinc and silver. The main gold mine at Poura, in western-central Burkina, has experienced production difficulties and the government planned in 1994 to sell part of its 60% stake in the company involved in its development, the Société de recherches et d'exploitations minières du Burkina (SOREMIB), in order to attract new capital to the mine, which had production of 3,461 kg in 1990, before it switched production from open-pit to underground operations. Bidders include Billiton of the Netherlands, Randgold of South Africa and the Bureau de recherches géologiques et minières of France. The privatization of SOREMIB is regarded as part of a wider programme to attract foreign mining interests. Other companies involved in gold prospecting in Burkina include BHP of Australia and Mutual Resources of Canada. A feature of the present mining regime is the official purchase of all gold production by the Comptoir burkinabè des métaux précieux; however there is substantial informal production, which is mostly sold after having been smuggled out of the country.

Trial exploitation of manganese deposits at Tambao, in the north-east, was begun by Interstar of Canada during 1993, although the project is hindered by the lack of a complete railway connection to the port of Abidjan. The deposits at Tambao are estimated at almost 18m. tons of ore, containing 51% manganese, and there are additional resources of carbonate ore. Interstar hopes to transport 30,000–80,000 tons per year in the initial phase of development. The government's railway extension project has been completed between Ouagadougou and Kaya, but this is more than 200 km short of the mining area, a distance which in the first phase will be served by road transport. Trial exports have been conducted via Côte d'Ivoire and Ghana.

The potential for zinc mining operations at Perkoa (in central Burkina), which would be well served by the existing railway through Koudougou, has been under investigation by Boliden International Mining AB of Sweden since 1990. There is a production potential of 1.3m. tons of zinc concentrate over 10 years, but commercial operations are not expected to begin until 1995. Burkina's other mineral prospects include titanium, vanadium, nickel, bauxite, lead and phosphates, although none of these are considered to be commercially viable at present. A more immediate development prospect is for the quarrying of limestone deposits at Tin Hrassan, near Tambao, which can be developed for cement production. In 1993 the Holderbank group of Switzerland bought a stake in the state-controlled cement clinker company, increasing the possibility that production at the plant may begin within a few years.

Electricity generation (all thermal) reached 157m. kWh in 1991, and considerable expansion is under way. A 15-MW hydroelectric station on the Kompienga river, in the east of the country, was inaugurated in early 1989. Construction of the dam, at a cost of $90m., was funded by the African Development Bank, the Federal Republic of Germany, France, Canada and Saudi Arabia. Work has begun on a 16-MW hydroelectric project on the Nankabe river, with a capacity of 7.5 MW; the installation was scheduled to come into operation in mid-1992. Meanwhile, a 60-MW scheme is planned at Noumbiel, on the Mouhoun (formerly Black Volta), at a cost of some $300m. (Under normal circumstances, however, none of these hydroelectric installations is likely to operate at full capacity, because of the low level of rainfall.) In addition, Burkina and Côte d'Ivoire plan to co-operate on the construction of a 225-km power transmission line to Banfora and Bobo-Dioulasso. Aid for the project is being sought from international donors. Programmes to improve distribution are currently under way, with assistance from France and the EU, while studies are being conducted into the possible extension of the Ghanaian electricity network to Ouagadougou.

MANUFACTURING

Manufacturing activity is still rudimentary but has been expanding, and its share of GDP increased from 8% in 1960 to about 12% in 1991. Growth has been modest because of the small size of the domestic market, the lack of indigenous raw materials, and because of shortages of finance and management skills, with investment deterred by political uncertainty. Production takes the form of agricultural processing and the substitution of consumer goods imports. The first industrial plant of any significance was the textile plant at Koudougou, which entered production in 1970 with an annual capacity of 500 tons of yarn and 760 tons of woven material, using local supplies of cotton. Cotton-ginning capacity was increased in 1989 with the expansion of the Société burkinabè de fibres textiles (SOFITEX) complex in Bobo-Dioulasso.

During the period of political revolution under Sankara, the Société des brasseries du Burkina Faso (BRAKINA) brewery concern was one of the few major industries to retain a substantial private holding. Under the 1986–90 development plan a total of 35 new industrial investments, valued at 19,600m. francs CFA, were planned, but the state was unable to raise the finance required for the wide range of activities identified. Only a few of the projects were completed, including a tomato concentrate plant, a cotton-seed oil and shea-nut butter plant and companies involved in the manufacture of medical solutions and animal feeds.

Other projects outside the scope of the development plan were pursued, but by 1990 the industrial sector was suffering from several general difficulties, including competition from imported (often smuggled) products from neighbouring countries. Industries that have hitherto remained viable include the Société industrielle du Faso (SIFA), an associate of the Cie française de l'Afrique occidentale, which produces motor cycles and bicycles (important methods of transport in this predominantly rural country). Part of the state's holding in SIFA (47.5% since 1985) was sold to private Burkinabè interests in 1993. Also of significance is the processing and sale of hides and skins, and the Aliz group—the dominant company in the sector—aims to expand its operations beyond Burkina (initially into Niger).

Since 1992 the government has been trying to stimulate new investment through its privatization programme. By early 1994 agreements had been reached on the sale of government shares in 10 companies, from an initial list of 20, and there were plans for further sales of the more strategic industries in the years ahead. These include the Société Sucrière de la Compé (SOSUCO), the Société des Huiles et Savons du Burkina (SHSB CITEC HUILERIE) and the Société Faso-Fani textiles concern.

TRANSPORT INFRASTRUCTURE

An important transport artery is the railway line from the border with Côte d'Ivoire through Bobo-Dioulasso, Koudougou and Ouagadougou to Kaya. The track, vehicles and services are, however, in need of maintenance and further investment. Work on the extension of the main line to Tambao is dependent upon the provision of external financing for its completion (see above), but foreign aid (through concessionary loans from the International Development Association) may be forthcoming for much-needed renovation of the main line, following the withdrawal, in 1987, of Côte d'Ivoire from the joint rail partnership. Burkina and Côte d'Ivoire subsequently established separate rail companies, and in January 1993 issued a joint tender for the transfer to private ownership of the two enterprises. In 1986 there were 13,117 km of classified roads, of which about one-third were main roads. Funding is being sought for the upgrading of the road between Bobo-Dioulasso and the Malian border, which will complete the Burkinabè section of the Trans-Sahelian highway linking Dakar (Senegal) and N'Djamena (Chad). Under its 1991–96 infrastructure development programme (funded by Arab and Islamic donors), the government aimed to improve Burkina's transport links with other countries of the region. The runways of the country's two international airports (at Ouagadougou and Bobo-Dioulasso) were extended during the 1980s to accommodate large cargo aircraft. In 1991 almost 194,000 passengers and 8,000 tons of freight passed through Ouagadougou airport.

DEVELOPMENT AND FINANCE

The expressed objective of the Compaoré administration, to achieve a balanced budget, will not easily be attained, for both political and economic reasons. The low level of commercial activity in the economy means that taxable capacity is still very limited. Since the early 1970s, when expenditure was held down and small budget surpluses were achieved, there has been a history of fiscal deficit. Expenditure on development, which reached a peak of 7,800m. francs CFA (one-sixth of total budget expenditure) in 1981, was reduced in subsequent years, in order to restrict the rise in budget spending. There was, however, a noticeable change in direction in 1985, with spending forecast to rise by one-fifth, as development expenditure more than doubled, reflecting work on the Kompienga and Bagre dams and on the Tambao rail link. The budget deficit was, none the less, almost eliminated, as the Sankara government introduced new taxes. There were further increases in taxation in both 1986 and 1987; however, the budget deficit (excluding the surge in debt-servicing arrears) rose dramatically, to 20,100m. francs CFA in 1986 and 33,600m. francs CFA in 1987, as a result of even higher increases in government current and capital outlays. The Compaoré government initially relaxed the unpopular austerity measures that had been introduced under Sankara. However, negotiations with the World Bank and the IMF, regarding the formulation of a structural adjustment programme, which were finally concluded in late 1990, meant that rigorous control of government finances again became a priority. Following a deficit of 31,500m. francs CFA in 1988, restrictions on expenditure during 1989 transformed the deficit into a surplus of 26,500m. francs CFA in that year. However, there was a disappointing budget out-turn in 1990, when a deficit of 16,000m. francs CFA was recorded. The shortfall widened to 36,400m. francs CFA in 1991, despite the modification of tax collection mechanisms and the stabilization of salary costs (the largest single item of expenditure), but narrowed to 17,800m. francs CFA in 1992.

The three-year (1991–93) structural adjustment programme aimed to achieve average economic growth of 4% per year, while curtailing the average annual rate of inflation at less than 4%, curbing the external current account deficit and eliminating arrears on external debt repayments. The programme included measures to reform taxation and customs duties, and a value-added tax was introduced with effect from the beginning of 1993. It was aimed to stabilize expenditure on wages and to channel funds into such areas as primary education, health and financial administration. In early 1993 the IMF approved a three-year (1993–95) enhanced structural adjustment facility, with more concessionary terms. The government's adjustment policies aim to restructure public expenditure and increase the effectiveness of public investments, while supporting private sector investment and privatization, and rationalizing import and export procedures. The devaluation of the CFA franc, from January 1994, is expected to make agricultural commodity exports more competitive in the medium term, but its first impact was to put pressure on costs of production in CFA franc terms, with the greatest impact being felt in transport and import costs generally. Wage rises were restrained, and special measures were taken to minimize the impact on prices of essential commodities. Financial objectives for 1994–96, as identified (following the devaluation) by the Burkinabè authorities and the IMF, included real GDP growth averaging 5.8% per year (the rate was 0.4% in 1993), the reduction of the overall budget deficit (excluding grants) from 16.2% of GDP in 1994 to 6.5% in 1996 (the ratio was 9.2% in 1993) and a decline in the rate of inflation (0.6% in 1993) from 31.2% in 1994 to 6.3% in 1996.

FOREIGN TRADE AND PAYMENTS

Burkina suffers a chronic and substantial trade deficit. This deficit averaged 5,000m. francs CFA per year during 1960–70, but began to rise sharply from 1969 onwards. The widening in the trade gap reflected a more rapid rate of import growth, while export earnings stagnated. This development is explained, in large part, by the drought which affected the whole area and which adversely affected shipments of livestock and cotton. Imports, on the other hand, were augmented by official investment programmes, the demand for raw materials, the effect of the droughts on food supplies, and the second round of petroleum price increases. In 1982 the trade deficit reached a peak of 95,902m. francs CFA: five times the value of exports, which totalled only 18,110m. francs CFA. In the two following years the trade gap narrowed, because of the increase in cotton earnings, which, at that time, accounted for around one-half of total export receipts, and the easing of the petroleum import bill because of lower world prices. By 1984 the deficit had declined to 76,392m. francs CFA, around twice the level of export receipts, but the subsequent sharp fall in world cotton prices and the increase in food imports, due to the drought, caused the trade gap to widen in 1985, to 115,086m. francs CFA (a new record, but relatively less severe than in 1982—import cover was one-fifth, compared with one-seventh). This level was broadly maintained in 1986; however, the deficit declined sharply in 1987, to some 84,000m. francs CFA. This reflected a doubling in revenue from sales of cotton (owing to an improvement in international prices for that commodity), together with increased production of gold and a decline in imports of cereals as domestic output recovered. These effects were sustained during 1988, when the trade deficit contracted by more than one-quarter, to 70,800m. francs CFA. However, the deficit regressed to 82,000m. francs CFA in 1989, and continued to widen in subsequent years, largely reflecting higher levels of imports of foodstuffs and capital goods: the deficit was 85,400m. francs CFA in 1990, 89,800m. francs CFA in 1991, and 95,800m. francs CFA in 1992.

There is an important offsetting factor on the current payments account—the remittances from emigrants, which raised private transfers to an average of $97m. (net) per year in 1980–85. These remittances were equivalent to more than two-thirds of export earnings and more than one-half of official aid in that period. Net private transfers totalled $159.6m. in 1986, but declined steadily thereafter, to total only $97.5m. in 1989, owing to economic and political problems in the countries to which Burkinabè workers have traditionally migrated (this has, moreover, imposed increased strain on the economy of Burkina, as migrant workers have returned). None the less, a considerable improvement was recorded in 1990 ($113.9m.), and, after a marginal decline in 1991, private transfers amounted to $123.5m. in 1992. Inflows of official development assistance averaged $296m. per year in 1985–91: the major sources of aid during this period were France, the Federal Republic of Germany, Italy, Canada and the Netherlands. Because a substantial part of these transfers has traditionally been in grant form, Burkina's external debt remained comparatively low—only $511m. at the end of 1985, according to the World Bank—and its debt-servicing burden moderate (equivalent to 9.9% of exports of goods and services in that year). By 1988 total external debt had increased by 65%, to $845m, although the level of debt-servicing declined to 9.3%, owing to the increasing proportion of loans from official sources (governments and multilateral agencies) on concessionary terms. At the end of 1988 almost three-quarters of the country's borrowing was on concessionary terms. Total debt outstanding declined to $717m. in 1989, before rising again, to $1,055m., in 1992. In 1991 (when the debt stood at $968m.) the cost of debt-servicing was equivalent to 9.2% of export earnings. A series of reschedulings and cancellations of debt in the early 1990s have meant that Burkina is not classified as 'debt-distressed', as are other, less poor, sub-Saharan African countries, and further concessions were made by multilateral and bilateral creditors following the devaluation of the CFA franc. None the less, its precarious balance-of-payments position and its continuing dependence on external funds to finance basic development necessitate the maintenance of special terms.

Statistical Survey

Source (except where otherwise stated): Institut National de la Statistique et de la Démographie, BP 374, Ouagadougou; tel. 33-55-37.

Area and Population

AREA, POPULATION AND DENSITY

Area (sq km)	274,200*
Population (census results)	
1–7 December 1975	5,638,203
10–20 December 1985	
Males	3,833,237
Females	4,131,468
Total	7,964,705
Population (official estimates at mid-year)	
1990	9,000,940
1991	9,242,166
1992	9,490,000
Density (per sq km) at mid-1992	34.6

* 105,870 sq miles.

PRINCIPAL TOWNS (population at 1985 census)

Ouagadougou (capital)	441,514	Ouahigouya	38,902
Bobo-Dioulasso	228,668	Banfora	35,319
Koudougou	1,926	Kaya	25,814

BIRTHS AND DEATHS (UN estimates, annual averages)

	1975–80	1980–85	1985–90
Birth rate (per 1,000)	47.2	47.1	47.0
Death rate (per 1,000)	21.4	19.7	18.5

Expectation of life (UN estimates, years at birth, 1985–90): 47.0 (males 45.3; females 48.8).

Source: UN, *World Population Prospects: The 1992 Revision.*

ECONOMICALLY ACTIVE POPULATION
(ILO estimates, '000 persons at mid-1980)

	Males	Females	Total
Agriculture, etc.	1,550	1,414	2,964
Industry	89	57	146
Services	145	165	310
Total	1,784	1,637	3,421

Source: ILO, *Economically Active Population Estimates and Projections, 1950–2025.*

1985 census: Total labour force 4,067,011 (males 2,078,360; females 1,988,651).

Mid-1992 (estimates in '000): Agriculture, etc. 4,125; Total 4,916 (Source: FAO, *Production Yearbook).*

Agriculture

PRINCIPAL CROPS ('000 metric tons)

	1990	1991	1992
Maize	258	315	310
Millet	449	849	785*
Sorghum	751	1,238	1,179*
Rice (paddy)	48	39	49
Sweet potatoes†	24	24	24
Yams	37	37	52†
Other roots and tubers	13	14	14†
Vegetables	229	236†	245†
Fruit	70	71	72
Pulses†	120	120	120
Groundnuts (in shell)	134	99	110†
Cottonseed	116*	107*	100†
Cotton (lint)†	77	77	71
Sesame seed	4	6	8†
Tobacco (leaves)	1	1†	1†
Sugar cane†	380	350	350

* Unofficial figure. † FAO estimate(s).

Source: FAO, *Production Yearbook.*

LIVESTOCK ('000 head, year ending September)

	1990	1991	1992
Cattle	3,937	4,015	4,096
Sheep	5,050	5,198	5,350
Goats	6,625	6,693	6,860
Pigs	516	518	530
Horses	22	22	22
Asses	411	419	427
Camels	12	12	12*

* FAO estimate.

Poultry (million): 17 in 1990; 17 in 1991; 18 in 1992.

Source: FAO, *Production Yearbook.*

LIVESTOCK PRODUCTS
(FAO estimates unless otherwise indicated, '000 metric tons)

	1990	1991	1992
Beef and veal	37	35	35
Mutton and lamb	11	11	12
Goats' meat	18	19	19
Pigs' meat	6	6	6
Poultry meat	19	19	20
Cows' milk	95*	116	118
Goats' milk	20	20	21
Butter	0.7	0.9	0.9
Hen eggs	15.4	15.4	16.0
Cattle hides	5.9	5.6	5.6
Sheep skins	2.6	2.7	2.9
Goat skins	4.8	4.9	5.0

* Official figure.
Source: FAO, *Production Yearbook*.

Forestry

ROUNDWOOD REMOVALS
(FAO estimates, '000 cubic metres, excluding bark)

	1990	1991	1992
Sawlogs, veneer logs and logs for sleepers*	1	1	1
Other industrial wood	394	405	417
Fuel wood	8,347	8,585	8,833
Total	8,742	8,991	9,251

* Estimated to be unchanged since 1985.
Source: FAO, *Yearbook of Forest Products*.

Fishing

(FAO estimates, '000 metric tons, live weight)

	1989	1990	1991
Total catch	8.0	7.0	7.0

Source: FAO, *Yearbook of Fishery Statistics*.

Mining

(mineral content of ore, metric tons)

	1991	1992	1993
Gold	6	5	4

Source: Gold Fields Mineral Services Ltd, *Gold 1994*.

Industry

SELECTED PRODUCTS

	1989	1990	1992
Cottonseed oil ('000 metric tons, refined)	9	14	18*
Wheat flour ('000 metric tons)	13	23	21*
Raw sugar ('000 metric tons)†	24	30	27
Beer ('000 hectolitres)	398	350	362
Soft drinks ('000 hectolitres)	117	108	99
Cigarettes (million)	609	822	983
Footwear ('000 pairs, excluding rubber)	500	500	1,271
Soap ('000 metric tons)	9.9	14.5	25.6*
Bicycle and motor cycle tyres ('000, including inner tubes)	1,377	3,483	29,674 *
Motor cycles and scooters ('000)	23	24	19
Bicycles ('000)	45	39	28
Electric energy (million kWh)	154	155	157

† Provisional or estimated figure.
* Data from FAO.
Source: UN, *Industrial Statistics Yearbook*.

Finance

CURRENCY AND EXCHANGE RATES

Monetary Units
100 centimes = 1 franc de la Communauté financière africaine (CFA).

French Franc, Sterling and Dollar Equivalents (31 March 1994)
1 French franc = 100 francs CFA;
£1 sterling = 846.40 francs CFA;
US $1 = 570.14 francs CFA;
1,000 francs CFA = £1.181 = $1.754.

Average Exchange Rate (francs CFA per US $)
1991 282.11
1992 264.69
1993 283.16

Note: An exchange rate of 1 French franc = 50 francs CFA, established in 1948, remained in force until January 1994, when the CFA franc was devalued by 50%, with the exchange rate adjusted to 1 French franc = 100 francs CFA.

BUDGET ESTIMATES (million francs CFA)

Revenue	1988	1989	1990*
Fiscal receipts	81,131	90,903	87,637
Taxes on income and profits	21,909	22,966	19,696
Individual taxes	10,655	13,046	10,963
Corporate and business taxes	8,900	8,000	7,000
Taxes on goods and services	29,955	32,907	31,227
Turnover taxes	16,432	17,480	17,084
Consumption taxes	10,775	10,889	9,229
Taxes on fiscal monopolies	940	2,600	2,600
Taxes on international trade and transactions	27,219	32,938	34,211
Import duties	25,040	30,684	31,957
Other current receipts	8,367	8,000	9,200
Administrative fees, charges and non-industrial sales	3,116	2,511	2,243
Capital receipts	798	1,630	1,734
Total	90,296	100,533	98,571

Expenditure	1988	1989	1990*
General public services	11,830	10,327	12,961
Defence	13,669	18,112	18,778
Public order and security	3,754	4,367	5,549
Education	17,523	19,747	21,602
Health	6,450	7,426	7,963
Social security and welfare	135	130	130
Housing and community amenities	735	357	716
Other community and social services	2,747	3,016	4,521
Economic services	15,296	19,277	13,749
Agriculture, forestry and fishing	6,201	5,708	5,702
Mining, manufacturing and construction	1,389	2,671	603
Transport and communications	6,596	9,010	5,295
Other economic services	1,110	1,888	2,149
Debt-repayment	15,557	17,150	18,407
Other purposes	8,570	7,305	6,737
Total	96,286	107,214	111,113

* In September 1990 the budget estimates for 1990 were revised as follows: Revenue 96,970 million francs CFA; Expenditure 105,270 million francs CFA.

Source: Banque centrale des états de l'Afrique de l'ouest.

1991 (Budget estimates, million francs CFA): Revenue 154,420; Expenditure 176,862.
1992 (Budget estimates, million francs CFA): Revenue 210,900; Expenditure 216,800.
1993 (Budget estimates, million francs CFA): Revenue 227,400; Expenditure 252,300.
1994 (Revised budget estimates, million francs CFA): Revenue 296,730; Expenditure 373,860.

CENTRAL BANK RESERVES (US $ million at 31 December)

	1991	1992	1993
Gold*	3.9	3.8	4.1
IMF special drawing rights	8.0	7.7	7.7
Reserve position in IMF	10.3	9.9	9.9
Foreign exchange	327.8	323.7	364.7
Total	350.0	345.1	386.4

* Valued at market-related prices.

Source: IMF, *International Financial Statistics*.

MONEY SUPPLY ('000 million francs CFA at 31 December)

	1991	1992	1993
Currency outside banks	60.94	66.24	79.32
Demand deposits at deposit money banks*	45.80	41.39	42.00
Checking deposits at post office	1.90	1.90	—
Total money (incl. others)	109.34	110.57	121.83

* Excluding the deposits of public establishments of an administrative or social nature.

Source: IMF, *International Financial Statistics*.

COST OF LIVING (Consumer Price Index for African households in Ouagadougou; base: 1983 = 100)

	1988	1989	1990
Food	103.3	99.0	97.6
Fuel and light	96.1	99.2	97.5
Clothing	114.9	117.6	117.4
Rent	105.6	102.7	105.6
All items (incl. others)	110.4	109.8	109.0

Source: ILO, *Year Book of Labour Statistics*.

All items (base: 1990 = 100): 102.5 in 1991; 100.5 in 1992; 101.1 in 1993 (Source: IMF, *International Financial Statistics*).

NATIONAL ACCOUNTS
(million francs CFA at current prices)

Composition of the Gross National Product

	1983	1984	1985
Gross domestic product (GDP) at factor cost	357,929	368,035	427,384
Indirect taxes, *less* subsidies	24,084	22,530	28,498
GDP in purchasers' values	381,013	390,565	455,882
Factor income received from abroad	3,986	4,162	4,241
Less Factor income paid abroad	5,636	5,884	5,996
Gross national product	379,362	388,845	454,126

Source: UN, *National Accounts Statistics*.

Expenditure on the Gross Domestic Product

	1989	1990	1991
Government final consumption expenditure	129,068	134,068	149,000
Private final consumption expenditure	650,640	668,640	684,900
Increase in stocks	21,900	21,000	21,500
Gross fixed capital formation	190,248	192,248	204,200
Total domestic expenditure	991,856	1,015,956	1,059,600
Exports of goods and services	73,458	76,376	77,900
Less Imports of goods and services	319,314	321,314	347,000
GDP in purchasers' values	746,000	771,018	790,500
GDP at constant 1980 prices	449,940	458,939	467,890

Source: UN Economic Commission for Africa, *African Statistical Yearbook*.

Gross Domestic Product by Economic Activity

	1983	1984	1985
Agriculture, hunting, forestry and fishing	152,052	164,205	213,968
Mining and quarrying	77	304	294
Manufacturing	48,053	47,457	50,901
Electricity, gas and water	4,055	4,246	3,192
Construction	7,749	4,934	5,333
Trade, restaurants and hotels	46,344	42,187	45,418
Transport, storage and communications	24,211	29,011	30,913
Finance, insurance, real estate and business services	14,009	14,510	15,488
Government services	67,556	67,455	67,405
Other community, social and personal services	1,877	1,771	2,026
Other services	3,675	5,788	6,552
Sub-total	369,658	381,868	441,490
Import duties	18,131	16,219	21,151
Less Imputed bank service charge	6,778	7,523	6,758
GDP in purchasers' values	381,013	390,565	455,882

Source: UN, *National Accounts Statistics*.

BALANCE OF PAYMENTS (US $ million)

	1990	1991	1992
Merchandise exports f.o.b.	272.2	283.2	280.3
Merchandise imports f.o.b.	−593.2	−601.5	−642.3
Trade balance	−321.0	−318.3	−361.9
Exports of services	49.6	48.6	57.0
Imports of services	−249.4	−246.7	−259.9
Other income received	15.4	14.9	16.6
Other income paid	−23.5	−30.8	−43.1
Private unrequited transfers (net)	113.9	106.4	123.5
Official unrequited transfers (net)	312.9	321.8	368.7
Current balance	−102.1	−104.2	−99.0
Capital (net)	89.5	−29.6	79.8
Net errors and omissions	−5.2	181.9	31.1
Overall balance	−17.7	48.1	11.8

Source: IMF, *International Financial Statistics.*

External Trade

Source: Banque centrale des états de l'Afrique de l'ouest.

PRINCIPAL COMMODITIES (million francs CFA)

Imports c.i.f.	1988	1989	1990
Dairy products	5,275	3,326	4,743
Unprocessed foods of plant origin	18,222	20,402	15,534
Cereals	12,372	15,413	9,375
Processed foodstuffs	3,103	4,010	5,060
Beverages and tobacco	2,577	2,775	2,911
Refined petroleum products	9,836	10,801	16,344
Inedible crude materials (except fuels)	3,515	2,744	3,104
Non-electrical machinery	14,750	13,569	13,220
Electrical machinery	7,826	6,653	9,017
Road transport equipment	14,823	11,549	12,554
Chemicals	15,767	15,252	20,912
Miscellaneous manufactured articles	35,814	31,127	38,759
Hydraulic cement	6,656	5,877	7,461
Total (incl. others)	134,944	125,352	145,833

Exports f.o.b.	1988	1989	1990
Livestock and livestock products	1,702	1,681	2,738
Cattle, beef and veal	1,141	1,142	1,938
Vegetables	679	519	654
Hides and skins	2,205	2,809	3,071
Cotton (ginned)	19,011	14,356	23,415
Machinery and transport equipment	2,525	1,048	325
Miscellaneous manufactured articles	14,153	8,236	9,539
Unworked gold	12,307	6,893	8,104
Total (incl. others)	41,947	30,269	41,282

PRINCIPAL TRADING PARTNERS (million francs CFA)

Imports	1988	1989	1990
Belgium/Luxembourg	2,410	1,969	2,728
Canada	527	968	1,975
China, People's Republic	1,930	1,482	1,320
Côte d'Ivoire	20,639	18,209	23,971
France	41,551	36,145	40,099
Germany, Federal Republic	7,107	5,933	6,949
Italy	5,852	5,312	5,057
Japan	8,554	5,931	6,181
Netherlands	6,962	4,314	4,949
Nigeria	1,798	1,839	3,252
Senegal	737	1,445	3,172
Spain	1,857	2,273	1,729
Taiwan	1,875	1,414	1,575
Thailand	5,453	11,595	2,561
Togo	4,389	3,611	4,816
United Kingdom	2,293	2,929	2,652
USA	6,073	5,649	9,198
Total (incl. others)	134,944	125,352	145,833

Exports	1988	1989	1990
Belgium/Luxembourg	3	1,555	623
China, People's Republic	410	342	3,218
Côte d'Ivoire	3,818	3,797	4,676
Denmark	389	351	246
France	15,640	8,848	9,535
Germany, Federal Republic	443	671	19
Italy	1,298	1,783	3,136
Japan	1,509	483	542
Portugal	1,263	836	1,624
Spain	1,139	986	1,008
Switzerland	99	161	4,392
Taiwan	8,898	5,112	3,113
Togo	2,678	1,846	1,283
United Kingdom	639	375	935
Total (incl. others)	41,947	30,269	41,282

Transport

RAILWAYS (traffic)

	1980	1981	1982
Passenger journeys ('000)	3,646	3,277	2,867
Passenger-km (million)	1,250	988	856
Freight ton-km (million)	600	634	668

Passengers carried: 2.4 million in 1985; 1.5 million in 1986.
Freight: 233,009 metric tons in 1985; 227,870 metric tons in 1986.

ROAD TRAFFIC (estimates, '000 motor vehicles in use)

	1989	1990	1991
Passenger cars	15	16	16
Commercial vehicles	14	14	15

Source: UN Economic Commission for Africa, *African Statistical Yearbook.*

CIVIL AVIATION (traffic on scheduled services)*

	1989	1990	1991
Kilometres flown (million)	3	3	3
Passengers carried ('000)	132	137	124
Passenger-km (million)	254	264	235
Freight ton-km (million)	18	18	16
Mail ton-km (million)	1	1	1

* Including an apportionment of the traffic of Air Afrique.

Source: UN, *Statistical Yearbook.*

Tourism

	1986	1987	1988
Tourist arrivals	60,704	68,308	74,053
Tourist receipts (million francs CFA)	2,212	2,300	5,883

1991: Tourist arrivals 110,327; Tourist receipts (million francs CFA) 6,170.

Source: Direction de l'Administration Touristique et Hôtelière, Ouagadougou.

Communications Media

	1989	1990	1991
Radio receivers ('000 in use)	225	235	245
Television receivers ('000 in use)	45	48	49
Telephones ('000 in use)*	16	17	17
Daily newspapers			
Number	n.a.	1	n.a.
Average circulation ('000 copies)	n.a.	3	n.a.
Non-daily newspapers			
Number	n.a.	10	n.a.
Average circulation ('000 copies)	n.a.	14	n.a.

Book production (1985): 9 titles.

* Estimates.

Sources: UNESCO, *Statistical Yearbook*; UN Economic Commission for Africa, *African Statistical Yearbook*.

Education

(1991, unless otherwise indicated)

	Institutions	Teachers	Students Males	Students Females	Students Total
Pre-primary*	95	259†	3,744	3,911	7,655
Primary	2,590	9,165	324,717	205,296	530,013
Secondary					
General	n.a.	3,162	64,568	32,602	97,170
Vocational	n.a.	474‡	4,412	3,610	8,022
Teacher training	n.a.	n.a.	350§	n.a.	n.a.
University level‡	n.a.	n.a.	3,978	1,108	5,086

* 1989 figures.

† State education only.

‡ 1990 figure(s).

§ Estimate.

Source: UNESCO, *Statistical Yearbook*.

Directory

The Constitution

The present Constitution was approved in a national referendum on 2 June 1991, and was formally adopted on 11 June. The following are its main provisions:

The Constitution of the 'revolutionary, democratic, unitary and secular' Fourth Republic of Burkina Faso guarantees the collective and individual political and social rights of Burkinabè citizens, and delineates the powers of the executive, legislature and judiciary.

Executive power is vested in the President, who is Head of State, and in the Government, which is appointed by the President. The President is elected, by universal suffrage, for a seven-year term, renewable only once.

Legislative power is exercised by the multi-party Assemblée des députés populaires (ADP). Delegates to the ADP are elected, by universal suffrage, for a five-year term. The President is empowered to appoint a prime minister; however, the ADP has the right to veto any such appointment. Provision is also made for the creation of a second, consultative chamber.

Both the Government and the ADP may initiate legislation.

The judiciary is independent. Judges are to be accountable to a Higher Council, under the chairmanship of the Head of State.

The Constitution denies legitimacy to any regime that might take power as the result of a *coup d'état*.

The Government

HEAD OF STATE

President: BLAISE COMPAORÉ (assumed power as Chairman of the Front populaire 15 October 1987; elected President 1 December 1991).

COUNCIL OF MINISTERS

(August 1994)

President: BLAISE COMPAORÉ.

Prime Minister: ROCH MARC CHRISTIAN KABORÉ.

Minister of State, with responsibility for Defence: KANIDOUA NABOHO.

Minister, with responsibility for African Integration and Solidarity: HERMAN YAMÉOGO.

Minister with responsibility for Special Duties at the Presidency: SALIF DIALLO.

Minister of the Economy, Finance and Planning: ZÉPHIRIN DIABRÉ.

Minister of Justice and Keeper of the Seals: YARGA LARBA.

Minister of External Relations: ABLASSEH OUÉDRAOGO.

Minister of Territorial Administration: VINCENT TE KABRÉ.

Minister of Industry, Trade and Mines: SOULEY MOHAMED.

Minister of Secondary and Higher Education and Scientific Research: MAURICE MÉLÉGUÉ TRAORÉ.

Minister of Primary Education and Mass Literacy: ALICE TIENDRÉBÉOGO.

Minister with responsibility for Relations with Parliament: THOMAS SANOU.

Minister of Public Works, Housing and Town Planning: JOSEPH KABORÉ.

Minister of Employment, Labour and Social Security: AREUIMA ALPHONSE OUÉDRAOGO.

Minister of the Civil Service and Administrative Modernization: JULIETTE BONKOUNGOU.

Minister of Agriculture and Animal Resources: JEAN-PAUL SAWADOGO.

Minister of Communications, Culture and Spokesperson for the Government: NOURCHOIR CLAUDE SOMDA.

Minister of Health: CHRISTOPHE DABIRÉ.

Minister of the Environment and Tourism: ANATOLE G. TIENDRÉBÉOGO.

Minister of Water Resources: JOSEPH NONGDO OUÉDRAOGO.

Minister of Youth and Sports: IBRAHIM TRAORÉ.

Minister of Transport: OUALA KOUTIEBOU.

Minister of Social Welfare and the Family: AKILA BELMBAONGO.

Minister-delegate, in charge of the Budget: CÉLÉSTIN TIENDRÉBÉOGO.

MINISTRIES

Office of the President: Ouagadougou

Office of the Prime Minister: Ouagadougou.

Ministry of Agriculture and Animal Resources: BP 7005, Ouagadougou.

Ministry of the Civil Service and Administrative Modernization: Ouagadougou.

Ministry of Communications and Culture: 01 BP 2507, Ouagadougou 01; tel. 30-70-52; telex 5237; fax 30-70-56.

Ministry of Defence: BP 496, Ouagadougou; telex 5297.

Ministry of Employment, Labour and Social Security: BP 7006, Ouagadougou.

Ministry of the Environment and Tourism: BP 7044, Ouagadougou; tel. 33-41-65; telex 5555.

Ministry of External Relations: BP 7038, Ouagadougou; telex 5222.

Ministry of Finance and Planning: BP 7012, Ouagadougou; tel. 33-40-74; telex 5256.

Ministry of Health: Ouagadougou; tel. 33-28-68; telex 5555.

Ministry of Industry, Trade and Mines: BP 365, Ouagadougou.

Ministry of Justice: BP 526, Ouagadougou.

Ministry of Primary Education and Mass Literacy: 01 BP 1179, Ouagadougou 01; tel. 30-12-94.

Ministry of Public Works, Housing and Town Planning: Ouagadougou.

Ministry of Secondary and Higher Education and Scientific Research: 03 BP 7130, Ouagadougou 03; tel. 31-29-11; telex 5555; fax 31-41-41.

Ministry of Social Welfare and the Family: c/o World Bank Resident Mission, BP 622, Ouagadougou; tel. 30-62-37; telex 5265; fax 30-86-49.

Ministry of Territorial Administration: BP 7034, Ouagadougou.

Ministry of Transport: BP 177, Ouagadougou.

Ministry of Water Resources: Ouagadougou.

Ministry of Youth and Sports: BP 7035, Ouagadougou.

Legislature

ASSEMBLÉE DES DÉPUTÉS POPULAIRES

President: Dr ARSÈNE YÈ BOGNESSAN.

General Election, 24 May 1992

Party	Seats
ODP/MT	78
CNPP—PSD	12
RDA	6
ADF	4
PAI	2
MDP	1
MDS	1
PSB	1
USD	1
USDI	1
Total	107

Advisory Council

Conseil Economique et Social: Ouagadougou; f. 1985 as Conseil Révolutionnaire Economique et Social, name changed 1992; 38 mems; Pres. PHILIPPE OUÉDRAOGO.

Political Organizations

At the May 1992 general election 62 political parties were reported to have been accorded legal status, although by mid-1994 there were believed to be about 28 active political parties. Among the first to be officially recognized were:

Front populaire (FP): Ouagadougou; f. Oct. 1987, restructured 1991; includes:

Mouvement des démocrates progressistes (MDP): f. 1990; Sec.-Gen. LASSANE OUANGRAOUA.

Organisation pour la démocratie populaire/Mouvement du travail (ODP/MT): f. 1989 by merger of Union des communistes burkinabè and a dissident faction of the Union des luttes communistes; Pres. Dr ARSÈNE YÈ BOGNESSAN; Sec.-Gen. NABAHO KANIDOUA.

Union des démocrates et patriotes burkinabè (UDPB): Sec.-Gen. JOSEPH OUÉDRAOGO.

Union des sociaux-démocrates (USD): f. 1990; Leader ALAIN YODA.

Among the political organizations outside the FP in mid 1994 were:

Alliance pour la démocratie et la fédération (ADF): 01 BP 2061 Ouagadougou 01; tel. 31-15-15; f. 1990 by breakaway faction of Mouvement des démocrates progressistes; Leader HERMAN YAMÉOGO.

Convention nationale des patriotes progressistes—Parti social-démocrate (CNPP—PSD): expelled from FP March 1991; Leader PIERRE TAPSOBA.

Mouvement pour la démocratie sociale (MDS): fmrly Groupe communiste burkinabè, name changed 1991; Sec.-Gen. JEAN-MARC PALM.

Parti pour la démocratie et le progrès (PDP): f. 1993, following split from CNPP—PSD; Leader JOSEPH KI-ZERBO.

Parti du travail du Burkina (PTB): f. 1990.

Rassemblement démocratique africain (RDA): pre-independence party; Leader GÉRARD KANGO OUÉDRAOGO.

Union des verts pour le développement du Burkina (UVDB): Sec.-Gen. RAM OUÉDRAOGO.

Other prominent political organizations include: the **Alliance pour la démocratie et l'émancipation sociale (ADES)**, the **Groupe des démocrates patriotes (GDP)**, the **Parti africain de l'indépendance (PAI)**, the **Parti de la convergence pour les libertés et l'intégration (PCLI)**, the **Parti écologiste pour le progrès (PEP)**, the **Parti socialiste burkinabè (PSB)**, and the **Union des sociaux-démocrates indépendants (USDI)**.

Diplomatic Representation

EMBASSIES IN BURKINA FASO

Algeria: BP 3893, Ouagadougou; telex 5359.

Cuba: BP 3422, Ouagadougou; telex 5360; Ambassador: REME REMIGIO RUIZ.

Egypt: BP 668, Ouagadougou; telex 5289; Ambassador: Dr MOHAMAD ALEY EL-KORDY.

France: 902 ave de l'Indépendance, 01 BP 504, Ouagadougou 01; tel. 30-67-70; telex 5211; Ambassador: GÉRARD SIMON.

Germany: 01 BP 600, Ouagadougou 01; tel. 30-67-31; telex 5217; fax 31-39-91; Ambassador: JOHANN WENZL.

Ghana: BP 212, Ouagadougou; tel. 33-28-75; Ambassador: (vacant).

Korea, Democratic People's Republic: BP 370, Ouagadougou; Ambassador: KIM SUN JE.

Libya: BP 1601, Ouagadougou; telex 5311; Secretary of People's Bureau: (vacant).

Netherlands: BP 1302, Ouagadougou; telex 5303; Ambassador: ALEXANDER HELDRING.

Nigeria: BP 132, Ouagadougou; tel. 33-42-41; telex 5236; Chargé d'affaires a.i.: A. K. ALLI ASSAYOUTI.

USA: 01 BP 35, Ouagadougou 01; tel. 30-67-23; telex 5290; fax 31-23-68; Ambassador: DONALD J. MCCONNELL.

Judicial System

The Constitution of 2 June 1991 provides for the independence of the judiciary. Judges are to be accountable to a Higher Council, under the chairmanship of the President of the Republic.

Religion

More than 50% of the population follow animist beliefs.

ISLAM

At 31 December 1986 there were an estimated 2,514,261 Muslims in Burkina Faso.

CHRISTIANITY

The Roman Catholic Church

Burkina comprises one archdiocese and eight dioceses. At 31 December 1992 there were an estimated 890,580 adherents (about 9.6% of the total population).

Bishops' Conference: Conférence des Evêques de Burkina Faso et du Niger, BP 1195, Ouagadougou; tel. 30-60-26; f. 1966, legally recognized 1978; Pres. Rt Rev. JEAN-MARIE UNTAANI COMPAORÉ, Bishop of Fada N'Gourma.

Archbishop of Ouagadougou: Cardinal PAUL ZOUNGRANA, 01 BP 1472, Ouagadougou 01; tel. 30-67-04.

Protestant Churches

At 31 December 1986 there were an estimated 106,467 adherents.

The Press

Direction de la presse écrite: Ouagadougou; govt body responsible for media direction.

DAILIES

Observateur Paalga (New Observer): 01 BP 584, Ouagadougou 01; tel. 33-27-05; fax 31-45-79; f. 1974; independent; Dir EDOUARD OUÉDRAOGO; circ. 8,000.

Le Pays: 01 BP 4577, Ouagadougou 01; tel. 31-35-46; fax 31-45-50; f. 1991; independent; Dir BOUREIMA JÉRÉMIE SIGUÉ; circ. 4,000.

Sidwaya (Truth): 5 rue du Marché, 01 BP 507, Ouagadougou 01; f. 1984; state-owned; Mossi; Editor-in-Chief YAMBA YAMÉOGO; circ. 5,000.

PERIODICALS

Le Berger: Zone commerciale, ave Binger, BP 2581, Bobo-Dioulasso; f. 1992; weekly; Dir BLAISE KUILIGA YAMÉOGO.

Bulletin de l'Agence d'Information du Burkina: 01 BP 2507, Ouagadougou 01; tel. 30-70-52; telex 5327; fax 30-70-56; 2 a week; Editor-in-Chief JAMES DABIRÉ; circ. 200.

La Clef: 01 BP 6113, Ouagadougou 01; tel. 31-38-27; f. 1992; weekly; Dir KY SATURNIN; circ. 3,000.

L'Intrus: 01 BP 2009, Ouagadougou 01; f. 1985; weekly; satirical; Dir JEAN HUBERT BAZIÉ; circ. 3,000.

Le Journal du Jeudi: 01 BP 3654, Ouagadougou 01; tel. 31-41-08; f. 1991; weekly; independent; Dir BOUBACAR DIALLO; circ. 8,000.

Le Matin: Bobo-Dioulasso; tel. 97-16-93; f. 1992; weekly; Dir FLORENT DOFINITI BONZI.

Yeelen (Light): Ouagadougou; monthly; organ of the ODP/MT.

Zoom: BP 8106, Ouagadougou; tel. 30-28-74; fax 31-44-68; f. 1992; fortnightly; Dir ABOU YACINE N. SIRIMA; circ. 2,500.

NEWS AGENCIES

Agence d'Information du Burkina (AIB): 01 BP 2507, Ouagadougou 01; tel. 30-70-52; telex 5327; fax 30-70-56; f. 1963; fmrly Agence Burkinabè de Presse; state-controlled; Dir Minister of Communication.

Foreign Bureaux

Agence France-Presse (AFP): BP 391, Ouagadougou; tel. 33-56-56; telex 5204; Bureau Chief KIDA TAPSOBA.

ITAR—TASS (Russia) is also represented in Burkina Faso.

Publishers

Presses Africaines SA: BP 1471, Ouagadougou; tel. 33-43-07; telex 5344; general fiction, religion, primary and secondary textbooks; Man. Dir A. WININGA.

Société Nationale d'Edition et de Presse (SONEPRESS): BP 810, Ouagadougou; f. 1972; general, periodicals; Pres. MARTIAL OUÉDRAOGO.

Government Publishing House

Imprimerie Nationale du Burkina Faso (INBF): route de l'Hôpital Yalgado, BP 7040, Ouagadougou; tel. 33-52-92; f. 1963; Dir LATY SOULEYMANE TRAORÉ.

Radio and Television

In 1991, according to UNESCO, there were an estimated 245,000 radio receivers and 49,000 television receivers in use.

RADIO

Radiodiffusion-Télévision Burkina: BP 7029, Ouagadougou; tel. 33-68-05; telex 5132; f. 1959; services in French and 16 vernacular languages; Dir BAYER BALAWO.

Radio Bobo-Dioulasso: BP 392, Bobo-Dioulasso; tel. 99-11-58; daily programmes in French and vernacular languages.

Radio Horizon FM: 01 BP 2714, Ouagadougou 01; tel. 31-28-58; fax 31-39-34; private commercial station; broadcasts in French, English and eight vernacular languages; Dir MUSTAPHA LAABLI THIOMBIANO.

Radio Tapoa: Diapaga; f. 1989; broadcasts to Tapoa province.

REP: Ouagadougou; f. 1987; private commercial station; Dir JEAN-HUBERT BAZIE.

TELEVISION

Télévision Nationale du Burkina: 29 blvd de la Révolution, 01 BP 2530, Ouagadougou; tel. 31-01-35; telex 5327; f. 1963; Dir SEYDOU AZAD SAWADOGO.

Finance

(cap. = capital; res = reserves; m. = million; brs = branches; amounts in francs CFA)

BANKING

Central Bank

Banque Centrale des Etats de l'Afrique de l'Ouest (BCEAO): ave Gamal-Abdel-Nasser, BP 356, Ouagadougou; tel. 30-60-15; telex 5205; fax 31-01-22; headquarters in Dakar, Senegal; f. 1955; bank of issue for the seven states of the Union monétaire ouest-africaine (UMOA), comprising Benin, Burkina Faso, Côte d'Ivoire, Mali, Niger, Senegal and Togo; cap. and res 379,881m. (Sept. 1992); Gov. CHARLES KONAN BANNY; Dir in Burkina Faso MOUSSA KONÉ; br. in Bobo-Dioulasso.

State Banks

Banque Arabe-Libyenne-Burkinabè pour le Commerce et le Développement (BALIB): ave Nelson Mandela, 01 BP 1336, Ouagadougou 01; tel. 30-78-78; telex 5501; fax 31-06-28; f. 1987, 50% state-owned, 50% owned by Govt of Libya; cap. 2,000m. (Sept. 1993); Pres. LUCAIN SOMÉ; Man. Dir IBRAHIM K. HELLAWI.

Banque Internationale du Burkina SAEM (BIB): rue de la Chance, angle rue Patrice Lumumba, 01 BP 362, Ouagadougou 01; tel. 31-01-00; telex 5372; fax 31-00-94; f. 1974; 40% owned by Meridien BIAO SA (Luxembourg), 25% state-owned; cap. 2,200m. (Sept. 1992); Pres. and Man. Dir GASPARD OUÉDRAOGO; 14 brs.

Banque Internationale pour le Commerce, l'Industrie et l'Agriculture du Burkina (BICIA—B): ave Dr Nkwamé N'Krumah, 01 BP 8, Ouagadougou 01; tel. 30-62-26; telex 5203; fax 31-19-55; f. 1973; 51% state-owned; cap. 2,500m. (Sept. 1992); Pres. DIE MARTIN SOW; Man. Dir HAMADÉ OUÉDRAOGO; 11 brs.

Banque Nationale de Développement du Burkina (BND–B): place de la Révolution, 01 BP 148, Ouagadougou 01; tel. 30-60-82; telex 5225; fax 30-60-89; f. 1961; placed in administrative receivership 1991; cap. 1,600m. (Sept. 1992); Receiver DENIS RAYNAUD; 7 brs.

Caisse Nationale de Crédit Agricole du Burkina (CNCAB): ave Gamal-Abdel-Nasser, 01 BP 1644, Ouagadougou 01; tel. 30-21-62; telex 5443; fax 31-43-52; f. 1979; 54% state-owned; cap. 1,300m. (Sept. 1990); Pres. Minister of State, in charge of Finance and Planning; Man. Dir NOËL KABORÉ; 4 brs.

Groupe BFCIB–UREBA–CAI: 01 BP 585, Ouagadougou 01; tel. 30-60-35; telex 5269; est. in progress 1994 entailing merger of Banque pour le Financement du Commerce et des Investissements du Burkina (BFCIB), Union Révolutionnaire de Banques (UREBA) and Caisse Autonome d'Investissements (CAI); proposed cap. 1,600m.; Dir DER AUGUSTIN SOMDA (acting).

Financial Institution

Caisse Autonome d'Amortissement du Burkina: BP 1309, Ouagadougou; tel. 33-51-37; manages state funds; Man. Dir DOUAMBA TINGA DIDACE.

INSURANCE

Fonci-Assurances (FONCIAS): ave Léo Frobénius, 01 BP 398, Ouagadougou 01; tel. 30-62-04; telex 5323; fax 31-01-53; f. 1978; 51% owned by Athena Afrique (France), 20% state-owned; cap. 140m.; Pres. El Hadj OUMAROU KANAZOE; Man. Dir GÉRARD G. MANTOUX.

Société Nationale d'Assurances et de Réassurances (SONAR): 01 BP 406, Ouagadougou 01; tel. 30-62-43; telex 5294; f. 1973; 25% state-owned; cap. 240m.; Man. Dir AUGUSTIN N. TRAORÉ.

Union des Assurances du Burkina (UAB): 08 BP 11041, Ouagadougou 08; tel. 31-26-15; fax 31-26-20; f. 1990; 80% owned by private Burkinabè interests, 20% by l'Union Africaine (Côte d'Ivoire); cap. 270m.; Maj. Dir. J. V. ALFRED YAMÉOGO.

Trade and Industry

GOVERNMENT REGULATORY BODIES AND ENTERPRISES

Bureau des Mines et de la Géologie du Burkina (BUMIGEB): 01 BP 601, Ouagadougou 01; tel. 30-01-94; telex 5340; fax 30-01-87; f. 1978; research into geological and mineral resources; Pres. SAFYATOU BA; Man. Dir KASSOUM JOSEPH KABORÉ.

Caisse de Stabilisation des Prix des Produits Agricoles (CSPPA): 01 BP 1453, Ouagadougou 01; tel. 30-62-17; telex 5202; f. 1964; responsible for stabilization of agricultural prices; supervises trade and export; Pres. BOUREIMA TIEN; br. at Bobo-Dioulasso.

Comptoir Burkinabè des Métaux Précieux (CBMP): Ouagadougou; govt agency responsible for purchase of all gold production.

Office National d'Aménagement des Terroirs (ONAT): BP 524, Ouagadougou; tel. 30-61-10; f. 1974; fmrly Autorité des Aménagements des Vallées des Voltas; integrated rural development, including economic and social planning; Man. Dir EMMANUEL NIKIEMA.

Office National des Céréales (OFNACER): BP 53, Ouagadougou; tel. 33-67-38; telex 5317; responsible for stabilization of the supply and price of cereals; Dir MOUSSA MILOGO.

Office National du Commerce Exterieur (ONAC): ave Léo Frobénius, 01 BP 389, Ouagadougou 01; tel. 31-13-00; telex 5258; fax 31-14-69; f. 1974; promotes and supervises external trade; Man. Dir ALI COULIBALY.

Office National de l'Eau et de l'Assainissement (ONEA): 01 BP 170, Ouagadougou 01; tel. 30-60-73; telex 5226; f. 1977; storage, purification and distribution of water; Dir ALI CONGO.

Office National de l'Exploitation des Ressources Animales: BP 7058, Ouagadougou; tel. 33-68-41; telex 5312.

Société Nationale Burkinabè d'Electricité (SONABEL): ave Nelson Mandela, BP 54, Ouagadougou; tel. 33-62-05; telex 5208; f. 1968; cap. 963m. francs CFA; state-owned; production and distribution of electricity and water; Dir-Gen. OUMARA IDANI.

CHAMBER OF COMMERCE

Chambre de Commerce, d'Industrie et d'Artisanat du Burkina: ave Nelson Mandela, 01 BP 502, Ouagadougou 01; tel. 30-61-14; telex 5268; fax 30-61-16; f. 1948; Pres. PAUL BALKOUMA; Sec.-Gen. ALBERT ELYSÉE KIEMDE; br. in Bobo-Dioulasso.

DEVELOPMENT AGENCIES

Caisse Française de Développement (CFD): ave Binger, BP 529, Ouagadougou; tel. 30-68-26; telex 5271; fmrly Caisse Centrale de Coopération Economique, named changed 1992; Dir M. GLEIZES.

Mission Française de Coopération: 01 BP 510, Ouagadougou 01; tel. 30-67-71; telex 5211; fax 30-89-00; centre for administering bilateral aid from France under co-operation agreements signed in 1961; Dir PIERRE JACQUEMOT.

EMPLOYERS' ORGANIZATIONS

Association Professionnelle des Banques et Établissements Financiers (APBEF): Ouagadougou; Pres. HAMADÉ OUÉDRAOGO.

Conseil National du Patronat Burkinabè: Ouagadougou; Pres. BRUNO IGBOUDO.

Groupement Professionnel des Industriels: BP 810, Ouagadougou; tel. 30-28-19; f. 1974; Pres. MARTIAL OUÉDRAOGO.

Syndicat des Commerçants Importateurs et Exportateurs (SCIMPEX): 01 BP 552, Ouagadougou 01; tel. 31-18-70; fax 31-04-11; Pres. JEAN-FRANÇOIS MEUNIER.

CO-OPERATIVES

Groupement Coopératif de Ventes Internationales des Produits du Burkina (Cooproduits): BP 91, Ouagadougou; telex 5224; exports groundnuts, sesame seeds, shea-nuts (karité nuts) and gum arabic; Chair. and Man. Dir KÉOULÉ NACOULIMA.

Société de Commercialisation du Burkina 'Faso Yaar': ave du Loudun, BP 531, Ouagadougou; tel. 30-61-28; telex 5274; f. 1967; 99% state-owned; import-export and domestic trade; Pres. Minister of Industry, Trade and Mines.

Union des Coopératives Agricoles et Maraîchères du Burkina (UCOBAM): 01 BP 277, Ouagadougou 01; tel. 30-65-27; telex 5287; f. 1968; comprises 8 regional co-operative unions (20,000 mems); production and marketing of fruit and vegetables.

MAJOR INDUSTRIAL COMPANIES

The following are some of the largest companies in terms of either capital investment or employment.

Compagnie Burkinabè pour la Transformation des Métaux (CBTM): BP 235, Bobo-Dioulasso; tel. 99-01-60; telex 8209; f. 1973; cap. 120m. francs CFA; mfrs of aluminium household goods; Pres. SIDI MADATALI; Man. Dir JEAN-PIERRE JOYEUX.

Compagnie des Mines d'Or de Kieré (COMIDOK): Kiéré; f. 1993; exploitation and exploration of gold deposits.

Compagnie Minière de Tambao (COMITAM): 01 BP 12, Ouagadougou 01; tel. 30-67-47; fax 31-27-58; f. 1975; cap. 200m. francs CFA; 65% owned by Interstar Mining Group Inc (Canada), 35% state-owned; exploitation of manganese deposits at Tambao; Pres. S. DONALD MOORE; Man. Dir K. H. E. REICHER.

Grands Moulins du Burkina (GMB): BP 64, Banfora; tel. 88-00-57; telex 8238; f. 1970; cap. 865m. francs CFA; 73% state-owned; flour-millers and mfrs of animal feed; Man. Dir JOSEPH ADAMA SOMBIE.

Groupe Aliz: Bobo-Dioulasso; processing and export of animal hides and skins; 2m. hides and skins processed, 600,000 raw hides exported annually.

Manufacture Burkinabè de Cigarettes (MABUCIG): BP 94, Bobo-Dioulasso; tel. 97-01-22; telex 8205; fax 97-21-62; f. 1966; cap. 935m. francs CFA; cigarette production of 1,000 metric tons per year; Pres. PIERRE IMBERT; Man. Dir BLONDE.

Société Africaine de Pneumatiques (SAP): BP 389, Bobo-Dioulasso; tel. 98-15-69; telex 8207; f. 1972; cap. 1,005m. francs CFA; tyres and inner tubes; Pres. and Man. Dir K. LAZARE SORE.

Société des Brasseries du Burkina Faso (BRAKINA): BP 519, Ouagadougou; tel. 30-13-55; telex 5331; fax 30-08-37; f. 1960; cap. 2,530m. francs CFA; brewers and mfrs of soft-drinks and ice; Pres. JEAN-CLAUDE PALU; Man. Dir MARC BEAUQUESNE.

Société Burkinabè des Ciments et Matériaux CIMAT): Ouagadougou; cap. 1,800m. francs CFA; 98.3% state-owned; exploitation of limestone deposits, cement production, clinker crushing; Man. Dir ALEXIS SIA.

Société Burkinabè des Fibres Textiles (SOFITEX): BP 147, Bobo-Dioulasso; tel. 98-22-03; telex 8208; fax 98-14-05; f. 1979; cap. 4,400m. francs CFA; 65% state-owned; development and processing of fibrous plants; Pres. DIEUDONNÉ YAMÉOGO; Man. Dir GUY SOMÉ.

Société de Construction et de Gestion Immobilière du Burkina (SOCOGIB): BP 148, Ouagadougou; tel. 30-01-97; f. 1961; cap. 1,843m. francs CFA; 36% state-owned; housing development; Man. Dir ANATOLE BELEMSAGHA.

Société de Fabrication des Piles du Faso (SOFAPIL): Zone Industrielle, BP 266, Bobo-Dioulasso; tel. 98-04-97; telex 8220; fax 98-21-54; f. 1971; cap. 683m. francs CFA; mfrs of batteries; Pres. SALIF OUÉDRAOGO; Man. Dir PATRICK LEYDET.

Société Faso-Fani: BP 105, Koudougou; tel. 44-01-33; telex 5250; f. 1965 as Société Voltaïque des Textiles; cap. 1,223m. francs CFA; 56% state-owned; weaving, spinning, dyeing and printing of textiles; Man. Dir FRANÇOIS KONSEÏBO.

Société des Huiles et Savons du Burkina (SHSB CITEC HUILERIE): BP 338, Bobo-Dioulasso; tel. 97-04-70; telex 8203; fax 98-11-12; f. 1967; cap. 1,500m. francs CFA; production of groundnut oil; mfrs of shea (karité) butter, soap and animal feed; Pres. ZAMA BANHORO; Man. Dir SIDIKI SIDIBE.

Société Industrielle du Faso (SIFA): Bobo-Dioulasso; affiliate of Cie française de l'Afrique Occidentale; mfrs of motor cycles and bicycles.

Société Nationale d'Exploitation et de Distribution Cinématographique du Burkina (SONACIB): BP 206, Ouagadougou; tel. 33-55-04; cap. 128m. francs CFA; 95% state-owned; Man. Dir M. TRAORÉ.

Société des Plastiques du Faso (FASOPLAST): Zone Industrielle de Gounghin, 01 BP 534, Ouagadougou 01; tel. 30-20-76; telex 5269; fax 30-27-40; f. 1986; cap. 681m. francs CFA; mfrs of plastics; Man. Dir SYLVAIN DOMBOUE; 138 employees.

Société de Recherches et d'Exploitations Minières du Burkina (SOREMIB): BP 5562, Ouagadougou; tel. 30-62-35; telex 5412; f. 1961; cap. 4,000m. francs CFA; 60% state-owned, transfer to private ownership of part of state holding pending in 1994; mineral exploration and exploitation; Pres. DIEUDONNÉ YAMÉOGO; Man. Dir JOSEPH OUÉDRAOGO.

Société Sucrière de la Compé (SOSUCO): BP 13, Banfora; tel. 88-00-18; telex 8212; f. 1969; fmrly Société Sucrière du Burkina Faso; cap. 6,031m. francs CFA; 69% state-owned; sugar refining; Man. Dir SOULEYMANE OUÉDRAOGO.

TRADE UNIONS

There are more than 20 autonomous trade unions. The five trade union syndicates are:

Confédération Générale du Travail Burkinabè (CGTB): Ouagadougou; f. 1988; confed. of several autonomous trade unions.

Confédération Nationale des Travailleurs Burkinabè (CNTB): BP 445, Ouagadougou; f. 1972; Leader of Governing Directorate ABDOULAYE BÂ.

Confédération Syndicale Burkinabè (CSB): BP 299, Ouagadougou; f. 1974; mainly public service unions; Sec.-Gen. YACINTHE OUÉDRAOGO.

Organisation Nationale des Syndicats Libres (ONSL): BP 99, Ouagadougou; f. 1960; 6,000 mems (1983).

Union Syndicale des Travailleurs Burkinabè (USTB): BP 381, Ouagadougou; f. 1958; Sec.-Gen. BONIFACE SOMDAH; 35,000 mems in 45 affiliated orgs.

Transport

RAILWAY

At the end of 1991 there were some 622 km of track in Burkina Faso. A 105-km extension from Donsin to Ouagadougou was inaugurated in December of that year. Plans exist for the construction of an extension to the manganese deposits at Tambao: in 1989 the cost of the project was estimated at 12,000m. francs CFA.

Société des Chemins de Fer du Burkina (SCFB): 01 BP 192, Ouagadougou 01; tel. 30-60-50; telex 5433; fax 30-77-49; f. 1989 to operate the Burkinabè railway network that was fmrly managed by the Régie du Chemin de Fer Abidjan–Niger; length of railway: 622 km; Pres. SIDIKI SIDIBE; Man. Dir ANDRÉ EMMANUEL YAMÉOGO.

ROADS

At 31 December 1986 there were 13,117 km of roads, including 4,633 km of main roads and 4,108 km of secondary roads; about 14% of the road network was paved. A major aim of current projects for the construction or upgrading of roads, as part of the Government's 1991–96 infrastructure development programme (funded by the Arab Bank for Economic Development in Africa, the Islamic Development Bank, the OPEC Fund for International Development and the Governments of Kuwait and Saudi Arabia), is to improve transport links with other countries of the region.

Régie X9: 01 BP 2991, Ouagadougou 01; tel. 30-42-96; telex 5313; f. 1984; urban, national and international public transport co; Dir FRANÇOIS KONSEIBO.

CIVIL AVIATION

There are international airports at Ouagadougou and Bobo-Dioulasso, 49 small airfields and 13 private airstrips. Ouagadougou airport handled 193,773 passengers and 7,986 metric tons of freight in 1991.

Air Afrique: BP 141, Ouagadougou; tel. 30-60-20; telex 5292; see under Côte d'Ivoire.

Air Burkina: ave Loudun, 01 BP 1459, Ouagadougou 01; tel. 30-76-76; telex 203; fax 31-31-65; f. 1967 as Air Volta, name changed 1984; 66% state-owned; operates domestic and regional services; Man. Dir PAUL ANTOINE GANEMTORE.

Air Inter-Burkina: Ouagadougou; f. 1994; operates domestic passenger and postal services.

Tourism

The principal tourist attraction is big game hunting in the east and south-west, and along the banks of the Mouhoun (Black Volta) river. There is a wide variety of wild animals in the game reserves. In 1991 there were 110,327 tourist arrivals at hotels, and receipts from tourism totalled 6,170m. francs CFA.

Direction de l'Administration Touristique et Hôtelière: BP 624, Ouagadougou; tel. 30-63-96; telex 5555; Dir-Gen. MOUSSA DIALLO.

Faso Tours: BP 1318, Ouagadougou; tel. 30-66-71; telex 5377; f. 1989; Dir-Gen. JEAN-CLAUDE BOUDA.

Defence

National service is voluntary, and lasts for two years on a part-time basis. In June 1993 the armed forces numbered 8,700 (army 7,000, air force 200, gendarmerie 1,500). Other units include a 'security company' of 250 and a part-time people's militia of 45,000.

Defence Expenditure: Budgeted at 37,800m. francs CFA in 1992.

Commander-in-Chief of the Armed Forces: Lt-Col BADAYE FAYAMA.

Education

Education is provided free of charge, and is officially compulsory for six years between the ages of seven and 14. Primary education begins at seven years of age and lasts for six years. Secondary education, beginning at the age of 13, lasts for a further seven years, comprising a first cycle of four years and a second of three years. In 1991 primary enrolment was equivalent to only 37% of children in the relevant age-group (males 46%; females 29%). Secondary enrolment in that year was equivalent to only 8% (males 10%; females 5%). There is a university in Ouagadougou (which had some 5,500 students in the early 1990s), while some students receive higher education in European and other African universities. A rural radio service has been established to further general and technical education in rural areas. In 1990, according to UNESCO estimates, adult illiteracy averaged 81.8% (males 72.1%; females 91.1%). Central government expenditure on education in 1990 was budgeted at 21,602m. francs CFA, representing some 19.4% of total government spending (the highest level of expenditure on any sector in that year).

Bibliography

Allen, C., Radu, M. S. and Somerville, K. (Eds). *Benin, The Congo, Burkina Faso: Economics, Politics and Society.* New York and London, Pinter Publishers, 1989.

Anderson, S. (Ed. and Trans.). *Thomas Sankara Speaks: The Burkina Faso Revolution 1983–87.* New York and London, Pathfinder Press, 1988.

Andrimirado, S. *Sankara le rebelle.* Paris, Jeune Afrique Livres, 1987.

Il s'appelait Sankara: Chronique d'une mort violente. Paris, Jeune Afrique Livres, 1988.

Audouin, J., and Deniel, R. *L'Islam en Haute-Volta à l'epoque coloniale.* Paris, L'Harmattan, 1979.

Cruise O'Brien, D. B., Dunn, J., and Rathbone, R. (Eds). *Contemporary West African States.* Cambridge, Cambridge University Press, 1989.

Duval, M. *Un totalitarisme sans état—essai d'anthropologie politique à partir d'un village burkinabè.* Paris, L'Harmattan, 1985.

Englebert, P. *La Révolution burkinabè.* Paris, L'Harmattan, 1986.

'Burkina Faso in Transition', in *CSIS Africa Notes,* No. 111. Washington, DC, Center for Strategic and International Studies, 1990.

Guion, J. R. *Blaise Compaoré: Réalisme et intégrité.* Paris, Mondes en devenir, 1991.

Harrison Church, R. J. *West Africa.* 8th Edn, London, Longman, 1979.

Izard, M. *Le Yatenga précolonial.* Paris, Editions Karthala, 1985.

Kargoubou, S. *Géographie de la Haute-Volta.* Ouagadougou, Ecole nationale d'administration.

Kayeba-Muase, C. *Syndicalisme et démocratie en Afrique noire. L'expérience de Burkina.* Paris, Editions Karthala, 1989.

Kiéthéga, J.-B. *L'or de la Volta noire.* Paris, Editions Karthala, 1983.

Labazée, P. *Entreprises et entrepreneurs du Burkina Faso.* Paris, Khartala, 1988.

McFarland, D. M. *Historical Dictionary of Upper Volta.* Metuchen, NJ, Scarecrow Press, 1978.

Obinwa Nnaji, B. *Blaise Compaoré: The Architect of Burkina Faso Revolution.* Ibadan, Spectrum Books, 1989.

Rimmer, D. *The Economies of West Africa.* London, Weidenfeld and Nicolson, 1984.

Savonnet-Guyot, C. *Etat et sociétés au Burkina: essai sur le politique africain.* Paris, Karthala, 1986.

Ye, B. A. *Profil politique de la Haute Volta coloniale et néocoloniale ou les origines du Burkina Faso révolutionnaire.* Ouagadougou, Imprimerie Nouvelle du Centre, 1986.

Ziegler, J. *Sankara, Un nouveau pouvoir africain.* Lausanne, Pierre-Marcel Favre/ABC, 1986.

BURUNDI

Physical and Social Geography

The Republic of Burundi, like its neighbour Rwanda, is exceptionally small in area, comprising 27,834 sq km (10,747 sq miles), but with a relatively large population of 5,786,000 (official estimate for mid-1992). The result is a high density of 208 persons per sq km. The principal towns are the capital, Bujumbura (population officially estimated at 215,243 in January 1987), and Gitega (population 15,943 in 1978).

Burundi is bordered by Rwanda to the north, by Zaire to the west and by Tanzania to the south and east. The natural divide between Burundi and Zaire is formed by Lake Tanganyika and the Ruzizi river on the floor of the western rift-valley system. To the east, the land rises sharply to elevations of around 1,800 m above sea-level in a range that stretches north into the much higher, and volcanic, mountains of Rwanda. Away from the edge of the rift valley, elevations are lower, and most of Burundi consists of plateaux of 1,400–1,800 m. Here the average temperature is 20°C and annual rainfall 1,200 mm. In the valley the temperature averages 23°C, while rainfall is much lower at 750 mm.

Population has concentrated on the fertile, volcanic soils at 1,500–1,800 m above sea-level, away from the arid and hot floor and margins of the rift valley. The consequent pressure on the land has resulted in extensive migration, mainly to Tanzania, Zaire and Uganda. However, measures adopted in these countries to discourage such migrations are closing these outlets. The ethnic composition of the population is much the same as that of Rwanda: about 85% Hutu, 14% Tutsi (later arrivals in the country and until recently unchallenged as the dominant group) and less than 1% Twa, pygmoid hunters. Historically, the kingdoms of Urundi and Ruanda were almost invariably enemies, and traditional rivalry remains strong. Thus the assimilation of their related languages, Kirundi and Kinyarwanda, has yet to be achieved.

Recent History

FILIP REYNTJENS

Revised for this edition by FRANÇOIS MISSER

Unlike most African states, Burundi and its northern neighbour Rwanda were not an artificial creation of colonial rule. When they were absorbed by German East Africa in 1899, they had been organized kingdoms for centuries, belatedly forced to open their borders to European intrusion. When, in 1916, Belgium occupied Ruanda-Urundi (as the League of Nations mandated territory encompassing both Rwanda and Burundi was designated), it continued the system of 'indirect rule' operated by the Germans. This choice of colonial policy had a particular impact, since an ethnic minority, the Tutsi (comprising about 14% of the population), had long been dominant over the majority Hutu (85%) and a pygmoid group, the Twa (1%). Unlike the situation in Rwanda, however, the potential for conflict between Hutu and Tutsi was contained by the existence of the ganwa, an intermediate princely class between the mwami (king) and the populace. The mwami and ganwa were Tutsi, standing apart from the Tutsi masses, who, in turn, comprised two main groups, the Banyaruguru and the Bahima. Relations between the ordinary Tutsi and the Hutu were on an equal footing, and intermarriage was common.

The exercise of its perceived duties under the League of Nations mandate led to arbitrary and disruptive intervention by Belgium in Burundi's social and political system. However, to fulfil the criteria imposed by the UN Trusteeship Council after 1948, the Belgian administration was moved towards some degree of democratization. Two main parties came to the fore. The Union pour le progrès national (UPRONA), led by Prince Louis Rwagasore (the eldest son of the mwami), was a progressive nationalist movement, aiming to unite all groups and interests. The rival Parti démocrate chrétien (PDC) was more conservative and maintained cordial links with the Belgian administration. At legislative elections held in September 1961 to precede the granting of internal self-government in January 1962, UPRONA won 58 of the 64 seats in the new national assembly. Rwagasore, who became prime minister, was assassinated two weeks later by agents of the PDC. His death was to prove a crucial event in the subsequent history of Burundi; the absence of his unifying influence was to lead to the division of UPRONA and to the emergence of open conflict between Hutu and Tutsi.

MICOMBERO AND BAGAZA

UPRONA proved unable to contain the ethnic tensions that followed the attainment of independence on 1 July 1962. The monarchy emerged as the only source of legitimacy to which both Hutu and Tutsi could relate in any meaningful fashion. In order to consolidate his own position, the mwami, Mwambutsa IV, sought to ensure a proper balancing of ethnic interests in government. Four governments held office during 1963–65, each comprising almost even proportions of Hutu and Tutsi. Tensions reached a climax when the Hutu prime minister, Pierre Ngendandumwe, was assassinated in January 1965, only a week after taking office. The ensuing political crisis was resolved by a decisive Hutu victory at parliamentary elections held in May. Mwambutsa nevertheless appointed a Tutsi prince as the new prime minister. Incensed by this and by other actions taken by the mwami, a faction of the Hutu-dominated gendarmerie attempted to seize power in October. The repression of this abortive *coup d'état* was extremely violent: virtually the entire Hutu political élite was massacred, together with thousands of rurally-based Hutu who had supported the revolt. These events effectively ended any significant participation by the Hutu in Burundi's political life for many years.

In July 1966 Mwambutsa was deposed by his son, who took the title of Ntare V. He appointed Capt. (later Lt-Gen.) Michel Micombero as prime minister. In November Ntare was himself overthrown by Micombero, who declared Burundi a republic. With the abolition of the monarchy, the most important stabilizing element in the political system was removed, and subsequent purges of Hutu officers and politicians further consolidated Tutsi supremacy. Following an abortive coup attempt in April 1972, massacres of unprecedented magnitude and brutality were carried out. It was estimated that 100,000–200,000 Hutu were killed, and that a further 200,000 fled the country, mainly to Zaire, Tanzania and Rwanda. All Hutu elements were eliminated from the armed forces.

In November 1976 Col Jean-Baptiste Bagaza, like Micombero a Tutsi-Hima from Rutovu, in the south, seized power in a bloodless coup. The new regime made strong efforts to encourage national reconciliation and integration. Under agrarian reforms introduced in the mid-1970s, former Tutsi overlords were compelled to cede much of their titular land to Hutu peasants, and refugees were encouraged to return to their lands. More significantly, the archaic system of land tenure was formally abolished, along with the requirement for peasants to render onerous services to their landlords, and proprietary rights over the land were vested in the hands of the peasantry. None the less, patron-client ties have persisted in various forms, with Tutsi elements generally in the role of patron.

Although the army remained a significant force, attempts were made by the Bagaza regime to increase democratic participation in government. A new constitution, adopted by national referendum in November 1981, provided for a national assembly to be elected by universal adult suffrage, and the first elections were held in October 1982. Having been re-elected president of UPRONA at the party's second national congress in July 1984, Bagaza was elected head of state in August, for the first time by direct suffrage, winning 99.63% of the votes cast; he was the sole candidate in both elections.

During the period 1984–87 there was a sharp deterioration in the government's attitude towards human rights. This was particularly marked in relation to religious freedom, and led Bagaza's regime into intense conflict with several Christian denominations. The number of political prisoners, which rose considerably during this period, included members of churches accused of criticizing government restrictions on religious activities, as well as people suspected of involvement in Hutu opposition groups. Many detainees were reported to have been subjected to torture. This intensification of authoritarian rule led to strained relations with a number of donor countries, which sought to bring pressure on Bagaza by withholding substantial amounts of development aid.

THE BUYOYA REGIME, 1987-93

On 3 September 1987, during a visit abroad, Bagaza was deposed by an army-led *coup d'état*, instigated by Maj. Pierre Buyoya, a close associate who accused the former president of corruption and formed a Military Committee for National Salvation (CMSN), comprising 31 army officers. UPRONA was dissolved and the 1981 constitution was suspended. On 2 October Buyoya was sworn in as president, at the head of a new 20-member government. Bagaza subsequently went into exile in Libya.

Apart from its adoption of a more liberal approach to the issue of religious freedoms, the new regime did not differ significantly from that of Bagaza. It remained dependent upon the support of a small Tutsi-Hima élite, prevalent in the army, the civil service, the judiciary and educational institutions. Although Buyoya emphasized a desire for *rapprochement* and released hundreds of political prisoners, it was clear that the major problem facing the new leadership, as had been the case with Bagaza's regime, was the claim by the Hutu majority for fuller participation in public life.

In August 1988 tribal tensions erupted in the north of the country when groups of Hutu, claiming Tutsi provocation, slaughtered hundreds of Tutsi in the towns of Ntega and Marangara. The Tutsi-dominated army was immediately dispatched to the region to restore order, and in the subsequent week large-scale tribal massacres, similar to those of 1972, occurred. More than 60,000 refugees, mainly Hutu, fled to neighbouring Rwanda, as the death toll rose to an estimated 20,000. (Most refugees had been resettled in Burundi by mid-1989.) In the aftermath of the killings, a group of Hutu intellectuals were arrested for protesting against the army's actions and for demanding the establishment of an independent commission of inquiry into the massacres. In October, however, Buyoya announced changes to the council of ministers, including the appointment of a Hutu, Adrien Sibomana, to the newly-restored post of prime minister. Significantly, the council comprised an equal number of Tutsi and Hutu representatives. In the same month a commission for national unity (again comprising an equal number of Tutsi and Hutu) was established to investigate the massacres and to make recommendations for national reconciliation.

The political situation remained tense during the first half of 1989. There were several attempted coups by hardline Tutsi activists and by supporters of ex-president Bagaza. Following the publication, in April, of the report of the commission for national unity, Buyoya announced plans to combat all forms of discrimination against the Hutu and to introduce new regulations to ensure equal opportunities in education, employment and in the armed forces.

In April 1990 the commission for national unity produced a draft charter on national unity, which, as with the 1989 report, was submitted to extensive national debate. Public discussion, however, was closely monitored and directed by UPRONA, and did little to satisfy the demands of internal (clandestine) and external opposition groups. Political tensions were renewed in August, when the exiled leader of the Parti de libération du peuple Hutu (PALIPEHUTU), the principal Hutu opposition party, died in prison in Tanzania, and the leader of a smaller dissident group was killed in a motor accident in Rwanda. Opponents of UPRONA alleged that both men had been assassinated by agents of Buyoya. Later in the same month, army barracks at Mabanda, in southern Burundi, were attacked by an armed group of exiled Hutu who had crossed the frontier from Tanzania.

Following a visit to Burundi in September 1990 by Pope John Paul II, internal attention focused on preparations for the UPRONA national congress, which took place in December. The congress, which was enlarged to include participation by non-party members, abolished the CMSN and transferred its functions to an 80-member party central committee, with a Hutu, Nicolas Mayugi, as its secretary-general. The draft charter on national unity, duly approved at a referendum held in February 1991 by an electoral margin of 89.2% to 10.2%, was rejected as a 'farce' by PALIPEHUTU and other opposition groups. Later in the same month the implementation of a cabinet reshuffle, whereby Hutus were appointed to 12 of the 23 government portfolios, was viewed with scepticism by political opponents. In March a 35-member commission was established to prepare a report on the 'democratization' of national institutions and political structures, in preparation for the drafting of a new constitution. President Buyoya insisted that transfer to a multi-party system of government was not implicit in the adoption of a new constitituion, but by mid-1991 both Buyoya and the prime minister, Adrien Sibomana, had expressed hopes that a new constitution, providing for a more democratic system of government, would be approved by referendum in early 1992 and would take effect from March of that year.

Constitutional Transition

In September 1991 Buyoya presented the report of the constitutional commission on 'national democratization'. Among the recommendations of the report, which was to provide the basis of a draft constitution, were the establishment of a parliamentary system to operate in conjunction with a presidential system of government, a renewable five-year presidential mandate, the introduction of proportional representation, freedom of the press, the compilation of a declaration of human rights and a system of 'controlled multipartyism' whereby political groupings seeking legal recognition would be forced to fulfil specific requirements, including acceptance of the charter on national unity. Further evidence of the government's apparent commitment to the process of 'democratization' was the abolition, in October, of the state security court, which hitherto had recognized no right of appeal.

In February 1992 the government announced that a referendum was to be held on 9 March to ascertain support for the constitutional reform proposals. It was stated that electoral endorsement of the draft constitution would be followed by legislative elections, and by a presidential poll in 1993. A swiftly-suppressed coup attempt, only days before the referendum, failed to disrupt the proceedings, and the proposals received the support of more than 90% of voters. The new constitution was promulgated on 13 March 1992. At the beginning of April, in an extensive ministerial reshuffle, seven ministers left the government, Buyoya relinquished the defence portfolio, and Hutus were appointed to 15 of the 25 portfolios. On 16 April Buyoya approved legislation relating to the creation of new political parties in accordance with the provisions of the new constitution. Under the terms of this legislation, new political parties were to demonstrate impartiality with regard to ethnic or regional origin, gender and religion, and were to refrain from militarization. By October eight political parties had received legal recognition. Later in the month, the president announced the creation of the National Electoral Preparatory Commission (NEPC), a 33-member body comprising representatives of the eight recognized political parties, together with administrative, judicial, religious and military officials. The commission, which was responsible for orchestrating the process of democratization, convened for the first time at the end of November. In mid-November Buyoya had rejected the demands of five political parties to participate in a transitional government to oversee preparations for the forthcoming legislative elections (tentatively scheduled for March 1993). In response, however, the president announced the creation of a national consultative commission on democratization, to function in a purely advisory capacity. By early December Buyoya had appointed a new 12-member technical commission, charged with drafting an electoral code and a communal law (two of the duties previously assigned to the NEPC), owing to the withdrawal from the NEPC of six political parties, in protest at the participation in negotiations of a representative of the new Confederation of Trade Unions of Burundi (CSB), which had yet to achieve legal status.

In February 1993 President Buyoya announced that presidential and legislative elections would take place in June, while elections for local government officials would be held in November. The presidential poll, conducted on 1 June, was won, with 64.8% of votes cast, by Melchior Ndadaye, the candidate of the Front pour la démocratie au Burundi (FRODEBU), with the support of the Rassemblement du peuple burundien (RPB), the Parti du peuple (PP) and the Parti liberal (PL), ahead of Buyoya, who received 32.4% of the votes, as the UPRONA candidate, with support from the Rassemblement pour la démocratie et le développement économique et social (RADDES) and the Parti social démocrate (PSD). A third candidate, Pierre-Claver Sendegeya of the Parti de réconciliation du peuple (PRP), received only 1.4% of the votes. Legislative elections for 81 seats in the new legislative body were conducted on 29 June. Once again, FRODEBU emerged as the most successful party, with 71% of the votes and 65 of the 81 seats in the new legislature. UPRONA, with 21.4% of the votes, secured the remaining 16 seats. The PRP, the PP, the RADDES and the PRB all failed to attract the minimum 5% of votes needed for representation in the legislature. While the presidential and legislative elections had been conducted without major disturbance, an attempted coup in early July was promptly contained, and resulted in the arrest of four army officers. Ndadaye assumed the presidency on 10 July, thus becoming Burundi's first ever Hutu head of state. A new 23-member council of ministers was subsequently announced. The new prime minister, Sylvie Kinigi, was one of seven newly-appointed Tutsi ministers.

NDADAYE, NTARYAMIRA AND ETHNIC UNREST

On 21 October 1993 more than 100 army paratroopers, supported by armoured vehicles, swiftly overwhelmed supporters of the government, and occupied the presidential palace and the headquarters of the national broadcasting company. Several prominent Hutu politicians and officials, including President Ndadaye, were detained and subsequently killed (presumably by execution) by the insurgents, who later proclaimed François Ngeze, one of the few Hutu members of UPRONA, and a minister in the government of former president Buyoya, as head of a national committee for public salvation (CPSN). While members of the government sought refuge abroad and in the offices of foreign diplomatic missions in Bujumbura, the armed forces declared a state of emergency, closing national borders and the capital's airport. However, immediate and unanimous international condemnation of the coup, together with the scale and ferocity of renewed tribal violence (fuelled by reports of Tutsi-dominated army units seeking out and eliminating Hutu intellectuals), undermined support for the insurgents from within the armed forces, and precipitated the collapse of the CPSN, which was disbanded on 25 October. The prime minister, Sylvie Kinigi, who had earlier refused the insurgents' offer of surrender in exchange for amnesty, announced an end to the curfew, but remained in hiding, urging the international community to sanction the deployment in Burundi of an international force to protect the civilian government. Communications were restored on 27 October, and on the following day the UN confirmed that the government had reassumed control of the country. Ngeze and 10 coup leaders were placed under arrest, while around 40 other insurgents were thought to have fled to Zaire. Although the coup was widely interpreted as an attempt by the Tutsi military élite to check the political advancement of Hutus, there was some speculation that supporters of ex-president Bagaza were responsible for the uprising, which may have been precipitated by suggestions that Ndadaye was attempting to establish an alternative, Hutu-dominated presidential gendarmerie. In early December a 27-member commission of judicial inquiry was created to investigate the insurgency.

Meanwhile, in early November 1993, several members of the government, including the prime minister, had left the French embassy (where they had remained throughout the uprising) with a small escort of French troops, and on 8 November Kinigi met with 15 of the 17 surviving ministers (the minister for territorial administration and communal development, Juvénal Ndayikeza, had been killed during the coup), in an attempt to address the humanitarian crisis arising from the massacre and displacement of thousands of Burundians, as a result of ethinic violence, provoked by the failed coup (see below). On the same day the constitutional court officially recognized the presidential vacancy resulting from the murder of both Ndadaye and his constitutional successor, Giles Bimazubute, the speaker of the national assembly, and stated that presidential power should be exercised by the council of ministers, acting in a collegiate capacity, pending fresh presidential elections, to be conducted within three months. However, the minister of external relations and co-operation, Sylvestre Ntibantunganya (who succeeded Ndadaye as leader of FRODEBU), expressed concern that no electoral timetable should be considered before the resolution of internal security difficulties and the initiation of a comprehensive programme for the repatriation of refugees. Ntibantunganya was subsequently elected speaker of the national assembly, and relinquished the foreign affairs portfolio, which was assumed by Jean-Marie Ngendahayo, minister of communications and government spokesman.

In early January 1994 the FRODEBU deputies in the national assembly approved a draft amendment to the constitution, whereby henceforth a president of the republic could be elected by the national assembly, in the event of a presidential vacancy having been recognized by the constitutional court. UPRONA deputies, who had boycotted the vote, challenged the constitutionality of the amendment, and expressed concern that such a procedure represented election by indirect suffrage, in direct contravention of the terms of the constitution. Although the continued boycott of the national assembly by UPRONA deputies, together with procedural impediments to the immediate ratification of the amendment, forced the postponement, on 10 January, of an attempt by FRODEBU deputies to elect their presidential candidate, the minister of agriculture and livestock, Cyprien Ntaryamira, three days later, following the successful negotiation of a political truce with opposition parties, Ntaryamira was elected president by the national assembly (with 78 of the 79 votes cast), and assumed the post on 5 February. A Tutsi prime minister, Anatole Kanyenkiko, was appointed two days later, while the composition of a new multi-party council of ministers was finally agreed in mid-February.

In November 1993, following repeated requests by the government for an international contribution to the protection of government ministers in Burundi, the OAU agreed to the deployment of a 200-strong protection force (MIPROBU), to be composed of civilian and military personnel, for a period of six months. In December opposition parties, including UPRONA and the RADDES, organized demonstrations in protest at the arrival of the military contingent of 180, scheduled for late January 1994, claiming that Burundi's sovereignty and territorial integrity were being compromised.

Although the commitment to establishing political stability was demonstrated by the representation of the main opposition parties in the new government (ministerial posts were occupied by members of UPRONA, RADDES, Inkinzo and the Parti indépendent des travailleurs—parties which had also secured a guaranteed percentage of future diplomatic, security and civil service posts), the apparent impunity of those responsible for the failed October coup and for reprisal attacks against Tutsis, perpetuated the volatile security situation. On 11 February 1994 an international commission of inquiry, established by a number of human rights organizations, concluded that a majority of members of the armed forces had been directly or indirectly involved in the October coup attempt. It was estimated that 25,000-50,000 Burundians had died as a result of the violence arising from the insurrection. (A UN-sponsored fact-finding mission to investigate the incident arrived in Burundi in March 1994.)

During February 1994 ethnic tension mounted as extremist factions of both Hutu and Tutsi groups attempted to establish territorial strongholds within the country. Reports that both sides had amassed considerable supplies of armaments aroused fears of a severe escalation of the conflict. (The minister of the interior, Léonard Nyangoma, claimed that the armed forces had been distributing weapons to Tutsi extremists since 1973, whereas Burundian Hutu refugees in Rwanda were thought to have received arms and military training from the Rwandan armed forces and the *Interahamwe* Hutu militia operating in Rwanda.) Fighting in the capital in early February resulted in the deaths of around 100 Burundians, prompting a delay in the deployment of MICROBU. (In mid-March the government persuaded the OAU to reduce the MICROBU military contingent from 180 to 47.) In early March security forces attempting to locate an opposition arms cache in the Kamengue district of the capital were fired upon by rebels, later identified as the self-styled 'people's army' of Hutu extremists. The armed forces, suspecting elements within FRODEBU, notably Nyangoma, of supporting the rebels in an attempt to establish an armed Hutu force to match the Tutsi-dominated national force (which had resisted all political initiatives for its reform), responded to the rebels' refusal to disarm with an uncompromising display of military strength, during which between 40 and 200 civilians were killed. Attempts by the armed forces to disable Hutu strongholds in and around the capital resulted in the imposition of a *de facto* curfew in Bujumbura in late March, exaggerating existing divisions between FRODEBU's moderate faction, headed by President Ntaryamira (who, anxious to sustain cordial relations with the armed forces, advocated a programme of forced disarmament of militia groups on both sides), and Nyangoma's hardline faction, which opposed further military action against the militias. However, Ntaryamira's insistence that several senior army personnel and the chief of the national gendarmerie should be replaced for having failed to address the security crisis, and that the armed forces should not overlook its own ranks in the enforcement of the pacification programme, provoked sections of the security forces to embark on a campaign of violent destruction in the capital, resulting in dozens of civilian deaths. Following the incident Nyangoma described the state of the capital as one of 'total confusion', and estimated that as many as 1,000 civilians had been killed by the errant soliders, claims which were denied by the government spokesman, Cyriaque Simbizi, (who estimated a death toll of around 400), prompting accusations that Nyangoma was exaggerating the security crisis in order to precipitate a large-scale civil confrontation.

On 6 April 1994, returning from a regional summit meeting in Dar es Salaam, Tanzania, President Ntaryamira was killed (together with the ministers of development, planning and reconstruction, and communications) when the aircraft of Rwandan President Juvénal Habyarimana, in which he was travelling at Habyarimana's invitation, was the target of a rocket attack above Kigali airport, and crashed on landing. Habyarimana was also killed in the crash, and was widely-acknowledged to have been the intended victim of the attack, apparently perpetrated by either the Tutsi-led rebel Front patriotique rwandais (FPR) or by a Hutu extremist faction within the Rwandan armed forces, although both sides denied responsibility for the incident. In contrast to the violent political and tribal chaos which erupted in Rwanda in the aftermath of the death of Habyarimana, Burundians responded positively to appeals for calm issued by Sylvestre Ntibantunganya, the speaker of the national assembly, who, on 8 April, was confirmed (in accordance with the constitution) as interim president for a three-month period, following which a presidential election would be conducted. Although considered to be a less compromising FRODEBU member than Ntaryamira, Ntibantunganya had demonstrated no affiliation to Nyangoma's extremist wing. Nevertheless, Ntibantunganya's statesmanship was immediately tested by several military hardliners who attempted to organize a coup, but were swiftly apprehended by loyalist troops on 25 April.

Meanwhile, sporadic violent exchanges between Hutu extremist rebels and factions of the armed forces were continuing to claim casualties (on 21 April 1994 the attorney general was killed during an exchange of gunfire). In late April, hoping to defuse mounting tensions within the lower ranks of the armed forces, and to impose his leadership over dissident factions of FRODEBU, the president issued an ultimatum to the warring militias, that all illegal arms should be surrendered by 1 May. Following unsuccessful attempts to negotiate the disarmament of the Kamengue 'people's army', the armed forces were authorized to bombard the district with mortar shells, forcing the withdrawal and surrender of many of the rebels. Relations between the government and the armed forces improved considerably as a result, prompting the president to indicate that the contentious reform of the armed forces would not be achieved through the imposition of ethnic quotas. The government and the military were further reconciled following a statement, issued by the prime minister in early May, that Nyangoma had forfeited his position in the council of ministers, having failed to return from government business abroad. During May UPRONA elected Charles Mukasi, the chief editor of a weekly newspaper, as its new leader. In the same month, former president Bagaza resumed political activity, at the head of a new party, the Parti pour le redressement national (PARENA).

Having discounted the possibility of organizing a general election, owing to the fragile security situation and the lack of available government funds, by early June 1994 all major political parties were engaged in negotiations to decide a procedure for the restoration of the presidency. While some FRODEBU members suggested that the new president should be elected by the national assembly, opposition parties considered that the full implementation of an agreement on power-sharing, concluded in February, would be a condition to their agreeing to any candidate proposed by FRODEBU. In mid-July a new agreement on power-sharing was negotiated, providing for the division of posts in local administration (including provincial governorships—nine of which were allocated to FRODEBU, while the remainder would be divided between the major opposition parties) and diplomatic missions abroad. However, the issue of presidential succession seemed likely to be further complicated by indications that Ntibantunganya, an obvious candidate for the office, would be reluctant to continue in the position, owing to party obligations, beyond the interim period, which was extended, on 11 July, for a further three months.

In August 1991 the detention, by security forces, of several Hutus thought to be members of PALIPEHUTU, for alleged 'incitement to massacre', was denounced by the human rights organization Amnesty International. In November continuing ethnic tension erupted into violent confrontations in Bujumbura and the north and north-west of the country between Hutus and Tutsis, involving armed men and civilians on both sides. In January 1992 the minister of the interior stated that order had been restored and announced an official total of 551 deaths resulting from the November disturbances. Unofficial sources, however, estimated that as many as 3,000 had been murdered, many of them Hutus killed by government security forces in reprisal attacks. Widespread concern was expressed, following the disturbances, at the large number of refugees fleeing to neighbouring Zaire and Rwanda. In late 1991 an estimated 30,000 refugees had fled to Zaire and by early 1992 some 10,000 Burundians were still seeking refuge in Rwanda. In late April 1992 further violent disturbances were reported in the north-west of the country, along the border with Rwanda. The government attributed responsibility for the unrest to an insurgency by PALIPEHUTU activists, whom they alleged had been trained and armed in Rwanda. Despite an undertaking, agreed by both countries in August 1992, to implement bilateral attempts to intensify border security and to co-operate more fully in attempts to repatriate refugees, border tension persisted into late 1992 and early 1993.

In October and November 1993, following an abortive coup by factions of the Tutsi-dominated armed forces (see above), ethnic violence erupted on a massive scale, throughout the country, claiming an estimated 50,000 lives. The UN High Commissioner for Refugees (UNHCR) appealed for financial assistance to help address the humanitarian crisis generated by an estimated 800,000 displaced persons, including 500,000 who had fled into neighbouring Tanzania, Rwanda and Zaire, and risked malnutrition and disease at makeshift refugee camps. The situation was compounded by reports of acute food shortages in Burundi. In November the World Food Programme (WFP) initiated an emergency relief operation, while in the same month the UNHCR was allocated US $5m. by the UN Department of Humanitarian Affairs, for the relief of the refugee crisis. However, limited relief resources were overburdened in April 1994 by the exodus of thousands of Rwandans, and by the repatriation of vast numbers of Burundians from refugee camps in Rwanda, following the political violence and accompanying massacres carried out by the presidential guard and Hutu militias, following the death of President Habyarimana.

Economy

Revised for this edition by FRANÇOIS MISSER

In terms of average income, Burundi is one of the poorest countries in the world, and its economic performance is heavily dependent on international prices for coffee. In 1992, according to estimates by the World Bank, Burundi's gross national product (GNP), measured at average 1990–92 prices, was US $1,193m., equivalent to $210 per head. During 1985–92, despite a high rate of population growth (2.9% annually), GNP per head increased, in real terms, at an average annual rate of 1.0%. Overall gross domestic product (GDP) increased, in real terms, at an average rate of 7.1% per year during 1965–80, and by an annual average of 4.0% in 1980–91. Real GDP rose by 3.5% in 1990, 5.0% in 1991 and 2.3% in 1992. The annual rate of inflation averaged 4.3% in 1985–92. The rate averaged 9.0% in 1991, declined to 4.5% in 1992, and increased again to 9.7% in 1993. Burundi is among the 30 African states designated by the fourth Lomé Convention as least developed and therefore qualifying for special treatment under that Convention's scheme to stabilize export earnings (Stabex) for products sold to the European Community (EC). At mid-1992 Burundi had a population density of 208 persons per sq km, the second highest in mainland Africa, and efforts are being made to move people from the over-populated hilly areas to the Ruzizi valley.

AGRICULTURE AND TRADE

At mid-1992 an estimated 90.9% of the labour force were engaged in agriculture (including forestry and fishing), mainly at subsistence level, and in 1992 the agricultural sector provided about 55% of GDP. Burundi's dominant cash crop and economic mainstay is coffee. However, the overwhelming dependence on coffee, which provided 68.9% of total export earnings in 1992, has caused difficulties with the balance of payments in times of falling world coffee prices. The Stabex scheme, introduced in 1975 under the first Lomé Convention and retained in the three subsequent Conventions, has helped to ease this difficulty. Additionally, in the early 1990s the government acted to attract private-sector investment in the coffee industry. The state monopoly on coffee exports was relaxed, and a restructuring of the two factories that process Burundi's entire coffee crop was undertaken. Although exports of coffee were valued at a record 17,057m. Burundi francs in 1986, the pattern of earnings from this source has been erratic, declining to 7,891m. francs in 1987 before recovering to 16,010m. francs in 1988. Revenue from coffee exports declined to 9,502m. francs in 1989 and totalled 9,567m. francs in 1990, reflecting downward trends in world coffee prices. In 1991, however, the value of exports of coffee improved to 13,482m. francs which represented $ 73m., according to World Bank statistics. But in 1992, coffee exports amounted to just $ 51m., owing to a 35% decrease in coffee prices on the world market. In 1990 coffee accounted for 75.6% of total exports by value, increasing to 81% in 1991, only to decrease sharply in 1992, to 68.9%.

Despite civil and political disturbances during 1993 and 1994, the mid-year crop was expected to exceed 30,000 metric tons, owing to favourable climatic conditions. It was hoped that an increase in the price of coffee on world markets would compensate for any future shortfall in volume of production, incurred as a result of civil instability and population displacement.

In 1992 Burundi's total export earnings amounted to US $74m., compared with $ 91m. in 1991 and $ 73m. in 1990. Imports, however, have also increased steadily in recent years, rising from $ 235m. in 1990 to $ 259m. in 1992. The principal imports are machinery and equipment, petroleum products and food. The EU countries (in particular Belgium, Luxembourg, France and Germany), together with the USA, are Burundi's main trading partners.

The credibility of a free export zone, established in 1992, was seriously undermined in August 1993, when the new administration withdrew the financial advantages being offered to a Belgian gold dealer and refiner under the scheme, having calculated that the company's use of the zone was depriving the state of $ 12m. per year in taxes.

Tea is now Burundi's second most important export commodity, and is continuing to increase its share of export earnings. Exports of tea accounted for 13.5% of total export earnings in 1992, compared with 9.1% in 1991 and 5.3% in

1985. During the early 1990s five tea plantations were undergoing development and expansion, with financial assistance from the Caisse française de développement and the European Development Fund (EDF).

In 1987 cotton became a significant export, accounting for 5.7% of total export receipts. Production has subsequently fallen sharply, following heavy rains which destroyed some 600 ha of plantations. However, it was hoped that production would begin to recover in 1992. Mainly grown in the plain of Ruzizi, the cotton crop is nearly all sold to Belgium.

Burundi has obtained foreign assistance for the development of other crops. On the Imbo plain, land is being reclaimed for the cultivation of cotton and rice in an integrated rural development scheme which is assisted by the UN Development Programme and the FAO. Irrigated rice cultivation is also being encouraged in the Mosso region. Plans to establish an integrated sugar scheme in the south-east of this region, with finance provided mainly by the African Development Bank, the OPEC Fund and the Arab Bank for Economic Development in Africa (BADEA), are proceeding. Plantations of sugar cane have been established on the Mosso plain, near Bujumbura, in association with a refinery, which was projected to satisfy 90% of Burundi's demand for sugar by the early 1990s, with further potential for exports. Cassava, sweet potatoes, bananas, pulses, maize and sorghum are other important, but mainly subsistence, crops.

The development of livestock is hindered by the social system, which encourages the maintenance of cattle herds that are both too large and too little exploited. However, the sale of hides has increased, and in 1991 was the fourth most valuable source of export earnings. Some fishing is practised in the waters of Lake Tanganyika.

MINERALS

Small quantities of bastnaesite and cassiterite have been exploited by the Karongo Mining Co (SOMIKA). Gold, tungsten and columbo-tantalite are mined in small quantities, and important deposits of vanadium and uranium are being surveyed. Petroleum has been detected beneath Lake Tanganyika and in the Ruzizi valley, for which test drillings were carried out in the late 1980s by US petroleum interests, in association with the Burundi government. In 1973 a UN survey discovered large nickel deposits, then estimated at 5% of world reserves, near Musongati. A three-year exploration agreement for the southern part of the area was signed in 1993 with a subsidiary of the British company, Rio Tinto Zinc, whereas the Australian BHP corporation has demonstrated interest in a similar project for the northern area of Musongati. Should the reserves eventually prove to have commercial potential, the processing of this ore could include the recovery of copper, cobalt and platinum-group metals, as well as nickel. An evaluation of the economic feasibility of exploiting identified deposits of phosphate rock was under way in 1991. Sufficient reserves of carbonatite to satisfy the domestic demand for cement have also been identified (Burundi is currently 100% dependent on imports.)

INDUSTRY AND TRANSPORT

There is little industrial activity in Burundi, apart from the processing of agricultural products, e.g. cotton, coffee, tea and vegetable oil extraction, and small-scale wood mills. Industry, comprising mining, manufacturing, construction and utilities, provided 16.1% of GDP in 1992. During 1980–91 industrial GDP increased by an annual average of 4.6%. Only 2.3% of the working population were employed in industrial activities in 1979, and this ratio had not increased by 1992. The Five-Year Plans for 1978–82 and 1983–87 aimed to revitalize the stagnant economy by increasing and diversifying production, both for export and for import-substitution, and by encouraging businesses in unfavourable areas. By the mid-1980s several small enterprises, including cement, footwear and insecticide factories and a brewery, had been established. A textile industry was also developed, with aid from the People's Republic of China. Industrial development is hampered by Burundi's distance from the sea (about 1,400 km to Dar es Salaam and 2,000 km to Mombasa), which means that only manufactures capable of absorbing the high costs of transport can be developed.

The International Development Association (IDA) is helping to finance a long-term programme to develop basic forestry services, and to promote tree-planting to supply wood for fuel, building-poles and timber. The project will benefit an estimated 60,000 rural families. The Irish Peat Development Authority has been assisting Burundi to exploit peat bogs as an alternative fuel source. An estimated 12,000 metric tons of peat were extracted in 1992.

The network of roads is dense, but few of the 6,300 km of routes are made up with asphalt, and these are the roads that connect Bujumbura with Gitega, Kayanza and Nyanza-Lac. In February 1992 the government revealed that 600 km of roads had been rehabilitated during the previous three years, and announced a four-year programme of future road improvements covering a further 1,000 km. A new crossing of the Ruzizi river, the Bridge of Concord (Burundi's longest bridge), was inaugurated in early 1992.

Lake Tanganyika (about 8% of which is the sovereign responsibility of Burundi) is a crucial component in Burundi's transport system, since most of the country's external trade is conducted along the lake between Bujumbura and Tanzania and Zaire. Plans to construct a railway linking Burundi with Uganda, Rwanda and Tanzania were announced in 1987. The proposed line would connect with the Kigoma–Dar es Salaam line in Tanzania, substantially improving Burundi's isolated trade position. There is an international airport at Bujumbura.

FOREIGN AID AND DEVELOPMENT PLANNING

Burundi is likely to remain dependent on foreign assistance for some time, not only for capital projects but also for budgetary support. The main bilateral donors of aid and technical assistance are Belgium, France, Japan and Germany. The multilateral agencies, such as the IDA and the EDF, are involved in schemes to increase Burundi's production of coffee, and BADEA has also been a substantial source of development loans. Burundi has also been a considerable beneficiary of aid from the EC through the Lomé Conventions. The main thrust of EC development aid has been in the rural sector, while Stabex transfers have been of pivotal importance to the coffee, tea and cotton industries. Under the current Lomé agreement, the EDF has allocated ECU 126m. for projects in Burundi during the period 1990–95, of which ECU 112m. is in grants and the balance in venture capital.

In 1977 Burundi, Rwanda and Tanzania established the Organization for the Management and Development of the Kagera River Basin, which was formed to continue projects started in 1971 to develop irrigation, electric power, navigation and mining in the basin. The Kagera river basin project, combined with a hydroelectric power station already completed at Mugere and another, of 18 MW, at Rwegura, which was inaugurated in 1986 and was expected to provide about one-third of Burundi's electricity requirements, will eventually free Burundi from dependence on electricity from outside sources, mainly Zaire. Eventual self-sufficiency in power should also promote mineral production.

In 1976 Burundi, Rwanda and Zaire established the Economic Community of the Great Lakes Countries (CEPGL). The energy directorate of CEPGL was established in Bujumbura in 1981, and a large joint hydroelectric scheme to benefit the three member-countries (the Ruzizi II project) was commissioned in 1987. Confronted by continued export shortfalls, however, the government has been forced to restrict infrastructural investment, raising the question of whether Burundi can make a significant contribution to regional integration schemes. Burundi became a full member of the Preferential Trade Area for Eastern and Southern African States (PTA) in 1985, and provides the headquarters for the organization's trade and development bank.

In November 1983 the Burundi franc, whose exchange rate had hitherto been fixed in relation to the US dollar, was effectively devalued by 23% when it was linked instead to the IMF's special drawing right (SDR). Burundi is currently one of the largest recipients per caput of low-interest loans from the World Bank, and, to satisfy criteria imposed by the Bank, the first of a series of devaluations of the Burundi franc took place in July 1986, when the currency was devalued by 15% as part of a structural adjustment programme (SAP) which was agreed with the IMF and the World Bank as a counter to Burundi's over-reliance on coffee export earnings, to the decline in economic growth and to the rapid increase in external indebtedness. This programme, which operated during 1986–89, sought to encourage diversification from coffee production, improve the rate of economic growth, reduce domestic inflation, strengthen the balance of payments and increase Burundi's reserves of foreign exchange. In February 1988 the Burundi franc was devalued by 9%, the first stage in a phased devaluation of 35%. In August the exchange rate was stabilized at SDR 1 = 201 Burundi francs. This remained in force until December 1989, when a rate of SDR 1 = 232.14 Burundi francs was established. By 1990, however, few of the programme's specific objectives had been achieved. Burundi remained dependent upon foreign resources to finance its external account deficits, no significant diversification of its productive base had taken place, and coffee remained the dominant export commodity. In August 1991 the Burundi franc was devalued by about 15%, and in November the World Bank agreed to extend the SAP arrangements. The currency's direct link with the SDR ended in May 1992, since when the value of the Burundi franc has been determined in relation to a 'basket' of the currencies of the country's principal trading partners. The Burundi government has declared its aim to achieve economic growth averaging at least 4.0% annually during 1991–94 and to reduce the rate of inflation to 4% per year in 1993.

During 1992, according to the IMF estimates, Burundi's GDP rose by about 2.3%, and the annual rate of inflation decreased to 4.5% from 9.0% in 1991. In 1993, however, the rate increased again, to 9.7%. In 1992 the budgetary deficit was estimated to be equivalent to 14% of GDP, compared with 9% of GDP in 1991, largely owing to increased defence spending. World Bank forecasts of economic growth for 1993 and the following years were expected to be undermined by increased ethnic and political instability in late 1993 and early 1994, and by the financial burden of repatriating and accommodating hundreds of thousands of refugees and displaced persons, in the aftermath of tribal violence arising from the failed coup of October 1993. In such a climate, it seemed unlikely that the successful implementation of plans to privatize one-half of all public enterprises and establish private management contracts for the remainder, by the end of 1995, would be achieved. (By mid-1992 some 24 of Burundi's 84 state-operated companies had been transferred to private ownership.) Foreign debt remains a major cause of economic concern. Burundi's external debt at the end of 1992 was $1,023m., of which $947m. was long-term public debt, although both France and Belgium recently cancelled repayment obligations amounting to some 13% of Burundi's total debt. In that year the cost of debt-servicing was equivalent to 39.9% of revenue from exports of goods and services.

Statistical Survey

Area and Population

AREA, POPULATION AND DENSITY

Area (sq km)	27,834*
Population (census results)	
15–16 August 1979	
Males	1,946,145
Females	2,082,275
Total	4,028,420
15–16 August 1990	5,139,073
Population (official estimates at mid-year)†	
1990	5,458,499
1991	5,620,000
1992	5,786,000
Density (per sq km) at mid-1992	207.9

* 10,747 sq miles.

† Not revised to take account of the 1990 census result.

PRINCIPAL TOWNS

Bujumbura (capital), population 215,243 (estimate, 1 January 1987); Gitega 15,943 (1978).

Source: Banque de la République du Burundi.

BIRTHS AND DEATHS (UN estimates, annual averages)

	1975–80	1980–85	1985–90
Birth rate (per 1,000)	44.7	46.1	46.6
Death rate (per 1,000)	18.8	17.5	17.1

Expectation of life (UN estimates, years at birth, 1985–90): 48.4 (males 46.7; females 50.1).

Source: UN, *World Population Prospects: The 1992 Revision.*

ECONOMICALLY ACTIVE POPULATION
(1983 estimates)

Traditional agriculture	2,319,595
Fishing	5,481
Traditional trades	22,820
Private sector (modern)	37,884
Public sector	95,061
Total labour force	2,480,841

1979 census: Total labour force 2,418,029 (males 1,137,042; females 1,280,987).

Sources: *Revue des statistiques du travail* and Centre de recherche et de formation en population.

1991 estimate (persons aged 10 years and over): Total labour force 2,779,777 (males 1,316,863; females 1,462,914), excluding unemployed persons not previously employed. Source: ILO, *Year Book of Labour Statistics*.

Mid-1992 estimates ('000): Agriculture, etc. 2,697; Total labour force 2,966. Source: FAO, *Production Yearbook*.

Agriculture

PRINCIPAL CROPS ('000 metric tons)

	1990	1991	1992
Wheat	9	9	9
Maize	168	172	178
Millet	13	13	14
Sorghum	64	65	67
Rice	40	40	41
Potatoes	45	46	46
Sweet potatoes	664	680	701
Cassava (Manioc)	569	584	597
Yams	8	8	8
Taro (Coco yam)	128	132	135
Dry beans	330	338	346
Dry peas	36	37	37
Palm kernels*	2.8	2.8	2.9
Groundnuts (in shell)*	97	98	98
Cottonseed	3	5†	5†
Cotton (lint)	2	3†	3†
Sugar cane	88*	131*	155*
Coffee (green)	34	29	34
Tea (made)	4	5	6*
Tobacco (leaves)*	4	4	3
Bananas and plantains	1,547	1,585	1,645

* FAO estimate(s). † Unofficial estimate.

Source: FAO, *Production Yearbook*.

LIVESTOCK ('000 head, year ending September)

	1990	1991*	1992*
Cattle	432	435	440
Sheep	361	365	370
Goats	927	930	932
Pigs	103	103	105

* FAO estimates.

Poultry (FAO estimates, million): 4 in 1990; 4 in 1991; 4 in 1992.

Source: FAO, *Production Yearbook*.

LIVESTOCK PRODUCTS (FAO estimates, '000 metric tons)

	1990	1991	1992
Beef and veal	11	11	11
Mutton and lamb	1	1	1
Goats' meat	3	3	3
Pig meat	4	4	4
Cows' milk	26	26	26
Goats' milk	7	7	7
Hen eggs	3.0	3.1	3.2

Source: FAO, *Production Yearbook*.

Forestry

ROUNDWOOD REMOVALS ('000 cubic metres)

	1989	1990	1991
Sawlogs, veneer logs and logs for sleepers	6	4	6
Other industrial wood*	43	44	46
Fuel wood*	4,044	4,162	4,291
Total	4,093	4,210	4,343

* FAO estimates.

Source: FAO, *Yearbook of Forest Products*.

Fishing

('000 metric tons, live weight)

	1989*	1990	1991
Dagaas	5.2	14.5	19.7
Freshwater perches	1.4	1.9	2.1
Others	5.1	1.0	1.2
Total catch	11.7	17.4	23.1

* FAO estimates.

Source: FAO, *Yearbook of Fishery Statistics*.

Mining

	1989	1990	1991
Gold (kilograms)	19	9	25
Tin ore (metric tons)*	62	60	70
Kaolin ('000 metric tons)†	4	5	5
Peat ('000 metric tons)	14	11	10

* Data from *International Tin Statistics* (UNCTAD, Geneva).
† Data from US Bureau of Mines.

Source: UN, *Industrial Statistics Yearbook*.

Industry

SELECTED PRODUCTS

	1989	1990	1991
Beer ('000 hectolitres)	919	1,010	1,084
Soft drinks ('000 hectolitres)	139	137	148
Cigarettes (million)	333	384	450
Blankets ('000)	280	326	276
Footwear ('000 pairs)	289	192	296

Source: Banque de la République du Burundi.

Finance

CURRENCY AND EXCHANGE RATES

Monetary Units

100 centimes = 1 Burundi franc.

Sterling and Dollar Equivalents (31 March 1994)

£1 sterling = 381.9 francs;
US $1 = 257.3 francs;
1,000 Burundi francs = £2.618 = $3.887.

Average Exchange Rate (Burundi francs per US dollar)

1991 181.51
1992 208.30
1993 242.78

Note: In November 1983 the Burundi franc was linked to the IMF's special drawing right (SDR), with the mid-point exchange rate initially fixed at SDR 1 = 122.7 francs. This remained in force until July 1986, after which the rate was frequently adjusted. A rate of SDR 1 = 232.14 francs was established in December 1989. This was in operation until August 1991, when the currency was devalued by about 15%, with the new rate set at SDR 1 = 273.07 francs. This arrangement ended in May 1992, when the Burundi franc was linked to a 'basket' of the currencies of the country's principal trading partners.

BUDGET (million Burundi francs)

Revenue	1989	1990	1991
Income tax	4,976.7	6,331.6	8,519.5
Property tax	141.8	154.0	182.5
Customs duties	9,153.8	6,017.0	7,183.5
Excise duties	4,869.3	5,447.3	6,198.5
Other indirect taxes	5,993.7	6,831.6	9,400.5
Administrative receipts	6,362.6	6,108.2	2,860.3
Total revenue	31,497.9	30,889.7	34,344.8

Expenditure	1989	1990	1991
Goods and services	17,100.3	19,373.9	19,338.6
Subsidies and transfers	6,825.4	6,898.3	7,414.1
Net loans	26.7	38.8	67.1
Other	8,391.8	7,572.5	8,934.0
Total expenditure	32,344.2	33,883.5	35,753.8

Source: Banque de la République du Burundi.

CENTRAL BANK RESERVES (US $ million at 31 December)

	1991	1992	1993
Gold*	6.44	5.79	n.a.
IMF special drawing rights	3.75	1.49	0.70
Reserve position in IMF	10.36	8.06	8.05
Foreign exchange	127.28	164.63	154.23
Total	147.83	179.96	n.a.

* Valued at market-related prices.

Source: IMF, *International Financial Statistics.*

MONEY SUPPLY (million Burundi francs at 31 December)

	1989	1990	1991
Currency outside banks	9,868	10,766	11,441
Official entities' deposits at Central Bank	1,377	1,103	792
Demand deposits at commercial banks	8,300	9,707	12,080
Demand deposits at other monetary institutions	696	769	913
Total money	20,241	22,345	25,226

Source: Banque de la République du Burundi.

COST OF LIVING (Consumer Price Index for Bujumbura; base: January 1980 = 100)

	1989	1990	1991
Food	180.5	193.9	207.0
Clothing	182.0	198.0	221.6
Rent, fuel and light	171.3	181.6	193.8
All items (incl. others)	195.9	209.7	228.5

Source: Banque de la République du Burundi.

NATIONAL ACCOUNTS (million Burundi francs at current prices)

Composition of the Gross National Product

	1991	1992	1993
GDP in purchasers' values	211,898	226,384	234,434
Net factor payments abroad	−2,041	−8,845	−2,694
Gross national product	209,857	217,539	231,740

Expenditure on the Gross Domestic Product

	1991	1992	1993
Government final consumption expenditure	36,112	35,212	41,324
Private final consumption expenditure	177,692	187,784	204,844
Increase in stocks	−1,043	1,005	1,037
Gross fixed capital formation	38,307	47,779	38,744
Total domestic expenditure	251,068	271,780	285,949
Exports of goods and services	21,231	20,309	17,746
Less Imports of goods and services	60,402	65,705	69,261
GDP in purchasers' values	211,897	226,384	234,434
GDP at constant 1990 prices	206,483	211,166	n.a.

Source: IMF, *International Financial Statistics.*

Gross Domestic Product by Economic Activity*

	1988	1989	1990
Agriculture, hunting, forestry and fishing	73,270	86,259	96,782
Mining and quarrying } Electricity, gas and water }	1,462	1,535	1,566
Manufacturing	6,949	6,836	8,006
Construction	6,176	6,639	7,774
Trade, restaurants and hotels	13,100	13,834	16,445
Transport, storage and communications	3,762	4,147	4,544
Other commercial services	2,599	2,638	3,232
Government services	19,331	22,803	27,158
Non-profit services to households	497	—	—
GDP at factor cost	127,146	144,691	165,507
Indirect taxes, *less* subsidies	16,891	20,488	17,098
GDP in purchasers' values	144,037	165,179	182,605

* Excluding GDP of the artisan branch (million francs): 8,870 in 1988; 8,223 in 1989; 9,637 in 1990.

Source: Banque de la République du Burundi.

BALANCE OF PAYMENTS (US $ million)

	1990	1991	1992
Merchandise exports f.o.b.	72.9	91.5	80.2
Merchandise imports f.o.b.	−189.0	−195.9	−181.8
Trade balance	−116.1	−104.5	−101.6
Exports of services	16.6	25.5	17.3
Imports of services	−125.4	−136.8	−133.7
Other income received	8.2	9.7	14.0
Other income paid	−23.1	−20.9	−27.7
Private unrequited transfers (net)	10.0	13.2	12.8
Official unrequited transfers (net)	163.6	182.5	164.9
Current balance	−66.2	−31.3	−53.8
Direct investment (net)	1.2	0.9	0.6
Other capital (net)	76.8	69.6	98.3
Net errors and omissions	−15.1	−101.7	−19.6
Overall balance	−3.2	−62.6	25.5

Source: IMF, *International Financial Statistics.*

External Trade

PRINCIPAL COMMODITIES (million Burundi francs)

Imports c.i.f.	1989	1990	1991
Intermediate goods	10,885.0	15,394.5	17,607.4
Capital goods	10,375.1	13,734.2	16,479.0
Consumer goods	8,649.6	11,050.6	12,067.8
Total	29,909.7	40,179.3	46,154.2

Exports f.o.b.	1989	1990	1991
Coffee	9,501.7	9,670.1	13,481.6
Cotton	31.3	27.8	—
Hides and skins	509.3	649.4	433.5
Tea	1,004.2	1,145.4	1,514.2
Minerals	39.0	34.3	34.7
Other products	1,218.9	1,256.6	1,180.9
Total	12,304.4	12,783.6	16,644.9

Source: Banque de la République du Burundi.

PRINCIPAL TRADING PARTNERS (million Burundi francs)

Imports	1989	1990	1991
Belgium/Luxembourg	4,630.1	5,825.5	6,535.6
France	3,036.1	3,969.8	4,528.9
Germany	4,059.5	5,165.5	4,078.4
Italy	1,185.7	1,463.9	1,590.4
Japan	2,427.9	2,926.5	3,847.2
Kenya	893.6	1,003.6	1,344.0
Netherlands	488.8	469.8	1,040.0
Tanzania	354.9	487.2	953.0
United Kingdom	602.7	654.6	743.7
USA	365.8	410.6	791.7
Zaire	320.0	266.0	374.2
Others	11,544.6	17,536.3	20,327.1
Total	29,909.7	40,179.3	46,154.2

Exports	1989	1990	1991
Belgium/Luxembourg	169.9	99.8	238.6
France	790.0	1,246.1	818.6
Germany	1,876.4	1,760.0	2,905.5
Italy	275.0	302.5	164.0
Netherlands	119.6	180.9	561.9
United Kingdom	280.0	808.2	410.3
USA	887.7	1,508.8	3,207.1
Others	7,905.8	6,878.0	8,338.9
Total	12,304.4	12,783.6	16,644.9

Source: Banque de la République du Burundi.

Transport

ROAD TRAFFIC (estimates, '000 motor vehicles in use)

	1989	1990	1991
Passenger cars	9	10	10
Commercial vehicles	6	7	7

Source: UN Economic Commission for Africa, *African Statistical Yearbook*.

LAKE TRAFFIC (Bujumbura—'000 metric tons)

	1989	1990	1991
Goods:			
Arrivals	150.4	152.9	188.4
Departures	33.0	32.5	35.1

Source: Banque de la République du Burundi.

CIVIL AVIATION (Bujumbura Airport)

	1989	1990	1991
Passengers:			
Arrivals	30,685	33,581	35,735
Departures	30,116	33,598	36,247
Freight (metric tons):			
Arrivals	4,198	4,510	4,183
Departures	1,868	1,664	1,652

Source: Banque de la République du Burundi.

Tourism

	1989	1990	1991
Tourist arrivals ('000)	82	109	125
Tourist receipts (US $ million)	3	4	4

Source: UN Economic Commission for Africa, *African Statistical Yearbook*.

Communications Media

	1989	1990	1991
Radio receivers ('000 in use)	300	320	340
Television receivers ('000 in use)	3	5	5
Telephones ('000 in use)*	10	10	10
Daily newspapers:			
Number	n.a.	1	n.a.
Circulation ('000 copies)	n.a.	20	n.a.

*Estimates.

Sources: UNESCO, *Statistical Yearbook*, and UN Economic Commission for Africa, *African Statistical Yearbook*.

Education

(1991)

	Teachers	Pupils
Pre-primary*	40	2,087
Primary	9,582	631,039
Secondary:		
General†	n.a.	40,334
Vocational	510	6,174
Higher	492	3,830

* Figures refer to 1988/89 (Source: Ministry of Primary and Secondary Education).

† Including first cycle of teacher training.

Source: UNESCO, *Statistical Yearbook*.

Directory

The Constitution

The Constitution was promulgated on 13 March 1992 and provided for the establishment of a plural political system. The Constitution seeks to guarantee human rights and basic freedoms for all citizens, together with the freedom of the press. Executive powers are vested in the president, who (under normal circumstances—see below) is elected directly, by universal adult suffrage, for a five-year term, renewable only once. Statutory power is shared with the prime minister, who appoints a council of ministers. Legislative power is exercised by a national assembly, whose members are elected directly, by universal adult suffrage, for a five-year renewable mandate.

The Government

HEAD OF STATE

Interim President: SYLVESTRE NTIBANTUNGANYA (assumed office 6 April 1994).

COUNCIL OF MINISTERS
(August 1994)

Prime Minister: ANATOLE KANYENKIKO.

Minister of State in charge of Development, Planning and Reconstruction: (vacant).

Minister of State in charge of External Relations and Co-operation: JEAN-MARIE NGENDAHAYO.

Minister of State for Interior and Public Security: LÉONARD NYANGOMA.

Minister of Finance: SALVATOR TOYI.

Minister of National Defence: Col GEDEON FYIROKO.

Minister of Justice and Keeper of the Seals: FULGENCE DWIMA BAKANA.

Minister of Territorial Administration: JEAN-BAPTISTE MANWANGARI.

Minister of Agriculture and Livestock: PIERRE-CLAVER NAHIMANA.

Minister of Basic Education and Adult Literacy: NICÉPHORE NDIMURUKUNDO.

Minister of Secondary and Higher Education: LIBOIRE NGENDAHAYO.

Minister of Labour and Professional Training: VENERAND BAKEVYUMUSAYA.

Minister of the Civil Service: MARGUERITE BUKURU.

Minister of Communal Development: AMBROISE NIYONSABA.

Minister of Commerce and Industry: JOSEPH NZEYIMANA.

Minister of Small- and Medium-Scale Industries and Tourism: ONESIME CIZA.

Minister of Energy and Mines: ERNEST KABUSHEMEYE.

Minister of Transport, Posts and Telecommunications: SHADRACK NIYONKURU.

Minister of Public Works and Equipment: LÉONIDAS NYAMWANA.

Minister of Territorial Management and Environment: SALVATOR NTIHABOSE.

Minister of Communications, and Government Spokesman: (vacant).

Minister of Human Rights and Refugees: ISSAH NGENDAKUMANA.

Minister of Public Health: JEAN MINANI.

Minister of Social Affairs and Women's Affairs: EMILIENNE MINANI.

Minister of Culture, Youth and Sport: ALPHONSE RUGUMBARARA.

Minister of Institutional Reform and National Assembly Relations: GAETHAN NIKOBAMYE.

Minister Delegate for Reconstruction: JACQUES NGENDAKUMANA.

Minister Delegate for Co-operation: ANTOINE NTAMOBWA.

MINISTRIES

Office of the President: Bujumbura; tel. (2) 26063; telex 5049.

Ministry of Agriculture and Livestock: Bujumbura; tel. (2) 22087.

Ministry of the Civil Service: BP 1480, Bujumbura; tel. (2) 23514; fax (2) 28715.

Ministry of Commerce and Industry: Bujumbura; tel. (2) 25330.

Ministry of Communal Development: Bujumbura.

Ministry of Communications: Bujumbura.

Ministry of Culture, Youth and Sport: Bujumbura; tel. (2) 26822.

Ministry of Development, Planning and Reconstruction: BP 1830, Bujumbura; tel. (2) 23988; telex 5135.

Ministry of Energy and Mines: Bujumbura.

Ministry of External Relations and Co-operation: Bujumbura; tel. (2) 22150; telex 5065.

Ministry of Finance: BP 1830, Bujumbura; tel. (2) 23988; telex 5135.

Ministry of Human Rights and Refugees: Bujumbura.

Ministry of the Interior and Public Security: Bujumbura.

Ministry of Justice: Bujumbura; tel. (2) 22148.

Ministry of Labour and Professional Training: Bujumbura.

Ministry of National Defence: Bujumbura.

Ministry of National Education: Bujumbura.

Ministry of Public Health: Bujumbura; tel. (2) 26020.

Ministry of Public Works and Equipment: BP 1860, Bujumbura; tel. (2) 26841; telex 5048; fax (2) 26840.

Ministry of Small- and Medium-Scale Industries and Tourism: Bujumbura.

Ministry of Social Affairs and Women's Affairs: Bujumbura; tel. (2) 25039.

Ministry of Territorial Administration: Bujumbura; tel. (2) 24242.

Ministry of Territorial Management and Environment: Bujumbura.

Ministry of Transport, Posts and Telecommunications: BP 2000, Bujumbura; tel. (2) 22923; telex 5103; fax (2) 26900.

President and Legislature*

PRESIDENT

Presidential election, 1 June 1993

Candidate	Valid votes cast	% valid votes cast
MELCHIOR NDADAYE (FRODEBU)	1,483,904	65.68
PIERRE BUYOYA (UPRONA)	742,360	32.86
PIERRE-CLAVER SENDEGEYA (PRP)	33,072	1.46
Total	2,259,336	100.00

NATIONAL ASSEMBLY

Speaker: SYLVESTRE NTIBANTUNGANYA (FRODEBU).

Legislative elections, 29 June 1993

Party	Votes cast	% of votes cast	Seats
FRODEBU	1,532,107	71.04	65
UPRONA	462,324	21.44	16
RPB	35,932	1.67	—
PRP	29,966	1.39	—
RADDES	26,631	1.23	—
PP	24,372	1.13	—
Independents	853	0.04	—
Invalid votes	44,474	2.06	—
Total	2,156,659	100.00	81

* Following the assassination of Ndadaye and his constitutional successor in October 1993, a constitutional amendment was adopted whereby a successor was to be elected by the National Assembly. On 13 January 1994 Cyprien Ntaryamira, a member of FRODEBU, was elected President by 78 of the 79 votes cast by the National Assembly. Following Ntaryamira's death in April 1994, the Speaker of the National Assembly, Sylvestre Ntibantunganya, assumed the presidency for an interim, three-month period (subsequently extended for a further three months), in accordance with the Constitution.

PROVINCIAL GOVERNORS*

(June 1994)

Bubanza: (vacant).

Bujumbura (Rural): ALOYS HAKIZIMANA.

Bururi: AUGUSTIN NZOJIBWAMI.

Cankuzo: VESTINE MBUNDAGU.

Cibitoke: NEPHTALI NIYIBIZI.

Gitega: JOACHIM NURWAKERA.

Karuzi: ANGLEBERT SENTAMO.

Kayanza: MALACHIE SURWAVUBA.

Kirundo: DEOGRATIAS BIZIMANA.

Makamba: JEAN-BAPTISTE GAHIMBARE.

Muramvya: LÉONCE NDARUBAGIYE.

Muyinga: BALTHAZAR NDIMURWANKO.

Ngozi: JOSEPH NTAKARUTIMANA.

Rutana: LÉONIDAS HAKIZIMANA.

Ruyigi: HENRI BUKUMBANYA.

* Under the terms of a multi-party agreement on power-sharing, concluded in July 1994, nine provincial governorships were allocated to FRODEBU, while the remainder were to be divided among the major opposition parties.

Political Organisations

Although the March 1992 constitution provided for the establishment of a multi-party system, political parties are required to demonstrate firm commitment to national unity, and impartiality with regard to ethnic or regional origin, gender and religion, in order to receive legal recognition.

Alliance nationale pour les droits et le développement (ANADDE): Bujumbura; f. 1992.

Front pour la démocratie au Burundi (FRODEBU): Bujumbura; f. 1992; Leader SYLVESTRE NTIBANTUNGANYA.

Inkinzo y'Ijambo Ry'abarundi (Guarantor of Freedom of Speech in Burundi): Bujumbura; f. 1993; Pres. Dr ALPHONSE RUGAMBARARA.

Parti indépendent de travailleurs: Bujumbura.

Parti libéral (PL): Bujumbura; f. 1992.

Parti du peuple (PP): Bujumbura; f. 1992; Leader SHADRAK NIYONKURU.

Parti de réconciliation du peuple (PRP): Bujumbura; f. 1992; Leader MATHIAS HITIMANA

Parti pour le redressement national (PARENA): Bujumbura; f. 1994; Leader JEAN-BAPTISTE BAGAZA.

Parti social démocrate (PSD): Bujumbura; f. 1993.

Rassemblement pour le démocratie et le développement économique et social (RADDES): Bujumbura; f. 1992.

Rassemblement du peuple burundien (RPB): Bujumbura; f. 1992.

Union pour le progrès national (UPRONA): BP 1810, Bujumbura; tel. (2) 25028; telex 5057; f. 1958; following the 1961 elections, the numerous small parties which had been defeated merged with UPRONA, which became the sole legal political party in 1966; party activities were suspended following the coup of Sept. 1987, but resumed in 1989; Leader CHARLES MUKASI.

The constitutional reforms, which exclude political organizations advocating 'tribalism, divisionalism or violence' and require party leaderships to be equally representative of Hutu and Tutsi ethnic groups, have been opposed by some externally-based opposition parties. These include the **Parti de libération du peuple hutu (PALIPEHUTU**, f. 1980 and based in Tanzania), which seeks to advance the interests of the Hutu ethnic group. An armed dissident wing of PALIPEHUTU, known as the **Force nationale de libération (FNL)**, led by KABORA KHOSSAN, is based in southern Rwanda.

Diplomatic Representation

EMBASSIES IN BURUNDI

Belgium: 9 ave de l'Industrie, BP 1920, Bujumbura; tel. (2) 23676; telex 5033; Ambassador: DENIS BANNEEL.

China, People's Republic: BP 2550, Bujumbura; tel. (2) 24307; Ambassador: JIANG KANG.

Egypt: 31 ave de la Liberté, BP 1520, Bujumbura; tel. (2) 23161; telex 5040; Ambassador: MUHAMMAD MOUSA.

France: 31 ave de l'UPRONA, BP 1740, Bujumbura; tel. (2) 26464; telex 5044; Ambassador: ROBERT RIGOUZZO.

Germany: 22 rue 18 septembre, BP 480, Bujumbura; tel. (2) 26412; telex 5068; Ambassador: KARL FLITTNER.

Holy See: 46 chaussée Prince Louis-Rwagasore, BP 1068, Bujumbura (Apostolic Nunciature); tel. (2) 22326; fax (2) 23176; Apostolic Pro-Nuncio: Most Rev. RINO PASSIGATO, Titular Archbishop of Nova Caesaris.

Korea, Democratic People's Republic: BP 1620, Bujumbura; tel. (2) 22881; Ambassador: AHN JAE BU.

Romania: rue Pierre Ngendandumwe, BP 2770, Bujumbura; tel. (2) 24135; Chargé d'affaires a.i.: ALEXANDRA ANDREI.

Russia: 78 blvd de l'UPRONA, BP 1034, Bujumbura; tel. (2) 26098; telex 5164; fax (2) 22984; Ambassador: ARTOUR VESSELOV.

Rwanda: 24 ave du Zaïre, BP 400, Bujumbura; tel. (2) 23140; telex 5032; Ambassador: SYLVESTRE UWIBAJIJE.

Tanzania: BP 1653, Bujumbura; Ambassador: NICHOLAS J. MARO.

USA: ave des Etats-Unis, BP 1720, Bujumbura; tel. (2) 23454; fax (2) 22926; Ambassador: ROBERT KREUGER.

Zaire: 5 ave Olsen, BP 872, Bujumbura; tel. (2) 23492; Ambassador: VIZI TOPI.

Judicial System

The 1981 Constitution prescribed a judicial system wherein the judges were subject to the decisions of UPRONA. Under a programme of legal reform, announced in 1986, provincial courts were to be replaced by a dual system of courts of civil and criminal jurisdiction. A network of mediation and conciliation courts was to be established to arbitrate in minor disputes arising among the rural population. Substantial reforms of the legal system were expected to follow the implementation of the 1992 Constitution.

Supreme Court: BP 1460, Bujumbura; tel. (2) 22571; fax (2) 22148. Court of final instance; four divisions: ordinary, cassation, constitutional and administrative.

Courts of Appeal: Bujumbura, Gitega and Ngozi.

Tribunals of First Instance: There are 17 provincial tribunals and 123 smaller resident tribunals in other areas.

Tribunal of Trade: Bujumbura.

Tribunals of Labour: Bujumbura and Gitega.

Administrative Courts: Bujumbura and Gitega.

Religion

More than 65% of the population are Christians, the majority of whom (an estimated 61%) are Roman Catholics. Anglicans number about 60,000. There are about 200,000 Protestants, of whom some 160,000 are Pentecostalists. Fewer than 40% of the population adhere to traditional beliefs, which include the worship of the God 'Imana'. About 1% of the population are Muslims. The Bahá'í Faith is also active in Burundi.

CHRISTIANITY

Conseil National des Eglises protestantes du Burundi (CNEB): BP 17, Bujumbura; tel. (2) 24216; fax (2) 27941; f. 1970; five mem. churches; Pres. Bishop JEAN-ALFRED NDORICIMPA; Gen. Sec. Rev. SYLVÈRE NIMPE.

The Anglican Communion

The Church of the Province of Burundi, inaugurated in 1992, comprises four dioceses.

Archbishop of Burundi and Bishop of Matana: Most Rev. SAMUEL SINDAMUKA, DS 12, Bujumbura; tel. (2) 24389; telex 5127; fax (2) 29129.

The Roman Catholic Church

Burundi comprises one archdiocese and six dioceses. At 31 December 1992 there were an estimated 3,455,998 adherents.

Bishops' Conference: Conférence des Evêques catholiques du Burundi, 5 blvd de l'UPRONA, BP 1390, Bujumbura; tel. (2) 23263; fax (2) 23270; f. 1980; Pres. Rt Rev. BERNARD BUDUDIRA, Bishop of Bururi.

Archbishop of Gitega: Most Rev. JOACHIM RUHUNA, Archevêché, BP 118, Gitega; tel. (40) 2160; fax (40) 2547.

Other Christian Churches

Union of Baptist Churches of Burundi: Rubura, DS 117, Bujumbura 1; Pres. PAUL BARUHENAMWO; Exec. Sec. OSIAS HABINGABWA.

Other denominations active in the country include the Evangelical Christian Brotherhood of Burundi, the Free Methodist Church of Burundi and the United Methodist Church of Burundi.

BAHÁ'Í FAITH

National Spiritual Assembly: BP 1578, Bujumbura.

The Press

NEWSPAPERS

Burundi chrétien: BP 232, Bujumbura; Roman Catholic weekly; French.

Le Renouveau du Burundi: BP 2870, Bujumbura; f. 1978; publ. by UPRONA; daily; French; circ. 20,000; Dir JEAN NZEYIMANA.

Ubumwe: BP 1400, Bujumbura; tel. (2) 23929; f. 1971; weekly; Kirundi; circ. 20,000.

PERIODICALS

Au Coeur de l'Afrique: Association des conférences des ordinaires du Rwanda et Burundi, BP 1390, Bujumbura; bimonthly; education; circ. 1,000.

Bulletin économique et financier: BP 482, Bujumbura; bimonthly.

Bulletin mensuel: Banque de la République du Burundi, Service des études, BP 705, Bujumbura; tel. (2) 25142; telex 5071; monthly.

Bulletin officiel du Burundi: Bujumbura; monthly.

Le Burundi en Images: BP 1400, Bujumbura; f. 1979; monthly.

Culture et Sociétés: BP 1400, Bujumbura; f. 1978; quarterly.

Ndongozi Y'uburundi: Catholic Mission, BP 690, Bujumbura; tel. (2) 22762; fax (2) 28907; fortnightly; Kirundi.

Revue administration et juridique: Association d'études administratives et juridiques du Burundi, BP 1613, Bujumbura; quarterly; French.

NEWS AGENCY

Agence burundaise de Presse (ABP): 6 ave de la Poste, BP 2870, Bujumbura; tel. (2) 25417; telex 5056; publ. daily bulletin.

Publishers

BURSTA: BP 1908, Bujumbura; tel. (2) 31796; fax (2) 32842; f. 1986; Dir RICHARD KASHIRAHAMWE.

GRAVIMPORT: BP 156, Bujumbura.

IMPARUDI: BP 3010, Bujumbura.

Imprimerie la Licorne: BP 2942, Bujumbura.

Imprimerie MAHI: BP 673, Bujumbura.

MICROBU: BP 645, Bujumbura.

Mister Minute Service: BP 1536, Bujumbura.

Imprimerie Moderne: BP 2555, Bujumbura.

Imprimerie du Parti: BP 1810, Bujumbura.

Les Presses Lavigerie: BP 1640, Bujumbura.

Régie de Productions Pédagogiques: BP 3118, Bujumbura.

SASCO: BP 204, Bujumbura.

Government Publishing House

Imprimerie nationale du Burundi (INABU): BP 991, Bujumbura; tel. (2) 24046; fax (2) 25399; f. 1978; Dir NICOLAS NIJIMBERE.

Radio and Television

In 1991 there were 340,000 radio receivers and about 5,000 television receivers in use. Colour television transmissions began in 1985.

Voix de la Révolution/La Radiodiffusion et Télévision Nationale du Burundi (RTNB): BP 1900, Bujumbura; tel. (2) 23742; telex 5119; f. 1960; govt-controlled; daily radio programmes in Kirundi, Swahili, French and English; Dir-Gen. DONATIEN NAHIMANA; Dirs (Radio) CHRISTINE NTAHE, ANTOINE NTAMIKEVYO; Dir (Television) DIDACE BARANDARAETSE.

Finance

(cap. = capital; res = reserves; dep. = deposits; m. = million; brs = branches; amounts in Burundi francs)

BANKING

Central Bank

Banque de la République du Burundi (BRB): BP 705, Bujumbura; tel. (2) 25142; telex 5071; fax (2) 23128; f. 1964 as Banque du Royaume du Burundi; state-owned; bank of issue; cap. and res 7,101.7m. (Dec. 1989), dep. 9,779m. (Dec. 1991); Gov. MATHIAS SINAMENYE; Vice-Gov. EVARISTE NIBASUMBA.

Commercial Banks

Banque Burundaise pour le Commerce et l'Investissement SARL (BBCI): blvd du 1 Novembre, BP 2320, Bujumbura; tel. (2) 23328; telex 5012; fax (2) 23339; f. 1988; cap. 330m. (Dec. 1992); Admin. CHARLES KABURAHE

Banque Commerciale du Burundi SARL (BANCOBU): 84 chaussée Prince Louis-Rwagasore, BP 990, Bujumbura; tel. (2) 22317; telex 5051; fax (2) 21018; f. 1988 by merger; 51% state-owned; cap. 330m. (Dec. 1992); Pres. JACQUES VAN EETVELDE; Dir-Gen. L. NDABAKWAJE

Banque de Crédit de Bujumbura SARL (BCB): ave Patrice Emery Lumumba, BP 300, Bujumbura; tel. (2) 22091; telex 5063; fax (2) 23007; f. 1964; cap. and res 933m., dep. 10,649m. (Dec. 1992); Pres. THACIEN NZEYIMANA; Man. ATHANASE GAHUNGU; 7 brs.

Caisse d'Epargne du Burundi (CADEBU): 40 chaussée Prince Louis-Rwagasore, BP 615, Bujumbura; tel. (2) 25462; telex 5071; fax (2) 23575; f. 1964; state-owned; cap. 90m. (Dec. 1992); Pres. Minister of Commerce and Industry; Man. Dir ARTHEMON MUHITIRA.

Development Banks

Banque Nationale pour le Développement Economique SARL (BNDE): 3 rue du Marché, BP 1620, Bujumbura; tel. (2) 22888; telex 5091; fax (2) 23775; f. 1966; cap. 740m. (Dec. 1992); Pres. LAURENT NIYUNGEKO; Dir-Gen. FRANÇOIS BARWENDERE.

Caisse de Mobilisation et de Financement (CAMOFI): 245 chausée Prince Louis-Rwagasore, BP 8, Bujumbura; tel. (2) 25642; telex 5082; f. 1979; 50% state-owned; finances public-sector development projects; cap. 200m. (Dec. 1991); Pres. Minister of Finance.

Meridien BIAO Bank Burundi SARL: 1 blvd de la liberté, BP 45, Bujumbura; tel. (2) 25712; telex 5151; fax (2) 25794; f. 1992 by merger; 30% owned by Meridien International Bank (Bahamas); cap. 800m., dep. 10,281m. (Dec. 1991); Pres. and Chair. M. DONATIEN BIHUTE; Man. Dir KEVIN HUGH CAIN; 4 brs.

Société Burundaise de Financement SARL (SBF): 6 rue de la Science, BP 270, Bujumbura; tel. (2) 22126; telex 5080; fax (2) 25437; f. 1981; cap. 860m. (Dec. 1991); Man. GASPARD SINDAYIGAYA.

Société de Gestion et de Financement (SOGEFI): Immeuble Ucar II, chaussée du Peuple Murundi, BP 1035, Bujumbura; tel. (2) 21346; fax (2) 21351; f. 1992; cap. 120m. (July 1992); Pres. DIDACE NZOHABONAYO; Dir-Gen. SÉVERIN MANDEVU.

INSURANCE

Burundi Insurance Corporation (BICOR): BP 2377, Bujumbura.

Société d'Assurances du Burundi (SOCABU): BP 2440, 14–18 rue de l'Amitié, Bujumbura; tel. (2) 26520; telex 5113; fax (2) 26803; f. 1977; partly state-owned; cap. 180m.; Chair. EGIDE NDAHIBESHE; Man. FRANÇOIS-XAVIER CIZA.

Société Générale d'Assurances et de Réassurance (SOGEAR): BP 2432, Bujumbura; tel. (2) 22345; fax (2) 29338; f. 1991.

Union Commerciale d'Assurances et de Réassurance (UCAR): BP 3012, Bujumbura; tel. (2) 23638; telex 5162; fax (2) 23695; f. 1986; cap. 150m. (June 1990); Chair. Lt-Col EDOUARD NZAMBIMANA; Man. Dir HENRY TARMO.

Trade and Industry

STATE TRADE ORGANIZATION

Office National du Commerce (ONC): Bujumbura; f. 1973; supervises international commercial operations between the Govt of Burundi and other states or private orgs; also organizes the import of essential materials; subsidiary offices in each province.

DEVELOPMENT ORGANIZATIONS

Comité de Gérance de la Reserve Cotonnière (COGERCO): Bujumbura; develops the cotton industry.

Fonds de Promotion Economique: PB 270, Bujumbura; tel. (2) 25562; telex 80; f. 1981 to finance and promote industrial, agricultural and commercial activities; Man. Dir BONAVENTURE KIDWINGIRA.

Institut des Sciences Agronomiques du Burundi (ISABU): BP 795, Bujumbura; tel. (2) 23384; f. 1962 for the scientific development of agriculture and livestock.

Office de la Tourbe du Burundi (ONATOUR): BP 2360, Bujumbura; tel. (2) 26480; telex 48; f. 1977 to promote the exploitation of peat deposits.

Office des Cultures Industrielles du Burundi (Office du Café du Burundi) (OCIBU): BP 450, Bujumbura; tel. (2) 26031; fax (2) 25532; supervises coffee plantations and coffee exports.

Office du Thé du Burundi (OTB): Bujumbura; tel. (2) 24228; telex 5069; fax (2) 24657; f. 1979 supervises production and marketing of tea.

Office National du Bois (ONB): BP 1492, Bujumbura; tel. (2) 24416; f. 1980 to exploit local timber resources and import foreign timber; Dir LAZARE RUNESA.

Office National du Logement (ONL): BP 2480, Bujumbura; tel. (2) 26074; telex 48; f. 1974 to supervise housing construction.

Société d'Economie Mixte pour l'Exploitation du Quinquina au Burundi (SOKINABU): 16 blvd Mwezi Gisabo, BP 1783, Bujumbura; tel. (2) 23469; telex 81; f. 1975 to develop and exploit cinchona trees, the source of quinine; Dir RAPHAËL REMEZO.

Société de Stockage et de Commercialisation des Produits Vivriers (SOBECOV): Bujumbura; f. 1977 to stock and sell agricultural products in Burundi.

Société Sucrière du Moso (SOSUMO): BP 835, Bujumbura; tel. (2) 26576; telex 35; fax (2) 23028; f. 1982 to develop and manage sugar cane plantations.

CHAMBER OF COMMERCE

Chambre de Commerce et de l'Industrie du Burundi: BP 313, Bujumbura; tel. (2) 22280; f. 1923; Chair. DONATIEN BIHUTE; 130 mems.

TRADE UNION

Union des Travailleurs du Burundi (UTB): BP 1340, Bujumbura; tel. (2) 23884; telex 57; f. 1967 by merger of all existing unions; closely allied with UPRONA; sole authorized trade union, with 18 affiliated nat. professional feds; Sec.-Gen. MARIUS RURAHENYE.

Transport

RAILWAYS

There are no railways in Burundi. Plans have been pending since 1987 for the construction of a line passing through Uganda, Rwanda and Burundi, to connect with the Kigoma–Dar es Salaam line in Tanzania. This rail link would relieve Burundi's isolated trade position.

ROADS

The road network is very dense and in 1991 there was a total of 14,473 km of roads, of which 1,950 km were national highways and 2,523 km secondary roads. A new crossing of the Ruzizi River, the Bridge of Concord (Burundi's longest bridge), was opened in early 1992. In February 1992 the Government revealed that 600 km of roads had been rehabilitated during the previous three years, and announced a four-year programme of future road improvements covering a further 1,000 km.

INLAND WATERWAYS

Bujumbura is the principal port for both passenger and freight traffic on Lake Tanganyika, and the greater part of Burundi's external trade is dependent on the shipping services between Bujumbura and lake ports in Tanzania, Zambia and Zaire.

CIVIL AVIATION

There is an international airport at Bujumbura, equipped to take large jet-engined aircraft.

Air Burundi: 40 ave du Commerce, BP 2460, Bujumbura; tel. (2) 23460; telex 5080; fax (2) 23452; f. 1971 as Société de Transports Aériens du Burundi; state-owned; operates scheduled passenger services to destinations throughout central Africa; Man. Dir Maj. ISAAC GAFUREO.

Tourism

Tourism is relatively undeveloped. Tourist arrivals were estimated at 125,000 in 1991, with receipts amounting to US $4m.

Office National du Tourisme: BP 902, Bujumbura; tel. (2) 22202; telex 5010; f. 1972; responsible for the promotion and supervision of tourism; Dir AMATUS BURIGUSA (acting).

Defence

Total armed strength in June 1993 was estimated at 7,150, comprising an army of 5,500, an air force of 150, and a paramilitary force of 1,500 gendarmes (including a 50-strong marine police force)

Defence Expenditure: Estimated at 4,500m. Burundi francs in 1988.

Chief of Staff of the Army: Lt-Col JEAN BIKOMAGU.

Chief of Staff of the Gendarmerie: Maj. EPITAPHE BAYAGANAKANDI.

Education

Education is provided free of charge. Kirundi is the language of instruction in primary schools, while French is used in secondary schools. Primary education, which is officially compulsory, begins at seven years of age and lasts for six years. Secondary education, which is not compulsory, begins at the age of 13 and lasts for up to seven years, comprising a first cycle of four years and a second of three years. In 1991 the total enrolment at primary and secondary schools was equivalent to 39% of the school-age population (males 44%; females 35%), whereas in 1980 the proportion had been only 15%. Enrolement at primary schools increased from 175,856 in 1980 to 631,039 in 1991. Enrolment at secondary schools, including pupils receiving vocational instruction and teacher training, rose from 19,013 in 1980 to 48,398 in 1991. However, the latter total was equivalent to only 6% of the population in the secondary age-group. There is one university, in Bujumbura, with 2,749 students in 1988/89. According to UNESCO estimates, the average rate of illiteracy among the population aged 15 years and over was 50.0% (Males 39.1%; females 60.2%) in 1990. In 1988 the International Development Association (IDA) awarded Burundi a credit of SDR 23m. to assist in financing a programme to achieve universal primary education by the 1995/96 school year. Expenditure on education was estimated at 17.7% of total government spending in 1991.

Bibliography

Chrétien, J.-P. 'La société du Burundi: Des mythes aux réalités', in *Revue Française d'Etudes Politiques Africaines*, July-August 1979, Nos. 163–4, pp. 94–118.

Histoire rurale de l'Afrique des Grands Lacs. Paris, Editions Karthala.

Chrétien, J.-P., Guichoua, A., and Le Jeune, G. *La crise d'août 1988 au Burundi.* Paris, Editions Karthala.

Gahama, J. *Le Burundi sous administration belge.* Paris, Editions Karthala, 1983.

Guillet, C., and Ndayishinguje, P. *Légendes historiques du Burundi.* Paris, Editions Karthala, 1987.

Hausner, K.-H., and Jezic, B. *Rwanda et Burundi.* Bonn, Kurt Schroeder, 1968.

Lambert, M. Y. *Enquête démographique Burundi* (1970–1971). Bujumbura, Ministère du Plan, 1972.

Lemarchand, R. *Rwanda and Burundi.* London, Pall Mall, 1970.

'Social Change and Political Modernisation in Burundi', in *Journal of Modern African Studies*, IV, No. 4, 1966, pp. 417–32.

Selective Genocide in Burundi. 1974.

African Kingships in Perspective. 1974.

Ethnocide as Discourse and Practice. Woodrow Wilson Center Press and Cambridge University Press, 1994.

Mpozagara, G. *La République du Burundi.* Paris, Berger-Levrault, 1971.

Mworoha, E. *Histoire du Burundi.* Paris, Hatier, 1987.

Nsanzé, T. *Le Burundi au carrefour de l'Afrique.* Brussels, Remarques africaines, 1970.

L'Edification de la République du Burundi. Brussels, 1970.

Ntahombaye, P. *Des noms et des hommes. Aspects du nom au Burundi.* Paris, Editions Karthala, 1983.

République du Burundi. *Plan quinquennal de développement économique et social du Burundi (1978–82).* Bujumbura.

Reyntjens, F. *Burundi 1972–1988. Continuité et changement.* Brussels, Centre d'étude et de documentation africaines (CEDAF–ASDOC), 1989.

University of Burundi. *Questions sur la paysannerie au Burundi. Actes de la table ronde: Sciences sociales, humaines et développement rural.* Bujumbura, 1985.

Vasina, J. *La légende du passé, traditions orales du Burundi.* Tervuren, Musée royale de l'Afrique centrale, 1972.

Weinstein, W. *Historical Dictionary of Burundi.* Metuchen, NJ, and London, Scarecrow Press, 1976.

World Bank. *Farming Systems in Africa: The Great Lakes Highlands of Zaire, Rwanda and Burundi.* Washington, DC, International Bank for Reconstruction and Development, 1984.

CAMEROON

Physical and Social Geography

JOHN I. CLARKE

PHYSICAL FEATURES

The Republic of Cameroon covers an area of 475,442 sq km (183,569 sq miles), and contains exceptionally diverse physical environments. A census in April 1987 recorded a population of 10,493,655. The population was officially estimated at 11,540,000 in mid-1989. Cameroon has a fairly central position within the African continent, with the additional advantage of a 200-km coastline. Owing to its location between west and central Africa, Cameroon incorporates many of the physical and social features of both.

The diversity of physical environments in Cameroon arises from various factors including its position astride the volcanic belt along the hinge between west and central Africa, its intermediate location between the great basins of the Congo, the Niger and Lake Chad, its latitudinal extent between 2° and 13°N, its altitudinal range from sea-level to more than 4,000 m, and its spread from coastal mangrove swamp to remote continental interior.

In the south and centre of the country a large undulating and broken plateau surface of granites, schists and gneisses rises northwards away from the Congo basin to the Adamawa plateau (900–1,520 m above sea-level). North of the steep Adamawa escarpment, which effectively divides northern from southern Cameroon, lies the basin of the Benue river, a tributary of the Niger, which is floored by sedimentary rocks, interspersed with inselbergs and buttes. In the west of the country a long line of rounded volcanic mountains and hills extends from Mt Cameroon (4,070 m), the highest mountain in west and central Africa, north-eastwards along the former boundary between East and West Cameroon and then along the Nigerian border. Volcanic soils derived from these mountains are more fertile than most others in the country and have permitted much higher rural population densities than elsewhere.

Cameroon has a marked south-north gradation of climates, from a seasonal equatorial climate in the south (with two rainy seasons and two moderately dry seasons of unequal length), to southern savannah and savannah climates (with one dry and one wet season), to a hotter drier climate of the Sahel type in the far north. Rainfall thus varies from more than 5,000 mm in the south-west to around 610 mm near Lake Chad. Corresponding to this climatic zonation is a south-north gradation of vegetal landscapes: dense rain forest, Guinea savannah, Sudan savannah and thorn steppe, while Mt Cameroon incorporates a vertical series of sharply divided vegetation zones.

POPULATION

The population of Cameroon is growing rapidly (by an average of 3.0% per year in 1985–92) and its composition and distribution are extremely diverse. In the southern forest regions Bantu peoples prevail, although there are also pygmy groups in some of the more remote areas. North of the Bantu tribes live many semi-Bantu peoples including the ubiquitous Bamiléké. Further north the diversity increases, with Sudanese Negroes, Hamitic Fulani (or Foulbe) and Arab Choa.

The population has a very uneven distribution, with concentrations in the west, the south-central region and the Sudan savannah zone of the north. An important religious and social divide lies across the country. While the peoples of the south and west have been profoundly influenced by Christianity and by the European introduction of an externally orientated colonial-type economy, the peoples of the north are either Muslim or animist and have largely retained their traditional modes of life. Consequently, the population of the south and west is much more developed, economically and socially, than that of the north, although the government has made efforts to reduce this regional disparity.

One aspect of this disparity is the southern location of the capital, Yaoundé (estimated population 649,000 at mid-1991), and the main port of Douala (810,000), as well as most of the other towns. Much of their growth results from rural-urban migration; many of the migrants come from overcrowded mountain massifs in the west, and the Bamiléké constitute about 37% of the inhabitants of Douala. Nevertheless, 65% of all Cameroonians remain rural village-dwellers.

One other major contrast in the social geography of Cameroon is between anglophone north-west and south-west Cameroon, with less than one-tenth of the area and just over one-fifth of the population, and the much larger, more populous francophone area of former East Cameroon. The contrasting effects of British and French rule are still evident in education, commerce, law and in many other ways, although unification of the civil services since 1972, official bilingualism and integration of transport networks and economies have contributed to a reduction in the disparities between the two zones.

Recent History

PIERRE ENGLEBERT

European interest in the Cameroon coast dates from the arrival of Portuguese explorers in about 1472. The Portuguese fished the Wouri river and caught a variety of seasonal crayfish, which they mistook for prawns (*camarões*). They named the river Rio dos Camarões, and the name, in various European forms (Camarones–Spanish; Kamerun–German; Cameroun–French; and Cameroons–English), came to designate the area between Mt Cameroon and the Río Muni (now the mainland component of the Republic of Equatorial Guinea).

For the next 300 years, Portuguese, Spanish, English, French, German and (in the late 18th century) US traders and slavers operated along the Cameroon coast, until the establishment of the German protectorate of Kamerun in 1884. The Germans laid the infrastructural foundation for the modern economy of the country: railways, roads, bridges, towns, hospitals and plantations. In 1916 the German administration was overthrown by combined French-British-Belgian military operations during the First World War.

MANDATES, TRUSTEESHIP AND INDEPENDENCE

In 1919, following the military occupation of the Kamerun protectorate during the First World War, the territory was divided into British and French spheres of influence. In 1922 both zones became subject to mandates of the League of Nations, which allocated four-fifths of the territory to French administration as French Cameroun, and the other one-fifth, comprising two long, non-contiguous areas along the eastern Nigerian border, to British administration as the Northern and Southern Cameroons.

In 1946 the mandates were converted into UN trust territories, still under their respective French and British administrations. However, growing anti-colonial sentiment made it difficult for France and Britain to resist the UN Charter's promise of eventual self-determination for all inhabitants of trust territories. Between 1948–60 more than 100 political associations were established in French Cameroun, including the Union des populations camerounaises (UPC), which was formed in 1948 by trade unionists and demanded the reunification of French Cameroun and the British Cameroons, and independence from France. By May 1955, unable to gain power legally, the UPC attempted to instigate a revolt, which was, however, unsuccessful. The UPC was banned, but initiated a guerrilla war against the administration. (In 1960, however, the administration again granted legal status to the UPC.) In 1957 French Cameroun became an autonomous state within the French Community, with André-Marie Mbida, leader of the Cameroun Democrats, as prime minister. Following a government crisis a year later, Ahmadou Ahidjo, the leader of the Union camerounaise (UC) and Mbida's vice-premier, acceded to power. Meanwhile, domestic and international pressure resulted in the territory's progression toward independence and on 1 January 1960 the Republic of Cameroon was established. Ahidjo was elected as the country's first president.

Political developments in the British Cameroons, which was attached for administrative purposes to neighbouring Nigeria, progressed more slowly. In 1955 the Kamerun National Democratic Party (KNDP) was formed by a Bamenda schoolteacher, John N. Foncha, with a programme of complete secession from Nigeria and unification with French Cameroun. Following the elections of January 1959, Foncha became premier. After discussions at the UN it was agreed that a plebiscite would be held in both parts of the trust territory to determine their future. In February 1961 the electorate in the Southern Cameroons voted in favour of union with the Republic of Cameroon (which took place on 1 October), while northern Cameroon voters chose to merge with Nigeria (becoming the province of Sardauna). The new Federal Republic of Cameroon comprised two states: the former French zone became East Cameroon, while the former British portion became West Cameroon. Shortly afterwards, Ahidjo and Foncha assumed, respectively, the presidency and vice-presidency of the federation.

After federation, Cameroon moved towards increasing political, economic and social integration. By 1966 most of the states' areas of jurisdiction were under central control. In the same year, the dominant parties in the two states, the UC and the KNDP, along with four minor parties, merged to form a single national organization, the Union nationale camerounaise (UNC). In 1968 Foncha was replaced as premier by Salomon Tandeng Muna, a strong supporter of Ahidjo. In 1970 Ahidjo was re-elected president, while Muna became vice-president.

In May 1972 the electorate overwhelmingly approved a new constitution, which abolished all the separate state institutions, as well as the office of federal vice-president, and provided for a strong executive president, a national executive council of ministers responsible to the president, a unicameral national assembly and a completely centralized administrative system. On 2 June the country was officially renamed the United Republic of Cameroon. Ahidjo retained the presidency and in May 1973 Muna became president of the newly-elected national assembly.

The United Republic of Cameroon adopted a non-aligned foreign policy and undertook to reduce its dependence on France and its Western allies. The UNC exercised full supremacy over all aspects of Cameroon's organized political and social life. In April 1975 Ahidjo was re-elected unopposed by more than 99% of registered voters. In June, Paul Biya, the former secretary-general in the president's office, was appointed to the new post of prime minister and a new cabinet was formed.

Despite dissatisfaction in some quarters with the single-party system and discontent among English-speaking politicians about their relatively low representation in government, the single list of candidates for the second national assembly chosen by the UNC was overwhelmingly approved by the electorate in May 1978. An increase in activity by clandestine opposition groups dissatisfied with Ahidjo's autocratic rule became evident in 1979, notably in the English-speaking south-western region of the country. In April 1980, however, Ahidjo was again re-elected as sole candidate for a further five-year term.

THE BIYA PRESIDENCY

In November 1982 President Ahidjo resigned on the grounds of ill-health, and transferred power to Biya. Biya was expected to continue the policies of national unity and non-alignment which characterized the former president's rule. The appointment of Bello Bouba Maigari, a northerner, as prime minister in the subsequent cabinet reshuffle confirmed the continuity of the new regime, and Ahidjo retained the chairmanship of the UNC. In April 1983, however, four prominent ministers were dismissed in an unexpected cabinet reshuffle. Following a further reorganization in June, rumours of division between Ahidjo and Biya emerged.

Tensions and Coup Attempts

On 22 August 1983 Biya announced that a conspiracy to overthrow the government had been suppressed, and that two close military advisers of Ahidjo had been arrested. Maigari and the minister for the armed forces—both northern Muslims—were subsequently dismissed and, in an administrative reorganization, the number of the country's provinces was increased from seven to 10. On 27 August it was announced that Ahidjo had resigned the chairmanship of the UNC. Biya was elected to the post at a special UNC congress in September; Ahidjo left the country, and remained in exile in France and Senegal until his death in November 1989. On 14 January 1984 Biya was re-elected president, as sole candidate, with 99.98% of the vote. The national assembly subsequently approved a constitutional amendment restoring the country's original official name, the Republic of Cameroon.

At the end of February 1984 Ahidjo and his two military advisers were tried (Ahidjo *in absentia*) for their alleged complicity in the August 1983 coup attempt. It was claimed that Ahidjo had been enraged by Biya's failure to consult him regarding the government reorganization in June, and had instructed his aides to eliminate Biya by any means available, including assassination. All three men received death sentences, which were, however, subsequently commuted to terms of life imprisonment.

On 6 April 1984 members of the élite republican guard attempted to overthrow the government. The coup attempt was suppressed by forces loyal to Biya, after intense fighting, in which a large number of people were reported to have been killed. In contrast to the February trials, the alleged instigators of the coup attempt were quickly tried by military tribunal, and 46 of the defendants were subsequently executed. However, the attempted coup had a destabilizing effect on the Biya government.

Reassertion of Presidential Power

In the following months Biya was able to maintain control, and confidence in the government was gradually restored. Further trials of those allegedly involved in the April coup attempt were conducted, but always in conditions of secrecy. Members of the government whose allegiance remained in doubt were gradually removed from office, most of the major public enterprises experienced a change of leadership, and in May 1984 the UNC central committee dismissed seven of the 12 members of its political bureau. In July six ministers were replaced in a government reshuffle. At a party congress, held in March 1985, the UNC was renamed the Rassemblement démocratique du peuple camerounais (RDPC).

In August 1985 Biya reshuffled the cabinet, removing 10 predominantly 'conservative' ministers. The reshuffle was followed by a number of changes in the senior management of the major parastatal organizations. The country's 10 governorships were also reorganized. From January to March 1986, elections took place for members of RDPC bodies on all levels; the choice of candidates for the first time since the creation of the party indicated that a measure of democratization was emerging. New candidates were elected to more than 50% of the posts, with the proportion rising to 70% at the lower levels of office. The gradual appointment to the administration, often to posts in the parastatal bodies, of a further number of the formerly influential functionaries of the Ahidjo period also indicated Biya's increasing confidence in the stability of his government. The return to Cameroon, from Ghana, of 55 former political dissidents in February 1986 was followed in August by the release of 14 supporters of the UPC, who had been detained since late 1985 on charges of organizing clandestine meetings and distributing tracts.

In November 1986 a government reshuffle was carried out. In January 1987 the minister of foreign affairs was dismissed, after signing an agreement to restore diplomatic relations with Hungary, allegedly without Biya's knowledge. The increasingly authoritarian nature of government policy was also demonstrated by the arrest of two journalists employed by the government-owned national daily newspaper, the *Cameroon Tribune*, following the unauthorized publication of details of a new presidential decree.

Elections to the national assembly took place in April 1988, together with a presidential election (brought forward from January 1989 for reasons of economy). Voters in the legislative elections were presented with a choice of RDPC-approved candidates; of the 180 candidates elected to the enlarged national assembly, 153 were new members. However, the abstention rate was estimated at 9.9% (compared with 0.8% at the previous general election, in May 1983). Biya, the sole candidate for the presidency, obtained 98.75% of the votes cast, compared with 99.98% recorded in the 1984 election.

In May 1988 24 ministers were dismissed, and several ministries were merged or abolished. In subsequent months the president's relations with the press became increasingly strained, as journalists who were critical of the government continued to be detained. The ensuing appointment of a reputable journalist as minister of information was intended to reduce tensions between the government and the media. In October there were widespread rumours, officially denied, of government complicity in the murder of a prominent lawyer who had been connected with many government officials. In a government reorganization in April 1989, an additional secretary of state for finance was appointed to assist in negotiations for the rescheduling of Cameroon's external debt, following the adoption of an IMF-approved structural adjustment programme (see Economy).

In early 1989 attention was focused on protest in legal circles at a perceived erosion of the rule of law. The formation, in February, of a special unit of the security forces to combat terrorism and organized crime, and the subsequent appointment of three reputedly 'hard-line' army generals to influential security posts, indicated that the government would continue to repress dissent. In August the human rights organization, Amnesty International, expressed concern about prison conditions in Yaoundé and Douala, and in March 1990 the same organization appealed for an inquiry into the deaths (allegedly from torture) in December 1989 of two prisoners who had been detained since April 1984.

Opposition and the Pro-Democracy Movement

In February 1990 a number of people were arrested and tried for subversion, as a result of their alleged involvement in an unofficial opposition organization, the Social Democratic Front (SDF). Twelve of the 18 defendants were imprisoned. Later that month, in an apparent attempt to strengthen national unity in the aftermath of the convictions, it was announced that an estimated 100 prisoners who had been detained following the April 1984 coup attempt were to be released.

Biya continued to oppose the establishment of a multi-party system, on the grounds that such a fundamental political change would undermine attempts to resolve the prevailing economic crisis. From March 1990 a series of demonstrations in support of the RDPC took place. In May six deaths were reported, after security forces violently suppressed a demonstration organized by the SDF, which took place in Bamenda (in the English-speaking north-west of the country) and was attended by at least 20,000 people. The SDF, led by John Fru Ndi, received the support of prominent writers and lawyers (and was alleged by the government to be receiving financial support from Nigeria). In the same month English-speaking students at the University of Yaoundé clashed with participants in a counter-demonstration: about 300 students were detained by the security forces. Also in May the authorities banned the publication of an independent weekly, the *Cameroon Post*, which had implied its support for the SDF.

In late June 1990 a congress of the RDPC re-elected Biya as president of the party and carried out a major reorganization of the central committee. In response to continued civil unrest, Biya stated that the future adoption of a multi-party system was envisaged, and subsequently announced a series of reforms, including the abolition of laws governing subversion, the relaxation of restraints on the press, and the reform of legislation prohibiting political associations. In the same month a committee was established to formulate legislation on human rights. In August several political prisoners were released. In early September Biya effected an extensive reorganization of the cabinet, and created a new ministry to oversee the country's programme for economic stabilization. Later in September the vice-president of the RDPC resigned, in protest at alleged corruption and violations of human rights by the government.

On 5 December 1990 the national assembly approved a constitutional amendment providing for the establishment of a multi-party system. Under the revised constitution, the government was required to grant (or refuse) registration within three months to any political association seeking legal recognition, and registered parties were to receive state support during election campaigns. However, the recruitment of party activists on a regional or ethnic basis and the financing of political parties from external sources was prohibited. Numerous political associations subsequently emerged.

During 1991 pressure for political reform intensified. In January anti-government demonstrators protested at Biya's failure (despite previous undertakings) to grant an amnesty to prisoners implicated in the April 1984 coup attempt. In the same month the trial of two journalists, who had published an article critical of Biya in the independent periodical, *Le Messager*, provoked violent rioting. Meanwhile, opposition leaders renewed their demands for the convening of a national conference to formulate a timetable for multi-party elections. In April Biya's continued opposition to the holding of such a conference provoked a series of demonstrations and widespread riots, which were violently suppressed by security forces; by the end of that month more than 100 people were reported to have been killed. Later in April in response to increasing pressure for constitutional reform, the national assembly formally granted a general amnesty to all political prisoners, and reintroduced the post of prime minister. Sadou Hayatou, hitherto secretary-general to the presidency, was appointed to the position. Hayatou subsequently formed a 32-member transitional government, which principally comprised members of the former cabinet. At the end of April, however, a newly-established alliance of 11 leading opposition groups, the National Co-ordination Committee of Opposition Parties (NCCOP), demanded an unconditional amnesty for all political prisoners (the existing arrangements for an amnesty excluded an estimated 400 political prisoners jailed for ostensibly non-political offences), and the convening of a national conference before 10 May.

In early May 1991 the University of Yaoundé was closed, after security forces suppressed demonstrations by students. The continuing refusal of the government to set a date for the national conference prompted the NCCOP to initiate a campaign of civil disobedience, initially comprising one-day strikes and demonstrations. Opposition leaders also demanded the resignation of Hayatou and his cabinet as a precondition to multi-party elections. Later that month seven of Cameroon's 10 provinces were placed under military rule, and in June the government prohibited meetings of opposition parties. In June the NCCOP intensified the campaign of civil disobedience, and orchestrated a general strike, which halted economic activity in most towns. In an attempt to end the campaign, the government prohibited opposition gatherings, and, following continued civil disturbances, banned the NCCOP, on the grounds that it was fomenting terrorist activity. Leaders of the opposition alliance announced that the campaign of civil disobedience was to continue. (However, the effect of the general strike declined in subsequent months.) In September several opposition leaders were temporarily detained, following further violent demonstrations, during which several hundred people were reportedly arrested.

In October 1991 Biya announced that legislative elections were to take place on 16 February 1992, and that a prime minister was to be appointed from the party that secured a majority in the national assembly. He also invited opposition leaders to meet Hayatou to discuss the proposed establishment of a new electoral code. Tripartite negotiations between the government, the opposition parties and independent officials commenced at the end of October, but were delayed by procedural disputes, owing to opposition demands that the agenda of the meeting be extended to include a review of the constitution. In mid-November, however, the government and about 40 of the 47 registered opposition parties signed an agreement providing for the establishment of a 10-member committee to draft constitutional reforms. The opposition pledged to suspend the campaign of civil disobedience, while the government agreed to end the ban on opposition meetings and to release all prisoners who had been arrested during the demonstrations earlier that year. However, several parties belonging to the NCCOP, including the SDF, subsequently declared the agreement to be invalid, resulting in increasing division within the opposition. Later in November the government revoked the ban on opposition gatherings, and, in December, ended the military rule which had been imposed in seven of the provinces. In the same month the national assembly approved a new electoral code. In January 1992 the government announced that legislative elections were to take place on 1 March, following demands from opposition leaders that elections be postponed in order to allow parties sufficient time for preparation. However, a number of opposition groups, including two of the four principal parties, the SDF and the Union démocratique du Cameroun (UDC), refused to participate in the elections, claiming that the scheduled date was too early and that the electoral code was biased in favour of the RDPC.

In February 1992 more than 100 people were killed in the northern town of Kousseri, following violent clashes between the Kokoto and Arab Choa ethnic groups, which had erupted during the registration of voters for elections. In the same month the opposition parties that had not accepted the tripartite agreement in November 1991 formed a political association, the Alliance pour le redressement du Cameroun (ARC), which was to boycott the elections. Later in February the former prime minister, Bello Bouba Maigari, was elected as chairman of one of the principal opposition movements, the Union nationale pour la démocratie et le progrès (UNDP); the UNDP subsequently announced that it would contest the elections.

At the legislative elections on 1 March 1992, which were contested by 32 political parties, the RDPC won 88 of the 180 seats in the national assembly, while the UNDP secured 68, the Union des populations camerounaises (UPC) 18, and the Mouvement pour la défense de la République (MDR) six seats. An estimated 61% of registered voters participated in the elections, although the proportion was only 10% in regions affected by the general strike. Following discussions between Biya and the leader of the MDR, Dakole Daissala, after the elections, the RDPC formed an alliance with the MDR, thereby securing an absolute majority in the national assembly. Biya subsequently appointed Joseph-Charles Doumbu as secretary-general of the RDPC, replacing Ebénézer Njoh Mouelle, who had failed to be re-elected to the national assembly. Later in March a French-speaking member of the RDPC, Djibril Cavayé Yeguie, was elected as president of the newly-established national assembly. On 9 April Biya formed a new 25-member cabinet, which, however, retained the majority of ministers from the previous government. Five members of the MDR, including Dakole Daissala, also received portfolios. Simon Achidi Achu, an anglophone member of the RDPC who had served in the Ahidjo administration, was appointed as prime minister.

In July 1992 Gen. Benoît Asso'o Emane, a prominent military officer and close associate of Biya, was dismissed, after publishing a book that was critical of the government. In August Biya announced that the forthcoming presidential election, due to take place in May 1993, was to be brought forward to 11 October 1992. This measure was widely believed to benefit the government, following the failure of a large number of opposition supporters to register earlier that year, as a result of the SDF boycott of the legislative elections. Later in August the minister of the civil service and administrative reform, who had been relieved of certain duties after his discovery of financial malpractice perpetrated by a number of civil servants, resigned. In September three independent publications, including *Le Messager*, were banned. Later that month the government introduced legislation regulating the election of the president, which prohibited political parties from forming electoral alliances, and stipulated that, contrary to the system in operation in the majority of francophone countries, the election was to comprise a single round of voting. Despite protracted negotiations, the opposition subsequently failed to select a single candidate to contest the presidential election, as planned; however, two of the seven opposition members who had presented their candidacy withdrew in favour of the leader of the SDF, John Fru Ndi, who received the support of the ARC alliance.

At the presidential election, which took place on 11 October 1992, Biya was re-elected by 39.9% of votes cast, while Fru Ndi secured 35.9%, and Maigari, the candidate of the UNDP, 19.2% of the vote. However, Fru Ndi disputed the official results, and claimed that he had won the election. A number of violent demonstrations, particularly in the north-west and in Douala, were subsequently staged by opposition supporters in protest at the alleged electoral irregularities by the government; several hundred people were reported to have been arrested in Bamenda, in the North-West Province. Later in October, however, the supreme court ruled against an appeal by Fru Ndi that the results of the election be declared invalid, despite confirmation from a US monitoring organization that widespread electoral malpractices had been detected. At the end of October, in response to continued unrest, the government placed Fru Ndi and a number of his supporters under house arrest, and declared a state of emergency in the North-West Province for a period of three months.

Constitutional Reform

On 3 November 1992 Biya was inaugurated as president. Although he pledged to institute further constitutional reforms, international criticism of the government increased, resulting in the suspension of economic aid by the USA and Germany in protest at the government's suppression of opposition activity and the continued enforcement of the state of emergency. In the same month an attempt by the South African archbishop, Desmond Tutu, to mediate between the government and the SDF ended in failure, after Fru Ndi rejected his proposal for the establishment of a government of national unity. At the end of

November Biya appointed a new 30-member cabinet, which included, for the first time, representatives of the UPC, the UNDP and the Parti national du progrès (PNP). In December order was restored in the North-West Province, and at the end of that month, the state of emergency was lifted, although Fru Ndi claimed that a number of troops remained in the region. In January 1993 the government granted amnesty to a number of political prisoners, who had been arrested in October 1992.

In March 1993 the Union pour le changement (UPC), an alliance of opposition parties, which included the SDF, co-ordinated a campaign of demonstrations and a boycott of French consumer goods (in protest at the French government's continuing support for Biya), to reinforce demands that a new presidential election take place. The government accused the UPC of attempting to incite civil disorder in order to destabilize the country. In the same month, however, in response to international pressure, the government announced that a national debate on constitutional reform was to take place by the end of May. In early April, following SDF demands that a revised constitution be submitted for approval at a national referendum by a stipulated date, Fru Ndi stated that he was to convene a national conference to determine the political future of Cameroon. In the same month a meeting organized by the Cameroon Anglophone Movement (CAM), which took place in Buea, the capital of the South-West Province, issued demands for the restoration of a federal system of government, in response to the dominance of the French-speaking section of the population in the country. (The SDF, however, was not in favour of the proposed establishment of a federal state.) Later in April reports of division within the SDF emerged, after a prominent party official, Bernard Muna, declared his support for SDF participation in the national debate that was to be organized by the government; Muna was subsequently dismissed from his post in the SDF.

Following a meeting with the French president, François Mitterrand, in early May 1993, Biya announced that the planned debate on the revision of the constitution was to take place in early June. Instead of the envisaged national conference, however, a technical, commission was established to prepare recommendations based on proposals from all sectors of the population. Later in May the government promulgated draft constitutional amendments, which provided for a democratic system of government, including the establishment of an upper legislative chamber, a council of supreme judiciary affairs, a council of state, and a high authority to govern the civil service. The constitutional provisions also restricted the powers of the president, whose tenure was to be limited to two five-year terms of office. Elections were to comprise two rounds of voting (a system more favourable to the opposition). The draft legislation retained a unitary state, but, in recognition of demands by supporters of federalism, introduced a more decentralized system of government. The constitutional proposals were subject to amendment, following the recommendations of the technical commission. However, three representatives of the English-speaking community subsequently resigned from the technical commission, in protest at the government's alleged control of the constitutional debate.

At a party congress, which took place in July 1993, the SDF adopted a draft constitution that provided for a decentralized federal state. At the end of August a two-day strike, which was organized by the SDF as part of its anti-government campaign, failed to attract the support of other prominent opposition parties, and was only partially observed; however, rioting by opposition supporters was reported in Bamenda. In September a number of opposition activists were arrested, in an effort by the government to pre-empt further strikes. Later that month, however, the UPC announced plans to organize a new series of demonstrations in support of opposition demands. In early November security forces prevented Fru Ndi from conducting a press conference in Yaoundé on the occasion of the first anniversary of Biya's re-election, while about 30 SDF members were arrested; Fru Ndi briefly took refuge at the residence of the Dutch ambassador. The SDF detainees were subsequently released, following the intervention of the French government.

In November 1993 the constitutional debate was effectively postponed, after the government annouced substantial reductions in public sector salaries, prompting strike action from teachers. In early December a general strike, which was organized with the support of the opposition, was observed by a limited number of civil servants. In early 1994 other public sector workers joined the strike; in response to the increase in labour unrest, the government began to adopt repressive measures, suspending the salaries of a number of striking teachers in January, and dismissing other teachers in February. Also in January renewed student unrest occurred, when a demonstration in support of demands for improved conditions was suppressed by the security forces.

In February 1994 six principal opposition parties (excluding the SDF) established an alliance, known as the Front démocratique et patriotique (FDP), to contest municipal elections, which were due to take place later that year. In April the authorities banned a conference by supporters of a federalist system of government, which, nevertheless, took place at Bamenda. In July an extensive government reorganization was carried out.

In September 1993, following renewed conflict between the Kokoto and Arab Choa ethnic groups in Kousseri, a peace agreement, which was mediated by government negotiators, was reached. In December more than 30 people were killed in further ethnic clashes in the region. Ethnic fighting was compounded by acts of armed banditry, which were attributed by the security forces to the Arab Choa ethnic group, and ensuing repression; in February 1994 security forces killed some 50 Arab Choa at the village of Karena, after clashing with bandits. The majority of the armed bandits in northern Cameroon were, however, widely believed to be former Chadian rebels. In late March more than 1,200 Cameroonians took refuge in Chad, in response to further clashes between armed bandits and security forces.

During 1989–91 President Biya pursued initiatives with the ultimate aim of securing Cameroon's admission to the Commonwealth. It was widely suggested that Biya's motives for joining that organization reflected both a wish to appease the English-speaking population at a time of increasing participation in the activities of francophone associations, and a means of obtaining additional development aid. (Cameroon continued to receive French support, as well as significant assistance from the USA.) In 1993, however, a second application by Cameroon for membership of the Commonwealth was rejected.

EXTERNAL RELATIONS

In June 1991 the Nigerian government claimed that Cameroon had annexed nine Nigerian fishing settlements, following a long-standing border dispute, based on a 1913 agreement between Germany and the United Kingdom that ceded the Bakassi peninsula in the Gulf of Guinea (a region of strategic significance) to Cameroon. Subsequent attempts to negotiate the dispute achieved little progress, and further incursions by Cameroon were reported in November. After a period of relative calm, relations between the two countries again deteriorated in early January 1994, following reports that members of the Cameroonian security forces had entered Nigeria and raided villages, killing several Nigerian nationals. Some 500 Nigerian troops subsequently occupied the two nominally Cameroonian islands of Diamant and Jabane in the Gulf of Guinea. Cameroon also dispatched troops to the region, while the two nations agreed to resume bilateral negotiations in an effort to resolve the dispute. In February the Cameroonian government announced that it was to submit the dispute for adjudication by the UN Security Council, the Organization of African Unity and the International Court of Justice. However, subsequent clashes between Nigerian and Cameroonian forces in the disputed region prompted fears of a full-scale conflict between the two nations. Shortly afterwards, a French diplomatic and military mission arrived in Cameroon, in response to a request for military assistance from the Cameroonian government in the context of the defence agreements between the two countries. Nevertheless, bilateral negotiations continued: in late March a proposal by the Nigerian government that a referendum be conducted in the contested areas was rejected by the Cameroon government. In the same month the OAU urged the withdrawal of troops from the disputed region; however Cameroon failed to obtain an official condemnation of Nigeria, and both governments indicated dissatisfaction with the resolution. In May two members of the Nigerian armed forces were killed in further clashes in the region. Later that month negotiations between the two nations, which were mediated by the Togolese government, resumed in Yaoundé. However, a summit meeting to discuss the dispute, which was scheduled to take place in July, was postponed, owing to social unrest in Nigeria.

Economy

MICHAEL CHAPMAN

Revised for this edition by the Editor

During the Ahidjo period, Cameroon followed a relatively centrist policy, with emphasis on the diversification of international economic relations, and the increase of effective government involvement in, and control over, economic development. Cameroon moved toward more detailed interventionism, including a cautious growth of state participation. The same moderate economic policies were pursued by President Biya until the economic crisis of 1989 (see below).

During the 1960s and 1970s Cameroon demonstrated a significant level of economic growth, which was based on a variety of agricultural exports and the development of self-sufficiency in food, and increased in the late 1970s, owing to a significant development of the petroleum sector. By 1980 petroleum had become the country's principal export commodity, a development that was to shield the economy from fluctuations in earnings from export crops. In the first half of the 1980s economic growth averaged 7%–8% annually (more than double the annual average in the previous two decades). Following a sharp decline in the international price for petroleum in 1986, however, the economy deteriorated, although the effects were initially limited by the government's policy of drawing on accumulated revenue from sales of petroleum in order to sustain the level of investment expenditure and imports. Nevertheless, owing to sustained weaknesses in international prices for petroleum products, these funds were exhausted by the end of the decade, and the Biya government was obliged to introduce austerity programmes, involving major reductions in both current and capital budgets. These measures resulted in a very sharp contraction in the economy, with the rate of decline in real gross domestic product (GDP) reaching 10.4% in the year ending 30 June 1988, but falling to 5.4% in 1988/89, and to 2.5% (estimated figure) in 1989/90. In view of this situation, and with the support of loans from the World Bank, the African Development Bank (ADB) and France, Cameroon undertook an extensive, five-year programme of economic restructuring in 1989/90. This entailed the reform of the country's parastatal organizations (through the liquidation of unprofitable enterprises and the transfer to private ownership of others) and of the cumbersome and inefficient administrative structure (by means of redundancies and reductions in salaries). Specifically, the role of the national agricultural marketing board, the Office national de commercialisation des produits de base (ONCPB), was reduced, and responsibility for marketing was gradually transferred to the private sector. However, the benefits of these measures failed to compensate for a reduction in export earnings and in investment, which resulted in a continued decline in real GDP of 6.0% in 1991, and of 5.7% in 1992. (Nevertheless, Cameroon retained a middle-income status among developing countries, with a gross national product (GNP) of US $820 per head in 1992.)

The implementation of reforms was further impeded by an opposition campaign of civil disobedience, which was initiated in 1991 (see Recent History). Political instability, in conjunction with widespread corruption within the civil service and increasing external debt, contributed to a severe deterioration in the economy in 1993. In November of that year the government announced substantial reductions in public sector salaries as part of its structural adjustment programme, prompting strike action by civil servants. The price of essential commodities was subsequently reduced in an attempt to alleviate economic hardship, which was, however, compounded by a devaluation of the CFA franc by 50% in January 1994. In April the government announced a programme of further retrenchment within the civil service, under the terms of a stand-by credit agreement with the IMF (see below).

AGRICULTURE

In the early 1980s, as the petroleum industry increased in importance, the contribution of agriculture, forestry and fishing to Cameroon's GDP declined, from 32% in the year ending 30 June 1979 to 21% in 1984/85. During the second half of the decade the sector's contribution increased, accounting for 27% of GDP in 1990 (owing to a decline in the petroleum industry), but subsequently registered a further reduction, to 22% of GDP, in 1992. An estimated 59.3% of the labour force were employed in the sector in 1992. Primary agricultural and forest products provide about 40% of total export earnings, with coffee and cocoa accounting for less than one-quarter. The government gives priority to agricultural development, maintaining the level of producer prices (using petroleum revenue for the purpose if necessary) and providing other incentives in the form of subsidies on fertilizers and pesticides, and bonuses for replanting coffee and cocoa. In late 1989, however, the official prices paid to producers of cocoa, coffee and cotton were reduced, to correspond with prevailing international prices for these commodities. Small-scale farmers dominate agricultural export production with the exception of rubber and palm oil. Despite efforts to develop Cameroonian participation, timber production remains dominated by large foreign firms.

Coffee is cultivated on some 400,000 ha, predominantly in the west and south. Output, which fluctuates according to climatic conditions, increased to 126,200 metric tons in 1988/89, but declined to 86,418 tons in 1989/90, and remained at the same level in 1990/91. Four-fifths of the coffee crop is robusta, the remainder being arabica. In 1991/92 production of robusta coffee totalled 85,409 tons, but declined to an estimated 45,000 tons in 1992/93. Output of cocoa, grown on around 350,000 ha, reached 140,300 tons in 1990/91, declining to 107,000 tons in 1991/92, and to an estimated 76,283 tons in 1992/93. Both coffee and cocoa yields have suffered as a result of the failure of replanting programmes to keep pace with the ageing of plantations. The annual production of bananas declined from more than 100,000 tons in the early 1960s to about two-thirds of this level in the early 1980s. The industry was adversely affected by the loss of British markets and the conversion to different banana varieties which steadily depleted export-oriented smallholder production. Following a major restructuring of the sector, which began in 1987, production increased substantially, and the state-owned enterprise, Organisation camerounaise de banane, was transferred to the private sector.

Cotton production, which is concentrated in the north, recovered from the drought of the late 1970s and early 1980s, and reached 165,400 metric tons of unginned (seed) cotton in 1988/89. However, production declined to 103,900 tons in 1989/90. The sharp reduction in producer prices in 1989 was expected to halt further expansion of cotton cultivation. However, production increased to 100,000 tons in 1990/91, as a result of favourable climatic conditions. Output of palm oil has recently fluctuated between 80,000 tons and 120,000 tons per year, about twice the level of the late 1970s, but the product is not competitive on world markets. Rubber, however, has good prospects, with yields competing with those of the major Asian producers. Output has increased in recent years, to 53,000 tons in 1989/90.

In 1991 an estimated 51.4% of the country was covered by forest, but an inadequate transport system has impeded the development of this sector. After declining during the early 1980s (reflecting the recession in world timber prices), production recovered to almost 2.1m. cu m in 1984/85 and 1985/86, while revenue from exports of logs and wood products totalled some 30,000m. francs CFA in 1986. However, the recovery in production was not sufficient to reactivate the pulp factory which was commissioned in 1981 but which ceased operation in the following year (see below). The structural adjustment programme undertaken in 1989 included measures to develop forestry; production of logs increased to 2.29m. cu m in 1991 compared with 1.97m. cu m in 1987/88.

Cameroon's food production has been increasing at a higher rate than population growth, despite the adverse effects of the droughts of the 1970s and the early 1980s, and the country is generally self-sufficient. In 1992 production of millet and sorghum reached an estimated 435,000 metric tons (compared with 408,000 tons in 1989), while maize production amounted to an estimated 380,000 tons (compared with 371,000 tons in 1989). According to FAO estimates, output of root crops totalled about 2m. metric tons in 1992. The annual harvest of paddy rice, which is grown under both traditional and modern methods, has increased dramatically, from only 15,000 tons in 1979/80 to 107,400 tons in 1984/85, reflecting the government's priority of achieving self-sufficiency in this cereal. Output declined in subsequent years, to only 63,800 tons in 1987/88, but increased to 70,000 tons in 1988/89 and 90,000 tons in 1990/91; the long-term target for annual rice production remains 280,000 tons by the year 2000. Commercial production of sugar began in 1966 and has since expanded steadily; output of raw sugar was estimated at some 1,400 tons in 1992. Livestock makes a significant contribution to the food supply. In 1992 the national herds were assessed at 4.7m. cattle, 7.1m. sheep and goats, and 1.4m. pigs, while commercial poultry farms had an estimated 19m. birds. The development of the fisheries industry has been constrained by the relatively small area available for exploitation (because of boundary disputes and the presence of the offshore island of Bioko, part of Equatorial Guinea) and the poor level of fish stocks in these waters, as well as by drought, which has affected yields from inland fishing areas. By the late 1980s the number of industrial fishing vessels was reduced, and the total fishing catch had declined substantially; in 1991 the total catch was estimated at 65,300 metric tons, of which the freshwater catch was 22,000 tons.

MINING AND POWER

In 1976 Elf, the French oil company, proved a commercial oilfield in shallow water near the Nigerian border. Production of crude petroleum reached 9.16m. tons in 1985, but declined in subsequent years, to 6.4m. tons in 1993. Exploration activity has remained minimal, although some new permits were granted in 1991. Total remaining identified resources amounted to 54.8m. tons in 1993, and are expected to be exhausted by the end of the decade. In 1982 the state corporation, Société nationale des hydrocarbures, obtained a 20% interest in all the petroleum-producing companies.

Natural gas has been located offshore, and in 1982 the construction of a major plant to produce liquefied natural gas (LNG) at Kribi was planned. However, more conservative estimates of offshore gas reserves and the decline in world demand in the late 1980s led to the abandonment of the project. In 1991, however, the government announced new feasibility studies for the construction of the LNG plant to meet domestic fuel requirements.

There are bauxite deposits of some 900m. tons at Minim-Martap, and of some 200m. tons at Ngaoundal, but these remain unexploited, and the Edéa smelter continues to depend on supplies from Guinea, although the opening of the Transcam railway towards the north has made development of the indigenous resources more likely. Deposits of iron ore near Kribi remain unexploited, and uranium reserves totalling 10,000 tons have been identified, but not developed, while large-scale limestone deposits near Garoua supply clinker and cement plants.

Hydroelectricity provides 85% of the country's electricity production, which was 2,702 kWh in 1989/90: heavy industry is the major consumer, with the aluminium plant taking nearly 50% of the total generation. The chief installations are at Edéa (total capacity 263 MW) and at Song-Loulou (total capacity 384 MW). These stations supply the network linking Yaoundé, Edéa, Douala and the west. The other major network supplies the north and draws principally on the 72-MW hydroelectric station at Lagdo, which was built with aid from the People's Republic of China (although operations are hindered in years of drought). A 200-MW hydroelectric installation is planned at the Nachtigal Falls on the Sanaga river.

MANUFACTURING

In 1992 manufacturing accounted for 22% of GDP; manufacturing GDP increased by an annual average of 10.6% in 1980-92. The sector is, however, dominated both by the processing of raw materials, and by the processing or assembly of imported raw materials and components. The national industry is therefore not deeply integrated into the economic structure and has limited linkage effects.

While the Edéa dam and aluminium-smelter complex (drawing on bauxite from Guinea) were completed in 1958, the bulk of the other export-processing and domestic consumer-goods industry is of post-independence origin. The government gave priority to industrial development aimed at national and regional markets as a means of accelerating growth. To this end, extensive tax and financing incentives were made available, while the state took substantial shareholdings in major ventures, held through the Société nationale d'investissement du Cameroon (SNI). During the economic crisis in the mid-1980s, many of the businesses in the SNI became unviable, and a major restructuring programme was announced. However, its implementation was slow and little progress was made until late 1990, when 15 companies were transferred to the private sector. Other parastatal enterprises were liquidated, and those remaining under the aegis of the state, such as the electricity corporation SONEL, were obliged to sign performance contracts with the government as part of the overall structural adjustment programme. An industrial free zone was established in 1991.

Under the fourth Five-Year Plan (1976–81), linkages between the raw material base and manufacturing were increased by the development of an integrated pulp and paper mill, a tyre factory based on local rubber, the expansion of cement production (quadrupling to 516,000 tons in 1981), the increase in aluminium production capacity, and the installation of a petroleum refinery. The Edéa pulp and paper plant operated from 1981 until its closure, following heavy financial losses, in late 1982. A petroleum refinery began production at Cap Limboh in 1981. Its initial annual capacity was increased to 2m. tons, but declined to 1.5m. tons, owing to a reduction in domestic demand. Cement production has expanded at a rate close to overall economic growth. Under the 1981–86 Development Plan, industry and energy were together allocated 17% of planned investment of 2,300,000m. francs CFA, although this target was later recognized as unrealistic. In the early 1990s tobacco and beverages, construction materials, shoes, furniture and textiles were the principal manufacturing sectors.

TRANSPORT

The rail network, totalling some 1,104 km, is the most important element of the transport infrastructure. The main line is the 885-km 'Transcameroonian', from Douala to Ngaoundéré. Reconstruction of the Douala-Yaoundé section was completed in 1987, with finance from France, the EC, the USA and Middle Eastern sources.

The road network totalled some 70,570 km in 1991, of which 7,720 km were classed as main roads and 14,450 as secondary roads. The World Bank is providing financial support for a $245m. programme of road improvement and upgrading, but the proposed construction under the sixth Development Plan of 3,000 km of tarred roads was postponed, owing to reductions in public expenditure necessitated by the economic recession.

Cameroon has seaports at Douala-Bonabéri, Limbe/Tiko and Kribi. Total traffic handled by the ports in 1990/91 was 3.7m. tons, of which 97% passed through Douala-Bonabéri. Feasibility studies have been conducted for deep-water ports at Cap Limboh (near Limbe and the oil refinery) and Grand Batanga, south of the existing port handling wood and minerals at Kribi. The latter, however, is dependent on the exploitation of the offshore gas reserve and iron ore reserves, neither of which seems likely in the near future.

The poor state of the road network has encouraged the development of internal air travel and of small domestic airports. Cameroon Airlines—75% owned by the government and 25% by Air France—has provided internal, French and regional services since Cameroon's withdrawal from Air Afrique in 1971. Services exist to a number of airports, including several European destinations. Douala airport was rebuilt in 1977 to take all subsonic aircraft, and there is a second international airport at Garoua. The construction of an international airport at Yaoundé was completed in 1991.

FINANCE AND INVESTMENT

Revenue from petroleum production profoundly changed the country's fiscal position, and allowed a rapid rise in both current and capital spending. Government expenditure increased dramatically over the period 1980/81–1985/86. Owing to the rise in petroleum royalties, no new borrowing or additional taxation was required to finance the budget. However, the decline in world petroleum prices during 1986 and the consequent fall in oil royalties, to 150,000m. francs CFA, caused the government to restrict the increase in total planned spending in 1986/87 to 8%, which represented a reduction in real terms, compared with 1985/86. In 1987/88 expenditure was due to fall for the first time in nominal values, by almost one-fifth, through initiating fewer projects and slowing work on those already begun. This austerity would seem to reflect the depletion of the *compte hors budget* (extra-budgetary account), a secret fund accumulated, over several years, from petroleum royalties. However, revenue declined at a faster rate than had been expected in 1987/88, while expenditure exceeded the projected 650,000m. francs CFA, to reach 813,000m. francs CFA. Revenue continued to decline for the next two years, falling to 562.8m. francs CFA in 1988/89 and to 516.8m. francs CFA in 1989/90. However, attempts to control expenditure have apparently had some success, with a 12.7% decline in 1988/89, to 714m. francs CFA, and a further small decline, to 705.1m. francs CFA, in 1989/90. In 1990/91 revenue increased to 540.6m. francs CFA, while expenditure declined slightly, to 701.7m. francs CFA, resulting in a reduced budget deficit of 161.1m. francs CFA. In 1991/92 revenue declined to 495.9m. francs CFA; however the budget deficit fell to 59.8m. francs CFA, owing to a dramatic reduction in expenditure, to 555.7m. francs CFA.

The fifth Five-Year Plan (1981–86) demonstrated a departure from previous plans. The private sector was expected to supply an increased share (40%) of the finance, while half of the 60% from public resources was to be raised domestically. The Plan covered investments totalling 2,300,000m. francs CFA. Agriculture and transport infrastructure were each allocated over one-fifth of total planned expenditure, and the Plan's overall target of a 7% real annual growth of GDP, giving a rise in per caput income of more than 4% annually, was achieved. The sixth Five-Year Plan (1986–91) projected a further rise in total investment, to 7,830,000m. francs CFA, of which the public sector was to provide 42% and foreign sources (public and private) 23%. The share of the rural sector (agriculture, fisheries and forestry) was to rise to 26% of total investment, and the target was average annual growth of 6.7%. As a result of the stringent reductions in the investment budget, and the prospect of continuing austerity, however, the 1986–91 investment target was not attained. In February 1992 a further structural adjustment programme, which included new tax measures, was introduced.

FOREIGN TRADE AND AID

Following a deterioration in the country's foreign trade position in the 1970s, the emergence of petroleum as Cameroon's major export (crude petroleum accounted for 55% of export earnings in 1985) increased the export total to 816,912m. francs CFA in 1985, and, even with a significant rise in import spending (to 513,898m. francs CFA in that year), Cameroon's foreign trade demonstrated a considerable and growing surplus in the early 1980s. In 1986/87, however, the sharp decline in petroleum earnings (reflecting reductions in both prices and output) caused export earnings to fall. In 1987 a trade surplus of $254m. was recorded, which increased to $620.5m. in 1988. Following a decline to $464m. in 1989, the trade surplus recovered to $599.3m. in 1990, but fell sharply, to $380.9m. in 1991.

Owing to the high level of earnings from the petroleum sector during the early 1980s, the rapid increase in development expenditure was financed without a substantial increase in the foreign debt. Between 1980 and 1985 the total external debt increased by only one-sixth, to $2,940m., equivalent to just over one-third of total annual GNP in 1985. Servicing of the foreign debt was thus manageable, representing about 15% of export earnings in most years during the first half of the decade. From 1986, however, there was a marked deterioration, owing to the sharp decline in revenue from the petroleum sector. The external debt increased by more than one-quarter in 1986, and continued to rise, albeit less rapidly, in the following years, to reach $4,743m. by the end of 1989. At the end of 1991, following an increase in arrears, external debt totalled $6,278m.

Although receipts of aid increased to an average of more than $240m. per year in 1986–87, the concessional element of the country's total borrowing declined from an annual average of 31% in 1980–85 to 24% in 1990. The debt-service ratio consequently increased to 29% in 1987 and 31% in 1988, but was reduced to 21.5% in 1990, as a result of debt rescheduling by the 'Paris Club' of Western official creditors. In May 1989, following the negotiation of agreements with the IMF, in late 1988, on stand-by and compensatory credits, and in the context of continuing budgetary restraint, Cameroon obtained a rescheduling of some $550m., to the end of March 1990, in liabilities to official creditors. However, both the agreement with the IMF and a $150m. structural adjustment loan (SAL) from the World Bank were suspended in 1990, when the government failed to comply with performance requirements. The World Bank SAL was resumed in April 1991, when a second $50m. tranche was disbursed. A further stand-by agreement with the IMF was reached in December, in exchange for a commitment by the government to reduce expenditure and to improve tax collection. In February 1992 the government concluded an agreement with the 'Paris Club', which provided for a further rescheduling of external debt. In September the IMF suspended the disbursement of credit, pending the payment of accumulated debt arrears. In 1993 Cameroon received assistance from the French government to enable it to pay debt-servicing arrears to the World Bank, after that organization also suspended disbursements in

December 1992, and indicated that it would alter Cameroon's debtor status. By the end of 1993 Cameroon's total external debt had reached an estimated $7,500m. (compared with $6,550m. at the end of 1992). In March 1994, however, the IMF approved a stand-by credit for Cameroon equivalent to $114m.; the IMF-endorsed structural adjustment programme laid emphasis on the continuation of retrenchment of public sector salaries, and an increase in non-petroleum revenue through customs and indirect tax reforms. In the same month Cameroon received a further structural adjustment loan of $50m. from the World Bank, and obtained a rescheduling of debt by the 'Paris Club', which involved a reduction of payments by 50%.

Statistical Survey

Source (unless otherwise stated): Direction de la Statistique et de la Comptabilité Nationale, BP 25, Yaoundé; tel. 22-07-88; telex 8203.

Area and Population

AREA, POPULATION AND DENSITY

Area (sq km)	475,442*
Population (census results)	
9 April 1976†	
Males	3,754,991
Females	3,908,255
Total	7,663,246
April 1987	10,493,655
Population (official estimates at mid-year)	
1986	10,457,000
1987	10,821,746
1989‡	11,540,000
Density (per sq km) at mid-1989	24.3

* 183,569 sq miles.

† Including an adjustment for underenumeration, estimated at 7.4%. The enumerated total was 7,090,115 (males 3,472,786; females 3,617,329).

‡ Figure for 1988 is not available.

PROVINCES (population at 1976 census)

	Urban	Rural	Total
Centre-South	498,290	993,655	1,491,945
Littoral	702,578	232,588	935,166
West	232,315	803,282	1,035,597
South-West	200,322	420,193	620,515
North-West	146,327	834,204	980,531
North	328,925	1,904,332	2,233,257
East	75,458	290,750	366,235
Total	2,184,242	5,479,004	7,663,246

Note: In August 1983 the number of provinces was increased to 10. Centre-South province became two separate provinces, Centre and South. The northern province was split into three: Far North, North and Adamoua.

PRINCIPAL TOWNS

1976 (population at census): Douala 458,426, Yaoundé (capital) 313,706, Nkongsamba 71,298, Maroua 67,187, Garoua 63,900, Bafoussam 62,239, Bamenda 48,111, Kumba 44,175, Limbe (formerly Victoria) 27,016.

Mid-1991 (estimated population): Douala 810,000, Yaoundé 649,000, Garoua 142,000, Maroua 123,000, Bafoussam 113,000.

Source: *La Zone Franc—Rapport 1991.*

BIRTHS AND DEATHS (UN estimates, annual averages)

	1975–80	1980–85	1985–90
Birth rate (per 1,000)	45.5	43.9	42.0
Death rate (per 1,000)	17.6	15.6	13.8

Source: UN, *World Population Prospects: The 1992 Revision.*

ECONOMICALLY ACTIVE POPULATION
(official estimates, persons aged six years and over, mid-1985)

	Males	Females	Total
Agriculture, hunting, forestry and fishing	1,574,946	1,325,925	2,900,871
Mining and quarrying	1,693	100	1,793
Manufacturing	137,671	36,827	174,498
Electricity, gas and water	3,373	149	3,522
Construction	65,666	1,018	66,684
Trade, restaurants and hotels	115,269	38,745	154,014
Transport, storage and communications	50,664	1,024	51,688
Financing, insurance, real estate and business services	7,447	562	8,009
Community, social and personal services	255,076	37,846	292,922
Activities not adequately defined	18,515	17,444	35,959
Total in employment	2,230,320	1,459,640	3,689,960
Unemployed	180,016	47,659	227,675
Total labour force	2,410,336	1,507,299	3,917,635

Source: International Labour Office, *Year Book of Labour Statistics.*

Mid-1992 (estimates in '000): Agriculture, etc. 2,729; Total 4,604 (Source: FAO, *Production Yearbook).*

Agriculture

PRINCIPAL CROPS ('000 metric tons)

	1990	1991	1992
Rice (paddy)	55	90*	90†
Maize	369	450*	380†
Millet and sorghum	413*	463*	435†
Potatoes†	32	32	32
Sweet potatoes†	154	154	160
Cassava (Manioc)†	1,200	1,230	1,230
Yams†	70	80	80
Other roots and tubers†	450	450	450
Dry beans†	50	70	70
Groundnuts (in shell)*	100	100	100
Sesame seed†	15	15	15
Cottonseed	66*	66*	60†
Cotton lint*	47	47	48
Palm kernels*	53	53	53
Sugar cane†	1,500	1,400	1,400
Vegetables†	454	455	459
Avocados†	35	36	37
Pineapples†	35	35	36
Bananas†	510	520	520
Plantains†	850	860	860
Coffee (green)*	101	87	85
Cocoa beans	122	100	94*
Tobacco (leaves)†	3	4	4
Natural rubber*	47	47	48

* Unofficial estimate(s). † FAO estimate(s).

Source: FAO, *Production Yearbook*.

LIVESTOCK ('000 head, year ending September)

	1990	1991*	1992*
Cattle	4,697	4,700	4,730
Pigs	1,364	1,370	1,380
Sheep	3,500†	3,550	3,560
Goats	3,520	3,550	3,560

* FAO estimates. † Unofficial estimate.

Poultry (million, FAO estimates): 18 in 1990; 18 in 1991; 19 in 1992.

Source: FAO, *Production Yearbook*.

LIVESTOCK PRODUCTS (FAO estimates, '000 metric tons)

	1990	1991	1992
Beef and veal	72	73	73
Mutton and lamb	14	15	15
Goats' meat	13	13	13
Pigmeat	16	17	17
Poultry meat	18	19	19
Other meat	45	43	45
Cows' milk	117	117	118
Hen eggs	12.0	12.0	12.4
Cattle hides	10.3	10.4	10.4
Sheepskins	2.4	2.5	2.5
Goatskins	1.3	1.3	1.3

Source: FAO, *Production Yearbook*.

Forestry

ROUNDWOOD REMOVALS ('000 cubic metres)

	1989	1990	1991
Sawlogs, veneer logs and logs for sleepers	2,120	2,363	2,290
Other industrial wood*	771	797	824
Fuel wood*	10,809	11,177	11,523
Total	13,700	14,337	14,637

* FAO estimates.

Source: FAO, *Yearbook of Forest Products*.

SAWNWOOD PRODUCTION
('000 cubic metres, incl. railway sleepers)

	1986	1987	1988
Total	665	577	574

1989–91: Annual production as in 1988 (FAO estimates).

Source: FAO, *Yearbook of Forest Products*.

Fishing

('000 metric tons, live weight)

	1989	1990*	1991*
Freshwater fishes	20.0	20.0	22.0
Bigeye grunt	3.3	3.3	3.2
Croakers and drums	2.8	2.8	2.7
Threadfins and tasselfishes	0.7	0.7	0.7
Sardinellas	18.0	18.0	17.5
Bonga shad	18.0	18.0	17.5
Other marine fishes (incl. unspecified)	1.9	1.9	1.8
Total fish	64.6	64.6	65.3
Crustaceans and molluscs	13.0	13.0	12.7
Total catch	77.6	77.6	78.0

* FAO estimates.

Source: FAO, *Yearbook of Fishery Statistics*.

Mining

('000 metric tons, unless otherwise indicated)

	1988	1989	1990
Crude petroleum	8,482	8,635	8,480
Tin (metric tons)†	6	5	5*
Limestone flux and calcareous stone*	57	n.a.	n.a.

* Provisional or estimated figure(s).

† Estimated metal content of ore (Source: International Tin Council).

Source: UN, *Industrial Statistics Yearbook*.

Crude petroleum ('000 metric tons): 6,588 in 1992 (Source: UN, *Monthly Bulletin of Statistics*).

Industry

SELECTED PRODUCTS
('000 metric tons, unless otherwise indicated)

	1988	1989	1990
Raw sugar	84	78	81
Cocoa butter (exports)	5.6	n.a.	n.a.
Beer ('000 hectolitres)	5,105	n.a.	n.a.
Soft drinks ('000 hectolitres)	1,172	n.a.	n.a.
Cigarettes (million)*	4,300	4,300	4,300
Soap	23.4	n.a.	n.a.
Jet fuels	93	94	95
Motor spirit (petrol)	395	397	380
Kerosene	297	298	301
Distillate fuel oils	430	432	434
Residual fuel oils	570	572	575
Lubricating oils	95	97	98
Cement	586	n.a.	n.a.
Aluminium (unwrought)†	80	87.3	87.5
Footwear ('000 pairs)	1,733	n.a.	n.a.
Electric energy (million kWh)	2,583	2,699	2,705

* Provisional or estimated figures.
† Using alumina imported from Guinea.
Source: UN, *Industrial Statistics Yearbook*.

Finance

CURRENCY AND EXCHANGE RATES

Monetary Units
100 centimes = 1 franc de la Coopération financière en Afrique central (CFA).

French Franc, Sterling and Dollar Equivalents (31 March 1994)
1 French franc = 100 francs CFA;
£1 sterling = 846.40 francs CFA;
US $1 = 570.14 francs CFA;
1,000 francs CFA = £1.181 = $1.754.

Average Exchange Rate (francs CFA per US $)
1991 282.11
1992 264.69
1993 283.16

Note: The exchange rate of 1 French franc = 50 francs CFA, established in 1948, remained in force until January 1994, when the CFA franc was devalued by 50%, with the exchange rate adjusted to 1 French franc = 100 francs CFA.

BUDGET ('000 million francs CFA, year ending 30 June)

Revenue	1989/90	1990/91	1991/92*
Taxation	360.81	327.46	311.66
Taxes on income, profits, etc.	90.59	87.38	90.50
General income tax	34.07	31.26	37.94
Corporate tax on profits	56.52	56.12	52.56
Social security contributions	33.33	30.01	—
Domestic taxes on goods and services	106.37	96.66	86.92
Sales taxes	61.69	57.11	49.19
Excises	44.68	39.55	36.98
Taxes on international trade and transactions	74.32	67.71	91.80
Import duties	68.14	64.07	87.77
Export duties	6.18	3.64	4.03
Other current revenue	145.45	190.10	172.30
Unclassified current revenue	10.52	23.05	11.95
Capital revenue	.01	—	—
Total	516.79	540.61	495.91

Expenditure†	1989/90	1990/91	1991/92
Current expenditure	492.84	545.92	464.80
Expenditure on goods and services	365.15	376.51	346.01
Wages and salaries	274.44	286.48	282.34
Other purchases of goods and services	90.71	90.03	63.67
Interest payments	38.11	43.05	39.40
Subsidies and other current transfers	89.58	126.36	79.39
Capital expenditure	180.05	133.40	78.64
Acquisition of fixed capital assets	180.05	133.40	78.64
Adjustment to cash expenditure	32.18	22.39	12.24
Total	705.07	701.71	555.68

* Excluding national social security funds.
† Excluding net lending ('000 million francs CFA, year ending 30 June): 6.24 in 1989/90; 3.02 in 1990/91; 1.20 in 1991/92.
Source: IMF, *Government Finance Statistics Yearbook*.

CENTRAL BANK RESERVES
(US $ million, excluding gold, at 31 December)

	1991	1992	1993
Gold*	10.58	9.95	11.91
IMF special drawing rights	5.56	0.28	0.09
Reserve position in IMF	0.33	0.40	0.47
Foreign exchange	37.15	19.70	1.90
Total	53.62	30.33	14.37

* Valued at market-related prices.
Source: IMF, *International Financial Statistics*.

MONEY SUPPLY ('000 million francs CFA at 31 December)

	1991	1992	1993
Currency outside banks	170.25	149.02	116.13
Demand deposits at deposit money banks	258.45	159.94	150.06
Total money (incl. others)	429.90	311.33	267.46

Source: IMF, *International Financial Statistics*.

COST OF LIVING (Consumer Price Index for Africans in Yaoundé; base: 1980 = 100)

	1987	1988	1989*
Food	171.7	172.5	160.4
Clothing	374.4	n.a.	n.a.
All items (incl. others)	220.0	223.7	218.6

* Average figures for January-April and September-December.
Source: ILO, *Year Book of Labour Statistics*.

NATIONAL ACCOUNTS

('000 million francs CFA at current prices)

National Income and Product (year ending 30 June)

	1982/83	1983/84	1984/85
Compensation of employees	747.4	875.5	989.5
Operating surplus	1,363.7	1,737.5	2,181.7
Domestic factor incomes	2,111.1	2,613.0	3,171.2
Consumption of fixed capital	158.1	165.2	194.7
Gross domestic product (GDP) at factor cost	2,269.2	2,778.3	3,365.9
Indirect taxes	355.0	434.1	485.4
Less Subsidies	6.1	17.4	12.4
GDP in purchasers' values	2,618.0	3,195.0	3,838.9
Factor income received from abroad	11.7	14.1	23.6
Less Factor income paid abroad	71.5	76.2	121.8
Gross national product	2,558.3	3,132.9	3,740.7
Less Consumption of fixed capital	158.1	165.2	194.7
National income in market prices	2,400.2	2,967.7	3,546.0
Other current transfers received from abroad	17.4	18.3	14.5
Less Other current transfers paid abroad	22.5	23.8	13.5
National disposable income	2,395.1	2,962.2	3,547.0

Expenditure on the Gross Domestic Product

	1987/88	1988/89	1989/90
Government final consumption expenditure	385.6	364.1	376.9
Private final consumption expenditure	2,486.7	2,348.3	2,402.4
Increase in stocks	20.1	18.9	22.0
Gross fixed capital formation	990.6	935.4	943.4
Total domestic expenditure	3,883.0	3,666.7	3,744.7
Exports of goods and services	579.3	547.1	553.4
Less Imports of goods and services	692.4	653.8	659.7
GDP in purchasers' values	3,769.9	3,560.0	3,638.3
GDP at constant 1980 prices	2,110.4	1,983.8	2,025.5

Source: UN, *National Accounts Statistics*.

Gross Domestic Product by Economic Activity

	1989	1990	1991
Agriculture, hunting, forestry and fishing	740	752	749
Mining and quarrying	428	435	407
Manufacturing	406	411	424
Electricity, gas and water	36	38	38
Construction	168	172	165
Wholesale and retail trade, restaurants and hotels	369	380	368
Transport and communications	196	418	417
Finance, insurance, real estate and business services	402	199	195
Public administration and defence	300	302	310
Other community, social and personal services	65	66	66
Sub-total	3,110	3,173	3,139
Less Statistical adjustment	34	34	34
GDP at factor cost	3,076	3,139	3,105
Indirect taxes, *less* subsidies	484	499	503
GDP in purchasers' values	3,560	3,638	3,608

Source: UN Economic Commission for Africa, *African Statistical Yearbook*.

BALANCE OF PAYMENTS (US $ million)

	1988	1990*	1991
Merchandise exports f.o.b.	1,841.2	1,615.7	1,317.8
Merchandise imports f.o.b.	–1,220.8	–1,016.3	–936.9
Trade balance	620.5	599.3	380.9
Exports of services	456.2	490.0	233.0
Imports of services	-901.4	–842.4	–527.6
Other income received	16.8	7.1	12.1
Other income paid	–515.0	–566.0	–443.4
Private unrequited transfers (net)	–134.9	–51.7	–7.5
Official unrequited transfers (net)	29.0	28.9	29.3
Current balance	–428.8	–334.8	–323.1
Direct investment (net)	38.6	–77.4	–22.0
Other capital (net)	13.1	–149.6	–142.9
Net errors and omissions	166.3	–301.1	323.6
Overall balance	–210.8	–862.9	–164.3

* Figurs for 1989 are not available.

Source: IMF, *International Financial Statistics*.

External Trade

PRINCIPAL COMMODITIES
(distribution by SITC, US $ million)

Imports c.i.f.	1986	1987	1989*
Food and live animals	208.0	202.6	179.6
Fish, crustaceans, molluscs and preparations	38.3	41.1	46.9
Fresh, chilled or frozen fish	30.2	32.5	41.2
Cereals and cereal preparations	89.0	79.1	76.8
Malt (incl. malt flour)	43.5	27.9	27.9
Beverages and tobacco	44.8	47.4	21.0
Crude materials (inedible) except fuels	44.5	42.7	47.9
Metalliferous ores and metal scrap	29.2	28.5	35.7
Alumina (aluminium oxide)	27.7	27.2	34.7
Chemicals and related products	248.1	258.9	193.9
Medicinal and pharmaceutical products	72.4	99.4	67.2
Medicaments (incl. veterinary medicaments)	66.7	91.9	62.2
Artificial resins, plastic materials, etc.	35.9	32.4	30.2
Disinfectants, insecticides, fungicides, etc.	31.1	31.1	24.0
Basic manufactures	342.6	378.9	292.8
Paper, paperboard and manufactures	46.7	44.0	36.3
Paper and paperboard	33.7	30.8	26.7
Textile yarn, fabrics, etc.	58.7	94.2	41.0
Woven fabrics of jute, etc.	4.7	41.2	9.7
Non-metallic mineral manufactures	49.4	70.6	49.0
Lime, cement, etc.	18.9	44.2	28.1
Cement	16.1	40.0	24.2
Iron and steel	54.8	36.6	41.9
Machinery and transport equipment	611.9	626.5	391.9
Power-generating machinery and equipment	45.8	43.2	20.3
Machinery specialized for particular industries	73.4	79.8	62.9
Civil engineering and contractors' plant and equipment	25.9	27.3	30.6
General industrial machinery, equipment and parts	117.3	119.8	87.0
Telecommunications and sound equipment	59.5	36.7	13.2
Other electrical machinery, apparatus, etc.	60.0	58.8	34.2
Road vehicles and parts†	185.8	193.0	100.8
Passenger motor cars (excl. buses)	72.1	75.4	43.2
Motor vehicles for the transport of goods, etc.	59.5	72.1	28.4
Goods vehicles (lorries and trucks)	56.2	66.0	25.9
Other transport equipment†	46.2	70.9	57.7
Aircraft, associated equipment and parts†	31.1	14.1	13.6
Ships, boats and floating structures	5.8	44.5	38.8
Tugs, special purpose vessels and floating structures	3.3	39.1	30.6
Miscellaneous manufactured articles	149.3	149.1	109.0
Printed matter	32.2	38.5	30.1
Total (incl. others)	1,704.7	1,749.0	1,273.3

* The distribution by commodities is not available for 1988 (total imports $1,271 million).

† Excluding tyres, engines and electrical parts.

Exports f.o.b.	1986	1987	1989*
Food and live animals	395.3	314.5	434.9
Coffee, tea, cocoa and spices	376.2	294.1	412.1
Coffee and coffee substitutes	198.4	129.5	214.7
Unroasted coffee and coffee husks and skins	194.7	129.2	214.1
Cocoa	176.1	162.6	196.2
Cocoa beans (raw or roasted)	144.8	125.1	168.7
Cocoa butter and cocoa paste	30.6	37.5	27.4
Crude materials (inedible) except fuels	102.8	131.4	245.6
Cork and wood	61.0	77.7	141.3
Rough or roughly squared wood (excl. fuel wood and pulpwood)	53.2	63.0	107.1
Non-coniferous sawlogs and veneer logs	52.7	63.0	107.1
Simply worked wood and railway sleepers	7.8	14.7	34.2
Shaped non-coniferous wood	6.9	13.0	32.8
Textile fibres and waste	19.1	26.9	68.7
Raw cotton (excl. linters)	19.0	26.8	68.6
Mineral fuels, lubricants, etc.	77.3	145.2	230.9
Petroleum, petroleum products, etc.	77.3	145.2	230.9
Crude petroleum oils, etc.	74.2	142.1	229.6
Basic manufactures	97.9	111.3	243.5
Non-metallic mineral manufactures	1.8	5.3	40.3
Lime, cement, etc.	0.8	4.0	36.5
Cement	0.8	4.0	36.5
Non-ferrous metals	61.6	69.4	144.6
Aluminium and aluminium alloys	61.5	69.4	144.5
Unwrought aluminium and alloys	47.2	55.8	126.1
Machinery and transport equipment	62.3	82.4	66.8
Transport equipment (excl. tyres, engines and electrical parts)	13.1	43.9	43.0
Ships, boats and floating structures	6.1	35.2	27.6
Tugs, special purpose vessels and floating structures	5.1	32.2	20.5
Total (incl. others)	780.8	829.4	1,281.6

* The distribution by commodities is not available for 1988 (total exports $924 million).

Source: UN, *International Trade Statistics Yearbook.*

1990 (million francs CFA): Total imports c.i.f. 449,100; Total exports f.o.b. 549,800.

PRINCIPAL TRADING PARTNERS (US $ million)

Imports c.i.f.	1986	1987	1989*
Bangladesh	0.0	19.4	11.0
Belgium/Luxembourg	59.0	71.4	39.9
Brazil	12.0	19.0	25.8
Canada	6.8	5.8	49.0
Denmark	9.4	15.8	—
France	718.7	655.5	464.7
Germany, Fed. Repub.	155.3	160.9	71.6
Guinea	26.5	27.2	34.7
Italy	80.7	74.4	38.5
Japan	130.0	143.9	72.6
Korea Repub.	16.7	15.3	8.4
Netherlands	45.3	40.7	116.4
Pakistan	10.0	15.0	8.6
Panama	0.0	26.1	5.0
Senegal	13.7	18.3	15.9
Spain	42.3	34.3	19.9
Switzerland	39.4	42.8	17.5
Tunisia	6.2	20.1	10.4
United Kingdom	62.7	56.9	7.0
USA	84.1	60.7	64.3
Total (incl. others)	1,704.7	1,749.0	1,273.3

* The distribution by countries is not available for 1988 (total imports $1,271 million).

Exports f.o.b.	1986	1987	1989*
Belgium/Luxembourg	7.3	26.5	246.9
Central African Repub.	12.3	12.5	22.8
Chad	15.4	18.0	6.4
Congo	16.1	17.9	17.3
Côte d'Ivoire	9.5	5.9	17.4
Equatorial Guinea	5.1	9.4	35.5
France	173.0	144.7	301.3
Gabon	34.8	47.7	30.1
Germany, Fed. Repub.	74.1	41.0	113.4
Italy	73.7	114.1	18.0
Japan	13.7	10.1	18.8
Netherlands	187.9	191.3	81.5
Nigeria	38.7	26.0	30.3
Portugal	4.1	9.0	16.1
Spain	29.5	22.2	64.0
USSR	24.5	12.9	6.6
USA	22.6	60.1	128.1
Total (incl. others)	780.8	829.4	1,281.6

* The distribution by countries is not available for 1988 (total exports $924 million).

Source: UN, *International Trade Statistics Yearbook*.

Transport

RAILWAYS (traffic, year ending 30 June)

	1985/86	1986/87	1987/88
Passengers carried ('000)	2,079	2,267	2,413
Passenger-km (million)	412	444	469
Freight carried ('000 tons)	1,791	1,411	1,375
Freight ton-km (million)	871	675	594

Source: Ministère des Travaux Publics et des Transports, Yaoundé.

Net ton-km (million): 622 in 1988; 743 in 1989; 684 in 1990.

Passenger-km (million): 466 in 1988; 458 in 1989; 442 in 1990.

Source: UN, *Statistical Yearbook*.

ROAD TRAFFIC (motor vehicles in use at 31 December)

	1984	1985	1986
Passenger cars	72,449	77,105	80,757
Commercial vehicles	41,301	43,510	44,875
Tractors and trailers	2,045	2,473	2,709
Motorcycles and scooters	41,579	41,807	40,961

1990: Passenger cars 63,400; Commercial vehicles 34,300 (Source: UN, *Statistical Yearbook*).

INTERNATIONAL SEA-BORNE SHIPPING (Douala)

	1986	1987	1988
Vessels entered	1,366	1,260	1,122
Freight loaded ('000 metric tons)	1,179	1,119	1,210
Freight unloaded ('000 metric tons)	3,189	2,715	2,558

Source: Ministère des Travaux Publics et des Transports, Yaoundé.

Freight loaded ('000 metric tons): 9,565 in 1989; 10,081 in 1990.

Freight unloaded ('000 metric tons): 3,298 in 1989; 3,396 in 1990.

Source: UN, *Monthly Bulletin of Statistics*.

CIVIL AVIATION (traffic on scheduled services)

	1987	1990*	1991
Kilometres flown (million)	5	6	5
Passengers carried ('000)	561	378	357
Passenger-km (million)	610	533	301
Freight ton-km (million)	37	9	10

* Figures for 1988 and 1989 are unavailable.

Source: UN, *Statistical Yearbook*.

Tourism

	1988	1989	1990
Tourist arrivals	99,312	85,942	99,157

Source: UN, *Statistical Yearbook*.

Communications Media

	1989	1990	1991
Radio receivers ('000 in use)	1,500	1,650	1,725
Television receivers ('000 in use)	250	270	279
Telephones ('000 in use)*	51	52	53

* Provisional figures.

Daily newspapers (1990): 2 (average circulation 80,000 copies).

Non-daily newspapers (1988): 25 (average circulation 315,000 copies).

Source: mainly UNESCO, *Statistical Yearbook*.

Education

(1990)

	Institutions	Teachers	Students Males	Students Females	Students Total
Pre-primary	807	3,567	46,953	46,818	93,771
Primary	6,709	38,430	1,059,967	904,179	1,964,146
Secondary					
General	388*	11,400†	239,888	169,841	409,729
Teacher training	183*	232	232	283	515
Vocational	n.a.	5,652†	52,666	37,362	90,028
Higher	n.a.	1,086	n.a.	n.a.	33,177
Universities	n.a.	761	n.a.	n.a.	31,360

* 1986/87 figure. † 1989 figure.

Source: mainly UNESCO, *Statistical Yearbook*.

Directory

The Constitution*

The Republic of Cameroon is a multi-party state. The main provisions of the 1972 Constitution, as amended, are summarized below:

The Constitution declares that the human being, without distinction as to race, religion, sex or belief, possesses inalienable and sacred rights. It affirms its attachment to the fundamental freedoms embodied in the Universal Declaration of Human Rights and the UN Charter. The State guarantees to all citizens of either sex the rights and freedoms set out in the preamble of the Constitution.

SOVEREIGNTY

1. The Republic of Cameroon shall be one and indivisible, democratic, secular and dedicated to social service. It shall ensure the equality before the law of all its citizens. Provisions that the official languages be French and English, for the motto, flag, national anthem and seal, that the capital be Yaoundé.

2–3. Sovereignty shall be vested in the people who shall exercise it either through the President of the Republic and the members returned by it to the National Assembly or by means of referendum. Elections are by universal suffrage, direct or indirect, by every citizen aged 21 or over in a secret ballot. Political parties or groups may take part in elections subject to the law and the principles of democracy and of national sovereignty and unity.

4. State authority shall be exercised by the President of the Republic and the National Assembly.

THE PRESIDENT OF THE REPUBLIC

5. The President of the Republic, as Head of State and Head of the Government, shall be responsible for the conduct of the affairs of the Republic. He shall define national policy and may charge the members of the Government with the implementation of this policy in certain spheres.

6–7. Candidates for the office of President must hold civic and political rights, be at least 35 years old and have resided in Cameroon for a minimum of 12 consecutive months, and may not hold any other elective office or professional activity. The President is elected for five years, by a majority of votes cast by the people, and may be re-elected. A presidential election may take place before the expiry of the five-year term, if the incumbent President so decides. Provisions are made for the continuity of office in the case of the President's resignation.

8–9. The Ministers and Vice-Ministers are appointed by the President to whom they are responsible, and they may hold no other appointment. The President is also head of the armed forces, he negotiates and ratifies treaties, may exercise clemency after consultation with the Higher Judicial Council, promulgates and is responsible for the enforcement of laws, is responsible for internal and external security, makes civil and military appointments, provides for necessary administrative services.

10. The President, by reference to the Supreme Court, ensures that all laws passed are constitutional.

11. Provisions whereby the President may declare a state of emergency or state of siege.

THE NATIONAL ASSEMBLY

12. The National Assembly shall be renewed every five years, though it may at the instance of the President of the Republic legislate to extend or shorten its term of office. It shall be composed of 180 members elected by universal suffrage.

13–14. Laws shall normally be passed by a simple majority of those present, but if a bill is read a second time at the request of the President of the Republic a majority of the National Assembly as a whole is required.

15–16. The National Assembly shall meet twice a year, each session to last not more than 30 days; in one session it shall approve the budget. It may be recalled to an extraordinary session of not more than 15 days.

17–18. Elections and suitability of candidates and sitting members shall be governed by law.

RELATIONS BETWEEN THE EXECUTIVE AND THE LEGISLATURE

19. Bills may be introduced either by the President of the Republic or by any member of the National Assembly.

20. Reserved to the legislature are: the fundamental rights and duties of the citizen; the law of persons and property; the political, administrative and judicial system in respect of elections to the National Assembly, general regulation of national defence, authorization of penalties and criminal and civil procedure etc., and the organization of the local authorities; currency, the budget, dues and taxes, legislation on public property; economic and social policy; the education system.

21. The National Assembly may empower the President of the Republic to legislate by way of ordinance for a limited period and for given purposes.

22–26. Other matters of procedure, including the right of the President of the Republic to address the Assembly and of the Ministers and Vice-Ministers to take part in debates.

27–29. The composition and conduct of the Assembly's programme of business. Provisions whereby the Assembly may inquire into governmental activity. The obligation of the President of the Republic to promulgate laws, which shall be published in both languages of the Republic.

30. Provisions whereby the President of the Republic, after consultation with the National Assembly, may submit to referendum certain reform bills liable to have profound repercussions on the future of the nation and national institutions.

THE JUDICIARY

31. Justice is administered in the name of the people. The President of the Republic shall ensure the independence of the

judiciary and shall make appointments with the assistance of the Higher Judicial Council.

THE SUPREME COURT

32–33. The Supreme Court has powers to uphold the Constitution in such cases as the death or incapacity of the President and the admissibility of laws, to give final judgments on appeals on the Judgment of the Court of Appeal and to decide complaints against administrative acts. It may be assisted by experts appointed by the President of the Republic.

IMPEACHMENT

34. There shall be a Court of Impeachment with jurisdiction to try the President of the Republic for high treason and the Ministers and Vice-Ministers for conspiracy against the security of the State.

THE ECONOMIC AND SOCIAL COUNCIL

35. There shall be an Economic and Social Council, regulated by the law.

AMENDMENT OF THE CONSTITUTION

36–37. Bills to amend the Constitution may be introduced either by the President of the Republic or the National Assembly. The President may decide to submit any amendment to the people by way of a referendum. No procedure to amend the Constitution may be accepted if it tends to impair the republican character, unity or territorial integrity of the State, or the democratic principles by which the Republic is governed.

* In May 1993 the Government promulgated draft constitutional amendments, which provided for a democratic system of government, with the establishment of an upper legislative chamber (to be known as the Senate), a council of supreme judiciary affairs, a council of state, and a civil service high authority, and restricted the power vested in the President, who was to serve a maximum of two five-year terms. The draft legislation was to be amended in accordance with the recommendations of a technical commission, which was to compile proposals from all sectors of the population.

The Government

HEAD OF STATE

President: PAUL BIYA (took office 6 November 1982; elected 14 January 1984; re-elected 24 April 1988 and 11 October 1992).

CABINET
(September 1994)

A coalition of the Rassemblement démocratique du peuple camerounais, the Mouvement pour la défense de la République, the Union des populations camerounaises, the Union nationale pour la démocratie et le progrès, and the Parti national du progrès.

Prime Minister: SIMON ACHIDI ACHU.

Deputy Prime Minister in charge of Territorial Administration: GILBERT ANDZE TSOUNGUI.

Deputy Prime Minister in charge of Housing and Town Planning: HAMADOU MOUSTAPHA.

Minister of State in charge of Posts and Telecommunications: DAKOLE DAISSALA.

Minister of State in charge of Communications: AUGUSTIN KONTCHOU KUOMENGUI.

Minister of State in charge of Agriculture: AUGUSTIN FREDERIC KODOCK.

Minister of Foreign Affairs: FERDINAND LEOPOLD OYONO.

Minister of Justice and Keeper of the Seals: DOUALA MOUTOME.

Minister of Livestock, Fisheries and Animal Husbandry: HAMADJODA ADJOUDJI.

Minister of Higher Education: Prof. PETER AGBOR-TABI.

Minister of Public Health: JOSEPH OWONA.

Minister of Labour and Social Security: SIMON MBILA.

Minister of Industrial and Commercial Development: PIERRE ELOUDOU MANI.

Minister of Public Service and Administrative Reforms: SALI DAIROU.

Minister of Social Affairs and Women's Affairs: BOUBAKARI AISSATOU YAOU.

Minister of Public Works: JEAN-BAPTISTE BOKAM.

Minister of Scientific and Technical Research: JOSEPH MBEDE.

Minister of Tourism: PIERRE SOUMAN.

Minister of Environment and Forests: DR BAVA DJINGOER.

Minister of Youth and Sports: JOSEPH-MARIE BIPOUN WOUM.

Minister of National Education: DR ROBERT MBELLA MBAPPE.

Minister of Mines, Water and Energy: VITA BELLO MBELLE.

Minister of Transport: ISSA BAKARI TCHIROMA.

Minister of Culture: TOKO MANGAN.

Minister of Economy and Finance: JUSTIN NAIRO.

Minister in charge of Special Duties: PETER ABETY.

Minister Delegate at the Presidency in charge of Defence: EDOUARD AKAME MFOUMOU.

Minister Delegate at the Ministry of Foreign Affairs: FRANCIS NKWAIN.

Minister Delegate at the Ministry of Economy and Finance in charge of the Budget: ROGER MILINGUI.

Minister Delegate at the Ministry of Economy and Finance in charge of the Stabilization Plan and Economy Recovery: NANA SINKAM.

Minister Delegate in charge of relations with the National Assembly: MAIDADI SADOU.

There are also 11 Secretaries of State.

MINISTRIES

Correspondence to ministries not holding post boxes should generally be addressed c/o the Central Post Office, Yaoundé.

Office of the President: Yaoundé; tel. 23-40-25; telex 8207.

Office of the Prime Minister: Yaoundé.

Ministry of Agriculture: Yaoundé; tel. 23-40-85; telex 8325.

Ministry of Communications: BP 1588, Yaoundé; tel. 22-31-55; telex 8215.

Ministry of Culture: Yaoundé.

Ministry of Defence: Yaoundé; tel. 23-40-55; telex 8261.

Ministry of Economy and Finance: BP 18, Yaoundé; tel. 23-40-00; telex 8260.

Ministry of Environment and Forests: Yaoundé.

Ministry of Foreign Affairs: Yaoundé; tel. 22-01-33; telex 8252.

Ministry of Higher Education: Yaoundé; telex 8418.

Ministry of Housing and Town Planning: Yaoundé; tel. 23-22-82; telex 8560.

Ministry of Industrial and Commercial Development: Yaoundé; tel. 23-40-40; telex 8638; fax 22-27-04.

Ministry of Justice: Yaoundé; tel. 22-01-97; telex 8566.

Ministry of Labour and Social Welfare: Yaoundé; tel. 22-01-86.

Ministry of Livestock, Fisheries and Animal Husbandry: Yaoundé; tel. 22-33-11.

Ministry of Mines, Water and Energy: Yaoundé; tel. 23-34-04; telex 8504.

Ministry of National Education: Yaoundé; tel. 23-40-50; telex 8551.

Ministry of Planning and Regional Development: Yaoundé; telex 8268.

Ministry of Posts and Telecommunications: Yaoundé; tel. 23-06-15; telex 8582; fax 23-31-59.

Ministry of Public Health: Yaoundé; tel. 22-29-01; telex 8565.

Ministry of the Public Service and Administrative Reform: Yaoundé; telex 8597.

Ministry of Public Works: Yaoundé; tel. 22-16-22; telex 8653.

Ministry of Scientific and Technical Research: Yaoundé.

Ministry of Social Affairs and Women's Affairs: Yaoundé; tel. 22-41-48.

Ministry of Territorial Administration: Yaoundé; tel. 23-40-90; telex 8503.

Ministry of Tourism: BP 266, Yaoundé; tel. 22-44-11; telex 8318.

Ministry of Transport: Yaoundé.

Ministry of Youth and Sports: Yaoundé; tel. 23-32-57; telex 8568.

President and Legislature

PRESIDENT

Election, 11 October 1992

Candidate	Votes (%)
PAUL BIYA (RDPC)	39.9
JOHN FRU NDI (SDF)	35.9
BELLO BOUBA MAIGARI (UNDP)	19.2
ADAMOU NDAM NJOYA (UDC)	3.6
JEAN-JACQUES EKINDI (MP)	0.5
EMA OTOU (RFP)	0.4

ASSEMBLÉE NATIONALE

President: DJIBRIL CAVAYÉ YEGUIE.

Vice-President: GABRIEL MBALLA BOUNOUNG.

General Election, 1 March 1992

Party	Seats
Rassemblement démocratique du peuple camerounais (RDPC)*	88
Union nationale pour la démocratie et le progrès (UNDP)	68
Union des populations camerounaises (UPC)	18
Mouvement pour la défense de la République (MDR)*	6
Total	180

* Following the elections, the RDPC formed an alliance with the MDR, thereby securing an absolute majority in the National Assembly.

Political Organizations

The Rassemblement démocratique du peuple camerounais (RDPC) was the sole legal party until the adoption, in December 1990, of a constitutional amendment permitting the formation of other political associations. By mid-1994 more than 70 political parties had been granted legal recognition. The most important of these are listed below:

Alliance pour la démocratie et le développement (ADD): Sec.-Gen. GARGA HAMAN ADJI.

Alliance démocratique pour le progrès du Cameroun (ADPC): Garoua; f. 1991.

Alliance pour le progrès et l'émancipation des dépossédés (APED): Yaoundé; f. 1991; Leader BOHIN BOHIN.

Alliance pour le redressement du Cameroun (ARC): f. Feb. 1992 by a number of opposition movements.

Association social-démocrate du Cameroun (ASDC): Maroua; f. 1991.

Congrès panafricain du Cameroun (CPC): Douala; f. 1991.

Convention libérale (CL): f. 1991; Leader PIERRE-FLAMBEAU NGAYAP.

Démocratie intégrale au Cameroun (DIC): Douala; f. 1991; Leader GUSTAVE ESSAKA.

Front démocratique et patriotique (FDP): f. 1994; alliance of six opposition parties.

Liberal Democratic Alliance (LDA): Buea; Pres. HENRI FOSSUNG.

Mouvement pour la démocratie et le progrès (MDP): Leader SAMUEL EBOYA.

Mouvement pour la défense de la République (MDR): f. 1991; Leader DAKOLE DAISSALA.

Mouvement progressif (MP): f. 1991; Leader JEAN-JACQUES EKINDI.

Mouvement social pour la nouvelle démocratie (MSND): Leader YONDO BLACK.

Parti de l'action du peuple (PAP): Leader VICTOR MUKUELLE NGOH.

Parti de l'alliance libérale (PAL): Leader CÉLÉSTIN BEDZIGUI.

Parti des démocrates camerounais (PDC): Yaoundé; f. 1991; Leader SALOMON ELOGO METOMO.

Parti libéral-democrate (PLD): f. 1991; Leader NJOH LITUMBE.

Parti national du progrès (PNP): Leader ANTAR GASSAGAY.

Parti ouvrier unifié du Cameroun (POUC): Leader DIEUDONNÉ BIZOLE.

Parti républicain du peuple camerounais (PRPC): Bertoua; f. 1991; Leader ATEBA NGOUA.

Parti socialiste camerounais (PSC): Leader JEAN-PIERRE DEMBELE.

Parti socialiste démocratique (PSD): Douala; f. 1991; Leader ERNEST KOUM BIN BILTIK.

Parti socialiste démocratique du Cameroun (PSDC): Leader JEAN MICHEL TEKAM.

Parti de la solidarité du peuple (PSP): f. 1991; Pres. WOUNGLY MASSAGA.

Rassemblement camerounais pour la République (RCR): Leader SAMUEL WOUAFFO.

Rassemblement démocratique du peuple camerounais (RDPC): BP 867, Yaoundé; tel. 23-27-40; telex 8624; f. 1966 as Union nationale camerounaise (UNC) by merger of the Union camerounaise, the Kamerun National Democratic Party and four opposition parties; renamed in March 1985; sole legal party 1972–90; Pres. PAUL BIYA; Sec.-Gen. JOSEPH-CHARLES DOUMBA.

Rassemblement des forces patriotiques (RFP): Leader EMA OTOU.

Rassemblement pour l'unité nationale (RUN): Yaoundé; f. 1991.

Social Democratic Front (SDF): Bamenda; f. 1990; Leader JOHN FRU NDI; Sec.-Gen. ASSANGA ASSIGA.

Union démocratique du Cameroun (UDC): f. 1991; Leader ADAMOU NDAM NJOYA.

Union des forces démocratiques du Cameroun (UFDC): Yaoundé; f. 1991; Leader VICTORIN HAMENI BIELEU.

Union nationale pour la démocratie et le progrès (UNDP): f. 1991; Leader BELLO BOUBA MAIGARI.

Union des populations camerounaises (UPC): Douala; f. 1948; Leader NDEH NTUMAZAH.

Union des républicains du Cameroun (URC): Douala; f. 1991.

Union pour le changement (UPC): coalition of opposition parties; Leader JOHN FRU NDI.

Union sociale démocratique (USD): Yaoundé; f. 1991.

Diplomatic Representation

EMBASSIES IN CAMEROON

Belgium: BP 816, Yaoundé; tel. 22-27-88; telex 8314; Ambassador: MARIELLE VEL ELST.

Brazil: BP 348, Yaoundé; tel. 23-19-57; telex 8587; Ambassador: ANNUNCIATA SALGADO DOS SANTOS.

Canada: Immeuble Stamatiades, BP 572, Yaoundé; tel. 23-02-03; telex 8209; Ambassador: ARSÈNE DESPRES.

Central African Republic: BP 396, Yaoundé; tel. 22-51-55; Ambassador: STANISLAS POLLOGBA.

Chad: BP 506, Yaoundé; tel. 22-06-24; telex 8352; Ambassador: OUANGMOTCHING HOMSALA.

China, People's Republic: BP 1307, Yaoundé; tel. 23-00-83; Ambassador: ZHANG LONGBAO.

Congo: BP 1422, Yaoundé; tel. 23-24-58; telex 8379; Ambassador: BERNADETTE BAYONNE.

Egypt: BP 809, Yaoundé; tel. 22-39-22; telex 8360; fax 20-26-47; Ambassador: ELDIN BAYOUMI.

Equatorial Guinea: BP 277, Yaoundé; tel. 22-41-49; Ambassador: ALFREDO ABESO NVONO ONGUENE.

France: Plateau Atémengué, BP 1631, Yaoundé; tel. 22-02-33; telex 8233; Ambassador: GILLES VIDAL.

Gabon: BP 4130, Yaoundé; tel. 22-29-66; telex 8265; Ambassador: YVES ONGOLLO.

Germany: BP 1160, Yaoundé; tel. 23-05-66; telex 8238; Ambassador: EBERHARD NOLDEKE.

Greece: BP 82, Yaoundé; tel. 22-39-36; telex 8364; Ambassador: EMMANUEL WLANDIS.

Holy See: rue du Vatican, BP 210, Yaoundé (Apostolic Nunciature); tel. 20-04-75; telex 8382; Apostolic Pro-Nuncio: Most Rev. SANTOS ABRIL Y CASTELLÓ, Titular Archbishop of Tamada.

Israel: BP 5934, Yaoundé; tel. 20-16-44; telex 8632; fax 21-08-23; Ambassador: MOSHE LIBA.

Italy: Quartier Bastos, BP 827, Yaoundé; tel. 20-33-76; telex 8305; fax 21-52-50; Ambassador: MARGHERITA COSTA.

Japan: Yaoundé; Ambassador: TADASHI SUZUKI.

Korea, Republic: BP 301, Yaoundé; Ambassador: HOON SOHN.

Liberia: Ekoudou, Quartier Bastos, BP 1185, Yaoundé; tel. 23-12-96; telex 8227; Ambassador: CARLTON ALEXWYN KARPEH.

Morocco: BP 1629, Yaoundé; tel. 20-50-92; telex 8347; fax 20-37-93; Ambassador: MIMOUN MEHDI.

Netherlands: BP 310, Yaoundé; tel. 22-05-44; telex 8237; Ambassador: MAX DAMME.

Nigeria: BP 448, Yaoundé; tel. 22-34-55; telex 8267; Ambassador: MAHMUD GEORGE BELLO.

Russia: BP 488, Yaoundé; tel. 22-17-14; telex 8859; fax 20-78-91; Ambassador: VITALY LITVINE.

Saudi Arabia: BP 1602, Yaoundé; tel. 22-39-22; telex 8336; Ambassador: HAMAD AL-TOAIMI.

Senegal: plateau Bastos, BP 1716, Yaoundé; tel. 22-03-08; telex 8303; Ambassador: SALOUM KANDE.

Spain: BP 877, Yaoundé; tel. 22-41-89; telex 8287; Ambassador: LUIS GARCÍA CEREZO.

Switzerland: BP 1169, Yaoundé; tel. 21-28-96; telex 8316; fax 20-62-20; Ambassador: WILLY HOLD.

Tunisia: rue de Rotary, BP 6074, Yaoundé; tel. 22-33-68; telex 8370; Ambassador: MOHAMED SAID EL-KATEB.

United Kingdom: ave Winston Churchill, BP 547, Yaoundé; tel. 22-05-45; telex 8200; fax 22-01-48; Ambassador: WILLIAM QUANTRILL.

USA: rue Nachtigal, BP 817, Yaoundé; tel. 23-40-14; telex 8223; Ambassador: HARRIET WINSAR ISOM.

Zaire: BP 632, Yaoundé; tel. 22-51-03; telex 8317; Ambassador: KUTENDAKANA BUMBULU.

Judicial System

Supreme Court: Yaoundé; consists of a president, nine titular and substitute judges, a procureur général, an avocat général, deputies to the procureur général, a registrar and clerks.

President of the Supreme Court: ALEXIS DIPANDA MOUELLE.

High Court of Justice: Yaoundé; consists of 9 titular judges and 6 substitute judges, all elected by the National Assembly.

Attorney-General: RISSOUCK A MOULONG MARTIN.

Religion

It is estimated that 53% of the population are Christians (mainly Roman Catholics), 25% adhere to traditional religious beliefs and 22% are Muslims.

CHRISTIANITY

Protestant Churches

There are about 1m. Protestants in Cameroon, with about 3,000 church and mission workers, and four theological schools.

Fédération des Eglises et missions évangéliques du Cameroun (FEMEC): BP 491, Yaoundé; tel. 22-30-78; f. 1968; 10 mem. churches; Pres. Rev. Dr JEAN KOTTO (Evangelical Church of Cameroon); Admin. Sec. Rev. Dr GRÉGOIRE AMBADIANG DE MENDENG (Presbyterian Church of Cameroon).

Eglise évangélique du Cameroun (Evangelical Church of Cameroon): BP 89, Douala; tel. 42-36-11; fax 42-40-11; f. 1957; independent since 1957; 500,000 mems (1992); Pres. Rev. CHARLES E. NJIKE; Sec. Rev. HANS EDJENGUELE.

Eglise presbytérienne camerounaise (Presbyterian Church of Cameroon): BP 519, Yaoundé; tel. 32-42-36; independent since 1957; comprises four synods and 16 presbyteries; 200,000 mems (1985); Gen. Sec. Rev. GRÉGOIRE AMBADIANG DE MENDENG.

Eglise protestante africaine (African Protestant Church): BP 26, Lolodorf; active among the Ngumba people; 8,400 mems (1985); Dir-Gen. Rev. ANTOINE NTER.

Presbyterian Church in Cameroon: BP 19, Buéa; tel. 32-23-36; telex 5310; 250,000 mems (1990); 211 ministers; Moderator Rev. HENRY ANYE AWASOM.

Union des Eglises baptistes au Cameroun (Union of Baptist Churches of Cameroon): BP 6007, New Bell, Douala; tel. 42-41-06; autonomous since 1957; 37,000 mems (1985); Gen. Sec. Rev. EMMANUEL MBENDA.

Among other denominations active in the country are the Cameroon Baptist Church, the Cameroon Baptist Convention, the Church of the Lutheran Brethren of Cameroon, the Evangelical Lutheran Church of Cameroon, the Presbyterian Church in West Cameroon and the Union of Evangelical Churches of North Cameroon.

The Roman Catholic Church

Cameroon comprises four archdioceses and 17 dioceses. At 31 December 1992 there were an estimated 3,852,123 adherents, representing about 29.5% of the total population. There are several active missionary orders, and four major seminaries for African priests.

Bishops' Conference: Conférence Episcopale Nationale du Cameroun, BP 807, Garoua; tel. 27-13-53; f. 1981; Pres. Rt Rev. JEAN-BAPTISTE AMA, Bishop of Ebolowa-Kribi.

Archbishop of Bamenda: Most Rev. PAUL VERDZEKOV, Archbishop's House, BP 82, Bamenda; tel. 36-12-41; fax 36-34-87.

Archbishop of Douala: Cardinal CHRISTIAN WIYGHAN TUMI, Archevêché, BP 179, Douala; tel. 42-37-14; fax 42-18-37.

Archbishop of Garoua: Most Rev. ANTOINE NTALOU, Archevêché, BP 272, Garoua; tel. 27-13-53; fax 27-29-42.

Archbishop of Yaoundé: Most Rev. JEAN ZOA, Archevêché, BP 207, Yaoundé; tel. 21-04-83; telex 8681; fax 23-50-58.

BAHÁ'Í FAITH

National Spiritual Assembly: BP 145, Limbe; tel. 33-21-46; mems in 1,744 localities.

The Press

Restrictions on the press have been in force since 1966. In 1993 there were about 40 newspapers and other periodical publications.

DAILY

Cameroon Tribune: BP 1218, Yaoundé; tel. 30-40-12; telex 8311; fax 30-43-62; f. 1974; govt-controlled; French and English; Dir PAUL C. NDEMBIYEMBE; Editor-in-Chief EBOKEM FOMENKY; circ. 20,000.

PERIODICALS

Afrique en Dossiers: BP 1715; Yaoundé; f. 1970; French and English; Dir EBONGUE SOELLE.

Cameroon Outlook: BP 124, Limbe; f. 1969; 3 a week; independent; English; Editor JEROME F. GWELLEM; circ. 20,000.

Cameroon Panorama: BP 46, Buéa; tel. 32-22-40; f. 1962; monthly; English; Roman Catholic; Editor Sister MERCY HORGAN; circ. 4,000.

Cameroon Post: Yaoundé; weekly; English; independent; Publr PADDY MBAWA; Editor JYLIUS WAMEY; circ. 50,000.

Cameroon Times: BP 200, Limbe; f. 1960; 3 a week; English; Editor-in-Chief JEROME F. GWELLEM; circ. 12,000.

Le Combattant: Yaoundé; weekly; independent; Editor BENYIMBE JOSEPH; circ. 21,000.

Courrier Sportif du Bénin: BP 17, Douala; weekly; Dir HENRI JONG.

Dikalo: Douala; independent; weekly; Man. Editor THOMAS PATRICK YONTO.

La Gazette: BP 5485, Douala; 2 a week; Editor ABODEL KARIMOU; circ. 35,000.

The Gazette: BP 408, Limbe; tel. 33-25-67; weekly; English edn of *La Gazette*; Editor JEROME F. GWELLEM; circ. 70,000.

The Herald: BP 3659, Yaoundé; tel. 31-55-22; fax 31-81-61; weekly; English; Dir Dr BONIFACE FORBIN; circ. 8,000.

Le Jeune Observateur: Yaoundé; f. 1991; Editor JULES KOUM.

Journal Officiel de la République du Cameroun: BP 1603, Yaoundé; tel. 23-12-77; telex 8403; fortnightly; official govt notices; circ. 4,000.

Le Messagère: Douala; fortnightly; independent; Editor PIUS NJAWE; circ. 19,000.

Nleb Bekristen: Imprimerie Saint-Paul, BP 763, Yaoundé; f. 1935; fortnightly; Ewondo; Dir PASCAL BAYLON MVOE; circ. 6,000.

La Nouvelle Expression: Douala; independent; weekly; Man. Editor SEVERIN TCHOUNKEU.

Presbyterian Newsletter: BP 19, Buéa; telex 5613; quarterly.

Recherches et Études Camerounaises: BP 193, Yaoundé; monthly; publ. by Office National de Recherches Scientifiques du Cameroun.

Le Serviteur: BP 1405, Yaoundé; monthly; Protestant; Dir Pastor DANIEL AKO'O; circ. 3,000.

Le Travailleur/The Worker: BP 1610, Yaoundé; tel. 22-33-15; f. 1972; monthly; French and English; journal of Organisation

Syndicale des Travailleurs du Cameroun/Cameroon Trade Union Congress; Sec.-Gen. LOUIS SOMBES; circ. 10,000.

L'Unité: BP 867, Yaoundé; weekly; French and English.

NEWS AGENCIES

CAMNEWS: c/o SOPECAM, BP 1218, Yaoundé; Dir JEAN NGANDJEU.

Foreign Bureaux

Agence France-Presse (AFP): Villa Kamdem-Kamga, BP 229, Elig-Essono, Yaoundé; telex 8218; Correspondent RENÉ-JACQUES LIGUE.

Agencia EFE (Spain): BP 11776, Yaoundé; Correspondent ANDREU CLARET.

Xinhua (New China) News Agency (People's Republic of China): ave Joseph Omgba, BP 1583, Yaoundé; tel. 20-25-72; telex 8294; Chief Correspondent SUN XINGWEN.

Reuters (UK) and Informatsionnoye Telegrafnoye Agentstvo Rossii-Telegrafnoye Agentstvo Suverennykh Stran (ITAR–TASS) (Russia) are also represented in Cameroon.

Publishers

Centre d'Edition et de Production pour l'Enseignement et la Recherche (CEPER): BP 808, Yaoundé; tel. 22-13-23; telex 8338; f. 1977; general non-fiction, science and technology, tertiary, secondary and primary textbooks; Man. Dir JEAN CLAUDE FOUTH.

Editions Buma Kor: BP 727, Yaoundé; tel. 23-13-30; telex 8438; fax 23-07-68; f. 1977; general, children's, educational and Christian; English and French; Man. Dir B. D. BUMA KOR.

Editions Clé: BP 1501, Yaoundé; tel. 22-35-54; telex 8438; fax 23-27-09; f. 1963; African and Christian literature and studies; school textbooks; Gen. Man. COMLAN PROSPER DEH.

Editions Le Flambeau: BP 113, Yaoundé; tel. 22-36-72; f. 1977; general; Man. Dir JOSEPH NDZIE.

Editions Semences Africaines: BP 5329, Yaoundé-Nlongkak; f. 1974; fiction, history, religion, textbooks; Man. Dir PHILIPPE-LOUIS OMBEDE.

Gwellem Publications: Presbook Compound (Down Beach), BP 408, Limbe; tel. 33-25-67; f. 1983; periodicals, books and pamphlets; Dir and Editor-in-Chief JEROME F. GWELLEM.

Government Publishing Houses

Imprimerie Nationale: BP 1603, Yaoundé; tel. 23-12-77; telex 8403; Dir AMADOU VAMOULKE.

Société de Presse et d'Editions du Cameroun (SOPECAM): BP 1218, Yaoundé; tel. 30-40-12; telex 8311; fax 30-43-62; f. 1977; under the supervision of the Ministry of Communications; Dir-Gen. PAUL CÉLESTIN NDEMBIYEMBE; Man. Editor PIERRE ESSAMA ESSOMBA.

Radio and Television

In 1991 there were an estimated 1.73m. radio receivers and 279,000 television receivers in use. In 1989 a total of 32 television transmitters were in service. Television programmes from France were broadcast by the Office de Radiodiffusion—Télévision Camerounaise from early 1990.

Office de Radiodiffusion-Télévision Camerounaise (CRTV): BP 1634, Yaoundé; tel. 21-40-88; telex 8888; f. 1987 by merger; broadcasts in French and English; Pres. HENRI BANDOLO; Dir-Gen. GERVAIS MENDO ZE.

Radio Buea: POB 86, Buéa; tel. 32-26-15; programmes in English, French and 15 other local languages; Man. PETERSON CHIA YUH; Head of Station GIDEON MULU TAKA.

Radio Douala: BP 986, Douala; tel. 42-60-60; programmes in French, English, Douala, Bassa, Ewondo, Bakoko and Bamiléké; Dir BRUNO DJEM; Head of Station LINUS ONANA MVONDO.

Radio Garoua: BP 103, Garoua; tel. 27-11-67; programmes in French, Hausa, English, Foulfouldé, Arabic and Choa; Dir BELLO MALGANA; Head of Station MOUSSA EPOPA.

There are also provincial radio stations at Abong Mbang, Bafoussam, Bamenda, Bertoua, Ebolowa, Maroua and Ngaoundéré, and there is a local radio station serving Yaoundé.

Finance

(cap. = capital; res = reserves; dep. = deposits; m. = million; brs = branches; amounts in francs CFA)

BANKING

Central Bank

Banque des Etats de l'Afrique Centrale (BEAC): BP 83, Yaoundé; tel. 23-04-88; telex 8204; fax 23-33-80; f. 1973 as the central bank of issue for mem. states of the Customs and Economic Union of Central Africa (UDEAC); 6 brs in Cameroon; cap. and res 203,500m. (Jan. 1993); Gov. JEAN-FÉLIX MAMALEPOT; Dir in Cameroon SADOU HAYATOU.

Commercial Banks

Amity Bank Cameroon SA: place Joss, BP 2705, Douala; tel. 43-20-53; telex 5639; fax 43-20-46; f. 1991; cap. 479.5m. (June 1993); Pres. BERNARD TAGNE TANTSE; Dir-Gen. LAWRENCE LOWETH TASHA.

Banque Internationale pour le Commerce et l'Industrie du Cameroun (BICIC): ave Charles de Gaulle, BP 4070, Douala; tel. 42-29-65; telex 5225; fax 42-41-16; f. 1962; 64% state-owned; cap. 6,000m. (June 1992); Pres. JEAN-BAPTISTE BOKAM; Dir-Gen. ETIENNE NTSAMA; 34 brs.

Banque Méridien BIAO Cameroun SA: BP 4001, Douala; tel. 42-80-11; telex 5218; fax 42-25-48; f. 1991; 10% state-owned; cap. 6,350m. (June 1993); Pres. DR ABDOULAYE SOUAIBOU; Man. Dir CONRAD G. TEPPEMA; 26 brs.

Banque Unie de Crédit (BUC): place Elig Essono, BP 122, Yaoundé; tel. 23-15-72; telex 8879; f. 1976; state-owned; cap. 400m. (Dec. 1987); Pres. and Man. Dir GUSTAVE LELE.

International Bank of Africa Cameroon SA: blvd de la Liberté, BP 3300, Douala; tel. 42-84-22; telex 5734; fax 42-84-23; f. 1982; transferred to the private sector; cap. 3,000m.; Chair. JAMES ONOBIONO; Dir-Gen. MAROUN KHALIFE.

Société Commerciale de Banque—Crédit Lyonnais Cameroun (SCB—CLC): ave Monseigneur Vogt, BP 700, Yaoundé; tel. 23-40-05; telex 8213; fax 22-41-32; f. 1989; 35% state-owned; cap. 6,000m. (June 1992); Pres. MARTIN OKOUDA; Dir-Gen. HALILOU YERIMA BOUBAKARY; 19 brs.

Société Générale de Banques au Cameroun (SGBC): 7 rue Joss, BP 4042, Douala; tel. 42-70-10; telex 5646; fax 42-87-72; f. 1963; 26.7% state-owned; cap. 4,900m. (June 1993); Pres. AMADOU MOULIOM NJIFENJOU; Gen. Man. GASTON NGUENTI; 29 brs.

Standard Chartered Bank Cameroon SA: 57 blvd de la Liberté, BP 1784, Douala; tel. 42-36-12; telex 5858; fax 42-27-89; f. 1981; 34% state-owned; cap. 1,000m. (June 1993); Chair. EPHRAIM INONI; Vice-Pres. FERDINAND MVENG NGWEBA; 2 brs.

Development Banks

Crédit Agricole du Cameroun: ave du Maréchal Foch, BP 11801, Yaoundé; tel. 23-23-60; telex 8332; fax 22-53-74; f. 1987; 41% state-owned; cap. 4,850m. (June 1993); agricultural development bank; Chair. GILBERT ANDZE TSOUNGUI; Dir-Gen. BERND STIEHL.

Crédit Foncier du Cameroun (CFC): BP 1531, Yaoundé; tel. 22-03-73; telex 8368; fax 23-52-21; f. 1977; 70% state-owned; cap. 6,000m. (June 1992); provides financial assistance for low-cost housing; Chair. GEORGES NGANGO; Dir-Gen. SYLVESTRE NAAH ONDOA.

Crédit Industriel et Commercial: BP 1591, Yaoundé; tel. 23-16-90; telex 8395; fax 23-12-21; f. 1987; industrial development bank.

Société Nationale d'Investissement du Cameroun (SNI): place de la Poste, BP 423, Yaoundé; tel. 22-44-22; telex 8205; fax 22-39-64; f. 1964; state-owned investment and credit agency; cap. 8,500m. (June 1993); Chair. VICTOR AYISSI MVODO; Dir-Gen. ESTHER BELIBI.

Finance Institutions

Caisse Autonome d'Amortissement du Cameroun: BP 7167, Yaoundé; tel. 22-01-87; telex 8858; fax 22-01-29; Dir-Gen. ISAAC NJIEMOUN.

Caisse Commune d'Epargne et d'Investissement (CCEI): ave de la Retraite, BP 11834, Yaoundé; tel. 22-32-34; telex 8907; fax 22-17-85; cap. 1,005m. (June 1992); Pres. PAUL KAMMOGNE FOKAM.

Fonds d'Aide et de Garantie des Crédits aux Petites et Moyennes Entreprises (FOGAPE): BP 1591, Yaoundé; tel. 23-38-59; telex 8395; fax 23-12-21; Pres. BERNARD BIDIAS NGON; Dir JACQUES MVUH LAMERO.

INSURANCE

Assurances Mutuelles Agricoles du Cameroun (AMACAM): BP 962, Yaoundé; tel. 22-49-66; telex 8300; f. 1965; cap. 100m.; Pres. Samuel Ngbwa Nguele; Dir-Gen. Luc Claude Nanfa.

Caisse Nationale de Réassurances (CNR): ave Foch, BP 4180, Yaoundé; tel. 22-37-99; telex 8262; fax 23-36-80; f. 1965; all classes of reinsurance; cap. 1,000m.; Pres. Jean Keutcha; Man. Dir Antoine Ntsimi.

Compagnie Camerounaise d'Assurances et de Réassurances (CCAR): 11 rue Franqueville, BP 4068, Douala; tel. 42-31-59; telex 5341; fax 42-64-53; f. 1974; cap. 499.5m.; Pres. Yvette Chassagne; Dir Gen. Christian Le Goff.

Compagnie Nationale d'Assurances (CNA): BP 12125, Douala; tel. 42-41-25; telex 5100; fax 42-47-27; f. 1986; all classes of insurance; cap. 600m.; Chair. Théodore Ebobo; Man. Dir. Protais Ayangma Amang.

General and Equitable Assurance Cameroon Ltd (GEACAM): 56 blvd de la Liberté, BP 426, Douala; tel. 42-59-85; telex 5690; fax 42-71-03; cap. 300m.; Pres. V. A. Ngu; Man. Dir J. Chebaut.

Société Camerounaise d'Assurances et de Réassurances (SOCAR): 86 blvd de la Liberté, BP 280, Douala; tel. 42-08-38; telex 5504; fax 42-13-35; f. 1973; cap. 800m.; Chair. J. Yonta; Man. Dir J. L. Hottevart.

Société Nouvelle d'Assurances du Cameroun (SNAC): rue Manga Bell, BP 105, Douala; tel. and fax 42-92-03; telex 5745; f. 1974; all classes of insurance; cap. 700m.; Dir-Gen. Jean Chebaut.

Trade and Industry

ADVISORY BODY

Economic and Social Council: BP 1058, Yaoundé; tel. 23-24-74; telex 8275; advises the Govt on economic and social problems; comprises 150 mems and a perm. secr.; mems serve a five-year term; Pres. Luc Ayang; Sec.-Gen. François Eyok.

PRINCIPAL DEVELOPMENT ORGANIZATIONS

Caisse Française de Développement (CFD): BP 46, Yaoundé; tel. 22-23-24; telex 8301; fax 23-57-07; Dir Dominique Dordain.

Cameroon Development Corporation (CAMDEV): Bota, Limbe; tel. 33-22-51; telex 5242; fax 33-26-54; f. 1947, reorg. 1982; cap. 12,241m. francs CFA; 91.7% state-owned; statutory agricultural corpn established to acquire and develop plantations of tropical crops; operates two oil mills, four banana packing stations, three tea and seven rubber factories; Chair. Siegfried Etame Massoma; Gen. Man. Peter Mafany Musonge.

Direction Générale des Grands Travaux du Cameroun (DGTC): BP 6604, Yaoundé; tel. 22-18-03; telex 8952; fax 22-13-00; f. 1988; commissioning, implementation and supervision of public works contracts; Chair. Jean Fouman Akame; Man. Dir Michel Kowalzick.

Hévéa-Cameroun (HEVECAM): BP 1298, Douala and BP 174, Kribi; tel. 42-75-64; telex 5880; f. 1975; cap. 56,000m. francs CFA; state-owned; development of 15,000 ha rubber plantation; 4,500 employees; Pres. Nyokwedi Malonga; Man. Dir Jean Remy.

Mission d'Aménagement et d'Equipement des Terrains Urbains et Ruraux (MAETUR): BP 1248, Yaoundé; tel. 22-31-13; telex 8571; f. 1977; Pres. Léopold Ferdinand Oyono; Dir-Gen. André Mama Fouda.

Mission de Développement de la Province du Nord-Ouest (MIDENO): BP 442, Bamenda; telex 5842; Dir Andrew Waindim Ndonyi.

Mission Française de Coopération et d'Action Culturelle: BP 1616, Yaoundé; tel. 22-44-43; telex 8392; fax 22-33-96; administers bilateral aid from France; Dir Jean Boulogne.

Office Céréalier dans la Province du Nord: BP 298, Garoua; tel. 27-14-38; telex 7603; f. 1975 to combat effects of drought in northern Cameroon and stabilize cereal prices; Pres. Alhadji Mahamat; Dir-Gen. Gilbert Gourlemond.

Société de Développement du Cacao (SODECAO): BP 1651, Yaoundé; tel. 22-09-91; telex 8574; f. 1974, reorg. 1980; cap. 425m. francs CFA; development of cocoa, coffee and food crop production in the Centre-Sud province; Pres. Joseph-Charles Doumba; Dir-Gen. Valentin Nlend.

Société de Développement de l'Elevage (SODEVA): BP 50, Kousseri; cap. 50m. francs CFA; Dir Alhadji Oumarou Bakary.

Société de Développement et d'Exploitation des Productions Animales (SODEPA): BP 1410, Yaoundé; tel. 22-24-28; f. 1974; cap. 375m. francs CFA; development of livestock and livestock products; Man. Dir Etienne Engueleguele.

Société de Développement de la Haute-Vallée du Noun (UNVDA): BP 25, N'Dop and BP 83, Bamenda; f. 1978; cap. 895m. francs CFA; rice, maize and soya bean cultivation; Dir-Gen. Samuel Bawe Chi Wanki.

Société de Développement de la Riziculture dans la Plaine des Mbo (SODERIM): BP 146, Melong; f. 1977; cap. 1,535m. francs CFA; cultivation and processing of rice and other agricultural products; Pres. Conrad Eyoum Essombe; Man. Dir Joseph-Jacques Nga.

Société d'Expansion et de Modernisation de la Riziculture de Yagoua (SEMRY): BP 46, Yagoua; tel. 29-62-13; telex 7655; f. 1971; cap. 4,580m. francs CFA; commercialization of rice products and expansion of rice-growing in areas where irrigation is possible; Pres. Albert Ekono; Dir-Gen. Limangana Tori.

Société Immobilière du Cameroun (SIC): BP 387, Yaoundé; tel. 23-34-11; telex 8577; fax 22-51-19; f. 1952; cap. 1,000m. francs CFA; housing construction and development; Pres. Enoch Kwayeb; Dir-Gen. Paul Djongouane.

CHAMBERS OF COMMERCE

Chambre d'Agriculture, d'Elevage et des Forêts du Cameroun: Parc Repiquet, BP 287, Yaoundé; tel. 22-38-85; telex 8243; f. 1955; 120 mems; Pres. René Gobé; Sec.-Gen. Solomon Nfor Gwei; other chambers at Yaoundé, Bafoussam, Bamenda, Douala and Garoua.

Chambre de Commerce, d'Industrie et des Mines du Cameroun: BP 4011, Douala; tel. 42-28-88; telex 5616; f. 1963; also at BP 12206, Douala; BP 36, Yaoundé; BP 211, Limbe; BP 59, Garoua; BP 944, Bafoussam; BP 551, Bamenda; 138 mems; Pres. Pierre Tchanqué; Sec.-Gen. Saïdou Abdoulaye Bobboy.

EMPLOYERS' ASSOCIATIONS

Groupement des Femmes d'Affaires du Cameroun (GFAC): BP 1940, Douala; tel. 42-4-64; telex 6100; Pres. Françoise Foning.

Groupement Interprofessionnel pour l'Etude et la Co-ordination des Intérêts Economiques au Cameroun (GICAM): ave Konrad Adenauer, BP 1134, Yaoundé; tel. 22-27-22; telex 8286; fax 20-27-22; also at BP 829, Douala; tel. 42-31-41; f. 1957; Pres. André Siaka; Sec.-Gen. Roland Laheuguere.

Syndicat des Commerçants Importateurs-Exportateurs du Cameroun (SCIEC): 16 rue Quillien, BP 562, Douala; tel. 42-03-04; Sec.-Gen. G. Toscano.

Syndicat des Industriels du Cameroun (SYNINDUSTRICAM): 92 blvd de Liberté, BP 673, Douala; tel. 42-30-58; telex 5342; fax 21-52-86; f. 1953; Pres. Samuel Kondo Ebelle; Sec.-Gen. N. Nsomo.

Syndicat des Producteurs et Exportateurs de Bois du Cameroun: BP 570, Yaoundé; tel. 20-27-22; telex 8998; fax 20-27-22; Pres. Carlo Oriani.

Syndicat Professionnel des Entreprises du Bâtiment, des Travaux Publics et des Activités Annexes: BP 1134, Yaoundé; also at BP 660, Douala; tel. 20-27-22; telex 8998; fax 20-27-22; Pres. Paul Soppo-Priso.

Syndicats Professionnels Forestiers et Activités connexes du Cameroun: BP 100, Douala.

Union des Syndicats Professionnels du Cameroun (USPC): BP 829, Douala; Pres. Moukoko Kingue.

West Cameroon Employers' Association (WCEA): BP 97, Tiko.

PRINCIPAL CO-OPERATIVE ORGANIZATIONS

Bakweri Co-operative Union of Farmers Ltd: Dibanda, Tiko; produce marketing co-operative for bananas, cocoa and coffee; 14 socs, 2,000 mems; Pres. Dr E. M. L. Endeley.

Cameroon Co-operative Exporters Ltd: BP 19, Kumba; f. 1953; mems: 8 socs; cen. agency for marketing of mems' coffee, cocoa and palm kernels; Man. A. B. Enyong; Sec. M. M. Eyoh (acting).

Centre National de Développement des Entreprises Coopératives (CENADEC): BP 120, Yaoundé; f. 1970; promotes and organizes the co-operative movement; bureaux at BP 43, Kumba and BP 26, Bamenda; Dir Jacques Sangue.

North-West Co-operative Association Ltd (NWCA): BP 41, Bamenda; tel. 36-12-12; telex 5842; Pres. Simon Achidi Achu; Dir Dr Robert Ghogomu Tapisi.

Union Centrale des Coopératives Agricoles de l'Ouest (UCCAO): ave Samuel Wonko, BP 1002, Bafoussam; tel. 44-14-39; telex 7005; fax 44-11-01; f. 1957; marketing of cocoa and coffee; 110,000 mems; Pres. Victor Gnimpieba; Dir-Gen. Pierre Nzefa Tsachoua.

West Cameroon Co-operative Association Ltd: BP 135, Kumba; founded as cen. financing body of the co-operative movement; provides short-term credits and agricultural services to mem. socs; policy-making body for the co-operative movement in West Cameroon; 142 mem. unions and socs with total membership of c. 45,000; Pres. Chief T. E. NJEA; Sec. M. M. QUAN.

There are 83 co-operatives for the harvesting and sale of bananas and coffee and for providing mutual credit.

MAJOR INDUSTRIAL COMPANIES

The following are some of the largest companies in terms of either capital investment or employment:

ALUCAM, Camerounaise de l'Aluminium: BP 54, Edéa; tel. 46-43-11; telex 5223; fax 42-47-74; f. 1954; cap. 17,388m. francs CFA; 39% state-owned; manufacture of aluminium by electrolysis using imported alumina; Pres. MAURICE LAPARRA; Man. Dir M. MALONG.

Cameroon Sugar Co, Inc (CAMSUCO): BP 1462, Yaoundé; tel. 23-09-56; telex 8309; f. 1975; cap. 10,691m. francs CFA; sugar plantations, refining and marketing; Pres. SALOMON ELOGO METOMO; Gen. Man. JOSEPH ZAMBO.

Céramiques Industrielles du Cameroun (CERICAM): BP 2033, Douala; tel. 42-37-71; telex 5637; f. 1969; cap. 1,200m. francs CFA; 20% state-owned; production of ceramic tiles, enamelled mosaics, etc.; Dir-Gen. MICHELANGELO BALDUCCI.

Cimenteries du Cameroun (CIMENCAM): BP 1323, Douala; tel. 39-11-19; telex 5325; fax 39-09-84; f. 1965; cap. 5,600m. francs CFA; cement works at Figuil and clinker-crushing plant at Douala-Bonabéri; Pres. ADAMA MODI; Dir-Gen. PIERRE REGENET.

Contreplaqués du Cameroun (COCAM): BP 154, Mbalmayo; tel. 28-11-20; telex 8242; fax 28-14-20; f. 1966; cap. 2,489m. francs CFA; 89% state-owned, of which 49% by Société nationale d'investissement du Cameroun; development of forest resources, production of plywood and slatted panels; Pres. PATRICE MANDENG; Dir-Gen. RAYMOND VINCENT ATAGANA ABENA.

Cotonnière Industrielle du Cameroun (CICAM): BP 7012, Douala-Bassa; tel. 42-62-15; telex 5253; fax 42-28-30; f. 1965; cap. 2,137m. francs CFA; factory for bleaching, printing and dyeing of cotton at Douala; Pres. ESTHER DANG; Dir-Gen. MICHEL VIALLET; 1,000 employees.

Dumez Camindustrie: BP 3476, Douala; tel. 42-79-24; telex 5883; f. 1982; cap. 1,250m. francs CFA; mfrs of construction materials; Pres. ANDRÉ KAMEL.

Les Grandes Huileries Camerounaises: Zone Industrielle de Bassa, BP 1642, Douala; f. 1982; cap. 1,400m. francs CFA; 50% state-owned; Pres. Alhadji BACHIROU; Man. Dir ERIC JACOBSEN.

Guinness Cameroun SA: BP 1213, Douala; tel. 40-27-58; telex 5327; fax 40-71-82; f. 1967; cap. 1,920m. francs CFA; production and marketing of beers; Chair. and Man. Dir G. V. HORNE; 927 employees.

International Brasseries (IB): BP 4237, Douala; cap. 2,400m. francs CFA; 34% owned by Heineken (Netherlands); mfrs of beer; Dir-Gen. PHILIPPE MATHIEU.

Nouvelles Brasseries Africaines (NOBRA): BP 2280, Douala; tel. 42-85-03; telex 5291; f. 1979; cap. 7,000m. francs CFA; mfrs of soft drinks; Pres. PIERRE TCHANQUE; Dir-Gen. ANDERS ANDERSEN.

Société Africaine Forestière et Agricole du Cameroun (SAFACAM): BP 100, Douala; tel. 42-97-58; fax 42-25-12; f. 1897; cap. 1,820m. francs CFA; plantation of natural rubber and production of rubber and latex; rubber and palm plantations at Dizangué; Pres. JACQUES ROULAND; Man. Dir PIERRE COOMANS; 1,900 employees.

Société Anonyme des Brasseries du Cameroun (SABC): BP 4036, Douala; tel. 42-91-33; telex 5305; fax 42-79-45; f. 1948; cap. 10,102m. francs CFA; production of beer and soft drinks; Dir Gen. ANDRÉ SIAKA; 2,631 employees.

Société Bernabe Cameroun SARL: BP 529, Douala; tel. 42-96-22; telex 5350; fax 42-50-33; f. 1950; cap. 1,276m. francs CFA; mfrs of metal goods, hardware and construction materials; Pres. ANDRÉ NICOLAS; Man. Dir GÉRARD BOUYER.

Société Camerounaise des Dépôts Pétroliers (SCDP): rue de la Cité Chardy, BP 2271, Douala; tel. 40-54-45; telex 5609; fax 40-47-96; f. 1978; cap. 3,500m. francs CFA; storage and distribution of Cameroon petroleum; Pres. BERNARD MOUDIO; Dir JEAN-BAPTISTE NGUINI EFFA.

Société Camerounaise de Fabrication de Piles Electriques (PILCAM): BP 1916, Douala; tel. 42-26-28; telex 5712; f. 1970; cap. 1,472m. francs CFA; Pres. VICTOR FOTSO; Dir ANDRÉ FONTANA; 745 employees.

Société Camerounaise de Métallurgie (SCDM): BP 706, Douala; tel. 42-42-56; telex 5316; fax 42-01-85; f. 1984; cap. 1,475m. francs CFA; steel processors and mfrs of metal products; Man. Dir ALAIN GILBERT-DESVALLONS.

La Société Camerounaise de Minoteries: BP 785, Douala; tel. 42-75-01; telex 5573; fax 42-17-61; f. 1986; cap. 1,000m. francs CFA; flour mill; Pres. BABA AHMADOU; Dir-Gen. NGOH LAMBERT.

Société Camerounaise de Palmeraies (SOCAPALM): blvd Leclerc, BP 691, Douala; tel. 42-81-38; telex 5576; f. 1968; cap. 9,470m. francs CFA; 68.1% state-owned; management of palm plantations and production of palm oil and manufactured products; Chair. JEAN-BAPTISTE YONKEU; Gen. Man. ROBERT MBELLA MBAPPE.

Société Camerounaise de Sacherie (SCS): Zone Industrielle de Bassa, BP 398, Douala; tel. 42-31-04; telex 5608; f. 1971; cap. 2,075m. francs CFA; 39% owned by ONCPB; production of sacks; Pres. GUILLAUME NSEKE; Dir THOMAS DAKAYI KAMGA.

Société Camerounaise des Tabacs (SCT): rue Joseph-Clerc, BP 29, Yaoundé; tel. 22-14-88; telex 8567; f. 1964; cap. 1,750m. francs CFA; tobacco cultivation and curing; Pres. PHILÉMON ADJIBOLO; Man. Dir LUCIEN KINGUE EBONGUE.

Société Camerounaise de Transformation de l'Aluminium (SOCATRAL): BP 291, Edéa; tel. 46-40-24; telex 5223; fax 46-47-74; f. 1960; cap. 750m. francs CFA; 49% owned by ALUCAM (q.v.); production of corrugated sheets, aluminium strips and rolled discs; Pres. M. CHARDON; Dir-Gen. M. NDIORO.

Société Camerounaise de Verrerie (SOCAVER): BP 1456, Douala; tel. 42-64-03; telex 6096; f. 1966; cap. 4,354m. francs CFA; 37% owned by SABC (q.v.); mfrs of glassware; Pres. MICHEL HUAS; Man. Dir CLAUDE PELLETREAU.

Société de Développement du Coton au Cameroun (SODECOTON): BP 302, Garoua; tel. 27-10-80; telex 7617; f. 1974; cap. 4,529m. francs CFA; 70% state-owned; cotton ginning and production of cottonseed oil; Pres. Alhadji MAHAMAT; Man. Dir MOHAMED IYA.

Société ELF de Recherches et d'Exploitation des Pétroles du Cameroun (ELF–SEREPCA): 83 blvd de la Liberté, BP 2214, Douala-Bassa; tel. 42-17-85; telex 5299; fax 42-13-66; f. 1951; cap. 1,000m. francs CFA; 20% state-owned; prospecting and exploitation of offshore petroleum; Pres. JEAN LOUIS VERMEULEN; Dir-Gen. MICHEL CHARLES.

Société Forestière et Industrielle de Belabo (SOFIBEL): BP 1762, Yaoundé; tel. 23-26-57; telex 5834; f. 1975; cap. 1,902m. francs CFA; 39% state-owned; sawmill; mfrs of plywood; Pres. SADOU DAOUDOU; Man. Dir DENIS KEEDI ATOK.

Société Générale des Travaux Métalliques (GETRAM): BP 3693, Douala; tel. 42-80-68; telex 5206; fax 42-77-61; f. 1980; cap. 1,200m. francs CFA; Pres. BERNARD MOUNDIO; Dir-Gen. OLIVIER BOUYGUES.

Société Industrielle Camerounaise des Cacaos (SIC CACAOS): BP 570, Douala; tel. 40-37-95; telex 5201; f. 1949; cap. 1,147.5m. francs CFA; production of cocoa and cocoa butter; Pres. JEAN-MARC DIEUDONNÉ OYONO; Man. Dir YVES SCHMUCK.

Société Industrielle des Tabacs du Cameroun (SITABAC): BP 1105, Douala; tel. 42-49-19; telex 6147; fax 42-59-49; cap. 2,641m. francs CFA; manufacture and sale of cigarettes; Pres. and Dir-Gen. JAMES ONOBIONO.

Société Nationale des Eaux du Cameroun (SNEC): BP 157, Douala; tel. 42-87-11; telex 5265; fax 42-29-45; f. 1967; cap. 6,500m. francs CFA; 73% state-owned, 22% by Société Nationale d'Electricité du Cameroun; production, storage and distribution of drinking water; Pres. AMADOU ALI; Dir-Gen. CLÉMENT OBOUH FEGUE; 2,340 employees.

Société Nationale d'Electricité du Cameroun (SONEL): 63 ave du Général de Gaulle, BP 4077, Douala; tel. 42-54-44; telex 5551; fax 42-22-47; f. 1974; 93.1% state-owned, 6.9% held by Caisse Française de Developpement; cap. 30,000m.; Pres. JEAN FALMAN AKAME; Dir-Gen. MARCEL NIAT NJIFENJI.

Société Nationale des Hydrocarbures (SNH): BP 955, Yaoundé; tel. 22-19-10; telex 8514; f. 1980; cap. 1,000m. francs CFA; national petroleum co; Pres. EDOUARD AKAME MFOUMOU; Dir-Gen. JEAN ASSOUMOU.

Société Nationale de Raffinage (SONARA): BP 365, Cap Limboh, Limbé; tel. 33-22-38; telex 5561; fax 42-41-99; f. 1976; cap. 17,800m. francs CFA; 66% state-owned; establishment and operation of petroleum refinery at Cap Limboh; Chair. ANDRÉ BOTTO À NGON; Gen. Man. BERNARD EDING; 527 employees.

Société de Palmeraies de la Ferme Suisse (SPFS): BP 06, Edéa-Ongué; tel. 42-34-18; telex 5745; f. 1976; cap. 1,525m. francs CFA; cultivation of products for industrial processing, operates factory for processing palm oil and palm kernels; Pres. and Man. Dir PHILIPPE PIECHAUD; Man. YVON LE FLOCH (acting).

Société Shell du Cameroun: BP 4082, Douala; tel. 42-24-15; telex 5221; fax 42-60-31; f. 1954; cap. 2,800,000m. francs CFA; import and distribution of petroleum products; Pres. and Dir-Gen. JAAP HOOGCARSPEL.

Société Sucrière du Cameroun (SOSUCAM): BP 857, Yaoundé; tel. 22-07-99; telex 8323; f. 1965; cap. 2,500m. francs CFA; 24% state-owned; sugar refinery at M'bandjock; Man. Dir. LOUIS YINDA.

Société des Tabacs, Cigares et Cigarettes J. Bastos de l'Afrique Centrale (SBAC): BP 94, Yaoundé; tel. 21-08-75; telex 8212; fax 20-04-00; f. 1946; cap. 3,290.9m. francs CFA; 93% owned by British American Tobacco; production of tobacco and manufacture of cigarettes; Pres. RICHARD HOWE; Dir TONY WILLIAM REID.

Société Textile du Cameroun pour le Linge de Maison (SOLICAM): BP 2413, Douala; tel. 42-97-20; telex 6024; f. 1979; cap. 3,000m. francs CFA; textile complex; Pres. SIMON NGANNYON; Dir-Gen. MICHEL VIALLET.

Total Cameroun: rue de la Cité Chardy, BP 4048, Douala; tel. 42-63-41; telex 5264; f. 1947; cap. 1,646m. francs CFA; exploration for, exploitation and distribution of petroleum reserves; Pres. J. GOUBEAU; Dir P. THIBAUD.

TRADE UNION FEDERATION

Confédération Syndicale des Travailleurs du Cameroun (CSTC): BP 1610, Yaoundé; tel. 23-00-47; f. 1985; fmrly the Union National des Travailleurs du Cameroun (UNTC); Pres. DOMINIQUE FOUDA IMAH; Sec.-Gen. ANDRE-JULES MOUSSENI.

Transport

RAILWAYS

There are some 1,104 km of track, the West Line running from Douala to Nkongsamba (166 km) with a branch line leading south-west from Mbanga to Kumba (29 km), and the Transcameroon railway which runs from Douala to Ngaoundéré (885 km), with a branch line from Ngoumou to Mbalmayo (30 km).

Office du Chemin de Fer Transcamerounais: BP 625, Yaoundé; tel. 22-44-33; telex 8293; supervises the laying of new railway lines and improvements to existing lines, and undertakes relevant research; Dir-Gen. LUC TOWA FOTSO.

Régie Nationale des Chemins de Fer du Cameroun (REGIFERCAM): BP 304, Douala; tel. 40-60-45; telex 5607; fax 42-32-05; f. 1947; rehabilitation programme announced 1989; Chair. SAMUEL EBOUA; Man. Dir SAMUEL MINKO.

ROADS

In 1991 there were an estimated 70,570 km of roads (including 7,720 km of main roads and 14,450 km of secondary roads), of which about 3,750 km were paved. In 1991 the African Development Bank approved a loan of $125m. towards the construction of a further 136 km of tarred roads.

SHIPPING

There are seaports at Kribi and Limbe/Tiko, a river port at Garoua, and an estuary port at Douala-Bonabéri, the principal port and main outlet, which has 2,510 m of quays and a minimum depth of 5.8 m in the channels, 8.5 m at the quays. In 1988 the port handled 3.8m. metric tons of cargo. Total handling capacity is 7m. metric tons annually. Plans are under way to increase the annual capacity of the container terminal from 1.5m. tons to 2m. tons.

Cameroon Shipping Lines SA (CAMSHIPLINES): Centre des Affaires Maritimes, 18 rue Joffre, BP 4054, Douala; tel. 42-00-38; telex 5615; fax 42-01-14; f. 1975; cap. 6,136m. francs CFA; 67% state-owned; 6 vessels trading with western Europe, USA, Far East and Africa; Chair. FRANÇOIS SENGAT KUO; Man. Dir RENÉ MBAYEN.

Compagnie Maritime Camerounaise SA (CMC): Douala.

Conseil National des Chargeurs du Cameroun (CNCC): BP 1588, Douala; tel. 42-32-06; telex 5669; fax 42-89-01; f. 1986; cap. 800m. francs CFA; promotion of the maritime sector; Gen. Man. GUSTAVE TCHETGEN.

Delmas Cameroun: rue Kitchener, BP 263, Douala; tel. 42-47-50; telex 5222; fax 42-88-51; f. 1977; cap. 6,000m. francs CFA; Pres. JEAN-GUY LE FLOCH; Dir-Gen. DANY CHUTAUX.

Office National des Ports/National Ports Authority: Centre des Affaires Maritimes, 18 rue Joffre, BP 4020, Douala; tel. 42-01-77; telex 5270; fax 42-67-97; f. 1971; cap. 12,040m. francs CFA; Chair. ISSA TCHIROMA BAKARY; Gen. Man. TCHOUTA MOUSSA.

Société Africaine de Transit et d'Affrètement (SATA): Vallée Tokoto, BP 546, Douala; tel. 42-82-09; telex 5239; f. 1950; cap. 625m. francs CFA; Man. Dir RAYMOND PARIZOT.

Société Agence Maritime de l'Ouest Africain Cameroun (SAMOA): 5 blvd de la Liberté, BP 1127, Douala; tel. 42-16-80; telex 5256; f. 1953; cap. 24m. francs CFA; agents for Lloyd Triestino, Gold Star Line, OT Africa Line, Spliethoff, Van Uden, Deco Line, Compagnie Maritime Camerounaise; Dir JEAN PERRIER.

Société Camerounaise de Manutention et d'Acconage (SOCAMAC): BP 284, Douala; tel. 42-40-51; telex 5537; f. 1976; cap. 1,114m. francs CFA; freight handling; Pres. MOHAMADOU TALBA; Dir-Gen. HARRY J. GHOOS.

Société Camerounaise de Transport et d'Affrètement (SCTA): BP 974, Douala; tel. 42-17-24; telex 6181; f. 1951; cap. 100m. francs CFA; Pres. JACQUES VIAULT; Dir-Gen. GONTRAN FRAUCIEL.

Société Ouest-Africaine d'Entreprises Maritimes—Cameroun (SOAEM—Cameroon): 5 blvd de la Liberté, BP 4057, Douala; tel. 42-52-69; telex 5220; fax 42-05-18; f. 1959; cap. 1,927m. francs CFA; Pres. JACQUES COLOMBANI; Man. Dir JEAN-LOUIS GRECIET.

Société de Transports Urbains du Cameroun (SOTUC): BP 1697, Yaoundé; tel. 21-38-07; telex 8330; fax 20-77-84; f. 1973; cap. 3,100m. francs CFA; 58% owned by Société Nationale d'Investissement du Cameroun; operates urban transport services in Yaoundé and Douala; Dir-Gen. MARCEL YONDO; Mans JEAN-VICTOR OUM (Yaoundé), GABRIEL VASSEUR (Douala).

SOCOPAO (Cameroun): BP 215, Douala; tel. 42-64-64; telex 5252; f. 1951; cap. 1,440m. francs CFA; agents for Palm/Elder/Hoegh Lines, Bank Line, CNAN, CNN, Comanav, Comasersa, Dafra Line, Grand Pale, Marasia SA, Maritima del Norte, Navcoma, Nigerian Shipping Line, Niven Line, Splosna Plovba, Rossis Maritime, SSSIM, Veb Deutsche Seereederei, Polish Ocean Lines, Westwind Africa Line, Nautilus Keller Line, Estonian Shipping Co, AGTI Paris, K-Line Tokyo; Pres. VINCENT BOLLORE; Man. Dir E. DUPUY.

Transcap Cameroun: BP 4059, Douala; tel. 42-72-14; telex 5247; f. 1960; cap. 342m. francs CFA; Pres. RENÉ DUPRAZ; Man. Dir MICHEL BARDOU.

CIVIL AVIATION

There are international airports at Douala, Garoua, Yaoundé and Bafoussam. There are 39 smaller airports and aerodromes.

Cameroon Airlines (Cam-Air): 3 ave du Général de Gaulle, BP 4092, Douala; tel. 42-25-25; telex 5345; f. 1971; 75% govt-owned and 25% by Air France; domestic flights and services to Africa and Europe; rehabilitation programme announced 1989; Chair. PAUL TESSA; Dir-Gen. CLAUDE KIENTZ.

Tourism

Tourists are attracted by the cultural diversity of local customs, and by the national parks, game reserves and sandy beaches. In 1990 an estimated 99,157 tourists visited Cameroon. In that year receipts from tourism totalled an estimated US $21m.

Société Camerounaise de Tourisme (SOCATOUR): BP 7138, Yaoundé; tel. 23-32-19; telex 8766; Pres. ABDOULAYE SOUAIBOU; Dir-Gen. MARC CHO NKWENTI.

Defence

In June 1993 Cameroon had an army of 6,600, a navy of 1,200 and an airforce of 300. Paramilitary forces numbered some 4,000. France has a bilateral defence agreement with Cameroon.

Defence Expenditure: Budgeted at 47,800m. francs CFA for 1991/92.

Commander-in-Chief of the Armed Forces: PAUL BIYA.

Education

Since independence, Cameroon has achieved one of the highest rates of school attendance in Africa, but provision of educational facilities varies according to region. Education, which is bilingual, is provided by the government, missionary societies and private concerns. Education in state schools is available free of charge, and the government provides financial assistance for other schools.

Primary education begins at six years of age. It lasts for six years in Eastern Cameroon (where it is officially compulsory), and for seven years in Western Cameroon. Secondary education, beginning at the age of 12 or 13, lasts for a further seven years, comprising two cycles of four years and three years in Eastern Cameroon, and of five years and two years in Western Cameroon. In 1989 an estimated 76% of children in the relevant age-group were enrolled at primary schools (82% of boys; 71% of girls). In 1990 secondary enrolment was equivalent to 28%

of children in the appropriate age-group (32% of boys; 23% of girls). In 1990, according to estimates by UNESCO, the average rate of adult illiteracy was 45.9% (males 33.4%; females 57.4%). The State University at Yaoundé, which was established in 1962, has been decentralized, and consists of five regional campuses, each devoted to a different field of study. In the budget for 1991/92 education was allocated 70,770m. francs CFA (22.7% of total projected current expenditure).

Bibliography

Bandolo, H. *La flamme et la fumée*. Yaoundé, Editions SOPECAM, 1988.

Bayart, J.-F. *L'Etat au Cameroun*. Paris, Presses de la Fondation Nationale des Sciences Politiques, 1985.

Belinga, E. *Cameroun: La Révolution pacifique du 20 mai*. Yaoundé, 1976.

Beti, M. *Lutte ouverte aux Camerounais*. Rouen, Editions des peuples noirs, 1986.

Biya, P. *Communal Liberalism*. London, Macmillan, 1987.

Biyiti bi Essam, J.-P. *Cameroun: Complots et Bruits de Bottes*. Paris, Harmattan, 1984.

Bouchaud, J. *La Côte du Cameroun dans l'histoire et la cartographie des origins à l'annexion allemande*. Yaoundé, Centre IFAN, 1952.

Cruise O'Brien, D. B., Dunn, J., and Rathbone, R. *Contemporary West African States*. Cambridge University Press, 1989.

De Lancey, M. W. *Cameroon: Dependence and Independence*. Westview Press, Boulder, CO, 1989.

De Lancey, M. W., and Schraeder, P. J. *Cameroon*. Oxford, Clio, 1986.

Donnat, G. *Afin que nul l'oublie*. Paris, Harmattan, 1986.

Epale, S. J. *Plantations and Development in Western Cameroon 1875–1975: A Study in Agrarian Capitalism*. New York, Vantage Press, 1985.

Eyinga, A. *Introduction à la politique camerounaise*. Paris, Harmattan, 1984.

Gabriel, R. *L'Administration publique camerounaise*. Paris, Librairie Générale de Droit et de Jurisprudence, 1986.

Gaillard, P. *Le Cameroun*. Paris, Editions L'Harmattan, 1989.

Hugon, P. *Analyse du sous-développement en Afrique noire: L'example de l'economie du Cameroun*. Paris, Presses Universitaires de France, 1968.

Joseph, R. A. *Radical Nationalism in Cameroon*. London, Oxford University Press, 1977.

Koenig, E. L., Chia, E., and Povey, J. (Eds). *A Socio-Linguistic Profile of Urban Centers in Cameroon*. Los Angeles, UCLA (Crossroads Press), 1983.

Konings, P. *Labour Resistance in Cameroon*. London, Currey, 1993.

Kuoh, C.-T. *Mon témoinage—Le Cameroun de l'indépendance, 1958–1970*. Paris, Editions Karthala, 1990.

Le Vine, V. T. and Nye, R. *Historical Dictionary of Cameroon*. Metuchen, NJ, Scarecrow Press, 1974.

Marc, A. *La Politique économique de l'Etat britannique dans la Région du Sud-Cameroon, 1920–60*. Paris, 1985.

Mbembe, J. A. *Ruben Um Nyobé: Le Problème national kamerunais*. Paris, Harmattan, 1984.

Ngoh, V. J. *Cameroon 1884–1985: A Hundred Years of History*. Yaoundé, Imprimerie Nationale, 1988.

Ngongo, L. *Histoire des forces religieuses au Cameroun*. Paris, Editions Karthala, 1982.

Ngwa, J. A. *A New Geography of Cameroon*. 2nd Edn, London, Longman, 1979.

Prévitali, S. *Le Cameroun par les ponts et par les routes*. Paris, Editions Karthala, 1988.

Schatzberg, M. G., and Zartmann, W. *The Political Economy of Cameroon*. New York, Praeger, 1986.

Stoecker, H. (Ed.). *German Imperialism in Africa*. London, Hurst Humanities, 1986.

Zeltner, J.-C., and Torneux, H. *L'arabe dans le bassin du Tchad*. Paris, Editions Karthala, 1986.

CAPE VERDE

Physical and Social Geography

RENÉ PÉLISSIER

The island Republic of Cape Verde, comprising 10 islands, of which nine are inhabited, and five islets, lies about 500 km west of Dakar, in the Atlantic Ocean. The archipelago comprises the windward islands of Santo Antão (754 sq km), São Vicente (228 sq km), Santa Luzia (34 sq km), São Nicolau (342 sq km), Boa Vista (622 sq km), and Sal (215 sq km) to the north, while to the south lie the leeward islands of Maio (267 sq km), Santiago (992 sq km), Fogo (477 sq km) and Brava (65 sq km).

The total area is 4,033 sq km (1,557 sq miles) and the administrative capital is Cidade de Praia (population of 62,000 at 1990 census) on Santiago Island. The other main centre of population is Mindelo (São Vicente), with 47,000 inhabitants in 1990, which is the foremost port and, with Praia, the economic centre of the archipelago. The 1990 census recorded a total population of 341,491 (84.7 inhabitants per sq km). Santiago is the most populous of the 10 main islands, with 175,000 inhabitants in 1990, followed by São Vicente (51,000), Santo Antão (44,000) and Fogo (34,000).

Except for the low-lying islands of Sal, Boa Vista and Maio, the archipelago is mountainous, craggy and deeply furrowed by erosion and volcanic activity. The highest point is Mt Fogo (2,829 m), an active volcano. Located in the semi-arid belt, the islands have an anaemic hydrography, and suffer from chronic shortages of rainfall, which, coupled with high temperatures (yearly average 22°–26° C at Praia), cause catastrophic droughts which have periodically devastated the islands, and since independence drought conditions have necessitated heavy dependence on international food aid, which accounts for most of Cape Verde's food requirements. A desalination plant in São Vicente serves the needs of Mindelo, which is otherwise without drinkable water.

Ethnically, about 71% of the inhabitants are of mixed descent, except on Santiago, where the majority is of pure African stock. Whites represent about 1% of the population. The vernacular is a creole Portuguese (*Crioulo*), which is influenced by African vocabulary, syntax and pronunciation. Illiteracy is still prevalent. In 1992 the average life expectancy at birth was 60 years for men and 64 years for women.

Since independence, a significant number of islanders have emigrated, principally to the USA, the Netherlands, Italy and Portugal, where Cape Verdeans have replaced Portuguese migrants to other countries of the European Community. In 1989 an estimated 700,000 Cape Verdeans were living abroad, and their remittances to the country formed an important source of development capital.

Recent History

JONATHAN GREPNE

Based on an earlier article by MILES SMITH-MORRIS

The Cape Verde islands were colonized by Portugal in the 15th century. In the movement during the 1950s for liberation from Portuguese rule, Cape Verde was linked with the mainland territory of Portuguese Guinea (now Guinea-Bissau) under a unified nationalist movement, the Partido Africano da Independência do Guiné e Cabo Verde (PAIGC). At Guinea-Bissau's independence in September 1974, however, the PAIGC leadership in Cape Verde decided to pursue its claims separately, rather than to seek an immediate federation with Guinea-Bissau, with which there were few unifying factors other than a common colonial heritage. In December 1974 the Portuguese government and representatives of the islands' PAIGC formed a transitional administration, from which members of other political parties were excluded. Elections to a national people's assembly took place in June 1975, with independence, as the Republic of Cape Verde, following on 5 July. Aristides Pereira, the secretary-general of the PAIGC, became the republic's first president. In 1980 the PAIGC was constitutionally established as the sole legal party, and in November of the same year prospects of unification with Guinea-Bissau were extinguished when Luis Cabral, the president of Guinea-Bissau (and himself a Cape Verdean), was removed in a *coup d'état*. At the beginning of 1981 the Cape Verdean branch of the PAIGC held a special congress at which the party renamed itself the Partido Africano da Independência de Cabo Verde (PAICV).

PEREIRA AND THE PAIGC, 1975–91

Cape Verde's political affairs have long been secondary to the islands' struggle for physical survival amid geographical and economic pressures that are perhaps unequalled in intensity anywhere else in the world. Substantial infusions of foreign aid (from sources including the EC, the USA, certain Arab states and, until the late 1980s, the former Eastern bloc countries) have been augmented by remittances from Cape Verdeans resident overseas (whose numbers greatly exceed those living in the country). While heavily reliant on periods of remission from persistent drought as well as on sustained international support, the government and people of Cape Verde have not been inactive. A dual strategy of agrarian reform and construction has been pursued, in an attempt to increase the country's agricultural capacity. In 1983 an agrarian reform law came into force, by which the government intended to dispossess absentee landlords. Although pre-legislation discussions had elicited some opposition, and even rioting, the government was not deflected from its course. It also made efforts to ensure that the land reforms were implemented with due regard to local conditions and with a minimum of bureaucracy (In 1993 the agrarian reform law was revoked by the MPD administration with considerable public support). Simultaneously, an ambitious programme of dike-construction and tree-planting was implemented, so that the islands' capacity for water-retention would be much increased. This generated considerable popular enthusiasm, which indicated favourable prospects for both the economic and political future of the country.

Since forecasts were made, in 1985, that the population of Cape Verde would reach 500,000 by the year 2000, the government made the promotion of birth control a priority during its second National Development Plan (1986–90), and aimed to reduce the average number of children per family from 6.3 to 4.7 by the year 2000. In July 1987 the national assembly approved legislation to legalize abortion, despite concerted opposition by the Roman Catholic Church. Tension developed, and 16 people were arrested following public demonstrations. In January 1993 the government announced that a referendum would be held that year on whether to revoke the legislation on abortion, but later withdrew the decision. Two motions to revoke the legislation, introduced by a small cross-party group of legislators, were unsuccessful in that year.

Although Cape Verde was, until September 1990, a one-party state (see below), government policies were generally pragmatic and sensitive, and in the mid-1980s non-PAICV members began to take an increasingly prominent role in public life. The requirement of civil servants to swear an oath of allegiance to the principles of the PAICV was abandoned, and three prominent Cape Verdean businessmen, who were not members of the PAICV, successfully sought election to the national people's assembly in December 1985. Control of the economy was eased, to allow a greater degree of private economic initiative, and in mid-1989 the government introduced legislation to encourage Cape Verdeans abroad to become involved in the process of development.

In a government reshuffle in January 1986, following the re-election of President Pereira by the national assembly for a further five-year term, most ministers and senior officials retained their posts, but several functions were redistributed: in particular, all aspects of economic management were centralized in the prime minister's office.

The government was reorganized in March 1988, when the main economic ministries were restructured. In October *Voz di Povo*, the state-controlled newspaper, published a manifesto signed by 24 lawyers, alleging that the government was failing to respect human rights. Later in that month the newspaper published a further document, signed by 24 judges, denying the allegations. In a ministerial reshuffle in December, the minister of foreign affairs, rural development and fisheries, and the minister of national education were replaced.

In February 1989 President Pereira returned from a month's convalescence, following a heart attack, to resume his role as a mediator in negotiations involving Namibian independence and the Angolan civil war, and in a maritime border dispute between Senegal and Guinea-Bissau. Relations with Portugal were enhanced by exchanges of ministerial visits in 1988 and 1989, and visits to Portugal by both Pereira and the prime minister, Gen. Pedro Pires, in 1990. In 1989 Cape Verde signed a civil aviation security agreement with the USA.

Moves towards a relaxation of the PAICV's political monopoly became apparent in early 1990, as Cape Verde became affected both by political changes in west Africa and by those overtaking the Eastern Bloc. A party congress held in November 1988 included discussions on constitutional reforms to end the supremacy of the ruling party, as well as on economic liberalization. In November 1989 two political commissions were established, to regulate legislative elections and to consider proposals for constitutional revision. Local elections, scheduled for 1990, were postponed until 1991 to allow the organization of legislative elections in the same year. The postponement was opposed by the influential Roman Catholic newspaper *Terra Nova*, which accused the government of perpetuating the imbalance of power.

In February 1990, in an apparent response to increasing pressure from church and academic circles, the PAICV announced the convening of an emergency congress to discuss the possible abolition of the constitutional provision which guaranteed the supremacy of the PAICV. In April a newly-formed political organization, the Movimento para a Democracia (MPD), issued a manifesto in Paris, which urged the immediate introduction of a multi-party system. Pereira subsequently announced that the next presidential election, which was planned for December 1990, would be held, for the first time, on the basis of universal adult suffrage.

The tempo of opposition activity on the islands increased in May 1990, with the presentation of a petition to the president of the national people's assembly, appealing for an immediate end to the single-party system of government. Later in the month, Pereira announced that he would retire as secretary-general of the PAICV at the party congress in July, intending to place himself above the fray of political campaigning in a future multi-party system. At the first public meeting of the MPD, held in Praia on 2 June, the movement's co-ordinator, Carlos Veiga, stated that the MPD was prepared to negotiate with the PAICV for a transition to political plurality. Participants at the meeting demanded immediate constitutional reform, the disbanding of the political police, the separation of the army from the PAICV and the holding of legislative elections prior to the presidential election.

Some of the opposition's demands were fulfilled in the following month. On 4 July 1990 Pereira announced that legislative elections would be held on a multi-party basis before the end of 1990. A cabinet reshuffle later in the month involved the creation of seven new state secretariats and the abolition of the ministry of the armed forces and security, with Pires assuming the new portfolio of minister of defence. The PAICV congress, which opened on 25 July, reviewed proposals for the termination of the one-party political system and elected Pires as secretary-general, in succession to Pereira.

On 28 September 1990 Cape Verde officially became a multi-party state, with the approval by the national people's assembly of the constitutional amendment abolishing the PAICV's monopoly of power. No limit was placed on the number of parties that could be registered, although it was stipulated that they should not be based on religious affiliation or purely regional interests. The assembly announced that legislative elections would be held in January 1991, with the presidential election to follow before the end of February. Following the announcement the MPD were formally registered, however an application made by the União Caboverdiana Independente e Democrática (UCID), led by John Wahnon, was rejected. The UCID, founded in 1974 and subsequently active mainly abroad (particularly among Cape Verdeans resident in the USA, Portugal and the Netherlands), subsequently announced that it was to co-operate with the MPD in the forthcoming elections. The MPD held its first congress in Praia on 3–4 November, at which Veiga was elected party chairman. It later announced that the party would endorse the candidacy of António Manuel Mascarenhas Gomes Monteiro, a former supreme court judge, for the presidency. On 13 November Pereira confirmed that he would seek re-election as president.

MASCARENHAS AND THE MPD

The legislative elections held on 13 January 1991, which were the first multi-party elections to take place in lusophone Africa, resulted in a decisive victory for the MPD, which secured 56 of the 79 seats in the national assembly. The PAICV held the remaining 23 seats. Pires submitted the resignation of his government on 15 January and announced the commitment of the PAICV to adopt a constructive role in opposition to the MPD. On 26 January Veiga was sworn in as prime minister at the head of an interim government, mostly comprising members of the MPD, pending the result of the presidential election. This was duly held on 17 February, and resulted in a decisive victory for Mascarenhas, who secured 73.5% of the votes cast. The new president was sworn in on 22 March, and a new government was officially inaugurated on 4 April. In his initial statements of the new government's policies, Veiga promised to curb public spending and to improve the poor living conditions which affect the majority of the population. Cape Verde would continue to follow a non-aligned foreign policy. In the economic sphere, Veiga cited fishing, tourism and service industries as areas for development priority.

The new government announced plans to redraft the constitution to include provision for fundamental human rights and a market economy, and it also established a commission to prepare a new national anthem and national flag. In August 1991, Dr David Hoppfer Almada, a deputy of the national assembly and former minister for information and culture under the PAICV government, resigned from the PAICV and declared himself independent, reducing the number of PAICV deputies in the national assembly to 22. The first multi-party local elections, held on 15 December 1991, resulted in another decisive victory for the MPD, which secured control of 10 of the 14 local councils, including that of the capital, Praia. The PAICV gained control of three councils, including those in Boa Vista and Fogo islands (respectively the birthplaces of ex-president Pereira and the former prime minister, Gen. Pires). An independent group, which was supported by the UCID, won control of the council in São Vicente. Despite the MPD's success in the elections, the government acknowledged that the high rate of abstention (about 40% of the electorate) reflected public disappointment with its achievements in its first months in power.

In January 1992 Veiga reshuffled the cabinet and created three new ministries which were intended to improve government efficiency. The new ministries were: infrastructure and transport, culture and communication, and tourism, industry and commerce. In accordance with Veiga's announcement of a strengthening of the role of the national assembly, which would convene more frequently and for longer periods in order to reduce legislative delays, a new ministry, for public administration and parliamentary affairs, was created under the charge of a newly appointed minister. This development had also been sought by the opposition PAICV.

On 25 September 1992 a new constitution came into force, enshrining the principles of multi-party democracy. Under the new Constitution of the Republic of Cape Verde (also referred to as the 'Second Republic'), a new national flag and emblem were adopted, with a new national anthem being adopted in January 1993.

In March 1993 the council of ministers was reorganized, and the number of ministers increased from 11 to 13. The number of secretaries of state was reduced from 10 to six. The ministry of finance and planning became solely the ministry of finance, while a new ministry, of economic co-ordination, was created. The posts of secretary of state for finance, fisheries, and tourism, industry and commerce were abolished, while the position of secretary of state for internal administration was upgraded to the status of minister.

At its annual national congress in August 1993 the PAICV elected Aristides Lima to the post of secretary-general of the party, replacing Pedro Pires, who was appointed to the newly-created post of party president. At the annual national conference of the UCID, held in the same month, Celso Celestino assumed control of the party, ousting the party president, Antero Barros, in what was described as an effective 'coup' by the 'Iberia Section' of the party. Celestino subsequently announced that should the UCID obtain office in the 1996 elections, he would reverse the privatization policy of the current government. In February 1994, as a result of the increasing division within the UCID, its former leader, John Wahnon, left the party. In late 1993 internal conflict within the ruling MPD prompted Veiga to announce an extraordinary national convention of the party to take place in late February 1994. In December 1993 the minister for health, Rui Alberto Figueiredo Soares, resigned following criticism of the government's health policies by the former health minister, Luís Sousa Nobre Leite. In the same month the minister of justice and labour, Eurico Correia Monteiro, was dismissed following his announcement that he would contend the leadership of the MPD at the forthcoming party convention. The minister of public administration and parliamentary affairs, Alfredo Gonçalves Teixeira, was dismissed at the same time. Responsibility for the justice and labour portfolio was assumed by the minister for internal administration, Mário Ramos Pereira da Silva, and that for the public administration and parliamentary affairs portfolio was assumed by the minister of culture and communication, Ondina Maria Fonseca Rodrigues Ferreira.

At the extraordinary national convention of the MPD held in February 1994, Carlos Veiga was re-elected president of the party. However, increasing conflict within the party resulted in some 30 party delegates, led by Eurico Monteiro and former minister of foreign affairs Jorge Carlos Almeida Fonseca, boycotting the convention and holding a convention of their own. Monteiro announced that he intended to form a new political party, to be named the Partido da Convergência Democrática (PCD), which would oppose the MPD at the 1996 elections.

In March 1994 Veiga announced a further reorganization of the council of ministers. Pedro Monteiro Freire de Andrade was appointed minister of justice and João Baptista Medina appointed minister of health. The ministry of internal administration was restyled the ministry of cabinet affairs. In addition, José António Mendes dos Reis was appointed minister of a newly created ministry, of employment, youth and social promotion. In May 1994, following the split within the ruling MPD, a motion of confidence in the government was debated by the legislature. The motion was carried in the government's favour by a narrow margin of 41 votes to 38.

Since coming to power in early 1991, the MPD government has endeavoured to enhance Cape Verde's international relations, conducting a series of meetings with foreign powers. President Mascarenhas visited Nigeria in June 1991, Senegal in July and Portugal in November. In February 1992 he held talks in Cape Verde with the president of South Africa. Following a meeting in Lisbon in January 1992 between the Cape Verdean and Israeli ministers of foreign affairs, it was announced that the two countries were to establish diplomatic relations. Also in that month, Cape Verde became a non-permanent member (for a statutory 2-year period) of the UN Security Council, which gave Veiga the opportunity to meet President Bush during a meeting of member heads of government in New York. Mascarenhas attended a 'summit' meeting of the leaders of the five African lusophone countries (Paises Africanos da Língua Oficial Portuguesa—PALOP) in São Tomé and Príncipe in March. The leaders discussed means of strengthening co-operation between Portugal's ex-colonies in Africa and the possibility of co-ordinating their relations with the EC. Further PALOP meetings, including representatives from the IMF and the African Development Bank, took place in Lisbon in October and November 1992. Mascarenhas visited Mozambique and Tanzania in April 1992, Mauritania in September and Botswana in October. In July Veiga attended a seminar in Dakar, Senegal, of the heads of government of the Economic Community of West African States (ECOWAS). In February 1993 Cape Verde and Senegal signed a treaty settling the demarcation of the countries' common maritime border. In May Mascarenhas visited Switzerland, and in the same month Cape Verde opened a consulate in Hong Kong. In October Mascarenhas made a state visit to Kuwait, opening channels for co-operation. In April 1994 diplomatic relations were formally established with South Africa.

Economy

JONATHAN GREPNE

Based on an earlier article by MILES SMITH-MORRIS

According to estimates by the World Bank, Cape Verde's real gross national product (GNP) increased at an average rate of 1.8% per year during 1985–92. In 1992 it was estimated that total GNP reached US $330m. (at average 1990–92 prices), the equivalent of $850 per head. Poverty is the dominant theme in this largely subsistence economy, which hinges on the vagaries of the rainfall and is threatened by local overpopulation in the wetter islands. The flat islands (Sal, Maio, Boa Vista), where the wind blows almost all the year round, have little arable farming, and livestock-breeding is their main occupation. The agricultural profile of the other seven main islands reflects outdated techniques of cultivation and animal husbandry, resistance to change, the lack of finance and government incentives, erosion and, above all, lack of rainfall. Only some 11% (37,000 ha) of the total surface area of the archipelago is suitable for agriculture (half of this is on Santiago) and of this only about 2,000 ha are irrigated. In early 1994 unemployment was estimated to affect about 24% of the labour force, with a further 26% underemployed. In 1985 an estimated 42% of the population lived below the official 'poverty line' ($170 per year).

According to FAO estimates, 41.7% of the economically active population were engaged in agriculture (including forestry and fishing) in 1992. However, in that year only 16% of food needs were met by local resources. About 54% of farms are smaller than 1 ha in area and less than 3% exceed 5 ha. Some large estates (mostly white-owned) have been nationalized, and an agrarian reform law took effect in 1983, eliminating indirect farming and favouring small individual holdings and the formation of co-operatives. Landholdings over 5 ha (or 1 ha, if irrigated) which were not farmed directly by their owners were to be distributed to their actual cultivators.

A 10-year drought eased in the autumn of 1978, but in 1979, 1981 and 1983 the drought was so severe that almost all crops were lost. In 1984 heavy rainfall caused catastrophic floods. A reafforestation plan has been put into effect: about 2.8m. drought-resistant trees were planted during 1978–81, and a further 1.5m. in 1982/83, bringing the total to 9m. by 1986. In that year a further 3m. trees were planted, and the government aimed to continue planting 3m. trees per year to ensure self-sufficiency in firewood by the year 2000. A five-year programme of soil conservation began in 1990, with the aim of planting a further 2m. trees on three islands. Finance totalling $3.5m. was provided by the EC. In 1991 some 16% of the total surface area of the archipelago was forested. About 7,200 rainwater dikes have been built, and well-sinking is a high priority in the government's programme, which aims to irrigate 8,000–10,000 ha by the end of the century. In 1987 a state-owned company, Empresa Pública de Abastecimentos (EMPA), bought 10,700 ha of fertile agricultural land for maize-growing, forestry and livestock raising in Paraguay, along the border with Brazil. The land cost $1.12m., and was to be used to produce food for domestic consumption in Cape Verde. However, the land has since been expropriated by the Paraguayan government, incurring a claim for compensation by the Cape Verde government.

Cape Verde's food crops are maize, beans, cassava and sweet potatoes, supplemented (wherever soils, terrain and rainfall permit) with bananas, vegetables, sugar cane, fruits, etc. The main staples are beans and maize, which are intercropped. In 1985 production of maize amounted to only 1,000 tons, and that of pulses 2,000 tons. In 1986, however, production recovered, and output increased to 12,000 tons of maize and 6,000 tons of pulses. There was an exceptionally abundant harvest in 1987/88, owing to high rainfall and greater availability of land for cultivation, and output of maize reached 21,000 tons. After two years of good rainfall, however, drought returned in 1988. In conjunction with damage by locusts, this led to a 50% fall in agricultural output. Production of maize declined to 16,000 tons in 1988/89 and to 7,300 tons in 1990/91, and was expected to be only 2,500 tons in 1991/92. Total cereal production in 1991/92 was expected to be only 4,000 tons, compared with 11,000 tons in the previous year. More than one-half of Cape Verde's total irrigated land is under sugar cane (production 18,000 tons in 1992, according to FAO estimates), most of which is used in the production of a popular alcoholic beverage for local consumption. The government is seeking to reallocate this land to staple and cash crops by encouraging the manufacture (and future export) of an alternative liquor using imported molasses. Santiago is the main agricultural producer, followed by Santo Antão, Fogo and São Nicolau. Cash crops, such as bananas (production 6,000 tons in 1992, according to an FAO estimate), arabica coffee, groundnuts, castor beans and pineapples, are encouraged, but poor inter-island communications, low educational attainment, the shortage of government funds, the lack of suitable available land and adverse climatic conditions militate against the development of a thriving agriculture.

International food aid has been required since independence in 1975. In 1986 70,000 tons of food aid were needed, and in 1987 these requirements reached an estimated 56,000 tons. Total food aid was reduced to 28,000 tons in 1988/89, following two years of good harvests. However, in January 1990 France dispatched 4,000 tons of maize, purchased from Togo, in response to an appeal at the end of 1989 for emergency food assistance; after poor harvests in both 1990 and 1991, food aid of 17,420 tons of cereals was expected to be needed in 1992. The only crop that the islands export to any significant extent is bananas (1,821 tons in 1992). These are shipped to Portugal, which operates a quota on Cape Verdean imports. A rather exotic commodity, locally known as *purgueira (Jatropha curcas)*, which grows wild, is also exported (for soap-making). In the past, Cape Verde exported coffee, castor beans and tomatoes, but quantities were minimal, owing to the prevailing climatic conditions. In 1987 Cape Verde received $10.8m. in aid from the Netherlands to finance a major land and water conservation project on Santo Antão, and a loan of $6.7m. from the African Development Fund (ADF) to finance an agricultural rehabilitation programme. In the same year, the US Agency for International Development (USAID) provided $1m. for a three-year programme of agricultural research. In 1988 the USA provided millet worth $2m. as part of a four-year food aid programme. The US government also provided $1.7m. for the continuation of water conservation projects, and for a locust-control programme.

Livestock herds have been reduced to one-quarter, or even one-tenth, of their pre-drought level, but are slowly recovering. In 1992, according to FAO estimates, about 19,000 cattle, 110,000 goats, 6,000 sheep and 86,000 pigs were raised for food and milk. Following the poor rains in 1990, the government announced emergency measures to maintain stocks of cattle fodder. About 14,000 horses, asses and mules provide the main form of transport in rural areas.

Fishing offers the greatest development potential, and modern appliances and boats are being slowly introduced to the sector. Fishing exports consist primarily of tuna and lobster. In 1981 a cold-storage plant was opened at Mindelo, with refrigeration capacity of 6,000 tons, and it is hoped that this can be raised to 9,000 tons in the future. In 1985 the Arab Bank for Economic Development in Africa (BADEA) granted a loan of $300,000 for the development of the fishing sector, and in 1986 the FAO agreed to provide assistance to increase production of fish and also of potatoes. In mid-1987 BADEA announced that it would provide a further $4m. loan to finance an industrial fisheries project, which aimed to increase the catch of tuna to 5,000–6,000 tons per year. In early 1988 the fishing sector received loans from the ADF ($8.5m.), the International Fund for Agricultural Development ($5.7m.) and Japan ($3.5m.). In 1987 the state-owned fishing company was reorganized as Empresa Caboverdiana de Pescas (PESCAVE), and given responsibility for increasing the catch of fish. Fishing remains very much a small-scale industry, employing about 7,000 local fishermen in 1993, representing some 6% of the economically active population, with a total fleet of 810 boats, of which about 60 are motorized. Cape Verde's annual potential catch has been estimated at 50,000 tons, although actual catches have fallen in recent years, from 14,730 tons in 1981 to about 10,000 tons in 1992. In 1992 Cape Verde exported 1,278 tons of fish and fish products, which provided 53.8% of export earnings. Negotiations with the EC on a fisheries agreement, expected to cover tuna fishing, were held in October 1989. A fishing agreement was signed with the EC for the first time in August 1990. The agreement, to operate initially for three years, established quotas for catches by boats from EC countries in Cape Verdean waters, in exchange for which the EC agreed to pay a total of $1.9m. In October 1993 Japan donated a fishing vessel, worth $5.6m., to Cape Verde.

The manufacturing sector is still marginal (fish conserving, textiles and rum making), with 5,520 employees in 1990 and a contribution of about 6% to GDP in 1991. Most enterprises remain under private control, and the authorities tend to favour immigrants who wish to create new enterprises. In 1984 plans were agreed to construct a cement factory on Maio, but the government cancelled the project in 1988, as it was no longer considered commercially viable. In 1987 the Federal Republic of Germany agreed to finance the expansion of a plant producing butane gas. Mining is of little significance, representing less than 1% of GDP in 1992, with pozzolana, a volcanic ash used in cement manufacture (10,000 tons per year in 1981–90, according to estimates by the US Bureau of Mines and the UN), and salt (7,000 tons in 1990) being the main products, albeit decreasing in output.

Until recently, Cape Verde failed to exploit its strategic economic position between Africa, Europe and America. After independence, sea transport was expanded significantly, to establish regular links between most of the islands and mainland Africa and Portugal. The main port of the islands, Porto Grande, at Mindelo on São Vicente, also plays a transatlantic role, although traffic has declined since 1976. A new shipbuilding and repairing yard was opened at Mindelo in 1983, and in 1987 the ADF provided a loan of $681,000 to finance feasibility studies on upgrading the shipyard. In 1982 work started on the construction of a port at Palmeira, on Sal. Agreements were signed with the USSR in 1988 to provide Soviet technical assistance for the port at Palmeira, together with development finance for a port under construction at Tarafal on São Nicolau island and for the construction of a new port at Sal-Rei on Boa Vista. In 1985 Cape Verde and Angola agreed on arrangements for the sharing of port facilities, and ship-repair and refrigeration services. In 1986 an accord was signed with Brazil, which made Cape Verde a commercial platform for Brazilian products destined for the west African coast and Europe. Under the accord, the Brazilian state-owned oil company, Petróleo Brasileiro (PETROBRAS), planned a joint venture with the Cape Verdean oil company, ENACOL, to develop a 'spot' market in light and heavy fuels, which would operate from Cape Verde. In 1988 the government rejected an offer of $65m. from a consortium of Western industrialized countries, including the USA and Australia, to dispose of their toxic waste. In March 1993 a World Bank programme was approved for the upgrading and maintenance of the infrastructure. The 'Programme for Infrastructure and Transport' was to include an upgrading of Porto Grande and of the port of Vale de Cavaleiros on the island of Fogo, as well as repairs to, and maintenance of, roads. The programme, which was expected to take four years to implement at a cost of $87m., was to be financed by donors including the World Bank ($12.5m.), the ADF ($11.3m.), BADEA ($7m.) and the European Investment Bank ($5.6m.).

The Amílcar Cabral international airport on Sal Island has a capacity of 1m. passengers per year. In 1991 Portugal announced a loan of $8m. to finance construction of a new terminal at the airport. Its facilities have been used as a strategic refuelling point, chiefly by the airlines of South Africa, Portugal, the USSR, Cuba, Guinea-Bissau and Angola. In April 1987 Cape Verde's airline, Transportes Aéreos de Cabo Verde (TACV), inaugurated a new weekly service to Boston, in the USA. By early 1990, TACV had expanded its international operations to 10 flights per week, and in November 1991 started direct flights to Lisbon. In 1987 Cape Verde suffered a reduction of about $6m. in revenue as a result of the curtailment by the US government of flights by South African Airways to the USA. These transatlantic flights, which had used Cape Verde as a stopover and had previously comprised 90% of air traffic through Sal, declined from 38 to six per month. Cape Verde attempted to attract other airlines to Sal: in early 1988 discussions were held with Italian, Zambian and Botswana airlines concerning the introduction of stop-over flights to the USA. However, following the repeal of US sanctions in late 1991, South African air traffic was resumed, with a resulting increase in revenue. In early 1992 BADEA announced that it would be granting a loan of $9m. for the construction of a new international airport at Praia. This was augmented in July by loans from the ADF, for $11.73m., and the African Development Bank, for $8.36m., with the Cape Verde government contributing $4.75m. The new airport will be able to accommodate Airbus and Boeing 757 type aircraft and is due for completion by mid-1997. The government is increasingly aware of the tourist potential of the islands, which has so far been limited primarily to Sal with its international airport and three international standard hotels. Currently, about 2,000 tourists per year, mostly Portuguese, Italian and French, visit the islands. Santiago will be accessible to tourism with the completion of the new airport at Praia and the construction of a major tourism centre, with marina, at São Francisco Bay by British developers. Several laws relating to the industry, granting guarantees and incentives to investors, have been enacted since December 1991, and in October 1992 the prime minister declared tourism to be the principal sector for private investment.

Government policy in recent years has emphasized efforts to increase foreign earnings from service industries and in 1989 legislation was approved to open the economy to external private investment. In 1990 the World Bank began preparation of a project to develop an industrial 'free zone' on the islands. The project, expected to benefit from an $8m. loan from the bank, aimed to exploit Cape Verde's strategic position to establish an international trade centre, based on transhipping, 'offshore' manufacturing and banking and financial services; the World Bank loan would be made available to private-sector developers. Cape Verde has also been attempting to develop a role as a centre for ship registration, hoping to profit from disruption in more established centres, such as Liberia and Panama. In April 1992 the government signed an agreement with investors from the USA, Saudi Arabia and Pakistan to establish an agency, based in Mindelo, to develop a ship registration system.

Cape Verde's principal export is fish, supplemented by small quantities of bananas and plantains. However, exports are on such a small scale that earnings have covered only 5%–10% of import costs in recent years. Cape Verde sustained a trade deficit of $97m. in 1988, $99m. in 1989 and $81m. in 1990, although the decline in the deficit was due to reductions in imports rather than any significant increase in exports. There was an increase in the deficit, to $117.23m., in 1991 and to $168.86m., in 1992. Portugal is the principal trading partner, although in the late 1980s its share of trade was declining in importance. In October 1987 Cape Verde held its first Portuguese trade fair. A further international trade fair took place in Praia in June 1993. Other prominent trading partners are the Netherlands and Spain. Trade liberalization was a priority of the new MPD government. By 1994 some 90% of imported goods that had previously been restricted to state importers, including construction materials, books, paper, transport equipment and parts, and textiles, were liberalized, with the result that several new import/export companies were established.

Remittances from about 700,000 Cape Verdeans living outside the country (principally in the USA, the Netherlands, Portugal, Italy and Angola), which were equivalent to almost 40% of the trade deficit in 1979, alleviate an otherwise desperate situation. Emigrant remittances stagnated in the mid-1980s, however, owing to the decline of the US dollar and a high rate of unemployment among Cape Verdean expatriates; by 1988 remittances were contributing only 11% of GDP, compared with 20% at independence in 1975. The government is attempting to attract expatriates' capital into the small industrial and fishing sectors by offering favourable tax conditions for investors. An agreement between Cape Verde and the USA, signed in 1985, formed the cornerstone of this new policy. In 1987 an organization was established to assess emigrants' financial and technical potential. However, the rate of emigration is expected to decline, as other countries introduce harsher restrictions on immigration.

Foreign aid has been indispensable to Cape Verde, and in 1986 EC aid covered about 53% of the country's total import bill. Cape Verde receives EC investment aid under the Lomé Conventions, and the EC also provides food aid: Cape Verde received 7,000 tons in 1982 and in 1983, and in May 1987 the EC agreed to provide 9,500 tons of food aid in 1987–89. However, despite international assistance, which amounted to $140m. in 1975–80 and $60m. per year in 1980–85, there were insufficient credits available to implement the Cape Verde government's economic policies. Total bilateral and multilateral aid to the country reached $110.2m. in 1986, but decreased to $86.3m. in 1987. This was principally due to a reduction in aid from Italy, which provided $8.6m. in 1987, in contrast to $37.9m. in 1986. Assistance from the other major donors, Sweden, the Netherlands, the Federal Republic of Germany, France and the USA, was consistent with previous years. Grants amounted to 94% of total aid in 1987. Under the third Lomé Convention, Cape Verde was allocated $28.1m. for 1986–90; this was to rise, under the fourth Convention, to $35m. during the period 1991–95. The EC aid programme aimed to improve supplies of water and electricity to Praia. In 1993 the EC granted $6m. for a project to provide a network of water pipelines connecting suburban groundwater sources and reservoirs to Praia by mid-1996. In 1993 Israeli technology was being employed to install water desalination units for Praia, with finance provided by the EC. A more comprehensive government scheme, estimated to cost some $82m., to be funded by major foreign donors, was announced in September 1993. The project aimed to provide access to drinking water for the entire population by 2005. In 1988 a project to upgrade the transport and energy sectors was initiated, at a cost of $5.1m. This was supported by a loan of $4.7m. from the International Development Association. Later in the year, the OPEC Fund for International Development agreed a $1.5m. loan to finance petroleum imports, as well as two additional grants to cover the country's subscription to the UNCTAD Common Fund for Commodities ($1m.) and to support water supply and sanitation ($500,000). At the end of 1988, Sweden, one of the principal donor countries, signed a three-year agreement to grant a loan of $26m. on concessionary terms. A further two-year agreement to grant a loan of $20m. was signed at the end of 1991. In 1989 the UN Capital Development Fund provided $2.2m. for a programme to develop primary schools, supported by the UN Development Programme (UNDP). The USA granted $1.4m. towards a four-year export promotion scheme at an estimated cost of $4m. In January 1990 France provided $1.8m., of which about two-thirds was to finance a water supply programme, and the remaining one-third to support research into cray-fishing. In June 1990 Luxembourg agreed to lend $1m. to help finance housing projects in Mindelo and Porto Novo. Spain agreed to provide $1.6m. in aid for 1991, with projects in health, education and veterinary medicine taking priority. In early 1993 the European Investment Bank agreed to lend more than $6m. towards the extension of the power plant at Mindelo.

A point worth noting is the low level of Cape Verde's debt-servicing costs, which the budget-conscious government has kept to a minimum. Cape Verde's total external debt at the end of 1992 was $159.9m., of which $151.4m. was long-term debt. As a proportion of the value of exports of goods and services, the debt-service ratio was 10.1% in 1991.

In 1986 Cape Verde initiated its second four-year National Development Plan, which aimed to expand tourism, light industry and the agricultural and fishing sectors, and to reduce the unemployment rate to 25% of the economically active population. The government intended to introduce reforms in agriculture, education and the civil service during the Plan period. About 31.6% of the financing was to come from external donors, with the balance funded by emigrants' remittances and revenue from the international airport on Sal Island.

Following the first multi-party elections of 1991, the new government indicated that it would, like its predecessor, emphasize the development of service industries. In one of his first policy statements, in April 1991, the prime minister, Carlos Veiga, said that his government must concentrate on areas such as fishing, tourism, services and industry to 'meet the challenge of economic development'.

A third four-year National Development Plan, adopted in August 1992, outlined the new government's plans for economic development, with a view to establishing Cape Verde as an open-market economy. At a meeting of international development partners in October 1992, the participants expressed their satisfaction with Cape Verde's management of its economic development—a view which has enabled the government to retain a large measure of control over the allocation of development aid. Under the plan, the government will concentrate on the development of service-sector industries to increase its export potential, in particular those of tourism, fishing, maritime services (including transhipping), air traffic and re-exporting. There are also plans to transfer a number of state enterprises to private ownership, including the telecommunications section of the state postal and telecommunications company, the state airline (TACV) and the main hotel in Praia (Praia-Mar). Partial privatization is also planned for state-owned shipping, paint, livestock, textiles, fuel and cereal import and distribution companies. In August 1992 the International Development Association agreed to provide a $4.7m. loan to finance technical assistance in preparation for privatization and private-sector economic development programmes. The development of private initiatives is also being assisted by the US government, which is financing the Centro do Promoção do Investimento e das Exportações (PROMEX), a body under partial government control, established to promote exports and foreign investment in Cape Verde. During 1993 new legislation was introduced with the aim of opening Cape Verde's economy more fully to external investment. This has included new measures for the promotion of exports and free trade enterprises. In October 1993 Cape Verde became a member of the Multilateral Investment Guarantee Agency (MIGA), an affiliate of the World Bank.

In July 1993 the first commercial and development bank was established, the Banco Comercial do Atlântico (BCA). Despite the fact that its capital was raised solely from state funds provided by the Banco de Cabo Verde, the BCA enjoys relative independence from the central bank and has a high degree of autonomy in its administration and management. The Banco de Cabo Verde now functions solely as a central bank. New legislation introduced in 1993 provides for the creation of financial institutions to offer loans and credit to small- and medium-sized entrepreneurs.

Measures were adopted in 1993 to reduce by 50% the size of the civil service, estimated at 12,000, by means of a voluntary redundancy scheme. Restructuring of the public administration is being implemented to introduce greater bureaucratic efficiency and to reduce public expenditure. In early 1994 the IDA approved a credit of $8.1m. to help finance a $9m. public sector reform and capacity building project which was due for completion in 1999.

Government spending for 1993 was budgeted at 19,500m. escudos. Increased revenue from fiscal sources was expected to begin accruing in January 1993, following the broadening of the scope of liability for income tax.

Statistical Survey

Source (unless otherwise stated): Statistical Service, Banco de Cabo Verde, Av. Amílcar Cabral, Santiago; tel. 61-31-53; telex 99350.

AREA AND POPULATION

Area: 4,033 sq km (1,557 sq miles).

Population: 272,571 at census of 15 December 1970; 295,703 (males 135,695, females 160,008) at census of 2 June 1980; 341,491 (males 161,494; females 179,997) at census of 23 June 1990. *By island* (1990 census, figures rounded to nearest '00): Boa Vista 3,500, Brava 7,000, Fogo 34,000, Maio 5,000, Sal 7,700, Santo Antão 44,000, São Nicolau 14,000, Santiago 175,000, São Vicente 51,000.

Density (1990): 84.7 per sq. km.

Principal Town: Cidade de Praia (capital), population 62,000 at 1990 census.

Births and Deaths (1990): Registered live births 9,669 (birth rate 28.3 per 1,000); Registered deaths 2,505 (death rate 7.3 per 1,000). Source: UN, *Population and Vital Statistics Report*.

Expectation of life (UN estimates, years at birth, 1985–90): 66.1 (males 65.0; females 67.0). Source: UN, *World Population Prospects: The 1992 Revision*.

Economically Active Population (persons aged 10 years and over, 1990 census): Agriculture, hunting, forestry and fishing 29,876; Mining and quarrying 410; Manufacturing 5,520; Electricity, gas and water 883; Construction 22,722; Trade, restaurants and hotels 12,747; Transport, storage and communications 6,138; Financing, insurance, real estate and business services 821; Community, social and personal services 17,358; Activities not adequately defined 24,090; Total labour force 120,565 (males 75,786, females 44,779), including 31,049 unemployed persons (males 19,712, females 11,337). Source: International Labour Office, *Year Book of Labour Statistics*.

AGRICULTURE, ETC.

Principal Crops ('000 metric tons, 1992): Maize 6, Potatoes 3, Cassava 2, Sweet potatoes 3, Pulses 4 (1990), Coconuts 10*, Dates 2*, Sugar cane 18, Bananas 6. Source: FAO, *Production Yearbook*.

Livestock (FAO estimates, '000 head, year ending September 1992): Cattle 19, Pigs 86, Sheep 6, Goats 110, Asses 11. Source: FAO, *Production Yearbook*.

Fishing ('000 metric tons, live weight): Total catch 8.6 in 1989; 7.7 in 1990; 8.5 in 1991. Source: FAO, *Yearbook of Fishery Statistics*.

* FAO estimate.

MINING

Production (metric tons, 1990): Salt (unrefined) 7,000; Pozzolana 10,000. Source: UN Economic Commission for Africa, *African Statistical Yearbook*.

INDUSTRY

Production (metric tons, unless otherwise indicated, 1991): Biscuits 348 (1990 figure), Bread 4,000, Canned fish 300, Frozen fish 3,700 (1990 figure), Manufactured tobacco 94, Alcoholic beverages 200,000 litres (1990 figure), Soft drinks 700,000 litres (1990 figure), Electric energy 36m. kWh. Source: UN, *Industrial Statistics Yearbook;* UN Economic Commission for Africa, *African Statistical Yearbook*.

FINANCE

Currency and Exchange Rates: 100 centavos = 1 Cape Verde escudo; 1,000 escudos are known as a conto. *Sterling and Dollar Equivalents* (31 March 1994): £1 sterling = 125.323 escudos; US $1 = 84.415 escudos; 1,000 Cape Verde escudos = £7.979 = $11.846. *Average Exchange Rate* (escudos per US dollar): 71.408 in 1991; 68.018 in 1992; 80.427 in 1993.

Budget (estimates, million escudos, 1984): Revenue 1,630; Expenditure 2,134.5.
Source: *Marchés Tropicaux et Méditerranéens*.

International Reserves (US $ million at 31 December 1992): IMF special drawing rights 0.07; Foreign exchange 75.69; Total 75.76. Source: IMF, *International Financial Statistics*.

Money Supply (million escudos at 31 December 1992): Currency outside banks 3,191.3. Source: IMF, *International Financial Statistics*.

Cost of Living (Consumer Price Index for Praia; base: 1990 = 100): 110 in 1991; 113 in 1992; 125 in 1993. Source: IMF, *International Financial Statistics*.

Expenditure on the Gross Domestic Product (million escudos at current purchasers' values, 1991): Government final consumption expenditure 4,703; Private final consumption expenditure 20,055; Increase in stocks 730; Gross fixed capital formation 8,750; *Total domestic expenditure* 34,238; Exports of goods and services 3,706; *Less* Imports of goods and services 13,620; *GDP in purchasers' values* 24,324. Source: UN Economic Commission for Africa, *African Statistical Yearbook*.

Gross Domestic Product by Economic Activity (million escudos at current prices, 1991): Agriculture, forestry and fishing 4,400; Mining and quarrying 60; Manufacturing 1,300; Electricity, gas and water 617; Construction 4,298; Trade, restaurants and hotels 5,090; Transport and communications 2,600; Finance, insurance, real estate and business services 890; Government services 1,770; Other community, social and personal services 200; *Sub-total* 21,225; Indirect taxes, *Less* Subsidies 3,099; *GDP in purchasers' values* 24,324. Source: UN, Economic Commission for Africa, *African Statistical Yearbook*.

Balance of Payments (US $ million, 1992): Merchandise exports f.o.b. 4.43; Merchandise imports f.o.b. –173.29; *Trade Balance* –168.86; Exports of services 53.47; Imports of services –26.69; Other income received 5.66; Other income paid –4.40; Private unrequited transfers (net) 69.86; Official unrequited transfers (net) 67.41; *Current balance* –3.55; Direct investment (net) –0.75; Other capital (net) 6.82; Net errors and omissions 5.49; Overall balance 8.01. Source: IMF, *International Financial Statistics*.

EXTERNAL TRADE

Principal Commodities (US $ '000): *Imports c.i.f.* (1990): Food and live animals 28,849 (Dairy products 5,434, Cereals and cereal preparations 7,377, Vegetables and fruit 4,229, Sugar, sugar preparations and honey 4,912); Beverages and tobacco 4,961 (Beverages 4,273); Crude materials excl. fuels 3,927; Mineral fuels, lubricants, etc. 10,220 (Petroleum, petroleum products, etc. 8,894); Animal and vegetable oil 4,155; Chemicals and related products 8,371; Basic manufactures 24,469 (Paper and paper manufactures 2,886, Iron and steel 3,453); Machinery and transport equipment 41,910 (Road vehicles and parts 8,854, Other transport equipment 18,219); Miscellaneous manufactured articles 9,431; Total (incl. others) 136,310. *Exports f.o.b.* (excl. parcel post, 1990): Food and live animals 5,166 (Fish and preparations 3,243, Bananas and plantains (fresh or dried) 1,894); Petroleum and petroleum products 18,592; Machinery and transport equipment 3,164; Total (incl. others) 28,564. Source: UN, *International Trade Statistics Yearbook*. **1992:** *Exports f.o.b.* (million escudos): Bananas 112; Fish 63; Crustaceans 97.7; Fish oils and fats 6.6; Basic manufactures 24.9; Pozzolana 59.8; Total (incl. others) 311. Source: General Directorate for Commerce, Ministry of Tourism, Industry and Commerce.

Principal Trading Partners (US $ '000, 1992): *Imports c.i.f.*: Brazil 10,252; Belgium and Luxembourg 4,676; Côte d'Ivoire 4,500; Denmark 3,058; France 6,475; Germany 6,665; Italy 7,734; Japan 8,993; Netherlands 18,706; Portugal 57,916; Romania 4,856; Spain 3,777; Sweden 3,957; Switzerland 3,058; USA 10,072; Total (incl. others) 179,864. *Exports f.o.b.:* Netherlands 462; Portugal 3,909; Spain 327; Total (incl. others) 4,808.

TRANSPORT

Road Traffic (motor vehicles in use, estimates, 1991): Passenger cars 2,000, Commercial vehicles 1,000. Source: UN Economic Commission for Africa, *African Statistical Yearbook*.

Shipping (international freight traffic, estimates, 1991): Goods loaded 87,000 metric tons; goods unloaded 580,000 metric tons (Source: UN, Economic Commission for Africa, *African Statistical Yearbook*); (1981): Passengers embarked 97,746; passengers disembarked 97,746. Source: mainly Direção Geral de Estatística, Praia, Santiago.

Civil Aviation (traffic on scheduled services, 1990): Kilometres flown 2,000,000; passengers carried 177,000; passenger-km 161,000,000; freight ton-km 1,000,000. Source: UN, *Statistical Yearbook*.

COMMUNICATIONS MEDIA

Radio receivers (1991): 61,000 in use. Source: UNESCO, *Statistical Yearbook*.

Television receivers (1991): 7,000 in use (estimate). Source: UN Economic Commission for Africa, *African Statistical Yearbook*.

Telephones (1994): 15,000 in use (estimate). Source: Empresa Pública dos Correios e Telecomunicações de Cabo Verde.

Newspapers (1988): 3 titles (average circulation 7,000 copies). Source: UNESCO, *Statistical Yearbook*.

Book production (1989): 10 titles. Source: UNESCO, *Statistical Yearbook*.

EDUCATION

Pre-primary (1986/87): 58 schools, 4,523 pupils, 136 teachers.

Primary (1989/90): 367 schools (provisional figure), 67,761 pupils, 2,028 teachers.

Total Secondary (1987/88): 6,413 pupils, 268 teachers.

General Secondary (1989/90): 7,114 pupils, 238 teachers.

Teacher training (1987/88): 141 pupils, 25 teachers.

Vocational schools (1989/90): 588 pupils, 56 teachers.

Source: UNESCO, *Statistical Yearbook*.

Directory

The Constitution

A new constitution of the Republic of Cape Verde ('the Second Republic') came into force on 25 September 1992. The Constitution defines Cape Verde as a sovereign, unitary and democratic republic, guaranteeing respect for human dignity and recognizing the inviolable and inalienable rights of man as a fundament of humanity, peace and justice. It recognizes the equality of all citizens before the law, without distinction of social origin, social condition, economic status, race, sex, religion, political convictions or ideologies and promises transparency for all citizens in the practising of fundamental liberties. The Constitution gives assent to popular will, and has a fundamental objective in the realization of economic, political, social and cultural democracy and the construction of a society which is free, just and in solidarity. The Republic of Cape Verde will create, progressively, the necessary conditions for the removal of all obstacles which impede the development of mankind and limit the equality of citizens and their effective participation in the political, economic, social and cultural organizations of the State and of Cape Verdean society.

The Head of State is the President of the Republic, who is elected by universal adult suffrage and must obtain two-thirds of the votes cast to win in the first round of the election. If no candidate secures the requisite majority, a new election is held within 21 days and contested by the two candidates who received the highest number of votes in the first round. Voting is conducted by secret ballot. Legislative power is vested in the Assembléia Nacional, which is also elected by universal adult suffrage. The Prime Minister is nominated by the Assembléia Nacional, to which he is responsible. On the recommendation of the Prime Minister, the President appoints the Council of Ministers, whose members must be elected deputies of the Assembléia Nacional. There are 14 local government councils, elected by universal suffrage for a period of five years.

The Government

HEAD OF STATE

President: ANTÓNIO MANUEL MASCARENHAS GOMES MONTEIRO (took office 22 March 1991).

COUNCIL OF MINISTERS
(August 1994)

Prime Minister, with responsibility for Defence: Dr CARLOS ALBERTO WAHNON DE CARVALHO VEIGA.

Minister of Foreign Affairs: Dr MANUEL CASIMIRO DE JESUS CHANTRE.

Minister of Economic Co-ordination: Dr JOSÉ TOMÁS WAHNON DE CARVALHO VEIGA.

Minister of Finance: Dr ULPIO NAPOLEÃO FERNANDES.

Minister of Tourism, Industry and Commerce: Dr JOÃO HIGINO DO ROSÁRIO SILVA.

Minister of Fisheries, Agriculture and Rural Activity: Dra HELENA NOBRE DE MORAIS SEMEDO.

Minister of Education and Sport: Dr MANUEL DA PAIXÃO SANTOS FAUSTINO.

Minister of Justice: PEDRO MONTEIRO FREIRE DE ANDRADE.

Minister of Health: Dr JOÃO BAPTISTA MEDINA.

Minister of Infrastructure and Transport: Eng. TEÓFILO FIGUEIREDO ALMEIDA SILVA.

Minister of Culture and Communication, with responsibility for Public Administration and Parliamentary Affairs: Dra ONDINA MARIA FONSECA RODRIGUES FERREIRA.

Minister of Cabinet Affairs: MÁRIO RAMOS PEREIRA DA SILVA.

Minister of Employment, Youth and Social Promotion: Dr JOSÉ ANTÓNIO MENDES DOS REIS.

Secretary of State for Foreign Affairs and Co-operation: Dr JOSÉ LUÍS BARBOSA LEÃO MONTEIRO.

Secretary of State for Employment, Youth and Social Promotion: Dr ARMANDO HOPFFER BARRETO.

Secretary of State for Agriculture: Dr JOSÉ ANTÓNIO PINTO MONTEIRO.

Secretary of State for Emigration and Communities: Dr ANTÓNIO PASCOAL SILVA SANTOS.

Secretary of State for the Navy and Ports: MANUEL VICENTE SILVA.

MINISTRIES

Office of the President: Presidência da República, Praia, Santiago; tel. 61-26-69; telex 6051.

Office of the Prime Minister: Palácio do Governo, Várzea CP 16, Praia, Santiago; tel. 61-04-05; telex 6054; fax 61-30-99.

Ministry of Defence: Palácio do Governo, Várzea, Praia, Santiago; tel. 61-35-91; telex 6077; fax 61-30-99.

Ministry of Culture and Communication: Rua Hospital-Praia, Praia, Santiago; tel. 61-57-61; telex 6030; fax 61-43-69.

Ministry of Economic Co-ordination: 107 Avda Amílcar Cabral, CP 30, Praia, Santiago; tel. 61-56-98; telex 6058; fax 61-38-97.

Ministry of Education and Sport: Palácio do Governo, Várzea, Praia, Santiago; tel. 61-05-07; telex 6057.

Ministry of Finance and Planning: 107 Avda Amílcar Cabral, CP 30, Praia, Santiago; tel. 61-56-96; telex 6058; fax 61-38-97.

Ministry of Fisheries, Agriculture and Rural Activity: Ponta Belém, Praia, Santiago; tel. 61-57-17; telex 6072; fax 61-40-54.

Ministry of Foreign Affairs and Co-operation: Praça Dr Lorena, Praia, Santiago; tel. 61-57-27; telex 6070; fax 61-39-52.

Ministry of Health: Palácio do Governo, Várzea, Praia, Santiago; tel. 61-05-01; telex 6059.

Ministry of Cabinet Affairs: Palácio do Governo, Várzea, Praia, Santiago; tel. 61-05-01; telex 6062.

Ministry of Justice: Rua Serpa Pinto, Praia, Santiago; tel. 61-56-91; telex 6025; fax 61-56-78.

Ministry of Public Administration and Parliamentary Affairs: Palácio do Governo, Várzea,Praia, Santiago; tel. 61-05-11; fax 61-30-99.

Ministry of Tourism, Industry and Commerce: Palácio do Governo, Várzea, Praia, Santiago; tel. 61-05-15; telex 6035; fax 61-44-16.

Ministry of Infrastructure and Transport: Ponta Belém, Praia, Santiago; tel. 61-57-09; telex 6060; fax 61-56-99.

Ministry of Employment, Youth and Social Promotion: Praia, Santiago; tel. 61-23-24.

President and Legislature

PRESIDENT

Election, 17 February 1991

	Percentage of votes cast
ANTÓNIO MASCARENHAS MONTEIRO (MPD)	73.5
ARISTIDES MARIA PEREIRA (PAICV)	26.5
Total	100.0

ASSEMBLÉIA NACIONAL (AN)

Legislative Election, 13 January 1991

Party	Seats
Movimento para Democracia (MPD)	56
Partido Africano da Independência de Cabo Verde (PAICV)	23
Total	79

Political Organizations

Movimento para a Democracia (MPD): Praia, Santiago; f. 1990; leadership comprises a nat. council of 45 mems, a nat. comm. of 15 mems, and a legal council; advocates administrative decentralization; obtained majority of seats in legis. elections held in Jan. 1991; Chair. Dr CARLOS ALBERTO WAHNON DE CARVALHO VEIGA.

Partido Africano da Independência de Cabo Verde (PAICV): CP 22, Praia, Santiago; telex 6022; fax 61-16-09; f. 1956 as the Partido Africano da Independência do Guiné e Cabo Verde (PAIGC); name changed in 1981, following the 1980 coup in Guinea-Bissau, which the Cape Verde Govt had opposed, having previously favoured an eventual union with Guinea-Bissau; sole authorized political party 1975–90; Pres. Gen. PEDRO VERONA RODRIGUES PIRES; Sec.-Gen. ARISTIDES LIMA.

Partido da Convergência Democrática (PCD): Praia, Santiago; f. 1994; Pres. Dr EURICO CORREIA MONTEIRO.

Partido Socialista Democrático (PSD): Praia, Santiago; f. 1992; Leader JOÃO ALÉM.

União Caboverdiana Independente e Democrática (UCID): Praia, Santiago; f. 1974 by emigrants opposed to the PAICV; legalized in 1991; Pres. CELSO CELESTINO.

União do Povo das Ilhas de Cabo Verde–Em Reconstrução (UPICV–R): CP 281, Praia, Santiago; tel. 61-37-63; f. 1958, revived in 1990; Leader JOSÉ LEITÃO DA GRAÇA.

Diplomatic Representation

EMBASSIES IN CAPE VERDE

Brazil: Chã de Areia, CP 93, Praia, Santiago; tel. 61-56-07; telex 6075; Ambassador: NUNO ALVARO G. D'OLIVEIRA.

China, People's Republic: Achada de Santo António, Praia, Santiago; tel. 61-55-86; Ambassador: CHEN DEHE.

Cuba: Prainha, Praia, Santiago; tel. 61-55-97; telex 6087; fax 61-55-90; Ambassador: JOSÉ MANUEL INCLÁN EMBADE.

France: CP 192, Praia, Santiago; tel. 61-55-89; telex 6064; fax 61-55-90; Ambassador: FRANÇOIS CHAPPELLET.

Portugal: Achada de Santo António, CP 160, Praia, Santiago; tel. 61-56-02; telex 6055; fax 61-40-58; Ambassador: EUGÉNIO ANACORETA CORREIA.

Russia: Achada de Santo António, CP 31, Praia, Santiago; tel. 61-21-32; telex 6016; Ambassador: VLADIMIR I. STOLYAROV.

Senegal: Prainha, Praia, Santiago; tel. 61-56-21; Ambassador: CHEIKH TIDIANE DIALLO.

USA: Rua Hoji Ya Yenna 81, CP 201, Praia, Santiago; tel. 61-56-16; telex 6068; fax 61-13-55; Ambassador: JOSEPH MONROE SEGARS.

Judicial System

Supremo Tribunal da Justiça: Praça Alexandre de Albuquerque, Platô, Praia, Santiago; tel. 61-58-10; telex 6025; fax 61-45-19; established 1975; the highest court.

President: Dr ÓSCAR GOMES.

Attorney-General: Dr HENRIQUE MONTEIRO.

Religion

CHRISTIANITY

At 31 December 1992 there were an estimated 362,350 adherents of the Roman Catholic Church, representing 95.8% of the total population. Protestant churches, among which the Church of the Nazarene is prominent, represent about 1% of the population.

The Roman Catholic Church

Cape Verde comprises the single diocese of Santiago de Cabo Verde, directly responsible to the Holy See. The Bishop participates in the Episcopal Conference of Senegal, Mauritania, Cape Verde and Guinea-Bissau, currently based in Senegal.

Bishop of Santiago de Cabo Verde: Rt Rev. PAULINO DO LIVRAMENTO EVORA, Avda Amílcar Cabral, Largo 5 de Outubro, CP 46, Praia, Santiago; tel. 61-11-19; telex 6088; fax 61-45-99.

The Anglican Communion

Cape Verde forms part of the diocese of The Gambia, within the Church of the Province of West Africa. The Bishop is resident in Banjul, The Gambia.

The Press

Agaviva: Mindelo, São Vicente; tel. 31-21-21; f. 1991; monthly; Editor GERMANO ALMEIDA; circ. 4,000.

Boletim Informativo: CP 126, Praia, Santiago; f. 1976; weekly; publ. by the Ministry of Foreign Affairs; circ. 1,500.

Boletim Oficial da República de Cabo Verde: Imprensa Nacional, CP 113, Praia, Santiago; tel. 61-41-50; weekly; official.

Contacto: CP 89C, Praia, Santiago; tel. 61-57-52; fax 61-14-42; f. 1993; quarterly; economic bulletin produced by Centro de Promoção do Investimento e das Exportações (PROMEX); circ. 1,000.

Económica: Avda 5 de Julho, 75, CP 36, Praia, Santiago; tel. and fax 61-23-93; f. 1992; quarterly; Editor JOSÉ ULISSES SILVA; circ. 2,500.

Novo Jornal Cabo Verde: Largo do Hospital Dr Agostinho Neto, CP 118, Praia, Santiago; tel. 61-39-89; fax 61-38-29; f. 1993; two a week; Editor JOSÉ TAVARES GOMES; circ. 5,000.

Opinião: Praia, Santiago; Editor DANIEL LOBO.

Raízes: CP 98, Praia, Santiago; tel. 319; f. 1977; quarterly; cultural review; Editor ARNALDO FRANÇA; circ. 1,500.

A Semana: CP 36C, Avda Cidade de Lisboa, Praia, Santiago; tel. 61-25-69; fax 61-39-50; weekly; organ of the PAICV; Editor JORGE SOARES; circ. 5,000.

Terra Nova: São Vicente; monthly; Roman Catholic; Editor P. FIDALGO BARROS.

Unidade e Luta: Praia, Santiago; organ of the PAICV.

NEWS AGENCIES

Cabopress: Achada Santo António, CP 40/A, Praia, Santiago; tel. 61-55-54; telex 6044; fax 61-55-55; f. 1991.

Foreign Bureaux

Agence France-Presse (AFP): CP 26/118 Praia, Santiago; tel. 61-38-89; telex 52; Rep. FÁTIMA AZEVEDO.

Agência Portuguesa de Noticias (LUSA): Prainha, Praia, Santiago; tel. 61-35-19.

Inter Press Service (IPS) (Italy): CP 14, Mindelo, São Vicente; tel. 31-45-50; Rep. JUAN A. COLOMA.

Publisher

Government Publishing House

Imprensa Nacional: CP 113, Praia, Santiago; tel. 61-42-09; Admin. JOÃO DE PINA.

Radio and Television

There were an estimated 61,000 radio receivers and 7,000 television receivers in use in 1991.

RADIO

Rádio Educativa de Cabo Verde: Achada de Santo António, Praia, Santiago; tel. 61-11-61.

Rádio Nacional de Cabo Verde (RNCV): Praça Albuquerque, CP 26, Praia, Santiago; tel. 61-57-55; govt-controlled; five transmitters and five solar relay transmitters; FM transmission only; broadcasts in Portuguese and Creole for 18 hours daily; Dir FONSECA SOARES.

Voz de São Vicente: CP 29, Mindelo, São Vicente; f. 1974; govt-controlled; Dir FRANCISCO TOMAR.

TELEVISION

Televisão Nacional de Cabo Verde (TNCV): Achada de Santo António, CP 2, Praia, Santiago; tel. 61-40-80; one transmitter and seven relay transmitters; broadcasts in Portuguese and Creole for five hours daily; Chair. DANIEL LIVRAMENTO.

Finance

(cap. = capital; res = reserves; dep. = deposits; m. = million; brs = branches; amounts in Cape Verde escudos)

BANKING

Central Bank

Banco de Cabo Verde (BCV): 117 Avda Amílcar Cabral, CP 101, Praia, Santiago; tel. 61-55-29; telex 99350; fax 61-44-47; f. 1976; bank of issue; cap. and res 1,796.2m., dep. 3,790.4m. (1984); Gov. OSWALDO MIGUEL SEQUEIRA.

Other Banks

Banco Comercial do Atlântico (BCA): 117 Avda Amílcar Cabral, Praia, Santiago; tel. 61-55-29; telex 99350; f. 1993; commercial and development bank; Gov. AMÉLIA FIGUEIREDO; 11 brs.

Caixa Económica de Cabo Verde (CECV): Avda Cidade de Lisboa, CP 199, Praia, Santiago; tel. 61-55-61; fax 61-55-60; commercial and development bank.

The **Fundo de Solidariedade Nacional** is the main savings institution; the **Fundo de Desenvolvimento Nacional** channels public investment resources; and the **Instituto Caboverdiano** administers international aid.

INSURANCE

Companhia Caboverdiana de Seguros (IMPAR): Avda Amílcar Cabral, CP 469, Praia, Santiago; tel. 61-14-05; fax 61-37-65; f. 1991; Pres. Dr CORSINO FORTES.

Garantia Companhia de Seguros: CP 138, Praia, Santiago; tel. 61-35-32; fax 61-25-55; f. 1991.

Trade and Industry

CHAMBERS OF COMMERCE

Associação Comercial Industrial e Agrícola de Barlavento (ACIAB): CP 62, Mindelo, São Vicente; tel. 31-31-18.

Associação Comercial de Sotavento (ACAS): Rua Serpa Pinto, Praia, Santiago; tel. 61-29-91; telex 6005; fax 61-29-64.

Centro de Promoção do Investimento e das Exportações (PROMEX): CP 89C, Fazenda, Praia, Santiago; tel. 61-57-52; fax 61-14-42; f. 1990; promotes foreign investment and exports.

STATE INDUSTRIAL ENTERPRISES

Empresa de Comercialização de Produtos do Mar—INTERBASE, EP: CP 59, Mindelo, São Vicente; tel. 31-46-68; fax 31-39-40; supervises marketing of fish; shipping agency and ship chandler.

Empresa Nacional de Administração dos Portos, EP (ENAPOR): Avda Marginal, CP 82, Mindelo, São Vicente; tel. 31-44-14; telex 3049; fax 31-46-61.

Empresa Nacional de Aeroportos e Segurança Aérea, EP (ASA): Aeroporto Amílcar Cabral, Ilha do Sal; tel. 41-13-94; telex 4036; fax 41-15-70; airports and aircraft security.

Empresa Nacional de Avicultura, EP (ENAVI): CP 135, Praia, Santiago; tel. 61-19-22; telex 6072; f. 1979; state enterprise for poultry farming.

Empresa Nacional de Combustíveis, EP (ENACOL): CP 1, Mindelo, São Vicente; tel. 31-31-49; telex 3086; fax 31-48-73; f. 1979; state enterprise supervising import and distribution of petroleum; Dir Dr MARIO A. RODRIGUES.

Empresa Nacional de Conservação e Reparação de Equipamentos (SONACOR): Praia, Santiago; tel. 61-25-57; telex 6080.

Empresa Nacional de Produtos Farmacêuticos (EMPROFAC): CP 59, Praia, Santiago; tel. 61-56-36; telex 6024; fax 61-58-72; f. 1979; state monopoly of pharmaceuticals and medical imports.

Empresa Pública de Abastecimento (EMPA): CP 107, Praia, Santiago; tel. 61-56-27; telex 6054; fax 61-37-37; f. 1975; state provisioning enterprise, supervising imports, exports and domestic distribution; Dir-Gen. MARIA DEOLINDA D. MONTEIRO.

Empresa Pública dos Correios e Telecomunicações de Cabo Verde (CTT): Direcção-Geral, Praia, Santiago; tel. 61-55-79; telex 6087; Dir-Gen. JOSÉ LUIS LIVRAMENTO.

Empresa Pública de Electricidad e Agua (ELECTRA): 10 Avda Unidade Africana, CP 137, Mindelo, São Vicente; tel. 31-44-48; telex 3045.

Instituto Nacional de Cooperativas: Praia, Santiago; central co-operative organization.

Ministério das Pescas, Agricultura e Animação Rural (MPAR): CP 206, Praia, Santiago; tel. 61-29-76; fax 61-17-70; oversees the development of the fishing industry; Dir-Gen. CARLOS ALBERTO ÉVORA ROCHA.

MAJOR INDUSTRIAL COMPANIES

Companhia da Pozolana de Cabo Verde: Porto Novo, Ilha de Santo Antão; pozzolan industry.

Companhia Fomento de Cabo Verde: Santa Maria, Ilha do Sal; salt industry.

Confecções Morabeza, SARL: CP 18, Mindelo, São Vicente; tel. 31-21-44; telex 3048; fax 31-28-19; f. 1978; textiles; 55% state-owned; exports to Africa, Europe and Canada; Man. Dir CESÁRIO J. G. LOPES.

Salins du Cap Vert: Pedra Lume, Ilha do Sal; salt industry.

SOCAL: Sociedade Industrial de Calçado, SARL: CP 92, Mindelo, São Vicente; tel. 31-50-59; telex 3089; fax 31-20-61; industrial shoe factory.

TRADE UNIONS

Sindicato dos Transportes, Comunicações e Turismo (STCT): Praia, Santiago.

União Nacional dos Trabalhadores de Cabo Verde—Central Sindical (UNTC—CS): Rua Dr Júlio Abreu, Praia, Santiago; tel. 61-31-48; telex 6002; fax 61-36-29; f. 1978; Chair. JULIO ASCENSÃO SILVA.

Transport

ROADS

In 1993 there were about 2,250 km of roads, of which 660 km were paved.

SHIPPING

Cargo-passenger ships call regularly at Porto Grande, Mindelo, on São Vicente, and Praia, on Santiago. Work began in 1982 on a port at Palmeira, on Sal island. New ports under construction at Sal-Rei, on Boa Vista, and at Tarrafal, on São Nicolau, received financial and technical assistance from the USSR. In 1993 plans were announced for a US $13.2m. upgrading of Porto Grande, and for the re-establishment of the port of Vale dos Cavaleiros, on Fogo island, at a cost of $10.6m.

Comissão de Gestão dos Transportes Marítimos de Cabo Verde: CP 153, São Vicente; tel and fax. 31-49-79; telex 3031.

Companhia Cabo-Verdiana de Transportes Marítimos: CP 150, Praia, Santiago; tel. 61-22-84; fax 61-60-95.

Companhia Nacional de Navegação Arca Verde: Rua 5 de Julho, CP 41, Praia, Santiago; tel. 61-10-60; telex 6067; fax 61-54-96; f. 1975.

Companhia de Navegação Estrela Negra: Avda 5 de Julho 17, CP 91, São Vicente; tel. 31-54-23; telex 3030.

Companhia Nacional de Navegação Portuguesa: Agent in Santiago: João Benoliel de Carvalho, Lda, CP 56, Praia, Santiago.

Companhia Portuguesa de Transportes Marítimos: Agent in Santiago: João Benoliel de Carvalho, Lda, CP 56, Praia, Santiago.

Linhas Marítimas (LINMAC): Dr João Battista Ferreira Medina, Praia, Santiago; tel. 61-40-99.

Seage Agência de Navegação de Cabo Verde: Avda Cidade de Lisboa, CP 232, Praia, Santiago; tel. 61-57-58; telex 6033; fax 61-25-24; Chair. CESAR MANUEL SEMEDO LOPES.

CIVIL AVIATION

The Amílcar Cabral international airport is at Espargos, on Sal Island, with capacity for aircraft of up to 50 tons. It can handle 1m. passengers per year. Expansion of the airport's facilities began in 1987, with EC and Italian aid. There is also a small airport on each of the other main islands. A second international airport, under construction on Santiago, was due for completion in mid 1997.

CABOVIMO: 32 Avda Unidade Guiné-Cabo Verde, Praia, Santiago; tel. 61-33-14; fax 61-55-59; f. 1992; internal flights; Gen. Man. JORGE DANIEL SPENCER LIMA.

Transportes Aéreos de Cabo Verde (TACV): Rua Guerra Mendes 11/13, CP 1, Praia, Santiago; tel. 61-32-73; telex 6065; fax 61-35-85; f. 1958; connects all nine inhabited islands; also operates service to Europe; Dir ALFREDO CARVALHO.

Tourism

The islands of Santiago, Santo Antão, Fogo and Brava offer attractive mountain scenery, and Santiago combines this with white sandy beaches. There are also extensive beaches on the islands of Sal, Boa Vista and Maio. There are three hotels on Sal, one on Boa Vista and two in Praia. Some 22,000 visitors arrived in Cape Verde during 1993; however, the majority of these were Cape Verdean emigrants returning on holiday. In that year some 2,500 tourists proper arrived, mainly from Portugal (about 67%), Germany and France. In 1993 a 15-year National Tourism Development Plan was adopted providing for a projected increase in tourist arrivals to some 400,000 annually by 2008

Instituto Nacional do Turismo—INATUR: Chã da Areia, CP 294, Praia, Santiago; tel and fax 61-44-75; Pres. Dr JOSÉ DUARTE.

Defence

The armed forces, initially formed from ex-combatants in the liberation wars, totalled about 1,100 (army 1,000, air force less than 100) in June 1993. There is also a police force, the Police for Public Order, which is organized by the local municipal councils. National service is by selective conscription.

Defence Expenditure: Budgeted at 242m. escudos (US $3.6m.) in 1992.

Education

Primary education, beginning at seven years of age and lasting for six years, is compulsory. Secondary education, beginning at 13 years of age, is divided into two cycles, the first comprising a three-year general course, the second a two-year pre-university course. In 1986/87 there were also three teacher-training units and one industrial and commercial school. In 1989 the total enrolment at primary and secondary schools was equivalent to 77% of all school-age children (males 80%; females 75%). In 1986/87 there was 4,523 children enrolled at pre-primary schools. In 1989/90 67,761 pupils attended primary schools, and 7,114 attended general secondary schools. Primary enrolment in 1989 included 95% of children in the relevant age-group (males 96%; females 94%). In 1987 the comparable ratio for secondary enrolment was only 11% (males 12%; females 11%). In 1989 the average rate of illiteracy among the population aged 15 years and over was estimated at 33.5%.

Bibliography

A.G.U. *Cabo Verde.* Lisbon, 1966.

Amaral, I. d. *Santiago de Cabo Verde.* Lisbon, 1964.

Cabral, N. E. *Le Moulin et le Pilon, les îles du Cap-Vert.* Paris, 1980.

Cape Verde Government Publication. *República de Cabo Verde: 5 Anos de Independência (1975–80).* Lisbon, 1980.

Carreira, A. *Cabo Verde, Formação e Extinção de uma Sociedade Escravocrata.* Bissau, 1972.

Migrações nas Ilhas de Cabo Verde. Lisbon, Universidade Nova, 1977.

Cabo Verde: Classes sociais, estructura familiar, migrações. Lisbon, Ulmeiro, 1977.

The People of the Cape Verde Islands: Exploitation and Emigration (trans. and edited by C. Fyfe). London, Hurst and Hamden, CT, Archon Books, 1983.

Davidson, B. *No Fist is Big Enough to Hide the Sky: The Liberation of Guinea-Bissau and Cape Verde.* 2nd Edn, London, Zed Press, 1984.

The Fortunate Isles: A Study of Cape Verde. London, Hutchinson, and Trenton, NJ, World Press, 1989.

de Pina, M.-P. *Les îles du Cap-Vert.* Paris, Karthala, 1987.

Foy, C. *Cape Verde: Politics, Economics and Society.* London, Printer Publishers, Marxist Regimes Series, 1988.

May, S. *Tourismus in der Dritten Welt: Das Beispiel Kapverde.* Frankfurt am Main, Campus Verlag, 1985.

Meintel, D. *Race, Culture and Portuguese Colonialism in Cabo Verde.* Syracuse, NY, Syracuse University Press, 1985.

THE CENTRAL AFRICAN REPUBLIC

Physical and Social Geography

DAVID HILLING

PHYSICAL FEATURES

Geographically, the Central African Republic forms a link between the Sudano-Sahelian zone and the Zaire (Congo) basin. The country consists mainly of plateau surfaces at 600–900 m above sea-level, which provide the watershed between drainage northwards to Lake Chad and southwards to the Oubangui/Zaire system. In the Bongo massif of the north-east, altitudes of 1,400 m are attained. There are numerous rivers, and during the main rainy season (July–October) much of the south-east of the country becomes inaccessible as a result of extensive inundation. The Oubangui river to the south of Bangui provides year-round commercial navigation and is the country's main outlet for external trade. However, development of the country is retarded by its land-locked location and the great distance (1,815 km) to the sea by way of the fluvial route from Bangui to Brazzaville, in the Congo, and thence by the Congo-Océan railway to Pointe-Noire.

POPULATION AND RESOURCES

The Central African Republic covers an area of 622,984 sq km (240,535 sq miles). At the census of December 1975 the population was 2,054,610. By December 1988, according to official estimates, the population had increased to 2,688,426, an average density of only 4.3 inhabitants per sq km. The greatest concentration of population is in the western part of the country, while large areas in the east are virtually uninhabited. There are numerous ethnic groups, but the Banda and Baya together comprise more than 50% of the population. Sango, a lingua franca, has been adopted as the national language.

Only in the extreme south-west of the country is the rainfall sufficient (1,250 mm) to give a forest vegetation. From the Lobaye region come coffee, cocoa, rubber, palm produce and timber. Forest extends northwards along watercourses beyond the main forest region, and in a belt beyond the forest, cotton is the main cash crop. This area could benefit substantially from a proposed rail link with the Transcameroon railway.

Alluvial deposits of diamonds occur widely and are exploited, but uranium is potentially of much greater economic importance in the future. The exploitation of ore-rich deposits at Bakouma, 480 km east of Bangui, which has been inhibited by inadequate access routes and by technical problems, now awaits a recovery in the present level of world uranium prices.

Recent History

PIERRE ENGLEBERT

The former French territory of Oubangui-Chari became the Central African Republic (CAR) on achieving internal self-government in 1958. Barthélemy Boganda, the first prime minister, died in 1959, and was succeeded by David Dacko, who became the CAR's first president at independence on 13 August 1960. The ruling Mouvement d'évolution sociale de l'Afrique noire (MESAN) was declared the sole legal party in December 1962. On 31 December 1966 the chief of staff of the army, Col Jean-Bédel Bokassa, staged a *coup d'état*, placing Dacko, his cousin, under house arrest. Bokassa's power was virtually absolute, and he involved himself in every aspect of national life. However, he was unpredictable and despotic, and the country suffered from frequent changes in policy and an inefficient and corrupt administration. Relations with France were turbulent. Little open opposition to Bokassa emerged, but twice, in 1969 and 1973, senior ministers were implicated in alleged coup attempts. Bokassa elevated his status from that of president to president for life in 1972 and to marshal of the republic in 1974. In September 1976 the council of ministers was replaced by the Council for the Central African Revolution (CRC), with Ange Patassé as prime minister and Dacko as personal adviser to Bokassa. Two months later Bokassa dissolved the CRC, and announced the foundation of the Central African Empire. His coronation as emperor took place in December 1977, at a cost estimated to have absorbed one-quarter of the country's annual foreign earnings. Following his coronation, Bokassa increasingly withdrew from public view.

Open opposition to Bokassa's rule mounted from the beginning of 1979, when student demonstrations in Bangui escalated into pitched battles between police and protesters. The failure of Bokassa's forces to stem growing unrest was illustrated in May by reports that a number of children had been murdered by the police. Several opposition groups were formed in exile, including the Mouvement pour la libération du peuple centrafricain (MLPC), led by Patassé, and in July these groups formed a common front. On the night of 20 September, while Bokassa was in Libya, he was deposed in a bloodless coup by Dacko, supported by a contingent of French troops flown in from Gabon. Dacko proclaimed the country once again a republic and himself its president. Bokassa initially sought refuge in France, but was granted asylum in Côte d'Ivoire. The government appointed by Dacko, which retained many of Bokassa's ministers, quickly became plagued by internal dissension and public opposition. A new multi-party constitution was approved by referendum on 1 February 1981 and a presidential election followed on 15 March. Dacko, who was able to influence the electorate by the timely distribution of essential commodities, was elected with 50% of the votes cast, while his main opponent, Patassé, received 38%, although all the opposition candidates challenged the result and protested about irregularities. Opposition to Dacko's rule increased during 1981; legislative elections were cancelled, and the government suppressed the opposition parties, in breach of its commitment to political pluralism. Deprived of French support by the change of government in Paris, Dacko was persuaded to transfer power to a military government. On 1 September Gen. André Kolingba, the army chief of staff, was declared head of state. All party-political activity was suspended.

KOLINGBA'S RULE, 1981–93

On the first anniversary of his assumption of power, Kolingba announced a programme of economic recovery covering the period to 1985, and said that a one-party system would be envisaged thereafter. However, disenchantment with the military regime had begun to spread. In March 1982 an unsuccessful coup attempt was staged by Patassé, who subsequently took refuge in the French embassy. A crisis in the two countries' relations followed when the French, although not involved in the coup attempt, insisted that Patassé be granted safe passage to exile in Togo. Kolingba, whose government remained dependent on French aid, was forced to comply, against his stated determination to bring Patassé to trial. Relations between the two countries improved, however, following an official visit by Kolingba to Paris in October. Kolingba's foreign policy has been guided by the awareness that the survival of his regime is dependent upon the continued goodwill of the French government. France is the country's principal source of economic and budgetary aid, and French advisers oversee the CAR's security services, while providing a buttress against Libyan adventurism. Indeed, the French military presence in the CAR is a vital element of France's strategy in the region, notably with regard to Chad.

In August 1982 Abel Goumba, the leader of the opposition Front patriotique oubanguien–Parti du travail (FPO–PT), was arrested, with another leading member of the party, on charges of plotting against the government. Following intense but discreet French pressure, they were released in September 1983 with some of the prisoners who had been arrested in the Patassé coup attempt. Other members of the FPO–PT, meanwhile, had appointed a new leadership which was committed to armed struggle. The two other political parties fell into a similar state of fragmentation: part of the membership of the MLPC rejected the leadership of Patassé; and sections of the Mouvement centrafricain pour la libération nationale (MCLN) rejected their leader, Iddi Lala. Some elements of the three parties agreed in August 1983 to form a united front, named the Parti révolutionnaire centrafricain. The government appeared to be less alarmed by this development, however, than by Bokassa's attempt, in November, to return from exile in Côte d'Ivoire. His departure was prevented by the Ivorian authorities, who then expelled him to France, where he was reluctantly allowed to take up residence. In early 1984 several civilian politicians, including Goumba and Henri Maidou, a former vice-president, were arrested for violating the ban on political parties. At a trial in July, sentences of up to 10 years' imprisonment were passed on those implicated in the 1982 coup attempt. Some of these were reduced by Kolingba in December 1984, when both Goumba and Maidou were also released. In that month several opposition leaders formed a 'government-in-exile' in Libya. Kolingba was extremely apprehensive about this development. Former Brig.-Gen. Alphonse Mbaikoua, the 'president', and former Brig.-Gen. François Bozize, the 'vice-president', were erstwhile members of the Kolingba regime who had helped to organize the 1982 coup attempt and had escaped arrest. In July 1986 the MLPC and the FPO–PT announced the formation of a Front uni (FU), which was to campaign for a democratic system of government.

In September 1985 Kolingba dissolved the cabinet and formed a new administration, in which civilians were not only appointed ministers for the first time since the military take-over, but also held the majority of portfolios. Nevertheless, military personnel held the major posts. At a referendum held in November 1986 some 91.17% of voters granted a further six-year mandate to Kolingba as president and approved a draft constitution which provided for wide-ranging powers for the head of state, with the legislature occupying a mainly advisory role. In December a government reshuffle took place, in which Kolingba assumed the defence portfolio. In February 1987, at the constitutive assembly of the Rassemblement démocratique centrafricain (RDC), the sole political party stipulated in the new constitution, a clear separation was defined between party and state, and membership of the party was made voluntary. In July the country's first legislative elections for 20 years were held, at which all candidates were nominated by the RDC. Whether or not because of an electoral boycott by the FU, only 50% of eligible voters balloted for the 142 candidates selected to contest the 52 seats in the national assembly.

In October 1986, with the economy under scrutiny from the IMF and moves towards an ostensibly more democratic regime in progress, the government had been highly embarrassed when Bokassa suddenly returned to the CAR. He was arrested upon his arrival at Bangui airport. Reluctant to administer the death sentence imposed on him in his absence for charges ranging from embezzlement to murder and cannibalism, the government ordered a new trial, to be held in public in the presence of international observers.

The reasons for Bokassa's return have remained unclear. He had apparently been led to suppose that his return would be followed by his reinstatement as emperor by popular acclaim. During his retrial, represented by French defence lawyers, he argued that he had returned of his own free will to clear his name. However, he subsequently accepted an element of responsibility for some of his actions. The prosecution was poorly organized, with several of its witnesses themselves being arrested after giving evidence, and the trial lasted for six months. In June 1987 Bokassa was found guilty of four of the 14 charges brought against him, and was sentenced to death. An appeal was lodged, but was rejected by the supreme court in November. In February 1988, however, Kolingba commuted the sentence to one of imprisonment for life. In August 1989 it was announced that all remaining death sentences were to be similarly commuted; however, the remission excluded those who had been sentenced to death *in absentia*. In September 1991 Bokassa's life sentence was commuted to 20 years' imprisonment and in December 1992 the length of the sentence was further reduced, to 10 years.

After the trial, Kolingba resumed his earlier attempts at democratization and national reconciliation. The first municipal elections were held in May 1988, at which voters were offered a choice of RDC-approved candidates. A government reshuffle followed in July. Kolingba sought a *rapprochement* with former opponents of his regime by inviting Brig.-Gen. François Bozize to return from exile. (Bozize chose to remain in Benin, where he had founded an opposition movement, the Rassemblement populaire pour la reconstruction de la Centrafrique.) In addition, Kolingba appointed Henri Maidou to an influential banking position. Members of Patassé's MLPC were also rehabilitated during 1988, although Patassé himself remained in exile in Togo. However, in July 1989 about 12 opponents of the Kolingba regime, including members of the FPO–PT and Brig.-Gen. Bozize, were arrested in Benin, and subsequently extradited to the CAR and imprisoned. Bozize was eventually released and officially pardoned in December 1991.

In January 1989, shortly after the CAR had recognized the declaration, by the Palestine Liberation Organization, of an independent state of Palestine, it was announced that diplomatic relations were to be re-established with Israel. In May, however, diplomatic relations with Sudan were suspended, and the border with that country closed, when Sudan, in accordance with the boycott by the Arab states of all links with Israel, refused to allow the aircraft in which Kolingba was travelling on an official visit to Israel to cross its airspace. Kolingba's visit was postponed until July, when he travelled to Israel via Zaire and Europe. Diplomatic relations between the CAR and Sudan were resumed in September. In 1991 the government appealed to the international donor community for relief aid for an estimated 20,000 refugees from Sudan.

In May 1990 the RDC ruled that the establishment of a multi-party system in the CAR would be 'incompatible' with the country's political and economic development. However, this ruling was immediately contested in the form of a petition for a national conference on the future of the country, signed by 253 prominent citizens. The petition claimed that society in the CAR was 'corrupted by tribal discrimination, nepotism, fraud and injustice'. In October there was an outbreak of rioting in Bangui when the police attempted to disperse a public meeting of opposition supporters; several people were detained, including Dacko, Maidou and Goumba.

From late 1990 the government's unpopularity intensified, owing to the implementation of further economic austerity measures. Public servants were unpaid for several months in 1990, and in December the trade union movement, the Union syndicale des travailleurs de la Centrafrique (USTC), appealed for a general strike. The RDC eventually agreed to pay the workers one-quarter of the arrears owed to them, as well as promising to re-establish the post of prime minister and to undertake a fundamental review of the constitution. In March 1991 most of those who had been detained after the riots of October 1990 were released. The new post of prime minister was created in March 1991, with Edouard Franck, a former minister of state at the presidency, as the first occupant.

From April onwards sporadic strikes plagued the government, as the political opposition sought refuge in the trade union movement. In early July a meeting organized by the USTC was dispersed by the security forces. At least 10 union leaders were arrested in the following days and charged with convening an illegal political assembly. Nevertheless, in early July the government finally conceded the restoration of a multi-party political system and the imminent legalization of political parties; President Kolingba admitted that the reforms were being made to meet the wishes of the international donor community, on which the CAR was dependent. However, public meetings remained illegal, opposition parties were prevented access to the state-controlled media and civil service unions were banned by decree until the end of October. In early August the USTC called a 48-hour general strike in protest at the arrests of its leaders, and at the suppression of civil service unions. During August President Kolingba resigned from the presidency of the RDC. In July 1991 the CAR established diplomatic relations with Taiwan, and those with the People's Republic of China were suspended.

At the end of October 1991 the government agreed to convene a national debate, comprising representatives of the government and opposition movements. Throughout the next few months negotiations on the reform process took place between the government and the opposition; the latter advocated the replacement of the planned national debate by a national conference, which would have sovereign powers to overrule the president's recommendations and to introduce reforms itself. Meanwhile, Kolingba continued to oscillate between repression and compromise. In December he pardoned Brig.-Gen. Bozize for his involvement in the attempted coup of March 1982, while in May 1992 an opposition politician was sentenced to six months' imprisonment for criticizing a speech by the president.

The negotiations on reform collapsed in early May 1992. Nevertheless, the government continued to make preparations for a national debate. Divisions emerged within the opposition at this time, as five centrist parties formed the Conseil de l'entente des partis modérés, which appeared more inclined towards compromise than the main opposition grouping, the Concertation des forces démocratiques (CFD).

In August Kolingba opened the 'grand national debate'. Boycotted by the CFD and the church, it was dominated by pro-Kolingba nominees from the RDC and local government. The opening of the debate coincided with the killing of a leading member of the CFD by the security forces during a peaceful anti-government protest: this incident provoked condemnation from Amnesty International and the US ambassador.

At the end of August 1992, the national assembly approved legislation in accordance with decisions taken by the grand national debate: constitutional amendments were introduced which provided for the strict separation of executive, legislative and judicial powers and for direct multi-party presidential and legislative elections. Kolingba was granted temporary powers to rule by decree pending the election of a multi-party legislature. In early September Kolingba announced that presidential and parliamentary elections would be held in the following month. The elections commenced in late October, but were suspended by decree of the president (himself a candidate at the presidential election) and subsequently annulled by the supreme court. Three other candidates (ex-president David Dacko, former premier Ange Patassé and Enoch Derant Lakoué, the leader of the Parti social-démocrate—PSD) supported the annullment, although it was opposed by Dr Abel Goumba, the CFD candidate and leader of the Front patriotique pour le progrès (FPP). The CFD eventually accepted the postponement, suggesting that the elections should be restaged in February 1993. All sides accepted this proposal, and Kolingba appointed Gen. Timothée Malendoma as prime minister of a transitional government. Malendoma's Forum civique had broken ranks with the CFD by participating in the grand national debate, but Malendoma nevertheless retained the support of the opposition, having been one of the founders of the campaign for democracy. However, the CFD chose not to participate in his government.

In January 1993 Malendoma was dismissed after complaining that Kolingba had curtailed his powers as prime minister. The elections were again postponed, and in May the new prime minister, Enoch Durant Lakoué, announced that polling would take place in October. However, after strong opposition protest and severe pressure exerted by the French government, Kolingba brought the elections forward to August. At the first round of the presidential election on 22 August, Patassé received 37.3% of the votes cast, followed by Goumba with 21.68%, and Dacko with 20.1%. Kolingba received just 10.1%. At the elections to the legislature, held concurrently, of the 31 seats won outright, 15 were won by the MLPC of Ange Patassé, four seats by supporters of Dacko, four by the RDC and eight by smaller parties, some of which were grouped in the CFD. Kolingba initially sought to prevent the publication of the first-round results by issuing decrees which modified the electoral code and altered the composition of the supreme court. However, strong pressure from France, including the threat to suspend all forms of bilateral co-operation, forced him to reverse his decision. Some 2,000 supporters of David Dacko also demonstrated in Bangui in September to demand the invalidation of the results of the first round. Two days later, however, Dacko officially accepted the results, thereby accepting his defeat.

DEMOCRATIC TRANSITION

Patassé won the second round of the ballot on 19 September 1993, receiving 52.47% of votes cast (Goumba received 45.62%) and was declared president by the supreme court on 27 September. After the second round of voting for seats in the national assembly the MLPC had a total of 34 seats (nine seats short of an absolute majority), the RDC had 13 seats, the FPP and the Parti libéral démocratique (PLD) had seven seats each, and the Alliance pour la démocratie et le progrès (ADP) and supporters of Dacko, had six seats each. The remaining 12 seats were shared among seven minor parties.

Former president Bokassa was freed by Kolingba on 1 September 1993, three years before the end of his sentence, in a general amnesty for prisoners decreed ostensibly in celebration of the 12th anniversary of Kolingba's accession to power, but nevertheless widely interpreted to have been an attempt by the president to disrupt the elections and remain in power. After his release Bokassa declared that he was still 'the emperor' and that he would return to power if public opinion supported him; on his release, however, the government banned him from participating in elections for life and demoted him from the rank of marshal. Patassé was sworn in as president on 22 October. In his inaugural address he stressed that the government would aim to promote decentralization and regionalization, and to improve political freedoms. He also pledged to address the outstanding problem of unpaid salaries for civil servants. In late October Patassé appointed Jean-Luc Mandaba, a former minister of health under Kolingba and vice-president of the MLPC, as prime minister. After appointing a 19-member cabinet at the end of October, which included three ministers from the outgoing administration, Mandaba emphasized the primacy of economic policy in his reform programme. In addition to the MLPC, the new members of the government included representatives of the PLD, the ADP and the MDD, giving the coalition government a working majority of 53 seats in the national assembly. On 27 October, Patassé appointed Gen. Jean-Roger Lako as chief of staff of the armed forces.

In December 1993 Dacko institutionalized the support he commanded in a new party, the Mouvement pour la démocratie et le développement (MDD), whose stated objectives were to consolidate and safeguard national unity, and to promote the equitable distribution of income. At the end of 1993 the government announced the establishment of a commission of enquiry (including an audit of the former administration's financial affairs) which would investigate Kolingba's conduct during his 12-year presidency. In March 1994, following the arrest of two senior members of the RDC accused of provoking popular discontent, Kolingba was stripped of his army rank.

At the end of December 1993 the new minister of foreign affairs in charge of francophone countries, Simon Bedaya-Ngaro, led a delegation to Zaire where discussions were held with President Mobutu on cross-border issues. In early 1994, the government denied rumours that it was aiding the Sudanese army in its operations against the Sudan People's Liberation Army (SPLA) by allowing weapons to cross its territory. Following suggested mediation in the Sudanese civil war the Patassé administration instead reasserted its desire to seek a solution to the conflict in Chad. In February the government sponsored peace negotiations in Bangui between the government of Chad and southern factions. In late March the Central African Republic was admitted as the fifth member of the Lake Chad Basin Commission, in acknowledgement that the CAR is the main watershed for two major rivers flowing north to Lake Chad. Diplomatic relations with South Africa were restored by Kolingba prior to his departure from office in October 1993.

Economy

DIANA HUBBARD

Revised for this edition by the Editor

From independence in 1960 until 1965, under the first government of President Dacko, the economy of the Central African Republic (CAR) stagnated and, in particular, showed a severe decline in the output of cotton. In 1966 the new military government, under Jean-Bédel Bokassa, introduced measures to revive agriculture, and to encourage rural development. These measures had some considerable success up to 1970; however, during the early 1970s economic stagnation and recession recurred, and these problems (which continue to beset the CAR) became increasingly severe during the three years of the 'Central African Empire' (1976–79). The country's economic plight was a prime factor in the military take-over in September 1981. Faced with declining output and worsening budgetary and balance-of-payments deficits, the new government of Gen. Kolingba concluded an agreement with the International Monetary Fund (IMF) for a stand-by loan, which had already been partly negotiated by the Dacko regime. Severe cuts in public expenditure, reducing wages and personnel numbers in the civil service, the army and the police, formed part of an austerity plan implemented in early 1982. This, in turn, led to political strains which prompted a coup attempt by opposition leader Ange Patassé in March 1982. The fear of further adverse political consequences led the Kolingba government to abrogate its undertaking to the IMF (in relation to the budget deficit) in late 1983. The IMF stand-by facility and the allied rescheduling of the foreign debt were consequently suspended, and by the end of 1983 the country's financial position was precarious. The government yielded to the economic circumstances and revised its budget and investment targets to comply with IMF requirements. Stand-by credits were resumed, allowing for the rescheduling of the foreign debt. In mid-1987 the CAR introduced a three-year structural adjustment programme, which aimed to liberalize the economy, to foster private enterprise and to improve public finances, primarily through policies of retrenchment in the civil service and the liquidation or transfer to private ownership of parastatal organizations. Considerable progress was made, and in May 1990 a new structural adjustment facility was agreed with the IMF, to cover the period mid-1991–mid-1992.

Since the mid-1980s growth in real gross domestic product (GDP) has been erratic, generally reflecting the effect of climatic factors and fluctuations in world market prices on, respectively, the supply of and receipts from the CAR's major exports. An exceptional rate of growth in GDP in 1986, amounting to 5.2% in real terms, was reversed in 1987 with a decline of 2.5%. In 1988 real GDP increased by 2.2%, and two years of steady real growth followed in 1989 and 1990, with rates of 1.9% and 1.5% respectively. In 1991, however, real GDP increased by only 0.1% and in 1992 registered a decline of 2.3%.

AGRICULTURE

In 1992 about 61% of the working population were engaged in agriculture, which provided 41% of GDP in 1991. Agriculture is concentrated in the tropical rain-forest area in the south-west and the savannah lands in the central and north-west. The food crops (mainly cassava, maize, millet, sorghum, groundnuts and rice) are grown principally for domestic consumption. The rise in agricultural production has failed to keep pace with population growth, partly owing to drought. In recent years, food has accounted for around one-tenth of import spending, with a deficit in domestic production of one-fifth of total consumption. As a result, the government has placed a greater emphasis on food production in its regional development programmes, and the cultivation of rice is being encouraged. Meanwhile, agricultural diversification is being encouraged, mainly to substitute imports. A US $20m. palm oil complex is in operation at Bossongo, with an oil mill with an annual capacity of 7,500 tons, servicing 2,500 ha of plantations. In 1988 production began at a sugar refinery, supplied from 1,300 ha of new plantations (see below).

Coffee is the CAR's major export crop. It was formerly produced on large, European-owned plantations, but, following the political instability of the late 1970s and 1980s, small-holder production has become increasingly important and now accounts for 75% of total output. The crop is cultivated mainly in the south-western and central-southern regions of the country, and more than 90% is of the *robusta* variety. The level of production varies widely and is influenced by drought and trends in international prices for coffee. Output totalled 20,200 tons in 1988/89 before falling back to 14,000 tons in 1989/90, 12,000 tons in 1990/91, recovering to an estimated 14,000 tons in 1991/92. The Agence de développement de la zone caféière (ADECAF) is the parastatal organization responsible for the purchase, transportation and marketing of this commodity. Yields were raised to 890 kg per ha in 1990, which is relatively high by world standards.

Cotton is the most widely-grown cash crop, and is cultivated by an estimated 280,000 small-holder farmers. Production fell to a low of around 17,000 tons in 1981/82, but showed a good recovery in following years, peaking at 45,660 tons in 1984/85. However, yields—normally below 500 kg per ha—are among the lowest in Africa. The sharp fall in world cotton prices in 1986 led the government to respond to World Bank prompting and to cut back subsidies to cotton farmers and close down three of the CAR's seven cotton ginning complexes, while concentrating planting on the most productive areas. As a result, production declined by more than one-third in 1987/88, to only 19,200 tons. However, the importance of cotton cultivation as a source of employment and to the economy of the northern area prompted President Kolingba, in 1988, to halt the reduction of the area under cultivation, and to maintain the level of producer prices. However, owing to reduced demand much cotton remained unsold in subsequent years, and producers responded by planting significantly less. Output totalled 13,000 tons in 1990, and was estimated to have fallen to 8,000 tons in 1991 before recovering to about 12,000 tons in 1991. The longer-term outlook for the CAR's cotton crop is favourable, particularly as it is less severely affected by drought than some other crops.

Tobacco makes a limited, but steady, contribution to export earnings. Production in 1990 was estimated at 1,000 tons. Cape tobacco was traditionally grown in western regions of the country, and cut tobacco in eastern regions; however, a rise in world demand for cape tobacco has led to progressively reduced outputs of cut varieties.

The livestock industry is of recent development. Its further growth is hindered by available fodder and by the prevalence of the tsetse fly. Since 1950 efforts have been made to develop the industry, and the number of cattle increased substantially despite the setback of the droughts. The herd has also grown as a result of migration from Chad and Sudan. In 1992 there were an estimated 2.7m. head of cattle and 1.3m. goats. Nevertheless, domestic meat production fails to satisfy demand, and around 100,000 head of cattle are imported annually, mainly from Chad and Sudan. Efforts are being made to improve marketing, and to encourage the sedentary raising of cattle to allow for treatment against disease. Abattoirs and factories to utilize the products of the animal industries are also being promoted.

The country's large forest resources (35.8m. ha of tropical rain-forest) are at present under-exploited commercially, largely as a result of a lack of adequate roads and low-cost means of transportation to the coast. Only about 10% of the forest area is accessible to river transport. In addition, large areas are held as private hunting reserves. Timber exploitation has nevertheless expanded considerably since the late 1960s, following the formation of new companies geared to export and the establishment of new sawmills. Fellings of industrial roundwood reached a peak of 846,000 cu m in 1974, but fell back sharply in subsequent years, partly owing to low water levels on the traditional transport route along the Congo river. Moreover, the rise in the value of the CFA franc in relation to the currencies of the major Asian producers has reduced the price competitiveness of the CAR product. Log production, which averaged some 330,000 cu m annually in 1980–85, declined to 154,000 cu m in 1987 and to 152,000 cu m in 1988, before recovering to 295,500 cu m in 1989. The decline reflected a decrease in the area under forest (in the absence of any timber conservation and in response to the demands of agriculture and pasture). In 1990 the IDA announced a loan of $19m. to support a new forestry policy, which included the preparation of an inventory of forests and tree types and a substantial forest management programme. In addition, a national park was to be established in the rain-forest in the south-west of the country.

MINING

Mining contributed only 3.6% of the CAR's GDP in 1987. Diamonds are the main mineral deposit, and are found in alluvial deposits, mainly in the south-west and west of the country. Until 1960 production was wholly in the hands of expatriate companies but, with the closure in 1969 by government decree of the principal companies, individual African prospectors were responsible by 1970 for the whole of production. The decline in recorded production since the late 1960s, from a peak of 609,000 carats in 1968 to an average of 480,000 carats per year in 1989–93, is partly attributable to smuggling to the Congo, a concomitant of which has been a decline in the quality of officially traded stones, in addition to substantial reductions in government revenue. Smuggled, unofficial output is thought to be double the official total. In the mid-1980s the government attempted to discourage smuggling by increasing customs surveillance and by reducing the relatively high export tax. Subsequently there was some improvement in recorded diamond exports, which were valued at 22,200m. francs CFA in 1989 and 19,700m. francs CFA in 1990. Recorded production was 417,000 carats in 1988, 529,000 carats in 1989, 415,000 carats in 1990 and 430,000 carats in 1991, of which 428,100 carats were exported. Output in 1992 and 1993 was around 400,000 carats annually. Local cutting and polishing industries are being developed; however, exports of diamonds are mostly in uncut form.

Gold is also mined, although production levels have fluctuated sharply, from a peak of 538 kg in 1980 to only 31 kg in 1982; output totalled 293.8 kg in 1989, but declined to 226.6 kg in 1990. Uranium has been discovered near Bakouma, 480 km east of Bangui. Reserves are estimated at 20,000 tons, with a concentration ratio of some 50%. It was hoped to start production during the 1980s at around 800 tons per year, but the weakening in international prices for uranium has obstructed development of the deposits, which would also necessitate the construction of a road to the border with Cameroon.

MANUFACTURING AND POWER

The industrial sector is little developed, and contributed only 16% of GDP in 1991. Manufacturing activity includes the processing of raw materials such as wood and cotton, and food-processing and the production of cigarettes, beer, soap and vegetable oil for the domestic market. A vehicle-assembly plant opened in 1981, but output levels have been very low, and operations were virtually suspended in 1986.

The textile and leather industries constitute the chief industrial sector. Cotton ginning takes place in 20 factories. A textile complex, undertaking spinning, weaving and dyeing, which formed the CAR's largest single industrial enterprise, was acquired by the state when it was on the point of liquidation in 1976. Four years later, it did close down, but in 1983 the European Investment Bank and the French government agreed to provide loans of 4,600m. francs CFA to rehabilitate the project, which now has a capacity of 4.4m. metres of cloth per year. The spinning plant began production at the end of 1984, and the weaving plant was completed in 1985, but the complex is still not operating at full capacity. In early 1994 the complex was reported to have closed again due to informal sector competition. Garments are made up in several factories, and shoes are also produced. Major projects that are envisaged include a plywood and chipboard factory, clinker-grinding and a cement factory, and a variety of food-processing industries. A new plant to refine cotton seed oil, with a treatment capacity of 20,000 tons of seed per year, is planned at Bambari, while an oil mill has been built at the Bossongo oil palm plantation (see above), with funding from the African Development Bank, France and the African Development Fund. A sugar-processing plant was opened at Ouaka in 1987 and is the first in the CAR, with cane supplied from 1,100 ha of new plantations. It has a planned annual output of 6,000 tons of sugar (for the domestic market).

The CAR is heavily dependent on imported petroleum as an energy source (70% of commercial supply). The remainder is provided by local hydroelectricity: the two Boali stations at the M'Bali falls supply about 80% of total electricity output, with about 10 smaller thermal stations accounting for the remainder. Plans are under way to construct a new hydroelectric plant at Kembe. In 1991 total output of electric energy was 96 kWh of which hydroelectricity accounted for the largest proportion.

TRANSPORT

The transport system is badly underdeveloped and a major constraint on the country's economic development. There is an extensive network of roads (23,738 km in 1991) but less than 460 km are paved. The road system suffered serious deterioration over the 1977–81 period, owing to lack of upkeep. In recent years, however, international development organizations have extended funds for the rehabilitation of the network. The CAR section of the Transafrican highway from Lagos to Mombasa was completed in 1984, providing a link with Cameroon; this route is now being upgraded. There is no railway, but there are long-standing plans to extend the Transcameroon line to Bangui and also to link the CAR with the rail system in Sudan and Gabon. However, for the foreseeable future any development in the land transport network will be in the form of roads rather than rail. A much larger volume of freight is carried by river; of a total of 7,000 km of inland waterways, some 2,800 km are navigable, most importantly the Oubangui river south of Bangui, which is the country's main outlet for external trade, and the Sangha and Lobaye rivers. Port facilities are being improved, with French and EC assistance.

The principal route for the import and export trade is the trans-equatorial route which involves 1,800 km by river from Bangui to Brazzaville, in the Congo and then rail from Brazzaville to Pointe-Noire. This route also handles traffic for Chad. It was formerly operated by a public corporation, jointly owned by the countries of the Union douanière et économique de l'Afrique centrale (UDEAC), but this was dissolved, and the CAR subsequently operated its own river transport authority. With river traffic falling as exporters and importers preferred the more efficient land route through Cameroon, and also because of poor navigation conditions on the Oubangui, river transport operations were returned to the private sector in 1980. The government has committed 4,300m. francs CFA to rehabilitation: in the mean time, however, traffic has not yet recovered to its 1980 level of 263,386 tons.

There is an international airport at Bangui–Mpoko, and there are 37 small airports. Internal services are, however, irregular and dependent on the availability of fuel.

A five-year programme for the modernization of the existing transport infrastructure, at a total projected cost of $139m. (to be financed by bilateral and multilateral donors), was announced in mid-1990.

PUBLIC FINANCE

The CAR's fiscal position is weak, with a narrow tax base which is vulnerable to adverse trends in international prices for coffee and cotton and prone to erosion as a result of smuggling, while bearing the burden of losses incurred by the parastatal organizations and of personnel expenditure for the cumbersome civil service. Consequently, substantial deficits have been incurred. France provided budgetary aid to the new Dacko government in December 1979, but the budget deficit continued to increase (reaching 8,200m. francs CFA in 1982). As part of its agreement with the IMF for payments support, the government implemented measures in 1982 to reduce the numbers of the 27,000-strong civil service and to cut the salaries of those remaining by 28%. Despite the partial success of this policy, a deficit of 7,500m. francs CFA was recorded in 1983, and France extended direct budgetary aid. In 1984 the government was obliged by the country's difficult payments situation to agree to another stabilization programme guided by the IMF. This provided for an increase in tax revenues and a restructuring of the parastatal organizations to reduce the drain on budget resources. The deficit was subsequently reduced (reaching its lowest level, of 2,000m. francs CFA on expenditure of 43,700m. francs CFA, in 1985), but rose again, to 43,400m. francs CFA in 1988 and to 49,906m. in 1989, as revenue stagnated while expenditure continued to rise, in spite of some success in the government's programme of voluntary redundancy for one-tenth of the civil service. France granted budgetary support in 1987–89, and such aid will be required for the foreseeable future. The deficit was estimated at 48,780m. francs CFA in 1990, and was projected to fall further, to 37,240m. francs CFA, in 1991, owing to the reduced expenditure on public-sector wages resulting from prolonged strikes.

TRADE, AID AND THE BALANCE OF PAYMENTS

The CAR's foreign trade accounts show a persistent deficit. While imports have tended to increase, export receipts have fluctuated widely, in response to trends in international prices for diamonds, coffee, timber and cotton. Diamonds remain the principal source of export earnings, accounting for 48% of total export revenue in 1990 followed by timber, cotton and coffee.

With a large net outflow on services, partly offset by transfer payments (i.e. official grants), the CAR has shown a substantial deficit on the current account of the balance of payments in recent years, totalling 10,958m. francs CFA in 1989, 22,700m. francs CFA in 1990 and 17,426m francs CFA in 1991.

Since independence, France has continued to be the major source of aid, providing two-thirds of all aid in the period 1982–87, and budgetary aid equivalent to more than one-half of the government's planned expenditure in 1988. Substantial aid funds have also been provided by the EDF through support for export earnings (under the Stabex provisions of the Lomé Conventions), aid to improve productivity and diversify the economy, and technical assistance. Aid from the US government totalled $3m. in 1990. In all, disbursements of official development assistance from non-communist countries and multilateral agencies averaged $124m. per year during the period 1982–87, equivalent to more than 95% of the CAR's export earnings and rose to $236m. in 1990, with France providing 44%. Although about two-thirds of this aid has been in grant form, the funds have not been sufficient to resolve the country's balance-of-payments difficulties, and the CAR has repeatedly sought stand-by credits from the IMF. In 1994 the IMF approved a stand-by credit of $23m. to support economic reform policies in the CAR. The total external debt increased rapidly throughout the 1980s, rising from $185m. in 1980 to $901m. at the end of 1992, in which year the cost of debt-servicing was equivalent to 10.2% of the value of exports of goods and services. In 1991 88% of the total external debt was owed to official creditors; concessionary terms with long maturity periods had been arranged for 78% of the total external debt. Beginning in 1989 the CAR was to benefit from debt relief under the terms of the June 1988 Toronto agreement, and the country's public debt to France was cancelled with effect from January 1990.

DEVELOPMENT PLANNING

The first Development Plan, covering the four-year period 1967–70, placed particular emphasis upon rural development and education. The second Development Plan covered the five-year period 1971–75. The development of productive capacity absorbed rather more than 50% of planned expenditure, economic infrastructure about 25% and social infrastructure about 15%. The CAR's third Development Plan, for 1976–80, was abandoned in 1978, with only one-sixth of the total investments realized. In early 1980 the CAR adopted, with IMF approval, an austerity Plan aimed at limiting the payments deficit and budgetary disequilibrium by concentrating resources on promoting agricultural production, and by monitoring public transfers more carefully. This short-term (1980–81) rehabilitation Plan was to cover investments of 45,000m. francs CFA but, partly due to political uncertainties, barely 25% were realized.

In 1982 Gen. Kolingba initiated a Recovery Plan for 1983–86, envisaging total expenditure of 169,000m. francs CFA and prepared within the framework of the IMF proposals for economic stabilization. A development plan, involving expenditure of 280,000m. francs CFA, was prepared for the period 1986–90, but later was formally superseded by the objectives of the 1987–89 structural adjustment programme. In May 1990 a new structural adjustment facility was agreed with the IMF. However, growing political instability during 1990 and 1991 hindered the progress achieved by the Kolingba government in pursuing economic adjustment targets. In 1992, according to estimates by the World Bank, the CAR's gross national product (GNP), measured at average 1990–92 prices, was $1,307m., equivalent to $410 per head. The World Bank has since revised its approach to francophone African countries, emphasizing support for agricultural and rural development and eliminating the need for a policy choice between favouring food crops or export crops.

In January 1994 the CAR and the other member countries of the CFA franc zone adopted a comprehensive macroeconomic strategy which included devaluation of the CFA franc against the French franc by 50%.

PROBLEMS AND PROSPECTS

In addition to its vulnerability to adverse climatic conditions and to unfavourable movements in world prices for its agricultural exports, the inadequacy of the CAR's transport facilities has been a severe handicap to sustained economic growth. The development of these facilities would benefit economic development in all sectors, particularly forestry. In the second part of the 1960s the country made determined efforts to address its economic problems, but during the 1970s, the economy lost its momentum, an outcome for which domestic policies and their administration must bear a large responsibility, although adverse climatic factors also played a part. Agricultural production declined, and marketing difficulties were experienced with domestic food crops. The diamond industry's lack of probity added to the government's own financial problems. Industry and commerce stagnated, an outcome to which the payments difficulties of the treasury contributed both directly and indirectly. To these various problems were added the damaging effects of high energy prices and the world economic recession of the early 1980s and the persistence of adverse economic conditions world-wide in the early 1990s. If significant economic progress is to be achieved, there will be a need for both continued foreign technical and financial assistance at high levels and for fundamental domestic economic, financial and administrative reforms. After his inauguration in October 1993 President Patassé announced an emergency programme of economic measures for 1994 which aimed to rehabilitate central government finances and eliminate the primary budget deficit. The new measures, supported by the IMF, included the liberalization of the economy's regulatory framework, restructuring public enterprises and implementing a new civil service statute.

Statistical Survey

Source (unless otherwise stated): Division des Statistiques et des Etudes Economiques, Ministère de Finance, du Plan, des Statistiques et de la Coopération Internationale, Bangui; tel. 61-45-74; telex 5280.

Area and Population

AREA, POPULATION AND DENSITY

Area (sq km)	622,984*
Population (census of 8–22 December 1975)	
Males	1,023,128
Females	1,064,872
Total	2,088,000
Population (official estimates at 31 December)	
1986	2,739,564
1988	2,688,426
1991	2,895,000
Density (per sq km) at 31 December 1991	4.6

* 240,535 sq miles.

PRINCIPAL TOWNS (official estimates at 31 December 1988)
Bangui (capital), population 451,690, Berbérati 41,891, Bouar 39,676, Bambari 38,633, Bossangoa 31,502, Carnot 31,324.

BIRTHS AND DEATHS (UN estimates, annual averages)

	1975–80	1980–85	1985–90
Birth rate (per 1,000)	44.1	45.0	44.9
Death rate (per 1,000)	20.6	19.3	18.2

Source: UN, *World Population Prospects: The 1992 Revision.*

ECONOMICALLY ACTIVE POPULATION
(ILO estimates, '000 persons at mid-1980)

	Males	Females	Total
Agriculture, etc.	436	432	868
Industry	56	20	76
Services	131	124	255
Total	623	576	1,200

Source: ILO, *Economically Active Population Estimates and Projections, 1950–2025.*

Mid-1992 (estimates in '000): Agriculture, etc. 878; Total 1,450 (Source: FAO, *Production Yearbook*).

Agriculture

PRINCIPAL CROPS ('000 metric tons)

	1990	1991	1992
Rice (paddy)	8	7	7*
Maize	57	58	50*
Millet and sorghum*	30	24	16
Cassava (Manioc)	547	575*	606*
Yams†	195	200	220
Taro (Coco yam)†	38	39	39
Groundnuts (in shell)	80	60	43*
Sesame seed	21*	23*	27*
Cottonseed	18	17†	18†
Pumpkins, squash and gourds	13	14†	16†
Oranges†	16	16	16
Mangoes†	8	8	8
Bananas†	92	93	94
Plantains†	67	68	68
Coffee (green)	14	12*	14*
Cotton (lint)	13	8*	12*

* Unofficial estimate(s). † FAO estimate(s).

Source: FAO, *Production Yearbook.*

LIVESTOCK ('000 head, year ending September)

	1990	1991	1992*
Cattle	2,595	2,677	2,700
Goats	1,242	1,270*	1,300
Sheep	134	135*	137
Pigs	405	441	460

Chickens (million): 3 in 1990; 3* in 1991; 3* in 1992.

* FAO estimate(s).

Source: FAO, *Production Yearbook*.

LIVESTOCK PRODUCTS (metric tons)

	1990	1991	1992*
Beef and veal	40,000†	42,000*	43,000
Mutton and lamb*	1,000	1,000	1,000
Goats' meat	4,000†	4,000*	5,000
Pig meat	8,000†	8,000†	8,000
Poultry meat	2,000†	3,000*	3,000
Other meat	8,000	7,000	7,000
Cows' milk	47,000†	48,000†	48,000
Cattle hides (fresh)*	6,512	6,769	7,040
Hen eggs*	1,332	1,332	1,341
Honey	9,034	9,300*	9,500

* FAO estimate(s). † Unofficial estimate.

Source: FAO, *Production Yearbook*.

Forestry

ROUNDWOOD REMOVALS ('000 cubic metres, excluding bark)

	1989	1990	1991
Sawlogs, veneer logs and logs for sleepers	227	171	118
Other industrial wood*	256	264	271
Fuel wood*	3,055	3,055	3,055
Total	3,538	3,490	3,444

* FAO estimates. Annual output of fuel wood is assumed to be unchanged since 1987.

Source: FAO, *Yearbook of Forest Products*.

SAWNWOOD PRODUCTION ('000 cubic metres)

	1989	1990	1991
Total	57	63	60

Source: FAO, *Yearbook of Forest Products*.

Fishing

('000 metric tons, live weight)

	1989	1990	1991
Total catch (freshwater fish)	13.0	13.0	13.5

Source: FAO, *Yearbook of Fishery Statistics*.

Mining

	1988	1989	1990
Gold (kg, metal content of ore)	382	328	241
Gem diamonds ('000 carats)	358	448	415
Industrial diamonds ('000 carats)	59	81	78

Industry

SELECTED PRODUCTS

	1985	1986	1987
Beer (hectolitres)	275,560	280,000	299,000
Soft drinks (hectolitres)	49,758	59,000	68,000
Cigarettes and cigars (million)	572	440	476
Footwear ('000 pairs)	611	544	159
Motor cycles (number)	4,515	3,000	3,000
Bicycles (number)	3,103	3,000	1,000
Electric energy (million kWh)	78	94	92

1988: Electric energy (million kWh) 93.

1989: Electric energy (million kWh) 93.

1990: Electric energy (million kWh) 95.

1991: Electric energy (million kWh) 96.

Source: UN, *Industrial Statistics Yearbook*.

Finance

CURRENCY AND EXCHANGE RATES

Monetary Units

100 centimes = 1 franc de la Coopération financière en Afrique centrale (CFA).

French Franc, Sterling and Dollar Equivalents (31 March 1994)

1 French franc = 100 francs CFA;
£1 sterling = 846.40 francs CFA;
US $1 = 570.14 francs CFA;
1,000 francs CFA = £1.181 = $1.754.

Average Exchange Rate (francs CFA per US $)

1991 282.11
1992 264.69
1993 283.16

Note: The exchange rate of 1 French franc = 50 francs CFA, established in 1948, remained in force until January 1994, when the CFA franc was devalued by 50%, with the exchange rate adjusted to 1 French franc = 100 francs CFA.

BUDGET (revised figures, million francs CFA)

Revenue	1991	1992	1993
Taxes	33,600	42,900	34,120
Other receipts	3,800	3,900	2,410
Total	37,400	46,800	36,530

Expenditure	1991	1992	1993
Current expenditure	48,100	47,300	37,100
Capital expenditure	34,900	32,800	29,700
Total	83,000	80,100	66,800

Source: Banque des Etats de l'Afrique Centrale, *Etudes et Statistiques*, August-September 1993.

CENTRAL BANK RESERVES (US $ million at 31 December)

	1990	1991	1992
Gold*	3.98	3.94	3.70
IMF special drawing rights	4.87	0.70	0.06
Reserve position in IMF	0.13	0.13	0.12
Foreign exchange	113.63	102.15	99.94
Total	122.61	106.92	103.82

* National valuation.

Source: IMF, *International Financial Statistics.*

MONEY SUPPLY ('000 million francs CFA at 31 December)

	1991	1992	1993
Currency outside banks	42.26	43.09	52.16
Demand deposits at commercial and development banks	10.77	9.06	7.27
Total money	53.03	52.16	59.43

Source: IMF, *International Financial Statistics.*

COST OF LIVING
(Consumer Price Index for Bangui; base: 1981 = 100)

	1989	1990	1991
Food	128.4	129.3	124.0
Fuel and light	153.8	143.4	141.3
Clothing	163.0	155.3	n.a.
All items (incl. others)*	135.2	134.9	131.0

* Excluding rent.

Source: ILO, *Year Book of Labour Statistics.*

NATIONAL ACCOUNTS (million francs CFA at current prices)
Gross Domestic Product by Economic Activity

	1988	1989	1990
Agriculture, hunting, forestry and fishing	120,540	121,900	123,990
Mining and quarrying	8,930	10,310	10,740
Manufacturing	22,530	28,590	29,570
Electricity, gas and water	1,270	1,310	1,360
Construction	6,960	5,350	5,670
Trade, restaurants and hotels / Transport, storage and communications }	69,200	71,040	73,610
Government services	29,950	29,480	28,960
Sub-total (incl. others)	283,270	291,770	297,630
Import duties	13,620	13,720	13,560
GDP in purchasers' values	296,890	305,490	311,190

BALANCE OF PAYMENTS (US $ million)

	1990	1991	1992
Merchandise exports f.o.b.	150.5	125.6	123.5
Merchandise imports f.o.b.	−241.6	−178.7	−165.1
Trade balance	−91.1	−53.0	−41.6
Exports of services	69.1	50.5	53.6
Imports of services	−168.5	−136.7	−143.9
Other income received	0.8	5.5	6.4
Other income paid	−22.4	−19.0	−25.3
Private unrequited transfers (net)	−32.9	−29.8	−32.1
Official unrequited transfers (net)	155.9	120.7	125.4
Current balance	−89.1	−61.8	−57.4
Direct investment (net)	−3.1	−8.4	−8.7
Other capital (net)	72.6	32.9	41.6
Net errors and omissions	1.0	−1.8	24.8
Overall balance	−18.6	−39.1	0.3

Source: IMF, *International Financial Statistics.*

External Trade

PRINCIPAL COMMODITIES (distribution by SITC, US $'000)

Imports c.i.f.	1989
Food and live animals	22,768
Cereals and cereal preparations	8,192
Wheat flour	4,320
Sugar, sugar preparations and honey	6,232
Sugar and honey	5,959
Refined sugars	5,945
Beverages and tobacco	5,706
Tobacco and tobacco manufactures	3,715
Mineral fuels, lubricants, etc	10,658
Petroleum and petroleum products	10,390
Refined petroleum products	10,273
Gas oils (distillate fuels)	3,358
Chemicals and related products	22,239
Medicinal and pharmaceutical products	10,333
Medicaments	6,705
Essential oils, perfume materials and cleansing preparations	3,009
Pesticides, disinfectants, etc.	3,104
Basic manufactures	28,364
Paper, paperboard and manufactures	3,325
Textile yarn, fabrics, etc.	5,737
Non-metallic mineral manufactures	6,780
Lime, cement, etc.	5,288
Cement	5,244
Machinery and transport equipment	52,876
Machinery specialized for particular industries	7,605
Civil engineering and contractors' plant and equipment	3,094
General industrial machinery, equipment and parts	7,712
Electrical machinery, apparatus, etc.	8,061
Road vehicles and parts (excl. tyres, engines and electrical parts)	23,638
Passenger motor cars (excl. buses)	5,510
Motor vehicles for goods transport and special purposes	7,395
Goods vehicles (lorries and trucks)	4,969
Parts and accessories for motor vehicles	6,625
Miscellaneous manufactured articles	11,722
Total (incl. others)	159,124

Source: UN, *International Trade Statistics Yearbook.*

1991 (million francs CFA): Total imports 40,853 (Source: IMF, *International Financial Statistics*).

Exports f.o.b.	1989
Food and live animals	40,341
Coffee, tea, cocoa and spices	40,204
Coffee (green and roasted)	40,204
Crude materials (inedible) except fuels	34,999
Cork and wood	18,204
Sawlogs and veneer logs	12,712
Sawn lumber	5,102
Textile fibres and waste	12,608
Cotton	12,608
Basic manufactures	59,232
Non-metallic mineral manufactures	58,972
Diamonds (non-industrial)	58,970
Total (incl. others)	140,287

Source: UN, *International Trade Statistics Yearbook*.

1990 (million francs CFA): Coffee 2,730; Wood 3,348; Cotton 3,837; Diamonds 15,970. (Source: IMF, *International Financial Statistics*.)

1991 (million francs CFA): Coffee 1,413; Wood 1,996; Cotton 5,799; Diamonds 15,714.

PRINCIPAL TRADING PARTNERS (US $'000)

Imports c.i.f.	1989
Belgium/Luxembourg	4,032
Cameroon	14,514
Chad	1,701
China	4,211
Congo	5,111
France	67,631
Gabon	2,469
Italy	2,681
Japan	12,043
Netherlands	3,338
United Kingdom	1,988
USA	2,037
Zaire	5,715
Total (incl. others)	159,124

Exports f.o.b.*	1989
Belgium/Luxembourg	71,353
France	48,242
Spain	2,482
Sudan	3,320
Switzerland	6,967
Total (incl. others)	137,903

* Excluding exports of gold (US $'000): 2,384 in 1989.

Source: UN, *International Trade Statistics Yearbook*.

Transport

ROAD TRAFFIC (motor vehicles in use at 31 December)

	1981	1982	1983
Passenger cars	23,750	38,930	41,321
Buses and coaches	79	103	118
Goods vehicles	3,060	3,190	3,720
Motorcycles and scooters	170	278	397
Mopeds	62,518	71,421	79,952

Source: IRF, *World Road Statistics*.

1988: Passenger cars 11,700; Commercial vehicles 3,700.
1989: Passenger cars 11,100; Commercial vehicles 3,400.
1990: Passenger cars 11,600; Commercial vehicles 3,600.

Source: UN, *Statistical Yearbook*.

INLAND WATERWAYS TRAFFIC—INTERNATIONAL SHIPPING (metric tons)

	1986	1987	1988
Freight unloaded at Bangui	152,000	113,300	126,300
Freight loaded at Bangui	75,500	57,200	53,100
Total	227,500	170,500	179,400

CIVIL AVIATION (traffic on scheduled services)*

	1989	1990	1991
Kilometres flown (million)	3	3	3
Passengers carried ('000)	128	130	118
Passenger-km (million)	236	245	216
Freight ton-km (million)	18	18	16

*Including an apportionment of the traffic of Air Afrique.

Source: UN, *Statistical Yearbook*.

Tourism

	1988	1989	1990
Foreign tourist arrivals	1,875	2,039	1,599

Communications Media

	1989	1990	1991
Radio receivers	180,000	200,000	210,000
Television receivers	10,000	13,000	14,000

Source: UNESCO, *Statistical Yearbook*.

Telephones: 5,712 in use in 1991.

Education

(1989)

	Teachers	Pupils
Primary	3,581	323,661
Secondary		
General	1,216	45,633
Vocational	101	3,514
Higher	386*	3,482

* Figure for 1988.

Source: UNESCO, *Statistical Yearbook*.

1991: Primary school teachers 4,004; Primary school pupils 308,409.

Directory

The Constitution

The present Constitution of the Central African Republic was adopted following its approval by referendum on 21 November 1986. In August 1992 the Constitution was amended to provide for the strict separation of executive, legislative and judicial powers.

THE PRESIDENCY

The President of the Republic is Head of State and Commander-in-Chief of the national armed forces. The President is elected for a six-year term by direct universal suffrage. He is elected by an absolute majority of votes cast. If such is not obtained at the first ballot, a second ballot is to take place, contested by the two candidates gaining the largest number of votes in the first ballot. The election of the new President is to take place not less than 20 days and not more than 40 days before the expiration of the mandate of the President in office. However, the President may choose to hold a referendum to determine whether or not his mandate is to be renewed. Should the electorate reject the proposal, the President is to resign and a new presidential election is to be held two weeks after the publication of the results of the referendum. The Presidency is to become vacant only in the event of the President's death, resignation, condemnation by the High Court of Justice or permanent physical incapacitation, as certified by a Special Committee comprising the presidents of the National Assembly, the Economic and Regional Council and the Supreme Court (see below). The election of a new President must take place not less than 20 days and not more than 40 days following the occurrence of a vacancy, during which time the president of the National Assembly is to act as interim President, with limited powers.

The President appoints the Prime Minister, who presides over the Council of Ministers. The President promulgates laws adopted by the National Assembly or by the Congress and has the power to dissolve the National Assembly, in which event legislative elections must take place not less than 20 and not more than 40 days following its dissolution.

PARLIAMENT

This is composed of the National Assembly and the Economic and Regional Council, which, when sitting together, are to be known as the Congress. The primary function of the Congress is to pass organic laws in implementation of the Constitution, whenever these are not submitted to a referendum.

The National Assembly

The National Assembly is composed of deputies elected by direct universal suffrage for a five-year term. Its president is designated by, and from within, its bureau. Legislation may be introduced either by the President of the Republic or by a consensus of one-third of the members of the Assembly. Provisions are made for the rendering inadmissible of any law providing for the execution of projects carrying a financial cost to the State which exceeds their potential value. The National Assembly holds two ordinary sessions per year of 60 days each, at the summons of the President of the Republic, who may also summon it to hold extraordinary sessions with a pre-determined agenda. Sessions of the National Assembly are opened and closed by presidential decree.

The Economic and Regional Council

The Economic and Regional Council is composed of representatives from the principal sectors of economic and social activity. One-half of its members are appointed by the President, and the remaining half are elected by the National Assembly on the nomination of that body's president. It acts as an advisory body in matters referred to it by the President, as well as in all legislative proposals of an economic and social nature.

The Congress

The Congress has the same president and bureau as the National Assembly. An absolute majority of its members is needed to pass organic laws, as well as laws pertaining to the amendment of the Constitution which have not been submitted to a referendum. It defines development priorities and may meet, at the summons of the President, to ratify treaties or to declare a state of war.

Additional clauses deal with sovereignty, the judiciary, the administration of the CAR's *collectivités territoriales* and with the procedure for constitutional amendments.

The Government

HEAD OF STATE

President: ANGE-FÉLIX PATASSÉ (inaugurated 22 October 1993).

COUNCIL OF MINISTERS
(August 1994)

Prime Minister: JEAN-LUC MANDABA.

Minister of Finance, Planning and International Co-operation: EMMANUEL DOKOUNA.

Minister of National Defence and Veterans: JEAN METTE-YAPENDE.

Minister of the Interior and National Security: JEAN-CLAUDE DOBANGA.

Minister of Foreign Affairs, in charge of Francophone Relations: SIMON BEDAYA-NGARO.

Minister of Justice and Law Reform and Keeper of the Seals: JACQUES MBOSSO.

Minister of Education, Co-ordination of Research and Technology: ETIENNE GOYEMIDE.

Minister of Public Health and Population: ANDRÉ ZANEFEI TOUMBONA.

Minister of Energy Resources and Minerals: CHARLES MAZI.

Minister of Agriculture and Livestock: GABRIEL BOTE BADEKARA.

Minister of Water Resources, Forests, Hunting, Fisheries, Tourism and Environment: MARTIN GBAFOLO.

Minister of Industry, Commerce and Crafts: LÉON ODOUFOU.

Minister of the Civil Service, Labour, Social Security and Vocational Training: FIDÈLE OGBAMI.

Minister of Communications, Posts and Telecommunications: JOSEPH-VERMOND TCHENDO.

Minister of Transport, Public Works, Housing and Territorial Administration: OLIVIER GABIRAULT.

Minister of Youth, Sport, Arts and Culture: ALBERT NDODET.

Minister of Social Action and the Promotion of Women: MARIE NOELLE KOYARA.

Minister in charge of General Secretariat of Government and Relations with Parliament: GÉRARD GABA.

MINISTRIES

Office of the President: Palais de la Renaissance, Bangui; tel. 61-03-23; telex 5253.

Ministry of Agriculture and Livestock: Bangui.

Ministry of the Civil Service, Labour, Social Security and Vocational Training: Bangui; tel. 61-01-44.

Ministry of Communications, Posts and Telecommunications: BP 1290, Bangui; telex 5301.

Ministry of Education, Co-ordination of Research and Technology: BP 791, Bangui; telex 5333.

Ministry of Energy Resources and Minerals: Bangui; telex 5243.

Ministry of Finance, Planning and International Co-operation: BP 912, Bangui; tel. 61-44-88; telex 5280.

Ministry of Foreign Affairs: Bangui; tel. 61-15-74; telex 5213.

Ministry of the Interior and National Security: Bangui.

Ministry of Industry, Commerce and Crafts: Bangui.

Ministry of Justice and Law Reform: Bangui; tel. 61-16-44.

Ministry of National Defence and Veterans: Bangui; tel. 61-46-11; telex 5298.

Ministry of Public Health and Population: Bangui; tel. 61-29-01.

Ministry of Transport, Public Works, Housing and Territorial Administration: BP 941, Bangui; tel. 61-23-07; telex 5335; fax 61-15-52.

Ministry of Water Resources, Forests, Hunting, Fisheries, Tourism and Environment: Bangui.

Ministry of Youth, Sport, Arts and Culture: Bangui.

President and Legislature

PRESIDENT

Presidential election, First Ballot, 22 August 1993

Candidate	Votes	% of votes
ANGE-FÉLIX PATASSÉ (MLPC)	302,004	37.31
Dr ABEL GOUMBA (CFD)	175,467	21.68
DAVID DACKO (Independent)	162,721	20.10
Gen. ANDRÉ KOLINGBA (RDC)	97,942	12.10
ENOCH DERANT LAKOUÉ (PSD)	19,368	2.39
Gen. TIMOTHÉE MALENDOMA (FC)	16,400	2.03
Brig.-Gen. FRANÇOIS BOZIZE (RPRC)	12,169	1.50
RUTH ROLLAND JEANNE MARIE (PRC)	8,068	1.00
Invalid votes	15,317	1.89
Total	809,456	100.00

Second Ballot, 19 September 1993

Candidate	% of votes
ANGE-FÉLIX PATASSÉ (MLPC)	52.47
Dr ABEL GOUMBA (CFD)	45.62
Invalid votes	1.91
Total	100.00

ASSEMBLÉE NATIONALE

Legislative power is vested in the bicameral Congress, comprising the National Assembly and the advisory Economic and Regional Council.

President: HUGUES DOBOZENDI.

General election, 27 August and 19 September 1993

	Seats
MLPC	34
RDC	13
FPP	7
PLD	7
ADP	6
Supporters of David Dacko*	6
CN	3
PSD	3
MESAN	1
FC	1
PRC	1
MDRERC	1
Independents	2
Total	85

* Formed the Mouvement pour la démocratie et le développement in December 1993.

Political Organizations

The Rassemblement démocratique centrafrican (RDC) was the sole legal political party from February 1987 until July 1991, when the Constitution was amended to enable the establishment of a plural political system.

Alliance pour la démocratie et le progrès (ADP): Bangui; f. 1991; Leader FRANÇOIS PEHONA.

Convention nationale (CN): Bangui; f. 1991; Leader DAVID GALIAMBO.

Forum civique (FC): Bangui; Leader Gen. TIMOTHÉE MALENDOMA.

Front patriotique pour le progrès (FPP): BP 259, Bangui; tel. and fax (236) 61-52-23; f. 1991; aims to promote political discourse and education; Leader Dr ABEL GOUMBA.

Mouvement centrafricain pour la libération nationale (MCLN): Lagos, Nigeria; Leader Dr IDDI LALA.

Mouvement pour la démocratie et le développement (MDD): Bangui; f. 1993; aims to promote national unity and the fair distribution of national revenue; Leader DAVID DACKO.

Mouvement démocratique pour la renaissance et l'évolution de la République Centrafricaine (MDRERC): Bangui.

Mouvement d'évolution sociale de l'Afrique noire (MESAN); f. 1949; comprises two separate factions, led respectively by PROSPER LAVODRAMA and JOSEPH NGBANGADIBO.

Mouvement pour la libération du peuple centrafricain (MLPC): f. 1979; Pres. ANGE-FÉLIX PATASSÉ; Vice-Pres. JEAN-LUC MANDABA.

Mouvement pour la libération de la République Centrafricaine: Bangui; Leader HUGUES DOBOZENDI.

Mouvement socialiste centrafricaine: Bangui.

Parti libéral-démocrat (PLD): Bangui; Leader NESTOR KOMBO-NAGUEMON.

Parti républicain centrafricain (PRC): Bangui; Leader RUTH ROLLAND JEANNE MARIE.

Parti social-démocrate (PSD): Bangui; Leader ENOCH DERANT LAKOUÉ.

Rassemblement démocratique centrafricain (RDC): BP 503, Bangui; tel. 61-53-75; f. 1987; sole legal political party 1987–91; Sec.-Gen. LAURENT GOMINA-PAMPALI.

Rassemblement populaire pour la reconstruction de la Centrafrique (RPRC): Leader Brig.-Gen. FRANÇOIS BOZIZE.

Union populaire pour le développement économique et social: Bangui; Leader HUBERT KATOSSI SIMANI.

In 1991 several political parties and associations united as the **Concertation des forces démocratiques (CFD),** under the leadership of Dr ABEL GOUMBA. Five parties left the CFD to form the **Conseil de l'entente des partis modérés (CEPM)** in 1992.

Diplomatic Representation

EMBASSIES IN THE CENTRAL AFRICAN REPUBLIC

Cameroon: BP 935, Bangui; telex 5249; Ambassador: CHRISTOPHER NSAHLAI.

Chad: BP 461, Bangui; telex 5220; Ambassador: El Hadj MOULI SEID.

Congo: BP 1414, Bangui; telex 5292; Chargé d'affaires: ANTOINE DELICA.

Côte d'Ivoire: BP 930, Bangui; telex 5279; Ambassador: JEAN-MARIE AGNINI BILE MALAN.

Egypt: BP 1422, Bangui; telex 5284; Ambassador: SAMEH SAMY DARWICHE.

France: blvd du Général de Gaulle, BP 884, Bangui; tel. 61-30-00; telex 5218; Ambassador: PAUL ANGELIER.

Gabon: BP 1570, Bangui; tel. 61-29-97; telex 5234; Ambassador: FRANÇOIS DE PAULE MOULENGUI.

Germany: ave G. A. Nasser, BP 901, Bangui; tel. 61-07-46; telex 5219; fax 61-19-89; Ambassador: RHEINHARD BUCHOLZ.

Holy See: ave Boganda, BP 1447, Bangui; tel. 61-26-54; fax 61-03-71; Apostolic Pro-Nuncio: Most Rev. DIEGO CAUSERO, Titular Archbishop of Meta.

Iraq: Bangui; telex 5287; Chargé d'affaires: ABDUL KARIM ASWAD.

Japan: BP 1367, Bangui; tel. 61-06-68; telex 5204; Chargé d'affaires: KIYOJI YAMAKAWA.

Libya: Bangui; telex 5317; Head of Mission: EL-SENUSE ABDALLAH.

Nigeria: BP 1010, Bangui; tel. 61-40-97; telex 5269; Chargé d'affaires: AYODELE J. BAKARE.

Romania: BP 1435, Bangui; Chargé d'affaires a.i.: MIHAI GAFTONIUC.

Russia: Bangui; Ambassador: YURI BALABANOV.

Sudan: Bangui; Ambassador: TIJANI SALIH FADAYL.

USA: blvd David Dacko, BP 924, Bangui; tel. 61-02-00; fax 61-44-94; Ambassador: ROBERT E. GRIBBIN, III.

Zaire: BP 989, Bangui; telex 5232; Ambassador: EMBE ISEA MBAMBE.

Judicial System

Supreme Court: BP 926, Bangui; tel. 61-41-33; highest judicial organ; acts as a Court of Cassation in civil and penal cases and as Court of Appeal in administrative cases; comprises four chambers: constitutional, judicial, administrative and financial.

President of the Supreme Court: FIDEL MANDABA GORME.

There is also a Court of Appeal, a Criminal Court, 16 tribunaux de grande instance, 37 tribunaux d'instance, six labour tribunals and a permanent military tribunal. A High Court of Justice was established under the 1986 Constitution, with jurisdiction in all cases of crimes against state security, including high treason by the President of the Republic.

In August 1992 constitutional amendments were introduced which provided for the strict separation of executive, legislative and judicial powers.

Religion

An estimated 60% of the population hold animist beliefs, 5% are Muslims and 35% Christians; Roman Catholics comprise about 20% of the total population.

CHRISTIANITY

The Roman Catholic Church

The Central African Republic comprises one archdiocese and five dioceses. There were an estimated 579,801 adherents at 31 December 1991.

Bishops' Conference: Conférence Episcopale Centrafricaine, BP 798, Bangui; tel. 61-31-48; fax 61-46-92; f. 1982; Pres. Mgr Joachim N'Dayen, Archbishop of Bangui.

Archbishop of Bangui: Mgr Joachim N'Dayen, Archevêché, BP 1518, Bangui; tel. 61-31-48; fax 61-46-21.

Protestant Church

Eglise Protestante de Bangui: Bangui.

The Press

DAILY

E Le Songo: Bangui; Sango; circ. 2,000.

PERIODICALS

Bangui Match: Bangui; monthly.

Le Courrier Rural: BP 850, Bangui; publ. by Chambre d'Agriculture.

Journal Officiel de la République Centrafricaine: BP 739, Bangui; f. 1974; fortnightly; economic data; Dir-Gen. Gabriel Agba.

Nations Nouvelles: BP 965, Bangui; irregular; publ. by Organisation Commune Africaine et Mauricienne.

Renouveau Centrafricain: Bangui; weekly.

Ta Tene (The Truth): BP 1290, Bangui; monthly.

Terre Africaine: BP 373, Bangui; weekly.

NEWS AGENCIES

Agence Centrafricaine de Presse (ACAP): BP 40, Bangui; tel. 61-10-88; telex 5299; f. 1974; Gen. Man. Victor Deto Teteya.

Informatsionnoye Telegrafnoye Agentstvo Rossii—Telegrafnoye Agentstvo Suverennykh Stran (ITAR—TASS) (Russia) and Agence France-Presse are the only foreign press agencies represented in the CAR.

Publisher

Government Publishing House

Imprimerie Centrafricain: BP 329, Bangui; tel. 61-00-33; f. 1974; Dir-Gen. Pierre Salamate-Koilet.

Radio and Television

There were an estimated 210,000 radio receivers in use in 1991. A 100-kW transmitter came into service at Bimbo in 1970, and two 50-kW transmitters were introduced in 1984. Television broadcasting began in 1983. There were an estimated 14,000 television receivers in use in 1991.

Radiodiffusion-Télévision Centrafrique: BP 940, Bangui; telex 2355; f. 1958 as Radiodiffusion Nationale Centrafricaine; govt-controlled; radio programmes in French and Sango; Man. Dir Paul Service.

Finance

(cap. = capital; res = reserves; dep. = deposits; m. = million; amounts in francs CFA)

BANKING

Central Bank

Banque des Etats de l'Afrique Centrale (BEAC): BP 851, Bangui; tel. 61-24-00; telex 5236; fax 61-19-95 headquarters in Yaoundé, Cameroon; f. 1973 as the central bank of issue for mem. states of the Customs and Economic Union of Central Africa (UDEAC), comprising Cameroon, the Central African Republic, Chad, the Congo, Equatorial Guinea and Gabon; cap. and res 203,500m. (Jan. 1993); Gov. Jean-Félix Mamalepot; Dir in CAR Auguste Tene-Koyzoa (acting).

Commercial Banks

Banque de Crédit Agricole et de Développement (BCAD): 1 place de la République, BP 801, Bangui; tel. 61-32-00; telex 5207; f. 1984; 50% owned by Banque de Participation et de Placement (Switzerland), 33.33% state-owned, 8.33% owned by Caisse Nationale de Crédit Agricole and 8.33% owned by Pacfinancial Consultants; cap. 600m. (Dec. 1987); Pres. Michel M. Chautard; Gen. Man. René Jaulin.

Banque Populaire Maroco-Centrafricaine (BPMC): rue Guerillot, BP 844, Bangui; tel. 61-31-90; telex 5244; fax 61-62-30; f. 1991; 50% owned by Banque Centrale Populaire, 12.5% owned by Banque Marocaine du Commerce Exterie and 37.5% state-owned; cap. 716m.; Pres. Abdellatif Laraki.

Banque Meridien BIAO Centrafrique SA: place de la République, BP 910, Bangui; tel. 61-36-33; telex 5233; fax 61-61-36; f. 1980; cap. 700m., dep. 6,551m. (Dec. 1992); Chair. Bertrand Le Bail; Gen. Man. François Epaye; 1 br.

Union Bancaire en Afrique Centrale: rue de Brazza, BP 59, Bangui; tel. 61-29-90; telex 5225; fax 61-34-54; f. 1962; 85% state-owned, 15% owned by Crédit Lyonnais; cap. 1,000m., res 660m. (Dec. 1991); Pres. Dieudonné Padoudji-Yadjoua; Gen. Man. Joseph Koyagbele; 1 br.

Investment Bank

Banque Centrafricaine d'Investissement (BCI): BP 933, Bangui; tel. 61-00-64; telex 5317; f. 1976; 34.8% state-owned; cap. 1,000m.; Pres. Alphonse Kongolo; Man. Dir Gérard Sambo.

Financial Institution

Caisse Autonome d'Amortissement des Dettes de la République Centrafricaine: Bangui; management of state funds; Dir-Gen. Joseph Pingama.

Caisse Nationale d'Epargne (CNE): Bangui; tel. 61-22-96; telex 5200; Pres. Jean Baptiste Koyassambia: Dir-Gen. André Bayoka Dieka.

Development Agencies

Caisse Française de Développement: BP 817, Bangui; tel. 61-36-34; telex 5291; Dir Nils Robin.

Mission Française de Coopération et d'Action Culturelle: BP 934, Bangui; tel. 61-53-63; fax 61-28-24; administers bilateral aid from France; Dir Alain Morel.

INSURANCE

Agence Centrafricaine d'Assurances (ACA): BP 512, Bangui; tel. 61-06-23; f. 1956; cap. 3.8m.; Dir Mme R. Cerbellaud.

Assureurs Conseils Centrafricains Faugère et Jutheau: rue de la Kouanga, BP 743, Bangui; tel. 61-19-33; telex 5331; fax 61-44-70; f. 1968; cap. 5m.; Dir Jean Claude Roy.

Entreprise d'Etat d'Assurances et de Réassurances (SIRIRI): ave du Président Mobutu, BP 852, Bangui; tel. 61-36-55; telex 5306; f. 1972; general; cap. 100m.; Pres. Emmanuel Dokouna; Dir-Gen. Jean-Marie Yollot.

Legendre, A. & Cie: rue de la Victoire, BP 896, Bangui; cap. 1m.; Pres. and Dir-Gen. André Legendre.

Trade and Industry

CHAMBERS OF COMMERCE

Chambre d'Agriculture, d'Elevage, des Eaux, Forêts, Chasses, Pêches et Tourisme: BP 850, Bangui; Pres. Maurice Methot; Sec.-Gen. Anatole Possiti.

Chambre de Commerce, d'Industrie, des Mines et de l'Artisanat (CCIMA): BP 813, Bangui; tel. 61-42-55; telex 5261; Pres. Bernard-Christian Ayandho; Sec.-Gen. Jean-Louis Giacometti (acting).

PRINCIPAL DEVELOPMENT ORGANIZATIONS

Agence de Développement de la Zone Caféière (ADECAF): BP 1935, Bangui; tel. 61-47-30; coffee producers' asscn; assists coffee marketing co-operatives; Dir-Gen. J. J. Nimiziambi.

Caisse de Stabilisation et de Péréquation des Produits Agricoles (CAISTAB): BP 76, Bangui; tel. 61-08-00; telex 5278; supervises pricing and marketing of agricultural products; Dir-Gen. M. Bounandele-Koumba.

Comptoir National du Diamant (CND): blvd B. Boganda, BP 1011, Bangui; tel. 61-07-02; telex 5262; f. 1964; cap. 195m. francs CFA; 50% state-owned, 50% owned by Diamond Distributors (USA): mining and marketing of diamonds; Dir-Gen. M. VASSOS.

Office National des Forêts (ONF): BP 915, Bangui; tel. 61-38-27; f. 1969; reafforestation, development of forest resources; Dir-Gen. C. D. SONGUET.

Société Centrafricaine de Développement Agricole (SOCADA): ave David Dacko, BP 997, Bangui; tel. 61-30-33; telex 5212; f. 1964; reorg. 1980; cap. 1,000m. francs CFA; 75% state-owned, 25% Cie Française pour le Développement des Fibres Textiles (France); purchasing, transport and marketing of cotton, and cotton ginning at 20 plants, also organizes the production of cotton oil (at two refineries) and groundnut oil; Pres. MAURICE METHOT; Man. Dir PATRICE ENDJINGBOMA.

Société Centrafricaine des Palmiers (CENTRAPALM): BP 1355, Bangui; tel. 61-49-40; fax 61-38-75; f. 1975; cap. 2,125m. francs CFA; state-owned; production and marketing of palm oil; operates the Bossongo agro-industrial complex (inaugurated 1986); Pres. THÉODORE BAGUA-YAMBO; Gen. Man. JEAN-PRIVAT MBAYE.

MAJOR INDUSTRIAL COMPANIES

The following are some of the largest companies in terms of either capital investment or employment.

Bata SA Centrafricaine: BP 364, Bangui; tel. 61-45-79; telex 5257; f. 1969; cap. 150m. francs CFA; footwear mfrs; Dir VICTOR DE RYCKE.

Centrafrique-Roumano-Bois (CAROMBOIS): BP 1159, Bangui; telex 5264; f. 1974; cap. 673m. francs CFA; 60% owned by FOREXIM (Romania); Dir-Gen. VICTOR IONESCU; 306 employees.

COLALU: rue Chavannes, BP 1326, Bangui; tel. 61-20-42; telex 5248; f. 1969; cap. 69m. francs CFA; 57% owned by ALUCAM (Cameroon); mfrs of household articles and sheet aluminium; Pres. CLAUDE MILLET; Dir-Gen. M. KAPPES.

Compagnie Industrielle d'Ouvrages en Textiles (CIOT): BP 190, Bangui; tel. 61-36-22; telex 5238; f. 1949; cap. 250m. francs CFA; mfrs of clothing and hosiery; Dir-Gen. MICHEL ROBERT.

Entreprise Forestière des Bois Africains Centrafrique (EFBACA): BP 205, Bangui; tel. 61-25-33; telex 5265; f. 1969; cap. 259m. francs CFA; 12% state-owned; exploitation of forests and wood processing; Pres. VICTOR BALET; Dir JEAN QUENNOZ.

Huilerie Savonnerie Centrafricaine (HUSACA): BP 1020, Bangui; tel. 61-58-54; telex 5234; fax 61-68-11; mfrs of soap, edible oil and animal feed; Dir B. ABDALLAH.

Industrie Centrafricaine du Textile (ICAT): BP 981, Bangui; tel. 61-40-00; telex 5215; f. 1965; cap. 586m. francs CFA; state-owned; textile complex; Man. Dir M. NGOUNDOUKOUA.

Industries Forestières de Batalimo (IFB): BP 517, Bangui; f. 1970; cap. 100m. francs CFA; Dir JACQUES GADEN.

Manufacture Centrafricaine de Cigares (MANUCACIG): BP 976, Bangui; tel. 61-23-14; f. 1976; cap. 163m. francs CFA; 13% state-owned; processes locally-grown tobacco leaf; capacity 10m. cigars per annum; Pres. ALBERT GOFFI; Dir JEAN-MARIE DECOURCHELLE; 130 employees.

Motte-Cordonnier-Afrique (MOCAF): BP 806, Bangui; tel. 61-04-77; telex 5224; f. 1951; cap. 1,123m. francs CFA; production of beer, soft drinks and ice; Pres. BERTRAND MOTTE; Dir-Gen. PHILIPPE MAGNAVAL.

Société Centrafricaine de Cigarettes (SOCACIG): BP 728, Bangui; tel. 61-03-00; fax 61-51-30; f. 1970; cap. 698.4m. francs CFA; cigarette mfrs; Pres. PIERRE IMBERT; Dir in Bangui ALAIN PERREARD.

Société Centrafricaine des Cuirs (CENTRA-CUIRS): BP 1769, Bangui; f. 1975; cap. 75m. francs CFA; 20% state-owned; mfrs of leather goods.

Société Centrafricaine de Déroulage (SCAD): BP 1607, Bangui; tel. 61-18-05; telex 5226; fax 61-56-60; f. 1972; cap. 700m. francs CFA; exploitation of forests, mfrs of plywood, operates a sawmill; Dir-Gen. J. KAMACH; 392 employees.

Société Centrafricaine du Diamant (SODIAM): BP 1016, Bangui; tel. 61-03-79; telex 5210; cap. 100m. francs CFA; export of diamonds; Dir DIMITRI ANAGNOSTELLIS.

Société Centrafricaine d'Exploitation Forestière et Industrielle (SOCEFI): BP 3, M'Bata-Bangui; f. 1947, nationalized 1974; cap. 880m. francs CFA; sawmill; timber exports, mfrs of prefabricated dwellings; Man. Dir PIERRE OPANZOYEN.

Société Centrafricaine des Gaz Industriels (SOCAGI): blvd du Général de Gaulle, BP 905, Bangui; tel. 61-19-11; telex 5205; f. 1965; cap. 53m. francs CFA; manufacture and sale of industrial and medical gases; Pres. and Dir-Gen. PAUL LALAGUE.

Société Centrafricaine des Tabacs (SCAT): ave B. Boganda, BP 1042, Bangui; tel. 61-37-11; telex 5326; f. 1966; cap. 1,050m. francs CFA; 66% state-owned, 33% by SEITA (France); technical supervision of plantations; collecting and curing of tobacco; restructuring programme under way in 1990; Pres. M. GBIANZA; Man. Dir JOËL BEASSEM; 95 employees.

Société d'Exploitation et d'Industrialisation Forestière en RCA (SLOVENIA-BOIS): BP 1571, Bangui; tel. 61-44-35; telex 5266; f. 1970; cap. 250m. francs CFA; partly Yugoslav-owned; sawmill; Dir FRANC BENKOVIĆ.

Société Industrielle Centrafricaine (SICA): BP 1325, Bangui; tel. 61-44-99; telex 5251; f. 1967; cap. 200m. francs CFA; sawmill at M'baiki in the Lobaye area, annual capacity 18,000 cu m; Dir CHARLES SYLVAIN.

Société Industrielle Forestière en Afrique Centrale (SIFAC): BP 156, Bangui; telex 5272; f. 1970; cap. 95m. francs CFA; sawmill and joinery; Dir JACQUES GADEN.

Société Nationale des Eaux (SNE): BP 1838, Bangui; tel. 61-20-28; telex 5341; state-owned water co; Dir-Gen. ALPHONSE KONGOLO.

Société de Plantations d'Hévéas et de Caféiers (SPHC): BP 1384, Bangui; f. 1974; cap. 160m. francs CFA; rubber and coffee plantations.

Total Centrafricaine de Gestion (TOCAGES): BP 724, Bangui; tel. 61-05-88; telex 5243; f. 1950; cap. 200m. francs CFA; 51% state-owned; storage, retailing and transport of petroleum products; Dir CHRISTIAN-DIMANCHE SONGUET.

TRADE UNION

Union Syndicale des Travailleurs de la Centrafrique (USTC): Bangui; Sec.-Gen. THÉOPHILE SONNY KOLLE.

Transport

A five-year programme for the modernization of the CAR's transport infrastructure, at a projected cost of US $139m. (to be funded by bilateral and multilateral creditors), was announced in 1990.

RAILWAYS

There are no railways at present. There are long-term plans to connect Bangui to the Transcameroon railway. A line linking Sudan's Darfur region with the CAR's Vakaga province is also planned.

ROADS

At 31 December 1991 there were about 23,738 km of roads, including 5,398 km of main roads and 3,909 km of secondary roads. Only about 1.8% of the total network is paved. Eight main routes serve Bangui, and those that are surfaced are toll roads. Both the total road length and the condition of the roads are inadequate for current requirements. A major project of road rehabilitation and construction is being assisted by France and the EC. The CAR is linked with Cameroon by the Transafrican Lagos–Mombasa highway.

Bureau d'Affrètement Routier Centrafricain (BARC): BP 523, Bangui; tel. 61-20-55; telex 5336; Dir-Gen. J. M. LAGUEREMA-YADINGUIN.

Compagnie Nationale des Transports Routiers (CNTR): Bangui; tel. 61-46-44; state-owned; Dir-Gen. GEORGES YABADA.

Compagnie de Transports Routiers de l'Oubangui Degrain & Cie (CTRO): Bangui; f. 1940; Man. NICOLE DEGRAIN.

INLAND WATERWAYS

There are some 2,800 km of navigable waterways along two main water courses. The first, formed by the Congo and Oubangui rivers, is open all year, except in the dry season, and can accommodate convoys of barges (of up to 800 tons load) between Bangui, Brazzaville and Pointe-Noire. The second is the river Sangha, a tributary of the Oubangui, on which traffic is also seasonal. There are two ports, at Bangui and Salo, on the rivers Oubangui and Sangha respectively. Efforts are being made to develop the stretch of river upstream from Salo to increase the transportation of timber from this area, and to develop Nola as a timber port. The 1990–95 transport development programme aims to improve the navigability of the Oubangui river.

Agence Centrafricaine des Communications Fluviales (ACCF): BP 822, Bangui; tel. 61-02-11; telex 5256; f. 1969; state-owned; development of inland waterways transport system; Man. Dir JUSTIN NDJAPOU.

Société Centrafricaine de Transports Fluviaux (SOCATRAF): BP 1445, Bangui; telex 5256; f. 1980; 51% owned by ACCF; Man. Dir FRANÇOIS TOUSSAINT.

CIVIL AVIATION

The international airport is at Bangui-Mpoko. There are also 37 small airports for internal services.

Air Afrique: BP 875, Bangui; tel. 61-46-60; telex 5281; see under Côte d'Ivoire; Dir in Bangui ALBERT BAGNERES.

Inter-RCA: BP 1413, Bangui; telex 5239; f. 1980 to replace Air Centrafrique; 52% state-owned, 24% by Air Afrique; extensive internal services; Man. Dir JULES BERNARD OUANDE.

Tourism

The main tourist attractions are the waterfalls, forests and wildlife. There are excellent hunting and fishing opportunities. There were an estimated 1,599 tourist arrivals in 1990.

Office National Centrafricain du Tourisme (OCATOUR): BP 655, Bangui; tel. 61-45-66.

Defence

In June 1993 the armed forces numbered about 3,800 men (army 3,500; air force 300), with a further 2,700 men in paramilitary forces. Military service is selective and lasts for two years. France maintains a force of 1,200 troops in the CAR.

Defence Expenditure: Estimated at 7,400m. francs CFA in 1992.

Chief of Staff of the Armed Forces: Gen. JEAN-ROGER LAKO.

Education

Education is officially compulsory for eight years between six and 14 years of age. Primary education begins at the age of six and lasts for six years. Secondary education begins at the age of 12 and lasts for up to seven years, comprising a first cycle of four years and a second of three years. In 1989 an estimated 56% of children in the relevant age-group (68% of boys; 44% of girls) attended primary schools, while secondary enrolment was equivalent to only 12% (boys 17%; girls 7%). According to estimates by UNESCO, the adult illiteracy rate in 1990 averaged 62.3% (males 48.2%; females 75.1%). French aid to the education sector totalled more than 1,000m. francs CFA in 1988/89. The provision of state-funded education was severely disrupted during the early 1990s, owing to the government's inadequate resources.

Bibliography

Bigo, D. *Pouvoir et obéissance en Centrafrique*. Paris, Editions Karthala, 1989.

Carter, G. M. (Ed.). *National Unity and Regionalism in Eight African States*. Ithaca, NY, Cornell University Press, 1966.

de Dreux Brezé, J. *Le Problème du regroupement en Afrique équatoriale*. Paris, Librairie Gale de Droit et de Jurisprudence, 1968.

Hance, W. A. 'Middle Africa from Chad to Congo (Brazzaville)', in *The Geography of Modern Africa*. New York and London, Columbia University Press, 1964.

O'Toole, T. *The Central African Republic. The Continent's Hidden Heart*. Boulder, CO, Westview Press, 1986.

Robson, P. 'Economic Integration in Equatorial Africa', in *Economic Integration in Africa*. London, Allen and Unwin, 1968.

UDEAC. *Bulletin des Statistiques Générales de l'UDEAC*. Bangui, Secrétariat-Général de l'UDEAC, 1976.

CHAD

Physical and Social Geography

DAVID HILLING

The Republic of Chad is bordered to the north by Libya, to the south by the Central African Republic, to the west by Niger and Cameroon and to the east by Sudan. The northernmost of the four independent states which emerged from French Equatorial Africa, Chad is, with an area of 1,284,000 sq km (495,800 sq miles), the largest in terms of size and population (officially estimated to be 6,288,000 at mid-1993). Traditionally a focal point for Saharan and equatorial African trade routes, the country's vast size, land-locked situation and great distance from the coast create problems for economic development.

The relief is relatively simple. From 240 m in the Lake Chad depression in the south-west, the land rises northwards through the Guéra massif at 1,800 m to the mountainous Saharan region of Tibesti at 3,350 m. Eastwards, heights of 1,500 m are attained in the Ouaddai massif. In the south the watershed area between the Chari and Zaire (Congo) rivers is of subdued relief and only slight elevation. The only rivers of importance, both for irrigation and seasonal navigation, are the Chari and Logone, which traverse the south-west of the country and join at N'Djamena, before flowing into Lake Chad.

Extending across more than 16° of latitude, Chad has three well-defined zones of climate, natural vegetation and associated economic activity. The southern third of the country has annual rainfall in excess of 744 mm (increasing to 1,200 mm in the extreme south), and has a savannah woodland vegetation. This is the country's principal agricultural zone, providing the two main cash crops, cotton and groundnuts, and a variety of local food crops (especially rice). Northwards, with rainfall of 250–500 mm per year, there is a more open grassland, where there is emphasis on pastoral activity, limited cultivation of groundnuts and local grains, and some collection of gum arabic. This marginal Sahel zone was adversely affected by drought during most of the 1970s and 1980s, and the cattle herds were greatly reduced in number. The northern third of the country has negligible rainfall and a sparse scrub vegetation, which grades north into pure desert with little apparent economic potential, although the 'Aozou strip', a region of 114,000 sq km in the extreme north, formerly claimed by Libya but returned to Chad in 1994 (see Recent History), is believed to contain substantial deposits of uranium and manganese.

Chad's total population is relatively small in relation to its large area, and is markedly concentrated in the southern half of the country. Religious and ethnic tensions between the people of the north and south have traditionally dominated the history of Chad. The population of the north is predominantly Islamic, of a nomadic or semi-nomadic character, and is largely engaged in farming and in breeding livestock. Rivalry between ethnic groups is strong. By contrast, the inhabitants of the south are settled farmers, who largely follow animistic beliefs. The Sara tribes, some 10 ethnic groups with related languages and cultural links, who inhabit the prefectures of Moyen-Chari, Logone Occidental and Logone Oriental, and part of the prefecture of Tandjilé, comprise a large section of the population of the south. The prefecture of Mayo-Kebbi and the remainder of Tandjilé are peopled with numerous ethnic groups (Moundang, Toubouri, Moussei, Nangchéré, Gabri, etc). Since the end of the Second World War, the population of the south has inclined towards a modern, Western culture; the rate of literacy has increased rapidly, and Christian churches have attracted a number of adherents. The population of the north, however, forms a traditional, Islamic society, and is largely unaffected by modern education. As a result, the majority of administrators and civil servants who were recruited after independence originated from the south. The state is secular and exercises neutrality in relation to religious affiliations. French and Arabic are the official languages, but local languages (Karembou, Ouadi, Teda, Daza, Djonkor) are also spoken.

Recent History

BERNARD LANNE

Formerly a province of French Equatorial Africa, Chad became an autonomous state within the French Community in November 1958. François Tombalbaye, a southerner and leader of the Parti progressiste tchadien (PPT), was elected prime minister in March 1959. Chad achieved independence on 11 August 1960, with Tombalbaye as president. However, the Saharan territory of the north, Borkou-Ennedi-Tibesti (BET), remained under French military administration until 1964. In January 1962 Tombalbaye dissolved all political parties except the PPT. In 1963 the PPT was declared the sole legal party, and its executive body, the Bureau politique national (BPN), became Chad's supreme political organ. The BPN was composed equally of Muslims and southerners, but was, in fact, increasingly dominated by Tombalbaye.

THE EMERGENCE OF FROLINAT

The political monopoly of the PPT was opposed by certain northern politicians who had exercised influence prior to independence, and in September 1963 civil disturbances occurred in the capital, Fort-Lamy (now N'Djamena). In 1964 mismanagement and corruption on the part of government officials prompted widespread discontent. In 1965 a full-scale rebellion began, concentrated mainly in the north. The Front de libération nationale du Tchad (FROLINAT), which was established in Sudan in 1966, later assumed leadership of the revolt. In August 1968 French military intervention on behalf of the government commenced; French reinforcements subsequently launched a number of successful military offensives against the rebels.

In 1969 elections to a new national assembly took place, and a Muslim was selected as president of the assembly. In 1971 many political prisoners were released, and the BPN and the government were reorganized to allow the inclusion of a number of former political detainees. However, the rebellion in the north of the country continued. In August Tombalbaye suspended diplomatic relations with Libya, which he accused of complicity in an attempted coup at Fort-Lamy. The Libyan leader, Col Qaddafi, subsequently transferred support to FROLINAT. As a result of the French military intervention, however, the rebellion was contained (although FROLINAT remained undefeated), and in 1972 the French reinforcements left the country. (In 1972 and 1973 diplomatic relations between Chad and France deteriorated, after Tombalbaye accused the French government of interference in Chad's internal affairs.) In November 1972, in an apparent attempt to isolate the rebels, Tombalbaye severed diplomatic relations with Israel, and signed a pact of friendship with Libya. However, FROLINAT continued to receive military assistance from Libya, which, in 1973, annexed the 'Aozou strip' in northern Chad; the Libyan claim to sovereignty over the region was based on an unratified treaty, which was signed by France and Italy in 1935.

In 1973 several prominent members of the government, including the army chief of staff, Gen. Felix Malloum, were imprisoned on conspiracy charges. In August of that year the PPT was reconstituted as the Mouvement national pour la révolution culturelle et sociale (MNRCS), and its executive council, which was composed equally of Muslims and southerners, was proclaimed the supreme political organ. Under the influence of the president of Zaire, Gen. Mobutu, Tombalbaye subsequently adopted the policy of 'authenticity', changing his first name from François to Ngarta, and ordering the abandonment of all Christian first names. Ritual initiation, known as *ndo* among the Sara, was reintroduced, and execution was decreed for those who refused to undergo the ordeal. (Muslims however, were not obliged to submit to the new policies.)

MALLOUM TAKES POWER

On 13 April 1975 Tombalbaye was killed in a military coup, which was organized by army officers originating from the south. Malloum was subsequently released, and became president of a supreme medical council. The national assembly and the MNRCS were dissolved, and a provisional government was formed. Despite initial popular support, the new government soon encountered difficulties. Following a disagreement with France over the continued detention of a French hostage by rebel forces, the French garrison at N'Djamena was closed in October 1975; however, new co-operation agreements were signed with France in March 1976. Although the government appealed for national reconciliation, a number of rebel groups, including FROLINAT, remained in opposition. However, divisions subsequently emerged within FROLINAT, and its leader, Hissène Habré, who opposed the Libyan annexation of the 'Aozou strip', was replaced by Goukouni Oueddei. (Habré continued, however, to claim leadership of a faction within FROLINAT.)

Following a deterioration in relations between Chad and Libya concerning the annexation of the 'Aozou strip', the Libyan government increased military aid to FROLINAT, which launched renewed offensives in 1977. In January 1978 an agreement was signed in Khartoum between Malloum and Habré, in an attempt to secure a cease-fire. However, FROLINAT unified its command under a revolutionary council, which was led by Goukouni, and continued to gain control of large areas of territory. After protracted negotiations, the government appealed to France for assistance, and in mid-1978 French reinforcements halted the advance of FROLINAT.

CIVIL CONFLICT

In August 1978, following negotiations between Malloum and Habré, a *charte fondamentale,* which provided for Habré's appointment to the post of prime minister, was promulgated. The military council was accordingly dissolved, and a new government was formed. However, central authority was soon undermined by disagreements between Malloum and Habré, and in February 1979 fighting erupted in N'Djamena between government forces (Forces armées tchadiennes—FAT) and Habré's troops, known as the Forces armées du nord (FAN). Members of the FAN seized control of the capital, with the support of the French government (which, however, officially pursued a policy of neutrality), while rebels, under the leadership of Goukouni, known as the Forces armées populaires (FAP), gained territory in northern Chad. Subsequent massacres of southerners in the north of the country, and of Muslims in the south, reflected the increasing division between the two communities. In March Malloum resigned and fled the country, leaving governmental responsibility with the former commander of the gendarmerie, Lt-Col (later Col) Wadal Abdelkader Kamougue.

In April 1979, following the failure of reconciliation conferences, which took place in Nigeria, a provisional government (Gouvernement d'union nationale de transition—GUNT) was formed, comprising members of FROLINAT, the FAN, the Mouvement populaire pour la libération du Tchad (MPLT), and the FAT. The leader of the MPLT, Lol Mahamat Choua was appointed president, while Goukouni and Habré received ministerial portfolios. However, the southern factions refused to recognize the new government, and a committee, under the presidency of Kamougue, was established at Moundou to govern the south. Attempts to capture the prefecture of Mayo-Kebbi from Kamougue's forces failed, and the GUNT became increasingly isolated by governments of neighbouring countries. In August a further conference, which took place in Nigeria, resulted in the creation of a second GUNT, under the presidency of Goukouni, with Kamougue as vice-president. In November a council of ministers, which represented the various groupings, was appointed. However, the fragmentation of the northern factions increased, while Goukouni's authority was undermined by continued disagreement with Habré.

In March 1980 fighting between the FAP and the FAN resumed in N'Djamena. Numerous attempts at mediation failed, and in April the GUNT dismissed Habré from his post as minister of state for defence. In accordance with the French government's policy of neutrality, all French troops were withdrawn from Chad in May. In June a treaty of friendship and co-operation was signed in Tripoli between Libya and a representative of Goukouni, without the prior consent of the GUNT. In October Libyan forces intervened in the hostilities, resulting in the defeat of Habré and the retreat of the FAN from N'Djamena by the end of that year. A Libyan contingent, numbering some 15,000 men, was subsequently established in the country.

In January 1981 Goukouni signed a further agreement in Tripoli, which provided for a gradual political union of Chad and Libya. However, the French government strongly opposed the proposed union, and French military personnel in the Central African Republic (CAR) were reinforced. In April the intervention of Libyan troops in skirmishes between members of Goukouni's FAP and the Conseil démocratique révolutionnaire (CDR), one of the breakaway factions of FROLINAT, at Abéché, the capital of the prefecture of Ouaddai, resulted in numerous casualties. Goukouni subsequently negotiated the withdrawal of Libyan forces stationed at N'Djamena airport. In September, at a meeting between Goukouni and the French president, François Mitterrand, in Paris, France affirmed its support for the GUNT; the French government subsequently hastened the departure of the Libyan troops by urging the president of the OAU to send a peace-keeping force to Chad. In November, at the request of the council of ministers, Libyan troops were withdrawn, and an Inter-African Force (IAC) was subsequently installed under the auspices of the OAU.

HABRÉ'S RETURN TO POWER

Following the departure of the Libyan troops, the FAN renewed its offensive, and by mid-January 1982 had gained control of several towns in northern Chad. In February, however, the OAU adopted a resolution, whereby a cease-fire was to be imposed later that month, elections were to take place under OAU supervision before 30 June and the IAF was subsequently to withdraw. However, Goukouni rejected the resolution, which was effectively a political victory for the FAN, and hostilities intensified. In subsequent months the FAN continued to advance, and finally captured N'Djamena on 7 June 1982. Goukouni fled to Cameroon and thence to Algeria, while the coalition of factions that constituted the GUNT began to fragment.

On 19 June 1982, following the capture of N'Djamena, the formation of a provisional council of state, with Habré as head of state, was announced. By the end of that month the IAF had withdrawn fully from Chad. A provisional constitution, the *acte fondamental*, was promulgated on 29 September. On 21 October Habré was inaugurated as president, dissolved the council of state and formed a new government, which included former members of the Tombalbaye and Goukouni administrations, with southerners occupying a large proportion of ministerial positions. However, Goukouni's troops regained control of the greater part of the BET, with Libyan support, and in October Goukouni announced the formation of a rival 'government of national salvation' at Bardai. Habré subsequently succeeded in obtaining international recognition, occupying Chad's seat at the UN and gaining the support of the majority of African states. By early 1983, however, Habré's forces had suffered defeats in the north, while tribal differences had caused divisions within the FAN. In January of that year a number of members of Kamougue's FAT joined the FAN to form the Forces armées nationales tchadiennes (FANT).

FRENCH INTERVENTION

In March 1983 negotiations took place between Habré and the Libyan government; however, Habré rejected Libyan demands for the recognition of Chad's Islamic character and of the annexation of the 'Aozou strip', and the signing of a treaty of alliance. In June Goukouni's rebel troops, with military assistance from Libya, captured the northern administrative centre of Faya-Largeau, and, in early July, occupied the entire BET region, and advanced to Abéché. Following Habré's appeals for aid to counter Libyan aggression, Zaire responded by sending a paratroop contingent, while the USA supplied armaments. Mitterrand, however, refused Habré's request for direct intervention. After a successful counter-offensive by the FANT at the end of July, Goukouni's forces, with Libyan air support, recaptured Faya-Largeau, and again advanced southwards. In early August, as a result of pressure from francophone African heads of state, Mitterrand dispatched some 3,000 French troops to Chad, in an attempt to separate the warring factions and open negotiations to resolve the civil war. The French troops subsequently imposed an 'interdiction line' from Salal to Arada, preventing Goukouni's forces and their Libyan allies from advancing further south; by mid-September all fighting between the Chadian factions had ceased.

In January 1984 a meeting of all factions, which took place at Addis Ababa, Ethiopia, under the aegis of the OAU, was abandoned. Later that month following an offensive against the post of Zigueï in the north of Kanem, Goukouni's troops were attacked by French military aircraft, one of which was destroyed. President Mitterrand subsequently decided to extend the limit of the exclusion zone to the 16th parallel (the 'Koro Toro–Oum Chalouba line').

THE FORMATION OF UNIR AND REORGANIZATION OF THE OPPOSITION

During early 1984 it became increasingly evident that Habré needed to regain support in southern Chad in order to consolidate political power. At a conference of *préfets* in April, the army's repression of civilians and military interference in administrative and judicial affairs were criticized, and in May several senior members of the security forces were removed from office. In June Habré dissolved the FROLINAT–FAN faction, and created a new official party, the Union nationale pour l'indépendance et la révolution (UNIR). Six of the 15 members of UNIR's executive bureau were southerners, but former FAN officials maintained a prominent role in the new party. The formation of UNIR was, however, regarded as a move towards national reconciliation and the creation of a democratic, unified government. In a government reshuffle, which took place in July, one-half of the ministerial posts (including the foreign affairs portfolio) were allocated to southerners, while a leader of the rebel commandos from the south was appointed minister of defence.

On 30 August 1984, however, the guerrilla commandos (*commandos rouges*, or *codos*), led by Col Alphonse Kotiga, suspended negotiations with the government, and resumed hostilities. The entire region of southern Chad, apart from Mayo-Kebbi, returned to civil war. The subsequent repression of the rebellion by government forces resulted in considerable suffering by the civilian population: widespread arrests and summary executions were carried out, and villages were destroyed. About 25,000 refugees fled to the CAR. The violence perpetrated by government forces effectively intensified religious and ethnic rivalries, and negated any political advantages that had been gained by the formation of UNIR.

Meanwhile, increasing dissension among anti-Habré forces emerged, resulting in the formation by GUNT factions of new 'splinter groups' and an anti-Goukouni movement. At a meeting of GUNT factions, which took place in August 1985, a Conseil suprême de la révolution (CSR), comprising seven anti-government groupings, under the presidency of Goukouni, was formed. Later that year, however, several former opposition factions declared support for the Habré regime, including the Front démocratique du Tchad (FDT) and the Comité d'action et de concertation (CAC-CDR), which had broken away from the pro-Goukouni CDR.

In November following offers of financial remuneration by Habré, some 1,200 *codos* joined government forces; by the end of that year hostilities had ceased.

THE FRENCH WITHDRAWAL

Negotiations between France and Libya, with mediation from the governments of Austria and Greece, resulted in an agreement, which was signed in September 1984, providing for the simultaneous withdrawal from Chad of French and Libyan forces. The evacuation of French forces was completed in early November, but Libyan troops remained, in contravention of the agreement. Following an unsuccessful meeting with Qaddafi, which took place at Elounda, Crete, later that month, Mitterrand conceded that the French government had been misled. He later declared that France would not enforce Libyan withdrawal from northern Chad, but would intervene if Libyan forces advanced towards N'Djamena. He recognized Chad's claim to the 'Aozou strip', while criticizing Habré for jeopardizing national unity, in favour of territorial gain. A national reconciliation conference, which took place at Brazzaville, the Congo, in October 1984, ended in failure.

LIBYAN INCURSIONS

From October 1985 Libya began to reinforce its military presence in the north of Chad, assembling an estimated 4,000 troops. In November President Mitterrand reiterated that France would respond to any Libyan military action in Chad. In February 1986, however, GUNT forces initiated Libyan-supported attacks on government positions to the south of the French interdiction line. The offensive was repelled by the FANT, and Habré appealed to France for increased military aid. Shortly afterwards French military aircraft, which were stationed in the CAR, bombed a Libyan-built airstrip at Ouadi Doum, north-east of Faya-Largeau. A retaliatory air strike on N'Djamena airport caused minor damage. France subsequently established an air strike force at N'Djamena to counteract any further Libyan attack (an intervention which was known as *Opération Epervier*), while the USA provided supplementary military aid to Habré's forces. Further incursions across the interdiction line in March were repelled by FANT ground forces. Later that month hostilities ceased temporarily, following the capture by government forces of a rebel base at Chicha.

HABRÉ'S RECAPTURE OF THE NORTH

In March 1986 Habré appointed several former opponents to the council of ministers. Meanwhile, divisions within the GUNT increased; Goukouni's refusal to attend OAU-convened reconciliation talks prompted the resignation in June of the vice-president of the GUNT, Col Wadal Abdelkader Kamougue, who declared his support for Habré in

February 1987 and joined the government in August of that year. In August 1986 Acheikh Ibn Oumar's CDR withdrew its support for Goukouni, leaving the latter virtually isolated. Later that month clashes between FAP and CDR troops occurred in the Tibesti region. By October Goukouni had declared himself willing to negotiate with Habré, and it was subsequently reported that the FAP had decided to join Habré's FANT. Goukouni was subsequently wounded during an alleged attempt at abduction by Libyan troops in Tripoli, and in mid-November, with Libyan support, Oumar assumed the presidency of a reconstituted GUNT coalition, comprising seven of the original 11 factions, including the Mouvement révolutionnaire du peuple (MRP), formerly led by Kamougue.

In December 1986 clashes took place in the Tibesti region between Libyan forces and the now pro-Habré FAP. FANT forces subsequently moved north of the interdiction line, and France increased its logistical support. In January 1987 FANT troops recaptured a number of strategic targets in the north of the country. Following a Libyan offensive on the southern town of Arada, France launched a retaliatory air attack against the airbase of Ouadi Doum; in March Ouadi Doum was recaptured by the FANT. Libyan forces subsequently began to retreat, evacuating Faya-Largeau, and by May Habré's troops had regained control of northern Chad, with Libya occupying only the Aozou region. In August the FANT seized control of the town of Aozou, the administrative centre of the region, but was later forced to withdraw to positions in Tibesti, following a series of Libyan air attacks on Chadian targets. In September Habré's forces entered south-eastern Libya, where they attacked and occupied the military base of Maaten-es-Sarra. A Libyan military aircraft was subsequently shot down over N'Djamena by the French defensive force, and French positions at Abéché were bombed. (In protest at this offensive, the French government suspended supplies of arms to Chad until December.) On 11 September a cease-fire, which had been mediated by the OAU, took effect. However, the Chadian government claimed that Libyan aircraft continued to infringe Chadian airspace, and that members of a Libyan-supported 'Islamic Legion' had clashed with members of the FANT near the Sudanese border. There was also a considerable reinforcement of the Libyan bases in the Aozou region and in Toummo (in Niger). Military engagements took place in November 1987, near Goz Beïda, and in March 1988, to the east of Ennedi.

RESTORATION OF DIPLOMATIC RELATIONS WITH LIBYA

A meeting between the heads of state of Chad and Libya, under the aegis of the OAU *ad hoc* committee (which had been established in 1977 to debate the question of the sovereignty of the Aozou region) was scheduled for May 1988. Shortly before the summit it was announced that Qaddafi (who had repeatedly boycotted meetings of the *ad hoc* committee) would not be attending, in protest at Chad's treatment of prisoners of war. However, Qaddafi subsequently announced his willingness to recognize the Habré régime, invited Habré and Goukouni to meet in Libya for discussions concerning reconciliation and offered to provide financial aid for the reconstruction of bombed towns in northern Chad. Habré reacted with caution to Qaddafi's proposals, but in early June announced that his government was prepared to restore diplomatic relations with Libya, which had been suspended in 1982. Following discussions between the ministers of foreign affairs of the two countries, which took place in Gabon in July 1988, both Chad and Libya agreed, in principle, to the restoration of diplomatic relations, although the questions of the fate of Libyan prisoners of war in Chad, the disputed sovereignty of the Aozou region and the future security of common borders remained unresolved. In October, following mediation by Togo, Chad and Libya issued a joint communiqué expressing their willingness to seek a peaceful solution to the territorial dispute, and to co-operate with the OAU committee appointed for that purpose. The cease-fire was reaffirmed, diplomatic relations were resumed, and the two countries exchanged ambassadors in November.

INTERNAL DEVELOPMENTS

In July 1987 reconciliation talks between Habré and Goukouni (who had been resident in Algiers since February) ended in failure. Following a government reshuffle in August, both Kamougue and the former leader of the *codos*, Col Kotiga Guerina, received ministerial portfolios. In February 1988 a number of former opposition parties, including the FAP and the CAC–CDR, merged with UNIR. In March the GUNT was reconstituted under Goukouni, following a dispute with Oumar regarding the leadership of the movement. In November, following the conclusion of a peace agreement in Iraq, forces led by Oumar declared support for Habré, and subsequently returned to Chad. In January 1989 it was announced that the GUNT was willing to resume negotiations with the Habré government.

Despite a semblance of unity, which was exemplified in March 1989 by the appointment of Oumar as minister of foreign affairs, political dissent remained. In early April the minister of the interior and territorial administration, Ibrahim Mahamat Itno, was arrested, following the discovery of an alleged plot to overthrow the Habré government. The c-in-c of the armed forces, Hassan Djamous, and his predecessor in that post, Idriss Deby (who were both implicated in the conspiracy), fled to Sudan with their supporters. FANT troops were dispatched to quell the mutiny, and it was later announced that Djamous had died in the ensuing conflict. Meanwhile, Deby escaped to Libya (with Sudanese assistance), and in June formed a new opposition movement, the 'Action du 1 avril' in Sudan. In July the unity of GUNT was undermined, when a number of factions announced their withdrawal from the coalition. A reorganization of the council of ministers took place in October, following the death of the minister of planning and co-operation, Soumaila Mahamat. (Mahamat was among 171 people who were killed when a French airliner exploded in September, shortly after leaving N'Djamena.) In February 1990 two ministers were dismissed from the government.

In July 1988 a presidential decree established a committee to formulate a new constitution. Constitutional proposals were submitted to Habré in June 1989, and a draft document was approved in a national referendum on 10 December (reportedly receiving the support of 99.94% of votes cast). The new constitution, which was promulgated on 20 December, endorsed Habré as president for a further seven-year term, upheld the principle of a sole ruling party, and envisaged the creation of a legislative body, the national assembly, which was to be elected, with a five-year mandate, by direct universal suffrage. At legislative elections, which took place in July 1990, 436 candidates (many of whom were members of UNIR) contested 123 seats; 56% of the registered electorate voted. However, several prominent members of UNIR failed to secure seats in the new legislature.

DIPLOMATIC ACTIVITY

Although a Libyan delegation attended the second UNIR congress in November 1988, relations between the two countries remained strained. Chad continued to accuse Libya of violating the cease-fire agreement: in November a Libyan aircraft that had entered Chadian airspace was shot down, and in December clashes between Chadian and pro-Libyan forces near the border with Sudan were reported. Relations between the two countries deteriorated further in mid-1989, when Habré accused Qaddafi of preparing a further military offensive against Chad (with the support of the al-Mahdi regime in Sudan). Subsequent negotiations between Habré and Qaddafi were inconclusive, owing to Habré's rejection of proposals made by President Chadli of Algeria, which envisaged the withdrawal of the *Opération Epervier* force from Chad. At the end of August, however, Oumar and the Libyan minister of foreign affairs, Jadellah Azouz at-Tali, signed a draft agreement (*accord cadre*), which envisaged the peaceful resolution of the dispute: if a political settlement were not achieved within one year, the issue would be submitted to arbitration by the International Court of Justice (ICJ). Provision was made for all armed forces to be withdrawn from the Aozou region, under the supervision of non-partisan African observers, and for the release of all prisoners of war. Chad and Libya reaffirmed their commitment to the principles of the September 1987 cease-fire agreement, and declared a policy of mutual non-interference in each other's internal affairs: hostile radio broadcasts and financial or military support for dissidents were to cease. In September, however, the first session of a Chad-Libya joint commission, which had been established to oversee the implementation of the agreement, ended in failure, following a dispute regarding the programme for the release of Libyan prisoners of war. Later that year the agreement was further undermined by the resumption of hostilities between the FANT and pro-Libyan forces along Chad's border with Sudan.

In March 1990 Deby and his supporters, the Forces patriotiques du salut (subsequently known as the Mouvement patriotique du salut, MPS), invaded eastern Chad from bases in Sudan. France dispatched military equipment and personnel to reinforce *Opération Epervier* at Abéché: although the French contingent did not participate in the military engagements, its presence undoubtedly induced the rebel forces to retreat. In late March discussions between Oumar and Libyan officials, which took place in Gabon, were undermined by a statement issued by the Chadian government, alleging Libyan and Sudanese support for the MPS; the accusations were denied by the leaders of both countries. In May the fifth session of the Chad-Libya joint commission was compromised by the seizure, by Chadian forces, of 10 Libyan vehicles on Sudanese territory; Libya subsequently protested to the UN and the OAU at this offensive against what were claimed to be civilian vehicles. Following an emergency session of the executive bureau of UNIR in late July, the Chadian government alleged that Libya and Sudan were massing forces in Sudan's Darfur region, in preparation for a major offensive against Chad. Subsequent discussions between Chadian and Libyan delegates failed to secure agreement. In late August, however, shortly before the stipulated deadline for a negotiated settlement, apparently successful negotiations between Habré and Qaddafi took place in Morocco. Both governments subsequently agreed to refer the territorial dispute for adjudication by the ICJ.

DEBY TAKES POWER

On 10 November 1990 forces led by Deby, which were believed to number some 2,000, again invaded Chad from Sudan, and launched an attack on positions held by Chadian government forces at Tiné, to the north-east of Abéché. The governments of Libya and Sudan again denied accusations of complicity in the offensive. The FANT initially forced the rebels to retreat to Sudan; however, the attacks were soon resumed, and by mid-November the MPS was reported to have captured Tiné. Despite an appeal by Habré to the French government for military assistance, the *Opération Epervier* contingent, which had been reinforced to protect French interests in the region, took no part in the military engagements. The MPS continued to consolidate its position in eastern Chad, and many FANT units reportedly transferred their allegiance to Deby. Negotiations concerning the sovereignty of the Aozou region, which had been scheduled for late November, were suspended by Qaddafi, who claimed that recent Chadian allegations of Libyan involvement in the rebel invasion had undermined conditions for the discussions. Although the US government declared its full support for Habré, France maintained its policy of non-intervention in Chad's internal affairs (it was widely believed that France's lack of support for the incumbent regime reflected Habré's failure to initiate a transition towards multi-party democracy).

On 29 November 1990 the MPS seized control of Abéché. On the following day, Habré, together with members of his family and of the council of ministers, fled to Maroua, in eastern Cameroon. Deby arrived in N'Djamena two days later. A curfew was immediately imposed, in an attempt to suppress the rioting and looting that had followed Habré's flight from the capital. Deby subsequently declared his commitment to the creation of a democratic multi-party political system. On 3 December the national assembly was dissolved, and the constitution suspended. Shortly afterwards a provisional council of state was established, and Deby assumed power as interim head of state. The new 33-member council of state mainly comprised members of the MPS and allied parties; however, Oumar (hitherto the minister of foreign affairs in the Habré government), was appointed special adviser to the head of state. A number of political organizations that had opposed Habré subsequently declared their support for the MPS. Goukouni Oueddei announced his willingness to initiate political discussions with the new government, despite persistent reports that he was massing forces in northern Chad. Also in December a report, compiled by the MPS, accused Habré of violations of human rights and of corruption. Deby subsequently sought Habré's extradition from Senegal (where he had been granted political asylum) so that he might be tried on criminal charges. Later that month the curfew was removed, and the government announced that the FANT was to be restructured to form a smaller republican army, to be known as the Armées nationales tchadiennes (ANT), and that a national gendarmerie was to replace the military police.

Following the accession to power of the MPS, it was announced that aid and co-operation agreements between France and the Habré government would be honoured, and that new accords would be formulated. The USA, however, refused to extend formal recognition to the new regime, on the grounds of Deby's allegedly close links with Libya, although it affirmed its commitment to honouring existing aid agreements. The Libyan and Sudanese governments declared support for the new regime and undertook not to allow forces hostile to Deby to operate in their territory. However, relations between Chad and Libya were temporarily strained, following the airlift, apparently organized by the USA and France, of an estimated 600 Libyan detainees, who had allegedly been trained by the USA to undertake military action against Qaddafi. A two-day official visit to Libya by Deby in February 1991 consolidated relations between the two countries; however, Deby refused to abandon Chad's claim to the sovereignty of the Aozou region, which remained under consideration by the ICJ.

On 1 March 1991 a national charter, which had been submitted by the executive committee of the MPS, was adopted for a 30-month transitional period, at the end of which a referendum was to be held to determine Chad's constitutional future. The charter confirmed Deby's appointment as president, head of state and chairman of the MPS, and required the government to institute measures to prepare for the implementation of a multi-party system. Under the terms of the charter, a new council of ministers and a 31-member legislative body, to be known as the council of the republic, were to replace the provisional council of state. On 4 March Deby was formally inaugurated as president. On the following day the council of state was dissolved, and the former president of the national assembly, Dr Jean Alingue Bawoyeu, was appointed prime minister in a new 29-member government, which included 16 new ministers. A number of influential portfolios were allocated to southerners. Later in March two political organizations which had opposed the Habré government amalgamated with the MPS.

POLITICAL REFORM

In early May 1991 an informal alliance of five principal opposition movements, led by Goukouni, demanded that the registration of political associations be immediately authorized, and that a national conference be convened to determine a programme for the transition to a multi-party system. Later that month Deby announced that a national conference, scheduled for May 1992, would prepare a new constitution to provide for the introduction of a multi-party system, and would be followed by legislative elections. Constitutional amendments permitting the registration of opposition movements would enter into force in January 1992; a commission would be established to draft legislation governing the future activity of political associations. Goukouni, who visited Chad (from Algeria) for the first time in nine years, subsequently met Deby to discuss the proposals for the introduction of a pluralist system. In early June a commission, which consisted of members of the council of the republic, was to submit recommendations concerning the authorization of political associations within 60 days. In July a minor reshuffle of the council of ministers was carried out.

On 1 October 1991 the council of ministers adopted the commission's recommendations, which stipulated conditions for the authorization of political associations. Under the new legislation, each political party was required to have a minimum of 30 founder members, three each from 10 of Chad's 14 prefectures; the formation of parties on an ethnic or regional basis was prohibited. The minister of the interior was obliged to approve the authorization of associations within three months of registration. However, the MPS was exempted from the conditions of registration, and opposition groups declared the legislation to be biased in its favour. In subsequent months a number of political organizations applied for legal recognition.

OPPOSITION TO THE DEBY GOVERNMENT

In September 1991 rebels attacked military garrisons in Tibesti, in northern Chad, killing 50 people. Deby subsequently alleged that the offensive was instigated by troops loyal to Habré, who had fled to Niger in December 1990. In October troops attacked an arsenal at N'Djamena airport in an attempt to seize power; some 40 people were killed in the ensuing fighting. Several officials, including the minister of the interior, Maldoum Bada Abbas, were arrested on suspicion of involvement in the coup attempt. Although the government subsequently announced that Abbas had been motivated by personal ambition, there was speculation that the coup attempt had been provoked by discontent within his ethnic group, the Hadjerai, who were under-represented in the council of ministers. The French government reaffirmed its support for the MPS, and announced that the *Opération Epervier* contingent would be reinforced by an additional 300 troops. Following the attempted coup, the Chadian government abrogated a co-operation agreement with Libya which Abbas had negotiated in September, on the grounds that the sovereignty of the Aozou region remained in dispute. In December the government announced an extensive ministerial reshuffle, in which two new portfolios were created. Later that month a national commission was established to determine the composition and agenda of the national conference.

On 24 December 1991 some 3,000 troops loyal to Habré attacked several towns in the region of Lake Chad, in the west of the country. The rebels were reported to be members of the Mouvement pour la démocratie et le développement (MDD), an opposition group based in Libya, led by Goukouni Guët, a former supporter of Habré. Government forces, which launched a counter-offensive, initially suffered heavy losses. By early January 1992 the rebels had captured the towns of Liwa and Bol, and were advancing towards N'Djamena. The French government dispatched some 450 troops to reinforce the *Opération Epervier* contingent (which numbered some 1,100), ostensibly to protect French citizens in the area. Shortly afterwards the government claimed that the rebels had been defeated, and that the ANT had regained control of Liwa and Bol. France subsequently withdrew some 150 of the additional troops which had been sent to the area.

Following the failure of the insurrection, a number of prominent members of the opposition and former ministers of the Habré government, who were suspected of complicity in the rebellion, were arrested; several of these were reported to have been summarily executed. The French government subsequently condemned the violence in N'Djamena, and warned that its continued support for Deby was dependent on the implementation of political reforms. Later in January 1992 Bawoyeu reaffirmed the government's commitment to the process of democratization, and announced an amnesty for political prisoners (which also applied to those accused of involvement in the coup attempt in October 1991, including Maldoum Bada Abbas). In February Abbas was appointed as president of a new provisional council of the republic. However, ethnic factions within the ANT continued to carry out acts of violence against civilians in the capital, particularly against southerners; in mid-February a prominent member of the human rights organization, the Ligue tchadienne des droits des hommes (LTDH), was killed, reportedly by soldiers loyal to Deby. The LTDH and other opposition groups subsequently organized demonstrations and a two-day strike in support of its demands for the resignation of the government.

In February 1992 government forces suppressed an alleged coup attempt, when a group of disaffected soldiers, reported to be members of the Comité de sursaut national pour la paix et la démocratie (CSNPD), attacked a police station in N'Djamena. The LTDH and other opposition groups claimed that the incident had been fabricated by the government, in an attempt to divert attention from the generally disorderly conduct of troops stationed in N'Djamena. In March four French citizens stated to have been involved in the incident were expelled from Chad. In early April the French government announced that the role of *Opération Eperview* as a defensive air-strike force was to cease, although French troops were to remain in the country to assist in the restructuring of the ANT. This change in policy was widely interpreted as a warning to Deby to end the human rights violations perpetrated against opponents of the government, and to continue with the implementation of democratic reform. In the same month the MDD claimed that more than 40 of its members, including Goukouni Guët, had been arrested in Nigeria in February, extradited to Chad, and subsequently imprisoned or executed. Later in April soldiers belonging predominantly to the Zaghawa ethnic group surrounded the presidential palace in protest at government plans to demilitarize N'Djamena and to reduce the number of personnel in the ANT, which, it was feared, would restrict the influence of the Zaghawa ethnic group in the armed forces. After mediation by the minister of state for public works and transport, Abbas Koti (himself a Zaghawa), the troops agreed to withdraw.

In May 1992 the national conference, which had been envisaged as the next stage in the process towards democracy, was postponed, on the grounds that the preparatory commission had not completed its work; it was indicated that the conference would take place in September of that year. During May a number of amendments to the national charter were adopted, in accordance with recommendations by the council of the republic. Under the revised charter, the prime minister was permitted to assume the interim presidency, in the absence of the president. On 20 May Joseph Yodoyman, a member of the Alliance nationale pour la démocratie et le développement (ANDD), was appointed as prime minister, replacing Bawoyeu. On 22 May Deby formed a new council of ministers, which included, for the first time, five members of the opposition. However, it was reported that other opposition leaders had refused to join the government, while the influence of southerners in the council of ministers was also reduced. By late May some 10 political parties had been granted legal recognition, including the Union pour la démocratie et la République (UDR), led by Bawoyeu.

In late May 1992 rebels affiliated to the MDD launched a further attack in the region of Lake Chad, which was reportedly led by a former minister in the GUNT, Moussa Medela. Government forces subsequently initiated counter-offensives from Nigerian territory. In mid-June an agreement between the government and the CSNPD, which was led by Lt Kette Nodji Moise, provided for the release of members of the CSNPD in detention. Later that month the government announced that it had pre-empted a coup attempt, led by Abbas Koti. Shortly afterwards supporters of Koti, known as the Conseil de redressement du Tchad (CNRT), attacked government forces in the region of Lake Chad; fighting was also reported at Chicha, near Faya-Largeau. At the end of June an agreement, which was signed in Libreville, Gabon, between the government and the MDD, provided for the end of hostilities between the two forces, and for the immediate release of prisoners detained as a result of their membership of the MDD. In July, however, government forces were reported to have launched renewed attacks against MDD troops in the region of Lake Chad.

In July 1992 the trade union federation, the Union syndicats du Tchad (UST), organized a series of strikes, in protest at government plans to reduce salaries and to increase taxes. Later that month Yodoyman was expelled from the ANDD for allegedly failing to support the process of democratic reform. Shortly afterwards the minister of the civil service and labour, Nabia Ndali (who was a member of the ANDD), resigned from the government. In early August three representatives of human rights organizations serving in the government, including a member of the LTDH, also resigned, in protest at the continued violent acts by security forces in N'Djamena. The council of ministers was subsequently reorganized. In the same month clashes between CSNPD forces and government troops were reported from Doba, in southern Chad. In September the government signed further peace agreements with the MDD, the CSNPD and an opposition movement based in Sudan, the Front national du Tchad (FNT).

In October 1992 public-sector workers staged a one-month general strike, which was organized by the UST, in support of demands for higher salaries and the convening of the national conference (which had been postponed since May). Two members of the opposition who held ministerial portfolios resigned in protest at the subsequent ban imposed by the government on the activities of the UST; a minor reorganization of the council of ministers followed. In mid-October, in response to increasing public pressure, the government announced that the national conference was to take place in January 1993. Later in October MDD forces launched a further offensive against the ANT at Bagassola, in the region of Lake Chad. At the end of October the MDD claimed that the government had received armaments from Libya, in preparation for the resumption of hostilities, and officially declared the peace agreement, signed in September, to be invalid. In November a number of prominent members of the UST were arrested, after the general strike was extended for a further month. Later in November the government ended the ban that had been imposed on the UST, but suspended the civil servants who continued to observe the general strike. In December renewed clashes between government forces and members of the MDD occurred near Lake Chad. In that month a co-operation agreement, signed by the governments of Chad and Libya, prompted criticism from opposition parties. In early January 1993 the government withdrew the sanctions that had been imposed on a number of civil servants, and the general strike effectively ended. Later that month FROLINAT announced that three of its long-standing leaders, including Goukouni Oueddei, had been removed, and party organs dissolved.

CONSTITUTIONAL TRANSITION AND CIVIL UNREST

In mid-January 1993 some 800 delegates (representing, among others, the organs of state and 30 political organizations, together with trade unions and other professional associations) attended the opening of the national conference, which was to prepare for the establishment of a democratic system of government. However, following disputes over a motion confirming the sovereign status of the conference, proceedings were temporarily delayed. In the same month it was reported that members of the CSNPD had attacked government forces at Gore, in the southern prefecture of Logone Oriental. Later in January an abortive coup attempt was mounted by troops loyal to Habré during a visit by Deby to Paris; several of the rebels were subsequently arrested. In February government troops, in conflict with the MDD in the region of Lake Chad, clashed with members of the Nigerien armed forces, after attacking rebel bases in Niger. In the same month, following renewed military engagements between government troops and the CSNPD in southern Chad, opposition groups claimed that members of the ANT had perpetrated retaliatory massacres of civilians in the region of Gore, prompting increased tension between the population of the north and south. By March some 15,000 civilians had fled from southern Chad to the CAR, following atrocities committed by government forces. Also in March it was reported that Koti (who had been arrested in Cameroon in December 1992) had escaped from detention.

MOUNGAR'S TRANSITIONAL GOVERNMENTS

The progress of the national conference was impeded by controversy over demands for the extension of the use of Arabic for official communications; on 6 April 1993, however, the conference adopted a transitional charter, elected Dr Fidèle Moungar, the minister of national and higher education, to be prime minister, and established a 57-member interim legislature, the conseil supérieur de la transition (CST). The leader of the Rassemblement pour la démocratie et le progrès, Lol Mahamat Choua (who had briefly served as president of Chad in 1979), was elected chairman of the CST. Under the terms of the transitional charter (which came into effect on 9 April), Deby was to remain in office as head of state and c-in-c of the armed forces for a period of one year (with provision for one extension), while a transitional government, under the supervision of the CST, was to implement economic, political and social programmes, drafted by the conference; multi-party elections were to take place at the end of this period. Later in April Moungar announced the appointment of a transitional government, which retained only four members of the former council of ministers and included representatives of a number of opposition parties.

In early May 1993, following a report by a commission of inquiry which had been dispatched to Logone Oriental, the transitional government confirmed that members of the ANT had carried out a number of massacres of civilians in southern Chad earlier that year, apparently in reprisal for hostilities initiated by the CSNPD. Moungar announced that officials implicated in the violence had been arrested, that military units in the region were to be replaced, and that a judicial investigation was to be instituted. In the same month, in accordance with the resolutions of the national conference, Deby dissolved the government intelligence service, which had attracted criticism from opposition and human rights groups. Later in May a human rights organization, Chad Non-Violence, withdrew its representative from the CST, in protest at the violence perpetrated by members of the ATN, and at the alleged failure of the government to comply with the decisions of the national conference. In June the CST refused to ratify the co-operation agreement that had been signed with Libya in November 1992, in view of the unresolved dispute over the sovereignty of the Aozou region (which was to be reviewed at the ICJ later that month). In late June Moungar announced the formation of a new transitional government, in which the number of members were reduced from 30 to 17. In the same month widespread concern at the increasing incidence of violent crime emerged, following the assassination of the director of the soldiers' reintegration committee, Mbailaou Miabe, by troops in N'Djamena. In an attempt to restore civil order, the transitional government subsequently introduced a number of new security measures, and in early July announced that the ANT and the security forces were to be reorganized. Violent crime continued throughout the country, however, and in early July a one-day general strike, organized by opposition parties, was staged in protest at the continuing civil disorder.

In early August 1993 some 82 civilians were killed in the region of Chokoyam, in Ouaddai, apparently as a result of ethnic differences. Shortly afterwards it was reported that some 41 people had been killed when a demonstration, staged by residents of N'Djamena (originating from Ouaddai) in protest at the massacre, was violently suppressed by the republican guard. The CST subsequently accused the government of exceeding its powers by deploying the republican guard to disperse the demonstration, and by imposing a national curfew in response to the unrest. In mid-August Koti (who had denied allegations by the government that CNRT troops had perpetrated the massacre in Ouaddai) returned to Chad, after a peace agreement was reached by the CNRT and the Chadian authorities. In September, despite efforts by the government to appease discontent in the south, the CSNPD threatened to impede plans to exploit petroleum reserves in the region of Doba, in southern Chad (which were considered to be essential to future prospects of economic development), unless the government complied with demands for the establishment of a federal state. In mid-October Koti signed a further agreement with the government, whereby the CNRT was to be granted legal status as a political party and its forces were to be integrated into the ANT. However, Koti was subsequently killed by security forces while allegedly resisting arrest on charges of involvement in a conspiracy to overthrow the government. The CNRT rejected claims by the authorities that documents, signed by Koti, detailing plans to stage an armed coup had been discovered, and announced that hostilities with government forces would be resumed.

KOUMAKOYE AND OPPOSITION PRESSURE

In September 1993 increasing disagreement between Deby and Moungar concerning government policy intensified, after Deby dismissed the minister of finance and computer sciences, Robert Roingam, without consulting Moungar. Although relations between Deby and Moungar appeared to improve following the appointment of a successor to Roingam, in October a motion expressing 'no confidence' in the Moungar administration, apparently initiated by supporters of Deby, was approved in the CST by 45 of the 56 votes cast. Moungar subsequently resigned and his government was dissolved. In early November the CST elected Delwa Kassire Koumakoye, hitherto the minister of justice and keeper of the seals, as prime minister. Later that month a new 16-member transitional government, which included 10 members of the former administration, was appointed.

In December 1993 a 17-member 'institutional committee' was established to prepare a draft constitution, an electoral code and legislation governing the registration of political organizations; the committee, which included representatives of the transitional organs and a number of political parties, was to submit recommendations within a period of two months. However, industrial action by public sector workers (particularly by teachers) in protest at the government's continued failure to pay arrears in salaries resumed, and in January 1994 the government banned an opposition demonstration and threatened to implement sanctions against striking civil servants. Later that month a reorganization of the transitional government took place. Meanwhile, opposition activity continued: the MDD and the Union nationale pour la démocratie et le socialisme announced that they were to unite against government forces, while members of the FNT, who apparently were to have been integrated into the army following a peace agreement, attacked a military garrison at Abéché. (It was subsequently reported that more than 200 people had been killed in ensuing clashes between the FNT and government forces.) Also in January Cameroon claimed that members of the CNRT, who were allegedly planning to initiate an offensive against N'Djamena, had killed members of the Cameroonian security forces in the north of that country. In February negotiations between the government and the CSNPD, which were mediated by the government of the CAR, resulted in a cease-fire agreement; the discussions subsequently ended in failure, however, and further clashes between government and CSNPD forces took place in the south of the country at the end of March.

CONSTITUTIONAL PROPOSALS

In March 1994 the institutional committee presented recommendations for a draft constitution, which included provisions for the election of a president for a term of five years, the installation of a bicameral legislative assembly and a constitutional court, and the establishment of a decentralized administrative structure. In April, in accordance with demands by the opposition, the CST extended the transitional period for one year, on the grounds that the government had achieved little progress in the preparation for democratic elections. A new electoral timetable was adopted, whereby the government was obliged to provide funds for the organization of the elections, reach an agreement with the UST in order to end industrial unrest, and implement further preparatory measures by June, including the adoption of an electoral code, the establishment of a national reconciliation council, which was to negotiate a peace settlement with rebel movements, and the appointment of electoral and human rights commissions. The constitutional recommendations were to be submitted for approval at a national referendum in December; in the event that the new constitution was adopted by the electorate, legislative elections would take place in January 1995, followed by a presidential election in March.

Subsequent government efforts to negotiate a settlement with the UST in accordance with the stipulations of the new electoral timetable were impeded by further strike action, which was initiated by public sector workers at the end of April, in support of demands for an increase in salaries to compensate for the effects of the devaluation of the CFA franc in January. Despite the promulgation of a presidential decree at the beginning of May declaring the strike to be illegal, industrial action continued throughout that month. Also in May, despite apparent opposition from Deby, the government established a 12-member national reconciliation council, which was to initiate negotiations with the opposition engaged in hostilities. Later that month Deby announced an extensive government reorganization, in which nine ministers were removed. However, one of the newly-appointed ministers, Salomon Ngarbaye Tombalbaye, the son of the former president and leader of the Mouvement pour la démocratie et le socialisme du Tchad, refused to join the government, owing to its continued failure to address social and economic hardship in the country. In June the CSNPD denied claims by the Chadian authorities that a number of its members had joined government forces. (Following the failure of the peace negotiations in March, the government of the CAR had prohibited the CSNPD from conducting military operations from CAR territory.) In early July the government and the UST reached a negotiated settlement, which provided for a limited increase in salaries and the payment of arrears. In early August peace negotiations between the government and the CSNPD resumed in the CAR.

THE RETURN OF THE AOZOU REGION

In February 1994 the ICJ ruled in favour of Chad in the dispute over the sovereignty of the Aozou region, thereby upholding the provisions of a treaty that had been signed in 1955 by the governments of France and Libya. Later that month, however, Chad claimed that Libya had deployed additional troops in the region. In March discussions between the governments of Chad and Libya to establish a timetable for the withdrawal of Libyan troops resulted in little progress, apparently owing to Libyan insistence on adherence to the agreement that had been reached in 1989, providing for repatriation of Libyan prisoners of war. Nevertheless, the Libyan government maintained that it would comply with the ICJ ruling, and in April agreed to commence the withdrawal of troops from the region, in an operation that was to be monitored by UN observers and officials from both countries. At the end of May Libya and Chad issued a joint statement confirming that the withdrawal of Libyan troops had been completed as scheduled. In June the two governments signed a co-operation agreement.

Economy

KOJO S. AMANOR

Revised for this edition by the Editor

Chad is one of the poorest and least developed countries of continental Africa, and its geographical isolation, climate and meagre natural resources have resulted in an economy of very narrow range. The agricultural sector has traditionally dominated the economy, accounting for 48% of Chad's gross domestic product (GDP), and employing about 72.5% of the labour force, in 1992. The industrial and commercial sectors are small, and virtually all production facilities of the modern sector are installed in the south or in N'Djamena, the capital. Much economic activity is illicit, and very few statistics are published. There are hardly any all-weather roads and no railways. The country is land-locked and its major economic centres are situated 1,400–2,800 km from the sea. Its structural problems of economic development, which are immense in any circumstances, have been rendered still more acute by civil conflict and by drought. In the early 1980s Chad's domestic production supplied only around three-quarters of the country's food requirements, necessitating substantial food aid.

According to estimates by the World Bank, GDP increased, in real terms, by an annual average of 5.3% in 1980–92. In 1992 Chad's gross national product (GNP), measured at average 1990–92 prices, was US $1,261m., equivalent to $220 per head (one of the lowest per caput levels in the world). During 1985–92, it was estimated, GNP per head increased, in real terms, at an average annual rate of 1.3%, while the population increased by an average of 2.5% annually.

AGRICULTURE

The main area of crop production is situated in the south of the country, with cattle production prevailing in the more arid northern zones. In the extreme north camel and sheep rearing, and date orchards are predominant. Subsistence agriculture accounts for three-quarters of annual crop production. The principal food crops are sorghum, millet and groundnuts. Cassava, rice, dates, maize and wheat are also grown for domestic consumption. Since the late 1970s there have been problems in meeting domestic food requirements. Between 1972–85 annual grain deliveries under aid programmes averaged 44,200 metric tons. As a result of drought, production of cereals in the 1984/85 crop year declined to 289,800 tons (the lowest annual total for twenty years), and a severe famine ensued. Owing to adequate rainfall in the following year, production increased to 676,600 tons and was maintained between 570–680 tons in the late 1980s. Despite adverse climatic conditions and serious food shortages in some parts of the country in 1990, grain production has continued to increase and in 1991 812,000 tons of cereal were harvested. Chad's entire groundnut crop (which amounted to 147,000 metric tons in 1992) is consumed or processed into groundnut oil locally. Some progress has been made in the cultivation of wheat and rice by modern methods. (Output of the latter reached 118,000 metric tons in 1991.) Rural development schemes, which have been implemented in southern Chad, with assistance from France, the EC, Canada and the World Bank, aim to increase production of cereals and livestock. In 1992, however, erratic climatic conditions adversely affected cereal output (particularly rice production, which declined to 52,000 tons). At the end of 1993 a deficit in cereal output of 154,000 tons was projected, prompting renewed fears of famine.

The sugar-processing sector has benefited from support from France and other donors. In the period 1977–79 15,000m. francs CFA was invested in the development of a sugar agro-industrial complex, based on 6,000 ha of irrigated cane fields and a sugar-processing refinery at Banda, with an annual capacity to process 30,000 tons of raw sugar. Between 1987–90 290,000 tons of sugar cane were harvested per annum. Raw sugar production has increased from 27,000 tons to over 30,000 in 1991, while sugar cane output reached 400,000 tons in 1992. In 1991 the national sugar-processing corporation, the Société national sucrière du Tchad (SONASUT) received an investment of 16m. francs CFA from France to expand raw sugar production to 45,000 tons, with the aim of creating national self-sufficiency in sugar production.

Cotton is the dominant crop and principal export commodity. Production of cotton has been widely encouraged since the 1920s, and the crop is currently grown on almost 150,000 ha in the south of the country. Annual yields fluctuate widely, mainly reflecting rainfall patterns, and in poor years production levels are less than one-half of those in neighbouring Cameroon. Owing to civil conflict in the south in late 1984 and early 1985, and the decline in international prices for cotton in the following years, production declined to 89,500 metric tons in 1986/87, contributing to the substantial losses already incurred by the marketing monopoly, the Société cotonnière du Tchad (COTONTCHAD), largely as a result of mismanagement and corruption. This agency, which is 75% state-owned, is responsible for the provision of inputs and the purchasing, transportation, ginning and marketing of the crop, and the manufacture of cottonseed oil. In response to the near bankruptcy of COTONTCHAD in 1986, a consortium of donors launched a programme to provide credit for crop purchases; France, the International Development Association (IDA), the European Development Fund and the Netherlands contributed $48.9m. towards the restructure of COTONTCHAD, which involved the closure of half of the cotton-ginning mills, and 60% of shelling installations, the reduction of the total number of employees from 3,000 to 1,700, and the elimination of the subsidies on fertilizers and pesticides for farmers. Following the introduction of new pricing policies to provide greater incentives for production, seed cotton output increased to an estimated 151,086 tons in 1989/90 and to 156,600 tons in 1990/91. In 1991/92 cotton production reached 174,000 tons; owing to a decline in the price of cotton in 1992, however, COTONTCHAD again incurred substantial losses, and in July of that year received emergency aid from France. In 1992/93 cotton output declined to 120,000 tons, apparently as a result of civil conflict in the south of the country, necessitating further emergency assistance from France.

Gum arabic, which is harvested from traditional plantations in the north, is a minor export product. Output has been adversely affected by drought and the unstable political situation: in the late 1980s annual production averaged 200 tons (compared with the record level of 1,100 tons produced in 1969).

Livestock production plays an important role in the Chadian economy, accounting for 13% of GDP, and engaging about 40% of the labour force. Cattle raising is concentrated mainly in the central part of the country; the herds, however, are moved long distances between the north and the south along traditional routes following a seasonal pattern. Livestock is often exported illicitly, without payment of taxes, and mainly to Nigeria where it is sold or bartered for consumer goods. In 1992, according to the FAO, there were 4.5m. cattle, 3m. goats and 2m. sheep. In the long term there is considerable potential for livestock production in Chad, but its realization would require the upgrading of the herds and improvements in marketing arrangements. As a result of drought cattle have moved southwards into the mainly crop-producing prefectures of Moyen Chari and Mayo-

Kebbi. In 1988 the IDA provided $37m. towards a five-year project, which aims to increase meat and milk production, improve rangeland management and veterinary services, and liberalize export trading and pricing policies. The construction of a large slaughterhouse in N'Djamena is under way, which is envisaged as the centre of an export-orientated frozen and canned meat industry.

MINING, MANUFACTURING AND POWER

Exploitation of the located deposits of petroleum have been inhibited by the high cost of importing plant and machinery long distances with poor or non-existent transport facilities. In response to the increase in the international price of petroleum during the 1970s, however, Conoco, in conjunction with Shell, began petroleum extraction in the Sedigi region, to the north of Lake Chad, in 1977. Amounts available during 1979/80 were small—about 1,500 barrels per day (b/d)—but nevertheless represented 80% of domestic requirements. The precarious security situation, however, resulted in the suspension of even this small output. In 1988 an agreement was signed with a consortium led by Exxon, Shell and Chevron, regarding the establishment of a petroleum refinery to exploit the reserves in the Sedigi region, estimated at 70m. tons. (In 1992 Elf Aquitaine replaced Chevron in the consortium.) In early 1991 the World Bank provided a loan of 3,340m. francs CFA towards the construction of a refinery with a production capacity of 3,300 b/d, an associated 12-MW electrical power station and a 320-km pipeline. The project was designed to reduce Chad's dependence on imports of petroleum and oil from Nigeria and Cameroon; in 1993, however, it was abandoned, after the World Bank failed to provide further loans. Following exploration in the region of the Doba Basin, in southern Chad, in 1993, additional reserves of petroleum amounting to an estimated 150m.—200m. barrels were discovered (increasing total estimated reserves in that region to 700m.—800m. barrels). In early 1994 initial discussions between a consortium, comprising Esso, Shell and Elf Aquitaine, and the governments of Chad and Cameroon took place regarding the construction of a pipeline, which would transport petroleum from the Doba region to the Cameroonian port of Kribi; however, the logistical difficulties appeared to be considerable while there was concern that rebel activity in the south of the country might jeopardize the project.

Natron, found in pans on the northern edge of Lake Chad, is at present the only mineral of importance exploited in Chad. It is used as salt, for human and animal consumption, in the preservation of meats and hides and in soap production. Evidence of other minerals—notably tungsten, cassiterite, uranium, bauxite and gold in the north—offers prospects for the future, but none has so far been exploited on a commercial scale. However, the Société tchadienne d'exploitation des carrières, has been established to exploit deposits of limestone for use as construction material. In 1994 the Aozou region, which was believed to contain significant reserves of uranium and other minerals, was returned to Chad.

Manufacturing (which accounted for 16% of GDP in 1992) is centred in N'Djamena and Moundou, and is mainly devoted to the processing of agricultural products. The processing of cotton is the principal industry; however, the importance of this sector declined during the 1980s, with the closure of one-half of COTONTCHAD's ginning mills (by the late 1980s annual ginning capacity was only 120,000 tons, compared with 184,000 tons at the beginning of the decade). Cotton thread and cloth were produced by the Société textile du Tchad (STT) in Sarh; by 1989, however, production had declined by 45% to 8.5m. metres of cloth, largely a result of increased competition from Nigerian imports (following the decline in the value of the naira), and in 1992 the STT was liquidated. In 1994 the French government pledged to grant 12,000m. francs CFA to support the cotton industry. Despite increases in sugar production in recent years to 30,000 tons, and plans to further increase output, production has also been affected by imports and smuggling of low-priced sugar from Nigeria and Cameroon. There is also a wide range of small-scale enterprises operating outside the recorded sector, including crafts and the production of agricultural implements, which make a significant contribution to employment and overall production.

Electricity in Chad is generated by two oil-powered plants operated by a public corporation, Société tchadienne d'eau et d'électricité (STEE). The annual output of electricity rose rapidly until the mid-1970s, but has since stagnated, because of the difficulties of importing petroleum. In 1989 production totalled some 81m. kWh, and electricity charges (at about six times the level in Nigeria) were among the highest in Africa.

TRANSPORT

Transportation within Chad is inadequate and expensive. Communications with the outside world are difficult, slow and costly because of the great distance from the sea, the character of the trade, and poor facilities in neighbouring countries. In 1991 only 430 km of the estimated 27,000 km of roads were paved. Transport limitations are a major obstacle to the country's economic development, and efforts are being made to improve the internal transport system (with help from the World Bank, the EDF and the USA), including the rehabilitation and construction of an ancillary road network as part of rural development in the south. In early 1990 the World Bank formulated a major road construction programme, involving 1,800 km and costing an estimated 100,000m. francs CFA. 250 km of tarred road between Abéché and N'Djamena were completed, in a project funded by French aid. The construction of a road linking N'Djamena to Mao is also under way. Transport infrastructural improvements in adjacent countries, especially in Cameroon, were expected to benefit Chad; however, an agreement, signed by the two countries in 1962, to extend the Transcameroon railway from N'Gaoundéré to Sarh, in southern Chad, has been indefinitely postponed. Major reconstruction of N'Djamena international airport had to be carried out in 1983 with the help of foreign loans, following severe damage during the previous year's struggle for control of the capital. Further improvements, including runway extensions, were completed in 1987. The renovation of the runway at Abéché commenced in 1988, while a programme to upgrade facilities at Faya-Largeau began in 1990; French financial and technical assistance was obtained for both projects.

PUBLIC FINANCE

Economic decline and civil strife have exacerbated Chad's severe public-finance difficulties, which can be relieved only by substantial contributions from both international agencies and the country's allies, notably France and the USA. The deterioration in the political situation in the 1970s effectively halted development expenditure, while expenditure on defence accounted for one-quarter of the total budget. Since 1983 the budgetary deficit has increased annually, and foreign aid has been needed to maintain basic government services. By 1985 the annual fiscal deficit had reached 29,163m. francs CFA, with expenditure more than double total revenue. The government, with the support of the IMF, the World Bank, France and the USA, aimed to restrict the 1986 budget deficit to 5,500m. francs CFA, which was to be almost entirely covered by funds from France and the USA. In return, Chad was to endeavour to increase revenue receipts (through increased taxes on petroleum products and luxury goods) and to reduce spending (for example, on subsidies for cotton production and on civil service employment). Following the financial crisis at COTONTCHAD (which normally made a major contribution to government revenue), however, the deficit increased to 9,329m. francs CFA in 1986. Although the government continued its efforts to generate additional revenue, and to reduce expenditure on personnel in the public sector, high deficits were recorded in subsequent years, reaching 25,458m. francs CFA in 1989, 22,451m. francs CFA in 1990, and 26,502m. francs CFA in 1991. In 1992, following serious economic and financial difficulty, an austerity budget, supported by international donors, was announced, and a programme to restructure the civil service and to transfer a number of banks and state-owned enterprises to the private sector was initiated. Later in 1992, in accordance with recommendations by the IMF, the government announced plans to increase taxes and to reduce the salaries of civil servant staff, prompting a protracted strike in the public sector. At the end of 1992 however, the budgetary deficit was estimated at 22,600m. francs CFA (equivalent to 6% of GDP), exacerbated by the continuing decline in custom revenues (which account for a high proportion of total government revenue), largely as a result of increased smuggling across the Nigerian and Cameroonian borders.

In January 1994 a devaluation of the CFA franc by 50% resulted in an increase in the price of essential commodities of 41% (in the year to May), prompting further strikes in the public sector. In March Chad and the other member states of the Union douanière et économique des états de l'Afrique centrale signed an agreement that established the Communauté économique et monétaire en Afrique centrale, providing for increased economic and monetary union. In the same month the IMF initiated a one-year stand-by programme, with credit equivalent to about US $23m., while the World Bank agreed to disbursements of the same amount (subject to the government's fulfilment of the conditions stipulated by the IMF). The programme was designed to restore public finance through (among other measures) improvement in the collection of taxes and other customs duties, the guaranteed payment of civil servants' salaries, and the continuation of a programme of retrenchment in the armed forces.

DEVELOPMENT PLANNING

From 1966 a series of Development Plans were implemented but proved largely unsuccessful, as a result of the lack of well-formulated projects and the difficulty in obtaining aid to the extent required. The 1986–88 interim development programme emphasized the attainment of self-sufficiency in foodstuffs and the provision of basic needs. This effort to establish more systematic planning was supported by the international community: in late 1987 the IMF pledged structural adjustment funds totalling SDR 21.42m., while external credit assistance was provided for the government's planning institutions. In 1990 the IMF disbursed the final loan of SDR 6.1m. francs CFA, under the three-year structural adjustment facility, approved in 1987. A new orientation plan was formulated in 1990, whereby donors made provisions for technical assistance to strengthen the capacities of the ministries to devise, implement and monitor economic and financial planning.

FOREIGN TRADE, AID AND PAYMENTS

While exports and imports have fluctuated widely as a result of the civil war, Chad's foreign trade has, almost without exception, shown a very large deficit, owing to the low level of production in the economy and the high cost of transport. The principal imports are food products (accounting for 17% of the cost of total imports in 1991) and petroleum. Cotton is the principal export commodity (contributing 80% of total export earnings in 1990) followed by meat and live animals. By the late 1980s the decline in international prices for cotton resulted in a significant reduction in export revenue, while imports increased sharply, resulting in a substantial rise in the trade deficit. Owing to the rise in output of cotton in recent years and the improvement in world market prices, export earnings reached 49,600m. francs CFA in 1989, and 51,200m. francs CFA in 1990. In 1989 a trade deficit of US $84.9m. was recorded, which declined to $29.2m. in 1990. In 1991, however, the deficit increased dramatically, to $100.2m.

In 1990 Chad's principal sources of imports were France (52%), Cameroon (9%), and the USA, Belgium, Luxembourg, and the Federal Republic of Germany (each accounting for under 6%). The main destination of exports in 1990 was the Federal Republic of Germany (24%), Portugal (19%), France (16%), and Japan (12%). However, illicit imports from Nigeria and Cameroon account for a high proportion of Chad's foreign trade.

Since independence in 1960, Chad has continued to rely heavily on foreign assistance, in order to finance the massive deficits on the trade and services account, and to provide funds for basic budgetary requirements and for any development expenditure. France has remained the principal supplier of aid, including direct budgetary assistance (more than one-half of the bilateral aid disbursed in 1987 was of French origin). EC and multilateral agencies and, more recently, Arab countries also provide substantial help, principally for agricultural and communication projects and for construction of the petroleum pipeline and refinery. At a conference of donor nations in November 1982 aid totalling $185m. was pledged (just over 50% of the amount requested by the new government of President Habré for an economic reconstruction programme). A further meeting, in December 1985, resulted in pledges of aid in excess of $424m., including $100m. from the World Bank and $50m. from the African Development Bank. The aid, in support of Chad's interim 1986–90 Development Programme, was expected to reach $450m. in total. The current programme of national reconstruction has received considerable support from the EDF (through funds to restore the road network and to reconstruct N'Djamena), France (both civil and military) and the USA (for road rehabilitation). In 1990 Chad received aid totalling $47.5m. from France, to finance the budget deficit. In 1992 and 1993 the French government supplied additional budgetary aid to enable the government to pay the salaries of civil servants.

In the 1980s about 90% of Chad's foreign aid was in grant form, and most of the country's borrowing was from government and the public sector, on highly concessionary terms, with arrears on payment. In 1984 official external aid totalled $87.7m. By 1989 external aid had risen to $242m., of which $179m. consisted of grants and $63m. of credits and loans. Consequently, while the country's external debt increased significantly, from $156m. in 1984 to $368m. by 1989, and while foreign exchange arrears rose from $16m. in 1984 to $129m. in 1989, debt-servicing remained relatively low, equivalent to 5.2% of exports of goods and services in 1989. At the end of 1990 external debt totalled $430.4m., while the cost of debt-servicing was equivalent to about 4.0% of earnings from exports of goods and services. Despite a cancellation, with effect from January 1990, of Chad's outstanding official liabilities to France, total external debt reached $606.3m. at the end of 1991 (of which $546.9m. was long-term public debt). In 1994, following the devaluation of the CFA franc, France agreed to cancel Chad's outstanding official debt.

PROBLEMS AND PROSPECTS

Following the accession to power of the Mouvement patriotique du salut in late 1990, Chad became increasingly dependent upon bilateral and multilateral credit, and highly vulnerable to any suspension in the flow of foreign aid.

Since 1991 the government has been unable to stabilize the fiscal situation, despite efforts to improve the collection of taxes and to control budgetary expenditure; the administration's lack of revenue has been further undermined by an increase in illicit trade. Protracted civil conflict has resulted in additional economic disruption. Austerity measures, which were adopted in accordance with recommendations by the IMF in 1992, prompted a prolonged strike in the public sector, which resulted in a further deterioration in the economy. The devaluation of the CFA franc in January 1994 was expected to result in a dramatic increase in the rate of inflation and decline in per capita GDP; according to projections by the IMF, however, real growth rates were to improve and the budgetary deficit was to be reduced by 1995. A new IMF stand-by programme, which was adopted in March 1994, was designed to restore public finance. Although strike action ended in mid-1994 (see Recent History), it was feared that continuing civil disorder would impede economic progress. However, substantial reserves of petroleum, which were discovered in the south of the country in 1993, were believed to have the potential to attract significant private investment and to transform Chad's long-term economic prospects.

Statistical Survey

Source (unless otherwise stated): Direction de la Statistique, des Etudes Economiques et Démographiques, BP 453, N'Djamena.

Area and Population

AREA, POPULATION AND DENSITY

Area (sq km)	
Land	1,259,200
Inland waters	24,800
Total	1,284,000*
Population (sample survey)	
December 1963–August 1964	3,254,000†
Population (official estimates at mid-year)	
1991	5,819,000
1992	5,961,000
1993	6,288,000
Density (per sq km) at mid-1993	5.0

* 495,800 sq miles.

† Including areas not covered by the survey.

PREFECTURES (official estimates, mid-1988)

	Area (sq km)	Population	Density (per sq km)
Batha	88,800	431,000	4.9
Biltine	46,850	216,000	4.6
Borkou-Ennedi-Tibesti (BET)	600,350	109,000	0.2
Chari-Baguirmi	82,910	844,000	10.2
Guera	58,950	254,000	4.3
Kanem	114,520	245,000	2.1
Lac	22,320	165,000	7.4
Logone Occidental	8,695	365,000	42.0
Logone Oriental	28,035	377,000	13.4
Mayo-Kebbi	30,105	852,000	28.3
Moyen Chari	45,180	646,000	14.3
Ouaddai	76,240	422,000	5.5
Salamat	63,000	131,000	2.1
Tandjilé	18,045	371,000	20.6
Total	1,284,000	5,428,000	4.2

PRINCIPAL TOWNS (officially-estimated population in 1988)

N'Djamena (capital)	594,000	Moundou	102,000
Sarh	113,400	Abéché	83,000

BIRTHS AND DEATHS (UN estimates, annual averages)

	1975–80	1980–85	1985–90
Birth rate (per 1,000)	44.1	44.2	43.9
Death rate (per 1,000)	23.1	21.4	19.5

Source: UN, *World Population Prospects: The 1992 Revision.*

ECONOMICALLY ACTIVE POPULATION
(ILO estimates, '000 persons at mid-1980)

	Males	Females	Total
Agriculture, etc.	1,043	318	1,361
Industry	72	4	76
Services	154	44	197
Total	1,269	366	1,635

Source: ILO, *Economically Active Population Estimates and Projections, 1950–2025.*

Mid-1992 (estimates in '000): Agriculture 1,446; Total 1,993 (Source: FAO, *Production Yearbook*).

Agriculture

PRINCIPAL CROPS ('000 metric tons)

	1990	1991	1992
Wheat*	2	3	2
Rice (paddy)*	66	118	52
Maize	29	48*	91*
Millet	168	226*	295*
Sorghum	280	286*	379*
Other cereals	57	131*	96*
Potatoes†	18	18	18
Sweet potatoes†	46	46	46
Cassava (Manioc)†	330	330	330
Yams†	240	240	240
Taro (Coco yam)†	9	9	9
Dry beans†	42	42	42
Other pulses†	18	18	18
Groundnuts (in shell)	108	97	147
Sesame seed	12	9	14
Cottonseed	98	104	110†
Cotton (lint)*	60	69	70
Dry onions†	14	14	14
Other vegetables†	60	60	60
Dates†	32	32	32
Mangoes†	32	32	32
Other fruit†	50	51	52
Sugar cane†	340	370	400

* Unofficial figure(s). † FAO estimate(s).

Source: FAO, *Production Yearbook.*

LIVESTOCK ('000 head, year ending September)

	1990	1991	1992
Cattle	4,297	4,400	4,507
Goats	2,800	2,923	3,012*
Sheep	1,964	1,983	2,043*
Pigs	14	15	14†
Horses	195	182	185†
Asses	264	269	270†
Camels	549	565	570†

Poultry (FAO estimates, million): 4 in 1990; 4 in 1991; 4 in 1992.

* Unofficial figure. † FAO estimate.

Source: FAO, *Production Yearbook.*

LIVESTOCK PRODUCTS (FAO estimates, '000 metric tons)

	1990	1991	1992
Total meat	89	87	94
Beef and veal	63	65	67
Mutton and lamb	8	4	9
Goats' meat	9	10	10
Poultry meat	4	4	4
Cows' milk	116	119	121
Sheep's milk	9	9	9
Goats' milk	14	14	14
Butter	0.3	0.3	0.3
Hen eggs	3.6	3.7	3.8
Cattle hides	9.0	9.2	9.5
Sheep skins	1.6	0.7	1.6
Goat skins	1.9	1.9	1.9

Source: FAO, *Production Yearbook.*

Forestry

ROUNDWOOD REMOVALS
('000 cubic metres, excluding bark)

	1990	1991	1992*
Sawlogs, etc.	3	5	5
Other industrial wood*	556	570	585
Fuel wood*	3,389	3,472	3,568
Total	3,948	4,047	4,158

* FAO estimate(s).
Source: FAO, *Yearbook of Forest Products.*

Fishing

(FAO estimates, '000 metric tons, live weight)

	1989	1990	1991
Total catch (freshwater fishes)	65	60	60

Source: FAO, *Yearbook of Fishery Statistics.*

Industry

SELECTED PRODUCTS
('000 metric tons, unless otherwise indicated)

	1989	1990	1991
Salted, dried or smoked fish*	19.0	19.2	n.a.
Raw sugar†	33	32	33
Beer ('000 hectolitres)	115	116	140
Soft drinks ('000 hectolitres)	32	35	n.a.
Cigarettes (million)	9,350	12,378	22,438
Woven cotton fabrics (million metres)	10.3	3.4	3.0
Radio receivers ('000)	9	13	n.a.
Electric energy (million kWh)	82	82	85

* Provisional or estimated figures.
† Source: International Sugar Organization.
Source: UN, *Industrial Statistics Yearbook.*

Finance

CURRENCY AND EXCHANGE RATES

Monetary Units

100 centimes = 1 franc de la Coopération financière en Afrique centrale (CFA).

French Franc, Sterling and Dollar Equivalents (31 March 1994)

1 French franc = 100 francs CFA;
£1 sterling = 846.40 francs CFA;
US $1 = 570.14 francs CFA;
1,000 francs CFA = £1.181 = $1.754.

Average Exchange Rate (francs CFA per US $)

1991	282.11
1992	264.69
1993	283.16

Note: The exchange rate of 1 French franc = 50 francs CFA, established in 1948, remained in force until January 1994, when the CFA franc was devalued by 50%, with the exchange rate adjusted to 1 French franc = 100 francs CFA.

BUDGET (million francs CFA)

Revenue*	1989	1990	1991
Tax revenue	26,347	29,027	25,209
Taxes on income, profits, etc.	6,174	5,903	7,287
Domestic taxes on goods and services	11,022	12,357	10,874
Taxes on international trade and transactions	6,766	7,692	4,929
Other current revenue	1,675	2,540	7,032
Property income	594	304	2,007
Administrative fees, charges, etc.	714	752	922
Total	28,022	31,567	32,241

Expenditure†	1989	1990	1991
Current expenditure	47,980	45,121	45,170
Expenditure on goods and services	37,615	42,797	46,500
Wages and salaries	25,989	28,584	27,159
Other purchases of goods and services	11,626	14,213	19,341
Interest payments	876	1,902	3,202
Subsidies and other current transfers	3,279	2,980	3,088
Capital expenditure	62,965	58,131	68,601
Total	110,945	103,252	113,771

* Excluding grants received (million francs CFA): 57,767 in 1989; 49,234 in 1990; 55,028 in 1991.
† Excluding net lending (million francs CFA): 302 in 1989.
Source: IMF, *Government Finance Statistics Yearbook.*

CENTRAL BANK RESERVES
(US $ million, at 31 December)

	1991	1992	1993
Gold*	3.94	3.70	4.42
IMF special drawing rights	0.16	0.03	0.01
Reserve position in IMF	0.39	0.37	0.38
Foreign exchange	119.25	80.08	38.54
Total	123.74	84.18	43.35

* Valued at market-related prices.
Source: IMF, *International Financial Statistics.*

MONEY SUPPLY ('000 million francs CFA at 31 December)

	1991	1992	1993
Currency outside banks	49.45	46.95	35.84
Demand deposits at commercial and development banks	19.32	15.79	9.19
Total money (incl. others)	68.86	62.86	45.47

Source: IMF, *International Financial Statistics.*

COST OF LIVING (Consumer Price Index for African households in N'Djamena; base: 1985 = 100)

	1990	1991	1992
All items	100.0	104.1	99.8

Source: IMF, *International Financial Statistics.*

NATIONAL ACCOUNTS (estimates, million francs CFA at current prices)

Expenditure on the Gross Domestic Product

	1989	1990	1991
Government final consumption expenditure	88,499	82,665	83,714
Private final consumption expenditure	293,007	273,692	267,592
Gross fixed capital formation	43,070	40,230	41,392
Total domestic expenditure	424,576	396,587	392,698
Exports of goods and services	66,430	62,085	63,934
Less Imports of goods and services	145,436	135,875	134,157
GDP in purchasers' values	345,570	322,797	322,475
GDP at constant 1980 prices	206,767	201,182	197,863

Gross Domestic Product by Economic Activity

	1989	1990	1991
Agriculture, hunting, forestry and fishing	133,458	135,150	134,609
Mining and quarrying	1,073	1,398	1,411
Manufacturing	52,712	30,950	27,886
Electricity, gas and water	2,223	1,908	1,990
Construction	5,214	5,270	5,808
Wholesale and retail trade, restaurants and hotels	90,970	91,220	91,311
Transport and communications	7,027	5,697	5,499
Finance, insurance, real estate and business services	2,447	2,500	2,522
Public administration and defence	30,480	29,695	31,674
Other community, social and personal services	2,311	2,600	2,912
GDP at factor cost	327,915	306,388	305,622
Indirect taxes, *less* subsidies	17,655	16,409	16,873
GDP in purchasers' values	345,570	322,797	322,495

Source: UN Economic Commission for Africa, *African Statistical Yearbook*.

BALANCE OF PAYMENTS (US $ million)

	1989	1990	1991
Merchandise exports f.o.b.	155.4	230.3	193.9
Merchandise imports f.o.b.	−240.3	−259.5	−294.1
Trade balance	−84.9	−29.2	−100.2
Exports of services	42.3	40.9	37.6
Imports of services	−210.0	−228.2	−254.5
Other income received	1.3	3.0	9.9
Other income paid	−10.8	−23.8	−25.8
Private unrequited transfers (net)	−20.2	−12.9	−13.8
Official unrequited transfers (net)	226.3	204.5	266.6
Current balance	−55.9	−45.6	−80.3
Direct investment (net)	6.2	n.a.	n.a.
Other capital (net)	55.8	56.1	116.5
Net errors and omissions	23.7	−33.3	−52.9
Overall balance	29.7	−22.9	−16.7

Source: IMF, *International Financial Statistics.*

External Trade

PRINCIPAL COMMODITIES (million francs CFA)

Imports	1983
Beverages	71.7
Cereal products	2,272.1
Sugar, confectionery, chocolate	292.7
Petroleum products	2,280.5
Textiles, clothing, etc.	392.1
Pharmaceuticals, chemicals	1,561.9
Minerals and metals	311.2
Machinery	843.2
Transport equipment	987.6
Electrical equipment	773.3
Total (incl. others)	13,539.6

Total imports (million francs CFA): 79,272 in 1984; 74,708 in 1985; 73,437 in 1986; 67,894 in 1987; 68,000 in 1988; 76,657 in 1989; 77,742 in 1990; 83,670 in 1991. (Source: IMF, *International Financial Statistics*).

Exports	1983
Live cattle	49.5
Meat	23.5
Fish	2.0
Oil-cake	8.1
Natron	8.1
Gums and resins	0.4
Hides and skins	16.6
Raw cotton	3,753.7
Total (incl. others)	4,120.0

Total exports (million francs CFA): 57,384 in 1984; 27,781 in 1985; 34,145 in 1986; 32,892 in 1987; 42,900 in 1988; 49,561 in 1989; 51,202 in 1990; 54,710 in 1991 (Source: IMF, *International Financial Statistics*).

PRINCIPAL TRADING PARTNERS (million francs CFA)

Imports	1984	1985	1986
Belgium/Luxembourg	435	520	1,712
Cameroon	3,461	12,371	8,777
China, People's Republic	n.a.	39	896
Congo	417	519	395
France	22,132	14,439	21,772
Germany, Fed. Republic	1,322	1,562	2,876
Italy	3,133	2,874	3,263
Netherlands	777	1,950	2,017
Nigeria	4,817	4,368	5,673
USA	4,095	9,247	7,670
Total (incl. others)	45,759	51,520	58,831

Exports	1984	1985	1986
Cameroon	929	1,711	2,661
Central African Republic	64	1,219	321
France	6,950	1,432	1,774
Nigeria	113	1,981	425
Sudan	8	47	101
Zaire	125	5	n.a.
Total (incl. others)	8,231	6,446	5,374

Transport

ROAD TRAFFIC (motor vehicles in use)

	1985
Private cars	2,741
Buses, lorries and coaches	4,000
Tractors	711
Scooters and motorcycles	3,442
Trailers	977
Total	11,871

Source: Ministère des Transports et de l'Aviation Civile.

CIVIL AVIATION (traffic on scheduled services*)

	1989	1990	1991
Kilometres flown ('000)	2,000	3,000	2,000
Passenger-km ('000)	231,000	240,000	211,000
Freight ton-km ('000)	18,000	18,000	16,000
Mail ton-km ('000)	1,000	1,000	1,000

* Including an apportionment of the traffic of Air Afrique.

Source: UN, *Statistical Yearbook.*

Tourism

	1989	1990	1991
Foreign tourist arrivals	12,000	9,000	21,000

Source: UN, *African Statistical Yearbook.*

1990: Foreign tourist arrivals 29,000. Source: *UN, Statistical Yearbook.*

Communications Media

	1989	1990	1991
Radio receivers ('000 in use)	1,310	1,350	1,385
Television receivers ('000 in use)	6	7	7
Telephones (estimates, '000 in use)	9	9	10

Daily newspapers: 1 in 1990 (average circulation 2,000).

Non-daily newspapers: 1 in 1988 (average circulation 1,000).

Sources: UNESCO, *Statistical Yearbook,* and UN, *Statistical Yearbook.*

Education

(1989)

	Institutions	Teachers	Pupils
Primary	1,868	7,327	492,231
Secondary:			
General	48*	1,422	54,751
Teacher training	18*	54†	1,017
Vocational	7*	231†	2,802
Higher	4*	329†	2,983†

* Figure refers to 1987. † Figure refers to 1988.

Primary (1991): Institutions 2,544; Teachers 9,238; Pupils 591,417.

General Secondary (1991): Teachers 2,062; Pupils 72,641.

Source: UNESCO, *Statistical Yearbook,* and Ministère de l'Education Nationale.

Directory

The Constitution

On 1 March 1991 the Government promulgated a National Charter, which was to remain in force for a 30-month transitional period and required the Government to institute reforms to prepare for the transition to a multi-party political system. A National Conference with sovereign status, which took place in January–April 1993, adopted a further Transitional Charter (with effect from 9 April), elected a Prime Minister and established a 57-member interim legislature, the Conseil supérieur de la transition (CST). The Transitional Charter was to remain in force for a period of one year (with provision for one extension), at the end of which democratic organs of government were to be elected in the context of a multi-party political system. Under the terms of the Charter, the Head of State (who was to remain in office for the transitional period), was to appoint the members of a Transitional Government on the recommendation of the Prime Minister. Subsequent Prime Ministers were to be elected by the CST. The Transitional Government, with the supervision of the CST, was to implement the resolutions of the conference.

In March 1994 an 'institutional committee' presented recommendations for a draft constitution, which included provisions for the election of a president for a term of five years, the installation of a bicameral legislature (comprising a national assembly and a senate) and a constitutional court, and the establishment of a decentralized administrative structure. In April the CST extended the transitional period for one year; according to a new electoral timetable, the constitutional recommendations were to be submitted for approval at a national referendum in December, and, in the event that the new constitution was adopted by the electorate, legislative elections were to take place in January 1995, followed by a presidential election in March.

The Government

HEAD OF STATE

President and Commander-in-Chief of the Armed Forces: IDRISS DEBY (assumed office 4 December 1990; inaugurated 4 March 1991).

TRANSITIONAL GOVERNMENT
(August 1994)

An interim coalition of the Mouvement patriotique du salut (MPS) and a number of former opposition parties.

Prime Minister: DELWA KASSIRE KOUMAKOYE.

Minister of Justice and Keeper of the Seals: Maj. LOUM HINASSOU LAINA.

Minister of Communications: KOMTOK LAOTEH DIENOBI.

Minister of Finance: PATAKE ALBERT PAHIMI.

Minister of Foreign Affairs: AHMAT ABDERAMANE HAGGAR.

Minister of the Interior and Security: ABDERAHMANE MISKINE IZO.

Minister of National Education, Youth and Sports: MAHAMAT SALEH ALABO.

Minister of Social and Women's Affairs: MAHAMAT MAMADOU REGUI.

Minister of Public Health: MAHAMAT AHAMAT ALHABO.

Minister of Agriculture and Environment: MAHAMAT ADOUM KALOBOUNE.

Minister of Planning and Co-operation: NOUR MARIAM MAHAMAT.

Minister of the Civil Service and Labour: SALIBOU GARBA.

Minister of Economy and Tourism: OUARDOUGOU BOLOU.

Minister of Mines and Energy: MAHAMAT GARFA.

Minister of Public Works and Transport: ESAIE TCHAKNA.

Minister of Livestock and Water Resources: MAHAMAT AHMAT SOUKOU.

Minister of the Armed Forces: ALI ABSAKINE.

MINISTRIES

Office of the President: N'Djamena; tel. 51-44-37; telex 5201.

Office of the Prime Minister: N'Djamena.

Ministry of Agriculture and the Environment: N'Djamena; tel. 51-37-52.

Ministry of the Civil Service and Labour: N'Djamena; tel. 51-56-56.

Ministry of Communications: N'Djamena; tel. 51-42-64; telex 5254.

Ministry of Economy and Tourism: N'Djamena.

Ministry of Finance: N'Djamena; tel. 51-21-61; telex 5257.

Ministry of Foreign Affairs: N'Djamena; tel. 51-50-82; telex 5238.

Ministry of the Interior and Security: N'Djamena; tel. 51-46-59.

Ministry of Justice: N'Djamena; tel. 51-56-56.

Ministry of Livestock and Animal Resources: N'Djamena; tel. 51-59-07.

Ministry of Mines and Energy: N'Djamena; tel. 51-20-96.

Ministry of National Defence: N'Djamena; tel. 51-58-89.

Ministry of National Education, Youth and Sports: BP 731, N'Djamena; tel. 51-44-76.

Ministry of Planning and Co-operation: N'Djamena; tel. 51-58-98.

Ministry of Public Health: N'Djamena; tel. 51-39-60.

Ministry of Public Works and Transport: BP 436, N'Djamena; tel. 51-20-96.

Ministry of Social and Women's Affairs: N'Djamena.

Legislature

A Transitional Charter, which took effect on 9 April 1993 for a period of one year, established a 57-member interim legislature, the Conseil supérieur de la transition. Following the extension of the transitional period for one year, elections to a new legislative body were rescheduled to take place in January 1995.

Chairman: LOL MAHAMAT CHOUA.

Political Organizations

In October 1991 legislation providing for the authorization of political associations, subject to certain conditions of registration, was adopted. Some 30 political organizations subsequently obtained legal status; the most prominent of these are listed below.

Action pour l'unité et le socialisme (ACTUS): N'Djamena; f. 1992.

Alliance nationale pour la démocratie et le développement (ANDD): N'Djamena; f. 1992; Leader SALIBOU GARBA.

Alliance nationale pour la démocratie et le renouveau (ANDR): N'Djamena; f. 1993.

Alliance nationale pour le progrès et le développement (ANT): N'Djamena; f. 1992.

Forum pour le changement démocratique (FCD): N'Djamena; f. 1992; alliance of 15 opposition parties; Leader JULIEN MARABI.

Front des forces d'action pour la République: Leader YORONGAR LEMOHIBAN.

Mouvement patriotique du salut (MPS): N'Djamena; f. 1990 as a coalition of several opposition movements, incl. the Action du 1 avril, the Mouvement pour le salut national du Tchad and the Forces armées tchadiennes; other opposition parties joined the MPS during the Nov. 1990 offensive against the govt of Hissène Habré, and after the movement's accession to power in the following month; Chair. IDRISS DEBY; Exec. Sec. NADJITA BEASSOUMAL.

Mouvement pour la démocratie et le socialisme du Tchad (MDST): N'Djamena; Leader Dr SALOMON NGARBAYE TOMBALBAYE.

Mouvement socialiste pour la démocratie du Tchad (MSTD): N'Djamena; Leader ALBERT MBAINAIDO DJOMIA.

Mouvement pour l'unité et la démocratie du Tchad (MUDT): f. 1992; Leader JULIEN MARABAYE.

Parti africain pour le progrès et la justice sociale (PAPJS): Leader NEATOBEI DIDIER VALENTIN.

Parti pour la liberté et le développement (PLD): N'Djamena; f. 1993; Leader IBN OUMAR MAHAMAT SALEH.

Parti social-démocrate tchadien (PSDT): Moundou; Leader NIABE ROMAIN.

Rassemblement pour la démocratie et le progrès: N'Djamena; f. 1992; Leader LOL MAHAMAT CHOUA.

Rassemblement démocratique du Tchad (RDT): N'Djamena; f. 1992.

Rassemblement pour le développement et le progrès: f. 1992; Leader MAMADOU BISSO.

Rassemblement national pour la démocratie et le progrès (RNDP): N'Djamena; f. 1992; Pres. KASSIRE DELWA KOUMAKOYE.

Rassemblement des nationalistes tchadiennes (RNT): N'Djamena; f. 1992.

Rassemblement du peuple du Tchad (RPT): N'Djamena; f. 1992; Leader DANGBE LAOBELE DAMAYE.

Union pour la démocratie et la République (UDR): N'Djamena; f. 1992; Leader Dr JEAN ALINGUE BAWOYEU.

Union démocratique pour le progrès du Tchad (UDPT): POB 1071, N'Djamena; f. 1992; Pres. ELIE ROMBA.

Union démocratique tchadienne (UDT): N'Djamena; Leader ABDERAHMANE KOULAMALLAH.

Union des forces démocratiques (UFD): N'Djamena; f. 1992; Sec.-Gen. Dr NAHOR MAHAMOUT.

Union des forces démocratiques—Parti républicain (UFD—PR): f. 1992; Leader GALI GATTA NGOTHE.

Union nationale: f. 1992; Leader ABDOULAYE LAMANA.

Union nationale pour la démocratie et le progrès (UNDP): N'Djamena; Leader YASSIN BAKIT.

Union nationale pour le développement et le renouveau (UNDR): Leader SALEH KEBZABO.

Union du peuple tchadien pour la reconstruction nationale (UPTRN): N'Djamena; f. 1992; Leader HAPPA KAROUMA.

Union pour le renouveau et la démocratie (URD): N'Djamena; f. 1992; Leader Col WADAL ABDELKADER KAMOUGUE.

A number of dissident factions (some based overseas) are also active. These include the **Comité de sursaut national pour la paix et la démocratie (CSNPD),** led by Lt KETTE NODJI MOISE; the **Conseil national de redressement du Tchad (CNRT),** led by IDRISS AGAR BICHARA; the Front d'action pour l'installation de la démocratie au Tchad; the **Front de libération nationale du Tchad (FROLINAT),** led by a provisional high council of the revolution (Chair. MAHMOUD ALI MAHMOUD); the **Front national du Tchad (FNT),** based in Sudan, and led by Dr FARIS BACHAR; the **Mouvement pour la démocratie et le développement (MDD),** based in Libya, and associated with the former president, HISSÈNE HABRÉ; with a military wing, the **Forces armées occidentales (FAO),** led by BRAHIM MALLAH MAHAMAT; and the **Union nationale pour la démocratie et le socialisme (UNDS),** led by YOUSSOU SOUGOUDI.

Diplomatic Representation

EMBASSIES IN CHAD

Algeria: N'Djamena; tel. 51-38-15; telex 5216; Ambassador: MAMI ABDERRAHMANE.

Central African Republic: BP 115, N'Djamena; tel. 51-32-06; Ambassador: DAVID NGUINDO.

China, People's Republic: ave Président Blanchart, BP 1133, N'Djamena; tel. 51-36-62; telex 5235; Ambassador: GUO TIANMIN.

Egypt: BP 1094, N'Djamena; tel. 51-36-60; telex 5216; Ambassador: AZIZ M. NOUR EL-DIN.

France: BP 431, N'Djamena; tel. 51-25-75; telex 5202; Ambassador: YVES AUBIN DE LA MESSUZIÈRE.

Germany: ave Félix Eboué, BP 893, N'Djamena; tel. 51-62-02; telex 5246; fax 51-48-00; Chargé d'affaires: HARMUT HEIDEMANN.

Iraq: N'Djamena; tel. 51-22-57; telex 5339; Chargé d'affaires: ALI MAHMOUD HASHIM.

Libya: N'Djamena; Ambassador: GHEITH S. SAIF-ANNASER.

Nigeria: 35 ave Charles de Gaulle, BP 752, N'Djamena; tel. 51-24-98; telex 5242; Chargé d'affaires: A. M. ALIYU BIU.

Sudan: BP 45, N'Djamena; tel. 51-34-97; telex 5235; Ambassador: TAHA MAKKAWI.

USA: ave Félix Eboué, BP 413, N'Djamena; tel. 51-40-09; telex 5203; fax 51-33-72; Ambassador: LAURENCE POPE.

Zaire: ave du 20 août, BP 910, N'Djamena; tel. 51-59-35; telex 5322; Ambassador: Gen. MALU-MALU DHANDA.

Judicial System

The Supreme Court was abolished after the coup of April 1975. Under the Government of Hissène Habré, there was a Court of Appeal at N'Djamena. Criminal courts sat at N'Djamena, Sarh, Moundou and Abéché, and elsewhere as necessary, and each of these four major towns had a magistrates' court. In October 1976 a permanent Court of State Security was established, comprising eight civilian or military members.

Religion

It is estimated that some 50% of the population are Muslims and about 7% Christians, mainly Roman Catholics. Most of the remainder follow animist beliefs.

ISLAM

Comité Islamique du Tchad: N'Djamena; tel. 51-51-80.

Head of the Islamic Community: Imam MOUSSA IBRAHIM.

CHRISTIANITY

The Roman Catholic Church

Chad comprises one archdiocese and four dioceses. At 31 December 1992 the estimated number of adherents represented about 6.5% of the total population.

Bishops' Conference: Conférence Episcopale du Tchad, BP 456, N'Djamena; tel. 51-44-43; telex 5360; fax 51-40-60; Pres. Most Rev. CHARLES VANDAME, Archbishop of N'Djamena.

Archbishop of N'Djamena: Most Rev. CHARLES VANDAME, Archevêché, BP 456, N'Djamena; tel. 51-44-43; telex 5360; fax 51-28-60.

Protestant Church

Entente des Eglises et Missions Evangéliques au Tchad: BP 2006, N'Djamena; tel. and fax 51-53-93; a fellowship of churches and missions working in Chad; includes Eglise évangélique au Tchad, Assemblées Chrétiennes, Eglise fraternelle Luthérienne and Eglise évangélique des frères.

BAHÁ'Í FAITH

National Spiritual Assembly: BP 181, N'Djamena; tel. 51-47-05; mems in 1,125 localities.

The Press

Al-Watan: BP 407, N'Djamena; tel. 51-57-96; weekly; Editor-in-Chief MOUSSA NDORKOÏ.

Bulletin Mensuel de Statistiques du Tchad: BP 453, N'Djamena; monthly.

Comnat: BP 731, N'Djamena; tel. 29-68; publ. by UNESCO.

Contact: N'Djamena; f. 1989; independent; current affairs; Dir KOULAMALO SOURADJ.

Info-Tchad: BP 670, N'Djamena; daily news bulletin issued by Agence Tchadienne de Presse; French.

Informations Economiques: BP 458, N'Djamena; publ. by the Chambre de Commerce, d'Agriculture et d'Industrie; weekly.

NEWS AGENCIES

Agence Tchadienne de Presse (ATP): BP 670, N'Djamena; tel. 51-58-67; telex 5240.

Foreign Bureaux

Agence France-Presse (AFP): BP 83, N'Djamena; tel. 51-54-71; telex 5248; Correspondent ALDOM NADJI TITO.

Reuters (United Kingdom): N'Djamena; tel. 51-56-57; Correspondent ABAKAR ASSIDIC.

Publisher

Government Publishing House: BP 453, N'Djamena.

Radio and Television

In 1991, according to UNESCO, there were an estimated 1,385,000 radio receivers and 7,000 television receivers in use.

RADIO

Radiodiffusion Nationale Tchadienne: BP 892, N'Djamena; tel. 51-60-71; state-controlled; programmes in French, Arabic and eight vernacular languages; there are four transmitters; Dir-Gen. MOUSSA DAGO.

Radio Sarh: BP 270, Sarh; daily programmes in French, Sara and Arabic; Dir DIMANANGAR DJAÏNTA.

Radio Moundou: BP 122, Moundou; tel. 69-13-22; daily programmes in French, Sara and Arabic; Dir (vacant).

TELEVISION

Télé-Chad: Commission for Information and Culture, BP 748, N'Djamena; tel. 51-29-23; state-controlled; broadcasts c. 12 hours per week in French and Arabic; Dir IDRISS AMANE MAHAMAT; Programme Man. MACLAOU NDILDOUM.

Finance

(cap. = capital; res = reserves; br. = branch; m. = million; amounts in francs CFA)

BANKING

Central Bank

Banque des Etats de l'Afrique Centrale (BEAC): BP 50, N'Djamena; tel. 51-41-76; telex 5220; fax 51-44-87; headquarters in Yaoundé, Cameroon; f. 1973 as central bank of issue for mem. states of the Customs and Economic Union of Central Africa (UDEAC), comprising Cameroon, the Central African Republic, Chad, the Congo, Equatorial Guinea and Gabon; cap. and res 203,500m. (Jan. 1993); Gov. JEAN-FÉLIX MAMALEPOT; Dir in Chad ADAM MADJI; 2 brs.

Other Banks

Banque de Développement du Tchad (BDT): rue Capitaine Ohrel, BP 19, N'Djamena; tel. 51-28-70; telex 5375; f. 1962; 58.4% state-owned; cap. 520m.; Dir-Gen. MOUTA ALI ZOUZERTI.

Banque Internationale pour le Commerce et l'Industrie du Tchad (BICIT): 15 ave Charles de Gaulle, BP 38, N'Djamena; telex 5233; 40% state-owned; Man. Dir HISSEINE LAMINE; activities temporarily suspended.

Banque Méridien BIAO Tchad: ave Charles de Gaulle, BP 87, N'Djamena; tel. 51-43-14; telex 5228; fax 51-23-45; f. 1980; 19.7% state-owned; cap. 1,350m. (Dec. 1992); Pres. RAOUL KONTCHOU; Dir-Gen. MICHEL LE BLANC.

Banque Tchadienne de Crédit et de Dépôts (BTCD): 2–6 rue Robert Lévy, BP 461, N'Djamena; tel. 51-41-90; telex 5212; fax 51-37-13; f. 1963; 40% state-owned; cap. 800m. (Dec. 1992); Pres. GUEALBAYE MANASSET; Dir-Gen. MICHEL LHOTE; br. at Moundou.

Financial Bank Tchad: ave Charles de Gaulle, BP 804; tel. 51-33-89; telex 5380; fax 51-29-05; f. June 1992; cap. 1,000m. (1992); Pres. CHARLES BAYSSET; Dir-Gen. HERVÉ LE HAGRE.

Bankers' Organizations

Association Professionnelle des Banques au Tchad: N'Djamena.

Conseil National de Crédit: N'Djamena; f. 1965 to formulate a national credit policy and to organize the banking profession.

INSURANCE

Assureurs Conseils Tchadiens Faugère et Jutheau et Cie: BP 139, N'Djamena; tel. 51-21-15; telex 5235; Dir PHILIPPE GARDYE.

Société de Représentation d'Assurances et de Réassurances Africaines (SORARAF): N'Djamena; Dir Mme FOURNIER.

Société Tchadienne d'Assurances et de Réassurances (STAR): BP 914, N'Djamena; tel. 51-56-77; telex 5268; Dir PHILIPPE SABIT.

Trade and Industry

CHAMBER OF COMMERCE

Chambre Consulaire: BP 458, N'Djamena; tel. 51-52-64; f. 1938; Pres. ELIE ROMBA; Sec.-Gen. SALEH MAHAMAT RAHMA; brs at Sarh, Moundou, Bol and Abéché.

DEVELOPMENT ORGANIZATIONS

Caisse Française de Développement: BP 478, N'Djamena; tel. 51-40-71; fax 51-28-31; Dir JACBIE BATHANY.

Mission Française de Coopération et d'Action Culturelle: BP 898, N'Djamena; tel. 51-42-87; telex 5340; fax 51-44-38; administers bilateral aid from France; Dir ANOLIE BAILLEUL.

Office National de Développement Rural (ONDR): BP 896, N'Djamena; tel. 51-48-64; f. 1968; Dir MICKAEL DJIBRAEL.

Société pour le Développement de la Région du Lac (SODELAC): BP 782, N'Djamena; tel. 51-35-03; telex 5248; f. 1967; cap. 180m. francs CFA; Pres. CHERIF ABDELWAHAB; Dir-Gen. MAHAMAT MOCTAR ALI.

TRADE

Office National des Céréales (ONC): BP 21, N'Djamena; tel. 51-37-31; f. 1978; production and marketing of cereals; Dir YBRAHIM MAHAMAT TIDEI; 11 regional offices.

Société Nationale de Commercialisation du Tchad (SONACOT): N'Djamena; telex 5227; f. 1965; cap. 150m. francs CFA; 76% state-owned; nat. marketing, distribution and import-export co; Man. Dir MARBROUCK NATROUD.

MAJOR INDUSTRIAL COMPANIES

The following are some of the largest private and state-owned companies in terms of capital investment or employment.

Boissons et Glacières du Tchad (BT): BP 656, N'Djamena; tel. 51-31-71; telex 5315; f. 1972; cap. 110m. francs CFA; production of mineral water, Coca-Cola, squashes and ice; Pres. MARCEL ILLE; Dir GASTON BONLEUX.

Brasseries du Logone: ave du Gouverneur Général Félix Eboué, BP 170, Moundou; telex 7204; f. 1962; cap. 800m. francs CFA; brewery; Man. Dir BRUNO DELORME; 145 employees.

Les Grands Moulins du Tchad: BP 173, N'Djamena; f. 1963; cap. 158.25m. francs CFA; milling of flour; mfrs of pasta, biscuits and cattle feed; Pres. EMILE MIMRAN; Man. Dir in N'Djamena JEAN-PAUL BAILLEUX.

Manufacture de Cigarettes du Tchad: BP 572, N'Djamena; tel. 51-21-45; telex 5278; f. 1968; cap. 288m. francs CFA; 15% state-owned; mfrs of cigarettes at Moundou; Pres. ANDRÉ THEVENIN; Man. Dir MICHEL IZAUTE.

Shell Tchad: route de Farcha, BP 110, N'Djamena; tel. 51-24-90; telex 5221; f. 1971; cap. 205m. francs CFA; Pres. LUC MINGUET; Dir-Gen. JEAN-PIERRE FIORENTINO.

Société Cotonnière du Tchad (COTONTCHAD): rue du Capitaine d'Abzac, BP 1116, N'Djamena; tel. 51-41-32; telex 5229; fax 51-31-71; f. 1971; cap. 4,256m. francs CFA; 75% state-owned; buying, ginning and marketing of cotton; owns six cotton gins and one cottonseed oil mill; Pres. NGARNAYAL MBAILEMDANA; Dir-Gen. HAROUN KABADI.

Société Nationale Sucrière du Tchad (SONASUT): BP 37, N'Djamena; tel. 51-32-70; telex 5263; f. 1963, 53% state-owned; cap. 5,871m. francs CFA; refining of sugar; mfrs of lump sugar and confectionery; Pres. YOUSSOUF SIDI SOUGOUNI; Dir-Gen. NOUSSA KADAM.

Société Tchadienne d'Eau et d'Electricité (STEE): 11 rue du Colonel Largeau, BP 44, N'Djamena; tel. 51-28-81; telex 5226; fax 51-21-34; f. 1968; cap. 4,989m. francs CFA; production and distribution of electricity and water; Pres. GOMON MAWATA WAKAG; Dir-Gen. ISMAEL MAHAMAT ADOUM.

Société des Télécommunications Internationales du Tchad (TIT): BP 1132, N'Djamena; tel. 51-57-82; telex 5200; fax 51-50-66; cap. 150m. francs CFA; 52% state-owned; study and development of international communications systems; Man. Dir KHALIL D'ABZAC.

TRADE UNION

Union Syndicats du Tchad (UST): BP 1143, N'Djamena; tel. 51-42-75; telex 5248; f. 1988 by merger of the Confédération Syndicale du Tchad, the Union Nationale des Travailleurs du Tchad and the Union Nationale des Syndicats du Tchad; Pres. DOMBAL DJIMBAGUE; Sec.-Gen. DJIBRINE ASSALI HAMDALLAH.

Transport

RAILWAYS

In 1962 Chad signed an agreement with Cameroon to extend the Transcameroon railway from N'Gaoundéré to Sarh, a distance of 500 km. Although the Transcameroon reached N'Gaoundéré in 1974, its proposed extension into Chad has been indefinitely postponed.

ROADS

In 1991 there were an estimated 27,000 km of roads, of which 430 km were paved roads. There are also some 20,000 km of tracks suitable for motor traffic during the October–July dry season. In July 1986 the World Bank provided a loan of US $21m. towards a major programme to rehabilitate 2,000 km of roads. In 1988 the International Development Association (IDA) granted $47m. to support the final stage of the programme: the rehabilitation of the 30-km N'Djamena–Djermaya road and the 146-km N'Djamena–Guelengdeng road. In the following year the IDA approved a further credit of $60m. for the rehabilitation of more than 1,800 km of main roads. The EC is contributing to the construction of a highway leading from N'Djamena to Sarh and Lere, on the Cameroon border.

Coopérative des Transportateurs Tchadiens (CTT): BP 336, N'Djamena; tel. 51-43-55; telex 5225; road haulage; Pres. SALEH KHALIFA; brs at Sarh, Moundou, Bangui (CAR), Douala and N'Gaoundéré (Cameroon).

INLAND WATERWAYS

The Chari and Logone rivers, which converge a short distance south of N'Djamena, are navigable. These waterways, connecting Sarh with N'Djamena on the Chari and Bongor and Moundou with N'Djamena on the Logone, are usable only during the wet season (August–December).

CIVIL AVIATION

The international airport at N'Djamena opened in 1967: an improvement programme was completed in 1987. The renewal of the runway at Abéché, with French aid, began in 1988, and the upgrading of facilities at Faya-Largeau, also with assistance from France, began in 1990. There are more than 40 smaller airfields.

Air Afrique: BP 466, N'Djamena; tel. 51-40-20; see under Côte d'Ivoire.

Air Tchad: 27 ave du Président Tombalbaye, BP 168, N'Djamena; tel. 51-50-90; telex 5345; f. 1966; govt-controlled; international charters and domestic passenger, freight and charter services; Dir-Gen. MAHAMAT NOURI.

Tourism

Chad's potential attractions for tourists include a variety of scenery from the dense forests of the south to the deserts of the north. There were an estimated 21,000 tourist arrivals in 1991. In 1990 revenue from tourism totalled an estimated US $12m.

Direction du Tourisme, des Parcs Nationaux et Réserves de Faune: BP 86, N'Djamena; tel. 51-23-03; telex 5358; fax 57-22-61; also Délégation Régionale au Tourisme, BP 88, Sarh; tel. 274; f. 1962; Dir MORKEMNGAR PASCAL.

Defence

In June 1993 the Armée nationale tchadienne (ANT) was estimated to number some 25,200 (army approximately 25,000, air force 200). In addition, there were paramilitary forces of as many as 4,500. Military service is by conscription for three years. The government's economic policy includes a gradual reduction in the number of members of the armed forces. Under defence agreements with France, the army receives technical and other aid: in mid-1993 France deployed an estimated 750 troops in Chad.

Defence Expenditure: Budgeted at 9.354.2m. francs CFA in 1992.

Commander-in-Chief of the Armed Forces: IDRISS DEBY.

Chief of Army Staff: Lt-Col MAHAMAT GARFA.

Chief of Naval Staff: Lt MORNADJI MBAISSANEBE.

Chief of Air Force: Lt-Col ZAKARIAH OUAOUEI JAHAAD.

Education

Education is officially compulsory for eight years between six and 14 years of age. Primary education begins at the age of six and lasts for six years. Secondary education, from the age of 12, lasts for a further seven years, comprising a first cycle of four years and a second cycle of three years. In 1991 primary enrolment was equivalent to 65% of children in the relevant age-group (89% of boys; 41% of girls), while the comparable ratio for secondary enrolment was only 9%. The Université du Tchad was opened at N'Djamena in 1971. In addition, there are several technical colleges. In 1989 the African Development Bank approved a loan of more than 3,500m. francs CFA for the construction of 40 primary schools. In 1990, according to estimates by UNESCO, the average rate of adult illiteracy was 70.2% (males 57.8%; females 82.1%).

Bibliography

Buijtenhuijs, R. *Le Frolinat et les révoltes populaires du Tchad (1965–1976).* The Hague, 1978.

Le Frolinat et les guerres civiles du Tchad (1977–1984). Paris, Editions Karthala, 1987.

Cruise O'Brien, D. B., Dunn, J., and Rathbone R. (Eds). *Contemporary West African States.* Cambridge, Cambridge University Press, 1989.

Decalo, S. *Historical Dictionary of Chad.* Metuchen, NJ, Scarecrow Press, 1977; new edn 1987.

Desjardins, T. *Avec les otages du Tchad.* Paris, 1975.

Diguimnbaye, G., and Langue, R. *L'Essor du Tchad.* Paris, Presses universitaires de France, 1969.

Foltz, W. J. 'Chad's Third Republic: Strengths, Problems and Prospects', in *CSIS Africa Notes,* Briefing Paper No. 77. Washington, DC, Center for Strategic and International Studies, 1987.

Hugot, P. *Le Tchad.* Paris, Nouvelles Editions Latines, 1965.

Lanne, B. *Tchad-Libye. La querelle des frontières.* Paris, Editions Karthala, 1982.

Le Cornec, J. *Histoire politique du Tchad de 1900 à 1962.* Paris, Librairie générale de Droit et Jurisprudence, 1963.

Le Rouvreur, A. *Sahariens et Sahéliens du Tchad.* Paris, Berger-Levrault, 1962.

Mbaïosso, A. *L'éducation au Tchad.* Paris, Editions Karthala, 1990.

N'Gangbet, M. *Peut-on encore sauver le Tchad?* Paris, Editions Karthala, 1984.

N'Gansop, G.-J. *Tchad: Vingt ans de crise.* Paris, Harmattan, 1986.

Secretariat General du Gouvernement. *Notes et Etudes,* No. 2696. Paris, 1960.

Sikes, S. *Lake Chad.* London, 1972.

Whiteman, K. *Chad.* London, Minority Rights Group (Report No. 80), 1988.

World Bank. *Chad: Development Potential and Constraints.* Washington, DC, 1974.

Zeltner, J.-C., and Tourneux, H. *L'arabe dans le bassin du Tchad.* Paris, Editions Karthala, 1986.

THE COMOROS*

Physical and Social Geography

R. J. HARRISON CHURCH

The Comoro Islands, an archipelago of four small islands, together with numerous islets and coral reefs, lie between the east African coast and the north-western coast of Madagascar. The four islands cover a total land area of only 2,236 sq km (863 sq miles) and are scattered along a NW–SE axis, a distance of 300 km separating the towns of Moroni in the west and Dzaoudzi in the east. The French names for the islands, Grande-Comore (on which the capital, Moroni, is situated), Anjouan, Mohéli and Mayotte were changed in May 1977 to Njazidja, Nzwani, Mwali and Mahoré respectively, although the former names are still widely used. The islands are volcanic in structure, and Mt Karthala (rising to 2,440 m above sea-level) on Njazidja is still active; its last serious eruption was in 1977. Climate, rainfall and vegetation all vary greatly from island to island. There are similar divergences in soil characteristics, although in this instance natural causes have been reinforced by human actions, notably in deforestation and exhaustion of the soil.

The ethnic composition of the population (officially estimated to be 484,000, including Mayotte, in December 1986) is complex. The first settlers were probably Melano-Polynesian peoples who came to the islands from the Far East by the sixth century AD. Immigrants from the coast of Africa, Indonesia, Madagascar and Persia, as well as Arabs, had all arrived by about 1600. The Portuguese (in the early part of the 16th century), the Dutch and the French further complicated the ethnic pattern, the latter introducing into the islands Chinese (who have since left) and Indians. The different sections of the population are still not fully integrated. In Mayotte and Mwali Arabic features are less evident, mainly because the two islands were settled by immigrants from the African coast and Madagascar. In fact, while Arab characteristics are strong in the islands generally, in particular in the coastal towns, the African is predominant in the territory as a whole. Historically, too, there was some unity between the islands, since members of the same noble family ruled each island. Islam is the predominant religion of the islands. Swahili and Arabic were the main languages spoken before French colonization began in 1843. As a French colony, French became the official language until independence when the new state returned to Arabic. The majority of the population speak Comoran, a mixture of Arabic and Swahili. Average population density (including Mayotte) was 216.5 inhabitants per sq km in December 1986, and is increasing rapidly in conjunction with growing pressure on the available land.

Recent History

Revised for this edition by the Editor

The Comoros, acquired as a French possession during 1841–1909, was administered with Madagascar and became a French Overseas Territory in 1947. The islands attained internal autonomy in December 1961, although substantial powers remained with a French resident commissioner. Local administration was carried out by an elected chamber of deputies and a government council.

A movement for full independence from France (while retaining French financial co-operation and support) gained momentum in the early 1970s and led to a referendum in December 1974, in which there was a 96% vote in favour of independence. This was strongly opposed, however, by the Mouvement populaire mahorais (MPM), which sought the status of a French overseas department for the island of Mayotte (Mahoré), where there was a 64% vote against independence. France sought to persuade the Comoran government to draft a constitution for the islands which would allow a large measure of decentralization and thus satisfy the population of Mayotte. It was also proposed by France that any constitutional proposals should be ratified by referendum in each island separately before independence could be granted. These proposals were rejected by the Comoran chamber of deputies, and on 6 July 1975 the chamber approved a unilateral declaration of independence, designated Ahmed Abdallah, president of the government council, as president of the republic and head of state, and constituted itself as the national assembly.

Although France made no attempt to intervene, it maintained control of Mayotte. President Abdallah was deposed in August 1975, and the assembly was abolished. A national executive council, headed by Prince Saïd Mohammed Jaffar, was established. Jaffar, leader of the Front national uni, a grouping of parties in favour of a more conciliatory policy towards Mayotte, was replaced as president in January 1976 by Ali Soilih, and was granted additional powers under the terms of a new constitution. In February Mayotte voted overwhelmingly to retain its links with France. (For further information on Mayotte, see p. 303).

Preparations for the referendum in Mayotte caused a deterioration in relations between France and the Comoros: the Comoran government nationalized all French administrative property and expelled French officials. On 31 December 1975 France formally recognized the independence of Grande-Comore (Njazidja), Anjouan (Nzwani) and Mohéli (Mwali), but all relations between the two governments, together with aid and technical assistance programmes, were effectively suspended.

The Soilih regime initiated a revolutionary programme, blending Maoist and Islamic philosophies, to create an economically self-sufficient and ideologically progressive state. The excesses of Soilih's methods aroused widespread resentment among traditional elements of society, and his economic reforms failed. Four unsuccessful coup attempts were staged during the rule of the Soilih administration.

* Most of the information contained in this chapter relates to the whole Comoran archipelago, which the Comoros claims as its national territory and has styled 'The Federal Islamic Republic of the Comoros'. The island of Mayotte, however, is administered by France as an Overseas Collectivité Territoriale, and is treated separately at the end of this chapter (p. 303).

PRESIDENTIAL GOVERNMENT

The Second Abdallah Presidency, 1978–89

In May 1978 Soilih was finally overthrown in an unopposed coup, accomplished by about 50 European mercenaries, led by a Frenchman, Col Robert Denard, on behalf of the exiled ex-president, Ahmed Abdallah. Soilih was killed a fortnight later, allegedly while trying to escape from house arrest. Power was assumed by a 'politico-military directory', with Abdallah and his former deputy, Muhammed Ahmed, as co-presidents; the new administration pledged to adopt a constitution and conduct elections, while Abdallah announced his intention of restoring good relations with members of the Arab League. Neighbouring African countries were, however, concerned by the role of mercenaries in effecting the coup, and the Comoros delegation was expelled from the ministerial council of the Organization of African Unity (OAU). The presence of Denard and his associates became increasingly embarrassing, and at the end of September they were asked to leave. Diplomatic relations with France were, however, restored shortly after the coup, and the French government, while it denied having given any official encouragement to the mercenaries, was clearly willing to support the new regime as being favourable to its strategic interests in the Indian Ocean. The resumption of French economic, cultural and military co-operation was accompanied by assistance from Arab countries (including Saudi Arabia, Kuwait and Iraq), the EC and the African Development Fund. In February 1979 the Comoran delegation was readmitted to the OAU, indicating that the new regime had eventually been accepted.

Meanwhile, at a referendum, which took place on 1 October 1978, a new constitution creating a Federal Islamic Republic (in which each island was to be granted some degree of autonomy under an elected governor) was adopted by more than 99% of votes cast. On 22 October Abdallah was elected president for a term of six years, and in December elections to a 38-member federal assembly (comprising 18 representatives of Njazidja, 15 of Nzwani and five of Mwali) took place. Although the new constitution provided for the free activity of all political parties, the federal assembly voted in January 1979 in favour of the establishment of a one-party system for a period of 12 years. The Union comorienne pour le progrès (Udzima) became the sole legal party in February 1982.

Under the terms of the 1978 constitution, it was envisaged that the island of Mayotte would rejoin the Comoran state at some later date, although Mayotte continued to demand the status of a French *département*. The Mayotte issue was not mentioned in five agreements which were signed with France in November; both governments were apparently willing to defer making a definite decision on the future of Mayotte and to give priority to the resumption of French aid to the other islands of the archipelago. In February 1984 negotiations were finally resumed between France and the Comoros on the future of Mayotte. (For further information on Mayotte, see p. 303.)

A federal balance in the Comoran government proved difficult to establish, with the people of Mwali, for example, complaining that they were under-represented in major posts. There were reports of political repression: Amnesty International and other groups expressed concern at the alleged ill-treatment of political prisoners. In February 1981 about 150 people were arrested, following reports (which were officially denied) of an attempted coup. The detainees were released in May, together with 31 of the 40 political prisoners who had been convicted of involvement in the coup in 1978. A number of unofficial opposition groups, which were based mainly in France, were established.

In January 1982, following allegations of government corruption and financial mismanagement, Abdallah dissolved the federal assembly and appointed a new prime minister, Ali Mroudjae, formerly minister of foreign affairs and co-operation. A new council of ministers, which was to implement the government's policy of economic revival, was appointed. Elections to a new federal assembly took place in March and it was announced that the civil service was to be reduced in size by one-third. Constitutional amendments, approved in October, increased the power of the president, while reducing that of the governors of the four islands; each governor was henceforth to be appointed by the president and no longer directly elected. In addition, the federal government became responsible for controlling the islands' economic resources. The term of office of the island councillors was, however, extended from four to five years.

In December 1983 a conspiracy to overthrow the government, involving a former Comoran diplomat, Saïd Ali Kemal, was discovered. The coup attempt was thwarted by the arrest of British mercenary leaders in Australia. At a presidential election, which took place in September 1984, Abdallah (who was the sole candidate) was re-elected for a further six-year term by 99.4% of votes cast. Despite appeals by opposition groups for voters to boycott the election, some 98% of the electorate participated. In January 1985, following the adoption of constitutional amendments, the position of prime minister was abolished, and President Abdallah assumed the powers of head of government. In March an attempt by members of the presidential guard to overthrow Abdallah (who was absent on a private visit to France) was thwarted. In November 17 people, including Mustapha Saïd Cheikh, the secretary-general of Front démocratique (FD), a banned opposition movement, were sentenced to forced labour for life and 50 others were imprisoned for their part in the coup attempt. In December, however, 30 political prisoners, many of whom were members of the FD, were granted amnesty, and in May 1986 a further 15 detainees were released.

In September 1985 a reform of the governmental structure was carried out, and was followed by a minor cabinet reshuffle in February 1986. In February 1987 the government announced that elections to the federal assembly would take place in March. Although Abdallah had indicated that all political groups would be permitted to participate, opposition candidates were allowed to contest seats only on Njazidja, where they obtained more than 35% of votes cast; Udzima retained full control of the legislature (in which the number of seats had been increased from 38 to 42. It was subsequently claimed by Comoran dissidents in Réunion that about 400 people were arrested during the election. There were also allegations of widespread electoral fraud.

In July 1987 Abdallah reinstated all the civil servants who had been dismissed or suspended following the coup attempt in 1985, in an apparent effort to gain favour with the traditional Comoran élite, which dominated the civil service. In late November, during Abdallah's absence at a meeting in France between African and French heads of state, the Comoran authorities suppressed an attempted coup by a left-wing group (comprising former members of the presidential guard and members of the armed forces, apparently with assistance from French mercenaries and South African military advisers. Three rebels were killed and several civilian fatalities occurred in the fighting. In March 1988 anti-government leaflets were distributed on Mwali by a dissident group based in Mayotte, the Echo mohélien. In April the president's son, Nassuf Abdallah, established the Union régionale pour la défense de la politique du Président Ahmed Abdallah, a pro-government party, which was based on the island of Njazidja.

In mid-1987 it was reported that Abdallah intended to secure a third elected term as president, following the expiry of his mandate in 1990, and that the constitution, which limited presidential tenure to two six-year terms, was to be revised accordingly. In November 1988 it was announced that commissions responsible for the revision of the constitution had been established on each of the three islands. In November 1989 the constitutional amendment permitting President Abdallah to serve a third six-year term was approved by 92.5% of votes cast in a popular referendum. However, this result was challenged by the president's opponents, and violent demonstrations ensued.

Mercenary Intervention

On the night of 26–27 November 1989 President Abdallah was assassinated in an attack on the presidential palace by members of the presidential guard (which included a number of European advisers), under the command of Col Denard. As stipulated in the constitution, the president of the supreme court, Saïd Mohamed Djohar, took office as interim head of state, pending a presidential election. Col Denard and his supporters however, staged a coup, in which 27 members of the security forces were reportedly killed. This effective seizure of power by Denard prompted immediate international condemnation; France and South Africa suspended aid to the islands, despite denials by Denard of any complicity in President Abdallah's death. France despatched a naval task force to Mayotte, with the stated aim of evacuating French citizens from the Comoros. In mid-December Denard agreed to withdraw peacefully from the islands, and, following the arrival of French paratroops in Moroni, was flown to South Africa with 25 other mercenaries. It was subsequently agreed that a French military presence would remain on the islands for up to two years in order to train local security forces.

The Djohar Presidency

At the end of December 1989 the main political groups agreed to form a provisional government of national unity. A general amnesty was granted to all political prisoners, and an inquiry was initiated into the assassination of President Abdallah. In January 1990 demonstrations were staged in protest at the postponement of the presidential election, due to be held that month, until February. The election duly took place on 18 February, but voting was abandoned, amid opposition allegations of widespread fraud. Balloting eventually took place on 4 and 11 March; after an inconclusive first round, Djohar, who was supported by Udzima, obtained 55.3% of the total votes cast, while Mohamed Taki, the leader of the Union nationale pour la démocratie aux Comores (UNDC), secured 44.7% of the vote. (Six other candidates, who had participated in the first round of voting, had withdrawn in favour of the two main candidates.) In late March Djohar appointed a new government, which included two of his minor opponents in the presidential election: Prince Saïd Ali Kemal (grandson of the last sultan of the Comoros), a former ambassador and the founder of the opposition Islands' Fraternity and Unity Party (CHUMA), and Ali Mroudjae, a former prime minister and the leader of the Parti comorien pour la démocratie et le progrès (PCDP). In April Djohar accused Taki, who was temporarily abroad, of attempting to destabilize the government, and threatened reprisals against him. In the same month Djohar announced plans for the formal constitutional restoration of a multi-party political system, and indicated that extensive economic reforms were to be undertaken.

On 18–19 August 1990 a coup attempt was staged by armed rebels, who attacked various French installations on the island of Njazidja. Two Comorans who were implicated in the plot, and subsequently arrested, were alleged to be supporters of Mohamed Taki. The revolt was apparently organized by a small group of European mercenaries, who intended to bring about Djohar's downfall through the enforced removal of French forces from the islands. In September the minister of the interior and administrative reform, Ibrahim Halidi, was accused of involvement in the conspiracy and dismissed from office. By mid-September more than 20 people had been detained in connection with the insurgency. It was reported in October that the leader of the conspirators, Max Veillard, had been killed by Comoran security forces.

A ministerial reshuffle, which took place in October 1990, was followed by a period of dissension within the leadership of Udzima. By December an unofficial contest for the chairmanship of the government party had emerged between the minister of foreign affairs, Mtara Maecha, and two former ministers from the Abdallah administration, Saïd Ahmed Saïd Ali (Sharif) and Omar Tamou. Two members of the council of ministers, Saïd Hassane Saïd Hachim and Saïd Ali Youssouf, transferred their allegiance from Udzima to a newly-formed party, the Rassemblement pour le changement et la démocratie, but remained in the government.

In March 1991 the government announced that a conference, comprising three representatives of each political association, was to be convened to discuss constitutional reform. The conference took place in May, but several principal opposition parties, which objected to arrangements whereby Djohar reserved the right to modify the conference's recommendations, refused to attend. However, the conference presented draft constitutional amendments, which were to be submitted for endorsement by a national referendum.

On 3 August 1991 the president of the supreme court, Ibrahim Ahmed Halidi, announced the dismissal of Djohar, on the grounds of negligence, with the support of the court, and proclaimed himself interim president. Opposition leaders declared the seizure of power to be legitimate under the terms of the constitution. The government, however, ordered the arrests of Halidi and several other members of the supreme court. A state of emergency was imposed, and remained in force until early September. A number of demonstrations in favour of Djohar took place in early August, although members of Udzima failed to express support for the government. Later that month the government announced a ban on all public demonstrations, following violent clashes between pro-government demonstrators and members of the opposition.

In late August 1991 Djohar announced the establishment of a new coalition government, which included the appointment of two members of the FD. In an attempt to appease increasing discontent on the island of Mwali, which had repeatedly demanded greater autonomy, Djohar also nominated two members of Mwalian opposition groups to the government. However, the two leading political associations represented in the coalition government, Udzima and the PCDP, objected to the ministerial reshuffle, and accused Djohar of attempting to reduce the power of the principal parties. Shortly afterwards the two members of the PCDP in the government were ordered to resign by their party. In early September the four ministers belonging to Udzima were also obliged to resign. Later that month Djohar appointed a further three ministers.

In November 1991 Udzima announced that it was to withdraw its support for Djohar and join the parties opposing the government coalition. It also condemned the proposed constitutional amendments, which had been drafted in May. Opposition leaders demanded the dissolution of the federal assembly, which they declared to be illegitimate on the grounds that it had been elected under the former one-party system, and the formation of a government of national unity. Later in November, however, Djohar reached an agreement with the principal opposition leaders, Mohamed Taki and Abdul Majdid, to initiate a process of national reconciliation, which would include the formation of a government of national unity and the convening of a constitutional conference. The agreement also recognized the legitimacy of Djohar's election as president.

In January 1992 a new transitional government of national unity was formed, under the leadership of Mohamed Taki, who was designated as its co-ordinator. Later in January a national conference, comprising representatives of political associations supporting Djohar and of opposition parties, was convened to draft a new constitution, which was subsequently to be submitted for endorsement by public referendum. However, the conference was boycotted by representatives of Mwali (which in late 1991 had announced plans to conduct a referendum on self-determination for the island). In April 1992 the conference submitted a number of constitutional proposals.

In May 1992 18 opposition parties demanded the resignation of Djohar's son-in-law, Mohamed M'Changama, as minister of finance, following allegations of irregularities in negotiating government contracts. Djohar subsequently redesignated Mohamed Taki as prime minister and formed a new interim cabinet, in which, however, M'Changama retained his portfolio, and a number of his supporters were represented. The constitutional referendum was postponed from late May until 7 June, when, despite concerted opposition by eight parties, led by Udzima and the FD, the reform proposals were accepted by 74.25% of those voting. The new constitutional provisions, which limited presidential tenure to a maximum of two five-year terms, also provided for a bicameral legislature, comprising a federal assembly, together with a 15-member senate, comprising five representatives from each island to be chosen by an electoral college. Elections at national and local level were to take place later in 1992. In early July the president removed Mohamed Taki from office on the grounds that he had allegedly appointed a former associate of Col Denard to a financial advisory post in the government. Later that month a new government was formed.

In mid-1992 social and economic conditions on the Comoros deteriorated, following renewed strikes in a number of sectors, in protest at economic austerity measures undertaken by the government in conjunction with the IMF and World Bank. In early September Djohar announced that legislative elections were to commence in late October (despite the recommendation of an electoral commission that they take place in December). However, opposition parties claimed that the schedule provided insufficient time for preparation, and threatened to boycott the elections. Later that month a demonstration, organized by Udzima, the UNDC and the FD, in support of demands for Djohar's resignation, was suppressed by security forces. In an attempt to allay unrest, Djohar announced a new electoral timetable, in which legislative elections would take place in early November, and local government elections in December.

In late September 1992, during a visit by Djohar to Paris, an abortive coup attempt was staged by disaffected members of the armed forces, who seized the radio station at Moroni and announced that the government had been overthrown. A number of the rebels, including two sons of ex-president Abdallah were subsequently arrested, and, in October, were charged with involvement in the insurgency. In mid-October rebel troops, led by a former member of Abdallah's presidential guard, attacked the military garrison of Kandani, in an attempt to release the detainees. Shortly afterwards, government forces attacked the rebels at Mbeni, to the north-east of Moroni; fighting was also reported on the island of Nzwani. Later in October a demonstration was staged in protest at the French government's support of Djohar, following speculation that, in addition to supplies of food rations, government forces had received consignments of armaments from France. By the end of October some 25 people had been killed in clashes between rebels and government troops in Moroni.

In October 1992 Djohar agreed to reschedule the legislative elections until late November, although opposition parties demanded a further postponement, and Udzima and the UNDC continued to support a boycott of the elections. Later that month, in accordance with a presidential decree, nine government ministers who intended to contest the elections officially resigned. The first round of the legislative elections, which took place on 22 November, was marred by widespread violence and electoral irregularities. Several of the 21 political parties that had contested the election demanded that the results be declared invalid, and joined the boycott implemented by Udzima and the UNDC. Election results in six constituencies were subsequently annulled, while the second round of voting on 29 November took place in only 34 of the 42 constituencies. Following partial elections on 13 and 30 December, reports indicated that candidates supporting the president, including seven members of the Union des démocrates pour le développement (UDD), had secured a narrow majority in the federal assembly. In accordance with the terms of the constitution, the leader of the UDD, Ibrahim Abdérémane Halidi, was appointed prime minister on 1 January 1993, and formed a new council of ministers. Later in January, in response to pressure from the Mwalian deputies in the federal assembly, a Mwalian, Amir Attoumane, was elected speaker.

Shortly after the new government took office, divisions between Djohar and Halidi began to emerge, while the political parties supporting Djohar, which commanded a majority in the federal assembly, fragmented into three dissenting factions. In early February 1993 a curfew was temporarily imposed in Moroni, in response to increasing tension over a land dispute between the inhabitants of Moroni and those of Ioni, 15 km to the south. In mid-February, following criticism of the appointment of a number of ministers, several representatives of the parties that supported Djohar in the federal assembly proposed a vote of censure against the government, which was, however, rejected by 23 of the 42 deputies. Later that month the council of ministers was extensively reshuffled, although the political parties that supported Djohar remained dissatisfied with the composition of the government.

In April 1993 nine people, including the two sons of ex-president Abdallah and two prominent members of Udzima, were convicted on charges of involvement with the coup attempt in September 1992, and sentenced to death. However, Djohar subsequently commuted the sentences to terms of imprisonment, following considerable domestic and international pressure. In May 1993 the government announced that local government elections were to take place in September. Later in May eight supporters of M'Changama, allied with a number of opposition deputies, proposed a motion of censure against the government (apparently with the tacit support of Djohar), which contested Halidi's competence as prime minister. Following the approval of the motion by 23 of the 42 deputies in the federal assembly, Djohar appointed an associate of M'Changama, Saïd Ali Mohamed, as prime minister, replacing Halidi. Mohamed subsequently formed a new council of ministers, which, however, received the support of only 13 of the 42 members of the federal assembly. In mid-June 19 parliamentary deputies affiliated to Halidi, who had established an informal alliance, known as the Rassemblement pour le triomphe et la démocratie, proposed a motion of censure against the new government, on the grounds that the prime minister had not been appointed from a party that commanded a majority in the federal assembly. However, Djohar declared the motion to be unconstitutional, and, in view of the continued absence of a viable parliamentary majority, dissolved the federal assembly, and announced that legislative elections were to take place within 40 days. Shortly afterwards, he appointed a former presidential adviser, Ahmed Ben Cheikh Attoumane, as prime minister. A new council of ministers was subsequently formed (although two of the newly-appointed ministers immediately announced their resignation).

Following the dissolution of the federal assembly, opposition parties declared Djohar to be unfit to hold office, in view of the increasing political confusion, and demanded that legislative elections take place within the period of 40 days stipulated in the constitution. In ealy July, however, Djohar announced that the elections were to be postponed until October, and requested that the 24 registered political parties form themselves into three main groupings. Despite pressure from the French government, Djohar failed to honour earlier pledges to grant amnesties to those imprisoned following the coup attempt in September 1992. Later in July 1993 opposition parties organized a one-day general strike (which was widely observed), apparently as a prelude to a campaign of civil disobedience that was designed to force Djohar to bring forward the date of the legislative elections or to resign. Shortly afterwards several members of the opposition, including two parliamentary deputies, who had allegedly participated in the campaign of civil disobedience, were temporarily detained.

In early September 1993 a number of opposition movements, led by Udzima and the UNDC, established an informal electoral alliance, known as the Union pour la République et le progrès. The FD, the PCDP, CHUMA and the Mouvement pour la démocratie et le progrès (MDP) also announced that they would present joint candidates. Later in September Djohar postponed the legislative elections until November, officially on the grounds that the government had inadequate resources to conduct the elections. There was, however, widespread speculation that Djohar was seeking to gain time to organize his supporters into a united alliance to contest the elections. In the same month security forces closed a private radio station, which was owned by Abbas Djoussouf, the leader of the MDP.

Having failed to obtain party political support for an electoral alliance, (owing to hostility towards M'Changama) Djohar announced in October 1993 the formation of a new party, the Rassemblement pour la démocratie et le renouveau (RDR), mainly comprising supporters of M'Changama and including several prominent members of the government. Later that month 16 political parties, including several organizations that supported Djohar, threatened to boycott the elections unless the government repealed legislation that redrew constituency boundaries and provided for the appointment of a new electoral commission. In an effort to disrupt the election campaign, opposition supporters subsequently prevented government candidates from convening political gatherings. In November the legislative elections were rescheduled for 12 and 19 December, and the local government elections were postponed indefinitely. Later in November Djohar reorganized the council of ministers, and established a new national electoral commission, in compliance with the demands of the opposition.

In the first round of the legislative elections, which took place in an orderly atmosphere on 12 December 1993, four opposition candidates secured seats in the federal assembly, apparently provoking official concern. However, in the second round of polling (which was postponed until 20 December), it was reported that three people had been killed in violent incidents on Nzwani, where the authorities had taken over supervision of the polling stations. The national electoral commission subsequently invalidated the election results in eight constituencies. Partial elections subsequently took place in these constituencies and at Moroni, where the second round of voting had been postponed at the demand of two government candidates; however, opposition candidates refused to participate on the grounds that voting was again to be conducted under government supervision rather than that of the national electoral commission. The RDR consequently secured all 10 contested seats in the partial elections, and 22 seats overall (thereby gaining a narrow majority in the federal assembly), while opposition candidates obtained the remaining 20 seats. In early January 1994 Djohar appointed the secretary-general of the RDR, Mohamed Abdou Madi, as prime minister. Abdou Madi subsequently formed a new council of ministers, which included several supporters of M'Changama. M'Changama was elected speaker of the federal assembly.

Following the isntallation of the new government, 12 prominent opposition parties adopted a joint resolution claiming that the RDR had obtained power illegally, and established a new alliance, known as the Forum pour le redressement national (FRN), led by Djoussouf. Later in January 1994 three opposition leaders, including Djoussouf, were temporarily prevented from leaving the Comoros. In February security forces seized the transmitters of a private radio station, owned by Udzima, which had broadcast independent news coverage. In the same month a demonstration took place in protest at the continued detention of an MDP candidate, Mohamed Ahmed Faud, who had been arrested in connection with one of the deaths that had occurred during the legislative elections. In March the Comoros protested to the French government, after a French periodical published an article claiming that M'Changama was implicated in a number of fraudulent business transactions. At a religious ceremony later that month, which was attended by Djohar, a former bodyguard of an RDR candidate was arrested by the security forces and stated to be in possession of a firearm. A former governor of Njazidja and member of the FRN, Mohamed Abdérémane, was subsequently arrested on suspicion of involvement in an assassination attempt against Djohar, while Djoussouf and Mroudjae (who was also a prominent member of the FRN) were also questioned in connection with the incident. Abdérémane was later released, however, and there was speculation that the government had orchestrated the incident in an attempt to discredit the opposition.

In April 1994 pressure both from the Comoran opposition and the French government in favour of an amnesty for political prisoners increased. In the same month disagreements emerged between M'Changama and Abdou Madi over the appointments of a number of prominent officials. In early May a court ruling in favour of Fuad's release led the government to dismiss the magistrate concerned. At the end of that month teachers initiated strike action (which was later joined by health workers) in support of an increase in salaries and the reorganization of the public sector. In early June a motion of censure against Abdou Madi, which was proposed by supporters of the FRN in the federal assembly, was rejected by 26 of the 42 deputies. In mid-June it was reported that five people had been killed on Mwali, following an opposition demonstration in support of the strike, which was violently suppressed by the security forces. Later that month an agreement by the government to sell the state-owned airline, Air Comores, to a private company based in France, was rescinded, following protests from both opposition and government supporters in the federal assembly. Under a compromise arrangement, the company agreed to take over the management of the airline's operations. Controversy over this issue resulted in further political tension, and there was increasing speculation that Djohar intended to replace Abdou Madi as prime minister.

Since the mid-1980s the Comoran administration has attempted to establish closer links with neighbouring states. In January 1985 the Comoros was admitted as the fourth member state of the Indian Ocean Commission (IOC), an organization founded in 1982 by Madagascar, Mauritius and Seychelles to promote regional co-operation and economic development. In 1988 diplomatic relations were established with Seychelles. Following his election as president, Djohar undertook a regional goodwill tour, and in 1990 formal diplomatic relations were established with the USA. In 1993 the League of Arab Nations (Arab League) accepted an application for membership from the Comoros.

Economy

Revised for this edition by the Editor

The Comoros, with few natural resources, a chronic shortage of cultivable land, a narrow base of agricultural crops and a high density of population, is among the poorest countries of sub-Saharan Africa, and is highly dependent on external trade and assistance. In 1992, according to estimates by the World Bank, the gross national product (GNP) of the Comoros (excluding Mayotte), measured at average 1990–92 prices, was US $262m., equivalent to $510 per head. During 1985–92, it was estimated, GNP per head declined, in real terms, at an average annual rate of 2.3%. Over the same period, the population increased by an annual average of 3.7%. The Comoros' gross domestic product (GDP) increased, in real terms, by an annual average of 4.5% between 1980–85, but the rate of growth declined to an annual average of 1.1% in 1985–90. GDP increased, in real terms, by 2.1% in 1991, and by 1.6% in 1992.

Agriculture is the dominant economic activity in the Comoros (contributing an estimated 39.6% of GDP and employing about 78.1% of the labour force in 1992). In 1986, despite large-scale emigration to neighbouring countries, overall population density was 259.9 per sq km (excluding Mayotte), and is particularly high on the island of Nzwani (Anjouan). The problem of overpopulation on the three independent islands has worsened since the break with Mayotte, which has the largest area of unexploited cultivable land in the archipelago. Settlers from Nzwani and Njazidja (Grande-Comore) have been forced to leave Mayotte and return to their already overpopulated native islands, where the potential for agricultural development is very limited.

Local subsistence farming, using primitive implements and techniques, is inadequate to maintain the population. Yields are poor, storage facilities lacking, and much of the best land is reserved for export cash-crop production. Cassava, sweet potatoes, rice and bananas are the main food crops, and yams, maize and coconuts are also cultivated. Almost all meat and vegetables are imported, as is most of the rice consumed on the islands. Rice is also the islands' principal import, accounting for US $7.2m. (equivalent to 28.8% of the cost of total imports).

The major export crops are vanilla, ylang-ylang and cloves. Prices for vanilla, of which the islands are the world's second largest producer (with an estimated commercial output of 214,000 metric tons in 1992), have been affected in recent years by competition from low-cost producers, notably Indonesia, and by synthetic substitutes. France accounts for about one-third of the Comoros' vanilla exports. Adverse conditions in the market for cloves have persisted since the mid-1980s; only 474 metric tons were exported in 1992 (compared with 2,750 tons in 1991). The Comoros is the world's main source of ylang-ylang, for which prices have been favourable in recent years. Ageing plantations and inadequate processing equipment, however, have prevented this export from achieving its full potential, and output declined from 72 metric tons in 1989 to an estimated 45 tons in 1992. Shortfalls in foreign exchange revenue from these three commodities have been met by funds, under the Stabex (Stabilization of Export Earnings) scheme provided for in the Lomé Convention. The commercial exploitation of copra, formerly a significant export crop, has virtually ceased, owing to lack of demand from the domestic and international market. Agricultural GDP increased by an annual average of 4.2% in 1980–85, and by 3.3% in 1985–90; in 1992, however, it declined by 0.8%.

The manufacturing sector contributed 4.4% of GDP in 1992. The sector consists primarily of the processing of export crops, particularly of vanilla and essential oils, and a few factories supplying the domestic market. Manufacturing GDP increased by 4.3% in 1980–85, and by 4.5% in 1985–90; the rate of growth declined to 1.8% in 1991, but increased to 5.6% in 1992.

Fishing is practised on a small scale, with a total catch of about 6,500 metric tons in 1991 (according to FAO estimates). According to recent studies, the Comoros has a potential annual catch of 25,000–30,000 tons of tuna, which could provide the basis for a processing industry. A two-year project, aiming to provide an infrastructure for a Comoran fishing industry, has been initiated. The Comoros' fishing industry has received substantial aid from Japan. In October 1987 the Comoros and the EC signed a fishing agreement which permitted 40 tuna-fishing vessels from EC countries to operate in Comoran waters for three years and allowed the implementation of a scientific programme. In July 1988 the Comoros signed a further three-year agreement with France and Spain.

The Comoros has a developing tourist industry. In 1991 16,942 tourists visited the islands (compared with 7,627 in 1990), of which 9,584 were European. In 1988 receipts from tourism totalled 800m. Comoran francs. In the late 1980s the government, with financial support from South Africa, implemented a number of hotel development projects; in 1991 hotel capacity increased fom 112 to 294 rooms.

Economic development in the Comoros is impeded by poor infrastructure, with a shortage of electricity, a very limited road system and a lack of reliable transportation between the islands and with the outside world. In the early 1990s, however, public investment laid emphasis on infrastructural development, with the initiation of a programme, financed by the EC, to construct a port at Fomboni, on Mwali, to improve shipping access to the island, and the expansion of the road network on all three islands.

France represents the main source of economic support (see below), while the other member states of the EU, Japan (see above), Saudi Arabia, Kuwait and the United Arab Emirates also provide financial assistance. The government's development priorities for the 1980s were: increased production of basic foodstuffs and energy; an improvement in inter-island communications, water supply, and housing and regional development; and the creation of more efficient public health and training facilities. The Comoros' first international aid donors' conference took place in Moroni in 1984: discussion focused on the Comoros Development Plan 1983–86, which aimed to achieve self-sufficiency in food, improved supplies of water and electricity, better health care, urban planning and housing, and a controlled rate of population growth. Donors pledged some $114m. of project finance, of which $15.25m. was allocated for the construction of a hydroelectric power plant on Nzwani. In 1985 the EC announced that it would channel 7,065m. Comoros francs into aid for the agricultural sector over the period 1986–90. In 1987 the EC provided loans for the fishing sector and to finance investment for small and medium-sized enterprises. In 1988 the European Development Fund approved loans to develop the port at Moroni; the project was completed in mid-1991. France, the Comoros' major bilateral donor, provided 29.5m. French francs in budgetary aid in 1988 and 30m. French francs in 1989. In 1990 the French government cancelled Comoran debt totalling 229m. French francs, and waived repayment of a state loan of a further 9m. French francs. In 1991 the Comoros government received substantial budgetary aid from France, which facilitated the repayment of about $14m. of debt arrears owed to the African Development Bank (ADB) (allowing the resumption of suspended disbursements). In 1992 France pledged some 60m. French francs towards co-operation projects, and budgetary aid totalling 20m. French francs. Following the devaluation of the Comoros franc in January 1994 (see below), the French government agreed to cancel outstanding debt arrears. In 1993 budgetary assistance from France contributed to the payment of civil servants' salaries, while French aid in 1994 was again expected to allow the repayment of arrears owed to the ADB, as a precondition to the resumption of credit from that organization.

The Comoros' foreign trade accounts have shown a persistent deficit; imports have tended to increase, while export receipts have fluctuated widely, in response to trends in international prices for vanilla, cloves and ylang-ylang. In 1987 the Comoros sustained a visible trade deficit of $34.6m. There was a sharp recovery in export earnings in 1988, with an increase of 84% on the 1987 level, bringing the total value of exports to 6,398m. Comoros francs. (This significant improvement was attributable to the disposal of a two-year accumulation of vanilla stocks.) By 1989 the visible trade deficit had declined to $17.6m., while there was a surplus of $2.9m. on the current account of the balance of payments. In 1990, however, the visible trade deficit increased to $27.3m., and there was a deficit of $9.3m. on the current account of the balance of payments. In 1991, despite an increase in the total value of exports of 44%, compared with 1990, a visible trade deficit of $29.2m. was recorded. In that year there was a deficit of $8.9m. on the current account of the balance of payments. In 1989 the principal source of imports (58%) was France, which was also the principal market for exports (44.5%). The USA, Bahrain, Kenya, Botswana, Brazil and South Africa were also major trading partners. The leading exports in 1991 were spices, particularly vanilla (63.8%), and essential oils (14.1%). The principal imports in that year were rice (28.8%), petroleum products (10.7%) and road vehicles (9.9%).

There were budget shortfalls of 1,608m. and 2,057m. Comoros francs in 1986 and 1987 respectively. A prime factor in this rise was the dramatic fall in export revenue in the first six months of 1987. The budgetary deficit in 1988 was 2,200m. Comoros francs, and in 1989 the estimated deficit was 2,779m. Comoros francs. In 1990, in an attempt to curtail increasing deficits in the budget and external current account, the government initiated measures to improve tax collection and reduce expenditure. Although these reforms were, in part, successful, domestic and external arrears remained high. In 1991, however, the budgetary deficit increased to the equivalent of 20% of GDP (compared with a level of 18% of GDP in 1990). As a result, the government suffered difficulties in meeting wage and other payment obligations. In 1993 the budgetary deficit was estimated at 1,000m. Comoros francs (equivalent to 12% of GDP). The average annual rate of inflation was 3.0% in 1985–92.

At the end of 1992 the Comoros' external public debt totalled US $173.2m. (of which $165.1m. was long-term public debt), while the cost of debt-servicing was equivalent to 6.6% of the value of exports of goods and services. Following negotiations with the IMF, a three-year structural adjustment programme for the period 1991–93 was agreed, providing facilities totalling almost $135m., whereby the Comoros government undertook to diversify exports, reduce public expenditure, promote export-orientated industries and transfer state-owned enterprises to private-sector ownership. Measures subsequently implemented under the programme included the abolishment of levies on export crops, the liberalization of imports of a number of commodities, the initiation of environmental projects to control soil erosion (particularly on Nzwani), the 'privatization' of a number of state-owned hotels, the liquidation of the state-owned meat-marketing company, the Société comorienne des viandes (SOCOVIA), and the dismissal of a number of civil servants. However, the restructure of the public sector prompted widespread strikes, which caused severe economic disruption. In 1992 it appeared that insufficient progress had been achieved under the programme, and in September of that year it was announced that IMF and World Bank delegations were to visit the Comoros to discuss new reform objectives. In early 1993 the World Bank and IMF agreed to continue disbursements, following the approval of government plans, which included further 'privatization' measures and reduction in civil service personnel. However, the continuing volubility of internal political conditions impeded the implementation of the structural adjustment programme, and, despite some success in reducing fiscal imbalances, economic prospects have remained unfavourable. In January 1994 the devaluation of the Comoros franc by 33% (in relation to the French franc) resulted in an increase in the price of imported goods, prompting strike action in the education and health sectors in support of higher salaries. In March, however, following the adoption of an economic reform programme for the period 1994–96, the IMF approved a one-year structural adjustment facility, equivalent to $1.9m., while the World Bank also agreed to further credit. The programme laid emphasis on the continuation of the restructuring of the public sector and the re-evaluation of price controls; the government aimed to achieve economic growth of 4%, to restrict the rate of inflation to 4%, and to reduce the current account deficit (excluding official transfers) to less than 15% of GDP by 1996.

Statistical Survey

Source (unless otherwise stated): Ministry of Finance and the Budget, BP 324, Moroni; tel. 2767; telex 219.

Note: Unless otherwise indicated, figures in this Statistical Survey exclude data for Mayotte.

AREA AND POPULATION

Area: 1,862 sq km (719 sq miles) *By island:* Njazidja (Grande-Comore) 1,146 sq km, Nzwani (Anjouan) 424 sq km, Mwali (Mohéli) 290 sq km.

Population: 335,150 (males 167,089; females 168,061), excluding Mayotte (estimated population 50,740), at census of 15 September 1980; 484,000 (official estimate), including Mayotte, at 31 December 1986.

Principal Towns (population at 1980 census): Moroni (capital) 17,267; Mutsamudu 13,000; Fomboni 5,400.

Births and Deaths (including figures for Mayotte, UN estimates): Average annual birth rate 48.8 per 1,000 in 1975–80, 48.5 per 1,000 in 1980–85, 48.5 per 1,000 in 1985–90; average annual death rate 15.9 per 1,000 in 1975–80, 14.4 per 1,000 in 1980–85, 13.0 per 1,000 in 1985–90. (Source: UN, *World Population Prospects: The 1992 Revision*).

Economically Active Population (ILO estimates, '000 persons at mid-1980, including figures for Mayotte): Agriculture, forestry and fishing 150; Industry 10; Services 20; Total 181 (males 104, females 77). Source: ILO, *Economically Active Population Estimates and Projections, 1950–2025*.

AGRICULTURE, ETC.

Principal Crops (FAO estimates, '000 metric tons, 1992): Rice (paddy) 10, Maize 4, Cassava (Manioc) 49, Sweet potatoes 10, Pulses 8, Coconuts 50, Bananas 53. Source: FAO, *Production Yearbook*.

Livestock (FAO estimates, '000 head, year ending September 1992): Asses 5, Cattle 47, Sheep 14, Goats 126. Source: FAO, *Production Yearbook*.

Livestock Products (FAO estimates, '000 metric tons, 1992): Meat 2 (beef and veal 1); Cows' milk 4. Source: FAO, *Production Yearbook*.

Fishing ('000 metric tons, live weight): Total catch 6.8 in 1989; 8.0 in 1990; 6.5 (FAO estimate) in 1991. Source: FAO, *Yearbook of Fishery Statistics*.

INDUSTRY

Electric energy (production by public utilities): 16 million kWh in 1991. Source: UN, *Industrial Statistics Yearbook.*

FINANCE

Currency and Exchange Rates: 100 centimes = 1 Comoros franc. *Sterling and Dollar Equivalents* (31 March 1994): £1 sterling = 634.8 Comoros francs; US $1 = 427.6 Comoros francs; 1,000 Comoros francs = £1.575 = $2.339. *Average Exchange Rate* (Comoros francs per US $): 282.11 in 1991; 264.69 in 1992; 283.16 in 1993. Note: The Comoros franc was introduced in 1981, replacing (at par) the franc CFA. The fixed link to French currency was retained, with the exchange rate set at 1 French franc = 50 Comoros francs. This remained in effect until January 1994, when the Comoros franc was devalued by 33.3%, with the exchange rate adjusted to 1 French franc = 75 Comoros francs.

Budget (provisional, million Comoros francs, 1987): *Revenue:* Taxation 5,302.3 (Import duties 3,069.4); Other current revenue 1,517.7; Total 6,820.0, excluding grants received from abroad (6,889.1). *Expenditure:* General public services 2,599.7; Defence 910.8; Education 5,287.6; Health 1,527.2; Recreational, cultural and religious affairs and services 1,035.9; Economic affairs and services 9,179.6 (Fuel and energy 1,002.0; Agriculture, forestry, fishing and hunting 3,794.2; Transportation and communication 2,438.6); Total (incl. others) 21,036.7, excluding net lending (67.2). Figures refer to the consolidated operations of the central Government, including extrabudgetary accounts. Source: IMF, *Government Finance Statistics Yearbook.*

International Reserves (US $ million at 31 December 1992): Gold 0.19; IMF special drawing rights 0.03; Foreign exchange 26.38; Total 26.60. Source: IMF, *International Financial Statistics.*

Money Supply (million Comoros francs at 31 December 1992): Currency outside deposit money banks 4,082; Demand deposits at deposit money banks 3,866; Total money (incl. others) 10,857. Source: IMF, *International Financial Statistics.*

Gross Domestic Product by Economic Activity (estimates, million Comoros francs at current factor cost, 1991): Agriculture, hunting, forestry and fishing 27,426; Manufacturing 2,944; Electricity, gas and water 549; Construction 4,730; Trade, restaurants and hotels 10,699; Transport, storage and communications 2,823; Finance, insurance, real estate and business services 1,368; Public administration and defence 12,380; Other services 366; GDP at factor cost 63,284; Indirect taxes (net of subsidies) 5,964; GDP in purchasers' values 69,248. Source: UN Economic Commission for Africa, *African Statistical Yearbook.*

Balance of Payments (US $ million, 1991): Merchandise exports f.o.b. 24.36; Merchandise imports f.o.b. –53.60; *Trade balance* –29.24; Exports of services 24.70; Imports of services –44.38; Other income received 2.81; Other income paid –3.74; Private unrequited transfers 3.73; Official unrequited transfers 37.21; *Current balance* –8.91; Direct investment (net) 2.51; Other capital (net) 1.64; Net errors and omissions 1.70; *Total* (net monetary movements) –3.06. Source: IMF, *International Financial Statistics.*

EXTERNAL TRADE

Principal Commodities (US $'000, 1991): *Imports:* Meat and meat products 4,471; Dairy products and eggs 1,691; Rice 7,182; Flour 797; Sugar and honey 797; Refined petroleum products 6,242; Pharmaceutical products 708; Cement 3,273; Iron and steel 1,717; Road vehicles 5,750; Clothes 11,671; Total (incl. others) 58,250. *Exports:* Spices 19,922 (Vanilla 15,889, Cloves 3,871); Essential oils 3,516; Total (incl. others) 24,914. Source: UN, *International Trade Statistics Yearbook.*

Principal Trading Partners (million French francs, 1977): *Imports:* People's Republic of China 4.0; France 33.6; Kenya and Tanzania 7.6; Madagascar 16.1; Pakistan 6.8; Total (incl. others) 81.1. *Exports:* France 28.8; Federal Republic of Germany 1.5; Madagascar 2.2; USA 9.4; Total (incl. others) 44.0. **1989** (US $ '000): *Imports:* 42,736. *Exports:* France 8,495; Germany 1,888; Netherlands 194; Singapore 373; USA 6,616; Total (incl. others) 17,566. **1991** (US $'000): *Imports* 58,250. *Exports:* France 7,615; USA 10,617; Total (incl. others) 24,914. Source: UN, *International Trade Statistics Yearbook.*

TRANSPORT

Road Traffic (1987): 5,000 motor vehicles in use. Source: UN, *Statistical Yearbook.*

International Shipping (estimated sea-borne freight traffic, '000 metric tons, 1991): Goods loaded 12; Goods unloaded 107. Source: UN, *Economic Commission for Africa, African Statistical Yearbook.*

Civil Aviation (1973): 15,227 passenger arrivals, 15,674 passenger departures, 909 tons of freight handled.

COMMUNICATIONS MEDIA

Radio receivers (1991): 72,000 in use. Source: UNESCO, *Statistical Yearbook.*

Television receivers (1991): 200 in use. Source: UNESCO, *Statistical Yearbook.*

Telephones (1991): 3,000 in use (estimated figure). Source: UN Economic Commission for Africa, *African Statistical Yearbook.*

EDUCATION

Pre-Primary (1980): 600 teachers; 17,778 pupils.

Primary (1987): 257 schools; 1,777 teachers; 64,737 pupils.

Secondary (1986): 449 (1980) teachers (general education 557 (1989); teacher training 10; vocational 31); 21,168 pupils (general education 14,472 (1989); teacher training 32; vocational 302).

Higher (1989): 32 teachers; 248 pupils.

Source: UNESCO, *Statistical Yearbook.*

Directory

The Constitution

Under the Constitution of the Federal Islamic Republic of the Comoros, which was approved by popular referendum on 7 June 1992, the President is directly elected for five years by universal adult suffrage, and may not serve more than two terms. Provision is made for a bicameral legislature, comprising a 42-member Federal Assembly, elected for a term of four years, and a 15-member Senate (five representatives from each island), selected for a six-year term by an electoral college. Legislative elections are to take place within a period of 40 days after the dissolution of the Federal Assembly. The office of Prime Minister is to be held by a member of the party commanding a majority of seats in the Federal Assembly. The Council of Ministers is nominated by the Prime Minister. The Constitution also provides for the creation of a Constitutional Council. The relevant provisions of the 1978 Constitution are summarized below:

The preamble affirms the will of the Comoran people to derive from the state religion, Islam, inspiration for the regulation of government, to adhere to the principles laid down by the Charters of the UN and the Organization of African Unity, and to guarantee the rights of citizens in accordance with the UN Declaration of Human Rights. Sovereignty resides in the people, through their elected representatives. All citizens are equal before the law.

ISLAND AND FEDERAL INSTITUTIONS

The Comoros archipelago constitutes a federal Islamic republic. Each island has autonomy in matters not assigned by the Constitution to the federal institutions. There is universal secret suffrage for all citizens of more than 18 years of age in full possession of their civil and political rights. The number of political parties may be regulated by federal law.

The Head of State is the President of the Republic. The Governor of each island is directly elected, and appoints not more than four Commissioners to whom administration is delegated. If the Presidency falls vacant, the President of the Supreme Court assumes the office on a temporary basis until a presidential election takes place.

Each electoral ward elects one deputy to the Federal Assembly, which meets for not more than 45 days at a time, in April and October, and if necessary in extraordinary sessions. Matters covered by federal legislation include defence, posts and telecommunications, transport, civil, penal and industrial law, external trade, federal taxation, long-term economic planning, education and health.

The Council of each island is directly elected for four years. Each electoral ward elects one councillor. Each Council meets for not more than 15 days at a time, in March and December and if necessary in extraordinary sessions. The Councils are responsible for non-federal legislation.

THE JUDICIARY

The judiciary is independent of the legislative and executive powers. The Supreme Court arbitrates in any case where the Government is accused of malpractice.

The Government

HEAD OF STATE

President: SAÏD MOHAMED DJOHAR (took office as acting President 27 November 1989; elected President by popular vote 11 March 1990; took office 20 March 1990).

COUNCIL OF MINISTERS
(August 1994)

Prime Minister, with responsibility for Public Works: MOHAMED ABDOU MADI.

Minister of Information, Culture, Youth, Sports, and Posts and Telecommunications, Spokesman for the Government, with responsibility for relations with the Federal Assembly: HOUMED MDAHOMA M'SAÏDIÉ.

Minister of Finance and the Budget: AHMED EL HARIF HAMIDI.

Minister of Foreign Affairs and Co-operation: SAÏD MOHAMED SAGAF.

Minister of Equipment, Energy, Town Planning and Housing: MOUSSA TOYBOU.

Minister of Justice and Islamic Affairs: MOUSLIM BEN MOUSSA.

Minister of National Education, and Professional and Technical Training: IBRAHIM HISSANI M'FOIHAYA.

Minister of Social Affairs, Labour and Employment: SITTOU RAGHADAT MOHAMED.

Minister of Public Health: ATTOUMANE BOINA ISSA.

Minister of Rural Development, Fishing and the Environment: IDAROUSSE ATTOUMANE.

Minister of Transport and Tourism: AHMED SAÏD ISSILAM.

Minister of the Economy, Industry, Crafts and Planning: AHMED BOURHANE.

Minister of the Interior and Decentralization: AHMED HOUMADI.

MINISTRIES

Office of the Prime Minister: BP 421, Moroni; tel. (73) 2413; telex 233.

Ministry of the Economy, Industry, Crafts and Planning: BP 41, Moroni; tel. (73) 2292; telex 240.

Ministry of Equipment, Energy, Town Planning and Housing: Moroni.

Ministry of Finance and the Budget: BP 324, Moroni; tel. (73) 2767; telex 219.

Ministry of Foreign Affairs and Co-operation: BP 482, Moroni; tel. (73) 2306; telex 219; fax (73) 2108.

Ministry of Information, Culture, Youth, Sports and Posts and Telecommunications: BP 421, Moroni; telex 219.

Ministry of the Interior and Decentralization: Moroni.

Ministry of Justice and Islamic Affairs: Moroni.

Ministry of National Education, and Professional and Technical Training: BP 446, Moroni; tel. (73) 2420; telex 229.

Ministry of Public Health: BP 42, Moroni; tel. (73) 2277; telex 219.

Ministry of Rural Development, Fishing and the Environment: Moroni.

Ministry of Social Affairs, Labour and Employment: BP 520, Moroni; tel. (73) 2411; telex 219.

Ministry of Transport and Tourism: Moroni; tel. (73) 2098; telex 244.

President and Legislature

PRESIDENT

In the first round of voting, which took place on 4 March 1990, none of the eight candidates received 50% of the total votes cast. A second round of voting took place on 11 March, when voters chose between the two leading candidates. SAÏD MOHAMED DJOHAR received 55.3% of the votes, while MOHAMED TAKI ABDULKARIM obtained 44.7%.

LEGISLATURE

The Constitution provides for a bicameral legislature, comprising a 42-member Federal Assembly, elected for a term of four years, and a 15-member Senate (five representatives from each island), selected for a six-year term by an electoral college.

Assemblée Fédérale

In elections to the Federal Assembly, which took place on 12 and 20 December 1993, members of President Djohar's political party, the Rassemblement pour la démocratie et le renouveau (RDR), secured 22 seats, while opposition candidates obtained 20 seats.

Speaker: MOHAMED SAÏD ABDALLAH M'CHANGAMA.

Political Organizations

The Union comorienne pour le progrès (Udzima) was the sole legal party between 1982 and November 1989, when formal restrictions on multi-party activity was ended. In mid-1994 there were more than 20 active political parties.

CHUMA (Islands' Fraternity and Unity Party): Moroni; Leader Prince SAÏD ALI KEMAL.

Forum pour le redressement national (FRN): f. 1994; alliance of 12 opposition parties; Leader ABBAS DJOUSSOUF.

Front démocratique (FD): BP 758, Moroni; tel. (73) 2939; f. 1982; Leader MOUSTAPHA SAÏD CHEIKH.

Front populaire comorien (FPC): Mwali; supports President Djohar; Leader MOHAMED HASSANALY.

Mayesha Bora: Moroni; supports President Djohar; Leader AHMED SAÏD ISLAM.

Mouvement pour la démocratie et le progrès (MDP): Moroni; Leader ABBAS DJOUSSOUF.

***Mouvement pour la rénovation et l'action démocratique (MOURAD):** Moroni; f. 1990; aims to promote economic and financial rehabilitation; Leader ABDOY ISSA.

Mzingara: f. 1993 by former supporters of the Union nationale pour la démocratie aux Comores; supports President Djohar; Chair. CHADDULI ABDOU BACAR.

Nguzo: Moroni; supports President Djohar; Leader TAKI MBOREHA.

Opposition unie (OU): Moroni.

Parti comorien pour la démocratie et le progrès (PCDP): Moroni; Leader ALI MROUDJAE.

***Parti socialiste des Comores (PASOCO):** POB 720, Moroni; tel. (73) 1328; Leader ALI IDAROUSSE.

Parti du salut national (PSN): f. 1993; breakaway faction of PCDP; Islamic orientation; supports President Djohar; Leader SAÏD ALI MOHAMED.

Rassemblement pour le changement et la démocratie (Rachad): Moroni; f. 1991 by a breakaway faction of Udzima; Leader SAÏD HASSANE SAÏD HACHIM.

Rassemblement pour la démocratie et le renouveau (RDR): f. 1993 by President Djohar to contest the legislative elections; Chair. IBRAHIM SAID NAÇR ED DINE.

Rassemblement pour le triomphe et la démocratie (RTD): f. 1993; parliamentary group of supporters of the fmr prime minister, Ibrahim Abdérémane Halidi; Leader ABDILLAH SOILIHI.

***Union comorienne pour le progrès (Udzima):** Moroni; sole legal party 1982–89; withdrew support from President Djohar in Nov. 1991; Leader CHAHER BEN SAID MASSOUNDI.

Union des démocrates pour le développement (UDD): Nzwani; supports President Djohar; Leader IBRAHIM ABDÉRÉMANE HALIDI.

***Union nationale pour la démocratie aux Comores (UNDC):** Moroni; Leader OMAR SAID BOURHANE.

Uwezo: Moroni; f. 1990; supports President Djohar ; Leader MOUAZOIR ABDULLAH.

* Contested the legislative elections in 1993 as the Union pour la République et le progrès (URP).

Diplomatic Representation

EMBASSIES IN THE COMOROS

China, People's Republic: Moroni; tel. (73) 2721; Ambassador: ZHU CHENHUAI.

France: blvd de Strasbourg, BP 465, Moroni; tel. (73) 0753; telex 220; Ambassador: JEAN-LUC SIBIUDE.

Italy: Moroni; Ambassador: FORQUATO CARDILLI.

Mauritius: Moroni.

Seychelles: Moroni.

South Africa: Moroni; Ambassador: MAPPEL DORAM.

USA: Moroni; Ambassador: KENNETH PELTIER.

Judicial System

The Supreme Court consists of two members chosen by the President of the Republic, two elected by the Federal Assembly, one by the Council of each island, and former Presidents of the Republic.

Religion

The majority of the population are Muslims. At 31 December 1992 there were an estimated 3,000 adherents of the Roman Catholic Church, equivalent to 0.5% of the total population.

CHRISTIANITY

The Roman Catholic Church

Office of Apostolic Administrator of the Comoros: Mission Catholique, BP 46, Moroni; tel. and fax (73) 0570; Apostolic Pro-Administrator Fr GABRIEL FRANCO NICOLAI.

The Press

Al Watwany: M'tsangani, BP 984, Moroni; tel. (73) 0861; f. 1985; weekly; state-owned; general; Dir ALLAOUI SAÏD OMAR; circ. 1,500.

L'Archipel: Moroni; f. 1988; weekly; independent; Publrs ABOUBACAR MCHANGAMA, SAINDOU KAMAL.

NEWS AGENCIES

Agence Comores Presse (ACP): Moroni.

Foreign Bureau

Agence France-Presse (AFP): BP 1327, Moconi; telex 242; Rep. ABOUBACAR MICHANGAMA.

Radio and Television

In 1991 there were an estimated 72,000 radio receivers and 200 television receivers in use. Transmissions to the Comoros from Radio France Internationale commenced in early 1994.

Radio-Comoros: BP 250, Moroni; tel. (73) 0531; telex 241; govt-controlled; domestic service in Comoran and French; international services in Swahili, Arabic and French; Tech. Dir KOMBO SOULAIMANA.

Radio Tropic FM: transmissions suspended in Sept. 1993; Chair ABBAS DJOUSSOUF.

Voix des Iles: owned by the Union comorienne pour le progrès (Udzima); transmissions suspended in Feb. 1994.

Finance

BANKING

(cap. = capital; dep. = deposits; res = reserves; m. = million; brs = branches; amounts in Comoros francs)

Central Bank

Banque Centrale des Comores: BP 405, Moroni; tel. (73) 1002; telex 213; f. 1981; bank of issue; cap. and res 2,202.8m. (Dec. 1989); Pres. AHMED ABDOU; Dir-Gen. MOHAMED HALIFA.

Commercial Bank

Banque pour l'Industrie et le Commerce—Comores (BIC): place de France, BP 175, Moroni; tel. (73) 0243; telex 242; fax (73) 1229; f. 1990; subsidiary of Banque nationale de Paris–Internationale; 34% state-owned; cap. 300m. (Dec. 1992), dep. 15,599.9m. (Dec. 1991); Pres. MOHAMED MOUMINI; Dir-Gen. MICHEL GRILLO; 6 brs.

Other Banks

Banque de Développement des Comores: place de France, BP 298, Moroni; tel. (73) 0818; telex 213; f. 1982; provides loans, guarantees and equity participation for small and medium-scale projects; 50% state-owned; cap. 300m. (Dec. 1992); Pres. DAROUECHE ABDALLAH; Dir-Gen. AZALI AMBARI DAROUECHE.

Trade and Industry

CHAMBER OF COMMERCE

Chambre de Commerce, d'Industrie et d'Agriculture: BP 763, Moroni.

DEVELOPMENT ORGANIZATIONS

CEFADER: a rural design, co-ordination and support centre, with brs on each island.

Mission Permanente de Coopération: Moroni; centre for administering bilateral aid from France; Dir GABRIEL COURCELLE.

Office National du Commerce: Moroni, Njazidja; state-operated agency for the promotion and development of domestic and external trade; Chair. (vacant).

Société de Développement de la Pêche Artisanale des Comores (SODEPAC): state-operated agency overseeing fisheries development programme.

STATE ENTERPRISES

Electricité et Eau des Comores (EEDC): Moroni; telex 251; production and distribution of electricity and water; ownership was to be transferred to Electricité de France-International in 1993.

Société Comorienne des Hydrocarbures (SCH): POB 28, Moroni; tel. (73) 0486; telex 226; fax (73) 1883; imports petroleum products.

Société Nationale des Postes et des Télécommunications: Moroni; operates posts and telecommunications services.

TRADE UNION

Union des Travailleurs des Comores: Moroni.

Transport

ROADS

In 1991 there were an estimated 900 km of roads in the Comoros (of which 650 km were paved). A major road-improvement scheme was launched in 1979, with foreign assistance, and by 1990 about 170 km of roads on Njazidja and Nzwani had been resurfaced.

SHIPPING

The port of Mutsamudu, on Njazidja, can accommodate vessels of up to 11 m draught. Goods from Europe come via Madagascar, and coastal vessels serve the Comoros from the east coast of Africa. The development of the port of Moroni, with EC support, was completed in mid-1991. In 1993 the EC pledged US $4m. to finance the construction of a port at Fomboni, on Mwali, to improve shipping access to the island.

Société Comorienne de Navigation: Moroni; services to Madagascar.

CIVIL AVIATION

The international airport is at Moroni-Hahaya on Njazidja and each of the three other islands has a small airfield..

Air Comores (Société Nationale des Transports Aériens): BP 417, Moroni; tel. (73) 2245; telex 218; f. 1975; state-owned; scheduled and cargo services linking Moroni to Nzwani, Mwali and Dzaoudzi; Man. Dir ROWLAND ASHLEY.

Tourism

The principal tourist attractions are the beaches, underwater fishing and mountain scenery. In 1988 receipts from tourism totalled 800m. Comoran francs. In 1991 16,942 tourists visited the Comoros. In that year hotel capacity increased from 112 to 294 rooms, following the implementation of a niumber of hotel development projects.

Société Comorienne de Tourisme et d'Hôtellerie (COMOTEL): Itsandra Hotel, Njazidja; tel. (73) 2365; national tourist agency.

Defence

The national army, the Forces comoriennes de défense (FCD), has a strength of 700–800 men.

Defence Expenditure: Budgeted at 910.8m. Comoros francs in 1987.

Chief of Staff of the Comoran Armed Forces: Commdr ASSOUMANI AZZALY.

Education

Education is officially compulsory for nine years between seven and 16 years of age. Primary education begins at the age of six and lasts for six years. Secondary education, beginning at 12 years of age, lasts for a further seven years, comprising a first cycle of four years and a second of three years. Enrolment at primary schools in 1989 was equivalent to an estimated 75% of children in the relevant age-group (boys 82%; girls 68%). Children may also receive a basic education through traditional Koranic schools, which are staffed by Comoran teachers. In 1989 enrolment at secondary schools was equivalent to 17% of children in the relevant age-group (males 20%; females 15%). Expenditure by the central government on education in 1987 was 5,287.6m. Comoros francs, representing 25.1% of total spending. In 1980, according to census results, the average rate of adult illiteracy was 52.1% (males 44.0%; females 60.0%).

MAYOTTE

Since the Comoros unilaterally declared independence in July 1975, Mayotte (Mahoré) has been administered separately by France. The independent Comoran state claims Mayotte as part of its territory and officially represents it in international organizations, including the UN. In December 1976, following a referendum in April (in which the population voted to renounce the status of an overseas territory), France introduced the special status of *collectivité territoriale* for the island. The French government is represented on Mayotte by an appointed prefect. There is a general council, with 17 members, who are elected by universal adult suffrage. Mayotte has one representative in the national assembly in Paris, and one in the senate.

Following the coup in the Comoros in May 1978, Mayotte rejected the new government's proposal that it should rejoin the other islands under a federal system, and reaffirmed its intention of remaining linked to France. The main political party on Mayotte, the Mouvement populaire mahorais (MPM), demands full departmental status for the island, but France has been reluctant to grant this, in view of Mayotte's underdeveloped condition. In December 1979 the French national assembly approved legislation to prolong Mayotte's special status for another five years, during which period a referendum was to be conducted on the island. In October 1984, however, the national assembly further extended Mayotte's status, and the referendum on the island's future was postponed indefinitely. The UN general assembly has adopted several resolutions reaffirming the sovereignty of the Comoros over the island, and urging France to reach an agreement with the Comoran government as soon as possible. The Organization of African Unity (OAU) has endorsed this view.

In March 1987 clashes between islanders and illegal Comoran immigrants were reported. Order was eventually restored, following the arrival of reinforcements of gendarmes from Réunion. In August the Comoros boycotted the Indian Ocean region's first 'Youth Games', in protest against the participation of Mayotte. In June 1989 Tanzania and the Comoros issued a joint communiqué urging an early resolution of the island's future status.

Following elections to the French national assembly in March 1986, a coalition of the Rassemblement pour la République (RPR) and the Union pour la démocratie française (UDF) formed a new government in mainland France. Henry Jean-Baptiste, representing an electoral alliance of the UDF and the Centre des démocrates sociaux (CDS), secured the Mayotte seat in the new assembly. In October Jacques Chirac became the first French prime minister to visit Mayotte, where he assured the islanders that they would remain French citizens for as long as they wished. Meanwhile, the French government announced a five-year Development Plan for Mayotte, which provided for the reform of land tenure, labour relations, town planning, public markets and penal procedure, reserving the power to implement these reforms by decree if necessary. However, relations between the MPM and the RPR/UDF government rapidly deteriorated following the Franco-African summit in November 1987, when Chirac expressed his reservations to the Comoran president concerning the elevation of Mayotte to the status of a full overseas department. These misgivings appeared to contradict an earlier assurance, given during the RPR/UDF alliance's election campaign in early 1986, that he endorsed the MPM's aim to improve the status of Mayotte.

In the first round of the 1988 French presidential election, which took place on 24 April, the islanders demonstrated their opposition to the prime minister's stance on Mayotte's constitutional future by favouring the candidacy of Raymond Barre to that of Chirac. The second round of the election, held on 10 May, was contested by Chirac and François Mitterrand, the incumbent president and candidate of the Parti socialiste (PS), who had received only 4% of the votes on Mayotte in the first round. Supporters of Barre on Mayotte transferred a large proportion of their votes to Mitterrand, rather than Chirac, and Mitterrand subsequently received 50.3% of votes cast on Mayotte. At elections to the French national assembly, which took place in June, the seat for Mayotte was retained by Henry Jean-Baptiste, the UDF/CDS deputy (who later that month joined the newly-formed centrist group in the French national assembly, the Union du centre.) At the cantonal election in September and October, the MPM retained a majority of seats in the general council.

In November 1989 the general council urged the French government to introduce measures to curb immigration to Mayotte from neighbouring islands, particularly from the Comoros. In January 1990 pressure by a group from the town of Mamoudzou resulted in increasing tension over the presence of Comoran refugees on the island. Later that month there was a demonstration in protest against illegal immigration to the island. A paramilitary organization, 'Caiman' (which demanded the expulsion of illegal immigrants), was subsequently formed, but was refused legal recognition by the authorities. In May the Comoran president, Saïd Mohamed Djohar, undertook to pursue peaceful dialogue to resolve the question of Mayotte's sovereignty, and issued a formal appeal to France to reconsider the island's status. Mayotte was used as a strategic military base in late 1990, in preparation for French troop participation in multinational operations during the 1991 Gulf War.

At elections to the general council in March 1991, the MPM secured an additional three seats. However, Younoussa Bamana, the president of the general council and leader of the MPM, was defeated in his canton, Keni-Keli, by the RPR candidate. In late July, however, Bamana secured the majority of votes cast in a partial election, which took place in the canton of Chicani.

In late June 1991 a demonstration on the islet of Pamandzi, in protest at the relocation of a number of people as a result of the expansion of the airfield, prevented an aircraft from Réunion from landing. Unrest among young people on Pamandzi escalated in early July; the mayor fled after demonstrators attempted to set fire to the town hall. Clashes took place between demonstrators and security forces, and the prefect requested that police reinforcements be dispatched from Réunion to restore order. An organization of young people, l'Association des jeunes pour le développement de Pamandzi (AJDP), accused the mayor of maladministration and demanded his resignation. The demonstrations, which threatened to destabilize the MPM, were generally viewed as a manifestation of general discontent among young people on Mayotte (who comprised about 60% of the population). Later in July five members of the AJDP, who had taken part in the demonstration at the airfield in June, received prison sentences.

In June 1992 increasing tension resulted in further attacks against Comoran immigrants resident in Mayotte. In early September representatives of the MPM met the French prime minister, Pierre Bérégovoy, to request the reintroduction of entry visas in order to restrict immigration from the Comoros. Later that month the MPM organized a boycott (which was widely observed) of Mayotte's participation in the French referendum on the Treaty on European Union, in protest at the French government's refusal to introduce entry visas. In December the prefect of Mayotte, Jean-Paul Costes, and a number of other prominent officials were charged in connection with the deaths of several people in domestic fires that had been caused by poor quality fuel imported from Bahrain. In February 1993 a general strike, staged in support of wage increases, culminated in violent rioting; security forces were subsequently dispatched from Réunion and mainland France to restore order. At the end of February Costes was replaced as prefect by Jean-Jacques Debacq.

At elections to the French national assembly, which took place in March 1993, Jean-Baptiste was returned by 53.4% of votes cast, while the secretary-general of the local branch of the RPR, Mansour Kamardine, obtained 44.3% of the vote. Kamardine subsequently accused Jean-Baptiste of illegally claiming the support of an electoral alliance of the RPR and the UDF, known as the Union pour la France (UPF), by forging the signatures of the secretary-general of the RPR and his UDF counterpart on a document. However, Jean-Baptiste denied the allegations, and, in turn, began legal proceedings against Kamardine for alleged forgery and defamation. At elections to the enlarged general council, which took place in March 1994, the MPM secured 12 seats, the local branch of the RPR four seats, and independent candidates three seats. In mid-1994 the French government introduced new regulations, in an effort to reduce illegal immigration to Mayotte.

Mayotte's gross domestic product (GDP) per head was estimated at 4,050 French francs in 1991. Between the censuses of 1985 and 1991 the population of Mayotte increased by an annual average of 5.8%. The economy of Mayotte is based almost entirely on agriculture. Rice, cassava and maize are cultivated for domestic consumption, and vanilla, ylang-ylang (an ingredient of perfume), coffee and copra are the main export products. Construction is the sole industrial sector. There are no mineral resources on the island. Imports of mineral products comprised 4.4% of the cost of total imports in 1988.

In 1992 France was the principal source of imports (74%), and the principal market for exports (70%). Other major trading partners were South Africa, Singapore, Thailand, the Comoros, and Réunion. Owing to its reliance on imports, Mayotte operates a substantial trade deficit, which totalled 437.8m. French francs in 1992. In 1988 the principal imports were foodstuffs (22%), machinery and transport equipment (20.7%) and metals (10.5%), and the main exports were oil of ylang-ylang (78%) and vanilla (21%). In 1986 Mayotte's external assets totalled 203.8m. francs. In 1991 Mayotte's budget expenditure was an estimated 365m. francs.

A five-year Development Plan (1986–91) included measures to improve infrastructure and to increase investment in public works. (The Plan was subsequently extended to the end of 1993.) Substantial aid from France during the period 1987–92 was designed to stimulate the development of tourism on the island through the construction of a deep-water port at Longoni and the expansion of the airfield at Dzaoudzi. Mayotte's remote location, however, remains an obstacle to the development of the tourist sector.

The principal towns are the capital, Dzaoudzi (population 5,865 in 1985), Mamoudzou (12,026) and Pamandzi-Labattoir (4,106). France is responsible for the defence of the island: in mid-1993 there were 3,400 French troops stationed on Mayotte and Réunion.

Statistical Survey

Source: mainly Office of the Prefect, Government Commissioner, Dzaoudzi.

AREA AND POPULATION

Area: 374 sq km (144 sq miles).

Population: 67,167 (census of August 1985); 94,410 (census of August 1991). *Principal towns* (population at 1985 census): Dzaoudzi (capital) 5,865, Mamoudzou 12,026, Pamandzi-Labattoir 4,106. *Dzaudzi* (estimated population at 1991 census): 8,300. Source: INSEE, *Annuaire Statistique de la France 1991–92*.

Births and Deaths (1985–90): Birth rate 35.6 per 1,000; Death rate 6.2 per 1,000. Source: Institut National de la Statistique et des Etudes Economiques, *L'Economie de la Réunion*.

AGRICULTURE, ETC.

Livestock (1990): Cattle 12,000; Sheep 3,000; Goats 15,000. Source: Secrétariat du Comité Monétaire de la Zone Franc, *La Zone Franc, Rapport 1990.*

Fishing (metric tons, 1989): Total catch 1,700. Source: Ministère des Départements et Territoires d'Outre-Mer.

FINANCE

Currency and Exchange Rates: 100 centimes = 1 French franc. *Sterling and Dollar Equivalents* (31 March 1994): £1 sterling = 8.4640 francs; US $1 = 5.7014 francs; 1,000 French francs = £118.15 = $175.40. *Average Exchange Rate* (French francs per US dollar): 5.642 in 1991; 5.294 in 1992; 5.663 in 1993.

Budget (estimates, million francs): Total expenditure 371.6 (current 197.2, capital 174.4) in 1989; 338 (current 236, capital 102) in 1990; 365 in 1991.

Money Supply (million French francs at 31 December 1989): Currency outside banks 341; Demand deposits 83; Total money 424.

EXTERNAL TRADE

Principal Commodities ('000 francs, 1988): *Imports:* Foodstuffs 65,014; Machinery and appliances 61,097; Metals and metal products 31,061; Transport equipment 50,097; Total (incl. others) 294,981. *Exports:* Oil of ylang-ylang 8,188; Vanilla 1,810; Coffee (green) 178; Total (incl. others) 10,189. Figures exclude re-exports (42.9 million francs in 1988). **1989** (million francs): Total imports 338.1; Total exports 35.5. **1990** (million francs): Total imports 327.7; Total exports 37.6.

Principal Trading Partners ('000 francs): *Imports* (1988): France 193,984; Singapore 9,507; South Africa 26,854; Thailand 12,617; Total (incl. others) 294,981. *Exports* (1983): France 4,405.

Source: Secrétariat du Comité Monétaire de la Zone Franc, *La Zone Franc, Rapport 1988.*

TRANSPORT

Roads (1984): 93 km of main roads, of which 72 km are tarred, 137 km of local roads, of which 40 km are tarred, and 54 km of tracks unusable in the rainy season; 1,528 vehicles.

Civil Aviation (1984): *Arrivals:* 7,747 passengers, 120 metric tons of freight; *Departures:* 7,970 passengers, 41 metric tons of freight.

EDUCATION

Primary (1986): 28 schools; 366 teachers; 15,632 pupils (20,836 in 1990).

Secondary (1990): 6 schools; 65 teachers (1986); 2,957 pupils.

Directory

The Constitution

Under the status of Collectivité Territoriale, which was adopted in December 1976, Mayotte has an elected General Council, comprising 19 members, which assists the Prefect in the administration of the island. In 1984 a referendum on the future of Mayotte was postponed indefinitely.

The Government

Représentation du Gouvernement, Dzaoudzi, 97610 Mayotte; tel. 60-10-54.

(August 1994)

Prefect: JEAN-JACQUES DEBACQ.

Secretary-General: JEAN-PIERRE LAFLAQUIÈRE.

Deputy to the French National Assembly: HENRY JEAN-BAPTISTE (UDF-CDS).

Representative to the French Senate: MARCEL HENRY (MPM).

GENERAL COUNCIL

Conseil Général, Mamoudzou, 97600 Mayotte; tel. 61-12-33.

The General Council comprises 19 members. At elections in March 1994, the Mouvement Populaire Mahorais (MPM) secured 12 seats, the Fédération de Mayotte du Rassemblement pour la République four seats, and independent candidates three seats.

President of the General Council: YOUNOUSSA BAMANA.

Political Organizations

Fédération de Mayotte du Rassemblement pour la République: Dzaoudzi, 97610 Mayotte; local branch of the French (Gaullist) RPR; Sec.-Gen. MANSOUR KAMARDINE.

Mouvement Populaire Mahorais (MPM): Dzaoudzi, 97610 Mayotte; seeks departmental status for Mayotte; Leader YOUNOUSSA BAMANA.

Parti pour le Rassemblement Démocratique des Mahorais (PRDM): Dzaoudzi, 97610 Mayotte; f. 1978; seeks unification with the Federal Islamic Republic of the Comoros; Leader DAROUÈCHE MAOULIDA.

Prior to the French general election of June 1988, the two major French right-wing political parties, the **Rassemblement pour la République (RPR)** and the **Union pour la Démocratie Française (UDF)**, formed an electoral alliance, the **Union du Rassemblement du Centre (URC)**. After the election, 40 UDF deputies, including the deputy from Mayotte, formed a new centrist parliamentary group, the **Union du Centre (UDC)**. In 1990 the UDF and the RPR formed a new electoral alliance, the **Union pour la France (UPF)**.

Judicial System

Tribunal Supérieur d'Appel: Mamoudzou, 97600 Mayotte; tel. 61-12-65; fax 61-19-63; Pres. JEAN-BAPTISTE FLORI.

Procureur de la République: PATRICK BROSSIER.

Tribunal de Première Instance: Pres. ARLETTE MEALLONNIER-DUGUE.

Religion

Muslims comprise about 98% of the population. Most of the remainder are Christians, mainly Roman Catholics.

CHRISTIANITY

The Roman Catholic Church

Mayotte is within the jurisdiction of the Apostolic Administrator of the Comoros.

The Press

Le Journal de Mayotte: BP 181, Mamoudzou, 97600 Mayotte; tel. 61-16-95; fax 61-08-88; f. 1983; weekly; circ. 15,000.

Radio and Television

In 1989 there were an estimated 30,000 radio receivers in use.

Société Nationale de Radio-Télévision Française d'Outre-Mer (RFO)—Mayotte: BP 103, Dzaoudzi, 97610 Mayotte; tel. 60-10-17; telex 915822; fax 60-18-52; f. 1977; govt-owned; radio broadcasts in French and Mahorian; television transmissions began in 1986; Regional Dir BERNARD I. REGIS; Technical Dir MARC E. BAUDIN.

Finance

BANKS

Institut d'Emission d'Outre-Mer: BP 500, Mamoudzou, 97600 Mayotte.

Banque Française Commerciale: Mamoudzou, 97600 Mayotte; br. at Dzaoudzi.

Transport

ROADS

The main road network totals approximately 93 km, of which 72 km are bituminized. There are 137 km of local roads, of which 40 km are tarred, and 54 km of minor tracks which are unusable during the rainy season.

SHIPPING

Coastal shipping is provided by locally-owned small craft. A deep-water port is under construction at Longoni.

CIVIL AVIATION

There is an airfield at Dzaoudzi, serving four-times weekly commercial flights to Réunion and twice-weekly services to Njazidja, Nzwani and Mwali. The expansion of the airfield commenced in 1991; a second stage of the programme was initiated in early 1994.

Tourism

The main tourist attraction is the natural beauty of the tropical scenery. In 1985 the island had six hotels, providing a total of approximately 100 beds. Tourist arrivals number an annual average of 1,200 (of whom two-thirds are from France).

Comité Territorial du Tourisme de Mayotte: rue de la Pompe, BP 169, Mamoudzou, 97600 Mayotte; tel. 61-09-09; fax 61-03-46.

Bibliography

Bourde, A. 'The Comoro Islands: problems of a microcosm', in *Journal of Modern African Studies*, No. 3, 1965.

Cornu, H. *Paris et Bourbon, La politique française dans l'Océan indien.* Paris, Académie des Sciences d'Outre-mer, 1984.

Dubins, B. 'The Comoro Islands: A Bibliographical Essay', in *African Studies Bulletin*, No. 12, 1969.

Mantoux, T. 'Notes socio-économiques sur l'archipel des Comores', in *Revue française d'études politiques africaines*, No. 100, 1974.

Marquardt, W. *Seychellen, Komoren und Maskarenen.* Munich, 1976.

Newitt, M. *The Comoros Islands: Struggle against Dependency in the Indian Ocean*, Aldershot, Gower, 1985.

Weinberg, S. *Last of the Pirates: The Search for Bob Denard.* London, Jonathan Cape, 1994.

World Bank. *Comoros: Current Economic Situation and Prospects.* Washington, DC, International Bank for Reconstruction and Development, 1983.

THE CONGO

Physical and Social Geography

DAVID HILLING

POPULATION

The Zaire (Congo) river forms approximately 1,000 km of the eastern boundary of the Republic of the Congo, the remainder of which is provided by the Oubangui river from just south of the point at which the Equator bisects the country. The area of 342,000 sq km (132,047 sq miles) supports a population of 1,843,421 (census of 1984), an average density of only 5.4 per sq km. About one-third of the population are dependent on agriculture, mainly of the bush-fallowing type, but this is supplemented where possible by fishing, hunting and gathering. The main ethnic groups are the Vili on the coast, the Kongo centred on Brazzaville, and the Téké, M'Bochi and Sanga of the plateaux in the centre and north of the country. At the 1984 census the principal centres of urban population were the capital, Brazzaville (population 596,200) and the main port of Pointe-Noire (population 298,014).

PHYSICAL FEATURES AND RESOURCES

Substantial deposits of petroleum have been found offshore, and their exploitation by US, French and Italian companies represents a major sector of the economy. The immediate coastal zone is sandy in the north, more swampy south of Kouilou, and in the vicinity of Pointe-Indienne yields small amounts of petroleum. A narrow coastal plain does not rise above 100 m, and the cool coastal waters modify the climate, giving low rainfall and a grassland vegetation. Rising abruptly from the coastal plain are the high-rainfall forested ridges of the Mayombé range, parallel to the coast and achieving a height of 800 m, in which gorges, incised by rivers such as the Kouilou, provide potential hydroelectric power sites. At Hollé, near the Congo-Océan railway and at the western foot of the range, there are considerable phosphate deposits. Mayombé also provides an important export commodity, timber, of which the main commercial species are okoumé, limba and sapele.

Eastwards the Niari valley has lower elevation, soils that are good by tropical African standards and a grassland vegetation which makes agricultural development easier. A variety of agricultural products such as groundnuts, maize, vegetables, palm oil, coffee, cocoa, sugar and tobacco, is obtained from large plantations, smaller commercial farms and also peasant holdings. These products provide the support for a more concentrated rural population and the basis for some industrial development.

A further forested mountainous region, the Chaillu massif, is the Zaire basin's western watershed, and this gives way north-eastwards to a series of drier plateaux, the Batéké region and, east of the Likoula river, a zone of Zaire riverine land. Here are numerous watercourses, with seasonal inundation, and dense forest vegetation, which supports some production of forest products, although the full potential has yet to be realized. The rivers Zaire and Oubangui, with tributaries, provide more than 6,500 km of navigable waterway, which are particularly important, owing to the lack of good roads.

Recent History

PIERRE ENGLEBERT

The Republic of the Congo became autonomous within the French Community in November 1958, with Abbé Fulbert Youlou as prime minister. Full independence followed on 15 August 1960; in March 1961 Youlou was elected president, and a new constitution was adopted, giving the president extensive executive powers. Youlou's domestic policies exacerbated ethnic tensions, and his attempt, in August 1963, to curtail trade union activity resulted in a general strike and the declaration of a state of emergency. In mid-August Youlou resigned, and a provisional government was formed under the premiership of Alphonse Massamba-Débat. In December a new constitution was approved by referendum, and Massamba-Débat was elected president. In 1964 the Mouvement national de la révolution (MNR) was established, on Marxist-Leninist principles, as the sole political party. In the following years, tension developed between the MNR and the army. This period saw the emergence of the paratroop commander, Capt. Marien Ngouabi, as the dominant figure in Congolese politics. In August 1968, following a series of confrontations between Massamba-Débat and the MNR, Ngouabi took power in a military coup. In January 1969 he became president. In December a new Marxist-Leninist party, the Parti congolais du travail (PCT), replaced the MNR, and in the following month the country was renamed the People's Republic of the Congo.

Abortive attempts to overthrow the government took place in February and May 1972 and in February 1973. The adoption of a new constitution in June was followed by elections to a new national assembly and the formation of a new government in August, with Henri Lopes as prime minister. Ethnic tensions, added to disagreements over political ideology and power struggles within the political élite, contributed to a continuing atmosphere of political instability. In December 1975 Ngouabi dismissed both the PCT's political bureau and the government, and appointed Maj. (later Gen.) Louis-Sylvain Goma, formerly the chief of staff of the armed forces, as prime minister. After several failed attempts on his life, Ngouabi was assassinated in March 1977 during an attempted coup by supporters of Massamba-Débat, who was arrested, tried and executed. In April Col (later Brig.-Gen.) Jacques-Joachim Yhombi-Opango, a former chief of staff of the armed forces, was appointed head of state. Yhombi-Opango improved relations with the USA and France, but his regime inherited severe economic problems and came into conflict with the left wing of the PCT. In February 1979, faced with a collapse in support, Yhombi-Opango surrendered his powers to a provisional committee appointed by the PCT. In the following month the president of the committee, Col (later Gen.) Denis Sassou-Nguesso, was appointed president of the republic and chairman of the PCT's central committee. A new council of ministers, led by Goma, was announced in April.

THE SASSOU-NGUESSO REGIME

In July 1979 elections were held for a national people's assembly and for regional councils, and a socialist constitution was overwhelmingly approved in a referendum. A month later, President Sassou-Nguesso agreed to release a number of political prisoners, including those implicated in the assassination of Ngouabi. The president also announced that Congolese living abroad who were opposed to the regime could return to their country without fear of repression. Later he rehabilitated some of those implicated in the coup plot of February 1973.

The revolutionary rhetoric of the Sassou-Nguesso regime was belied by an increasingly pro-Western foreign policy, a correspondingly liberal economic policy, and a relative marginalization of some left-wing factions within the PCT. At the PCT congress in July 1984 Sassou-Nguesso was re-elected chairman of the PCT central committee and president of the republic for a further five-year term. The congress also adopted a constitutional amendment, by which the head of state assumed additional powers as the head of the government. The new politburo and central committee, and the government (which was reshuffled shortly afterwards), revealed a consolidation of the pro-Western faction and of Sassou-Nguesso's personal supporters. However, the main branch of the radical wing of the PCT, M-22, retained its influence, both within the party and the government. Sassou-Nguesso further consolidated his position by assuming the post of minister of defence and of security. Legislative elections were held in September. In November Yhombi-Opango, who had been imprisoned since March 1979, was placed under house arrest.

Persistent ethnic rivalries, together with dissillusionment with the government's response to the country's worsening economic situation, resulted in an increase in opposition to the Sassou-Nguesso regime during the late 1980s. During July 1987 20 army officers were arrested on suspicion of undermining state security. They were mostly members of the northern Kouyou ethnic group (prominent members of which have included Ngouabi and Yhombi-Opango: Sassou-Nguesso is from a different northern group, the Mboshi). A commission of enquiry, established by the government, identified the affair as a coup attempt. Although the plot had apparently been instigated by a right-wing army group, it seemed to have some links with M-22. The findings of the enquiry also implicated Yhombi-Opango and his former colleague, Pierre Anga, both of whom were under house arrest in their native village of Owando, about 400 km to the north of Brazzaville. Yhombi-Opango agreed to appear before the commission of enquiry, but Anga responded to the demand by inciting an armed uprising in Owando during which, in late August and early September, up to 60 people were reported to have been killed. Under the terms of the Franco-Congolese military co-operation treaty, a French aircraft was dispatched from Gabon to transport troops to Owando; Anga, however, evaded arrest, and remained at large until July 1988, when he was killed by Congolese security forces.

In August 1988 an amnesty was announced for political prisoners sentenced before July 1987. However, the continued detention of two political prisoners who were members of southern ethnic groups was widely perceived as an indication of the persistence of the country's ethnic divisions.

At the PCT congress in July 1989 Sassou-Nguesso was re-elected chairman of the PCT and president of the republic for a further five-year term. In August Alphonse Mouissou Poaty-Souchalaty (who had, in the previous month, been elected to the politburo of the ruling party) was appointed prime minister, and a new government was announced. At legislative elections, held in September, the single list of 133 candidates was approved by 99.19% of those who used their vote. For the first time the list included candidates who were not members of the PCT: 66 seats were allocated to youth, women's, religious and professional organizations, while eight nominations were reserved for independent candidates. In November Sassou-Nguesso announced a series of extensive reforms, whose aim would be to achieve a liberalization of the economy: state intervention was to be reduced, while private enterprise was to be fostered. In the following month it was reported that more than 40 prisoners, who had been detained without charge since July 1987, had been released.

POLITICAL TRANSITION

In February 1990 a committee was appointed to examine the possible repercussions for the Congo of the political changes taking place in Eastern Europe. In early July the PCT announced that an extraordinary congress would be held in 1991 to introduce a multi-party system and that the PCT's role in mass and social organizations would be reduced.

In mid-August 1990, on the occasion of the 30th anniversary of the country's independence, Sassou-Nguesso announced the release of several political prisoners, including the former head of state, Yhombi-Opango. In early September a reorganization of some minor government posts was carried out. During that month the Confederation of Congolese Trade Unions (CSC) was refused permission by the government to disaffiliate itself from the PCT. The CSC had also demanded an immediate transition to a multi-party political system and increased salaries for workers in the public sector. However, in response to a general strike, called in protest by the CSC, the government agreed to permit free elections to the leadership of the trade union organization, and in late September the central committee of the PCT resolved to permit the immediate registration of new political parties, and the assumption of power in early 1991 by a transitional government, in preparation for the convocation of a national conference on the country's constitutional future.

In December 1990 Alphonse Poaty-Souchalaty resigned as prime minister over a 'conflict of views' within the party on finding a solution to the national crisis. In the same month the PCT's extraordinary congress (originally scheduled for 1991) abandoned Marxism-Leninism and legalized the formation of a multi-party system (effective from January 1991). A new central committee and politburo were also elected. Ambroise Noumazalay was elected secretary-general and Sassou-Nguesso re-elected chairman of the central committee.

From early January 1991 the army was instructed to dissociate itself from the PCT, and to remain neutral in its support of democracy. In early January Gen. Goma was appointed prime minister, and shortly afterwards an interim government was installed.

The national conference, convened in February 1991, was immediately adjourned until mid-March, owing to a dispute over the number and representations of attendant organizations. In a settlement to the dispute opposition movements were allocated seven of 11 seats on the conference's governing body and were represented by 700 of the 1,100 delegates; the Roman Catholic bishop of Owando, Ernest N'Kombo, was elected chairman. The conference voted itself a sovereign body whose decisions were to be binding and not subject to government approval. In April the conference announced that the constitution was to be abrogated and the national people's assembly and other national and regional institutions were to be dissolved. In June a 153-member legislative higher council of the republic was established under N'Kombo's chairmanship, in order to supervise the implementation of these measures, pending the adoption of a new constitution and the holding of elections. In the same month the prime minister replaced the president as head of the government, and the country reverted to the name Republic of the Congo. André Milongo, a former World Bank official without formal political affiliation, succeeded Gen. Goma as prime minister. Independent trade unions were also legalized.

In December the higher council of the republic adopted a draft constitution, which provided for legislative power to be vested in an elected national assembly and senate and for executive power to be held by an elected president. A reshuffle of cabinet posts was announced at the end of December.

In mid-January 1992, following a reorganization of senior army posts by the prime minister, members of the army, who were allegedly supporters of Sassou-Nguesso, occupied strategic positions in Brazzaville and demanded the reinstatement of military personnel who had allegedly been dismissed because of their ethnic affiliations, the removal of the newly appointed secretary of state for defence and payment of overdue salaries. The government rejected these demands, whereupon the mutinous soldiers demanded Milongo's resignation as prime minister. Armed clashes in Brazzaville at that time between government supporters and mutinous troops resulted in at least five civilian deaths. The crisis was resolved when the secretary of state for defence resigned, and Milongo agreed to reorganize the council of ministers, appointing a candidate preferred by the army as minister of defence and dismissing all the remaining secretaries of state. Milongo appointed himself supreme chief of the armed forces.

Electoral Discord

The draft constitution was approved by 96.3% of those who voted at a referendum in mid-March 1992. Municipal elections took place in early May, amid accusations against the government of electoral irregularities. The Union panafricaine pour la démocratie sociale (UPADS) and the Mouvement congolais pour la démocratie et le développement intégral (MCDDI) won most seats, while the PCT did not achieve wide support. In late May Milongo appointed a new cabinet, whose membership was drawn from each of the country's regions, in order to avoid accusations of domination by any one ethnic group. Elections to the future national assembly took place on 24 June and 19 July. The UPADS became the majority party, winning 39 of the 125 contested seats, followed by the MCDDI (29 seats) and the PCT (18 seats). At elections to the senate, held on 26 July, the UPADS again won a majority (23) of the contested seats (60), followed by the MCDDI, with 13 seats. In August, Pascal Lissouba, the leader of the (UPADS) and a former prime minister, won 36% and 61% of the votes respectively at two rounds of presidential elections, defeating Bernard Kolelas, the leader of the MCDDI, and President Sassou-Nguesso. Lissouba, whose election campaign had promised the devolution of power from Brazzaville to the regions and the continued implementation of economic reforms, was inaugurated as president at the end of August. At the beginning of September he appointed Maurice-Stéphane Bongho-Nouarra (a member of the UPADS) as prime minister, with a mandate to form a coalition government based on a UPADS–PCT parliamentary alliance. However, shortly after a new cabinet had been named, the PCT terminated the pact, on the grounds that Lissouba had not given it as many ministerial posts as he had promised. The PCT then formed an alliance with the Union pour le renouveau démocratique (URD), a new grouping of seven parties, including the MCDDI. The URD–PCT alliance, which now had a majority of seats in parliament, demanded the right to form a new administration and, at the end of October, won a vote of no confidence in the government. In mid-November Bongho-Nouarra announced the resignation of his government. Soon afterwards President Lissouba, in defiance of demands by the URD–PCT, dissolved the national assembly and announced that new legislative elections would be held in 1993. In response, the URD–PCT coalition commenced a protest campaign of civil disobedience. In early December the chief of staff of the armed forces intervened and, with the barely veiled threat of a military take-over in the background, demanded that the two sides form a transitional government, pending the holding of legislative elections. Claude Antoine Dacosta, a former FAO and World Bank official, was appointed prime minister of the new transitional administration. In March 1993 it was announced that the fresh parliamentary elections would be held in May and June.

At the first round of legislative elections, which took place in early May 1993, the 'Presidential Group', comprising the UPADS and its allies, won 62 of the 125 seats in the National Assembly, while the URD–PCT coalition secured 49. Protesting that serious electoral irregularities had occurred, the URD–PCT refused to contest the second round of elections in early June (for seats where a clear majority had not been achieved in the first round) and demanded that some of the first-round polls should be repeated. At the second round the 'Presidential Group' secured an absolute majority (69) of seats in the national assembly. In late June Lissouba appointed a new cabinet, with ex-president Yhombi-Opango as prime minister. During June Bernard Kolelas, the leader of the MCDDI and of the URD–PCT coalition, nominated a rival cabinet and urged his supporters to force the government to call new elections by means of a campaign of civil disobedience. However, the political crisis soon precipitated violent conflict between armed militias (representing opposition and ethnic interests) and the security forces, resulting in at least 30 deaths during June and July. At the end of June the supreme court ruled that electoral irregularities had occurred at the first round of elections. In mid-July Lissouba declared a state of emergency. In late July the government and the opposition negotiated a truce, and in early August, following mediation by the OAU, France and President Bongo of Gabon, the two sides agreed that the disputed first-round election results should be examined by a committee of impartial international arbitrators and that the second round of elections should be restaged (the second round that had been held in June was consequently annulled by the supreme court). The state of emergency was revoked in mid-August.

Following the repeated second round of legislative elections, which took place at the beginning of October 1993, the 'Presidential Group', which had secured 65 seats, retained its overall majority in the national assembly. (Therefore the cabinet that had been appointed in June, with Yhombi-Opango as prime minister, remained unchanged.) The URD–PCT, which had amassed 57 seats, agreed to participate in the new assembly. In November, however, confrontations between opposition militias and the security forces erupted once again, resulting in serious social and economic disruption and more than 100 fatalities. A cease-fire was eventually agreed by the 'Presidential Group' and the opposition at the end of January 1994. In the following month the committee of international arbitrators, which had been investigating the conduct of the first round of legislative elections held in May 1993, ruled that the results in eight constituencies were unlawful.

In late February 1994 the government and the opposition jointly agreed to the deployment of a buffer force to help maintain order in the southern suburbs of Brazzaville, and by the following month the clashes had abated sufficiently for Lissouba to leave on a brief official visit to France. During April, however, scattered clashes were reported between the armed forces and supporters of Sassou-Nguesso. Contacts between the 'Presidential Group' and the opposition were maintained during the months following the January cease-fire. Kolelas, who was elected mayor of Brazzaville in July, appeared at a public rally in the following month with senior representatives of the presidency, during which tribute was paid to those on both sides who had died in the 1993 disorders.

FOREIGN RELATIONS

After the mid-1970s the Congo moved away from the sphere of influence of the former USSR, fostering links with neighbouring francophone countries, and also with France, the USA and the People's Republic of China. France is the source of more than one-half of total assistance to the Congo, and is the major supplier of imports and business partner in the extraction of petroleum. Nevertheless, Cuban troops were stationed in the Congo from 1977 until April 1991. In 1988 the Congo mediated in negotiations between Angola, Cuba, South Africa and the USA, which resulted in the signing, in December, of the Brazzaville accord, regarding the withdrawal of Cuban troops from Angola and progress towards

Namibian independence. In April 1989 relations between the Congo and Zaire became strained, following reciprocal expulsions from those countries of Congolese and Zairean nationals, who were alleged to be illegal residents. Further expulsions of Zairean nationals from the Congo took place during 1991. Diplomatic relations with the Republic of Korea (severed in 1964) were restored in June 1990, and relations with Israel (severed in 1973) were resumed in August 1991.

The Congo established diplomatic relations with South Africa in March 1993.

Economy

EDITH HODGKINSON

Revised for this Edition by the Editor

For several years after independence in 1960 a systematic policy of state participation in productive enterprise was pursued, but the private sector was permitted to continue its activities, especially in mining, forestry and transport. During the early 1970s, however, President Ngouabi introduced the policy of 'scientific socialism'. All public services and transport systems were nationalized and more government control introduced throughout the economy. Upon becoming head of state in 1977, Joachim Yhombi-Opango emphasized that the Congo needed a 'mixed' economy and would benefit from the expertise which private investment could provide. Under his successor, Sassou-Nguesso, who ousted him two years later, the serious inefficiency of many of the nationalized companies was soon recognized, and foreign management consortia were introduced, while the petroleum sector was further opened to private foreign investment. In 1989, following a pronouncement in 1988 on the failure of the public sector to stimulate economic growth, the government of Sassou-Nguesso implemented a new policy of economic liberalization. Revised taxation procedures were intended to foster private-sector activity (notably through the even application of value added tax). In addition, retrenchment in the civil service was planned. In January 1994 the government and the IMF agreed on a programme of economic retrenchment. Among the more important measures was government's undertaking to privatize the major public-sector industries; these reforms, which were reported to be under way in June, included rail, air and water transport, electricity, the petroleum industry and postal services. More immediately, the government dismissed over 8,000 civil employees and undertook to abolish a further 1,000 civil service jobs by the end of the year.

Partly as a result of Brazzaville's former position as the capital of French Equatorial Africa, and partly because the Congo and Oubangui rivers have long provided the main access to the Central African Republic (CAR) and Chad, the Congo's economic structure has evolved rather differently from that of most countries of comparable levels of economic development; transport, services and administration in particular have been disproportionately important. These sectors accounted for nearly one-third of gross domestic product (GDP) in 1989, and more than one-half of the population reside in urban areas, with almost one-third in Brazzaville. The next most significant sector is mining (mainly petroleum, which is the country's principal export commodity): the sector, which was of negligible importance at independence, accounted for 29% of GDP in 1989. Around one-third of the country's inhabitants are dependent on agriculture and forestry. Despite the development of commercial agriculture, this sector contributed only 13% to GDP in 1992. Manufacturing developed relatively well at an early stage, partly to serve the markets of the CAR and Chad. In recent years, however, its performance has been very disappointing, to which inefficient management in the public sector, increased competition for industry among the member countries of the Union douanière et économique de l'Afrique centrale (UDEAC), and ill-advised investments all contributed. The manufacturing sector accounted for only 8% of GDP in 1991.

Economic growth has fluctuated widely in the recent past. The mid- and late 1970s saw overall stagnation, and regression in some sectors, as output of petroleum declined and production of potash ceased altogether. However, improved output of petroleum, from 1979 onwards, coincided with increases in international prices for that commodity, thus stimulating very high rates of investment by both the public sector and the petroleum companies. Consequently, GDP expanded by 21.3% in 1981 and by 18.9% in the following year. However, economic growth fell sharply, to only 3.4% in 1983 and 7% in 1984, as petroleum prices declined and public investment was severely curtailed (see below). GDP declined by 6.8% in 1986, owing to budgetary retrenchment (in accordance with the IMF-sponsored programme for economic stabilization), in conjunction with the decline in petroleum production and the collapse, in that year, of international prices for petroleum. Limited GDP growth occurred in 1987 (0.7%) and 1988 (0.2%), rising to 3.7% in 1989 and to 2.2% in 1990, mainly as a result of increased petroleum output and improved international prices for that commodity. The annual rate of inflation averaged −0.3% in 1985-92; in 1992 consumer prices increased by an annual average of 2.9%.

The 50% devaluation of the Congo's currency, the CFA franc, in January 1994, will substantially influence the country's economic prospects. On the one hand, export competitiveness, particularly for primary products, should be significantly enhanced, while the substantial rise in import costs should stimulate domestic import-substitution, particularly in the manufacturing sector. However, the immediate reduction in purchasing power inherent in the devaluation will impose economic hardship on vulnerable sections of the population and could necessitate temporary price subsidies on staple foods and the creation of labour-intensive public works programmes at a time when the government is faced with the implementation of IMF economic structures. Foreign financial support will thus be essential in the short term, both in new funds and debt relief.

AGRICULTURE AND FORESTRY

Since the early 1970s the agricultural sector has suffered from relative neglect, hasty nationalizations and the abandonment of farmwork in favour of salaried employment in the towns. Cash crops are much less important as exports than minerals or timber, and the country is far from self-sufficient in food. (Some 27% of the population cannot reliably fulfil their food requirements.) Spending on food imports almost trebled in the early 1980s, and in 1985 accounted for almost one-fifth of total expenditure on imports. With the exception of palm products, sugar and tobacco, which are grown on modern plantations (particularly in the Niari valley), most agricultural crops are grown by families on small farms. Government policy has aimed at increasing both productivity and acreage under cultivation, and to these ends it has attempted an ambitious agricultural extension programme, but progress has been limited. In 1971 'Operation Manioc' was launched, which aimed to make the country self-sufficient in cassava, its staple food crop; three farms of 3,000 ha were organized. Shortly afterwards, the Congo's first state farm (about 600 ha) was opened, and 9,000 ha eventually came under state farms, most of them poorly managed and requiring subsidy. By 1987 several of these farms were being sold to the private sector, and the state agencies' monopoly on the marketing of agricultural products was abolished. In 1992 output of cassava reached an estimated 790,000 metric tons and that of maize totalled an estimated 26,000 tons. Secondary food crops are plantains, yams and sweet potatoes. According to the FAO, total food crop production in 1991 was 28% higher than the average level in 1979–81; however, food crop production per head decreased by more than 8% during the same period.

Export crops contribute very little to foreign earnings. In the past the most important cash crops have been sugar cane and tobacco, with exports going almost wholly to other UDEAC countries. In 1978 output of refined sugar was only 5,700 tons, and imports were necessary. In that year the sugar industry was put under the control of a newly-formed state corporation, the Sucrerie du Congo (SUCO). The restructuring of management led to a sharp recovery in production, which was some 33,000 tons in 1990. In 1989 the Congo had quotas for the export of refined sugar at guaranteed prices to the EC and the USA of 10,000 tons and 16,070 tons respectively. In February 1991 it was announced that SUCO was to be transferred to the private sector.

Other export crops include cocoa, coffee, groundnuts and the oil palm. The quality of Congolese cocoa has recently been improved. Output declined from an estimated 2,305 tons in 1987/88 to 1,611 tons in 1988/89, and it declined further, to 957 tons in 1989/90. Coffee production averaged some 2,300 tons in most years in the 1980s, but fell to 1,931 tons in 1988/89, and to 1,030 tons in 1989/90. Output appeared to recover in 1990/91, with 1,028 tons recorded in the first nine months of the season. Groundnut production for the commercial market has fallen since 1969 to around 1,800 tons per year, but palm groves are being extended in an attempt to improve the production rate of palm oil. This saw a severe decline, from 2,460 tons (refined) in 1982 to only 1,093 tons in 1984. A programme to plant a total of 10,000 ha of palm groves near Ouesso was undertaken in 1982–85. In 1991 output of palm oil was estimated at 17,000 tons.

Animal husbandry has developed slowly, owing to the prevalence of the tsetse fly and the importance of the forestry sector: although numbers of livestock are increasing, the country is not self-sufficient in meat and dairy products. Grants from the European Development Fund and the World Food Programme have enabled stock-rearing farms to be established. Fishing is not well developed but is carried out commercially on a small scale, especially for tuna. The total fish catch was about 45,600 tons in 1991.

Forestry

Forests cover more than 60% of the country's total area and are a significant natural resource. Forestry is a major economic activity and timber was the Congo's main export until 1973. Exploitation began at the coast and penetrated inland following the line of the Congo-Océan railway. There is further activity in the Congo basin from where rough timber is floated out. The purchase and sale of logs was, until 1987, a monopoly of the state-owned Office Congolaise des Bois, but 95% of production was carried out by the private sector, with foreign companies accounting for 58% of the total in 1984. The exploitation by foreign investors of forest resources in the north of the country is being encouraged, while the more accessible but heavily depleted southern forests have been reserved for local interests. It is hoped that the ending of the state monopoly over the marketing of timber, the inauguration of new concessions in the north and improvements in the transport infrastructure will eventually stimulate further increases in both production and exports of timber. The principal woods exploited are okoumé, limba and sapele. Since 1979 some 25,000 ha have been planted with eucalyptus, and planting is to continue on a further 35,000 ha.

Output of timber was 399,982 cu m in 1989, and, owing to the disposal of stocks, 407,482 cu m were exported in that year. Production fell to 348,000 cu m in 1990, while exports totalled 349,000 cu m, as further stocks were sold. In 1991 output and exports declined further, to 223,600 cu m and 222,900 cu m respectively. Government regulations require that at least 60% of log output be processed: the major products are sawn timber (approximately one-half for export), veneer (primarily for export) and plywood (mainly for the local market). Production of these items averaged 130,000 cu m per year in the late 1980s. It is believed that pressure from environmentalists may adversely affect the international market for tropical timber. In 1991 the World Bank announced that strict environmental assessments were to be carried out before funding would be granted for forestry-related projects. In 1993 the World Bank's Global Environment Facility was providing assistance to the Congo for the Conservation of its virgin forests. The United Nations Food and Agriculture Organization provided the Congo with a grant of 36m. francs CFA in 1994 to aid in the further privatization of forestry enterprises.

MINING AND POWER

Until the 1970s mining was of little significance in the Congo, and in 1969 mineral exports accounted for less than 5% of total exports. By 1984, however, mineral sales provided 90% of export earnings and mining accounted for 43% of GDP, reflecting the development of the petroleum sector.

Production of petroleum has fluctuated since onshore deposits were discovered, at Pointe-Indienne, in 1957. In 1971, when these deposits were almost exhausted, new offshore oilfields were discovered. The Emeraude field went into production in 1972: output reached 2.5m. tons in 1974, but declined subsequently. Reserves of 600m. tons of heavy viscous petroleum in the Emeraude field, which would require expensive steam-injection procedures for recovery, have remained unexploited. Production at the Loango field was delayed until 1977. The latter field is being worked by AGIP Recherches Congo and Elf Congo, and its maximum production of 2m. tons annually was reached in 1982. It now produces 800,000 tons per year. Another field, Likouala, which is estimated to have reserves of 40m. tons, began production in 1980, and two further offshore fields, Sendji Marine and Yanga, came on stream in 1981 and 1982. Output of crude petroleum, which had eased since 1975, consequently rose sharply from 1978 onwards, reaching 6.32m. tons in 1987, with the Sendji and Yanga fields accounting for about one-half of the total. At the end of that year operations began at the Tchibouela field, which has an estimated 12m. tons of recoverable reserves, and which was expected to yield about 2m. tons per year by 1990. In late 1988 production began at the Zatchi Marine field, output from which reached 360,000 tons in 1992. Total production was 7.04m. tons in 1988, rising to 7.96m. tons in 1989, 8.03m. tons in 1990 and 8.2m. tons in 1992. In 1993 production declined slightly to 8.06m. tons. With major exploration and development planned at off-shore deposits including Elf-Congo's Nkossa field and at the Kitina deposit where Agip-Research have a concession, in 1994 the Congo's annual output of petroleum was expected to reach some 15m. tons by 1996/97. In 1990 the monopoly of the state-owned Société nationale de recherches et d'exploitation pétrolière (HYDRO-CONGO) over the distribution of petroleum products in the Congo was ended. The international conflict which followed the invasion and annexation of Kuwait by Iraq in August 1990 benefited the Congo's petroleum industry by boosting international petroleum prices and by encouraging exploration by oil companies in petroleum-producing areas outside the Middle East. In late 1990 Elf Congo drilled its first onshore exploration well for seven years.

The petroleum refinery at Pointe-Noire initially opened in 1976. Technical problems then enforced a six-year closure. The refinery was rebuilt by a French firm and, under its new name CORAF, came into operation in 1982. The refinery produces for the domestic and export (fuel oil) markets, but has produced at substantially below its capacity of 1m. tons per year, with output reaching 580,000 tons in 1987, and the IMF and the World Bank have put pressure on the government to dispose of its majority holding in the company.

Deposits of natural gas are exploited at Pointe-Indienne. Production reached 15m. cu m in 1977, but fell to 500,000 cu m by 1980, as the deposits neared exhaustion. New gas reserves were discovered off Pointe-Noire in 1981. Gaz-Congo, in which Elf and AGIP each hold a one-third share, was formed to exploit the reserves, and the government hoped that a plant producing liquefied natural gas, operated by Elf, would be established. However, no progress was achieved in this proposal, and almost all production, currently some 760m. cu m annually, is flared. Feasibility studies for a gas condensation and ammonia plant at Pointe-Noire finally began in late 1990.

The hydrocarbons sector is the only significant mining activity. In the late 1950s rich deposits of potassium chloride were discovered at Hollé, near Pointe-Noire. Facilities were built to mine, refine and transport the potassium to the Atlantic coast, and a pier to accommodate large bulk-carrying ships was constructed near Pointe-Noire. However, the project was beset with technical and marketing difficulties, and production consistently fell well below the planned 800,000 tons capacity. The potassium mines have been closed since serious flooding took place in 1977, but a joint-venture company, the Société des Potasses du Congo (SPC), has been formed to prospect for potash deposits along the coast.

Lead, zinc, gold and copper are produced in small quantities, and deposits of high-grade iron ore, phosphate and bauxite are known. Bulgaria has provided assistance to develop the phosphate deposits (estimated at 4.5m. tons). In 1985 the Congo and Gabon signed an agreement for joint exploitation of the High Ivingo iron ore deposits (estimated at some 1,000m. tons), but this project will require substantial external funds, together with an improvement in the international market for that commodity, for its implementation.

Production and distribution of electricity have been in the hands of a state-owned corporation since 1967. Total generating capacity was 149 MW in 1990, mainly from the hydroelectric stations on the Bouenza (74 MW) and Djoué (15 MW). The former was built with Chinese aid and entered production in 1980. Work has begun on a second major hydroelectric plant, also with Chinese assistance, on the Lefini river at Imboulou, with capacity planned at 100 MW.

MANUFACTURING

The contribution of manufacturing to GDP has declined as the petroleum sector has expanded. Production is concerned mainly with the processing of agricultural and forest products and most of the industry is in Brazzaville, Pointe-Noire and N'Kayi. Many of the larger manufacturing companies are state-owned. However, several have been transferred to private ownership, in accordance with the country's obligations to the IMF.

The industrial development of the 1970s and 1980s had little success. A cement plant was established at Loutété in 1968, reached its peak output in 1971, but subsequently showed a sharp fall in production, despite strong demand from construction programmes. The plant closed in 1985, reopened, and then ceased production again in 1987, because of cash-flow problems. In 1988 the company's assets were transferred to a new, partly Norwegian-owned, concern. An associated project, costing US $8.1m., involved the construction of cement silos at Pointe-Noire, which were opened in 1985 to store both imported and domestically-produced cement. The textile industry is represented by two operations, a textile complex at Kinsoundi, which was established in 1968, and a textile printing works, using both local and imported cloth, which was inaugurated in Brazzaville in 1975. A long-standing project for the construction of a plant to produce paper pulp, with an annual production capacity of 290,000 tons, was abandoned because of a lack of foreign finance, and the newly-developed eucalyptus plantations are being used instead to supply a telegraph-pole factory, production at which commenced in 1988. In 1989 it was announced that a vegetable oil refinery was to be constructed at Brazzaville, largely financed by multilateral development agencies, with the aim of reducing the Congo's dependence on imported vegetable oils. Plans are being considered for the construction of a gas-fed urea and chemicals plant.

TRANSPORT

The Congo plays an important role in the trans-equatorial transport system (formerly operated on an inter-state basis) which links Chad, the CAR and parts of Cameroon and Gabon with the Atlantic coast; all of the rail and much of the river portion of the system is located in the Congo. In 1986 the port of Pointe-Noire handled 9.5m. tons of freight, including 5.4m. tons of petroleum, some 552,100 tons of timber (most of this extracted in the CAR and floated downstream to the smaller port of Brazzaville, from which it is transported by rail to Pointe-Noire), and about 2.46m. tons of manganese ore from Gabon. Thus 60–70% of the traffic on the Congo-Océan railway is of an international nature. The manganese ore from Gabon reaches the line via a 286-km spur from Louboumo to the Gabon border. The saturation of the existing railway capacity and the constraint that this represented on the further development of timber exports prompted a major scheme to increase capacity by two-fifths. Work started on realignment in 1976, was finally completed in 1985, having cost 150,000m. francs CFA. With the acquisition of new rolling stock, the railway increased its freight handling to 1.4m. tons (excluding manganese) in 1986, compared with 1.15m. tons in 1984. However, the railway will, ultimately, lose about one-half of the manganese transit traffic from Gabon, following the opening of the Transgabonais railway line in late 1986, and the inauguration of minerals-handling facilities at the port of Owendo, in that country, in 1988. It was hoped that Gabon would maintain manganese traffic at a level of 2m. tons annually, while the Congolese government sought finance for a project to increase timber traffic on the spur to Gabon by planting commercial timber along the line. However, culpability for a serious rail crash on the line in 1991 was disputed by the two countries, leading Gabon to route all manganese exports through Owendo. At the end of 1993 the Brazzaville-Pointe Noire railway link was forced to close following clashes between presidential supporters and opposition groups in Brazzaville. The closure, which lasted until early 1994, led to fuel rationing in the capital and increased prices on many consumer commodities. In 1994 Germany provided eight locomotives and promised a further six at a later date, bringing the total number of locomotives to 44. The Congo-Ocean Railways (CFCO) was one of a number of companies, including the airline company Lina Congo, scheduled for privatization in 1994.

Other transport facilities, and especially the road network, are little developed, owing to the great distances and dense equatorial forest. Large areas in the north of the country have no road access. Only about 835 km of the total 12,000 km of roads and tracks are asphalted. During the 1980s a project was initiated to construct a long-distance all-weather road from Ouesso, in the north, to Port Rousset and Brazzaville, crossed by another road between Belinga, in Gabon, and Bangui, in the CAR. In 1988 the World Bank provided $35m. to support a road rehabilitation programme. Pressure from environmental groups may deter donors from financing any future road improvement projects in the north of the country. In general, poor communications continue to constitute a major obstacle to economic development. There are international airports at Brazzaville and Pointe-Noire, as well as airports at six regional capitals and 37 smaller airfields.

DEVELOPMENT PLANNING

The Congo's first Development Plan covered the period 1964–70. Further Plans covered the periods 1970–74 and 1975–79. A new five-year Development Plan for 1982–86 aimed to reduce the economy's dependence on oil exports by using petroleum income to develop infrastructure, increase agricultural production, rehabilitate the state industrial sector and make social investments in health and education. Infrastructural investments alone were allocated 48% of planned expenditures. However, the fall in world prices for petroleum, after the Plan was prepared, meant that expenditures had to be reduced in 1983, 1984 and 1985. While the core of the programme (i.e. the main infrastructural projects) was retained, some projects were postponed, and agricultural development was adversely affected. Spending in the 1982–86 Plan was limited to 830,000m. francs CFA, and, as part of the structural adjustment plan designed to restore balance to public finances, the launch of the next five-year plan was postponed, while an 'interim investment programme' (envisaging reduced levels of expenditure) was formulated for 1987 and 1988. Only in 1989 was the government able to draw up a further medium-term development plan (the Economic and Social Action Plan—PAES), covering the period 1990–94. The plan emphasized the reduction of the economy's dependence on petroleum and the public sector, by stimulating primary production (farming, forestry and fishing) and the reform of the parastatal organizations. In late 1990 the government signed a structural adjustment programme with the IMF, for which it received $40m. in funding. However, political unrest during the early 1990s has severely disrupted all sectors of the economy, particularly with respect to liberalization and austerity measures.

Implementation of economic measures agreed in a letter of intent with the IMF began in 1994 and was supported by a stand-by credit of $33m. The programme aimed to arrest the decline in non-oil real GDP, while overall real GDP was estimated to decline by approximately 2.5% because of a projected fall in petroleum output. Two further goals were to limit the inflationary surge to approximately 40% for the year, which was expected following the currency devaluation, and to contain the current account deficit at approximately 28% of GDP.

The rise in petroleum taxes and royalties from 1978 onwards (at some 110,000m. francs CFA, they constituted 70% of budget revenue in 1981) stimulated a sharp rise in budget development spending at the beginning of the 1980s. This increased seventeenfold between 1979–83. While current spending continued to rise in both 1984 and 1985 (with debt-service costs in the latter year comprising nearly one-half of the total), the capital budget was restrained. With petroleum revenues down, the overall deficit nearly doubled in 1986, to 141,200m. francs CFA. Both current and capital spending were decreased substantially in that year. The reduction in current spending was to be achieved by means of a wide range of measures, including a 'freeze' on government salaries (the payroll had been increasing steadily during the early 1980s) and the rationalization (including sale to private interests) of several state-owned companies, whose losses had depleted budget resources. The deficit was reduced, but remained high (at 86,100m. francs CFA). In 1987, therefore, there were further substantial reductions in current and capital spending, with the latter totalling less than one-half of its level in 1984. However, the deficit continued to rise in both 1987 and 1988, to reach 98,400m. francs CFA in the latter year, owing to the contraction in the economy and in spite of further reductions in capital spending. Provisional figures for 1989 showed an impressive fall in the budgetary deficit, to 43,000m. francs CFA, equivalent to 5.6% of GDP. This resulted from a twofold increase in petroleum revenues. Although petroleum revenues increased by a further 50% in 1990, the deficit soared to 188,100m. francs CFA (representing a record 23.5% of GDP), owing to the repayment of a substantial amount of debt arrears. Under the stabilization programme agreed with the IMF, the government was to reduce the public-sector deficit by 1992, by imposing further restrictions on both current and capital spending, and by selling its interests in all but seven parastatal bodies (classified as strategic) and closing those for which there were no buyers. In 1992, however, the government's fiscal receipts fell to 59,900m. francs CFA, from 64,500m. in 1991 and the budget deficit was estimated to be equal to 20% of GDP in that year. None the less, although the government remains far from attaining its fiscal targets, it has taken major steps towards the reform of the state-owned corporate sector, with 76 companies due to be sold to private interests, closed down or restructured. If the country's official creditors were to agree to substantial debt relief (either in the form of a cancellation or of a reduction in interest rates), pressure on the current budget would be greatly eased: the figures for 1989 demonstrate that this would have an impact far outweighing that of government budgetary restraint. France has provided $100m. in supplementary budgetary assistance for 1992. In 1994 France granted the Congo 10m. French francs to help offset the effects of the CFA franc devaluation and would help to fund health, educational and food projects.

FOREIGN TRADE AND PAYMENTS

Whereas the Congo's foreign trade was in chronic deficit during the 1960s and 1970s, the expansion of the petroleum sector which began in the late 1970s transformed the situation. In 1978 the Congo recorded a foreign trade deficit of 24,090m. francs CFA, and in 1979 a surplus of 46,150m. As a result of petroleum sales, export receipts increased from only 34,200m. francs CFA in 1978 to 552,600m. in 1984, to exceed import spending by 282,600m. The reduction in petroleum prices in 1986 resulted in a more than halving of export earnings, and, although imports declined as a result of budget austerity, the trade surplus narrowed to only 50,100m. francs CFA. This, in conjunction with higher interest payments on the rapidly-escalating foreign debt, prompted a sharp deterioration in the current account of the balance of payments, from a surplus of $210m. in 1984 to a deficit of $601m. in 1986. The recovery in export revenue in 1987, as petroleum prices and output rose, in conjunction with a decline in imports, resulted in an improvement in the trade surplus (to $457m.), and thus in a narrowing of the current-payments deficit, to $223m. The deficit increased in 1988, to $445.5m., as a result of a decline in the trade surplus. In 1989 the value of exports increased by 35% to $1,138m., while austerity measures restricted the value of imports to $534m.: the deficit on the current account of the balance of payments shrank to $85m. in that year. Export earnings improved further in 1990, to $1,388.7m., and import restraint continued; an increased debit on the services and other income account, however, led to a current account deficit of $250.5m. In 1991 export earnings declined to $1,136m. and the value of imports was $458m. The deficit on the current account fell to $168.7m. At the end of 1991 international reserves stood at $4.8m., sufficient to cover only four days of merchandise imports. In 1992 there was a visible trade surplus of $649.8m. and the deficit on the current account increased to $307.9m.

In recent years the Congo has received considerable amounts of foreign aid. In 1986–89 official development assistance from the non-communist countries and multilateral agencies averaged $115m. per year. France reduced its disbursements in 1987–89, but provided an exceptional disbursement of $169m. in 1990, which raised total development assistance to a record level of $230m. Financial and technical assistance from the People's Republic of China has also been important. While borrowing from official creditors (multilateral and bilateral) expanded only slowly in the early 1980s, borrowing from private creditors rose sharply, mainly reflecting the expansion in imports, and exceeded that from official sources, to give an external debt of $3,031m. at the end of 1985. This was equivalent to 157% of the country's gross national product (GNP) in that year. The cost of servicing the debt was equivalent to one quarter of the country's foreign earnings in both 1983 and 1984, and to one-third in 1985—a very substantial burden, which necessitated a rescheduling of the debt. The country's foreign creditors, both official and commercial, insisted that the Congo first obtain a stand-by credit from the IMF. In mid-1986, after lengthy negotiations, the Congo obtained IMF approval for a structural adjustment programme, which facilitated agreement on a rescheduling, over 10 years (with three years' grace), of a total of $700m. in debt arrears for 1985 and obligations for 1986 and 1987. Further reschedulings gave relief for 1988 and 1989. However, the external debt had risen to $4,351m. by the end of 1987, or 213% of GNP, making the Congo the most heavily indebted African nation (on a per caput basis). Debt relief and additional funds were essential. In order to secure such concessions, the Congo entered negotiations for a new structural adjustment programme with the IMF and the World Bank in 1989. Although finalization was delayed by slow progress in reducing the fiscal deficit (as previously agreed), and hence by the need for additional foreign assistance, a programme of support by external donors, led by France, was operational by mid-1990. Meanwhile, as a result of a sharp fall in short-term indebtedness, from $901m. in 1987 to $597m. in 1988, the Congo's total external debt declined by 4% in 1988 to $4,158m. In 1989, despite the first ever decline in the level of outstanding public and publicly guaranteed long-term debt (no bank has sufficient confidence in the Congolese economy to lend without a public guarantee), a 29% increase in short-term debt caused the total external debt to increase by 4%. In 1989 debt service payments (as a proportion of foreign earnings) fell to the lowest level (27%) since 1984; however, this was achieved by building up arrears on long-term debt service payments, which reached $353m. in that year. The substantial repayment of arrears in 1990 reduced their level to $172m. The consequent fall in short-term indebtedness was, however, eradicated by an increase in long-term borrowing during that year, causing the Congo's total external debt to rise to $5,118m. As a result of improved economic growth, this represented the same proportion of GNP as in the previous year (203%). Earlier reschedulings produced a debt service—foreign earnings ratio of 18.2% in 1990 (excluding the arrears repayment). At the end of 1991 the total external debt stood at $4,744m. and had increased only marginally, to $4,751m. (of which total $3,878m. was long-term public debt), by the end of 1992. In August 1993 the 'Paris Club' of official creditors (to which the Congo owes almost 70% of its external debt) agreed to rescheduling arrangements under which a period of up to 20 years was to be allowed for the repayment of loans extended for development projects. The repayment term for other loans was increased to 15 years, with an eight-year grace period.

Statistical Survey

Source (unless otherwise stated): Centre National de la Statistique et des Etudes Economiques, Ministère de l'Economie de la Finance et du Plan, BP 2031, Brazzaville; tel. 83-43-24; telex 5210.

Area and Population

AREA, POPULATION AND DENSITY

Area (sq km)	342,000*
Population (census results)	
7 February 1974	1,319,790
22 December 1984	1,843,421
Density (per sq km) at December 1984	5.4

* 132,047 sq miles.

REGIONS (estimated population at 1 January 1983)*

Brazzaville	456,383	Kouilou	78,738
Pool	219,329	Lékoumou	67,568
Pointe-Noire	214,466	Sangha	42,106
Bouenza	135,999	Nkayi	40,419
Cuvette	127,558	Likouala	34,302
Niari	114,229	Loubomo	33,591
Plateaux	110,379	**Total**	1,675,067

* Figures have not been revised to take account of the 1984 census results.

PRINCIPAL TOWNS (population at 1984 census)

Brazzaville (capital)	596,200
Pointe-Noire	298,014

BIRTHS AND DEATHS (UN estimates, annual averages)

	1975–80	1980–85	1985–90
Birth rate (per 1,000)	45.8	43.9	44.4
Death rate (per 1,000)	17.4	15.8	14.8

Expectation of life (UN estimates, years at birth, 1985-90): 52.0 (males 49.4; females 54.7).
Source: UN, *World Population Prospects: The 1992 Revision*.

EMPLOYMENT
('000 persons at 1984 census)

	Males	Females	Total
Agriculture, etc.	105	186	291
Industry	61	8	69
Services	123	60	183
Total	289	254	543

Mid-1992 (FAO estimates, '000 persons): Agriculture, etc. 523; Total labour force 886 (Source: FAO, *Production Yearbook*).

Agriculture

PRINCIPAL CROPS ('000 metric tons)

	1990	1991	1992
Maize*	25	25	26
Sugar cane*	450	450	450
Sweet potatoes*	17	20	21
Cassava (Manioc)*	770	780	790
Yams*	12	12	13
Other roots and tubers*	33	33	33
Dry beans*	5	6	6
Tomatoes*	9	9	9
Other vegetables*	33	34	34
Avocados*	23	23	24
Pineapples*	12	12	12
Bananas*	38	40	42
Plantains*	75	80	85
Palm kernels*	0.5	0.5	0.5
Groundnuts (in shell)*	26	27	28
Coffee (green)	1†	1†	1*
Cocoa beans	2†	2*	2*
Tobacco leaves	2†	2†	2*
Natural rubber*	2	2	2

* FAO estimate(s). † Unofficial estimate.
Source: FAO, *Production Yearbook*.

LIVESTOCK ('000 head, year ending September)

	1990	1991*	1992*
Cattle	68	68	69
Pigs	50*	52	55
Sheep	105*	108	110
Goats	270*	272	275

* FAO estimate(s).

Poultry (FAO estimates, million): 2 in 1990; 2 in 1991; 2 in 1992.

Source: FAO, *Production Yearbook*.

LIVESTOCK PRODUCTS (FAO estimates, '000 metric tons)

	1990	1991	1992
Beef and veal	2	2	2
Pig meat	2	2	2
Poultry meat	5	5	5
Other meat	12	13	13
Cows' milk	1	1	1
Hen eggs	1.2	1.2	1.2

Source: FAO, *Production Yearbook*.

Forestry

ROUNDWOOD REMOVALS ('000 cubic metres, excluding bark)

	1989	1990	1991*
Sawlogs, veneer logs and logs for sleepers	809	833	833
Pulpwood	465	477	477
Other industrial wood*	284	293	303
Fuel wood	2,009	2,079	2,147
Total	3,567	3,682	3,760

* FAO estimates.

Source: FAO, *Yearbook of Forest Products*.

SAWNWOOD PRODUCTION ('000 cubic metres)

	1989	1990	1991
Total (incl. boxboards)	46	46*	49*

* FAO estimate.

Source: FAO, *Yearbook of Forest Products*.

Fishing

('000 metric tons, live weight)

	1989	1990	1991
Freshwater fishes	24.1	26.3	27.2
Common sole*	1.0	1.0	0.8
Sea catfishes*	0.8	0.8	0.6
Boe drum*	1.1	1.2	0.9
West African croakers*	2.6	2.8	2.2
Sardinellas	11.0*	10.5*	9.2
Other marine fishes (incl. unspecified)*	5.2	5.6	4.3
Total catch	45.8	48.2	45.6

* FAO estimate(s).

Source: FAO, *Yearbook of Fishery Statistics*.

Mining

('000 metric tons, unless otherwise indicated)

	1988	1989	1990
Crude petroleum	7,038	7,962	8,076
Copper ore*	1.0†‡	1.0†‡	—
Gold (kg)*	5	16†	16
Lead ore*†‡	1.8	1.4	1.0
Zinc ore*†‡	1.7	1.0	1.0

* Figures refer to the metal content of ores.

† Provisional or estimated figures.

‡ Data from the US Bureau of Mines.

Source: UN, *Industrial Statistics Yearbook*.

Crude petroleum ('000 metric tons): 7,596 in 1991; 9,000 in 1992 (Source: UN, *Monthly Bulletin of Statistics*).

Industry

SELECTED PRODUCTS

('000 metric tons, unless otherwise indicated)

	1988	1989	1990
Raw sugar	31	35*	33
Beer ('000 hectolitres)	744	n.a.	n.a.
Soft drinks ('000 hectolitres)	178	n.a.	n.a.
Cigarettes (metric tons)	770	1,000	1,000
Veneer sheets ('000 cu metres)	56	52	52*†
Soap	1.5	n.a.	n.a.
Jet fuels	12	12	12
Motor spirit (petrol)	51	51	51
Distillate fuel oils	107	102	103
Residual fuel oils	335	342	345
Cement	58†	58†	58
Electric energy (million kWh)	292	397	398
Footwear ('000 pairs)	296	n.a.	n.a.

* Data from the FAO.

† Provisional or estimated figures.

Source: UN, *Industrial Statistics Yearbook*.

Finance

CURRENCY AND EXCHANGE RATES

Monetary Units

100 centimes = 1 franc de la Coopération financière en Afrique centrale (CFA).

French Franc, Sterling and Dollar Equivalents (31 March 1994)

1 French franc = 100 francs CFA;
£1 sterling = 846.40 francs CFA;
US $1 = 570.14 francs CFA;
1,000 francs CFA = £1.181 = $1.754.

Average Exchange Rate (francs CFA per US $)

1991 282.11
1992 264.69
1993 283.16

Note: The exchange rate of 1 French franc = 50 francs CFA, established in 1948, remained in force until January 1994, when the CFA franc was devalued by 50%, with the exchange rate adjusted to 1 French franc = 100 francs CFA.

BUDGET ('000 million francs CFA)

Revenue	1990*	1991	1992
Petroleum receipts	119.4	109.4	87.9
Non-petroleum receipts	86.5	88.5	84.7
Aid	2.6	1.5	2.4
Total	208.5	199.4	175.0

Expenditure	1990†	1991	1992
Current expenditure	227.1	279.2	267.4
Salaries	79.4	130.0	134.8
Transfers, subsidies, goods and services	69.6	83.2	70.4
Interest	78.1	66.1	62.6
Capital expenditure	32.4	10.4	12.5
Others	2.6	8.2	34.3
Total	262.1	297.8	314.2

* Provisional figures.

Source: *La Zone Franc–Rapport 1992.*

CENTRAL BANK RESERVES (US $ million at 31 December)

	1990	1991	1992
Gold*	3.98	3.94	3.70
IMF special drawing rights	1.66	0.06	0.06
Reserve position in IMF	0.67	0.67	0.65
Foreign exchange	3.58	4.03	6.27
Total	9.89	8.70	10.70

* National valuation.

Source: IMF, *International Financial Statistics.*

MONEY SUPPLY ('000 million francs CFA at 31 December)

	1990	1991	1992
Currency outside banks	66.20	53.28	60.39
Demand deposits at commercial and development banks	54.10	58.73	64.64

Source: IMF, *International Financial Statistics.*

COST OF LIVING (Consumer Price Index for Africans in Brazzaville; base: 1980 = 100)

	1988	1989	1990
Food	160.3	159.6	162.0
Fuel, light and water	150.6	137.3	137.8
Clothing	184.6	193.0	205.5
Rent	172.6	172.2	192.2
All items	167.7	167.8	172.7

Source: ILO, *Year Book of Labour Statistics.*

NATIONAL ACCOUNTS (million francs CFA at current prices)

National Income and Product

	1986	1987	1988
Compensation of employees	264,296	253,198	245,033
Operating surplus	133,347	183,843	188,612
Domestic factor incomes	397,643	437,041	433,645
Consumption of fixed capital	156,074	164,360	144,647
Gross domestic product (GDP) at factor cost	553,717	601,401	578,292
Indirect taxes	91,444	90,790	82,358
Less Subsidies	4,754	1,668	1,686
GDP in purchasers' values	640,407	690,523	658,964
Factor income from abroad	2,781	9,333	3,112
Less Factor income paid abroad	44,717	86,030	93,328
Gross national product	598,471	613,826	568,748
Less Consumption of fixed capital	156,074	164,360	144,647
National income in market prices	442,397	449,466	424,101
Other current transfers from abroad	17,470	25,403	24,100
Less Other current transfers paid abroad	25,512	36,255	36,264
National disposable income	434,355	438,614	411,937

Source: UN, *National Accounts Statistics.*

Expenditure on the Gross Domestic Product

	1987	1988	1989
Government final consumption expenditure	142,115	138,722	144,600
Private final consumption expenditure	390,669	396,328	408,500
Increase in stocks	−7,811	−6,518	−3,776
Gross fixed capital formation	144,016	129,158	126,700
Total domestic expenditure	668,989	657,690	676,024
Exports of goods and services	288,254	267,723	368,100
Less Imports of goods and services	266,720	266,448	270,600
GDP in purchasers' values	690,523	658,964	773,524
GDP at constant 1978 prices	388,843	395,711	402,694

Source: UN, *National Accounts Statistics.*

Gross Domestic Product by Economic Activity

	1987	1988	1989
Agriculture, hunting, forestry and fishing	82,434	91,384	100,839
Mining and quarrying	155,188	110,399	216,192
Manufacturing	59,757	56,917	54,483
Electricity, gas and water	10,614	12,714	14,014
Construction	21,580	17,117	13,955
Trade, restaurants and hotels	102,153	107,588	111,321
Transport, storage and communication	71,294	72,600	70,075
Finance, insurance, real estate, business, community, social and personal services	70,975	71,108	70,503
Government services	102,716	102,603	104,306
Other services	1,395	1,400	1,400
Sub-total	678,106	643,830	757,088
Import duties	25,533	28,188	28,936
Less Imputed bank service charge	13,116	13,054	12,500
GDP in purchasers' values	690,523	658,964	773,524

Source: UN, *National Accounts Statistics.*

BALANCE OF PAYMENTS (US $ million)

	1990	1991	1992
Merchandise exports f.o.b.	1,388.7	1,028.7	1,190.4
Merchandise imports f.o.b.	−512.7	−553.0	−540.6
Trade balance	876.0	475.7	649.8
Exports of services	99.5	93.2	97.9
Imports of services	−769.1	−737.3	−746.5
Other income received	14.7	12.8	11.3
Other income paid	−474.9	−350.9	−343.0
Private unrequited transfers (net)	−62.8	−59.2	−71.8
Official unrequited transfers (net)	65.7	138.6	94.4
Current balance	−250.9	−427.1	−307.9
Capital (net)	−23.9	−159.2	−222.9
Net errors and omissions	−45.4	55.4	—
Overall balance	−320.1	−530.9	−530.8

Source: IMF, *International Financial Statistics.*

External Trade

Note: Figures exclude trade with other states of the Customs and Economic Union of Central Africa (UDEAC).

PRINCIPAL COMMODITIES (million francs CFA)

Imports c.i.f.	1986	1987	1988
Machinery	50,027	32,264	36,252
Transport equipment	20,090	16,791	17,532
Petroleum products	3,438	4,985	3,978
Chemicals and related products	17,437	15,445	20,290
Textile materials and manufactures	6,540	5,174	5,564
Iron and steel	19,332	13,271	12,377
Food, beverages and tobacco	37,270	28,954	34,466
Plastic and rubber goods	14,701	15,459	5,394
Precision instruments, watches, etc.	5,724	3,276	4,591
Total (incl. others)	199,394	151,738	161,958

Exports f.o.b.	1986	1987	1988
Petroleum and petroleum products	239,395	123,034	178,289
Wood	18,240	23,077	34,935
Diamonds	3,678	5,900	4,768
Coffee	642	198	202
Iron and steel	897	415	251
Total (incl. others)	268,757	155,303	223,744

PRINCIPAL TRADING PARTNERS (US $ '000)

Imports c.i.f.	1985	1986	1987
Belgium/Luxembourg	13,831	16,036	n.a.
France	264,030	303,630	258,295
Germany, Fed. Republic	27,098	18,488	11,827
Italy	48,018	26,854	25,305
Japan	19,845	24,578	16,851
Netherlands	15,601	14,525	15,717
Spain	26,008	32,410	21,313
United Kingdom	19,869	19,214	n.a.
USA	38,430	30,168	7,759
Total (incl. others)	580,231	578,635	504,832

Exports f.o.b.	1985	1986	1987
Belgium/Luxembourg	11,440	12,413	n.a.
France	118,539	100,569	130,242
Germany, Fed. Republic	2,941	7,080	12,330
Italy	19,930	69,997	85,341
Morocco	15,423	10,894	n.a.
Netherlands	65,793	33,555	44,156
Spain	150,810	89,008	37,395
USA	652,349	420,942	111,628
Total (incl. others)	1,087,215	776,854	516,693

Source: UN, *International Trade Statistics Yearbook.*

Transport

RAILWAYS (traffic)

	1988	1989	1990
Passenger-km (million)	419	434	410
Freight ton-km (million)	477	467	421

Source: UN, *Statistical Yearbook.*

ROAD TRAFFIC ('000 motor vehicles in use)

	1988	1989	1990
Passenger cars	26.0	26.0	26.0
Commercial vehicles	20.0	20.0	20.0

Source: UN, *Statistical Yearbook.*

INLAND WATERWAYS (freight traffic, '000 metric tons)

Port of Brazzaville	1985	1986	1987
Goods loaded	77	77	62
Goods unloaded	407	309	331

INTERNATIONAL SEA-BORNE SHIPPING
(freight traffic, '000 metric tons)

	1988	1989	1990
Goods loaded	9,400	9,295	8,987
Goods unloaded	686	707	736

Source: UN, *Monthly Bulletin of Statistics.*

CIVIL AVIATION (traffic on scheduled services)*

	1989	1990	1991
Kilometres flown (million)	3	3	3
Passengers carried ('000)	234	239	227
Passenger-km (million)	272	282	253
Freight ton-km (million)	19	18	17

* Including an apportionment of the traffic of Air Afrique.
Source: UN, *Statistical Yearbook.*

Tourism

	1988	1989	1990
Foreign tourist arrivals	39,000	40,000	46,000
Tourist receipts (million US dollars)	6	6	7

Source: UN, *Statistical Yearbook.*

Communications Media

	1989	1990	1991
Radio receivers ('000 in use) .	240	250	260
Television receivers ('000 in use)	10	13	14
Telephones ('000 in use) . .	26	n.a.	n.a.
Daily newspapers	n.a.	5	n.a.

Sources: UNESCO, *Statistical Yearbook*; UN, *Statistical Yearbook*.

Education

(1990)

	Teachers	Pupils
Primary	7,626	502,918
Secondary		
General	4,924	170,465
Teacher training	169	280
Vocational	1,758	12,278
Higher	1,112	10,671

1991: Higher education teachers 1,159; Higher education pupils 12,045.

Source: UNESCO, *Statistical Yearbook*.

Directory

The Constitution

The Constitution, which was approved by a national referendum in March 1992, provides for legislative power to be exercised by an elected National Assembly and Senate and for executive power to be held by a President, elected by universal adult franchise, who is also the Supreme Commander of the Armed Forces. The President appoints a Prime Minister from the political party with the majority of parliamentary seats. The President, acting on the advice of the Prime Minister, also appoints a Cabinet. Elections to the presidency and the 125-member National Assembly are to take place every five years, and elections to the 60-member Senate are to be held every six years. Further provisions guarantee an independent judiciary and the freedom of the media.

The Government

HEAD OF STATE

President: Pascal Lissouba (took office 31 August 1992).

COUNCIL OF MINISTERS
(August 1994)

Prime Minister and Chairman of the Priorities Committee: Brig.-Gen. Jacques-Joachim Yhombi-Opango.

Chairman of the Development Committee: Claude Antoine Dacosta.

Chairman of the Socio-Cultural Development Committee: Maurice-Stéphane Bongho-Nouarra.

Chairman of the National Defence Committee: Gen. Raymond Damasse Ngollo.

Chairman of the Legislation, Judicial Affairs and Administrative Reform Committee: Aimé Matsika.

Minister of State for the Interior in charge of Security, Regional Development and Relations with Parliament: Martin M'Beri.

Minister of Foreign Affairs and Co-operation in charge of Francophone Affairs: Benjamin Bounkoulou.

Minister of Finance: N'Guila Moungounga Nkombo.

Minister of Economy and Planning: Clement Mouamba.

Minister of Communication, Posts and Telecommunications and Government Spokesman: Albertine Lipou Massala.

Minister of Industrial Development, Mines and Energy: Jean Itadi.

Minister of Equipment and Public Works: Lambert Galibali.

Minister of Agriculture and Animal Husbandry: Grégoire Lefouoba.

Minister of Civil Service and Administrative Reform: Jean-Prosper Koyo.

Minister of Transport and Civil Aviation: Maurice Niaty Mouamba.

Minister of Commerce, Consumer Affairs and Small- and Medium-sized Enterprises: Marius Mouambenga.

Minister of Health and Social Welfare: Jean-Roger Ekoundzola.

Minister of Labour, Social Security and Solidarity: Anaclet Tsomambet.

Minister of Petroleum Resources: Benoît Koukebene.

Minister of Tourism and Environment: François-Auguste Tchitchele.

Minister of Culture: Dandou Abel Dibindou.

Minister of Water, Forestry and Fisheries: Rigobert Ngouolali.

Minister of National Education: Noutete Nasone Tangui.

Minister of Democratic Culture and Human Rights: Gabriel Matsiola.

MINISTRIES

All Ministries are in Brazzaville.

Office of the President: Palais du Peuple, Brazzaville; telex 5210.

Ministry of Finance: Centre Administratif, Quartier Plateau, BP 2031, Brazzaville; tel. 81-06-20; telex 5210.

Ministry of National Education and Culture: BP 169, Brazzaville; tel. 83-24-60; telex 5210.

Ministry of Foreign Affairs and Co-operation: BP 2070, Brazzaville; tel. 83-20-28; telex 5210.

Ministry of Health and Social Welfare: Palais du Peuple, Brazzaville; tel. 83-29-35; telex 5210.

Ministry of Industrial Development, Mines and Energy, Commerce and Small and Medium-sized Enterprises: Brazzaville; tel. 83-18-27; telex 5210.

President and Legislature

PRESIDENT

Presidential Election, First Ballot, 2 August 1992

Candidate	% of votes
Pascal Lissouba	35.89
Bernard Kolelas	22.89
Gen. Denis Sassou-Nguesso	16.87
André Milongo	10.18
Others (12 candidates)	14.17
Total	100.00

Second Ballot, 16 August 1992

Candidate	% of votes
Pascal Lissouba	61.32
Bernard Kolelas	38.68
Total	100.00

SÉNAT

General Election, 26 July 1992

Party	Seats
UPADS	23
MCDDI	13
RDD	8
RDPS	5
PCT	3
UDR	1
Independents	7
Total	60

ASSEMBLÉE NATIONALE*

Speaker: ANDRÉ MILONGO.

General Election, 2 May 1993 and 3 October 1993*

Party	Seats
UPADS	47
MCDDI	28
PCT	15
RDPS	10
RDD	6
UFD	3
Other parties	14
Independents	2
Total	125

*In January 1994 an independent electoral committee annulled the results in eight constituencies where there was found to be evidence of electoral fraud; three of the seats were held by supporters of the government and the remaining five by opposition members.

Political Organizations

Mouvement africain pour la réconstruction sociale: Leader JEAN ITADI.

Mouvement congolais pour la démocratie et le développement intégral (MCDDI): f. 1990; Leader BERNARD KOLELAS.

Mouvement patriotique du Congo (MPC): Paris, France.

Parti congolais du travail (PCT): Brazzaville; telex 5335; f. 1969; sole legal political party 1969–90; socialist orientation; Pres. of Cen. Cttee Gen. DENIS SASSOU-NGUESSO; Sec.-Gen. AMBROISE NOUMAZALAY.

Parti congolais pour la réconstruction (PCR): Brazzaville.

Parti libéral congolais: f. 1990; Gen. Sec. MARCEL MAKON.

Parti populaire pour la démocratie sociale et la défense de la République: f. 1991; Leader STANISLAS BATHEUS-MOLLOMB.

Parti du renouvellement et du progrès: Leader HENRI MARCEL DOUMANGUELE.

Parti social-démocrate congolais (PSDC): f. 1990; Pres. CLÉMENT MIERASSA.

Parti du travail: f. 1991; Leader DR AUGUSTE MAYANZA.

Rassemblement pour la défense des pauvres et des chômeurs au Congo: Leader ANGÈLE BANDOU.

Rassemblement pour la démocratie et le développement (RDD): f. 1990; advocates a mixed economy; Leader Brig.-Gen. JACQUES-JOACHIM YHOMBI-OPANGO.

Rassemblement pour la démocratie et le progrès social (RDPS): f. 1990; Leader JEAN-PIERRE THYSTÈRE-TCHICAYA.

Rassemblement démocratique et populaire du Congo: Leader JEAN-MARIE TASSOUA.

Union du centre: Leader OKANA MPAN.

Union pour la démocratie congolaise (UDC): f. 1989; advocates economic liberalization; Chair. FÉLIX MAKOSSO.

Union pour la démocratie et la République (UDR): f. 1992; Leader ANDRÉ MILONGO.

Union pour la démocratie et le progrès social (UDPS): f. 1994 in a merger between the Union pour le développement et le progrès social (UDPS), led by JEAN-MICHEL BOUKAMBA-YANGOUMA and the Parti populaire pour la démocratie sociale et la défense de la République led by STANISLAS BATHEUS-MOLLOMB; Leader JEAN-MICHEL BOUKAMBA-YANGOUMA.

Union écologique du Congo: Pres. MANDZENGUE YOUNOUS.

Union des forces démocratiques (UFD): Leader DAVID CHARLES GANAO.

Union nationale pour la démocratie et le progrès (UNDP): f. 1990; Leader PIERRE NZE.

Union panafricaine pour la démocratie sociale (UPADS): Pres. PASCAL LISSOUBA.

Union patriotique pour la démocratie et le progrès: Sec.-Gen. CÉLESTIN NKOUA.

Union patriotique pour la réconstruction nationale: Leader MATHIAS DZON.

Union pour le progrès: Pres. JEAN-MARTIN M'BEMBA.

Union pour le progrès du peuple congolais: f. 1991; seeks national unity and democracy; Leader ALPHONSE NBIHOULA.

Union pour le progrès social et la démocratie (UPSD): Brazzaville; f. 1991; Pres. ANGE-EDOUARD POUNGUI.

Union pour le renouveau démocratique (URD): f. 1992 as an alliance of seven political parties (incl. the MCDDI and the RDPS); Leader BERNARD KOLELAS.

Diplomatic Representation

EMBASSIES IN THE CONGO

Algeria: BP 2100, Brazzaville; tel. 83-39-15; telex 5303; Ambassador: MOHAMED NACER ADJALI.

Angola: BP 388, Brazzaville; tel. 81-14-71; telex 5321; Ambassador: JOSÉ AGOSTINHO NETO.

Belgium: BP 225, Brazzaville; tel. 83-29-63; telex 5216; Ambassador: JOHAN VERKERCKE.

Cameroon: BP 2136, Brazzaville; tel. 83-34-04; telex 5242; Ambassador: JEAN-HILAIRE MBEA MBEA.

Central African Republic: BP 10, Brazzaville; tel. 83-40-14; Ambassador: CHARLES GUEREBANGBI.

Chad: BP 386, Brazzaville; tel. 81-22-22; Chargé d'affaires: NEATOBEI BIDI.

China, People's Republic: BP 213, Brazzaville; tel. 83-11-20; Ambassador: YE HONGLIANG.

Cuba: BP 80, Brazzaville; tel. 81-29-80; telex 5308; Ambassador: JUAN CÉSAR DÍAZ.

Czech Republic: BP 292, Brazzaville; tel. 82-08-37.

Egypt: BP 917, Brazzaville; tel. 83-44-28; telex 5248; Ambassador: MOHAMED ABDEL RAHMAN DIAB.

France: rue Alfassa, BP 2089, Brazzaville; tel. 83-14-23; telex 5239; Ambassador: MICHEL ANDRÉ.

Gabon: ave Fourneau, BP 2033, Brazzaville; tel. 81-05-90; telex 5225; Ambassador: CONSTANT TSOUMOU.

Germany: BP 2022, Brazzaville; tel. 83-29-90; telex 5235; Ambassador: ADOLF EDERER.

Guinea: BP 2477, Brazzaville; tel. 81-24-66; Ambassador: BONATA DIENG.

Holy See: rue Colonel Brisset, BP 1168, Brazzaville; tel. 83-15-46; fax 83-65-39; Apostolic Pro-Nuncio: Most Rev. DIEGO CAUSERO, Titular Archbishop of Meta.

Italy: 2-3 blvd Lyautey, BP 2484, Brazzaville; tel. 83-40-47; telex 5251; Ambassador: TIBOR HOOR TEMPIS LIVI.

Korea, Democratic People's Republic: BP 2032, Brazzaville; tel. 83-41-98; Ambassador: CHA JONG UNG.

Libya: BP 920, Brazzaville; Secretary of People's Bureau: (vacant).

Nigeria: BP 790, Brazzaville; tel. 83-13-16; telex 5263; Ambassador: LAWRENCE OLUFOLAHAN OLADEJO OYELAKIN.

Romania: BP 2413, Brazzaville; tel. 81-32-79; telex 5259; Chargé d'affaires a.i.: DIACONESCO MILCEA.

Russia: BP 2132, Brazzaville; tel. 83-44-39; telex 5455; fax 83-69-17; Ambassador: ANATOLY SAFRONOVICH ZAITSEV.

USA: ave Amílcar Cabral, BP 1015, Brazzaville; tel. 83-20-70; telex 5367; fax 83-63-38; Ambassador: WILLIAM RAMSAY.

Viet Nam: BP 988, Brazzaville; tel. 83-26-21; Ambassador: BUI VAN THANH.

Zaire: 130 ave de l'Indépendance, BP 2450, Brazzaville; tel. 83-29-38; Ambassador: (vacant).

Judicial System

Supreme Court: Brazzaville; telex 5298; acts as a cour de cassation; Pres. CHARLES ASSEMEKANG.

Revolutionary Court of Justice: Brazzaville; f. 1969; has jurisdiction in cases involving state security.

Religion

About one-half of the population follow traditional animist beliefs. Most of the remainder are Christians. In 1978 the Government banned all religions and sects, except the Roman Catholic Church, the Congo Evangelical Church, the Salvation Army, Islam and the followers of Simon Kimbangu Prophète, Lassy Zephirin Prophète and Terynkyo.

CHRISTIANITY

The Roman Catholic Church

The Congo comprises one archdiocese and five dioceses. At 31 December 1992 there were an estimated 948,500 adherents.

Bishops' Conference: Conférence Episcopale du Congo, BP 200, Brazzaville; tel. 83-06-29; f. 1967; Pres. Rt Rev. BERNARD NSAYI, Bishop of Nkayi.

Archbishop of Brazzaville: Most Rev. BARTHÉLÉMY BATANTU, Archevêché, BP 2301, Brazzaville; tel. 83-17-93.

Other Christian Churches

Protestant Churches: In all four equatorial states (the Congo, the Central African Republic, Chad and Gabon) there are nearly 1,000 mission centres with a total personnel of about 2,000.

Eglise Evangélique du Congo: BP 3205, Bacongo-Brazzaville; tel. 83-43-64; f. 1909; autonomous since 1961; 110,461 mems (1985); Pres. Rev. JEAN MBOUNGOU.

ISLAM

In 1991 there were an estimated 25,000 Muslims and 49 mosques in the Congo.

Comité Islamique du Congo: 77 Makotipoko Moungali, BP 55, Brazzaville; tel. 82-87-45; f. 1988; Leaders HABIBOU SOUMARE, BACHIR GATSONGO, BOUILLA GUIBIDANESI.

The Press

DAILIES

ACI: BP 2144, Brazzaville; tel. 83-05-91; telex 5285; daily news bulletin publ. by Agence Congolaise d'Information; circ. 1,000.

Aujourd'hui: BP 1171, Brazzaville; tel. and fax 83-77-44; f. 1991; Dir CHRISTIAN N'DINGA; Chief Editor FYLLA DI FUA DI SASSA.

L'Eveil de Pointe-Noire: Pointe-Noire.

Mweti: BP 991, Brazzaville; tel. 81-10-87; national news; Dir MATONGO AVELEY; Chief Editor HUBERT MADOUABA; circ. 8,000.

PERIODICALS

Bakento Ya Congo: BP 309, Brazzaville; tel. 83-27-44; quarterly; Dir MARIE LOUISE MAGANGA; Chief Editor CHARLOTTE BOUSSE; circ. 3,000.

Bulletin de Statistique: Centre Nationale de la Statistique et des Etudes Economiques, BP 2031, Brazzaville; tel. 83-36-94; f. 1977; quarterly; Dir-Gen. MARCEL MOUELLE.

Bulletin Mensuel de la Chambre de Commerce de Brazzaville: BP 92, Brazzaville; monthly.

Combattant Rouge: Brazzaville; tel. 83-02-53; monthly; Dir SYLVIO GEORGES ONKA; Chief Editor GILLES OMER BOUSSI.

Congo-Magazine: BP 114, Brazzaville; tel. 83-43-81; monthly; Dir GASPARD MPAN; Chief Editor THÉODORE KIAMOSSI; circ. 3,000.

Effort: BP 64, Brazzaville; monthly.

Jeunesse et Révolution: BP 885, Brazzaville; tel. 83-44-13; weekly; Dir JEAN-ENOCH GOMA-KENGUE; Chief Editor PIERRE MAKITA.

La Semaine Africaine: BP 2080, Brazzaville; tel. 83-03-28; f. 1952; weekly; general information and social action; circulates widely in francophone equatorial Africa; Dir JEAN-PIERRE GALLET; Chief Editor JOACHIM MBANZA; circ. 6,500.

Le Madukutsekele: Brazzaville; f. 1991; weekly; satirical; Editor MATHIEU BAKIMA-BALIELE; circ. 5,000.

Le Pays: f. 1991; weekly; Dir ANTOINE MALONGA.

Le Soleil: f. 1991; weekly; organ of the Rassemblement pour la démocratie et le développement; Chief Editor BERNARD KOLELA.

Le Stade: BP 114, Brazzaville; tel. 81-47-18; telex 5285; f. 1985; weekly; sports; Dir HUBERT-TRÉSOR MADOUABA-NTOUALANI; Chief Editor BERTIN EBINDA; circ. 12,000.

Voix de la Classe Ouvrière (Voco): BP 2311, Brazzaville; tel. 83-36-66; six a year; Dir MICHEL JOSEPH MAYOUNGOU; Chief Editor MARIE-JOSEPH TSENGOU; circ. 4,500.

NEWS AGENCIES

Agence Congolaise d'Information (ACI): BP 2144, Brazzaville; tel. 83-46-76; telex 5285; f. 1961; Dir RIGOBERT DOUNIAMA-ETOUA.

Foreign Bureaux

Agence France-Presse (AFP): c/o Agence Congolaise d'Information, BP 2144, Brazzaville; tel. 83-46-76; telex 5285; Correspondent JOSEPH GOUALA.

Associated Press (AP) (USA): BP 2144, Brazzaville; telex 5477; Correspondent ARMAND BERNARD MASSAMBA.

Informatsionnoye Telegrafnoye Agentstvo Rossii—Telegrafnoye Agentstvo Suverennykh Stran (ITAR—TASS) (Russia): BP 379, Brazzaville; tel. 83-44-33; telex 5203; Dir YURI ULYANOVSKY.

Inter Press Service (IPS) (Italy): POB 964, Brazzaville; tel. 810565; telex 5285.

Pan-African News Agency (PANA) (Senegal): BP 2144, Brazzaville; tel. 83-11-40; telex 5285; fax 83-70-15.

Reuters (United Kingdom): BP 2144, Brazzaville; telex 5477; Correspondent ANTOINE MOUYAMBALA.

Rossiyskoye Informatsionnoye Agentstvo—Novosti (RIA—Novosti) (Russia): BP 170, Brazzaville; tel. 83-43-44; telex 5227; Bureau Chief DMITRI AMVROSIEV.

Xinhua (New China) News Agency (People's Republic of China): 40 ave Maréchal Lyauté, BP 373, Brazzaville; tel. 83-44-01; telex 5230; Chief Correspondent XU ZHENQIANG.

Publishers

Imprimerie Centrale d'Afrique (ICA): BP 162, Pointe-Noire; f. 1949; Man. Dir M. SCHNEIDER.

Société Congolaise Hachette: Brazzaville; telex 5291; general fiction, literature, education, juvenile, textbooks.

Government Publishing House

Imprimerie Nationale: BP 58, Brazzaville; Man. KIALA MATOUBA.

Radio and Television

IN 1991 THERE WERE AN ESTIMATED 260,000 RADIO SETS AND 14,000 TELEVISION RECEIVERS IN USE.

Radiodiffusion-Télévision Congolaise: BP 2241, Brazzaville; tel. 83-16-76; telex 5299; Dir JEAN-FRANÇOIS SYLVESTRE SOUKA.

Télévision Nationale Congolaise: BP 2241, Brazzaville; tel. 81-51-52; began transmission in 1963; operates for 46 hours per week, with most programmes in French but some in Lingala and Kikongo; Dir JEAN-GILBERT FOUTOU.

Radio Congo: BP 2241, Brazzaville; tel. 83-03-83; radio programmes in French, Lingala, Kikongo, Subia, English and Portuguese; transmitters at Brazzaville and Pointe-Noire; also broadcasts to Namibia in English and vernacular languages; Dir LUCIL OBA.

Finance

(cap. = capital; res = reserves; dep. = deposits; br. = branch; m. = million; amounts in francs CFA)

BANKING

Central Bank

Banque des Etats de l'Afrique Centrale (BEAC): BP 126, Brazzaville; tel. 83-28-14; telex 5200; fax 83-63-42; headquarters in Yaoundé, Cameroon; f. 1973 as the central bank of issue for mem. states of the Customs and Economic Union of Central Africa (UDEAC), comprising Cameroon, the Central African Republic, Chad, the Congo, Equatorial Guinea and Gabon; cap. and res 203,500m. (Jan. 1993); Gov. JEAN-FÉLIX MAMALEPOT; Dir in the Congo ANGE-EDOUART POUNGUI; br. at Pointe-Noire.

Commercial Banks

Banque Française Intercontinentale (FIBA): BP 14579, Brazzaville; tel. 83-62-24; telex 5556; fax 83-62-25; f. 1975; 37.3%

owned by Elf Aquitaine, 5.3% by Banque Indosuez, 57.4% owned by others.

Banque Internationale du Congo (BIDC): ave Amílcar Cabral, BP 33, Brazzaville; tel. 83-03-08; telex 5339; fax 83-53-82; f. 1983; 72% state-owned; cap. and res 2,287m., dep. 32,180m. (Dec. 1991); Pres. and Chair. MATHIAS DZON; Gen. Man. MICHEL JOSIEN.

Union Congolaise de Banques SA (UCB): ave Amílcar Cabral, BP 147, Brazzaville; tel. 83-30-00; telex 5206; fax 83-68-45; f. 1974; 95% state-owned, 5% by the Banque Belgolaise, Belgium; cap. 3,000m. (Dec. 1992); Pres. JOSEPH KOMBO-KINTOMBO; Gen. Man. MATHIEU AKONGO; 8 brs.

Development Bank

Banque de Développement des États de l'Afrique Centrale: (see Franc Zone, p. 107).

Financial Institution

Caisse Congolaise d'Amortissement: 410 allée du Chaillu, BP 2090, Brazzaville; tel. 83-32-41; telex 5294; f. 1971; management of state funds; Man. Dir FELIX BOUENO.

INSURANCE

Assurances et Réassurances du Congo (ARC): ave Amílcar Cabral, BP 977, Brazzaville; tel. 83-01-71; telex 5236; f. 1973 to acquire the businesses of all insurance cos operating in the Congo; 50% state-owned; cap. 500m.; Dir-Gen. RAYMOND IBATA; brs at Pointe-Noire, Loubomo and Ouesso.

Trade and Industry

DEVELOPMENT AGENCIES

Caisse Française de Développement: BP 96, Brazzaville; tel. 83-15-95; telex 5202; French fund for economic co-operation; Dir JACQUES BENIER.

Mission Française de Coopération: BP 2175, Brazzaville; tel. 83-15-03; f. 1959; administers bilateral aid from France; Dir JEAN-BERNARD THIANT.

Office des Cultures Vivrières (OCV): BP 894, Brazzaville; tel. 82-11-03; f. 1979; state-owned; food-crop development; Dir-Gen. GILBERT PANA.

STATE MARKETING BOARDS

Office Congolais des Bois (OCB): 2 ave Moe Vangoula, BP 1229, Pointe-Noire; tel. 94-22-38; telex 8248; f. 1974; cap. 1,486m. francs CFA; monopoly of purchase and marketing of all timber products; Man. Dir ALEXANDRE DENGUET-ATTIKI.

Office du Café et du Cacao (OCC): BP 2488, Brazzaville; tel. 83-19-03; telex 5273; f. 1978; cap. 1,500m. francs CFA; marketing and export of coffee and cocoa; Man. Dir PAUL YORA.

Office National de Commercialisation des Produits Agricoles (ONCPA): BP 144, Brazzaville; tel. 83-24-01; telex 5273; f. 1964; marketing of all agricultural products except sugar; promotion of rural co-operatives; Dir JEAN-PAUL BOCKONDAS.

Office National du Commerce (OFNACOM): BP 2305, Brazzaville; tel. 83-43-99; telex 5309; f. 1964; proposals for transfer to private-sector ownership announced in 1987; cap. 2,158m. francs CFA; importer and distributor of general merchandise; monopoly importer of salted and dried fish, cooking salt, rice, tomato purée, buckets, enamelled goods and blankets; Dir-Gen. VALENTIN ENOUSSA NCONGO.

Office National d'Importation et de Vente de Viande en Gros (ONIVEG): Brazzaville; tel. 82-30-33; telex 5240; f. 1975; cap. 177m. francs CFA; monopoly importer and distributor of wholesale meats; Man. Dir ROBERT PAUL MANGOUTA.

CHAMBERS OF COMMERCE

Chambre de Commerce, d'Agriculture et d'Industrie de Brazzaville: BP 92, Brazzaville; tel. 83-21-15; Pres. MAURICE OGNAOY; Sec.-Gen. FRANÇOIS DILOU-YOULOU.

Chambre de Commerce, d'Agriculture et d'Industrie de Loubomo: BP 78, Loubomo.

Chambre de Commerce, d'Industrie et d'Agriculture du Kouilou: 8 ave Charles de Gaulle, BP 665, Pointe-Noire; tel. 94-12-80; f. 1948; Chair. FRANÇOIS-LUC MACOSSO; Sec.-Gen. JEAN-BAPTISTE SOUMBOU.

PROFESSIONAL ORGANIZATION

Union Patronale et Interprofessionnelle du Congo (UNICONGO): BP 42, Brazzaville; tel. 83-05-51; fax 83-68-16; f. 1960; employers' union; Pres. G. BOUR; Sec.-Gen. J. FUMEY.

NATIONALIZED INDUSTRIES

Minoterie, Aliments de Bétail, Boulangerie (MAB): BP 789, Pointe-Noire; tel. 94-19-09; telex 8283; f. 1978; cap. 2,650m. francs CFA; monopoly importer of cereals; production of flour and animal feed; Man. Dir DENIS TEMPERE.

Régie Nationale des Palmeraies du Congo (RNPC): BP 8, Brazzaville; tel. 83-08-25; f. 1966; cap. 908m. francs CFA; production of palm oil; Man. Dir RENÉ MACOSSO.

Société Nationale de Construction (SONACO): BP 1126, Brazzaville; tel. 83-06-54; f. 1979; cap. 479m. francs CFA; building works; Man. Dir DENIS M'BOMO.

Société Nationale de Distribution d'Eau (SNDE): rue du Sergent Malamine, BP 229 and 365, Brazzaville; tel. 83-73-26; telex 5272; fax 83-38-91; f. 1967; proposals for transfer to private-sector ownership announced in 1994; water supply and sewerage; holds monopoly over wells and import of mineral water; Chair. and Man. Dir S. MPINOU.

Société Nationale d'Elevage (SONEL): BP 81, Loutété, Massangui; f. 1964; cap. 80m. francs CFA; development of semi-intensive stock-rearing; exploitation of by-products; Man. Dir THÉOPHILE BIKAWA.

Société Nationale d'Exploitation des Bois (SNEB): Pointe-Noire; tel. 94-02-09; f. 1970; cap. 1,779m. francs CFA; production of timber; Pres. RIGOBERT NGOULOU; Man. Dir ROBERT ZINGA KANZA.

Société Nationale de Recherches et d'Exploitation Pétrolières (HYDRO-CONGO): Cnr ave Paul Doumer and ave du Camp, BP 2008, Brazzaville; tel. 83-40-22; telex 5300; fax 83-12-38; f. 1973; proposals for transfer to private-sector ownership announced in 1994; cap. 710m. francs CFA; research into and production of petroleum resources; monopoly distributor of petroleum products in the Congo until 1990; refinery at Pointe-Noire; also mfrs of lubricants; Dir-Gen. AIMÉ PORTELLA.

Société des Verreries du Congo (SOVERCO): BP 1241, Pointe-Noire; tel. 94-19-19; telex 8288; f. 1977; cap. 500m. francs CFA; mfrs of glassware; Chair. A. E. NOUMAZALAYE; Man. Dir NGOYOT IBARRA.

Unité d'Afforestation Industrielle du Congo (UAIC): BP 1120, Pointe-Noire; tel. 94-04-17; telex 8308; f. 1978; eucalyptus plantations to provide wood-pulp for export; Dir ROLAND JAFFRÉ.

MAJOR INDUSTRIAL COMPANIES

The following are some of the largest companies in terms of either capital investment or employment.

AGIP Recherches Congo: BP 2047, Brazzaville; tel. 83-11-52; telex 6010; f. 1969; cap. 2,000m. francs CFA; 20% state-owned, 80% by AGIP (Italy); exploration and exploitation of petroleum resources; Chair. PIETRO CAVANNA; Man. Dir ANTONIO ROSSANI.

BATA SA Congolaise: ave du Général de Gaulle, BP 32, Pointe-Noire; tel. 94-03-26; telex 8232; f. 1965; cap. 250m. francs CFA; mfrs of shoes using plastic, rubber and leather; Pres. GEORGES MAREINE; Man. Dir MICHEL DUMOULIN.

Boissons Africaines de Brazzaville (BAB): BP 2193, Brazzaville; tel. 83-20-06; telex 5266; f. 1964; cap. 350m. francs CFA; mfr and sale of carbonated drinks and syrups; Man. Dir J. SERVAIS.

Brasserie de Brazzaville: ave du Nouveau Port, BP 105, Brazzaville; tel. 83-17-65; telex 5305; fax 83-25-64; f. 1968; cap. 1,250m. francs CFA; production of beer and soft drinks; Man. Dir ROLAND DIERCKX DE CASTERLE; 253 employees.

La Congolaise des Bois Impregnés (CBI): BP 820, Pointe-Noire; f. 1986; cap. 800m. francs CFA; 49% owned by UAIC (see Nationalized Industries); production of electricity poles from eucalyptus trees; Pres. AMBROISE NOUMAZALAY; Man. Dir JOHN F. BRIDGES.

Elf Congo: BP 761, Pointe-Noire; tel. 94-17-95; telex 8239; also at BP 405, Brazzaville; tel. 83-41-24; f. 1969; cap. 5,000m. francs CFA; 20% state-owned, 80% by Elf Aquitaine; exploration and exploitation of petroleum resources; Dir-Gen. (at Brazzaville) SERGE NAVILLE; Dir at Pointe-Noire EMMANUEL YOKA.

Impressions de Textiles de la République du Congo (IMPRECO): BP 188, Brazzaville; tel. 81-02-74; telex 5218; fax 83-01-96; f. 1973; cap. 720m. francs CFA; 30% state-owned; textile printing factory; Chair. FRANÇOIS VRINAT; Man. Dir LOUIS DEFFOND.

PLACONGO SA: BP 717, Pointe-Noire; tel. 94-02-79; telex 8224; f. 1965 as Société des Placages du Congo; cap. 4,400m. francs CFA; 36% state-owned; rotary peeling of logs; Pres. Dr DOUNIAM OSSEBI; Man. Dir DOMINIQUE TOURANCHET.

Savonnerie du Congo (SAVCONGO): Brazzaville; tel. 83-10-17; telex 5221; f. 1958; cap. 1,100m. francs CFA; mfrs of soap and domestic cleaning products; Pres. PIERRE OTTO MBONGO; Dir JUSTIN ELENGA.

Société Cimentière du Congo (SOCICO): BP 72, Loutété; tel. 92-61-26; telex 5244; f. 1968 as Cimenterie Domaniale de Loutété (CIDOULOU); cap. 900m. francs CFA; 50% owned by Scancem (Norway); Man. Dir OLE KULSETH.

Société Congolaise des Bois (SOCOBOIS): BP 300, Loubomo; tel. 91-02-04; telex 8257; f. 1964; cap. 400m. francs CFA; timber mills; Dir OTTO SCHLUMBOHM.

Société Congolaise des Brasseries Kronenbourg (SCBK): blvd Bitelika Dombi, BP 1147, Pointe-Noire; tel. 94-02-45; telex 8237; fax 94-37-40; f. 1963; cap. 1,872m. francs CFA; production and sale of beer and soft drinks, fruit juices, soda, ice and carbon dioxide; Pres. ARMAND SERFATY; Man. Dir GÉRARD BOUR; 409 employees.

Société Congolaise Industrielle des Bois (CIB): BP 145, Brazzaville; tel. 83-11-31; telex 5255; fax 83-33-79; cap. 2,070m. francs CFA; logs and timber production; Pres. Dr HEINRICH LÜDER STOLL; Dir-Gen. JEAN-MARIE MEVELLEC.

Société Congolaise Industrielle des Bois d'Ouesso: Ouesso; f. 1981; cap. 2,500m. francs CFA; 51% state-owned; extraction of forestry products.

Société Congolaise de Pêches Maritimes (COPEMAR): Pointe-Noire; tel. 94-20-32; telex 8322; f. 1981; cap. 860m. francs CFA; processing of fish products; Man. Dir PASCAL ISSANGA.

Société Forestière Algéro-Congolaise (SFAC): BP 5109, Brazzaville; tel. 83-46-40; telex 5420; f. 1983; cap. 3,000m. francs CFA; timber production and marketing; Dir-Gen. ARMAND BIENVENU VOUIDIBIO.

Société des Huiles du Congo (HUILCA SA): BP 103, N'Kayi; tel. 92-11-60; telex 5565; f. 1988; cap. 700m. francs CFA; 40% state-owned; production of oils and fats, vegetable oil refinery at Brazzaville; Pres. ANTOINE TABET; Man. Dir EMMANUEL PAMBOU.

Société Industrielle et Agricole du Tabac Tropical (SIAT): BP 50, Brazzaville; tel. 83-16-15; telex 5211; fax 83-16-72; f. 1945; cap. 1,550m. francs CFA; mfrs of cigarettes; Dir-Gen. YVON MEREAUX.

Société Industrielle des Bois de Mossendjo (SIBOM): Pointe-Noire; f. 1984; cap. 1,782m. francs CFA; 35% state-owned.

Société Industrielle de Déroulage et de Tranchage (SIDETRA): BP 1202, Pointe-Noire; tel. 94-20-07; telex 8206; f. 1966; cap. 950m. francs CFA; 35% state-owned; forestry, production of sawn wood and veneers; Pres. JACQUES SERVAIS; Dir-Gen. MARIE-ALPHONSE ONGAGOU-DATCHOU; 650 employees.

Société Mixte Bulgaro-Congolaise de Recherche et d'Exploitation des Phosphates (SOPHOSCO): Brazzaville; f. 1976; cap. 250m. francs CFA; 51% state-owned, 49% by govt of Bulgaria; mining of phosphate.

Société d'Economie Mixte de Construction (SEMICO): BP 13022, Brazzaville; f. 1983; cap. 1,050m. francs CFA; 25% state-owned; construction.

Société des Silos à Ciment du Congo (SIACIC): Pointe-Noire; cap. 600m. francs CFA; Dir Lt-Col FLORENT TSIBA.

Société des Textiles du Congo (SOTEXCO): BP 3222, Brazzaville; tel. 83-33-83; f. 1966; cap. 1,700m. francs CFA; operates cotton-spinning mills, dyeing plants and weaving plants in Kinsoundi; Man. Dir M. KOMBO-KITOMBO.

TRADE UNIONS

In June 1991 legislation was enacted which permitted the formation of independent trade unions.

Confédération Syndicale Congolaise (CSC): BP 2311, Brazzaville; tel. 83-19-23; telex 5304; f. 1964; Sec.-Gen. JEAN-MICHEL BOUKAMBA-YANGOUMA; 80,000 mems.

Confédération Syndicale des Travailleurs Congolais: Brazzaville; f. 1993; federation of 13 trade unions; Sec.-Gen. LOUIS GOUNDOU.

Transport

Agence Transcongolaise des Communications (ATC): BP 711, Pointe-Noire; tel. 94-15-32; telex 8345; f. 1969; proposals for transfer to private-sector ownership announced in 1994; cap. 23,888m. francs CFA; three divisions: Congo-Océan Railway, inland waterways and Brazzaville inland port, and the Atlantic port of Pointe-Noire; Man. Dir Col JEAN-FÉLIX ONGOUYA.

RAILWAYS

There are 510 km of track from Brazzaville to Pointe-Noire. A 286-km section of privately-owned line links the manganese mines at Moanda (in Gabon), via a cableway to the Congo border at M'Binda, with the main line to Pointe-Noire.

ATC—Chemin de Fer Congo-Océan (CFCO): BP 651, Pointe-Noire; tel. 94-11-84; telex 8231; fax 94-12-30; Dir DÉSIRÉ GOMA.

INLAND WATERWAYS

The Congo and Oubangui rivers form two axes of a highly developed inland waterway system. The Congo river and seven tributaries in the Congo basin provide 2,300 km of navigable river and the Oubangui river, developed in co-operation with the Central African Republic, an additional 2,085 km.

ATC—Direction des Voies Navigables, Ports et Transports Fluviaux: BP 2048, Brazzaville; tel. 83-06-27; waterways authority; Dir MÉDARD OKOUMOU.

Compagnie Congolaise de Transports: BP 37, Loubomo; f. 1960; cap. 36m. francs CFA; Pres. and Dir-Gen. ROBERT BARBIER.

Société Congolaise de Transports (SOCOTRANS): BP 617, Pointe-Noire; tel. 94-23-31; f. 1977; cap. 17m. francs CFA; Man YVES CRIQUET.

Transcap-Congo: BP 1154, Pointe-Noire; tel. 94-01-46; telex 8218; f. 1962; cap. 100m. francs CFA; Chair. J. DROUAULT.

SHIPPING

Pointe-Noire is the major port of the Congo. Brazzaville, on the Congo river, is an inland port. A major expansion programme for Brazzaville port, undertaken during the 1980s, aimed at establishing the port as a container traffic centre for several central African countries. In 1989 Congolese seaports handled 10m. metric tons of goods for international transport.

ATC—Direction du Port de Brazzaville: BP 2048, Brazzaville; tel. 83-00-42; nationalized in 1977; port authority; Dir JEAN-PAUL BOCKONDAS.

ATC—Direction du Port de Pointe-Noire: BP 711, Pointe-Noire; tel. 94-00-52; telex 8318; fax 94-20-42; nationalized in 1977; port authority; Dir DOMINIQUE BEMBA.

La Congolaise de Transport Maritime (COTRAM): f. 1984; national shipping co; state-owned.

ROADS

In 1992 there were 12,000 km of roads and tracks, of which only a small proportion were bituminized. The principal routes link Brazzaville to Pointe-Noire, in the south, and to Ouesso, in the north.

Régie Nationale des Transports et des Travaux Publics: BP 2073, Brazzaville; tel. 83-35-58; f. 1965; civil engineering, upkeep of roads and public works; Man. Dir HECTOR BIENVENU OUAMBA.

CIVIL AVIATION

There are international airports at Brazzaville (Maya-Maya) and Pointe-Noire. There are airports at six regional capitals, as well as 37 smaller airfields.

Afri-Congo: Brazzaville; f. 1986; private airline operating flights to Rwanda and Burundi.

Agence Nationale de l'Aviation Civile (ANAC): BP 128, Brazzaville; tel. 81-09-94; telex 5388; f. 1970; Gen. Man. GILBERT M'FOUO-OTSIALLY.

Air Afrique: BP 1126, Pointe-Noire; tel. 94-17-00; telex 8342; see under Côte d'Ivoire; Dir at Pointe-Noire JEAN-CLAUDE NDIAYE; Dir at Brazzaville I. CISSÉ DEMBA.

Lina Congo (Lignes Nationales Aériennes Congolaises): ave Amílcar Cabral, BP 2203, Brazzaville; tel. 83-30-66; telex 5243; fax 83-17-21; f. 1965; state-owned; operates an extensive internal network; also services to the Central African Republic; Man. Dir JEAN-JACQUES ONTSA-ONTSA.

Tourism

Brazzaville has three international hotels. There is a shortage of accommodation in Pointe-Noire, where the petroleum and business sectors have increased demand. A regional hotel chain is to be established to cater for travellers in the provinces. There are plans to convert Mbamou Island into a tourist resort. An estimated 46,000 tourists visited the Congo in 1990, when earnings from the sector totalled an estimated US $7m.

Direction Générale du Tourisme et des Loisirs: BP 456, Brazzaville; tel. 83-09-53; telex 5210; f. 1980; Dir-Gen. ANTOINE KOUNKOU-KIBOUILOU.

Defence

In June 1993 the army numbered 10,000, the navy about 350 and the air force 500. There were 6,100 men in paramilitary forces. National service is voluntary for men and women, and lasts for two years.

Defence Expenditure: Estimated at 33,250m. francs CFA for 1992.

Supreme Chief of the Armed Forces: Brig.-Gen. JACQUES-JOACHIM YHOMBI-OPANGO.

Chief of General Staff of the National People's Army: Col EMMANUEL ETA-ONKA.

Education

Education is officially compulsory for 10 years between six and 16 years of age. Primary education begins at the age of six and lasts for six years. Secondary education, from 12 years of age, lasts for seven years, comprising a first cycle of four years and a second of three years. Private education was legalized in 1990. In 1990 there were 502,918 pupils enrolled at primary schools, while 170,465 pupils were receiving general secondary education. In addition, there were 169 secondary students at teacher-training colleges and 1,758 students attending vocational institutions. The Marien Ngouabi University, at Brazzaville, was founded in 1971. In 1991 there were 12,045 students at university level. Some Congolese students go to France for technical instruction. In 1990, according to estimates by UNESCO, the average rate of adult illiteracy was 43.4% (males 30.0%, females 56.1%), one of the lowest in Africa. Expenditure on education by the central government was about 37,899m. francs CFA (14.4% of total spending) in 1990.

Bibliography

Allen, C., Radu, M. S., Somerville, K., et al. *Benin, The Congo, Burkina Faso: Economics, Politics and Society.* New York, Columbia University Press, 1989.

Amin, S., and Coquery-Vidrovitch, C. *Histoire économique du Congo 1880–1968.* Paris, Anthropos, 1969.

Asch, S. *L'Eglise du Prophète Kimbangu.* Paris, Editions Karthala, 1983.

Bertrand, H. *Le Congo.* Paris, Maspero, 1975.

Coquery-Vidrovich, C. *Le Congo au temps des grandes compagnies concessionnaires, 1898–1930.* Paris, Mouton, 1972.

Ekondy, A. *Le Congo-Brazzaville: essai d'analyse et d'explication sociologiques selon la méthode pluraliste.* Berne, Lang, 1983.

Gakosso, G-F. *La réalité congolaise.* Paris, La Pensée Universelle, 1983.

Gauze, R. *The Politics of Congo Brazzaville.* Stanford, CA, 1973.

Gide, A. *Voyage au Congo.* 1926.

Lissouba, P. *Conscience du développement et démocratie.* Dakar, 1975.

M'Kaloulou, B. *Dynamique paysanne et développement rural au Congo.* Paris, L'Harmattan, 1984.

Rabut, E. *Brazza, commissaire général. Le Congo français (1886–1897).* Paris, Editions de L'ecole des hauts études en sciences sociales, 1989.

Rey, P. P. *Colonialisme, néo-colonialisme et transition au capitalisme. Exemple de la Comilog au Congo-Brazzaville.* Paris, 1971.

Soret, M. *Les Kongo nord occidentaux.* Paris, Presses universitaires de France, 1959.

Histoire du Congo. Paris, Berger-Levrault, 1978.

Thompson, V., and Adloff, R. *Historical Dictionary of the People's Republic of the Congo.* Revised Edn, Metuchen, NJ, Scarecrow Press, 1984.

Vennetier, P. *Géographie du Congo-Brazzaville.* Paris, Gauthier Villars, 1966.

'Population et économie du Congo-Brazzaville', in *Cahiers d'Outre Mer.* Bordeaux, 1962.

'Problems of Port Development in Gabon and Congo', in Hoyle, B. S., and Hilling, D. (Eds), *Seaports and Development in Tropical Africa.* London, 1970.

Wagret, J.-M. *Histoire et sociologie politiques du Congo.* Paris, Librairie générale de droit et de jurisprudence, 1963.

West, R. *Brazza of the Congo.* Newton Abbot, 1973.

CÔTE D'IVOIRE

Physical and Social Geography

R. J. HARRISON CHURCH

The Republic of Côte d'Ivoire is situated on the west coast of Africa, between Ghana to the east and Liberia to the west, with Guinea, Mali and Burkina Faso to the north. Côte d'Ivoire is economically the most important of the states of sub-Saharan francophone Africa. The country has an area of 322,462 sq km (124,503 sq miles), and at the 1988 census the population was 10,815,694. There is a diversity of peoples, with the Agni and Baoulé having cultural and other affinities with the Ashanti of Ghana.

From the border with Liberia eastwards to Fresco, the coast has cliffs, rocky promontories and sandy bays. East of Fresco the rest of the coast is a straight sandbar, backed, as in Benin, by lagoons. None of the seaward river exits is navigable, and a canal was opened from the sea into the Ebrié lagoon at Abidjan only in 1950, after half a century's battle with nature.

Although Tertiary sands and clays fringe the northern edge of the lagoons, they give place almost immediately to Archaean and Pre-Cambrian rocks, which underlie the rest of the country. Diamonds are obtained from gravels south of Korhogo, and near Séguéla, while gold is mined at Ity, in the west, and at Aniuri, in the south-east. The Man mountains and the Guinea highlands on the border with Liberia and Guinea are the only areas of vigorous relief in the country. Substantial deposits of haematite iron ore may be developed near Man for export through the country's second deep-water port of San Pedro. The development of small offshore oilfields south-east of Abidjan had virtually ceased by the late 1980s, although there is considerable potential for the exploitation of further deposits of petroleum and also of natural gas.

Except for the north-western fifth of Côte d'Ivoire, the country has an equatorial climate. This occurs most typically in the south, which receives annual rainfall of 1,250–2,400 mm, with two maxima, and where the relative humidity is high. Much valuable rain forest survives in the south-west, but elsewhere it has been extensively planted with coffee, cocoa, bananas, pineapple, rubber and oil palm. Tropical climatic conditions prevail in the north-west, with a single rainy season of five to seven months, and 1,250–1,500 mm of rain annually. Guinea savannah occurs here, as well as in the centre of the country, and projects southwards around Bouaké.

Recent History

PIERRE ENGLEBERT

By independence in 1960 the Parti démocratique de la Côte d'Ivoire (PDCI) had achieved a virtual monopoly of political life in Côte d'Ivoire. As party leader and a representative of the PDCI in the French national assembly, Félix Houphouët-Boigny dominated the grouping known as the Rassemblement démocratique africain, which had affiliates in other francophone countries. Throughout the 1950s Houphouët-Boigny supported French colonial rule and strongly opposed the formation of an independent West African federation. When, in 1960, it became clear that most colonies would be granted independence, Houphouët-Boigny pre-empted negotiations on federation by declaring unilateral independence on 7 August. Houphouët-Boigny was the sole candidate for the presidency at every election until 1990, and (despite constitutional provision for the existence of more than one political organization) his party, for historical reasons retaining the name Parti démocratique de la Côte d'Ivoire–Rassemblement démocratique africain (PDCI–RDA), was the only legal political party until the same year.

THE HOUPHOUËT-BOIGNY ERA

President Houphouët-Boigny dictated the course of Ivorian politics from independence until his death—officially at 88 years of age—in December 1993, guiding the economic and political evolution of the country without any effective challenge to his rule. Political unrest occurred sporadically, although usually without effective leadership, and Houphouët-Boigny responded to public discontent by holding 'dialogues' which brought together different strands of opinion to allow grievances to be aired. Prominent personalities were periodically removed from positions of influence, but most eventually returned to office or were rehabilitated by means of patronage. Political opponents were at times awarded government posts as a means of defusing potential unrest. The principal guarantee of the security of the state remains in the form of a French military base and joint French-Ivorian military exercises.

Student unrest in 1968 and 1969 coincided with the beginning of an attempt to 'Ivorianize' public administration and the economy. French influence in Côte d'Ivoire has grown throughout the years since independence, and French investment has been favoured, creating a quasi-permanent French community numbering about 50,000 (although the number of French advisers working in the country has been reduced in recent years. Many important sectors of the economy are French-managed, and the security of French financial backing, together with membership of the Franc Zone, has contributed to economic growth.

Speculation about the succession to Houphouët-Boigny accompanied each of the electoral campaigns since the 1960s. Following Houphouët-Boigny's re-election for a fourth five-year term in 1975, a constitutional amendment was passed providing for the president of the national assembly, Philippe Yacé, to succeed as executive head of state in the event of the president's death, resignation or incapacity. A period of economic and social *malaise*, beginning in 1978, coincided with the beginning of Yacé's loss of presidential favour, after he was accused of manipulating mayoral elections. Houphouët-Boigny annulled the elections and Yacé did not appear in public for several months.

Houphouët-Boigny supervised wide-ranging economic and political changes in 1980, following rumours of a coup plot in April. Prior to presidential and legislative elections the order of succession was again revised with a further constitutional amendment allowing the president to nominate a vice-president who would automatically succeed him. The 1980 legislative elections involved considerable changes in leadership at national and local levels. For the first time voters were presented with a choice of candidates. At the outset of the election campaign in September Yacé was removed from political prominence by the abolition of his post as secretary-general of the PDCI–RDA. In a further diminution of Yacé's influence, Henri Konan Bédié, a former ambassador to the USA and finance minister who was being increasingly mentioned as a likely successor to the presidency, was named president of the new 147-member national assembly. However, Houphouët-Boigny, re-elected as president in October, refrained from designating a vice-president and delayed appointing a new government until February 1981. The growing economic problems of the early 1980s were accompanied by evidence of social discontent; strikes by students and teachers in 1982 and 1983, respectively, led to the temporary banning of their unions and to closures of educational establishments.

The succession issue re-emerged prior to the October 1985 presidential election, with the abolition of the still-vacant post of vice-president in a constitutional amendment which allowed only for the president of the legislature to succeed to the presidency on an interim basis. The official result of the presidential election recorded a 100% vote for Houphouët-Boigny. However, at legislative elections in the following month, in which 546 candidates (all PDCI–RDA members) contested the assembly's 175 seats, only 64 of the incumbent deputies were returned. In January 1986 Konan Bédié was re-elected president of the national assembly, and Yacé returned to political prominence with his election as president of the economic and social council, the country's third most senior political post. In April it was announced that the country wished to be known internationally by its official French name of 'Côte d'Ivoire', rather than having the name translated.

Tensions between the government and the secondary schoolteachers' union, SYNESCI (until this time the country's only independent trade union) reached a crisis in September 1987, when government-supported teachers seized control of the union's national executive. A number of union leaders were arrested and detained until July 1988. In December 1987 the dismissal of the minister of maritime affairs, Lamine Fadika, and of four PDCI–RDA officials was rumoured to be linked to the discovery of a plot to overthrow the government.

By the end of the 1980s Houphouët-Boigny's persistent refusal to designate a successor, and the absence of any clear indication of his willingness to retire, continued to suppress open political debate, while engendering considerable rivalry among potential successors. An opportunity for the airing of grievances was provided by the 'days of national dialogue', a series of meetings convened by the president in September 1989 and attended by representatives of the government and PDCI–RDA, armed forces and representatives of trade unions and professional organizations. Despite this atmosphere of apparent openness, Houphouët-Boigny rejected appeals to activate constitutional provisions permitting a multi-party system, on the grounds that political pluralism would impede progress towards national unity.

In early 1990 Côte d'Ivoire experienced unprecedented political upheaval, doubtless influenced by events elsewhere in the region and compounded by the continuing succession crisis and the prospect of economic austerity (as a result of agreements concluded with international creditors in 1989). Demonstrations in February and March 1990 among students and workers centred on the government's austerity policies, in particular the announcement in March of reductions in salaries of as much as 40% for public servants and the imposition of a new tax on private sector incomes. Many academic institutions were closed, and persistent anti-government demonstrations, as well as the circulation of leaflets calling for strike action, led to the deployment of troops in Abidjan. In early April, following the death of a student when troops intervened to disperse demonstrators, all educational establishments were closed and the 1989/90 academic year declared invalid.

By mid-April 1990 it was evident that the continued imposition of levies on income entailed too great a political risk and, moreover, would generate only a small proportion of Côte d'Ivoire's revenue requirements. Houphouët-Boigny appointed Alassane Ouattara, the governor of the Banque centrale de l'Afrique de l'ouest, to head a commission whose function would be to formulate adjustment measures that would be both more economically effective and more politically acceptable. In early May Houphouët-Boigny accepted a recommendation of the PDCI–RDA political bureau that constitution sanction be given to a plural political system. The status of hitherto unofficial opposition movements was subsequently formalized, and many new parties were formed. The government adopted a conciliatory attitude towards further instances of unrest, including a mutiny by army conscripts during May. At the end of the month a less stringent programme of austerity measures was announced, in accordance with the recommendations of the Ouattara commission.

Presidential and legislative elections were scheduled, respectively, for late October and late November 1990. Although the elections were to be held in the context of the country's new multi-party political system, tensions between the PDCI–RDA and the emerging political parties were evident. Opposition leaders accused the government of impeding the reform process, as Houphouët-Boigny refused to accede to demands that a transitional government be established and that a national conference be convened to discuss Côte d'Ivoire's political future. Security forces intervened at several rallies organized by the opposition, and in late September Houphouët-Boigny accused his opponents of complicity in an alleged plot to assassinate Pope John Paul II at the time of his visit to Côte d'Ivoire. (During his visit the Pope consecrated a basilica in Yamoussoukro, Houphouët-Boigny's birthplace, constructed—officially at Houphouët-Boigny's own expense—at a cost of some 40,000m. francs CFA.)

In October 1990 a congress of the PDCI–RDA endorsed Houphouët-Boigny as the party's presidential candidate. In the previous month Laurent Gbagbo had been chosen as the candidate of the Front populaire ivoirien (FPI), the leading opposition party. Côte d'Ivoire's first contested presidential election thus took place on 28 October. Houphouët-Boigny was elected for a seventh term of office, having, by the official count, received the support of 81.7% of those who voted (69.2% of the electorate). The FPI and its allies, claiming that Gbagbo had secured more than one-half of the votes cast, alleged electoral malpractice, and appealed unsuccessfully to the supreme court to invalidate the election.

In early November 1990 the legislature approved two constitutional amendments. The first (an amendment to Article 11) strengthened Konan Bédié's position by providing for the president of the national assembly to assume the functions of the president of the republic, should this office become vacant, until the expiry of the mandate of the previous incumbent. The second made provision for the appointment of a prime minister, a post which was subsequently given to Alassane Ouattara.

Almost 500 candidates, representing some 17 parties, contested legislative elections on 25 November 1990. According to the official results, the PDCI–RDA secured 163 seats in the new legislature, while the FPI won nine (Gbagbo was among the successful FPI candidates). Francis Wodié, the leader of the Parti ivoirien des travailleurs (PIT), was also elected, as were two independent candidates. Konan Bédié was subsequently reconfirmed as president of the legislature.

The composition of the new council of ministers, announced in late November 1990, indicated that priority would be given to economic considerations, with Ouattara, as prime minister, also taking the economy and finance portfolio. Several long-serving government members left office, and the total number of ministers was reduced from 29 to 20. A number of administrative changes were instituted in the first half of 1991, including policies of retrenchment in the public sector and the replacement of senior civil servants with younger technocrats. In April an extraordinary session of the PDCI–RDA appointed Laurent Dona-Fologo, a former government minister who had failed to secure election to the legislature in the 1990 elections, to the revived post of party secretary-general.

DISSENSION, REPRESSION AND SUCCESSION

The greatest source of opposition to the new administration was the education sector. In May 1991 security forces used violent methods to disperse a students' meeting at the University of Abidjan. About 180 students were said to have been arrested. Students and academic staff staged demonstrations in protest against the armed forces' brutality (many of which were dispersed by the security forces). There was further violence in June, when members of a students' association, the Fédération estudiantine et scolaire de Côte d'Ivoire (FESCI), attacked a student who had defied an order to boycott classes (and who was alleged to have been engaged by the PDCI–RDA to foment student unrest). In response, the government ordered that FESCI be disbanded and deployed security forces on the campus. In late June the Syndicat national de la recherche et de l'enseignement supérieur, an organization representing academic staff in higher education, organized an indefinite strike. The arrest in early July of 11 FESCI members, on suspicion of involvement in the attack on their fellow-student, prompted further protests, and it was not until August, when the government agreed to withdraw troops from the campus, to suspend legal proceedings against FESCI activists and to restore the right of 'non-academic assembly' at the university (although the ban on FESCI remained), that tensions were temporarily dispelled.

Amnesty measures during 1991 for a reported 11,000 detainees contrasted with the continued suppression of opponents of the Houphouët-Boigny regime and the implementation of far-reaching legislation governing the press. The political and social climate deteriorated following the publication, in late January 1992, of the findings of a commission of inquiry that had been appointed by Houphouët-Boigny to investigate the security forces' actions at the University of Abidjan in May 1991. Although the commission found the chief of the general staff of the armed forces, Gen. Robert Gueï, directly responsible for the acts of violence committed by his troops, Houphouët-Boigny expressed his support for Gueï, and emphasized that neither he nor any of those incriminated in the commission's report would be subject to disciplinary proceedings. Violent demonstrations by FESCI supporters immediately erupted on the university campus, prompting the authorities to close the university for 48 hours in early February, and opposition parties demanded sanctions against Gueï and called on the government to resign. Student unrest continued, and in mid-February 16 FESCI leaders, including the union's secretary-general, Martial Ahipeaud, were arrested. Shortly afterwards a 20,000 strong demonstration, organized by the FPI, degenerated into violence. More than 100 people were arrested following clashes between protesters and the security forces. Among those detained were Laurent Gbagbo and René Degny-Segui (the president of the national human rights organization). It was announced that they and other opposition leaders would be prosecuted under the term of a presidential ordinance, which, according to the government, had been signed by Houphouët-Boigny (who had been in Europe since early February) on the eve of the demonstration. The ordinance, which was rumoured among the opposition to have been introduced retrospectively, rendered political leaders responsible for violent acts committed by their supporters.

In late February 1992 Martial Ahipeaud was fined and sentenced to three years' imprisonment, after having been convicted of reconstituting a banned organization and of responsibility for acts of vandalism committed by students earlier in the month. In early March Gbagbo, Degny-Segui and seven others were each fined and sentenced to two-year prison terms; three others received lesser sentences, and the trials of opposition supporters continued during the following weeks. In late April the seven remaining FPI deputies began a boycott of the national assembly, in protest against the imprisonment of Gbagbo and another FPI member of parliament, and in the following month Francis Wodié similarly withdrew from the legislature.

Houphouët-Boigny returned to Côte d'Ivoire, after an absence of almost five months (most of which had been spent in France), in late June 1992. One month later he proclaimed an amnesty for all those convicted of political offences since the time of the 1990 disturbances. The amnesty was approved by PDCI–RDA deputies in the legislature later in the month. Opposition deputies maintained their boycott, protesting that, not only did the amnesty prevent detainees from pursuing the right of appeal, but that it also exempted members of the security forces from charges relating to offences allegedly committed during the period covered by the measure. In early August Houphouët-Boigny declared an amnesty for almost 2,500 minor offenders.

Discontent re-emerged in the education sector in the second half of 1992. The abolition of free public transport for those in higher education prompted violent protests in Abidjan in September, as a result of which about 15 students were arrested, and in November security forces were reported to have used tear gas to disperse students who were refusing to sit examinations at the University of Abidjan. There was further student unrest in April 1993, when a gathering of some 3,000 students at the University of Abidjan, organized by radical members of FESCI to demand increased access to grants and accommodation, as well as changes in the curricula of tertiary institutions outside Abidjan, was dispersed by security forces. As many as 45 students were later reported to have been arrested, as the meeting degenerated into violence. A boycott of classes was maintained until May, and in August students staged a two-week hunger strike outside the cathedral in Abidjan, following rumours (subsequently denied by the government) that university accommodation was to be privatized and to demand the payment of grant arrears.

Meanwhile, tensions between the Ouattara administration and elements of the military emerged in late March 1993, when about 45 members of the élite presidential guard staged a brief rebellion, taking two NCOs hostage at the presidential palace in Abidjan. The mutineers, who were demanding pay increases commensurate with those recently granted to civilian employees at the presidency, ended their protest following discussions with Houphouët-Boigny (who had not been at his official residence at the time of the incident). In early April, however, some 250 presidential guards, again demanding salary increases, mutinied in Yamoussoukro, returning to barracks only after negotiations with Houphouët-Boigny, Col Gueï and the minister of defence. The guards' actions were cited by Ouattara's opponents (notably, within the PDCI–RDA, supporters of Konan Bédié) as evidence of the prime minister's ineffectiveness in reconciling the demands of economic austerity with the need to maintain domestic harmony. In early March, moreover, the legislature had voted effectively to deprive Ouattara of control of the proceeds of the sale of state assets, recommending that a parliamentary committee be established to scrutinize the government's privatization programme: Ouattara's opponents had maintained that some state holdings, in particular the electricity and water utilities, had been undervalued prior to their sale to private interests.

Houphouët-Boigny left Côte d'Ivoire in mid-May 1993; he subsequently spent six months receiving medical treatment in France and Switzerland. As it became increasingly evident that the president's health was failing, controversy arose concerning the issue of succession. Many prominent politicians, including Ouattara and Gbagbo (both of whom were known to have presidential ambitions), denounced the process defined in the constitution, alleging that Article 11 effectively endorsed an hereditary presidency—Konan

Bédié, like Houphouët-Boigny, was a member of the Baoulé ethnic group from a family of chiefs and cocoa-planters—and demanding that the constitution be revised once more to permit the president of the legislature to assume the post of president of the republic on an interim base only, pending new elections.

President Houphouët-Boigny died in Yamoussoukro on 7 December 1993. Later the same day Konan Bédié made a television broadcast announcing that he was assuming the duties of president of the republic, with immediate effect, in accordance with the constitution. Ouattara initially refused to recognize Konan Bédié's right of succession; however, France assumed what was widely regarded as a decisive role in the matter, promptly acknowledging Konan Bédié's legitimacy as president and conveying official condolences to him in his capacity as the new head of state. Ouattara resigned the premiership two days after Houphouët-Boigny's death, and the supreme court confirmed Konan Bédié as president on 10 December. The armed forces formally declared allegiance to the new head of state, and Konan Bédié met with Gbagbo and Wodié, although both declined to endorse his accession to the presidency.

Daniel Kablan Duncan, formerly minister-delegate, responsible for the economy, finance and planning, was appointed to succeed Ouattara as prime minister. His government, named in mid-December 1993, retained senior members of the previous administration in charge of defence, foreign affairs, the interior and raw materials, and included two close associates of Konan Bédié, Laurent Dona-Fologo and Thimothée N'Guetta Ahoua, as ministers of state. Lamine Fadika returned to the government as minister of mines and energy, while the new minister of culture, Bernard Zadi Zaourou (the leader of the Union des sociaux-démocrates), had earlier expressed his opposition to Konan Bédié's unelected accession to the presidency.

During a two-month period of official mourning following Houphouët-Boigny's death, Konan Bédié conducted an effective purge of Ouattara sympathizers, appointing his own supporters to positions of influence in government agencies, the judiciary and in the state-owned media. Supporters of the former prime minister were prevented by security forces from welcoming him at the airport in Abidjan when he returned from an overseas visit in January 1994. Ouattara was, moreover, subject of virulent attacks in the official daily newspaper, *Fraternité Matin*, which emphasized both his Muslim and Burkinabè origins. The first months of Konan Bédié's presidency were notable for the prosecution of several journalists, deemed to have been disrespectful to the president or other state officials: among those who received custodial sentences were the editor of a pro-Ouattara weekly, *Le Patriote*, and the director and journalists of the FPI daily, *La Voie*.

Houphouët-Boigny's state funeral, which took place in the basilica in Yamoussoukro in early February 1994, was attended by 24 African heads of state, as well as Presidents Mitterrand of France (leading an 80-strong delegation from that country) and Hrawi of Lebanon.

Several months of sporadic labour unrest were brought to an end by Houphouët-Boigny's death, and, largely owing to the period of national mourning, reactions to the devaluation, in January 1994, of the CFA franc were generally more muted in Côte d'Ivoire than in other countries of the region. Opposition leaders did, none the less, denounce the measure, and workers' representatives denounced salary increases of 5%–15%, together with compensatory tax reductions and price controls, as insufficient to offset the adverse effects of the currency's depreciation. In May and June, moreover, a new campaign by students, who staged demonstrations and strikes in an attempt to secure the payment of grant arrears, resulted in numerous arrests. Despite Konan Bédié's earlier criticism of Ouattara's economic policies, notably the dismantling of the state-owned sector, the new president and prime minister confirmed their commitment to adjustment measures initiated under Ouattara, and the pursuit of the privatization process was a major element of financial programmes agreed with international creditors in early 1994.

Konan Bédié was elected chairman of the PDCI–RDA in late April 1994. His position as head of state was further strengthened by Ouattara's appointment, in May, to the post of deputy managing director of the IMF, based in Washington, DC. None the less, rumours of divisions within the PDCI–RDA were confirmed in June, when disaffected members left the party to form a new organization, the Rassemblement des républicains.

FOREIGN RELATIONS

Throughout his presidency Houphouët-Boigny was active in regional and international affairs, assisting in the peace process in Angola and, despite strong criticism by the Organization of African Unity, favouring black African dialogue with the apartheid regime in South Africa. Prime minister Vorster and President Botha of South Africa visited Côte d'Ivoire while in office, and President de Klerk had also been received by Houphouët-Boigny before the dismantling of apartheid legislation began. South African financial assistance was granted for the Ivorian gold-mining, agricultural and agro-industrial sectors following a visit by de Klerk in December 1989. In April 1992 Côte d'Ivoire became the first black African country to establish diplomatic relations with South Africa.

In regional affairs, Côte d'Ivoire under Houphouët-Boigny exerted a strong conservative influence, and tended to favour the maintenance of close links with the West, although Houphouët-Boigny was particularly critical in the final years of his regime of what he regarded as attempts by 'Anglo-Saxon' countries to depress the prices of Africa's major commodities. Relations with France were generally close, despite the apparent support of the French socialists for Gbagbo and the FPI, and relations were expected to remain cordial under Konan Bédié.

In late 1989 the government of Liberia alleged that rebel forces, who were involved in an attempt to overthrow the incumbent regime, had entered the country through Côte d'Ivoire. Despite evidence to the contrary, Houphouët-Boigny consistently denied that his government was supporting Charles Taylor's National Patriotic Front of Liberia (NPFL), which was instrumental in the overthrow of President Doe in mid-1990. During 1991 Côte d'Ivoire assumed a prominent role in attempts to achieve a peaceful dialogue between opposing forces in Liberia. A series of negotiations involving the rival factions was initiated in Yamoussoukro in the second half of the year. In December, none the less, the Liberian interim president, Dr Amos Sawyer, accused Côte d'Ivoire and Burkina of providing the NPFL with arms and training facilities. Although Côte d'Ivoire did not initially contribute troops to the ECOMOG military observer group that was dispatched to Liberia by the Economic Community of West African States (ECOWAS) in August 1990, Houphouët-Boigny attended the ECOWAS summit meeting, convened in November 1992 in Abuja, Nigeria, to discuss the Liberian issue, and supported a communiqué proposing that ECOMOG be extended to all ECOWAS member states and appealing for UN intervention in the peace process. However, relations with other ECOWAS members deteriorated in late February 1993, when (following recent allegations that NPFL units were operating from Ivorian territory) aircraft under ECOMOG command bombed the Ivorian border region of Danané. Côte d'Ivoire formally protested to ECOWAS, which expressed its regret at the incident, claiming that the area attacked had been mistaken for Liberian territory. Rumours persisted that Ivorian authorities were violating the international economic and military blockade of Liberia by (either actively or passively) allowing the NPFL access to the sea via the port of San Pedro in south-western Côte d'Ivoire, and there were reports that several of Taylor's close and influential associates had taken up residence in Abidjan. In late May Côte d'Ivoire protested that ECOMOG jets had again bombed territory in the Danané region, although this was denied by the ECOMOG command. In early August, at the request of the UN special representative for Liberia, the Ivorian government announced that convoys transporting humanitarian aid to Liberia would no longer be permitted to travel through Côte d'Ivoire—ECOMOG and the Liberian interim government had for some time alleged that such convoys were being used to channel military assistance to the NPFL. Shortly afterwards it was announced that humanitarian aid transfers would resume via Côte d'Ivoire, subject to inspection by UN or ECOMOG representatives. Côte d'Ivoire deployed additional troops near the border with Liberia in September, following an attack on a refugee camp on Ivorian territory. According to the office of the UN High Commissioner for Refugees, some 185,000 people who had fled the Liberian conflict were sheltering in Côte d'Ivoire in early 1993.

Relations with neighbouring Ghana deteriorated in late October and early November 1993, when attacks in Ghana on Ivorian footballers and their supporters provoked violent reprisals against the Ghanaian community (and also against other immigrant groups) in Côte d'Ivoire, as a result of which 25 people (mostly Ghanaians) were killed. As many as 2,000 people were reported to have taken refuge at the Ghanaian ambassador's residence in Abidjan, while some 200 Ivorians were said to have been detained in Ghana. Later in November operations began to repatriate some 3,000 Ghanaians, although by the end of the year there were reports that many of these were returning to Côte d'Ivoire.

Economy

EDITH HODGKINSON

For some 20 years following its independence, Côte d'Ivoire was remarkable for its very high rate of economic growth—with gross domestic product (GDP) increasing, in real terms, by an annual average of 11% in 1960–70 and 6%–7% in 1970–80—which brought it into the ranks of middle-income developing countries. During the 1980s, however, the economy entered a period of decline, owing mainly to a weakening in international prices for the country's major export commodities (coffee and cocoa) and the serious drought of 1982–84. GDP stagnated in 1982, and fell by just over 2% per year in 1983 and 1984. Economic growth was resumed in 1985, with record harvests of cocoa and cotton and a recovery in coffee output (owing to the ending of the drought), and higher world prices for most export commodities. Growth of GDP reached 4.9% in that year, and 3.4% in 1986. However, the economy's sensitivity to developments in international markets for cocoa and coffee was revealed when the sharp fall in export prices for both commodities in 1987 (to below Ivorian production costs), for cocoa in subsequent years and for coffee since 1989 resulted in a decline in GDP for five consecutive years (1987–91), representing a cumulative decline of one-seventh. Gross national product (GNP), according to estimates by the World Bank, was US $8,655m. in 1992, equivalent to $670 per head—one-fifth lower than in 1980.

A new phase in the development of the Ivorian economy began in 1991 with the implementation of a far-reaching programme of structural reform, involving the acceptance by Côte d'Ivoire of an IMF/World Bank programme of fiscal austerity and market liberalization (including the disengagement of the state from both production and service sectors). The 'Plan Ouattara' had ambitious targets: an increase of 5% in GDP by 1995 and the achievement of an average annual growth rate of 3.2% in 1992–95; a doubling in the rate of investment growth, and a reduction by more than one-half in the deficit on the current account of the balance of payments. However, even with financial support from foreign donors and creditors, GDP stagnated in 1992 and declined once more (by 1.1%) in 1993.

Alassane Ouattara's departure from the post of prime minister, following the death of President Houphouët-Boigny in December 1993, did not entail any change in Côte d'Ivoire's overall economic strategy. The objective remains a return to economic growth, with real growth projected at 2.0% for 1994, 5.7% for 1995 and 6.4% for 1996. The devaluation, by 50%, of the CFA franc, in January 1994, should aid this process, since it will enhance the competitiveness of Ivorian exports (to the extent that, after an initial surge, inflation is held in check) and stimulate the production of agricultural goods, both for export (as higher earnings in local currency terms are, at least in part, passed on to producers) and for the domestic market (to substitute imports which have become suddenly and substantially more expensive). The adverse consequence of the devaluation—the immediate reduction in purchasing power, which some sectors of the population cannot easily remedy—will necessitate new measures of income protection, such as temporary price subsidies on staple foods and the implementation of labour-intensive public works programmes, which will strain budget resources. Foreign financial support at a higher level than in recent years will thus be essential, in the form of both new funds and the relief of debt liabilities, if the structural objectives of the programme (the reduction of the fiscal deficit, accelerated privatization and the liberalization of foreign trade) are to be achieved.

A return to strong economic growth is all the more exigent given the very high rate of population growth. At about 3.8% per year since 1983, this is one of the fastest in the world (bringing the total population to an estimated level of 12.9m. by mid-1992). The rate of urbanization has been rapid (one-half again the overall rate of population growth), with 40% of the population residing in urban areas in 1984—more than double the proportion in 1960. Abidjan's population was thought have reached 2.5m. by 1989, i.e. eight times its level of 25 years earlier, and urban unemployment (registered at 22.4%—excluding foreigners—in 1988) is a growing problem. This pressure on Abidjan was a significant factor in the designation of Yamoussoukro as the country's future political capital, although it is envisaged that Abidjan will remain the major centre for economic activity. A major factor in population growth has been immigration from less prosperous neighbouring countries, particularly Burkina Faso, Guinea and Mali, and these immigrants now constitute almost one-third of the population, providing vital manpower for plantations and urban services.

AGRICULTURE

Although the Ivorian economy is relatively diversified, it remains dependent on agriculture, which contributes almost one-half of GDP and employs about 54% of the economically active population. Agriculture provides about three-quarters of export earnings, and the sector's rapid growth was the basis for the economic expansion of the 1960s and 1970s.

The principal cash crops are coffee and cocoa. The cultivation and processing of coffee is the main source of income for about one-half of all Ivorians, and it employs more than 2.5m. people. In 1992 Côte d'Ivoire was the second largest African producer, after Ethiopia. The record crop of 366,838 metric tons was registered in 1980/81, and was grown on about 280,000 small, family-owned plantations covering some 1m. ha. Output has since been in overall decline. Drought reduced the crop to only 85,200 tons in 1983/84, but after a strong recovery in the following year the crop has fluctuated in the range 186,000–284,000 tons, while official forecasts for 1993/94 envisaged output of as little as 140,000 tons. By the early 1990s about three-quarters of the country's coffee plants were more than 15 years old, and were thus producing well below potential capacity.

Government plans provide for extensive replanting of the old robusta plantations with a cross between robusta and arabica varieties: the total area under cultivation is projected to increase by 270,000 ha to 1.3m. ha by the end of the century, and production is expected to consolidate at 300,000 tons per year.

Production of cocoa beans doubled between 1970 and 1979, making Côte d'Ivoire the largest exporter in the world. The country became the world's largest producer when its level of production overtook Ghana's in 1977/78. (It had overtaken Nigeria's production in 1974.) Overall output continued to increase, to reach a record 848,900 tons in 1988/89. This level has not been matched since, with the crop averaging some 763,000 tons per year in 1989/90–1992/93 and estimated at 750,000 tons in 1993/94. The government has implemented a major replanting programme, eliminating ageing cultivation in the traditional cocoa belt, in the south-east, and developing it in the west, where rainfall is abundant. The expansion in cocoa production was also attributable to the transfer to the cultivation of cocoa by many former coffee producers: until 1989 the two crops attracted virtually the same producer price, although the latter was more heavily taxed and is more difficult to grow. However, the decline in prices in 1987 and the unfavourable outlook for 1988 prompted the government to suspend the replanting campaign at the end of 1987 and to abandon its production target of 1m. tons annually by the end of the century.

A state marketing agency, the Caisse de stabilisation et de soutien des prix des productions agricoles (Caistab), traditionally purchased all cocoa and coffee production, and during the boom years of 1975–77 this agency bought the crops from producers at prices that were significantly below world market levels, so providing a surplus for investment in other sectors of the economy. Subsequently, however, the fall in prices on the world market meant that the government was unable to maintain the real income of producers, and purchase prices remained unchanged for four years until 1983/84 (before the presidential election was due to take place). Purchase prices were increased in that year and in the following two years, but the steep fall in world prices (by 40% for coffee and 20% for cocoa) caused another 'freeze' in 1986/87 and 1987/88. In early 1988 the government imposed an embargo on sales of cocoa, in an unsuccessful attempt to bring about an increase in international prices for that commodity. However, the expected further rise in output in 1988/89, together with the country's limited storage capacity, obliged the government to modify its policy. In late 1988 an agreement was concluded with a French commodity broker, the Cie financière sucres et denrées (Sucden), under the terms of which the latter was to buy 400,000 tons of Ivorian cocoa. Half of this consignment was to be sold to end-users, while the rest was to be stored in Europe for a two-year period. In all, Sucden purchased 550,000 tons of the 1988/89 crop, while a US commodity trader, Philipp Brothers, bought 280,000 tons. However, this policy of bulk sales to major buyers was abandoned in late 1989, by which time the collapse of international prices for cocoa, in conjunction with pressure from the IMF to end the drain on budget resources that Caistab's operations represented, had obliged the Ivorian government to impose very steep reductions in the official prices payable to producers of cocoa. Producer prices for the 1989/90 season were thus reduced from 400 francs CFA (a level that had been maintained since 1985/86) to 200 francs CFA per kg—their lowest level since 1978, while the price payable to producers of robusta coffee was adjusted from 200 francs CFA to 100 francs CFA per kg; these prices were maintained during 1990/91–1992/93. However, there was a significant new development in the 1991/92 season, with the abolition of export quotas for cocoa and coffee, while the liberalization of the sector was completed when Caistab was opened to participation by private interests and its quality-control function was eliminated. The agency now concentrates on forward selling on the international market, and forecast a return to profitability in 1993 for the first time since 1984. Producer prices for both cocoa and coffee were increased immediately after the January 1994 devaluation, although not to the full extent of the depreciation in the currency's value: the cocoa price was set at 240 francs CFA per kg for the 1993/94 season and 290 francs CFA for 1994/95, while prices for coffee were to rise to 220 francs CFA and 265 francs CFA per kg respectively.

With about one-half of Côte d'Ivoire's total export earnings provided by sales of these two crops, both highly vulnerable to international market trends, the government has emphasized the need for diversification in agricultural production. Since the 1960s Côte d'Ivoire has become a major producer of palm oil, and since the mid-1970s there has been greater emphasis on the local processing of palm products. A series of replanting programmes has been supported by the World Bank, the EC (now European Union), France and the United Kingdom, and in the mid-1980s the replanting rate was 10,000 ha per year. The current programme, which began in 1986, aimed, initially, to clear and replant 65,000 ha, and to construct two processing mills: the target was to make Côte d'Ivoire the world's leading producer of palm oil. Although production of palm oil reached a record 200,313 tons in 1987, the steep fall in world prices in that year prompted the government to reduce the planting target and to postpone the construction of one of the mills. The first processing mill was inaugurated in 1990, but construction of the second has been postponed and the planting target lowered. However, output rose to more than 260,000 tons in 1990 and 1991, declining marginally, to 244,038 tons, in 1992.

Cotton cultivation has done particularly well in recent years. Production had increased only slowly until the mid-1970s, when the government embarked on a deliberate policy of helping the farmers in the north of the country. The programme exceeded its target of 100,000 metric tons of seed cotton (set for 1980) during the season of 1977/78; production reached a record 290,600 tons in 1988/89, before declining slightly, to 241,700 tons in 1989/90 (mainly owing to unfavourable weather and the inadequacy of official prices paid to producers). Output has since averaged almost 245,000 tons per year and Côte d'Ivoire vies with Sudan and Mali for the position as Africa's second largest cotton producer (after Egypt). Most of the cotton is processed locally in eight ginning complexes (total capacity 300,000 tons per year), both for export (some 80% of total production) and for the local textile industry.

The rubber industry has shown considerable success in recent years, and the government has ambitious plans to become Africa's most important rubber producer by the end of the century, with a projected annual output of 130,000 tons (almost twice the 1992/93 level of 74,000 tons) by the mid-1990s. It is hoped to bring 42,000 ha of new land under cultivation. Côte d'Ivoire is also a significant producer of pineapples. Output was severely affected by the drought of 1982–84, before recovering briefly during the mid-1980s, but exports then declined from 149,700 tons in 1986 to their lowest level of 78,700 tons by 1988. Since then exports have gradually recovered, reaching 114,100 tons in 1992.

In recent years the government stressed the need to increase production of basic food crops, in which Côte d'Ivoire was not self-sufficient. The country is normally self-sufficient in maize (with harvests averaging 505,000 tons per year in 1989/90–1991/92) and in cassava, yams and plantains (producing an annual average of some 5m. tons over the same period). Farmers in the traditional cocoa belt are increasingly engaged in food production, while two of the country's sugar complexes have been converted to rice cultivation. By the mid-1980s the rice development programme was showing an effect, and output reached 668,000 tons in 1990/91. None the less, the rapid rise in demand, reflecting the pace of urbanization (which entails a switch in grain preference to rice), meant that Côte d'Ivoire continued to import rice; it was, however, expected that the devaluation of the currency would depress purchases of the foreign product.

A deficiency in sugar supply and the need to save foreign exchange on sugar imports led the government to launch a sugar programme in 1973. The objective was to meet the growing level of internal consumption and to allow a surplus for export. Production began at the first complex in 1977, and by 1980 the two schemes in operation could supply most of internal demand, estimated at 80,000 tons of raw sugar per year. However, permission had already been given to build further sugar complexes at four other sites. The cost of sugar production in the local complexes proved to be unexpectedly high, and was at least double the world market price at the beginning of 1980. This situation, in conjunction with the need to reduce foreign borrowing, led to the cancellation of six more planned complexes and the reduction of planned areas of sugar cane plantations on those units already sanctioned. Output of raw sugar from the six sugar schemes in the country increased steadily, from 52,500 metric tons in 1978/79 to a record 186,000 tons in 1982/83, but fell in subsequent years, to 111,500 tons in 1984/85, owing partly to drought and partly to the closure of two sugar complexes for conversion to the cultivation of staple crops. Recovery in subsequent years was fairly steady, reaching an estimated 136,000 tons in 1991/92. Under a $112m. investment programme, supported by French credits, production is due to be restored to some 186,000 tons annually.

Forestry provided the country's third main source of export earnings, from both logs and sawn timber, until it was overtaken by petroleum products in 1984. Most production is carried out by large integrated firms, many of which are foreign-owned. The area of exploitable timber had fallen to only about 1m. ha in 1987, compared with some 15.6m. ha at independence, because of inadequate reafforestation and the encroachment of agriculture on forest areas. In an attempt to conserve resources, the government therefore restricted commercial production to 3m. cu m per year. With domestic demand rising, the volume available for export is expected to decline further. Exports fell from 3.1m. cu m (logs) in 1980 to only 221,000 cu m in 1992. Meanwhile, the World Bank and other external agencies are supporting a reafforestation programme, with a projected cost of 70,000m. francs CFA, which includes replanting on 22,000 ha, with a production target of 6.6m. cu m over 35 years. Progress has, however, been disappointing (replanting has recently averaged only 5,000 ha per year), and the government has committed itself to a ban on exports of timber once the country's foreign payments position has improved.

Livestock herds are small: in 1992 there were some 1.2m. cattle, an estimated 2.1m. sheep and goats and 382,000 pigs—and meat production satisfies only one-third of national demand. Fishing is a significant activity (Abidjan is the largest tuna-fishing port in Africa, with an annual catch of about 96,000 tons). However, most of the catch is made by foreign ships and merely transits through the port, and Ivorian participation in this sector is still low, with Côte d'Ivoire's own fishing fleet numbering only 38 vessels, and most traditional fishing being undertaken by non-Ivorians.

MANUFACTURING AND MINING

The manufacturing sector, which (according to some estimates) accounted for 17% of GDP in 1985, is dominated by agro-industrial activities—such as the processing of cocoa, coffee, cotton, oil palm, pineapples and fish. It was stimulated, immediately after independence, by the need to replace goods traditionally imported from Senegal, the manufacturing centre for colonial French West Africa, and it formed one of the most dynamic areas of the economy during the period of its most rapid growth. In 1965–74 Côte d'Ivoire's manufacturing output expanded, in real terms, at an average rate of 8.9% per year, with growth easing to 5.4% per year in the following decade, after the main industrial opportunities had been exploited. However, this sector continues to be sustained by the high rate of growth of domestic demand, arising from the rapid increase in the country's population. Since the late 1980s the emphasis of government policy has shifted from import substitution to export promotion.

A significant strand in government policy has been the attempt to 'Ivorianize' both equity and management. Ivorian-held equity in industrial firms, virtually nil in 1960, had reached almost two-thirds of the total by late 1982. However, this was almost entirely held by the government (51.5%), while the private-sector Ivorian share was very small (13.6%). This reflected the development of parastatal organizations, during the 1970s, as a means of restructuring and diversifying the economy. However, a succession of government reports drew attention to the low level of profitability in state-owned companies and the excessive use of foreign finance, in addition to mismanagement, corruption and general lack of managerial flair. The financial losses being incurred by the parastatal companies became so serious that in 1980 the government reversed its policy regarding these organizations and began to dispose of its interests through outright sale, leasing, or the creation of autonomous co-operatives. An important element of the stabilization programme that was introduced by Alassane Ouattara in 1990 was an acceleration of the 'privatization' process. Several major companies had been sold off by the end of 1992, including the electricity and water utilities, and the telecommunications agency. The government holding in the petroleum refinery was scheduled for sale to majority private interests, as were Palmindustrie, the 'centrepiece' of the oil palm sector, and the three major companies involved in rubber production. The government aimed to dispose of 80 of a total of about 140 public sector companies by the end of 1995. However, the programme, particularly the sale of majority holdings in the electricity and water utilities to subsidiaries of the Bouygues group of France, caused considerable public disquiet. The new president, Henri Konan Bédié, had formerly led the parliamentary opposition to such sales; however, following his accession to the presidency he confirmed his administration's commitment to the programme of divestment, and the terms of the IMF credit agreed in early 1994 referred to 'accelerated' privatization.

The only significant activity in the mining sector (apart from petroleum production) is diamond extraction, but the output from two mines, at Tortiya and Séguéla, has significantly declined from the levels of the early 1970s (some 15,000 carats are produced annually, compared with 209,000 carats in 1975), and this sector is now operated by small-scale private companies. Figures for diamond production in the late 1980s ranged from 20,000 carats per year (legal exports) to 250,000 carats annually (including illicit production). The exploitation of deposits of gold-bearing rock at Ity, in the west, began in January 1991, in a joint venture with the Cie française des mines (a subsidiary of the Bureau de recherches géologiques et minières); production reached 1,000 kg in 1992. A second gold mine has been developed at Aniuri, in a joint venture between Eden Roc Mineral Corporation (of Canada) and the state mining company. Operations began in mid-1993.

ENERGY

Electricity generating capacity rose very rapidly, from only 41 MW in 1962 to 675 MW in the early 1980s, as the result of the development of hydroelectric capacity. However, plans to build a massive dam and generating station at Soubré on the Sassandra river, with an installed capacity of 328 MW, were jeopardized when the 1982–84 drought meant that water levels at hydroelectric installations were too low to allow power generation. New thermal capacity was installed to make up the deficit. The contribution of hydroelectric plant to total electricity production fell to 23% in 1984, compared with 90% at the beginning of the decade. Although it recovered to 67% in 1985 (a share it has broadly maintained since), the future of the Soubré scheme remains uncertain. Meanwhile, negotiations for the exploitation of offshore reserves of natural gas, estimated at 550,000m. cu ft (15,600m. cu m), to fuel the 100-MW thermal plant at Vridi collapsed, and the easing in petroleum prices during the mid-1980s made the project less attractive. The government has been engaged in lengthy negotiations with a consortium headed by Apache International of the

USA for the development of the field, with a production capacity of 1.5m. cu m per day. In addition, a new enterprise, Cie des énergies de Côte d'Ivoire (CENCI), in which private French interests have a majority stake, signed an agreement in late 1992 to lay a pipeline and construct a gas treatment plant and power station. Total investment in the development is estimated at $220m., with CENCI providing one-quarter and the World Bank a loan of $40m. Work on the scheme was due to start in late 1993, but was delayed pending clarification of Konan Bédié's attitude to foreign ownership of strategic sectors.

A significant development was the discovery of small-scale reserves of offshore petroleum in 1975. Total reserves of the Bélier field, located 15 km south of Grand Bassam, were estimated to be 75m. tons. A larger discovery was made in the Espoir field (also offshore) in 1980, but production failed to meet expectations. Output from Bélier attained a maximum of 457,000 tons in 1982, and that from Espoir reached a peak of 771,000 tons in 1984, to give a record total output of 1.1m. tons in that year. However, output declined in subsequent years, to 975,000 tons in 1986, and operations at the Espoir field were suspended in early 1989, while those at the Bélier field ceased one year later. In addition, offshore exploration for petroleum had virtually ceased by 1984, with the oil rigs moving to potentially more interesting offshore fields further south. The Ivorian continental shelf had proved difficult to drill, with oil reserves scattered in small pockets. None the less, there was considerable optimism during the first half of 1994 with regard to the viability of deposits of petroleum and natural gas to the south-west of Abidjan.

Exports of petroleum, which began in 1982, slackened in line with production trends from their peak of 366,000 tons in 1984 to 170,000 tons in 1985, but imports (principally from Nigeria) have risen to meet the requirements of the petroleum refinery at Abidjan. This is operated by the Société ivoirienne de raffinage, currently jointly owned by the government and foreign oil companies, and is designed to meet the needs of Côte d'Ivoire, Mali and Burkina Faso. For several years, it operated at only around one-half of its annual capacity (of 3.2m. tons) because of reduced demand in these economies, and the resulting financial difficulties were exacerbated by large outstanding debts from the government and the national electricity company. Capacity was therefore reduced, with the elimination of an 800,000-ton distillation unit.

TRANSPORT

The most important transport facility is the deep-water port of Abidjan, rivalled in francophone West Africa only by the iron ore-handling port of Nouadhibou in Mauritania. In 1986–92 Abidjan handled an average of 9.8m. tons of freight per year, including shipments to and from Burkina Faso and Mali. This represents a recovery to near the levels recorded in 1980, after several years during which the volume of traffic fell, mainly because of a decline in timber exports and oil imports. Major improvements have been carried out, including the installation of large-scale container-handling facilities. The government has obtained funding from the World Bank for a development programme, to include the construction of a terminal for sawn timber, a clinker conveyor belt and mooring berth and an internal road, as well as the enlargement of the Vridi canal (which allows passage through the reef). Work on these projects began in 1988. Another major port has been developed since 1971 at San Pedro, mainly to handle timber exports. This handled total traffic of almost 755,000 tons in the first nine months of 1991 (about one-half of the level of 1983, owing to the decline in exports of logs).

Côte d'Ivoire has some 55,000 km of classified roads. A programme to construct some 1,300 km of new roads and upgrade the network was completed in 1988. A further scheme, to be financed by the African Development Bank (ADB), under which 600 km of roads were to be built or upgraded, was initiated in 1989, while 350 km were to be upgraded in 1991–94, and a four-year (1994–97) programme for the repair and extension of the road network was to be supported by the World Bank, the ADB, the West African Development Bank and the governments of Germany and Japan. A railway line links Abidjan to Ouagadougou, with 638 km of line in Côte d'Ivoire. The line was managed by a single authority, the Régie du chemin de fer Abidjan–Niger (RAN), but experienced financial and technical difficulties, with both freight and passenger traffic in decline. In 1986 the Ivorian government requested that each national participant manage its portion of the line. The separation was effected in 1989: RAN was liquidated, and its Ivorian activities were assumed by the Société ivoirienne des chemins de fer—the sale of which was envisaged under the privatization programme. Côte d'Ivoire has international airports at Abidjan and Yamoussoukro; in addition, there are several regional airports.

TOURISM

Tourism developed strongly in the 1970s, with a newly-created ministry stimulating diversification in location (away from the Abidjan area) and in type of visitor (away from business executives, who previously accounted for almost two-thirds of arrivals). Special tax incentives and government guarantees on loans were offered for hotel construction. By late 1982 the country's hotel capacity was some 9,500 rooms, of which some 4,300 were in classified establishments, while a new form of tourism has developed with holiday villages set in rural areas. The annual number of tourists increased from some 93,000 in 1974 to 198,900 in 1979, with business visitors accounting for 40% of arrivals. However, arrivals have since remained at about 200,000 per year, reflecting world trends in tourism. With hotel capacity continuing to rise, occupancy rates averaged only 33% in 1990. Nevertheless, this sector, although now much less buoyant, continues to make a useful contribution to Côte d'Ivoire's earnings of foreign exchange (some $70m. per year), and employs about 10,000 people.

FINANCE AND DEVELOPMENT

Budget spending has risen in parallel with economic growth, with current spending in the past covered from internal sources and investment spending largely financed by foreign borrowing. The deterioration in the economy during the early 1980s, and the associated fall in tax receipts, threatened serious disequilibrium. In response, a series of austerity budgets was adopted, with total spending declining, in real terms, each year from 1982 onwards. Reductions were initially limited to the investment budget, which fell from 379,000m. francs CFA in 1982 to only 187,000m. francs CFA in 1985, halving its value in real terms. Although Yamoussoukro, Houphouët-Boigny's birthplace, was designated as the new capital of Côte d'Ivoire in 1983, all new projects in the town were suspended. There was no investment in new projects in 1985, and local sources were to finance 42% of the capital budget, compared with only 19% in the previous year. (A major aim of the austerity programme was to reduce external borrowing.) In 1986 current spending declined, in real terms, for the first time, with restrictions being applied to recruitment to the civil service and reductions in salaries for staff in parastatal bodies. These austerity measures transformed the budget balance from a record deficit of 361,000m. francs CFA (equivalent to 13% of GDP) in 1982 to a small surplus (83,000m. francs CFA) in 1985, permitting a slight relaxation in 1986, when investment spending rose to 201,000m. francs CFA. However, the sharp fall in commodity prices in that year resulted in continuing fiscal austerity in 1987 and 1988, with investment expenditure declining again, to 123,000m. and 143,000m. francs CFA respectively, and current spending slightly lower in real terms. None the less, the fiscal deficit widened again, to 449,000m. francs CFA in 1988 (equivalent to 14.3% of GDP), as a result of the decline in revenue owing to lower international prices for Côte d'Ivoire's principal commodities, together with increased expenditure to compensate Caistab for the decline in prices. Fiscal austerity was reimposed in 1989: current expenditure was held marginally below the 1988 level, while the investment budget was reduced by more than one-third, to bring total spending to 1,169,000m. francs CFA (little changed from 1988). However, budget receipts declined significantly, to 670,000m. francs CFA, resulting in a deficit of 499,000m. francs CFA (16.9% of GDP). A reduction in expenditure in 1990 more than offset the further decline in revenues, to reduce the budget deficit to 341,000m. francs CFA (12.9% of GDP), while in 1991 a small reduction in current spending and a marginal rise in revenue (in part generated by increased income taxes), narrowed the deficit to 330,000m. francs CFA. Since this was the sum allocated to interest payments, the new government of Alassane Ouattara could claim to have achieved its aim of eliminating the deficit excluding interest payments on government debt. However, in terms of the more usual definition of budgetary balance, Côte d'Ivoire was still recording a very substantial fiscal deficit, and was far from achieving the restructuring of public finance that was being strongly advocated by the IMF. The budgets for 1992 and 1993 forecast deficits of 419,000m. francs CFA and 375,000m. francs CFA respectively. The 1994 budget had to be redrafted following the currency devaluation. The focus of IMF pressure continues to be spending on public sector salaries, which accounts for about two-thirds of total current expenditure. Ouattara resisted the implementation of salary cuts, seeking instead to reduce expenditure on salaries by means of 'natural wastage' and voluntary redundancies. The new administration has proposed an effective cut in public sector salaries by setting pay increases at only 5%–15% in 1994—far below the expected level of inflation arising from the currency depreciation.

FOREIGN TRADE AND PAYMENTS

Despite its very rapid economic growth during the period 1950–75, Côte d'Ivoire, in the past, had fewer problems with the balance of payments than most comparable African economies. Exports increased at a faster rate than GNP, with real expansion averaging 9% per year in 1962–75, and they remain the main factor contributing to the growth of GNP.

Côte d'Ivoire's balance of trade has always been in surplus because of the strength of its exports, which have largely been determined by the level of earnings from sales of coffee and cocoa. With the recovery in coffee and cocoa output after the 1982–84 drought, the surplus increased more than fivefold in 1984, to 525,700m. francs CFA, and reached a new record level of 545,100m. francs CFA in 1985, despite a relaxation of the import restraints that had been imposed to offset the decline in commodity earnings. The surplus had been halved by 1987, and was only 206,600m. francs CFA in 1988, owing to the severe decline in international prices for cocoa and coffee, and in spite of the reduction in expenditure on imports (because of the contraction in the economy). The recovery in the volume of cocoa exports in 1989, following the ending of the moratorium on exports of that commodity, contributed to an increase in total earnings that was not entirely counterbalanced by a recovery in import spending, resulting in a marginally higher surplus, of 222,100m. francs CFA. Balance-of-payments figures (a slightly different measure of foreign trade, which understates the total cost of imports) show a limited improvement in export earnings in 1990, before a regression to 1989 levels in 1991 and a slight upturn in both 1992 and 1993. Meanwhile, imports showed only minor fluctuations, and in 1993 were probably little changed from their value in 1989, implying a trade surplus in the region of $1,000m.

The sharp increase in the surplus up to 1985, as well as the decline in private transfers of funds, reduced the substantial deficit on the current account of the balance of payments that Côte d'Ivoire recorded at the beginning of the decade ($1,827m. in 1980). In 1985 the balance actually showed a marginal surplus, of $64m. However, current payments deteriorated markedly in the following three years, reflecting the diminishing trade surplus and the heavy burden of interest payments, owing to earlier, very substantial, foreign borrowing (particularly in the late 1970s), as high prices for cocoa and coffee stimulated ambitious capital investment programmes by the government, and particularly by the state corporations. The deficit had reached $1,241m. by 1988, and after a decline in 1989 increased once more to a peak of $1,590m. in 1991. The rescheduling of debt-servicing payments by the 'Paris Club' of creditor governments in November 1991 facilitated a small reduction in the current account deficit in 1992, to $1,424m. A major aim of the stabilization programme for 1994–96 is a reduction by almost one-half of this deficit as a proportion of GDP (from 13.1% in 1992 to 7.7% in 1996, excluding official grant inflows).

Reflecting the difficulties of the 1980s, the external debt has escalated sharply since the beginning of that decade, and at the end of 1992 was more than twice the level of 1980, at $17,997m. This was equivalent to 207% of GNP in that year, while the debt-service ratio has been about 35% of the value of exports of goods and services in almost every year since 1981. Both are unmanageable proportions, and by the end of 1992 Côte d'Ivoire's arrears on its long term debt totalled more than $3,300m., of which one-third was overdue interest.

Côte d'Ivoire's compliance with economic retrenchment programmes agreed with the IMF has enabled the government to negotiate a series of debt-reschedulings. Such an agreement in mid-1984 covered $775m. in payments of debt interest and principal that were due to official creditors, and principal due to private creditors, for the period up to the end of 1985. In 1986, despite a slight improvement in its payments position (owing to a strong export performance and a decline in both interest rates and the value of the US dollar), the country negotiated an extended rescheduling of most of its commercial and official debts falling due in 1986–89. In May 1987, however, faced with a sudden, substantial reduction in export earnings as a result of the sharp decline in world prices for coffee and cocoa, the government suspended debt payments. A new agreement was finalized in early 1988 for the rescheduling of all debt principal and 80% of interest due in 1987–88 to the 13 major creditor countries in the 'Paris Club', over a 10-year period (including six years' grace). Agreement was also reached for the rescheduling, over 15 years (with five years' grace), of repayment due in 1988–95 on liabilities to the 350 commercial bank creditors of the 'London Club'. However, the government failed to resume payments of interest, with the result that the supporting standby funding from the IMF was suspended. None the less, following Côte d'Ivoire's agreement (in mid-1989) to an 18-month economic adjustment and fiscal stabilization programme—devised by the IMF and the World Bank—the country's official creditors agreed, in December of that year, to reschedule outstanding arrears and a further $750m. due in principal and interest to the end of 1990, over 14 years with an eight-year grace period; they also pledged $380m. in quickly-disbursing funds. Negotiations with commercial creditors failed to achieve any formula, but further debt-relief was obtained from official creditors in November 1991, with a rescheduling of $829m. over 15–20 years.

While Côte d'Ivoire, with its middle-income status, depends substantially on private commercial sources for external borrowing (about one-quarter of public external debt is due to commercial banks), it has received significant sums of aid. In 1987–92 official development assistance from non-communist countries and multilateral agencies averaged $652m. per year with a sudden rise (to $859m.) in 1990 reflecting French support for the introduction of multi-party politics in the form of a $300m. increase in its assistance. A significant form of development assistance in the recent past has been structural adjustment loans from the World Bank (reaching $650m. in the 1980s) and sectoral loans in support of the adjustment programme. The release of these loans has been linked to Côte d'Ivoire's implementation of reforms in the economic structure and to the imposition of fiscal austerity. With the economy continuing to be highly vulnerable to trends in commodity prices and the very substantial burden of debt, Côte d'Ivoire has been anxious to maintain its co-operation with the World Bank and the IMF. The stabilization programme that was introduced in mid-1990 was well received by the IMF, which subsequently reinstated stand-by facilities. A new stand-by credit, for drawings of a maximum of $113m. over the following twelve months, was granted in September 1991. Far more substantial support from the country's creditors was forthcoming when, as long urged by the IMF and the World Bank, the CFA franc was devalued in January 1994. A three-year credit, of some $467m., was granted by the IMF under its enhanced structural adjustment facility, while France cancelled debts of 8,500m. French francs (then $1,500m.) and the 'Paris Club' rescheduled some $1,600m., of which it was expected that one-half would subsequently be cancelled. The halving of external debt denominated in foreign currency terms would thus restore it to its previous equivalent in domestic currency terms, but Côte d'Ivoire hopes that its foreign earning capacity, and hence its ability to service debt in the longer term, will have been enhanced by the devaluation.

Statistical Survey

Source (unless otherwise stated): Direction de la Statistique, Ministère de l'Economie, des Finances et de la Planification, Immeuble SCIAM, ave Marchand, BP V163, Abidjan; tel. 21-05-66; telex 23747.

Area and Population

AREA, POPULATION AND DENSITY

Area (sq km)	322,462*
Population (census results)	
30 April 1975	6,702,866
1 March 1988	
Males	5,527,343
Females	5,288,351
Total	10,815,694
Density (per sq km) at census of 1988	33.5

* 124,503 sq miles.

PROVINCES

	Area (sq km)	Population (1975 census)
Abengourou	6,900	177,692
Abidjan*	14,200	1,389,141
Aboisso	6,250	148,823
Adzopé	5,230	162,837
Agboville	3,850	141,970
Biankouma	4,950	75,711
Bondoukou	16,530	296,551
Bouaflé	8,500	263,609
Bouaké*	23,670	808,048
Bouna	21,470	84,290
Boundiali	10,095	132,278
Dabakala	9,670	56,230
Daloa	15,200	369,610
Danané	4,600	170,249
Dimbokro	14,100	475,023
Divo	10,650	278,526
Ferkessedougou	17,728	90,423
Gagnoa	6,900	259,504
Guiglo	14,150	137,672
Katiola	9,420	77,875
Korhogo	12,500	276,816
Man	7,050	278,659
Odienné	20,600	124,010
Sassandra	25,800	191,994
Séguéla	21,900	157,539
Touba	8,720	77,786
Total	320,633†	6,702,866

* Including commune.
† Other sources give the total area as 322,462 sq km.

Source: *La Côte d'Ivoire en Chiffres*, 1979.

(Note: Following a reorganization of local government in 1985, Côte d'Ivoire comprised a total of 49 provinces.)

PRINCIPAL TOWNS (population at 15 June 1979)
Abidjan 1,423,323; Bouaké 272,640.

BIRTHS AND DEATHS (UN estimates, annual averages)

	1975–80	1980–85	1985–90
Birth rate (per 1,000)	50.7	50.2	49.9
Death rate (per 1,000)	17.5	15.7	14.7

Expectation of life (UN estimates, years at birth, 1985–90): 51.9 (males 50.3; females 53.7).

Source: UN, *World Population Prospects: The 1992 Revision*.

ECONOMICALLY ACTIVE POPULATION
(ILO estimates, '000 persons at mid-1980)

	Males	Females	Total
Agriculture, etc.	1,385	928	2,314
Industry	231	62	293
Services	693	248	940
Total	2,309	1,238	3,547

Source: ILO, *Economically Active Population Estimates and Projections, 1950–2025*.

Mid-1992 (estimates, '000 persons): Agriculture, etc. 2,590; Total 4,826 (Source: FAO, *Production Yearbook*).

Agriculture

PRINCIPAL CROPS ('000 metric tons)

	1990	1991	1992
Maize	497	515	425†
Millet	47	49	40*
Sorghum	26	27	20*
Rice (paddy)	660	687	700†
Sweet potatoes*	18	18	16
Cassava (Manioc)	1,393	1,465	1,350*
Yams	2,528	2,556	2,450†
Taro (Coco yam)	282	311	280*
Pulses*	8	8	8
Tree nuts*	11	11	11
Sugar cane*	1,500	1,600	1,600
Palm kernels	44.3	36.9	41.1
Groundnuts (in shell)	134	139	140†
Cottonseed	121	137	110†
Coconuts	363	328†	270†
Copra*	62	54	42
Tomatoes*	40	40	40
Aubergines (Eggplants)*	40	40	40
Chillies, peppers*	23	23	23
Other vegetables*	352	363	343
Oranges*	28	28	28
Other citrus fruit	18	28	28*
Bananas	146	151	185†
Plantains	1,086	1,150†	1,170†
Mangoes*	14	14	14
Pineapples	196	174	240†
Other fruit*	12	12	13
Coffee (green)	286	199	240‡
Cocoa beans	781	804	700†
Tobacco (leaves)	2†	2†	2*
Cotton (lint)	105	116	87†
Natural rubber (dry weight)	70	71	76†

* FAO estimate(s).
† Unofficial figure.
‡ The official figure for production of green coffee in 1992 was subsequently revised to 125,000 metric tons.

Source: FAO, *Production Yearbook*.

LIVESTOCK ('000 head, year ending September)

	1990	1991	1992
Cattle	1,108	1,145	1,183
Pigs	360	372	382*
Sheep	1,134	1,161	1,200*
Goats	888	908	919*

* Unofficial figure.

Poultry (million): 24 in 1990; 25 in 1991; 26 (FAO estimate) in 1992.

Source: FAO, *Production Yearbook*.

LIVESTOCK PRODUCTS (FAO estimates, '000 metric tons)

	1990	1991	1992
Beef and veal	33	36	47
Mutton and lamb	5	5	5
Goats' meat	4	4	4
Pig meat	14	15	15
Poultry meat	42	43	43
Other meat	28	27	28
Cows' milk	22	23	25
Hen eggs	13.8	15.2	15.8
Cattle hides	4.3	4.7	6.1
Sheepskins	1.1	1.2	1.2
Goatskins	1.0	1.1	1.1

Source: FAO, *Production Yearbook*.

Forestry

ROUNDWOOD REMOVALS ('000 cubic metres)

	1990	1991	1992
Sawlogs, veneer logs and logs for sleepers	2,811	2,219	1,994
Other industrial wood*	755	784	814
Fuel wood*	9,739	10,111	10,494
Total	13,305	13,114	13,302

* FAO estimates.

Source: FAO, *Yearbook of Forest Products*.

SAWNWOOD PRODUCTION
('000 cubic metres, including railway sleepers)

	1990	1991	1992
Total	753	608	611

Source: FAO, *Yearbook of Forest Products*.

Fishing

('000 metric tons, live weight)

	1989	1990	1991
Freshwater fishes	28.5	25.5	21.8
Bigeye grunt	0.5	7.4	6.1
Lookdown fish	1.1	1.3	0.8
Sardinellas	18.1	22.9	20.6
Bonga shad	13.0	14.0	11.0
Other clupeoids	1.6	1.3	0.9
Atlantic black skipjack	4.9	2.8	0.1
Largehead hairtail	5.7	0.2	0.2
Chub mackerel	1.1	1.3	1.0
Other marine fishes (incl. unspecified)	22.0	25.1	20.4
Total fish	96.6	101.8	83.0
Crustaceans	2.6	2.6	2.2
Total catch	99.2	104.4	85.2
Inland waters	30.7	27.7	23.8
Atlantic Ocean	68.5	76.8	61.4

Source: FAO, *Yearbook of Fishery Statistics*.

Mining

	1989	1990	1991
Crude petroleum ('000 metric tons)*	190	315	320
Diamonds ('000 carats)†	12	12	15

* Provisional or estimated figures.
† Data from the US Bureau of Mines.

Source: UN, *Industrial Statistics Yearbook*.

Industry

SELECTED PRODUCTS
('000 metric tons, unless otherwise indicated)

	1989	1990	1991
Salted, dried or smoked fish*	15.0	15.2	n.a.
Tinned fish*	38.3	41.4	n.a.
Palm and palm kernel oil†	167	208	218
Raw sugar*	145	154	155
Cigarettes (million)	4,500†	4,500	4,500
Cotton yarn (pure and mixed)	24.7†	n.a.	n.a.
Plywood ('000 cubic metres)	44	42	42*†
Jet fuel	48	51	53
Motor spirit (Petrol)	215	235	237
Kerosene	331	335	339
Distillate fuel oils	593	595	520
Cement‡	700	500	499
Electric energy (million kWh)	2,361	2,365	2,376

Cocoa powder (exports, '000 metric tons): 22.1*† in 1988.
Cocoa butter (exports, '000 metric tons): 28.2*† in 1988.

* Data from the FAO.
† Provisional or estimated figure(s).
‡ Data from the US Bureau of Mines.

Source: UN, *Industrial Statistics Yearbook.*

Finance

CURRENCY AND EXCHANGE RATES

Monetary Units

100 centimes = 1 franc de la Communauté financière africaine (CFA).

French Franc, Sterling and Dollar Equivalents (31 March 1994)

1 French franc = 100 francs CFA;
£1 sterling = 846.40 francs CFA;
US $1 = 570.14 francs CFA;
1,000 francs CFA = £1.181 = $1.754.

Average Exchange Rate (francs CFA per US $)

1991 282.11
1992 264.69
1993 283.16

Note: An exchange rate of 1 French franc = 50 francs CFA, established in 1948, remained in force until January 1994, when the CFA franc was devalued by 50%, with the exchange rate adjusted to 1 French franc = 100 francs CFA.

BUDGET (million francs CFA)

Revenue*	1988	1989	1990†
Fiscal receipts	517,750	497,710	509,018
Taxes on income and profits	90,360	99,929	102,940
Individual taxes	52,700	53,101	54,715
Corporate and business taxes	30,460	38,656	39,300
Employers' contributions	42,030	35,588	36,100
Taxes on goods and services	120,880	144,634	169,933
Turnover taxes	61,460	63,791	64,770
Consumption taxes	44,100	61,800	79,953
Taxes on international trade and transactions	263,100	216,068	198,495
Import duties	183,420	177,557	193,400
Export duties	79,680	38,511	5,095
Other current receipts	15,936	8,484	15,233
Aid, grants and subsidies	2,965	18,681	5,000
Total	536,651	524,875	529,251

Expenditure	1988	1989	1990†
General public services	137,029	126,772	144,948
Defence	38,155	41,369	42,042
Public order and security	32,267	31,209	32,608
Education	191,040	190,242	191,153
Health	44,971	41,018	42,496
Social security and welfare	4,822	5,319	5,529
Housing and community amenities	37,898	30,128	40,931
Other community and social services	11,911	4,716	4,952
Economic services	142,738	111,219	113,179
Agriculture, forestry and fishing	64,925	60,133	68,687
Mining, manufacturing and construction	3,833	4,282	4,365
Electricity and other energy resources	—	90	25
Transport and communications	66,590	41,650	36,242
Other economic services	7,390	5,064	3,860
Debt repayment	1,700	4,247	1,582
Other purposes	2,117	—	—
Total	642,948	586,239	619,420

* Revenue excludes borrowing (million francs CFA): 106,297 (internal 20,500, external 85,797) in 1988; 61,364 (internal 9,500, external 51,864) in 1989; 90,169 (internal 23,000, external 67,169) in 1990.
† Estimates.

Source: Banque centrale des états de l'Afrique de l'ouest.

1991 (draft budget, million francs CFA): Current expenditure 449,800; Investment expenditure 107,940.
1992 (draft budget, million francs CFA): Current expenditure 442,500; Investment expenditure 113,500.
1993 (draft budget, million francs CFA): Current expenditure 442,500; Investment expenditure 141,200.
1994 (draft budget, million francs CFA): Current expenditure 500,010; Investment expenditure 220,728.

CENTRAL BANK RESERVES (US $ million at 31 December)

	1991	1992	1993
Gold*	15.8	15.4	16.6
IMF special drawing rights	2.0	0.3	1.1
Foreign exchange	11.4	6.7	1.1
Total	29.2	22.3	18.9

* Valued at market-related prices.

Source: IMF, *International Financial Statistics.*

MONEY SUPPLY ('000 million francs CFA at 31 December)

	1991	1992	1993
Currency outside banks	258.3	252.1	273.2
Demand deposits at deposit money banks*	250.1	234.5	220.8
Checking deposits at post office	1.4	2.5	—
Total money (incl. others)	510.1	489.4	494.6

* Excluding the deposits of public establishments of an administrative or social nature.

Source: IMF, *International Financial Statistics.*

COST OF LIVING (Consumer Price Index for low-income Africans in Abidjan; base: 1980 = 100)

	1989*	1990†	1991
Food	176.7	152.7	155.3
Fuel and light	145.5	145.5	145.5
Clothing	244.5	244.5	243.9
Rent	153.7	153.7	153.7
All items†	166.5	165.2	168.0

* January to August only.
† March to December only.
Source: ILO, *Year Book of Labour Statistics.*

NATIONAL ACCOUNTS
('000 million francs CFA at current prices)
Expenditure on the Gross Domestic Product

	1989	1990	1991
Government final consumption expenditure	482	519	564
Private final consumption expenditure	2,015	2,164	2,243
Increase in stocks	−30	−34	−39
Gross fixed capital formation	357	407	429
Total domestic expenditure	2,824	3,056	3,197
Exports of goods and services	951	1,061	1,439
Less Imports of goods and services	786	861	1,149
GDP in purchasers' values	2,989	3,256	3,487
GDP at constant 1980 prices	2,659	2,553	2,596

Source: UN Economic Commission for Africa, *African Statistical Yearbook.*

Gross Domestic Product by Economic Activity

	1989	1990	1991
Agriculture, hunting, forestry and fishing	826	733	752
Mining and quarrying	67	68	70
Manufacturing	435	365	381
Electricity, gas and water	63	60	62
Construction	89	90	93
Trade, restaurants and hotels	310	301	313
Transport, storage and communications	260	238	247
Finance, insurance, real estate and business services	86	80	81
Public administration and defence	350	305	313
Other services	580	504	518
GDP at factor cost	3,066	2,744	2,829
Indirect taxes, *less* subsidies	−77	512	658
GDP in purchasers' values	2,989	3,256	3,487

Source: UN Economic Commission for Africa, *African Statistical Yearbook.*

BALANCE OF PAYMENTS (US $ million)

	1990	1991	1992
Merchandise exports f.o.b.	3,027.9	2,686.2	2,880.0
Merchandise imports f.o.b.	−1,700.6	−1,706.8	−1,885.6
Trade balance	1,327.4	979.4	994.4
Exports of services	557.9	529.9	550.5
Imports of services	−1,737.3	−1,636.6	−1,466.6
Other income received	23.9	23.0	18.9
Other income paid	−1,130.5	−1,219.4	−1,245.6
Private unrequited transfers (net)	−553.5	−464.4	−492.3
Official unrequited transfers (net)	207.5	197.8	217.2
Current balance	−1,304.7	−1,590.2	−1,423.5
Direct investment (net)	20.9	20.2	21.5
Other capital (net)	−206.4	278.6	−79.3
Net errors and omissions	−75.4	27.5	143.4
Overall balance	−1,565.6	−1,263.8	−1,337.9

Source: IMF, *International Financial Statistics.*

External Trade

Source: Banque centrale des états de l'Afrique de l'ouest.

PRINCIPAL COMMODITIES (million francs CFA)

Imports c.i.f.	1987	1988	1989
Dairy products	24,445	24,587	22,320
Cereals	45,091	32,186	48,268
Beverages and tobacco	16,003	12,506	11,156
Fuels	100,900	85,952	143,121
Crude petroleum	93,438	79,978	136,705
Machinery and transport equipment	143,649	129,596	110,600
Electrical machinery	25,560	23,607	24,529
Non-electric machinery	60,956	62,783	54,804
Road vehicles	53,946	41,660	29,718
Chemicals	93,152	90,261	99,862
Miscellaneous manufactured articles	169,112	151,617	153,327
Cotton yarn and fabrics	15,066	10,195	5,802
Total (incl. others)	673,899	619,920	673,447

Exports f.o.b.	1987	1988	1989
Pineapples	21,040	15,914	12,019
Green coffee	118,053	115,644	73,545
Cocoa beans	312,615	207,388	325,192
Cocoa paste and cocoa butter	54,456	37,481	41,625
Coffee extracts and essences	18,230	30,219	22,304
Canned fish	22,457	27,060	24,760
Fuels	101,175	88,266	86,176
Latex	16,201	19,875	18,461
Wood	63,043	55,004	58,948
Cotton (ginned)	25,678	41,846	35,676
Fats and oils	18,042	15,414	17,811
Machinery and transport equipment	14,069	32,238	25,581
Chemicals	21,606	23,892	30,589
Miscellaneous manufactured articles	68,392	68,639	72,600
Cotton yarn and fabrics	16,869	14,602	12,392
Total (incl. others)	929,143	826,467	895,571

PRINCIPAL TRADING PARTNERS (million francs CFA)

Imports	1987	1988	1989
Belgium/Luxembourg	17,481	16,479	16,645
Brazil	4,823	9,106	7,260
China, People's Repub.	17,120	10,384	4,793
France	213,313	193,451	193,180
Germany, Fed. Repub.	35,340	34,303	36,153
Italy	36,396	31,304	35,944
Japan	37,275	28,194	18,123
Mauritania	6,114	8,049	6,423
Netherlands	34,356	34,612	31,580
Nigeria	73,128	58,993	107,473
Pakistan	13,541	6,781	3,473
Senegal	9,862	7,380	5,933
Spain	23,321	28,836	25,651
Switzerland	11,298	8,992	7,438
United Kingdom	15,546	21,965	16,281
USA	29,719	24,034	28,745
Total (incl. others)	673,899	619,920	673,447

Exports	1987	1988	1989
Belgium/Luxembourg	41,372	43,496	38,594
Burkina Faso	22,295	28,909	27,008
France	141,567	131,549	121,936
Germany, Fed. Repub.	56,881	38,585	66,886
Ghana	15,429	16,111	15,510
Italy	67,465	59,696	53,169
Japan	5,732	6,101	11,966
Mali	24,036	23,273	23,494
Netherlands	156,585	130,893	201,329
Niger	8,714	7,953	9,401
Nigeria	20,490	21,564	12,793
Portugal	6,510	9,020	6,660
Senegal	15,519	17,297	14,827
Spain	25,196	23,073	25,138
Togo	13,657	6,469	8,425
USSR	47,660	39,943	44,360
United Kingdom	32,889	24,537	30,821
USA	97,746	61,390	59,262
Total (incl. others)	929,143	826,467	895,571

Transport

RAILWAYS (including Burkina Faso traffic)

	1982	1983	1984
Passengers ('000)	3,171.8	2,941.0	2,574.9
Passenger-km (million)	892.6	971.8	857.8
Freight ('000 metric tons)	731	601	702
Freight (million net ton-km)	610.6	468.7	530.2

ROAD TRAFFIC (estimates, '000 motor vehicles in use)

	1989	1990	1991
Passenger cars	181	182	185
Commercial vehicles	94	96	97

Source: UN Economic Commission for Africa, *African Statistical Yearbook.*

INTERNATIONAL SEA-BORNE SHIPPING (freight traffic at Ports of Abidjan and San Pedro, '000 metric tons)

	1987	1988	1989
Goods loaded	4,319	4,195	4,667
Goods unloaded	6,137	6,134	6,454

1990 (freight traffic at Abidjan, '000 metric tons): Goods loaded 4,063; Goods unloaded 5,775.
1991 (freight traffic at Abidjan, '000 metric tons): Goods loaded 3,995; Good unloaded 6,048.
1992 (freight traffic at Abidjan, '000 metric tons): Goods loaded 3,984; Goods unloaded 6,178.

Source: Banque centrale des états de l'Afrique de l'ouest.

CIVIL AVIATION (traffic on scheduled services)*

	1989	1990	1991
Kilometres flown (million)	4	4	4
Passengers carried ('000)	218	200	175
Passenger-km (million)	319	317	286
Freight ton-km (million)	18	18	16
Mail ton-km (million)	1	1	1

* Including an apportionment of the traffic of Air Afrique.

Source: UN, *Statistical Yearbook.*

Tourism

	1989	1990*	1991*
Tourist arrivals ('000)*	180	184	188
Tourist receipts (US $ million)	67	68	70

* Estimates.

Source: UN Economic Commission for Africa, *African Statistical Yearbook.*

Communications Media

	1989	1990	1991
Radio receivers ('000 in use)	1,600	1,700	1,765
Television receivers ('000 in use)	675	728	730
Telephones ('000 in use)*	123	126	127
Daily newspapers			
Number	n.a.	1	n.a.
Average circulation ('000 copies)	n.a.	90	n.a.

* Estimates.

Book production (1983, excluding pamphlets): 46 titles; 3,766,000 copies.

Sources: UNESCO, *Statistical Yearbook*; UN Economic Commission for Africa, *African Statistical Yearbook*.

Education

PUPILS ENROLLED (1991, unless otherwise indicated)

	Males	Females	Total
Pre-primary	5,795	5,422	11,217
Primary	844,293	603,492	1,447,785
Secondary			
General	267,828	128,778	396,606
Teacher training	n.a.	n.a.	3,094
Vocational*	14,361	8,500	22,861
Higher†	n.a.	n.a.	19,660
University level†	8,967	2,333	11,300

* 1985 figures. Data refer to schools attached to the then Ministry of National Education and Scientific Research.

† 1984 figures.

Source: UNESCO, *Statistical Yearbook*.

Directory

The Constitution

The Constitution was promulgated on 31 October 1960. It was amended in June 1971, October 1975, August 1980, November 1980, October 1985, January 1986 and November 1990.

PREAMBLE

The Republic of Côte d'Ivoire is one and indivisible. It is secular, democratic and social. Sovereignty belongs to the people who exercise it through their representatives or through referenda. There is universal, equal and secret suffrage. French is the official language.

HEAD OF STATE

The President is elected for a five-year term by direct universal suffrage and is eligible for re-election. He is Head of the Administration and the Armed Forces and has power to ask the Assemblée nationale to reconsider a Bill, which must then be passed by two-thirds of the members of the legislature; he may also have a Bill submitted to a referendum. In case of the death or incapacitation of the President of the Republic, the functions of the Head of State are assumed by the President of the Assemblée nationale, until the expiry of the previous incumbent's mandate.

EXECUTIVE POWER

Executive power is vested in the President. He appoints the Prime Minister, who, in turn, appoints the Council of Ministers. Any member of the Assemblée nationale appointed minister must renounce his seat in the legislature, but may regain it on leaving the Government.

LEGISLATIVE POWER

Legislative power is vested in the 175-member Assemblée nationale, elected for a five-year term of office. Legislation may be introduced either by the President or by a member of the National Assembly.

JUDICIAL POWER

The independence of the judiciary is guaranteed by the President, assisted by the High Council of Judiciary.

ECONOMIC AND SOCIAL COUNCIL

This is an advisory commission of 120 members, appointed by the President because of their specialist knowledge or experience.

POLITICAL ORGANIZATIONS

Article 7 of the Constitution stipulates that political organizations can be formed and can exercise their activities freely, provided that they respect the principles of national sovereignty and democracy and the laws of the Republic.

The Government

HEAD OF STATE

President: HENRI KONAN BÉDIÉ (took office 7 December 1993).

COUNCIL OF MINISTERS
(August 1994)

Prime Minister and Minister of the Economy, Finance and Planning: DANIEL KABLAN DUNCAN.

Minister of State, with responsibility for Relations with the Organs of State: THIMOTHÉE N'GUETTA AHOUA.

Minister of State, with responsibility for National Integration: LAURENT DONA-FOLOGO.

Minister of Defence: LÉON KONAN KOFFI.

Minister of Foreign Affairs: AMARA ESSY.

Minister of the Interior: EMILE CONSTANT BOMBET.

Minister of Justice and Keeper of the Seals: Me FAUSTIN KOUAMÉ.

Minister of Agriculture and Animal Resources: LAMBERT KOUASSI KONAN.

Minister with responsibility for Raw Materials: GUY-ALAIN EMMANUEL GAUZE.

Minister of Higher Education and Scientific Research: SALIOU TOURÉ.

Minister of National Education: PIERRE KIPRE.

Minister of Equipment, Transport and Telecommunications: EZAN AKELE.

Minister of Security: GASTON OUASSÉNAN KONÉ.

Minister of Public Health and Social Welfare: MAURICE KAKOU GUIKAHUE.

Minister of Mines and Energy: LAMINE FADIKA.

Minister of Industry and Trade: FERDINAND KACOU ANGORA.

Minister of Construction and Town Planning: ALBERT KAKOU TIAPANI.

Minister of Employment and the Civil Service: ACHI ATSAIN.

Minister of Communications: DANIÈLE BONI-CLAVERIE.

Minister of the Environment and Tourism: LANCINÉ GON COULIBALY.

Minister of Culture: BERNARD ZADI ZAOUROU.

Minister of the Family and Women's Promotion: ALBERTINE GNANAZAN HEPIE.

Minister of Youth and Sports: KOMENAN ZAKPA.

Minister-delegate to the Prime Minister, with responsibility for the Economy, Finance and Planning: N'GORAN NIAMIEN.

Director of the Presidential Cabinet: NOËL NÉMIN.

MINISTRIES

Ministry of Agriculture and Animal Resources: BP V82, Abidjan; telex 23612.

Ministry of Communications: BP V138, Abidjan; telex 23501.

Ministry of Culture: Abidjan.

Ministry of Defence: BP V11, Abidjan; telex 22855.

Ministry of the Economy, Finance and Planning: Immeuble SCIAM, ave Marchand, BP V163, Abidjan; tel. 21-05-66; telex 23747.

Ministry of Employment and the Civil Service: BP V93, Abidjan 01; tel. 21-04-00.

Ministry of the Environment and Tourism, Construction and Town Planning: ave Jean Paul II, BP V6, Abidjan 01; tel. 29-13-67; telex 22108.

Ministry of Equipment, Transport and Telecommunications: BP V184, Abidjan; tel. 21-29-92; telex 23438.

Ministry of the Family and Women's Promotion: Abidjan.

Ministry of Foreign Affairs: BP V109, Abidjan; telex 23752.

Ministry of Higher Education and Scientific Research: BP V151, Abidjan.

Ministry of Industry and Trade: Abidjan.

Ministry of the Interior: BP V241, Abidjan; telex 22296.

Ministry of Justice: BP V107, Abidjan.

Ministry of Mines and Energy: BP V50, Abidjan; tel. 21-50-03; telex 22262; fax 21-53-20.

Ministry of National Education: BP V120, Abidjan; tel. 21-12-31.

Ministry of Public Health and Social Welfare: Cité Administrative, Tour C, 16e étage, BP V4, Abidjan; tel. 21-08-71; telex 22597; fax 21-10-85.

Ministry of Security: Abidjan.

Ministry of Youth and Sports: BP V136, Abidjan; telex 22719; fax 22-48-21.

President and Legislature

PRESIDENT

Presidential Election, 28 October 1990

Candidate	Votes	% of votes
Dr Félix Houphouët-Boigny	2,445,365	81.68
Laurent Gbagbo	548,441	18.32
Total	2,993,806	100.00

Note: In accordance with the constitution, following the death of President Houphouët-Boigny, on 7 December 1993, Henri Konan Bédié—hitherto President of the Assemblée nationale—assumed the office of President of the Republic.

ASSEMBLÉE NATIONALE

President: Charles Donwahi.

General Election, 25 November 1990

Party	Seats
PDCI—RDA	163
FPI	9
PIT	1
Independent	2
Total	175

Advisory Council

Conseil Economique et Social: 04 BP 301, Abidjan; tel. 21-20-60; reconstituted 1982; govt advisory body; Pres. Philippe Grégoire Yacé; Vice-Pres Félicien Konian Kodjo, B. Beda Yao, Gladys Anoma; 120 mems.

Political Organizations

Despite constitutional provision for the existence of more than one political organization, President Houphouët-Boigny's Parti démocratique de la Côte d'Ivoire—Rassemblement démocratique africain (PDCI—RDA) was the sole legal party until May 1990. By mid-1994 about 40 political organizations had gained legal status. The following parties won seats in the Assemblée nationale at the November 1990 elections:

Front populaire ivoirien (FPI): 22 BP 302, Abidjan 22; f. 1982 in France; Sec.-Gen. Laurent Gbagbo.

Parti démocratique de la Côte d'Ivoire—Rassemblement démocratique africain (PDCI—RDA): Maison du Parti, Abidjan; f. 1946 as the local section of the Rassemblement démocratique africain; Chair. Henri Konan Bédié; Sec.-Gen. Laurent Dona-Fologo.

Parti ivoirien des travailleurs (PIT): 20 BP 43, Abidjan 20; f. 1990; First Nat. Sec. Francis Wodié.

Other legalized parties include:

The **Alliance pour la social-démocratie (ASD–CNIPO):** Pres. Achi Koman; the **Congrès démocrate national (CDN)):** Nat. Exec. Sec. Moctar Haidara; the **Front ivoirien du salut (FIS):** Sec.-Gen. N'Takpe Auchoret Monnon'Gba; the **Front de redressement national (FRN):** Sec.-Gen. Victor Atsepi; the **Mouvement démocratique et social (MDS):** First Nat. Sec.-Gen. Siaka Touré; the **Mouvement indépendantistes ivoirien (MII):** Pres. Adou Yapi; the **Mouvement progressiste de Côte d'Ivoire (MPCI):** Sec.-Gen. Augustin Nangone Bi Doua; the **Organisation populaire de la jeunesse (OPJ):** Sec.-Gen. Denis Latta; the **Parti africain pour la renaissance ivoirienne (PARI):** Sec.-Gen. Daniel Anikpo; the **Parti communiste ivoirien (PCI):** Sec.-Gen. Denis Gueu Dro; the **Parti fraternel des planteurs, des parents d'élèves et industriels ivoiriens (PFPPEI):** Pres. Ernest Amessan; the **Parti ivoirien pour la démocratie (PID):** Sec.-Gen. Faustin Botoko Léka; the **Parti ivoirien de justice et de solidarité (PIJS):** Pres. Kekongo N'Dien; the **Parti libéral de Côte d'Ivoire (PLCI):** Sec.-Gen. Yady Soumah; the **Parti pour la libération totale de la Côte d'Ivoire (PLTCI):** Sec.-Gen. Elise Alloufou Niamien; the **Parti pour les libertés et la démocratie (PLD):** Pres. Jean-Pierre Ouya; the **Parti national socialiste (PNS):** Pres. Raphaël Yapi Beda; the **Parti ouvrier et paysan de Côte d'Ivoire (POPCI):** Exec. Pres. Kouassi Adolphe Blokon; the **Parti progressiste ivoirien (PPI):** Pres. Soumahoro Kassindou; the **Parti pour la protection de l'environnement (PPE):** Sec.-Gen. Dioba Coulibaly; the **Parti du rassemblement du peuple pour la jeunesse de Côte d'Ivoire (PRJCI):** Sec.-Gen. Philippe Essis Khol; the **Parti pour la reconstruction nationale et la démocratie (PRND):** Pres. Marc Joseph Behed; the **Parti réformiste démocratique ivoirien (PRDI):** Sec.-Gen. Raphaël Beugré Koamé; the **Parti pour la réhabilitation ivoirienne du social et de l'économie (PRISE):** Exec. Pres. Georges Grahou; the **Parti républicain de Côte d'Ivoire (PRCI):** Sec.-Gen. Robert Gbai Tagro; the **Parti socialiste ivoirien (PSI):** First Nat. Sec. Mandouadjoa Kouakou; the **Rassemblement des forces démocratiques (RFD):** Pres. Fakourou Touré; the **Rassemblement pour le progrès social (RPS):** Pres. Mamadou Koné; the **Rassemblement des républicains (RDR):** Sec.-Gen. Djeny Kobina; the **Rassemblement pour la République (RPR):** Sec.-Gen. Blaise Bonoua Kodjo; the **Rassemblement des sociaux-démocrates (RSD):** Sec.-Gen. Mahi Guina; the **Union des libéraux pour la République (ULR):** Pres. Céléstin Amon; the **Union des paysans, des ouvriers et des salariés de Côte d'Ivoire (UPOSCI):** Sec.-Gen. Coa Kiémoko; the **Union pour le progrès social (UPS):** Sec.-Gen. Albert Séhé; and the **Union des sociaux-démocrates (USD):** Sec.-Gen. Bernard Zadi Zaourou.

Diplomatic Representation

EMBASSIES IN CÔTE D'IVOIRE

Algeria: 53 blvd Clozel, 01 BP 1015, Abidjan 01; tel. 21-23-40; telex 23243; Ambassador: Benattallah Halim.

Angola: Lot 19, Cocody-les-Deux-Plateaux, derrière l'Ecole Nationale d'Administration, 16 BP 1734, Abidjan 16; tel. 41-38-79; telex 27187; fax 41-28-89; Ambassador: Simeão Adão Manuel Kafuxi.

Austria: Immeuble N'Zarama, blvd Lagunaire-Charles de Gaulle, Plateau, 01 BP 1837, Abidjan 01; tel. 21-25-00; telex 22664; fax 22-19-23; Ambassador: Dr Georg Znidaric.

Belgium: Immeuble Alliance, ave Terrasson de Fougères, 01 BP 1800, Abidjan 01; tel. 21-00-88; telex 23633; Ambassador: Jacques Henin.

Benin: rue des Jardins, 09 BP 238, Abidjan 09; tel. 41-44-14; telex 27103; Ambassador: (vacant)

Brazil: Immeuble Alpha 2000, rue Gourgas, 01 BP 3820, Abidjan 01; tel. 22-23-41; telex 23443; Ambassador: Italo M. A. Mastrogiovanni.

Burkina Faso: 2 ave Terrasson de Fougères, 01 BP 908, Abidjan 01; tel. 32-13-55; telex 23453; fax 32-66-41; Ambassador: Léandre Bassole.

Cameroon: 01 BP 2886, Abidjan 01; tel. 32-33-31; Ambassador: Paul Kamga Njike.

Canada: Immeuble Trade Centre, 01 BP 4104, Abidjan 01; tel. 32-20-09; telex 23593; Ambassador: DENIS BELISLE.

Central African Republic: rue des Combattants, 01 BP 3387, Abidjan 01; tel. 21-36-46; telex 22102; Ambassador: JEAN-PAUL NGOUPANDÉ.

China, People's Republic: 01 BP 3691, Abidjan 01; tel. 44-59-00; telex 22104; Ambassador: CAI ZAIDU.

Colombia: 01 BP 3874, Abidjan 01; tel. 33-12-44; fax 32-47-31; Ambassador: CARLOS ADOLFO ARENAS CAMPOS.

Czech Republic: Immeuble Tropique III, 01 BP 1349, Abidjan 01; tel. 21-20-30; telex 22110; fax 22-19-06.

Denmark: Immeuble Le Mans, 5e étage, blvd Botreau Roussel, angle ave Noguès, Plateau, 01 BP 4569, Abidjan 01; tel. 21-17-66; telex 23871; fax 21-41-89; Chargé d'affaires: PETER TJERK.

Egypt: Immeuble El Nasr, ave du Général de Gaulle, 01 BP 2104, Abidjan 01; tel. 32-79-25; telex 23537; Ambassador: AHMED RASHAD.

Ethiopia: Immeuble Nour Al-Hayat, 01 BP 3712, Abidjan 01; tel. 21-33-65; telex 23848; Ambassador: (vacant).

France: rue Lecoeur, quartier du Plateau, 17 BP 175, Abidjan 17; tel. 21-67-49; telex 23699; fax 22-42-54; Ambassador: CHRISTIAN DUTHEIL DE LA ROCHÈRE.

Gabon: Cocody Danga Nord, derrière la Direction de la Géologie, 01 BP 3765, Abidjan 01; tel. 41-51-54; telex 27188; fax 44-75-05; Ambassador: VICTOR MAGNAGNA.

Germany: Immeuble Le Mans, blvd Botreau Roussel, 01 BP 1900, Abidjan 01; tel. 32-47-27; telex 23642; fax 32-47-29; Ambassador: R. ZIMMERMAN.

Ghana: Résidence de la Corniche, blvd du Général de Gaulle, 01 BP 1871, Abidjan 01; tel. 33-11-24; Chargé d'affaires: JOSEPH NWANEAMPEH.

Guinea: Immeuble Crosson Duplessis, 08 BP 2280, Abidjan 08; tel. 32-86-00; telex 22865; Ambassador: MAMADY KOLY KOROUMA.

Holy See: 08 BP 1347, Abidjan 08 (Apostolic Nunciature); tel. 44-38-35; fax 44-72-40; Apostolic Nuncio: Most Rev. JANUSZ BOLONEK, Titular Archbishop of Madaurus.

India: Lot 36, impasse Ablaha Pokou, Cocody, Danga Nord, 06 BP 318, Abidjan 06; tel. 44-52-31; telex 28103; fax 44-01-11; Chargé d'affaires a.i.: DEVI CHARAN BANSAL.

Israel: Immeuble Nour Al-Hayat, 01 BP 1877, Abidjan 01; tel. 21-49-53; fax 21-87-04; Ambassador: JAACOV REVAH.

Italy: 16 rue de la Canebière, Cocody, 01 BP 1905, Abidjan 01; tel. 44-61-70; telex 26123; fax 44-35-87; Ambassador: RAFFAELE CAMPANELLA.

Japan: ave Chardy, 01 BP 1329, Abidjan 01; tel. 21-28-63; telex 23400; fax 21-30-51; Ambassador: MOTOHIKO NISHIMURA.

Korea, Democratic People's Republic: BP V48, Abidjan; tel. 44-22-75; Ambassador: YI JAE RIM.

Korea, Republic: Immeuble Le Général, 01 BP 3950, Abidjan 01; tel. 32-22-90; telex 23638; Ambassador: YANG TAE-KYU.

Lebanon: 01 BP 2227, Abidjan 01; tel. 33-28-24; telex 22245; Ambassador: MOHAMED DAHER.

Liberia: Immeuble La Symphonie, 30 ave du Général de Gaulle, Abidjan; tel. 22-23-59; telex 23535; Chargé d'affaires: TIAHKWEE JOHNSON.

Libya: Immeuble Shell, 48 ave Lamblin, 01 BP 5725, Abidjan 01; tel. 22-01-27; Chargé d'affaires a.i.: BADREDDIN M. RABIE.

Mali: Maison du Mali, rue du Commerce, 01 BP 2746, Abidjan 01; tel. 32-31-47; telex 23429; Ambassador: (vacant).

Mauritania: Abidjan; tel. 44-16-43; telex 27181; Ambassador: Col AHMEDOU OUM ABDALLAH.

Morocco: 24 rue de la Canebière, Cocody, 01 BP 146, Abidjan 01; tel. 44-58-78; telex 26147; Ambassador: ABDELHAKIM SEMLALI.

Netherlands: Immeuble Les Harmonies, angle blvd Carde et ave Dr Jamot, 01 BP 1086, Abidjan 01; tel. 22-77-12; telex 23694; Ambassador: ANTHONIE PIJPERS.

Niger: 01 BP 2743, Abidjan 01; tel. 26-28-14; telex 43185; Ambassador: MADI KONATÉ.

Nigeria: 35 blvd de la République, 01 BP 1906, Abidjan 01; tel. 21-38-17; telex 23532; Ambassador: JONATHAN OLUWOLE COKER.

Norway: Immeuble N' Zarama, blvd du Général de Gaulle, 01 BP 607, Abidjan 01; tel. 22-25-34; telex 23355; fax 21-91-99; Ambassador: KJELL ØSTREM.

Poland: 04 BP 308, Abidjan 04; tel. 44-12-25; telex 26114; Chargé d'affaires: KRZYSZTOF SLIWINSKI.

Russia: Riviera SQ-1 Sud, 01 BP 7646, Abidjan 01; tel. 43-09-59; Ambassador: MIKHAIL VLADIMOROVICH MAIOROV.

Senegal: Résidence Nabil, blvd du Général de Gaulle, 08 BP 2165, Abidjan 08; tel. 32-28-76; telex 23897; Ambassador: AHMED TIJANE KANÉ.

Spain: impasse Ablaha Pokou, Cocody, Danga Nord 08 BP 876, Abidjan 08; tel. 44-48-50; telex 28120; fax 44-71-22; Ambassador: VICENTE FERNÁNDEZ TRELLES.

Sweden: Immeuble N'Zarama, 4e étage, blvd Lagunaire, 04 BP 992, Abidjan 04; tel. 21-24-10; telex 23293; fax 21-21-07; Ambassador: PETER BRUCE.

Switzerland: Immeuble Alpha 2000, rue Gourgas, 01 BP 1914, Abidjan 01; tel. 21-17-21; telex 23492; fax 21-27-70; Ambassador: PIERRE DE GRAFFENRIED.

United Kingdom: Immeuble Les Harmonies, 3e étage, angle blvd Carde et ave Dr Jamot, Plateau, 01 BP 2581, Abidjan 01; tel. 22-68-50; telex 23706; fax 22-32-21; Ambassador: MARGARET ROTHWELL.

USA: 5 rue Jesse Owens, 01 BP 1712, Abidjan 01; tel. 21-09-79; telex 23660; fax 22-32-59; Ambassador: HUME HORAN.

Zaire: 29 blvd Clozel, 01 BP 3961, Abidjan 01; tel. 22-20-80; telex 23795; Ambassador: BAMBI MAVUNGU.

Judicial System

Since 1964 all civil, criminal, commercial and administrative cases have come under the jurisdiction of the Tribunaux de première instance (Magistrates' courts), the assize courts and the Court of Appeal, with the Supreme Court as supreme court of appeal.

The Supreme Court: rue Gourgas, BP V30, Abidjan; has four chambers: constitutional, judicial, administrative and auditing; Pres. MICHEL KOUI MAMADOU.

Courts of Appeal: Abidjan and Bouaké; hear appeals from courts of first instance; Abidjan: First Pres. YANON YAPO, Attorney-Gen. LOUIS FOLQUET; Bouaké: First Pres. AHIOUA MOULARE, Attorney-Gen. ANOMAN OGUIE.

The High Court of Justice: composed of Deputies elected from and by the National Assembly; has jurisdiction to impeach the President or other member of the Government; Pres. (vacant).

State Security Court: composed of a president and six regular judges, all appointed for five years; deals with all offences against the security of the State; Pres. (vacant).

Courts of First Instance: Abidjan, Pres. ANTOINETTE MARSOUIN; Bouaké: Pres. KABLAN AKA EDOUKOU; Daloa: Pres. WOUNE BLEKA; there are a further 25 courts in the principal centres.

Religion

It is estimated that 60% of the population follow traditional animist beliefs, while 20% are Muslims and 20% are Christians, mainly Roman Catholics.

CHRISTIANITY

The Roman Catholic Church

Côte d'Ivoire comprises one archdiocese and 12 dioceses. At 31 December 1992 there were an estimated 1,610,000 adherents (about 14.2% of the total population).

Bishops' Conference: Conférence Episcopale de la Côte d'Ivoire, 01 BP 1287, Abidjan 01; tel. 33-22-56; f. 1973; Pres. Rt Rev. AUGUSTE NOBOU, Bishop of Korhogo.

Archbishop of Abidjan: Cardinal BERNARD YAGO, Archevêché, ave Jean Paul II, 01 BP 1287, Abidjan 01; tel. 21-12-46.

Protestant Churches

Assemblée de Dieu: 04 BP 266, Abidjan 04; Pres. ADAMO OUEDRAOGO.

Christian and Missionary Alliance: BP 585, Bouaké 01; tel. 63-23-12; fax 63-54-12; f. 1929; 13 mission stations; Dir Rev. WESLEY NEVIUS.

Conservative Baptist Foreign Mission Society: BP 109, Korhogo; tel. 86-00-33; f. 1947; active in evangelism, medical work, translation, literacy and theological education in the northern area and in Abidjan.

Eglise du Nazaréen (Church of the Nazarene): 22 BP 623, Abidjan 22; tel. 43-16-99; fax 43-02-60; f. 1988; ministerial training and medical work; Dir. DOUGLAS RUNYAN.

Eglise Protestante Baptiste Oeuvres et Mission: 03 BP 1032, Abidjan 03; tel. 45-28-18; fax 45-56-41; f. 1975; active in evangelism, teaching and social work; medical centre, 298 places of worship, 215 missionaries and 60,366 mems; Pres. DION YAYE ROBERT.

Eglise Protestante Méthodiste: 41 blvd de la République, 01 BP 1282, Abidjan 01; tel. 21-17-97; c. 120,000 mems; Pres. LAMBERT AKOSSI N'CHO.

Mission Baptiste Méridionale: 01 BP 3722, Abidjan 01.

Mission Evangélique de l'Afrique Occidentale: BP 822, Bouaflé; tel. 68-93-70; fax 44-58-17; f. 1934; 11 mission centres, 59 missionaries; Field Dir SHOERD VAN DONGE; affiliated church: Alliance des Eglises Evangéliques de Côte d'Ivoire; 192 churches, 38 full-time pastors; Pres. BOAN BI ZRÉ EMMANUEL.

Mission Evangélique Luthérienne en Côte d'Ivoire (MELCI): BP 196, Touba; tel. and fax 70-70-58; f. 1984; active in evangelism and social work; Dir OSCAR NORDBØ.

Union des Eglises Evangéliques du Sud-Ouest de la Côte d'Ivoire and **Mission Biblique:** 08 BP 20, Abidjan 08; f. 1927; c. 250 places of worship.

The Press

DAILIES

Bonsoir la Côte d'Ivoire: Abidjan; f. 1993; Editor GEORGES AMANI.

La Chronique du Soir: 09 BP 150, Abidjan 09; tel. 22-15-12; general information; Dir. ROCH D'ASSOMPTION TIETI.

Fraternité-Matin: blvd du Général de Gaulle, 01 BP 1807, Abidjan 01; tel. 21-27-27; telex 23718; f. 1964; organ of the PDCI–RDA; Man. Dir MICHEL KOUAMÉ; circ. 80,000.

Ivoir 'Soir: blvd du Général de Gaulle, 01 BP 1807, Abidjan 01; tel. 21-27-27; telex 23718; f. 1987; organ of the PDCI–RDA; social, cultural and sporting activities; Man. Dir MICHEL KOUAMÉ; circ. 50,000.

La Voie: 17 BP 656, Abidjan 17; tel. 25-85-25; organ of the FPI; Dir ABOU DRAHAMANE SANGARÉ (imprisoned April 1994).

PERIODICALS

Abidjan 7 Jours: 01 BP 1965, Abidjan 01; tel. 35-39-39; telex 43171; f. 1964; weekly; local information; circ. 10,000.

L'Agouti Panseur: 01 BP 5117, Abidjan 01; tel. 21-51-36; weekly; general information; Dir ABOUBAKAR DIAY.

Le Combattant: 09 BP 664, Abidjan 09; tel. 22-19-90; weekly; general information; Dir JEAN-CLAUDE LIKRE KOGORÉ.

Le Démocrate: 01 BP 1212, Abidjan 01; tel. 24-25-61; organ of the PDCI; weekly; Dir JEAN-PIERRE AYE.

La Dépêche: 05 BP 1924, Abidjan 05; weekly; general information; Dir AUGUSTIN LEKPA.

Le Dialogue: 01 BP 89, Abidjan 01; tel. 24-35-77; weekly; general information; Dir MAMADOU N'GODJIGUI DOUKOURÉ.

Djeliba—le journal des jeunes Chrétiens: 01 BP 1287, Abidjan 01; tel. 21-69-79; f. 1974; 5 a year; Editor PIERRE TRICHET; circ. 7,000.

Eclosion: 08 BP 668, Abidjan 08; tel. 42-42-43; weekly; general information; Dir BOA EHUI.

Entente Africaine: Cocody-les-Deux-Plateaux, rue des Jardins, 01 BP 8534, Abidjan 01; tel. 41-04-76; fax 41-04-15; f. 1969; publ. by Centre Africain de Presse et d'Edition; quarterly; illustrated; Editor JUSTIN VIEYRA; circ. 10,000.

Forum Economique: 04 BP 488, Abidjan 04; tel. 24-09-07; monthly; Dir M. TALEB.

Fraternité-Hebdo: 01 BP 1212, Abidjan 01; tel. 21-29-15; organ of the PDCI; weekly; Editor GUY PIERRE NOUAMA.

Le Guido (Abidjan Jour et Nuit): 01 BP 1807, Abidjan 01; tel. 37-06-66; telex 372545; f. 1987; weekly; local information; Dir LAURENT DONA-FOLOGO.

Ivoire-Dimanche (ID): 01 BP 1807, Abidjan 01; f. 1971; weekly; circ. 75,000.

Le Jeune Démocrate: 08 BP 1866, Abidjan 08; tel. 45-69-22; weekly; general information; Dir IGNACE DASSOHIRI; Editor-in-Chief JEAN-SYLVESTRE LIA.

Journal Officiel de la Côte d'Ivoire: Service Autonome des Journaux Officiels, BP V70, Abidjan; tel. 22-67-76; weekly; circ. 1,000.

Liberté: 05 BP 1118, Abidjan 05; tel. 25-65-58; organ of the FPI; weekly; Dir JACQUES KACOU.

Le Messager: BP 1776, Abidjan; 6 a year; Editor ANDRÉ LEROUX.

Notre Temps: Abidjan; tel. 37-01-97; fax 43-00-74; f. 1991; weekly; circ. 15,000.

Le Nouvel Horizon: Abidjan; f. 1990; organ of the FPI; weekly; circ. 15,000.

La Nouvelle: 01 BP 1287, Abidjan 01; tel. 21-69-79; f. 1989; 6 a year; Editor PIERRE TRICHET; circ. 4,500.

La Nouvelle Presse: Cocody-les-deux-Plateaux, rue des Jardins, 01 BP 8534, Abidjan 01; tel. 41-04-76; fax 41-04-15; f. 1992; publ. by Centre Africain de Presse et d'Edition; weekly; current affairs; Editors JUSTIN VIEYRA, JÉRÔME CARLOS; circ. 25,000.

Le Patriote: 22 BP 1398, Abidjan 22; tel. 37-65-65; organ of the PDCI; weekly; Dir HAMED BAKAYOKO.

Réalités: 06 BP 100, Abidjan 06; tel. 41-41-79; organ of the PRCI; weekly; Dir RAPHAËL KOUAME BEUGRÉ.

Revue Ivoirienne de Droit: BP 3811, Abidjan; f. 1969; publ. by the Centre ivoirien de recherches et d'études juridiques; legal affairs; circ. 1,500.

Téré: 20 BP 43, Abidjan 20; organ of the PIT; weekly; Dir ANGÈLE GNONSOA.

Tribune du Banco: 22 BP 302, Abidjan 22; organ of the FPI; weekly; Dir JEAN KADIO-MOROKRO.

L'Union: 04 BP 2295, Abidjan 04; tel. 22-49-59; weekly; Dir YACOUBA BALLO.

La Voix d'Afrique: Cocody-les-Deux-Plateaux, rue des Jardins, 01 BP 8534, Abidjan 01; tel. 41-04-76; fax 41-04-15; publ. by Centre Africain de Presse et d'Edition; monthly; Editor-in-Chief GAOUSSOU KAMISSOKO.

NEWS AGENCIES

Agence Ivoirienne de Presse (AIP): 04 BP 312, Abidjan 04; telex 23781; f. 1961; Dir KONÉ SEMGUÉ SAMBA.

Foreign Bureaux

Agence France-Presse (AFP): 18 ave du Docteur Crozet, 01 BP 726, Abidjan 01; tel. 21-90-17; telex 22481; Dir (vacant).

Agenzia Nazionale Stampa Associata (ANSA) (Italy): 01 BP 90, Abidjan 01; tel. 22-40-61.

Associated Press (AP) (USA): 01 BP 5843, Abidjan 01; tel. 41-37-49; telex 28129; Correspondent ROBERT WELLER.

Reuters (United Kingdom): Résidence Les Acacias, 20 blvd Clozel, 01 BP 2338, Abidjan 01; tel. 21-12-22; telex 23921; fax 21-30-77; Chief Correspondent N. M. KOTCH.

Xinhua (New China) News Agency (People's Republic of China): Cocody Danga Nord Lot 46, 08 BP 1212, Abidjan 08; tel. 44-01-24; Chief Correspondent XIONG SHANWU.

Central News Agency (Taiwan) is also represented in Abidjan.

Publishers

Le Bureau Ivoirien des Nouvelles Editions Africaines (BINEA): 01 BP 3525, Abidjan 01; tel. 24-08-25; telex 42543; f. 1972 as Nouvelles Editions Africaines; bibliography, fiction, poetry, theatre, religion, art, juveniles, history, textbooks; Dir KROAH-BILÉ N'DABIAN.

Centre Africain de Presse et d'Edition: Cocody-les-Deux-Plateaux, rue des Jardins, 01 BP 8534, Abidjan 01; tel. 41-04-76; fax 41-04-15; fmrly Société Inter Afrique Presse Communications; Man. JUSTIN VIEYRA.

Centre d'Edition et de Diffusion Africaines (CEDA): square Aristide Briand, 04 BP 541, Abidjan 04; tel. 32-60-02; telex 22451; fax 32-72-62; f. 1961; general non-fiction; Chair. and Man. Dir VENANCE KACOU.

Centre de Publications Evangéliques: 08 BP 900, Abidjan 08; tel. 44-48-05; fax 44-58-17; f. 1970; religious; Dir ROBERT BRYAN.

Société Nouvelle de Presse et d'Editions: Abidjan; Dir MICHEL KOUAME.

Université Nationale de Côte d'Ivoire: 01 BP V34, Abidjan 01; tel. 44-08-59; telex 26138; f. 1964; general non-fiction and periodicals; Publications Dir GILLES VILASCO.

Government Publishing House

Imprimerie Nationale: BP V87, Abidjan; telex 23868.

Radio and Television

In 1991, according to UNESCO, there were an estimated 1.8m. radio receivers and 730,000 television receivers in use. Legislation to end the state monopoly of the broadcast media was enacted in late 1991.

Radiodiffusion Ivoirienne: BP V191, Abidjan 01; tel. 21-48-00; telex 22635; f. 1962; govt radio station broadcasting in French, English and local languages; MW station at Abidjan, relay at Bouaké; VHF transmitters at Abidjan, Bouaflé, Man and Koun-Abbrosso; Dir MAMADOU BERTÉ.

Radio Espoir: Port Bouët; f. 1991; private Catholic station.

Radio Nostalgie: Abidjan; f. 1993; subsidiary of Radio Nostalgie (France); FM station; Dirs HAMED BAKAYOKO, YVES ZOGBO, Jr.

Télévision Ivoirienne: 08 BP 883, Abidjan 08; tel. 43-90-39; telex 22293; f. 1963; broadcasts in French; two channels; stations at Abidjan, Bouaflé, Bouaké, Binao, Digo, Dimbokro, Koun, Man, Niangbo, Niangué, Séguéla, Tiémé and Touba; Man. (vacant).

A private television channel, operated by Canal Horizon, a subsidiary of Canal+ (France), was expected to commence broadcasts from Abidjan during the early 1990s. Broadcasts from Abidjan by **BBC Afrique**, the British Broadcasting Corporation's first FM station outside Europe, began in April 1994.

Finance

(br. = branch; cap. = capital; res = reserves; dep. = deposits; m. = million; amounts in francs CFA)

BANKING

Central Bank

Banque Centrale des Etats de l'Afrique de l'Ouest (BCEAO): angle blvd Botreau Roussel et ave Delafosse, 01 BP 1769, Abidjan 01; tel. 21-04-66; telex 23474; fax 22-28-52; headquarters in Dakar, Senegal; bank of issue and central bank for the seven states of the Union monétaire ouest africaine (UMOA), comprising Benin, Burkina Faso, Côte d'Ivoire, Mali, Niger, Senegal and Togo; f. 1955; cap. and res 379,881m. (Sept. 1992); Gov. CHARLES KONAN BANNY; Dir in Côte d'Ivoire TIÉMOKO KONÉ; 5 brs.

Other Banks

Afribail-Côte d'Ivoire SA: 8–10 ave Joseph Anoma, 01 BP 1274, Abidjan 01; tel. 22-07-22; telex 23641; fax 21-24-66; f. 1980; fmrly BIAO-Côte d'Ivoire; 51% owned by Meridien BIAO SA (Luxembourg); cap. 5,000m. (Sept. 1991); Chair. and Man. Dir NIAMIEN N'GORAN; 37 brs in Côte d'Ivoire.

Banque Atlantique-Côte d'Ivoire: angle ave Botreau Roussel et rue du Commerce, 04 BP 1036, Abidjan 04; tel. 21-82-18; telex 23834; fax 21-68-52; f. 1978; cap. and res 1,998m., dep. 16,147m. (Sept. 1992); Chair. DOSSONGUI KONÉ; Man. Dir P. PEETERS.

Banque de l'Habitat de la Côte d'Ivoire (BHCI): 22 ave Joseph Anoma, 01 BP 2325, Abidjan 01, tel. 22-60-00; telex 22544; fax 22-58-18; f. 1993 to finance housing projects, operations commenced 1994; cap. 1,030m; Chair. and Man. Dir KONÉ KAFONGO.

Banque Internationale pour le Commerce et l'Industrie de la Côte d'Ivoire SA (BICICI): ave Franchet d'Espérey, 01 BP 1298, Abidjan 01; tel. 20-16-00; telex 23651; fax 20-17-00; f. 1962; 28% owned by Société Financière pour les Pays d'Outre-Mer (comprises BNP, Banque Bruxelles Lambert and Dresdner Bank, 24% state-owned, 21% by Banque Nationale de Paris); cap. and res 15,199m., dep. 257,072m. (Sept. 1992); Chair. JOACHIM RICHMOND; Man. Dir FRANÇOIS DENIS; 38 brs.

Banque Paribas Côte d'Ivoire (PARIBAS CI): Immeuble Alliance, 6e étage, 17 ave Terrasson de Fougères, 17 BP 09, Abidjan 17; tel. 21-86-86; telex 22870; fax 21-88-23; f. 1984; 84% owned by Paribas International (France); cap. 1,000m. (Sept. 1993); Chair. DANIEL BÉDIN; Man. Dir BERNARD PANNETIER.

Banque Real de Côte d'Ivoire SA: Immeuble Botreau Roussel, 5e étage, angle ave Delafosse et blvd Botreau Roussel, 04 BP 411, Abidjan 04; tel. 21-84-52; telex 22430; fax 21-85-99; f. 1976; owned by Banco Real SA (Brazil); cap. 1,000m. (Sept. 1992); Chair. ANCEDE RICARDO GRIBEL; Man. Dir DOMINGO SAVIO GONÇALVES.

Compagnie Financière de la Côte d'Ivoire (COFINCI): Tour BICICI, 15e étage, rue Gourgas, 01 BP 1566, Abidjan 01; tel. 21-27-32; telex 22228; fax 20-17-00; f. 1974; 72.2% owned by BICICI; cap. 1,400m. (Sept. 1992); Chair. and Man. Dir JOACHIM RICHMOND.

Ecobank–Côte d'Ivoire: Immeuble Alliance, 17 ave Terrasson de Fougères, 01 BP 4107, Abidjan 01; tel. 21-10-41; telex 23266; fax 21-88-16; f. 1989; 85% owned by Ecobank Transnational Inc (operating under the auspices of the Economic Community of West African States); cap. 2,000m. (Sept. 1993); Chair. ABDOULAYE KONÉ; Man. Dir LOUIS NALLET; 1 br.

Société Générale de Banques en Côte d'Ivoire SA (SGBCI): 5–7 ave Joseph Anoma, 01 BP 1355, Abidjan 01; tel. 20-12-34; telex 23437; fax 20-14-86; f. 1962; 37.2% owned by Société Générale (France); cap. 11,500m. (March 1993); Chair. TIÉMOKO YADÉ COULIBALY; Man. Dir LUC BARAS; 55 brs.

Société Générale de Financement et de Participations en Côte d'Ivoire (SOGEFINANCE): 5–7 ave Joseph Anoma, 01 BP 3904, Abidjan 01; tel. 22-55-30; telex 23813; fax 20-14-86; f. 1978; 58% owned by SGBCI; cap. 1,000m. (Sept. 1993); Chair. and Man. Dir TIÉMOKO YADÉ COULIBALY; Man. LUC BARAS.

Société Ivoirienne de Banque (SIB): 34 blvd de la République, 01 BP 1300, Abidjan 01; tel. 20-00-00; telex 22283; fax 21-97-41; f. 1962; 80% owned by Crédit Lyonnais (France); 20% state-owned, cap. 4,000m. (Sept. 1993); Chair. ABOU DOUMBIA; Man. Dir ROBERT SABATIER; 37 brs.

Financial Institution

Caisse Autonome d'Amortissement: Immeuble SCIAM, ave Marchand, 01 BP 670, Abidjan 01; tel. 21-06-11; telex 23798; f. 1959; management of state funds; Chair. ABDOULAYE KONÉ; Man. Dir VICTOR KOUAMÉ.

Bankers' Association

Association Professionnelle des Banques et Etablissements Financiers de Côte d'Ivoire (APBEFCI): 01 BP 3810, Abidjan 01; tel. 21-20-08; Pres. JEAN PIERRE MEYER.

STOCK EXCHANGE

Bourse d'Abidjan: Abidjan 01; tel. 21-57-42; fax 22-16-57; Pres. M. NAKA LÉON.

INSURANCE

Assurances Générales de Côte d'Ivoire (AGCI): Immeuble AGCI, ave Noguès, 01 BP 4092, Abidjan 01; tel. 21-99-32; telex 22502; fax 33-25-79; f. 1979; cap. 1,290m.; Chair. JOACHIM RICHMOND; Man. Dir PIERRE DE POMPIGNAN.

Assurances Générales de Côte d'Ivoire—Vie (AGCI—Vie): Immeuble AGCI, ave Nogues, 01 BP 4092, Abidjan 01; tel. 33-11-31; telex 22502; fax 33-25-79; f. 1988; cap. 300m.; life; Chair. JOACHIM RICHMOND; Man. Dir PIERRE DE POMPIGNAN.

Assurmafer SA: 11 ave Joseph Anoma, 01 BP 62, Abidjan 01; tel. 21-10-52; telex 23231; f. 1941; cap. 160m.; Chair. PIERRE DE POMPIGNAN; Dir GILBERT HIS.

Colina SA: Immeuble Colina, blvd Roume, 01 BP 3832, Abidjan 01; tel. 21-65-05; telex 23570; fax 22-59-05; f. 1980; cap. 600m.; Chair. MICHEL PHARAON; Dir-Gen. RAYMOND FARHAT.

Mutuelle Universelle de Garantie (UNIWARRANT): 01 BP 301, Abidjan 01; tel. 32-76-32; telex 22120; fax 32-55-36; f. 1970; cap. 400m.; Chair. and Man. Dir FATIMA SYLLA.

La Nationale d'Assurances (CNA): 30 ave du Général de Gaulle, 01 BP 1333, Abidjan 01; tel. 22-08-00; fax 22-49-06; f. 1972; cap. 400m.; insurance and reinsurance; Chair. LÉON AMON; Man. Dir RICHARD COULIBALY.

La Sécurité Ivoirienne: Immeuble La Sécurité Ivoirienne, blvd Roume, 01 BP 569, Abidjan 01; tel. 21-50-63; telex 23817; fax 21-05-67; f. 1971; cap. 300m.; general; Chair. DIA HOUPHOUËT-BOIGNY; Dir-Gen. JACQUES BARDOUX.

Société Africaine d'Assurances et de Réassurances en République de Côte d'Ivoire (SAFFARRIV): Résidence Longchamp, blvd Roume, 01 BP 1741, Abidjan 01; tel. 21-91-57; telex 22159; fax 21-82-72; f. 1975; cap. 700m.; Pres. TIÉMOKO YADÉ COULIBALY; Man. Dir PATRICK MANTOUX.

Société Ivoirienne d'Assurances Mutuelles—Mutuelle d'Assurances Transports (SIDAM—MAT): Immeuble SIDAM, ave Houdaille, 01 BP 1217, Abidjan 01; tel. 21-97-82; telex 22670; fax 32-94-39; f. 1970, restructured 1985; cap. 150m.; Chair. ABOU DOUMBIA; Dir-Gen. SOULEYMANE MEITE.

L'Union Africaine-IARD (UA): ave de la Fosse Prolongée, 01 BP 378, Abidjan 01; tel. 21-73-81; telex 23568; fax 32-15-03; f. 1981; cap. 1,500m.; insurance and reinsurance; Chair. ERNEST AMOS DJORO; Dir JEAN-KACOU DIAGOU.

Union Africaine Vie: ave Houdaille, 01 BP 2016, Abidjan 01; tel. 22-25-15; telex 22200; fax 22-37-60; f. 1985; cap. 825m.; life assurance; Chair. ERNEST AMOS DJORO; Dir JEAN-KACOU DIAGOU.

Trade and Industry

DEVELOPMENT AGENCIES

Caisse Française de Développement: 01 BP 1814, Abidjan 01; tel. 44-53-05; telex 28113; fmrly Caisse Centrale de Coopération Economique, name changed 1992; Dir in Côte d'Ivoire ANTOINE BAUX.

Mission Française de Coopération: 01 BP 1839, Abidjan 01; tel. 21-60-45; administers bilateral aid from France; Dir ROGER BOURDIL.

STATE COMPANIES

Caisse de Stabilisation et de Soutien des Prix des Productions Agricoles (Caistab): BP V132, Abidjan; tel. 20-27-

00; telex 23712; fax 21-89-94; f. 1964; cap. 4,000m. francs CFA; until 1991 controlled price, quality and export of agricultural products; now responsible for forward selling of agricultural commodities on the international market; offices in Paris, London and New York; Man. Dir RENÉ AMANI.

Compagnie Ivoirienne pour le Développement des Cultures Vivrières (CIDV): 01 BP 2049, Abidjan 01; tel. 21-00-79; telex 23612; f. 1988; production of food crops; Man. Dir BENOÎT N'DRI BROU.

Direction et Controle des Grands Travaux (DCGTX): blvd de la Corniche, Cocody, 04 BP 945, Abidjan 04; tel. 44-28-05; telex 26193; fax 44-56-66; f. 1978; commissioning, implementation and supervision of public works contracts; Man. Dir PHILIPPE SEREY-EIFFEL.

Palmindustrie: 01 BP V239, Abidjan 01; tel. 36-93-88; telex 43100; f. 1969; cap. 3,365m. francs CFA; transfer to private ownership pending in 1993; development of palm, coconut and copra products; Man. Dir BONIFACE BRITO.

Société de Développement des Plantations Forestières (SODEFOR): blvd François Mitterrand, 01 BP 3770, Abidjan 01; tel. 44-46-16; telex 26156; fax 44-02-40; f. 1966; cap. 50m. francs CFA; establishment and management of plantations, reafforestation, marketing of timber products; Pres. Minister of Agriculture and Animal Resources; Man. Dir KONAN SOUNDELE.

Société pour le Développement Minier de la Côte d'Ivoire (SODEMI): 31 blvd André Latrille, 01 BP 2816, Abidjan 01; tel. 44-29-94; telex 26162; fax 44-08-21; f. 1962; cap. 600m. francs CFA; geological and mineral research; Pres. NICOLAS KOUANDI ANGBA; Man. Dir JOSEPH N'ZI.

Société pour le Développement des Plantations de Canne à Sucre, l'Industrialisation et la Commercialisation du Sucre (SODESUCRE): 16 ave du Docteur Crozet, 01 BP 2164, Abidjan 01; tel. 21-04-79; telex 23451; fax 21-07-75; f. 1971; cap. 30,500m. francs CFA; transfer to private ownership pending in 1994; management of sugar plantations, refining, marketing and export of sugar and by-products; Chair. and Man. Dir JOSEPH KOUAMÉ KRA.

Société pour le Développement des Productions Animales (SODEPRA): Immeuble Les Harmonies, angle blvd Carde et ave Dr Jamot, 01 BP 1249, Abidjan 01; tel. 21-13-10; telex 22123; f. 1970; cap. 404m. francs CFA; rearing of livestock; Chair. CHARLES DONWAHI; Man. Dir PAUL LAMIZANA.

Société Nationale d'Opérations Pétrolières de la Côte d'Ivoire (PETROCI): Immeuble les Hévéas, BP V194, Abidjan 01; tel. 21-85-58; telex 22135; fax 21-68-24; f. 1975; transfer to private ownership pending in 1994; cap. 20,000m. francs CFA; all aspects of petroleum development; Pres. and Man. Dir MOUSSA FANNY.

CHAMBERS OF COMMERCE

Chambre d'Agriculture de la Côte d'Ivoire: 11 ave Lamblin, 01 BP 1291, Abidjan 01; tel. 32-16-11; Sec.-Gen. GBAOU DIOMANDÉ.

Chambre de Commerce et d'Industrie de Côte d'Ivoire: 6 ave Joseph Anoma, 01 BP 1399, Abidjan 01; tel. 33-16-00; telex 23224; fax 32-39-46; Pres. SEYDOU DIARRA; Dir-Gen. KONAN KOFFI.

EMPLOYERS' ASSOCIATIONS

Fédération Maritime de la Côte d'Ivoire (FEDERMAR): 04 BP 723, Abidjan 04; tel. 21-25-83; Sec.-Gen. VACABA DE MOVALY TOURÉ.

Fédération Nationale des Industries de la Côte d'Ivoire: 01 BP 1340, Abidjan 01; tel. 35-71-42; f. 1993 to replace Syndicat des Industriels de la Côte d'Ivoire; Pres. PIERRE MAGNE; Sec.-Gen. PHILIPPE MEYER; 150 mems.

Groupement Interprofessionnel de l'Automobile (GIPA): Immeuble Jean Lefèbvre, 14 blvd de Marseille, 01 BP 1340, Abidjan 01; tel. 35-71-42; telex 42380; f. 1953; 30 mems; Pres. DANIEL DUBOIS; Sec.-Gen. PHILIPPE MEYER.

Syndicat des Commerçants Importateurs, Exportateurs et Distributeurs de la Côte d'Ivoire (SCIMPEX): 01 BP 3792, Abidjan 01; tel. 21-54-27; Pres. JACQUES ROSSIGNOL; Sec.-Gen. M. KOFFI.

Syndicat des Entrepreneurs et des Industriels de la Côte d'Ivoire (SEICI): Immeuble Jean Lefèbvre, 14 blvd de Marseille, 01 BP 464, Abidjan 01; tel. 21-83-85; f. 1934; Pres. ABDEL AZIZ THIAM.

Syndicat des Exportateurs et Négociants en Bois de Côte d'Ivoire: Immeuble CCIA, 5e étage, Porte 8, 01 BP 1979, Abidjan 01; tel. 21-12-39; fax 21-26-42; Pres. JEAN-CLAUDE BERNARD.

Syndicat des Producteurs Industriels du Bois (SPIB): Immeuble CCIA, 5e étage, Porte 8, 01 BP 318, Abidjan 01; tel. 21-12-39; fax 21-26-42; f. 1973; Pres. BRUNO FINOCCHIARO.

Union des Entreprises Agricoles et Forestières: Immeuble CCIA, 5e étage, Porte 8, 01 BP 2300, Abidjan 01; tel. 21-12-39; fax 21-26-42; f. 1952; Pres. JEAN-BAPTISTE AMETHIER.

Union Patronale de Côte d'Ivoire (UPACI): 01 BP 1340, Abidjan 01; tel. 35-71-42; telex 43280; Pres. JOSEPH AKA-ANGHUI; Sec.-Gen. PHILIPPE MEYER.

MAJOR INDUSTRIAL COMPANIES

The following are some of the largest companies in terms of either capital investment or employment.

Blohorn SA: 01 BP 1751, Abidjan 01; tel. 24-90-60; telex 42279; fax 25-11-05; f. 1960; cap. 6,040m. francs CFA; 80% owned by Unilever Group; management of industrial complex for processing oil-seeds; production of palm oil and products derived from it, including soap, margarine and glycerine; Chair. PIERRE BONNEIL; Vice-Chair. MARTIN RUSHWORTH; 1,000 employees.

Carnaud Metalbox SIEM: blvd Giscard d'Estaing, 01 BP 1242, Abidjan 01; tel. 35-89-74; telex 634000; fax 35-03-94; f. 1954; subsidiary of Carnaud Metalbox (France); cap. 1,889m. francs CFA; fmrly Société Ivoirienne d'Emballage Métallique; mfrs of cans; Chair. B. JÜRGEN HINTZ; Man. Dir PHILIPPE EYMARD.

Compagnie des Caoutchoucs du Pakidie (CCP): 01 BP 1191, Abidjan 01; tel. 35-73-14; telex 23605; f. 1960; cap. 856m. francs CFA; rubber plantations; Chair. GÉRARD MARCHAL; Dir FULGENCE KOFFY.

Compagnie Ivoirienne pour le Développement des Textiles (CIDT): route de Béoumi, BP 622, Bouaké; tel. 63-30-13; telex 69121; fax 63-41-67; f. 1974; cap. 7,200m. francs CFA; 75% state-owned; development of cotton production, cotton ginning; Pres. and Man. Dir COULIBALY SAMBA; 1,722 employees.

Compagnie Ivoirienne d'Electricité (CIE): 01 BP 6932, Abidjan 01; f. 1990 to assume electricity distribution network fmrly operated by Energie Electrique de la Côte d'Ivoire, transferred to majority private ownership 1992; 20% state-owned, 51% controlled by Société Bouygues group (France) and Electricité de France; Pres. MARCEL ZADI KESSY; Man. Dir GÉRARD THEURIAU.

Entreprise Forestière des Bois Africains (EFBA): Résidence Neuilly, 19 blvd Angoulvant, 01 BP 958, Abidjan 01; tel. 22-74-31; telex 23689; cap. 516m. francs CFA; sawmills in Agboville, Boubélé and Zagné; Dirs ALAIN BOUNEAU, MARCEL KUNG.

Eveready Côte d'Ivoire SA: Zone Industrielle de Vridi, 15 BP 611, Abidjan 15; tel. 27-33-84; telex 43390; f. 1969; cap. 894m. francs CFA; wholly-owned subsidiary of Eveready Battery Co (USA); mfrs of batteries; Dir A. CORVEZ.

Ets R. Gonfreville (ERG): route de l'Aéroport, BP 584, Bouaké; tel. 63-32-13; telex 69105; fax 63-46-65; f. 1921; cap. 2,999m. francs CFA; 10.5% state-owned; transfer to private ownership of state holding pending in 1993; spinning, weaving, dyeing and printing of cotton textiles; clothing mfrs; Chair. SOUNKALO DJIBO; Man. Dir CLAUDE TRESCOL; 2,452 employees.

Filatures, Tissages, Sacs–Côte d'Ivoire SA (FILTISAC): Km 8, route d'Adzopé, 01 BP 3962, Abidjan 01; tel. 37-13-02; telex 23273; fax 37-09-67; f. 1965; transferred to private ownership 1994; cap. 1,587m. francs CFA; mfrs of polythene and jute bags and other packaging; Pres. SIDI MADATALI; 1,300 employees.

Grands Moulins d'Abidjan (GMA): Quai 1, Zone Portuaire, 01 BP 1743, Abidjan 01; tel. 21-28-33; telex 23740; f. 1963; cap. 2,000m. francs CFA; flour milling and production of animal feed; Dir KOUASSI KOUADIO.

Industrie de Transformation des Produits Agricoles (API): Zone Industrielle de Vridi, 15 BP 431, Abidjan 15; tel. 35-20-09; telex 43159; f. 1968; cap. 900m. francs CFA; wholly owned by Cacao Barry Group (France); marketing of cocoa products, processing of cocoa beans; Man. Dir HONORÉ AKPANGNI.

Mobil Oil-Côte d'Ivoire: impasse Paris-Village, 01 BP 1777, Abidjan 01; tel. 21-73-20; telex 23779; f. 1974; cap. 2,000m. francs CFA; distribution of petroleum products; Chair. MICHEL BONNET; Dir J. LABAUNE.

Moulin du Sud-Ouest (MSO): 04 BP 1218, Abidjan 04; tel. 21-20-62; telex 23230; f. 1979; cap. 1,105m. francs CFA; flour milling at San Pedro; Chair. VICTOR AMAGOU; Man. Dir JEAN-CLAUDE FRAPPIER.

Nandjelait: Zone Industrielle de Vridi, 01 BP 2149, Abidjan 01; f. 1986; cap. 600m. francs CFA; production, packaging and sale of dairy products and by-products; Chair. and Man. Dir ROGER ABINADER.

National Electric-Côte d'Ivoire (NELCI): 16 BP 131, Abidjan 16; f. 1983; cap. 1,000m. francs CFA; assembly of radio and television receivers; Chair. TAMADA TAKASHI.

Nestlé Côte d'Ivoire: rue du Lycée Technique, 01 BP 1840, Abidjan 01; tel. 44-44-44; telex 27194; fax 44-43-43; f. 1959;

cap. 5,518m. francs CFA; subsidiary of Nestlé SA (Switzerland); production of coffee and cocoa products, manufacture and sale of food products; Chair. GEORGES N'DIA KOFFI; Man. Dir FRANÇOIS PRÉVOT.

Omnium Chimique et Cosmétique (COSMIVOIRE): Zone Industrielle de Vridi, 01 BP 3576, Abidjan 01; tel. 27-57-32; telex 43223; fax 27-28-13; f. 1974; cap. 702m. francs CFA; mfrs of soaps, cosmetics, oils, margarine, butter and alcohol; Pres. ALAIN YACOUBA BAMBARA; Man. Dir YAO KOFFI NOËL.

PPB–Côte d'Ivoire: Yopougon, 05 BP 2131, Abidjan 05; tel. 35-32-83; telex 23107; f. 1978; cap. 550m. francs CFA; mfrs of prefabricated concrete floors; Man. Dir JEAN-FRANÇOIS MOREAU.

Sadofoss SA: 01 BP 3867, Abidjan 01; tel. 35-75-09; telex 43372; f. 1975; cap. 524m. francs CFA; mfrs of paint and industrial adhesives; Man. Dir BERNARD THEUSS.

Société Africaine de Cacao (SACO): rue Pierre et Marie Curie, 01 BP 1045, Abidjan 01; tel. 35-44-10; telex 43293; f. 1956; cap. 1,733m. francs CFA; 35% state-owned, 65% owned by Cacao Barry Group (France); mfrs of cocoa powder, chocolate products, cocoa butter and oil-cake; Pres. and Man. Dir SEYDOU DIARRA; 670 employees.

Société Africaine de Plantations d'Hévéas (SAPH): 14 blvd Carde, 01 BP 1322, Abidjan 01; tel. 21-18-91; telex 23696; fax 22-18-67; f. 1956; cap. 8,771m. francs CFA; 60.4% state-owned; transfer to private ownership of part of state holding pending in 1993; production of rubber on 24,000 ha of plantations; Pres. and Man. Dir YVES ROLAND.

Société des Brasseries de la Côte d'Ivoire (BRACODI): 25 blvd de Marseille, 01 BP 1855, Abidjan 01; tel. 24-13-94; telex 23432; fax 24-01-345; f. 1949; cap. 3,363m. francs CFA; manufacture and sale of beer, soft drinks and ice; Pres. PIERRE CASTEL; Man. Dir JEAN-MARIE DURAND.

Société des Caoutchoucs de Grand-Béréby (SOGB): 17 BP 18, Abidjan 17; tel. 21-99-47; telex 23888; fax 33-25-80; f. 1979; cap. 21,602m. francs CFA; rubber plantations; 94.8% state-owned; transfer to private ownership of part of state holding pending in 1993; Pres. and Gen. Man. ALEXIS KOUASSI DETOH.

Société des Ciments d'Abidjan (SCA): 01 BP 3751, Abidjan 01; tel. 21-32-63; telex 23610; f. 1965; cap. 2,000m. francs CFA; 40% state-owned; cement mfrs; Chair. and Man. Dir PIERRE AMIDA.

Société de Conserves de Côte d'Ivoire (SCODI): Quai de Pêche, Zone Industrielle de Vridi, 01 BP 677, Abidjan 01; tel. 25-66-74; telex 43254; fax 27-05-52; f. 1960; cap. 908m. francs CFA; tuna canning; Chair. PAUL ANTONIETTI; Gen. Man. YVON RIVA.

Société de Construction et d'Exploitation d'Installations Frigorifiques (SOCEF): Port de Pêche, 04 BP 154, Abidjan 04; tel. 35-54-42; f. 1962; cap. 900m. francs CFA; mfrs of refrigeration units; Dir GÉRARD CLEMENT.

Société Cotonnière Ivoirienne (COTIVO): BP 244, Agboville; tel. 51-70-01; telex 51002; fax 51-73-34; f. 1972; cap. 3,600m. francs CFA; textile complex; Pres. MICHEL HEMONNOT; Man. Dir MICHEL DUTRONC.

Société de Distribution d'Eau de la Côte d'Ivoire (SODECI): 1 ave Christiani-Treichville, 01 BP 1843, Abidjan 01; tel. 23-30-00; fax 24-20-33; f. 1959; cap. 2,000m. francs CFA; production, treatment and distribution of drinking water; Chair. MARCEL ZADI KESSY; Man. Dir PIERRE LE TAREAU; 1,330 employees.

Société de Galvanisation de Tôles en Côte d'Ivoire (TOLES-IVOIRE): 15 BP 144, Abidjan 15; tel. 27-53-38; telex 43184; f. 1969; cap. 975m. francs CFA; mfrs of galvanized corrugated sheets and other roofing materials; Chair. SIDI MADATALI; Man. Dir PHILIPPE GODIN.

Société Ivoirienne de Béton Manufacturé (SIBM): 12 rue Thomas Edison, 01 BP 902, Abidjan 01; tel. 35-52-71; fax 35-82-27; f. 1978; cap. 800m. francs CFA; mem. of Société Africaine de Béton Manufacturé group; mfrs of concrete; Man. Dir DANIEL PAUL.

Société Ivoirienne de Cables (SICABLE): Zone Industrielle de Vridi, 15 BP 35, Abidjan 15; tel. 27-57-35; fax 27-12-34; f. 1975; cap. 740m. francs CFA; 35% state-owned, 51% owned by Cables Pirelli; transfer to private ownership of state holding pending in 1993; mfrs of electricity cables; Chair. ROGER AGNIEL; Man. Dir HERVÉ JACOTOT.

Société Ivoirienne de Ciments et Matériaux (SICM): blvd du Port, 01 BP 887, Abidjan 01; tel. 24-17-34; telex 42382; fax 24-27-21; f. 1962; cap. 507m. francs CFA; clinker-crushing plant; Chair. DANIEL GORGUES; Man. Dir O. RONIN.

Société Ivoirienne de Construction et de Gestion Immobilière (SICOGI): 01 BP 1856, Abidjan 01; tel. 37-03-40; telex 24122; f. 1962; cap. 2,000m. francs CFA; 54% state-owned; planning and construction; Man. Dir KONÉ BANGA.

Société Ivoirienne d'Oxygène et d'Acetylène (SIVOA): 131 blvd de Marseille, 01 BP 1753, Abidjan 01; tel. 35-44-71; telex 43394; fax 35-80-96; f. 1962; cap. 873m. francs CFA; 20% state-owned, 72% by Air Liquide (France); mfrs of industrial and medical gases; Dir JEAN-PIERRE DESSALLES; 120 employees

Société Ivoirienne de Raffinage (SIR): route de Vridi, blvd de Petit-Bassam, 01 BP 1269, Abidjan 01; tel. 27-01-60; telex 43442; fax 21-17-98; f. 1962; cap. 26,000m. francs CFA; 47% owned by PETROCI; transfer to private ownership of state holding pending in 1993; operates petroleum refinery at Abidjan; Chair. and Man. Dir DAOUDA THIAM; 736 employees.

Société Ivoirienne des Tabacs (SITAB): Zone Industrielle, 01 BP 607, Bouaké 01; tel. 63-35-31; telex 61116; f. 1971; cap. 4,449m. francs CFA; mfrs of cigarettes; Chair. FRANÇOISE AIDARA; Vice-Chair. and Man. Dir PIERRE MAGNE; 849 employees.

Société Ivoirienne de Trituration de Graines Oléagineuses et de Raffinage d'Huiles Végétales (TRITURAF): 15 BP 324, Abidjan 15; tel. 25-92-93; telex 42279; fax 25-11-05; f. 1973; cap. 1,300m. francs CFA; 75% owned by Blohorn SA; Chair. PIERRE BONNEIL; Man. Dir GEORGES BROU KOUASSI.

Société de Limonaderies et Brasseries d'Afrique (SOLIBRA): 27 rue du Canal, 01 BP 1304, Abidjan; tel. 24-91-33; telex 43192; fax 35-97-91; f. 1955; cap. 3,000m. francs CFA; mfrs of beer, lemonade and ice at Abidjan, Bouaflé and Yopougon; Chair JOHNNY THIJS; Man. Dir JACQUES GOCHELY.

Société des Mines d'Afema (SOMIAF): Abidjan; jt venture by SODEMI and Eden Roc Mineral Corpn (Canada); exploitation of gold deposits at Aniuri.

Société des Mines d'Ity (SMI): Ity; regd office 08 BP 872, Abidjan 08; f. 1989; cap. 600m. francs CFA; 60% owned by SODEMI, 40% by Cie Française des Mines; development of gold reserves at Ity; Pres. ABDOULAYE KONÉ; Man. Dir M. PALANQUE.

Société Multinationale de Bitumes (SMB): blvd de Petit-Bassam, Zone Industrielle de Vridi, 12 BP 622, Abidjan 12; tel. 27-01-60; telex 42539; fax 27-05-18; f. 1976; cap. 1,218m. francs CFA; 93% owned by PETROCI; Chair. and Man. Dir MOUSSA TOURÉ; 50 employees.

Société Nationale Ivoirienne de Travaux (SONITRA): route d'Anyama, 01 BP 2609, Abidjan 01; tel. 37-13-68; telex 24105; f. 1963; cap. 2,273m. francs CFA; 55% state-owned; building and construction; Chair. FERNAND KONAN KOUADIO; Man. Dir AMOS SALOMON; 1,393 employees.

Société Nouvelle Abidjanaise de Carton Ondulé (SONACO): Zone Industrielle de Yopougon, 01 BP 1119, Abidjan; tel. 46-49-70; telex 29164; fax 46-45-06; f. 1964; cap. 1,200m. francs CFA; mfrs of paper goods and corrugated cardboard; Chair. DANIEL FORGET; Man. Dir FÉLIX DADIE; 406 employees.

Société Nouvelle Sifca: rue des Galions, 01 BP 1289, Abidjan 01; tel. 24-26-52; telex 43453; fax 24-07-90; f. 1964; cap. 2,000m. francs CFA; export of cocoa and coffee; Pres. and Man. Dir YVES LAMBELIN; 235 employees.

Société Shell-Côte d'Ivoire: Zone Industrielle de Vridi, 15 BP 378, Abidjan 15; tel. 27-00-18; telex 43362; fax 27-24-99; f. 1928; cap. 1,800m. francs CFA; 50% holding by PETROCI; distribution of petroleum products; Pres. and Man. Dir EDOUARD ETTE.

Société de Stockage de Côte d'Ivoire (STOCACI): rue des Thoniers, Zone Portuaire, 01 BP 1798, Abidjan 01; f. 1980; cap. 1,000m. francs CFA; treatment and storage of cocoa and other products; Chair. JEAN ABILE GAL; Vice-Chair. and Man. Dir MADELEINE TCHICAYA.

Société de Tubes d'Acier et Aluminium en Côte d'Ivoire (SOTACI): Zone Industrielle de Yopougon, 01 BP 2747, Abidjan 01; tel. 45-39-22; telex 29110; fax 45-39-25; f. 1978; cap. 1,029m. francs CFA; mfrs of steel and aluminium tubing and pipes; Chair. and Man. Dir MOUSTAPHA KHALIL; Dir JOSÉ HURTADO.

Star Auto: rue Pierre et Marie Curie, 01 BP 4054, Abidjan 01; tel. 25-43-06; telex 43324; fax 25-44-15; f. 1983; cap. 1,400m. francs CFA; subsidiary of Mercedes-Benz AG (Germany); mfrs and distributors of motor vehicles; Chair. H. UTESS; Gen. Man. GÉRARD FAU.

Union Industrielle Textile de Côte d'Ivoire (UTEXI): Zone Industrielle de Vridi, 15 BP 414, Abidjan 15; tel. 27-44-81; telex 43264; fax 27-16-16; f. 1972; cap. 3,700m. francs CFA; 12.75% state-owned; spinning and weaving mill at Dimbokro; Chair. JACQUES ROSSIGNOL; Man. Dir NOBOYUKI YOSHIDA.

Union Ivoirienne de Traitement de Cacao (UNICAO): 15 BP 406, Abidjan 15; tel. 27-14-49; telex 42343; fax 27-56-82; cap. 1,100m. francs CFA; processing of cocoa beans; Chair. YVES LAMBELIN; Man. Dir HENRI KORNER.

UNIWAX: Zone Industrielle de Yopougon, 01 BP 3994, Abidjan 01; tel. 45-44-12; telex 29100; fax 46-49-42; f. 1967; cap. 1,000m. francs CFA; mfrs of batik fabrics; Chair. PIERRE BONNEIL; Man. Dir GILLES MOISAN; 520 employees.

Usine de Traitement de Produits Agricoles (UTPA): rue des Thonniers, Zone Portuaire, 01 BP 1798, Abidjan 01; tel. 21-16-55; telex 23657; f. 1977; cap. 2,000m. francs CFA; coffee packaging at Abengourou, Kotobi and Daloa; Chair. EMILE ABILE-GAL; Man. Dir ALAIN PERILLAUD.

TRADE UNIONS

Union Générale des Travailleurs de Côte d'Ivoire (UGTCI): 05 BP 1203, Abidjan 05; tel. 21-26-65; f. 1962; Sec.-Gen. HYACINTHE ADIKO NIAMKEY; 100,000 individual mems; 190 affiliated unions.

There are also several independent trade unions, the most prominent independent federation being the Fédération des Syndicats Autonomes de la Côte d'Ivoire.

Transport

RAILWAYS

Société Ivoirienne des Chemins de Fer (SICF): 01 BP 1551, Abidjan 01; tel. 21-02-45; telex 23564; fax 21-39-62; f. 1989, following dissolution of Régie du Chemin de Fer Abidjan–Niger (a jt venture with the Govt of Burkina Faso); state-owned; transfer to private ownership pending in 1994; 660 km of track; Pres. and Man. Dir ABDEL AZIZ THIAM.

ROADS

There are some 68,000 km of roads, of which some 5,290 km are surfaced. Financial constraints have resulted in the postponement of several construction and rehabilitation projects. However, a four year (1994–97) programme for the repair and extension of the road network, valued at 147,000m. francs CFA, was to be supported by the World Bank, the African Development Bank, the Banque ouest-africaine de développement and the Governments of Germany and Japan.

Société des Transports Abidjanais (SOTRA): 01 BP 2009, Abidjan 01; tel. 36-90-11; telex 43101; f. 1960; 60% state-owned; urban transport; Chair. MAURICE BAHI ZAHIRI; Dir-Gen. JEAN-BAPTISTE COFFI.

SHIPPING

Côte d'Ivoire has two major ports, Abidjan and San Pedro, both of which are industrial and commercial establishments with financial autonomy. Abidjan, which handles some 10m. metric tons of goods annually (10.2m. tons in 1992), is the largest container and trading port in west Africa. Access to the port is via the 2.7 km-long Vridi Canal. Rehabilitation works undertaken in the late 1980s were expected to contribute to a continued increase in Abidjan's traffic. The port at San Pedro, which handled 754,417 tons of goods in the first nine months of 1991, remains the main gateway to the south-western region of Côte d'Ivoire.

Port Autonome d'Abidjan (PAA): BP V85, Abidjan; tel. 24-26-40; telex 42318; fax 24-23-28; f. 1950; public undertaking supervised by the Ministry of Equipment, Transport and Telecommunications; Man. Dir JEAN-MICHEL MOULOD.

Port Autonome de San Pedro (PASP): BP 339/340, San Pedro; tel. 71-16-79; telex 99102; f. 1971; Man. Dir OGOU ATTEMENE (acting).

Compagnie Maritime Africaine-Côte d'Ivoire (COMAF-CI): rond-point du Nouveau Port, 08 BP 867, Abidjan 08; tel. 32-40-77; telex 23357; f. 1973; navigation and management of ships; Dir FRANCO BERNARDINI.

SAGA-CI: rond-piont du Nouveau Port, 01 BP 1727, Abidjan 01; tel. 23-23-23; telex 43312; fax 24-25-06; merchandise handling, transit and storage; Chair. CHARLES BENITAL; Dir DANIEL CHARRIER.

Société Agence Maritime de l'Ouest Africain-Côte d'Ivoire (SAMOA-CI): rue des Gallions, 01 BP 1611, Abidjan 01; tel. 21-29-65; telex 23765; f. 1955; shipping agents; Man. Dir CLAUDE PERDRIAUD.

Société Ivoirienne de Navigation Maritime (SIVOMAR): 5 rue Charpentier, zone 2b, Treichville, 01 BP 1395, Abidjan 01; tel. 21-73-23; telex 22226; fax 32-38-53; f. 1977; shipments to ports in Africa, the Mediterranean and the Far East; Dir SIMPLISSE DE MESSE ZINSOU.

Société Ivoirienne de Transport Maritime (SITRAM): rue des Pétroliers, 01 BP 1546, Abidjan 01; tel. 36-92-00; telex 42254; fax 35-73-93; f. 1967, nationalized 1976; return to private ownership pending in 1994; services between Europe and west Africa and the USA; Chair. BONIFACE PEGAWAGNABA; Dir Commdt FAKO KONÉ.

Société Ouest-Africaine d'Entreprises Maritimes en Côte d'Ivoire (SOAEM-CI): 01 BP 1727, Abidjan 01; tel. 21-59-69; telex 23654; fax 32-24-67; f. 1978; merchandise handling, transit and storage; Chair. JACQUES PELTIER; Dir JACQUES COLOMBANI.

SOCOPAO-Côte d'Ivoire: km 1 blvd de Marseille, 01 BP 1297, Abidjan 01; tel. 24-13-14; telex 43261; fax 24-21-30; shipping agents; Shipping Dir OLIVIER RANJARD.

CIVIL AVIATION

There are two international airports, Abidjan—Houphouët-Boigny and Yamoussoukro. In addition, there are regional airports at Berebi, Bouaké, Daloa, Korhogo, Man, Odienne, San Pedro, Sassandra and Tabou.

Air Afrique (Société Aérienne Africaine Multinationale): 3 ave Joseph Anoma, 01 BP 3927, Abidjan 01; tel. 21-09-00; telex 23785; f. 1961; owned jtly by Air France and the Govts of Benin, Burkina Faso, the Central African Republic, Chad, the Congo, Côte d'Ivoire, Guinea-Bissau, Mali, Mauritania, Niger, Senegal and Togo; extensive regional flights and services to Europe, North America and the Middle East; Dir-Gen. YVES ROLAND-BILLECART.

Air Ivoire: 13 ave Barthe, 01 BP 1027, Abidjan 01; tel. 21-34-29; telex 23727; fax 27-88-03; f. 1960, govt-owned since 1976; internal flights and services within West Africa; Man. Dir Col ABDOULAYE COULIBALY.

Tourism

The game reserves, forests, lagoons, rich tribal folklore and the lively city of Abidjan are all of interest to tourists. Some 188,000 tourists visited Côte d'Ivoire in 1991; receipts from tourism in that year totalled an estimated US $70m.

Direction de la Promotion Touristique: BP V184, Abidjan; tel. 21-49-70; telex 22108; fax 21-73-06; Dir EUGÈNE KINDO-BOUADI.

Defence

In June 1993 Côte d'Ivoire had 5,500 men in the army, 900 in the air force and 700 in the navy. In addition, there were paramilitary forces of approximately 7,800 men (including a presidential guard of 1,100 men and a 4,400-strong gendarmerie). Service is by selective conscription and lasts for six months. France supplies equipment and training, and maintains a force of about 500 men.

Defence Expenditure: Estimated at 21,390m. francs CFA in 1992.

Chief of General Staff of the Armed Forces: Gen. ROBERT GUEÏ.

Education

In 1990, according to UNESCO estimates, adult illiteracy averaged 46.2% (males 33.1%; females 59.8%). Education at all levels is available free of charge. Primary education, which is officially compulsory, usually begins at seven years of age and lasts for six years. Enrolment at primary schools in 1991 was equivalent to 69% of all children in the relevant age-group (81% of boys; 58% of girls). In the towns, however, average attendance is more than 90%. Secondary education, usually beginning at the age of 13, lasts for up to seven years, comprising a first cycle of four years and a second cycle of three years. In 1991 the total enrolment at secondary schools was equivalent to 24% of children in the relevant age-group (32% of boys; 16% of girls). The National University at Abidjan has six faculties, and in 1993/94 had 40,000–50,000 enrolled students. University-level facilities have been constructed in Yamoussoukro; in addition, many students attend French universities. About 1,300 teachers and researchers of French nationality were estimated to be working in Côte d'Ivoire in 1991. Expenditure on education in 1990 was projected at 191,153m. francs CFA (30.9% of total budget spending), the highest allocation to any sector.

Bibliography

Affou, Y. S. *La relève paysanne en Côte d'Ivoire.* Paris, Editions Karthala, 1990.

Amin, S. *Le développement du capitalisme en Côte d'Ivoire.* Paris, 1966.

Amondji, M. *Félix Houphouët-Boigny et La Côte d'Ivoire.* Paris, Editions Karthala, 1984.

Avenard, J.-M. *Le milieu naturel de la Côte d'Ivoire.* Bondy, France, ORSTOM, 1972.

Cowan, L. G. 'Côte d'Ivoire at 27'. *CSIS Africa Notes,* Briefing Paper No. 71. Washington, DC, Center for Strategic and International Studies, 1987.

Cruise O'Brien, D. B., Dunn, J., and Rathbone, R. (Eds.). *Contemporary West African States.* Cambridge, Cambridge University Press, 1989.

David, P. *Côte d'Ivoire.* Paris, Editions Karthala, 1986.

Domergue-Cloarec. *La Santé en Côte d'Ivoire.* 2 vols. Paris, Académie des Sciences d'Outre-Mer, 1987.

Dozon, J.-P. *La Société bété en Côte d'Ivoire.* Paris, Editions Karthala, 1983.

Duruflé, G. *L'ajustement structurel en Afrique (Sénégal, Côte d'Ivoire, Madagascar).* Paris, Editions Karthala, 1987.

Fauré, Y. A., and Médard, J.-F. *Etat et bourgeoisie en Côte d'Ivoire.* Paris, Editions Karthala, 1983.

Foster, P., and Zolberg, A. R. (Eds). *Ghana and the Ivory Coast, Perspectives and Modernization.* University of Chicago Press, 1972.

Gombeaud, J.-L., Moutout, C., and Smith, S. *La Guerre du cacao, histoire secrète d'un embargo.* Paris, Calmann-Lévy, 1990.

Harrison Church, R. J. *West Africa.* 8th Edn, London, Longman, 1979.

Lisette, G. *Le Combat du Rassemblement Démocratique Africain.* Paris, Présence Africaine, 1983.

Loucou, J.-N. *Histoire de la Côte d'Ivoire.* Paris, Editions Karthala.

Rapley, J. *Ivorien Capitalism: African Entrepreneurs in Côte d'Ivoire.* London, Lynne Rienner, 1993.

Rimmer, D. *The Economies of West Africa.* London, Weidenfeld and Nicolson, 1984.

Rougerie, G. *La Côte d'Ivoire.* Paris, Presses universitaires de France, 1964.

Siriex, P. H. *Félix Houphouët-Boigny: L'homme de la paix.* Paris, Seghers, 1975.

Sy, M. S. *Recherches sur l'exercice du pouvoir politique en Afrique noir (Côte d'Ivoire, Guinée, Mali).* Paris, 1965.

Touré, A. *La Civilisation quotidienne en Côte d'Ivoire.* Paris, Editions Karthala, 1983.

Wilde, J. de, et al. *Agricultural Development in Tropical Africa.* Baltimore, MD, Johns Hopkins Press, 1967.

World Bank. *Côte d'Ivoire Living Standards Survey: Design and Implementation.* Washington, DC, International Bank for Reconstruction and Development, 1986.

Zartman, I. W. *The Political Economy of the Ivory Coast.* New York, Praeger, 1984.

DJIBOUTI

Physical and Social Geography

I. M. LEWIS

The Republic of Djibouti is situated at the southern entrance to the Red Sea. It is bounded on the far north by Eritrea, on the west and south by Ethiopia, and on the south-east by Somalia. Djibouti covers an area of 23,200 sq km (8,958 sq miles), consisting mostly of volcanic rock-strewn desert wastes, with occasional patches of arable land, and spectacular salt lakes and pans. The climate is torrid, with high tropical temperatures and humidity during the monsoon season. The average annual rainfall is less than 125 mm. Only in the upper part of the basaltic range north of the Gulf of Tadjourah, where the altitude reaches more than 1,200 m above sea-level, is there continuous annual vegetation.

At 31 December 1990 the population was officially estimated at 519,900, including refugees and other resident non-nationals. In 1981 the capital town, Djibouti (whose port and rail-head constitute the territory's *raison d'être*), had a population of about 200,000. The indigenous population is almost evenly divided between the Issa (who are of Somali origin) and the Afar, the former having a slight predominance. Both are Muslim Cushitic-speaking peoples with a traditionally nomadic economy and close cultural affinities, despite frequent local rivalry. The Afar inhabit the northern part of the country, the Issa the southern, and both groups span the artificial frontiers separating the Republic of Djibouti from Ethiopia and Somalia.

Since the development of the port of Djibouti in the early 1900s, the indigenous Issas have been joined by immigrants from the adjoining regions of Somalia. The Afar generally follow more restricted patterns of nomadic movement than the Issa, and a more hierarchical traditional political organization. While they formed a number of small polities, these were linked by the pervasive cleavage running throughout the Afar population between the 'noble' Asaimara (or 'red') clans and the less prestigious Asdoimara (or 'white') clans. There is also a long-established Arab trading community. European expatriates are mainly French, mostly in government employment, commerce and the armed forces.

Recent History

MILES SMITH-MORRIS

Revised for this edition by the Editor

French involvement in the territory that now comprises the Republic of Djibouti dates from the mid-19th century, and was stimulated by subsequent Anglo-French rivalry for control of the entrance to the Red Sea. During 1897–1917 a Franco-Ethiopian railway was constructed to carry Ethiopia's trade through the French port.

The territory's indigenous inhabitants, the Afar and the Issa, have strong connections with Ethiopia and Somalia respectively. Until the 1960s, divisions between the two communities were not marked; subsequently, however, conflicting international interests in the Horn of Africa, together with France's policy of favouring the minority Afar community, combined to create tensions in the territory, then known as French Somaliland (renamed the French Territory of the Afars and the Issas in 1967).

Demands for independence were led by the Issa community, while numbers of Afars, who favoured maintenance of the French connection, were significantly enlarged in the mid-1970s by immigration from Somalia. Support by the Organization of African Unity (OAU) for the granting of full independence to Djibouti added to the pressures on France, which attempted to foster a more harmonious relationship between the two ethnic groups. A unified political movement, the Ligue populaire africaine pour l'indépendance (LPAI), was formed, and, following an overwhelming vote favouring independence at a referendum held in May 1977, the territory became independent on 27 June. Hassan Gouled Aptidon, a senior Issa politician and leader of the LPAI, became the first president of the newly-proclaimed Republic of Djibouti.

Initial intentions to maintain a careful ethnic balance in government were not sustained. In March 1979 Gouled replaced the LPAI with a new political party, the Rassemblement populaire pour le progrès (RPP), whose leadership and policies were to be determined by himself. The two principal Afar-dominated pre-independence parties responded by merging into a unified, and clandestine, opposition movement, the Front démocratique pour la libération de Djibouti (FDLD).

RPP SUPREMACY

In June 1981 the first presidential election was held; Gouled, as the sole candidate, received 84% of the popular vote and was thus elected for a further six-year term. The FDLD rejected the results of the presidential election and, from its base in Addis Ababa, demanded a return to democracy and the release of political prisoners. Soon afterwards, a new opposition party—the Parti populaire djiboutien (PPD)—was formed under the leadership of ex-premier Ahmed Dini. The leadership was arrested in September and the party banned, but in October, following the adoption of legislation to establish a one-party state, the PPD leaders were released.

At legislative elections held in May 1982, 90% of the electorate endorsed the single list of candidates presented by the RPP. A new government, formed in June, differed little from its predecessor, and Gourad Hamadou continued in the post of prime minister. One potential source of dissent was removed when, in September, members of the MPL and the UNI returned from exile in Ethiopia, under the terms of an amnesty.

Until the mid-1980s, there was little overt opposition to the RPP under Gouled's leadership. In January 1986 a bomb was exploded at the headquarters of the RPP, killing two people. The bombing and the subsequent assassination of a prominent local businessman were followed by intensive security operations, in which more than 1,000 people were arrested. Although most of the detainees were later released, more than 300 of them were deported to their 'countries of origin'.

Evidence of open opposition to President Gouled received wider international attention in May 1986, when Aden Robleh Awalleh, a former cabinet minister, was charged with conducting 'massive propaganda campaigns' against the RPP, and was expelled from the party. Aden Robleh fled to Ethiopia, from where he announced the formation of a new opposition group, the Mouvement national djiboutien pour l'instauration de la démocratie (MNDID), with the stated aim of restoring a multi-party parliamentary democracy.

At the presidential election held in April 1987 Gouled, the sole candidate, received just over 90% of the votes cast. Concurrently, a single list of candidates for the chamber of deputies was endorsed by 87% of those voting. In November President Gouled dissolved the government and appointed an enlarged council of ministers comprising 16 members. In February 1988 an attack on the border town of Balho was attributed to the MPL and was widely seen as a sign of increasing ethnic tensions.

In April 1989 inter-tribal hostilities erupted in Djibouti city and the Afar town of Tadjourah. Tension increased in Afar-inhabited areas in May, when, in a speech to coincide with the end of the Islamic month of Ramadan, Gouled instructed the army to deal firmly with tribal disturbances. At the same time he announced that measures were to be taken against illegal refugees (see below), who were both an economic burden on the country and a source of instability.

In October 1989 violent clashes occurred between members of rival clans in Balbala, Djibouti city. Ten people were believed to have been killed and more than 100 injured. Security forces subsequently arrested several hundred people, some of whom were stated to have been deported to Gesdir, a remote border region between Djibouti, Ethiopia and Somalia. Sizeable numbers of these deportees were later reported to have been killed by the Somali National Movement (SNM) and Issa militia men.

In January 1990 the FDLD, the MNDID and independent members of the opposition merged to form a new opposition party, the Union des mouvements démocratiques (UMD). The group's declaired aim was to 'unite all the ethnic groups and different political persuasions' and to resolve 'the chaotic situation' existing in the country. In May inter-ethnic strife broke out between the Issa and the Gadabursi communities in Djibouti city. In June units of the Djibouti armed forces raided the town of Tadjourah and arrested Afars who were suspected of involvement in the MPL.

In November 1990 the president reshuffled his council of ministers, introducing one new member and reallocating several portfolios. In so doing, he was believed to have strengthened his position in the ministry of finance, and to have reduced the influence of the erstwhile minister of finance, Mohamed Djama Elabe (a member of the Fourlaba branch of the Issa clan), who was regarded as a potential candidate in the presidential election scheduled for 1992.

In early January 1991 Ali Aref Bourhan, who had led the council of ministers in the period prior to independence, was detained, together with about 100 Afar dissidents, on suspicion of having conspired to assassinate political leaders and senior army officers. Meanwhile, members of the Issa clan were also reported to be discontented at the relegation of Elabe from the ministry of finance and national economy to that of health and social affairs in the cabinet reshuffle of the previous November, and at the strengthening of the influence of the Mamasan branch of the Issa clan, to which the president belonged. In mid-February Bourhan was formally charged with murder, attempted murder and with attempting to destabilize the country. Stricter security measures were applied against disaffection among the Afar community, but the government denied allegations that some Afars who had been arrested had been tortured.

At the fifth RPP congress, held in March 1991, the party resolved that it would remain Djibouti's sole legal political organization. This rejection of political pluralism was widely interpreted as a sign of its increasing insecurity in response to mounting discontent among Djibouti's various clans and clan branches—especially the Afar—at their exclusion from political power.

In April 1991 a former presidential adviser, Mohamed Moussa Kahin, was arrested on suspicion of involvement with the proscribed Mouvement pour l'unité et pour la démocratie (MUD), and in the following month Gouled dismissed the minister of the interior, posts and telecommunications, Khaireh Allaleh Hared, and the minister of youth, sports and cultural affairs, Hussein Barkat Siraj, from the council of ministers.

CIVIL CONFLICT

A serious challenge to President Gouled's government appeared in April 1991 with the formation of a new and powerful armed opposition group, the Front pour la restauration de l'unité et de la démocratie (FRUD), which was composed of three militant Afar groups, the Front pour la restauration des droits et de la legalité, the Front pour la résistance patriotique djiboutienne and the Action pour la révision de l'ordre à Djibouti. In mid-November the FRUD, with a force of about 3,000 men, launched a full-scale insurrection, and by the end of the month controlled many towns and villages in the north of the country, and was besieging the northern cities of Tadjourah and Obock, which were held by the national army. The government conscripted all men between 18 and 25 years of age, and requested military assistance from France (see below) to repel what it described as external aggression by soldiers loyal to the deposed President Mengistu of Ethiopia. The FRUD denied that it constituted a foreign aggressor (although many of its officers had received training in Ethiopian military camps), claiming that its aim was to win fair representation for all ethnic groups in Djibouti's political system. In mid-December 75 civilians in the north of the country and about 40 in Arhiba, the Afar quarter of Djibouti city, were killed by the security forces. Afar opinion viewed the latter deaths as reprisals for the killing of government soldiers by the FRUD in the Tadjourah area.

In late December 1991 Gouled announced that a national referendum regarding proposed changes in the system of government would be held, but only when the 'external aggressors' had been expelled from the country. At the end of the month, 14 Afar deputies resigned from the RPP (and, therefore, from the chamber of deputies), claiming that its leaders were seeking to protect their privileges rather than the national interest. In January 1992 the ministers of health and social affairs and of the civil service and administration reform resigned, in protest at the government's policy of continuing the war, and subsequently formed the nucleus of a new political movement. In the same month, Gouled appointed a committee to draft a new constitution, intended to provide for a multi-party political system. Following a meeting in January 1992 with senior French officials, the FRUD said that it was willing to open a dialogue with the government, based on an immediate bilateral cease-fire and progress on the promised democratic reforms. The government, however, continued to insist that the FRUD was controlled by foreign interests, describing its military activities as an 'invasion' and responded to French mediation attempts with complaints that France had failed to honour its defence agreement. By the end of January the government had lost control of most of northern Djibouti, with its garrisons in Tadjourah and Obock kept supplied from the sea.

Attempts by France at achieving a *rapprochement* appeared more promising in the second half of February 1992, when, following meetings with the FRUD and the Djibouti government it was announced that the FRUD would declare a cease-fire, that France would deploy troops from its Djibouti garrison as a peace-keeping force in the north and that the government would release the FRUD's spokesman in the capital, Abbate Ebo Adou, who had been arrested in December. However, initial hopes that the agreement would open the way for a negotiated settlement were soon disappointed, despite sustained diplomatic efforts by France. At the end of March the FRUD announced that it was ending its cease-fire, stating that the deployment of the

French peace-keeping forces, which it had initially agreed to, was merely protecting a 'blood-stained dictatorship'. In April Abbate Ebo was re-arrested, ostensibly for contravening the terms of his release.

Constitutional Manoeuvres

The presidential commission on constitutional reform submitted its report at the end of March 1992 and on 4 April the president announced his plans for reform, which, while conceding the principle of a multi-party system, proposed few other changes and retained a strong executive presidency. The proposals were rejected as inadequate by the opposition, which demanded the holding of a national constitutional conference, and by the FRUD, although cautiously welcomed by France. The changes would, the president announced, be voted on in a national referendum, to be held on 17 June, with legislative elections to follow a month later. It was later announced that the mandate of the chamber of deputies, which had been due to expire at the end of May, had been extended for a further five years. The election timetable that the president announced was quickly seen to be unrealistic, especially with large areas of the country outside government control. In late June President Gouled announced that the referendum would be held on 4 September, followed by the introduction of a multi-party system on 20 September. Legislative elections would then take place on 20 November.

In early July 1992 Gouled announced pardons for a number of opposition figures, including Aden Robleh Awalleh, the exiled leader of the Parti national démocratique (PND), and the leader of the Front des forces démocratiques, Omar Elmi Khaireh. However, Ali Aref Bourhan and five others (who had been arrested in January 1991 and accused of plotting to overthrow the government) were, in July 1992, sentenced to 10 years' imprisonment. Others among the 47 accused received prison sentences of up to six years. The government sustained another defection in August with the announcement that Elaf Orbiss Ali, an Afar, had resigned as minister of labour, in protest against the continuing civil war and deteriorating economic situation, and was joining the Front uni de l'opposition djiboutienne (FUOD), a coalition of opposition parties, including the FRUD.

The draft constitution that the president prepared was approved by referendum on 4 September 1992, with 96.84% voting in favour, according to the ministry of the interior, which claimed a turnout of 75.16% of the 120,000 eligible voters. A proposition to restrict the number of political parties to four was approved by 96.79% of those who voted. However, with two-thirds of the country controlled by the FRUD, which had urged its supporters to boycott the referendum, and no independent observers present, the voting figures were received with some scepticism, notably by France, which refused to endorse the results. The referendum nevertheless facilitated the holding of multi-party elections on 20 November, following the registration of political parties, but in mid-October it was announced that these would be postponed until 18 December. Applications for registration were initially accepted from only two of the five parties applying: the ruling RPP and the Parti pour le renouveau démocratique (PRD), led by Djama Elabe (a former minister), which had split Mohamed from the FUOD in September. Applications from the FRUD and the FUOD were rejected. The application from the PND, which had withdrawn from the FUOD following Awalleh's pardoning and return from exile, was initially rejected, on the grounds that it did not possess sufficiently broad ethnic support, but the party was legalized in mid-October.

Attempts by France to bring about negotiations between the government and FRUD appeared to have achieved success when it was announced, after a meeting between Presidents Gouled and Mitterrand, in November 1992 that the two sides would meet face to face for the first time on board a French ship later in the month. However, the meeting was cancelled at the last minute by the government, which claimed that the FRUD had failed to honour preconditions, including the release of prisoners of war. In late November France withdrew its troops from northern Djibouti, where they had acted as a buffer between government and rebel forces. With the opposition largely excluded from the process, the 18 December elections, which were monitored by observers from France, the OAU and the Arab League, provided an easy victory for the RPP, which won all 65 seats in the chamber of deputies and 76.71% of the popular votes. Only the PRD contested the elections (taking one-third of the votes cast in the capital), Awalleh having withdrawn the PND after protesting about irregularities and demanding a postponement of the elections. More than 51% of the electorate failed to vote in the elections, leading to charges from the PND that the chamber was unrepresentative. Renewed fighting was reported in January 1993, with dozens of people said to have been killed in what appeared to be a new government offensive against the FRUD in the Tadjourah area. The army claimed a series of successes during February and March, recapturing the FRUD strongholds in the south of the country and severing the rebels' supply routes to the sea. Nevertheless, the FRUD achieved a propaganda victory with its first guerrilla attack on Djibouti city itself in mid-March.

Gouled reshuffled the cabinet in early February 1993, preserving the traditional ethnic balance, with Issa ministers receiving eight portfolios, and Afar representatives seven (including the foreign affairs and economy and commerce portfolios, which went to Mohamed Bolok Abdou and Mohamed Ali respectively) and one portfolio each held by members of the Arab, Issaq and Gadabursi minorities. However, other changes suggested no relaxation of the government's policy, with the former minister of the interior, Ahmed Bulaleh Barreh (an opponent of negotiations with the FRUD), moving to the ministry of defence. The former minister of foreign affairs, Moumin Bahdon Farah, was appointed minister of justice and Islamic affairs, but retained his post as secretary-general of the RPP. Five candidates stood in Djibouti's first contested presidential election, which was held on 7 May: Gouled himself, Elabe (for the PRD), Awalleh (PND) and two independents, Mohamed Moussa Ali 'Tourtour' (actually of the still proscribed MUD, but not representing his party) and Ahmed Ibrahim Abdi. The level of electoral participation was low (at 49.9% of those registered to vote), indicating an Afar boycott. Official results showed that Gouled obtained 60.76% of the votes cast, compared with 22.03% for Elabe and 12.25% for Awalleh, while 'Tourtour' and Abdi won 2.99% and 1.97% of the votes cast respectively. The opposition alleged that there had been widespread fraud in the conduct of the elections.

Military and Political Initiatives

Following his re-election as president, Gouled appealed to FRUD to negotiate with the government. His appeal was rejected, as he proposed that discussions should take place in Djibouti itself, while the FRUD insisted that it would only meet the government abroad, in the presence of foreign mediators. In early July 1993 the army launched a full-scale offensive on the FRUD positions in the centre and north of the country. The campaign was successful, and within a week the army had captured the FRUD's headquarters on the plateau of Asa Gayla, as well as other towns and areas held by the rebel group. As a result of the hostilities, thousands of the inhabitants of these largely Afar-populated areas fled towards the Ethiopian border. Many of the rebels were reported to have retreated into the mountains in the far north of the country. The FRUD continued its struggle, however, and in mid-July it launched armed attacks on government forces, including an assault on the army's camp at Tajourah. French dissatisfaction with Gouled's military tactics was expressed by the cancellation of a planned visit to Djibouti by the French minister of co-operation and development who pledged to take action to obtain the release of Ali Aref Bourhan. Under sustained pressure from the French government, Gouled agreed in December to an exchange of prisoners with FRUD, and this was followed later in the month by the release of Aref

Bourhan and his immediate associates in the alleged coup conspiracy of January 1991.

Relations with France came under further strain in early 1993 as the result of threats by the French government to withhold financial aid, in an attempt to persuade Gouled to negotiate with the FRUD. Counter-insurgency operations were intensified, with the result that, by July, an estimated 80,000 civilians had been displaced by the fighting. In September the Djibouti government was strongly criticized by Amnesty International for abuses of human rights, inflicted by the army.

The extent of the military reverses inflicted on the FRUD was reflected in the intensification of political activity during late 1993. In October the PRD and the FRUD issued joint proposals for a cease-fire, to be followed by negotiations aimed at forming a transition 'government of national unity' to supervise the implementation of democratic reforms. These objectives were also defined by two new parties formed in the same month: the Organisation des masses Afars (OMA) and the Parti centriste et des reformes démocratiques (PCRD). The PCRD, whose leadership comprised former members of the FRUD, announced that it was to seek official registration from the government. In December the PRD and the PND launched a co-ordinated campaign to persuade the government to agree to new parliamentary elections under the supervision of an independent electoral commission.

In early 1994, again under economic pressure from France, the government agreed to reduce the scale of its military expenditure, although operations against the FRUD continued in February. During March, however, a split developed within the FRUD leadership, several of whose members, led by Ougoureh Kifle Ahmad, began to seek support within the movement for a negotiated political settlement of the conflict. In May, Kifle Ahmad was expelled from the FRUD executive committee, but re-emerged in the following month, with the claimed support of the majority of FRUD members, as the party's secretary-general. Ali Mohamed Daoud was declared to be president of the FRUD. The new leaders, who were stated to hold office on a 'provisional' basis, continued to be opposed by several senior FRUD activists, including the party's former president, Ahmed Dini, based in Addis Ababa. In late June, Kifle Ahmad and the Djibouti government agreed terms for an immediate cease-fire, and formal negotiations for a peace settlement began in July.

REFUGEES AND EXTERNAL RELATIONS

A source of international discontent has been the substantial flow of refugees from the Eritrean and Ogaden conflicts in Ethiopia (see below), which has greatly added to Djibouti's economic problems. In April 1984 a new scheme for repatriating Ethiopian refugees (estimated to number 35,000), under the aegis of the UN High Commissioner for Refugees (UNHCR), was begun. By December 1984 it was estimated that around 16,000 had returned to Ethiopia. However, the recurrence of drought and the political situation in Ethiopia caused some refugees to return, and by June 1987 the number of 'official' refugees in Djibouti was 17,200. In August 1986 a new repatriation programme was announced by the Djibouti government in consultation with the Ethiopian government and UNHCR. According to Djiboutian sources, the number of voluntary repatriations under this programme had reached 2,000 by the end of March 1987. The burden that 'official' refugees have imposed on the economy has been exacerbated by an influx of illegal immigrants from Somalia and Ethiopia, and in June 1987 the government announced tighter controls on border crossings and identity papers. Following discussion in February 1988, Djibouti and Ethiopia agreed to control movements across their common border and to curb the influx of refugees into Djibouti. In January 1989, President Gouled announced that measures were to be taken against illegal refugees, who were not only an economic burden on the country, but also a source of instability. At the beginning of June 1991 there were an estimated 35,000 Somali and 5,000 Ethiopian official refugees in Djibouti. By August about 4,000 of the Ethiopians had registered to return, under a repatriation scheme administered by UNHCR. By early 1993, it was estimated, the number of Somali refugees in Djibouti had reached 120,000 and UNHCR was investigating ways to repatriate the majority of them to the north of Somalia, to the self-declared 'republic of Somaliland' (formed by insurgent forces in northern Somalia in April 1991).

Because of its geographical position, the maintenance of peaceful relations with both Ethiopia and Somalia has been a vital consideration in Djibouti's foreign policy. The key economic goal of maintaining its share in the rail and sea transport of Ethiopian trade, which was intermittently disrupted by guerrilla action and regional unrest during the late 1970s, was partially realized in 1985 when the governments of Ethiopia and Djibouti agreed to create an independent railway company.

During 1979 Djibouti concluded agreements with both Ethiopia and Somalia for closer co-operation in transport, communications and trade. Regular meetings of frontier boundary commissioners were proposed with Ethiopia in that year, and official visits to Djibouti by high-ranking Ethiopian delegations took place in 1980 and again in 1983. In May 1985 the two countries concluded a trade and development co-operation agreement, although relations became clouded in the following year when Ethiopia granted asylum to Aden Robleh and the MNDID. However, since the removal of the Ethiopian president, Mengistu Haile Mariam, in May 1991, Djibouti has maintained good relations with the successor transitional government in that country. In April 1994 an agreement providing for bilateral co-operation in a number of economic spheres was signed by the two countries.

As a result of Gouled's wish to reconcile the vying factions in the Horn of Africa, Djibouti took an important role in promoting the creation in 1985 of the six-nation Intergovernmental Authority on Drought and Development (IGADD), with a permanent secretariat in Djibouti. IGADD's first summit meeting, in January 1986, brought both the Ethiopian and Somali heads of state to Djibouti, marking a significant step towards an eventual settlement of regional conflicts. In April 1988, following a further meeting in Djibouti, between the two leaders, Ethiopia and Somalia agreed to re-establish diplomatic relations, to withdraw troops from their common border and to exchange prisoners of war.

Relations with Somalia deteriorated following an attack by the SNM on border posts along the Somali-Djibouti border. The Somali government had always regarded with suspicion Djibouti's declared neutrality in respect of the Somali-Ethiopian conflict. Following the outbreak of armed insurgency in northern Somalia, Somalia accused the Djibouti government of openly supporting the SNM, whose opposition to the Siad Barre regime had many sympathizers among Issa and Issaq clansmen in Djibouti. In March 1990, when inter-tribal conflict erupted into heavy fighting in Loya Adde and Zeila on the Somali side of the border with Ethiopia, Somalia accused Djibouti of waging armed aggression in its territory. A denial by the Djibouti government did not prevent a further deterioration in relations, and the maritime border between Djibouti and Somalia was closed in October.

In June 1991 Djibouti hosted a preliminary conference of groups from southern Somalia, aimed at forming a transitional Somali government. In October the land borders between Djibouti and Somalia were reopened for the first time since May 1989, when they had been closed as a result of civil unrest in Somalia. Relations between Djibouti and the government of 'Somaliland' deteriorated sharply in early 1992 following contacts between the 'Somaliland' authorities and the FRUD. Tensions involving the presence of refugee Issas in the border area were reported in July 1994.

In December 1987 President Mitterrand visited Djibouti: the first visit by a French president since 1977. President Gouled made an official visit to France in June 1989, during which he described relations with France as of an 'exceptional quality' and praised the stabilizing influence of the French military presence in Djibouti. However, the French military presence became more controversial following Iraq's invasion of Kuwait in August 1990 and the onset of the 'Gulf crisis'. French troops in Djibouti were reinforced and Djibouti became the operational base for France's participation in the multinational force deployed in Saudi Arabia. By supporting the UN resolutions which were formulated against Iraq, Djibouti jeopardized its future relations with Iraq, which was emerging as an important supplier of economic and military aid. However, Djibouti's stance during the Gulf War of January–February 1991 strengthened its ties with France, and in February the two countries signed two defence treaties which extended military co-operation. In January 1992, however, there was serious disagreement between France and Djibouti over France's refusal to intervene militarily in the conflict between government forces and the FRUD. Relations between the two countries remained tense during 1992 and 1993, with France using the threat of withholding its aid, in an attempt to persuade the government to negotiate with the rebels, and showing dissatisfaction with the pace and extent of Gouled's political reforms. A meeting betweeen the two presidents in November 1992 led to the release of French budgetary aid, but France later made clear its irritation at the government's failure to attend a planned meeting with the FRUD. From December 1992 Djibouti became the operational centre for French troops participating in multinational (and subsequently United Nations) operations in Somalia. The facilities of Djibouti airport were also made available for US troop transport.

Djibouti became a member of UN Security Council, for a two-year period, on 1 January 1993. In February the Egyptian minister of foreign affairs visited Djibouti, and ties were strengthened with the signing of an agreement on co-operation in economic, technical, cultural, religious and trade sectors. Since 1991 Djibouti has had diplomatic relations with Eritrea, which became a *de facto* independent state (breaking away from Ethiopia) in that year. In May 1993 President Gouled attended celebrations in Eritrea on the occasion of that country's official transition to independence.

Economy

MILES SMITH-MORRIS

Revised for this edition by the Editor

The economy is based on trade through the international port of Djibouti, and its developing service sector, which account for almost three-quarters of the country's gross domestic product (GDP). In addition to the expanding port, there is a railway, which links Djibouti to Addis Ababa in Ethiopia, and a modern airport that is capable of landing large jet-engined aircraft. The banking sector is growing in importance, aided by the stable and freely convertible Djibouti franc and the absence of exchange controls. A substantial share of the country's receipts derive from the provision of services to the French military garrison (with about 4,000 men in 1994) and other expatriates.

There is little arable farming in Djibouti, as the land is mainly volcanic desert, one of the least hospitable and most unproductive terrains in Africa, and the country is able to produce only about 3% of its food requirements. More than one-half of the population are pastoral nomads, herding goats, sheep and camels. A 10-year programme to develop fishing was started in 1980, supported by the International Fund for Agricultural Development and it was hoped to increase catches to 1,200 metric tons per year, and in 1990 the Islamic Development Bank agreed to finance the construction of a fish-canning factory with an annual capacity of 1,500 metric tons.

The development of underground water supplies for irrigation is being studied, and deep-water wells have been sunk in an attempt to alleviate the effects of periodic drought. A loan was received in 1987 from the African Development Bank to finance a project to supply water to the towns of Djibouti, Ali-Sabieh, Tadjourah and Obock. Relief assistance during periods of periodic drought and flooding has been forthcoming from the EC, France, Japan, Saudi Arabia, and Germany.

Industry is limited to a few small-scale concerns. Regional political uncertainties and high labour costs have discouraged the creation of new industries, despite the existence of a free zone and the major liberalization of investment legislation in 1984, and almost all consumer goods have to be imported. A power station supplying a mineral-water bottling factory at Tadjourah, the first major industrial project outside the capital, was commissioned in 1981, and a dairy plant (on the outskirts of Djibouti town), a government printing press and an extension to the Boulaos power station were all opened in 1984–85. Plans to privatize the Tadjourah mineral water plant were announced in 1991, but the plant was later reported to have been damaged in fighting between government and rebel forces.

Work began in 1986 on a major geothermal exploration project, financed by foreign aid, in the Hanle Gaggade area. Conditions there proved to be unsuitable for the development of this form of energy, but more favourable results were reported after tests had been conducted in the Goubet-Lac-Assal region in 1987. The object of this scheme is to make Djibouti self-sufficient in energy, and possibly able to export gas to neighbouring countries. This remains a distant goal, however, and in the early 1990s Djibouti relied on imported fuels for 90% of its energy requirements. Italy has donated $22m. towards the purchase of equipment for the first phase of the project, whose total cost has been estimated at $38m. France is also participating in the project, which is co-financed by the World Bank, OPEC and the UN Development Programme.

Work on Djibouti's first petroleum refinery at Dorale, began in 1990, with Saudi Arabian private-sector assistance. The $800m. refinery was expected to produce 100,000 barrels per day of petrol, kerosene and liquified gas. The project, which was to become operational in 1994, was reported to have been delayed by the conflict between the government and the insurgent Front pour la restauration de l'unité et de la démocratie (FRUD).

Djibouti's establishment as a free port, in 1981, has helped to arrest a relative decline in total port business, which, affected by competition from rising Arab ports nearby, was virtually stagnant until the completion, in 1985, of a deep-water container terminal, with 'roll-on, roll-off' facilities and a refrigerated warehouse, capable of handling 40,000 tons. The rehabilitation of the port's berth facilities, together with dredging and reclamation work, has been proceeding. In 1992 France agreed to lend $8m. towards continuing modernization of the port facilities, including internal transport and management. As Djibouti has good bunkering and watering facilities and is well placed for transhipment, it was hoped that the addition of these facilities would help the port to regain some of the business that it lost during the closure of the Suez Canal (1967–75), and to increase its competitiveness with the expanding Arab ports. The Gulf crisis of 1990–91 acted as a major stimulus to the port, with total traffic rising to nearly 1.5m. tons in 1990, compared with only 870,000 tons in the previous year. In 1992 Djibouti established a 'flag of convenience' registry, with the aim of attracting international shipowners seeking such facilities. Tax incentives were also being offered to shipping companies reinvesting their profits in Djibouti. The port was expected to benefit from an expected increase in Ethiopian traffic, following the independence in 1992 of Eritrea, whose facilities at Assat and Massawa are less developed than those available in Djibouti.

Several other developments in communications infrastructure in the 1980s enhanced Djibouti's competitiveness on trading routes. These included the inauguration, in 1985, of a second earth station, linking Djibouti to the telecommunications network of the Arab Satellite Communication Organization, and the laying of an undersea telecommunications cable to Saudi Arabia. An underwater telephone cable to Aden, Yemen, was expected to come into service in 1994.

For many years, the Djibouti government was anxious about its lack of control over the railway linking Djibouti city with Addis Ababa; 660 km of the line's 778 km pass through the territory of Ethiopia, which employs more than three-quarters of the railway staff. The signing of a new railway agreement with Ethiopia in 1981 brought some improvement, which was further enhanced in July 1985, when a joint ministerial meeting between the two countries decided to grant autonomous status to the railway company, with the aim of improving its profitability. A major programme for the replacement of rolling stock and the rehabilitation of track was begun in 1986, with funding from the EC. Further financial assistance from this source was received in 1993.

The government's first Development Plan (1982–84) was undertaken to channel foreign aid into a cohesive development strategy. Potential has been constrained, however, by the lack of infrastructure, of trained labour and of natural resources. Nevertheless, a highly successful conference of aid donors was held in Djibouti in 1983, when most of the funds that the country needed for its 1984–89 Development Plan (which envisaged total expenditure of $570m.) were raised, including more than $100m. from Arab sources. Development projects that had already started included the construction by a Yugoslav contractor of a 114-km 'unity' highway linking Djibouti to Tadjourah. There are also plans for an improved road through Loyada into northern Somalia.

Djibouti remains heavily dependent on foreign assistance, which, because of the country's strategic position, is readily forthcoming. The main donors are the EU, France and Saudi Arabia. The Saudi Fund for Development was to provide funds for the renovation of Djibouti's port facilities, and was also to finance housing and educational projects and road construction. Djibouti is a member of the African Development Bank, the IMF, the Islamic Development Bank, the World Bank and its affiliate, the International Finance Corporation, and also receives considerable financial support from these organizations. After some years of declining levels of overseas aid, which combined with stagnating government receipts to create serious financial problems, aid disbursements to Djibouti rose sharply in 1990 to $129.1m., an increase of 57% on 1989 levels. France provided 45% of the total, but there was a marked increase in aid from Arab countries.

In 1989, according to UN estimates, Djibouti's GDP, measured at current prices, was $492m., equivalent to $1,236 per head. Djibouti's overall GDP expanded, in real terms, at an average annual rate of 1.2% in 1980–85 and 2.0% in 1985–89, reversing an average annual decline of 2.7% in 1977–79. However, as a result of rapid population increase, GDP per head declined, in real terms, during 1980–86. During 1985–92 the population rose by 2.9% annually (according to World Bank estimates), owing partly to the influx of refugees from Ethiopia and Somalia.

Djibouti's external debt was estimated to total $189.5m. at the end of 1992, of which $173.8m. was long-term public debt. Debt-servicing has remained at manageable levels, representing 7.7% of exports of goods and services in 1988, 4.8% in 1990 and 4.4% in 1992. The annual rate of inflation averaged 4.5% in 1985–92.

In the 1988 budget, expenditure was fixed at 23,267m. Djibouti francs, an increase of 4.8% over the 1987 level, owing to higher provisions for external public debt, personnel and administrative costs. In an attempt to maximize revenue, the government planned in January 1988 to introduce, among other measures, a tax on profits from public industrial and commercial establishments and on companies; and a surtax on qat (a narcotic shrub), alcohol and tobacco. In the 1989 budget, expenditure was fixed at 24,300m. Djibouti francs, while revenue was fixed at 23,900m. Djibouti francs. At the same time, the government adopted new tax laws which sought to improve the collection of government revenues and thus assist in the reduction of the budgetary deficit. The 1990 budget fixed ordinary government expenditure at 25,200m. Djibouti francs, while total revenue was fixed at 24,000m. Djibouti francs. The 1991 budget was projected to balance at 26,000m. Djibouti francs. The budget gave priority to education, health and security, and also provided for 12,500m. Djibouti francs to be devoted to development projects. The IMF has, since 1992, repeatedly warned the government about the seriousness of its growing budget and balance-of-payments deficits. In 1993 ordinary expenditure was forecast at 28,321m. Djibouti francs, and expenditure in 1994 was estimated to reach 32,500m. Djibouti francs.

The Djibouti franc has, since early 1986, fluctuated in value, along with the US dollar, to which it is linked. During that year inflation emerged as a problem for the first time since Djibouti's independence, reaching 22.5% in the 12 months ending June 1986. Current budgetary aid for 1989 totalling 37.5m. French francs was promised by the French government. The aid was provided under the terms of an agreement, signed in 1980, which expired in 1989. In that year, France indicated a change of policy with regard to budgetary aid to Djibouti: aid would no longer extend over a 10-year period, but would be fixed annually. At the same time, the French government requested Djibouti to reduce its public expenditure and to intensify its revenue-raising efforts. Since the commencement of the military insurrection in late 1991 by the FRUD, France has used its aid as a lever in persuading the government to negotiate with the insurgents: budgetary aid of 23.5m. French francs for 1992 was not disbursed until November of that year. The French government has dealt similarly with subsequent tranches of aid; in March 1994 an allocation of 11.5m. French francs for rebuilding war-damaged infrastructure was added to a budgetary aid allocation of 8.5m. French francs.

It was planned to increase substantially public investment in 1990. A total of 10,788m. Djibouti francs was to be invested in projects in the communications, agricultural and fisheries sectors, and in social, environmental and urban improvement schemes. Almost 40% of total expenditure on public projects (about twice the level of 1989) was allocated to projects in the communications sector. It was also proposed to invest 2,058m. Djibouti francs in agriculture and fisheries. Capital expenditure in 1991 was fixed at 13,850m. Djibouti francs, most of which would, again, be directed towards the communications sector; the total budget was projected to balance at 26,000m. Djibouti francs. The conflict with FRUD has since had a noticeable impact on investment, with capital spending allocated only 540m. Djibouti francs out of total expenditure of 28,320m. Djibouti francs planned in the 1993 budget. Capital spending was forecast to account for only 3% of the 1994 budget.

It was initially feared that the crisis in the Persian (Arabian) Gulf region, which began in August 1990 as a result of Iraq's invasion and annexation of Kuwait, would seriously damage the economy of Djibouti. Development projects which had been funded by Iraq and Kuwait, for instance, were immediately suspended. However, Djibouti's decision to support the UN's efforts to liberate Kuwait ensured that its relations with its three principal benefactors, France, Saudi Arabia and Kuwait, were unharmed. Moreover, the ensuing war in the Gulf region emphasized Djibouti's strategic importance to the USA, from whose Economic Support Fund Djibouti receives some $3m. annually.

In September 1990 the government estimated that losses resulting from the crisis in the Gulf would amount (in 1990) to $218m. This estimate took into account increases in the price of imports (especially petroleum), which were expected to average 15%; increases in transport expenses; and the postponement of investments pledged by Kuwait, Saudi Arabia and Iraq. Losses of state revenues in 1990 were forecast at $23m. There was, however, a doubling of official revenues from Djibouti port, deriving from the war-related traffic. Djibouti's role as a service centre was also enhanced by the Western military entervention in Somalia in 1992. The FRUD insurgency has been a major hindrance to economic activity and a considerable burden on government expenditure. Economic development and revenue collection has been brought to a standstill in areas of the country outside government control, and the resultant uncertainties have discouraged foreign investment.

Statistical Survey

Source (unless otherwise stated): Ministère de l'Economie et du Commerce, BP 1846, Djibouti; tel. 351682; telex 5871.

AREA AND POPULATION

Area: 23,200 sq km (8,958 sq miles).

Population: 220,000 (1976 estimate), including Afars 70,000, Issas and other Somalis 80,000, Arabs 12,000, Europeans 15,000, other foreigners 40,000; 519,900 (including refugees and resident foreigners) at 31 December 1990 (official estimate).

Density (1990): 22.4 per sq km.

Principal Towns: Djibouti (capital), population 200,000 (1981); Dikhil; Ali-Sabieh; Tadjourah; Obock.

Births and Deaths (UN estimates, 1985–90): Average annual birth rate 47.0 per 1,000; Average annual death rate 17.9 per 1,000; Expectation of life (years at birth 1989–90): 61.0 (males 59.4% females 62.6). Source: UN, *World Population Prospects: The 1992 Revision.*

AGRICULTURE, ETC.

Principal Crops (FAO estimate, '000 metric tons, 1992): Vegetables 22.

Livestock (FAO estimates, '000 head, year ending September 1992): Cattle 180, Sheep 450, Goats 506, Asses 8, Camels 61.

Livestock Products: (FAO estimates, metric tons, 1992): Meat 7,000; Cows' milk 6,000; Cattle hides 440; Sheep skins 336; Goatskins 460.

Fishing (metric tons, live weight): Total catch 391 in 1989; 359 in 1990; 380 in 1991 (FAO estimate). Source: FAO, *Yearbook of Fishery Statistics.*

INDUSTRY

Electric energy (million kWh): 175 in 1989; 175 in 1990; 178 in 1991.

FINANCE

Currency and Exchange Rates: 100 centimes = 1 Djibouti franc. *Sterling and Dollar Equivalents* (31 March 1994): £1 sterling = 263.84 Djibouti francs; US $1 = 177.72 Djibouti francs; 1,000 Djibouti francs = £3.790 = $5.627. *Exchange Rate:* Fixed at US $1 = 177.721 Djibouti francs since February 1973.

Budget (million Djibouti francs, 1990): *Revenue:* Taxation 18,864, Non-tax current revenue 1,881, Grants 5,123, Repayment of loans 8, Total 25,876; *Expenditure:* General administration 11,476, Defence 4,709, Education 1,981, Youth and Sport 172, Health 1,778, Economic services 1,796, Debt servicing 1,058, Other current expenditure 1,657, Capital expenditure 1,176, Total 25,803; **1993** (forecast, million Djibouti francs): Expenditure 28,321; **1994** (forecast, million Djibouti francs): Expenditure 32,500m.

International Reserves (US $ million at 31 December 1993): IMF special drawing rights 0.21; Foreign exchange 74.89; Total 75.10. Source: IMF, *International Financial Statistics.*

Money Supply (million Djibouti francs at 31 December 1992): Currency outside banks 11,331; Demand deposits at commercial banks 21,595; Total money (incl. others) 34,981. Source: IMF, *International Financial Statistics.*

Gross Domestic Product by Economic Activity (million Djibouti francs at current prices, 1983): Agriculture, hunting, forestry and fishing 2,580; Manufacturing 4,910; Electricity, gas and water 1,914; Construction 4,550; Trade, restaurants and hotels 9,410; Transport, storage and communications 5,900; Finance, insurance, real estate and business services 6,630; Government services 16,200; Other community, social and personal services 920; Sub-total 53,014; Import duties 10,713; *Less* Imputed bank service charge 3,730; GDP in purchasers' values 59,997. Source: UN, *National Accounts Statistics.*

Balance of Payments (million Djibouti francs, 1982): Exports f.o.b. (incl. re-exports) 20,830, Imports c.i.f. −38,523, *Trade Balance* −17,693; Services, port 847, Unrequited transfers (net) 8,909, *Current Balance* −4,366; Capital movements 1,942, Changes in reserves −2,424.

EXTERNAL TRADE

Principal Commodities (million Djibouti francs): *Imports* (1991, distribution by BTN): Live animals and animal products 1,659; Vegetable products 5,596 (cereals 1,404, oil seeds and oleaginous fruits 2,260); Prepared foodstuffs, beverages, vinegar and tobacco 5,212; Mineral products 4,013 (mineral fuels and oils 3,524); Chemical products 2,358; Textiles and textile articles 4,465; Base metals and articles of base metal 2,396; Machinery, mechanical appliances and electrical equipment 3,246 (boilers, machinery and mechanical appliances 1,465); Transport equipment 2,703 (cars, tractors and bicycles 2,630); Total (incl. others) 38,103. *Exports* (1991): Live animals 477, Food 395; Total (incl. others) 3,083.

Total imports (million Djibouti francs): 34,920 in 1989; 38,174 in 1990; 38,103 in 1991.

Total exports (million Djibouti francs): 4,423 in 1989; 4,420 in 1990; 3,083 in 1991.

Principal Trading Partners (million Djibouti francs, 1991): *Imports:* Bahrain 1,013; Belgium and Luxembourg 915; China, People's Republic 1,181; Ethiopia 3,154; France 9,954; Italy 2,469; Japan 2,739; Netherlands 1,327; Saudi Arabia 1,920; Singapore 955; Thailand 1,151; United Arab Emirates 865; United Kingdom 1,028; USA 1,405; Total (incl. others) 38,103. *Exports:* France 1,760; Italy 100; Saudi Arabia 171; Somalia 127; Yemen Arab Republic 494; Total (incl. others) 3,083.

TRANSPORT

Railways (Djibouti-Ethiopian Railway, 1990): Freight traffic ('000 metric tons): 301.9; Passengers 957,000.

Road Traffic ('000 motor vehicles, 1987): Passenger cars 7; Commercial vehicles 1. Source: UN, *Statistical Yearbook.*

Shipping (Djibouti port, 1988): Goods loaded 409,000 metric tons; Good unloaded 840,000 metric tons; (Djibouti port, 1989) Goods loaded 430,000 metric tons; Goods unloaded 958,000 metric tons; (Djibouti port, 1990): Goods loaded 414,000 metric tons; Goods unloaded 958,000 metric tons. Source: UN, *Monthly Bulletin of Statistics.*

Civil Aviation (Djibouti airport, 1990): Freight loaded 1,145 metric tons; Freight unloaded 6,381 metric tons; Passenger arrivals 61,727; Passenger departures 62,494.

TOURISM

Visitors (arrivals at hotels): 29,400 in 1988; 40,762 in 1989; 32,699 in 1990.

COMMUNICATIONS MEDIA

Radio Receivers (1991): 39,000 in use.

Television Receivers (1991): 24,000 in use.

Source: UNESCO, *Statistical Yearbook.*

Telephones (1990): 5,666 subscribers.

EDUCATION

Primary (1990/91): 69 schools; 31,926 pupils; 737 teachers.

Secondary (1990/91): 26 schools (10 state schools, 16 private schools); 9,363 pupils; 329 teachers (state schools only).

Teacher Training (1990/91): 108 pupils; 13 teachers.

Source: Direction Générale de l'Education.

Directory

The Constitution

In February 1981 the National Assembly approved the first constitutional laws controlling the election and terms of office of the President, who is elected by universal adult suffrage for six years and may serve for no more than two terms. Candidates for the presidency must be presented by a regularly constituted political party and represented by at least 25 members of the Chamber of Deputies. The Chamber, comprising 65 members, is elected for a five-year term.

In October 1984 a new constitutional law was proposed, specifying that, when the office of President falls vacant, the President of the Supreme Court will assume the power of Head of State for a minimum of 20 days and a maximum of 35 days, during which period a new President shall be elected.

Laws approving the establishment of a single-party system were adopted in October 1981. A new Constitution, providing for the establishment of a maximum of four political parties, was approved by national referendum on 4 September 1992 and entered into force on 15 September.

The Government

HEAD OF STATE

President and Commander-in-Chief of the Armed Forces: HASSAN GOULED APTIDON (took office 27 June 1977; re-elected June 1981, April 1987 and May 1993).

COUNCIL OF MINISTERS
(August 1994)

Prime Minister: BARKAD GOURAD HAMADOU.

Minister of Justice and Islamic Affairs: MOUMIN BAHDON FARAH.

Minister of the Interior and Extension of Regional Administration: IDRIS HARBI FARAH.

Minister of Defence: AHMED BULALEH BARREH.

Minister of Planning, Lands and Co-operation: MUHAMMAD MUSA CHEHEM.

Minister of Foreign Affairs: MOHAMED BOLOK ABDOU.

Minister of Finance: AHMED ADEN YUSSUF.

Minister of Economy and Commerce: MOHAMED ALI MOHAMED.

Minister of Ports and Maritime Affairs: MUSA BURALEH ROBLEH.

Minister of Transport, Tourism and Communications: AHMED WABERI DINI.

Minister of Education: AHMED GIREH WABERI.

Minister of Labour and Manpower Training: IBIROW AHMED HAMADOU.

Minister of the Civil Service and Administrative Reform: OUGOURE HASSAN IBRAHIM.

Minister of Health and Social Affairs: MOHAMED SAID SALAH.

Minister of Public Works, Housing and Construction: OUGOUREH HASSAN IBRAHIM.

Minister of Agriculture and Nomadic Development: UMAR CHIRDON ABBAS.

Minister of Industry, Energy and Minerals: ALI MOHAMED HUMAD.

Minister of Youth, Sports and Culture: MOHAMED IBRAHIM MUHAMMAD.

MINISTRIES

Office of the Prime Minister: BP 2086, Djibouti; tel. 351494; telex 5871; fax 355049.

Ministry of Agriculture and Nomadic Development: BP 453, Djibouti; tel. 351297; telex 5871.

Ministry of the Civil Service and Administrative Reform: BP 155, Djibouti; tel. 351464; telex 5871.

Ministry of Defence: BP 42, Djibouti; tel. 352034; telex 5871.

Ministry of Economy and Commerce: BP 1846, Djibouti; tel. 351682; telex 5871.

Ministry of Education: BP 2102, Djibouti; tel. 350850; telex 5871.

Ministry of Finance: BP 13, Djibouti; tel. 350297; telex 5871; fax 35601.

Ministry of Foreign Affairs: BP 1863, Djibouti; tel. 352471; telex 5871.

Ministry of Health and Social Affairs: BP 296, Djibouti; tel. 353331; telex 5871.

Ministry of Industry, Energy and Minerals: BP 175, Djibouti; tel. 350340; telex 5871.

Ministry of the Interior and Extension of Regional Administration: BP 33, Djibouti; tel. 350791; telex 5990.

Ministry of Justice and Islamic Affairs: BP 12, Djibouti; tel. 351506; telex 5871; fax 354012.

Ministry of Labour and Manpower Training: BP 170, Djibouti; tel. 350497; telex 5871.

Ministry of Planning, Lands and Co-operation: Djibouti.

Ministry of Ports and Maritime Affairs: BP 2107, Djibouti; tel. 350105; telex 5871.

Ministry of Tourism, Transport and Communications: Djibouti; tel. 350971; telex 5871.

Ministry of Public Works, Housing and Construction: BP 11, Djibouti; tel. 350006; telex 5871.

Ministry of Youth, Sports and Culture: Djibouti.

President and Legislature

PRESIDENT

Presidential Election, 7 May 1993

Candidates	Votes	%
HASSAN GOULED APTIDON (RPP)	45,470	60.76
MOHAMED DJAMA ELABE (PRD)	16,485	22.03
ADEN ROBLEH AWALLEH (PND)	9,170	12.25
MOHAMED MOUSSA ALI 'TOURTOUR' (Independent)	2,239	2.99
AHMED IBRAHIM ABDI (Independent)	1,474	1.97
Total	74,838	100.00

CHAMBRE DES DÉPUTÉS

Elections for the 65-seat Chamber of Deputies were held on 18 December 1992. The election was contested by the governing Rassemblement populaire pour le progrès (RPP) and the opposition Parti du renouveau démocratique (PRD). All 65 seats were won by the RPP.

President of the Chamber: SAID IBRAHIM BADOUL.

Political Organizations

Constitutional reforms allowing the registration of a maximum of four political parties took effect in September 1992. By mid-1994 three parties had obtained legal status:

Parti national démocratique (PND): f. 1992; seeks formation of 'govt of national unity' to supervise implementation of democratic reforms; Chair. ADEN ROBLEH AWALLEH.

Parti du renouveau démocratique (PRD): Djibouti; f. Sept. 1992 to succeed the Mouvement pour la paix et la réconciliation (f. 1992); seeks to establish democratic parliamentary govt; Pres. MOHAMED DJAMA ELABE; Sec.-Gen. MAKI HOUMED GABA.

Rassemblement populaire pour le progrès (RPP): Djibouti; f. 1979 to succeed the Ligue populaire africaine pour l'indépendance; sole legal party 1981–92; Pres. HASSAN GOULED APTIDON; Sec.-Gen. MOUMIN BAHDON FARAH.

The following organizations are banned:

Front des forces démocratiques (FFD): Leader OMAR ELMI KHAIREH.

Front de libération de la côte des Somalis (FLCS): f. 1963; Issa-supported; has operated from Somalia; Chair. ABDALLAH WABERI KHALIF; Vice-Chair. OMAR OSMAN RABEH.

Front pour la restauration de l'unité et de la démocratie (FRUD): f. 1991 by merger of three militant Afar groups: the Action pour la révision de l'ordre à Djibouti, the Front pour la restauration des droits et de la légalité, and the Front pour la résistance patriotique djiboutienne; advocates fair representation in government of Djibouti's different ethnic groups; commenced armed insurgency in Nov. 1991; split into two factions in March 1994; the dominant group, which favours a negotiated settlement with the Govt, recognizes the following leaders: Pres. **Ali Mohamed Daoud**; Sec.-Gen. **Ougoureh Kifleh Ahmed.**

Front uni de l'opposition djiboutienne (FUOD): f. 1992; based in Ethiopia; united front of internal opposition groups, incl. some fmr mems of RPP; Leader MOHAMED AHMED ISSA ('CHEIKO').

Mouvement de la jeunesse djiboutienne (MJD): Leader ABDOULKARIM ALI AMARKAK.

Mouvement populaire pour la libération de Djibouti (MPLD): f. 1964; Afar-supported; based in Dire Dawa, Ethiopia; Leader SHEHEM DAOUD.

Mouvement pour l'unité et la démocratie (MUD): advocates political pluralism; Leader MOHAMED MOUSSA ALI (TOURTOUR).

Organisation des masses Afar (OMA): f. 1993 by mems of the fmr Mouvement populaire de libération (f. 1975); Chair. AHMED MALCO.

Parti centriste et des reformes démocratiques (PCRD): f. 1993 in Addis Ababa, Ethiopia, by breakaway faction of the FRUD; seeks official registration as an opposition party; Chair. HASSAN ABDALLAH WATTA.

Parti populaire djiboutien: f. 1981; mainly Afar-supported; Leader MOUSSA AHMED IDRIS.

Union démocratique pour le progrès (UDP): f. 1992; advocates democratic reforms; Leader FARAH WABERI.

Union des mouvements démocratiques (UMD): f. 1990 by merger of the fmr Front démocratique pour la libération de Djibouti and the Mouvement national djiboutien pour l'instauration de la démocratie; Pres. MOHAMED ADOYTA.

Diplomatic Representation

EMBASSIES IN DJIBOUTI

China, People's Republic: Djibouti; tel. 352246; telex 5926; Ambassador: SUN ZHIRONG.

Egypt: BP 1989, Djibouti; tel. 351231; telex 5880; Ambassador: MOHSEN T. AZMI.

Ethiopia: BP 230, Djibouti; tel. 350718; Ambassador: BERHANU DINKA.

France: 45 blvd du Maréchal Foch, BP 2039, Djibouti; tel. 350963; telex 5861; Ambassador: RÉGIS DE BÉLENET.

Iraq: BP 1983, Djibouti; tel. 353469; telex 5877; Ambassador: ABDEL AZIZ AL-GAILANI.

Libya: BP 2073, Djibouti; tel. 353339; telex 5874; Ambassador: JALAL MUHAMMAD AL-DAGHELY.

Oman: BP 1996, Djibouti; tel. 350852; telex 5876; Ambassador: SAOUD SALEM HASSAN AL-ANSI.

Russia: BP 1913, Djibouti; tel. 352051; telex 5906; fax 355990; Ambassador: PULAT ABDULLAEV.

Saudi Arabia: BP 1921, Djibouti; tel. 351645; telex 5865; fax 352284; Chargé d'affaires: MOWAFFAK AL-DOLIGANE.

Somalia: BP 549, Djibouti; tel. 353521; telex 5815; Ambassador: MOHAMED SHEK MOHAMED MALINGUR.

Sudan: Djibouti; tel. 351483; Ambassador: TAG EL-SIR MOHAMED ABASS.

USA: Villa Plateau du Serpent, blvd du Maréchal Joffre, BP 185, Djibouti; tel. 353995; fax 353940; Ambassador: MARTIN CHESCHES.

Yemen: BP 194, Djibouti; tel. 352975; Ambassador: MUHAMMAD ABDOUL WASSI HAMID.

Judicial System

The Supreme Court was established in 1979. There is a high court of appeal and a court of first instance in Djibouti; each of the five administrative districts has a 'tribunal coutumier'.

President of the Court of Appeal: KADIDJA ABEBA.

Religion

ISLAM

Almost the entire population are Muslims.

Qadi of Djibouti: MOGUE HASSAN DIRIR, BP 168, Djibouti; tel. 352669.

CHRISTIANITY

The Roman Catholic Church

Djibouti comprises a single diocese, directly responsible to the Holy See. There were an estimated 8,225 adherents in the country at 31 December 1991.

Bishop of Djibouti: Mgr GEORGES PERRON, Evêché, blvd de la République, BP 94, Djibouti; tel. 350140; fax 354834.

The Anglican Communion

Within the Episcopal Church in Jerusalem and the Middle East, Djibouti lies within the jurisdiction of the Bishop in Egypt.

Other Christian Churches

Eglise Protestante: blvd de la République, BP 416, Djibouti; tel. 351820; f. 1957; Pastor PASCAL VERNIER.

Greek Orthodox Church: blvd de la République, Djibouti; tel. 351325; c. 350 adherents; Archimandrite STAVROS GEORGANAS.

The Ethiopian Orthodox Church is also represented in Djibouti.

The Press

L'Atout: Palais du peuple, Djibouti; twice a year; publ. by the Centre National de la Promotion Culturelle et Artistique.

Carrefour Africain: BP 393, Djibouti; fax 354916; fortnightly; publ. by the Roman Catholic mission; circ. 500.

La Nation: place du 27 juin, BP 32, Djibouti; tel. 352201; weekly; Dir ISMAEL H. TANI; circ. 3,500.

Le Progrès: Djibouti; weekly; publ. by the RPP; Publr ALI MOHAMED HUMAD.

Revue de l'ISERT: BP 486, Djibouti; tel. 352795; telex 5811; three a year; publ. by the Inst. Supérieur d'Etudes et de Recherches Scientifiques.

NEWS AGENCIES

Agence Djiboutienne de Presse (ADP): place du 27 juin, BP 32, Djibouti; tel. 350201; telex 5871.

Foreign Bureau

Agence France-Presse (AFP): BP 97, Djibouti; tel. 352294; telex 5863; Correspondent KHALID HAIDAR ABDALLAH.

Radio and Television

There were an estimated 39,000 radio receivers and 24,000 television receivers in use in 1991. In 1980 Djibouti became a member of the Arab Satellite Communication Organization, and opened an earth station for radio, television and telecommunications; a second earth station opened in June 1985.

Radiodiffusion-Télévision de Djibouti (RTD): BP 97, Djibouti; tel. 352294; telex 5863; f. 1957; state-controlled; programmes in French, Afar, Somali and Arabic; 24 hours radio and 7 hours television daily; Dir-Gen. OJAMA ADEN.

Finance

(cap. = capital; dep. = deposits; m. = million; res = reserves; br. = branch; amounts in Djibouti francs)

BANKING

Central Bank

Banque Nationale de Djibouti: BP 2118, Djibouti; tel. 352751; telex 5838; fax 356288; f. 1977; bank of issue; Gov. ADEN LUC.

Commercial Banks

Banque al-Baraka Djibouti: ave Pierre Pascal, BP 2607, Djibouti; tel. 355046; telex 5739; fax 355038; Dir-Gen. AHMED OULD SALEM.

Banque de Djibouti et du Moyen-Orient SA: place Lagarde, BP 2112, Djibouti; tel. 353291; telex 5943; fax 355828; f. 1983; 55% owned by Middle East Bank; cap. 300m. (Dec. 1987); Man. Dir LÉONIDE LAVAL.

Banque Indosuez Mer Rouge (France): 10 place Lagarde, BP 88, Djibouti; tel. 353016; telex 5829; fax 351638; f. 1908; cap. and res 1,650m., dep. 19,235m. (Dec. 1992); Chair. and CEO FRANÇOIS GRIFFE; 5 brs.

Banque pour le Commerce et l'Industrie-Mer Rouge (BCIMR): place Lagarde, BP 2122, Djibouti; tel. 380857; telex 5821; fax 354260; f. 1977; 51% owned by Banque Nationale de Paris Intercontinentale; cap. and res. 4,070m., dep. 24,866m. (Dec. 1992); Pres. VINCENT DE ROUX; 7 brs.

Commercial and Savings Bank of Somalia: place Lagarde, BP 2004, Djibouti; tel. 351282; telex 5879.

Commercial Bank of Ethiopia: rue de Marseilles, BP 187, Djibouti; tel. 352101; telex 5835; fax 356777; f. 1980; Man. ASSEBEWORK ZEGEYE.

Development Bank

Banque de Développement de Djibouti: angle ave Georges Clemenceau et rue Pierre Curie, BP 520, Djibouti; tel. 353391; telex 5717; fax 355022; f. 1983; 39.2% govt-owned; cap. 1,557m. (Dec. 1992); Pres. AHMED WALIEH SAMATAR

Banking Association

Association Professionnelle des Banques: c/o Banque pour le Commerce et l'Industrie (Mer Rouge), place Lagarde, BP 2122, Djibouti; tel. 350857; telex 5821; fax 354260; Pres. MOHAMED ADEN.

INSURANCE

Assurances Générales de France (AGF): 3 rue Marchand, Djibouti; tel. 350839.

Ethiopian Insurance Co: rue de Bruxelles, BP 3457, Djibouti; tel. 354065.

Ets Marill 'La Prudence': rue Marchand, BP 57, Djibouti; tel. 351650.

State Insurance Co of Somalia (SICOS): BP 50, Djibouti; tel. 352707; telex 5819; all classes of insurance.

Union des Assurances de Paris (UAP): blvd Bonhour, Djibouti; tel. 355470.

About 10 European insurance companies maintain agencies in Djibouti.

Trade and Industry

Chambre Internationale de Commerce et d'Industrie: place Lagarde, BP 84, Djibouti; tel. 351070; telex 5957; f. 1906; 24 mems; 12 assoc. mems; Pres. SAID ALI COUBECHE; First Vice-Pres. MOHAMED ADEN.

TRADE UNION

Union générale du travail: Djibouti; f. 1992 to succeed Union générale des travailleurs de Djibouti; confed. of 22 unions; Chair. AHMED DJAMA EGUEH (OBOLEY); Sec.-Gen. ADEN MOHAMED ARDOU.

Transport

RAILWAYS

Compagnie du Chemin de Fer Djibouti-Ethiopien: BP 2116, Djibouti; tel. 350353; telex 5953; fax 351256; POB 1051, Addis Ababa; tel. 517250; telex 21414; fax 513533; f. 1908, adopted present name in 1981; jtly-owned by Govts of Djibouti and Ethiopia; plans to grant autonomous status were announced by the two Govts in 1985; 781 km of track (100 km in Djibouti) linking Djibouti with Addis Ababa; Pres. W. GUEMACHOU; Gen.-Man. SEGED BIRHANE (acting).

ROADS

In 1989 there were 3,067 km of roads, including 1,130 km of main roads, 1,800 km of regional roads and 125 km of urban roads. More than 400 km of the roads are bitumen-surfaced, including the 185-km road along the Ethiopian frontier. Of the remainder, 1,000 km are serviceable throughout the year, the rest only during the dry season. Half the roads are usable only by heavy vehicles. In 1981 the 40-km Grand Bara road was opened, linking the capital with the south. In 1986 the Djibouti—Tadjourah road, the construction of which was financed by Saudi Arabia, was opened, linking the capital with the north.

SHIPPING

Djibouti was established as a free port in 1981. In 1991 the port handled 1.7m. metric tons of freight.

Port Autonome International de Djibouti: BP 2107, Djibouti; tel. 352331; telex 5836; fax 356187; Dir ADEN AHMED DOUALE.

Maritime and Transit Service: rue de Marseille, BP 680, Djibouti; tel. 35-32-04; telex 5845; fax 354149.

Principal Shipping Agents

Compagnie Générale Maritime: 3 rue Marchand, BP 182, Djibouti; tel. 353825; telex 5817; fax 354778; agents for Mitsui OSK, CGM, CGM-SUD, SNC, Capricorne, WAKL, Hapaglloyd, Sea Consortium, Total Transport and others; Gen. Man. HENRI FERRAND.

Compagnie Maritime et Manutention de Djibouti: ave des Messageries Maritimes, BP 89, Djibouti; tel. 351028; telex 5825; fax 350466; agents for Wec Nederland BV, Tsavliris, Ogden Marine Inc., Seahawk Ship Management Inc., Global Maritime, Western Bulk Carriers, Acomante Maritime; also stevedores and freight forwarders; Man. Dir A. A. HETTAM.

Inchcape Shipping Services & Co (Djibouti) SA: 9–11 rue de Genève, BP 81, Djibouti; tel. 353844; telex 3856; fax 353294; f. 1942; Lloyd's and DHL's agents, and shipping agents for Nippon Yusen Kaisha, Waterman Steamship Co, P & OCL, Cosco, Harrison Lines, Ellerman Lines, DSR, Shell, Mobil, Seachem, JSP and others; Dir-Gen. JOHN MCCAULEY.

J. J. Kothari & Co Ltd: rue d'Athens, BP 171, Djibouti; tel. 350219; telex 5860; fax 351778; agents for American President Lines, Shipping Corpn of India, Pacific International Lines, Shipping Corpn of Saudi Arabia, Egyptian Navigation, Sealift NV, India Shipping Co, Geepee Lines, VOSCO Line and others; also ship managers, stevedores, freight forwarders; Dirs S. J. KOTHARI, NALIN KOTHARI.

Mitchell Cotts Djibouti SARL: blvd de la République, BP 85, Djibouti; tel. 351204; telex 5812; fax 355851; agents for Adriatic Tankers, Beacon, Central Gulf, Cunard Ellerman, Dan Bunkering Denmark, Dry Tank/Piraeus, Harrison, Khan Shipping, Marship Operators, Mobil/Fairfax/London, Naftomar, Pand OCL, Scan-Shipping/Denmark and others; Dir FAHMY SAID CASSIM.

Société Maritime L. Savon et Ries: blvd Cheikh Osman, BP 2125, Djibouti; tel. 352351; telex 5823; fax 351103; agents for DRML, Conti Lines, SUDGARCO, Lloyd Triestino, Messina, Polish Ocean Lines and others; Gen. Man. J. P. DELARUE.

CIVIL AVIATION

The international airport is at Ambouli, 6 km from Djibouti, and there are six other airports providing domestic services.

Air Djibouti (Red Sea Airlines): BP 505, rue Marchand, Djibouti; tel. 352651; telex 5820; fax 354363; f. 1971, when Air Somalie took over the fmr Air Djibouti (f. 1963); the Djibouti Govt holds 62.5% of shares, and Air France 32.3%; placed in liquidation in Jan. 1991; internal flights and international services to points in the Middle East and Europe; Gen. Man. PAUL BOTBOL.

Tourism

Djibouti offers desert scenery in its interior and watersport facilities on its coast. In 1990 there were 32,699 hotel visitors.

Office National du Tourisme et de l'Artisanat: place du 27 juin, BP 1938, Djibouti; tel. 353790; telex 5938; fax 356322.

Defence

Arrangements for military co-operation exist between Djibouti and France, and in June 1993 there were about 4,000 French military personnel stationed in Djibouti. In June 1993 the total armed forces of Djibouti itself, in which all services form part of the army, numbered 3,900 (including 100 naval and 200 air force personnel). There were also paramilitary forces numbering 600 gendarmes, as well as a 3,000-strong national security force. Conscription of all men between 18 and 25 years of age was introduced in late 1991.

Defence Expenditure: 4,709m. Djibouti francs in 1990.

Commander-in-Chief of the Armed Forces: Pres. HASSAN GOULED APTIDON.

Education

The government has overall responsibility for education. Primary education generally begins at seven years of age and lasts for six years. Secondary education, usually starting at the age of 13, lasts for seven years. Budgetary expenditure on education in 1991 was 2,872m. Djibouti francs, equivalent to 11.1% of total government expenditure. In 1992 there were 30,589 primary school pupils and 9,740 pupils receiving general secondary and vocational education (including teacher training). As Djibouti has no university, students seeking further education go abroad to study, mainly to France.

Bibliography

Cassanelli, L. V. *The Shaping of Somali Society: Reconstructing the History of a Pastoral People, 1600–1900*. Philadelphia, Pennsylvania University Press, 1982.

Chailley, M. *Note sur les Afar de la région de Tadjoura*. Paris, Académie des Sciences d'Outre-mer, 1984.

Laudouze, A. *Djibouti, Nation carrefour*. Paris, Editions Karthala, 1982.

Lewis, I. M. *A Modern History of Somalia: Nation and State in the Horn of Africa*, 1979.

Peoples of the Horn of Africa: Somali, Afar and Saho. London, International African Institute, 1969.

Poinsot, J. P. *Djibouti et la côte française des Somalis*. Paris, 1965.

Saint-Veran, R. *A Djibouti avec les Afars et les Issas*. Published by the author at Parc Saint-Véran, 06800 Cagnes-sur-Mer, France, 1977.

Thompson, V., and Adloff, R. *Djibouti and the Horn of Africa*. London, Oxford University Press, 1968.

EQUATORIAL GUINEA

Physical and Social Geography

RENÉ PÉLISSIER

The Republic of Equatorial Guinea occupies an area of 28,051 sq km (10,831 sq miles). Geographically, the main components of the republic are the islands of Bioko (formerly Fernando Póo), covering 2,017 sq km, and Annobón (also known as Pagalu), 17 sq km; and, on the African mainland, bordered to the north by Cameroon, to the south and east by Gabon and westwards by the Gulf of Guinea, lies the province of Río Muni (Mbini), 26,017 sq km, including three coastal islets, Corisco (15 sq km), and the Great and Little Elobeys (2.5 sq km).

Bioko is a parallelogram-shaped island, 72 km by 35 km, formed from three extinct volcanoes. To the north lies the Pico de Santa Isabel (rising to 3,007 m above sea-level), with an easy access. In the centre of the island are the Moka heights, while, further south, the Gran Caldera forms the remotest and least developed part of the island. The coast is steep to the south. Malabo is the only natural harbour. Crop fertility is high, owing to the presence of volcanic soils. At the southern extremity of the Guinean archipelago lies the remote island of Annobón, south of the island of São Tomé.

Mainland Río Muni is a jungle enclave, from which a coastal plain rises steeply toward the Gabonese frontier. Its main orographic complexes are the spurs of the Monts de Cristal of Gabon. The highest peaks are Piedra de Nzas, Monte Mitra and Monte Chime, all rising to 1,200 m. The main river is the Mbini (also known as the Río Benito), non-navigable except for a 20-km stretch, which bisects Río Muni. On the Cameroon border is the Río Campo; its tributary, the Kye, is the *de facto* eastern border with Gabon. The Río Muni is not itself a river but the mouth of several Gabonese and Río Munian rivers. The coast is a long beach, with low cliffs towards Kogo. There is no natural harbour.

The country has an equatorial climate with heavy rainfall, especially in Bioko. The average temperature of Malabo is 25°C and the average rainfall is in excess of 2,000 mm. Humidity is high throughout the island, except on the Moka heights. Río Muni has less debilitating climatic conditions.

According to the 1983 census, which recorded a total population of 300,000, there were 57,190 inhabitants on Bioko, 240,804 in Río Muni and 2,006 on Annobón. The population was officially estimated to be 356,000 at mid-1991. The main city is Malabo (with 15,253 inhabitants at the July 1983 census), the capital of Bioko and of the republic, as well as the main economic, educational and religious centre. The other town of some note is Luba. Bubi villages are scattered in the eastern and western parts of the island. On the mainland the only urban centre is the port of Bata, which had 24,100 inhabitants in 1983. Other ports are Mbini and Kogo. Inland, Mikomeseng, Niefang, Ebebiyin and Evinayong are small market and administrative centres. The country is divided into seven administrative provinces: Bioko Norte, Bioko Sur and Annobón for the two main islands; Centro-Sur, Kié-Ntem, Litoral and Wele-Nzas for the mainland and its adjacent islets.

The ethnic composition of Equatorial Guinea is unusually complex for so small a political unit. The Fang are the dominant group in Río Muni, where they are believed to account for between 80%–90% of the population. North of the Mbini river are the Ntumu Fang, and to the south of it the Okak Fang. Coastal tribes—the Kombe, Balengue, Bujeba, etc.—have been pushed towards the sea by Fang pressure. Both Fang and coastal peoples are of Bantu origin. In recent years, continental Río Munians (mostly Fang) have flocked to Bioko, where they now dominate the civil and military services. The Bubi, who are the original inhabitants of Bioko, may now number about 15,000. The Fernandino, of whom there are a few thousand, are the descendants of former slaves liberated by the British, mingled with long-settled immigrants from coastal west Africa. The working population of Annobón are principally fishermen and sailors.

The official language is Spanish. In Río Muni the Fang language is spoken, as well as those of coastal tribes. In Bioko the principal local language is Bubi, although pidgin English and Ibo are widely understood.

Recent History

W. G. CLARENCE-SMITH

Revised for this edition by the Editor

The Republic of Equatorial Guinea, comprising the province of Río Muni (Mbini), on the African mainland, and the islands of Fernando Póo (Bioko), Corisco, Annobón and the Elobyes, was granted independence on 12 October 1968, after 190 years of Spanish colonial rule. Francisco Macías Nguema, a mainland Fang from the Esangui clan, took office as president of the new republic, following multi-party elections in which he had received the support of a moderate coalition grouping.

In office, Macías Nguema moved swiftly to suppress democracy, and to assert his absolute power through a 'reign of terror'. In 1970 all political parties were fused into a single party, which came to be known as the Partido Unico Nacional de los Trabajadores (PUNT). The brutal and increasingly capricious nature of the regime led to the flight of as many as one-third of the total populace, including nearly all of the skilled and educated elements of Equato-Guinean society. Macías Nguema obtained much of his economic and military aid from Eastern bloc countries; contacts with Spain deteriorated, and serious quarrels arose regionally with Gabon and Nigeria. The country's economy, centred on cocoa plantations on Fernando Póo and relying on imported African labour, was devastated by the excesses of Macías Nguema's regime.

OBIANG NGUEMA'S PRESIDENCY

On 3 August 1979 Lt-Col (later Brig.-Gen.) Teodoro Obiang Nguema Mbasogo, the commander of the national guard and a nephew of the president, staged a successful *coup d'état*. Macías, who fled from the capital, was eventually captured and executed on 29 September. Obiang Nguema announced the restoration of the rule of law, but banned all political parties and ruled through a supreme military council (SMC), which continued to be dominated by the Esangui clan. An alleged attempt to depose the new regime in April 1981 was followed by some 150 arrests and reports of serious violations of human rights. However, sustained pressure from exiled opposition groups, together with the government's need to secure foreign economic assistance, compelled Obiang Nguema to grant political concessions. In December 1981 the first civilians were appointed to the SMC, and in August 1982 a new constitution was submitted to a referendum, being approved by 95% of voters. Provisions for the protection of human rights and for a limited form of popular representation were incorporated in the constitution, and Obiang Nguema was appointed to a seven-year term as president. In May 1983 a coup attempt involving military personnel close to the president was foiled, and in August elections were held. An estimated 50,000 voters balloted for 41 candidates, nominated by the president, to serve for a term of five years in a unicameral legislature, with virtually no independent legislative powers.

In 1986 there was a third attempted coup, promoted by the minister of defence, Lt-Col Fructuoso Mba Onaña Nchama, an uncle of the president. Obiang Nguema responded in the following year by creating a 'governmental party', the Partido Democrático de Guinea Ecuatorial (PDGE), while still resisting calls for multi-party democracy. The higher ranks of the civil service and armed forces remained firmly in the hands of the Esangui clan, and elections continued to be overtly manipulated by the government. At legislative elections held in July 1988, all of the PDGE candidates were returned, receiving 99.2% of the votes cast. A further coup attempt followed in September.

The first presidential elections since 1968 took place in June 1989, with Obiang Nguema, the sole candidate, receiving 99% of the votes cast. The election was not conducted by secret ballot. An amnesty for political detainees was proclaimed in August. Nevertheless, the international human rights organization Amnesty International has repeatedly accused the government of wrongfully arresting political opponents and mistreating detainees. The Roman Catholic church, which claims the allegiance of the majority of the population, emerged in 1990 from many years of official silence to criticize the regime's record of human rights abuses.

Opposition Pressures

Under growing internal and international pressure, the president finally conceded the principle of political plurality in July 1991. A new constitution, embodying provisions for a multi-party system and the observance of human rights, was approved by referendum in mid-November, and in early January 1992 a new electoral law was promulgated, followed by the implementation of a general amnesty covering all political exiles, in mid-January, when a new transitional government was formed. However, these reform measures failed to meet the opposition's expectations. Provisions of the new constitution exempted Obiang Nguema from any judicial procedures arising from his tenure, while Equato-Guinean citizens who also hold foreign passports and persons not continuously resident in Equatorial Guinea for 10 years were barred from standing as election candidates. This measure thus effectively excluded virtually all exiled political opponents from participation in national political life. The electoral law also required all political parties to submit a deposit of 30m. francs CFA as a condition of registration, and prohibited the use of funds from abroad for this purpose. Moreover, the president declared that legislative and presidential elections would not be held until 1993 and 1996 respectively, when the current mandates of the legislature and of the president had expired. The transitional government included only PDGE members, although the party's 'liberal' wing was represented, notably by the new foreign minister, Benjamín Mba Ekua.

During January 1992 the United Nations published a report that adversely criticized the human rights record of the Equato-Guinean authorities and some of the provisions incoporated in the new constitution. Throughout 1992 the security forces continued to arrest members of opposition parties. In early November two Spanish businessmen were charged with plotting against the government; they were found guilty in late November and sentenced to 12 years' imprisonment, but were pardoned on the same day. In mid-December about 100 anti-government protesters were arrested in Malabo; however, they were released soon afterwards. Further arrests of opposition members occurred in mid-January 1993. In early February the UN published another report alleging a serious disregard for human rights by the Obiang Nguema regime. During February and March the government and several opposition organizations negotiated a national pact that established conditions for the conduct of the forthcoming legislative elections; these included the freedom to organize political activity, equal access by all parties to the media and a revision of the legislation governing the financing of political organizations. However, the government was soon accused of violating the pact. In late May five opposition members were arrested while attending a political meeting. In mid-July Obiang Nguema announced that the parliamentary elections would take place in mid-September, following the dissolution of the legislative assembly in August. Violent clashes were reported between anti-government demonstrators and security forces on the island of Annobón during August. The administration accused Spain of inciting the demonstrations, a claim which was strenuously denied by the Spanish government. In the same month Amnesty International published a report in which it was stated that the Obiang Nguema regime had allegedly sanctioned the arrests and torture of its political opponents.

Multi-party legislative elections scheduled for September 1993 were eventually held in mid-November, although they were boycotted by the opposition alliance Plataforma de la Oposición Conjunta (POC) in protest at Nguema's refusal to review contentious clauses of the electoral law or to permit international observers to inspect the electoral register. Although OAU representatives attended as observers the UN declined a request by the authorities to monitor the elections, asserting that correct procedures were evidently not being implemented. Following a turn-out variously estimated at between 30%-50% of the electorate, the PDGE won 68 of the 80 seats in the house of representatives; six opposition parties which presented candidates, the Convención Socialdemocrática Popular, won six seats, the Unión Democrática y Social de Guinea Ecuatorial won five seats and the Convención Liberal Democrática obtained one seat.

Prior to the elections, opposition politicians were reported to have been harassed by the security forces and during the polling irregularities in procedures were allegedly widespread. In early December 1993 the government announced that henceforth all party political gatherings would be subject to prior official authorization. In mid-December Silvestre Siale Bileka, who had been prime minister of the interim government and was appointed prime minister of the new government, nominated a council of ministers in which there were no opposition representatives.

At the beginning of June 1994 up to six people were reported to have been killed in an alleged attack on a military barracks on the Koyon peninsula which the government referred to as a 'plot to destabilize the country'. Voter registration for the municipal elections, due to be held in November, took place between early April and early June. Opposition parties were urged by the government to register and to assign representatives to each polling station to check the registration of activists. At the end of June the first session of the new house of representatives was opened by the president.

Equato-Guinean exiles have reacted cautiously to Obiang Nguema's efforts to encourage their return. His regime's authoritarian ethos, together with reports of persistent human rights abuses, corruption and economic stagnation, have tended to discourage the great majority of emigrés. During the Macías period, the most influential exiled opposition party had been the Alianza Nacional para la Restauración Democrática de Guinea Ecuatorial (ANRDGE). Based in Geneva, Switzerland, it achieved a semi-representative, if unofficial, standing with UN bodies. During Obiang Nguema's rule, however, ANRDGE's influence declined, and the exiled opposition split into numerous small and shifting groups, many of which were based in Spain. The Partido del Progreso de Guinea Equatorial (PPGE), founded in 1983 and led by Severo Moto Nsa, emerged as a particularly influential opposition platform during the 1980s. Moto Nsa was appointed secretary-general of the Junta Coordinadora de las Fuerzas de Oposición Democrática, which was formed in Zaragoza, Spain, in 1983, as a co-ordinating body for exiled opposition groups. Moto Nsa did not, however, return to Equatorial Guinea until April 1994. Smaller concentrations of exiled politicians continue to operate from France and Portugal and political liberalization in Gabon led during 1990 to the emergence of Libreville as a new centre of activity for the Equato-Guinean opposition in exile. The most significant of these groups was the Unión para la Democracia y el Desarollo Social (UDDS), founded in September 1990 and led by Antonio Sibacha Bueicheku. A coalition of parties dominated by the UDDS was formed in Libreville in April 1991, under the title of Coordinación Democrática de los Partidos de Oposición de Guinea Ecuatorial. Following the government's amnesty for political exiles in January 1992 and the enactment of legislation in that month legalizing a multi-party political system, the opposition began to prepare for the legislative elections due to take place in 1993 (see above). The POC, grouping nine opposition parties based in Spain, was formed in 1992.

Foreign Relations

In its foreign relations since 1979, Equatorial Guinea has sought generally to enhance its contacts with the Western powers, and particularly with Spain and France. Relations with Spain, which has consistently provided substantial economic aid, have been strained throughout the 1980s and early 1990s by reports of internal corruption, the misuse of aid funds and abuses of human rights in Equatorial Guinea. In mid-December 1993 the Spanish consul in Bata was expelled 'for interference in the country's internal affairs', following an alleged meeting between the consul and members of opposition parties. The Spanish government recalled its ambassador for consultations and in retaliation cut further aid to the country, excluding humanitarian assistance, from the beginning of January 1994. The ban was extended to all forms of aid at the end of the month.

From the early 1980s Obiang Nguema attempted to move the country away from Spanish influence and into France's economic sphere. In December 1983 Equatorial Guinea became a member of the Union douanière et économique de l'Afrique centrale (UDEAC), and in August 1984 it joined the Banque des états de l'Afrique centrale (BEAC). Full entry to the Franc Zone followed in January 1985, when the CFA franc replaced the epkwele as the national currency. The increasing level of French economic influence was reflected in the president's regular attendance at Franco-African summit meetings, and in an extended curriculum of French-language classes in Equato-Guinean schools. Faced in the late 1980s by increasing French impatience with the economic and political shortcomings of his regime, however, Obiang Nguema turned once more to Spain. In February 1990 the two countries finalized a four-year co-operation accord (see Economy). In addition, Obiang Nguema has sought to establish amicable relations with China and the Democratic People's Republic of Korea. Military aid from Morocco, which replaced that from Cuba after 1979, has remained crucial to the maintenance of his regime.

Regionally, Obiang Nguema has encountered difficulties with Nigeria, which in 1988 threatened to invade Bioko to eject South African personnel, whom Nigeria alleged to be installing a satellite-tracking station and extending Malabo airport, in preparation for a military assault on the Niger delta oilfields. The affair was eventually resolved in 1990 by reciprocal state visits by the two heads of state. In mid-1994 following a visit to Nigeria by Obiang Nguema, the two countries agreed to co-operate in the establishment of an international committee to demarcate maritime borders in the Gulf of Guinea. Cameroon and São Tomé and Príncipe were also expected to become members. Relations with Gabon have come under strain, as the result of unresolved frontier disputes, revived by petroleum exploration activity in southern Río Muni. In May 1993 Equatorial Guinea and South Africa established diplomatic relations and in January 1994 diplomatic relations with Israel were re-established.

Economy

W. G. CLARENCE-SMITH

Revised for this edition by the Editor

The economy of Equatorial Guinea is based on agriculture and forestry, the principal products being timber, cocoa, coffee, palm oil, bananas and cassava. In 1992, according to estimates by the World Bank, Equatorial Guinea's gross national product (GNP), measured at average 1990–92 prices, was US $146m., equivalent to $330 per head. During 1985–92, it was estimated, GNP per head decreased, in real terms, at an average annual rate of 0.3%. In 1985–92 the population increased by an annual average of 2.3%. According to estimates by the World Bank, Equatorial Guinea's gross domestic product (GDP) increased, in real terms, by an annual average of 2.4% in 1985–90. GDP per head totalled $391, at current prices, in 1989. Real GDP appears to have declined in aggregate terms in 1991. However, the government is hoping that oil exports will lead to an economic boom from the mid-1990s.

AGRICULTURE, FORESTRY AND FISHING

Timber from Río Muni has been the country's most important export since 1987, with some 800,000 ha estimated to be suitable for lumbering operations. The main lumbering areas have tended to be situated close to the coast and larger rivers. The principal exploited species of wood are *okoumé* and *akoga*, which together account for about one-half of total exports. In 1967, the year before independence, production by Spanish concessionaires reached nearly 340,000 metric tons. Output subsequently declined sharply, and amounted to a mere 1,000 tons in 1978. Production and exports recovered quickly after the overthrow of Macías in 1979, although production has remained considerably below the level of 300,000 cu m which the FAO considers to be a realistic goal. Exports have levelled out at around 150,000 cu m annually since 1987. Moreover, the government's wish to increase the proportion of processed to unprocessed exports has largely failed to materialize, despite the construction in 1982, with Italian aid, of a sawmill with an annual capacity of 20,000 cu m. Exploitation rights to sizeable areas of forest were granted by Obiang Nguema to foreign (mainly French and Spanish) concessionaires. Some of these, however, have ceased operations and others have become insolvent. In 1989 Israeli timber interests leased the 90,000 ha of Semge, the largest concession, which was formerly held by French interests. The timber companies have blamed their difficulties on high and insufficiently differentiated export taxes, expensive and inadequate port facilities in Bata, high tax on fuels, poor roads, and the lack of local credit facilities. The saturation of the world market for *okoumé* wood and competition from more efficient South-

East Asian producers have compounded their problems. In 1990 the government adopted a forestry action plan, which aimed to revitalize timber production and emphasized the necessity of implementing reafforestation measures.

Cocoa is Equatorial Guinea's principal agricultural export and is the main crop of Bioko, where its cultivation accounts for about 90% of the country's total output. An area in excess of 41,000 ha was under cocoa cultivation before independence, underpinned by high guaranteed prices on the Spanish domestic market. More than 800 plantations belonged to Africans, but most of the land and production was controlled by Europeans. Political upheavals during the regime of President Macías Nguema contributed to a sharp decline in cocoa output, which fell from about 38,000 tons annually before independence to less than 5,500 tons by 1979/80. Production has stagnated since then, totalling 5,200 tons in 1991, when it provided more than one-third of total exports by value. Production in 1992 was unofficially estimated to be 5,000 tons. The cocoa plantations, nationalized by Macías Nguema, were offered back to their former owners after the coup of 1979, but many owners either failed to reclaim their lands or had them re-confiscated. Most of the plantations are now owned by members of the presidential entourage, and are managed by two Spanish companies. They are worked on a sharecropping basis by local small farmers. However, only about one-third of the land that was cultivated before independence is now exploited, and most of the trees are old and poorly tended. The main problem remains that of labour, as Nigerian plantation workers who were repatriated during the mid-1970s have not wished to return and forced labourers who were brought from Río Muni were sent home after 1979. A five-year cocoa rehabilitation project for 7,550 ha, initiated in 1985 by the World Bank and supported by a variety of donors, achieved little success. In 1991 the World Bank initiated a 10-year cocoa rehabilitation scheme, under which strictly commercial criteria were to be applied, to preclude any accusations of uneconomic subsidies. Under the programme, it was hoped that yields would be increased through replanting and the control of plant pests and diseases. The programme also provides for a gradual expansion in the areas under cultivation, with the promotion of diversification into other crops in areas of marginal cocoa production. The cocoa rehabilitation scheme is part of a wider agricultural project, which has attracted a pledge of $18m. from the World Bank and lesser sums from other donors. The government is carrying out a survey of land tenure on Bioko, and has promised to follow this up with a land reform programme. Nevertheless, the outlook for cocoa remains poor. In early 1992, international prices for the commodity reached their lowest point, in real terms, since 1975. However, the prospect of at least a short-term recovery arose after the 50% devaluation of Equatorial Guinea's currency, the CFA franc, in line with other members of the CFA franc zone, (see below) in January 1994. As a result, Equatorial Guinea's cocoa exports may become more cost-competitive in relation to those of South-East Asian producers, who are aggressively expanding their share of the market.

Coffee is the third most important export commodity, but it lags far behind timber and cocoa. The Spanish administration encouraged smallholder cultivation in Río Muni for the Spanish market during the 1940s. In 1968, the year of independence, exports stood at just under 8,500 metric tons, part of which represented coffee from Gabon and Cameroon (smuggled over the frontier to benefit from higher Spanish prices). By 1979–80, exports had dwindled to just over 100 tons. Production recovered to more than 1,000 tons per year by the end of the 1980s, but it is estimated that about two-thirds of the harvest is smuggled into Gabon to benefit from that country's higher producer prices. In 1988 it was estimated that there were nearly 20,000 ha planted with coffee, divided among some 25,000 households. The quality is poor and the yields are extremely low, as the bushes are mainly old and ill-tended. However, France and the EU are currently financing a project to rejuvenate coffee smallholdings in Río Muni.

France and the EU are also encouraging the growth of food production as part of their rural development aid programme, aimed at enhancing production of cassava, cocoyam, plantain, bananas, rice, maize, palm oil, and eggs for the domestic market. There are also eventual prospects of substantial food exports to Gabon, which is persistently short of foodstuffs and which already imports about 3,000 tons of plantain a year from Río Muni.

Livestock raising almost disappeared from the country during the Macías Nguema period. In 1986 the African Development Bank (ADB) provided a loan of $12.6m. to revive the raising of cattle on the high pastures of Moka, in Bioko, to the situation prevailing prior to independence, when the island was self-sufficient in beef and dairy products. The cattle herd was estimated at 5,000 head in 1992, and a slaughterhouse was in operation. In Río Muni the emphasis has been on poultry raising, again with ADB support, and by the end of the 1980s Río Muni was again well supplied with chickens and eggs.

At independence, some 5,000 people worked in the fishing industry, and the people of Annobón were renowned as skilled fishermen. Tuna from Annobón waters and shellfish from Bioko were processed locally and exported. Under Macías Nguema, the fishing industry collapsed, and the former USSR was granted a fishing monopoly. This was terminated in January 1980, and replaced by agreements with Spain in 1980, with Nigeria in 1982 (renewed in 1991), and with the EC in 1983 (renewed in 1986 and 1989). In 1989 the EC paid 6m. European Currency Units (ECU) for an agreed monthly tonnage catch by European fishing vessels, mainly Spanish and French. The EC has also financed research and training schemes to improve Equatorial Guinea's own artisanal fishing operations. The overall catch rose from around 1,000 tons in 1981–82 to an estimated 3,500 tons in 1991, of which a negligible proportion came from artisanal fisherman. Shellfish constituted nearly one-half of the total catch. A tuna-processing factory at the port of Luba on Bioko, which was financed by Spanish aid, was due to begin production in the early 1990s; it was hoped that the plant would stimulate local involvement in the fishing industry.

INDUSTRY, MINING, POWER AND COMMUNICATIONS

In 1984 the offshore Alba gas and condensate field was discovered by Spain's Repsol on behalf of Empresa Guineano-Española de Petroleos (Gepsa), a joint venture between the government and Repsol. However, Gepsa was dissolved in June 1990, and the concession was taken over, on a production-sharing basis, by a consortium of US independent operators, led by Walter International. Production began in late 1991, at a rate of 1,200 barrels per day (b/d), and was shipped to a storage complex near Malabo. The first consignment of condensates left Bioko in early 1992. Output was expected to rise to 4,000 b/d by 1994, and to remain at that level throughout the decade. The government hopes that petroleum will become the country's main export, earning in the region of $25m. a year. Walter International carried out further successful exploration work in neighbouring blocs near Bioko and between April 1992 and March 1993 it was reported that the company had exported some 1.2m. barrels of high grade petroleum valued at $23m. Various companies are exploring in concessions in Río Muni. Altogether, 18 exploration and appraisal wells had been drilled by late 1991.

Equatorial Guinea has reserves of gold, iron, manganese, tantalum and uranium, but these have yet to be exploited. In 1987 funding was finalized for the construction of a 3.6-MW hydroelectric power station on the Riaba river (Bioko), at a total cost of $32.1m., and the project was officially opened by the president in 1989. There have been commissioning problems with the power station, and disputes over electricity tariffs with a French company, Saur-Afrique, which manages the distribution of electricity on the island. A further power station, to be constructed with aid from the People's Republic of China, is planned for Bikomo, near Bata.

Before independence, there was a diversified and flourishing light industrial sector, centred in Malabo; this infrastructure was effectively ruined by President Macías Nguema and has yet to be fully restored. The manufacturing sector contributed only 1.3% of GDP in 1989. Two sawmills in Bata currently account for most of the country's industrial activity; the town also has a small cement works and a bleach factory. Food-processing and soap production are carried out on a small scale.

Since independence the entire Equato-Guinean road network has fallen into disrepair. During the early 1990s Spain allocated much of its economic aid towards the repair of roads on Bioko, in order to allow the cocoa plantations in the Luba and Riaba areas to re-enter production. A group of international donors are providing assistance for the upgrading of a road from the Mbini area to Cogo on the Gabonese frontier, much of which is currently impassable in the rainy season; this should boost exports of foodstuffs to Gabon. 'Food for work' programmes are also being introduced, in order to maintain the network of feeder roads. There are no railways.

The harbour which handles by far the largest volume of exports is Bata, in Río Muni, which is used by the timber companies and which handled nearly 125,990 metric tons of exports in 1990. The Italian government provided some $5m. for the rehabilitation of the port in 1987, on condition that the facility be operated by a joint Italo-Equato-Guinean company. The initial aim is to increase the handling capacity of Bata to 500,000 tons per year, and eventually to 1m. tons. There have been long and unexplained delays in implementing this project. Malabo has an excellent natural harbour (formed by a sunken volcanic crater), which has been rehabilitated by a French company. Malabo handled only 12,659 tons of exports in 1990, but dealt with 42,804 tons of imports, well above Bata's total of 28,558 tons. There are regular shipping services to Europe, but maritime communications between Malabo, Bata and Annobón are erratic, and there is little traffic by sea with neighbouring states.

There is an international airport at Malabo and a smaller airport at Bata. South African assistance to extend and modernize Malabo airport, which has a runway of 3,000 m, was halted after Nigerian protests (see Recent History), but France has provided funds to upgrade facilities, A project, funded by Arab sources, greatly to extend and upgrade Bata airport is opposed by the World Bank, which views the scheme as of questionable economic value. Attempts to form a national airline have been bedevilled by mismanagement and alleged corruption. Aerolíneas Guinea Ecuatorial, founded in 1982, had collapsed by 1985. Its successor, the Compañía Ecuato-Guineana de Aviación, was established in 1986 as a partnership between the government (70%) and Air Inter-Gabon (30%). After incurring heavy losses, the company went into liquidation in early 1990, seriously disrupting communications between Malabo and Bata. In late November 1990 the government signed an agreement with a private Nigerian carrier, Concord Airlines, in order to maintain essential services; however, there were problems with the implementation of this agreement.

AID AND DEVELOPMENT

The economy continues to rely to a great extent on good relations with Spain, which supplied aid totalling 17,000m. pesetas over the period 1979–86. In addition to aid of 2,000m. Spanish pesetas in 1989, Spain also cancelled repayment of one-third of Equatorial Guinea's debt of 5,000m. pesetas, with the remaining two-thirds to be repaid over 14 years, with eight years' grace. In February 1990 Spain signed an agreement to provide a further $100m. of aid, to be disbursed over four years, covering education, health, administrative reform and economic infrastructure. The Spanish government stated that this involved expenditure amounting to 11 times as much per caput as for any of the other hispanophone countries which receive Spanish assistance. In 1991 Spain cancelled a further one-third of the country's debt. However, in January 1994 Spain suspended aid to Equatorial Guinea following the expulsion of the spanish consul to Bata in December 1993 (see Recent History). France is the country's second main provider of aid, with French assistance rising steeply after Equatorial Guinea joined the various French-sponsored regional economic associations for Central Africa in 1983–85. French aid for 1988 totalled approximately $18m. However, France has been displeased by Equatorial Guinea's inability to fulfil IMF loan conditions (see below) and by a persistent tendency for it to draw too heavily on the resources of the BEAC, without providing adequate national accounts. Loans and grants have come from a variety of other Western and Middle Eastern sources, as well as from China and Nigeria, but none on the scale of those provided by Spain and France. An international aid conference, held in Geneva in April 1982, aimed to provide $140m. for development projects. In November 1988 a second international aid conference pledged a total of $63m. in support of Equatorial Guinea's medium-term investment programme (1989–91). In December 1988 the IMF granted a structural adjustment facility (SAF) of SDR 11.7m. (Equatorial Guinea had received its first IMF stand-by credit, totalling SDR 9.2m., in July 1985.) However, in February 1990 the IMF refused to make any further payments, and shortly afterwards a World Bank mission announced that it was not prepared to make any recommendation for the implementation of a structural adjustment programme. Both multilateral agencies declared themselves particularly dissatisfied with the government's inability to eradicate the budgetary deficit, which stood at 2,512m. francs CFA in 1989. In 1990, when the budget deficit fell to an estimated 252m. francs CFA, the government adopted measures to reduce the deficit further which included liberalizing import prices, stimulating private investment and raising the tariffs charged by public utilities. By 1993 the budget, according to an optimistic estimate by the BEAC, showed a surplus of 579m. francs CFA. However, the multilateral agencies have expressed concern at the continuing deficit on the current account of the balance of payments, which stood at $24.66m. in 1991, although this has been offset, to some extent, by inflows of foreign aid.

The commencement of petroleum exports is expected to generate a significant improvement in both the balance of payments and budgetary deficits from the early 1990s. As a result of this amelioration in the economic situation, the IMF agreed to unblock the disbursement of SAF funds in December 1991. The government has introduced an economic programme for 1993–95, supported by an SDR 12.9m. three-year enhanced structural adjustment facility (ESAF) from the IMF, which aims to accelerate the diversification of the economy and the reform of the public sector, and to restructure the financial sector. Under the programme, the education and social welfare systems are to be developed.

In May 1994 the government announced a budget of 29,000m. francs CFA. It was estimated that at least 50% of budgetary expenditure would go towards servicing the national debt. In the same month the IMF announced the disbursement of the second SAF tranche worth $5.2m., the first disbursement of which had been made in 1993. The 1993 reform programme which had accompanied the SAF loan had, however, been largely deemed a failure on account of the government's expansionary fiscal and monetary policies and slower than expected progress in carrying out structural reforms. Under the 1994 programme it was expected that the real rate of economic growth could be increased while containing inflation at 35% and reducing the current account deficit.

In January 1985 Equatorial Guinea entered the Franc Zone. The Banco de Guinea Ecuatorial (the former central bank and bank of issue) ceased operation, and the epkwele, which had been linked to the Spanish peseta, was replaced by the franc CFA at a rate of 4 bipkwele = 1 franc CFA. It was hoped that Equatorial Guinea's entry into the Franc Zone would bring the country out of isolation by encouraging foreign trade and investment. In July 1985 the 'Paris Club' of Western creditor governments granted a rescheduling, over 10 years, of 246m. French francs of debt, with a five-year period of grace. According to the World Bank,

Equatorial Guinea's total external debt approached $250m. at the end of 1991, imposing a heavy burden on such an underdeveloped economy.

The devaluation of the CFA franc will substantially affect the country's economic prospects. Export competitiveness for primary products should be significantly enhanced, while the substantial rise in the cost of imports could in the longer term stimulate domestic import substitution and the expansion of Equatorial Guinea's manufacturing sector. However, the immediate reduction in consumer purchasing power inherent in the devaluation will impose economic hardship on vulnerable sections of the population. To alleviate some of these social costs the government has temporarily frozen the price of bread and medicine, restrained petroleum prices and is seeking to implement special employment schemes to help cope with an expected increase in the numbers of the unemployed. Foreign financial support will thus be essential in the short term, both in new funds and debt relief.

Statistical Survey

Source (unless otherwise stated): Dirección Técnica de Estadística, Secretaría de Estado para el Plan de Desarrollo Económico y Cooperación, Malabo.

AREA AND POPULATION

Area: 28,051 sq km (Río Muni (Mbini) 26,017 sq km, Bioko 2,017 sq km, Annobón 17 sq km).

Population: 246,941 (Río Muni 200,106, Bioko 44,820, Annobón 2,015) at December 1965 census; 300,000 (Río Muni 240,804, Bioko 57,190, Annobón 2,006), comprising 144,268 males and 155,732 females, at census of 4–17 July 1983 (Source: Ministerio de Asuntos Exteriores, Madrid); 356,000 (official estimate) at mid-1991.

Provinces (population, census of July 1983): Kié-Ntem 70,202, Litoral 66,370, Centro-Sur 52,393, Wele-Nzas 51,839, Bioko Norte 46,221, Bioko Sur 10,969, Annobón 2,006.

Principal towns (population at 1983 census): Malabo (capital) 15,253, Bata 24,100.

Births and Deaths (UN estimates, annual averages): Birth rate 43.3 per 1,000 in 1980–85, 43.8 per 1,000 in 1985–90; Death rate 21.1 per 1,000 in 1980–85, 19.6 per 1,000 in 1985–90; Expectation of life (UN estimates, years at birth, 1985–90): 46.0 (males 44.4; females 47.6) (Source: UN, *World Population Prospects: The 1992 Revision*).

Economically Active Population (persons aged 6 years and over, 1983 census): Agriculture, hunting, forestry and fishing 59,390; Mining and quarrying 126; Manufacturing 1,490; Electricity, gas and water 224; Construction 1,929; Trade, restaurants and hotels 3,059; Transport, storage and communications 1,752; Financing, insurance, real estate and business services 409; Community, social and personal services 8,377; Activities not adequately defined 984; Total employed 77,740 (males 47,893, females 29,847); Unemployed 24,825 (males 18,040, females 6,785); Total labour force 102,565 (males 65,933, females 36,632). Note: Figures are based on unadjusted census data, indicating a total population of 261,779. The adjusted total is 300,000 (Source: International Labour Office, *Year Book of Labour Statistics*).

AGRICULTURE, ETC.

Principal Crops (FAO estimates, '000 metric tons, 1992): Sweet potatoes 35; Cassava 47; Coconuts 8; Palm kernels 3; Bananas 17; Cocoa beans (unofficial estimate) 5; Green coffee 7 (Source: FAO, *Production Yearbook*).

Livestock (FAO estimates, '000 head, year ending September 1992): Cattle 5; Pigs 5; Sheep 36; Goats 8 (Source: FAO, *Production Yearbook*).

Forestry (1991): Roundwood removals (FAO estimates, '000 cu m): Fuel wood 447; Sawlogs, veneer logs and logs for sleepers 160; Total 607 (Source: FAO, *Yearbook of Forest Products*).

Fishing (FAO estimates, metric tons, live weight): Total catch 4,000 in 1989; 3,700 in 1990; 3,500 in 1991 (Source: FAO, *Yearbook of Fishery Statistics*).

INDUSTRY

Palm oil (FAO estimates, '000 metric tons): 5.0 in 1990; 5.0 in 1991; 5.0 in 1992 (Source: FAO, *Production Yearbook*).

Veneer sheets (FAO estimates, '000 cubic metres): 10 in 1989; 10 in 1990; 10 in 1991 (Source: FAO, *Yearbook of Forest Products*).

Electric energy (million kWh): 17 in 1988; 17 in 1989; 18 in 1990 (Source: UN, *Industrial Statistics Yearbook*).

FINANCE

Currency and Exchange Rates: 100 centimes = 1 franc de la Coopération financière en Afrique centrale (CFA). *French Franc, Sterling and Dollar Equivalents* (31 March 1994): 1 French franc = 100 francs CFA; £1 sterling = 846.40 francs CFA; US $1 = 570.14 francs CFA; 1,000 francs CFA = £1.181 = $1.754. *Average Exchange Rate* (francs CFA per US dollar): 282.11 in 1991; 264.69 in 1992; 283.16 in 1993. *Note:* An exchange rate of 1 French franc = 50 francs CFA, established in 1948, remained in force until January 1994, when the CFA franc was devalued by 50%, with the exchange rate adjusted to 1 French franc = 100 francs CFA.

Budget (estimates, million francs CFA, 1992): *Revenue:* Fiscal receipts 6,000, Other receipts 3,900; Total 9,900. *Expenditure:* Compensation of employees 2,400; Interest payments 3,200; Other goods and services 3,100; Capital expenditure 800; Total 9,500 (Source: *La Zone Franc—Rapport 1992*).

1993: (estimates, million francs CFA): Total revenue 9,638, Total expenditure 9,059 (Source: BEAC, *Etudes et Statistiques*).

International Reserves (US $ million at 31 December 1993): IMF special drawing rights 0.38; Foreign exchange 0.10; Total 0.48 (Source: IMF, *International Financial Statistics*).

Money Supply ('000 million francs CFA at 31 December 1993): Currency outside deposit money banks 1.21; Demand deposits at deposit money banks 1.34; Total money 2.55 (Source: IMF, *International Financial Statistics*).

Cost of Living (Consumer price index for Africans in Malabo; base: November 1984 = 100): 77.6 in 1989; 78.48 in 1990; 76.00 in 1991 (Source: IMF, *International Financial Statistics*).

Expenditure on the Gross Domestic Product (million francs CFA at current prices, 1991): Government final consumption expenditure 6,696; Private final consumption expenditure 35,225; Increase in stocks −1,091; Gross fixed capital formation 8,525; *Total domestic expenditure* 49,355; Exports of goods and services 13,174; *Less* Imports of goods and services 16,100; *GDP in purchasers' values* 46,429 (Source: UN, *National Accounts Statistics*).

Gross Domestic Product by Economic Activity (million francs CFA at current prices, 1991): Agriculture, hunting, forestry and fishing 23,328; Manufacturing 597; Electricity, gas and water 1,358; Construction 1,299; Trade, restaurants and hotels 3,319; Transport and communications 855; Finance, insurance, real estate and business services 1,005; Government services 6,354; Other services 5,817; Sub-total 43,932; Import duties 2,497; GDP in purchasers' values 46,429 (Source: UN, *National Accounts Statistics*).

Balance of Payments (US $ million, 1991): Merchandise exports f.o.b. 35.75; Merchandise imports f.o.b. −59.56; *Trade balance* −23.81; Exports of services 6.19; Imports of services −43.03; Other income paid (net) −9.41; private unrequited transfers (net) −16.55; Official unrequited transfers (net) 61.96; *Current balance* −24.66; Capital (net) 32.19; Net errors and omissions −30.72; *Overall balance* −23.19 (Source: IMF, *International Financial Statistics*).

EXTERNAL TRADE

Principal Commodities (distribution by SITC, US $'000, 1990): *Imports c.i.f.:* Food and live animals 4,340, Beverages and tobacco 3,198, Petroleum and petroleum products 4,738, Chemical products 2,378, Basic manufactures 3,931, Machinery and transport equipment 35,880; Total (incl. others) 61,601.

Exports f.o.b.: Cocoa 6,372, Coffee 316, Sawlogs and veneer logs 12,839, Textile fibres and waste 7,078, Ships and boats, etc. 23,852; Total (incl. others) 61,705 (Source: UN, *International Trade Statistics Yearbook.*)

Principal Trading Partners (US $'000, 1991): *Imports c.i.f.:* Cameroon 29,141, Liberia 22,032, Spain 11,640, USA 33,366; Total (incl. others) 113,545. *Exports f.o.b.:* Cameroon 47,212, Nigeria 8,955, Spain 11,645; Total (incl. others) 86,151 (Source: UN, *International Trade Statistics Yearbook.*)

TRANSPORT

Shipping (international sea-borne freight traffic, '000 metric tons, 1989): Goods loaded 100, Goods unloaded 60 (Source: UN, *Monthly Bulletin of Statistics*).

Civil Aviation (traffic on scheduled services, 1990): Passengers carried 14,000, Passenger-km 7,000,000 (Source: UN, *Statistical Yearbook*).

COMMUNICATIONS MEDIA

Radio receivers 153,000 in use in 1991; Television receivers 3,000 in use in 1991; Daily newspapers 2 in 1990, estimated circulation 2,000; Book production 17 titles in 1988 (Source: UNESCO, *Statistical Yearbook*).

EDUCATION

Primary (1980/81): Schools 511; Teachers 647; Pupils 40,110.

Secondary and Further (1980/81): Schools 14; Teachers 288; Pupils 3,013. There were 175 pupils studying abroad.

1982: Primary school pupils 52,021; Secondary school pupils 4,368.

1983: Primary school pupils 61,532.

Source for 1982 and 1983: UNESCO, *Statistical Yearbook.*

Directory

The Constitution

The present Constitution was approved by a national referendum on 16 November 1991. It provides for the introduction of multi-party democracy, for the separate posts of President (in whom executive power is vested and who is also Supreme Commander of the Armed Forces) and Prime Minister (Head of the Government) and for an 80-member legislative House of Representatives. The term of office of the President is seven years, renewable on an indefinite number of occasions. The House of Representatives is to serve for a term of five years.

The Government

HEAD OF STATE

President and Supreme Commander of the Armed Forces: Brig.-Gen. (TEODORO) OBIANG NGUEMA MBASOGO (assumed office 25 August 1979; elected President 25 June 1989).

COUNCIL OF MINISTERS
(August 1994)

Prime Minister and Head of Government: SILVESTRE SIALE BILEKA.

Deputy Prime Minister and Minister of the Economy and Finance: ANATOLIO NDONG MBA.

Minister of State in Charge of Special Duties: ALEJANDRO EVUNA OWONO ASANGONO.

Minister of State for Transport, Information and Communications and Spokesman for the Government: ANTONIO FERNANDO NVE NGU.

Minister of State for Foreign Affairs and Co-operation: MIGUEL OYONO NDONG MIFUMU.

Minister of State for the Interior: JULIO NDONG ELA MANGUE.

Secretary-General of the Presidency: FRANCISCO PASCUAL EYEGUE OBAMA ASUE.

Minister of Justice and Religion: FRANCISCO JAVIER NDONGO BENGONO.

Minister of Public Works, Housing and Town Planning: ALEJANDRO ENVORO OVONO.

Minister of Education and Science: RICARDO MANGUE OBAMA NFUBE.

Minister of Labour and Social Development: CONSTANTINO CONGUE.

Minister of Industry, Energy and Small and Medium-sized Enterprises: SEVERINO OBIANG BENGONO.

Minister of Mines and Hydrocarbons: JUAN OLO MBA NSENG.

Minister of Agriculture, Fisheries and Food: ALFREDO MOKUDI NANGA.

Minister of Health and the Environment: BERNABE NGORE.

Minister of Women's Promotion and Social Affairs: BALBINA NCHAMA NVO.

Minister of Culture, Tourism and Francophone Affairs: AGUSTÍN NSE NFUMU.

MINISTRIES

All Ministries are in Malabo.

Ministry of Agriculture, Fisheries and Food: Apdo 504, Malabo.

Ministry of the Economy and Finance: Bioke Norte Malabo; tel. 31-05; fax 32-05.

Ministry of Foreign Affairs and Co-operation: Malabo; tel. 32-20.

Legislature

CÁMARA DE REPRESENTANTES DEL PUEBLO

Speaker: FELIPE ONDO OBIANG ALOGO.

General Election, 21 November 1993

Party	Seats
Partido Democrático de Guinea Ecuatorial (PDGE)	68
Convención Socialdemocrática Popular (CSDP)	6
Unión Democrática y Social de Guinea Ecuatorial (UDSGE)	5
Convención Liberal Democrática (CLD)	1
Total	80

Political Organizations

Legislation was enacted in January 1992 permitting a multiparty political system to operate.

Convención Liberal Democrática (CLD): Pres. ALFONSO ESIE MIFUMU.

Convención Socialdemocrática Popular (CSDP).

Coordinación Democrática de los Partidos de Oposición de Guinea Ecuatorial: Libreville, Gabon; f. 1991; coalition of the following political groups:

- **Movimento Nacional para la Nueva Liberación de Guinea Ecuatorial.**
- **Movimiento para la Unificación Nacional de Guinea Ecuatorial (MUNGE):** Kinshasa, Zaire; f. 1990.
- **Partido de Reunificación (PR).**
- **Partido Republicano.**
- **Unión para la Democracia y el Desarrollo Social (UDDS):** Libreville, Gabon; f. 1990; Sec.-Gen. ANTONIO SIBACHA BUEICHEKU.
- **Frente Democrático para la Reforma:** Libreville, Gabon; Sec.-Gen. BIYONGO BI-TUNG.

Junta Coordinadora de las Fuerzas de Oposición Democrática: Zaragoza, Spain; f. 1983; Pres. TEODORO MACKUANDJI BONDJALE OKO; comprises:

- **Alianza Nacional para la Restauración Democrática de Guinea Ecuatorial (ANRDGE):** BP 335, 1211 Geneva 4, Switzerland; f. 1974; Sec.-Gen. MARTÍN NSOMO OKOMO.
- **Frente de Liberación de Guinea Ecuatorial (FRELIGE).**

Movimiento de Liberación y Futuro de Guinea Ecuatorial (MOLIFUGE).

Partido Democrático de Guinea Ecuatorial (PDGE): Malabo; f. 1987; sole legal party 1987–92; Chair. Brig.-Gen. (TEODORO) OBIANG NGUEMA MBASOGO.

Plataforma de la Oposición Conjunta (POC): Madrid, Spain; Leader TOMÁS MACHEBA; alliance including the following political parties:

Convergencia para la Democracia Social (CPDS): Leader CELESTINO BACALE.

Partido de Coalición Social Democráticos.

Partido del Progreso de Guinea Ecuatorial (PPGE): Madrid, Spain; f. 1983; Pres. SEVERO MOTO NSA; Sec.-Gen. JOSÉ LUIS JONES.

Partido Socialdemócrata de Guinea Ecuatorial: Madrid, Spain; f. 1990; Pres. MARCELINO MANGUE MBA; Gen. Sec. TOMÁS MECHEBA FERNÁNDEZ.

Partido Socialista de Guinea Ecuatorial (PSGE): Madrid, Spain; maintains an office in Libreville, Gabon; Sec.-Gen. TOMÁS MACHEBA.

Unión Nacional para la Democracia.

Unión Socialdemocrática: Sec.-Gen. ANGEL MIKO ALO NCHAMA.

Unión Popular (UP): f. 1992; Pres. EUSEBIO EBOGA.

Reunión Democrática para la Liberación de Guinea Ecuatorial (RDLGE): Paris, France: f. 1981; formed 12-mem. provisional govt-in-exile in 1983; Pres. MANUEL RUBÉN NDONGO.

Unión Democrática y Social de Guinea Ecuatorial (UDSGE): Lisbon, Portugal; f. 1990; Pres. CARMELO MODÚ AKUSE.

Diplomatic Representation

EMBASSIES IN EQUATORIAL GUINEA

Cameroon: BP 292, Malabo; tel. and fax 22-63; Ambassador: JOHN NCHOTU AKUM.

China, People's Republic: Malabo; Ambassador: WANG YONGCHENG.

Cuba: Malabo; Ambassador: (vacant).

France: Carreterra del Aeropuerto, Malabo; tel. 20-05; Ambassador: JACQUES GAZON.

Gabon: Apdo 648, Douala, Malabo; tel. 420; telex 1125; Ambassador: JEAN-BAPTISTE MBATCHI.

Korea, Democratic People's Republic: Malabo; Ambassador: RYOM THAE RYUL.

Nigeria: 4 Paseo de los Cocoteros, Apdo 78, Malabo; tel. 23-86; Ambassador: JOHN SHINKAME.

Russia: Malabo; Ambassador: LEV ALEKSANDROVICH VAKHRAMEYEV.

Spain: Malabo; Ambassador: ARTURO AVELLÓ.

USA: Calle de Los Ministros, Apdo 597, Malabo; tel. 24-06; Ambassador: JOHN E. BENNETT.

Judicial System

The structure of Jucicial Administration was established in February 1981. The Supreme Tribunal in Malabo, consisting of a President of the Supreme Tribunal, the Presidents of the three chambers (civil, criminal and administrative), and two magistrates from each chamber, is the highest court of appeal, There are Territorial High Courst in Malabo and Bata, which are also courts of appeal. courts of the first instance exist in Malabo and bata, and may be convened in the other provincial capitals, and local courts may be convened when necessary.

President of the Supreme Tribunal: JULIO ELA NDONG.

Religion

An estimated 99% of the population are adherents of the Roman Catholic Church. Traditional forms of worship are also followed.

CHRISTIANITY

The Roman Catholic Church

Equatorial Guinea comprises one archdiocese and two dioceses. There were an estimated 361,100 adherents in the country at 31 December 1992.

Bishops' Conference: Arzobispado, Apdo 106, Malabo; f. 1984; Pres. Rt Rev. ANACLETO SIMA NGUA, Bishop of Bata.

Archbishop of Malabo: Most Rev. ILDEFONSO OBAMA OBONO, Arzobispado, Apdo 106, Malabo; tel. 29-09.

Protestant Church

Iglesia Evangélica de Guinea Ecuatorial (Evangelical Church of Equatorial Guinea): Apdo 195, Malabo; f. 1960; c. 8,000 mems; Sec.-Gen. Rev. SAMUEL OKE ESONO ATUGU.

The Press

Africa 2000: Apdo 180, Malabo; tel. 27-20; Spanish; cultural review; quarterly; publ. by Centro Cultural Hispano-Guineano; Editor DONATO NDONGO-BIDYOGO.

Ebano: Malabo; Spanish; irregular; circ. 1,000.

EL-Sol: Malabo; Spanish; weekly.

Hoja Parroquial: Malabo; weekly.

Potopoto: Apdo 236, Bata; Fang and Spanish; irregular; Dir FRANCISCO DE ANTA FRANCO.

Unidad de la Guinea Ecuatorial: Malabo; irregular.

La Verdad: Malabo; weekly; opposes Govt; publ. by the Convergencia para la Democracia Social; banned by Govt in Sept. 1993; Editor PLACIDO MIKO ABOGO.

FOREIGN NEWS BUREAU

Agencia EFE (Spain): 50 Calle del Presidente Nasser, Malabo; tel. 31-65; Bureau Chief DONATO NDONGO-BIDYOGO.

Publisher

Centro Cultural Hispano-Guineano: Apdo 180, Malabo; tel. 27-20.

Radio and Television

There were an estimated 153,000 radio receivers and 3,000 television receivers in use in 1991.

RADIO

Africa 2000: Camino de Basilé, Malabo; tel. 24-90; f. 1988; govt-controlled; cultural and educational programmes in Spanish; broadcasts suspended in Dec. 1993; Dir ANTONIO JOSÉ MÍNGUEZ PONS.

Radio Ecuatorial Bata: Apdo 749, Bata; tel. 182; govt-controlled; commercial station; programmes in Spanish, French and vernacular languages; Dir JESÚS OBIANG NGUEMA NDONG.

Radio Santa Isabel: Apdo 195, Malabo; tel. 382; govt-controlled; programmes in Spanish, French, Fang, Bubi, Annobonés and Combe; Dir JUAN EYENE OPKUA NGUEMA.

TELEVISION

Director of Television: MAXIMILIANO MBA.

Finance

(cap. = capital; p.u. = paid up; res = reserves; m. = million; br. = branch; amounts in francs CFA)

BANKING

Central Bank

Banque des Etats de l'Afrique Centrale (BEAC): Apdo 510 Malabo; tel. 20–10; telex 5407; fax 20–06; headquarters in Yaoundé, Cameroon; f. 1973 as the bank of issue for mem. states of the Customs and Economic Union of Central Africa (UDEAC), comprising Cameroon, the Central African Republic, Chad, the Congo, Equatorial Guinea and Gabon; cap. and res 203,500m. (Jan. 1993); Gov. JEAN-FÉLIX MAMALEPOT; Dir in Equatorial Guinea MARTÍN-CRISANTO EBE MBA; brs in Bata and Malabo.

Commercial Bank

Banco Meridien BIAO Guinea Ecuatorial (BMB-GE): 6 Calle de Argelia, Apdo 686, Malabo; tel. 28-87; telex 5403; fax 27-42; f. 1986; cap. p.u. 300m. (Dec. 1993); Pres. CASTRO NVONO AKELE; Gen. Man. CHARLES SANLAVILLE; 2 brs.

Financial Institution

Caja Autónoma de Amortización de la Deuda Pública: Ministry of the Economy and Finance, Malabo; tel. 31-05; fax 32-05; management of state funds; Dir PATRICIO EKA NGUEMA.

Trade and Industry

Cámara de Comercio, Agrícola y Forestal de Malabo: Apdo 51, Malabo; tel. 151.

Cámaras Oficiales Agrícolas de Guinea: Bioko and Bata; buys cocoa and coffee from indigenous planters, who are partially grouped in co-operatives.

Empresa General de Industria y Comercio (EGISCA): Malabo; f. 1986; parastatal body jtly operated with the French Société pour l'Organisation, l'Aménagement et le Développement des Industries Alimentaires et Agricoles (SOMDIA); import-export agency.

INPROCAO: Malabo; production, marketing and distribution of cocoa.

Oficina para la Cooperación con Guinea Ecuatorial (OCGE): Malabo; f. 1981; administers bilateral aid from Spain.

Sociedad Anónima de Desarrollo del Comercio (SOADECO-Guinée): Malabo; f. 1986; parastatal body jtly operated with the French Société pour l'Organisation, l'Aménagement et le Développement des Industries Alimentaires et Agricoles (SOMDIA); development of commerce.

Total-Guinée Equatoriale: Malabo; f. 1984; cap. 150m. francs CFA; 50% state-owned, 50% by CFP-Total (France); petroleum marketing and distribution; Chair. of Board of Dirs Minister of Public Works, Housing and Town Planning.

TRADE UNIONS

Union of Central African Workers (USTC): Malabo; Sec.-Gen. THEOPHILE SONNY-COLLE.

Transport

RAILWAYS

There are no railways in Equatorial Guinea.

ROADS

Bioko: a semi-circular tarred road serves the northern part of the island from Malabo down to Batete in the west and from Malabo to Bacake Grande in the east, with a feeder road from Luba to Moka and Bahía de la Concepción; total length of roads: about 160 km.

Río Muni: a tarred road links Bata with Mbini (Río Benito) in the west; another road, partly tarred, links Bata with the frontier post of Ebebiyin in the east and then continues into Gabon; other earth roads join Acurenam, Mongomo de Guadelupe and Nsork; total length of roads: 1,015 km.

SHIPPING

The main ports are Bata (general cargo), Malabo (general), Luba (bananas, timber), Mbini and Kogo (timber). A regular monthly service is operated by the Spanish Compañía Transmediterránea from Barcelona, calling at Malabo and Bata, and by other carriers.

CIVIL AVIATION

There is an international airport at Malabo, and a smaller airport at Bata. The national carrier, Compañia Ecuato-Guineana de Aviación, went into liquidation in early 1990. The regional airline, Air Afrique, agreed to maintain the country's national and regional flights, pending the establishment of a new carrier. In November 1990 the Government signed an agreement with a Nigerian private airline, Concord Airlines, providing for the operation of a service between Lagos and Bata, as well as domestic flights.

Tourism

Prior to the overthrow of President Macías Nguema in 1979, few foreigners visited Equatorial Guinea. Tourism remains undeveloped.

Defence

In June 1993 there were 1,100 men in the army, 120 in the navy and 100 in the air force. There was also a paramilitary force of 2,000. Military service is voluntary. Spain has provided military advisers and training since 1979, and the presidential guard is provided by Morocco, which maintains about 360 troops in the country. Military aid has also been received from the USA. Foreign military aid totalled US $150,000 in 1988.

Defence expenditure: Estimated at US $6m. in 1982.

Supreme Commander of the Armed Forces: Brig.-Gen. (TEODORO) OBIANG NGUEMA MBASOGO.

Education

Education, which is provided free of charge, is officially compulsory and free for eight years between the ages of six and 14 years. Primary education starts at six years of age and normally lasts for six years. Secondary education, beginning at the age of 12, also spans a six-year period, comprising a first cycle of four years and a second cycle of two years. In 1982 the total enrolment at primary and secondary schools was equivalent to 81% of the school-age population. In 1986 primary education in nine grades was provided for 65,000 pupils in 550 schools. More advanced education for 3,013 pupils was provided in 14 centres, with 288 teachers, in 1980/81.

Since 1979, assistance in the development of the educational system has been provided by Spain, which had 100 teaching staff working in Equatorial Guinea in 1986. Two higher education centres, at Bata and Malabo, are administered by the Spanish Universidad Nacional de Educación a Distancia and had 500 students in 1986. The French government also provides considerable financial assistance, and French was expected to become a compulsory subject in Equato-Guinean schools during the early 1990s. In 1983 the average rate of adult illiteracy was 38% (males 22.6%; females 51.5%). In 1988 budgetary expenditure on education by the central government amounted to 620m. francs CFA (3.9% of total expenditure).

Bibliography

Agencia Española de Cooperación Internacional. *Segundo plano marco de cooperación entre el Reino de España y la República de Guinea Ecuatorial.* Madrid, AECI, 1990.

Castro A., Mariano, and de la Calle Muñoz, M. L. *Geografía de Guinea Ecuatorial.* Madrid, Programa de Colaboración Educativa con Guinea Ecuatorial, 1985.

Castroviejo Bolívar, Javier, Juste Balleste, Javier, and Castelo Alvarez, Ramón. *Investigación y conservación de la naturaleza en Guinea Ecuatorial.* Madrid, Oficina de Cooperación con Guinea Ecuatorial, 1986.

Cohen, R. (Ed.) *African Islands and Enclaves.* London, Sage Publications, 1983.

Cronjé, S. *Equatorial Guinea: The Forgotten Dictatorship.* London, 1976.

Economist Intelligence Unit. *Congo, Gabon, Equatorial Guinea, Country Report.* London, quarterly.

Economist Intelligence Unit. *Gabon, Equatorial Guinea, Country Profile.* London, annual.

Eman, A. *Equatorial Guinea during the Macías Nguema régime.* Washington DC, 1983.

Fegley, R. *Equatorial Guinea: An African tragedy.* New York, Peter Lang, 1989.

Fernández, R. *Guinea: Materia reservada.* Madrid, 1977.

García Domínguez, R. *Guinea: Macías, la ley del silencio.* Barcelona, 1977.

González-Echegaray, C. *Estudios Guineos: Filología.* Madrid, IDEA, 1964.

Estudios Guineos: Etnología. Madrid, IDEA, 1964.

Jakobeit, C. 'Äquatorialguinea' in Hanisch, R. and Jakobeit, C. (Eds). *Der Kakaoweltmarkt,* Vol. 2. Hamburg, Deutsches Überseeinstitut, 1991.

Klitgaard, R. *Tropical Gangsters.* London, I. B. Tauris, 1990.

Kobel, A. E. *La République de Guinée Equatoriale, ses resources potentielles et virtuelles, et possibilités de développement.* Bern 1976.

Liniger-Goumaz, M. *Guinea Ecuatorial: Bibliografía General.* 5 vols. Berne and Geneva, 1976–85.

Equatorial Guinea: An African Historical Dictionary. Metuchen, NJ, Scarecrow Press, 1979.

La Guinée équatoriale, un pays méconnu. Paris, 1980.

De la Guinée équatoriale nguemiste. Eléments pour le dossier de l'afro-fascisme. Geneva, Editions du Temps, 1983.

Connaître la Guinée équatoriale. Rouen, Editions des Peuples Noirs, 1985.

Statistics of Nguemist Equatorial Guinea. Geneva, Editions du Temps, 1986.

Small is not always Beautiful: The Story of Equatorial Guinea. London, Hurst, 1988.

Martín de Molino, A. *Los Bubis, ritos y creencias.* Malabo, Centro Cultural Hispano-Guineano, 1989.

Miranda Díaz, M. *España en el continente africano.* Madrid, IDEA, 1963.

Moreno Moreno, A. *Reseña histórica de la presencia de España en el golfo de Guinea.* Madrid, IDEA, 1952.

Ndongo Bidyogo, D. *Historia y Tragedia de Guinea Ecuatorial.* Madrid, Cambio, 1977.

Nguema-Obam, P. *Aspects de la religion fang.* Paris, Editions Karthala, 1984.

Pélissier, R. *Los Territorios Españoles de Africa.* Madrid, 1964.

Etudes hispano-guinéennes. Orgeval, Editions Pélissier, 1969.

Africana. Bibliographies sur l'Afrique luso-hispanophone (1800–1980). Orgeval, Editions Pélissier, 1981.

Servicio Informativo Español. *España y Guinea Ecuatorial.* Madrid, 1968.

de Teran, M. *Sintesis geográfica de Fernando Póo.* Madrid, IDEA, 1962.

de Unzueta y Yuste, A. *Islas del Golfo de Guinea (Elobeyes, Corisco, Annobón, Príncipe y Santo Tomé).* Madrid, Institito de Estudios Políticos, 1945.

Historia geográfica de Fernando Póo. Madrid, IDEA, 1947.

ERITREA

Physical and Social Geography

MILES SMITH-MORRIS

The State of Eritrea, which formally acceded to independence on 24 May 1993, covers an area of 121,144 sq km (46,774 sq miles). Its territory includes the Dahlak islands, a low-lying coralline archipelago offshore from Massawa. Eritrea, which has a coastline on the Red Sea extending for almost 1,000 km, is bounded to the north-west by Sudan, to the south and west by the Ethiopian administrative regions of Gondar, Tigre and Wollo, and to the south-east by Djibouti. The terrain consists of the northern end of the Ethiopian plateau (rising to more than 2,000 m above sea-level), where most cultivation takes place, and a low-lying semi-desert coastal strip, much of which supports only pastoralism. Lowland areas have less than 500 mm of rainfall per year, compared with 1,000 mm in the highlands. Average annual temperatures range from 17°C in the highlands to 30°C in Massawa. The Danakil depression in the south-east descends to more than 130 m below sea-level and experiences some of the highest temperatures recorded on earth, frequently exceeding 50°C. Much of the coniferous forest that formerly covered the slopes of the highlands has been destroyed because of settlement and cultivation; soil erosion is a severe problem.

The country's natural resources await study and exploration. Copper ores and gold were mined from the Eritrean plateau in prehistoric times and there has been some extraction of iron ore, but exploration and exploitation of the country's mineral resources were halted by the war for independence. The Dallol depression, south of Massawa, is known to have valuable potash deposits. Some exploration for petroleum has taken place in Red Sea coastal areas; oil seepages and offshore natural gas finds have been recorded.

The population of Eritrea was enumerated at just over 2.7m. in the Ethiopian census of 1984, but the war for independence has resulted in large-scale population movements. Some 500,000 refugees are thought to be in neighbouring Sudan and a large, but unknown, number of Eritreans still live in Ethiopia. A total of 1.2m. people registered to vote in the April 1993 referendum, 860,000 of them within Eritrea, leading to estimates of a current domestic population of about 2m. The population is fairly evenly divided between Tigrinya-speaking Christians, the traditional inhabitants of the highlands, and the Muslim communities of the western lowlands, northern highlands and east coast.

Recent History

DAVID POOL

Revised for this edition by ALAN RAKE

Modern Eritrea dates from the establishment of an Italian colony at the end of the 19th century. From a small concession gained near Assab in 1869, the Italians extended their control to Massawa in 1885 and to most of Eritrea by 1889. In the same year the Ethiopian emperor, Menelik, and the Italian government signed the Treaty of Uccialli, which effectively recognized Italian control over Eritrea (and from which Italy derived its subsequent claim to a protectorate over Ethiopia). The Eritrea colony was formed in an area where, at times in the past, the peoples had had varying and discontinuous tributary relations with Ethiopian empires to the south, the Ottoman empire and Egypt on the Red Sea coast and various Sudanic empires to the west and north-west. Eritrea's entanglement with these different neighbouring political units prior to colonial rule brought forth highly contested versions of pre-colonial history, the most contentious of which was the Ethiopian claim that all of Eritrea had been an integral part of historic Ethiopia. This claim for sovereignty was as spurious as the claim that Eritrea had previously constituted a distinct entity. There were and are religious beliefs and practices common to Ethiopian and Eritrean Orthodox Christians, and Tigrinya, an Ethiopian language, is spoken both in highland Eritrea and in the northern-most Ethiopian province of Tigre. These cultural and religious ties, however, do not extend to other communities in Ethiopia. Similarly, large parts of Eritrea, notably the north and west, have had, at most, no more than minimal historic and cultural links to Ethiopia. Nevertheless, history provided the setting for the subsequent political and military struggle between Eritrean nationalists and Ethiopia.

The period of Italian rule (1889–1941) and the temporary British military administration (1941–1952) created a society, economy and polity more advanced than in the semi-feudal Ethiopian empire. Under Italian rule the rudiments of an urban social and economic order were founded, and in the British period political parties and trade unions were permitted and a free press was established as, successively, the victorious Allied powers and the UN discussed the future of the former Italian colony. Ethiopia pressed its territorial claims and mobilized support for political union largely among the Christian highlanders. The strategic interests of the USA and its influence in the newly-founded UN resulted in a compromise, in the form of a federation between Eritrea and Ethiopia. There was, however, no provision for proper federal institutions. Emperor Haile Selassie, an autocratic ruler, set about stifling Eritrean autonomy until, in 1962, its status was reduced to that of an Ethiopian province.

The dissolution of the federation brought forth a more militant Eritrean nationalism, whose political roots had been established during the process of consultation for the disposal of the Italian colony in the latter part of the period of British rule. The Eritrean Liberation Movement, founded in 1958, was succeeded by the Eritrean Liberation Front (ELF), which began an armed struggle in September 1961. Organizational and ideological differences erupted into violence within the ELF in the mid-1960s, as the result of demands for reform from the increasing numbers of educated guerrilla fighters, particularly those from the Christian highlands and the Muslim eastern lowland towns. A reformist group separated from the ELF and formed the

Popular Liberation Forces (renamed the Eritrean People's Liberation Front—EPLF, in 1977). A major consequence of the split was the civil war of 1972–74. Some reformists, however, remained within the ELF, although most of these eventually left in two stages, the first group breaking away in 1977–78 and the second (the Sagem group joining the EPLF) in 1985, following a second civil war. These desertions destroyed the ELF as a coherent military organization, although a number of disaffected factions remained loyal to it and suspicious of the EPLF. The most influential groups remaining outside the EPLF have been those associated with Ahmed Nasser, leader of the ELF—Revolutionary Council, and an Islamic movement which emerged during the 1980s among refugees in Sudan. The EPLF leadership consolidated a highly centralized and disciplined political and military organization, in contrast to the more loosely organized and factionalized ELF.

The course of the 1974 revolution in Ethiopia and its violent aftermath brought thousands of new recruits into the resistance groups. Even greater numbers of recruits joined the EPLF after the Mengistu regime launched its 'red terror' campaign in Asmara, and following its capture of smaller cities such as Keren and Decamhare in 1977. The retreat from the cities and liberated highland areas in 1978 brought with it thousands of young peasants, both male and female. From 1978 onwards the EPLF consolidated the defence of its base area in the north. Through the 1980s the EPLF pushed back the Ethiopian forces on all fronts, capturing large quantities of heavy artillery and tanks, and transforming itself from a guerrilla force into a regular army. Ethiopian defeats gave the EPLF control of the north, the west (formerly the ELF's heartland) and, finally, the east coast with the capture of Massawa port in 1990. The EPLF broke through the Decamhare front in May 1991 and entered Asmara, the capital. The retreating Ethiopian forces left the city largely undamaged. The discipline of the Eritrean People's Liberation Army (EPLA) and the extensive network of secret cells in the capital helped to ensure a smooth transition from liberation movement to government.

Concurrent with the liberation of Asmara in 1991 was the London Conference under the chairmanship of Herman Cohen, the US assistant secretary of state for Africa. Representatives of the EPLF attended in a delegation separate from the Ethiopian People's Revolutionary Democratic Front (EPRDF), now in control of Ethiopia and sympathetic to Eritrean nationalist aspirations. Both the USA and the Ethiopian delegation accepted the EPLF as the provisional government, and the latter agreed to hold a referendum on independence in 1993. Ethiopian assent to this process played an important role in the international legitimation of Eritrea's path to independence. In advance of the referendum, the EPLF formed a government and established ministries, most of whose key personnel were drawn from the EPLF. Although the international and regional political context was favourable for the transition to independence, the international economic context, prolonged warfare, drought and the legacy of neglect and destruction left by the Ethiopian forces placed the new government in straitened circumstances; 80% of the population were still dependent on food aid and urban economic activity was almost at a standstill. Over and above these domestic problems was the task of attracting back and reintegrating around 750,000 refugees. Of these, there are 500,000 in neighbouring Sudan, 90% of whom are very poor and will require comprehensive assistance to return. An additional legacy of war is the scale of fatalities, which have been estimated at 60,000–75,000.

In the absence of any significant sources of domestic revenue for reconstruction, the task of rebuilding fell largely on the 75,000-strong EPLA, the members of which received a small stipend for their work. Administrative and technical cadres have taken government positions, skilled fighter-workers have been used to reconstruct manufacturing industry and many ordinary fighters have been drafted to undertake the arduous work of road and other infrastructural repair. Finance for reconstruction has come largely from contributions by Eritreans abroad and from assistance by foreign governments and non-governmental organizations. Foreign assistance amounted to US $140m. 'in the past year', according to the new head of state, Issaias Afewerki, in a speech in June 1993. Without full legal sovereignty, access to loans and assistance from international financial institutions was limited, but in 1993 this formal constraint was removed. During 23–25 April a UN-supervised referendum took place in an atmosphere of national celebration. Of the 1,102,410 Eritreans who voted, 99.8% endorsed national independence. The anniversary of the liberation of Asmara, 24 May, was proclaimed Independence Day, and on 28 May the State of Eritrea became the 182nd member of the UN.

Following Eritrea's formal accession to independence, a four-year transitional period was declared, during which preparations were to proceed for establishing a constitutional and pluralist political system. At the apex of the transitional government were three state institutions: the consultative council (the executive authority formed from the ministers, provincial governors and heads of government commissions); the national assembly (the legislative authority formed from the central committee of the EPLF with the addition of 30 members from the provincial assemblies and an additional 30 individuals selected by the central committee); and the judiciary. One of the national assembly's first acts was the election of a head of state. To little surprise, Issaias Afewerki, the secretary-general of the EPLF, was elected, by a margin of 99 votes to five.

President Afewerki appointed a new state council in early June 1993, comprising 14 ministers (all members of the EPLF politburo) and 10 regional governors. Ramadan Muhammed Nur was removed from the politically sensitive post of governor of Danakil province (where he had successfully contained Afar nationalism) and was appointed minister of local government, a post which was expected to assume increasing importance during the transition process. Another prominent EPLF member, Petros Solomon, was allocated the defence portfolio. The third congress of the EPLF was convened at Nakfa, in Sahel province, in early February 1994. There the EPLF effected the formal transformation from a military front to a national movement for peace and democracy (the People's Front for Democracy and Justice—PFDJ), hoping to embrace all Eritreans (with the exception of those accused of collaboration during the liberation struggle). The party congress also confirmed its support for a plural political system which was to be included in the final draft of a new constitution, which (together with legislation to regulate the formation of political parties) was to be submitted for approval by a national referendum. Afewerki was elected chairman of an 18-member executive committee (while remaining head of state, and leader of the PFDJ). A 75-member PFDJ central committee was also elected (an additional 75 members were to be elected by PFDJ regional committees).

In early March 1994 the national assembly adopted a series of resolutions (Decree No 52), including an amendment to Decree No 37 (which had defined the structure of the executive administration), whereby the former executive body, the consultative council, was formally superseded by a 16-member cabinet. (Former government authorities with responsibility for transport and tourism were to be upgraded to ministerial level.) Other measures adopted by resolutions of the assembly included the creation of a 50-member constitutional commision, and the establishment of a committee charged with the reorganization of the country's administrative divisions. It was also decided that the national assembly would henceforth comprise 75 members of the PFDJ central committee, and 75 directly elected members. However, all but eight of the 50-member constitutional commission were government appointees, and there was no provision for any opposition participation in the interim system. Democratic elections were not expected before 1997 at the earliest. Afewerki implemented a ministerial reshuffle in March following the resignation of veteran nationalist Ramadan Muhammad Nur. All members of the new state council were EPLF stalwarts. Petros Solomon was moved to the foreign ministry and Mesfin Hagos became minister of defence. However, the reorganization was widely interpreted as an attempt to formalize a separation of the functions of the government and the PFDJ executive. Amin Muhammad Sa'id, who had occupied the information and culture portfolio, was omitted from the new state council, having been recently nominated secretary-general of the PFDJ. One of the first actions of the new state council was to draft new legislation governing investment, which was expected to result in a significant liberalization of trade.

In April 1994 26 members of the opposition Eritrean Liberation Front—Revolutionary Council (ELF-RC) were arrested and detained in Ethiopia, where the men had previously been allowed to live peacefully. Their sudden arrest was interpreted as a direct result of defence agreements signed between Eritrea and Ethiopia in 1993. Other ELF-RC leaders were reported to have been forcibly repatriated to Eritrea.

Eritrea gradually increased its international contacts during 1993. Diplomatic ties were established with Sudan, Ethiopia, Israel, Australia and Pakistan, and several international organizations, shortly after independence. Relations with Ethiopia improved considerably during 1993. An agreement for the joint use of the ports of Assab and Massawa was signed in July, while in August it was reported that 90,000 Ethiopian prisoners of war had been released by the Eritrean government. In late September the first meeting of the Ethiopian-Eritrean joint ministerial commission was held in Asmara, during which agreement was reached on measures to allow the free movement of nationals between each country, and on co-operation regarding foreign affairs and economic policy. However, cordial relations with several Arab states deteriorated following the publication and dissemination of articles critical of the Afewerki administration by the militant Islamic fundamentalist organization, Jihad Islamiyya, based in Sudan. Following a border incident in December 1993 during which some 20 alleged fundamentalist infiltrators from Sudan were killed by Eritrean security forces (three Eritrean soldiers and two civilians were also killed), in early 1994 Afewerki suggested to the UN Security Council that the Sudanese government was supporting subversion by Islamic fundamentalists of the Eritrean Islamic Jihad operating from bases in Sudan. Afewerki accused the Sudanese National Islamic Front (NIF) under the leadership of Dr Hassan El Turabi, of fomenting unrest among the nearly 1m. Eritrean refugees resident in Sudan. While the Sudanese government denied that it or the NIF were involved in such actions, reports that nationals of Afghanistan, Pakistan, Morocco and Tunisia (apparently trained by Iranian instructors within Sudan) had been among the 20 victims of the December 1993 invasion, appeared to substantiate rumours of several such training camps, close to Sudan's borders, arousing considerable concern in Uganda and Kenya.

Sudan is burdened by the number of Eritrean refugees remaining within its borders and in January 1994 announced that it would repatriate up to half a million Eritrean refugees from 30 camps within its territory, over a period of months.

In early May 1994, following a three-day official visit to France (the first such visit undertaken to a Western nation since independence), President Afewerki announced that financial commitments amounting to some 20m. francs had been secured, from the French government, for the rehabilitation of the airport and the water-supply system in Asmara.

Economy

Revised for this edition by the Editor

There is little statistical information available on the Eritrean economy. However, it is estimated that Eritrea is one of the poorest countries in Africa, with an annual income of between US $75–$150 per head. Although Eritrea has the distinction of being one of the very few non-debtor states in Africa, many of its people are without even a basic subsistence income; at the end of the war in 1991 it was estimated that more than 85% of the population were surviving on international relief. The need for the government to redevelop the economy is, therefore, the greatest challenge facing the country. In 1993 it was estimated that it would cost about $3,000m. to begin the reconstruction of the economy and infrastructure. However, in 1992, according to the government relief co-ordination office, Eritrea received less than $32m. in overseas aid. Moreover, in early 1994 there was virtually no foreign investment in the country.

By far the most important sector of the economy is agriculture, which, despite a reduction in food production of roughly 40% between 1980 and 1990, still sustains 90% of the population. Most sedentary agriculture is practised in the highlands, where rainfall is sufficient to cultivate the main crops: teff (an indigenous grain), maize, wheat, sorghum and millet. In 1992, which was described as a satisfactory year in agricultural terms, some 315,000 ha of land were cultivated, and the harvest was good enough to satisfy an estimated 54% of Eritrea's food requirements. The grain harvest increased from some 70,000 metric tons in 1991 to between 250,000 and 300,000 tons in 1992, but 1993 was a disastrous year, following the almost complete failure of the rains and the persistent problems caused by crop pests. As a result, 80% of the grain crop was estimated to have been lost, and there was a cereal deficit of almost 200,000 tons. Much of the country, therefore, required the distribution of emergency food aid. In June 1993 the World Food Programme announced the launch of a six-month emergency food operation (including several food-for-work projects) to assist more than 500,000 Eritreans suffering serious food shortages.

In an effort to stimulate production, the Eritrean authorities have exempted agricultural (and industrial) exports from sales tax, although they will continue to be subject to export duty. However, lack of animal power, seed grains and capital equipment (in 1993 Eritrea had only 47 tractors) will certainly hamper the long-term development of the agricultural sector. Serious environmental degradation, caused directly and indirectly by the war, also presents a huge problem. Owing to the problem of water scarcity and unreliable rainfall, careful water management and conservation are essential. In 1992 17 water reservoirs and 20 small dams were built as part of an effort to improve water harvesting. In an attempt to prevent soil erosion, more than 40,000 km of badly eroded hillsides have been terraced and 22m. new trees planted.

Fisheries are a potential growth area for the Eritrean economy and have been given serious consideration. An FAO-sponsored conference was held in Massawa in March 1993 to discuss measures to develop Eritrea's marine fishery resources. Fishing of sardines, anchovies, tuna, shark and mackerel is practised in the waters of the Red Sea. UN fishery experts have estimated an annual yield of around 70,000 metric tons. However, much of the catch is smuggled abroad, since government price controls and a poor transport infrastructure have discouraged the development of a domestic market, in the past. In May 1994 the China State Construction and Engineering Co was awarded a 3.7m. birr contract to build a new fishing centre at the port of Massawa.

Eritrea's shattered industrial base traditionally centered on the production of glass, cement, footwear and canned goods. Although some of the 40 public-sector factories—producing textiles, footwear, beverages and other light industrial goods—were operating in 1991, they were doing so at only one-third capacity. The industrial sector is believed to require at least an initial $30m. of capital investment in order to begin operating to capacity. The government has calculated that the cost of industrial recovery would be $20m. for the private sector and $66m. for the state sector. A new investment code has been issued, which prescribes tax allowances on income, low import and export duties for up to five years, and duty-free imports of materials required to establish industrial enterprises. In a further effort to encourage foreign investment and the development of a free market, the government has guaranteed that property will not be nationalized or confiscated, prices will not be fixed and the state will not hold monopolies.

Although the government has stated that its aim is to create a free-market economy, there has, as yet, been little international aid provided by large bilateral donors such as the USA. Suspicions aroused by the ruling party's former Marxist ideology are believed to have been one factor in this delay. Aside from lack of investment, two major structural problems hamper the expansion of Eritrea's manufacturing base: firstly, the acute lack of local demand for all but the most basic manufactures; and, secondly, the absence of domestic energy resources. Unless reserves of petroleum or natural gas are discovered off shore, Eritrea will have to import all of its energy needs for the foreseeable future.

Eritrea's mineral resources are believed to be of significant potential value. Of particular importance, in view of Eritrea's acute energy shortage, is the possibility of large reserves of petroleum and natural gas beneath the Red Sea. In early 1993 the government made petroleum exploration regulations more stringent, and British Petroleum, which had signed a contract for petroleum exploration with the former Ethiopian regime, had its exploration rights invalidated. A US petroleum company, Amoco, and the International Petroleum Corporation of Canada are the only two remaining companies with concessions. The latter has operating rights in the 31,000 sq km Danakil block along the Eritrean coast, where there are believed to be good prospects for petroleum and gas discoveries. However, the two companies are still waiting for the legal status of their contracts, signed under the Mengistu regime, to be determined. In November 1993 a new code of practise regulating the petroleum sector was promulgated, hoping to attract investors. Conditions are considered to be liberal, providing for a 25-year licence with renewal periods of 10 years. Several prominent petroleum companies, including Amoco, Andarko, Total, Chevron, Mobil and Shell have expressed an interest in exploration and distribution. A local company, Prima, backed by expatriate Eritrean shareholders and Shell-Eritrea, is expected to handle internal distribution.

Gold-bearing seams exist in many of the igneous rocks forming the highlands of Eritrea. There are at least 15 gold mines and a large number of prospects close to Asmara, and the potential for new discoveries in the area is considered good. In the vicinity of Barentu, 150 km west of Asmara, there is also a region of widespread gold mineralization.

In March 1993 the International Development Association approved a credit of SDR 18.1m. (US $25m.) to support Eritrea's $147m., two-year Recovery and Rehabilitation Programme, which was to be funded by a series of loans on concessionary terms. The second largest contributor was Italy, which pledged $24.3m. Contributions were also promised by a number of other European countries, the EU and the UN Development Programme. The main components in the programme were: agricultural and industrial input, equipment for infrastructural development, mechanical, electrical and telecommunications spare parts, construction materials for social utilities and cottage industries, and support for administration and economic planning.

Steps towards international economic assimilation were taken in May 1993, when Eritrea was admitted to the group of African, Caribbean and Pacific (ACP) countries party to the Lomé Convention. In September an IMF delegation visited Asmara and held talks with the government regarding Eritrea's application to join the Fund, and in August 1994 Eritrea became the 179th member of the IMF, with an initial quota of SDR 11.5m. Eritrea is eager to show the international donor community its commitment to implementing a liberal trade and exchange regime and developing an export-orientated domestic economy. As early as January 1992 Eritrea and Ethiopia signed an agreement whereby the port of Assab became a free port for Ethiopia, and which provided for tax-free trade between the two countries, using the Ethiopian birr as currency. International donors are fully aware that the future of Eritrea's economy will very much depend on economic relations with Ethiopia.

Statistical Survey

Area and Population

AREA, POPULATION AND DENSITY*

Area (sq km)	121,144†
Population (provisional census results)	
9 May 1984	2,703,998
Density (per sq km) at 9 May 1984	22.3

* Including the Assab district.
† 46,774 sq miles.

Note: In 1993 the domestic population was estimated to be about 2m., based on the total of 1.2m. people who registered to vote in the April 1993 referendum, 860,000 of whom lived in Eritrea.

PRINCIPAL TOWN
(population at 1984 census)

Asmara (capital)	275,385

Finance

CURRENCY AND EXCHANGE RATES

Monetary Units
100 cents = 1 birr.

Sterling and Dollar Equivalents (31 March 1994)
£1 sterling = 7.423 birr;
US $1 = 5.000 birr;
100 birr = £13.472 = $20.000.

Note: Following its secession from Ethiopia in May 1993, Eritrea retained the Ethiopian currency. The exchange rate of US $1 = 5.000 birr was introduced in October 1992 and remained in force until April 1994, when it was adjusted to $1 = 5.130 birr. The currency was further devalued in May 1994.

Directory

The Constitution

In May 1993 the transitional Government issued Decree No. 37, defining the structure, powers and duties of the executive administration during a four-year transitional period. The Decree also created a legislature, the National Assembly, comprising the Central Committee of the Eritrean People's Liberation Front (later restyled the People's Front for Democracy and Justice) and 60 additional representatives. During the transitional period the National Assembly was to be the supreme legislative authority. The Government established a commission to initiate the drafting of a constitution. Decree No 52, adopted in March 1994, included an amendment to Decree No 37, providing for the establishment of a 16-member State Council.

The Government

HEAD OF STATE

President: ISSAIAS AFEWERKI (assumed power May 1991; elected President by National Assembly 8 June 1993).

STATE COUNCIL
(August 1994)

President: ISSAIAS AFEWERKI.
Minister of Defence: MESFIN HAGOS.
Minister of Internal Affairs: ALI SAYYID ABDULLAH.
Minister of Justice: FAWZIYYAH HASHIM.
Minister of Foreign Affairs: PETROS SOLOMON.
Minister of Information and Culture: BARAKI GEBRE SELASSIE.
Minister of Finance and Development: HAILE WOLDE TENSAE.
Minister of Trade and Industry: EKUBA ABRAHA.
Minister of Agriculture: TESFAY GIRMATZION.
Minister of Local Government: MUHAMMAD AHMED SHARIFO.
Minister of Marine Resources: DR SALIH MEKKI.
Minister of Construction: ABRAHA ASFEW.
Minister of Energy, Mining and Water Resources: TESFAY GEBRE SELASSIE.
Minister of Education: OSMAN SALIH MUHAMMAD.
Minister of Health: SEBHAT EPHREM.
Minister of Transport: DR GIORGIS TEKLE MIKAEL.
Minister of Tourism: WORKU TESFAY MIKAEL.

MINISTRIES AND COMMISSIONS

Ministry of Agriculture: POB 1024, Asmara; tel. 118699; fax 118193.
Ministry of Construction: POB 841, Asmara; tel. 119077.
Ministry of Defence: POB 629, Asmara; tel. 113349; fax 114920.
Ministry of Education: POB 5610, Asmara; tel. 113044; fax 113866.
Ministry of Energy, Mining and Water Resources: POB 5285, Asmara; tel. 116872; fax 117652.
Ministry of Finance and Development: POB 896, Asmara; tel. 113633; fax 117947.
Ministry of Foreign Affairs: POB 190, Asmara; tel. 113556; fax 113788.
Ministry of Health: POB 212, Asmara; tel. 112877; fax 112899.
Ministry of Information and Culture: POB 242, Asmara; tel. 115171; fax 119847.
Ministry of Internal Affairs: POB 250, Asmara; tel. 119299; fax 114920.
Ministry of Justice: POB 241, Asmara; tel. 111822.
Ministry of Local Government: POB 225, Asmara; tel. 113006.
Ministry of Marine Resources: POB 923, Asmara; tel. 114271; fax 112185.
Ministry of Tourism: Asmara.
Ministry of Trade and Industry: POB 1844, Asmara; tel. 123910; fax 120586.
Ministry of Transport: POB 204, Asmara; tel. 110144.
Commission for Eritrean Refugee Affairs: POB 198, Asmara; tel. 112495; fax 112861.
Housing Commission: POB 348, Asmara; tel. 117400.
Land Commission: POB 976, Asmara; tel. 110125.

Provincial Administrators

Administrator of Ademhar Province: IBRAHIM IDRIS TOTIL.
Administrator of Akele Guzay Province: SALIH AHMED IYAYE.
Administrator of Asmara Province: SEBHAT EPHREM (acting).
Administrator of Barka Province: AMIN SHEIKH SALIH.
Administrator of Danakil Province: HAMID AHMED KARIKAREH.
Administrator of Gash and Setit Province: GERMANO NATI.
Administrator of Hamasien Province: BERHANE GEBRE EGZIABHIER.
Administrator of Sahel Province: MUHAMMAD SA'ID NAWID.
Administrator of Senhit Province: ASMEROM GEBRE EGZIABHIER.
Administrator of Seraye Province: ADHANOM GEBRE MARIAM.

Legislature

NATIONAL ASSEMBLY

In accordance with transitional arrangements formulated in Decree No. 37 of May 1993, the National Assembly consists of the Central Committee of the People's Front for Democracy and Justice (PFDJ) and 60 other members: 30 from the Provincial Assemblies and an additional 30 members, including a minimum of 10 women, to be nominated by the PFDJ Central Committee. The legislative body 'outlines the internal and external policies of the government, regulates their implementation, approves the budget and elects a president for the country'. The National Assembly is to hold regular sessions every six months under the chairmanship of the President. In his role as Head of the Government and Commander-in-Chief of the Army, the President nominates individuals to head the various government departments. These nominations are ratified by the legislative body. In March 1994 the National Assembly voted to alter its composition, to include 75 members of the Central Committee of the PFDJ and 75 directly elected members.
Chairman of the National Assembly: ISSAIAS AFEWERKI.

Political Organizations

At independence in May 1993, many of the rival political organizations to the Eritrean People's Liberation Front (now the People's Front for Democracy and Justice) declared their support for the transitional Government.

Democratic Movement for the Liberation of Eritrea: opposition group; Leader HAMID TURKY.

Eritrean Islamic Jihad: extremist opposition group; in Aug. 1993 split into a mil. wing and a political wing, led by Sheikh MOHAMED ARAFA.

Eritrean Liberation Front (ELF): f. 1958; commenced armed struggle in 1961; subsequently split into numerous factions (see below); mainly Muslim support; rivals to PFDJ.

Eritrean Liberation Front—Central Command (ELF—CC): f. 1982; Chair. ABDALLAH IDRISS.

Eritrean Liberation Front—National Council (ELF—NC): Leader ABDULKADER JAILANY.

Eritrea Liberation Front—Revolutionary Council (ELF—RC): Leader AHMED NASSER.

People's Front for Democracy and Justice (PFDJ): Asmara; f. 1970 as the Eritrean People's Liberation Front, by secession from the Eritrean Liberation Front; adopted present name in Feb. 1994; Christian and Muslim support; in May 1991 took control of Eritrea and formed provisional Govt; maintains Eritrean People's Liberation Army (EPLA) numbering c. 85,000; formed transitional Govt in May 1993; 18-mem. Exec. Cttee, 75-mem. Cen. Cttee; Chair. ISSAIAS AFEWERKI; Sec.-Gen. AMIN MUHAMMAD SA'ID.

Judicial System

The judicial system is being reorganized by the transitional Government. At present the legal system incorporates laws adopted by the Eritrean People's Liberation Front prior to and following liberation, together with elements of customary law and Islamic law. Decree No. 37, issued in May 1993, stated that Eritrean courts 'perform their duties according to the law and independently of the legislative and executive bodies of the Eritrean Government and safeguard the rights, interests and freedoms of the Government, associations and individuals, which are stated by the law.'

Diplomatic Representation

EMBASSIES IN ERITREA

China, People's Republic: POB 204, Asmara; tel. 116988.

Djibouti: Asmara; tel. 114189; Ambassador: OMER SAID AHMED.

Egypt: 45 Degiat Afwerk St, Asmara; tel. 119935; Ambassador: MOHAMED AFIFI BADER.

Ethiopia: Franklin D. Roosevelt St, Asmara; tel. 115962; Ambassador: AWALOM WOLDU.

Israel: Asmara; Ambassador: MENASHE ZIPORI.

Italy: 45 Shemelis Habte St, Asmara; tel. 118914; fax 111115; Ambassador: GIOVANNI GERMANO.

Sudan: POB 371, Asmara; tel. 118176; fax 110287; Ambassador: JAFER HASSAN SALEH.

USA: POB 211, Asmara; tel. 113720; fax 117584; Ambassador: ROBERT HOUDEK.

Yemen: POB 5566, Asmara; tel. 112396; fax 118871; Ambassador: AHMED ABDALLA BOSHO.

Religion

Eritrea is almost equally divided between Muslims and Christians. Most Christians are adherents of the Orthodox Church, although there are Protestant and Roman Catholic communities. A small number of the population follow traditional beliefs.

CHRISTIANITY

The Eritrean Orthodox Church

Following meetings held in Asmara in September 1993, the Ethiopian Orthodox and Eritrean Orthodox church leaders agreed to recognize the Eritrean Orthodox Church as a separate entity from the Ethiopian Orthodox Church. The Eritrean Orthodox Church announced plans to appoint a bishop for each of the country's 10 provinces.

Leader: Bishop PHILIPPOS.

The Roman Catholic Church

Alexandrian-Ethiopian Rite

At 31 December 1992 the diocese of Asmara contained an estimated 72,081 adherents.

Bishop of Asmara: Rt Rev. ZEKARIAS YOHANNES, 19 Gondar St, POB 244, Asmara; tel. 110206.

Latin Rite

The Apostolic Vicariate of Asmara, covering the whole of Eritrea, had 32,621 adherents at 31 December 1992.

Apostolic Administrator: Fr LUCA MILESI, 107 National Ave, POB 224, Asmara; tel. 110631; fax 112322.

The Anglican Communion

Within the Episcopal Church in Jerusalem and the Middle East, Eritrea forms part of the diocese of Egypt.

Leader: ASFAHA MAHARY.

ISLAM

There are substantial Muslim communities in the western lowlands, the northern highlands and the eastern coastal region.

Leader: Sheikh AL-AMIN OSMAN AL-AMIN.

The Press

Chamber News: POB 856, Asmara; tel. 111388; Tigrinya and English; publ. by Asmara Chamber of Commerce.

Eritrea Profile: POB 247, Asmara; f. 1994; weekly; English; publ. by the Ministry of Information and Culture.

Hadas Eritra (New Eritrea): Asmara; f. 1991; twice a week; in English, Tigrinya and Arabic; govt publ. Editor YITBAREK ZEROM; circ. 25,000.

Trade and Development Bulletin: POB 856, Asmara; tel. 110814; telex 42079; monthly; Tigrinya and English; publ. by the Asmara Chamber of Commerce; Editor TAAME FOTO.

Radio and Television

Communications and Postal Authority: POB 234, Asmara; tel. 112900; fax 110938; Dir LEULE GEBREAB.

RADIO

Voice of the Broad Masses of Eritrea (Dimseehafash): Asmara; govt station; programmes in Arabic, Tigrinya, Tigre, Afar and Kunama.

TELEVISION

ERI-TV: Asmara: f. 1992; govt station providing educational, tech. and information service; broadcasting began in Jan. 1993 in Arabic and Tigrinya; transmissions limited to Asmara and surrounding areas.

Finance

The unit of currency in Eritrea is the Ethiopian birr. Negotiations on future arrangements were proceeding in 1994 between the Governments of Eritrea and Ethiopia.

BANKING

Bank of Eritrea: POB 849, Asmara; tel. 123033; telex 42065; fax 123162; f. 1993; Gov. ANDEBERHANE WOLDE GIORGIS.

Trade and Industry

During the war of independence much of Eritrea's industrial base was either destroyed or dismantled and removed to Ethiopia. The authorities in Asmara have estimated the initial cost of industrial regeneration to be US $20m. for the private sector and $66m. for the public sector. As part of its commitment to a free-market system, the Government plans to divest itself of some 40 public enterprises which have recommenced production, but only at about one-third capacity. The greatest challenge facing Eritrean industry remains the acute shortage of energy. Large offshore petroleum deposits beneath the Red Sea and substantial natural gas reserves in the Danakil depression have yet to be effectively exploited.

CHAMBER OF COMMERCE

Asmara Chamber of Commerce: POB 856, Asmara.

Transport

Eritrea's original transport infrastructure was severely damaged during the three decades of war. As part of the Government's Recovery and Rehabilitation Programme, US $27m. has been allocated to road reconstruction and $10.2m. to improving port facilities.

Ministry of Transport: POB 204, Asmara; tel. 110144.

RAILWAYS

The railway connection between Agordat, Asmara and the port of Massawa was dismantled during the war, and the Government has not allocated any funds, under its current programme, to reconstruct the line.

ROADS

Most of Eritrea's road system is unpaved. Roads that are paved require considerable repair, as do many of the bridges across seasonal water courses destroyed in the war. Road construction between Asmara and the port of Massawa is being given particular priority in the Recovery and Rehabilitation Programme.

SHIPPING

Eritrea has two major seaports: Massawa, which was heavily bombed in 1990 after being captured by forces of the Eritrean People's Liberation Front; and Assab, which, in the past, principally served Addis Ababa, in Ethiopia. Under an agreement signed between the Ethiopian and Eritrean Governments in 1993, the two countries will share the facilities of both ports. Since the end of the war, activity in Massawa has increased. In 1992 a total of 228 vessels docked there, unloading 559,000 metric tons of goods; 11,000 tons of export goods passed through the port. Traffic and revenues have risen by 20% since 1991.

Port and Maritime Transport Authority: POB 851, Asmara; tel. 111399; fax 113647; Dir WELDE MIKAEL ABRAHAM.

CIVIL AVIATION

The international airport is at Asmara. Air Eritrea operates an internal service between Assab and Asmara.

Civil Aviation Authority: POB 252, Asmara; tel. 113769; fax 110665; Dir PAULOS KAHSAY.

Tourism

With Eritrea's transport infrastructure still requiring massive repair, the prospects for tourism seem to be limited. However, the country possesses many areas of scenic and scientific interest, including the Dahlak Islands (a coral archipelego rich in marine life), off the coast from Massawa, and the massive escarpment rising up from the coastal plain, with its own unique climate and wildlife. In late 1993 the transitional Government inaugurated a programme of privatization of state-operated hotels in Asmara, Massawa, Keren and Assab. Responsibility for tourism now resides with the Ministry of Tourism.

Defence

In mid-1993 the forces of the Eritrean People's Liberation Front (which dominated the government formed at independence) were estimated to number about 80,000 men and women. By late 1993 some 26,000 combatants—those who had joined after 1990—had been demobilized. The Eritrean authorities are widely believed to have assumed control of the Ethiopian navy, based in the ports of Massawa and Assab. Military service is compulsory for all Eritreans between 18 and 40 years of age, for a period of 12–18 months.

Education

Education, which is not compulsory, is provided free of charge in government schools and at the University of Asmara. There are also some fee-paying private schools. Owing to the severe disruption to many people's education caused by the war, there are no strict age-groups at any particular level. However, as an approximate guide, nursery education begins at four years of age, elementary (grades 1–6) is from six to 10 years of age, junior secondary (grades 7–8) is from 10 to 13 years of age, and secondary (grades 9–12) is from 13 to 17 years of age.

Bibliography

Cliffe, L., and Davidson, B. (Eds). *The Long Struggle of Eritrea for Independence and Constructive Peace*. London, Spokesman, 1988.

Erlich, H. *The Struggle over Eritrea 1962–78*. Stanford, CA, Hoover Institution, 1983.

Gebregergis, T. *Eritrea: An Account of an Eritrean Political Exile on his Visit to Liberated Eritrea: December 1991–March 1992*. Amsterdam, Liberation Books, 1993.

Gebre-Medhin, J. *Peasants and Nationalism in Eritrea*. Trenton, NJ, Red Sea Press, 1989.

Legum, C., and Lee, B. *Conflict in the Horn of Africa*. London, Rex Collings, 1977.

Lewis, I. M. (Ed.). *Nationalism in the Horn of Africa*. London, Ithaca Press, 1983.

Markakis, J. *National and Class Conflict in the Horn of Africa*. Cambridge, Cambridge University Press (African Studies Series No. 55), 1988.

Medhanie, T. *Eritrea: The Dynamics of a National Question*. Amsterdam, B. R. Grunner, 1986.

Pateman, R. *Eritrea: Even the Stones are Burning*. Trenton, NJ, Red Sea Press, 1990.

Sherman, R. *Eritrea: The Unfinished Revolution*. New York, Praeger, 1980.

ETHIOPIA

Physical and Social Geography

G. C. LAST

The People's Democratic Republic of Ethiopia is a land-locked country in the Horn of Africa. Its boundaries stretch from latitude 3°N to 15°N and from longitude 33°E to 48°E, enclosing an area of 1,130,138 sq km (436,349 sq miles). Ethiopia's western neighbour is Sudan; to the south it shares a border with Kenya; and to the east and south-east lie the Republic of Djibouti and Somalia. To the north and north-east lies Eritrea (the former Ethiopian state gained independence in May 1993).

Boundary changes announced in November 1991 divided Ethiopia (excluding Eritrea) into 12 self-governing regions and two chartered cities (Addis Ababa and Harar). These arrangements were based on those in operation prior to 1987, when Ethiopia (inclusive of Eritrea) was divided into 24 Administrative Regions and five Autonomous Regions.

PHYSICAL FEATURES

Elevations range from around 100 m below sea-level in the Dallol Depression (Kobar Sink), on the north-eastern border with Eritrea, to a number of mountain peaks in excess of 4,000 m above sea-level, which dominate the plateaux and of which the highest is Ras Dashen, rising to 4,620 m, in the Semien mountain massif, north-east of Lake Tana.

The southern half of Ethiopia is bisected by the rift valley, which has a range of 40–60 km in width and whose floor is occupied by a number of lakes (Zwai, Langano, Abiata, Shala, Awasa, Abaya or Margherita and Chamo). In the latitude of Addis Ababa, the western wall of the rift turns north and runs parallel to the west coast of Arabia, leaving a wide plain between the escarpment and the Red Sea coast of Eritrea. The eastern wall of the rift turns to the east in the latitude of Addis Ababa, forming an escarpment looking north over the Afar plains. The escarpments are nearly always abrupt, commanding extensive views over the lowlands some 1,000 m below, and are broken at only one point near Addis Ababa where the Awash river descends from the rim of the plateau. It is at this point that the railway from Djibouti reaches the highlands.

The plateaux to the west of the rift system dip gently towards the west and are drained by right bank tributaries of the Nile system, which have carved deep and spectacular gorges. The plateaux to the north of Lake Tana are drained by the Tekeze and Angareb rivers, headwaters of the Atbara. The central plateaux are drained by the Abbai (Blue Nile) river and its tributaries. The Abbai rises in Lake Tana and is known as the Blue Nile in Sudan. Much of the flood water in the Blue Nile system comes from the left bank tributaries (e.g. Didessa and Dabus), which rise in the high rainfall region of south-west Ethiopia. This southern region is also drained by the Akobo, Gilo and Baro rivers which form the headwaters of the Sobat river. The only river of significance to the west of the rift valley which is not part of the Nile system is the Omo, which drains southwards into Lake Turkana and is known in its upper course as the Gibie. The lower trough of the Omo has, in recent years, been the site of interesting archaeological discoveries of early human occupation, pre-dating the early remains at Olduvai in Tanzania. The rift valley itself contains a number of closed river basins, including the largest, the Awash, which flows north from the rift valley proper into the Afar plain and terminates in Lake Abe. It is in the middle and lower Awash regions of the rift valley that even earlier remains of man have been discovered, in the locality of Hadow, below the escarpment to the east of Dessie. The highlands to the east of the rift are drained south-eastwards by the headstreams of the Webi-Shebelli and Juba river systems.

As a result of earth movements, associated volcanic activity and subsequent erosion, the plateau surfaces are generally covered by thick deposits of Tertiary lavas, but the deep gorges, protected from widening by the hard lava cap, have often cut down through Cretaceous, Jurassic and Triassic sedimentaries to the Pre-Cambrian basement. However, in the north in Tigre Administrative Region, the Tertiary lavas have been removed over wide areas, exposing limestones and sandstones. In the rift valley and Afar plains, Quaternary volcanics cover much of the surface and overlie the Quaternary basalts. In the area to the south of the Dallol Depression, there are a number of active cones and vents. To the south-east of the rift valley the plateaux are less extensive but high mountain areas capped by plateau basalts overlook the wide plains of the Ogaden, where sandstones and limestones predominate. The location of Ethiopia across a series of major fault lines and its association with earth movements, particularly in the Afar plains, which are related to the continuing drift of the African continent away from the Asian blocks, makes it very susceptible to earth tremors, most of which are fortunately of a low magnitude.

NATURAL RESOURCES

Although the exploitation of gold and copper ores dates from prehistoric times on the Eritrean plateau, little is known of the potential mineral resources of Ethiopia. There are alluvial gold workings in the Adola area of the Sidamo region, and platinum deposits near Yubdo in the Wollega region. Probably the area with the highest mineral potential lies in the west and south-west (in Wollega, Illubabor and Kaffa regions). However, this area is largely inaccessible and much of it is covered by rain forest.

Valuable potash deposits have been proven in the Dallol Depression. These await the development of other infrastructure in this desolate region, but represent a potential source of mineral exports.

Exploration for petroleum was carried out for some years in the Ogaden region without success. More recently, however, attention has been diverted to the southern borders of Ethiopia. In the Bale region between the rivers Web and Webi-Shebelli, it has been reported that promising strikes of oil have been obtained. These, however, await official confirmation and suggestions on how effective exploitation can be achieved. Finally, estimates are now being made of the geothermal power potential of extensive sources in the Afar plain region.

With its high rainfall and precipitous relief, Ethiopia is well-endowed with hydroelectric power potential. A number of plants are already in operation along the course of the Awash river, south of Addis Ababa. Along the Blue Nile river basin, numerous sites have been identified at which power production could be coupled with irrigation schemes.

CLIMATE AND VEGETATION

Ethiopia lies within the tropics but the wide range of altitude produces considerable variations in temperature conditions which are reflected in the traditional zones of the *dega* (the temperate plateaux), the *kolla* (hot lowlands) and the intermediate frost-free zone of the *woina dega*. The boundaries between these three zones lie at approximately 2,400 m and

1,700 m above sea-level. Average annual temperature in the *dega* is about 16°C, in the *woina dega* about 22°C and in the *kolla* at least 26°C.

The seasonal oscillation of the inter-tropical convergence zone over Ethiopia causes a main rainy season over most of the country during June, July and August, when moist equatorial air is drawn in from the south and west.

Ethiopia is extremely vulnerable to drought conditions, particularly in the low-lying pastoral areas, and along the eastern escarpment where there is a widespread dependence upon the spring rains (*belg*) which failed completely during the Wollo-Tigre famine of 1973. The development of cultivation in areas of marginal rainfall has accentuated this problem.

Despite the significant variations in local climates and in the duration and intensity of rainfall, Ethiopia's climatic conditions can be described generally in terms of well-watered highlands and uplands, mostly receiving at least 1,000 mm of rain a year with the exception of the Tigrean plateau, and dry lowlands, generally having less than 500 mm of rain, with the significant exception of the Baro and Akobo river plains in the south-west, which lie in the path of summer rain-bearing winds.

The natural vegetation of the plateaux and highlands above 1,800 m is coniferous forest (notably *zigba* and *tid)*, but these forests have now largely disappeared and are found today only in the more inaccessible regions, e.g. in the Bale highlands and on the slopes of Mt Jiba, to the west of Addis Ababa. In the south-west higher rainfall with lower elevations and higher temperatures has produced extensive broad-leafed rain forests with a variety of species including abundant *karraro*. Although there has been a steady encroachment by shifting cultivators, these forested areas in the former Illubabor and Kaffa Administrative Regions of the south-west are relatively remote and have not yet been subjected to extensive commercial exploitation. Their main significance is the presence of the coffee bush which grows wild as part of the natural undergrowth and supplies a significant proportion of Ethiopia's exports.

Above the tree line on the plateaux are wide expanses of mountain grassland. The highlands are the site of settled agriculture in which approximately 4m. farmers produce a variety of grain crops. Unfortunately, the growth of population and the depletion of resources in forest cover and soil has led to the practice of farming in areas which are very marginal and unreliable in rainfall, particularly along the eastern escarpment. This has exacerbated the drought and famine conditions which have developed in the period since 1973. In the lowlands, dependent on rainfall conditions, there is a range of dry-zone vegetation, from limited areas of desert through thorn scrub to acacia savannah. The extensive natural range-lands, particularly in the Borena and Ogaden plains in the south, are an important natural resource in Ethiopia, a fact which is responsible for the country's estimated cattle population of around 26m. head.

However, the drought conditions, which began in 1972–73, in association with abnormal conditions affecting the whole Sahel region of Africa, have completely disrupted the pastoral economy in many areas. There has been a high mortality rate both of humans and livestock, while the vegetation cover has suffered a long-term set-back.

POPULATION AND CULTURES

There has never been a full population census in Ethiopia, but a census that was conducted in May 1984 was estimated to have reached 85% of the population. The results showed the total population (excluding Eritrea, but including an estimate for areas not covered by the census) to be 39,868,501 (males 20,061,453, females 19,806,048). Based on these figures, the country's estimated total population was 49,947,400 at mid-1991. The average annual population growth rate for Ethiopia and Eritrea in 1987–91 was 3.1%. Before the census results were published, the country's total population had been projected (on the basis of sample surveys) to reach 27m. by 1975 and 35m. by 1985, assuming a rural growth rate of around 2% per annum and an urban growth in excess of 7%. More than 50% of the population are aged 19 years or less, and more than 70% are under 29 years of age. This distribution, coupled with the early age of marriage in Ethiopia, implied a rapidly increasing population growth rate.

At the 1984 census the country's capital, Addis Ababa, was the largest city (with a population of 1,412,577), followed by Asmara (now the capital of Eritrea—275,385) and Dire Dawa (98,104). There were also nine towns with between 50,000 and 90,000 inhabitants each. The growth rates in these larger urban settlements are high. Overall density of population at mid-1991 was 44.2 per sq km. However, this average concealed a very wide variation among the regions, as might be expected from the multiplicity of natural environments.

Generally speaking, the distribution of population reflects the pattern of relief. The highlands, having a plentiful rainfall, are the home of settled agriculture. Land more than 2,000 m above sea-level is free of the malarial mosquito, a factor contributing to the non-occupation of lowlands which are suitable for farming. It would not be unreasonable to assume that 10% of the population live below 1,000 m, 20% at 1,000 m–1,800 m and 70% above the 1,800 m contour line. Nearly all the major settlements are in the highlands. The notable exceptions are special cases such as the border post of Moyale, the river port of Gambela and the railway creations, Dire Dawa and Nazret. The distribution of population has been affected by recurrent droughts since the mid 1980s, which have forced many people to leave their traditional areas in search of emergency aid; and by the erstwhile government's policy of resettling famine victims from the former Tigre and Wollo Administrative Regions in newly-established villages in the lowlands of the south-west; additionally, the civil war which intensified in 1989–91, resulted in the displacement of large numbers of people.

Recent History

PATRICK GILKES

THE ETHIOPIAN EMPIRE

Ethiopia's history as an organized and independent polity dates from about 100 BC with a kingdom at Axum in the northern part of the present state. The Axumite empire, as it later became, was converted to Christianity in the fourth century. In the fourth and sixth centuries AD, it extended across the Red Sea, but its core lay in the northern Ethiopian highlands. When Axum collapsed in the eighth century, power shifted south to Lasta, and later to Shoa. In the 16th century, 50 years of conflict with the Muslim Sultanate of Adal exhausted both; they fell an easy prey to the Oromos, a pastoral people who expanded out of a small area to the south. Adal was reduced to the city of Harar; the Ethiopian rulers moved to Gondar in the north-west.

In the latter part of the 18th century as the monarchy weakened, central government broke down, though the position of emperor, however enfeebled, and the Ethiopian Coptic (Orthodox) Church, provided an element of continuity. Real power was in the hands of provincial nobles from the highlands, Tigrean, Oromo and Amhara, who fought for control of the throne, though none seized it until 1855. Tewodros, a minor noble from Gondar, and then Yohannes IV from the northern Tigre region tried to restore imperial power. Yohannes spent most of his reign fending off Egyptians, Italians and Dervishes: he died in battle with the Dervishes in 1889. His successor, Menelik of Shoa, reunited and expanded the empire to the east, south and west of Shoa. It was from these largely Oromo-inhabited areas that virtually all Ethiopia's resources came, in particular coffee, gold, ivory and slaves. Menelik's successes coincided with the arrival of the European colonial powers. He defeated the Italians at the battle of Adua in 1896, but under the subsequent treaty Italy retained control of Eritrea, which it had formally colonized in 1890.

Menelik's conquests had shifted the balance of the empire south again and in the 1880s he had founded a new capital, Addis Ababa, where the first bank, hospital, modern school and printing press were established in the 1900s. A new railway, from Djibouti, reached Dire Dawa in 1902 and Addis Ababa in 1918. In 1907, also as part of Menelik's programme of modernizing and unifying Ethiopia, he established a cabinet, although it was largely disregarded following his death in 1911, when his grandson, Lij Yasu, assumed imperial control. Suspicious of the Christian Amhara nobility of Shoa, he tried to put together an alternative coalition of support, composed of Oromos (the ethnic group of his father) and Muslims; and, in the hope of gaining access to the sea (cut off by the Italian colony of Eritrea), he looked for support to Germany and Turkey as enemies of France, Britain and Italy. Still uncrowned, Lij Yasu was deposed in 1916, following his conversion to Islam. Zauditu, a daughter of Menelik, became empress while Ras Teferi, later Emperor Haile Selassie, became regent and heir. As regent he obtained Ethiopia's entry into the League of Nations and issued the first anti-slavery decrees. Once emperor (1930), Haile Selassie began the process of wresting power from the nobility and turning Ethiopia into a modern autocracy. His efforts were interrupted in 1935 by the Italian invasion. Mussolini had imperial ambitions and Italy wanted revenge for the defeat of Adua. In May 1936 with his armies defeated, partly because of Italy's use of poison gas, Haile Selassie left Ethiopia to appeal to the League of Nations. On his departure the Italian army entered Addis Ababa and a five-year period under Italian fascist occupation began. The liberation of Ethiopia was facilitated by the Second World War, with Britain eventually adopting Haile Selassie's cause as part of the Allies' campaign against Germany and Italy. In May 1941, with South African troops already having captured it, Haile Selassie re-entered his capital. The Italians left little behind except an extensive road network, though their administrative divisions, ethnically based, influenced post-war attitudes.

After 1941, Haile Selassie continued his largely successful policy of centralization, playing off the British, who came close to occupying Ethiopia after 1941 (they only withdrew from the Ogaden in 1948 and the Reserved Haud area in 1954) against the USA. In 1952, after protracted discussions, Eritrea, which had been made a UN mandated territory after the war, was federated with Ethiopia. Almost immediately Haile Selassie set about dismantling its institutions, including the press, the trade unions and the elected parliament, all anathema to his own highly centralized system of government. In 1962 Eritrea became the 14th province of Ethiopia: a development that essentially sparked off the Eritrean independence struggle. Originally led by the Eritrean Liberation Front (ELF) which drew most of its support from Muslim pastoralists from the lowland areas, it was joined in the early 1970s by the Eritrean People's Liberation Front (EPLF), which was more representative of the Christian highland agriculturalists.

Haile Selassie provided the trappings of a modern state, including, in 1955, a constitution with parliament elected by universal adult suffrage; but it had no power. Similarly, he made no real attempt to carry out necessary changes in land policy, or adjust the hierarchies of administrative power to lessen the dominance of Christian Amharas (who constituted no more than 35% of the population). Ethiopia remained essentially feudal, with small Amhara-dominated modern sectors in the bureaucracy and in industry. These provided the impetus for the outbreak of opposition among non-Amhara nationalities, in Tigre region in 1943, among Oromos and Somalis in Bale in 1963–70, and from 1961 in Eritrea. Haile Selassie himself dismissed the revolt of his own bodyguard in 1960 as no more than a minor problem, and remained bemused by annual student demonstrations which took place from 1965 onwards. He preferred to concentrate on international affairs, securing Addis Ababa as the headquarters of the Organization of African Unity, and of the UN Economic Commission for Africa. His main ally was the USA, with Ethiopia being the principal recipient of US aid in Africa in the 1950s and 1960s and providing the USA with a major communications base at Kagnew, near Asmara. Haile Selassie failed, however, to quell Somali irredentism or to prevent Sudan assisting the Eritrean rebels, even though he helped negotiate the settlement of 1972 between Northern and Southern Sudan.

The long-term weaknesses of the regime included the growing agrarian crisis, inequitable distribution of land, and lack of development. More immediately, the costs of revolts in Bale and Eritrea, drought and famine in Wollo in 1972–74 when 200,000 people died, and, by 1973, Haile Selassie's own near incapacity (owing to old age) and his failure to designate an heir, fuelled the grievances of the military, students (with no employment prospects), and workers. A series of mutinies in the army started in January 1974, and were paralleled at once by strikes in the civilian sector. A new prime minister was appointed with a mandate to introduce real constitutional change. Matters seemed to settle down briefly; but behind the scenes more radical political groups and elements within the armed forces were gaining prominence. By June when it was clear reform was stagnating, a newly formed co-ordinating committee of the armed forces, police and territorial army took action, arresting leading aristocrats and political figures, including the emperor's closest associates and advisers. After a series of revelations concerning financial manipulation, Haile Selassie was deposed in September, with hardly a murmur of dissent. In March 1975 the constitution was abrogated, parliament dissolved and the monarchy was formally abolished.

REVOLUTION AND MILITARY RULE

The imperial regime was replaced by the co-ordinating committee, as a provisional military administrative council (PMAC), known as the Dergue. A popular soldier, Lt-Gen.

Aman Andom, was drafted in as head of state and chairman of the Dergue, but the Dergue itself, a group of 120 soldiers up to the rank of major, held the real power. Internal disputes over whether to take a hard line against the ongoing Eritrean revolt (Gen. Aman was himself Eritrean) led to the deaths of Aman and two other Dergue members in November 1974. At the same time 57 former high-ranking military and civilian officials were summarily shot without trial, including two ex-prime ministers and 17 generals. A new head of state was appointed, Brig.-Gen. Teferi Banti, who also became the nominal chairman of the Dergue. His two vice-chairmen were Maj. (later Lt.-Col) Mengistu Haile Mariam and Lt-Col Atnafu Abate.

The PMAC now began to see itself as the vanguard of the Ethiopian Revolution, and under the influence of left-wing intellectuals returning from abroad, opted for a socialist model of government. In December 1974, Ethiopia was declared a socialist state, and a programme of revolutionary reforms called *Ethiopia Tikdem* ('Ethiopia First') was initiated. Most of the major reforms were implemented in the first months of 1975. More than 100 companies were nationalized or partly taken over by the state. Rural land was nationalized in March 1975, and urban land four months later. Thousands of students were dispatched to the countryside as part of a national campaign for development, designed to provide education in health, literacy and to organize the land reform. (Later, in 1979, an impressive and highly successful national literacy campaign was launched.) Over 30,000 local, electively-led peasant associations were created with responsibility for their own tax collection, judicial affairs and administration. Similar associations, *kebeles*, were set up in towns, with pyramids of higher level organizations, district, regional and national. In December 1975 a new trade union body was created, the All-Ethiopia Trade Union.

It was not until April 1976, however, that the theory of the revolution was outlined in the 'national democratic revolution programme'. This was essentially the work of a Marxist-Leninist group, the All-Ethiopia Socialist Movement (MEISON) which wanted a Soviet-style communist party, and, more important, was prepared to accept the need for military rule for the time being. It was therefore allowed to operate through a political office and an ideological school, both established in May 1976. Its rival was the Ethiopian People's Revolutionary Party (EPRP), another and more popular Marxist-Leninist grouping, which argued for the immediate creation of a civilian government, and also supported the Eritrean struggle. Both groups had supporters within the Dergue; both were involved in the struggle to control the new institutions. Their disputes intensified into urban terrorism and spilt over into the Dergue. Lt-Col Mengistu (who in 1975 had emerged as the most influential member of the Dergue) came under threat in December 1976 when the structure of the Dergue was reorganized. Six weeks later Mengistu retaliated: in February 1977 Gen. Teferi Banti and five other leading members of the Dergue were executed and Mengistu took over as head of state and chairman of the PMAC. He subsequently launched, originally on behalf of his ally MEISON, the 'red terror' campaign, aimed at eliminating the EPRP. Tens of thousands of people were killed or tortured, particularly in urban areas. MEISON did not benefit and in mid-1977, Mengistu turned against it too. By late 1978 both organizations had been virtually eliminated.

These ideological and power struggles were intensified by the deteriorating military situation in both Eritrea in the north and in the south and south-east where Somalia was also attempting to take advantage of the weakness of the central administration and of the Ethopian army, whose structure and effectiveness had been virtually destroyed by the revolution. In Eritrea the collapse of the government position was first apparent in January 1975 when a joint attack (almost their first and last) by the ELF and the EPLF on Asmara, the Eritrean capital, nearly succeeded in capturing the city. The government response was substantial and brutal, and for the first time many Tigrean Christians in Eritrea joined the liberation fronts. In 1976, the Dergue made its first effort to raise a 'people's army', organizing a force of some 20,000 ill-armed and untrained peasants who were easily defeated by the Eritreans. It quickly learnt from the disaster, with Cuba, persuaded of Ethopia's revolutionary authenticity by Mengistu, training over 300,000 men in six months in 1977.

The new units proved to be necessary. By the end of 1977 in Eritrea there were only five garrisons left—in Adi Caieh, Asmara, Barentu, Massawa, and Assab far to the south. Some of the new militia were moved in to hold these five towns; most had to be rushed down to the south-east where guerrilla operations were reinforced by a Somali invasion in July 1977. Somalia claimed the Somali-inhabited area of the Ogaden, arguing that it had been colonized by the Ethiopians in the late 19th century. For Ethiopia, the issue was simply one of an undefined border. There was a brief undeclared war in 1964, followed by an OAU cease-fire, but as Ethiopia's internal security weakened in 1975–76, Somalia reorganized the Western Somali Liberation Front (WSLF), and increased arms supplies and training. Cuba made an unsuccessful effort to mediate between the two states in March 1977. In July Somali forces crossed the border, and by November the city of Harar was under attack. However the overstretched Somali army ran out of supplies, just as Ethiopia received a massive influx of Soviet weapons, including hundreds of tanks, and fighter aircraft. Somalia, until then a close ally of the USSR (which had tried to remain on good terms with both countries), expelled Soviet military advisers and severed relations with Cuba, correctly convinced that the USSR had decided for Ethiopia. (In early 1977 Mengistu had formally broken with the USA after criticisms of Ethiopia's human rights record and its failure to supply the arms he needed.) With its new weaponry and some 16,000 Cuban troops, the Ethiopian army went on the offensive in February 1978. In early March the Somali army was forced to withdraw.

In June 1978 a revitalized Ethiopian army moved back into Eritrea. Within three months, it had recaptured most of the towns and reopened the roads south. By the end of the year the ELF, largely subdued, had reverted to guerrilla operations, while the EPLF had withdrawn to the far north to the proximity of the remote town of Nacfa. There, however, advancing Ethiopian forces lost their momentum, and over several years accumulated severe losses in a series of unsuccessful offensives. The largest, undertaken as part of 'Operation Red Star', was personally commanded by Mengistu. Launched when a government campaign to win hearts and minds in Eritrea had had some effect, the operation was to have combined military and development activity and was designed to integrate the province with the rest of Ethiopia. It was, however, another failure (resulting in 30,000 casualties) despite the continuing religious, ethnic and ideological differences among the Eritrean movements which had erupted into civil war in 1981. (The EPLF, in alliance with the Tigre People's Liberation Front (TPLF) from neighbouring Tigre region, drove the ELF into Sudan in 1982, where they were disarmed and later fragmented.)

THE NATIONALITIES ISSUE

The successes of 1978 allowed Mengistu to turn his attention to organizing a political party of government. The removal of MEISON left several small Marxist-Leninist political organizations, but disputes among them and within the PMAC led Lt-Col Mengistu to opt for a party of individuals. The Commission for Organizing the Party of the Working People of Ethiopia (COPWE) was established in 1979. The composition of its central committee was 70% military. Loyalty rather than ideology became the prime criterion for membership. In order to reinforce COPWE, revolutionary women's and youth movements were founded in 1980, and the All Ethiopia Peasant Association and the All Ethiopia Trade Union were restructured in 1982. In September 1984, the Workers' Party of Ethiopia (WPE) was formally inaugurated, and for the first time representatives from the workers', peasants' and local organizations were included in the central committee. The WPE failed to attract either support or loyalty from the general population, being seen, rightly, as a vehicle for the regime's control. Nor did it have the hoped for effect on the PMAC's major problem in the 1970s: the continued failure to solve the nationality issue.

From the beginning the rhetoric of the revolution raised expectations among various nationalities, particularly

Oromos, Somalis, Afars and Tigreans. (Eritrea, with nine nationalities, was seen less as a nationalist issue by the EPLF than as a colonial issue, a more acceptable reason for independence to the international community.) The government had one partial success, the Afars. The Afar Liberation Front (ALF) was founded in 1975 after an unsuccessful revolt by the traditional ruler, Sultan Ali Mirreh; but a 'progressive' Afar National Liberation Movement (ANLM) appeared, which was prepared to accept the PMAC's version of regional autonomy. A successful Afar congress was held in Gewane in April 1977. Subsequently ANLM members were appointed local administrators, but the speed of progress towards autonomy satisfied no-one. No progress was made in increasing the autonomy of the Somalis or Oromos. The Somalis, despite the defeat of Somalia in 1978, had the great advantage of an open border, and the Somali government continued its support for the WSLF and the Somali Abo Liberation Front (which operated in Bale and Sidamo regions) until the mid-1980s when both movements, suffering from internal splits, virtually ceased operations. The Ethiopian government, similarly, backed Somali opposition groups, holding two Somali villages in 1982–88. Relations between the two governments improved in 1986 as a result of Italian and Djiboutian mediation; and in 1988, faced by a desperate need for extra troops in Eritrea, Mengistu abandoned his insistence on border demarcation as a precondition to the cessation of hostilities with Somalia. By the early 1980s, the Oromo Liberation Front (OLF), which advocates self-determination for the Oromo people and emphasizes the use of Oromo culture and language, was gaining support from peasants critical of government efforts to set up co-operatives. Prior to this the regime's greatest area of support had been among Oromo peasantry who had benefited from the land reforms of 1975. Government responses to Oromo opposition included widespread arrests of Oromos in Addis Ababa and other towns, but the OLF remained militarily small, operating along the Sudan border of western Wollega, and in an area south-west of Harar.

Most serious for the government was the growth of the Tigre People's Liberation Front (TPLF). Established in 1975, it gained the support of the EPLF from which it received training and arms. The TPLF had other opponents besides the central government: the Ethiopian Democratic Union (EDU), a group based in exile which included members of the former aristocracy, and the Ethiopian People's Revolutionary Party (EPRP) which had taken up armed struggle in Tigre in 1975. The TPLF drove them out in 1977–78, and later gained considerable support from the effects of the 'red terror' campaign, and from its calls for Tigrean self-determination. It became increasingly left wing, setting up the Marxist-Leninist League of Tigre in the mid-1980s. Like the Eritreans and Oromos, the TPLF gained substantially from using the border with Sudan. Throughout the 1980s Ethio-Sudanese relations were poor, with each country supporting the other's dissidents. The regime's response to the growth of the nationality movements and their guerrilla operations was at first military, though operations against the TPLF and other groups always took second place to those in Eritrea. A political response finally came in a constitution endorsed by referendum in February 1987. This set up an 835-seat elected legislature, the national shengo, and in September, the People's Democratic Republic of Ethiopia was proclaimed with Mengistu as president, chief executive, c-in-c of the armed forces, and chairman of the council of ministers, the defence council and the state council. Ethiopia was declared a unified socialist state under the democratic centralism of the WPE. A new administrative structure allowed for five autonomous regions, four based on ethnicity: Tigre for the Tigrean people; Dire Dawa for the Issa Somalis; the Ogaden region for all other Somalis; Assab for the Afars; and Eritrea (with nine different nationalities). The EPLF and the TPLF at once rejected the new structure. By then both were determined to depose Mengistu, regarding his removal as a prerequisite for achievement of their aims.

Political failure was paralleled by economic and military disasters. Efforts to mobilize production after 1979 made some progress, but the state farms proved extremely inefficient, and the catastrophic drought of 1984–85 wiped out any gains. The international community's response to the disaster was slow, partly because of Ethiopia's degree of commitment to the USSR, which in total, provided the regime with some US $8,000m. of military equipment. How many died is unknown. The government, as part of its relief measures, moved about 600,000 people into the south and west in a highly unpopular resettlement campaign, while the TPLF (Tigre was the worst-hit area) moved 200,000 into Sudan. The resettlement scheme, ill-prepared and less than voluntary, was terminated in 1986 as a result of international criticism. Another major famine threatened in 1989–90, following the highly unpopular villagization policy, bringing together several villages as single units for security and political reasons. This policy and resettlement adversely affected agricultural production. Provision of aid was complicated by the conflicts, with both sides using food as a weapon.

OVERTHROW OF MENGISTU'S REGIME

The military situation deteriorated after 1988 with defeats in Eritrea followed by the loss to the TPLF of all Tigre region in the following year. Disillusionment grew in the army, which previously had been prepared to accept Mengistu because of his detemination to keep Eritrea and his commitment to a united Ethiopia; but by 1989 his refusal to contemplate a political solution was regarded as a liability. In May most senior army officers took part in an attempted *coup d'état*. Sweeping changes to the command structure and the appointment of unqualified commanders, coupled with a further series of defeats at the hands of the rebels, further demoralized the army. Within weeks of the attempted coup Mengistu agreed to more talks with the EPLF, which itself only accepted under heavy international pressure, since meetings held in 1982–85 had been fruitless. In 1989, utilizing the provisions of the 1987 constitution, the government offered autonomy to the regions whereby regional assemblies with control over health, education, development, finance and taxation would be elected. This was not enough for the EPLF, nor did they trust Mengistu. Neither side was prepared to compromise on the issue of Eritrean independence. Talks with the TPLF made equally little progress.

Once in control of Tigre in 1989, the TPLF established a united front, the Ethiopian People's Revolutionary Democratic Front (EPRDF), with the Ethiopian People's Democratic Movement, a largely Amhara organization that the TPLF had itself created as a surrogate organization to fight in non-Tigrean areas. As the EPRDF advanced further south it created other organizations: the Oromo People's Democratic Organization was created after the OLF refused to join the EPRDF, and an officers' movement (EDORM). The TPLF remained the major element in the front, but its own original demands for self-determination were replaced by its commitment to the removal of Mengistu and the establishment of a democratic government in Addis Ababa. By November 1989, the EPRDF had reached within 160 km of Addis Ababa. For a time it looked as if Mengistu might be able to obtain Israel's support in return for allowing Falashas to leave (13,000 had been flown from Sudan to Israel in a secret airlift in 1984). Relations were restored in November and Israel provided Ethiopia with cluster bombs and anti-guerrilla training; but under strong US pressure this support was stopped. (In May 1991 with government consent, the Israelis briefly took control of Addis Ababa airport for 36 hours to fly out the remaining Falasha population, numbering about 14,000.)

By February 1990, when the EPLF captured Massawa, cutting off supply lines for the Ethiopian army in Eritrea. Mengistu made further concessions. Ethiopian socialism was abandoned; opposition groups were invited to participate in a unity party; free market principles replaced economic planning; and peasants were allowed to bequeath land to their children. It was insufficient. The economy was collapsing as rapidly as the military and political situation. The price of coffee was falling, and supplies of low-cost Soviet oil had ceased in May 1989. The revolution in Eastern Europe brought about a complete collapse of Ethiopia's overseas alliances. In January 1991, the EPRDF produced a new political programme which did not mention Marxism and was moderate and democratic enough to be acceptable to the USA. As the guerrillas closed in on Addis Ababa, Mengistu's armies ceased to fight. On 21

May, Mengistu fled to Zimbabwe where he was granted political asylum. The USA presided over peace talks in London in an attempt to provide an orderly transfer of power from the government. The government delegation could not even surrender before the USA, fearing a collapse of law and order in Addis Ababa, invited the EPRDF to form a government, much to the irritation of the OLF delegation which felt it was premature. The EPLF attended the conference but as observers only, to mark Eritrea's *de facto* independence. On 28 May the EPRDF entered the capital and subsequently established an interim government. The EPLF likewise established a provisional government in Eritrea, pending the holding of a referendum on the issue of independence. This was successfully conducted in April 1993, when 99.8% of voters demonstrated overwhelming support for independence.

THE EPRDF AND ETHNIC POLITICS

In July 1991 the EPRDF convened a national conference attended by representatives of some 20 political organizations to discuss Ethiopia's political future and establish a transitional government. It was carefully stage-managed, with the EPRDF preparing the agenda, drawing up a national charter providing for an 87-seat council of representatives to govern during a two-year transition period, creating some of the political groups which attended, and organizing seat allocations. The chairman of the EPRDF, Meles Zenawi, was elected head of state; the vice-chairman of the EPRDF, Tamrat Layne, became prime minister. Some 32 political organizations were subsequently represented on the council, with the EPRDF's component parts occupying 32 of the 87 seats. The next largest group on the council was the OLF with 12 seats. The Oromos were allocated a total of 27 seats but they were divided between five different organizations. The portfolios of the council of ministers were similarly distributed with 17 ministers from 7 different organizations being appointed.

From the outset, the EPRDF made it clear it would support Eritrean independence, and emphasized self-determination for Ethiopia's nationalities within a federal system as the answer to the political problem of a multi-ethnic state. In November the EPRDF drew up new boundaries for 12 self-governing regions with two chartered cities, Addis Ababa and Harar. The basis was ethnicity and language, although equally they reflected political power. Tigre region, the home of the TPLF (the dominant organization within the EPRDF), lost a large area of desert, and gained the rich farming lands of Setit Humera along the Sudanese border. The Oromo region brought together most of four former regions, while nationalities that were widely spread, like the Amhara and the Gurage, and those who sought a centralized state, were not favoured by the new system.

The first stage of implementation of the new policies was the organization of local administrative elections, conducted in 1992, followed by regional nationality elections. By mid-1993 most regions had elected assemblies which were functioning to a greater or lesser extent. Budgets came from the central government for 1992/93, but regions were expected to raise their own funding thereafter. In fact the threat of large-scale famine in 1994 (with nearly 7 million people reportedly at risk by April) following poor rains and a significant decline in agricultural production, made this impossible.

Numerous political parties emerged, mostly ethnically based. (More than 100 parties existed in early 1993.) As Tigreans make up no more than seven per cent of the population, the EPRDF created surrogate parties or 'democratic organizations' further complicating the political process. The existence of the EPRDF's Oromo People's Democratic Organization was a major reason for the breakdown in relations with the OLF, despite the OLF's position in government. In the build-up to the elections, there were numerous clashes as the two organizations manoeuvred for position in the Oromo regions. Both also sought to drive other nationalities out of their areas. Just before the elections, the OLF and several other groups pulled out, and the OLF also withdrew from the government. Its criticisms of the election were supported by international observers who reported harassment, intimidation, failures to deliver registration and voting cards or to organize election committees. The EPRDF and its supporting parties did extremely well in almost every region, and even in Addis Ababa it won a surprising 81 of 84 regional seats. The two areas where elections were postponed, the Afar and Somali regions, were those where the EPRDF had not succeeded in organizing its own political support. After its withdrawal the OLF attempted to revive guerrilla conflict in several parts of the Oromo region into 1994, though only on a small scale and with little effect. Western ambassadors and the former US president, Jimmy Carter, made a number of efforts to reconcile the OLF and the EPRDF, but the EPRDF refused to compromise over such issues as its control of the armed forces, and no significant progress was made.

In June 1994 elections were conducted for a constituent assembly to ratify a draft constitution which had already been approved by the council of representatives. The election was much better organized than in 1992 and there were no reports of obvious intimidation. The EPRDF again triumphed decisively, while the main opposition groups boycotted the election. The main issues for consideration by the assembly concerned the definition of self-determination—whether the constitution should include a guaranteed right to independence or if this should only be allowed under certain well-defined circumstances. Following approval of the constitution, the final stage in the creation of the proposed Federal Democratic Republic of Ethiopian Peoples will be national elections for a federal government, scheduled for 1995.

Opposition to EPRDF policies was twofold. The Oromo Liberation Front (OLF) and the Ogaden National Liberation Front (ONLF), a Somali organization, sought a firmer and faster commitment to the possibility of secession, and a genuine devolution of power which they claimed was not the intention of the EPRDF. (The constitutent assembly election had to be postponed in the Somali region for some weeks because of unrest following arrests and security operations by the EPRDF to weaken the position of the ONLF.) Other opposition groups, which supported Ethiopia's unity and opposed Eritrean independence, feared ERPDF policies would partition the state. Among these were externally-based parties, including the Coalition of Ethiopian Democratic Forces (COEDF) composed of former opponents of Mengistu including the EPRP, MEISON and one faction of the Ethiopian Democratic Union (EDU), and the Ethiopian Medhin Democratic Party (MEDHIN), founded by a former foreign minister under Mengistu, Col Goshu Wolde.

Internally, opposition emerged in the university at Addis Ababa. In January 1993, one student died in a demonstration protesting against UN support for Eritrean independence, and in April, 41 staff were dismissed or were refused new contracts. Since the majority were Amhara, there was widespread suspicion the EPRDF was trying to silence Amhara critics of Eritrean independence. Dismissals from the civil service and from government companies were also suspected of being ethnically motivated. Amhara organizations, notably the All Amhara People's Organization (AAPO), came under pressure for criticising EPRDF policies over Eritrea. In June 1994, its leader, Prof. Asrat Woldeyes, was accused of inciting violence and given a two-year jail sentence. In fact, the April 1993 referendum and the subsequent declaration of Eritrean independence occurred without incident, and there was a general, if reluctant acceptance of the *fait accompli*.

The EPRDF also encountered opposition regarding other aspects of policy. Its decision to continue government ownership of land, though coupled with 'security of usage', was deeply resented. Nor was there support for the introduction of a new system of leasehold, with rates fixed by government assessors. The economy, after two good years in 1991–2 and 1992–3, looked less promising with the serious food shortages and the failure to implement a realistic privatization programme. The EPRDF remained divided on the desirability of a full-scale market economy, leaving many unanswered questions over the financing of its proposed federal system.

Human rights emerged as a crucial issue in 1993–94 as discrepancies appeared between EPRDF rehtoric and policy. In 1992 the EPRDF approved a press law which was subsequently invoked to arrest or detain dozens of editors, owners and journalists over a period of months from late 1993, largely, it appeared, on the basis of criticism or questioning of government policy. The Ethiopian Human Rights Council, set up in 1992, claimed that it suffered harassment in response to allegations of government abuses. The long delays in bringing senior officials of the former regime to trial also raised comment, though few disagreed with the special prosecutor's intention to charge them with crimes against humanity. In February 1994 Ethiopia requested the extradition of the former leader, Col Mengistu, but the Zimbabwe government appeared reluctant to comply.

Following an opposition meeting in Paris in March 1993, bringing together COEDF, MEDHIN, and the OLF as well as Afar and Tigrean parties, the opposition, called for a national reconciliation conference to be held in Addis Ababa in December, 1993. The EPRDF, although refusing to become involved, did not prevent convention of the conference, but proceeded to arrest some participants on arrival. There was considerable international condemnation of the incident, and the conference went ahead under intense media scrutiny. The only significant development, however, was the emergence of yet another opposition grouping, the Coalition of Alternative Forces for Peace and Democracy in Ethiopia (CAFPDE). There is still little evidence, whether within or beyond Ethiopia, of the opposition producing any coherent alternative to the EPRDF, or seriously threatening the EPRDF's position.

Internationally, the EPRDF continued to maintain good relations with the USA, and with European powers, but there were indications in 1994 that some international observers had begun to doubt the EPRDF's commitment to pluralism and human rights. But neither this nor questions regarding EPRDF economic policies prevented a meeting of the 'Paris Club' of creditor governments, in March 1994, pledging a further US $1,000m. in loans and grants, in addition to earlier pledges of $3,000m. Relations with Eritrea have remained cordial. They are likely to remain so as long as Ethiopia continues to enjoy access to the port of Assab (which has free port status) and its oil refinery. Both countries are well aware of their need to co-operate, and both continue to show interest in the possibilities of wider economic co-operation within the Horn of Africa.

In 1993, President Meles led efforts by the OAU to foster a peace settlement in Somalia, and Addis Ababa provided the venue for three conferences which sought to reconcile the warring Somali factions.

Economy

JAMES PICKETT

With revisions by the Editor

Ethiopia is one of the poorest countries in the world. Taking the standard welfare measure of income per head, it is, on World Bank statistics, on a par with Tanzania and Somalia, marginally better placed than Mozambique, and poorer than all other countries. Two-thirds of the world's poorest countries are in sub-Saharan Africa. Yet Ethiopia is poor, even by the standards of that depressed region. Compared to an average for Africa of 72.4% in 1991, enrolment in primary schools in Ethiopia was equivalent to just 25% of children in the relevant age-group. In the same year there were 79,000 people per doctor in Ethiopia, against 27,000 in sub-Saharan Africa as a whole and 3,000 in middle-income countries. On such varied indicators as life expectancy at birth, fertilizer use, calories per head, domestic savings and the share of primary commodities in total exports, Ethiopian data compare unfavourably with the sub-Saharan averages.

AGRICULTURE

The proximate cause of Ethiopian poverty is the weight of traditional, low-productivity, agriculture in total economic activity. In truth, however, Ethiopia is not poor because its agriculture is backward. On the contrary, its agriculture is backward because the country is poor. Ethiopia has long been lacking extensive and sustained commercial and cultural contact with others, and has only recently begun to develop the institutions and attitudes that would enable it to emulate the ways of technologically more advanced economies. Indeed it was not until after the Second World War that a sustained effort was made to achieve modern economic growth.

Comprehensive estimates of production and expenditure date from 1960. These indicate that between 1960–73 gross domestic product (GDP) grew, in real terms, at an average annual rate of 4.3%. As population increased in the same period by 2.6% per year, real income per head rose at an annual rate of 1.7%. It should, however, be noted that agricultural output advanced at an average annual rate of 2.3%, more rapidly than in many other African countries. Nevertheless, agricultural supply still increased more slowly than the population.

By the early 1970s, agricultural improvement was spreading. In 1974, however, the new, left-wing military government that deposed Emperor Haile Selassie moved rapidly to nationalize the land, all major industries, much of the distribution system and the banks, together with large-scale commercial farms; to the latter were added a number of hastily-created state farms. Land reform aspired to grant peasants security of tenure. State farms had privileged access to investible funds, improved seeds and fertilizers, and in the prices paid by the state for their output. Similar privileges were granted to producer co-operatives in an unsuccessful attempt to make these attractive to small-scale producers. From first to last, peasant production accounted for well over 90% of coffee and the highland food grains—barley, wheat, teff, maize and sorghum.

Yields were higher on state farms than on peasant plots, although these were more productive per hectare than the producer co-operatives. However, since the state farms were grossly inefficient their unit costs were greater than those of the peasant. Peasants were, nevertheless, forced to sell to the state-run Agricultural Marketing Corporation (AMC) at lower prices than those given to the state farms. Quotas were set by the government in Addis Ababa and enforced on location by the service co-operatives to which most peasants belonged. The quotas were arbitrarily determined, and prices, which were initially, if loosely, related to costs, went unchanged for more than a decade. The system was, and was seen to be, coercive. The peasant did his or her best to sell as much as possible in private markets, even if this meant cheating the AMC. Private markets operated with difficulty. In some areas private merchants were prohibited, and they were harassed everywhere.

One-third of the rural population was forced into newly-created village structures, mainly to be more easily controlled politically. This programme was also unpopular and peasants fled it as soon as they were free to do so.

Ethiopa's gross domestic product (GDP) increased, in real terms, by an annual average of 1.6% in 1980–91. During 1985–92, however, per capita gross national product (GNP) decreased, in real terms, at an average annual rate of 2.0%, as population increased by an annual average of 3.4% over the same period. Among the causes of this disappointing performance were growing civil strife, a less buoyant post-1973 world economy, and the failure of the rains. These exogenous factors should not, however, be allowed to mask the major cause, which was misconceived government policy. The lack of sufficient skilled and experienced personnel, for example, would in itself have been sufficient to have caused central planning to fail in Ethiopia. Moreover, the advent of the Mengistu regime led to a substantial initial exodus of educated people, while many others fled during his 17-year rule.

It is not surprising Ethiopia remains largely pre-modern. Agriculture accounted for 48% of GDP in 1992 and engaged 73% of the economically active population in that year. The sectoral share of agriculture, however, understates its importance. Carrying and marketing agricultural commodities account for much domestic transport and domestic trade, and manufacturing largely takes the form of adding value to agricultural raw materials. In 1992 the share of industry was 13%, and that of services was 39%. The large share of the service sector is explained by an enlarged bureaucracy, the needs of the military, and the fact that domestic service industry is the main mechanism for spreading what little income there is.

The continuing fragility of the economy and the low productivity of its farms are reflected in changes in agricultural trade. In 1974 Ethiopia imported 118,000 metric tons of cereals on commercial terms. By 1990 the figure had become 687,000 tons, an increase of 482%. Again, imports of food aid increased from 54,000 tons in 1974 to 538,000 tons in 1990, a rise of almost 900%. The ratio of aid to commercial imports also went up, from 46% in 1974 to 78% in 1990.

In the late 1980s, a ministry of agriculture survey revealed that the average size of a peasant holding was a mere 1.3 ha. It also recorded that fewer than 14% of the farmers surveyed used any sort of fertilizer; that no more than 2% used improved seeds; that less than 5% and fewer than 1% applied herbicides and pesticides respectively; and that irrigation was available to fewer than 5% of the peasant farms. These farms mostly use little capital—sickles, hoes, crude wooden ploughs, and machetes—and virtually no skills that result from systematic training. Power requirements are produced by people and animals. Sowing practices have remained unchanged for years and the crop is harvested by sickle, trampled by oxen, and winnowed by tossing into the wind. The marketable surplus is small, and much production is for own consumption.

The pressure of population and traditional agricultural practices exacerbate soil erosion and degradation, and have contributed to the denudation of tree cover. The UN Food and Agricultural Organization and the Ethiopian ministry of agriculture believe that about one-half of the highland soils (270,000 sq km) has already been eroded.

Coffee accounts for about one-half of the agricultural value added, and represented 44% of export earnings in 1990. Production is largely in peasant hands. During the Mengistu period, however, farm-gate prices were so low that many coffee farmers switched to other crops. In addition, state marketing was inefficient, and Ethiopia had difficulty in meeting its quotas under the International Coffee Agreement.

Ethiopia has the largest cattle population in Africa, and ranks about 10th in the world in terms of cattle numbers. Most of the livestock is in the hands of the peasants. Animals are generally in poor health, and largely untouched by a fledgling veterinary service. Yet they are the most easily realizable of peasant assets, and their utility under conditions of drought is perhaps the most powerful reason for keeping them.

In Ethiopia drought almost inevitably leads to famine. Thus, in 1985 a general failure of the rains, which had cumulated in some regions in successive years, led to hunger over much of the country. Throughout that year 8m. people were in need of relief, and in 1986 there were still 6m. in the same plight. From the population statistics it may be inferred that there were 1m. additional deaths in 1985. This may be compared to the estimated 200,000 who died in the 1972–73 famine that played a part in the downfall of Haile Selassie.

There are 8m. or more peasant households. The peasant's rain-fed agriculture, his unsophisticated techniques of production, and his lack of tradeable assets leave him vulnerable to the vagaries of the weather, the international economy, the government, and insect pests. Yet it is not possible to transform the Ethiopian economy without there first being substantial technical progress in the dominant peasant sector. The size constraint of the domestic market means that manufacturing enterprises are generally below the minimum economic size. Moreover, lack of experience often results in low productivity, which negates any advantage gained by low wages. It is therefore highly unlikely that Ethiopian manufactured goods could attract substantial foreign orders. Indeed, it is doubtful if the small, but highly-protected, industrial sector would fend off foreign goods in the domestic economy if the trade regime were more liberal. The promise of tourism notwithstanding, the service sector could not become the driving force of the economy until after many years have passed. Thus, although a weak farming sector gives rise to many problems, it is there that future hopes largely lie.

Economic failure led the Mengistu government to take this truth seriously if belatedly. From 1988 onwards market forces were progressively reinstated. Agricultural policy was reformed. Private merchants were again allowed to operate, the harshness of the AMC regime wass tempered by reform and downgrading of the quota system. Farm-gate prices paid by the government were raised, and the peasant given greater freedom to undertake private trade. In 1990 it was announced that the economy would be market-driven, so that private investment—domestic and foreign—would be welcomed.

The transitional government that took power following Mengistu's overthrow in 1991 is committed to extending the market economy. With the help of the World Bank, the IMF, the African Development Bank and bilateral donors, a programme of economic reconstruction and rehabilitation is under way. An ambitious structural adjustment effort is also in place; to date, the government's attention has focused on the highland economy, where most of the population is and most economic activity takes place. At lower altitudes in the southwest of the country the 'false' banana plant (*enset*) is a staple crop. It is, moreover, one that has attracted technical progess, and so has helped sustain dense and growing populations. In this relatively wet area much of Ethiopia's coffee is grown. Lower still, and down to sea level, the population is sparse and scattered. The nomads it comprises are mainly pastoralists.

The closing stages of the civil war had a strongly adverse effect on the economy. Thus, according to official figures, in the fiscal year to 7 July 1991 real GDP fell by 0.3%. This was followed by a decline of more than 10% in the year 1991/92. The drop in agricultural output was 3% in the first, and 8% in the second of the successive years.

ECONOMIC POLICY REFORM

The Economic Relief and Rehabilitation Programme (ERRP) aims to make good the ravages of war, including the resettlement of Mengistu's disbanded army. The programme aims to create a largely market-driven economy, to foster the conditions for sustained economic growth. Wide-ranging macro-economic changes are central to this effort. The government will, however, retain responsibility for economic progress, will keep more or less direct control of strategic enterprises, and will contribute to growth through the provision of public and merit goods. To date, policies towards private investment have been made more liberal, a new labour code has been introduced, economic freedom has been restored to the peasants, public enterprises have been reorganized and required to meet commercial performance criteria, prices have been widely freed, transport has been deregulated, positive real interest rates have been contrived, the tax and tariff systems have been reformed, and the birr has been devalued. Other measures in the making include the divestiture of most of the public enterprises, including all state farms other than experimental farms that have an extension role.

The basis of internal administration has changed. National transitional and regional transitional governments have been established by proclamation. Regional and lower self-governments exercise legislative, executive and judicial powers within their areas, except for matters such as defence, foreign affairs, economic policy, citizenship and the printing of money, which are reserved for the central government. More generally devolved powers are determined by a central council of representatives. The second-tier governments are empowered to raise money from domestic lenders and to levy dues and taxes. In general, the decentralized governments, must act in concert with central economic and other policies. These arrangements aim to bring economic federalism to Ethiopia. This is, however, normally a less efficient system than a unitary one. The new mode of government will certainly strain the country's stock of skilled manpower and, in particular, will place heavy demands on central government; and considerable skill will be required if it is to co-ordinate spending and borrowing at each level of government in such a way as to bring consistency to its overall economic policy. This task will be eased, but not be made easy, if there is maximum reliance on the market at all levels of government. The demands that will result from the restructuring of government reinforce the importance that attaches to the economic freedom of the peasants.

The devaluations of the birr in October 1992 and in April and May 1994, as well as the introduction in May 1993 of a fortnightly foreign exchange auction, together with other measures, including the partial reform of taxation and the elimination of all export taxes (except on coffee), the removal of the capital charge on subsidies to public enterprises and the encouragement of private-sector merchant trading, are substantial steps in the direction of restoring a market economy. While it will take time for the full impact of these measures to be felt, the short-term evidence is encouraging. The immediate effect of the 1992 devaluation was an improvement in the real exchange rate. Defined as the nominal rate multiplied by the ratio of domestic to foreign inflation, this is perhaps the most important single factor in the reform programme. It determines the allocation of resources between tradeable and non-tradeable goods in the domestic economy, and greatly influences the scope for trade. Following a period in which domestic price rises were outpacing inflation elsewhere, devaluation of the nominal rate removes the disability under which the economy had been operating. The longer-term effectiveness of these exchange rate corrections will depend upon the trend in prices in their wake. Thus, the control of inflation is critical.

In the short-term, however, it is difficult to increase output directly or by the more efficient use of resources as these are switched from lower to higher productivity, even in the favourable conditions created by devaluation. It takes time to organize an increase in exports and to seize the increased opportunity for efficient import substitution. There is, therefore, a danger that inflationary expectations can become entrenched before growth-producing measures are in operation.

Ethiopian price data are incomplete, although available statistics indicate that between devaluation and the first quarter of 1993 prices of cereals, pulses and oilseeds all declined, by 25%, 18.9%, and 23.5%, respectively. Food purchases do not exhaust household expenditure. Even in the Addis Ababa retail price index, however, they account for almost one-half the total. Food prices, which are subject to marked seasonal fluctuations, are normally at their peak in October and at their lowest in January. It is, therefore, likely that the seasonal factor is at least partly responsible for the favourable changes just reported. Nevertheless, their size is sufficiently great as to suggest that not all of the price improvement was seasonal. Moreover if the worst fears had been realized, prices could have risen sufficiently to offset more than the seasonal fall. That did not occur.

Another significant pointer was the lack of movement in building material prices in the quarter following devaluation. Yet significant rises could have been expected from devaluation, higher interest rates, and economic recovery. The price stagnation could, however, have had causes other than devaluation. For example, stocks might have been increased beyond prudence in anticipation of the realignment of the currency. And government-controlled public prices might have caused private merchants to buy most of the public stocks at fixed prices for future sale at higher ones. Inflation would be thus deferred rather than avoided.

Recent inflationary pressures in the period have been constrained by a good harvest and the willingness of the peasants to bring their produce to the market and by the fact that the full impact of devaluation has yet to be felt in the domestic economy. Moreover, manufacturing and services are still largely in public hands, so that price controls have almost certainly led to some suppression of inflation. This remains, therefore, a real threat, particularly since reweighting the Addis Ababa Consumer Price Index (the weights of which are still based on a 1963 survey) by data from household budgets in 1980 shows that prices in the first quarter of 1992/93 were at least 11% higher than in the same period of 1991/92.

There has been encouraging increase in output, particularly of cereals. Against this, the early impact of devaluation on exports has been somewhat disappointing. Coffee deliveries in Addis Ababa did rise, but not dramatically. Leather goods earned more foreign exchange than in the pre-devaluation period. Exports of sesame seed and haricot beans, for which floor prices had been set, were disappointing, although a fall in world prices clearly had an impact on their earnings.

Devaluation has had one important result. The Washington DC based institutions, the EC, the UN and other major donors took the willingness to devalue as a sign that Ethiopia was serious in seeking economic reform, and so deserving of external support. The decision taken, one of the most immediate benefits was a rescheduling of external debt at a meeting of the 'Paris Club' of official creditors in December 1992. Ethiopia's external debt was then $3,670m. Servicing this in 1992/93 would have needed more than $300m. and some 8% of GDP or 60% of estimated export earnings. Rescheduling will save at least $500m. in the next three years. As a result, however, debt servicing in later years will rise. Rescheduling grants respite, and will be justified if, in consequence, the economy becomes stronger and so more able to carry the burden of earlier debts.

There has been a significant deficit in the balance of trade in recent years. This reached its peak in 1991/92, when the effects of the war were greatest, and the inducement to smuggle exports (including those of coffee) was at its height. In the first quarter of 1992/93 the gap widened to birr 118.2m. This still did not match the imbalance of 1990/91, when the deficit was birr 602.2m. The level of exports and imports in 1992/93 were higher than in 1991/92, but still had not recovered that of the late 1980s and the early 1990s. In the corresponding period of 1988/89, for example, exports and imports stood at birr 256.3m. and birr 612.2m. respectively. These data compare with exports of birr 93.1m. and imports of birr 211.3m. in the first quarter of 1992/93.

The encouraging feature of the latest export figures is that coffee exports recovered significantly, as farmers took advantage of renewed stability and higher cash prices. These also attracted previously smuggled coffee back to normal channels. General importers were kept down by a sharp drop in *franco valuta* goods. Over all, it is still too early to assess the impact of devaluation on the balance of payments, but it is already clear that the restoration of external balance will not be easy.

ECONOMICS OF THE PUBLIC SECTOR

In tandem with devaluation and the freeing of peasant producers, the transitional government has formulated a strategy of agriculture-led industrialization. To succeed, this calls for macro-economic policies that will restore and sustain internal and external balance. At least of equal importance, is that public expenditure must be within the limits of what the economy can afford, and give clear priority to peasant agriculture. The hope is then that peasant agriculture will make a growing contribution to food security, make increased savings available to finance general capital formation, release labour for off-farm activities, and, above all, provide growing markets for industrial firms. Moreover, the pattern of demand that is likely to flow from rising peasant incomes should call for goods and services that can be provided by viable small-scale businesses using relatively labour-intensive production techniques and located in small market towns.

The level and composition of government spending and the ways in which it is financed are very important. If government expenditure is financed by the domestic banking system the money supply is automatically increased. Thus in 1989/90 and 1990/91 the budget deficits were the highest ever, amounting respectively to 17% and 15% of GDP. These were financed by credit from the domestic banks, and broad money expanded by some 18% in each of the two years. In 1991/92 money growth slowed to 13% but much of this still derived from government borrowing. In 1992/93 the broad money supply grew by 11% in the first eight months. Unfortunately, indications at the end of that period were that the annual rate could be as high as 16%.

This continuing expansion of the money supply owed much to an increase in foreign assets. These were some birr 400m. in 1991/92, but had risen to about birr 900m. in 1992/93. Growth in government credits was relatively modest, although facilities given to non-government sectors of the economy rose significantly. Carried forwards, as it were, there is excess liquidity in the economy. If this is to be eliminated, the money supply should grow at a rate below that of the nominal GDP.

Hitherto Ethiopia has been financially prudent. Repayment and servicing have been on time; and careful control of fiscal deficits has kept down inflation, particularly by sub-Saharan standards. From late 1990, however, the rate of inflation rose sharply as the needs of a war economy were increasingly met by domestic credit. Interruption of agricultural production also caused the prices of food grains to rise. Given the importance of imported inputs to both agriculture and industry, because of delays in the arrival of imports financed by the ERRP and because devaluation has increased the price of imports, in birr terms, by 142%, the economy is working at less than its capacity. This has made a drop in government revenues more manageable than otherwise would have been the case since the shortfall in revenue has been offset, to some extent, by a lower-than-normal expenditure. Indeed, by the first quarter of 1992/93 capital and current expenditure were outpaced by income from taxes and grants to the extent of birr 29m. This contrasts with first quarter deficits in the three previous fiscal years of birr 60.5m., birr 180.5m. and birr 143.9m. respectively. The surplus did not last, however, and in the second quarter of 1992/93 a deficit of birr 498m. was recorded.

The change between the two quarters was due to a marked increase in capital spending. This was not matched by a reduction in current expenditure, which was birr 795.3m. in the second quarter of 1992/93, or 36% higher than in the same period of 1991/92. More than two-thirds of the total deficit was financed by domestic bank credit. There must, therefore, be a lingering fear that as the economy expands the fiscal deficit will grow also.

Education and health spending are often taken as prime targets when structural adjustment calls for financial retrenchment. Thus far, they do not seem to have been so treated in Ethiopia. In the first half of 1992/93 expenditure on education and health was birr 251.5m. and birr 69.7m. respectively. In the corresponding period of 1991/92 the respective amounts were birr 198.9m. and birr 47.8m.

Too much should not be read into limited data. Reform is proceeding. And as the economy grows revenues will rise under a reformed as well as under an unreformed system. Receipts, however, will still be limited, so that priorities must be resolutely applied to capital and current spending. Not only must resources be left for private sector development, but public spending has to be supportive of private markets. An efficient network of rural credit, an improved system of roads, a marked increase and refocusing of agricultural research and extension services, basic health and education provision in all regions, an agricultural intelligence system, vastly improved financial institutions (including the development of a capital market), a legal system geared to the sanctity of contract and the inviolability of private property, and a reformed and efficient civil service that, *inter alia*, can manage a rising flow of aid and foreign investment, conduct timely and competent policy analysis and so offer sound advice to government, and set up the institutions needed if economic federalism is to be effective—these are among the tasks for government. The role of the state in Ethiopian economic affairs has never been as challenging.

RECENT ECONOMIC DEVELOPMENTS

Not surprisingly in the economic and political conditions of the time, the Ethiopian economy in 1991–92 was in a state of near collapse. In the four years from 1988–89 to 1991–92 real output fell at an average annual rate of 3%. Moreover, the decline was particularly marked in the fiscal year 1991–92, when the GDP was more than 7% lower than that of the previous year.

Economic rehabilitation and reform programmes were quickly put in place in the second half of 1991 and in 1992. The obvious question is: how successful have these new policies been? Before answering this directly, it should be remarked that even the most radical reforms cannot be expected to make good years of economic mismanagement overnight. Still, in 1992–93 the economy recovered the ground that had been lost in the year before by growing by 7.6% in real terms. Given its weight in total economic activity, the increase in agricultural output of almost 5% was particularly welcome. The other main sectors—industry, distribution, and services—rose by 12.0%, 8.9% and 9.3% respectively.

Welcome as it was, this improved economic performance should be seen as recovery rather than long-term growth. That has still to come. To say this is not to disparage the achievement that recovery represents. If a traveller is going in the wrong direction, the first step he or she has to take is to turn around if the proper destination is to be reached.

Nevertheless, it is important to be aware of the special character of the achievement. Peasant agriculture, which remains the most important economic activity in Ethiopia, was helped by several factors that should continue to operate and make a substantial contribution to future growth. The first, and most important of these, is the restoration of economic freedom to the peasants. Related to this, the second is the fact that private merchants are back in the grain trade. Devaluation should also have helped agriculture since it would make imported food more expensive and agricultural exports more profitable than before.

For all that, peasant farming is still overwhelmingly rainfed, so that it was helped greatly by rains that was plentiful and timely in relation to the farm calendar. It is, therefore, not surprising that cereals, pulses and oil seeds all posted positive rates of growth—of 9%, 10% and 3.4% respectively. Food imports on commerical terms fell by 75% in 1992–93, but food aid rose by 26%.

Following the devaluation of the birr in October 1992, the government introduced a foreign exchange auction, which was intended to ease the way for more financial liberalization. The amounts auctioned at the weekly sale have been increasing, and by July 1994 the rate had moved from birr 5 = US $1.00 to birr 6.22 = US $1.00. Prospective business entrepreneurs were among those successful at the auction, and there have been clear signs of increasing imports of spare parts and raw materials. The return of public enterprises to the private sector has been moving slowly. These enterprises have, however, been reorganized and are now run on commercial lines.

It is not possible from available data to be sure of how much of the increased industrial output has been due to new ventures, and how much from greater capacity utilization in existing firms. There is, however, no doubt that as access to foreign currency increased, capacity utilization did likewise. In a sample of factories, there were three with low changes in utilization between 1991–92 and 1992–93, but others recorded gains in the range of 15% to 54%.

Trade statistics are almost always among the first available. It is thus possible to compare performance in the first half of 1993–94 with that of the corresponding period in the previous year. Thus the value of exports fell by some 10%. Non-coffee export earnings fell, however, by less than 1%, so that most of the decline was due to falling coffee sales. This decline was most marked in Saudi Arabia, where Harar and Wellega had long enjoyed a monopoly, and so had sold at above-average prices. These attracted others, however, and North Yemen has now become a supplier of this type of coffee, ending the Ethiopian monopoly. There was also some hesitancy in the growing Japanese market as the yen weakened against the US dollar. Imports declined by 17.4% in the relevant period.

In the first half of 1993–94, government revenue rose by 25%. As expenditure rose by 34%, the overall deficit (with capital expenditure included) increased by 26%. Narrow money was remarkably stable in this period—rising by less than 1%. Quasi-money increased, however, by 16%. As measured by the Addis Ababa retail price index, prices fell by 4.3% in this period.

Present indications are that the run of good harvests that have marked the last few years may not remain unbroken. It is already estimated that there are 7m. people threatened by famine, because of failure of the rains. Drought does not have to lead to famine, if the economy is well enough integrated to enable well-directed food transfers to take place. There has of course to be an adequate supply of food to be transferred. Food previously stored has been used, and supplies and pledges from foreign donors are considerable. Much of the food, however, is in Assab, in Eritrea, and its impact will depend on the speed with which it is cleared from the port and distributed to the people who so badly need it. Life can never be secure when it depends on rain-fed farming.

Statistical Survey

Source (unless otherwise stated): Central Statistical Authority, POB 1143, Addis Ababa; tel. 553010.

Note: Unless otherwise indicated, figures in this Survey refer to the territory of Ethiopia prior to the secession of Eritrea in May 1993.

Area and Population

AREA, POPULATION AND DENSITY (excluding Eritrea)

Area (sq km)	1,130,138*
Population (census of 9 May 1984)†	
Males	20,062,453
Females	19,806,048
Total	39,868,501
Population (official estimates at mid-year)	
1989	46,927,600
1990	48,359,800
1991	49,947,400
Density (per sq km) at mid-1991	44.2

* 436,349 sq miles.

† Including an estimate for areas not covered by the census.

ADMINISTRATIVE REGIONS
(excluding Eritrea, census of 9 May 1984)*

	Area (sq km)	Population	Density (per sq km)
Addis Ababa	222.0	1,423,111	6,410.4
Arussi	23,674.7	1,662,790	70.2
Bale	127,052.7	1,017,336	8.0
Gemu Goffa	40,347.8	1,267,477	31.5
Gojam	61,224.3	3,273,524	53.5
Gondar	79,579.5	3,018,909	37.9
Hararge	272,636.9	4,192,898	15.4
Illubabor	46,367.2	975,658	21.0
Kefa (Kaffa)	56,633.5	2,478,957	43.8
Shoa	85,093.7	8,102,326	95.2
Sidamo	119,760.4	3,813,075	31.8
Tigre	64,921.2	2,415,871	37.2
Wollega	70,480.9	2,478,425	35.2
Wollo	82,143.6	3,746,144	45.6
Total	1,130,138.4	39,868,501	35.3

* Following the adoption of a new Constitution in 1987, the 15 existing regions were replaced by 24 Administrative Regions and five Autonomous Regions. In November 1991, however, the new transitional Government announced the division of the country (excluding Eritrea) into 14 new Administrative Regions, based on the pre-1987 divisions.

PRINCIPAL TOWNS (excluding Eritrea, population at 1984 census)

Addis Ababa (capital)	1,423,111	Harar	63,070
Dire Dawa	99,980	Mekele	62,662
Gondar (incl. Azeso)	80,675	Jimma	60,218
Nazret	77,237	Debre Zeit	55,655
Dessie	71,537	Akaki	55,244
		Bahir Dar	54,766

BIRTHS AND DEATHS (UN estimates, annual averages)

	1975–80	1980–85	1985–90
Birth rate (per 1,000)	48.3	44.5	49.5
Death rate (per 1,000)	21.5	23.5	20.0

Expectation of life (UN estimates, years at birth, 1985–90): 45.0 (males 43.4; females 46.6).

Source: UN, *World Population Prospects: The 1992 Revision.*

ECONOMICALLY ACTIVE POPULATION* (ISIC Major Divisions, persons aged 10 years and over, 1984 census)

	Males	Females	Total
Agriculture, hunting, forestry and fishing	9,486,409	6,614,602	16,101,011
Mining and quarrying	9,062	3,281	12,343
Manufacturing	167,649	119,249	286,898
Electricity, gas and water	11,071	1,681	12,752
Construction	41,822	3,947	45,769
Trade, restaurants and hotels	250,870	445,148	696,018
Transport, storage and communications	65,812	11,251	77,063
Financing, insurance, real estate and business services	10,857	3,660	14,517
Community, social and personal services	581,936	351,560	933,496
Total labour force	10,625,488	7,554,379	18,179,867

* Data have been adjusted to include estimates for areas not covered by the census. The figures exclude persons seeking work for the first time, totalling 55,841 (males 30,066; females 25,775), but include other unemployed persons.

Source: ILO, *Year Book of Labour Statistics.*

Agriculture

PRINCIPAL CROPS ('000 metric tons)

	1990	1991	1992
Wheat*	867	890	900
Barley*	899	925	1,000
Maize*	1,636	1,530	1,650
Oats*	71	70	70
Millet (Dagusa)*	273	260	280
Sorghum*	787	810	1,100
Other cereals*	1,924	1,820	2,000
Potatoes*	380	384	388
Sweet potatoes*	152	153	154
Yams*	260	261	262
Other roots and tubers*	1,250	1,280	1,270
Dry beans	83	130*	130*
Dry peas	97	110*	110*
Dry broad beans	279	282*	282*
Chick-peas	101	120*	120*
Lentils	30	35*	35*
Other pulses	121	147	138*
Sugar cane*	1,650	1,530	1,620
Soybeans	21	20*	21*
Groundnuts (in shell)*	52	53	54
Castor beans*	13	14	14
Rapeseed	78	80*	81*
Sesame seed	33†	35†	36*
Linseed	34	34†	35*
Safflower seed*	34	35	35
Cottonseed	42†	42†	26*
Cotton (lint)†	19	19	12
Vegetables and melons*	591	594	599
Bananas*	78	79	80
Other fruit (excl. melons)*	151	152	154
Tree nuts*	63	64	65
Coffee (green)	204	210†	216†
Tobacco (leaves)	4†	4†	4*
Fibre crops (excl. cotton)*	17	17	18

* FAO estimate(s). † Unofficial estimate(s).

Source: FAO, *Production Yearbook*.

LIVESTOCK ('000 head, year ending September)

	1990	1991	1992
Cattle†	30,000	30,000	31,000
Sheep	22,960*	23,000†	23,200†
Goats	17,200*	18,000†	18,100†
Asses†	5,000	5,100	5,200
Horses†	2,650	2,700	2,750
Mules†	590	610	630
Camels†	1,050	1,060	1,070
Pigs†	20	20	20

* Unofficial estimate. † FAO estimate(s).

Poultry (FAO estimates, million): 58 in 1990 and 1991; 59 in 1992.

Source: FAO, *Production Yearbook*.

LIVESTOCK PRODUCTS
(FAO estimates, unless otherwise indicated; '000 metric tons)

	1990	1991	1992
Beef and veal	245*	245*	210
Mutton and lamb	82*	82	82
Goats' meat	67	67	68
Pig meat	1	1	1
Poultry meat	76	77	77
Other meat	130	133	133
Edible offals	98	98	95
Cows' milk	748	752	774
Goats' milk	95	99	100
Sheep's milk	57	58	58
Butter	9.9	10.4	10.8
Cheese	4.4	4.6	4.8
Hen eggs	78.9	79.1	79.4
Honey	23.0	23.4	23.7
Wool:			
greasy	12.2	12.2	12.3
clean	6.3	6.3	6.4
Cattle hides	47.0	47.0	44.1
Sheep skins	14.7	14.7	15.0
Goat skins	14.1	14.2	14.3

* Unofficial estimate.

Source: FAO, *Production Yearbook* and *Quarterly Bulletin of Statistics*.

Forestry

ROUNDWOOD REMOVALS
('000 cubic metres, excluding bark)

	1990	1991	1992
Sawlogs, etc.	32	20	20*
Other industrial wood*†	1,693	1,693	1,693
Fuel wood*	41,283	42,563	43,890
Total	43,008	44,276	45,603

* FAO estimate(s).

† Assumed to be unchanged since 1983.

Source: FAO, *Yearbook of Forest Products*.

SAWNWOOD PRODUCTION
('000 cubic metres, incl. railway sleepers)

	1990	1991	1992
Total	22	12	12*

*FAO estimate.

Source: FAO, *Yearbook of Forest Products*.

Fishing

('000 metric tons, live weight)

	1989	1990*	1991*
Inland waters	2.7	3.0	2.8
Indian Ocean	1.6	2.0	1.7
Total catch	4.3	5.0	4.5

* FAO estimates.

Source: FAO, *Yearbook of Fishery Statistics*.

Mining

('000 metric tons, unless otherwise indicated)

	1989	1990	1991
Gold (kilograms)*	745	800	3,038
Salt	110	110	110
Limestone	150	100	n.a.
Sand	775	1,250	n.a.
Kaolin	0	1	1

* Twelve months ending 30 June. † Estimate.

Sources: US Bureau of Mines, given in UN, *Industrial Statistics Yearbook.*

Industry

SELECTED PRODUCTS ('000 metric tons, unless otherwise indicated; year ending 7 July)

	1989/90	1990/91
Flour	242.5	238.6
Macaroni	8.1	7.5
Raw sugar	178	171.4
Wine ('000 hectolitres)	101.5	100.2
Beer ('000 hectolitres)	776.6	627.5
Soft drinks ('000 boxes containing 7.2 litres)	11,265	10,765
Mineral waters ('000 bottles containing 0.65 litre)	36,047	36,443
Cigarettes (million packets)	2,711	2,396
Cotton yarn	5.9	7.9
Woven cotton fabrics ('000 sq metres)	70,459	76,195
Blankets ('000 sq metres)	3,919	3,548
Nylon fabrics ('000 sq metres)	5,433	5,007
Footwear ('000 pairs)	9,361	7,385
Leather footwear	2,035	1,884
Rubber and canvas footwear	4,013	3,555
Plastic footwear	3,313	1,946
Soap	11.3	10.1
Ethyl alcohol ('000 hectolitres)	5.8	4.5
Quicklime (metric tons)	1,998.8*	2,310.4*
Cement	413	345

* Estimate.

Source: Ministry of Labour.

Finance

CURRENCY AND EXCHANGE RATES

Monetary Units

100 cents = 1 birr.

Sterling and Dollar Equivalents (31 March 1994)

£1 sterling = 7.423 birr;
US $1 = 5.000 birr;
100 birr = £13.472 = $20.000.

Exchange Rate

An official rate of US $1 = 2.070 birr was established in February 1973. This remained in force until October 1992, when a rate of $1 = 5.000 birr was introduced. That rate was in effect until April 1994, when it was adjusted to $1 = 5.130 birr. The currency was further devalued in May 1994.

GENERAL BUDGET (million birr, year ending 7 July)

Revenue*	1987/88	1988/89	1989/90
Taxation	1,984.8	1,864.3	2,190.4
Taxes on income, profits, etc.	796.0	805.2	945.0
Sales taxes	102.0	95.0	100.0
Excises	466.3	353.5	498.1
Import duties	213.0	155.3	177.5
Export duties	114.4	141.6	79.8
Stamp taxes	28.8	25.0	30.0
Entrepreneurial and property income	697.8	670.6	557.0
Administrative fees and charges, etc.	28.0	47.5	36.0
Other current revenue	1,258.1	1,718.3	1,607.2
Capital revenue	27.0	27.5	27.0
Total revenue	3,995.7	4,328.2	4,417.6

Expenditure†	1987/88	1988/89	1989/90
General public services and defence	1,426.0	1,865.3	2,132.2
Education	421.7	453.1	488.5
Health	133.4	141.4	149.8
Social security and welfare	82.0	109.0	79.1
Economic affairs and services	809.6	893.3	998.1
Agriculture, forestry and fishing	485.0	447.0	572.6
Transport and communication	219.4	221.5	187.8
Other purposes	2,260.5	2,580.1	2,691.4
Total expenditure	5,133.2	6,042.2	6,539.1
Current‡	3,097.2	3,758.5	4,153.5
Capital	2,036.0	2,283.7	2,385.6

* Excluding grants received from abroad (million birr): 635.9 in 1987/88 (estimate).

† Excluding net lending (million birr): 101.4 in 1987/88 (estimate).

‡ Including interest payments (million birr): 244.7 in 1987/88 (estimate).

NATIONAL BANK RESERVES (US $ million at 31 December)

	1991	1992	1993
Gold*	15.1	11.4	11.4
IMF special drawing rights	0.2	0.1	0.3
Reserve position in IMF	—	9.5	9.6
Foreign exchange	54.3	222.8	445.9
Total	69.6	243.8	467.2

* National valuation.

Source: IMF, *International Financial Statistics.*

MONEY SUPPLY (million birr at 31 December)

	1991	1992	1993
Currency outside banks	4,007	4,709	4,776
Demand deposits at commercial banks	2,192	2,433	2,674
Total money	6,199	7,142	7,450

Source: IMF, *International Financial Statistics.*

COST OF LIVING (General Index of Retail Prices for Addis Ababa, excluding rent; base: 1980 = 100)

	1990	1991	1992
Food	149.5	211.2	236.3
Fuel, light and soap*	196.3	267.0	266.4
Clothing	103.4	117.6	160.3
All items (incl. others)	153.9	209.0	230.9

* Including certain kitchen utensils.

Source: ILO, *Year Book of Labour Statistics*.

NATIONAL ACCOUNTS
(million birr at current prices, year ending 7 July)

Expenditure on the Gross Domestic Product

	1990/91	1991/92	1992/93
Government final consumption expenditure	2,936	2,165	3,208
Private final consumption expenditure*	10,685	11,706	13,951
Gross fixed capital formation	1,421	1,215	3,502
Total domestic expenditure	15,032	15,086	20,661
Exports of goods and services	1,124	1,039	3,165
Less Imports of goods and services	2,520	2,617	7,018
GDP in purchasers' values	13,646	13,508	16,809

* Including increase in stocks. The figures are obtained as a residual.

Source: IMF, *International Financial Statistics*.

Gross Domestic Product by Economic Activity (provisional)

	1986/87	1987/88	1988/89
Agriculture, hunting, forestry and fishing	4,317.9	4,326.7	4,665.7
Mining and quarrying	12.3	13.5	14.3
Manufacturing	1,167.3	1,199.5	1,230.1
Electricity, gas and water	134.8	143.6	159.0
Construction	422.6	418.8	439.8
Wholesale and retail trade	1,056.9	1,068.0	1,121.2
Transport, storage and communications	713.0	721.4	783.0
Finance, insurance and real estate*	624.6	704.8	668.7
Public administration and defence	850.6	1,142.0	1,339.1
Other community, social and personal services†	626.9	676.5	704.6
Other services	72.4	73.1	73.9
GDP at factor cost	9,999.3	10,487.9	11,199.4
Indirect taxes, *less* subsidies	1,196.5	1,279.1	1,291.6
GDP in purchasers' values	11,195.8	11,767.0	12,491.0

* Including imputed rents of owner-occupied dwellings.
† Including, restaurants, hotels and business services.

Source: UN, *National Accounts Statistics*.

BALANCE OF PAYMENTS (US $ million)

	1990	1991	1992
Merchandise exports f.o.b.	292.0	167.6	169.9
Merchandise imports f.o.b.	-912.1	-470.8	-992.7
Trade balance	-620.1	-303.2	-822.9
Exports of services	304.6	268.3	267.9
Imports of services	-358.8	-284.3	-368.3
Other income received	9.2	14.4	22.3
Other income paid	-77.7	-96.7	-104.1
Private unrequited transfers (net)	229.1	222.4	341.5
Official unrequited transfers (net)	211.3	353.0	543.9
Current balance	-302.4	173.9	-119.7
Capital (net)	230.0	-204.1	94.2
Net errors and omissions	-125.9	-254.9	-43.3
Overall balance	-198.3	-285.1	-68.8

Source: IMF, *International Financial Statistics*.

External Trade

PRINCIPAL COMMODITIES
(distribution by SITC, US $ '000)

Imports c.i.f.	1989	1990	1991
Food and live animals	77,787	129,824	20,151
Cereals and cereal preparations	58,216	102,272	14,172
Wheat and meslin (unmilled)	46,836	76,311	10,059
Crude materials (inedible) except fuels	25,918	34,483	5,689
Mineral fuels, lubricants, etc.	107,933	128,082	50,196
Petroleum, petroleum products, etc.	107,847	128,073	50,134
Crude petroleum oils, etc.	86,451	112,892	29,148
Refined petroleum products	19,855	13,224	20,543
Chemicals and related products	170,553	108,810	72,735
Inorganic chemicals	20,612	20,372	6,629
Medicinal and pharmaceutical products	33,538	25,383	8,812
Medicaments	28,124	22,129	16,150
Manufactured fertilizers	60,849	16,115	23,613
Basic manufactures	148,167	172,897	76,327
Rubber manufactures	25,103	17,835	9,250
Iron and steel	37,538	28,121	15,558
Machinery and transport equipment	338,402	427,255	210,482
Machinery specialized for particular industries	109,621	115,650	28,652
Textile and leather machinery	18,421	25,350	6,457
General industrial machinery, equipment and parts	34,950	40,727	13,268
Telecommunications and sound equipment	32,199	23,250	13,028
Other electrical machinery, apparatus, etc.	34,269	38,714	9,963
Road vehicles and parts*	108,061	121,752	77,506
Passenger motor cars (excl. buses)	23,972	42,097	26,561
Motor vehicles for goods transport, etc.	28,115	32,889	26,929
Goods vehicles (lorries and trucks)	24,264	30,528	25,906
Parts and accessories for cars, buses, lorries, etc.*	42,432	34,300	16,223
Other transport equipment*	4,116	56,077	54,633
Aircraft, etc., and parts*	1,161	53,138	53,056
Miscellaneous manufactured articles	44,012	45,314	30,092
Total (incl. others)	952,739	1,076,105	471,810

* Excluding tyres, engines and electrical parts.

Exports f.o.b.	1989	1990	1991
Food and live animals	323,446	181,978	126,325
Vegetables and fruit	11,186	25,881	6,292
Fresh or simply preserved vegetables	10,193	25,256	3,724
Coffee, tea, cocoa and spices	296,061	132,864	117,169
Coffee and coffee substitutes	293,839	131,508	116,233
Crude materials (inedible) except fuels	91,466	76,329	32,311
Raw hides, skins and furskins	65,942	60,776	25,068
Raw hides and skins (excl. furs)	65,941	60,775	25,068
Goat skins	17,225	11,818	5,088
Sheep skins with the wool on	38,575	39,980	16,202
Mineral fuels, lubricants, etc.	18,048	20,504	1,836
Petroleum, petroleum products, etc.	18,048	20,504	1,836
Total (incl. others)*	451,706	296,544	188,609

* Excluding platinum.

PRINCIPAL TRADING PARTNERS (US $ '000)

Imports c.i.f.	1989	1990	1991
Belgium-Luxembourg	12,027	20,606	9,635
Canada	22,134	9,743	5,349
France	21,637	30,805	13,853
German Dem. Rep.	8,625	13,260	36,335
Germany, Fed. Rep.	102,759	101,409	53,734
Greece	7,948	12,951	1,686
Italy	133,287	177,858	48,034
Japan	62,244	70,416	45,374
Kenya	22,894	18,911	20,349
Korea, Rep.	4,897	13,680	2,001
Netherlands	32,731	30,392	15,684
Saudi Arabia	12,211	17,144	46,773
Sweden	32,200	19,339	10,097
Switzerland	16,781	21,918	5,613
USSR	129,380	139,549	4,493
United Kingdom	84,622	81,588	26,482
USA	53,393	57,805	61,888
Yugoslavia	5,106	10,688	4,124
Total (incl. others)	952,740	1,076,105	471,810

Exports f.o.b.	1989	1990	1991
Austria	2,671	8,459	8,038
Belgium-Luxembourg	14,723	8,900	8,033
Djibouti	25,852	35,294	7,285
France	21,917	8,032	11,475
Germany, Fed. Rep.	105,141	50,674	46,713
Italy	29,964	22,304	11,304
Japan	48,175	43,706	38,291
Netherlands	25,828	7,685	3,921
Saudi Arabia	29,838	32,301	14,095
USSR	41,846	10,511	1,022
United Kingdom	7,975	8,616	26,737
USA	65,151	31,726	8,183
Total (incl. others)	451,702	296,529	188,609

Transport

RAILWAYS (traffic, excluding Eritrea, year ending 7 July)*

	1988/89	1989/90	1990/91
Addis Ababa–Djibouti:			
Passenger-km (million)	342	298	277
Freight (million net ton-km)	141	129	126

* Including traffic on the portion of the Djibouti–Addis Ababa line which runs through the Republic of Djibouti. Data pertaining to freight include service traffic.

Source: UN, *Statistical Yearbook*.

ROAD TRAFFIC (motor vehicles in use at 31 December)

	1989	1990	1991
Cars	39,942	37,054	37,799
Buses and coaches	4,515	4,460	5,999
Goods vehicles	12,615	12,890	14,940
Motorcycles and scooters	1,708	1,440	1,515
Total	58,780	55,844	60,253

Source: IRF, *World Road Statistics*.

INTERNATIONAL SEA-BORNE SHIPPING
(estimated freight traffic, '000 metric tons)

	1989	1990	1991*
Goods loaded	615	520	592
Goods unloaded	3,190	3,014	3,120

* Estimates.

Source: Economic Commission for Africa, *African Statistical Yearbook*.

CIVIL AVIATION (traffic on scheduled services)

	1989	1990	1991
Kilometres flown (million)	23	21	21
Passengers carried ('000)	651	620	636
Passenger-km (million)	1,606	1,529	1,568
Freight ton-km (million)	93	67	79

Source: UN, *Statistical Yearbook*.

Tourism

	1989	1990	1991*
Tourist arrivals ('000)	74	73	82
Tourist receipts (US $ million)	21	25	19

* Unofficial estimates.

Communications Media

	1988	1989	1990
Telephones ('000 in use)	138	153	159
Radio receivers ('000 in use)	8,700	9,000	9,400
Television receivers ('000 in use)	n.a.	100	115
Book production: titles*	560	n.a.	385
Daily newspapers:			
Number	3	3	3
Average circulation ('000 copies)	42	n.a.	n.a.
Non-daily newspapers:			
Number	4	4	4
Average circulation ('000 copies)	40	n.a.	n.a.

* Including pamphlets (213 in 1988; 220 in 1990).

1991: 9.7m. radio receivers in use; 130,000 television receivers in use; 240 book titles (incl. 93 pamphlets) produced.

Source: mainly UNESCO, *Statistical Yearbook*.

Education

	Teachers		Pupils/Students	
	1990	1991	1990	1991
Pre-primary	2,091	1,531	73,668	58,444
Primary	68,370	68,399	2,466,375	2,063,636
Secondary: general	22,721	23,110	858,716	775,211
Vocational*	480	492	5,300	4,101
Universities	1,439	1,440	29,066	20,948
Other higher	251	257	5,010	1,590

* Figures refer to 1987 and 1988, respectively.

Source: UNESCO, *Statistical Yearbook*.

Directory

The Constitution

In July 1991 a national conference elected a transitional Government and approved a charter under the provisions of which the Government was to operate until the holding of democratic elections. The charter provided guarantees for freedom of association and expression, and for self-determination for Ethiopia's different ethnic constituencies. The transitional Government was to be responsible for drafting a new constitution to replace that introduced in 1987. A constituent assembly, dominated by representatives of the EPRDF was elected in June 1994 and was expected to ratify the draft constitution (already approved by the Council of Representatives).

The Government

HEAD OF STATE

President: MELES ZENAWI (assumed power May 1991; elected President 23 July 1991).

COUNCIL OF MINISTERS OF TRANSITIONAL GOVERNMENT
(August 1994)

Prime Minister: TAMIRAT LAYNE.

Minister of Foreign Affairs: SEYOUM MESFIN.

Minister of Health: ADANECH KIDANE MARIAM.

Minister of Mines and Energy: EZEDIN ALI.

Minister for External Economic Co-operation: ABDUL-MEJID HUSSEN.

Minister of State Farms and Development of Coffee and Tea: HASAN ABDELA.

Minister of Internal Affairs: KUMA DEMEKSA.

Minister of Defence: SIYE ABRAHA.

Minister of Planning and Economic Development: Dr DOURI MOHAMMED.

Minister of Culture and Sport: LEULE SELASSIE TEMAMO.

Minister of Education: GENET ZEWDE.

Minister of Information: Dr NEGASSO GIDADA.

Minister of Agriculture: ELIAS NEGASSA.

Minister of Trade: YOSEF KUMELO.

Minister of Finance: ALEMAYEHU DABA.

Minister of Justice: MAHETEME SOLOMON.

Minister of Works and Urban Development: HAILE SELASSIE ASEGIDE.

Minister of Transport and Communications: WAKJIRA GEMECHU.

Minister of Labour and Social Affairs: MEMBERE ALEMAYEHU.

Minister of Industry: ASEFA KEDEBE.

Minister of Development of Natural Resources and Environmental Protection: MESFIN ABEBE.

Commissioner for Relief and Rehabilitation: SIMON MECHALE.

MINISTRIES AND COMMISSIONS

Office of the Prime Minister: POB 1013, Addis Ababa; tel. 123400.

Ministry of Agriculture: POB 1223, Addis Ababa; tel. 448040; fax 513042.

Ministry of Construction: Addis Ababa; tel. 155406.

Ministry of Culture and Sport: POB 1902, Addis Ababa; tel. 446338.

Ministry of Defence: POB 125, Addis Ababa; tel. 445555; telex 21261.

Ministry of Development of Natural Resources and Environmental Protection: Addis Ababa.

Ministry of Education: POB 1367, Addis Ababa; tel. 553133.

Ministry of Energy and Mines: POB 486, Addis Ababa; tel. 448250; telex 21448; fax 517874.

Ministry for External Economic Co-operation: POB 2559, Addis Ababa; tel. 151066; telex 21320.

Ministry of Finance: POB 1905, Addis Ababa; tel. 113400; telex 21147.

Ministry of Foreign Affairs: POB 393, Addis Ababa; tel. 447345; telex 21050.

Ministry of Health: POB 1234, Addis Ababa; tel. 516156.

Ministry of Industry: POB 704, Addis Ababa; tel. 518025; telex 21514; fax 515411.

Ministry of Information: POB 1020, Addis Ababa; tel. 111124.

Ministry of Internal Affairs: POB 2556, Addis Ababa; tel. 113334.

Ministry of Justice: POB 1370, Addis Ababa; tel. 447390.

Ministry of Labour and Social Affairs: POB 2056, Addis Ababa; tel. 517080.

Ministry of State Farms and Development of Coffee and Tea: POB 3222, Addis Ababa; tel. 518088; telex 21130.

Ministry of Town Planning: POB 3386, Addis Ababa; tel. 150000.

Ministry of Trade: POB 1769, Addis Ababa; tel. 448200.

Ministry of Transport and Communications: POB 5780, Addis Ababa; tel. 514055; fax 150744.

Commission for Hotels and Tourism: POB 2183, Addis Ababa; tel. 447470; telex 21067.

Commission for National Water Resources: POB 486, Addis Ababa; tel. 447597; telex 21219.

Commission for Relief and Rehabilitation: POB 5686, Addis Ababa; tel. 153011; telex 21281.

Legislature

COUNCIL OF REPRESENTATIVES

In accordance with the provisions of a transitional government charter (approved by a national conference in July 1991), an 87-member Council of Representatives, consisting of deputies from national freedom movements, other political organizations and well-known personalities, was established to govern Ethiopia during a 24-month period of transition. The Council elected its own Chairman, to be the head of the transitional Government; its Vice-Chairman; and its Secretary-General. The Council was charged with approving the appointment, by its Chairman, of a Prime Minister; and with approving the appointment, by the Prime Minister, of other members of a Council of Ministers. The Council of Representatives was also to 'lead the country towards a completely democratic system' by establishing a constitutional drafting commission; by approving and submitting to public scrutiny a draft constitution prepared by the commission (due to be published in late 1994); and by preparing the country for elections to a new National Assembly, in accordance with the provisions of a new constitution.

Elections to a Constituent Assembly were conducted in June 1994. Elections to a new legislature were expected to take place in 1995.

Chairman: MELES ZENAWI.

Vice-Chairman: Dr FEKADU GEDAMU.

Secretary-General: TESFAYE HABISO.

Political Organizations

Afar Liberation Front (ALF): based in fmr Hararge and Wollo Administrative Regions; supports transitional Govt; Leader ALI MIRAH.

Coalition of Alternative Forces for Peace and Democracy in Ethiopia (CAFPDE): f. 1993, broad-based coalition of groups in opposition to the EPRDF; Chair. BEYENE PETROS.

Coalition of Ethiopian Democratic Forces (COEDF): f. 1991 in USA by the Ethiopian People's Revolutionary Party—EPRP (the principal party involved), a faction of the Ethiopian Democratic Union (EDU) and the Ethiopian Socialist Movement (MEISON); opposes EPRDF; Chair. MERSHA YOSEPH.

Ethiopian Democratic Unity Party (EDUP): Addis Ababa; f. 1984 as Workers' Party of Ethiopia; adopted present name in March 1990, when its adherence to Marxist-Leninist ideology was relaxed and membership opened to non-Marxist and opposition groups; sole legal political party until May 1991; Sec.-Gen. Lt-Gen. TESFAYE GEBRE KIDAN.

Ethiopian National Democratic Party (ENDP): f. 1994 by merger of five pro-government organizations with mems in the Council of Representatives; comprises: the Ethiopian Democratic Organization, the Ethiopian Democratic Organization Coalition (EDC), the Gurage People's Democratic Front (GPDF), the Kembata People's Congress (KPC), and the Wolaita People's Democratic Front (WPDF); Chair. FEKADU GEDAMU.

Ethiopian People's Revolutionary Democratic Front (EPRDF): Addis Ababa; f. 1989 by the TPLF as an alliance of insurgent groups seeking regional autonomy and engaged in armed struggle against the EDUP Govt; Leader MELES ZENAWI; in May 1991 took control of Addis Ababa and, with other organizations, formed transitional Govt; alliance comprises:

Ethiopian People's Democratic Movement (EPDM): based in Tigre; represents interests of the Amhara people; reported to have changed its name to the Amhara National Democratic Movement in January 1994; Sec.-Gen. TAMIRAT LAYNE.

Oromo People's Democratic Organization (OPDO): f. 1990 by the TPLF to promote its cause in Oromo areas; based among the Oromo people in the Shoa region; Dep. Sec.-Gen. KUMA DEMEKSA.

Tigre People's Liberation Front (TPLF): f. 1975; the dominant organization within the EPRDF; Leader MELES ZENAWI.

Ethiopian Somali Democratic League (ESDL): f. 1994 by merger of 11 Ethiopian Somali organizations; comprises: Somali Democratic Union Party, the Issa and Gurgura Liberation Front, the Gurgura Independence Front, the Eastern Gabooye Democratic Organization, the Eastern Ethiopian Somali League, the Horyal Democratic Front, the Social Alliance Democratic Organization, the Somali Abo Democratic Union, the Shekhash People's Democratic Movement, the Ethiopian Somalis' Democratic Movement and the Per Barreh Party; 127-member central cttee and 15-member exec. cttee; Chair. ABDUL-MAEJID HUSSEIN.

Oromo Liberation Front (OLF): seeks self-determination for the Oromo people; participated in the Ethiopian transitional Govt until June 1992; Sec.-Gen. GELASSA DILBO; Vice Sec.-Gen. LENCHO LETTA.

Somali Abo Liberation Front (SALF): operates in fmr Bale Administrative Region; has received Somali military assistance; Sec.-Gen. MASURAD SHU'ABI IBRAHIM.

Southern Ethiopian People's Democratic Union (SEPDU): f. 1992 as an alliance of 10 ethnically-based political groups from the south of the country; represented in the Council of Representatives, although five of the 10 groups were expelled from the Council in April 1993, after having attended an opposition 'Peace for Ethiopia' conf. in Paris at the end of March; Chair. BEYENE PETROS.

Western Somali Liberation Front (WSLF): POB 978, Mogadishu, Somalia; f. 1975; aims to unite the Ogaden region with Somalia; maintains guerrilla forces of c. 3,000 men; has received support from regular Somali forces; Sec.-Gen. ISSA SHAYKH ABDI NASIR ADAN.

In November 1991 a coalition of Oromo organizations was formed, comprising:

Oromo People's Democratic Organization (OPDO): see above.

Islamic Front for Liberation of Oromia (IFLO): Chair. JARRE ABAGEDA.

United Oromo People's Liberation Front (UOPLF).

Oromo Abo Liberation Front (OALF): Chair. MOHAMMED SIRAGE.

Other organizations in opposition to the Ethiopian transitional Government include: the **Democratic Unity Party (DUP):** Chair. AHMAD ABD AL-KARIM; the **Ethiopian Medhin Democratic Party:** Leader GOSHU WOLDE; the **Ethiopian National Democratic Organization,** the **Ethiopian People's Democratic Unity Organization (EPDUO):** Leader TADESE TILAHUN; the **Ethiopian People's Revolutionary Party (EPRP)**; the pro-monarchist **Moa Ambessa Party** and the **National Democratic Union.**

Other ethnic organizations seeking self-determination for their respective groups include: the **Abugda Ethiopian Democratic Congress**; the **Afar Revolutionary Democratic Union**; the **All-Amhara People's Organization (AAPO):** Chair. Prof. ASRAT WOLDEYES; the **Burji People's Democratic Organization**; the **Daworo People's Democratic Movement**; the **Gedeo People's Democratic Organization (GPDO):** Leader ALESA MENGESHA; the **Hadia People's Democratic Organization**; the **Harer National League**; the **Jarso Democratic Movement**; the **Kaffa People's Democratic Union (KPDU)**; the **Kefa People's Democratic Movement**; the **Ogaden National Liberation Front (ONLF)**; and the **Yem Nationality Movement.**

Other political organizations include the **Ethiopian Democratic Action Group:** Chair. EPHREM ZEMIKAEL; and **Forum 84.**

Diplomatic Representation

EMBASSIES IN ETHIOPIA

Algeria: POB 5740, Addis Ababa; tel. 652300; telex 21799 fax 650187; Ambassador: AMAR BENDJAMA.

Argentina: Addis Ababa; telex 21172; Ambassador: Dr H. R. M. MOGUES.

Austria: POB 1219, Addis Ababa; tel. 712144; telex 21060; Ambassador: Dr HORST-DIETER RENNAU.

Bulgaria: POB 987, Addis Ababa; tel. 612971; telex 21450; Chargé d'affaires: VLADIMIR MOUTAFOV.

Burundi: POB 3641, Addis Ababa; tel. 651300; telex 21069; Ambassador: THARCISSE MIDONZI.

Cameroon: Bole Rd, POB 1026, Addis Ababa; telex 21121; Ambassador: DOMINIQUE YONG.

Canada: African Solidarity Insurance Bldg, 6th Floor, Churchill Ave, POB 1130, Addis Ababa; tel. 511100; telex 21053; fax 512818; Ambassador: D. S. STOCKWELL.

Chad: Addis Ababa; telex 21419; fax 612050; Ambassador: J. B. LAOKOLE.

China, People's Republic: POB 5643, Addis Ababa; telex 21145; Ambassador: GU JIAJI.

Congo: POB 5571, Addis Ababa; tel. 154331; telex 21406; Ambassador: (vacant).

Côte d'Ivoire: POB 3668, Addis Ababa; tel. 711213; telex 21061; Ambassador: ANTOINE KOUADIO-KIRINE.

Cuba: Jimma Road Ave, POB 5623, Addis Ababa; tel. 202010; telex 21306; Ambassador: ANTONIO PÉREZ HERRERO.

Czech Republic: POB 3108, Addis Ababa; tel. 516132; telex 21021; fax 513471.

Djibouti: POB 1022, Addis Ababa; tel. 613200; telex 21317; fax 612504; Ambassador: DJIBRIL DJAMA ELABE.

Egypt: POB 1611, Addis Ababa; tel. 113077; telex 21254; Ambassador: SAMIR AHMED.

Equatorial Guinea: POB 246, Addis Ababa; Ambassador: SALVADOR ELA NSENG ABEGUE.

Finland: Tedla Desta Bldg, Bole Rd, POB 1017, Addis Ababa; tel. 513900; telex 21259; Chargé d'affaires a.i.: ERIK BREHMER.

France: Kabana, POB 1464, Addis Ababa; tel. 550066; telex 21040; fax 551793; Ambassador: LOUIS AMIGUES.

Gabon: POB 1256, Addis Ababa; tel. 181075; telex 21208; Ambassador: DENIS DANGUE REWAKA.

Germany: Kabana, POB 660, Addis Ababa; tel. 550433; telex 21015; fax 551311; Ambassador: Dr HORST WINKELMAN.

Ghana: POB 3173, Addis Ababa; tel. 711402; telex 21249; fax 712511; Ambassador: KOBINA WUDU.

Greece: Africa Ave, POB 1168, Addis Ababa; tel. 110612; telex 21092; Chargé d'affaires: M. DIAMANTOPOULOS.

Guinea: POB 1190, Addis Ababa; tel. 449712; Ambassador: PIERRE BASSAMBA CAMARA.

Holy See: POB 588, Addis Ababa (Apostolic Nunciature); tel. 712100; fax 711499; Apostolic Pro-Nuncio: Most Rev. PATRICK COVENEY, Titular Archbishop of Satriano.

Hungary: Abattoirs Rd, POB 1213, Addis Ababa; tel. 651850; telex 21176; Ambassador: Dr SÁNDOR ROBEL.

India: Kabana, POB 528, Addis Ababa; tel. 552100; telex 21148; fax 552521; Ambassador: GURCHARAN SINGH.

Indonesia: Mekanisa Rd, POB 1004, Addis Ababa; tel. 202104; telex 21264; Ambassador: T.M. MOCHTAR MOHAMAD THAJEB.

Iran: 317/02 Jimma Rd, Old Airport Area, POB 1144, Addis Ababa; tel. 200369; telex 21118; Chargé d'affaires: HASSEN DABIR.

Israel: New Tafari Makonnen School, POB 1075, Addis Ababa; Ambassador: URI NOI.

Italy: Villa Italia, POB 1105, Addis Ababa; tel. 551565; telex 21342; fax 550218; Ambassador: SERGIO ANGELETTI.

Jamaica: National House, Africa Ave, POB 5633, Addis Ababa; tel. 613656; telex 21137; Ambassador: OWEN A. SINGH.

Japan: Finfinne Bldg, Revolution Sq., POB 5650, Addis Ababa; tel. 511088; telex 21108; fax 511350; Ambassador: SUKETORO ENOMOTO.

Kenya: Fikre Mariam Rd, POB 3301, Addis Ababa; tel. 610303; telex 21103; Ambassador: JACK BEN IAH TUMWA.

Korea, Democratic People's Republic: POB 2378, Addis Ababa; Ambassador: JANG HAK SU.

Korea, Republic: Jimma Rd, Old Airport Area, POB 2047, Addis Ababa; tel. 444490; telex 21140; Ambassador: DEUK PO KIM.

Liberia: POB 3116, Addis Ababa; tel. 513655; telex 21083; Ambassador: THOMAS C. T. BESTMAN.

Libya: POB 5728, Addis Ababa; telex 21214; Secretary of People's Bureau: K. BAZELYA.

Malawi: POB 2316, Addis Ababa; tel. 712440; telex 21087; fax 710490; Ambassador: W. R. CHIMUZU.

Mexico: Tsige Mariam Bldg 292/21, 4 Piso, Churchill Rd, POB 2962, Addis Ababa; tel. 443456; telex 21141; Ambassador: CARLOS FERRER.

Mozambique: Addis Ababa; telex 21008; Ambassador: ALBERTO SITHOLE.

Netherlands: Old Airport Area, POB 1241, Addis Ababa; tel. 711100; telex 21049; fax 711577; Ambassador: JAN M. JONKMAN.

Niger: Debrezenit Rd H-18 K-41 N-057, POB 5791, Addis Ababa; tel. 651175; telex 21284; Ambassador: MOULOUL AL-HOSSEIN.

Nigeria: POB 1019, Addis Ababa; tel. 120644; telex 21028; Ambassador: ASSANE IGODOE.

Poland: Bole Rd, POB 1123, Addis Ababa; tel. 610197; telex 21185; Ambassador: TADEUSZ WUJEK.

Romania: Africa Ave, POB 2478, Addis Ababa; tel. 181191; telex 21168; Ambassador: BARBU POPESCU.

Russia: POB 1500, Addis Ababa; tel. 552061; telex 21534; fax 613795; Ambassador: LEV MIRONOV.

Rwanda: Africa House, Higher 17 Kelele 20, POB 5618, Addis Ababa; tel. 610300; telex 21199; fax 610411; Ambassador: ROMUALD MUGEMA.

Saudi Arabia: Old Airport Area, POB 1104, Addis Ababa; tel. 448010; telex 21194; Chargé d'affaires: ABD AR-RAHMAN AL-FUAD.

Senegal: Africa Ave, POB 2581, Addis Ababa; tel. 611376; telex 21027; Ambassador: PAPA LOUIS FALL.

Sierra Leone: POB 5619, Addis Ababa; tel. 710033; telex 21144; Ambassador: ALIMAMY PALLO BANGURA.

Slovakia: POB 3108, Addis Ababa; tel. 516152; telex 21021; fax 513471.

Somalia: Addis Ababa; Ambassador: ABRAHIM HAJI NUR.

Spain: Entoto St, POB 2312, Addis Ababa; tel. 550222; telex 21107; Ambassador: A. MARTÍNEZ-MORCILLO.

Sudan: Kirkos, Kabele, POB 1110, Addis Ababa; telex 21293; Ambassador: UTHMAN AL-SAID.

Sweden: Ras Tesemma Sefer, POB 1029, Addis Ababa; tel. 516699; telex 21039; Ambassador: BIRGITTA KARLSTROM DORPH.

Switzerland: Jimma Rd, Old Airport Area, POB 1106, Addis Ababa; tel. 711107; telex 21123; fax 712177; Ambassador: PETER A. SCHWEIZER.

Tanzania: POB 1077, Addis Ababa; tel. 441064; telex 21268; Ambassador: FATUMA TATU NURU.

Tunisia: Kesetegna 20, Kebele 39, POB 10069, Addis Ababa; Ambassador: MOHAMED BACHROUCH.

Turkey: POB 1506, Addis Ababa; tel. 612321; telex 21257; Ambassador: ERHAN ÖĞÜT.

Uganda: POB 5644, Addis Ababa; tel. 513088; telex 21143; fax 514355; Ambassador: JOVAN KULANY.

United Kingdom: Fikre Mariam Abatechan St, POB 858, Addis Ababa; tel. 612354; telex 21299; fax 610588; Ambassador: ROBIN CHRISTOPHER.

USA: Entoto St, POB 1014, Addis Ababa; tel. 550666; telex 21282; fax 551166; Ambassador: IRVING HICKS (designate).

Venezuela: Debre Zeit Rd, POB 5584, Addis Ababa; tel. 654790; telex 21102; Chargé d'affaires: ALFREDO HERNÁNDEZ-ROVATI.

Viet Nam: POB 1288, Addis Ababa; Ambassador: NGUYEN DUY KINH.

Yemen: POB 664, Addis Ababa; telex 21346; Ambassador: Lt-Col HUSSEIN MOHASIN AL-GHAFFARI.

Yugoslavia: POB 1341; Addis Ababa; tel. 517804; telex 21233; Ambassador: IGOR JOVOVIĆ.

Zaire: Makanisa Rd, POB 2723, Addis Ababa; tel. 204385; telex 21043; Ambassador: BOMINA-N'SONI LONGANGE.

Zambia: POB 1909; Addis Ababa; tel. 711302; telex 21065; Ambassador: BASIL R. KABWE.

Zimbabwe: POB 5624, Addis Ababa; tel. 183872; telex 21351; Ambassador: TICHAONA J. B. JOKONYA.

Judicial System

Special People's Courts were established in 1981 to replace the former military tribunals. Judicial tribunals are elected by members of the urban dwellers' and peasant associations. In 1987 the Supreme Court ceased to be administered by the Ministry of Law and Justice and became an independent body. In October 1993, however, the Council of Representatives approved draft amendments empowering the Ministry of Justice to assume, additionally, the status of prosecutor; the office of prosecutor was to operate as a division under the Ministry.

The Supreme Court: Addis Ababa; comprises civil, criminal and military sections; in 1987 its jurisdiction (previously confined to hearing appeals from the High Court) was extended to include supervision of all judicial proceedings throughout the country; the Supreme Court is also empowered, when ordered to do so by the Procurator-General or at the request of the President of the Supreme Court, to review cases upon which final rulings have been made by the courts, including the Supreme Court, but where basic judicial errors have occurred; prior to May 1991, judges were elected by the National Shengo (the former national legislature); Pres. ASEFA LIBEN.

The High Court: Addis Ababa; hears appeals from the Provincial and sub-Provincial Courts; has original jurisdiction.

Awraja Courts: Regional courts composed of three judges, criminal and civil.

Warada Courts: Sub-regional; one judge sits alone with very limited jurisdiction, criminal only.

Religion

About 45% of the population are Muslims and about 40% belong to the Ethiopian Orthodox (Tewahido) Church. There are also significant Evangelical Protestant and Roman Catholic communities. The Pentecostal Church and the Society of International Missionaries carry out mission work in Ethiopia. There are also Hindu and Sikh religious institutions. Most of Ethiopia's small Jewish population was evacuated by the Israeli Government in May 1991. An estimated 5%–15% of the population adhere to animist rites and beliefs.

CHRISTIANITY

Ethiopian Orthodox (Tewahido) Church

The Ethiopian Orthodox (Tewahido) Church is one of the five oriental orthodox churches. It was founded in AD 328, and in 1989 had more than 22m. members, 20,000 parishes and 290,000 clergy. The Supreme Body is the Holy Synod and the National Council, under the chairmanship of the Patriarch. The Church comprises 25 archdioceses and dioceses (including those in Jerusalem, Sudan, Djibouti and the Western Hemisphere). There are 32 Archbishops and Bishops. The Church administers 1,139 schools and 12 relief and rehabilitation centres throughout Ethiopia.

Patriarchate Head Office: POB 1283, Addis Ababa; tel. 116507; telex 21489; Patriarch Archbishop Abune ABUNE PAULOS; Gen. Sec. L. M. DEMTSE GEBRE MEDHIN.

The Roman Catholic Church

At 31 December 1992 Ethiopia contained an estimated 65,700 adherents of the Alexandrian-Ethiopian Rite and 208,780 adherents of the Latin Rite.

Bishops' Conference: Ethiopian Episcopal Conference, POB 2454, Addis Ababa; tel. 550300; telex 21381; fax 553113; f. 1966; Pres. Cardinal PAULOS TZADUA, Archbishop of Addis Ababa.

Alexandrian-Ethiopian Rite

Adherents are served by one archdiocese (Addis Ababa) and one diocese (Adigrat).

Archbishop of Addis Ababa: Cardinal POULOS TZADUA, Catholic Archbishop's House, POB 21903, Addis Ababa; tel. 111667; fax 553113.

Latin Rite

Aherents are served by the five Apostolic Vicariates of Awasa, Harar, Meki, Nekemte and Soddo-Hosanna.

Other Christian Churches

The Anglican Communion: Within the Episcopal Church in Jerusalem and the Middle East, the Bishop in Egypt has jurisdiction over seven African countries, including Ethiopia.

Armenian Orthodox Church: Deacon VARTKES NALBANDIAN, St George's Armenian Church, POB 116, Addis Ababa; f. 1923.

Ethiopian Evangelical Church (Mekane Yesus): Pres. Ato FRANCIS STEPHANOS, POB 2087, Addis Ababa; tel. 552966; telex 21528; fax 552966; f. 1958; affiliated to Lutheran World Fed., All Africa Conf. of Churches and World Council of Churches; 1,028,630 mems (1991).

Greek Orthodox Church: Metropolitan of Axum Most Rev. PETROS GIAKOUMELOS, POB 571, Addis Ababa.

Seventh-day Adventist Church: Pres. Pastor BEKELE BIRI, POB 145, Addis Ababa; tel. 511199; telex 21549; f. 1907; 64,000 mems.

ISLAM

Leader: Haji MOHAMMED AHMAD.

JUDAISM

Following the secret airlifts to Israel in 1984–85 of about 13,000 Falashas (Ethiopian Jews), and further emigrations during 1989–91, there are estimated to be fewer than 2,000 Falashas still in the country.

The Press

DAILIES

Addis Zemen: POB 30145, Addis Ababa; f. 1941; Amharic; publ. by the Ministry of Information; Editor-in-Chief MERID BEKELE; circ. 40,000.

Ethiopian Herald: POB 30701, Addis Ababa; tel. 119050; f. 1943; English; publ. by the Ministry of Information; Editor-in-Chief KIFLOM HADGOI; circ. 37,000.

PERIODICALS

Abyotawit Ethiopia: POB 2549, Addis Ababa; fortnightly; Amharic.

Addis Tribune: Tambek International, POB 2395, Addis Ababa; f. 1993; weekly; English; Editor-in-Chief T. BEKELE; circ. 5,000.

Addis Zimit: POB 2395, Addis Ababa; f. 1993; weekly; Amharic; Editor-in-Chief T. BEKELE; circ. 8,000.

Al-Alem: POB 30232, Addis Ababa; weekly; Arabic; publ. by the Ministry of Information; Editor-in-Chief TELSOM AHMED; circ. 2,500.

Berisa: POB 30232, Addis Ababa; f. 1976; weekly; Oromogna; publ. by the Ministry of Information; Editor BULO SIBA; circ. 3,500.

Birhan Family Magazine: POB 2248, Addis Ababa; monthly; women's magazine.

Birritu: National Bank of Ethiopia, Documentation Division, POB 5550, Addis Ababa; six a year; Amharic and English; business, insurance and financial news; circ. 6,000.

Ethiopian Trade Journal: POB 517, Addis Ababa; tel. 518240; telex 21213; quarterly; English; publ. by the Ethiopian Chamber of Commerce; Editor-in-Chief GETACHEW ZICKE.

Ethiopis Review: Editor-in-Chief TESFERA ASMARE.

Meskerem: POB 80001, Addis Ababa; quarterly; theoretical politics; circ. 100,000.

Negarit Gazzetta: POB 1031, Addis Ababa; irregularly; Amharic and English; official gazette of laws, orders and notices.

Negradas: Ethiopian Chamber of Commerce, POB 517, Addis Ababa; Amharic.

Nigdina Limat: POB 517, Addis Ababa; tel. 158039; telex 21213; monthly; Amharic; publ. by the Ethiopian Chamber of Commerce.

Tinsae (Resurrection): POB 1283, Addis Ababa; tel. 116507; telex 21489; Amharic and English; publ. by the Ethiopian Orthodox Church.

Wetaderna Alamaw: POB 1901, Addis Ababa; fortnightly; Amharic.

Yezareitu Ethiopia (Ethiopia Today): POB 30232, Addis Ababa; weekly; Amharic and English; publ. by the Ministry of Information; Editor-in-Chief IMIRU WORKU; circ. 30,000.

NEWS AGENCIES

Ethiopian News Agency (ENA): Patriots' St, POB 530, Addis Ababa; tel. 120014; telex 21068; Chief AMARE AREGAWI.

Foreign Bureaux

Agence France-Presse (AFP): POB 3537, Addis Ababa; tel. 511006; telex 21031; Chief SABA SEYOUM.

Agenzia Nazionale Stampa Associata (ANSA) (Italy): POB 1001, Addis Ababa; tel. 111007; Chief BRAHAME GHEBREZGHI-ABIHER.

Associated Press (AP): Addis Ababa; tel. 161726; Correspondent ABEBE ANDUALAM.

Deutsche Presse-Agentur (dpa) (Germany): Addis Ababa; tel. 510687; Correspondent GHION HAGOS.

Informatsionnoye Telegrafnoye Agentstvo Rossii—Telegrafnoye Agentstvo Suverennykh Stran (ITAR—TASS) (Russia): POB 998, Addis Ababa; tel. 181255; telex 21091; Chief GENNADI G. GABRIELYAN.

Prensa Latina (Cuba): Gen. Makonnen Bldg, 5th Floor, nr Ghion Hotel, opp. National Stadium, POB 5690, Addis Ababa; tel. 519899; telex 21151; Chief HUGO RIUS BLEIN.

Reuters (UK): Addis Ababa; tel. 156505; telex 21407; Correspondent TSEGAYE TADESSE.

Rossiyskoye Informatsionnoye Agentstvo—Novosti (RIA—Novosti) (Russia): POB 239, Addis Ababa; telex 21237; Chief VITALI POLIKARPOV.

Xinhua (New China) News Agency (People's Republic of China): POB 2497, Addis Ababa; tel. 151064; telex 21504; Correspondent TENG WENQI.

PRESS ASSOCIATION

Ethiopian Journalists' Association: POB 5911, Addis Ababa; tel. 128198; Chair. IMERU WORKU (acting).

Publishers

Addis Ababa University Press: POB 1176, Addis Ababa; tel. 119148; telex 21205; f. 1968; educational and reference works in English; Editor INNES MARSHALL.

Ethiopia Book Centre: POB 1024, Addis Ababa; tel. 116844; f. 1977; privately-owned; publr, importer, wholesaler and retailer of educational books.

Kuraz Publishing Agency: POB 30933, Addis Ababa; tel. 551688; telex 21512; state-owned.

Government Publishing House

Government Printing Press: POB 1241, Addis Ababa.

Radio and Television

In 1991, according to UNESCO, there were an estimated 9.7m. radio receivers and 130,000 television receivers in use.

Telecommunications Authority of Ethiopia: POB 1047, Addis Ababa; tel. 510500; telex 21000; Gen. Man. FIKRU ASFAW.

RADIO

Voice of Ethiopia: POB 1020, Addis Ababa; tel. 121011; f. 1941; Amharic, English, French, Arabic, Afar, Oromifa, Tigrinya and Somali; Gen. Man. MOGUS TAFFESSE.

Voice of the Broad Oromo Masses: in Oromifa.

TELEVISION

Ethiopian Television: POB 5544, Addis Ababa; tel. 116701; telex 21429; f. 1964; state-controlled; commercial advertising is accepted; programmes are transmitted from Addis Ababa to 18 regional stations; broadcasts are receivable in all except two regions of Ethiopia; Dir-Gen. WOLE GURMU.

Finance

(cap. = capital; p.u. = paid up; dep. = deposits; m. = million; res = reserves; brs = branches; amounts in birr)

BANKING

All privately-owned banks and other financial institutions were nationalized in 1975.

Central Banks

National Bank of Ethiopia: POB 5550, Addis Ababa; tel. 517430; telex 21020; fax 514588; f. 1964; bank of issue; cap. and res 317.6m., dep. 731.5m. (June 1992); Gov. LEIKUN BERHANU; 4 brs.

Other Banks

Agricultural and Industrial Development Bank: Joseph Broz Tito St, POB 1900, Addis Ababa; tel. 511188; telex 21173; fax 511606; provides development finance for industry and agriculture, technical advice and assistance in project evaluation; cap. p.u. 100m. (June 1992); Gen. Man. GEBREMARIAM BEYENE; 21 brs.

Commercial Bank of Ethiopia: Unity Square Rd, POB 255, Addis Ababa; tel. 515000; telex 21037; fax 514522; f. 1964, reorg. 1980; cap. and res 104.1m., dep. 6,234.0m. (June 1993); Gen. Man. TILAHUN ABBAY; 144 brs.

Housing and Savings Bank: Higher 21 Kebele 04, POB 3480, Addis Ababa; tel. 512300; telex 21869; f. 1975; provides credit for construction of houses and commercial bldgs; cap. p.u. 18.3m. (June 1993); Gen. Man. LULSEGED TEFERI; 16 brs.

INSURANCE

Ethiopian Insurance Corporation: POB 2545, Addis Ababa; tel. 516488; telex 21120; fax 517499; f. 1976 to undertake all insurance business; Gen. Man. AYALEW BEZABEH.

Trade and Industry

CHAMBER OF COMMERCE

Ethiopian Chamber of Commerce: Mexico Sq., POB 517, Addis Ababa; tel. 518240; telex 21213; f. 1947; city chambers in Addis Ababa, Asella, Awassa, Bahir Dar, Dire Dawa, Nazret, Jimma, Gondar, Dessie and Lekempte; Pres. WOUBISHET WORKALEMAHU; Sec.-Gen. KASSAHUN JEMBERE.

AGRICULTURAL ORGANIZATION

Ethiopia Peasants' Association (EPA): f. 1978 to promote improved agricultural techniques, cottage industries, education, public health and self-reliance; comprises 30,000 peasant asscns with c. 7m. mems; Chair. (vacant).

TRADE AND INDUSTRIAL ORGANIZATIONS

Ethiopian Beverages Corporation: POB 1285, Addis Ababa; tel. 186185; telex 21373; Gen. Man. MENNA TEWAHEDE.

Ethiopian Cement Corporation: POB 5782, Addis Ababa; tel. 552222; telex 21308; fax 551572; Gen. Man. REDI GEMAL.

Ethiopian Chemical Corporation: POB 5747, Addis Ababa; tel. 184305; telex 21011; Gen. Man. ASNAKE SAHLU.

Ethiopian Coffee Marketing Corporation: POB 2591, Addis Ababa; tel. 515330; telex 21174; fax 510762; f. 1977; Gen. Man. GETACHW HAILE LEUL.

Ethiopian Food Corporation: Higher 21, Kebele 04, Mortgage Bldg, Addis Ababa; tel 158522; telex 21292; fax 513173; f. 1975; produces and distributes food items including edible oil, ghee substitute, pasta, bread, maize, wheat flour etc.; Gen. Man. BEKELE HAILE.

Ethiopian Fruit and Vegetable Marketing Enterprise: POB 2374, Addis Ababa; tel. 519192; telex 21106; f. 1980; sole wholesale domestic distributor and exporter of fresh and processed fruit and vegetables, and floricultural products; Gen. Man. YOHANES AGONAFER.

Ethiopian Handicrafts and Small-Scale Industries Development Agency: POB 5758, Addis Ababa; tel. 157366.

Ethiopian Import and Export Corporation (ETIMEX): POB 2313, Addis Ababa; tel. 512400; telex 21235; fax 514396; f. 1975; state trading corpn under the supervision of the Ministry of Trade; import of building materials, foodstuffs, stationery and office equipment, textiles, clothing, chemicals, general merchandise, capital goods; Gen. Man. ASCHENAKI G. HIWOT.

Ethiopian Livestock and Meat Corporation: POB 5579, Addis Ababa; tel. 159341; telex 21095; f. 1984; state trading corpn responsible for the development and export of livestock and livestock products; Gen. Man. GELANA KEJELA.

Ethiopian National Metal Works Corporation: Addis Ababa; fax 510714; Gen. Man. ALULA BERHANE.

Ethiopian Oil Seeds and Pulses Export Corporation: POB 5719, Addis Ababa; tel. 550597; telex 21133; fax 553299; Gen. Man. EPHRAIM AMBAYE.

Ethiopian Petroleum Corporation: POB 3375, Addis Ababa; telex 21054; fax 512938; f. 1976; Gen. Man. ZEWDE TEWOLDE.

Ethiopian Pharmaceuticals and Medical Supplies Corporation: POB 21904, Addis Ababa; tel. 134577; telex 21248; fax 752555; f. 1976; manufacture, import, export and distribution of pharmaceuticals, chemicals, dressings, surgical and dental instruments, hospital and laboratory supplies; Gen. Man. BERHANU ZELEKE.

Ethiopian Sugar Corporation: POB 133, Addis Ababa; tel. 519700; telex 21038; fax 513488; Gen. Man. ABATE LEMENGH.

National Leather and Shoe Corporation: POB 2516, Addis Ababa; tel. 514075; telex 21096; fax 513525; f. 1975; produces and sells semi-processed hides and skins, finished leather, leather goods and footwear; Gen. Man. GIRMA W. AREGAI.

National Textiles Corporation: POB 2446, Addis Ababa; tel. 157316; telex 21129; fax 511955; f. 1975; production of yarn, fabrics, knitwear, blankets, bags, etc.; Gen. Man. FIKRE HUGIANE.

Natural Gums Processing and Marketing Enterprise: POB 62322, Addis Ababa; tel. 159930; telex 21336; Gen. Man. YEWONDWOSSEN FASIL.

TRADE UNIONS

Ethiopian Trade Union (ETU): POB 3653, Addis Ababa; tel. 514366; telex 21618; f. 1975 to replace the Confed. of Ethiopian Labour Unions; comprises nine industrial unions and 22 regional unions with a total membership of 320,000 (1987); Chair. (vacant).

Transport

RAILWAYS

Djibouti-Ethiopian Railway (Chemin de Fer Djibouto-Ethiopien — CDE): POB 1051, Addis Ababa; tel. 517250; telex 21414; fax 513997; f. 1908, adopted present name in 1981; jtly-owned by Govts of Ethiopia and Djibouti; plans to grant autonomous status were announced by the two Govts in July 1985; 781 km of track, of which 681 km in Ethiopia, linking Addis Ababa with Djibouti; Pres. WAKJIRA GEMECHU; Vice-Pres. AHMED WABERI GEDIE.

ROADS

In 1991 the total road network comprised 27,972 km of primary, secondary and feeder roads and trails, of which 19,017 km were main roads. A highway links Addis Ababa with Nairobi in Kenya, forming part of the Trans-East Africa Highway. In November 1992 the Ethiopian Road Transport Authority (see below) secured approximately US $96m. in loans from the World Bank and the African Development Bank for a programme of road repairs.

Ethiopian Road Transport Authority: POB 2504, Addis Ababa; fax 510715; enforcement of road transport regulations, registering of vehicles and issuing of driving licences.

Ethiopian Transport Construction Authority: POB 1770, Addis Ababa; tel. 447170; telex 21180; f. 1951; constructs roads, bridges, airfields, ports and railways, and maintains roads and bridges throughout Ethiopia; Gen. Man. KELLETTA TESFA MICHAEL.

National Freight Transport Corporation: POB 2538, Addis Ababa; tel. 151841; telex 21238; f. 1974; truck and tanker operations throughout the country.

Public Transport Corporation: POB 5780, Addis Ababa; tel. 153117; telex 21371; fax 510720; f. 1977; urban bus services in Addis Ababa and Jimma, and services between towns; Gen. Man. TESFAYE SHENKUTE.

SHIPPING

The formerly Ethiopian-controlled ports of Massawa and Assab now lie within the boundaries of the State of Eritrea (q.v.). There is, however, an agreement between the two Governments allowing Ethiopian access to the port of Assab, formerly the port for Addis Ababa. There are irregular services by foreign vessels to Massawa and Assab, which can handle over 1m. metric tons of merchandise annually. Assab, a free port, has a petroleum refinery with an annual capacity of 800,000 metric tons. Much trade passes through Djibouti (in the Republic of Djibouti) to Addis Ababa, and Ethiopia has access to the Kenyan port of Mombasa. The Ethiopian merchant shipping fleet totalled 28,409 grt in July 1983.

Ethiopian Shipping Lines: POB 2572, Addis Ababa; tel. 518280; telex 21045; fax 519525; f. 1964; serves Red Sea, Europe and Far East with its own and chartered vessels; Chair. WAKJIRA GEMECHU; Gen. Man. G. KIDAN KAHSAY.

Marine Transport Authority: POB 1861, Addis Ababa; tel. 446448; telex 21280; fax 516015; f. 1978; manages inland waterways, handles cargo.

Maritime and Transit Services Corporation: POB 1186, Addis Ababa; tel. 510666; telex 21057; fax 514097; f. 1979; handles cargoes for import and export; operates shipping agency service.

CIVIL AVIATION

Ethiopia has two international airports (at Addis Ababa and Bahir Dar) and around 40 airfields. Bole International Airport in the capital handles 95% of international air traffic and 85% of domestic flights. A programme to modernize the airport, at an estimated cost of 466m. birr (US $144m.), was to be undertaken in 1993–96.

Civil Aviation Authority: POB 978, Addis Ababa; tel. 610277; telex 21162; fax 612533; constructs and maintains airports; provides air navigational facilities; Gen.-Man. BEKELE SERBESSA.

Ethiopian Airlines: Bole International Airport, POB 1755, Addis Ababa; tel. 612222; telex 21012; fax 611474; f. 1945; operates regular domestic services and flights to 40 international destinations in Africa, Europe, Middle East, India and the People's Republic of China; Chair. Minister of Defence; Gen. Man. Capt. ZELEKE DEMISSIE.

Tourism

Ethiopia's tourist attractions include the early Christian monuments and churches, the ancient capitals of Gondar and Axum, the Blue Nile Falls and the National Parks of the Semien and Bale Mountains. Tourist arrivals at Addis Ababa airport in 1991 totalled 81,581. Tourism provided an estimated US $19m. in foreign exchange in that year.

Ethiopian Tourism Commission: POB 2183, Addis Ababa; tel. 517470; telex 21067; fax 513899; f. 1961; Commr REZENE ARAYA.

Defence

Following the fall of Mengistu's government and the defeat of his army in May 1991, troops of the Eritrean People's Liberation Front (EPLF) and the Ethiopian People's Revolutionary Democratic Front (EPRDF) were deployed in Eritrea and in Ethiopia respectively. In June 1993 EPRDF forces were estimated at about 100,000. In October 1993 it was announced that preparations were under way to create a 'multi-ethnic defence force'.

Education

Education in Ethiopia is free and, after a rapid growth in numbers of schools, it is hoped to introduce compulsory primary education shortly. Since September 1976 most primary and secondary schools have been controlled by local peasant associations and urban dwellers' associations. Primary education begins at seven years of age and lasts for six years. Secondary education, beginning at 13 years of age, lasts for a further six years, comprising a first cycle of two years and a second of four years. In 1991 total enrolment at primary schools was equivalent to 25% of children in the relevant age-group (29% of boys; 21% of girls); the comparable ratio for secondary enrolment was only 12% (13% of boys; 11% of girls). The 1989/90 budget allocated 7.5% (488.5m. birr) of total expenditure to education. A major literacy campaign was launched in 1979. By 1990 more than 23m. people had been enrolled for tuition programmes, and the rate of adult illiteracy had reportedly been reduced to 23% (compared with 96% in 1970). Ethiopia has two universities. In 1990 some 16,116 students were enrolled at Addis Ababa University. There is an agricultural university at Alemaya and a polytechnic institute at Bahir Dar. There is a considerable shortage of qualified teachers, which is particularly acute in secondary schools relying heavily on expatriate staff.

Bibliography

Abir, M. *Ethiopia and the Red Sea: The Rise and Decline of the Solomonic Dynasty and Muslim-European Rivalry in the Region.* London, Frank Cass, 1980.

Balsvik, R. R. *Haile Selassie's Students: The Intellectual and Social Background to Revolution, 1952–77.* East Lansing, Michigan State University, 1985.

Bureau, J. *Ethiopie, un drame impérial et rouge.* Paris, Ramsay, 1987.

Clapham, C. *Haile-Sellassie's Government.* London, 1969.

Transformation and Continuity in Revolutionary Ethiopia. Cambridge, Cambridge University Press, 1988.

Clarke, J. *Ethiopia's Campaign against Famine.* London, Harney and Jones, 1987.

Cohen, J. M., and Koehn, P. *Ethiopian Provincial and Municipal Government.* Michigan State University, 1980.

Del Boca, A. *The Ethiopian War 1935–1941.* Chicago, University of Chicago Press, 1969.

Donham, D., and James, W. (Eds). *The Southern Marches of Imperial Ethiopia.* Cambridge, Cambridge University Press, 1986.

Dugan, J., and Lafore, L. *Days of Emperor and Clown, The Italo-Ethiopian War 1935–1936.* New York, Doubleday, 1973.

Ethiopian Relief and Rehabilitation Commission. *The Challenges of Drought.* Addis Ababa, Relief and Rehabilitation Commission, 1985.

Faye, B. *Eleveurs d'Ethiopie.* Paris, Editions Karthala, 1990.

Gebre-Medhin, J. *Peasants and Nationalism in Eritrea.* Trenton, NJ, Red Sea Press, 1989.

Gilkes, P. *The Dying Lion: Feudalism and Modernization in Ethiopia.* London, Julian Friedmann, 1974.

Ginzberg, E., and Smith, H. A. *A Manpower Strategy for Ethiopia.* Addis Ababa, 1966.

Greenfield, R. *Ethiopia, A New Political History.* New York, Praeger, 1955.

Griffin, K. (Ed.). *The Economy of Ethiopia.* New York, St Martin's Press, 1992.

Haile Sellassie I. *The Autobiography of Emperor Haile Sellassie I. 'My Life and Ethiopia's Progress.'* Oxford, Oxford University Press, 1976.

Halliday, F., and Molyneux, M. *The Ethiopian Revolution.* London, Verso Editions, 1981.

Hancock, G. *Ethiopia: The Challenge of Hunger.* London, Gollancz, 1985.

Harbeson, J. W. *The Ethiopian Transformation.* Boulder, CO, Westview Press, 1988.

Hess, R. L. *The Modernization of Autocracy.* Ithaca, NY, and London, Cornell University Press, 1972.

(Ed.). *Proceedings of the 5th International Conference on Ethiopian Studies: Session B.* Chicago, University of Illinois, 1979.

Katsuyoski, F., and Markakis, J. (Eds). *Ethnicity and Conflict in the Horn of Africa.* London, Currey, 1994.

Korn, D. A. *Ethiopia, the United States and the Soviet Union 1974–85.* London, Croom Helm, 1986.

Last, G. C. 'Introductory Notes on the Geography of Ethiopia', *Ethiopia Observer,* Vol. VI, No. 2, pp. 82–134, 1962.

Levine, D. N. *Wax and Gold: Tradition and Innovation in Ethiopian Culture.* University of Chicago Press, 1965.

Greater Ethiopia: The Evolution of a Multi-Ethnic Society. University of Chicago Press, 1974.

McCann, J. *From Poverty to Famine in Northeast Ethiopia.* Philadelphia, University of Pennsylvania Press, 1987.

Marcus, H. G. *The Life and Times of Menelik II.* Oxford, Clarendon Press, 1975.

Ethiopia, Great Britain and the United States 1941–74. Los Angeles, University of California Press, 1983.

Haile Selassie I: The Formative Years 1892–1936. Los Angeles, University of California Press, 1987.

Markakis, J. *Ethiopia: Anatomy of a Traditional Polity.* London, Oxford University Press, 1974.

National and Class Conflict in the Horn of Africa. Cambridge, Cambridge University Press (African Studies Series, No. 55), 1988.

Medhanie, T. *Eritrea: the Dynamics of a National Question.* Amsterdam, B. R. Grunner, 1986.

Mockler, A. *Haile Selassie's War.* Oxford, Oxford University Press, 1985.

Mosley, L. O. *Haile Sellassie.* London, Weidenfeld and Nicolson, 1964.

Ottaway, M. *Soviet and American Influence in the Horn of Africa.* New York, Praeger, 1982.

Ottaway, M. (Ed.). *The Political Economy of Ethiopia.* New York, Praeger, 1990.

Ottway, D. and M. *Ethiopia: Empire in Revolution.* New York and London, African Publishing Co, 1978.

Pankhurst, R. *Economic History of Ethiopia, 1880–1935.* Addis Ababa, 1968.

History of Ethiopian Towns. London, 1982.

Prouty, C. *Empress Taytu and Menilek II: Ethiopia 1883–1910.* London, Ravens Educational and Development Services, 1986.

Prouty, C., and Rosenfeld, E. *Historical Dictionary of Ethiopia.* Metuchen, NJ, Scarecrow Press, 1981.

Sbacchi, A. *Ethiopia under Mussolini: Fascism and the Colonial Experience.* London, Zed Press, 1985.

Sellassie, H. B. *Conflict and Intervention in the Horn of Africa.* New York and London, Monthly Review Press, 1980.

Spencer, J. H. *Ethiopia, The Horn of Africa and US Policy.* Cambridge, MA, Institute for Foreign Policy Analysis, 1977.

Ethiopia at Bay. Michigan, Reference Publications, 1984.

Tareke, G. *Ethiopia: Power and Protest—Peasant Revolts in the Twentieth Century.* Cambridge, Cambridge University Press, 1991.

Thompson, B. *Ethiopia, The Country That Cut off Its Head, A Diary of the Revolution.* London, Robson Books, 1975.

Tubiana, J. (Ed.). *Modern Ethiopia from the Accession of Menelik II to the Present.* Rotterdam, A. A. Balkema. Proceedings of the 5th International Conference of Ethiopian Studies: Session A, 1980.

Ullendorff, E. *The Ethiopians, An Introduction to Country and People.* Oxford University Press, 1960.

Wolde, M. M. *A Preliminary Atlas of Ethiopia.* Addis Ababa, 1962.

GABON

Physical and Social Geography

DAVID HILLING

Lying along the Equator, on the west coast of Africa, the Gabonese Republic covers an area of 267,667 sq km (103,347 sq miles) and comprises the entire drainage basin of the westward-flowing Ogooué river, together with the basins of several smaller coastal rivers such as the Nyanga and Como.

The low-lying coastal zone is narrow in the north and south but broader in the estuary regions of the Ogooué and Gabon. South of the Ogooué numerous lagoons, such as the N'Dogo, M'Goze, and M'Komi, back the coast, and the whole area is floored with Cretaceous sedimentary rocks, which at shallow depth yield oil. The main producing oil fields are in a narrow zone stretching southwards from Port-Gentil, both on- and off-shore. The interior consists of Pre-Cambrian rocks, eroded into a series of plateau surfaces at heights of 450–600 m and dissected by the river system into a number of distinct blocks, such as the Crystal mountains, the Moabi uplands and the Chaillu massif. This area is one of Africa's most mineralized zones, and traditional small-scale mining of gold and diamonds has been replaced in importance by large-scale exploitation of manganese at Moanda and uranium at Mounana. There are numerous deposits of high-grade iron ore.

Gabon has an equatorial climate, with uniformly high temperatures, high relative humidities and mean annual rainfalls of 1,500–3,000 mm. About three-quarters of the country's surface is covered with forests, and wood from the okoumé tree provided the basis for the country's economy until superseded by minerals in the 1960s. Grassland vegetation is restricted to the coastal sand zone south of Port-Gentil and parts of the valleys of the Nyanga, upper N'Gounié and upper Ogooué.

Agricultural development in the potentially rich forest zone has been limited by the small size of the country's population. The July 1993 census recorded a total of 1,011,710, with an average population density of only 3.8 inhabitants per sq km. As the population is small in relation to national income, Gabon has the highest level of income per head in sub-Saharan Africa, although many of the country's enterprises depend on labour imported from neighbouring countries. Gabon also has a French resident population estimated at 20,000. Greater rural concentrations are found in Woleu N'Tem, where coffee and cocoa are the main cash crops, and around Lambaréné, where palm oil and coffee are important. The country's principal ethnic groups are the Fang (30%) and the Eshira (25%). The three main urban concentrations are believed to account for more than one-half of the population; in 1988 Libreville, the capital, had more than 352,000 inhabitants, Port-Gentil, the centre of the petroleum industry, 164,000, and Franceville/Moanda, the mining centres, 75,000.

Recent History

PIERRE ENGLEBERT

Gabon was granted internal autonomy in November 1958, with Léon M'Ba, leader of the Bloc démocratique gabonais (BDG) as prime minister. The country became fully independent on 17 August 1960 and M'Ba was elected president of the republic in February 1961.

M'Ba appointed Jean-Hilaire Aubame, leader of the Union démocratique et sociale gabonaise, as foreign affairs minister. In 1963, however, the long-standing rivalry between the two men culminated in Aubame's removal from the post and appointment as head of the supreme court. In January 1964 M'Ba dissolved the national assembly and announced that elections were to take place in February. A week before the scheduled election, M'Ba was deposed in a military coup, which installed a revolutionary committee, under the leadership of Aubame. After French military intervention, M'Ba was reinstated, and at elections in April the BDG secured a majority of seats in the national assembly. During the next two years Gabon effectively became a one-party state: most opposition members of the assembly joined the BDG, which contested the 1967 elections unopposed. M'Ba died in November 1967 and was succeeded by Albert-Bernard Bongo, the vice-president he had appointed earlier that year. In March 1968 Bongo announced the formal creation of a one-party state, and of a new ruling party, the Parti démocratique gabonais (PDG).

ONE-PARTY GOVERNMENT

Gabon enjoyed political stability during the 1970s, with the PDG taking an increasingly dominant role in political life. Legislative and presidential elections took place in February 1973; all PDG candidates for the national assembly, and Bongo, the sole candidate for the presidency, were elected with 99.56% of the votes cast. In 1975 Bongo abolished the post of vice-president and appointed Léon Mébiame, who had been vice-president, to the new post of prime minister. Gabon experienced rapid economic growth under a liberal system which encouraged and protected foreign capital investment; in 1975 Gabon became a full member of the Organization of the Petroleum Exporting Countries (OPEC). In September of that year Bongo converted to Islam, changing his forename to Omar.

Despite unprecedented criticism of inefficiency in national administration at the PDG's second extraordinary congress in January 1979, Bongo was selected as sole candidate for the presidency, and in December was re-elected for a further seven-year term, with 99.96% of the votes cast. Legislative elections in February were followed by a government reshuffle, in which several new ministers were appointed to the cabinet, although Bongo's most trusted allies continued to hold the most influential positions. In mid-1981 Bongo transferred his functions as head of government to Mébiame, and relinquished his other ministerial portfolios.

Social and political strains, deriving from the rapid growth of the economy in the mid-1970s and the subsequent decline, became evident after 1980. The Mouvement de redressement national (MORENA), a moderate opposition group which emerged in late 1981, accused Bongo of corruption and personal extravagance and demanded the restoration of multi-party democracy. In November 1982 37 MORENA members were convicted of offences against state security. However, Bongo maintained his commitment to one-party rule, appealing to exiles to return to Gabon to participate in democratic debate within the single-party framework.

Relations with France, which were traditionally close, deteriorated, following the election of the French socialist president in 1981. However, the prospect of other countries, notably the USA, becoming involved in Gabon's economy prompted France to initiate a reconciliation, and in January 1983 President Mitterrand visited Gabon. In October of that year relations again became strained, following the publication in France of a book which asserted that Gabon was ruled by French and Gabonese masonic secret societies. Bongo subsequently ordered the Gabonese media to suspend all coverage of events in France. The ban was eventually lifted in December, but relations between the two countries remained tense until April 1984, when the French prime minister visited Libreville.

At elections to an enlarged national assembly in March 1985, PDG candidates received 99.5% of votes cast. In May Bongo repeated his invitation to opposition members to return to Gabon; in August, however, MORENA formed a government-in-exile in Paris. A MORENA candidate contested the presidential election of November 1986, but was prevented from organizing a campaign, and the movement's exiled leadership appealed to voters to boycott the election. Nevertheless, Bongo was re-elected for a further seven-year term, with 99.97% of the vote. Despite the provision of more than one list of PDG-approved candidates in the local government elections in June 1987, the incumbent officials were re-elected in most cases. Bongo subsequently commented that, since the element of choice had resulted in division within communities, the establishment of a multi-party system would lead to further conflict.

Following a deterioration in the economy, compulsory reductions in salaries for public-sector employees in October 1988 provoked strike action. Bongo's subsequent announcement that economic reforms and austerity measures would, henceforth, be pursued only to the extent that they did not undermine social and political stability had a detrimental effect on the country's negotiations with its external creditors.

MORENA, which had been preoccupied with internal divisions since 1987, resumed its campaign against the government in early 1989. In May, however, the movement's chairman, Fr Paul M'Ba Abessole, visited Gabon and, after a meeting with Bongo, announced that he and many of his supporters would return to the country in the near future. M'Ba Abessole later declared his support for Bongo's regime and in early 1990, following his removal from the leadership of MORENA, formed a new organization, MORENA des bûcherons (renamed Rassemblement des bûcherons in February 1991 to avoid confusion with the rival MORENA-originels).

A number of arrests took place in October 1989, following an alleged conspiracy to overthrow the government. It was claimed that the detainees, who included senior members of the security forces and prominent public officials, had acted on behalf of Pierre Mamboundou, the leader of the Paris-based Union du peuple gabonais (UPG). Further arrests followed in November 1989, after the alleged discovery of a second plot against the government.

CONSTITUTIONAL TRANSITION

A series of strikes and demonstrations by students and workers in early 1990 reflected increasing public discontent with economic austerity measures. On 22 February a 'special commission for democracy', established in January by the PDG central committee, submitted a report, which contained an explicit condemnation of the one-party system. On the following day, Bongo announced that immediate and fundamental political reforms would be introduced. However, his proposal to replace the ruling party by a Rassemblement social-démocrate gabonais (RSDG), which would cover a diverse ideological spectrum, did little to appease the workforce.

In early March 1990, following a joint session of the central committee of the PDG and the national assembly, legislative elections, scheduled for April, were postponed for six months to allow time for the constitution to be amended. On 9 March the PDG political bureau announced that a multi-party system was to be introduced, under the supervision of the RSDG, at the end of a five-year transitional period. However, a national conference of some 2,000 delegates, which was convened in late March to formulate a programme for the transfer to multi-party democracy, rejected Bongo's proposals, and voted instead for the immediate creation of a multi-party system and the formation of a new government, which would hold office only until the October legislative elections. Bongo acceded to the conference's decisions, and in April, Casimir Oye Mba, the governor of the Banque des états de l'Afrique centrale, was appointed prime minister in a transitional administration, which included several opposition members.

On 22 May 1990 the central committee of the PDG and the national assembly approved constitutional amendments that would facilitate the transition to a multi-party system. The existing presidential mandate (effective until January 1994) was to be respected; thereafter, elections to the presidency would be contested by more than one candidate and the tenure of office would be reduced to five years, renewable only once. At the same time, Bongo resigned as secretary-general (claiming that such a partisan role was now incompatible with his position as head of state), and the post was assumed by Jean Adiahenot. These far-reaching changes, however, were overshadowed by the repercussions of the death, in suspicious circumstances, of Joseph Rendjambe, the secretary-general of the opposition movement, the Parti gabonais du progrès (PGP). Demonstrators, who alleged Bongo's complicity in the death, attacked property belonging to the president and his associates. A country-wide curfew was imposed as unrest spread. French troops were dispatched to Gabon to protect the interests of the 20,000 resident French nationals, and several hundred Europeans were evacuated. The strength of the Gabonese economy was for a time jeopardized by severe disruption in the petroleum sector. A state of emergency was imposed in Port-Gentil and its environs, and at least two deaths were reported after Gabonese security forces intervened to restore order. In early June it was announced that the French military reinforcements were to be withdrawn. The national curfew was repealed in early July; however, the state of emergency remained in force in the area surrounding Port-Gentil.

Legislative Elections

Legislative elections were scheduled for 16 and 23 September 1990; however, only political parties which had registered during the national conference in March were allowed to present candidates. The first round of multi-party elections on 16 September was disrupted by violent protests by voters, who claimed that electoral fraud was being practised in favour of the PDG. Following allegations by opposition parties of widespread electoral malpractices, results in 32 constituencies were declared invalid, although the election of 58 candidates (of whom 36 were members of the PDG) was confirmed. The transitional government subsequently conceded that irregularities had taken place, and the second round of the elections was postponed until 21 and 28 October. A commission representing both the PDG and opposition parties was established to prevent further irregularities. At the elections in October, the PDG won an overall majority, with 62 seats, while opposition candidates secured 55 seats. The formation of a government of national unity was announced on 27 November; Casimir Oye Mba, the head of the former interim government, was appointed as prime minister. Sixteen portfolios were allocated to members of the PDG, with the remaining eight distributed among members of five opposition parties. Three other opposition movements refused Bongo's offer of inclusion in the government. A new draft constitution, which was promulgated on 22 December, endorsed reforms included in the transitional constitution introduced in May. Further measures included the proposed establishment of an upper house, to be known as the senate, which was to control the balance and regulation of power. This proposal, however, was strongly opposed by the opposition parties. A constitutional council was also to replace the administrative chamber of the supreme court and a national communications council was to be formed to ensure the impartial treatment of information by the state media.

The final composition of the national assembly was determined in March 1991, when elections took place in five constituencies where the results had been annulled, owing to alleged irregularities. Following the completion of the elections, the PDG secured 66 seats, while the PGP obtained 19, the Rassemblement national des bûcherons (RNB, formerly MORENA des bûcherons) 17, MORENA-originels seven, the Association pour le socialisme au Gabon (APSG) six, the Union socialiste gabonais (USG) three, and two smaller parties one seat each.

Political Realignments and Social Unrest

In May 1991 six opposition parties formed an alliance, known as the Coordination de l'opposition démocratique (COD). The COD announced its withdrawal from the national assembly, and demanded the immediate and total implementation of the new constitution, the appointment of a new prime minister, the submission of constitutional proposals for consideration by the national assembly, and access to the state-controlled media. Following a general strike, which was orchestrated by the COD, Bongo announced the dissolution of the council of ministers. He also declared that he was prepared to implement fully the new constitution, and affirmed that, in accordance with the constitution, a constitutional court and a national communications council had been created. In a further attempt to appease public discontent, Bongo pardoned more than 200 political prisoners. However, opposition parties belonging to the COD refused to participate in a proposed government of national unity. On 18 June Bongo re-appointed Oye Mba as prime minister. Later that month, opposition deputies, who had resigned from the national assembly, resumed parliamentary duties. On 22 June a new coalition government was formed, which retained 14 members of the previous council of ministers. Members of MORENA-originels, the USG and the APSG were also represented in the government.

In September 1991 clashes took place between demonstrators supporting the RNB and members of the PDG. In October a minor reorganization of the council of ministers was carried out. In December two deputies in the national assembly resigned from the PGP, owing to its alleged political affiliation with the PDG. In the same month a vote of censure against the government was proposed in the national assembly, following opposition complaints at the sale of one of the aircraft belonging to the national airline, Air Gabon, and at inadequate financing of political parties. However, the motion was rejected by 68 of the 118 votes cast. At the end of December two prisoners implicated in the attempted coup in 1985 were released; the government subsequently claimed that all political prisoners in Gabon had been pardoned. In February 1992 three political associations, MORENA-originels, the Parti socialiste gabonais (PSG) and the USG formed an alliance, known as the Forum africain pour la reconstruction (FAR). Later in February the government announced that a multiparty presidential election would take place in December 1993, two months before the expiry of Bongo's term of office.

Widespread strikes and demonstrations continued in 1992; in February, following protests by students demanding additional scholarship grants, the university was closed, and a ban on public demonstrations and gatherings was imposed. In the same month a meeting of supporters of the RNB was dispersed by security forces; several injuries were reported. Later in February the COD organized a one-day general strike in Port-Gentil (which was only partially observed), followed by a one-day 'dead city' campaign in Port-Gentil and Libreville. At the end of February the government reopened the university, and ended the ban on political gatherings and demonstrations, purportedly in the interests of democracy. In March, however, a protester was killed, when a demonstration by teachers in support of improvements in salary and working conditions was suppressed by security forces. The COD subsequently instigated a further one-day 'dead city' campaign in Libreville. In early April, in an attempt to regain public support, the PDG organized a pro-government demonstration in the capital.

In early July 1992 the national assembly adopted a new electoral code (which had been submitted by the government), despite protests by the FAR that the government had failed to comply with the demands presented by the COD in October 1991. In the same month a motion of censure against the government, proposed by opposition deputies in the national assembly in response to the postponement of local government elections, was defeated. In mid-July members of the UPG demonstrated in support of demands that their leader, Pierre Mamboundou, be permitted to return to Gabon. In August the council of ministers was reorganized. In December three members of the PDG, including a former minister, were expelled from the party, after establishing a faction, known as the Cercle des libéraux réformateurs (CLR).

Social unrest continued during the first half of 1993. In April there were widespread protests and demonstrations in central and southern Gabon at the poor quality of living conditions that had resulted from the lack of social infrastructure, particularly road facilities and reliable water supplies in rural areas; security forces were dispatched to restore order. In the same month Jules Bourdès-Ogouliguendé (who had resigned from the PDG in January) relinquished his post as president of the national assembly, prior to presenting his candidacy for the forthcoming presidential election. Ogouliguendé, who had for some time adopted an independent stance on controversial political issues, voting on occasion against the government, formally announced his candidacy in May, when Pierre Maganga-Moussavou, the leader of the PSD, and Alexandre Sambat, a former ambassador to the USA, declared that they were also to contest the presidential election. Pierre Mamboundu, although sentenced *in absentia* in 1990 to a 10-year term of imprisonment, was expected to return from exile in Senegal to contest the election on behalf of the UPG. In July Bongo reorganized the council of ministers, following the resignation of the minister with responsibility for labour and employment, Simon Oyono-Aba'a, who had been nominated as the presidential candidate of MORENA-originels. In September the government established a commission to supervise the organization of the presidential election, which was scheduled for 5 December; the opposition was granted a consultative role in the commission. In October Bongo finally announced that he was to contest the presidential election; by the end of that month 16 candidates had emerged (of which three subsequently withdrew in favour of Bongo), including M'Ba Abessole, the leader of the PGP, Pierre-Louis Agondjo-Okawé, and a former prime minister, Léon Mébiame. (Mamboundou had been prevented from returning to Gabon within the scheduled period for the registration of presidential candidates.)

In early November 1993 five political associations, the PDG, the USG, the APSG, the CLR and the Parti de l'unité du peuple gabonais, agreed to support Bongo's candidacy in the presidential election, while eight opposition candidates established an informal alliance, known as the Convention des forces du changement (CFC). Later that month a number of demonstrations were staged by members of the CFC, in protest at alleged irregularities in the electoral register, which were attributed by the opposition to deliberate malpractice on the part of the government. Clashes between opposition and government supporters ensued, and in early December the government agreed to revise the register in part (but failed to comply with opposition demands that the election be postponed).

Presidential Election and Political Retrenchment

At the presidential election, which took place on 5 December 1993, Bongo was re-elected by 51.18% of votes cast, while M'Ba Abessole secured 26.51% of the votes; some 86% of the registered electorate participated. The official announcement of the results provoked rioting by opposition supporters, in which several foreign nationals were attacked (apparently as a result of dissatisfaction with international observers, who declared that no electoral malpractice had taken place). Security forces suppressed the unrest, reportedly killing five people, and a national curfew and state of alert (which included a ban on demonstrations) were subsequently imposed. M'Ba Abessole, however, rejected the election results, and established the 'high council of the Republic' (HCR), which included the majority of the presidential candidates, as part of a parallel government. Despite the reports by international observers that the elections had been conducted fairly, the opposition appealed to the constitutional court to annul the results, on the grounds that the government had perpetrated electoral malpractice. In mid-December Bongo condemned M'Ba Abessole's establishment of a parallel administration, and invited the other candidates who had contested the election to participate in a government of national consensus. As a result of the administrative confusion, local government elections, which were due to take place in late December, were postponed until March 1994.

In early January 1994 the USA criticized the government for infringement of human rights, after three opposition leaders, including two presidential candidates, were prevented from leaving the country. Later that month the constitutional court rejected the appeal by the opposition, and endorsed the election results. On 22 January Bongo was officially inaugurated as president. M'Ba Abessole subsequently redesignated the HCR as the 'high council for resistance', and urged his supporters to refuse to pay taxes and to boycott the local government elections (which were again postponed, to August). In mid-February the national curfew and the state of alert, which had been declared in December 1993, were repealed, but were reimposed later that month, after a general strike, in support of demands for an increase in salaries to compensate for a devaluation of the CFA franc in January, degenerated into violence. Security forces destroyed the transmitters of Radio Liberté, a radio station owned by the RNB (which had supported the strike), and attacked M'Ba Abessole's private residence, resulting in further clashes with protesters. Strike action was suspended after four days, following negotiations between the government and trade unions; nine people had been killed during that period, according to official figures (although the opposition claimed that a total of 38 had died). At the end of February the minister of state control, in charge of parastatal affairs, announced his resignation from the government and from the PDG, owing to disagreement with the increasingly authoritarian stance adopted by Bongo. In the same month the government initiated an inquiry, after it was reported that 67 alleged illegal immigrants, mainly Ghanaian and Nigerian nationals, had died in detention (apparently as a result of poor prison conditions).

In March 1994 Oye Mba submitted his resignation and dissolved the council of ministers; later that month he was reappointed as prime minister and, following the opposition's rejection of his offer to participate in a government of national unity, a 38-member administration was formed, solely comprising representatives of the presidential majority (apart from one member of the PGP, who was expected to be expelled from that party). The size of the new government, in view of the deterioration in the economy, prompted widespread criticism, and two of the newly-appointed members, including the minister with responsibility for state control, subsequently refused to assume their allocated posts, apparently owing to disagreement with the composition of the portfolios. Also in March, 80 of the 120 deputies in the national assembly approved a constitutional amendment providing for the establishment of a senate (which the opposition had resisted) and repealing legislation that prohibited unsuccessful presidential candidates from participating in the government within a period of 18 months.

In June 1994 opposition parties agreed to a further postponement of the local government elections, to early 1995, owing to general lack of preparation. In the same month the authorities closed the Université Omar Bongo, after strike action by students, which was initiated in late May in support of demands for an increase in grants, led to violent incidents.

Economy

JANET E. LEWIS

Based on an earlier article by MICHAEL CHAPMAN

INTRODUCTION

The rapid development of Gabon's petroleum resources, together with the exploitation of other minerals and of forest products, has produced an impressive rate of economic growth. As a result of economic expansion, combined with a small population, Gabon has the highest level of gross domestic product (GDP) per caput in sub-Saharan Africa (estimated at US $4,660 in 1992), and ranks as an upper-middle-income country. However, the growth rate of the economy has been erratic, with periods of strong growth, recession and stagnation. With the economy largely dependent on petroleum the fall in international prices for that commodity in early 1986 caused a sharp contraction of GDP during the following two years. The petroleum sector was the first to be affected during 1986, and the decline then spread to other, non-oil, sectors. Between 1980–92, it was estimated, real GDP increased by an annual average of 0.5%, compared with an average annual growth rate of 9.5% between 1965–80. GDP increased, in real terms, by 6.6% in 1991, but declined by 2.0% in 1992, following a decline in international prices for petroleum.

Private investment (mainly foreign) has been dominant, but public investment in infrastructure and agriculture has risen substantially in recent years. Economic growth has been accompanied by important structural changes. With the depletion of coastal forests, the share of forest products in GDP has been declining, although, after a period of stagnation, production of wood products began to increase in the mid-1980s. However, the main source of growth since the mid-1960s has been the petroleum sector, which accounted for 30% of GDP and 80% of export earnings in 1992. Despite attempts to diversify the economy, the development of the hydrocarbon and other mineral industries, notably uranium and manganese, remain the major catalysts for sustained economic growth.

In December 1986 the government embarked upon a structural adjustment policy, covering the period to December 1988, which was supported by a stand-by loan of SDR 98.7m. from the IMF. Negotiations between the Gabonese government and the IMF were suspended in November 1988, following a failure to concur over performance targets, but in September 1989 a new stand-by arrangement, totalling SDR 43m., was agreed. In March 1990, however, the programme was suspended, following considerable political instability. None the less, the new government continued to adhere to adjustment criteria, such as the restructuring of public corporations and restraints on wage increases. In the early 1990s widespread strikes and demonstrations disrupted economic activity throughout the country. A new stand-by credit, which was approved by the IMF, was frozen in 1992, with the recommendation that a medium term (1993–1997) adjustment strategy be adopted to ensure a budgetary surplus. Following the devaluation of the CFA franc in January 1994 (see below), a reform that was favoured by the IMF but strenuously opposed by the Gabonese government, a new stand-by agreement of SDR 38m. was reached with the IMF, with a further 21m. to follow, to compensate for the inflationary effects of the devaluation and support the government's attempts to control public expenditure.

AGRICULTURE

Owing to the density of the tropical rain forest, only a small proportion of land area is suitable for agricultural activity, and, of this area, only 0.5% was under cultivation in the late 1980s. In 1992 agriculture (including forestry and fishing) contributed 9% of GDP, and employed 65.9% of the economically active population. Gabon has yet to achieve self-sufficiency in staple crops: imports of foodstuffs accounted for 17% of the value of total imports in 1992. Despite the government's aim of reducing expenditure on food imports and diversifying the economy by giving priority to the expansion of the agricultural sector, government policy had been directed mainly towards encouraging development in other sectors of the economy. Despite sharp reductions in total public investment in 1987 and 1988 compared with previous years, the agricultural sector's allocation was about one-quarter in each year. This compares with a share of less than 10% in previous years.

An important objective has been to limit the rural exodus, for labour shortages in some areas have been so acute that former plantations have been unworkable, and even subsistence production is barely sustained. In 1988 a three-year interim investment programme replaced the traditional Development Plan and was designed to complement structural adjustment programmes worked out with the IMF and the World Bank. Under the 1988–91 interim programme, the 'productive' sector of the economy was to receive 40% (27,000m. francs CFA) of planned investment, with agriculture receiving 64% of the allocation.

The principal cash crops are palm oil, cocoa, coffee and refined sugar. Of these, palm oil is the most important, although export potential is limited, owing to unfavourable competition from producers in the Far East. A parastatal organization, the Société de développement de l'agriculture au Gabon (Agrogabon), manages three plantations near Lambaréné with a total of 7,500 ha under cultivation. Production of raw palm oil totalled 51,376 tons in 1988 and increased to 58,766 tons in 1989. Domestic palm oil production is gradually substituting for imports of cooking oil. The main agricultural export is cocoa; however, its contribution to export revenue is minimal, with exports amounting to only some 1,600 metric tons by the early 1980s. In 1988/89 cocoa output totalled 1,887 tons, declining to 1,780 tons in 1989/90, to 1,309 tons in 1990/91, and to 1,242 tons in 1991/92. A cocoa-reprocessing plant, with a capacity of 400 tons per year, operates at Koulamoutou. Commercial output of coffee declined from 1,218 metric tons in 1988/89, to 232 tons in 1989/90; production recovered slightly, to 444 tons in 1990/91, but declined to 198 tons in 1991/92. Depressed world prices for both coffee and cocoa since the late 1980s, together with the government's reduction of producer prices in 1990, has adversely affected export performance. Production of refined sugar increased from negligible levels to 18,535 tons in 1987, as a result of the partial success of a large-scale mechanized sugar complex at Franceville, designed to produce 30,000 tons annually. Internal demand is about 11,000 tons per year: the surplus is exported. It is hoped to continue the export trade in refined sugar, which began with the supply of 4,000 tons to the USA and the Central African Republic during 1985. In the 1980s the government decided actively to promote the development of rubber as an export crop. Three of the country's four plantations are managed by the state-run Hevegab. Two of these are at Mitzic, covering a total area of 5,000 ha, and the third is at Bitam, with an area of 3,000 ha. The fourth plantation is managed by Agrogabon at Kango in the Estuaire province and covers an area of 4,000 ha.

Animal husbandry was, for many decades, hindered by the prevalence of the tsetse fly. In 1980, however, the first tsetse-resistant cattle were imported from Senegal, The Gambia and Zaire. Agrogabon now manages three cattle ranches at Lekabi, Nyanga and N'Gounié with a total of 29,000 in 1992. Poultry farming is mainly on a smallholder basis but there is one industrial poultry farm at Boumango which produced 2,856 tons of poultry meat in 1988. In 1992, according to FAO estimates, there were 29,000 cattle, 164,000 pigs and 252,000 sheep and goats.

FORESTRY

Virgin forests cover some 75% of Gabon's total land area. Until the commencement of mineral exploitation in the early 1960s, the economy was virtually dependent upon the timber industry. Okoumé and, to a lesser extent, ozigo (tropical softwoods used in the manufacture of plywood and furniture) are the most important timbers, accounting for 80% of Gabon's timber exports. Gabon's forests contain an estimated 100 other species of commercially exploitable hard and soft woods. Gabon currently ranks as Africa's fourth largest producer of tropical wood, and the world's largest exporter of okoumé wood. About 50 companies are active in the forestry sector, which is dominated by a small number of European enterprises. Gabonese enterprises, including both family concessions on a non-mechanized basis and mechanized enterprises of various sizes, are also involved in small-scale timber production. In 1993 the forestry sector engaged 15% of the working population, partially compensating for unemployment in rural areas.

For the purpose of granting licences, the government has divided Gabon into three distinct logging regions. With the depletion of forests in the accessible 'first zone' (which is reserved exclusively for Gabonese firms), exploitation has been expanded in the 'second zone', which covers the central part of the country. The completion of the second section of the Transgabon railway, in 1986, improved the accessibility of the 'third zone'.

Output of timber has fluctuated since independence, mainly in response to international demand and to movements in the value of the US dollar in relation to the franc CFA. Output of its principal export commodity, okoumé wood, declined between 1972–77, reflecting the world economic recession. Production levels improved in the late 1970s, but were adversely affected, from 1984 onwards, by increasing competition from South-East Asia, in conjunction with the decline in the value of the US dollar against the franc CFA, and the loss of some traditional markets. Following a strong recovery in demand for Gabon's timber, in 1990 production totalled 1.19m. cu m (of which 1.13m. cu m comprised okoumé), while exports amounted to 1.1m. cu m. In 1991, however, output declined to 895,100 cu m (of which 821,600 cu m comprised okoumé), and exports to 884,400 cu m. In 1992 production recovered slightly, to 952,900 cu m, while exports totalled 927,200 cu m.

The organization of the forestry sector, in particular the quasi-monopoly at marketing level of the state-owned Société nationale des bois du Gabon (SNBG), has been widely criticized. In 1988 the government announced a restructuring of the SNBG, which has been implemented with some success. However, in 1993 the SNBG still maintained its monopoly on the marketing of okoumé, although sales of other types of wood had been liberalized. Several forestry companies have yet to recuperate the financial losses that were incurred during the recessionary years, and the industry, as a whole, still suffers from the lack of internal outlets and from a rigid pricing system which is not adapted to fluctuations on the world timber market.

In the early 1980s exports of timber benefited from shifts in the value of the franc CFA against the US dollar, reaching their highest level, of 57,100m. francs CFA (equivalent to 6.5% of the value of total export earnings), in 1984. By 1987 earnings had declined to 46,900m. francs CFA; however, in the context of the 1986 slump in international prices for petroleum, the percentage share had increased to 12.1%. Earnings from timber exports increased to 49,900m. francs CFA in 1989, and to 55,500m. francs CFA in 1990 (equivalent to 8.4% of the value of total export earnings). In 1991 the decline in European construction activity resulted in a decline of 28% in these exports, and the government introduced a system of production quotas to seek to maintain producer prices at $200 per cu m. In 1992 timber accounted for 7.5% of Gabon's total export revenue (or 40% of export revenue, excluding oil). In 1992 restrictions on logging imposed in Asian countries resulted in high demand and an increase in prices. After the government relaxed quotas, production rose sharply to 1.5m. cu m, still just below the volume recorded in 1990, but higher in value (53,000m. francs CFA, compared with the 1990 figure.) In early 1994 world prices continued to rise, as did Gabon's production, particularly production of okoumé and ozigo. France, Israel and Greece have traditionally been the principal markets for Gabonese timber. Exports comprise sawlogs, plywood, blockboard and veneer sheets. In 1987 the SNBG announced that it had secured orders from France, Hong Kong, Turkey and India for more than 1.6m. cu m of timber annually over the following three years, with France purchasing around 60% of the total. France is the principal market for okoumé, although in 1991–92 its share of okoumé exports declined by 6%, to 32%; over the same period, sales to Japan almost doubled. Reforestation has been under way for some years, and the programme, which is designed to enable Gabon's output of okoumé to be maintained, accounts for the major part of the government's investment in forestry, amounting to 2,000m. francs CFA in the period 1980–82. Gabon, like most African timber producers, exports the vast majority of its wood in the form of raw logs. One of the government's aims is to raise the share of locally processed wood from its present level of about 25%. An investment plan had been designed to automate the factory of the Compagnie forestière du Gabon (CFG), which operates the largest sawmill in the country and is a major producer of plywood. However, the CFG's production declined by more than 60% during the 1980s; the state became the major shareholder in 1989, but supply and production difficulties continued in the early 1990s.

MINING

The main source of Gabon's considerable economic growth since the 1970s has been the exploitation of the country's mineral wealth, principally petroleum and, to a lesser extent, manganese and uranium. In 1993 Gabon was the fourth largest producer of petroleum in Africa, and 13th in the world. A member of OPEC, Gabon accounted for only 1.3% of that organization's total production in 1991.

The petroleum industry has emerged as the principal sector of the economy, accounting for 43% of GDP, 83% of total export earnings and 65% of government revenue in 1985. The sector is vulnerable to fluctuations in world petroleum prices and in the value of the US dollar. Rapidly increasing petroleum revenues resulted in a fivefold increase in GDP in 1974-85; although production rose by 70% in 1985-92, petroleum export earnings declined by 30%.

Exploitation started in 1956, but significant growth only commenced after 1967, with the coming into production of the Gamba-Ivinga deposits and the exploitation of the offshore Anguille deposit. Until 1989 production was largely offshore, with the main areas of reserves located around Port-Gentil, near Gamba and in the south, around Mayumba. Annual output fluctuated widely between 1966–87. In December 1987 the Obando Marin concession entered production, increasing output by 11,000 barrels per day (b/d) and thus prompting a recovery in production. In January 1989 the massive Rabi-Kounga onshore deposit entered production. Output rapidly exceeded projections, and by July the field was producing 50,000 b/d. Total oil output for 1989 was 10.2m. tons, an increase of 29% compared with 1988. By early 1990 Rabi-Kounga was producing 135,000 b/d and national output for the year reached 13.5m. tons, with exports totalling 12.5m. tons (compared with 8.6m. tons in 1989). In 1991 production increased to 14.7m. tons and exports to 13.8m. tons. In 1992, however, output declined to 14.5m. tons, with exports totalling 13.3m. tons, as a result of reduced output from Rabi-Kounga. In 1993 production improved following heavy investment in Rabi-Kounga, which accounted for 49% of total oil exports. Government policy is to maintain overall production levels, but no major discoveries have been made in recent years and exploration costs are high.

Reflecting the decline in international prices for petroleum, the value of Gabon's exports of that commodity fell to 244,500m. francs CFA in 1986, compared with 731,800m. francs CFA in the previous year. Income recovered modestly in 1987, but declined, to an estimated 227,500m. francs CFA, in 1988. After an increase in production in 1988, government revenue from the petroleum sector recovered to 376,000m. francs CFA in 1989, and, following the substantial rise in oil prices precipitated by the war in the Persian (Arabian) Gulf, to 540,900m. francs CFA in 1990. Oil prices declined by 14.8% in 1991, and by a further 6.4% in 1992.

Gabon's exports of crude petroleum are mainly destined for the USA (which became Gabon's largest market in 1992), France, Argentina and Brazil. A new link was established in 1984 for the supply of 10,000 b/d to Taiwan. Elf-Gabon, in which the state is in partnership with the French company, Elf-Aquitaine, was responsible for more than 70% of Gabon's production throughout the 1970s and most of the 1980s. However, by 1993 the principal operator was Shell Gabon, which operated the Rabi-Kounga field in association with Elf-Gabon and Amerada Hess. Foreign-owned companies have proved eager to invest in Gabon, and by 1988 a total of 28 companies had exploration interests: these included Agip, Conoco, Phillips, Norsk Hydro and British Gas. Agip withdrew in 1993; in 1992 25 oil companies, of which nine were operators, were present in Gabon, but Shell Gabon and Elf-Gabon remained the largest producers. Production by Elf-Gabon, in which the state had a 25% shareholding, declined by 2.5% between 1991 and 1992. In 1992 it began production at two new offshore fields, Hylia and Vanneau, off Port-Gentil, with production transported by pipeline to Elf-Gabon's terminal at Cap Lopez, and in 1994 a new onshore field, Avocette, was opened. Shell Gabon increased production between 1991 and 1992, and in 1993 began exploration at a new offshore field, Kenguerie Marin, between Port-Gentil and Libreville. In 1987 expenditure on exploration was estimated at 34,800m. francs CFA. In 1991 Gabon's estimated reserves totalled 100m. tons. Gabon's two petroleum refineries at Port-Gentil are operated by the Société gabonaise de raffinage (SOGARA), designed to supply the central African market, and by the Cie Gabon-Elf de raffinage (COGER), marketing principally in Western Europe. By the late 1980s, following modifications to its facilities, SOGARA's annual refining capacity was 800,000 tons. In 1992 an agreement between Elf-Aquitaine and British Petroleum (BP) provided for the acquisition by Elf-Aquitaine of a number of BP's refining and distribution activities. Gabon's annual refining capacity was 1.2m. tons in 1993; more than 700,000 tons of crude oil are processed annually.

Since 1962, manganese ore has been mined at Moanda, near Franceville, by the Cie minière de l'Ogooué (COMILOG). Gabon is estimated to have about 6.5% of world reserves of manganese. In 1992 Gabon's reserves were estimated at 52m. tons, and in the early 1990s production averaged 1.6m. tons per year, almost all of which was exported. In 1989 manganese output rose by 11% to 2.5m. tons, of which 2.4m. tons were exported. In 1990, however, production declined to 2.4m. tons, of which 2.2m. tons was exported, resulting in an estimated export revenue of 60,000m. francs CFA. In that year, however, Gabon overtook South Africa as the world's principal exporter of manganese ore; in 1993 the South African group, Gencor, acquired a 15% holding in COMILOG. Manganese output declined further, to 1.6m. tons in 1991, and to 1.4m. tons in 1992, with exports totalling 1.8m. tons and 1.5m. tons respectively (the difference in volume being attributable to reserves held in Gabon). Most of the extracted ore has traditionally been transported through the neighbouring Congo to the port at Pointe-Noire. However, the inauguration of the Transgabon railway and the opening of a new minerals-handling terminal at Owendo, near Libreville, in 1988 has provided additional facilities for the conveyance of manganese. Manganese is exported by the Société ferro-manganèse de Paris-Outreau (SFPO), in which COMILOG only has a minority holding.

The exploitation of uranium began in 1958. Deposits are exploited at Mounana and two other sites and the ore is concentrated before export by the Cie des mines d'uranium de Franceville (COMUF), a consortium largely controlled by French interests but with a 25% share held by the Gabonese government. COMUF offers Gabonese uranium on world markets, through the French Atomic Energy Commission. Uranium accounted for 3% of total export earnings in 1985, and for 7% in 1986, as the petroleum sector's share of export earnings fell. A reduction in world demand caused the volume of exports to decline from 999 tons in 1980 to 752 tons in 1987, before recovering to 899 tons in 1988, and to 983 tons in 1989. Following a further decline in world demand in 1990, exports fell to 624 tons. Earnings from exports of uranium, which totalled 22,000m. francs CFA in 1988, declined to 21,200m. francs CFA in 1989, and to 14,200m. francs CFA in 1990. Production increased from only 210 tons in 1972 to 1,006 tons in 1983. Output subsequently declined, to 793 tons in 1987, but recovered to 912 tons in 1988. In 1989 production fell to 867.7 tons but exports increased, as COMUF drew on stocks held locally. Production declined even further in 1990, to 710 tons, and, owing to the low level of world prices, Gabon reduced its uranium production to 680 tons in 1991, to 540 tons in 1992, and to 556 tons in 1993. Output has thus consistently fallen short of the total productive capacity of 1,500 tons of uranium metal per year and is unlikely to improve, owing to the depressed level of demand on the world market since 1985. In 1994 the world price for uranium was equivalent to only 13% of its level in 1978. Between 1991 and 1993 COMUF recorded annual losses, and the consortium has imposed staff reductions each year from 1989. Known reserves of uranium are sufficient for about 50 years' output at current production rates. About 80% of Gabon's output is sold to France, with the remainder going mainly to Belgium and Japan. Future prospects are poor as a consequence of the resistance to nuclear power and the end of the arms race, the large volume of production arriving on the world market from Eastern Europe and the high level of stocks held internationally.

One of the largest iron-ore deposits in the world, which is situated at Belinga, in the north-east of Gabon, remains economically unviable, in view both of depressed international price levels, and of the government's inability to secure the funds necessary to develop the third section of the Transgabon railway (that would facilitate the conveyance of the iron ore). Lead, zinc and phosphate deposits are known to exist, and further prospecting, for gold and diamonds, is in progress. A few individual diggers mine gold, with a total recorded output of 138 kg in 1988. The government is keen to promote the mining of niobium (columbium), phosphates, rare earths and titanium at Mabounie; the European Investment Bank (EIB) has shown interest in the scheme. Foreign investment is also being sought for a project to extract barytes. Marble is quarried at Doussé-Oussou, and reserves of copper and talc have also been identified.

MANUFACTURING, POWER AND TRANSPORTATION

Gabon's manufacturing sector is relatively small, accounting for 5.2% of GDP in 1991. Manufacturing GDP increased by an annual average of 6.4% in 1980–85, and by 11.8% in 1985–90; in 1992, however, manufacturing GDP increased by only 0.6%. A substantial part of this contribution was represented by oil refining and timber processing. Other manufacturing industries include the production of mineral concentrates, plants for processing agricultural products (coffee hulleries, a flour mill, several breweries and a soft drinks plant), cement, soap, paint, industrial gas, cigarettes, textile printing and clothing, and cement clinker. Factories for the manufacture of electric batteries, plastic articles and steel cables have also been constructed. Gabon has sought to develop large-scale natural-resource-based industries, but since its own domestic market is very small, these can for the most part be viable only in the context of the Union douanière et économique de l'Afrique centrale (UDEAC), of which Gabon is one of the six member countries. Gabon imports substantial quantities of manufactures from other UDEAC countries, but exported little to its UDEAC partners until the completion of the petroleum refineries. Cement output increased by 18% in 1985, to 245,000 tons. Production declined, to 129,000 metric tons, in 1991, significantly below annual capacity of 400,000 tons.

Gabon's sugar industry has been slow to develop. Production of refined sugar at the new Sosuho plant reached 18,535 tons in 1987; about one-third of this was exported.

In 1993 the government sought to encourage the development of Gabonese small and medium-sized businesses, which account for one-quarter of Gabon's firms and contribute between 5%-10% of GDP. An African Development Bank (ADB) loan of 19,000m. francs CFA was agreed, allowing such firms to borrow at a maximum interest rate of 12% (when local rates were 18%) over a period of 15 years, with a grace period of five years.

Electricity is produced and distributed in eleven urban centres by a semi-public company, the Société d'énergie et d'eau du Gabon (SEEG). Production was mainly on the basis of thermal plants utilizing oil or natural gas at Libreville and Port-Gentil, until the completion of the first hydroelectric plant at Kinguélé, near Libreville. An electricity and water supply programme was launched in 1984 to improve facilities in 30 regional centres. There is considerable potential hydroelectric power in Gabon, and output from the M'Bei valley is being increased by extensions to the Kinguélé system and by new installations at Tchimbélé. Over the period 1968–80 annual production of electricity increased from 74m. kWh to 569m. kWh for an installed capacity of 208,700 kW in 1980. In 1988 SEEG produced 908m. kWh, of which about one-fifth was generated thermally and the remainder produced by hydroelectric installations. In 1990 Gabon had an installed capacity of 279,000 kW, of which 73% was hydroelectric.

Gabon's surface transportation system is inadequate. Until 1979 there were no railways except for the cableway link between the Congo border and the Moanda manganese mine, and the main rivers are navigable only for the last 80–160 km of their course to the Atlantic Ocean. The road network is poorly developed and much of it is unusable during the rainy seasons. In 1992 there were an estimated 8,590 km of roads, of which only about 680 km were paved. In order to overcome the obstacles which the poor transport system presents to economic development, substantial investment in transport was undertaken in the 1980s. In 1989 the World Bank approved a loan of $30m., in support of a three-year programme for the repair and maintenance of the road network. In 1992 a project to surface some 1,400 km of road by the year 2000 was announced; in 1994 the ADB granted a loan of $99m. to finance road improvement.

The Transgabon railway scheme is among the most prestigious achievements of the Bongo presidency. External donors, none the less, have been highly critical of the expenditure involved. It proved difficult to find financial backing for even the first 340-km section of the rail line, linking Owendo and Booué; work eventually began in 1974, and was completed in January 1983. Work on the 330-km second section of the Transgabon, from Booué to Franceville, began in 1983 and was undertaken by Eurotrag, a West European consortium. Intended to provide access to new areas of forestry, as was the first section, and also to facilitate the transportation of minerals, the second section was completed in December 1986. The total cost of the railway was then estimated to have reached nearly $3,000m. Plans for a third section of 235 km, from Booué to Belinga, intended to enable exploitation of large iron-ore deposits in the north-east of the country, were suspended, owing to lack of finance, and available resources reallocated to the completion of the Booué–Franceville stretch. By 1989 the 648-km line linking Libreville and Franceville was fully operational. The inauguration, in late 1988, of the minerals-handling terminal at Owendo was expected to result in an increase in revenue for the operator of the railway, the Office du chemin de fer transgabonais (OCTRA). In 1993 OCTRA had a budget of 15,000m. francs CFA, and received a subsidy of 2,000m. francs CFA from the state. It derives 50% of its income from the transport of wood, 20% from passengers, 20% from general freight and 10% from manganese. The Owendo timber port opened in 1979, with a capacity of 1.5m. cu m per year. General improvements to the deep-water ports were undertaken at Owendo and at Port-Gentil during the 1980s. The construction of a deep-water port at Mayumba is planned.

Air transport plays an extremely important role in the economy, particularly because the dense forest, which covers much of the country, makes other modes of transport impracticable. The second phase of a programme to modernize and extend Libreville's Léon M'Ba international airport, needed to accommodate the large number of international flights for both freight and passengers, was completed in early 1988. In July 1988 a new company, the Société de gestion de l'aéroport de Libreville, was established to complete the rehabilitation of, and to manage, the airport. The third phase of the project, which was intended to raise annual capacity to 1m. passengers from a previous level of 600,000, was completed in 1990. In 1991 650,000 passengers arrived at Leon M'Ba airport, and 15,000 tons of freight was handled. As well as five domestic airports (Libreville, Port-Gentil, Franceville, Lambaréné and Moanda), there are several small airfields owned mainly by large companies working in the region. In 1977, following its withdrawal from Air Afrique, Gabon established its own international air service, Air Gabon, in which the state has an 80% interest. In 1993 Air Gabon made a loss of 3,500m. francs CFA.

FOREIGN TRADE AND PAYMENTS

Gabon has enjoyed a sustained surplus on its registered foreign trade. In 1986, however, the sharp decline in oil prices had a dramatic effect on export earnings, which fell to 372,000m. francs CFA, a reduction of more than 50% on the previous year. With imports falling much less sharply (to 339,100m. francs CFA), the trade surplus declined to only 33,000m. francs CFA. Export earnings recovered slightly in 1987, to 386,600m. francs CFA, and imports declined sharply to 219,900m. francs CFA, producing a trade surplus of 166,700m. francs CFA. In 1988 a reduction in revenue from oil exports resulted in a reduced trade deficit of 120,400m. francs CFA, with export earnings of 356,100m. francs CFA and imports of 235,700m. francs CFA. However, in 1989 the value of exports rose by 46% to 518,700m. francs CFA, encouraged by rising world prices and increased oil output from Rabi-Kounga. Imports in 1989 totalled 239,800m. francs CFA, with a healthy trade surplus of 278,900m. francs CFA. In 1990, following a further improvement in oil prices, exports were estimated at 675,700m. francs CFA, and imports at 210,200m. francs CFA, resulting in a trade surplus of 465,500m. francs CFA, which reached levels attained in the mid-1980s. Exports fell to 632,700m. francs CFA in 1991, when imports increased to 235,400m. francs CFA, producing a trade surplus of 397,300m. francs CFA. In 1992 it was estimated that exports declined to 613,500m. francs CFA, and imports to 230,000m. francs CFA, resulting in a slightly reduced trade surplus of 383,500m. francs CFA.

Gabon's favourable trade balance is normally reinforced by an inflow of aid and intermittently by substantial inflows of private long-term capital investment, mainly for the exploitation of petroleum. However, there is normally a substantial recurrent outflow in respect of profit remittances by foreign enterprises, debt service and other payments. Interest and repayments in respect of official short- and medium-term borrowings mounted alarmingly during the early 1980s, producing a substantial fall in reserves of foreign exchange. The success of austerity measures, implemented in accordance with IMF credit facilities in 1982, temporarily halted the decline in external currency reserves and reduced the country's debt-service ratio from 17% of export earnings in 1980 to 12% in 1985. The decline in earnings from exports of petroleum, combined with rising imports and an increasing deficit on services, caused the overall current account to fall into deficit in 1985, after being in surplus since 1978. Current account surpluses of 37,700m. francs CFA and 49,300m. francs CFA, respectively, in 1983 and 1984 were followed by a deficit on the current account of the balance of payments of 72,900m. francs CFA in 1985. Compounded by the decline in international prices for petroleum, the deficit reached 366,100m. francs CFA in 1986, but contracted to 135,000m. francs CFA in 1987, owing, in part, to a further rescheduling of debt by international creditor governments. Following agreement of a medium-term stand-by loan from the IMF in December 1986 (see below), the government's economic adjustment programme aimed to achieve a considerable reduction in the current-account deficit. However, owing to the deterioration in the trade balance in 1988 the current-account deficit increased to 183,300m. francs CFA. In 1989 the deficit declined sharply to 61,200m. francs CFA, and in 1990 the exceptionally high trade surplus resulted in a surplus in the current account of 58,300m. francs CFA. In 1991 the surplus on the current account declined to 54,500m. francs CFA, while a deficit was recorded in 1992 (according to the IMF).

In 1990 France was Gabon's principal market for exports (35.4%) and supplier of imports (47%). Trade with neighbouring UDEAC countries remains modest: the region purchased 0.2% of Gabon's exports and provided 5.5% of imports in 1990. A reform of customs duties on imported raw materials, which was proposed by UDEAC in 1993, aimed to lower the production costs of locally produced goods and to stimulate regional trade. In 1994 a treaty was signed by the six member countries of UDEAC, providing for the creation of the Communauté économique et monétaire en Afrique centrale, which was designed to encourage trade between member countries, initially through the standardization of transport policies, with the long-term target of free circulation of goods and services.

Since independence Gabon has been the recipient of considerable foreign aid from the West, particularly 'tied' aid from France. Grants from successive European Development Funds account for much of the other aid, with most of the remainder coming from Germany, the USA, the World Bank and the ADB. Of the 20,000m.–30,000m. francs CFA that Gabon receives in foreign aid each year, approximately two-thirds originates from France. Gabon has a surplus trade balance with France; in 1988-92 exports to France were almost 50% higher in value than imports from France. However, capital flows between the two countries have been negative for Gabon since 1989, when the balance moved from a surplus of 19,834m. francs CFA in 1988, to a deficit of 2,556m. francs CFA, declining further to a deficit of 32,573m. francs CFA in 1990 and 39,071m. francs CFA in 1991. In 1994 Japan granted aid of nearly 9,000m. francs CFA to finance a social action programme. The EC provided aid, amounting to 7,000m. francs CFA, to improve health services (conditional upon the introduction of health charges).

Tourism is greatly encouraged and has expanded in recent years. Luxurious hotel and conference facilities were built during the 1970s, and by 1987 there were 74 hotels, with a total of 3,077 rooms; 108,000 tourists visited Gabon in 1990.

PUBLIC FINANCE

During the 1960s Gabon achieved substantial surpluses on its ordinary budget, enabling considerable contributions to be made to the development budget. Nevertheless, until the early 1970s, substantial overall deficits resulted, which were financed in part by suppliers' credits and expensive short- and medium-term borrowing. Since 1977 the external debt repayments due in respect of these borrowings have increased dramatically and, despite buoyant oil revenues, the government's budgetary situation became grave. The government's budgetary difficulties had widespread repercussions on the private sector, and the extensive curtailment of less essential public expenditure projects became inevitable when in 1978 Gabon obtained an $18m. IMF credit under the stand-by arrangement to meet immediate financial obligations.

In 1979 budgetary expenditure was 328,000m. francs CFA, giving priority to financial recovery, debt-servicing and maintenance of economic activity, to the detriment of new investment. Debt-servicing remained a major item in the 1980 budget, fixed at 334,100m. francs CFA and in the 1981 budget, in which expenditure totalled 424,800m. francs CFA. The 1982 budget rose further to 457,200m. francs CFA, of which 175,400m. was intended for development spending. The 1983 budget was originally set at 562,000m. francs CFA, of which 266,000m. was for investment, notably in the Transgabon railway project. However, falling world prices for petroleum necessitated a reduction of 20,000m. francs CFA in investment. A more favourable economic climate allowed for an 11% increase in the 1984 budget, to 597,000m. francs CFA. Additional petroleum revenues prompted the government to revise its 1984 budget, and in June 1984 the total was raised to 624,000m. francs CFA. This figure was not achieved, owing to outstanding debts to the oil companies and the cost of servicing the foreign debt.

The 1985 budget was increased to 679,000m. francs CFA, with the slight decline in oil revenues offset by an additional 19,000m. francs CFA in tax receipts and a 50,000m. francs CFA fall in expenditure on debt-servicing. Recurrent expenditure for 1985 was increased by 22,500m. francs CFA, to 219,000m. francs CFA. Total revenues, meanwhile, reached an estimated 594,000m. francs CFA, leaving a deficit of 85,000m. francs CFA. The revised 1986 budget proposed a reduction in total expenditure of 8%–10% in real terms, to 670,000m. francs CFA, with the investment budget most severely affected. Priority continued to be given to development projects already under way, especially the Transgabon railway (which was allocated 116,200m. francs CFA of the total investment budget of 279,000m. francs CFA), agricultural development projects and road-building. Revenue in 1986 was adversely affected by the decline in international petroleum prices (with government revenues from the petroleum sector falling by 24%, compared with the previous year), reaching 550,000m. francs CFA and leading to an increased budget deficit of 120,000m. francs CFA. In the context of the continuing depression in the international petroleum market, revenue in the 1987 budget was almost halved, to 263,300m. francs CFA: revenue from petroleum, at 64,500m. francs CFA, was less than one-quarter of the 1986 level. Recurrent expenditure of 263,800m. francs CFA was only about 10% less than that of the previous year, reflecting the constraints of the high level of debt-servicing. Operating expenses, in contrast, were reduced by more than 15%. With the completion of the Transgabon railway, the government was able to reduce the investment budget by 73.6%, to 97,300m. francs CFA, with an overall final budget deficit of 105,700m. francs CFA. Only agriculture was excluded from wide-ranging reductions in public investment, in which the most substantial cuts were made in infrastructural development, public administration and education.

In early 1987 the 'Paris Club' of Western official creditors agreed to reschedule official debt repayments falling due between 1986 and 1988, following the Gabonese government's suspension of payments on both official and commercial debt in September 1986. Agreement was also reached with the 'London Club' of commercial creditors in 1987. The 1987 budget deficit of 126,900m. francs CFA was to be financed by loans for capital projects, advances from the central bank and drawings from an SDR 98.7m. stand-by loan that had been approved by the IMF in December 1986. The 1988 budget aimed for increased revenues from non-petroleum sources, such as higher duties on alcohol and tobacco, and a rise in sales taxes. Continued austerity in 1988 resulted in a further slight decline in revenue, to 246,600m. francs CFA, although revenue from petroleum recovered to 74,500m. francs CFA. Despite extensive reductions in public-sector expenditure (including the imposition of redundancies and salary cuts), current expenditure rose to 267,500m. francs CFA. The investment budget was kept to a minimal 66,200m. francs CFA, although this still entailed an overall budget deficit of 83,500m. francs CFA (allowing for the increase in arrears on interest payments). In March 1988 the 'Paris Club' agreed to reschedule US $344m. of official debt principal and interest due in that year, contributing to a reduction in the debt-servicing burden. Revenue was estimated at 282,500m. francs CFA and expenditure at 351,700m. francs CFA in 1989, resulting in an overall budget deficit of 64,100m. francs CFA. In 1990 an increase in petroleum receipts contributed to a rise of total revenue to 373,300m. francs CFA, while expenditure declined slightly, to 326,700m. francs CFA; an overall budget surplus of 51,000m. francs CFA was recorded. In 1991, despite a further increase in total revenue, to 441,700m. francs CFA (following continued high receipts from petroleum), a sharp rise in expenditure, to 465,500m. francs CFA, resulted in an overall budget deficit of 25,200m. francs CFA. In mid-1990 President Mitterrand of France announced unilateral debt-relief measures for middle-income developing countries, such as Gabon, that had previously been excluded from concessionary relief. In September 1991 the government's concerted efforts to rectify Gabon's finances were recognized by the 'Paris Club', which agreed to reschedule a further $545m. of debt. This, in turn, resulted in a further arrangement with the IMF, which granted a $40m. stand-by facility. The World Bank subsequently released the second tranche ($50m.) of a structural adjustment loan, while the ADB disbursed $60m. (the second tranche of a similar loan). In 1992, following a rise in total revenue of 13.8%, an increased budget deficit of 32,100m. francs CFA was recorded. In that year a structural adjustment programme, which was to be financed by a stand-by credit arrangement with the IMF, was suspended following delays in the implementation of austerity measures, resulting in additional difficulties in financing the budget deficit. At the end of 1992 external debt totalled US $3,799m., while the cost of debt-servicing was equivalent to 16.9% of revenue from exports of goods and services.

The budget for 1993 of 398,500m. francs CFA was increased slightly in 1994, to 415,000m. francs CFA. It was expected that revenue from the country's own resources would amount to 372,000m. francs CFA in 1994, nearly half of which would be derived from oil revenue, as a result of increased production. However, with heavy administrative expenditure (246,000m. francs CFA, an increase of 10.5% compared with 1993, owing to public sector wage costs), investment of 100,000m. francs CFA and the servicing of the public debt (69,000m. francs CFA), the budget was estimated to produce a deficit of 43,000m. francs CFA. The investment budget represented an increase of 16% compared with 1993, with priority given to health and human resource infrastructure.

Throughout 1993 Gabon's considerable economic and political difficulties were compounded by fears of a possible devaluation of the franc CFA, creating uncertainties for government, investors and foreign creditors. The devaluation of the franc CFA by 50%, which was announced in January 1994, had an immediate impact. As imported food prices began to increase, the government adopted stabilization measures: a price freeze on basic food commodities, an adjustment of the customs duty reform agreed by UDEAC and some relief measures for businesses. Widespread demands for an increase in wage rates inevitably ensued, with social and industrial unrest and strike action by trade unions. In April the government acceded to pressure from within the civil service and awarded salary increases of 10% to compensate for the worst effects of the devaluation, increasing the public sector wage bill by 15,000m. francs CFA.

In 1993, prior to the devaluation, Gabon's indebtedness had become acute. The total public debt was estimated at 850,000m. francs CFA, of which 415,000m. francs CFA was owed to France. The government was unable to make the debt repayments due in 1993, amounting to some 405,000m. francs CFA; the budget for 1994 provided only 69,000m. francs CFA for debt repayment. Following the devaluation the IMF, the 'Paris Club' and the 'London Club' of Western commercial creditors renegotiated their agreements with Gabon to support the government's efforts to sustain its adjustment strategies. The 'London Club' of private banks announced a restructuring of all Gabon's commercial debt contracted before 1986. A debt of some US $110m. was renegotiated, with concessions applicable to past arrears as well as future liabilities. The IMF agreed to credit of SDR 60.1m. (equivalent to US $85m.) in two tranches, of which SDR 38.6m. (US $55m.) was to be released immediately. The organization accepted that the devaluation of the CFA franc, the limited sources of outside investment over the previous two years, the slow pace of reductions in public expenditure and of diversification of non-petroleum revenues and unpaid debt arrears had weakened the government in its attempts to apply structural reforms (including limited privatization, the lowering of tariff barriers and measures to improve the labour market). Following the IMF agreement, the 'Paris Club' agreed to reschedule 740,000m. francs CFA of Gabon's public debt. (Gabon had repaid virtually nothing since 1992.) Repayment was to resume in 1997 for a period of 13 years (following a three-year period of grace). The Gabonese government and the IMF signed a structural adjustment agreement, whereby the government hoped to attract 1,058,000m. francs CFA of external finance, including the rescheduling of public debt previously agreed by the 'Paris Club'. At the same time France cancelled 70,000m. francs CFA of debt, which was due in 1994, and the French Development Fund released 35,000m. francs CFA to support the government's structural adjustment programme.

DEVELOPMENT PLANNING

In its development policies, Gabon has consistently sought to encourage private foreign investment. There have been modest attempts to promote the 'Gabonization' of management and attempts to improve the performance of parastatal corporations, but a new investment code published in July 1989, to complement structural adjustment policies, strongly encourages private foreign and local investors.

In the first Five-Year Development Plan (1966–70) total investment was estimated at 90,000m. francs CFA. For the second Five-Year Development Plan (1971-75) total planned investment was 150,000m. francs CFA. The third Five-Year Plan, which had to be curtailed as part of the IMF agreement, envisaged a huge investment of 1,269,000m. francs CFA in 1976–80, based on the availability of oil revenues from present known reserves. An interim Plan for the three years 1980–82 was produced to cover investments of 879,000m. francs CFA (almost $4,000m.). The objective of this Plan was to restructure the Gabonese economy by developing agriculture, infrastructure and processing industries (specifically those based on domestic extractive industries) in preparation for the eventual diminution of the country's dependence on earnings from petroleum. The fifth Plan (originally formulated to cover the years 1984–88, but subsequently extended to 1990) was similar to the previous interim Plan, and was in keeping with the government's overall policy of planned economic liberalism. Approximately 1,230,000m. francs CFA was to be invested during the Plan period, with infrastructure, notably the Transgabon railway, receiving 50% of the total proposed investment. About 20% of investment was allocated to rural development (including agriculture and energy), and 17% to social services and education. Under the Plan, high priority was to be given to the diversification of the country's productive sector. Following the fall in petroleum revenues in 1985 and 1986, however, several projects were affected by the government's austerity programme, as spending on development was reduced. A two-year stabilization programme was implemented in 1986–88, and the government also embarked on a structural adjustment programme, with guidance from the IMF, the World Bank and the ADB. The programme aimed to reduce dependence on the petroleum sector, in the medium term, to direct investment towards productive sectors unrelated to that commodity, to restructure the parastatal sector and to monitor borrowing by public companies. New measures for the liberalization of external trade and of the pricing regime were introduced between October 1988 and May 1989, and a new investment code was published in 1990. During 1990, however, political upheaval diverted attention from the economy, although an unexpected increase in petroleum revenues was achieved, mainly as a result of the unexpectedly large volume of production from Rabi-Kounga. The government has since introduced three-year 'rolling' plans, with the emphasis on agriculture and forestry, infrastructural rehabilitation and maintenance, education and training and the promotion of small and medium-sized enterprises.

In a wider context, Gabon has achieved very creditable rates of growth since the 1970s. Nevertheless, the country's heavy dependence on petroleum revenues has led it to suffer considerably from the depressed international prices for petroleum of the mid-1980s, and the economic situation is not without its difficulties. Foreign investment has been constrained in recent years by high wages and acute labour shortages. Long-term prospects for petroleum, on which so much depends, are uncertain. In addition, growth is dependent on the possibilities of maintaining export earnings by expanding manganese and uranium production, increasing forest exploitation and, eventually, on exploiting the immense iron ore reserves in the Mekambo region. For all these, however, adequate transport and handling facilities require to be developed. Secondary sources of growth may be found in the further development of processing industries and of manufacturing but success is dependent on creating a regional market for such goods, given the constraints imposed by the limited size of the domestic market. In view of its small population, Gabon is likely to remain principally an exporter of raw materials for some time.

Statistical Survey

Source (unless otherwise stated): Direction Générale de l'Economie, Ministère de la Planification, de l'Economie et de l'Administration Territoriale, Libreville.

Area and Population

AREA, POPULATION AND DENSITY

Area (sq km)	267,667*
Population (census results)	
8 October 1960–May 1961	
Males	211,350
Females	237,214
Total	448,564
January 1993	1,011,710
Density (per sq km) at mid-1993	3.8

* 103,347 sq miles.

REGIONS

Region	Population (1976 estimate)	Chief town
Estuaire	311,300	Libreville
Haut-Ogooué	187,500	Franceville
Moyen-Ogooué	50,500	Lambaréné
N'Gounié	122,600	Mouila
Nyanga	89,000	Tchibanga
Ogooué-Ivindo	56,500	Makokou
Ogooué-Lolo	50,500	Koula-Moutou
Ogooué-Maritime	171,900	Port-Gentil
Woleu-N'Tem	162,300	Oyem
Total	1,202,100	

PRINCIPAL TOWNS (population in 1988)

Libreville (capital)	352,000	Franceville	75,000
Port-Gentil	164,000		

BIRTHS AND DEATHS (UN estimates, annual averages)

	1975–80	1980–85	1985–90
Birth rate (per 1,000)	30.9	33.8	38.9
Death rate (per 1,000)	18.9	18.1	16.8

Expectation of life (UN estimates, years at birth, 1985–90): 51.5 (males 49.9; females 53.2).

Source: UN, *World Population Prospects: The 1992 Revision*.

ECONOMICALLY ACTIVE POPULATION
(ILO estimates, '000 persons at mid-1980)

	Males	Females	Total
Agriculture, etc.	205	174	379
Industry	49	5	54
Services	50	19	69
Total labour force	305	198	502

Source: ILO, *Economically Active Population Estimates and Projections, 1950–2025*.

Mid-1992 (estimates, '000 persons): Agriculture, etc. 352; Total 534. Source: FAO, *Production Yearbook*.

Agriculture

PRINCIPAL CROPS ('000 metric tons)

	1990	1991	1992
Maize	22*	23*	24
Cassava (Manioc)*	250	250	260
Yams*	110	110	115
Taro (Coco yam)*	65	68	70
Vegetables*	30	31	31
Bananas*	9	9	9
Plantains*	235	240	245
Cocoa beans	2	1†	2†
Coffee (green)*	2	2	2
Groundnuts (in shell)*	15	16	16
Sugar cane*	210	210	160

* FAO estimate(s). † Unofficial figure.

Source: FAO, *Production Yearbook.*

LIVESTOCK
(FAO estimates, '000 head, year ending September)

	1990	1991	1992
Cattle	27	28	29
Pigs	160	162	164
Sheep	160	165	170
Goats	80	81	82

Poultry (FAO estimates, million): 2 in 1990; 2 in 1991; 2 in 1992.

Source: FAO, *Production Yearbook.*

LIVESTOCK PRODUCTS

1992 (FAO estimates, '000 metric tons): Meat 27; Hen eggs 1.5.

Forestry

ROUNDWOOD REMOVALS ('000 cubic metres)

	1990	1991*	1992*
Sawlogs, veneer logs and logs for sleepers	1,633	1,633	1,633
Fuel wood*	2,539	2,623	2,711
Total	4,172	4,256	4,344

* FAO estimates.

Source: FAO, *Yearbook of Forest Products.*

SAWNWOOD PRODUCTION
('000 cubic metres, incl. railway sleepers)

	1990	1991	1992
Total	37*	32*	32†

* Unofficial figure.
† FAO estimate.

Source: FAO, *Yearbook of Forest Products.*

Fishing

('000 metric tons, live weight)

	1989	1990	1991
Freshwater fishes*	1.9	2.0	2.0
West African croakers	1.2	1.5	1.5*
Lesser African threadfin	1.3	0.4	0.4*
Bonga shad*	10.0	9.5	9.3
Other marine fishes (incl. unspecified)*	3.9	4.8	4.7
Total fish*	18.3	18.2	17.8
Southern pink shrimp	4.6	4.3	4.2
Total catch*	22.9	22.5	22.0

* FAO estimate(s).

Source: FAO, *Yearbook of Fishery Statistics.*

Mining

('000 metric tons, unless otherwise indicated)

	1989	1990	1991
Crude petroleum	10,227	13,493	17,355*
Natural gas (petajoules)	4	4	4
Uranium ore (metric tons)†	870	710	600
Manganese ore†‡	1,196.5	1,118.5	961.6
Gold (kilograms)†‡	81	80	80

Source: UN, *Industrial Statistics Yearbook.*
* Provisional or estimated figure.
† Figures refer to the metal content of ores.
‡ Data from the US Bureau of Mines.

1992: Crude petroleum 15,372,000 metric tons. Source: UN, *Monthly Bulletin of Statistics.*

Industry

PETROLEUM PRODUCTS ('000 metric tons)

	1989	1990	1991
Liquefied petroleum gas*	5	5	7
Motor spirit (petrol)	72	75	78
Kerosene	70	72	75
Jet fuel	67	68	70
Distillate fuel oils	208	205	212
Residual fuel oil	193	195	198
Bitumen (asphalt)	1	1	1

* Provisional or estimated figures.

Source: UN, *Industrial Statistics Yearbook.*

SELECTED OTHER PRODUCTS
(metric tons, unless otherwise indicated)

	1987	1988	1989
Palm oil (refined)	8,349	10,346	2,307
Flour	27,428	23,105	25,976
Refined sugar	19,232	18,459	20,905
Soft drinks ('000 hectolitres)	395.7	318.6	297.2
Beer ('000 hectolitres)	571.5	511.3	460.2
Cement ('000 metric tons)	139	131	117
Electric energy (million kWh)	894.9	910.0	901.0

Plywood ('000 cu metres): 49 in 1990 (Unofficial figure); 50 in 1991 (Unofficial figure); 50 in 1992 (FAO estimate) (Source: FAO, *Yearbook of Forest Products*).

Veneer sheets ('000 cu metres): 65 in 1990 (FAO estimate); 60 in 1991 (Unofficial figure); 60 in 1992 (FAO estimate) (Source: FAO, *Yearbook of Forest Products*).

Finance

CURRENCY AND EXCHANGE RATES

Monetary Units

100 centimes = 1 franc de la Coopération financière en Afrique centrale (CFA).

French Franc, Sterling and Dollar Equivalents (31 March 1994)
1 French franc = 100 francs CFA;
£1 sterling = 846.40 francs CFA;
US $1 = 570.14 francs CFA;
1,000 francs CFA = £1.181 = $1.754.

Average Exchange Rate (francs CFA per US $)
1991 282.11
1992 264.69
1993 283.16

Note: An exchange rate of 1 French franc = 50 francs CFA, established in 1948, remained in force until January 1994, when the CFA franc was devalued by 50%, with the exchange rate adjusted to 1 French franc = 100 francs CFA.

BUDGET ('000 million francs CFA)

Revenue*	1989	1990	1991
Tax revenue	197.8	226.4	311.9
Taxes on income, profits, etc.	54.8	81.3	121.7
Domestic taxes on goods and services	65.4	75.8	104.5
Taxes on international trade and transactions	67.2	59.3	76.6
Other current revenue	84.6	107.0	129.0
Property income	3.1	7.1	16.9
Administrative fees, charges, etc.	49.8	81.7	81.2
Capital revenue	0.1	39.9	0.8
Total	282.5	373.3	441.7

* Excluding grants received ('000 million francs CFA): 6.0 in 1989; 5.0 in 1990; 6.0 in 1991.

Expenditure†	1989	1990	1991
Current expenditure	212.8	222.5	253.4
Expenditure on goods and services	196.7	204.2	235.5
Subsidies and other current transfers	16.1	18.2	17.8
Capital expenditure	138.9	104.2	212.1
Acquisitions of fixed capital assets	63.3	54.3	58.2
Purchase of land and intangible assets	7.2	6.1	14.0
Capital transfers	68.4	43.8	139.9
Total	351.7	326.7	465.5

† Excluding net lending ('000 million francs CFA): 1.0 in 1989; 0.7 in 1990; 7.4 in 1991.

Source: IMF, *Government Finance Statistics Yearbook*.

CENTRAL BANK RESERVES (US $ million at 31 December)*

	1991	1992	1993
Gold*	4.55	4.28	5.11
IMF special drawing rights	6.35	0.10	0.03
Reserve position in IMF	0.07	0.07	0.07
Foreign exchange	321.05	71.04	0.64
Total	332.02	75.49	5.85

* Valued at market-related prices.

Source: IMF, *International Financial Statistics*.

MONEY SUPPLY ('000 million francs CFA at 31 December)

	1991	1992	1993
Currency outside banks	62.88	56.79	50.47
Demand deposits at commercial and development banks	132.48	84.71	86.92
Total money (incl. others)	189.92	139.01	134.61

Source: IMF, *International Financial Statistics.*

COST OF LIVING (Retail Price Index for African families in Libreville; base: 1985 = 100)

	1991	1992	1993
All items	100.0	100.3	90.7

Source: IMF, *International Financial Statistics.*

NATIONAL ACCOUNTS

('000 million francs CFA at current prices)

Expenditure on the Gross Domestic Product

	1987	1988	1989
Government final consumption expenditure	247.0	229.5	220.0
Private final consumption expenditure	499.5	510.6	524.8
Increase in stocks	-7.0	-12.1	-10.0
Gross fixed capital formation	301.1	325.0	298.1
Total domestic expenditure	1,040.6	1,053.0	1,032.9
Exports of goods and services	415.1	369.1	534.1
Less Imports of goods and services	412.0	441.4	454.8
GDP in purchasers' values	1,043.7	980.7	1,112.2

Gross Domestic Product by Economic Activity

	1987	1988	1989
Agriculture, stock-breeding and fishing	88.9	91.3	90.3
Forestry	21.9	22.3	18.8
Petroleum exploitation and research	256.2	195.8	345.7
Mining and quarrying	42.7	42.6	51.6
Timber industry	11.2	10.4	10.7
Refining	24.8	25.7	23.8
Processing industries	52.5	52.5	50.5
Electricity, water, gas and steam	27.5	29.5	28.8
Construction	68.2	57.2	44.5
Trade	87.6	89.1	86.8
Hotels, cafés and restaurants	11.8	12.2	12.2
Transport	54.7	54.6	54.5
Financial institutions	33.2	30.4	31.9
Public administration and services to households	134.9	134.3	129.5
Other services	82.6	83.6	84.3
Sub-total	998.7	931.5	1,063.9
Import duties	64.4	66.2	68.2
Less Imputed bank service charge	19.4	17.0	19.9
Total	1,043.7	980.7	1,112.2

BALANCE OF PAYMENTS (US $ million)

	1990	1991	1992
Merchandise exports f.o.b.	2,481.6	2,243.1	2,297.4
Merchandise imports f.o.b.	−772.0	−834.4	−885.9
Trade balance	1,709.6	1,408.7	1,411.5
Exports of services	241.6	226.9	252.0
Imports of services	−1,002.5	−830.9	−813.8
Other income received	20.1	28.0	47.2
Other income paid	−620.1	−529.6	−890.1
Private unrequited transfers (net)	−158.5	−125.5	−154.1
Official unrequited transfers (net)	24.2	5.7	12.1
Current balance	214.4	183.3	−135.3
Direct capital investment (net)	44.6	−116.3	−62.0
Other capital (net)	−182.4	−337.5	−715.9
Net errors and omissions	−45.4	73.1	4.6
Overall balance	31.1	−197.4	−908.5

Source: IMF, *International Financial Statistics*.

External Trade

Note: Figures exclude trade with other countries in the Customs and Economic Union of Central Africa (UDEAC): Cameroon, the Central African Republic, Chad (since January 1984), the Congo and Equatorial Guinea (since January 1985).

PRINCIPAL COMMODITIES ('000 million francs CFA)

Imports	1987	1988	1989
Machinery and apparatus	42.3	48.8	70.6
Transport equipment	31.1	21.2	24.2
Food products	42.1	33.9	31.8
Metals and metal products	24.2	32.8	27.2
Chemical products	8.0	8.9	13.1
Vegetable and animal products (non-food)	4.2	3.3	3.5
Precision instruments	5.7	9.1	14.4
Textiles and textile products	6.2	5.3	4.3
Hygiene and cleaning products	9.5	8.9	10.5
Vehicles	3.9	5.8	6.0
Mineral products	3.5	3.6	3.8
Total (incl. others)	216.7	215.8	241.8

Exports	1987	1988	1989
Petroleum and petroleum products	266.6	222.6	361.0
Manganese	32.4	45.0	59.3
Timber	46.9	48.3	48.1
Uranium	24.0	22.1	21.1
Total (incl. others)	386.9	356.1	509.6

PRINCIPAL TRADING PARTNERS ('000 million francs CFA)

Imports	1983	1984	1985*
Belgium/Luxembourg	4.7	10.1	15.1
France	141.5	172.5	176.2
Germany, Fed. Republic	13.3	18.0	22.2
Italy	8.2	14.9	16.1
Japan	19.3	22.1	24.5
Netherlands	9.9	9.4	8.8
Spain	6.5	7.5	6.1
United Kingdom	9.4	11.7	16.0
USA	28.8	25.1	38.9
Total (incl. others)	276.5	320.4	387.0

Exports	1983	1984	1985*
Canada	24.9	54.6	34.3
France	171.0	271.8	295.3
Germany, Fed. Republic	6.3	33.2	6.0
Italy	30.8	9.9	20.8
Netherlands	26.9	20.3	30.0
Spain	37.6	60.6	62.8
United Kingdom	22.9	16.2	37.1
USA	144.1	195.5	164.8
Total (incl. others)	762.2	881.7	887.0

* Estimated figures.

Source: *La Zone Franc-Rapport 1988*.

Transport

RAILWAYS (traffic)

	1984	1985	1986*
Passengers carried	135,913	137,111	125,816
Freight carried (metric tons)	664,605	723,034	666,412

* Estimated figures.

ROAD TRAFFIC (motor vehicles in use)

	1983	1984	1985
Passenger cars	15,150	15,650	16,093
Buses and coaches	479	508	546
Goods vehicles	9,240	9,590	9,960

Source: the former Ministère des Transports Terrestres, Ferroviaires, Fluviaux et Lagunaires.

INTERNATIONAL SEA-BORNE SHIPPING (freight traffic, '000 metric tons)

	1988	1989	1990
Goods loaded	8,890	10,739	12,828
Goods unloaded	610	213	212

Source: UN, *Monthly Bulletin of Statistics*.

CIVIL AVIATION (traffic on scheduled services)

	1988	1989	1990
Kilometres flown (million)	6	6	6
Passengers carried ('000)	383	407	398
Passenger-kilometres (million)	418	447	445
Freight ton-kilometres (million)	27	29	26

Source: UN, *Statistical Yearbook*.

Tourism

	1988	1989	1990
Tourist arrivals ('000)	20	113	108

Source: UN, *Statistical Yearbook*.

Communications Media

	1989	1990	1991
Radio receivers ('000 in use)	155	165	171
Television receivers ('000 in use)	40	43	45
Daily newspapers:			
Number	n.a.	1	n.a.
Average circulation ('000 copies)	n.a.	20	n.a.
Telephones ('000 in use)*	20	20	20

* Estimated figures.

Source: UNESCO, *Statistical Yearbook*; UN, *African Statistical Yearbook*.

Education

(1991)

	Institutions	Teachers	Pupils: Males	Pupils: Females	Pupils: Total
Pre-primary	9	37	465	485	950
Primary	1,024	4,782	105,819	104,181	210,000
Secondary:					
General	n.a.	1,356	n.a.	n.a.	42,871
Vocational	n.a.	476	n.a.	n.a.	8,477
Teacher training*	n.a.	284	2,422	2,963	5,385
University level	2	299	2,148	852	3,000
Other higher	n.a.	257†	864‡	247‡	1,111‡

* 1987 figures. † 1983 figure. ‡ 1988 figure.

Source: UNESCO, *Statistical Yearbook*.

Directory

The Constitution

The Constitution of the Gabonese Republic was adopted on 14 March 1991. The main provisions are summarized below:

PREAMBLE

Upholds the rights of the individual, liberty of conscience and of the person, religious freedom and freedom of education. Sovereignty is vested in the people, who exercise it through their representatives or by means of referenda. There is direct, universal and secret suffrage.

HEAD OF STATE

The existing presidential mandate is valid for a period of seven years (until 1994). Thereafter, the President will be elected by direct universal suffrage for a five-year term, renewable only once. The President is Head of State and of the Armed Forces. The President may, after consultation with his ministers and leaders of the National Assembly, order a referendum to be held. The President appoints the Prime Minister, who is Head of Government and who is accountable to the President. The President is the guarantor of national independence and territorial sovereignty.

EXECUTIVE POWER

Executive power is vested in the President and the Council of Ministers, who are appointed by the Prime Minister, in consultation with the President.

LEGISLATIVE POWER

The National Assembly is elected by direct universal suffrage for a five-year term. It may be dissolved or prorogued for up to 18 months by the President, after consultation with the Council of Ministers and President of the Assembly. The President may return a bill to the Assembly for a second reading, when it must be passed by a majority of two-thirds of the members. If the President dissolves the Assembly, elections must take place within 40 days.

The Constitution also provides for the establishment of an upper chamber (the Senate), to control the balance and regulation of power.

POLITICAL ORGANIZATIONS

Article 2 of the Constitution states that 'Political parties and associations contribute to the expression of universal suffrage. They are formed and exercise their activities freely, within the limits delineated by the laws and regulations. They must respect the principles of democracy, national sovereignty, public order and national unity'.

JUDICIAL POWER

The President guarantees the independence of the Judiciary and presides over the Conseil Supérieur de la Magistrature. Supreme judicial power is vested in the Supreme Court.

The Government

HEAD OF STATE

President: El Hadj OMAR (ALBERT-BERNARD) BONGO (took office 2 December 1967, elected 25 February 1973, re-elected December 1979, November 1986 and December 1993).

COUNCIL OF MINISTERS

(August 1994)

Prime Minister: CASIMIR OYE MBA.

Minister of State for Equipment and Construction: ZACHARIE MYBOTO.

Minister of State for Communications, Posts and Telecommunications: JACQUES ADIAHENOT.

Minister of State Control, Decentralization, Territorial Administration and Regional Integration: (vacant).

Minister of Justice and Keeper of Seals: SERGE MBA BEKALE.

Minister of Social and Family Affairs and National Solidarity: VICTOR MAPANGOU MOUKANI MUETSA.

Minister of the Interior, Local Communities and Mobile Security: ANTOINE MBOUMBOU-MIYAKOU.

Minister of Transport, and of Tourism and National Parks: MARTIN FIDÈLE MAGNAGA.

Minister of Foreign Affairs and Co-operation: JEAN PING.

Minister of National Defence, Public Security and Immigration: Gen. IDRISS NGARI.

Minister of Mines, Energy and Hydraulic Resources: PAUL TOUNGUI.

Minister of National Education, Professional Training and Government Spokesman: PAULETTE MOUSSAVOU MISSAMBO.

Minister of Merchant Marine and Fishing: JOACHIM MAGOUINDI-MAHOTES.

Minister of the Civil Service and Administrative Reform: PIERRE-CLAVER NZONG.

Minister of Water, Forestry Resources and the Environment: EUGENE KAKOU MAYAGA.

Minister of Labour and Human Resources: JEAN-REMY PENDY-BOUYIKI.

Minister of Culture, Arts, Mass Education and Human Rights: LAZARE DINGOMBE.

Minister of Finance, the Budget and State Shareholdings: MARCEL DOUPAMBY MATOKA.

Minister of Commerce, Industry and Scientific Research: PATRICE NZIENGUI.

Minister of the Economy, Planning, Reform of the Parastatal Sector and Privatization: ANDRÉ DIEUDONNÉ BERRE.

Minister of Public Health: JEROME NGOUA-BEKALE.

Minister of Youth and Sports: YOLANDE BIKE.

Minister of Higher Education: RENE NDEMEZO'O.

Minister of Small and Medium-sized Enterprises, and Handicrafts: PIERRE NZIENGUI-MABILA.

Minister of Habitat, Lands and Urban Planning: EMMANUEL AKOGHE MBA.

Minister Delegate at the Office of the Prime Minister, in charge of relations with Parliament and Official Organizations: FIDÈLE TOUCK ADIGAW.

Minister Delegate for Finance, the Budget and State Shareholdings: FAUSTIN BOUKOUBI.

Minister Delegate for Commerce, Industry and Scientific Research: Gen. ALBERT NDJAWE NJOY.

There are also nine secretaries of state.

MINISTRIES

Office of the Prime Minister: BP 546, Libreville; telex 5409.

Ministry of Agriculture, Livestock and Rural Development: BP 551, Libreville; tel. 76-29-43; telex 5587.

Ministry of the Civil Service and Administrative Reform: Libreville.

Ministry of Commerce, Industry and Scientific Research: BP 3906, Libreville; tel. 76-30-55; telex 5347.

Ministry of Communications, Posts and Telecommunications: BP 2280, Libreville; tel. 76-16-92; telex 5361.

Ministry of Culture, Arts, Mass Education and Human Rights: Libreville.

Ministry of the Economy, Planning, Reform of the Parastatal Sector and Privatization: Libreville.

Ministry of Equipment and Construction: BP 371, Libreville; tel. 76-14-87.

Ministry of Finance, the Budget and State Shareholdings: BP 165, Libreville; tel. 72-12-10; telex 5238.

Ministry of Foreign Affairs and Co-operation: BP 2245, Libreville; tel. 76-22-70; telex 5255.

Ministry of Habitat, Lands and Urban Planning: Libreville.

Ministry of the Interior, Local Communities and Mobile Security: Libreville.

Ministry of Justice: Libreville; tel. 72-26-95.

Ministry of Labour and Human Resources: BP 4577, Libreville; tel. 74-32-18.

Ministry of Merchant Marine and Fishing: Libreville.

Ministry of Mines, Energy and Hydraulic Resources: Libreville; tel. 72-31-96; telex 5629.

Ministry of National Defence, Public Security and Immigration: Libreville; tel. 76-25-95; telex 5453.

Ministry of National and Higher Education, and Professional Training: BP 6, Libreville; tel. 72-17-41; telex 5501.

Ministry of Public Health: Libreville; tel. 76-35-90; telex 5385.

Ministry of Small and Medium-sized Enterprises, and Handicrafts: Libreville.

Ministry of Social Affairs and Family Affairs and National Solidarity: Libreville.

Ministry of State Control, Decentralization, Territorial Administration and Regional Integration: BP 178, Libreville; tel. 76-34-62; telex 5711.

Ministry of Territorial Administration, Local Communities and Decentralization: BP 2110, Libreville; tel. 74-35-06; telex 5638.

Ministry of Tourism and National Parks: BP 403, Libreville; tel. 72-42-34; fax 72-43-90.

Ministry of Transport: BP 3974, Libreville; tel. 72-11-62; telex 5479; fax 77-33-31.

Ministry of Water, Forestry Resources and the Environment: Libreville.

Ministry of Youth and Sports: Libreville; tel. 76-35-76; telex 5642.

President and Legislature

PRESIDENT

Presidential Election, 5 December 1993

Candidate	% of votes
El Hadj OMAR (ALBERT-BERNARD) BONGO	51.18
Fr PAUL M'BA ABESSOLE	26.51
PIERRE LOUIS AGONDJO-OKAWÉ	4.78
PIERRE CLAVIER MAGANGA-MOUSSAVOU	3.64
JULES BOURDÈS-OGOULIGUENDÉ	3.38
ALEXANDRE SAMBAT	2.59
LIDJOB DIVUNGI DI DINGE	2.20
Prof. LÉON MBOYEBI	1.83
JEAN-PIERRE LEPANDOU	1.38
MARC SATURNIN NAN NGUEMA	0.86
SIMON OYONO-ABA'A	0.83
ADRIEN NGUEMA ONDO	0.44
LÉON MÉBIAME	0.38
Total	100.00

ASSEMBLÉE NATIONALE

President: ELOI-MARCEL RAHANDI CHAMBRIER.

Secretary-General: PIERRE N'GUEMA-MVÉ.

General Election, September 1990–March 1991

Party	Seats*
Parti démocratique gabonais	66
Parti gabonais du progrès	19
Rassemblement national des bûcherons	17
MORENA-originels	7
Association pour le socialisme au Gabon	6
Union socialiste gabonais	3
Cercle pour le renouveau et le progrès	1
Union pour la démocratie et le développement Mayumba	1
Total	120

* Subsequent to the election, a number of deputies transferred political affiliations.

Political Organizations

Constitutional amendments providing for the introduction of a multi-party system took effect in May 1990. Political associations in existence in mid-1994 included:

Association pour le socialisme au Gabon (APSG).

Cercle des libéraux réformateurs (CLR): f. 1993 by breakaway faction of the PDG; Leader JEAN-BONIFACE ASSELE.

Cercle pour le renouveau et le progrès (CRP).

Convention des forces du changement: f. 1993 as an informal alliance of eight opposition presidential candidates.

Coordination de l'opposition démocratique (COD): f. 1991 as an alliance of eight principal opposition parties; Chair. SEBASTIEN MAMBOUNDOY MOUYAMA.

Forum d'action pour le renouveau (FAR): f. 1992; a factional alliance within the COD; Leader Prof. LÉON MBOYEBI; comprises three political parties:

Mouvement de redressement national (MORENA-originels): f. 1981 in Paris, France; Leader JEAN-PIERRE ZONGUE-NGUEMA.

Parti socialiste gabonais (PSG): f. 1991; Leader Prof. LÉON MBOYEBI.

Union socialiste gabonais (USG): Leader VINCENT ESSOLO MENGE.

Front national (FN): f. 1991; Leader MARTIN EFAYONG.

Parti démocratique gabonais (PDG): BP 268, Libreville; tel. 70-31-21; fax 70-31-46; f. 1968; sole legal party 1968–90; Sec.-Gen. JEAN ADIAHENOT.

Parti des libéraux démocrates (PLD): Leader MARC SATURNIN NAN NGUEMA.

Parti gabonais du centre indépendent (PGCI): Leader JEAN-PIERRE LEPANDOU.

Parti gabonais du progrès (PGP): f. 1990; Pres. PIERRE LOUIS AGONDJO-OKAWÉ; Sec.-Gen. ANSELME NZOGHE.

Parti social-démocrate (PSD): f. 1991; Leader PIERRE CLAVIER MAGANGA-MOUSSAVOU.

Parti de l'unité du peuple gabonais (PUP): Libreville; f. 1991; Leader LOUIS GASTON MAYILA.

Rassemblement des démocrates (RD): f. 1993.

Rassemblement des Gaubis: Libreville; f. 1994; Leader MAX ANICET KOUMBA-MBADINGA.

Rassemblement national des bûcherons (RNB): f. 1990; fmrly MORENA des bûcherons; Leader Fr PAUL M'BA ABESSOLE; First Sec. ANDRÉ KOMBILA KOUMBA.

Union du peuple gabonais (UPG): f. 1989 in Paris, France; Leader PIERRE MAMBOUNDOU.

Union nationale pour la démocratie et le développement (UNDD): f. 1993; supports President Bongo.

Union pour la démocratie et le développement Mayumba (UDD).

Diplomatic Representation

EMBASSIES IN GABON

Algeria: BP 4008, Libreville; tel. 73-23-18; telex 5313; Ambassador: BENYOUCEF BABA-ALI.

Angola: BP 4884, Libreville; tel. 73-04-26; telex 5565; Ambassador: BERNARDO DOMBELE M'BALA.

Argentina: BP 4065, Libreville; tel. 74-05-49; telex 5611; Ambassador: HUGO HURTUBEI.

Belgium: BP 4079, Libreville; tel. 73-29-92; telex 5273; Ambassador: PAUL DE WULF.

Brazil: BP 3899, Libreville; tel. 76-05-35; telex 5492; fax 74-03-43; Ambassador: JAIME VILLA-LOBOS.

Cameroon: BP 14001, Libreville; tel. 73-28-00; telex 5396; Chargé d'affaires a.i.: NYEMB NGUENE.

Canada: BP 4037, Libreville; tel. 74-34-64; telex 5527; Ambassador: JEAN NADEAU.

Central African Republic: BP 2096, Libreville; tel. 72-12-28; telex 5323; Ambassador: FRANÇOIS DIALLO.

China, People's Republic: BP 3914, Libreville; tel. 74-32-07; telex 5376; Ambassador: YANG SHANGHUH.

Congo: BP 269, Libreville; tel. 73-29-06; telex 5541; Ambassador: PIERRE OBOU.

Côte d'Ivoire: BP 3861, Libreville; tel. 72-05-96; telex 5317; Ambassador: JEAN-OBEO COULIBALY.

Egypt: BP 4240, Libreville; tel. 73-25-38; telex 5425; fax 73-25-19; Ambassador: SALAH ZAKI.

Equatorial Guinea: BP 14262, Libreville; tel. 76-30-15; Ambassador: CRISANTOS NDONGO ABA MESSIAN.

France: BP 2125, Libreville; tel. 74-04-75; telex 5249; Ambassador: LOUIS DOMINICI.

Germany: BP 299, Libreville; tel. 76-01-88; telex 5248; fax 72-40-12; Ambassador: (vacant).

Guinea: BP 4046, Libreville; tel. 70-11-46; Chargé d'affaires: MAMADI KOLY KOUROUMA.

Iran: BP 2158, Libreville; tel. 73-05-33; telex 5502; Ambassador: Dr ABBASSE SAFARIAN.

Italy: Immeuble Personnaz et Gardin, rue de la Mairie, BP 2251, Libreville; tel. 74-28-92; telex 5287; fax 74-80-35; Ambassador: VITTORIO FUMO.

Japan: BP 2259, Libreville; tel. 73-22-97; telex 5428; fax 73-60-60; Ambassador: HIDEO KAKINUMA.

Korea, Democratic People's Republic: BP 4012, Libreville; tel. 73-26-68; telex 5486; Ambassador: YIM KUN CHUN.

Korea, Republic: BP 2620, Libreville; tel. 73-40-00; telex 5356; fax 73-00-79; Ambassador: PARK CHANG-IL.

Lebanon: BP 3341, Libreville; tel. 73-14-77; telex 5547; Ambassador: MAMLOUK ABDELLATIF.

Mauritania: BP 3917, Libreville; tel. 74-31-65; telex 5570; Ambassador: El Hadj THIAM.

Morocco: BP 3983, Libreville; tel. 73-31-03; telex 5434; Chargé d'affaires a.i.: TAGMA MOHA OUALI.

Nigeria: BP 1191, Libreville; tel. 73-22-03; telex 5605; Ambassador: JOE-EFFIONG UDOH EKONG.

Philippines: BP 1198, Libreville; tel. 72-34-80; telex 5279; Chargé d'affaires: ARCADIO HERRERA.

Russia: BP 3963, Libreville; tel. 72-48-68; telex 5797; fax 72-48-70; Ambassador: YOURI LEYZARENKO.

São Tomé and Príncipe: BP 409, Libreville; tel. 72-15-46; telex 5557; Ambassador: JOSEPH FRET LAU CHONG.

Senegal: BP 3856, Libreville; tel. 73-26-87; telex 5332; Ambassador: OUMAR WELE.

South Africa: BP 4063, Libreville; tel. 73-93-39; fax 73-93-41; Ambassador: WILHELM STEENKAMP.

Spain: BP 2105, Libreville; tel. 72-12-64; telex 5258; fax 74-88-73; Ambassador: MIGUEL ANTONIO ARIAS ESTÉVEZ.

Togo: BP 14160, Libreville; tel. 73-29-04; telex 5490; Ambassador: AHLONKO KOFFI AQUEREBURU.

Tunisia: BP 3844, Libreville; tel. 73-28-41; Ambassador: EZZEDINE KERKENI.

USA: blvd de la Mer, BP 4000, Libreville; tel. 76-20-03; telex 5250; Ambassador: JOSEPH C. WILSON.

Uruguay: BP 5556, Libreville; tel. 74-30-44; telex 5646; Ambassador: Dr ALVARO ALVAREZ.

Venezuela: BP 3859, Libreville; tel. 73-31-18; telex 5264; fax 73-30-67; Ambassador: VÍCTOR CROQUER-VEGA.

Yugoslavia: BP 930, Libreville; tel. 73-30-05; telex 5329; Ambassador: ČEDOMIR STRBAC.

Zaire: BP 2257, Libreville; tel. 74-32-54; telex 5335; Ambassador: KABANGI KAUMBU BULA.

Judicial System

Supreme Court: BP 1043, Libreville; tel. 72-17-00; three chambers: judicial, administrative and accounts; Pres. BENJAMIN PAMBOU-KOMBILA.

Constitutional Court: Libreville; Pres. MARIE MADELEINE BORANSOUO.

Courts of Appeal: Libreville and Franceville.

Court of State Security: Libreville; 13 mems; Pres. FLORENTIN ANGO.

Conseil Supérieur de la Magistrature: Libreville; Pres. El Hadj OMAR BONGO; Vice-Pres. Pres. of the Supreme Court (ex officio).

There are also Tribunaux de Première Instance (County Courts) at Libreville, Franceville, Port-Gentil, Lambaréné, Mouila, Oyem, Koula-Moutou, Makokou and Tchibanga.

Religion

About 60% of Gabon's population are Christians, mainly adherents of the Roman Catholic Church. About 40% are animists, and fewer than 1% are Muslims.

CHRISTIANITY

The Roman Catholic Church

Gabon comprises one archdiocese and three dioceses. At 31 December 1991 there were an estimated 645,653 adherents in the country, equivalent to 53.2% of the total population.

Bishops' Conference: Conférence Episcopale du Gabon, BP 209, Oyem; tel. 98-63-20; f. 1989; Pres. Rt Rev. BASILE MVÉ ENGONE, Bishop of Oyem.

Archbishop of Libreville: Most Rev. ANDRÉ-FERNAND ANGUILÉ, Archevêché, Sainte-Marie, BP 2146, Libreville; tel. 72-20-73.

Protestant Churches

Christian and Missionary Alliance: active in the south of the country; 16,000 mems.

Eglise Evangélique du Gabon: BP 10080, Libreville; tel. 72-41-92; f. 1842; independent since 1961; 120,000 mems; Pres. Pastor SAMUEL NANG ESSONO; Sec. Rev. EMILE NTETOME.

The Evangelical Church of South Gabon and the Evangelical Pentecostal Church are also active in the country.

The Press

Le Bûcheron: BP 6424, Libreville; official organ of the Rassemblement national des bûcherons; Pres. PIERRE ANDRÉ KOMBILA.

Bulletin Evangélique d'Information et de Presse: BP 80, Libreville; monthly; religious.

Bulletin Mensuel de la Chambre de Commerce, d'Agriculture, d'Industrie et des Mines: BP 2234, Libreville; tel. 72-20-64; telex 5554; fax 74-64-77; monthly.

Bulletin Mensuel de Statistique de la République Gabonaise: BP 179, Libreville; monthly; publ. by Direction Générale de l'Economie.

L'Economiste Gabonais: BP 3906, Libreville; quarterly; publ. by the Centre gabonais du commerce extérieur.

Gabon d'Aujourd'hui: BP 750, Libreville; weekly; publ. by the Ministry of Communications, Posts and Telecommunications.

Gabon Libre: BP 6439, Libreville; tel. 74-42-22; weekly; Dir DZIME EKANG; Editor RENÉ NZOVI.

Gabon-Matin: BP 168, Libreville; daily; publ. by Agence Gabonaise de Presse; Man. HILARION VENDANY; circ. 18,000.

La Griffe: BP 4928, Libreville; tel. 74-73-45; weekly; independent; satirical; Pres. JÉRÔME OKINDA; Editor NDJOUMBA MOUSSOCK.

Journal Officiel de la République Gabonaise: BP 563, Libreville; f. 1959; fortnightly; Man. EMMANUEL OBAMÉ.

Ngondo: BP 168, Libreville; monthly; publ. by Agence Gabonaise de Presse.

Le Progressiste: blvd Léon-M'Ba, BP 7000, Libreville; tel. 74-54-01; publ. by Multipress Gabon; Dir BENOÎT MOUITY NZAMBA; Editor JACQUES MOURENDE-TSIOBA.

La Relance: BP 268, Libreville; tel. 70-31-66; weekly; organ of the Parti démocratique gabonais; Pres. JACQUES ADIAHENOT; Dir RENÉ NDEMEZO'O OBIANG.

Sept Jours: BP 213, Libreville; weekly.

L'Union: BP 3849, Libreville; tel. 73-21-84; telex 5305; fax 73-83-26; f. 1975; 75% state-owned; daily; official govt publication; Man. Dir ALBERT YANGARI; Dir RENÉ KOUPANGOYE; circ. 15,000.

NEWS AGENCIES

Agence Gabonaise de Presse (AGP): BP 168, Libreville; tel. 21-26; telex 5628.

Foreign Bureau

Agence France-Presse (AFP): Immeuble Sogapal, Les Filaos, BP 788, Libreville; tel. 76-14-36; telex 5239; fax 72-45-31; Correspondents LAURENT CHEVALLIER, MICHEL CARRIOU.

Publishers

Imprimerie Centrale d'Afrique (IMPRIGA): BP 154, Libreville; tel. 70-22-55; fax 70-05-19; f. 1973; Chair. ROBERT VIAL; Dir FRANCIS BOURQUIN.

Multipress Gabon: blvd Léon-M'Ba, BP 3875, Libreville; tel. 73-22-33; telex 5389; f. 1973; Chair. PAUL BORY.

Société Imprimerie de l'Ogooué (SIMO): BP 342, Port-Gentil; f. 1977; Man. Dir URBAIN NICOUE.

Société Nationale de Presse et d'Edition (SONAPRESSE): BP 3849, Libreville; tel. 73-21-84; telex 5391; f. 1975; Pres. and Man. Dir JOSEPH RENDJAMBE.

Radio and Television

In 1991, according to UNESCO, there were an estimated 171,000 radio receivers and 45,000 television receivers in use.

RADIO

The national network, 'La Voix de la Rénovation', and a provincial network broadcast for 24 hours each day in French and local languages. Plans to construct 13 new FM radio stations were announced in 1986.

Africa No. 1: BP 1, Libreville; tel. 76-00-01; telex 5558; fax 74-21-33; f. 1980; 35% state-controlled; international commercial radio station; broadcasts began in 1981; daily programmes in French and English; Pres. LOUIS BARTHÉLEMY MAPANGOU; Mans MICHEL KOUMBANGOYE, GILLES MARQUET.

Radiodiffusion-Télévision Gabonaise (RTG): BP 150, Libreville; tel. 73-20-25; telex 5342; f. 1959; state-controlled; Dir-Gen. WILLIAM OYONNE; Dir of Radio CHARLES NGUIENDET.

Radio Liberté: Libreville; owned by Rassemblement national des bûcherons; transmissions suspended in Feb. 1994.

TELEVISION

Television transmissions can be received as far inland as Kango and Lambaréné; in 1986 proposals were announced for the extension and modernization of the network to cover the whole of Gabon, including the construction of 13 new TV broadcasting stations. Programmes are also transmitted by satellite to other African countries. Colour broadcasts began in 1975.

Radiodiffusion-Télévision Gabonaise (RTG): BP 150, Libreville; tel. 73-20-25; telex 5342; fax 73-21-53; f. 1959; state-controlled; Dir-Gen. WILLIAM OYONNE; Dir of Television HENRI-JOSEPH KOUMBA.

Télé-Africa: Libreville; tel. 76-20-33; private channel; daily broadcasts in French.

Finance

(cap. = capital; res = reserves; dep. = deposits; brs = branches; m. = million; amounts in francs CFA)

BANKING

Central Bank

Banque des Etats de l'Afrique Centrale (BEAC): BP 112, Libreville; tel. 76-13-52; telex 5215; fax 74-45-63; headquarters in Yaoundé, Cameroon; f. 1973 as central bank of issue for mem. states of the Customs and Economic Union of Central Africa (UDEAC); cap. and res 203,500m. (Jan. 1993); Gov. JEAN-FÉLIX MAMALEPOT; Dir in Gabon JEAN-PAUL LEYIMANGOYE; 3 brs.

Commercial Banks

Banque Internationale pour le Commerce et l'Industrie du Gabon, SA (BICIG): ave du Colonel Parant, BP 2241, Libreville; tel. 76-26-13; telex 5526; fax 74-40-34; f. 1973; 26.4% state-owned; cap. 6,390m. (Dec. 1991); Pres. GUY-ETIENNE MOUVAGHA-TCHIOBA; Man. Dir EMILE DOUMBA; 9 brs.

Banque Meridien BIAO Gabon, SA: Immeuble Concorde, blvd de l'Indépendance, BP 106, Libreville; tel. 76-26-27; telex 5221; fax 76-20-63; 28.6% state-owned; cap. 1,260m. (Dec. 1992); Pres. PAUL OKUMBA D'OKWATSEGUE; Dir-Gen. JEAN-URBAIN MINKO OBIANG; 9 brs.

Banque Paribas-Gabon: blvd de l'Indépendance, BP 2253, Libreville; tel. 76-23-26; telex 5265; fax 74-08-94; f. 1971; 33.4% state-owned; cap. 7,892m. (Dec. 1992); Pres. ALFRED MABIKA; Dir-Gen. HENRI-CLAUDE OYIMA; br. at Port-Gentil.

Crédit Foncier de Gabon: blvd de l'Indépendance, BP 3905, Libreville; tel. 72-47-45; 75% state-owned; Pres. HENRI MINKO; Dir-Gen. EMMANUEL NTOUTOUME.

Union Gabonaise de Banque, SA (UGB): ave du Colonel Parant, BP 315, Libreville; tel. 77-70-00; telex 5232; fax 76-46-16; f. 1962; 25% state-owned; cap. and res 6,569.3m., dep. 64,123.5m. (Dec. 1992); Pres. and Dir-Gen. MARCEL DOUPAMBY-MATOKA; 6 brs.

Development Banks

Banque Gabonaise de Développement (BGD): rue Alfred Marche, BP 5, Libreville; tel. 76-24-89; telex 5430; fax 74-26-99; f. 1960; 69% state-owned; cap. 10,500m. (Dec. 1992); Pres. JEAN-BAPTISTE OBIANG ETOUGHE; Dir-Gen. RICHARD ONOUVIET; 3 brs.

Banque Nationale de Crédit Rural (BNCR): ave Bouet, BP 1120, Libreville; tel. 72-47-42; telex 5830; fax 74-05-07; f. 1986; 74% state-owned; cap. 1,350m. (Dec. 1992); Pres. GÉRARD MEYO M'EMANE; Man. Dir JACQUES DIOUF.

Société Gabonaise de Participation et de Développement (SOGAPAR): blvd de l'Indépendance, BP 2253, Libreville; tel. 73-23-26; telex 5265; fax 74-08-94; f. 1971; studies and promotes projects conducive to national economic development; 35% state-owned; cap. 2,063m. (Dec. 1992); Pres. DANIEL BEDIN; Man. Dir HENRI-CLAUDE OYIMA.

Société Nationale d'Investissements du Gabon (SONADIG): BP 479, Libreville; tel. 72-09-22; fax 74-81-70; f. 1968; cap. 500m.; state-owned investment co; Pres. ANTOINE OYIEYE; Dir-Gen. S. EDOU-EYENE.

Financial Institution

Caisse Autonome d'Amortissement du Gabon: BP 912, Libreville; tel. 76-41-43; telex 5537; management of state funds; Dir-Gen. MAURICE EYAMBA TSIMAT.

INSURANCE

Agence Gabonaise d'Assurance et de Réassurance (AGAR): BP 1699, Libreville; tel. 74-02-22; fax 76-59-25; f. 1987; cap. 50m.; Man. Dir LOUIS GASTON MAYILA.

Assurances Générales Gabonaises (AGG): ave du Colonel Parant, BP 2148, Libreville; tel. 76-09-73; telex 5473; f. 1974; cap. 66.5m.; Chair. JEAN DAVIN, JACQUES NOT.

Assureurs Conseils Franco-Africains du Gabon (ACFRA-GABON): BP 1116, Libreville; tel. 72-32-83; telex 5485; cap. 43.4m.; Chair. FRÉDÉRIC MARRON; Dir M. GARNIER.

Assureurs Conseils Gabonais-Faugère et Jutheau & Cie: Immeuble Shell-Gabon, rue de la Mairie, BP 2138, Libreville; tel. 72-04-36; telex 5435; fax 76-04-39; cap. 10m.; represents foreign insurance cos; Dir GÉRARD MILAN.

Groupement Gabonais d'Assurances et de Réassurances (GGAR): Immeuble les Horizons, blvd Triomphal Omar Bongo, BP 3949, Libreville; tel. 74-28-72; telex 5673; f. 1985; cap. 225m.; Chair. RASSAGUIZA AKEREY; Dir-Gen. DENISE OMBAGHO.

Mutuelle Gabonaise d'Assurances: ave du Colonel Parant, BP 2225, Libreville; tel. 72-13-91; telex 5240; Sec.-Gen. M. YENO-OLINGOT.

Omnium Gabonais d'Assurances et de Réassurances (OGAR): blvd Triomphal Omar Bongo, BP 201, Libreville; tel. 76-15-96; telex 5505; fax 76-58-16; f. 1976; 10% state-owned; cap. 340m.; general; Pres. MARCEL DOUPAMBY-MATOKA; Man. Dir EDOUARD VALENTIN; brs in Oyem, Port-Gentil, Franceville.

Société Nationale Gabonaise d'Assurances et de Réassurances (SONAGAR): ave du Colonel Parant, BP 3082, Libreville; tel. 76-28-97; telex 5366; f. 1974; owned by l'Union des Assurances de Paris (France); Dir-Gen. JEAN-LOUIS MESSAN.

SOGERCO-Gabon: BP 2102, Libreville; tel. 76-09-34; telex 5224; f. 1975; cap. 10m.; general; Dir M. RABEAU.

L'Union des Assurances du Gabon (UAG): ave du Colonel Parant, BP 2141, Libreville; tel. 74-34-34; telex 5404; fax 74-14-53; f. 1976; cap. 280.5m.; Chair. ALBERT ALEWINA CHAVIOT; Dir EKOMIE AFENE.

Trade and Industry

GOVERNMENT ADVISORY BODY

Conseil Economique et Social de la République Gabonaise: BP 1075, Libreville; tel. 76-26-68; comprises representatives from salaried workers, employers and Govt; commissions on economic, financial and social affairs and forestry and agriculture; Pres. EDOUARD ALEXIS M'BOUY-BOUTZIT.

CHAMBER OF COMMERCE

Chambre de Commerce, d'Agriculture, d'Industrie et des Mines du Gabon: BP 2234, Libreville; tel. 72-20-64; telex 5554; fax 74-64-77; f. 1935; regional offices at Port-Gentil and Franceville; Pres. JEAN-BAPTISTE NGOMO-OBIANG; Sec.-Gen. DOMINIQUE MANDZA.

EMPLOYERS' FEDERATIONS

Confédération Patronale Gabonaise: BP 410, Libreville; tel. 76-02-43; fax 74-86-52; f. 1959; represents the principal industrial, mining, petroleum, public works, forestry, banking, insurance, commercial and shipping concerns; Pres. EMILE DOUMBA; Sec.-Gen. ERIC MESSERSCHMITT.

Conseil National du Patronat Gabonais (CNPG): Libreville; Pres. RAHANDI CHAMBRIER; Sec.-Gen. THOMAS FRANCK EYA'A.

Syndicat des Entreprises Minières du Gabon (SYNDIMINES): BP 260, Libreville; telex 5388; Pres. ANDRÉ BERRE; Sec.-Gen. SERGE GREGOIRE.

Syndicat des Importateurs Exportateurs du Gabon (SIMPEX): BP 1743, Libreville; Pres. ALBERT JEAN; Sec.-Gen. R. TYBERGHEIN.

Syndicat des Producteurs et Industriels du Bois du Gabon: BP 84, Libreville; tel. 72-26-11; Pres. CLAUDE MOLENAT.

Syndicat Professionnel des Usines de Sciages et Placages du Gabon: BP 417, Port-Gentil; f. 1956; Pres. PIERRE BERRY.

Union des Représentations Automobiles et Industrielles (URAI): BP 1743, Libreville; Pres. M. MARTINENT; Sec. R. TYBERGHEIN.

Union Nationale du Patronat Syndical des Transports Urbains, Routiers et Fluviaux du Gabon (UNAPASYFTUROGA): BP 1025, Libreville; f. 1977; Pres. LAURENT BELLAL BIBANG-BI-EDZO; Sec.-Gen. MARTIN KOMBILA-MOMBO.

PRINCIPAL DEVELOPMENT ORGANIZATIONS

Agence Nationale de Promotion de la Petite et Moyenne Entreprise (PROMO-GABON): BP 3939, Libreville; tel. 74-31-16; telex 000576; f. 1964; state-controlled; promotes and assists small and medium-sized industries; Pres. SIMON BOULAMATARI; Man. Dir JEAN-FIDÈLE OTANDO.

Caisse Française de Développement: BP 64, Libreville; tel. 74-33-74; telex 5362; fax 74-51-25; Dir ANTOINE BAUX.

Centre Gabonais de Commerce Extérieur (CGCE): BP 3906, Libreville; tel. 76-11-67; telex 5347; promotes foreign trade and investment in Gabon; Man. Dir MICHEL LESLIE TEALE.

Commerce et Développement (CODEV): BP 2142, Libreville; tel. 76-06-73; telex 5214; f. 1976; cap. 2,000m. francs CFA; 95% state-owned, future transfer to private ownership announced 1986; import and distribution of capital goods and food products; Chair. and Man. Dir JÉRÔME NGOUA-BEKALE.

Mission Française de Coopération: BP 2105, Libreville; tel. 76-10-56; telex 5249; fax 74-55-33; administers bilateral aid from France; Dir JEAN-CLAUDE QUIRIN.

Office Gabonais d'Amélioration et de Production de Viande (OGAPROV): BP 245, Moanda; tel. 66-12-67; f. 1971; development of private cattle farming; manages ranch at Lekedi-Sud; Pres. PAUL KOUNDA KIKI; Dir-Gen. VINCENT EYI-NGUI.

Palmiers et Hévéas du Gabon (PALMEVEAS): BP 75, Libreville; f. 1956; cap. 145m. francs CFA; state-owned; palm-oil development.

Société de Développement de l'Agriculture au Gabon (AGROGABON): BP 2248, Libreville; tel. 76-40-82; fax 76-44-72; f. 1976; cap. 2,788m. francs CFA; 92% state-owned; Man. Dir ANDRÉ PAUL-APANDINA.

Société de Développement de l'Hévéaculture (HEVEGAB): BP 316, Libreville; tel. 70-03-43; telex 5615; fax 70-19-89; f. 1981; cap. 5,500m. francs CFA; 99.9% state-owned; development of rubber plantations in the Mitzic, Bitam and Kango regions; Chair. EMMANUEL ONDO-METHOGO; Man. Dir GUY DE ROQUEMAUREL.

Société Gabonaise de Recherches et d'Exploitations Minières (SOGAREM): blvd de Nice, Libreville; state-owned; research and development of gold mining; Chair. ARSÈNE BOUNGUENZA; Man. Dir SERGE GASSITA.

Société Gabonaise de Recherches Pétrolières (GABOREP): BP 564, Libreville; tel. 75-06-40; telex 8268; fax 75-06-47; exploration and exploitation of hydrocarbons; Chair. HUBERT PERRODO; Man. Dir P. F. LECA.

Société Nationale de Développement des Cultures Industrielles (SONADECI): BP 256, Libreville; tel. 76-33-97; telex 5362; f. 1978; cap. 600m. francs CFA; state-owned; agricultural development; Chair. PAUL KOUNDA KIKI; Man. Dir GEORGES BEKALÉ.

MAJOR INDUSTRIAL COMPANIES

The following are some of the largest private and state-owned companies in terms of either capital investment or employment.

L'Auxiliaire du Bâtiment J.-F. Aveyra (ABA): BP 14382, Libreville; tel. 70-44-80; telex 5454; f. 1977; cap. 1,000m. francs CFA; production of construction materials, plastics; Chair. JEAN-FRANÇOIS AVEYRA; Man. Dir G. DUTILH.

Compagnie Forestière du Gabon (CFG): BP 521, Port-Gentil; tel. 55-20-45; telex 8209; fax 55-36-43; f. 1953; cap. 6,785m. francs CFA; 60% state-owned; production of okoumé plywood and veneered quality plywoods; Chair. RAYMOND NDONG SIMA; Man. Dir HERMAN VAN DER KOLFF.

Compagnie Gabon—Elf de Raffinage (COGER): BP 564, Port-Gentil; tel. 75-36-52; telex 8217; f. 1976; cap. 2,500m. francs CFA; 30% state-owned, 70% owned by Elf-Gabon; petroleum refining; Chair. RENÉ RADEMBINO CONIQUET; Man. Dir EMMANUEL SIPAMIO-BERRE.

Compagnie des Mines d'Uranium de Franceville (COMUF): BP 260, Libreville; tel. 76-43-10; telex 5388; f. 1958; cap. 5,050m. francs CFA; 25% state-owned; uranium mining at Mounana; Chair. MAURICE DELAUNEY; Man. Dir HENRI BASSET; 998 employees.

Compagnie Minière de l'Ogooué (COMILOG): BP 27-28, Moanda; tel. 66-10-00; telex 6213; fax 66-11-57; f. 1953; cap. 10,938m. francs CFA; 30% owned by private Gabonese interests; manganese mining at Moanda; Pres. SYLVIO RODOZ; Man. Dir MICHEL LEVEAU; 1,738 employees.

Elf-Gabon: BP 525, Port-Gentil; tel. 75-60-00; telex 8210; f. 1934; cap. 22,500m. francs CFA; 25% state-owned, 54% owned by Elf-Aquitaine group; prospecting for and mining of petroleum; Chair. ANDRÉ TARALLO; Man. Dir MARC COSSÉ; 1,157 employees.

Gabo-Ren: Port-Gentil; f. 1975; cap. 1,600m. francs CFA; 33% state-owned, 32% owned by Elf-Gabon, 35% owned by N'Ren Corpn; mfrs of artificial ammonia and urea.

Leroy-Gabon: BP 69, Libreville; tel. 72-14-14; telex 5252; fax 76-15-94; f. 1976; cap. 2,080m. francs CFA; forestry; Chair. and Man. Dir JEAN LEPRINCE.

Mobil Oil Gabon: Zone Industrielle Sud Owendo, BP 145, Libreville; tel. 70-05-48; telex 5562; fax 70-05-87; f. 1974; cap. 547m. francs CFA; storage and distribution of petroleum products; Chair. MICHEL BONNET; Man. Dir RÉGIS D'HUART.

Rougier Océan Gabon SA (ROG): BP 130, Libreville; tel. 74-31-50; telex 5257; cap. 1,200m. francs CFA; forestry and mfr of plywood; Chair. MAURICE ROUGIER; Dir HERVÉ BOZEC.

Shell Gabon: BP 146, Port-Gentil; tel. 55-26-62; telex 8206; f. 1960; cap. 15,000m. francs CFA; owned 75% by Royal Dutch-Shell group, 25% state-owned; prospecting for and mining and distribution of petroleum; Chair. and Man. Dir PHILIPPE EMERY.

Société Bernabé Gabon: BP 2084, Libreville; tel. 74-34-32; telex 5351; fax 76-05-21; cap. 1,000m. francs CFA; metallurgical products, construction materials, hardware; Man. Dir ROBERT Y. LESPES.

Société des Brasseries du Gabon (SOBRAGA): 20 blvd Léon M'Ba, BP 487, Libreville; tel. 73-23-66; telex 5275; fax 73-36-12; f. 1966; cap. 1,500m. francs CFA; mfrs of beer and soft drinks; Chair. and Man. Dir PIERRE CASTEL; Dir M. PALU.

Société des Ciments du Gabon: BP 477, Libreville; tel. 70-20-25; telex 5483; fax 70-27-05; f. 1976; cap. 12,505m. francs CFA; 91.44% state-owned, 8.55% owned by Elf-Gabon; clinker crushing works at N'Toum, Owendo (Libreville) and Franceville; Chair. Pierre Nziengui Mabila; Man. Dir Serge Lasseni Duboze.

Société d'Exploitation des Produits Oléagineux du Gabon (SEPOGA): BP 1491, Libreville; tel. 76-01-92; telex 5494; fax 74-15-67; f. 1977; cap. 732m. francs CFA; 25% state-owned, 14% owned by Shell Gabon; production and marketing of vegetable oils; Chair. Paul Kounda-Kiki; Man. Dir Edmund Scheffler.

Société Gabonaise des Ferro-Alliages (SOGAFERRO): BP 2728, Moanda; telex 5218; f. 1974; cap. 1,000m. francs CFA; 10% state-owned; manganese processing; Chair. Dr Hervé Moutsinga; Man. Dir Gilles de Seauve.

Société Gabonaise de Raffinage (SOGARA): BP 530, Port-Gentil; tel. 75-36-52; telex 8217; f. 1965; cap. 1,200m. francs CFA; 25% state-owned; refines locally-produced crude petroleum; Man. Dir Emmanuel Sipamio-Berre; 455 employees.

Société Gabonaise des Textiles (SOGATEX): f. 1987; 36.5% state-owned; mfrs of garments.

Société de la Haute Mondah (SHM): BP 69, Libreville; tel. 72-22-29; telex 5252; f. 1939; cap. 888m. francs CFA; forestry, plywood and sawmilling; Etienne Guy Mouvagha-Tchioba; Man. Dir M. Dejoie.

Société Industrielle d'Agriculture et d'Elevage de Boumango (SIAEB): BP 68, Franceville; tel. 67-72-88; telex 3301; f. 1977; cap. 1,740m. francs CFA; 35% state-owned; maize, soya, rice and poultry production; Man. Dir Jean-Jacques Dubois.

Société Industrielle Textile du Gabon (SOTEGA): blvd Léon M'Ba, BP 2171, Libreville; tel. 72-19-29; telex 5236; f. 1968; cap. 260m. francs CFA; 15% state-owned; textile printing; Chair. Raphaël Eboboca; Man. Dir M. Marescaux.

Société Italo-Gabonaise des Marbres (SIGAMA): BP 3893, Libreville; tel. 72-25-83; telex 5384; f. 1974; cap. 542m. francs CFA; operates a marble quarry and factory at Doussé Oussou; Man. Dir Franco Marchio.

Société Meunière et Avicole du Gabon (SMAG): BP 462, Libreville; tel. 70-18-76; telex 5298; fax 70-28-12; f. 1968; cap. 910m. francs CFA; partly state-owned; production of eggs, cattle-food, flour, bread; Chair. J. Louis Vilgrain; Dir X. Thomas; 475 employees.

Société des Mines de Fer de Mekambo (SOMIFER): BP 3965, Libreville; tel. 73-28-58; f. 1960; cap. 900m. francs CFA; 49% state-owned; mineral prospecting and mining; Chair. Adama Diallo; Dir Jean Audibert.

Société de Mise en Valeur du Bois (SOMIVAB): BP 3893, Libreville; tel. 78-18-27; telex 5384; cap. 1,550m. francs CFA; forestry, sawmill, mfrs of sleepers for Transgabon railway; Chair. Hervé Moutsinga; Man. Dir Franco Marchio.

Société Nationale des Bois du Gabon (SNBG): BP 67, Libreville; tel. 76-47-94; telex 5201; f. 1944; cap. 1,000m. francs CFA; 51% state-owned; has a monopoly of marketing all okoumé production; Chair. and Man. Dir Mamadou Diop; 500 employees.

Société National de Distribution de Produits Pétroliers (PIZO): BP 4030, Libreville; tel. 72-01-21; telex 5526; f. 1975; cap. 1,500m. francs CFA; 50% state-owned, future transfer to private ownership announced 1986; Chair. and Man. Dir Jean-Bernard Saulnerond-Mapangou.

Société National Immobilière (SNI): BP 515, Libreville; tel. 76-05-81; f. 1976; cap. 750m. francs CFA; 77% state-owned; development and maintenance of housing; Chair. and Man. Dir Georges Issembe.

Société Pizo de Formulation de Lubrifiants (PIZOLUB): BP 699, Port-Gentil; tel. 55-28-40; telex 8299; fax 55-03-82; f. 1978; cap. 500m. francs CFA; 49% state-owned; mfrs of lubricating materials; Chair. Marcel Sandoungout; Dir-Gen. Pierre Ripoll.

Société Sucrière du Haut-Ogooué (SOSUHO): BP 1180, Libreville; tel. 72-00-51; telex 5298; f. 1974; cap. 500m. francs CFA; sugar production and agro-industrial complex at Ouélé; Chair. L. Saba; Man. Dir P.-Y. le Maout.

Société des Télécommunications Internationales Gabonaises (TIG): BP 2261, Libreville; tel. 78-77-56; telex 5200; fax 74-19-09; f. 1971; cap. 3,000m. francs CFA; 61% state-owned; study and development of international telecommunications systems; Man. Dir A. N'Gouma Mwyumala.

TRADE UNIONS

Confédération Gabonaise des Syndicats Libres (CGSL): Libreville; Sec.-Gen. Francis Mayombo.

Confédération Syndicale Gabonaise (COSYGA): BP 14017, Libreville; telex 5623; f. 1969, by the Govt, as a specialized organ of the PDG, to organize and educate workers, to contribute to social peace and economic development, and to protect the rights of trade unions; Gen. Sec. Martin Allini.

Transport

RAILWAYS

The construction of the Transgabon railway, which comprises a section running from Owendo (the port of Libreville) to Booué (340 km) and a second section from Booué to Franceville (330 km), was completed in December 1986. By 1989 regular services were operating between Libreville and Franceville. More than 829,000 metric tons of freight (including 584,000 tons of timber) and 118,400 passengers were carried on the network in 1988.

Office du Chemin de Fer Transgabonais (OCTRA): BP 2198, Libreville; tel. 70-24-78; telex 5307; fax 70-33-18; f. 1972; state-owned; Chair. Alexandre Ayo Barro; Dir Gen. Célestin Ndolia-Nhaud.

ROADS

In 1992 there were an estimated 8,590 km of roads, including 3,290 km of main roads and 1,950 km of secondary roads; about 680 km of the road network was paved. In 1992 a seven-year project to surface some 1,400 km of road by the year 2000 was announced. In the same year a programme was initiated to construct a further 1,851 km of roads, at an estimated cost of some US $528m.

INLAND WATERWAYS

The principal river is the Ogooué, navigable from Port-Gentil to Ndjolé (310 km) and serving the towns of Lambaréné, Ndjolé and Sindara.

Compagnie de Navigation Intérieure (CNI): BP 3982, Libreville; tel. 72-39-28; telex 5289; f. 1978; cap. 500m. francs CFA; state-owned; inland waterway transport; agencies at Port-Gentil, Mayumba and Lambaréné; Chair. Jean-Pierre Mengwang me Ngyema; Dir Mathurin Anotho-Onanga.

SHIPPING

The principal deep-water ports are Port-Gentil, which handles mainly petroleum exports, and Owendo, 15 km from Libreville, which services mainly barge traffic. The principal ports for timber are at Owendo, Mayumba and Nyanga, and there is a fishing port at Libreville. The construction of a deep-water port at Mayumba is planned. A new terminal for the export of minerals, at Owendo, was opened in December 1988. In 1989 the merchant shipping fleet had a total displacement of 25,000 grt, compared with a displacement of 98,000 grt in 1985.

Compagnie de Manutention et de Chalandage d'Owendo (COMACO): BP 2131, Libreville; tel. 70-26-35; telex 5208; f. 1974; Pres. Georges Rawiri; Dir in Libreville M. Raymond.

Office des Ports et Rades du Gabon (OPRAG): BP 1051, Libreville; tel. 70-00-48; telex 5319; fax 70-37-35; f. 1974; state-owned; national port authority; Pres. Ali Bongo; Dir-Gen. Martin Louri.

Société Nationale d'Acconage et de Transit (SNAT): BP 3897, Libreville; tel. 70-04-04; telex 5420; fax 70-13-11; f. 1976; 51% state-owned; freight transport; Dir-Gen. Claude Ayo-Iguendha.

Société Nationale de Transports Maritimes (SONATRAM): BP 3841, Libreville; tel. 74-06-32; telex 5289; fax 74-59-67; f. 1976; 51% state-owned; river and ocean cargo transport; Man. Dir Raphael Moara Walla.

Société Ouest Africaine d'Entreprises Maritimes (SOAEM-GABON): BP 518, Port-Gentil; tel. 75-21-71; telex 8205; 10% state-owned; freight shipping; Chair. J. Peltier; Man. Dir G. Trotereau.

Société du Port Minéralier d'Owendo: f. 1987; cap. 4,000m. francs CFA; majority holding by COMILOG; management of new terminal for minerals at Owendo.

SOCOPAO-Gabon: BP 4, Libreville; tel. 70-21-40; telex 5212; fax 70-02-76; f. 1963; freight transport and storage; Dir Henri Lecordier.

CIVIL AVIATION

There are international airports at Libreville, Port-Gentil and Franceville, 65 other public and 50 private airfields linked mostly with the forestry and petroleum industries.

Air Affaires Gabon: BP 3962, Libreville; tel. 73-25-13; telex 5360; fax 73-49-98; f. 1975; domestic passenger chartered and scheduled flights; Chair. Raymond Bellanger; Dir Ange Agostini.

Air Service Gabon (ASG): BP 2232, Libreville; tel. 73-24-08; telex 5522; fax 73-60-69; f. 1965; charter flights; Chair. Jérôme Okinda; Gen. Man. Francis Lascombes.

Compagnie Nationale Air Gabon: BP 2206, Libreville; tel. 73-00-27; telex 5371; fax 73-01-11; f. 1951 as Cie Aérienne Gabonaise; began operating international services in 1977, following Gabon's withdrawal from Air Afrique (see under Côte d'Ivoire); 80% state-owned; internal and international cargo and passenger services; Chair. MARTIN BONGO; Dir-Gen. Commdr RENÉ MORVAN.

Société de Gestion de l'Aéroport de Libreville (ADL): BP 363, Libreville; tel. 73-62-44; telex 5459; fax 73-61-28; f. 1988; 26.5% state-owned; management of airport at Libreville; Pres. CHANTAL LIDJI BADINGA; Dir-Gen. PIERRE ANDRÉ COLLET.

Tourism

Tourist arrivals totalled 108,000 in 1990. The tourist sector is being extensively developed, with new hotels and associated projects and the promotion of national parks. In 1987 there were 74 hotels, with a total of 3,077 rooms.

Centre de Promotion Touristique du Gabon (GABONTOUR): BP 2085, Libreville; tel. 74-67-90; f. 1988; Dir-Gen. JUSTE LAMBERT LOUMBANGOYE.

Ministère du Tourisme et des Parcs Nationaux: BP 403, Libreville; tel. 72-42-34; fax 72-43-90.

Office National Gabonais du Tourisme: BP 161, Libreville; tel. 72-21-82.

Defence

In June 1993 the army consisted of 3,250 men, the air force of 1,000 men, and the navy of 500 men. Paramilitary forces numbered 4,800 (including a gendarmerie of 2,000). Military service is voluntary. In 1993 France deployed a military detachment of 500 in Gabon; in early 1994, however, it was announced that the French government was to reduce military assistance to Gabon.

Defence Expenditure: Estimated at 46,510m. francs CFA in 1989.

Commander-in-Chief of the Armed Forces: Maj.-Gen. ANDRÉ OYINI.

Education

Education is officially compulsory for 10 years between six and 16 years of age: in 1984 an estimated 75% of children in the relevant age-group attended primary and secondary schools (78% of boys; 72% of girls). Primary and secondary education is provided by the state and mission schools. Primary education begins at the age of six and lasts for six years. Secondary education, beginning at 12 years of age, lasts for up to seven years, comprising a first cycle of four years and a second of three years. The Université Omar Bongo, at Libreville, had 2,741 students in 1986. The Université des Sciences et des Techniques de Masuku, at Franceville, was opened in 1986, with an enrolment of 550 students. Many students go to France for university and technical training. In 1990, according to estimates by UNESCO, adult illiteracy averaged 39.3% (males 26.5%; females 51.5%). The 1994 budget allocated 78,850m. francs CFA (19% of total administrative spending) to expenditure on education.

Bibliography

Aicardi de Saint-Paul, M. *Le Gabon du roi Denis à Omar Bongo.* Paris, Editions Albatros, 1987. Trans. (Palmer, A. F., and Palmer, T.) as *Gabon: The Development of a Nation.* London, Routledge, 1989.

Ambouroué-Avaro, J. *Un peuple gabonais à l'aube de la colonisation.* Paris, Editions Karthala, 1983.

Bongo, O. *El Hadj Omar Bongo par lui-même.* Libreville, Multipress Gabon, 1988.

Bory, P. *The New Gabon.* Monaco, 1978.

Bouquerel, J. *Le Gabon.* Paris, Presses universitaires de France, 1970.

Deschamps, H. *Traditions orales et archives du Gabon.* Paris, Berger-Levrault, 1962.

Fernandez, J. W. *Bwiti.* Princeton, NJ, Princeton University Press, 1982.

Gaulme, F. *Le Pays de Cama Gabon.* Paris, Editions Karthala, 1983.

Le Gabon et son ombre. Paris, Editions Karthala, 1988.

McKay, J. 'West Central Africa', in Mansell Prothero, R. (Ed.), *A Geography of Africa*, London, 1969.

Péan, P. *Affaires africaines.* Paris, Fayard, 1983.

Raponda-Walker, A. *Notes d'histoire du Gabon.* Montpellier, Imprimerie Charité, 1960.

Vennetier, P. 'Problems of port development in Gabon and Congo', Ch. II in Hoyle, B. S. and Hilling, D. (Eds), *Seaports and Development in Tropical Africa.* London, 1970.

Les Plans de Développement des Pays d'Afrique Noire. 4th Edn, Paris, Ediafric, 1977.

L'Economie Gabonaise. Ediafric, Paris, 1977.

THE GAMBIA

Physical and Social Geography

R. J. HARRISON CHURCH

The Republic of The Gambia is one of mainland Africa's smallest states, with an area of 11,295 sq km (4,361 sq miles). Its population (enumerated at 1,025,867 in April 1993, according to provisional census results) is, however, one of the fastest-growing. Apart from a very short coastline, The Gambia is a semi-enclave in Senegal. The two countries have common physical and social phenomena, but differ in history, colonial experience and certain economic affiliations.

The Gambia essentially comprises the valley of the navigable Gambia river. Around the estuary (3 km wide at its narrowest point) and the lower river, the state is 50 km wide, and extends eastward either side of the navigable river for 470 km. In most places the country is only 24 km wide with but one or two villages within it on either bank, away from mangrove or marsh. The former extends about 150 km upstream, the limit of the tide in the rainy season, although in the dry season and in drought years the tide penetrates further upstream. Annual rainfall in The Gambia averages 1,150 mm.

Small ocean-going vessels can reach Kaur, 190 km upstream, throughout the year; Georgetown, 283 km upstream, is accessible to some small craft. River vessels regularly call at Fatoto, 464 km upstream, the last of 33 wharf towns served by schooners or river boats. Unfortunately, this fine waterway is underutilized because it is separated from most of its natural hinterland by the nearby frontier with Senegal.

Some mangrove on the landward sides has been removed for swamp rice cultivation. Behind are seasonally flooded marshes with freshwater grasses, and then on the upper slopes of Tertiary sandstone there is woodland with fallow bush and areas cultivated mainly with groundnuts and millet, the important cash and food crops.

The Gambia has few mineral resources, although reserves of petroleum have been identified.

The principal ethnic groups are the Mandinka, Fula, Wollof, Jola and Serahuli. There is also a small but influential Creole (Aku) community. Each ethnic group has its own vernacular language, although the official language is English.

Recent History

ARNOLD HUGHES

Revised for this edition by John A. Wiseman

Although the British had been active on the Gambia river since the mid-17th century, it was not until 1888 that the administration of The Gambia was separated from that of Sierra Leone and a Gambia legislature was established. In the following year agreements with France delimiting the boundaries between Senegal and The Gambia gave the British control over most of the river valley. By 1901 Britain had extended the protectorate over all of the major chieftaincies along the river.

It was not until after the Second World War that any significant measure of social and economic change occurred. The export of groundnuts provided sufficient revenue for the territory's administration, but left little for spending on welfare facilities or infrastructure. There was little pressure, or need felt, to allow the populace any meaningful participation in political life. The inhabitants of the protectorate were given limited representation in the legislative council in 1932, but it was only after 1946 that the populace of the interior was allowed greater participation in the political process. The earliest political parties, such as the United Party, founded in 1951, derived their support principally from the electorate of Banjul and tended to represent urban interests. With its enfranchisement in 1959, the rural electorate expressed a growing preference for the Protectorate People's Party, founded in that year and led by Dawda (later Sir Dawda) Jawara, a senior government veterinary officer. Despite its initial identification with the Mandinka, the party sought to integrate the country's ethnic groups, changing its name to the People's Progressive Party (PPP) and endeavouring to distribute political offices on an inter-communal basis. The PPP won the 1962 elections, which ushered in self-government, with Jawara as prime minister. On 18 February 1965 the PPP led the country to independence as a constitutional monarchy. On 24 April 1970 The Gambia became a republic, with Jawara as its first president.

THE JAWARA PRESIDENCY, 1970–94

New forms of opposition to the PPP emerged in the 1970s. The National Convention Party (NCP), founded by the former vice-president, Sherif Mustapha Dibba, in 1975, drew its support from Mandinka who resented power-sharing with other ethnic groups and replaced the United Party as the largest opposition party in the 1977 elections, although making only a limited inroad into the PPP's large majority. Complaints of corruption and inertia in the PPP and a deteriorating economy helped to fuel support for more extreme opponents, notably two self-styled Marxist groups, the Gambia Socialist Revolutionary Party (GSRP) and the Movement for Justice in Africa–The Gambia (MOJA–G). The murder of the deputy commander of the small paramilitary field force by a mutinous police officer in October 1980 provoked a crisis. Senegalese troops were flown in (under the terms of the two countries' 1965 defence agreement) to prevent further military disaffection; the GSRP and MOJA–G were proscribed, and the leaders of the latter organization arrested and charged with sedition. The Libyan diplomatic mission, suspected of being in contact with local dissidents, was closed and its staff expelled.

Hopes that violent opposition had been dispelled were abruptly shattered in less than a year. On 30 July 1981, taking advantage of Jawara's absence in London, a small group of civilian conspirators, led by Kukoi Samba Sanyang (who was rumoured to have connections with MOJA–G), made common cause with disaffected members of the field force to take over the government. They seized several strategic points in Banjul and the surrounding area but failed to attract much support among the populace. Senegalese military help was again forthcoming: nearly 3,000 Senegalese troops entered The Gambia and within a week had routed the rebel forces. Some of the rebel leaders, including Sanyang, escaped to Guinea-Bissau but more than 1,000 people were detained under the state of emergency declared on Jawara's return to the country.

The major sequel of these events was the formation of the Senegambia confederation, which came into being in February 1982, a product of Senegalese fears of continuing instability and the Gambian government's own security concerns. In some respects a logical extension of the close ties already existing between the two countries, the confederation also represented a novel departure, with uncertain consequences for Gambian autonomy. The main source of disagreement between the two partners was the political and economic evolution of the relationship. Senegal envisaged a united Senegambian state with a common economy, while The Gambia wished to limit integration with its much larger neighbour.

Although the eight-day insurrection, in which as many as 1,000 people were killed, briefly marred The Gambia's overseas prestige, the country soon returned to political normality. Among the measures taken to reassert democratic practice, perhaps the most prominent was the holding of the country's first popular presidential election in May 1982. Jawara's overwhelming victory over Dibba (at the time in detention for his alleged involvement in the previous year's coup attempt) in the presidential election testified to his continuing personal popularity. In the simultaneous legislative election, none the less, the government vote fell substantially, mainly because a large number of former PPP supporters stood as independent candidates: the PPP secured 27 seats, the NCP three and independents five.

The state of emergency was ended in 1985, enabling the NCP to mount a strong campaign for the general and presidential elections of May 1987, in which it sought to capitalize on revelations of corruption in official circles and on the financial hardships resulting from the government's economic recovery programme (see Economy). The PPP was also challenged by the Gambia People's Party (GPP), formed in 1986 by three former PPP ministers and led by a former vice-president, Assan Musa Camara, who—together with Dibba—rivalled Jawara for the presidency. However, the legislative election decisively confirmed the PPP in power, with 31 of the 36 directly elected seats in the house of representatives, despite a further fall (to about 57%) in its share of the vote; the NPC, with 28% of the vote, won the remaining five seats. Jawara was re-elected to the presidency, although his share of the vote also declined (to 59%, as against 72% in 1982).

In February 1988, despite government reluctance to divulge details of the affair, it became generally known that a coup plot had been discovered, involving both Gambian and Senegalese nationals. Of the four individuals subsequently tried on charges of treason and conspiracy to overthrow the Gambian government, two were members of the separatist movement in the southern Senegalese region of Casamance. The involvement in the conspiracy of Kukoi Samba Sanyang, who was now resident in Libya, was alleged at the trial.

A Senegambian free trade zone was agreed in 1988, but Senegal's dissatisfaction at protracted delays in achieving even limited integration, together with its frustration at the failure of the confederation to halt cross-border smuggling, was compounded in August 1989 when Jawara requested that the confederal presidency (hitherto the privilege of the Senegalese head of state) be alternated between the two countries. In the same month President Diouf of Senegal announced that his country's troops were to be withdrawn from The Gambia, ostensibly in response to military commitments in the border region with Mauritania and to avoid Gambian involvement in any conflict with that country. On 23 August Diouf stated that, in view of The Gambia's reluctance to proceed towards full political and economic integration with Senegal, the confederal agreement, having failed to achieve its aims, should be suspended, and the two countries should try to formulate more attainable co-operation accords. The confederation was formally dissolved in September.

In mid-1990, in his capacity as chairman of the conference of heads of state and government of the Economic Community of West African States (ECOWAS), President Jawara contributed to attempts to mediate in the civil conflict in Liberia. Gambian troops subsequently participated in the ECOWAS Monitoring Group that was dispatched to Liberia in August of that year. In mid-June 1991 60 members of a Gambian military unit that had recently returned from Liberia staged a protest in Banjul, demanding that outstanding allowances be paid. The protesters returned to barracks after assurances had been given that their grievances would be examined, and a commission of inquiry was duly appointed to investigate the circumstances surrounding the incident. (In early September seven officers were dismissed from the armed forces, in accordance with the findings of the inquiry.) Meanwhile, the commander of the national gendarmerie and army, Lt-Col Momodou N'Dow-N'Jie, resigned in the aftermath of the demonstration, after admitting that he had lost the confidence and co-operation of the forces under his command. A Nigerian national was named as his successor in late July, and a defence co-operation agreement was signed with Nigeria in early 1992. In February of that year about 30 soldiers (again newly-returned from Liberia) staged a brief protest to demand the payment of salary arrears.

Presidential and legislative elections took place on 29 April 1992. Although challenged by four other candidates for the presidency, Jawara (who had initially announced that he would not be seeking a sixth presidential mandate) was re-elected, with his share of the vote (at 58%) remaining much the same as in 1987. His closest rival, Dibba, took 22% of the votes. The PPP lost six seats; however, the government party retained a comfortable legislative majority, with 25 elective seats. The NCP secured six seats, and the GPP two; three independent candidates were also elected to the legislature.

A reorganization of the cabinet, announced at the time of the presidential inauguration in May 1992, suggested that Jawara was preparing to cede some of his political powers. Among the most notable changes was his relinquishing of the defence portfolio to Saihou Sabally, who had been transferred from the finance ministry to the hitherto largely ceremonial vice-presidency. Also at his inauguration, Jawara announced an amnesty for members of MOJA–G, although Kukoi Samba Sanyang was believed to be excluded from the clemency measures. In November Jawara revoked the ban, in force since 1980, on MOJA–G and the GSRP.

In April 1993 parliament approved the abolition of the death penalty: although a total of 87 death sentences had been imposed (mostly in cases of treason) since independence, only one execution had been carried out.

In January 1994 Jawara announced that an independent public complaints commission was to be established, with the aim of combating corruption in public life. Allegations of impropriety had intensified in recent months: Sabally had been linked to an embezzlement scandal at the Gambia Co-operative Union, and in December 1993 the Roman Catholic bishop of Banjul had issued a vehement condemnation of corruption in the public sector.

MILITARY GOVERNMENT

President Jawara was deposed in an abrupt but bloodless coup in July 1994, shortly after his return from a visit to the United Kingdom. On 22 July soldiers (apparently angered at having been disarmed by their Nigerian commanding officers at Banjul airport, where they had assembled to welcome Jawara) staged protests in the capital, again demanding payments outstanding from a tour of duty with peace-keeping forces in Liberia. Strategic positions including the airport and power installations were taken by rebels, and telecommunications links were suspended. In the evening the first broadcasts were made announcing that Jawara had been overthrown by a group of young army officers, led by Lt Yaya Jammeh, styling themselves the armed forces provisional ruling council (AFPRC). Jawara and members of his government and entourage left The Gambia aboard a US navy vessel (which had been anchored off Banjul in preparation for manoeuvres with the Gambian fleet) and were subsequently granted asylum by the Senegalese government. Among members of the Jawara administration who were reported to have been arrested was Sabally, although he was subsequently said to have departed for Senegal.

The AFPRC suspended the constitution and announced a ban on all political activity; a night-time curfew was imposed, and the country's borders were temporarily closed. The AFPRC undertook to recover state funds which it alleged had been misappropriated by former state officials, and promised a return to democratic rule once the process of eliminating the corruption which it claimed had been fostered under Jawara's rule was in progress. On 26 July Jammeh pronounced himself head of state, and named a government which included both civilians and representatives of the military. (Two ministers were dismissed almost immediately, accused of colluding with the deposed regime.) Among the members of the new cabinet was Bakary Dabo, the former regime's minister of finance and economic affairs, who had initially fled with Jawara but who later returned to Banjul to resume the finance portfolio. Fafa Idriss M'bye, who as minister of justice in 1982–84 had been responsible for the drafting of anti-corruption legislation, but who had been forced to resign after having himself been implicated in allegations of financial impropriety, was reappointed minister of justice and attorney-general. It was announced that an executive committee, comprising the AFPRC and certain government ministers, would be established as the highest political authority. Those members of Jawara's government who had been arrested were released from detention at the beginning of August, and the new authorities gave assurances that all members of the former regime would be welcome to return to The Gambia to participate in the reform process. About 20 members of the military remained in custody, and were subject to a new decree that authorized the detention for up to six months of any member of the army or police considered to be a threat to state security.

FOREIGN RELATIONS

Relations with Senegal deteriorated appreciably following the dissolution of the Senegambia confederation. While both countries expressed a desire to maintain a privileged relationship, the Senegalese reportedly imposed customs duties and travel restrictions that were unfavourable to Gambian interests, and prevented supplies of important commodities from entering The Gambia through Senegal. By January 1991 relations had improved sufficiently for a meeting of the Gambian minister of external affairs, Alhaji Omar Sey, and his Senegalese counterpart to culminate in the conclusion of a bilateral treaty of friendship and co-operation. However, Senegal's abrupt, unilateral decision to close the Senegalese–Gambian border in September 1993, apparently to reduce smuggling between the two countries, again strained relations. Negotiations subsequently took place between representatives of Senegal and The Gambia, in an attempt to minimize the adverse effects of the closure on The Gambia's regional trading links, and in February 1994 it was announced that President Meles Zenawi of Ethiopia had been invited to mediate between the two countries.

Beginning in mid-1992, the escalation of the conflict between government and separatist forces in Senegal's southern Casamance province (which is effectively cut off from the rest of Senegal by the Gambian enclave) prompted a large influx of refugees from the region into The Gambia. By January 1993 more than 3,000 refugees had crossed into The Gambia. Negotiations between the two governments, and assurances by the Senegalese authorities that the refugees were safe to return, failed to resolve the situation as unrest in Casamance persisted. The refugee problem was intensified by the return to The Gambia of more than 6,000 Gambian nationals, resident in diamond-mining areas of Sierra Leone since the 1950s, following attacks by local rebels.

Diplomatic relations with Israel, severed at the time of the 1973 Arab–Israeli war, were restored in September 1992, despite objections made by Gambian Muslim leaders. It was expected that Israel would provide agricultural assistance. In the previous month Jawara had visited Iran, apparently with the aim of obtaining Iranian support for The Gambia's petroleum-exploration programme.

Although the overthrow of President Jawara and suspension of constitutional government, in July 1994, was condemned by many of The Gambia's external creditors, including the Commonwealth and the European Union, the appointment to the new administration of Bakary Dabo, who had previously enjoyed cordial relations with the international financial community, was expected to enhance the Jammeh regime's international standing. The new government received messages of support from several west African states, including Ghana, Nigeria and Sierra Leone. Senegal, despite having granted asylum to Jawara and his associates, also conveyed a message of good will to the new regime, while negotiations with Nigeria regarding the future of the bilateral defence agreement were described as 'fruitful'. Attending a summit meeting of the Economic Community of West African States in early August, a delegation led by the vice-chairman of the AFPRC, Lt Sana Sabally, gave further assurances of an early return to democratic rule. In September it was reported that Jawara was seeking asylum in the United Kingdom.

Economy

ARNOLD HUGHES

Revised for this edition by JOHN A. WISEMAN

Even by tropical African standards, The Gambia is minute as a national economy, with a population in April 1993 of 1,025,867, according to provisional census results, contained in an area of 11,295 sq km along the banks of the Gambia river. According to estimates by the World Bank, The Gambia's gross national product (GNP) per head (measured at average 1990–92 prices) was US $370 in 1992—the same level, in nominal terms, as in 1981. Between 1980–92, it was estimated, GNP per head declined, in real terms, at an average annual rate of 0.4%. Gambian government figures indicate that the rate of growth of the gross domestic product (GDP), which averaged 3.4% in 1985–90, declined from 4.2% in the financial year ending 30 June 1992 to an estimated 2.1% in 1992/93, reflecting disappointing performance in the agriculture and tourism sectors. Real GDP growth of about 5% was forecast for 1993/94.

The cultivation and processing of groundnuts constitute the principal agricultural and industrial activities. Although groundnuts and groundnut products account for the major part of domestic exports (78.6% in 1985/86), by the early 1990s tourism had overtaken this sector as the principal source of foreign exchange. Fishing is also significant, and there is an important re-export trade to neighbouring countries. Fluctuations in international prices for groundnuts (which are unaffected by The Gambia's own output levels) are a significant influence on the country's prosperity, as is the value, relative to the dalasi, of the CFA franc, since 'black market' currency rates encourage the smuggling of much of the groundnut production into neighbouring Senegal. The further diversification of the economy is important, given the high rate of population growth (an average 3.9% per year in 1983–93). Indications of the existence of petroleum reserves may eventually provide a degree of future economic security. In the mean time, external development assistance, from both bilateral and multilateral donors, is essential.

The agricultural sector (including forestry and fishing) contributed 23.1% of GDP in 1990/91. Much of the groundnut crop is from subsistence farming and does not reach the export market, especially during periods of drought. Production of groundnuts was estimated at 151,000 metric tons in 1982, declining to 106,000 tons in 1983. According to unofficial figures, annual output had recovered slightly by 1989, to 120,000 tons; however, in 1990/91 the groundnut harvest reportedly declined to only 74,500 tons, owing to late and inadequate rains and to the low price paid to groundnut producers (which is almost 40% less than the price paid to farmers in Senegal). Following a marginal increase, to 84,000 tons, in 1991/92, output was reported to have suffered a further severe decline, to 55,000 tons, in 1992/93.

Other food crops have demonstrated a similar vulnerability to adverse climatic conditions. Output of millet and sorghum was estimated to have fallen from 49,000 tons in 1982 to 29,000 tons in 1983, before rising to a level estimated by the FAO at 77,000 tons in 1991. Production of paddy rice fell from 37,000 tons in 1982 to 19,000 tons in 1983, with 1991 output estimated at 22,000 tons, while maize output dwindled from 17,000 tons in 1982 to only 6,000 tons in 1983, before recovering to 24,000 tons in 1991, according to unofficial figures. The cultivation of such crops as citrus fruits, avocados and sesame seed has been encouraged by the government, and has proved to be commercially useful. The total fishing catch declined from 18,092 tons in 1977 to 9,212 tons in 1982, before recovering to some 23,743 tons in 1991. Exports of fish and fish products were valued at D23.1m. in 1989/90, compared with D20.1m. in 1988/89.

FINANCE AND DEVELOPMENT

The West African Currency Board pound was replaced by the Gambian pound in 1965, without change in the one-for-one parity with sterling. The Gambian pound was devalued along with sterling in November 1967. In March 1971 the Central Bank of The Gambia was inaugurated, and in July a new, decimalized currency unit, the dalasi, was adopted, replacing the old at the rate of D5 = £1. Following the floating of the British pound in June 1972, the parity with sterling was maintained until March 1973, when the dalasi was revalued to D4 = £1 in order to arrest increases in prices of imports from non-sterling sources. The worsening economic situation led to a devaluation of the dalasi to the earlier rate of D5 = £1 in March 1984. In January 1986 the fixed rate was abandoned, and a 'floating' rate was adopted as part of the IMF-supported economic recovery programme (ERP). By 31 March 1994 the exchange rate was approximately D14.4 = £1.

Development finance is obtained very largely from outside sources. The relative importance of the United Kingdom has declined as aid has become diversified by contributions from the International Development Association, the European Development Fund, France, Switzerland, Germany, Japan and Arab donors. In September 1985 The Gambia was the subject of a donors' conference in London, attended by the United Kingdom, the Netherlands and representatives of the European Commmunity (now European Union), among others, to discuss support for the balance of payments. Among the projects proposed, which were in line with IMF and World Bank recommendations, were measures to improve productivity in the agricultural sector, reforms of the civil service and parastatal organizations, and financial restructuring.

Development objectives since the mid-1980s have been to improve transport and communications and to raise yields of groundnuts and rice (the staple food), along with some attempt to diversify production. Rice imports have reached 30,000 tons per year and their price to local consumers has enjoyed a substantial government subsidy (reduced in 1982 and 1984), but the cultivation of both swamp and irrigated rice is being developed with some success. The Jahali-Pacharr rice scheme, involving 1,500 ha and using imported rice strains and irrigated land, supplied one-quarter of The Gambia's total production in 1984, reportedly affording the highest yields of any rice farm in the world. In 1988 The Gambia received a loan of $6.8m. from the African Development Bank (ADB), in support of a further five-year rice development project. Food production still falls short of demand, with gross production of food-grains declining from 104,000 tons in 1982/83 to 68,000 tons in 1983/84. An estimated 60,000 tons of cereals were imported in 1986. A cotton development project, financed by the ADB, is also under way, and operation of a ginnery began in 1977, although results have so far disappointed expectations.

Initial doubts about the potential of tourism have been overcome. In the early 1990s this sector contributed about 10% of annual GDP. An estimated 7,500 people were employed in the sector, either directly or indirectly, at that time. Following steady growth, of about 10% per year, in tourist numbers throughout the 1980s and early 1990s, there was an unexpected decline, of some 12% in arrivals in the main (July–February) 1992/93 season, which was largely attributed to the economic recession in Europe. The 1993/94 season was reported to have been particularly successful, and the Jawara administration was optimistic about prospects for the Gambian tourist industry, placing particular emphasis on the development of 'eco-tourism' activities and the promotion of tourism outside the main season. It was expected, however, that the July 1994 coup would have a detrimental effect on the sector, at least in the early part of the 1994/95 season.

The river serves as a major artery of trade and transport, and the length of all-weather roads has more than doubled since 1960. In 1990 there were 2,386 km of roads, although only 21% of the network was paved. The port of Banjul has been modernized and is being further enlarged: in early 1994 the ADB approved a loan of $22m. in support of the Banjul Port Development Project, the total cost of which was estimated at $33m. Facilities at the Yundum international airport have been upgraded by the US National Aeronautics and Space Administration (NASA), to enable the airport to serve as an emergency landing site for space shuttle vehicles.

Since the coup attempt in July 1981, The Gambia has experienced a growing deficit in its budget, which has been largely financed by overseas aid. An IMF loan of SDR16.9m. was granted for 1981–83, to stabilize the economy, but its effect was eroded by the Jawara government's expansionary fiscal policies, increased arrears in external debt repayments and the growth in food imports, brought about by reduced agricultural production, due to drought. The revised estimate for the 1983/84 budget showed recurrent revenue at D150.5m. and expenditure at D164.9m. Government development spending contributed significantly to the growing deficit, having increased at an average annual rate of 19.3% in the years 1978–84. There was a small budget surplus, of D8.6m., in 1987/88. However, this was expected to narrow to D0.5m. in 1988/89: budget estimates for that financial year envisaged revenue of D405.1m., compared with D386.7m. in 1987/88, and recurrent expenditure of D404.6m., compared with D380.0m. in 1987/88. The increased development budget, of D205.0m., compared with D169.6m. in 1987/88, was to be financed largely by external aid contributions, which continued to be granted in recognition of the government's adherence to measures imposed by the IMF, and of its partial success in achieving economic recovery. Following a deficit of D19.3m. in 1989/90, budget estimates for 1990/91 envisaged a deficit of D59.4m. Development expenditure was estimated at D195m., of which D175m. was to be financed by external loans (D120m.) and grants. By mid-1991 the actual recurrent budgetary deficit for 1990/91 was projected at D82m. This represented slightly more than 4% of annual GDP, a significant improvement compared with the previous year, when the deficit was equivalent to almost 11% of annual GDP. The reduction in the shortfall was achieved by means of the exercise of strict control over recurrent expenditure, in conjunction with a high level of revenue collection; expenditure on public-sector employees increased by only 10%, while for the first time no transfers or loans were made to parastatal organizations. Budget estimates for 1991/92 envisaged development expenditure of D226m., of which D141m. was to be derived from external loans and D58m. from external grants. The 1994/95 budget, delivered shortly before the *coup d'état*, envisaged total expenditure of D958.0m., including development expenditure of D278.2m.

The ERP envisaged reductions in public expenditure, in conjunction with the diversification of the agricultural sector and the stimulation of the private sector (in part by the transfer to private ownership of several parastatal organizations). In December 1988 existing agreements with the IMF were superseded by a three-year enhanced structural adjustment facility of SDR 20.52m., in support of measures to consolidate the achievements of the ERP. Despite continuing economic difficulties, by mid-1990 both the Gambian government and the IMF felt sufficiently encouraged by the success of the ERP in bringing about basic fiscal and economic discipline for it to be replaced by a programme for sustained development (PSD), which aimed to create an environment that would foster sustained growth. Among the major components of the PSD was the furtherance of the privatization programme: to this end, two former mainstays of the state sector, The Gambia Produce Marketing Board (until 1990 the monopoly exporter of groundnuts) and The Gambia Utilities Corporation, were sold to private interests in mid-1993.

Such adjustment efforts achieved considerable success in curtailing the rate of inflation: from an increase of 56.6% in 1986, inflation slowed to 23.5% in 1987, and by 1991 the average annual rate of inflation was only 8.6%; the rate increased slightly, to 9.5% in 1992, but declined to 6.5% in 1993.

It was unclear at mid-1994 to what extent The Gambia's relations with the international financial community would be affected by the military take-over. Meanwhile, long-term impediments to growth remain The Gambia's reliance on imports and its external debt, which (while classified by the World Bank as 'moderate') represents a considerable drain on government funds. The visible trade deficit, which averaged $86.5m. per year in 1980–81 (reflecting a sudden increase in expenditure on imports), narrowed to $35.5m. per year in 1982–83 and reached a low point of $8.7m. in 1984, following a 66% increase in the value of exports in that year. The deficit widened to $12.1m. in 1985 and continued to increase, by an average of almost 20% per year, for the remainder of the decade—reaching $29.9m. in 1990—as the average annual increase in exports (12.0%) failed to keep pace with the growth in imports (13.4%). The deficit rose to $42.1m. in 1991, reflecting a 31.7% increase in the cost of imports, but declined again, to $30.8m., in 1992. The current account of the balance of payments has, none the less, been in surplus in every year since 1984, largely reflecting improved receipts from services and an increase in income from private transfers, while the overall balance of payments has shown an annual surplus since 1987. In the absence of any new debt relief since January 1988 (when the 'London Club' of commercial creditors agreed to reschedule some $19m. of debt), The Gambia's external debt has increased steadily, from $326.8m. in 1988 to $379.4m.—equivalent to 102% of GNP—at the end of 1992. In the latter year the cost of debt-servicing was equivalent to 13.3% of the value of exports of goods and services.

RELATIONS WITH SENEGAL

The formal dissolution, in September 1989, of the Senegambia confederation (see Recent History), and subsequent allegations regarding Senegal's economic 'harrassment' of The Gambia, raised serious questions regarding future economic relations between the two countries. During 1990 the Senegalese authorities eased restrictions on cross-border traffic, and the conclusion, in January 1991, of a new co-operation treaty confirmed several existing bilateral agreements governing such areas as defence and security, transport and telecommunications, health, trade, fishing, agriculture and energy. None the less, Senegal's closure, in September 1993, of the border between the two countries prompted protests by The Gambia that its overland trading links had been blocked. Moreover, The Gambia's re-export trade was, in particular, adversely affected by the 50% devaluation, in January 1994, of the CFA franc.

Both countries have also maintained their membership of the sub-regional Gambia River Basin Development Organization, to which Guinea and Guinea-Bissau also belong. This organization is principally concerned with promoting development by means of regional co-operation and the joint exploitation of shared natural resources.

Statistical Survey

Source (unless otherwise stated): Directorate of Information and Broadcasting, 14 Hagan St, Banjul; tel. 27230.

Area and Population

AREA, POPULATION AND DENSITY

Area (sq km)	11,295*
Population (census results)	
15 April 1983	
Males	342,134
Females	345,683
Total	687,817
15 April 1993	
Total	1,025,867†
Density (per sq km) at census of 1993	90.8

* 4,361 sq miles. † Provisional.

PRINCIPAL TOWNS (population at 1983 census)

Banjul (capital)	44,188	Farafenni	10,168
Serrekunda	68,433	Sukuta	7,227
Brikama	19,584	Gunjur	7,115
Bakau	19,309		

BIRTHS AND DEATHS (UN estimates, annual averages)

	1975–80	1980–85	1985–90
Birth rate (per '000)	48.8	48.2	47.4
Death rate (per '000)	24.9	23.1	21.4

Expectation of life (UN estimates, years at birth, 1985–90): 43.0 (males 41.4; females 44.6).

Source: UN, *World Population Prospects: The 1992 Revision*.

ECONOMICALLY ACTIVE POPULATION*
(persons aged 10 years and over, 1983 census)

	Total
Agriculture, hunting, forestry and fishing	239,940
Quarrying	66
Manufacturing	8,144
Electricity, gas and water	1,233
Construction	4,373
Trade, restaurants and hotels	16,551
Transport, storage and communication	8,014
Public administration and defence	8,295
Education	4,737
Medical services	2,668
Personal and domestic services	6,553
Activities not adequately defined	25,044
Total	325,618†

* Figures exclude persons seeking work for the first time.
† Males 174,856; females 150,762.

Mid-1992 (estimates in '000): Agriculture, etc. 326; Total 406 (Source: FAO, *Production Yearbook*).

Agriculture

PRINCIPAL CROPS ('000 metric tons)

	1990	1991	1992
Millet and sorghum	55	70	77*
Rice (paddy)	21	21	22*
Maize	14	20	24*
Cassava (Manioc)†	6	6	6
Palm kernels†	2	2	2
Groundnuts (in shell)	75	84	80*
Seed (unginned) cotton†	5	6	7

* Unofficial figure. † FAO estimates.

Source: FAO, *Production Yearbook.*

LIVESTOCK ('000 head, year ending September)

	1990	1991	1992*
Cattle*	400	390	400
Goats	180	156	150
Sheep	121	121	121
Pigs*	11	11	11
Asses	37	31	30
Horses	16	16	16

Poultry (million)*: 1 in 1990; 1 in 1991; 1 in 1992.

* FAO estimates.

Source: FAO, *Production Yearbook.*

LIVESTOCK PRODUCTS (FAO estimates, '000 metric tons)

	1990	1991	1992
Beef and veal	6	6	6
Poultry meat	1	1	1
Goats' meat	1	1	n.a.
Other meat	1	1	2
Cows' milk	7	7	7

Source: FAO, *Production Yearbook.*

Forestry

ROUNDWOOD REMOVALS
(FAO estimates, '000 cubic metres, excluding bark)

	1990	1991	1992
Sawlogs, veneer logs and logs for sleepers*	14	14	14
Other industrial wood*	7	7	7
Fuel wood	907	919	925
Total	928	940	946

* Assumed by the FAO to be unchanged since 1983.

Source: FAO, *Yearbook of Forest Products.*

Fishing

('000 metric tons, live weight)

	1989	1990	1991
Tilapias	1.2	1.2	1.1
Other freshwater fishes	1.5	1.5	1.4
Croakers and drums	0.4	0.9	0.5
Sardinellas	3.5	0.9	1.8
Bonga shad	9.3	8.0	14.8
Sharks, rays, skates, etc.	0.4	0.6	0.4
Other marine fishes (incl. unspecified)	0.9	2.2	1.3
Total fish	17.3	15.4	21.4
Southern pink shrimp	0.3	1.3	1.0
Cuttlefishes and bobtail squids	0.6	0.7	0.4
Octopuses	1.5	0.3	0.8
Other crustaceans and molluscs	0.1	0.2	0.1
Total catch	19.8	17.9	23.7
Inland waters	2.7	2.7	2.5
Atlantic Ocean	17.1	15.2	21.2

Source: FAO, *Yearbook of Fishery Statistics.*

Industry

SELECTED PRODUCTS

	1989	1990	1991
Salted, dried or smoked fish ('000 metric tons)*	0.7	0.7	n.a.
Vegetable oils—unrefined ('000 metric tons)	7	3†	3†
Electric energy (million kWh)	61	67	68

* Data from the FAO.

† Provisional or estimated figure.

Finance

CURRENCY AND EXCHANGE RATES

Monetary Units

100 butut = 1 dalasi (D).

Sterling and Dollar Equivalents (31 March 1994)

£1 sterling = 14.402 dalasi;
US $1 = 9.701 dalasi;
1,000 dalasi = £69.43 = $103.08.

Average Exchange Rate (dalasi per US $)

1991 8.803
1992 8.888
1993 9.129

BUDGET (million dalasi, year ending 30 June)

Revenue*	1989/90
Current revenue	485.77
Revenue from taxation	454.81
Taxes on income, profits and capital gains	62.40
Domestic taxes on goods and services	181.48
Taxes on international trade and transactions	208.12
Other current revenue	30.96
Entrepreneurial and property income	11.16
Administrative fees and charges, non-industrial and incidental sales	17.72
Capital revenue	0.40
Total	486.17

Expenditure†	1989/90
General public services	99.44
Defence	23.58
Public order and safety	24.83
Education	67.47
Health	38.18
Social security and welfare	16.32
Housing and community amenities	25.47
Recreational, cultural and religious affairs and services	8.05
Economic affairs and services	173.82
Fuel and energy	16.61
Agriculture, forestry, fishing and hunting	35.20
Mining, manufacturing and construction	0.16
Transport and communications	78.59
Other economic affairs and services	43.26
Other purposes	112.44
Total	589.60
Current	388.21
Capital	201.39

* Excluding grants received from abroad (million dalasi): 155.79 (current 104.32; capital 51.47).
† Excluding lending minus repayments (million dalasi): 71.66.
Source: IMF, *Government Finance Statistics Yearbook*.

CENTRAL BANK RESERVES (US $ million at 31 December)

	1990	1991	1992
IMF special drawing rights	1.76	0.77	0.62
Reserve position in IMF	0.04	0.04	2.04
Foreign exchange	53.58	66.80	91.38
Total	55.39	67.62	94.03

Source: IMF, *International Financial Statistics*.

MONEY SUPPLY (million dalasi at 31 December)

	1990	1991	1992
Currency outside banks	152.17	182.28	207.08
Demand deposits at commercial banks	137.90	211.30	228.09
Total money (incl. others)	296.19	393.58	435.17

Source: IMF, *International Financial Statistics*.

COST OF LIVING (Consumer Price Index for low-income families in Banjul and Kombo St Mary; base: 1990 = 100)

	1991	1992	1993
All items	108.6	118.9	126.6

Source: IMF, *International Financial Statistics*.

NATIONAL ACCOUNTS
('000 dalasi at current prices, year ending 30 June)
Gross Domestic Product by Economic activity

	1988/89	1989/90	1990/91
Agriculture, hunting, forestry and fishing	493,711	642,751	639,880
Mining and quarrying	373	405	486
Manufacturing	90,127	140,521	160,965
Electricity, gas and water	14,994	17,000	19,200
Construction	84,204	93,672	130,607
Trade, restaurants and hotels	947,507	861,207	1,062,375
Transport, storage and communications	190,574	211,195	247,000
Finance, insurance, real estate and business services	190,453	205,550	236,455
Community, social and personal services	56,000	64,000	74,000
Government services	146,229	174,151	193,398
Sub-total	2,014,172	2,410,452	2,764,366
Less Imputed bank service charge	71,862	65,209	75,000
Total	1,942,310	2,345,243	2,689,366

Source: UN, *National Accounts Statistics*.

BALANCE OF PAYMENTS (US $ million)

	1990	1991	1992
Merchandise exports f.o.b.	110.62	142.87	146.95
Merchandise imports f.o.b.	-140.51	-185.00	-177.76
Trade balance	-29.88	-42.13	-30.81
Exports of services	69.78	80.53	80.86
Imports of services	-51.83	-72.23	-66.93
Other income received	1.59	3.78	4.85
Other income paid	-13.04	-11.30	-7.31
Private unrequited transfers (net)	-14.13	-15.12	-13.28
Official unrequited transfers (net)	43.17	39.38	43.23
Current balance	33.93	13.15	37.16
Direct investment (net)	—	10.20	6.16
Other capital (net)	-6.09	10.57	12.55
Net errors and omissions	-24.01	-16.69	-36.65
Overall balance	3.83	17.22	19.22

Source: IMF, *International Financial Statistics*.

External Trade

PRINCIPAL COMMODITIES
(distribution by SITC, US $ '000)

Imports c.i.f.	1989	1990	1991
Food and live animals	44,570	61,316	61,500
Wheat meal and flour	7,094	3,072	6,044
Beverages and tobacco	6,666	7,897	9,231
Mineral fuels and lubricants	8,033	12,117	21,729
Motor spirit (gasoline) and other light oils	2,399	3,999	6,513
Kerosene (incl. jet fuel)	1,205	1,719	6,879
Gas oils	2,364	4,246	6,380
Animal and vegetable oils, fats, etc.	2,368	2,865	4,269
Chemicals and related products	8,211	13,601	13,656
Basic manufactures	27,493	36,052	36,524
Machinery and transport equipment	26,558	30,601	29,787
Miscellaneous manufactured articles	12,289	14,588	21,377
Total (incl. others)	139,241	182,715	202,208

Exports f.o.b.	1989	1990	1991
Food and live animals	4,849	5,019	5,595
Fish and fish preparations	3,065	2,876	3,445
Vegetables and fruits	1,056	1,278	1,432
Oilcakes	728	865	718
Groundnuts (green)	2,680	6,520	4,699
Raw cotton	872	1,832	1,713
Groundnut oil	4,426	4,411	2,072
Total (incl. others)	44,550	32,305	39,770

Source: UN, *International Trade Statistics Yearbook*.

PRINCIPAL TRADING PARTNERS (US $ '000)

Imports c.i.f.	1989	1990	1991
Belgium/Luxembourg	5,099	6,793	8,551
China, People's Republic	1,532	23,041	29,537
Côte d'Ivoire	898	740	3,333
Denmark	740	4,672	977
France (incl. Monaco)	13,592	21,907	16,814
Germany	15,614	12,771	13,619
Hong Kong	5,693	4,105	13,136
Italy	3,897	6,472	5,367
Japan	5,719	5,843	8,103
Myanmar	1,532	2,811	1,149
Netherlands	12,866	1,714	21,331
Senegal	4,729	5,991	5,229
Thailand	6,010	2,515	6,137
United Kingdom	26,259	31,806	26,572
USA	6,327	10,639	6,804
Total (incl. others)	139,241	182,715	202,208

Exports f.o.b.	1989	1990	1991
Belgium/Luxembourg	1,382	2,875	1,782
China, People's Republic	n.a.	n.a.	880
France (incl. Monaco)	2,303	2,705	2,982
Germany	962	121	400
Ghana	284	752	320
Guinea	135	667	754
Guinea-Bissau	n.a.	2,560	6,866
Mali	n.a.	206	1,234
Netherlands	2,899	5,386	3,062
Senegal	528	1,128	948
Switzerland (incl. Liechtenstein)	n.a.	4,355	914
United Kingdom	2,343	2,608	5,827
Total (incl. others)	44,500	32,305	39,770

Source: UN, *International Trade Statistics Yearbook*.

Transport

ROAD TRAFFIC (estimates, '000 motor vehicles in use)

	1989	1990	1991
Private cars	5	6	6
Commercial vehicles	6	6	6

Source: UN Economic Commission for Africa, *African Statistical Yearbook*.

INTERNATIONAL SEA-BORNE SHIPPING
(freight traffic, '000 metric tons)

	1988	1989	1990
Goods loaded	155	158	169
Goods unloaded	210	214	212

Source: UN, *Monthly Bulletin of Statistics*.

CIVIL AVIATION (estimated traffic)

	1989	1990	1991
Freight loaded (metric tons)	280	290	303
Freight unloaded (metric tons)	1,100	1,200	1,300
Passenger arrivals ('000)	63	63	64
Passenger departures ('000)	63	63	64
Transit passengers ('000)	28	28	29

Source: UN Economic Commission for Africa, *Statistical Yearbook*.

Tourism

TOURIST ARRIVALS (year ending 30 June)

	1991/92
Total	63,131

Communications Media

	1989	1990	1991
Radio receivers ('000 in use)	140	146	150
Telephones ('000 in use)*	7	7	8
Daily newspapers	n.a.	2	n.a.
Non-daily newspapers	n.a.	6	n.a.
Periodicals	n.a.	10	n.a.
Books published (first editions)†			
Titles	n.a.	n.a.	21
Copies ('000)	n.a.	n.a.	7

* Estimates.

† Including pamphlets: 6 titles, 1,000 copies in 1991.

Sources: UNESCO, *Statistical Yearbook*; UN Economic Commission for Africa, *African Statistical Yearbook*.

Education

(1991/92)

	Teachers	Pupils: Males	Pupils: Females	Pupils: Total
Pre-primary	408	n.a.	n.a.	13,118
Primary	2,876	53,775	36,870	90,645
Secondary	n.a.	14,263	7,523	21,786

Source: UNESCO, *Statistical Yearbook*.

Post-secondary (1984/85): 8 schools; 179 teachers; 1,489 pupils.

Directory

The Constitution

Following the seizure of power by the Armed Forces Provisional Ruling Council (AFPRC) in July 1994, the 1970 Constitution was suspended and the presidency and legislature, as defined therein, dissolved. It was announced that an executive committee, comprising the members of the AFPRC and certain government ministers, would be established to act as the hieghest political authority.

The Government

HEAD OF STATE

Chairman of the Armed Forces Provisional Ruling Council: Lt YAYA A. J. J. JAMMEH (proclaimed Head of State 26 July 1994).

ARMED FORCES PROVISIONAL RULING COUNCIL
(September 1994)

Lt YAYA A. J. J. JAMMEH (Chairman)
Lt S. B. SABALLY (Vice-Chairman)
Lt EDWARD SINGATEH
Lt SADIBOU HYDARA
Lt YANKUBA TOURAY

THE CABINET
(September 1994)

Chairman of the Armed Forces Provisional Ruling Council: Lt YAYA A. J. J. JAMMEH.
Vice-Chairman of the Armed Forces Provisional Ruling Council: Lt S. B. SABALLY.
Minister of Defence: Lt EDWARD SINGATEH.
Minister of the Interior: Lt SADIBOU HYDARA.
Minister of Local Government: Lt YANKUBA TOURAY.
Minister of Information and Tourism: SUSAN WAFFA-OGOOH.
Minister of Trade, Industry and Employment: JOHN P. BOJANG.
Minister of Health and Social Welfare: FATOUMATA TAMBAJANG.
Minister of External Affairs: BOLONG L. SONKO.
Minister of Finance and Economic Affairs: BAKARY B. DABO.
Minister of Justice and Attorney-General: FAFA IDRISS M'BYE.
Minister of Education: SATANG JOW.
Minister of Works and Communications: MBEMBA TAMBEDU.
Minister of Youth, Sports and Culture: AMINA FAAL-SONKO.
Minister of Agriculture and Natural Resources: MUSA MBENGA.
Secretary-General and Head of the Civil Service: MUSTAPHA B. WADDA.

MINISTRIES

Office of the Chairman of the Armed Forces Provisional Ruling Council: State House, Banjul; tel. 227208; telex 2204; fax 227034.

Ministry of Agriculture and Natural Resources: The Quadrangle, Banjul; tel. 22147; fax 229546.

Ministry of Defence: Banjul.

Ministry of Education: Bedford Place Bldg, POB 989, Banjul; tel. 228522; telex 2264; fax 225066.

Ministry of External Affairs: 4 Marina Parade, Banjul; tel. 228291; telex 2351; fax 228060.

Ministry of Finance and Economic Affairs: The Quadrangle, Banjul; tel. 228291; telex 2264.

Ministry of Health and Social Welfare: The Quadrangle, Banjul; tel. 227872; telex 2357; fax 228505.

Ministry of Information and Tourism: The Quadrangle, Banjul; tel. 228496; telex 2204.

Ministry of the Interior: 71 Dobson St, Banjul; tel. 228611.

Ministry of Justice: Marina Parade, Banjul; tel. 228181.

Ministry of Local Government: The Quadrangle, Banjul; tel. 228291.

Ministry of Trade, Industry and Employment: Central Bank Bldg, Banjul; tel. 228229; telex 2293.

Ministry of Works and Communications: Half-Die, Banjul; tel. 228251.

Ministry of Youth, Sports and Culture: Bedford Place Bldg, POB 989, Banjul; tel. 228522; telex 2264; fax 225066.

President and Legislature

The Constitution of 1970 was suspended following the July 1994 *coup d'état*. The elected organs of state provided for in the Constitution were:

PRESIDENT

A presidential election took place on 29 April 1992. Alhaji Sir DAWDA JAWARA was elected for a sixth term of office, securing 58.4% of the votes cast. His closest rival, SHERIF MUSTAPHA DIBBA, won 22% of the votes. The other candidates were ASSAN MUSA CAMARA, Dr MOMODOU LAMIN BOJANG and SIDIA JATTA.

HOUSE OF REPRESENTATIVES

Speaker: Alhaji MOMODOU B. N'JIE.

Election, 29 April 1992

Party	Seats
People's Progressive Party	25
National Convention Party	6
Gambia People's Party	2
Independent	3
Total	36

In addition to the 36 members directly elected, the House had 14 other members: the Attorney-General, five Chiefs and eight nominated (non-voting) members.

Political Organizations

All political activity was banned following the *coup d'état* of July 1994. The organizations listed below were active prior to the assumption of power by the military:

Gambia People's Party (GPP): Banjul; f. 1986 by fmr mems of the PPP; socialist; Leader ASSAN MUSA CAMARA.

National Convention Party (NCP): 4 Fitzgerald St, Banjul; f. 1975; advocates social reform and more equitable distribution of national wealth; 50,000 mems; Leader SHERIF MUSTAPHA DIBBA.

People's Democratic Organisation for Independence and Socialism (PDOIS): Banjul; f. 1986; radical socialist; Leaders HALIFA SALLAH, SAM SARR, SIDIA JATTA.

People's Democratic Party (PDP): Bojang Kunda, Brikama, Kombo Central; tel. 84190; f. 1991; advocates promotion of agricultural self-sufficiency, mass education and infrastructural development; Pres. Dr MOMODOU LAMIN BOJANG; First Sec. JABEL SALLAH.

People's Progressive Party (PPP): 21 OAU Blvd, Banjul; f. 1959; merged in 1965 with Democratic Congress Alliance and in 1968 with Gambia Congress Party; Nat. Pres. I. A. A. KELEPHA SAMBA; Sec.-Gen. Alhaji Sir DAWDA KAIRABA JAWARA.

The following opposition groups were banned between November 1980 and November 1992:

Gambia Socialist Revolutionary Party (GSRP).

Movement for Justice in Africa–The Gambia (MOJA–G).

Diplomatic Representation

EMBASSIES AND HIGH COMMISSIONS IN THE GAMBIA

China, People's Republic: Fajara, Banjul; tel. 223835; Chargé d'affaires: LIN TINGHAI.

Nigeria: Garba Jahumpa Ave, Banjul; tel. 95805; High Commissioner: MARK NNABUGWU EZE.

Senegal: 10 Nelson Mandela St, Banjul; tel. 227469; Ambassador: MOKTAR KÉBÉ.

Sierra Leone: 67 Hagan St, Banjul; tel. 228206; High Commissioner: AROUN BOHARE.

United Kingdom: 48 Atlantic Rd, Fajara, POB 507, Banjul; tel. 495133; telex 2211; fax 496134; High Commissioner: MICHAEL J. HARDIE.

USA: Kairaba Ave, Fajara, POB 19, Banjul; tel. 92858; fax 92475; Ambassador: ANDREW WINTER.

Judicial System

The judicial system of The Gambia is based on English Common Law and legislative enactments of the Republic's Parliament which include an Islamic Law Recognition Ordinance whereby an Islamic

Court exercises jurisdiction in certain cases between, or exclusively affecting, Muslims.

Supreme Court of The Gambia: Law Courts, Independence Drive, Banjul; tel. 227383; fax 228380; consists of the Chief Justice and puisne judges; has unlimited jurisdiction; appeal lies to the Court of Appeal.

Chief Justice: BRAIMAH AMEN OMOSUN.

The Gambia Court of Appeal is the Superior Court of Record and consists of a president, justices of appeal and other judges of the Supreme Court ex officio. Final appeal, with certain exceptions, to the Judicial Committee of the Privy Council in the United Kingdom.

President: PATRICK DANKWA ANIN.

The Banjul Magistrates Court, the Kanifing Magistrates Court and the **Divisional Courts** are courts of summary jurisdiction presided over by a magistrate or in his absence by two or more lay justices of the peace. There are resident magistrates in all divisions. The magistrates have limited civil and criminal jurisdiction, and appeal lies from these courts to the Supreme Court.

Islamic Courts have jurisdiction in matters between, or exclusively affecting, Muslim Gambians and relating to civil status, marriage, succession, donations, testaments and guardianship. The Courts administer Islamic (Shari'a) Law. A cadi, or a cadi and two assessors, preside over and constitute an Islamic Court. Assessors of the Islamic Courts are Justices of the Peace of Islamic faith.

District Tribunals are appeal courts which deal with cases touching on customs and traditions. Each court consists of three district tribunal members, one of whom is selected as president, and other court members from the area over which it has jurisdiction.

Religion

About 85% of the population are Muslims. The remainder are mainly Christians, and there are a few animists, mostly of the Jola and Karoninka ethnic groups.

ISLAM

Imam Ratib of Banjul: Alhaji ABDOULIE M. JOBE, King Fahd Bun Abdul Aziz Mosque, 39 Lancaster St, POB 562, Banjul; tel. 228094.

CHRISTIANITY

The Gambia Christian Council: POB 27, Banjul; tel. and fax 392092; telex 2290; f. 1966; six mems (churches and other Christian bodies); Chair. Rev. JOHN A. STEDMAN (Chair. and Gen. Supt of the Methodist Church of The Gambia); Sec.-Gen. HANNAH ACY PETERS.

The Anglican Communion

The diocese of The Gambia, which includes Senegal and Cape Verde, forms part of the Church of the Province of West Africa. The Metropolitan of the Province is the Archbishop of West Africa. There are about 1,500 adherents in The Gambia.

Bishop of The Gambia: Rt Rev. SOLOMON TILEWA JOHNSON, Bishop's Court, POB 51, Banjul; tel. 227405; telex 2203; fax 229312.

The Roman Catholic Church

The Gambia comprises a single diocese, directly responsible to the Holy See. At 31 December 1992 there were an estimated 21,400 adherents in the country (about 2.6% of the total population). The diocese administers a development organization (Caritas, The Gambia), and runs 63 schools and training centres. The Bishop of Banjul is a member of the Inter-territorial Catholic Bishops' Conference of The Gambia, Liberia and Sierra Leone (based in Freetown, Sierra Leone).

Bishop of Banjul: Rt Rev. MICHAEL J. CLEARY, Bishop's House, POB 165, Banjul; tel. 393437; fax 390998.

Other Christian Churches

Methodist Church: POB 288, Banjul; f. 1821; tel. 227425; Chair. and Gen. Supt Rev. K. JOHN A. STEDMAN; Sec. Rev. TITUS K. A. PRATT.

The Press

Publication of newspapers and journals by political organizations was officially suspended following the July 1994 *coup d'état*.

The Daily Observer: PMB 131, Banjul; tel. 496608; fax 496878; f. 1992; daily; independent; Man. Dir KENNETH Y. BEST.

Foroyaa (Freedom): Bundunka Kunda, POB 2306, Serrekunda; publ. by the PDOIS; Editors HALIFA SALLAH, SAM SARR, SIDIA JATTA.

The Gambia Onward: 48 Grant St, Banjul; Editor RUDOLPH ALLEN.

The Gambia Outlook: 29 Grant St, Banjul; Editor M. B. JONES.

The Gambia Weekly: 14 Hagan St, Banjul; tel. and fax 227230; telex 2204; f. 1943; govt bulletin; Editor A. F. SAGNIA; circ. 500.

The Gambian: 60 Lancaster St, Banjul; Editor NGAING THOMAS.

The Gambian Times: 21 OAU Blvd, POB 698, Banjul; tel. 445; f. 1981; fortnightly; publ. by the PPP; Editor MOMODOU GAYE.

The Nation: People's Press, 3 Boxbar Rd, POB 334, Banjul; fortnightly; Editor W. DIXON-COLLEY.

Newsmonth: Banjul; f. 1993; weekly; Editor BARBUCARR GAYE.

The Point: Banjul; f. 1991; weekly.

The Toiler: 31 OAU Blvd, POB 698, Banjul; Editor PA MODOU FALL.

The Worker: 6 Albion Place, POB 508, Banjul; publ. by the Gambia Labour Union; Editor M. M. CEESAY.

PRESS ORGANIZATION

Press Council: Banjul; f. 1991; comprises a president (nominated by the Minister of Information and Tourism) and 10 other appointed members, all of whom serve for a period of three years; charged with preparing a new press code, considering charges of defamation, ordering the publication of apologies to aggrieved persons or institutions, facilitating a 'right of reply' for such parties, and imposing fines where appropriate.

NEWS AGENCIES

Gambia News Agency (GAMNA): Information Office, 14 Hagan St, Banjul; tel. 226621; telex 2204; fax 227230; Dir EBRIMA SAGNIA.

Foreign Bureau

Agence France-Presse (AFP): 14 Hagan St, Banjul; tel. 228873; Correspondent DEYDA HYDARA.

Associated Press (USA) and Inter Press Service (Italy) are also represented in The Gambia.

Publisher

Government Printer: MacCarthy Sq., Banjul; tel. 227399; telex 2204.

Radio and Television

In 1991, according to UNESCO estimates, there were some 150,000 radio receivers in use. There is no national television service, but transmissions can be received from Senegal. A programme for the modernization of the Gambian telecommunications system, with financial assistance from France, was inaugurated in 1985, and, upon completion (scheduled for 1992), was expected to facilitate the development of a national television service.

Radio Gambia: Mile 7, Banjul; tel. 95101; telex 2204; f. 1962; non-commercial govt service of information, education and entertainment; broadcasts c. 14 hours daily in English, Mandinka, Wolof, Fula, Jola, Serer and Serahuli; Dir ABDOULIE A. NJIE (acting).

Radio 1 FM; Fajara; f. 1990; private station broadcasting FM music programmes to the Banjul area; Dirs GEORGE CHRISTENSEN, VICKIE CHRISTENSEN.

Radio Syd: POB 279/280, Banjul; tel. and fax 226490; commercial station broadcasting 20 hours a day, mainly music; programmes in English, French, Spanish, Wolof, Mandinka, Fula, Jola and Serahuli; also tourist information in Swedish; Dir CONSTANCE WADNER ENHÖRNING.

Finance

(cap. = capital; res = reserves; dep. = deposits; m. = million; brs = branches; amounts in dalasi)

BANKING

Central Bank

Central Bank of The Gambia: 1–2 Buckle St, Banjul; tel. 228103; telex 2218; fax 226969; f. 1971; bank of issue; cap. and res 4.0m., dep. 917.6m. (June 1992); Gov. ABDOU A. B. NJIE; Gen. Man. M. C. BAJO.

Other Banks

Continent Bank Ltd: 61 Buckle St, POB 142, Banjul; tel. 226986; telex 2257; fax 229711; f. 1990; privately-owned; cap. 4m. (Dec. 1992); Chair. Dr MUHAMMAD NADER BAYZID; Man. Dir Alhaji ABDOU A. FAAL.

Meridien BIAO Bank Gambia Ltd: 3–4 Buckle St, POB 1018, Banjul; tel. 225777; telex 2382; fax 225781; f. 1992 (acquired certain assets of The Gambia Commercial and Development Bank); wholly-owned subsidiary of Meridien BIAO SA (Luxembourg); cap. 12.5m.; Chair. R. K. Kontchou; Man. Dir J. K. Donnan; 3 brs.

Standard Chartered Bank Gambia Ltd: 8 Buckle St, POB 259, Banjul; tel. 228681; telex 2210; fax 227714; f. 1978; 75% owned by Standard Chartered Bank Africa PLC (UK), 25% by private Gambian interests; cap. and res 24.8m., dep. 490.2m. (Dec. 1993); Chair. Dr Peter John N'Dow; Man. Dir C. I. Buchanan; 3 brs.

INSURANCE

Capital Insurance Co Ltd: 22 Anglesea St, POB 485, Banjul; tel. 228544; telex 2320; fax 229219; f. 1986; Man. Dir Joseph C. Fye.

The Gambia National Insurance Co Ltd: 6 OAU Blvd, POB 750, Banjul; tel. 228412; telex 2268; f. 1979; Man. Dir Kawsu K. Darbo.

Greater Alliance Insurance Co: 10 Nelson Mandela St, Banjul; tel. 227839; telex 2245; fax 226687; f. 1989.

Senegambia Insurance Co Ltd: 7 Nelson Mandela St, POB 880, Banjul; tel. 228866; telex 2314; fax 226820; f. 1984; Man. Dir Alhaji Babou A. M. Ceesay; Gen. Man. Fye K. Ceesay.

Trade and Industry

CHAMBER OF COMMERCE

Gambia Chamber of Commerce and Industry: 78 Wellington St, POB 33, Banjul; tel. 765; f. 1961; Exec. Sec. Pierre W. F. N'Jie.

GOVERNMENT REGULATORY BODIES

National Environmental Agency (NEA): 5 Fitzgerald St, Banjul; tel. 228056; fax 229701; Dir Ndey-Isatou Njie.

National Investment Board (NIB): Banjul; Chief Exec. Abdoulai Touray.

National Trading Corporation of The Gambia Ltd (NTC): 1–3 Wellington St, POB 61, Banjul; tel. 228395; telex 2252; f. 1973; transfer to private ownership pending in 1993; Chair. and Man. Dir Momodou Cham; 15 brs.

EMPLOYERS' ASSOCIATION

Gambia Employers' Association: POB 333, Banjul; f. 1961; Vice-Chair. G. Madi; Sec. P. W. F. N'Jie.

MAJOR COMPANIES

Banjul Breweries Ltd: POB 830, Kombo Saint Mary, Banjul; tel. 392566; telex 2244; fax 392266; f. 1975; owned by Brauhaase (Germany); 160 employees.

CFAO (Gambia): Banjul; general merchants; Chair. R. P. Couerbe; Man. H. Berge; 100 employees.

Chellaram Group (Gambia) Ltd: POB 275, Banjul; tel. 392912; telex 2240; fax 392910; importers and general merchants, bottling of soft drinks; Man. Dir Mahesh T. Gopalaney; 150 employees.

Gambia Oilseeds Processing and Marketing Co Ltd: Marina Foreshore, Banjul; tel. 227572; telex 2205; fax 228037; assumed 'core' assets of The Gambia Produce Marketing Board in 1993.

The Gambia River Transport Co Ltd: 61 Wellington St, POB 215, Banjul; tel. 228490; river transport of groundnuts and general cargo; Man. Dir. Lamin Juwara; 200 employees.

S. Madi (Gambia) Ltd: 10c Nelson Mandela St, POB 225/226, Banjul; tel. 227372; telex 2209; fax 226192; general merchants, garage operators, agents for Lloyd's of London; Man. Dir A. B. Dandeh-N'Jie.

Maurel and Prom: 22 Buckle St Banjul; telex 2309; fax 228942; general merchants; Man. J. Eschenlohr.

The Milky Way: 4 Wellington St, POB 95, Banjul; tel. 227378; telex 2227; f. 1983; general merchants; Mans Kamal Melki, Nawal Melki, Boundia S. Dibba, Jere Sanyang.

Utilities Holding Corporation (UHC): NIB Bldg, Independence Dr, POB 609, Banjul; telex 2302; fax 228260; fmrly The Gambia Utilities Corpn, transferred to private ownership in 1993; distribution of electricity and water; Man. Dir Shola Joiner; 450 employees.

Zingli Manufacturing Co Ltd: Kanifing Industrial Estate, POB 2402, Serrekunda; tel. 392282; telex 2291; mfrs of corrugated iron and wire.

TRADE UNIONS

Gambia Labour Union: 6 Albion Place, POB 508, Banjul; tel. 641; f. 1935; 25,000 mems; Pres. B. B. Kebbeh; Gen. Sec. Mohamed Ceesay.

Gambia Workers' Confederation: Banjul; f. 1958 as The Gambia Workers' Union, present name adopted in 1985; govt recognition was withdrawn between 1977–85; Sec.-Gen. Pa Modou Fall.

The Gambia Trades Union Congress: POB 307, Banjul; Sec.-Gen. Sam Thorpe.

Transport

Gambia Public Transport Corporation: Factory St, Kanifing Industrial Estate, POB 801, Kanifing; tel. 392230; telex 2243; fax 392454; f. 1979; operates road transport and ferry services; Chair. Kekoto B. S. Maane; Man. Dir Ismailla Ceesay.

RAILWAYS

There are no railways in The Gambia.

ROADS

In 1990 there were 2,386 km of roads in The Gambia. Of this total, 756 km were main roads, and 453 km were secondary roads. Only 32% of the road network was paved in that year, rendering some roads impassable in the rainy season. The South Bank Trunk Road links Banjul with the Trans-Gambia Highway, which intersects it at Mansakonko. The South Bank Trunk Road is bituminized as far as Basse, about 386 km from Banjul. The North Bank Trunk Road connects Barra with Georgetown. A road linking Banjul and Serrekunda was completed in early 1990. The construction of a road linking Lamin Koto with Passimas, funded by the Gambian Government, the Arab Bank for Economic Development in Africa, the Islamic Development Bank and the OPEC Fund for International Development, began in early 1993.

SHIPPING

The River Gambia is well suited to navigation. The port of Banjul receives about 300 ships annually, and there are intermittent sailings to and from North Africa, the Mediterranean and the Far East. In early 1994 the African Development Bank approved a loan of US $22m. in support of a project (the total cost of which was estimated at $33m.) for the expansion of port facilities at Banjul. A weekly river service is maintained between Banjul and Basse, 390 km above Banjul, and a ferry connects Banjul with Barra. Construction of a barrage across the river at Balingho is planned. Small ocean-going vessels can reach Kaur, 190 km above Banjul, throughout the year.

Gambia Ports Authority: Wellington St, POB 617, Banjul; tel. 227266; telex 2235; fax 227268; transfer to private ownership pending in 1993; Man. Dir Alhaji O. B. Cham.

The Gambia Shipping Agencies Ltd: Wellington St, Banjul; tel. 227432; telex 2202; fax 227929; shipping agents and forwarders; Man. Sten C. Hedemann; 30 employees.

The **Gambia River Basin Development Organization** (Organisation de mise en valeur du fleuve Gambie), a jt project with Senegal, Guinea and Guinea-Bissau to develop the river and its basin, was f. in 1978 and is based in Dakar, Senegal (see p. 123).

CIVIL AVIATION

There is an international airport at Yundum, 27 km from Banjul. Facilities at Yundum have been upgraded by the US National Aeronautics and Space Administration (NASA), to enable the airport to serve as an emergency landing site for space shuttle vehicles.

Gambia Airways: City Terminal, 68–69 Wellington St, POB 535, Banjul; tel. 226733; telex 2214; f. 1964; 60% state-owned, 40% owned by British Airways; operates regional services and weekly flights to London (UK); sole handling agent at Yundum, sales agent; Man. Dir Salifu M. Jallow.

Tourism

Tourists are attracted by The Gambia's beaches and also by its abundant birdlife. According to provisional figures, 63,131 tourists visited The Gambia in the 1991/92 season (July–June). Tourists come mainly from the United Kingdom (54.4% of the total in 1988/89), Sweden, France and Germany. In 1987/88 there were 4,500 hotel beds in resort areas. A major expansion of tourism facilities was under way in the early 1990s, despite a decline in the sector caused by the world-wide economic recession and by the 1990–91 crisis in the region of the Persian (Arabian) Gulf.

Ministry of Information and Tourism: The Quadrangle, Banjul; tel. 228496; telex 2204; Dir of Tourism SHEIK NYANG.

Defence

In June 1993 the Gambian armed forces comprised 800 men. A bilateral military co-operation agreement, under which Nigeria provided 70 military advisers (including the commanding officer) of the Gambian armed forces, came into operation in early 1992. Negotiations between the new Gambian military administration and the Nigerian authorities regarding the future of this accord were in progress in mid-1994. Military service is mainly voluntary.

Defence Expenditure: Estimated at D20.1m. in 1988/89.

Commander of the Army: Col LAWAN GWADABE.

Education

Primary education, beginning at eight years of age, is free but not compulsory and lasts for six years. On completion of this period, pupils may sit an entrance examination, leading either to five years of secondary high school or to four years of secondary technical school. The country's eleven high schools offer an academic-based curriculum, leading to examinations at the 'Ordinary' level of the General Certificate of Education (GCE) of the West African Examinations Council (WAEC). Two high schools provide two-year courses, leading to GCE 'Advanced' level examinations. In 1989/90 a total of 18,118 candidates from The Gambia were examined by the WAEC. Gambia College, at Brikama, offers post-secondary courses in teacher training, agriculture and health; other post-secondary education is provided by technical training schools. University education must be obtained abroad. In 1991 52% of children in the relevant age-group were enrolled at primary schools (boys 61%; girls 42%). Secondary enrolment in that year included only 15% of children in the appropriate age-group (boys 20%; girls 10%). According to UNESCO estimates, adult illiteracy in 1990 averaged 72.8% (males 61.0%; females 84.0%). A long-term restructuring of the education system was undertaken in 1990. In 1977 Koranic studies were introduced at all stages of education, and many children attend Koranic schools (daara). Central government expenditure on education in 1991/92 was D78m. (12.9% of total budget expenditure in that year).

Bibliography

Bridges, R. C. (Ed.). *Senegambia.* Aberdeen University African Studies Group, 1974.

Dieke, P. U. C. *Tourism in The Gambia: Some Issues in Development Policy*, in World Development, Vol. 21 No. 2, Oxford, Pergamon Press, 1993.

Gailey, H. A. *A History of The Gambia.* London, Routledge and Kegan Paul, 1964.

Historical Dictionary of The Gambia. Metuchen, NJ, Scarecrow Press, 1975.

Gamble, D. P. *A General Bibliography of The Gambia.* Boston, G. K. Hall and Co, 1979.

The Gambia, World Bibliographical Series, Vol. 91. Oxford, Clio Press, 1988.

Gray, J. M. *A History of the Gambia.* New York, Barnes and Noble, and London, Cass, 1966.

Harrison Church, R. J. *West Africa.* 8th Edn, London, Longman, 1979.

Hughes, A. 'From Colonialism to Confederation: the Gambian Experience of Independence 1965–1982', in Cohen, R. (Ed.), *African Islands and Enclaves.* London, Sage Publications, 1983.

The Senegambian Confederation, in Contemporary Review, February 1984.

(Ed.). *The Gambia: Studies in Society and Politics.* University of Birmingham Centre of West African Studies, 1991.

The Collapse of the Senegambian Confederation, in The Journal of Commonwealth and Comparative Politics, Vol. 30 No. 2, London, Frank Cass, 1992.

Jarrett, H. R. *A Geography of Sierra Leone and Gambia.* Harlow, Longman, 1981.

People's Progressive Party Special Editorial Commission. *The Voice of the People, the Story of the PPP, 1959–1989.* Banjul, The Gambia Communications Agency and Barou-Ueli Enterprises, 1992.

Quinn, C. A. *Mandingo Kingdoms of the Senegambia.* Evanston, IL, Northwestern University Press, 1972.

Radelet, S. *Reform without Revolt: The Political Economy of Economic Reform in The Gambia*, in World Development, Oxford, Pergamon Press, Vol. 28 No. 8, 1992.

Rice, B. *Enter Gambia: the Birth of an Improbable Nation.* London, Angus and Robertson, 1968.

Rimmer, D. *The Economies of West Africa.* London, Weidenfeld and Nicolson, 1984.

Robson, P. *Integration, Development and Equity: Economic Integration in West Africa.* London, Allen and Unwin, 1983.

Sallah, T. M. *Economics and Politics in The Gambia*, in The Journal of Modern African Studies, Vol. 28 No. 4, 1990.

Tomkinson, M. *Gambia.* London, Michael Tomkinson Publishing, 1987.

Wiseman, J. A. *Democracy in Black Africa: Survival and Revival.* New York, Paragon House, 1990.

Wright, D. R. *The Early History of Niumi.* Ohio University Center for International Studies, 1977.

GHANA

Physical and Social Geography

E. A. BOATENG

PHYSICAL FEATURES

Structurally and geologically, the Republic of Ghana exhibits many of the characteristics of sub-Saharan Africa, with its ancient rocks and extensive plateau surfaces marked by prolonged sub-aerial erosion. About half of the surface area is composed of Pre-Cambrian metamorphic and igneous rocks, most of the remainder consisting of a platform of Palaeozoic sediments believed to be resting on the older rocks. These sediments occupy a vast area in the north-central part of the country and form the Voltaic basin. Surrounding this basin on all sides, except along the east, is a highly dissected peneplain of Pre-Cambrian rocks at an average of 150–300 m above sea-level but containing several distinct ranges of up to 600 m. Along the eastern edge of the Voltaic basin and extending right down to the sea near Accra is a narrow zone of highly folded Pre-Cambrian rocks forming the Akwapim-Togo ranges. These ranges rise to 300–900 m above sea-level, and contain the highest points in Ghana. Continuing northwards across Togo and Benin, they form one of west Africa's major relief features, the Togo-Atakora range.

The south-east corner of the country, below the Akwapim-Togo ranges, is occupied by the Accra-Ho-Keta plains, which are underlain by the oldest of the Pre-Cambrian series (known as the Dahomeyan) and contain extensive areas of gneiss, of which the basic varieties weather to form heavy but agriculturally useful soils. Extensive areas of young rocks, formed between the Tertiary and Recent ages, are found only in the broad delta of the Volta in the eastern part of the Accra plains, and in the extreme south-west corner of the country along the Axim coast; while in the intervening littoral zone patches of Devonian sediments combine with the rocks of the Pre-Cambrian peneplain to produce a coastline of sandy bays and rocky promontories.

Most of the country's considerable mineral wealth, consisting mainly of gold, diamonds, manganese and bauxite, is associated with the older Pre-Cambrian rocks, although there are indications that petroleum may be available in commercial quantities in some of the younger sedimentaries. For a brief period in the 1980s actual exploitation, in relatively small quantities, of offshore deposits took place at Saltpond.

The drainage is dominated by the Volta system, which occupies the Voltaic basin and includes the vast artificial lake of 8,502 sq km formed behind the hydroelectric dam at Akosombo. A second dam is sited at Kpong, 8 km downstream from Akosombo. Most of the other rivers in Ghana, such as the Pra, Birim, Densu, Ayensu and Ankobra, flow between the southern Voltaic or Kwahu plateau and the sea. Most are of considerable local importance as sources of drinking water, but are hardly employed for irrigation purposes.

CLIMATE AND VEGETATION

Climatic conditions are determined by the interaction of two principal airstreams: the hot, dry, tropical, continental air mass or harmattan from the north-east, and the moist, relatively cool, maritime air mass or monsoon from the south-west across the Atlantic. In the southern part of the country, where the highest average annual rainfall (of 1,270–2,100 mm) occurs, there are two rainy seasons (April–July and September–November), while in the north, with annual averages of 1,100–1,270 mm, rainfall occurs in only a single season between April and September, followed by a long dry season dominated by the harmattan. There is much greater uniformity as regards mean temperatures, which average 26°–29°C. These temperatures, coupled with the equally high relative humidities, which fall significantly only during the harmattan, tend to produce oppressive conditions, relieved only by the relative drop in temperature at night, especially in the north, and the local incidence of land and sea breezes near the coast.

Vegetation in Ghana is determined mainly by climate and soil conditions. The area of heavy annual rainfall broken by one or two relatively short dry seasons, to be found in the south-west portion of the country and along the Akwapim-Togo ranges, is covered with evergreen forest in the wetter portions and semi-deciduous forest in the drier portions, while the area of rather lower rainfall, occurring in a single peak in the northern two-thirds of the country and the anomalously dry area around Accra, are covered with savannah and scrub. Prolonged farming activities and timber exploitation have reduced the original closed forest vegetation of some 82,000 sq km to about 24,000 sq km, while in the savannah areas prolonged cultivation and bush burning have also caused serious degradation of the vegetation. Truly edaphic vegetation types are found mostly in swampy or estuarine areas and on isolated lateritic hardpans in the savannah zone.

POPULATION

Ghana covers an area of 238,537 sq km (92,100 sq miles). The March 1984 census recorded a population of 12,296,081, giving an approximate density of 51.5 inhabitants per sq km. During 1985–92 the population increased by an annual average of 3.3%, and, in mid-1991, according to official estimates, was 15,400,000, with a density of 64.6 inhabitants per sq km. The high rate of population growth, together with the influx of large numbers—mostly youth from the rural areas into the urban centres—coupled with a virtually stagnant economy and the lack of adequate employment openings, has created serious social and political problems. In view of these demographic trends, the government has initiated a campaign of family planning and population control, and aims to improve living standards through increased economic development. The highest densities occur in the urban and cocoa-farming areas in the southern part of the country, and also in the extreme north-eastern corner, where intensive compound farming is practised.

Altogether there are no less than 75 different languages and dialects, each more or less associated with a distinct ethnic group. The largest of these groups are the Akan, Mole-Dagbani, Ewe and the Ga-Adangbe, which in 1960 formed respectively 44.1%, 15.9%, 13.0% and 8.3% of the population. Any divisive tendencies which might have arisen from this situation have been absent, largely as a result of governmental policies; however, a distinction can be made between the southern peoples, who have come most directly and longest under the influence of modern European life and the Christian religion, and the northern peoples, whose traditional modes of life and religion have undergone relatively little change, owing mainly to their remoteness from the coast. One of the most potent unifying forces has been the adoption of English as the official national language, although it is augmented officially by some five major local languages.

Recent History

T. C. McCASKIE

Revised for this edition by the Editor

Longstanding protest within the Gold Coast against British rule, chiefly expressed by the educated professional classes, resulted in the formation in 1947 of the United Gold Coast Convention (UGCC), led by a lawyer, Dr J. B. Danquah. In 1949 the secretary of the UGCC, Dr Kwame Nkrumah, formed the more radical Convention People's Party (CPP), which demanded immediate self-government. In 1950 the British authorities sentenced Nkrumah to a term of imprisonment, but later that year permitted the drafting of a constitution, which provided for indigenous ministerial government under the British crown. A general election, which took place in 1951, was won by the CPP, and in the following year Nkrumah became prime minister; subsequent elections in 1954 and 1956 were also won by the CPP. Ghana was formed as the result of a UN-supervised plebiscite in May 1956, when the British-administered part of Togoland, a UN Trust Territory, voted to join the Gold Coast in an independent state. On 6 March 1957 Ghana was granted independence within the Commonwealth, becoming the first British dependency in sub-Saharan Africa to attain independence under majority rule.

NKRUMAH AND THE CPP

Nkrumah (who became prime minister of the new state) espoused 'African socialism' and maintained close relations wih the USSR and its allies, while remaining economically dependent on Western countries. In 1957 the opponents of the CPP merged to form the United Party (UP), led by Dr Kofi Busia, a former university professor. The government introduced repressive measures, in particular the Preventive Detention Act (1958), which allowed the imprisonment of opponents without trial for five years. In accordance with a referendum held earlier in the year, Ghana became a republic on 1 July 1960, with Nkrumah as executive president. In 1964 Ghana officially became a 'socialist single-party state'.

Following widespread discontent at the country's economic difficulties, and at alleged corruption within the CPP, however, Nkrumah was deposed by the army and police on 24 February 1966. The CPP was abolished and replaced by a National Liberation Council (NLC), which comprised four army officers and four police officers: its chairman was Gen. Joseph Ankrah. (He was replaced in April 1969, following disputes within the NLC, by Brig.—later Lt-Gen.—Akwasi Afrifa.) After assuming power, the NLC declared its intention of restoring civilian rule: it established commissions of inquiry into the alleged crimes of the CPP administration, and formed a constituent assembly to draft a new constitution. The official ban on party politics was removed in May 1969, and a general election took place in August. The Progress Party (PP), led by Busia, secured 105 of the 140 seats in the new national assembly, and Busia assumed office as prime minister on 1 October. A three-man commission, comprising members of the former NLC, held presidential power until 31 August 1970, when Edward Akufo-Addo, a lawyer, took office as a non-executive civilian president.

ACHEAMPONG AND THE NRC

The Busia government proved unable to resolve Ghana's economic problems; increasing hardship prompted renewed discontent, while the PP was also widely perceived as corrupt. On 13 January 1972 the armed forces again seized power, under the leadership of Lt-Col (later Gen.) Ignatius Kutu Acheampong. A National Redemption Council (NRC), comprising senior army and police officers, assumed control of the country, and political parties were once again banned. The NRC subsequently achieved a modest improvement in Ghana's economic situation (principally by the restriction of unnecessary imports and the encouragement of agricultural production, as part of its stated policy of self-reliance). It also attempted to decentralize the government, establishing 58 new district councils in 1974. Following the NRC's seizure of power, several abortive coup attempts were made by members of the armed forces or supporters of the banned political parties.

In response to increasing rivalry within the NRC, Acheampong replaced it in October 1975 with a seven-member Supreme Military Council (SMC). In 1976 he proposed the formation of a 'union government' (UNIGOV), which would comprise a tripartite power-sharing arrangement between the armed forces, the police and civilians, without political parties. In July 1977, despite strong opposition to the plans from lawyers and other professional groups, and indications of dissent within the armed forces, the SMC announced a timetable for relinquishing power, stating that a referendum on the formation of UNIGOV would be conducted in March 1978 and would be followed by a general election in June 1979. The referendum, which took place in March 1978, as scheduled, endorsed the proposed system by 55.6% of votes cast; however, the result was widely believed to have been obtained by malpractice. The Ghana Bar Association subsequently staged a strike in protest at the alleged electoral fraud. In April selected opposition groups were proscribed; by May nearly 300 opponents of the government had been placed in preventive detention. In July Lt-Gen. (later Gen.) Frederick Akuffo, the chief of the defence staff, assumed power in a bloodless coup. Akuffo subsequently dismissed all but three members of the SMC, and a number of leading officials of state agencies (including the Cocoa Marketing Board). Shortly afterwards, Acheampong was placed under arrest.

THE FIRST RAWLINGS COUP AND THE LIMANN GOVERNMENT

On 1 January 1979 the ban on the formation of political associations was ended, and 16 parties were registered, in preparation for the general election, which was still scheduled for June. In May, however, junior military officers staged an unsuccessful coup attempt. Flight-Lt Jerry Rawlings, the alleged leader of the conspirators, was imprisoned, but was subsequently released by other officers. On 4 June he and his associates successfully seized power, amid great popular acclaim. They subsequently established an Armed Forces Revolutionary Council (AFRC), headed by Rawlings, and initiated a campaign to eradicate corruption. In the same month Acheampong, Akuffo, Afrifa and other senior officers were convicted on charges of corruption, and executed.

The AFRC indicated that its assumption of power was temporary, and the general election, which took place in June 1979, as scheduled, was contested by five parties: the Action Congress Party (ACP); the People's National Party (PNP); the Popular Front Party (PFP); the Social Democratic Front (SDF); and the United National Convention (UNC). The PNP secured 71 of the 140 seats, and agreed to form a governing coalition with the UNC, which obtained 13 seats. The leader of the PNP, Dr Hilla Limann, was elected to the presidency, and was inaugurated on 24 September.

Almost immediately serious disagreements developed within the ruling coalition and within the PNP itself. In October 1980 the UNC ended the alliance with the PNP, which subsequently retained a majority of only one seat in the legislature. In September 1981 the other parties represented in the legislature (including the UNC) amalgamated to form the All People's Party, electing the leader of the PFP, Victor Owusu, as their leader. Measures implemented by the government in an attempt to stimulate the economy, proved unsuccessful, and public discontent was manifested in widespread strikes and riots over the escalating price of food. In March and May 1980 and February 1981 several attempts to seize power by members of the armed forces were reported. A second coup by Rawlings, who retained enormous personal popularity, was widely anticipated.

THE SECOND RAWLINGS COUP AND THE PNDC

On 31 December 1981 Rawlings seized power for the second time. The constitution was abolished, parliament dissolved, and civilian political parties proscribed. Rawlings assumed chairmanship of a Provisional National Defence Council (PNDC), comprising four military personnel and three civilians. Limann and a number of prominent members of the PNP were imprisoned or placed in preventive detention. The PNDC subsequently appointed a national administration.

In direct contrast to the events of June 1979, Rawlings expressed no intention of restoring power to civilian politicians; instead, the PNDC decided to implement measures to 'democratize' political decision-making and to decentralize power. In March 1982 city and district councils were replaced by People's Defence Committees (PDC), in an attempt to create mass participation at the local level in the 'revolution' (as the PNDC described the coup), and to create and foster public awareness and vigilance. The PDC were to form the basic structure of the new government.

The 'democratization' of the army led to the creation of factions, and to the consequent threat of constant instability; in March 1982 a number of military personnel staged an abortive coup against the PNDC. By mid-1982 the armed forces were increasingly divided along ethnic lines, with the Ewes supporting Rawlings, and the majority of northerners backing Sgt Alolga Akata-Pore (a member of the PNDC). In October erroneous rumours that Rawlings had been killed in armed ethnic clashes between soldiers at Burma Camp, in Accra, resulted in an increase in ethnic confrontation and policy disagreements, and on 22 November the chief of the defence staff, Brig. Joseph Nunoo-Mensah, resigned, publicly voicing his disagreement with the policies of the PNDC. On the following day soldiers staged a coup attempt, which was suppressed by troops loyal to the PNDC. Akata-Pore was arrested, but other conspirators, together with Chris Bukari-Atim (a member of the PNDC), managed to escape to neighbouring Togo, from where, together with groups based in the United Kingdom, they continued to plan to overthrow Rawlings.

In February and March 1983 there were minor attempts to overthrow the government, and widespread rumours of numerous other minor disturbances. On 19 June Ghanaian military exiles from Togo, led by Sgt Malik (former bodyguard to Nunoo-Mensah), infiltrated Accra and released more than 50 prisoners from jail; many of the Togo-based exiles and the freed prisoners had been participants in the attempted coup of 23 November 1982. They briefly seized the Ghana Broadcasting Corporation, from where they broadcast a statement. Troops loyal to Rawlings quickly suppressed the coup, but many of the leading conspirators escaped. In August the perpetrators of the coup attempts of 23 November and 19 June were put on trial (many of them *in absentia*). Of the 20 who were sentenced to death, only five were actually in custody; four of these were executed on 13 August. In March 1984 three of the leading conspirators were apprehended and executed.

In June 1983, in the aftermath of the coup attempt, the Ghana People's Solidarity Organization (GHAPSO) demanded the abolition of the judicial system, on the grounds that it was class-based and undemocratic. In October the PNDC reprimanded PDC members for using relatives in the armed forces to exact 'judicial' retribution from selected individuals. In the same month the PNDC disciplined PDC units in the Western Region for exceeding their authority. The moderation of the PNDC's position was attributed, in part, to the kidnap and murder of three high court judges in June 1982; a number of army personnel were implicated in the incident.

The process of 'democratization' also affected Ghana's student community; by May 1983, university students, initially supporters of Rawlings, were engaged in violent protests regarding a number of issues: discontent with the apparent ineffectiveness of the government's economic policies; demands for a return to civilian rule; and resentment at the government's links with Libya and Cuba. Major clashes between workers and students ensued, and the PNDC closed the universities and converted them into training schools for revolutionary cadres. Despite an improvement in the economic situation during 1984, demands by the Trade Union Congress (TUC) for better wages and living standards became more insistent. The universities were reopened in March, amid concern about their much-depleted staffing levels and sources of funding. Dissent continued throughout the year, between the Ghana Bar Association (GBA) and the tribunal structure of the PNDC, over issues of ultimate national judicial authority, with much of the argument devolving upon the question of 'political' detainees.

In 1985 adverse economic conditions prompted renewed unrest. In March of that year the TUC protested vehemently against low wages and general economic policy. In the same month students strongly opposed proposals that they might assist the economy by paying for their education. Rawlings subsequently urged the creation of more efficient and nationally relevant universities. In May a conference of the National Union of Ghanaian Students (NUGS) criticized the PNDC, its fiscal policies and its record on human rights. Fraud and corruption were also endemic; in May three people were executed for the embezzlement of substantial sums from the Ghana Commercial Bank.

During 1985 elements of the army, with periodic support from groups outside the country, were reported to be conspiring against the PNDC. In February a number of alleged plotters were arrested in Kumasi (Ashanti), and were accused of planning to assassinate Rawlings. Later that month a coup plot was detected in the army, and two majors and three sergeants were subsequently tried in camera. Five conspirators, allegedly linked to dissidents in Togo, were executed in May. In September Maj.-Gen. (later Lt-Gen.) Arnold Quainoo, the c-in-c of the armed forces, and Brig. (later Maj.-Gen.) Winston M. Mensa-Wood, the commandant of the military academy training school, were appointed to the PNDC, which was expanded from eight to 10 members.

INTERNAL AFFAIRS

The PNDC became increasingly preoccupied with domestic security in 1986 and 1987, possibly as a result of the dissident political activity abroad. In March 1986 a number of people were tried for involvement in a conspiracy to overthrow the government by dissident Ghanaians; several death sentences were subsequently carried out. In August Victor Owusu, the leader of the disbanded PFP and a former minister and presidential candidate, was arrested for alleged subversion. In June 1987 the PNDC announced further arrests in connection with an alleged conspiracy to overthrow the government. Seven further arrests took place in November; on this occasion the detainees included former officials of the PNDC.

Various administrative reforms were carried out by the PNDC from late 1984 to 1988. In December 1984 the PDC were redesignated Committees for the Defence of the Revolution (CDR). In April 1986 there was an extensive review of the judiciary, resulting in the summary retirement of some judges for alleged incompetence and corruption. In December Rawlings announced that the PNDC was to seek a national mandate through district assembly elections, scheduled for mid-1987. It was envisaged that each district assembly would have an elected chairman, while the district secretary would continue to be appointed by the PNDC and would retain responsibility for routine administration. In July 1987, however, district council elections were postponed until the final quarter of 1988, and it was announced that the ban on political parties was to remain. In April there was an extensive government reshuffle, in which a new post to co-ordinate the work of the CDR was created, and secretaries for information, political programmes and for the national commission for women and development were appointed. During 1988 the number of districts was increased from 65 to 110, and in October these were grouped into three electoral zones.

The district assembly elections took place in three stages, between December 1988 and February 1989. More than 60% of the registered electorate voted, a far higher percentage than in any comparable ballot for many years. The PNDC reserved one-third of seats for its own nominees, and retained the power to scrutinize and disqualify individual candidates, although it was envisaged that the elected district assemblies would move towards regional representation, and ultimately form a national body which would supersede the PNDC.

However, the envisaged adoption of democratic reforms continued to be threatened by the effects of the grave economic situation. In 1988 the three universities were closed for four months, following a student boycott over subsidies and the proposed introduction of student loans. In December of that year the PNDC discontinued free secondary and university education, and in the following month inaugurated a student loan scheme, provoking considerable student discontent. In addition, the PNDC's attempts to implement economic reforms were impeded by widespread mismanagement and corruption in the commercial sector. In 1989 further controls were imposed on the media; in March of that year newspaper and magazine licences became subject to review under new legislation

In September 1989 an attempted coup took place, led by Maj. Courage Quashigah, a former commander of the military police and a close associate of Rawlings. Quainoo was subsequently dismissed as commander of the armed forces, although he remained a member of the PNDC. (Rawlings himself assumed control of the armed forces until June 1990, when Mensa-Wood was appointed to that post.) Quashigah (who had taken a leading part in suppressing the June 1983 coup attempt) and four other members of the security forces were charged with conspiring to assassinate Rawlings. In November a board of enquiry, which investigated the charges of treason, concluded that most of the conspirators were motivated by personal grievances and ambition. A minor government reshuffle was announced in December, and in January 1990 five further arrests were made in connection with the coup attempt. In August the human rights organization, Amnesty International, criticized the continued detention of Quashigah and six other members of the security forces, and claimed that they were imprisoned for political dissension. Amnesty also expressed concern over the death in custody of one of the alleged conspirators, Flt-Lt Domie.

TRANSITION TO MULTI-PARTYISM

In 1990 there were increasing demands for an end to the ban, imposed by the PNDC, on political activities and associations, and for the abolition of a number of laws, particularly those concerning the detention of suspects. In July of that year, in response to pressure from Western donors to increase democracy in return for a continuation in aid, the PNDC announced that a national commission for democracy (NCD), under the chairmanship of Justice Annah, a member of the PNDC, would organize a series of regional debates, which would review the decentralization process, and consider Ghana's political and economic future. In August, however, a newly-formed political association, the Movement for Freedom and Justice (MFJ), criticized the NCD, claiming that it was too closely associated with the PNDC. In addition, the MFJ demanded the abolition of a number of laws, the release of political prisoners, the end of press censorship, and the imminent restoration of a multi-party system. The PNDC, however, advocated a national consensus, rather than a return to the discredited political system. In September the MFJ accused the PNDC of intimidation, after security forces suppressed its inaugural meeting. Both students and trade unionists voiced support for the MFJ's general objectives. However, the PNDC maintained that it would not permit the emergence of political associations, despite toleration of more generalized political activities.

On 30 December 1990 Rawlings announced proposals for the establishment of a constitution by the end of 1991. The NCD was to present a report on the democratic process with reference to the series of regional debates. The PNDC was to consider the recommendations, and then convene a consultative body to determine constitutional reform. However, the MFJ and other critics of the PNDC protested that no definite schedule for political reform had been presented, and that no criteria had been established for the composition of the proposed consultative body. The MFJ continued to demand the immediate restoration of a multi-party system, while the PNDC maintained that such a model was inappropriate, and accused the MFJ of ignoring the economic constraints on political reform. In late January 1991 two new ministers were appointed in a minor reshuffle of cabinet posts.

In late March 1991 the NCD presented its report on the democratic process, which recommended the election of an executive president for a fixed term, the establishment of a national assembly, and the creation of the post of prime minister. Rawlings announced that the PNDC would consider the report and submit recommendations to the proposed national consultative body, which was to be established in May, and to start work in July. On 10 May, contrary to previous expectations, the PNDC endorsed the restoration of a multi-party system, and approved the NCD's recommendations. It was emphasized, however, that the formation of political associations remained prohibited. The MFJ immediately challenged the veracity of the PNDC's announcement, and the state-controlled press accused the MFJ of planning subversive action. In late May a 260-member consultative assembly was established, which was to review recommendations by a government-appointed committee of constitutional experts. A new constitution was subsequently to be submitted for endorsement by a national referendum.

In June 1991 the government reiterated denials that a number of political prisoners were detained in Ghana, and announced that it had invited Amnesty International to investigate the allegations. In the same month the PNDC announced an amnesty for political exiles, excepting those implicated in acts of subversion against the government. In early August a newly-formed alliance of opposition movements, human rights organizations and trade unions, including the MFJ and the NDM, known as the Co-ordinating Committee of Democratic Forces of Ghana (CCDFG), demanded that a constitutional conference be convened to determine a schedule for the transition to democracy, and that legislation prohibiting political activities be immediately repealed. Later in August the committee submitted a series of recommendations for constitutional reform, which included the establishment of a legislature, a council of state and a national security council. It was proposed that a president, who would also be c-in-c of the armed forces, would be elected by universal suffrage for a four-year term of office; the leader of the party which commanded a legislative majority would be appointed to the post of prime minister. However, the subsequent review of the draft constitution by the consultative assembly was impeded by opposition demands for a boycott, on the grounds that the number of government representatives in the assembly was too high. Two organizations, the GBA and NUGS (which each had one seat in the assembly), refused to attend. In the same month Rawlings announced that presidential and legislative elections would take place in late 1992.

In early December 1991 Rawlings ordered the arrest of the secretary-general of the MFJ, John Ndebugre, for allegedly failing to stand when the national anthem was played. Amnesty International subsequently reiterated claims that a number of prisoners in Ghana were detained for political dissension. In the same month the government announced the establishment of an interim national electoral commission (INEC), which was to assume functions formerly allocated to the NCD: the demarcation of electoral regions, and the supervision of public elections and referenda. In January 1992 the government extended the allocated period for the review of the draft constitution, originally scheduled for completion by the end of 1991, to the end of March 1992, provoking widespread speculation that Rawlings planned to delay the democratic process. In February, however, preparations for the forthcoming multi-party elections commenced; the PNDC subsequently carried out a government reshuffle. In March Rawlings announced a programme for the transition to democracy, which was to be completed on 7 January 1993. The new constitution was to be submitted for endorsement by national referendum on 28 April 1992. Legislation permitting the formation of political associations was to be introduced on 18 May, despite opposition demands that a multi-party system be adopted prior to the referendum. A presidential election was to take place on 3 November, and was to be followed by legislative elections on 8 December. Later in March the government granted an amnesty to 17 prisoners, who had been convicted on charges of alleged subversion, including Quashigah.

At the end of March 1992 the consultative assembly endorsed the majority of the constitutional recommendations, which were subsequently presented for approval by the PNDC. However, the proposed creation of the post of prime minister was rejected by the assembly; executive power was to be vested solely in the president, who would appoint a vice-president. In addition, the draft constitution included a provision that members of the government be exempt from prosecution for acts committed during the PNDC's rule; opposition groups subsequently condemned the legislation, on the grounds that it contravened human rights. At the national referendum held on 28 April, however, the adoption of the draft constitution was approved by 92% of votes cast, with 43.7% of the electorate voting.

In May 1992 the government introduced legislation which ended the ban on the formation of political associations imposed in 1981; political parties were required to apply to INEC for legal recognition. Under the terms of the legislation, however, 21 former political organizations remained proscribed, while emergent parties were not permitted to use the names or slogans of these organizations. Moreover, the permitted amounts of individual monetary contributions to parties were restricted. Later in May Komla A. Gbedemah, a former member of the Nkrumah government, and 28 other prominent opposition figures, applied to the high court to disallow the legislation, which, it was claimed, was biased in favour of the PNDC. However, the high court ruled in favour of INEC, which subsequently began to issue documentation for registration to prospective political parties. At the end of May the government announced that the legislation had been amended to allow INEC to impose a new limit for individual monetary contributions. In the same month it was reported that a large number of people had been killed in clashes between the Gonja and Nawuri ethnic groups in northern Ghana.

In June 1992 a number of political associations emerged, many of which were established by supporters of former politicians; six opposition movements were subsequently granted legal recognition. In the same month a coalition of pro-government organizations, the National Democratic Congress (NDC), was formed to contest the elections on behalf of the PNDC. However, an existing alliance of supporters of Rawlings, known as the Eagle Club, refused to join the NDC, and created its own political association, the Eagle Party of Ghana, subsequently known as the EGLE (Every Ghanaian Living Everywhere) Party. In July Rawlings denied that he was associated with the Eagle Club, and rejected an offer by the EGLE Party to represent it in the presidential election. In August the government promulgated legislation regulating the conducting of the forthcoming elections, which included a stipulation that, if no presidential candidate received more than 50% of votes cast, a second election between the two candidates with the highest number of votes would take place within 21 days.

In September 1992, in accordance with the new constitution, Rawlings retired from the armed forces (although he retained the title of c-in-c of the armed forces in his capacity as head of state), and was subsequently nominated as the presidential candidate of the NDC. (The NDC later formed an electoral coalition with the EGLE Party and the National Convention Party—NCP). A member of the NCP, Kow Nkensen Arkaah, became Rawlings' vice-presidential candidate. Four other political associations presented candidates to contest the presidency: the People's Heritage Party (PHP); the National Independence Party (NIP); the People's National Convention (PNC—which nominated a former president, Dr Hilla Limann); and the New Patriotic Party (NPP). Although the establishment of a united opposition to Rawlings was discussed, the parties failed to achieve agreement, owing, in part, to the apparent conviction of the NPP (which was recognized as the strongest of the movements) that its presidential candidate, Prof. A. A. Boahen, could win unaided against Rawlings.

In preparation for the November 1992 election, INEC divided Ghana into 200 constituencies. Despite controversy over the accuracy of the high number of registered voters, the PNDC, acting through INEC, refused to carry out a revision of the electoral register. However, INEC did arrange for the forthcoming election to be monitored by Commonwealth observers. During the electoral period, Rawlings enacted a number of popular measures, which included, in September, the announcement of substantial wage increases for civil servants and other public sector workers, and, in October, the introduction of legislation that restricted (but did not abolish) the PNDC's right to detain citizens without trial. However, these measures were widely perceived to be electoral bribes, and their popular impact was limited. Later in October the high court dismissed an application by the MFJ for an injunction to prevent Rawlings from contesting the presidential election, on the grounds that he was not a Ghanaian national (his father was Scottish), and that he remained accountable for charges in connection with the coups he had staged. Shortly before the election, large NPP and NDC rallies took place in Kumasi and Accra respectively, while widespread outbreaks of sporadic violence between NPP and NDC supporters were reported.

Less than 48.3% of the registered electorate voted in the presidential election, which took place, as scheduled, on 3 November 1992. Rawlings secured 58.3% of the vote, while Boahen obtained 30.4%, Limann 6.7%, the NIP candidate, Kwabena Darko, 2.8%, and the PHP candidate, Lt-Gen. (retd) E. A. Erskine, 1.7% of votes cast. Rawlings, with more than 50% of the votes cast, was therefore declared the winner. Regional voting patterns confirmed pre-election assumptions: Rawlings—head of the PNDC (which was widely considered to be dominated by the Ewe ethnic group)—gained 93.3% of the vote in the Ewe heartland of the Volta Region, but obtained only 32.9% of the vote in Ashanti, while Boahen, who originated from Shanti, received most support in that region. The Commonwealth observers subsequently declared that the conducting of the election had been both free and fair. However, the opposition parties, led by the NPP, claimed that widespread electoral irregularities had taken place. A curfew was imposed in Kumasi, in Ashanti, following incidents of violence, and rioting by opposition supporters, in which a NDC ward chairman was killed; in addition, a series of explosive devices were detonated in Accra and Tema. The government subsequently rescheduled the legislative elections for 22 December. Later in November a prominent member of the PHP was detained, together with other opposition supporters, on the grounds of complicity in the bombings.

At a rally held in Accra in early December 1992, Boahen announced that the opposition had direct evidence of electoral fraud perpetrated by the government, and that this would be made public in due course. The opposition parties declared, however, that they would not contest the results of the presidential election in court, but that they would boycott the forthcoming elections. Accordingly, the legislative elections (which had been postponed until 29 December) were contested only by the NDC and its allies, the EGLE Party and the NCP. In 23 of the 200 constituencies the single candidate was returned unopposed; 29% of the registered electorate voted in the remaining 177 constituencies. The NDC won 189 of the 200 seats in the parliament, while the NCP secured eight seats, the EGLE Party one seat, and independent candidates two seats. On 7 January 1993 Rawlings was sworn in as president of the Fourth Republic, the PNDC was officially dissolved and the new parliament was inaugurated.

THE FOURTH REPUBLIC

In early January 1993 a number of the severe economic austerity measures, introduced under the 1993 budget, resulted in an immediate increase in transport and supply costs, and food prices. The NPP, the PNC, the NIP and the PHP subsequently formed an alliance, known as the Inter-Party Co-ordinating Committee (ICC), which strongly criticized the budget (widely believed to have been formulated under the terms of the World Bank and the IMF), and announced that it was to act as an official opposition to the government, despite its lack of representation in the parliament. In March Rawlings submitted nominations for members of the cabinet and other ministers for approval by the parliament. In the same month the two main perpetrators of the bombings in November 1992 were fined and sentenced to 10 years' imprisonment. In early

April the NPP published a book, entitled *The Stolen Verdict*, which provided detailed evidence of malpractice perpetrated by the NDC and INEC in the presidential election. On 14 April elections were held for the 10 regional seats in the council of state, and in May a 17-member cabinet (which included a number of members of the former PNDC administration) was sworn in. International approval of the series of election results was apparently indicated by subsequent pledges, undertaken at a meeting of donor nations, of economic assistance for Ghana. However, the constituent parties of the ICC continued to dispute the results of the presidential election. In June Rawlings urged a boycott of products manufactured by companies that supported the opposition. In the same month the supreme court upheld a claim by the NPP that certain existing legislation was in contravention of the constitution. In August the NPP (which had apparently been adversely affected by discrimination in the allocation of government contracts) announced that it was prepared to recognize the legitimacy of the election results, thereby undermining the solidarity of the ICC. In October the minister of justice, who in his capacity as public prosecutor had failed to win several trials in the supreme court, resigned after a state-controlled newspaper questioned his competence. In November, in accordance with the constitution, a 20-member national security council, chaired by Arkaah, was established. In December the PHP, the NIP and a faction of the PNC (all of which represented supporters of ex-president Nkrumah) merged to form a new organization, known as the People's Convention Party.

In February 1994 longstanding hostility between the Konkomba ethnic group, which originated in Togo, and the landowning Nanumba intensified, following demands by the Konkomba for traditional status that would entitle them to own land; some 500 people were killed in ethnic clashes in the Northern Region, which were apparently precipitated by a market quarrel that arose from the sale of a guinea-fowl. The government subsequently dispatched troops to the Northern Region to restore order and imposed a state of emergency in seven districts for a period of three months; however, skirmishes between a number of ethnic factions continued, and it was reported that some 6,000 Konkomba had fled to Togo. In early March 12 people were killed at Tamale, 420 km north of Accra, when security forces fired on demonstrators belonging to the Dagomba ethnic group, who had allegedly attacked a group of Konkomba.

In March 1994 a minor government reorganization was effected. Later that month district assembly elections took place (except in the seven districts where the state of emergency remained in force); although the elections were contested on a non-party basis, it was reported that candidates who were unofficially supported by the NPP had secured the majority of seats in a number of the district assemblies. Negotiations between representatives of the various ethnic groups involved in the conflict in the Northern Region were initiated in April, under the aegis of the government. In the same month it was reported that the authorities had discovered a conspiracy to overthrow the government, which apparently involved threats to kill Quashigah (the instigator of the coup attempt in 1989) and editors of two private newspapers; the opposition, however, questioned the veracity of these claims. In May the NPP announced that it was to withdraw from reconciliation discussions between the government and the opposition, owing to lack of progress. In the same month a minor reshuffle of the government was carried out, and the state of emergency in force in the Northern Region (where a total of 1,000 people had been killed, and a further 150,000 displaced) was extended for one month. In early June, however, the seven ethnic factions involved in the fighting signed a peace agreement that provided for the imposition of an immediate cease-fire and renounced violence as a means of settling disputes over land-ownership. The government subsequently announced that troops were to be permanently stationed in the Northern Region in order to pre-empt further conflict, and appointed a negotiating team, which was to attempt to resolve the inter-ethnic differences. The state of emergency was extended for a further month in June, and again in July. In early August, however, the government announced that order had been restored in the region, and ended the state of emergency.

FOREIGN POLICY UNDER THE RAWLINGS GOVERNMENTS

In 1984 the PNDC established close links with the government of Capt. Thomas Sankara in the neighbouring state of Burkina Faso. Sankara, who seized power in August 1983, based the working structure of his 'revolution' on that of the PNDC. During 1984 Ghana also revived its involvement with the foreign policy structures of the African community, and in September of that year was elected to the chairmanship of the OAU liberation committee. In August 1986 the governments of Ghana and Burkina Faso agreed to establish a high-level political commission which would be responsible for preparing a 10-year timetable for the political union of the two countries. Agreements were also made to harmonize their currencies and their energy, transport, trade and educational systems, and in September and October a joint military exercise was held. Following a military coup in Burkina Faso in October 1987, relations between the two countries were temporarily strained, but subsequently improved, after meetings between Rawlings and Sankara's successor, Capt. Blaise Compaoré.

In July 1985 relations between Ghana and the USA became strained when a distant relative of Rawlings, Michael Agbotui Soussoudis, was arrested by the US authorities and charged with espionage. He was subsequently convicted, and sentenced to 20 years' imprisonment. Shortly afterwards, four members of the diplomatic missions in Accra and Washington were expelled by the respective governments. In December, however, following secret negotiations between the PNDC and the Reagan administration, Boussoudis was exchanged for a number of identified CIA agents in Ghana. In the same month Joseph H. Mensah, the leader of the exiled Ghana Democratic Movement, was arrested in the USA, with two other Ghanaians, and put on trial for attempting to purchase military equipment for shipment to dissidents in Ghana. (However, charges against Mensah were invalidated by legal technicalities.) Tension between the two countries increased in March 1986, when it was discovered that a Panamanian-registered freighter en route from Buenos Aires, Argentina, to Rio de Janeiro was transporting arms and ammunition, while its 18-member crew comprised a number of known mercenaries and US veterans of the Viet Nam war. The PNDC claimed that the vessel had been destined for subversive operations against Ghana, and had been financed by a Ghanaian dissident with alleged links with the CIA. During their trial in Brazil, eight members of the crew admitted that the charges were substantially true and that the dissident, named as Godfrey Osei, had purchased the weaponry in Argentina by posing as an agent of the Ghanaian government. The eight men were sentenced to terms of imprisonment, but three of them subsequently escaped to the USA, with, according to the Ghanaian government, the assistance of the CIA.

Relations with Togo deteriorated sharply in May 1986, following the arrest in Ghana of eight people on charges of subversion: they had allegedly been operating from a base in Togo. In June seven of the defendants were executed. In September an attempted coup in Togo was blamed, in turn, by the Togolese government on infiltrators from Ghana. The frontiers were closed, and in the following month the PNDC accused the Togolese authorities of maltreating the Ghanaians who had been detained in connection with the coup attempt. Although the borders were reopened in February 1987, relations between the two states remained strained.

Between December 1988 and January 1989 more than 130 Ghanaians were deported from Togo, where they were alleged to be residing illegally. In October 1991 the governments of Ghana and Togo signed an agreement on the free movement of goods and persons between the two countries. In October 1992, however, Ghana denied claims by the Togo government that it was implicated in subversive activity by Togolese dissidents based in Ghana. (By late 1992 more than 100,000 Togolese had taken refuge in Ghana, following the deterioration in the political situation in Togo). In January 1993 Ghana announced that its armed forces were to be mobilized, in reaction to concern at the increasing civil unrest in Togo. In March the Togo government accused Ghana of supporting an armed attack on the military camp at Lomé, where the Togolese president, Gen. Gnassingbe Eyadéma, resided. In January 1994 relations with Togo again became strained, following a further attack on Eyadéma's residence, which was claimed by the Togolese authorities to have been staged by armed dissidents based in Ghana. The Ghanaian chargé d'affaires in Togo was subsequently arrested, while Togolese forces killed 12 Ghanaians and bombarded a customs post at Aflao and several villages near the border between the two countries. Ghana, however, denied the accusations of involvement in the coup attempt, and threatened to retaliate against further acts of aggression. In May allegations by the Togolese government that Ghana had been responsible (owing to lack of border security) for bomb attacks in Togo resulted in further tension between the two nations.

In November 1993 attacks in Ghana on Ivorian footballers and their supporters prompted violent reprisals against the Ghanaian community in Côte d'Ivoire, leading to 25 deaths. More than 10,400 Ghanaians resident in Côte d'Ivoire were subsequently repatriated, while Ghana formally protested to the Ivorian authorities. However, relations with Côte d'Ivoire improved, following the establishment of a joint commission to investigate the violence in December.

Ghana has participated in the Monitoring Group (ECOMOG) of the Economic Community of West African States (ECOWAS, see p. 104), which was dispatched to Liberia in August 1990 following the outbreak of conflict between government and rebel forces in that country (see chapter on Liberia). In mid-1993 some 1,000 Ghanaian troops remained in Liberia. In August 1994, however, Rawlings, who replaced the Beninois president as chairman of the conference of heads of state and government of ECOWAS, indicated that Ghana was to consider the withdrawal of troops from Liberia.

Economy

RICHARD SYNGE

The Ghanaian economy is based primarily on agriculture, although mining has also traditionally been of significance, especially in foreign trade. The dominant commercial and export activity is cocoa production, which was established in the country, mainly as an African smallholder crop, in the latter part of the 19th century. In the late 1950s, at the time of its political independence, Ghana was the world's leading exporter of cocoa, and this crop has continued to account for between 45%–70% of commodity exports in most years since the early 1970s. Ghana's other cash crops for export include coffee, bananas, palm kernels, copra, limes, kola nuts and shea nuts. Agricultural raw materials are also grown for processing by local manufacturing industries. Rubber, cotton, oil palms and kenaf are the most important, though productivity has been badly affected in recent years by the lack of foreign exchange for imported inputs and by poor planning. Food farming is based on the production of maize, millet, sorghum, rice, cassava, taro, yams and plantains. Secondary export activities are gold and timber production, which were first established in the 1880s.

At independence in 1957 Ghana possessed one of the strongest economies in Africa. However, the economy declined sharply in the following 25 years. During that period real per caput income fell, bringing about large reductions in the production of most of the main food crops, as well as the agricultural and mineral exports. The government tax base was diminished by a combination of falling incomes and production, and an increase in smuggling, and this in turn created large deficits, which led to rising inflation and enlarged external debts. It also contributed to lower expenditure on, and a general neglect of the country's infrastructure, as well as its education and health services.

This process of decline commenced during the Nkrumah years (1957–66), and was characterized by ambitious expenditure, a major nationalization programme, and the alignment of Ghana's trade with Eastern Europe. The military government which displaced Nkrumah, inherited serious economic problems, including crippling debts, and initiated austerity campaigns and other economic reforms. The successor civilian government headed by Dr Kofi Busia, which assumed power in 1969, continued these efforts and also attempted to liberalize the trade and other policies, which had been tightly regulated from the early days of the Nkrumah administration. However, the unpopularity of many of Busia's economic measures precipitated a coup in January 1972, which established a lengthy period of military government. Following the establishment of the first Rawlings government, efforts to reduce corruption and restore the basis of economic production and growth culminated in the first Economic Recovery Programme (ERP I), which the second Rawlings government introduced in 1983. This programme, which was developed in close collaboration with the World Bank and the IMF, was essentially designed as the stabilization phase of the economy's recovery. A second programme, covering the period 1987–90, (ERP II) was regarded as the structural adjustment and development stage of that recovery. Most of the subsequent policy initiatives of the government were designed under the two ERP.

With the introduction in 1992 of its new multi-party constitution, followed by elections at the end of the year, Ghana suffered a brief period of economic uncertainty, compounded by difficulties in fiscal management and reduced earnings from cocoa and gold. Government expenditure briefly exceeded stipulated levels, after pay increases were awarded to civil servants, resulting in a suspension of programmed assistance from a number of donor agencies. In the aftermath of the elections, President Rawlings' new constitutional government (little changed from its predecessor) was forced to adopt unpopular measures in its 1993 budget, and imposed sharp increases in the price of fuel, which prompted protests from trade unions and from the political parties that had boycotted the parliamentary elections.

In 1993 the government succeeded in re-establishing fiscal control, improving the efficiency of revenue-raising agencies, particularly the customs and excise service, and accelerated its divestiture of state holdings, nominating for sale some parastatals that had previously been considered 'strategic'. Under the new Rawlings government, the emphasis of economic policy has shifted more fully towards the stimulation of the private sector as an essential part of its declared strategy of accelerated growth and poverty alleviation. In 1993 the government announced that the investment code would be further liberalized, and that there would be radical revisions to a number of tax and price control laws. The sale of part of the government's stake in Ashanti Goldfields Corpn on the London and Accra stock markets in April 1994 represented a new stage in the opening up of the economy to foreign portfolio investment. Government shares in a number of other companies were also sold, and in 1994 it was expected that shares in public enterprises would progressively be made available to private investors. The government is, however, aware that it is still some way from alleviating poverty or significantly raising standards of living for most Ghanaians, and has announced that it intends to maintain expenditure on education and basic health.

The continuing financial support of the international community for Ghana's reform efforts was reinforced by a new commitment by donors, undertaken at a meeting in Paris in June 1993, to provide finance of US $2,100m. in 1993 and 1994 to meet Ghana's anticipated balance-of-payments difficulties. Although borrowing under an IMF structural adjustment facility came to an end in 1992, the vagaries of international commodity markets have necessitated further drawings on IMF resources.

POLICY OBJECTIVES OF THE ERP

Exchange rate and trade policy reforms were given priority in the recovery programmes, resulting in a progressive nominal devaluation of the official cedi from between early 1983 and early 1986. A weekly foreign exchange auction for specified transactions, but excluding cocoa exports, was introduced in September 1986 and remained in operation until mid-1990 (see below). This two-tier structure was unified in February 1987, thereby ending discrimination against cocoa exports and an unrealistically low cedi exchange rate for certain specified imports, particularly petroleum. In conjunction with these exchange-rate changes the long-established quantitative restrictions on imports, which were still necessary in 1986 because of continued currency over-valuation, were lifted and replaced by a fairly uniform rate of customs tariff on most imports. In late 1986 quantitative restrictions were removed from almost all raw materials, spare parts and capital goods. There were two further main reforms in exchange and trade arrangements. The first was the release of foreign exchange to consumer goods by allowing their participation in the auction. The second was the licensing of a number of foreign exchange bureaux, which were empowered to buy and sell foreign exchange independently.

In the area of public finance the ERP aimed to raise the revenue base of the government, which had declined sharply by the early 1980s. They placed emphasis on a series of policies to simplify and rationalize the major taxes, particularly the sales and customs taxes, improve tax administration, and achieve prompter adjustment of petroleum and other administered prices to reduce the subsidy burden associated with higher import prices. In the case of direct taxes, a main objective was to amend tax brackets and exemptions in order to reduce the degree of progressivity, which was seen as a main incentive for non-compliance. In the case of indirect taxes, the main objective was the integration of the *ad hoc* excise taxes on a wide range of goods with an expanded sales tax to establish the reformed sales tax as the major source of indirect tax revenues. In addition, measures were taken to rationalize the import tariff as the central instrument of trade protection. Finally, and as a by-product of exchange rate policies, the major devaluations of the currency have significantly enhanced tax revenues on cocoa earnings.

In the area of budgetary expenditure, the successive IMF programmes have sought to monitor and limit government expenditure while changing the structure of that expenditure; the number of personnel in the civil service and parastatal sector has also been progressively reduced. Overall, the recovery programmes have achieved some success, both in raising the revenue and expenditure shares of GDP, and in achieving reduced fiscal deficits.

Major changes have been introduced in price and subsidy policies. In the case of cocoa prices, ERP I introduced a series of rises in producer prices as a key element of the attempt to achieve a recovery of production levels. The World Bank structural adjustment credit of 1987 consolidated this process by introducing a scheme to relate Ghanaian producer prices to world prices on a formula basis.

In relation to consumer prices, recent policies focused on the elimination of the endemic price control, under which by 1970, some 6,000 prices, relating to about 700 separate items, were restricted. This formed part of the dissolution of the implicit social contract on wages and prices, which operated through the 1970s and the early 1980s. The liberalization of prices achieved by the recovery programmes achieved improved availability of many items, although for some groups it led to a widening division between the levels of prices and wages. In conjunction with price reforms, there was also a systematic programme of subsidy removal. Reductions in fertilizer and pesticide subsidies were implemented under the ERP from an early stage and the fertilizer subsidy ceased entirely in 1989.

A final area of policy reform since the 1983 ERP was that of state ownership. At an early stage a consultant study recommended that 80 of 235 state enterprises be either converted into joint ventures with the private sector, be completely divested, or in a few cases be liquidated. Although progress was initially slow, some 52 enterprises had been divested by mid-1993, of which 33 were sold to foreign investors. In addition, some parastatal companies, previously considered to be 'strategic', such as Ghana Airways and the Posts and Telecommunications Corpn. were designated for transfer to the private sector.

In late 1989 measures agreed under the terms of the enhanced structural adjustment facility (ESAF) included the unification, in mid-1990, of the auction and foreign bureau exchange rates, an increase in privatization, a further relaxation of trade restrictions, and the liberalization of fuel prices. Ghana's first stock exchange, based in Accra, began functioning in late 1990; three stockbroking firms were initially registered.

Policies adopted in 1992 included the abolition in March of the weekly foreign auction, with the aim of making exchange rate determination a function of a freely operating interbank market, and the introduction of a new range of tax and import duty rates. Emphasis was placed on reducing inflation, which had increased dramatically by 1990.

In view of adverse economic conditions in the second half of 1992, with a decline in cocoa earnings and a temporary loss of donor support, the government adopted new objectives to restore the macro-economic balance during 1993. The target for growth was set at 4.5%. The new policy orientation has become one of accelerated privatization, liberalization and encouragement of foreign investment. Cocoa purchasing was opened to private competition at the end of 1992 and the privatization of the government's stake in banks was initiated. The government has studied examples of rapid economic growth in East Asian nations, and can be expected to make further adjustments towards this end, with renewed emphasis on developing human resources.

ECONOMIC PERFORMANCE UNDER THE ERP

By 1983, the economy of Ghana was severely flawed as a consequence of two decades or more of economic mismanagement, falling incomes, lower exports, reduced imports, deteriorating infrastructure, endemic corruption and a serious distortion of most incentives. Thus, specific imbalances—excessive inflation and unsustainable fiscal and external deficits—were largely symptomatic of the economic recession in the productive sectors. Against this general background, economic performance since 1983 can be considered very successful, although further progress is necessary to achieve broad-based growth at all levels of the economy.

GDP increased by an annual average of 3.2% in 1980–91, but reached an average of nearly 5% towards the end of that period. The growth rate declined to 3.9% in 1992, but was estimated at 5.0% in 1993, and projected at 5.2% in 1994. Although there has been success in some areas, and Ghana's economy grew overall by 40% between 1984 and 1991, there is still concern about the sustainability of the structural adjustment process. The services sector, in particular trading activity, demonstrated substantial growth over the reform period, while mining also made an important contribution. However, growth in both the agricultural and manufacturing sectors proved disappointing. The services represented some 77% of the growth in the economy between 1984 and 1991, with mining and industry contributing 19% and agriculture 5%.

The recovery in the output of cocoa that might have been expected to result from the government's reforms was constrained by the collapse of world prices for the commodity. Government efforts to increase progressively the share of international prices received by cocoa farmers were impeded by the necessity of maintaining the flow of revenue, by the high marketing costs and by the decline in world prices. The failure of the domestic private sector to invest in productive activity, which was partially attributable to the high cost of credit and generally low level of savings, also proved disappointing. The influx of foreign exchange from aid programmes and a growth in tourism has stimulated trade in imported goods, but manufacturing output has failed to respond to the new conditions.

In relation to the balance of payments, the major success has been the reversal of the chronic reduction in imports which had restricted the economy for several years, and the release of enlarged import volumes for both productive sectors and consumers. Imports have increased sharply, from $499.7m. in 1983 to $1,457m. in 1992, and world inflationary trends have had an adverse effect in some years. Overall, the current account deficit, excluding official transfers, increased from less than 1% of GDP in 1983 to more than 8% by 1990. Although the rise in gold production increased the value of gold exports to more than $300m., and the total value of exports to $986m. in 1992, the growth of cocoa and other exports remained slow. Substantial inflows of external concessional assistance were expected to maintain the overall balance of payments surplus at around $168m. in 1993. The inflows of official grants and long-term concessional loans increased from less than 1% of GDP in 1983 to about 10% of GDP by 1990, facilitating the elimination of external payments arrears and of official reserves.

The government's efforts to reduce inflation have been only partially successful. After reaching 122.8% in 1983, partly as a result of the severe drought of that year, the rate declined to 10.4% in 1985, but averaged more than 30% in each of the following five years. The rate declined to 18.0% in 1991, and to 10.1% in 1992, but again increased, to 25.0%, in 1993. The overall consumer price index was dominated by food prices, which were determined largely by domestic food output. Fuel prices and developments in the exchange rate of the cedi were also important factors.

POPULATION

According to the result of the March 1984 census, Ghana's population had increased by 43% since 1970, to reach 12.3m. The heaviest concentrations were in the regions of Ashanti (2.1m.), Eastern (1.7m.), Greater Accra (1.4m.), and Volta (1.2m.). The least populous regions were Upper East and Upper West. About 50% of the population are under 15 years of age, and 40% live in and around the principal metropolitan areas. Ghana's population is becoming increasingly urbanized, with an estimated 5.5% rise in the average annual growth rate of the urban population in 1980–85, compared with an average annual growth rate of 3.4% for the whole country over the same period. During 1985–92, according to World Bank estimates, the population increased by an annual average of 3.3%

At the 1984 census the Ghanaian labour force was about 5.6m., of whom an estimated 41% were in the agricultural sector, and 23% were engaged in service industries. Unemployment in 1983 was officially estimated at 12%–15% of the workforce, although the real level was believed to be considerably higher, owing to the slump in economic activity, the operation of a three-day week in certain sectors and the large influx of returnees from Nigeria. Despite opposition from trade unions, the recognition of chronic over-employment in the public sector resulted in attempts to reduce the public-sector workforce, while raising the wages of remaining employees, by redeployment of labour to the agricultural sector, by voluntary redundancies and by temporary lay-offs. In order to help those affected by its economic retrenchment policies, the government launched the Programme of Action to Mitigate the Social Costs of Adjustment (PAMSCAD) in 1988 and obtained pledges of $140m. from donors to finance it. The first part of the PAMSCAD comprised a series of schemes to generate employment for those (about 45,000) affected by the job losses in the public sector during 1988–90. The second part aimed to strengthen community social programmes, including self-help groups. The final part was intended to provide the most vulnerable groups in society with basic needs, such as water and sanitation, health care, nutrition and housing.

AGRICULTURE

In 1992 the agricultural sector accounted for 48.6% of GDP and employed 48.7% of the working population. Cocoa is traditionally Ghana's most important cash crop, occupying more than one-half of all the country's cultivated land and providing, on average, around 65% of total export earnings. Output, however, declined steadily during the 1970s, owing to a combination of factors, which included a lack of financial incentives for farmers, caused by fluctuating world cocoa prices, an overvalued cedi, unreliable payment procedures and low producer prices; ageing and diseased trees; shortages of fertilizers and vital pesticides; and poor transport and distribution services. The decline continued into the 1980s, exacerbated by drought, bush fires and smuggling (the latter activity, mainly into Côte d'Ivoire, Togo and Burkina Faso, led to losses of about 50,000 tons of cocoa per year).

In October 1983 the government launched a $130m. campaign under ERP I to revitalize the cocoa sector, based on an earlier programme for reform and rehabilitation, drafted in 1979. The CMB was reorganized to implement the campaign more efficiently. Cash incentives were offered to farmers to replant crops, and producer prices were increased by 67%. Essential inputs, such as insecticides, building materials and sprayers, were made available, and improvements were made to transport and distribution services. Financial assistance was provided by the World Bank. Attention was also focused on estate rehabilitation and disease control in the major growing areas in the Ashanti and Western regions (although the areas worst affected by disease were the Eastern and Central regions). Progress was slow, owing to shortages of labour, resistance by farmers to the uprooting of old trees in order to prevent the spread of disease to new pods, and continued doubts about the adequacy of price incentives. Although more than 3m. hybrid cocoa pods were distributed to private farms for planting in mid-1985, many farmers chose to plant food crops rather than cocoa. Later in the year the CMB was reorganized as the Ghana Cocoa Board (COCOBOD) and in July 1986 a new agreement, proposed by the World Bank, fixed the level of producer prices. In Ghana 320,000 ha of cocoa farming land were designated as special zones for rehabilitation and spraying to prevent black pod disease. Under ERP II, the government aimed to increase cocoa production to more than 350,000 tons per year. However, this target proved to be over-optimistic, and output has remained below 300,000 tons per year, totalling only 243,000 tons in 1991/92. With world prices continuing to decline the government's measures to increase producer prices have proved unsuccessful. Subsidies on fertilizers have been abolished and high rates of interest have discouraged farmers from seeking credit from the commercial banks. In early 1993 Rawlings promised to maintain appropriate prices for cocoa farmers, and in July COCOBOD was deprived of its monopoly, and three trading companies were licensed to purchase cocoa direct from farmers. However, COCOBOD retained exclusive control over Ghanaian cocoa exports.

Droughts in 1976, 1977 and 1982 necessitated huge imports of staple foodstuffs and increased Ghana's dependence on international food aid. Adverse weather conditions, bush fires and the return of some 1m. Ghanaian migrants from Nigeria led to acute food shortages in 1983, but the return of favourable weather conditions in 1984, combined with new price incentives, helped to increase crop yields considerably. The rise in food production was not, however, sufficient to meet local demand, and 257,000 tons of food aid (of which a considerable proportion came from Eastern Europe) was needed to compensate for the food deficit in 1984. Even the excellent maize harvest in 1984 was substantially below consumption requirements of 1.1m. metric tons. Excess production of maize in Ghana's main producing areas, around the Ashanti and Brong-Ahafo Regions, created added problems for the government. The state-owned Food Distribution Corporation has limited storage facilities, and lacks the resources to purchase and distribute excess stocks. With maize prices declining sharply, consumers were virtually forced to buy maize in the new 'people's shops'. This development, in turn, further depressed prices and led to the accumulation of large unsold stocks. By 1988, however, staple food production had increased to 6.8m. tons. Despite severe floods, crop surpluses were reported in 1989. In 1991 maize production increased to 932,000 tons, compared with 574,000 tons in 1985. In that year production of paddy rice reached 151,000 tons, while output of cassava and yams also increased significantly. In 1992, however, according to unofficial figures, maize production declined to

580,000 tons, while output of paddy rice was estimated to have fallen to 100,000 tons. In 1994 ethnic conflict in the north of the country (a principal agricultural region) necessitated emergency food aid, and it was feared that the harvest in the following year would be adversely affected.

To maintain the continuity of food supplies throughout the year, the government operates a national food security and buffer stock system. A price-support structure, to combat fluctuating producer prices, was introduced in 1985, and moves were under way to sell state farms back to the private sector. The ministry of agriculture has also set up a national resource allocation committee, which aims to rationalize the distribution of inputs and equipment. The ministry has drawn up a pilot scheme for intensive food crop production in the Accra plains, on previously unused land. The area under oil palms is also to be increased to 2,500 ha, and the IDA is granting $25m. towards the second stage of a large palm oil project. Production of palm oil rose to an estimated 55,000 tons in 1987, compared with 13,000 tons in 1982.

In 1987 the government introduced a four-year agricultural programme, which included proposals to 'privatize' certain services provided by the secretariat for agriculture and to reorganize its planning and research unit. In 1991 the government implemented a Medium Term Agricultural Development Programme (1991–2000), which aimed to achieve complete self-sufficiency in food by the year 2000. The programme included proposals to diversify staple crops and improve livestock production; farmers were to receive subsidized loans from local banks to purchase high yield seed and fertilizers.

Cattle farming is restricted to the Northern region and the Accra plains. Production of meat is insufficient to meet local annual demand of about 200,000 tons. Imports of livestock from adjacent countries have been considerable, though declining in recent years, owing to shortages of foreign exchange. Domestic fisheries (marine and Volta Lake) supply only about one-half of the country's total annual demand of 600,000 tons. The total catch in 1988 was 362,000 tons, increasing to 365,000 in 1991.

Ghana has extensive forests, mostly in the south-west, and developed a substantial timber export industry during the 1960s. The establishment of a Timber Marketing Board (TMB), with powers to fix minimum contract prices, marked the beginning of a decline in this sector, and in 1985 the TMB was replaced by the Forest Products Inspection Bureau and the Timber Export Development Board. Efforts are proceeding to promote timber exports, which are projected eventually to reach 700,000 cu m per year. The government aims to phase out exports of raw logs and to encourage local processing of timber products, following the introduction in late 1993 of duty incentives for imports of sawmilling and other equipment. Forest replanting, which was being carried out at an annual rate of 11,000 ha in the early 1970s, had declined to 4,000 ha per year by the late 1980s. Ghana, however, possesses enough timber to meet its foreseeable domestic and export requirements until the year 2030. In early 1989 a forest management programme was initiated, financed by $30.6m. from the IDA. The World Bank also made $39.4m. available for forest protection. Export earnings from timber declined to $88m. in 1989, but increased by 35%, to $120m., in 1990. In 1991 the forestry sector accounted for 6% of GDP and 8% of total export earnings.

MANUFACTURING

Apart from traditional industries such as food processing, Ghana has a number of long-established large and medium-sized enterprises, including a petroleum refinery and plants producing textiles, vehicles, cement, paper, chemicals and footwear, and some export-based industries, such as cocoa processing and timber plants.

The manufacturing industries have traditionally been under-used, high-cost and strongly dependent on imported equipment and materials. Expansion has been deterred by low levels of investment, by transport congestion and by persistent shortages of imported materials and spares. Moreover, the consistent overvaluation of the cedi and the irregularity of supply increased the attractiveness of imports relative to home-produced goods.

Manufacturing output stagnated in the 1970s and then declined sharply in the early 1980s, and the sector's contribution to Ghana's total GDP fell from 22% in 1973 to under 5% before the start of ERP I in 1983. There was an increase to 8% in 1986, and to nearly 10% of GDP in 1990. This recovery has been assisted by freer access to imports, following the liberalization measures implemented under the adjustment programme. Almost all industries have continued to be affected by shortages of raw materials, spare parts and other imported machinery, irregular electricity supplies, and inflation. These factors, together with poor planning, lack of co-ordination, and duplication, especially in the soap, textile and beverage industries, reduced average capacity utilization to as low as 20% in 1985. However, manufacturing output recovered somewhat in 1986, as more capital equipment was purchased by producers, using the new foreign exchange 'auctions'. In 1988 the rate of capacity utilization reached 62%. In 1983–90 manufacturing output increased by an annual average of 9.5%. The contribution of the industrial sector to total GDP increased from less than 12% in 1983 to more than 14% in 1990. However, the performance of the manufacturing sector was again impeded in 1991 by continuing structural problems, and the dramatic increase in the costs of spare parts and raw materials.

According to an IMF study in 1991, the response of the private sector to the improved macro-economic environment remained unsatisfactory, reflecting the time needed to restore confidence in a sector undermined by earlier policy mistakes. The process of reform itself has also forced the closure of many industries that had previously been sheltered from foreign and domestic competition. New policy measures implemented since 1990, which were designed to promote private investment in manufacturing, included reductions in tax rates, and an extension of the capital allowances provided under the Investment Code to all manufacturing enterprises.

Among the largest capital-intensive industries in Ghana is an aluminium smelter at Tema, operated by the Volta Aluminium Co (VALCO), which is owned by the multinational Kaiser Aluminium and Chemical Corpn (90%) and the Reynolds Metals Co (10%). Although the Tema plant has a potential output capacity of 200,000 metric tons of primary aluminium per year, production was running at less than 50,000 tons annually in the mid-1980s, owing to lower world demand and reduced energy supplies from the drought-stricken Akosombo hydroelectricity plant. Other developments in the manufacturing sector have included the reopening of a glass factory at Aboso, with a capacity of 25,000 tons per year; a $36m. project to increase palm oil production, including the opening of a new $15m. palm oil mill in 1987, with a capacity of 25,000 tons per year; a new cement factory using local raw materials; the rehabilitation of Ghana Sugar Estates to produce alcohol; Chinese funding for three rice mills; and the construction of a citronella distillation plant at Bonso. Privatization of the manufacturing sector accelerated in 1993, and the Divestiture Implementation Committee has undertaken to sell the government's shares in a number of enterprises, including the Tema oil refinery, the Tema food complex, the Ghana Industrial Holding Co's pharmaceutical subsidiary, the Bonsa Tyre Co (including its rubber estate) and cocoa processing factories in Tema and Takoradi.

Evidence of increasing foreign investor confidence is apparent in the repurchase by multinationals, such as Unilever and Guinness, of shares in their Ghanaian operations that had been held by government. In an attempt to encourage new investments by US corporations, the government has repealed some restrictive legislation, and in early 1993 prepared a new investment bill for presentation to parliament. The bill has sharply reduced the minimum capital requirements for new foreign investment and reserves very few activities exclusively for Ghanaians. Dividends, profits and the original investment capital can be repatriated freely in convertible currency, and tax incentives and benefits have been improved. There is a target of an annual growth rate in investment of 11.4% between 1990–95, with private sector investment alone increasing at 13.5% a year.

MINING

Gold is Ghana's principal mineral export, accounting for an increasing proportion of total export earnings in recent years. Ghana's export earnings from gold, totalling about $92m. per year in 1985 and 1986, increased to $300m. in 1991. The principal mine is situated at Obuasi, operated by the Ashanti Goldfields Corpn, which is 43% owned by Lonrho PLC, a British-based multinational company. The high value of Ashanti Goldfields was demonstrated by the successful flotation of 26% of its shares on the London and Accra stock exchanges in April 1994. With the shares selling at more than $20 per unit, the government received more than $300m. and the company more than $50m. The government retained a 31% share in the company.

In 1992 substantial new investment was under way in the gold mining sector, with Ashanti Goldfields (which accounts for 75% of Ghana's official production) implementing a number of measures to expand its output. The company has initiated a programme, at an estimated cost of $250m., to increase production capacity from underground sources to 600,000 oz per year, established a new open-pit sulphide operation, and developed a new surface operation, with an estimated output of 38,000 oz per year. Gold replaced cocoa as Ghana's principal export commodity in 1992. In the year to September 1993 Ashanti Goldfields produced a record 765,250 oz (exceeding projected output), compared with 654,298 oz in 1992, and 569,480 oz in 1991. The other major investments in gold were largely from private sources, while the activities of the government-owned State Gold Mining Corporation (SGMC) have been hindered by technical difficulties. Recent discoveries of viable mining projects on new concessions have tended to discourage investors from entering into joint ventures with SGMC or implementing privatization measures. In addition, expensive rehabilitation of the mines is required. Production from the SGMC and its joint venture with the Australian company, Southern Cross Mining, was negligible in 1991.

Following exploration and development by private investors from 1985, several medium-scale producers, mainly using open-pit methods, commenced a stage of production in 1991/92. These included the following companies: Teberebie Goldfields, Billiton Bogosu, Ghana Australia Goldfields, Goldenrae Mining Company and Bonte. Some have received financial support and equity contributions from development finance companies, particularly the International Finance Corporation (IFC) and European bilateral institutions. Gold mining investment in the period 1987–91 totalled some $600m., and the further investment of $500m. was predicted. New investment proposals were also planned. Total gold production was estimated at 1.2m. oz in 1993, and was expected to reach 2m. oz by 1996.

In 1991 production from Teberebie Goldfields and Billiton Bogosu amounted to some 70,000 oz each, according to preliminary figures. Teberebie's annual production capacity was estimated at 100,000 oz; the company was controlled by Pioneer Group of the USA, which invested some $40m. in the project. Teberebie was committed to observing the government's increasingly stringent environmental conditions, and to allocating revenue to rehabilitate mined-out areas at the conclusion of mining. Billiton has also been obliged to consider the environmental hazards of its project to increase annual production to 150,000 oz, at an estimated cost of $100m. In 1993 Gold Fields of South Africa assumed control of the SGMC property at Tarkwa, with a commitment to spend $11m. on improved production and further exploration. In 1992 Rawlings announced that the government intended to initiate consultations and discussions with the mining companies in order to draft legislation to regulate the conduct of the companies, following a report on the impact of gold mining on the environment.

Diamonds, which are mainly industrial stones, are mined, both by Ghana Consolidated Diamonds (formerly Consolidated Africa Selection Trust) at Akwatia and by local diggers. Total recorded production has dwindled from 3.2m. carats in 1960 to 442,000 carats in 1987, and to only 300,000 carats in 1988. Diamond output remained at around 200,000 carats annually between 1989–91. In 1993 the South African company, De Beers, acquired a 40% stake in Ghana Consolidated Diamonds (which was to be reconstituted as Birim River Diamonds Ltd in 1995), with Lazare Kaplan International of the USA holding 40% and the government 20% of the remaining shares. Development was to continue at Akwatia, and diamond output was expected to increase to 400,000 carats in 1994.

Ghana became a petroleum producer in 1978, when a US company, Agri-Petco International, began extracting petroleum from the continental shelf near Saltpond. Reserves at the Saltpond oilfield were estimated at 7m. barrels, but average output during the early 1980s was only 1,250 barrels per day (b/d). In 1986 another US company, Primary Fuel of the USA (which had acquired Agri-Petco International), halted production at Saltpond, owing to a decline in profits. In 1983 the government established the Ghana National Petroleum Corpn (GNPC) to develop offshore areas under production-sharing contracts. In 1984 foreign oil companies were invited to bid for exploration and production licences in 70% of its offshore blocks. Exploration and production rights were set out under the 1984 Petroleum Law, which allows the government to take an initial 10% share in any venture, with the option of buying 50% of production and holding a 50% royalty on output. As of 1993, however, following some exploratory drilling, no commercial quantities of oil had been identified, although various gas projects for power generation were in the process of being developed.

The country's sole refinery is operated by the Ghanaian–Italian Petroleum Co and is located at Tema. Capacity at the refinery, in which the government holds a 50% share, is just over 1.3m. metric tons. Nigeria is the principal supplier of crude petroleum to Ghana. Other suppliers include Iran, Libya and Algeria.

Ghana possesses substantial reserves of bauxite, although only a small proportion, at Awaso in the Western region, is currently mined. Exploitation of these deposits is carried out by the Ghana Bauxite Co (GBC), in which the government holds a 55% interest. Bauxite output, which is all exported, fell from more than 300,000 metric tons per year during the 1950s to less than 30,000 tons by the mid-1980s, owing to the rapid deterioration of the railway line linking Awaso with port facilities at Takoradi. Following the virtual closure of the line in 1984, the GBC temporarily ceased operations, although output recovered to 170,000 tons in 1985, as repairs to the rail link progressed. In 1990 production increased further to 400,000 tons, but declined to 324,000 tons in 1991. Plans to utilize the large bauxite deposits at Kibi for the VALCO aluminium smelter at Tema have failed to materialize because of funding difficulties and opposition from Kaiser Aluminium, which currently imports bauxite from Jamaica for use at the Tema plant.

Manganese ore is mined at Nsuta, in the Western Region, by Ghana National Manganese Corpn. Despite obsolete equipment and limited transport facilities at Takoradi Port and the main railway, ore production of 230,000–260,000 tons annually was achieved in the second half of the 1980s, increasing to 319,000 tons in 1991. Albeit that these figures represent about one-half of the output levels in the 1960s, Ghana ranks as the world's eighth largest producer of manganese.

In 1986 the government introduced a new mineral code, whereby new mining projects were required to be self-financing in foreign exchange and were granted external account status. The new code made Ghana highly attractive to foreign investors, but almost all of their interest has been focused on gold, with remaining finance being directed to the diamond industry.

ELECTRICITY

Until the Akosombo hydroelectricity plant was opened on the Volta Lake in 1966, electricity production came solely from diesel generators that were operated by the State Electricity Corpn or by the mines. In 1986 the Akosombo plant, with an installed generating capacity of 912 MW, and the recently opened 160-MW Kpong plant together provided virtually all of Ghana's electricity needs, and allowed electricity to be exported to Togo and Benin. In the early 1980s the Volta River Authority (VRA), which operates electricity supply from the Volta Lake, was forced to restrict output, owing to a reduction of water levels after two years of drought. Sporadic interruptions in the electricity supply ensued, and major commercial consumers, such as the Volta Aluminium Company (VALCO—which takes, on average, more than 60% of the power supply from Akosombo), were forced to reduce production levels. An improvement in rainfall from 1984 allowed a return to full output. A project to extend the electricity supply to the Northern, Upper West and Upper East regions from Brong Ahafo, in order to save reliance on diesel generators in the north, is being financed by bilateral and multilateral credits. In May 1994, however, following poor rainfall, the VRA was again obliged to restrict output, with VALCO agreeing to a reduction of 22% in its energy allocation.

The expansion of the Kpong hydroelectricity plant and the linking of the power systems of Ghana and Côte d'Ivoire is expected to facilitate a growth in electricity exports. However, plans to build a 450-MW hydroelectricity plant at Bui, on the Black Volta, to provide electricity for export and to supply northern Ghana, have been delayed, owing to funding difficulties. The construction of the country's first thermal power generation plant (at a projected cost of $400m.) at Takoradi was due to commence in late 1994 and was expected to be completed by 1997.

PUBLIC FINANCE

Ghana's fiscal base is extremely narrow. Traditionally, the country's high levels of development spending have been funded by revenues from excises (mainly on cocoa) and sales taxes, but, to an increasing extent, these funds proved to be inadequate, in relation to expenditure. The loss of cocoa revenues, as a result of smuggling and a downturn in export volumes, added to the already rapid decline in revenues from other trade transactions, caused by the overvaluation of the cedi and persistent shortages of foreign exchange. However, this decline was to some extent reversed, following the introduction of reform programmes.

Since 1983 fiscal policies have been designed to lower the imbalances in government finances and to foster economic growth. Capital spending, and the proportion of both revenue and expenditure to GDP, have increased significantly. From 1987 increasing emphasis has been laid on improving economic incentives and tax administration, with the result that, in 1992, corporate tax rates were considerably lower than before the reform process . Receipts from import duties expanded during 1987–90, increasing from 16% to 25% of total revenue. Another important source of revenue was petroleum taxes, which represented some 10% of revenue. Export duties, recently levied exclusively on cocoa, have declined as a percentage of total revenue, from 35% in 1983 to 10% in 1990. The declining contribution of receipts from the cocoa tax to total revenue reflected the reduction in world cocoa prices, as well as substantial real increases in producer prices paid to farmers.

Government expenditure has been realigned, with the aim of increasing both civil service wages and capital expenditure on infrastructure, agriculture, education and health. The rationalization of the civil service involved the redeployment of some 50,000 civil servants in the period 1987–90. Defence expenditure has remained low, representing 7.5% of total expenditure in 1985, according to official statistics, and declining to 3.1% of total expenditure by 1989.

The budget deficit (including foreign grants) remained fairly stable between 1983–90, fluctuating between 2.1% and 3.3% as a percentage of GDP. Excluding grants, the deficit increased to 5.5% in 1990, partly as a result of the declining share of grants in project-related aid. After considerable financing of the deficit (which reached C118,175m. in 1993) the budget for 1994 aimed to achieve a surplus of C68,000m., despite substantial interest payments of C114,200m. on domestic debts and C61,300m. on foreign debts. Priorities for government expenditure in 1994 included education, health, and the stimulation of employment in the private sector, with the aim of reducing poverty.

Ghana's heavy use of IMF facilities has contributed significantly to the country's foreign debts, which totalled $4,209m. in 1991, of which obligations to the IMF accounted for $834m. Most of the country's other borrowings are long-term and at concessionary rates, but the debt-servicing burden remains substantial; the ratio of debt service to foreign exchange earnings in 1993 was estimated at 38%. The government has, nevertheless, given priority to its debt-servicing obligations, resulting in an improvement in the country's credit rating. Private banks have proved increasingly willing to extend short-term credit to Ghana for a variety of financial operations, including the purchase of the cocoa crop for the 1993/94 season.

DOMESTIC COMMERCE AND FINANCE

A small number of large and long-established foreign companies continue to be important in the import trade, though they have now largely withdrawn from retail transactions, except for department stores in the major towns and for certain 'technical' goods. Since 1962 the publicly-owned Ghana National Trading Corpn (GNTC), created by purchase of A. G. Leventis and Co, has existed alongside the expatriate companies. At the retail level, independent Ghanaian and other African traders compete with the GNTC and with Lebanese and a few Indian businesses. The complex and highly fragmented trade in locally produced foodstuffs is almost wholly in African ownership.

In 1968 the government announced that small-scale retail and wholesale trade and the representation of overseas manufacturers (together with taxi services and small-scale manufacturing) would henceforth be reserved for Ghanaian enterprise. Most of these restrictions came into force in August 1970. Under an investment policy decree of April 1975, Ghanaian participation of 40%–55% was required by December 1976 in the equities of larger foreign businesses in a range of activities including distribution, banking and some manufacturing processes. Insurance was later brought into these arrangements. In 1986 the government introduced a new investment code, offering a range of fiscal and trade incentives and inducements. The priority sectors, designated for special treatment under the new code, are agriculture, import substitution industries, construction and tourism. The government continues to stress the importance of private investment and has reduced public-sector investment in the development of basic key industries. Public-sector investment accounted for only 28% of total proposed investment under ERP I.

The banking sector has expanded, and undergone substantial reform since the mid-1980s. In 1992 there were five commercial banks as well as three development banks, three merchant banks and a number of rural banks. The Bank of Ghana has strengthened its supervisory role and in June 1992 assumed control of the assets of the Ghana Co-operative Bank.

TRANSPORT

The country's two major ports are both artificial: Takoradi, built in the 1920s, and Tema, which was opened in 1961 to replace the Accra roadstead, and which has become an industrial centre. The rehabilitation of the two ports, at an estimated cost of $100m., was completed in 1990. The Ghana merchant shipping fleet had a total displacement of 225,000 gross registered tons in 1982, but its size was subsequently reduced, as the national Black Star Line disposed of some of its ships, owing to recurrent labour disputes and an increasing debt burden.

There are 947 km of railway, forming a triangle between Takoradi, Kumasi and Accra-Tema. Exports traditionally accounted for the greater part of railway freight tonnage, but cocoa and timber were diverted to the roads as rail facilities deteriorated, and the railways have required a regular government subsidy since 1976. In 1988 the IDA and the African Development Bank provided a credit of $42m. towards a project to rehabilitate the Western Line railway from Kumasi to Takoradi. Equipment worth $12.8m. was also provided by the IDA to help to repair faulty track.

In 1992 there were about 36,700 km of classified roads, of which 7,300 km were paved. The road system is good by tropical African standards, but its maintenance has been a constant problem since the early 1960s. Vehicle spare parts were also scarce, and the internal distributive system deteriorated physically. In 1991 the government initiated a major five-year programme of road development and rehabilitation, at an estimated cost of $142.3m.

The creation of the Volta Lake, stretching some 400 km inland from the Akosombo dam, opened up new possibilities for internal transportation, but lake transport is still relatively modest. In the late 1980s the Federal Republic of Germany financed a project to construct new ports on the lake, and to establish a new cargo and passenger service.

There is an international airport at Kotoka, near Accra, and other airports at Kumasi, Sunyani, Takoradi and Tamale serving inland traffic. The national airline is Ghana Airways. In 1988 the government received a loan of $12m. from France to finance the rehabilitation of Kotoka Airport (at a total cost of $55.5m.), which commenced in 1991.

FOREIGN TRADE AND AID

Ghana is essentially an exporter of primary products, mainly cocoa, timber and gold, and an importer of capital goods, foodstuffs and mineral fuels. The propensity to import is high, both among consumers and producers, although trade flows fluctuate in response to variations in the cocoa harvest and world commodity prices.

The continued decline in earnings of convertible currency, a growing food deficit and rising world prices for petroleum increased the pressure on import costs and on Ghana's reserves of foreign exchange. The country's terms of trade seriously deteriorated, and 'visible' trade surpluses in 1979 (US $262.6m.) and 1980 ($195.3m.) were followed by a deficit of $243.6m. in 1981, a small surplus in 1982, and a further deficit of $60.6m. in 1983. The trade balance again moved into surplus in 1984; from 1987, however, deficits were recorded, reaching $321.1m. in 1991, $470.3m. in 1992, and $643m. in 1993. Substantial deficits on 'invisible' trade (services and transfers), accentuated by increased payments to service the external debt, caused the current account to follow the 'visibles' into deficit in 1981. Following surpluses on the current account of the balance of payments in 1979 ($122m.) and 1980 ($29.2m.), the current account has remained in deficit in each year since 1981. The deficit on the current account increased to $252.7m. in 1991, to $377.8m. in 1992, and to $545m. in 1993.

In the early 1990s Western industrial nations comprised Ghana's major trading partners, although useful links have been maintained with countries of the former Eastern bloc, with which Ghana developed trade relations in the early 1980s (in 1984 the USSR accounted for one-quarter of Ghanaian exports). In 1989 the principal export destinations were Germany (representing 21.7% of the total), the United Kingdom (13%), the USA (11.4%) and Japan (6%). The major sources of imports in 1989 were Nigeria (22.3%), which provided most of Ghana's petroleum imports, the United Kingdom (16.7%), the USA (10%) and Germany (8%).

Since the mid-1970s, the Ghanaian economy has become increasingly reliant upon external finance. Bilateral aid and loans from traditional trading partners, such as the UK, Germany and the USA, have fluctuated with political changes in the country, and in recent years these sources of funds have been replaced by increasing financial support from World Bank affiliates and the IMF. In early 1993 a consortium of international donor organizations, including the World Bank, pledged $2,100m. to support the government's economic policies.

Although the level of donor pledges has risen dramatically since 1980, the disbursement of funds has been slow, owing to the complexity of donor agreements, and the lack of local expertise in administering aid. The repayment of the short-maturity credits from the IMF, which has contracted since 1983, has increased the pressure on the capital account of the balance of payments. In addition, Ghana's total external debt increased dramatically, to exceed $4,100m. in 1992, of which $1,347m. was medium-term and $2,797m. long-term debt. In 1994 ethnic conflict in the north of the country (see Recent History) necessitated additional assistance from the international community to compensate for the increase in budgetary expenditure.

Statistical Survey

Source (except where otherwise stated): Central Bureau of Statistics, POB 1098, Accra; tel. 66512.

Area and Population

AREA, POPULATION AND DENSITY

Area (sq km)	238,537*
Population (census results)	
1 March 1970	8,559,313
11 March 1984	
Males	6,063,848
Females	6,232,233
Total	12,296,081
Population (official estimate at mid-year)	
1991	15,400,000
Density (per sq km) at mid-1991	64.6

* 92,100 sq miles.

POPULATION BY REGION (1984 census)

Western	1,157,807
Central	1,142,335
Greater Accra	1,431,099
Eastern	1,680,890
Volta	1,211,907
Ashanti	2,090,100
Brong-Ahafo	1,206,608
Northern	1,164,583
Upper East	772,744
Upper West	438,008
Total	12,296,081

Principal Ethnic Groups (1960 census, percentage of total population): Akan 44.1, Mole-Dagbani 15.9, Ewe 13.0, Ga-Adangbe 8.3, Guan 3.7, Gurma 3.5.

PRINCIPAL TOWNS (population at 1984 census)

Accra (capital)	867,459
Kumasi	376,249
Tamale	135,952
Tema	131,528
Takoradi	61,484
Cape Coast	57,224
Sekondi	31,916

BIRTHS AND DEATHS (UN estimates, annual averages)

	1975-80	1980-85	1985-90
Birth rate (per 1,000)	45.1	45.2	44.3
Death rate (per 1,000)	15.3	14.3	13.1

Expectation of life (UN estimates, years at birth, 1985–90): 54.0 (males 52.2; females 55.8).

Source: UN, *World Population Prospects: The 1992 Revision.*

ECONOMICALLY ACTIVE POPULATION (1984 census)

	Males	Females	Total
Agriculture, hunting, forestry and fishing	1,750,024	1,560,943	3,310,967
Mining and quarrying	24,906	1,922	26,828
Manufacturing	198,430	389,988	588,418
Electricity, gas and water	14,033	1,404	15,437
Construction	60,692	3,994	64,686
Trade, restaurants and hotels	111,540	680,607	792,147
Transport, storage and communications	117,806	5,000	122,806
Financing, insurance, real estate and business services	19,933	7,542	27,475
Community, social and personal services	339,665	134,051	473,716
Total employed	2,637,029	2,785,451	5,422,480
Unemployed	87,452	70,172	157,624
Total labour force	2,724,481	2,855,623	5,580,104

Source: ILO, *Year Book of Labour Statistics.*

Agriculture

PRINCIPAL CROPS ('000 metric tons)

	1990	1991	1992
Maize	553	932	580*
Millet	75	112	80*
Sorghum	136	241	210*
Rice (paddy)	81	151	100†
Sugar cane†	110	110	110
Cassava (Manioc)	2,717	3,600*	4,000*
Yams	877	1,000†	1,000†
Taro (Coco yam)	815	1,297	1,200†
Onions†	28	28	28
Tomatoes	86	92†	100†
Eggplants (Aubergines)	6	6†	6†
Pulses	14	20†	20†
Oranges	50	50†	50†
Lemons and limes†	30	30	30
Bananas†	4	4	4
Plantains	799	1,178	1,200†
Pineapples	10	12†	12†
Palm kernels	29*	31*	34†
Groundnuts (in shell)	113	67*	100*
Coconuts†	220	225	220
Copra†	9	9	9
Coffee (green)*	1	2	2
Cocoa beans	284	243*	280*
Tobacco (leaves)	2*	2*	2†

* Unofficial figure(s). † FAO estimate(s).

Source: FAO, *Production Yearbook.*

LIVESTOCK ('000 head, year ending September)

	1990	1991*	1992*
Horses	1	1	1
Asses	10	10	10
Cattle	1,145	1,300	1,400
Pigs	474	500	500
Sheep	2,224	2,500	2,500
Goats	2,019	2,600	2,600

* FAO estimates.

Poultry (million): 10 in 1990; 11 (FAO estimate) in 1991; 12 (FAO estimate) in 1992.

Source: FAO, *Production Yearbook.*

LIVESTOCK PRODUCTS (FAO estimates, '000 metric tons)

	1990	1991	1992
Beef and veal	20	22	24
Mutton and lamb	6	7	7
Goat meat	5	7	7
Pig meat	11	11	11
Poultry meat	12	14	15
Other meat	90	90	91
Cows' milk	22	25	27
Hen eggs	12.7	12.7	13.5
Cattle hides	2.5	2.8	3.0

Source: FAO, *Production Yearbook.*

Forestry

ROUNDWOOD REMOVALS ('000 cubic metres)

	1990	1991	1992
Sawlogs, veneer logs and logs for sleepers	1,290	1,229	1,318
Other industrial wood*	381	381	381
Fuel wood	16,068*	15,512	15,512*
Total	17,739	17,122	17,211

* FAO estimate(s).

Source: FAO, *Yearbook of Forest Products.*

SAWNWOOD PRODUCTION ('000 cubic metres, incl. railway sleepers)

	1990	1991	1992
Total	472	400	410

Source: FAO, *Yearbook of Forest Products.*

Fishing

('000 metric tons, live weight)

	1989	1990	1991
Inland waters	57.7	58.0	57.0
Atlantic Ocean	303.5	333.6	308.0
Total catch	361.2	391.6	365.0

Source: FAO, *Yearbook of Fishery Statistics.*

Mining

('000 metric tons, unless otherwise indicated)

	1989	1990	1991
Gold (kilograms)*	13,265	16,840	26,310
Diamonds ('000 carats)†	370	446	490
Manganese ore*	160.4	98.0	104.3
Bauxite	347	381	400

* Figures refer to the metal content of ores.
† Data from the US Bureau of Mines.
Source: UN, *Industrial Statistics Yearbook*.

Industry

SELECTED PRODUCTS
('000 metric tons, unless otherwise indicated)

	1988	1989	1990
Wheat flour	95.2	88.1	108.4
Beer ('000 hectolitres)	614	639	628
Soft drinks ('000 crates)	1,377	1,553	8,147
Cigarettes (millions)	1,831	1,616	1,805
Motor spirit (petrol)	142.4	252	203.6
Kerosene	110.0	136.5	117.8
Diesel and gas oil	290.2	262.2	204.7
Cement	412.1	560.7	678.6
Aluminium (unwrought)*	161	169	174
Electric energy (million kWh)	4,807.8	5,230.5	5,801.4

* Primary metal only.

1991 ('000 metric tons, unless otherwise indicated): Cigarettes (million) 2,100; Motor spirit (petrol) 210; Kerosene 120; Cement 675 (provisional or estimated figure); Aluminium (unwrought) 175; Electric energy (million kWh) 6,152.
Source: UN, *Industrial Statistics Yearbook*.

Finance

CURRENCY AND EXCHANGE RATES

Monetary Units
100 pesewas = 1 new cedi.

Sterling and Dollar Equivalents (31 March 1994)
£1 sterling = 1,387.5 cedis;
US $1 = 934.6 cedis;
10,000 cedis = £7.207 = $10.700.

Average Exchange Rate (cedis per US $)
1991 367.83
1992 437.09 (estimate)
1993 649.06

GENERAL BUDGET (provisional, million cedis)

Revenue*	1988	1989	1990
Taxation	125,779	179,139	214,254
Taxes on income, profits, etc.	39,689	46,640	51,693
Employees' income tax	6,016	7,572	10,855
Self-employed income tax	5,080	5,060	6,085
Company tax	27,648	32,534	32,711
Domestic taxes on goods and services	36,318	52,673	72,706
General sales taxes	12,363	17,893	23,406
Excises	15,019	18,998	22,917
Petroleum tax	8,485	15,078	25,397
Taxes on international trade	49,772	79,826	89,855
Import duties	17,010	32,415	36,013
Export duties	24,465	31,243	26,185
Other current revenue	16,459	14,037	25,272
Total	142,238	193,170	239,526

Expenditure†	1988	1989	1990
General public services	19,474	25,789	33,376
Defence	4,603	6,106	9,006
Public order and safety	8,581	10,171	13,470
Education	36,995	47,692	64,835
Health	12,880	19,853	25,706
Social security and welfare	9,904	14,379	18,389
Housing and community amenities	5,002	5,170	6,607
Recreational, cultural and religious affairs	2,195	3,857	6,872
Economic services	25,753	33,124	38,282
Agriculture, forestry and fishing	5,004	9,142	10,438
Mining, manufacturing and construction	1,617	2,184	2,625
Roads and waterways	12,444	14,883	16,081
Other transport and communications	2,535	2,352	3,248
Other purposes	18,511	30,327	37,931
Interest payments	11,961	18,744	27,318
Transfers to other levels of government	3,543	1,960	2,633
Total	143,897	196,466	254,473
Current	116,009	153,359	201,238
Capital	27,888	43,107	53,235

* Excluding grants received, mainly from abroad (million cedis): 11,553 in 1988; 21,343 in 1989; 27,821 in 1990.
† Excluding net lending (million cedis): 5,983 in 1988.

INTERNATIONAL RESERVES (US $ million at 31 December)

	1991	1992	1993
Gold*	74.0	78.1	77.2
IMF special drawing rights	12.5	4.4	0.5
Foreign exchange	537.7	291.6	316.7
Total	624.2	374.1	394.4

* National valuation.
Source: IMF, *International Financial Statistics*.

MONEY SUPPLY ('000 million new cedis at 31 December)

	1991	1992	1993
Currency outside banks	89.93	183.48	222.20
Deposits of non-financial public enterprises	13.09	2.18	3.30
Demand deposits at deposit money banks	132.01	174.82	235.32
Total money (incl. others)	235.75	360.69	461.35

Source: IMF, *International Financial Statistics*.

COST OF LIVING (Consumer Price Index for Accra; average of monthly figures. Base: 1980 = 100)

	1990	1991	1992
Food	2,711	2,955	3,261
Clothing and footwear	4,371	5,052	5,488
Rent, fuel and light	5,802	8,373	10,097
All items (incl. others)	3,575	4,219	4,644

Source: ILO, *Year Book of Labour Statistics.*

NATIONAL ACCOUNTS (million new cedis at current prices)

National Income and Product

	1988	1989*	1990†
GDP in purchasers' values	1,051,196.3	1,417,214.4	2,031,700
Net factor income from abroad	-26,526.8	-28,188.0	-36,700
Gross national product	1,024,669.5	1,389,026.4	1,995,000
Less Consumption of fixed capital	68,740.9	86,142.4	110,700
National income in market prices	955,928.6	1,302,884.0	1,884,300
Other current transfers from abroad (net)	70,029.9	115,344.0	n.a.
National disposable income	1,025,958.5	1,418,228.0	n.a.

* Provisional figures.

† Source: UN, *National Accounts Statistics.*

Expenditure on the Gross Domestic Product*

	1990	1991	1992
Government final consumption expenditure	222,000	294,200	400,100
Private final consumption expenditure	1,736,100	2,159,400	2,544,300
Increase in stocks	1,400	1,600	1,900
Gross fixed capital formation	247,700	326,400	386,100
Total domestic expenditure	2,207,200	2,781,600	3,332,400
Exports of goods and services	312,600	404,700	482,900
Less Imports of goods and services	488,000	611,500	806,400
GDP in purchasers' values	2,031,700	2,574,800	3,008,800
GDP at constant 1985 prices	433,700	456,800	474,600

* Figures are rounded to the nearest 100m. new cedis.

Source: IMF, *International Financial Statistics.*

Gross Domestic Product by Economic Activity

	1988	1989	1990*
Agriculture and livestock	459,114.8	607,651.2	860,033.7
Forestry and logging	47,604.1	64,376.6	85,716.8
Fishing	14,810.2	21,946.6	26,573.3
Mining and quarrying	20,795.6	26,309.7	35,824.2
Manufacturing	100,534.6	141,814.9	187,523.9
Construction	30,247.4	42,577.7	62,210.7
Transport, storage and communications	44,430.4	60,524.2	89,417.2
Finance, insurance, real estate and business services	28,562.4	38,040.8	78,421.2
Government services	72,993.0	97,564.9	151,701.6
Other community, social and personal services	7,405.0	10,881.7	20,311.2
Producers of private non-profit services	1,057.8	1,463.1	2,158.4
Sub-total	1,048,996.3	1,404,263.2	2,022,313.4
Import duties	17,010.2	32,414.7	36,013.3
Less Imputed bank service charge	14,810.2	19,463.5	26,640.4
GDP in purchasers' values	1,051,196.3	1,417,214.4	2,031,686.3

* Provisional figures.

BALANCE OF PAYMENTS (US $ million)

	1990	1991	1992
Merchandise exports f.o.b.	890.6	997.6	986.4
Merchandise imports f.o.b.	-1,198.9	-1,318.7	-1,456.7
Trade balance	-308.3	-321.1	-470.3
Exports of services	79.3	95.1	110.3
Imports of services	-295.4	-318.8	-371.3
Other income received	13.8	15.2	18.6
Other income paid	-133.6	-144.0	-133.8
Private unrequited transfers (net)	201.9	219.5	254.9
Official unrequited transfers (net)	213.8	201.4	213.8
Current balance	-228.5	-252.7	-377.8
Direct investment (net)	14.8	20.0	22.5
Other capital (net)	310.2	318.1	299.1
Net errors and omissions	8.8	23.8	-0.4
Overall balance	105.3	109.2	-56.6

Source: IMF, *International Financial Statistics.*

External Trade

PRINCIPAL COMMODITIES ('000 cedis)

Imports	1985	1986*	1987*
Food and live animals	1,892,024	5,007,394	9,127,837
Beverages and tobacco	733,593	438,751	741,541
Crude materials (inedible) except fuels	827,421	2,115,119	2,924,354
Mineral fuels, lubricants, etc.	13,786,623	14,419,751	24,530,573
Animal and vegetable oils and fats	301,553	466,977	934,842
Chemicals	5,896,400	11,008,098	20,902,140
Basic manufactures	5,060,599	10,950,023	38,761,716
Machinery and transport equipment	12,436,517	28,630,065	49,137,239
Miscellaneous manufactured articles	4,890,964	4,240,493	25,567,087
Other commodities and transactions	1,329,592	16,081,335	2,152,507
Total	47,155,286	93,358,006	174,779,836

Exports	1986	1987	1988
Cocoa	41,895,579	67,872,726	n.a.
Logs	2,682,012	n.a.	n.a.
Sawn timber	1,995,159	n.a.	n.a.
Bauxite	547,412	851,442	2,351,894
Manganese ore	894,811	1,205,743	1,738,043
Diamonds	561,231	696,996	710,094
Gold	11,915,233	24,205,589	49,417,526
Total (incl. others)	76,948,000	147,275,000	n.a.

* Provisional figures.

PRINCIPAL TRADING PARTNERS ('000 cedis)

Imports	1985	1986*	1987*
Canada	384,680	1,540,593	2,020,834
China, People's Repub.	445,812	811,612	1,545,731
France	1,036,690	2,669,607	6,222,440
Germany, Federal Repub.	5,394,777	10,738,609	19,049,744
Italy	1,561,173	2,836,425	3,047,137
Japan	2,845,424	3,714,632	7,188,215
Libya	7,433	34,489	233,279
Netherlands	1,216,629	3,517,359	5,598,598
Nigeria	10,601,454	11,495,206	21,806,475
Norway	201,533	354,515	535,642
United Kingdom	11,843,832	16,361,776	68,495,538
USA	2,725,773	9,065,604	18,310,717
Total (incl. others)	43,142,515	86,366,800	165,463,210

Exports	1985	1986*	1987*
Germany, Federal Repub.	2,035,879	4,512,882	8,625,993
Japan	3,249,391	5,361,443	9,377,516
Netherlands	3,400,444	8,554,502	14,005,545
USSR	2,156,475	7,453,808	9,515,974
United Kingdom	6,806,297	10,547,658	27,934,600
USA	2,743,024	12,283,339	19,243,017
Yugoslavia	328,770	690,310	2,061,718
Total (incl. others)	24,733,619	70,021,623	103,679,585

* Provisional figures.

Transport

RAILWAYS (traffic)

	1988	1989	1990
Passengers carried ('000)	3,259.4	2,890.4	1,896.8
Freight carried ('000 metric tons)	774.0	751.4	724.1
Passenger-km (million)	389.3	330.5	277.5
Net ton-km (million)	125.5	130.8	126.9

ROAD TRAFFIC (vehicles in use at 31 December)

	1988	1989
Passenger cars	51,627	57,897
Motor cycles	4,309	4,661
Buses and coaches	17,470	20,434
Goods vehicles	7,723	9,691

Source: International Road Federation, *World Road Statistics.*

INTERNATIONAL SEA-BORNE SHIPPING
(estimated freight traffic, '000 metric tons)

	1988	1989	1990
Goods loaded	1,485	1,475	1,810
Goods unloaded	2,640	2,688	2,842

Source: UN, *Monthly Bulletin of Statistics.*

CIVIL AVIATION (traffic on scheduled services)

	1989	1990	1991
Kilometres flown (million)	4	4	5
Passengers carried ('000)	232	188	192
Passenger-km (million)	382	366	331
Freight ton-km (million)	14	16	19
Total ton-km (million)	48	49	58

Source: UN, *Statistical Yearbook.*

Tourism

	1988	1989	1990
Tourist arrivals ('000)	114	125	146

Source: UN, *Statistical Yearbook.*

Communications Media

	1989	1990	1991
Radio receivers ('000 in use)	n.a.	4,000	4,150
Television receivers ('000 in use)	211	225	235
Telephones ('000 in use)	83	84	85
Daily newspapers			
Number	n.a.	2	n.a.
Average circulation ('000 copies)	n.a.	200	n.a.

Sources: UNESCO, *Statistical Yearbook;* UN Economic Commission for Africa, *African Statistical Yearbook.*

Education

(1989)

	Institutions	Teachers	Students
Pre-primary	4,735	15,152	323,406
Primary*	11,165	66,946	1,945,422
Secondary			
General (public only)*	n.a.	39,903	768,603
Teacher training	38†	1,001	15,723
Vocational (public only)	20‡	1,247	20,777
University	3‡	700§	9,609*

* 1990 figure(s).
† 1988 figure.
‡ 1988/89 figure.
§ Excluding the University of Ghana.
Source: mainly UNESCO, *Statistical Yearbook.*

Directory

The Constitution

Under the terms of the Constitution of the Fourth Republic, which was approved by national referendum on 28 April 1992, Ghana has a multi-party political system. Executive power is vested in the President, who is Head of State and Commander-in-Chief of the Armed Forces. The President is elected by universal adult suffrage for a term of four years, and appoints a Vice-President. The duration of the President's tenure of office is limited to two four-year terms. It is also stipulated that if no presidential candidate receives more than 50% of votes cast a new election between the two candidates with the highest number of votes is to take place within 21 days. Legislative power is vested in a 200-member unicameral Parliament, which is elected by direct adult suffrage for a four-year term. The Council of Ministers is appointed by the President, subject to approval by the Parliament. The Constitution also provides for a 25-member Council of State, principally comprising presidential nominees and regional representatives, and a National Security Council, mainly comprising senior ministers and members of the security forces, both of which act as advisory bodies to the President.

The Government

HEAD OF STATE

President and Commander-in-Chief of the Armed Forces: Flt-Lt (retd) JERRY RAWLINGS (assumed power as Chairman of Provisional National Defence Council 31 December 1981; elected President 3 November 1992).

Vice-President: KOW NKENSEN ARKAAH.

COUNCIL OF MINISTERS
(August 1994)

Minister of Defence: Alhaji MAHAMA IDDRISU.

Attorney-General and Minister of Justice: Dr OBED ASAMOAH (acting).

Minister of Finance and Economic Planning: Dr KWESI BOTCHWEY.

Minister of Foreign Affairs: Dr OBED ASAMOAH.

Minister of the Interior: Col (retd) E. M. OSEI-WUSU.

Minister of Health: Cdre (retd) STEVE OBIMPEH.

Minister of Food and Agriculture: IBRAHIM ISSAKA ADAM.

Minister of Education: HARRY SAWYERR.

Minister of Information: KOFI TOTOBI QUAKYI.

Minister of Local Government and Rural Development: KWAMENA AHWOI.

Minister of Mines and Energy: RICHARD KWAME PEPRAH.

Minister of Trade and Industries: EMMA MITCHEL.

Minister of Transport and Communications: EDWARD SALIA.

Minister of Parliamentary Affairs: J. H. OWUSU-ACHEAMPONG.

Minister of Employment and Social Welfare: DAVID SARPONG BOATENG.

Minister of the Environment, Science and Technology: Dr CHRISTINE AMOAKO-NUAMAH.

Minister of Lands and Forestry: Dr KWABENA ADJEI.

There are, in addition, nine non-cabinet ministers, of which four are responsible, respectively, for roads and highways, works and housing, tourism, and youth and sports.

REGIONAL MINISTERS

Ashanti: DANIEL OHENE AGYEKUM.

Brong Ahafo: I. K. ADJEI-MENSAH.

Central: EBENEZER KWABENA FOSU.

Eastern: Maj. EMMANUEL TETTEH.

Greater Accra: MICHAEL AFEDI GIZO.

Northern: Lt-Col (retd) ABDULAI IBRAHIM.

Upper East: SHERIF A. GUMA.

Upper West: J. YELEH CHIREH.

Volta: MODESTUS AHIABLE.

Western: Dr JOHN ABU.

MINISTRIES

Office of the President: Accra.

Ministry of Defence: Burma Camp, Accra; tel. (21) 777611; telex 2077.

Ministry of Education: POB M45, Accra; tel. (21) 665421.

Ministry of Employment and Social Welfare: Accra.

Ministry of the Environment, Science and Technology: POB M232, Accra; tel. (21) 66679; fax (21) 666828.

Ministry of Finance and Economic Planning: POB M40, Accra; tel. (21) 665421; telex 2132.

Ministry of Food and Agriculture: POB M37, Accra; tel. (21) 665421.

Ministry of Foreign Affairs: POB M53, Accra; tel. (21) 665421; telex 2001.

Ministry of Health: POB M44, Accra; tel. (21) 665421.

Ministry of Information: POB M41, Accra; tel. (21) 228011; telex 2201.

Ministry of the Interior: POB M42, Accra; tel. (21) 665421.

Ministry of Justice: Accra.

Ministry of Lands and Forestry: POB M212, Accra; tel. (21) 665421.

Ministry of Local Government and Rural Development: POB M50, Accra; tel. (21) 665421.

Ministry of Mines and Energy: POB M212, Accra; tel. (21) 665421.

Ministry of Parliamentary Affairs: Accra.

Ministry of Roads and Highways: POB M57, Accra; tel. (21) 221822; fax (21) 223908.

Ministry of Tourism: Accra.

Ministry of Trade and Industry: POB M47, Accra; tel. (21) 665421; telex 2105.

Ministry of Transport and Communications: POB M38, Accra; tel. (21) 665421.

Ministry of Works and Housing: Accra.

President and Legislature

PRESIDENT

Presidential election, 3 November 1992

Candidates	Votes	%
Flt-Lt (retd) JERRY RAWLINGS (Progressive Alliance*)	2,327,600	58.3
Prof. ALBERT ADU BOAHEN (NPP)	1,213,073	30.4
Dr HILLA LIMANN (PNC)	266,728	6.7
KWABENA DARKO (NIP)	113,615	2.8
Lt-Gen. (retd) E. A. ERSKINE (PHP)	68,099	1.7
Total	3,989,115	100.0

* An electoral coalition comprising the National Democratic Congress (NDC), the National Convention Party (NCP) and the EGLE (Every Ghanaian Living Everywhere) Party.

PARLIAMENT

Speaker: Justice DANIEL F. ANNAN.

Legislative election, 29 December 1992

	Seats
National Democratic Congress (NDC)	189
National Convention Party (NCP)	8
Independents	2
EGLE (Every Ghanaian Living Everywhere) Party	1
Total	200

COUNCIL OF STATE

Chairman: Alhaji MUMUNI BAWUMIA.

Political Organizations

The ban on the operation of political associations, which had been in force since December 1981, was lifted in May 1992. The most prominent political organizations in mid-1994 were:

Democratic People's Party (DPP): Accra; f. 1992; Chair. T. N. WARD-BREW.

EGLE (Every Ghanaian Living Everywhere) Party: Accra; alliance of supporters of Pres. Jerry Rawlings; Chair. NANA OFORI ATTA.

Ghana Democratic Republican Party (GDRP): Accra; f. 1992; Leader Dr KOFI AMOAH.

National Convention Party (NCP): Accra; f. 1992; pro-Govt; Chair. Rev. KWAKU BOATENG; Sec.-Gen. Alhaji ABUBAKAR B. ZIBLIM.

National Democratic Congress (NDC): Accra; f. 1992; coalition of pro-Govt organizations; Chair. ISSIFU ALI.

New Generation Alliance (NGA): Accra; f. 1992.

New Patriotic Party (NPP): Accra; f. 1992 by supporters of the fmr Prime Minister, Dr Kofi Busia; Chair. BERNARD JOAO DA ROCHA; Sec.-Gen. AGYENIM BOATENG.

People's Convention Party (PCP): f. Dec. 1993 by the National Independence Party, the People's Heritage Party and a faction of the People's National Convention; Chair. Alhaji ASUMAH BANDA (acting).

People's National Convention (PNC): Accra; f. 1992 by supporters of the fmr President, Dr Kwame Nkrumah; Leader Dr HILLA LIMANN.

Popular Party for Democracy and Development (PPDD): Accra; f. 1992 by supporters of the fmr President, Dr Kwame Nkrumah; Chair. KWAME WIAFE; Sec.-Gen. KWESI PRATT.

The opposition movements listed below, some of which operate mainly from outside Ghana, were in existence prior to the restoration of a plural political system:

Campaign for Democracy in Ghana (CDG): London, England.

Co-ordinating Committee of Democratic Forces of Ghana (CCDFG): f. 1991; an alliance of 11 opposition movements and other orgs; Chair. Maj. (retd) KOJO BOAKYE GYAN.

Democratic Alliance of Ghana (DAG): based in London, England; Chair. BRIGHT ODURO KWARTENG.

Free Democrats' Union (FDU): Leader Maj. (retd) KOJO BOAKYE DJAN.

Ghana Democratic Movement (GDM): London, England; f. 1983.

Ghana Democratic Union: Nigeria; Leader Dr EDUKU QUARFO.

Kwame Nkrumah Revolutionary Guards (KNRG): Accra; African socialist; Chair. SONNIE PROVENCAL.

Movement for Freedom and Justice (MFJ): Accra; f. 1990 to campaign for the restoration of a civilian-led democratic system; Sec.-Gen. JOHN NDEBUGRE.

New Democratic Movement (NDM): Accra; socialist; Chair. KWAME KARIKARI.

United Party (UP): centre-right; Leader J. H. MENSAH.

United Revolutionary Front (URF): London, England; coalition of Marxist-Leninist groups.

Diplomatic Representation

EMBASSIES AND HIGH COMMISSIONS IN GHANA

Algeria: F606/1, off Cantonments Rd, Christiansborg, POB 2747, Accra; tel. (21) 776828; Ambassador: HAMID BOURKI.

Benin: C175 Odoi Kwao Crescent, POB 7871, Accra; tel. (21) 225701; Chargé d'affaires: L. TONOUKOUIN.

Brazil: 5 Volta St, Airport Residential Area, POB 2918, Accra; tel. (21) 777154; telex 2081; Ambassador: CARLOS NORBERTO DE OLIVEIRA PARES.

Bulgaria: 3 Kakramadu Rd, East Cantonments, POB 3193, Accra; tel. and fax (21) 774231; telex 2709; Chargé d'affaires a.i.: ALEXANDER PEYTCHEV.

Burkina Faso: 772/3, Asylum Down, off Farrar Ave, POB 651, Accra; tel. (21) 221988; telex 2108; Ambassador: EMILE GOUBA.

Canada: No. 46, Independence Ave, POB 1639, Accra; tel. (21) 228566; telex 2024; High Commissioner: C. D. FOGERTY.

China, People's Republic: No. 7, Agostinho Neto Rd, Airport Residential Area, POB 3356, Accra; tel. (21) 777073; Ambassador: GUO JINGAN.

Côte d'Ivoire: House No. 9, 8th Lane, off Cantonments Rd, POB 3445, Christiansborg, Accra; tel. (21) 774611; telex 2131; Ambassador: KONAN NDA.

Cuba: 20 Amilcar Cabral Rd, Airport Residential Area, POB 9163 Airport, Accra; tel. (21) 775868; telex 2234; Ambassador: LAUREANO CARDOSO.

Czech Republic: C260/5, Kanda High Rd No. 2, POB 5226, Accra-North; tel. (21) 223540; Ambassador Dr JOSEPH JANEČEK.

Egypt: 27 Noi Fetreke St, Roman Ridge, POB 2508, Accra; tel. (21) 776854; telex 2691; fax (21) 776795; Ambassador: MOHAMED EL-ZAYAT.

Ethiopia: House No. 6, Adiembra Rd, East Cantonment, POB 1646, Accra; tel. (21) 775928; Chargé d'affaires a.i.: BEIDE MELAKU.

France: 12th Rd, off Liberation Ave, POB 187, Accra; tel. (21) 228571; telex 2733; fax (21) 775904; Ambassador: JEAN-CLAUDE BROCHENIN.

Germany: Valdemosa Lodge, Plot No. 18, North Ridge Residential Area, 7th Ave Extension, POB 1757, Accra; tel. (21) 221311; telex 2025; fax (21) 221349; Ambassador: HANS-JOACHIM HELOT.

Guinea: 11 Osu Badu St, Dzorwulu, POB 5497, Accra-North; tel. (21) 777921; Ambassador: DORE DIALE DRUS.

Holy See: Airport Residential Area, POB 9675, Accra; tel. (21) 777759; fax (21) 774019; Apostolic Nuncio: Most Rev. ANDRÉ DUPUY, Titular Archbishop of Selsea.

Hungary: 14 West Cantonment, POB 3027, Accra; tel. (21) 777234; telex 2543; Chargé d'affaires a.i.: IMRE SOSOVICSKA.

India: 9 Ridge Rd, Roman Ridge, POB 3040, Accra; tel. (21) 775601; telex 2154; fax (21) 772176; High Commissioner: DILJIT SINGH PANNUN.

Iran: 10 Agbaamo St, Airport Residential Area, POB 1260073, Accra; tel. (21) 74474; telex 2117; Ambassador: SHAMEDDIN KHAREGHANI.

Italy: Jawaharlal Nehru Rd, POB 140, Accra; tel. (21) 775621; telex 2039; Ambassador: MARIO FUGAZZOLA.

Japan: Josif Broz Tito Ave, off Jawaharlal Nehru Ave, POB 1637, Accra; tel. (21) 775616; telex 2068; Ambassador: TOSHIRO KOJIMA.

Korea, Democratic People's Republic: 139 Roman Ridge, Ambassadorial Estate, Nortei Ababio Estate, POB 13874, Accra; tel. (21) 777825; Ambassador: RI JAE SONG.

Korea, Republic: 3 Abokobi Rd, East Cantonments, POB 13700, Accra; tel. (21) 777533; Ambassador: HONG-WOO NAM.

Lebanon: 864/1 off Cantonments Rd, OSU RE, POB 562, Accra; tel. (21) 776727; telex 2118; Ambassador: HICHAM DIMACHKIEH.

Liberia: F675/1, off Cantonments Rd, Christiansborg, POB 895, Accra; tel. (21) 775641; telex 2071; Ambassador: T. BOYE NELSON.

Libya: 14 Sixth St, Airport Residential Area, POB 6995, Accra; tel. (21) 774820; telex 2179; Secretary of People's Bureau: Dr FATIMA MAGAME.

Mali: Crescent Rd, Block 1, POB 1121, Accra; tel. (21) 666421; telex 2061; Ambassador: MUPHTAH AG HAIRY.

Netherlands: 89 Liberation Rd, Sankara Circle, POB 3248, Accra; tel. (21) 773644; telex 2128; fax (21) 773655; Ambassador: S. H. BLOEMBERGEN.

Nigeria: Rangoon Ave, POB 1548, Accra; tel. (21) 776158; telex 2051; High Commissioner: T. A. OLU-OTUNLA.

Pakistan: 11 Ring Rd East, POB 1114, Accra; tel. (21) 776059; telex 2426; High Commissioner: Dr ABDUL KABIR.

Poland: 2 Akosombo St, Airport Residential Area, POB 2552, Accra; tel. (21) 775972; telex 2558; fax (21) 776108; Chargé d'affaires a.i.: KAZIMIERZ MAURER.

Romania: North Labone, Ward F, Block 6, House 262, POB M112, Accra; tel. (21) 774076; telex 2027; Chargé d'affaires: GHEORGHE V. ILIE.

Russia: F856/1, Ring Rd East, POB 1634, Accra; tel. (21) 775611; Ambassador: (vacant).

Saudi Arabia: F868/1, off Cantonments Rd, OSU RE, Accra; tel. (21) 776651; Chargé d'affaires: ANWAR ABDUL FATTAH ABDRABBUH.

Singapore: Accra.

Slovakia: C260/5, Kanda High Rd No. 2, POB 5226, Accra-North; tel. (21) 223540.

Spain: Airport Residential Area, Lamptey Ave Extension, POB 1218, Accra; tel. (21) 774004; telex 2680; fax (21) 776217; Ambassador: LORENZO GONZÁLEZ ALONSO.

Switzerland: 9 Water Rd S.I., North Ridge Area, POB 359, Accra; tel. (21) 228125; telex 2197; fax (21) 223583; Ambassador: PIERRE MONOD.

Togo: Togo House, near Cantonments Circle, POB 4308, Accra; tel. (21) 777950; telex 2166; Ambassador: LARBLI TCHINTCHIBIDJA.

United Kingdom: Osu Link, off Gamel Abdul Nasser Ave, POB 296, Accra; tel. (21) 221665; telex 2323; fax (21) 664652; High Commissioner: D. C. WALKER.

USA: Ring Road East, POB 194, Accra; tel. (21) 775346; fax (21) 776008; Ambassador: KENNETH L. BROWN.

Yugoslavia: 47 Senchi St, Airport Residential Area, POB 1629, Accra; tel. 775761; Ambassador: LAZAR COVIĆ.

Judicial System

The civil law in force in Ghana is based on the Common Law, doctrines of equity and general statutes which were in force in England in 1874, as modified by subsequent Ordinances. Ghanaian customary law is, however, the basis of most personal, domestic and contractual relationships. Criminal Law is based on the Criminal Procedure Code, 1960, derived from English Criminal Law, and since amended. The Superior Court of Judicature comprises a Supreme Court, a Court of Appeal and a High Court of Justice; Inferior Courts include Circuit Courts, District Courts and such other Courts as may be designated by law.

Supreme Court: The Supreme Court consists of the Chief Justice and not fewer than four other Justices of the Supreme Court. It is the final court of appeal in Ghana and has jurisdiction in matters relating to the enforcement or interpretation of the Constitution.

Chief Justice: PHILLIP E. N. K. ARCHER.

The Court of Appeal: Consists of the Chief Justice and not fewer than five Judges of the Court of Appeal. It has jurisdiction to hear and determine appeals from any judgment, decree or order of the High Court.

The High Court: Comprises the Chief Justice and not fewer than 12 Justices of the High Court. It exercises original jurisdiction in all matters, civil and criminal, other than those for offences involving treason. Trial by jury is practised in criminal cases in Ghana and the Criminal Procedure Code, 1960, provides that all trials on indictment shall be by a jury or with the aid of Assessors.

The Circuit Court: Circuit Courts exercise original jurisdiction in civil matters where the amount involved does not exceed C100,000. They also have jurisdiction with regard to the guardianship and custody of infants, and original jurisdiction in all criminal cases, except offences where the maximum punishment is death or the offence of treason. They have appellate jurisdiction from decisions of any District Court situated within their respective circuits.

District Courts: To each magisterial district is assigned at least one District Magistrate who has original jurisdiction to try civil suits in which the amount involved does not exceed C50,000. District Magistrates also have jurisdiction to deal with all criminal cases, except first-degree felonies, and commit cases of a more serious nature to either the Circuit Court or the High Court. A Grade I District Court can impose a fine not exceeding C1,000 and sentences of imprisonment of up to two years and a Grade II District Court may impose a fine not exceeding C500 and a sentence of imprisonment of up to 12 months. A District Court has no appellate jurisdiction, except in rent matters under the Rent Act.

Juvenile Courts: Jurisdiction in cases involving persons under 17 years of age, except where the juvenile is charged jointly with an adult. The Courts comprise a Chairman, who must be either the District Magistrate or a lawyer, and not fewer than two other members appointed by the Chief Justice in consultation with the Judicial Council. The Juvenile Courts can make orders as to the protection and supervision of a neglected child and can negotiate with parents to secure the good behaviour of a child.

National Public Tribunal: Considers appeals from the Regional Public Tribunals. Its decisions are final and are not subject to any further appeal. The Tribunal consists of at least three members and not more than five, one of whom acts as Chairman.

Regional Public Tribunals: Hears criminal cases relating to prices, rent or exchange control, theft, fraud, forgery, corruption or any offence which may be referred to them by the Provisional National Defence Council.

Special Military Tribunal: Hears criminal cases involving members of the armed forces. It consists of between five and seven members.

Religion

At the 1960 census the distribution of religious groups was: Christians 42.8%, traditional religions 38.2%, Muslims 12.0%, unclassified 7.0%. In August 1989 the Government introduced a law requiring religious bodies to obtain registration from the Religious Affairs Committee of the National Commission for Culture.

CHRISTIANITY

Christian Council of Ghana: POB 919, Accra; tel. (21) 776725; f. 1929; advisory body comprising 14 Protestant churches; Chair. Rt Rev. D. A. KORANTENG; Gen. Sec. Rev. D. A. DARTEY.

The Anglican Communion

The Church of the Province of West Africa has six dioceses in Ghana.

Provincial Secretary: B. A. TAGOE, POB 8, Accra; tel. (21) 662292.

Archbishop of West Africa and Bishop of Koforidua: Most Rev. ROBERT OKINE, POB 980, Koforidua; tel. (81) 2329.

Bishop of Accra: Rt Rev. FRANCIS W. B. THOMPSON, Bishopscourt, POB 8, Accra; tel. (21) 662292.

Bishop of Cape Coast: Rt Rev. KOBINA ADDUAH QUARSHIE, Bishopscourt, POB 38, Cape Coast; tel. (42) 2018.

Bishop of Kumasi: Rt Rev. EDMUND YEBOAH, Bishop's House, POB 144, Kumasi; tel. (51) 4117.

Bishop of Sekondi: Rt Rev. THEOPHILUS ANNOBIL, POB 85, Sekondi; tel. (31) 6048.

Bishop of Sunyani and Tamale: Rt Rev. JOSEPH KOBINA DADSON, Bishop's House, POB 110, Tamale; tel. (71) 2018.

The Roman Catholic Church

Ghana comprises three archdioceses and seven dioceses. At 31 December 1992 there were 1,801,096 adherents in the country, equivalent to 12.1% of the total population.

Ghana Bishops' Conference: National Catholic Secretariat, POB 9712, Airport, Accra; tel. (21) 776491; telex 2471; fax (21) 776492; f. 1960; Pres. Rt Rev. FRANCIS A. K. LODONU, Bishop of Keta-Ho.

Archbishop of Accra: Most Rev. DOMINIC ANDOH, Chancery Office, POB 247, Accra; tel. (21) 222728.

Archbishop of Cape Coast: Most Rev. PETER K. APPIAH-TURKSON, Archbishop's House, POB 112, Cape Coast; tel. (42) 2593.

Archbishop of Tamale: Most Rev. PETER POREKU DERY, Gumbehini Rd, POB 42, Tamale; tel. (71) 2924; fax (71) 2425.

Other Christian Churches

African Methodist Episcopal Zion Church: POB 239, Sekondi; Pres. Rev. Dr ZORMELO.

Christian Methodist Episcopal Church: POB 3906, Accra; Pres. Rev. YENN BATA.

Evangelical-Lutheran Church of Ghana: POB 197, Kaneshie; tel. 223487; telex 2134; fax 223353; Pres. Rev. PAUL KOFI FYNN; 21,000 mems.

Evangelical-Presbyterian Church: POB 18, Ho; tel. 755; f. 1847; Moderator Rt Rev. D. A. KORANTENG; 294,848 mems.

Ghana Baptist Convention: POB 1979, Kumasi; tel. (51) 5215; f. 1963; Pres. Rev. FRED DEEGBE; Sec. Rev. FRANK ADAMS.

Mennonite Church: POB 5485, Accra; f. 1957; Moderator Rev. S. T. OKRAH; Sec. ABRAHAM K. WETSEH; 800 mems.

Methodist Church of Ghana: Liberia Rd, POB 403, Accra; tel. (21) 228120; independent since 1961; Pres. Rt Rev. Prof. K. A. DICKSON; Sec. Rev. Dr EBENEZER RIVERSON; 332,804 mems.

Presbyterian Church of Ghana: POB 1800, Accra; tel. (21) 662511; telex 2525; f. 1828; Moderator Rt Rev. D. A. KORANTENG; Sec. Rev. I. K. FOKUO; 422,438 mems.

Seventh-day Adventists: POB 1016, Accra; tel. (21) 223720; telex 2119; f. 1943; Pres. P. K. ASAREH; Sec. SETH A. LARYEA.

The African Methodist Episcopal Church, the F'Eden Church, and the Society of Friends (Quakers) are also active in Ghana.

In June 1989 the activities of the Church of Jesus Christ of Latter-day Saints (Mormons) and the Jehovah's Witnesses were banned. The groups were alleged to have conducted themselves in a manner not conducive to public order.

ISLAM

There is a substantial Muslim population in the Northern Region. The majority are Malikees.

Chief Imam: Alhaji MUKITAR ABASS.

The Press

In 1992 a commission was established to regulate the media.

NEWSPAPERS

Daily

Daily Graphic: Graphic Rd, POB 742, Accra; tel. (21) 228911; f. 1950; state-owned; Editor ELVIS ARYEH; circ. 100,000.

The Ghanaian Times: New Times Corpn, Ring Rd West, POB 2638, Accra; tel. (21) 228282; f. 1958; state-owned; Editor CHRISTIAN AGGREY; circ. 40,000.

The Pioneer: Abura Printing Works Ltd, POB 325, Kumasi; tel. (51) 2204; f. 1939; Editor T. H. EWUSI-BROOKMAN; circ. 100,000.

Weekly

Champion: POB 6828, Accra-North; tel. (21) 229079; Man. Dir MARK D. N. ADDY; Editor FRANK CAXTON WILLIAMS; circ. 300,000.

Christian Chronicle: Accra; English; Editor GEORGE NAYKENE.

Christian Messenger: Presbyterian Book Depot Bldg, POB 3075, Accra; tel. (21) 662415; telex 2525; f. 1883; English, Twi and Ga edns; Editor G. B. K. OWUSU; circ. 60,000.

Echo: POB 5288, Accra; f. 1968; Sundays; Man. Editor M. K. FRIMPONG; circ. 30,000.

Entertaining Eye: Kad Publication, POB 125, Darkuman-Accra; Editor NANA KWAKYE YIADOM; circ. 40,000.

Evening News: POB 7505, Accra; tel. (21) 229416; Man. Editor OSEI POKU; circ. 30,000.

Experience: POB 5084, Accra-North; Editor ALFRED YAW POKU; circ. 50,000.

Free Press: Accra; independent; English; Editor EBEN QUARCOO.

Ghanaian Chronicle: POB 16369, Airport, Accra; Editor NANA KOFI COOMSON; circ. 60,000.

The Ghanaian Voice: Newstop Publications, POB 514, Mamprobi, Accra; Editor DAN K. ANSAH; circ. 100,000.

Graphic Sports: POB 742, Accra; tel. (21) 228911; circ. 60,000.

The Mirror: Graphic Rd, POB 742, Accra; tel. (21) 228911; telex 2475; fax (21) 669886; f. 1953; state-owned; Sat.; Editor E. N. O. PROVENCAL (acting); circ. 90,000.

New Nation: POB 6828, Accra-North; Man. Dir MARK D. N. ADDY; Editor S. N. SASRAKU; circ. 300,000.

Sporting News: POB 5481, Accra-North; f. 1967; Man. Editor J. OPPONG-AGYARE.

Standard: POB 247, Accra: Editor Rev. CHARLES PALMER-BUCKLE; circ. 50,000.

Statesman: Accra; official publication of the New Patriotic Party; Editor HARUNA ATTAH.

Weekend: Newstop Publications, POB 514, Mamprobi, Accra; Editor DAN K. ANSAH; circ. 40,000.

Weekly Insight: Accra; f. 1993; independent; English; Editor KWESI PRATT.

Weekly Spectator: New Times Corpn, Ring Road West, POB 2638, Accra; state-owned; f. 1963; Sun.; Editor YAW BOAKYE OFORI ATTA; circ. 165,000.

PERIODICALS

Fortnightly

Ideal Woman (Obaa Sima): POB 5737, Accra; tel. (21) 221399; f. 1971; Editor KATE ABBAM.

Legon Observer: POB 11, Legon; telex 2556; fax (21) 774338; f. 1966; publ. by Legon Society on National Affairs; Chair. J. A. DADSON; Editor EBOW DANIEL.

New Ghana: Information Services Dept, POB 745, Accra; English; political, economic and cultural affairs.

Monthly

Africa Flamingo: POB 9194, Airport Emporium Ltd, Accra; Editor FELIX AMANFU; circ. 50,000.

African Woman: Ring Rd West, POB 1496, Accra.

Boxing and Football Illustrated: POB 8392, Accra; f. 1976; Editor NANA O. AMPOMAH; circ. 10,000.

Chit Chat: POB 7043, Accra; Editor ROSEMOND ADU.

Drum: POB 1197, Accra; general interest.

Ghana Journal of Science: Ghana Science Asscn, POB 7, Legon; Editor Dr A. K. AHAFIA.

Police News: Police HQ, Accra; Editor S. S. APPIAH; circ. 20,000.

The Post: Ghana Information Services, POB 745, Accra; tel. (21) 228011; telex 2201; f. 1980; current affairs and analysis; circ. 25,000.

The Scope: POB 8162, Tema; Editor EMMANUEL DOE ZIORKLUI; circ. 10,000.

Students World: POB M18, Accra; tel. (21) 774248; telex 2171; f. 1974; educational; Man. Editor ERIC OFEI; circ. 10,000.

The Teacher: Ghana National Asscn of Teachers, POB 209, Accra; tel. (21) 221515; fax (21) 226286; f. 1931; quarterly; circ. 20,000.

Quarterly

Akwansosem: Ghana Information Services, POB 745, Accra; tel. (21) 228011; telex 2201; Akuapim Twi, Asanti Twi and Fante; Editor KATHLEEN OFOSU-APPIAH.

Armed Forces News: General Headquarters, Directorate of Public Relations, Burma Camp, Accra; f. 1966; Editor Maj. E. W. K. NIBO; circ. 8,000.

Ghana Enterprise: c/o Ghana National Chamber of Commerce, POB 2325, Accra; tel. (21) 662427; telex 2687; fax (21) 662210; f. 1961; Editor J. B. K. AMANFU.

Ghana Manufacturer: c/o Asscn of Ghana Industries, POB 8624, Accra-North; tel. (21) 777283; f. 1974; Editor (vacant); circ. 1,500.

Insight and Opinion: POB 5446, Accra; Editorial Sec. W. B. OHENE.

Radio and TV Times: Ghana Broadcasting Corpn, Broadcasting House, POB 1633, Accra; tel. (21) 221161; telex 2114; f. 1960; Editor ERNEST ASAMOAH; circ. 5,000.

NEWS AGENCIES

Ghana News Agency: POB 2118, Accra; tel. (21) 665135; telex 2400; fax 669840; f. 1957; Gen. Man. KWAO LOTSU; 10 regional offices, 110 district offices and 1 overseas office.

Foreign Bureaux

Associated Press (AP) (USA): POB 6172, Accra; Bureau Chief P. K. COBBINAH-ESSEM.

Informatsionnoye Telegrafnoye Agentstvo Rossii—Telegrafnoye Agentstvo Suverennykh Stran (ITAR—TASS) (Russia): POB 9141, Accra; Agent IGOR AGEBEKOV.

United Press International (UPI) (USA): POB 9715, Accra; tel. (21) 225436; telex 2340; Bureau Chief R. A. QUANSAH.

Xinhua (New China) News Agency (People's Republic of China): 2 Seventh St, Airport Residential Area, POB 3897, Accra; tel. (21) 772042; telex 2314.

Deutsche Presse-Agentur (Germany) is also represented.

Publishers

Advent Press: POB 0102, Osu, Accra; tel. (21) 777861; telex 2119; f. 1937; Gen. Man. EMMANUEL C. TETTEH.

Adwinsa Publications (Ghana) Ltd: Advance Press Bldg, 3rd Floor, School Rd, POB 92, Legoh Accra; tel. (21) 221654; f. 1977; general, educational; Man. Dir KWABENA AMPONSAH.

Afram Publications: 72 Ring Rd East, POB M18, Accra; tel. (21) 774248; telex 2171; f. 1974; textbooks and general; Man. Dir ERIC OFEI.

Africa Christian Press: POB 30, Achimota; tel. and fax (21) 220271; f. 1964; religious, biography, paperbacks; Gen. Man. RICHARD A. B. CRABBE.

Asempa Publishers: POB 919, Accra; tel. (21) 221706; f. 1970; religion, social issues, African music, fiction, children's; Gen. Man. Rev. EMMANUEL B. BORTEY.

Baafour and Co: POB K189, Accra New Town; f. 1978; general; Man. B. KESE-AMANKWAA.

Benibengor Book Agency: POB 40, Aboso; fiction, biography, children's and paperbacks; Man. Dir J. BENIBENGOR BLAY.

Black Mask Ltd: POB 7894, Accra North; tel. (21) 229968; f. 1979; textbooks, plays, novels, handicrafts; Man. Dir YAW OWUSU ASANTE.

Editorial and Publishing Services: POB 5743, Accra; general, reference; Man. Dir M. DANQUAH.

Educational Press and Manufacturers Ltd: POB 9184, Airport-Accra; tel. (21) 220395; f. 1975; textbooks, children's; Man. G. K. KODUA.

Emmanuel Publishing Services: POB 5282, Accra; tel. (21) 225238; f. 1978; educational and children's; Dir EMMANUEL K. NSIAH.

Encyclopaedia Africana Project: POB 2797, Accra; tel. (21) 776939; f. 1962; reference; Dir J. O. VANDERPUYE.

Frank Publishing Ltd: POB M414, Accra; f. 1976; secondary school textbooks; Man. Dir FRANCIS K. DZOKOTO.

Ghana Publishing Corpn: PMB Tema; tel. (221) 2921; f. 1965; textbooks and general fiction and non-fiction; Man. Dir F. K. NYARKO.

Ghana Universities Press: POB 4219, Accra; tel. (21) 225032; f. 1962; scholarly and academic; Dir A. S. K. ATSU.

Goodbooks Publishing Co: POB 10416, Accra North; tel. (21) 665629; f. 1968; children's; Man. A. ASIRIFI.

Miracle Bookhouse: POB 7487, Accra North; tel. (21) 226684; f. 1977; general; Man. J. APPIAH-BERKO.

Moxon Paperbacks: POB M160, Accra; tel. (21) 665397; fax (21) 774358; f. 1967; travel and guide books, fiction and poetry, Africana; quarterly catalogue of Ghanaian books and periodicals in print; Man. Dir JAMES MOXON.

Sedco Publishing Ltd: Sedco House, Tabon St, North Ridge, POB 2051, Accra; tel. (21) 221332; telex 2456; fax 220107; f. 1975; educational; Man. Dir COURAGE K. SEGBAWU.

Sheffield Publishing Co: Accra; tel. (21) 667480; fax (21) 665960; f. 1970; religion, politics, economics, science, fiction; Publr RONALD MENSAH.

Unimax Publishers Ltd: 42 Ring Rd South Industrial Area, POB 10722, Accra-North; tel. (21) 227443; telex 2515; fax (21) 225215; atlases, educational and children's; Dir EDWARD ADDO.

Waterville Publishing House: POB 195, Accra; tel. (21) 663124; f. 1963; general fiction and non-fiction, textbooks, paperbacks, Africana; Man. Dir A. S. OBUAM.

Woeli Publishing Services: POB K601, Accra New Town; tel. and fax (21) 229294; f. 1984; children's, fiction, academic; Dir W. A. DEKUTSEY.

PUBLISHERS' ASSOCIATIONS

Ghana Book Development Council: POB M430, Accra; tel. (21) 229178; f. 1975; govt-financed agency; promotes and co-ordinates writing, production and distribution of books; Exec. Dir D. A. NIMAKO.

Ghana Book Publishers' Association: c/o Africa Christian Press, POB 40, Achimota; Sec. E. B. BORTEY.

Private Newspaper Publishers' Association of Ghana (PRINPAG): POB 125, Darkuman, Accra; Gen. Sec. K. AGYEMANG DUAH.

Radio and Television

In 1991 there were an estimated 4,150,000 radio receivers and 235,000 television receivers in use.

There are internal radio broadcasts in English, Akan, Dagbani, Ewe, Ga, Hausa and Nzema; there is an external service in English and French. There are three sound transmitting stations and 53 relay stations.

Television transmissions began in 1965; there are two studios in Accra and four transmission stations: Ajangote (about 32 km from Accra), Kissi in the Central Region, Jamasi in Ashanti and Bolgatanga in the Northern Region.

Ghana Broadcasting Corporation: Broadcasting House, POB 1633, Accra; tel. (21) 221161; telex 2114; f. 1935; Dir-Gen. DAVID ANAGLATE; Dir of TV JAMES CROMWELL; Dir of Radio KWASI AMOAKO.

Finance

(cap. = capital; res = reserves; dep. = deposits; m. = million; brs = branches; amounts in cedis)

BANKING

Central Bank

Bank of Ghana: High St, Accra; tel. (21) 662395; telex 2052; fax (21) 662996; f. 1957; bank of issue; cap. and res 1,535.2m., dep. 138,540.9m. (Dec. 1989); Chair. Dr GODFRIED K. AGAMA.

State Banks

Agricultural Development Bank: Cedi House, Liberia Rd, POB 4191, Accra; tel. (21) 662758; telex 2295; fax (21) 229620; f. 1965; state-owned; credit facilities for farmers and commercial banking; cap. 1,334m. (1992), dep. 11,600m. (1991); Chair. NATHAN QUAO; Man. Dir P. A. KURANCHIE; 29 brs.

Bank for Housing and Construction (BHC): Okofoh House, 24 Kwame Nkrumah Ave, POB M1, Adabraka, Accra; tel. (21) 220033; telex 2096; fax (21) 229631; f. 1983; 50% state-owned; cap. 1,000m. (Dec. 1992); Chair. GLORIA NIKOI; Man. Dir Dr A. B. AHMAD.

Ghana Commercial Bank: POB 134, Accra; tel. (21) 664914; telex 2034; fax (21) 662168; f. 1953; state-owned; cap. and res 36,755m., dep. 208,649.8m. (Dec. 1992); Chair. S. K. APEA; Man. Dir HELEN K. LOKKO; 145 brs.

Ghana Co-operative Bank: Kwame Nkrumah Ave, POB 5292, Accra-North; tel. (21) 228735; telex 2446; fax (21) 222292; f. 1970; 82% state-owned; cap. 120.2m. (Dec. 1990), dep. 3,200m. (August 1989); Chair. GEORGE K. HAGAN; Man. Dir K. K. MENSAH; 21 brs.

National Investment Bank Ltd (NIB): 37 Kwame Nkrumah Ave, POB 3726, Accra; tel. (21) 669301; telex 2161; fax (21) 669307; f. 1963; 75% state-owned; provides long-term investment capital, jt venture promotion, consortium finance man. and commercial banking services; cap. and res 4,146.8m., dep 3,482.4m. (Dec. 1990); Chair. JOHN K. RICHARDSON; Man. Dir STEVE DADZIE; 9 brs.

National Savings and Credit Bank: Ring Rd Central, Accra; tel. (21) 228322; telex 2383; fax (21) 228346; f. 1972; 75% state-owned; cap. 642m., dep. 10,617m. (June 1992); Chair. E. F. ANNO; Man. Dir J. A. NUAMAH; 17 brs.

National Trust Holding Co: Dyson House, Kwame Nkrumah Ave, POB 9563, Airport, Accra; tel. (21) 229664; f. 1976 to finance Ghanaian acquisitions of indigenous cos; also assists in their development and expansion, and carries out trusteeship business; cap. 116.5m. (1992); Chair. B. A. GOGO; Man. Dir E. J. A. ARYEE.

Social Security Bank (SSB): POB 13119, Accra; tel. (21) 221726; telex 2209; fax (21) 668651; f. 1976; cap. and res 7,469.2m., dep. 43,400.8m. (Dec. 1992); Chair. ISSIFU ALI; Man. Dir PRYCE K. THOMPSON.

Merchant Banks

Continental Acceptances Ltd: 47 Independence Ave, POB 14596, Accra; tel. (21) 221056; telex 2675; fax (21) 668657; f. 1990; cap. and res 2,275.4m., dep. 18,380.2m. (Dec. 1992); Chair. E. P. L. GYAMPOH; Gen. Man. DAVID C. PEACOCK.

Ecobank Ghana (EBG): 19 Seventh Ave, Accra; tel. (21) 221103; telex 2718; fax (21) 667127; f. 1989; cap. and res 2,111.3m., dep. 20,360.6m. (Dec. 1992); Chair. JOHN SACKAH ADDO; Man. Dir WILLIAM KNOX WHITWORTH.

Merchant Bank (Ghana) Ltd: Swanmill, Kwame Nkrumah Ave, POB 401, Accra; tel. (21) 666331; telex 2191; fax (21) 667305; f. 1972; 30% state-owned; cap. and res 1,432.2m., dep. 6,520.5m. (1991); Chair. YAW MANU SARPONG; Man. Dir CHRIS N. NARTEY; 3 brs.

Foreign Banks

Barclays Bank of Ghana Ltd (UK): High St, POB 2949, Accra; tel. (21) 664901; telex 2721; fax (21) 667420; f. 1971; 40% state-owned; cap. and res 5,541.3m., dep. 52,586.3m. (Dec. 1992); Chair. NANA WEREKO AMPEM; Man. Dir R. I. A. KNAPMAN; 39 brs.

Standard Chartered Bank Ghana Ltd (UK): Standard Bank Bldg, High St, POB 768, Accra; tel. (21) 664590; telex 2671; fax (21) 667751; f. 1896; cap. 500m. (Dec. 1992), dep. 26,969.4m. (Dec. 1990); Chair. DAVID ANDOH; Man. Dir A. R. HOLDEN; 28 brs.

STOCK EXCHANGE

Ghana Stock Exchange (GSE): Kingsway Bldg, Second Floor, Kwame Nkrumah Ave, Accra; tel. (21) 669908; telex 2722; fax (21) 669913; Dir YEBOA AMOA.

INSURANCE

Ghana Union Assurance Co Ltd: POB 1322, Accra; tel. (21) 664421; telex 2008; fax (21) 664988; f. 1973; Man. Dir KWADWO DUKU.

The Great African Insurance Co Ltd: POB 12349, Accra North; tel. (21) 227459; telex 3027; fax (21) 228905; f. 1980; Man. Dir KWASI AKOTO.

The State Insurance Corporation of Ghana: POB 2363, Accra; tel. (21) 666961; telex 2171; fax (21) 662205; f. 1962; state-owned; undertakes all classes of insurance; also engages in real estate and other investment; Man. Dir B. K. QUASHIE.

Social Security and National Insurance Trust: POB M149, Accra; f. 1972; covers over 1.25m. employees; Chief Admin. A. AWUKU.

Vanguard Assurance Co Ltd: Insurance Hall, Derby House, Derby Ave, POB 1868, Accra; tel. (21) 666485; telex 2005; fax (21) 668610; f. 1974; general accident, marine, motor and life insurance; Man. Dir NANA AWUAH-DARKO AMPEM; 7 brs.

Several foreign insurance companies operate in Ghana.

Trade and Industry

PUBLIC BOARDS AND CORPORATIONS

Atomic Energy Commission: POB 80, Legon/Accra; construction of a nuclear reactor at Kwabenya, near Accra, which was begun in 1964, was suspended during 1966–74; the commission's present activities are primarily concerned with the applications of radioisotopes in agriculture and medicine; Chair. Dr A. K. AHAFIA.

Bast Fibres Development Board: POB 1992, Kumasi; f. 1970; promotes the commercial cultivation of bast fibres and their processing, handling and grading.

Food Production Corporation: POB 1853, Accra; f. 1971; state corpn providing employment for youth in large scale farming enterprises; controls 76,900 ha of land (16,200 ha under cultivation); operates 87 food farms on a co-operative and self-supporting basis, and rears poultry and livestock.

Ghana Cocoa Board (COCOBOD): POB 933, Accra; telex 2082; f. 1985 to replace the Cocoa Marketing Board; responsible for purchase, grading and export of cocoa, coffee and shea nuts, and encourages production and scientific research aimed at improving quality and yield of cocoa, coffee and shea nuts; CEO DAVID ANINAKWA.

Ghana Consolidated Diamond Co Ltd: POB M108, Accra; telex 2058; f. 1986 to replace Diamond Marketing Corpn, to grade, value and process diamonds, buy all locally won, produced or processed diamonds; engages in purchasing, grading, valuing, export and sale of local diamonds; Chair. KOFI AGYEMAN; Man. Dir JOSEPH ANSAFO-MENSAH.

Ghana Cotton Co Ltd: f. 1986 to replace Cotton Development Board; Govt holds 70% interest, private textile cos 30%; 15 regional offices; Chair. HARRY GANDA.

Ghanaian Enterprises Development Commission: Accra; f. 1975; assists the indigenization of the economy, especially small and medium-scale industrial and commercial enterprises, by providing loans and advisory services.

Ghana Food Distribution Corporation: POB 4245, Accra; tel. (21) 228428; f. 1971; buys, stores, preserves, distributes and sells foodstuffs through 10 regional centres; Man. Dir E. H. K. AMANKWA.

Ghana Industrial Holding Corporation (GIHOC): POB 2784, Accra; tel. (21) 664998; telex 2109; f. 1967; controls and manages 26 state enterprises, including steel, paper, bricks, paint, pharmaceuticals, electronics, metals, canneries, distilleries and boatbuilding factories; also has three subsidiary cos and four jt ventures; managed since 1989 by an interim superintending secr.

Ghana Investment Centre: Central Ministerial Area, POB M193, Accra; tel. (21) 665125; telex 2229; fax 663801; f. 1981 to replace Capital Investments Board; negotiates new investments, approves projects, registers foreign capital and decides extent of govt participation; Chair. P. V. OBENG (Chair. Cttee of Secs); Vice-Chair. Dr KWESI BOTCHWEY (Sec. for Finance and Economic Planning).

Ghana National Manganese Corporation: POB M183, Ministry PO, Accra; telex 2046; f. 1975 following nationalization of African Manganese Co mine at Nsuta; Chair. P. O. AGGREY; Man. Dir EBENEZER OKLAM.

Ghana National Petroleum Corporation: Private Mail Bag, Tema, Accra-North; tel. (221) 6020; telex 2188; fax (221) 712916; f. 1983; exploration, development, production and disposal of petroleum; Chair. TSATSU TSIKATA.

Ghana National Trading Corporation (GNTC): POB 67, Accra; tel. (21) 664871; f. 1961; organizes exports and imports of selected commodities; over 500 retail outlets in 12 admin. dists.

Ghana Standards Board: c/o POB M245, Accra; tel. (21) 776231; telex 2545; fax (21) 776092; f. 1967; establishes and promulgates standards; promotes standardization, industrial efficiency and development and industrial welfare, health and safety; operates certification mark scheme; 363 mems; Dir Dr E. K. MARFO.

Ghana Water and Sewerage Corporation: POB M194, Accra; f. 1966 to provide, distribute and conserve water for public, domestic and industrial use, and to establish, operate and control sewerage systems.

Grains and Legumes Development Board: POB 4000, Kumasi; tel. (51) 4231; f. 1970; state-controlled; promotes and develops production of cereals and leguminous vegetables.

Minerals Commission: 10 Sixth St, Airport Residential Area, Accra; tel. (21) 772783; telex 2545; fax (21) 773324; f. 1984; supervises, promotes and co-ordinates the minerals industry.

Posts and Telecommunications Corporation: Posts and Telecommunications Bldg, Accra-North; tel. (21) 221001; telex 3010; fax (21) 667979; f. 1974; provides both internal and external postal and telecommunication services; Dir-Gen. JOSEPH AGGREY-MENSAH.

State Construction Corporation: Ring Rd West, Industrial Area, Accra; f. 1966; state corpn with a labour force of 7,000; construction plans give priority to enhancing agricultural production; Man. Dir J. A. DANSO, Jr.

State Farms Corporation: Accra; undertakes agricultural projects in all regions but Upper Region; Man. Dir E. N. A. THOMPSON (acting).

State Fishing Corporation: POB 211, Tema; tel. (221) 6177; telex 2043; fax (221) 2336177; f. 1961; govt-sponsored deep-sea fishing, distribution and marketing (incl. exporting) org.; transfer to private-sector ownership pending in 1991; owns 5 deep-sea fishing trawlers; CEO Dr ISAAC C. N. MORRISON.

State Gold Mining Corporation: POB 109, Tarkwa; Accra Office, POB 3634; tel. 775376; telex 2348; f. 1961; manages four gold mines; CEO F. AWUA-KYEREMATEN.

State Hotels Corporation: POB 7542, Accra-North; tel. (21) 664646; telex 2113; f. 1965; responsible for all state-owned hotels, restaurants, etc. in 10 major centres; Man. Dir S. K. A. OBENG; Gen. Man. EBEN AMOAH.

State Housing Construction Co: POB 2753, Accra; f. 1982 by merger; oversees govt housing programme.

Timber Export Development Board: POB 515, Takoradi; tel. (31) 29216; telex 2189; f. 1985; promotes the sale and export of timber; CEO SAMUEL KWESI APPIAH.

CHAMBER OF COMMERCE

Ghana National Chamber of Commerce: POB 2325, Accra; tel. (21) 662427; telex 2687; fax (21) 662210; f. 1961; promotes and protects industry and commerce, organizes trade fairs; 2,500 individual mems and 8 mem. chambers; Pres. ISHMAEL E. YAMSON; Exec. Sec. JOHN B. K. AMANFU.

COMMERCIAL AND INDUSTRIAL ORGANIZATIONS

Ghana Export Promotion Council: Republic House, POB M146, Accra; tel. (21) 228813; telex 2289; fax (21) 668263; f. 1972; Chair. and mems appointed by Ghana Mfrs' Asscn, Ghana Nat. Chamber of Commerce, Ghana Export Co, Capital Investment Bd, Ministry of Trade and Industry, Ministry of Food and Agriculture and Ghana Armed Forces; Exec. Sec. KWESI AHWOI.

The Indian Association of Ghana: POB 2891, Accra; tel. (21) 776227; f. 1939; Pres. ATMARAM GOKALDAS.

Institute of Marketing (IMG): POB 102, Accra; tel. (21) 226697; telex 2488; fax (21) 222171; f. 1981; reorg. 1989; seeks to enhance professional standards; Chair. I. E. YAMSON; Pres. FRANK APPIAH.

EMPLOYERS' ASSOCIATION

Ghana Employers' Association: Kojo Thompson Rd, POB 2616, Accra; tel. (21) 228455; fax (21) 228405; f. 1959; 400 mems; Pres. I. E. YAMSON; Vice-Pres. H. R. AMONOO.

Affiliated Bodies

Association of Ghana Industries: Trade Fair Centre, POB 8624, Accra-North; tel. (21) 777283; telex 3027; fax (21) 773143; f. 1957; Pres. Dr Justice ATTA ADDISON; Exec. Sec. EDDIE IMBEAH-AMOAKUH.

Ghana Booksellers' Association: POB 10367, Accra-North; tel. (21) 773002; fax (21) 773242; Pres. SAMPSON BRAKO; Gen. Sec. FRED J. REIMMER.

The Ghana Chamber of Mines: POB 991, Accra; tel. (21) 665355; telex 2036; fax (21) 662926; f. 1928; Pres. EBEN T. OKLAH; Dir SAM POKU.

Ghana Electrical Contractors' Association: POB 1858, Accra.

Ghana National Association of Teachers: POB 209, Accra; tel. (21) 221515; fax (21) 226286; f. 1931; Pres. G. N. NAASO; Gen. Sec. PAUL OSEI-MENSAH.

Ghana National Contractors' Association: c/o J. T. Osei and Co, POB M11, Accra.

Ghana Timber Association (GTA): POB 246, Takoradi; f. 1952; promotes, protects and develops timber industry; Chair. TETTEH NANOR.

CO-OPERATIVES

The co-operative movement in Ghana began in 1928 among cocoa farmers, and evolved into the country's largest farmers' organization. In 1944 the co-operative societies were placed under government supervision. The co-operative movement was suspended during 1960–66, and is now under the direction of a government-appointed secretary-general. In 1986 there were 8,387 co-operative societies. The structure of the movement places the co-operative associations at the top, co-operative unions in a secondary position of seniority in the towns, and village co-operative societies at the base.

Department of Co-operatives: POB M150, Accra; tel. (21) 666212; f. 1944; govt-supervised body, responsible for registration, auditing and supervision of co-operative socs; Registrar R. BUACHIE-APHRAM; Sec.-Gen. J. M. APPIAH.

Ghana Co-operatives Council Ltd: POB 4034, Accra; f. 1951; co-ordinates activities of all co-operative socs; comprises 15 nat. co-operative asscns and five central socs; Sec.-Gen. JOHN MARTIN APPIAH.

The 15 co-operative associations include the Ghana Co-operative Marketing Asscn Ltd, the Ghana Co-operative Credit Unions Asscn Ltd, the Ghana Co-operative Agricultural Producers and Marketing Asscn Ltd, and The Ghana Co-operative Consumers' Asscn Ltd.

MAJOR INDUSTRIAL COMPANIES

The following are among the largest companies in terms of either capital investment or of employment.

Achimota Brewery Co Ltd: POB 114, Achimota, Accra; f. 1973, as Tata Brewery; beer and soft drinks; Chair. P. S. KPODO; Man. Dir M. W. WAAS.

Ashanti Goldfields Co Ltd: POB 10, Obuasi; f. 1897, reorg. 1994; gold mining; leases mining and timber concessions from the govt, which holds 31.3% of the shares; 43.1% is held by Lonrho PLC and 25.6% by private investors; Chair. R. K. PEPRAH; Man. Dir SAM JONAH; 9,500 employees.

BP Ghana Ltd: 95 Kojo Thompson Rd, POB 553, Accra; tel. (21) 221445; telex 2093; fax (21) 221453; f. 1965; shares held by BP Africa Ltd, National Investment Bank, National Trust Holding Co Ltd; distribution of petroleum products, fuelling marine vessels at Tema and Takoradi, and aircraft at Kotoka International Airport, Accra; Man. Dir F. J. Mouchet; 173 employees.

The Cocoa Processing Co (GCMB) Ltd: Effia Junction Industrial Estate, POB 218, Takoradi; f. 1964; cap. C2m.; responsible to the Ghana Cocoa Board; processes high-grade cocoa products for export; Gen. Man. I. K. van der Puije; 600 employees.

Ghana Bauxite Co Ltd: POB 1, Awaso; 55% state-owned; fmrly British Aluminium Co Ltd; mining of bauxite at Awaso with loading facilities at Takoradi; Man. Dir T. Cregg.

Ghana Consolidated Diamonds Ltd: c/o 34 Seymour St, London, W1H 5WD, England; tel. (071) 724-9398; telex 262899; fax (071) 723-8384; 20% govt-owned; operates diamond mine at Akwatia; change of name to Birim River Diamonds Ltd planned in 1995.

Lever Bros Ghana Ltd: POB 1648, Accra; mfrs of household and toilet soaps, non-soap detergents, scourers, toothpaste, margarine and other edible fats; Man. Dir A. K. Jesani.

Tema Oil Refinery (TOR) Ltd: POB 599, Tema; telex 2011; fax (221) 2884; f. 1963; sole oil refinery in Ghana; state-controlled since 1977; Man. Dirs W. S. Parker, A. S. K. Aidoo, L. Prempeh; 330 employees.

Total Ghana Ltd: 3 Yiyiwa St, Abelenkpe, Accra; tel. (21) 772309; telex 2681; fax (21) 773662; f. 1960; subsidiary of Total Paris; distribution of petroleum products, incl. liquefied petroleum gas; Man. Dir Frank Haettel.

UAC of Ghana Ltd: POB 64, Kwame Nkrumah Ave, Accra; tel. (21) 664985; telex 2008; fax (21) 664808; f. 1955 as United Africa Co of Ghana Ltd; comprises 5 divisions and assoc. cos; subsidiary of UAC International Ltd, London; agricultural, industrial, specialized merchandising, distributive and service enterprises; Chair. I. E. Yamson; 770 employees.

Volta Aluminium Co Ltd (VALCO): POB 625, Tema; tel. (221) 228156; telex 2160; fax (221) 667605; owned by Kaiser Aluminium and Chemical Corpn (90%) and the Reynolds Metal Co (10%); operates an aluminium smelter at Tema (annual capacity 200,000 tons); Chair. J. V. L. Phillips; Man. Dir Ted Frostenson.

TRADE UNIONS

Ghana Trades Union Congress (GTUC): Hall of Trade Unions, POB 701, Accra; tel. (21) 662568; fax (21) 667161; f. 1945; 17 affiliated unions; all activities of the GTUC were suspended in March 1982; Chair. Interim Man. Cttee E. K. Aboagye; Sec.-Gen. Christian Appiah-Agyei.

Transport

State Transport Corporation: Accra; f. 1965 to succeed Govt Transport Dept; Man. Dir Lt-Col Akyea-Mensah.

RAILWAYS

There were 947 km of railways in 1986, connecting Accra, Kumasi and Takoradi. In 1988 the Italian Government agreed to provide US $30m., and the World Bank approved a loan of $9.4m., towards a project to rehabilitate the railway network. In 1990 Ghana received a further loan of $32m. from France.

Ghana Railway Corporation: POB 251, Takoradi; tel. (31) 2181; telex 2297; f. 1977; responsible for the operation and maintenance of all railways; Gen. Man. Amponsah Ababio.

ROADS

In 1992 there were about 36,700 km of classified roads in Ghana. Of this total, 14,430 km were trunk roads and 21,264 km were feeder roads. Of the total road network, 7,300 km were paved in 1992. A major five-year programme of road development and rehabilitation, costing US $142.3m., was initiated in 1991. In 1992 the Government allocated a projected 26.7% of total expenditure to the rehabilitation of roads.

Ghana Highway Authority: POB 1641, Accra; tel. (21) 666591; telex 2359; fax (21) 665571; f. 1974 to plan, develop, classify and maintain roads and ferries; CEO H. O. A. Quaynor.

SHIPPING

The two main ports are Tema (near Accra) and Takoradi, both of which are linked with Kumasi by rail. The rehabilitation of the two ports, at an estimated cost of US $100m., was completed in 1990. In 1990 goods loaded totalled an estimated 1.8m. metric tons, and goods unloaded an estimated 2.8m. tons.

Alpha (West Africa) Line Ltd: POB 451, Tema; telex 2184; operates regular cargo services to west Africa, the UK, the USA, the Far East and northern Europe; agents for Mercandia (West Africa) Line, Cameroon National Line, Pakistan National Lines, Uiterwyk West Africa Lines and Great South America Line; Man. Dir E. Collingwoode-Williams.

Black Star Line Ltd: 4th Lane, Kuku Hill Osu, POB 248, Accra; tel. (21) 28879; telex 2019; fax (21) 775140; f. 1957; state-owned; operates passenger and cargo services to Europe, the UK, Canada, the USA, the Mediterranean and west Africa; agents for Gold Star Line, Zim West Africa Lines, Société Ivoirienne de Transport Maritime (SITRAM), and Cie Maritime Zaïroise (CMZ); fleet of 4 freighters; displacement 52,016 grt; Man. Dir Victor Nu Attuquay-efio.

Holland West-Afrika Lijn N.V.: POB 269, Accra; POB 216, Tema; and POB 18, Takoradi; cargo services to and from North America and the Far East; agents for Royal Interocean Lines and Dafra Line.

Liner Agencies (Ghana) Ltd: POB 66, Accra; tel. (21) 228436; telex 2396; fax (21) 228461; freight services to and from UK, Europe, USA, Canada, Japan and Far East; intermediate services between west African ports; agents for Barber W.A. Line, Elder Dempster Lines, Guinean Gulf Line, Kawasaki Kisen Kaisha, Mitsui OSK Lines, Nigerian National Shipping Line, Marine Chartering of San Francisco, A/S Bulkhandling of Oslo, Botany Bay Shipping Co, SITRAM, CMZ and Palm Line; Man. Dir Lloyd C. Piper.

Remco Shipping Lines Ltd: POB 3898, Accra; tel. (21) 224609; displacement 11,880 grt.

Scanship (Ghana) Ltd: CFAO Bldg, High St, POB 1705, Accra; tel. (21) 664314; telex 2181; agents for Maersk Line, Splosna Plovba Line, Hoegh Line, Jadranska Slobodna Plovidba-Split, Keller Shipping, Polish Ocean Line, DSR Line, Estonian Shipping Co, Euro-Africa Line, Spliethoffs Shipping Corpn of India.

CIVIL AVIATION

The main international airport is at Kotoka (Accra). There are also airports at Takoradi, Kumasi, Sunyani and Tamale. In 1988 Ghana received a loan of US $12m. from France to finance the rehabilitation of Kotoka Airport (at a total cost of $55.5m.), which began in 1991.

Gemini Airlines Ltd: America House, POB 7328, Accra-North; tel. (21) 665785; f. 1974; operates once-weekly cargo flight between Accra and London; Dir V. Owusu; Gen. Man. P. F. Okine.

Ghana Airways Corporation: Ghana House, POB 1636, Accra; tel. (21) 773321; telex 2489; fax (21) 777675; f. 1958; state-owned; transfer to the private sector pending in 1994; operates domestic services and international routes to West African and European destinations; Chair. E. A. B. Mayne; Man. Dir Capt. Alex Sam (acting).

Tourism

Ghana's attractions include fine beaches, game reserves, traditional festivals, and old trading forts and castles. In 1992/93 tourist arrivals were estimated at 210,000, and revenue from tourism totalled US $288m. In 1990 a government programme to expand tourism was initiated, with the aim of increasing tourist arrivals to 334,000 per year by 1995.

Ghana Tourist Board: POB 3106, Accra; tel. (21) 665441; telex 2714; f. 1968; Exec. Dir Edmund Y. Ofosu-Yeboah.

Ghana Association of Tourist and Travel Agencies: Ramia House, Kojo Thompson Rd, POB 7140, Accra; Pres. Joseph K. Ankumah; Sec. Johnnie Moreaux.

Ghana Tourist Development Co Ltd: POB 8710, Accra; tel. (21) 772084; telex 2714; fax (21) 772093; f. 1974; develops tourist infrastructure, including hotels, restaurants and casinos; operates foreign exchange, duty-free and diplomatic shops; Man. Dir Betty Akuffo-Amoabeng.

Defence

In June 1993 Ghana had total armed forces of 6,850 (army 5,000, navy 850 and air force 1,000) and a paramilitary force of 5,000. The headquarters of the Defence Commission of the OAU is in Accra.

Defence Expenditure: Budgeted at C20,700m. in 1992.

Commander-in-Chief of the Armed Forces: Flt-Lt (retd) Jerry Rawlings.

Chief of Defence Staff: Air Marshal Achilles H. K. Dumashie.

Commander of the Navy: Commdr TOM K. ANNAN.

Commander of the Air Force: Air Vice-Marshal J. A. BRUCE.

Education

Education is officially compulsory for 10 years, between the ages of six and 16 years. Primary education begins at the age of six and lasts for six years. Secondary education, from the age of 12, lasts for seven years, comprising a first cycle of four years and a second of three years. Under the Junior Secondary School Programme, introduced in 1989, a levy of 500 cedis per pupil was charged to finance the rehabilitation of junior secondary schools. At the junior secondary schools pupils are examined to determine admission to senior secondary school courses, which lead to examinations at the 'ordinary' level of the general certificate of education, and technical and vocational courses. In 1990 primary enrolment was equivalent to 77% of children in the relevant age-group (84% of boys; 69% of girls), while the comparable ratio for secondary enrolment was 38% (48% of boys; 29% of girls). There are three universities. Expenditure on education by the central government in 1990 was estimated at 64,835m. cedis (25.5% of total spending). According to UNESCO estimates, the average rate of adult illiteracy in 1990 was 39.7% (males 30%; females 49%). In 1990 the government introduced a five-year programme, financed by the USA, to improve conditions in primary schools.

Bibliography

Adjei, M. *Death and Pain: Rawlings Ghana: The Inside Story.* London, Black Line Publishing Ltd, 1994.

Afrifa, A. A. *Ghana Coup d'Etat.* London, Frank Cass, 1967.

Agbodeka, F. *An Economc History of Ghana from the Earliest Times.* Accra, Ghana Universities Press, 1994.

Armah, K. *Nkrumah's Legacy.* London, Rex Collings, 1974.

Austin, D. *Politics in Ghana 1946–60.* Oxford University Press, 1964.

Babatope, E. *The Ghana Revolution from Nkrumah to Jerry Rawlings.* Enugu, Fourth Dimension Publishers, 1984.

Bank of Ghana. *Annual Report* and *Quarterly Economic Bulletin.*

Baynham, S. *The Military and Politics in Nkrumah's Ghana.* Boulder, CO, Westview Press, 1988.

Boateng, E. A. *A Geography of Ghana.* 2nd Edn, Cambridge University Press, 1970.

Brown, C. K. (Ed.). *Rural Development in Ghana.* Accra, Ghana University Press, 1986.

Busia, K. A. *Africa in Search of Democracy.* London, Routledge and Kegan Paul, 1967.

Central Bureau of Statistics. *Annual Economic Survey.* Accra.

Chazan, N. *An Anatomy of Ghanaian Politics: Managing Political Recession 1969–1982.* Boulder, CO, Westview Press, 1983.

Cruise O'Brien, D. B., Dunn, J., and Rathbone, R. (Eds). *West African States.* Cambridge, Cambridge University Press, 1989.

Davidson, B. *Black Star. A View of the Life and Times of Kwame Nkrumah.* London, Panaf Books, 1974.

Dickson, K. B. *A Historical Geography of Ghana.* Cambridge University Press, 1969.

Economic Society of Ghana. *Economic Bulletin of Ghana.* Published quarterly. Legon.

Foster, P., and Zolberg, A. R. (Eds). *Ghana and the Ivory Coast: Perspectives and Modernization.* University of Chicago Press, 1972.

Graham, R. *The Aluminium Industry and the Third World: Multinational Corporations and Underdevelopment.* London, Zed Press, 1982.

Greenhalgh, P. *West African Diamonds: An Economic History 1919–83.* Manchester University Press, 1985.

Gyimah-Boardi, E. (Ed.). *Ghana under PNDC Rule.* Dakar, Codesria, 1993.

Harrison Church, R. J. *West Africa.* 8th Edn, London, Longman, 1979.

Hayward, M. F. *Elections in Independent Africa.* Boulder, CO, Westview Press, 1987.

Huq, M. M. *The Economy of Ghana: The First 25 Years since Independence.* London, Macmillan, 1988.

Jeffries, R. *Class, Power and Ideology in Ghana.* Cambridge University Press, 1978.

Jones, T. *Ghana's First Republic.* London, Methuen, 1976.

Kay, G. (Ed.). *The Political Economy of Colonialism in Ghana: A Collection of Documents and Statistics 1900–60.* Cambridge University Press, 1972.

Killick, A. *Development Economics in Action: A Study of Economic Policies in Ghana.* London, Heinemann, 1978.

Killick, A., and Szereszewski. 'The Economy of Ghana', in Robson, P., and Lury, D. A. (Eds). *The Economies of Africa*, pp. 79–126. London, George Allen and Unwin, 1969.

Kimble, D. *Political History of Ghana.* London, Oxford University Press, 1963.

Ninsin, K. A., and Drah, F. K. (Eds). *The Search for Democracy in Ghana: A Case Study in Political Instability in Africa.* Accra, Asempa Publishers, 1987.

Nkrumah, K. *Autobiography.* London, Nelson, 1958.

Dark Days in Ghana. London, Lawrence and Wishart. 1968.

Revolutionary Path. London, Panaf Books, 1974.

Okeke, B. E. *4 June: A Revolution Betrayed.* Enugu, Ikenga Publishers, 1982.

Oquaye, M. *Politics in Ghana 1972–1979.* Accra, Tornado Publications, 1980.

Pinkney, R. *Ghana under Military Rule 1966–1969.* London, Methuen, 1972.

Rimmer, D. 'The Crisis in the Ghana Economy', in *Journal of Modern African Studies*, May 1966.

The Economies of West Africa. London, Weidenfeld and Nicolson, 1984.

Ward, W. E. F. *A History of Ghana.* London, Allen and Unwin, 1958.

Yeebo, Z. *Ghana: The Struggle for Popular Power—Rawlings: Saviour or Demagogue?* Accra, New Beacon Books, 1992.

GUINEA

Physical and Social Geography

R. J. HARRISON CHURCH

The Republic of Guinea covers an area of 245,857 sq km (94,926 sq miles), containing exceptionally varied landscapes, peoples and economic conditions. A census at mid-1992 recorded a population of some 5.6m. (giving an average density of 22.8 inhabitants per sq km), although the actual population is believed to be somewhat higher.

Guinea's coast is part of the extremely wet south-western sector of west Africa, which has a monsoonal climate. Thus Conakry, the capital, has five to six months with almost no rain, while 4,300 mm fall in the remaining months. The coastline has shallow drowned rivers and estuaries with much mangrove growing on alluvium eroded from the nearby Fouta Djallon mountains. The Baga people have removed much of the mangrove and bunded the land for rice cultivation. Only at two places, Cape Verga and Conakry, do ancient hard rocks reach the sea. At the latter they have facilitated the development of the port, while the weathering of these rocks has produced bauxite for quarrying on the offshore Los Islands.

Behind the swamps a gravelly coastal plain, some 65 km wide, is backed by the steep, often sheer, edges of the Fouta Djallon, which occupies the west-centre of Guinea. Much is over 900 m high, and consists of level Primary sandstones (possibly of Devonian age) which cover Pre-Cambrian rocks to a depth of 750 m. The level plateaux, with many bare lateritic surfaces, are the realm of Fulani herders. Rivers are deeply incised in the sandstone. These more fertile valleys were earlier cultivated with food crops by slaves of the Fulani, and then with banana, coffee, citrus and pineapple on plantations under the French. Falls and gorges of the incised rivers have great hydroelectric power potential. This is significant in view of huge deposits of high-grade bauxite located at Fria and Boké. The climate is still monsoonal but, although the total rainfall is lower—about 1,800 mm annually—it is more evenly distributed than on the coasts as the rainy season is longer. In such a mountainous area there are sharp variations in climatic conditions over a short distance, and from year to year.

On the Liberian border the Guinea highlands rise to 1,752 m at Mt Nimba, where substantial deposits of haematite iron ore are to be developed in co-operation with Liberia. These rounded mountains contrast greatly with the level plateaux and deep narrow valleys of the Fouta Djallon. Rainfall is heavier than in the latter, but is again more evenly distributed, so that only two or three months are without significant rain. Coffee, kola and other crops are grown in the forest of this area, unfortunately remote from Conakry but accessible by road from Monrovia or by mineral railway from Buchanan, Liberia. Diamonds of exceptional quality are mined north of Macenta and west of Beyla, and the exploitation of gold reserves is in progress.

Recent History

PIERRE ENGLEBERT

INDEPENDENCE AND THE TOURÉ ERA, 1958–84

In a referendum held in French Guinea on 28 September 1958, 95% of the voters rejected membership of a proposed community of self-governing French overseas territories, to be established under the constitution of the new French republic. French Guinea was the only French colony to reject the proposal. A powerful influence was exerted on the voters by Ahmed Sekou Touré, a trade union leader and the secretary-general of the Parti démocratique de Guinée (PDG), which had won 58 of the 60 seats in the territorial assembly in 1957, and which demanded complete independence from France. Thus, on 2 October 1958 the territory became independent as the Republic of Guinea; Sekou Touré became its first president, and the PDG the sole political party. Punitive economic reprisals were taken by the departing French authorities, and French aid and investment were suspended.

President Sekou Touré pursued a policy of socialist revolution, and any opposition was ruthlessly suppressed. Purges of various groups, including traders, civil servants and the military, were conducted intermittently, and numerous opponents of the government were forced into exile. Sekou Touré's survival in office was attributable to his dominance of all central government activities, his reliance on a group of close collaborators, and his ability to balance the authority of the armed forces against that of the PDG 'people's militia', which was used to enforce government policies.

Guinea withdrew from the Franc Zone in 1960 as a gesture of economic independence, but, as a result, the Guinea franc became worthless outside the country, and there was widespread trafficking in foreign currency. In 1964 severe measures were adopted to prevent smuggling and unauthorized currency-dealing, and to increase state control of both internal and external trade. Following independence the government initially obtained assistance from the USSR, but after 1961 (when the Soviet ambassador was expelled for allegedly interfering in Guinea's internal affairs) the USA became a more significant source of aid.

The presence of many thousands of Guinean exiles abroad, especially in the neighbouring states of Côte d'Ivoire and Senegal and in France, prompted Sekou Touré to make repeated allegations of foreign plots to overthrow him: a reported coup attempt in April 1960, for example, was ascribed to the French government, while senior French officials and President Houphouët-Boigny of Côte d'Ivoire were accused of complicity in an 'assassination plot' in October 1965. In 1965 exiles based in Abidjan, Dakar and Paris formed an opposition front, provoking allegations by Sekou Touré that the three countries were training 'mercenaries' for an invasion of Guinea.

In November 1970 an abortive invasion did take place: it originated in the neighbouring territory of Portuguese Guinea (now Guinea-Bissau), where Sekou Touré's government had been supporting a nationalist movement, the Partido Africano da Independência da Guiné e Cabo Verde (PAIGC). Some 350 troops, comprising mainly Guinean exiles led by Portuguese officers, landed from the sea off Conakry: during two days of sporadic fighting they destroyed the offices of the PAIGC and freed some political prisoners, but failed to overthrow Sekou Touré. Severe reprisals followed: many prominent Guineans, including seven former ministers and the Roman Catholic archbishop of Conakry, were arrested, and about 90 were sentenced to death. In February 1973 the assassination in Conakry of the PAIGC leader, Amílcar Cabral, gave rise to renewed suspicion of plots against the Touré regime.

In 1973 there was a reorganization of local government structures, with an increase in the mandate of the Pouvoirs révolutionnaires locaux, introduced in 1968 as executive bodies at village level and which were now given the role of planning the production and marketing of commodities. In 1975 all private trading was forbidden. Transactions were to be conducted through official co-operatives, under the supervision of the 'economic police' of the PDG. These measures apparently encountered opposition in northern Guinea among the nomadic Fulani ethnic group, and in 1976 the government announced the discovery of a 'Fulani plot', organized by Diallo Telli, the minister of justice and a former secretary-general of the OAU. He died in a prison camp in 1977, having 'confessed' his collusion in the plot, which had, it was alleged, been sponsored by the US Central Intelligence Agency. In the same year a UN report revealed maltreatment of Guinean political prisoners, and in 1978 the human rights organization, Amnesty International, published details of torture, political executions and imprisonment without trial. The Guinean government subsequently claimed that such abuses had ceased.

In 1977 there was widespread unrest and demonstrations against the PDG's 'economic police', who were widely suspected of extortion and smuggling. In response, Sekou Touré disbanded the 'economic police' and permitted the resumption (from July 1979) of small-scale private trading. In late 1978 it was agreed to increase the membership of the central organs of the PDG and to merge the functions of the party and the state. In January 1979 the country was renamed the People's Revolutionary Republic of Guinea.

Diplomatic relations with France (which had been effectively severed in 1965) were restored in 1976, and in the following year the two countries reached an agreement on economic co-operation, including an undertaking by the French government to curb the activities of Guinean dissidents in Paris. In 1978 Sekou Touré declared a policy of 'co-operation with capitalist as well as socialist states'. At the same time the government sought to improve relations with Côte d'Ivoire and Senegal, and increased its participation in regional organizations.

CONTÉ AND THE CMRN

Sekou Touré died suddenly in March 1984. Before the Guinean authorities could choose a successor, the army staged a *coup d'état* in April, and a Comité militaire de redressement national (CMRN) took power. Although the CMRN was composed mainly of middle- and lower-ranking officers, its principal leaders, Col (later Gen.) Lansana Conté and Col Diarra Traoré, who became president and prime minister respectively, had both held senior positions for some years. A semi-civilian government was appointed, and efforts were made to improve relations with neighbouring countries and with potential creditors (most notably France). In May the country resumed the designation of Republic of Guinea.

The PDG and organs of state of the Sekou Touré era were dismantled under this second republic, which was initially greeted with great enthusiasm. State surveillance and control were ended, and many political detainees were freed and their places taken by a few former leaders of the PDG. Corruption involving Sekou Touré and his senior officials was revealed, and the CMRN was eloquent in its denunciations of Touré's 'bloody and pitiless dictatorship', promising a new era of freedom. Exiled groups of Guineans were eager to return but, with an estimated 2m. exiles scattered through neighbouring states, Guinea's new rulers showed no willingness to accommodate them all at once.

Major difficulties confronted the CMRN, particularly in its management of the economy. Given the parlous economic situation and uncertain internal situation, major political decisions had to be contained within the bounds of fiscal austerity and social acceptability. A devaluation of the currency was long overdue, and local political opinion and external creditors favoured the liberalization of trading practices (a process already initiated in the later years of the Sekou Touré regime) and fostering of private enterprise. There was, however, an inertia in the administrative system, where corruption and tax evasion had had damaging effects.

Undercurrents of Opposition

In the first months of his presidency Conté adopted an open and magnanimous style of government, inviting constructive advice and criticism from all quarters. In a government reshuffle in December 1984, however, Conté abolished the post of prime minister, demoting Traoré to a lesser cabinet post. Noting that some of his colleagues had used power only to 'satisfy their personal interests', Conté warned that there might be further changes, with the emphasis being placed on competence.

On 4 July 1985, while Conté was attending a regional summit meeting in Togo, Traoré attempted a *coup d'état*, supported mainly by members of the police force. However, troops loyal to Conté swiftly regained control, and the president returned, to public acclaim, two days later. Traoré and many of his family were arrested, and the armed forces conducted a purge of his suspected sympathizers; in all, more than 200 arrests were made. Traoré and the late president's half-brother, Ismaël Touré, were among those executed in the immediate aftermath of the coup attempt. About 60 other military officers were later sentenced to death, following secret trials. (In January 1988 an amnesty for 67 political prisoners, including Sekou Touré's widow and son, was announced.)

The coup attempt strengthened Conté's position, allowing him to pursue the extensive economic reforms that were demanded by the World Bank and the IMF as a prerequisite for the disbursement of new funds. The national currency, the syli, was devalued and replaced in January 1986 by a revived Guinea franc. A 'streamlining' of the cumbersome civil service was initiated, with inevitable redundancies, many state-owned enterprises were dissolved or offered for sale, and the banking system was overhauled. In December 1985 Conté reorganized the council of ministers, introducing a majority of civilians for the first time since he took power and creating 'regional' ministries.

By late 1987 opposition to Conté's reform programme was revealed by unrest within the armed forces and the civil service, while high levels of inflation provoked demonstrations in Conakry in January 1988. Conté reorganized the government in the same month, transferring two high-ranking ministers to regional ministries. Further reshuffles were implemented in April of that year and in June 1989.

Meanwhile, a process of limited democratization was proceeding. In October 1988, in a speech to commemorate the 30th anniversary of the country's independence, Conté declared an amnesty for 39 political prisoners, including some of those who had been implicated in the 1985 coup attempt. The president also announced the establishment of a committee to draft a new constitution, which would, upon completion, be submitted for approval in a national referendum. In October 1989 Conté announced that, following the adoption of the document, the CMRN would be replaced by a new supreme political body, the Comité transitoire de redressement national (CTRN), which was to oversee a five-year transitional period prior to the establishment of a two-party political system. Thus, it was envisaged that elections would be held in the mid-1990s, by universal suffrage, for the post of president of the republic and for a unicameral legislature. In February 1990 an amnesty was announced for all political detainees and exiled dissidents. Among those to benefit were former associates of Sekou Touré and those implicated in the July 1985 coup attempt.

The austerity measures necessitated by the government's economic adjustment efforts were widely unpopular, but, as elsewhere in the region, it was in the education sector that discontent tended most frequently to manifest itself. Teachers staged a strike in early 1990, in protest at inadequate pay and conditions, forcing the government to replace an unpopular education minister. Tensions resurfaced in November, when the authorities closed the University of Conakry in response to a boycott of classes by students who were demanding the reform of the system for the allocation of grants, together with improved educational standards and facilities, and two students were killed by security forces at a demonstration in the capital. The government ordered the resumption of classes in late November, but two further demonstrators were killed in December, as disturbances continued.

Despite an appeal made by Conté, in early November 1990, for the return to Guinea of political exiles, three members of an illegal opposition movement, the Rassemblement populaire guinéen (RPG) were imprisoned later in the same month. One was convicted of forging official documents, while his co-defendants were found guilty of distributing banned newspapers on Guinean territory; all three had been detained since August, and had been classified as political prisoners by Amnesty International.

Rejecting widespread demands for an accelerated programme of political reform, the Conté government proceeded with its plan for a gradual transition to a two-party political system. The draft constitution (*loi fondamentale*) was submitted to a national referendum in December 1990. According to official results, the document received the support of 98.7% of those who voted (some 97.4% of the registered electorate). The period of transition to civilian rule thus began, and in late February 1991 the 36-member CTRN was inaugurated, under the chairmanship of President Conté. A reorganization of the council of ministers earlier in the month had entailed the removal from the government of two close associates of Conté, who were now appointed to the CTRN (the new constitution stipulated that membership of the CTRN was incompatible with ministerial status). Military officers continued to hold the most sensitive posts in the new government, implying that the president intended to ensure the continued loyalty of the armed forces.

Academic staff renewed strike action in May 1991. Shortly afterwards, the government announced a doubling of civil servants' salaries, together with increases in some social allowances and a halving of the salaries of members of the council of ministers and of the CTRN. However, the trade union confederation, the Confédération des travailleurs de Guinée (CTG), deemed these concessions to be insufficient, and organized a widely-observed general strike, which effectively paralysed the capital. Most workers heeded a recommendation by the CTG for an early return to work, although academic staff withheld their labour until early June.

In May 1991 the leader of the RPG, Alpha Condé, returned to Guinea after a long period of exile in France and Senegal. Three arrests were made when a meeting of his supporters was dispersed by the security forces, and in late May the government imposed a ban on unauthorized meetings and demonstrations. In mid-June one person was killed when security forces opened fire on a group of demonstrators who had gathered outside the police headquarters in Conakry, to where Condé had been summoned to answer questions relating to the seizure, at the country's main airport, of a consignment of allegedly subversive materials. As many as 60 people were reported to have been detained, while Condé sought refuge in the Senegalese embassy, where he remained for several weeks before being granted political asylum in Senegal.

In October 1991 Conté indicated that, contrary to earlier proposals for political change, the registration of an unlimited number of political parties would come into effect on 3 April 1992 (the eighth anniversary of the coup that had brought him to power), and that legislative elections would take place before the end of 1992 in the context of a full multi-party political system. However, tensions between the government and opposition remained, and Conté refused to accede to demands that a national conference be convened to prepare for the forthcoming elections. In late October 1991 three people were killed during anti-government demonstrations in the eastern city of Kankan. Moreover, in December the Conté administration was obliged to refute allegations, made by Amnesty International, of the persecution, imprisonment and torture of political opponents.

THE THIRD REPUBLIC

The constitution of the third republic was promulgated on 23 December 1991. In January 1992 Conté ceded the presidency of the CTRN (whose membership was, at the same time, reduced to 15), in accordance with the provisions of the constitution, which envisaged the separation of the powers of the executive and legislature. In the following month the government was extensively reorganized, with most military officers and all those who had returned from exile after the 1984 coup (*Guinéens de l'extérieur*) leaving the cabinet—although it later appeared that some long-serving ministers had been removed from office in order that they might establish a pro-Conté political party; in addition, the resident ministries were abolished.

The RPG was among the first parties to be legalized in April 1992, and Alpha Condé returned to Guinea in June. Other than the RPG, the most prominent challengers to the pro-Conté Parti de l'unité et du progrès (PUP) were the Parti pour le renouveau et le progrès (PRP), led by a prominent journalist, Siradiou Diallo, and the Union pour la nouvelle République, led by Mamadou Bâ. However, the increasing fragmentation of the opposition movement undermined its attempts to persuade the government to convene a national conference in advance of the legislative elections. Political tensions were heightened by opposition allegations that the PUP was benefiting from state funds, and by apparent government efforts to coerce civil servants into joining the party. Moreover, there was evidence that the government was undertaking development projects in areas of potential PUP support. Clashes between pro- and anti-Conté activists (seemingly fuelled by ethnic rivalries) occurred frequently from mid-1992, and in October prompted the government to impose a ban on all unauthorized public gatherings. In that month Conté escaped an assassination attempt when gunmen opened fire on the vehicle in which he was travelling. Amadou Oury Bah, the leader of the opposition Union des forces démocratiques, was briefly detained in connection with the incident, but allegations of his involvement were deemed to be unfounded.

In December 1992 the government announced the indefinite postponement of the legislative elections, which had been scheduled for the end of the month, citing technical and financial difficulties. It was later indicated that the elections would be organized during the final quarter of 1993, and that (contrary to the preference of most opposition parties) they would be preceded by a presidential election. The delay provoked further discontent, and in late May shops were looted and vehicles damaged in Conakry when about 30,000 people joined a demonstration to demand that the legislative elections take place at an earlier date. As many as three people were said to have been killed, and 50 injured, during the protest: witnesses claimed that PUP sympathizers had assaulted demonstrators. Opposition leaders were subsequently summoned by the authorities to account for their supporters' actions. In early July opposition rallies took place in Conakry, and in several regions outside the capital, to demand the establishment of a transitional government of national unity and an independent electoral commission.

During the second half of 1993 opposition parties failed in their attempts to form an electoral alliance, with the aim of preventing a divided opposition vote from benefiting Conté and the PUP at the forthcoming elections, and in late October the supreme court approved candidates for the presidential election, which had been scheduled for 5 December. Conté was to represent the PUP, his major challengers being Alpha Condé, Siradiou Diallo and Mamadou Bâ.

In late September 1993 the government imposed a ban on all political gatherings and street demonstrations, following violent incidents in Conakry when police opened fire on demonstrators, as a result of which, according to official figures, some 18 people were killed—other reports claimed as many as 63 deaths—and almost 200 injured. Such repression of the opposition (together with the detention of several foreign journalists in the same month) called into question the extent of the Conté regime's commitment to the demilitarization of the political process and the establishment of democratic institutions. In mid-October, at a meeting between Conté and representatives of 43 political organizations (the first such meeting since the legalization of political parties), it was reportedly agreed to establish an independent electoral commission. However, controversy arose regarding the composition of such a body, and the opposition denounced the government's decision to place it under the jurisdiction of the ministry of the interior and security. By mid-November opposition candidates were demanding that the presidential election be postponed, citing irregularities in the compilation of electoral lists, as well as delays in the issuing of voting cards and in the appointment of the electoral commission. It was also claimed that the PUP was able to hold electoral rallies, while the opposition remained subject to the ban announced in September. In late November the government announced a two-week postponement of the presidential poll, admitting that technical preparations for voting were incomplete. The opposition, in common with trade union and religious leaders, continued to appeal for a two-month delay.

In the days preceding the election there was violence in Conakry and in the interior, involving supporters of the PUP and opposition activists, as a result of which at least four deaths were recorded. A further six people were reported to have been killed in the suburbs of the capital as voting proceeded on 19 December 1993. Despite confused appeals for a boycott of the poll by several opposition leaders (and the absence of voters' lists in some polling centres), the rate of participation by voters was, officially, 78.5% of the registered electorate, with supporters of all candidates voting. According to official results, which were confirmed by the supreme court in early January 1994, Conté was elected at the first round of voting (the constitution requires that the president be elected by an absolute majority), securing 51.70% of the votes cast. Condé, his nearest rival, took 19.55% of the votes; however, a supreme court ruling that the results of voting in the Kankan and Siguiri prefectures, in both of which Condé had won more than 90% of the votes, was invalid (owing to alleged malpractice by RPG activists in the conduct of the poll) fuelled opposition claims that the poll had been fraudulent and the result manipulated in favour of Conté. Of the other candidates, Bâ took 13.37% of the votes and Diallo 11.86%. Many Guineans residing abroad were unable to participate in the election, as a consequence of the inadequate distribution of voting cards, and there was violence among Guinean communities elsewhere in the region, as demonstrators destroyed polling stations at Guinean embassies, alleging electoral fraud.

Conté was inaugurated as president on 29 January 1994. Although he indicated that a new government would be appointed, which would be 'representative and composed of more competent Guineans', he resisted opposition appeals that the new administration should include representatives of diverse political trends. Conté announced that his priorities would be to strengthen national security and unity and to promote economic growth. In May Mamadou Bâ announced his lack of confidence in the Guinean opposition movement, and stated his willingness to recognize Conté as the country's legitimately elected head of state. However, relations between the government and opposition remained generally poor, and the RPG in particular protested at the harassment of its activists by members of the armed forces. Moreover, the Association guinéenne des droits de l'homme was severely critical of the Conté regime, denouncing a recent increase in the ill-treatment of prisoners' and attempts by the authorities to deprive individuals of basic rights and freedoms. The brief detention, in June, of eight senior armed forces officers, including the deputy chief of staff of the air force, prompted rumours that a coup attempt had been discovered; the government confirmed that certain members of the armed forces had participated in a 'political' meeting, in contravention of their terms of service, but denied the existence of a destabilization plot.

Conté announced a major restructuring of the government in late August 1994. The composition of the new council of ministers, which was substantially larger than the previous administration, apparently reflected Conté's stated intention to base economic growth on the promotion of the primary sector.

France has assumed an increasingly active role in the Conté regime's strategy for aid and investment. French interests have predominated in taking control of the newly-privatized state companies, and there has been a substantial inflow of French advisers and teachers. In addition, Guinea is dependent on France for the provision of civilian and military intelligence.

In June 1993 the Guinean authorities estimated that some 620,000 refugees had fled from Liberia and Sierra Leone to Guinea. In April 1990 President Conté denied suggestions that Guinean troops were supporting the Doe regime in Liberia. In August of that year Guinean armed forces were deployed along the border with Liberia, following a series of incursions by deserters from the Liberian army. Guinean army units also participated in the ECOMOG monitoring group of the Economic Community of West African States that was dispatched to Liberia in that month, and in April 1991 it was annnounced that a Guinean contingent was to be deployed in Sierra Leone to assist that country in repelling violations of its territory by the National Patriotic Front of Liberia (NPFL), led by Charles Taylor. Following the *coup d'état* in Sierra Leone in April 1992, ex-president Momoh of that country was granted asylum in Guinea, although the Conté government expressed its wish to establish 'normal' relations with the new regime and announced that Guinean forces would remain in Sierra Leone. None the less, the fears of the new Strasser administration in Sierra Leone that Momoh might seek to organize a counter-coup from Guinean territory caused some strain in the two countries' relations.

In October 1992 the Conté government confirmed for the first time that Liberian forces were being trained in Guinea; however, assurances were given that those receiving military instruction were not, as had been widely rumoured, members of the anti-Taylor United Liberation Movement of Liberia for Democracy (ULIMO), but that they were to constitute the first Liberian government forces following the eventual restoration of peace. In March 1993 the NPFL protested to the UN that ULIMO had launched an armed attack on NPFL-held territory from Guinea, and threatened reprisals should further offensives occur. Although Guinea continued to deny support for ULIMO, it was admitted later in the same month that, contrary to earlier indications, Liberian forces trained in Guinea (at the request of the Liberian interim government) had already returned to Liberia. Efforts were undertaken during early 1994 to reinforce security along Guinea's borders, following recent incursions by both ULIMO and NPFL fighters.

Economy

EDITH HODGKINSON

Revised for this edition by the Editor

With substantial mineral deposits and excellent agricultural potential, Guinea could be one of the richest countries in west Africa. Yet the economic record since independence has been disappointing. The country's gross domestic product (GDP) expanded, in real terms, at an average rate of 3.0% per year in 1970–80, reflecting the rapid development of the bauxite sector during that decade, but declined by 1.4% per year in 1980–85. The causes of Guinea's relatively poor performance were largely political. First, there was the abrupt severance of the country's links with France in 1958. Some of the short-term difficulties arising from the sudden withdrawal of French officials, and the discontinuance of aid, were overcome by support from Eastern bloc countries, while the immediate and substantial flight of capital was stemmed when Guinea created its own currency, the Guinea franc (FG), after withdrawing from the Franc Zone in 1960. However, other consequences—the need to find alternative markets for Guinea's exports and alternative sources of capital and technical assistance, and to build up the country's indigenous skills and supplies—took longer to resolve.

Second, the newly independent Guinea immediately sought to set up a socialist economy, with direct state control of production and consumption in virtually every sector—an objective demanding managerial input that Guinea lacked, and which resulted in great inefficiency and waste. Mining, the one economic sector where state control was diluted, developed as an enclave, with admittedly major benefits for Guinea's export earnings but little linkage and feedback into the rest of the economy, which remained essentially based on agriculture and which suffered from Sekou Touré's system of highly centralized management. The economy consequently became even more dualistic, with the development of a large informal sector in response to the near monopoly of the state over formal economic activity. In an attempt to remove at least the domestic constraints on growth, the Conté administration has introduced a series of policy reforms, agreed with the IMF and the World Bank. These include the transfer to private interests, or elimination, of the parastatal organizations, the liberalization of foreign trade and the abolition of price controls, monetary and banking reforms, and the reduction in the number of civil service personnel. The recovery programme received substantial international support, in the form of debt-relief and of new funds from both bilateral and multilateral sources. Such reforms have enjoyed considerable success, and real GDP growth in 1988–92 averaged 4.1% per year. Although the rate slowed in 1991, and has since been further impeded by social and political unrest, growth rates of 3.8% and 3.5%, respectively, were recorded in 1992 and 1993. Gross national product (GNP) per head in 1992, at US $510, was among the lowest levels in the world.

POPULATION AND EMPLOYMENT

Population growth has been relatively slow, owing to the high level of emigration during the Sekou Touré regime. Therefore, while the population was stated to be 4.5m. (excluding adjustment for underenumeration) at the 1983 census, a further 2m. Guineans (some of whom returned following the 1984 coup) were estimated to be living abroad. Census results from mid-1992 showed a total population of some 5.6m., of whom about 10% were believed to be refugees from Liberia and Sierra Leone. However, more recent estimates have been significantly higher, and the government has admitted that it considers the population to be somewhat greater.

The population is concentrated in the plateau area of central Guinea: about 23% of the population was estimated to be living in Conakry and its environs in 1990. The active labour force in the early 1990s was estimated at about 3m. Employment in the industrial and service sectors increased from 12% of the total economically active population in 1965 to 23% in 1988, while employment in the agricultural sector eased from 85% of the total in 1970 to about 73% in 1992. Some 70% of salaried employees are concentrated in the public sector, which has rendered more difficult the Conté government's aim of reducing the number of civil service personnel by one-half. By the end of 1989 the number of permanent employees in the public sector had been reduced to about 51,000 (with a further 5,000 contractual employees), compared with some 90,000 employees in 1986. However, the real contraction is less significant, as some of the losses resulted from the transfer to private ownership of state-owned interests. Employment in the public sector has since stabilized at about 50,000.

AGRICULTURE

Despite the rapid development and potential of the mining sector, agriculture remains the most important economic activity, in terms both of value of output 23.2% of GDP in 1991) and of employment (see above). Its slow growth (3% per year between 1970–77, and only around 1% per year during the final years of the Sekou Touré regime) has offset the much stronger performance of mining. Agricultural production was depressed by the low official prices paid to producers, government controls on marketing, and the production tax on crops and livestock, which led to large-scale smuggling of produce by peasant farmers. The collective agricultural units (FPA), which occupied a dominant role in agriculture, and the Pouvoirs révolutionnaires locaux (PRL), which controlled the transport and marketing of agricultural production, were highly inefficient. Thus, although the Sekou Touré government gave priority to the agricultural sector in its development spending, the target rate of growth was modest—an average of 3% per year in the period 1981–85. The government of Lansana Conté has also given priority to agriculture, and is looking to foreign investment to revive plantation agriculture. However, it has made important institutional changes, abolishing the FPA and the PRL. It has substantially raised producer prices, and abolished the production tax. Farmers have, however, been slow to react to the changes, and production in 1991 was only 9% higher than in 1986. The drastic currency devaluation that occurred in late 1985 (see below) aimed to stimulate production for export, while management practices within the rural development ministry have been reformed with assistance from the World Bank and France.

There are few official figures for crop production. In 1992 output of paddy rice (cultivated mainly in the Forest Guinea area) was unofficially put at 757,000 metric tons, while production of cassava (in the Soussou coastal region) was estimated by the FAO at 660,000 tons, sweet potatoes at 100,000 tons and maize (unofficially) at 94,000 tons. In the past, Guinea was a net exporter of food grains but during the early 1980s it imported about 130,000 tons of grain per year, equivalent to more than one-quarter of its requirements and accounting for around 30% of export revenues. A programme was inaugurated in 1980 to develop rice-growing in the Forest Guinea region, aided by the World Bank and the African Development Bank (ADB), and the two agencies proceeded to assist the second-stage Guéckédou project, which developed upland and swamp rice at a cost of $25.2m. Another project, the Siguiri scheme, involved the rehabilitation of 5,820 ha of alluvial land near the Niger river, and the development of 1,000 ha adjacent. In late 1990 the Caisse centrale de coopération économique (the official French development agency, subsequently renamed the Caisse française de développement—CFD), announced that it was to provide funding of 43.4m. French francs in support of a new, three-year programme that aimed to encourage the expansion of rice cultivation. None the less, large quantities of rice are still imported, although the figure was almost halved in 1990, to 112,000 tons (from 195,000 tons in the previous year); rice imports increased to 182,000 tons in 1991. Overall results for food production, disappointing in the first years of the 1980s (the FAO estimates that production increased by an annual average of only 0.9% in 1981–85), have since been more encouraging, with output increasing by an average of 3.0% per year in 1985–93. The staple crops are supplemented by the substantial livestock herd (raised by traditional methods), estimated by the FAO in 1992 at 1.8m. cattle, 510,000 sheep and 460,000 goats. In 1986 the government initiated a major livestock project, aiming to provide credit and extension services, including a vaccination programme, to 160,000 families. The target was a 75% rise in meat production over a 20-year period. The total cost of the seven-year scheme was estimated at $22m., of which nearly $20m. was to be covered by the International Development Association (IDA), France and the Arab Bank for Economic Development in Africa (BADEA).

The major commercial crops are bananas, coffee, pineapples, oil palm, groundnuts and citrus fruit. The banana plantations, which suffered in the late 1950s from disease and, with independence, from the withdrawal of European planters and the closing of the protected French market, showed a slow rise in output during the 1960s. During the 1980s, however, the plantations yielded more than 100,000 tons per year. Coffee output has fluctuated widely, with the exportable production of 4,000 tons in 1982/83 being followed by a net import in 1983/84, mainly reflecting the incidence of smuggling to neighbouring countries, where higher prices were obtainable. Before independence Guinea exported about 20,000 tons of coffee annually. Higher prices paid to producers in the late 1980s prompted more output to be sold on the official domestic market: exportable production rose strongly, from 6,900 tons in 1985/86 to 13,000 tons in 1986/87. Annual output of 30,000 tons was recorded in the early 1990s. The IDA has lent $7m. for pineapple development, and production, which, having fallen from 25,000 tons per year in the late 1960s to about one-half of this level in 1970, had recovered to more than 80,000 tons per year by the early 1990s. Production of groundnuts declined to 75,000 tons (unshelled) per year in 1983–88, from its previous annual level of about 83,000 tons, and output remained at much the same level (78,000 tons per year) in 1990–92. Output of unrefined palm oil was 45,000 tons in 1988, and had increased to some 52,000 tons by 1992. A modest export trade in horticultural produce has also been developed: during the 1988/89 season Guinea exported 2,265 tons of pineapples and 300 tons of mangoes, as well as small quantities of tomatoes, green beans, dried fruit and flowers. Such exports have increased significantly in recent years, as quality-control and transportation links have improved. Because of the overvaluation of the currency until 1985, exports of bananas, coffee, palm and other crops were subsidized out of the proceeds of import taxes. This practice has ceased under the Conté regime, and it is hoped that the production of cash crops will henceforth be stimulated by improved producer prices and the more realistic exchange rate. In late 1986 a nine-year project was launched to plant 13,000 ha with rubber and oil palm in Forest Guinea, with the aim of re-establishing, in a modified form, the plantation agriculture that was characteristic of the colonial period, and of attracting foreign investment to this sector. Meanwhile, a project in Haute Guinée, aided by France, has encouraged the cultivation of cotton, by smallholders, on 2,500 ha: output was 2,260 tons in 1988/89. Under a second phase, it was hoped that production would have increased to 33,000 tons by 1995.

There is considerable potential for timber production, with forests covering more than two-thirds of the land area. Timber resources are currently used mainly for fuel, with total production of roundwood (by small-scale producers) estimated at 4.2m. cu m in 1992. However, an integrated forestry industry is planned, and in 1989 foreign credits were pledged for a programme of forest conservation.

The fishing sector remains relatively undeveloped. The total catch was about 35,000 tons per year in 1987–91; however, only a small proportion of the total catch from Guinean waters has been accounted for by indigenous fleets, the rest having been taken by factory ships and industrial trawlers. Since 1983 the Guinean government has concluded a series of fishing accords with the European Community (now European Union—EU). The two-year agreement which took effect in January 1990 allowed European trawlers to land an average of 12,000 tons of fish per year, in return for compensation paid to Guinea of ECU 750,000 annually, and it has since been agreed to award future foreign licences exclusively to EU fleets. The fishing sector has considerable potential (the catch could be increased substantially), and there has been some development in recent years. The ADB is helping to finance a five-year project, costing an estimated $35m., to develop fish supplies for the domestic market, including the establishment of onshore facilities and the supply of equipment for small-scale fishermen. The government has entered into two private ventures with US and French interests. The first will have a fleet of 18 vessels and onshore processing facilities, and will concentrate on exports. The second, which operates three vessels (and plans to increase its fleet to 25), intends to secure an annual fish catch of 40,000 tons, with some 25,000 tons going to the domestic market. In addition, a project for the rehabilitation of the port of Conakry includes the installation of deep-freeze equipment to serve the fishing industry, as well as for the construction of a deep-water port.

MINING AND POWER

Guinea's most dynamic sector and most important source of foreign exchange, providing more than 90% of recorded export revenues for much of the 1980s, is mining, which contributed 22.0% of GDP in 1991. Since 1990, none the less, the sector has suffered great upheavals, as operations have been disrupted by industrial disputes and technical difficulties, and has declined in importance in both relative and absolute terms. The country possesses more than one-quarter of the world's known bauxite reserves, with a very high-grade ore. Guinea ranks second only to Australia in terms of ore production and is the world's largest exporter of bauxite. Since the mid-1980s, however, bauxite revenues have been affected by a slump in world demand for aluminium and the considerable surplus in world production capacity. Annual output averaged 13.5m. tons in the period 1981–86 and increased thereafter, reaching a record level of 17.9m. tons in 1988; production in 1989–91 averaged 17.4m. tons per year. It is planned to upgrade and develop the country's mines, with the aim of increasing annual output to 20m. tons.

The exploitation of bauxite reserves at Fria, by the Cie internationale pour la production de l'alumine Fria (an international consortium that included Pechiney) began in the 1930s. Processing into alumina began in 1960, at what remains the country's only smelter. Following independence, the government took a 49% share in the company, which was renamed Friguia. Production from the reserves has recently averaged 1.25m. tons per year, while the smelter's output has eased from a peak of 692,000 tons (recorded in 1980, and close to the plant's total capacity of 700,000 tons annually) to an annual average of 631,000 tons in 1989–91. A rehabilitation programme, costing $80m., is under way. Some Guinean alumina is exported to Cameroon for refining.

The country's principal bauxite mine is at Boké, in the north-west, which was commissioned in 1973 by the Cie des bauxites de Guinée, a joint venture between the government and the Halco group (an international consortium of US, Canadian, Dutch, French, German and Italian aluminium companies). The government holds 49% of the capital and receives 65% of the mine's net profits. The scheme involved investment of $400m., including infrastructural development—142 km of railway and a port at Kamsar. Finance came from the World Bank and the US Agency for International Development, as well as from Halco itself. Output increased from around 900,000 tons per year to the complex's full capacity (at that time) of 10m. tons in 1981, eased subsequently, before recovering to 9.9m. tons in 1987; output reached 11.5m. tons per year in 1990 and 1991, and the plant's capacity is to be expanded to 13.5m. tons by 1996.

A similar agreement to that signed with Halco was concluded in 1969 by Guinea and the USSR for the working of bauxite deposits at Debélé, near Kindia, where reserves are estimated at 44m. tons. Production by the Office des Bauxites de Kindia began in 1974, with capacity of 2.5m. tons per year, and, after initial rail transport problems, output increased to 3m. tons in 1984, declined slightly in the two following years, but returned to full capacity in 1987. Following the dissolution of the USSR, the company suffered severe financial difficulties: it was reorganized as the Société des Bauxites de Kindia in 1992, and was scheduled for privatization in 1994. Agreements have also been signed with Yugoslav and Swiss companies for the exploitation of the Dabola and Tougué bauxite deposits (although prospects for agreements signed with Yugoslavia are uncertain). These are estimated at 425m. tons, and it is planned to build an alumina plant with an annual capacity of 300,000 tons and an aluminium smelter to handle 150,000 tons per year. Production is projected at 8m. tons of bauxite at Tougué and 5m. tons at Dabola. Another agreement was signed in 1976 with official agencies from six Arab countries, to exploit the Ayé-Koyé deposits in the Boké region of north-western Guinea. It is planned to establish a mine producing 9m. tons per year, and also a smelter. In 1980 a consortium of Swiss, Algerian, Romanian and Yugoslav interests signed an agreement with the government for the smelter complex at the site, with an annual capacity of 1.2m. tons of alumina and 150,000 tons of aluminium. However, this scheme must await the coming into operation of the Konkouré river dam (see below).

Working of the iron-ore deposits on the Kaloum peninsula (near Conakry) was begun in 1953 by an Anglo-French group, and provided a stable output of about 700,000 tons per year between 1960–69, when working at Kaloum was abandoned. An ambitious project for the exploitation of the far superior deposits at Mt Nimba, which has proven reserves of 350 tons of high-grade (66.7%) ore (total reserves have been estimated at as much as 1,000m. tons), has been studied and much discussed for more than a decade. However, as the transport of ore through neighbouring Liberia is an essential element of the project, development has been delayed by the civil conflict in that country, as well as international concerns regarding the potential environmental impact of the project (Mt Nimba is included on UNESCO's 'World Heritage List'). It was originally proposed that a consortium of the government (50%) and companies from Japan, the USA, France, Spain, Romania, Yugoslavia, Nigeria, Algeria and Liberia would undertake the project, which, with associated infrastructure, was to cost an estimated $900m. Initial production of 2m. tons per year, beginning in the late 1980s, was scheduled to rise to 15m. tons by 1992. However, the original proposals failed to attract sufficient capital, since commitments by potential customers for the ore were far below the planned level of output, and a scaled-down revision of the project was prepared in co-operation with the Liberian authorities prior to the overthrow of President Doe in September 1990. This envisaged shipment via an 18-km rail spur for processing in Liberia, with export through that country's port of Buchanan. There are plans for the eventual construction of a railway (at an estimated cost of $555m.) to Conakry, where a new deep-water port would be constructed. In late 1989 Guinea and Liberia agreed to establish a joint-venture company the Nimba International Mining Co (Nimco) to manage the scheme. Guinea is the principal shareholder in the project, together with the government of Liberia, Euronimba (a consortium of French, South African, Japanese and Kuwaiti investors) and the United Kingdom's African Mining Consortium Ltd. New arrangements, announced in early 1994, envisaged annual output of 12m. tons.

Production of diamonds rose in the late 1960s, to reach 80,000 carats per year in the early 1970s: the official figure did not include substantial illicit production, and mining was suspended in the late 1970s to prevent smuggling and theft. In 1980 the government allowed the resumption of diamond mining by private companies. Two companies have so far been established: the Société de Diamant de Guinée, founded in 1984 (with US and French participation), and AREDOR-Guinée, founded in 1981 as the Association pour la recherche et l'exploitation de diamants et de l'or (with Australian, Swiss, British and—for the first time in Guinea—International Finance Corporation participation). In each, the government has a 50% holding and takes 65% of net profits. The former company plans to produce 120,000–240,000 carats per year, while the latter commenced production in 1984, in the Banankoro region. AREDOR-Guinée has enjoyed considerable success, unearthing some of the largest diamonds ever found in Guinea. According to the US Bureau of Mines, diamond output in 1987 was 175,000 carats, but by 1991 production had declined to 91,000 carats. Mining of diamonds was suspended following violent incidents in 1991, and in 1992 the government revoked the ban on small-scale prospecting and liberalized the gem-stones trade. Production in that year was 100,000 carats, and in 1993 output was stated by De Beers' Central Selling Organisation to have risen to 400,000 carats.

Gold is mined both industrially and by individuals. Three joint-venture companies have been established since 1984: between the Guinea government and French, Saudi Arabian and US interests (in the Société Minière du Niandan), between Guinea and Norwegian and French interests (in the Société Minière du Dinguiraye) and between Guinea and Belgian interests (in the Société Aurifère de Guinée—SAuG). In late 1988 SAuG began exploitation of the gold reserves at Koron, in the Siguiri district. Annual production from the mine, which was developed at a cost of some $30m., was forecast at 2,000–3,000 kg of unrefined gold. Output in 1989 totalled 2,000 kg. Alluvial gold extraction at Siguiri ceased in 1992; however, Golden Shamrock Mines of Australia has since acquired the concession, and plans to exploit hard-rock gold deposits. A large prospecting area to the south of Siguiri has been acquired by Cyprus Amax Minerals of the USA. The Société Minière de Dinguiraye was due to begin production, at 2,000 kg per year, in 1989, while the Société Minière du Niandan is exploiting reserves of gold and diamonds at Kéniéro, near Kouroussa. Cambrian Resources of Australia also intends to develop a concession at Kouroussa. AREDOR-Guinée has also produced gold from gravel processed for diamonds. Officially recorded output of gold by individual diggers in 1989 totalled 1,500 kg, declining to 1,000 kg in 1990. Overall national production (including that by SAuG) was estimated at 7,000 kg, taking into account smuggling and unregulated local dealing. There were reports in mid-1994 that diamond- and gold-mining operations by AREDOR-Guinée had been suspended, following the withdrawal of Guinea's investment partners in response to insecurity in diamond-mining areas.

The country possesses no known resources of fossil fuels, but there is continuing exploration for petroleum offshore. Currently, the Société guinéenne des hydrocarbures (SGH), a joint venture by the Guinean government and a subsidiary of Mobil Oil, is carrying out exploration on 35,300 sq km, and all other areas are being evaluated by a Swiss company under contract to the ministry of mines. Three groups are engaged in uranium prospecting: COGEMA of France, the Japanese Power Reactor and Nuclear Fuel Development Corporation and Italy's AGIP; and two consortia with government participation and including Nigerian, Moroccan, Yugoslav, Romanian, Belgian, French, Arab and US interests.

Reflecting the demands of the alumina sector and the development of hydroelectric power, production of electricity rose fivefold between 1960 and 1976, to 500m. kWh, of which about two-thirds was consumed by Friguia. Net installed capacity is 176 MW, of which 36 MW is operated by the mining enterprises. Supplies of energy outside the mining and industrial sector are vastly inadequate, despite an estimated hydroelectric potential of 63,000 GWh. Non-mining and industrial power supplies are equivalent to about 330 GWh, compared with an estimated demand of some 450 GWh. Yugoslavia financed the construction of a 100-MW hydroelectric dam on the Bafing river, designed to supply power for the Dabola-Tougué bauxite project. There were also plans, under the Touré regime, to build a 750-MW hydroelectric complex on the Konkouré river, with an aluminium smelter, but financing was not settled. The Conté administration has agreed to continue this project, but has halved the capacity of the plant and has scaled down the smelter's maximum annual output to 100,000 tons. The whole revised project is now estimated to cost $2,200m., which will need to be met by foreign sources. In 1989 French consultants conducted initial studies for a 75-MW installation at Garafiri, on the Konkouré river, close to Conakry. Funding for the project, whose total cost is estimated at $238m. (of which Guinea is to contribute $16m.), has already been pledged by the World Bank, the ADB, CFD, Saudi Arabia, the Islamic Development Bank, the European Development Bank and BADEA, and construction was scheduled to begin in June 1995. The dam was expected to enter into operation by the end of 1998, and, it was envisaged, would satisfy the electricity needs of the Middle and Lower Guinea regions and part of Upper Guinea until 2002. Meanwhile, a 750-MW project is planned for Télimelé, also with World Bank and French support for the estimated cost of more than $1,000m., while the IDA has agreed to provide $35m., in support of hydroelectric projects. As part of the economic reform programme, the national power corporation is being restructured, with international financial assistance, and foreign investors have been sought for this utility; the Société Guinéenne d'Electricité, owned by the Guinean government, in participation with Hydro-Québec of Canada, Electricité de France and SAUR of France, was formed in 1994 to oversee the production and distribution of electricity. It was envisaged that the electricity network would be extended to cover the whole country by 2004.

MANUFACTURING

The principal aim of Guinea's small manufacturing sector, which accounted for only 4.4% of GDP in 1991, has been import-substitution, but the experience of the state-run projects that were established under Sekou Touré was disappointing. Lack of foreign exchange for raw materials, of skilled workers and of technical expertise, combined with poor management and low domestic purchasing power, meant that most of the plants were, and are still, operating substantially below capacity. A French evaluation made in 1985 estimated that utilization was equivalent to only one-tenth of capacity. The industrial units include a textile factory (with an annual capacity of 24m. m of fabrics), construction materials plant, food and agricultural processing facilities, and a cement factory. The Conté government has liberalized the investment code, giving equal treatment to foreign capital and individuals, with guarantees against expropriation, and has a more positive attitude to the private sector as a whole than the Touré regime. Of 135 state enterprises in existence in 1985, all but 24 had been sold to the private sector or dissolved by mid-1992. Further divestments were scheduled for the mid-1990s.

TRANSPORT INFRASTRUCTURE

The inadequacy of Guinea's transport infrastructure has been cited by the World Bank as the 'single most severe impediment to output recovery'. The network is to be almost entirely reconstructed, in order to restore links between Conakry and the country's interior. In 1991 there were 29,750 km of roads and tracks, including 4,050 km of main roads and 7,760 km of secondary roads; about 4,500 km of the network was paved. The IDA has supported programmes of road rehabilitation and maintenance. In 1988 the agency pledged a credit of $55m., in support of a long-term programme for the rehabilitation of 10,000 km of roads. The rail network is better developed: a 662-km line links Conakry with Kankan and Fria, while a 135-km heavy-gauge railway links the Boké bauxite deposits with the deep-water port at Kamsar, which handles around 9m. tons per year and is thus the country's major export outlet in tonnage terms. The port of Conakry, which handled 5.6m. tons of foreign trade in 1991, has been extended and modernized as part of a programme that envisages the construction of naval-repair and deep-water port facilities. A petroleum terminal is also planned for Conakry. There is an international airport at Conakry, and a number of smaller airstrips.

FINANCE AND ECONOMIC POLICY

Government revenue is heavily reliant on income from the mining companies, which contributed 60% of fiscal receipts in the late 1980s. These revenues had risen sharply in the mid- and late 1970s, reflecting the growth of the bauxite sector. However, current expenditure exceeded revenue, owing to the government's policy of providing jobs in the public sector to all graduates, combined with the rising losses of the state enterprises, and the growing burden of servicing the foreign debt.

By 1981 the growing deficit of the public sector was equivalent to around one-fifth of GDP, with parastatal enterprises alone accounting for some three-quarters of the deficit. As part of Guinea's programme for economic stabilization, inaugurated in 1986 with support from the IMF, consumer subsidies were reduced or eliminated, while the activities of state enterprises were curtailed (see above) and employment in the civil service was to be reduced by more than one-half. This severe fiscal austerity proved difficult to implement, and the government was obliged to rescind some of the price increases resulting from the devaluation of the currency in 1986, while the reduction in civil service personnel has yet to be fully implemented. The overall deficit in the public sector, while much reduced, to about 10% of annual GDP in 1986–88, thus remained substantial. By mid-1990, the adjustment programme that had been agreed with the IMF and the World Bank was under severe strain, and disbursements of external credits were suspended.

The 1991 budget, which was introduced (after some delay) in May of that year, provided for expenditure of FG 610,900m., compared with projected revenue of FG 286,300m. Despite this considerable financing deficit, the budget received support from the IMF and the World Bank; negotiations regarding further credits from these organizations resumed, but were again suspended soon after, when the Conté government announced that the salaries of civil servants were to be doubled. None the less, a new agreement, for an enhanced structural adjustment facility (ESAF) of SDR 57.9m., was finally achieved in November 1991, in support of a three-year (1991–94) programme of reform. The programme (which was revised in early 1992) aimed to achieve real average GDP growth of at least 5% in each year of the plan period, while reducing the annual rate of inflation to 8% by 1994 and narrowing the external current account deficit to 4.2% of GDP over the same period. In the event, moreover, the budget deficit for 1991, at an estimated FG 104,000m., was considerably smaller than had been envisaged, owing to higher than expected revenues and successful control of government spending. The deficit widened to FG 225,900m. in 1992 (equivalent to 7.5% of GDP), as targets for fiscal revenue failed to be met, and was expected to have increased in 1993 (and to a lesser extent in 1994), owing to a decline in net receipts from the mining sector—most notably from sales of bauxite and alumina.

At all times, the implementation of development policies has been heavily dependent on external funds. Almost two-thirds of development expenditure in the 1960s was covered by foreign aid, with funding for the first (1960–64) Development Plan originating almost exclusively from the Eastern bloc. However, the second (1965–71) Plan received substantial funding from Western countries, principally from the USA. Since the 1984 *coup d'état*, financial support from multilateral agencies and Western governments has been critical to the economic recovery programme. The 1987–89 programme of public investment gave priority to the rehabilitation of infrastructure and rural development. The same priorities were retained in the public investment programme for 1991–93, which envisaged expenditure of FG 845,000m., of which more than 85% was to be sought from external donors.

The latter years of the Touré regime saw a near-reversal of government policies on the private sector. Private trade, discouraged since independence, had stopped altogether by 1975. Farmers were obliged to deliver their crops to PRL co-operative stores, and all transactions were supervised by the state's 'economic police'. In 1977 market selling resumed after riots by women in Conakry and other towns, and in 1978 it was announced that producers would themselves market their produce. Private trade was reintroduced in 1979, under stringent conditions. By 1981 traders were permitted to purchase agricultural produce which was previously a monopoly of official trading organizations, and in 1983 measures were introduced to support private trading. Such recognition and encouragement of private trading aimed to reduce the extent of 'black market' transactions and smuggling. The commitment of the Conté administration is much greater: it has abolished the PRL and the state export and import agency, closed the six state banks and introduced laws allowing the establishment of private banking institutions, and is transferring the assets of state-owned companies to private ownership.

FOREIGN TRADE AND PAYMENTS

With the development of bauxite resources since the early 1970s, the country's external trade position has greatly improved. Previously, exports had stagnated because the initial rise in earnings from bauxite and alumina, to account for nearly two-thirds of exports in 1969, was offset by the ending of iron ore sales after 1967 and the overall poor performance of export crops. Another factor which held down export growth—at least in the official statistics—was the overvaluation of the country's currency. Exporters were required to surrender their foreign exchange earnings at a rate that effectively reduced their value by around three-quarters. Smuggling was rife, with about one-third of the coffee crop thought to leave the country illicitly. The sharp rise in bauxite exports resulted in strong growth in export earnings after 1975, and sales of bauxite and alumina contributed more than 90% of recorded earnings in the early 1980s. (Diamonds and gold have since made a significant contribution to export revenue—16.5% of the total in 1990). Exports were provisionally valued at $788m. in 1990, of which about 57% was from sales of bauxite; export earnings were estimated at $772m. in 1991. Such increases have financed the growth in imports, from $65m. in 1969 to an estimated $707m. in 1991—a rise which, in large part, reflects capital investment in the mining sector. The trade account has consequently shown a small surplus in recent years—an average of some $100m. annually in 1982–88, declining to $65m. by 1991; however, some estimates indicated a deficit of more than 100m. for 1992. The value of illicit exports to neighbouring countries (consisting largely of agricultural products) was, in the past, estimated at some $100m. per year, with the proceeds being used mainly to finance illicit imports. It had been hoped that the devaluation of the currency and increases in agricultural producer prices would attract more trade into legal channels. By the early 1990s, however, these measures seemed to have had relatively little effect.

Guinea has relied heavily on foreign capital (in the form of mining investment) and aid. The country's *rapprochement* with France and adherence to the Lomé Conventions (the aid and trade agreements with the EC), in conjunction with the change of political regime in 1984, resulted in a rapid increase in the flow of official development assistance, which averaged $254m. per year in 1985–91. In 1977 Guinea made its first drawing from the IMF, while its admission in the following year to the regional sub-committee of the Association of African Central Banks and the West African Clearing House enhanced contacts with the Franc Zone. Reflecting its dependence on foreign sources to finance the government's capital spending programme, Guinea's foreign debt rose very sharply, from $137m. in 1960 to $1,387m. at the end of 1981 (equivalent to 86% of the country's GNP in that year), a level that was broadly maintained in the following four years. Although the burden of servicing the debt was alleviated by concessionary interest rates on most of the borrowing and by the buoyancy of Guinean exports, it remained at a high level throughout this period, fluctuating within the range of 14%–24% of exports of goods and services, and obligations were not discharged in full. Arrears on both repayment and interest had apparently reached $300m. at the time of the 1984 coup. With debt-service payments projected to rise steeply over the next few years, and with foreign exchange reserves nearing depletion, a rescheduling of the foreign debt was a necessity.

In early 1986, following final agreement between the IMF and the Conté administration on the terms of the economic stabilization programme (which included a 93% devaluation of the syli and its replacement by a revived Guinea franc), the country's Western creditors agreed to a rescheduling of debt. Some $200m. in debt liabilities were rescheduled over 10 years, with five years' grace: this arrangement covered all arrears and debt-servicing due up to early 1987. However, the external debt increased strongly again in the late 1980s, to reach $2,257m. at the end of 1988, when the cost of debt-servicing was equivalent to 19.5% of export earnings. In early 1989 the 'Paris Club' of creditor governments agreed to reschedule a further portion of Guinea's external debt. Three creditor governments—most significantly France ($259m.) but also the Federal Republic of Germany ($33m.) and the USA ($5m.)—subsequently cancelled part of the Guinean debt. By the end of 1992, however, despite rescheduling agreements covering $110m. in 1990, $29m. in 1991 and $157m. in 1992, the total external deficit had increased to $2,652m. (86% of GNP), although the burden of debt-servicing (12.3% of export earnings) was at its lowest level since 1985 and the proportion of borrowing on concessionary terms had increased to 77.3% (from 64.2% in 1989). Further debt-relief is essential to the Guinean economy, since, in spite of the prospect of increased revenue from the diamond- and gold-mining and agricultural sectors, the country remains highly dependent on revenue from the exploitation of its bauxite reserves, and is thus vulnerable to fluctuations in international prices for that commodity. The current account of Guinea's balance of payments (having recorded an estimated deficit of $291m. in 1992) is expected to continue in deficit during the mid-1990s. New funding is vital to the success of economic adjustment efforts however, the Conté administration's attempts to reconcile the need for economic austerity, as advocated by the international financial community, with domestic social and political pressures may continue to undermine the efficacy of the reform programme.

Statistical Survey

Source (unless otherwise stated): Service de la Statistique Générale, Conakry; tel. 44-21-48.

Area and Population

AREA, POPULATION AND DENSITY

Area (sq km)	245,857*
Population (census results)	
4–17 February 1983	4,533,240†
1992	5,600,000‡
Density (per sq km) at 1992	22.8

* 94,926 sq miles.

† Excluding adjustment for underenumeration.

‡ Provisional figure, including refugees from Liberia and Sierra Leone (estimated at about 10% of the total).

PRINCIPAL TOWNS (population at December 1972)

Conakry (capital) 525,671 (later admitted to be overstated); Kankan 60,000.

BIRTHS AND DEATHS (UN estimates, annual averages)

	1975–80	1980–85	1985–90
Birth rate (per 1,000)	51.6	51.3	51.0
Death rate (per 1,000)	25.4	23.8	22.0

Expectation of life (UN estimates, years at birth, 1985–90): 42.5 (males 42.0; females 43.0).

Source: UN, *World Population Prospects: The 1992 Revision.*

ECONOMICALLY ACTIVE POPULATION
(persons aged 10 years and over, census of 1983)

	Males	Females	Total
Agriculture, hunting, forestry and fishing	856,971	566,644	1,423,615
Mining and quarrying	7,351	4,890	12,241
Manufacturing	6,758	4,493	11,251
Electricity, gas and water	1,601	1,604	3,205
Construction	5,475	3,640	9,115
Trade, restaurants and hotels	22,408	14,901	37,309
Transport, storage and communications	17,714	11,782	29,496
Finance, insurance, real estate and business services	2,136	1,420	3,556
Community, social and personal services	82,640	54,960	137,600
Activities not adequately defined*	101,450	54,229	155,679
Total labour force	1,104,504	718,563	1,823,067

* Includes 18,244 unemployed persons (not previously employed), whose distribution by sex is not available.

Source: International Labour Office, *Year Book of Labour Statistics.*

Mid-1992 (estimates in '000): Agriculture, etc. 1,880; Total labour force 2,590 (Source: FAO, *Production Yearbook*).

Agriculture

PRINCIPAL CROPS ('000 metric tons)

	1990	1991	1992
Maize	78	79	94*
Millet†	48	40	41
Sorghum†	24	19	20
Rice (paddy)	616	638	757*
Other cereals†	101	101	110
Sweet potatoes	81	99	100†
Cassava (Manioc)	658	658	660†
Yams	80	95	100†
Taro (Coco yam)	34	35	25†
Pulses†	60	60	60
Coconuts	18*	18†	18†
Vegetables†	420	420	420
Sugar cane†	225	225	225
Citrus fruits	210	210	230†
Bananas	165	165	170†
Plantains	400	410	420
Pineapples	81	81	85†
Other fruits†	37	37	37
Palm kernels†	40	40	40
Groundnuts (in shell)	78	78	78†
Coffee (green)	30	30	30†
Cocoa beans	2	2	2†
Tobacco (leaves)†	2	2	2

* Unofficial figure. † FAO estimate(s).

Source: FAO, *Production Yearbook.*

LIVESTOCK
(FAO estimates, '000 head, year ending September)

	1990	1991	1992
Cattle	1,800	1,800	1,800
Sheep	510	510	510
Goats	460	460	460
Pigs	33	33	33
Horses	2	2	2
Asses	1	1	1

Poultry (FAO estimates, million): 13 in 1990; 13 in 1991; 13 in 1992.

Source: FAO, *Production Yearbook.*

LIVESTOCK PRODUCTS (FAO estimates, '000 metric tons)

	1990	1991	1992
Beef and veal	18	18	18
Poultry meat	18	18	18
Other meat	7	7	7
Cows' milk	42	42	42
Goats' milk	4	4	4
Hen eggs	13.9	13.9	14.5
Cattle hides	3.2	3.2	3.2

Source: FAO, *Production Yearbook.*

Forestry

ROUNDWOOD REMOVALS
('000 cubic metres, excluding bark)

	1990	1991	1992
Sawlogs, veneer logs and logs for sleepers	140	140	140
Other industrial wood*	401	414	426
Fuel wood*	3,453	3,559	3,669
Total	3,994	4,113	4,235

* FAO estimates.

Source: FAO, *Yearbook of Forest Products*.

SAWNWOOD PRODUCTION
('000 cubic metres, including railway sleepers)

	1990	1991	1992
Total	70	70	63

Source: FAO, *Yearbook of Forest Products*.

Fishing

(FAO estimates, '000 metric tons, live weight)

	1989	1990	1991
Freshwater fishes	3.0	3.0	3.5
Sardinellas	22.0	21.0	22.0
Other marine fishes	9.0	11.0	12.0
Total catch	34.0	35.0	37.5

Source: FAO, *Yearbook of Fishery Statistics*.

Mining

	1989	1990	1991
Bauxite ('000 metric tons)*	17,547	17,524	17,054
Diamonds ('000 carats)†	148‡	135	91

* Data from *World Metal Statistics*, London.
† Data from the US Bureau of Mines.
‡ Provisional or estimated figure.

Source: UN, *Industrial Statistics Yearbook*.

Bauxite (estimates, '000 metric tons): 16,000 in 1992 (Source: UN, *Monthly Bulletin of Statistics*).

Industry

SELECTED PRODUCTS
('000 metric tons, unless otherwise indicated)

	1989	1990	1991
Raw sugar*	15	20	20
Palm oil (unrefined)*†	47	50	51
Alumina (calcined equivalent)‡	619	642	632
Electric energy (million kWh)	514	518	521

* Data from the FAO.
† Provisional or estimated figure(s).
‡ Data from the US Bureau of Mines.

Source: UN, *Industrial Statistics Yearbook*.

Finance

CURRENCY AND EXCHANGE RATES

Monetary Units
100 centimes = 1 franc guineén (FG or Guinea franc).

Sterling and Dollar Equivalents (31 March 1994)
£1 sterling = 1,449.4 Guinea francs;
US $1 = 976.3 Guinea francs;
10,000 Guinea francs = £6.899 = $10.243.

Average Exchange Rate (Guinea francs per US $)
1990 660.2
1991 753.9
1992 903.0

Note: The Guinea franc was reintroduced in January 1986, replacing (at par) the syli. At the same time, the currency was devalued by more than 90%. The syli had been introduced in October 1972, replacing the original Guinea franc (at 10 francs per syli).

BUDGET (million Guinea francs)

Revenue*	1988	1989	1990
Tax revenue	110,000	168,000	231,000
Taxes on goods and services	23,000	38,000	42,000
Taxes on international trade and transactions	83,000	125,000	183,000
Import duties	11,000	15,000	32,000
Export duties	72,000	110,000	151,000
Other current revenue	14,000	14,000	15,000
Total	124,000	182,000	246,000

Expenditure	1988	1989	1990
Current expenditure	135,000	170,000	203,000
Expenditure on goods and services	83,000	117,000	145,000
Wages and salaries	46,000	61,000	79,000
Interest payments	31,000	29,000	41,000
Subsidies and other current transfers	21,000	24,000	17,000
Capital expenditure	115,000	152,000	218,000
Total	250,000	322,000	421,000

* Excluding grants from abroad (million Guinea francs): 37,000 in 1988; 52,000 in 1989; 68,000 in 1990.

Source: IMF, *Government Finance Statistics Yearbook*.

COST OF LIVING
(Consumer Price Index for Conakry; base: 1987 = 100)

	1990	1991	1992
Food	198.5	231.1	267.8
Fuel and light	160.8	207.5	232.9
Clothing	153.1	170.5	181.8
Rent	173.5	195.9	235.1
All items (incl. others)	194.9	232.4	271.9

* Including certain household equipment.

Source: International Labour Office, *Year Book of Labour Statistics*.

NATIONAL ACCOUNTS
(million Guinea francs at current prices)

Expenditure on the Gross Domestic Product*

	1989†	1990	1991
Government final consumption expenditure	125,320	172,850	204,560
Private final consumption expenditure	1,085,690	1,320,560	1,704,220
Increase in stocks / Gross fixed capital formation	275,830	356,690	426,530
Total domestic expenditure	1,486,840	1,850,100	2,335,310
Exports of goods and services	415,820	547,920	686,720
Less Imports of goods and services	463,800	573,540	748,480
GDP in purchasers' values	1,438,860	1,824,480	2,273,550
GDP at constant 1980 prices	431,830	452,080	473,240

* Figures are rounded to the nearest 10m. Guinea francs.
† Estimates.

Gross Domestic Product by Economic Activity*

	1989	1990	1991
Agriculture, hunting, forestry and fishing	339,150	429,080	506,380
Mining and quarrying	321,970	407,350	480,740
Manufacturing	63,990	80,950	95,540
Electricity, gas and water	3,270	4,140	4,880
Construction	88,370	111,810	131,950
Trade, restaurants and hotels	347,130	439,180	518,300
Transport, storage and communications	72,180	91,320	107,780
Finance, insurance, real estate and business services	67,800	94,650	110,970
Public administration and defence	96,140	110,240	192,600
Other services	19,720	27,460	33,150
GDP at factor cost	1,419,710	1,796,190	2,182,270
Indirect taxes; *less* subsidies	19,150	28,290	91,280
GDP in purchasers' values	1,438,860	1,824,480	2,273,550

* Figures are rounded to the nearest 10m. Guinea francs.

Source: UN Economic Commission for Africa, *African Statistical Yearbook*.

BALANCE OF PAYMENTS (US $ million)

	1990	1991	1992
Exports of goods and services	842	813	684
Imports of goods and services	864	886	918
Other income (net)	-228	-204	-138
Private unrequited transfers (net)	-40	-31	-53
Official unrequited transfers (net)	101	110	134
Current balance	-189	-198	-291
Long-term capital (net)	118	115	179
Short-term capital (net) / Net errors and omissions	109	151	196
Overall balance	38	68	84

Source: World Bank, *Trends in Developing Economies*.

External Trade

PRINCIPAL COMMODITIES (US $ million)

Imports	1986	1987	1988*
Food products	73.0	62.8	62.8
Consumer goods	88.8	69.4	61.9
Semi-manufactured goods	163.7	194.5	215.7
Petroleum and petroleum products	55.0	65.8	67.3
Capital goods	70.7	75.1	83.5
Total	451.2	467.6	491.2

Exports	1986	1987	1988*
Bauxite and alumina	461.8	479.3	428.2
Diamonds	50.9	59.3	59.4
Gold	11.2	17.8	24.5
Coffee	19.3	14.1	17.1
Fish	n.a.	n.a.	3.5
Total (incl. others)	554.5	583.9	548.1

* Estimates.

Source: *Africa Research Bulletin*.

PRINCIPAL TRADING PARTNERS (million Guinea francs)

Imports	1988	1989	1990
Africa	5,933	9,225	12,215
China, People's Republic*	2,938	4,588	7,111
European Community	131,629	194,233	246,605
France*	66,588	91,928	123,045
Germany, Federal Republic*	10,332	18,649	21,407
United Kingdom*	8,578	15,635	14,974
Japan*	4,787	5,555	14,201
USA*	16,493	27,247	31,988

Exports	1988	1989	1990
Africa	14,735	28,971	41,383
European Community	114,412	201,301	238,505
France*	16,648	35,883	41,017
Germany, Federal Republic*	15,549	30,806	26,986
United Kingdom*	5,287	9,901	12,574
USA*	54,563	90,682	87,010

* Estimates.

Source: UN Economic Commission for Africa, *African Statistical Yearbook*.

Transport

RAILWAYS (estimates, traffic)

	1989	1990	1991
Freight ton-km (million)	605	640	660

Source: UN Economic Commission for Africa, *African Statistical Yearbook*.

ROAD TRAFFIC
(estimates, '000 motor vehicles in use)

	1989	1990	1991
Passenger cars	12	12	12
Commercial vehicles	13	13	13

Source: UN Economic Commission for Africa, *African Statistical Yearbook.*

INTERNATIONAL SEA-BORNE SHIPPING
(estimated freight traffic, '000 metric tons)

	1988	1989	1990
Goods loaded	9,920	10,500	12,210
Goods unloaded	690	715	712

Source: UN, *Monthly Bulletin of Statistics.*

CIVIL AVIATION (traffic on scheduled services, '000)*

	1981	1982
Kilometres flown	3,100	3,100
Passengers carried	128	131
Passenger-km	142,000	144,000
Freight ton-km	600	700

* UN estimates.
Source: UN, *Statistical Yearbook.*

Communications Media

	1989	1990	1991
Radio receivers ('000 in use)	230	240	248
Television receivers ('000 in use)	30	40	42
Telephones ('000 in use)	18	19	20

Newspapers: 1 daily (average circulation 13,000) in 1988; 1 non-daily (estimated average circulation 1,000) in 1990.

Sources: UNESCO, *Statistical Yearbook*; UN Economic Commission for Africa, *African Statistical Yearbook.*

Education

(1990/91, unless otherwise indicated)

	Institu-tions	Teachers	Students		
			Males	Females	Total
Primary	2,476	8,699	237,456	109,351	346,807
Secondary General	n.a.	4,846	57,935	17,739	75,674
Teacher training	n.a.	128	1,081	985	2,066
Vocational	n.a.	1,002	5,997	2,205	8,202
University level*	n.a.	805	5,608	637	6,245

* 1988/89 figures.
Source: UNESCO, *Statistical Yearbook.*

Directory

The Constitution

The Constitution that had been adopted in May 1982 was suspended in April 1984 by the Comité militaire de redressement national (CMRN), which had assumed power in a coup. A new Constitution (the *Loi fondamentale*) was adopted in a national referendum on 23 December 1990, and the Constitution of the Third Republic of Guinea was promulgated on 23 December 1991.

The new Constitution defines a clear separation of the powers of the executive, legislative and judicial organs of state. Article 19 provided for the dissolution of the CMRN and for the creation, in its place, of a Comité transitoire de redressement national (CTRN). The CTRN was to oversee a transitional period (of not more than five years), at the end of which civilian rule, in the context of a two-party political system, would be established. However, on 3 April 1992 an 'organic law', permitting the legalization of an unlimited number of political parties, came into effect. The Constitution provides for elections, by universal adult suffrage, for a civilian President and a unicameral legislature. The President of the Republic must be elected by an absolute majority of the votes cast, and a second round of voting is held should no candidate obtain such a majority at a first round.

The Government

HEAD OF STATE

President: Gen. (retd) LANSANA CONTÉ (took office 4 April 1984; elected 19 December 1993).

COMITÉ TRANSITOIRE DE REDRESSEMENT NATIONAL

The Comité transitoire de redressement national (CTRN) replaced the Comité militaire de redressement national on 21 February 1991. The function of the CTRN, which comprises 15 civilian and military representatives, is to oversee a transitional period to civilian rule (see Constitution, above).

COUNCIL OF MINISTERS

(September 1994)

President of the Republic and Head of Government: Gen. LANSANA CONTÉ.

Minister of Foreign Affairs: KOZO ZOMANIGUI.

Minister of the Interior: ALSENY RENÉ GOMEZ.

Minister of Justice and Keeper of the Seals: SALIFOU SYLLA.

Minister of Planning and Co-operation: MICHEKL KAMANO.

Minister of Finance: El Hadj CAMARA.

Minister of Mines and Geology: FACINET FOFANA.

Minister of Energy and the Environment: DORANK ASSIFAT DIASSENY.

Minister of Urban Affairs and Housing: Lt-Col JEAN TRAORÉ.

Minister of Health: KANDJOURA DRAME.

Minister of Administrative Reform: GERMAIN DUALAMU.

Minister of Youth, Arts and Sports: TOUMANI DAKOUM SAKO.

Minister of Secondary Education: AICHA DIALLO BAH.

Minister of Higher Education and Scientific Research: ALIOUNE BANIRE DIALLO.

Minister of Public Works: CELLOU DALEN DIALLO.

Minister of Trade and Industry: SEKOU KONATÉ.

Minister of Transport: IBRAHIMA SYLLA.

Minister of Agriculture: MAKALE CAMARA.

Minister of Fishing: MAMADI DIARRÉ.

Minister of Labour and Social Affairs: JOSÉPHINE GUILAVO.

Minister of Childhood: YVONNE CONDE.

Minister of Post and Telecommunications: EMMANUEL GNAN.

Minister of Defence: Lt-Col ABDOURAHMANE DIALLO.

Minister of Economic and Financial Control: KAZALIOU BALDE.

High Commissioner for Information: ALPHA CAMARA.

High Commissioner for Tourism: SIDI CISSOKO.

MINISTRIES

All ministries and high commissions are in Conakry.

Office of the President: Conakry; tel. 44-11-47; telex 623.

Ministry of Agriculture: BP 576, Conakry; tel. 44-19-66.

Ministry of Energy and the Environment: BP 1217, Conakry; tel. 44-50-01; telex 22350.

Ministry of Foreign Affairs: Conakry; tel. 40-50-55; telex 634.

Ministry of the Interior: Conakry; telex 621.

Ministry of Justice: Conakry; tel. 44-16-04.

Ministry of National Education: Conakry; tel. 44-19-01; telex 631.

Ministry of Planning and Co-operation: BP 707, Conakry; tel. 44-16-37; telex 22311; fax 44-21-48.

President and Legislature

PRESIDENT

Election, 19 December 1993

Candidate	% of votes
LANSANA CONTÉ (PUP)	51.70
ALPHA CONDÉ (RPG)	19.55
MAMADOU BOYE BÂ (UNR)	13.37
SIRADIOU DIALLO (PRP)	11.86
FACINÉ TOURÉ (UNPG)	1.40
MOHAMED MANSOUR KABA (Djama)	
ISMAËL MOHAMED GASSIM GUSHEIN (PDG—RDA)	2.12
JEAN-MARIE DORÉ (UPG)	
Total	100.00

ASSEMBLÉE NATIONALE

The National Assembly was dissolved following the military coup of April 1984. A unicameral legislative body was expected to be elected, on a multi-party basis, before the end of 1994.

Political Organizations

Following the military coup of April 1984, the country's sole political party, the Parti démocratique de Guinée (PDG), was dissolved, and party political activity officially ceased until April 1992, when legislation providing for the existence of an unlimited number of political parties came into effect. By mid-1994 about 45 parties had obtained official status. The most influential of these include the following:

Parti démocratique de Guinée—Rassemblement démocratique africain (PDG—RDA): Leader El Hadj ISMAËL MOHAMED GASSIM GUSHEIN.

Parti Djama: Leader MOHAMED MANSOUR KABA.

Parti guinéen des écologistes (PGE): Leader OUMAR SYLLA.

Parti guinéen pour le progrès (PGP): Leader ABDOULAYE 'PORTOS' DIALLO.

Parti pour le renouveau et le progrès (PRP): Sec.-Gen. SIRADIOU DIALLO.

Parti de l'unité et du progrès (PUP): supports Pres. Conté.

Rassemblement guinéen pour le développement (RGD): Leader ALKHAMLY TAHEY CONDÉ.

Rassemblement populaire guinéen (RPG): Leaders ALPHA CONDÉ, AHMED TIDIANE CISSÉ.

Union démocratique de Guinée (UDG): Leader SEKOU SYLLA.

Union des forces démocratiques (UFD): Leader AMADOU OURY BAH.

Union nationale démocratique de Guinée (UNDG): Leader ISSIAGA MARA.

Union pour la nouvelle République (UNR): Sec.-Gen. MAMADOU BOYE BÂ.

Union pour le progrès de Guinée (UPG): Sec.-Gen. JEAN-MARIE DORÉ.

Union nationale pour la prospérité de la Guinée (UNPG): Leader Lt-Col (retd) FACINÉ TOURÉ.

Diplomatic Representation

EMBASSIES IN GUINEA

Algeria: BP 1004, Conakry; tel. 44-15-03; Chargé d'affaires a.i.: BOUCHERIT NACEUR.

Benin: BP 787, Conakry; Ambassador: JONAS GBOHOUNDADA.

Bulgaria: BP 429, Conakry; tel. 46-13-29; Ambassador: BONET NIKOLOV STOILOV.

Canada: Corniche Sud, BP 99, Coleah, Conakry; tel. 46-36-26; telex 2170; Chargé d'affaires a.i.: ANDRÉE DUBOIS.

China, People's Republic: BP 714, Conakry; Ambassador: KONG MINGHUI.

Côte d'Ivoire: Conakry; telex 2126; Chargé d'affaires a.i.: ATTA YACOUBA.

Cuba: BP 71, Conakry; Ambassador: COLMAN FERREI.

Czech Republic: BP 2097, Conakry; tel. 46-14-37.

Egypt: BP 389, Conakry; Ambassador: HUSSEIN EL-NAZER.

France: BP 373, Conakry; tel. 44-16-55; telex 600; Ambassador: JEAN-PIERRE GUIDON.

Germany: BP 540, Conakry; tel. 41-15-06; telex 22479; fax 41-22-18; Ambassador: WALTER JÜRGEN SCHMID.

Ghana: BP 732, Conakry; Ambassador: LAARY BIMI.

Guinea-Bissau: BP 298, Conakry; Ambassador: ARAFAN ANSU CAMARA.

Iraq: Conakry; telex 2162; Chargé d'affaires a.i.: MUNIR CHIHAB AHMAD.

Italy: BP 84, Village Camayenne, Conakry; tel. 46-23-32; telex 636; Ambassador: FAUSTO MARIA PENNACCHIO.

Japan: Mayorai, Corniche Sud, BP 895, Conakry; tel. 44-36-07; telex 22482; Ambassador: TSUKASA ABE.

Korea, Democratic People's Republic: BP 723, Conakry; Ambassador: HANG CHANG-RYOL.

Lebanon: BP 342, Conakry; telex 2106; Ambassador: MOHAMED ISSA.

Liberia: BP 18, Conakry; telex 2105; Chargé d'affaires a.i.: ANTHONY ZEZO.

Libya: BP 1183, Conakry; telex 645; Chargé d'affaires a.i.: MUFTAH MADI.

Mali: Conakry; telex 2154; Ambassador: KIBILI DEMBA DIALLO.

Morocco: BP 193, Conakry; telex 22422; Ambassador: MOHAMED AYOUCH.

Nigeria: BP 54, Conakry; telex 633; Ambassador: P. N. OYEDELE.

Romania: BP 348, Conakry; tel. 44-15-68; Ambassador: MARCEL MĂMULARU.

Russia: BP 329, Conakry; Ambassador: VLADIMIR N. RAYEVSKY.

Saudi Arabia: BP 611, Conakry; telex 2146; Chargé d'affaires a.i.: WAHEEB SHAIKHON.

Senegal: BP 842, Conakry; tel. and fax 44-44-13; Ambassador: MAKHILY GASSAMA.

Sierra Leone: BP 625, Conakry; Ambassador: Commdr MOHAMED DIABY.

Switzerland: BP 720, Conakry; tel. 46-26-12; telex 22416; Chargé d'affaires a.i.: PIERRE RIEM.

Syria: BP 609, Conakry; tel. 46-13-20; Chargé d'affaires a.i.: BECHARA KHAROUF.

Tanzania: BP 189, Conakry; tel. 46-13-32; telex 2104; Ambassador: NORMAN KIONDO.

USA: angle 2e blvd et 9e ave, BP 603, Conakry; tel. 44-15-20; fax 44-15-22; Ambassador: JOSEPH A. SALOOM, III.

Yugoslavia: BP 1154, Conakry; Ambassador: DANILO MILIĆ.

Zaire: BP 880, Conakry; telex 632; Ambassador: B. KALUBYE.

Judicial System

The Constitution of the Third Republic embodies the principle of the independence of the judiciary, and delineates the competences of each component of the judicial system, including the Higher Magistrates' Council, the Supreme Court, the High Court of Justice and the Magistrature. In late 1993 France granted 10m. French francs, in support of a programme for the restructuring of the judicial system.

Chief Justice of the Supreme Court: LAMINE SIDIME.

Director of Public Prosecutions: ANTOINE IBRAHIM DIALLO.

Religion

It is estimated that 95% of the population are Muslims and 1.5% Christians.

ISLAM

Islamic League: Conakry; Sec.-Gen. El Hadj AHMED TIDIANE TRAORÉ.

CHRISTIANITY

The Anglican Communion

Anglicans in Guinea are adherents of the Church of the Province of West Africa, comprising 11 dioceses. The diocese of Guinea (formerly the Río Pongas), inaugurated in August 1985, is the first French-speaking diocese in the Province. The Bishop of Guinea also has jurisdiction over Guinea-Bissau.

Bishop of Guinea: Rt Rev. PRINCE THOMPSON (acting), Bishop of Freetown, Sierra Leone, BP 105, Conakry.

The Roman Catholic Church

Guinea comprises the archdiocese of Conakry and the dioceses of N'Zérékoré and Kankan. There were some 68,500 Roman Catholics in Guinea in 1992.

Bishops' Conference: Conférence Episcopale de la Guinée, BP 2016, Conakry; tel. 44-33-70; fax 44-33-70; Pres. Most Rev. ROBERT SARAH, Archbishop of Conakry.

Archbishop of Conakry: Most Rev. ROBERT SARAH, Archevêché, BP 1006 bis, Conakry; tel. 44-32-70; fax 44-33-70.

The Press

Ecole Nouvelle: Conakry; monthly; education.

L'Evénement de Guinée: BP 796, Conakry; monthly; independent; Dir BOUBACAR SANKARELA DIALLO.

Fonike: BP 341, Conakry; sport and general; Dir IBRAHIMA KALIL DIARE.

Horoya (Liberty): BP 191, Conakry; weekly; Dir MOHAMED MOUNIR CAMARA.

Journal Officiel de Guinée: BP 156, Conakry; fortnightly; organ of the Govt.

La Guinéenne: Conakry; monthly; women's interest.

L'Observateur: Conakry; independent; Dir SEKOU KONE.

Le Travailleur de Guinée: Conakry; monthly; trade union organ.

NEWS AGENCIES

Agence Guinéenne de Presse: BP 1535, Conakry; tel. 46-54-14; telex 640; f. 1960; Man. Dir MOHAMED CONDÉ.

Foreign Bureaux

Rossiyskoye Informatsionnoye Agentstvo—Novosti (RIA—Novosti) (Russia): BP 414, Conakry; Dir VASILI ZUBKOV.

Xinhua (New China) News Agency (People's Republic of China): BP 455, Conakry; tel. 46-13-47; telex 2128; Correspondent ZHANG ZHENYI.

Agence France-Presse, ITAR—TASS (Russia) and Reuters (UK) are also represented in Guinea.

PRESS ASSOCIATION

Association Guinéenne des Editeurs de la Presse Indépendante (AGEPI): Conakry; f. 1991; an asscn of independent newspaper publishers; Chair. BOUBACAR SANKARELA DIALLO.

Publisher

Editions du Ministère de l'Education Nationale: Direction nationale de la recherche scientifique, BP 561, Conakry; tel. 44-19-50; telex 22331; f. 1959; general and educational; Dir Prof. KANTÉ KABINÉ.

Radio and Television

In 1991, according to UNESCO, there were an estimated 248,000 radio receivers and 42,000 television receivers in use.

Radiodiffusion-Télévision Guinéenne (RTG): BP 391, Conakry; tel. 44-22-05; telex 22341; radio broadcasts in French, English, Créole-English, Portuguese, Arabic and local languages; television transmissions in French and local languages; Dir-Gen. JUSTIN MOREL.

A network of rural radio stations was scheduled to begin broadcasts during the early 1990s.

Finance

(cap. = capital; m. = million; brs = branches; amounts in Guinea francs unless otherwise stated).

BANKING

Central Bank

Banque Centrale de la République de Guinée: 12 blvd du Commerce, BP 692, Conakry; tel. 44-26-51; telex 22225; fax 44-48-98; f. 1960; bank of issue; Gov. KERFALLA YANSANA; 4 brs.

Commercial Banks

Banque Internationale pour l'Afrique en Guinée (BIAG): blvd du Commerce, BP 1419, Conakry; tel. 41-42-65; telex 22180; fax 41-22-97; f. 1985; 85% state-owned; cap. 10m. French francs (Dec. 1992); provides 'offshore' banking services; Pres. (vacant); Man. Dir ALAIN-CHARLES CAUBÈRE.

Banque Internationale pour le Commerce et l'Industrie de la Guinée (BICI-GUI): ave de la République, BP 1484, Conakry; tel. 44-32-50; telex 22175; fax 44-39-62; f. 1985; 39.6% state-owned; cap. 8,393m. (Dec. 1992); Pres. TAFSIR CAMARA; Man. Dir THIERRY JULIEN; 11 brs.

Banque Populaire Maroco-Guinéenne (BPMG): ave de la République, BP 4400, Conakry; tel. 44-36-98; telex 22146; fax 44-32-61; f. 1991; 35% owned by Banque Centrale Populaire (Morocco), 30% state-owned, 30% owned by Société Internationale pour le Développement Economique de la Guinée; cap. 1,683m. (Aug. 1993); Pres. SORIBA TOURÉ; Man. Dir ABDERRAFIA BENNANI; 3 brs.

Société Générale de Banques en Guinée: ave de la République, BP 1514, Conakry 1; tel. 44-17-41; telex 22212; fax 44-25-65; f. 1985; 34% owned by Société Générale (France); cap. 3,345m. (Dec. 1992); Pres. J. L. MATTEI; Man. Dir CLAUDE SOULE.

Union Internationale de Banque en Guinée (UIBG): 5e blvd, angle 6e ave, centre ville, BP 324, Conakry; tel. 44-20-96; telex 23135; fax 44-42-77; f. 1987; 51% owned by Crédit Lyonnais (France); cap. 2,000m. (Dec. 1992); Pres. ALPHA AMADOU DIALLO; Man. Dir ROBERT ETCHEBARNE.

Islamic Bank

Banque Islamique de Guinée: 6 ave de la République, BP 1247, Conakry; tel. and fax 44-50-71; telex 22184; f. 1983; 62% owned by Dar al-Maal al-Islami (DMI Trust); cap. 4,915m. (Dec. 1992); provides Islamic banking services; Pres. Dr MAHMOUD EL HEW; Man. MOHAMED YAYA KOROMA.

INSURANCE

Union Guinéenne d'Assurance et de Réassurance (UGAR): BP 179, Conakry; tel. 44-48-41; telex 23211; fax 44-17-11; f. 1989; 60% state-owned, 40% owned by L'Union des Assurances de Paris; cap. 2,000m.; Man. Dir MAURICE GIBOUDOT.

Trade and Industry

DEVELOPMENT AGENCY

Caisse Française de Développement (CFD): Conakry; telex 780; fmrly Caisse Centrale de Coopération Economique, name changed 1992; Dir in Guinea GUY TERRACOL.

Mission Française de Coopération: Conakry; administers bilateral aid; Dir in Guinea ANDRÉ BAILLEUL.

CHAMBERS OF COMMERCE

Chambre de Commerce, d'Industrie et d'Agriculture de Guinée: BP 545, Conakry; tel. 44-44-95; telex 609; f. 1985; Chair. Capt. THIANA DIALLO; 70 mems.

Chambre Economique de Guinée: BP 609, Conakry.

TRADE ORGANIZATION

Entreprise Nationale Import-Export (IMPORTEX): BP 152, Conakry; tel. 44-28-13; telex 625; state-owned import and export agency; Dir MAMADOU BOBO DIENG.

MAJOR INDUSTRIAL COMPANIES

The following are among the largest companies in terms either of capital investment or employment.

AREDOR-Guinée: BP 1218, Conakry; tel. 44-31-12; telex 22132; f. 1981 (as Association pour la recherche et l'exploitation de diamants et de l'or), entered production in 1984; 50% state-owned, 50% held jtly by Bridge Oil Ltd (Australia), Industrial Diamond Co (UK), Simonius, Vischer and Co (Switzerland), Bankers' Trust; (withdrawal of overseas investors reported in mid-1994); diamond mining and gold; Gen. Man. J. PIERRE MORITZ; 1,200 employees.

BONAGUI: Z.I. Matoto, BP 3009, Conakry; tel. 41-18-92; telex 23358; fax 41-24-91; f. 1986; cap. 2,607m. FG; privately owned; soft-drinks bottling factory. Man. ERIC BOULANGER; 147 employees.

Compagnie des Bauxites de Guinée: BP 523, Conakry; f. 1964; cap. US $2m.; 49% state-owned, 51% owned by Halco (Mining) Inc (a consortium of interests from USA, Canada, France, Germany, the Netherlands and Italy); bauxite mining at Boké; Pres. JOHN L. PERVOLA; Vice-Pres. NAVA TOURÉ; 2,796 employees.

Compagnie des Eaux Minérales de Guinée: Conakry; f. 1987; owned by Compagnie générale des eaux (France); mineral water bottling plant.

Entreprise Nationale d'Electricité de Guinée (ENELGUI): Immeuble Cherif Diallo, blvd Telly Diallo, BP 322, Conakry; tel. 41-18-57; telex 23287; fax 41-17-51; fmrly Société Nationale d'Electricité; national electricity utility; transfer to private ownership pending in 1994; Man. Dir PIERRE LA LIBERTÉ (acting).

Friguia: BP 334, Conakry; tel. 41-31-13; fax 44-34-63; f. 1957; cap. 13,602m. FG; 49% state-owned, 51% owned by Holding Frialco; alumina plant at Fria; Man. Dir ALAIN MORALÉS; 1,500 employees.

Nimba International Mining Co (Nimco): BP 837, Conakry; telex 622; f. 1989; principal shareholding by govt of Guinea, with participation by Liberia, Euronimba and African Mining Consortium Ltd; development of high-grade iron deposit at Mt Nimba, (12m. tons annually, to be shipped via Buchanan, Liberia).

Nouvelle Société Africaine de Plastiques (SAP): BP 63 bis, Conakry; f. 1958; cap. 25m. FG; mfrs of plastic tiles, shoes, bags, rainwear, etc.; Dir MOMO KEITA.

Office de Développement de la Pêche artisanale et de l'Aquaculture en Guinée (ODEPAG): 6 ave de la République, BP 1581; Conakry; tel. 44-19-48; telex 22315; development of fisheries and fish-processing.

Société d'Aquaculture de Koba (SAKOBA): BP 4834, Conakry; tel. 44-24-75; telex 22111; fax 41-46-43; f. 1991; 49% state-owned, 51% owned by private Guinean and French interests; prawn-farming venture with a planned annual capacity of 1,300 metric tons of frozen shrimps for export by 1997; 700 employees; Mans SEPIA International (France).

Société Aurifère de Guinée (SAuG): BP 1006, Conakry; tel. 44-45-18; telex 23237; f. 1985; cap. US $4.9m.; 49% state-owned, balance controlled by Belgian interests; gold prospecting and exploitation at Koron and Didi; Dir-Gen. RICHARD WINBY.

Société des Bauxites de Dabola (SBD): Conakry; f. 1971; 51% state-owned; bauxite mining at Dabola and Tougué.

Société des Bauxites de Kindia (SBK): Conakry; telex 2148; f. 1969, as Office des Bauxites de Kindia (a jt-venture with the USSR), production began 1974; named changed 1992; state-controlled; transfer to private ownership pending in 1994; bauxite mining at Debélé; Dir MAMADOU SYLLA; 1,700 employees.

Société de Diamant de Guinée: f. 1984 to exploit diamond reserves in Kouroussa province; 50% state-owned.

Société d'Exploitation des Eaux de Guinée (SEEG): BP 150, Conakry; tel. 44-43-67; fax 44-43-68; f. 1988; national water authority.

Société Guinéenne des Carburants: Conakry; f. 1988; distribution of petroleum products.

Société Guinéenne d'Electricité (SOGEL): Conakry; f. 1994; 49% state-owned, 51% held jtly by Hydro-Québec (Canada), Electricité de France and SAUR (France); intended to oversee production, transport and distribution of electricity.

Société Guinéenne des Hydrocarbures (SGH): BP 892, Conakry; tel. 46-12-56; telex 776; f. 1980; 50% state-owned; research into and exploitation of offshore petroleum reserves.

Société Guinéenne des Palmiers à Huile et Hévéas (SGPH): Conakry; cultivation and processing of palms and heveas.

Société Guinéenne de Pêche (SOGUIPECHE): Conakry; f. 1987; 51% state-owned, 49% owned by Jego-Query (France); fishing and processing of fish products.

Société Guinéenne des Plastiques (SOGUIPLAST): Conakry; plastics; privately-owned.

Société Guinéo-Arabe d'Alumine: BP 554, Conakry; f. 1975 by Guinean govt and six Arab govts; to open and develop production of aluminium at Ayekoe; estimated production 1m. tons annually.

Société Industrielle de Peintures et de Cosmétiques (SIPECO): Conakry; privatized 1986; mfrs of industrial paints.

Société Libyo-Guinéenne pour le Développement Agricole et Agro-industrielle (SALGUIDIA): BP 622, Conakry; 44-31-34; telex 22117; fax 41-13-09; cap. 15m. FG; fmrly Société Industrielle des Fruits Africains; fruit growing (pineapples, grapefruit and oranges); fruit canning and juice extracting; marketing.

Société Minière de Dinguiraye: Dinguiraye; 85% owned by Delta Gold Mining (owned jtly by Kenor AS (Norway) and Bureau de Recherches Géologiques et Minières (France), 15% state-owned; exploitation of gold deposits at Dinguiraye.

Société Minière de Niandan (SMN): Kénéro; f. 1986; cap. US $5m.; 50% state-owned, balance controlled by French, Saudi Arabian and US interests; gold and diamond mining at Kéniéro.

Société Minière et de Participation Guinée-Alusuisse: Conakry; f. 1971; owned by Guinean govt and Alusuisse (Switzerland); to establish bauxite mine and aluminium smelter at Tougué; estimated production of bauxite 8m. tons annually.

Société Nationale de Carrière de Granite (SONACAG): Conakry; 30% state-owned; quarrying and granite company.

Société de Pêche de Kamsar (SOPEKAM): Kamsar Free Zone; f. 1984; 40% govt-owned, 40% Universal Marine & Shark Products (USA); fishing and processing of fish products; fleet of 18 fishing vessels.

SOPROCIMENT: Conakry; owned by Koch Manutention Mécanique; construction of clinker crusher; capacity 250,000 tons annually.

TRADE UNIONS

Confédération des travailleurs de Guinée (CTG): BP 237, Conakry; f. 1984; Sec.-Gen. Dr MOHAMED SAMBA KÉBÉ.

Transport

RAILWAYS

There are 662 km of 1-m gauge track from Conakry to Kankan in the east of the country, crossing the Niger at Kouroussa. Three lines for the transport of bauxite link Sangaredi with the port of Kamsar in the west, and Conakry with Kindia and Fria, a total of 383 km. Plans exist for the eventual use of a line linking the Nimba iron ore deposits with the port of Buchanan in Liberia.

Office National des Chemins de Fer de Guinée (ONCFG): BP 589, Conakry; tel. 44-46-13; telex 22349; f. 1905; Man. Dir FOFANA M. KADIO.

ROADS

In 1991 there were an estimated 29,750 km of roads, including 4,050 km of main roads and 7,760 km of secondary roads; 4,490 km of the road network were paved in 1990. An 895-km cross-country road links Conakry to Bamako, in Mali, and the main highway connecting Dakar (Senegal) to Abidjan (Côte d'Ivoire) also crosses Guinea. The road linking Conakry to Freetown (Sierra Leone) forms part of the Trans West African Highway, extending from Morocco to Nigeria.

La Guinéenne-Marocaine des Transports (GUIMAT): Conakry; f. 1989; owned jtly by Govt of Guinea and Hakkam (Morocco); operates national and regional transport services.

Société Générale des Transports de Guinée (SOGETRAG): Conakry; f. 1984; state-owned; bus operator.

SHIPPING

Conakry and Kamsar are the international seaports. In 1987 3.1m. tons of bauxite were exported through Conakry and 9m. tons through Kamsar. A naval repair dockyard and deep-water port facilities were to be constructed at Conakry, at a cost of US $60m., as part of a four-year (1989–92) port extension programme.

Port Autonome de Conakry: BP 715, Conakry; tel. 44-27-37; telex 22276.

Port de Kamsar OFAB: Kamsar.

ENTRAT International—Société d'Economie Mixte: BP 315, Conakry; stevedoring and forwarding; Dir-Gen. JEAN-MARIE DORÉ.

Société Navale Guinéenne: BP 522, Conakry; telex 644; f. 1968; shipping agents; Dir-Gen. NABY SYLLA.

SOTRAMAR: Kamsar; f. 1971; exports bauxite from mines at Boké through port of Kamsar.

CIVIL AVIATION

There is an international airport at Conakry-Gbessia, and smaller airfields at Labé, Kankan and Faranah.

Air Guinée: 6 ave de la République, BP 12, Conakry; tel. 44-46-02; telex 22349; f. 1960; regional and internal services; Dir-Gen. El Hadj NFA MOUSSA DIANE.

Société de Gestion et d'Exploitation de l'Aéroport de Conakry (SOGEAC): Conakry; f. 1987; manages Conakry-Gbessia international airport; 51% state-owned.

Tourism

Secrétariat d'Etat au Tourisme et à l'Hôtellerie: square des Martyrs, BP 1304, Conakry; tel. 44-26-06; f. 1989.

Defence

In June 1993 Guinea had an army of 8,500, a navy of 400 and an air force of 800. Paramilitary forces numbered some 9,600, and included a 7,000-strong people's militia. Military service is by conscription and lasts for two years.

Defence Expenditure: Estimated at US $27m. in 1989.

Chief of Staff of Armed Forces: Lt-Col Samoussa Kondé.

Education

Education is provided free of charge at every level. Primary education, which begins at seven years of age and lasts for six years, is officially compulsory. In 1990, however, enrolment at primary schools was equivalent to only 37% of children in the relevant age-group (males 50%; females 24%). A project that was inaugurated in mid-1990, with financial assistance from the World Bank, aimed to create 70,000 new primary-school places. Secondary education, from the age of 13, lasts for seven years, comprising a first cycle of four years and a second of three years. Enrolment at secondary schools in 1990 was equivalent to only 10% of children in the appropriate age-group (males 15%; females 5%). There are universities at Conakry and Kankan. In 1990, according to estimates by UNESCO, the average rate of adult illiteracy was 76.0% (males 65.1%; females 86.6%). Under a six-year transitional education plan, announced in June 1984, ideological education was eliminated and French was adopted as the language of instruction in schools. Teaching of the eight national languages has been suspended. A ban on private schools operated between 1961–84. Government expenditure on education in 1988 was equivalent to 21.5% of total budget spending.

Bibliography

Adamolekun, L. *Sekou Touré's Guinea.* London, Methuen, 1976.

Ameillon, B. *La Guinée, bilan d'une indépendance.* Paris, Maspero, 1964.

Amnesty International. *Guinea.* London, 1978.

Canale, J. S. *La République de Guinée.* Paris, Editions Sociales, 1970.

Diallo, A. *Le mort de Diallo Telli.* Paris, Editions Karthala, 1983.

Europe Outremer. *La Guinée d'aujourd'hui.* Paris, 1979.

Kake, I. B. *Sékou Touré, le héros et le tyran.* Paris, Jeune Afrique Livres, 1987.

Lewin, A. *La Guinée.* Paris, Presses Universitaires de France, 1984.

O'Toole, T. E. *Historical Dictionary of Guinea.* Metuchen, NJ, Scarecrow Press, 1988.

Rimmer, D. *The Economies of West Africa.* London, Weidenfeld and Nicolson, 1984.

Rivière, C. *Guinea: The Mobilization of a People* (trans. by Thompson, V., and Adloff, R.). Ithaca, NY, Cornell University Press, 1977.

Soriba Camara, S. *La Guinée sans la France.* Paris, Presse de la Fondation nationale des sciences politiques, 1977.

Touré, S. *L'expérience guinéenne et l'unité africaine.* Paris, Présence africaine, 1959.

L'action politique du parti démocratique en Guinée. Conakry, 1962.

GUINEA-BISSAU

Physical and Social Geography

RENÉ PÉLISSIER

The Republic of Guinea-Bissau, formerly Portuguese Guinea, is bounded on the north by Senegal and by the Republic of Guinea to the east and south. Its territory includes a number of coastal islands, together with the Bissagos or Bijagós archipelago, which comprises 18 main islands. The capital is Bissau, although plans have been pending since independence in 1973 to move the seat of government to Madina de Boé, in the north-eastern part of the country.

The country covers an area of 36,125 sq km (13,948 sq miles), including some low-lying ground which is periodically submerged at high tide. Except for some higher terrain (rising to about 300 m above sea-level), close to the Guinea border, the relief consists of a coastal plain deeply indented by *rias* which play a useful role in internal communications, and a transition plateau, forming the *planalto* de Bafatá in the centre, and the *planalto* de Gabú, which abuts on the Fouta Djallon.

The country's main physical characteristics are its meandering rivers and wide estuaries, where it is difficult to distinguish mud, mangrove and water from solid land. The main rivers are the Cacheu, also known as Farim on part of its course, the Mansôa, the Geba and Corubal complex, the Rio Grande and, close to the Guinean southern border, the Cacine. Ocean-going vessels of shallow draught can reach most of the main population centres, and flat-bottomed tugs and barges can penetrate to nearly all significant outposts except in the north-eastern sector.

The climate is tropical, hot and wet with two seasons. The rainy season lasts from mid-May to November and the dry season from December to April. April and May are the hottest months, with temperatures ranging from 20°C to 38°C, and December and January are the coldest, with temperatures ranging from 15°C to 33°C. Rainfall is abundant (1,000–2,000 mm per year in the north), and excessive on the coast. The interior is savannah or light savannah woodland, while coastal reaches are covered with mangrove, swamps, rain forest and tangled forest.

The first official census since independence, conducted in April 1979, recorded a population of 753,313. According to official estimates, the population had increased to 810,000 by mid-1981 and to 943,000 at January 1989. According to UN estimates, however, the total was 833,000 at mid-1981, rising to 966,000 at mid-1989 and to 1,028,000 at mid-1993. The main population centre is Bissau, which had 109,214 inhabitants at the 1979 census. Bafatá, Bolama, Farim, Cantchungo, Mansôa, Gabú, Catió and Bissorã are the other important towns. Prior to the war of independence, the main indigenous groups were the Balante (about 32% of the population), the Fulani or Fula (22%), the Mandyako (14.5%), the Malinké or Mandingo (13%), and the Pepel (7%). The non-Africans were mainly Portuguese civil servants and traders, and Syrian and Lebanese traders. Although Portuguese is the official language, a Guinean *crioulo* is the lingua franca.

Recent History

MILES SMITH-MORRIS

The campaign for independence in Portuguese Guinea (now Guinea-Bissau) began in the 1950s with the formation of the Partido Africano da Independência da Guiné e Cabo Verde (PAIGC). Armed resistance began in the early 1960s, and by 1972 the PAIGC was in control of two-thirds of the country. The conflict necessitated the deployment of some 40,000 Portuguese combatants, and their heavy losses in 1973–74 have been cited as a contributory factor in the military *coup d'état* in Portugal in April 1974. Guinea-Bissau became independent on 10 September, under the leadership of Luiz Cabral, brother of the assassinated founder of the PAIGC, Amílcar Cabral.

Despite its Marxist-Leninist orientation, the PAIGC government adopted a non-aligned stance in its foreign relations, receiving military aid from the Eastern bloc and economic assistance from Western countries and Arab states. Friendly relations with Portugal were renewed.

By 1980, however, Guinea-Bissau's economic situation had deteriorated, owing partly to drought, but also to the policies of the Cabral regime. Agricultural production had fallen below pre-independence levels, the state-controlled retail network had proved inadequate, and sparse economic resources were being deployed in projects of questionable utility.

Until 1980, the PAIGC supervised both Cape Verde and Guinea-Bissau, the two constitutions remaining separate, but with a view to eventual unification. These arrangements were abruptly terminated in November 1980, when Cabral was overthrown by the prime minster, João Vieira, and a military-dominated revolutionary council took control of government.

THE VIEIRA REGIME

The period following the coup was one of considerable political ferment, with major shifts in the leadership, although President Vieira has remained the dominant force. The unrest was attended by further economic decline, which was as much an effect of the regime's economic policies as of the international economic situation.

A special PAIGC congress in 1981 reaffirmed the regime's commitment to socialism and rebuked the previous administration for deviation from the policies of Amílcar Cabral. The party hierarchy was changed, and some former opponents of the regime were brought into the government, while Portuguese-trained civil servants returned to the bureaucracy.

These events were followed, in May 1982, by the postponement of promised elections and by a government reshuffle in which President Vieira assumed the portfolios of defence and security, while Vasco Cabral and Mário Cabral, who represented the party's radical left wing, lost their ministerial posts, although they remained influential within the PAIGC. In July, following rumours of plots, several members of the pre-coup leadership were arrested, and later in that year they were put on trial. In August 1983 three ministers were dismissed, on the grounds of embezzlement, and the chief of staff of the armed forces was suspended. These departures were apparently part of a struggle for primacy between Vieira and Vítor Saúde Maria, the prime minister. The issue was eventually decided in Vieira's favour, and in 1984 it was proposed that a new constitution would abolish the office of prime minister. In March, having been dismissed from office both for corruption and allegedly plotting a coup, Saúde Maria sought asylum in the Portuguese embassy. Several other party members were subsequently accused of colluding with Saúde Maria and were expelled from the PAIGC.

The new constitutional arrangements took effect in May 1984. Elections had been held in March for eight regional councils (comprising PAIGC-approved candidates only) which, in turn, elected 150 members of a new legislative assembly. This body approved the new constitution and selected a council of state to discharge legislative functions when the assembly was not in session. A government reshuffle ensued, which reduced the number of ministers and brought the return to office both of Vasco Cabral, as secretary of the council of state and minister in the presidency for economic affairs, and of Mário Cabral, as minister of trade and tourism. A number of younger and better-trained officials were also appointed, and Bartolomeu Pereira, perhaps the most prominent of the 'technocratic' group and formerly a secretary of state, became minister of economic co-ordination, planning and international co-operation. The overall effect of these changes was to formalize the position of Vieira as head of state, chief of government, c-in-c of the armed forces and head of the PAIGC, and to assemble a government in which the emphasis was placed on economic competence.

Political instability returned in November 1985, in the form of an attempted coup, led by the first vice-president, Col Paulo Correia, and several senior army officers. Although the plot was swiftly thwarted and its leaders were arrested, the involvement of so many senior figures seriously alarmed the Vieira regime. The precise background of the plot was never clarified, but personal animosities, ethnic resentment among Balantes in the army and the president's campaign against corruption in the ruling élite were certainly contributory factors. In July 1986 six people, accused of involvement in the conspiracy, were reported to have died in prison. Later in the same month, 12 alleged plotters were condemned to death, and 41 were sentenced to hard labour. Correia and five others were executed, but the remaining six had their death sentences commuted, following international appeals for clemency. In order to discourage the creation of personal power-bases, Vieira replaced a number of multi-functional ministries with smaller administrative portfolios. Three ministries for the provinces were created, and the council of ministers was enlarged from 15 to 19 members. In December 1988 four of those imprisoned following the 1985 attempted coup were released under an amnesty. All the remaining prisoners had been released by January 1990.

The policy of economic liberalization, initiated in 1983 in an attempt to halt economic decline, was accelerated in the late 1980s. In August 1986 the government abolished trading restrictions and allowed private traders to import and export goods. At the fourth PAIGC congress, held in November, Vieira introduced further proposals to reduce state controls over trade and the economy, and to increase foreign investment. These moves were supported by the congress, which re-elected him as secretary-general of the PAIGC for a further four years. In February 1987 Vieira ensured future PAIGC support for economic liberalization by appointing Vasco Cabral as permanent secretary of the central committee of the PAIGC. In a subsequent government reshuffle, a new minister of justice and two new secretaries of state for justice and foreign affairs were appointed. In April the government and the World Bank agreed on a structural adjustment programme which included further liberalization measures for the economy. These were accompanied by a restructuring of the state investment programme and a reduction in levels of public-sector employment, and were followed in May by a 41% devaluation of the Guinea peso. Although Vieira promised that the domestic effects of the latter would be offset by government subsidies on essential commodities, political tension increased, amid rumours that about 20 army officers had been arrested for plotting against the president. In August Vieira denied rumours that a *coup d'état* had been attempted while he was receiving medical treatment in France.

In February 1989 a minor reshuffle of the government took place, and in the same month it was announced that the PAIGC had set up a six-member national commission to revise the constitution. Regional elections were held in early June, at which all candidates were nominated by the PAIGC. The electoral commission reported a 95.8% turnout of eligible voters, although this figure was disputed by other sources. The 473 councillors convened in mid-June to elect the national assembly, which in turn elected the council of state. Vieira was confirmed as president for a second five-year term. In January 1990 Vieira announced the formation of two commissions to review, respectively, the programme and statutes of the PAIGC and the laws on land ownership, in preparation for the fifth PAIGC congress, due to be held in November. In March an extensive government reshuffle took place, in which Vasco Cabral became second vice-president, in charge of social affairs. Several ministries were restructured, and their number was increased from 19 to 24.

Constitutional Transition

In April 1990, from its base in Lisbon, the Resistência da Guiné-Bissau–Movimento Bafatá (RGB–MB) proposed political negotiations with the PAIGC, with the implication that civil war might ensue should its demands for reform not be met. Shortly afterwards, President Vieira gave approval in principle to the introduction of a multi-party political system. It was stated that the necessary constitutional amendments would be implemented in late 1990, following a special congress of the PAIGC, and that the next presidential election, due in 1994, could be contested by two or more candidates. In early June 1990 another external opposition movement, the Frente da Luta para a Libertação da Guiné (FLING), demanded an immediate conference of all political parties. In August President Vieira informed a meeting of the PAIGC central committee that multi-partyism was the only system that could bring democratic freedom to Guinea-Bissau. He also announced that members of the national assembly would in future be elected by universal adult suffrage. A national conference on the transition to democracy was held in October, attended by 350 representatives of the government, the ruling party and private organizations. The conference voted in favour of the holding of a national referendum on the nature of political reforms to be introduced. There was also support for the establishment of a transitional government to oversee the democratization process, and for the abolition of the PAIGC's political monopoly. Criticism of the government at the conference was acknowledged by the minister of justice, Mário Cabral, who admitted that the PAIGC had made mistakes, particularly in regard to economic management.

Rumours of an attempted coup were widespread in November and December 1990, although these were consistently denied by the government. Vieira returned early from a visit to Taiwan in early November, cancelling a planned trip to Japan; some observers linked his return to the flight of the former prime minister, Vítor Saúde Maria, and the former armed forces minister, Umaru Djalo, to Portugal, where they were granted political asylum.

At an extraordinary conference of the PAIGC, which opened in January 1991, Vieira confirmed that the transition to multiparty democracy would be completed by 1993, when a presidential election would be held. During the transitional period, the armed forces would become independent of the PAIGC, and the party would cease to be the country's dominant social and political force. Vieira appealed to all Guineans, both at home and abroad, to participate in the democratization process.

Constitutional amendments, bringing one-party rule to a formal end, were approved unanimously by the national assembly in May 1991. The reforms terminated the PAIGC's role as the leading political force and Vieira indicated that legislative elections would be held before 1993. The new arrangements also severed the link between the party and the armed forces, and guaranteed the operation of a freemarket economy. To prevent the formation of regionally-based or separatist organizations, it was stipulated that new parties seeking registration must obtain at least 100 signatures from each of the nine provinces, with a total of 2,000 signatures required for registration; these regulations were revised in August, when the numbers of signatures required were halved to 50 and 1,000 respectively. A number of opposition parties were created following the introduction of the legislation. The Frente Democrática Social (FDS), set up clandestinely in 1990 and led by Rafael Barbosa, gave rise to two splinter groups in mid-1991: the Frente Democrática (FD), led by Aristides Menezes, and the Partido Unido Social Democrático (PUSD), led by former prime minister Vítor Saúde Maria. On 18 November the FD became the first party to be legalized by the supreme court, bringing to a formal end 17 years of one-party politics.

The PAIGC held its fifth ordinary congress from 16–23 December 1991, at which delegates discussed ways to broaden the party's support in advance of the first democratic elections. As part of this process, President Vieira undertook an extensive cabinet reshuffle at the end of December. The post of prime minister, abolished in 1984, was revived with the appointment of Carlos Correia, previously minister of state for agriculture and rural development, to the position. Other cabinet changes included the appointment of Samba Lamine Mane as minister of defence, a portfolio formerly held by Vieira himself, and of João Cruz Pinto as minister of justice, replacing Vasco Cabral, who also lost his position as second vice-president. In addition Vieira relinquished the post of minister of the interior to Abubacar Baldé. Filinto de Barros, formerly minister of natural resources and industry, was appointed minister of finance. The reshuffle included the removal of Col Camara, the first vice-president, who had been accused of involvement in smuggling of arms to separatist guerrillas in Senegal's southern Casamance region.

Three further opposition parties were legalized by the supreme court in December and January: the RGB – MB, led by Domingos Fernandes Gomes, the FDS, and the PUSD. Three other parties had yet to achieve recognition and another was formed in mid-January, following a further split in the FDS: the Partido para a Renovação Social (PRS), led by former FDS vice-chairman Koumba Yalla. At the FD's first public rally in mid-January, party leader Menezes called on the PAIGC to set up a caretaker government bringing in representatives of the opposition. In late January, four opposition parties: the RGB – MB, FDS, PUSD and the Partido da Convergência Democrática (PCD), led by Vítor Mandinga, agreed to set up a 'democratic forum' for consultations. They demanded that the government dissolve the political police and cease using state facilities for political purposes. They also called for a revision of press law, free access to media, the creation of an electoral commission and the declaration of election dates in consultation with all the opposition parties.

An opposition demonstration, the first to be permitted by the government, was held in Bissau on 7 March 1992, attended by an estimated 30,000 people. Speakers at the demonstration denounced the corruption of the PAIGC leadership and accused the security forces of human rights abuses. Election dates were announced on 9 March, following a meeting of the PAIGC national council. Presidential elections were to be held on 15 November, followed by legislative elections on 13 December, despite demands by the opposition that the elections be held in June, with the legislative elections held first. The national council meeting also elected Saturnino Costa as the new permanent secretary to the party's central committee, replacing Vasco Cabral, who had held the post since 1987. At the end of March 1992 the supreme court rejected as incomplete the application for registration as a political party by the FLING; following a second application, the FLING was legalized in May. In that month a dissident group known as the 'Group of 121' broke away from the PAIGC to form a new party, the Partido de Renovação e Desenvolvimento (PRD). The PRD called for the establishment of a transitional government pending democratic elections and for the dissolution of the political police. In mid-May the leader of the RGB – MB, Domingo Fernandes, returned from a six year exile in Portugal. Following his return Fernandes and the leaders of the FD, PCD, FDS and the PUSD met President Vieira to discuss the democratic process. As a result of the talks it was decided that commissions would be set up to oversee and facilitate the organization of the forthcoming elections.

In July 1992 the leader and founder of the FLING, François Kankoila Mendy, returned to Guinea-Bissau after 40 years in exile. In the following month, in response to opposition demands for the establishment of a national conference to oversee the transition to multi-party democracy, Vieira inaugurated the Comissão Multipartidária de Transição (Multiparty Transition Commission), charged with drafting legislation in preparation for the country's first democratic elections. All officially recognized parties were to be represented on the commission, although it was boycotted by the recently recognized Partido Democrático do Progresso (PDP), led by Amine Michel Saad, which alleged that the commission's work would be biased in favour of the PAIGC. Several other political parties achieved official recognition in the second half of 1992, including the PRD (under the leadership of former health minister João da Costa), the Movimento para a Unidade e a Democracia (MUDE), led by former education minister Filinto Vaz Martins, and the PRS.

In October 1992 Vieira carried out a major reshuffle of the council of ministers. Eight ministers who had served in the cabinet since the country's independence in 1974 were dismissed, including the minister of foreign affairs, Júlio Semedo, the minister of justice, João Cruz Pinto, and the minister of industry and natural resources, Manuel dos Santos. Other changes included the establishment of a new ministry of territorial administration, replacing the three resident ministries for the provinces.

In early November 1992 the government announced that the presidential and legislative elections, scheduled for that month, were to be postponed until March 1993. The postponement was caused by a disagreement concerning the sequence in which the two sets of elections should be held; contrary to government proposals, the opposition parties insisted that the legislative elections take place prior to the presidential elections.

Legislation preparing for the transition to a pluralist democracy was approved by the national assembly in February 1993, and in the following month a four-member commission was appointed to supervise the forthcoming elections. However, reports in mid-March of a coup attempt against the Vieira government threatened to disrupt the transition to democracy. Initial reports indicated that Maj. Robalo de Pina, commander of the Forças de Intervenção Rápida (an élite guard of some 30 soldiers responsible for protecting the president), had been assassinated in what appeared to be an army mutiny, provoked by disaffection at poor standards of pay and living conditions. After initial denials, the government confirmed that a coup attempt had taken place. About 50 people were arrested, including the leader of the PRD, João da Costa. Opposition politicians claimed that the incident had been contrived by the government in an effort to discredit the opposition and to maintain Vieira's hold on power. It was announced that the suspects would be brought to trial in August. Da Costa and nine other members of the PRD in detention were released in mid-June, but banned from political activity. In mid-April public-sector unions organized a three-day general strike in support of demands for wage increases and payment of arrears. In May, following a further split in the FDS, a new political party, the Partido da Convenção Nacional (PCN), was formed. In July Vieira announced that simultaneous presidential and legislative multi-party elections would be held on 27 March 1994. In early August da Costa was rearrested for allegedly violating the conditions of his parole, prompting renewed accusations by opposition politicians that the government's actions were politically motivated. Following a threatened boycott of the national electoral commission by the opposition, da Costa was released.

In January 1994, when da Costa came to trial, several of his co-defendents retracted statements implicating him in the coup attempt, and it was claimed that accusations against him had been fabricated by the director-general of state security, Col João Monteiro, who had presided over the military commission of inquiry which had investigated the coup attempt. In early February da Costa was acquitted.

Multi-Party Elections

One week before the designated election date, set for 27 March 1994, Vieira announced the postponement of the elections owing to financial and technical difficulties, including delays in the electoral registration process and inadequacies in the functioning of the regional electoral commissions. Voter registration for the postponed elections was conducted between 11–23 April. On 11 May it was announced that the elections would be held on 3 July, with a 21-day period of electoral campaigning to begin on 11 June. In early May six opposition parties, the FD, FDS, MUDE, PDP, PRD and the Liga para a Proteção da Ecologia (LIPE), formed a coalition in order jointly to contest the forthcoming elections. Later that month a further five opposition parties, the FLING, PRS, PUSD, RGB – MB and the Foro Cívico da Guiné (FCG), announced the establishment of an informal alliance under which each party reserved the right to present its own candidates in the elections.

The elections took place on schedule on 3 July, although voting was extended for two days owing to logistical problems. Eight candidates contested the presidency, while 1,136 candidates contested the 100 legislative seats. The PAIGC secured a clear majority in the national people's assembly, winning 64 seats, but the results of the presidential election were inconclusive, with Vieira winning 46.17% of the votes, while his nearest rival, Koumba Yalla of the PRS, secured 21.89% of the votes. As no candidate had obtained an absolute majority, a second round presidential election between the two leading candidates was conducted on 7 August, in which Vieira obtained a narrow victory, winning 52% of the vote to Yalla's 48%. Vieira was to be inaugurated as President in late September.

FOREIGN AFFAIRS

In its foreign relations, the Vieira regime is motivated primarily by the need to solicit aid, and secondly by a sense of vulnerability to the economic interests of its larger and more prosperous francophone neighbours, Senegal and Guinea. As a result, the country has actively promoted co-operation with Portugal, even to the point of proposing an 'escudo zone' (an idea in which other lusophone African countries have shown no interest). Relations with Portugal deteriorated in October 1987, after patrol boats detained six Portuguese vessels for alleged illegal fishing in Guinea-Bissau's territorial waters. Portugal retaliated by suspending non-medical aid, but reversed this decision in early November, after the vessels were released. Shortly afterwards, the head of security at the embassy of Guinea-Bissau in Lisbon sought political asylum, alleging that the diplomatic mission was preparing to organize the assassinations of prominent members of the exiled RGB–MB, which had its headquarters in Lisbon. These allegations were vigorously denied by the government of Guinea-Bissau. During a brief visit to Lisbon in October 1988, President Vieira raised the question of the RGB–MB's activities with President Soares of Portugal. As a sign of further commitment to *rapprochement* between the two countries the Portuguese prime minister, Cavaco Silva, paid a four-day visit to Guinea-Bissau in March 1989, when both governments promised increased bilateral co-operation, and agreed to continue to promote relations between African lusophone states. President Soares' visit to Guinea-Bissau in November 1989 included discussions on the issue of dual nationality for Guinea-Bissau residents. In January 1990 a co-operation agreement between Portugal and Guinea-Bissau allowed a credit facility in conversions of the Guinea peso to the Portuguese escudo at an agreed rate. Links with Portugal were strengthened further by visits during 1990 by the Portuguese prime minister, Cavaco Silva, and by the Portuguese ministers for foreign affairs and the environment. In September 1989 President Mubarak of Egypt and President Vieira signed a friendship and co-operation treaty. Diplomatic relations were established with Taiwan in May 1990. In August it was announced that full diplomatic relations were to be established with Iran.

Relations with neighbouring countries have been improving in recent years and those between Guinea-Bissau and Cape Verde, which had deteriorated following the coup in 1980, have gradually become closer. The two countries signed a bilateral co-operation agreement in February 1988 and agreed to liquidate certain joint shipping interests which predated the 1980 coup. A boundary dispute with the Republic of Guinea was resolved in Guinea-Bissau's favour by the International Court of Justice in February 1985. In August 1989 a similar dispute arose between Guinea-Bissau and Senegal over the demarcation of maritime borders, which had been based on a 1960 agreement between the former colonial powers, France and Portugal. Guinea-Bissau brought proceedings against Senegal in the International Court of Justice (ICJ), after rejecting an international tribunal's ruling in favour of Senegal. Guinea-Bissau requested direct negotiations with Senegal and invited President Mubarak of Egypt (as president of the OAU) and President Soares of Portugal to act as mediators. In April 1990 Guinea-Bissau accused Senegal of repeated territorial violations, following the seizure of a Soviet vessel operating in Guinea-Bissau territorial waters and several infringements of Guinea-Bissau's air-space. In early May Guinea-Bissau and Senegal appeared close to military conflict after a reconnaissance platoon of the Senegalese army entered Guinea-Bissau territory. However, the detachment was withdrawn, and military confrontation was avoided. Following a meeting between President Vieira and President Diouf of Senegal in late May, the two heads of state affirmed their commitment to seeking a peaceful solution to the dispute. A meeting of the two countries' joint commission in July failed to make any significant progress towards determining an agreed maritime boundary. The meeting, the first for nine years, did result in an agreement to establish a commission to monitor security on the common land border (a response to claims by Senegal that Guinea-Bissau had supported separatists in Senegal's Casamance region). Action by the Senegalese armed forces against the separatists led to the flight of several hundred refugees to Guinea-Bissau in late 1990. The Bissau government has been involved in negotiations between the Senegal government and the Casamance separatists which led to the signing in Bissau of a cease-fire agreement in May 1991. However, violence again erupted in Casamance in the second half of 1991.

In November 1991 the ICJ ruled that the agreement concluded between France and Portugal in 1960 regarding the demarcation of maritime borders between Guinea-Bissau and Senegal remained valid. In October 1993 the presidents of Guinea-Bissau and Senegal signed an agreement providing for the joint management and exploitation of the countries' maritime zones (see Economy). The agreement, which was for a renewable 20-year period, was expected to put a definitive end to the countries' dispute over the demarcation of their common maritime borders.

Relations with Senegal have, however, continued to be strained by separatist violence in the Casamance region. In December 1992, following an attack by separatists that resulted in the deaths of two Senegalese soldiers, Senegalese aircraft bombarded border villages in Guinea-Bissau, killing two people and injuring three. President Vieira protested to the Senegalese authorities and denied Senegalese claims that the government was providing support for the rebels. The Senegalese government apologized and offered assurances that there would be no repetition of the incident. In March 1993, in an apparent attempt to convince Senegal that it did not support the rebels, the government handed over Fr Diamacounce Sengor, one of the exiled leaders of the Casamance separatists, to the Senegalese authorities. In early 1993 the number of Senegalese refugees in Guinea-Bissau was estimated to total 11,000.

Economy

MILES SMITH-MORRIS

INTRODUCTION

In terms of average income, Guinea-Bissau is among the 15 poorest countries in the world. In 1992, according to estimates by the World Bank, Guinea-Bissau's gross national product (GNP), measured at average 1990–92 prices, was US $217m., equivalent to only $210 per head. During 1985–92, it was estimated, GNP per head increased, in real terms, at an average rate of only 0.4% per year. Over the same period the population increased by an annual average of 2.1%. Guinea-Bissau's gross domestic product (GDP) increased by 2.5% in 1992.

Following independence in 1974, the government established a centrally-planned economy, and an ambitious investment programme, financed mainly by foreign borrowing, was initiated, with emphasis on the industrial sector. However, the economy, which had been adversely affected by the campaign for independence, continued to deteriorate, partly as a result of the government's policies, and by the late 1970s Guinea-Bissau had an underdeveloped agricultural sector, a growing external debt, dwindling exports and escalating inflation.

In the 1980s the government initiated a policy of economic liberalization, in an attempt to reverse the decline in the economy. In 1983 measures were initiated to liberalize the trading sector, to increase producer prices and to encourage private enterprise. Although the measures of adjustment succeeded in increasing agricultural production and exports in 1984, the momentum behind the reforms slowed in 1985–86. By the end of 1986, export earnings had fallen, and the production of many goods had been halted, as the depletion of the country's reserves of foreign exchange made it difficult to import fuel or spare parts. In response to the deteriorating economic situation, the government adopted a structural adjustment programme (SAP) for 1987–90 (see below), which aimed to strengthen the role of the private sector by removing controls over prices and marketing, and by reforming the public sector.

AGRICULTURE AND FISHING

Agriculture is the principal economic activity, and the agricultural sector (including forestry and fishing) engaged 77.8% of the working population in 1992. Agriculture in Guinea-Bissau is entirely an African activity, since there are no European settlers. In 1992 agriculture accounted for about 44% of the country's GDP, and in 1991, according to the World Bank, the sector provided about half of total export earnings. Among food crops, rice is the staple food of the population. The southern region of Tombali accounts for about 70% of the country's rice production. Production of swamp rice and upland rice amounted to about 70,000 metric tons per annum in the pre-war period, and some rice was exported in years of good harvests. The FAO estimate for the production of paddy rice in 1992 was 123,000 tons. The government is promoting a project aimed at achieving an annual harvest of 30,000 tons of rice from new fields. The droughts of 1977, 1979–80 and 1983 drastically reduced rice production, and in 1986/87 the overall food deficit reached an estimated 17,000 tons. By 1989 it had risen to 165,700 tons, owing to locust depredation and late and insufficient rain for the 1988/89 crop. In response to this situation the World Food Programme (WFP) was to provide $13.8m. for imports of 21,000 tons of food for the period 1989–91. Agricultural output was maintained in 1990, despite another year of inadequate rains. Estimates by the Comité permanent Inter-etats pour la Lutte contre la secheresse au Sahel (CILSS) assessed production at 160,000 metric tons of rice, 23,000 tons of maize and 64,000 tons of millet and sorghum. Nevertheless, President Vieira appealed in January 1991 for international assistance to compensate for the remaining food deficit of 31,000 tons. Cereal output in 1991 declined by 58.2% compared to the previous year, from 250,400 tons in 1990 to 104,704 tons in 1991, and was estimated to have remained at a similar level in 1992. Maize, beans, cassava, sorghum and sweet potatoes play an important part at the village level. Rice imports increased sharply in recent years, to some 60,000 tons in 1991, depressing the market for domestic produce.

Traditional exports are groundnuts (20,000 tons produced in 1992, according to FAO estimates), grown in the interior as an extension of the Senegalese cultivation, oil-palm products in the islands and on the coast, and coconuts. In 1977 groundnut exports of 16,335 tons, accounted for 60% of total export earnings. In 1986 only about 4,000 tons, worth $1.3m., were exported. Exports of palm kernels amounted to 10,600 tons, worth $1.3m., in 1983, but declined to an estimated 6,000 tons, worth about $1m., in 1986. Cashew nuts are a relatively recent crop, with an expanding production, estimated at 6,000 tons in 1987, rising to an estimated 30,000 tons per year in 1990, 1991 and 1992. In 1988 export earnings from cashew nuts totalled $8.4m., or 53% of total export revenue. Most of Guinea-Bissau's cashew nuts are purchased by India.

In the government's development plans, priority has been given to agriculture, with the aim of achieving self-sufficiency in food. A sugar refinery (with an annual capacity of 10,000 tons), capable of satisfying domestic needs, is being built at Gambiel and will be supplied from new irrigated plantations covering an area of 6,000 ha. An agro-industrial complex at Cumeré is capable of processing 50,000 tons of rice and 70,000 tons of groundnuts annually. It is estimated that these schemes, together with the projected construction of a thermo-electric power station, will require an investment of $200m., mainly from external sources. The government has nationalized most of the land but does grant private concessions to work the land and has maintained the rights of those tilling their fields. The regime also confiscated the property of former pro-Portuguese Guineans and introduced state control over foreign trade and domestic retail trade through 'people's shops', whose inefficiency and corruption led to serious shortages of consumer goods and contributed to the downfall of President Cabral in 1980. In 1983/84 the government partially 'privatized' the state-controlled trading companies, and raised producer prices by about 70%, in an attempt to accelerate agricultural output. Despite the introduction of these measures, Guinea-Bissau continues to operate a 'war economy', superimposed upon a typically backward peasant economy where most products are bought and sold by the state. Since 1987, however, plans have been accelerated for the removal of price controls on most agricultural products, except essential goods, and for the liberalization of internal marketing systems. In 1992 the government disbanded the People's Militia, a paramilitary corps charged with monitoring the economic sector inside the country. Checkpoints within the country were subsequently dismantled, thus facilitating the distribution of farm products.

The fishing industry has expanded rapidly since the late 1970s, and it has been estimated that the potential annual catch in Guinea-Bissau's waters could total nearly 250,000 tons, although by 1990 only 5%–7% of this level was actually being realized. Fish exports earned an estimated $2.2m. in 1991. If illegal fishing could be effectively prevented, fishing could become Guinea-Bissau's main source of revenue. In 1986 fish products provided 11.5% of export earnings. Guinea-Bissau established joint fishing ventures with the USSR, Algeria and France, and agreed to allow vessels from the EC and Algeria to fish in its maritime zone. In 1987 the USA financed a programme for patrolling Guinea-Bissau's waters to prevent illegal fishing. In March 1989 an agreement was signed with Portugal for the creation of a joint fishing company. Portugal also provided a grant of $2.1m. towards a fisheries project, and in December 1990 the African Development Bank (ADB) agreed to lend $15m. for a project to develop fishing for export at Cacine, in the south. A new fishing agreement was signed with the EC in 1991, increasing the quotas allowed to EC vessels in Guinea-Bissau's waters. In October 1993 an agreement was signed with Senegal providing for the joint management of the countries' maritime zones, with fishing resources to be divided equally (see below).

Cattle-breeding is a very important activity among Balante and Muslim tribes of the interior. In 1992 there were 450,000 head of cattle, 250,000 goats, 250,000 sheep and 300,000 pigs, according to FAO estimates. Meat consumption is significant, and some hides and skins are exported. Tree-felling was temporarily halted while a full assessment of resources was made, but exports resumed in 1986, reaching $1m., and production totalled 572,000 cu m in 1992 according to FAO estimates. Exports of rough and processed timber are estimated to have earned $1.2m. in 1991. In the 1988–91 Development Plan, forestry was allocated a high priority by the government, and a reafforestation programme was to be implemented.

INDUSTRY, MINING AND TRANSPORT

There is little industrial activity other than food-processing, brewing and cotton-processing. A car assembly plant, with a capacity of 500 vehicles per year, was reopened in 1986, following the government's encouragement of the private sector. The factory was opened in 1979, but was forced to close in 1984, owing to lack of components. In 1987 the government attempted to attract foreign investment for the rehabilitation and expansion of a fish-processing plant, and the establishment of a factory to produce plywood and furniture. An agreement between Guinea-Bissau, Portugal and the USA was signed in 1987 for the establishment of an experimental credit fund to encourage private enterprise. In July 1989 an agreement was signed with Portugal, under which a Portuguese company was to reopen a plastics factory which had ceased production in 1984. Electricity consumption totalled 14m. kWh in 1985, according to UN estimates. In 1987 work began on the construction of an 8,000-kW diesel-electric power station, funded by the USSR; its completion, together with the rehabilitation of the Bissau thermal power station and purchase of a new 3.5 MW generating unit, formed part of a project aimed at increasing total generating capacity to 15.4 MW. In 1992 the European Investment Bank (EIB) agreed to provide ECU 7.5m. towards financing the project.

The mining sector has still to be developed, and prospecting for bauxite, petroleum and phosphates is in progress. A large deposit of 200m. tons of bauxite was reported in the Boé area in 1972, but exploitation has not yet become economic. In 1981 a French exploration team announced the discovery of 200m. tons of phosphates in Cacheu and Oio. In 1987 the government negotiated for financial backing to exploit phosphate deposits in the northern region. Petroleum exploration has resumed; an offshore zone, contested with Guinea until 1985, may contain significant deposits. A second maritime zone, on the border with Senegal, was being claimed by the Senegalese government. However, in October 1993 an agreement was signed with Senegal providing for the joint management of the countries' maritime zones (see also above), with Senegal to receive an 85% share of petroleum resources to Guinea-Bissau's 15%. The agreement, which was for a renewable 20-year period, was expected to put a definitive end to the countries' dispute over the demarcation of their common maritime borders. In 1984 the government reached agreement with a group of foreign oil companies concerning petroleum prospecting in an offshore concession covering 4,500 sq km, and in 1985 licences for exploration of some 40 offshore blocks were offered on favourable terms, following the relaxation of Guinea-Bissau's hydrocarbons law. A US petroleum company, Pecten, began exploratory drilling in its offshore permits in 1990. In July of that year the government announced that a new oil exploration programme was to begin in 1991; a joint commission had been formed with Guinea to facilitate exploration in the two countries' maritime border area.

For strategic reasons, an impressive network of 3,500 km of roads (540 km tarred) was built from Bissau to the north and north-east in 1972. The EU is interested in an international project to construct a road linking Banjul, in The Gambia, to Bissau. The road system is poor, especially during the rainy season. In 1989 the World Bank approved a loan of $23.6m. towards a $43m. infrastructural rehabilitation scheme. Other donors included the UN Capital Development Fund, the Kuwait Fund for Arab Development, the ADB and the Islamic Development Bank. In early 1989 grants totalling $31.3m. were provided by the ADB, the Arab Bank for Economic Development in Africa and the EC for road improvements. The road from São Domingos to M'Pack in Senegal, built with aid from the EC and Italy, opened in 1990. Water transport could be much developed, as 85% of the population live within 20 km of a navigable waterway. In 1984 work began on a project, expected to cost $47.4m., to enlarge Bissau harbour and to rehabilitate four river ports. The ADB was to lend $2.5m. in 1991 for the purchase of port equipment. The construction of a new river port at N'Pungda began in 1986, to improve rice distribution to the northern region. There are also plans to expand the international airport at Bissalanca. In 1991 Guinea-Bissau and Portugal signed an air transport agreement, under which the Portuguese national airline, TAP, would provide equipment and technicians to help Air Bissau to improve internal services, as well as increasing the frequency of Lisbon-Bissau flights from two to three per week. An experimental television service, financed by Portugal (with equipment provided by a Portuguese company, Radio Marconi), was introduced in 1989. A joint company, Guiné-Telecom, was established in 1989 by Radio Marconi and the government to improve the country's telecommunications services.

EXTERNAL TRADE, FINANCE AND DEVELOPMENT

Serious external trade imbalances persist. Exports rose from about $12m. in 1982 to $17.4m. in 1984, but fell to $7.5m. in 1986. In 1987 exports rose dramatically to $15.3m., as a result of the devaluation of the peso in May, and to $15.9m. in 1988. The value of exports continued to rise, to $17.5m. in 1989, $21.5m. in 1990 and $23m. in 1991, but this did not keep pace with the devaluation of the Guinea peso, which at 3,659 pesos = $1 in 1991 was worth barely half its value of two years earlier. According to IMF figures, the value of exports totalled only $6.5m. in 1992. Devaluation of the peso continued, reaching 6,934 pesos = $1 in 1992 and 10,082 pesos = $1 in 1993. Meanwhile, the demand for manufactured goods, machinery, fuel and food has ensured a high level of imports, averaging $60m. per year in the 1980s. However, foreign exchange controls and the closure of some state enterprises caused a large fall in imports of industrial raw materials. Imports totalled $51.2m. in 1986, falling to $48.8m. in 1987 and rising again in 1988 to about $57m., according to IMF figures. Imports continued to rise reaching $78m. in 1989 and $93m. in 1990 before falling slightly to $78m. in 1991. According to IMF figures, the value of imports totalled $83.5m. in 1992. Portugal is still Guinea-Bissau's principal trading partner, accounting for 34% of exports and 23% of imports in 1989. In 1988, Italy replaced Portugal as the main supplier of manufactured goods, providing 21% of Guinea-Bissau's total imports that year, and 27% in 1989. In 1988, India received an estimated 40% of exports, as it is a major importer of cashew nuts. In 1988 the budgetary deficit was equivalent to 18.4% of GDP and stood at 31,557m. Guinea pesos, rising to 53,558m. pesos in 1989. This sharp rate of increase was largely attributable to the devaluation of the Guinea peso. Grants from abroad continue to be the major source of revenue, accounting for 71.2% of the total for 1989. The deficit on the current account of the balance of payments reached $31.4m. in 1990, increasing to $48.6m. in 1991 and $79.3m. in 1992. The average annual rate of inflation was 17% in 1987/88. According to the central bank, inflation reached 110% in 1992. The shortfalls in the economy are offset by inflows of foreign aid, which averaged more than $60m. per year in 1981–85, increasing from $72.2m. in 1986 to $106.3m. in 1987. The increase was due principally to a rise in multilateral assistance, especially from the World Bank, the African Development Fund (ADF) and the EC. The level of aid fell slightly in 1988, to $100m. In recent years, the Netherlands and the Scandinavian countries have been important aid-donors. Guinea-Bissau has attended various Franco-African summit conferences and has been a signatory to successive Lomé Conventions. In November 1987 Guinea-Bissau applied to join the Franc Zone, but withdrew its application in January 1990 following the formulation of an exchange rate agreement with Portugal linking the Guinea peso rate to that of the Portuguese escudo. This accord was considered to form the initial stage in the creation of an 'escudo zone'. However, in August 1993, Guinea-Bissau renewed its application to join the Franc Zone. An extensive re-organization of Guinea-Bissau's banking system has been under way since 1989, involving the replacement of Banco Nacional da Guiné-Bissau by three institutions: a central bank, a commercial bank (Banco Internacional da Guiné-Bissau, which began operations in March 1990), and a national credit bank, established in September 1990, to channel investment. A fourth financial institution, responsible for managing aid receipts, was created with assistance from the EC, the US Agency for International Development, Sweden and Portugal, under the terms of a memorandum signed in 1990. In 1991 the government authorized the establishment of privately-operated foreign exchange bureaux.

President Vieira's government aimed to downgrade many of the prestigious projects that had been initiated by Cabral's administration, and to emphasize rural development. In order to achieve a coherent policy, a Development Plan for 1983–86 was prepared in 1982. In December 1983 the peso was devalued by 50%, with the new official exchange rate set at 88 pesos = SDR 1, as part of a programme of economic stabilization, which aimed to liberalize trade and to increase activity in the private sector. In 1986 trading restrictions were lifted, allowing private traders to import and export goods, although the two state-owned enterprises continued to control trading in rice, petroleum products, pesticides and various other commodities.

After consultations with the World Bank, the IMF and other external donors, Guinea-Bissau initiated a Structural Adjustment Programme (SAP) covering the period 1987–90. The programme was to be wholly financed by external aid totalling $46.4m. The SAP included proposals to liberalize the economy and to reform public administration and enterprises. It aimed to achieve a real GDP growth rate of at least 3.5% per year, a lower annual inflation rate (of about 8%) and a reduction in the current account and budgetary deficits. In May 1987 the peso was devalued by about 60%, with the official rate set at 650 pesos = US $1, and new taxes and higher tariffs were introduced. Civil servants' salaries were increased by 25% in 1987, and by 50% in 1988, although one-third of the 16,623 state employees were to be gradually redeployed in the agricultural sector and in public works projects. At the end of 1990, civil servants were granted an extra month's salary to ameliorate the stringencies imposed by the SAP. In 1988 the government reduced subsidies on petroleum products, and thus increased their average price by 40%.

The Development Plan (1989–92) aimed to consolidate the progress made under the SAP in the reduction of the state's role in the economy, and the growth of private investment. Emphasis was on social development. The agricultural and fishing sectors were to be given priority as a means of achieving self-sufficiency and reducing the balance-of-payments deficit. By the end of 1989, Guinea-Bissau's total external debt was estimated at $458m., of which $427m. was public and publicly-guaranteed long-term debt. Overall debt-servicing charges for that year totalled $11.6m., or 43% of exports. By the end of 1992 total external debt had risen to $634.0m., of which $580.1m. was long-term public debt. In that year the cost of debt servicing was equivalent to 93.4% of the total value of exports of goods and services. In October 1989, the 'Paris Club' of Western official creditors, including Belgium, France, Sweden and Switzerland, agreed to reschedule $21m. of principal and interest due from end-October 1989 to December 1990. In September 1989 Belgium agreed to reschedule $2.5m. of Guinea-Bissau's debt. Portugal announced in October 1990 that it would convert Guinea-Bissau's debt of $14.5m. into a Guinea peso fund to be used to support development projects. At the end of the year Portugal released a $6m. credit to the government as part of the financial agreement concluded in January (see above). In January 1989, following the removal of subsidies, fuel prices rose a further 40%, and this was quickly followed by a 33% increase in the price of bread. Further fuel price increases followed in January, July and October 1990 and February 1991, linked to the depreciation of the Guinea peso against the US dollar and in response to the rise in world petroleum prices that accompanied the Gulf crisis.

In January 1989 the government announced the adoption of a $104.6m. investment programme, to be funded entirely by external donors, which was to supplement development projects already proceeding under the SAP. In an attempt to stimulate foreign trade, restrict 'black market' activity and restrain inflation, customs duties and general taxes on imported goods were reduced in April. In the following month international donor countries pledged to allocate Guinea-Bissau $120m., of which 40% was to assist in financing the balance-of-payments deficit, and the remainder to meet general financing requirements. In accordance with these agreements, the World Bank approved a $23.4m. loan to support the second stage of the SAP, introduced in 1987. Joint financing was expected from, among others, the Netherlands ($4.8m.), the USA ($4.5m.) and the ADF ($17.2m.). Under the second stage of the SAP, the government undertook to extend the aims of its economic liberalization programme. A particular focus was to be the privatization of state-owned enterprises.

In June 1990 President Vieira initiated new measures to attract domestic and foreign private investment. It was stated that most of the 50 public enterprises were to be restructured and made more efficient although some strategic sectors, such as telecommunications, electricity and infrastructure, were expected to remain under state control. A decree on privatization was adopted in March 1991, defining areas of state intervention in the economy and outlining the rules for transferring state holdings in public enterprises to the private sector. Nine enterprises were listed for initial privatization, including the 'people's shops', the national brewery and the fishing enterprise, SEMAPESCA. The government's failure to meet some of the targets of the adjustment programme led, however, to a suspension of international financing when the IMF declined to renew its structural adjustment facility. Among funding suspended as a result was the third tranche of the World Bank's structural adjustment loan, totalling $6.5m.; negotiations on a resumption of World Bank funding began in July 1992 and, in July 1993, it was announced that credits were finally to be resumed. However, in the following month, the World Bank reversed its decision, owing to the government's delay in making repayments on its external debt. In April 1992 the International Development Association announced a loan of $7.2m. to help finance an economic management project. The project, which aimed to improve the government's management and monitoring of economic policy, was to cost a total of $8m. Among the measures involved in the project were a modernizing of the budget process and reform of the tax structure. In April 1993 the government initiated a $63m. public investment programme. The programme, which concentrates predominantly on public works, was to be funded by $32.5m. in aid and $29.5m. in loans contracted by the government, which was itself to provide the remaining $1m.

Statistical Survey

Area and Population

AREA, POPULATION AND DENSITY

Area (sq km)	36,125*
Population (census results)	
16–30 April 1979	
Males	362,589
Females	390,724
Total	753,313
Population (UN estimates at mid-year)†	
1991	984,000
1992	1,006,000
1993	1,028,000
Density (per sq km) at mid-1993	28.5

* 13,948 sq miles.

† Source: UN, *World Population Prospects: The 1992 Revision.*

POPULATION BY REGION (1979 census, provisional)

Bafatá	116,032
Biombo	56,463
Bissau	109,214
Bolama/Bijagos	25,743
Cacheu	130,227
Gabú	104,315
Oio	135,114
Quinara	35,532
Tombali	55,099
Total	767,739

PRINCIPAL TOWNS (population at 1979 census)

Bissau (capital)	109,214	Catió	5,170
Bafatá	13,429	Cantchungo	4,965
Gabú	7,803	Farim	4,468
Mansôa	5,390		

BIRTHS AND DEATHS (UN estimates, annual averages)

	1975–80	1980–85	1985–90
Birth rate (per 1,000)	42.4	43.3	42.9
Death rate (per 1,000)	26.2	24.7	23.0

Expectation of life (UN estimates, years at birth, 1985–90): 41.5 (males 39.9; females 43.1).

Source: UN, *World Population Prospects: The 1992 Revision.*

ECONOMICALLY ACTIVE POPULATION
(ILO estimates, 1000 persons at mid-1980)

	Males	Females	Total
Agriculture, etc.	174	158	332
Industry	12	3	14
Services	46	11	57
Total	231	172	403

Source: ILO, *Economically Active Population Estimates and Projections, 1950–2025.*

Mid-1992 (estimates in '000): Agriculture etc. 359; Total 461 (Source: FAO, *Production Yearbook*).

Agriculture

PRINCIPAL CROPS ('000 metric tons)

	1990	1991	1992
Rice (paddy)	123	123	123
Maize	14	13	12
Millet	17	28	25
Sorghum	11	13	10
Roots and tubers	67	62	61*
Groundnuts (in shell)	18	20	20
Cottonseed	2	2	1
Coconuts*	25	25	25
Copra*	5	5	5
Palm Kernels*	10	10	8
Vegetables and melons*	20	20	20
Plantains*	33	33	33
Other fruits*	31	34	34
Sugar cane	6	6*	6
Cashew nuts	30	30	30
Cotton (lint)	1†	1*	n.a.

* FAO estimate(s). † Unofficial figure.

Source: FAO, *Production Yearbook.*

LIVESTOCK ('000 head, year ending September)

	1990	1991	1992
Cattle	410	425*	450
Pigs	290*	290	300
Sheep	242	245*	250
Goats	208	220	250

* FAO estimates.

Source: FAO, *Production Yearbook.*

LIVESTOCK PRODUCTS (FAO estimates, '000 metric tons)

	1990	1991	1992
Beef and veal	3	3	3
Pig meat	9	9	9
Cows' milk	12	12	12
Goats' milk	2	2	2

Source: FAO, *Production Yearbook.*

Forestry

ROUNDWOOD REMOVALS
(FAO estimates, '000 cubic metres, excluding bark)

	1990	1991	1992
Sawlogs, veneer logs and logs for sleepers*	40	40	40
Other industrial wood	105	107	110
Fuel wood†	422	422	422
Total	567	569	572

* Assumed to be unchanged since 1971.

† Assumed to be unchanged since 1979.

Source: FAO, *Yearbook of Forest Products.*

SAWNWOOD PRODUCTION
(FAO estimates, '000 cubic metres, incl. railway sleepers)

	1990	1991	1992
Total*	16	16	16

* Assumed to be unchanged since 1971.

Source: FAO, *Yearbook of Forest Products.*

Fishing

(FAO estimates, '000 metric tons, live weight)

	1989	1990	1991
Inland waters	0.2	0.2	0.2
Atlantic Ocean	5.2	5.2	4.8
Total catch	5.4	5.4	5.0

Source: FAO, *Yearbook of Fishery Statistics.*

Industry

SELECTED PRODUCTS

	1989	1990	1991
Palm oil ('000 metric tons)*	5	5	5
Electric energy (million kWh)	31	40	41

* FAO estimates.

Source: UN, *Industrial Statistics Yearbook.*

Finance

CURRENCY AND EXCHANGE RATES

Monetary Units

100 centavos = 1 Guinea peso.

Sterling and Dollar Equivalents (31 March 1994)

£1 sterling = 18,363.5 pesos;
US $1 = 12,369.3 pesos;
100,000 Guinea pesos = £5.446 = $8.085.

Average Exchange Rate (Guinea pesos per US dollar)

1991 3,659
1992 6,934
1993 10,082

BUDGET (million pesos)

Revenue*	1986	1987	1988
Taxation	2,232†	7,818†	16,240
Taxes on income, profits etc	598	877	1,243
Social security contributions	109	145	204
Taxes on property	5	13	40
Excises	976	3,680	5,615
Import duties	580	1,436	3,547
Export duties	101	3,394	4,879
Other taxes	252	674	712
Other current revenue	1,587	4,322	6,457
Capital revenue	9	13	14
Total	3,828	12,153	22,711

Expenditure‡	1985	1986	1987
General public services	1,540	5,199	13,414
Defence	738	1,251	2,168
Education	1,476	1,408	2,541
Health	754	1,298	2,638
Social security and welfare	160	699	4,273
Housing and community amenities	337	2,129	4,067
Other community and social services	738	68	198
Economics services	7,862	7,179	19,523
Other purposes	1,379	n.a.	n.a.
Adjustments	−464	n.a.	n.a.
Total	14,520	19,231	48,822

* Excluding grants received (million pesos): 7,675 in 1986; 22,443 in 1987; 36,338 in 1988.

† Including adjustments.

‡ Excluding net lending (million pesos): 1,056 in 1985; −198 in 1986; 3,667 in 1987.

Source: IMF, *Government Finance Statistics Yearbook.*

CENTRAL BANK RESERVES (US $ million at 31 December)

	1991	1992	1993
IMF special drawing rights	—	—	0.01
Foreign exchange	14.58	17.75	14.16
Total	14.58	17.75	14.17

Source: IMF, *International Financial Statistics.*

MONEY SUPPLY ('000 million Guinea pesos at 31 December)

	1991	1992	1993
Currency outside banks	54.52	104.22	132.53
Demand deposits at deposit money banks	31.01	54.20	68.25
Total money (incl. others)	86.58	158.61	201.91

Source: IMF, *International Financial Statistics.*

COST OF LIVING (Consumer Price Index; base: 1990 = 100)

	1991	1992	1993
Food, beverages and tobacco	157.6	267.3	395.8

Source: IMF, *International Financial Statistics.*

NATIONAL ACCOUNTS
(million Guinea pesos at current prices)

Expenditure on the Gross Domestic Product

	1989	1990	1991
Government final consumption expenditure	46,925	58,013	108,032
Private final consumption expenditure	351,049	514,670	860,458
Increase in stocks	6,337	4,591	7,695
Gross fixed capital formation	66,197	70,546	89,125
Total domestic expenditure	470,508	647,820	1,065,310
Exports of goods and services	28,924	61,211	114,568
Less Imports of goods and services	140,557	198,937	324,894
GDP in purchasers' values	358,875	510,094	854,985
GDP at constant 1986 prices	55,434	57,263	58,981

Gross Domestic Product by Economic Activity

	1989	1990	1991
Agriculture, hunting, forestry and fishing	160,016	227,508	382,400
Mining and quarrying; Manufacturing; Electricity, gas and water	28,465	41,930	72,556
Construction	34,645	50,937	71,874
Trade, restaurants and hotels	92,338	131,250	220,356
Transport, storage and communications	12,824	18,874	33,364
Finance, insurance, real estate, etc.; Community, social and personal services (excl. government)	11,697	16,626	27,914
Government services	18,891	22,969	46,522
GDP in purchasers' values	358,875	510,094	854,985

Source: UN, *National Accounts Statistics.*

BALANCE OF PAYMENTS (US $ million)

	1990	1991	1992
Merchandise exports f.o.b.	19.3	20.4	6.5
Merchandise imports f.o.b.	-68.1	-67.5	-83.5
Trade balance	-48.8	-47.0	-77.0
Services (net)	-24.8	-30.2	-30.3
Other income (net)	-10.6	-17.0	-13.3
Private unrequited transfers (net)	1.0	-4.1	-0.6
Official unrequited transfers (net)	51.8	49.8	42.0
Current balance	-31.4	-48.6	-79.3
Capital (net)	1.2	-8.8	2.2
Net errors and omissions	-4.5	-13.9	33.7
Overall balance	-34.7	-71.3	-43.4

Source: IMF, *International Financial Statistics.*

External Trade

PRINCIPAL COMMODITIES (US $ million)

Imports c.i.f.	1990	1991
Food	25	19
Fuel and energy	8	10
Capital goods	36	27
Total (incl. others)	93	78

Exports f.o.b.	1990	1991
Groundnuts	1	0
Other food	12	14
Total (incl. others)	19	28

Source: World Bank, *Trends in Developing Economies.*

PRINCIPAL TRADING PARTNERS

Imports (million pesos)	1984
France	232.7
Germany, Fed. Repub.	213.7
Italy	110.4
Netherlands	215.6
Portugal	924.0
Senegal	362.0
Sweden	70.2
USSR	462.7
USA	192.4
Total (incl. others)	3,230.7

Source: Ministry of Planning, Bissau.

Exports (US $ '000)	1981
China, People's Repub.	1,496
France	1,376
Portugal	2,890
Senegal	1,122
Spain	4,058
Sweden	1,627
Switzerland	1,617
United Kingdom	1,211
Total (incl. others)	15,730

Source: UN, *International Trade Statistics Yearbook.*

Transport

ROAD TRAFFIC (UN estimates, '000 motor vehicles in use)

	1989	1990	1991
Passenger cars	4	4	4
Commercial vehicles	3	3	3

Source: UN Economic Commission for Africa, *African Statistical Yearbook.*

INTERNATIONAL SEA-BORNE SHIPPING
(freight traffic, '000 metric tons)

	1989	1990	1991
Goods loaded	33	35	40
Goods unloaded	305	310	315

Source: UN Economic Commission for Africa, *African Statistical Yearbook.*

CIVIL AVIATION (traffic on scheduled services)

	1990
Kilometres flown (million)	1
Passengers carried ('000)	21
Passenger-km (million)	10
Total ton-km (million)	1

Source: UN, *Statistical Yearbook.*

Communications Media

	1989	1990	1991
Radio receivers ('000 in use)	37	38	39
Telephones ('000 in use)*	7	7	8
Daily newspapers:			
Number	n.a.	1	n.a.
Average circulation ('000 copies)	n.a.	6	n.a.

* UN estimates.

Sources: UNESCO, *Statistical Yearbook*; UN Economic Commission for Africa, *African Statistical Yearbook.*

Education

(1988)

	Institutions	Teachers	Students Males	Students Females	Students Total
Pre-Primary	5	43	384	370	754
Primary	632*	3,065*	50,744	28,291	79,035
Secondary:					
General	n.a.	617†	3,588	1,917	5,505
Teacher training	n.a.	33	137	39	176
Vocational	n.a.	74	593	56	649
Tertiary	n.a.	n.a.	380	24	404

* 1987 figures. † 1986 figure.

Source: UNESCO, *Statistical Yearbook.*

Directory

The Constitution

A new Constitution for the Republic of Guinea-Bissau was approved by the National People's Assembly on 16 May 1984 and amended in May 1991 (see below). The main provisions of the 1984 Constitution were:

Guinea-Bissau is an anti-colonialist and anti-imperialist Republic and a State of revolutionary national democracy, based on the people's participation in undertaking, controlling and directing public activities. The Partido Africano da Independência da Guiné e Cabo Verde (PAIGC) shall be the leading political force in society and in the State. The PAIGC shall define the general bases for policy in all fields.

The economy of Guinea-Bissau shall be organized on the principles of state direction and planning. The State shall control the country's foreign trade.

The representative bodies in the country are the National People's Assembly and the regional councils. Other state bodies draw their powers from these. The members of the regional councils shall be directly elected. Members of the councils must be more than 18 years of age. The National People's Assembly shall have 150 members, who are to be elected by the regional councils from among their own members. All members of the National People's Assembly must be more than 21 years of age.

The National People's Assembly shall elect a 15-member Council of State, to which its powers are delegated between sessions of the Assembly. The Assembly also elects the President of the Council of State, who is also automatically Head of the Government and Commander-in-Chief of the Armed Forces. The Council of State will later elect two Vice-Presidents and a Secretary. The President and Vice-Presidents of the Council of State form part of the Government, as do Ministers, Secretaries of State and the Governor of the National Bank.

The Constitution can be revised at any time by the National People's Assembly on the initiative of the deputies themselves, or of the Council of State or the Government.

Note: Constitutional amendments providing for the operation of a multi-party political system were approved unanimously by the National People's Assembly in May 1991. The amendments stipulated that new parties seeking registration must obtain a minimum of 2,000 signatures, with at least 100 signatures from each of the nine provinces. (These provisions were adjusted in August to 1,000 and 50 signatures, respectively.) In addition, the amendments provided for the National People's Assembly to be elected by universal adult suffrage, for the termination of official links between the PAIGC and the armed forces, and for the operation of a free market economy. Multi-party elections took place in July 1994.

The Government

HEAD OF STATE

Head of Government, President of the Council of State and Commander-in-Chief of the Armed Forces: Commdr João Bernardo Vieira (assumed power 14 November 1980; elected President of the Council of State 16 May 1984, and re-elected 19 June 1989; elected President in multi-party democratic elections 3 July and 7 August 1994, to be inaugurated in late September 1994).

COUNCIL OF STATE
(August 1994)

President: Commdr João Bernardo Vieira.

Permanent Secretary: Carlos Correia.

Members:

Carlos Correia.
Filinto de Barros.
Júlio Semedo.
Francisca Pereira.
Mário Mendes.
Teoboldo Barboza.
M'Bana Match.
Carmen Pereira.
Col Manuel Mário Monteiro dos Santos.
Fatima Fati.
Mamadu Fore Balde.

COUNCIL OF MINISTERS
(August 1994)

Head of Government, President of the Council of State, Commander-in-Chief of the Armed Forces: Commdr João Bernardo Vieira.

Prime Minister: Carlos Correia.

Minister of Justice: Mamadu Saliu Djalo Pires.

Minister of Rural Development and Agriculture: Filinto de Barros.

Minister of the Interior: Dr Abubacar Baldé.

Minister of Natural Resources: João Cardoso.

Minister of Foreign Affairs and Co-operation: Bernadino Cardoso.

Minister of Defence: Samba Lamine Manè.

Minister of Health: Henriqueta Godinho Gomes.

Minister of Education and Culture: Dr Fernando Delfim da Silva.

Minister of Trade and Industry: Assumane Manè.

Minister of Social Affairs and Women's Affairs: Francisca Pereira.

Minister of Fishing: Eduardo Fernandes.

Minister of Transport and Communications: Luis Oliveira Sanca.

Minister of Public Works: Alberto Lima Gomes.

Minister of Administrative Reform and Civil Service: Malam Bacai Sanha.

Minister of Information: Augusto Viegas.

Minister of Territorial Administration: Manuel Manè.

There are seven Secretaries of State.

MINISTRIES

All Ministries are in Bissau.

President and Legislature

PRESIDENT

Presidential Election, First Ballot, 3 July 1994

Candidate	Votes	% of Votes
João Bernardo Vieira (PAIGC)	141,836	46.17
Koumba Yalla (PRS)	67,257	21.89
Domingos Fernandes Gomes (RGB — MB)	53,277	17.34
Carlos Domingos Gomes (PCD)	15,575	5.07
François Kankoila Mendy (FLING)	8,594	2.80
Bubacar Djalo (UM)	8,447	2.75
Vítor Saúde Maria (PUSD)	6,687	2.18
Antonieta Rosa Gomes (FCG)	5,538	2.18
Total	307,211	100.00

Second Ballot, 7 August 1994

Candidate	Votes	%
João Bernardo Vieira (PAIGC)	161,083	52.00
Koumba Yalla (PRS)	148,664	48.00
Total	309,747	100.00

NATIONAL PEOPLE'S ASSEMBLY

Election, 3 July 1994

	% of Votes	Seats
Partido Africano da Independência da Guiné e Cabo Verde (PAIGC)	46.0	64
Resistência da Guiné-Bissau—Movimento Bafatá (RGB — MB)	19.2	17
Partido para a Renovação Social (PRS)	10.3	12
União para a Mudança (UM)	12.8	6
Frente da Luta para a Libertação da Guiné (FLING)	2.5	1
Partido da Convergência Democrática (PCD)	5.3	—
Partido Unido Social Democrático (PUSD)	2.9	—
Foro Cívico da Guiné (FCG)	0.2	—
Total (incl. others)	100.0	100

Political Organizations

Constitutional provision for the establishment of a plural political system was approved in May 1991. In order to attain legal status, each party was required to obtain registration by the Supreme Court. These procedures commenced in November 1991.

Foro Cívico da Guiné (FCG): Bissau; Leader Antonieta Rosa Gomes.

Frente da Luta para a Libertação da Guiné (FLING): Bissau; f. 1962; legalized in May 1992; Leader François Kankoila Mendy.

Partido Africano da Independência da Guiné e Cabo Verde (PAIGC): CP 106, Bissau; f. 1956; fmrly the ruling party in both Guinea-Bissau and Cape Verde; although Cape Verde withdrew from the PAIGC following the coup in Guinea-Bissau in Nov. 1980, Guinea-Bissau has retained the party name and initials; in Dec. 1990 the party cen. cttee assented to the establishment of a multi-party system; Pres. Commdr João Bernardo Vieira; Perm. Sec. of Cen. Cttee Saturnino Costa.

Partido da Convenção Nacional (PCN): Bissau; f. 1993 by breakaway faction of the FDS.

Partido da Convergência Democrática (PCD): Bissau; Leader Vítor Mandinga.

Partido para a Renovação Social (PRS): Bissau; f. 1992 by breakaway faction of the FDS; legalized in Oct. 1992; Leader Koumba Yalla.

Partido Unido Social Democrático (PUSD): Bissau; f. 1991; legalized in Jan. 1992; Leader Vítor Saúde Maria.

Resistência da Guiné-Bissau—Movimento Bafatá (RGB—MB): Bissau; f. 1986 in Lisbon, Portugal; maintains offices in Paris (France), Dakar (Senegal) and Praia (Cape Verde); legalized in Dec. 1991. Chair. Domingos Fernandes Gomes.

União para a Mudança (UM): Bissau; f. 1994 as coalition to contest presidential and legislative elections of July 1994; Leader Rafael Barbosa (FDS); Sec. Manuel Rambout Barcelos (PRD); comprises following parties:

Frente Democrática (FD): Bissau; f. 1991; legalized in Nov. 1991; Leader Marcelino Baptista.

Frente Democrática Social (FDS): Bissau; f. 1991; legalized in Dec. 1991; Leader Rafael Barbosa.

Liga para a Proteção da Ecologia (LIPE): Bissau; f. 1993; ecology party.

Movimento para a Unidade e a Democracia (MUDE): Bissau; legalized in Aug. 1992; Leader Filinto Vaz Martins.

Partido Democrático do Progresso (PDP): Bissau; f. 1991; legalized in Aug. 1992; Pres. of Nat. Council Amine Michel Saad.

Partido de Renovação e Desenvolvimento (PRD): Bissau; f. 1992 by PAIGC dissidents; fmrly known as 'Group of 121'; legalized in Oct. 1992; Leaders Manuel Rambout Barcelos, Agnelo Regala, João da Costa.

Diplomatic Representation

EMBASSIES IN GUINEA-BISSAU

Algeria: Rua 12 de Setembro 12, CP 350, Bissau; tel. 211522; Ambassador: R. Benchikh el Fegoun.

Brazil: Rua São Tomé, Bissau; tel. 201327; telex 245; fax 201317; Ambassador: Marcelo Didier.

Cape Verde: Bissau; Ambassador: António Lima.

China (Taiwan): Avda Amilcar Cabral 35, CP 66, Bissau; tel. 201501; fax 201466.

Cuba: Rua Joaquim N'Com 1, Bissau; tel. 213579; Ambassador: Diosdado Fernández González.

Egypt: Rua 12 de Setembro, CP 72, Bissau; tel. 213642; Ambassador: Fadel Fadel Atta.

France: Rua Eduardo Mondlane 67-A, Bissau; tel. 212633; Ambassador: Eric Lem.

Germany: Avda Osvaldo Vieira 28, Bissau; tel. 212992; Ambassador: Erich Meske.

Guinea: Rua 14, no. 9, CP 396, Bissau; tel. 212681; Ambassador: Mohamed Laminé Fodé.

Libya: Rua 16, CP 362, Bissau; tel. 212006; Representative: Dokali Ali Mustafa.

Portugal: Rua de Lisboa 6, Apdo 76, Bissau; tel. 201261; telex 248; fax 201269; Ambassador: João Rosa Lã.

Russia: Avda 14 de Novembro, Bissau; tel. 251036; fax 251050; Ambassador: Viktor M. Zelenov.

Senegal: Bissau; tel. 212636; Ambassador: Ahmed Tijane Kane.

USA: CP 297, 1067 Bissau; tel. 201159; fax 201159; Ambassador: Roger A. McGuire.

Judicial System

Under the provisions of the 1984 Constitution, Judges of the Supreme Court are appointed by the President of the Council Of State.

President of the Supreme Court: Manuel Lopes.

Religion

About 54% of the population are animists, 38% are Muslims and 8% are Christians, mainly Roman Catholics.

CHRISTIANITY

The Roman Catholic Church

Guinea-Bissau comprises a single diocese, directly responsible to the Holy See. At 31 December 1992 there were an estimated 70,500 adherents in the country.

Bishop of Bissau: Mgr Settimio Arturo Ferrazzetta, CP 20, 1001 Bissau; tel. 251057; fax 251058.

The Anglican Communion

Within the Church of the Province of West Africa, Guinea-Bissau forms part of the diocese of Guinea, established in 1985. The Bishop of Guinea is resident in Conakry, Guinea. The Archbishop of the Province is the Bishop of Koforidua (Ghana).

The Press

A new national policy on information took effect in December 1989. It was subsequently announced that all areas of the press were to be reorganized in 1990. In 1991 the National Assembly approved laws allowing greater press freedom.

Baguerra: Bissau; owned by the Convergência Democrática.

Expresso-Bissau: Bissau; f. 1992; independent private weekly; Publr João de Barros.

Nô Pintcha: Bissau; daily; Dir Sra Cabral; circ. 6,000.

NEWS AGENCY

Agência Noticiosa da Guinea (ANG): CP 248, Bissau; tel. 212151; telex 96900.

Radio and Television

According to UNESCO estimates, there were 39,000 radio receivers in use in 1991. An experimental television service began transmissions in November 1989. Regional radio stations were to be established at Bafatá, Cantchungo and Catió in 1990. In September 1990 Radio Freedom, which broadcast on behalf of the PAIGC during Portuguese rule and had ceased operations in 1974, resumed transmissions.

Radiodifusão Nacional da República da Guiné-Bissau: CP 191, Bissau; govt-owned; broadcasts on short-wave, MW and FM in Portuguese; Dir Francisco Barreto.

Finance

(cap. = capital; m. = million; brs = branches; amounts in Guinea pesos)

BANKING

The decentralization of banking activities began in 1989.

Central Bank

Banco Central da Guiné-Bissau: Avda Amílcar Cabral, CP 38, Bissau; tel. 212434; telex 241; fax 201305; f. 1975 as Banco Nacional da Guiné-Bissau; bank of issue; also operates as a commercial bank; cap. 100m.; Gov. Luis Candido Ribeiro; 2 brs.

Other Banks

Banco Internacional da Guiné-Bissau: Avda Amílcar Cabral, CP 74, Bissau; tel. 213662; telex 204; fax 201033; f. 1989; cap. 3,260m. (Dec. 1992); 26% state-owned, 25% by Guinea-Bissau enterprises and private interests, 49% by Portuguese interests; Chair. Alvito José da Silva; Gen. Man. José Aníbal Tavares.

Banco Totta e Açores (Portugal): Rua 19 de Setembro, CP 618, Bissau; tel. 214794; fax 201591; Gen. Man. Carlos Alberto Morais.

Caixa de Crédito da Guiné: Bissau; govt savings and loan institution.

Caixa Económica Postal: Avda Amílcar Cabral, Bissau; tel. 212999; telex 979; postal savings institution.

INSURANCE

In 1979 it was announced that a single state-owned insurer was to replace the Portuguese company Ultramarina.

Trade and Industry

Since independence the Government has been actively pursuing a policy of small-scale industrialization to compensate for the almost total lack of manufacturing capacity. It adopted a comprehensive programme of state control, and in late 1976 acquired 80% of the capital of a Portuguese company, **Ultramarina,** a large firm specializing in a wide range of trading activities, including ship-repairing and agricultural processing. The Government also holds a major interest in the **CICER** brewery and has created a joint-venture company with the Portuguese concern **SACOR** to sell petroleum products. Since 1975 three fishing companies have been formed with foreign participation: **GUIALP** (with Algeria), **Estrela do Mar** (with the former USSR) and **SEMAPESCA** (with France). In December 1976 **SOCOTRAM,** an enterprise for the sale and processing of timber, was inaugurated. It operates a factory in Bissau for the production of wooden tiles and co-ordinates sawmills and carpentry shops throughout the country. In 1979 the **Empresa de Automóveis da Guiné** opened a car-assembly plant at Bissau, capable of producing 500 vehicles per year. A plan to restructure several public enterprises was being implemented in the early 1990s, as part of the Government's programme to attract private investment.

Empresa Nacional de Pesquisas e Exploração Petrolíferas e Mineiras (PETROMINAS): Rua Eduardo Mondlane 58, Bissau; tel. 212279; state-owned; regulates all prospecting for hydrocarbons and other minerals; Dir-Gen. António Cardoso.

CHAMBER OF COMMERCE

Associação Comercial, Industrial e Agrícola da Guiné-Bissau: Bissau; f. 1987.

TRADE UNION

União Nacional dos Trabalhadores de Guiné (UNTG): 13 Avda Ovai di Vievra, CP 98, Bissau; tel. 212094; telex 900; Sec.-Gen. Mário Mendes Correa.

Legislation permitting the formation of other trade unions was approved by the National People's Assembly in October 1991.

Transport

RAILWAYS

There are no railways in Guinea-Bissau.

ROADS

In 1991, according to UN estimates, there were about 4,150 km of roads, of which 360 km were paved. A major road rehabilitation scheme is proceeding, and in 1989 donors provided US $31.3m. for road projects. An international road, linking Guinea-Bissau with The Gambia and Senegal, is planned. In 1989 the Islamic Development Bank granted more than US $2m. towards the construction of a 111-km road linking north and south and a 206-km road between Guinea-Bissau and Guinea. A five-year rehabilitation project, funded by international donors, was due to begin in 1990. The programme included repair work on roads, the management and supply of equipment to transport companies, and town planning.

SHIPPING

Under a major port modernization project, the main port at Bissau was to be renovated and expanded, and four river ports were to be upgraded to enable barges to load and unload at low tide. The total cost of the project was estimated at US $47.4m., and finance was provided by the World Bank and Arab funds. In 1986 work began on a new river port at N'Pungda, which was to be partly funded by the Netherlands.

Empresa Nacional de Agências e Transportes Marítimos (Guinémar): Sociedade de Agências e Transportes da Guiné Lda, Rua Guerra Mendes, 4-4A, CP 244, Bissau; tel. 212675; telex 240; nationalized 1976; shipping agents and brokers; Gen. Man. Marcos T. Lopes; Asst Gen. Man. Noël Correia.

CIVIL AVIATION

There is an international airport at Bissalanca, which there are plans to expand, and 10 smaller airports serving the interior.

Transportes Aéreos da Guiné-Bissau (TAGB): Aeroporto Osvaldo Vieira, CP 111, Bissau; tel. 245802; telex 268; f. 1977; domestic services and flights to France, Portugal, the Canary Islands (Spain), Guinea and Senegal; Dir Capt. Eduardo Pinto Lopes.

Tourism

Centro de Informação e Turismo: CP 294, Bissau; state tourism and information service.

Defence

In June 1993 the armed forces totalled 9,200 men: army 6,800, navy 300, air force 100, and the paramilitary gendarmerie 2,000.

Defence Expenditure: Estimated at 8,027m. Guinea pesos in 1989.

Commander-in-Chief of the Armed Forces: Commdr João Bernardo Vieira.

Education

Education is officially compulsory only for the period of primary schooling, which begins at seven years of age and lasts for six years. Secondary education, beginning at the age of 13, lasts for up to five years (a first cycle of three years and a second of two years). In 1988 the total enrolment at primary and secondary schools was equivalent to 38% of the school-age population (males

49%; females 27%). In that year enrolment at primary schools of children in the relevant age-group was equivalent to 60% (males 77%; females 42%). The comparable figures for secondary schools was 7% (males 9%; females 4%). Expenditure on education by the central government in 1989 was 5,051m. pesos (2.7% of total spending). In 1988 the IDA approved a credit of US $4.3m. for a project to expand the primary education system. Mass literacy campaigns have been introduced: according to UNESCO estimates, the average rate of adult illiteracy in 1980 was 81.1% (males 75.4%; females 86.6%), but by 1990 the rate had declined to 63.5% (males 49.8%; females 76.0%). In 1991 plans were announced for the establishment of the country's first university.

Bibliography

Andreini, J.-C., and Lambert, M.-L. *La Guinée-Bissau.* Paris, 1978.

Cabral, A. *Unity and Struggle* (collected writings) (trans. by M. Wolfers). London, Heinemann Educational, 1979.

Cabral, L. *Crónica da Libertação.* Lisbon, O Jornal, 1984.

Chabal, P. *Amílcar Cabral—Revolutionary Leadership and People's War.* Cambridge, Cambridge University Press, 1983.

Chaliand, G. *Lutte armée en Afrique.* Paris, Maspero, 1967. As *Armed Struggle in Africa.* New York and London, Monthly Review Press, 1969.

Guinée 'portugaise' et Cap-Vert en Lutte pour leur Indépendance. Paris, Maspero, 1964.

Davidson, B. *The Liberation of Guiné.* Harmondsworth, Penguin Books, 1969.

No Fist is Big Enough to Hide the Sky: The Liberation of Guinea-Bissau and Cape Verde. 2nd Edn, London, Zed Press, 1984.

Fisas Armengol, V. *Amílcar Cabral y la Independencia de Guinea-Bissau.* Barcelona, Nova Terra, 1974.

Freire, P. *Pedagogy in Progress: Letters to Guinea-Bissau.* London, W. & R. Publ. Co-operative, 1978.

Galli, R., and Jones, D. *Guinea-Bissau: Politics, Economics and Society.* New York and London, Pinter Publishers, 1987.

Lobban, R. *Historical Dictionary of the Republics of Guinea-Bissau and Cape Verde.* Folkestone, Kent, Bailey Bros and Swinfen, 1981.

Lopes, C. *Guinea-Bissau: From Liberation Struggle to Independent Statehood.* Boulder, CO, Westview Press, 1987.

Mettas, J. *La Guinée portugaise au vingtième siècle.* Paris, Académie des Sciences d'Outre-mer.

da Mota Teixeira, A. *Guiné Portuguesa.* 2 vols. Lisbon, 1964.

Paulini, T. *Guinea-Bissau, Nachkoloniale Entwicklung eines Agrarstaates.* Göttingen, 1984.

Pereira, L. T., and Moita, L. *Guiné-Bissau: Três Anos de Independencia.* Lisbon, CIDAC, 1976.

Rimmer, D. *The Economies of West Africa.* London, Weidenfeld and Nicolson, 1984.

Rudebeck, L. *Guinea-Bissau.* Uppsala, 1974.

Problèmes de pouvoir populaire et de développement. Uppsala, Scandinavian Institute of African Studies, Research Report 63.

Urdang, S. *Fighting Two Colonialisms.* London, Monthly Review Press, 1979.

World Bank. *Guinea-Bissau: A Prescription for Comprehensive Adjustment.* Washington DC, 1988.

KENYA

Physical and Social Geography

W. T. W. MORGAN

PHYSICAL FEATURES

The total area of the Republic of Kenya is 580,367 sq km (224,081 sq miles) or 569,137 sq km (219,745 sq miles) excluding inland waters (mostly Lake Turkana and part of Lake Victoria). Kenya is bisected by the Equator and extends from approximately 4°N to 4°S and 34°E to 41°E.

The physical basis of the country is of extensive erosional plains, cut across ancient crystalline rocks of Pre-Cambrian age. These are very gently warped—giving an imperceptible rise from sea level towards the highlands of the interior which have their base at about 1,500 m. above sea-level.

The height of the Kenya highlands has been greatly augmented by outpourings of Tertiary lavas, giving plateaux at 2,500–3,000 m and with isolated extinct volcanoes yet higher: Mt Kenya (5,199 m) and Mt Elgon (4,321 m). The Great Rift Valley bisects the country from north to south and is at its most spectacular in the highlands, where it is some 65 km across and bounded by escarpments 600–900 m high. The trough is dotted with lakes and volcanoes which are inactive but generally associated with steam vents and hot springs. Westward the plains incline beneath the waters of Lake Victoria, and eastwards they have been down-warped beneath a sediment-filled basin, which is attracting exploration for petroleum.

CLIMATE

Although Kenya is on the Equator, its range of altitude results in temperate conditions in the highlands above 1,500 m, with temperatures which become limiting to cultivation at about 2,750 m, while Mt Kenya supports small glaciers. Average temperatures may be roughly calculated by taking a sea-level mean of 26°C and deducting 1.7°C for each 300 m of altitude. For most of the country, however, rainfall is more critical than temperature. Only 15% of the area of Kenya can be expected to receive a reliable rainfall adequate for cultivation (750 mm in four years out of five). Rainfall is greatest at the coast and in the west of the country, near Lake Victoria and in the highlands, but the extensive plains below 1,200 m are arid or semi-arid. In the region of Lake Victoria and in the highlands west of the Rift Valley, rain falls in one long rainy season. East of the Rift Valley there are two distinct seasons: the long rains (March–May) and the short rains (September–October).

NATURAL RESOURCES

The high rainfall areas tend to be intensively cultivated on a small-scale semi-subsistence basis with varying amounts of cash cropping. Food crops are in great variety, but most important and widespread are maize, sorghum, cassava and bananas. The principal cash crops, which provide the majority of exports, are tea, coffee (*arabica*), pyrethrum and sisal. The first three are particularly suited to the highlands and their introduction was associated with the large-scale farming on the alienated lands of the former 'White Highlands'. The herds of cattle, goats, sheep and camels of the dry plains are as yet of little commercial value and support a low density of mainly subsistence farmers.

Forests are largely restricted to the rainy upper levels of the highlands, where the limited output possible from the natural forests led to the introduction of plantations of conifers and of wattle. Fisheries are of local importance around Lake Victoria and are of great potential at Lake Turkana.

Soda ash is mined at Lake Magadi in the Rift Valley. Deposits of fluorspar, rubies, gold, salt, vermiculite and limestone are also exploited. However, mineral resources make a negligible contribution to Kenya's economy.

POPULATION AND CULTURE

A total population of 10,942,705 was recorded at the census of August 1969. At the August 1979 census the figure had risen to 15,327,061, excluding estimated underenumeration of 5%. The provisional results of the August 1989 census indicated a total population of 21,443,636. The resultant overall density of 36.7 per sq km is extremely unevenly distributed, with approximately 75% of the population contained in only 10% of the area; densities approach 400 per sq km on the small proportion of the land that is cultivable. With such pressure on cultivable land, the high rate of population increase (an annual average of 3.6% during the 1980s) is causing concern, although the rate of increase has declined since 1989. About 15% of the population live in urban areas, and most of these are in Nairobi (population provisionally estimated to be 1,346,000 at the 1989 census) and Mombasa (provisionally estimated to be 465,000 at the 1989 census). The towns also contain the majority of the non-African minorities of some 89,185 Asians, 34,560 Europeans and 41,595 Arabs (1989 census).

Kenya has been a point of convergence of major population movements in the past, and, on a linguistic and cultural basis, the people have been divided into Bantu, Nilotic, Nilo-Hamitic (Paranilotic) and Cushitic groups. Persian and Arab influence at the coast is reflected in the Islamic culture. Kiswahili is the official language, although English, Kikuyu and Luo are widely understood.

Recent History

RICHARD WALKER

Revised for this edition by ALAN RAKE

COLONIAL RULE TO THE KENYATTA ERA, 1895–1978

Kenya, formerly known as British East Africa, was declared a British protectorate in 1895, primarily to secure a route to Uganda. By 1902 the government was encouraging white settlement in the central highlands. Although by 1914 there were no more than 1,000 European land-holders, significant African armed resistance had arisen. In 1907 a legislative council was established, comprising mainly European settlers. By the early 1920s some African political activity had begun to be organized, particularly among the Kikuyu in the capital, Nairobi, and among the Luo. Local native councils were introduced in 1925. By the 1940s the white settler farmers had achieved considerable prosperity, but agriculture in the African lands could not sustain the rapidly-increasing population, and many migrated to the towns in search of work.

In 1944 the Kenya African Union (KAU), an African nationalist organization, was formed, demanding African access to white-owned land. The movement comprised the educated elite of several tribes, and commanded little popular support, except among the Kikuyu. In 1947 Jomo Kenyatta (a Kikuyu and previously the KAU's representative in the United Kingdom) became president of the organization. In 1952 a campaign of terrorism was initiated by the Mau Mau, a predominantly Kikuyu secret society. A state of emergency was declared by the British authorities in October. The disturbances took the form of a Kikuyu civil war, as well as a challenge to colonial authority: by 1956, when the terrorist campaign ceased, 32 European civilians had been killed, but the number of Africans who died totalled about 13,000. In June 1953 Kenyatta was imprisoned for alleged involvement in Mau Mau activities, and the KAU was banned. All political activity was proscribed until 1955. During the period of this ban two Luo political activists, Tom Mboya and Oginga Odinga, came to prominence. In 1957 African members were elected to the legislative council, on a limited franchise (covering 60% of the adult African population). Mboya was the unofficial leader of these members, who refused to accept government posts and demanded a universal adult franchise.

The state of emergency was revoked in January 1960. A transitional constitution, drafted in January and February of that year, allowed Africans a large majority in the legislative council, and legalized political parties. African members of the council subsequently formed the Kenya African National Union (KANU). James Gichuru, a former president of the KAU, was elected acting president of KANU, and Mboya and Odinga were also elected to the party's leadership.

At a general election in 1961 KANU candidates won a majority of seats in the legislative council, but refused to form an administration before the release of Kenyatta. A coalition government was formed under Ronald Ngala. Following his release in August 1961, Kenyatta assumed the presidency of KANU. KANU won a decisive victory in the general election of May 1963, and Kenyatta became prime minister in June, when internal self-government began. Kenya became independent on 12 December. The country was declared a republic (with Kenyatta as president) exactly one year later. After independence Kenya remained dependent on the United Kingdom for military assistance and for financial aid to compensate European settlers for their land.

By 1965 there was a clear division within KANU, between the party's 'conservative' wing, led by Tom Mboya, and the 'radicals', led by Oginga Odinga, who was the country's vice-president until his resignation in April 1966. In 1966 Odinga formed a new party, the Kenya People's Union (KPU), which accused the government of furthering the interests of a small privileged class. Legislation requiring the 30 KPU members of the house of representatives to contest by-elections was immediately approved: only nine KPU members were re-elected. Security legislation was also enacted, giving the government powers of censorship and the right to hold suspects in detention without trial. In December Kenya's two legislative chambers, the senate and the house of representatives, were amalgamated to form a unicameral national assembly. Daniel arap Moi, the minister of home affairs, became vice-president in January 1967.

In July 1969 Tom Mboya (then minister for economic planning and secretary-general of KANU) was assassinated by a Kikuyu. Luo demonstrations against Kenyatta followed, and in the same week the KPU was banned and Odinga was placed in detention, where he remained for 15 months. At a general election in December, in which only KANU members took part, two-thirds of the members of the previous national assembly lost their seats.

During the early 1970s President Kenyatta became increasingly reclusive and autocratic, although he was elected, unopposed, for a third five-year term in September 1974. At a general election in October (in which, once again, only KANU members were presented as candidates), more than one-half of the members of the previous assembly were defeated. President Kenyatta died in August 1978.

THE MOI PRESIDENCY

Programme of Reform

With the support of Charles Njonjo, the attorney-general and an influential associate of the elderly Kenyatta, the presidency passed to Daniel arap Moi, the vice-president, in October 1978. A programme to purge Kenya's corrupt bureaucracy was initiated, and in December all political detainees were released, provoking the first pro-government student demonstrations since independence. President Moi, a Kalenjin, emphasized regional representation in the new style of government, devising new authorities to stimulate regional development. In the general election of November 1979, however, Odinga and four other former KPU members were barred from standing. The election was fiercely contested—by up to 12 candidates in some constituencies—and substantially revitalized the political scene. The new cabinet, in which Moi took the defence portfolio, included a pro-Western minister of foreign affairs, Dr Robert Ouko, whose appointment reflected the trend towards a closer relationship with the USA. This was confirmed when a US military delegation visited Kenya to negotiate the use of Kenyan military facilities by US forces. The election also marked the end of the president's period of grace: student protest began, with predominantly Luo participation, prompted by the KPU bannings. This period also saw the systematic strengthening of Kenya's armed forces.

In April 1980 Njonjo resigned as attorney-general, and in June he was elected at a by-election to the national assembly, later becoming minister of home and constitutional affairs. A 'de-tribalization' drive commenced in mid-1980, whereby virtually every Kenyan organization title which had a tribal implication was renamed.

Parliamentary criticism of President Moi's government intensified during 1980. Moi initiated an attempt to bring Odinga and his substantial following back into KANU, and Odinga was finally granted life membership of the party. Although KANU rejected his candidature for a by-election held in April, Odinga continued to attack the US military presence in Kenya, and to denounce the 'systematic plunder' of national resources, and resultant mass unemployment.

During 1981 there were intense factional disputes betweem supporters of one or other of the president's two lieutenants, as disagreements between Mwai Kibaki, the vice-president, and Njonjo became unbridgeable. The issue was resolved by the cabinet reshuffle of February 1982, when Njonjo lost the home affairs portfolio to Kibaki. During this period, Moi appeared to be growing increasingly intolerant of criticism: Odinga and another former MP were expelled from KANU for advocating the formation of a new party. In June Kenya constitutionally became a one-party state.

Coup Attempt

In August 1982 a section of the Kenya air force attempted to overthrow the government. The revolt (which was supported by a number of university students) was swiftly crushed by the army, although sporadic firefights and looting continued for several days. The instigators of the revolt (who cited corruption and the restriction of freedom as the causes of the insurrection) escaped to Tanzania, but were subsequently deported to Kenya and sentenced to death. The official death toll of the day's fighting was given as 159, but unofficial sources asserted that the true total was much higher.

Following the coup attempt, about 2,000 air force personnel and 1,000 civilians were detained; the air force was disbanded, and the university was closed. The commander of the air force, the commissioner of police and the commandant of the General Service Unit, an élite military force, were dismissed and detained. By March 1983 the government had sufficiently recovered from the political paralysis which followed the revolt to suspend the courts martial which had sentenced 12 airmen to death, and an amnesty was granted to most of the remaining detainees. The considerable degree of Luo involvement in the coup attempt also had political repercussions: Odinga was placed under house arrest (from which he was freed in October 1983), and the Luo information minister, Peter Aringo, was dismissed. Conciliatory moves, aimed at some of the sources of political unrest, included a new code of conduct for politicians in office, and an investigation of the civil service.

The 'Njonjo Affair'

The country was distracted from the persistent mood of political uncertainty by the spectacular fall from power of Charles Njonjo. In May 1983 Moi alleged that certain unspecified foreign powers were grooming an unnamed Kenyan politician to take over as president. Moi then announced that a general election would be held in September—a year earlier than constitutionally required—in order to 'cleanse the system' of any corruption. After Njonjo's name was mentioned in the national assembly in connection with the allegation, there followed a storm of accusation and invective against him. Denying all charges, Njonjo was suspended from the cabinet and from KANU, and in June he resigned his seat in the assembly, while the president appointed a judicial commission to inquire into the 'Njonjo affair'. Meanwhile, the September election which returned Moi unopposed for a second term as president attracted only 48% of the electorate. A major cabinet reshuffle followed the election. The Njonjo inquiry commission began its work in October 1983 and was eventually closed in August 1984, when Njonjo withdrew from public life (when the report finally appeared, he was pardoned but not rehabilitated). The immediate aftermath of the inquiry was a purge of figures associated with the Njonjo faction. By October, however, the Njonjo affair appeared to be effectively closed.

Moi's Authority Reasserted

While intensive press coverage of the Njonjo inquiry had been absorbing public attention, there were indications that the coup attempt had persuaded the Moi government of the need to respond more flexibly to opposition. The problem of student opposition was approached on several fronts. A programme of national youth service, originally announced soon after Moi's accession but then indefinitely postponed, was finally introduced in 1984. During that year, a controversial restructuring of the education syllabus was also introduced, placing renewed emphasis on technical and vocational studies. During 1984, after the education minister had advocated 'dialogue' between students and government, there were unprecedented meetings between student leaders and President Moi at Nairobi university. In February 1985, however, renewed clashes between students and the police left one student dead and 65 injured. The university was then closed and re-opened in April 1985 but, following further student unrest, was again closed from March until May 1986.

During the progress of the Njonjo inquiry, there were also signs that President Moi intended henceforth to control his government within certain firm limits, although against a background of freer public debate than had been possible before the attempted coup. Presidential authority over the parliamentary front bench was reaffirmed when cabinet ministers (over 40% of members of the assembly) were required to endorse a letter from the president, stating that they were not at liberty to criticize, or differ from, the government outside immediate government circles. Some conciliation was offered to the political left-wing with a presidential amnesty for fugitives abroad.

After dismissals, in late 1984, of prominent civil servants for abuse of office, rationalizations of major parastatal organizations, and a minor cabinet reshuffle in January 1985 (followed by a reshuffle of appointments in the provincial administration), political life in early 1985 was dominated by a recruitment drive to revitalize the membership of KANU as a prelude to local and national KANU elections, held in June. By the end of 1985 a considerable revitalization of the party had taken place, consolidating Moi's pre-eminent position. During February 1986, however, there were indications of lingering political discontent, including a series of unprecedented verbal attacks on the vice-president, Mwai Kibaki, by members of the national assembly.

The 'Mwakenya Conspiracy'

In March 1986 it was revealed that several Kenyans had been detained under the provisions of the Public Security Act, and that others were to face charges of publishing seditious documents: during the ensuing 12 months, a 'conspiracy' known as 'Mwakenya' (a Swahili acronym for the Union of Nationalists to Liberate Kenya) became the focal point of Kenyan politics. Although President Moi alleged that 'Mwakenya' comprised the same 'tribalistic élite' that had fostered the 1982 coup attempt, it became apparent that 'Mwakenya' embraced a wide spectrum of opposition to the Moi presidency.

In August 1986 the annual KANU party conference approved a new open 'queue-voting' system, to replace the secret ballot, in the candidate selection stage of the general election scheduled for early 1988. This new system, whereby voters were to queue publicly in support of the candidate of their choice, was opposed by the National Council of Churches of Kenya on the grounds that it would discourage voting by church ministers, civil servants and others whose political impartiality was necessary for their work. In December the national assembly adopted constitutional amendments which increased the power of the president by transferring control of the civil service to the president's office, and reduced the independence of the judiciary by giving the president the power to dismiss the attorney-general and the auditor-general without endorsement by a legal tribunal. No votes were cast in opposition to the amendments, but two MPs who had openly questioned the virtue of the changes were briefly detained in January 1987. By early 1987, more than 100 people had been detained in connection with 'Mwakenya', some of them receiving lengthy terms of imprisonment, and the political climate had become reminiscent of the months preceding the 1982 coup attempt. In April 1987 Oginga Odinga, still the most prestigious opponent of the government, made an unprecedented public declaration of opposition to Moi's political management; the government, opting for caution, took no action against Odinga, who repeated his criticism of the Moi administration in July and August. The administration did, however, make allegations of involvement with 'Mwakenya' against several influential church leaders. The government's uncompromising response to opposition suggested that Moi was thoroughly aware that he was confronted by the most serious challenge yet to his authority. In March 1988 Mwakenya distributed a statement accusing the authorities of corruption and electoral malpractice in the first stage of the general election held in February 1988.

Although the government may have over-reacted in its anxieties about 'Mwakenya', the movement none the less represented genuine undercurrents of discontent. Its followers comprised an amorphous affiliation of opposition elements, including Kikuyu peasants, urban intellectuals (often, but not exclusively, Luo), and elements of the established political network. Most threatening for the government was the fact that 'Mwakenya' was apparently confined to no particular region.

Political Retrenchment

From early 1987, international criticism of President Moi's government was intensified, as further allegations emerged of human rights abuses in Kenya. The government's response to this criticism reflected, for the most part, its continuing hostility both to external pressure and internal opposition. In April, however, Moi ordered the dismissal of members of the police force found to be guilty of corruption, criminal activity or brutality, and two months later the minister of foreign affairs was replaced, reportedly on the grounds that he was failing effectively to defend Kenya's record on human rights. In July Amnesty International published a report which accused the Kenyan authorities of seeking to silence political opposition by detention without trial and by torture.

In October and November 1987 serious rioting broke out among Muslims in Mombasa, following a government ban on an Islamic public meeting. The government's fear of destabilization by foreign powers was reflected in the detention, in November, of seven student leaders, one of whom was imprisoned for allegedly spying on behalf of Libya. These arrests led to mass student demonstrations during December; clashes between students and riot police resulted, to the dismay of the government, in the temporary detention and alleged mistreatment of four Western journalists. Nairobi university was then closed, and its student organization banned.

In early 1988 the government made some minor concessions to international criticism of its conduct towards its opponents. In January the president demoted Justus Ole Tipis, the minister of state for security, following a controversy over the brief detention of two US human rights activists who were allegedly in possession of 'subversive' documents, and in February the president ordered the release of nine political detainees, several of whom later claimed that they had been tortured while in custody.

A general election to the national assembly, held in March 1988, provided only limited indication of Moi's popularity. Prior to the parliamentary polling, the president was returned unopposed for a third term of office. The open-air 'queue-voting' technique of candidate selection, conducted in February, produced a KANU-approved list to contest 123 of the 188 elective seats (65 candidates, including the president, were returned unopposed). Potential candidates who were unpopular with the Moi administration (such as Oginga Odinga) were excluded from seeking election, and seats were largely contested on local and personality issues rather than on national policies. In an extensive government reshuffle following the election, the vice-president, Mwai Kibaki, was demoted to the post of minister of health (it was widely believed that the president was disquieted by Kibaki's popularity among the Kikuyu), and replaced by Josephat Karanja, a relatively obscure politician with no popular following.

The independence of the judiciary from the executive was effectively removed in July 1988, when the national assembly assented to constitutional amendments which allowed the president to dismiss judges at will, and which increased the period of detention, from 24 hours to 14 days, of people suspected of capital offences. These measures led to an intensification of criticism of the government's record on human rights, especially from church leaders and lawyers. President Moi subsequently accused foreigners of acting in concert with Kenyan church leaders against the government, and he therefore proposed the arrest of 'roaming' foreigners and threatened to curtail freedom of worship.

Elections to the leadership of KANU were held in September 1988; Moi was confirmed as president of the party, and Kibaki was replaced by Karanja as party vice-president. Allegations of malpractice in the KANU elections were made by Kibaki, among others, and in December Kenneth Matiba, the minister of transport and communications, resigned and was expelled from KANU after criticizing the conduct of party elections.

Karanja's period of influence was short-lived: in February 1989 he became the subject of a campaign of vilification by fellow MPs, which culminated, in late April, in a unanimous parliamentary vote expressing 'no confidence' in him. He was widely accused of attempting to establish himself as a rival to President Moi and of pursuing tribal interests. In addition, he encountered allegations from some quarters of conspiring with the Ugandan government to destabilize Kenya. At the beginning of May, Karanja, who had denied the charges against him, resigned from the posts of Kenyan vice-president and vice-president of KANU. Moi appointed Prof. George Saitoti, the minister of finance, as the country's new vice-president and announced a major cabinet reshuffle. Shortly afterwards, Karanja resigned from the national assembly, and in mid-June he was expelled from KANU.

In early June 1989 President Moi, who was clearly sensitive to continuing international criticism of his human rights record, released all political prisoners who were being detained without trial, and offered an amnesty to dissidents living in exile. While this action was applauded by Amnesty International, that organization repeated allegations that many convicted Kenyan political prisoners had received unfair trials. In early November part of Nairobi university was closed, owing to student unrest.

In February 1990, the minister of foreign affairs and international co-operation, Dr Robert Ouko, died in circumstances suggesting that he had been murdered. Accusations that the government was implicated in Ouko's death led to anti-government riots in Nairobi and the western town of Kisumu, following the minister's funeral. The government responded by banning all demonstrations from the beginning of March, and requested an investigation by British police into Dr Ouko's death (the results of this were presented to the Kenyan authorities in September 1990, and in October President Moi ordered a judicial inquiry into the affair). In April the minister of information and broadcasting, Waruru Kanja, was dismissed, following allegations on his part that Ouko's death was politically motivated. Pressure on the government to terminate KANU's political monopoly increased in May with the formation of a broad alliance of intellectuals, lawyers and church leaders (under the leadership of the former cabinet minister, Kenneth Matiba) which sought to legalize political opposition. In early July Moi ordered the arrests of several of the alliance's leaders, including Matiba and Raila Odinga, the son of the former vice-president. Serious rioting ensued in Nairobi and its environs, and sporadic disorders were reported in the hinterland of the Kikuyu-dominated Central province; more than 20 people were killed in the disturbances, and more than 1,000 rioters were reportedly arrested. The KANU leadership responded to international criticism by denouncing the advocates of multi-party political reform as 'tribalists' in the pay of 'foreign masters', seeking to undermine Kenyan unity. Moi accused the US government of interfering in the country's internal politics after one of the dissident leaders was granted refuge in the US embassy in Nairobi. In mid-August a prominent Anglican bishop, who had publicly criticized the government, died in a car crash, following threats to his life from members of the cabinet; the most senior of these, Peter Okondo, the minister of labour, subsequently resigned his post. The government ordered a public inquest into the bishop's death. In November Amnesty International reported that several hundreds of people detained at the time of the July riots remained in custody, and accused the Kenyan authorities of torturing some prisoners. During late 1990 seven people were arrested and charged with treason.

In early December 1990, having considered the findings of a political review committee, which had tested public opinion in mid-1990, KANU abolished the system of 'queue-voting' which had been approved by the party in 1986, and resolved to cease expulsions of party members. In January 1991 KANU agreed to readmit to the party a number of people who had previously been expelled. In the following month Oginga Odinga founded the National Democratic Party (NDP) and was subsequently harrassed by the Kenyan authorities: he was arrested briefly in May, shortly before the court of appeal rejected his application to register the NDP as a political party.

In March 1991 a prominent human rights lawyer and magazine editor was arrested and charged with sedition, having accused President Moi of promoting the interests of his native Kalenjin tribe, and having published the manifesto of the banned NDP. The charge was withdrawn in May, following widespread exposure of the case in the international media. In that month President Moi reiterated his offer of an amnesty for dissident Kenyans in exile abroad. In early June the government announced the release from imprisonment of Kenneth Matiba, who was reportedly suffering from ill health. During that month several religious leaders and lawyers formed a body, known as the Justice and Peace Convention, which aimed to promote freedom of political expression. In July four of those arrested during the unrest of July 1990 were found guilty of sedition and each sentenced to seven years' imprisonment. In late July 1991 the human rights organization, Africa Watch, published allegations that the government was permitting the torture of detainees and exerting undue influence on the judiciary. At the beginning of August six opposition leaders, including Oginga Odinga, formed a new political movement, the Forum for the Restoration of Democracy (FORD); the government immediately outlawed the grouping, but it continued to operate.

In late September 1991 the judicial inquiry into the death (in February 1990) of Dr Robert Ouko was presented with evidence that Dr Ouko had been murdered. In mid-November 1991 President Moi dismissed Nicholas Biwott from the post of minister of industry, in response to widespread suspicion that Biwott was implicated in the alleged assassination of Dr Ouko. Later in the same month, Biwott and a former chief of state security were arrested in connection with the case. However, the two suspects were released in early December, owing to a lack of evidence against them. Meanwhile, President Moi ordered the dissolution of the judicial inquiry. It was announced in May 1992 that a former civil servant was to stand trial for the murder of Dr Ouko.

In mid-November 1991 several members of FORD were arrested prior to a planned pro-democracy rally in Nairobi; protestors at the rally (which took place despite a government ban) were dispersed by the security forces. The Kenyan authorities were condemned internationally for suppressing the demonstration, and most of the opposition figures who had been detained were subsequently released. In late November bilateral and multilateral creditors suspended aid to Kenya for 1992, pending the acceleration of both economic and political reforms; the donors emphasized, in particular, the desirability of an improvement in Kenya's human rights record.

Political Pluralism and Ethnic Tensions

In early December 1991 a special conference of KANU delegates, chaired by President Moi, acceded to the domestic and international pressure for reform, and resolved to permit the introduction of a multi-party political system. Soon afterwards the national assembly approved appropriate amendments to the constitution. It was announced that presidential and legislative elections would take place, in the context of a multi-party political system, by March 1993. Several new political parties were registered in early 1992.

In mid-December 1991 President Moi dismissed the minister of manpower development and employment, Peter Aringo, who had publicly criticized the government; Aringo subsequently resigned as chairman of KANU. Later in December Mwai Kibaki, the minister of health and a former vice-president, resigned from the government, in protest against alleged electoral malpractice by KANU and against the unsatisfactory outcome of the judicial inquiry into the death of Dr Ouko. Kibaki immediately founded the Democratic Party. Five other ministers and deputy ministers resigned their posts in December 1991 and January 1992.

In mid-January 1992 several members of the newly-legalized FORD were charged with having spread malicious rumours, following claims by that party that a military coup, which would eliminate the democracy movement, was being plotted. In early March the security forces used violent methods to suppress a hunger strike in Nairobi by women who were demanding the release of political prisoners.

During the first half of 1992 as many as 2,000 people were reportedly killed and some 20,000 made homeless as a result of tribal clashes in western Kenya. Opposition leaders accused the government of covertly inciting the violence as a means of discrediting the progress towards a multi-party political system, while the government countered that the exacerbation of existing ethnic tensions was an inevitable result of the new political freedoms. In mid-March the government banned all political rallies, purportedly in a bid to suppress the unrest. In late March restrictions were placed on the activities of the press. A two-day general strike, organized by FORD to demand the release of political prisoners and the removal of the ban on political rallies, was held in early April: the government acceded to the latter demand shortly afterwards.

In mid-May 1992 some 34 members of the opposition were arrested, following the publication in the national media of unsubstantiated allegations that elements within the government were plotting to assassinate government opponents. Later in that month the security forces suppressed a pro-Islamic demonstration in Mombasa, killing two people. The period of voter registration for the forthcoming elections commenced in early June; this was initially boycotted by opposition parties, who iterated a number of demands, including the establishment of an independent commission to supervise the electoral process and an amnesty for political prisoners and exiles. At the beginning of July, however, the boycott was abandoned. In mid-June KANU published draft legislation restricting the president to no more than two terms of office and stipulating that the successful presidential candidate must receive at least one-quarter of all votes cast in at least five of the country's eight provinces: this measure was to encourage political participation along national rather than ethnic lines.

From mid-1992 FORD was weakened by mounting internal divisions; in August the organization split into two opposing factions, and in October these were registered as separate political parties, FORD—Asili and FORD—Kenya, respectively led by Kenneth Matiba and Oginga Odinga.

In early November 1992 President Moi announced that the elections would take place in early December; soon afterwards, however, they were rescheduled to late December, owing to a ruling by the high court that the opposition parties required more time to nominate candidates. At the presidential election Moi was re-elected, winning 36.35% of the votes, ahead of Kenneth Matiba (26.00%), Mwai Kibaki (19.45%) and Oginga Odinga (17.48%). Of the 188 elective seats in the national assembly, KANU won 100 (including 16 which were not contested), FORD—Asili and FORD—Kenya secured 31 each, the DP took 23, and the remaining seats were divided between the Kenya Social Congress, the Kenya National Congress and an independent candidate. Some 15 former cabinet ministers lost their seats. Votes were cast predominantly in accordance with ethnic affiliations, with the two largest tribes, the Kikuyu and Luo, overwhelmingly rejecting KANU. The leaders of FORD—Asili, FORD—Kenya and the DP initially launched a campaign to have the results declared invalid, alleging that gross electoral irregularities had taken place. In mid-January 1993, however, a Commonwealth monitoring group stated that the outcome of the elections reflected 'the will of the people' despite accusing the government of corruption, intimidation and incompetence. Soon afterwards opposition parties announced that they were to contest the results in 31 seats in the national assembly and that they were preparing challenges regarding a further 30 seats.

In early January 1993 Moi was sworn in for a further five-year term as president. An extensive reshuffle of cabinet posts was implemented in mid-January. In February the government impounded copies of three opposition publications which allegedly contained seditious material. In early April four opposition members, including Raila Odinga, were arrested and charged with participating in an illegal demonstration. In mid-April the World Bank agreed to release foreign aid which had been suspended since November 1991. At the beginning of May 1993 a general strike was called by the Central Organization of Trade Unions (COTU) to demand wage increases and the dismissal of the vice-president and minister of planning and national development, Prof. George Saitoti; the former demand was partially acceded to. COTU's secretary-general was arrested and charged with inciting industrial unrest.

In May 1993 Sheikh Khalid Balala, the former leader of the banned Islamic Party of Kenya threatened to declare a 'jihad' against the government and called for the assassination of government ministers. KANU responded by attacking what it termed 'Arab fundamentalists' and Balala was arrested on charges of incitement. In an attempt to counter the support for Balala KANU sponsored a rival Muslim party, the United Muslims of Africa, led by a former KANU politician from Mombasa, Emmanuel Maitha, whose stated objective was to end 'the domination and oppression of indigenous African tribes by rich Arabs'. Behind the ethnic rivalry, however, lay a serious economic conflict centred on local feelings about the purchase of high-value land in tourist coastal areas by 'outsiders'—namely Asians, whites and certain government ministers.

Tribal clashes which occurred in the first half of 1993, described by church organizations as the most serious since independence, were most acute in the Rift Valley and on the borders between land occupied by the Masai and the Kikuyu tribes. In May, during serious riots and clashes with the police in Nakuru, the capital of the Rift Valley province, a number of prominent opposition MPs were arrested. The rapid escalation in violence prompted a group of opposition MPs to call on the UN to intervene. By August 900 people had been killed and 130,000 made homeless; opposition MPs accused the government of fomenting the troubles. Kalenjin leaders from the Rift Valley, meanwhile, warned the Kikuyu not to create conflict whilst themselves alledgedly conniving in the dispossession of Kikuyu farms. Where eviction was successful, title deeds were often then burnt and the land then occupied by Kalenjins. Hundreds of Kikuyu families, some of whom had lived in the Rift Valley since the 1920s, and others who arrived in the 1960s after independence, sought safety in squatter camps and churches.

Foreign observers who toured the Rift Valley in mid-1993 accused the government of failing to contain the fighting and of pursuing a policy of 'ethnic cleansing'. President Moi sealed off part of the Rift Valley in September (in the Molo, Burnt Forest and Londiani areas) ostensibly to prevent further hostilities, although the opposition claimed that his real aim was to suppress criticism of the government. In October some 500 Masai fighters killed a number of Kikuyu who had taken refuge in churches near Narok. Church sources blamed government troops of involvement in the violence. After three attacks on police stations in different parts of the country, at the end of October President Moi accused his opponents of fomenting a civil war and gave the police wide-ranging powers to respond to the spiralling violence. Although most of the raids were by the Kikuyu, one raid on a police base near Nairobi was carried out by Masai. Five prominent Kikuyu who were arrested in connection with the other raids included the human rights activist Kiogi Wa Wamwere who had been released earlier in the year following his arrest on charges of treason.

William ole Ntimama, the minister of local government, openly supported the Masai in their conflict with the Kikuyu and became increasingly active both as a champion of his own Masai people and as a defender of the government position. Critics, however, including 12 Roman Catholic bishops, blamed the government for the tribal conflicts; one human rights organization, Africa Watch, even claimed that the ethnic violence had been deliberately exploited by Moi and his associates in order to undermine the move towards political pluralism. The organization estimated that 1,500 people had been killed and 300,000 displaced since the clashes began.

The conflict and subsequent recriminations in the Rift Valley aggravated the confrontation between the government and the opposition; with the latter beginning to feel marginalized. In July Oginga Odinga was officially designated the leader of the opposition and immediately appointed a 'shadow cabinet' from his FORD–Kenya party. A Luo, and relatively uninvolved in the Rift Valley troubles, Odinga was drawn closer to the government by Moi. However, some of Odinga's leading Kikuyu supporters, including his deputy, Paul Muite, became dissatisfied with the course his leadership was taking; Muite finally resigned when Odinga dismissed his fellow Kikuyu human rights activist Gitobu Imanyara. Many of Odinga's Kikuyu supporters subsequently left FORD–Kenya and joined the rival Kikuyu-dominated FORD–Asili Party; some joined KANU.

In August 1993 Odinga admitted to having accepted a large donation from an Asian businessman who had close connections with the government and of having failed, subsequently, to pay the money into party funds. At the time of his death in late January 1994, the rift between his party and that of Kenneth Matiba's FORD–Asili had widened considerably. A young lawyer and political unknown, Kijana Wamalwa took over the leadership of FORD–Kenya. President Moi used the change in leadership to end the co-operation between KANU and FORD–Kenya which had begun when Odinga was recognized as leader of the opposition in July. After Odinga's death FORD–Kenya acquired a more even ethnic and regional balance and attracted supporters from FORD–Asili, whose influence began to decline.

In early January 1994 Richard Leakey, director of the Kenya Wildlife Service (KWS), resigned after coming under attack from a number of ministers, including Noah Katana Ngala, the minister of tourism. Although Leakey was respected internationally for his efforts at ending the poaching of elephants and for obtaining substantial financial support for the protection of Kenya's game reserves (a vital element in the country's tourism industry), some government ministers complained that he was doing little to protect the people on and around the reserves whose crops were being ravaged by the wildlife. Initially President Moi refused to accept his resignation and instead set up a commission of inquiry which subsequently recommended that three-quarters of all the KWS expenditure should be spent on the people nearest to the game reserves and that the game rangers should be taken away from the KWS and placed under the control of the police. Leakey accepted neither of these recommendations and confirmed his resignation. He was replaced by another white Kenyan, David Western, who managed to retain financial autonomy for the KWS and to ensure that game rangers within the Wildlife Protection Unit remain outside the control of the commissioner of police.

In further outbreaks of violence between the Kikuyu and the Kalenjin in April 1994 which took place in the Burnt Forest area of the Rift Valley a further 20 people were killed and 65 houses (mostly Kikuyu) were destroyed. Moi responded by reimposing a security zone and curfew on the area. Roman Catholic bishops again issued a statement in which they said that the government was fully responsible and that the attacks on the Kikuyus were led by trained men determined to drive out non-Kalenjins. In a show of rare unanimity shortly afterwards opposition leaders accused Moi of deliberately instigating the clashes.

Anonymous bomb threats in April 1994 to the US embassy were widely attributed to government supporters critical of the US stance over tribal violence and the human rights issue in Kenya. In late May the attorney-general, Amos Wako warned the political opposition not to make derogatory remarks about President Moi. In June the main opposition parties, except for FORD–Asili, agreed to unite to form the United Democratic Alliance and to present an agreed list of candidates in future elections.

EXTERNAL RELATIONS

President Moi has resumed presidential direction of foreign affairs: Kenyatta, uniquely in Africa, left the conduct of foreign relations to his ministers of foreign affairs, and never travelled outside the country. Throughout the years of Kenyatta's presidency, Kenya remained unconvinced of the benefits of close integration with its neighbours through the East African Common Services Organization and its successor, the East African Community (EAC). During the early 1970s major political and economic tensions developed between the EAC member states, and by July 1977 the Community had ceased to function. Throughout the period of Idi Amin's regime in Uganda, President Kenyatta maintained an official stance of strict neutrality towards that country, although relations with Tanzania gradually deteriorated to a level of outright hostility by the time of Kenyatta's death in 1978. The collapse in April

1979 of the Amin regime raised hopes of better relations generally in east Africa, but Kenya was deeply suspicious of Tanzania's military role in Uganda. A meeting at Arusha, Tanzania, in January 1980 between President Moi and Presidents Nyerere of Tanzania and Binaisa of Uganda failed to allay these anxieties. The accession of Dr Milton Obote to the presidency of Uganda in December 1980, however, was followed by a sustained improvement in Kenya's relations with both Uganda and Tanzania. In November 1983 the three countries reached agreement on the distribution of the assets and liabilities of the EAC. Shortly afterwards, the border between Kenya and Tanzania (closed in 1977) was reopened, and in December the two countries agreed to establish full diplomatic relations. In 1986 agreement was reached on a trade treaty and on the establishment of a joint co-operation commission.

When the National Resistance Army (NRA) seized power in Uganda in January 1986, Moi accepted the inevitable and offered full co-operation to the new Ugandan president, Yoweri Museveni. However, relations became less cordial as Moi became increasingly distrustful of the radical nature of the new regime in Kampala. Additionally, the Kenyan authorities became anxious that continued unrest in Uganda could provide a source of arms for 'Mwakenya' supporters in Kenya. Tension grew during 1986 over alleged Kenyan interference in freight deliveries to Uganda that were routed through Mombasa, developing into an open dispute over alleged ill-treatment of Ugandans resident in Kenya after a Ugandan national died in Kenyan police custody in early 1987. At least 500 Ugandans were among numbers of foreigners to be detained in March, following a speech made by President Moi, assailing 'illegal aliens' who were allegedly creating unrest in Kenya. In May Uganda lodged further complaints over Kenya's alleged closing of the land frontier at Busia and Malaba. The tension eased somewhat in June, when it appeared that the movement of traffic between the two countries was possible.

The détente however, proved to be short-lived. In September 1987 Uganda claimed that Kenya was harbouring anti-Museveni rebels, and stationed troops at its border with Kenya. These claims were denied, and Moi warned that any infiltration by Ugandan troops in Kenya would encounter fierce retaliation. The influx of some 2,000 Ugandan refugees into Kenya strained relations further. In December Ugandan troops were alleged to have entered Kenya illegally in pursuit of rebels, and for several days the Ugandan and Kenyan armed forces exchanged fire across the border, which was temporarily closed to traffic. The Kenyan government expelled the Ugandan high commissioner and a number of other Ugandan citizens. Later in December, Presidents Moi and Museveni agreed to withdraw troops from either side of the border and to allow the resumption of normal traffic. In January 1988 the two countries signed a joint communiqué which provided for co-operation between them in resolving problems relating to the flow of traffic across the common border. This *rapprochement* was disrupted in July, when the Ugandan government accused Kenya of complicity in smuggling weapons to a rebel group in northern Uganda, and security was tightened along the Kenya–Uganda border to prevent alleged incursions by Ugandan troops. In late October Uganda complained that Kenya had been intermittently obstructing the movement of Ugandan traffic across the border. In March 1989 the Ugandan government strongly denied Kenyan allegations that Ugandan troops had been involved in an attack by Ugandan cattle-rustlers on Kenyan security forces earlier in that month, and that a Ugandan military aircraft had been responsible for the bombing of a town in north-western Kenya shortly afterwards. In February 1991 the Kenyan government accused Uganda of plotting to invade Kenya; the Ugandan government refuted the allegation. In November 1991, however, the presidents of Kenya, Uganda and Tanzania met in Nairobi, and declared their commitment to developing mutual co-operation.

In December 1980 and May 1981 Lt-Col Mengistu Haile Mariam of Ethiopia made state visits to Kenya; the two countries subsequently signed a treaty of friendship and co-operation, and a mutual defence pact. Somalia has traditionally laid claim to part of north-eastern Kenya, where there is a large ethnic Somali population. In mid-1981, however, President Moi held talks with the Somali president, Siad Barre, at which the latter renounced these territorial claims. In July 1984, during a state visit to Somalia by the Kenyan leader, Presidents Moi and Siad Barre pledged to increase bilateral co-operation between their respective countries and discussed arrangements for monitoring the Kenya–Somalia border. In November 1987 ministers from both countries signed a joint communiqué in which they undertook to consolidate existing good relations. In early 1989, however, friction developed between the Kenyan government and ethnic Somalis from both north-eastern Kenya and Somalia, when Somali poachers were alleged to be largely responsible for the rapid depletion of Kenyan elephant numbers in recent years; it was reported that several thousand ethnic Somalis had been ordered to evacuate areas near the game parks. In late 1989 the Kenya government began to scrutinize the status of ethnic Somalis, in order to determine whether they held Somali or Kenyan citizenship. In April 1991, following the overthrow and flight of President Siad Barre in January of that year, the new Somali government accused the Kenyan government of providing assistance to Barre and his supporters, who had taken refuge in Kenya. In March 1994 Kenya provided the venue for talks between rival Somali factions which ended with the signing of a reconciliation accord calling for the establishment of a government of national unity by May of that year. In May 1992 the Kenyan government negotiated permanent asylum for Barre in Nigeria. Relations between Kenya and Libya deteriorated in April 1987, when five Libyan diplomats were expelled for alleged subversive activities. In the following month a Kenyan newspaper published an unsubstantiated report that Libya was training dissidents from Kenya to overthrow the government. In December the government closed the Libyan diplomatic mission in Nairobi. Relations between Kenya and Sudan deteriorated in June 1988, as they exchanged mutual accusations of aiding rebel factions. In early 1989 Sudan renewed a long-standing dispute with Kenya over the sovereignty of territory on the Kenyan side of the Kenya–Sudan border, known as the 'Elemi triangle', which was believed to contain substantial deposits of petroleum. By May 1994, however, relations between the two countries had improved sufficiently for the Sudanese president, Mohammad Omar el-Bashir, to participate in celebrations held in Nairobi to mark the 30th anniversary of the African Development Bank.

By January 1993 Kenya was sheltering about 500,000 refugees, including an estimated 400,000 from Somalia, 80,000 from Ethiopia and 20,000 from Sudan. During that month the Moi Government claimed that the refugees were placing an intolerable burden on the country's resources; the UN, however, refused a request by Kenya to repatriate the total refugee population with immediate effect. Some 44,000 Ethiopian refugees were repatriated by March 1993.

In November 1990 a visit to Kenya by the South African minister of foreign affairs constituted the first direct contact at ministerial level between the Kenyan and South African governments since Kenya became independent. The improvement in relations between the two countries was consolidated when President Frederik de Klerk of South Africa made a state visit to Kenya in June 1991, and when President Moi reciprocated the visit in June 1992.

Since becoming president, Moi has made a number of overseas visits and has taken an active interest in continental affairs. In 1989 he offered his services as mediator between vying forces in Ethiopia and Mozambique, and in 1991 he chaired peace talks between the factions involved in the Somali civil war. An important development in foreign affairs under Moi has been Kenya's support of US military commitments in the Indian Ocean. In mid-1980 Kenya permitted the USA to use port and air base facilities in Kenya, in return for increased US military assistance to Kenya.

In recent years Kenya has received international criticism of its records on human rights, particularly from the USA. Following the violent disruption by Kenyan security forces of a meeting in Kenya between a US congressman and a Kenyan church leader in January 1987 the USA temporarily suspended aid allocations to Kenya. In August the US administration suspended military aid of US $5m. to Kenya, in protest at the Kenyan government's arrest of opposition figures in July of that year; the funds were eventually released in February 1991. In October 1990 Kenya severed diplomatic relations with Norway, following protests by the Norwegian government to Kenya about the arrest on treason charges during that month of a Kenyan dissident who had been exiled in Norway; Norway subsequently suspended aid allocations to Kenya. Diplomatic relations were restored in February 1994 although Norway refused to resume aid to the country. In mid-November 1991, following protests by several overseas governments against arrests by the Kenyan security forces of opposition leaders who had organized a pro-democracy rally (see above), the Kenyan government accused US, German and Swedish diplomats of assisting Kenyan dissidents (allegations which were vigorously denied). In response, Germany withdrew its ambassador for 'consultations'. Later in the same month, following the decision by donor nations and organizations to withhold aid to Kenya (see above), the USA announced that it was suspending assistance worth $28m. Nevertheless, strategic considerations continue to ensure that the informal military alliance between Kenya and the USA will remain intact for the foreseeable future. In May 1994 the USA announced the disbursement of development assistance worth K£23.95m. for agricultural research, rural infrastructure and health care programmes.

Economy

LINDA VAN BUREN

INTRODUCTION

The population of Kenya at the August 1989 census was 21,400,000, producing an average population density of 36.9 per sq km. Much of Kenya's population is concentrated in the south-western highlands, the coastal strip and the lake area. The rate of population increase in 1980–92 was estimated to be 3.6% per annum. In 1985 the country's average annual birth rate, at 5.4%, was the highest in the world; by 1992, however, the rate stood at 3.7%, the sixth lowest in sub-saharan Africa. The rate of infant mortality (64 per 1,000 live births in 1992, compared with 102 per 1,000 in 1970) is the third lowest in continental sub-Saharan Africa.

Agriculture is the main occupation and source of income of the majority of the people, but the service and manufacturing sectors are substantially more important than would normally be expected in a country of Kenya's income level. The disproportionate development of manufacturing, processing and service industries was bound up with the early presence in Kenya of a substantial number of non-African settlers, whose high incomes generated demand.

At independence in 1963, the export-orientated agriculture in Kenya was based upon large-scale commercial agriculture of the settled 'White Highlands' and on European- and Asian-owned plantations. Much of the government's agricultural effort in the early years of independence was devoted to a land reform programme designed to transfer land from the European settlers and to resettle Africans upon it. Later, the government turned its attention to the Kenyanization of commerce, which at that time was dominated by non-African and frequently non-citizen businesses.

Kenya's record in the 15 years or so after independence placed it, in terms of the growth of output, among the most successful of African developing countries. From independence until 1980, the economy progressed at a cumulative annual rate of growth of 6.8% in real terms, with growth in the industrial sector reaching 9.7% per year during the 1970s. This expansion was financed by a substantial inflow of capital as well as by domestic sources.

During the period 1970–78 Kenya's gross domestic product (GDP) expanded at an average rate of more than 5% per annum in real terms. In the early 1980s, indications of weakness in the once-booming economy became increasingly evident. Deteriorating terms of trade led to a growing balance-of-payments deficit and a sharp decline in reserves of foreign exchange; burgeoning government expenditure, which was encouraged by the earlier high prices for Kenya's exports of tea and coffee, resulted in substantial budgetary deficits; and the government's high rate of borrowing on the international market created a debt-service ratio of more than 27% of export earnings by 1984. During 1983, however, some degree of economic recovery was achieved as a result of measures introduced by the government, in accordance with conditions imposed by the International Monetary Fund (IMF), and also by way of an inflow of aid from a variety of multilateral and bilateral donors, as well as from funds from the IMF itself. The improved world outlook, together with buoyant tea prices, led observers to take a more optimistic view of Kenya's economic prospects by the start of 1984. Prospects were ruined, however, by the severe drought of that year (the most severe for 50 years): harvests were drastically reduced, necessitating large cereal imports, and growth in GDP fell to only 0.9%. However, as a result of improved rainfall and favourable coffee prices in 1985 and 1986, real GDP expanded by 4.1% and 5.5%, respectively, in those years. The growth rate eased to 4.8% in 1987, owing to a decline in coffee prices and a rise in petroleum prices; however, favourable weather conditions and higher commodity prices led to an increase, to 5.2%, in the growth rate of GDP in 1988. A reversal of these factors resulted in an estimated decline in GDP growth to 5% in 1989, 4.3% in 1990 and 1.7% in 1991. GDP growth was estimted to be 1.8% in 1992. The annual inflation rate, according to government estimates, was reduced from 10.7% in 1985 to 5.7% in 1986, and to slightly below that level in 1987, but rose to 11.8% in 1988. It averaged 10.5% in 1989, and rose again in 1990 and 1991, to 15.8% and 19.6% respectively. During the first three months of 1993 the annual rate of inflation soared to 60%, owing to the effects of the suspension of international donor aid and the deregulation of prices in 1992 (see below). In the last quarter of 1993 inflation 'declined sharply' according to the IMF. In 1991, according to estimates by the World Bank, Kenya's gross national product (GNP), measured at average 1989–91 prices, was US $8,505m., equivalent to $340 per head. During 1980–92, it was estimated, GNP per head increased, in real terms, by 0.2% per year. In 1992 GNP per head declined by 1.6%.

AGRICULTURE

Agriculture continues to dominate Kenya's economy, although its share of GDP has declined slightly in recent years; in 1992 the agricultural sector (including forestry and fishing) contributed 27% of GDP. The principal cash crops, tea and coffee, ranked second and third respectively, behind tourism, as sources of foreign exchange in 1992. About 75% of the working population make their living on the land. More than one-half of total agricultural output is subsistence production.

Agricultural output is greatly dependent upon the weather since there is as yet little irrigated production, although the area under irrigation is being increased. The huge Bura scheme on the Tana river was designed to grow mainly cotton. The project, having been beset by financial and management problems, fell several years behind schedule. The main donors were the World Bank, the UK, the European Development Fund and the Netherlands. By early 1986 about 2,000 families had been settled.

In the early 1960s, as a result of land reform and increased coffee production on African farms, the share of small farms in marketed output grew rapidly. Since 1976 this share has stood at about one-half. There are around 1.7m. smallholders in the monetary sector and 3,200 large farms, ranches and plantations. There is an acute shortage of arable land, and only 7% of the country is classified as first-class land. The majority of smallholders have plots of less than 2 ha, and successive subdivisions of plots among farmers' sons impels large numbers of people to towns in search of employment.

Between 1972–81 annual growth of the agricultural sector lagged far behind the net population growth rate, except in 1976 and 1977, when improved performance was largely the result of unprecedentedly high world prices for coffee. In 1981, however, agricultural output grew by 6.2%, partly as a result of better weather conditions. Growth rates of 4.4% and 4.5% were recorded for 1982 and 1983 respectively. Disappointing 'short' rains in late 1983, followed by the severe drought of 1984, seriously affected almost all crops and created near-famine conditions in many parts of the country. Fortunately, rain returned at the end of 1984 and, with heavy rainfall in early 1985, the agricultural sector made a strong recovery in 1985/86. The output of the sector increased by 4.8% in 1986, but the rate of expansion declined to 3.8% in 1987, when crops were adversely affected by the premature end of the 'long' rains. Agricultural production increased by 4.4% in 1988, but the growth rate retreated to 3.9% in 1989, owing mainly to low international coffee prices and unfavourable weather conditions. The same factors contributed to growth of only 3.4% in 1990. There was a modest recovery in the growth of agricultural production, to 4.3%, in 1991. Between 1991 and 1993, however, output declined by an estimated 6%, owing partly to the onset of a severe drought and low world prices for coffee.

The principal cash crops are coffee, tea, sugar cane, maize, wheat, sisal, pyrethrum and cotton.

Kenya's leading export crop is coffee, almost all of it high-grade arabica. Until October 1992 the Coffee Board of Kenya controlled coffee production and handled much of its marketing. Since then, however, the marketing of coffee has been liberalized and the role of the Coffee Board has been confined to licensing, regulation and research. In addition, coffee auctions are now conducted in US dollars. Small-holders accounted for 117,677 ha of the total 156,304 ha planted with coffee in 1986, and they produce about 60% of the crop. Until the abandonment of coffee quotas by the International Coffee Organization (ICO) in July 1989, Kenya's production consistently exceeded its quota allocations, with the result that buyers were sought on the open market, mainly in the Middle East. Drought in Brazil caused world prices to soar by the end of 1985, and in early 1986 Kenya was able to take advantage of the price boom and earned K£388.5m. from coffee exports in 1986, compared with K£230.6m. in the previous year. However, prices fell sharply again from late 1986, which, compounded by lower output, resulted in a decline in export earnings, to an estimated K£194.6m., in 1987. Despite low market prices, export earnings rose to almost K£245m. in 1988, when a record marketed output of 124,600 metric tons was achieved. Following the suspension of ICO quota arrangements in 1989, together with a decline in production to 119,000 tons in the 1988/89 crop year, coffee export revenue was reduced to K£255.8m. in 1989. Output was 114,000 tons in the 1989/90 season, with exports earning K£180m. in 1990. Output of coffee declined sharply, to 87,000 metric tons, in 1990/91, owing to unfavourable weather conditions. Although Kenya's rich arabica coffee has long commanded a premium price, the instability of the coffee market (in April 1992, world coffee prices were, in nominal terms, at a 22-year 'low') acted as a disincentive to Kenyan producers, many of whom were proposing to abandon coffee-growing in favour of more profitable crops. In late 1989, however, a coffee development scheme, aimed at raising productivity and improving farmers' access to credit, was initiated with the support of the Commonwealth Development Corporation and the World Bank. The seven-year scheme, expected to cost $107m., also provides for the construction of 65 processing factories and the rehabilitation of a further 275 such installations. Since October 1993 Kenya has taken part in the stock-withholding arrangements of the Association of Coffee Producing Countries, which have gradually generated an improvement in prices. The outlook for coffe production received a significant boost in May 1994, however, when world coffee prices reached a five-year high. In 1992/93 coffee output was 73,000 metric tons, in which year the sector accounted for 16% of exports.

Kenya's second export crop is tea. High-quality tea has been a rapidly expanding crop since the early 1970s, and Kenya now ranks as the world's third largest exporter of tea, behind India and China. The share of tea in Kenya's export earnings rose from 13.7% in 1982 to over 28% in 1984. However, with the onset of sharply falling prices, the proportion fell to 18% in 1986, recovering to 21.7% in 1987 and again declining, to 20.2%, in 1988. Although the 1987 harvest reached 155,808 tons, the continuing decline in world prices led to a fall in export earnings, to an estimated K£163.4m. Production of tea rose to 164,030 tons in 1988, to 181,000 tons in 1989, to 197,000 tons in 1990 and to a record 204,000 tons in 1991. As a result of drought in all growing areas and the disruption to farming caused by ethnic clashes in western regions, output in 1992 fell to 188,100 tons. However, by 1993 tea production had risen again, to 211,200 tons. Kenya benefited from a rising trend in tea prices in 1989, when revenue from tea, at K£266.2m., exceeded that from coffee for the first time. Kenyan tea commands the second highest price premium on international markets. In 1993 tea sales accounted for 28% of Kenya's exports.

The United Kingdom takes more than 45% of Kenya's exported tea, and Pakistan is the next most important customer, taking 26%. The share of small farms in total area under tea has expanded rapidly under the high-density settlement schemes of the Kenya Tea Development Authority (KTDA), which has more than 40 tea factories in 14 districts. In July 1992 the government announced the forthcoming transferral of tea factories to the private sector. About 170,000 smallholders grow tea on 68,810 ha, and production of tea from their land accounts for 55% of total output. Estates, grouped in the Kenya Tea Growers' Association, cover about 31,017 ha. Smallholders' yields (at 1,638 kg per ha) are still lower than those of the large plantations (2,929 kg per ha), but are increasing as their bushes start to reach maturity.

The Kenya Sugar Authority was established in 1971 to develop the growing and processing of sugar cane. In 1980 there was a surplus of 150,000 metric tons of sugar for export after domestic demand of 275,000 tons had been met. By the late 1980s, domestic consumption had increased, and annual imports of sugar exceeded 120,000 tons in some years. Output of sugar cane was about 4.7m. tons annually in both 1987 and 1988. Production of raw sugar achieved successive record levels in 1989, 1990 and 1991, estimated at 457,000, 467,000 and 532,000 tons respectively. Cane is sold to the sugar companies by smallholders and co-operatives. There are five parastatal sugar companies. During the early 1990s sugar produced in western Kenya was being smuggled into Uganda on a scale large enough to cause shortages on the Kenyan market.

Production of cotton increased steadily in the 1970s, but output of lint slumped from 62,179 bales (each of 480 lb or 218 kg) in 1978/79 to 37,555 bales in 1982/83. Thereafter, only 40,000–60,000 bales have been produced annually, although potential output of lint is estimated at more than 220,000 bales. Imported lint is necessary to satisfy the demand of the domestic textiles industry; in 1991 imports of lint amounted to 8,000 metric tons, costing US $13m. The reasons for the poor performance include low prices, an erratic payments system, inefficient marketing, and drought.

Kenya became self-sufficient in tobacco in 1983, with production at about 6,600 metric tons. Production of tobacco rose by 24% in 1987, and included 5,212 tons of flue-cured, 126 tons of burley and 1,658 tons of fire-cured tobacco. In 1991 about 4,000 ha of land was planted with tobacco, yielding a total crop of 9,756 metric tons (an average of 2,439 kg per ha).

Kenya is the world's second largest producer of sisal, after Brazil. However, production of sisal, which reached a peak of 86,526 metric tons in 1974, was only an estimated 45,000 tons in 1990 and has successively fallen, to 39,000 tons in 1991 and 34,000 tons in 1992. Revenue from this crop totalled K£12.9m. in 1990. The number of large estates has fallen to 19, from about 60 in 1954. Kenya benefited from buoyant sisal prices in the first half of 1993.

Kenya supplies 65%–70% of the world market for pyrethrum. There are currently about 30,000 ha under pyrethrum, and its output is mainly linked to co-operatives.

The Pyrethrum Board of Kenya allocates quotas and attempts to improve production and its quality. In the late 1980s production ranged from 7,500 tons to about 10,000 tons annually. By the early 1990s, however, the increasing use of biological insecticides (particularly in the USA, the mainstay of Kenyan pyrethrum exports), had resulted in declining levels of demand for this commodity.

Horticultural produce is now a significant source of foreign exchange. Fresh flowers, fruit and vegetables are air-freighted to Europe and the Middle East. Production increased from 1.5m. kg in 1968 to 548m. kg in 1993, while earnings rose from $76m. in 1980 to $139m. in 1990, and to an estimated $157m. in 1991. The vegetables and fruit, but not pineapples, are grown mainly by smallholders; two large companies account for most of the cut flowers. Kenya exports about 60,000 metric tons of canned pineapple products and 11,000 tons of pineapple juice per year, and started exporting fresh pineapples in 1988. The United Kingdom imports 44% of the vegetables and fruit. Kenya is the world's fourth-largest exporter of cut flowers, which are grown mainly on large-scale farms in the Naivasha region of Central province. Horticultural produce accounted for 10% of total export earnings in 1988, compared with 3% of export earnings in 1983. The sector has great potential and is a highly successful example of export diversification, but lack of air-freight space and inadequate cold-storage facilities at Jomo Kenyatta International Airport has placed a major constraint on further expansion, as did the high cost of aviation fuel during the 1980s. Kenya is also faced with growing competition from other new exporters of horticultural products.

Kenya's principal food crop is maize. Imports were needed in 1980 and 1981 to compensate for serious shortfalls, caused by drought, low producer prices and the fact that maize exports were authorized despite low stocks. There were improved harvests in the following two years, but the drought which started in the latter part of 1983 led to a very serious shortfall in maize, as well as other cereals, in 1984. As a result, large quantities of food aid had to be imported. However, improved rainfall enabled Kenya to dispense with emergency famine relief by mid-1985. In 1985/86 there was a record maize harvest of 2.9m. metric tons, and in 1987 some maize was exported. In 1986/87 the harvest declined to an estimated 1.9m. tons, but the excellent harvests in the two preceding years had resulted in a substantial stockpile. Good rains produced a crop of 2.8m. tons in 1989, increasing maize stocks to 1m. tons, and a record crop of 3m. tons in 1990. However, drought adversely affected output in 1991/92, necessitating the importation of food aid valued at K£0.425m. by June 1992. The loss-making National Cereals and Produce Board (NCPB) was to be restructured under an agreement that Kenya signed with the World Bank in 1986 for a $71.5m. agricultural adjustment programme, and with additional aid from the EC. The government liberalized grain marketing in 1993 to allow more private-sector involvement, though it reserved for itself the power to 'make selected targeted interventions where market forces may not be effective'.

The country is not, even in good years, self-sufficient in wheat, and normally has to import 30% of its needs. Consumer demand for bread is steadily rising. It is an unfortunate trend, since maize yields are much higher than those for wheat, and its production costs have a foreign exchange component of about 50%, compared with 80% for wheat production.

Livestock and dairy production are important both for domestic consumption and for export. The bulk (90%) of marketed milk production is handled by Kenya Co-operative Creameries. The country had an estimated 13.8m. cattle in 1990, 13m. in 1991, 11m. in 1992 and just 9m. in 1993; drought accounts for most of the decline in stocks. A substantial proportion of dairy cattle are in small herds of up to 10 animals. Kenya has traditionally exported butter, cheese and skimmed milk powder, and maintains strategic stocks of these products. Output of fresh whole cows' milk fell from 2.14m. metric tons in 1991 to 1.81m. metric tons in 1992 and to 1.56m. metric tons in 1993.

INDUSTRY

Kenya is the most industrially developed country in east Africa, with a good infrastructure, extensive transport facilities and considerable private-sector activity. Nevertheless, the manufacturing sector contributed only 12% of GDP in 1992. The annual increase in the output of the sector averaged 10.5% in 1965–80. The rate subsequently slowed considerably, to only 2.7% in 1982, recovering to 4% in 1984, 4.5% in 1985 and 5.9% in 1986. Growth declined slightly in 1987, to 5.7%, but increased to 6% in 1988, retreating to 5.9% in 1989, 4.9% in 1990 and to 3.7% in 1991, as a result of selective price increases and diminished domestic demand. Growth in manufacturing output recovered to 4.9% in 1992, partly owing to the effects of the liberalization of foreign exchange controls in that year (see below). The manufacturing sector employs fewer than 200,000 people. It suffered from stringent import controls during the late 1970s and the 1980s, with 60%–70% of its inputs having to be imported, and has also been hindered by delays in the issuing of import licences and by controls on ex-factory prices. In addition the steady devaluation of the shilling in recent years has increased the costs of those manufacturers heavily dependent on imported inputs. Manufacturing is, in practice, based on import-substitution, although the government is now putting great emphasis on developing export-orientated industries. In 1990 imports of goods intended for the manufacture of exports were exempted from import duty and value added tax. Kenyan manufacturers hope to find new markets among the member countries of the Preferential Trade Area for Eastern and Southern African States (PTA). Major industries include petroleum refining (using imported crude petroleum), the processing of agricultural products, vehicle assembly, the exploitation of soda-ash reserves, the production of chemicals, publishing and printing and the manufacture of textiles and clothing, cement, electrical equipment, tyres, batteries, paper, ceramics, machinery, metal products, rubber, wood and cork products and leather goods. Petroleum refining provided 10.9% of export earnings in 1990. About one-half of the investment in the industrial sector is foreign-owned, and, of this, the United Kingdom owns about one-half. The USA is the second most important foreign investor.

The giant Panafrican Paper Mills' plant at Webuye started production in early 1975. A major expansion raised annual production capacity from 66,000 metric tons to 90,000 tons. The government owns 40% of the company's shares. A partly Swedish-owned company, Tetra Pak Converters, began production of laminated milk cartons in late 1983.

The textile industry has performed relatively well, and diversification has begun in the clothing and leather industries. Some clothing is exported to the EC. Mount Kenya Textiles (Mountex) at Nanyuki is to be transferred to private sector ownership by mid-1995, and its output is to be increased from 500,000 m of cloth per month in 1992 to 1.2m. m per month by 1995. There are three vehicle assembly plants: Associated Vehicle Assemblers, General Motors Kenya and Leyland Kenya. They produce trucks, commercial vehicles, pickups, minibuses and four-wheel drive vehicles and passenger cars from kits supplied by General Motors, British Leyland, Ford, Volvo, Fiat, Isuzu, Toyota and Volkswagen. General Motors Kenya started assembly of a passenger car, the Uhuru, in 1985. Domestic sales of locally-produced vehicles reached 13,600 in 1987, an increase of more than 30% from 1986. Already a small proportion of Kenyan-assembled vehicles are exported to Uganda, Sudan and Malawi. About 30% of components are produced locally and this proportion is to be increased. The government has a 35% interest in Leyland Kenya, and a 51% interest in the other two assembly firms. Tyres are manufactured by Firestone East Africa. The parent company, the US-based Firestone Corporation, reduced its share in the enterprise from 80% to 18% in 1985. An expansion programme for 1989–92, with a projected cost of K£22.5m., sought to increase production capacity from the current level of 500,000 tyres per year to 700,000 tyres per year. Cement, produced by the Bamburi Portland Cement Co and East African Portland Cement, was one of the most successful industries during the 1980s. However, this industry has been suffering the effects of irregular supplies of imported inputs, an increasingly competitive export market and the fall in the value of the US dollar (the currency in which cement earnings are denominated). Foreign companies own 74% of the Bamburi plant, the government 16% and local private investors 10%. There are two steel rolling mills, in Nairobi and Mombasa, and a re-rolling mill using scrap steel is being built in Nairobi. An aluminium rolling mill is to be constructed at Mombasa by Kaluworks; some of the output will be exported. There are three glassware factories, two owned by the Madhvani Group, and one by Kenya Breweries Ltd. There is a sheet glass factory at Mombasa. Charcoal is produced from coffee husks by Kenya Planters' Co-operative Union at Nairobi and is exported to the Middle East, as well as being used locally to replace some of the wood charcoal. The Bata Shoe Co has constructed a factory at Voi, from which it exports to Tanzania and to markets in central Africa. A machine-tool manufacturing plant is being set up at Nairobi, in a joint venture with an Indian firm, and will include a training centre. Kenya Breweries Ltd, part of the East African Breweries Group, has four brewing plants, and it exports a small percentage of its beer.

The Mombasa petroleum refinery, which is half-owned by the state and half by a group of international oil companies (BP, Caltex, Exxon and Shell), first went into production in 1963 and is capable of handling 4.2m. tons of crude petroleum annually, although only 2.1m. tons were handled in 1987. Refined petroleum products were, until recently, Kenya's largest source of foreign exchange, but the refinery needs a huge injection of funds to modernize it. Plans to extend the Mombasa-to-Nairobi oil pipeline as far as the Ugandan border were pledged financing of $120m. in 1990; the scheme had been in abeyance since mid-1987, owing to trade and political disputes between the two countries.

MINERALS

Mining activity in Kenya is so far limited, but prospecting is continuing. Soda ash, Kenya's principal mineral export, is extracted at Lake Magadi, in the Rift Valley; about 240,000 tons were produced in 1991. The other principal products are gold, salt, vermiculite and limestone. A fluorspar ore deposit in the Kerio valley in Rift Valley province has been mined since 1975: it produced 95,000 metric tons in 1990, and has a total capacity of 102,000 metric tons. The extraction of extensive deposits of rubies began in 1974; gems of up to 30 kg have been reported. Deposits of garnet crystals discovered at Tsavo have received high valuations. Other minerals identified in the region include apatite, graphite, kaolin, kyanite, rubies, topazes, green tourmalines and tsavolite. Searches for chromite, nickel, fluorspar and vermiculite in Central province, and for chromite, nickel and copper in the Kerio valley are being undertaken. Prospecting for petroleum and gas has continued intermittently on and off shore, but so far without significant results. Under an Oil Exploration Act, introduced in 1984, exploitation by foreign oil companies would be on a production-sharing basis. Exploration concessions have been taken by Amoco, Compagnie Française des Pétroles (CFP–Total), Marathon Oil Co, Mobil, Fina (of Belgium) and Petro-Canada, operating either independently or in consortia. In 1988 CFP–Total discovered traces of gas and oil in a test well drilled in Isiolo district, in the north-west. It was the 20th well to be drilled in Kenya since exploration began in the 1950s; the others, mostly in coastal areas, had all been dry. Several concessions came due for renewal in 1988, and Total's discovery, and the discovery of a deposit in Turkana district, revived the oil companies' flagging interest, although the commercial value of these finds is not yet known. The first exploration agreement since 1985 was awarded in 1989 to a consortium comprising Total, Amoco, Marathon and Texaco. The four-year agreement relates to an area covering 32 sq km of the Wajit and Mandera districts in the north-east of the country. New agreements were finalized in mid-1990 with Amoco and Shell Exploration. Energy imports accounted for 19% of merchandise exports in 1992.

POWER

Electricity, apart from small local stations, is supplied inland by hydroelectric plants in the Tana river basin and by the geothermal station at Olkaria, and at the coast by an oil-fired plant. This is supplemented by a bulk supply of 30 MW from Owen Falls in Uganda under a 50-year agreement signed in 1958. Hydroelectric plants supply about 75% of total generating capacity. There are five major stations on the Tana river: Gitaru, Kamburu, Kindaruma, Masinga and Kiambere. The 140-MW station at Kiambere was commissioned in 1988, increasing Kenya's total generating capacity to 715 MW. Another station, with a capacity of 105 MW, operates at Turkwel Gorge in Turkana district. The Olkaria geothermal scheme in the Rift valley, 90 km from Nairobi, began production in 1981 and now has three 15-MW generators in operation. The World Bank is lending $27m. for further geothermal exploration in the Rift Valley and Coast provinces. Two 30-MW power stations are to be built at Olkaria. A major study of the development of rivers in the Lake Victoria basin, for irrigation and hydropower, was begun in 1983. In 1987 the Kenya Power and Lighting Co, which is responsible for generation, transmission and distribution of electric power, announced a plan to improve and expand its operations, at an expected cost of K£350m., to meet projected growth in demand of 6% per year to the year 2000.

COMMUNICATIONS

Kenya's extensive transport system includes road, rail, coastal and inland water and air. Full container-handling facilities have been added at Mombasa, the chief port, to deal with the volume of containers, which expanded from 50,000 20-ft (6-m) equivalent units (TEU) in 1982 to nearly 103,000 TEU in 1985. The modern container-handling terminal was opened in 1983, and the country's first inland clearance depot for containers, at Embakasi on the outskirts of Nairobi, began operating in 1984. In early 1993 it was announced that Mombasa's Kilindini port was to be expanded by 1,200 ha. Mombasa provides access to the sea for Uganda, eastern Zaire, Burundi and Rwanda. Although faced with competition from Dar es Salaam, in Tanzania, which has been undergoing modernization, Mombasa handled 7,991,822 metric tons in 1992, compared with 7,143,876 tons in 1991. Transit cargo passing through the port to neighbouring states (including northern Tanzania) increased sharply from 527,418 tons in 1991 to 1,209,977 tons in 1992.

Kenya Airways has operated its own international services since the break-up of East African Airways. In April 1989 the airline inaugurated a freighter service to Europe: fresh flowers and vegetables were the main outward cargo. In 1992 Kenya Airways underwent a major reorganization in preparation for privatization which is expected to take place before the end of 1994. African Express Airkenya, a private passenger airline, began operating regular services between Kenya and Europe in 1986.

A 590-km road between Kitale and Juba, in Southern Sudan, provides an all-weather road link between the two countries. Rebuilding of 175 km of Kenyan roads began in 1990 as part of the 'northern corridor' scheme to improve access for land-locked countries to Mombasa port. The scheme is being financed by the EC and Germany. In early 1990 Japan promised to provide almost $200m. in concessionary finance to help develop road infrastructure and airports.

The railway in Kenya runs from the coast at Mombasa, through Nairobi, to western Kenya, and on to points in Tanzania and Uganda. A three-year project to improve Kenya Railways Corporation's operations, at an expected cost of $45.5m., was started in 1987, and was aimed, in particular, at making the railways more competitive in the freight market.

Under a major telecommunications development project, funded by the World Bank and started in 1983, international subscriber dialling was introduced in 1984, and between 1970 and 1984 the number of exchange lines rose from 70,000 to 106,000. A further 130,000 lines are planned, which will produce a ratio of one telephone for every 100 people. In August 1992 a K£119m. radio transmitter, in the Ngong hills near Nairobi, was inaugurated, reportedly bringing 95% of the population within range of radio transmissions. There is an earth satellite station at Longonot. Kenya Posts and Telecommunications Corporation is to be transferred to private sector ownership.

TOURISM

In 1989 tourism became Kenya's largest source of foreign exchange, in terms of gross receipts. Earnings from the sector amounted to K£349.3m. in 1989, and to K£595m. in 1991. Over the period 1983–90 the number of visitors increased steadily. Arrivals totalled 729,000 in 1989 and 814,400 in 1990. However, the number of visitors declined to 804,600 in 1991, and to an estimated 650,000 in 1992. A number of well-publicized attacks on foreign tourists and reports of political unrest in the country were believed to have contributed to this decline. Earnings from the sector declined to $295m. in 1992. Germany and the United Kingdom provide the largest number of tourists.

FOREIGN TRADE, BALANCE OF PAYMENTS AND AID

Kenya typically has a substantial deficit in visible trade with countries outside Africa. Its terms of trade have fluctuated quite widely since the mid-1970s, but, overall, there has been a general decline. In 1977 the trade deficit was less than K£30m., but this rose to K£267m. in 1978, with the end of the coffee boom and soaring import costs. Reduced imports and higher export earnings meant that the 1983 deficit was reduced to K£250.5m., from K£375.2m. in 1982. In 1984 export earnings rose by about 19%, owing to high prices for tea and coffee, to K£777.8m., but imports also rose (to K£1,114.8m.), partly because of liberalization measures but also because of additional food imports, made necessary by drought. In 1985 exports increased further, to K£802.4m., but the import bill rose to K£1,201.5m., so that the trade gap widened to K£398.8m., 18% more than in 1984. Higher coffee earnings helped to increase 1986 export earnings to K£958m. (including re-exports worth about K£29m.), while the import bill rose less steeply, to K£1,338m., producing a smaller deficit than in 1985, at K£380m. In 1987, however, export earnings declined sharply to K£790m. (of which K£36m. derived from re-exports), while imports increased to K£1,431m., producing a deficit of K£641m. Although exports improved to K£1,184m. in 1990, the value of imports soared to K£2,434m., producing a trade deficit of K£1,250m. Merchandise exports of US $1,053.7m. and imports of $1,712.9m. produced a visible trade deficit of $659.2m. in 1991. Merchandise imports of $1,713m. exceeded merchandise exports of $1,339m. by 28% in 1992, yielding a visible trade deficit in that year of $374m.

The government is making efforts to stimulate non-traditional exports, in an attempt to reduce dependence on fluctuating world prices for its main agricultural commodities. Non-traditional exports include horticultural produce, canned pineapple products, handicrafts, clothing, leather, cement, soda ash and fluorspar. The government is also putting great effort into stimulating exports of manufactured goods, including textiles, paper and vehicles. Manufacturing was hampered by restrictions on imports of raw materials, parts and machinery until 1992, when these restrictions began to be removed gradually. After crude oil and petroleum products, the largest import bill is for industrial machinery and transport equipment. Consumer goods account for only about 15% of the total.

Pattern of Trade

The major outlet for Kenya's exports, outside east Africa, continues to be Europe. The United Kingdom is still the most important trading partner, accounting for 13.3% of Kenyan exports in 1990 and 15.7% of its imports in 1991. The main supplier, after the UK and the United Arab Emirates (Kenya's main supplier of crude oil) is Japan. Regional trade is important to Kenya, which has consistently had a favourable trade balance with its neighbours, to which it exports petroleum products, food and basic manufactures in particular. Since the re-opening of the Kenya/Tanzania border (closed from 1977–83) trade with Tanzania has been limited by that country's lack of foreign exchange. Official trade with Uganda was depressed during the 1970s and early 1980s because of that country's internal troubles, but in 1986 agreements were signed between the two countries to re-open the direct rail link across the border and to re-start the Kisumu–Jinja lake services. In early 1987, however, a trade dispute developed between the two countries, centring on the decision by Uganda to use rail trade routes in place of road routes, thereby reducing the earnings of Kenyan trucking firms. Strict controls were then imposed on both sides of the border, hampering the movement of traffic from Uganda to Kenya. Cross-border traffic subsequently resumed, but a degree of tension has remained between the two countries (see Recent History), as a result of which official bilateral trade has declined. A vast amount of goods are smuggled into Uganda from Kenya.

Balance of Payments

Kenya's formerly strong balance of payments has been weak in most years since the early 1970s.

In September 1981 the government obtained a $115m. eight-year Euroloan as balance-of-payments support. In January 1982 the IMF authorized a stand-by arrangement, worth $175.7m. over 12 months, to support the government's economic stabilization programme. However, the government was unable to fulfil the IMF's conditions, and the arrangement was suspended in mid-year. Following a 15% devaluation of the shilling in December 1982, a new arrangement, for SDR 175.95m. over 18 months, was finally approved in March 1983. This, together with additional balance-of-payments aid from bilateral donors, helped to reduce the deficit on the current account from $304.7m. in 1982 to $48.1m. in 1983. Subsequently the effects of drought and the high cost of debt-servicing combined to increase the current account deficit. A 12-month stand-by facility from the IMF, worth SDR 85.2m., was agreed in January 1985, to support the government's 1985 economic programme. The current account deficit was reduced from $173.8m. in 1985 to $68.5m. in 1986; in 1987, however, there was a sharp deterioration in Kenya's terms of trade, and this, combined with the government's somewhat over-inflationary policies, resulted in an overall balance-of-payments deficit of nearly $100m., compared with a surplus of $116.9m. in 1986. The deficit on the current account widened to $579.6m. in 1989, following a period of import-led growth, but was reduced to $502.1m. in 1990 and to $230.9m. in 1991. The current account deficit in 1992 was $312m. before official transfers, which reduced the deficit to $98m. Although there was a surplus of $122m. on the overall balance-of-payments account in 1989, deficits of $92.5m., $51.1m. and $65m. were registered in 1990, 1991 and 1992 respectively. In January 1988 a new IMF arrangement, worth SDR 175.2m., was agreed. Of the total, SDR 85m. was a stand-by facility, to be drawn over 18 months, and SDR 90.2m. was a three-year structural adjustment facility (SAF). In accordance with IMF requirements, the government maintained a flexible exchange rate policy and the value of the shilling was allowed to move steadily downwards in relation to the major international currencies. Kenya received the approval of the IMF for its management of the economy during the late 1980s, particularly for having reduced the rate of increase in money supply. However, the budget deficit remained a problem, as did the losses incurred by the country's parastatal bodies. In April 1989 the government reached agreement with the IMF and the World Bank on the release of funds to support an economic programme for 1989–91: the funds included an enhanced structural adjustment facility (ESAF) worth SDR 240m., which was made available in late May, and replaced the SAF that had been arranged in January 1988. In December 1991 the 'Paris Club' of official creditors suspended aid to Kenya (see below).

Kenya's reserves of foreign exchange stood at $80m. at the end of 1992, compared with $460m. in 1985, having been deliberately depleted to relieve pressure on the balance of payments. The government has bowed to pressure from the IMF and the World Bank to liberalize the sale of foreign exchange, and in May 1994 the IMF estimated the country's foreign exchange reserves to be approximately $700m. It is estimated that overseas holdings by Kenyan residents amount to at least $4,000m.

At the end of 1992 Kenya's total external debt was $6,367m., down from $7,014m. in 1991. Of the 1992 total, $5,214m. was long-term public debt. The debt-service ratio has declined from 41.7% of export earnings in 1987 to 34.6% in 1990, to

32.7% in 1991 and to 27.1% in 1992, owing to debt cancellations and to the granting of concessionary loans.

Aid

Since independence, Kenya has received substantial amounts of development aid. In 1982 Kenya asked its main donors to provide additional balance-of-payments support to help to halt the serious economic decline. A series of donors' meetings was held, in London and Nairobi, over the next few months and more than $77m. was subsequently pledged. Early in 1984 the World Bank-sponsored Consultative Group of aid donors to Kenya met in Paris to discuss the government's 1984–88 Development Plan, which required external financing of about $520m. in both 1984 and 1985. At a further meeting, held in April 1986, $900m. was pledged for the following two years. In October 1988 donors' commitments for 1989 totalled $1,100m. The sources of aid have diversified considerably in recent years. The share provided by the United Kingdom has fallen, while multilateral agencies, particularly the World Bank and the European Development Fund, have increased their share. In July 1982 the World Bank approved a $131m. structural adjustment programme, the second that it had made to Kenya. However, disbursement of the second tranche of this loan was suspended in 1983, because Kenya had not yet fulfilled the Bank's conditions on de-controlling maize marketing, and it was not completed until early 1984. Discussions concerning a third structural adjustment loan subsequently collapsed, since agreement had still not been reached on grain marketing, and the World Bank decided to revert to sectoral loans from 1986. Following an improvement in relations with the Bank, donors were encouraged to provide larger amounts. In early 1989 the Federal Republic of Germany, Kenya's principal bilateral creditor, announced that it would cancel the total debt of $435m. in return for increased Kenyan investment in projects aimed at protecting the environment. Japan also increased its aid to Kenya, becoming the country's largest official donor. The ESAF agreement, concluded with the IMF in April 1989, resulted in the World Bank's approval for two credits, totalling $89m., in October. Of the total amount, $45m. was the second tranche of a $110m. industrial sector adjustment credit (ISAC), which commenced during the previous year. The remaining $44m. was to supplement a $115.3m. financial sector credit approved in mid-1989. Relations with the international donor community were strained towards the end of 1989, when the government proposed building a 60-storey media complex at a cost of $200m., with 'offshore' commercial financing. At a special January 1990 donors' meeting to discuss levels of external commercial borrowing proposed by the Kenyan government since mid-1989, donors expressed concern that the new loans would raise the debt-service ratio and would slow productive investment. The USA agreed to cancel Kenya's debt on condition that the government agreed to abandon the plans, which it subsequently did. In November 1991, however, the 'Paris Club' declared a moratorium on aid to Kenya, pending the implementation of economic and political reforms. Following the holding of multi-party elections in December 1992 (see Recent History), lending resumed in April 1993. In December 1993 the IMF agreed to a one-year ESAF arrangement totalling $61.97m., of which one half was disbursed immediately. A further 'Paris Club' rescheduling took place in January 1994. A total of $850m. was pledged by donors for 1994.

PUBLIC FINANCE

The main features of the 1982/83 budget were increases in many import duties, a halving of capital gains tax and the withdrawal of the export compensation scheme, which had given exporters rebates of up to 20% of the value of their exported goods. In September 1982 President Moi announced that the scheme was to be reintroduced as part of the programme to stimulate manufactured exports. In the 1983/84 budget import duties on raw materials were reduced and rises in sales tax and the price of beer were introduced. Among the main features of the 1984/85 budget were a reduction of import duties on raw materials and capital equipment, the lowering of the commercial bank lending rate, and a reduction in withholding tax, to encourage foreign investment. The cautiously expansionary 1985/86 budget added 300 items of consumer goods to the import priority schedule (with the aim of making local industry more competitive) and abolished capital gains tax. It reduced tariffs on some imported raw materials and capital goods, and introduced a unified rate of export compensation in the hope of speeding up the payment procedure. Under the 1986/87 budget duty was increased on beer and cigarettes, while sales tax on diesel fuel, cooking fats and soap was reduced. The actual budgetary deficit was K£404m. (equivalent to 7% of GDP).

The 1987/88 budget proposals included measures to boost investment, with some reductions in taxes and duties on imported capital goods and raw materials for the manufacturing sector, and incentives for new industries located outside Nairobi and Mombasa. The actual budget deficit was K£328.6m., equivalent to 6.7% of GDP. The 1988/89 budget aimed to reduce the deficit by 20%, and to encourage foreign investment by allowing investors to deduct foreign exchange losses on their investments. Other new measures in the budget included the simplification of the tariff structure, the doubling of airport taxes and increase in levies on cigarettes, beer, soft drinks and petrol, and the reduction of import duties on motor vehicles and on television and radio receivers. The actual budgetary deficit for 1988/89 was equivalent to 4.5% of GDP. The 1989/90 budget envisaged recurrent expenditure of K£2,472.8m. (an increase of 21% over actual expenditure in 1988/89) and development expenditure of K£922.1m. (14.4% higher than the out-turn for the previous year). Total revenue was forecast at K£2,493.9m. The actual budgetary deficit was equivalent to 4.2% of GDP. The 1990/91 budget envisaged a rapid expansion of exports, based on fiscal management and incentives to the private sector. The actual budgetary deficit was equivalent to 5.3% of GDP.

The budget proposals for 1991/92 envisaged total expenditure of K£4,500m., and included the restructuring of the taxation system. The budgetary deficit was forecast to fall to 2% of GDP. Expenditure under the 1992/93 budget was forecast at K£5,500m.

DEVELOPMENT PLANNING

Development policy in Kenya emphasizes the role of private enterprise in industry and commerce, and foreign investment is actively encouraged. Direct participation by the state in productive enterprises is limited, and in recent years the government has been withdrawing from unprofitable joint ventures. In 1991 the government announced that all remaining unproductive, 'non-strategic' state-owned companies were to be transferred to private-sector ownership; details of the impending privatization of some 207 such companies had been released by mid-1993.

Kenya's first Development Plan, revised in 1966, covered the period 1964–70. Important objectives of the plan included the Kenyanization of the economy, until then largely in expatriate hands. The second Development Plan (1969/70–1973/74) had as a basic objective the acceleration of rural development and the rectification of the imbalance between rural and urban incomes. Annual growth targets under the third Development Plan (1974–78) were assisted by the rise in world coffee prices during 1976 and 1977. One of the main themes of Kenya's fourth Development Plan (1979–83) was the fight against rural poverty. However, the deteriorating economic situation led the government to revise the Plan in May 1980, lowering the target annual growth rate of GDP from 6.3% to 5.4%.

The fifth Development Plan (1984–88) envisaged an average annual growth rate of 4.9%, showing a much more cautious approach than in the previous Plan. It placed greater reliance on domestic resources for financing development. There was to be continued emphasis on projects for the benefit of the poor and on attaining a better balance between urban and rural areas.

In 1986 the government published details of a programme for economic reform (Sessional Paper No. 1), which aimed at increasing productivity, providing incentives and stimulating investment in the private sector, developing and diversifying agricultural and industrial exports, creating jobs in rural areas and achieving an annual GDP growth rate of 5.6%–6% up to the year 2000.

A sixth Development Plan, covering the period 1989–93, aimed primarily to increase earnings of foreign exchange and to generate employment through the expansion of the industrial sector. The targeted average annual growth rate for the economy as a whole was 5.4%; an annual increase of 4.5% was projected for the agricultural sector, and growth of 6.4% per year for the manufacturing sector. Some reforms of the health and education sectors, including the introduction of charges to users, were to be introduced in order to reduce the budgetary deficit. The plan also aimed to reduce the rate of population growth, by promoting family planning. In 1990 import duty and value added tax were withdrawn from goods intended for the manufacture of exports, in order to stimulate industrial expansion. During the first half of 1992, however, following the imposition by foreign donors in November 1991 of a moratorium on aid (see above), the government implemented a sweeping programme of economic reforms: these included the liberalization of imports, exports and exchange control, the streamlining of government ministries, price deregulation and a reduction in the bureaucracy surrounding incoming foreign investment. Although the reform measures were briefly suspended in March 1993, having been denounced by President Moi as 'dictatorial and suicidal', they were reintroduced in May, following the announcement by the World Bank in April that it would resume aid allocations to Kenya. In a speech delivered for him in early May 1994, President Moi vowed to continue with the policy of economic liberalization already under way. The Kenyan currency was devalued by 32% between July 1991 and June 1992, by 37% in February 1993, and by 23% in April 1993. According to an assessment made by the IMF in May 1994 Kenya has made 'important headway' in tightening monetary conditions. The Kenya shilling, the IMF pointed out, had 'appreciated' from over KSh. 80 per US dollar to about KSh. 60 per US dollar during the previous 12 months. In May 1994 the government announced the liberalization of foreign exchange controls which would allow commercial banks to undertake foreign exchange transactions without reference to the Central Bank. The new measures, which took immediate effect, meant that the Kenyan shilling became fully convertible against other world currencies.

REGIONAL ARRANGEMENTS AND PROBLEMS

In 1967 Kenya, Tanzania and Uganda founded the East African Community (EAC), which comprised a customs union and a range of public services, including the East African Development Bank, operated on a collectively-managed basis. During the early 1970s, however, major economic and political tensions developed between the EAC's member countries. By the beginning of 1977 the railways had effectively become national enterprises, East African Airways had broken up and Kenya had launched its own Kenya Airways. In February Tanzania closed its border with Kenya, and trade between the two countries virtually ceased. In July 1977, for practical purposes, the EAC ceased to exist. The East African Development Bank, however, has continued to function.

Negotiations concerning the distribution of the EAC's assets and liabilities among the former member states continued intermittently for six years, under the chairmanship of a World Bank-appointed mediator. Agreement was eventually reached in November 1983, and a new era of improved relations between the three countries seemed at least a possibility. Kenya was allocated a 42.5% share of the assets, whose value was put at $898m., while Tanzania received 32.5% and Uganda 25%. Long-term external debts totalled about $220m., and a creditors' meeting was arranged to discuss possible rescheduling. In addition, Uganda was to be paid compensation of $191m. by the other two partners, because their shares of the assets were calculated as greater than the equity shares which they held in the former community corporations. Kenya started to pay this compensation by transferring some of its railway rolling stock to Uganda. An immediate result of the settlement was the re-opening of the Kenya/Tanzania border, which has provided some limited opportunities for Kenyan exporters. The two countries' airlines resumed inter-state flights in 1984 and there have been agreements on overland transport, the cross-border transport of tourists, an expanded air service and co-operation in shipping and port services.

PROBLEMS AND PROSPECTS

Kenya's high rate of population growth has imposed major strains upon the economy, in terms of public expenditure, as well as threatening social stability. However, government initiatives to encourage family planning have had significant success in reducing the rate in recent years. Another major constraint to growth has been the balance-of-payments problem. The period of rapid growth had ended by 1978. External factors contributing to the sharp slowdown have been deteriorating terms of trade, with rising prices for petroleum and other imports and generally low world prices for Kenya's commodities. Internal factors have included: lack of incentives to agricultural producers; severe shortages of imported inputs for manufacturers; high government spending; an overvalued currency; low wages, which have declined in real terms, and consequent poor productivity; and too much stress on industries relying heavily on expensive imported materials and equipment.

Pressure from the IMF, the World Bank and bilateral donors helped to persuade the government to take a firm grip on the economy and on public spending by late 1982. In September of that year President Moi stressed the government's commitment to encouraging the private sector and foreign investment, both public and private. In June 1986 a radical departure from Kenya's previously liberal policy on foreign investment was indicated in a speech by President Moi, in which he declared that Kenyans should henceforth hold controlling interests in joint ventures with foreigners. The government attempted, however, to dispel fears that this policy would endanger existing foreign investments. Following the collapse of a number of financial institutions, owing to the malpractice and mismanagement of their directors, the government formed a committee in August to investigate the scandal and to restore public confidence in Kenya's financial system. A further wave of bank collapses led the government to take action again in 1994 to strengthen the sector.

There remain many serious flaws in the economy's basic structure, and pressure on land and the lack of alternative employment for the growing numbers of landless people represent serious long-term difficulties. The sweeping programme of economic reforms implemented by the government in 1992 should make substantial headway in addressing these problems, although the positive effects of the reforms may take some time to permeate through the economy. By early 1993, measures to liberalize agricultural marketing had produced mixed results, but the introduction of foreign exchange retention accounts had clearly facilitated the importation of raw materials by manufacturers.

Statistical Survey

Source (unless otherwise stated): Central Bureau of Statistics, POB 30256, Nairobi; tel (2) 33970.

Area and Population

AREA, POPULATION AND DENSITY

Area (sq km)	580,367*
Population (census results)†	
24 August 1989	
Males	10,628,368
Females	10,815,268
Total	21,443,636
Density (per sq km) at August 1989	36.7

* 224,081 sq miles. Total includes 11,230 sq km (4,336 sq miles) of inland water.
† Provisional.

PRINCIPAL ETHNIC GROUPS (at census of August 1989)

African	21,163,076	European	34,560
Arab	41,595	Other	115,220*
Asian	89,185	**Total**	21,443,636

*Includes persons who did not state 'tribe' or 'race'.

PRINCIPAL TOWNS (population at census of August 1989)

Nairobi (capital)	1,346,000	Meru	78,100
Mombasa	465,000	Thika	57,100
Kisumu*	185,100	Kitale	53,000
Nakuru	162,800	Kisii	44,000
Eldoret*	104,900	Kericho	40,000
Nyeri*	88,600	Malindi*	35,200

* Boundaries extended between 1979 and 1989.

BIRTHS AND DEATHS (UN estimates, annual averages)

	1975-80	1980-85	1985-90
Birth rate (per 1,000)	53.6	48.8	45.6
Death rate (per 1,000)	15.5	13.2	11.4

Expectation of life (UN estimates, years at birth, 1985–90): 57.9 (males 55.9; females 59.9).

Source: UN, *World Population Prospects: The 1992 Revision.*

ECONOMICALLY ACTIVE POPULATION
(ILO estimates, '000 persons at mid-1980)

	Males	Females	Total
Agriculture, etc.	3,174	2,555	5,729
Industry	403	81	484
Services	534	324	859
Total	4,111	2,961	7,072

Source: ILO, *Economically Active Population Estimates and Projections, 1950–2025.*

Mid-1992 (estimates in '000): Agriculture, etc. 8,038; Total labour force 10,563. (Source: FAO, *Production Yearbook.*)

EMPLOYMENT* ('000 registered employees at June each year)

	1990	1991	1992
Agriculture and forestry	269.7	272.0	272.3
Mining and quarrying	4.2	4.3	4.4
Manufacturing	187.7	188.9	189.6
Electricity and water	22.4	22.4	22.3
Construction	71.4	72.4	73.4
Trade, restaurants and hotels	114.0	116.7	118.4
Transport, storage and communications	74.2	76.2	76.9
Financing, insurance, real estate and business services	65.2	66.3	66.9
Community, social and personal services	600.2	622.4	638.4
Total	1,409.0	1,441.8	1,462.6
Males	1,100.5	1,117.1	1,133.5
Females	308.5	324.6	329.1

* This table refers only to employment in the modern sector. There were an estimated 347,892 self-employed and unpaid family workers and employees at small-scale establishments registered at June 1991.

Agriculture

PRINCIPAL CROPS ('000 metric tons)

	1990	1991	1992
Wheat	190	195	200*
Rice (paddy)†	59	60	58
Barley	31	37†	34†
Maize	2,290	2,340	2,561*
Millet	70	52	55*
Sorghum	111	98	107*
Potatoes	242	230†	240†
Sweet potatoes	537*	550†	600†
Cassava (Manioc)	723	761	770†
Pulses	235	240†	235†
Cottonseed	18*	20*	19†
Cotton lint	9*	10*	9†
Coconuts	42	42	43†
Vegetables	631	643†	655†
Sugar cane†	4,750	4,580	4,430
Pineapples*	225	245	270
Bananas†	200	210	220
Plantains†	340	350	360
Cashew nuts	7*	15†	15†
Coffee (green)	104	86	70*
Tea (made)	197	204	188*
Sisal	40	39	35†

* Unofficial figure(s). † FAO estimate(s).

Source: FAO, *Production Yearbook.*

LIVESTOCK ('000 head, year ending September)

	1990	1991*	1992*
Cattle	13,793	13,000	11,000
Sheep	6,516†	6,500	6,000
Goats	8,000†	8,000	7,500
Pigs	105	105	105
Camels*	810	820	810

* FAO estimates. † Unofficial figure.

Poultry (FAO estimates, million): 25 in 1990; 25 in 1991; 25 in 1992.

Source: FAO, *Production Yearbook.*

LIVESTOCK PRODUCTS ('000 metric tons)

	1990	1991	1992*
Beef and veal*	250	239	216
Mutton and lamb*	26	26	24
Goats' meat*	31	31	30
Pig meat*	5	5	5
Poultry meat*	48	48	48
Other meat*	29	29	29
Edible offals*	61	58	53
Cows' milk*	2,320	2,139	1,810
Sheep's milk*	29	29	26
Goats' milk*	100	100	94
Butter and ghee	4.6†	3.5†	3.5
Cheese	0.2	0.3	0.2
Poultry eggs*	42.0	42.0	42.0
Honey*	17.0	18.0	19.0
Wool:			
greasy*	2.2	2.2	2.0
clean*	1.1	1.1	1.0
Cattle hides*	39.4	37.2	33.6

* FAO estimates. † Unofficial figure.

Source: FAO, mainly *Production Yearbook.*

Forestry

ROUNDWOOD REMOVALS
(FAO estimates, '000 cubic metres, excluding bark)

	1990	1991	1992
Sawlogs, veneer logs and logs for sleepers*	460	460	460
Pulpwood*	357	357	357
Other industrial wood*	930	961	993
Fuel wood*	33,190	34,328	35,501
Total	34,937	36,106	36,897

* FAO estimates.

Source: FAO, *Yearbook of Forest Products.*

SAWNWOOD PRODUCTION
(FAO estimates, '000 cubic metres)

	1990	1991	1992
Total	185	185	185

* FAO estimate.

Source: FAO, *Yearbook of Forest Products.*

Fishing

('000 metric tons, live weight)

	1989	1990	1991
Silver cyprinid	45.5	46.7	58.1
Nile tilapia	13.1	38.3	27.5
Nile perch	56.9	71.9	57.3
Other fishes (incl. unspecified)	29.9	43.8	54.7
Other aquatic animals	1.0	1.0	1.1
Total catch	146.4	201.8	198.6
Inland waters	138.8	191.9	191.2
Indian Ocean	7.6	9.9	7.4

Source: FAO, *Yearbook of Fishery Statistics.*

Mining

(metric tons)

	1990	1991	1992
Soda ash	231,900	219,500	181,330
Fluorspar	80,529	77,402	80,630
Salt	70,318	72,441	72,494
Limestone products†	35,733	32,017	30,656

† Excluding limestone used for production of cement.

Industry

SELECTED PRODUCTS
('000 metric tons, unless otherwise indicated)

	1990	1991	1992
Wheat flour	172	186	222
Raw sugar	414	427	397
Beer ('000 hectolitres)	3,311	3,140	3,686
Cigarettes (million)	6,648	6,473	7,031
Cement	1,512	1,423	1,507
Motor spirit (petrol)	335	328	348
Kerosene and jet fuel	492	421	455
Distillate fuel oils	563	542	580
Residual fuel oil	670	648	670
Electric energy (million kWh)	3,044	3,237	3,215

Finance

CURRENCY AND EXCHANGE RATES

Monetary Units

100 cents = 1 Kenya shilling (Ks.);
Ks. 20 = 1 Kenya pound (K£).

Sterling and Dollar Equivalents (31 March 1994)

£1 sterling = Ks. 96.29;
US $1 = Ks. 64.86;
Ks. 1,000 = £10.385 = $15.418.

Average Exchange Rate (Ks. per US $)

1991 27.508
1992 32.217
1993 58.001

Note: The foregoing information refers to the Central Bank's mid-point exchange rate. However, with the introduction of a foreign exchange bearer certificate (FEBC) scheme in October 1991, a dual exchange rate system is in effect. In May 1994 foreign exchange transactions were liberalized and the Kenya shilling became fully convertible against other world currencies.

BUDGET (K£ million, year ending 30 June)

Revenue	1990/91	1991/92*	1992/93*
Current:			
Direct taxes	713.08	851.39	921.96
Import duties	334.68	329.04	425.56
Excise duties	185.16	330.07	388.45
Sales tax	766.07	993.16	1,074.79
Other indirect taxes	103.89	100.22	77.03
Interest, profits and dividends (incl. rent)	149.51	186.24	220.55
Current transfers	18.02	10.76	6.10
Sales of goods and services	83.11	71.00	93.46
Loan repayments	7.53	12.41	12.05
Compulsory fees, fines and penalties	43.82	35.36	35.18
Other	39.48	5.72	20.38
Total current	2,444.35	2,925.37	3,275.51
Capital:			
Long-term borrowing	206.50	11.50	177.25
Internal borrowing	530.05	344.90	795.00
Loan repayments	7.53	12.41	12.05
Capital transfers	59.48	62.20	214.22
Withdrawals from funds	0.74	—	—
Total capital	804.30	431.01	1,198.52
Total	3,248.65	3,356.38	4,474.03

Expenditure	1990/91	1991/92*	1992/93*
Current:			
General public services	368.54	422.26	580.25
Defence	261.57	206.52	210.79
Education	619.96	643.29	799.84
Health	133.39	152.44	181.55
Housing, community and social welfare	46.41	51.54	68.57
Economic services	309.77	325.28	410.93
Other services	1,538.43	1,971.58	2,251.85
Total current	3,278.07	3,772.91	4,503.78
Development:			
General public services	191.99	166.47	314.31
Mining, manufacturing and construction	40.23	8.82	23.00
Housing, social and community welfare	52.00	40.90	78.40
Roads	91.20	84.16	131.77
Education	66.99	59.09	106.01
Health	39.52	37.58	113.37
Agriculture and forestry	104.88	110.77	398.90
Defence	33.92	25.86	27.88
Electricity, gas and water	57.84	41.01	58.53
Total development (incl. others)	828.13	651.69	1,333.06
Total	4,106.20	4,424.60	5,836.84

* Provisional.

Sources: Central Bank of Kenya, Nairobi; Central Bureau of Statistics, Nairobi.

INTERNATIONAL RESERVES (US $ million at 31 December)

	1990	1991	1992
Gold*	13.5	15.0	12.2
IMF special drawing rights	3.9	1.4	0.8
Reserve position in IMF	17.4	17.5	16.8
Foreign exchange	184.1	98.1	35.4
Total	218.9	132.0	65.2

* National valuation of gold reserves (80,000 troy oz in each year).

Source: IMF, *International Financial Statistics.*

MONEY SUPPLY (Ks. million at 31 December)

	1990	1991	1992
Currency outside banks	10,829	12,761	17,205
Demand deposits at commercial banks	16,773	19,155	26,621

Source: IMF, *International Financial Statistics.*

COST OF LIVING (Consumer Price Index for low-income group in Nairobi; annual averages; base: 1990 = 100.)

	1991	1992
Food	123.5	166.9
Fuel and light	114.7	122.6
Clothing	114.5	134.9
Rent	119.3	154.5
All items (incl. others)	119.3	154.5

Source: ILO, *Year Book of Labour Statistics.*

NATIONAL ACCOUNTS (K£ million at current prices)

Composition of the Gross National Product

	1990	1991*	1992*
Compensation of employees	3,643.2	4,026.3	4,812.2
Operating surplus Consumption of fixed capital }	4,897.4	5,773.6	6,792.9
Gross domestic product (GDP) at factor cost†	8,540.6	9,799.9	11,605.1
Indirect taxes	1,399.0	1,562.4	1,815.7
Less Subsidies	0.1	0.1	0.1
GDP in purchasers' values	9,939.3	11,362.1	13,420.8
Factor income received from abroad	5.5	8.2	2.8
Less Factor income paid abroad	461.5	597.9	731.6
Gross national product (GNP)	9,483.2	10,772.4	12,691.9

* Figures are provisional.

† Includes non-monetary economy.

Source: Central Bureau of Statistics.

Expenditure on the Gross Domestic Product

	1990	1991	1992
Government final consumption expenditure	1,831.0	1,889.5	2,102.0
Private final consumption expenditure	6,245.2	7,226.2	9,245.5
Increase in stocks	345.3	217.6	44.9
Gross fixed capital formation	2,030.3	2,133.6	2,122.0
Total domestic expenditure*	10,455.6	11,529.4	13,514.4
Exports of goods and services	2,553.3	3,021.8	3,464.4
Less Imports of goods and services	3,069.6	3,189.1	3,557.9
GDP in purchasers' values	9,939.3	11,362.1	13,420.9

Source: Central Bureau of Statistics.

Gross Domestic Product by Economic Activity
(at factor cost)

	1989	1990	1991
Agriculture, hunting, forestry and fishing	2,271	2,375	2,797
Mining and quarrying	19	23	28
Manufacturing	855	987	1,167
Electricity, gas and water	109	79	100
Construction	477	539	749
Trade, restaurants and hotels	829	948	1,133
Transport, storage and communication	486	598	682
Finance, insurance, real estate and business services	1,170	1,589	1,518
Government services	1,167	1,299	1,459
Other community, social and personal services	228	251	331
Other producers	97	114	132
Sub-total	7,708	8,803	10,096
Less Imputed bank service charge	282	263	296
Total	7,426	8,541	9,800

Source: UN, *National Accounts Statistics.*

BALANCE OF PAYMENTS (US $ million)

	1990	1991	1992
Merchandise exports f.o.b.	1,010.5	1,053.7	1,004.0
Merchandise imports f.o.b.	-2,005.3	-1,697.6	-1,594.5
Trade balance	-994.9	-643.9	-590.5
Exports of services	1,208.6	1,132.7	1,139.7
Imports of services	-693.7	-631.1	-575.1
Other income received	14.3	17.0	8.7
Other income paid	-429.2	-438.5	-362.9
Private unrequited transfers (net)	167.8	144.4	68.3
Official unrequited transfers (net)	206.9	204.5	214.2
Current balance	-520.3	-214.8	-97.7
Direct investment (net)	57.1	18.8	6.4
Other capital (net)	303.8	77.8	-276.5
Net errors and omissions	66.9	74.3	110.9
Overall balance	-92.5	-43.9	-256.9

Source: IMF, *International Financial Statistics.*

External Trade

PRINCIPAL COMMODITIES
(distribution by SITC, US $'000)*

Imports c.i.f.	1987	1988	1990
Food and live animals	69,371	46,650	139,462
Crude materials (inedible) except fuels	47,841	56,509	79,321
Mineral fuels, lubricants, etc	348,735	290,566	424,471
Petroleum and petroleum products	344,373	284,369	412,188
Animal and vegetable oils and fats	50,512	71,458	45,549
Chemicals and related products	310,174	355,147	234,798
Plastic materials, etc	68,447	91,074	62,617
Basic manufactures	245,711	320,538	272,080
Iron and steel	102,613	135,780	119,213
Machinery and transport equipment	596,459	763,908	856,476
Machinery specialized for particular industries	130,719	147,638	124,041
General industrial machinery, equipment and parts	83,925	99,002	99,286
Telecommunications and sound equipment	61,507	96,346	104,809
Other electrical machinery, apparatus, etc	59,007	81,665	95,378
Road vehicles and parts	164,207	201,425	236,513
Passenger motor cars (excl. buses)	42,034	48,670	76,805
Motor vehicles for goods transport and special purposes	77,298	88,046	95,881
Aircraft and aircraft parts	17,631	47,539	132,729
Miscellaneous manufactured articles	63,520	75,152	64,580
Total (incl. others)	1,737,805	1,986,741	2,135,583

Exports f.o.b.†	1987	1988	1990
Food and live animals	589,893	655,243	480,114
Cereals and cereal preparations	26,546	25,838	23,243
Vegetables and fruit	93,892	106,807	79,042
Coffee (green and roasted)	236,743	275,964	143,551
Tea	216,215	227,179	195,761
Crude materials (inedible) except fuels	97,010	121,820	184,742
Textile fibres and waste	15,322	15,963	23,140
Mineral fuels, lubricants, etc	125,571	136,634	134,821
Petroleum and petroleum products	125,225	136,230	134,644
Chemicals and related products	38,950	31,531	42,697
Basic manufactures	57,896	78,726	118,227
Machinery and transport equipment	24,278	20,599	108,978
Road vehicles and parts	10,432	9,946	59,620
Motor vehicles for goods transport and special purposes	3,362	2,692	24,080
Miscellaneous manufactured goods	17,172	18,916	37,828
Total (incl. others)	961,042	1,072,524	1,028,393

* Figures for 1989 are not available. Not all data for 1990 are comparable with those for previous years.

Source: UN, *International Trade Statistics Yearbook.*

PRINCIPAL TRADING PARTNERS (US $'000)

Imports c.i.f.	1989	1990	1991
Belgium/Luxembourg	n.a.	51,086	n.a.
Finland	n.a.	29,977	n.a.
France*	190,902	116,617	112,791
Germany, Federal Republic	192,950	152,010	171,376
India	40,537	33,192	37,682
Italy	97,198	96,397	68,793
Japan	238,341	243,285	227,177
Malaysia	n.a.	40,269	n.a.
Netherlands	62,883	70,082	45,226
Saudi Arabia	41,207	58,836	99,560
Sweden	n.a.	27,842	n.a.
United Arab Emirates	245,912	154,537	246,104
United Kingdom	340,762	310,536	310,536
USA	159,402	172,599	98,834
Total (incl. others)	2,173,423	2,135,853	1,980,199

Exports f.o.b.	1988	1989	1990
Belgium/Luxembourg	29,017	n.a.	17,155
Burundi	13,111	6,180	20,313
Djibouti	1,234	998	22,798
Egypt	11,318	10,563	15,165
France*	19,763	20,807	17,301
Germany, Federal Republic	128,355	86,451	79,111
Italy	36,913	26,369	16,377
Netherlands	54,993	48,452	40,606
Pakistan	30,305	n.a.	59,754
Rwanda	26,425	16,428	75,207
Somalia	7,891	7,789	16,190
Spain	12,583	n.a.	8,559
Sudan	24,532	20,427	14,926
Sweden	23,946	n.a.	12,356
Tanzania	27,433	26,764	22,295
Uganda	94,226	64,212	190,322
United Kingdom	210,585	193,563	136,320
USA	52,036	48,101	28,341
Zaire	12,093	6,567	24,636
Total (incl. others)	1,072,498	993,338	1,028,393

* Including Monaco.

Source: UN, *International Trade Statistics Yearbook.*

Transport

RAILWAYS (traffic)

	1990	1991	1992*
Passengers carried ('000)	3,109	2,635	2,563
Passenger-km (million)	677	658	557
Freight carried ('000 metric tons)	3,317	3,581	2,821
Freight ton-km (million)	1,865	1,627	1,755

* Provisional.

ROAD TRAFFIC (motor vehicles in use at 31 December)

	1990	1991	1992*
Motor cars	156,851	164,234	171,813
Buses and coaches	13,445	14,740	16,323
Goods vehicles	32,183	32,794	35,344
Vans	88,396	92,585	95,967
Tractors, trailers and semi-trailers	37,908	39,264	40,699
Motor cycles and mopeds	23,536	24,895	25,912

* Provisional.

INTERNATIONAL SEA-BORNE SHIPPING
(estimated freight traffic, '000 metric tons)

	1990	1991	1992*
Goods loaded	2,297	1,791	2,083
Goods unloaded	5,192	5,310	5,810

* Provisional.

CIVIL AVIATION (traffic on scheduled services)

	1989	1990	1991
Kilometres flown (million)	14	16	13
Passengers carried ('000)	760	794	760
Passenger-km (million)	1,399	1,652	1,479
Freight ton-km (million)	48	52	39

Source: UN, *Statistical Yearbook.*

Tourism

	1988	1989	1990
Tourist arrivals ('000)	677	714	801
Tourist receipts (million US dollars)	410	375	443

Source: UN, *Statistical Yearbook.*

Communications Media

	1988	1989	1990
Radio receivers ('000 in use)	2,100	2,200	3,000
Television receivers ('000 in use)	135	200	225
Telephones ('000 in use)	337	357	383
Book production (titles)	n.a.	n.a.	348
Daily newspapers:			
Titles	5	n.a.	5
Average circulation ('000 copies)	303*	n.a.	350†

* Figure refers to four dailies only. † Estimate.

1991 ('000 in use): Radio receivers 2,100; Television receivers 234.

Sources: UNESCO, *Statistical Yearbook*; UN, *Statistical Yearbook.*

Education

(1990)

	Institutions	Teachers	Pupils
Primary	14,691	172,117	5,392,319
General secondary	2,758	35,097	614,161
Technical*	36	1,147	11,700
Teacher Training	24	n.a.	17,914
Universities	4	4,392	35,421

* 1988 figures.

Sources: Ministry of Education, Nairobi; UNESCO, *Statistical Yearbook.*

Directory

The Constitution

The Constitution was introduced at independence on 12 December 1963. Subsequent amendments, including the adoption of republican status on 12 December 1964, were consolidated in 1969. A further amendment in December 1991 permitted the establishment of a multi-party system. The Constitution can be amended by the affirmative vote on Second and Third Reading of 65% of the membership of the National Assembly (excluding the Speaker and Attorney-General).

The central legislative authority is the unicameral National Assembly, in which there are 188 directly elected Representatives, 12 members nominated by the President and two ex-officio members, the Attorney-General and the Speaker. The maximum term of the National Assembly is five years from its first meeting (except in wartime). It can be dissolved by the President at any time, and the National Assembly may force its own dissolution by a vote of 'no confidence', whereupon Presidential and Assembly elections have to be held within 90 days.

Executive power is vested in the President, Vice-President and Cabinet. Both the Vice-President and the Cabinet are appointed by the President, who must be a member of the Assembly and at least 35 years of age. Election of the President, for a five-year term, is by direct popular vote; the winning candidate at a presidential election must receive no less than 25% of the votes in at least five of Kenya's eight provinces. If a President dies, or a vacancy otherwise occurs during a President's period of office, the Vice-President becomes interim President for up to 90 days while a successor is elected.

The Government

HEAD OF STATE

President: DANIEL ARAP MOI (took office 14 October 1978; elected August 1983, commenced further term of office February 1988, re-elected December 1992).

CABINET
(September 1994)

President and Commander-in-Chief of the Armed Forces: DANIEL ARAP MOI.

Vice-President and Minister of Planning and National Development: Prof. GEORGE SAITOTI.

Minister of Agriculture, Livestock and Marketing: SIMEON NYACHAE.

Minister of Finance: WYCLIFF MUDAVADI.

Minister of Foreign Affairs: STEPHEN MUSYOKA.

Minister of Education: JOSEPH KAMOTHO.

Minister of Land Reclamation, Regional and Water Development: DARIUS MBELA.

Minister of Energy: JOHN KYALO.

Minister of Environment and Natural Resources: JOHN SAMBU.

Minister of Transport and Communication: DALMAS OTIENO.

Minister of Commerce and Industry: KIRUGI M'MUKINDIA.

Minister of Tourism: NOAH NGALA.

Minister of Health: JOSHUA ANGATIA.

Minister of Local Government: WILLIAM OLE NTIMAMA.

Minister of Home Affairs and National Heritage: FRANCIS LOTODO.

Minister of Lands and Urban Development: JACKSON MULINGE.

Minister of Labour and Manpower Development: PHILIP MASINDE.

Minister of Information and Broadcasting: JOHNSTONE MAKAU.

Minister of Culture and Social Services: JACKSON KALWEO.

Minister of Co-operative Development: KAMWITHI MUNYI.

Minister of Public Works and Housing: Prof. JONATHAN NG'ENO.

Minister of Research, Technical Training and Technology: ZACHARY ONYONKA.

Minister of State in the President's Office: HUSSEIN MOHAMED, KIPKALIA KONES.

Attorney-General: AMOS WAKO.

MINISTRIES

Office of the President: Harambee House, Harambee Ave, POB 30510, Nairobi; tel. (2) 27411.

Office of the Vice-President and Ministry of Planning and National Development: Treasury Bldg, Harambee Ave, POB 30007, Nairobi; tel. (2) 338111; telex 22696.

Ministry of Agriculture, Livestock and Marketing: Kilimo House, Cathedral Rd, POB 30028, Nairobi; tel. (2) 728370; telex 33042.

Ministry of Commerce and Industry: Co-operative House, Haile Selassie Ave, POB 47024, Nairobi; tel. (2) 340010.

Ministry of Co-operative Development: Kencom House, Moi Ave, Nairobi; tel. (2) 340081.

Ministry of Culture and Social Services: Reinsurance Plaza, Taifa Rd, POB 45958, Nairobi; tel. (2) 339650.

Ministry of Education: Jogoo House 'B', Harambee Ave, POB 30040, Nairobi; tel. (2) 28411.

Ministry of Energy: Nyayo House, Kenyatta Ave, POB 30582, Nairobi; tel. (2) 331242; telex 23094.

Ministry of Environment and Natural Resources: Kencom House, POB 30126, Nairobi; tel. (2) 29261.

Ministry of Finance: Treasury Bldg, Harambee Ave, POB 30007, Nairobi; tel. (2) 338111; telex 22696.

Ministry of Foreign Affairs: Harambee House, POB 30551, Nairobi; tel. (2) 334433; telex 22003.

Ministry of Health: Medical HQ, Afya House, Cathedral Rd, POB 30016, Nairobi; tel. (2) 720030; fax (2) 725902.

Ministry of Home Affairs and National Heritage: Nairobi.

Ministry of Information and Broadcasting: Jogoo House, POB 30025, Nairobi; tel. (2) 28411; telex 22244.

Ministry of Labour and Manpower Development: National Social Security House, POB 40326, Nairobi; tel. (2) 729800.

Ministry of Land Reclamation, Regional and Water Development: Maji House, Ngong Rd, POB 49720 Nairobi; tel. (2) 723103.

Ministry of Lands and Settlement: POB 30450, Nairobi; tel. (2) 718050.

Ministry of Local Government: Jogoo House 'A', POB 30004, Nairobi; tel. (2) 28411.

Ministry of Public Works and Housing: POB 30260, Nairobi; tel. (2) 723101.

Ministry of Research, Technical Training and Technology: Utalii House, Uhuru Highway, POB 30623, Nairobi; tel. (2) 336173.

Ministry of Tourism and Wildlife: Utalii House, 5th Floor, Uhuru Highway, POB 54666, Nairobi; tel. (2) 331030; telex 25016.

Ministry of Transport and Communication: Transcom House, Ngong Rd, POB 52692, Nairobi; tel. (2) 729200; telex 22272; fax (2) 726326.

President and Legislature

PRESIDENT

Election, 29 December 1992

Candidates	Votes	%
DANIEL ARAP MOI	1,962,866	36.35
KENNETH MATIBA	1,404,266	26.00
MWAI KIBAKI	1,050,617	19.45
OGINGA ODINGA	944,197	17.48
GEORGE MOSETI ANYONA	14,273	0.26
CHIBULE WA TSUMA	10,221	0.19
JOHN HARUN MWAU	8,118	0.15
MUKARU NG'ANG'A	5,776	0.11
Total	5,400,334	100.00

NATIONAL ASSEMBLY

Speaker: FRANCIS OLE KAPARO.

General Election, 29 December 1992

Party	Seats
KANU	100*
FORD—Asili	31*
FORD—Kenya	31
DP	23
KSC	1
KNC	1
Independent	1
Total	188

* In June 1993 a representative of FORD—Asili defected to KANU.

In addition to the 188 directly elected seats, 12 are held by nominees of the President. The Attorney-General and the Speaker are, ex officio, members of the National Assembly.

Political Organizations

Kenya was a *de facto* one-party state between 1969 and June 1982, when it became a *de jure* one-party state. In December 1991 the Constitution was amended to legalize a multi-party political system.

Democratic Party (DP): Nairobi; f. 1991; Pres. MWAI KIBAKI; Sec.-Gen. JOHN KEEN.

Forum for the Restoration of Democracy—Asili (FORD—Asili): Nairobi; f. 1992; Chair. KENNETH MATIBA; Sec.-Gen. MARTIN SHIKUKU.

Forum for the Restoration of Democracy—Kenya (FORD—Kenya): Nairobi; f. 1992; Chair. MICHAEL KIJANA WAMALWA; Sec.-Gen. MUNYUA WAIYAKI.

Islamic Party of Kenya (IPK): Mombasa; f. 1992; Islamic fundamentalist; banned; Chair. OMAR MWINYI; Sec.-Gen. ABDULRAHMAN WANDATI.

Kenya African National Union (KANU): POB 72394, Nairobi; f. 1960; sole legal party 1982–91; c. 4.3m. mems (1988); Pres. DANIEL ARAP MOI; Chair. WILSON NDOLO AYAH; Sec.-Gen. JOSEPH KAMOTHO.

Kenya National Congress (KNC): f. 1992.

Kenya National Democratic Alliance Party (KENDA): f. 1991; Chair. MUKARU NG'ANG'A.

Kenya Social Congress (KSC): f. 1992; Chair. GEORGE MOSETI ANYONA.

Labour Party Democracy: Chair. MOHAMED IBRAHIM NOOR.

National Development Party (NDP): f. 1994; Chair. STEPHEN OMONDI OLUDHE.

Party for Independent Candidates of Kenya (PICK): Leader: HARUN MWAU.

People's Union of Justice and New Order: Kisumu; Islamic support; Leader WILSON OWILI.

Rural National Democratic Party: f. 1992; supports farmers' interests; Chair. SEBASTIAN MUNENE.

Social Democratic Party: Nairobi; f. 1992.

United Democratic Alliance (UDA): f. 1994; an informal coalition of main opposition parties (excl. FORD–Asili) formed to present an agreed list of candidates in future elections.

United Muslims of Africa (UMA): f. 1993; Leader EMMANUEL MAITHA.

Youth Associated with the Restoration of Democracy (YARD): Chair. ELIUD AMBANI MULAMA.

Diplomatic Representation

EMBASSIES AND HIGH COMMISSIONS IN KENYA

Argentina: POB 30283, Nairobi; tel. (2) 335242; telex 22544; Ambassador: JOSÉ MARÍA CANTILO.

Australia: POB 30360, Nairobi; tel. (2) 445034; telex 22203; fax (2) 444617; High Commissioner: L. W. HERRON.

Austria: City House, Wabera St, POB 30560, Nairobi; tel. (2) 228281; telex 22076; Ambassador: Dr PAUL HARTIG.

Bangladesh: POB 41645, Nairobi; tel. (2) 562815; telex 25077; High Commissioner: SHARIFUL HAQ.

Belgium: Limuru Rd, POB 30461, Nairobi; tel. (2) 741564; telex 222269; fax (2) 741568; Ambassador: CRISTIAN FELLENS.

Brazil: Jeevan Bharati Bldg, Harambee Ave, POB 30751, Nairobi; tel. (2) 337722; telex 22498; fax (2) 336245; Ambassador: LUÍS FELIPE TEIXEIRA SOARES.

Burundi: Development House, Moi Ave, POB 44439, Nairobi; tel. (2) 218458; telex 22425; Ambassador: VANANT BAATAKANWA.

Canada: Comcraft House, Haile Selassie Ave, POB 30481, Nairobi; tel. (2) 214804; telex 22198; fax (2) 226987; High Commissioner: LUCIE GENEVIEVE EDWARDS.

Chile: International House, Mama Ngina St, POB 45554, Nairobi; tel. (2) 331320; telex 22348; fax (2) 215648; Ambassador: Dr VICENTE SÁNCHEZ.

China, People's Republic: Woodlands Rd, POB 30508, Nairobi; tel. (2) 722559; telex 22235; Ambassador: WU MINGLIAN.

Colombia: Muthaiga Rd, POB 48494, Nairobi; tel. (2) 765927; fax (2) 765911; Ambassador: Dr GERMÁN GARCÍA-DURÁN.

Costa Rica: POB 76639, Nairobi; tel. and fax (2) 569078.

Cyprus: Eagle House, Kimathi St, POB 30739, Nairobi; tel. (2) 220881; telex 22436; High Commissioner: MICHAEL SPANOS.

Czech Republic: Harambee Ave, POB 48785; tel. (2) 223448; telex 25115; fax (2) 223447.

Denmark: HFCK Bldg, Koinange St, POB 40412, Nairobi; tel. (2) 331088; telex 22216; fax (2) 331492; Ambassador: HENNING KJELDGAARD.

Djibouti: POB 59528, Nairobi; tel. (2) 229633; Ambassador: SALEH HAJI FARAH.

Egypt: Harambee Plaza, 7th Floor, POB 30285, Nairobi; tel. (2) 225991; telex 22335; Ambassador: MARAWAN ZAKI BADR.

Ethiopia: State House Ave, POB 45198, Nairobi; tel. (2) 723027; telex 22864; fax (2) 723401; Ambassador: OFATO ALEW.

Finland: International House, City Hall Way, POB 30379, Nairobi; tel. (2) 334777; telex 22010; Ambassador: DAVID JOHANSSON.

France: Embassy House, Harambee Ave, POB 41784, Nairobi; tel. (2) 339783; telex 22279; fax (2) 339421; Ambassador: MICHEL ROUGAGNOU.

Germany: Williamson House, 4th Ngong Ave, POB 30180, Nairobi; tel. (2) 712527; telex 22221; fax (2) 714886; Ambassador: BERND MÜTZELBURG.

Greece: IPS Bldg, Kimathi St, POB 30543, Nairobi; tel. (2) 340722; telex 22008; Ambassador: ELIAS KATSAREAS.

Holy See: Apostolic Nunciature, Manyani Rd West, POB 14326, Nairobi; tel. (2) 442975; fax (2) 446789; Apostolic Pro-Nuncio: Most Rev. CLEMENTE FACCANI, Titular Archbishop of Serra.

Hungary: Agip House, 2nd Floor, POB 30523, Nairobi; tel. (2) 226914; telex 22364; fax (2) 569433; Chargé d'affaires: ZSIGMOND D. PATAY.

India: Jeevan Bharati Bldg, Harambee Ave, POB 30074, Nairobi; tel. (2) 222361; telex 22079; fax (2) 334167; High Commissioner: KIRAN DOSHI.

Indonesia: Utalii House, Uhuru Highway, POB 48868, Nairobi; tel. (2) 215873; telex 23171; Ambassador: DALINDRA AMAN.

Iran: POB 49170, Nairobi; tel. (2) 720343; telex 22563; Ambassador: HAMID MOAYYER.

Iraq: Matungulu House, POB 49213, Nairobi; tel. (2) 580262; telex 22176; Chargé d'affaires: HILKMAT AL-ALANI.

Israel: POB 30354, Nairobi; tel. (2) 722182; telex 22412; fax (2) 715966; Ambassador: ARIEH ODED.

Italy: International Life House, Mama Ngina St, POB 30107, Nairobi; tel. (2) 337356; telex 22251; fax (2) 337056; Ambassador: Dr RENATO VOLPONI.

Japan: Kenyatta Ave, POB 60202, Nairobi; tel. (2) 332955; telex 22286; Ambassador: GINKO SATO.

Korea, Republic: Anniversary Towers, University Way, POB 30455, Nairobi; tel. (2) 333581; telex 22300; Ambassador: RAH WON-CHAN.

Kuwait: Muthaiga Rd, POB 42353, Nairobi; tel. (2) 767144; telex 22467; Chargé d'affaires: JABER SALEM HUSSAIN EBRAHEEM.

Lesotho: International House, Mama Ngina St, POB 44096, Nairobi; tel. (2) 337493; telex 22489; High Commissioner: (vacant).

Malawi: Waiyaki Way (between Mvuli and Church Rds), POB 30453, Nairobi; tel. (2) 440569; telex 22749; fax 440568; High Commissioner: M. V. L. PHIRI (acting).

Mexico: POB 14145, Nairobi; tel. (2) 582850; telex 23065; fax (2) 581500; Ambassador: A. GONZÁLEZ.

Morocco: POB 61098, Nairobi; tel. (2) 222264; telex 22531; Ambassador: MEHDI BENNANI.

Mozambique: POB 66923, Nairobi; tel. (2) 581857; Chargé d'affaires: EDWARDO ADRIANO.

Netherlands: Uchumi House, Nkrumah Ave, POB 41537, Nairobi; tel. (2) 227111; telex 22285; fax (2) 339155; Ambassador: ROBERT FRUIN.

Nigeria: Hurlingham, POB 30516, Nairobi; tel. (2) 564116; telex 22194; fax (2) 562776; High Commissioner: CLARKSON N. UMELO.

Norway: Nairobi; Ambassador: ARMAN AARDAL.

Pakistan: St Michel Rd, Westlands, POB 30045, Nairobi; tel. (2) 443911; telex 25907; fax (2) 446507; High Commissioner: AMIR M. KHAN.

Poland: Kabarnet Rd, POB 30086, Nairobi; tel. (2) 566288; telex 22266; fax (2) 562588; Ambassador: ADAM T. KOWALEWSKI.

Portugal: POB 34020, Nairobi; tel. (2) 338990; telex 22634; Ambassador: Dr PAULO COUTO BARBOSA.

Romania: POB 48412, Nairobi; tel. (2) 227515; Chargé d'affaires: GHEORGHE DRAGOS.

Russia: Lenana Rd, POB 30049, Nairobi; tel. (2) 722559; telex 25261; fax (2) 721888; Ambassador: VLADIMIR S. KITAYEV.

Rwanda: International Life House, Mama Ngina St, POB 48579, Nairobi; tel. (2) 334341; telex 22463; Ambassador: CYPRIEN HABIMANA.

Saudi Arabia: POB 58297, Nairobi; tel. (2) 762781; telex 22990; Chargé d'affaires: GHORM SAID MAWHAN.

Slovakia: Milimani Rd, POB 30204, Nairobi; tel. (2) 721896; telex 25371; fax (2) 721898.

Spain: Bruce House, Standard St, POB 45503, Nairobi; tel. (2) 336330; telex 22157; Ambassador: LUIS G. MERINO.

Sri Lanka: International Life House, Mama Ngina St, POB 48145, Nairobi; tel. (2) 227577; telex 25081; High Commissioner: Dr G. G. M. SIKURAJAPATHY.

Sudan: Minet ICDC House, 7th Floor, POB 48784, Nairobi; tel. (2) 720853; Ambassador: Dr ABDEL LATIF ABDEL HAMID IBRAHIM.

Swaziland: Silopark House, POB 41887, Nairobi; tel. (2) 339231; telex 22085; High Commissioner: Prince CHURCHILL B. H. DLAMINI.

Sweden: International House, Mama Ngina St, POB 30600, Nairobi; tel. (2) 229042; telex 22264; fax (2) 218908; Ambassador: NILS GUNNAR REVELIUS.

Switzerland: International Life House, Mama Ngina St, POB 30752, Nairobi; tel. (2) 228735; telex 22181; Ambassador: Dr ARMIN KAMER.

Tanzania: Continental House, POB 47790, Nairobi; tel. (2) 331056; High Commissioner: MIRISHO SAM HAGGAI SARAKIKYA.

Thailand: POB 58349, Nairobi; tel. (2) 715800; telex 22836; Ambassador: APIPHONG JAYANAMA.

Turkey: Gigiri Rd, off Limuru Rd, POB 30785, Nairobi; tel. (2) 520404; telex 22346; fax (2) 521237; Chargé d'affaires: CUNEYT YAVUZCAN.

Uganda: POB 60855, Nairobi; tel. (2) 330801; telex 22732; High Commissioner: J. TOMUSANGE.

United Kingdom: Bruce House, Standard St, POB 30465, Nairobi; tel. (2) 335944; telex 22219; fax (2) 333196; High Commissioner: Sir KIERAN PRENDERGAST.

USA: cnr Moi and Haile Selassie Aves, POB 30137, Nairobi; tel. (2) 334141; telex 22964; fax (2) 340838; Ambassador: AURELIA BRAZEAL.

Venezuela: International House, Mama Ngina St, POB 34477, Nairobi; tel. (2) 341078; telex 22671; fax (2) 337487; Ambassador: ALBERTO LIZARRALDE MARADEY.

Yemen: Ngong Rd, POB 44642, Nairobi; tel. (2) 564379; Ambassador: Dr HUSSEIN AL-GALAL.

Yugoslavia: State House Ave, POB 30504, Nairobi; tel. (2) 720671; telex 22515; Ambassador: LJUBE ZAFIROV.

Zaire: Electricity House, Harambee Ave, POB 48106, Nairobi; tel. (2) 229771; telex 22057; Ambassador: ATENDA MONGEBE OMWANGO.

Zambia: Nyerere Rd, POB 48741, Nairobi; tel. (2) 724850; telex 22193; fax (2) 718494; High Commissioner: ENESS CHISHALA CHIYENGE.

Zimbabwe: Minet ICDC House, Mamlaka Rd, POB 30806, Nairobi; tel. (2) 711071; telex 25033; High Commissioner: ANGELINA MAKWAVARARA.

Judicial System

The Kenya Court of Appeal: POB 30187, Nairobi; the final court of appeal for Kenya in civil and criminal process; sits at Nairobi, Mombasa, Kisumu, Nakuru and Nyeri.

Chief Justice: FRED KWASI APALOO.

Justices of Appeal: MATHEW MULI, J. M. GACHUHI, J. R. O. MASIME, J. E. GICHERU, R. O. KWACH, A. M. COCKAR.

The High Court of Kenya: Harambee Ave, POB 40112, Nairobi; tel. (2) 21221; has unlimited criminal and civil jurisdiction at first instance, and sits as a court of appeal from subordinate courts in both criminal and civil cases. The High Court is also a court of admiralty. There are two resident puisne judges at Mombasa, and a resident puisne judge at Nakuru, Eldoret, Kakamega, Kisumu and Nyeri. Regular sessions are held in Kisii and Meru.

Resident Magistrates' Courts: have country-wide jurisdiction, with powers of punishment by imprisonment up to five years or by fine up to K£500. If presided over by a chief magistrate or senior resident magistrate the court is empowered to pass any sentence authorized by law. For certain offences, a resident magistrate may pass minimum sentences authorized by law.

District Magistrates' Courts: of first, second and third class; have jurisdiction within districts and powers of punishment by imprisonment for up to five years, or by fines of up to K£500.

Kadhi's Courts: have jurisdiction within districts, to determine questions of Islamic law.

Religion

Most of the population hold traditional African beliefs, although there are significant numbers of African Christians. The Arab inhabitants are Muslims, and the Indian population is partly Muslim and partly Hindu. The Europeans and Goans are almost entirely Christian. Muslims are found mainly along the coastline; however, the Islamic faith has also established itself among Africans around Nairobi and among some ethnic groups in the northern districts. East Africa is also an important centre for the Bahá'í faith.

CHRISTIANITY

National Council of Churches of Kenya: Church House, Moi Ave, POB 45009, Nairobi; tel. (2) 338211; f. 1943 as Christian Council of Kenya; 35 full mems and eight assoc. mems; Chair. Rev. Dr GEORGE WANJAU; Sec.-Gen. Rev. SAMUEL KOBIA.

The Anglican Communion

Anglicans are adherents of the Church of the Province of Kenya, comprising 20 dioceses. It became a separate church in 1970, and had some 2m. members in 1994.

Archbishop of Kenya and Bishop of Nairobi: Most Rev. Dr MANASSES KURIA, POB 40502, Nairobi; tel. (2) 714755; fax (2) 718442.

Greek Orthodox Church

Archbishop of East Africa: NICADEMUS of IRINOUPOULIS, Nairobi; jurisdiction covers Kenya, Tanzania and Uganda.

The Roman Catholic Church

Kenya comprises four archdioceses and 15 dioceses. At 31 December 1993 there were an estimated 7.25m. adherents in the country, representing nearly 29% of the total population.

Kenya Episcopal Conference: National Catholic Secretariat, POB 48062, Nairobi; tel. (2) 443133; fax (2) 442910; f. 1976; Pres. Most Rev. ZACCHAEUS OKOTH, Archbishop of Kisumu.

Archbishop of Kisumu: Most Rev. ZACCHAEUS OKOTH, POB 1728, Kisumu; tel. (35) 43881; fax (35) 42415.

Archbishop of Mombasa: Most Rev. JOHN NJENGA, Catholic Secretariat, Nyerere Ave, POB 83131, Mombasa; tel. (11) 228217; fax (11) 473166.

Archbishop of Nairobi: Cardinal MAURICE OTUNGA, Archbishop's House, POB 14231, Nairobi; tel. (2) 441919.

Archbishop of Nyeri: Most Rev. NICODEMUS KIRIMA, POB 288, Nyeri; tel. (171) 2366.

Other Christian Churches

African Christian Church and Schools: POB 1365, Thika; tel. (151) 47; f. 1948; 50,000 mems; Moderator Rt Rev. JOHN NJUNGUNA; Gen. Sec. Rev. SAMUEL MWANGI.

African Church of the Holy Spirit: POB 183, Kakamega; f. 1927; 20,000 mems; Exec. Sec. Rev. PETER IHAJI.

African Israel Nineveh Church: Nineveh HQ, POB 701, Kisumu; f. 1942; 350,000 mems; High Priest Rt Rev. JOHN KIVULI, II; Gen. Sec. Rev. JOHN ARAP TONUI.

Baptist Convention of Kenya: Pres. Rev. ELIUD MUNGAI, POB 14907, Nairobi.

Evangelical Lutheran Church in Kenya: Pres. Pastor JOHN KURURIA, POB 874, Kisii; tel. (381) 20237; 28,000 mems.

Methodist Church in Kenya: POB 47633, Nairobi; tel. (2) 724841; f. 1862 (autonomous since 1967); 300,000 mems (1994); Presiding Bishop Prof. ZABLON NTHAMBURI.

Presbyterian Church of East Africa: POB 48268, Nairobi; tel. (2) 504417; fax (2) 504442; Moderator Rt Rev. BERNARD MUINDI; Sec.-Gen. Rev. Dr SAMUEL MWANIKI.

Other denominations active in Kenya include the Africa Gospel Church, the Africa Inland Church, the African Brotherhood Church, the African Independent Pentecostal Church, the African Interior Church, the Church of God in East Africa, the Episcopal Church of Kenya, the Free Pentecostal Fellowship of Kenya, the Full Gospel Churches of Kenya, the Lutheran Church in Kenya, the National Independent Church of Africa, the Pentecostal Assemblies of God, the Pentecostal Evangelistic Fellowship of God and the Reformed Church of East Africa.

BAHÁ'Í FAITH

National Spiritual Assembly: POB 47562, Nairobi; tel. (2) 725447; mems resident in 9,654 localities.

ISLAM

Supreme Council of Kenyan Muslims: Nat. Chair. A. H. S. AL-BUSAIDY; Sec.-Gen. Alhaji SHABAN BAKARI.

The Press

PRINCIPAL DAILIES

Daily Nation: POB 49010, Nairobi; tel. (2) 337691; English; f. 1960; banned by Govt in June 1989 from reporting parliamentary proceedings; Editor-in-Chief WANGETHI MWANGI; Man. Editor TOM MSHINDI; circ. 165,000.

Kenya Leo: POB 30958, Nairobi; tel. (2) 337798; f. 1983; Kiswahili; KANU party newspaper; Man. Editor JOB MUTUNGI.

Kenya Times: POB 30958, Nairobi; tel. (2) 24251; telex 25008; f. 1983; English; KANU party newspaper; Editor-in-Chief JOHN KHAKHUDU AGUNDA; circ. 52,000.

The Standard: POB 30080, Nairobi; tel. (2) 540280; telex 24032; fax (2) 553939; English; f. 1902; Editor-in-Chief (vacant); Man. Editor KAMAU KANYANGA; circ. 70,000.

Taifa Leo: POB 49010, Nairobi; tel. (2) 337691; Kiswahili; f. 1960; daily and weekly edns; Editor ROBERT MWANGI; circ. 57,000.

SELECTED PERIODICALS

Weeklies and Fortnightlies

Coast Week: weekly; Editor ADRIAN GRIMWOOD; circ. 40,000.

Kenrail: POB 30121, Nairobi; tel. (2) 221211; telex 22254; English and Kiswahili; publ. by Kenya Railways Corpn; Editor J. N. LUSENO; circ. 20,000.

Kenya Gazette: POB 30746, Nairobi; tel. (2) 334075; f. 1898; official notices; weekly; circ. 8,000.

The People: Nairobi; Editor-in-Chief BEDAN MBUGUA.

Society: Changamwe Rd, Industrial Area, Nairobi; weekly; Editor-in-Chief PIUS NYAMORA.

The Standard on Sunday: POB 30080, Nairobi; tel. (2) 540280; telex 24032; fax (2) 553939; English; Man. Editor ESTHER KAMWERU; circ. 90,000.

Sunday Nation: POB 49010, Nairobi; f. 1960; English; Man. Editor BERNARD NDERITU; circ. 170,000.

Sunday Times: POB 30958, Nairobi; tel. (2) 337798; telex 25008; ROBERT OTANI.

Taifa Jumapili: POB 49010, Nairobi; f. 1987; Kiswahili; Editor ROBERT K. MWANGI; circ. 56,000.

Taifa Weekly: POB 49010, Nairobi; tel. (2) 337691; f. 1960; Kiswahili; Editor ROBERT K. MWANGI; circ. 68,000.

The Weekly Review: POB 42271, Nairobi; f. 1975; English; Editor AMBOKA ANDERE; circ. 32,000.

What's On: Rehema House, POB 49010, Nairobi; tel. (2) 27651; telex 25092; Editor NANCY KAIRO; circ. 10,000.

Monthlies

Afrika ya Kesho: PO Kijabe; Kiswahili; Editor J. N. SOMBA; circ. 4,000.

Autonews: POB 30339, Nairobi; tel. (2) 25502; journal of the Automobile Asscn of Kenya; Editor PATRICIA HUGHES-SCOTT; circ. 13,000.

East African Medical Journal: POB 41632, Nairobi; tel. (2) 724617; English; f. 1923; Editor-in-Chief Prof. E. G. KASILI; circ. 4,000.

East African Report on Trade and Industry: POB 30339, Nairobi; journal of Kenya Asscn of Mfrs; Editor GORDON BOY; circ. 3,000.

Executive: POB 47186, Nairobi; tel. (2) 555811; telex 24095; fax (2) 557815; f. 1980; business; Editor ALI ZAIDI; circ. 16,000.

Kenya Export News: POB 30339, Nairobi; tel. (2) 25502; English; publ. for Kenya External Trade Authority, Ministry of Commerce and Industry; Editor Prof. SAMUEL NJOROGE; circ. 5,000.

Kenya Farmer (Journal of the Agricultural Society of Kenya): c/o English Press, POB 30127, Nairobi; tel. (2) 20377; f. 1954; English and Kiswahili; Editor ROBERT IRUNGU; circ. 20,000.

Kenya Yetu: POB 8053, Nairobi; tel. (2) 223201; telex 22244; f. 1965; Kiswahili; publ. by Ministry of Information and Broadcasting; Editor M. NDAVI; circ. 10,000.

Nairobi Handbook: POB 30127, Accra Rd, Nairobi; Editor Mrs R. OUMA; circ. 20,000.

The Nairobi Law Monthly: Tumaini House, 4th Floor, Nkrumah Ave, POB 53234, Nairobi; tel. (2) 330480; f. 1987; banned by Govt March–July 1991; English; Editor-in-Chief GITOBU IMANYARA.

News from Kenya: POB 8053, Nairobi; tel. (2) 28411; telex 22244; publ. by Ministry of Information and Broadcasting.

Other Periodicals

African Ecclesial Review: POB 4002, Eldoret; scripture, religion and development; 6 a year; Editor AGATHA RADOLI; circ. 2,500.

Afya: POB 30125, Nairobi; tel. (2) 501301; telex 23254; fax (2) 506112; journal for medical and health workers; quarterly.

Busara: POB 30022, Nairobi; literary; 2 a year; Editor KIMANI GECAU; circ. 3,000.

East African Agricultural and Forestry Journal: POB 30148, Nairobi; f. 1935; English; quarterly; Editor J. O. MUGAH; circ. 1,000.

Eastern African Economic Review: POB 30022, Nairobi; f. 1954; 2 a year; Editor J. K. MAITHA.

Economic Review of Agriculture: POB 30028, Nairobi; tel. (2) 728370; telex 33042; f. 1968; publ. by Ministry of Agriculture, Livestock and Marketing; quarterly; Editor OKIYA OKOITI.

Education in Eastern Africa: POB 5869, Nairobi; f. 1970; 2 a year; Editor JOHN C. B. BIGALA; circ. 2,000.

Finance: Nairobi; monthly; Editor-in-Chief NJEHU GATABAKI.

Inside Kenya Today: POB 8053, Nairobi; tel. (2) 223201; telex 22244; English; publ. by Ministry of Information and Broadcasting; quarterly; Editor M. NDAVI; circ. 10,000.

Journal of the Language Association of Eastern Africa: POB 30571, Nairobi; tel. (2) 28411; telex 22244; publ. by Ministry of Information and Broadcasting; 2 a year; Editor T. P. GORMAN; circ. 2,000.

Kenya Education Journal: POB 2768, Nairobi; f. 1958; English; 3 a year; Editor W. G. BOWMAN; circ. 5,500.

Kenya Statistical Digest: POB 30007, Nairobi; tel. (2) 338111; telex 22696; publ. by Ministry of Finance; quarterly.

Target: POB 72839, Nairobi; f. 1964; English; 6 a year; religious; Editor REBEKA NJAU (acting); circ. 17,000.

NEWS AGENCIES

Kenya News Agency (KNA): Information House, POB 8053, Nairobi; tel. (2) 223201; telex 22244; f. 1963; Dir S. MUSANDU.

Foreign Bureaux

Agence France-Presse (AFP): International Life House, Mama Ngina St, POB 30671, Nairobi; tel. (2) 332043; telex 22243; Bureau Chief DIDIER LAPEYRONIE.

Agenzia Nazionale Stampa Associata (ANSA) (Italy): Agip House, POB 20444, Nairobi; tel. (2) 711338; telex 23251; fax (2) 229383; Representative ADOLFO D'AMICO.

Associated Press (AP) (USA): Chester House, Koinange St, POB 47590, Nairobi; tel. (2) 340663; telex 25101; Bureau Chief REID G. MILLER.

Deutsche Presse-Agentur (dpa) (Germany): Chester House, 1st Floor, Koinange St, POB 48546, Nairobi; tel. (2) 330274; telex 22330; fax (2) 221902; Bureau Chief Dr HUBERT KAHL.

Informatsionnoye Telegrafnoye Agentstvo Rossii—Telegrafnoye Agentstvo Suverennykh Stran (ITAR—TASS) (Russia): Likoni Lane, POB 49602, Nairobi; tel. (2) 721978; telex 22192; fax (2) 721978; Correspondent VLADIMIR MANVELOV.

Inter Press Service (IPS) (Italy): Press Centre, Chester House, Koinange St, POB 54386, Nairobi; tel. (2) 335418; Correspondent HORACE AWORI.

Kyodo Tsushin (Japan): Mbaaz Ave, POB 58281, Nairobi; tel. (2) 339504; telex 22915; Bureau Chief JUNJI MIURA.

United Press International (UPI) (USA): POB 76282, Nairobi; tel. (2) 337349; fax (2) 213625; Correspondent JOE KHAMISI.

Xinhua (New China) News Agency (People's Republic of China): Ngong Rd at Rose Ave, POB 30728, Nairobi; tel. (2) 722494; telex 23241; Dir and Chief Correspondent YE ZHIXIONG.

Publishers

Camerapix: POB 45048, Nairobi; tel. (2) 223511; telex 22576; fax (2) 217244; f. 1960; architecture and design, travel, topography, natural history; CEO MOHAMED AMIN.

East African Educational Publishers Ltd: cnr Mpaka Rd and Woodvale Grove, Westlands, POB 45314, Nairobi; tel. (2) 444700; f. 1965; academic, educational, creative writing in Kenyan languages; Man. Dir HENRY CHAKAVA.

East African Publishing House Ltd: POB 30571, Nairobi; tel. (2) 557417; f. 1965; educational, academic and general; also publs periodicals; Man. Dir EDWARD N. WAINAINA.

Evangel: POB 28963, Nairobi; tel. (2) 802033; f. 1952; Gen. Man. RICHARD ONDENG.

Foundation Books: Kencom House, Moi Ave, POB 73435, Nairobi; tel. (2) 761520; f. 1974; Man. Dir F. O. OKWANYA.

Gaba Publications: Amecea Pastoral Institute, POB 4002, Eldoret; tel. (321) 33286; religious; Dir Sister AGATHA RADOLI.

Kenya Literature Bureau: Belle Vewarea, off Mombasa Rd, POB 30022, Nairobi; tel. (2) 506142; f. 1977; parastatal body under Ministry of Education; literary, educational, cultural and scientific books and journals; Chair. JANE KIANO; Man. Dir S. C. LANG'AT.

Jomo Kenyatta Foundation: POB 30533, Nairobi; tel. (2) 557222; f. 1966; primary, secondary, university textbooks; Man. Dir HERBERT CHABALA.

Longman Kenya Ltd: POB 18033, Nairobi; tel. (2) 541345; telex 24101; fax (2) 540037; f. 1965; textbooks and educational materials; Man. Dir Dr E. M. MUGIRI.

Macmillan Kenya (Publishers) Ltd: POB 30797, Nairobi; tel. (2) 224485; telex 22574; fax (2) 212179; Man. Dir DAVID MUITA.

Newspread International: POB 46854, Nairobi; tel. (2) 331402; telex 22143; fax (2) 333448; reference, economic development; Exec. Editor KUL BHUSHAN.

Oxford University Press (Eastern Africa): Waiyaki Way, ABC Place, POB 72532, Nairobi; tel. (2) 440555; fax (2) 443972; f. 1954; educational and general; Regional Man. ABDULLAH ISMAILY.

Paulines Publications-Africa: POB 49026, Nairobi; tel. (2) 442319; fax (2) 442144; religious.

Transafrica Press: Kenwood House, Kimathi St, POB 48239, Nairobi; tel. (2) 331762; f. 1976; general, educational and children's; CEO JOHN NOTTINGHAM.

Government Publishing House

Government Printing Press: POB 30128, Nairobi.

PUBLISHERS' ORGANIZATION

Kenya Publishers' Association: POB 72532, Nairobi; tel. (2) 336377; Sec. ABDULLAH ISMAILY (acting).

Radio and Television

In 1991, according to UNESCO, there were an estimated 2.1m. radio receivers and 234,000 television receivers in use.

Kenya Broadcasting Corporation (KBC): Broadcasting House, POB 30456, Nairobi; tel. (2) 334567; telex 25361; f. 1989 as a state corpn to succeed Voice of Kenya (f. 1959); responsible for radio and television broadcasting; Chair. Dr JULIUS KIANO; Man. Dir PHILIP OKUNDI; Dir of Broadcasting DAVID OLE NASIEKU.

Radio: three services: National (Kiswahili); General (English); Vernacular (Hindustani, Kikuyu, Kikamba, Kimeru, Kimasai, Somali, Borana, Luhya, Kalenjin, Kisii, Kuria, Rendile, Burji, Teso, Turkana and Luo).

Television: broadcasting financed by licence fees, commercial advertisements and a state subsidy; services in Kiswahili and English; operates on four channels for approximately 50 hours per week. In June 1994 it was announced that a private television station, Cable Television Network (CTN), would begin broadcasting later in the year.

Finance

(cap. = capital; p.u. = paid up; res = reserves; dep. = deposits; brs = branches; amounts in Kenya shillings)

BANKING

Central Bank

Central Bank of Kenya: Haile Selassie Ave, POB 60000, Nairobi; tel. (2) 226431; telex 22324; fax (2) 340192; f. 1966; bank of issue; cap. and res 2,057.6m., dep. 21,900.4m. (June 1992); Gov. ERIC C. KOTUT; Dep. Gov. ELIPHAZ RIUNGU.

Commercial Banks

Barclays Bank of Kenya Ltd: Bank House, Moi Ave, POB 30120, Nairobi; tel. (2) 332230; telex 22210; fax (2) 335219; f. 1978; cap. 572m. (Dec. 1990); Chair. SAMUEL WARUHIU; Man. Dir R. A. BIRD; 54 brs.

Biashara Bank of Kenya Ltd: Investment House, Muindi Mbingu St, POB 30831, Nairobi; tel. (2) 221064; telex 25161; fax 221679; f. 1984; cap. and res 134.3m., dep. 1,471.3m. (Sept. 1992); Chair. S. B. R. SHAH.

Commercial Bank of Africa Ltd: Commercial Bank Bldg, cnr Wabera and Standard Sts, POB 30437, Nairobi; tel. (2) 228881; telex 23205; fax (2) 335827; f. 1967; 100% owned by Kenyan shareholders; cap. and res 371m., dep. 3,108m. (Dec. 1993); Chair. M. H. DA GAMA ROSE; Man. Dir E. J. SILVA; 6 brs.

Consolidated Bank of Kenya Ltd: POB 51133, Nairobi; tel. (2) 220175; telex 22482; fax (2) 340213; f. 1989; state-owned; cap. and res 400.2m., dep. 953.8m. (March 1993); Man. Dir E. K. MATHIU.

Delphis Bank Ltd: Koinange St, POB 44080, Nairobi; tel. (2) 228461; telex 22493; fax (2) 219469; f. 1991; CEO F. H. J. BARNES.

Kenya Commercial Bank Ltd: Kencom House, Moi Ave, POB 48400, Nairobi; tel. (2) 339441; telex 23085; fax (2) 338006; f. 1970; 70% state-owned; cap. and res 2,183m., dep. 31,367m. (Dec. 1993); Exec. Chair. A. T. KAMINCHIA; Gen. Man. E. K. ARAB BII; 264 brs and sub-brs.

Meridien BIAO Bank Kenya Ltd: Windsor House, Muindi Mbingu St, POB 30132, Nairobi; tel. (2) 219411; telex 22116; fax (2) 219392; f. 1992.

Middle East Bank Kenya Ltd: Kenyatta Ave, POB 47387, Nairobi; tel. (2) 335168; telex 23132; fax (2) 336182; f. 1981; 100% owned by Kenyan shareholders; cap. p.u. 75m., dep. 1,223.4m. (Dec. 1993); Chair. A. ESMAIL; Man. Dir S. S. DINAMANI; 2 brs.

National Bank of Kenya Ltd (Banki ya Taifa La Kenya Ltd): National Bank Bldg, Harambee Ave, POB 72866, Nairobi; tel. (2) 226472; telex 22619; fax (2) 330784; f. 1968; 100% state-owned; cap. and res 1,289m., dep. 10,671m. (June 1994); Exec. Chair. JOHN SIMBA; Gen. Man. A. H. AHMED; 18 brs.

Pan African Bank Ltd: ICEA Bldg, 14th Floor, Kenyatta Ave, POB 45334, Nairobi; tel. (2) 225325; telex 23058; fax (2) 218490; f. 1982; cap. p.u. 100m. (Dec. 1990); Chair. and Man. Dir MOHAMMAD ASLAM; 8 brs.

Stanbic Bank Kenya Ltd: Kenyatta Ave, POB 30550, Nairobi; tel. (2) 335888; telex 22397; fax (2) 330227; f. 1970 as Grindlays Bank International (Kenya); 40% state-owned; cap. p.u. 15m. (Sept. 1992), dep. 366.7m. (Sept. 1986); Chair. A. D. B. WRIGHT; 2 brs.

Standard Chartered Bank Kenya Ltd: Stanbank House, Moi Ave, POB 30003, Nairobi; tel. (2) 330200; telex 22209; fax (2) 330506; 74.5% owned by Standard Chartered Bank Africa; cap. and res 1,747m., dep. 21,426.6m. (Dec. 1993); Chair. JULIUS GECAU; Man. Dir and CEO ALAN CLEARY; 43 brs.

Trust Bank Ltd: Trustforte Bldg, Moi Ave, POB 46342, Nairobi; tel. (2) 226413; telex 25143; fax (2) 334995; f. 1988; cap. and res 365m., dep. 4,000m. (Sept. 1993); Chair. AJAY SHAH; Gen. Man. H. V. BHATT; 5 brs.

Union Bank of Kenya Ltd: Postbank House, Banda St, POB 34823, Nairobi; tel. (2) 28705; telex 23263; fax (2) 720925; f. 1984; cap. 51m., dep. 120m. (1987); CEO C. K. MURAYA, D. M. KAVUU, D. G. MBATIA; 3 brs.

Merchant Banks

Diamond Trust of Kenya Ltd: Moi Ave, POB 61711, Nairobi; tel. (2) 337445; telex 23294; fax (2) 336836; f. 1945; cap. p.u. 56.5m. (Dec. 1990); Chair. ZAHER AHAMED; Man. Dir NIZAR MERUANI.

Kenya Commercial Finance Co Ltd: POB 48400, Nairobi; tel. (2) 339074; telex 23085; f. 1971; cap. p.u. 100m. (1991), dep. 2,666m. (1990); Chair. A. ABDALLAH; Chief Man. J. K. MUTHUNDO.

Kenya National Capital Corporation Ltd: POB 73469, Nairobi; tel. (2) 336077; telex 22159; f. 1977; 60% owned by National Bank of Kenya, 40% by Kenya National Assurance Co; cap. 80m., dep. 940m. (1991); Chair. WANJOHI MURIITHI; Gen. Man. J. P. OKORA.

Pan African Credit and Finance Ltd: ICEA Bldg, 5th Floor, Kenyatta Ave, POB 47529, Nairobi; tel. (2) 25325; telex 23058; fax (2) 722410; 98.65% owned by Pan African Bank; cap. p.u. 40m. (Dec. 1990); Chair. and Man. Dir MOHAMMAD ASLAM.

Standard Chartered Financial Services Ltd: International House, 1st Floor, Mama Ngina St, POB 40310, Nairobi; tel. (2) 336333; telex 22089; fax (2) 334934; 100% owned by Standard Chartered Bank Kenya; cap. and res 161.7m. (Dec. 1992), dep. 1,700m. (Dec. 1992); Chair. A. CLEARY; Man. Dir W. VON ISENBURG.

Foreign Banks

ABN AMRO Bank NV (Netherlands): Nyerere Rd, POB 30262, Nairobi; tel. (2) 710455; telex 22262; fax (2) 713391; Gen. Man. W. A. E. J. LEMSTRA; 2 brs.

Bank of Baroda (India): Bank of Baroda Bldg, cnr Mondlane St and Tom Mboya St, POB 30033, Nairobi; tel. (2) 337611; telex 22250; fax (2) 333089; Exec. Chair. AFUL DESAI; 6 brs.

Bank of India: Kenyatta Ave, POB 30246, Nairobi; tel. (2) 221414; telex 22725; fax (2) 334545; Chief Man. P. V. PALSOKAR.

Bank of Oman: ICEA Bldg, Kenyatta Ave, POB 11129, Nairobi; tel. (2) 330562; telex 22596; fax (2) 330792; Man. MUHAMMAD RAFIQUE.

Banque Indosuez (France): Reinsurance Plaza, Taifa Rd, POB 69562, Nairobi; tel. (2) 215859; telex 23091; fax (2) 214166; Regional Man. JEAN-MICHEL BROCATO.

Citibank NA (USA): Fehda Towers, 6th Floor, Muindi Mbingu St, POB 30711, Nairobi; tel. (2) 334286; telex 22051; fax (2) 337340; Gen. Man. TERENCE DAVIDSON.

First American Bank of Kenya Ltd (USA): ICEA Bldg, Kenyatta Ave, POB 30691, Nairobi; tel. (2) 333960; telex 222398; fax (2) 333868; f. 1987; cap. and res 167m., dep. 1,557m. (1992); Chair. N. N. MERALI; Man. Dir MANLIO BLASETTI; 1 br.

Habib Bank AG Zurich (Switzerland): National House, Koinange St, POB 30584, Nairobi; tel. (2) 334984; telex 22982; fax (2) 726774; Gen. Man. BAKIRALI NASIR.

Co-operative Bank

Co-operative Bank of Kenya Ltd: Co-operative House, Haile Selassie Ave, POB 48231, Nairobi; tel. (2) 287112; telex 22938; fax (2) 336073; f. 1968; cap. and res 235.7m., dep. 2,622m. (June 1992); Chair. HENRY MULLI; Gen. Man. ERASTUS MUREITHI; 17 brs.

Development Banks

East African Development Bank: Bruce House, Standard St, POB 47685, Nairobi; tel. (2) 340642; telex 22689; fax (2) 21665; loan finance to, and promotion of regional projects; Man. J. F. OWITI.

Industrial Development Bank Ltd: National Bank Bldg, Harambee Ave, POB 44036, Nairobi; tel. (2) 337079; telex 22339; fax (2) 334594; f. 1973; 49% state-owned; finances industrial projects; cap. p.u. 258m. (June 1991); Chair. J. K. NDOTO; Man. Dir Dr YUSUF NZIBO.

STOCK EXCHANGE

Nairobi Stock Exchange: IPS Bldg, Kimathi St, POB 43633, Nairobi; tel. (2) 230692; fax (2) 224200; f. 1954; 6 mems; Chair. J. M. MBATU; CEO J. K. KIHUMBA.

INSURANCE

American Life Insurance Co: American Life House, POB 49460, Nairobi; tel. (2) 721124; telex 22621; general.

Blue Shield Insurance Co Ltd: POB 49610; Nairobi; tel. (2) 227932; fax (2) 337808; f. 1983; life and general.

Cannon Assurance (Kenya) Ltd: Haile Selassie Ave, POB 30216, Nairobi; tel. (2) 335478; telex 25482; f. 1974; life and general; cap. 20m.; CEO I. J. TALWAR.

Corporate Insurance Co Ltd: Postbank House, Koinange and Banda Sts, POB 34172, Nairobi; tel. (2) 25302; telex 25134; f. 1983; life and general; cap. 10m.; CEO WILLIAM MURUNGU.

Heritage Insurance Co Ltd: Norwich Union Bldg, Mama Ngina St, POB 30390, Nairobi; tel. (2) 725303; telex 22476; fax (2) 722835; f. 1975; general; CEO T. C. GOSS.

Insurance Co of East Africa Ltd (ICEA): ICEA Bldg, Kenyatta Ave, POB 46143, Nairobi; tel. (2) 21652; life and general; CEO R. C. WOOTTON.

Intra Africa Assurance Co Ltd: Williamson House, 4th Ngong Ave, POB 43241, Nairobi; tel. (2) 712607; f. 1977; CEO H. G. MKANGI.

Jubilee Insurance Co Ltd: POB 30376, Nairobi; tel. (2) 340343; telex 22199; fax (2) 216882; f. 1937; life and general; Chair. ABDUL JAFFER.

Kenindia Assurance Co Ltd: Kenindia House, Loita St, POB 44372, Nairobi; tel. (2) 333100; telex 23173; fax (2) 218380; f. 1979; life and general; CEO D. SWAMINATHAN.

Kenya National Assurance Co Ltd: Bima House, Harambee Ave, POB 20425, Nairobi; tel. (2) 338660; telex 23057; fax (2) 210617; f. 1964; state-owned; all classes of insurance and reinsurance; cap. 10m.; Exec. Chair. HENRY KOSGEY; Gen. Man. E. G. BUNYASSI.

Kenya Reinsurance Corporation: Reinsurance Plaza, Taifa Rd, POB 30271, Nairobi; tel. (2) 332690; telex 22046; fax (2) 339161; f. 1970; CEO WILLIAM MBOTE.

Lion of Kenya Insurance Co Ltd: POB 30190, Nairobi; tel. (2) 338800; telex 22717; f. 1978; general; CEO I. A. GALLOWAY.

Pan African Insurance Co Ltd: Pan Africa House, Kenyatta Ave, POB 62551, Nairobi; tel. (2) 339544; telex 22750; f. 1946; life and general; cap. 10m.; CEO D. K. NGINI.

Phoenix of East Africa Assurance Co Ltd: Ambank House, University Way, POB 30129, Nairobi; tel. (2) 338784; telex 23050; fax (2) 211848; general; Gen. Man. M. J. ADAMS; Exec. Dir MOYEZ ALIBHAI.

Provincial Insurance Co of East Africa Ltd: Old Mutual Bldg, Kimathi St, POB 43013, Nairobi; tel. (2) 330173; telex 22852; f. 1980; general; cap. 5m.; CEO E. C. BATES.

Prudential Assurance Co of Kenya Ltd: Yaya Centre, Argwings Kodhek Rd, POB 76190, Nairobi; tel. (2) 567374; telex 22280; f. 1979; general; cap. 8m.; CEO E. THOMAS.

Royal Insurance Co of East Africa Ltd: Mama Ngina St, POB 40001, Nairobi; tel. (2) 330171; telex 23249; fax (2) 727396; f. 1979; general; CEO S. K. KAMAU.

Taisho Monarch Insurance Co Ltd: Longonot Place, Kijabe St, POB 44003, Nairobi; tel. (2) 330042; f. 1979; general; cap. 5m.; CEO N. J. G. DONNE.

Trade and Industry

Kenya National Trading Corporation Ltd: Uchumi House, Nkrumah Ave, POB 30587, Nairobi; tel. (2) 29141; telex 22298; f. 1965; promotes national control of trade in both locally produced and imported items; exports coffee and sugar; CEO S. W. O. OGESSA.

CHAMBER OF COMMERCE

Kenya National Chamber of Commerce and Industry: Ufanisi House, Haile Selassie Ave, POB 47024, Nairobi; tel. (2) 334413; f. 1965; 46 brs; Nat. Chair. DAVID GITAU; CEO C. K. GATHIRIMU.

TRADE ASSOCIATIONS

East African Tea Trade Association: Rex House, Moi Ave, POB 85174, Mombasa; tel. (11) 315687; fax (11) 225823; f. 1957; organizes Mombasa weekly tea auctions; CEO MARK RADOLI; 167 mems.

Export Processing Zones Authority: POB 50563, Nairobi; tel. (2) 712800; fax (2) 713704; established by the govt. to promote investment in Export Processing Zones; CEO SILAS ITA.

Export Promotion Council: POB 43137, Nairobi; tel. (2) 333555; telex 22468; fax (2) 226036; promotes exports; Chair. SAM MUUMBI.

Kenya Association of Manufacturers: POB 30225, Nairobi; tel. (2) 746005; fax (2) 746028; Chair. R. BRENNEISEN; CEO JOHN W. KURIA; 560 mems.

STATUTORY BOARDS

Central Province Marketing Board: POB 189, Nyeri.

Coffee Board of Kenya: POB 30566, Nairobi; tel. (2) 332896; telex 25706; fax (2) 330546; f. 1947; Chair. PITHON MWANGI; Gen. Man. AGGREY MURUNGA.

Kenya Dairy Board: POB 30406, Nairobi.

Kenya Meat Corporation: POB 30414, Nairobi; tel. (2) 340750; telex 22150; f. 1953; purchasing, processing and marketing of beef livestock; Chair. H. P. BARCLAY.

Kenya Sisal Board: Mutual Bldg, Kimathi St, POB 41179, Nairobi; tel. (2) 223457; f. 1946; CEO J. H. WAIRAGU; Man. Dir KENNETH MUKUMA.

Kenya Sugar Authority: Hill Plaza Bldg, Ngong Rd, POB 51500, Nairobi; tel. (2) 710600; telex 25105; fax (2) 723903; Chair. R. O. OTUTU; CEO J. A. MUDAVADI.

National Cereals and Produce Board: POB 30586, Nairobi; tel. (2) 555288; telex 22769; f. 1966; Chair. JAMES MATUA; Dir Maj. W. K. KOITABA.

Pyrethrum Board of Kenya: POB 420, Nakuru; tel. (37) 211567; telex 33080; fax (37) 45274; f. 1935; 18 mems; Chair. T. O. OMATO; CEO J. M. G. WAINAINA.

Tea Board of Kenya: POB 20064, Nairobi; tel. (2) 220241; fax (2) 331650; f. 1950; regulates tea industry on all matters of policy, licenses tea planting and processing, combats pests and diseases, controls the export of tea, finances research on tea, promotes Kenyan tea internationally; 21 mems; Chair. ELIUD MAHIHU; CEO GEORGE M. KIMANI.

DEVELOPMENT ORGANIZATIONS

Agricultural Development Corporation: POB 47101, Nairobi; tel. (2) 338530; telex 22856; fax (2) 336524; f. 1965 to promote agricultural development and reconstruction; CEO Dr WALTER KILELE.

Agricultural Finance Corporation: POB 30367, Nairobi; tel. (2) 333733; telex 22649; a statutory organization providing agricultural loans; Gen. Man. G. K. TOROITICH.

Development Finance Company of Kenya Ltd: Finance House, 16th Floor, Loita St, POB 30483, Nairobi; tel. (2) 340401; telex 22662; fax (2) 338426; f. 1963; private co with govt participation; paid-up cap. Ks. 139m. (1991); Chair. H. N. K. ARAP MENGECH; Gen. Man. J. V. BOSSE.

Horticultural Crops Development Authority: POB 42601, Nairobi; tel. (2) 337381; telex 22687; fax (2) 228386; f. 1968; invests in production, dehydration, processing and freezing of fruit and vegetables; exports of fresh fruit and vegetables; Chair. KASANGA MULWA; Man. Dir M. A. S. MULANDI.

Housing Finance Co of Kenya Ltd: Rehani House, Kenyatta Ave, POB 30088; Nairobi; tel. (2) 333910; f. 1965; cap. Ks 20m., dep. 2,300m. (1989); Man. Dir WALTER MUKURIA.

Industrial and Commercial Development Corporation: Uchumi House, Aga Khan Walk, POB 45519, Nairobi; tel. (2) 229213; telex 22429; fax (2) 333880; f. 1954; govt-financed; assists industrial and commercial development; Chair. REUBEN CHESIRE; Exec. Dir CHARLES MBINDYO.

Investment Promotion Centre: National Bank Bldg, 8th Floor, Harambee Ave, POB 55704, Nairobi; tel. (2) 221401; telex 25460; fax (2) 336663; promotes and facilitates local and foreign investment; Exec. Chair. MARTIN P. KUNGURU.

Kenya Fishing Industries Ltd: Nairobi; cap. Ks. 5m.; Man. Dir ABDALLA MBWANA.

Kenya Industrial Estates Ltd: Nairobi Industrial Estate, Likoni Rd, POB 78029, Nairobi; tel. (2) 542300; telex 24191; fax (2) 553124; f. 1967 to finance and develop small-scale industries.

Kenya Industrial Research and Development Institute: POB 30650, Nairobi; tel. (2) 557762; f. 1942, reorg. 1979; research and advisory services in scientific, technical and industrial development; Dir Dr R. O. ARUNGA.

Kenya Planters' Co-operative Union: Nairobi; coffee cultivation and processing; Chair. A. MWANGI; Man. Dir JAMES NYAGA.

Kenya Tea Development Authority: POB 30213, Nairobi; tel. (2) 21441; telex 22645; f. 1960 to develop tea growing, manufacturing and marketing among African smallholders; in 1987 it supervised an area of 56,500 ha, cultivated by 150,414 registered growers, and operated 39 factories; Chair. ERIC KOTUT; Man. Dir CYRUS IRUNGU.

Settlement Fund Trustees: POB 30449, Nairobi; administers a land purchase programme involving over 1.2m. ha for resettlement of African farmers.

EMPLOYERS' ASSOCIATIONS

Federation of Kenya Employers: Waajiri House, Argwings Kodhek Rd, POB 48311, Nairobi; tel. (2) 721929; telex 22642; Chair. J. P. N. SIMBA; Exec. Dir TOM D. OWUOR; the following are affiliates:

Association of Local Government Employers: POB 52, Muranga; Chair. S. K. ITONGU.

Distributive and Allied Industries Employers' Association: POB 30587, Nairobi; Chair. P. J. MWAURA.

Engineering and Allied Industries Employers' Association: POB 48311, Nairobi; tel. (2) 721929; Chair. D. M. NJOROGE.

Kenya Association of Building and Civil Engineering Contractors: POB 43598, Nairobi; Chair. G. S. HIRANI.

Kenya Association of Hotelkeepers and Caterers: POB 46406, Nairobi; tel. (2) 726640; fax (2) 721505; f. 1944; Chair. J. MWENDWA.

Kenya Bankers' (Employers') Association: POB 30003, Nairobi; tel. (2) 330200; Chair. J. A. M. DOCHERTY.

Kenya Sugar Employers' Union: POB 262, Kisumu; Chair. L. OKECH.

Kenya Tea Growers' Association: POB 320, Kericho; tel. (2) 21010; telex 22070; fax (2) 339559; Chair. M. K. A. SANG.

Kenya Vehicle Manufacturers' Association: POB 1436, Thika; Chair. G. J. PULFER.

Motor Trade and Allied Industries Employers' Association: POB 48311, Nairobi; tel. (2) 721929; fax (2) 721990; Exec. Sec. G. N. KONDITI.

Sisal Growers' and Employers' Association: POB 47523, Nairobi; tel. (2) 720170; telex 22642; fax (2) 721990; Chair. A. G. COMBOS.

Timber Industries Employers' Association: POB 18070, Nairobi; Chair. H. S. BAMBRAH.

MAJOR INDUSTRIAL COMPANIES

The following are among the largest companies in terms either of capital investment or employment.

BAT (Kenya) Ltd: POB 30000, Nairobi; tel. (2) 533555; telex 24131; fax (2) 531717; f. 1957; subsidiary of British American Tobacco Co Ltd, United Kingdom; mfrs of tobacco products; Man. Dir T. P. G. MCDOWELL.

Bata Shoe Co (Kenya) Ltd: POB 23, Limuru; tel. (2) 41253 telex 22386; fax (2) 41209; f. 1943; mfrs of footwear; CEO A. FERNANDEZ.

A. Baumann and Co Ltd: POB 40538, Nairobi Baumann House, Haile Selassie Ave, Nairobi; tel. (2) 140538; fax (2) 210315; f. 1926; cap. K£640,011; res K£1.68m.; brs and subsidiaries in Kenya, Tanzania and Uganda; steamship agents, warehousemen, clearing and forwarding agents, exporters and importers of electrical, engineering and agricultural products, and mfrs of carbon brushes and soft alloys; also involved in the air-conditioning business in Kenya, paint manufacture in Uganda, and has substantial investments in a large number of local cos and industries; Chair. N. NGANGA; Man. Dir H. RANA.

Consolidated Holdings Ltd: POB 11854, Nairobi; telex 22204; fax (2) 553939; f. 1919; cap. K£2,140,410; holding co with interests in Kenya in newspaper publication and the distribution of foreign newspapers and magazines; Chair. M. W. HARLEY; Man. Dir R. S. HOLT.

East Africa Industries: POB 30062, Nairobi; tel. (2) 542000; telex 22507; fax (2) 543912; f. 1943; mfrs of soaps, detergents and edible oils; CEO J. B. WANJUI.

East African Portland Cement Co Ltd: POB 40101, Nairobi; tel. (2) 226551; telex 22151; fax (2) 211936; f. 1933; cement mfrs; Chair. A. LULU; Man. Dir J. G. MAINA.

Firestone East Africa (1969) Ltd: POB 30429, Nairobi; tel. (2) 559922; telex 24052; fax (2) 544241; f. 1969; tyre and tube mfrs; CEO N. N. MERALI.

General Motors East Africa Ltd: Enterprise Rd, Mombasa Rd, POB 30527, Nairobi; tel. (2) 556588; telex 24071; fax (2) 544178; f. 1975; motor vehicle assembly; CEO D. D. MCCARTHY.

Kenya Breweries Ltd: POB 30161, Nairobi; tel. (2) 802701; telex 22628; fax (2) 802054; f. 1920; mfr of lager beers, Guinness stout and malted barley; Chair. J. G. KIEREINI; Man. Dir M. J. KARANJA.

Kenya Co-operative Creameries Ltd: Dakar Rd, POB 30131, Nairobi; tel. (2) 532535; telex 24128; fax (2) 544879; f. 1925; processes and markets the bulk of dairy produce; Dir JOB MUKULE.

Magadi Soda Co Ltd: POB 1, Magadi; f. 1926; processors of soda ash for export.

Panafrican Paper Mills (East Africa) Ltd: POB 30221, Nairobi; tel. (2) 335489; telex 22083; f. 1970; printing and packaging; CEO A. J. RIJHWANI.

TRADE UNIONS

Central Organization of Trade Unions (Kenya) (COTU): Solidarity Bldg, Digo Rd, POB 13000, Nairobi; tel. (2) 23733; f. 1965 as the sole trade union fed.; Chair. P. MWANGI-KIBIRIBIRI; Sec.-Gen. JOHNSON OGENDO; the following unions are affiliates:

Amalgamated Union of Kenya Metalworkers: POB 73651, Nairobi; Gen. Sec. F. E. OMIDO.

Dockworkers' Union: POB 98207, Mombasa; tel. (11) 491427; f. 1954; Gen. Sec. J. KHAMIS.

Kenextelcoms Workers' Union: Nairobi; Gen. Sec. CHARLES J. NGUTA.

Kenya Building, Construction, Civil Engineering and Allied Trades Workers' Union: POB 49628, Nairobi; Gen. Sec. JOHN MURUGU.

Kenya Chemical and Allied Workers' Union: POB 73820, Nairobi; Gen. Sec. WERE DIBI OGUTO.

Kenya Engineering Workers' Union: POB 90443, Mombasa; Gen. Sec. JUSTUS MULEI.

Kenya Game Hunting and Safari Workers' Union: POB 47509, Nairobi; Gen. Sec. J. M. NDOLO.

Kenya Local Government Workers' Union: POB 55827, Nairobi; Gen. Sec. WASIKE NDOMBI.

Kenya Management Staff Association: POB 13195, Nairobi; Gen. Sec. W. K. ADELL.

Kenya Petroleum and Oil Workers' Union: POB 10376, Nairobi; Gen. Sec. JACOB OCHINO.

Kenya Quarry and Mine Workers' Union: POB 48125, Nairobi; tel. (2) 332120; f. 1961; Gen. Sec. WAFULA WA MUSAMIA.

Kenya Railways and Harbours Union: POB 72029, Nairobi; Gen. Sec. RAPHAEL OKANGO.

Kenya Scientific Research, International Technical and Allied Institutions Workers' Union: Ngumba House, Tom Mboya St, POB 55094, Nairobi; tel. (2) 339964; Sec.-Gen. SAMSON OWEN KUBAI.

Kenya Shoe and Leather Workers' Union: POB 49629, Nairobi; Gen. Sec. JAMES AWICH.

Kenya Timber and Furniture Workers' Union: POB 50099, Nairobi; Gen. Sec. D. N. MATHERU.

Kenya Union of Entertainment and Music Industry Employees: POB 47043, Nairobi; Gen. Sec. JAMES YONGO.

Kenya Union of Journalists: POB 47035, Nairobi; Gen. Sec. GEORGE ODIKO.

Kenya Union of Printing, Publishing, Paper Manufacturers and Allied Workers: POB 12144, Nairobi; Gen. Sec. JOHN BOSCO.

Kenya Union of Sugar Plantation Workers: POB 174, Muhoroni; Gen. Sec. ONYANGO MIDIKA.

National Seamen's Union of Kenya: POB 81123, Mombasa; Gen. Sec. I. S. ABDALLAH MWARUA.

Plantation and Agricultural Workers' Union: POB 1161, Nakuru; Gen. Sec. P. MWANGI-KIBIRIBIRI.

Transport and Allied Workers' Union: POB 74108, Nairobi; tel. (2) 23618; Gen. Sec. JULIAS MALII.

Independent Unions

Kenya National Union of Teachers: POB 30407, Nairobi; f. 1957; Sec.-Gen. A. A. ADONGO.

Union of Postal and Telecommunication Workers (K): POB 48155, Nairobi; Gen. Sec. ALI I. MOHAMED; 11,000 mems.

Transport

RAILWAYS

In 1993 there were 2,740 km of track open for traffic including sidings.

Kenya Railways Corporation: POB 30121, Nairobi; tel. (2) 221211; telex 22254; fax (2) 340049; f. 1977; Exec. Chair. Prof. J. K. MUSUVA; Gen. Man. E. Y. HARIZ (acting).

ROADS

At the end of 1993 there were 63,120 km of classified roads, of which 6,438 km were main roads and 18,982 km were secondary roads. Some 13.7% of road surfaces were paved. An all-weather road links Nairobi to Addis Ababa, in Ethiopia, and there is a 590-km road link between Kitale (Kenya) and Juba (Sudan).

Abamba Public Road Services: POB 40322, Nairobi; tel. (2) 556062; fax (2) 559884; operates bus services from Nairobi to all major towns in Kenya and to Kampala in Uganda.

East African Road Services Ltd: POB 30475, Nairobi; tel. (2) 764622; telex 23285; f. 1947; operates bus services from Nairobi to all major towns in Kenya; Chair. S. H. NATHOO; Gen. Man. E. H. MALIK.

Nyayo Bus Service Corp.: POB 47174, Nairobi; tel. (2) 803588; f. 1986; operates bus services within and between major towns in Kenya.

Speedways Trans-Africa Freighters: POB 75755, Nairobi; tel. (2) 544267; telex 23000; largest private road haulier in East Africa, with over 200 trucks; CEO HASSAN KANYARE.

SHIPPING

Major shipping operations in Kenya are handled at the international seaport of Mombasa which has 16 deep-water births with a total length of 3,044 m and facilities for the off-loading of bulk carriers, tankers and container vessels. An inland container depot with a potential full capacity of 120,000 20-ft (6-m) equivalent units was opened in Nairobi in 1984. Two further inland depots were scheduled to begin operating in early 1994 at Eldoret and Kisumu.

Kenya Ports Authority: POB 95009, Mombasa; tel. (11) 565222; telex 21243; fax (11) 311867; f. 1977; sole operator of coastal port facilities and inland container depots; Chair. SAJJAD RASHID; Man. Dir ALBERT C. MUMBA.

Kenya Cargo Handling Services Ltd: POB 95187, Mombasa; tel. (11) 25955; telex 20047; division of Kenya Ports Authority; Man. Dir JOSHUA KEGODE.

Inchcape Shipping Services Kenya Ltd: POB 90194, Mombasa; tel. (11) 314245; telex 21278; fax (11) 314224.

Kenya Shipping Agency Ltd: Southern House, Moi Ave, POB 84831, Mombasa; tel. (11) 20501; telex 21013; fax (11) 314494; subsidiary of Kenya National Trading Corpn Ltd; dry cargo, container, bulk carrier and tanker agents.

Lykes Lines: POB 30182, Nairobi; tel. (2) 332320; telex 22317; fax (2) 723861; services to USA ports.

Mackenzie Maritime Ltd: POB 90120, Mombasa; tel. (11) 221273; telex 21205; fax (11) 316260; agents for Amada Shipping, Ellerman Lines PLC, Deutsche Ost-Afrika Linie, Thos and Jas Harison, P & O Containers Ltd, Mitsui OSK Lines.

Marship Ltd: Jubilee Bldg, Moi Ave, POB 80443, Mombasa; tel. (11) 314705; telex 21442; fax (11) 316654; f. 1986; shipbrokers, ship management and chartering agents.

Mitchell Cotts Kenya Ltd: Cotts House, Wabera St, POB 30182, Nairobi; tel. (2) 221273; telex 22317; fax (2) 214228; agents for DOAL, Cie Maritime Belge SA, Nippon Yusen Kaisha.

Southern Line Ltd: POB 90102, Mombasa; tel. (11) 20507; telex 21288; operating dry cargo and tanker vessels between East African ports, Red Sea ports, the Persian (Arabian) Gulf and Indian Ocean islands.

Spanfreight Shipping Ltd: Kimathi House, Kimathi St, POB 52612, Nairobi; tel. (2) 715400; telex 25262; fax (2) 722196.

Specialized Shipping Agencies: Mombasa.

Star East Africa Co: POB 86725, Mombasa; tel. (11) 314060; telex 21251; fax (11) 312818; shipping agents and brokers.

Wigglesworth and Co Ltd: POB 90501, Mombasa; tel. (11) 25241; telex 21246.

CIVIL AVIATION

Jomo Kenyatta International Airport, at Nairobi, was inaugurated in 1978. Moi International Airport, at Mombasa, also handles international traffic. Wilson Airport in Nairobi services domestic flights as do airports at Malindi and Kisumu. Kenya has about 400 airstrips. In 1991 the Government announced a US $10.9m. programme to rehabilitate and expand Jomo Kenyatta International and Moi International Airports. This work began in November 1993 at Moi International Airport. The expansion and updating of facilities at Jomo Kenyatta Airport was completed in 1994.

Kenya Airports Authority: Jomo Kenyatta International Airport, POB 19001, Nairobi; tel. (2) 822950; telex 25552; fax (2) 822078; f. 1991; responsible for the provision and management of aerodromes and services and facilities thereof, approves and controls private airstrips; Man. Dir B. S. OMUSE.

Air Kenya Aviation: Wilson Airport, POB 30357, Nairobi; tel. (2) 501601; telex 22939; fax (2) 500845; f. 1985; operates internal scheduled and charter passenger services; Man. Dir JOHN BUCKLEY.

Kenya Airways Ltd: Jomo Kenyatta International Airport, POB 19002, Nairobi; tel. (2) 822171; telex 22771; fax (2) 822480; f. 1977 following the dissolution of East African Airways; passenger services to Africa, Asia and Europe; freight service to the United Kingdom and the Netherlands; internal services from Nairobi to Kisumu, Mombasa and Malindi; has a freight subsidiary (Kenya Airfreight Handling Ltd) and a charter subsidiary (Kenya Flamingo Airways); Chair. PHILIP NDEGWA; Man. Dir BRIAN DAVIES.

CIVIL AVIATION AUTHORITY

Kenya Directorate of Civil Aviation: Jomo Kenyatta International Airport, POB 30163, Nairobi; tel. (2) 822950; telex 25239; f. 1948; under Kenya govt control since 1977; responsible for the conduct of civil aviation; advises the Govt on civil aviation policy; Dir J. P. AYUGA.

Tourism

Kenya's main attractions as a tourist centre are its wildlife, with 25 National Parks and 23 game reserves, the Indian Ocean coast and a good year-round climate.

Tourist arrivals numbered 814,400 in 1990, but declined to 804,600 in 1991 and to an estimated 650,000 in 1992, when earnings from the sector totalled US $295m. (compared with $595m. in 1991).

Kenya Tourist Development Corporation: Utalii House, Uhuru Highway, POB 42013, Nairobi; tel. (2) 330820; telex 23009; fax (2) 227815; f. 1965; Chair. PAUL KITOLOLO; Man. Dir ELIAS MUSYOKA.

Defence

In June 1993 Kenya's armed forces numbered 24,400, comprising an army of 20,500, an air force of 2,500 and a navy of 1,400. Military service is voluntary. There is a paramilitary force of 5,000 police. Military assistance is received from the United Kingdom, and from the USA, whose Rapid Deployment Force uses port and onshore facilities in Kenya.

Defence Expenditure: Estimated at K£518.5m. for 1993/94.

Commander-in-Chief of the Armed Forces: DANIEL ARAP MOI.

Chief of Armed Forces General Staff: Gen. MAHMOUD HAJI MOHAMMED.

Education

Education is not compulsory. The government provides, or assists in the provision of schools. Primary education is provided free of charge. The education system involves eight years of primary education (beginning at five or six years of age), five years at secondary school and four years of university education. The total enrolment at primary schools increased from about 900,000 in 1963 to 5,392,319 in 1990. The number of pupils in secondary schools increased from 31,923 in 1963 to 614,161 in 1990. In 1990 the total enrolment at primary and secondary schools was equivalent to 77% of the school-age population (boys 79%; girls 74%). In 1990, according to estimates by UNESCO, the adult literacy rate was 69% (males 79.8%; females 58.5%). There are four state universities, with total enrolment of 35,421 students in 1990. The education sector was allocated 15.5% of total government expenditure in the provisional budget for 1992/93.

Bibliography

Works on Kenya, Tanzania and Uganda generally

Gregory, R. G. *India and East Africa. A History of Race Relations within the British Empire, 1890–1939.* Oxford University Press, 1972.

Livingstone, I., and Ord, H. A. *An Introduction to Economics for Eastern Africa.* London, Heinemann, 1980.

Mangat, J. S. *A History of the Asians in East Africa, c. 1886–1945.* Oxford, Clarendon Press, 1969.

Morgan, W. T. W. *East Africa.* London, Longman, 1973.

(Ed.). *East Africa: its Peoples and Resources.* 2nd Edn, Oxford University Press, 1972.

Nicholls, C. S. *The Swahili Coast.* London, Allen and Unwin, 1972.

Oxford History of East Africa. Oxford University Press, Vol. 2, 1965; Vol. 3, 1976.

Report of the East African Royal Commission, 1953–1955, Cmd 9475. London, HMSO, 1955.

Treaty for East African Co-operation. Nairobi, Government Printer, 1967.

Kenya

arap Moi, D. T. *Kenya African Nationalism: Nyayo Philosophy and Principles.* London, Macmillan, 1986.

Arnold, G. *Modern Kenya.* London, Longman, 1981.

Bennett, G. *Kenya, A Political History; the Colonial Period.* London, Oxford University Press, 1963.

Berman, B., and Lonsdale, J. *Unhappy Valley: Clan, Class and State in Colonial Kenya.* London, James Currey, 1988.

Bourmand, D. *Histoire politique du Kenya.* Paris, Editions Karthala, 1988.

Gerzel, C. *The Politics of Independent Kenya.* London, Heinemann; Nairobi, East Africa Publishing House, 1970.

(Ed.) *Government and Politics in Kenya.* Nairobi, East African Publishing House, 1969.

Greer, J., and Thorbecke, E. *Food Poverty and Consumption Patterns in Kenya.* Geneva, International Labour Office, 1986.

Hayward, M. F. *Elections in Independent Africa.* Boulder, CO, Westview Press, 1987.

Kanogo, T. *Squatters and the Roots of Mau Mau, 1905 – 63.* London, James Currey, 1987.

Kenyatta, J. *Facing Mount Kenya.* London, Heinemann, 1979.

Killick, T. (Ed.). *Papers on the Economy of Kenya: Performance, Problems and Politics.* London, Heinemann Educational, 1983.

Kitching, G. N. *Class and Economic Change in Kenya: The Making of an African Bourgeoisie 1905–1970.* Yale University Press, 1980.

Leys, C. *Underdevelopment in Kenya: The Political Economy of Neo-Colonialism.* London, Heinemann Educational, 1975.

Mboya, T. *The Challenge of Nationhood.* London, André Deutsch, 1970.

Miller, N. N. *Kenya: The Quest for Prosperity.* Westview/Gower, 1984.

Mungeam, G. H. *British Rule in Kenya, 1898–1912.* London, Clarendon Press, 1966.

Ogot, B. A. (Ed.). *Politics and Nationalism in Colonial Kenya.* Nairobi, East African Publishing House, 1972.

Ojany, F. F., and Ogendo, R. B. *Kenya: A Study in Physical and Human Geography.* London, Longman, 1973.

Pulfrey, W. *Geology and Mineral Resources of Kenya.* Nairobi, Government Printer, 1960.

Swainson, N. *The Development of Corporate Capitalism in Kenya, 1918–1977.* London, Heinemann, 1980.

Throup, D. W. *Economic and Social Origins of Mau Mau, 1945 – 53.* London, James Currey, 1987.

LESOTHO

Physical and Social Geography

A. MacGREGOR HUTCHESON

PHYSICAL FEATURES

The Kingdom of Lesotho, a small, land-locked country of 30,355 sq km (11,720 sq miles), is enclosed on all sides by South Africa. It is situated at the highest part of the Drakensberg escarpment on the eastern rim of the South African plateau. About two-thirds of Lesotho is very mountainous. Elevations in the eastern half of the country are generally more than 2,440 m above sea-level, and in the north-east and along the eastern border they exceed 3,350 m. This is a region of very rugged relief, bleak climate and heavy annual rainfall (averaging 1,905 mm), where the headstreams of the Orange river have cut deep valleys. Westwards the land descends through a foothill zone of rolling country, at an altitude of 1,830–2,135 m, to Lesotho's main lowland area. This strip of land along the western border, part of the high veld, averages 40 km in width and lies at around 1,525 m. Annual rainfall averages in this region are 650–750 mm, and climatic conditions are generally more pleasant. However, frost may occur throughout the country in winter, and hail is a summer hazard everywhere. The light, sandy soils which have developed on the Karoo sedimentaries of the western lowland compare unfavourably with the fertile black soils of the Stormberg basalt in the uplands. The temperate grasslands of the west also tend to be poorer than the montane grasslands of the east.

POPULATION AND NATURAL RESOURCES

The population at mid-1989 was estimated to be 1,700,000, most of whom were Basotho, but also including some Europeans and Asians. The noticeable physical contrasts between east and west are reflected in the distribution and density of the population. While large parts of the mountainous east (except for valleys) are sparsely populated, most of the fertile western strip, which carries some 70% of the population, has densities in excess of 200 per sq km (the national average in 1989 was 56.0 per sq km). Such population pressure, further aggravated by steady population growth, has resulted (i) in permanent settlement being pushed to higher levels (in places to 2,440 m) formerly used for summer grazing, and on to steep slopes, thus adding to the already serious national problem of soil erosion; (ii) in an acute shortage of cultivable land and increased soil exhaustion, particularly in the west; (iii) in land holdings which are too small to maintain the rural population; and (iv) in the country's inability, in its current stage of development, to support all its population, thus necessitating the migration of large numbers of workers to seek paid employment in South Africa. It was estimated in 1992 that about 38% of the adult male labour force were employed in South Africa, mainly in the mines. Lesotho's economy depends heavily on their remitted earnings, and a migratory labour system on this scale has grave social, economic and political implications for the country.

Lesotho's long-term development prospects largely depend on making optimum use of its soil and water resources. Less than 13% of the country is cultivable and, since virtually all of this is already cultivated, only more productive use of the land can make Lesotho self-sufficient in food (20% of domestic needs are currently imported from South Africa). The high relief produces natural grasslands, well suited for a viable livestock industry, but this has been hindered through inadequate pasture management, excessive numbers of low-quality animals and disease. Lesotho and South Africa are jointly implementing the Highlands Water Project (see Economy), which will provide employment for thousands of Basotho and greatly improve Lesotho's infrastructure. Reserves of diamonds have been identified in the mountainous north-east, and there are small surface workings at Lemphane, Liquobong and Kao. The search for other minerals is continuing, the most promising to date being uranium, found in rhyolitic rocks near Teyateyaneng in the north-west.

Recent History

RICHARD BROWN

Lesotho, formerly known as Basutoland, became a British protectorate in 1868, at the request of the Basotho people's chief, who feared Boer expansionism. Basutoland was annexed to Cape Colony (now part of South Africa) in 1871 but detached in 1884. It became a separate British colony, and was administered as one of the high commission territories in southern Africa (the others being the protectorates of Bechuanaland, now Botswana, and Swaziland). The British Act of Parliament that established the Union of South Africa in 1910 also provided for the possible inclusion in South Africa of these territories, subject to the consent of the local inhabitants. Until 1960, successive South African governments asked for the transfer of the three territories, but the native chiefs always objected to such a scheme.

Modern party politics began in 1952 with the founding of the Basutoland Congress Party (BCP, renamed the Basotho Congress Party in 1966) by Dr Ntsu Mokhehle. A revised constitution, which established the territory's first legislative council, was introduced in 1956, and a new constitution, granting limited powers of self-government, was adopted in 1959.

The BCP decisively won elections to the legislative council, held in 1960. Basutoland's first general election, held on the basis of universal adult suffrage, took place on 29 April 1965, and full internal self-government was achieved on the following day. Moshoeshoe II, the paramount chief, was recognized as king. The majority of seats in the new legislative assembly were won by the Basutoland National Party (BNP, renamed the Basotho National Party at independence), a conservative group which received financial and organizational support from the South African government. The BNP's leader, Chief Leabua Jonathan, failed to win a seat, but won a by-election in July 1965, whereupon he became prime minister. Basutoland became independent, as Lesotho, on 4 October 1966.

JONATHAN AND THE BNP

A constitutional crisis arose in December, when Moshoeshoe attempted to obtain wider personal powers. In January 1967, however, the king signed an undertaking, on pain of enforced abdication, to abide by the constitution, which gave effective executive power to the prime minister. A general election was held in January 1970, when the opposition BCP appeared to have won a majority of seats in the national assembly. However, Chief Jonathan declared a state of emergency, suspended the constitution and arrested Mokhehle and other leaders of the BCP. The election was annulled, and the assembly prorogued. Some 500 people were reported to have been killed by the police during the ensuing disturbances.

King Moshoeshoe was placed under house arrest and later exiled, although he returned in December 1970, after accepting a government order which prohibited him from taking part in politics. From January 1970 the country was effectively under the prime minister's personal control. In March 1973, as a result of pressure from members of his own party (as well as from political opponents), Jonathan established an interim national assembly, comprising chiefs and nominated members, with the declared aim of drafting a new constitution. The state of emergency was revoked in July. The BCP split into an 'internal' faction, whose members were willing to accept nomination to the interim assembly, and an 'external' faction, whose members demanded a return to normal political life: the latter group was led by Mokhehle and was held responsible for an attempted coup in January 1974. Mokhehle and other leading BCP members fled the country, and some 35 supporters of the BCP were sentenced to terms of imprisonment. Strict new security laws were subsequently introduced.

Although Lesotho was economically dependent on South Africa, and the government's official policy during the 1970s was one of 'dialogue' with its neighbour, Chief Jonathan repeatedly criticized the South African government's policy of apartheid, and declared his support for the prohibited African National Congress of South Africa (ANC). During the late 1970s he accused the South African government of supporting the Lesotho Liberation Army (LLA), the military wing of the 'external' faction of the BCP, which was conducting a campaign of violence: this was denied by South Africa. In 1982 the LLA was blamed for the murder of a government minister and of the secretary-general of the BCP's 'internal' faction. In December of that year South African commando troops launched a raid on Maseru, the capital of Lesotho, killing some 30 ANC members and about 12 Losotho citizens. The UN Security Council unanimously condemned the action. In August 1983 South Africa delivered an ultimatum to Lesotho, either to expel (or repatriate) 3,000 South African refugees or be subjected to economic sanctions. Two groups of refugees left Lesotho, reportedly voluntarily, after the ultimatum.

In March 1983 Chief Jonathan announced that elections would be held, and in May of that year legislation was introduced to repeal the emergency order of 1970 that had suspended the constitution. In January 1985 the national assembly was dissolved, and in July the government announced that the elections would take place in September. However, the elections were cancelled in August, when no candidates from the five opposition parties were nominated to contest them: the opposition parties maintained that the government refused to publish the electoral roll, thus preventing opposition candidates from securing sufficient signatures to qualify for nomination. It was announced that Chief Jonathan and the BNP candidates in all 60 constituencies had been returned to office unopposed. In addition to arousing considerable domestic political opposition, the government's cancellation of the elections also appeared to have increased the hostility of the LLA, which launched a number of attacks on BNP targets during late 1985.

Lesotho's continued refusal to sign a joint non-aggression pact led South Africa to impound consignments of armaments destined for Lesotho, and to threaten to impose further economic sanctions in August 1984. On 1 January 1986 South Africa imposed a blockade on the border with Lesotho, impeding access to vital supplies of food and fuel. Five leading Lesotho politicians opposed to the government were arrested on their return from talks in Pretoria, and there were reports of fighting between factions of the armed forces, some members of which had apparently become dissatisfied at the Lesotho government's contacts with socialist states and at the radical policies of the BNP's influential Youth League.

MILITARY RULE, 1986–93

On 15 January 1986 troops of the Lesotho paramilitary force, led by Maj.-Gen. Justin Lekhanya, surrounded government buildings and the Youth League headquarters. Five casualties were reported in the ensuing fighting, and on 20 January Lekhanya (who had recently returned from 'security consultations' in South Africa), together with Maj.-Gen. S. K. Molapo, the commander of the security forces, and S. R. Matela, the chief of police, deposed the Jonathan government.

The new regime established a military council, headed by Lekhanya and including five other senior officers of the paramilitary force (which was subsequently replaced by the Royal Lesotho Defence Force–RLDF). On 27–28 January 1986 a council of ministers was sworn in, comprising three officers and 17 civilians, predominantly civil servants and professional men, and including one former member of Jonathan's cabinet. The national assembly was dissolved, and all executive and legislative powers were vested in the king, acting on the advice of the military council. One week after the coup, about 60 members of the ANC were deported from Lesotho, and on the same day the South African blockade was lifted.

The initial response of opposition groups was favourable to the coup. The exception was Mokhehle's wing of the BCP, which demanded the immediate restoration of the 1966 constitution, the integration of the LLA into Lesotho's armed forces and the holding of free elections within six months. All formal political activity was suspended by the military council on 27 March. In August Chief Jonathan, together with six of his former ministers, was placed under house arrest, but in September the high court declared the initial detention order, and then a second detention order, to be invalid. Chief Jonathan died in April 1987.

In September 1986 the council of ministers was restructured (giving increased responsibility to Maj.-Gen. Lekhanya), and the military council held discussions with the leaders of the five main opposition parties. The suspension of political activity continued, however, and opposition to the military council was discouraged. In April 1988 the five main opposition parties appealed to the Organization of African Unity (OAU), the Commonwealth and the South African government to restore civilian rule. In the following month Mokhehle, after 14 years of exile, was allowed to return to Lesotho for peace talks, together with other members of the BCP. The government agreed to guarantee the personal security of those returning, on certain conditions, the most important of these being that members of the LLA, were to be prohibited from joining the RLDF. It was widely believed that the South African government had played a part in promoting this reconciliation. In 1989 the LLA was reported to have been disbanded, and by 1990 the two factions of the BCP had apparently reunited under the leadership of Mokhehle.

In mid-1989 some elements within the government were reported to have sought the removal of Lekhanya from the chairmanship of both the military council and the council of ministers, following reports in the international media that implicated him in the fatal shooting of a civilian at Maseru in December 1988: it was claimed that Lekhanya had falsely attributed responsibility for the incident to a subordinate. In September 1989, at an inquest into the civilian's death (which was reportedly instigated at the request of some members of the military council), Lekhanya admitted the truth of the allegations. Nevertheless, in October a verdict of justifiable homicide was returned.

In early 1990 a power struggle developed between Lekhanya and King Moshoeshoe. In February Lekhanya dismissed three members of the military council and one member of the council of ministers, reportedly owing to their alleged involvement in a coup plot. Following the king's refusal to approve the changes to the military council, Lekhanya suspended his executive and legislative powers. Shortly afterwards, Lekhanya promised that a return to civilian government would take place in 1992, and, to reassure business interests, a programme for privatizing state enterprises was announced. In early March 1990 the military council assumed the executive and legislative powers which were previously vested in the king, and Moshoeshoe (who remained head of state) went into exile, in England. Later in March one of the dismissed members of the military council, Lt-Col Sekhobe Letsie, was charged with the murder in 1986 of two former government ministers (who had been regarded as leading opponents of Lekhanya) and their wives. In June a national constituent assembly was inaugurated to draft a new constitution acceptable to the majority of Basotho; its members included Lekhanya, together with members of the council of ministers, traditional chiefs, local councillors, businessmen and representatives of banned political parties.

In October 1990 Maj.-Gen. Lekhanya invited King Moshoeshoe to return to Lesotho from exile. However, the king announced that his return would be conditional upon the lifting of military rule and the formation, by representatives of all political parties, of an interim government, pending the restoration of the 1966 constitution and the holding of an internationally-supervised general election. On 6 November 1990 Lekhanya responded by promulgating an order which deposed the king with immediate effect. On 8 November Lesotho's 22 principal chiefs elected Moshoeshoe's eldest son, Prince Bereng Seeisa, as the new king, and on 12 November he succeeded to the throne, as King Letsie III, having undertaken not to involve himself in the political life of the country.

On 30 April 1991 Lekhanya was removed as chairman of the military council in a coup led by Col (later Maj.-Gen.) Elias Phitsoane Ramaema, a member of the military council. Col Ramaema succeeded Lekhanya as chairman of that body, which was immediately reorganized, along with the council of ministers; Ramaema's announcement that there would be no changes in government policy indicated that the coup resulted from a conflict of personalities rather than from a divergence of political aims. In mid-May Ramaema announced the repeal of the law which had banned party political activity in 1986. However, a tense atmosphere prevailed following the coup, and in late May resentment of foreign-owned businesses precipitated riots in Maseru and other major towns, which resulted in some 34 deaths and 425 arrests.

In early June 1991 20 officers were dismissed from the RLDF, following an unsuccessful attempt to overthrow Ramaema and to reinstate Lekhanya; the latter was placed under house arrest during August-September, owing to allegations that a further counter-coup was being plotted. By July the national constituent assembly had drafted a new constitution. In September the council of ministers was restructured.

In April 1992 relatives of ex-king Moshoeshoe announced that he intended to return to Lesotho from exile, in defiance of the wishes of the military council. In early June it was announced that elections would take place in late November. The council of ministers was reshuffled in late June. Following talks in England between Moshoeshoe and Ramaema, under the auspices of the secretary-general of the Commonwealth, the former king returned to Lesotho in July. In August two members of the military council were dismissed, following allegations against them of corruption.

ELECTED GOVERNMENT AND ARMY UNREST

The transition from military rule to democratic government, which had been scheduled to take place in November 1992, was postponed at short notice; the general election finally took place in late March 1993. The BCP swept to power, winning all 65 seats in the new national assembly (gaining 54% of the votes, compared with the BNP's 16%). Mokhehle, the leader of the BCP, was sworn in as prime minister at the beginning of April, and, on the same day, King Letsie was reported to have sworn allegiance to the new constitution (which took effect following the election). Although independent local and international observer teams pronounced the general election to be broadly free and fair, the BNP, which is supported by members of the former military regime, alleged widespread irregularities and refused to accept the results; the BNP also subsequently declined the BCP government's offer of two seats in the newly established senate.

There was a short-lived period of political reconciliation before a serious outbreak of fighting within the army in mid-January 1994 brought contentious issues to the fore. In addition to soldiers' grievances about pay and conditions, one army faction supported the opposition BNP while another favoured a return to military rule, with troops loyal to the government constituting a minority. In spite of intense shelling by the rival factions around Maseru, there were few casualties. The episode received a notably rapid regional response, with support both from the Commonwealth and the OAU for the prime minister's request for external mediation to end the conflict. Reflecting changes in the wider political situation in southern Africa, the presidents of Botswana, South Africa and Zimbabwe, together with Nelson Mandela, the president of the ANC, met in Maseru within two weeks of the outbreak of fighting and agreed to establish a regional task force to monitor a cease-fire. This historic initiative succeeded in containing the crisis, resulting in a truce in late January, although lawlessness within the army continued. In mid-April, rebel troops assassinated Selometsi Baholo, the deputy prime minister and minister of finance who had been kidnapped along with four other cabinet ministers. This action may have been connected with the unresolved problem of political succession in Lesotho's leadership arising from the age and health of Mokhehle. In May the minister for natural resources, Monyane Moleleki, abruptly resigned from the cabinet and left for South Africa. Public security concerns were intensified in the same month by a three-week police and prison officers' strike during which striking police abducted and subsequently released the minister of information, Mpho Malie. The strike ended when a salary agreement was reached in late May. Uncertainty remains concerning the position of former members of the LLA, who were to have been integrated into the regular defence force. Moreover, the government's request for external assistance during the army unrest was widely criticized inside Lesotho, and in July a commission of inquiry was established, comprising members of the defence forces of Botswana, South Africa and Zimbabwe.

The issue of the monarchy, which remains unresolved, provoked a serious political crisis in mid-August 1994, following an abortive attempt by King Letsie to remove the government and suspend certain sections of the constitution. The king (who acknowledges his father's claim to the throne) stated that he had acted in response to 'national dissatisfaction' with the government, and announced that a provisional council was to be formed to govern the country pending national elections in 12 months' time. Internally, the king's action provoked a large pro-government demonstration, and disturbances in which at least four people died. Externally, the crisis brought together Botswana, South Africa and Zimbabwe in concerted diplomatic efforts to reinstitute constitutional government in Lesotho. Military intervention by the regional powers was considered, and international donors threatened to withdraw aid. The king and Mokhehle were summoned to a meeting in South Africa in late August, at which the monarch was given a one-month deadline to restore the government or face economic sanctions. The Mokhehle administration was formally reinstated in mid-September, with a contingent agreement providing for King Letsie's eventual abdication in favour of Moshoeshoe II.

FOREIGN RELATIONS

Crucial to Lesotho's external affairs has been its relationship with South Africa, to whose support the Jonathan regime owed some of its initial success. In 1970 Lesotho and Malawi were the only countries to abstain on an OAU resolution calling on Western powers not to supply arms to South Africa. Perhaps aware of the extent to which his pro-South African policies were losing him support among the Basotho population, the majority of whom had first-hand experience of apartheid, Jonathan made a number of increasingly sharp criticisms of the South African government from 1972, and in November 1974 revived Lesotho's claim to 'conquered territory' in South Africa's Orange Free State (OFS). A vigorous anti-South African stance at the UN and OAU in the first half of 1975 increased tensions between the two countries. Lesotho's refusal to recognize South Africa's proclamation of an 'independent' Transkei in October 1976 led the Transkeian authorities to demand visas from visiting Lesotho nationals. In December Lesotho protested to the UN that this action had effectively closed the border with Transkei and was seriously disrupting internal communications because the mountainous terrain between Maseru and the south-west of the country made transport impossible except by air. Tension was exacerbated by a South African decision to terminate subsidies on exports of wheat and maize to Lesotho, and by Chief Jonathan's renewed claim to lands in the OFS. In February 1978 the Transkei authorities imposed stringent border controls, which virtually halted all cross-border traffic. In addition to cutting off Basotho migrant workers from mines in South Africa, these measures posed a threat of serious food shortages in the south-eastern region of Lesotho, which is dependent upon supplies transported through the Transkei from South Africa. In August Lesotho was host to a UN symposium on human rights, focusing mainly on southern Africa. Jonathan added to South African ire when he attended the non-aligned conference in Havana, Cuba, in September 1979 and again attacked apartheid. The first meeting of the leaders of Lesotho and South Africa since 1967 took place in August 1980 and produced a preliminary agreement on the Highlands Water Project (see Economy), an advantageous scheme for Lesotho to supply water to South Africa.

During 1982–83 relations with South Africa deteriorated sharply, following allegations of South African armed raids against ANC sympathizers in Lesotho. In April 1983 Jonathan announced that Lesotho was effectively in a state of war with South Africa. These tensions, together with the development of closer relations between Lesotho and several socialist countries, probably contributed to South Africa's application of strict border controls on its main frontier with Lesotho at the end of May, resulting in food shortages. The border controls were eased in June, after a meeting between both countries in which they agreed to curb cross-border guerrilla infiltration, but were re-imposed in July. Further talks with South Africa followed, and, soon afterwards, Lesotho declared that it had received an ultimatum from the republic, either to expel (or repatriate) some 3,000 refugees or to face the economic consequences. In September two groups of refugees left the country.

Relations with South Africa remained at a low ebb for most of 1984. In March Chief Jonathan alleged that the South African government had encouraged dissident exiles to form a new opposition party, the Basotho Democratic Alliance (BDA), as part of a conspiracy to overthrow the government. In April the BDA was officially registered as a political party, and its chairman reportedly confirmed that South Africa had promised to provide financial support to the BDA for the forthcoming election campaign. Relations between the two countries were further marred during 1984 by South African attempts to coerce Lesotho into signing a joint non-aggression pact, similar to the Nkomati Accord, agreed in March 1984 with Mozambique. Lesotho's continued refusal to sign such a pact led South Africa to impound consignments of armaments destined for Lesotho, and to threaten further economic sanctions in August, including the suspension of the Highlands Water Project. However, after talks between the two countries in the following month, and an announcement by Lesotho that the ANC had agreed to withdraw completely from its territory, relations improved slightly in October, when South Africa released the arms that it had been impounding and resumed talks on the Highlands Project.

Tension was renewed during 1985, as, with unrest spreading in South Africa, Jonathan refused South African requests to expel ANC refugees and to discuss a mutual security pact with South Africa. In October the South African minister of foreign affairs visited Maseru in an unsuccessful attempt to persuade the government to take action against the ANC. Subsequently the South African government threatened to deport Basotho workers in South Africa. In December there was a raid on Maseru, ostensibly carried out by the LLA, for which Jonathan publicly blamed Pretoria, again refusing to hand over refugees or to discuss a security treaty. South Africa again warned Lesotho against harbouring members of the ANC, and blamed Lesotho for attacks in South Africa. On 1 January 1986 South Africa imposed strict checks at border crossing-points (see above), claiming the need to exclude 'terrorists'.

Following the military coup of January 1986, the new government sent a delegation to South Africa. Although the South African government denied having any part in the coup, Lesotho's new rulers proved to be more amenable to South Africa's policy on regional security. It was agreed that neither country would allow its territory to be used for attacks on the other; South African refugees began to be flown out, and South Africa withdrew its special border checks on 25 January. By August more than 200 South African refugees, believed to be ANC members, were reported to have been expelled from Lesotho (although the Lesotho government did not permit their extradition directly to South Africa). Additionally, the new government agreed to create a joint security committee and to proceed with the Highlands water scheme. Technicians from the Democratic People's Republic of Korea were expelled from Lesotho, and the new regime announced that it would resume relations with the Republic of Korea. In March Lekhanya travelled to Pretoria and met President Botha of South Africa. The two leaders reiterated the principles of mutual respect and non-interference. The North Korean embassy was closed in September. In the following month the treaty for the Highlands Water Project was signed by Lesotho and South Africa. In April 1987 the two countries signed an agreement to establish a joint trade mission. In May Lekhanya visited the USA, where he held talks with the US secretary of state. Lesotho and South Africa concluded 'friendly and successful' negotiations on issues relating to their common border in March 1988. In April 1990 Lesotho established diplomatic relations with Taiwan, and those with the People's Republic of China were severed but were resumed in January 1994. Lesotho and South Africa agreed to establish diplomatic relations, at ambassadorial level, in May 1992.

In December 1992 South Africa alleged that terrorist attacks on South African targets were being launched from Lesotho. In April 1993, however, the new Lesotho government declared its intention to co-operate closely with South Africa, which, following the election of an ANC-dominated government in April 1994, will continue to exercise a powerful influence on the affairs of Lesotho.

Economy

RICHARD BROWN

Lesotho is, economically, one of the world's least developed countries. Its resources have been listed as 'people, water and scenery'. The country's population in 1992 was estimated at 1.85m, of whom about 95% were residing in rural areas. Between 1985–92 the population increased at an average rate of 2.7% per year. About 38% of the male labour force were employed as migrant workers in South Africa in 1992 (compared with an estimated 45% in 1987) and the remittances of Basotho migrant workers constitute more than 40% of Lesotho's gross national product (GNP). This phenomenon reflects a continuing lack of opportunities in the domestic formal sector, despite government attempts to develop manufacturing and services, and severe pressure on agricultural land, which continues to support about 80% of the resident labour force. This pressure is reflected in the wide disparity of population density, which reaches 200 per sq km in the west, where virtually all arable land and 70% of the population are concentrated, compared with a national average density of 56.0 per sq km. at mid-1989. The resulting problems of land shortage, soil erosion and falling productivity have been compounded by recurrent drought.

Lesotho's economic performance has also been adversely affected by the problems of the intimately linked South African economy—particularly in terms of the depreciation in the value of the South African rand, which is at par with the Lesotho currency unit, the loti (plural: maloti). Nevertheless, the country's gross domestic product (GDP) increased, in real terms, by an annual average of 5.5% in 1980–91, and is estimated to have increased by about 2.5% in 1992 and 1993. In 1992, according to estimates by the World Bank, Lesotho's GNP, measured at average 1990–92 prices, was US $1,090m., equivalent to $580 per head. During 1985–92, it was estimated, GNP increased, in real terms, at an average annual rate of 0.8%.

The country's internal tensions (see Recent History) probably underlie the record budget of $436m. presented on 2 May 1994. Expenditure in 1994/95 was to rise by 14%, while spending on development was to increase by 25.3% and on education by nearly one-third. Buoyant customs revenues, largely due to the construction of the Highland Water Project (see below) underpin the increases, but will diminish in the next few years as the main construction work is completed.

AGRICULTURE

Although only about 10% of the total land area of 30,355 sq km is suitable for arable cultivation (with a further 66% usable for pasture), agriculture is the primary occupation for the great majority of Basotho (78% of the labour force in 1992) and accounts for about one-fifth of export earnings. The sector's contribution to GDP has declined, from 47% in 1970 to 15% in 1991, owing to a fall in yields by an average of 3% per year, caused by soil erosion, the prevalence of poor agricultural practices, and by the impact of drought (most recently during 1982–85 and from 1990). Apart from increases in the use of fertilizers and tractors since 1970, the sector remains largely unmodernized. Most crops continue to be produced, using traditional methods, by peasant farmers who have little security of tenure under existing laws.

Maize is the staple crop, accounting for 60% of the total planted area, followed by sorghum with 30%. Sorghum, beans and sunflower oil are also cultivated. Summer wheat is so far the only crop to have been exported in significant quantities, with most exports sold to South Africa. Food imports have been required in recent years. In 1991/92 only 20% of basic needs were met from domestic production, owing to exceptionally severe drought conditions. A maize shortfall of 242,000 tons was forecast in the 1992/93 season. Adequate rains in 1993/94 were expected to restore output, but the drought emergency programme was to continue in 1994/95. Compared with its potential, the livestock sector has been little exploited, although cattle exports have traditionally accounted for about one-third of agricultural exports, with wool and mohair providing a further 30% each. In 1992 the national herd was estimated at 536,000 cattle, 1.5m. sheep and 1.1m. goats, having suffered severe depletion during the early 1980s as a result of the drought. The Livestock Products Marketing Service was established in 1973 as a state monopoly for marketing and improving production. One of its major projects, construction of an export-orientated abattoir in Maseru, was completed in 1983. This facility, and associated fattening pens, aimed initially to cater for local demand, but extending eventually into exports to regional and EU markets. Milk production is also being promoted.

The government is implementing a programme for food security, based on the development of small-scale irrigated agricultural schemes and the general improvement of rural water supplies. The Lesotho Agricultural Development Bank (LADB), established in 1980 and the sole source of farmers' credit, plays an important part in the self-sufficiency programme. The slow pace of agricultural improvement led the government, in September 1987, to threaten to expropriate land from inefficient farmers. Traditional chiefs in village councils were ordered to monitor land-use and to set annual production targets and producer prices each October. In 1988 the World Bank also agreed to provide a $16m. credit to finance a project to support reform in land management and conservation, while agriculture and rural development were to receive the bulk of the ECU 41m. that was allocated to Lesotho by the EC under the provisions of the third Lomé Convention.

MANUFACTURING, MINING AND TOURISM

Confronted by the chronic problems of agriculture, and by the need to create jobs for a rapidly expanding population, Lesotho has promoted development in other sectors, with varying degrees of success. Its main assets are proximity and duty-free access to the South African market, and abundant labour. Lesotho enjoys one of the lowest average rates of adult illiteracy in Africa (30%, according to the population census of 1986), and emigrant Basotho workers command an excellent reputation in South Africa. However, South Africa has, until recently, actively discouraged the development of competing industries in Lesotho.

The Lesotho National Development Corpn (LNDC), founded in 1967, and the Basotho Enterprises Development Corpn (BEDCO), which provides finance to local entrepreneurs, have been the main bodies stimulating manufacturing development, promoting a wide variety of small industries, including tyre retreading, tapestry weaving, electric lamp assembly, diamond cutting and polishing and the production of clothing, candles, ceramics, explosives, furniture, fertilizers and jewellery. Inducements to foreign companies have included generous allowances and tax 'holidays', duty-free access to the EC and Southern African Customs Union (SACU, see below) markets, the provision of industrial infrastructure and the construction of industrial estates in Maseru and Maputsoe (with further estates planned elsewhere in the country). During the late 1980s, when economic sanctions were imposed against South Africa by the international community, the government intensified its efforts to encourage the involvement of South African firms in Lesotho. Industrial developments during the 1980s which were supported by the LNDC included a project designed to double the capacity of the Basotho Fruit and Vegetable Cannery at Mazenod, and the establishment of the Maseru Tyre Co, a concern manufacturing parachutes for sporting and military purposes, a brewery and soft drinks plant in Maseru and two new steel plants and a wire products factory near the capital. By 1989 the LNDC was promoting 51 companies which employed more than 10,000 workers. In 1991 a Chinese company opened a television assembly plant.

For its part, BEDCO has had some success in encouraging small-scale enterprises, with strong financial support from Canada. Up to 2,000 new jobs are estimated to have been created since its foundation in 1975. As a result of these efforts, the manufacturing sector grew by an annual average of 12.8% in 1980–91, and its contribution to GDP has increased from about 6% in 1986 to 15.3% in 1991/92. In 1991 the UN Development Fund provided up to M1.5m. in assistance for a project to develop small industries.

There has also been significant development of tourism, which is now both a major source of employment and the second largest source of 'invisible' earnings, after workers' remittances. Tourist arrivals increased from 4,000 in 1968 to 171,000 in 1990; most visitors are South African. The sector has been adversely affected by competition from leisure and gambling resorts in the former South African 'homelands'.

Diamond mining was limited to small diamond diggings, exploited by primitive methods, until 1977, when a small modern mine at Letseng-la Terai, developed and administered by De Beers Consolidated Mines of South Africa, began full production. Most of the diamonds that the mine produced were of industrial quality, although a few unusually large gemstones were also found. Recovery rates, at only 2.8 carats per 100 metric tons, proved to be the lowest of any mine in the De Beers group, and operations ceased in 1982, depriving Lesotho of some 50% of its visible export earnings. Plans to reopen the mine have, however, been under consideration since 1984, and the possibility of residual diamond mining from the slag at Letseng-la-Terai has been suggested as a low-cost alternative. Lesotho is also believed to possess uranium and petroleum deposits but exploration and survey work for both minerals has yet to be undertaken.

POWER

Lesotho's major undeveloped resource is water. After much uncertainty over economic and technical feasibility, the final details of the controversial Highlands Water Project (HWP) were agreed with South Africa in March 1988 (see below). A massive undertaking for any country (particularly for one as small as Lesotho), with costs originally estimated at $3,770m., the HWP involves the diversion of water from Lesotho's rivers for export to South Africa, with self-sufficiency in hydro-generated electricity as the major by-product. The prospective throughput of water is projected at 77 cu m per second by the time the scheme is completed in the year 2017, although at the end of the first phase, planned for 1997, the rate will be about 18 cu m per second. The HWP is expected to have a generating capacity of 200 MW by the year 2003. The first phase of the scheme is now expected to cost $2,415m. Approximately three-quarters of this sum was raised in southern Africa (including some 57% from banks), with diversified external sources providing the balance. The commercial segment of the debt is to be met from royalty payments received on water sales to South Africa. Excavation began in 1991, with completion of the first stage, which includes the Katse dam, scheduled for 1997.

The water treaty negotiated with South Africa covers the legal framework of the project and the pricing and volume of water to be sold. One of the most contentious aspects of the treaty was the control of water delivery. There were strong fears, both in Lesotho and among its neighbours, that, unless Maseru controlled the 'tap', the country would be even more dependent on South Africa as the republic could delay the transfer of water payments as a form of leverage. The treaty addresses part of the problem, with South Africa due to pay monthly royalties in cash, regardless of water delivered, plus a unit cost component based on each cu ft of water delivered.

TRANSPORT AND COMMUNICATIONS

Owing to its mountainous terrain, much of Lesotho was, until recently, virtually inaccessible except by horse or light aircraft. However, a substantial network of tracks, passable by four-wheel drive vehicles, has now been built up, largely by 'food for work' teams in the mountain areas, and more than 570 km of tarred roads have been constructed. The road between Leribe, in the north, and Tsoaing, beyond Maseru, has been bituminized. In 1983 the first section of the southern perimeter road from Tsoloane to Mohale's Hoek was completed with aid from BADEA, and in 1984 the EC agreed to finance the next stage, to the Mekaling river. Finance from the EC was also made available in 1984 for the third stage, from Mekaling to Quthing. Several other road-building and rehabilitation projects have received funding: these include the construction of a new road linking Mohale's Hoek to Quthing. Construction of 300 km of new roads under the HWP commenced in 1987. In 1990 a bilateral agreement was reached with South Africa to jointly construct a bridge over the Caledon river, for the transportation of equipment to the HWP. Lesotho's economic development has depended heavily on South African road and rail outlets, a dependence which was graphically illustrated in 1983, 1984 and early 1986, when Pretoria instituted road blocks and checks, as a form of economic sanctions, which had severely debilitating effects on the Lesotho economy. A greater degree of independence in international communications was reached after the Maseru international airport became operational in mid-1986. The national carrier, Lesotho Airways, operates internal flights as well as international services via South Africa and Swaziland.

EMPLOYMENT, WAGES AND MIGRANT LABOUR

Lesotho's dependence on South Africa is also reflected in the earnings of the Basotho migrant labour force. Nearly two-fifths of the adult male labour force (113,000 workers) were employed in South African gold and coal mines in 1992. This has been necessitated by land shortage and the depressed state of agriculture in Lesotho, and by lack of employment opportunities and low wages in the formal sector (Lesotho's unemployment rate was 41% in 1991, 20% higher than in 1986). During 1990–91 some 10,000 Basotho were dismissed from South African mines, owing to a decline in international prices for gold and the high unemployment rate in that country.

The Lesotho economy's dependence on receipts from services and transfers, in the form of migrants' remittances, is reflected in the fact that the country's GNP is generally more than double GDP. (In most other African states the net outflow of services means that GDP is larger than GNP.) Apart from their obvious role in financing the large trade gap, the remittances are central to the income of up to 60% of families and are also used by the government to finance development. Some 30% of miners' cash income (reduced from 60% in 1991) has, by law, to be remitted direct to the Lesotho Bank (where it earns less than the commercial rates of interest). Workers' families are permitted to draw one-half of this immediately, with the remainder being retained until the workers return to Lesotho after completing their contracts.

The decline in the number of migrant workers since 1990 holds potentially grave consequences for Lesotho's economy. If South Africa were to carry out its often repeated threat to repatriate all migrants, the economic impact on Lesotho would be devastating. In 1985 the government invited the International Labour Office's Southern African Team for employment to report on alternative employment prospects. The resulting report emphasized the creation of small-scale enterprises, employing up to 50 people each, as the main area of potential job development, although such a policy would need far more active investment efforts from government than in the past.

SACU AND THE MONETARY AGREEMENTS

Together with Botswana, Namibia, South Africa and Swaziland, Lesotho is a member of the Southern African Customs Union (SACU), which dates formally from 1910, when the Union (now the Republic) of South Africa was established. The most recent SACU agreement, made in 1969, provides for payments to Botswana, Swaziland and Lesotho (the BSL countries) to be made on the basis of their share of goods imported by SACU countries, multiplied by an 'enhancement' factor of 1.42 as a form of compensation for the BSL countries' loss of freedom to conduct a completely independent economic policy, and for the costs that this restriction involves in trade diversion and loss of investment. SACU revenue is paid two years in arrears and earns no interest, but for Lesotho it has formed up to 70% of government recurrent revenues in recent years. Lesotho has resisted attempts by South Africa to renegotiate the terms governing SACU.

In December 1974 the governments of Lesotho, Swaziland and South Africa concluded the Rand Monetary Agreement (RMA). Under this agreement, Lesotho received interest on rand currency circulating in Lesotho, at a rate of two-thirds of the current yield to redemption of the most recent issues of long-dated South African government stock offered the previous year. In January 1980, however, Lesotho followed Botswana and Swaziland in their moves towards monetary independence by introducing its own currency, the loti (plural: maloti), replacing the South African rand at par. This measure was designed to give Lesotho greater control over factors influencing its development and over cash outflows by Basotho visiting South Africa. In July 1986 the RMA was superseded by a new agreement, establishing a Tripartite Monetary Area (TMA) comprising Lesotho, Swaziland and South Africa (including Namibia, which became independent in 1990). Under the TMA arrangement, Lesotho may determine the exchange rate of its own currency, but to date the loti has remained at par with the rand.

EXTERNAL TRADE AND PAYMENTS

Until the 1980s, Lesotho was largely able to ignore its balance of payments, since, as a *de facto* member of the South African rand monetary area, situations which in other countries would have shown up as a balance-of-payments problem would, in Lesotho, have appeared as a general credit shortage. In fact, this happened only rarely until the 1980s, as Lesotho's chronic trade deficit, resulting from a limited export base and large requirements of food imports, was more than offset by current transfers, migrant remittances and surpluses on the capital account of the balance of payments. As a result of a sharp decline in export earnings from 1980, combined with a reduction in aid receipts and an increase in imports, deficits on the current account of the balance of payments were incurred in some of the subsequent years. A deficit of $10m. in 1983 was followed in 1984 by a small surplus of $2m., and in 1985 receipts and payments were roughly in balance. Lesotho's external position subsequently deteriorated again, with the current account registering a deficit of $17m. in 1986. However, a current account surplus of $24m. was recorded in 1987. Although exports reached $47m. in 1987, imports also increased substantially, to $397m. As donors became concerned about the government's management of the economy, aid disbursements began to be withheld. A deficit of $25m. on the current account was recorded in 1988. During that year an IMF programme of reforms was implemented. In 1989 the current account registered a surplus of $10.4m., and further surpluses were reported in 1990 and 1991, of $65m. and $63.3m. respectively. The combined effects of drought and the decline in the level of workers' remittances are expected to make it difficult to sustain this performance. In 1990 workers' remittances totalled M1,102m., more than 600% of the value of Lesotho's exports and equivalent to 73% of GDP (compared with 105% of GDP in 1984).

South Africa is Lesotho's main trading partner within SACU. In 1991 SACU was the source of 94% of Lesotho's imports and the destination for 42% of its exports, while a further 30% of exports went to the EC. Like Botswana and Swaziland, Lesotho is associated with the EU under the provisions of the Lomé Convention, according duty-free access to EU markets for all exports except those covered by the EU's Common Agricultural Policy, which will benefit only from a small preference. The short-term effect on Lesotho's exports has been small, although there are hopes of eventual beef exports.

PUBLIC FINANCE

Since the renegotiation of the SACU agreement in 1969, revenue from this source has increased, from R1.9m. in 1968/69 to an estimated M548m. in 1992/93. Successive budget deficits during the 1980s (which were exacerbated by high spending on defence, in response to regional uncertainty) led to substantial cuts, in real terms, in other sectors.

In July 1988 the IMF approved a loan of SDR 9.6m. under its structural adjustment facility (SAF), to support a three-year economic programme agreed with the World Bank. The programme aimed to achieve an annual increase in GDP to 4%; to reduce the budget deficit from 18.8% of GDP in 1987/88 to 4.1% in 1990/91; to lower the debt-service ratio; and to reduce the rate of inflation. The government undertook to adopt policies which would increase the supply of credit from commercial banks to the private sector, encourage private investment in industry (particularly in industrial enterprises which would produce goods for export or provide substitutes for imports) and increase agricultural productivity. Initial delays in the Lesotho government's negotiations with the IMF were caused by the International Development Association's approval, in May, of an SDR 15m. ($20.7m.) credit for urban development and an SDR 11.7m. ($16.2m.) credit for land management, which led to concern about Lesotho's ability to meet the targets set for the SAF. In December 1988 a meeting of donor governments and organizations, convened by the UN Development Programme, agreed to provide $390m. in assistance for Lesotho's three-year programme. In the first year of the programme its targets were not met. The budgetary deficit increased to M181.1m. in 1988/89. However, the deficit was equivalent to only 0.6% of GNP in 1990/91. It was announced in early 1990 that some state enterprises, including Lesotho Airways and Lesotho Freight Air Transport, were to be transferred to the private sector.

In June 1991 the IMF agreed to provide SDR 18.1m. under its enhanced structural adjustment facility (ESAF) in support of an economic development programme covering the period 1991–94. The programme aimed to diversify manufacturing production and exports, to promote the role of the private sector in the economy and to improve the balance-of-payments position. By early 1993 Lesotho was exceeding the targets set by the ESAF. Current financing was to conclude in August 1994, and Lesotho's progress and further needs are under review by the IMF.

Between 1980–86 Lesotho's receipts of net development assistance fell by over 40% in real terms. The budget allocation for servicing the national debt increased from M36m. in 1982/83 to M60m. in 1984/85, although in 1985/86 and 1986/87 the upward trend in debt servicing costs appeared to have been stemmed, with a drop in real allocations. Lesotho's disbursed public debt more than doubled between 1980–84 to $134m., or 24.3% of GNP. The total external public debt was $471.6m. at the end of 1992, resulting in a debt-service ratio of 5.6%, as a percentage of exports of goods and services; this was equivalent to 42% of GNP, the highest level ever recorded.

The first Five-Year Development Plan (1970/71–1974/75) concentrated on the development of roads and agriculture. The second Five-Year Plan (1975/76–1979/80) exceeded its public investment target of R112m., although investment was still insufficient to stimulate economic growth. Under the third Development Plan, originally scheduled to cover 1980/81–1984/85 but extended to 1985/86, long-term investments were targeted at M700m. The plan was pessimistic about the prospects for job creation but did aim to spread economic growth and to make improvements in social welfare and the conservation of resources. In December 1988 donors pledged $390m. in support of a fourth Plan, covering the period 1988/89–1990/91. The severe drought in recent years has, however, interfered with the plan's implementation.

Lesotho continues to face formidable economic problems. The acute shortage of fertile land, the problem of soil erosion, and the backward state of agriculture make it highly unlikely that this sector can absorb the increase in population. Much will depend on the attitudes of the new government in South Africa and on the benefits to be derived from the HWP.

Statistical Survey

Source (unless otherwise stated): Bureau of Statistics, POB 455, Maseru 100; tel. 3852.

Area and Population

AREA, POPULATION AND DENSITY

Area (sq km)	30,355*
Population (census results)†	
12 April 1976	
Males	458,260
Females	605,928
Total	1,064,188
12 April 1986 (provisional)	1,447,000
Population (official estimates at mid-year)‡	
1985	1,528,000
1987	1,619,000
1989	1,700,000
Density (per sq km) at mid-1989	56.0

* 11,720 sq miles.
† Excluding absentee workers in South Africa, numbering 152,627 (males 129,088; females 23,539) in 1976.
‡ Including absentee workers in South Arica. Mid-year estimates for 1986 and 1988 are not available.

DISTRICT POPULATIONS
(Each district* has the same name as its chief town)

	1976†	1979‡	1981§
Berea	146,124	155,616	162,400
Butha-Buthe	77,178	81,926	84,800
Leribe	206,558	222,180	234,400
Mafeteng	154,339	166,644	175,900
Maseru	257,809	277,307	292,200
Mohale's Hoek	136,311	144,013	152,300
Mokhotlong	73,508	78,237	80,900
Qacha's Nek	76,497	81,060	84,700
Quthing	88,491	93,769	98,300
Total	1,216,815	1,301,575	1,365,900

* A new district, Thaba-Tseka, was created in 1981, for which no population figures were available.
† Census of 12 April, including absentee workers in South Africa.
‡ Mid-year estimate.
§ Mid-year estimate, projected from the 1976 census.

Capital: Maseru, population 45,000 in 1976.

BIRTHS AND DEATHS (UN estimates, annual averages)

	1975–80	1980–85	1985–90
Birth rate (per 1,000)	41.9	40.4	36.3
Death rate (per 1,000)	16.5	12.6	11.0

Expectation of life (UN estimates, years at birth, 1985–90): 58.0 (males 55.5; females 60.5).

Source: UN, *World Population Prospects: The 1992 Revision.*

ECONOMICALLY ACTIVE POPULATION
(ILO estimates, '000 persons at mid-1980)

	Males	Females	Total
Agriculture, etc.	300	271	571
Industry	21	6	27
Services	38	26	64
Total labour force	359	303	662

Source: ILO, *Economically Active Population Estimates and Projections, 1950–2025.*

Mid-1992 (estimates in '000): Agriculture, etc. 674; Total 864 (Source: FAO, *Production Yearbook*).

In 1992 about 38% of the total adult male labour force were in employment in South Africa.

Agriculture

PRINCIPAL CROPS ('000 metric tons)

	1990	1991	1992
Wheat	29	18	15*
Maize	172	108	61
Sorghum	36	12	10*
Roots and tubers†	7	8	8
Pulses†	7	7	6
Vegetables†	26	27	26
Fruit†	18	19	18

* Unofficial figure. † FAO estimates.

Source: FAO, *Production Yearbook.*

LIVESTOCK (FAO estimates, '000 head, year ending September)

	1990	1991	1992
Cattle	535	540	536
Sheep	1,460	1,470	1,460
Goats	1,050	1,060	1,060
Pigs	74	75	75
Horses	121	122	122
Asses	128	129	129

Source: FAO, *Production Yearbook.*

LIVESTOCK PRODUCTS ('000 metric tons)

	1990	1991	1992
Cows' milk*	24	24	24
Beef and veal*	13	14	13
Mutton and lamb*	4	4	4
Goats' meat*	3	3	3
Pig meat*	3	3	3
Hen eggs*	0.8	0.8	0.8
Wool:			
greasy	3.0†	3.0†	2.9*
clean*	1.5*	1.5*	1.5

* FAO estimate(s). † Unofficial figure.

Source: FAO, *Production Yearbook.*

Forestry

ROUNDWOOD REMOVALS
(FAO estimates, '000 cubic metres, excluding bark)

	1990	1991	1992
Total (all fuel wood)	604	619	635

Source: FAO, *Yearbook of Forest Products.*

Mining

	1979	1980	1981
Diamonds (carats)	64,886	105,245	52,291

1982: 39,000 carats (estimate) (Source: UN, *Industrial Statistics Yearbook).*

Finance

CURRENCY AND EXCHANGE RATES

Monetary Units
100 lisente (singular: sente) = 1 loti (plural: maloti).

Sterling, Dollar and Rand Equivalents (31 March 1994)
£1 sterling = 5.167 maloti;
US $1 = 3.481 maloti;
R1 = 1 loti;
100 maloti = £19.35 = $28.73.

Average Exchange Rate (US $ per loti)
1991 0.36280
1992 0.35092
1993 0.30641

Note: The loti is fixed at par with the South African rand.

BUDGET ('000 maloti, year ending 31 March)

Revenue*	1989/90	1990/91	1991/92
Taxation	444,347	558,033	700,721
Taxes on income, profits, etc.	59,366	70,802	138,300
Taxes on property	201	352	585
Domestic taxes on goods and services	119,331	130,344	137,198
Sales tax	102,510	112,300	112,700
Excises	12,300	13,120	16,300
Taxes on international trade	264,764	355,985	424,336
Import duties†	263,770	355,000	424,000
Other taxes	685	550	302
Other current revenue	80,761	69,531	118,934
Property income	42,578	40,694	70,494
Administrative fees, charges, etc.	16,602	15,154	17,941
Capital revenue	85	115	300
Total	525,193	627,679	819,955

Expenditure‡	1989/90	1990/91	1991/92
General public services	63,400	63,097	91,400
Defence	66,235	61,262	62,770
Public order and safety	32,805	35,409	44,950
Education	113,257	144,168	212,671
Health	67,587	88,266	111,173
Social security and welfare	13,502	13,411	14,965
Housing and community amenities	36,288	39,856	37,916
Other community and social services	4,940	4,906	6,528
Economic services	271,099	278,846	306,620
Fuel and energy	14,485	13,686	18,900
Agriculture, forestry, fishing and hunting	77,758	80,599	106,341
Mining, manufacturing and construction	74,473	67,180	47,695
Transportation and communication	77,825	82,759	96,134
Other economic services	26,558	34,622	37,550
Other purposes	101,060	94,305	80,965
Total	770,173	823,526	969,958
Current	435,184	456,155	622,340
Capital	334,989	367,371	347,618

* Excluding grants received from abroad ('000 maloti): 151,925 in 1989/90; 188,000 in 1990/91; 149,200 in 1991/92.

† Including Lesotho's allocated share of the Southern African Customs Union's collections of customs duties, excise duties and sales taxes not separately identifiable.

‡ Excluding net lending ('000 maloti): 10,313 in 1989/90; 8,950 in 1990/91; 9,050 in 1991/92.

Source: IMF, *Government Finance Statistics Yearbook.*

INTERNATIONAL RESERVES (US $ million at 31 December)

	1991	1992	1993
IMF special drawing rights	0.29	0.66	0.56
Reserve position in IMF	1.87	4.83	4.82
Foreign exchange	112.88	152.00	n.a.
Total	115.04	157.49	n.a.

Source: IMF, *International Financial Statistics.*

MONEY SUPPLY (million maloti at 31 December)

	1991	1992	1993
Currency outside banks	35.01	37.96	43.75
Demand deposits at commercial banks	304.00	337.53	389.43
Total money	339.01	375.49	433.18

Source: Central Bank of Lesotho.

COST OF LIVING
(Consumer Price Index for low-income group; base: 1980 = 100)

	1990	1991	1992
Food	342.2	404.8	500.3
All items	350.9	413.6	484.0

Source: UN, *Monthly Bulletin of Statistics.*

NATIONAL ACCOUNTS
(million maloti at current prices, year ending 31 March)

Expenditure on the Gross Domestic Product

	1990/91	1991/92	1992/93
Government final consumption expenditure	234.6	314.2	380.5
Private final consumption expenditure	1,756.7	2,304.3	2,660.3
Increase/decrease in stocks	−10.3	−6.9	−7.7
Gross fixed capital formation	1,162.4	1,248.8	1,424.0
Total domestic expenditure	3,143.4	3,860.4	4,457.1
Exports of goods and services	216.0	250.1	378.3
Less Imports of goods and services	1,850.2	2,371.8	2,809.5
GDP in purchasers' values	1,509.2	1,738.7	2,025.9

Source: IMF, *International Financial Statistics.*

Gross Domestic Product by Economic Activity

	1989/90	1990/91	1991/92*
Agriculture, forestry and fishing	215.0	249.9	219.4
Mining and quarrying	4.4	6.2	3.1
Manufacturing	150.3	166.7	217.7
Electricity, gas and water	13.3	24.5	31.3
Building and construction	214.2	291.7	236.3
Trade, restaurants, and hotels	100.7	123.0	165.5
Transport and communication	39.1	46.7	54.8
Finance, insurance and real estate	139.4	158.6	190.0
Public administration and defence	90.2	96.9	123.4
Other services	111.5	119.2	177.4
Sub-total	1,078.1	1,283.4	1,418.9
Less Imputed bank service charge	51.1	65.0	53.0
GDP at factor cost	1,027.0	1,218.4	1,365.9
Indirect taxes, *less* subsidies	260.3	286.3	277.9
GDP in purchasers' values	1,287.3	1,504.7	1,643.8

* Estimates.

Sources: UN, *National Accounts Statistics*; UN Economic Commission for Africa, *African Statistical Yearbook.*

BALANCE OF PAYMENTS (US $ million)

	1990	1991	1992
Merchandise exports f.o.b.	59.5	67.2	109.2
Merchandise imports f.o.b.	−672.6	−803.5	-932.6
Trade balance	−613.2	−736.4	−823.4
Export of services	40.6	40.9	41.3
Imports of services	−80.5	−83.5	−81.7
Other income received	455.0	476.8	496.3
Other income paid	−22.8	−20.9	−33.7
Private unrequited transfers (net)	4.8	2.7	3.9
Official unrequited transfers (net)	281.1	403.5	434.9
Current balance	65.0	83.1	37.6
Direct investment (net)	17.1	7.5	2.7
Other capital (net)	−62.1	−68.2	−65.2
Net errors and omissions	−2.8	20.1	74.8
Overall balance	17.2	42.4	49.9

Source: IMF, *International Financial Statistics.*

External Trade

PRINCIPAL COMMODITIES

Imports c.i.f. ('000 maloti)	1979	1980	1981
Food and live animals	68,559	76,918	82,902
Beverages and tobacco	13,725	16,233	21,761
Clothing	31,652	34,452	36,733
Machinery and transport equipment	44,084	58,397	74,647
Petroleum products	22,848	31,633	37,766
Chemicals	16,372	18,853	28,229
Footwear	10,556	12,423	14,338
Total (incl. others)	303,612	360,757	439,375

Total imports (million maloti): 567.2 in 1982; 539.7 in 1983; 634.5 in 1984; 751.0 in 1985; 803.3 in 1986; 954.8 in 1987; 1,327.5 in 1988; 1,406.5 in 1989; 1,801.3 in 1990; 2,255.7 in 1991; 3,013.9 in 1992 (Sources: Central Bank of Lesotho; IMF, *International Financial Statistics).*

Exports f.o.b. (million maloti, distribution by SITC)	1989	1990	1991*
Food and live animals	26.0	22.6	21.6
Beverages and tobacco	0.9	3.0	n.a.
Inedible crude materials	33.7	15.5	16.9
Chemicals and related products	2.9	2.2	2.9
Basic manufactures	10.8	17.6	10.2
Machinery and transport equipment	1.2	1.6	5.2
Miscellaneous manufactured articles	89.7	90.3	129.3
Other commodities and transactions	7.4	0.9	0.1
Total	172.6	153.7	186.2

* Provisional figures.

Source: Bureau of Statistics and Customs Department.

Total exports (million maloti): 178.4 in 1989; 152.7 in 1990; 166.9 in 1991; 185.6 in 1992 (Source: IMF, *International Financial Statistics*).

PRINCIPAL TRADING PARTNERS (estimates, million maloti)

Imports	1990	1991	1992
SACU*	1,711.3	2,195.3	2,469.7
EC	41.6	35.6	127.2
Other	55.4	101.5	304.8

Source: Bureau of Statistics and Customs Department.

Exports	1979	1980	1981
SACU*	12,955	18,379	20,130
EC	3,580	5,152	4,462
Switzerland	21,070	21,345	18,024
Other	311	401	508

* Southern African Customs Union, of which Lesotho is a member; also including Botswana, Namibia, South Africa and Swaziland.

Transport

ROAD TRAFFIC (estimates, '000 motor vehicles in use)

	1989	1990	1991
Passenger cars	6	6	6
Commercial vehicles	14	14	14

Source: UN Economic Commission for Africa, *African Statistical Yearbook.*

CIVIL AVIATION (traffic on scheduled services)

	1989	1990	1991
Kilometres flown (million)	1	1	1
Passengers carried ('000)	63	53	56
Passenger-km (million)	33	13	14
Freight ton-km (million)	1	0	0

Source: UN, *Statistical Yearbook.*

Tourism

	1988	1989	1990
Tourist arrivals ('000)	110	169	171
Tourist receipts (US $ million)	8	8	9

Source: UN, *Statistical Yearbook.*

Communications Media

	1989	1990	1991
Radio receivers ('000 in use)	46	48	51
Television receivers ('000 in use)	5	10	11
Telephones ('000 in use)*	12	12	12
Daily newspapers			
Number	n.a.	4	n.a.
Average circulation ('000 copies)	n.a.	20	n.a.

* Estimates.

Sources: UNESCO, *Statistical Yearbook;* UN Economic Commission for Africa, *African Statistical Yearbook.*

Education

(1991)

	Institutions	Teachers	Students
Primary	1,198	6,685	361,144
General secondary	179	2,407	46,572
Teachers' training college	1	87	567
Technical and vocational schools	9	140	1,600
University	1	204	1,421

Source: Ministry of Education, Maseru.

Directory

The Constitution

The Constitution of the Kingdom of Lesotho, which took effect at independence in October 1966, was suspended in January 1970. A new Constitution was promulgated following the March 1993 general election. Its main provisions are summarized below:

Lesotho is an hereditary monarchy. The King, who is Head of State, has no executive or legislative powers. Executive authority is vested in the Cabinet, which is headed by the Prime Minister, while legislative power is exercised by the 65-member National Assembly, which is elected, at intervals of no more than five years, by universal adult suffrage in the context of a multi-party political system. There is also a Senate, comprising traditional chiefs and eight nominated members.

The Government

HEAD OF STATE

HM King Letsie III (succeeded to the throne 12 November 1990).

CABINET
(September 1994)

Prime Minister and Minister of Defence and Public Service: Dr Ntsu Mokhehle.

Deputy Prime Minister and Minister of Finance and Economic Planning and Manpower Development: (vacant).

Minister of Trade, Industry and Tourism: Shakhane Robong Molhlehle.

Minister of Labour and Employment: Not'si Molopo.

Minister of Agriculture, Co-operatives and Marketing: Ntsukunyane Mphanya.

Minister of Home Affairs, Local Government, Rural and Urban Development: Lesao Lehohla.

Minister of Education and Training, Sports, Culture and Youth Affairs: Pakalitha Mosisili.

Minister of Health and Social Welfare: Dr Khauhelo Deborah Raditapole.

Minister of Natural Resources, Water, Highlands Water, Energy, Mining, Technology and the Environment: Monyane Moleleki.

Minister of Works, Transport, Post and Telecommunications: David Mochochoko.

Minister of Information and Broadcasting: Mpho Malie.

Minister of Justice and Human Rights, Law and Constitutional Affairs: Kelebone Maope.

Minister of Foreign Affairs: Molapo Qhobela.

MINISTRIES

Office of the Prime Minister: Maseru.

Ministry of Agriculture, Co-operatives and Marketing: POB 24, Maseru 100; tel. 322741; telex 4330.

Ministry of Defence and Public Service: POB 527, Maseru 100; tel. 323861; telex 4330.

Ministry of Education and Training, Sports, Culture and Youth Affairs: POB 47, Maseru 100; tel. 323045; telex 4330.

Ministry of Finance and Economic Planning and Manpower Development: POB 395, Maseru 100; tel. 311101; telex 4330; fax 310157.

Ministry of Foreign Affairs: POB 1387, Maseru 100; tel. 323861; telex 4330.

Ministry of Health and Social Welfare: Private Bag A116, Maseru 100; tel. 322564; telex 433010.

Ministry of Home Affairs, Local Government, Rural and Urban Development: Maseru.

Ministry of Information and Broadcasting: POB 36, Maseru 100; tel. 323561; telex 4450; fax 310003.

Ministry of Justice and Human Rights, Law and Constitutional Affairs: POB 402, Maseru 100; tel. 322683; telex 4330.

Ministry of Natural Resources, Water, Highlands Water, Energy, Mining, Technology and the Environment: POB 772, Maseru 100; tel. 322491; telex 4253.

Ministry of Trade, Industry and Tourism, Labour and Employment: POB 747, Maseru 100; tel. 322802; telex 4384; fax 310121.

Ministry of Works, Transport, Post and Telecommunications: POB 20, Maseru 100; tel. 323761; telex 4258; fax 310125.

Legislature

NATIONAL ASSEMBLY

Elections to the 65-member National Assembly took place in March 1993. The Basotho Congress Party won all of the seats.

Political Organizations

Party political activity was banned during the period March 1986–May 1991.

Basotho Congress Party (BCP): POB 111, Maseru; f. 1952; Leader Dr NTSU MOKHEHLE; 75,000 mems.

Basotho Democratic Alliance (BDA): Maseru; f. 1984; Pres. S. C. NCOJANE.

Basotho National Party (BNP): POB 124, Maseru 100; f. 1958; Nat. Chair. EVARISTUS RETSELISITSOE SEKHONYANA; Sec.-Gen. (vacant); 280,000 mems.

Communist Party of Lesotho (CPL): Maseru; f. 1962 (banned 1970–91); supported mainly by migrant workers employed in South Africa; Leader MOKHAFISI JACOB KENA.

Kopanang Basotho Party (KBP): Maseru; f. 1992; campaigns for women's rights; Leader LIMAKATSO NTAKATSANE.

Lesotho Labour Party (LLP): Maseru; f. 1991; Leader MAMOLEFI RANTHIMO.

Marematlou Freedom Party (MFP): POB 0443, Maseru 105; tel. 315804; f. 1962; Leader VINCENT MOEKETSE MALEBO; 300,000 mems.

National Independence Party: Maseru; f. 1984; Pres. ANTHONY C. MANYELI.

Popular Front for Democracy: Maseru; f. 1991.

United Democratic Party (UDP): POB 776, Maseru 100; f. 1967; Chair. BEN L. SHEA; Leader CHARLES D. MOFELI; Sec.-Gen. MOLOMO NKUEBE; 26,000 mems.

Diplomatic Representation

EMBASSIES AND HIGH COMMISSIONS IN LESOTHO

Germany: Maseru; telex 4379; Ambassador: HANS GUENTER GNOSTKE.

South Africa: Lesotho Bank Centre, Private Bag A266, Maseru 100; tel. 315758; fax 310128; Ambassador: P. GERHARD VISSER.

United Kingdom: POB 521, Maseru 100; tel. 313961; telex 4343; fax 310120; High Commissioner: JAMES ROY COWLING.

USA: POB 333, Maseru 100; tel. 312666; fax 310116; Ambassador: LEONARD H. O. SPEARMAN.

Judicial System

HIGH COURT

The High Court is a superior court of record, and in addition to any other jurisdiction conferred by statute it is vested with unlimited original jurisdiction to determine any civil or criminal matter. It also has appellate jurisdiction to hear appeals and reviews from the subordinate courts. Appeals may be made to the court of appeal.

Chief Justice: BRENDAN PETER CULLINAN.

Judges: M. L. LEHOHLA, J. L. KHEOLA, B. K. MOLAI.

COURT OF APPEAL

Judges: ISMAIL MAHOMED (President), J. BROWNE, G. P. KOTZE, R. N. LEON, J. H. STEYN.

SUBORDINATE COURTS

Each of the 10 districts possesses subordinate courts, presided over by magistrates.

JUDICIAL COMMISSIONERS' COURTS

These courts hear civil and criminal appeals from central and local courts. Further appeal may be made to the high court and finally to the court of appeal.

CENTRAL AND LOCAL COURTS

There are 71 such courts, of which 58 are local courts and 13 are central courts which also serve as courts of appeal from the local courts. They have limited civil and criminal jurisdiction.

Religion

About 90% of the population profess Christianity.

CHRISTIANITY

Christian Council of Lesotho: POB 547, Maseru 100; tel. 323639; telex 4512; f. 1964; six mem. and four assoc. mem. churches; Chair. Rev. L. N. KHEEKHE.

The Anglican Communion

Anglicans in Lesotho are adherents of the Church of the Province of Southern Africa, comprising 22 dioceses. The Metropolitan of the Province is the Archbishop of Cape Town, South Africa. Lesotho forms a single diocese.

Bishop of Lesotho: Rt Rev. PHILIP STANLEY MOKUKU, Bishop's House, POB MS 87, Maseru 100; tel. 311974; fax 310161.

Lesotho Evangelical Church

President: Rev. G. L. SIBOLLA, PO Morija; Exec. Sec. Rev. THEBE, POB 260, Maseru 100; tel. 3942; independent since 1964; c. 207,000 mems.

The Roman Catholic Church

Lesotho comprises one archdiocese and three dioceses. At 31 December 1991 there were an estimated 692,548 adherents in the country.

Lesotho Catholic Bishops' Conference: Catholic Secretariat, POB 200, Maseru 100; tel. 312525; telex 4540; f. 1980; Pres. Rt Rev. EVARISTUS THATHO BITSOANE, Bishop of Qacha's Nek.

Archbishop of Maseru: Most Rev. BERNARD MOHLALISI, Archbishop's House, 19 Orpen Rd, POB 267, Maseru 100; tel. 312565.

Other Christian Churches

Denominations active in Lesotho include the African Methodist Episcopal Church, the Assembly of God and the Methodist Church.

BAHÁ'Í FAITH

National Spiritual Assembly: POB 508, Maseru 100; tel. 312346; mems resident in 476 localities.

The Press

Lentsoe la Basotho: POB 36, Maseru 100; tel. 323561; telex 4450; fax 310003; f. 1986; Sesotho; publ. by Ministry of Information and Broadcasting; Editor K. LESENYA; circ. 5,000.

Leselinyana la Lesotho: POB 7, Morija 190; tel. 360244; f. 1863; fortnightly; Sesotho, with occasional articles in English; publ. by Lesotho Evangelical Church; Editor A. B. THOALANE; circ. 15,000.

Lesotho Today: POB 36, Maseru 100; tel. 323561; telex 4450; fax 310003; f. 1986; English; publ. by Ministry of Information and Broadcasting; Editor S. K. MAKHAKHE; circ. 2,500.

Moeletsi oa Basotho: Mazenod Institute, POB MZ 18, Mazenod 160; tel. 62224; telex 4271; f. 1933; weekly; Roman Catholic; Sesotho; Editor WILLIAM LESENYA; circ. 12,000.

Mphatlatsane: Maseru; daily; independent newspaper.

NEWS AGENCIES

Lesotho News Agency (LENA): POB 36, Maseru 100; tel. 315317; telex 4598; fax 310003; f. 1986; Dir LEBOHANG LEJAKANE; Editor KHOELI PHOLOSI.

Foreign Bureau

Inter Press Service (IPS) (Italy): c/o Lesotho News Agency, POB 36, Maseru; Correspondent LEBOHANG LEJAKANE.

Publishers

Macmillan Boleswa Publishers Lesotho (Pty) Ltd: POB 7545, Maseru 100; tel. 317340; fax 310047.

Mazenod Institute: POB MZ 18, Mazenod 160; tel. 62224; telex 4271; f. 1931; Roman Catholic; Man. Fr B. MOHLALISI.

Morija Sesuto Book Depot: POB 4, Morija 190; f. 1861; owned by the Lesotho Evangelical Church; religious, educational and Sesotho language and literature.

St Michael's Mission: The Social Centre, POB 25, Roma; f. 1968; religious and educational; Man. Dir Fr M. FERRANGE.

Government Publishing House

Government Printer: Maseru.

Radio and Television

In 1991 there were an estimated 51,000 radio receivers and 11,000 television receivers in use.

Lesotho National Broadcasting Service: POB 552, Maseru 100; tel. 323561; telex 4450; fax 310003; programmes in Sesotho and English; television transmissions began in 1988; Dir of Broadcasting MCENI TENTE.

Finance

(cap. = capital; p.u. = paid up; res = reserves; dep. = deposits; m. = million; brs = branches; amounts in maloti)

BANKING

Central Bank

Central Bank of Lesotho: POB 1184, Maseru 100; tel. 314281; telex 4367; fax 310051; f. 1980; bank of issue; cap. and res 75.4m., dep. 507.8m. (Dec. 1992); Gov. and Chair. Dr ANTHONY M. MARUPING; Gen. Man. ALEMU ABERRA.

Commercial Banks

Barclays Bank PLC: POB 115, Kingsway, Maseru 100; tel. 312423; telex 4346; fax 310068; Gen. Man. W. G. PRICE; 4 brs and 3 agencies.

Lesotho Bank: POB 1053, Maseru 100; tel. 315737; telex 4206; fax 310268; f. 1972; state-owned; commercial bank, also carries out development banking functions; cap. and res 65m., dep. 532m. (Dec. 1992); Chair. Dr MOKETE; Gen. Man. N. MONYANE; 6 brs and 15 agencies.

Standard Chartered Bank Lesotho Ltd: Standard Bank Bldg, 1st Floor, Kingsway, POB 1001, Maseru 100; tel. 312696; telex 4332; fax 310025; Chief Man. W. C. IRWIN; 3 brs and 7 agencies.

Development Banks

Lesotho Agricultural Development Bank (LADB): 58 Kingsway Rd, POB 845, Maseru 100; tel. 313277; telex 4269; fax 310139; f. 1980; state-owned; cap. p.u. 5m. (Dec. 1991); Chair. L. T. TYOANE; Man. Dir C. S. MOLELLE; 7 brs and 12 agencies.

Lesotho Building Finance Corporation (LBFC): Private Bag A59, Maseru 100; tel. 313514; telex 4326; state-owned; Man. Dir N. MONYANE; 3 brs.

INSURANCE

Lesotho National Insurance Co (Pty) Ltd: Private Bag A65, Lesotho Insurance House, Kingsway, Maseru; tel. 323032; telex 4220.

Trade and Industry

DEVELOPMENT ORGANIZATIONS

Lesotho Highlands Development Authority: POB 7332, Maseru 100; tel. 311280; telex 4523; fax 310060; f. 1986 to supervise the Highlands Water Project, being undertaken jtly with South Africa; CEO MASUPHA SOLE.

Lesotho National Development Corporation (LNDC): Development House, 1st Floor, Kingsway Rd, Private Bag A96, Maseru 100; tel. 312012; telex 4341; fax 311038; f. 1967; 90% govt-owned; candle, carpet, tyre-retreading, explosives and furniture factories, potteries, two diamond prospecting operations, a fertilizer factory, an abattoir, a clothing factory, a diamond-cutting and polishing works, a jewellery factory, a housing co, a brewery, an international hotel with a gambling casino, Lesotho Airways Corpn and a training centre for motor mechanics; cap. p.u. M20m. (March 1993); Chair. Minister of Trade, Industry and Tourism; Man. Dir A. M. MONYAKE.

Basotho Enterprises Development Corporation (BEDCO): POB 1216, Maseru 100; tel. 312094; telex 4370; f. 1980; promotes and assists with the establishment and development of small-scale Basotho-owned enterprises; Man. Dir S. K. PHAFANE.

Lesotho Co-operatives Handicrafts: Maseru; f. 1978; marketing and distribution of handicrafts; Gen. Man. KHOTSO MATLA.

CHAMBER OF COMMERCE

Lesotho Chamber of Commerce and Industry: POB 79, Maseru; tel. 323482.

MARKETING ORGANIZATIONS

Livestock Products Marketing Service: POB 800, Maseru; telex 4344; f. 1973; sole organization for marketing livestock and livestock products; liaises closely with marketing boards in South Africa; projects include an abattoir, tannery, poultry and wool and mohair scouring plants; Gen. Man. S. R. MATLANYANE.

Produce Marketing Corporation: Maseru; telex 4365; f. 1974; Gen. Man. M. PHOOFOLO.

EMPLOYERS' ORGANIZATION

Association of Lesotho Employers: POB 1509, Maseru; tel. 315736; telex 4368; f. 1961; represents mems in industrial relations and on govt bodies, and advises the Govt about employers' concerns; Pres. L. J. MATSELA; Exec. Dir T. MAKEKA.

TRADE UNIONS

Construction and Allied Workers Union of Lesotho (CAWULE): Maseru.

Lesotho General Workers' Union: POB 322, Maseru; f. 1954; Chair. J. M. RAMAROTHOLE; Sec. T. MOTLOHI.

Lesotho Transport and Telecommunication Workers' Union: POB 266, Maseru; f. 1959; Pres. M. BERENG; Sec. P. MOTRAMAI.

National Union of Construction and Allied Workers: POB 327, Maseru; f. 1967; Pres. L. PUTSOANE; Sec. T. TLALE.

National Union of Printing, Bookbinding and Allied Workers: PO Mazenod 160; f. 1963; Pres. G. MOTEBANG; Gen. Sec. CLEMENT RATSIU.

Union of Shop Distributive and Allied Workers: POB 327, Maseru; f. 1966; Pres. P. BERENG; Sec. J. MOLAPO.

CO-OPERATIVE SOCIETIES

Co-op Lesotho Pty Ltd: Ministry of Agriculture, Co-operatives and Marketing, POB 24, Maseru 100; tel. 322741; telex 4330.

Registry of Co-operatives: POB 89, Maseru; Registrar P. MOEKETSI.

Transport

RAILWAYS

Lesotho is linked with the South African railway system by a short line (2.6 km in length) from Maseru to Marseilles, on the Bloemfontein/Natal main line.

ROADS

At 31 December 1992 Lesotho's road network totalled 5,242 km, of which 1,347 km were main roads and 1,003 km were secondary roads. About 840 km were paved. Construction of 300 km of new roads, under the Highlands Water Project, began in 1987. In the 1993/94 budget M80m. (5.7% of total expenditure) was allocated for the improvement of the road network.

CIVIL AVIATION

The international airport is at Thota-Moli, about 20 km from Maseru. There are 40 airstrips in Lesotho, of which 14 receive charter and regular scheduled air services.

Lesotho Airways Corporation: Mejametalana Airport, POB 861, Maseru 100; tel. 312453; telex 4347; fax 310126; f. 1971; govt-owned; internal flights and scheduled international services via South Africa and Swaziland; Chair. T. MAKHAKE; Man. Dir MICHAEL MACDONAGH.

Tourism

In 1990 there were some 171,000 tourist arrivals, an increase of 55.5% compared with 1988. Receipts from tourism in 1990 totalled about US $9m. in the latter year. Spectacular mountain scenery is the principal tourist attraction. The majority of visitors come from South Africa.

Lesotho Tourist Board: POB 1378, Maseru 100; tel. 323760; telex 4280; fax 310108; f. 1983; Man. Dir Mrs C. M. MOSAE.

Defence

Military service is voluntary. The Royal Lesotho Defence Force comprised 2,000 men in June 1993.

Defence Expenditure: Projected at M111.4m. (5.3% of total expenditure) for 1992/93.

Commander of the Royal Lesotho Defence Force: Maj.-Gen. S. K. MOLAPO.

Education

All primary education is available free of charge, and is provided mainly by the three main Christian missions (Lesotho Evangelical, Roman Catholic and Anglican), under the direction of the Ministry of Education and Training, Sports, Culture and Youth Affairs. Lesotho has one of the highest levels of literacy among African countries: according to the population census of 1986, the average rate of adult illiteracy was 30% for males and 11% for females. Education at primary schools is officially compulsory for seven years between six and 13 years of age. Secondary education, beginning at the age of 13, lasts for up to five years, comprising a first cycle of three years and a second of two years. Of children in the relevant age-group in 1993 an estimated 63.8% of males and 77.7% of females were enrolled at primary schools, while in 1991 49.5% of males and 60.8% of females were enrolled at secondary schools. The National University of Lesotho had 1,360 students in 1990. Of projected expenditure by the central government in the 1994/95 financial year, M332m. (20.9%) was allocated to education.

Bibliography

For works on the former High Commission territories generally, see Botswana bibliography, p. 190

Bureau of Statistics. *Annual Statistical Bulletin*. Maseru.

Hailey, Lord. *South Africa and the High Commission Territories*. London, Oxford University Press, 1965.

Halpern, J. *South Africa's Hostages: Bechuanaland, Basutoland and Swaziland*. Harmondsworth, Penguin Books, 1965.

IBRD. *Lesotho: A Development Challenge*. Washington, IBRD, 1975.

Jones, D. *Aid and Development in Southern Africa*. London, Croom Helm/Overseas Development Institute, 1977.

Khaketla, B. M. *Lesotho 1970: An African Coup Under the Microscope*. London, Hurst, 1974.

Konczacki, Z. A., Parpart, J. L., and Shaw, T. M. *Studies in the Economic History of Southern Africa*. Vol. II. London, Cass, 1991.

Marres, P., and van der Wiel, A. *Poverty Eats My Blanket. A Poverty Study: The Case of Lesotho*. Maseru, Lesotho Government Printer, 1977.

Moody, E. *Growth Centres in Lesotho*. Pretoria, Africa Institute of South Africa, 1975.

Sanders, P. *Moshoeshoe, Chief of the Sotho*. London, Heinemann/Philip, 1975.

Selwyn, P. *Industries in the Southern African Periphery: A Study of Industrial Development in Botswana, Lesotho and Swaziland*. London, Croom Helm/Overseas Development Institute, 1977.

Spence, J. E. *Lesotho: the Politics of Dependence*. London, Oxford University Press, for the Institute of Race Relations, 1967.

Stevens, R. P. *Lesotho, Botswana and Swaziland*. London, Pall Mall, 1967.

LIBERIA

Physical and Social Geography

CHRISTOPHER CLAPHAM

The Republic of Liberia was founded in 1847 by freed black slaves from the southern USA who settled along the western Guinea coast between Cape Mount (11° 20′ W) and Cape Palmas (7° 40′ W) from 1821 onwards. Liberia extends from 4° 20′ N to 8° 30′ N with a maximum breadth of 280 km between Buchanan and Nimba. The country occupies an area of 97,754 sq km (37,743 sq miles) between Sierra Leone to the west, the Republic of Guinea to the north, and Côte d'Ivoire to the east.

PHYSICAL FEATURES AND POPULATION

An even coastline of 570 km, characterized by powerful surf, rocky cliffs and lagoons, makes access from the Atlantic Ocean difficult, except at the modern ports. The flat coastal plain, which is 15–55 km wide, consists of forest and savannah. The interior hills and mountain ranges, with altitudes of 180–360 m, form part of an extended peneplain, covered by evergreen (in the south) or semi-deciduous (in the north) rain forests. The northern highlands contain Liberia's greatest elevations, which include the Nimba mountains, reaching 1,752 m above sea-level, and the Wologisi range, reaching 1,381 m. The descent from the higher to the lower belts of the highlands is characterized by rapids and waterfalls.

Liberia has two rainy seasons near Harper, in the south, and one rainy season (from May to October) in the rest of the country. From Monrovia, on the coast in north-west Liberia, with an average of 4,650 mm per year, rainfall decreases towards the south-east and the hinterland, reaching 2,240 mm per year at Ganta. Average temperatures are more extreme in the interior than at the coast. Monrovia has an annual average of 26°C, with absolute limits at 33°C and 14°C respectively. At Tappita temperatures may rise to 44°C in March and fall to 9°C during cool harmattan nights in December or January. Mean water temperature on the coast is 27°C.

The drainage system consists of 15 principal river basins, of which those of the Cavalla river, with an area of 30,225 sq km (including 13,730 sq km in Liberia), and of the St Paul river, with an area of 21,910 sq km (11,325 sq km in Liberia), are the largest. The water flow varies considerably and may reach over 100,000 cubic feet per second (cfs) at the Mt Coffee gauge of the St Paul river in August or decrease to 2,000 cfs during the dry season in March.

The first Liberian census enumerated a population of 1,016,443 in April 1962. According to the second census, in February 1974, an increase of 47.9%, to 1,503,368, had taken place, indicating an average annual growth rate of 3.36%, one of the highest in Africa. A third census, held in February 1984, enumerated a total population of 2,101,628. According to official estimates, the population had increased to 2,580,000 at mid-1992.

The main groups comprising the Liberian population at the 1974 census were the 16 indigenous African tribes (totalling 1,402,950), 42,834 non-tribal Liberians (mainly descendants of the settlers), 47,654 non-Liberian Africans (including 26,337 Guineans, 8,068 Fanti from Ghana, and 6,440 Sierra Leoneans), 3,430 Lebanese, 2,399 US citizens, and 4,101 Europeans. The major ethnic group is the Kpelle (numbering 298,500 in 1974), who occupy the central section of the country, particularly Bong County. The Bassa in the Buchanan region (214,150) and the Gio in Nimba County (130,300) are the second and third largest groups. Other well-known groups are the seafaring Kru (121,400) and the Vai.

Prior to 1990 the demographic pattern of Liberia was characterized by a number of features typical of developing countries: a high proportion of children under 15 years of age (47% in 1984); a low average population density (26.4 per sq km at mid-1992); a high growth rate in the capital (the population of Monrovia, including Congotown, increased from 80,992 in 1962 to 208,629 in 1978, and to 421,058 in 1984), and in coastal districts; a high rate of migration towards urban centres, and the resulting social problems of slum formation, increasing crime and unemployment. Considerable social and demographic disruption has attended the civil disorder that has dominated Liberian affairs since December 1989. In November 1993 some 400,000–500,000 people (about 20% of the total population) had taken refuge in the Monrovia area. According to estimates by the United Nations High Commissioner for Refugees, there were then about 415,000 Liberian refugees in Guinea, 250,000 in Côte d'Ivoire, 20,000 in Ghana, 16,000 in Sierra Leone, and 4,000 in Nigeria.

Recent History

CHRISTOPHER CLAPHAM

Liberia was founded by liberated black slaves from the southern USA. During 1822–92 some 16,400 former slaves were settled along the 'Malagueta' or 'Grain Coast' of west Africa, under the auspices of US philanthropic organizations. They were joined by some 5,700 Africans who had been freed from slaving vessels by the British and US navies. Conditions on the coast were harsh, and many of the settlers died, moved elsewhere or returned to the USA. Liberia was never officially a US colony, and it became an independent republic on 26 July 1847, with a constitution based on that of the USA. For most of the 19th century the republic controlled only scattered coastal settlements with their immediate hinterland. Control was extended inland from the 1890s onwards, in response to encroachment by British and French colonialism, although the people of the interior were not fully subdued until the 1920s. In 1926, however, European influence was reduced when the US-owned Firestone Plantations Co began operations in Liberia, establishing massive rubber estates, and becoming the country's principal private-sector employer.

TUBMAN AND TOLBERT

For more than 130 years after independence Liberian politics was dominated by descendants of the original settlers, known as Americo-Liberians; the True Whig Party (TWP) maintained uninterrupted rule between 1871-1971. In contrast to his predecessors, President William Tubman, who was inaugurated in 1944, advocated the development of the economy through the encouragement of foreign investment, and a policy of assimilating Liberia's different ethnic groups. Amendments to the constitution of 1847 gave representation in the legislature to the hinterland provinces and the right of suffrage to all adults, subject to a property qualification. The three hinterland provinces were reorganized into four countries in 1964.

President Tubman died in July 1971 and was succeeded by the vice-president, William Tolbert, who was re-elected in 1975. While maintaining Liberia's close links with Western countries, Tolbert established diplomatic relations with the USSR in 1972. In 1973 the Mano River Union, which provided for increased economic co-operation with Sierra Leone, was established, and Liberia became a member of the Economic Community of West African States (ECOWAS). Although the economy continued to expand, Liberia was adversely affected during the late 1970s by declining world demand for its principal exports, iron ore and rubber, and by a sharp increase in international prices.

In July 1979 a demonstration in protest at a proposed increase in the price of rice, which was organized by the Progressive Alliance of Liberia (PAL), an opposition group formed in the previous year, resulted in riots and looting. President Tolbert assumed emergency powers and postponed the forthcoming municipal elections. Shortly afterwards, the government subsidized the price of rice and in December allowed the PAL to register as an official opposition party, under the name of the Progressive People's Party (PPP). Support for the PPP increased rapidly, and, in March 1980 its chairman, Gabriel Baccus Matthews, advocated a general strike; he and some 70 supporters were subsequently arrested.

THE PEOPLE'S REDEMPTION COUNCIL

On 12 April 1980 President Tolbert was assassinated in a military coup, led by Master Sgt (later Gen.) Samuel Doe. A People's Redemption Council (PRC), which comprised military personnel, with Doe as chairman, was established; the constitution was suspended and political parties were banned. The PRC assumed the government of the country, in conjunction with a 17-member council of ministers, five of whom were soldiers, while the remainder were members of the three movements that had been politically active before the coup: the TWP, the PPP and the radical Movement for Justice in Africa (MOJA). The new regime publicly executed 13 leading officials of the previous administration, including six ministers, the chief justice, the speaker of the house of representatives and the president of the senate. Although popular within Liberia, the executions were condemned internationally: the Liberian delegation was excluded from a summit meeting of the Organization of African Unity (OAU) in Lagos, later in the same month, and Doe's claim to Tolbert's chairmanship of the OAU was rejected. Doe promised that no further executions would take place, however, and Liberia's international standing was gradually restored. The PRC retained Liberia's traditionally close links with Western countries, and US aid was substantially increased.

In April 1981 a commission was established to draft a new constitution. During 1981–82 there were frequent resignations and dismissals from the PRC and the council of ministers, as Doe demonstrated his avowed intention to eradicate official corruption (while also gradually removing those with a different ideological outlook). In August 1981 five members of the PRC, including the vice-chairman, Thomas Weh Syen, were executed for conspiring against the government, and, shortly afterwards, the principal representative of MOJA in the council of ministers, Togba-Nah Tipoteh, resigned as minister of economics. The minister of justice, Chea Cheapoo, was dismissed in September for alleged dishonesty, and Matthews was removed as minister of foreign affairs in November. In 1982 several other ministers and heads of public companies were dismissed, following allegations of malpractice. In October 1983 the army commander, Brig.-Gen. Thomas Quiwonkpa (who had been accused of plotting against the government), was dismissed from the PRC, and fled the country. A number of other members of the PRC, however, continued to attract public criticism, and the government's increasingly conservative orientation proved to be unpopular.

CIVILIAN RULE

The draft constitution was approved by the PRC in March 1983, and subsequently adopted by 78.3% of registered voters in a referendum, which took place in July 1984. The new constitution again provided for a bicameral legislature and the separation of executive and legislative powers, and abolished property qualifications for voters. Also in July President Doe dissolved the PRC and replaced it with an interim national assembly, under his chairmanship, which comprised the members of the former PRC, together with 36 appointed civilians, mainly former supporters of the TWP. In the same month the ban on political organizations was removed, in anticipation of presidential and legislative elections, which were due to take place in 1985.

In August 1984 Doe formed the National Democratic Party of Liberia (NDPL) and formally announced his intention to contest the presidential elections. Other newly-established parties included the Liberian People's Party (LPP), the successor to MOJA; the United People's Party (UPP), a reconstituted PPP; the Unity Party (UP), the Liberian Action Party (LAP); and the Liberian Unification Party (LUP). However, the registration of political associations was impeded by considerable legal difficulties (including a prohibitive financial qualification). Opposition leaders were briefly detained, following an attempt to assassinate Doe in April 1985. Only three parties besides the NDPL—the LAP, the LUP and the UP—were eventually registered to contest the elections, which took place in October. There were allegations of electoral fraud and intimidation of voters, and the chairman of the government-appointed electoral commission declared that extensive irregularities had taken place. It was later announced that Doe had been elected to the presidency, with 50.9% of the votes cast. (Neutral observers, however, believed the leader of the LAP, Jackson Doe, to have been the actual winner.) At concurrent elections to the bicameral national assembly, the NDPL secured 22 of the 26 seats in the senate and 51 of the 64 seats in the house of representatives. The LAP rejected the results, and refused to occupy the seats assigned to them.

In November 1985 an attempted military coup, led by Brig.-Gen. Quiwonkpa, was suppressed by troops loyal to the government. Quiwonkpa and a number of his supporters were killed, and subsequent fighting between rebels and government forces resulted in at least 600 deaths. Opposition leaders were detained, and meetings of students and others likely to be critical of the government were banned.

The formal installation of a civilian government in January 1986 failed to achieve internal stability and international acceptance, as President Doe had hoped. Although Doe appealed for national reconciliation, only a few members of the opposition parties agreed to accept posts in his government. In March the LAP, LUP and UP formed an alliance, known as the Liberia Grand Coalition. In March 1988 Gabriel Kpolleh, the leader of the LUP, was arrested on charges of conspiring to overthrow the government; in October he and nine others were sentenced to 10 years' imprisonment. In July 1988 Doe announced that a former PRC vice-chairman, Nicholas Podier, had been killed while purportedly staging an attempted coup from bases in Côte d'Ivoire. In the same month the constitution was amended to allow the presidential tenure to be extended for more than two terms. Following the installation of the civilian government, there was a rapid succession of ministerial appointments; four ministers of finance were replaced in 1987–89. The government's suppression of political opponents and the press was restrained only by US threats to withdraw economic aid. Following allegations of economic mismanagement and diversion of aid funds, a team of US experts arrived in Liberia in late 1987 to supervise government finances, but was withdrawn in December 1988. Liberia's relations with neighbouring countries became strained, following Doe's accession to power, although links were established with Nigeria.

CIVIL CONFLICT AND INTERIM GOVERNMENT

In late December 1989 an armed insurrection by rebel forces began in the north-eastern border region of Nimba County. The rebels claimed to be members of a hitherto unknown opposition group, the National Patriotic Front of Liberia (NPFL), led by Charles Taylor, a former government official who was being sought for trial on charges of corruption. In early 1990 several hundred deaths ensued in the course of fighting between the Liberian army (the Armed Forces of Liberia—AFL) and the rebels, which swiftly developed into a conflict between President Doe's ethnic group, the Krahn, and the local Gio and Mano tribes. Both the Krahn-dominated army and the rebel forces were responsible for numerous atrocities against civilians; a large proportion of the local population took refuge in neighbouring Côte d'Ivoire and Guinea. By April the NPFL had overcome government resistance in Nimba County, and in May it extended its control to the remainder of the country, apart from the capital, Monrovia. The NPFL military offensive on Monrovia began in early July, and Taylor repeatedly demanded Doe's resignation as a precondition for a cease-fire. Taylor's authority as self-proclaimed head of a 'National Patriotic Reconstruction Assembly' (NPRA) was, however, challenged by a breakaway faction, known as the Independent National Patriotic Front of Liberia (INPFL), led by Prince Yormie Johnson, whose troops, estimated to number less than 500, rapidly gained control of parts of Monrovia. During August a number of foreign nationals and diplomatic staff were evacuated by a US naval force. Repeated efforts by ECOWAS to negotiate a cease-fire proved unsuccessful, and in late August it dispatched a seaborne force, comprising some 4,000 troops, provided by Ghana, Nigeria, Sierra Leone, The Gambia, Togo and Guinea, to enforce peace in the region. Doe and Johnson agreed to accept the ECOWAS monitoring group (ECOMOG), but its initial occupation of the port area of Monrovia (which had been under Johnson's control), encountered armed opposition by Taylor's forces.

On 30 August 1990 ECOWAS convened a national conference in the Gambian capital, Banjul, although the NPFL refused to attend. Exiled representatives of Liberia's principal political parties, churches and other groups elected Dr Amos Sawyer, the leader of the LPP, as president of an interim government of national unity (IGNU), with a representative of the Liberian Council of Churches, Bishop Ronald Diggs as vice-president. In late August it was reported that the AFL, which supported Doe, and Johnson's INPFL, had formed an alliance against the NPFL. In September, however, discussions, supervised by ECOMOG, between the AFL and INPFL resulted in armed clashes; Doe was subsequently captured and killed by the INPFL.

In October 1990 ECOMOG launched an armed offensive, with the aim of establishing a neutral zone in Monrovia to separate the three warring factions, and subsequently gained control of central Monrovia. Thus, Liberia became effectively divided between two administrations: Monrovia was placed under the jurisdiction of the IGNU, which was maintained in power by ECOMOG, while most of the remainder of the country was controlled by the NPFL. Taylor continued to assert his claim to the presidency, and, later that month, established his own rival administration, the National Patriotic Reconstruction Assembly (NPRA), based at Gbarnga, in Bong County (in central Liberia). On 22 November Sawyer was formally installed as interim president in Monrovia. Numerous attempts were made to negotiate a cease-fire and the restoration of a single elected administration for the whole country. An initial cease-fire, signed at the Malian capital, Bamako, in late November, effectively recognized the division of the country into two parts.

Following a series of negotiations, under the auspices of ECOWAS, a peace agreement was signed in Yamoussoukro, Côte d'Ivoire, in October 1991, whereby all Liberian warring factions were to be encamped and disarmed, and national elections were to be conducted under ECOWAS supervision. Although the cease-fire was maintained, efforts to re-establish a national government proved unsuccessful, largely as a result of Taylor's refusal to disarm NPFL forces and to submit to the authority of ECOMOG, which he believed to be prejudiced in favour of Sawyer. Taylor also cited the increasing military threat presented by ULIMO (see below) as a reason not to disarm.

Progress towards a settlement was also inhibited by the rival sources of external support for ECOMOG and the NPFL. ECOMOG, though formally representing ECOWAS as a whole, largely comprised forces of the anglophone states within that organization, dominated by Nigeria. Guinea also supported ECOMOG, while Senegalese troops (financed by the USA) participated in the force from September 1991 (but were withdrawn in early 1993, owing to the need for an increased security presence within Senegal). The NPFL received supplies and consignments of armaments from neighbouring Côte d'Ivoire, and from Burkina Faso, although support from both countries was periodically restrained as a result of diplomatic pressure. ECOMOG and the IGNU were backed by the USA, which provided both military and financial assistance, while the NPFL appeared to receive at least tacit support from French interests in Côte d'Ivoire.

A number of other Liberian factions and groupings were also involved in the conflict. The INPFL initially co-operated with the IGNU, and participated in a 28-member interim national assembly, which was established in January 1991; in April of that year, when Amos Sawyer was re-elected as interim president, a member of the INPFL, Peter Naigow, became vice-president, replacing Bishop Diggs. In August, however, the INPFL withdrew from the interim government, following criticism by Sawyer of the execution (reportedly at Prince Johnson's instigation) of four INPFL members accused of criminal activities, and Naigow resigned. The INPFL subsequently attempted to re-establish links with Taylor's NPFL, but its role in the conflict declined. Meanwhile, it was reported that the AFL (which comprised the remaining troops of the late President Doe) continued to perpetrate acts of brutality against civilians. Nominally, at least, both the INPFL and the AFL were disarmed and confined to barracks, under the terms of the agreement reached in Yamoussoukro. (The INPFL was subsequently dissolved in September 1992.)

A further movement, the United Liberation Movement of Liberia for Democracy (ULIMO), led by Raleigh Seekie, was formed in June 1991 by former supporters of the late President

Doe, who had taken refuge in Sierra Leone. ULIMO immediately announced its opposition to the NPFL, and refused to comply with the Yamoussoukro accord. ULIMO forces entered north-western Liberia in September 1991, and, from November, were also involved in clashes with the NPFL in the Mano River Bridge area, in the south-west of the country. The Sierra Leonean government refuted allegations by Taylor that its troops had participated in ULIMO offensives in retaliation for NPFL incursions into Sierra Leone and support for the Sierra Leonean opposition group, the Revolutionary United Front (RUF).

In early 1992 there appeared to be some prospect of a peaceful settlement. Roads linking Monrovia and territory under the control of the NPFL were opened, and, in April, ECOMOG began to deploy troops in NPFL-controlled areas, with the aim of disarming all factions and creating conditions that would allow elections to take place. In May, however, six Senegalese soldiers were captured and executed by NPFL forces; ECOMOG forces were subsequently withdrawn to Monrovia. This incident further exacerbated relations between ECOMOG and NPFL, and, in late July, ECOWAS announced that it would impose economic sanctions on the NPFL if Taylor did not fully comply with the conditions of the Yamoussoukro agreement within 30 days. In August ULIMO attacked the NPFL from Sierra Leone, with considerable success, gaining control of large areas of Lofa and Cape Mount Counties in western Liberia.

In September 1992, following the expiry of the stipulated date for the implementation of the Yamoussoukro agreement, ECOMOG threatened to enforce the terms of the peace accord. In mid-October the NPFL launched a major offensive against ECOMOG positions in the outskirts of Monrovia, and captured a number of strategic areas, effectively besieging the capital and resulting in the temporary closure of the James Spriggs Payne Airport, the city's principal link with the international community. The NPFL recruited boys, some as young as eight, and executed large numbers of civilians who refused to join its forces; mass graves were subsequently discovered in the suburbs of Monrovia, which had been occupied by NPFL forces, and at the Firestone plantations. The murder of five American nuns by the NPFL in late October attracted particular international condemnation.

Following the NPFL offensive, ECOMOG abandoned its previous peace-keeping stance for a directly combatant role; Nigerian aircraft under ECOMOG command bombed NPFL positions. Aerial attacks on the border with Côte d'Ivoire, designed to impede NPFL supply routes, prompted protests from the Ivorian government. In late November 1992 the UN security council imposed a mandatory arms embargo on all factions in the conflict (excluding ECOMOG), and authorized the UN secretary-general to send a special envoy, Trevor Gordon-Somers, to Liberia. A former president of Zimbabwe, Canaan Banana, was appointed as OAU representative, but the combined efforts of the two delegates appeared to have little effect. In early January 1993, following a new offensive, ECOMOG forces (which had been reinforced by Nigerian and Ghanaian troops) regained control of the outskirts of Monrovia, and advanced along the coast, capturing the airport at Robertsfield later that month, the Firestone rubber plantation at Harbel in mid-February, and the principal port of Buchanan in early April. NPFL claims that Nigerian aircraft had destroyed medical facilities in Buchanan proved to be unfounded.

In early 1993 ULIMO intensified its attacks in western Liberia, gaining control of Cape Mount and Bomi Counties and the greater part of Lofa County, thereby preventing the RUF in Sierra Leone from receiving support from the NPFL. In March ULIMO accepted an invitation to join the IGNU, although its relations with the government and ECOMOG remained uneasy, and, in early April, ECOMOG disarmed ULIMO forces in Monrovia, in the interests of public safety. (ULIMO had divided into two factions, of which one, led by Raleigh Seekie, principally comprised Krahn, and operated from Sierra Leone, while the other, led by Alhaji G. V. Kromah, was principally Islamic and Mandingo, and operated from Guinea.) In April the UN security council adopted a further resolution, which condemned attacks on ECOMOG, and declared that the UN was prepared to take further measures against any faction unwilling to implement the Yamoussoukro accord. Although the NPFL was evidently in retreat, and, in mid-May, Taylor announced the adoption of guerrilla warfare tactics, it remained capable of inflicting casualties on both ULIMO and ECOMOG. Several leading members of the Taylor administration fled to Côte d'Ivoire, and Taylor himself was reported to be attempting to recruit mercenary forces. Also in May ECOMOG announced that all relief supplies to NPFL-controlled areas would be diverted through a 'humanitarian corridor' from Monrovia, to prevent Taylor from taking advantage of aid convoys from Côte d'Ivoire to import consignments of fuel and armaments for NPFL forces, in contravention of the UN security council embargo of November 1992; this decision, which ECOMOG was unable to enforce, was opposed by non-governmental organizations operating in NPFL territory, and Taylor announced that he would accept humanitarian relief only through Côte d'Ivoire. In June more than 600 refugees were killed by troops (alleged to be members of the NPFL) at the Harbel rubber plantation. Following initial investigations, the IGNU announced that Taylor and his associates were implicated in the massacre, and would be charged with violations of human rights.

In July 1993 a peace conference, attended by all factions involved in the hostilities, was convened, under the auspices of the UN and ECOWAS, in Geneva, Switzerland. After several days of negotiations, the IGNU, the NPFL and ULIMO agreed to a cease-fire (which was to take effect at the end of that month and was to be monitored by UN observers and a reconstituted peace-keeping force), and to the formation of a transitional government. The peace accord was formally signed on 25 July at an ECOWAS summit meeting, held in Cotonou, Benin. Under the terms of the agreement, the IGNU was to be replaced by the Liberian national transitional government (LNTG), which was to include a five-member council of state, and the existing legislature by a 35-member transitional parliament (comprising 13 representatives of the IGNU, 13 of the NPFL, and nine of ULIMO), pending presidential and legislative elections, which were to take place in February 1994. In response to demands by Taylor, the dominance of the Nigerian contingent in ECOMOG was to be considerably reduced; the new peace-keeping force, which was to be reconstituted as the ECOWAS cease-fire monitoring group, was to be supplemented with additional troops from other West African nations.

At the end of July 1993 the cease-fire was successfully implemented; in early August, however, ECOMOG claimed that the NPFL had violated the peace agreement by repeatedly entering territory under the control of the peace-keeping force. In mid-August the IGNU, the NPFL and ULIMO each appointed one representative to the transitional council of state, while the remaining two members (representatives of the IGNU and ULIMO respectively) were elected by a list of candidates who had been nominated by the three factions. Shortly afterwards, the former speaker of the interim national assembly, Bismark Kuyon, was elected as chairman of the council of state. However, Kuyon announced that the inauguration of the council of state (originally scheduled for 24 August) was to be postponed, pending the disarmament of all warring factions in accordance with the peace agreement. The NPFL criticized this decision, and accused Kuyon of violating the peace agreement, which required that the transitional institutions be installed within a period of 30 days. Subsequent delays in the deployment of UN observers and additional peace-keeping troops resulted in a protracted impasse: Taylor refused to permit the disarmament of NPFL forces prior to the arrival of the additional troops (owing to his scepticism regarding ECOMOG's neutrality) while the IGNU continued to insist that the installation of the transitional authorities take place in conjunction with the disarmament process. In August ECOWAS imposed an economic embargo against territory under the control of the NPFL, in an attempt to enforce disarmament.

In early September 1993 the IGNU expressed concern following an announcement by the new Nigerian administration that it was to withdraw its contingent from ECOMOG by March 1994. Later in September a UN investigation, which was led by a Kenyan lawyer, concluded that AFL troops had perpetrated the massacre at Harbel (which had been previously ascribed to the NPFL), and implied that ECOMOG had deliberately failed to identify those responsible. A number of AFL units were subsequently withdrawn to Monrovia and disarmed, while three members of the AFL were arrested for alleged participation in the massacre. The IGNU, however, disputed the results of the inquiry. In the same month the UN security council approved the establishment of the UN observer mission in Liberia (UNOMIL), which was to co-operate with ECOMOG and the OAU in supervising the transitional process. In early October a transitional legislative assembly was established, in accordance with the peace agreement (although its installation, was also delayed, pending the implementation of the disarmament process). Later in October it was announced that the governments of Tanzania, Uganda and Zimbabwe were to contribute troops to ECOMOG, in response to a request from the OAU. (Zimbabwe subsequently failed to send troops, owing to financial difficulties.)

In late October 1993 attempts to establish a council of ministers, as part of the LNTG, were delayed, owing to the failure of the IGNU, the NPFL and ULIMO to reach an agreement regarding the distribution of ministerial portfolios. Following a consultative meeting, which took place in Cotonou in early November, however, the three factions agreed to the allocation of a number of portfolios in the LNTG. Later in November the NPFL accused the IGNU of further delaying the transitional process, after Sawyer dismissed Kuyon (who had reportedly dissociated himself from the IGNU's refusal to relinquish power prior to disarmament) and appointed Philip Banks, hitherto minister of justice, in his place. (Both the NPFL and ULIMO had previously replaced their representatives in the council of state.)

Meanwhile, it was feared that renewed hostilities in several areas of the country would jeopardize the peace accord. An armed faction, known as the Liberia Peace Council (LPC), comprising members of the Krahn ethnic group from Grand Gedeh County, together with a number of disaffected AFL troops, emerged in September 1993, and subsequently entered into conflict with the NPFL in south-eastern Liberia. A large number of civilians fled to Buchanan from Rivercess and Grand Bassa Counties, in response to fighting in the region. The LPC, which was led by Dr George Boley, a prominent member of ULIMO, claimed to be a non-partisan movement, which had been established in response to what it claimed to be continued atrocities perpetrated by the NPFL. In December fighting between ULIMO and a newly-formed movement, the Lofa Defence Force (LDF), was also reported in Lofa County (in western Liberia), apparently in retaliation against alleged acts of violence committed by ULIMO forces in the region. The NPFL denied involvement with the LDF, which occupied territory previously controlled by ULIMO in north-western Liberia.

In late December 1993 the contingents of additional ECOMOG troops from Tanzania and Uganda began to arrive. In February 1994 further negotiations took place between the IGNU, the NPFL and ULIMO, with the aim of resolving outstanding differences regarding the implementation of the peace accord. At the end of February the council of state elected David Kpomakpor, a representative of the IGNU, as its chairman. In early March units belonging to UNOMIL and the new ECOMOG force were deployed, and the disarmament of all factions commenced. Following an ethnic dispute involving Kromah and a military commander of ULIMO, Gen. Roosevelt Johnson (who had effectively replaced Seekie), however, some ULIMO troops refused to relinquish their armaments, on the grounds that they had received no instructions to do so. ECOMOG subsequently threatened to enforce the disarmament process if ULIMO continued to fail to co-operate with peace-keeping troops. On 7 March the council of state was inaugurated; it was envisaged that the presidential and legislative elections (which were originally scheduled for February) would take place in September. However, the disarmament process was subsequently impeded by an increase in rebel activity; in addition to continuing hostilities involving the LPC and the NPFL (despite a cease-fire agreement, which was mediated by ECOMOG in March), more than 200 people were killed in clashes between members of the Krahn and Mandingo ethnic groups within ULIMO, particularly in the region of Tubmanburg, north of Monrovia (where the organization was based). The hostilities (which followed the dispute earlier that month between Kromah, a Mandingo, and Johnson, a Krahn) were prompted by resentment within the Krahn at the predominance of the Mandingo among ULIMO representatives in the transitional institutions. In early April discussions between Kromah and Johnson, which were mediated by the Sierra Leonean head of state, resulted in a peace agreement, however, fighting continued throughout that month in western Liberia. In early May the two factions agreed to a cease-fire, in response to the intervention of ECOMOG and UNOMIL; however, subsequent negotiations regarding the ethnic distribution of the posts allocated to ECOMOG within the transitional institutions were unsuccessful, and it was reported that the cease-fire had not been implemented.

By early April 1994 only 1,447 of the estimated 30,000 troops in Liberia had disarmed, of whom the majority were members of the AFL. The mandate of UNOMIL to remain in the country (which was due to expire in that month) was extended until October, pending the completion of the transitional process; however, the UN security council was to review the role of UNOMIL in Liberia in May, with regard to the progress that had been achieved in the peace process. Also in April the nomination of several cabinet ministers by the IGNU, the NPFL and ULIMO was approved by the transitional legislative assembly. The subsequent discovery that a letter (which was purportedly signed by the chairman of ECOWAS and Beninois head of state, Nicéphore Soglo), upholding the allocation of the principal portfolios of justice and foreign affairs to members of the NPFL, was a forgery prompted widespread speculation regarding the motivation of a number of elements involved in the peace process. Later in April Taylor declared that the NPFL would not participate in the LNTG unless all his cabinet nominees were accepted, following continued controversy regarding the portfolios of justice and foreign affairs. In May, however, a 19-member cabinet was installed, comprising seven members of the NPFL (which held the disputed portfolios of justice and foreign affairs), seven of ULIMO and five of the IGNU. Following its scheduled review of progress in the implementation of the peace settlement, the UN security council declared itself to be satisfied with the installation of the LNTG, but expressed concern at the factional violence, which continued to impede the disarmament process. In the same month the USA condemned the widespread violations of human rights perpetrated by a number of factions, particularly by the LPC (which had reportedly massacred civilians, believed to be NPFL supporters, in south-eastern Liberia).

In May 1994 the Nigerian government indicated that it was to commence the withdrawal of its troops from ECOMOG, following allegations by the NPFL that it had provided logistical support to the LPC. In June Tanzania announced that it was to remove its contingent from ECOMOG, on the grounds that it had not received funds pledged by the UN, while Ghana also envisaged the withdrawal of its troops, as a result of financial difficulties. In mid-June, following threats by the US government to suspend assistance to Liberia, owing to continued lack of progress in the implementation of the peace agreement, members of the transitional legislative assembly met NPFL officials at Gbarnga to discuss the disarmament process. In the same month Kpomakpor suspended the minister of finance, owing to his continued failure to submit financial reports to the council of state. At the end of June some 50 people were killed in hostilities between the two ULIMO factions at the border with Sierra Leone; clashes between Kromah's forces and ECOMOG, which had attempted to prevent a massacre of civilians, were also reported. In early July Kromah's faction initiated an offensive to recapture Tubmanburg, which was under the control of Johnson's forces. In the same month Taylor claimed that the Nigerian troops under the command of ECOMOG had launched further attacks against the NPFL.

In early August 1994, following secret negotiations, representatives of the five factions involved in civil conflict (the AFL, the LDF, the LPC, ULIMO and the NPFL) signed an agreement providing for the cessation of hostilities, and pledged to co-operate in the process of disarmament; it was further agreed that the LPC and the LDF (which had not been party to the Cotonou accord) be allowed to participate in the LNTG. (However, further clashes between the LPC and the NPFL were reported in the region of Buchanan.) Later in August some 800 members of ULIMO based in Sierra Leone were disarmed, following complaints by traditional chiefs that they had attacked military posts in the south-east of that country. In the same month the chief of staff, Lt-Gen. Hezekiah Bowen, officially rejected the results of the UN inquiry that implicated the AFL in the massacre in June 1993, and demanded that the LNTG, in conjunction with the international community, establish a committee to investigate allegations that the AFL had committed numerous violations of human rights during the civil conflict. Meanwhile, indications by the Ghanaian president, Jerry Rawlings (who became chairman of the conference of heads of state and government of ECOWAS in early August), that ECOMOG might be withdrawn if the progress achieved by the end of that year was judged to be insufficient prompted fears of the resumption of full-scale conflict. In late August Taylor demanded the removal of three representatives of the NPFL in the cabinet, who had allegedly refused to attend meetings convened by the NPFL leadership to discuss the peace process, thereby demonstrating increasing inter-party division; Taylor further claimed that the three ministers had been involved in the organization of attacks against NPFL positions. Kpomakpor, however, criticized Taylor, and declared his opposition to the replacement of the ministers.

In early September 1994 (when the original mandate of the LNTG was due to expire), a meeting of the NPFL, the AFL and the ULIMO faction led by Kromah was convened, under the aegis of Rawlings, at Akosombo, Ghana. Meanwhile, following clashes between dissident members of the NPFL and troops loyal to Taylor in the region of Gbarnga, the minister of labour, Thomas Woeweiyu, claimed that Taylor had fled the country and announced his deposition as leader of the NPFL. On 12 September, however, Taylor, Kromah and the chief of staff of the AFL, Lt.-Gen. Hezekiah Bowen, signed a peace accord, which provided for an immediate cessation of hostilities and the establishment later that month of a reconstituted council of state, in which four of the members were to be nominated by the three warring factions, while the remaining member was to be selected by a national conference of prominent civilians; presidential and general elections were rescheduled for October 1995, and the new government was subsequently to be installed in January 1996. However, the proposed installation of a principally military council of state prompted widespread criticism. In mid-September dissident members of the AFL staged an abortive coup attempt, seizing the presidential mansion; ECOMOG forces subsequently attacked the building and arrested a number of the rebels. Later that month the NPFL dissidents, who were reportedly in alliance with elements of the AFL, ULIMO, the LPC and the LDF, succeeded in gaining control of Gbarnga; forces loyal to Taylor had retreated to the town of Palala, some 20 km east of Gbarnga. At the end of September the warring factions had failed to establish a new council of state, as provided for in the agreement.

Economy

CHRISTOPHER CLAPHAM

Revised for this edition by the Editor

In 1987, according to estimates by the World Bank, Liberia's gross national product (GNP), measured at average 1985–87 prices, was US $1,051m., equivalent to $450 per head. During 1980–87, it was estimated, GNP declined, in real terms, at an average annual rate of 2.1%, while real GNP per head declined by 5.2% per year. During 1985–92 the population increased by an annual average of 3.1%. During 1985–89, according to UN estimates, Liberia's gross domestic product (GDP) increased, in real terms, by an annual average of 1.5%, compared with an average annual decline of 1.5% in 1980–85. Although Liberia appears in world markets as pre-eminently a mineral producer, with iron ore accounting for 57% of its export earnings in 1987, the country remains basically agricultural, with about 69% of the working population employed in the sector in 1992.

Following the outbreak of civil war in December 1989, considerable damage was done to Liberia's economic infrastructure, most foreign nationals left the country, and about one-half of the Liberian population became refugees or were internally displaced. GDP was estimated to have declined, in real terms, by 9% in 1990, and by 10% in 1991. In early 1992, however, some economic activity was reported to have resumed under the aegis of the National Patriotic Reconstruction Assembly (NPRA), an alternative administration formed by Charles Taylor, whose forces, the National Patriotic Front of Liberia (NPFL), controlled the greater part of Liberian territory; the NPRA, rather than the interim government based in Monrovia, received taxes and export duties from timber, rubber and mining operations. Following the peace agreement that was signed in July 1993 and the subsequent installation of the Liberian national transitional government (see Recent History), Liberia was expected to benefit from the resumption of official exports of rubber and timber to increase foreign exchange revenue. However, continuing factional violence proved an impediment to economic reconstruction.

AGRICULTURE, FORESTRY AND FISHING

Agriculture (including forestry and fishing) contributed 36.7% of the country's GDP in 1989. Rubber, coffee and cocoa are the main cash crops. The principal food crops are rice and cassava (manioc); with palm oil and some fish or meat, these form the basis of the national diet. Other crops, such as yams, eddoes, sweet potatoes, okra and groundnuts, and fruit such as plantains, oranges, mangoes, avocados or grapefruits are of secondary or local importance. Some of the main problems of Liberian subsistence agriculture are the low yields of rice (less than 900 kg per ha on average), the low total production of less than 300,000 metric tons per year, and the destruction of some 12,000 ha per year of valuable timber by the method of land rotation with bush fallowing. Agricultural production, according to the FAO, increased by an annual average of 2.0% in 1980–89, but declined by 35.3% in 1990 and by 7.8% in 1991. Output increased by 4.1% in 1992.

In order to increase total production and reduce rice imports, the government initiated an 'operation production' campaign in 1963, which was followed by several projects introduced by President Tolbert. An expanded rice programme was initiated to provide technical assistance, credits and other help to individual farmers, while special rice projects of more than 40 ha were started in different regions. Farmer co-operatives were established at these projects and elsewhere. A project costing US $17.4m., supported by the International Development Association (IDA), to improve the incomes of about 7,500 farm families was announced in 1984. Imports of rice increased to 74,013 metric tons (costing $26m.) by 1979. In 1988 imports of rice amounted to $27.9m. (equivalent to 10.2% of the total cost of imports). Following the outbreak of war, production of paddy rice was estimated to have declined from 290,000 tons in 1989 to 110,000 tons in 1992, and much of the population became dependent on relief grain. Nimba County and Lofa County were particularly badly affected, and distribution of relief was impeded by looting by members of the armed factions. Food shortages were also reported in Monrovia, where the population had increased considerably, owing to the influx of refugees from country areas, and riots in protest at the rise in food prices occurred in September 1993.

In 1983 the Firestone Plantations Co, formerly Liberia's largest private-sector employer, closed the smaller of its two rubber plantations, at Cavalla in Maryland County, but continued to operate the huge Harbel plantation of more than 30,000 ha until 1988, when it sold its Liberian interests to the Japanese tyre company Bridgestone, although Firestone continued to be responsible for local management. With continued weakness in the world rubber market, all of the Liberian companies have found it difficult to compete with South-East Asian producers, and the level of production has stagnated. Output in 1985, which earned $77m. and accounted for 18% of Liberia's exports, represented only 2% of world production. All of the major rubber companies incurred financial losses on their Liberian operations in the 1980s; and B. F. Goodrich sold its 8,100-ha plantation to the British-Malaysian Guthrie group in 1983, while many of the small Liberian-owned farms were forced out of production. The war resulted in a severe disruption of exports, and rubber production was estimated to have declined from 118,000 metric tons in 1989 to 22,000 tons in 1992. Firestone resumed operations at Harbel in February 1992 (following an agreement with the NPRA), but these were interrupted by the ECOMOG capture of Harbel and Buchanan in early 1993. In mid-1993 Buchanan was officially reopened to shipping, and exports of rubber were expected to resume, under the aegis of the Liberian national transitional government.

Coffee production is centred in northern Liberia, between Voinjama and Kolahun, where mainly *Coffea robusta* is cultivated. Figures for annual coffee exports indicate substantial fluctuations, dependent on the level of prices on the world market and the quantities smuggled to and from neighbouring countries. Production has remained fairly stable since 1967, totalling 8,000–10,000 metric tons per year, of which about one-half is consumed locally.

Cocoa has been introduced into Maryland County from Bioko (Equatorial Guinea), but an attempt to develop a cocoa plantation near Ganta ended in failure, and rubber is now grown there. Production has remained at about 5,000 metric tons per year, almost all of which is exported.

Experiments with tobacco in Nimba County were initially promising. However, owing to increasing difficulties, they were practically discontinued and the big tobacco-drying sheds were dismantled. Problems also arose with the Liberia Sugar Corpn's plantation at Barrake in Maryland County, to the south of Firestone's Cavalla rubber plantation. By 1980 an area of 600 ha had been cultivated with sugar cane. However, the original Taiwanese management withdrew after Liberia recognized the People's Republic of China. In January 1983 Chinese advisers arrived to assist in the management and rehabilitation of the plantation. By 1987, however, the plantation was in need of further rehabilitation, and Cuba agreed to provide the necessary assistance.

Liberia possesses substantial forest reserves; a national forest inventory made from 1960 to 1967 indicated that there was an average timber potential of 10,000–15,000 cu metres per sq km on a closed forest area of 2.5m. ha, and that 1 sq km contained an average number of 15,000–20,000 trees. From the mid-1960s there was a great increase in timber production, and in 1980 about 450,000 cu m of logs, with a value of $72.5m., were exported. Exports declined in the early 1980s, owing to the exhaustion of accessible timber, but recovered to reach 787,000 cu. m in 1988. Further depletion took place after 1990, as a result of the export of timber to support NPFL operations.

Reafforestation in Liberia began in 1971 and was centralized later on at the independent Forestry Development Authority (FDA), created in 1974 to provide for a more effective forest management and improved training and conservation practices. There are five major reforestation areas. In the mid-1970s a large sawmill and a plywood mill near Greenville began production.

Another important forest product is palm nuts, from which, according to unofficial figures, some 25,000 metric tons of palm oil were produced in 1992. In addition to some 1,620 ha of smaller plantations (mainly in the Kakata area), there is a large estate at New Cess, near Buchanan in Grand Bassa County, with some 2,940 ha planted; it is operated by the Liberia Industrial Corpn (LIBINC). Another large estate of some 1,860 ha at Wangakor, near Robertsport in Grand Cape Mount County, belonging to the Liberian-owned West African Agricultural Corpn (WAAC) started production in 1972. In south-eastern Liberia the Liberian Palm Products Corpn (LPPC), a subsidiary of the Liberian Produce Marketing Co (LPMC), has been developing two larger programmes at Buto, near Juarzon in Sinoe County (3,040 ha), and at Dube in Grand Gedeh County (4,050 ha), with technical assistance from SODEPALM of Côte d'Ivoire. An agreement to establish a palm oil factory for the Buto project, financed by the Belgian government and a vegetable oil processing firm, was signed in March 1984, and aid of $3.36m. for various palm oil projects was granted by the European Development Fund in 1985. A palm kernel oil mill has been constructed by the LPMC, and in 1987 a French company, Finex International, agreed to construct Liberia's first palm oil refinery and to assume the management of the National Palm Oil Corpn for five years, in an attempt to reorganize and rehabilitate the sector.

FAO estimates indicate that in 1992 there were some 220,000 sheep, 220,000 goats, 120,000 pigs and 38,000 head of cattle. In the same year, the FAO estimated that Liberia produced some 17,000 tons of meat.

Fish production increased from 1,180 metric tons in 1960 to 18,731 tons in 1987, but by 1991, according to FAO estimates, it had decreased to 9,600 tons (including a catch of 4,000 tons in inland waters).

MINING

Since the opening of the Bomi Hills iron ore mine by the Liberia Mining Co (LMC) in 1951, the mining sector has become increasingly important to the Liberian economy, although by 1980 it employed only 5.1% of the labour force. In 1989 mining contributed 10.9% of GDP. Discoveries of diamonds in the lower Lofa river area in 1957 resulted in an influx of thousands of plantation workers to Weasua and other places in the Gola forest. The value of diamond exports achieved a record US $49.4m. in 1973, when 812,000 carats were exported. By the mid-1980s, however, exports were averaging about 200,000 carats annually; much of this volume has been attributed to stones smuggled from adjoining countries and attracted to Liberia by its currency link with the US dollar. In 1988 diamonds accounted for only $8.8m. (2.2%) of total exports. According to data from the US Bureau of Mines, diamond production totalled 67,000 carats in 1988, and had declined further, to 40,000 carats, by 1991.

Gold mining is concentrated in the Tchien area, where 50 of the 67 mining licences were granted in 1976. An extensive gold mining concession was awarded to the Liberia Gold and Diamond Corpn. Gold production increased from 359 kg in 1982, to 700 kg in 1989, but declined slightly, to 600 kg, in 1991.

There have been several other mineral discoveries, notably of bauxite, copper, columbite-tantalite, corundum, lead, manganese, tin and zinc. Of economic significance are the deposits of barite in the Gibi range near Kakata, and kyanite reserves. The discovery of deposits of uranium in Bong and Lofa Counties was announced in July 1981. In 1981, Kantana Resources of Canada signed a production-sharing agreement with the Liberian government for petroleum exploration in the coastal area between Robertsfield and Grand Bassa County. Further exploration agreements were signed with Amoco in 1983, and with the Henry Resources Corpn in 1985. Amoco, however, suspended operations in 1986.

Iron ore mining has been the principal extraction industry of Liberia since 1961, when, in terms of value, iron ore replaced rubber as the leading export commodity. Liberia soon became one of the world's main exporters of iron ore. In the 1980s, however, the reduction in international demand for iron ore severely depressed production and export earnings; in 1989 iron ore accounted for 51% of total export earnings, compared with 62.1% in 1981. The National Iron Ore Co mine, which is 85% Liberian-owned, was opened on the Mano river in Grand Cape Mount County, in 1961. Liberia's largest deposits of iron ore—probably more than 1,000m. metric tons, including at least 235m. tons of high-grade ore of 65%–70% iron content—were exploited by the Liberian-American-Swedish Minerals Co (LAMCO) from 1963. With investments of more than $300m., covering the construction of Africa's first pelletizing plant at Buchanan (opened in 1968), a new port and a 274-km railway, the Nimba project comprised one of the largest private enterprises in the whole of Africa. Its main shareholders were the Grängesberg Co of Sweden, together with five other Swedish companies, and the US Bethlehem Steel Corpn (25%). Owing to the world recession, LAMCO's production declined sharply in the 1980s, from over 10m. tons in 1981 to 2m. tons in 1989. LAMCO ceased production in July 1989, and in September was transferred to a government-owned holding company, Liberian Mining Co (LIMICO), which reached agreement with the British-based African Mining Consortium (AMC) to assume control of operations at Yekepa. The civil conflict in the area started two months later, and mining operations were suspended. The fourth of Liberia's open-cast mines, in the Bong range north of Kakata, was opened in 1965 by the Bong Mining Co (70% Federal German, 25% Italian) on behalf of the German-Liberian Mining Co (DELIMCO), of which the Liberian government held a 50% interest. Operations were suspended in June 1990. As a result of the civil conflict, production of iron ore declined from 8,011,000 tons in 1988 to 2,490,000 tons in 1990.

In March 1991 mining operations resumed under the aegis of the NPRA, which granted concessions to a number of foreign-owned export companies for the exploitation of diamonds and gold. LIMICO was reported to have resumed exports of iron ore to Europe, paying the NPRA $10m. per month to keep open the railway to Buchanan; this trade was suspended, following the ECOMOG capture of the port, in early 1993.

INDUSTRY

Companies such as Firestone and LAMCO assisted in the development of Liberia's technical and social infrastructure by constructing roads, ports, airfields, schools and hospitals. Their contribution to economic development in general was nevertheless limited, as few secondary industries based on iron ore or rubber were established. Small enterprises predominate in the manufacturing sector, mainly construction firms, saw mills, repair shops, and tailors' shops; over 80% have less than 10 employees. Many enterprises were seriously affected by the depressed state of the economy in the 1980s. The few larger plants with over 50 employees include the rubber factories at the concession sites and the beverage industry, represented by a Coca-Cola and other bottling plants and by a brewery.

The principal Liberian-owned company is the Mesurado Group, which, in addition to its fishing interests, manufactures detergents, soap, industrial gases and animal foods. A chemicals and explosives factory was established near Robertsfield in 1964. In the same year the Industrial Park near Paynesville was created by the Liberian Development Co on behalf of the Liberian government, initially comprising a shoe factory and a metallo-plastics firm. A cement factory was constructed in 1968 in Monrovia by the Lebanese-owned Liberian Cement Corpn (LCC), with a capacity of 125,000 tons of clinker cement per year. In the same year a petroleum refinery with an annual capacity of 650,000 tons was constructed by the Liberian Petroleum Refining Corpn (LPRC). A steel rolling mill, using scrap metal from ships broken in Liberia, was constructed by Hong Kong shipping interests and began operations in 1988. Other small industrial enterprises include oilseed and rice mills, a sugar factory, a rum distillery, and factories producing umbrellas, aluminium parts, batteries, foam rubber, hand tools, candles, detergents, biscuits and confectionery. The import substitution effect, however, remains small because over 95% of the raw materials are imported; only cement, matches and batteries have been eliminated from the Liberian import list. In January 1991 the cost of rehabilitating the LPRC's facilities after war damage was projected at $7m.

The main impediments to industrialization are the restricted interest in investments, the small number of Liberian entrepreneurs, the concentration of industry in the Monrovia region, and the limited size of the domestic market. In an attempt to overcome the domestic market handicap, the government established an industrial free zone area as an expansion of the Monrovia 'free port', with the assistance of UNIDO. It was hoped that the industrial free zone would provide facilities for 50 factories with direct contacts with the world market and create 10,000 new jobs. The restricted significance of the manufacturing sector in the Liberian economy is indicated by its contribution of 7.3% to the country's GDP in 1989, and by the size of its work-force, which represented about 1.2% of the working population in 1980.

TRANSPORT, POWER AND TELECOMMUNICATIONS

In 1991 there were an estimated 6,095 km of classified roads, including 2,030 km of main roads and 1,540 km of secondary roads; about 2,400 km of the total network were paved. Agreements to reconstruct the Gbarnga–Voinjama and Ganta–Harper highways were announced in 1988. A main road between Monrovia and Freetown, completed in 1988, reduced the distance between the two capitals from 1,014 to 544 km, and was eventually to form part of a planned highway from Nouakchott, in Mauritania, to Lagos. The principal roads in Liberia were closed as a result of the civil conflict of 1989–91, but were reported to have reopened in 1992.

The railways from Monrovia to Mano River via Bomi Hills (145 track-km), from Monrovia to the Bong Mine (78 track-km) and from Buchanan to Nimba (267 track-km) have all been constructed for the transport of iron ore. The latter railway, owned by LAMCO, is also utilized for the transport of logs and rubber and for the Guinea transit trade. It also operates a passenger line from Buchanan to Yekepa.

In 1992 the Liberian-registered merchant fleet comprised 1,672 vessels, with a total displacement of about 55.2m. gross registered tons (grt). Although it remained the largest national fleet in the world, it had decreased from 81.5m. grt in 1982, reflecting the decline in the number of oil tankers, competition from other 'open registry' states, and growing international opposition to 'open registry' shipping. In September 1989, in an attempt to attract more ships, the government announced a change from a registration fee based on tonnage to a uniform rate of $2,500 per vessel. In 1987 the Liberian National Shipping Line, formed in association with a Federal German company, began operations. Liberia's principal ports are Monrovia Free Port, Buchanan, Greenville and Harper. The EC has contributed aid for the development of Harper port. In 1992 the resumption of armed conflict in the region of Monrovia resulted in the suspension of most shipping activity. In mid-1993, however, the port of Buchanan was officially reopened to shipping.

Liberia's principal airports are Roberts Field International Airport, at Harbel, 56 km east of Monrovia, and James Spriggs Payne Airport, at Monrovia. International air traffic reached 52,954 passengers arriving and 55,541 departing in 1985, as compared with 24,724 arriving and 28,281 departing in 1970. During the same period the quantities of cargo loaded and unloaded increased from 242 to 1,247 tons and from 1,142 to 1,624 tons respectively. In 1990 the civil conflict in Monrovia resulted in the suspension of air services, although one small company, Weasua Air, maintained services from Freetown and Abidjan to James Spriggs Payne Airport. In 1992 the resumption of armed conflict in the region of Monrovia again resulted in the suspension of most air services.

Public power production rose from 328.8m. kWh in 1972 to 904m. kWh in 1985, but dependence on hydroelectric power, especially from the Mt Coffee plant, resulted in shortages of electricity during the dry season. Power production declined to 565m. kWh in 1990, and to 450m. kWh in 1991; in December 1990 the Mt Coffee dam was reported to have been completely destroyed.

PUBLIC FINANCE

A substantial rate of growth in government revenues between 1945–81 failed to keep pace with increased levels of government spending, which, especially with the decline in the growth rate of revenue during the recession of the late 1970s, led to heavy budgetary deficits. Following the 1980 coup, the Doe government inherited a foreign debt of US $800m. and a budgetary deficit of $71m. Increased domestic expectations after the coup of April 1980, together with a decline in foreign business confidence and the weakness of the international iron ore market, placed further strains on the economy. In addition, private-sector liquidity fell sharply, as both local and foreign investors moved their convertible assets abroad. Such disinvestment has continued. Government spending on public order and defence increased from $21m. to $52m. between 1979 and 1981, and civil service salaries were also raised. The reliability of the budgets was in doubt, with extra-budgetary spending reportedly being about 25% of the level of total budget expenditure in 1984 and 1985. Drastic attempts to reduce government spending culminated in a reduction of 25% in the wages of all government employees (except the armed forces) from December 1985. In 1988 the fiscal year was changed to correspond to the calendar year. An overall budgetary deficit of L $91.9m. (equivalent to 7.8% of GDP) was recorded in 1988. In 1991–93 the national budget related only to the small part of the national territory controlled by the interim government of national unity (IGNU), while the NPRA in the interior imposed levies on the local population and on companies exporting through the port of Buchanan and through Côte d'Ivoire. The IGNU budget for 1992 envisaged expenditure of $167m. and income of $129m. arising largely from 'currency gain', or printing money. The 1993 budget of $273,930,000, which was approved in April 1993, was to be funded by taxes of $79,225,000, of which 44.3% was to come from the merchant shipping registry, and 'currency gain' of $170.6m. Defence accounted for 12.9% of projected expenditure, and education for 11.6%. In March 1994 the transitional legislative assembly adopted an interim budget of L $273m. for the months of April and May, pending the approval of the 1994 budget.

Since 1940 the Liberian dollar has been nominally maintained at par with the US dollar, and US banknotes are used in Liberia alongside Liberian coins. Following the military coup in 1980, the value of US dollar notes in circulation declined from $10.5m. in that year to $4.2m. in 1984, while Liberian coins in circulation rose from $11.6m. to $31.3m. over the same period, and to $46.6m. by the end of 1985. This resulted in the creation of a two-tier currency, with a substantial premium for US notes, and rapid inflation in local currency terms. By April 1993 the 'black' market exchange rate was reported to be US $1 = L $20. Liberian coins had begun to be officially withdrawn from circulation in July 1989, being replaced by local bank notes which further emphasized the effective separation of Liberian and US currencies. In early 1992 the government introduced new banknotes, in an attempt to demonetize currency held by the NPRA, and a fluctuating exchange rate emerged between new and old notes, depending on local political control. In October 1993 the exchange rate increased to US $1=L $50, later declining to US $1=L $40.

The willingness of the USA to increase its aid, from some US $10m. in 1979 to $64m. in 1985, undoubtedly encouraged the Doe government to maintain Liberia's traditional alignment with Western countries. However, US aid was sharply reduced to $43m. in 1986. In February 1987 a US federal agency reported that $12m. of aid had been diverted to unauthorized use, with a further $16.5m. unaccounted for. The release of further US aid was subsequently made conditional upon Liberian acceptance of 17 US-appointed operational experts to supervise revenue collection and government expenditure. The experts arrived in Liberia in late 1987 but left after only one year of a projected two-year stay, owing to their failure to control unauthorized presidential allocations, or the revenues of public corporations. In 1988 US aid was further reduced, to $31m. From 1990, however, the USA provided emergency assistance to counteract the effects of the civil conflict; in 1990–91 economic aid from the USA was estimated at $140m. In mid-1994 the US government was considering the adoption of an additional relief programme for Liberia, which would authorize the provision of supplementary emergency food assistance, at an estimated cost of $90m. for the 1994 and 1995 fiscal years.

Other major aid donors have been the EC, under the Lomé agreements, and the World Bank. In addition, Liberia received successive stand-by credits from the IMF: for SDR 82.7m. in October 1982, for SDR 55m. in September 1983, and for SDR 42.8m. in November 1984, the last of these being suspended within a week, owing to repayment arrears on a previous loan. Successive debt-rescheduling timetables were agreed in December 1981, December 1983 and December 1984. In January 1986 Liberia was declared ineligible for further drawings on the IMF, and in February 1988 the Fund closed its mission in Monrovia, claiming that the government had not seriously attempted to reform the economy. The World Bank suspended disbursements in February 1986. In March 1990 the IMF declared Liberia a 'non-co-operating' country, and threatened expulsion, owing to the government's failure to pay outstanding arrears; Liberia owed an estimated US $396m. to the IMF and $65m. to the African Development Bank (ADB). An appeal for $13.8m. in emergency aid received virtually no response, although emergency donations totalling $127m. were made between December 1989 and May 1991 by individual governments and private charities. Total external debt increased from $437m. in 1978 to $1,439m. in 1986 and to $1,989m. in 1991, with interest payment arrears on long-term public debt rising from $27m. in 1984 to $483m. in 1991; since there were no new disbursements after 1989, accumulated arrears were the sole source of increasing indebtedness. By the end of 1992 external debt had declined slightly, to $1,952m., of which $1,101m. was long-term public debt. In mid-1994 it was reported that a donor conference of international financial institutions was to be convened in Liberia.

ECONOMIC PROSPECTS

Liberia's economic growth since the Second World War was reflected in the increase in overseas trade turnover (imports plus exports) from $32.2m. in 1950 to $151.8m. in 1960, and to $1,130.5m. in 1980. However, following the recession and the 1980 coup, the economy declined. Over the period 1979–83 real GDP fell at an average annual rate of 4.4%, and in subsequent years GDP continued to decline, although at a slower rate. The value of imports fell from $411.6m. in 1983 to $286.3m. in 1985, reflecting a dramatic decline in local purchasing power. Liberia's economic growth was achieved principally by the export of primary products to the industrial economies, and involved a high level of dependence, firstly on rubber (which accounted for 88.1% of total export value in 1951) and then on iron ore (64% of total export value in 1985). In both cases, prices varied considerably.

In 1987 Liberia recorded a visible trade surplus of US $63m., although there was a deficit of $118m. on the current account of the balance of payments. In 1988 the principal source of imports (21.2%) was the USA, while the principal market for exports (27.3%) was the Federal Republic of Germany. Although a little 'downstream' processing of primary products was achieved, manufacturing was inhibited by a very small domestic market, and exports to neighbouring west African countries remained negligible. Economic development was further inhibited by strong social and political pressures, resulting in a shift in resources towards imported consumer goods and the public sector.

The civil war resulted in considerable destruction, looting and deterioration in the modern sector of the country's economy, although the relative openness of the country's borders enabled some trade to continue. The hinterland area from which all the export crops and minerals were extracted remained under the control of the NPFL administration based in Gbargna, which was able to export limited amounts of iron ore and rubber through the port of Buchanan. Charitable agencies imported food and medical supplies through Buchanan and other ports, including Monrovia, although the commercial import-export and distribution network had broken down. The subsistence economy was maintained, despite political collapse, while local crops such as cassava to some extent compensated for the shortfall in imported rice. Following the peace agreement that was signed in July 1993 and the subsequent installation of the Liberian national transitional government (see Recent History), it was hoped that conditions in the country would allow economic reconstruction to commence. However, plans by the United Nations High Commissioner for Refugees, under the terms of the peace accord, to repatriate Liberian refugees proved unsuccessful, owing to continuing factional violence, while further civilians fled to neighbouring countries or became internally displaced, necessitating increased emergency assistance.

Statistical Survey

Sources (unless otherwise stated): the former Ministry of Planning and Economic Affairs, POB 9016, Broad Street, Monrovia; tel. 222622.

Area and Population

AREA, POPULATION AND DENSITY

Area (sq km)	97,754*
Population (census results)	
1 February 1974	
Males	759,109
Females	744,259
Total	1,503,368
1–14 February 1984	2,101,628
Population (official estimates at mid-year)	
1990	2,460,000
1991	2,520,000
1992	2,580,000
Density (per sq km) at mid-1992	26.4

* 37,743 sq miles.

ADMINISTRATIVE DIVISIONS
(population at 1984 census)

Counties:		Nimba	313,050
Bomi	66,420	Rivercess	37,849
Bong	255,813	Sinoe	64,147
Grand Bassa	159,648	Territories:	
Grand Cape Mount	79,322	Gibi	66,802
Grand Gedeh	102,810	Kru Coast	35,267
Lofa	247,641	Marshall	31,190
Maryland	85,267	Sasstown	11,524
Montserrado	544,878	**Total**	2,101,628

PRINCIPAL TOWN

Monrovia (capital), population 421,058 at 1984 census.

BIRTHS AND DEATHS (UN estimates, annual averages)

	1975–80	1980–85	1985–90
Birth rate (per 1,000)	47.4	47.2	47.3
Death rate (per 1,000)	18.1	16.7	15.8

Expectation of life (UN estimates, years at birth, 1985–90): 53.0 (males 52.0; females 54.0).

Source: UN, *World Population Prospects: The 1992 Revision.*

ECONOMICALLY ACTIVE POPULATION

	1978	1979	1980
Agriculture, forestry, hunting and fishing	355,467	366,834	392,926
Mining	25,374	26,184	28,047
Manufacturing	6,427	6,631	7,102
Construction	4,701	4,852	5,198
Electricity, gas and water	245	246	263
Commerce	18,668	19,266	20,636
Transport and communications	7,314	7,549	8,086
Services	49,567	51,154	54,783
Others	28,555	29,477	31,571
Total	496,318	512,193	548,615

Mid-1992 (estimates in '000): Agriculture, etc. 690; Total 1,000 (Source: FAO, *Production Yearbook*).

Agriculture

PRINCIPAL CROPS ('000 metric tons)

	1990	1991	1992
Rice (paddy)*	100	109	110
Sweet potatoes*	18	18	18
Cassava (Manioc)*	300	300	300
Yams*	15	15	15
Taro (Coco yam)*	15	15	18
Coconuts*	7	7	7
Palm kernels*	7	7	7
Vegetables and melons*	71	71	71
Sugar cane*	225	225	225
Oranges*	7	7	7
Pineapples*	7	7	7
Bananas*	80	80	80
Plantains*	33	33	33
Cocoa beans†	3	1	1
Natural rubber (dry weight)†	40	19	22

* FAO estimates. † Unofficial figures.

Source: FAO, *Production Yearbook.*

LIVESTOCK
(FAO estimates, '000 head, year ending September)

	1990	1991	1992
Cattle	38	38	38
Pigs	120	120	120
Sheep	220	220	220
Goats	230	220	220

Poultry (FAO estimates, million): 4 in 1990; 4 in 1991; 4 in 1992.

Source: FAO, *Production Yearbook.*

LIVESTOCK PRODUCTS (FAO estimates, metric tons)

	1990	1991	1992
Pig meat	4,000	4,000	4,000
Poultry meat	5,000	5,000	5,000
Other meat	8,000	8,000	8,000
Cows' milk	1,000	1,000	1,000
Hen eggs	4,032	4,032	4,032

Source; FAO, *Production Yearbook*.

Forestry

ROUNDWOOD REMOVALS
('000 cubic metres, excluding bark)

	1990	1991	1992
Sawlogs, veneer logs and logs for sleepers	1,008*	593	890
Other industrial wood*	158	164	169
Fuel wood*	4,890	4,962	5,040
Total	6,056*	5,719	6,099

* FAO estimate(s).
Source: FAO, *Yearbook of Forest Products*.

SAWNWOOD PRODUCTION
('000 cubic metres, including railway sleepers)

	1985	1986	1987
Total	169	191	411

1988–92: Annual production as in 1987 (FAO estimates).
Source: FAO, *Yearbook of Forest Products*.

Fishing

('000 metric tons, live weight)

	1989	1990	1991
Inland waters	4.0	4.0	4.0
Atlantic Ocean	10.8	2.5	5.6
Total catch	14.8	6.5	9.6

Source: FAO, *Yearbook of Fishery Statistics*.

Mining

	1989	1990	1991
Iron ore ('000 metric tons)*	7,450	2,490	n.a.
Industrial diamonds ('000 carats)	93	60	60
Gem diamonds ('000 carats)†	62	40	40
Gold (kilograms)*	700	700	600

* Figures refer to the metal content of ores.
† Data from the US Bureau of Mines.
Source: UN, *Industrial Statistics Yearbook*.

Industry

SELECTED PRODUCTS
('000 metric tons, unless otherwise indicated)

	1988	1989	1990
Palm oil*	35	35	30
Beer ('000 hectolitres)	158	n.a.	n.a.
Soft drinks ('000 hectolitres)	171	n.a.	n.a.
Cigarettes (million)†	22	22	22
Cement	130	85‡	50
Electric energy (million kWh)	834	818	565

* FAO estimates.
† Data from the US Department of Agriculture.
‡ Provisional or estimated figure.
Source: mainly UN, *Industrial Statistics Yearbook*.
1991: Palm oil 25 ('000 metric tons, unofficial figure); Cigarettes (million) 22; Electric energy (million kWh) 450.
1992 ('000 metric tons): Palm oil 25 (unofficial figure).

Finance

CURRENCY AND EXCHANGE RATES

Monetary Units
100 cents = 1 Liberian dollar (L $).

Sterling and Dollar Equivalents (31 March 1994)
£1 sterling = L $1.4846;
US $1 = L $1.000;
L $100 = £67.36 = US $100.00.

Exchange Rate
Since 1940 the Liberian dollar has been officially at par with the US dollar.

BUDGET
(public sector accounts, L $ million, year ending 30 June)

Revenue*	1985/86	1986/87	1988†
Tax revenue	172.7	172.4	203.8
Taxes on income and profits	71.7	61.5	72.1
Taxes on property	1.1	2.3	2.6
Taxes on domestic transactions	44.9	57.7	53.3
Taxes on foreign trade	51.6	48.6	73.6
Other taxes	3.4	2.3	2.2
Other current revenue	7.7	8.0	8.9
Capital revenue	0.3	0.2	0.1
Total	180.7	180.6	212.8

Expenditure‡	1985/86	1986/87	1988†
General public services	51.3	51.3	67.8
Defence	21.0	23.5	26.5
Education	38.8	42.8	31.3
Health	15.6	18.7	14.5
Social security and welfare	2.3	2.5	2.9
Housing and community amenities	2.7	2.6	2.1
Recreational, cultural and religious affairs and services	7.2	6.4	4.2
Economic affairs and services	94.4	72.8	79.8
Fuel and energy	7.3	4.5	17.4
Agriculture, forestry, fishing and hunting	21.0	23.6	14.1
Mining, manufacturing and construction	13.1	6.4	2.1
Transport and communications	19.8	18.2	15.0
Other purposes	40.6	42.9	54.3
Total	273.9	263.5	283.4
Current§	205.3	226.1	244.7
Capital	68.6	37.4	38.7

* Excluding grants received from abroad (L $ million): 25.0 (current 17.0, capital 8.0) in 1985/86; 18.0 (current 12.2, capital 5.8) in 1986/87.

† Beginning in 1988, the fiscal year was changed to coincide with the calendar year.

‡ Excluding net lending (L $ million): 22.7 in 1985/86; 19.0 in 1986/87; 21.3 in 1988.

§ Including interest payments (L $ million): 40.6 in 1985/86; 42.9 in 1986/87; 41.2 in 1988.

Source: IMF, *Government Finance Statistics Yearbook.*

INTERNATIONAL RESERVES (US $ million at 31 December)

	1991	1992	1993
Reserve position in IMF	0.04	0.04	0.04
Foreign exchange	1.27	0.94	2.33
Total	1.31	0.98	2.37

Source: IMF, *International Financial Statistics.*

MONEY SUPPLY (L $ million at 31 December)

	1991	1992	1993
Currency outside banks	189.28	154.94	277.55
Demand deposits at commercial banks	92.32	111.12	149.95
Total money (incl. others)	281.67	266.11	427.58

Source: IMF, *International Financial Statistics.*

COST OF LIVING
(Consumer Price Index for Monrovia; base: 1980 = 100)

	1986	1987	1988
Food	107.8	108.0	128.8
Fuel and light	127.2	127.4	128.1
Clothing	124.9	144.8	157.5
Rent	103.8	104.1	105.1
All items (incl. others)	123.2	129.4	141.8

1989: Food 141.2 (average for January–October); All items 150.2.
1990 (January–June): Food 160.7; All items 162.4.

Source: ILO, *Year Book of Labour Statistics.*

NATIONAL ACCOUNTS (L $ million at current prices)
Expenditure on the Gross Domestic Product

	1987	1988	1989
Government final consumption expenditure	143.9	136.3	141.6
Private final consumption expenditure	713.9	733.3	656.8
Increase in stocks*	7.0	3.5	4.0
Gross fixed capital formation	120.4	115.3	96.8
Statistical discrepancy	22.9	39.1	48.2
Total domestic expenditure	1,008.1	1,027.5	947.4
Exports of goods and services	438.2	452.3	521.4
Less Imports of goods and services	356.8	321.5	275.2
GDP in purchasers' values	1,089.5	1,158.3	1,193.6
GDP at constant 1981 prices	1,015.0	1,043.7	1,072.8

* Figures refer only to stocks of iron ore and rubber.

Gross Domestic Product by Economic Activity

	1987	1988	1989
Agriculture, hunting, forestry and fishing	381.8	412.0	410.7
Mining and quarrying	105.0	115.0	122.3
Manufacturing	73.1	80.4	81.6
Electricity, gas and water	19.0	18.8	19.0
Construction	32.7	28.8	26.3
Trade, restaurants and hotels	60.1	64.2	63.3
Transport, storage and communications	75.3	79.1	79.1
Finance, insurance, real estate and business services	119.2	136.1	141.8
Government services	108.5	109.7	139.4
Other community, social and personal services	34.4	35.5	35.5
Sub-total	1,009.1	1,079.6	1,119.0
Less Imputed bank service charge	18.3	27.1	36.5
GDP at factor cost	990.8	1,052.5	1,082.5
Indirect taxes, *less* subsidies	99.0	105.8	111.3
GDP in purchasers' values	1,089.5	1,158.3	1,193.6

Source: UN, *National Accounts Statistics.*

BALANCE OF PAYMENTS (US $ million)

	1985	1986	1987
Merchandise exports f.o.b.	430.4	407.9	374.9
Merchandise imports f.o.b.	−263.8	−258.8	−311.7
Trade balance	166.6	149.1	63.2
Exports of services	34.6	56.9	52.5
Imports of services	−80.2	−80.5	−74.2
Other income received	3.7	2.1	5.2
Other income paid	−131.0	−183.3	−188.3
Private unrequited transfers (net)	−28.0	−25.4	−21.4
Official unrequited transfers (net)	90.4	96.4	45.4
Current balance	56.1	15.3	−117.6
Direct investment (net)	−16.2	−16.5	38.5
Portfolio investment (net)	4.4	5.6	—
Other capital (net)	−139.0	−191.6	−223.8
Net errors and omissions	−108.7	−73.8	30.3
Overall balance	−203.4	−261.0	−272.6

Source: IMF, *International Financial Statistics.*

External Trade

PRINCIPAL COMMODITIES

Imports c.i.f. (US $ million)	1986	1987	1988
Food and live animals	53.6	58.7	47.3
Rice	12.1	17.7	27.9
Mineral fuels, lubricants, etc.	52.9	69.8	55.3
Refined petroleum products	52.5	67.1	n.a.
Motor spirit and other light fuels	12.1	14.2	n.a.
Chemicals and related products	26.3	22.1	15.3
Basic manufactures	36.0	55.3	48.0
Machinery and transport equipment	59.1	73.5	82.3
Miscellaneous manufactured articles	18.1	14.2	15.4
Total (incl. others)	259.0	307.6	272.3

1989 (US $ million): Total imports c.i.f. 323.0.

Exports f.o.b. (US $ million)	1986	1987	1988
Coffee and substitutes	16.3	9.0	5.6
Cocoa	9.0	5.9	6.3
Natural rubber and gums	70.9	89.4	110.2
Wood in the rough or roughly squared	33.1	35.5	32.0
Iron ore and concentrates	248.4	218.0	219.7
Diamonds	6.6	11.0	8.8
Total (incl. others)	408.4	382.2	396.3

Source: UN, *International Trade Statistics Yearbook*.

1989 (L $ million): Total exports f.o.b. 461.16 (iron ore 235.05, rubber 119.93, logs 91.98). Source: National Bank of Liberia, *Quarterly Statistical Bulletin*.

PRINCIPAL TRADING PARTNERS (US $ million)*

Imports c.i.f.	1986	1987	1988
Belgium/Luxembourg	8.5	11.2	15.0
China, People's Republic	7.1	14.7	4.8
Denmark	10.6	7.6	5.9
France (incl. Monaco)	6.5	6.4	4.7
Germany, Federal Republic	32.7	52.3	39.5
Italy	2.5	2.2	7.3
Japan	20.1	15.0	12.0
Netherlands	20.6	26.8	14.4
Spain	2.5	6.6	3.1
Sweden	2.4	0.6	4.6
United Kingdom	24.2	18.4	12.7
USA	42.5	58.0	57.7
Total (incl. others)	259.0	307.6	272.3

Exports f.o.b.	1986	1987	1988
Belgium/Luxembourg	29.2	23.2	28.2
France (incl. Monaco)	33.1	33.2	33.2
Germany, Federal Republic	114.5	109.2	108.1
Italy	70.3	63.4	63.2
Japan	4.9	1.0	4.8
Netherlands	14.4	11.5	10.5
Spain	16.4	17.8	13.4
United Kingdom	7.2	8.8	6.3
USA	93.2	73.9	74.6
Total (incl. others)	408.4	382.2	396.3

* Imports by country of origin; exports by country of last consignment.

Source: UN, *International Trade Statistics Yearbook*.

Transport

ROAD TRAFFIC (vehicles in use at 31 December)

	1979	1986	1987
Cars	13,070	10,788	7,148
Buses and coaches	3,415	1,572	1,078
Goods vehicles	8,999	4,639	2,953
Total	25,484	16,999	11,179

Source: International Road Federation, *World Road Statistics*.

SHIPPING

Merchant Fleet (at 30 June)

	1990	1991	1992
Number of vessels	1,688	1,605	1,672
Displacement ('000 gross registered tons)	54,699.6	52,426.5	55,166.9

Source: Lloyd's Register of Shipping.

International Sea-borne Shipping
(freight traffic, '000 metric tons)

	1988	1989	1990
Goods loaded	15,000	15,200	14,900
Goods unloaded	1,430	1,490	1,520

Source: UN, *Monthly Bulletin of Statistics*.

CIVIL AVIATION (traffic on scheduled services)

	1989	1990
Passengers carried ('000)	32	32
Passenger-km (million)	7	7

Source: UN, *Statistical Yearbook*.

Communications Media

	1989	1990	1991
Radio receivers ('000 in use)	560	580	600
Television receivers ('000 in use)	45	47	49
Telephones ('000 in use)*	23	24	25
Daily newspapers (number)	n.a.	8	n.a.

* Estimates.

Sources: UNESCO, *Statistical Yearbook;* UN Economic Commission for Africa, *African Statistical Yearbook*.

Education

	1983	1984	1985
Schools	1,284	1,830	1,691
Teachers	7,202	9,817	9,856
Students	245,673	275,243	260,560

1986: Students 250,322.

Source: Ministry of Education, Monrovia.

Directory

The Constitution

The Constitution, promulgated on 6 January 1986 (and amended in July 1988), provides for the division of state authority into three independent branches: the executive, the legislature and the judiciary. Executive powers are vested in the President, who is Head of State, Head of Government and Commander-in-Chief of the Liberian armed forces, and who is elected by universal adult suffrage for a six-year term (renewable more than once). Legislative power is vested in the bicameral National Assembly, comprising the Senate and the House of Representatives. Members of both houses are directly elected by popular vote. The Constitution provides for a multi-party system of government, and incorporates powers to prevent the declaration of a one-party state, the dissolution of the legislature or the suspension of the judiciary. The Constitution may be amended by a two-thirds majority of both houses of the National Assembly.

An Interim President was inaugurated in November 1990, and an Interim Government of National Unity (IGNU) was appointed in Monrovia in January 1991. Under the terms of a peace agreement, which was signed in July 1993, the IGNU was replaced by a Council of State, and the existing legislature by a Transitional Legislative Assembly, pending presidential and general elections (which were subsequently rescheduled for September 1994). In September 1994, however, an agreement between the principal warring factions provided for the establishment of a reconstituted council of state, and rescheduled the elections for October 1995 (see Recent History).

The Government

LIBERIAN NATIONAL TRANSITIONAL GOVERNMENT

Council of State
(September 1994)

A transitional executive council, comprising representatives of the former Interim Government of National Unity (IGNU), the National Patriotic Forces of Liberia (NPFL) and the United Liberation Movement of Liberia for Democracy (ULIMO).

DAVID D. KPOMAKPOR (Chairman) (IGNU)

Gen. (retd) ISAAC MUSA (Vice-Chairman) (NPFL)

Dr EL-MOHAMED SHERIF (Vice-Chairman) (ULIMO)

PHILIP A. Z. BANKS (IGNU)

DEXTER TAHYOR (ULIMO)

Cabinet
(September 1994)

An interim coalition of the IGNU, the NPFL and ULIMO.

Minister of Foreign Affairs: DOROTHY M. COOPER.

Minister of Finance: JOSIAH GBON (acting).

Minister of Justice: LAVELI SUPUWOOD.

Minister of Defence: Gen. SANDEE WARE.

Minister of Posts and Telecommunications: ROOSEVELT JAYJAY.

Minister of Commerce and Industry: LOSINEE F. KAMARA.

Minister of Agriculture: Dr ROLAND C. MASSAQUOI.

Minister of Internal Affairs: SAMUEL SAYE DOKIE.

Minister of Health and Social Welfare: Dr VAMBA KANNEH.

Minister of Education: Dr LEVI ZANGAI.

Minister of Planning and Economic Affairs: AMELIA WARD.

Minister of Information, Culture and Tourism: JOE W. MULBAH.

Minister of Lands, Mines and Energy: ZEHYEE KEKIE.

Minister of Public Works: Brig.-Gen. ACHEAPHON BESTMAN.

Minister of Labour: THOMAS J. WOEWEIYU.

Minister of State for Presidential Affairs: MANYU KAMARA.

Minister of Youth and Sports: COMMENY B. WESSEH.

Minister of Rural Development: SAMUEL BROWNELL.

Minister of Transport: SAM MAHN.

Ministers without Portfolio: MANYU KAMARA, ANSUMANA KROMAH.

MINISTRIES

Ministry of Agriculture: Tubman Blvd, POB 9010, Monrovia.

Ministry of Commerce and Industry: Ashmun St, POB 9014, Monrovia.

Ministry of Defence: Benson St, POB 9007, Monrovia.

Ministry of Education: Broad St, POB 1545, Monrovia.

Ministry of Finance: Broad St, POB 9013, Monrovia.

Ministry of Foreign Affairs: Mamba Point, Monrovia.

Ministry of Health and Social Welfare: POB 9004, Sinkor, Monrovia.

Ministry of Information, Culture and Tourism: 110 United Nations Drive, POB 9021, Monrovia.

Ministry of Internal Affairs: cnr Warron and Benson Sts, POB 9008, Monrovia.

Ministry of Justice: Ashmun St, POB 9006, Monrovia.

Ministry of Labour: Mechlin St, POB 9040, Monrovia.

Ministry of Lands, Mines and Energy: Capitol Hill, POB 9024, Monrovia.

Ministry of Planning and Economic Affairs: Broad St, POB 9016, Monrovia.

Ministry of Posts and Telecommunications: Carey St, Monrovia.

Ministry of Presidential Affairs: Executive Mansion, Capitol Hill, Monrovia.

Ministry of Public Affairs: Lynch St, POB 9011, Monrovia.

Ministry of Rural Development: Monrovia.

Ministry of Transport: Monrovia.

Ministry of Youth and Sports: POB 9040, Sinkor, Monrovia.

Legislature

NATIONAL ASSEMBLY

The 1986 Constitution vests legislative authority in a bicameral National Assembly, comprising a Senate of 26 members and a House of Representatives of 64 members. Under the terms of the peace agreement that was signed in July 1993, the existing 28-member Interim National Assembly was replaced by a 35-member Transitional Legislative Assembly in October of that year (comprising representatives of the principal warring factions), pending legislative elections.

Speaker of the Transitional Legislative Assembly: MORRIS M. DUKULY.

Political Organizations

Labour Party (LP).

Liberia New Horizons: f. 1994; supports social and political development in Liberia.

Liberia Unification Party (LUP): aims include free enterprise, national self-sufficiency in food, economic revival, freedom of press and speech; official registration reported to have been revoked in 1987; Leader WILLIAM GABRIEL KPOLLEH.

Liberian Action Party (LAP): aims include freedom of press, speech and religion, accountability of public officials, and national economic reconstruction; draws support mainly from the middle classes and business interests; Leader Dr S. BYRON TARR; Chair. EMMANUEL KOROMA; Sec.-Gen. Prof. LEVI REEVES-ZANGAI.

Liberian Liberal Party (LLP): f. 1987; co-operates with the NDPL; Leader PAUL YANSEN.

Liberian People's Party (LPP): f. by fmr mems of the Movement for Justice in Africa, a Pan-African political grouping active prior to the 1980 coup; banned in 1985; Chair. DUSTY WOLOKOLLIE; Leader Dr AMOS SAWYER.

National Patriotic Front of Liberia (NPFL): f. in Abidjan, Côte d'Ivoire; began mil. operations in Dec. 1989; Leader CHARLES TAYLOR.

National Patriotic Party (NPP): f. Dec. 1991 as the political wing of the NPFL.

True Whig Party (TWP): f. 1868; ruling party prior to the April 1980 coup; banned 1980–91; Sec.-Gen. MAXWELL CARTER.

United Liberation Movement of Liberia for Democracy (ULIMO): Tubmanburg; f. 1991 by supporters of the late Pres. Samuel Doe; split into two ethnic factions (subsequently led by Alhaji G. V. KROMAH and Gen. ROOSEVELT JOHNSON) which engaged in conflict in early 1994.

United People's Party (UPP): f. by fmr mems of the Progressive People's Party, which led opposition prior to the April 1980 coup; banned 1985–86; Leader GABRIEL BACCUS MATTHEWS.

Unity Party (UP): Chair. JOSEPH KOFA.

The following dissident factions were active in 1994:

Liberia Peace Council (LPC): f. 1993; mainly Krahn support; in conflict with NPFL forces in south-eastern Liberia; Chair. Dr GEORGE BOLEY; Sec.-Gen. OCTAVIUS WALKER.

Lofa Defence Force: f. 1993; in conflict with ULIMO forces in Lofa County.

Diplomatic Representation

Note: Following the advance of the NPFL on Monrovia in May 1990, all embassy staff were evacuated. By mid-1994 a number of embassies were reported to have reopened.

EMBASSIES IN LIBERIA

Algeria: Capitol By-Pass, POB 2032, Monrovia; tel. 224311; telex 44475; Chargé d'affaires: MUHAMMAD AZZEDINE AZZOUZ.

Cameroon: 18th St and Payne Ave, Sinkor, POB 414, Monrovia; tel. 261374; telex 44240; Ambassador: VICTOR E. NDIBA.

Côte d'Ivoire: Tubman Blvd, Sinkor, POB 126, Monrovia; tel. 261123; telex 44273; Ambassador: CLÉMENT KAUL MELEDJE.

Cuba: 17 Kennedy Ave, Congotown, POB 3579, Monrovia; tel. 262600; Ambassador: M. GAUNEANO CARDOSO TOLEDO.

Egypt: POB 462, Monrovia; tel. 261953; telex 44308; Ambassador: MUHAMMAD SALEH EL-DIN EL-DAOUR.

Germany: Oldest Congotown, POB 34, Monrovia; tel. 261460; telex 44230; Ambassador: Dr JÜRGEN GEHL.

Ghana: cnr 11th St and Gardiner Ave, Sinkor, POB 471, Monrovia; tel. 261477; Ambassador: G. R. NIPAH.

Guinea: Tubman Blvd, Sinkor, POB 461, Monrovia; tel. 261182; Ambassador: (vacant).

Holy See: Apostolic Nunciature, Sinkor, POB 4211, Monrovia; tel. 262948; Apostolic Pro-Nuncio: Most Rev. LUIGI TRAVAGLINO, Titular Archbishop of Lettere (temporarily resident at 23 Jomo Keyatta Rd, POB 526, Freetown, Sierra Leone; tel. 242131; fax 240509).

Israel: Gardiner Ave, between 11th and 12th Sts, Sinkor, Monrovia; tel. 262861; telex 44415; Ambassador: MOSHE ITAN.

Italy: Mamba Point, POB 255, Monrovia; tel. 224580; telex 44438; Ambassador: Dr. ENRIC'ANGIOLO FERRONI-CARLI.

Korea, Republic: 10th St and Payne Ave, Sinkor, POB 2769, Monrovia; tel. 261532; telex 44241; Ambassador: KIM YONG-JIP.

Lebanon: 12th St, Monrovia; tel. 262537; telex 44208; Ambassador: MICHEL BITAR.

Libya: Monrovia.

Morocco: Tubman Blvd, Congotown, Monrovia; tel. 262767; telex 44540; Chargé d'affaires a.i.: Dr MOULAY ABBES AL-KADIRI.

Nigeria: Tubman Blvd, Sinkor, POB 366, Monrovia; tel. 261093; telex 44278; Ambassador: HENRY AJAKAIYE.

Poland: cnr 10th St and Gardiner Ave, Sinkor, POB 860, Monrovia; tel. 261113; Chargé d'affaires: ZBIGNIEW REJMAN.

Romania: 81 Sekou Touré Ave, Sinkor, POB 2598, Monrovia; tel. 261508; Chargé d'affaires: SILVESTRA ZUGRAV.

Russia: Payne Ave, Sinkor, POB 2010, Monrovia; tel. 261304; Ambassador: VASILI STEPANOVICH BEBKO.

Senegal: Monrovia, Ambassador MOCTAR TRAORE.

Sierra Leone: Tubman Blvd, POB 575, Monrovia; tel. 261301; Ambassador: DENNIS RANSFORD WOODE.

Spain: Capitol Hill, POB 275, Monrovia; tel. 221299; telex 44538; Ambassador: MANUEL DE LUNA.

Sweden: POB 335, Monrovia; tel. 261646; telex 44255; Chargé d'affaires: OVE SVENSSON.

Switzerland: Old Congo Rd, POB 283, Monrovia; tel. 261065; telex 44559; Chargé d'affaires: CHARLES HALLER.

United Kingdom: Mamba Point, POB 120, Monrovia; tel. 221491; telex 44287; Ambassador: STEPHEN SEAMAN.

USA: 111 United Nations Drive, Mamba Point, POB 98, Monrovia; tel. 222994; Ambassador: WILLIAM H. TWADDELL.

Zaire: Spriggs Payne Airport, Sinkor, POB 1038, Monrovia; tel. 261326; Ambassador: MUABI M. S. KUMUANBA.

Judicial System

In February 1982 the People's Supreme Tribunal (which had been established following the April 1980 coup) was renamed the People's Supreme Court, and its chairman and members became the Chief Justice and Associate Justices of the People's Supreme Court. The judicial system also comprised People's Circuit and Magistrate Courts. The five-member Supreme Court (composed of representatives of the interim Government and of the NPFL) was established in January 1992 to adjudicate in electoral disputes.

Chief Justice of People's Supreme Court: EMMANUEL GBALAZEH.

Religion

Liberia is officially a Christian state, although complete religious freedom is guaranteed. Christianity and Islam are the two main religions. There are numerous religious sects, and many Liberians hold traditional beliefs.

CHRISTIANITY

Liberian Council of Churches: 182 Tubman Blvd, POB 2191, Monrovia; tel. 262820; f. 1982; six full mems and two assoc. mems.; Pres. Bishop ARTHUR F. KULAH; Gen. Sec. IMOGENE M. COLLINS.

The Anglican Communion

Anglicans in Liberia are adherents of the Church of the Province of West Africa, incorporating the local Protestant Episcopal Church. Anglicanism was established in Liberia in 1836, and the diocese of Liberia was admitted into full membership of the Province in March 1982. In 1985 the Church had 125 congregations, 39 clergy, 26 schools and about 20,000 adherents in the country.

Bishop of Liberia: (vacant), Protestant Episcopal Church, Randall St, POB 277, Monrovia; tel. 224760.

The Roman Catholic Church

Liberia comprises the archdiocese of Monrovia and the dioceses of Cape Palmas and Gbarnga. At 31 December 1992 there were an estimated 83,778 adherents in the country, equivalent to 2.9% of the total population. The Bishops participate in the Inter-territorial Catholic Bishops' Conference of the Gambia, Liberia and Sierra Leone (based in Freetown, Sierra Leone).

Archbishop of Monrovia: Most Rev. MICHAEL KPAKALA FRANCIS, Catholic Mission, POB 2078, Monrovia; tel. 221389; telex 44529; fax 221399.

Other Christian Churches

Assemblies of God in Liberia: POB 1297, Monrovia; f. 1908; 14,578 adherents, 287 churches; Gen. Supt JIMMIE K. DUGBE, Sr.

Lutheran Church in Liberia: POB 1046, Monrovia; 25,600 adherents; Pres. Bishop RONALD J. DIGGS.

Providence Baptist Church: cnr Broad and Center Sts, Monrovia; f. 1821; 2,500 adherents, 300 congregations, 6 ministers, 8 schools; Pastor Rev. A. MOMOLUE DIGGS; associated with:

The Liberia Baptist Missionary and Educational Convention, Inc: POB 390, Monrovia; tel. 222661; f. 1880; Pres. Rev. J. K. LEVEE MOULTON; Nat. Vice-Pres. Rev. J. GBANA HALL; Gen. Sec. CHARLES W. BLAKE.

United Methodist Church in Liberia: cnr 12th St and Tubman Blvd, POB 1010, 1000 Monrovia 10; tel. 223343; f. 1833; c. 70,000 adherents, 487 congregations, 450 ministers, 300 lay pastors, 38 schools; Resident Bishop Rev. ARTHUR F. KULAH; Sec. Rev. JULIUS SARWOLO NELSON.

Other active denominations include the National Baptist Mission, the Pentecostal Church, the Presbyterian Church in Liberia, the Prayer Band and the Church of the Lord Aladura.

ISLAM

The total community numbers about 670,000.

National Muslim Council of Liberia: Monrovia; Leader Shaykh KAFUMBA KONNAH.

The Press

NEWSPAPERS

Daily Observer: 117 Broad St, Crown Hill, POB 1858, Monrovia; tel. 223545; f. 1981; independent; 5 a week; Editor-in-Chief STANTON B. PEABODY; circ. 30,000.

Herald: Monrovia; f. 1987; Catholic weekly; Editor RUFUS DARPOH.

The Inquirer: Monrovia; Man. Editor GABRIEL WILLIAMS.

New Times: Monrovia; Man. Editor RUFUS DARPOH; Editor JEFF MUTADA.

Sunday Express: Mamba Point, POB 3029, Monrovia; weekly; Editor JOHN F. SCOTLAND; circ. 5,000.

Sunday People: POB 3366, Monrovia; 2 a week; Editor D. G. PYNE-DRAPER.

PERIODICALS

Daily Listener: POB 35, Monrovia; monthly; Man. CHARLES C. DENNIS; circ. 3,500.

The Eye: POB 4692, Monrovia; daily; Editor H. B. KINBAH.

Journal of Commerce, Industry & Transportation: POB 9041, Monrovia; tel. 222141; telex 44331.

The Kpelle Messenger: Kpelle Literacy Center, Lutheran Church, POB 1046, Monrovia; Kpelle-English monthly; Editor Rev. JOHN J. MANAWU.

Liberian Star: POB 691, Monrovia; f. 1954; monthly; Editor HENRY B. COLE; circ. 3,500.

Palm: Johnson and Carey Sts, POB 1110, Monrovia; 6 a year; Editor JAMES C. DENNIS.

The People Magazine: Bank of Liberia Bldg, Suite 214, Carey and Warren Sts, POB 3501, Monrovia; tel. 222743; f. 1985; monthly; Editor and Publr CHARLES A. SNETTER.

Plain Talk: POB 2108, Monrovia; daily; Editor-in-Chief N. MACAULAY PAYKUE.

X-Ray Magazine: c/o Liss Inc, POB 4196, Monrovia; tel. 221674; f. 1985; monthly; health; Man. Editor NMAH BROPLEH.

PRESS ORGANIZATION

Press Union of Liberia: Monrovia; f. 1985; Pres. LAMINI A. WARITAY.

NEWS AGENCIES

Liberian News Agency (LINA): POB 9021, Capitol Hill, Monrovia; tel. 222229; telex 44249; Dir-Gen. ERNEST KIAZOLY (acting).

Foreign Bureaux

Agence France-Presse (AFP): Monrovia; telex 44211; Rep. JAMES DORBOR.

Informatsionnoye Telegrafnoye Agentstvo Rossii—Telegrafnoye Agentstvo Suverennykh Stran (ITAR—TASS) (Russia): 10th St and Payne Ave, Monrovia; Correspondent GENNADY TALALAYEV.

United Press International (UPI) (USA): Monrovia; Correspondent T. K. SANNAH.

Xinhua (New China) News Agency (People's Republic of China): Adams St, Old Rd, Congotown, POB 3001, Monrovia; tel. 262821; telex 44547; Correspondent SUN BAOYU.

Publisher

Government Publishing House

Government Printer: Government Printing Office, POB 9002, Monrovia; tel. 221029; telex 44224.

Radio and Television

In 1991, according to UNESCO estimates, there were 600,000 radio receivers and 49,000 television receivers in use.

RADIO

ELBC—The Voice of Peace, Harmony and Reconcilation: Liberian Broadcasting System, POB 594, Monrovia; tel. 224984; f. 1960, reorg. 1990, under the aegis of the interim Govt; broadcasts in English, French and Liberian vernaculars; Dir-Gen. WEADE KOBBAH WUREH; Asst Dir-Gen. (Radio) NOAH A. BORDOLO.

LAMCO Broadcasting Station (ELNR): LAMCO Information and Broadcasting Service, Nimba; Liberian news, music, cultural, political and educational programmes in English; carries national news and all nation-wide broadcasts from ELBC, and local news in English and African languages (Mano, Gio, Bassa, Vai, Lorma, Kru, Krahn, Grebo and Kpelle); also relays BBC World Service and African Service news programmes; Dir T. NELSON WILLIAMS.

Liberia Rural Communications Network: POB 10-02176, 1000 Monrovia 10; tel. 271368; f. 1981; govt-operated; rural development and entertainment programmes; operates three medium-wave stations and central administrative and programming unit; broadcasts in principal Liberian languages; Dir JEROME DAVIS.

Radio ELWA: POB 192, Monrovia; tel. 271669; f. 1954; operated by the Sudan Interior Mission; religious, cultural and educational broadcasts in English, French, Arabic and 42 west African vernaculars; Broadcasting Dir LEE J. SONIUS.

Voice of America: Monrovia; telex 44365; broadcasts in English, French, Swahili, Hausa and Portuguese.

TELEVISION

ELTV: Liberian Broadcasting System, POB 594, Monrovia; tel. 224984; telex 44249; f. 1964; commercial station, partly govt-supported; broadcasts $5\frac{1}{2}$ hours daily Mon.–Fri., $9\frac{1}{2}$ hours daily Sat. and Sun.; Dir-Gen. WEADE KOBBAH WUREH.

Finance

(cap. = capital; p.u. = paid up; res = reserves; dep. = deposits; m. = million; br. = branch; amounts in Liberian dollars)

BANKING

Most banking operations in Liberia were suspended in 1990, as a result of the disruption caused by the civil conflict, although several banks reopened in mid-1991.

Central Bank

National Bank of Liberia: Broad St, POB 2048, Monrovia; tel. 222497; telex 44215; f. 1974; bank of issue; cap. and res 17.1m., dep. 70.7m. (1986); Gov. DAVID K. WINTER; Dep. Gov. LINDSAY M. HAINES.

Other Banks

Agricultural and Co-operative Development Bank: Carey and Warren Sts, POB 3585, Monrovia; tel. 224385; telex 44535; fax 221500; f. 1977; cap. p.u. 6.6m. (Dec. 1989), res. 6.7m., dep. 30.6m. (Dec. 1987); Chair. Dr NAH-DOE P. BROPLEM; Pres. and Gen. Man. JEROME M. HODGE; 6 brs.

Citibank (Liberia): Ashmun St, POB 280, Monrovia; tel. 224991; telex 44274; f. 1935; cap. 0.5m.; Gen. Man. THIERRY BUNGINER; 1 br.

Eurobank Liberia Ltd: Broad and Warren Sts, POB 2021, 1000 Monrovia; tel. 224873; telex 44455; fax 225921; Chair. GEORGES PHILIPPE; Pres. DONALD S. REYNOLDS; cap. 1m. (Dec. 1992).

First Commercial and Investment Bank: Cnr Ashmun and Mechlin Sts, POB 1442, Monrovia; tel. 222498; telex 44431; fax 222351; cap. 3.6m. (Dec. 1991); Chair. and Pres. EDWIN J. COOPER.

International Trust Co of Liberia: 80 Broad St, POB 292, Monrovia; tel. 221600; telex 44588; f. 1948; cap. p.u. 2m., dep. 30m. (Dec. 1989); Pres. DAVID CLARK; Gen. Man. RAYMOND M. ABOU SAMRA; 1 br.

Liberia Finance and Trust Corporation: Broad St, POB 3155, Monrovia; tel. 221020; telex 44386; cap. 790,487 (Dec. 1984); Chair. G. ALVIN JONES; Pres. C. T. O. KING, III.

Liberian Bank for Development and Investment (LBDI): Ashmun and Randall Sts, POB 0547, Monrovia; tel. 223998; telex 44345; fax 223044; f. 1961; cap. and res 1,832.1m., dep. 34.1m. (Dec. 1993); Chair. FRANCIS T. KARPEH; Pres. JAMES S. P. COOPER

Liberian Trading and Development Bank Ltd (TRADEVCO): 57 Ashmun St, POB 293, Monrovia; tel. 221800; telex 44270; fax 225035; f. 1955; wholly-owned subsidiary of Mediobanca SpA (Italy); cap. and res 3.2m., dep. 45.0m. (Dec. 1992); Chair. and Pres. GIORGIO PICOTTI.

Meridien BIAO Bank Liberia Ltd: Meridien House, Randall and Ashmun Sts, POB 0408, Monrovia; tel. 221500; telex 44565; fax 224087; cap. p.u. 7m. (Sept. 1993); Chair. J. C. KAPOTWE; Pres. RAHAMAT HOSEIN.

National Housing and Savings Bank: UN Drive, Waterside, POB 818, Monrovia; tel. 224495; telex 44337; fax 224498; f. 1972; priority financing for low-cost govt housing programmes; cap. p.u. 5.1m. (Dec. 1986); Pres. PATRICK D. KUTO-AKOI.

Banking Association

Liberia Bankers' Association: POB 292, Monrovia; an asscn of commercial and development banks; Pres. LEN MAESTRE.

INSURANCE

American International Underwriters, Inc: Carter Bldg, 39 Broad St, POB 180, Monrovia; tel. 224921; telex 44389; general; Gen. Man. S. B. MENSAH.

American Life Insurance Co: Carter Bldg, 39 Broad St, POB 60, Monrovia; life and general; f. 1969; Vice-Pres. ALLEN BROWN.

Insurance Co of Africa: 80 Broad St, POB 292, Monrovia; f. 1969; life and general; Pres. GIZAW H. MARIAM.

Lone Star Insurances Inc: 51 Broad St, POB 1142, Monrovia; tel. 222257; telex 44394; non-life (property and casualty).

Minet James Liberia Inc: POB 541, Monrovia; Man. Dir EDWARD MILNE.

National Insurance Corporation of Liberia (NICOL): LBDI Bldg Complex, POB 1528, Sinkor, Monrovia; tel. 262429; telex 44228; f. 1984; state-owned; sole insurer for Govt and parastatal bodies;

also provides insurance for the Liberian-registered merchant shipping fleet; Man. Dir MIATTA EDITH SHERMAN.

Royal Exchange Assurance: Ashmun and Randall Sts, POB 666, Monrovia; all types of insurance; Man. RONALD WOODS.

United Security Insurance Agencies Inc: Randall St, POB 2071, Monrovia; telex 44568; personal (life, accident and medical); Dir EPHRAIM O. OKORO.

Trade and Industry

CHAMBER OF COMMERCE

Liberia Chamber of Commerce: POB 92, Monrovia; tel. 223738; telex 44211; f. 1951; Pres. DAVID A. B. JALLAH; Sec.-Gen. LUESETTE S. HOWELL.

DEVELOPMENT ORGANIZATIONS

Forestry Development Authority: POB 3010, 1000 Monrovia; tel. 224940; responsible for forest management and conservation; Man. Dir BENSON S. GWYAN.

Liberia Industrial Free Zone Authority: Bushrod Island, POB 9047, Monrovia; f. 1975; 98 mems; Man. Dir GBAI M. GBALA.

National Investment Commission (NIC): Former Executive Mansion Bldg, POB 9043, Monrovia; tel. 225163; telex 44560; f. 1979; autonomous body negotiating investment incentives agreements on behalf of Govt; promotes agro-based and industrial development; Chair. G. E. SAIGBE BOLEY; Exec. Dir P. SEBASTIAN SMITH.

MARKETING ORGANIZATION

Liberian Produce Marketing Corporation: POB 662, Monrovia; tel. 222447; telex 44590; f. 1961; govt-owned; exports Liberian produce, provides industrial facilities for processing of agricultural products and participates in agricultural development programmes; Man. Dir ALETHA JOHNSON-FRANCIS.

EMPLOYERS' ASSOCIATION

National Enterprises Corporation: POB 518, Monrovia; tel. 261370; importer, wholesaler and distributor of foodstuffs, and wire and metal products for local industries; Pres. EMMANUEL SHAW, Sr.

MAJOR INDUSTRIAL COMPANIES

The following are among the largest companies in terms either of capital investment or employment. In 1990 the majority of industrial companies were forced to suspend activity, owing to the disruption caused by the civil war. A number of companies resumed operations in 1992.

Bong Mining Co Ltd: POB 538, Monrovia; tel. 225222; telex 44269; fax 225770; f. 1958; cap. $26.5m.; engages in iron ore mining, upgrading of crude ore and transportation of concentrate and pellets to Monrovia Free Port for shipment abroad; capacity: 4.5m. tons of concentrate and 3m. tons of pellets annually; Pres. HANSJOERG RIETZSCH; Gen. Man. HANS-GEORG SCHNEIDER; 2,200 employees.

Firestone Plantations Co: POB 140, Harbel; telex 44499; f. 1926; operated the world's largest natural rubber plantation until 1988, when its Liberian interests were acquired by the Japanese co, Bridgestone; resumed operations in 1992; 8,117 employees.

Liberia Cement Corporation (CEMENCO): POB 150, Monrovia; tel. 222650; telex 44558; mfrs of Portland cement.

The Liberia Co: POB 45, Broad St, Monrovia; f. 1947; cap. $1m; shipping agents Delta Steamship Lines; owns COCOPA rubber plantations; Pres. J. T. TRIPPE (New York); Vice-Pres. J. M. LIJNKAMP (Monrovia); 850 employees.

Liberian International American Corporation (LIAC): mining of iron ore.

Liberian Iron and Steel Corporation (LISCO): POB 876, Monrovia; f. 1967; mining of iron ore.

Liberian Mining Co (LIMICO): Monrovia; govt-owned; mining of iron ore; assumed control of LAMCO JV Operating Co in 1989; operations suspended between 1990–92.

Liberia Petroleum Refining Corporation (LPRC): POB 90, Monrovia; sole producer of domestically produced fuels, with designed capacity of 15,000 b/d; products include diesel fuel, fuel oils, liquid petroleum gas; supplies domestic market and has limited export facilities for surplus products.

Mesurado Industrial Complex: POB 142, Monrovia; Liberian-owned cos; products include detergents, soap, industrial gases, windows and animal feeds; Pres. P. BONNER JALLAH.

National Iron Ore Co Ltd: POB 548, Monrovia; f. 1958; 85% govt-owned co mining iron ore at Mano river; Gen. Man. S. K. DATTA RAY.

Shell Liberia Ltd: Bushrod Island, POB 360, Monrovia; f. 1920; inc in Canada; distributors of petroleum products; Man. M. Y. KUENYEDZI; 15 employees.

United States Trading Co: POB 140, Monrovia; f. 1949; distribution of Firestone products; Ford USA and UK vehicle sales and service, wholesalers and retailers of foodstuffs and beverages.

TRADE UNIONS

Congress of Industrial Organizations: 29 Ashmun St, POB 415, Monrovia; Pres. Gen. J. T. PRATT; Sec.-Gen. AMOS N. GRAY; 5 affiliated unions.

Labor Congress of Liberia: 71 Gurley St, Monrovia; Sec.-Gen. P. C. T. SONPON; 8 affiliated unions.

Liberian Federation of Labor Unions: J. B. McGill Labor Center, Gardnersville Freeway, POB 415, Monrovia; f. 1980 by merger; Sec.-Gen. AMOS GRAY; 10,000 mems (1983).

Transport

RAILWAYS

Bong Mining Co Ltd: POB 538, Monrovia; tel. 225222; telex 44269; fax 225770; operates 78 km of standard track, transporting iron ore concentrates and pellets from Bong mine to Monrovia; Gen. Man. H.-G. SCHNEIDER.

Liberian Mining Co: Monrovia; govt-owned; assumed control of LAMCO JV Operating Co in 1989; operates 267 track-km between Buchanan and the iron ore mine at Nimba; also operates a passenger railway between Buchanan and Yekepa.

National Iron Ore Co Ltd: POB 548, Monrovia; 145 km of track, Mano River to Monrovia, for transport of iron ore; Gen. Man. S. K. DATTA RAY.

ROADS

In 1991 there were an estimated 6,095 km of classified roads, including 2,030 km of main roads and 1,540 km of secondary roads; about 2,400 km of the total network were paved. The main trunk road is the Monrovia–Sanniquellie motor road, extending north-east from the capital to the border with Guinea, near Ganta, and eastward through the hinterland to the border with Côte d'Ivoire. Trunk roads run through Tapita, in Nimba County, to Grand Gedeh County and from Monrovia to Buchanan. A bridge over the Mano river connects with the Sierra Leone road network, while a main road links Monrovia and Freetown (Sierra Leone). The principal roads in Liberia, which were closed throughout 1990 as a result of the armed conflict, were reported to have been reopened in early 1992.

SHIPPING

In January 1993 Liberia's open-registry fleet (1,568 vessels), the largest in the world in terms of gross tonnage, had a total displacement of 55.1m. grt. In 1992 the resumption of armed conflict in Monrovia resulted in the suspension of most shipping activity. In mid-1993, however, the principal port of Buchanan was officially reopened to shipping.

Liberia National Shipping Line (LNSL): Monrovia; f. 1987; jt venture by the Liberian Govt and private German interests; routes to Europe, incl. the UK and Scandinavia.

National Port Authority: POB 1849, Monrovia; tel. 221454; telex 44275; f. 1967; administers Monrovia Free Port and the ports of Buchanan, Greenville and Harper; Man. L. A. KROMAH.

CIVIL AVIATION

Liberia's principal airports are Roberts Field International Airport, at Harbel, 56 km east of Monrovia, and James Spriggs Payne Airport. There are more than 100 other airfields and airstrips. In 1992 the resumption of armed conflict in Monrovia resulted in the suspension of most air services.

ADC Liberia Inc: Monrovia; f. 1993; services to the United Kingdom, the USA and destinations in West Africa.

Air Liberia: POB 2076, Monrovia; telex 44298; f. 1974 by merger; state-owned; scheduled passenger and cargo services; Man. Dir JAMES K. KOFA.

Tourism

Bureau of Tourism: Sinkor, Monrovia; Dir-Gen. JALLAH K. KAMARA.

Defence

In June 1993 the Armed Forces of Liberia (comprising troops of the former president, Samuel Doe) were estimated to number 2,000, troops of the National Patriotic Front of Liberia 5,000 and those of the United Liberation Movement of Liberia for Democracy 3,400. In early 1994 some 20,000 troops under under the command of the ECOWAS Cease-fire Monitoring Group, and 368 members of the UN Observer Mission in Liberia were deployed in Liberia.

Defence Expenditure: Projected at US $38.1m. (12.9% of total expenditure) for 1993.

Chief of Staff of the Armed Forces: Lt-Gen. HEZEKIAH BOWEN.

Education

Primary and secondary education are available free of charge, except for an annual registration fee, and the government provides a 50% subsidy for university tuition. Education is officially compulsory for nine years, between seven and 16 years of age. Primary education begins at seven years of age and lasts for six years. Secondary education, beginning at 13 years of age, lasts for a further six years, divided into two cycles of three years each. In 1984 the total enrolment at primary schools was equivalent to only 40% of children in the relevant age-group (boys 51%; girls 28%), while the comparable ratio for secondary schools was 18%. The University of Liberia, in Monrovia, had about 3,300 students in 1988. Other higher education institutes include the Cuttington University College (controlled by the Protestant Episcopal Church), a college of technology and a computer science institute. Expenditure on education by the central government in 1988 was L $31.3m., representing 11.0% of total spending. UNESCO estimated that 60.5% of the adult population (males 50.2%; females 71.2%) remained illiterate in 1990.

Bibliography

Clapham, C. *Liberia and Sierra Leone: An Essay in Comparative Politics*. Cambridge University Press, 1976.

Corder, S. H. *Liberia under Military Rule*. Monrovia, 1980.

Cruise O'Brien, D. B., Dunn, J., and Rathbone, R. (Eds). *Contemporary West African States*. Cambridge, Cambridge University Press, 1989.

Dunn, D. E. *The Foreign Policy of Liberia During the Tubman Era 1944–71*. Hutchinson Benham, 1979.

Dunn, D. E., and Holsoe, S. E. *Historical Dictionary of Liberia*. Metuchen, NJ, Scarecrow Press, 1986.

Dunn, D. E., and Tarr, S. B. *Liberia: A National Polity in Transition*. Metuchen, NJ, Scarecrow Press, 1988.

Fahnbulleh, H. B., Jr. *The Diplomacy of Prejudice: Liberia in International Politics 1945–1970*. Vantage Press, 1986.

Givens, W. *Liberia: The Road to Democracy under the Leadership of Samuel Kanyon Doe*. London, Kensal Press, 1986.

Holsoe, S. E. *A Bibliography on Liberia, Part I: Books*, 1971; *Part II: Publications Concerning Colonization*, 1971; *Part III: Articles*, 1975. (Liberian Studies Research Working Papers No. 1, 3, 5). Newark, DE, University of Delaware.

Huberich, C. H. *The Political and Legislative History of Liberia*. 2 vols. New York, 1947.

Kappel, R., Korte, W., and Mascher, R. F. *Liberia, Underdevelopment and Political Rule in a Peripheral Society*. Hamburg, Institut für Afrika-Kunde, 1986.

Kappel, R., and Korte, W. (Eds). *Books and Articles on Liberia*. Bremen, Liberia Working Group, 1989.

Liebenow, J. G. *Liberia: The Quest for Democracy*. Bloomington, Indiana University Press, 1987.

Republic of Liberia, Ministry of Planning and Economic Affairs. *Indicative Manpower Plan of Liberia for the Period 1972–1982*. Monrovia, 1974.

1974 *Census of Population and Housing, Population Bulletin No. 2: Final Population Totals and Related Percentages with some Salient Demographic Characteristics*. Monrovia, 1978.

1974 *Population and Housing Census of Liberia, Population Characteristics of Major Areas, Liberia and Major Political Divisions*. Monrovia, 1977, 1979.

Economic Survey of Liberia 1980. Monrovia, 1981.

Rimmer, D. *The Economies of West Africa*. London, Weidenfeld and Nicolson, 1984.

Schulze, W. *A New Geography of Liberia*. London, Longman, 1973.

Sisay, H. B. *Big Powers and Small Nations*. Lanham, MD, University Press of America, 1985.

US Library of Congress. *Liberia during the Tolbert Era: A Guide*. Washington, DC, 1984.

van Mourik, D. *Land in Western Liberia. A Reconnaissance. Agricultural Land Evaluation of the Mano River Union Project Area in Liberia*. Freetown, Mano River Secretariat, 1979.

Vogt, M. A. (Ed.). *Liberian Crisis and ECOMOG: A Bold Attempt at Regional Peace-keeping*. Lagos, Gabumo Publishing Co, 1992.

Wonkeryor, E. L. *Liberia's Military Dictatorship: A 'Fiasco' Revolution*. Chicago, Smugglers' Press, 1985.

MADAGASCAR

Physical and Social Geography

VIRGINIA THOMPSON

PHYSICAL FEATURES

The Democratic Republic of Madagascar comprises the island of Madagascar, the fourth largest island in the world, and several much smaller offshore islands. Madagascar lies 390 km from the east African mainland across the Mozambique channel. It extends 1,600 km from north to south and up to 570 km wide. The whole territory covers an area of 587,041 sq km (226,658 sq miles). Geologically, the main island is composed basically of crystalline rock, which forms the central highlands that rise abruptly from the narrow eastern coastal strip but descend gradually to the wide plains of the west coast.

Topographically, Madagascar can be divided into six fairly distinct regions. Antsiranana province, in the north, is virtually isolated by the island's highest peak, Mt Tsaratanana, rising to 2,800 m above sea level. Tropical crops can be grown in its fertile valleys, and the natural harbour of Antsiranana is an important naval base. Another rich agricultural region lies in the north-west, where a series of valleys converge on the port of Mahajanga. To the south-west along the coastal plains lies a well-watered region where there are large animal herds and crops of rice, cotton, tobacco, and manioc. The southernmost province, Toliary (Tuléar), contains most of Madagascar's known mineral deposits, as well as extensive cattle herds, despite the almost total lack of rainfall. In contrast, the hot and humid climate of the east coast favours the cultivation of the island's most valuable tropical crops—coffee, vanilla, cloves, and sugar-cane. Although this coast lacks sheltered anchorages, it is the site of Madagascar's most important commercial port, Toamasina. Behind its coral beaches a continuous chain of lagoons, some of which are connected by the Pangalanes Canal, provides a partially navigable internal waterway. The island's mountainous hinterland is a densely populated region of extensive rice culture and stock raising. Despite its relative inaccessibility, this region is Madagascar's administrative and cultural centre, the focal point being the capital city of Antananarivo.

Climatic conditions vary from tropical conditions on the east and north-west coasts to the hotness and dryness of the west coast, the extreme aridity of the south and the temperate zone in the central highlands. Forests have survived only in some areas of abundant rainfall, and elsewhere the land has been eroded by over-grazing and slash-and-burn farming methods. Most of the island is savannah-steppe, and much of the interior is covered with laterite. Except in the drought-ridden south, rivers are numerous and flow generally westward, but many are interspersed by rapids and waterfalls, and few are navigable except for short distances.

POPULATION AND CULTURE

Geography and history account for the diversity and distribution of the population, which, according to official estimates, was 12,092,000 at mid-1993. The island's 18 principal ethnic groups are the descendants of successive waves of immigrants from such diverse areas as south-east Asia, continental Africa and Arab countries. The dominant ethnic groups, the Merina (1,993,000 at the 1974 census) and the Betsileo (920,600), who inhabit the most densely populated central provinces of Antananarivo and Fianarantsoa, are of Asian-Pacific origin. In the peripheral areas live the tribes collectively known as *côtiers*, of whom the most numerous are the Betsimisaraka (1,134,000) on the east coast, the Tsimihety (558,100) in the north, and the Antandroy (412,500) in the south. Population density ranges from 30 inhabitants per sq km on the central plateaux to 2 per sq km along much of the west coast. At mid-1993 the average density was officially estimated to be 20.6 inhabitants per sq km. Although continuous migrations, improved means of communication, and a marked cultural unity have, to some extent, broken down geographical and ethnic barriers, traditional tribal antagonisms—notably between the Merina and the *côtiers*—remain close to the surface.

Increasing at an average annual rate of 3.1% during 1985–92, the Malagasy are fast exceeding the island's capacity to feed and employ them. Estimates from the 1974/75 census indicated that more than half the population was under 20 years of age, that the large foreign element was rapidly declining, and that the urban component was steadily growing. French nationals, who numbered some 50,000 before 1972, dwindled to fewer than 15,000 by 1986. In 1981 there were some 5,000 Indians holding French nationality and an equal number of creoles. The Comorans, who were formerly the second largest non-indigenous population group and were concentrated in the Mahajanga area (60,000 in 1976), have become an almost negligible element there, owing to the repatriation of about 16,000 after the clashes between them and the Malagasy in December 1976. Also inhabiting the west coast are the 10,000 or so Indian nationals, who are also unpopular with the Malagasys because of their social clannishness and their wealth, acquired through control of the textile and jewellery trades and of urban real estate. Administratively, the Asians are organized into *congrégations*, each headed by a representative chosen by them but appointed by and responsible to the government. A Chinese community, numbering about 10,000, is dispersed throughout the east-coast region, where they are principally employed as grocers, small-scale bankers, and traders in agricultural produce.

More than 82% of the Malagasy still live in rural areas, but the towns are attracting an ever-larger percentage of the fast-growing youthful population, thus aggravating urban socio-economic problems. Antananarivo, the capital, is by far the largest city (estimated population 662,585 in 1985) and continues to expand, as do all the six provincial capitals.

Recent History

MERVYN BROWN

FRENCH RULE

In 1896 France invaded and annexed Madagascar. The imposition of colonial rule did not, however, resolve the basic ethnic conflict between the dominant Merina tribe, based on the central plateau, and the coastal peoples (*côtiers*), most of whom had been forcibly incorporated into the Merina kingdom in the early 19th century. The work of British Protestant missionaries had been mainly confined to the plateau area and tended to reinforce the differences between the Merina and the *côtiers*.

By 1904 the French had completed their conquest of the island and integrated it with France's economy. Nationalist feeling among the educated Merina was subsequently demonstrated by increasing demands for French citizenship. However, the slow pace of the official policy of assimilation caused their leaders to aim instead for independence. Nationalist hopes were encouraged by the institution in 1946 of a more liberal system of government, whereby Madagascar elected deputies to the French parliament. A predominantly Merina party in favour of independence, the Mouvement démocratique pour la rénovation malgache (MDRM), won all three Malagasy seats in the French national assembly in that year. However, fears of a resumption of Merina domination resulted in the formation by *côtiers* of the Parti des déshérités de Madagascar (PADESM), which was opposed to early independence. The subsequent rapid growth of PADESM was one of the factors that provoked a violent revolt in 1947, organized by extremist factions of the MDRM, in which about 80,000 people were killed. The MDRM was suppressed, its three deputies sentenced to death or life imprisonment (later commuted to exile in France) and political activity suspended.

INDEPENDENCE

In 1956 the French *loi cadre* instituted universal suffrage and transferred a significant share in executive power to the Malagasy. The predominantly *côtier*-supported Parti social démocrate (PSD), formed from progressive elements of PADESM, and led by a schoolteacher, Philibert Tsiranana, emerged as the principal party. In October 1958 Madagascar became, as the Malagasy Republic, an autonomous state within the French Community, and in 1959 Tsiranana was elected president. Full independence was achieved on 26 June 1960.

Opposition to the PSD

Following Tsiranana's accession to power, the PSD, which practised a moderate, pragmatic socialism, was joined by nearly all of its early rivals. The only significant opposition was the left-wing Parti du congrès de l'indépendance de Madagascar (AKFM), led by Richard Andriamanjato, a Merina Protestant pastor and mayor of Antananarivo. The rivalry between the two parties reinforced the long-standing conflict between Merina and *côtiers*; however, the PSD's political dominance was maintained throughout the decade following independence.

In the late 1960s, however, the economy deteriorated, and there was increasing opposition to the government's authoritarianism and subservience to French interests. In April 1971 peasants in the region of Toliary, in the south-west, provoked by excessive taxation and abuses committed by local officials, attacked a number of police posts. Tsiranana attributed this revolt, and the first overt student unrest, a medical students' strike in March 1971, to a 'Maoist plot'. Following the suppression of the uprising by the government, a regional left-wing group, the Mouvement national pour l'indépendence de Madagascar (MONIMA), led by Monja Jaona, became a significant opposition movement, attracting support from students and urban radicals.

Tsiranana, increasingly intolerant of opposition, persisted in strengthening relations with South Africa, and, contrary to the demands of striking students, maintained economic and cultural links with France. As the sole candidate in the presidential election of January 1972, Tsiranana was re-elected with 99.9% of the votes cast, but this result bore little relation to the true state of political opinion. In response to increasing dissatisfaction with government policies, particularly with the continuing French domination of education, students staged a series of strikes, which were joined later by other groups. In May, after 34 people were killed in a violent confrontation between security forces and members of a coalition of students, teachers, workers and urban unemployed, Tsiranana relinquished powers to Gen. Gabriel Ramanantsoa, the Merina chief of staff of Madagascar's armed forces.

MILITARY GOVERNMENT

Under Ramantsoa's leadership, order was quickly restored in the country. At a referendum, which was conducted in October 1972 to determine the future form of Madagascar's government, Ramanantsoa received a mandate from 96% of the voters to govern for a transitional period of five years, pending the establishment of new institutions and a new constitution.

The promotion of Malagasy as the official language and the 'Malagasization' of education was welcomed by student and nationalist opinion, but led to riots and strikes in coastal areas, owing to revived fears of Merina domination. Nationalists and radicals, including the extreme left-wing Mouvement pour le pouvoir prolétarien (MFM), led by Manandafy Rakotonirina, supported the major changes in foreign policy: the establishment of diplomatic relations with the People's Republic of China, the Soviet bloc countries and Arab nations; the withdrawal from the Franc Zone and the Organisation commune africaine et mauricienne (OCAM); and, in particular, the renegotiation of the co-operation agreements with France, which resulted in the evacuation of French air and naval bases.

However, Ramanantsoa's authority was undermined by the worsening trade and financial position, disunity in the armed forces and the government, and continuing disaccord between *côtiers* and Merina. The cabinet was divided between moderates, led by Col Roland Rabetafika, and radicals, led by Col Richard Ratsimandrava, the minister of the interior. The principal cause of dissension was the latter's plans for radical administrative and political reform, based on a revival of the traditional communities, known as *fokontany*.

Ratsimandrava and Ratsiraka

On 31 December 1974 the mobile police, a mainly *côtier* force, staged an attempted coup in protest at Merina domination of the armed forces, resulting in a prolonged crisis. In February 1975 Ramanantsoa transferred power to Col Richard Ratsimandrava, who was, however, assassinated six days later. Gen. Gilles Andriamahazo immediately assumed power, and formed an 18-member directorate. Martial law and press censorship were imposed, and political parties suspended.

In June 1975 some 300 men who had been charged with involvement in Ratsimandrava's assassination were acquitted, except for three men discovered at the scene of the murder. Later that month Andriamahazo was succeeded as head of state by Lt-Commdr Didier Ratsiraka, a *côtier* and a former minister of foreign affairs. Ratsiraka subsequently established a supreme revolutionary council (CSR), originally entirely military, to supervise a government that principally comprised civilians. Martial law was lifted, but press censorship was retained. Banks, insurance and shipping companies, the petroleum refinery and mineral resources were nationalized, followed by the leading foreign trading company, the Société Marseillaise. In September Ratsiraka published details of his policy, entitled *boky mena* (Little Red Book) or 'Charter of the Malagasy Socialist Revolution', in which he pledged to carry out administrative and agrarian reforms based on the *fokontany*, reorganize the armed forces as an 'army of development' and pursue a non-aligned foreign policy. At a referendum, which took place in December, 94.66 of voters approved a new constitution, which incorporated the tenets of the Charter, and the appointment of Ratsiraka as president for a term of seven years. The country was renamed the Democratic Republic of Madagascar, and the 'Second Republic' was proclaimed.

THE SECOND REPUBLIC

The new 'revolutionary' institutions were the presidency, the CSR (which soon became predominantly civilian), the military committee for development (CMD) with purely advisory functions, a constitutional high court, a national people's assembly, and a cabinet of ministers appointed by the president. In March Ratsiraka formed the Avant-garde de la révolution malgache (AREMA) as the nucleus of the Front national pour la défense de la révolution socialiste malgache (FNDR), the only political organization permitted by the constitution. Several existing parties subsequently joined the FNDR, including the AKFM, MONIMA, the MFM and the Elan populaire pour l'unité nationale, known as the Vonjy which comprised left-wing elements of the former PSD).

With the help of the administrative network and the traditional support given to the government party in the rural areas, AREMA won the majority of seats in local government elections, which took place between March and June 1977, resulting in division within the FNDR. MONIMA withdrew from the FNDR, and was subsequently proscribed. In legislative elections in June, AREMA won 112 of the 137 seats in the national assembly. Nevertheless, a number of disparate right-wing and left-wing factions had emerged within the body of AREMA. The main conservative elements were the Merina bourgeoisie, based in Antananarivo, and the Council of Malagasy Churches (FFKM), representing both Protestants and Catholics. Neither group differed openly with Ratsiraka's version of socialism but, for different reasons, criticized its application. Religious leaders complained of the widespread corruption, while Merina businessmen, albeit pleased with the nationalization of the economy, felt that the government had unduly favoured the *côtiers* in the distribution of the profits and had been incompetent in economic management. In August the membership of the CSR was extended to include leaders of the former political parties, and more *côtiers*, in an effort to restore political equilibrium.

During 1978–79 sporadic violence occurred in the rural provinces, which suffered from extreme drought. The unrest increased in late 1980, after Monja Jaona called for a general strike and was arrested, prompting demonstrations by university students, who clashed violently with security forces in early February 1981. Ratsiraka, however, released Jaona from detention; MONIMA subsequently rejoined the FNDR, and Jaona was appointed to the CSR. Ratsiraka, meanwhile, attempted to establish himself in the international community as a spokesman for the developing countries and as the leading advocate of the demilitarization of the Indian Ocean. His 'non-aligned' foreign policy manifested itself chiefly in hostility to what he perceived as Western imperialism, in conjunction with close relations with the USSR and other Eastern bloc countries. A specially close link was established with the Democratic People's Republic of Korea, which provided soldiers for Ratsiraka's personal bodyguard.

Political and Economic Challenges

In January 1982 Ratsiraka announced his candidature for a second term as president. Later that month a conspiracy to overthrow the government was discovered. Following a severe deterioration in the economy, Ratsiraka was obliged to adopt austerity measures imposed by the IMF. Consequently, with his prestige impaired and the island's economy weakened, Ratsiraka appeared vulnerable to the challenge raised by Monja Jaona's declaration of his candidacy for election to the presidency. At the presidential election, which took place in November, however, Ratsiraka was re-elected by 80.17% of the vote, while Jaona won only 19.83% of the votes cast. Jaona refused to accept the result, attributing it to electoral fraud. In December Jaona called for a general strike in support of demands that the results of the election be annulled, and a new poll conducted. Following rioting in mid-December, Jaona was arrested and removed from the CSR.

In August 1983 elections to the 137-member national assembly took place. Political apathy, rather than active opposition to the FNDR leadership, accounted for the high abstention rate; AREMA won nearly 65% of the votes cast, and secured 117 seats in the national assembly. However, MONIMA attracted considerable support in the capital. A new government (which closely resembled the previous cabinet) was subsequently appointed.

Social Unrest

Urban violence increased dramatically in the 1970s and early 1980s, with groups of unemployed harassing and extorting money from people in the capital, especially those opposed to the government. To counter their activities, students and other youths mainly of bourgeois families organized vigilante groups who practised the oriental martial art of kung-fu. Clashes between the two groups resulted in a ban on the practice of kung-fu in September 1984, which provoked further rioting from kung-fu adherents. In December some 50 people were killed in fighting between TTS and exponents of kung-fu. In February 1985 a reorganization of the council of ministers, which included new appointments to four ministries responsible for economic reform and development, was intended to confirm the regime's socialist direction in the face of 'deviationist' tendencies and increased liberalism in the economic sector. In August security forces attacked the headquarters of the kung-fu societies, which the government accused of planning a coup attempt; some 50 people were killed and over 200 arrested. (At the trial of 245 kung-fu adherents in March 1988, the majority of the defendants were acquitted.)

In November 1986 Ratsiraka provoked renewed opposition through proposals for a number of reforms of higher education. Following a series of protests and boycotts by students and university authorities, the government decided to postpone the introduction of the reforms for a further academic year. Nevertheless, unrest continued through the early months of 1987, owing to the government's failure to comply with demands for the release of 40 students arrested during the disturbances, the withdrawal of the security forces from the university campus and the abandonment of the entire reform programme. Order was restored only after the government agreed to withdraw the proposed reforms.

In the rural south of Madagascar there were further outbreaks of violence in 1986–87, following severe famine in the region. In November 1986 violent demonstrations, resulting in a number of deaths, took place at Toamasina, the principal Malagasy port, in protest at food shortages and the introduction of measures to rationalize the port. Violence erupted again in early 1987, when Indian and Pakistani traders in southern towns were attacked, and their shops and houses were burnt and looted. During the disturbances there were about 14 deaths, and Indian families, many holding French nationality, took refuge at the French consulate or fled to Réunion. The Asian community had long been unpopular with the Malagasys, who resented its control of the retail sector and relative prosperity. In June 56 people who had taken part in the riots against the Indo-Pakistani community received prison sentences.

In 1987 opposition to Ratsiraka appeared to be increasing within the FNDR, partly as a result of disagreement with the government's reaction to the student strikes and other disturbances. The MSM and the Vonjy, joined later by the Parti socialiste monima (VSM), began to co-operate openly with MONIMA in opposing government policies and, from May 1987, in demands for the resignation of the government and the holding of new elections. MSM, Vonjy and MONIMA also decided to contest the presidential elections, which were due to take place in 1989. Ratsiraka subsequently announced that legislative and local government elections, scheduled for 1988, would be postponed respectively until May and September 1989. In February 1988 the prime minister, Gen. Désiré Rakotoarijaona, resigned, ostensibly on grounds of ill-health, and was succeeded by the minister of public works, Lt-Col Victor Ramahatra. In January 1989 the constitution was amended to allow Ratsiraka to bring forward the presidential election from November to March. In February the MFM, Vonjy and VSM announced the formation of an opposition alliance, the Alliance démocratique de Madagascar (ADM), but retained separate presidential candidates. Restrictions on the freedom of the press were relaxed in February, and in the following month Ratsiraka announced the permanent abolition of press censorship.

At the presidential election, which took place in March 1989, Ratsiraka was returned for a third term of office, receiving 62% of the total votes cast (compared with more than 80% at the previous election). Manandafy Rakotonirina of the MFM (which had now moved from the extreme left to a market-orientated liberalism) obtained 20% of the poll, while the Vonjy candidate, Dr Jérôme Marojama Razanabahiny secured 15% and Monja Jaona of MONIMA only 3%. Later in March a new political movement, the AKFM/Fanavaozana, was formed by Richard Andriamanjato, in response to the failure of the AKFM to support his presidential candidature. In mid-April five people were killed in rioting, following allegations by the ADM of serious irregularities in balloting during the presidential election. The membership of the cabinet remained unchanged following Ratsiraka's inauguration, but six members of the CSR, including Manandafy and Andriamanjato, were dismissed for opposing his re-election. At the end of April the ADM declared its intention to boycott the forthcoming legislative elections, but this threat was withdrawn when Ratsiraka promised to allow representatives of the opposition parties to observe polling procedures. At the legislative elections in May, AREMA increased its previously substantial parliamentary majority by a further three seats, winning 120 of the 137 parliamentary seats. The MFM, which obtained seven seats, rejected the results, alleging fraud. The Vonjy secured four seats, the AKFM/Fanavaozana three seats, the original AKFM two seats and MONIMA only one. The abstention rate was high, averaging 25% of registered voters and reaching almost 35% in some urban constituencies.

Political Reform

Despite AREMA's electoral success, widespread disillusionment with the government continued among the intellectual and urban classes. In August 1989 Ratsiraka reorganized both the CSR and the government, removing members of doubtful loyalty to himself and replacing them with strong supporters. The fragile opposition alliance was divided by the reappointment of Monja Jaona to the CSR, together with the vice-president of the Vonjy and some minor opposition figures, while several economic and technical specialists were appointed to the government. Shortly before the reorganization, Ratsiraka convened a meeting of the FNDR, the first since 1982, at which the constituent parties were invited to submit proposals for the future of the FNDR and a possible revision of the 1975 constitution. He also consulted privately with leaders of the churches and other opinion groups. However, demands by the Council of Malagasy Churches for the abolition of the FNDR's monopoly on political activity, as well as the elimination of socialist references in the constitution, received wide support.

In the first round of local government elections (to the *fokontany*) in September 1989, AREMA again gained the majority of votes, except in Antananarivo, but the average abstention rate was 30%. AREMA's electoral strength and the divisions among his opponents enabled Ratsiraka to limit constitutional changes. The amendments adopted by parliament in December abolished the requirement for political parties to be members of the FNDR, and thus effectively dissolved the FNDR itself. However, the privileged status of socialism in the constitution was retained. Nevertheless, provisions were made for a multi-party democracy, backed by the economic liberalism imposed by the IMF and the new freedom of the press, which opposition newspapers were using increasingly to criticize the government. In the early months of 1990 the formation of a number of new parties was announced. Two former PSD ministers established a centre-right party, the Mouvement des démocrates chrétiens malgaches (MDCM), while the Vonjy was seriously weakened by the defection of André Resampa and nine other leading members to form a new Parti socio-démocrate, with Resampa as secretary-general.

In March 1990 the government formally permitted the resumption of multi-party politics. Numerous organizations subsequently emerged, some of them small left-wing parties supporting the president which joined with AREMA, the old AKFM and elements of Vonjy and MONIMA, to form a new coalition, the Mouvement militant pour le socialisme malagasy (MMSM). Other new parties, notably the Union nationale pour le développement et la démocratie (UNDD), led by a medical professor, Albert Zafy, joined the MFM, AKFM/Fanavaozana and the newly-formed MDC and PSD in opposition to the government. The MFM now changed its name from Mouvement pour le pouvoir prolétarien to Mouvement pour le progrès de Madagascar, while retaining the same Malagasy initials, MFM.

On 13 May 1990 a group of armed rebels seized control of the radio station at Antananarivo and broadcast a statement announcing that Ratsiraka's regime had been overthrown; and an opposition crowd gathered outside the station to demonstrate their support. Six people were killed and 50 injured in the subsequent suppression of the revolt by security forces. Of the 11 rebels arrested and brought to trial in December, several were acquitted and the others received short prison sentences.

Meanwhile, the withdrawal of Soviet support following the collapse of communism in the USSR compelled Ratsiraka to become more dependent on Western nations, particularly France, for economic aid. Improved relations with France were demonstrated by a state visit by President Mitterrand in June 1990, during which it was announced that Madagascar's $750m. debt to France had been cancelled and that France would be permitted to resume use of the facilities at the naval base at Antsiranana.

In mid-1990 the Conseil chrétien des églises de Madagascar (FFKM) invited all political associations to attend conferences, which were to take place in August and December 1990, to discuss a programme of reform. However, Ratsiraka criticized the FFKM's intervention, and parties belonging to the MMSM refused to attend the conferences. At the conference, which took place in December, 16 opposition factions, together with trade unions and other groups, established an informal alliance, under the name Forces vives (FV) to co-ordinate proposals for constitutional reform. The leading figures of FV were Zafy (UNDD), Manandafy (MFM) and Andriamanjato (AKFM/Fanavaozana). In the same month the national people's assembly adopted legislation that abolished press censorship, ended the state monopoly of radio and television and permitted the establishment of private broadcasting stations in partnership with the government. In January 1991 Ratsiraka announced that further constitutional amendments would be adopted by the assembly at its next meeting in May. It was later indicated that the main change would be the replacement of the supreme revolutionary council by an elected senate.

Confrontation and General Strike

At the session of the national people's assembly in May 1991, FV supporters forced their way into the chamber to submit their alliance's proposals for amending the constitution; these included the elimination of references to socialism, a reduction in the powers of the president and a limit on the number of terms he could serve. However, the only amendments considered were those presented by the government, which, although numerous, did not meet the FV's basic demands. In early June the FV leadership demanded that a constitutional conference be convened. When the government failed to respond, the FV called a general strike from 10 June, and began a series of peaceful demonstrations, in support of demands for the resignation of the president and the replacement of the government by a new 'provisional government', which would include opposition leaders. The army and police did not intervene in the demonstrations, and similar gatherings took place in the provincial capitals.

The strike was widely supported in the civil service, banks, major firms and transport and, together with the daily demonstrations, resulted in the suspension of economic activity in the capital. In July 1991 various negotiations between the FV and the MMSM, with the mediation of the FFKM or the French embassy, failed, owing to the FV's insistence on the resignation of the president. Ratsiraka refused to resign, on the grounds that he had been democratically elected. In response, the FV maintained that the 1989 elections were not democratic (since only political parties adhering to the FNDR were allowed to operate), and denounced abuses of human rights and widespread corruption in the government and in the president's family. In mid-July the FV appointed its own provisional government, with a retired general, Jean Rakotoharison, as president and Zafy as prime minister. 'Ministers' of the provisional government then began to occupy various ministry buildings, with the assistance of civil servants observing the strike. Later in July Ratsiraka announced a state of emergency, reimposed censorship, and prohibited mass meetings. This had little effect, however, as the army and police took no action to enforce it. In the next few days Zafy and three other FV 'ministers' were abducted and held in various army camps. There were also murders of several FV leaders in Toamasina and Antsiranana.

On 28 July 1991 Ratsiraka announced the dismissal of his government and pledged to organize a referendum on a new constitution by the end of the year. At a demonstration on the folllowing day, however, the FV insisted on the president's resignation, the lifting of the state of emergency and the release of their 'ministers' (they were released unharmed on the following day). On 8 August Ratsiraka nominated a new prime minister Guy Razanamasy, the mayor of Antananarivo, who invited the FV to participate in the government. The offer was rejected and on 10 August the FV organized a large but peaceful protest march on the president's residence to demand his resignation. The president's bodyguard fired into the crowd, killing 100 and wounding many more. On the same day a further 20 people were killed in the suppression of a similar demonstration in Mahajanga. The French government subsequently suspended military aid and advised Ratsiraka to resign, offering him asylum in France. The Roman Catholic archbishop of Antananarivo joined those calling for the president's resignation, and the FFKM announced that it was abandoning its role as mediator and would henceforth support the FV. Later that month Ratsiraka declared Madagascar to be a federation of six states, under his presidency, and claimed to command the support of five provinces, where AREMA continued to hold the majority of seats in regional councils. On 26 August Razanamasy formed a government, which contained some defectors from the FV, including Resampa. He also modified the state of emergency, but threatened that civil servants would be dismissed unless they returned to work by 4 September. On that day, however, the FV, which had denounced the new government as 'puppets' of Ratsiraka, organized a massive demonstration, which halted all economic activity in Antananarivo.

During September and October the FV continued to organize frequent demonstrations and maintain the general strike at an effective level, ensuring the closure of all ports except for Toamasina. Ratsiraka was sustained by support from the provinces and was able to exploit divisions within the opposition, notably between Manandafy's MFM, which favoured a constitutional settlement, and the majority of radicals led by Zafy. Meanwhile, the army and the aid donors increased their pressure on all parties to reach a settlement including a consensus government.

Interim Settlement

Finally, after an ultimatum from the army, an interim agreement, signed on 31 October 1991 by Razanamasy and representatives of the FV, MMSM and FFKM, provided for the suspension of the constitution and the creation of a transitional government, which was to remain in office for a maximum period of 18 months, pending the adoption of a new constitution and the holding of elections. Under the agreement, Ratsiraka remained as president with the ceremonial duties of head of state and titular head of the armed forces, but relinquished all executive powers. A 31-member Haute autorité de l'état (HAE), under Zafy, and a 130-member advisory Conseil de redressement économique et social (CRES), headed jointly by Andriamanjato and Manandafy, replaced the CSR and the national people's assembly, while Razanamasy's government was to be expanded to include members of the FV.

In February 1992 the interim authorities suspended the elected bodies (nearly all AREMA and supporting Ratsiraka) at the various levels of local government and replaced them with special delegations. In the same month proposals for a new constitution and electoral code were compiled at a series of regional forums, and delegates were elected to attend a national forum, which was convened in Antananarivo in late March. After attacks against the conference hall and an attempt to assassinate Zafy, the forum was moved to a military camp. At the end of March security forces fired at supporters of Ratsiraka, led by Monja Jaona, who had marched on the camp; eight people, including a former minister, were killed.

Ratsiraka continued to maintain his intention to stand for re-election, and called for a federalist draft constitution to be submitted to a referendum as an alternative to the unitary draft being considered by the forum. After much debate, a clause was included in the electoral code excluding the candidature of anyone who had been elected president twice under the second republic. The constitution adopted by the forum, subject to approval by the transitional authorities and at a national referendum, was of a parliamentary type, with a constitutional president, a senate and a national assembly elected by proportional representation, and executive power vested in a prime minister elected by the assembly. The referendum on the constitution was scheduled for 21 June 1992, and was to be followed by presidential elections in August and the legislative elections two months later. However, continuing lack of agreement within the government and the HAE regarding the exclusion of Ratsiraka from the presidential elections and the extent of the future president's powers delayed the publication of the draft constitution and therefore caused the referendum to be postponed. Despite attempts by federalist supporters of Ratsiraka to disrupt the referendum, the new constitution was approved on 19 August by 73% of votes cast.

The federalists subsequently intensified pressure for Ratsiraka's right to stand for re-election. After a number of violent incidents involving federalists, including the temporary seizure of the airport at Antsiranana and the bombing of the railway track linking Toamasina and the capital, the transitional authorities agreed to allow Ratsiraka to contest the election. A further seven candidates, including Zafy and Manandafy, were also to participate in the elections. In the first round of the presidential election, which was conducted peacefully under international supervision on 25 November, Zafy secured 45% of votes cast, while Ratsiraka obtained 29% and Manandafy 10% of the vote. The second round, which was contested by the two leading candidates, took place on 10 February 1993. Most of the other candidates transferred their support to Zafy, who obtained a substantial majority of 67% of the vote, against 33% for Ratsiraka. Zafy was formally invested as president in late March, amid violent clashes between security forces and federalists in northern Madagascar. However, the transitional authorities remained in place, pending the formation of a new government after the legislative elections (which were rescheduled for 16 June). In accordance with a constitutional stipulation, Zafy resigned as president of the UNDD in May.

In early June 1993 two people were killed and 40, including Monja Jaona, arrested, after security forces attacked federalists who had seized the prefecture building in Toliary. On 16 June the elections to the national assembly (which had been reduced from 184 to 138 seats) were contested under a system of proportional representation by 121 political parties and some 4,000 candidates. Several elements of the FV coalition presented separate lists of candidates; however, the remaining parties in the alliance, known as the Cartel HVR, proved the most successful group, securing 45 seats; Manandafy's MFM obtained 16 seats, while a new pro-Ratsiraka movement, FAMIMA, won only 11 seats. Intensive inter-party negotiations prior to the first meeting of the assembly resulted in some shifting in party support for the various candidates contesting the post of prime minister. In the election on 9 August, Manandafy obtained 32 votes and Roger Ralison (the candidate of the Cartel) 45 votes. The winner, with 55 votes, was Francisque Ravony, who was the favoured candidate of President Zafy and the business community. Ravony, a respected lawyer, and a son-in-law of the former president, Philibert Tsiranana, had served as deputy prime minister in the transitional government. The leader of the AKFM/ Fanavaozana, Richard Andriamanjato, was elected president of the national assembly.

THE THIRD REPUBLIC

At the end of August 1993 Ravony formed a new council of ministers, which was endorsed by 72% of deputies in the national assembly, together with his programme, which laid emphasis on economic recovery based on free-market policies, and measures to eradicate corruption. The latter resulted in the arrest in September of 12 senior civil servants, who were accused of misappropriating World Bank credits equivalent to US $10m. In October Ravony appointed a further three ministers to the government. Effective action regarding economic recovery subsequently proved difficult, however, owing, in part, to the fragmented nature of the national assembly, which comprised some 25 separate parties; these became grouped into two informal coalitions of equal size (and a small number of independent deputies), but neither was specifically a government or opposition organization, and ministers were appointed from both alliances and also from the independent members. Despite the immediate necessity for substantial assistance from the World Bank and the IMF to sustain the economy, a number of deputies opposed the acceptance of structural adjustment measures, imposed by the World Bank and IMF as a precondition to the approval of financial credit, owing to the additional widespread hardship that would ensue. A strike by civil servants in January 1994 demonstrated the difficulty in accepting IMF demands for substantial retrenchment in the civil service and a 'freeze' of public sector salaries. In early 1994 a number of severe cyclones resulted in a further deterioration in the economy, and weakened the government's ability to resist the demands of the World Bank and IMF. In May agreement was reached on the implementation of reforms, and a structural adjustment programme was subsequently adopted (see Economy).

Local government elections, scheduled to take place in October 1993, were repeatedly postponed, owing to lack of agreement concerning proposals to restructure and decentralize government by the establishment of some 28 regional authorities, which would replace the six existing provinces. Although there was general agreement on the aim of decentralization, the substantial cost involved was perceived to be an impediment at a time of severe economic difficulty.

In April 1994 it was reported that the Malagasy authorities had demanded the expulsion of the French ambassador in Antananarivo, Gilles d'Humières, on the grounds that he was involved in attempts to destabilize the government. In June a programme of economic reforms, which had been drafted by the government in conjunction with the World Bank and the IMF, was opposed by a majority of deputies in the national assembly. In July 31 deputies (including Razanamasy and Rakotonirina), belonging to one of the parliamentary coalitions, known as G6, proposed a motion of censure against Ravony's government, which was, however, rejected by 94 of the 138 deputies. In August Ravony reorganized the council of ministers.

As a result of economic considerations and the need to encourage foreign investment, the new government established relations with Israel, South Africa, the Republic of Korea and (for trade and economic purposes only) Taiwan, in a complete reversal of Ratsiraka's original foreign policies.

Economy

MICHAEL CHAPMAN

Revised for this edition by the Editor

Madagascar was classified by the World Bank in 1992 as one of the world's 13 poorest countries. In that year, according to estimates by the World Bank, Madagascar's gross national product (GNP), measured at average 1990–92 prices, was US $2,809m., equivalent to about $230 per head. In 1985–92, it was estimated, GNP per head declined, in real terms, by an annual average of 1.7%, while the population increased by an annual average of 3.1%. Madagascar's gross domestic product (GDP) increased, in real terms, by an average of 1.1% per year in 1980–92. In the mid-1980s it was estimated that 65% of the population were in the subsistence sector. However, the urban population represented more than 23% of this total in 1990.

THE RURAL SECTOR

The rural economy accounts for 80% of Madagascar's export revenues and supplies most of the raw materials needed for industry. In 1992 the agricultural sector (including forestry and fishing) accounted for 33% of GDP and engaged an estimated 75.6% of the country's labour force. The production of both food and export crops, except cotton, either stagnated or declined after President Ratsiraka took power in 1975, mainly as a result of the imposition of doctrinaire socialist principles and natural disasters. The island's agricultural sector also suffered from adverse climatic conditions, a lack of insecticides, spare parts and fertilizers, and the poor maintenance of rural roads. The imposition of co-operative societies and state farms on a reluctant peasantry also contributed to the agricultural sector's poor performance. During 1980–92 agricultural GDP increased by an annual average of 2.4%, considerably below the population growth rate. The introduction of higher producer prices during the 1980s aimed to increase output of food crops, in particular, and eventually to achieve self-sufficiency in food. However, in view of the problems of quotas, low world prices and international competition, a major policy objective is to improve the quality of export crops, while limiting the expansion in output. The diversification of both food and export crops is also a priority. The forestry sector has been badly neglected, and 81% of domestic fuel needs are supplied by wood and charcoal. In 1991, according to FAO estimates, about 26% of the land area was covered by forests. A $66m. aid arrangement was agreed at a donors' meeting in Paris in February 1990 to support the first stage of a long-term environmental action plan. In August 1989 a 'debt-for-nature' exchange, the first for Africa, was arranged: the USA gave the Worldwide Fund For Nature $1m. to buy $2.1m. of government commercial debts at a 55% discount from a consortium of international banks, and to use the money for environmental projects. The experiment proved successful, and further debt-conversion agreements, involving international organizations, were subsequently negotiated.

Paddy rice is the main crop grown by 70% of the population, whose basic food is rice (the average annual per caput consumption is about 135 kg, the highest of any country in the world), and it occupies about 1.25 ha, or approximately one-half the area under cultivation. Output of paddy remained constant at an average annual level of about 2m. metric tons for some years but the cyclones of January 1982 caused flooding which damaged the paddy crop and necessitated imports of about 356,000 tons of rice, at great cost, during that year. In early 1984 a further four cyclones destroyed some 40,000 ha of rice fields, and in March 1986 a cyclone destroyed rice fields and damaged Toamasina, the major port. A further cyclone in January 1990 destroyed rice fields and coffee plantations, especially in the south-east. The area planted to rice was subsequently reduced, while output of potatoes and maize was increased. In 1986 the government abolished virtually all controls on the rice trade, except for a minimum purchasing price of 90 FMG per kg and the maintenance of buffer stocks by the state. The estimated harvest in 1986 was 2.1m. tons, and in 1987 2.2m. tons. Imports of about 162,000 tons were necessary in both years but these were reduced to 75,000 tons in 1989, and to 50,000 tons in 1990 (with production reaching an estimated 2.4m. tons in that year). Severe drought in 1991–92 necessitated some 60,000 tons of imports. Rice production totalled 2.3m. tons in 1991, but increased to 2.5m. tons in 1992. There is a need for improved husbandry and for the introduction of higher-yielding varieties, as well as an improved distribution system. Other important staple crops are maize, cassava, bananas and sweet potatoes.

Madagascar's main cash crops are coffee, vanilla and cloves. The most important is coffee (97% of it robusta, although arabica production is encouraged), which, in the 1980s, accounted for about 24% of total export earnings and engaged 25% of the working population. Output in the 1980s was generally about 80,000–84,000 metric tons per year, almost double the export quota allocated by the International Coffee Organization (ICO). Madagascar thus had considerable quantities for disposal on the non-quota market. Domestic consumption has risen steadily in recent years, to about 15,000 tons per year. There was a dramatic decline in world coffee prices after the ICO agreement collapsed in July 1989, leading to a loss in export revenue of over $20m. that year. Despite a recovery in prices, export earnings from coffee declined further, to 57,965.5m. francs MG, owing, in part, to cyclone damage, and a reduction in quality. Export revenue from coffee amounted to 51,902.0m. francs MG in 1991, increasing slightly to 58,844.1m. francs MG in 1992 (equivalent to 11.8% of total export revenue). A National Coffee Trading Committee was established, with World Bank assistance, in October 1988 to determine pricing and other policies.

Madagascar is the world's largest exporter of vanilla (which accounted for 19.1% of total export revenue in 1992). The USA and France are the main purchasers. Output has fluctuated between 600 metric tons and 1,800 tons a year. Owing to competition from very cheap synthetic substitutes, the value of vanilla is determined by its scarcity, so the government is planning to reduce annual production. Madagascar operates a quota and price cartel system with Réunion and the Comoros. It exported only 967 tons in 1988, although in 1989 exports were about 1,200 tons. In 1991 revenue from exports of vanilla totalled $46m., increasing to $60m. in 1992. In 1993 it was reported that the price of vanilla had increased substantially, despite the cartel system, while illicit exports of the crop reflected disaffection, among farmers.

Production of cloves in the early 1980s was at a level of 10,000–12,000 metric tons per year and accounted for about a quarter of export earnings, but in 1983 the main buyer, Indonesia, suspended purchases and Madagascar was left with large quantities of unsold stocks. New markets were found in Sri Lanka and the Far East, and exports recovered by 1985 to 11,600 tons. In 1987 there was a collapse in world prices, following the emergence of Indonesia as a clove exporter, while liberalization of marketing in Madagascar caused an excess of cloves on the market, depressing prices further. Output declined to 7,100 tons in 1989, when cloves were overtaken by vanilla as the island's principal export crop. Production of cloves declined further, to 8,000 tons in 1992 (a fall of 39% compared with 1991), owing, in part, to the emergence of new exporters, including Brazil.

Small quantities of pepper and ylang-ylang (an essence used in the perfume industry) are also exported. Production of seed cotton declined steadily, from 42,900 metric tons in 1984/85 to 27,000 tons in 1987/88. However, 41,000 tons were harvested in 1988/89 and exports resumed, after a period of several years. Sisal is a minor export crop, adversely affected for a number of years by synthetic substitutes. World prices have improved, but drought in the south in 1988 caused the closure of three major sisal estates. Annual production is 20,000 tons. There are five sugar factories, of which four have been rehabilitated with French aid, increasing their output from 80,000 tons a year to an average of some 120,000 tons in the late 1980s. The fifth factory, near Morondava on the west coast, was built with Chinese assistance and began operating in 1987, with an annual capacity of 22,000 tons. All factories are managed by the state-owned Société Siramamy Malagasy. Production of raw sugar reached 120,000 tons in 1989, but declined to 111,000 tons in 1990, and to 96,000 tons in 1992. Imports of sugar are necessary to meet domestic requirements (which amount to some 130,000 tons per year); in 1992 11,092 tons were imported from Mauritius and Réunion. Most sugar is consumed domestically. Groundnuts, pineapples, coconuts, butterbeans and tobacco are also grown.

Sea fishing by coastal fishermen is being industrialized, with assistance from Japan and France. Shrimp fishing has expanded considerably, and represents the second largest source of export revenue (after vanilla); the shrimp catch reached 8,700 metric tons in 1993. Small quantities of lobster are also exported. In 1991 the total catch amounted to 101,000 tons. Vessels from EC (now European Union—EU) countries fish by agreement for tuna and prawns in Madagascar's exclusive maritime zone, extending to 370 km (200 nautical miles) of the coast. An $18m. tuna canning complex has been established as a joint venture with a French company at Antsiranana, financed predominantly by France and the European Investment Bank (EIB). The EIB, the International Finance Corpn and France are providing funds for Pêcheries de Nossy Bé to replace three trawlers and to modernize the shrimp-processing plant at Hellville in the north-west.

Madagascar has about 10.3m. head of cattle; however, cattle are generally regarded as an indication of wealth rather than as sources of income, and the development of a commercial beef sector is difficult. Nevertheless, there is some ranching and 142,000 metric tons of beef and veal were produced commercially in 1992, according to FAO estimates. Some beef is exported, but volumes have declined in recent years, to about 800 tons a year, despite an EC quota of 11,000 tons. There is an urgent need to revive veterinary sevices, improve marketing and rehabilitate abattoirs, partly to meet EC import standards. Live animals and some canned corned beef are exported to African countries, the Gulf states and Indian Ocean islands. There are scarcely any dairy cattle and the three milk processing plants use imported milk powder. There were some 1.5m. pigs in 1992, according to FAO estimates, but pigmeat is a luxury item and only about 40,000 tons were produced commercially in that year. According to FAO estimates, there were some 1.3m. goats in that year. Poultry is kept on a small-scale, non-commercial basis.

INDUSTRY

Industry accounted for 14% of Madagascar's GDP in 1992; the sector employs only about 3% of the working population. The island's major industrial centres, other than mines, are located in the High Plateaux or near Toamasina port. Food processing accounts for 49% of all industrial value added. Textiles was formerly the second largest sector but has now been superseded by brewing, paper and soap. There are cement plants at Mahajanga and Toamasina. However, in the late 1980s average annual production of cement was only about 40,000 metric tons, necessitating imports of about 250,000 tons per year; by 1990 production had declined to 20,000 tons. A fertilizer plant at Toamasina, which began operations in 1985, produces 90,000 tons per year of urea- and ammonia-based fertilizers. Other industries include the manufacture of wood products and furniture, tobacco, agricultural machinery and the processing of agricultural products. Industrial GDP increased by an annual average of 0.8% in 1980–92, and most plants have been operating at less than one-third of their capacity.

In June 1986 the government introduced a new investment code, which provided incentives for domestic and foreign private investment in activities outside the public sector, particularly in manufacturing for the export market. All military and strategic industries, including those in the energy sector, dockyards and ship repair yards, have remained in the control of the Office militaire national pour les industries stratégiques (OMNIS). The country's fifth investment code, which came into force in January 1990, introduced incentives to attract foreign private investors, in particular. This enactment was strongly opposed by many politicians and also by local business people. Rules regarding foreign exchange and the number of expatriate employees have been relaxed and private investors are granted tax incentives. In the case of small and medium-sized enterprises, profits are exempt from corporation tax for the first five years, after which there is tax relief for a further five years. A number of export processing zones (EPZ) have been established, and have attracted foreign investor's interest, particularly from South-East Asia, Mauritius and France. A preliminary agreement has been signed with a consortium of Hong Kong countries, involving projected investment totalling $650m. over 15 years. A Mauritian firm has commenced production of textile products for the EC market while another Mauritius entrepreneur plans to manufacture paints. Labour is cheaper and corporation tax lower in the Malagasy EPZ than in those in Mauritius, but there are much higher risks for companies producing for export. Between May 1990 and October 1992, 69 new enterprises, financed by foreign capital, were established in Madagascar. The creation of a further 18 companies was expected in the following four years.

In March 1990 the IDA approved a credit of $48m. to finance the government's project to develop private enterprises. The money was to be loaned to private business people, or allocated to the development of training and extension services, to the restructuring of the chamber of commerce and to the establishment of an investment promotion agency. In mid-1994 the International Finance Corporation (IFC) approved an equity investment amounting to about $1.1m. in the Madagascar Capital Development Fund (an investment fund established by a French bank), which was to assist export-orientated companies.

MINING

Madagascar has sizeable deposits of a wide range of minerals, but in many cases they are in remote areas, making commercial exploitation difficult and expensive. However, chromite, graphite and mica are all exported, as are small quantities of semi-precious stones, such as topaz, garnet and amethyst. Chromite output (chromium ores and concentrates) before 1976 was approximately 200,000 metric tons per year, although in the early 1980s production had declined to very low levels. In 1989 output increased to 153,000 tons, compared with 64,200 tons in 1988, but declined to 129,000 tons in 1991 (despite a maximum annual capacity of 160,000 tons. The main deposits of chrome ore are at Andriamena, but it is also mined at Befandriana Nord. Graphite output was also very low in the early 1980s; after increasing to 14,100 tons in 1989, and to 18,500 tons in 1990, production again declined, to 13,500 tons in 1991. Production of mica reached 1,800 tons in 1986, declining to 693 tons in 1988, but recovering to 1,800 tons in 1990. The government is inviting private mining companies to exploit the country's gold deposits, which were nationalized in 1975. Official production has been only a few kilograms a year, but considerable quantities are sold unofficially by small prospectors. France is providing about $1m. towards the study of existing workings and further prospecting. A major project to resume the mining of ilmenite (titanium ore), which ceased in 1977, was launched in 1986. The World Bank is providing partial financial assistance for the project, which is being managed by OMNIS and a subsidiary of Rio Tinto-Zinc (RTZ). Strict environmental restrictions were placed on further World Bank funding and were expected to delay exports from the mine. Zircon and rutile will also be produced, and annual export earnings of $40m. are projected. Other continuing projects include the establishment of a nickel-processing plant, with assistance from the Democratic People's Republic of Korea, and platinum discovered at Andriamena was to be developed with French assistance. In the early 1990s there were also plans to exploit an estimated 100m. tons of bauxite at Manantenina in the south-east of the country.

ENERGY

Madagascar's prospects for reducing fuel imports have been improved by the development of hydroelectric power, a reduction in the cost of imported petroleum (which in 1992 absorbed 11.3% of the country's total export earnings, compared with 16% in 1989) and by the discovery of offshore petroleum deposits. The Andekaleka hydroelectric scheme, which began operations in 1982, supplies Antananarivo and Antsirabe areas, as well as the Andriamena chrome mine. A second stage to extend this grid to Toamasina is planned, but finance has yet to be secured. There are seven hydroelectric stations, providing over two-thirds of electricity demand, while the remainder is generated by thermal installations. However, oil imports in 1991 totalled 340,000 tons, whereas hydroelectricity output represented the energy equivalent of only about 90,000 tons of oil. Fuel wood and charcoal is estimated to provide 80% of the country's total energy needs. Many mines and factories have their own small diesel- or steam-powered generators. In April 1994 the government announced plans for the construction of a solar-energy electricity power plant, at a projected cost of US $3,400m.

In 1980 the government announced that deposits of petroleum had been discovered and that the Petroleum Code would be revised. In the following decade several foreign companies signed concession agreements with the government to prospect in a number of areas, particularly in the Morandava basin, in western Madagascar. In 1990 BHP Australia signed an agreement to explore the Mahajanga area in the north west. As a result of the war in the Persian Gulf in late 1990 and early 1991, interest among Western oil companies in locating deposits of petroleum outside the Gulf region increased and, in Madagascar, Shell began drilling at three onshore sites in mid-1991. In early 1992, however, it appeared that the deposits in the Morandava region were commercially insignificant. Studies are continuing on heavy oil deposits at Tsimororo, but earlier plans to exploit oil shale at Bemolanga have been abandoned, in view of the cost and technical problems involved.

For some years the USSR provided about two-thirds of Madagascar's imports of petroleum, some on a concessionary financing basis. However, in 1988 the USSR suspended deliveries of petroleum to Madagascar, owing to unpaid bills totalling some $240m. Madagascar was subsequently obliged to buy Iranian crude petroleum, without any concessionary terms. Petroleum is also supplied by Libya and Gabon. The Toamasina refinery produces about 350,000 tons of products per year and exports about 70,000–80,000 tons. In early 1994 the government announced that the petroleum sector was to be liberalized, after the Toamasina refinery was damaged by cyclones.

TRANSPORT

Madagascar's mountainous topography has hindered the development of adequate communications. In 1991 there were 34,750 km of classified roads, of which 8,539 km were main roads and 18,382 km were secondary roads; only 5,352 km of the road network were paved. In 1987 there were 39,500 km of unclassified roads, used only in favourable weather. In 1988 a programme to rehabilitate 4,781 km of roads (of which 1,500 km tarred) by 1993 was initiated. The $144m. project was to be financed by the IDA, the EC, Switzerland and Norway. In June 1989 the European Development Fund (EDF) granted $10m. for road rehabilitation in the north and west of the country. In mid-1994 a programme to rehabilitate a further 500 km of main roads, at an estimated cost of $81m., was under consideration by the EDF.

In 1993 there were 1,095 km of railway. Three lines in the north of the country primarily served the capital, while the fourth (in the south) linked Fianarantsoa to Manakara port. In 1986 the World Bank agreed to lend $12m. to finance the rehabilitation of the northern railway network, and the 40-km extension of one line. A 72-km extension to a line on the northern system was opened in 1986.

Domestic air services are important to Madagascar, on account of its size, difficult terrain and poor quality of road and rail networks. There are 211 airfields, two-thirds of which are privately owned. The international airport is at Antananarivo. The national airline, Air Madagascar, is two-thirds owned by the government and one-third by Air France. Under the government's new liberalization measures, Air Madagascar lost its monopoly on domestic services. In October 1992 external services were substantially reduced.

Toamasina and Mahajanga, the principal seaports, suffer from lack of storage space and equipment. Toamasina port handles about 70% of Madagascar's foreign trade and was in the process of being enlarged and modernized, until 80% of the port was destroyed by a cyclone in March 1986. In January 1987 the IDA agreed to provide a $16m. credit for a $34.8m. project to rehabilitate 10 ports. France, Germany and the UK are also financing the project. Toamasina is independently managed but the other ports are operated by the Malagasy Ports Authority. The parastatal Société Malgache de Transports Maritimes has four ocean-going ships, while coastal shipping is mostly handled by private firms. The country's 18 ports handled a total of 791,700 tons of freight in 1989. In 1984 the government initiated a development project to restore more than 200 km of the Pangalanes canal, which runs for 600 km near the east coast from Toamasina to Farafangana. In early 1990 432 km of the canal between Toamasina and Mananjary were navigable.

TOURISM

In 1989 the government introduced a tourism investment programme, which aimed to achieve 100,000 tourist arrivals by 1995. The government planned to exploit specialist markets represented by the growing number of visitors who are attracted by Madagascar's unusual varieties of wildlife. A number of state-owned hotels were transferred to private-sector ownership, and a French adviser was appointed to prepare a new tourism plan. The French group Savana and its parent-company Pullman–International Hotels were to implement the tourism project at a total cost of $234m., of which $30m. was provided by the government, mainly for infrastructural costs. An hotel group, partly owned by Mauritian interests, began the construction of a 200-room luxury hotel in the capital. In 1989 net tourism receipts were estimated at $22m. The number of tourist arrivals rose from 35,400 in 1988, to 39,000 in 1989. There were 4,208 hotel rooms and 52,923 tourist arrivals in 1990, when tourist receipts increased to $37m.; in 1991, however, the number of tourist arrivals declined by 34%, to 34,891, in reaction to the country's internal unrest.

EXTERNAL TRADE AND BALANCE OF PAYMENTS

During the period 1977 to 1987 Madagascar's unfavourable trade balance steadily worsened. Despite a brief rise in the value of exports in 1980, imports increased even faster than before, owing to the official policy of industrialization and overriding emphasis on investment.

As the balance-of-payments problems became increasingly severe, the government was obliged to yield to pressure from the IMF, the World Bank and Western aid donors and creditors to liberalize trade and to adjust the Malagasy franc exchange rate. The reforms succeeded in reducing the external current account deficit from 14.6% of GDP in 1980 to 8.7% in 1986, when it was $136m. The deficit declined from $149m. in 1988, to $82m. in 1989, as a result of improved export earnings in that year. Following a sharp increase in imports, the deficit on the current account rose to $251m. in 1990, but declined to $188m. in 1991, and to $136m. in 1992. The government has aimed to reduce import restrictions and to introduce comprehensive tariff reforms. In February 1988 simplified import procedures were introduced, and the government also announced the removal of export duties from all goods except those, such as coffee, handled by state marketing boards. The trade deficit was converted to a surplus of $1m. in 1989; in 1990, however, a deficit of $248m. was recorded, which declined to $102m. in 1991, but increased to $138m. in 1992. The principal exports in 1992 were vanilla, shrimps, coffee, and cloves and clove oil. The principal imports in that year included minerals (chiefly crude petroleum), chemical products, machinery, and vehicles.

The principal source of imports in 1992 was France (30.3%); other major suppliers were Germany, the USA and Japan. France was also the principal market for exports (accounting for 26.6% of exports in that year); other important purchasers were the USA, Germany and Japan. The importance of the USSR as a source of imports began to decline in the second half of 1988, following the expiry of petroleum oil supply contracts.

ECONOMIC POLICY, PLANNING AND AID

Ratsiraka's 'strategy for development', initially embodied in a Plan covering three stages over the period 1978–2000, proved unsuccessful after only two years, principally as a result of the government's failure to take into consideration Madagascar's inadequate supply of the raw materials which were needed to operate some of the projected (or even existing) factories, the growing rice deficit, and the lack of spare parts and consumer-goods inducements. By mid-1980 the external debt had risen to $680m., and Ratsiraka appealed successfully to the IMF for an $85m. loan, and later asked France to cancel Madagascar's debt. By 1981 many of Madagascar's traditional suppliers refused to grant credit to its government.

In return for a further stand-by loan of about $80m. in May 1982, the IMF required the government to devalue the Malagasy franc by 15%; to channel state investments into the agricultural sector, to increase payments to farmers for paddy rice and cotton; and to restrict any increase in the minimum wage to 4.5%. Fulfilment of these and other drastic demands was immediately visible in the 1983 budget allocations, and was also reflected by a revision of national policies under which the state would either retain its monopoly or hold a majority share in certain vital sectors such as mining and hydrocarbons, but in most other areas would allow private entrepreneurs to invest in, and initiate, new projects. Although there was an improvement in the supply of provisions to urban consumers, as a result of the increase in payments to farmers and the liberalization of the rice trade in 1983–84, there was a noticeable rise in the cost of living, while successive devaluations of the Malagasy franc, together with the failure to make any appreciable increase in the wages of non-agricultural workers, placed the cost of basic necessities beyond the means of the average Malagasy. Even with the overall improvements in Madagascar's economic situation, the declining level of production, especially in export crops, caused an increasing dependence on costly imports (particularly fuel and rice) and on foreign aid.

In April 1985 the IMF approved a stand-by arrangement of SDR 29.5m. to support Madagascar's economic and financial programme during 1985–86. At a World Bank-sponsored Consultative Group meeting in April 1986 donors made commitments of about $600m. for 1986–87. In May the IMF agreed to grant Madagascar two facilities, totalling SDR 32.7m., to offset the effects of the cyclone in March and the shortfalls in export earnings during the previous year. A devaluation of the Malagasy franc in August (see below), and further liberalization of trade and distribution, encouraged the IMF to provide a three-year stand-by arrangement of SDR 30m. in September. In October the 'Paris Club' of Western creditor governments agreed to reschedule SDR 73.8m. of debts for 1986 and SDR 99.2m. for 1987.

In June 1986 a new investment code was introduced, providing incentives for domestic and foreign investment, particularly in manufacturing for the export market. Also in 1986 the government abolished most state controls on the internal rice trade. In 1987 further measures were introduced to encourage exports by allowing exporters to fix prices directly with foreign purchasers, and imposing a duty, equal to 10% of the import licence, on importers. The Malagasy franc was devalued by 20% in August 1986. There were several subsequent adjustments, and in June 1987 the currency was devalued by a further 41%. The government's reform measures resulted in the approval of a $100m. structural adjustment loan arrangement from the World Bank and several bilateral donors. In August 1987 the IMF agreed to provide a new stand-by facility of SDR 42.2m. over three years, which included a structural adjustment facility. In the same month the 'London Club' of Western commercial creditors agreed to reschedule $59.4m. of debt.

At a meeting in Paris in January 1988, the World Bank-sponsored Consultative Group agreed to provide Madagascar with $700m. in quick-disbursing aid, conditional upon the rescheduling of debts due to the 'Paris Club' later in the year. The donors strongly commended the Malagasy government's structural adjustment programme. The budget deficit had been reduced to the equivalent of 4% of GDP in 1986 (compared with 18.4% in 1980), and price controls had been lifted from most products and fixed profit margins had been virtually abolished by the end of 1987. In early 1988 the government stated its commitment to rationalize the public sector by closing loss-making nationalized enterprises and selling off many others. At the end of 1988 the IMF approved a 10-month stand-by facility of SDR 13.3m. to replace a credit of SDR 30m. which had expired in March 1988, without being fully drawn. Conditions of the new arrangement included further trade liberalization, stricter controls on government spending, the return of state banks to private-sector ownership, the opening up of financial markets to foreign competition, and improved credit access for producers. This was in addition to the three-year structural adjustment facility due to expire in August 1990. The IDA released $125m. in July 1988 to support the government's plan to reform the public sector, and made available a credit of $22m. for social programmes.

The new IMF agreement opened the way for further pledges from donors attending a meeting in October 1988 of the 'Paris Club' of Western official creditors, who agreed to reschedule $212m. of debt and to cancel $37m. of principal. The Federal Republic of Germany cancelled $116m. of debt in 1988, and in 1989 France decided to write off one-third of the debt owed to it, or about $471.4m. Debt-servicing costs were reduced from $271m. in 1987 to $221m. in 1988. The latest debt relief measures decreased further costs, but in 1988 debt servicing still represented 53.7% of export earnings. In May 1989 the IMF gave approval for a three-year enhanced structural adjustment facility (ESAF), to replace the 10-month stand-by agreement. The credit of SDR 76.9m. was to give support to the programme covering the period 1989–1991 which aims to promote growth of per caput income in real terms and to stabilize the financial sector. As part of the liberalization programme the government removed all price subsidies in March 1989.

Total external debt was estimated at $3,400m. at the end of 1989, although this represented a decline in US dollar terms compared with 1987, a result of devaluation since the middle of that year. However, total external debt had increased to $3,805m. by the end of 1992. Despite the 'Paris Club' rescheduling of debt-service arrangements in 1988, debt-service payments still represented 34.3% of the value of exports of goods and services in 1991; however, the cost of debt-servicing declined to 20.7% in 1992. Madagascar received a total of $557m. in official development assistance from members of the OECD's development assistance committee in 1991, of which $342m. was in grant form. The main bilateral donors were France and Germany, while the World Bank's IDA and the EC were the principal multilateral donors. In 1988 the rate of inflation (which had declined to an average of 9.9% in 1984) increased by an average of 27%, owing to the abolition of price controls and the devaluation of the currency, which resulted in higher prices for imported goods. According to IMF estimates, however, the rate declined to an average of 11.8% in 1990, and to 8.6% in 1991; consumer prices increased by 14.5% in 1992, and by 10.0% in 1993.

Liberalization of the banking sector has attracted foreign private banks to Madagascar. Banque Nationale de Paris is the main shareholder owning 55% of Banque Malgache de l'Océan Indien (BMOI), which was officially opened in January 1990. Belgian and German banks own 20% of BMOI, and about 300 Malagasy shareholders own 25%. In mid-1994 the government announced plans to establish five new banks and a stock exchange in Madagascar.

In 1991 a public investment programme (1991–1993), financed by the World Bank, IMF and other international donors, was initiated. The programme, which cost an estimated US $1,000m., again placed emphasis on the liberalization of trade and the financial sector, the encouragement of foreign and domestic investment, a reduction in the role of parastatal bodies, and increased producer prices. Following a prolonged general strike in the second half of 1991 (see Recent History), however, the programme was deferred, pending the fulfilment of certain conditions, which included the transfer of a number of parastatal organizations to the private sector and a reduction in public expenditure.

The general strike in 1991 resulted in a severe deterioration in the financial sector: despite a substantial decline in capital expenditure, the ensuing fall in tax revenue, in conjunction with increased expenditure on personnel, prompted a rise in the budgetary deficit in 1991, to 272,400m. francs MG (equivalent to 5.2% of GDP). Reserves of foreign exchange, which totalled US $223.7m. at the end of 1988 (excluding gold), declined to $89m. Economic conditions failed to improve in 1992, owing to the continued lack of political stability. In 1993 the new government initiated negotiations with the Bretton Wood institutions to obtain funding for a further economic reform programme. Following a report by a joint mission (which was dispatched to Madagascar by the World Bank and IMF in early 1994), however, the organizations insisted that a number of economic reforms be implemented as a precondition to the disbursement of funds to support a new structural adjustment programme. Severe cyclones in early 1994 resulted in a further deterioration in economic conditions, increasing the necessity for substantial assistance, while the French government indicated that continuing aid for reforms was conditional on an agreement between Madagascar and the Bretton Wood institutions. In May the government accepted the conditions imposed by the World Bank and IMF, notably the 'floating' of the Malagasy franc (which resulted in an immediate devaluation), the removal of price controls, further 'privatization', and measures to reduce budgetary expenditure, including substantial retrenchment in the civil service. A structural adjustment programme was subsequently adopted, and credit agreements with the World Bank and IMF were to be signed later that year. However, continuing opposition within the national assembly to the economic reforms was expected to prove an impediment to the implementation of the new measures. Also in 1994 the government initiated an emergency rehabilitation project, at an estimated cost of $17m., to repair the severe damage to physical and economic infrastructure that had been caused by the cyclones.

Statistical Survey

Source (unless otherwise stated): Banque des Données de l'Etat, BP 485, Antananarivo; tel. 21613.

Area and Population

AREA, POPULATION AND DENSITY

Area (sq km)	587,041*
Population (census results)	
9 May 1966	6,200,000
1974–75†	
Males	3,805,288
Females	3,798,502
Total	7,603,790
Population (official estimates at mid-year)	
1990	11,197,000
1991	11,493,000
1993	12,092,000
Density (per sq km) at mid-1993	20.6

* 226,658 sq miles.

† The census took place in three stages: in provincial capitals on 1 December 1974; in Antananarivo and remaining urban areas on 17 February 1975; and in rural areas on 1 June 1975.

PRINCIPAL ETHNIC GROUPS (estimated population, 1974)

Merina (Hova)	1,993,000	Sakalava	470,156*
Betsimisaraka	1,134,000	Antandroy	412,500
Betsileo	920,600	Antaisaka	406,468*
Tsimihety	558,100		

* 1972 figure.

PRINCIPAL TOWNS (population at 1975 census)

Antananarivo (capital)	406,366	Mahajanga (Majunga)	65,864
Antsirabé	78,941	Toliary (Tuléar)	45,676
Toamasina (Tamatave)	77,395	Antsiranana (Diégo-Suarez)	40,443
Fianarantsoa	68,054		

The population of Antananarivo was estimated to be 662,585 in 1985.

BIRTHS AND DEATHS (UN estimates, annual averages)

	1975–80	1980–85	1985–90
Birth rate (per 1,000)	45.7	45.9	45.8
Death rate (per 1,000)	16.7	15.4	14.0

Expectation of life (UN estimates, years at birth, 1985–90): 53.5 (males 52.0; females 55.0).

Source: UN, *World Population Prospects: The 1992 Revision*.

ECONOMICALLY ACTIVE POPULATION
(ILO estimates, '000 persons at mid-1980)

	Males	Females	Total
Agriculture etc.	1,731	1,583	3,314
Industry	216	28	244
Services	457	82	539
Total labour force	2,405	1,693	4,098

Source: ILO, *Economically Active Population Estimates and Projections, 1950–2025*.

Mid-1985 (official estimates, '000 persons): Total labour force 3,929 (males 2,194; females 1,735) (Source: ILO, *Year Book of Labour Statistics*).

Mid-1992 (estimates in '000): Agriculture, forestry and fishing 4,096; Total labour force 5,421 (Source: FAO, *Production Yearbook*).

Agriculture

PRINCIPAL CROPS ('000 metric tons)

	1990	1991	1992
Maize	155	145	165
Rice (paddy)	2,420	2,342	2,450
Sugar cane	2,000	1,950	1,900
Potatoes	272	274	276
Sweet potatoes	486	487*	440*
Cassava (Manioc)	2,292	2,307	2,320
Taro (Coco yam)*	98	99	100
Dry beans	37	37*	37*
Vegetables and melons*	330	330	296
Oranges*	85	84	85
Bananas*	220	218	220
Avocados*	21	21	22
Mangoes*	205	205	170
Pineapples*	50	50	50
Other fruits*	204	203	206
Groundnuts (in shell)	30	29	34
Cottonseed†	20	16	17
Cotton (lint)*	12	10	10
Coconuts*	84	84	85
Copra*	10	10	10
Coffee (green)	85	85	87
Cocoa beans	4	4	4
Tobacco (leaves)*	4	4	4
Sisal	20	20	19

* FAO estimate(s). † Unofficial figures.

Source: FAO, *Production Yearbook*.

LIVESTOCK ('000 head, year ending September)

	1990	1991*	1992*
Cattle	10,254	10,265	10,276
Pigs	1,431	1,461	1,493
Sheep*	737	753	770
Goats*	1,256	1,283	1,311

* FAO estimates.

Chickens (million): 22 in 1990; 22 in 1991 (FAO estimate); 23 in 1992 (FAO estimate).

Ducks (FAO estimates, million): 6 in 1990; 6 in 1991; 6 in 1992.

Turkeys (FAO estimates, million): 4 in 1990; 4 in 1991; 4 in 1992.

Source: FAO, *Production Yearbook*.

LIVESTOCK PRODUCTS (FAO estimates, '000 metric tons)

	1990	1991	1992
Cows' milk	473	472	475
Beef and veal	142	142	142
Pigs' meat	39	39	40
Poultry meat	86	88	91
Hen eggs	17.1	17.4	18.2
Honey	3.7	3.8	3.8
Cattle hides	20.0	20.0	20.1

Source: FAO, *Production Yearbook*.

Forestry

ROUNDWOOD REMOVALS
(FAO estimates, '000 cubic metres, excluding bark)

	1990	1991*	1992*
Sawlogs, veneer logs and logs for sleepers	468	468	468
Other industrial wood*	339	339	339
Fuel wood*	7,293	7,537	7,790
Total	8,100	8,344	8,597

* Assumed to be unchanged since 1977.
Source: FAO, *Yearbook of Forest Products*.

SAWNWOOD PRODUCTION
('000 cubic metres, including railway sleepers)

	1990	1991	1992
Total	234	233*	233*

Source: FAO, *Yearbook of Forest Products*.

Fishing

('000 metric tons, live weight)

	1989	1990	1991
Inland waters:			
Freshwater fishes	30.2	32.0	27.7
Indian Ocean:			
Marine fishes	58.5	61.5	60.7
Marine crabs	1.0	1.2	1.0
Tropical spiny lobsters	0.3	0.3	0.4
Shrimps and prawns	7.3	9.2	10.2
Molluscs	0.1	0.1	0.3
Other aquatic animals	0.1	0.2	0.6
Total catch	97.6	104.5	101.0

Source: FAO, *Yearbook of Fishery Statistics*.

Mining

(metric tons)

	1988	1989	1990
Graphite	14,565	15,865	17,920
Salt (unrefined)	30,000*	30,000	30,000
Mica	693	1,182	1,800
Chromite†	49,000	47,000	35,000

* Provisional figures.
† Figures refer to the chromium content of ores mined.
Source: UN, *Industrial Statistics Yearbook*.

Industry

SELECTED PRODUCTS
(metric tons, unless otherwise indicated)

	1989	1990	1991
Raw sugar	120,000	111,000	96,000
Palm oil*	3,800	3,800	3,800
Beer (hectolitres)	232,000	298,000	n.a.
Cigarettes	2,341	1,955	n.a.
Woven cotton fabrics (million sq m)	59.5	49.1	n.a.
Cement	24,000	20,000	23,000
Liquefied petroleum gas	1,000	1,000†	1,000†
Motor spirit (petrol)	29,000	25,000	35,000
Kerosene	19,000	20,000	21,000
Distillate fuel oils	46,000	43,000	45,000
Residual fuel oils	86,000	65,000	67,000
Paints	1,900	2,400	n.a.
Soap	14,500	14,900	n.a.
Electric energy (for public use) (million kWh)	447	450	452

* FAO estimates. † Provisional figure.
Source: UN, *Industrial Statistics Yearbook*.

Finance

CURRENCY AND EXCHANGE RATES

Monetary Units
100 centimes = 1 franc malgache (Malagasy franc).

Sterling and Dollar Equivalents (31 January 1994)
£1 sterling = 2,938.0 francs MG;
US $1 = 1,960.1 francs MG;
10,000 francs MG = £3.404 = $5.102.

Average Exchange Rate (Malagasy francs per US $)
1991 1,835.4
1992 1,864.0
1993 1,913.8

BUDGET ('000 million francs MG)

Revenue*	1989	1990	1991
Taxation	354.0	434.2	336.1
Taxes on income, profits, etc.	45.5	68.0	64.0
General income tax	16.2	22.5	21.6
Corporate tax on profits	25.1	37.2	35.2
Domestic taxes on goods and services	98.8	102.5	81.4
Sales taxes	44.0	47.5	28.4
Excises	35.3	34.0	20.8
Profits of fiscal monopolies	15.2	16.0	28.3
Taxes on international trade and transactions	201.7	254.6	186.0
Import duties	154.5	217.7	150.6
Export duties	47.2	36.9	35.4
Other current revenue	106.8	112.8	81.5
Capital revenue	—	—	11.6
Total	460.8	547.0	429.2

* Excluding grants received ('000 million francs MG): 55.8 in 1989; 66.8 in 1990; 38.2 in 1991.

Expenditure	1989	1990	1991
General public services	122.3	142.0	147.8
Defence	51.3	53.5	55.8
Education	92.5	110.6	127.5
Health	42.0	45.1	48.7
Social security and welfare	11.1	17.5	10.9
Economic affairs and services	338.1	295.4	265.8
Agriculture, forestry, fishing and hunting	135.8	122.6	95.7
Mining, manufacturing and construction	151.6	116.5	114.6
Transportation and communication	27.2	21.3	19.2
Other purposes	130.6	119.7	148.7
Sub-total	788.1	784.1	805.4
Adjustment for expenditure financed by grants in kind	-108.2	-135.4	-65.6
Total	679.9	648.7	739.8
Current	399.8	418.8	480.0
Capital	280.1	229.9	259.8

Source: IMF, *Government Finance Statistics Yearbook*.

CENTRAL BANK RESERVES (US $ million at 31 December)

	1989	1990	1991
IMF special drawing rights	0.1	0.2	0.1
Foreign exchange	245.2	91.9	88.8
Total	245.3	92.1	88.9

Source: IMF, *International Financial Statistics*.

MONEY SUPPLY ('000 million francs MG at 31 December)

	1990	1991	1992
Currency outside banks	214.9	287.3	317.2
Demand deposits at deposit money banks	358.7	465.3	598.1
Total money	574.5	752.6	915.3

Source: IMF, *International Financial Statistics*.

COST OF LIVING (Consumer Price Index, excluding rent, for Madagascans in Antananarivo; base: 1980 = 100)

	1989	1990	1991
Food	420.2	479.1	523.2
Fuel and light	462.6	501.3	n.a.
Clothing	564.7	608.7	n.a.
All items (incl. others)	454.0	507.5	551.0

Source: ILO, *Year Book of Labour Statistics*.

1992: Food 610.2; All items 631.1 (Source: UN, *Monthly Bulletin of Statistics*).

1993: Food 660.9; All items 694.3 (Source: UN, *Monthly Bulletin of Statistics*).

NATIONAL ACCOUNTS
('000 million francs MG at current prices)

Expenditure on the Gross Domestic Product

	1989	1990	1991
Government final consumption expenditure	350.9	359.6	432.4
Private final consumption expenditure	3,254.8	3,874.9	4,632.8
Increase in stocks } Gross fixed capital formation }	536.3	861.9	291.1
Total domestic expenditure	4,142.0	5,096.3	5,356.2
Exports of goods and services	720.9	714.8	867.2
Less Imports of goods and services	857.6	1,209.5	1,316.9
GDP in purchasers' values	4,005.3	4,601.6	4,906.4

Source: UN Economic Commission for Africa, *African Statistical Yearbook*.

Gross Domestic Product by Economic Activity

	1989	1990	1991
Agriculture, hunting, forestry and fishing	1,181.7	1,334.3	1,488.4
Mining and quarrying	16.1	14.9	14.8
Manufacturing	471.6	492.6	530.6
Electricity, gas and water	42.7	78.7	87.0
Construction	48.7	61.7	52.6
Trade, restaurants and hotels	351.6	426.2	498.0
Transport, storage and communications	623.9	721.6	747.9
Finance, insurance, real estate and business services	58.7	64.6	70.0
Public administration and defence	190.9	240.7	284.4
Other services	658.7	756.9	791.9
GDP at factor cost	3,644.6	4,192.0	4,565.5
Indirect taxes, *less* subsidies	360.7	409.6	340.9
GDP in purchasers' values	4,005.3	4,601.6	4,906.4

Source: UN Economic Commission for Africa, *African Statistical Yearbook*.

BALANCE OF PAYMENTS (US $ million)

	1990	1991	1992
Merchandise exports f.o.b.	319	338	328
Merchandise imports f.o.b.	-566	-440	-466
Trade balance	-248	-102	-138
Exports of services	194	147	172
Imports of services	-274	-239	-266
Other income received	15	4	6
Other income paid	-176	-178	-145
Private unrequited transfers (net)	49	52	88
Official unrequited transfers (net)	188	127	148
Current balance	-251	-188	-136
Direct investment (net)	22	14	21
Other capital (net)	-40	-56	-109
Net errors and omissions	-9	-4	-52
Overall balance	-278	-235	-276

Source: IMF, *International Financial Statistics*.

External Trade

PRINCIPAL COMMODITIES
(million francs MG, excluding gold and military goods)

Imports	1990	1991	1992
Chemical products	116,471.9	88,345.8	116,056.6
Mineral products	187,554.3	144,312.0	168,925.0
Crude petroleum	80,453.5	91,076.9	95,880.9
Textiles	13,907.0	12,743.2	13,041.1
Metal products	72,674.3	53,232.1	59,571.3
Machinery	111,921.7	132,212.0	88,273.3
Electrical equipment	53,549.6	43,995.0	61,024.9
Vehicles and parts	106,990.9	98,527.0	81,502.0
Total (incl. others)	881,328.0	785,689.5	844,935.6

Exports	1990	1991	1992
Coffee (green)	57,965.5	51,902.0	58,844.1
Vanilla	85,012.3	84,887.0	95,540.7
Sugar	30,400.7	19,125.2	17,058.3
Cloves and clove oil	32,359.4	46,025.6	21,060.3
Petroleum products	14,993.9	20,551.5	17,412.9
Shrimps	50,381.1	74,772.5	70,581.0
Lobsters	4,615.8	6,901.9	5,941.1
Cotton fabrics	12,931.2	24,971.7	17,609.8
Chromium	18,507.6	17,288.1	14,373.7
Total (incl. others)	460,343.2	559,073.3	499,805.9

PRINCIPAL TRADING PARTNERS (million francs MG)

Imports	1990	1991	1992
Belgium/Luxembourg	19,501.6	17,390.5	14,946.6
France	259,664.7	246,479.2	256,193.2
Germany	59,324.0	65,947.0	51,253.1
Italy	25,070.7	25,367.0	24,839.4
Japan	53,232.8	51,722.3	49,352.7
Netherlands	15,552.9	14,528.8	18,539.9
United Kingdom	40,560.1	21,787.4	42,582.6
USA	34,662.3	53,689.0	49,683.2
Total (incl. others)	881,328.0	785,689.5	844,935.6

Exports	1990	1991	1992
Belgium/Luxembourg	9,259.4	5,483.2	16,469.3
France	126,248.8	143,531.9	133,064.2
Germany	38,093.8	55,810.3	49,592.8
Italy	11,641.0	15,788.9	15,647.3
Japan	41,133.1	47,526.9	42,974.0
Netherlands	21,317.8	16,365.1	10,890.4
United Kingdom	6,959.7	17,086.0	12,830.6
USA	77,669.7	78,009.9	77,617.0
Total (incl. others)	460,343.2	559,073.3	499,805.9

Transport

RAILWAYS (traffic)

	1985	1986	1987
Passengers carried ('000)	2,564	3,161	2,974
Passenger-km (millions)	178	208	209
Freight carried ('000 metric tons)	808	735	693
Ton-km (millions)	208.5	188	174

Passenger-km (million): 242 in 1988; 204 in 1989; 198 in 1990. Ton-km (million): 174 in 1988; 207 in 1989; 209 in 1990 (Source: UN, *Statistical Yearbook*).

ROAD TRAFFIC (vehicles in use at 31 December)

	1988	1989	1990
Cars	27,739	37,363	41,900
Buses and coaches	2,015	2,586	2,700
Goods vehicles	5,103	7,329	7,900
Vans	13,426	17,715	18,500
Tractors, trailers and semi-trailers	120	272	290
Motor cycles and mopeds	3,128	n.a.	n.a.

Source: International Road Federation, *World Road Statistics*.

INTERNATIONAL SEA-BORNE SHIPPING
(freight traffic, '000 metric tons)

	1987	1988	1989
Goods loaded:			
Mahajanga	17	18	29.4
Toamasina	252	350	360.6
Other ports	79	100	137.4
Total	348	468	527.4
Goods unloaded:			
Mahajanga	37	32	30.8
Toamasina	748	778	708.9
Other ports	48	53	52.0
Total	833	863	791.7

1990 ('000 metric tons): Goods loaded 540; Goods unloaded 984 (Source: UN, *Monthly Bulletin of Statistics*).

CIVIL AVIATION (traffic)

	1988	1989	1990
Kilometres flown (million)	5.5	5.5	4.7
Passengers carried ('000)	386.8	342.4	347.1
Passenger-km (million)	434	442	362
Freight ton-km (million)	23.3	28.9	23.4
Mail ton-km (million)	1.2	1.2	1.1

Tourism

	1988	1989	1990
Hotel rooms	2,991	3,656	4,208
Tourist arrivals	35,405	38,954	52,923
Receipts (million US $)	18	28	37

Source: Ministère des Transports, de la Météorologie et du Tourisme, Antananarivo.

Communications Media

	1989	1990	1991
Radio receivers ('000 in use)	2,300	2,400	2,480
Television receivers ('000 in use)	230	240	248
Book production*:			
Titles	146	154	46
Copies ('000)	731	541†	111
Daily newspapers:			
Number	n.a.	5	n.a.
Circulation ('000 copies)	n.a.	50	n.a.
Non-daily newspapers:			
Number	n.a.	27	n.a.
Circulation	n.a.	105	n.a.

* Including pamphlets (88 titles and 343,000 copies in 1989; 10 titles and 29,000 copies in 1991).

† Estimate.

Source: UNESCO, *Statistical Yearbook.*

Telephones ('000 in use, estimate): 54 in 1991 (Source: UN Economic Commission for Africa, *African Statistical Yearbook*).

Education

(1990)

	Insti-tutions	Teach-ers	Pupils		
			Males	Females	Total
Primary	13,791	38,933	796,924	773,797	1,570,721
Secondary:					
General	n.a.	14,856	162,439	160,333	322,772
Teacher training	n.a.	36	210	176	386
Vocational	n.a.	1,448	10,110	6,923	17,033
Universities, etc.	n.a.	939	19,745	16,079	35,824

Source: UNESCO, *Statistical Yearbook.*

Directory

The Constitution

The Constitution of the Democratic Republic of Madagascar, which was endorsed by national referendum on 19 August 1992, enshrines a unitary state, and provides for a bicameral legislature, comprising a Senate and a National Assembly. Two-thirds of the members of the Senate are selected by an electoral college for a term of four years, and the remaining one-third of the members are appointed by the President. The 138-member National Assembly is elected by universal adult suffrage, under a system of proportional representation, for a four-year term of office. The constitutional Head of State is the President, who is elected for a term of five years. If no candidate obtains an overall majority in the presidential election, a second round of voting is to take place a maximum of 30 days after the publication of the results of the first ballot. Executive power is vested in the Prime Minister, who is elected by the National Assembly, and appoints a Council of Ministers.

The Government

HEAD OF STATE

President: Prof. ALBERT ZAFY (took office 27 March 1993).

COUNCIL OF MINISTERS
(September 1994)

Prime Minister and Minister of Defence: FRANCISQUE RAVONY.

Minister of State for Agriculture and Rural Development: EMMANUEL RAKOTOVAHINY.

Minister of Foreign Affairs: JACQUES SYLLA.

Minister of Civil Service, Labour and Social Legislation: HENRI RAKOTOVOLOLONA.

Minister of the Economy and Town Planning: TOVONANAHARY RABETSITONTA.

Minister of Industrial Promotion and Craftmanship: GEDEON RAJAONSON.

Minister of the Interior and Decentralization: CHARLES CLEMENT SEVERIN.

Minister of Energy and Mining: BRUNO BETIANA.

Minister of Transport and Meteorology: DANIEL RAMAROMISA.

Minister of Finance and the Budget: JOSE YVON RASERIJAONA.

Minister of National and Regional Development: HENRI RAKOTONIRAINY.

Minister of Culture, Communications and Leisure Activities: TSILAVINA RALAINDIMBY.

Minister of Research and Development: ROGER ANDRIANASOLO.

Minister of Public Works: ROYAL ROELFILS.

Minister of Commerce and Supply: JEROME SAMBALLIS.

Minister of Primary and Secondary Education: FULGENCE FANONY.

Minister of Higher Education: ADOLPHE RAKOTOMANGA.

Minister of Health: ANDRIAMBAO DAMASY.

Minister of Tourism: ALPHONSE RALISON.

Minister of Population, Youth and Sports: THERESA RAVAO.

Minister of the Environment: GEORGES ALDINE RABELAZA.

Minister of Posts and Telecommunications: NY HASINA ANDRIAMANJATO.

Minister Delegate at the office of the Prime Minister, Keeper of the Seals, in charge of Judicial Affairs and Relations to Institutions: RABENIRAINY RAMANOELISON.

Minister Delegate at the Office of the Prime Minister, in charge of the National Police: BERTIN RAZAFINDRAZAKA.

Minister Delegate at the Office of the Prime Minister, in charge of the Armed Forces: Gen. CHARLES RAMENJA.

MINISTRIES

Office of the Prime Minister: BP 248, Mahazoarivo, 101 Antananarivo; tel. (2) 25258; telex 22339; fax (2) 35258.

Ministry of Agriculture and Rural Development: BP 500, Anosy, 101 Antananarivo; tel. (2) 24710; telex 22508; fax (2) 26561.

Ministry of the Civil Service, Labour and Social Legislation: Tsaralalana, 101 Antananarivo; tel. (2) 24816.

Ministry of Commerce and Supply: Ambohidahy, 101 Antananarivo; tel. (2) 27292; telex 22378; fax (2) 31280.

Ministry of Culture, Communications and Leisure Activities: BP 305, 101 Antananarivo; tel. (2) 27092; fax (2) 29448.

Ministry of the Economy and Town Planning: BP 674, Antananarivo 101; tel. (2) 20284.

Ministry of Energy and Mining: BP 527, Antananarivo; tel. (2) 25515; telex 22540.

Ministry of the Environment: Antananarivo.

Ministry of Finance and the Budget: BP 61, Antaninarenina, 101 Antananarivo; tel. (2) 21632; telex 22489.

Ministry of Foreign Affairs: Anosy, 101 Antananarivo; tel. (2) 21198; telex 22236; fax (2) 34484.

Ministry of Health: Ambohidahy, 101 Antananarivo; tel. (2) 23697.

Ministry of Higher Education: BP 4163, Tsimbazana, 101 Antananarivo; tel. (2) 27185; fax (2) 23897.

Ministry of Industrial Promotion and Craftmanship: BP 527, 101 Antananarivo; tel. (2) 25515; telex 22540.

Ministry of the Interior and Decentralization: Anosy, 101 Antananarivo; tel. (2) 23084.

Ministry of Justice: BP 231, Faravohitra, 101 Antananarivo; tel. (2) 24030.

Ministry of National and Regional Development: BP 3378, Anosy, Antananarivo; tel. (2) 35617.

Ministry of Population, Youth and Sports: Ambohijatovo, 101 Antananarivo; tel. (2) 23129.

Ministry of Posts and Telecommunications: Antaninarenina, 101 Antananarivo; tel. (2) 26121; telex 22250.

Ministry of Primary and Secondary Education: BP 267, Anosy, 101 Antananarivo; tel. (2) 21325.

Ministry of Public Works: Anosy, 101 Antananarivo; tel. (2) 24224; telex 22343.

Ministry of Research and Development: 27 rue Fernand Kasanga, BP 6224, Andoharano-Tsimbazaza, 101 Antananarivo; tel. (2) 33288; telex 22539; fax (2) 24075.

Ministry of Tourism: Antananarivo.

Ministry of Transport and Meteorology: Anosy, 101 Antananarivo; tel. (2) 24604; telex 22301; fax (2) 24001.

President and Legislature

PRESIDENT

Presidential Election, First Ballot, 25 November 1992

Candidate	Votes	%
Prof. ALBERT ZAFY (FV)	1,846,842	45.16
DIDIER RATSIRAKA (MMSM)	1,195,026	29.22
MANANDAFY RAKOTONIRINA (MFM)	417,504	10.21
EVARISTE MARSON (RPSD)	188,235	4.60
RUFFINE TSIRANANA (PSD)	142,571	3.49
JACQUES RABEMANANJARA (Independent)	117,273	2.87
RAZAFINDRAKOTO ANDRIAMANALINA (Independent)	92,061	2.25
TOVONANAHARY RABETSITONTA (Independent)	89,715	2.19
Total	4,089,227	100.00

Second Ballot, 10 February 1993

Candidate	Votes	%
Prof. ALBERT ZAFY (FV)	2,766,704	66.74
DIDIER RATSIRAKA (MMSM)	1,378,640	33.26
Total	4,145,344	100.00

LEGISLATURE

The August 1992 Constitution provides for a bicameral legislature, comprising a Senate and a National Assembly.

National Assembly

President: Pastor RICHARD ANDRIAMANJATO.

General Election, 16 June 1993

Party	Seats
Cartel HVR	46
MFM	15
Leader—Fanilo	13
FAMIMA	11
Fihaonana	8
RPSD	8
AKFM—Fanavaozana	5
UNDD—Rasalama forces vives	5
UNDD	2
CSDDM	2
Farimbona	2
Accord	2
Fivoarana	2
Rasalama forces vives—Teachers and Educators	1
GRAD—Iloafo	1
Vatomizana	1
Others	14
Total	138

Political Organizations

Legislation permitting the resumption of multi-party politics took effect in March 1990; more than 120 political associations subsequently emerged. The principal political organizations in 1994 were:

AKFM—Fanavaozana: Antananarivo; f. 1989 by a breakaway group from the former Parti du congrès de l'indépendance de Madagascar (AKFM); supports liberal policies; Leader Pastor RICHARD ANDRIAMANJATO.

Cartel HVR (Hery Velona Rasalama—Forces vives Rasalama): f. 1991 as the Forces vives (FV) alliance; reconstituted in 1993; supported Prof. Albert Zafy in the presidential election; Pres. ALAIN RAMAROSON.

Committee for the Support of Democracy and Development in Madagascar (CSDDM): f. 1993; Leader FRANCISQUE RAVONY.

Elan Populaire pour l'Unité Nationale (Vonjy Iray Tsy Mivaky—Vonjy): 101 Antananarivo; f. 1973; centrist; Leader Dr JÉRÔME MAROJAMA RAZANABAHINY.

FAMIMA: f. 1993; supports fmr President, Didier Ratsiraka.

Fihaonana: f. 1993; Leader GUY RAZANAMASY.

Leader—Farito: f. 1993; comprises 'non-politicians'; Leader HERIZO RAZAFIMAHALEO.

Mouvement pour le progrès de Madagascar (Mpitolona ho amin'ny Fandrosoan'ny Madagasikara—MFM): 101 Antananarivo; f. 1972 as Mouvement pour le pouvoir prolétarien (MFM), adopted present name in 1990; advocates liberal and market-orientated policies; Leader MANANDAFY RAKOTONIRINA; Sec.-Gen. GERMAIN RAKOTONIRAINY.

Parti social démocrate (PSD): Antananarivo; f. 1957, relaunched 1990; Sec.-Gen. RUFFINE TSIRANANA.

Rassemblement pour le socialisme et la démocratie (RPSD): breakaway faction from the PSD; Leader EVARISTE MARSON.

Union nationale pour la démocratie et le développement (UNDD): f. 1991 by Prof. ALBERT ZAFY; Leader EMMANUEL RAKOTOVAHINY.

Other parties represented in the legislature were Accord, Farimbona, Fivoarana, GRAD—Iloafa (Leader TOVONANAHARY RABETSITONJA, Ralama forces vives—Teachers and Educators, and Vatomizana.

Diplomatic Representation

EMBASSIES IN MADAGASCAR

China, People's Republic: Ancien Hôtel Panorama, BP 1658, 101 Antananarivo; Ambassador: ZHAO BAOZHEN.

Egypt: 47 ave Lénine, BP 4082, Ankadifotsy, 101 Antananarivo; tel. (2) 25233; telex 22364; Ambassador: EL-GAMAL F. DAIEF.

France: 3 rue Jean Jaurès, BP 204, 101 Antananarivo; tel. (2) 23700; telex 22201; Ambassador: (vacant).

Germany: 101 route circulaire, BP 516, Ambodirotra; tel. 23802; telex 22203; Ambassador: GÜNTER HELD.

Holy See: Amboniloha Ivandry, BP 650, 101 Antananarivo; tel. (2) 42376; telex 22432; fax (2) 42384; Apostolic Pro-Nuncio: Most Rev. BLASCO FRANCISCO COLLAÇO, Titular Archbishop of Octava.

India: 4 làlana Emile Rajaonson, BP 1787, 101 Antananarivo; tel. (2) 23334; telex 22484; Ambassador: A. K. BASU.

Indonesia: 15 rue Radama I Tsaralalana, 101 Antananarivo; tel. (2) 24915; telex 22387; Chargé d'affaires a.i.: Dr SAMUSI.

Iran: route circulaire, Lot II L43 ter, 101 Antananarivo; tel. (2) 28639; telex 22510; fax (2) 22298; Chargé d'affaires a.i.: MOSTAFA BOROUJERDI.

Italy: 22 rue Pasteur Rabary, BP 16, Ankadivato; tel. 21217; telex 22293; Ambassador: FRANCESCO SCIORTINO.

Japan: 8 rue du Dr Villette, BP 3863, Isoraka, 101 Antananarivo; tel. (2) 26102; telex 22308; fax (2) 21769; Ambassador: MASAHIKO IWASAKI.

Korea, Democratic People's Republic: Ambohibao; tel. 44442; telex 22494; Ambassador: KIM RYONG-YONG.

Libya: Lot IIB, 37A route Circulaire Ampandrana-Ouest, 101 Antananarivo; tel. (2) 21892; Secretary of People's Bureau: SALEM ALI SALEM DANNAH.

Mauritius: Antananarivo; Ambassador: (vacant).

Russia: Ampefiloha, Lot O, BP 4006; tel. 27070; Ambassador: YURI NIKOLAYEVICH MARZLIAKOV.

Switzerland: BP 118, 101 Antananarivo; tel. (2) 22846; telex 22300; fax (2) 28940; Chargé d'affaires: FRANCIS COUSIN.

United Kingdom: Immeuble 'Ny Havana', Cité de 67 Ha, BP 167, 101 Antananarivo; tel. (2) 27749; telex 22459; fax (2) 26690; Ambassador: PETER J. SMITH.

USA: 14–16 rue Rainitovo, Antsahavola, BP 620, 101 Antananarivo; tel. (2) 21257; telex 22202; fax (2) 34539; Ambassador: DENNIS BARRETT.

Judicial System

CONSTITUTIONAL HIGH COURT

Haute Cour Constitutionnelle: 101 Antananarivo; interprets the constitution and rules on constitutional issues; seven mems; Pres. NORBERT RATSIRAHONANA.

SUPREME COURT

Cour Suprême: Palais de Justice, Anosy, 101 Antananarivo; Pres. ALICE RAJAONAH (interim); Attorney-General COLOMBE RAMANANTSOA (interim); Chamber Pres. YOLANDE RAMANGASOAVINA, FRANÇOIS RAMANANDRAIBE.

COURT OF APPEAL

Cour d'Appel: Palais de Justice, Anosy, 101 Antananarivo; Pres. AIMÉE RAKOTONIRINA; Chamber Pres CHARLES RABETOKOTANY, PÉTRONILLE ANDRIAMIHAJA, BAKOLALAO RANAIVOHARIVONY, BERTHOLIER RAVELONTSALAMA, LUCIEN RABARIJHON, NELLY RAKOTOBE, ARLETTE RAMAROSON, CLÉMENTINE RAVANDISON, GISÈLE RABOTOVAO, JEAN-JACQUES RAJAONA.

OTHER COURTS

Tribunaux de Première Instance: at Antananarivo, Toamasina, Antsiranana, Mahajanga, Fianarantsoa, Toliary, Antsirabé, Ambatondrazaka, Antalaha, Farafangana, Maintirano; for civil, commercial and social matters, and for registration.

Cours Criminelles Ordinaires: tries crimes of common law; attached to the Cour d'Appel in Antananarivo but may sit in any other large town. There are also 31 Cours Criminelles Spéciales dealing with cases concerning cattle.

Tribunaux Spéciaux Economiques: at Antananarivo, Toamasina, Mahajanga, Fianarantsoa, Antsiranana and Toliary; tries crimes specifically relating to economic matters.

Tribunaux Criminels Spéciaux: judges cases of looting and banditry; 31 courts.

Religion

It is estimated that more than 50% of the population follow traditional animist beliefs, some 43% are Christians (about one-half of whom are Roman Catholics) and the remainder are Muslims.

CHRISTIANITY

Fiombonan'ny Fiangonana Kristiana eto Madagasikara (FFKM)/Conseil Chrétien des Eglises de Madagascar (Christian Council of Churches in Madagascar): Vohipiraisama, Ambohijatovo-Atsimo, BP 798, 101 Antananarivo; tel. (2) 29052; f. 1980; four full mems and one assoc. mem.; Pres. Pastor RABENOROLAHY; Gen. Sec. Rev. LALA ANDRIAMIHARISOA.

Fiombonan'ny Fiangonana Protestanta eto Madagasikara (FFPM)/Fédération des Eglises Protestantes à Madagascar (Federation of the Protestant Churches in Madagascar): VK 2 Vohipiraisana, Ambohijatovo-Atsimo, 101 Antananarivo; tel. (2) 20144; f. 1958; two mems; Pres. Rev. JOSEPH RAMAMBASOA; Gen. Sec. Rev. CHARLES RAKOTOSON.

The Anglican Communion

Anglicans are adherents of the Church of the Province of the Indian Ocean, comprising five dioceses (three in Madagascar, one in Mauritius and one in Seychelles). The Archbishop of the Province is the Bishop of Seychelles. The Church has about 160,000 adherents in Madagascar, where it embraces the Eklesia Episkopaly Malagasy (Malagasy Episcopal Church), founded in 1874.

Bishop of Antananarivo: Rt Rev. RÉMI JOSEPH RABENIRINA, Evêché Anglican, Ambohimanoro, 101 Antananarivo; tel. (2) 20827.

Bishop of Antsiranana: Rt Rev. KEITH BENZIES, Evêché Anglican, BP 278, Antsiranana; tel. (8) 22650.

Bishop of Toamasina: Rt Rev. DONALD SMITH, La Mission Anglicane, rue de la Fraternité, Toamasina; tel. (5) 32163.

The Roman Catholic Church

Madagascar comprises three archdioceses and 15 dioceses. At 31 December 1992 the number of adherents in the country represented about 20.3% of the total population.

Bishops' Conference: Conférence Episcopale de Madagascar, 102 bis ave Maréchal Joffre, Antanimena, BP 667, 101 Antananarivo; tel. (2) 20478; f. 1969; Pres. Rt Rev. JEAN-GUY RAKOTONDRAVAHATRA, Bishop of Ihosy.

Archbishop of Antananarivo: Most Rev. ARMAND RAZAFINDRATANDRA, Archevêché, Andohalo, 101 Antananarivo; tel. (2) 20726.

Archbishop of Antsiranana: Most Rev. ALBERT JOSEPH TSIAHOANA, Archevêché, BP 415, 201 Antsiranana; tel. (8) 21605.

Archbishop of Fianarantsoa: Most Rev. PHILIBERT RANDRIAM-BOLOLONA, Archevêché, place Mgr Givelet, BP 1440, 301 Fianarantsoa; tel. (7) 50672; fax (7) 24854.

Other Christian Churches

Fiangonan' i Jesoa Kristy eto Madagasikara/Eglise de Jésus-Christ à Madagascar: Lot 11 B18, Tohatohabato Ranavalona 1, Trano 'Ifanomezantsoa', BP 623, 101 Antananarivo; tel. (2) 26845; telex 22467; fax (2) 27033; f. 1968; Pres. Rev. EDMOND RAZAFIMAHEFA; Gen. Sec. Rev. LALA RASENDRAHASINA; 2m. mems.

Fiangonana Loterana Malagasy (Malagasy Lutheran Church): BP 1741, 101 Antananarivo; tel. (2) 22347; telex 22544; Pres. Rev. RANAIVOJAONA RAZAFIMANANTSOA; 600,000 mems.

The Press

In December 1990 the National People's Assembly adopted legislation guaranteeing the freedom of the press and the right of newspapers to be established without prior authorization.

PRINCIPAL DAILIES

Bulletin de l'Agence Nationale d'Information 'Taratra' (ANTA): 3 rue du R. P. Callet, Behoririka, BP 386, 101 Antananarivo; tel. (2) 21171; telex 22506; f. 1977; French; Man. Dir JEANNOT FENO.

Imongo Vaovao: 11K 4 bis Andravoahangy, BP 7014, 101 Antananarivo; tel. (2) 21053; f. 1955; Malagasy; Dir CLÉMENT RAMAMONJISOA; circ. 10,000.

Madagascar Tribune: Immeuble SME, rue Ravoninahitriniarivo, BP 659, Ankorondrano, 101 Antananarivo; tel. (2) 22635; telex 22340; fax (2) 22254; f. 1988; independent; French and Malagasy; Editor RAHAGA RAMAHOLIMIHASO; circ. 12,000.

Maresaka: 12 làlana Ratsimba John, Isotry, 101 Antananarivo; tel. (2) 23568; f. 1953; independent; Malagasy; Editor M. RALAIARIJAONA; circ. 5,000.

Midi-Madagascar: làlana Ravoninahitriniarivo, BP 1414, Ankorondrano, 101 Antananarivo; tel. (2) 30038; telex 22543; f. 1983; French; Dir JULIANA RAKOTOARIVELO; circ. 25,489.

Nouveau Journal de Madagascar: Cité Batimord; Ankorondrano; 101 Antananarivo; French and English; Dir JOHARY RAKOTONIRINA; circ. 12,000.

PRINCIPAL PERIODICALS

Afaka: BP 1475, 101 Antananarivo; Malagasy and French; Dir MAX RATSIMANDISA; circ. 5,000.

Basy Vava: Lot III E 96, Mahamasina Atsimo, 101 Antananarivo; tel. (2) 20448; f. 1959; Malagasy; Dir GABRIEL RAMANANJATO; circ. 3,000.

Bulletin de la Société du Corps Médical Malgache: Imprimerie Volamahitsy, 101 Antananarivo; Malagasy; monthly; Dir Dr RAKOTOMALALA.

Dans les Media, Demain: Immeuble Jeune Afrique, 58 rue Tsiombikibo, BP 1734, Ambatovinaky, 101 Antananarivo; tel. (2) 27788; telex 22225; fax (2) 30629; f. 1986; independent; weekly; Dir HONORÉ RAZAFINTSALAMA; circ. 2,500.

Feon'ny Mpiasa: Lot M8, Isotry, 101 Antananarivo; trade union affairs; Malagasy; monthly; Dir M. RAZAKANAIVO; circ. 2,000.

Fiaraha-Miasa: BP 1216, 101 Antananarivo; Malagasy; weekly; Dir SOLO NORBERT ANDRIAMORASATA; circ. 5,000.

Gazetinao: Lot IPA 37 ter, Anosimasina, 101 Antananarivo; tel. 33177; Malagasy; monthly; Dir ETIENNE M. RAKOTOMAHANINA; circ. 3,000.

La Gazette d'Antsirabé: Lot 12 C-190, Antsenakely, 110 Antsirabé; f. 1989; Dir VOLOLOHARIMANANA RAZAFIMANDIMBY; circ. 7,000.

Gazety Medikaly: Lot 12B, Ampahibe, 101 Antananarivo; tel. (2) 27898; f. 1965; medical; monthly; Dir PAUL RATSIMISETA; circ. 2,000.

Isika Mianakavy: Ambatomena, 301 Fianarantsoa; f. 1958; Roman Catholic; Malagasy; monthly; Dir J. RANAIVOMANANA; circ. 21,000.

Journal Officiel de la République Démocratique de Madagascar: BP 248, 101 Antananarivo; tel. (2) 25258; f. 1883; official announcements; French; weekly; Dir SAMÜEL RAMAROSON.

Journal Scientifique de Madagascar: Antananarivo; f. 1985; Dir Prof. MANAMBELONA; circ. 3,000.

Jureco: Immeuble SOMAGI, 120 rue Rainandriamampandry, 101 Antananarivo; tel. (2) 24145; telex 22365; fax (2) 20397; law and economics; monthly; Dir MBOARA ANDRIANARIMANANA.

Lakroan'i Madagasikara: Maison Jean XXIII, Mahamasina Sud, 101 Antananarivo; tel. (2) 21158; f. 1927; Roman Catholic; French and Malagasy; weekly; Dir LOUIS RASOLO; circ. 25,000.

Mada-Économie: 15 rue Ratsimilaho, BP 3464, 101 Antananarivo; tel. (2) 25634; f. 1977; reports events in south-east Africa; monthly; Editor RICHARD-CLAUDE RATOVONARIVO; circ. 5,000.

Mpanolotsaina: BP 623, 101 Antananarivo; tel. (2) 26845; religious, educational; Malagasy; quarterly; Dir PAUL SOLOHERY.

Ny Mpamangy-FLM: 9 rue Grandidier Isoraka, BP 538, Antsahamanitra, 101 Antananarivo; tel. (2) 32446; telex 22544; f. 1882; monthly; Dir Pastor MAMY ANDRIAMAHENINA; circ. 3,000.

Ny Sakaizan'ny Tanora: BP 538, Antsahaminitra, 101 Antananarivo; tel. (2) 32446; telex 22544; f. 1878; monthly; Editor-in-Chief DANIEL PROSPER ANDRIAMANJAKA; circ. 5,000.

PME Madagascar: rue Hugues Rabesahala, BP 953, Antsakaviro, 101 Antananarivo; tel. (2) 22536; telex 22261; fax (2) 34534; f. 1989; French; monthly; economic review; Dir ROMAIN ANDRIANARISOA; circ. 3,500.

Recherche et Culture: BP 907, 101 Antananarivo; tel. (2) 26600; f. 1985; publ. by French dept of the University of Antananarivo; 2 a year; Dir GINETTE RAMAROSON; circ. 1,000.

Revue Ita: BP 681, 101 Antananarivo; tel. (2) 30507; f. 1985; controlled by the Ministry of Population; quarterly; Dir FILS RAMALANJAONA; circ. 1,000.

Revue de l'Océan Indien: Communication et Médias Océan Indien, rue H. Rabesahala, BP 46, Antsakaviro, 101 Antananarivo; tel. (2) 22536; telex 22225; fax (2) 34534; f. 1980; quarterly; Man. Dir GEORGES RANAIVOSOA; Sec.-Gen. HERY M. A. RANAIVOSOA; circ. 3,250.

Sahy: Lot VD 42, Ambanidia, 101 Antananarivo; tel. (2) 22715; f. 1957; political; Malagasy; weekly; Editor ALINE RAKOTO; circ. 9,000.

Sosialisma Mpiasa: BP 1128, 101 Antananarivo; tel. (2) 21989; f. 1979; trade union affairs; Malagasy; monthly; Dir PAUL RABEMANANJARA; circ. 5,000.

Vaovao: BP 271, 101 Antananarivo; tel. (2) 21193; f. 1985; French and Malagasy; weekly; Dir MARC RAKOTONOELY; circ. 5,000.

Vaovao FJKM: BP 623, 101 Antananarivo; tel. (2) 30553; religious; 10 Malagasy edns a year, 5 French and English; Dir RAKOTO ARMAND MANITRA.

NEWS AGENCIES

Agence Nationale d'Information 'Taratra' (ANTA): 3 rue du R. P. Callet, Behoririka, BP 386, 101 Antananarivo; tel. (2) 21171; telex 22395; f 1977; Man. Dir JEANNOT FENO.

Foreign Bureaux

Agence France-Presse (AFP): 31 ave Andriba, Mahamasina, 101 Antananarivo; tel. (2) 20515; telex 22204; Correspondent STÉPHANE JACOB.

Associated Press (AP) (USA): BP 73, 101 Antananarivo; tel. (2) 40115; Correspondent CHRISTIAN CHADEFAUX.

Informatsionnoye Telegrafnoye Agentstvo Rossii—Telegrafnoye Agentstvo Suverennykh Stran (ITAR—TASS) (Russia): 18 bis rue Rainitivo, Antasahavola, 101 Antananarivo; tel. (2) 26371; telex 22347; Dir VALENTIN RAIKER.

Korean Central News Agency (KCNA) (Democratic People's Republic of Korea): BP 4276, 101 Antananarivo; tel. (2) 44795; Dir KIM YEUNG KYEUN.

Rossiyskoye Informatsionnoye Agentstvo—Novosti (RIA—Novosti) (Russia): BP 3840, 101 Antananarivo; tel. (2) 20411; telex 22272; Chief of Bureau BORIS IVANOV.

Xinhua (New China) News Agency (People's Republic of China): BP 1656, 101 Antananarivo; tel. (2) 29927; telex 22360; Chief of Bureau WU HAIYUN.

Publishers

Editions Ambozontany: BP 40, 301 Fianarantsoa; tel. (7) 50603; f. 1962; religious and school textbooks; Dir R. F. GIAMBRONE.

Foibe Filankevitry Ny Mpampianatra (FOFIPA): BP 202, 101 Antananarivo; tel. (2) 27500; f. 1971; school and educational texts; Dir Frère RAZAFINDRAKOTO.

Madagascar Print and Press Co (MADPRINT): rue Rabesahala, Antsakaviro, BP 953, 101 Antananarivo; tel. (2) 22536; telex 22226; fax (2) 34534; f. 1969; literary, technical and historical; Dir GEORGES RANAIVOSOA.

Maison d'Edition Protestante Antso (Librairie-Imprimerie): 19 rue Venance Manifatra, Imarivolanitra, BP 660, 101 Antananarivo; tel. (2) 20886; f. 1865; religious, school, social, political and general; Dir HANS ANDRIAMAMPIANINA.

Imprimerie Nouvelle: PK 2, Andranomahery, route de Majunga, 101 Antananarivo; tel. (2) 23330; Dir EUGÈNE RAHARIFIDY.

Nouvelle Société de Presse et d'Edition (NSPE): Immeuble Jeune Afrique, 58 rue Tsiombikibo, BP 1734, Ambatorinaky, 101 Antananarivo; tel. (2) 27788; telex 22225; fax (2) 30629.

Office du Livre Malgache: Lot 111 H29, Andrefan' Ambohijanahary, BP 617, 101 Antananarivo; tel. (2) 24449; f. 1970; children's and general; Sec.-Gen. JULIETTE RATSIMANDRAVA.

Edisiona Salohy: BP 7124, 101 Antananarivo; Dir JEAN RABENALISOA RAVALITERA.

Société de Presse et d'Edition de Madagascar: BP 1570, 101 Antananarivo; non-fiction, reference, science, university textbooks; Man. Dir Mrs RAJAOFERA ANDRIAMBELO.

Société Malgache d'Edition (SME): BP 659, Ankorondrano, 101 Antananarivo; tel. (2) 22635; telex 22340; fax (2) 33864; f. 1943; general fiction; university and secondary textbooks; Man. Dir RAHAGA RAMAHOLIMIHASO.

Société Nouvelle de l'Imprimerie Centrale (SNIC): làlana Ravoninahitriniarivo, BP 1414, 101 Antananarivo; tel. (2) 21118; f. 1959; science, school textbooks; Man. Dir MARTHE ANDRIAMBELO.

Imprimerie Takariva: 4 rue Radley, BP 1029, Antanimena, 101 Antananarivo; tel. (2) 22128; f. 1933; fiction, languages, school textbooks; Man. Dir PAUL RAPATSALAHY.

Trano Printy Fiangonana Loterana Malagasy (TPFLM): BP 538, 9 ave Grandidier, Antsahamanitra, 101 Antananarivo; tel. (2) 23340; f. 1875; religious, educational and fiction; Man. ABEL ARNESA.

Government Publishing House

Imprimerie Nationale: BP 38, 101 Antananarivo; tel. (2) 23675; all official publs; Dir JEAN DENIS RANDRIANIRINA.

Radio and Television

In December 1990 the state monopoly of broadcasting was abolished, and legislation was adopted which allows the establishment of private radio and television stations 'in partnership with the Government or its agencies'. According to UNESCO, there were an estimated 2,480,000 radio receivers and 248,000 television receivers in use in 1991.

RADIO

Radio Nasionaly Malagasy: BP 442, 101 Antananarivo; tel. (2) 21784; fax 22381; state-controlled; broadcasts in French and Malagasy; Dir SIMON SEVA MBOINY.

TELEVISION

Télévision Nasionaly Malagasy: BP 1202, 101 Antananarivo; tel. (2) 22381; telex 22506; f. 1931 as Radio-Télévision Malagasy; broadcasts in French and Malagasy; one transmitter; Dir-Gen. MAMY RAMIASINARIVO.

Finance

(cap. = capital; dep. = deposits; m. = million; brs = branches; amounts in Malagasy francs)

All commercial banks and insurance companies were nationalized in 1975, but in 1988 a process of restructuring was begun, allowing private and foreign investment.

BANKING

Central Bank

Banque Centrale de la République Malgache: ave de la Révolution Socialiste Malgache, BP 550, 101 Antananarivo; tel. (2) 21751; telex 22317; fax (2) 34532; f. 1973; bank of issue; cap. 1,000m.; Gov. RAOUL J. RAVELOMANANA; Dir-Gen. GASTON RAVELOJAONA.

Other Banks

Bankin'ny Tantsaha Mpamokatra (BTM): place de l'Indépendance, BP 183, 101 Antananarivo; tel. (2) 20251; telex 22208; fax (2) 33749; f. 1976 by merger; specializes in rural development; 90% state-owned; cap. 13,500m. (1992), dep. 193,485m. (1987); Man. BRUNO DISAINE; 75 brs.

Banky Fampandrosoana ny Varotra (BFV): 14 làlana Jeneraly Rabehevitra, BP 196, 101 Antananarivo; tel. (2) 20691; telex 22257; fax (2) 33645; 73.7% state-owned; f. 1977 by merger; cap. 11,500m. (1992), dep. 151,778.5m. (1990); Man. IGNACE RAMAROSON; Sec.-Gen. MAMY RABEMILA; 27 brs.

Banque Malgache de l'Océan Indien (BMOI) (Indian Ocean Malagasy Bank): place de l'Indépendance, BP 25, Antananarivo 101;

tel. (2) 34609; telex 22381; fax (2) 34610; f. 1990; cap. 10,000m. (March 1993); Pres. GASTON RAMENASON; Dir-Gen. MICHEL GUYON; 8 brs.

BNI—Crédit Lyonnais Madagascar: 74 rue du 26 Juin 1960, BP 174, 101 Antananarivo; tel. (2) 23951; telex 22205; fax (2) 33749; fmrly Bankin'ny Indostria; cap. 4,500m. (March 1993), dep. 207,209.2m. (1990); Pres. TANTELY ANDRIANARIVO; Dir-Gen. BERNARD FOURNIER; 27 brs.

Union Commercial Bank (UCB): 77 làlana Solombavambahoaka, BP 197, 101 Antananarivo; tel. (2) 27262; telex 22528; fax (2) 28740; f. 1992; cap. 1,500m. (March 1993); Pres. RAYMOND HEIN; Dir-Gen. JOCELYN THOMASSE.

INSURANCE

ARO (Assurances Réassurances Omnibranches): Antsahavola, BP 42, 101 Antananarivo; tel. (2) 20154; telex 22265; fax (2) 34464; Pres. DÉSIRÉ RAJOBSON; Dir-Gen. PASCAL RAKOTOMAVO.

Assurance France-Madagascar: 7 rue Rainitovo, BP 710, 101 Antananarivo; tel. (2) 23024; telex 22321; fax (2) 33673; f. 1951; Dir I. RATSIRA.

Compagnie Malgache d'Assurances et de Réassurances: Immeuble 'Ny Havana', Zone des 67 Ha, BP 3881, 101 Antananarivo; tel. (2) 26760; telex 22377; fax (2) 24303; f. 1968; cap. 13,482m. (1993); Pres. EVARISTE VAZAHA; Dir-Gen. JOCELYN RAKOTOMAVO.

Mutuelle d'Assurances Malagasy (MAMA): 1F, 12 bis, rue Rainibetsimisaraka, Ambalavao-Isotry, BP 185, 101 Antananarivo; tel. (2) 22508; Pres. RAKOTOARIVONY ANDRIAMAROMANANA.

Société Malgache d'Assurances, Faugère, Jutheau et Cie: 13 rue Patrice Lumumba, BP 673, 101 Antananarivo; f. 1952; tel. (2) 23162; telex 22247; Dir ANDRIANJAKA RAVELONAHIANA.

Trade and Industry

CHAMBER OF COMMERCE

Fédération des Chambres de Commerce, d'Industrie et d'Agriculture de Madagascar: 20 rue Colbert, BP 166, 101 Antananarivo; tel. 21567; 12 mem. chambers; Pres. HENRY RAZANATSHENEHO; Sec.-Gen. H. RATSIANDAVANA.

TRADE ORGANIZATION

Société d'Intérêt National Malgache des Produits Agricoles (SINPA): BP 754, rue Fernand-Kasanga, Tsimbazaza; tel. 20558; telex 22309; fax 20665; f. 1973; monopoly purchaser and distributor of agricultural produce; Chair. GUALBERT RAZANAJATOVO; Gen. Man. JEAN CLOVIS RALIJESY.

DEVELOPMENT ORGANIZATIONS

Société d'Etude et de Réalisation pour le Développement Industriel (SERDI): 78 bis, ave Lénine Ankaditapaka, BP 3180, 101 Antananarivo; tel. (2) 21335; telex 22453; fax (2) 29669; f. 1966; Dir-Gen. DAVID RAFIDISON.

Office militaire national pour les industries stratégiques (OMNIS): 21 làlana Razanakombana, BP 1 bis, 101 Antananarivo; tel. (2) 24439; telex 22370; fax (2) 22985; f. 1976; oversees the management of major industrial orgs and exploitation of mining resources; Dir-Gen. RAKOTO ANDRIANTSILAVO.

PRINCIPAL EMPLOYERS' ORGANIZATIONS

Groupement des Entreprises de Madagascar: Kianja MDRM sy Tia Tanindrazana, BP 1338, 101 Antananarivo; f. 1973; 22 syndicates and 26 individual cos; Sec.-Gen. AUGUSTIN RAFIDISON.

Syndicat des Entrepreneurs: 101 Antananarivo, 407 route Circulaire, BP 522.

Syndicat des Exportateurs de Vanille de Madagascar: Antalaha; 23 mems; Pres. M. BOURDILLON.

Syndicat des Importateurs et Exportateurs de Madagascar: 2 rue Georges Mandel, BP 188, 101 Antananarivo; Pres. M. FONTANA.

Syndicat des Industries de Madagascar: Kianja MDRM sy Tia Tanindrazana, BP 1695, 101 Antananarivo; tel. (2) 23608; f. 1958; Chair. CHARLES ANDRIANTSITOHAINA.

Syndicat des Planteurs de Café: 37 làlana Razafimahandry, BP 173, 101 Antananarivo.

Syndicat des Riziers et Producteurs de Riz de Madagascar: 2 rue Georges Mandel, BP 1329, 101 Antananarivo.

Syndicat Professionnel des Agents Généraux d'Assurances: Antananarivo; f. 1949; Pres. SOLO RATSIMBAZAFY; Sec. IHANTA RANDRIAMANDRANTO.

MAJOR INDUSTRIAL COMPANIES

The following are some of the largest companies in terms either of capital investment or employment.

Brasseries STAR Madagascar: BP 3806, Antananarivo; tel. (2) 27711; telex 22315; fax (2) 34682; f. 1953; cap. 10,090.9m. FMG; mfrs of beer and carbonated drinks. Pres. H. FRAISE; Gen. Man. YVAN COUDERC.

Compagnie des Ciments Malgaches: BP 302, Mahajanga; cap. 625m. FMG; cement works; Pres. JULES PLAQUET; Dir J. SCHNEEBERGER.

Cie Salinière de Madagascar: BP 29, Antsiranana; cap. 375m. FMG; exploitation of salt marshes.

La Cotonnière d'Antsirabé (COTONA): route d'Ambositra, BP 45, Antsirabé; tel. (2) 49422; telex 44800; fax (2) 49222; f. 1952; cap. 7,928m. FMG; spinning, weaving, printing and dyeing of textiles; Dirs-Gen. SALIM ISMAIL and AZIZ HASSAM ISMAIL.

Ets Gallois: BP 159, Antananarivo; cap. 220m. FMG; production of graphite and sisal; Pres. and Dir-Gen. HENRY GALLOIS.

Jiro sy Rano Malagasy (JIRAMA): BP 200, 149 rue Rainandriamampandry, Antananarivo; tel. (2) 20031; telex 22235; fax (2) 33806; f. 1975; state-owned; controls production and distribution of electricity and water; Dir Gen. CALEB RAKOTOARIVELO.

Kraomita Malagasy (KRAOMA): BP 936, Antananarivo; tel. (2) 24304; telex 22234; fax (2) 24654; f. 1966 as Cie Minière d'Andriamena (COMINA); cap. 1,540m. FMG; 100% state-owned; chrome mining and concentration; Dir-Gen. WILLY RANJATOELINA.

Omnium Industriel de Madagascar: BP 207, Antananarivo; tel. (2) 22373; telex 22303; fax (2) 28064; f. 1929; cap. 1,300m. FMG; mfrs of shoes and luggage; operates a tannery; Pres. and Dir-Gen. H. J. BARDAY.

Papeteries de Madagascar (PAPMAD): BP 1756, Ambohimanambola, 101 Antananarivo; tel. (2) 20635; telex 22229; fax (2) 24394; f. 1963; cap. 1,308m. FMG; paper-making; Pres. and Dir-Gen. P. RAJAONARY; Asst Dir-Gen. M. RAZAFIMIHARY.

Société Agricole du Domaine de Pechpeyrou: BP 71, Tolagnaro; f. 1947; cap. 192m. FMG; sisal growing.

Société Américaine, Grecque et Malgache 'Industrie de la Viande': Antananarivo; cap. 300m. FMG; abattoir, meat-canning, mfrs of meat products; Pres. and Dir-Gen. G. S. REPAS; Dir-Gen. T. C. BACOPOLOUS.

Société Commerciale Laitière (SOCOLAIT): BP 4126; Antananarivo; tel. (2) 22849; fax (2) 46467; cap. 800m. FMG; dairy products; Pres. SOCOTALY KARMALY.

Société des Cigarettes Melia de Madagascar: route d'Ambositra 110, BP 128, Antsirabé; tel. (2) 48241; telex 44803; f. 1956; cap. 881m. FMG; mfrs of cigarettes; Pres. and Dir-Gen. PHILIPPE DE VESINNE LARUE; Dir GUY RAVELOMANANTSOA.

Société d'Etudes de Constructions et Réparations Navales (SECREN): BP 135, Antsiranana; tel. (8) 21265; telex 93103; fax (8) 29326; f. 1975; cap. 2,600m. FMG; ship-building and repairs; Gen. Man. KILOBO RÉGIS.

Société de Filature et de Tissage de Madagascar (FITIM): BP 127, Mahajanga; f. 1930; cap. 1,444m. FMG; spinning and weaving of jute; Pres. AMADOU NDIAYE; Dir-Gen. GEORGES DIBERT.

Société Malgache de Collecte et de Distribution: BP 188, 101 Antananarivo; tel. (2) 24871; telex 22207; fax (2) 25024; f. 1972; fmrly Cie Lyonnaise de Madagascar; Chair. HENRI RASAMOELINA; Gen. Man. NORBERT RAZANAKOTO.

Société Malgache d'Exploitations Minières: BP 266, Antananarivo; f. 1926; cap. 130m. FMG; mining of graphite and mica; Pres. JEAN SCHNEIDER; Dir-Gen. LUCIEN DUMAS.

Société Malgache de Pêcherie (SOMAPECHE): BP 324, Mahanga; cap. 200m. FMG; sea fishing; Pres. J. RABEMANANJARA; Dir-Gen. J. BRUNOT.

Société Malgache de Raffinage: BP 433, Toamasina; f. 1964; cap. 750m. FMG; 51% state-owned; refinery for petroleum imported from the Middle East, chiefly Iran; production from offshore petroleum in Madagascar is planned; Dir-Gen. JACQUES GLANTENET.

Société Siramamy Malagasy (SIRAMA): BP 1633, Antananarivo; f. 1949; state-owned; cap. 2,500m. FMG; sugar refinery at St Louis; Pres. GABRIEL DAHER; Dir-Gen. Y. GROUITCH.

Société Textile de Majunga (SOTEMA): BP 375, Mahajanga; tel. (8) 2682; telex 62704; f. 1967; cap. 2,624m. FMG; spinning, weaving, printing and finishing textiles, finished garments; Pres. ALFRED RAKOTONJANAHARY; Vice-Pres. EDOUARD SEROUSSI.

Société Verrerie Malagasy (SOVEMA): BP 84, Toamasina; f. 1970; cap. 235.6m. FMG; bottles and glass articles; Pres. and Dir-Gen. A. SIBILLE.

Solitany Malagasy (SOLIMA): 2 ave Grandidier; BP 140, Antananarivo; tel. (2) 20633; telex 22222; fax (2) 26693; f. 1976; cap. 2,505m. FMG; importing and refining of crude petroleum, production and export of petroleum products; Dir-Gen. JEAN-BAPTISTE RENÉ.

TRADE UNIONS

Cartel National des Organisations Syndicales de Madagascar (CARNOSYAMA): BP 1035, 101 Antananarivo.

Confédération des Travailleurs Malgaches (Fivomdronamben'ny Mpiasa Malagasy—FMM): 3 ave Lénine, Ambatomitsanga, BP 1558, 101 Antananarivo; tel. (2) 24565; f. 1957; Sec.-Gen. JEAN RASOLONDRAIBE; 30,000 mems.

Fédération des Syndicats des Travailleurs de Madagascar (Firaisan'ny Sendika eran'i Madagaskara—FISEMA): Lot III, rue Pasteur Isotry, 101 Antananarivo; f. 1956; Pres. DESIRÉ RALAMBOTAHINA; Sec.-Gen. M. RAZAKANAIVO; 8 affiliated unions; 60,000 mems.

Fédération des Travailleurs Malagasy Révolutionnaires (FISEMARE): Lot IV N 77, Ankadifots, BP 1128, Antananarivo-Befelatanana; tel. (2) 21989; f. 1985; Pres. PAUL RABEMANANJARA.

Sendika Kristianina Malagasy—SEKRIMA (Christian Confederation of Malagasy Trade Unions): Soarano, route de Mahajanga, BP 1035, 101 Antananarivo; tel. (2) 23174; f. 1937; Pres. MARIE RAKOTOANOSY; Gen. Sec. RAYMOND RAKOTOARISAONA; 158 affiliated unions; 40,000 mems.

Sendika Revolisakionera Malagasy (SEREMA): 101 Antananarivo.

Union des Syndicats Autonomes de Madagascar (USAM): Ampasadratsarahoby, Lot 11 H67, Faravohitra, BP 1038, 101 Antananarivo; Pres. NORBERT RAKOTOMANANA; Sec.-Gen. VICTOR RAHAGA; 46 affiliated unions; 30,000 mems.

Transport

RAILWAYS

In 1993 there were 1,095 km of railway, all 1-m gauge track. The northern system, which comprised 729 km of track, links Toamasina, on the east coast, with Antsirabé, in the interior, via Brikaville, Moramanga and Antananarivo, with a branch line from Moramanga to Vohidiala which divides to Lake Alaotra and Morarano to collect chromium ore. The southern system, which comprised 170 km of track, links Manakara, on the south-east coast, and Fianarantsoa.

Réseau National des Chemins de Fer Malagasy: 1 ave de l'Indépendance, BP 259, Soarano, 101 Antananarivo; tel. (2) 20521; telex 22233; fax (2) 22288; f. 1909; Dir-Gen. RANAIVOHARITAFIKA ANDRIANTSOAVINA.

ROADS

In 1991 there were 34,750 km of classified roads, of which 8,539 km were main roads and 18,382 km were secondary roads; 5,352 km of the road network were paved. In 1987 there were 39,500 km of unclassified roads, used only in favourable weather.

INLAND WATERWAYS

The Pangalanes Canal runs for 600 km near the east coast from Toamasina to Farafangana. In 1984 the Government initiated a development project which was to restore more than 200 km of the canal by 1988, at a cost of 18.5m. FMG. In early 1990 432 km of the canal between Toamasina and Mananjary were navigable.

SHIPPING

There are 18 ports, the largest being at Toamasina, which handles about 70% of total traffic, and Mahajanga. In 1987 Madagascar received foreign loans totalling US $34.8m., including a credit of $16m. from the World Bank, to finance a project to rehabilitate 10 ports.

Compagnie Générale Maritime (CGM): BP 69, 501 Toamasina; tel. (5) 32312; telex 55612; f. 1976 by merger; Rep. J. P. BERGEROT.

Compagnie Malgache de Navigation (CMN): rue Toto Radona, BP 1621, 101 Antananarivo; tel. (2) 25516; telex 22263; f. 1960; coasters; 13,784 grt; transfer to private-sector ownership pending in 1994; Pres. Mme ELINAH BAKOLY RAJAONSON; Dir-Gen. ARISTIDE EMMANUEL.

Navale et Commerciale Havraise Peninsulaire (NCHP): rue Rabearivelo Antsahavola, BP 1021, 101 Antananarivo; tel. (2) 22502; telex 22273; Rep. JEAN PIERRE NOCKIN.

Société Nationale Malgache des Transports Maritimes (SMTM): 6 rue Indira Gandhi, BP 4077, 101 Antananarivo; tel. (2) 27342; telex 22277; fax (2) 33327; f. 1963; services to Europe; Chair. ALEXIS RAZAFINDRATSINA; Dir-Gen. RAMANANTSOA ANDRIONOVO.

Solitany Malagasy (SOLIMA): 2 ave Grandidier, BP 140, 101 Antananarivo; tel. (2) 20633; telex 22222; fax (2) 26693; f. 1976; transports and refines petroleum and its products; Chair. (vacant); Dir-Gen. CHRISTIAN LOUIS NTSAY.

CIVIL AVIATION

The international airport is at Antananarivo, while the airports at Mahajanga, Toamasina and Nossi-Bé can also accommodate large jet aircraft. There are more than 200 airfields, of which 57 are open to public air traffic.

Société Nationale Malgache des Transports Aériens (Air Madagascar): 31 ave de l'Indépendance, BP 437, 101 Antananarivo; tel. (2) 22222; telex 22232; f. 1962; 89.58% state-owned; extensive internal routes connecting all the principal towns; external services to the Comoros, France, Mauritius and Réunion; Chair. EMMANUEL RAKOTOVAHINY; Dir-Gen. RANDRIAMASY ZACKY.

Direction des Transports Aériens: BP 921, Anosy, 101 Antananarivo; tel. (2) 24604; telex 22301; fax (2) 24001.

Tourism

Madagascar's attractions include unspoiled scenery and many unusual varieties of wildlife. In 1990 receipts from tourism totalled US $37m., and there were 4,208 hotel rooms. In 1991 34,891 tourists visited Madagascar (a decline of 34% compared with 1990). In January 1989 a tourism investment programme was approved, in an effort to increase the number of visitors to 138,000 per year and to provide 5,000 extra hotel beds by 1995.

Direction du Tourisme de Madagascar: Tsimbazaza, BP 610, 101 Antananarivo; tel. (2) 26298; telex 26298; fax (2) 26719.

Defence

In June 1993 total armed forces numbered 21,000 men: army 20,000, navy 500 and air force 500. There is a paramilitary gendarmerie of 7,500.

Defence Expenditure: Budgeted at 59,175m. francs MG in 1992.

Chief of Armed Forces General Staff: Air Cdre ROBERT RABEMANANTSOA.

Education

Education is officially compulsory between six and 11 years of age. Madagascar has both public and private schools, although legislation that was enacted in 1978 envisaged the progressive elimination of private education. Primary education generally begins at the age of six and lasts for five years. Secondary education, beginning at 11 years of age, lasts for a further seven years, comprising a first cycle of four years and a second of three years. In 1990 primary enrolment was equivalent to 92% of children in the relevant age-group (males 93%; females 91%), while the comparable ratio for secondary education was 18% (males 18%; females 18%). Enrolment in tertiary education in that year was equivalent to 3.4% of the relevant age-group (males 3.8%; females 3.1%). According to UNESCO estimates, 19.8% of the adult population (males 12.3%; females 27.1%) remained illiterate in 1990: one of the lowest rates of illiteracy in Africa. In 1991 expenditure by the central government was 127,500m. francs MG (15.8% of total expenditure).

Bibliography

Archer, R. *Madagascar depuis 1972, la marche d'une révolution.* Paris, Editions l'Harmattan, 1976.

Bastian, G. *Madagascar, étude géographique et économique.* Nathan, 1967.

Brown, Sir M. *Madagascar Rediscovered.* London, Damien Tunnacliffe, 1978.

Cadoux, C. *La République malgache.* Paris, Berger-Levrault, 1970.

Covell, M. *Madagascar. Politics, Economics and Society.* London, Frances Pinter, 1987.

Deleris, F. *Ratsiraka: Socialisme et Misère à Madagascar.* Paris, L'Harmattan, 1986.

Deschamps, H. *Histoire de Madagascar.* 4th Edn, Paris, Berger-Levrault, 1972.

Drysdale, H. *Dancing with the Dead: A Journey through Zanzibar and Madagascar.* London, Hamish Hamilton, 1991.

Duruflé, G. *L'ajustement structurel en Afrique (Sénégal, Côte d'Ivoire, Madagascar).* Paris, Editions Karthala, 1987.

Ellis, S. *Un complot colonial à Madagascar: L'affaire Rainandriamampandry.* Paris, Editions Karthala, 1990.

Feeley-Harnick, G. *A Green Estate: Restoring Independence in Madagascar.* Washington, DC, Smithsonian Institution Press, 1991.

de Gaudusson, J. *L'Administration malgache.* Paris, Berger-Levrault, 1976.

Heseltine, N. *Madagascar.* London, Pall Mall, 1971.

Hugon, P. *Economie et enseignement à Madagascar.* Paris, Institut International de Planification de l'Education, 1976.

Litalien, R. *Madagascar 1956–1960, Etape vers la décolonisation.* Paris, Ecole Pratique des Hautes Etudes, 1975.

Massiot, M. *L'organisation politique, administrative, financière et judiciaire de la République malgache.* Antananarivo, Librairie de Madagascar, 1970.

Mutibwa, P. *The Malagasy and the Europeans: Madagascar's Foreign Relations 1861–95.* London, Longman, 1974.

Pascal, R. *La République malgache: Pacifique indépendance.* Paris, Berger-Levrault, 1965.

Pavageau, J. *Jeunes paysans sans terre: l'exemple malgache.* Paris, Editions l'Harmattan, 1981.

Rabemananjara, J. *Nationalisme et problèmes malgaches.* Paris, 1958.

Rabenoro, C. *Les relations extérieures de Madagascar, de 1960 à 1972.* Paris, Editions l'Harmattan, 1986.

Raison-Jourde, F. *Les souverains de Madagascar.* Paris, Editions Karthala, 1983.

Rajémis-Raolison, R. *Dictionnaire historique et géographique de Madagascar.* Fianarantsoa, Librairie Ambozontany, 1966.

Rajoelina, P. *Quarante années de la vie politique de Madagascar, 1947–1987.* Paris, L'Harmattan, 1988.

Rajoelina, P. and Ramelet, A. *Madagascar, la grande ile.* Paris, L'Harmattan, 1989.

Ralaimihoatra, E. *Histoire de Madagascar.* 2 vols. Antananarivo, Société Malgache d'Editions, 1966–67.

Ramahatra, O. *Madagascar: Une économie en phase d'ajustement.* Paris, Editions l'Harmattan, 1989.

Spacensky, A. *Madagascar: Cinquante ans de vie politique (de Ralaimongo à Tsiranana).* Paris, Nouvelles Editions Latines, 1970.

Thompson, V., and Adloff, R. *The Malagasy Republic.* Stanford University Press, 1965.

Tronchon, J. *L'insurrection malgache de 1947.* Paris, Editions Karthala, 1986.

Vérin, P. *Madagascar.* Paris, Editions Karthala, 1990.

Vindard, G. R., and Battistini, R. *Bio-geography and Ecology of Madagascar.* The Hague, 1972.

MALAWI

Physical and Social Geography

A. MACGREGOR HUTCHESON

The land-locked Republic of Malawi extends some 840 km from north to south, varying in width from 80 to 160 km. It has a total area of 118,484 sq km (45,747 sq miles), including 24,208 sq km (9,347 sq miles) of inland water, and is aligned along the southern continuation of the east African rift valley system.

Malawi occupies a plateau of varying height, bordering the deep rift valley trench which averages 80 km in width. The northern two-thirds of the rift valley floor are almost entirely occupied by Lake Malawi, which is 568 km in length and varies in width from 16 km to 80 km. The lake covers an area of 23,310 sq km, and has a mean surface of 472 m above sea-level. The southern third of the rift valley is traversed by the River Shire, draining Lake Malawi, via the shallow Lake Malombe, to the River Zambezi. The plateau surfaces on either side of the rift valley lie mainly at 760–1,370 m, but very much higher elevations are attained; above the highlands west of Lake Malawi are the Nyika and Viphya plateaux and the Dedza mountains and Kirk Range, which rise to between 1,524 and 2,440 m in places. South of Lake Malawi are the Shire highlands and the Zomba and Mulanje mountain ranges; the Zomba plateau rises to 2,100 m, and Mt Mulanje, the highest mountain in central Africa, to 3,050 m above sea-level.

The great variations in altitude and latitudinal extent are responsible for a wide range of climatic, soil and vegetational conditions within Malawi. There are three climatic seasons. During the cool season, from May to August, there is very little cloud, and mean temperatures in the plateau areas are 15.5°C–18°C, and in the rift valley 20°C–24.5°C. The coldest month is July, when the maximum temperature is 22.2°C and the minimum 11.7°C. In September and October, before the rains, a short hot season occurs when humidity increases: mean temperatures range from 27°C–30°C in the rift valley, and from 22°C–24.5°C on the plateaux at this time. During October/November temperatures exceeding 37°C may be registered in the low-lying areas. The rainy season lasts from November to April, and over 90% of the total annual rainfall occurs during this period. Most of Malawi receives an annual rainfall of 760–1,015 mm, but some areas in the higher plateaux experience over 1,525 mm.

Malawi possesses some of the most fertile soils in south-central Africa. Of particular importance are those in the lake-shore plains, the Lake Chilwa-Palombe plain and the upper and lower Shire valley. Good plateau soils occur in the Lilongwe-Kasungu high plains and in the tea-producing areas of Thyolo, Mulanje and Nkhata Bay districts. Although just over half the land area of Malawi is considered suitable for cultivation, rather less than 50% of this area is cultivated at present; this is an indication of the agricultural potential yet to be realized. The lakes and rivers have been exploited for their considerable hydroelectric and irrigation potential.

Malawi is one of the more densely populated countries of Africa, with 7,982,607 inhabitants (an average density of 67.4 per sq km of land) at the 1987 census. There were an estimated 8,823,000 inhabitants at mid-1992. According to UN projections, Malawi's population will increase to 11.4m. by the middle of the year 2000. However, population patterns are expected to be affected by the high rate of incidence of AIDS, which is particularly prevalent in urban areas. In mid-1994 there were estimated to be 600,000 Mozambican refugees in Malawi. Labour has been a Malawian resource for many years, and thousands of migratory workers seek employment in neighbouring countries, particularly in South Africa.

As a result of physical, historical and economic factors, Malawi's population is very unevenly distributed. The Southern Region, the most developed of the three regions, possesses over half the population, while the Northern Region has only about 12%. New investment in the Northern and Central Regions and the movement of the capital from Zomba to a new site at Lilongwe in the early 1970s are helping to redress these regional imbalances.

Recent History

RICHARD BROWN

THE COLONIAL PERIOD

In 1891 the British government declared a protectorate over the area that came to be known as Nyasaland. An agricultural economy was established by white settlers, while many Africans were made tenants-at-will, with few legal rights to the land they cultivated. Grievances against the injustices of the colonial system led to an unsuccessful uprising by Africans in early 1915. In 1944 the Nyasaland African Congress (NAC) was formed, linking, on a non-ethnic basis, native associations, independent churches and other groups of educated Africans. In 1951 the British government gave its assent to proposals by white settlers for a federation with the territories of Northern and Southern Rhodesia. Despite the opposition of Africans, who feared that the plan would prevent the achievement of independence, the Federation of Rhodesia and Nyasaland (FRN) was formally established in October 1953.

By 1955 the influence of a radical element within the NAC, led by Henry Chipembere and Kanyama Chiume, had become evident. In July 1958 Dr Hastings Kamuzu Banda, a physician who had retained close links with the NAC despite being resident abroad for nearly 40 years, returned to assume the leadership of the party. His vigorous denunciations of the federation, combined with the forceful campaigning of his followers, provoked an outbreak of civil disorder in March 1959: a state of emergency was declared, the NAC was banned and its leaders were arrested. After the emergence of the new Malawi Congress Party (MCP) in September 1959, led by the imprisoned Dr Banda, the British authorities were obliged to choose between maintaining control through the continued use of armed force, or leaving Malawi completely: they chose the latter alternative. Dr Banda was released in April 1960. Elections held in August 1961 gave the MCP a decisive victory. Full self-government was attained in January 1963; Dr Banda became prime minister in February, and the FRN was dissolved in December. On 6 July 1964 the protectorate of Nyasaland became the independent state of Malawi.

Dr Banda's reluctance to hasten the 'Africanization' of the economy or to pursue stronger anti-colonial policies was opposed by a significant proportion of educated Malawians; the prime minister reacted by giving greater responsibilities to white expatriates and by eliciting popular support from the less educated sections of the population. The dispute degenerated into open revolt, and in February 1965 Henry Chipembere led an unsuccessful uprising which resulted in his withdrawal into exile.

THE BANDA REGIME

On 6 July 1966 Malawi officially became a republic and a one-party state, with Banda as president: he was voted president-for-life in 1971. In the ensuing years no political opposition was tolerated, and the various exiled opposition groups, of which the most prominent were the Socialist League of Malawi (LESOMA) and the Malawi Freedom Movement (MAFREMO), remained ineffectual, although they claimed to command strong support. In March 1979 Banda admitted that a letter-bomb which had injured the leader of LESOMA, Dr Attati Mpakati, had been sent in accordance with his instructions; the Malawi government, however, denied any responsibility for the murder of Mpakati in March 1983, while he was on a private visit to Zimbabwe. In May 1983 the leader of MAFREMO, Orton Chirwa, and his wife Vera were sentenced to death for treason (having, it was alleged, been kidnapped in Zambia and brought to Malawi by force). Following appeals for clemency by international organizations and heads of state, Banda commuted the sentence to one of life imprisonment. (Orton Chirwa died in prison in October 1992 and Vera Chirwa was released in January 1993.) In October 1989 10 people, including a senior official of MAFREMO and members of his family, were killed in a bomb attack in Lusaka, Zambia; the Malawi government denied responsibility for the incident. In the following month the government rejected allegations by Amnesty International, that several Malawian political detainees had been subjected to torture. In October 1990 another international human rights organization accused the Malawi government of using detention without trial, torture and assassination to suppress political opposition; it was also alleged that Malawi security forces had shot dead 20 anti-government protesters in March of that year. In February 1991 a new opposition movement, the Malawi Socialist Labour Party, was formed by Malawians living in exile in Tanzania.

Within Malawi no political figure was permitted to emerge as an obvious successor to the ageing president. In 1983 a dispute was reported to have developed between Dick Matenje, the secretary-general of the MCP and a minister without portfolio, and John Tembo, the governor of the Reserve Bank of Malawi, concerning the eventual succession. Matenje and three other senior politicians died in May, reportedly in a motor accident, but exiled opposition members claimed that they had been shot while trying to leave the country. (An inquiry into the affair was opened in 1994.) The post of MCP secretary-general has remained vacant since then, and the dissolution and reorganization of the government has become virtually an annual occurrence, apparently to prevent ministers from establishing secure power bases. At a general election held in May 1987 (as in the previous elections of 1978 and 1983) only MCP candidates were allowed to participate: a total of 213 candidates contested 69 of the 112 elective seats in the national assembly.

In March 1992 the government was exposed to unprecedented opposition from the influential Roman Catholic church in Malawi, with the publication by its bishops of an open letter criticizing the state's alleged abuses of human rights. Pressure on the government intensified later in that month, when about 80 Malawian political exiles gathered in Lusaka to devise a strategy to precipitate political reforms. In early April Chakufwa Chihana, a prominent trade union leader who had demanded multi-party elections, returned to Malawi from exile and was immediately detained by the security forces. The Banda regime was seriously threatened from within the country in early May, when industrial unrest in the southern city of Blantyre escalated into violent anti-government riots; these spread to Lilongwe, and reportedly resulted in at least 40 deaths. Shortly afterwards international donors suspended all non-humanitarian aid to Malawi, pending an improvement in the government's human rights record. It was announced in early June that several hundred people had been arrested and charged with circulating anti-government literature.

Elections to an enlarged legislature took place in June 1992, at which 675 MCP candidates contested 141 elective seats in the national assembly: 45 candidates were returned unopposed, five seats remained vacant, owing to the disqualification of some candidates, and 62 former members of the national assembly lost their seats. The government claimed a turnout of about 80% of the electorate, although the opposition deemed this figure to be exaggeratedly high. At the end of June the president nominated 10 additional members to the national assembly. Chakufwa Chihana was released from detention in July, but was re-arrested soon afterwards and charged with sedition. (In December Chihana was found guilty and sentenced to two years' hard labour; the sentence was, however, subsequently reduced on appeal to nine months, and he was released from prison in June 1993.)

In September 1992 a group of opposition politicians formed the Alliance for Democracy (AFORD), a pressure group operating within Malawi under the chairmanship of Chihana, which aimed to campaign for democratic political reform. Another opposition organization, the United Democratic Front (UDF), was formed in the same month. In the October Banda reluctantly agreed that a national referendum by secret ballot on the introduction of multi-party democracy should be held. In early January 1993 more than 100,000 anti-government demonstrators attended a rally in Blantyre. During that month LESOMA and another party, the Malawi Democratic Union, merged to form the United Front for Multi-party Democracy, based in Zambia. In March MAFREMO dissolved itself and its membership joined AFORD.

TRANSITION TO DEMOCRACY

The referendum on the introduction of multi-party democracy took place in mid-June 1993. Although the government had disrupted the activities of opposition groups prior to the referendum, the latter secured a decisive victory, with 63.2% of voters demanding an end to single-party rule. A turnout of 67% of the electorate was recorded. The opposition received especially strong support in the north and south of the country, while voters in the central region mainly remained loyal to the MCP. Following the referendum, Banda rejected opposition demands for the immediate installation of a government of national unity. He agreed, however, to establish a multi-party national executive council, to oversee the transition to a multi-party system, and a national consultative council to draft a new constitution. A one-year interim constitution was introduced in May 1994, prior to the holding of multi-party elections. In October 1993 Dr Banda underwent major surgery in South Africa. Although believed to be more than 90 years of age, he was able to resume full presidential duties in December, shortly after violent clashes between the army and the 'Young Pioneers', the militant youth movement operated by the MCP (in which the 'Young Pioneers' were forcibly disarmed).

Banda's domination of the country finally ended with the multi-party elections held on 17 May 1994. In the four-candidate presidential contest, Bakili Muluzi, leader of the UDF, obtained 47.3% of the vote and was sworn in as president on 21 May; Banda himself won 33.6%, and Chakufwa Chihana (of AFORD) 18.6%. The UDF won 84 of the 177 parliamentary seats, the MCP 55 seats and AFORD 36 seats (the results of voting in two constituencies were invalidated). In the absence of strong ideological differences between the parties, regional and ethnic allegiances predominated: AFORD won all 33 of the Northern Region's seats; the MCP was strongly supported in the Central Region; and the UDF won most of the seats in the Southern Region. The expected UDF–AFORD coalition did not materialize, however, and one month after the elections AFORD agreed instead to work with the MCP, thus compelling the UDF to form a government without a parliamentary majority. The return of serious drought in June added to the immediate problems facing the government. The new president, a Muslim businessman and a former secretary-general of the MCP, has declared his intention to uphold democratic reforms, to work for political reconciliation and to alleviate poverty and reverse environmental degradation. President

Muluzi has also stated that his government will continue to pursue the economic liberalization policies initiated during the Banda period. Dr Banda's retirement from political life was announced in August 1994.

REGIONAL RELATIONS

President Banda's establishment of diplomatic relations with South Africa in 1967 alienated him for a time from most other African leaders, as did his promotion of friendly relations with Portugal under the pre-1974 right-wing regime. Following independence, Malawi's relations with its neighbours, Tanzania and Zambia, were strained by disputes over territorial boundaries: during the late 1960s Malawi claimed that its natural boundaries included the whole of the northern half of Lake Malawi, and extended at least 160 km north of Tanzania's Songwo river, as well as east and west into Mozambique and Zambia. Full diplomatic relations with Zambia were established in 1971, but it was not until 1985 that diplomatic relations were established with Tanzania. However, Malawi did become a member of the Southern African Development Community (SADC).

Dr Banda gave support neither to the Frente de Libertação de Moçambique (Frelimo) nor to the Patriotic Front (PF), during their respective independence struggles in Mozambique and Zimbabwe, and in 1982 the Mozambique government alleged that its opponents, members of the Resistência Nacional Moçambicana (Renamo, also known as the MNR), were operating from bases in Malawi. In October 1984 Malawi and Mozambique signed a general co-operation agreement, establishing a joint commission to regulate their relations. In July 1986, however, the chief of staff of Mozambique's armed forces alleged that Malawi was actively assisting the guerrillas of Renamo. Despite Banda's denial of these allegations, President Machel of Mozambique warned that, if Malawi continued to assist Renamo, he would close the border between the two countries, thereby denying Malawi its most direct access to the sea. In October 1986 President Machel was killed in an aeroplane crash in South Africa. The South African government claimed that documents which had been discovered in the crash wreckage revealed a plot by Mozambique and Zimbabwe to overthrow the Malawi government. Angry protests from the Malawi government to Mozambique and Zimbabwe were met by denials of the accusations. In December Malawi and Mozambique signed a further agreement on defence and security matters, which was believed to include co-operation in eliminating Renamo operations. In April 1987 it was confirmed that Malawi troops had been stationed in Mozambique to protect the strategic railway line linking Malawi to the Mozambican port of Nacala. In July 1988 relations between the two countries were consolidated when President Chissano of Mozambique made a state visit to Malawi, during which he stated that he did not believe Malawi to be supporting Renamo. In December Malawi, Mozambique and the UN High Commissioner for Refugees signed an agreement to promote the voluntary repatriation of an estimated 650,000 Mozambican refugees who had fled into Malawi over the previous two years, as a result of the continuing unrest in Mozambique, and who were placing a considerable burden on the country's resources; the number of refugees continued to rise, however, reaching about 1m. by mid-1992. Following the peace settlement in Mozambique in October 1992, a repatriation programme began, to be completed over a three-year period. However, in mid-1994 an estimated 600,000 Mozambican refugees still remained in Malawi.

Malawi's relations with Zimbabwe improved during the 1980s, despite the Banda regime's hostility to the PF before Zimbabwe's independence, and his failure to attend the independence celebrations in 1980. Diplomatic relations were subsequently established, and in 1986 a joint permanent commission was formed. In April 1990 Banda was a guest of honour at celebrations for Zimbabwe's 10th anniversary of independence.

As part of a more active foreign policy, the new government has offered troops for the UN peace-keeping operation in Rwanda and undertaken joint military exercises with US troops within Malawi.

Economy

RICHARD BROWN

INTRODUCTION

In terms of average income, Malawi is still among the world's poorest countries, with a gross domestic product (GDP) of about K959 (US $218) per head in 1993. According to UN figures, 80% of the estimated population of 9.3m. live below the poverty line. Nevertheless, Malawi has had some development successes since independence in 1964, despite problems of subsistence agriculture, low educational levels, shortage of skilled personnel, lack of mineral resources, inadequate infrastructure and import-dependent industries, compounded by the limitations of a land-locked position and a small domestic market.

ECONOMIC BACKGROUND

During the 1970s Malawi benefited from a sharp rise in investment, supported by favourable government policies and an influx of foreign aid and capital. The concurrent expansion of commercial output led to a doubling of production of export crops, and also placed Malawi among the few countries of sub-Saharan Africa where food production kept pace with population growth. In the social services sector there were extensive donor-supported programmes to improve the provision of education, health services, water supply and sanitation. Rapid growth in the domestic economy was, however, paralleled by a poor performance of the economy externally.

Malawi was beset by drought during 1979–81. The resulting decline in agricultural output adversely affected export earnings and necessitated the import of food, while associated industries began to experience severe reductions in revenue. With virtually no sector of the economy unaffected, GDP growth, in real terms, declined to 3.1% per year during the period 1980–91. In 1981, in an effort to restore growth, the government, supported by the IMF and the World Bank, initiated a programme of reform

The economy responded rapidly, helped by the return of favourable rains in 1982 and a resurgence of agricultural output. Restraint in the level of imports and an increase in inflows of aid helped to reduce Malawi's current account deficit while also enabling levels of external borrowing to decline. However, Malawi's terms of trade continued to decline during the period, and the complete closure of the routes through wartorn Mozambique in 1984 created excessively high freight costs for exports. A further reform programme began in 1986. Although a number of the anticipated measures were implemented during the year (including a reduction in subsidies and the reorganization of some major parastatal bodies) the economy began to falter again, with GDP growth falling to 2.8%, compared with the target of 4.2% and the budget deficit amounting to 11% of GDP, compared with a target of 3.5%. As a result of the economy's disappointing performance, the government cancelled its three-year extended facility with the IMF in August 1986, shortly before it was due to expire in October, pending a reassessment of the reform programme. In March 1988 agreement was reached on a 14-month stand-by facility, the government having agreed in August 1987, under pressure from the IMF, to reschedule its debt repayments. In July 1988 the government obtained a four-year enhanced structural adjustment facility (ESAF) from the IMF. A statement of development policies for the period to 1996 was published in 1988. Real GDP decreased at an average annual rate of 0.3% in 1985-92. Economic performance in 1992 was adversely affected by severe drought conditions, an unprecedented level of industrial unrest and the decision by international donors in May to link all future non-humanitarian aid to progress in upholding human rights. According to government figures, GDP declined by 7.9% in 1992, while (following two devaluations of the national currency) the annual inflation rate reached 22%. More than one-half of the population experienced food shortages in that year. Favourable weather conditions in 1992–93 restored the situation, and growth in real GDP reached 9.3% in 1993. The return of drought in the 1993–94 season is expected to reduce growth by 6.5% in 1994. The prospect of increased aid from the international community following the restoration of democracy may mittigate the worst effects of the downturn.

AGRICULTURE

Agriculture is the most important sector of the economy, accounting for some 27.5% of GDP in 1992. During 1980–91 agricultural GDP increased by an annual average of 2.4%. An estimated 73.3% of the working population are engaged in agriculture. The vast majority of these work in the smallholder sector, which accounts for nearly 80% of the cultivated area and of agricultural output, which is mostly on a subsistence basis. The principal cash crop is tobacco. Maize is the principal food crop, and is grown by virtually all smallholders. There have been some exports of maize, although imports of cereals have been required in years when unfavourable weather conditions have adversely affected output. Other food crops include cassava, millet, sorghum, groundnuts, rice and pulses. Malawi's principal agricultural exports are tobacco, tea and sugar. Large, hand-shelled, confectionary-grade groundnuts, coffee, cassava, rice, medium staple cotton and sunflower seed are also exported. Smallholder crops are marketed for export by the Agricultural Development and Marketing Corpn (ADMARC). Since the implementation, after 1981, of more favourable pricing arrangements, together with the introduction of new hybrid varieties, efforts have been made to diversify the range of commercial smallholder crops, to improve the productivity of food and export crops and to raise rural incomes. Assistance has been obtained from several donors, led by the International Development Association (IDA). The IDA is also helping to finance, in association with the International Fund for Agricultural Development (IFAD), a scheme, instigated in 1988, to improve the availability of credit to small-scale farmers. This scheme forms part of government plans to double the coverage of seasonal credit to about 30% of smallholders by 1995. Efforts to expand commercial production of crops, especially for export, and to raise rural incomes have taken two forms—the expansion of commercial smallholding schemes and the National Rural Development Programe (NRDP). Among the wide range of donor-supported smallholder schemes is an EU-sponsored project to develop the cultivation of tobacco and coffee in the north, and a tobacco scheme, financed by the Commonwealth Development Corporation (CDC) of the United Kingdom, near Mt Kasungu on the central plateau. The latter, started in 1970, has involved more than 1,500 growers, cultivating 1,200 ha of flue-cured tobacco and an equivalent area of maize. The 20-year NRDP, introduced in 1977, centred on eight agricultural development regions, covering one-fifth of the country; by 1985 more than 80% of Malawi's smallholders were involved in the programme. The scheme was aimed at increasing crop yields by encouraging simple improvements in farming techniques, with greater use of fertilizers, pest control and irrigation. This was intended to stimulate farmers with very small plots (40% of all smallholders) to achieve self-sufficiency in food production, and to enable larger smallholders to produce a surplus for market. However, growth in smallholder output lost momentum during the late 1980s, and the programme was suspended in 1988 (growth in smallholder output was only 2.6% in that year, compared with growth of 7% in the estate sector). This decline in the rate of growth resulted from the limited access of the majority of peasants to improved credit facilities and crop varieties; a government decision to phase out fertilizer subsidies from 1986; rising transport costs; and, most significantly, the small size of most plots of land.

Various livestock improvement projects have also been launched, resulting in a considerable drop in beef imports. Pilot dairies have been established in Blantyre and Lilongwe. Almost all livestock is kept by smallholders. In 1988 the total catch of fish from the lakes and the upper Shire river was about 83,000 tons, of which almost 8,000 tons were caught by the commercial sector. The EC and the UK are major donors to the sector, and are providing finance to help to fund research into small-scale fishing and the development of fish-farming.

Timber and pulpwood plantations have been developed since the early 1970s, with the area under state plantations totalling 20,800 ha in 1985. In addition, 54,000 ha of pine and eucalyptus have been planted on the Viphya plateau, in the north, to supply a pulp and paper project. The project focuses on development of part of the Viphya plantation, and the construction of processing facilities. The scheme will eventually provide employment for several thousand people, not only in forestry but also in infrastructural development, which includes the construction of a port on the lake at Chinteche and a new town.

Major Exports

Malawi is the second largest producer of tobacco in Africa, after Zimbabwe. The crop sustains some 6,500 estates and provides a cash income for about 66,000 tenant smallholders. It is by far the most important export, accounting for 75.6% of domestic export earnings in 1991. Malawi is the only significant African producer of burley, which is the most important of the six types of tobacco cultivated in Malawi. Output of this variety has achieved record levels in each year since 1991, the first year in which its cultivation on smallholdings was permitted (the production of burley had previously been confined to estates). The importance of burley has increased greatly since the early 1980s, when strong world demand encouraged a major expansion in output. Output of flue-cured tobacco, which is only grown on estates, and of the four types of tobacco traditionally cultivated by smallholders (Northern and Southern fire-cured, sun/air cured and oriental) is declining. The government is trying to improve smallholder production and output of flue-cured tobacco through a combination of improved prices and instructional and training programmes aimed at improving yields.

Malawi is, after Kenya, Africa's second largest producer and exporter of tea. In 1989 Malawi had about 18,000 ha planted with tea: 90% of the land under cultivation was controlled by large estates, and the remainder by 4,800 smallholders. Output of tea reached a record 40,500 tons in 1991. Export earnings from tea, which are vulnerable to international price factors, accounted for 8% of total export earnings in 1991. The United Kingdom is the main foreign purchaser.

Much of Malawi's sugar is consumed locally. The principal foreign customer is the EU, followed by the USA. Production is centered on the Dwangwa sugar project, covering some 5,250 ha of the Central Region, which started operations in 1979. Export earnings from sugar were adversely affected in the mid-1980s by low world prices and transport problems. They improved, however, from 1987, owing to a recovery in world prices. In 1991 export earnings from sugar provided about 6% of total export receipts. A sugar expansion project to meet increasing local demand was announced by the British based trading group Lonrho in 1992.

INDUSTRY

Development of Malawi's extremely limited industrial base was accorded high priority at independence, and subsequent rapid expansion increased manufacturing output by an average of 11% per year in the 1970s. During the early 1980s growth slowed to less than 3% per year, owing to a combination of factors, including the impact of drought on domestic demand and the scarcity of foreign exchange for imports (the sector is heavily dependent on imports). Manufacturing entered a recession after 1985, but by 1988 the sector recovered slightly, benefiting from the effects of the trade and industrial policy adjustment programme, and from the associated influx of donor funds. Output subsequently contracted, in part due to the aid ban. Industry (including manufacturing, construction and power) contributed 21.2% of GDP in 1992. Industrial GDP increased by an annual average of 3.3%. In 1992 manufacturing contributed 14.1% of GDP. During 1980–91 manufacturing GDP increased by an annual average of 3.9%.

Government encouragement of private enterprise led initially to the attraction of foreign private direct investment and management expertise, especially in collaboration with the government-owned Malawi Development Corporation (MDC), established in 1964. In common with other major parastatal bodies, however, the MDC has been subject to major reorganization and management restructuring since 1985. Small-scale industrial development has been promoted by the Small Enterprise Development Organisation of Malawi (SEDOM). The single largest industrial sector concern is Press Corporation. Nominally a private company, Press is indirectly controlled by Dr Banda and has interests throughout the modern sector of the economy. Often in joint-venture arrangements with foreign companies, these interests include tobacco and sugar estates, cattle ranching, ethanol production, civil engineering, transport, retail and wholesale trade, property development and banking and insurance.

Malawi has provided an attractive range of incentives for potential investors, including low-cost estate sites, tariff protection, exclusive licensing where justified, generous investment allowances and unrestricted repatriation of capital, profits and dividends. However, the rate of new investment has been inhibited partly by the small size of the local market and the limited possibilities for exports. Although new investment has not created as many new jobs as the government had hoped, owing to the capital-intensive nature of some operations, employment in the manufacturing sector has expanded significantly in recent years.

The government has also aimed to promote employment in the tourism sector, which has grown substantially since Malawi began seriously to develop its considerable tourist potential in the mid-1970s. The sector has, however, been adversely affected since the early 1980s by recession in South Africa, which accounts for the majority of visitors to Malawi. However, tourism earnings in 1986, at K4.4m., were double those of 1985. The number of visitors reached 76,100 in 1987, rising further to 99,400 in 1988 and to a record 129,912 in 1990.

Mining

Deposits of a number of minerals, including bauxite, asbestos, coal, gemstones, uranium, vermiculite and graphite, have been discovered, but only a few industrial minerals have so far been exploited to any extent, notably limestone by the Portland Cement Co (Malawi), a subsidiary of the MDC. During the 1980s the company's clinker and cement works were rehabilitated and its quarries were expanded; following these improvements, it is hoped that a small surplus of limestone would be produced for export. There has been small-scale exploitation of Malawi's coal reserves at the Kaziwiziwi mine near Livingstonia, in northern Malawi. Coal production at Kaziwiziwi was terminated in 1984, after less than a year's operation, because it was deemed to be uneconomic. The state-owned Mining Investment and Development Corpn (MIDCOR), however, reopened the mine. MIDCOR is also developing a coal mine at Rumphi, and exploitation of larger, but lower-grade, deposits at Ngana, in the north, and at Mwabi and Lengwe in the south, is under consideration. Much will depend, however, on the government's success in establishing coal as an alternative domestic fuel to wood. In 1989 large high-quality phosphate reserves were discovered, which could be utilized for local fertilizer production.

Considerations of cost have prevented the exploitation of Malawi's most important mineral discovery so far, the bauxite reserves in the Mulanje area, which are believed to amount to nearly 29m. metric tons of ore, containing an average of 43.9% alumina. Exploitation would involve heavy internal transport costs, owing to the remote location of the area, supplemented by transport costs to the coast, making development of the reserves uneconomic in present world market conditions. The feasibility of the project could improve if development of Malawi's hydroelectric capacity results in sufficient low cost power to meet the substantial requirements of alumina smelting.

Power

The Electricity Supply Commission of Malawi (ESCOM) operates both thermal and hydroelectric power stations in its grid, although the latter supply 85% of the central grid's generating capacity of 169 MW. Three plants on the Middle Shire river account for 99% of hydro capacity: Tedzani (40 MW); Nkula A (24 MW), which was completed in 1985; and Nkula B (80 MW). Outside the grid, ESCOM operates four small diesel sets in remote areas in the north, and there are 30 MW of privately-owned capacity, of which about 50% is operated by the sugar estates. Although the central grid is currently operating at below capacity (with sales of 626m. kWh in 1991), ESCOM is planning major investments in new capacity, to meet projected demand in the 1990s, as well as in reinforcing the existing grid. Even with the expansion of electricity output, the majority of Malawi's energy requirements are supplied from fuelwood, which accounted for some 90% of energy needs (compared with 3% for hydro-power, 4% for petroleum products and 1% for coal) in recent years. Nevertheless, petroleum and diesel fuel constitute Malawi's principal imports; in 1991 fuels comprised 16% of the value of total imports. In 1982 a factory to produce ethyl alcohol (ethanol) from molasses went into production, and in its first five years of operation it produced 6.8m. litres of ethanol annually, for 20% blending with petrol, equivalent to 10% of Malawi's gasoline needs. Full design capacity of 8.5m. litres per year was reached in 1988. The government intended to increase ethanol production to 20m. litres per year by the mid-1990s, subject to its commercial value. Just over 16,000 tons of coal were imported in 1988 (compared with 70,000 tons in 1982).

Transport

Malawi Railways operates 465 km of the 830-km single-line rail link from Salima, on the central lake-shore, to the Mozambique port of Beira, Malawi's traditional trade outlet on the Indian Ocean. Another rail link provides access to the port of Nacala, north of Beira. However, increased guerrilla activity in Mozambique after 1981 caused a major disruption in these routes, with freight traffic declining from 745,000 metric tons in 1980 to 274,000 tons in 1983, and to zero from 1984, when the routes were closed. The enforced re-routing of trade through South Africa, a journey of 3,000 km, has had a severe impact on the economy. Additional transport costs surged from \$50m. annually between 1984–86, to \$75m. in 1987 and to \$100m. in 1988. This was partly due to increased import volumes.

The first moves to provide Malawi with a cheaper alternative outlet began in 1983, when the United Kingdom agreed to upgrade the 65-km dirt road linking Karonga, near the northern end of Lake Malawi, to Mbeya, in southern Tanzania, so providing Malawi with access to the Tanzania–Zambia railway as far as the port of Dar es Salaam. Work on the Karonga–Mbeya road was completed in 1984. In 1985 a new priority 'northern corridor' scheme was proposed, involving a 750-km section of the Tazara railway line between Dar es Salaam and Mbeya, a 250-km road link from Mbeya to Chilumba port, at the northern end of Lake Malawi, and a 400-km journey along the lake to Chipoka port, to link with the southern transport network. The project (costing an estimated \$110m. and co-ordinated by the IDA) was completed in 1992, and was expected to carry up to 30% of Malawi's external trade.

Malawi will also benefit from the \$600m. Beira 'corridor' scheme, supported by a group of international donors under the guidance of the Southern African Development Community. Regional political developments have led to recent improvements at the port of Beira and an upgraded road network in the area. Work on the Beira railway line began in late 1985. At the same time rehabilitation of Malawi's rail link to Nacala was being undertaken. An escalation in Mozambican rebel attacks on the line led to the suspension of rehabilitation work for one year from early 1988. In August 1989 a cease-fire was agreed along the line, and in October the Nacala link was reopened. Traffic resumed slowly, owing to the disrepair of the line and to the uncertain security situation.

Malawi's road network, totalling 12,215 km in 1988, is being steadily upgraded, in particular the lakeshore Kamuzu Highway, which will provide the main link between the remote Northern Region and the Central and Southern Regions. Feeder and crop-extraction roads are also being extended. Road transport has shown a steady rate of growth, stimulated by the closure of Malawi's rail outlets.

Malawi has one main international airport at Lilongwe, three domestic airports and the former main international airport at Blantyre, which still serves some regional airlines. Lilongwe is regularly served by a number of international and regional airlines, as well as by the national carrier Air Malawi.

EXTERNAL TRADE AND PAYMENTS

Malawi's prospects for sustained development depend upon the achievement of improved export performance, especially in the industrial sector. The primary producer's dependence on international commodity trade is heightened in Malawi's case by an absence, so far, of exportable minerals. Agricultural products still account for more than 90% of domestic export receipts, with tobacco providing more than two-thirds of total foreign exchange earnings. Exports of manufactured goods, mainly clothing, footwear and cattle cake, increased during the 1980s, but still provide only about 5% of all export earnings. The principal imports are diesel fuel and petroleum (by far the largest item, accounting for 9% of all imports in 1989), machinery and transport equipment, piece goods and medical and pharmaceutical goods. In 1989 the principal imports were machinery and transport equipment, mineral fuels and miscellaneous manufactured articles.

Malawi's major trading partners have not changed over the years, although the volume of trade with the United Kingdom has declined. In 1992 Germany both accounted for 21% of exports, Japan 14%, the USA 13%, the United Kingdom 8% and South Africa 6%. The major suppliers of imports (1991) were South Africa (33%), the United Kingdom and Japan (both 7%) and Germany (6%).

Malawi has sustained a deficit on the current account of its balance of payments in every year since 1966, with a particularly sharp deterioration in 1979 and 1980, when it increased from an average of 8% of GDP to 23.5%. However, following the introduction of the economic stabilization programme in 1981 and an improvement in the trade balance, there was some recovery over the next two years. None the less, the current account deficit increased sharply from \$48.9m. in 1984 to \$124.7m. in 1985. There was subsequently an improvement in the level of the deficit, to \$89.9m. in 1986 and to \$53.1m. by 1988. However, a deficit of \$135.5m. was recorded in 1992, equivalent to 7.3% of GDP.

As a result of increases in debt-service costs and a reduction in concessionary assistance from 1980, Malawi operated a substantial overall balance-of-payments deficit in most years until 1987, when there was a surplus of K85m., reflecting the marked improvement in the merchandise trade surplus and the impact of the government's decision to suspend debt-service payments pending the conclusion of negotiations on new reschedulings with both the Paris and London 'Clubs' of government and private creditors. The signing of the rescheduling agreements in April and May 1988 (see below) contributed significantly to the K247m. overall balance-of-payments surplus recorded in that year. The surplus also reflected the impact of increased concessionary assistance: the capital account surplus increased by 67%, to K363.7m. in 1988.

PUBLIC FINANCE AND BANKING

In the three years after 1978/79 there was a rapid deterioration in the budgetary position, reflecting the worsening balance-of-payments situation and the decline in domestic growth. In 1980/81 the overall budget deficit reached 16.5% of GDP. With the introduction of the first economic adjustment programme in 1981, the overall deficit began to improve, and by 1985/86 it had fallen to 6.6% of GDP. However, this was largely attributable to a sharp fall in development expenditure, which declined by an annual average of 2% in real terms. Owing to a rise in the costs of debt-servicing and transport, and to an increase in losses by parastatal enterprises, recurrent expenditure expanded, in real terms, by 10% per year, resulting in a deficit that had to be financed by domestic and foreign borrowing. In 1985/86 total borrowing reached K242m.

The overall deficit deteriorated again in 1986/87, when, because revenues were lower than anticipated (owing to economic recession), it reached 11% of GDP. To arrest this trend, the 1987/88 budget proposals were particularly stringent, and it was hoped to reduce the overall deficit to K172.6m., or 6.5% of GDP. However, although an actual deficit of K171.5m. was recorded in that year, recession in the domestic economy (caused by drought and the impact on manufacturing of reduced imports) resulted in the deficit being equivalent to 8.2% of GDP. The budget for 1988/89 was also stringent, with the overall deficit falling to 3.1% of GDP. In 1989/90 the overall deficit rose again, to an estimated 4.9% of GDP. In that financial year the government undertook to keep development expenditure in line with availability of foreign funding, in order to prevent a major increase in future debt-service repayments. In 1990/91 the budget deficit represented 5.6% of GDP and rose to 9.1% in 1992/93, but was expected to be under 4% in 1993/4. The 1994/95 budget, presented in March, was widely seen as an attempt to influence the election by its emphasis on social expenditure and the reduction in the number of income-tax payers. The budget anticipated a decline of 6.2% in real GDP as a result of the drought.

The network of banking services includes a central bank, two commercial banks, the Post Office Savings Bank (POSB) and a development bank. The Reserve Bank of Malawi began issuing its own notes in 1965, the basic currency unit then being the Malawi pound, which stood at par with sterling. In February 1971 a decimal currency was introduced, with the kwacha (divided into 100 tambala) as the unit of exchange. The exchange rate of the kwacha was originally linked to that of sterling, but an active exchange rate policy was introduced in 1974. Since 1984 the kwacha exchange rate has been related to a 'basket' of the currencies of Malawi's seven principal trading partners. As part of the Reserve Bank's management of the exchange rate, the kwacha has been subject to regular trade-related devaluations since 1982. In February 1994 the Kwacha was 'floated', with the result that it depreciated by 25% in three months, relative to the US dollar. This depreciation is expected to contribute to an inflation level of around 30% in 1994, but will provide a stimulus to Malawi's exports.

FOREIGN AID, GOVERNMENT DEBT AND DEVELOPMENT PLANNING

Malawi began to undertake significant commercial borrowing in the mid-1970s, initially to finance development programmes. International organizations have replaced bilateral donors as the main source of foreign funding, with the IDA as the leading multilateral creditor. As a proportion of outstanding debt, commercial borrowing increased from less than 2% in 1976 to more than 24% in 1980. After 1979, non-concessionary borrowing rose sharply, as the government resorted to the banks to help to finance the budget deficit. This led to a substantial increase in total public debt-service payments. The 1982 and 1983 debt reschedulings, arranged with the 'Paris Club', resulted in a substantial fall in payments. By 1984 the effects of this relief were coming to an end, and in 1984/85 service payments increased sharply. In 1986/87 they were equivalent to 41% of total export earnings.

As a result of the high level of the debt-service ratio in 1987, the government came under pressure from the IMF to undertake a new rescheduling. With the scarcity of foreign exchange acting as an increasing constraint on recovery, the government finally agreed in mid-1987, and rescheduling agreements were eventually finalized in April 1988, when the 'Paris Club' agreed to reschedule debt due for repayment in 1988, over 20 years, including 10 years' grace. No details of the amount rescheduled were disclosed, but the World Bank estimated that publicly guaranteed debt due for repayment in 1988 was \$88m., of which \$59m. was principal owed to official and private creditors. The 'London Club' agreed to an eight-year rescheduling arrangement, including four years' grace.

As a result of the reschedulings, service payments were reduced to 31% of export earnings in 1988, falling to an average of 25.9% over the following five years.

The United Kingdom was Malawi's major aid donor in the years after independence, and has remained an important source of funding. Similarly, South Africa has been a significant source of donor aid, particularly in providing finance for the new capital of Lilongwe. Other major donors are the EC, France, Canada, the USA, Germany, Denmark, Japan, the African Development Bank, the IDA and the World Bank. In real terms, foreign grants and concessionary loans fell sharply between 1980 and 1987, with overall external support in the latter year totalling just $170m. In June 1988 the consultative group on Malawi approved $555m. in external support for Malawi's economic recovery programme, of which $265m. was to be released in 1988 and $290m. in 1989. The funding arrangements (which also included the April debt reschedulings, the IMF's March stand-by facility and its planned extended facility) represented an increase of almost 60% in external assistance. In May 1990 the consultative group on Malawi approved $508m. for 1990/91 in support of the economic recovery programme. In May 1992, however, the consultative group suspended all non-humanitarian aid, linking future assistance to an improvement in Malawi's human rights record. Following the multi-party elections in 1994 (see Recent History), Germany, the USA and the United Kingdom all indicated that they would provide increased future levels of aid.

Unlike many African states, Malawi has never attempted to determine a detailed economic plan as the basis for development policies. Instead, the government has opted for statements of objectives, policies and budget forecasts as an illustration of possible trends, rather than as a framework for control and direction.

In 1981 a five-year programme (for 1981/82–1985/86) was introduced, with an initial target of growth in real GDP of 5% per year. This was subsequently reduced to 3.4%. Under a three-year economic development programme, covering 1985/86–1987/88, transport was the priority, taking 32% of projected investment, with the 'northern corridor' constituting the main project. Agriculture was scheduled to receive 19%, education 9.6%, and industry and commerce 6.4%. A further statement of development policies was published in March 1988, covering the period 1987–96. It projected a limited range of objectives, outlining policies aimed at maintaining a realistic pace of growth in real GDP until the early 1990s, when the major constraints on foreign exchange and economic recovery (debt payments and transport costs) were expected to ease, and when the 'northern corridor' was due to become operational. Thereafter, growth was expected to accelerate, as a result of policies aimed at encouraging increased and diversified agricultural and industrial production for the domestic and export markets, facilitated by an increased liberalization of the economy.

Statistical Survey

Source (unless otherwise stated): Department of Information, POB 494, Blantyre; Office of the President and Cabinet, National Statistical Office, POB 333, Zomba; tel. 522377.

Area and Population

AREA, POPULATION AND DENSITY

Area (sq km)	118,484*
Population (census results)	
20 September 1977	5,547,460
1–21 September 1987	
Males	3,867,136
Females	4,121,371
Total	7,988,507
Population (official estimates at mid-year)†	
1990	8,288,946
1991	8,556,151
1992	8,823,000
Density (per sq km) at mid-1992	74.5

* 45,747 sq miles. The area includes 24,208 sq km (9,347 sq miles) of inland water.

† Not revised to take account of the results of the 1987 census.

Ethnic groups (1977 census): Africans 5,532,298; Europeans 6,377; Asians 5,682; others 3,103.

REGIONS (1987 census)

Region	Population
Southern	3,959,448
Central	3,116,038
Northern	907,121

Capital: Lilongwe, population 233,973 (including suburbs) at 1987 census.

Other Principal Town: Blantyre, population 331,588 (including Limbe) at 1987 census.

BIRTHS AND DEATHS (UN estimates, annual averages)

	1975–80	1980–85	1985–90
Birth rate (per 1,000)	57.2	56.6	55.6
Death rate (per 1,000)	24.0	22.3	21.4

Expectation of life (UN estimates, years at birth, 1985–90): 45.4 (males 44.6; females 46.2).

Source: UN, *World Population Prospects: The 1992 Revision.*

ECONOMICALLY ACTIVE POPULATION
(persons aged 10 years and over, 1987 census)

	Males	Females	Total
Agriculture, hunting, forestry and fishing	1,205,491	1,494,409	2,699,900
Mining and quarrying	1,662	—	1,662
Manufacturing	76,095	19,499	95,594
Electricity, gas and water	6,380	428	6,808
Construction	47,962	4,139	52,101
Trade, restaurants and hotels	64,999	38,204	103,203
Transport, storage and communications	15,682	1,044	16,726
Financing, insurance, real estate and business services	5,468	1,674	7,142
Community, social and personal services	97,041	40,101	137,142
Activities not adequately defined	—	657	657
Total employed	1,520,780	1,600,155	3,120,935
Unemployed	78,630	100,633	179,263
Total labour force	1,599,410	1,700,788	3,300,198

Source: ILO, *Year Book of Labour Statistics.*

Mid-1992 (estimates in '000): Agriculture, etc. 3,053; Total 4,167 (Source: FAO, *Production Yearbook*).

Agriculture

PRINCIPAL CROPS ('000 metric tons)

	1990	1991	1992
Rice (paddy)	45	61*	20*
Maize	1,343	1,590*	657*
Sorghum	15	19	4*
Potatoes†	330	340	330
Cassava (Manioc)	145	168*	129*
Dry beans†	85	82	78
Chick-peas	43	40†	35†
Other pulses	155	149†	145†
Groundnuts (in shell)*	37	57	23
Cottonseed*	22	27	13
Cotton (lint)*	9	11	5
Vegetables†	251	255	237
Bananas†	89	90	85
Plantains†	142	145	140
Other fruit†	214	217	207
Sugar cane†	1,790	1,800	1,950
Tea (made)	39	41	28*
Tobacco (leaves)	101	113	139*

* Unofficial figure(s). † FAO estimate(s).

Source: FAO, *Production Yearbook.*

LIVESTOCK
(unofficial figures, '000 head, year ending September)

	1990	1991	1992
Cattle	836	899	967
Pigs	233	235	238
Sheep	177	186	195
Goats	807	846	887

Poultry (FAO estimates, million, year ending September): 9 in 1990; 9 in 1991; 9 in 1992.

Source: FAO, *Production Yearbook.*

LIVESTOCK PRODUCTS (FAO estimates, '000 metric tons)

	1990	1991	1992
Beef and veal	17	17	17
Goats' meat	3	3	3
Pig meat	9	9	10
Poultry meat	9	9	9
Cows' milk	36	39	40
Poultry eggs	11.2	11.3	11.3

Source: FAO, *Production Yearbook.*

Forestry

ROUNDWOOD REMOVALS ('000 cubic metres, excluding bark)

	1990	1991	1992
Sawlogs, veneer logs and logs for sleepers	80	80*	80*
Other industrial wood	351	366*	380*
Fuel wood*	8,554*	8,912*	9,246*
Total	8,985	9,358*	9,706*

* FAO estimate(s).

Source: FAO, *Yearbook of Forest Products.*

SAWNWOOD PRODUCTION (unofficial estimates, '000 cubic metres, incl. railway sleepers)

	1990	1991	1992
Coniferous (soft wood)	28	28	28*
Broadleaved (hard wood)	15	15	15*
Total	43	43	43*

* FAO estimate(s).

Source: FAO, *Yearbook of Forest Products.*

Fishing

('000 metric tons, live weight)

	1989	1990	1991
Carps, barbels, etc.	9.9	15.8	3.0
Tilapias	15.1	15.3	15.3
Other freshwater fishes	45.8	43.0	45.5
Total catch	70.8	74.1	63.7

Source: FAO, *Yearbook of Fishery Statistics.*

Mining

('000 metric tons, unless otherwise indicated)

	1989	1990	1991
Limestone	125	143	184
Coal	37	41	52
Lime	3	4	5
Quarry stone	145	65	100
Gemstones	2	8	4

Industry

SELECTED PRODUCTS
('000 metric tons, unless otherwise indicated)

	1989	1990	1991
Raw sugar	162	189	191
Beer ('000 hectolitres)	757	752	763
Cigarettes (million)	1,080*	1,061	951
Blankets ('000)	836	988	1,126
Cement	79	101	112
Electric energy (million kWh)	586	718	750

* Data from the US Department of Agriculture.

Source: UN, *Industrial Statistics Yearbook.*

Finance

CURRENCY AND EXCHANGE RATES

Monetary Units

100 tambala = 1 Malawi kwacha (K).

Sterling and Dollar Equivalents (31 March 1994)

£1 sterling = 9.798 kwacha;
US $1 = 6.600 kwacha;
1,000 Malawi kwacha = £102,06 = $151.52.

Average Exchange Rate (kwacha per US $)

1991	2.8033
1992	3.6033
1993	4.4028

RECURRENT BUDGET
(revised estimates, K million, year ending 31 March)

Revenue	1991/92	1992/93	1993/94
Taxes on income and profits:			
Companies	252.1	222.6	250.1
Individuals	163.5	218.8	262.3
Taxes on goods and services:			
Surtax	349.9	372.3	468.5
Excise duties	29.8	37.7	57.6
Licences	12.2	7.4	12.3
Import duties	214.2	251.0	269.3
Other tax revenue	10.1	13.9	12.7
Total tax revenue	1,031.8	1,123.7	1,332.8
Non-tax revenue	132.4	279.1	281.2
Total	1,164.2	1,402.8	1,614.0

Expenditure	1991/92	1992/93	1993/94
Wages and salaries	258.4	415.6	533.7
Goods and other services	481.4	706.2	761.5
Grants and subsidies to statutory bodies	80.3	119.4	149.6
Debt servicing	390.5	418.9	530.3
Interest payments	173.3	254.1	272.9
Debt amortization	217.2	164.8	257.4
Other expenditure	110.8	140.1	177.7
Total (incl. extra-budgetary expenditure)	1,321.4	1,800.2	2,152.8

Source: Ministry of Finance, Lilongwe.

DEVELOPMENT BUDGET (K million, year ending 31 March)

1992/93 (projected figures): Total receipts 254.2; Total expenditure 294.6.

1993/94 (revised estimates): Total receipts 355.3; Total expenditure 455.7.

1994/95 (projected figures): Total receipts 559.7; Total expenditure 700.4.

Source: Ministry of Finance, Lilongwe.

INTERNATIONAL RESERVES (US $ million at 31 December)

	1991	1992	1993
Gold	0.54	0.54	0.54
IMF special drawing rights	0.26	0.08	0.75
Reserve position in IMF	3.18	3.05	2.96
Foreign exchange	149.77	36.82	53.59
Total	153.75	40.49	57.84

Source: IMF, *International Financial Statistics.*

MONEY SUPPLY (K million at 31 December)

	1991	1992	1993
Currency outside banks	222.69	289.79	414.21
Official entities' deposits with monetary authorities	65.17	22.01	45.58
Demand deposits at commercial banks	346.00	444.90	505.94
Total money	633.86	756.70	965.73

Source: IMF, *International Financial Statistics.*

COST OF LIVING (Consumer Price Index, excluding rent, for low-income families in Blantyre; base: 1980 = 100)

	1990	1991	1992
Food	422.5	477.8	613.3
Clothing	501.8	536.3	634.6
All items (incl. others)	444.4	492.2	616.1

Source: ILO, *Year Book of Labour Statistics.*

NATIONAL ACCOUNTS

Expenditure on the Gross Domestic Product
(K million in current prices)

	1991	1992	1993
Government final consumption expenditure	852.4	1,240.9	1,487.4
Private final consumption expenditure	4,770.8	5,323.3	7,236.2
Increase in stocks	200.0	180.0	200.0
Gross fixed capital formation	1,030.0	1,077.0	890.0
Total domestic expenditure	6,853.2	7,821.2	9,813.6
Exports of goods and services	1,437.2	1,504.3	1,472.4
Less Imports of goods and services	2,184.8	2,631.6	2,404.4
GDP in purchasers' values	6,105.6	6,693.9	8,881.6

Source: Reserve Bank of Malawi, Lilongwe.

Gross Domestic Product by Economic Activity
(K million at constant 1978 prices)

	1991	1992	1993
Agriculture, forestry and fishing	367.5	275.2	422.2
Manufacturing	137.5	141.6	126.8
Electricity and water	24.5	26.3	27.2
Construction	43.9	43.0	41.2
Trade, restaurants and hotels	132.1	129.5	118.4
Transport and communications	60.0	59.4	56.7
Finance, insurance and business services	71.7	71.4	67.3
Ownership of dwellings	43.6	44.4	44.9
Private social services	43.9	44.9	45.1
Government services	149.8	154.8	154.2
Sub-total	1,074.5	990.5	1,104.0
Less Imputed bank service charges	18.8	18.4	27.1
GDP at factor cost	1,055.7	972.1	1,076.9

Source: Reserve Bank of Malawi, Lilongwe.

BALANCE OF PAYMENTS (US $ million)

	1986	1987	1988
Merchandise exports f.o.b.	248.4	278.5	297.0
Merchandise imports f.o.b.	-154.1	-177.6	-253.0
Trade balance	94.3	100.9	43.9
Exports of services	27.8	43.7	37.8
Imports of services	-254.3	-243.8	-230.3
Balance on goods and services	-132.2	-99.2	-148.6
Private unrequited transfers (net)	13.1	13.8	15.1
Government unrequited transfers (net)	29.3	30.1	80.4
Current balance	-89.9	-55.3	-53.1
Direct capital investment (net)	—	0.1	—
Other long-term capital (net)	34.8	69.8	124.7
Short-term capital (net)	13.8	6.6	6.7
Net errors and omissions	40.7	24.2	-18.0
Total (net monetary movements)	-0.6	45.4	60.2
Valuation changes (net)	-20.3	-16.8	-2.6
Exceptional financing (net)	3.3	22.8	47.4
Changes in reserves	-17.6	51.4	105.0

Source: IMF, *International Financial Statistics.*

External Trade

SELECTED COMMODITIES (K'000)

Imports c.i.f.	1987	1988	1989
Piece goods	8,341	21,064	29,864
Other garments	741	1,055	4,773
Passenger cars and motorcycles	7,124	13,226	31,600
Commercial road vehicles	19,820	47,886	69,098
Medical and pharmaceutical goods	21,067	24,967	28,247
Dairy products	2,210	6,506	12,521
Agricultural machinery	5,718	10,272	24,701
Printed matter and stationery	4,585	7,123	11,049
Footwear	1,593	2,281	4,443
Petrol	27,316	42,207	52,478
Diesel fuel	42,348	59,677	67,764
Total (incl. others)	653,939	1,080,151	1,398,803

Total imports (K million): 1,715.3 in 1990; 2,184.8 in 1991; 2,562.2 in 1992 (Source: IMF, *International Financial Statistics*).

Exports f.o.b. (excl. re-exports)*	1989	1990	1991
Tobacco	458,286	769,569	982,059
Tea	101,234	127,432	103,808
Sugar	65,266	76,925	79,674
Groundnuts	1,011	66	1,742
Beans and peas	6,247	5,700	6,986
Rice	4,229	3,995	2,468
Total (incl. others)	730,169	1,097,906	1,299,330

* Total exports, including re-exports, were (K million): 824.1 in 1989; 1,220.6 in 1990; 1,437.2 in 1991; 1,547.1 in 1992 (Source: IMF, *International Financial Statistics*).

PRINCIPAL TRADING PARTNERS (K'000)

Imports	1989	1990
France	17,000	45,502
Germany, Federal Republic	88,600	95,584
Japan	88,100	119,036
Netherlands	52,700	51,617
South Africa	514,400	486,222
United Kingdom	238,500	362,136
USA	47,800	33,808
PTA*	147,800	124,162
Total (incl. others)	1,398,800	266,151

Exports (excl. re-exports)	1989	1990
France	26,900	37,178
Germany, Federal Republic	76,400	175,697
Japan	93,300	146,382
Netherlands	57,000	75,676
South Africa	70,700	77,733
United Kingdom	153,100	169,458
USA	93,300	129,523
PTA*	31,000	46,427
Total (incl. others)	730,200	225,787

* Preferential Trade Area for Eastern and Southern African States, of which Malawi is a member.

Source: Reserve Bank of Malawi, Lilongwe.

Transport

RAILWAYS (traffic)

	1991	1992	1993
Passengers carried ('000)	1,368	892	692
Passenger-kilometres ('000)	91,680	54,477	45,547
Freight ('000 ton-km, net)	59,569	68,186	42,264

Source: Malawi Railways, Limbe.

ROAD TRAFFIC (motor vehicles in use at 31 December)

	1990	1991	1992
Cars	11,266	11,548	13,898
Goods vehicles	9,807	10,052	12,113
Tractors	3,697	3,782	3,629
Motor cycles	3,536	3,624	3,580

Source: Road Traffic Commission, Blantyre.

SHIPPING

Inland waterways (lake transport)

	1991	1992	1993
Freight ('000 ton-km, net)	6,818	5,933	3,682
Passenger-kilometres ('000)	18,606	20,379	10,332

Source: Malawi Railways, Limbe.

CIVIL AVIATION

	1991	1992	1993
Chileka Airport (Blantyre)			
Passengers	77,840	85,769	95,075
Freight (metric tons)	1,293	7,042	1,328
Mail (metric tons)	57	57	97
Kamuzu International Airport (Lilongwe)			
Passengers	282,899	265,721	257,219
Freight (metric tons)	9,285	8,611	6,677
Mail (metric tons)	413	374	406

Tourism

	1988	1989	1990
Number of departing visitors	99,424	117,069	129,912
Average expenditure per person (kwacha)	276	299	328

Communications Media

	1988	1989	1990
Radio receivers ('000 in use)	1,907	2,000	2,080
Telephones ('000 in use)	49	50	50
Book production (titles)	123	141	n.a.
Daily newspapers:			
Titles	1	n.a.	1
Average circulation ('000 copies)	25	n.a.	25

Radio receivers ('000 in use): 2,200 in 1991.

Telephones ('000 in use): 54 in 1991.

Sources: UNESCO, *Statistical Yearbook*; National Statistical Office, Zomba.

Education

(Government, government-aided and unaided schools, 1989)

	Teachers	Pupils
Primary	20,580	1,325,453
Secondary (general)	1,096	29,326
Technical schools	60	770
Teacher training	190	2,909
University of Malawi	235	2,685

1990: Primary schools 2,906; Primary pupils 1,400,682; Secondary (general) pupils 31,495; Technical school pupils 780.

Source: UNESCO, *Statistical Yearbook*.

Directory

The Constitution

A new Constitution, replacing the (amended) 1966 Constitution, was approved by the National Assembly on 16 May 1994, and promulgated on 18 May.

THE PRESIDENT

The President is both Head of State and Head of Government. He has the right to participate in parliamentary debates and may refuse his assent to any Bill; if the Bill is passed again within six months he must either assent or dissolve Parliament and thus submit himself to an election. The President is elected for five years, by universal adult suffrage, in the context of a multi-party political system. The Chief Justice is appointed by the President, as are senior civil servants and members of the armed forces. The President may proclaim a state of emergency.

PARLIAMENT

Parliament comprises the President and the National Assembly. The National Assembly has 177 elective seats, elections being by universal adult suffrage, in the context of a multi-party system, and an unlimited number of additional members may be nominated by the President. The Speaker is appointed from among the ordinary members of the Assembly. The Assembly may change the Constitution by a two-thirds majority on the second and third readings. The parliamentary term is normally five years. The President has power to prorogue or dissolve Parliament.

EXECUTIVE POWER

Executive power is exercised by the President. Ministers are responsible to the President.

The Government

HEAD OF STATE

President: BAKILI MULUZI (took office 22 May 1994).

CABINET

(September 1994)

President and Head of Government: BAKILI MULUZI.

Vice-President: JUSTIN MALEWEZI.

Minister of Finance: ALEKE BANDA.

Minister of Commerce, Industry and Tourism: HARRY THOMSON.

Minister of External Affairs: EDWARD BWANALI.

Minister of Economic Planning and Development: TIM MANGWAZU.

Minister of Information and Broadcasting: JAMES MPINGANJIRA.

Minister of Home Affairs: PETER FACHI.

Minister of Defence: Dr CASSIM CHILUMPHA.

Minister of Education, Science and Technology: SAM MPASU.

Minister of Justice and Attorney-General: WEHNAM NAKANGA.

Minister of Transport and Communications: COLLINS CHIZUMILA.

Minister of Agriculture and Livestock Development: Dr JOHN NANKUMBA.

Minister of Health and Environmental Affairs: Dr GEORGE MTAFU.

Minister of Local Government and Rural Development: JAMES MAKHUMULA.

Minister of Works, Supplies and Water Development: PATRICK MBEWE.

Minister for Women's and Children's Affairs: EDDA CHITALO.

Minister of Lands and Housing: ALHAJI ITIMU.

Minister of Energy and Mining: ROLPH PATEL.

Minister of Youth, Sports and Culture: ZILIRO CHIBAMBO.

Minister of Labour and Manpower Development: GEORGE KANYANYA.

Minister of Forestry and Natural Resources: (vacant).

Minister of Community Services and Social Welfare: (vacant).

Minister of Physical Planning and Surveys: (vacant)

MINISTRIES

Office of the President: Private Bag 301, Capital City, Lilongwe 3; telex 44389.

Ministry of Agriculture and Livestock Development: POB 30134, Capital City, Lilongwe 3; tel. 733300; telex 44648.

Ministry of Commerce, Industry and Tourism: POB 30366, Capital City, Lilongwe 3; tel. 732711; telex 44873; fax 732551.

Ministry for Education, Science and Technology: Private Bag 328, Capital City, Lilongwe 3; tel. 733922; telex 44636; fax 782873.

Ministry of Energy and Mining: Private Bag 309, Capital City, Litengwe 3.

Ministry of External Affairs: POB 30315, Capital City, Lilongwe 3; tel. 782211; telex 44113; fax 782434.

Ministry of Finance: POB 30049, Capital City, Lilongwe 3; tel. 731311; telex 44407.

Ministry of Forestry and Natural Resources: Private Bag 350, Capital City, Lilongwe 3; telex 44465; fax 731452.

Ministry of Health and Environmental Affairs: POB 30377, Capital City, Lilongwe 3; telex 44558.

Ministry of Information and Broadcasting: POB 494, Blantyre.

Ministry of Justice: Private Bag 333, Capital City, Lilongwe 3; tel. 731533; fax 731776.

Ministry of Labour and Manpower Development: Private Bag 344, Capital City, Lilongwe 3.

Ministry of Local Government and Rural Development: POB 30366, Capital City, Lilongwe 3.

Ministry of Transport and Communications: Private Bag 322, Capital City, Lilongwe 3; tel. 730122.

Ministry for Women's and Children's Affairs: Private Bag 330, Capital City, Lilongwe 3; tel. 732222; telex 44361.

Ministry of Works, Supplies and Water Development: Private Bag 316, Capital City, Lilongwe 3: tel. 733188; telex 44285.

President and Legislature

PRESIDENT

Presidential Election, 17 May 1994

Candidate	Votes	% of votes
BAKILI MULUZI	1,404,754	47.3
Dr HASTINGS KAMUZU BANDA	996,363	33.6
CHAKUFWA CHIHANA	552,862	18.5
KAMPELO KALUA	15,624	0.5

NATIONAL ASSEMBLY

General Election, 17 May 1994

Party	Seats
UDF	84
MCP	55
AFORD	36
Others	2
Total	177

Political Organizations

The Malawi Congress Party was the sole party during 1966–93. In June 1993 the Constitution was amended to provide for the introduction of a multi-party political system. Eight political parties were authorized to participate in the multi-party elections of May 1994.

Alliance for Democracy (AFORD): f. 1992 to secure democratic reforms; in March 1993 absorbed membership of fmr Malawi Freedom Movement; legalized mid-1993; Pres. CHAKUFWA CHIHANA; Sec-.Gen. Dr DENIS NKWASI.

Christian-Islamic Alliance for Democracy: Lusaka, Zambia; f. 1992; Chair. ERMUS ARIEL KAMBALE.

Congress for the Second Republic (CSR): Dar es Salaam, Tanzania; Leader KANYAMA CHIUME.

Malawi Congress Party (MCP): Lilongwe; tel. 730388; f. 1959; sole legal party 1966–93; Pres. (vacant); Sec.-Gen. GWANDA CHAKUAMBA; Admin. Sec. MAXWELL PASHANE.

Malawi Democratic Party (MDP): legalized mid-1993.

Malawi Democratic Union: POB 34754, Lusaka, Zambia; Sec.-Gen. M. DZIKOLIDO.

Malawi National Democratic Party (MNDP): legalized mid-1993.

Malawi Socialist Labour Party (MSLP): Dar es Salaam, Tanzania; f. 1991; has a mil. wing, known as the Malawi Republican Army (MRA); Leader Dr CROSSROADS SAMBANEMANJA.

United Democratic Front (UDF): f. 1992; legalized mid-1993; obtained majority in May 1994 parl. elections; Pres. BAKILI MULUZI.

United Front for Multi-party Democracy (UFMD): POB 34754, Lusaka, Zambia; f. 1992; legalized mid-1993; Chair. Dr HARRY BWANAUSI.

Diplomatic Representation

EMBASSIES AND HIGH COMMISSIONS IN MALAWI

China (Taiwan): Area 40, Plot No. 9, POB 30221, Capital City, Lilongwe 3; tel. 730611; telex 44317; Ambassador: ROBERT C. J. SHIH.

Egypt: POB 30451, Lilongwe 3; tel. 730300; telex 44538; Ambassador: F. M. Y. ELKHADI.

France: Area 40, Road No. 3, POB 30054, Lilongwe 3; tel. 730579; telex 44141; Ambassador: MARCEL REY.

Germany: POB 30046, Lilongwe 3; tel. 782555; telex 44124; fax 780250; Ambassador: ULRICH NITZSCHKE.

Israel: POB 30319, Lilongwe 3; tel. 782923; fax 780436; Ambassador: MOSHE ITAN.

Korea, Republic: POB 30583, Lilongwe 3; telex 44834; Ambassador: PAK YONG-CHOL.

Mozambique: POB 30579, Lilongwe 3; telex 44793; Ambassador: AMOS MAHANJANE.

South Africa: Mpico Bldg, City Centre, POB 30043, Lilongwe 3; tel. 783722; telex 44255; fax 782571; High Commissioner: LLEWELLYN CREWE-BROWN.

United Kingdom: POB 30042, Lilongwe 3; tel. 782400; telex 44727; fax 782657; High Commissioner: JOHN F. R. MARTIN.

USA: Area 40, Flat 18, POB 30016, Lilongwe 3; tel. 730166; telex 44627; Ambassador: MICHAEL T. F. PISTOR.

Zambia: POB 30138, Lilongwe 3; tel. 731911; telex 44181; High Commissioner: AMMON UMBANDA.

Zimbabwe: POB 30183, Lilongwe 3; tel. 733988; High Commissioner: J. S. MVUNDURA.

Judicial System

The courts administering justice are the Supreme Court of Appeal, High Court and Magistrates' Courts.

The High Court, which has unlimited jurisdiction in civil and criminal matters, consists of the Chief Justice and five puisne judges. Traditional Courts were abolished under the 1994 Constitution. Appeals from the High Court are heard by the Supreme Court of Appeal in Blantyre.

High Court of Malawi: POB 30244, Chichiri, Blantyre 3; tel. 670255; Registrar D. F. MWAUNGULU.

Chief Justice: RICHARD A. BANDA.

Puisne Judges: H. M. MTEGHA, L. A. UNYOLO, M. P. MKANDAWIRE, D. G. TAMBALA, G. MUNLO.

Religion

About one-half of the population are Christians. The Asian community includes Muslims and Hindus, and there is a small number of African Muslims. Traditional beliefs also retain a significant following.

CHRISTIANITY

Christian Council of Malawi: POB 30068, Capital City, Lilongwe 3; tel. 730499; f. 1939; 13 mems and seven associates; Chair. Rev. Dr. S. D. CHIPHANGWI; Gen. Sec. Rev. M. M. MAPUTWA.

The Anglican Communion

The Church of the Province of Central Africa has about 80,000 adherents in its two dioceses in Malawi.

Bishop of Lake Malawi: Rt Rev. PETER NATHANIEL NYANJA, POB 30349, Capital City, Lilongwe 3; fax 731966.

Bishop of Southern Malawi: Rt Rev. NATHANIEL BENSON AIPA, PO Chilema, Zomba; fax 531243.

Protestant Churches

The Baptist Convention in Malawi: POB 51083, Limbe; tel. 643224; Chair. Rev. S. L. MALABWANYA; Gen. Sec. Rev. M. T. KACHASO GAMA.

Church of Central Africa (Presbyterian): Blantyre Synod: POB 413, Blantyre; tel. 636744; Gen. Sec. Rt Rev. Dr SILAS S. NCOZANA; 92,000 adherents in Malawi.

Evangelical Fellowship of Malawi: POB 2120, Blantyre; tel. 633543; Chair. K. M. LUWANI; Sec. W. C. MUSOPOLE.

The Lutheran Church of Central Africa: POB 120, Blantyre; tel. 630347; f. 1953; evangelical and medical work; Supt R. G. COX; 14,500 mems.

Seventh-day Adventists: POB 951, Blantyre; tel. 620264; telex 44216; Dir Mr MASOKA; Exec. Sec. Pastor G. S. MOYO.

The African Methodist Episcopal Church, the Churches of Christ, the Free Methodist Church, the Pentecostal Assemblies of God and the United Evangelical Church in Malawi are also active.

The Roman Catholic Church

Malawi comprises one archdiocese and six dioceses. At 31 December 1992 there were an estimated 1.9m. adherents in the country, representing about 20% of the total population.

Episcopal Conference of Malawi: Catholic Secretariat of Malawi, Chimutu Rd, POB 30384, Capital City, Lilongwe 3; tel. 782066; telex 44174; fax 782019; f. 1969; Pres. Most Rev. JAMES CHIONA, Archbishop of Blantyre.

Archbishop of Blantyre: Most Rev. JAMES CHIONA, Archbishop's House, POB 385, Blantyre; tel. 633905; telex 43515; fax 606107.

BAHÁ'Í FAITH

National Spiritual Assembly: POB 5849, Limbe; tel. 640996; fax 640910; f. 1970; mems resident in nearly 1,500 localities.

The Press

Boma Lathu: POB 494, Blantyre; tel. 620266; f. 1973; monthly; Chichewa; publ. by the Dept of Information; circ. 80,000.

Chitukuko cha Amayi n'Malawi: POB 494, Blantyre; tel. 620266; telex 44471; fax 620807; f. 1964; monthly; Chichewa (English—This is Malawi); publ. by the Dept of Information; circ. 12,000.

The Daily Times: PB 39, Ginnery Corner, Blantyre; tel. 671566; telex 44112; f. 1895; Mon.–Fri.; English; Editor-in-Chief Poulton Mtenje; circ. 20,000.

Financial Post: Blantyre; f.1992; weekly; English; independent; Editor Alaudin Osman.

The Independent: Blantyre; f.1993; weekly; English; independent; Editor Janet Karim.

Kuunika: PO Nkhoma, Lilongwe; f. 1909; monthly; Chichewa; Presbyterian; Editor Rev. M. C. Nkhalambayausi.

Malawi Government Gazette: Government Printer, POB 37, Zomba; tel. 523155; f. 1894; weekly.

Malawi News: PB 39, Ginnery Corner, Blantyre; f. 1959; weekly; English, Chichewa; circ. 13,500.

Moni: POB 5592, Limbe; tel. 651139; telex 44814; f. 1964; monthly; Chichewa and English; circ. 40,000.

Moyo: POB 3, Blantyre; monthly; English; publ. by Ministry of Health.

Nation: Blantyre; f.1993; weekly; English; independent; Editor Ken Lipanga.

New Express: Blantyre; f.1993; weekly; English; independent; Editors Willie Zingani, Felix Mponda.

Odini: POB 133, Lilongwe; tel. 721388; fax 721141; f. 1950; weekly; Chichewa and English; Roman Catholic; Dir S. P. Kalilombe; circ. 12,000.

This is Malawi: POB 494, Blantyre; tel. 620266; telex 44471; fax 620807; f. 1964; monthly; English; also Chichewa edn: Chitukuko cha Amayi n'Malawi; publ. by the Dept of Information; circ. 12,000.

NEWS AGENCY

Malawi News Agency (MANA): Mzuza; tel. 636122; telex 44234; f. 1966.

Publishers

Christian Literature Association in Malawi: POB 503, Blantyre; tel. 620839; f. 1968; general and religious books in Chichewa and English; Gen. Man. Willie Zingani.

Likuni Press and Publishing House: POB 133, Lilongwe; tel. 721388; fax 721141; f. 1949; publs in English and Chichewa; Gen. Man. (vacant).

Popular Publications: POB 5592, Limbe; tel. 651139; telex 44814; f. 1961; general and religious.

Government Publishing House

Government Printer: POB 37, Zomba; tel. 523155.

Radio

There were an estimated 2.2m. radio receivers in use in 1991. There is no television service in Malawi.

Malawi Broadcasting Corporation: POB 30133, Chichiri, Blantyre 3; tel. 671222; telex 44425; fax 671257; f. 1964; statutory body; semi-commercial, partly state-financed; domestic service in English and Chichewa; Gen. Man. Henry R. Chirwa; Head of Production Thennis Sineta; Editor-in-Chief Molland Nkhata.

Finance

(cap. = capital; p.u. = paid up; res = reserves; m. = million; dep. = deposits; brs = branches; amounts in kwacha)

BANKING

Central Bank

Reserve Bank of Malawi: POB 30063, Capital City, Lilongwe 3; tel. 732488; telex 44788; fax 731145; f. 1965; bank of issue; cap. and res 88m., dep. 755m. (1991); Gov. F. Z. Pelekamoyo; br. in Blantyre.

Commercial Banks

Commercial Bank of Malawi Ltd: POB 1111, Blantyre; tel. 620144; telex 44340; fax 620360; f. 1970 to encourage Malawian participation in business; cap. and res 63m., dep. 403m. (Dec. 1992); Chair. John Z. U. Tembo; CEO Dennis G. Lawrence; 14 brs; agencies throughout Malawi.

National Bank of Malawi: Victoria Ave, POB 945, Blantyre; tel. 620622; telex 44142; fax 620606; f. 1971; cap. and res 74.2m., dep. 712.7m. (Dec. 1992); Chair. C. W. Freyer; CEO E. G. Bell; 14 brs; agencies throughout Malawi.

Development Bank

Investment and Development Bank of Malawi Ltd (INDEBANK): Delamere House, Victoria Ave, POB 358, Blantyre; tel. 620055; telex 45201; fax 623353; f. 1972; cap. p.u. 17.4m. (Dec. 1992); provides loans to statutory corpns and to private enterprises in the agricultural, industrial, tourism, transport and commercial sectors, on a joint-financing basis; Chair. C. Barrow; Gen. Man. C. L. Mphande.

Merchant Banks

Leasing and Finance Co of Malawi Ltd: Delamere House, 6th Floor, Victoria Ave, POB 1963, Blantyre; tel. 620233; telex 44179; fax 620275; f. 1986; cap. and res 14.7m. (1993); Gen. Man. M. J. Taylor.

National Mercantile Credit Ltd: Plantation House, POB 821, Blantyre; tel. 623670; telex 44308; fax 620606; f. 1958; cap. p.u. 0.4m. (Jan. 1992); Chair. E. G. Bell; Gen. Man. M. Banford.

Savings Bank

Post Office Savings Bank: POB 521, Blantyre; tel. 620944; telex 44437.

INSURANCE

National Insurance Co Ltd: NICO House, Private Bag 30421, Capital City, Lilongwe 3; tel. 730366; telex 44622; f. 1971; cap. and res 8.9m. (1988); offices at Blantyre, Lilongwe and Mzuzu, agencies country-wide; Chair. J. Z. U. Tembo; Gen. Man. J. M. W. Bowles.

Premier Life Office: POB 393, Blantyre; tel. 620677; telex 44690.

Trade and Industry

CHAMBER OF COMMERCE

Associated Chambers of Commerce and Industry of Malawi: Chichiri Trade Fair Grounds, POB 258, Blantyre; tel. 671988; telex 43992; fax 671147; f. 1892; 550 mems; Chair. H. I. Thomson.

INDUSTRIAL AND COMMERCIAL ORGANIZATIONS

Agricultural Development and Marketing Corporation (ADMARC): POB 5052, Limbe; tel. 640044; telex 44121; fax 640486; statutory trading org. that markets the agricultural crops produced by smallholder farmers; exporter of confectionery, groundnut kernels, maize, cassava and sunflower seed; primary marketing of tobacco, wheat and a wide variety of beans, peas and other seeds; co-operates with commercial cos in the cultivation and processing of agricultural produce; Gen. Man. E. B. Kadzako.

Malawi Export Promotion Council: Delamere House, POB 1299, Blantyre; tel. 620499; telex 44589; fax 635429; f. 1974; Gen. Man. J. B. L. Malange.

Smallholder Coffee Authority: POB 230, Mzuzu; tel. 332899; fax 332902; producers of arabica coffee.

Smallholder Sugar Authority: Blantyre; telex 44647.

Smallholder Tea Authority: POB 80, Thyolo.

Tea Association of Malawi Ltd: POB 930, Blantyre; tel. 671182; telex 44320; f. 1936; 20 mems; Chair. A. Schwarz.

Tobacco Association of Malawi: POB 31360, Lilongwe 3; tel. 783099; telex 44598; fax 783493; f. 1929; 25,000 mems; Chair. H. B. J. Ntaba.

Tobacco Exporters' Association of Malawi: Private Bag 403, Kanengo, Lilongwe 4; tel. 765663; telex 44360; fax 765668; f. 1930; 9 mems; Chair. V. Cole.

DEVELOPMENT CORPORATIONS

Malawi Development Corporation (MDC): MDC House, Glyn Jones Rd, POB 566, Blantyre; tel. 620100; telex 44146; fax 620584; f. 1964; cap. 20m. kwacha (Dec. 1991); 100% state-owned; provides finance and management advice to commerce and industry; 15 subsidiary and assoc. cos; Chair. L. S. K. Msiska; Gen. Man. P. G. Partridge.

Mining Investment and Development Corporation Ltd (MIDCOR): POB 565, Lilongwe; f. 1985; state-owned; operates coal mines at Kaziwiziwi and Mchenga and explores for other mineral deposits; Gen. Man. Stanley Kalyati.

Small Enterprise Development Organization of Malawi (SEDOM): POB 525, Blantyre; tel. 622555; telex 44666; fax

622781; f. 1982; tech. and management advice to indigenous small-scale businesses.

EMPLOYERS' ASSOCIATIONS

Employers' Consultative Association of Malawi: POB 2134, Blantyre; tel. 671337; f. 1963; 300 mems; Chair. E. E. Gwazantini.

Master Builders', Civil Engineering Contractors' and Allied Trades' Association: POB 950, Blantyre; tel. 636966; f. 1955; 73 mems (1990); Chair. B. Clow.

Master Printers' Association of Malawi: POB 2460, Blantyre; f. 1962; 18 mems; Chair. G. M. Phoso.

Motor Traders' Association of Malawi: POB 311, Blantyre; tel. 622966; fax 621215; f. 1954; 42 mems (1989); Chair. M. Scott.

MAJOR INDUSTRIAL COMPANIES

The following are some of the largest companies in terms of capital investment or employment.

BATA Shoe Company (Malawi) Ltd: POB 936, Blantyre; tel. 670511; telex 44252; mfrs of shoes; Man. Dir H. Strohmayer.

B.A.T. (Malawi) Ltd: POB 428, Blantyre; tel. 670033; telex 44114; fax 670808; mfrs of cigarettes; Gen. Man. J. E. Kettle.

Brown and Clapperton: POB 1582, Limbe; tel. 634677; telex 44243; fax 635198; mfrs of engineering products.

Carlsberg Malawi Brewery Ltd: POB 1050, Heavy Industrial Area, Blantyre; tel. 670133; telex 44405; fax 671362; mfrs of beer; CEO H. H. Vasby.

Chilling Agrimal (Malawi) Ltd: POB 143, Heavy Industrial Area, Blantyre; tel. 670933; telex 44750; fax 670651; mfrs of agricultural implements; Gen. Man. J. Hicks.

CTM (Malawi) Ltd: POB 5350, Limbe; telex 44183; mfrs of textiles; Man. Dir K. Btyan.

Grain and Milling Co Ltd: POB 5847, Limbe; tel. 651055; telex 44868; grain millers.

Import and Export Co of Malawi (1984) Ltd: POB 1106, Blantyre; tel. 670999; telex 44214; fax 671160; mfrs and wholesalers of brushes.

International Timbers Ltd: POB 5050, Limbe; tel. 640399; telex 4248; f. 1907; cap. K6.6m.; foresters and sawmillers of home-grown eucalyptus timber; mfrs of tobacco packing material, structural laminated timber, woodblock flooring, pallets and wooden packaging material, commercial plywood, blockboard, tea chests and flush panel doors; Man. Dir David G. Lloyd.

Lever Brothers (Malawi) Ltd: POB 5151, Tsiranana Rd, Limbe; tel. 641100; telex 44253; fax 645720; f. 1963; mfrs of soaps, detergents, cooking oils, foods, beverages and chemicals; Chair. C. Foy.

Lonrho (Malawi) Ltd: POB 5498, Churchill Rd, Limbe; tel. 640000; telex 441127; fax 640427; f. 1963; cap. K5m.; total issued cap. of Lonrho group cos in Malawi: c. K70m.; Jt Man. Dirs K. N. Roberts and J. E. Smith; controls the following subsidiaries:

- **Alumina Corporation of Malawi Ltd, Corundum Mining Corporation Ltd:** Mining.
- **The Central Africa Co Ltd:** Tea and tobacco.
- **The Central African Transport Co:** Motor trading.
- **Chibuku Products Ltd:** Brewing.
- **David Whitehead and Sons (Malawi) Ltd:** Textiles.
- **Dwangwa Sugar Corporation Ltd:** Sugar.
- **Farming and Engineering Services Ltd:** Agricultural equipment.
- **General Construction Co Ltd:** Construction.
- **Halls' Garage Ltd:** Motor trading.
- **Leopard Developments Ltd:** Petroleum products.
- **Makandi Aviation Ltd:** Crop spraying.
- **RAISE Ltd:** Television assembly, steel construction.
- **The Sugar Corporation of Malawi Ltd:** Sugar.

Malawi Distilleries Ltd: POB 924, MacLeod Rd, Heavy Industrial Site, Blantyre; tel. 670722; telex 44820; fax 670813; f. 1967; cap. K0.45m.; sole producer of potable spirits for local consumption and export; Gen. Man. W. L. Shepherd.

Malawi Iron and Steel Corporation: POB 2165, Blantyre.

National Oil Industries Ltd: POB 567; Macleod Rd, Blantyre, tel. 670155; telex 44334; mfrs of cooking oils, cotton-seed cake and millers of rice; Gen. Man. F. A. Jumbe.

Packaging Industries (Malawi) Ltd: POB 30533, Chichiri, Blantyre 3; tel. 670533; telex 44601; fax 671283.

Pipe Extruders Ltd: POB 30041, Lilongwe 3; tel. 765388; telex 44871; fax 765410; mfrs of PVC.

Plastic Products Ltd: POB 907, Blantyre.

Plumbing and Engineering Works (PEW): POB 30038, Chichiri, Blantyre 3; tel. 671155; telex 44836; fax 671437; mfrs of trailer, bus and truck bodies and structural steel works; Gen. Man. George French.

The Portland Cement Co (1974) Ltd: POB 532, Heavy Industrial Area, Blantyre; tel. 671933; telex 44841; fax 671026; f. 1974; cap. K8m. (Dec. 1989); mfrs and distributors of cement; projected annual capacity: 140,000 metric tons; Gen. Man. M. A. R. Phiri.

Press and Shine Clothing Ltd: POB 306, Lilongwe; tel. 720566; telex 44819; mfrs of garments; Gen. Man. M. Chikankheni.

Press Steel Industries Ltd: POB 30116, Lilongwe 3; tel. 765088; telex 44859; fax 765848; metal rollers.

Southern Bottlers Ltd: POB 406, Blantyre; tel. 670022; telex 44229; mfrs of soft drinks.

Universal Industries Ltd: POB 507, Blantyre; tel. 670055; telex 44402; mfrs of confectionery; Man. Dir D.K. Amin.

Viply: POB 30717, Lilongwe 3; tel. 733387; telex 43354; fax 733512; mfrs of plywood.

TRADE UNIONS

Trades Union Congress of Malawi (TUCM): POB 5094, Limbe; f. 1964; 6,500 mems; Chair. W. C. Chimphanga; Gen. Sec. L. Y. Mvula; the following are among the principal affiliated unions:

- **Building Construction, Civil Engineering and Allied Workers' Union:** POB 110, Limbe; tel. 650598; f. 1961; 6,000 mems; Chair. W. I. Soko; Gen. Sec. G. Sitima.
- **Railway Workers' Union of Malawi:** POB 5393, Limbe; tel. 640844; f. 1954; 3,000 mems; Chair. W. C. Chimphanga; Gen. Sec. F. L. Mattenje.

Other unions affiliated to the TUCM are the Local Government Employees' Union, the Plantation and Agricultural Employees' Union, and the Transport and General Workers' Union.

Unaffiliated Union

Teachers' Association of Malawi: Limbe; f. 1964; 3,000 mems.

Transport

RAILWAYS

Malawi Railways and the Central African Railway Co, its wholly-owned subsidiary, operate between Nsanje (near the southern border with Mozambique) and Mchinji (near the border with Zambia) via Blantyre, Salima and Lilongwe, and between Nkaya and Nayuci on the eastern border with Mozambique, covering a total of about 789 km. Malawi Railways and Mozambique State Railways provide the links from the Mozambique ports of Beira and Nacala to Malawi. These links traditionally form Malawi's principal trade routes. However, they were effectively closed between 1983–85, owing to Mozambican insurgent activity. The rehabilitation of the rail link to Nacala was completed in October 1989.

There is a rail/lake interchange station at Chipoka on Lake Malawi, from where Malawi Railways vessels operate services to other lake ports in Malawi.

Malawi Railways: POB 5144, Limbe; tel. 640844; telex 44810; fax 640683; Chair. (vacant); Gen Man. F. W. Markham.

ROADS

The total length of roads in 1988 was 12,215 km, of which 2,662 km were bituminized. All main roads, and most secondary roads, are all-weather roads. Major routes link Lilongwe and Blantyre with Harare, Zimbabwe, Lusaka, Zambia, and Mbeya and Dar es Salaam in Tanzania. A 480-km highway runs along the western shore of Lake Malawi. A project to create a new trade route, or 'northern corridor', through Tanzania involved road construction and improvements in Malawi, and was completed in 1992.

Road Transport Operators' Association: Makata Industrial Site, Manica Bldg, POB 30740, Chichiri, Blantyre 3; tel. 670422; telex 44275; fax 671423; f. 1956; 204 mems (1993); Chair. R. R. Patel.

CIVIL AVIATION

Kamuzu International Airport (at Lilongwe) was opened in 1982. There is another main airport, at Blantyre, which serves a number of regional airlines, and three domestic airports.

Air Malawi Ltd: Chibisa House, Glyn Jones Rd, POB 84, Blantyre; tel. 620177; telex 44245; fax 620042; f. 1967; domestic and scheduled regional services; charter flights are also operated; Chair. John Z. U. Tembo; CEO Capt. Lewis Mbilizi.

Tourism

Big game, beaches on Lake Malawi, fine scenery and an excellent climate from the basis of the country's tourist potential. In 1990 an estimated 129,912 tourists visited Malawi.

Department of Tourism: POB 402, Blantyre; tel. 620300; telex 44645; fax 620947; f. 1969; responsible for Malawi tourist policy, administers govt rest-houses, sponsors training of hotel staff; publs tourist literature; Chief Tourism Officer M. M. MATOLA (acting).

Tourism Development and Investment Co (TDIC): Blantyre; f. 1988 by Malawi Development Corpn to operate hotels and tours.

Defence

Malawi's defence forces numbered 10,000 men in June 1993. All services form part of the army. There is also a paramilitary police force of 1,500.

Defence Expenditure: Estimated at K90.8m. in 1992/93.

Commander-in-Chief of the Armed Forces: Ngwazi Dr HASTINGS KAMUZU BANDA.

Army Commander: Gen. ISAAC YOHANE.

Inspector-General of Police: MC. J. KAMWANA.

Education

Primary education, which is officially compulsory, begins at six years of age and lasts for up to eight years. Secondary education, which begins at 14 years of age, lasts for four years, comprising two cycles of two years. In 1989 there were 1,325,453 pupils enrolled at primary schools, while the total enrolment in general secondary education was 29,326. In 1990 primary school enrolment was equivalent to an estimated 66% of children in the relevant age-group (males 72%, females 60%), but secondary enrolment was equivalent to only 2% of children in the appropriate age-group. Primary education is administered by local education authorities, and secondary education by the central government, The University of Malawi had 2,685 students in 1989. Some students attend institutions in the United Kingdom and the USA. Education was allocated 10.3% of total recurrent government expenditure in 1990. In 1987, according to census results, the average rate of adult illiteracy was 51.5% (males 34.7%; females 66.5). A five-year adult literacy programme was launched in 1986, and in 1987 two teacher-training colleges, built with the assistance of the World Bank were opened as part of the government's Second Educational Plan (1985–95).

Bibliography

Agnew, Lady S. (Ed.). *Malawi in Maps.* London, University of London Press, 1972.

Banda, H. K., and Nkumbula, H. M. *Federation in Central Africa.* London, 1951.

Hanna, A. J. *The Beginnings of Nyasaland and North-Eastern Rhodesia 1859–95.* Oxford, Clarendon Press, 1956.

L'Hoiry, P. *Le Malawi.* Paris, Editions Karthala, 1988.

Konczacki, Z. A., Parpart, J. L., and Shaw, T. M. *Studies in the Economic History of Southern Africa.* Vol. I. London, Cass, 1990.

McCracken, J. 'The Nineteenth Century in Malawi' and 'African Politics in Twentieth Century Malawi', in Ranger, T. O. (Ed.) *Aspects of Central African History.* London, Heinemann, 1968.

Politics and Christianity in Malawi 1875–1940. Cambridge University Press, 1977.

McMaster, C. *Malawi Foreign Policy and Development.* London, Julian Friedmann Publishers, 1974.

National Statistical Office. *Malawi Population Census 1977: Final Report.* Zomba, Government Printer, 1980.

Pachai, B. *Malawi: The History of the Nation.* London, Longman, 1973.

Pike, J. G., and Rimmington, G. T. *Malawi: A Geographical Study.* London, Oxford University Press, 1965.

President's Office, Economic Planning Division. *Economic Report.* Published annually. Zomba.

Reserve Bank of Malawi. *Economic and Financial Review.* Quarterly.

Stokes, E. T., and Brown, R. (Eds). *The Zambesian Past.* Manchester University Press, 1966.

Williams, T. D. *Malawi: The Politics of Despair.* Ithaca, NY, and London, Cornell University Press, 1978.

MALI

Physical and Social Geography

R. J. HARRISON CHURCH

With an area of 1.24m. sq km (478,767 sq miles), the Republic of Mali is only slightly smaller than Niger, west Africa's largest state. Like Niger and Burkina Faso, Mali is land-locked. It extends about 1,600 km from north to south, and roughly the same distance from east to west, with a narrowing at the centre. The population was 7,696,348 at the census of April 1987, and was officially estimated at 8,156,000 in mid-1990 (giving an average density of 6.6 inhabitants per sq km).

The ancient Basement Complex rocks of Africa have been uplifted in the mountainous Adrar des Iforas of the north-east, whose dry valleys bear witness to formerly wetter conditions. Otherwise the Pre-Cambrian rocks are often covered by Primary sandstones, which have bold erosion escarpments at, for example, Bamako and east of Bandiagara. At the base of the latter live the Dogon people, made famous by Marcel Griaule's study. Where the River Niger crosses a sandstone outcrop below Bamako, rapids obstruct river navigation, giving an upper navigable reach above Bamako, and another one below it from Koulikoro to Ansongo, near the border with Niger.

Loose sands cover most of the rest of the country and, as in Senegal and Niger, are a relic of drier climatic conditions. They are very extensive on the long border with Mauritania and Algeria.

Across the heart of the country flows the River Niger, a vital waterway and source of fish. As the seasonal floods retreat, they leave pasture for thousands of livestock desperate for food and water after a dry season of at least eight months. The retreating floods also leave damp areas for man, equally desperate for cultivable land in an arid environment. Flood water is sometimes retained for swamp rice cultivation, and has been made available for irrigation, particularly in the 'dead' south-western section of the inland Niger delta.

The delta is the remnant of an inland lake, in which the upper Niger once terminated. In a more rainy era this overflowed to join the then mighty Tilemsi river, once the drainage focus of the now arid Adrar des Iforas. The middle and lower courses of the Tilemsi now comprise the Niger below Bourem, at the eastern end of the consquential elbow turn of the Niger. The eastern part of the delta, which was formed in the earlier lake, is intersected by 'live' flood-water branches of the river, while the relic channels of the very slightly higher western part of the delta are never occupied naturally by flood water and so are 'dead'. However, these are used in part for irrigation water retained by the Sansanding barrage, which has raised the level of the Niger by an average of 4.3 m.

Mali is mainly dry throughout, with a rainy season of four to five months and a total rainfall of 1,120 mm at Bamako, and of only seven weeks and an average fall of 236 mm at Gao. North of this there is no rain-fed cultivation, but only semi-desert or true desert, which occupies nearly one-half of Mali. There the main hope is of finding petroleum. The mining of gold reserves, most of which are located in southern regions, is becoming an increasingly important activity.

Distances to the nearest foreign port from most places in Mali are at least 1,300 km, and, not surprisingly, there is much seasonal and permanent emigration.

Recent History

PIERRE ENGLEBERT

The former French colony of Soudan merged with Senegal in April 1959 to form the Federation of Mali, which became independent on 20 June 1960. Senegal seceded two months later, and the Republic of Mali was proclaimed on 22 September. Led by President Modibo Keita and his Union soudanaise party, Mali was declared a one-party state and pursued socialist policies, severing links with France and developing close relations with the Soviet bloc. Mali's withdrawal from the Franc Zone in 1962 adversely affected the economy, despite government efforts to regulate commerce. In 1967, despite radical internal opposition, the government reached agreement with France for an eventual return to the Franc Zone.

The internal disputes of 1967 and 1968 impelled Keita to take decisive action, dissolving the party's political bureau in August 1967 and the national assembly in January 1968, and replacing them with new bodies. The emergence of a militant youth movement, which undertook purges within the party and administration, caused concern in the army, especially after the arrest of several officers. A group of young officers staged a successful *coup d'état* in November 1968. The constitution was abrogated, and all political parties were banned. A 14-member Comité militaire pour la libération nationale (CMLN) was formed, with Lt (later Gen.) Moussa Traoré as president and Capt. Yoro Diakité as head of government.

THE TRAORÉ PERIOD, 1968–91

The new regime promised a return to civilian rule when Mali's economic problems (attributed to the drought in the Sahel region) had been overcome. Relations with France improved after the coup, and French aid helped to balance the budget. In September 1969, following the discovery of a military plot to reinstore Keita, Diakité was demoted to a lesser government post. (He was arrested in 1971, and died in detention in 1973.) Traoré, who had assumed personal leadership of the government, also encountered opposition among civil servants, state employees and students loyal to the former regime; however, such disaffection was overshadowed by the ravages of the 1968–74 drought.

In June 1974 a new constitution was approved by referendum. This provided for the establishment of a one-party state, with the CMLN to remain in power for a five-year transitional period. In September 1976 the formation of the future ruling party, the Union démocratique du peuple malien (UPDM), was announced. The political changes encountered persistent opposition both from supporters of the old regime and from proponents of multi-party democracy, and hostile demonstrations followed Keita's death in detention in May 1977. In 1978 a number of high-ranking officers were tried and imprisoned on charges of threatening state security.

Presidential and legislative elections were held in June 1979, with Traoré, as sole candidate for the presidency, winning a reported 99% of the votes cast and a single list of UDPM candidates being elected to the legislature. Unrest among students and teachers continued in 1980 and 1981, prompted by the dissolution of the students' union—following its refusal to affiliate with the UDPM—and the subsequent death in custody of a student leader. An alleged coup attempt in December 1980 led to death sentences for three gendarmes. A constitutional amendment, adopted in September 1981, increased the presidential term from five to six years, and reduced that of the national assembly from four years to three. Legislative elections followed in June 1982, again with a single list of UDPM candidates.

Beginning in 1981 the Traoré regime undertook a programme of economic liberalization, formulated in co-operation with the World Bank and other Western donors. The reforms were pursued in spite of severe drought conditions in 1983–84. None the less, Traoré's position was reinforced following his re-election to the presidency in June 1985 (obtaining, as sole candidate, 98% of the votes), with his power unchallenged by the youth, women's and trade union movements. In June 1986 Traoré appointed his personal physician, Dr Mamadou Dembélé (hitherto the minister of public health and social affairs), to the post of prime minister, thus recreating an office that had been dormant since 1971. Traoré also ceded the defence portfolio to a close associate, Gen. Sékou Ly. However, following a further ministerial reshuffle in June 1988, the post of prime minister was again abolished, and Dembélé returned to his former position in the council of ministers, while Traoré reassumed the defence portfolio. (Dembélé was dismissed from the government one year later, following allegations of his involvement in the smuggling of gold.)

The government's decision, in 1987, to curtail elements of its programme of austerity, in response to an increase in popular discontent, resulted in the suspension by the IMF and the World Bank of financing negotiations. However, capital inflows resumed in August 1988, following the introduction of new economic reforms. An anti-corruption commission was established in April 1987, and in December nine people were sentenced to death following the trial of 47 defendants accused of embezzling public funds. In mid-1989 four others were given death sentences, and a further 30 defendants were imprisoned for corruption. In August 1987 the minister of finance and trade, Soumana Sacko, was forced to resign, apparently as a result of the unpopularity in official circles of his efforts to eliminate corruption. Sacko was rehabilitated in late 1988, when he was appointed auditor-general, but he subsequently left Mali to work for the UN Development Programme.

Elections to the national assembly were held in June 1988, with provision being made for up to three candidates, nominated by UDPM regional party offices, to contest each of the 82 seats. The government reported that the UDPM candidates were endorsed by 98.56% of those who voted. Forty new members were elected to the assembly.

In September 1988 Traoré closed down the detention facilities at the Taoudenni salt mines, in northern Mali, and reduced the sentences of (or released) its 78 prisoners. Among those freed were several political detainees who had been implicated in the 1978 coup attempt.

In March 1990 President Traoré, doubtless influenced by political events elsewhere in the region, initiated a nationwide series of conferences to consider the exercise of democracy within and by the UDPM. Although the legitimacy of the ruling party was largely upheld outside the capital, it was reported that many speakers at the Bamako conference favoured political change. In response, Traoré stated that diverse political opinions must be expressed within the framework of the UDPM.

During the second half of 1990, Mali's first cohesive opposition movements began to emerge. Among the most prominent were the Comité national d'initiative démocratique (CNID, representing many lawyers) and the Alliance pour la démocratie au Mali (ADEMA, founded by the authors of the August 'open letter'), which organized mass pro-democracy demonstrations in December.

In a government reorganization in early January 1991, Traoré relinquished the defence portfolio to Brig.-Gen. Mamadou Coulibaly, the air force chief of staff. (Traoré, while remaining president of the council of ministers, would henceforth occupy no ministerial post.) Gen. Sékou Ly was designated minister of the interior and basic development.

One of Ly's first actions in his new capacity was to issue warnings to the CNID and ADEMA, as well as to a recently-formed unofficial students' organization, the Association des élèves et étudiants du Mali (AEEM), that their political activities must cease, thus bringing to an end a period of apparent political openness. Rallies were organized in protest against the restrictions, and the arrest of the leader of the AEEM, Oumar Mariko, prompted further unrest. Students, school pupils and lawyers led anti-government demonstrations. According to official reports, two demonstrators were killed, and 35 injured, when security forces intervened to suppress violent protests. Educational establishments throughout Mali were closed by the authorities, in response to widespread unrest, and the government deployed armoured vehicles in the capital. Some 250 demonstrators were reported to have been arrested during five days of protests, although officials stated that Mariko had been released from custody before the outbreak of violence. Further arrests were made in late January 1991, although most detainees had been released by the end of the month, and the government ordered the resumption of classes in mid-February.

ARMY INTERVENTION AND POLITICAL REFORM

Violent pro-democracy demonstrations on 22–24 March 1991 were harshly repressed by the security forces: official figures later revealed that 106 people were killed, and 708 injured, during the unrest. In response, President Traoré promised that political reforms would be introduced, but refused to accede to demands for his resignation. On 26 March it was announced that Traoré had been arrested. A military Conseil de réconciliation nationale (CRN), led by Lt-Col (later Brig.-Gen.) Amadou Toumani Touré, assumed power, and the constitution, government, legislature and the UDPM were dissolved. Negotiations between the CRN and those organizations that had opposed Traoré culminated in the disbanding of the CRN and the establishment of a 25-member Comité de transition pour le salut du peuple (CTSP), chaired by Touré, whose function would be to oversee a transition to a democratic, civilian political system. It was announced that municipal, legislative and presidential elections would be organized by the end of 1991, and that the armed forces would withdraw from political life on 20 January 1992 (the date of the annual 'Armed Forces Day' national holiday). The CTSP also promised to convene a national conference to seek a consensus view on constitutional, electoral and political reform. In early April 1991 Soumana Sacko, the former minister of finance and trade, was invited to return to Mali as a transitional prime minister. Upon his return, Sacko nominated a civilian-dominated council of ministers.

The CTSP, while affirming its commitment to the policies of economic adjustment that had been adopted by the Traoré administration in consultation with international creditors, undertook the reform of Malian political life, and sought to remove from positions of influence all those considered to have been implicated in the corrupt practices of the previous regime. Efforts were initiated, in the months that followed Traoré's downfall, to recover funds allegedly embezzled by his regime, rumoured to total some US $2,000m. (a sum comparable to the country's foreign debt), which were said to have been deposited in bank accounts overseas. Many of Traoré's military associates, including Sékou Ly, Mamadou Coulibaly and Ousmane Coulibaly, the chief of staff of the army, were arrested in connection with the brutality of the security forces in repressing the unrest that had preceded the overthrow of the Traoré government, while others were accused of 'economic crimes'. In June it was announced that Traoré was to be tried on charges that included having been an accessory to murder and assault, and illegal self-enrichment. None the less, the fragility of the new regime was demonstrated in mid-July, when it was announced that a coup attempt had been foiled. Those alleged to have promoted the plot, led by the minister of territorial administration, Maj. Lamine Diabira, were arrested, and the council of ministers and the CTSP were reorganized. Immediate increases in remuneration for military personnel and civil servants were announced in the aftermath of the attempt, and an amnesty was proclaimed for most political prisoners detained by the Traoré administration.

Provision was made for the registration of political parties: the CNID was registered as the Congrès national d'initiative démocratique, while ADEMA adopted the additional title of Parti africain pour la solidarité et la justice (while generally retaining its original acronym). The late president Modibo Keita was posthumously rehabilitated in early May, and his Union soudanaise, now known as the Union soudanaise—Rassemblement démocratique africain (US—RDA), in recognition of the party's original links with the Ivorian-dominated RDA, became an important political force in the immediate post-Traoré era.

The national conference, convened in Bamako on 29 July–12 August 1991, was attended by some 1,800 delegates, who prepared a draft constitution for what was to be designated the third republic of Mali, together with an electoral code and a charter governing political parties. The document provided for the separation of the powers of the executive, legislature and independent judiciary, and envisaged five-yearly presidential and legislative elections (by universal suffrage, in the context of a multi-party political system). It was emphasized that Touré would not contest the presidency. In late August seven government ministers and about one-half of the members of the CTSP were replaced, following allegations of their implication in the security forces' repressive actions prior to Traoré's downfall. Further government changes followed in December.

In November 1991 it was announced that the period of transition to civilian rule was to be extended until 26 March 1992. The delay was attributed principally to the CTSP's desire first to secure an agreement with Tuareg groups in the north (see below), but it was also admitted that the foreign assistance hitherto granted was insufficient to finance the electoral processes. The constitutional referendum, originally scheduled for 1 December 1991, thus took place on 12 January 1992, when the document was approved by 99.76% of those who voted (only about 43% of the electorate).

Municipal elections, which followed on 19 January 1992, were contested by 23 of the country's 48 authorized parties. Of these, ADEMA enjoyed the greatest success, winning 214 of the 751 municipal seats, while the US—RDA took 130 seats and the CNID 96. The rate of abstention by voters was almost 70%. Legislative elections took place, after some delay, on 23 February and 8 March, amid allegations that the electoral system was unduly favourable to ADEMA. Of the 21 parties that contested the elections, 10 secured seats in the 129-member national assembly: ADEMA won 76 seats (with 48.4% of the votes cast), the CNID nine (with 5.5% of the votes) and the US—RDA eight (with 17.6% of the votes). Overall, only about one-fifth of the electorate were said to have voted. Thirteen of the remaining seats were reserved for representatives of Malians resident abroad.

Nine candidates contested the first round of the presidential election, which finally took place on 12 April 1992 (the date for the transition to civilian rule having again been postponed). The largest share of the votes (44.95%) was won by the leader of the ADEMA, Alpha Oumar Konaré. A second round of voting, contested by Konaré and his nearest rival, Tiéoulé Mamadou Konaté of the US—RDA, followed two weeks later, at which Konaré won 69.01% of the votes cast. Again, participation by voters was little more than 20%.

THE KONARÉ PRESIDENCY

Konaré, a prominent historian, archaeologist and founder of an influential cultural co-operative, who had briefly served as a government minister in the late 1970s, was sworn in as president of the third republic on 8 June 1992 (having in the previous month resigned as chairman of ADEMA, in accordance with the provisions of the constitution). Younoussi Touré, hitherto the national director of the Banque centrale des états de l'Afrique de l'ouest, was immediately designated prime minister. While most strategic posts in Touré's government were allocated to members of ADEMA, opposition parties were represented, with members of the US—RDA and of the Parti pour la démocratie et le progrès (PDP) being assigned, respectively, to the national education and the justice and human rights ministries. In July (in the absence of opposition deputies, who boycotted the vote in protest against their lack of influence in a political system which they perceived to be excessively dominated by ADEMA) Aly Nouhoun Diallo, ADEMA's political secretary, was elected president of the national assembly.

The trial of ex-president Moussa Traoré and 32 of his associates began four days before Konaré's inauguration. However, proceedings were immediately adjourned, owing to a boycott of the trial by more than 70 defence lawyers, who were protesting against the lack of security for the accused. Hearings resumed in November, and in February 1993 Traoré, Sékou Ly, Mamadou Coulibaly and Ousmane Coulibaly were sentenced to death, after having been convicted of 'premeditated murder, battery and voluntary manslaughter'; the other defendants were acquitted. Appeal proceedings were immediately initiated against the sentences: although the death sentences were upheld by the supreme court in May, and Traoré declined to seek clemency from Konaré, it was widely expected that Konaré would commute them (no execution was known to have taken place since 1980). Charges relating to 'economic crimes' remained against Traoré, his wife and other members of the discredited regime. There was an attempt to revive the UDPM in June 1993, when the former ruling party held a constituent assembly, but the authorities refused to accord it legal status.

A political crisis was provoked in early 1993 by dissatisfaction in the education sector at the impact of the government's economic austerity programme on the payment of grants. In March students and school pupils attacked public buildings and vehicles in Bamako, and security forces intervened as the offices of the state radio service were besieged by protesters. There were further clashes in early April (as a result of which at least one person was killed, and 45 injured), when students, apparently protesting against government attempts to impose a new leader on their union, set fire to public buildings, including the seat of the national assembly, the official residence of the minister of state for national education and the headquarters of ADEMA. Younoussi Touré resigned shortly afterwards, and was replaced by Abdoulaye Sekou Sow. The new prime minister, who, while not affiliated to any political party, was known to be sympathetic to Konaré's policies, implemented an extensive government reorganization: his council of ministers remained dominated by ADEMA and its supporters, but also included opposition representatives—with, most notably, three ministries (among them the justice portfolio) being allocated to the CNID.

During the second half of 1993 there was evidence of increasing tensions among the parties participating in government. Members of ADEMA, the CNID and the US—RDA expressed dissatisfaction at their exclusion from the decision-making process, which they believed to be dominated by Konaré and the council of ministers. There was concern, moreover, that members of the Traoré regime retained positions of influence, while parties outside the government coalition protested that trial for 'economic crimes' of the ousted president and his associates had not yet begun. A reorganization of the government, in early November, was prompted by the resignation of ADEMA's vice-president, Mohamed Lamine Traoré, from his ministerial post. Sow's 'streamlined' council of ministers included new ministers responsible for finance (a controversial programme of austerity measures, announced in September, had failed to prevent the suspension of assistance by the IMF and the World Bank) and for foreign affairs. ADEMA remained the dominant party in the government, which also included representatives of the CNID, the PDP and the Rassemblement pour la démocratie et le progrès (RDP). Two of the US—RDA's three ministers left the government at the time of the reshuffle, and the party withdrew from the coalition shortly afterwards.

In early December 1993 it was revealed that a plot to assassinate Konaré, Sow and Aly Nouhoun Diallo, orchestrated by Oumar Diallo (Traoré's former aide-de-camp, who had been detained since July, accused of the misappropriation of state funds), had been thwarted. Five junior armed forces officers were arrested for their part in the conspiracy.

Political and social tensions were exacerbated by the devaluation, in January 1994, of the CFA franc (see Economy), despite the announcement of measures to offset the immediate adverse effects of the currency's depreciation. Sow, who had been experiencing increasing difficulty in securing support for his policies from ADEMA, resigned in early February; he was replaced by Ibrahim Boubacar Keita, since November 1993 the minister of foreign affairs, Malians abroad and African integration, who was said to be both a member of ADEMA's radical tendency and a close associate of Konaré. The president and the new prime minister, whose foreign affairs portfolio was assumed by Sy Kadiatou Sow, initially intended that the composition of the council of ministers should remain otherwise unaltered; however, the CNID and the RDP withdrew from the coalition, protesting that they had not been consulted about the recent changes. A new, ADEMA-dominated government was appointed, from which the PDP subsequently withdrew (although its representative in the council of ministers resigned from the party, in order that he might retain his portfolio).

Sow's resignation coincided with renewed unrest in the education sector, as students and school pupils protested against the effects of the currency's depreciation and demanded compensatory grant increases. Violent demonstrations in Bamako in mid-February 1994, which resulted in many arrests, prompted the closure of educational establishments (and a temporary ban on transmissions by an independent radio station that was believed by the authorities to have incited the unrest). In early March the detention, for his alleged involvement in the previous month's violence, of Yéhia Ould Zarawana, the leader of the AEEM, provoked further disturbances, during which public buildings were attacked. A day of 'inaction', organized by opposition groups in late March, in an attempt to secure the reopening of secondary and tertiary establishments (the resumption of classes at primary schools had been announced shortly beforehand) and the release of Zarawana and about 30 co-defendants, was deemed by the authorities to have been poorly supported, although the opposition claimed that much of the economic life of the capital had been disrupted. An attack, the same day, on the residence of the French consul-general in Bamako (attributed by some sources to a self-styled 'armed resistance group', which had recently distributed pamphlets threatening attacks on Western interests in Mali) was followed in early May by an offensive involving about 100 students and school pupils against the Bamako offices of the official French development agency. In mid-July the government agreed to the release on bail of Zarawana and the other detained students, shortly after they had begun a hunger strike in an attempt to secure their unconditional release.

ETHNIC TENSIONS

In late June 1990 Tuareg nomads mounted an attack on the sub-prefecture of Menaka (in eastern Mali, near the border with Niger), as a result of which 14 deaths were reported. The Malian authorities, who claimed that Tuareg rebels were attempting to establish a secessionist state in north-eastern Mali, responded in early July by imposing a state of emergency in the Gao and Tombouctou regions, while the armed forces conducted a repressive campaign against the nomads. Tuareg forces launched a further offensive near Bouressa in early September, which resulted in an estimated 200 Malian army casualties. Meanwhile, the repression of the Tuaregs by the Malian authorities resulted in the deaths of hundreds of nomads. Similar tension was being experienced in Niger, as large numbers of light-skinned Tuaregs, who had migrated to Algeria and Libya during periods of drought, began to return to west Africa. Shortly after the attack near Bouressa the heads of state of Algeria, Libya, Mali and Niger met in Algeria, where they agreed measures governing border controls and facilitating the return of refugees to their region of origin. In the same month it was announced that a new administrative region was to be established in the Kidal area of north-eastern Mali. In January 1991 representatives of the Traoré government met leaders of two Tuareg groups, the Mouvement populaire de l'Azaouad (MPA) and the Front islamique-arabe de l'Azaouad (FIAA), at Tamanrasset, in Algeria: a peace accord was signed, providing for an immediate cease-fire and for the eventual granting of a status of 'internal autonomy' for the Adrar region of northern Mali. The state of emergency was revoked in late January, and in early March Tuareg military prisoners were released.

Following the overthrow of the Traoré regime, the transitional administration affirmed its commitment to the Tamanrasset accord, and representatives of the Tuareg nomads were included in the CTSP. However, unrest continued in the north of the country, and in June 1991 the human rights organization, Amnesty International, reported incidences of the harsh repression of Tuaregs by the armed forces. By the time of the national conference it was reported that at least 150 members of the armed forces had been killed since the outbreak of the unrest. Meanwhile, thousands of Tuaregs, Moors and Bella (the descendants of the Tuaregs' black slaves), had fled to neighbouring countries to escape retaliatory attacks by the black population.

Attacks and skirmishes continued during the second half of 1991: the MPA was reported to have lost the support of more militant members, and a further group, the Front populaire de libération de l'Azaouad (FPLA), emerged to claim responsibility for several attacks. In mid-December 1991 a 'special conference on the north' (in preparation for negotiations that were to take place in Algeria) was convened in Mopti. With Algerian mediation, representatives of the transitional government and of four Tuareg groups—the MPA, the FIAA, the FPLA and the Armée révolutionnaire de libération de l'Azaouad (ARLA)—agreed in principle to a peace settlement. The accord envisaged an end to hostilities, the establishment of a commission of inquiry to examine the acts of violence perpetrated and losses suffered in areas affected by the conflict, and a reciprocal exchange of prisoners. Despite continued attacks, the negotiations resumed in the Algerian capital in late January 1992, at which the Malian authorities and the MPA, the FIAA and the ARLA (now negotiating together as the Mouvements et fronts unifiés de l'Azaouad—MFUA) formally agreed to implement the Mopti accord; the FPLA was reported not to have attended the Algiers sessions. A truce entered into force in early February, and the commission of inquiry was inaugurated in Gao shortly afterwards. Further talks in Algiers culminated, in late March, in the drafting of a 'national pact', which was signed in Bamako by the Malian authorities and the MFUA on 11 April (shortly after the exchange of prisoners and the repatriation of refugees, as envisaged in the accord, had been initiated). In addition to the provisions of the Mopti accord, the pact envisaged special administrative structures for the country's three northern regions, the incorporation of Tuareg fighters into the Malian armed forces, the demilitarization of the north and the instigation of efforts more fully to integrate Tuaregs in the economic and political fields.

Sporadic attacks, particularly against members of the northern majority Songhai, were reported. None the less, the implementation of the national pact was pursued, and in late October 1992 representatives of the government and the national assembly attended a congress of the MFUA at Taouardeï. Joint patrols were established, and Konaré visited the north in November to inaugurate the new administrative structures. In February 1993 the Malian government and the MFUA signed an accord facilitating the integration of an initial 600 Tuaregs into the national army. None the less, the refusal of the FPLA (whose leadership was based in Burkina) to participate in the application of the national pact undermined the peace process. It was not until May that the FPLA's secretary-general, Rhissa Ag Sidi Mohamed, declared the rebellion at an end and returned to Mali, urging FPLA fighters to participate in the implementation of the national pact.

During the second half of 1993 Tuareg leaders expressed concern that difficulties in repatriating refugees and in the implementation of the national pact were the cause of renewed attacks in the north. Indications of a breakdown in security were apparently confirmed by the assassination (allegedly by members of the ARLA) in the Kidal region, in early February 1994, of Col Bilal Saloum (the military leader of the MPA, regarded as a principal architect of the peace process, who had joined the Malian army in compliance with the national pact), and clashes between the MPA and the ARLA continued for several weeks before the two groups were reconciled. A meeting in Tamanrasset, in mid-April, between representatives of the Malian government and the MFUA (with Algerian mediation), intended to assess progress in the implementation of the national pact, was complicated by new demands, made by the MFUA, regarding the full integration of Tuaregs into Mali's military and civilian structures—which was, the Malian authorities maintained, governed by the constraints of the austerity programme. In mid-May, none the less, agreement was reached in the Algerian capital regarding the integration of 1,500 former rebels into the regular army and of a further 4,860 Tuaregs into civilian sectors; the MFUA undertook to dismantle its military bases in the north, while the government reaffirmed its commitment to the pursuit of development projects in northern areas.

The success of the Algiers agreement was, however, undermined by an intensification of clashes and acts of banditry in the north, as a result of which several hundred people, including many civilians, were reported to have been killed in the first half of 1994. Tensions, periodically escalating into violence, were reported between the so-called 'integrated' Tuareg fighters and regular members of the Malian armed forces, while the emergence of a Songhai resistance movement, Ganda Koi, further threatened the restoration of calm. Malian trade union leaders, moreover, expressed their opposition to the recruitment of Tuaregs into the civil service at a time of economic austerity. Violence continued, despite the stated commitment of the Malian government and the MFUA to the national pact, with the adherence of the FIAA, in particular, being called into question after the death of one of its leaders, in early June, as a result of a clash with members of the armed forces. Also in June Amnesty International expressed concern that members of the army were involved in the apparently arbitrary attacks on Tuareg civilians, while the Malian national assembly adopted a resolution demanding that the MFUA exert its authority over the rebel movement and urging the government to bring an end to insecurity in the north. Meeting in Tamanrasset, in late June, the Malian authorities and the MFUA agreed on the need for the reinforcement (initiated in previous weeks) of the army presence in areas affected by the violence, and established modalities for the more effective integration of Tuareg fighters. None the less, there was considerable concern regarding the future of the national pact following an escalation of violence in July. At the end of that month security forces acted to disperse an unauthorized anti-Tuareg demonstration in Bamako, and in early August, as Ibrahim Keita began a tour of northern regions, with the stated aim of reassuring residents of his administration's commitment to their security, a grenade attack took place on the home of a prominent Tuareg official in the capital.

The persistence of unrest during 1993–94, together with the poor infrastructure in the north, undermined attempts to repatriate refugees. In mid-1994, despite the existence of agreements between the Malian authorities and the governments of Algeria, Burkina Faso and Mauritania regarding the return of those who had fled Mali since 1990, it was estimated that as many as 100,000 Malian refugees remained in neighbouring countries.

EXTERNAL RELATIONS

In September 1983 the governments of Mali and Burkina Faso agreed to refer their long-standing boundary dispute over the Agacher strip, an area believed to contain significant mineral deposits, to the International Court of Justice (ICJ) for adjudication. In addition, Burkina withdrew its opposition to the readmission of Mali to the Franc Zone and the Union monétaire ouest-africaine (UMOA), which finally took place in 1984. The CFA franc was reintroduced as Mali's unit of currency in that year. On 25 December 1985, however, the dispute between Mali and Burkina, compounded by ideological differences, suddenly escalated into armed conflict, resulting in the six-day 'Christmas war'. During this brief conflict, Malian forces demonstrated their military superiority, but both sides were willing to submit to a cease-fire, agreed on 31 December, under the auspices of the Communauté économique de l'Afrique de l'Ouest (CEAO) (for more details, see Recent History of Burkina Faso). Throughout 1986 there was a gradual, and finally successful, reconciliation with Burkina: prisoners were exchanged in February, and full diplomatic relations, which had been broken off in 1974, were re-established in June. A ruling by the ICJ in December awarded Mali sovereignty over the western part of the Agacher strip, comprising about one-half of the disputed area. Both countries expressed satisfaction with this adjudication.

Following the overthrow of Moussa Traoré, members of the new administration travelled extensively in west Africa, where they generally received pledges of support for their actions. It was noted that the government of France, which had extended no military support to the Traoré regime as the influence of the Malian opposition movement increased, granted financial support for the recovery efforts that were necessary in the aftermath of the recent changes, and promised continued aid for Mali's programme of economic adjustment. French financial assistance was also forthcoming for the implementation of the national pact between the Malian government and Tuareg leaders.

Mali's relations with its immediate neighbours were largely dominated in the early 1990s by the presence in those countries of refugees from the conflict in northern Mali (see above). Diplomatic relations were established with Equatorial Guinea in November 1993 and with South Africa in May 1994. In June 1994 it was announced that Mali was to commit 150 troops to the UN Assistance Mission in Rwanda.

Economy

EDITH HODGKINSON

Revised for this edition by JANET E. LEWIS

Mali, the second largest country in francophone west Africa, is sparsely populated (with a density of 6.6 inhabitants per sq km in 1990) and land-locked, and most parts are desert or semi-desert, with the economically viable area confined to the Sahelian-Sudanese regions irrigated by the River Niger, which comprise about one-fifth of the total land area. The rate of economic growth in recent decades has been affected by drought, which caused declines in agricultural output in 1968–74, and again in 1982–85, thus prompting very wide fluctuations in gross domestic product (GDP). During 1980–85 GDP declined by an annual average of 0.5%. Mali enjoyed a strong economic recovery in 1987, when GDP growth of 11.8% was recorded, owing to an improvement in rainfall levels; however, the economy stagnated in the following two years, before showing a further marked recovery (of 12.5%) in 1989, but GDP eased down marginally in 1991. The situation was exacerbated by poor economic management throughout most of this period. There was a significant recovery in 1992, as the new regime implemented a programme of economic reform (in co-operation with the IMF and the World Bank), with real GDP growth of 7.8%. However, several targets were missed in 1993, despite the introduction of new austerity measures in the second half of that year, and GDP declined by 0.8%. Mali thus remains among the world's poorest countries.

In 1992, according to estimates by the World Bank, Mali's gross national product (GNP) was equivalent to only $310 per head. Mali's population, which was 7,696,348 at the census of April 1987, is (according to official figures) increasing at a rate of 1.8% per year, and was officially estimated to be 8.2m. at mid-1990. However, the UN estimates that the rate of population growth for the corresponding period was in the region of 3% per year. About 5% of the population are nomadic, and 25% urban, with the only significant agglomerations at the capital, Bamako, and the regional capitals. Persistent drought conditions throughout the Sahelian region during the 1970s and early 1980s drew a significant part of the nomadic population to the settled areas, with the result that parts of the Gao and Tombouctou (Timbuktu) regions are now deserted.

In the absence of strong economic growth or structural change, employment patterns have changed little since independence. In 1992 about 80% of the total labour force were estimated to be engaged in agriculture, largely at subsistence level, compared with 90% in 1965. Among these, there is significant seasonal migration (during the agricultural off-season) to Côte d'Ivoire and Senegal, and a total of some 2m. Malians are thought to work abroad, with France also an important host country. Wage employment is very low.

AGRICULTURE

Agricultural production has been affected by the persistent drought and also by institutional failings, low prices for producers, and the drift of population to the towns. In 1991 agriculture accounted for about 47.4% of GDP, compared with some 65% in the early 1960s. The sector is dominated by peasant farming, with minimal mechanization. Millet and sorghum are essentially produced at subsistence level. Output of cereals was severely affected by the droughts of the early 1970s and early 1980s: production of millet, sorghum and maize, which had been 1.3m. metric tons in 1976/77, declined to less than one-half of this level in 1984/85, while that of rice, at 103,400 tons in that year, continued to be substantially below earlier levels (269,000 tons in 1978/79 and an average of 170,000 tons per year in 1979–82). In the following two years, as a result of the return of adequate rainfall, the output of cereals showed a strong recovery, to more than 1.5m. tons of millet, sorghum and maize and 229,200 tons of rice in 1986/87. Output of cereals declined in 1987/88, owing to poor rains. However, there was a further good recovery in 1988/89, when total production of cereals reached 2.2m. tons. Mali thus achieved the target of self-sufficiency that had originally been set for 1978, and, in contrast to 1985 (when there was a shortfall of 481,000 tons in domestic cereal supply), had an exportable surplus of 600,000 tons. A slightly lower harvest was recorded in both 1989/90 and 1990/91, although the crop, at about 2m. tons in each year, was sufficient to fulfil domestic requirements. However, the rate of population growth since the late 1980s has meant that cereal imports (estimated at 90,000 tons in 1992/93) are still required, despite annual output of some 2.3m. tons.

The recurrent drought has also taken its toll of livestock: numbers of cattle were down to 3.9m. in 1975 and sheep 4m., from 5.35m. and 5.75m. respectively in 1969/70, which were easily the largest herds in francophone west Africa. Livestock numbers recovered to 5.8m. cattle and 11.5m. sheep and goats, following the implementation of a programme to rebuild herds which included the temporary suspension of livestock exports in 1975. However, the 1983–85 drought is thought to have caused the deaths of 40%–80% of the livestock, and has accelerated the movement of livestock-rearing from the north to the south, where it is geared towards export to Côte d'Ivoire. In 1992 there were 5.4m. cattle and 13.3m. sheep and goats.

Fishing on the Niger produces an annual catch of about 60,000 tons, but the sector is very vulnerable to drought and to the effects of large-scale dam building on the upper reaches of the river. The principal agency active in the cultivation of food crops is the Office du Niger, which administers 53,300 ha of irrigated land along the River Niger. For many years, however, the agency operated at a substantial financial loss, with about one-third of its irrigated area remaining uncultivated. In 1986 a rehabilitation programme was initiated which, at a cost of $39.8m., aimed to rationalize the organization's management and to increase the total cultivable area to more than 100,000 ha, of which 46,730 ha were to be planted with rice. However, yields of rice remain low (largely owing to poor levels of rainfall), and the Office du Niger has ceased cotton cultivation. In 1988 a programme was inaugurated with the aim of improving the irrigation network for the cultivation of rice both on the Office du Niger land and in the inland delta of the Niger in the Segou region. The cost of the programme, estimated at $84m., is being supported by the World Bank and France and other European donors. Overall, production of paddy rice, which averaged just over 300,000 tons per year in 1988/89–1990/91, increased to 444,500 tons in 1991/92 before declining slightly, to 404,500 tons, in 1992/93.

Until the early 1980s production of Mali's two major cash crops, cotton and groundnuts, rose appreciably (although erratically in the case of the latter). Cotton yields increased sixfold over 30 years, reaching 1,290 kg/ha in 1992/93. Mali accounted for 0.6% of world output in 1992, and the country is Africa's second largest cotton producer (after Egypt). About 2.3m. people were engaged in cotton production in 1993. In the case of both cotton and groundnuts, growth in output reflected government development programmes and external capital support. However, both crops fared badly in the difficult climatic conditions of the early 1980s: output of cotton fell to 96,500 tons in 1981/82. Production levels recovered well in subsequent years, with output of cotton reaching 276,023 tons in 1991/92 and 320,000 tons in 1992/93. This expansion can, in part, be attributed to the development programmes in the southern regions: Mali-Sud, an integrated project (including food crops) and Opération Haute-Vallée. Groundnut production, which had reached a record level of 205,000 tons in 1975/76, saw a general decline in subsequent years, but recovered to an annual average of some 123,300 tons in 1988/89–1990/91, as a result of more favourable weather. Output increased to 148,400 tons in 1991/92, before declining slightly, to 141,100 tons, in 1992/93. Following the devaluation, in January 1994, of the CFA franc, the official price paid to cotton growers was increased from 85 francs CFA per kg to 115 francs CFA/kg.

MINING AND POWER

Deposits of bauxite, copper, iron ore, nickel, manganese, uranium, diamonds and phosphates, of varying quality, have been located but not yet exploited, largely because of the country's land-locked position and lack of infrastructure. Prospecting is under way for petroleum, uranium, tungsten (wolfram), manganese, diamonds and gold. Marble is currently mined at Bafoulabé, and phosphate rock at Gao, but the most important mineral currently being exploited is gold. After considerable delay, production at the Kalana gold deposit began in 1985, supported by credits from the USSR. Planned capacity was 2,000 kg per year, from reserves estimated at 30 tons, but official output averaged only 400 kg per year in 1985–90. Exploitation of the reserves was suspended in early 1992, amid rumours that much of the production had bypassed official channels under the Traoré regime. Production at the Syama gold deposit, in southern Mali, began in early 1990. A joint-venture company was established with Australian and US interests to exploit the reserves, and annual output was scheduled to average 2,200 kg per year in 1990–93, increasing to 6,200 kg in 1994 under second-phase development. A third-phase project is planned to begin in 1997. The same company is to participate in a project to exploit gold deposits at Loulo, in the Kéniéba area, in co-operation with a Franco-Malian joint venture which envisages the production of 800 kg of gold per year. Other gold deposits are under investigation, and in late 1993 it was confirmed that a joint venture involving Canadian and South African mining companies and the Malian government is to open-mine gold reserves near Sadiola, with commencement due before 1996. The deposit, which is estimated to contain some 50m. tons of treatable ore, at a grade of 2 g of gold per ton of ore, was expected to yield an annual average of 4m. tons of ore over a period of about 13 years. There are long-established salt mines in the extreme north, with an annual production of 5,000 tons.

About 276m. kWh of electricity were generated in 1991, almost four-fifths of which were hydroelectric in origin. Since the commencement of production at the 45-MW capacity Selingué hydroelectric plant in 1982, electricity imports have no longer been necessary: in 1982 these amounted to 46m. kWh. However, the dependence on hydroelectric generation means that the supply is very unreliable, and in 1989 production at the Selingué plant was frequently suspended, owing to the low level of water in its reservoir. The construction of a dam at Manantali was completed in 1988. The operation of this dam is to be supervised by the Organisation pour la mise en valeur du fleuve Sénégal, in which both Mauritania and Senegal participate. Mali is to receive about one-half of the annual output of the hydroelectric plant (projected at 800m. kWh). However, the installation of generating equipment was delayed by disagreements over supply routes, and work was suspended for 10 months during 1989–90, owing to the deterioration in relations between Mauritania and Senegal, with the effect that the dam was not formally inaugurated until October 1992.

MANUFACTURING

Manufacturing activity, largely directed to meet local demand, is concentrated in Bamako, mainly taking the form of agricultural processing and the manufacture of consumer goods. Manufacturing contributed an estimated 8.7% of GDP in 1991, while industry as a whole accounted for 14.2% of the total. During the mid-1980s more than 75% of industrial turnover was accounted for by state companies, which operated nine of the 12 major food sector plants—a legacy of the Keita era. The 40 parastatal bodies generally proved to be inefficient and unprofitable, amassing debts of more than 100,000m. francs CFA by late 1987. Following the failure of successive governments to improve its performance, the sector is now being reorganized, under pressure from the IMF and other foreign creditors. It is planned to sell full or part-ownership in 30 of the companies, to dissolve some and, with foreign assistance (notably from the People's Republic of China), to improve the management of the remainder. The World Bank is providing funds for a programme to train management personnel in state enterprises and to assist planning. However, rationalization would mean either the loss of many jobs (10,000 were employed by these companies in 1986) or an increase in prices to the domestic consumer, or both.

The incomplete statistics available suggest general stagnation in industry throughout the 1970s and much of the 1980s, with several agricultural processing plants (particularly oilseed-crushing mills) operating well below capacity owing to a lack of supply. None the less, the indications are of some upturn during the second half of the 1980s, with the development of gold-mining and the success of schemes, including the two sugar refineries operated under the auspices of the Office du Niger, involving Chinese co-management. In accordance with the government's policy of disengagement from non-strategic industries, the state textiles producers were transferred to private ownership in 1990, and in 1994 it was announced that the country's main sugar producer was to be privatized. Also in 1994 the African Development Bank accorded its first loan to the Malian private sector, in the form of financing for a new food-processing enterprise in Bamako.

TRANSPORT INFRASTRUCTURE

The first years of the 1960s saw very substantial investment (one-fifth of total planned investment spending) in road-building, after the dissolution of the short-lived federation with Senegal in 1960, followed by Mali's withdrawal from the Franc Zone in 1962, disrupted traditional trading outlets. There are some 18,000 km of classified roads, of which about 6,000 km are all-weather roads and some 2,000 tarred. Mali's main access to the sea is via the Bamako–Abidjan (Cote d'lvoire) road. The 575-km all-weather road between Sévaré and Gao, which was opened in 1987, forms part of the Trans-Sahara Highway connecting Algeria with Nigeria. Financial support for the construction of the Mali section, which cost $142m., was provided by the OPEC Fund for International Development and the Arab Bank for Economic Development in Africa. A major programme for the modernization of the transport infrastructure, in progress in the mid-1990s, aims to maintain some 9,000 km of roads and restore 3,000 km of roads and tracks. The project is also to include the restoration of part of the 1,286-km rail link from Bamako to Dakar (Senegal). The cost of the programme ($305.7m.) is to be financed by the Malian government, the West African Development Bank, the African Development Fund, the European Development Fund, the Islamic Development Bank, the European Investment Bank and the OPEC Fund, together with the governments of Germany, Canada and France. There are long-standing plans to build a new railway line to link the capital with Kouroussa and Kankan, in Guinea, but these are unlikely to be realized in the near future. Owing to the inadequacy of the road and rail facilities, the country's inland waterways are of great importance to the transport infrastructure. The River Niger is used for transport during the rainy season, while traffic on the Senegal is expected to improve as a result of the completion of the Manantali dam, which should stabilize the water level and facilitate uninterrupted access to the sea.

FINANCE

At independence, Mali adopted a very ambitious capital spending programme. During the period 1960–65 it was planned to achieve annual growth of 8%, to develop nearly 90,000 ha of land (bringing in the peasant population through rural co-operatives) and to use state companies to operate the main sectors of the economy (including foreign trade, transport and mineral exploration). In the event, the bureaucratic superstructure became highly developed—administrative spending rose by an average 11%–12% per year in 1959–68 while the economy grew by a small fraction of this rate. Most state enterprises were operating at a loss, incurring an overall annual deficit of around 2,400m. Mali francs. The budgetary shortfall was bridged by creating money, and currency in circulation doubled between 1960–67. The simultaneous, and related, deterioration in the payments situation led Mali to seek to rejoin the Franc Zone and the Union monétaire ouest-africaine (UMOA), from which it had withdrawn in 1962. The conditions of the agreement providing for such a reintegration included a reduction in the activities of state enterprises and a 'freeze' on wages, to reduce the budget deficit. Mali eventually returned to the Franc Zone (as a *de facto* participant) in 1967. The recovery programme to cover the period 1970–73, drawn up with French advice, provided for a reduction in infrastructure and social investment, the dismantling of co-operatives, the abandonment of mineral exploration, and the winding up of some state industries. In the event, the budget deficit continued, and French subsidies were substantially in excess of the agreed upper limit, as any serious reduction in spending would have alienated the large and influential bureaucracy.

Initially, the military government that came to power in November 1968 pursued Modibo Keita's economic policies. Beginning in 1981, however, the Traoré government, under pressure from the IMF, the World Bank and bilateral donors, undertook a programme of economic reform. Adjustment measures included the ending of state monopolies, the restructuring or transfer to private ownership of parastatal organizations, the liberalization of the marketing of agricultural products and the easing of price controls. One objective of these measures was to curtail budgetary expenditure. However, the budget deficit remained at a high level, reaching 42,100m. francs CFA in 1985, since revenues were depressed by the weak foreign trade performance. The sharp decline in world cotton prices in 1986 resulted in a deficit of 43,900m. francs CFA in that year. The deficit was halved in 1987, as the government failed to fulfil its debt-servicing obligations, but increased again in 1988, to 48,900m. francs CFA, when Mali paid off its debt arrears in order to secure the resumption of credits (suspended since 1987) from the IMF and the World Bank. The deficit rose to 64,500m. francs CFA in 1989, reflecting the incorporation into the overall expenditure figures of certain hitherto separate budgets (for example, that for price stabilization). The deficit contracted sharply in 1990, to only 23,000m. francs CFA, as a result of higher tax revenue in conjunction with a decline in current expenditure (as employment in the civil service was rationalized and the functions of the state agricultural produce boards were scaled down). A shortfall of 30,100m. francs CFA was recorded in 1991. Compliance with the adjustment programme that had been agreed with the IMF and the World Bank was essential if Mali was to secure the external funds, mostly in the form of grants, needed for the budget. However, the unpopularity of the austerity programme, particularly as it affected employment among graduates, contributed to the popular opposition to President Traoré that ultimately resulted in the downfall of his regime in March 1991. The new regime affirmed its commitment to structural adjustment (the 1992 budget envisaged a deficit of less than 8,000m. francs CFA), although the forecast had to be revised to 10,900m. francs CFA following the disappearance of funds received at the national treasury. Despite this reverse, in August 1992 the government signed a structural adjustment agreement with the IMF and the World Bank, which provided loans equivalent to some $90m. in support of the programme for 1992–95.

During 1993 there was renewed internal opposition, notably from the trade unions, to the adverse effects of structural adjustment, while the IMF and the World Bank urged further financial restraint. In September 1993, following a recent visit by a World Bank mission, the government announced new austerity measures which included a reduction in state employees' and students' benefits (non-monetary benefits, notably housing and petrol allowances for civil servants, tend to form an important element of union demands), increases in taxes on hydrocarbons and in duties on alcohol and tobacco, new measures against fraud (which has contributed to a major decline in fiscal revenue) and an acceleration of the transfer to private ownership of public enterprises. By such measures, it was stated, the budget deficit for 1993 could be reduced from an envisaged 30,000m. francs CFA to 26,000m. francs CFA; state spending would decline by 2,000m. francs CFA in 1993, and by 14,000m. francs CFA in 1994. None the less, the IMF and the World Bank suspended all assistance to Mali in October 1994, in protest against the extent of the budgetary deficit. The IMF demanded that the shortfall be reduced to 17,000m. francs CFA in 1994, to 16,000m. francs CFA in 1995 and to less than 10,000m. francs CFA in 1996. For its part, the World Bank required that Mali reduce annual expenditure on civil servants' salaries from 48,000m. francs CFA to 39,000m. francs CFA, together with an improvement (by 5,000m. francs CFA per year) in tax collection. However, improved financial management would not substantially reduce Mali's independence on external support—the World Bank had already agreed to provide 125,000m. francs CFA for the investment budget, 80%–85% of which was to be funded by external donors in 1993. Meanwhile, trade unions continued to demand the payment of salary arrears and wage increases to offset inflation. The government rejected IMF pressure for a moratorium on pay increases for state employees and for the cancellation of a project to establish a national university.

Negotiations with the Bretton Woods institutions resumed following the 50% devaluation, in January 1994, of the CFA franc. Recognizing the government's need for assistance in pursuing a programme of structural adjustment at a time of potential social unrest, the World Bank and the IMF agreed, respectively, to provide 157,000m. and 50,000m. francs CFA in budgetary support for 1994–96, thereby allowing the government to allocate 13,000m. francs CFA to a special fund designed to assist those social groups most severely affected by the devaluation, to increase state employees' salaries by 10% with effect from April 1994. The official minimum wage, which (apart from a temporary increase in 1991) had remained at the same nominal level—67.22 francs CFA per hour—since March 1985, was increased by 8%. The 1994 budget, approved by parliament in March, envisaged a deficit of 83,000m. francs CFA, with revenue increasing from 188,000m. francs CFA under the 1993 budget to 291,000m. francs CFA (reflecting an anticipated increase in receipts from exports), and expenditure from 204,000m. to 374,000m. francs CFA. The government of France pledged assistance of 15,000m. francs CFA to help offset the adverse effects of the currency's depreciation.

FOREIGN TRADE AND PAYMENTS

Mali's trade balance is in chronic deficit, although there has been an overall improvement since the early 1970s, when exports typically represented only one-half of the value of imports. The sharp deterioration in the country's balance-of-payments position following independence led, in 1967, to Mali's *de facto* return to the Franc Zone and a consequent devaluation of the Mali franc by 50%. (The final stage in the return to financial integration with other francophone countries of the region came in 1984, when Mali rejoined UMOA and readopted the CFA franc as its currency.) However, Mali's current payments position remained weak, with the rise in international prices for petroleum coinciding with the decline in the country's agricultural production owing to drought. The trade deficit subsequently eased slightly during the mid-1970s, as earnings improved, owing to an increase in cotton production, while expenditure on imports stagnated or fell, as a result of a reduction in requirements for imported food. By 1977 the deficit was equivalent to about one-quarter of export receipts. The situation then deteriorated, however, as a result of the second round of petroleum price increases and the impact of drought on domestic agricultural production, and by 1985 the visible trade deficit (a record $152.4m.) was equivalent to 86.5% of the value of merchandise exports. Significantly lower deficits, averaging some $96.2m. were recorded annually in 1986–91, as rising sales of gold and an increase in the volume of cotton exports helped to offset weaknesses in international prices for these commodities while imports showed only modest growth, owing to the reduced need for foreign supplies of foods. In 1992, however, a marked increase in expenditure on imports, accompanied by lower export earnings, resulted in a visible trade deficit of $144.7m. It was hoped that the devaluation of the CFA franc, in January 1994, would improve the competitiveness of Malian exports and compensate for the loss of revenue arising notably from the rapid decline in demand for cotton in Eastern Europe (formerly a major trading region for Mali).

There are two important offsets to the trade deficit, namely aid inflows and emigrants' remittances. The latter averaged $23m. per year in the late 1980s, slightly below one-third of the average trade deficit. Aid inflows are substantially higher. Disbursements by non-communist countries and from multilateral agencies averaged $434m. per year in 1987–92, about one-half more than the level of previous years (owing to financing for drought-relief and the resumption, in 1988, of adjustment credits from the World Bank). France specifically has maintained a high level of support for the structural adjustment programme, in the form of budgetary grants as well as loans for specific projects and programmes, with its aid averaging $115m. per year in 1989–91. There is no prospect of Mali's being able to reduce its dependence on aid funds in the near future: these have been equivalent to one-fifth of its GNP in recent years. Because of the high grant element in the development assistance that Mali receives, its debt-servicing payments had, until the mid-1980s, remained low—8.3% of total foreign earnings in 1983. However, the drought of 1983–85 necessitated a rapid increase in external borrowing, from $879m. at the end of 1982 (equivalent to less than 75% of GNP) to $1,468m. by the end of 1985 (120% of GNP in that year). Despite the cancellation of significant amounts of bilateral debt during this period, the burden of servicing the debt rose substantially, owing to the decline in international prices for cotton. In the absence, after 1986, of a formal agreement with the IMF, there were no formal debt-relief concessions. Thus, as the external debt continued to accumulate (reaching $2,039m. by the end of 1988), so did arrears on the servicing of the debt. In October 1988, however, following a new agreement with the IMF on a programme of economic adjustment, Mali became the first debtor country to benefit from a system of exceptional debt-relief that had been agreed in principle at the summit meeting of industrialized nations, held in Toronto, Canada, in June of that year, which made provision for preferential debt-relief for countries with persistent debt-servicing difficulties. Without rescheduling, the servicing of the Malian external debt was projected to exceed 30% of foreign earnings in the period 1988–90, thus placing Mali among the 22 countries classified by the World Bank as 'debt-distressed'. Under the terms of the agreement, the 'Paris Club' of Western official creditors rescheduled $70m. in repayment and interest due to October 1989. These donors agreed to a further rescheduling (of an unspecified portion of debt) in November 1989, while the USA cancelled $7m. of official debt. More significantly, Mali was one of the world's 35 poorest countries whose official debt to France was cancelled at the beginning of 1990 (when Mali's debt of $240m. to that country was forgiven). None the less, the external debt, which had risen again, to $2,587, by the end of 1991, continues to represent a substantial burden on this poor economy. The debt-service ratio in that year was reduced to a tolerable level—5.0%, from 11.5% in 1990—only because of the non-payment of some obligations. Thus there remained a continuing need for both debt relief and new funding, and the 'Paris Club' agreed in November 1992 to a further round of rescheduling, on enhanced Toronto terms. By the end of 1992 the external debt ($2,595m.), expressed as a proportion of GNP, had declined to 93%, from 107% in 1991, while some 93% of lending was on concessional terms. However, the price for such support is the maintenance of an economic reform programme which has been shown to entail considerable political risk.

Statistical Survey

Source (unless otherwise stated): Direction de la Statistique et de l'Informatique, Ministère des Finances et du Commerce, BP 234, Koulouba, Bamako; tel. 22-56-87; telex 2559; fax 22-88-53.

Area and Population

AREA, POPULATION AND DENSITY

Area (sq km)	1,240,192*
Population (census results)	
16 December 1976	6,394,918
1–30 April 1987	
Males	3,760,711
Females	3,935,637
Total	7,696,348
Population (official estimates at mid-year)	
1989	7,960,000
1990	8,156,000
Density (per sq km) at mid-1990	6.6

*478,841 sq miles.

PRINCIPAL ETHNIC GROUPS (estimates, 1963)

Bambara	1,000,000	Malinke	200,000
Fulani	450,000	Tuareg	240,000
Marka	280,000	Sénoufo	375,000
Songhai	230,000	Dogon	130,000

ADMINISTRATIVE DIVISIONS
(estimated population at 1987 census)

District			
Bamako	646,163		
Regions*			
Ségou	1,328,250	Kayes	1,058,575
Sikasso	1,308,828	Tombouctou	453,032
Mopti	1,261,383	Gao	383,734
Koulikoro	1,180,260		

* A new region, Kidal, was formally established on 15 May 1991.

PRINCIPAL TOWNS
(population at 1976 census)

Bamako (capital)	404,000	Sikasso	47,000
Ségou	65,000	Kayes	45,000
Mopti	54,000		
(population at 1987 census)			
Bamako	658,275		

BIRTHS AND DEATHS (UN estimates, annual averages)

	1975–80	1980–85	1985–90
Birth rate (per 1,000)	50.7	50.8	51.0
Death rate (per 1,000)	24.1	22.3	20.7

Expectation of life (UN estimates, years at birth, 1985–90): 44.0 (males 42.4; females 45.6);.

Source: UN, *World Population Prospects: The 1992 Revision.*

ECONOMICALLY ACTIVE POPULATION
(ILO estimates, '000 persons at mid-1980)

	Males	Females	Total
Agriculture, etc.	1,649	314	1,963
Industry	32	14	46
Services	214	72	287
Total labour force	1,896	400	2,296

Source: ILO, *Economically Active Population Estimates and Projections, 1950–2025.*

Mid-1992 (estimates in '000): Agriculture, etc. 2,472; Total 3,100 (Source: FAO, *Production Yearbook).*

Agriculture

PRINCIPAL CROPS ('000 metric tons)

	1990	1991	1992
Millet, sorghum and fonio	1,268	1,660*	1,500*
Rice (paddy)	282	454*	405*
Maize	197	257*	219*
Other cereals	25	44*	32*
Sugar cane*	255	309	305
Sweet potatoes†	55	55	55
Cassava (Manioc)†	73	73	73
Other roots and tubers†	17	17	17
Vegetables†	253	258	261
Fruit	15	15	15
Pulses	61	61†	61†
Groundnuts (in shell)	180	170†	165†
Cottonseed†	121	160	180
Cotton (lint)	99	116*	114*

* Unofficial figure(s). † FAO estimate(s).

Source: FAO, *Production Yearbook.*

LIVESTOCK ('000 head, year ending September)

	1990	1991	1992
Cattle	4,996	5,198	5,373
Sheep	6,086	6,359	6,658
Goats	6,086	6,359	6,658
Pigs	56	67	75
Horses	77	83	85
Asses	575	590	600
Camels	245	246	250

Poultry (million): 22 in 1990; 22 in 1991; 22 in 1992.

Source: FAO, *Production Yearbook.*

LIVESTOCK PRODUCTS (FAO estimates, '000 metric tons)

	1990	1991	1992
Cows' milk	122	122	122
Sheep's milk	70	70	70
Goats' milk	140	140	140
Beef and veal	71	74	78
Mutton and lamb	20	20	20
Goat meat	22	22	22
Poultry meat	24	24	24
Poultry eggs	11.9	11.9	11.9
Cattle hides	11.0	11.4	12.0
Sheep skins	4.6	4.6	4.6
Goat skins	3.2	3.2	3.2

Source: FAO, *Production Yearbook.*

Forestry

ROUNDWOOD REMOVALS
(FAO estimates, '000 cubic metres, excluding bark)

	1990	1991	1992
Sawlogs, veneer logs and logs for sleepers*	13	13	13
Other industrial wood	344	355	367
Fuel wood	5,232	5,399	5,573
Total	5,589	5,767	5,953

* Estimated to be unchaged since 1988.
Source: FAO, *Yearbook of Forest Products.*

Fishing

('000 metric tons, live weight)

	1989	1990*	1991*
Total catch (freshwater fishes)	71.8	65.0	60.0

* FAO estimate.
Source: FAO, *Yearbook of Fishery Statistics.*

Mining

	1990	1991	1992
Gold (kilograms)*	2,355	2,597	3,467
Salt ('000 metric tons)†	5	5	n.a.

* Source: La Zone Franc, *Rapport 1992.*
† Data from the US Bureau of Mines in UN, *Industrial Statistics Yearbook.*

Industry

SELECTED PRODUCTS
('000 metric tons, unless otherwise indicated)

	1989	1990	1991
Salted, dried or smoked fish*	3.4	3.5	n.a.
Raw sugar*	22	24	27
Cement†	20	20	22
Electric energy (million kWh)	246	273	276

* Data from the FAO.
† Data from the US Bureau of Mines.
Source: UN, *Industrial Statistics Yearbook.*

Finance

CURRENCY AND EXCHANGE RATES

Monetary Units
100 centimes = 1 franc de la Communauté financière africaine (CFA).

French Franc, Sterling and Dollar Equivalents (31 March 1994)
1 French franc = 100 francs CFA;
£1 sterling = 846.40 francs CFA;
US $1 = 570.14 francs CFA;
1,000 francs CFA = £1.181 = $1.754.

Average Exchange Rate (francs CFA per US $)
1991 282.11
1992 264.69
1993 283.16

Note: An exchange rate of 1 French franc = 50 francs CFA, established in 1948, remained in force until January 1994, when the CFA franc was devalued by 50%, with the exchange rate adjusted to 1 French franc = 100 francs CFA.

BUDGET (estimates, million francs CFA)

Revenue	1988	1989	1990
Fiscal receipts	95,095	94,944	104,903
Taxes on income and profits	10,499	11,781	11,121
Individual taxes	4,919	5,299	5,171
Corporate and business taxes	5,280	6,082	5,350
Taxes on goods and services	42,791	44,394	46,216
Turnover taxes	21,880	21,300	23,218
Consumption taxes	18,350	20,148	19,692
Taxes on international trade and transactions	21,553	18,842	16,920
Import duties	12,266	8,850	10,529
Other current receipts	17,609	45,253	48,981
Capital receipts	45	45	1,661
Aid, grants and subsidies	304	38,842	37,992
Total	113,053	179,084	193,537

Expenditure	1988	1989	1990
General public services	8,773	9,021	•10,576
Defence	14,274	14,724	14,183
Public order and security	1,631	2,806	2,018
Education	13,223	13,554	17,201
Health	3,535	12,024	9,154
Housing and community services	634	21,359	17,736
Other community and social services	2,043	2,788	2,905
Economic services	7,274	100,039	107,901
Agriculture, forestry and fishing	3,908	35,918	46,126
Mining, manufacturing and construction	963	8,632	8,491
Electricity and other energy resources	13	6,931	10,475
Transport and communications	1,153	33,569	29,235
Other economic services	1,237	14,989	13,574
Debt-servicing	47,889	52,558	34,004
Other purposes	48,691	46,618	45,350
Total	147,967	275,491	261,028

Note: Estimates for 1988 refer to the current budget only, and include revenue from the Caisse Autonome d'Amortissement and the Office de Régulation et de Stabilisation des Prix. Estimates for 1989 and 1990 represent a consolidation of the current and investment budgets, and exclude borrowing from abroad (39,273m. francs CFA in 1989 and 51,855m. francs CFA in 1990).

Source: Banque centrale des états de l'Afrique de l'ouest.

1991 (estimates, million francs CFA): Revenue 224,950; Expenditure 230,795.
1992 (revised estimates, million francs CFA): Revenue 206,273; Expenditure 217,147.
1993 (estimates, million francs CFA): Revenue 188,000; Expenditure 204,000.
1994 (estimates, million francs CFA): Revenue 291,000; Expenditure 374,000

CENTRAL BANK RESERVES (US $ million at 31 December)

	1991	1992	1993
Gold*	6.7	6.5	7.0
IMF special drawing rights	0.4	0.1	0.1
Reserve position in IMF	12.4	11.9	12.0
Foreign exchange	306.5	295.9	320.3
Total	326.1	314.4	339.4

* Valued at market-related prices.

Source: IMF, *International Financial Statistics.*

MONEY SUPPLY ('000 million francs CFA at 31 December)

	1991	1992	1993
Currency outside banks	59.97	60.84	65.07
Demand deposits	47.40	47.36	52.72
Total money	107.37	108.20	117.79

Source: IMF, *International Financial Statistics.*

COST OF LIVING
(National Consumer Price Index; base: 1988 = 100)

	1990	1991	1992
Food	98.4	101.8	92.0
All items (incl. others)	100.5	101.9	95.9

Source: ILO, *Year Book of Labour Statistics.*

NATIONAL ACCOUNTS
('000 million francs CFA at current prices)

Expenditure on the Gross Domestic Product

	1989*	1990	1991*
Government final consumption expenditure	98.5	96.4	118.3
Private final consumption expenditure	499.6	562.0	591.2
Increase in stocks	15.4	13.3	-14.5
Gross fixed capital formation	122.0	123.3	122.9
Total domestic expenditure	735.5	795.0	817.9
Exports of goods and services	106.6	114.8	120.0
Less Imports of goods and services	207.4	225.6	225.6
GDP in purchasers' values	634.7	684.2	712.3

* Provisional.

Source: Banque centrale des états de l'Afrique de l'ouest.

Gross Domestic Product by Economic Activity

	1989*	1990	1991*
Agriculture, hunting, forestry and fishing	275.9	305.4	322.2
Manufacturing and mining	53.3	57.4	58.8
Water and electricity	7.8	8.6	9.5
Construction and public works	28.4	27.9	27.9
Transport and telecommunications	31.2	32.7	35.9
Trade	99.2	113.2	108.7
Other services	43.0	45.6	45.6
Public administration	65.9	60.4	70.6
Sub-total	604.7	651.2	679.2
Import duties	34.8	37.9	38.1
Less Imputed bank service charge	4.8	4.9	5.0
Total	634.7	684.2	712.3

* Provisional.

Source: Banque centrale des états de l'Afrique de l'ouest.

BALANCE OF PAYMENTS (US $ million)

	1990	1991	1992
Merchandise exports f.o.b.	337.9	354.5	339.3
Merchandise imports f.o.b.	-432.4	-447.1	-484.0
Trade balance	-94.5	-92.7	-144.7
Exports of services	80.1	84.4	74.4
Imports of services	-395.1	-377.0	-407.6
Other income received	19.5	20.9	24.6
Other income paid	-61.0	-63.8	-54.8
Private unrequited transfers (net)	66.9	70.0	94.4
Official unrequited transfers (net)	250.8	336.3	323.0
Current balance	-133.3	-22.0	-90.7
Direct investment (net)	-6.6	3.5	-7.6
Other capital (net)	84.3	62.6	15.2
Net errors and omissions	1.1	-3.5	-42.8
Overall balance	-54.6	40.7	-125.8

Source: IMF, *International Financial Statistics.*

External Trade

PRINCIPAL COMMODITIES (million francs CFA)

Imports c.i.f.	1988	1989	1990
Dairy products	6,558	2,957	6,817
Food products of plant origin	7,682	4,786	10,725
Cereals	3,958	2,420	6,463
Processed foodstuffs	19,096	10,373	16,418
Sugar and confectionery	10,518	5,577	9,641
Beverages and tobacco	3,183	5,301	5,880
Refined petroleum products	10,926	19,199	31,827
Other raw materials	21,653	13,776	23,587
Electrical machinery	15,867	10,361	15,467
Non-electrical machinery	6,319	4,091	8,764
Transport equipment	10,484	7,329	11,722
Chemicals	16,628	14,181	18,174
Miscellaneous manufactured articles	28,238	12,941	11,641
Cotton yarn and fabrics	2,211	890	2,826
Total (incl. others)	150,230	108,468	164,020

Exports f.o.b.	1988	1989	1990
Live animals	5,031	26,785	227,455
Food products of plant origin	1,799	481	886
Other raw materials	40,675	47,350	59,028
Cotton (ginned)	37,844	44,309	55,684
Fats and oils	4,621	20	1,104
Miscellaneous manufactured articles	10,542	3,862	7,805
Total (incl. others)	63,888	78,777	97,683

Source: Banque centrale des états de l'Afrique de l'ouest.

Gold (exports f.o.b., '000 million francs CFA): 11.9 in 1990; 14.0 in 1991; 15.2 (provisional) in 1992 (Source: Secrétariat du Comité Monétaire de la Zone Franc, *Rapport 1992*).

PRINCIPAL TRADING PARTNERS (million francs CFA)

Imports	1988	1989	1990
Austria	2,098	112	263
Belgium/Luxembourg	7,997	4,513	7,771
Canada	95	1,952	2,328
China, People's Republic	3,927	2,057	5,366
Côte d'Ivoire	12,467	21,793	29,720
France	44,725	26,599	37,163
Germany, Fed. Republic	10,504	7,394	9,128
Hong Kong	2,223	460	2,118
Italy	8,795	3,014	5,257
Japan	3,677	3,337	7,016
Netherlands	9,552	5,384	6,183
Nigeria	2,663	3,310	3,416
Poland	1,744	51	250
Senegal	7,379	7,611	15,275
Spain	6,502	2,636	4,482
Switzerland	2,317	1,173	1,491
Thailand	870	747	1,273
USSR	1,764	996	1,457
United Kingdom	2,821	3,713	4,721
USA	3,432	4,104	7,886
Total (incl. others)	150,230	108,468	164,019

Exports	1988	1989	1990
Belgium/Luxembourg	5,960	892	463
Canada	2,364	2,414	—
China, People's Republic	4,959	5,803	396
Côte d'Ivoire	4,824	21,831	47,855
France	5,740	3,871	23,981
Germany, Fed. Republic	3,469	3,416	9
Ireland	2,622	2,234	—
Italy	1,027	948	72
Japan	843	851	—
Morocco	2,083	1,789	—
Netherlands	1,334	615	126
Portugal	3,254	2,671	—
Senegal	1,577	7,914	16,991
Spain	1,140	1,625	33
Switzerland	8,627	3,612	6,678
Thailand	1,134	1,835	—
Tunisia	743	1,302	—
United Kingdom	1,563	1,546	114
Total (incl. others)	63,888	78,777	97,683

Source: Banque centrale des états de l'Afrique de l'ouest.

Transport

RAILWAYS (traffic)

	1986	1987	1988
Passenger-km (million)	176.9	772.8	731.9
Freight ton-km (million)	225.1	429.3	432.2

Source: Banque centrale des états de l'Afrique de l'ouest.

ROAD TRAFFIC (estimates, '000 motor vehicles in use)

	1989	1990	1991
Passenger cars	22	23	24
Commercial vehicles	13	13	14

Source: UN Economic Commission for Africa, *African Statistical Yearbook*.

CIVIL AVIATION (traffic handled at Bamako Airport)

	1989	1990	1991
Passengers (number)*	236,966	278,573	253,022
Freight (metric tons)	7,122	8,290	7,894
Mail (metric tons)	70	76	80

* Includes passengers in transit.

Source: Banque centrale des états de l'Afrique de l'ouest.

Communications Media

	1989	1990	1991
Radio receivers ('000 in use)	350	400	415
Television receivers ('000 in use)	4	10	11
Telephones ('000 in use)*	16	17	18
Daily newspapers			
Number	n.a.	2	n.a.
Average circulation ('000 copies)	n.a.	10*	n.a.

* Estimate(s).

Book production (textbooks, government publications and university theses, including pamphlets): 160 titles (92,000 copies) in 1984.

Sources: UNESCO, *Statistical Yearbook*; UN Economic Commission for Africa, *African Statistical Yearbook*.

Tourism

	1988	1989	1990
Tourist arrivals ('000) . .	36	32	44
Tourist receipts (US $ million)	38	28	32

Source: UN, *Statistical Yearbook.*

Education

(1991, unless otherwise indicated)

	Institu-tions	Teach-ers	Students		
			Males	Females	Total
Primary . . .	1,514	7,963	236,004	139,127	375,131
Secondary					
General . . .	n.a.	4,854	52,473	26,447	78,920
Teacher training*	n.a.	182	721	173	894
Vocational . .	n.a.	762*	5,798	2,917	8,715
University level* .	n.a.	701	5,798	905	6,703

* 1990 figure(s).

Source: UNESCO, *Statistical Yearbook.*

1993: Teacher training: Institutions 3; Teachers 73; Students 439 (Males 368; Females 73) (Source: Ministère de l'Education Nationale, Bamako).

Directory

The Constitution

Following the overthrow of President Moussa Traoré in March 1991, the Constitution of June 1979 was suspended. A new Constitution was approved in a national referendum on 12 January 1992:

The Constitution of the Third Republic of Mali upholds the principles of national sovereignty and the rule of law in a secular, multi-party state. The document provides for the separation of the powers of the executive, legislative and judicial organs of state.

Executive power is vested in the President of the Republic, who is elected for five years by universal adult suffrage. The President appoints the Prime Minister, who, in turn, appoints other members of the Council of Ministers.

Legislative authority is exercised by the unicameral Assemblée nationale, which is elected for five years by universal adult suffrage. Of the chamber's 129 deputies, 13 are elected to represent the interests of Malians resident abroad.

The Constitution guarantees (for the first time) the independence of the judiciary, and provides for the establishment of a Constitutional Court.

The rights, freedoms and obligations of Malian citizens are enshrined in the Constitution. Freedom of the press and of association are guaranteed.

The Government

HEAD OF STATE

President: ALPHA OUMAR KONARÉ (took office 8 June 1992).

COUNCIL OF MINISTERS

(September 1994)

Prime Minister: IBRAHIM BOUBACAR KEITA.

Minister of State for Defence: DJONKOUMA TRAORÉ.

Minister of Employment, the Civil Service and Labour: MOHAMED AG ERLAF.

Minister of Health, Solidarity and the Elderly: Maj. MODIBO SIDIBÉ.

Minister of Handicrafts and Tourism: FATOU HAIDARA.

Minister of Youth and Sports: BOUBACAR KARAMOKO COULIBALY.

Minister of Rural Development and the Environment: Dr BOUBACAR SADASSI.

Minister of Secondary and Higher Education and Scientific Research: MOUSTAPHA DICKO.

Minister of Territorial Administration and Security: Lt-Col SADA SAMAKÉ.

Minister of Culture and Communications: CHEIKNA DETTEBA KAMISSOKO.

Minister of Equipment and Transport: BAKARY KONIMBA TRAORÉ.

Minister of Finance and Trade: SOUMEYLA CISSÉ.

Minister of Basic Education: ADAMA SAMASSEKOU.

Minister of Foreign Affairs, Malians Abroad and African Integration: SY KADIATOU SOW.

Minister of Mines, Energy and Water Resources: CHEIKNA SEYDOU DITIANI DIAWARA.

Minister of Justice and Keeper of the Seals: BOUBACAR GAOUSSOU DIARRA.

MINISTRIES

Office of the President: BP 1463, Bamako; tel. 22-24-61; telex 2521.

Office of the Prime Minister: Bamako.

Ministry of Culture and Communications: Bamako.

Ministry of Defence: BP 215, Bamako; tel. 22-26-17.

Ministry of Employment, the Civil Service and Labour: BP 80, Bamako; tel. 22-59-51.

Ministry of Equipment and Transport: c/o World Bank Resident Mission, BP 1864, Bamako; tel. 22-66-82.

Ministry of Finance and Trade: BP 234, Koulouba, Bamako; tel. 22-56-87; telex 2559; fax 22-88-53.

Ministry of Foreign Affairs, Malians Abroad and African Integration: Koulouba, Bamako; tel. 22-54-89; telex 2560.

Ministry of Handicrafts and Tourism: BP 234; Koulouba, Bamako; tel. 22-56-87; telex 2559.

Ministry of Health, Solidarity and the Elderly: Koulouba, Bamako; tel. 22-53-01.

Ministry of Justice: BP 97, Bamako; tel. 22-24-36.

Ministry of Mines, Energy and Water Resources: BP 238, Bamako; tel. 22-35-47.

Ministry of National Education: BP 71, Bamako; tel. 22-24-50.

Ministry of Rural Development and the Environment: BP 1676, Bamako; tel. 22-60-24.

Ministry of Territorial Administration and Security: BP 78, Bamako; tel. 22-39-37.

Ministry of Youth and Sports: Bamako.

President and Legislature

PRESIDENT

Presidential Election, First Ballot, 12 April 1992

Candidate	% of votes
ALPHA OUMAR KONARÉ	44.95
TIÉOULÉ MAMADOU KONATÉ	14.51
MOUNTAGA TALL	11.41
ALAMY SYLLA	9.44
BABA AKHIB HAIDARRA	7.37
IDRISSA TRAORÉ	4.10
AMADOU ALI NIAGANDOU	4.01
MAMADOU (MARIBATO) DIABY	2.16
BAMBA MOUSSA DIALLO	2.04
Total	100.00

Second Ballot, 26 April 1992

Candidate	% of votes
ALPHA OUMAR KONARÉ	69.01
TIÉOULÉ MAMADOU KONATÉ	30.99
Total	100.00

ASSEMBLÉE NATIONALE

President: ALY NOUHOUN DIALLO.

General Election, 23 February and 8 March 1992

Party	Seats
ADEMA	76
CNID	9
US—RDA	8
PMD	6
RDP	4
UDD	4
UFDP	3
RDT	3
PDP	2
UMDD	1
Total	116*

* An additional 13 deputies were to be elected to represent the interests of Malians resident abroad.

Advisory Council

Conseil Economique et Social: Bamako; f. 1987.

Political Organizations

Following the dissolution in March 1991 of the Union démocratique du peuple malien, which had been the sole legal party since 1979 provision was made for the registration of an unlimited number of political parties. At the 1992 municipal and legislative elections some 48 organizations had been officially registered. The following parties were among the most prominent in these elections:

Alliance pour la démocratie au Mali—Parti africain pour la solidarité et la justice (ADEMA): BP 1791, Bamako; tel. 22-03-68; f. 1990 as Alliance pour la démocratie au Mali; Sec.-Gen. MOUHAMEDOU DICKO.

Congrès national d'initiative démocratique (CNID): Bamako; f. 1990 as Comité national d'initiative démocratique; Chair. Me MOUNTAGA TALL; Sec.-Gen. AMIDA DIABATÉ.

Parti pour la démocratie et le progrès (PDP): Bamako; Leader: Me IDRISSA TRAORÉ.

Parti malien pour le développement (PMD): Bamako.

Rassemblement pour la démocratie et le progrès (RDP): BP 2110, Bamako; tel. 22-30-92; fax 22-67-95; f. 1990; Leader ALMAMY SYLLA.

Rassemblement pour la démocratie et le travail (RDT): Bamako.

Union pour la démocratie et le développement (UDD): Bamako; f. 1991 by fmr supporters of ex-President Traoré; Leader MOUSSA BALLA COULIBALY.

Union des forces démocratiques pour le progrès (UFDP): f. 1991; Sec.-Gen. Me DEMBA DIALLO.

Union malienne pour la démocratie et le développement (UMDD): Bamako.

Union soudanaise—Rassemblement démocratique africain (US—RDA): Bamako; sole legal party 1960–68; revived 1991; Sec.-Gen. MAMADOU BECHIR GOLOGO.

Diplomatic Representation

EMBASSIES IN MALI

Algeria: Derrière le Fleuve, Badalabougou; Ambassador: ABDEL-MADJID BOULGHUI.

Burkina Faso: BP 9022, Bamako; Ambassador: HAMADOU KONE.

Canada: route de Koulikoro, BP 198, Bamako; telex 2530; Chargé d'affaires a.i.: GUY GAGNON.

China, People's Republic: BP 112, Bamako; telex 2455; Ambassador: LIU LIDE.

Egypt: BP 44, Badalabougou; tel. 22-35-03; fax 22-08-91; Ambassador: ABDELSALAM YEHIA EL-TAWIL.

France: square Patrice Lumumba, BP 17, Bamako; tel. 22-29-51; telex 2569; fax 22-03-29; Ambassador: JEAN-DIDIER ROISIN.

Germany: Badalabougou-Est, Lotissement A6, BP 100, Bamako; tel. 22-32-99; telex 2529; fax 22-96-50; Ambassador: HANS-HENNING BRUHN.

Guinea: BP 118, Bamako; tel. 22-29-75; telex 2576; Ambassador: MAMADOU MASS DIALLO.

Iran: quartier de l'Hippodrome, BP 2136, Bamako; Ambassador: MOJTABA SHAFII.

Iraq: BP 2512, Bamako-Badalabougou; tel. 22-38-06; telex 2416; Chargé d'affaires a.i.: JASSIM N. MSAWIL.

Korea, Democratic People's Republic: BP 765, Sogoniko, Bamako; Ambassador: KIM GI HAN.

Libya: quartier de l'Hippodrome, Bamako; telex 2420; Ambassador: FARAGE INAYA.

Malaysia: Badalabougou-Ouest, BP 98, Bamako; tel. 22-27-83; telex 2423; fax 22-32-32; Ambassador: CHOO SIEW-KIOH.

Mauritania: BP 135, Bamako; telex 2415; Ambassador: BILAL OULD WERZEG.

Morocco: BP 2013, Bamako; tel. 22-21-23; telex 22430; fax 22-77-87; Ambassador: LARBI ROUDIÉS.

Nigeria: BP 57, Badalabougou; tel. 22-57-71; Chargé d'affaires a.i.: F. F. ADEGUNLOYE.

Russia: BP 300, Bamako; Ambassador: PAVEL PETROVSKI.

Saudi Arabia: BP 81, Badalabougou; telex 2408; Chargé d'affaires: MUHAMMAD RAJAMIRI.

Senegal: ave Kassé Keïta, BP 42, Bamako; tel. 22-82-74; fax 23-17-80; Ambassador: MAMADOU LAITY NDIAYE.

USA: angle rue Rochester NY et rue Mohamed V, BP 34, Bamako; tel. 22-54-70; telex 2248; fax 22-37-12; Ambassador: WILLIAM H. DAMERION, III.

Judicial System

The 1992 Constitution provides for an independent judiciary, and for the establishment of a Constitutional Court.

Supreme Court: BP 7, Bamako; tel. 22-24-06; f. 1969; 25 mems; judicial section comprises two civil chambers, one commercial chamber, one social chamber and one criminal chamber; in addition, there are administrative and financial regulatory sections; Pres. LOUIS BASTIDE; Sec.-Gen. HENRIETTE BOUNSLY.

Court of Appeal: Bamako.

President of the Bar: Me MAGATTÉ SÈYE.

There are two Tribunaux de première instance (Magistrates' Courts) and also courts for labour disputes.

Religion

It is estimated that about 80% of the population are Muslims, while 18% follow traditional animist beliefs and 1.2% are Christians.

ISLAM

Chief Mosque: Bagadadji, place de la République, Bamako.

CHRISTIANITY

The Roman Catholic Church

Mali comprises one archdiocese and five dioceses. At 31 December 1992 there were an estimated 98,334 adherents in the country (1.1% of the total population).

Bishops' Conference: Conférence Episcopale du Mali, BP 298, Bamako; tel. 22-54-99; fax 22-52-14; f. 1973; Pres. Rt Rev. JEAN-MARIE CISSÉ, Bishop of Sikasso.

Archbishop of Bamako: Most Rev. LUC AUGUSTE SANGARÉ, Archevêché, BP 298, Bamako; tel. 22-54-99; fax 22-52-14.

Other Christian Churches

There are numerous Protestant mission centres, mainly administered by US societies, with a total personnel of about 370.

The Press

Restrictions on press freedom were formally ended under a new statute which entered force during December 1992 and January 1993.

DAILY NEWSPAPER

L'Essor—La Voix du Peuple: BP 141, Bamako; tel. 22-47-97; f. 1949; pro-Government newspaper; Editor SOULEYMANE DRABO; circ. 3,500.

PERIODICALS

There were some 60 periodicals in late 1993.

L'Afro-Arabe Revue: rue Mohamed V, BP 2044, Bamako; quarterly; Editor MOHAMED BEN BABA AHMED; circ. 1,000.

L'Aurore: BP 2043, Bamako; f. 1990; fortnightly; independent; Editor CHOUAHIBOU TRAORÉ.

Barakela: Bamako; monthly; publ. by the Union nationale des travailleurs du Mali.

Citoyen: Bamako; f. 1992; fortnightly; independent.

Concorde: BP 2043, Bamako; weekly; French and Arabic; Editor AL-MAMOUN KEITA; circ. 500.

Danbe: Bamako; f. 1990; organ of the CNID.

Les Echos: Bamako; f. 1989; fortnightly; publ. by Jamana cultural co-operative; circ. 25,000.

Jamana—Revue Culturelle Malienne: BP 2043, Bamako; f. 1983; quarterly; organ of Jamana cultural co-operative (f. by ALPHA OUMAR KONARÉ).

Kabaaru: Mopti; monthly; Fulbé language; rural interest; Editor BADAMA DOUCOURÉ; circ. 5,000.

Kibaru: BP 1463, Bamako; monthly; Bambara and three other languages; rural interest; Editor AMADOU GAGNY KANTÉ; circ. 5,000.

Journal Officiel de la République du Mali: BP 1463, Bamako; official announcements.

Mali Muso (Women of Mali): Bamako; quarterly; publ. by the Union des femmes du Mali; circ. 5,000.

Podium: BP 141, Bamako; weekly; culture and sports.

Le Républicain: Bamako; f. 1992; weekly; supports CNID; Publr TIÉBILÉ DRAME.

La Roue: BP 2043, Bamako; pre-independence journal, revived 1990; independent.

Sunjata: BP 141, Bamako; monthly; social, economic and political affairs; Editor SOUMEYLOU MAÏGA; circ. 3,000.

Yiriwa: BP 2043, Bamako; f. 1990; independent.

NEWS AGENCIES

Agence Malienne de Presse et Publicité (AMAPP): BP 116, Bamako; tel. 22-26-47; telex 2421; f. 1977; Dir GAOUSSOU DRABO.

Foreign Bureaux

Agence France-Presse (AFP): BP 778, Bamako; telex 2480; Correspondent CHOUAÏBOU BONKANE.

Rossiyskoye Informatsionnoye Agentstvo—Novosti (RIA—Novosti) (Russia): BP 193, Bamako; tel. 22-45-25; telex 2528; Correspondent BORIS TARASOV.

Xinhua (New China) News Agency (People's Republic of China): c/o Ambassade de la République Populaire de Chine, BP 112, Bamako; telex 2455; Correspondent NI MANHE.

IPS (Italy) and ITAR—TASS (Russia) are represented in Mali.

Publisher

EDIM SA: ave Kassé Keïta, BP 21, Bamako; tel. 22-40-41; f. 1972 as Editions Imprimeries du Mali, reorg. 1987; general fiction and non-fiction, textbooks; Chair. and Man. Dir IBRAHIMA BERTHE.

Radio and Television

In 1991, according to UNESCO, there were an estimated 415,000 radio receivers and 11,000 television receivers in use. Legislation authorizing the establishment of private radio and television stations was promulgated in early 1992, and in late 1993 seven independent radio stations were operating in Bamako. Radio France International and the Gabonese-based Africa No. 1 began FM broadcasts in Mali in March 1993.

Office de Radiodiffusion-Télévision Malienne (ORTM): BP 171, Bamako; tel. 22-24-74; f. 1957; state-owned; radio programmes in French, English, Bambara, Peulh, Sarakolé, Tamachek, Sonrai, Moorish, Wolof; about 37 hours weekly of television broadcasts; Man. Dir ABDOULAYE SIDIBE; Dir of Television CHEICK HAMALLA TOURÉ.

Chaîne 2: Bamako; f. 1993; radio broadcasts to Bamako.

Fréquence 3: Bamako; f. 1992; commercial radio station.

Radio-Bamakan: Bamako; f. 1991; pro-ADEMA.

Radio Kayira: Bamako; f. 1992; pro-CNID.

Radio Kledu: Bamako; f. 1992; commercial; Prop. MAMADOU COULIBALY.

Radio Liberté: Bamako; f. 1992; commercial.

Radio Tabalé: Bamako; f. 1992.

Finance

(cap. = capital; res = reserves; m. = million; brs = branches; amounts in francs CFA)

BANKING

Central Bank

Banque Centrale des Etats de l'Afrique de l'Ouest (BCEAO): square Patrice Lumumba, BP 206, Bamako; tel. 22-37-56; telex 2574; fax 22-47-86; headquarters in Dakar, Senegal; bank of issue and central bank for the seven states of Union monétaire ouest-africaine (UMOA), comprising Benin, Burkina Faso, Côte d'Ivoire, Mali, Niger, Senegal and Togo; cap. and res 379,881m. (Sept. 1992); Gov. CHARLES KONAN BANNY; Dir in Mali MANDÉ SIDIBÉ; br. at Mopti.

Commercial Banks

Bank of Africa-Mali (BOA): ave Kassé Keïta, BP 2249, Bamako; tel. 22-46-72; telex 2581; fax 22-46-53; f. 1982; 73% owned by private Malian interests; cap. 1,400m. (Sept. 1993); Chair. BOUREIMA SYLLA; Man. Dir XAVIER ALIBERT; 4 brs.

Banque Commerciale du Sahel (BCS): ave Kassé Keïta, BP 2372, Bamako; tel. 22-55-20; telex 2580; fax 22-55-43; f. 1982; fmrly Banque Arabe Libyo-Malienne pour le Commerce Extérieur et le Développement; 76.9% owned by Libyan Arab Foreign Bank, 22.6% state-owned; cap. 1,100m. (Sept. 1993); Chair. SEDDIK EL HAJJAJI; Man. Dir MOHAMED OMAR JABALLAH.

Banque Malienne de Crédit et de Dépôts SA (BMCD): ave du Fleuve, BP 45, Bamako; tel. 22-53-36; telex 2572; fax 22-79-50; f. 1961; 50.02% state-owned, 49.98% owned by Crédit Lyonnais (France); cap. 1,000m. (Sept. 1992); Chair. and Man. Dir AMIDOU OUMAR SY.

Banque Meridien BIAO Mali SA: Immeuble de Bolibana, blvd de l'Indépendance, BP 15, Bamako; tel. 22-50-66; telex 2501; fax 22-45-66; f. 1981; 51% owned by Meridien BIAO SA (Luxembourg), 49% by private Malian interests; cap. 3,403m. (Sept. 1993); Man. Dir ASSAMA SY; 4 brs.

Financial Bank Mali: ave Kassé Keïta, BP 1813, Bamako; tel. 22-72-00; telex 2713; fax 22-51-15; f. 1990; 100% Swiss-owned; Chair. and Man. Dir CHARLES BAYSSET.

Development Banks

Banque de Développement du Mali SA (BDM): ave du Fleuve, BP 94, Bamako; tel. 22-20-50; telex 2522; fax 22-50-85; f. 1968; 23% owned by private Malian interests, 20% state-owned, 20% owned by BCEAO, 20% by Banque ouest-africaine de développement; cap. 3,000m. (Sept. 1992); Chair. Minister of Finance and Trade; Man. Dir MOHAMED SLAOUI; 11 brs.

Banque Nationale de Développement Agricole (BNDA): Immeuble Caisse Autonome d'Amortissement, quartier du Fleuve, BP 2424, Bamako; tel. 22-64-64; telex 2638; fax 22-29-61; f. 1981; 39.5% state-owned; cap. 3,772m. (March 1993); Chair. Minister of Finance and Trade; Man. Dir BAKARY TRAORÉ; 2 brs.

Financial Institution

Caisse Autonome d'Amortissement du Mali: Immeuble Caisse Autonome d'Amortissement, Quartier du Fleuve, BP 1617, Bamako; telex 2676; management of state funds; Dir Minister of Finance and Trade.

INSURANCE

Caisse Nationale d'Assurance et de Réassurance (CNAR): Immeuble CNAR, square Patrice Lumumba, BP 568, Bamako; tel. 22-64-54; telex 2549; fax 22-23-29; state-owned; cap. 50m.; Man. Dir Founeke Keita; 10 brs.

La Soutra: BP 52, Bamako; telex 2469; fax 22-55-23; f. 1979; cap. 150m.; Chair. Amadou Niono.

Trade and Industry

DEVELOPMENT ORGANIZATIONS

Caisse Française de Développement (CFD): BP 32, Bamako; tel. 22-28-42; telex 2502; fmrly Caisse Central de Coopération Economique, name changed 1992; Dir Robert Chahinian.

Compagnie Malienne pour le Développement des Textiles (CMDT): BP 487, Bamako; tel. 22-24-62; telex 2554; fax 22-81-41; f. 1975; cap. 1,000m. francs CFA; 60% state-owned, 40% owned by Cie Française pour le Développement des Fibres Textiles; restructuring in progress in 1994; cotton cultivation, ginning and marketing; Chair. and Man. Dir Drissa Keita.

Mission Française de Coopération et d'Action Culturelle: BP 84, Bamako; tel. 22-64-29; telex 2653; fax 22-83-39; administers bilateral aid from France; Dir Jean Monlaü.

Office de Développement Intégré du Mali-Ouest (ODIMO): PB 38, Kita; tel. 57-31-41; fmrly office de Développement Intégré des Productions Arachidières et Céréalières; development of diversified forms of agricultural production; Man. Dir Zana Sanogo.

Office du Niger: BP 106, Ségou; tel. 32-00-93; fax 32-01-43; f. 1932; taken over from the French authorities in 1958; restructuring in progress in 1993–94; cap. 7,139m. francs CFA; the original project involved a major dam, 72 km above Ségou, directing water into irrigation networks covering 1m. ha on the left bank of the Niger; since 1960 the irrigated area has been extended to only 53,300 ha, but a rehabilitation scheme, announced in 1986, was to upgrade the existing networks and increase the total cultivable area; the scheme is being executed with assistance from several international donor organizations; the Office du Niger also operates four rice-processing plants; Pres. and Man. Dir Fernand Traoré.

Office des Produits Agricoles du Mali (OPAM): BP 132, Bamako; tel. 22-37-55; telex 2509; fax 22-04-06; f. 1965; cap. 5,800m. francs CFA; state-owned; manages National (Cereals) Security Stock, administers food aid, responsible for sales of cereals and distribution to deficit areas; Man. Dir Abdoulaye Koita.

Société Nationale de Recherches et d'Exploitation des Ressources Minières du Mali (SONAREM): BP 2, Kati; tel. 27-20-42; state-owned; Man. Dir Makan Kayentao.

CHAMBER OF COMMERCE

Chambre de Commerce et d'Industrie du Mali: place de la Liberté, BP 46, Bamako; tel. 22-50-36; telex 2435; fax 22-21-20; f. 1906; Pres. Drahamane Hamidou Touré; Sec.-Gen. Daba Traoré.

EMPLOYERS' ASSOCIATIONS

Association Malienne des Exportateurs de Légumes (AMELEF): BP 1996, Bamako; f. 1984; Pres. Badara Fagand Traoré; Sec.-Gen. Birama Traoré.

Association Malienne des Exportateurs de Ressources Animales (AMERA): Centre Malien de Commerce Extérieur, BP 1996, Bamako; tel. 22-56-83; f. 1985; Pres. Ambarké Yermangore; Admin. Sec. Ali Hacko.

MAJOR INDUSTRIAL COMPANIES

The following are among the major private and state-owned companies in terms of capital investment or employment.

Abattoir Frigorifique de Bamako: Zone Industrielle, BP 356, Bamako; tel. 22-24-67; telex 2992; f. 1965; cap. 339m. francs CFA; state-owned; Man. Dir El Hadj Youssouf Camara.

Béton Mali: BP 2410, Bamako; cap. 350m. francs CFA; mfrs and distributors of construction materials; Chair. and Man. Dir Mamadou Diatigui Diarra.

Compagnie Malienne des Textiles (COMATEX): route de Markala, BP 52, Ségou; tel. 32-01-83; telex 2584; f. 1968; cap. 4,250m. francs CFA; production of unbleached fibre and textiles; Man. Dir Lassana Sacko; 2,027 employees.

Energie du Mali (EDM): square Patrice Lumumba, BP 69, Bamako; tel. 22-30-20; telex 2587; fax 22-84-30; f. 1961; cap. 2,500m. francs CFA; 55% state-owned, 39% owned by CFD; planning, construction and operation of all power-sector facilities; Pres. Moctar Touré; Man. Dir Hamidou Diallo; 1,350 employees.

Ets Peyrissac—Mali: ave de la République, BP 168, Bamako; tel. 22-20-62; telex 2561; f. 1963; cap. 300m. francs CFA; distributors of motor vehicles; Dir François Grulois.

Grands Moulins du Mali (GMM): BP 324, Bamako; tel. 22-36-64; telex 2513; f. 1979; cap. 600m. francs CFA; mfrs of flour and animal feed; Chair. and Man. Dir Gérard Achcar.

Huilerie Cotonnière du Mali (HUICOMA): c/o CMDT, BP 487, Bamako; tel. 22-24-62; telex 2554; fax 22-81-41; f. 1979; cap. 500m. francs CFA; 50% owned by CMDT, 40% state-owned; production and marketing of cottonseed oil; Dir Fagnanama Koné.

Mobil Oil Mali: quartier TSF, Zone Industrielle, BP 145, Bamako; tel. 22-25-98; telex 2562; f. 1974; cap. 321m. francs CFA; distribution of petroleum products; Chair. and Man. Dir J. L. Villalba.

Pharmacie Populaire du Mali (PPM): ave Houssa Travele, BP 277, Bamako; tel. 22-46-25; telex 2523; f. 1960; cap. 400m. francs CFA; majority state-owned; import and marketing of medicines and pharmaceutical products; Man. Dir Dr Abdoulaye Diallo.

Société des Brasseries du Mali (BRAMALI): BP 442, Bamako; f. 1981; cap. 500m. francs CFA; mfrs of beer and soft drinks; Chair. and Man. Dir Seydou Djim Sylla.

Société de Gestion et d'Exploitation des Mines d'Or de Kalana (SOGEMORK): BP 2541, Bamako; tel. 22-44-46; BP 2, Kati; f. 1983; cap. 625m. francs CFA; state-owned; gold mining at Kalana; Man. Dir Abdou Karim Diop.

Société Industrielle de Karité (SIKAMALI): Bamako; telex 2476; f. 1980; cap. 938m. francs CFA; processors of shea-nuts (karité nuts); Dir Drissa Sangaré.

Société Karamoko Traoré et Frères (SOKATRAF): BP 88, Mopti; telex 2428; f. 1975; cap. 318m. francs CFA; import/export; Chair. and Man. Dir Dramane Traoré.

Société Malienne d'Etudes et de Construction de Matériel Agricole (SMECMA): BP 1707, Bamako; tel. 22-40-71; f. 1974; cap. 251.4m. francs CFA; mfrs of agricultural equipment; Chair. Ahmed Ag Hamani; Man. Dir Boubacar Nantégué Malle.

Société Malienne de Piles Electriques (SOMAPIL): route de Sotuba, Zone Industrielle, BP 1546, Bamako; tel. 22-46-87; telex 2401; fax 22-29-80; f. 1975; cap. 500m. francs CFA; mfrs of batteries; Chair. Kouman Doumbia; Man. Dir Gérard Helix.

Société Malienne de Produits Chimiques: BP 1560, Bamako; f. 1987; cap. 250m. francs CFA; mfrs and distributors of insecticides; Chair. and Man. Dir Issa Konda.

Société Malienne de Profilage et de Transformation des Métaux (TOLMALI): quartier TSF, Zone Industrielle, Bamako; tel. 22-33-35; telex 2547; fax 22-53-77; f. 1978; cap. 250m. francs CFA; mfrs of iron and steel construction materials and aluminium utensils.

Société Malienne de Sacherie (SOMASAC): BP 74, Bamako; tel. 22-49-41; telex 2564; f. 1971; cap. 462.5m. francs CFA; production of sacking from dah and kenaf fibre and manufacture of sacks; Chair. Dossolo Traoré; Man. Dir Ernest Richard.

Société Minière de Loulo (SOMILO): Loulo; f. 1987; cap. 2,133m. francs CFA; 51% state-owned, 49% by Bureau de Recherches Géologiques et Minières (France); exploitation of gold deposits; Chair. Mamadou Touré; Dir-Gen. Jean-Marie Bouffière.

Société Minière de Syama (SOMISY): Syama; f. 1990, as a jt venture by the govt of Mali (20%), BHP-Utah International (Australian- and US-owned—65%) and the International Finance Corpn (15%); exploration and exploitation of gold reserves at Syama; Man. David Higgins.

Société Nationale des Tabacs et Allumettes du Mali (SONATAM): route de Sotuba, Zone Industrielle, BP 59, Bamako; tel. 22-49-65; telex 2537; fax 22-23-72; f. 1968; cap. 2,177m. francs CFA; state-owned; production of cigarettes and matches; Chair. Moussa Baba Diarra; Man. Dir Boubacar Dembélé; 1,034 employees.

Société Nationale de Travaux Publics du Mali (SNTP-MALI): quartier du Fleuve, BP 1624, Bamako; tel. 22-22-48; telex 2419; cap. 500m. francs CFA; Dir R. Roy.

Tanneries Maliennes (TAMALI): route de Sotuba, BP 188, Bamako; tel. 22-28-26; telex 2616; f. 1970; cap. telex 2616; 254m. francs CFA; processing of skins and hides; Man. Dir Du Mong Ying.

TRADE UNION FEDERATION

Union nationale des travailleurs du Mali (UNTM): Bourse du Travail, blvd de l'Indépendance, BP 169, Bamako; tel. 22-20-31; f. 1963; Sec.-Gen. Issé Doucouré; mems in 12 affiliated national industrial-sector unions.

Transport

RAILWAYS

Mali's only railway runs from Koulikoro, via Bamako, to the Senegal border (642 track-km). The line continues to Dakar, a total distance of 1,286 km. Some 500,000 tons of freight were handled on the Malian railway in 1990. Plans exist for the construction of a new rail line linking Bamako with Kouroussa and Kankan, in Guinea.

Régie du Chemin de Fer du Mali (RCFM): rue Baba Diarra, BP 260, Bamako; tel. 22-29-68; telex 2586; fax 22-83-88; f. 1960; Pres. DIAKARIDIA SIDIBÉ; Man. Dir Mme CISSE OUMOU.

ROADS

The Malian road network in the early 1990s totalled some 18,000 km, of which about 6,000 km were all-weather roads and some 2,000 km were tarred. A bituminized road between Bamako and Abidjan (Côte d'Ivoire) provides Mali's main economic link to the coast.

Compagnie Malienne de Transports Routiers (CMTR): BP 208, Bamako; tel. 22-33-64; telex 2539; f. 1970; state-owned; Man. Dir MAMADOU TOURÉ.

INLAND WATERWAYS

The River Niger is navigable in parts of its course through Mali (1,693 km) during the rainy season from July to late December. The River Senegal was, until the early 1990s, navigable from Kayes to Saint-Louis (Senegal) only between August and November, but its navigability was expected to improve following the inauguration, in October 1992, of the Manantali dam, and the completion of works to deepen the river-bed.

Compagnie Malienne de Navigation (CMN): BP 10, Koulikoro; tel. 26-20-94; telex 3002; f. 1968; state-owned; river transport and shipbuilding; Pres. and Man. Dir LASSINÉ MARIKO (KONÉ).

Société Navale Malienne (SONAM): Bamako; f. 1981; transferred to private ownership in 1986; Chair. ALIOUNE KEÏTA.

CIVIL AVIATION

The principal airport is at Bamako-Senou. The other major airports are at Bourem, Gao, Goundam, Kayes, Kita, Mopti, Nioro, Ségou, Tessalit and Tombouctou. There are about 40 small airfields.

Air Afrique: BP 2651, Bamako; tel. 22-58-01; see under Côte d'Ivoire; Dir in Mali TH. AGONVINON.

Mali Tombouctou Air Service (MALITAS): Bamako; f. 1988 to succeed Air Mali; 20% state-owned, 80% owned by private Malian interests; domestic services; Chair. AMADOU OUSMANE SIMAGA.

Société des Transports Aériens (STA): BP 1809, Bamako; f. 1984; privately-owned; local services; Man. Dir MELHEM ELIE SABBAGUE.

Tourism

Some 44,000 tourists visited Mali in 1990; receipts from tourism in that year totalled US $32m. Mali's cultural heritage is promoted as a tourist attraction, although unrest in the north after 1990 adversely affected the sector.

Société Malienne d'Exploitation des Ressources Touristiques (SMERT): place de la République, BP 222, Bamako; tel. 22-59-42; telex 2433; f. 1975; 25% state-owned; Man. Dir HAMADY SOW.

Defence

In June 1993 the Malian armed forces numbered some 7,350 men: there was a land army of 6,900, a naval force of about 50 (with three patrol boats on the River Niger) and an air force of 400 men. Paramilitary forces numbered 7,800 men. There were, in addition, 20 Russian military advisers stationed in Mali in mid-1993. Military service is selective and lasts for two years.

Defence Expenditure: Estimated at 16,320m. francs CFA in 1993.

Chief of Staff of the Armed Forces: Col TOUMANI CISSOKO.

Chief of Staff of the Army: Lt SILIMA KEITA.

Education

Education is provided free of charge and is officially compulsory for seven years between seven and 16 years of age. Primary education usually begins at the age of seven and lasts for a minimum of six years and a maximum of eight years. Secondary education, from 13 years of age, lasts for a further six years, comprising two cycles of three years each. The rate of school-enrolment in Mali is among the lowest in the world, and in 1991 enrolment at primary schools included only 15% of children in the relevant age-group (males 17%; females 14%). Secondary enrolment in that year was equivalent to only 7% of children in the appropriate age-group (males 10%; females 5%). Although some higher education facilities are available in Mali, many students receive higher education abroad, mainly in France and Senegal; in mid-1993 the government announced plans for the construction of a university. In 1990, according to estimates by UNESCO, adult illiteracy averaged 68.0% (males 59.2%; females 76.1%). Budget estimates for 1990 allocated 17,201m. francs CFA to the education sector (6.6% of consolidated budget expenditure).

Bibliography

de Benoist, J.-R. *Eglise et pouvoir colonial au Soudan français.* Paris, Editions Karthala, 1987.

Brasseur, P. *Bibliographie générale du Mali (Anciens Soudan Français et Haut-Sénégal-Niger).* Dakar, Institut français d'Afrique noire, 1964.

Cisse, Y. T., and Kamissoko, W. *La grande geste du Mali, des origines à la fondation de l'empire.* Paris, Editions Karthala, 1988.

Cola Cissé, M., et al. *Le Mali: Le Paysan et L'Etat.* Paris, L'Harmattan, 1981.

Decraene, P. *Le Mali.* Paris, Presses universitaires de France, 1980.

Diarrah, Cheikh O. *Le Mali de Modibo Keita.* Paris, L'Harmattan, 1986.

Diop, M. *Histoire des classes sociales dans l'Afrique de l'Ouest. Tome 1: Le Mali.* Paris, L'Harmattan.

Dumont, R. *Afrique noire: développement agricole, reconversion de l'économie agricole: Guinée, Côte d'Ivoire, Mali.* Paris, Presses universitaires de France, 1962.

Foltz, W. J. *From French West Africa to Mali Federation.* Yale University Press, 1965.

Gaudio, A. *Le Mali.* Paris, Editions Karthala, 1988.

Harrison Church, R. J. *West Africa.* 8th Edn, London, Longman, 1979.

Imperato, P. J. *Historical Dictionary of Mali.* Metuchen, NJ, Scarecrow Press, 1987.

Maharaux, A. *L'Industrie au Mali.* Paris, L'Harmattan, 1986.

Mariko, K. *Les Touaregs Ouelleminden.* Paris, Editions Karthala, 1984.

Raimbault, M., and Sanogo, K. (Eds). *Recherches archaéologiques au Mali.* Paris, Editions Karthala, 1991.

Rimmer, D. *The Economies of West Africa.* London, Weidenfeld and Nicolson, 1984.

Snyder, F. G. *One-Party Government in Mali: Transition towards Control.* New Haven and London, Yale University Press, 1965.

Sy, M. S. *Recherches sur l'exercice du pouvoir politique en Afrique noire (Côte d'Ivoire, Guinée, Mali).* Paris, 1965.

MAURITANIA

Physical and Social Geography

DAVID HILLING

Covering an area of 1,030,700 sq km (397,950 sq miles), the Islamic Republic of Mauritania forms a geographical link between the Arab Maghreb and Black West Africa. Moors, heterogeneous groups of Arab/Berber stock, form about two-thirds of the population, which totalled 1,864,236 at the April 1988 census. According to official estimates, the population totalled 2,036,000 at mid-1991 (giving an average population density of 2 persons per sq km).

The Moors are divided on social and descent criteria, rather than skin colour, into a dominant group, the Bidan or 'white' Moors, and a group, probably of servile origin, known as the Harratin or 'black' Moors. All were traditionally nomadic pastoralists. The country's black African inhabitants traditionally form about one-third of the total population, the principal groups being the Fulani (20%) and the Wolof (12%). They are mainly sedentary cultivators and are concentrated in a relatively narrow zone in the south of the country.

During the drought of the 1970s and early 1980s, there was mass migration to the towns, and the urban population increased from 18% of the total in 1972 to as much as 35% in 1984. The population of Nouakchott was 135,000 at the time of the 1977 census, but this was estimated to have risen to 350,000 by 1984. Towns such as Nouadhibou (population 22,000 in 1977), Kaédi (21,000), Zouérate (17,500) and Rosso (16,500) have since grown considerably. There has been a general exodus from rural areas and an associated growth of informal peri-urban encampments. In 1963 about 83% of the population was nomadic, and 17% sedentary, but by 1988 only 12% remained nomadic, while 88% were settled, many of them in the larger towns.

In 1991 Arabic was declared to be the official language. The principal vernacular languages, Poular, Wolof and Solinke were, with Arabic, recognized as 'national languages'. French is widely used, particularly in the commercial sector.

Geologically, Mauritania is a part of the vast western Saharan 'shield' of crystalline rocks, but these are overlain in parts with sedimentary rocks, and some 40% of the country has a superficial cover of unconsolidated sand. Relief has a general north-east/south-west trend, and a series of westward-facing scarps separate monotonous plateaux, which only in western Adrar rise above 500 m. Locally these plateaux have been eroded, so that only isolated peaks remain, the larger of these being known as *kedia* and the smaller as *guelb*. These are often minerally enriched, the most famous being the *djbel le-hadid* ('iron mountains') of the Kédia d'Idjil, whose reserves of high-grade iron ore are expected to have been exhausted by the late 1990s. Mining at a neighbouring *guelb*, El Rhein (some 40 km to the north), began in 1984, while the exploitation of the important M'Haoudat deposit (55 km to the north of Zouérate) began in 1994. Development of reserves of gold at Akjoujt, also in the Adrar region, began in 1992. Copper may also eventually be extracted from the same deposit.

Two-thirds of the country may be classed as 'Saharan', with rainfall absent or negligible in most years and always less than 100 mm. In parts vegetation is inadequate to graze even the camel, which is the main support of the nomadic peoples of the northern and central area. Traditionally this harsh area has produced some salt, and dates and millet are cultivated at oases such as Atar. Southwards, in the 'Sahelian' zone, the rainfall increases to about 600 mm per year; in good years vegetation will support sheep, goats and cattle, and adequate crops of millet and sorghum can be grown. There is evidence that the 250 mm precipitation line has moved 200 km further south since the early 1960s, as Saharan conditions encroach on Sahelian areas. In 1983 rainfall over the whole country reached an average of only 27% of that for the period 1941–70, and was only 13% in the pasturelands of the Hodh Oriental region. Average annual rainfall in the early 1990s was reported to be only 100 mm. The Senegal river has been at record low levels, and riverine cultivation in the seasonally inundated *chemama* lands has been greatly reduced. Larger areas of more systematic irrigation could be made possible by dams which have been constructed for the control of the river.

Recent History

PIERRE ENGLEBERT

Mauritania achieved independence from France on 28 November 1960, with Moktar Ould Daddah, whose Parti du regroupement mauritanien (PRM) had won all the seats in the previous year's general election, as head of state. After independence all parties merged with the PRM to form the Parti du peuple mauritanien (PPM), and Mauritania was declared a one-party state in 1964. The 1961 constitution provided for an executive presidency, to which Ould Daddah was duly elected. A highly centralized and tightly controlled political system was imposed on a diverse political spectrum. Some elements among the Moorish population favoured union with Morocco, and, although every government included a small minority of black Mauritanians, the southern population feared Arab domination. In the early years of independence the majority of Arab states refused to recognize Mauritania, which Morocco claimed as part of its own territory. Mauritania relied heavily on the diplomatic support of France, while forming other international alliances, concentrating initially on black African countries. Morocco officially recognized Mauritania in 1969.

OULD DADDAH AND THE PPM

In the early 1970s the Ould Daddah government undertook a series of measures to strengthen Mauritania's political and economic independence. Economic and cultural agreements signed with France at independence were renegotiated, and Mauritania announced its intention to withdraw from the Franc Zone and introduce its own currency, the ouguiya. In 1974 the foreign-controlled operator of the iron-ore mines which provided 80% of national exports was nationalized. The period of reform culminated in a PPM congress in August 1975, at which Ould Daddah presented a charter for an Islamic, national, central and socialist democracy.

For the next four years Mauritanian political life was dominated by the question of the Spanish-controlled territory of the Western Sahara, sovereignty of which was claimed by both Morocco and Mauritania. In November 1975, despite a ruling made in the previous month by the International Court of Justice that the territory's people were entitled to self-determination, Spain, Morocco and Mauritania concluded the Madrid Agreement, whereby Spain agreed to cede the territory in February 1976 for division between its northern and southern neighbours. Occupation of the territory by Mauritania and Morocco met with fierce resistance from guerrillas of the Frente Popular para la Liberación de Sakiet el Hamra y Río de Oro, known as the Frente Polisario (Polisario Front), which had, with Algerian support, proclaimed a 'Sahrawi Arab Democratic Republic' (SADR). With the assistance of Moroccan troops, Mauritania occupied Tiris el Gharbia, the province it had been allocated under the Madrid agreement, but resistance by Polisario forces continued. Guerrilla attacks were mounted both in the new province and inside Mauritania's 1960 frontiers (most notably on the economically vital railway linking the iron-ore deposits near Zouérate with the port of Nouadhibou).

Despite a rapid expansion of its army, Mauritania became increasingly dependent on support from Moroccan troops and on financial assistance from France and conservative Arab states. Within Mauritania the war was popular only with the pro-Moroccan tendency: large sections of the Moorish population had ties of kinship with the Sahrawi insurgents and felt no commitment to the conflict. Mauritania proved impossible to defend, and its economy was in ruins.

SALEK AND HAIDALLA

In July 1978 Ould Daddah was overthrown and detained in a bloodless military coup. Power was assumed by a self-styled military committee for national recovery (CMRN), headed by the chief of staff, Lt-Col (later Col) Moustapha Ould Mohamed Salek, which suspended the constitution and dissolved the national assembly and PPM. Two days after the coup Polisario announced a cease-fire with Mauritania; this was accepted by the new government but proved difficult to maintain with Moroccan troops still on Mauritanian territory. With an eruption of racial tensions between blacks and Moors in early 1979 adding to political instability, Salek assumed absolute power in March, dissolving the CMRN in the following month and replacing it with a military committee for national salvation (CMSN). Salek continued to head the CMSN, but relinquished the post of prime minister to Lt-Col Ahmed Ould Bouceif. The new premier was, however, killed in an air crash in May, and the CMSN appointed Lt-Col Mohamed Khouna Ould Haidalla, the minister of defence since April, in his place. In the following month Salek resigned, and the CMSN appointed Lt-Col Mohamed Mahmoud Ould Ahmed Louly as his successor. In July Polisario announced an end to the ceasefire; later in the month the OAU called for a referendum to be held in Western Sahara. These events provided the impetus for Mauritania's withdrawal from the war: Haidalla declared that Mauritania had no territorial claims in Western Sahara, a decision that was formalized in the Algiers Agreement, signed with Polisario in August. King Hassan of Morocco then announced that his country had taken over Tiris el Gharbia 'in response to local demand'.

Haidalla displaced Louly as president in January 1980, and dismissed several members of the CMSN who were allegedly 'impeding national recovery'. Some of those dismissed were to form the nucleus of exiled opposition movements, including the Paris-based Alliance pour une Mauritanie démocratique, led by Ould Daddah, who had been released from prison in 1979. Following growing tensions within the CMSN, Haidalla formed a civilian government in December 1980, with Sid Ahmed Ould Bneijara as prime minister, and published a draft constitution with provision for a multi-party system. In March 1981 Haidalla's forces defeated an attempted coup led by former members of the CMSN. Allegations of Moroccan involvement led to the suspension of diplomatic relations. In April Ould Bneijara was replaced as prime minister by the army chief of staff, Lt-Col (later Col) Maawiya Ould Sid'-Ahmed Taya, who also took the defence portfolio; a new military government was formed and the draft constitution abandoned. A further alleged coup attempt was foiled in February 1982, as a result of which Salek and Ould Bneijara were imprisoned.

Mauritania, which had recognized the legitimacy of Polisario but not that of the SADR, found it increasingly difficult to maintain neutrality in the Western Sahara conflict, especially after October 1981, when Morocco bombed Sahrawi bases in northern Mauritania and threatened reprisals against Mauritania itself. During the OAU crisis in 1982 Mauritania refrained from formally recognizing the SADR but supported its admission to the OAU. It was not until February 1984 that Haidalla took the decisive step of recognizing the SADR—a move which had little impact on Morocco but did provoke unrest, notably among students, inside Mauritania. The fear of being 'destabilized' by Morocco or Libya apparently prompted Haidalla to resume the posts of prime minister and defence minister in a reshuffle in March, as a result of which Col Taya returned to his previous post as chief of staff. The country was simultaneously weakened by the effects of severe drought.

THE TAYA PRESIDENCY

Frustration with the impasse to which Haidalla's rule had brought Mauritania led to the quiet and bloodless *coup d'état* in December 1984, when Taya deposed Haidalla (who was attending a Franco-African summit meeting in Burundi). Haidalla was berated for extravagance and corruption, but nevertheless returned home to face detention. Taya instituted major economic reforms, which attracted support from bilateral and multilateral donors, and, in what was seen as an attempt to achieve a reconciliation with supporters of Ould Daddah, three members of the former president's government were appointed to ministerial posts in 1985. Ould Daddah was himself officially pardoned and invited to return home, but chose to remain in exile. In April 1985 diplomatic relations with Morocco were resumed.

Ethnic Unrest

The second half of the 1980s witnessed growing unrest among the black Mauritanian population—resentful at what they claimed to be the increasing Arabicization of the country by the Moorish community—as well as the government's first attempts at democratization. The distribution of an 'Oppressed Black African Manifesto' in April 1986 provoked the arrest, in September, on charges of 'undermining national unity', of a number of prominent black Mauritanians, 20 of whom were imprisoned. Civil disturbances involving the black community led to further arrests. The government responded by stressing the Islamic, rather than Arab, character of Mauritanian culture and by accelerating the introduction of Shari'a (Islamic) law. At municipal council elections in December 1986, provision was made for up to four lists of candidates in each municipality, although formal political organizations remained illegal. The Taya government pledged a continuation of the process of democratization, with the eventual introduction of direct legislative and presidential elections.

Ethnic tensions were again highlighted by the arrest, in October 1987, of 51 members of the black Toucouleur ethnic group, following the discovery of a coup plot. Three armed forces officers were sentenced to death, and 41 others were imprisoned. The Dakar-based Forces de libération africaine de Mauritanie (FLAM) alleged that some detainees had been tortured. In January 1988 it was claimed that more than 500 black NCOs had been dismissed from the army, gendarmerie and national guard, as a result of disturbances that had followed the executions of the three Toucouleur officers.

In mid-1988 it was reported that about 600 people, including members of the armed forces, were arrested, as part of a short-lived purge of light-skinned Bidan supporters of the Baath Arab Socialist organization, a movement sympathetic to the governments of Iraq and Morocco which had hitherto been influential in the CMSN. In September 13 opponents of the government, all alleged to have Baathist links, were convicted of undermining state security and of recruiting military personnel on behalf of an unnamed country. This estrangement of the pro-Moroccan faction was viewed in some quarters as a shift in the government's position to that which had been advocated by Haidalla (who was released from detention in December), and raised questions concerning Mauritania's professed neutrality in the Western Sahara question.

Friction with Senegal

The persistence of ethnic divisions within Mauritania was exemplified by the conduct of the three-year border dispute with Senegal. The deaths, in April 1989, of two Senegalese, following a disagreement over grazing rights with Mauritanian livestock-breeders, provoked a crisis that was exacerbated by long-standing ethnic and economic rivalries. In the aftermath of the border incident Mauritanian nationals residing in Senegal were attacked, and their businesses ransacked (the retail trade in Senegal had hitherto been dominated by some 300,000 mainly light-skinned Mauritanians resident in that country). Senegalese nationals in Mauritania (an estimated 30,000, many of whom were employed in the manufacturing sector), together with black Mauritanians, suffered similar attacks. Estimates of the number of casualties varied, but it was believed that by early May several hundred people, mainly Senegalese, had been killed. Operations to repatriate nationals of both countries commenced, with international assistance. Meanwhile, Mauritania was reported to be exploiting the crisis to expel members of its black indigenous population, while light-skinned Senegalese were being allowed to remain in their host country. Many others fled, or were expelled, from Mauritania to Mali. In July the human rights organization, Amnesty International, expressed concern that violations of human rights had occurred in Mauritania at the time of the expulsions, and in November it recommended that the Taya government conduct an inquiry into allegations of the torture and murder of black Mauritanians.

Despite international mediation attempts, and both countries' expressed commitment to the principle of a negotiated settlement to the dispute, Senegal's insistence on the inviolability of the border, as defined at the time of French colonial rule, and Mauritania's demand that its traders returning from Senegal receive compensation from the government of that country remained the greatest impediments to a solution. The two countries suspended diplomatic relations in August 1989. Further outbreaks of violence were reported later in the year, when black Mauritanians sheltering in Senegal crossed the frontier (with, the Taya government asserted, the complicity of the Senegalese armed forces) with the intention of reclaiming their property. In early 1990 attempts at mediation by the OAU were thwarted by military engagements in the border region, as a result of which several deaths were reported. Subsequent initiatives were equally unsuccessful, and in July telephone connections between the two countries were severed. (All transport links between Mauritania and Senegal had been suspended during 1989.)

Hopes of a *rapprochement* were further undermined in late 1990, when the Mauritanian authorities accused Senegal of complicity in an alleged attempt to overthrow President Taya. In December several sources, including Amnesty International, reported the arrests of large numbers of black Halpulaars in Mauritania. The government confirmed that many arrests (of both military personnel and civilians) had taken place in connection with an alleged coup conspiracy, but denied suggestions that detainees had been tortured. Although the Senegalese government denied any involvement in the alleged plot, relations between the two countries deteriorated, and in January and February 1991 incidents were reported in which Mauritanian naval vessels had opened fire on Senegalese fishing boats, apparently in Senegal's territorial waters. In March several deaths were reported to have resulted from a confrontation, on Senegalese territory, between the two countries' armed forces.

In March 1991 60 of those who had been detained following the alleged coup plot were released. This was followed by a general amnesty, in which all those who had been convicted of undermining state security were stated to have been released from custody. The Taya government claimed that almost all the country's political prisoners had thus been freed, but other sources maintained that several hundred of those who had been arrested in late 1990 remained in detention, and in the following month Amnesty International requested that the government respond to reports of the torture and execution of detainees.

Constitutional Reform

In April 1991 Taya announced that proposals for a new constitution, which would permit the establishment of a multiparty political system, were to be submitted for approval in a national referendum. This unexpected announcement coincided with an upsurge in overt political opposition. In May and June women who were demanding to know the fate of their relatives who had 'disappeared' following the alleged coup plot in November 1990 staged a demonstration in Nouakchott, and in June there were anti-government protests in Nouadhibou. Tracts and open letters, condemning the Taya government and demanding that a national conference be convened to deliberate the country's political evolution, began to circulate. The draft constitution was submitted to a national referendum on 12 July 1991. According to official figures, 97.9% of those who voted (85.3% of the registered electorate) endorsed the proposals. However, opposition movements claimed that the turn-out had been as low as 8% of registered voters. The new constitution accorded extensive powers to the president of the republic, who was to be elected, by universal suffrage, for a period of six years, with no limitation placed on further terms of office. Provision was made for a bicameral legislature (comprising a national assembly, to be elected by universal suffrage every five years, and a senate, to be appointed by municipal leaders with a six-year mandate), as well as for a constitutional council, an economic and social council and a supreme Islamic council. The CMSN would remain in power pending the inauguration of the new organs of state. Under the constitution, Arabic was designated as the sole official language.

Shortly after the adoption of the new constitution, legislation permitting registration of political parties took effect. Among the first parties to be accorded official status was the pro-government Democratic and Social Republican Party (DSRP), which was criticized by the opposition for its privileged access to the state apparatus; also influential in the first months of political pluralism were the Mauritanian Party for Renewal (which included ex-president Haidalla among its members) and the Union of Democratic Forces (UDF).

A general amnesty for all those accused or convicted of undermining state security was announced in July 1991, prompting FLAM (which had maintained a sporadic campaign of attacks on official targets) to suspend its military operations. However, the limitations of the democratization process became evident in August, when a further women's demonstration was violently dispersed by the security forces. Later in the month Amnesty International published a list of 339 people (mostly Halpulaars), who were alleged to have died in detention following the disclosure of the November 1990 coup plot.

Four candidates, including Taya, Ahmed Ould Daddah (the half-brother of the country's first president), who, while not at the time affiliated to any party, was supported by the UDF, and former CMRN chairman Salek, participated in the presidential election, which took place on 17 January 1992. According to official results, Taya obtained 62.7% of the poll (51.7% of the registered electorate voted); his nearest rival, Ahmed Ould Daddah, received 32.8% of the votes cast. The defeated candidates denounced Taya's victory as fraudulent, and appealed unsuccessfully to the supreme court to declare the election invalid. (Independent observers stated that some 'administrative' errors had undoubtedly occurred, but otherwise agreed that the election had been fairly conducted.) Unrest following the election led to at least two deaths and more than 160 arrests, and prompted the government to impose a temporary dusk-to-dawn curfew in Nouakchott and Nouadhibou. By early February all those who had been detained in the post-election violence had been released. Shortly before the presidential election FLAM had announced that it was to resume military operations.

'Democratized' Government

By late February 1992 six opposition parties that had initially intended to contest elections to the national assembly had withdrawn their candidates, claiming that the electoral process was unduly favourable to the DSRP. At the elections, which took place on 6 and 13 March, the DSRP won 67 of the chamber's 79 seats, with all but two of the remaining seats being secured by independent candidates. The rate of participation by voters was reported to have been low. It was stated that each of the country's ethnic groups was represented in the assembly. Other than the DSRP, only one party presented candidates for the senate (elections to which followed on 3 and 10 April). The DSRP emerged with a majority in the upper house, with 36 senators; 17 independent candidates were elected, the remaining three seats being reserved for representatives of Mauritanians resident abroad.

At his inauguration, on 18 April 1992, President Taya designated Sidi Mohamed Ould Boubacar, who had been minister of finance since October 1990, as prime minister. The only military officer in the new government was Col Ahmed Ould Minnih, as minister of defence. Included in the new government were three black ministers and one opposition representative. Ould Boubacar, a French-trained technocrat, was known to have extensive experience of financial management and had previously been involved in the country's negotiations with the IMF. However, his relative lack of experience in other areas of government suggested that Taya intended to retain a dominant role in the political process. The new government announced plans to restructure the judicial system and to reform the civil service. The two legislative chambers were inaugurated in late April 1992. The national assembly elected Cheikh Sid'Ahmed Ould Baba (a Harratin former minister of the interior, posts and telecommunications) as its president, while Dieng Boubou Farba (a Toucouleur who had previously been a national director of Air Afrique) became president of the senate. Ahmed Ould Daddah and his supporters formally joined the principal opposition to Taya's administration, the UDF (which was renamed the UDF–New Era), in June 1992.

The devaluation of the ouguiya, in early October 1992 (as part of an IMF-supported programme of economic adjustment), precipitated violent protests in the capital, as traders immediately imposed sharp increases in the prices of basic household commodities. Security forces intervened to restore order, and a night-time curfew was enforced in the Nouakchott region for a two-week period. The government gave assurances that measures would be taken to offset the adverse social consequences of the currency's depreciation, and compensatory salary increases were introduced in all sectors in January 1993.

Although the government placed particular emphasis on the multi-ethnic character of its administration, tensions remained. In late May 1993 parliament approved legislation pardoning all those (specifically including members of the army and security forces) convicted of crimes committed in connection with 'armed operations and acts of violence and terrorism' during the three years preceding Taya's inauguration as elected president. Security forces forcibly dispersed a demonstration in Nouakchott that had been organized by opponents of the measure, who protested that the period covered by the amnesty had been one of severe repression by the armed forces of black dissidents.

Several long-serving ministers were removed from the council of ministers in January 1993, and in June Mouhamedou Ould Michel left the ministry of planning and development to become governor of the central bank. Government changes in November included the departure from the post of minister of foreign affairs and co-operation of Mohamed Abdrahmane Ould Moine, regarded as a principal architect of Mauritania's recent *rapprochement* with Kuwait and its regional allies in the Gulf conflict (see below). His successor, Mohamed Salem Ould Lekhel, latterly the country's ambassador to Japan, was a former member of the CMSN and minister of the economy and finance under Taya's military regime.

Mauritania's first multi-party municipal elections took place in late January and early February 1994, at which the DSRP won control of 172 of the country's 208 administrative districts. Opposition groups, including the UDF–New Era (which took control of 17 districts, the remainder being won by independents), protested that the elections had been conducted fraudulently, and had been unduly favourable to the DSRP. (Prior to the elections several people, reported to be activists of both the DSRP and opposition parties, had been arrested in connection with alleged electoral malpractice, while several parties, anticipating fraud, boycotted the polls.) A disputed result was reported to have been the cause of ethnic clashes in eastern Mauritania.

Shortly before the first round of municipal voting the president of the unauthorized Mauritanian Human Rights Association (MHRA), Cheikh Sadibou Camara (who was also a member of the prominent Union for Democracy and Progress opposition party) was arrested and detained for several days, reportedly on charges of incitement to agitation. Camara had recently reported to a visiting delegation of international human rights organizations that children of Harratin (black Moors, who had formerly been slaves) had been abducted and sold into slavery—Mauritanian law regards any reference to slavery, which was formally abolished in 1980, as injurious to national unity. Overseas human rights monitors, who appealed for Camara's release, protested that the government's assertion that he belonged to an unrecognized organization was invalid, since the MHRA had made several applications for legal status, which had been withheld despite constitutional guarantees of the right of free association. Earlier in January 1994 Mauritania's first independent trade union confederation had been legalized, following a protracted dispute between its leaders and the authorities.

There was renewed concern regarding Mauritania's observance of civil rights following the seizure, in May 1994, by the ministry of the interior, posts and telecommunications of copies of an independent journal, *Le Calame* (publication of which was subsequently temporarily suspended by the authorities). The banned editions had included a report by the International Federation of Human Rights that was severely critical of the Taya regime, as well as an unfavourable article concerning the conduct while in a previous local government post of Mohamed Lemine Salem Ould Dah, who had assumed the interior portfolio in a government reshuffle earlier in the month. Publication of another independent journal, *Eveil Hebdo*, was temporarily suspended by the ministry of the interior in July.

The DSRP's control of the political process was confirmed at elections to renew one-third of the senate's membership in April and May 1994. At the same time the UFD–New Era's influence was undermined by internal tensions, as dissident groups complained of the party's loss of credibility as an opposition force and excessive centralization around Ahmed Ould Daddah's leadership.

External Issues

Renewed diplomatic initiatives resulted in a meeting, in July 1991 in Guinea-Bissau, of the foreign ministers of Mauritania and Senegal, at which it was agreed in principle to reopen the Mauritania–Senegal border and to resume diplomatic relations. (However, the issues of the demarcation of the border and the fate of Mauritanian refugees in Senegal were not discussed.) Bilateral contacts continued during the second half of the year, and in November Presidents Taya and Diouf met while attending the francophone summit meeting in France. Diplomatic links, at ambassadorial level, were finally restored in late April 1992, and the process of reopening the border began in early May. None the less, the contentious issues that had hitherto impeded the normalization of relations remained to be resolved. In June representatives of the refugees published an open letter in which they appealed for international assistance for repatriation efforts, together with the return of property confiscated by the Mauritanian authorities and payment compensation for the 'humiliation' suffered as a result of their earlier expulsion. Moreover, Mauritanian refugees in Senegal insisted that, as long as their national identity (*Mauritanité*) were not recognized by the Taya government, they would not return to Mauritania. Further tensions were reported in September 1993, when the Mauritanian authorities announced that Senegalese nationals would henceforth be required to fulfil certain criteria, including currency-exchange requirements, before being allowed to remain in (or enter) Mauritania. Concern was expressed that such conditions might be used to prevent black

Mauritanians who had fled to Senegal in 1989 from returning to Mauritania. In early 1994 it was estimated that as many as 50,000 Mauritanian refugees remained in Senegal.

The issue of refugees was also the subject of a series of senior-level negotiations with Mali (including meetings between the presidents of the two countries) in 1992–94. The problem of Mauritanian refugees in Mali was compounded by the presence in Mauritania of light-skinned Malian Tuaregs and Moors and also Bella (for further details, see Recent History of Mali), who, the Malian authorities asserted, were launching raids on Malian territory from bases in Mauritania. Following reports that Malian troops had, in turn, crossed into Mauritania in pursuit of rebels, the two countries agreed in early 1993 to begin work on a precise demarcation of their joint border, which was concluded in September 1993 (at which time there were some 13,000 black Mauritanian refugees in Mali. In April 1994 Mauritania, Mali and representatives of the UN High Commissioner for Refugees signed an agreement for the eventual voluntary repatriation of Malian refugees (estimated to number more than 40,000) from Mauritania. In the same month the governments of Mauritania, Mali and Senegal agreed to strengthen military co-operation, with the aim of improving joint border security. However, an escalation of unrest in northern Mali in July prompted the Mauritanian authorities, fearing a renewed influx of refugees, to dispatch military reinforcements to the border region.

Although France has remained an important aid-donor and provider of technical assistance, the Taya regime has sought increasingly to enhance links with the other countries of the Maghreb and with the Arab world as a whole. In February 1989 Mauritania was a founder member, together with Algeria, Libya, Morocco and Tunisia, of a new regional economic organization, the Union of the Arab Maghreb (UMA). The member states subsequently formulated 15 regional co-operation conventions. In February 1993, however, it was announced that, given the differing economic orientations of each signatory, no convention had actually been implemented, and the organization's activities were to be 'frozen'. A meeting of UMA leaders was, however, convened in April 1994.

Meanwhile, Mauritania has generally enjoyed cordial relations with Iraq (exemplified by the prominent role of the Baathist movement in Mauritanian public life). In April and May 1990 the government denied persistent rumours that it was allowing Iraq to test long-range missiles on Mauritanian territory. Following Iraq's forcible annexation of Kuwait, in August of that year, Mauritania condemned the deployment of troops in the region of the Persian (Arabian) Gulf by those countries that opposed the Iraqi action. On the outbreak of hostilities in that region, Mauritanians volunteered to support Iraq's armed forces, and demonstrations in protest against what was perceived to be a US-led offensive took place in Nouakchott. Mauritanian support for Iraq during the 1990–91 crisis resulted in the loss of financial assistance from other countries of the Gulf region. During 1993, however, Mauritania sought an improvement in relations with Kuwait and its allies, and there was a perceived loss of influence for Iraqi sympathizers. In April 1994 Kuwait's first deputy prime minister and minister of foreign affairs visited Mauritania, and the two countries issued a joint communiqué in which the Taya government emphasized its recognition of Kuwait's borders, as defined by the UN in 1993.

Mauritania's relations with France improved significantly in the early 1990s, following the introduction of multi-party institutions. Taya made an official visit to France in December 1993, during which he held discussions, described as 'fruitful' with President Mitterrand and the prime minister, Edouard Balladur. The Mauritanian authorities expressed the hope that bilateral co-operation would be improved as a result of such contacts. Conversely, in mid-1993 the USA suspended Mauritania's benefits under its generalized system of preferences—a programme whereby developing nations enjoy privileged access to US markets—on account of the Taya administration's poor record on workers' rights.

Economy

EDITH HODGKINSON

Revised for this edition by the Editor

Mauritania has few natural resources other than minerals, and its economy was almost entirely traditional and rural, based on livestock and agriculture, until the rapid development of the mining industry, in the 1960s and 1970s, enormously increased export earnings and government revenues. The country's gross domestic product (GDP) increased, in real terms, at an average rate of 8% per year during the 1960s. The growth rate fluctuated in the 1970s as a result of drought, trends in demand for iron ore, and disturbances in output, owing to the activities of the Polisario Front (see Recent History).

During the early 1980s the economy contracted (by an annual average of 1.0% in 1981–84) in the wake of a world recession in demand for iron ore and the burden of servicing a high level of foreign debt, much of it arising from ill-considered investments that Mauritania had made during the more prosperous years of the mid-1970s. Persistent drought was also a factor. The sole offsetting element was the dynamic growth of the fishing sector. The further expansion of this sector, together with the recovery in agricultural production when the drought ended, resulted in a recovery in GDP growth in 1985–88, to an average of 3.2% annually (slightly below the target of real GDP growth of 4% per year that had been envisaged in the programme for economic and financial recovery for that period). The rate of growth accelerated to 4.2% in 1989; however, decline in revenue from the fishing sector, together with disruption caused by the dispute with Senegal and the withdrawal of funding from Middle Eastern sources—as a consequence of Mauritania's support for Iraq at the time of the crisis in the region of the Persian (Arabian) Gulf—resulted in a decline, of 2.1%, in the rate of GDP growth in 1990. The following year saw growth of 2.8%, despite lower output in both the fishing and mining sectors. There was modest growth, estimated at 1.8%, in 1992, while a growth rate of 4.9% in 1993 was attributed to successes achieved under the government's programme of economic adjustment. In 1992, according to estimates by the World Bank, Mauritania's gross national product (GNP) was US $1,109m., equivalent to $530 per head. This level of GNP per head places Mauritania in the category of low-income developing countries (in earlier years, Mauritania had been classified as a lower middle-income developing country).

The Taya regime formulated a one-year economic recovery programme, in agreement with the IMF, when it came to power at the end of 1984. This was incorporated in the 1985–88 programme, which aimed to reduce budget and balance-of-payments deficits by means of more stringent criteria for selecting public investment projects. Emphasis was given to immediately productive schemes in fishing and agriculture, and to the rehabilitation of existing capacity and infrastructure in mining and transport. The achievements of the programme were to be consolidated under the terms of the 1989–91 economic support and revival programme, supported by an enhanced structural adjustment facility from the IMF (that was awarded in May 1989). The programme aimed to achieve real average GDP growth of 3.5% per year during 1989–91 by fostering private enterprise while restructuring and rehabilitating the banking system. As indicated above, there was in fact an overall contraction (of about 6%) in the economy during this period. However, the broad terms of the programme, and its GDP growth targets, have been maintained for the next (October 1992–September 1995) IMF-supported period of reform.

The total population of Mauritania was 1,864,236 at the census of April 1988, implying an average population growth of about 3% per year during the preceding decade. Official estimates for mid-1991 indicate a population of 2,036,000, although some uncertainty has been caused by population movements arising from the dispute with Senegal. Mauritania's average population density (about 2 per sq km) is the lowest in west Africa. The severe drought of the early 1970s, with its destruction of livestock, and the growth of the modern sector caused a significant diminution in numbers of those living a nomadic or semi-nomadic way of life. In 1965 these were estimated to total 83% of the population, but by 1988 the proportion had declined to 12%. A trend towards settlement in urban areas has been apparent. About 50% of the population was urban in 1992, compared with 14% in 1970; of these, more than 80% live in the capital, Nouakchott.

AGRICULTURE

As mining has developed, the contribution of agriculture and livestock-rearing to GDP has declined—from about 44% in 1960 to just under 30% in 1991 (although almost 64% of the labour force were employed in the sector in the latter year). Less than 1% of the land receives sufficient rainfall to sustain crop cultivation, which is largely confined to the Senegal river region in the extreme south.

The serious drought of the early 1970s destroyed a large part of the livestock herds (cattle numbered 2m. in 1970), while the harvest of millet and sorghum fell to below its normal level. The return of drought in subsequent years resulted in a further decline in production and livestock numbers, and the grain crop was estimated at 35,000 metric tons in 1979/80. In 1980/81 and 1981/82 there was a good recovery in output of cereals, but the severe drought of 1982–84 caused production to decline sharply, to only one-tenth of domestic requirements in 1983/84. Improved rainfall brought a very strong recovery in subsequent years, while the introduction of paddy rice cultivation proved highly successful, contributing to a total cereal crop of 183,600 tons in 1989/90. However, inadequate rains reduced the crop out-turn to an average of just over 100,000 tons in the following three years. Even in non-drought years imports are needed to satisfy domestic demand (which has increased as a result of urbanization). In the drought years 1982–84 commercial grain imports were as high as 300,000 tons, supplemented by over 100,000 tons of food aid. In 1992/93 the import requirement was forecast at 210,000 tons. Herding (which is the main occupation of the rural population, and whose contribution to GDP is five times greater than that of crop cultivation) was even more adversely affected by the droughts: in 1984 cattle numbers had fallen to about 1m., and sheep and goats to 5.7m. They have since recovered to near pre-drought levels. In 1992, according to FAO estimates, there were 1.4m. cattle and 9.0m. sheep and goats.

The military regime committed itself to a comprehensive rural development programme, concentrating on rebuilding livestock herds and providing reliable water supplies. The 1985–88 economic and financial recovery programme gave priority to the rural sector, which was allocated 35% of total investment, compared with only 10% in the previous (1981–85) plan. The major project in the 1980s was the Gorgol valley irrigation scheme, representing investment of $100m., with the World Bank, the EC (now European Union—EU), Saudi Arabia, Libya and France providing more than 85% of the funds. The scheme has provided irrigation for 3,600 ha of rice, sugar, wheat and maize since the inauguration of the dam in 1985. Two similar projects are in progress: one at Boghé, on the Senegal river, and the other based on a number of small dams in the centre and west of the country. In total, the three schemes are projected to bring some 30,000 ha into cultivation. The construction of dams at Djama, in Senegal (completed in 1985), and at Manantali (completed in 1988), in Mali, under the auspices of the Organization for the Development of the Senegal River (OMVS), is expected eventually to provide a further 16,000 ha of irrigated land.

FISHING

The fishing sector provides an important contribution to both local food supply and exports, and was the most dynamic sector of the economy in the 1980s. The potential annual catch in Mauritanian waters is estimated at as much as 600,000 tons. The rapid extension of foreign participation in the industry during the 1970s, which exceeded the growth of the fish-processing sector at Nouadhibou, obliged the government to reformulate its fishing policy in 1980. Thus, it abrogated existing agreements permitting foreign-based vessels to fish Mauritanian waters, and required foreign companies or governments fishing therein to form joint ventures with Mauritanian interests, with the latter holding a majority of the equity capital. Since 1983 all catches made in Mauritanian waters have had to be landed in the country for processing and export, and from mid-1984 until the monopoly was ended in 1992 all sales had to be directed through the state fishing company. Agreements have been reached with fishing companies from the EC, Japan, Ukraine and the People's Republic of China, among others. After protracted negotiations, a fishing agreement with the EC was signed in 1987. Covering a three-year period, the agreement granted fishing rights to vessels of EC countries in return for $23.7m. in compensation, but excluded some categories of fish and vessels. The subsequent three-year accord, concluded in 1990, maintained broadly the same terms, but made provision for the protection of fish stocks and for monetary compensation of $64m. A further arrangement with the EC was negotiated in 1993. The requirement that foreign enterprises land and process their catch in Mauritania has boosted fish exports and earnings, which in 1983 reached 312,100 tons (from only 14,600 in 1979) and UM 8,773m., causing fish to become, for the first time, a more important source of export earnings than iron ore—a position that was maintained in 1984, despite a recovery in sales of iron ore in that year, and in 1985. In 1986 the value of exports of fish reached a record UM 20,330m. and their volume a record 388,400 tons. In that year the fishing sector (including processing) accounted for about one-tenth of GDP, and the 1985–88 recovery programme allocated almost 9% of total new project investment (UM 3,520m.) to further fisheries development, with around one-half destined for a ship-repair yard in Nouadhibou, which was inaugurated in late 1989. However, the volume and value of catches declined in the late 1980s, as some international operators moved their operations elsewhere and because of the depletion of stocks earlier in the decade. By 1991 the sector's contribution to GDP had declined to 5%, with fish exports (of 251,800 tons) valued at UM 16,750m. Earnings improved by almost 10% in 1992, and by 1993, when exports of fish and fish products accounted for some 56% of the value of total exports, the contribution of fishing to GDP had recovered to 7%. The sector's future is compromised by the over-exploitation of stocks and by the poor state of the Mauritanian fleet (only about one-half of which was operational in 1992), although external assistance (such as a loan of $14.2m., granted by the African Development Fund in late 1993) has been made available for the expansion of fishing activities.

MINING AND POWER

While the vast majority of the population still depends on agriculture and livestock for its livelihood, the country's economic growth prospects were transformed during the 1960s by the discovery and exploitation of reserves of iron ore and copper, which made Mauritania one of west Africa's wealthier countries in terms of per caput income. The Guelbs region has workable reserves of iron ore estimated at 5,000m.–6,000m. tons. They are being developed by the former Société anonyme des mines de fer de Mauritanie (MIFERMA), established in 1959 by the French government, which held 24% of the capital, and French steel interests (32%) in association with British, Italian and Federal German concerns. Mauritania nationalized these holdings in 1974, and they became part of the state mining corporation, the Société nationale industrielle et minière (SNIM), which had been formed in 1972 and which later became the Société nationale industrielle et minière—Société d'économie mixte (SNIM—SEM). Between 1960–72 about 70,800m. francs CFA was invested in the development of the

Kédia d'Idjil mines, including the construction of a 670-km railway and a mineral port. Production of ore, which began in 1963, reached 11.7m. tons (gross weight) in 1974, eased to 8.8m. tons in the following year and then recovered to 9.5m. tons in 1976. In 1977 and 1978 annual output declined to 7.3m. tons, owing to depressed export demand and attacks on the supply line by guerrillas of the Polisario Front.

After the cease-fire of 1978, production recovered to over 8.9m. tons per year in 1979 and 1980. However, the fall in foreign demand, because of economic recession, meant that production was reduced in the following years, to an estimated 7.4m. tons in 1983. Meanwhile, SNIM began exploitation of the lower-grade (36%., compared with a metal content of as much as 60% at Kédia d'Idjil) *guelbs* iron ore deposits some 40 km north of the Kédia d'Idjil mines, which were expected to have been exhausted by the late 1990s. Production under the first stage of the project, at El Rhein, at an estimated cost of $360m., began in 1984, increasing total national output to 9.2m. tons in 1985 and to 11.6m. tons in 1990. However, production declined to 10.3m. tons in 1991 and to only 8.3m. tons in 1992, as technical problems (notably the cost of enrichment and separation in this isolated region) at El Rhein meant that the deposit yielded little more than 2m. tons per year, far less than the 'break-even' level of 3m. tons annually. The second stage of the project, a new mine at Oum Arwagen, was thus allowed to lapse. The company's main interest was transferred to the deposits at M'Haoudat, near Zouérate (estimated to contain recoverable reserves of 100m. tons), which have revealed potential for annual production of about 6m. tons of high-grade (60%–65%) ore. Financing for the project, the total value of which was put at $172m., was supplied by the African Development Bank, the European Investment Bank the Caisse française de développement and SNIM—SEM. Work on the scheme began in December 1991, and the mine was inaugurated in April 1994. As part of the project the mineral port at Point-Central, 10 km south of Nouadhibou, has been modernized and expanded, with new plant to mix different concentrate types. With the entry into production of the M'Haoudat scheme, the government hopes to sustain overall output averaging 12m. tons of ore annually, over at least 25 years. Exports of iron ore, which declined from 11.3m. tons in 1990 to 8.1m. tons in 1992, before recovering to 9.6m. tons in 1993, were forecast to increase to 10.5m. tons in 1994.

In 1967 the Société minière de Mauritanie (SOMIMA) was formed to exploit the copper reserves at Akjoujt, then estimated at 32m. tons. Partners included Charter Consolidated (45%), the Mauritanian government (22%) and private French interests (18%). The government took full control in 1975. Production began in 1970, with 3,000 tons of copper concentrate. Output rose to a peak of 28,982 tons in 1973, but ceased altogether in 1978, owing to the low grades of the deposit. A new company, the Société arabe des mines d'Inchiri, was formed in 1981 by the government and Arab interests in order to reopen the mine, at a projected annual production of 105,000 tons, exploiting more extensive reserves than earlier estimated, at a cost of $100m. Projected annual output has since been lowered to 65,000 tons, and investment reduced to $40m.; however, funding has yet to be secured. In early 1991 SOMIMA established a joint-venture company, Mines d'or d'Akjoujt (MORAK), with Australian interests and the International Finance Corp, to extract gold from Akjoujt. Operations began in April 1992, with total potential output forecast at 5,670 kg; the exploitation of other nearby deposits is envisaged. It was anticipated that production of gypsum would rise substantially with the reopening in 1984 of the N'Drahamcha quarry, north of Nouakchott, by the Société arabe des industries métallurgiques mauritano-koweïtienne (SAMIA). Total reserves are estimated at 4,000m. tons, among the largest in the world. Total output reached a peak of 19,400 tons in 1987, but technical and transportation problems caused a decline in subsequent years, with production of only 3,000 tons recorded in 1991.

As part of the reduction in the government's role in the economy, SNIM was opened to private participation in 1978, and Arab governments and institutions now hold 29% of the renamed concern SNIM—SEM is involved in prospecting for tungsten (wolfram), iron, petroleum, phosphates and uranium (the latter, in the north of the country, was temporarily interrupted by the guerrilla war). Phosphate reserves of 95m.–150m. tons have been located at Bofal, near the Senegal river. A consortium was established in 1990 to develop the deposit, although initial attempts to secure external financial support failed, and it is planned to construct a fertilizer plant to process eventual output.

Following the completion of seismic surveys, exploratory drilling for petroleum began at the offshore Autruche field in 1989, the economic viability of findings has not yet been proven. Reserves of gold, sulphur and peat are also being considered for exploitation.

Reflecting the needs of mineral development, electricity generation has expanded rapidly since the late 1960s, from 38.4m. kWh in 1967 to 143m. kWh in 1991; capacity of some 129 MW, has been almost entirely thermal. However, hydroelectric installations have been built on the Senegal river under the OMVS scheme (see above). A power line that will enable Mauritania to utilize electricity generated at the Manantali installation (which was inaugurated in October 1992) is to be constructed; none the less, it now seems unlikely that the target of generation of 800m. kWh (of which Mauritania would receive 15%) will be achieved. Existing plant, notably the power station at Nouadhibou and the distribution network, is currently being rehabilitated with World Bank support.

MANUFACTURING

There is, as yet, no significant industrial development outside the mining sector, but the manufacturing sector has expanded because of the development of the fish-processing industry. Initially, development had concentrated on import substitution. However, as income from iron mining rose during the early 1970s, the government promoted the development of large-scale, capital-intensive manufacturing projects, in which it participated directly. These included the petroleum refinery at Nouakchott, which entered production in 1978, with an annual capacity of 1m. tons. In the event, this wholly government-financed project was closed by the new regime. After reopening in 1982 (with Algerian assistance), the refinery closed again after only six months. However, an agreement on rehabilitation was reached with Algeria in 1985, and operations resumed in mid-1987. About two-thirds of its total annual output of 800,000 tons are scheduled for export. A sugar refinery was completed in 1977, but it was closed after less than one year's operation because its dependence on imported sugar made it uneconomic. However, the plant was reactivated in 1982, with assistance from Algeria, as a sugar-packaging operation. The government also planned to establish plants to produce 500,000 tons of steel and 30,000 tons of copper by 1979/80. SAMIA (see above) was formed in 1974, with Kuwaiti participation, to build the plants, and operations at the steel mill, which has product capacity of 36,000 tons and uses both scrap and imported billets, began in 1981. The mill failed to reach capacity production, and closed in 1984, but reopened in 1987 as a joint venture with Jordanian and Kuwaiti participation. In total, however, these projects proved to be unprofitable and a major burden on state finances. Although government enterprises remain of major importance, the Taya government is no longer placing emphasis on large-scale capital-intensive projects, but is, instead, encouraging development by the private sector and the establishment of small- and medium-scale operations, aimed at low-level import substitution. Long-term tax agreements are offered, and an industrial zone is planned for Nouakchott. Meanwhile, the development of fish-processing units at Nouadhibou, as a result of the government's fisheries policy, made this sub-sector into the single most important manufacturing activity, accounting for as much as 4% of annual GDP. In 1991 the manufacturing sector as a whole contributed almost 7% of GDP.

A major strand in current policy is the rationalization of the public sector. In mid-1990 the World Bank, in co-operation with Arab donors, Spain and the Federal Republic of Germany, agreed to provide $40m. in support of a programme to reduce, or eliminate, state monopolies, to transfer some state enterprises to private ownership, and to restructure some strategic enterprises (such as SNIM—SEM, the fish-export monopoly and the power utility). It was envisaged that one-half of Mauritania's 80 parastatal organizations would have been thus 'privatized' or liquidated by mid-1991. Although this target was not attained, there has been solid progress. The reform of the banking system, under the 1989–91 programme, had already entailed the streamlining of government banking institutions. The sugar refinery was finally closed, after no private buyer could be found, five textile and fishing companies were liquidated, the petroleum-products sector was fully liberalized, and the monopolies in fish-marketing, insurance and tea-importing have been ended.

TRANSPORT INFRASTRUCTURE

Transport infrastructure related to mineral development is of a high standard. The iron ore port of Point-Central, 10 km to the south of Nouadhibou, can accommodate 150,000-ton bulk carriers (a 670-km rail line links the port with the iron-ore deposits at Zouérate and has been extended by 40 km to the El Rhein deposit and by 30 km to M'Haoudat), while Nouakchott's capacity was expanded to 950,000 tons with the completion, in 1986, of a 500,000-ton deep-water facility, financed and constructed by the People's Republic of China. This development reduced the country's dependence on transportation through Senegal, and the excess capacity that the port currently represents could be used for gypsum and copper exports, and for traffic to Mali. Outside the mineral shipment network, communications are at present still poor: in 1986 there were some 7,500 km of roads and tracks, of which about 2,700 km were main roads. Only about 1,700 km of the road network were tarred. The 1,100-km Trans-Mauritania highway, linking Nouakchott with the south-eastern part of the country, was completed in 1985. Its construction was aided by foreign, principally Arab, funds. The Senegal river is navigable for 210 km throughout the year (navigability should eventually be extended, with the completion of the Manantali dam), and there are three major river ports, at Rosso, Kaédi and Gouraye. However, tensions with Senegal disrupted river traffic in 1989–92. There are international airports at Nouakchott and Nouadhibou.

FINANCE

Mauritania's budget situation was transformed by mineral development. The MIFERMA contract allowed the temporary liquidation of the chronic budget deficit and commitment of funds to capital development. Spending was also boosted by the guerrilla war and the administrative costs associated with the annexed territory of Western Sahara (abandoned in 1979). Consequently, ordinary expenditure rose by 11% in 1977 and was predicted to rise by 18% in 1978. The ceasefire allowed a much slower rise in current spending in 1978 (only 7%) and a projected fall of 9% in 1980, to UM 9,948m. However, the budget continued in deficit, reaching UM 5,423m. on current spending and UM 8,095m. on total spending in 1979. In return for IMF stand-by credits, successive Mauritanian governments have since 1980 attempted to restrain the level of budgetary spending and to raise current revenue. The overall deficit fell sharply, to around UM 1,800m. per year in both 1982 and 1983, but rose to an estimated UM 4,000m. in 1984, owing to the rising cost of servicing the foreign debt and to the impact of the drought. The 1985–88 recovery programme aimed to balance the current budget in 1986 and to generate a surplus by 1988. In its first year, however, the overall deficit reached an unprecedented UM 9,341m., as debt arrears were discharged. None the less, the current budget did achieve the intended balance, and the overall deficit eased to about UM 900m. in 1986, before widening to UM 2,000m. in 1987. The deficit increased again in the following two years, to reach UM 6,300m. in 1989. Improvements in revenue from taxes, in conjunction with strict controls on expenditure, reduced the deficit to an average of UM 3,100m. per year in 1990–91, while the budget remained in modest deficit in 1992. The deficit widened in 1993, largely reflecting the costs of restructuring the banking sector and of servicing the external debt (see below), together with increased social costs, and, in its economic programme for 1994 the government aimed to reduce the overall budget deficit to the equivalent of 3.3% of GDP, compared with 11% in 1993. Fiscal deficits have been overwhelmingly financed by external funds (largely in the form of debt-relief), while only a small proportion of public investment has been funded from domestic sources.

FOREIGN TRADE AND PAYMENTS

Foreign trade has been transformed by the development, firstly, of the mineral sector and, secondly, of fishing. The value of Mauritania's exports increased from 3,200m. francs CFA (mainly cattle)—equivalent to UM 650m.—in 1959 to UM 8,013m. in 1976, of which 6,919m. came from iron ore. Despite the heavy import requirements of mining development, imports rose less rapidly—from 7,000m. francs CFA (UM 1,400m.) in 1959 to UM 8,072m. in 1976. International reserves, which were only $3m. at the end of 1970, reached $143m. in early 1975. However, the trade account deteriorated in subsequent years, recording a deficit of UM 5,137m. in 1979, on exports of UM 6,733m. (of which iron ore accounted for UM 6,074m.). The major reasons were a weakening in the demand for iron ore, and increased spending on imports of petroleum. Tighter control on the growth in imports of capital equipment and consumer goods, the recovery in iron-ore prices and the sevenfold increase in earnings from fish exports (to UM 4,428m. in 1981) resulted in a narrowing in the trade gap in subsequent years, to only UM 294m. in 1981. After a sharp rise in the deficit in 1982, as a result of the decline in earnings from iron ore and the increase in petroleum imports with the opening of the refinery, foreign trade moved into surplus in 1983. Import spending was held down by the government's austerity programme and by a decrease in the import of petroleum products, while export revenue benefitted from the near-doubling in earnings from fish, to UM 8,773m. The trade surplus almost doubled in 1984, and again in 1985, as export totals were enlarged by the rise in iron ore shipments and imports eased further, with an increase in food aid (reducing the need for commercial purchases) and the completion of the first stage of investment at the *guelbs* mine project. The devaluation of the ouguiya in 1985 reinforced these trends. The surplus was maintained in 1986, and increased in 1987–89, as expenditure on imports was contained, while higher earnings from sales of iron ore and the further devaluation of the ouguiya in relation to the US dollar effectively doubled ouguiya-dominated export receipts during 1984–89. However, the balance of trade moved into deficit (of UM 770m.) in 1990, before returning to a modest surplus (of UM 1,512m.) in 1991. This recovery proved short-lived, as a sharp full in earnings from iron ore (resulting from both lower volumes and international prices) caused a regression into deficit, of some UM 870m., in 1992. (It must be borne in mind that significant cross-border trade is not recorded in these statistics.) Such fluctuations in the trade balance were largely responsible for changes in the deficit (before official transfers) on the current account of the balance of payments, although this remained substantial throughout the late 1980s and into the 1990s, averaging some $143m. per year in 1990–92 (equivalent to about 14% of GNP—a very high ratio). Net of official transfers, the current-account deficit averaged $146m. per year in 1986–88, but declined to $75.5m. in 1989–91 before regressing sharply, to an estimated $104.5m., in 1992. Further variations will undoubtedly be caused by the new devaluation (by 28%) of the ouguiya in late 1992.

The substantial trade surpluses that occurred every year between 1965 and 1974 enabled Mauritania to service its extensive foreign borrowing, while reaching a payments surplus in 1971–74. This allowed Mauritania to leave the West African Monetary Union in 1973 and establish its own currency, the ouguiya, not linked to the franc. In the less favourable payments situation in subsequent years, Mauritania's reserves were sustained by continuing capital borrowing. The country's external public debt reached $632.2m. (disbursed) at the end of 1976, and its service payments in that year reached 33% of total foreign earnings, compared with only 3.8% in 1974. The foreign debt declined in the following years, reaching $590m. at the end of 1979, but the burden of repayment and interest remained at the same level because of the country's substantial borrowing of commercial funds. Despite a rescheduling of debt obtained by the regime that came to power in 1978, indebtedness continued to rise, totalling $1,342m. at the end of 1984, which was almost double the level of GNP in that year. In addition, arrears of more than $100m., not agreed with lenders, had accrued by the end of 1984, and the debt burden was forecast to rise again in subsequent years. Against the background of the economic stabilization programme agreed with the IMF, the Taya government secured reschedulings of its debt to official creditors in 1985, 1986 and 1987, on the latter occasion obtaining a 15-year rescheduling (including five years' grace) on repayment. Moreover, Mauritania continued to receive substantial aid, of which more than one-half was in grant form, from non-communist countries and multilateral agencies: such funding averaged $242m. per year in 1985–88. However, the debt rose inexorably, to $2,054m. at the end of 1987 (equivalent to 247% of annual GNP), and arrears on interest payments had doubled by 1988, to $52m. The debt-service ratio neared 25% of foreign earnings during most of this period. Mauritania was one of the African countries classified by the World Bank as 'debt-distressed' (i.e., without rescheduling, its debt-service ratio would exceed more than 30% of external earnings in 1988–90) and was thus eligible for the system of exceptional debt-relief that was agreed in principle at the summit meeting of industrialized nations, held in Toronto, Canada, in June 1988. Accordingly, in June 1989 the 'Paris Club' of Western official creditors agreed to reschedule $52m. of the country's external debt. Some bilateral donors agreed to relief: in both 1988 and 1989 the Federal Republic of Germany cancelled official trade obligations, and in mid-1990 France cancelled official loans, totalling $60m., contracted before the end of 1988. In all, debts totalling $180m. were cancelled in 1989. While the foreign debt continued to rise, to $2,232m. by the end of 1991, debt-rescheduling agreements meant that the debt-service ratio was reduced to 19.4% of the value of exports of goods and services in that year—although this continued to represent a considerable burden on the Mauritanian economy. Moreover, interest arrears continued to accumulate, and totalling $115m. by the end of 1992 (in which year the external debt amounted to $2,303m.). Mauritania's failure to pay off debt arrears or to achieve the fiscal targets agreed with the IMF for 1989–91 meant that no further debt relief was accorded until early 1993, when, following the IMF's agreement to extend an enhanced structural adjustment facility for the period to September 1995, the 'Paris Club' agreed to cancel one-half of the interest due on non-concessional debt and to reschedule the remainder over 23 years, with payment due to begin only after 10 years. This round of debt relief represents savings for Mauritania amounting to more than $200m. However, in the absence of a massive improvement in its export-earning capacity (which is unlikely to arise), the fragility of the Mauritanian economy means that the country's ability to service foreign debt will remain uncertain.

Statistical Survey

Figures exclude Mauritania's section of Western Sahara, annexed in 1976 and relinquished in 1979.

Source (unless otherwise stated): Office National de la Statistique, BP 240, Nouakchott; tel. 514-77.

Area and Population

AREA, POPULATION AND DENSITY

Area (sq km)	1,030,700*
Population (census results)†	
1 January 1977	1,338,830
5–20 April 1988	
Males	923,175
Females	941,061
Total	1,864,236
Population (official estimates at mid-year)	
1989	1,919,858
1991‡	2,036,000
Density (per sq km) at mid-1991	2.0

* 397,950 sq miles.

† Figures include estimates for Mauritania's nomad population (444,000 in 1977; 224,095 in 1988).

‡ No estimate is available for mid-1990.

REGIONS

Region	Chief town	Area ('000 sq km)	Population (1977 census, '000)
Hodh el Charqui	Néma	183	157
Hodh el Gharbi	Aïoun el Atrous	53	124
Assaba	Kiffa	37	129
Gorgol	Kaédi	14	149
Brakna	Aleg	33	151
Trarza	Rosso	68	216
Adrar	Atar	215	55
Dakhlet-Nouadhibou	Nouadhibou	22	23
Tagant	Tidjikja	95	75
Guidimaka	Sélibaby	10	83
Tiris Zemmour	F'Derik	253	23
Inchiri	Akjoujt	47	18
Nouakchott	Nouakchott	1	135
Total		1,030	1,338

PRINCIPAL TOWNS (population at census of January 1977)

Nouakchott (capital)	134,986*	Zouérate	17,947
Nouadhibou (Port-Etienne)	22,365	Atar	16,394
Kaédi	20,356	Rosso	15,888

* Estimated at 350,000 in 1984.

BIRTHS AND DEATHS (UN estimates, annual averages)

	1975–80	1980–85	1985–90
Birth rate (per 1,000)	46.7	46.5	46.2
Death rate (per 1,000)	22.1	20.5	19.0

Expectation of life (UN estimates, years at birth, 1985–90): 46.0 (males 44.4; females 47.6).

Source: UN, *World Population Prospects: The 1992 Revision.*

ECONOMICALLY ACTIVE POPULATION
(ILO estimates, '000 persons at mid-1980)

	Males	Females	Total
Agriculture, etc.	268	90	358
Industry	43	3	46
Services	101	11	112
Total	413	103	516

Source: ILO, *Economically Active Population Estimates and Projections, 1950–2025*.

Mid-1992 (estimates in '000): Agriculture, etc. 436; Total 685 (Source: FAO, *Production Yearbook*).

Agriculture

PRINCIPAL CROPS ('000 metric tons)

	1990	1991	1992
Millet and sorghum	49	60	53*
Rice (paddy)	52	42	18*
Maize	3	2	2*
Potatoes†	1	1	1
Sweet potatoes†	3	3	2
Yams†	3	3	3
Pulses	20	28	19†
Dates†	13	14	12
Watermelons	4	7	7†
Groundnuts (in shell)†	2	2	2

* Unofficial figure. † FAO estimate(s).

Source: FAO, *Production Yearbook*.

LIVESTOCK ('000 head, year ending September)

	1990	1991	1992
Cattle	1,350	1,400*	1,400*
Goats*	3,320	3,500	3,600
Sheep	5,100†	5,300*	5,400*
Asses*	151	153	154
Horses*	18	18	18
Camels	950	990	990*

Poultry (million)*: 4 in 1990; 4 in 1991; 4 in 1992.

* FAO estimate(s). † Unofficial figure.

Source: FAO, *Production Yearbook*.

LIVESTOCK PRODUCTS
(FAO estimates unless otherwise indicated, '000 metric tons)

	1990	1991	1992
Beef and veal	17*	20*	20
Mutton and lamb	10	10	10
Goats' meat	8	8	8
Poultry meat	4	4	4
Other meat	21	21	23
Cows' milk	97	98	96
Sheeps' milk	70	70	70
Goats' milk	80	81	80
Poultry eggs	4.3	4.4	4.3
Cattle hides	2.2	2.5	2.5
Sheep skins	1.4	1.4	1.4
Goat skins	0.9	1.0	1.0

* Unofficial figure.

Source: FAO, *Production Yearbook*.

Forestry

ROUNDWOOD REMOVALS
(FAO estimates, '000 cubic metres, excluding bark)

	1990	1991	1992
Sawlogs, veneer logs and logs for sleepers*	1	1	1
Other industrial wood†	4	4	4
Fuel wood	7	8	8
Total	12	13	13

* Assumed by the FAO to be unchanged since 1977.
† Assumed by the FAO to be unchanged since 1987.

Source: FAO, *Yearbook of Forest Products*.

Fishing

(FAO estimates unless otherwise indicated, '000 metric tons, live weight)

	1989	1990	1991
Freshwater fishes	6.0*	6.0	6.0
Flatfishes	2.0	2.0	2.0
Groupers and seabasses	6.7	6.6	6.5
Meagre	5.6	5.5	5.5
Porgies, seabreams, etc.	6.6	6.5	6.4
Sardinellas	2.8	2.8	2.7
Other marine fishes (incl. unspecified)	22.1	21.7	21.4
Total fish	51.9	51.1	50.5
Marine crustaceans	0.3*	0.3	0.3
Cuttlefishes and bobtail squids	3.6	3.5	3.5
Octopuses	30.1*	29.6	29.2
Other cephalopods	6.7	6.6	6.5
Total catch	92.6	91.0	90.0

* Official figure.

Source: FAO, *Yearbook of Fishery Statistics*.

Mining

('000 metric tons)

	1989	1990	1991
Iron ore: gross weight*	11,300	11,600	10,300
metal content†	7,874	7,250	n.a.
Gypsum (crude)†	6	8	3

* Estimates.
† Data from the US Bureau of Mines.

Sources: UN, *Monthly Bulletin of Statistics* and *Industrial Statistics Yearbook*.

Industry

SELECTED PRODUCTS
('000 metric tons, unless otherwise indicated)

	1988	1989	1990
Frozen and chilled fish*	33.7	34.0	34.0
Salted, dried and smoked fish*	0.7	0.8	1.2
Fish oils	2	2	3
Electric energy (million kWh)	121	129	140

* Data from the FAO.

1991: Electric energy (million kWh) 143.

Sources: UN, *Industrial Statistics Yearbook*; UN Economic Commission for Africa, *African Statistical Yearbook*.

Finance

CURRENCY AND EXCHANGE RATES

Monetary Units
5 khoums = 1 ouguiya (UM).

Sterling and Dollar Equivalents (31 March 1994)
£1 sterling = 181.91 ouguiyas;
US $1 = 122.53 ouguiyas;
1,000 ouguiyas = £5.497 = $8.161.

Average Exchange Rate (ouguiyas per US $)
1991 81.946
1992 87.027
1993 120.806

BUDGET* (million ouguiyas)

Revenue	1978	1979
Tax revenue	3,875	4,937
Taxes on income and profits	1,049	1,551
Social security contributions	385	426
Taxes on goods and services	850	1,177
Turnover taxes	590	740
Excises	204	188
Taxes on services	35	213
Import duties	1,461	1,678
Other current revenue	1,810	768
Property income	141	176
Fines and forfeits	788	282
Capital revenue	862	679
Sales of fishing rights	816	662
Other items (net)†	–118	97
Grants from abroad	3,341	3,182
Total	9,770	9,663

Expenditure	1978	1979
General public services	2,405	2,490
Defence	3,541	3,238
Education	1,036	1,147
Health	318	310
Social security and welfare	379	423
Other community and social services	153	172
Economic services	1,125	1,485
Agriculture, forestry and fishing	631	781
Roads	132	261
Other transport	263	281
Other purposes	728	627
Sub-total	9,685	9,892
Less: Contributions to social security	–69	–78
Other items (net)†	–545	1,199
Lending (minus repayments)	1,570	114
Total	10,641	11,127

* Figures refer to the consolidated accounts of the general budget, the National Social Security Fund, the Mauritanian Red Crescent and the Ecole Nationale d'Administration.

† Including adjustment of accounts to a cash basis.

1983 (general budget only, million ouguiyas): Revenue 8,963 (excluding grants 161); Expenditure 10,109 (excluding net lending 233).

Source: IMF, *Government Finance Statistics Yearbook.*

1984 (estimates, million ouguiyas): Revenue 11,056; Expenditure 13,741.

1986‡ (revised estimates, million ouguiyas): Revenue 14,655; Expenditure 19,742 (recurrent 12,949; debt-servicing 4,516).

1987 (estimates, million ouguiyas): Budget balanced at 19,842.

1988 (estimates, million ouguiyas): Budget balanced at 20,504.

1989 (estimates, million ouguiyas): Budget balanced at 22,000.

1990 (estimates, million ouguiyas): Budget balanced at 22,119.

1991 (estimates, million ouguiyas): Budget balanced at 23,200.

1992 (estimates, million ouguiyas): Budget balanced at 24,723.

1993 (estimates, million ouguiyas): Budget balanced at 32,200.

1994 (estimates, million ouguiyas): Budget balanced at 38,169 (investment expenditure 19,781).

‡ Figures for 1985 are not available.

CENTRAL BANK RESERVES (US $ million at 31 December)

	1990	1991	1992
Gold*	4.4	4.2	3.8
IMF special drawing rights	0.8	0.1	0.1
Foreign exchange	53.3	67.5	61.1
Total	58.5	71.8	65.0

* Valued at market-related prices.

Source: IMF, *International Financial Statistics.*

MONEY SUPPLY (million ouguiyas at 31 December)

	1991	1992	1993
Currency outside banks	7,335	7,898	9,097
Demand deposits at deposit money banks	11,646	11,986	11,508
Total money (incl. others)	19,376	20,202	20,938

Source: IMF, *International Financial Statistics.*

COST OF LIVING (Consumer Price Index for Mauritanian households in Nouakchott; base: 1990 = 100)

	1991	1992	1993
All items	105.6	116.3	127.2

Source: IMF, *International Financial Statistics.*

NATIONAL ACCOUNTS
(million ouguiyas in current prices)

Expenditure on the Gross Domestic Product

	1989	1990	1991
Government final consumption expenditure	15,000	16,748	17,619
Private final consumption expenditure	54,580	60,582	65,065
Increase in stocks	200	228	222
Gross fixed capital formation	14,670	16,363	17,091
Total domestic expenditure	84,450	93,921	99,997
Exports of goods and services	46,350	51,404	56,647
Less Imports of goods and services	48,300	53,625	59,194
GDP in purchasers' values	82,500	91,700	97,450
GDP at constant 1980 prices	38,609	40,154	41,681

Gross Domestic Product by Economic Activity

	1989	1990	1991
Agriculture, hunting, forestry and fishing	19,500	21,100	23,421
Mining and quarrying	6,290	8,590	9,234
Manufacturing	3,600	4,700	5,264
Electricity, gas and water	650	720	809
Construction	3,770	4,020	4,193
Trade, restaurants and hotels	8,670	9,670	10,608
Transport, storage and communications	6,800	7,400	8,140
Finance, insurance, real estate and business services	3,480	4,080	4,525
Government services	8,620	9,520	10,129
Other services	2,070	2,260	2,446
GDP at factor cost	63,450	72,060	78,770
Indirect taxes, *less* subsidies	19,050	19,640	18,680
GDP in purchasers' values	82,500	91,700	97,450

Source: UN Economic Commission for Africa, *African Statistical Yearbook.*

BALANCE OF PAYMENTS (US $ million)

	1989	1990	1991
Merchandise exports f.o.b.	447.9	443.9	435.8
Merchandise imports f.o.b.	-349.3	-382.9	-399.1
Trade balance	98.6	61.0	36.7
Exports of services	33.6	26.8	31.2
Imports of services	-196.0	-136.8	-139.4
Other income received	5.6	3.8	2.0
Other income paid	-55.6	-50.2	-34.9
Private unrequited transfers (net)	-25.0	-15.6	-17.2
Official unrequited transfers (net)	120.3	101.5	103.3
Current balance	-18.6	-9.6	-18.3
Direct investment (net)	3.5	6.7	2.3
Other capital (net)	13.4	-7.2	23.6
Net errors and omissions	-3.6	-62.3	8.6
Overall balance	-5.3	-72.5	16.3

Source: IMF, *International Financial Statistics.*

External Trade

PRINCIPAL COMMODITIES (million ouguiyas)

Imports c.i.f.	1978	1979	1980
Consumer goods	3,999.4	5,438.4	6,111.0
Tea, sugar and rice	1,530.8	1,604.6	2,275.0
Other foodstuffs	1,196.9	2,308.8	2,132.0
Other consumer goods	1,271.7	1,524.6	1,704.0
Transport equipment	657.8	795.6	1,332.6
Vehicles	351.8	268.6	569.4
Spare parts and tyres	306.0	527.0	704.7
Investment goods	1,023.9	1,475.7	2,320.4
Building materials	609.8	670.7	778.9
Capital goods	414.1	805.0	1,541.5
Fuels	606.1	2,053.8	1,557.0
Others	2,077.6	2,456.5	1,797.0
Total	8,364.8	12,219.6	13,118.9

Total imports (million ouguiyas): 12,793 (Petroleum 1,773) in 1981; 14,213 (Petroleum 3,334) in 1982; 12,411 (Petroleum 2,278) in 1983; 13,201 (Petroleum 3,161) in 1984; 17,806 (Petroleum 2,487) in 1985; 16,429 (Petroleum 3,439) in 1986; 17,392 (Petroleum 2,639) in 1987; 18,029 (Petroleum 2,074) in 1988; 18,462 (Petroleum 2,630) in 1989.

1990 (imports, million ouguiyas): Petroleum 4,493.

Source (for 1981–90): IMF, *International Financial Statistics.*

Total imports (million ouguiyas): 18,412 in 1991.

Exports f.o.b.	1987	1988	1989
Iron ore	9,815	10,599	15,035
Fish and fish products	20,088	16,056	21,297
Total (incl. others)	31,608	26,655	36,332

1990 (exports, million ouguiyas): Iron ore 11,355; Fish and fish products 26,373.

Source: IMF, *International Financial Statistics.*

1991 (total exports, million ouguiyas): 18,231.

PRINCIPAL TRADING PARTNERS (US $'000)

Imports c.i.f.	1982	1983	1984
France	45,632	52,929	39,435
Senegal	21,082	20,201	18,570
Spain	25,792	22,850	31,694
Other Europe	40,338	33,837	38,304
Others	140,177	96,687	85,368
Total	273,021	226,504	213,371

Exports f.o.b.	1982	1983	1984
France	41,751	29,205	35,221
Japan	14,846	34,859	37,239
Senegal	2,055	1,153	540
Spain	25,333	35,031	29,613
Others	149,283	204,453	189,712
Total	233,268	304,701	297,325

Source: UN, *International Trade Statistics Yearbook.*

Transport

RAILWAYS

1984: Passengers carried 19,353; Passenger-km 7m.; Freight carried 9.1m. metric tons; Freight ton-km 6,142m.

Freight ton-km (million): 6,365 in 1985; 6,411 in 1986; 6,473 in 1987; 6,535 in 1988; 6,610 in 1989; 6,690 in 1990; 6,720 in 1991 (figures for 1988–91 are estimates) (Source: UN Economic Commission for Africa, *African Statistical Yearbook*).

ROAD TRAFFIC
(estimates, '000 motor vehicles in use)

	1989	1990	1991
Passenger cars	13	13	14
Commercial vehicles	6	6	7

Source: UN Economic Commission for Africa, *African Statistical Yearbook.*

INTERNATIONAL SEA-BORNE SHIPPING
(estimated freight traffic, '000 metric tons)

	1988	1989	1990
Goods loaded	8,960	9,010	10,037
Goods unloaded	610	616	674

Source: UN, *Monthly Bulletin of Statistics.*

CIVIL AVIATION (traffic on scheduled services)*

	1989	1990	1991
Kilometres flown (million)	3	4	3
Passengers carried ('000)	220	223	210
Passenger-km (million)	298	307	278
Freight ton-km (million)	18	18	16
Mail ton-km (million)	1	1	1

* Including an apportionment of the traffic of Air Afrique.

Source: UN, *Statistical Yearbook.*

Tourism

Tourist Arrivals (estimates, '000): 12 in 1984; 13 in 1985; 13 in 1986.

Receipts from Tourism (US $ million): 7 in 1984; 5 in 1985; 8 in 1986; 14 in 1987; 14 in 1988; 15 in 1989; 14 in 1990; 13 in 1991 (figures for 1989–91 are estimates).

Source: UN Economic Commission for Africa, *African Statistical Yearbook.*

Communications Media

	1989	1990	1991
Radio receivers ('000 in use)	282	291	300
Television receivers ('000 in use)	45	47	49
Telephones ('000 in use)*	15	16	17
Daily newspapers			
Number	n.a.	1	n.a.
Average circulation ('000 copies)	n.a.	1*	n.a.

* Estimate(s).

Sources: UNESCO, *Statistical Yearbook*; UN Economic Commission for Africa, *African Statistical Yearbook*.

Education

(1991/92)

	Institutions	Teachers	Students		
			Males	Females	Total
Primary	1,309	3,967	106,573	80,629	187,202
Secondary					
General	56	1,905	24,396	12,486	36,882
Teacher training	2	51	559	193	752
Vocational	3	118	885	145	1,030
Higher	4	176	4,983	867	5,850

Source: Ministère de l'Education Nationale, Nouakchott.

Directory

While no longer an official language under the terms of the 1991 Constitution (see below), French is still widely used in Mauritania, especially in the commercial sector. Many organizations are therefore listed under their French names, by which they are generally known.

The Constitution

The Constitution of the Arab and African Islamic Republic of Mauritania was approved in a national referendum on 12 July 1991.

The Constitution provides for the establishment of a multi-party political system. The President of the Republic is elected, by universal adult suffrage (the minimum age for voters being 18 years), for a period of six years: no limitations regarding the renewal of the presidential mandate are stipulated. Legislative power is vested in a National Assembly (elected by universal suffrage for a period of five years) and in a Senate (elected by municipal leaders with a six-year mandate—part of its membership being elected every two years). The President of the Republic is empowered to appoint a head of government. Provision is also made for the establishment of a Constitutional Council and a Supreme Islamic Council (both of which were inaugurated in 1992), as well as an Economic and Social Council.

The Constitution states that the official language is Arabic, and that the national languages are Arabic, Poular, Wolof and Solinke.

The Government

HEAD OF STATE

President: Col MAAWIYA OULD SID'AHMED TAYA (took office 12 December 1984; elected President 17 January 1992).

COUNCIL OF MINISTERS

(September 1994)

Prime Minister: SIDI MOHAMED OULD BOUBACAR.

Minister of State Control: ETHMANE SID'AHMED YESSA.

Minister of Foreign Affairs and Co-operation: MOHAMED SALEM OULD LEKHEL.

Minister of Defence: Col AHMED OULD MINNIH.

Minister of Justice: ADAMA SAMBA SOW.

Minister of the Interior, Posts and Telecommunications: MOHAMED LEMINE SALEM OULD DAH

Minister of Finance: LEMRABET SIDI MAHMOUD OULD CHEIKH AHMED..

Minister of Fisheries and Marine Economy: CHEIKH MOHAMED FALL KANE.

Minister of Planning and Employment: TAKI OULD SIDI.

Minister of Trade, Handicrafts and Tourism: CHEIKH MALAININE OULD CH'BIH.

Minister of Industry and Mines: SIDI MOHAMED OULD MOHAMED FALL.

Minister of Equipment and Transport: DIAGANA MOUSSA.

Minister of National Education: MOKHTAR OULD HAYE.

Minister of the Civil Service, Labour, Youth and Sports: ABDALLAHI OULD ABDI.

Minister of Water and Energy: MOHAMED LEMINE OULD AHMED.

Minister of Rural Development and the Environment: SGHAIER OULD MBAREK.

Minister of Health and Social Affairs: MOHAMED OULD LAMAR.

Minister of Culture and Islamic Orientation: LIMAM OULD TAGADDI.

Minister of Information: AHMED OULD KHALIFAH OULD JIDDOU.

Minister of Women's Affairs: MARIAM BINT AHMED AICHE.

Minister in charge of Relations with Parliament: RACHID OULD SALEH.

Minister-Adviser to the President of the Republic: Lt-Col N'DIAYE KANE.

Secretary-General of the Government: BA SILAY.

Assistant Secretary-General of the Government: BA ALASSANE YERO.

Secretary of State for Literacy and Basic Education and for the Union of the Arab Maghreb Affairs: CHEIKH OULD ALI.

Secretary of State, in charge of Civil Status: KHATTAR OULD CHEIKH AHMED.

MINISTRIES

Office of the President: Présidence de la République, BP 184, Nouakchott; tel. 523-17; telex 580.

Ministry of the Civil Service, Labour, Youth and Sports: Nouakchott.

Ministry of Culture and Islamic Orientation: BP 223, Nouakchott; tel. 511-30; telex 585.

Ministry of Defence: BP 184, Nouakchott; tel. 520-20; telex 566.

Ministry of Finance: BP 181, Nouakchott; tel. 520-20; telex 572.

Ministry of Equipment and Transport: BP 237, Nouakchott; telex 585.

Ministry of Fisheries and Marine Economy: BP 137, Nouakchott; tel. 524-76; telex 595; fax 531-46.

Ministry of Foreign Affairs and Co-operation: BP 230, Nouakchott; tel. 520-20; telex 585.

Ministry of Health and Social Affairs: BP 177, Nouakchott; tel. 518-58.

Ministry of Industry and Mines: BP 183, Nouakchott; tel. 513-18.

Ministry of Information: BP 223, Nouakchott.

Ministry of the Interior, Posts and Telecommunications: Nouakchott; tel. 529-34; telex 844.

Ministry of Justice: BP 350, Nouakchott; tel. 510-83.

Ministry of National Education: BP 387, Nouakchott; tel. 518-98.

Ministry of Planning and Employment: Nouakchott.

Ministry of Rural Development and the Environment: BP 366, Nouakchott; tel. 520-20 (ext. 386).

Ministry of State Control: Nouakchott.

Ministry of Trade, Handicrafts and Tourism: Nouakchott.

Ministry of Water and Energy: Nouakchott.

President and Legislature

PRESIDENT

Election, 17 January 1992

	Votes	% of total
MAAWIYA OULD SID'AHMED TAYA	345,583	62.65
AHMED OULD DADDAH	180,658	32.75
MOUSTAPHA OULD MOHAMED SALEK	15,735	2.85
MOHAMED MAHMOUD OULD MAH	7,506	1.36
Total*	551,575	100.00

* Included in the total number of valid votes are 2,093 'neutral votes'.

SENATE

President: DIENG BOUBOU FARBA.

Elections to the 56-member Senate took place on 3 and 10 April 1992. It was reported that 36 candidates of the Democratic and Social Republican Party (DSRP) were elected; 17 seats were won by independent candidates, and a further three senators were to represent the interests of Mauritanians resident abroad. Part of the Senate is subject to re-election every two years: accordingly, elections for 17 senators took place on 15 and 22 April 1994, while elections for the three representatives of Mauritanians abroad were conducted by the Senate on 14 May. The DSRP retained its majority in the upper house following the elections.

NATIONAL ASSEMBLY

President: Commdt (retd) CHEIKH SID'AHMED OULD BABA.

General Election, 6 and 13 March 1992

	Seats
Democratic and Social Republican Party	67
Mauritanian Party for Renewal	1
Rally for Democracy and National Unity	1
Independent	10
Total	79

Advisory Councils

Constitutional Council: f. 1992; includes six mems, three nominated by the Head of State and three designated by the Presidents of the Senate and National Assembly; Pres. DIDI OULD BOUNAAMA; Sec.-Gen. MOHAMED OULD MREHIB.

Supreme Islamic Council (al-Majlis al-Islamiya al-A'la'): f. 1992.

The 1991 Constitution also provides for the establishment of an Economic and Social Council.

Political Organizations

Following the adoption of the July 1991 Constitution, legislation to permit the authorization of political parties was promulgated. By mid-1994 at least 18 parties had been accorded official status. Among these were:

Democratic and Social Republican Party (DSRP): f. 1991; party of President Taya; Leader Cheikh SID'AHMED OULD BABA.

El Hor: f. 1994, following split from UDF—NE; Leader MESSAOUD OULD BOULKHEIR.

Mauritanian Party for Renewal (MPR): f. 1991; Leader MOULAYE EL HASSAN OULD JEYID.

Movement of Independent Democrats (MID): f. 1994, following split from UDF—NE; Leader ABEL-AID OULD KEBDE.

People's Progressive Party (PPP): f. 1991; Leader TALEB OULD JIDDOU.

Rally for Democracy and National Unity (RDNU): f. 1991; Chair. AHMED OULD SIDI BABA.

Socialist and Democratic People's Union (SDPU): f. 1991; Leader MOHAMED MAHMOUD OULD MAH.

Union for Democracy and Progress (UDP): f. 1993; Pres. HAMDI OULD MOUKNASS; Sec.-Gen. AHMED KILLI.

Union of Democratic Forces—New Era (UDF—NE): f. 1991 as Union of Democratic Forces, renamed 1992, restructured (following splits) 1994; Sec.-Gen. AHMED OULD DADDAH.

Unauthorized but influential is the Islamic **Ummah Party** (the Constitution prohibits the authorization of religious political organizations), founded in 1991. The clandestine anti-government **Forces de libération africaine de Mauritanie (FLAM)**, formed in 1983 to represent black Africans in Mauritania, remained active in 1993, while a further outlawed group, the **Rassemblement pour la renaissance des nègres-africains de la Mauritanie**, has conducted a sporadic campaign of violence against the Government and its supporters.

Diplomatic Representation

EMBASSIES IN MAURITANIA

Algeria: Nouakchott; telex 871; Ambassador: ZERGUINE MOHAMED.

China, People's Republic: BP 196, Nouakchott; Ambassador: LIU BAI.

Egypt: BP 176, Nouakchott; telex 520; Ambassador: (vacant).

France: BP 231, rue Ahmed Ould M'Hamed, Nouakchott; tel. 517-40; telex 582; Ambassador: MICHEL RAIMBAUD.

Gabon: BP 38, Nouakchott; tel. 529-19; telex 593; Ambassador: JACQUES BONAVENTURE ESSONGHE.

Germany: BP 372, Nouakchott; tel. 510-32; telex 5555; fax 517-22; Ambassador: FRITZ HERMANN FLIMM.

Korea, Republic: BP 324, Nouakchott; tel. 537-86; fax 544-43; Chargé d'affaires a.i.: WON CHOL-KIM.

Libya: Nouakchott; telex 534; Ambassador: NASSER ABASS OTHMANE.

Morocco: BP 621, Nouakchott; tel. 514-11; telex 550; Ambassador: ABDERRAHMANE EL KOUHEN.

Nigeria: BP 367, Nouakchott; telex 869; Ambassador: ABUBACAR MAHAMED.

Russia: BP 251, Nouakchott; tel. 519-73; Ambassador: VLADIMIR S. SHISHOV.

Saudi Arabia: Nouakchott; telex 813; Ambassador: MOHAMED AL FADH EL ISSA.

Senegal: BP 611, Nouakchott; Ambassador: DOUDOU DIOP.

Spain: BP 232, Nouakchott; tel. 510-28; telex 563; Ambassador: MANUEL GÓMEZ DE VALENZUELA.

Tunisia: BP 681, Nouakchott; tel. 528-71; telex 857; Ambassador: MOHAMED H'SAIRI.

USA: BP 222, Nouakchott; tel. 526-60; telex 558; fax 525-89; Ambassador: GORDON S. BROWN.

Zaire: BP 487, Nouakchott; tel. 528-36; telex 812; Ambassador: KYALWE MIHAMBO.

Judicial System

The Code of Law was promulgated in 1961 and subsequently modified to integrate modern law with Islamic institutions and practices. The main courts comprise a magistrate's court with six regional sections, 42 departmental civil courts and labour courts.

Shari'a (Islamic) law was introduced in February 1980. A special Islamic court was established in March of that year, presided over by a magistrate of Islamic law, assisted by two counsellors and two *ulemas* (Muslim jurists and interpreters of the Koran).

Supreme Court: Palais de Justice, Nouakchott; tel. 521-20; f. 1961; intended to ensure the independence of the judiciary; the court is competent in juridical, administrative and electoral matters; Pres. AHMEDOU OULD ABDELKADER.

Religion

ISLAM

Islam is the official religion, and the population are almost entirely Muslims of the Malekite rite. The major religious groups are the Tijaniya and the Qadiriya. Chinguetti, in the district of Adrar, is the seventh Holy Place in Islam.

CHRISTIANITY

Roman Catholic Church

Mauritania comprises the single diocese of Nouakchott, directly responsible to the Holy See. The Bishop participates in the Bishops' Conference of Senegal, Mauritania, Cape Verde and Guinea-Bissau, based in Dakar, Senegal. At 31 December 1992 there were an estimated 4,500 adherents, mainly non-nationals, in the country.

Bishop of Nouakchott: Mgr ROBERT DE CHEVIGNY, Evêché, BP 353, Nouakchott; tel. 515-15; fax 537-51.

The Press

Bulletin de la Chambre de Commerce: BP 215, Nouakchott; tel. 522-14; telex 581.

Ach-Chaab: BP 371, Nouakchott; tel. 535-23; telex 583; daily; French and Arabic; publ. by Agence Mauritanienne de l'Information; Dir-Gen. HADEMINE OULD SADY.

Al-Bayane: Nouakchott; f. 1991; independent; Arabic and French; Dir YAHYA OULD BECHIR.

Le Calame: Nouakchott; weekly; French and Arabic; independent.

Eveil-Hebdo: Nouakchott; weekly; independent.

Journal Officiel: Ministry of Justice, BP 350, Nouakchott; fortnightly.

Mauritanie Demain: Nouakchott; monthly; independent; Editor MUBARAK OULD BEIROUK.

Le Peuple: BP 371, Nouakchott; 6 a year; French and Arabic.

NEWS AGENCIES

Agence Mauritanienne de l'Information (AMI): BP 371, Nouakchott; tel. 529-70; telex 525; fmrly Agence Mauritanienne de Presse, name changed 1990; state-controlled; Dir RACHID OULD SALEH.

Foreign Bureau

Xinhua (New China) News Agency (People's Republic of China): Nouakchott; telex 541; Correspondent WANG TIANRUI.

Agence France-Presse is also represented in Mauritania.

Publishers

Imprimerie Commerciale et Administrative de Mauritanie: BP 164, Nouakchott; textbooks, educational.

Société Mauritanienne de Presse et d'Impression (SMPI): BP 371, Nouakchott; tel. 527-19; telex 877; f. 1978; state-owned; Pres. MOHAMED OULD BOUBACAR; Man. Dir MOUSSA OULD EBNOU.

Société Nationale d'Impression: BP 618, Nouakchott; govt publishing house; Pres. MOUSTAPHA SALECK OULD AHMED BRIHIM.

Société Nouvelle d'Impression et de Presse Professionnelles: Nouakchott.

Radio and Television

In 1991, according to estimates by UNESCO, there were 300,000 radio receivers and 49,000 television receivers in use.

Office de Radiodiffusion et Télévision de Mauritanie (ORTM): BP 200, Nouakchott; tel. 521-64; telex 515; f. 1958; state-owned; five transmitters; radio broadcasts in Arabic, French, Sarakolé, Toucouleur and Wolof; Dir SIDI OULD CHEIKH.

Finance

(cap. = capital; res = reserves; dep. = deposits; m. = million; br. = branch; amounts in UM)

BANKING

Central Bank

Banque Centrale de Mauritanie (BCM): ave de l'Indépendance, BP 623, Nouakchott; tel. 522-06; telex 532; fax 527-59; f. 1973; bank of issue; cap. 200m.; Gov. MOUHAMEDOU OULD MICHEL; 4 brs.

Commercial Banks

Banque al-Baraka Mauritanienne Islamique (BAMIS): ave du Roi Fayçal, BP 650, Nouakchott; tel. 514-24; telex 535; fax 516-21; f. 1985; 84% owned by al-Baraka Group (Saudi Arabia); cap. 3,000m. (1994); Chair. Dr HASSAN ABDALLAH KAMEL; Man. Dir MOHAMED LEMINE JEILANI.

Banque Mauritanienne pour le Commerce International (BMCI): Immeuble BMCI, ave Gamal-Abdel-Nasser, BP 622, Nouakchott; tel. 524-69; telex 5543; fax 520-45; f. 1974; privately-owned; cap. 750m., res 912m., dep. 7,323m. (Dec. 1990); Chair. and Man. Dir SIDI MOHAMED ABASS; brs at Nouadhibou, Nema and Aioun.

Banque Nationale de Mauritanie (BNM): ave Gamal-Abdel-Nasser, BP 614, Nouakchott; tel. 526-02; telex 567; fax 533-95; f. 1988 by merger; privately-owned; cap. 500m. (Sept. 1988); Man. Dir MOHAMED O. A. O. NOUEIGUED.

Chinguitty Bank: ave Gamal-Abdel-Nasser, BP 626, Nouakchott; tel. 521-42; telex 5562; fax 533-82; f. 1972 as Banque Arabe Libyenne-Mauritanienne pour le Commerce Extérieur et le Développement, name changed 1993; 50% state-owned, 50% owned by Libyan Arab Foreign Bank; cap. 1,500m. (Dec. 1993); Chair. HASSEN OULD SALEH; Man. Dir OMAR MOHAMED SEGHAYER; br. at Nouadhibou.

INSURANCE

Société Mauritanienne d'Assurances et de Réassurances (SMAR): 12 ave Gamal-Abdel-Nasser, BP 163, Nouakchott; tel. 526-50; telex 527; fax 518-18; f. 1974; 51% govt-owned, 49% owned by BCM; cap. 1,000m.; Chair. MAOULOUD OULD SIDI ABDALLA; Man. Dir ANNE AMADOU BABALY.

In late 1992 the Government approved proposals to end SMAR's insurance monopoly.

Trade and Industry

CHAMBER OF COMMERCE

Chambre de Commerce, d'Agriculture, d'Elevage, d'Industrie et des Mines de Mauritanie: BP 215, Nouakchott; tel. 522-14; telex 581; f. 1954; Chair. KANE YAYA.

DEVELOPMENT ORGANIZATIONS

Caisse Française de Développement (CFD): quartier des Ambassades, BP 211, Nouakchott; fmrly Caisse Centrale de Coopération Economique, name changed 1992; tel. 523-09; telex 516; Dir M. CATTIN.

Mission Française de Coopération: BP 203, Nouakchott; tel. 521-21; telex 582; administers bilateral aid; Dir JEAN HABERT.

Office Mauritanien des Céréales (OMC): BP 368, Nouakchott; tel. 528-30; telex 513; f. 1975; state-owned; Pres. WALY N'DAO; Dir MOHAMED BOCOUM.

Société Arabe Mauritano-Libyenne de Développement Agricole (SAMALIDA): BP 658, Nouakchott; tel. 537-15; f. 1980; cap. 350m. UM; 51% state-owned, 49% owned by Govt of Libya; Dir-Gen. O. TURKI.

Société Nationale de Développement Rural (SONADER): BP 321, Nouakchott; tel. 521-61; telex 807; Dir ABDERRAHMANE OULD SAIBOTT.

TRADE ORGANIZATIONS

Bureau d'Achats pour la République Islamique de Mauritanie (BARIM): ave du Président J. F. Kennedy, BP 272, Nouakchott; tel. 510-57; telex 810; f. 1969; cap. 6m. UM; importer and exporter; Dir-Gen. D. DIABIRA.

Société Mauritanienne de Commercialisation du Poisson (SMCP): BP 259, Nouadhibou; tel. 452-81; telex 420; f. 1984; cap. 500m. UM; state-owned; partial transfer to private ownership pending in 1994; until 1992 monopoly exporter of demersal fish and crustaceans; Pres. MOHAMED SALEM OULD LEKHAL; Dir-Gen. MOHAMED OULD MOCTAR.

Société Mauritanienne de Commercialisation des Produits Pétroliers (SMCPP): BP 679, Nouakchott; tel. 526-61; telex 849; f. 1980; cap. 120m. UM; state-owned; partial transfer to private ownership pending in 1994; import and distribution of petroleum products; Dir-Gen. ABDALLAHI OULD MOUHAMADEN.

Société Nationale d'Importation et d'Exportation (SONIMEX): BP 290, Nouakchott; tel. 514-72; telex 561; f. 1966; cap. 914m. UM; 74% state-owned; import of foodstuffs and textiles; export of gum-arabic; Pres. MOHAMED KHATTRY OULD SEGANE; Dir-Gen. MOUSSA FALL.

EMPLOYERS' ORGANIZATIONS

Confédération Générale des Employeurs de Mauritanie (CGEM): BP 383, Nouakchott; telex 859; f. 1974; professional asscn for all employers active in Mauritania; Sec.-Gen. MOHAMED ALI OULD SIDI MOHAMED.

Union Nationale des Industries et Entreprises de Mauritanie (UNIEMA): BP 215, Nouakchott.

MAJOR INDUSTRIAL COMPANIES

The following are some of the largest companies in terms of either capital investment or employment:

Compagnie Mauritano-Coréenne de Pêche (COMACOP): BP 527, Nouakchott; tel. 537-47; telex 592; f. 1977; cap. 230m. UM;

fishing and freezer complex; Chair. and Man. Dir ABDOU OULD AL HACHEME.

Complexe Minier du Nord (COMINOR): BP 1260, Nouadhibou; tel. 451-74; telex 426; fmrly MIFERMA, nationalized 1974; cap. 2,660m. UM; 100m. tons of iron ore are available for exploitation, yielding 66% pure iron; Operations Man. (at Zouérate) M. MILLIOTTE.

Mines d'Or d'Akjoujt (MORAK): BP 9, Akjoujt; f. 1991; cap. 459m. UM; 45% owned by SAMIN, 42.5% by General Gold Resources (Australia), 12.5% by International Finance Corpn; exploitation of gold deposits and exploration of copper reserves at Akjoujt; Chair. CHEIKH SID'EL MOKTAR OULD CHEIKH ABDELLAHI.

Société Algéro-Mauritanienne des Pêches (ALMAP): BP 321, Nouadhibou; tel. 451-48; telex 424; f. 1974; cap. 180m. UM; 51% state-owned, 49% owned by govt of Algeria; fishing, processing of fishery products; Dir BRAHIM OULD BOIDAHA; 500 employees.

Société Arabe du Fer et de l'Acier (SAFA): BP 114, Nouadhibou; tel. 453-89; telex 444; f. 1984; cap. 450m. UM; 33% owned by SNIM—SEM; steel rolling mill; Chair. MOHAMED SALECK OULD HEYINE; Man. Dir AHMEDOU OULD JIDDOU.

Société Arabe des Industries Métallurgiques Mauritano-Koweïtienne (SAMIA): BP 6247, Nouakchott; tel. 526-41; telex 508; f. 1974; cap. 1,400m. UM; 50% state-owned, 50% owned by Kuwait Foreign Trade, Contracting and Investment Co; copper refining; Chair. and Man. Dir MOHAMED YEHDIH OULD EL HACEN; Man. Dir AHMED WAFI.

Société Arabe Libyenne-Mauritanienne des Ressources Maritimes (SALIMAUREM): BP 75, Nouadhibou; tel. 452-41; telex 452; f. 1978; cap. 2,300m. UM; 50% state-owned, 50% owned by Libyan-Arab Finance Co; fishing and fish processing; freezer factory; Chair. AHMED OULD GHNAHALLA; Dir-Gen. SALA MOHAMED ARIBI.

Société Arabe des Mines d'Inchiri (SAMIN): BP 9, Akjoujt; tel. 671-04; telex 715; f. 1981; cap. 3,276m. UM; 37.5% state-owned, 62.5% owned by Arab interests; Chair. TAHER TABET; Man. Dir ABDERRAHMANE TAYEB.

Société de Construction et de Gestion Immobilière de Mauritanie (SOCOGIM): BP 28, Nouakchott; tel. 517-75; f. 1974; cap. 583m. UM; 89% state-owned; Chair. ABDALLAH OULD MOHAMEDEN; Man. Dir AHMED OULD MOHAMED KHAIROU.

Société Industrielle Mauritano-Roumaine pour la Mise en Valeur et l'Exploitation des Produits Aquatiques (SIMAR): Nouakchott; tel. 529-24; telex 823; f. 1980; cap. 180m. UM; transfer to state private ownership pending in 1993; fishing enterprise; Dir CONSTANTIN FLORIN.

Société Mauritanienne des Industries de Raffinage (SOMIR): BP 73, Nouadhibou; tel. 452-40; telex 439; f. 1981; cap. 4,600m. UM; operates a petroleum refinery and negotiates overseas transactions; Chair. MOUSTAFA KANE; Man. Dir MOUSSA FALL.

Société Nationale d'Eau et d'Electricité (SONELEC): ave de l'Indépendance, BP 355, Nouakchott; tel. 523-08; telex 587; f. 1968; cap. 400m. UM; state-owned; production and distribution of electricity and water; Man. Dir Capt. MOHAMED OULD BOUEÏDA.

Société Nationale Industrielle et Minière—Société d'Economie Mixte (SNIM—SEM): BP 42, Nouadhibou; tel. 451-90; telex 426; f. 1972; cap. 9,059.5m. UM; 71% state-owned; opened to foreign investment in 1978; research, exploitation, processing and marketing of minerals; Chair. CHEIKH SID'EL MOKTAR OULD CHEIKH ABDALLAHI; Man. Dir MOHAMED SALECK OULD HEYINE; 4,400 employees.

TRADE UNIONS

Confédération Générale des Travailleurs de Mauritanie: Nouakchott; f. 1992, officially recognized as Mauritania's first independent trade union confederation January 1994.

Union des Travailleurs de Mauritanie (UTM): Bourse du Travail, BP 630, Nouakchott; f. 1961; Sec.-Gen. MOHAMED BRAHIM (acting); 45,000 mems.

Transport

RAILWAYS

A 670-km railway connects the iron-ore deposits at Zouérate with Nouadhibou; a 40-km extension services the reserves at El Rhein, and a 30-km extension those at M'Haoudat. Motive power is diesel-electric. The Société Nationale Industrielle et Minière—Société d'Economie Mixte (SNIM—SEM) operates one of the longest (2.4 km) and heaviest (22,000 metric tons) trains in the world.

SNIM—Direction du Chemin de Fer et du Port: BP 42, Nouadhibou; tel. 451-74; telex 426; fax 453-96; f. 1963, present ownership (SNIM—SEM) since 1974; Gen. Man. MOHAMED SALECK OULD HEYINE; Dir KHALIA OULD BEYAH.

ROADS

In 1986 there were about 7,500 km of roads and tracks, of which main roads comprised some 2,700 km, and 22.5% of the road network (about 1,686 km) was tarred. The 1,100-km Trans-Mauritania highway, completed in 1985, links Nouakchott with Néma in the east of the country. Plans exist for the construction of a 7,400-km highway, linking Nouakchott with the Libyan port of Tubruq (Tobruk).

Société des Transports Publics de Nouakchott: BP 342, Nouakchott; tel. 529-53; f. 1975; Pres. CHEIKH MALAININE ROBERT; Dir-Gen. MAMADOU SOULEYMANE KANE.

INLAND WATERWAYS

The River Senegal is navigable in the wet season by small coastal vessels as far as Kayes (Mali) and by river vessels as far as Kaédi; in the dry season as far as Rosso and Boghé, respectively. The major river ports are at Rosso, Kaédi and Gouraye.

SHIPPING

The principal port is at Point-Central, 10 km south of Nouadhibou. Operational since 1963, it is almost wholly occupied with mineral exports. There is a commercial and fishing port at Nouadhibou, which handled 393,716 metric tons in 1983. The deep-water Port de l'Amitié at Nouakchott, built and maintained with assistance from the People's Republic of China, was inaugurated in 1986. The port, which has a total capacity of 1m. tons annually, handled 636,842 tons in 1991 (compared with 479,791 tons in 1990); the number of ships using the port in 1991 was 281 (compared with 244 in 1990).

Port de l'Amitié de Nouakchott: BP 267, Nouakchott; tel. 514-53; telex 538; f. 1986; deep-water port; Dir-Gen. KONÉ OULD MAHMOUD.

Port Autonome de Nouadhibou: BP 236, Nouadhibou; tel. 451-34; telex 441; f. 1973; state-owned; Pres. HABIB ELY; Dir-Gen. AMAR OULD H'MOÏDHA.

Shipping Companies

Compagnie Mauritanienne de Navigation Maritime (COMAUNAM): 119 ave Gamal-Abdel-Nasser, BP 799, Nouakchott; tel. 536-34; telex 5862; fax 525-04; f. 1973; 51% state-owned, 49% owned by Govt of Algeria; nat. shipping co; forwarding agent, stevedoring; Chair. MOHAND TIGHILT; Dir-Gen. KAMIL ABDELKADER.

Société d'Acconage et de Manutention en Mauritanie (SAMMA): BP 258, Nouadhibou; tel. 452-63; telex 433; f. 1960; freight and handling, shipping agent, forwarding agent, stevedoring; Chair. MOHAMED OULD ZEÏDANE; Man. Dir MOHAMED MAHMOUD OULD MATY.

Société Générale de Consignation et d'Entreprises Maritimes (SOGECO): BP 351, Nouakchott; tel. 527-40; telex 5557; fax 539-03; f. 1973; Chair. and Man. Dir ISMAIL OULD ABEIDNA.

CIVIL AVIATION

There are international airports at Nouakchott and Nouadhibou, an airport at Néma, and 23 smaller airstrips. Facilities at Nouakchott were expanded considerably in the late 1980s and early 1990s.

Air Afrique: BP 51, Nouakchott; tel. 525-45; fax 549-44; see under Côte d'Ivoire.

Société d'Economie Mixte Air Mauritanie: BP 41, Nouakchott; tel. 521-46; telex 573; fax 538-15; f. 1974; 60% state-owned, 20% owned by Air Afrique; domestic and regional passenger and cargo services; Dir-Gen. SIDI OULD ZEIN.

Tourism

Mauritania's principal tourist attractions are its historical sites, several of which have been listed by UNESCO under its World Heritage Programme, and its game reserves and national parks. Some 13,000 tourists visited Mauritania in 1986. Receipts from tourism in 1991 totalled an estimated US $13m.

Direction du Tourisme: BP 246, Nouakchott; tel. 533-37; f. 1988; Dir M'BOYE OULD ARAFAT.

Société Mauritanienne de Tourisme et d'Hôtellerie (SMTH): BP 552, Nouakchott; tel. 533-51; f. 1969; 50% owned by Air Afrique; promotes tourism, manages hotels and organizes tours; Man. Dir MOUSTAPHA TEFFAHI.

Defence

In June 1993 the total armed forces numbered 15,550 men: army 15,000, navy 400, air force 150. Full-time membership of paramilitary forces totalled about 5,000. Military service is by authorized conscription, and lasts for two years.

Defence Expenditure: Estimated at 3,220m. UM in 1992.

Chief of Staff of the Armed Forces: Col. MOULAYE OULD BOULKHREIS.

Chief of Staff of the National Gendarmerie: Lt-Col DE OULD NE.

Education

Formal education is not compulsory in Mauritania. At the time of the 1988 census the average rate of adult illiteracy was 64.3% (males 54.1%; females 73.5%). Primary education begins at six years of age and lasts for six years. In 1991 total enrolment at primary schools was equivalent to only 55% of children in the relevant age group (63% of boys; 48% of girls). It is aimed to increase primary enrolment to 90% of all children in Mauritania by 2000. Secondary education begins at 12 years of age and lasts for six years, comprising two cycles of three years each. The total enrolment at secondary schools in 1991 was equivalent to only 14% of children in the appropriate age-group (19% of boys; 10% of girls). A plan to make Arabic the compulsory first language in all schools (which had been postponed in 1979, following protests from the French-speaking south) was reintroduced in April 1988. In 1991/92 a total of 5,850 students were enrolled at Mauritania's four higher education institutions (including the University of Nouakchott, opened in 1983). Expenditure on education in 1988 was 3,188m. UM (22% of current expenditure in that year).

Bibliography

Bader, C. and Lefort, F. *Mauritanie, la vie réconciliée.* Paris, Fayard, 1990.

Balta, P. and Rulleau, C. *Le Grand Maghreb, des indépendances à l'an 2000.* Paris, Editions La Découverte, 1990.

Belvaude, C. *La Mauritanie.* Paris, Editions Karthala, 1989.

de Chassey, C. *Mauritania 1900–1975.* Paris, Harmattan, 1984.

Garnier, C., and Ermont, P. *Désert fertile: un nouvel état, la Mauritanie.* Paris, Hachette, 1960.

Gerteiny, A.G. *Mauritania.* London, Pall Mall; New York, Praeger, 1967.

Hudson, S. *Travels in Mauritania.* London, Virgin Books, 1990.

Rimmer, D. *The Economies of West Africa.* London, Weidenfeld and Nicolson, 1984.

Toupet, C. 'Les grands traits de la République Islamique de Mauritanie', in *L'Information Géographique.* Paris, 1962.

Toupet, C., and Pitte, J.-R. *La Mauritanie.* Paris, PUF, 1977.

Westebbe, R. M. *The Economy of Mauritania.* New York and London, Praeger, 1971.

MAURITIUS

Physical and Social Geography

The Republic of Mauritius lies in the Indian Ocean 800 km east of Madagascar between latitudes 19° 58′ and 20° 32′ S, covering 1,865 sq km (720 sq miles) in area. It is a volcanic island, consisting of a plain rising from the north-east to the Piton de la Petite Rivière Noire (826 m above sea-level) in the south-west, interspersed by abrupt volcanic peaks and gorges, and is almost completely surrounded by a coral reef. Including Rodrigues and its other islands, the whole territory covers a land area of 2,040 sq km (788 sq miles).

The climate is sub-tropical maritime, but with two distinct seasons; additionally, the warm dry coastal areas contrast with the cool rainy interior. Mauritius and Rodrigues are vulnerable to cyclones, particularly between September and May.

The population of Mauritius was enumerated at 1,058,942 at the July 1990 census, and was officially estimated at 1,084,000 in mid-1992, giving a density of 550.5 inhabitants per sq km. During 1985–92 the population increased by an annual average of only 1.1% (compared with a rise of 3% in 1963), owing, in part, to higher emigration and a decline in the birth rate. The population is of mixed origin, including people of European, African, Indian and Chinese descent. Almost 42% of the population inhabit the urban area extending from Port Louis (the capital and business centre) on the north-west coast, to Curepipe in the island's centre.

Rodrigues, a volcanic island of 104 sq km (40 sq miles) surrounded by a coral reef, lies 585 km east of the island of Mauritius (19°S, 63°E) and is an integral part of the Republic. Its population was enumerated at 34,204 in the 1990 census.

Mauritius has two dependencies (together covering 71 sq km and having 167 inhabitants at the 1990 census): Agalega, two islands 935 km north of Mauritius (10°S, 56°E); and the Cargados Carajos Shoals (or St Brandon Islands), 22 islets without permanent inhabitants but used as a fishing station, 370 km north-north-east of Mauritius (16°S, 59°E).

Mauritius claims sovereignty over Tromelin, a small island without permanent inhabitants, 556 km to the north-west. This claim is disputed by Madagascar and France. Mauritius also seeks the return of Diego Garcia, a coral atoll in the Chagos Archipelago, about 1,900 km to the north-east. The archipelago was formerly administered by Mauritius but in 1965 became part (and in 1976 all) of the British Indian Ocean Territory (see p. 632).

Recent History

ADELE SIMMONS

Revised for this edition by the Editor

Following unsuccessful attempts at colonization by the Dutch in the 17th century, the uninhabited islands of Mauritius and Rodrigues were occupied during the subsequent century by French settlers from the neighbouring island of Réunion, who established sugar plantations. Mauritius passed into British control in 1810. Subsequent settlement came mainly from east Africa and India, and the European population has remained largely French-speaking.

The Indian community in Mauritius took little part in politics until 1947, when the franchise was extended to adults over the age of 21 years who could establish simple literacy in any language. This expansion of the electorate deprived the Franco-Mauritian and Creole communities of their political dominance, and between 1948–59 the Mauritius Labour Party (MLP), led by Dr (later Sir) Seewoosagar Ramgoolam, consolidated the new political role of the Indian community. Following intense political debate between the MLP and the Ralliment Mauricien, the party representing the traditional Franco-Mauritian and Creole interests (which later became the Parti Mauricien Social-Démocrate—PMSD), a new constitution, providing for universal adult suffrage, was introduced in 1959; elections, which took place in March of that year, were won by the MLP. Ramgoolam became chief minister in September 1961, and was restyled premier in March 1964. In November 1965 the United Kingdom transferred the Chagos Archipelago (including the atoll of Diego Garcia), a Mauritian dependency about 2,000 km (1,250 miles) north-east of the main island, to the newly-created British Indian Ocean Territory (see p. 632).

Between 1960–65, with impetus from the MLP, Mauritius progressed steadily towards independence. The PMSD, led by Gaëtan (later Sir Gaëtan) Duval, sought unsuccessfully to rally support for a form of 'association' with the United Kingdom instead of full independence, which the Franco-Mauritian and Creole communities feared would lead to Hindu domination. At elections in August 1967, however, a newly-formed alliance of the MLP and the Comité d'Action Musulman (CAM), known as the Independence Party (IP), led by Ramgoolam, secured a majority of seats in the legislature, and a new constitution, providing for internal self-government, was introduced. On 12 March 1968 Mauritius became independent, within the Commonwealth, with Ramgoolam as prime minister. Ramgoolam subsequently formed an extended coalition government, in which the PMSD agreed to participate.

From 1970, the strongest opposition to the Ramgoolam government came from a newly-formed left-wing group, the Mouvement Militant Mauricien (MMM), led by Paul Bérenger. The MMM demanded a more equitable distribution of wealth, and attracted most support from the young unemployed, student groups and trade unions. In response to a period of intense labour unrest in the early 1970s, the government declared a state of emergency and detained leading members of the MMM. Following the dissolution of the coalition of the MLP and the PMSD in December 1973, the MLP continued in office in alliance with the CAM. At the general election, which had been postponed until December 1976, the MMM emerged as the largest single party in the legislative assembly, although with insufficient seats to form a government. Ramgoolam subsequently formed a new coalition with the PMSD. Despite renewed outbreaks of unrest and public disorder, and further arrests of MMM activists, the coalition retained power for the full term of the legislative assembly.

COALITION POLITICS

At elections to the legislative assembly in June 1982, an alliance of the MMM and Parti Socialiste Mauricien (PSM) won all 60 elective seats on the main island (42 to the MMM and

18 to the PSM). Anerood (later Sir Anerood) Jugnauth became prime minister and appointed Bérenger as minister of finance. In March 1983, however, following opposition within the cabinet to Bérenger's stringent economic policies and his attempts to make Creole (Kreol) the national language (despite the Indian descent of the majority of the population), twelve ministers, including Bérenger, resigned. Jugnauth subsequently formed a new government, but he and his supporters were excluded from meetings of the MMM central committee. At the end of March Bérenger was officially designated leader of the opposition. In early April Jugnauth formed a new party, the Mouvement Socialiste Militant (MSM), which, in May, amalgamated with the PSM, and was renamed the Mouvement Socialiste Mauricien. However, the new government controlled only 29 of the 66 seats in the legislative assembly, and Jugnauth was obliged to dissolve the assembly in June.

At a general election in August 1983 an alliance comprising the MSM, the MLP and the PMSD, led by Sir Gaëtan Duval, won 41 of the 62 elective seats, while the MMM won only 19 seats. (The Organisation du Peuple Rodriguais (OPR) secured the remaining two seats.) Bérenger was defeated in his home constituency, but he later secured an appointive seat in the assembly. Jugnauth remained prime minister, with Duval as deputy prime minister.

In December 1983 draft legislation that would allow Mauritius to become a republic failed to gain sufficient support in the legislative assembly, owing, in part, to disagreement between the government and the opposition over the nature of the powers to be granted to the president of the proposed republic. In the same month Sir Seewoosagur Ramgoolam was appointed governor-general. Satcam (later Sir Satcam) Boolell subsequently assumed the leadership of the MLP, but was dismissed from the cabinet in February 1984. In response, the MLP withdrew from the ruling coalition; however, 11 MLP deputies continued to support the government and formed a faction within the MLP, the Rassemblement des Travaillistes Mauriciens (RTM).

In March 1984 proposed restrictions on the press prompted considerable protest, particularly after the arrest of journalists at a public demonstration. The government eventually agreed to establish a joint commission, with representatives of the press, to examine the proposed legislation. On the commission's recommendation, the government withdrew the legislation and abandoned the legal proceedings against the arrested journalists. In April 1985, however, the government introduced similar legislation, which prohibited the publication of material that was judged to be damaging to the government.

In December 1985 the MMM won 118 of the 126 contested seats in municipal elections, demonstrating the increasing public dissatisfaction with the Jugnauth government. In the same month four members of the legislative assembly were arrested in the Netherlands on charges of drug smuggling. In January 1986, following Jugnauth's refusal to comment on allegations that other deputies were involved in the affair, four cabinet ministers announced their resignation. Shortly afterwards, Boodhoo relinquished the coalition's parliamentary leadership, and Jugnauth formed a new government, which retained the political balance of his previous administration. In the same month Sir Veerasamy Ringadoo, a former minister of finance and a supporter of Jugnauth, was appointed governor-general, following the death of Ramgoolam. In March the MMM, after initially boycotting the new session, unsuccessfully introduced a motion of censure against the government. Following the vote, however, five MSM deputies, including three who had resigned as ministers in January, withdrew their support from the coalition and sat as independents in the assembly.

In June 1986, in response to criticism from within the MSM, Jugnauth announced the creation of a commission of enquiry to investigate the drugs scandal. In the following month, however, three ministers resigned, citing lack of confidence in Jugnauth's leadership of the MSM and of the country. The government retaliated by expelling 11 MSM dissidents from the party. In August Jugnauth reshuffled the council of ministers and appointed Boolell as minister of foreign affairs and one of the three deputy prime ministers. In November, however, following a report by the commission of inquiry into the drugs affair, Boodhoo, who was implicated in the scandal, was formally expelled from the MSM and resigned from the legislative assembly, together with two other MSM deputies, thus reducing the MSM/PMSD coalition's strength in the legislature to only 30 of the 62 elective seats. In the subsequent political realignment, the MMM gained the support of several deputies who had abandoned the government coalition, although the allegiances of certain other deputies remained uncommitted. In January 1987 Jugnauth announced that a general election, scheduled for 1988, would take place later that year.

In March 1987 the commission of inquiry issued a further report stating that six deputies of the MSM/PMSD alliance had been directly implicated in drug-trafficking. In the same month further allegations associated Duval, one of the three deputy prime ministers, with the affair. However, Duval's subsequent offer of resignation was rejected by Jugnauth. In May Diwakar Bundhun, the minister of industry, was dismissed, after openly criticizing Jugnauth. Owing to the lack of majority support in the legislative assembly, Jugnauth announced that a general election was to take place in August, and postponed the presentation of the 1987/88 budget proposals until October.

At the general election on 30 August 1987 an electoral alliance formed by the MSM, the PMSD and the MLP won 39 of the 60 elective seats on the main island, although it received only 49.8% of total votes cast. The MMM, which campaigned within an opposition coalition, the 'Union', with two smaller parties (the Mouvement des Travaillistes Démocrates and the Front des Travailleurs Socialistes), won 21 seats, obtaining 48.1% of votes cast. Dr Prem Nababsingh subsequently became the leader of the MMM and of the opposition in the assembly, replacing Bérenger, who had failed to secure a seat. In September Jugnauth appointed a new council of ministers. Later that month the new government announced plans to make Mauritius a republic within the Commonwealth.

In July 1988 Boodhoo announced that the PSM had been revived, and that the party had withdrawn its support for the MSM. In August, following a disagreement over employment policies, the coalition was weakened, when Sir Gaëtan, the leader of the PMSD, left the government, together with his brother, Hervé Duval, the minister of industry. In January 1989 Boodhoo was briefly detained in connection with a scandal involving forged passports. The opposition demanded Jugnauth's resignation in February, following his expression of support for Soo Soobiah, the former high commissioner to the United Kingdom, who had been arrested on drug-smuggling charges. Two attempts on Jugnauth's life (in November 1988 and March 1989) were attributed by him to criminals involved in drug-trafficking. The coalition parliamentary majority was increased by one seat in June, following a by-election. In the same month Sir Gaëtan Duval was arrested on suspicion of involvement in a political assassination in 1971, but was later released.

In July 1990 the MMM and MSM agreed to form an alliance to contest the next general election, and to proceed with constitutional measures, which would allow Mauritius to become a republic. Under the proposed new constitution, Bérenger would assume the presidency, while Jugnauth would remain as executive prime minister, with Nababsingh as deputy prime minister. However, the draft amendments, which were submitted to the legislative assembly in mid-August, were opposed by members of the MLP (who formed an alliance with the PMSD), and Jugnauth failed to secure the necessary parliamentary majority. He subsequently dismissed Boolell, as well as two ministers belonging to the MSM, who had refused to support the proposed amendments. A further three ministers representing the MLP also resigned, leaving only one MLP member in the government. Boolell subsequently relinquished the leadership of the MLP to Dr Navin Ramgoolam (the son of Sir Seewoosagur). In September Jugnauth announced the formation of a new coalition government, in which the six vacant ministerial posts were allocated to members of the MMM, while Nababsingh was appointed as one of the three deputy prime ministers. In November, despite strong criticism by the MLP, the legislative assembly adopted a constitutional amendment to facilitate the removal of the speaker, Chattradhari Daby, who had opposed the proposed transition to a republican system of government.

In August 1991 Jugnauth dissolved the legislative assembly; the ensuing general election took place on 15 September. An alliance of the MSM, the MMM and the Mouvement des Travaillistes Démocrates (MTD) won 57 of the 62 elective seats, while the alliance of the MLP and the PMSD secured only three seats. (Members of the Organisation du Peuple Rodriguais were returned to the remaining two seats.) However, members of the opposition, including Dr Ramgoolam and Duval, alleged electoral malpractice, and refused to attend the inaugural session of the legislative assembly. Jugnauth subsequently formed a new government, to which nine representatives of the MMM (including Bérenger, who became minister of external affairs) and one representative of the MTD were appointed. Later in September Duval resigned from the legislative assembly. In the following month the MLP/PMSD alliance boycotted municipal elections, in which the MSM/MMM/MTD alliance won 125 of the 126 contested seats.

In October 1991 Jugnauth announced that, subject to the approval of constitutional amendments by a majority of 75% of members of the legislative assembly, Mauritius would become a republic within the Commonwealth on 12 March 1992. However, Duval asserted that the creation of a republic would allow Jugnauth to assume absolute power, and demanded that the proposed amendments be submitted to a national referendum. On 10 December 1991 the constitutional changes were approved by 59 of the 66 deputies in the legislative assembly. (The seven members of the MLP/PMSD alliance in the assembly refused to vote, on the grounds that the amendments provided for an increase in executive power, to the detriment of the legislature.) Under the terms of the revised constitution, the governor-general, Sir Veerasamy Ringadoo, who had been nominated by Jugnauth, was to assume the presidency for an interim period, pending the election of a president and vice-president, for a five-year term, by a simple majority of the legislative assembly (which would be renamed the national assembly). However, the MLP/PMSD alliance criticized these provisions, and demanded that the president be elected by universal suffrage. The constitution vested executive power in the prime minister, who would be appointed by the president, and would be the deputy best able to command a majority in the national assembly. On 12 March 1992 Ringadoo officially became interim president, replacing the British monarch, Queen Elizabeth II, as head of state. Later that month the government announced that Cassam Uteem, the minister of industry and industrial technology and a member of the MMM, was to be nominated to the presidency after a period of three months. (Under the terms of the alliance between the MSM and the MMM, members of the MMM were to be appointed to the presidency and vice-presidency, while Jugnauth was to remain as prime minister.)

In April 1992 opposition members demanded the resignation of Jugnauth, following the issue of a new bank note depicting his wife; it was reported that the ensuing criticism of Jugnauth had weakened the MSM/MMM alliance. In June, following the resignation of Ringadoo, officially on grounds of ill health, Uteem was elected to the presidency by the national assembly Sir Robindranooth Ghurburrun, a member of the MMM, was nominated to the vice-presidency. A minor reshuffle of the council of ministers was subsequently carried out.

In October 1992 Ramgoolam announced that he was to return to the United Kingdom to complete legal studies, despite a constitutional stipulation that the mandate of a parliamentary deputy who failed to attend sessions of the national assembly for a period of more than three months be suspended. Plans by Ramgoolam to return to Mauritius in time to attend subsequent meetings of the national assembly, were thwarted by the curtailment of a parliamentary session in December and the convening of a further session, in January 1993, without prior notice. In June, however, a proposal that Ramgoolam's parliamentary mandate be invalidated was rejected by the supreme court, which criticized the 'unreasonable' timing of the parliamentary session in January.

Following a number of disputes between the MMM and MSM in the first half of 1993, the government coalition was further destabilized in early August, when members of the PMSD secured the three vacant seats in a municipal by-election (in a constituency where the MMM traditionally attracted most support). Later in August, following an unexpected success by the PMSD in municipal elections in a constituency that traditionally supported the MMM, a meeting between Bérenger and Ramgoolam prompted speculation that an alliance between the MMM and MLP was contemplated. Shortly afterwards, Jugnauth dismissed Bérenger from the council of ministers, on the grounds that he had repeatedly criticized government policy.

The removal of Bérenger precipitated a serious crisis within the MMM, whose political bureau decided that the other nine members of the party who held ministerial portfolios should remain in the coalition government. Led by the deputy prime minister, Paramhansa Nababsing, and the minister of industry and industrial technology, Jean-Claude de l'Estrac, supporters of the pro-coalition faction announced in October 1993 that Bérenger had been suspended as secretary-general of the MMM. Bérenger and his supporters responded by expelling 11 MMM officials from the party, and subsequently obtaining a legal ban on Nababsing and de l'Estrac from using the party name. The split in the MMM led in November to a government reshuffle, in which the remaining two MMM ministers supporting Bérenger were replaced by members of the party's pro-coalition faction.

In April 1994 the MLP and the MMM announced that they had agreed terms for an alliance to contest the next general elections. Under its provisions, Ramgoolam was to be prime minister, Bérenger deputy prime minister, with cabinet portfolios allocated on the basis of 12 ministries to the MLP and nine to the MMM. In the same month, three MPs from the MSM, who had been close associates of a former minister of agriculture who had been dismissed two months earlier, withdrew their support from the government.

Nababsing and the dissident faction of the MMM, having lost Bérenger's legal challenge for the use of the party name, formed a new party, the Renouveau Militant Mauritien (RMM), which formally commenced political activity in June 1994. In the same month, Jugnauth declared that the government, which retained a cohesive parliamentary majority, would remain in office to the conclusion of its mandate in September 1996. In August 1994 a number of cabinet posts were reallocated.

Economy*

DONALD L. SPARKS

Mauritius* is a relatively small island (less than 800 square miles), which shares many of the economic problems of other states in sub-Saharan Africa, but also has unusual diversity and strength, and ranks among middle income countries. In 1980–91 Mauritius' gross domestic product (GDP) increased, in real terms, by an annual average of 6.7%. Mauritius was traditionally dependent on sugar production, and economic growth was therefore vulnerable to adverse climatic conditions and changes in international prices for sugar. However, the dominance of sugar in the economy has been eroded by the steadily expanding manufactured exports sector and by tourism; the contribution of revenue from sugar to the gross domestic product (GDP) declined from 13% in 1979 to less than 7% in 1993, when it accounted for 27.5% of total export earnings. In 1992, according to estimates by the World Bank, Mauritius' gross national product (GNP), measured at average 1990–92 prices, was $2,965m., equivalent to $2,700 per head. During 1985–92, it was estimated, GNP increased, in real terms, at an average annual rate of 6.3%. During the same period, the population rose by an annual average of 1.1%.

SUGAR

Until recently, agriculture was the backbone of Mauritius' economy, and sugar dominated the sector. Sugar cane is grown on a total of 84,400 ha (almost one-half of the entire surface area of the island and 87% of arable land). There are 21 large estates, covering 48,000 ha, all but one privately owned and each with a factory for processing the estate sugar and the cane grown by planters in the surrounding areas. The other land under sugar cane, producing over 40% of the total crop, is owned by 452 'big' planters and 35,000 'small' planters. Many of the latter, who are mostly Indo-Mauritian and who cultivate about one-quarter of the total land under cane, have grouped themselves into co-operatives to facilitate the consignment of cane to the factories on the estates. Some 70,000 workers (15% of the labour force in 1987) are employed in the sugar industry during the crop season between July and December, and 60,000 during the inter-crop period. A bulk sugar terminal, opened in 1980 with an annual capacity of 350,000 metric tons, is the third largest in the world. The Mauritius Sugar Syndicate markets all manufactured sugar, while the main estates are grouped into the Mauritius Sugar Producers' Association (MSPA).

In 1986, when the output of raw sugar totalled 707,000 metric tons, yields achieved an all-time record average of 9 tons of raw sugar per ha, reaching 12 tons per ha on some estates. Such yields exceeded those of European sugar beet producers, and were comparable with those of many Asian sugar-growing countries. Sugar output fell in 1987 and 1988, to 691,134 tons and an estimated 568,000 tons respectively, as a result of poor weather and a price 'freeze' imposed by the EC. Cyclones in January and April 1989 caused very severe damage to the crop. However, sugar production totalled 643,168 tons in 1992 (an increase of 5.2% compared with 1991). Owing to poor weather conditions, output fell in 1993 to 550,000 tons, the lowest level since 1980.

Most of the island's sugar was formerly sold to the UK at a guaranteed price, under the Commonwealth Sugar Agreement, but in 1975 this arrangement was replaced by a protocol of the first Lomé Convention, which was signed in that year by the EC and 46 developing countries, including Mauritius. Under this protocol and its two successors, Mauritius receives an annual quota of 500,000 metric tons of raw cane sugar, and is the principal exporter of sugar to European countries. Other important customers are the USA, Canada and New Zealand. Local consumption is about 37,000 tons per year. Mauritius has benefited from the EC quota arrangement in that, for these exports, the guaranteed price has been much higher than the 'spot' price on the world market. However, since 1982 the EC price has remained almost static, despite annual rounds of protracted and often acrimonious negotiations. In 1989 the price was reduced by 2%. Sugar import quotas operated since 1982 by the USA have been extremely detrimental to Mauritius.

Apart from poor weather in some years, problems affecting the industry in recent years have included low world prices ageing machinery in the factories, and the high level of the sugar export levy, which was introduced in 1980. Following the report of a commission set up to examine the sugar sector's problems, the government drew up a plan for restructuring the industry, and in 1984, as an initial step, it created the Mauritius Sugar Authority (MSA) to co-ordinate the plan and to monitor its effects. The resulting Sugar Action Plan (SAP) covered the period 1985–90, and one of its main features was the easing of the levy. Five factories were to be closed during that period, and the area planted with sugar was to be reduced by 1% per year, to encourage the growing of more food crops. Under the SAP, the island has been divided into five sugar regions, each supervised by a public company in which small planters will be encouraged to buy shares. The SAP also covered the modernization of sugar factories and the development of power stations fired by bagasse (the fibrous remnants of sugar cane after milling). In December 1988 the legislative assembly approved the Sugar Industry Efficiency Act, which provided for a programme of incentives and other measures. The export levy was to be set at a flat rate of 18.75% (instead of on a sliding scale corresponding to the amount exported) and the threshold raised from 1,000 tons to 3,000 tons. The export tax on molasses and the sugar milling tax were abolished. To combat absenteeism, a bonus related to attendance levels was to be paid to workers.

Progress has been made in improving yields through the introduction of irrigation and new strains of sugar cane. The large-scale Northern Plains irrigation scheme is expected to increase yields per acre from 25 metric tons of cane to 42 tons. However, there is little value in increasing overall output unless world markets can be found. Molasses and rum are important sugar by-products, and are also exported by Mauritius. A five-year agricultural development plan, launched in 1989–90, was aimed to increase the significance of the agricultural sector. About one-half of the programme's new funds (Rs 7,300m.) was to be allocated to the sugar industry, with much of it specifically going to bagasse energy production, a by-product of the sugar industry. Also under the programme, small farmers were to receive subsidized loans to buy mechanized planting and harvesting equipment. In 1992 the government initiated a new agricultural plan, and in 1993, approved legislation that provided additional agricultural incentives, and reduced the sugar export duty rate.

AGRICULTURE AND FISHING

Following a significant decline in sugar production, agriculture's contribution to GDP declined to 10.4% in 1992 (compared with 20% in 1970). Nevertheless, food crop production increased by 11% in 1989. Owing to a prolonged drought in 1990/91, however, many crops were planted late; as a result, maize production declined by 13.6%, and tomato production by 19.3%, while onion and potato output decreased by 50% and 55% respectively. Total agricultural output declined by approximately 2.5% in 1991. In 1992 agricultural employment represented 15.3% of the engaged labour force, compared with 18.3% in 1990.

Tea production, once a significant factor in the island's economy, has been adversely affected since the late 1980s by rising production costs and the low level of prices on world

* Although Rodrigues is an integral part of the Republic of Mauritius, most economic data refer to the island of Mauritius only. The figures in this section therefore refer to the main island only, unless otherwise stated.

markets. Export revenue from this source fell by 67%, between 1984–88, although the volume of tea exported remained fairly constant, at between 4,500–5,500 tons annually. Exports of tea in 1993, however, declined to less than 4,400 tons. In 1989 tea output, at 5,500 tons, stood at its lowest level since 1982, although since 1990 production has remained fairly constant at around 5,900 tons. Tea is grown in the humid highlands, which are unsuitable for sugar, and since 1959 the government has been expanding the area and distributing it to smallholders grouped into co-operatives. The area under tea is about 3,760 ha and the number of tea smallholders is 1,500. The Tea Development Authority (TDA), created by the government in 1971, made substantial financial losses, and in 1986 most of its functions were transferred to a new public company, the Mauritius Tea Factories Co (TeaFac), owned jointly by several state bodies and by tea producer co-operatives. TeaFac currently operates the TDA's four factories, which account for about 75% of tea exports, and is responsible for exporting tea, while the TDA's activities are restricted to training and extension services. The tea industry receives support from state subsidies.

Tobacco is the other main cash crop, after sugar and tea. Production has been expanded to the point where locally manufactured cigarettes are composed entirely of local tobacco apart from certain luxury grades. Output, which was 422 tons in 1970, has been expanded to about 1,000 tons per year. Practically all tobacco is grown and processed by British-American Tobacco (BAT—Mauritius).

Subsistence farming is conducted on a small scale, although the cultivation of food crops is becoming more widespread in view of the need to diversify the economy and reduce food imports. Food accounted for 12.1% of the total cost of imports in 1992. The expansion of vegetable cultivation and experiments in intercropping with sugar have resulted in self-sufficiency in potatoes and nearly all other vegetables. Other crops now being experimentally intercropped with sugar are maize, rice, vanilla and groundnuts. A tree-planting programme, started in 1982, aimed to produce one-half of the country's timber needs by the mid-1990s.

In the livestock sector, poultry farming has been the most successful, the production of poultry meat, in which, with eggs, Mauritius is self-sufficient, rising from 11,850 tons in 1991 to 14,850 tons in 1992. However, the island produces only 10% of its total beef requirements, and about 20% of its total consumption of dairy products, the remainder having to be imported mainly from New Zealand, Australia and South Africa. A National Dairy Board was established in 1985, and several projects were initiated, including a cattle improvement scheme and a study on the potential of deer farming. Most cattle fodder has to be imported, in particular maize from South Africa, at a very high cost. Studies have been carried out on the possible production of high-protein feeding-stuffs, manufactured from cane tops and molasses.

The fishing industry is being regenerated, with assistance from Japan and Australia in particular, and commercial fishing is gradually expanding. In 1991 coastal fishing increased by 26.6%, and ocean fishing by 32.7%; however, nearly 80% of fish consumed in Mauritius was imported in that year. Vessels from Japan, Taiwan and the Republic of Korea fish in offshore waters and tranship about 15,000 tons of fish, mostly tuna, every year. Since the mid-1970s, there has been a noticeable increase in illegal fishing by foreign companies in Mauritian waters. A joint-venture tuna-canning factory, owned 49% by Japanese interests, was set up in 1972 and exports to EU countries. A second tuna-canning plant, with an initial capacity of 10,000 tons per year, was opened in 1988. A new fishing port at Trou Fanfaron, built with Japanese grant aid, was opened in 1985, with a handling capacity of about 6,000 tons of fish per year. The experimental farming of prawns has been a success, and there are hopes for export potential in this field.

INDUSTRY

Until the 1970s, the industrial sector was very small and concentrated on import substitution of basic consumer products, such as food, beverages, tobacco, footwear, clothing, metal products, paints and board for furniture, made from bagasse. There is a fertilizer plant producing up to 100,000 tons per year, which also exports small quantities of the product, and a refinery to produce ethyl alcohol (ethanol) from molasses is under construction.

However, in view of the limited domestic market, the high level of unemployment and the emphasis on reducing dependence on the sugar sector, the government adopted a policy of export promotion by developing the Export Processing Zone (EPZ), a sector which concentrates on labour-intensive processing of imported goods for the export market. Within the EPZ, the government offers both local and foreign investors attractive packages of incentives, including tax 'holidays', exemption from import duties on most raw materials and capital goods, free repatriation of capital, profits and dividends, low-price electricity, etc. About 60% of invested capital is locally-owned, a further 25% is owned by Hong Kong entrepreneurs, and the remainder is supplied mainly by Pakistani, Indian, French, German and British interests. By September 1988 there were 586 enterprises in the EPZ, employing about 90,700 workers. However, the growth of employment subsequently slowed, and in 1993, when there were 554 enterprises (down from 556 in 1992), EPZ employment declined to 83,500, its lowest level since 1987. The EPZ's decline was due mostly to low productivity, increased competition, slow rates of modernization in the textile firms due to a lack of investment, high absenteeism rates and increasing protectionism in the industrial market economies.

The fastest-growing EPZ sectors have been textiles and clothing, which now account for 80% of total EPZ exports, more than 68% of EPZ enterprises, and 91% of EPZ labour. Mauritius is the world's third largest exporter of new woollen goods. Other rapidly growing sectors include electronics components and diamonds, and emphasis has been put on the development of precison engineering (electronics, watch and instrument making, etc.) and skilled crafts (diamond cutting and polishing, furniture, quality goods, etc.). Other products include toys, razor blades, nails, industrial chemicals, detergents, rattan furniture, plastic goods, tyres and assembly of recording cassettes. In 1991 the government aimed to diversify the EPZ, with particular emphasis on the textile sector.

Total exports from the EPZ increased steadily from Rs 3.9m. in 1971 to Rs 4,959.6m. in 1986, when they accounted for 55.5% of total export earnings and replaced sugar as the main source of export receipts. However, net earnings are much lower, as a result of the high cost of imported materials and components, and net foreign exchange revenue in 1986 was only Rs 1,100m. The import content represents about 70%–75% of EPZ export earnings. In 1990 EPZ exports rose to Rs 11,474m., compared with Rs 8,179m. in the previous year. (Of total EPZ exports, clothing accounted for Rs 9,080m.) However, the rate of EPZ export growth has fallen; EPZ imports also declined during the late 1980s, from 42% of total imports in 1986, to 30.6% in 1990. After a decline in 1991, the zone's exports increased by 11.2% in 1992, to Rs 13,500m. EPZ exports grew by over 18% in 1993, to Rs 15,500m. In 1992 EPZ exports accounted for 63.6% of the value of all of Mauritius' exports. According to the World Bank, however, poor training and lack of modernization restrict the zone's productivity.

As a result of increasing labour costs, many firms in the EPZ are using more capital-intensive technologies; this may affect employment in the next few years. In 1989 a shortage of unskilled labour arose in the sugar industry, and of skilled manual labour in the service and construction industries. The demand for skilled personnel in various business sectors, including marketing, management, accounting and computing, also exceeded the number of suitable candidates. The government has allocated Rs 260m. for training and education, as part of an initiative to regain international competitiveness, particularly in the EPZ. The Development Bank of Mauritius has created a Rs 200m. fund to modernize textile equipment. In order to promote industry, the government has also proposed a tax remission equivalent to 200% of expenditure by private companies on training. A centre of textile technology has also been established by the University of Mauritius

Mauritius has a large, and growing, informal sector. Women represent about one-third of total employment, although they comprise 65% of the workers in the EPZ. Official unemployment has declined in recent years, from a high of 75,000 in 1982, to a current level of approximately 18,000. In 1992 agriculture employed 44,300 workers, manufacturing 76,800 and government 56,100. The total work-force, in the formal sector, was 282,400 in 1992.

TOURISM

Mauritius is an attractive destination for European visitors, and tourism is now the third most important source of foreign exchange, after sugar and textiles. Arrivals of foreign tourists increased from 27,650 in 1970 to 245,000 in 1988, and to 375,000 in 1993. In 1989 revenue from tourism totalled $184m., an increase of 17.8% on the level of the previous year. Expenditure per tourist, however, rose very slowly, by only 7%, compared with 15% in the previous year. In 1992, when tourism receipts totalled Rs 4,460m., the greatest number of visitors were from Réunion (24.9%), France (20.6%) and South Africa (13.0%). Germany, the United Kingdom and Italy were also important markets. In 1990 there were an estimated 4,603 hotel rooms in Mauritius. Room occupancy in the large hotels declined from 82.9% in 1988 to 77.8% in 1989, and to 75.1% in 1990. The government intends to develop the sector further and to build new resorts, but is now taking measures to prevent environmental damage which has been caused by the uncontrolled expansion of tourism in recent years. In an attempt to limit environmental damage and to improve room occupancy rates, the government stopped issuing permits to build new hotels in 1990; however, small private hotels are exempt from the ban. Although the tourism sector provides employment, directly and indirectly, for more than 12,000 people in 1993, it has also contributed to the rise in costly imports, especially foodstuffs.

COMMUNICATIONS

There are approximately 1,831 km of classified roads, of which 886 km are main roads and 577 km are secondary roads. The road network is good, considering the mountainous terrain, and about 93% of the roads have been asphalted. There are a number of road projects planned or under way, including the motorway between Port Louis and the Plaisance international airport, and a new road from Pamplemousse to Grande Baie, and the reconstruction of the Nouvelle France–Mahébourg road. Port Louis, the major commercial port, was modernized and expanded, with a loan of $10m. from the World Bank. The port is currently undergoing an additional development project (at a total cost of Rs 314m., which was to be completed in 1994.

The international airport at Plaisance is served by 15 airlines. In 1992 the airport handled about 34,000 tons of freight and 950,000 passengers. It is being expanded, at a cost of about Rs 450m., and this work was due to be completed in 1994. The expansion was necessitated by a 50% increase in the number of international arrivals during the past decade. Air Mauritius, which is 51% government-owned, accounts for about one-half of total passenger traffic.

POWER AND WATER

Owing to the normally abundant rainfall and precipitous water courses, about 25% of electricity is generated from hydro sources, but most of the supply comes from diesel-powered thermal stations. The sugar estates generate electricity from bagasse. The 30-MW Champagne hydroelectric scheme started operating in late 1984. A 20-MW gas-powered generating plant in the north, built with French aid, came on stream in 1988. Energy demand is increasing at about 12% per year. In 1986 438m. kWh of electricity were generated. It is estimated that Mauritius could produce up to 350m. kWh of electricity per year by using bagasse as a fuel, compared with current annual production of about 34m. kWh. There is a 21.7-MW bagasse-fuelled station attached to the Flacq United Estates sugar factory, and a French-financed bagasse pelletization pilot plant, Bagapel, operates at the nearby Deep River–Beau Champ sugar estate. The object is to establish bagasse as a year-round fuel; currently it is available only in the harvesting season. Two 15-MW bagasse-fired power stations are planned. Studies on wave power and wind power are also being carried out. Water supply and distribution are well developed, with only 0.75% of the population without piped provision. Subterranean reserves are tapped to supply industry, the principal consumer. Energy imports, principally petroleum, generally represent less than 10% of total imports. In 1989, however, the import costs increased to almost 40%, owing to the Gulf War. In 1992 oil imports increased by 18.5%, compared with 1991, to 570,000 tons.

BALANCE OF PAYMENTS, PUBLIC FINANCE AND AID

Following the dramatic increase in world sugar prices in the mid-1970s, Mauritius was able to close its trade gap for the first time in 1974. In 1975 the trade balance went back into deficit, mainly as a result of an escalating bill for imports, particularly for petroleum products. It continued in deficit until 1986, when a surplus of Rs 214m. was recorded. The excellent trade figures that year were the result of high sugar output, the advance in EPZ export volume and also the decline in international petroleum prices and in the value of the US dollar. In 1987, however, a sharp increase in imports resulted in a deficit of Rs 1,000m. While exports rose by 12% in 1989, this was not enough to offset an increase of 15.8% in imports. Thus, the trade deficit in that year was Rs 4,700m. This record deficit was attributed to significant increases in import prices (22%), compared with lower increases in export prices (15%). In 1990 and 1991 trade deficits of Rs 5,700m. and Rs 5,300m. respectively were recorded, increasing to Rs 5,800m. in 1992. The visible trade deficits have been caused by increases in EPZ imports for manufacturing inputs, and in imported fuel costs, disappointing sugar harvests and a price freeze on sugar exports to the EC. The trade deficit for 1993 is expected to be at least as large as 1992, owing to limited gains in manufacturing productivity and adverse weather conditions.

The principal domestic exports are sugar, tea and molasses, and the principal imports are textile yarn and fabrics, petroleum products and motor vehicles. In 1993 the principal source of imports was South Africa (13.5%); other major suppliers were France, the United Kingdom and Japan. The principal market for exports (taking 32.4% of exports in that year) was the United Kingdom; other significant purchasers were France, Germany and the USA. The importance of South Africa in Mauritius' trade with Southern Africa is expected to increase significantly when the newly created Common Market for Eastern and Southern Africa (COMESA) becomes fully operational.

The overall balance of payments was in deficit between 1975/76–85/86 when a surplus of about Rs 260m. was achieved. The surplus rose to an estimated Rs 2,600m. in 1987/88. In 1990, however, a deficit of $119.1m. on the current account of the balance of payments was recorded, declining to $37m. in 1991. Mauritius' external debt totalled $1,080m. at the end of 1992; in that year the cost of debt-servicing was equivalent to 8.4% of the value of exports of goods and services. Mauritius has an excellent international credit rating. In November 1988 it completed the early repayment of a $40m. Eurodollar loan contracted in May 1982, and in 1989 aimed to liquidate a further Eurodollar loan, also for $40m., which was not due to mature until 1992.

Mauritius' economic problems in the early 1980s led the government to introduce harsh austerity measures in 1982. In August 1983 the newly-elected government was obliged to continue policies which would broadly satisfy conditions imposed by the IMF and the World Bank. The economic boom of the mid-1980s, precipitated by the growth of the EPZ sector, enabled the government to introduce more far-reaching measures to encourage economic expansion, and reduced the 1985/86 budget deficit to only 3.7% of GDP. Recurrent spending in the 1986/87 budget was projected to rise by only 3% but planned capital expenditure was increased by 46% and the overall budget deficit was estimated to total almost 5% of GDP. After four years of austerity, the new budget was generally welcomed by commercial interests and by the general public, owing to its proposals to maintain taxes at their existing level, to extend welfare benefits (particularly to workers in the EPZ sector) and to reduce customs duties on many items. In the 1987/88 budget current expenditure increased by 28%, in order to finance wage increases in the public sector, averaging 30%. The budget envisaged a defict of Rs 1,070m., equivalent to 4% of GDP. Total budgetary expenditure for 1988/89 was estimated at Rs 7,554m., of which current expenditure was to account for Rs 7,170m. The budgetary deficit for that financial year was projected at Rs 451m. The budget included proposals to liberalize banking regulations and to provide tax incentives, in order to stimulate international trading interest in the newly established stock exchange and to develop offshore banking activities (see below). The government's estimated budget deficit for 1989/90 was Rs 317.4m. To lessen this budgetary shortfall, the government introduced increased taxes on cigarettes, rum and beer and maintained subsidies on food staples such as rice and flour. Proposals were announced to introduce a harmonized system of customs tariffs and to develop re-export and transhipment activities by establishing a duty-free processing zone for bulk imports. In 1990/91 there was an estimated budgetary deficit of Rs 877m. (equivalent to 1.9% of GDP), which the government financed by increased borrowing on the domestic market. In 1991/92 however, the budgetary deficit declined to Rs 67.2m. In 1992 the government proposed reforms of the income tax system, with the introduction of a pay-as-you-earn scheme for employers, and a current payment system for the self-employed, both modelled on the British tax system. The changes were aimed at broadening the country's tax base. Mauritius' annual rate of inflation averaged 8.1% in 1980–91. Consumer prices increased by an average of 7% in 1991, and by 4.6% in 1992. The rate of inflation was estimated to have risen to 11% in 1993, as a consequence of the removal of government subsidies on flour and rice imports.

Mauritius' budget proposals in the early 1980s were, to a large extent, designed to fulfil conditions stipulated by the IMF and the World Bank, regardless of changes in government. The IMF had agreed a 27 month stand-by facility in October 1979, which required a 23% devaluation of the rupee and a reduction in government expenditure. When the trade balance continued to deteriorate during 1980, however, the IMF arrangement was abandoned, and a further agreement was negotiated.

In June 1981 the government obtained a Structural Adjustment Loan (SAL) of $15m. from the World Bank, to finance the three-year economic programme introduced in 1979. In December 1981 a second one-year stand-by credit of about $30m. was approved by the IMF, but was suspended in May 1982, as a result of the government's failure to meet IMF conditions. Agreement was reached with the IMF in May 1983 for a further facility of SDR 49.8m., and in December the World Bank finally approved a new SAL of $45m. Meanwhile, Mauritius' other main aid donors showed their confidence in the government's austerity programme when, in June 1983, at a meeting of the World Bank-sponsored consultative group, they pledged some $53m. in balance-of-payments support. In early 1984 disagreement arose between Mauritius and the IMF over the release of the remaining half of the stand-by facility. Disbursement of the remainder of the World Bank's second SAL was also delayed until March 1985, when the sugar restructuring plan was finally introduced. Sectoral loans of about $25m. for the sugar sector and $25m. for the industrial sector were agreed with the World Bank, following lengthy negotiations during late 1985 and throughout 1986. Agreement was reached with the IMF in late 1984 (finalized in March 1985) for an SDR 49m. stand-by facility, over 18 months, and SDR 7.5m. in compensatory financing for the shortfall in export earnings. Owing to the delay in negotiating the new arrangement, the government turned to European money markets for balance-of-payments support to enable the country to meet its immediate external debt-servicing obligations. In September 1984 the government signed a $40m. Euroloan agreement with a consortium of banks. When the IMF arrangement expired in August 1986, the government decided to defer negotiations on a new facility, owing to the country's strong economic performance. At a special donors' meeting organized by the World Bank, held in Paris in January 1989, $90m. was made available to finance a five-year environment protection programme, which laid emphasis on improvements to water and sewage treatment.

A new three-year Development Plan was introduced in April 1993, with the object of achieving further modernization and diversification of the economy. The plan envisages an increased pace of privatization of public enterprises, and provides for the creation of new incentives and institutions to assist the private sector.

As part of a long-term strategy to establish Mauritius as an international financial centre, controls on the movement of foreign exchange were relaxed in December 1986. From July 1988 commercial banks were allowed to settle all import payments without having to refer to the central bank. In 1989 the government also announced further measures to liberalize foreign exchange controls. An offshore banking facility was established in that year, under legislation adopted in December 1988. Barclays Bank of Mauritius, the Bank of Baroda and the Banque Privée Edmond de Rothschild were initially granted licences. A total of seven offshore banks were operating in early 1994. The government has also implemented a series of incentives to encourage companies to incorporate locally and to offer a minimum of 25% of their shares on the stock exchange, which opened in Port Louis in July 1989. Investors in these companies were to be exempt from tax on 35% of all dividend payments, and annual profits of up to Rs 100,000 from the sale of these securities were also to be exempt. Mauritius strengthened trade and investment relations with South Africa during 1990. Several textile firms have since opened offices in Madagascar, and other firms in the food and tourism sectors were also considering investment. China and Mauritius signed a technical co-operation and economic agreement in 1990, which provides Mauritius with an interest-free loan of $5.3m. for infrastructure projects; it is hoped that capital from Hong Kong, after that territory's return to Chinese sovereignty in 1997, might be attracted to Mauritius.

ECONOMIC PROSPECTS

Despite its relatively favourable economic performance during the 1980s, Mauritius faces a number of problems and uncertainties. Prominent among these is the rate of population growth, which projects a population of more than 1.5m. people by the year 2010, exclusive of the numbers of émigré Mauritians, estimated at about 50,000, who are expected to return to the island following retirement. This demographic trend is expected to pose the economy with considerable challenges.

The EPZ sector, which has led the island's industrial expansion in recent years, is expected to show growth of less than 8% annually in the 1990s. Since the base of export diversification is unlikely to be widened in the short term, a further decline in this sector can be expected. The government, however, is proceeding with proposals to diversify the EPZ's industrial base and to improve vocational, technical and professional training for the industrial sector. Inflation, which has so far been held within manageable levels, totalled 7% in 1991, and fell to 4.6% in 1992. Tourism, an economic mainstay of recent years, is becoming confronted by the prospect of overcrowding and environmental damage.

Mauritius' infrastructure is beginning to show need of heavy investment in projects such as roads, telecommunications and public utilities. A World Bank report, published in 1989, stressed the need for economic diversification to minimize the country's vulnerability to fluctuations in the international economy. Moreover, if GATT negotiations result in increased competition in the international textile market, Mauritius could lose its privileged access to the EU markets; the industry would therefore have to become more competitive, with the use of newer, costly technology. Recent changes by the EU, under its Common Agricultural Policy, and a decline in European sugar prices are also expected to have adverse effects on local sugar producers. Foreign direct investment into Mauritius increased during the 1980s, owing primarily to the expansion in the EPZ. By 1991, however, this investment fell sharply, following a slow-down in EPZ growth. This decreased investment led in turn to a further decline in the EPZ. However, the government remains committed to a free market economy, with the liberalization of foreign exchange controls and foreign exchange travel allowances, the rehabilitation of the port and establishment of a free port, strengthening the manufacturing sector in the EPZ. The government has also extended a number of privileges which were previously granted only to firms in the EPZ, and has abolished import permits for the majority of goods. With the implementation of such policies, and the inception of economic diversification, Mauritius can expect to experience much higher growth and per caput income levels than elsewhere in sub-Saharan Africa.

Statistical Survey

Source (unless otherwise stated): Central Statistical Office, Toorawa Centre, cnr Sir Seewoosagur Ramgoolam and J. Mosque Sts, Port Louis; tel. 2122316.

Area and Population

AREA, POPULATION AND DENSITY

Area (sq km)	2,040*
Population (census results)	
2 July 1983†	
Males	499,360
Females	502,818
Total	1,002,178
1 July 1990‡	1,058,942
Population (official estimates at mid-year)§	
1991	1,070,000
1992	1,084,000
Density (per sq km) at mid-1992§	550.5

* 788 sq miles.
† Including an adjustment of 1,746 for underenumeration.
‡ Including an adjustment of 2,115 for underenumeration.
§ Islands of Mauritius and Rodrigues only (area 1,969 sq km, population 1,058,775 at 1990 census).

ISLANDS

	Area (sq km)	Population: 2 July 1983 Census*	Population: 1 July 1990 Census†
Mauritius	1,865	968,609‡	1,024,571‡
Rodrigues	104	33,082	34,204
Other islands	71	487	167

* Figures relate to the *de facto* population.
† Figures relate to the *de jure* population.
‡ Including adjustment for underenumeration.

ETHNIC GROUPS

Island of Mauritius, mid-1982: 664,480 Indo-Mauritians (507,985 Hindus, 156,495 Muslims), 264,537 general population (incl. Creole and Franco-Mauritian communities), 20,669 Chinese.

LANGUAGE GROUPS (census of 1 July 1990)*

Arabic	1,686
Bhojpuri	343,832
Chinese	17,652
Creole	379,288
English	888
French	22,367
Hindi	38,181
Marathi	17,732
Tamil	47,953
Telegu	21,033
Urdu	45,311
Other languages	120,737
Total	1,056,660

* Figures refer to the usual languages spoken by the population on the islands of Mauritius and Rodrigues only. The data exclude an adjustment for underenumeration. The adjusted total was 1,058,775.

PRINCIPAL TOWNS (estimated population at mid-1993)

Port Louis (capital)	143,509	Curepipe	75,483
Beau Bassin/Rose Hill	95,140	Quatre Bornes	72,402
Vacoas-Phoenix	93,288		

BIRTHS, MARRIAGES AND DEATHS*

	1991	1992	1993
Registered live births:			
Number	22,197	22,902	22,329
Rate (per 1,000)	20.7	21.2	20.3
Registered marriages:			
Number	11,295	11,408	11,579
Rate (per 1,000)	10.6	10.5	10.6
Registered deaths:			
Number	7,027	7,023	7,433
Rate (per 1,000)	6.6	6.5	6.8

* Figures refer to the islands of Mauritius and Rodrigues only.

EMPLOYMENT
(persons aged 12 years and over)

	1991	1992	1993
Agriculture, hunting, forestry and fishing	72,000	71,500	71,000
Mining and quarrying	1,000	1,200	1,200
Manufacturing	139,400	141,300	139,100
Electricity, gas and water	3,400	3,400	3,500
Construction	30,700	31,700	32,900
Trade, restaurants and hotels	56,900	61,300	66,800
Transport, storage and communications	31,000	33,500	34,700
Financing, insurance, real estate and business services	12,100	12,900	14,100
Community, social and personal services	105,200	107,800	113,200
Activities not adequately defined	4,400	3,600	3,000
Total employed	456,100	468,200	479,500
Males	303,400	310,100	314,500
Females	152,700	158,100	165,000

Agriculture

PRINCIPAL CROPS ('000 metric tons)

	1990	1991	1992*
Maize	2	2	2
Potatoes	18	16	15
Coconuts*	3	2	3
Tomatoes	12	9	12
Sugar cane	5,548	5,621	6,400
Bananas	6	6	6
Tobacco (leaves)	1	1	1
Groundnuts (in shell)	2	1	2

* FAO estimates.

Source: FAO, *Production Yearbook*.

Tea (made) ('000 metric tons): 5.9 in 1991; 5.8 in 1992; 5.9 in 1993 (Source: International Tea Committee).

LIVESTOCK ('000 head, year ending September)

	1990	1991	1992*
Cattle	33	34*	34
Pigs	10	14	10
Sheep	7	7*	7
Goats*	95	96	95

* FAO estimate(s).

Source: FAO, *Production Yearbook*.

LIVESTOCK PRODUCTS ('000 metric tons)

	1990	1991*	1992*
Meat	14	15	15
Cows' milk*	25	25	25
Hen eggs*	4.2	4.2	4.3

* FAO estimates.

Source: FAO, *Production Yearbook*.

Forestry

ROUNDWOOD REMOVALS ('000 cubic metres, excluding bark)

	1989	1990	1991
Sawlogs, veneer logs and logs for sleepers	8	6	9
Other industrial wood	6	5	5
Fuel wood	17	16	3
Total	31	27	17

Source: FAO, *Yearbook of Forest Products*.

SAWNWOOD PRODUCTION ('000 cubic metres)

	1989	1990	1991
Total	5	4	5

Source: FAO, *Yearbook of Forest Products*.

Fishing

('000 metric tons, live weight)

	1989	1990	1991
Emperors (Scavengers)	4.3	3.7	4.0
Skipjack tuna	5.6	4.1	6.5
Yellowfin tuna	1.8	1.4	2.7
Other fishes (incl. unspecified)	5.0	5.1	5.2
Crustaceans and molluscs	0.5	0.4	0.4
Total catch	17.2	14.7	18.9

Source: FAO, *Yearbook of Fishery Statistics*.

Industry

SELECTED PRODUCTS (metric tons, unless otherwise indicated)

	1990	1991	1992
Raw sugar	624,302	611,340	643,168
Molasses	168,023	174,933	173,000
Manufactured tea	5,751	5,918	5,828
Beer and stout (hectolitres)	281,243	291,453	295,100
Electric energy (million kWh)*	667	737	n.a.

Rum (hectolitres): 53,000 in 1987; 59,000 in 1988; 64,000 in 1989 (Source: UN, *Industrial Statistics Yearbook*).

Ethyl alcohol (hectolitres): 22,292 in 1987; 29,000 in 1988; 26,000 in 1989 (Source: mainly UN, *Industrial Statistics Yearbook*).

Finance

CURRENCY AND EXCHANGE RATES

Monetary Units

100 cents = 1 Mauritian rupee.

Sterling and Dollar Equivalents (31 March 1994)

£1 sterling = 27.00 rupees;
US $1 = 18.19 rupees;
1,000 Mauritian rupees = £37.03 = $54.98.

Average Exchange Rate (Mauritian rupees per US $)

1991	15.652
1992	15.563
1993	17.648

BUDGET (million rupees, year ending 30 June)*

Revenue†	1990/91	1991/92	1992/93
Taxation	9,516.7	9,957.1	11,013.8
Taxes on income, profits and capital gains	1,387.1	1,565.4	1,464.7
Individual taxes	544.1	552.2	696.8
Corporate taxes	843.0	1,013.2	767.9
Social security contributions	419.1	574.3	690.5
Taxes on property	609.8	568.7	716.1
Taxes on financial and capital transactions	599.3	559.1	704.8
Domestic taxes on goods and services	2,297.9	2,585.3	2,939.8
General sales, turnover or value-added taxes	846.0	951.2	1,044.5
Excises	831.3	886.2	1,075.6
Alcoholic beverages	492.6	536.7	620.0
Taxes on specific services	471.5	576.6	573.7
Taxes on international trade and transactions	4,719.2	4,587.6	5,119.1
Import duties	4,247.9	4,159.5	4,685.2
Customs duties	2,789.4	2,708.6	3,222.4
Other import charges	1,458.5	1,450.9	1,462.8
Export duties	427.6	416.3	433.8
Other current revenue	598.2	1,420.9	1,366.4
Entrepreneurial and property income	248.1	991.4	957.2
From non-financial public enterprises and public financial institutions	213.1	934.8	896.3
Administrative fees and charges, non-industrial and incidental sales	260.1	314.8	306.4
Total	10,114.9	11,378.0	12,363.2

Expenditure‡	1990/91	1991/92	1992/93
General public services	1,042.8	1,226.1	1,240.3
Defence	153.0	175.6	180.1
Public order and safety	901.9	882.9	1,093.8
Education	1,444.0	1,684.0	1,810.3
Health	870.6	930.9	1,145.8
Social security and welfare	1,458.4	1,764.7	1,966.2
Housing and community amenities	328.3	500.4	738.7
Recreational, cultural and religious affairs and services	164.5	340.3	234.4
Economic affairs and services	1,489.5	1,880.8	1,886.1
Agriculture, forestry, fishing and hunting	623.9	683.0	715.2
Mining, manufacturing and construction	35.3	40.5	67.1
Transport and communication	433.1	689.4	665.2
Other purposes	2,090.5	2,131.9	1,846.1
Public debt interest	1,564.0	1,469.8	1,182.3
Transfers to local government	353.6	409.6	437.5
Development works	100.2	114.0	106.5
Total	9,943.5	11,517.6	12,141.8
Current	8,218.2	9,246.4	9,779.5
Capital	1,725.3	2,271.2	2,362.3

* Figures represent a consolidation of the General Budget, the National Pensions Fund and the operations of 13 extrabudgetary units of the central Government. Local government councils are excluded.

† Excluding grants received from abroad (million rupees): 25.2 in 1991/92; 78.0 in 1992/93.

‡ Excluding net lending (million rupees): 244.0 in 1991/92; 274.7 in 1992/93.

BANK OF MAURITIUS RESERVES
(US $ million at 31 December)

	1991	1992	1993
Gold*	4.9	4.2	3.9
IMF special drawing rights	25.7	24.3	28.9
Reserve position in IMF	1.8	8.6	10.1
Foreign exchange	865.8	787.3	718.1
Total	898.2	824.4	760.9

* Valued at market-related prices.

Source: IMF, *International Financial Statistics.*

MONEY SUPPLY (million rupees at 31 December)

	1991	1992	1993
Currency outside banks	3,407.5	3,820.1	4,230.9
Demand deposits at deposit money banks	3,262.8	3,383.4	3,188.3

Source: IMF, *International Financial Statistics.*

COST OF LIVING (Consumer Price Index, average of monthly figures. Base: June 1992 = 100)

	1991*	1992	1993
Food	149.2	102.4	116.5
Fuel and light	118.3	103.2	107.4
Rent	126.4	102.9	106.4
All items (incl. others)	149.5	103.5	114.4

* Base: 1987 = 100.

NATIONAL ACCOUNTS (million rupees in current prices)

Components of the Gross National Product

	1991	1992	1993*
Compensation of employees	17,228	19,455	22,800
Operating surplus; Consumption of fixed capital	18,720	20,960	23,550
Gross domestic product (GDP) at factor cost	35,948	40,415	46,350
Indirect taxes	7,221	7.765	8,630
Less Subsidies	403	465	330
GDP in purchasers' values	42,766	47,715	54,650
Factor income received from abroad; *Less* Factor income paid abroad	89	180	50
Gross national product (GNP) at market prices	42,855	47,895	54,700

Expenditure on the Gross Domestic Product

	1991	1992	1993*
Government final consumption expenditure	5,005	5,560	6,600
Private final consumption expenditure	27,500	30,156	34,400
Increase in stocks	–453	140	310
Gross fixed capital formation	12,385	13,630	15,600
Total domestic expenditure	44,437	49,486	56,910
Exports of goods and services	27,861	29,902	33,350
Less Imports of goods and services	29,532	31,673	35,610
GDP in purchasers' values	42,766	47,715	54,650
GDP at constant 1987 prices	29,367	31,164	32,721

Gross Domestic Product by Economic Activity
(at factor cost)

	1991	1992	1993*
Agriculture, forestry, hunting and fishing	4,093	4,495	4,625
Mining and quarrying	45	55	70
Manufacturing	8,274	9,200	10,315
Electricity, gas and water	775	975	1,240
Construction	2,590	3,005	3,500
Trade, restaurants and hotels	6,100	6,900	8,150
Transport, storage and communications	4,200	4,810	5,550
Financing, insurance, real estate and business services	4,354	4,825	5,500
Government services	3,640	3,985	4,825
Other services	1,877	2,165	2,575
Total	35,948	40,415	46,350

* Figures are provisional.

BALANCE OF PAYMENTS (US $ million)

	1991	1992	1993
Merchandise exports f.o.b.	1,215.1	1,302.6	1,304.4
Merchandise imports f.o.b.	–1,419.1	–1,473.4	–1,558.6
Trade balance	–204.0	–170.9	–254.2
Exports of services	566.6	609.6	609.9
Imports of services	–467.9	–543.3	–551.2
Other income received	82.5	91.0	70.0
Other income paid	–76.9	–80.1	–66.4
Private unrequited transfers (net)	79.5	86.6	91.7
Official unrequited transfers (net)	1.9	5.4	4.4
Current balance	–18.2	–1.5	–95.8
Direct investment (net)	8.1	–28.6	–25.5
Portfolio investment (net)	–0.4	—	–2.2
Other capital (net)	34.2	13.8	39.9
Net errors and omissions	167.2	59.7	90.6
Overall balance	190.8	43.3	7.0

Source: IMF, *International Financial Statistics.*

External Trade

PRINCIPAL COMMODITIES (million rupees)

Imports c.i.f.*	1991	1992	1993
Dairy products	547	598	667
Rice	314	277	464
Wheat flour	76	53	45
Petroleum products	1,783	1,766	1,771
Fixed vegetable oils	200	218	199
Textile yarn and thread	1,717	1,825	2,256
Textile fabrics	2,910	3,174	4,300
Cement	523	554	630
Iron and steel goods	700	689	777
Power-generating machinery	843	531	179
Machinery for particular industries	1,149	977	1,601
General industrial machinery	739	793	918
Road motor vehicles	1,188	1,310	1,396
Total (incl. others)	24,383	25,313	30,342

Exports f.o.b.†	1990	1991	1992
Sugar, raw	5,298	5,668	5,770
Molasses	96	91	93
Tea	83	95	113
Total (incl. others)	5,948	6,432	6,622

* Figures are provisional.
† Figures refer to domestic exports, excluding exports (mainly clothing) from the Export Processing Zone (EPZ), totalling (in million rupees): 12,136 in 1991; 13,081 in 1992; 15,821 in 1993.

PRINCIPAL TRADING PARTNERS (million rupees)

Imports c.i.f.*	1991	1992	1993
Australia	795	804	897
Bahrain	628	240	13
Belgium	306	362	747
China, People's Repub.	949	844	1,276
France	3,283	3,372	3,831
Germany	1,358	1,249	1,457
Hong Kong	1,068	1,082	1,393
India	1,115	1,323	1,773
Indonesia	144	227	403
Italy	781	744	1,026
Japan	1,770	2,176	1,792
Korea, Repub.	277	367	447
Kuwait	n.a.	n.a.	n.a.
Malaysia	539	664	835
New Zealand	337	337	361
Pakistan	309	305	462
Singapore	730	808	894
South Africa	2,870	3,272	4,112
Switzerland	349	433	556
Taiwan	1,104	948	1,262
United Kingdom	1,677	1,834	2,143
USA	530	553	707
Total (incl. others)	24,363	25,313	30,542

Exports f.o.b.*	1991	1992	1993
Belgium	328	357	496
Canada	96	163	122
France	3,727	4,207	4,709
Germany	2,055	1,778	1,633
Italy	918	937	917
Netherlands	368	368	480
Réunion	364	453	483
United Kingdom	6,750	6,992	7,440
USA	2,209	2,500	4,117
Total (incl. others)	18,700	20,072	22,992

* Figures are provisional.

Transport

ROAD TRAFFIC

	1991	1992	1993
Private vehicles:			
Cars	30,882	32,751	34,449
Motorcycles and mopeds	68,090	77,227	85,540
Commercial vehicles:			
Buses	2,021	2,097	2,217
Taxis	3,965	4,014	4,050
Goods vehicles	27,425	30,952	33,829
Government vehicles	3,912	4,136	4,378

Source: Ministry of Works, Port Louis.

SEA-BORNE SHIPPING
(freight traffic, '000 metric tons)

	1991	1992	1993
Goods unloaded	2,024	2,232	2,375
Goods loaded	851	956	830

Source: Ministry of Works, Port Louis.

CIVIL AVIATION (traffic)

	1991	1992	1993
Aircraft landings	5,265	5,322	5,577
Passenger arrivals	426,680	475,920	526,000*
Freight unloaded (metric tons)	11,198	11,200	11,066
Freight loaded (metric tons)	18,191	15,704	14,674

*Provisional.

Source: Ministry of Works, Port Louis.

Tourism

FOREIGN TOURIST ARRIVALS

Country of Residence	1991	1992	1993*
France	58,370	74,300	86,300
Germany, Federal Republic	24,140	29,800	40,600
Italy	13,290	14,990	15,000
Madagascar	6,010	7,260	7,600
Réunion	77,890	81,260	89,000
South Africa	43,020	39,790	42,000
Switzerland	8,930	10,150	11,000
United Kingdom	20,660	24,510	29,100
Total (incl. others)	300,670	335,400	375,000

*Provisional.

Communications Media

	1989	1990	1991
Radio receivers ('000 in use)	380	385	390
Television receivers ('000 in use)	230	233	236
Book production*:			
Titles	100	75	56
Copies ('000)	242	216	157
Daily newspapers:			
Number	n.a.	7	n.a.
Average circulation ('000 copies)	n.a.	80	n.a.
Non-daily newspapers:			
Number	n.a.	24	n.a.
Average circulation ('000 copies)	n.a.	75	n.a.

* Including pamphlets (26 titles and 47,000 copies in 1989; 22 titles and 109,000 copies 1990; 20 titles and 92,000 copies in 1991).

Source: UNESCO, *Statistical Yearbook*.

Telephones ('000 in use): 74 in 1989; 75 in 1990 (Source: UN *Statistical Yearbook*).

Education

(1993)

	Institutions	Students
Primary	281	125,543
Secondary	123	87,661
University	1	2,161
Institute of Education	1	2,645
Lycée Polytechnique	1	395

Directory

The Constitution

The Mauritius Independence Order, which established a self-governing state, came into force on 12 March 1968, and was subsequently amended. Constitutional amendments providing for the adoption of republican status were approved by the Legislative Assembly (henceforth known as the National Assembly) on 10 December 1991, and came into effect on 12 March 1992. The main provisions of the revised Constitution are listed below:

HEAD OF STATE

The Head of State is the President of the Republic, who is elected by a simple majority of the National Assembly for a five-year term of office. The President appoints the Prime Minister (in whom executive power is vested) and, on the latter's recommendation, other ministers.

COUNCIL OF MINISTERS

The Council of Ministers, which is headed by the Prime Minister, is appointed by the President and is responsible to the National Assembly.

THE NATIONAL ASSEMBLY

The National Assembly, which has a term of five years, comprises the Speaker, 62 members elected by universal adult suffrage, a maximum of eight additional members and the Attorney-General (if not an elected member). The island of Mauritius is divided into 20 three-member constituencies for legislative elections. Rodrigues returns two members to the National Assembly, one of whom is designated Minister for Rodrigues. The official language of the National Assembly is English, but any member may address the Speaker in French.

The Government

HEAD OF STATE

President: Cassam Uteem (took office 30 June 1992).

Vice-President: Sir Rabindrah Ghurburrun.

COUNCIL OF MINISTERS
(September 1994)

A coalition of the Mouvement Socialiste Mauricien (MSM), the Renouveau Militant Mauricien (RMM) and the Mouvement des

Travaillistes Démocrates (MTD). The Organisation du Peuple Rodriguais (OPR) is also represented.

Prime Minister, Minister of Defence and Internal Security, Information, Internal and External Communications and the Outer Islands, Minister of Justice and Attorney-General: Sir ANEROOD JUGNAUTH (MSM).

Deputy Prime Minister and Minister of Economic Planning and Development, Minister of Information and of Internal and External Communications: Dr PARAMHANSA NABABSING (RMM).

Minister of Health: JEAN REGIS FINETTE (MSM).

Minister of Trade and Shipping: ANIL KUMAR BACHOO (MTD) (until 15 Nov. 1994); DWARKANATH GUNGAH (MSM) (from 15 Nov. 1994).

Minister of Women's Rights, Child Development and Family Welfare: SHEILABHAI BAPPOO (MSM).

Minister of External Affairs: AHMUD SWALAY KASENALLY (RMM) (until 15 Nov. 1994); RAMDATHSING JADDOO (MSM) (from 15 Nov. 1994).

Minister of Arts, Culture, Leisure and Youth Development: MOOKHESSWUR CHOONEE (MSM).

Minister for Rodrigues: LOUIS SERGE CLAIR (OPR).

Minister of Housing, Lands and Town and Country Planning: LOUIS AMEDÉE DARGA (RMM).

Minister of Agriculture and Natural Resources: KEERTEE COOMAR RUHEE (RMM).

Minister of Local Government: PREMDUT KOONJOO (MMM).

Minister of Labour and Industrial Relations: KARL AUGUSTE OFFMANN (MSM).

Minister of Sports and Leisure: MICHAEL GLOVER (MSM).

Minister of Co-operatives and Handicraft: JAGDISHWAR GOBURDHUN (MSM).

Minister of Works: ANIL KUMAR BACHOO.

Minister of Manpower Resources and Vocational and Technical Training: RAMDUTHSING JADDOO (MSM) (until 15 Nov. 1994); MAHYENDRAH UTCHANAH (MSM) (from 15 Nov. 1994).

Minister of the Environment and Quality of Life: BASHIR AHMUD KHODABUX (RMM).

Minister of Tourism: NOE AH-QWET LEE CHEONG LEM (MMM).

Minister of Social Security and National Solidarity: DHARMANAND GOOPT FOKEER (RMM).

Minister of Education and Science: ARMOOGUM PARSURAMEN (MSM).

Minister of Civil Service Affairs and Employment: ASHOK KUMAR JUGNAUTH (MSM).

Minister of Finance: RAMAKRISHNA SITHANEN (MSM).

Minister of Energy, Water Resources and Postal Services, and of Scientific Research and Technology: AHMUD SWALAY KASENALLY (RMM).

Minister of Industry and Industrial Technology: JEAN-CLAUDE DE L'ESTRAC (RMM).

Minister of Fisheries and Marine Resources: MATHIEU ANGE LACLÉ (RMM).

MINISTRIES

Prime Minister's Office: Government Centre, Port Louis; tel. 2011001; telex 4249; fax 2088619.

Ministry of Agriculture and Natural Resources: NPF Bldg, 9th Floor, Port Louis; tel. 2127946; fax 2124427.

Ministry of Arts, Culture, Leisure and Reform Institutions: Government Centre, Port Louis; tel. 2012032.

Ministry of Civil Service Affairs and Employment: Government Centre, Port Louis; tel. 2011035.

Ministry of Co-operatives and Handicraft: Life Insurance Corpn of India Bldg, 3rd Floor, John Kennedy St, Port Louis; tel. 2084812; fax 2089265.

Ministry of Economic Planning and Development: Emmanuel Anquetil Bldg, Sir Seewoosagur Ramgoolam St, Port Louis; tel. 2011576; fax 2124124.

Ministry of Education and Science: Sun Trust Bldg, Edith Cavell St, Port Louis; tel. 2128411; fax 2123783.

Ministry of Energy, Water Resources and Postal Services: Government Centre, Port Louis; tel. 2011087; fax 2086497.

Ministry of the Environment and Quality of Life: Barracks St, Port Louis; tel. 2128332; fax 2129407.

Ministry of External Affairs: Government Centre, Port Louis; tel. 2011416; fax 2088087.

Ministry of Finance: Government Centre, Port Louis; tel. 2011145; fax 2088622.

Ministry of Fisheries and Marine Resources: Port Louis.

Ministry of Health: Emmanuel Anquetil Bldg, Sir Seewoosagur Ramgoolam St, Port Louis; tel. 2011910; fax 2080376.

Ministry of Housing, Lands and Town and Country Planning: Moorgate House, Port Louis; tel. 2126022; fax 2127482.

Ministry of Industry and Industrial Technology: Government Centre, Port Louis; tel. 2011221; fax 2128201.

Ministry of Information: Government Centre, Port Louis; tel. 2011278; fax 2088243.

Ministry of Internal and External Communications: Emmanuel Anquetil Bldg, 10th Floor, Sir Seewoosagur Ramgoolam St, Port Louis; tel. 2011089; fax 2121673.

Ministry of Justice: Jules Koenig St, Port Louis; tel. 2085321.

Ministry of Labour and Industrial Relations: Government Centre, Port Louis; tel. 2011195; fax 2089265.

Ministry of Local Government: Government Centre, Port Louis; tel. 2011215.

Ministry of Manpower Resources and Vocational and Technical Training: Jade House, Remy Ollier St, Port Louis; tel. 2421462.

Ministry for Rodrigues: Fon Sing Bldg, Edith Cavell St, Port Louis; tel. 2088472; fax 2126329.

Ministry of Social Security and National Solidarity: cnr Maillard and Jules Koenig Sts, Port Louis; tel. 2123006.

Ministry of Tourism: Emmanuel Anquetil Bldg, Sir Seewoosagur Ramgoolam St, Port Louis; tel. 2012286; fax 2086776.

Ministry of Trade and Shipping: Government Centre, Port Louis; tel. 2011067; fax 2126368.

Ministry of Women's Rights, Child Development and Family Welfare: Rainbow House, cnr Edith Cavell and Brown Sequard Sts, Port Louis; tel. 2082061; fax 2088250.

Ministry of Works: Treasury Bldg, Port Louis; tel. 2080281; fax 2128373.

Ministry of Youth and Sports: Emmanuel Anquetil Bldg, Sir Seewoosagur Ramgoolam St, Port Louis; tel. 2011242; fax 2126506.

Legislature

NATIONAL ASSEMBLY*

Speaker: ISWARDEO SEETARAM.

General Election, 15 September 1991

Party	Seats†
Mouvement Socialiste Mauricien	29
Mouvement Militant Mauricien‡	26
Mauritius Labour Party Parti Mauricien Social-Démocrate	3
Mouvement des Travaillistes Démocrates	2
Organisation du Peuple Rodriguais	2

* The legislature was elected as the Legislative Assembly. It was renamed the National Assembly in accordance with the constitutional amendments that took effect in March 1992.

† Four additional members (unsuccessful candidates who attracted the largest number of votes) were appointed from the MLP/PMSD alliance.

‡ Split in Oct. 1993. Faction supporting the coalition government was reconstituted in June 1994 as the Renouveau Militant Mauricien.

Political Organizations

Comité d'Action Musulman (CAM): POB 882, Port Louis; f. 1958; Indo-Mauritian Muslim support; Pres. YOUSSUF MOHAMMED.

Mauritius Labour Party (MLP): 7 Guy Rozemont Sq., Port Louis; tel. 2126691; f. 1936; Leader Dr NAVIN RAMGOOLAM; Sec.-Gen. JOSEPH TSANG MAN KIN.

Mouvement des Démocrates Libéraux: f. 1994 by VISHNU LUTCHMEENARAIDOO; seeks to replace the MLP in an electoral alliance with the PMSD to contest parl. elections in 1996.

Mouvement des Travaillistes Démocrates: Port Louis; Leader ANIL KUMAR BACHOO.

Mouvement Militant Mauricien (MMM): Port Louis; f. 1970; Leader: PAUL BÉRENGER.

Mouvement Socialiste Mauricien (MSM): Port Louis; f. 1983 by breakaway group from MMM; dominant party in subsequent coalition Govts; Leader Sir ANEROOD JUGNAUTH; Sec.-Gen. V. SAJADAH.

Organisation du Peuple Rodriguais (OPR): Port Mathurin, Rodrigues; represents the interests of Rodrigues; Leader LOUIS SERGE CLAIR.

Parti Mauricien Social-Démocrate (PMSD): POB 599, Port Louis; Pres. ALAN DRIVER; Leader LUC XAVIER DUVAL.

Parti Socialiste Mauricien (PSM): Port Louis; breakaway faction from the Mauritius Labour Party; joined the MSM in 1983; reconstituted as a separate party in 1988; Leader HARISH BOODHOO.

Renouveau Militant Mauricien (RMM): f. 1994 by breakaway faction of Mouvement Militant Mauricien; Chair. DHARMANAND FOKEER; Leader Dr PARAMHANSA (PREM) NABABSING; Gen. Sec. JEAN-CLAUDE DE L' ESTRAC.

Union Démocratique Mauricienne (UDM): 10 Barracks St, Port Louis; tel. 2124945; advocates proportional representation; affiliated to International Christian Democrats; Leader GUY OLLIVRY; Sec.-Gen. ELWYN CHUTEL.

Minor left-wing parties include the **Front des Travailleurs Socialistes** and **Lalit**, a Marxist-Leninist party.

Diplomatic Representation

EMBASSIES AND HIGH COMMISSIONS IN MAURITIUS

Australia: Port Louis; tel. 2081700; telex 4414; fax 2088878; High Commissioner: M. L. MCCARTER.

China, People's Republic: Royal Rd, Belle Rose, Quatre Bornes, Port Louis; tel. 4549111; Ambassador: YANG YIHUAI.

Egypt: King George V Ave, Floreal, Port Louis; tel. 6965012; telex 4332; Ambassador: H. ELBITAR.

France: St George's St, Port Louis; tel. 2083755; telex 4233; fax 2088145; Ambassador: J. DE ZORZI.

India: Life Insurance Corporation of India Bldg, President John F. Kennedy St, Port Louis; tel. 2083775; telex 4523; fax 2086859; High Commissioner: SHYAM SARAN.

Madagascar: Queen Mary Ave, Floreal, Port Louis; tel. 6865015; Ambassador: C. ZENY.

Pakistan: Anglo-Mauritius House, Intendance St, Port Louis; tel. 2126547; telex 4609; fax 2126548; High Commissioner: TASAWAR KHAN (acting).

Russia: Queen Mary Ave, Floreal, POB 509, Port Louis; tel. 6961545; telex 4826; Ambassador: V. I. TRIFONOV.

United Kingdom: POB 186, Curepipe; tel. 6865795; telex 4266; fax 6865792; High Commissioner: JOHN C. HARRISON.

USA: Rogers House, President John F. Kennedy St, Port Louis; tel. 2082347; fax 2089534; Ambassador: LESLIE M. ALEXANDER.

Judicial System

The laws of Mauritius are derived both from the old French Codes, suitably amended, and from English Law. The Judicial Department consists of the Supreme Court, presided over by the Chief Justice and eight other Judges who are also Judges of the Court of Criminal Appeal and the Court of Civil Appeal, the Intermediate Court, the Industrial Court and 10 District Courts. Final appeal is to the Judicial Committee of the Privy Council in the United Kingdom.

Chief Justice: Sir VICTOR GLOVER.

Senior Puisne Judge: R. LALLAH.

Puisne Judges: J. FORGET, A. G. PILLAY, R. PROAG, V. BOOLELL, Y. K. J. YEUNG SIK YUEN, A. M. G. AHMED.

Religion

At the 1972 census, Hindus comprised 51.0% of the population on the island of Mauritius, with Christians accounting for 31.3%, Muslims 16.6% and Buddhists 0.6%.

CHRISTIANITY

The Anglican Communion

Anglicans in Mauritius are within the Church of the Province of the Indian Ocean, comprising five dioceses (three in Madagascar, one in Mauritius and one in Seychelles). The Archbishop of the Province is the Bishop of Seychelles. In 1983 the Church had 5,438 members in Mauritius.

Bishop of Mauritius: Rt Rev. REX DONAT, Bishop's House, Phoenix; tel. 6865158.

Presbyterian Church of Mauritius

Minister: Pasteur ANDRÉ DE RÉLAND, 11 Poudrière St, Port Louis; tel. 2082386; f. 1814.

The Roman Catholic Church

Mauritius comprises a single diocese, directly responsible to the Holy See. At 31 December 1992 there were an estimated 287,853 adherents in the country, representing about 27% of the total population.

Bishop of Port Louis: Rt Rev. MAURICE PIAT, Evêché, 13 Mgr Gonin St, Port Louis; tel. 2083068; fax 2086607.

BAHÁ'Í FAITH

National Spiritual Assembly: POB 538, Port Louis; tel. 2122179; mems resident in 190 localities.

ISLAM

Mauritius Islamic Mission: Noor-e-Islam Mosque, Port Louis; Imam S. M. BEEHARRY.

The Press

DAILIES

China Times: 34 Emmanuel Anquetil St, POB 325, Port Louis; tel. 2403067; f. 1953; Chinese; Editor-in-Chief LONG SIONG AH KENG; circ. 3,000.

Chinese Daily News: 32 Rémy Ollier St, POB 316, Port Louis; tel. 2400472; f. 1932; Chinese; Editor-in-Chief WONG YUEN MOY; circ. 5,000.

L'Express: 3 Brown Sequard St, POB 247, Port Louis; tel. 2124365; telex 4384; fax 2088174; f. 1963; English and French; Editor-in-Chief YVAN MARTIAL; circ. 30,000.

Global News: Résidence des 5 Palmiers, 198 Royal Rd, Beau-Bassin; tel. 4543353; fax 4543420; English and French; daily, excl. Thurs. and Sun.; Editor FINLAY SALESSE.

Le Mauricien: 8 St George's St, POB 7, Port Louis; tel. 2083252; fax 2087059; f. 1908; English and French; Editor-in-Chief SIDNEY SELVON; circ. 30,000.

Le Socialiste: Manilall Bldg, 3rd Floor, Brabant St, Port Louis; tel. 2088003; English and French; Editor-in-Chief DÉSIRÉ APPOU; circ. 6,000.

The Sun: 31 Edith Cavell St, Port Louis; tel. 2089516; fax 2089517; English and French; Editor-in-Chief SUBASH GOBIN; circ. 22,000.

WEEKLIES AND FORTNIGHTLIES

Le Défi: 43 Lord Kitchener St, Port Louis; tel. 2110843; English and French; Editor-in-Chief YVON BRULECOEUR.

Le Dimanche: 5 Jemmapes St, Port Louis; tel. 2121177; f. 1961; English and French; Editor RÉGIS NAUVEL; circ. 20,000.

L'Evénement: 1 Victoria Bldg, Corderie St, Port Louis; tel. 2081400; English and French; Editor PERCY MCGAW.

L'Indépendant: 104 Chancery House, Port Louis; English and French; Editor-in-Chief NAMASSIWAYAM RAMALINGUM.

Lalit da Klas: 153B Royal Rd, G.R.N.W., Port Louis; tel. 2082132; Creole; Editor ASHOK SUBRON.

Mauritius Times: 23 Bourbon St, POB 202, Port Louis; tel. 2121313; telex 4409; fax 2121743; f. 1954; English and French; Editor-in-Chief BICKRAMSINGH RAMLALLAH; circ. 15,000.

Mauritius Today: 16 Conti St, Port Louis; English and French; Editors K. RAMSAHYE, D. BEEKHARRY.

Mirror: 39 Emmanuel Anquetil St, Port Louis; tel. 2403298; Chinese, English and French; Editor-in-Chief NG KEE SIONG; circ. 4,000.

Le Nouveau Militant: 21 Poudrière St, Port Louis; tel. 2126553; fax 2082291; f. 1979; publ. by the Mouvement Militant Mauricien; English and French; Editor-in-Chief J. RAUMIAH.

Le Rassembleur: 7 D'Estaing St, Port Louis; tel. 2089543; English and French; Editor DESIRÉ APPOU.

Le Rodriguais; Saint Gabriel, Rodrigues; tel. 8311613; fax 8311484; f. 1989; Creole, English and French; Editor JACQUES EDOUARD; circ. 2,000.

Sportamo: Nouvelle Imprimerie Mauricienne, 5 Jemmapes St, Port Louis; French.

Star: 43 Lord Kitchener St, Port Louis; tel. 2126110; English and French; Editor-in-Chief Dr H. RUHOMALLY.

Sunday Star: 38 Labourdonnais St, Port Louis; tel. 2420649; English and French; Editor-in-Chief A. A. SOHAWON.

Le Travailleur: POB 545, Port Louis; f. 1968; French and English.

Tzu Chiang Pao: 12 Arsenal St, Port Louis; f. 1972; Chinese; Editor H. S. M. YAN.

La Vie Catholique: 28 Nicolay Rd, Port Louis; tel. and fax 2420975; f. 1930; English and French; Editor-in-Chief MONIQUE DINAN; circ. 15,000.

Week-End: 8 St George's St, Port Louis; tel. 2083252; f. 1966; French and English; Editor-in-Chief GÉRARD CATEAU; circ. 35,000.

Zamana: 14 Vallonville St, Port Louis; f. 1948; English, French, Hindi; circ. 1,000.

MONTHLIES

Le Croissant: cnr Noor-e-Islam Mosque and Velore Sts, Port Louis; tel. 2407105; f. 1979; publ. by the Mauritius Islamic Mission; English and French; Dir Imam S. M. BEEHARRY; Editor BASHIR A. OOZEER; circ. 3,000.

Education News: Edith Cavell St, Port Louis; tel. 2121303; English and French; Editor-in-Chief GIAN AUBEELUCK.

Le Message: c/o Ahmadiyya Muslim Asscn, Dar es Salaam, POB 6, Rose Hill; tel. 4641747; fax 4542223; French; Editor ZAFRULLAH DOMUN.

Perspectives: 13 Jemmapes St, Port Louis; tel. 2081754; English and French; Editor T. TSANG KWAI KEW.

Le Progrès Islamique: 51 Solferino St, Rose Hill; f. 1948; English and French; Editor N. SOOKIA.

PROSI: Plantation House, Port Louis; tel. 2123302; telex 4214; f. 1969; sugar industry journal; circ. 2,000.

La Voix d'Islam: Parisot Rd, Mesnil, Phoenix; f. 1951; English and French.

PERIODICALS

5-Plus Magazine: Résidence des 5 Palmiers, 198 Royal Rd, Beau Bassin; tel. 4543353; fax 4543420; English and French; Editor-in-Chief PIERRE BENOIT.

Business Magazine: TN Tower, 1st Floor, 13 St George's St, Port Louis; tel. 2111925; fax 2111926; Editor-in-Chief LYNDSAY RIVIÈRE.

Femme des Iles: 43 Lord Kitchener St, Port Louis; tel. 2082126; Editor S. MAULLOO.

Le Mag: Industrial Zone, Tombeau Bay; tel. 2471005; fax 2471061; English and French; Editor ALAIN GORDON-GENTIL.

Mapbin News: cnr Jummah Mosque and Sir Virgil Naz Sts, Port Louis; tel. 2420892; English and French; quarterly; Editor-in-Chief YOUSOUF JUGROO.

Virginie: Azalées Ave, Quatre Bornes, Port Louis; women's interest; 6 a year.

Publishers

Best Graphics Ltd: Le Mauricien Bldg, 2nd Floor, 8 St George's St, Port Louis; tel. 2086283; Gen. Man. CLIFFORD LILYMAN.

Bukié Banané: 5 Edwin Ythier St, Rose Hill; tel. 4542327; f. 1979; Creole literature, poetry and drama; Man. Dir DEV VIRAHSAWMY.

Editions Le Printemps: 4 Club Rd, Vacoas; tel. 6961017; fax 6867302; Man. Dir ISLAM SULLIVAN.

Editions Nassau: Barclay St, Rose Hill; f. 1970; general fiction and paperbacks; Gen. Man. E. H. DENNEMONT.

Editions de l'Océan Indien Ltée: Stanley, Rose Hill; tel. 4646781; telex 4739; fax 4643445; f. 1977; textbooks, literature; English and French; Chair. S. BISSOONDOYAL.

Radio and Television

In 1991, according to UNESCO estimates, there were 390,000 radio receivers and 236,000 television receivers in use.

Mauritius Broadcasting Corporation: Broadcasting House, Louis Pasteur St, Forest Side; tel. 6865001; telex 4230; fax 6757332; f. 1964; independent corpn operating the national radio and television services; Dir-Gen. NANDO BODA.

Finance

(cap. = capital; p.u. = paid up; res = reserves; m. = million; dep. = deposits; br. = branch; amounts in Mauritian rupees)

BANKING

Central Bank

Bank of Mauritius: Sir William Newton St, POB 29, Port Louis; tel. 2084164; telex 4253; fax 2089204; f. 1967; bank of issue; cap. and res 33m., dep. 3,406.8m. (June 1993); Gov. Sir INDURDUTH RAMPHUL; Man. Dir RANAPARTAB TACOURI.

Commercial Banks

Banque Nationale de Paris Intercontinentale: 1 Sir William Newton St, POB 494, Port Louis; tel. 2084147; telex 4231; fax 2088143; Pres. MICHEL PÉBEREAU; Man. Dir YANN OZANNE.

Barclays Bank PLC, Mauritius: Sir William Newton St, POB 284, Port Louis; tel. 2121816; telex 4215; fax 2082720; Gen. Man. PATRICK NOBLE; 21 brs.

Delphis Bank Ltd: 16 Sir William Newton St, POB 485, Port Louis; tel. 2085061; telex 4294; fax 2085388; Man. Dir VIJAY K. RAMPHUL RAHMAN KHAN.

Habib Bank Ltd: 26 Sir William Newton St, POB 505, Port Louis; tel. 2080848; telex 4226; fax 2123829; Sr Vice-Pres. MOHAMMAD PARVEZ.

Hongkong and Shanghai Banking Corporation Ltd: Place d'Armes, POB 50, Port Louis; tel. 2081801; telex 4235; fax 2088449; Man. RICHARD INGLIS.

Indian Ocean International Bank Ltd: 34 Sir William Newton St, POB 863, Port Louis; tel. 2080121; telex 4390; fax 2080127; cap. p.u. 29.5m., dep. 751.2m. (June 1993); Chair. and Man. Dir SAM CUNDEN.

Mauritius Commercial Bank Ltd: 9–15 Sir William Newton St, POB 52, Port Louis; tel. 2082801; telex 4218; fax 2087054; f. 1838; cap. 427.4m., dep. 23,716.3m. (June 1993); Pres. Sir MAURICE LATOUR-ADRIEN; Gen. Man. YVAN LAGESSE; 40 brs.

Mauritius Co-operative Central Bank Ltd: 3 Dumas St, POB 572, Port Louis; tel. 2081059; telex 4248; fax 2087698; f. 1948; cap. p.u. 26.8m. (Feb. 1990), dep. 605.3m. (1989); Man. Dir SIVARAMEN PALAYATHEN; 1 br.; 352 mem. socs.

South East Asian Bank Ltd: 26 Bourbon St, POB 13, Port Louis; tel. 2088826; telex 5328; fax 2088825; Gen. Man. RAMLI AWANG.

The State Commercial Bank Ltd: Chancery House, 4th Floor, Lislet Geoffroy St, POB 152, Port Louis; tel. 2088909; telex 4292; fax 2088209; f. 1973; cap. and res 916.5m., dep. 8,952.8m. (June 1992); Chair. DHARAMDEV MANRAJ; Man. Dir T. M. KRISHNA REDDY; 46 brs.

Union International Bank Ltd: 22 Sir William Newton St, POB 1076, Port Louis; tel. 2088080; telex 4894; fax 2088085; cap. and res 39.1m., dep. 425.3m. (Dec. 1992); CEO K. P. CHANDRA HEGDE.

Development Bank

Development Bank of Mauritius: Chaussée St, POB 157, Port Louis; tel. 2080241; telex 4248; fax 2088498; f. 1964; cap. p.u. 125m., dep. 137.4m. (June 1991); 65% govt-owned; Chair. B. G. GHURBURRUN; Man. Dir RADHA LUXMUN PRABHU.

'Offshore' Banks

'Offshore' banking operations commenced in 1989.

Bank of Baroda (Mauritius): Nirmal House, Sir William Newton St, POB 553, Port Louis; tel. 2125082; fax 2083901; CEO CYRIL ALVARES.

Banque Internationale des Mascareignes: Moorgate House, 4th Floor, Sir William Newton St, POB 489, Port Louis; tel. 2124978; telex 4701; fax. 2124983; f. 1991; cap. p.u. 6m. (1993); Chair. A. WOLKENSTEIN; Gen. Man. FRÉDÉRIC DUNTZE.

Banque Privée Edmond de Rothschild (Océan Indien) Ltée: Chancery House, 3rd Floor, Lislet Geoffroy St, Port Louis; tel. 2122784; telex 4547; fax 2084561; Dir LUDOVIC VERBIST.

STOCK EXCHANGE

Stock Exchange Commission: SICOM Bldg, Sir Célicourt Antelme St, Port Louis; tel. 2088735; telex 5291; fax 2088676; f. 1993; Chair. COULDIP BASANTA; CEO SHARDA DINDOYAL.

Stock Exchange of Mauritius: Cascades Bldg, 6th Floor, Edith Cavell St, Port Louis; tel. 2129541; fax 2088409; f. 1989; Chair. KUSHAL KHUSHIRAM; Man. DARMANAND VIRAHSAWMY.

INSURANCE

Albatross Insurance Co Ltd: 22 St George's St, POB 116, Port Louis; tel. 2122874; telex 4299; fax 2084800; f. 1975; Chair. DEREK TAYLOR.

Anglo-Mauritius Assurance Society Ltd: Swan Group Centre, Intendance St, Port Louis; tel. 2089844; telex 4542; fax 2088956; inc. 1951; Chair. J. M. ANTOINE HAREL; Gen. Man. JEAN DE FONDAUMIÈRE.

British American Insurance Co (Mauritius) Ltd: BAI Bldg, 25 Pope Hennessy St, POB 331, Port Louis; tel. 2083637; fax 2083713; Man. Dir ALAIN C. Y. CHEONG.

Indian Ocean General Assurance Ltd: cnr Rémy Ollier and Corderie Sts, Port Louis; tel. 2124125; telex 4318; fax 2080127; f. 1970; Chair. S. CUNDEN; Man. Dir Mrs D. A. CUNDEN.

Island Insurance Co Ltd: Ken Lee Tower, 8th Floor, cnr Barracks and St George's Sts, Port Louis; tel. 2128594; fax 2088762; Chair. CARRIM A. CURRIMJEE; Man. A. K. ROY.

Lamco International Insurance Ltd: 12 Barracks St, Port Louis; tel. 2120233; telex 4407; fax 2080612; f. 1978; Chair. S. M. LATIFF; Gen. Man. A. S. KARKHANIS.

Life Insurance Corporation of India: Bank of Baroda Bldg, Sir William Newton St, Port Louis; tel. 2081485; telex 4726; fax 20863; Chief Man. Mr ATIMBAH.

Mauritian Eagle Insurance Co Ltd: 10 Dr Ferrière St, POB 854, Port Louis; tel. 2124877; telex 4867; fax 2088608; f. 1973; Exec. Dir GUY LEROUX.

Mauritius Union Assurance Co Ltd: 4 Léoville l'Homme St, POB 233, Port Louis; tel. 2084185; telex 4310; fax 2122962; f. 1948; Chair. Sir MAURICE LATOUR-ADRIEN; Man. Dir GERVAIS SALAÜM.

The New India Assurance Co Ltd: 32 Sir William Newton St, POB 398, Port Louis; tel. 2081442; telex 4834; fax 2082160; Man. Dir S. A. KUMAR.

Rainbow Insurance Co Ltd: 23 Edith Cavell St, POB 389, Port Louis; tel. 2081739; telex 4356; fax 2088750; f. 1976; Chair. B. GOKULSING; Gen. Man. L. RAMBURN.

Seagull Insurance Ltd: Blendax House, 3rd Floor, Dumat St, Port Louis; tel. 2120867; telex 4593; fax 2082417; Chair. Y. V. LAI FAT FUR; Man. Dir O. GUNGABISSOON.

Sparrow Insurance Co Ltd: 24 bis rue Bourbon, POB 1148, Port Louis; tel. 2085410; telex 4271; fax 2080947; f. 1978; Chair. SUBHOD CHAND ROY; Gen. Man. LEWIS MARIE.

State Insurance Corporation of Mauritius (SICOM) Ltd: SICOM Bldg, Sir Célicourt Antelme St, Port Louis; tel. 2126702; telex 4396; fax 2087662; f. 1975; Chair. R. JUGURNATH; Man. Dir P. J. BLACKBURN.

Stella Insurance Co Ltd: 17 Sir Seewoosagur Ramgoolam St, POB 852, Port Louis; tel. 2086051; telex 4719; fax 2081639; f. 1977; Chair. and Man. Dir R. KRESHAN JHOBOO.

Sun Insurance Co Ltd: Sunny House, cnr Barracks and St George's Sts, Port Louis; tel. 2122522; telex 4452; fax 2082052; f. 1981; Chair. Sir KAILASH RAMDANEE; Man. Dir Lady (URSULA) RAMDANEE.

Swan Insurance Co Ltd: 6–10 Intendance St, POB 364, Port Louis; tel. 2086881; telex 4393; fax 2086898; incorp. 1955; Chair. J. M. ANTOINE HAREL; Gen. Man. GILLES DE SORNAY.

L. and H. Vigier de Latour Ltd: Les Jamalacs Bldg, Old Council St, Port Louis; tel. 2122034; telex 4386; fax 2126056; Chair. and Man. Dir L. J. D. HENRI VIGIER DE LATOUR.

Trade and Industry

CHAMBER OF COMMERCE

Mauritius Chamber of Commerce and Industry: 3 Royal St, Port Louis; tel. 2083301; telex 4277; fax 2080076; f. 1850; 391 mems; Pres. PETER WHITE; Sec.-Gen. JEAN-CLAUDE MONTOCCHIO.

TRADING ORGANIZATIONS

Chinese Chamber of Commerce: 35 Dr Joseph Rivière St, Port Louis; tel. 2080946; telex 4300; fax 2421193; Pres. VINCENT AH CHUEN.

Indian Traders' Association: POB 367, Port Louis; tel. 2403509.

Mauritius Chamber of Merchants: Louis Pasteur St, Port Louis; tel. 2121477; telex 4619; fax 2087088; Pres. A. A. AHMED.

State Trading Corpn: Fon Sing Bldg, Edith Cavell St, Port Louis; tel. 2085440; telex 4537; fax 2088359; f. 1982 to manage import and distribution of rice, wheat, flour, petroleum products and cement; cap. Rs 10m.; 99% state-owned; Pres. B. DOOLOOA; Gen. Man. BEEJAYE GHOORAH.

DEVELOPMENT ORGANIZATIONS

Mauritius Development Investment Trust Company (MDITC): Anglo-Mauritius House, 7th Floor, Intendance St, Port Louis; tel. 2123251; telex 4212; fax 2088263; Chair. PETER WHITE; Man. Dir GEORGES LEUNG SHING.

Mauritius Export Development and Investment Authority (MEDIA): B.A.I. Bldg, 2nd Floor, 25 Pope Hennessy St, POB 1184, Port Louis; tel. 2087750; telex 4597; fax 2085965; f. 1985 to promote exports of goods and services and to encourage export-orientated investment; Chair. FAKHRU CURRIMJEE; CEO CHAND BHADAIN.

Mauritius Freeport Authority: Deramann Tower, 3rd Floor, 30 Sir William Newton St, Port Louis; tel. 2129626; fax 2129627; f. 1990 to promote freeport activities; Chair. Prof. EDOUARD LIM FAT; Dir-Gen. GÉRARD SANSPEUR.

Mauritius Offshore Business Activities Authority: Deramann Tower, 1st Floor, 30 Sir William Newton St, Port Louis; tel. 2129650; fax 2129459; manages and promotes 'offshore' commercial activities; Dir IQBAL RAJABALLY.

State Investment Corporation Ltd (SIC): Fon Sing Bldg, 2nd Floor, 12 Edith Cavell St, Port Louis; tel. 2122978; telex 4635; fax 2088948; provides support for new investment and transfer of technology, in agriculture, industry and tourism; Chair. Sir BHINOD BACHA; Man. Dir M. N. KISTNASSAMY.

EMPLOYERS' ASSOCIATION

Mauritius Employers' Federation: Cerné House, Chaussée St, Port Louis; tel. 2121599; fax 2126725; f. 1962; Pres. P. R. DE CHASTEIGNEUR DU MÉE; Dir Dr AZAD JEETUN.

TRADE UNIONS

Federations

Federation of Civil Service Unions (FCSU): 33 Corderie St, Port Louis; tel. 2426621; f. 1975; 52 affiliated unions with 16,500 mems (1992); Pres. D. BHURUTH; Gen.-Sec. R. SUNGKUR.

General Workers' Federation: 19B Poudrière St, Port Louis; tel. 2123338; Pres. BEEDIANAND JHURRY; Sec.-Gen. FAROOK AUCHOYBUR.

Mauritius Federation of Trade Unions: Etienne Pellereau St, Port Louis; tel 2401486; f. 1958; four affiliated unions; Pres. FAROOK HOSSENBUX; Sec.-Gen. R. MAREEMOOTOO.

Mauritius Labour Congress: 8 Louis Victor de la Faye St, Port Louis; tel. 2124343; telex 4611; fax 2088945; f. 1963; 55 affiliated unions with 70,000 mems (1992); Pres. R. ALLGOO; Gen. Sec. K. HURRYNAG.

Principal Unions

Government Servants' Association: 107A Royal Rd, Beau Bassin; tel. 4644242; f. 1945; 14,000 mems (1984); Pres. A. H. MALLECK-AMODE; Sec.-Gen. S. P. TORUL.

Government Teachers' Union: 3 Mgr Gonin St, POB 1111, Port Louis; tel. 2080047; f. 1945; 4,625 mems (1992); Pres. JUGDISH LOLLBEEHARRY; Sec. SHIVCOOMAR BAICHOO.

Nursing Association: Royal Rd, Beau Bassin; tel. 4645850; f. 1955; 2,040 mems (1980); Pres. CASSAM KUREEMAN; Sec.-Gen. FRANCIS SUPPARAYEN.

Organization of Artisans' Unity: 42 Sir William Newton St, Port Louis; tel. 2124557; f. 1973; 2,874 mems (1994); Pres. AUGUSTE FOLLET; Sec. ROY RAMCHURN.

Plantation Workers' Union: 8 Louis Victor de la Faye St, Port Louis; tel. 2121735; f. 1955; 13,726 mems (1990); Pres. C. BHAGIRUTTY; Sec. N. L. ROY.

Port Louis Harbour and Docks Workers' Union: 19B Poudrière St, Port Louis; tel. 2082276; 2,198 mems (1980); Pres. M. VEERABADREN; Sec.-Gen. GERARD BERTRAND.

Sugar Industry Staff Employees' Association: 1 Rémy Ollier St, Port Louis; tel. 2121947; f. 1947; 1,472 mems (1987); Chair. R. DE CHASTEAUNEUF; Sec.-Gen. JEAN MACLOU.

Textile, Clothes and Other Manufactures Workers' Union: Thomy d'Arifat St, Curepipe; tel. 6765280; Pres. PADMATEE TEELUCK; Sec.-Gen. DÉSIRÉ GUILDAREE.

Union of Bus Industry Workers: 19B Poudrière St, Port Louis; tel. 2123338; 1,783 mems (1980); Pres. BABOOA; Sec.-Gen. F. AUCHOYBUR.

Union of Employees of the Ministry of Agriculture and other Ministries: Royal Rd, Curepipe; tel. 6861847; f. 1989; 2,131 mems (1988); Sec. P. JAGARNATH.

Union of Labourers of the Sugar and Tea Industry: Royal Rd, Curepipe; f. 1969; 2,150 mems (1980); Sec. P. RAMCHURN.

Union of Municipality Workers: 23 Brabant St, Port Louis; 1,991 mems (1980); Sec. M. V. RAMSAMY.

Union of Workers of the Development Works Corporation: 23 Brabant St, Port Louis; 2,651 mems; Sec. E. VARDEN.

CO-OPERATIVE SOCIETIES

Mauritius Co-operative Agricultural Federation Ltd: Co-operation House, 3 Dumas St, Port Louis; tel. 2121360; f. 1950; supplies agricultural materials; promotes the interests of 209 mem. socs; Chair. N. BASANT RAI; Sec. R. HEMOO.

Mauritius Co-operative Union Ltd: Co-operation House, 3 Dumas St, Port Louis; tel. 2122922; telex 4348; f. 1952; educational and promotional activities; 303 mem. socs (1983); Pres. TOOVAN RAMPHUL; Sec.-Gen. DHARAMJEET BUCKTOWER.

Transport

RAILWAYS

There are no railways in Mauritius.

ROADS

In 1991 there were 1,831 km of classified roads, of which 886 km were main roads, and 577 km were secondary roads. About 93% of the road network is paved. The construction of an urban highway, linking the motorways approaching Port Louis, and the extension of one of the motorways to Plaisance airport were completed in 1988. Of total projected expenditure by the Government in 1990/91, Rs 190m. was allocated to the rehabilitation of roads.

SHIPPING

Mauritius is served by numerous foreign shipping lines. In 1990 Port Louis was established as a free port to expedite the development of Mauritius as an entrepôt centre. A programme to rehabilitate the port, at a total cost of Rs 314m., was due for completion in 1994.

Islands Service Ltd: c/o Rogers and Co Ltd, 5 President John F. Kennedy St, POB 60, Port Louis; tel. 2086801; telex 4312; services to Indian Ocean islands; Chair. R. H. MAINGARD.

Mauritius Marine Authority: Port Administration Bldg, POB 379, Mer Rouge, Port Louis; tel. 2400415; telex 4238; fax 2400856; f. 1976; port authority; Chair. H. RAMNARAIN; Dir-Gen. J. H. NAGDAN.

Mauritius Shipping Corporation Ltd: Nova Bldg, 1 Military Rd, Port Lous; tel. 2425255; telex 4874; fax 2425245; Pres. RAJESH DAUMOO; Dir SUREN RAMPHUL.

Société Mauricienne de Navigation, Ltée: 1 rue de la Reine, POB 53, Port Louis; tel. 2083241; telex 4213; fax 2088931; Chair. ARMAND BARUCH; Dir YVES BELLEPEAU.

CIVIL AVIATION

Sir Seewoosagur Ramgoolam international airport is at Plaisance, 4 km from Mahébourg; work on upgrading the airport started in 1984 and was completed in 1987, providing facilities to handle 1.1m. passengers annually. In early 1993 a further expansion programme, which was projected to cost more than US $30m., was initiated.

Air Mauritius: Rogers House, 5 President John F. Kennedy St, POB 441, Port Louis; tel. 2087700; telex 4415; fax 2088331; f. 1967; 51% state-owned; services to destinations in Europe, Asia, Australia and Africa; Chair. and Man. Dir Sir HARRY TIRVENGADUM.

Tourism

Tourists are attracted to Mauritius by its scenery and beaches, the pleasant climate and the blend of cultures. Accommodation capacity totalled 10,895 beds in 1992. The number of visitors increased from 139,670 in 1984 to 330,880 in 1992, when receipts totalled an estimated Rs 4,400m. In 1992 the greatest numbers of visitors were from Réunion (24.9%) and France (20.6%).

Mauritius Government Tourist Office: Emmanuel Anquetil Bldg, Sir Seewoosagur Ramgoolam St, Port Louis; tel. 2011703; telex 4249; fax 2125142; Gen. Man. CYRIL VADAMOOTOO.

Defence

The country has no standing defence forces, although there is a special 1,300-strong police mobile unit to ensure internal security.

Defence Expenditure: Budgeted at Rs 180.1m. in 1992/93.

Education

Educational standards are relatively high, and in 1990, according to census results, the average rate of adult illiteracy was only 20.1% (males 14.8%; females 25.3%), although education is not compulsory. Primary education begins at five years of age and lasts for six years. Secondary education, beginning at the age of 11, lasts for up to seven years, comprising a first cycle of three years and a second of four years. Primary and secondary education are available free of charge. In 1991 an estimated 89% of children in the relevant age-group (males 87%; females 90%) were attending primary school. In the same year the number of children attending secondary schools was equivalent to 54% of the appropriate age-group (males 52%; females 56%). Control of the large private sector in secondary education was indirectly assumed by the government in 1977. The University of Mauritius, founded in 1965, had 1,789 students in 1992/93, and a large number of students receive further education abroad. Of total expenditure by the central government in 1992/93, Rs 1,810.3m. (14.9%) was for education.

Bibliography

Baker, P. *Kreol: A Description of Mauritian Creole*. London, Hurst, 1972.

Benedict, B. *Indians in a Plural Society: A Report on Mauritius*. London, HMSO, 1961.

Mauritius, A Plural Society. London, 1965.

Bissoonoyal, B. *A Concise History of Mauritius*. Bombay, Bharatiya Vidya, 1963.

Cohen, R. *African Islands and Enclaves*. London, Sage Publications, 1983.

Favoreu, L. *L'île Maurice*. Paris, Berger-Levrault, 1970.

Food and Agriculture Organization. *Mauritius: Land and Water Resources Survey*. New York, UN, 1966.

Government of Mauritius. *Mauritius Economic Survey*. Port Louis, Ministry of Economic Planning and Development, annual.

Ingrams, W. H. *A Short History of Mauritius*. London, Macmillan, 1931.

International Monetary Fund. *Mauritius: Recent Economic Developments*. Washington, DC, 1984.

Jones, P., and Andrews, B. *A Taste of Mauritius*. London, Macmillan, 1982.

Lehembre, B. *L'île Maurice*. Paris, Editions Karthala, 1984.

Meade, J. E., et al. *The Economic and Social Structure of Mauritius*. London, Sessional Paper No. 7 of 1960, Methuen, reprinted by Frank Cass, 1968.

Ramgoolam, Sir S. *Our Struggle: 20th Century Mauritius*. New Delhi, Vision Books, 1982.

Simmons, A. S. *Modern Mauritius: The Politics of Decolonization*. Bloomington, IN, Indiana University Press, 1982.

Titmuss, R. M., and Abel-Smith, B. *Social Policies and Population Growth in Mauritius*. Sessional Paper No. 6 of 1960, London, Methuen, reprinted by Frank Cass, 1968.

Toussaint, A. *Port Louis, deux siècles d'histoire (1735–1935)*. Port Louis, 1946.

Bibliography of Mauritius 1501–1954. Port Louis, 1956.

Histoire des îles Mascareignes. Paris, Berger-Levrault, 1972.

World Bank. *Mauritius: Economic Memorandum: Recent Developments and Prospects*. Washington, DC, 1983.

Mauritius: Managing Success. Washington DC, 1989.

Wright, C. *Mauritius*. Newton Abbot, David and Charles, 1974.

OTHER ISLANDS

Rodrigues

Rodrigues (area 104 sq km, population 34,204 at the 1990 census) is administered by a resident commissioner. Rodrigues is represented in the legislative assembly by two members, one of whom is minister for the island. Fishing and farming are the principal activities, while the main exports are cattle, salt fish, sheep, goats, pigs and onions. The island is linked to Mauritius, 585 km to the west, by thrice-weekly air and monthly boat services.

The Lesser Dependencies

The Lesser Dependencies (area 71 sq km, population 167 at the 1990 census) are the Agalega Islands, two islands about 935 km north of Mauritius, and the Cargados Carajos Shoals (St Brandon Islands), 22 uninhabited islets 370 km north-north-east. Mauritius also claims sovereignty over Tromelin Island, 556 km to the north-west. This claim is disputed by Madagascar, and also by France, which maintains an airstrip and weather station on the island.

THE BRITISH INDIAN OCEAN TERRITORY (BIOT)

The British Indian Ocean Territory (BIOT) was formed in November 1965, through the amalgamation of the former Seychelles islands of Aldabra, Desroches and Farquhar with the Chagos Archipelago, a group of islands 1,930 km north-east of Mauritius, and previously administered by the governor of Mauritius. Aldabra, Desroches and Farquhar were ceded to Seychelles when that country was granted independence in June 1976. Since then BIOT has comprised only the Chagos Archipelago, including the coral atoll Diego Garcia, with a total land area of 60 sq km (23 sq miles), together with a surrounding area of some 54,400 sq km (21,000 sq miles) of ocean.

BIOT was established to meet British and US defence requirements in the Indian Ocean. Previously, the principal economic functions of the islands were fishing and the production of copra: the islands, together with the coconut plantations, were owned by a private company. After the purchase of the islands by the British crown in 1967, the plantations ceased to operate, and the population were offered the choice of resettlement in Mauritius or in the Seychelles. The majority (which numbered about 1,200) went to Mauritius, the resettlement taking place between 1969–71, prior to the construction of the military facility. Mauritius subsequently campaigned for the immediate return of the Territory, and received support from the Organization of African Unity and India. The election victory of the Mouvement Militant Mauricien in 1982 led to an intensification of these demands. Mauritius supported the former island population in a protracted dispute with the United Kingdom over compensation for those displaced, which ended in 1982 when the British government agreed to an *ex gratia* payment of £4m. In early 1984, however, it was reported that people who had been displaced from Diego Garcia were seeking $6m. from the US government to finance their resettlement in Mauritius. The US administration declined to accept any financial responsibility for the population.

A 1966 agreement between the United Kingdom and the USA provides for BIOT to be used by both countries over an initial period of 50 years, with the option of extending this for a further 20 years. The United Kingdom undertook to cede the Chagos Archipelago to Mauritius when it was no longer required for defence purposes. All US activities in BIOT are conducted in consultation with the British government. Originally the US military presence was limited to a communications centre on Diego Garcia. In 1972, however, construction of a naval support facility was begun, apparently in response to the expansion of the Soviet maritime presence in the Indian Ocean. This plan was expanded in 1974, the agreement being formalized by an 'exchange of notes' in 1976, and again following Soviet military intervention in Afghanistan in December 1979. Facilities on Diego Garcia include a communications centre, a runway with a length of 3,650 m, anchorage, refuelling and various ancillary services. During the 1980s the US government undertook a programme of expansion and improvement of the naval support facility which was to include a space-tracking station. In August 1987 the US navy began to use Diego Garcia as a facility for minesweeping helicopters taking part in operations in the Persian (Arabian) Gulf. Following Iraq's invasion of Kuwait in August 1990, Diego Garcia was used as a base for US B-52 aircraft, which were deployed in the Gulf region.

In January 1988 Mauritius renewed its campaign to regain sovereignty over the atoll of Diego Garcia, and reiterated its support for a 'zone of peace' in the Indian Ocean. In November 1989, following an incident in which a military aircraft belonging to the US air force accidentally bombed a US naval vessel near Diego Garcia, a demonstration was held outside the US embassy in Mauritius, demanding the withdrawal of foreign military forces from the area. The Mauritius government announced that it would draw the attention of the UN Security Council to the dangers that it perceived in the execution of US military air exercises. However, the US assistant secretary of state for african affairs reiterated during an official visit to Mauritius, in the same month, that the US would maintain its military presence in the Indian Ocean.

In January 1992 the Mauritius government demanded again that the UK recognize its sovereignty over the Chagos Archipelago, failing which it would raise the matter at the UN and seek adjudication by the International Court of Justice. The British government has subsequently maintained its refusal to cede the Territory, but in January 1994 arrangements were agreed for the establishment of a joint British-Mauritian fisheries commission to promote and co-ordinate conservation and scientific research within the territorial waters of BIOT. In May the Mauritius government ministers of foreign affairs and fisheries paid a two-day official visit to the Chagos Archipelago.

The civil administration of BIOT is the responsibility of a non-resident commissioner in the foreign and commonwealth office in London, represented on Diego Garcia by a royal naval commander and a small British naval presence. A chief justice, a senior magistrate and a principal legal adviser (who performs the functions of an attorney-general) are resident in the United Kingdom.

Land Area: about 60 sq km.

Population: There are no permanent inhabitants. In 1991 there were about 1,200 US and British military personnel and 1,700 civilian contractors in the Territory.

Currency: The pound sterling and the US dollar are both used.

Commissioner: DAVID MACLENNAN, Head of African Dept (Equatorial), Foreign and Commonwealth Office, King Charles St, London, SW1A 2AH, England; tel. (071) 270-3000.

Administrator: DON CAIRNS, African Dept (Equatorial), Foreign and Commonwealth Office, King Charles St, London, SW1A 2AH, England; tel. (071) 270-3000.

Commissioner's Representative: Commdr P. A. W. RAINE, RN, Diego Garcia, c/o BFPO Ships; telex 938 6903.

MOZAMBIQUE

Physical and Social Geography

RENÉ PÉLISSIER

PHYSICAL FEATURES

The Republic of Mozambique covers a total area of 799,380 sq km (308,641 sq miles). This includes 13,000 sq km of inland water, mainly comprising Lake Niassa, the Mozambican section of Lake Malawi. Mozambique is bounded to the north by Tanzania, to the west by Malawi, Zambia and Zimbabwe, and to the south by South Africa and Swaziland.

With some exceptions towards the Zambia, Malawi and Zimbabwe borders, it is generally a low-lying plateau of moderate height, descending through a sub-plateau zone to the Indian Ocean. The main reliefs are Monte Binga (2,436 m above sea-level), the highest point of Mozambique, on the Zimbabwe border in Manica province, Monte Namúli (2,419 m) in the Zambézia province, the Serra Zuira (2,227 m) in the Manica province, and several massifs which are a continuation into northern Mozambique of the Shire highlands of Malawi. The coastal lowland is narrower in the north but widens considerably towards the south, so that terrain less than 1,000 m high comprises about 45% of the total Mozambican area. The shore-line is 2,470 km long and generally sandy and bordered by lagoons, shoals and strings of coastal islets in the north.

Mozambique is divided by at least 25 main rivers, all of which flow to the Indian Ocean. The largest and most historically significant is the Zambezi, whose 820-km Mozambican section is navigable for 460 km. Flowing from eastern Angola, the Zambezi provides access to the interior of Africa from the eastern coast.

Two main seasons, wet and dry, divide the climatic year. The wet season has monthly averages of 26.7°–29.4°C, with cooler temperatures in the interior uplands. The dry season has June and July temperatures of 18.3°–20.0°C at Maputo.

POPULATION AND URBAN CENTRES

The census taken by the Portuguese authorities in December 1970 recorded a total population of 8,168,933, and the population increased to 11,673,725, excluding underenumeration (estimated at 3.8%), by the census of 1 August 1980. The population was officially estimated to be 16,593,500 in August 1992. The population density was 20.8 inhabitants per sq km. Mozambique's population increased by an annual average of 2.7% between 1985–92.

Mozambique was adversely affected by drought and famine during the 1980s: this was most severe during 1982–84 (when it was reported that about 100,000 people had died of starvation) and during 1986–87. In late 1992 it was estimated by international aid agencies that 3.2m. people were threatened with food shortages as a result of drought.

North of the Zambezi, the main ethnic groupings among the African population, which belongs to the cultural division of Central Bantu, are the Makua-Lomwe groups, who form the principal ethno-linguistic subdivision of Mozambique and are believed to comprise about 40% of the population. South of the Zambezi, the main group is the Thonga, who feature prominently as Mozambican mine labourers in South Africa. North of the Thonga area lies the Shona group, numbering more than 1m. Southern ethnic groups have tended to enjoy greater educational opportunities than those of other regions. The government has sought to balance the ethnic composition of its leadership, but the executive is still largely of southern and central origin.

Mozambique is divided into 11 administrative provinces, one of which comprises the capital, Maputo, a modern seaport whose population was estimated to be 1,006,765 at 1 January 1987. The second seaport of the country is Beira. Other towns of importance include Nampula, on the railway line to Niassa province and Malawi, and Quelimane.

Recent History

MILES SMITH-MORRIS

EMERGENCE OF FRELIMO

Following the Portuguese coup of April 1974, the Frente de Libertação de Moçambique (Frelimo) demanded full independence for Mozambique and the total assumption of power by itself. Frelimo, formed in 1962, maintained a sizeable armed force, by guerrilla standards, and had an effective and politically astute leadership, although it controlled only a small proportion of the territory. It faced no challenge from the Portuguese settlers, who were politically just as alienated as the Mozambicans by the administration in Lisbon. A transitional government, with Joaquim Chissano as prime minister, was formed in September and led the country to independence on 25 June 1975, when the Frelimo leader, Samora Machel, became the republic's first president.

The situation in 1974–75 was chaotic, as the Portuguese, who had operated the administration and the economy, fled the country. The exclusion of Africans by the colonial regime from almost all positions in the modern sector created a dearth of middle-level managers and others who could fill the vacuum left by the exodus of the Portuguese. Frelimo faced formidable problems in restructuring its internal organization, in setting up new state structures and in maintaining a minimal level of economic activity. In addition, Frelimo's strong support for exiled Rhodesian nationalists exposed it to increasingly heavy attacks from Rhodesian forces. The government's decision in March 1976 to close the border with Rhodesia and apply economic sanctions put an end to the transit traffic that had been a mainstay of the economy.

In 1977 Frelimo transformed itself from a relatively broad political grouping into a 'Marxist-Leninist vanguard party' and declared that its long-term goal was a socialist Mozambique. A political commissariat was formed to oversee the armed forces, along with mass organizations of women, workers and young people. A new electoral law created a system of indirectly elected bodies, by which lower assemblies in turn elected higher tiers, with the people's assembly as, nominally at least, the fount of political power.

From 1980 onwards, national life was increasingly dominated by the effects of appalling drought and the escalating political crisis in the region. For Mozambique this took the form of direct South African aggression and indirect attacks by that country through its support for the Resistência Nacional

Moçambicana (Renamo), an organization established by the Rhodesian government intelligence organization during the undeclared war between Rhodesia and Mozambique in 1976–79.

INTERNAL CONFRONTATION

By 1981, the collapse of the illegal regime in Rhodesia and internal dissension had reduced Renamo to little more than a gang of armed brigands, but substantial infusions of aid from South Africa later that year transformed it into an agent of economic devastation, lacking any serious political programme. By late 1981 Renamo had resumed its activities in northern Manica and Sofala provinces and northern Inhambane and had begun attacks on the Beira railway. From 1982 onwards, Zimbabwean troops were deployed along the oil pipeline from Mutare to Beira to prevent sabotage attempts by Renamo.

The Frelimo leadership exercised considerable diplomatic skill in pursuit of its national goals and regional stability, balancing relations with the Soviet bloc with contacts made with Western powers in the interests of bringing pressure to bear on South Africa to desist from the constant destabilization of its neighbours. In 1984 Mozambique joined the World Bank and the IMF, while the government announced a new and liberal foreign investment code.

Frelimo's achievements at this time in the fields of social welfare and education were considerable. Progress was made in expanding school enrolment and in reducing adult illiteracy; there were sharp increases in spending on health care, including successful vaccination campaigns. In 1983 the party's central committee was expanded from 57 to 130 members, with the bulk of the new recruits coming from the provinces, or from outside the state apparatus. Further administrative reforms followed in 1986 when President Machel appointed four leading members of the Frelimo politburo to oversee the activities of government ministries. In July Mário da Graça Machungo was appointed prime minister, taking responsibility for day-to-day administration and freeing the president to concentrate on military operations against Renamo.

Elections to the people's assembly, due in 1982, were finally begun in August 1986 but interrupted by the intensity of the internal conflict and the sudden death, in October, of President Machel (see below). In November, Frelimo's central committee appointed Joaquim Chissano, the former minister of foreign affairs, as president. The elections were completed by December 1986, with 299 Frelimo nominees standing for the 250 seats; all government and political leaders were re-elected.

Fundamental changes in Frelimo's political and economic philosophy began to emerge at the fifth party congress in July 1989, when the party renounced its Marxist-Leninist orientation and agreed to extend the right of membership to religious believers and property owners. In January 1990 draft proposals for a new constitution were published, providing for the direct election of the president and people's assembly by universal suffrage. The eligibility of Renamo to contest the elections was recognized, provided that it abandoned violence and acknowledged the legitimacy of the state. The draft constitution, which was submitted to public debate during 1990, provided for the separation of Frelimo and the state, the independence of the judiciary and the right to strike.

These political developments appeared to represent attempts to create a famework within which to find a diplomatic solution to the civil war, by reducing the disparity between the aims of the government and those of Renamo. The process of political change was further advanced in August 1990, when the central committee of Frelimo announced that multi-party legislative elections were to take place in 1991, and that the country's name was to be changed from the People's Republic of Mozambique to the Republic of Mozambique.

The new constitution was formally approved by the people's assembly at the beginning of November 1990 and took effect at the end of the month. Provisions outlawing censorship and enshrining freedom of expression had been added to the earlier draft after representations by local journalists; the constitution also abolished the death penalty, making Mozambique only the fourth African country to do so. The new constitution was welcomed by Western aid donors but immediately rejected by Renamo, which described it as the product of an unrepresentative, unelected assembly.

The renamed assembly of the republic met for the first time in December. One of its first acts was to pass legislation allowing the formation of new political parties, which took effect in February 1991. In March President Chissano announced that general elections would be held in 1992, although no specific date was given. A number of political parties announced their intention to apply for legal status under the new legislation. Among those issuing manifestos or holding press conferences in early 1991 were: the Partido Liberal e Democrático de Moçambique (Palmo), which described iself as 'anti-socialist' and whose manifesto expressed views critical of white, mixed race and Asian Mozambicans; the União Nacional Moçambicana (Unamo), described as 'social democratic' and composed of former anti-government guerrillas who had split from Renamo, and the Social Democratic Mozambique National Movement (Monamo), based in Portugal. A fourth party, the Congresso Independente de Moçambique (Coimo), held a press conference in Maputo in March 1991. Founded in Kenya in 1985, Coimo was led by Victor Marcos Saene, son of a Frelimo dissident who went into exile in 1969.

Evidence of opposition to the change-over to multi-party democracy came with reports in late June 1991 that a plot to overthrow the government had been thwarted. The government announced on 22 June that a number of serving and retired army officers, as well as civilians, had been arrested. Among those held by the authorities was a former chief of staff of the armed forces, Col-Gen. Sebastião Mabote. In August, the minister of the interior, Col Manuel José António, was detained and questioned in connection with the alleged coup conspiracy. His portfolio was temporarily transferred to Edmundo Carlos Alberto. The case against António was dropped in February 1992, on the grounds that he had been instrumental in bringing the coup attempt to the attention of the authorities, and he returned to his duties in April. Mabote was acquitted of all charges by the supreme court in September, and 13 others still in detention in connection with the alleged conspiracy were released under a general amnesty in October.

Frelimo held its sixth congress on 12–13 August 1991, re-electing Chissano as party chairman and electing its central committee by secret ballot for the first time. Feliciano Gundana, the minister of the presidency, was appointed to the new post of party secretary-general. New legislation on trade union activity was passed by parliament in December, allowing workers to form trade unions of their choice, to join and resign from unions at will and establishing unions as self-regulating and autonomous organizations, free from outside interference.

New political parties continued to organize during late 1991 and early 1992 in preparation for the forthcoming elections, with several of the newly established parties, including Renamo, holding conventions, one of the conditions for registration. The formal end to one-party politics came in March with the announcement that Unamo had fulfilled the conditions for registration as the first legal opposition party. Earlier, a long-standing opponent of Frelimo, Domingos Arouca, in exile in Portugal since 1975, returned to launch the local organization of his Frente Unido de Moçambique (Fumo), formed in exile in 1976. Arouca, imprisoned by the Portuguese in the 1960s for his opposition to colonial rule, left Mozambique at independence because of his opposition to Frelimo's then Marxist-Leninist orientation. On his return he declared his intention to form a 'third force', between Frelimo and Renamo on the political spectrum, and said he welcomed co-operation with other opposition parties. In late June 1992 the leader of Palmo, Martins Bilal, announced that eight parties, including Palmo, had agreed to work together to present a 'third force' in opposition to Frelimo and Renamo.

Following the signing, in October 1992, of the general peace agreement between the government and Renamo (see below), political activity intensified in preparation for the presidential and legislative elections, initially scheduled for October 1993. The government published a draft electoral law in March 1993 proposing the establishment of a 21-member national electoral commission, chaired by a member of the supreme court, to organize and supervise the elections. A multi-party conference convened in late April to discuss the law, broke down, however, when 12 opposition parties announced that they would boycott the conference until their demands for accommodation and logistical support were met. Following the collapse of the discussions, the 12 opposition parties called for the establishment of a transitional coalition government pending the elections. The demand was rejected by the government, which described it as anti-democratic. The conference met again in late July, after the opposition parties agreed to end their boycott in return for promises of state funding in 1994, but was again disrupted by the withdrawal of Renamo, which alleged that the draft electoral law contravened the peace agreement.

'DÉTENTE' WITH SOUTH AFRICA

The need to devote increased resources to the struggle against South African intervention eventually forced Mozambique to enter into discussions with the South African government in late 1983 and early 1984. Negotiations in February and March 1984 culminated in the Nkomati Accord, a non-aggression treaty in which both sides bound themselves not to give material aid to opposition movements in each other's countries, and to establish a joint security commission. Effectively, this meant that Mozambique would prevent the African National Congress of South Africa (ANC) from conducting military operations from its territory, while South Africa would cease to support Renamo. It was hoped that, under the accord, Mozambique would be in a position to begin the reconstruction of its shattered economy. The government immediately took steps to limit the activities of the ANC, restricting the organization's presence to a diplomatic mission in Maputo. By late 1984 there had been a noticeable reduction in ANC guerrilla activity in South Africa. For its part, however, the South African government effectively ignored the accord. The disruption resulting from continuing Renamo operations in Mozambique was considerable, and by August 1984, despite major government offensives against the rebels between March and July, Renamo forces were active in all 10 of Mozambique's provinces and the capital came increasingly under threat. While refraining from accusing South Africa directly of contravening the Nkomati Accord, the Mozambique leadership nevertheless made increasingly forthright statements demanding that the accord be implemented. For its part, the South African government repeatedly denied any involvement in the continuing Renamo activity.

The escalating internal conflict led the Frelimo government, none the less, to warn South Africa in August 1984 that both the accord and associated plans for economic co-operation were under threat unless Renamo activity was halted. In a bid to resolve the situation, South Africa responded by convening a number of separate but parallel talks with Renamo and Frelimo government representatives during August and September, which culminated in the so-called 'Pretoria Declaration' of early October, in which a cease-fire was agreed in principle between the Frelimo government and the rebels, and a tripartite commission, comprising Frelimo, Renamo and South African representatives, was established to implement the truce. In November, however, Renamo withdrew from the peace negotiations, citing the Frelimo government's continued refusal to recognize Renamo's legitimacy. The rebel movement also announced the launching of a major country-wide offensive. In December President Machel reportedly accused South Africa of abrogating the Nkomati Accord by continuing to support Renamo. Pretoria denied this, and made further, unsuccessful attempts in early 1985 to persuade Renamo to negotiate with the Frelimo government.

Meanwhile, the joint security commission, established between South Africa and Mozambique under the provisions of the accord, continued to meet to review the situation, but Renamo activity in Mozambique continued. In March 1985 the two countries reiterated their continued commitment to the accord, and South Africa announced that a restricted air space, partly aimed at preventing support from reaching Renamo guerrillas from South African territory, would be established in the South Africa-Mozambique border area. This was followed in April by an announcement that a joint operational centre, to be used by both countries to deal with security and other matters relating to the Nkomati Accord, would be established on the border between Mozambique and South Africa. However, in the same month, Renamo guerrilla activity effectively severed rail links between the two countries.

The worsening security situation precipitated a meeting in June 1985 in Harare, Zimbabwe, between President Machel, Robert Mugabe (the prime minister of Zimbabwe) and President Nyerere of Tanzania, at which it was agreed that Tanzania and Zimbabwe would support Mozambique, and, in particular, that Zimbabwe would augment its military presence in Mozambique. This arrangement resulted in the capture, in August, of the largest Renamo base, the so-called 'Casa Banana' in Sofala province, and of other major rebel bases in the area. Not only were large quantities of weapons captured, but also incriminating documentation concerning South African support for Renamo since the signing of the Nkomati Accord. Some of these documents were published, making it virtually impossible for the South African government to continue to deny what had been widely assumed among observers of South African affairs. The South African government confirmed the allegations, but claimed that continued contacts with Renamo were designed to promote peace negotiations between the guerrillas and the Frelimo government. In mid-October Mozambique unilaterally suspended the joint security commission.

South African embarrassment at the disclosure of its activities led Pretoria to make thinly-veiled accusations against other parties, providing partial confirmation of what many had suspected. Portuguese private interests were involved in supporting Renamo, and some leaders of the organization were said to possess Portuguese passports. There were reports that Renamo was supplied from Middle Eastern sources, via the Comoros, although the possible motivation for this was somewhat unclear. It was also apparent that some Renamo groups were operating from bases in Malawi.

In early 1986 Mozambique's military situation was becoming desperate. This was most graphically illustrated by the recapture in February of the 'Casa Banana' base by Renamo forces, who encountered no serious opposition from fleeing government troops. This military reverse dismayed the Zimbabweans, who had been instrumental in capturing the base; it was eventually recaptured by them in April.

The second half of 1986 was dominated both by a deterioration in the military situation and by the sudden death of President Samora Machel: in October a Soviet civilian aircraft carrying the president, on his return from a meeting in Zambia of leaders of the 'front-line' states, crashed just inside South African territory, killing the president, together with two of his aides and the minister of transport, Luís Santos. Controversy has continued to surround the causes of the crash, especially over the strong possibility of South African involvement. Following the disaster, Mozambican demonstrators attacked the South African trade mission in Maputo, in protest against South Africa's suspected involvement in the incident. In October the South African government announced that it was to ban recruitment of Mozambican miners, and was to repatriate some 60,000 Mozambicans already employed in South African mines, in retaliation for an alleged increase in activity by ANC guerrillas in the Mozambique border region. (However in January 1987 the repatriation decision was relaxed in respect of about 30,000 of the Mozambican mineworkers.) In January 1987 a joint report, compiled by Mozambican, Soviet and South African experts, was presented to an international board of inquiry, established to investigate the crash. The board concluded that pilot error, and not sabotage, had caused the accident, although some observers suggested that the examination of the course of events was not sufficiently thorough.

Following the death of Machel, Mozambique applied intense pressure on Malawi, including threats of military action, to induce its neighbour to cease complying with Renamo, and in December 1986 a joint security agreement was signed between the two states. In April 1987 President Chissano confirmed the presence of some 300 Malawian troops guarding part of the railway line from the Malawi frontier to Nacala, in northern

Mozambique. Malawi's willingness to co-operate with Mozambique was endangered in November 1987, when it was reported that Mozambique government forces had shot down a Malawian civilian aircraft (which they claimed to have been violating Mozambican airspace), killing 10 people. The Mozambique government expressed its regret, and a joint investigation by the two countries into the incident led to the drafting of new regulations on air safety. By mid-1988 the number of Malawian troops in Mozambique had increased to 600, and in July, during a state visit to Malawi, President Chissano praised the country for its support of his government. In December 1988 Mozambique, Malawi, and the United Nations High Commissioner for Refugees (UNHCR) signed an agreement to promote the voluntary repatriation of Mozambican refugees in Malawi.

The Mozambican army was so ill-equipped and malnourished that it was often unable to hold even well-defended positions. However, government troops became more successful at repulsing rebel attacks during 1987, although Renamo continued to cause widespread disruption. In February Zimbabwean and Mozambican troops recaptured five towns in northern Mozambique which Renamo had seized in late 1986. This signified a general shift in the balance of power, with Renamo increasing its operations in the south, while government troops registered important successes in the north and along the coastline. In March 1987 the government expressed cautious optimism about its military position; this followed a substantial reorganization of the armed forces, including the establishment of highly-trained commandos and the participation of reinforcements from Zimbabwe and Tanzania. The apparent cessation of covert aid by Malawi to Renamo may also have been significant. An open raid in late May by South African security forces on alleged ANC bases in metropolitan Maputo effectively signalled the demise of the Nkomati Accord. Renewed accusations of South African support for Renamo were made in July, when the rebels were allegedly responsible for the massacre of 424 civilians in the southern Mozambican town of Homoine. South Africa denied any involvement in the incident, however, and offered to investigate its circumstances jointly with Mozambique. International opinion was further outraged by successive attacks attributed to Renamo, including the ambush, in October, of a convoy travelling from Maputo on the main north–south road, in which more than 270 people were killed. The rebels were also reported to have conducted a series of cross-border raids into Zambia and, especially, Zimbabwe; between June and December some 80 Zimbabwean civilians were allegedly killed by Renamo guerrillas.

In December 1987 President Chissano announced a 'law of pardon', whereby convicted prisoners who showed repentance were to be released on parole or served with lenient sentences, and an amnesty for members of Renamo who surrendered their arms. By December 1988 it was claimed by the Mozambican authorities that more than 3,000 rebels had defected; these included two prominent members of the European branch of Renamo, both of whom accused South Africa of continuing complicity in the affairs of the organization. The amnesty was initially to have expired in December 1988, but was extended for a further 12 months. Meanwhile, government troops made important advances against the rebels.

The defection of some Renamo members appeared to have been prompted by bitter divisions within the organization. The main disagreement was between the proponents and opponents, such as Afonso Dhlakama (the leader of Renamo), of a peaceful resolution of the armed conflict by means of negotiation with the Frelimo government and by a reduction of links with South Africa.

Relations between Mozambique and South Africa were severely strained following the death of President Machel, the South African raid on Maputo and the massacre at Homoine. In late 1987 and early 1988, however, the two countries held discussions aimed at reviving the Nkomati Accord. A bomb attack in Maputo in April 1988, in which an exiled South African anti-apartheid activist was severely injured, threatened to undermine the progress made in negotiations. However, following initiatives from President Chissano to resume discussions, Mozambique and South Africa agreed in May to re-establish, 'as soon as possible', a joint security commission, and thereby effectively to revive the Nkomati Accord. In addition, a series of discussions between Mozambique, South Africa and Portugal led to an agreement by these countries, signed in November 1987, to restore the Cahora Bassa dam in Mozambique (see Economy). In September 1988 President Chissano met the then South African president, P. W. Botha, in Mozambique. As a result of this meeting, Mozambique and South Africa established a joint commission for co-operation and development, and South Africa agreed to provide non-lethal military aid for the protection of the Cahora Bassa power lines. In addition, South Africa agreed to give assistance for improvements to Maputo harbour and to the road and rail links between Mozambique and South Africa, and in November restrictions on the recruitment of Mozambican mineworkers in South Africa were withdrawn. In February 1989 South Africa proposed a peace initiative for Mozambique, whereby the USA was to mediate a settlement between the Mozambican government and Renamo; however, the two parties in the conflict rejected this offer. In the following month a senior US government official claimed that supplies were still reaching Renamo from South Africa. Nevertheless, during a visit to Mozambique in July by the leader of the South African National Party, F. W. de Klerk, President Chissano announced that he accepted that the South African government no longer supported the rebel organization.

Renamo announced a unilateral cease-fire in April 1989, in order to allow aid to reach people affected by famine, but this was reportedly not observed.

PEACE INITIATIVES

In June 1989 the government launched a peace initiative, publicizing a set of 12 principles, which demanded the cessation of acts of terrorism, guaranteed the right of political participation to all 'individuals' who renounced violence, recognized the principle that no group should impose its will on another by force and demanded that all parties should respect the legitimacy of the state and of the constitution. It was announced in mid-1989 that President Moi of Kenya and President Mugabe of Zimbabwe had agreed to mediate between Renamo and the Mozambique government. In August officials from the Mozambique Christian Council met representatives from Renamo (with whom they had previously had contact) in Nairobi to discuss the government peace proposals. Renamo rejected the proposals, demanding recognition as a political entity, the introduction of multi-party elections and the withdrawal of Zimbabwean troops from Mozambique. Nevertheless, there was indirect contact between Renamo and the government during late 1989. In mid-November Presidents Moi and Mugabe invited both parties to hold direct negotiations. Although the government subsequently agreed to this offer in principle, it continued to deny formal recognition to Renamo. The role of Presidents Mugabe and Moi as mediators came to an end after Renamo refused to attend a meeting between the protagonists that had been arranged to take place in Malawi in June 1990. However, the first direct talks between the two sides were held the following month in Rome, Italy; the Frelimo delegation was led by the minister of transport and communications, Armando Guebuza, and Renamo was represented by its foreign affairs spokesman, Raul Manuel Domingos. Further talks were held in August.

A third round of talks, due to start in September 1990, was postponed after Renamo alleged that the government had begun a new military offensive. The two sides met again in Rome in November when Renamo presented a list of demands as conditions for a cease-fire, including the withdrawal of all foreign troops from the country and the abandonment of the new constitution. Three weeks of talks culminated in the signing on 1 December of a partial cease-fire agreement. This provided for the withdrawal of Zimbabwean forces to within 3 km of the Beira and Limpopo transport 'corridors'. In exchange, Renamo agreed to cease hostilities and refrain from attacking the 'corridors'. The cease-fire was to be monitored by a joint verification commission (JVC) comprising representatives from 10 countries. The withdrawal of Zimbabwean troops to the 'corridors' was completed by the end of December but a number of violations of the cease-fire, mostly attributed to Renamo, were reported in January 1991.

A brief round of the peace talks was held in mid-December 1990, but proved inconclusive; the fifth round, in late January and early February 1991, collapsed after Renamo rejected a JVC report accusing it of breaching the cease-fire provisions. Later in February, Renamo announced that it would resume attacks. However, in March Renamo was reported to be ready to resume negotiations and declared a unilateral cease-fire over the Easter period. Attacks by Renamo during the early months of 1991 included the first, for more than a year, on the transport 'corridor' from Nacala port in northern Mozambique to Malawi. This had not been covered by the partial cease-fire agreement because of the lack of rebel activity in the area at the time.

Following a meeting between Renamo and members of the JVC in mid-April 1991 to discuss alleged violations of the cease-fire, direct talks resumed in Rome on 6 May. The talks, which ended on 10 June, were reported to have agreed on a timetable for the discussion of outstanding issues, including setting a date for the cessation of hostilities and for the calling of general elections.

The seventh round of peace talks, originally scheduled for July 1991, began in Rome on 1 August and was suspended on 9 August, to give Renamo time to consider proposals made by the mediators which would allow it to begin political activities in Mozambique as soon as a cease-fire had been agreed, but requiring it to recognize the existing constitution. Renamo was, however, reported to have made a new demand: that the UN should take control of the administration during the period between a cease-fire and the elections. This demand was abandoned at the next round of talks, in October, which ended with clear signs of progress, including the signing by the two sides of a protocol said to represent a recognition by Renamo of the government's legitimacy and its agreement to begin operating as an opposition political party. In return, the government was reported to have undertaken not to enact legislation before the elections on any of the issues under discussion at the talks. The establishment of a commission to oversee the eventual cease-fire was also agreed. A further protocol, in which Renamo agreed to start operating as a political party immediately after a cease-fire, was signed the following month.

Relations with Malawi deteriorated sharply at the end of December 1991, when Mozambique protested about Malawi's sudden closure of the border crossing at Milange, one of the major entry points to Mozambique. The closure halted international relief consignments to Mozambique's Zambézia province. No official explanation was given for the closure, although observers speculated that it was linked to internal opposition to the Malawi government. Following discussions between the two countries, the border crossing re-opened in mid-January 1992.

The role of President Mugabe of Zimbabwe as a mediator resumed following talks with Chissano in December 1991. In mid-January 1992, Mugabe and President Banda of Malawi held direct discussions with Renamo leader Afonso Dhlakama in Malawi in an effort to accelerate the progress of the peace talks, although it was reported that one of Renamo's main demands—the withdrawal of the 7,000 Zimbabwean troops from Mozambique—was not discussed. The ninth round of peace talks began in Rome on 21 January but were deadlocked for several weeks because of demands by Renamo that the government commit itself to a revision of the constitution. Evidence of progress emerged, however, with the signing on 12 March of a third protocol establishing the principles for the country's future electoral system. The protocol provided for a system of proportional representation for the legislature, with legislative and presidential elections to take place simultaneously within one year of the signing of a cease-fire. A national electoral commission was to be set up to oversee the elections, with one-third of its members appointed by Renamo. The protocol also guaranteed freedom of the press and media and of association, expression and movement.

Rebel activity continued within Mozambique, with attacks on the fringes of major cities, including Maputo, Beira and Chimoio, during March 1992. Convoys carrying relief supplies were also attacked and in April the Red Cross sought guarantees from Renamo that it would not attack relief shipments. Following appeals by Chissano and the Italian minister of foreign affairs for other countries, including the USA, Portugal, France and Britain, to participate in the peace talks as observers, US assistant secretary of state Herman Cohen met Dhlakama in Malawi in late April, at which he was understood to have persuaded the rebel leader to concentrate on discussing proposals for a cease-fire, rather than political issues, at the next round of talks. There was speculation that the increasingly severe drought in Mozambique (see below) was having an impact on Renamo's forces, and increasing the chances for a peaceful settlement. However, when, after a series of delays, the peace talks re-opened in Rome in mid-June Renamo's negotiators immediately departed from the agreed agenda to revive the constitutional issue, resulting in a further deadlock. An offer by Dhlakama of an immediate cease-fire, made after talks held in Botswana with President Mugabe and President Masire of Botswana on 5 July, was greeted with scepticism by the government, which pointed out that the rebel leader's condition for a cease-fire—guarantees of political freedom for Renamo supporters—had already been met in the October 1991 protocol. After meetings in mid-July with President F. W. de Klerk of South Africa and President Mugabe, Chissano announced on 19 July that he was prepared to meet Dhlakama. On 7 August, following three days of discussions in Rome (in the presence of President Mugabe, Lonrho chief executive Tiny Rowland, and representatives of the Italian government and of the Roman Catholic Church), Chissano and Dhlakama signed a joint declaration committing the two sides to a total cease-fire by 1 October 1992, as part of a general peace agreement which would provide for presidential and legislative elections within one year. Dhlakama rejected Chissano's offer of an immediate armistice, on the grounds that the mechanisms necessary to guarantee such a truce had first to be implemented. The two leaders did agree, however, to guarantee the political rights and freedoms and personal security of all Mozambican citizens and political parties, and to accept the role of the international community, particularly the UN, in monitoring and guaranteeing the peace agreement.

In mid-September 1992 Chissano and Dhlakama met in Gaborone, Botswana, to attempt to resolve the military and security issues which had remained deadlocked since the first substantive talks on the subjects in early July. At the talks Chissano offered to establish an independent commission to monitor and guarantee the impartiality of the Serviço de Informação e Segurança do Estado (SISE, State Information and Security Service), a body which Renamo claimed to be merely a successor to the disbanded political police, the Serviço Nacional de Segurança Popular (National Service of People's Security). In addition, it was agreed that the joint national defence force would comprise a total of 30,000 troops. As the talks continued, aid agencies warned that up to 3.2m. people in Mozambique were threatened with food shortages due to the drought. In mid-September Renamo agreed to open two transport corridors to allow food aid to reach some of those in need in areas under its control in central Mozambique, although it insisted that most areas could be supplied by air.

The General Peace Agreement

Following a slight delay (during which Dhlakama raised further questions regarding the commission monitoring the SISE and the administration of Renamo-occupied territory pending elections), the general peace agreement was finally signed on 4 October 1992. Under the terms of the agreement, a general cease-fire was to come into force immediately after ratification of the treaty by the assembly of the republic. Both the Renamo and the government forces were to withdraw to assembly points within seven days of ratification. A new 30,000-strong national defence force, the Forças Armadas de Defesa de Moçambique (FADM), would then be created, drawing on equal numbers from each side, with the remaining troops surrendering their weapons to a UN peace-keeping force within six months. A cease-fire commission, incorporating representatives from the government, Renamo and the UN, would be established to assume responsibility for supervising the implementation of the truce regulations. In overall political control of the peace process would be the Comissão de Supervisão e Controle (CSC, Supervision and Control Commission), comprising representatives of the government, Renamo and the UN, with responsibilities including the supervision of the cease-fire commission and other commissions charged with establishing the joint armed forces and reintegrating demobilized soldiers into society, as well as verifying the withdrawal of foreign troops from Mozambique. In addition, Chissano was to appoint a national commission with the task of supervising the SISE. Presidential and legislative elections were to take place, under UN supervision, one year after the signing of the general peace agreement, provided that it had been fully implemented and the demobilization process completed.

The general peace agreement was duly ratified by the assembly of the republic, and came into force on 15 October 1992. However, in the week that followed, the government accused Renamo of systematically violating the accord. The rebels had reportedly occupied four strategically-positioned towns in central and northern Mozambique. Dhlakama subsequently claimed that Renamo's actions had been defensive manoeuvres, and, in turn, accused government forces of violating the accord by advancing into Renamo territory. However, there was speculation as to the extent to which the Renamo leader was able to control his forces. The UN Security Council, meanwhile, agreed to appoint a special representative for Mozambique, former Italian parliamentarian and UN development programme official Aldo Ajello, and dispatch 25 military observers, the first of whom arrived in Maputo on 15 October.

In early November 1992, owing to considerable delays in the formation of the various peace commissions that were envisaged in the general peace agreement, the timetable for the cease-fire operations was redrafted. In mid-December the UN Security Council finally approved a plan for the establishment of the UN Operation in Mozambique (ONUMOZ), providing for the deployment of some 7,500 troops, police and civilian observers to oversee the process of demobilization and formation of the new national armed forces, and to supervise the forthcoming elections. A meeting of aid donors in Rome on 15 December agreed to commit most of the estimated US $330m. cost of the operation.

ONUMOZ Intervention

The commander of the UN military force, Maj.-Gen. Lélio Gonçalves Rodrigues da Silva, assumed his post in February 1993. There were continued delays in the deployment of the peace-keeping force, with the UN experiencing difficulty in persuading member nations to commit troops. Renamo, in turn, refused to begin demobilizing its forces until the UN force was in place. The location of the 49 assembly points was not agreed until late February. Renamo withdrew from the CSC and the cease-fire commission in mid-March, protesting that its officials had not been provided with necessary accommodation, transport and food. In early April Dhlakama announced that his forces would begin to report to assembly points only when Renamo received $15m. to support its political activities. The first UN troops, an Italian battalion, became operational in the Beira corridor on 1 April, and in mid-April the Zimbabwean troops guarding the Beira and Limpopo corridors finally withdrew, six months behind schedule, following their replacement by UN forces. Problems in financing the UN operation were also reported, with only $140m. of the $330m. budget having been approved. On 14 April the UN Security Council unanimously adopted Resolution 818, expressing serious concern at the delays, calling for the timetable for implementation of the peace treaty to be finalized and for both sides to guarantee freedom of movement for ONUMOZ. On 25 April Ajello confirmed that, due to the delays, the elections were unlikely to be held before mid-1994.

By early May 1993 the ONUMOZ force was approaching full strength, with units contributed by 19 countries totalling 4,721 armed and 150 unarmed personnel. Renamo, meanwhile, continued to use its demands for finance to delay the demobilization process, claiming, in late May, that it needed $100m. from the international community to transform itself into a political party. In early June a meeting in Maputo of the CSC announced a formal postponement of the election date to October 1994 (one year behind the original schedule), and called for immediate action on establishing assembly points and commencing the formation of the new national armed forces. A new timetable published by ONUMOZ envisaged assembly points opening in July–August 1993, with demobilization of the two forces beginning in September. Training of the new armed forces would take place from September 1993 to February 1994. Electoral registers would be prepared between 1 April and 30 June 1994, with the election campaign conducted between 1 September and 14 October, followed by the elections in mid-October. The CSC meeting was followed by a meeting of aid donors which revealed growing impatience among the international community with the repeated delays in the peace process and with Renamo's escalating demands for logistical and financial support. The meeting produced additional promises of support for the peace process, bringing the total pledged by donors to $520m., including support for the repatriation of 1.5m. refugees from neighbouring countries, the resettlement of 4m.–5m. displaced people and the reintegration of some 80,000 former combatants into civilian life, as well as for emergency relief and reconstruction. The UN also agreed to establish a trust fund of $10m. to finance Renamo's transformation into a political party, with use of the funds requiring approval by both Renamo and the UN. A second trust fund, accessible to all political parties, was to be established once the national electoral commission had been formed, following the eventual approval of a new electoral law.

In July 1993 Renamo announced new conditions to the advancement of the peace process, initially insisting on the recognition of its own administration, to operate parallel to that of the government. This demand was later revised, with Renamo asking for its members to be appointed to five of the country's 11 provincial governorships. However, in early September, following direct talks between Chissano and Dhlakama which began in Maputo in late August, an agreement was signed resolving the question of the control of provincial administrations. Under the terms of the agreement, Renamo was to appoint three advisers to each of the incumbent provincial governors to advise on all issues relating to the reintegration of areas under Renamo control into a single state administration. In addition, it was agreed that a request be made to the UN to send a police corps to supervise the activities of the national police and ensure neutrality in areas under Renamo control.

In late October 1993 the CSC approved a new timetable covering all aspects of the peace process, including the elections in October 1994. The timetable stipulated the approval of the new electoral law by the end of November 1993. Troops were to be confined to assembly points between November and December, with demobilization beginning in January 1994 and completed by May. Training of the FADM was also to begin in January 1994 and it was to be fully operational by September. However, at the time of announcement of the new timetable only 36 of the 49 designated assembly points had been approved, and only 23 were ready to begin accommodating troops.

In early November 1993 the UN Security Council adopted a resolution renewing the mandate of ONUMOZ for a further six months. In addition, it responded to the joint request by the government and Renamo for a UN police corps by authorizing the deployment of 128 police observers. In mid-November consensus was finally reached on the text of the electoral law following agreement that Mozambicans living abroad would be permitted to vote wherever the national electoral commission considered suitable conditions to exist. The new law was promulgated on 29 December.

At a meeting of the CSC in mid-November 1993 an agreement was signed providing for the confinement of troops to begin on 30 November. The process was to have concluded by the end of December. However, by that date less than 15% of the total number of troops for confinement had entered assembly points. In January 1994 the UN expressed concern at the slow pace at which government troops were assembling. In mid-January 540 military instructors arrived in Mozambique to begin training the FADM. The instructors consisted of government and Renamo troops who had been trained by British instructors in Zimbabwe. However, owing to logistical problems, the formal date for the initial cycle of training to begin was repeatedly postponed. In late February the definitive date was finally set for 21 March, some two months later than envisaged in the revised timetable for the peace process agreed in October 1993.

In early February 1994, following a protracted dispute concerning the level of representation of the respective parties in the national electoral commission, its members were finally inaugurated. The composition of the commission, which had finally been agreed in late October, 1993, included 10 members from the government, seven from Renamo, three from the other opposition parties and an independent chairman. On 23 February the UN Security Council announced that, in response to demands made by Dhlakama for a reinforcement of the UN police corps monitoring the confinement areas, it would be increasing their number from 128 to 1,144 (with simultaneous reductions in the number of UN military personnel to avoid extrabudgetary expenditure). In addition, the UN Security Council urged the government and Renamo to set a specific date for the October general election and called for a rapid conclusion to the demobilization process. By the end of February only 50% of troops had entered assembly points and none had officially been demobilized. In early March, in an effort to expedite the confinement process (which, to an extent, had been hampered by the inadequate capacity of assembly points), the government announced its decision to begin the unilateral demobilization of its troops. Renamo responded by beginning the demobilization of its troops on 18 March. In early April Lt-Gen. Lagos Lidimo, the nominee of the government, and former Renamo guerrilla commander Lt-Gen. Mateus Ngonhamo were inaugurated as the high command of the FADM.

On 11 April 1994 Chissano issued a decree establishing the date of the general election as 27–28 October; the announcement was widely welcomed, although there was criticism from leading bishops, who maintained that two days were insufficient to allow the entire electorate to vote. On 5 May the UN Security Council adopted a resolution renewing the mandate of ONUMOZ for the final period, ending on 15 November, subject to review in July and September. Voter registration for the elections began on 1 June and was due to continue until 15 August, with the total potential electorate estimated at some 7.89m. people. In late July the national electoral commission announced that as a consensus could not be reached on the issue of the enfranchizement of Mozambicans living abroad, emigrants would not be granted the right to vote in the forthcoming general election.

The confinement and demobilization processes continued to make slow progress and consequently the deadline for troop confinement was extended, beyond the beginning of the electoral process, to 8 July 1994, with demobilization to be completed by 15 August. By the end of July, according to official figures, the government had demobilized 28,878 troops of a total of 64,466 in the confinement areas. Renamo had demobilized 11,131 of a total of 22,637 troops, thus making it impossible for Renamo to supply its quota of 15,000 troops to the FADM. At that point only 6,406 troops from both sides had enlisted in the FADM and the prospect of the force being completed and operational before the conduct of elections in October was becoming increasingly remote. During July and August a series of mutinies took place among troops in confinement areas protesting at poor conditions and the slow pace of demobilization. In early August a mission was dispatched by the UN Security Council to impress upon the country's political leaders the importance of completing the demobilization process and conducting the elections on schedule.

The Refugee Problem

In January 1993 the office of the United Nations High Commissioner for Refugees (UNHCR) estimated that there were 1.7m. Mozambican refugees in neighbouring countries. As a consequence of the signing of the General Peace Agreement in October 1992, an estimated 800,000 refugees were expected to return to the country in 1993. In mid-June 1993 the UNHCR began its official voluntary repatriation programme with the return of a contingent of 254 from an estimated total of 140,000 refugees in Zimbabwe. In August Mozambique, the UNHCR and Swaziland signed a tripartite agreement providing for the return of 24,000 refugees from Swaziland, and in mid-October the first contingent, of 513, arrived in Mozambique (the programme was completed in June 1994). The first 300 of an estimated 25,000 refugees in Zambia also returned in October. In the same month a tripartite agreement was signed with South Africa, providing for the voluntary repatriation of some 350,000 Mozambican refugees. However, in January 1994 it was reported that South Africa had expressed its intention to begin expelling refugees from April. In February 1994 the UNHCR reported that some 600,000 refugees had returned from neighbouring countries in 1993, although the majority had done so spontaneously (with the largest number of spontaneous refugees coming from Malawi). By January 1994 only 20,167 refugees were reported to have returned through UNHCR repatriation schemes. In 1994 a further 600,000–700,000 refugees were expected to return. The complete repatriation programme was expected to last a total of three years and to cost $203m.

Economy

MILES SMITH-MORRIS

INTRODUCTION

Mozambique's post-independence economy has suffered the damaging effects of a guerrilla war, drought, floods, famine, the displacement of population, and a severe scarcity of skilled workers and foreign exchange. These difficulties are compounded by a large visible trade deficit, with export earnings covering only about 12% of import costs, and high levels of debt repayments, equivalent to about 60% of the value of Mozambique's exports of goods and services in 1988, despite rescheduling agreements. As a result, Mozambique is heavily reliant on foreign credits. Following the signing of the Nkomati Accord with South Africa in March 1984, the US government announced that its ban on direct bilateral aid to Mozambique had been lifted. In the same year Mozambique acceded to the third Lomé Convention, thus becoming eligible for assistance from the EC, and became a member of the IMF and the World Bank.

In 1992, according to estimates by the World Bank, Mozambique's gross national product (GNP), measured at average 1990–92 prices, was US $1,034m., equivalent to only $60 per head. Between 1985–92, it was estimated, GNP per head declined, in real terms, at an average rate of 1.3% per year. Signs of economic recovery began to emerge at the end of the 1980s with real growth in gross domestic product (GDP) averaging 5.4% in 1987–89. Economic growth declined during 1990–92, owing to drought, the effects of the war on production and reduced foreign support; GDP growth averaged only 0.8% during this period, according to the World Bank. With an end to the drought and prospects for sustained peace, GDP increased by an estimated 5.6% in 1993 and a similar rate of growth was projected for 1994. The annual average rate of inflation was estimated at 38.0% in 1980–92. With the impact of economic reforms, the rate of inflation fell from 160% in 1987 to 35.2% in 1991, before increasing to 45.2% in 1992 and to 76.2% in 1993, owing to an acute devaluation of the currency.

In January 1987 the government initiated an economic recovery programme (ERP) for 1987–90, which was supported by the IMF, and which aimed to increase economic efficiency and to reduce internal and external deficits, by a 'liberalization' of the economy (see below). In June the IMF approved an allocation of SDR 38.74m. in support of the ERP. As a consequence, other donors, both bilateral and multilateral, increased aid to $700m. for 1987.

Meanwhile, the implementation of the ERP began with two substantial devaluations of the metical, from US $1 = 40 meticais to US $1 = 200 meticais in January 1987, and to US $1 = 400 meticais in June 1987. Subsequent devaluations, by 12.5% in January 1988, 22.4% in July 1988, 6.9% in October 1988, and through subsequent monthly adjustments brought the exchange rate to US $1 = 2,700 meticais by the end of 1992. Other major components of the ERP include fiscal measures, with a planned reduction of the budget deficit from 50% of expenditure in 1986 to 25% in 1987, an increase in income taxes, and a reduction in government wage costs and government subsidies, and monetary measures, including the maintenance of stringent control on the rate of credit growth and the increased linkage of wages to productivity. Other measures under the programme include a deregulation of some prices previously controlled by the government, the stimulation of the private sector in industry and agriculture, the focusing of resources on activities of import-substitution or those yielding a high level of value added, the stimulation of exports and a review of procedures, for the allocation of foreign exchange. Price rises were duly introduced in April 1988, during the second phase of the ERP, when basic commodity prices were increased. In urban centres the price of maize rose by nearly 300%, that of rice by nearly 600%, and that of sugar by 400%. In an effort to offset the impact of these rises, the government announced an increase in minimum wages. However, enterprises were expected to limit overall increases in wage costs to 45%. The prices of petroleum, electricity and meat were increased in early 1989. In February 1990 further increases in food prices were announced.

In June 1990 the IMF approved an enhanced structural adjustment facility (ESAF) of SDR 85.40m. to support a further programme of economic reforms (1990–92), which aimed to increase the role of the private sector, to promote foreign investment and to improve access to imports and supplies of industrial inputs. The programme was intended to raise the annual growth rate of GDP to 6.0%, and to limit the current account deficit on the balance of payments to 30% of GDP (compared to an estimated 74.4% in 1989). In June 1994 the IMF announced a further loan of SDR 29.4m. under the ESAF to support economic reforms in 1994/5. A meeting of the consultative group of aid donors in Paris in December 1990 resulted in pledges of nearly $1,200m. for 1991: $400m. for debt relief (including the writing off of $19m. of debt), and $761m. in food and project aid (of which $200m. would be used in the rehabilitation of the Nacala railway). A number of reforms linked to the ERP were introduced in late 1990 and early 1991, including the establishment of a secondary foreign exchange market and the introduction of new incentives for foreign investors. Pledges totalling $1,125m.—48% in grant form—were made at the December 1991 consultative group meeting, although 80% of this consisted of debt relief, rather than new finance. In March 1992 the government unveiled a three-year plan for sharp cuts in public expenditure. The plan, prepared in consultation with the IMF, provided for reductions in investment in agriculture, mining and manufacturing, accompanied by a programme of privatizations in these areas, with the emphasis shifting to rehabilitation of infrastructure. Plans to sell off a number of major state-owned enterprises were announced in early 1992, including cashew nut processor Cajú de Moçambique, engineering company Cometal and forestry project Ifloma. By mid-1993 some 180 state enterprises had been transferred to private ownership, 80% of which were sold to Mozambican investors. A new investment code was approved by the legislature in June 1993, providing identical fiscal and customs benefits to both local and foreign investors.

A World Bank report, prepared for the December 1992 consultative group meeting of donors in Paris, estimated that Mozambique would require external funding totalling $1,198m. in 1993 in order to continue with the ERP, including $419m. in debt-rescheduling. The report added that the peace process would require additional financing of between $123m.–$231m. to meet the cost of demobilization, assistance to returning refugees and displaced people and the conduct of elections. Pledges made at the meeting fell short of the bank's estimates of the country's requirements, totalling about $760m., of which some $137m. was in the form of food aid. External funding requirements for 1994 were set at $1,400m., of which $405m. was for debt rescheduling. External financing requirements were expected to fall, according to World Bank projections, to $1,200m. in 1995 and $1,100m. in 1996.

AGRICULTURE

In periods of stability, 80%–90% of the total working population have been engaged in agriculture, and about 80% of exports in the late 1960s were of agricultural origin. Although only 5% of arable lands are cultivated, agriculture accounts for as much as 65% of Mozambique's GDP. The major cash crops are cashew nuts (accounting for 12.6% of export earnings in 1992), cotton and sugar cane. Maize, bananas, rice, tea, sisal and coconuts are also grown, and the main subsistence crop is cassava. Large-scale modern agriculture before independence was mainly under Portuguese control. About 3,000 farms and plantations were known to exist, employing more than 130,000 people on more than 1.6m. ha, while African plots covered some 2.8m. ha. Since independence, agricultural production has been adversely affected by several factors: the continuing internal conflict which has prevented nearly 3m. Mozambicans from farming the land; the scarcity of skilled labour, following the post-independence exodus by the Portuguese; low crop yields from some state farms; the collapse of rural transport and marketing systems, owing to general insecurity and disorganization; drought, flooding, cyclones and insect pests which have combined to destroy food crops in large areas of the country (notably in the south and the Zambézia region). During 1980–92 agricultural GDP increased by an estimated annual average of 1.3%.

The development of the cultivation of cashew nuts is a relatively recent occurrence. Production of cashew nuts was 204,000 metric tons in 1974. Output decreased by 44% between 1973 and 1976 and continued to decline until 1984, owing to inefficient marketing practices by state enterprises, lack of transportation and the effects of drought. Unofficial estimates assessed the production of cashew nuts at only 20,300 metric tons in 1984. In an attempt to increase production levels, the government doubled producer prices for the crop. Output of cashews was estimated at 25,000 tons in 1985 and, according to official figures, totalled 40,200 tons in the 1986/87 crop year. Output was estimated at 47,000 tons in 1987/88, and at 50,000 tons in 1988/89 but fell to 22,000 tons in 1989/90 due to poor weather conditions and security problems. The expansion in production resulted largely from a French-financed rehabilitation programme. Production rose to 31,000 tons in 1990/91 and to 35,000 tons in 1992/93; in late 1991 the government authorized the export of cashews in unprocessed form, for the first time since 1976, because of the inability of processing plants to cope with increased output. The processing plant in Nacala was due to be renovated in 1992–93, with Portuguese assistance. In April 1993 the African Development Bank granted $20m. for a five-year programme to rehabilitate the industry; annual production was expected to increase to 70,000 tons by the mid-1990s. In recent years cashew nuts have been the second most important export product, after prawns: exports of cashews earned $17.6m. in 1992.

Cotton has traditionally been the main cash crop of northern Mozambique, with more than 500,000 African growers in the Cabo Delgado, Niassa, Nampula and Zambézia provinces. Production of seed (unginned) cotton was 144,000 metric tons in 1973, but by 1984 had fallen to less than 20,000 tons, and in 1985 marketed production reached only 5,700 tons. A programme for rehabilitating the cotton sector is under way, with help from foreign companies. Some state farms are being transferred to peasant cultivation. The 1990 cotton harvest was reported to have been the best since the early 1980's, with 36,600 tons marketed. Cotton exports earned $10.8m. in 1992.

Sugar was produced by large cane-growing companies, such as the Sena Sugar Estates Ltd, on a tributary of the Zambezi, the Companhia Colonial do Buzi, south of Beira, and the

Sociedade Agrícola do Incomati, north of Maputo. This formerly monopolistic system produced 227,823 metric tons of sugar in 1975, but export earnings fell from 575m. escudos in 1975 to 260m. escudos in 1977. All the companies were nationalized and entrusted to Cuban experts, who sought unsuccessfully to restore pre-independence levels of production. Climatic conditions, combined with production difficulties, reduced raw sugar production to 126,000 tons in 1982, and to a record 'low' of 17,000 tons in 1986. However, output increased to about 55,000 tons in 1987. In 1992 exports of sugar earned $6.7m. As part of government plans to rehabilitate the industry, the African Development Fund provided $45m. for the rehabilitation of the Mafambisse sugar complex in Sofala province. Plans to rehabilitate the Marromeu and Luabo plantations and factories were announced in early 1990 by the Commonwealth Development Corporation.

In 1986 Mozambique ranked eighth, after Kenya, Malawi, Tanzania, Zimbabwe, Rwanda, South Africa and Mauritius, among African producers of tea. The Zambézia hills and mountains, close to the Malawi border, are the main producing area. The country produced 18,795 metric tons of made tea in 1973 but output fell to 13,143 tons in 1975. It rose to 22,190 tons in 1981 but declined again, to an estimated 11,000 tons in 1984, and to an estimated 3,000 tons in 1987 and 1,500 tons in 1988. The destruction by Renamo, in February 1987, of equipment at five tea-processing factories, which had been rehabilitated at a cost of about $30m., was expected to aggravate the decline of output for the forseeable future. The principal markets for Mozambican tea are the United Kingdom and the USA, and exports earned 1,212m. meticais in 1981, when shipments totalled 18,000 tons. Following the sharp fall in production since 1981, the value of tea exports declined, to 460m. meticais in 1984 and to only 51m. meticais in 1986, according to government figures. Exports of tea earned less than $10m. a year between 1985–88 but rose again towards the end of the decade, earning $22m. in 1989 and $24m. in 1990. In 1991 the Arab Bank for Economic Development in Africa (BADEA) agreed to lend $6.4m. towards an $8m. project to rehabilitate tea production.

Copra is produced mainly on immense coconut plantations on the coastal belt of the Zambézia and Nampula provinces. It is also a popular crop among Africans who use the oil and other copra products in daily life. In 1972 copra exports totalled 43,938 metric tons. Production levels have fluctuated in recent years, reaching an estimated 60,000 tons in 1980, falling to 50,000 tons in 1982, but rising to an estimated 69,000 tons in 1989, and to an estimated 70,000 tons in 1990 and 72,000 tons in 1991 and 1992. Local reports, however, put 1990 production at only 12,000 tons, due largely to a fall in prices. In 1992 exports of copra earned $4.2m. As in Angola, sisal was introduced by German planters. It is a typical plantation crop, concentrated on about 20 estates west of the ports of Moçambique, Nacala and Pemba. About 22,000 metric tons were produced in 1974 but only an estimated 1,000 tons in 1992.

The normal maize crop is far below the level needed to meet domestic requirements. According to the FAO, the harvest totalled 453,000 tons in 1990, 327,000 tons in 1991 and an estimated 133,000 tons in 1992, although reliable figures are unavailable. In 1986 only 21,500 tons were available on the market, compared with 76,000 tons in 1985. Marketed production rose to 43,100 tons in 1987, 60,400 tons in 1988 and 78,000 tons in 1989. In 1987 the cereal shortage was estimated at 800,000 tons, and was expected to be at least 700,000 tons in 1988. About 120,000 tons of rice were produced in the irrigated lowlands in 1974 falling to an estimated 33,000 tons in 1992. The government estimated marketed production of rice at about 43,500 tons in 1986 and 1987, falling to 41,300 tons in 1988. Oil seeds, such as sesame and sunflower seeds and, above all, groundnuts (estimated at 80,000 tons in 1992), allow for some exports to Portugal. Processing of vegetable oils produces more than 25,000 tons annually. Bananas (estimated at 80,000 tons in 1992) and citrus fruits are exported, as well as potatoes (estimated at 72,000 tons in 1992), tobacco and kenaf (a jute-like fibre).

Livestock is still of secondary importance, owing partly to the prevalence of the tsetse fly over about two-thirds of the country. Most of the cattle are raised south of the Save river, particularly in the Gaza province which has about 500,000 head. In 1992 estimated figures were: 1.25m. cattle; 118,000 sheep; 385,000 goats and 170,000 pigs. The Limpopo *colonato* and the area surrounding Maputo had European cattle ranches to provide the capital with meat and dairy products. Mozambique has to import fresh and prepared meat.

Since independence in 1975, the government has favoured communal agriculture at the village level. From 1976 onwards, more than 1,500 communal villages were formed, and agricultural co-operatives and state farms established, in an effort to 'socialize' the rural sector. In 1985 it was estimated that the state and co-operative sectors together accounted for about 40% of marketed production. However, several state farms proved to be uneconomic, and since 1983 the government has given increased priority to improving production from small farms in the family sector. From 1984 onwards, several state farms were divided into individual peasant holdings. In 1985 the government prepared a basic programme for agricultural rehabilitation, including the involvement of foreign enterprises in joint ventures. Further reforms have taken place as part of the 1987–90 ERP: subsidies have been reduced, and the prices of some agricultural products have been deregulated. Private producers and traders were encouraged with higher producer prices. In October 1987 a fund for agricultural and rural development was established by the Banco Popular de Desenvolvimento, with the aim of assisting peasant farmers and co-operatives to improve their output. Between 1987–90 the number of state farms was reduced from 150 to 109. In April 1988 and February 1990 the consumer prices of many basic commodities were sharply increased.

During 1981–84 a severe drought prevailed in eight out of the 10 provinces and 4m. people were seriously affected. Further problems were caused by floods and cyclones in 1984, and in both 1983 and 1984 there was a steady deterioration in the overall situation in the agricultural sector. In 1983 an estimated 1m. tons of cassava, equivalent to about one-third of the total annual crop, were lost because of drought. In the six southern provinces, agricultural production had declined by about 70%–80%, and some 550,000 tons of cereals were required to offset crop losses in 1983/84. In 1984 it was estimated that 600,000–900,000 tons of maize imports would be required for 1984/85, and the total cereal import requirement for that period (including commercial imports) was estimated at 620,000 tons. Mozambique received considerable international assistance during the drought. However, distribution of food supplies was persistently hampered by security and transport problems, owing to Renamo guerrilla activity. Because of the ravaged state of agriculture, FAO experts believed that a long-term modernization programme of agricultural methods was needed to reduce the national food production deficit.

In 1986 a combination of drought conditions and the escalation of rebel activity in the latter part of the year resulted in a famine: some 4m. people were threatened with starvation. In February 1987 the UN launched an appeal for $247m. in humanitarian aid to ease the problem; it was estimated that 800,000 tons of food aid would be required in 1987/88. As a result of a meeting of UN member-states held in March 1987, international donors increased their pledges of aid: of increased shipments of cereals pledged, the USA was to send 194,000 tons, and the EC 105,000 tons, in 1987. The outlook was equally bleak in the following year. Agricultural production was further hampered by the inadequate level of rainfall over much of the country in late 1987, and by floods in early 1988. Locusts were reported to have destroyed 80% of the cereal crop in Inhambane province in May 1988. In March of that year the UN launched an appeal, on behalf of the government, for $380m. in emergency aid; it was estimated that 710,000 tons of cereals were needed for 1988/89. In February 1989 the government appealed, through the UN, for $383m. in emergency funding for 1989/90. It was estimated that 916,000 tons of food aid were required to meet the needs of some 7.7m. people who were facing chronic food shortages. The government requested a further $136m. in emergency aid for 1990/91. The food supply situation continued to deteriorate during 1990. In December the World

Bank warned that half the population faced starvation or serious deprivation. In April 1991 the overall food deficit was put at 1.1m. tons.

With much of southern Africa suffering from severe drought, the food supply situation in Mozambique deteriorated further in 1992, with that year's harvests expected to yield only 30% of normal levels. Total cereal production was estimated at 236,000 tons, compared to 724,000 tons in 1990, the last year of normal rainfall. Almost complete harvest failure was reported from the south and centre of the country. A report prepared by the government and UN agencies to support an appeal for international assistance in May put the number of people threatened with famine at 3.15m., with a further 6m. in need of additional food supplies. The report estimated Mozambique's total food aid needs for the next 12 months at more than 1.3m. tons valued at US $270.7m.; the government appealed for total emergency assistance of $457.5m. to cover food aid and logistical needs. The first deaths from starvation were reported in late May. Conditions among Mozambican refugees in Malawi were also reported to be deteriorating as their numbers continued to grow, reaching 985,000 by June, with the number increasing by 8,000 a month. With the return of normal rains and the establishment of a cease-fire, the food supply improved in 1993, although the UN estimated that 1m. people, excluding refugees, would still require direct food aid in 1993–94. By the end of 1993, however, with hostilities at an end, there were indications that Mozambique was recovering its capacity to support itself. Although noting that it would be premature to declare an end to the emergency, a report prepared with UN assistance put the country's emergency needs for 1994/95 at $211m., less than half the figure for 1993/94, with an estimated 119,340 tons of food aid needed for 500,000 – 800,000 people.

Forestry has developed chiefly along the Beira railway and in the wetter Zambézia district. Important reafforestation programmes, using eucalyptus trees, have been launched around Maputo. Most of the exports are sawn timber, construction timber, etc., with a ready market in South Africa. In 1990 a South African company formed a joint venture with the Banco Popular de Desenvolvimento to produce timber products in Beira. Fishing is a relatively recent development on this extensive coast. An estimated 32,000 tons of fish and shrimps were landed in 1980, and a promising future seems likely for industrial fishing. Shrimps and prawns provided 29% of export earnings in 1984, valued at 1,199.1m. meticais. In 1992 exports of prawns accounted for 46.3% of total export revenue of $139.3m. In 1991 fish catches, including prawns, totalled an estimated 34,000 tons. Although Mozambique is still not self-sufficient in fish, domestic catches cover about 34% of consumption at present, compared with 6% in 1979. The potential catch is estimated at 500,000 tons of fish and 14,000 tons of prawns. In 1984 South Africa and Mozambique signed a three-year fisheries agreement, under which South Africa provided a credit worth R2m. for the development of the fishing sector. In May 1988 it was announced that the EC and Italy were to provide $40.7m. to finance a fisheries development project in Nampula, Sofala and Inhambane provinces. In April 1991 Japan announced a loan of $5m. for an experimental fishing project.

MINERALS

Mozambique has considerable mineral resources, although exploitation has been limited by internal unrest. The value of mineral exports was $1.1m. in 1987, $2.4m. in 1988 and $1m. in 1989. Mining contributed only 0.21% of GDP in 1991. There are confirmed coal reserves of some 6,000m. tons, but so far output has remained relatively low. The Moatize coal mine, near Tete has an annual production capacity of 600,000 tons, although output was only 84,500 tons in 1989 (compared with 574,800 tons in 1975), owing to a lack of facilities for transporting the coal to Beira port, and to rebel attacks against the railway to Beira. Exports of coal from Moatize declined from pre-independence levels of some 100,000 tons per year to only 9,000 tons in 1986. Coal exports totalled about 7,000 tons in 1991, falling well short of the target of 19,000 tons owing to disruptions resulting from the security situation. However, there are plans to revive the industry, with a new coal-handling terminal at Beira increasing annual capacity from 400,000 tons to 1.2m. tons. Renovation work on the railway to the port, having been repeatedly delayed as a result of the security situation, resumed in July 1990. The EC was providing funding of $72m. for the project. The government has signed bilateral agreements which envisage an increase in annual coal production levels to about 3m. tons by 1995. The rehabilitation project envisages foreign investment in mining projects of more than $600m., and in railway and port infrastructural work of almost $500m. The loans are to be repaid in coal. An agreement worth $700m. over seven years for coal prospecting and mining rights at Mucanha Vuzi was concluded with Brazilian companies in 1982. Mozambique has large reserves of tantalite, but only small quantities are exported; the value of exports was only $400,000 in 1987. There are deposits of ilmenite in the area north of the mouth of the Zambezi river. In 1987, following a five-year survey by the Geological Survey of Yugoslavia (GEO), the Irish-based Kenmare Resources Co entered a joint venture with GEO, aiming to extract heavy minerals from coastal sand dune deposits in the north-east of the country, between Angoche and Sangage. A second drilling programme was initiated in April 1988 to confirm the deposits of ilmenite, zircon and titano-magnetite, and smaller reserves of rutile and monazite. Preliminary assessments estimate the heavy mineral content at 2.2m.–5m. tons, depending upon the method of extraction, with possible revenues of $44m. a year. Production of graphite was due to begin at Ancuabe in Cabo Delgado province in early 1994. The project, which was to cost $11.5m., was funded by the European Investment Bank and the Commonwealth Development Corporation. The mining of iron ore began in the mid-1950s and production of ore averaged about 6m. tons (60%–65% iron) annually in the early 1970s. Production was disrupted by the civil war and ceased altogether between 1975 and 1984. At present, output is stockpiled and the resumption of exports of iron ore depends upon the eventual rehabilitation of the rail link between the mines at Cassinga and the coast. A major deposit of 360m. tons estimated reserves exists near Namapa in the Moçambique province. Bauxite deposits near Tete were reported to be awaiting the completion of the Cahora Bassa power complex to be processed in Vila Fontes on the Zambezi. New deposits of manganese, graphite, fluorite, platinum, nickel, radioactive minerals (e.g. uranium), asbestos, iron, diamonds and natural gas (of which there are confirmed reserves of about 60,000m. cu m) have been found. In 1985 a protocol was signed with the multinational company, Lonrho, regarding the possible development of gold mines in Manica province. In October 1987 Lonrho signed a 25-year agreement for rights in five blocks on a seam in Manica; in 1990 the company announced the formation of a joint venture with the Mineral Resources Ministry, Aluviões de Manica, with plans to produce 20 kilos of gold per month from alluvial deposits in the Revuè and Chua river basins. Reserves in the province are estimated at 50 metric tons. In June 1993 Italy agreed to provide $19m. to rehabilitate the Montepuez marble quarry in Cabo Delgado province and to build a processing factory in Pemba. Annual production from the quarry was projected at 8,100 cubic metres, with Portugal and South Africa identified as potential export markets.

Mozambique imports all its petroleum supplies. The Maputo refinery has an annual capacity of 800,000 tons of crude oil; production was 683,000 tons in 1981, compared with 518,716 tons in 1974. Oil prospecting was actively pursued by US, French, Federal German and South African companies, both offshore near the Rovuma river basin and Beira and on the mainland, but so far only gas has been found. Extraction of gas from the Pande field in southern Inhambane province was to begin with the assistance of a $30m. loan from the World Bank agreed in April 1994. The field's reserves are estimated at 40,000m. cubic metres. In early 1992 agreement was reached on sales of the gas to South Africa, involving the construction of a 900-km pipeline. The state-owned Empresa Nacional de Hidrocarbonetos de Moçambique controls concessions for petroleum production and exploration, although many foreign petroleum companies have been deterred from exploring for petroleum in Mozambique by the country's security situation and the fall in the world price of petroleum.

Petroleum prospecting was expected to resume in late 1994, following a three-year hiatus, with initial exploration focusing on the Rovuma basin. In recent years a critical shortage of foreign exchange has drastically reduced Mozambique's imports of crude petroleum, and severe shortages of fuel have ensued. The government has aimed to encourage foreign investment in the minerals sector, and during the period 1986–89 foreign mining investment in Mozambique increased from $5m. to $50m.

POWER

Electricity production, totalling 658m. kWh in 1975, increased to 4,940m. kWh in 1977, of which 4,490m. was hydroelectric. Total production reached 14,000m. kWh in 1980, but by 1991 had dwindled to 490 kWh, according to UN estimates. Eventually, however, the Cahora Bassa dam should provide great benefits for Mozambique's economy. (The dam, which has always operated at a loss, is owned and administered by the Portuguese government but by the end of the century, when the capital is reimbursed, the plant will have reverted to Mozambique.) By 1982 Cahora Bassa had a generating capacity of 2,075 MW. The supply of power to South Africa started belatedly in mid-1977, and by 1983 South Africa was receiving about 98% of Cahora Bassa's output. In March–April 1984 tripartite talks between Mozambique, Portugal and South Africa resulted in an agreement whereby Mozambique was to receive a share of the revenues, which had previously been paid exclusively to Portugal. Under the new agreement, Mozambique was to receive 5m.–10m. rand per year from South African electricity purchases. However, frequent sabotage of power lines by Renamo subsequently halted supplies from the dam to the South African grid. By March 1987 Cahora Bassa was reported to be operating at only 0.5% of its potential capacity. However, following six months of negotiations, Mozambique, Portugal and South Africa signed an agreement in June 1988 to restore operations at the dam. Under the agreement, 1,400 km of power lines (of which 900 km traversed areas under Renamo control) were to undergo rehabilitation (financed in part by the South African government), and an armed force was to be established to protect the lines, following the completion of the repair work. In September 1988 it was announced that South Africa would provide military aid to Mozambique for the protection of the lines. However, rehabilitation was continually delayed as a result of the security situation. In November 1991 a contract was awarded to an Italian-South African consortium to carry out the rehabilitation work. Funding for the rehabilitation was offered in early 1993 by South Africa ($65m.), Italy ($50m.) and Portugal ($20m.); Italy later withdrew its funding when its foreign aid programme came under investigation for corruption, but it was expected that EU funding would be found to cover the shortfall. Completion of the rehabilitation work, which was expected to take three years, would make Cahora Bassa the country's greatest source of export earnings, with an estimated $56m. a year. An agreement for Zimbabwe, which faces power shortages, to buy electricity from Cahora Bassa was signed in April 1992. The $200m. project would involve constructing a 350-km transmission line to Harare and was expected to take three years to complete. France, the European Investment Bank and the African Development Bank were among those being approached for financing.

The 240-km lake that has been created with the dam reaches the Zambian border, and grandiose plans have been made to irrigate 1.5m. ha in this otherwise economically backward salient of Mozambique. Tete could be developed as an iron and steel industrial centre, and the Zambezi made navigable from Tete to the sea. A second phase of the Cahora Bassa project opened in 1981, including installation of additional generating capacity of 1,750 MW directed to domestic needs.

Other main hydroelectric plants are on the Revuè river, west of Beira at Chicamba Real and Mavúzi. Further south, on the Limpopo, is the dam which helps to irrigate the *colonato*. Another dam at Massingir was expected to increase the irrigation potential of the Limpopo. However, the Massingir dam has been empty since soon after its completion in 1977, owing to the discovery of defects. In January 1988 a French company was contracted to undertake preventive maintenance on the dam and its rehabilitation is planned. A dam at Corumana, costing $250m., was inaugurated in July 1989; the dam's 15-MW power station, financed by Sweden and Norway at a cost of $20m., opened in September 1990. In 1977 a new state company was given the monopoly of production, transport and distribution of electric energy. Mozambique is connected to the South African grid, and by early 1988, in the absence of regular power supplies from Cahora Bassa, was importing an estimated 1,500m. kWh annually from South Africa, costing R15m. per year and absorbing almost 10% of Mozambique's annual export earnings. In February 1991 an agreement was signed with South Africa and Swaziland to build three dams for power generation and irrigation in the joint Komati river basin.

There is also a coal-fired power station in Maputo with a capacity of 60 MW, which is supplied by imports of coal from South Africa. A new turbine, donated by France, was installed at the Maputo station in 1991. It is estimated that 400,000 tons of timber are used annually as fuel wood in Mozambique. In 1989 the government instigated a project which aimed to protect the environment by promoting the domestic use of gas, paraffin and coal in place of fuel wood.

INDUSTRY

Industries are mainly devoted to the processing of primary materials, and Mozambique remains dependent on South African industrial products. About 47% of Mozambican manufacturers are located in and around Maputo, although the government is encouraging decentralization towards Beira and northern Mozambique. Under the colonial administration, investments from Portugal, South Africa, Italy and the UK established export-oriented industries. Food processing formed the traditional basis of this sector, with sugar refining, cashew- and wheat-processing predominating. However, textile production and brewing gained in importance during the 1980s. Other industries include the manufacture of cement, fertilizers and agricultural implements. Cotton spinning and weaving are undertaken at Chiomo, Maputo, and in Nampula province. In mid-1987 the Companhia Agro-Industrial Lonrho Moçambique, a joint venture that had been formed in 1985, received a loan of ECU 3m. ($3.5m.) from the European Investment Bank towards a project for the rehabilitation of its cotton ginnery at Chokwe and its vegetable-processing plant at Chilembene (which supplies Maputo).

The cement industry is operating at a reduced level, producing an estimated 80,000 metric tons in 1991, compared with 611,000 tons in 1973. Cement exports reached 192,000 tons in 1978 but dropped dramatically, to 70,000 tons, in 1982, and to a negligible level in 1986. A programme to rehabilitate the cement plant at Matola, enabling it to produce 400,000 tons a year, was expected to be completed by the end of 1993, with finance provided by the World Bank, European Development Bank, France, Norway, Sweden and Denmark. Construction of a small cement factory in Tete City, with a capacity of 2,500 tons per year, was under way during the late 1980s. This is for local use, and is funded by Germany. The construction sector expanded by 25% between 1977–81, by a further 4.4% in 1982 (when most other sectors were in decline), and by 5% in 1987. A fertilizer plant is in production at Matola. Preliminary studies were completed in early 1987 for a $180m. project for the construction of an ammonia plant at Inhassoro. Following the contraction of the industrial sector by an annual average of 8.4% during 1980–86, official sources estimated that industrial output increased by 6% in 1987, owing partly to restructuring of the sector under the ERP and partly to increased imports of raw materials. In 1988 industrial output increased by 5.1%, according to the government. Under the ERP, resources are to be focused on industries with high domestic added value, and on import-substitution products. Government control of prices was relaxed in several industrial sectors in 1987. The transfer to private-sector ownership of state-owned enterprises was a feature of the economic reforms of the early 1990s: by mid-1993 some 180 enterprises had been privatized.

Other secondary industries produce glass, ceramics, paper, tyres and railway carriages. Industrial output may have fallen to less than 50% of its pre-independence level, owing to the exodus of skilled whites, shortages of imported raw materials and spare parts, and the disruption to transport systems. The 1983–85 State Plan aimed to encourage small-scale industries, placing emphasis on the production of basic consumer goods and of import substitutes, using local materials. In 1990 the International Development Association (IDA) provided $38m. for the rehabilitation and promotion of small- and medium-scale enterprises.

TRANSPORT

Under normal conditions Mozambique derives much of its income from charges on goods carried between Zimbabwe, Zambia, Malawi, Swaziland and South Africa and its ports. Railways play a dominant part in this middle-man economy. In 1987 Mozambique had 3,131 km of track, excluding the Sena Sugar Estates railway (90 km), which serves only the company's properties. In 1986 6.6m. passengers and 303.3m. ton-km of freight were carried by rail. Main lines are: from Maputo, the Maputo–Ressano Garcia line to the South African border, the Maputo - Goba line to the Swaziland border, and the Maputo - Chicualacuala line to the Zimbabwe border (the Limpopo rail link) in the south; from Beira, the Beira–Mutare line to the Zimbabwe border, the Trans-Zambézia line to the Malawi border, and the Tete line. In the north the main route is the Nacala–Malawi line, with a branch-line to Lichinga. All these lines are intended primarily to export the products of land-locked countries, and secondarily to transport Mozambican goods. The whole of Mozambique's rail network has been subject to frequent disruption by Renamo guerrilla sabotage.

Most of the international lines are controlled by international conventions, since their effective functioning is vital to Mozambique's neighbours. The operation of the Beira and Maputo lines was highly profitable to the Mozambican treasury. In February 1979 Mozambique concluded an agreement with South Africa that was to raise South African exports through Mozambique from the 1978 level of 15,000 tons per day, to 30,000–35,000 tons per day by 1981. Revenue from South African use of Mozambican railways and harbours amounted to $93m. in 1977. By the late 1980s South African rail traffic through Mozambique had declined. In 1980 the Harare–Beira line was reopened but, owing to lack of maintenance, the port of Beira could no longer accommodate ships of over 5,000 tons.

In 1983 Mozambique secured several grants for making improvements to the railway network, including the rehabilitation of the vital 450-km rail link between the Moatize coal-fields and Beira port.

In October 1986 a short-term programme to reinstate the 'Beira Corridor', linking Zimbabwe to the Beira harbour, was initiated, at a cost of over $300m., financed mainly by the Netherlands, Scandinavia and the USA. A major project to rebuild the transport network in the corridor was announced in May 1987, under which Western European countries were to provide most of the $589m. cost. The project was expected to span an eight-year period. In 1987 there was an increase of 25% in traffic through the 'Beira Corridor', although the turnover in the transport sector overall declined by 8%, owing to continued disruption by Renamo and a decline in South African traffic. In March 1988 the volume of traffic through the corridor was 42% greater than in the corresponding period of the previous year. The rehabilitation of the Limpopo railway, which began in 1986, was completed in early 1993, at a cost of some $200m.

In December 1992 the government announced the proposed restructuring of the administration of the Beira, Maputo and Nacala transport corridors, with a view to encouraging private-sector involvement in investment and management. A survey of the Maputo network, financed by the IDA, was to be completed by the end of 1993.

This railway-dominated country lacks good roads. In 1991 there were only 27,287 km of roads and tracks. Unfortunately, the main roads are penetration lines toward the border and are grossly insufficient for Mozambique's purposes. Attempts are being made to construct a paved road from the Tanzanian border to the south. Most of the northern provinces are lacking in roads. There is a bridge across the Zambezi river at Tete, on the Zimbabwe–Malawi route, which was completed in 1972, and a tarred road links Malawi to Maputo via Tete. Prior to the end of hostilities in 1992 the poor security situation all but halted normal road transport to and from most cities, and it was necessary to organize military guards for convoys. Between 1977–82 about 550 km of paved roads were built, as well as 450 km of tracks and 50 bridges, and a major programme, supervised by the Southern African Development Co-ordination Conference (SADCC, now the Southern African Development Community—SADC), was under way in 1989 to improve the road links between Mozambique and neighbouring countries. UN agencies are helping to fund a programme to rehabilitate roads within the country. In April 1994 the IDA announced a credit of $188m. towards an $814.6m. programme to rehabilitate the country's roads. The five-year programme, covering 3,450 km of main roads, 11,700 km of unasphalted roads and 3,200 Bailey bridges, was also to receive finance from the African Development Bank, EU, USA, France, Germany and Kuwait.

The main ports are Maputo (the second largest port in Africa, with its annexe at Matola), Beira, Nacala and Quelimane. Maputo and Beira ports exist chiefly as outlets for South Africa, Swaziland, Zimbabwe, Zambia, Malawi and Zaire. However, because of the security situation, most of their potential traffic has been re-routed to the South African ports of Durban, East London and Port Elizabeth. The total freight traffic handled by Mozambique's ports was only 4.2m. tons in 1986, but increased to 9m. tons in 1988. In 1991 an estimated 6.2m. tons of cargo were handled. Maputo has an excellent, multi-purpose harbour and rehabilitation of its facilities, which aimed to increase the port's annual handling capacity from 7m. tons to 12m. tons, was completed in 1989. The first phase of the rehabilitation of Beira port, which included a joint terminal for petroleum and 'roll on, roll off' traffic and an increase in the capacity of the coal terminal, was completed in 1987, increasing its overall capacity by one-third, to 3.2m. tons per year. The second phase of the rehabilitation, which included the deepening of the entrance channel, was expected to raise capacity to 5m. tons per year on completion. Goods traffic handled at Beira in 1991 was stated to total 2.4m. tons, compared with 1.8m. tons in 1987. Repairs to the port of Nacala, damaged by a cyclone in early 1994, were to cost an estimated $14m. Foreign assistance was being sought to fund the repairs.

With the closure of most roads, coastal and river shipping have tended to increase since 1983. Oil is transported along a strategic pipeline from Beira to Mutare in Zimbabwe. The pipeline was embargoed from 1966 until 1980, but recommenced operations in 1982; it has been a frequent target of guerrilla disruption, in spite of its protection by Zimbabwean troops operating inside Mozambique.

International air transport is operated by the state-owned LAM, and domestic routes by TTA. There are 16 airports, of which three are international. In August 1990 LAM agreed to buy one Boeing 767 and one 737 and to lease a further 767 and two 737 aircraft. The first of the 737 was delivered in February 1991. A project to provide equipment to seven airstrips, which was supported by the Danish International Development Agency (Danida), was carried out in 1983–85; Danida agreed in March 1988 to expand the project and provide maintenance services for the original work. A $4.7m. rehabilitation programme was planned for Maputo airport. The project included the rebuilding of the terminal to increase handling capacity to 1m. passengers a year. Since 1983 most provincial capitals have been accessible from Maputo only by air (when fuel is available).

The improvement of Mozambique's ports and railways is a priority of the SADC (see p. 117), which aims to reduce the dependence of southern African states on South Africa.

TOURISM

Formerly a highly profitable activity, tourism relied on the influx of Rhodesians and South Africans to Beira and the southern beaches. Gorongosa Park, half-way between Zimbabwe and Beira, was also a great attraction. In 1972 Mozambique had 282 hotels, motels and boarding houses, containing 5,195 rooms, and received 291,574 visitors. In 1978 it was reported that all organized tourist travel had ceased, but in early 1984 Frelimo received a South African delegation for talks on a resumption of tourism, and in that year a joint-venture tourism company was established with South Africa in order to develop tourism on Inhaca island. Meanwhile, efforts have been made to attract tourists from Zimbabwe again. An estimated 1,000 tourists visited the country in 1981. However, the hopes of an actual resumption of South African tourism in 1984 proved to be premature, and, except on coastal islands and in the immediate vicinity of Maputo, the security situation has hampered any improvement in this highly volatile sector. During the late 1980s some hotels were rehabilitated.

TRADE AND GOVERNMENT FINANCE

Mozambique's severe balance-of-payments problem (the current deficit was $381m. in 1992) has been accentuated by high defence spending (which was projected to account for 35% of budget expenditure in 1994), much of it in already scarce foreign exchange, and by the drastic decline in tourism. Mozambique has also suffered from adverse movements in the terms of trade. Export volumes have also declined sharply as a result of guerrilla sabotage and unfavourable weather conditions. The value of exports was an estimated $104m. in 1989, compared with total imports of an estimated $805m. Exports increased to $126.4m. in 1990, but still covered only 13% of imports. Exports were estimated to have earned $162m. in 1991 and $139m. in 1992, with imports remaining at about $800m. a year. The employment of Mozambicans in South African mines also declined from a pre-independence peak of 118,000 to about 60,000 in 1986, creating a major unemployment problem. In October 1986 the South African government ordered the repatriation of Mozambican miners, thereby exacerbating the level of unemployment and reducing earnings of foreign exchange by about one-third. However, in January 1987 South Africa announced that about 30,000 of the miners would be permitted to remain, and in November 1988 restrictions on the recruitment of Mozambican mine-workers in South Africa were withdrawn.

Agreements on the rescheduling of Mozambique's debts, covering more than $400m. of repayments and arrears repayable in the period up to December 1988, were signed in May and June 1987 with Western official and commercial creditors, in order to reduce repayments on the country's external debt. Despite the 1987 reschedulings, the cost of debt-servicing in 1989 exceeded 200% of the value of Mozambique's exports of goods and services. In June 1990 Western official and commercial creditors agreed a further rescheduling of the country's debts. Mozambique's total external public debt was estimated by the World Bank at $4,928m. at the end of 1992, of which $4,136m. was long-term public debt. In that year the cost of debt-servicing was equivalent to 9.4% of the total value of exports of goods and services. In March 1993 a restructuring of bilateral debt resulted in $180m. of the $440m. Mozambique was due to pay its official creditors over the next two years being written off. Mozambique's total debt was estimated at $5,700m. in 1994, with servicing costs totalling 26.6% of export revenues, after rescheduling.

The budget proposals for 1994 envisaged current expenditure of 1,303,000m. meticais, investment expenditure of 1,211,000m. meticais and income of 1,107,000m. meticais. The entire investment budget and 15% of the current budget was to be financed through foreign grants and loans. Expenditure projections were 11% higher than in 1993 although revenue was expected to increase by only 7%. Defence and security continued to account for the largest share of the budget, at 35% of total spending, despite the end of the war.

Statistical Survey

Source (unless otherwise stated): Direcção Nacional de Estatística, Commissão Nacional do Plano, Avda Ahmed Sekou Touré 21, CP 493, Maputo; tel. 743117.

Area and Population

AREA, POPULATION AND DENSITY

Area (sq km)	799,380*
Population (census results)	
15 December 1970	8,168,933†
1 August 1980‡	
Males	5,670,484
Females	6,003,241
Total	11,673,725
Population (official estimates at 1 August)	
1990	15,730,900
1991	16,156,500
1992	16,593,500
Density (per sq km) at 1 August 1992	20.8

* 308,641 sq miles. The area includes 13,000 sq km (5,019 sq miles) of inland water.

† Covering only those areas under Portuguese control.

‡ Excluding an adjustment for underenumeration, estimated at 3.8%. The adjusted total is 12,130,000 (males 5,908,500; females 6,221,500).

PROVINCES (at 1 January 1987)

Province	Area (sq km)	Population	Density (per sq km)
Cabo Delgado	82,625	1,109,921	13.4
Gaza	75,709	1,138,724	15.0
Inhambane	68,615	1,167,022	17.0
Manica	61,661	756,886	12.3
City of Maputo	602	1,006,765	1,672.4
Maputo province	25,756	544,692	21.1
Nampula	81,606	2,837,856	34.8
Niassa	129,056	607,670	4.7
Sofala	68,018	1,257,710	18.5
Tete	100,724	981,319	9.7
Zambézia	105,008	2,952,251	28.1
Total	799,380	14,360,816	18.0

PRINCIPAL TOWN

Maputo (capital), population 755,300 (including adjustment) at census of 1 August 1980; estimated population 1,006,765 at 1 January 1987.

BIRTHS AND DEATHS (UN estimates, annual averages)

	1975–80	1980–85	1985–90
Birth rate (per 1,000)	45.4	45.7	45.0
Death rate (per 1,000)	20.8	20.0	18.8

Expectation of life (UN estimates, years at birth, 1985–90): 46.1 (males 44.5; females 47.8).

Source: UN, *World Population Prospects: The 1992 Revision.*

ECONOMICALLY ACTIVE POPULATION
(persons aged 12 years and over, 1980 census)

	Males	Females	Total
Agriculture, forestry, hunting and fishing	1,887,779	2,867,052	4,754,831
Mining and quarrying Manufacturing	323,730	23,064	346,794
Construction	41,611	510	42,121
Commerce	90,654	21,590	112,244
Transport, storage and communications	74,817	2,208	77,025
Other services*	203,629	39,820	243,449
Total employed	2,622,220	2,954,244	5,576,464
Unemployed	75,505	19,321	94,826
Total labour force	2,697,725	2,973,565	5,671,290

* Including electricity, gas and water.

Source: ILO, *Year Book of Labour Statistics.*

1991 (estimates, '000 persons): Agriculture 6,870; Industry 766; Services 798; Total labour force 8,434 (Source: UN Economic Commission for Africa, *African Statistical Yearbook*).

Agriculture

PRINCIPAL CROPS ('000 metric tons)

	1990	1991	1992
Rice (paddy)	96	56	33†
Maize	453	327	133†
Sorghum	175	155	66
Potatoes*	70	71	72
Sweet potatoes*	55	55	55
Cassava (Manioc)	4,056	3,690	3,239†
Pulses	92	78	56†
Groundnuts (in shell)	113†	115*	80*
Sunflower seed*	20	20	20
Cottonseed	64*	60	30*
Cotton (lint)	28†	25*	13†
Coconuts*	420	420	300
Copra	70*	72†	72†
Vegetables and melons*	200	165	115
Sugar cane*	330	330	320
Oranges*	20	18	18
Mangoes*	34	32	32
Bananas*	85	80	80
Papayas*	45	44	44
Other fruits*	191	172	132
Cashew nuts	49†	40*	40*
Tea (made)*	2	2	1
Tobacco (leaves)	3†	3†	3*
Jute and jute-like fibres*	4	4	4
Sisal*	1	1	1

* FAO estimate(s). † Unofficial estimate.

Source: FAO, *Production Yearbook.*

LIVESTOCK
(FAO estimates, '000 head, year ending September)

	1990	1991	1992
Asses	20	20	20
Cattle	1,380	1,370	1,250
Pigs	170	165	170
Sheep	121	118	118
Goats	385	380	385

Chickens (FAO estimates, million): 22 in 1990; 22 in 1991; 22 in 1992.

Source: FAO, *Production Yearbook.*

LIVESTOCK PRODUCTS (FAO estimates, '000 metric tons)

	1990	1991	1992
Beef and veal	41	45	36
Goats' meat	2	2	2
Pig meat	11	11	11
Poultry meat	21	21	21
Cows' milk	68	68	68
Goats' milk	10	10	10
Hen eggs	12.8	12.8	12.8
Cattle hides	5.4	6.0	4.8

Source: FAO, *Production Yearbook.*

Forestry

ROUNDWOOD REMOVALS ('000 cubic metres)

	1989	1990	1991
Sawlogs, veneer logs and logs for sleepers	46	47	50
Other industrial wood*	942	967	993
Fuel wood*	15,022	15,022	15,022
Total	16,010	16,036	16,065

* FAO estimates.

Source: FAO, *Yearbook of Forest Products.*

SAWNWOOD PRODUCTION
('000 cubic metres, incl. railway sleepers)

	1989	1990	1991
Coniferous (soft wood)	8*	8	6
Broadleaved (hard wood)	21	18	10
Total	29	26	16

* FAO estimate.

Source: FAO, *Yearbook of Forest Products.*

Fishing

('000 metric tons, live weight)

	1989	1990	1991
Inland waters:			
Freshwater fishes*	0.3	0.3	0.5
Indian Ocean:			
Marine fishes*	27.8	28.3	27.3
Shrimps and prawns	5.0	6.0	5.8*
Other crustaceans*	0.2	0.2	0.2
Molluscs*	0.2	0.2	0.2
Total catch*	33.3	35.0	34.0

* FAO estimate(s).

Source: FAO, *Yearbook of Fishery Statistics.*

Mining

('000 metric tons)

	1990	1991	1992
Coal	122.2	112.0	27.0
Bauxite	6.6	7.9	9.3
Salt (unrefined)	46.9	45.3	22.8

Source: Ministry of Mineral Resources.

Industry

SELECTED PRODUCTS
('000 metric tons, unless otherwise indicated)

	1988	1989	1990
Margarine	6	6	6
Wheat flour	61	56	50
Raw sugar	19	24	33
Beer ('000 hl)	297	158	117
Cigarettes (million)	670	3,500	1,864
Footwear (thousand pairs)	477	347	217
Sulphuric acid	13	13	13
Cement	64	80	100
Radio receivers ('000)	91	103	103
Electric energy (million kWh)	475	485	485

Source: UN Economic Commission for Africa, *African Statistical Yearbook*.

1991 ('000 metric tons, unless otherwise indicated): Raw sugar 33 (FAO figure); Cigarettes (million) 1,060; Cement 80 (estimate); Electric energy (million kWh) 490 (Source: UN, *Industrial Statistics Yearbook*).

Finance

CURRENCY AND EXCHANGE RATES

Monetary Units

100 centavos = 1 metical (plural: meticais).

Sterling and Dollar Equivalents (31 March 1994)

£1 sterling = 8,444.5 meticais;
US $1 = 5,688.1 meticais;
10,000 meticais = £1.184 = $1.758.

Average Exchange Rate (meticais per US $)

1991 1,764.0
1992 2,550.4
1993 3,874.2

BUDGET ('000 million meticais)

Revenue	1990	1991	1992
Taxation	266.4	379.9	573.9
On income	52.9	79.0	102.9
On goods and services	136.8	177.4	281.5
Customs duties	65.3	108.9	168.8
Import duties	40.0	68.0	112.3
Other taxes	11.4	14.6	20.8
Non-tax revenue	31.6	67.2	86.9
Total	298.0	447.1	660.8

Expenditure	1990	1991	1992
Current expenditure*	342.5	457.4	764.7
Defence and security	136.0	178.0	259.3
Civil service salaries	65.0	101.0	142.5
Education	34.1	n.a.	n.a.
Health	10.2	n.a.	n.a.
Goods and services	62.0	89.6	172.4
Education	11.0	n.a.	n.a.
Health	9.0	n.a.	n.a.
Interest on public debt	44.7	46.2	120.1
Others	37.0	50.4	69.3
Investment expenditure†	323.9	464.9	688.0
Liquidation of debt of enterprises	26.4	36.0	37.4
Total	692.8	958.3	1,490.1

* Including adjustments relating to preceding or following periods ('000 million meticais): −2.2 in 1990; −7.8 in 1991; 1.1 in 1992.

† Including adjustments relating to preceding or following periods ('000 million meticais): −17.4 in 1990; −26.0 in 1991; −60.0 in 1992.

Source: Ministry of Finance, Maputo.

CENTRAL BANK RESERVES
(US $ million at 31 December)

	1989	1990	1991
IMF special drawing rights	0.03	0.03	0.04
Reserve position in IMF	0.01	0.01	0.01
Foreign exchange	162.34	207.43	217.53
Total	162.38	207.48	217.58

Source: IMF, *International Financial Statistics*.

MONEY SUPPLY ('000 million meticais at 31 December)

	1989	1990	1991
Currency outside banks	94.1	147.1	189.6
Demand deposits at commercial banks	129.3	178.2	224.1

Source: IMF, *International Financial Statistics*.

COST OF LIVING
(Consumer Price Index for Maputo; base: 1990=100)

	1991	1992	1993
All items	133.3	193.5	340.9

Source: IMF, *International Financial Statistics*.

NATIONAL ACCOUNTS

National Income and Product
('000 million meticais at current prices)

	1984	1985	1986
Domestic factor incomes*	95.7	137.2	146.3
Consumption of fixed capital	4.0	4.0	4.0
Gross domestic product (GDP) at factor cost	99.7	141.2	150.3
Indirect taxes	9.8	6.9	8.7
Less Subsidies	0.4	0.5	0.5
GDP in purchasers' values	109.1	147.6	158.4
Net factor income from abroad	0.3	0.2	0.6
Gross national product	109.4	147.8	159.0
Less Consumption of fixed capital	4.0	4.0	4.0
National income in market prices	105.4	143.8	155.0

* Compensation of employees and the operating surplus of enterprises.

Source: UN, *National Accounts Statistics.*

Expenditure on the Gross Domestic Product
('000 million meticais at current prices)

	1991	1992	1993
Government final consumption expenditure	378	598	889
Private final consumption expenditure	1,779	2,584	4,006
Gross capital formation	802	1,202	2,018
Total domestic expenditure	2,959	4,384	6,913
Exports of goods and services	444	739	1,194
Less Imports of goods and services	1,436	2,359	4,085
GDP in purchasers' values	1,967	2,764	4,022

Source: IMF, *International Financial Statistics.*

Gross Domestic Product by Economic Activity
(estimates, million meticais at current prices)

	1989	1990	1991
Agriculture, hunting, forestry and fishing	555,480	668,150	801,780
Mining and quarrying	2,610	3,600	4,320
Manufacturing	305,240	420,700	504,840
Electricity, gas and water	54,360	74,920	89,910
Construction	86,030	225,000	270,000
Trade, restaurants and hotels	60,920	83,970	100,760
Transport and communications	124,350	162,400	194,880
Finance, insurance, real estate, etc.	4,460	6,140	7,370
Public administration and defence	37,730	52,000	62,410
Other services	7,120	9,810	11,770
GDP at factor cost	1,238,300	1,706,700	2,048,040
Indirect taxes, *less* subsidies	106,570	146,540	175,840
GDP in purchasers' values	1,344,870	1,853,240	2,223,880

Source: UN Economic Commission for Africa, *African Statistical Yearbook.*

BALANCE OF PAYMENTS (US $ million)

	1990	1991	1992
Merchandise exports f.o.b.	126	162	139
Merchandise imports f.o.b.	790	809	799
Trade balance	-663	-647	-659
Exports of services	103	147	165
Imports of services	206	237	246
Other income received	70	56	58
Other income paid	168	166	198
Official unrequited transfers (net)	448	502	499
Current balance	-415	-344	-381
Direct investment (net)	9	23	25
Other capital (net)	-93	-210	-148
Net errors and omissions	66	-4	32
Overall balance	-433	-536	-472

Source: IMF, *International Financial Statistics.*

External Trade

PRINCIPAL COMMODITIES (US $'000)

Imports c.i.f.	1988	1989	1990
Consumer goods:			
Foodstuffs	176,298	173,629	253,924
Other	104,597	155,927	83,888
Primary materials:			
Chemicals	48,547	52,185	31,953
Metals	35,465	42,472	29,808
Crude petroleum and petroleum products	61,104	71,523	95,860
Other	70,893	81,693	97,723
Machinery and spare parts	101,183	87,509	83,628
Capital goods	137,513	142,736	200,736
Total	735,600	807,674	877,520

Total imports (million meticais): 1,289,588 in 1991 (Source: UN, *Monthly Bulletin of Statistics*).

Exports f.o.b.	1990	1991	1992
Cashew nuts	14,288	16,033	17,592
Shrimps, prawns, etc.	43,365	60,779	64,550
Raw cotton	8,694	8,777	10,805
Sugar	7,862	9,765	6,655
Copra	2,603	4,657	4,188
Lobsters	3,835	2,814	4,885
Total (incl. others)	126,426	162,350	139,304

PRINCIPAL TRADING PARTNERS (US $'000)

Imports c.i.f.	1987	1988	1989
Belgium/Luxembourg	4,824	9,668	8,148
Canada	4,917	24,027	11,504
France	35,558	29,200	32,789
German Democratic Republic	8,677	17,093	29,140
Germany, Federal Republic	31,547	31,831	30,594
Italy	85,023	68,092	48,355
Japan	34,581	24,011	45,309
Portugal	31,049	42,627	55,130
Netherlands	27,398	29,313	16,475
South Africa	85,809	110,179	187,652
Sweden	27,653	28,875	24,406
Switzerland	9,685	5,024	4,590
USSR	54,896	73,228	78,842
United Kingdom	29,228	39,750	38,533
USA	62,888	56,222	57,279
Zimbabwe	15,366	31,337	22,858
Total (incl. others)	642,000	735,600	807,676

Exports f.o.b.	1989	1990	1991
France	1,070	653	4
German Democratic Republic	9,328	1,229 }	1,732
Germany, Federal Repub.	480	1,407* }	
Japan	12,249	13,092	19,635
Netherlands	1,452	479	218
Portugal	10,061	7,061	9,745
South Africa	5,426	8,868	14,148
Spain	22,789	22,634	31,238
USSR	4,743	2,635	4,580
United Kingdom	883	5,067	743
USA	12,609	14,553	21,409
Zimbabwe	1,153	273	5,283
Total (incl. others)	104,808	126,427	162,350

* Figure includes trade with the former German Democratic Republic from October 1990.

Transport

RAILWAYS (traffic)

	1984	1985	1986
Freight carried ('000 metric tons)	3,698.6	2,899.5	2,949.3
Freight ton-km (million)	536.3	289.6	303.3
Passengers carried ('000)	5,296.0	6,723.0	6,619.0
Passenger-km (million)	284.1	225.4	263.6

1987: Passenger-km 105m.; Freight ton-km 353m.
1988: Passenger-km 75m.; Freight ton-km 306m.

Source: UN, *Statistical Yearbook*.

1989: Passenger-km 73.5m.; Freight ton-km 402.2m.
1990: Passenger-km 78.9m.; Freight ton-km 421.4m.
1991: Passenger-km 79.0m.; Freight ton-km 306.7m.
1992: Passenger-km 26.0m.; Freight ton-km 616.0m.

ROAD TRAFFIC (motor vehicles in use at 31 December)

	1987	1988
Passenger cars	23,810	24,700
Buses and coaches	1,641	1,380
Goods vehicles	10,250	11,300
Vans	28,370	29,500

Source: International Road Federation, *World Road Statistics*.

INTERNATIONAL SEA-BORNE SHIPPING
(freight traffic, '000 metric tons)

	1989	1990	1991*
Goods loaded	2,430	2,578	2,800
Goods unloaded	3,254	3,379	3,400

* Estimates.

Sources: UN, *Monthly Bulletin of Statistics*, and UN Economic Commission for Africa, *African Statistical Yearbook*.

CIVIL AVIATION (traffic on scheduled services)

	1989	1990	1991
Kilometres flown (million)	5	5	5
Passengers carried ('000)	243	280	283
Passenger-km (million)	494	502	465
Freight ton-km (million)	10	9	9

Source: UN, *Statistical Yearbook*.

1992: Passenger-km 406.3m.; Freight ton-km 11.8m.

Communications Media

	1989	1990	1991
Radio receivers ('000 in use)	620	650	680
Television receivers ('000 in use)	35	40	42
Telephones ('000 in use)	64	66	n.a.
Daily newspapers:			
Number	n.a.	2	n.a.
Average circulation ('000)	n.a.	81	n.a.

Non-daily newspapers (1988): 2 (estimated average circulation 85,000).

Periodicals (1988): 5 (average circulation 2,263,000).

Book Production (1984): 66 titles (including 37 pamphlets); 3,490,000 copies (including 360,000 pamphlets).

Source: mainly UNESCO, *Statistical Yearbook*.

Education

(1992)

	Insti-tutions	Teachers	Students Males	Students Females	Students Total
Pre-primary*	n.a.	n.a.	24,278	20,822	45,100
Primary	3,384	22,132	693,352	506,495	1,199,847
Secondary:					
General	n.a.	3,614	87,599	57,072	144,671
Vocational†	n.a.	846	7,849	1,880	9,729
Teacher training	n.a.	280	2,589	1,431	4,020
Higher‡	2	457	n.a.	n.a.	2,562

* 1986 figures; Data refer to initiation classes.
† 1991 figures.
‡ 1988 figures; Source: Ministry of Education, Maputo.

Source: UNESCO, *Statistical Yearbook*.

Directory

The Constitution

The Constitution came into force on 30 November 1990, replacing the previous version, introduced at independence on 25 June 1975 and revised in 1978. It is summarized below.

GENERAL PRINCIPLES

The Republic of Mozambique is an independent, sovereign, unitary and democratic state of social justice. Sovereignty resides in the people, who exercise it according to the forms laid down in the Constitution. The fundamental objectives of the Republic include:

The defence of independence and sovereignty;

the defence and promotion of human rights and of the equality of citizens before the law; and

the strengthening of democracy, of freedom and of social and individual stability.

POLITICAL PARTICIPATION

The people exercise power through universal, direct, equal, secret, personal and periodic suffrage to elect their representatives, by referenda and through permanent democratic participation. Political parties are prohibited from advocating or resorting to violence.

FUNDAMENTAL RIGHTS AND DUTIES OF CITIZENS

All citizens enjoy the same rights and are subject to the same duties, irrespective of colour, race, sex, ethnic origin, place of birth, religion, level of education, social position or occupation. In realizing the objectives of the Constitution, all citizens enjoy freedom of opinion, assembly and association. All citizens over 18 years of age are entitled to vote and be elected. Active participation in the defence of the country is the duty of every citizen. Individual freedoms are guaranteed by the State, including freedom of expression, of the press, of assembly, of association and of religion. The State guarantees accused persons the right to a legal defence. No Court or Tribunal has the power to impose a sentence of death upon any person.

STATE ORGANS

Public elective officers are chosen by elections through universal, direct, secret, personal and periodic vote. Legally-recognized political parties may participate in elections.

THE PRESIDENT

The President is the Head of State and of the Government, and Commander-in-Chief of the armed forces. The President is elected by direct, equal, secret and personal universal suffrage on a majority vote, and must be proposed by at least 10,000 voters, of whom at least 200 must reside in each province. The term of office is five years. A candidate may be re-elected on only two consecutive occasions, or again after an interval of five years between terms.

THE ASSEMBLY OF THE REPUBLIC

Legislative power is vested in the Assembly of the Republic. The Assembly is elected by universal direct adult suffrage on a secret ballot, and is composed of between 200 and 250 Deputies. The Assembly is elected for a maximum term of five years, but may be dissolved by the President before the expiry of its term. The Assembly holds two ordinary sessions each year.

THE COUNCIL OF MINISTERS

The Council of Ministers is the Government of the Republic. The Prime Minister assists and advises the President in the leadership of the Government and presents the Government's programme, budget and policies to the Assembly, assisted by other ministers.

LOCAL STATE ORGANS

The Republic is administered in provinces, districts, cities and localities. The highest state organ in a province is the provincial government, presided over by a governor, who is answerable to the central Government. There shall be assemblies at each administrative level.

THE JUDICIARY

Judicial functions shall be exercised through the Supreme Court and other courts provided for in the law on the judiciary, which also subordinates them to the Assembly of the Republic. Courts must safeguard the principles of the Constitution and defend the rights and legitimate interests of citizens. Judges are independent, subject only to the law.

The Government

HEAD OF STATE

President of the Republic and Commander-in-Chief of the Armed Forces: JOAQUIM ALBERTO CHISSANO (took office 6 November 1986).

COUNCIL OF MINISTERS
(September 1994)

Prime Minister and Minister of Planning: MÁRIO FERNANDES DA GRAÇA MACHUNGO.

Minister for Foreign Affairs: PASCOAL MANUEL MOCUMBI.

Minister of National Defence: Gen. ALBERTO JOAQUIM CHIPANDE.

Minister of the Interior: Col MANUEL JOSÉ ANTÓNIO.

Minister of State for Administration: AGUIAR JONASSANE REGINALDO REAL MAZULA.

Minister of Co-operation: Maj.-Gen. JACINTO SOARES VELOSO.

Minister of Justice: USSUMANE ALI DAUTO.

Minister of Finance: ENEAS DA CONCEIÇÃO COMICHE.

Minister of Education: ANICETO DOS MUCHANGOS.

Minister of Information: RAFAEL BENEDITO AFONSO MAGUNI.

Minister of Health: LEONARDO SANTOS SIMÃO.

Minister of Mineral Resources: JOHN WILLIAM KACHAMILA.

Minister of Construction and Water: JOÃO MÁRIO SALOMÃO.

Minister of Trade: DANIEL FILIPE GABRIEL TEMBE.

Minister of Culture and Youth: JOSÉ MATEUS MUARIA KATHUPA.

Minister of Labour: TEODATO MONDIM DA SILVA HUNGUANA.

Minister of Agriculture: ALEXANDRE JOSÉ ZANDAMELA.

Minister of Industry and Energy: OCTÁVIO FILIANO MUTHEMBA.

Minister of Transport and Communications: Lt-Gen. ARMANDO EMÍLIO GUEBUZA.

Minister of the Presidency: FELICIANO SALOMÃO GUNDANA.

Minister without Portfolio: Maj.-Gen. MARIANO DE ARAÚJO MATSINHA.

There are also nine secretaries of state.

MINISTRIES

Office of the President: Avda Julius Nyerere, Maputo; tel. 491121; telex 6243.

Ministry of Agriculture: Praça dos Heróis Moçambicanos, CP 1406, Maputo; tel. 460010; telex 6195; fax 460145.

Ministry of Construction and Water: Avda Karl Marx 606, CP 268, Maputo; tel. 430028; telex 6572; fax 421369.

Ministry of Co-operation: Avda Ahmed Sekou Touré 21, CP 2787, Maputo; tel. 491966; telex 6485; fax 491995.

Ministry of Culture and Youth: Avda Patrice Lumumba 1217, CP 1742, Maputo; tel. 420068; telex 6621.

Ministry of Education: Avda 24 de Julho 167, Maputo; tel. 492006; telex 6148.

Ministry of Finance: Praça da Marinha Popular, CP 272, Maputo; tel. 425071; telex 6569.

Ministry of Foreign Affairs: Avda Julius Nyerere 4, Maputo; tel. 490218; telex 6418.

Ministry of Health: Avdas Eduardo Mondlane e Salvador Allende, CP 264, Maputo; tel. 430814; telex 6239.

Ministry of Industry and Energy: Avda 25 de Setembro 1218, Maputo; tel. 431029; telex 6235.

Ministry of Information: Avda Francisco Orlando Magumbwe 780, Maputo; tel. 491087; telex 6487.

Ministry of the Interior: Avda Olof Palme 46/48, Maputo; tel. 420130; telex 6487.

Ministry of Justice: Avda Julius Nyerere 33, Maputo; tel. 490940; telex 6594; fax 492106.

Ministry of Labour: Avda 24 de Julho 2351-2365, CP 281, Maputo; tel. 427051; telex 6392.

Ministry of Mineral Resources: Avda Fernão de Magalhães 34, Maputo; tel. 429615.

Ministry of National Defence: Avda Mártires de Mueda, Maputo; tel. 492081; telex 6331.

Ministry of Planning: Avda Ahmed Sekou Touré 21, Maputo; tel. 491054; telex 6398.

Ministry for the Presidency: Avda Julius Nyerere, Maputo; tel. 491121; telex 6485.

Ministry of Trade: Praça 25 de Junho, CP 1831, Maputo; tel. 426091; telex 6374.

Ministry of Transport and Communications: Avda Mártires de Inhaminga 306, Maputo; tel. 430151; telex 6466.

PROVINCIAL GOVERNORS

Cabo Delgado Province: ANTÓNIO SIMBINE.

Gaza Province: EUGÉNIO NUMAIO.

Inhambane Province: FRANCISCO JOÃO PATEGUANA.

Manica Province: ARTUR USSENE CANANA.

Maputo Province: RAIMUNDO MANUEL BILA.

Nampula Province: ALFREDO MARIA DE SÃO CEPEDA GAMITO.

Niassa Province: JÚLIO ALMOÇO N'CHOLA.

Sofala Province: FRANCISCO DE ASSIS MASQUIL.

Tete Province: CADMIEL FILIANO MUTHEMBA.

Zambézia Province: CARLOS AGOSTINHO DO ROSÁRIO.

City of Maputo: JOÃO BAPTISTA COSMÉ.

Legislature

ASSEMBLY OF THE REPUBLIC

The 250-member Assembly of the Republic, elected as the 'Peoples Assembly' in December 1986, comprises the 160-member Central Committee of the Frente de Libertação de Moçambique (Frelimo), the Executive Committee, the 15-member Political Commission, ministers and vice-ministers, provincial governors, representatives of the armed forces, representatives from each of the provinces and 10 other citizens. With the introduction of the new Constitution in November 1990, the People's Assembly was renamed the 'Assembly of the Republic'. Elections for a new Assembly were initially scheduled to take place in October 1993, one year after the signing of the General Peace Agreement between the Government and the Resistência Nacional Moçambicana (Renamo), but were subsequently postponed until October 1994.

President of the Assembly of the Republic: MARCELINO DOS SANTOS.

Political Organizations

Frente de Libertação de Moçambique (Frelimo): Rua Pereiro do Lago, Maputo; f. 1962 by the merger of three nationalist parties: the União Democrática Nacional de Moçambique, the União Nacionalista Africana de Moçambique and the União Africana de Moçambique Independente; reorg. 1977 as a 'Marxist-Leninist vanguard party'; in July 1989 abandoned its exclusive Marxist-Leninist orientation; Chair. JOAQUIM ALBERTO CHISSANO; Sec.-Gen. FELICIANO SALOMÃO GUNDANA.

The November 1990 Constitution provided for the introduction of a multi-party system. Enabling legislation took effect in February 1991, and by August 1994 the following parties had announced their intention to apply for, or had obtained, legal status:

Aliança Democrática de Moçambique (ADM): f. 1994; Co-ordinator JOSÉ PEREIRA BRANQUINHO.

Confederação Democrática de Moçambique (Codemo): f. 1991; Leader DOMINGOS CARDOSO.

Congresso Independente de Moçambique (Coinmo): Pres. VÍTOR MARCOS SAENE; Sec.-Gen. HILDA RABECA TSININE.

Frente de Ação Patriótica (FAP): f. 1991; Pres. JOSÉ CARLOS PALAÇO.

Frente Unido de Moçambique—Partido de Convergência Democrática (Fumo—PCD): Pres. DR DOMINGOS AROUCA.

Movimento Nacionalista Moçambicana—Partido Moçambicano da Social Democracia (Monamo): Sec.-Gen. DR MAXIMO DIAS.

Partido Agrário de Moçambique (PAM): f. 1991.

Regedores e Camponeses de Moçambique (Recamo): f. by ARONE SIJAMO.

Partido de Convenção Nacional (PCN): obtained legal status Dec. 1992; Co-ordinator-Gen. DR ABEL MABUNDA; Leaders LUTERO SIMANGO, INACIO CHIRE, LUIS GUIMARÃES.

Partido Democrático de Libertação de Moçambique (Padelimo): based in Kenya; Pres. JOAQUIM JOSÉ NIOTA.

Partido Democrático de Moçambique (Pademo): f. 1991; obtained legal status 1993; Co-ordinator WEHIA MONAKACHO RIPUA.

Partido Independente de Moçambique (Pimo): f. 1993; Pres. AYACOB SIMBINDE.

Partido Internacionalista Democrático de Moçambique (Pidemo): f. 1993; Leader JOÃO KAMACHO.

Partido Liberal e Democrático de Moçambique (Palmo): obtained legal status 1993; Chair. MARTINS BILAL; Dep. Chair. ANTÓNIO PALANGE.

Partido Nacional Democrático (Panade): obtained legal status July 1993; Leader JOSÉ MASSINGA.

Partido de Progresso Liberal Federal das Comunidades Religiosas de Moçambique (PPLFCRM): f. 1992; Pres. NEVES SERRANO.

Partido de Progresso Popular de Moçambique (PPPM): f. 1991; obtained legal status Dec. 1992; Pres. DR PADIMBE KAMATI ANDREA.

Partido de Renovação Democrático (PRD): obtained legal status Jan. 1994; Pres. MARIANO JANEIRO BORDINA.

Partido Revolucionário do Povo Socialista Unido de Moçambique (Prepsumo): f. 1992.

Partido Social, Liberal e Democrático: breakaway faction from Palmo; Leader CASIMIRO NYAMITAMB.

Partido do Trabalho (PT): f. 1993; breakaway faction from PPPM; Pres. MIGUEL MABOTE.

Social-Liberal e Democrático (SLD): f. 1991 by breakaway faction from Palmo; Leader CASIMIRO NHAMITHAMBO.

União Democrática de Moçambique (Udemo): f. 1987 as the mil. wing of Unamo, from which it broke away in 1991; adopted present name in April 1992; Leader GIMO PHIRI.

União Nacional Moçambicana (Unamo): f. 1987; breakaway faction from Renamo; social democratic; obtained legal status March 1992; Pres. CARLOS ALEXANDRE REIS; Sec.-Gen. FLORENCIA JOÃO DA SILVA.

The following group has been in conflict with the government since 1976, but in October 1992 signed a peace agreement with the Government, providing for a cessation of hostilities.

Resistência Nacional Moçambicana (Renamo): also known as Movimento Nacional da Resistência de Moçambique (MNR); f. 1976; has conducted guerrilla operations in all 10 provinces; receives support from Arab sources and from right-wing groups in USA and Europe, and has received support from South Africa; operates 'Voz da Renamo' radio station; Pres. and C-in-C AFONSO DHLAKAMA; Sec.-Gen. VICENTE ULULU.

In 1994 the government confirmed reports that the following armed separatist group was operating in Zambézia province.

Rombezia: aims to establish separate state in northern Mozambique between Rovuma and Zambezi rivers; reported to receive support from Malawi-based Portuguese; Leader MANUEL ROCHA.

Diplomatic Representation

EMBASSIES IN MOZAMBIQUE

Algeria: CP 1709, Maputo; tel. 492070; telex 6554; fax 490582; Ambassador: BRAHIM TAÏBI.

Angola: Maputo; Ambassador: PAULO CONDENÇA DE CARVALHO.

Belgium: CP 1500, Maputo; tel. 490077; telex 6511; Ambassador: MICHEL VANTROYEN.

Brazil: Avda Kenneth Kaunda 296, CP 1167, Maputo; tel. 492388; telex 6454; fax 490986; Ambassador: LUCIANO OZORIO ROSA.

Bulgaria: CP 4689, Maputo; tel. 491471; telex 6324; Ambassador: IVAN MARINOV SOKOLARSKI.

China, People's Republic: CP 4668, Maputo; tel. 491560; Ambassador: XIAO SIJIN.

Congo: Avda Kenneth Kaunda 783, CP 4743, Maputo; tel. 490142; telex 6207; Ambassador: EMILIENNE BOTOKA.

Cuba: CP 387, Maputo; tel. 491905; telex 6359; Ambassador: JOSÉ ESPINOSA.

Czech Republic: CP 1463, Maputo; tel. 491484; telex 6216.

Denmark: Avda 24 de Julho 1500, CP 4588, Maputo; tel. 420172; telex 6164; fax 420557; Chargé d'affaires: STIG BARLYNG.

Egypt: CP 4662, Maputo; tel. 491118; telex 6417; Ambassador: MOHAMED HINDAM.

France: CP 4781, Maputo; tel. 490444; telex 6307; Ambassador: GÉRARD CROS.

Germany: Rua de Mapulangwene 506, CP 1595; Maputo; tel. 492714; telex 6489; fax 494888; Ambassador: HELMUT RAU.

Greece: CP 714, Maputo; tel. 490481; telex 6299; fax 491397; Ambassador: ALEXANDROS SANDIS.

Guinea: CP 1125, Maputo; tel. 491478; telex 6527; Ambassador: (vacant).

Holy See: Avda Julius Nyerere 882, CP 2738, Maputo; tel. 491144; telex 6097; fax 492217; Apostolic Delegate: Most Rev. PETER STEPHAN ZURBRIGGEN, Titular Archbishop of Glastonia (Glastonbury).

Hungary: Avda Kenneth Kaunda 714, CP 1245, Maputo; tel. 492953; telex 6431; fax 490880; Ambassador: MIHÁLY TERJÉK.

India: Avda Kenneth Kaunda 167, Maputo; tel. 492437; telex 6452; fax 492364; Ambassador: SURENDRA KUMAR.

Iran: Avda Mártires da Machava 1630, Maputo; tel. 490700; telex 6159; Chargé d'affaires: SAYED MOUFRED.

Italy: Avda Kenneth Kaunda 387, CP 976, Maputo; tel. 491605; telex 6442; Ambassador: MANFREDO INCISCA DI CAMERANA.

Korea, Democratic People's Republic: CP 4694, Maputo; tel. 491482; Ambassador: RYANG KI RAK.

Lesotho: CP 1477, Maputo; tel. 492473; telex 6439; Ambassador: B. NTS'OHI.

Libya: CP 4434, Maputo; tel. 490662; telex 6475; Ambassador: MUHAMMAD AHMAD AL-AMARY.

Malawi: CP 4148, Maputo; tel. 491468; telex 6300; Ambassador: BERNARD KACHAMA.

Netherlands: CP 1163, Maputo; tel. 490031; telex 6178; fax 490429; Ambassador: R. A. VORNIS.

Nicaragua: Maputo; tel. 490810; telex 6245; Ambassador: CARLOS JOSÉ GARCÍA CASTILLO.

Nigeria: CP 4693, Maputo; tel. 490105; telex 6414; Ambassador: S. O. OGUNDELE.

Pakistan: CP 4745, Maputo; tel. 491265; Ambassador: MOHAMMAD NASSER KHAN.

Poland: Rua D. João IV 22, Maputo; tel. 490284; Ambassador: MIROSŁAW DACKIEWICZ.

Portugal: CP 4696, Maputo; tel. 490431; telex 1172; Ambassador: MANUEL LOPES DA COSTA.

Romania: CP 4648, Maputo; tel. 492999; telex 6397; Chargé d'affaires a.i.: TOMAS BALASOIU.

Russia: Avda Agostinho Neto 1103, CP 4666, Maputo; tel. 420091; telex 6635; Ambassador: VLADIMIR KORNEYEV.

Somalia: CP 4715, Maputo; telex 6354; Ambassador: YUSUF HASSAN IBRAHIM.

South Africa: Avda Julius Nyerere 745, CP 1120, Maputo; tel. 493030; telex 6376; fax 493029; Ambassador: JOHN SUMDY.

Spain: Rua Damião de Gois 347, CP 1331, Maputo; tel. 492025; telex 6579; fax 492055; Ambassador: FRANCISCO J. VIQUEIRA.

Swaziland: CP 4711, Maputo; tel. 492117; telex 6353; Ambassador: ALPHABET NKAMBULE.

Sweden: CP 338, Maputo; tel. 490091; telex 6272; fax 490056; Ambassador: LARS-OLOF EDSTRÖM.

Switzerland: CP 135, Maputo; tel. 492432; telex 6233; Chargé d'affaires: JEAN PIERRE BALLAMAR.

United Kingdom: Avda Vladimir I. Lénine 310, CP 55, Maputo; tel. 420111; telex 6265; fax 421666; Ambassador: RICHARD EDIS.

USA: CP 783, Maputo; tel. 492797; Ambassador: DENNIS C. JETT.

Yugoslavia: CP 4759, Maputo; tel. 490819; telex 6516; Ambassador: MIODRAG LEKIĆ.

Zaire: CP 2407, Maputo; tel. 492354; telex 6316; Ambassador: W'EBER M.-B. ANGELO.

Zambia: CP 4655, Maputo; tel. 492452; telex 6415; fax 491893; Ambassador: Maj.-Gen. B. CHISUTA.

Zimbabwe: CP 743, Maputo; tel. 490404; telex 6542; Ambassador: JOHN MAYOWE.

Judicial System

The Constitution of November 1990 provides for a Supreme Court and other judicial courts, an Administrative Court, courts-martial, customs courts, maritime courts and labour courts. The Supreme Court consists of professional judges, appointed by the President of the Republic, and judges elected by the Assembly of the Republic. It acts in sections, as a trial court of primary and appellate jurisdiction, and in plenary session, as a court of final appeal. The Administrative Court controls the legality of administrative acts and supervises public expenditure.

Religion

Many inhabitants follow traditional beliefs, but there are an estimated 5m. Christians and 4m. Muslims. There is a small Hindu community.

CHRISTIANITY

In 1975 educational and medical facilities that had hitherto been administered by churches were acquired by the State. In June 1988 the Government announced that these facilities were to be returned.

Conselho Cristão de Moçambique (Christian Council of Mozambique): Avda Ahmed Sekou Touré 1822, Maputo; tel. 422836; telex 6119; f. 1948; 18 mems; Pres. Rev. LUÍS WANELA; Gen. Sec. Rev. FILIPE SIQUE MBANZE.

The Roman Catholic Church

Mozambique comprises three archdioceses and eight dioceses. At 31 December 1992 the country had an estimated 2,176,488 adherents.

Bishops' Conference: Conferência Episcopal de Moçambique, Secretariado Geral, CP 286, Maputo; tel. 490766; telex 6101; f. 1982; Pres. Rt Rev. FRANCISCO JOÃO SILOTA, Bishop of Chimoio.

Archbishop of Beira: Most Rev. JAIME PEDRO GONÇALVES, Cúria Arquiepiscopal, CP 544, Beira; tel. 322313; fax 327639.

Archbishop of Maputo: Cardinal ALEXANDRE JOSÉ MARIA DOS SANTOS, Paço Arquiepiscopal, Avda Eduardo Mondlane 1448, CP 258, Maputo; tel. 426240; fax 421873.

Archbishop of Nampula: Most Rev. MANUEL VIEIRA PINTO, Paço Arquiepiscopal, CP 84, Nampula; tel. 213025; fax 214194.

The Anglican Communion

Anglicans in Mozambique are adherents of the Church of the Province of Southern Africa. There are two dioceses in Mozambique. The Metropolitan of the Province is the Archbishop of Cape Town, South Africa.

Bishop of Lebombo: Rt Rev. DINIS SALOMÃO SENGULANE, CP 120, Maputo; tel. 734364; telex 6119; fax 401093.

Bishop of Niassa: Rt Rev. PAULINO TOMÁS MANHIQUE, Missão Anglicana de Messumba, Metangula, CP 264, Lichinga, Niassa.

Other Churches

Baptist Convention of Mozambique: Avda Maguiguane 386, CP 852, Maputo; tel. 26852; Pres. Rev. BENTO BARTOLOMEU MATUSSE.

Free Methodist Church: Pres. Rev. LUÍS WANELA.

Presbyterian Church of Mozambique: CP 21, Maputo; tel. 423139; telex 6119; 50,000 adherents; Pres. of Synodal Council Rev. AMOSSE BALTAZAR ZITA.

Other denominations active in Mozambique include the Church of Christ, the Church of the Nazarene, the Reformed Church in Mozambique, the United Congregational Church of Mozambique, the United Methodist Church of Mozambique, and the Wesleyan Methodist Church.

ISLAM

Islamic Congress of Mozambique: represents Sunni Muslims; Chair. HASSANE MAKDÁ.

Islamic Council of Mozambique: Leader Sheikh ABOOBACAR ISMAEL MANGIRÁ.

The Press

DAILIES

Diário de Moçambique: Rua D. João de Mascarenhas, CP 81, Beira; tel. 322501; telex 7347; f. 1981; under state management since Sept. 1991; Dir EZEQUIEL AMBROSIO; Editor FARUCO SADIQUE; circ. 16,000.

Mediafax: Avda Mártires da Machava 1002, Maputo; tel. 490906; telex 6233; fax 490063; f. by co-operative of independent journalists Mediacoop; news-sheet by subscription only, distribution by fax; Editor CARLOS CARDOSO.

Notícias: Rua Joaquim Lapa, CP 327, Maputo; tel. 420119; telex 6453; f. 1926; morning; under state management since Sept. 1991; Dir-Gen. and Editor ALBINO MAGAIA; circ. 33,000.

WEEKLIES

Boletim da República: Avda Vladimir Lénine, CP 275, Maputo; govt and official notices; publ. by Imprensa Nacional da Moçambique.

Domingo: Rua Joaquim Lapa, CP 327, Maputo; tel. 431026; telex 6453; f. 1981; Sun.; Dir BENJAMIN FADUCO; Editor JORGE MATINE; circ. 40,000.

Savana: c/o Mediacoop, Avda Amílcar Cabral 1049, CP 73, Maputo; tel. 430106; fax 430721; f. 1994; Dir KOK NAM; Editor SALOMÃO MOYOANA.

Tempo: Avda Ahmed Sekou Touré 1078, CP 2917, Maputo; tel. 26191; telex 6486; f. 1970; magazine; under state management since Sept. 1991; Dir SIMEÃO CACHAMBA; circ. 40,000.

PERIODICALS

Agricultura: Instituto Nacional de Investigação Agronómica, CP 3658, Maputo; tel. 30091; f. 1982; quarterly; publ. by Centro de Documentação de Agricultura, Silvicultura, Pecuária e Pescas.

Moçambique—Informação Estatística: Comissão Nacional do Plano, CP 2051, Maputo; f. 1982; publ. by Centro de Documentação Económica.

Portos e Caminhos de Ferro: CP 276, Maputo; English and Portuguese; ports and railways; quarterly.

Revista Médica de Moçambique: Instituto Nacional de Saúde, Ministério da Saúde e Faculdade de Medicina, Universidade Eduardo Mondlane, CP 264, Maputo; tel. 427131; telex 6239; fax 423726; f. 1982; 4 a year; medical journal; Dir RUI GAMA VAZ.

NEWS AGENCIES

Agência de Informação de Moçambique (AIM): Rua da Radio Moçambique, CP 896, Maputo; tel. 430795; telex 6430; fax 421906; f. 1975; daily reports in Portuguese and English; monthly bulletin in English; Dir RICARDO MALATE.

Foreign Bureaux

Agence France-Press (AFP): c/o AIM, Rua da Radio Moçambique, CP 896, Maputo; tel. 430723; telex 6430; fax 421906; Correspondent PAUL FAUVET.

Agência Lusa de Informação (Portugal): Avda Ho Chi Min 111, Maputo; tel. 427591; fax 421690; Bureau Chief CARLOS LOBATO.

Agenzia Nazionale Stampa Associata (ANSA) (Italy): c/o AIM, Rua da Radio Moçambique, CP 896, Maputo; tel. 430723; telex 6252; fax 421906; Correspondent PAUL FAUVET.

Allgemeiner Deutscher Nachrichtendienst (ADN) (Germany): Rua Damião de Gois 177, CP 1144, Maputo; telex 6416; Correspondent MATTHIAS KUNERT.

Informatsionnoye Telegrafnoye Agentstvo Rossii—Telegrafnoye Agentstvo Suverennykh Stran (ITAR—TASS) (Russia): 1013 Rua F. Engels, Maputo; tel. 490212; Correspondents BORIS BOGDANOV, YURI CHITOV.

Inter Press Service (IPS) Italy: c/o AIM, Rua da Radio Moçambique, CP 896, Maputo; tel. 430795; telex 6430; fax 429253; Correspondent GIL LAURENCIANO.

Reuters (UK): Rua Daniel Napatima 275, Maputo; tel. 490845; telex 6696; Correspondent IAIN CHRISTIE.

Rossiyskoye Informatsionnoye Agentstvo—Novosti (RIA—Novosti) (Russia): CP 4692, Maputo; tel. 491034; telex 6285; Correspondent YURI BOGOMOLOV.

Xinhua (New China) News Agency (People's Republic of China): Avda Mártires da Machava 1309, CP 4675, Maputo; tel. 741560; telex 6449; Correspondent YANG ZHIGANG.

Publishers

Editora Minerva Central: Rua Consiglieri Pedroso 84, CP 212, Maputo; telex 6561; f. 1908; stationers and printers, educational, technical and medical textbooks; Man. Dir J. F. CARVALHO.

Empresa Moderna Lda: Avda 25 de Setembro, CP 473, Maputo; tel. 424594; f. 1937; fiction, history, textbooks; Gen. Dir FERNANDO HENRIQUE DOS SANTOS ANTÓNIO.

Instituto Nacional do Livro e do Disco: Avda 24 de Julho 1921, CP 4030, Maputo; tel. 34870; telex 6288; govt publishing and purchasing agency; Dir ARMÉNIO CORREIA.

Government Publishing House

Imprensa Nacional de Moçambique: CP 275, Maputo.

Radio and Television

There were an estimated 680,000 radio receivers and 42,000 television receivers in use in 1991.

RADIO

Rádio Moçambique: CP 2000, Maputo; tel. 427325; telex 6712; fax 421816; f. 1975; state-controlled; programmes in Portuguese, English and vernacular languages; Gen. Dir MANUEL JORGE TOMÉ; Admin. Dir MANUEL FERNANDO VETERANO.

TELEVISION

Televisão Experimental (TVE): Avda Julius Nyerere 930, CP 2675, Maputo; tel. 744788; telex 6346; f. 1981; transmissions on Wed., Thurs., Sat. and Sun. only; Dir ANTÓNIO JÚLIO BOTELHO MONIZ.

Finance

(cap. = capital; p.u. = paid up; res = reserves; dep. = deposits; m. = million; brs = branches; amounts in meticais)

BANKING

Central Bank

Banco de Moçambique: Avda 25 de Setembro 1695, CP 423, Maputo; tel. 428151; telex 6251; fax 429718; f. 1975; bank of issue; cap. 100,000m. (1993); Gov. ADRIANO AFONSO MALEIANE.

Commercial Banks

Banco Comercial de Moçambique: Avda 25 de Setembro 1695, CP 865, Maputo; tel. 428151; telex 6240; fax 421915; f. 1992 to take over commercial banking activities of Central Bank; cap. 30,000m., dep. 1,054,445m. (1993); Pres. AUGUSTO JOAQUIM CÂNDIDA; Exec. Dir and Gen. Man. ALBERTO DA COSTA CALÚ; 46 brs and agencies.

Banco Popular de Desenvolvimento: Avda 25 de Setembro 1184, CP 757, Maputo; tel. 428125; telex 6250; fax 423470; f. 1977; state-owned; cap. 16,000m., res 2,765m., dep. 441,203m. (1993); Chair. HERMENEGILDO MARIA CEPÊDA GAMITO; 193 brs and agencies.

Banco Standard Totta de Moçambique, SARL: Praça 25 de Junho 1, CP 2086, Maputo; tel. 420719; telex 6223; fax 426967; f. 1966; 20% Mozambican owned; cap. 9,375m., res 2,014,528m., dep. 199,502m. (1993); Man. Dir Dr ANTÓNIO JOSÉ MARTINS GALAMBA; 11 brs and agencies.

The relaxation of the banking laws in the early 1990s facilitated the establishment in Mozambique of branches of foreign banks including Banco de Fomento e Exterior SA and Banco Português do Atlântico.

DEVELOPMENT FUND

Fundo de Desenvolvimento AgrÍcola e Rural: Maputo; f. 1988 to provide credit for small farmers and rural co-operatives.

INSURANCE

In December 1991 the legislation was approved terminating the state monopoly of insurance and reinsurance activities.

Empresa Moçambicana de Seguros, EE (EMOSE): Avda 25 de Setembro 1383, CP 1165, Maputo; tel. 422095; telex 6280; f. 1977 as state insurance monopoly; took over business of 24 fmr cos; cap. 150m.; Gen. Dir VENANCIO MONDLANE.

Trade and Industry

CHAMBER OF COMMERCE

Câmara de Comércio de Moçambique: Rua Mateus Sansão Mutemba 452, CP 1836, Maputo; tel. 491970; telex 6498; Pres. AMÉRICO MAGAIA; Sec.-Gen. JOÃO ALBASINI.

INVESTMENT ORGANIZATION

Centro de Promoção de Investimentos (CPI): POB 4635, Maputo; tel. 422456; telex 6876; fax 422459; encourages foreign investment and jt ventures with foreign firms; evaluates and negotiates investment proposals; Dir AUGUSTO SUMBURANE.

STATE FOREIGN-TRADING ENTERPRISES

Cimentos de Moçambique: Avda Fernão de Magalhães 34, 2° Andar, CP 270, Maputo; tel. 424061; telex 6336; cement; transfer to private ownership pending; Dir HELDER RODRIGUES.

Citrinos de Manica, EE: Avda 25 de Setembro, Chimoio, CP 15, Manica; tel. 42316; exports citrus and tropical fruit; Dir OSIAS M. MANJATE.

Citrinos de Maputo, EE: Avda 25 de Setembro 1509, 6° Andar, CP 1659, Maputo; tel. 421857; telex 6538; exports citrus fruits; Dir Gen. MAURÍCIO MOTY CARIMO.

Companhia de Desenvolvimento Mineiro (CDM): Avda 24 de Julho 1895, 1°—2° Andares, CP 1152, Maputo; tel. 429170; telex 6413; fax 428921; exports marble, tantalite, asbestos anthophylite, beryl, bentonite, agates, precious and semi-precious stones; Dir LUÍS JOSSENE.

Companhia Industrial de Cordoarias de Moçambique (CICOMO), SARL: Avda Zedequias Manganhela 520, 4° Andar, CP 4113, Maputo; tel. 427272; telex 6347; sisal; Dir CARLOS CORDEIRO.

Distribuidora de Materiais de Construção (DIMAC): Avda Zedequias Manganhela 520, 11° Andar, CP 222, Maputo; tel. 423308; telex 6343; fax 422805; f. 1979; building materials; transfer to private ownership pending; Dir RUI FERNANDES.

Empresa de Comércio Externo de Equipamentos Industriais (INTERMÁQUINA): Rua Consiglieri Pedroso 165, CP 808, Maputo; tel. 424056; telex 6543; industrial equipment and accessories; Dir KONG LAM.

Empresa Distribuidora de Equipamento Eléctrico e Electrónico e Componentes (INTERELECTRA): Avda Samora Machel 162, CP 1159, Maputo; tel. 427091; telex 6203; fax 420723; electrical equipment and components; Dir FRANCISCO PAULO CUCHE.

Empresa Distribuidora e Importadora de Metais (INTERMETAL): Rua Com. Baeta Neves 53, CP 1162, Maputo; tel. 422770; telex 6372; metals and metal products; Man. Dir JORGE SILVESTRE LUÍS GUINDA.

Empresa Estatal de Hidráulica (HIDROMOC): Avda do Trabalho 1501, CP 193, Maputo; tel. 400181; telex 6234; fax 400043; irrigation equipment and chemicals for water treatment; transfer to private ownership pending; Dir EDUARDO J. NHACULE.

Empresa Estatal de Importação e Exportação de Medicamentos (MEDIMOC): Avda Julius Nyerere 500, 1° Andar, CP 600, Maputo; tel. 491211; telex 6260; fax 490168; pharmaceuticals, medical equipment and supplies; Gen. Dir RENATO RONDA.

Empresa Moçambicana de Apetrechamento da Indústria Pesqueira (EQUIPESCA): Avda Zedequias Manganhela 520, CP 2342, Maputo; tel. 27630; telex 6284; fishing equipment; Dir JOAQUIM MARTINS DA CRUZ.

Empresa Moçambicana de Importação e Exportação de Produtos Pesqueiros (PESCOM Internacional): Rua Consiglieri Pedroso 343, 4° Andar, CP 1570, Maputo; tel. 421734; telex 6409; fax 24961; f. 1978; imports and exports fish products; Dir FELISBERTO MANUEL.

Empresa Moçambicana de Importação e Exportação de Produtos Químicos e Plásticos (INTERQUIMICA): Rua de Bagamoyo 333, CP 2268, Maputo; tel. 423168; telex 6274; fax 21229; chemicals, fertilizers, pesticides, plastics, paper; Dir AURÉLIO RICARDO CHIZIANE.

Empresa Nacional de Carvão de Moçambique (CARBOMOC): Rua Joaquim Lapa 108, CP 1152, Maputo; tel. 24251; telex 6491; mineral extraction and export; Dir JAIME RIBEIRO.

Empresa Nacional de Importação e Exportação de Veículos Motorizadas (INTERMECANO): Rua Consiglieri Pedroso 165, CP 1280, Maputo; tel. 430221; telex 6505; motor cycles, cars, trucks, buses, construction plant, agricultural machinery, spare parts; Dir RODRIGO DE OLIVEIRA.

Empresa Nacional Petróleos de Moçambique (PETROMOC): Praça dos Trabalhadores 9, CP 417, Maputo; tel. 427191; telex 6382; fax 430181; f. 1977 to take over the Sonarep oil refinery and its associated distribution co; state directorate for liquid fuels within Mozambique, including petroleum products passing through Mozambique to inland countries; Dir MANUEL PATRÍCIO DA CRUZ VIOLA.

ENACOMO, SARL (Empresa Nacional de Exportação): Avda Samora Machel 285, CP 698, Maputo; tel. 430172; telex 6387; fax 428484; f. 1976; imports and exports; Man. Dir CARLOS PACHECO FARIA.

Importadora de Bens de Consumo (IMBEC): Rua da Mesquita 33, CP 4229, Maputo; tel. 421455; telex 6350; fax 423650; f. 1982; import of consumer goods; Man. Dir CARLOS COSSA.

Lojas Francas de Moçambique (INTERFRANCA): Rua Timor Leste 106, CP 1206, Maputo; tel. 425199; telex 6403; fax 431044; music equipment, motor cars, handicrafts, furniture; Gen. Dir CARLOS E. N. RIBEIRO.

Riopele Têxteis de Moçambique, SARL: Rua Joaquim Lapa 21, CP 1658, Maputo; tel. 31331; telex 6371; fax 422902; textiles; Dir CARLOS RIBEIRO.

OTHER MAJOR STATE ENTERPRISES

Comércio Grossista de Produtos Alimentares (COGROPA): Avda 25 de Setembro 874–896, CP 308, Maputo; tel. 428655; telex 6370; food supplies; transfer to private ownership pending; Dir ANTÓNIO BAPTISTA DO AMARAL.

Companhia da Zambézia, SARL: Avda Samora Machel 245, 4° Andar, CP 617, Maputo; tel. 420639; telex 6380; fax 421507; f. 1892; agriculture; Dirs JOSÉ BENTO VEDOR, JOÃO FORTE, CARLOS DE MATOS.

Companhia do Cajú do Monapo, SARL: Avda do Trabalho 2106, CP 1248, Maputo; tel. 400290; telex 6249; fax 401164; cashew nuts; CEO Dr LACERDA FERREIRA.

Companhia Siderurgica de Moçambique (CSM), SARL: Avda Nuno Alvares 566, CP 441, Maputo; tel. 401281; telex 6262; fax 400400; steel; Technical Man. HERLANDER PEDROSO.

Companhia Industrial do Monapo, SARL: Avda do Trabalho 2106, CP 1248, Maputo; tel. 400290; telex 6249; fax 401164; animal and vegetable oils and soap; CEO CARMEN RAMOS.

Electricidade de Moçambique: Avda Agostinho Neto 70, CP 2447, Maputo; tel. 492011; telex 6407; production and distribution of electric energy; Dir FERNANDO RAMOS JULIÃO.

Empresa de Construções Metálicas (ECOME): Avda das Industrias-Machava, CP 1358, Maputo; tel. 752282; agricultural equipment; Dir JUSTINO LUCAS.

Empresa Estatal de Maquinaria Agrícola (AGRO-ALFA): Avda 24 de Julho 2755, CP 1318, Maputo; tel. 422928; telex 6405; fax 30889; f. 1978; agricultural equipment; Dir ALFREDO MACAMO.

Empresa de Gestão e Assistência Técnica ao Equipamento Agrícola (MECANAGRO): Avda das FPLM 184, CP 2727, Maputo; tel. 460016; telex 6344; agricultural machinery; Dir RAGENDRA DE SOUSA.

Empresa Metalúrgica de Moçambique, SARL: Avda de Moçambique 1500, CP 1316, Maputo; tel. 475189; telex 6499; fax 475149; f. 1951; metallurgical products; Dir ANTÓNIO CAEIRO.

Empresa Moçambicana de Malhas (EMMA), SARL: Avda Zedequias Manganhela 488, CP 2663, Maputo; tel. 423112; telex 6813; textiles; Admin. AMADE OSSUMANE.

Empresa Moçambicana de Chá (EMOCHÁ): Avda Zedequias Manganhela 250, Maputo; tel. 424779; telex 6519; tea production; Dir MARCOS BASTOS.

Empresa Nacional de Cajú (CAJÚ): Avda das Industrias, CP 124, Maputo; tel. 753009; telex 6326; cashew nuts; Dir JÚLIO CUAMBA.

Empresa Nacional de Calçado e Têxteis (ENCATEX): Avda 24 de Julho 2969, CP 67, Maputo; tel. 731258; telex 6421; footwear and textiles; Dir SOVERANO BELCHIOR.

Empresa Nacional de Hidrocarbonetos de Moçambique (ENHM): Avda Fernão de Magalhães 34, CP 2904, Maputo; tel. 460083; telex 6478; controls concessions for petroleum exploration and production; Dir MÁRIO MARQUES.

Empresa Provincial (AVICOLA) EE: Avda 25 de Setembro 1676, CP 4202, Maputo; tel. 34738; Dir MÁRIO BERNARDO.

Fábricas Associadas de Óleos (FASOL), SARL: Avda de Namaacha, CP 1128, Maputo; tel. 723186; telex 6070; oils; transfer to private ownership pending; Dir CARLOS COSTA.

Forjadora EE—Fábrica Moçambicana de Equipamentos Industriais: Avda de Angola 2850, CP 3078, Maputo; tel. 465298; telex 6107; fax 465948; metal structures; Gen. Man. CARLOS SIMBINE.

Indústria Moçambicana de Aço (IMA), SARL: Avda 24 de Julho 2373, 12° Andar, CP 2566, Maputo; tel. 421141; telex 6323; fax 423446; steel; Dir MANUEL JOSÉ SEREJO.

Moçambique-Industrial, SARL: Rua Aruangua 39, 1° Andar, CP 432, Beira; tel. 322123; telex 7352; fax 325347; oils; Dir JORGE SOEIRO.

Química-Geral, SARL: Língamo-Matola, CP 15, Maputo; tel. 424713; telex 6448; fertilizers; Dir ALFREDO BADURU.

Sena Sugar Estate Lda: Avda 25 de Setembro 2801, CP 361, Maputo; tel. 427610; telex 6422; fax 426753; fmrly British-owned; govt-administered since 1978; plantations and mills in Sofala and Zambézia provinces; Dir HERMINIO MACHADO.

Texlom, SARL: Avda Filipe Samuel Magaia 514, CP 194, Maputo; telex 6289; textiles; Dir JOSÉ AUGUSTO TOMO PSICO.

TRADE UNIONS

Freedom to form trade unions, and the right to strike, are guaranteed under the 1990 Constitution.

Organização Nacional dos Jornalistas (OJN): Avda 24 de Julho, 231, Maputo; tel. 492031; f. 1978; Sec.-Gen. HILÁRIO M. E. MATUSSE.

Organização dos Trabalhadores de Moçambique—Central Sindical (OTM—CS) (Mozambique Workers' Organization—Trade Union Headquarters): Rua Manuel António de Sousa 36, Maputo; tel. 426477; telex 6116; fax 421671; f. 1983 as trade union fed. to replace fmr production councils; officially recognized in 1990; 200,000 mems (1993); Sec.-Gen. AUGUSTO MACAMO; Sec.-Gen. SOARES BUNHAZA NHACA.

Sindicato Nacional dos Trabalhadores Agro-Pecuários e Florestais (SINTAF): Avda 25 de Setembro 1676, 1°, Maputo; tel. 431182; Sec.-Gen. EUSÉBIO LUÍS CHIVULELE.

Sindicato Nacional dos Trabalhadores da Aviação Civil, Correios e Comunicações (SINTAC): Avda 25 de Setembro 1509, 2° andar, No 5, Maputo; tel. 30996; Sec.-Gen. MANUEL SANTOS DOS REIS.

Sindicato Nacional dos Trabalhadores do Comércio, Banca e Seguros (SINTCOBASE): Avda Ho Chi Min 365, 1° andar, CP 2142, Maputo; tel. 426271; Sec.-Gen. AMÓS JÚNIOR MATSINHE.

Sindicato Nacional dos Trabalhadores da Indústria do Açúcar (SINTIA): Avda das FPLM 1912, Maputo; tel. 460108; Sec.-Gen. DINIS SALOMÃO MUHAI.

Sindicato Nacional dos Trabalhadores da Indústria Alimentar e Bebidas (SINTIAB): Avda Eduardo Mondlane 1267, CP 394, Maputo; tel. 424709; Sec.-Gen. SAMUEL FENIAS MATSINHE.

Sindicato Nacional dos Trabalhadores da Indústria de Cajú (SINTIC): Rua do Jardim 574, 1° andar, Maputo; tel. 475300; Sec.-Gen. BOAVENTURA MONDLANE.

Sindicato Nacional dos Trabalhadores da Indústria de Construção Civil, Madeira e Minas (SINTICIM): Avda 24 de Julho 2341, 5° andar dt°, Maputo; tel. 421159; Sec.-Gen. JOSÉ ALBINO.

Sindicato Nacional dos Trabalhadores da Indústria Hoteleira, Turismo e Similares (SINTHOTS): Avda Eduardo Mondlane 1267, CP 394, Maputo; tel. 420409; Sec.-Gen. ALBERTO MANUEL NHAPOSSE.

Sindicato Nacional dos Trabalhadores da Indústria Metalúrgica, Metalomecânica e Energia (SINTIME): Avda Samora Machel 30, 6° andar, No 6, Maputo; tel. 430202; Sec.-Gen. ZAQUEU FRANCISCO.

Sindicato Nacional dos Trabalhadores da Indústria Química, Borracha, Papel e Gráfica (SINTIQUIGRA): Avda Karl Marx 414, 1° andar, CP 4433, Maputo; tel. 421553; Sec.-Gen. JOAQUIM M. FANHEIRO.

Sindicato Nacional dos Trabalhadores da Indústria Têxtil Vestuário, Couro e Calçado (SINTEVEC): Avda Maria José de Albuquerque 70, 11° andar, CP 2613, Maputo; tel. 415623; Sec.-Gen. PEDRO JOAQUIM MANDLAZE.

Sindicato Nacional dos Trabalhadores da Marinha Mercante e Pesca (SINTMAP): Rua Joaquim Lapa 4° 22-5° andar, No 6, Maputo; tel. 421148; Sec.-Gen. DANIEL MANUEL NGOQUE.

Sindicato Nacional dos Trabalhadores dos Portos e Caminhos de Ferro (SINPOCAF): Avda Guerra Popular, CP 2158, Maputo; tel. 420531; Sec.-Gen. DINIS EFRAIME FRANCISCO NHANGUMBE.

Sindicato Nacional dos Trabalhadores dos Transportes Rodoviários e Assistência Técnica (SINTRAT): Avda Paulo Samuel Kankhomba 1568, 1° andar, 14, Maputo; tel. 402390; Sec.-Gen. ALCANO HORÁCIO MULA.

Transport

Mozambique's transport system has been disrupted by guerrilla attacks and sabotage. The 'Beira Corridor', where rail and road links and a petroleum pipeline run from Manica, on the Zimbabwean border, to the Mozambican port of Beira, forms a vital outlet for the land-locked southern African countries, particularly Zimbabwe. The development of this route is a major priority of the Southern African Development Community (SADC). A scheme to rehabilitate the transport network along the 'Beira Corridor', at a projected cost of US $589m., was announced in May 1987.

RAILWAYS

In 1987 the total length of track was 3,131 km, excluding the Sena Sugar Estates Railway (90 km), which serves only the company's properties. The railways are all state-owned. There are both internal routes and rail links between Mozambican ports and South Africa, Zimbabwe and Malawi. Many lines and services have been disrupted by Renamo guerrilla operations. Improvement work on most of the principal railway lines began in the early 1980s. The rehabilitation of the 534-km Limpopo railway, linking Chicualacuala, at the Zimbabwe border, with the port of Maputo, was completed in March 1993. In September 1993 it was announced that the implementation of plans, initiated in 1990 but later disrupted, to rehabilitate the railway linking the port of Beira with the coal-mining centre of Moatize had resumed. In November 1993, following the rehabilitation of some 538 km of the total 610 km railway linking the port of Nacala with Blantyre, in Malawi, the completed section, which runs from Nacala to Entre Lagos on the Malawi border, was reopened.

Direcção Nacional dos Portos e Caminhos de Ferro de Moçambique (CFM): Avda Mártires de Inhaminga 336, CP 276, Maputo; tel. 430151; telex 6438; f. 1929; 3,131 km open; there are five separate systems linking Mozambican ports with the country's hinterland, and with other southern African countries, including Malawi, Zimbabwe and South Africa. These systems are administered from Nampula, Beira, Maputo, Inhambane and Quelimane respectively; Dir MÁRIO ANTÓNIO DIMANDE.

Empresa Nacional dos Portos e Caminhos de Ferro de Moçambique (CFM), SARL: Praça dos Trabalhadores, CP 2158, Maputo; tel. 427173; telex 6208; Dir-Gen. MÁRIO ANTÓNIO DIMANDE.

ROADS

In 1991 there were 27,287 km of roads in Mozambique, of which 4,693 km were paved. In that year a major programme, supervised by the SADCC (now SADC), was in progress to improve the road links between Mozambique and neighbouring countries. In early 1994 the Government announced a five-year road rehabilitation programme to reopen 11,000 km of roads closed during the hostilities, and to upgrade 3,000 km of paved roads and 13,000 km of secondary and tertiary roads. The programme, which was to cost an estimated US $24,000m., was to be financed mainly by international donors and the World Bank.

SHIPPING

The main ports are Maputo, Beira, Nacala and Quelimane. Some 6.2m. tons of cargo were handled in 1991. The port of Beira is undergoing modernization and expansion, aimed at increasing its cargo-handling capacity to 5m. tons annually. Rehabilitation of the port of Maputo was completed in 1989, as part of the SADCC (now SADC) transport programme. Repairs to the port of Nacala, damaged by a cyclone in early 1994, were to cost an estimated $14m. Foreign assistance was being sought to finance the repairs.

Agência Nacional de Frete e Navegação (ANFRENA): Rua Consiglieri Pedroso 396, CP 492, Maputo; tel. 428111; telex 6258; fax 427822; Dir FERDINAND WILSON.

Companhia Nacional de Navegação: CP 2064, Maputo; telex 6237.

Companhia Portuguesa de Transportes Marítimos: Avda Samora Machel 239, CP 2, Maputo; tel. 426912.

Empresa Moçambicana de Cargas (MOCARGO): Rua Consiglieri Pedroso 430, 1°–4° Andar, CP 888, Maputo; tel. 431022; telex 6581; fax 421438; f. 1984; shipping, chartering and road transport; Man. Dir MANUEL DE SOUSA AMARAL.

Manica Freight Services, SARL: Praça dos Trabalhadores 51, CP 557, Maputo; tel. 425048; telex 6221; fax 431084; international shipping agents; Dir W. A. VERPLOEGH.

Navique EE (Empresa Moçambicana de Navegação): Rua de Bagamoyo 366, CP 145, Maputo; tel. 425316; telex 6424; fax 426310; Chair. DANIEL C. LAMPIAO; Man. Dir JORGE DE SOUSA COELHO.

CIVIL AVIATION

There are 16 airports, of which three are international airports.

Aerocondor Moçambique: Beira.

Empresa Nacional de Transporte e Trabalho Aéreo, EE (TTA): Aeroporto Internacional de Maputo, CP 2054, Maputo; tel. 465292; telex 6539; fax 465484; scheduled services to 35 domestic points; also operates air taxi services, agricultural and special aviation services; Dir ESTEVÃO ALBERTO JUNIOR.

Linhas Aéreas de Moçambique (LAM): Aeroporto Internacional de Maputo, CP 2060, Maputo; tel. 734111; telex 6386; fax 735601; f. 1980; operates domestic services and international services within Africa and to Europe; Chair. and Dir-Gen. JOSÉ RICARDO ZUZARTE VIEGAS.

Tourism

Tourism, formerly a significant source of foreign exchange, ceased completely following independence, and was resumed on a limited scale in 1980. There were 1,000 visitors in 1981 (compared with 292,000 in 1972 and 69,000 in 1974). In 1984 a joint-venture company was established with South Africa in order to develop tourism on Inhaca island. Security problems continue to impede the recovery of the tourism industry.

Empresa Nacional de Turismo (ENT): Avda 25 de Setembro 1211, CP 614, Maputo; tel. 25011; telex 6303; f. 1985; hotels and tourism; Gen. Dir HELDER PATEGUANA.

Defence

In June 1990 the National Defence Force totalled an estimated 72,000, with 60,000 in the army, 1,000 in the navy and 6,000 in the air force, and a paramilitary force of 5,000; there were also provincial and people's militias, and local militias in villages. In September 1991 the Serviço Nacional de Segurança Popular (National Service of People's Security) was officially disbanded and replaced by the Serviço de Informação e Segurança do Estado (SISE, State Information and Security Service) with powers restricted to intelligence and counter-intelligence. In 1989 there were reported to be as many as 12,000 Zimbabwean troops in Mozambique, to guard the Mutare-Beira oil pipeline and to assist in offensives against Renamo rebel movement. In December 1990, in accordance with a partial cease-fire agreement between the government and Renamo, all Zimbabwean troops in Mozambique were confined to the two transport 'corridors' leading from Manica and Chicualacuala in Zimbabwe to the ports of Beira and Maputo, respectively. In 1989 some 600 Malawian troops were also reported to be in Mozambique, deployed along the transport 'corridor' leading from Malawi to the port of Nacala. In December 1991 the Government announced plans to reduce the armed forces by 45,000 in anticipation of the signing of a cease-fire agreement when, it was proposed, a single armed force incorporating Renamo guerrillas would be created. Under the provisions of the General Peace Agreement signed on 4 October 1992, the joint armed forces, Forças Armadas de Defesa de Moçambique (FADM), were to number 30,000, comprising equal numbers of government and Renamo troops. All remaining members of the National Defence Force and the paramilitary forces and militias were to be demobilized. In accordance with the provisions of the General Peace Agreement, all Zimbabwean and Malawian troops were withdrawn from Mozambique—in April 1993 and June 1993, respectively—prior to the holding of presidential and legislative elections, scheduled for October 1994 (postponed from October 1993). According to the official timetable for the peace process, the formation of the FADM was to have been completed by September 1994. However, owing to delays in the confinement and demobilization processes, only 6,406 troops from both sides had enlisted in the FADM by late July.

Defence Expenditure: Budgeted at 349,600m. meticais for 1993.

Commander-in-Chief of the Armed Forces: Pres. JOAQUIM ALBERTO CHISSANO.

Joint High Command: Lt-Gen. LAGOS LIDIMO; Lt-Gen. MATEUS NGONHAMO.

Education

At independence, between 85%–95% of the adult population were illiterate. In the early 1980s there was a major emphasis on campaigns for adult literacy and other adult education. By 1990, according to estimates by UNESCO, 67.1% of the adult population were illiterate (males 54.9%; females 78.7%). Education is officially compulsory for seven years from the age of seven. Primary schooling lasts for five years, and secondary schooling for seven years comprising two cycles of two and five years. The number of children receiving primary education increased from 634,000 in 1973 to 1,495,000 in 1979, but declined to 1,199,847 in 1992, owing to the security situation. As a proportion of the school-age population, the total enrolment at primary and secondary schools increased from 30% in 1972 to 52% in 1979, but declined to the equivalent of 32% in 1992 (males 38%; females 27%). There were 2,562 students at the university in 1988. A second university was expected to open in 1995. Education was allocated 17.5% of current budget expenditure in 1990. In early 1991 the government introduced a programme to improve primary education and strengthen the overall management of the education sector, at a cost of US $67.9m. (to be provided mainly by the World Bank).

Bibliography

Christian Aid Report. *Mozambique: Caught in the Trap.* Birmingham, UK, Third World Publications, 1988.

Coccia, G. *The Scorpion Sting.* Johannesburg, 1976.

Egerö, B. *Mozambique—A Dream Undone: The Political Economy of Democracy 1975–84.* Uppsala, Nordiska Afrikainstitutet.

Finnegan, W. *A Complicated War: The Harrowing of Mozambique.* Berkeley, University of California Press, 1992.

Geffray, C. *La cause des armes au Mozambique—Anthropologie d'une guerre civile.* Paris, Editions Karthala, 1990.

Hanlon, J. *Mozambique: The Revolution Under Fire.* London, Zed Press, 1990.

Mozambique: Who Calls the Shots? London, James Currey, 1991.

Henriksen, T. H. *Revolution and Counterrevolution: Mozambique's War of Independence 1964–74.* Westport, CT, Greenwood Press, 1983.

Mozambique: A History. London, Rex Collings, 1978.

Isaacman, A., and Isaacman, B. *Mozambique from Colonialism to Revolution 1900–82.* Boulder, CO, Westview Press, 1983.

ISCSPU. *Moçambique.* Lisbon, 1965.

Jardim, J. *Moçambique, terra queimada.* Lisbon, 1976.

Konczacki, Z. A., Parpart, J. L., and Shaw, T. M. (Eds). *Studies in the Economic History of Southern Africa.* Vol. I. London, Cass, 1990.

Machel, S. *Sowing the Seeds of Revolution.* London, 1974, and Harare, Zimbabwe Publishing House, 1981 (re-issue).

Middlemas, K. *Cabora Bassa.* London, 1975.

Mondlane, E. *The Struggle for Mozambique.* London and Baltimore, MD, Penguin Books, 1969.

Munslow, B. *Mozambique: The Revolution and its Origins.* London, Longman, 1983.

Nelson, H. D. (Ed.). *Mozambique: A Country Study.* Washington, DC, US Government Printing Office, 1985.

Pélissier, R. *Africana. Bibliographies sur l'Afrique luso-hispanophone (1800–1980).* Orgeval, Editions Pélissier, 1982.

Naissance du Mozambique (1854 – 1918). 2 vols. Orgeval, Editions Pélissier, 1984.

Rita-Ferreira, A. *Os povos de Moçambique.* Oporto, 1976.

de Saavedra, R. *Aqui Moçambique livre.* Johannesburg, 1975.

Saul, J. *State and Revolution in Eastern Africa.* London, Heinemann Educational, 1979.

A Difficult Road: The Transition to Socialism in Mozambique. New York, Monthly Review Press, 1985.

Schaedel, M. *Eingeboren-Arbeit.* Cologne, 1984.

Torp, E., Denny, L. M., and Ray, D. I. (Eds). *Mozambique and São Tomé and Príncipe: Politics, Economics and Society.* New York, Pinter, 1989.

Vail, L., and White, L. *Capitalism and Colonialism in Mozambique.* London, Heinemann Educational, 1981.

Verschuur, C., Corrêa Lima, M., Lamy, P., and Velasquez, G. *Mozambique: Dix ans de solitude.* Paris, Harmattan, 1986.

Weimer, B. *Die Mozambiquanische Aussenpolitik 1975–1982.* Baden-Baden, 1983.

NAMIBIA

Physical and Social Geography

A. MacGREGOR HUTCHESON

The Republic of Namibia, lying across the Tropic of Capricorn, covers an area of 824,292 sq km (318,261 sq miles). It is bordered by South Africa on the south and south-east, by Botswana on the east and Angola on the north, while the narrow Caprivi Strip, between the two latter countries, extends Namibia's boundaries to the Zambezi river and a short border with Zambia.

The Namib Desert, a narrow plain 65–160 km wide and extending 1,600 km along the entire Atlantic seaboard, has a mean annual rainfall of less than 100 mm; long lines of huge sand dunes are common and it is almost devoid of vegetation. Behind the coastal plain the Great Escarpment rises to the plateau which forms the rest of the country. Part of the Southern African plateau, it has an average elevation of 1,100 m above sea-level but towards the centre of the country there is a rise to altitudes of 1,525–2,440 m. A number of mountain masses rise above the general surface throughout the plateau. Eastwards the surface slopes to the Kalahari Basin and northwards to the Etosha Pan. Much of Namibia's drainage is interior to the Kalahari. There are no perennial rivers apart from those such as the Okavango and the Cuando, which cross the Caprivi Strip, and the Orange, Kunene and Zambezi, which form parts of the southern and northern borders.

Temperatures of the coastal areas are modified by the cool Benguela Current, while altitude modifies plateau temperatures (cf. Walvis Bay: January 19°C, July 14.5°C; and Windhoek (1,707 m): January 24°C, July 14°C). Mean annual rainfall varies from some 50 mm on the coast to 550 mm in the north. Most rain falls during the summer, but is unreliable and there are years of drought. Grasslands cover most of the plateau; they are richer in the wetter north but merge into poor scrub in the south and east.

Most of the population (totalling 1,033,196 at the May 1981 census, and provisionally enumerated at 1,401,711 at the census of October 1991) reside on the plateau. Figures for the density of population (1.7 inhabitants per sq km at the 1981 census) are misleading, as the better-watered northern one-third of the plateau contains more than one-half of the total population and about two-thirds of the African population, including the Ovambo (the largest single ethnic group), Kavango, East Caprivians and Kaokovelders. Almost the entire European population (80,000 in 1988, including the European population of Walvis Bay, then a South African exclave, but transferred to Namibia in March 1994) live in the southern two-thirds of the plateau, chiefly in the central highlands around Windhoek, the capital, together with the other main ethnic groups, the Damara, Herero, Nama, Rehoboth and Coloured. Excluding ports and mining centres in the Namib and small numbers of Bushmen in the Kalahari, these regions are largely uninhabited.

Namibia possesses scattered deposits of valuable minerals, and its economy is dominated by the mining sector. Of particular importance are the rich deposits of alluvial diamonds, which are exploited by surface mining, notably in the area between Oranjemund and Lüderitz. Operations at the Oranjemund mine are not, however, expected to remain economic after the year 2000, and development of an 'offshore' diamond field, extending 300 m from the coast, is therefore proceeding. Uranium ore (although of a low grade) is mined open-cast at Rössing, 39 km north-east of Swakopmund, which is the world's largest open-pit uranium oxide complex. There is another, smaller uranium deposit about 80 km south of Rössing, which is thought to be of a higher grade. Tin, copper, lead and zinc are also mined, and Namibia is believed to have significant reserves of coal, iron ore and platinum, although these have yet to be assessed. Other minerals currently produced or awaiting exploitation include vanadium, manganese, gold, silver, tungsten (wolfram), cadmium, limestone and rock salt. The existence of considerable reserves of offshore natural gas could be of great benefit to Namibia's future economic development.

Despite the limitations imposed by frequent drought, agriculture is a significant economic activity. With the help of water from boreholes, large areas are given over to extensive ranching. Rivers, notably the Orange, Kunene and Okavango, are potential water resources for irrigation and hydroelectric power, while swamps, such as those situated in the Caprivi Strip, could be drained to enhance arable output.

Namibia possesses potentially the richest inshore and deep-water fishing zones in tropical Africa as a consequence of the rich feeding provided by the Benguela Current. Measures are being taken to counter the effects of decades of over-fishing by both domestic and foreign fleets.

Recent History

CHRISTOPHER SAUNDERS

HISTORICAL BACKGROUND AND PROGRESS TOWARDS INDEPENDENCE, 1884–1981

South West Africa (SWA), declared a German protectorate in 1884, was occupied by South Africa following the outbreak of the First World War. In 1919 the League of Nations entrusted South Africa with a mandate to administer the territory. In 1925 the South African government granted limited self-government to the territory's European inhabitants. No trusteeship agreement was concluded with the United Nations after the Second World War, and the UN's refusal in 1946 to agree to South Africa's request to annex SWA marked the beginning of a protracted dispute. In 1949 South Africa granted the territory's European voters representation in the South African parliament. In 1950 the International Court of Justice (ICJ) ruled that South Africa was not legally obliged to place the territory under the UN trusteeship system, but that it was not competent to alter the legal status of the territory unilaterally. In 1966 the UN General Assembly voted to terminate South Africa's mandate and to assume responsibility for the territory; a Council for South West Africa was appointed in 1967, and in the following year the UN resolved that the territory should be renamed Namibia. The South African government, however, refused to allow the UN to take control of the territory's administration.

The UN activity was founded on an upsurge of resistance within the territory. In 1957 the Ovamboland People's Congress was formed. It was subsequently renamed the Ovamboland People's Organisation, and in 1960 the South West Africa People's Organisation (SWAPO). Its leaders included Sam Nujoma and Herman (later Andimba) Toivo ja Toivo. From 1963 onwards, SWAPO meetings were effectively banned, although it remained technically a legal organization. In 1966 SWAPO's military wing, the People's Liberation Army of Namibia (PLAN), began an armed struggle against South African rule. In 1968 SWAPO restyled itself as the South West Africa People's Organisation of Namibia.

In 1971 the ICJ ruled that South Africa's presence in Namibia was illegal and that it should withdraw immediately. The South African government's rejection of the ruling provoked a massive strike in the territory in December, to which the administration responded with arrests and the imposition of a partial state of emergency. In early 1973 South Africa set up a short-lived multiracial council for the territory. In December, after the failure of a UN attempt to establish negotiations with South Africa, the UN General Assembly voted to recognize SWAPO as the 'authentic representative of the people of Namibia', and appointed the first UN commissioner for Namibia to undertake 'executive and administrative tasks'.

South Africa's unsuccessful intervention in Angola in the second half of 1975 set the scene for the escalation of the Namibian armed struggle, and, by illegally using Namibia as a military base, South Africa made its position at the UN more vulnerable. With the accession to power in Angola of the pro-SWAPO Movimento Popular de Libertação de Angola, PLAN was able to establish bases close to the borders of Namibia. South Africa reacted to this threat by greatly expanding counter-insurgency forces in the territory.

At this time South Africa began to take initiatives on the political front. In September 1975 the South African prime minister, B. J. Vorster, convened a constitutional conference to discuss the territory's future. The Turnhalle conference, as it became known, designated 31 December 1978 as the target date for Namibian independence and, in March 1977, it produced a draft constitution for a pre-independence interim government. The constitution, providing for 11 ethnic administrations, was denounced by the UN and SWAPO, which issued its own constitutional proposals based on a parliamentary system with universal suffrage.

In order to persuade South Africa to reject the Turnhalle scheme and to adopt instead a plan which would be acceptable to the UN, a 'contact group' comprising the five western members of the UN Security Council was established. The group held talks with both the South African government and SWAPO beginning in April 1977. In September of that year South Africa appointed an administrator-general for Namibia, and the territory's representation in the South African parliament came to an end. By April 1978 the contact group was able to present proposals for a settlement providing for UN-supervised elections, a reduction in the numbers of South African troops from Namibia and the release of political prisoners. These proposals were accepted by South Africa in late April and by SWAPO in July, after a delay caused in part by a South African raid on a SWAPO refugee centre at Cassinga in Angola, during which a large number of civilians were massacred. The proposals were then incorporated into UN Security Council Resolution 435 of 28 September 1978. South Africa insisted on holding its own election for a Namibian constituent assembly in the territory in December; this was denounced by the international community, which, however, declined to impose sanctions in protest at the action. With SWAPO boycotting the election, 41 of the 50 seats were won by the Democratic Turnhalle Alliance (DTA), a conservative coalition of the ethnic groups involved in the conference under the leadership of Dirk Mudge, who thereafter chaired a ministerial council which was granted limited executive powers. A separate South West African Territory Force (SWATF) was established in 1980, although control of defence and security matters and external affairs remained in the hands of the South African government.

In January 1981 the UN convened a conference at Geneva which was attended by SWAPO, South Africa, the DTA and other internal parties. The contact group and the 'front-line' states (Angola, Botswana, Mozambique, Tanzania, Zambia and Zimbabwe) were present as observers. South Africa and the internal parties could not agree on a cease-fire date and the implementation of the UN plan. It was apparent that the South African prime minister, P. W. Botha, believed that SWAPO was communist-controlled and that therefore it could not be allowed to come to power. The DTA for its part needed more time to establish itself as a credible alternative to SWAPO; the South African government, meanwhile, hoped that the newly-elected Reagan administration in the USA would be sympathetic to South African policy.

Under US leadership, the contact group resumed consultations with South Africa and SWAPO during 1981. In July 1982 constitutional guidelines were agreed to by the two parties, which provided that the post-independence constitution should include a bill of rights and be approved by two-thirds of the members of a constituent assembly. Although South Africa and SWAPO were unable to agree on whether the election should be conducted wholly on the basis of proportional representation, the UN secretary-general was able to report that all other points at issue had been resolved. By then, however, a more formidable obstacle to the implementation of the UN plan had arisen. South Africa now insisted that the Cuban troops withdraw from Angola. This idea, known as 'linkage', was first introduced in 1981 by the US government, which viewed the war in Namibia and southern Angola as a buffer against Soviet expansionism. This view was not shared by the other members of the 'contact group', particularly France, which eventually left the group in December 1983. The US then continued the negotiations alone.

Within the territory, the DTA was seriously weakened in February 1982 by the resignation of Peter Kalangula, the leader of the only significant movement supported by the Ovambo (the largest ethnic group in Namibia) other than SWAPO. After several months of disagreement with the South African government over the future role of the DTA in the territory, Mudge resigned as chairman of the ministerial council in January 1983, and the council itself was automatically dissolved. The administrator-general, in turn, dissolved the national assembly, and assumed direct rule of Namibia on behalf of the South African government.

Even more disturbing to the internal settlement plans, perhaps, was the contempt with which the ethnic administrations came to be regarded. The attempt to enhance support by channelling state funds through these administrations went disastrously wrong. In 1983 South Africa appointed a commission of inquiry to investigate allegations of inefficiency and corruption: this revealed major irregularities, and in 1984 the administrator-general assumed powers to allow the central department of finance to control the spending of the ethnic authorities where necessary.

ARMED CONFLICT

During the early 1980s, South African troops and police, based in the north of the territory, were augmented by units from the locally-recruited SWATF, including mercenary and covert police detachments. The result was a severe deterioration in respect for human rights, initially in Ovamboland, but spreading in 1982–83 into the Kavango and Caprivi regions. Internal church reports of torture and killings were supported by a succession of international church delegations visiting Namibia during the period 1981–84. Such criticism, however, failed to moderate the harsh security policies operated by the territorial administration.

South Africa conducted extensive raids across the frontier into southern Angola from 1981, and parts of southern Angola were effectively occupied, with South Africa admitting that its troops were 200 km inside Angolan territory. In February 1984 a cease-fire agreement was concluded in Lusaka, Zambia, following talks between South African and US government officials. Under the terms of the agreement, a joint commission was established to monitor the withdrawal of South African troops from Angola, and Angola undertook to permit neither SWAPO nor Cuban forces to move into the areas vacated by South African troops. SWAPO declared that it would abide by the agreement, but made it clear that it would continue PLAN operations until a cease-fire was established in Namibia as the first stage in the implementation of Resolution 435. US negotiators continued, meanwhile, to focus their hopes on securing a regional accord, in which a settlement in Namibia along the lines of Resolution 435 would be counter-balanced by a removal of the Cuban troops from Angola. In November 1984, in response to US proposals, Angola's President dos Santos suggested a timetable for the withdrawal of Cuban troops from the south of Angola. South African withdrawal from Angola was completed in April 1985, but soon afterwards South Africa established an interim internal government in Namibia.

SOUTH AFRICAN STRATEGY

After the fall of the DTA ministers' council in January 1983, there was a hiatus until an informally-constituted Multi-Party Conference (MPC) began to meet in November of that year. At that time, its membership extended beyond the DTA to include the Damara Council, the Rehoboth Liberation Front, the SWAPO–Democrats (SWAPO–D, a breakaway faction of SWAPO), the right-wing National Party of South West Africa (SWANP) and the mainly Herero South West African National Union (SWANU). SWAPO, however, refused to join, and denounced the MPC as 'another South African puppet show'. In October 1984 the MPC called for an all-party meeting by 31 December of that year, failing which it would negotiate unilaterally with Pretoria for independence.

The credibility of the MPC was not high, owing to the past history of the DTA, the corruption and mismanagement of ethnic authorities under the control of MPC member parties, its failure to attract any Ovambo party, and its readiness to deal with South Africa. Aware of the lack of support for the MPC, the South African government sought to involve at least part of SWAPO in an internal settlement. In March 1984 it released Andimba Toivo ja Toivo, who had been imprisoned in South Africa since 1968. A number of SWAPO activists who had been detained since 1978 were also freed. In May 1984 formal talks were held in Lusaka between the administrator-general, SWAPO and the internal parties, under the joint chairmanship of President Kaunda of Zambia and the administrator-general. SWAPO, however, refused to capitulate, insisting on implementation of the internationally recognized Resolution 435 and the talks collapsed. The members of the MPC then proceeded with their own plans.

On 17 June 1985 the South African government installed a 'Transitional Government of National Unity' (TGNU) in Windhoek, pending independence, although the arrangement was condemned in advance by the contact group governments and was declared 'null and void' by the UN Secretary-General. This interim government consisted of a cabinet and a national assembly. Neither was elected and appointments were made from among the constituent parties of the MPC. A 'bill of rights', drawn up by the MPC, prohibited racial discrimination, and a constitutional council was established, under a South African judge, to prepare a constitution for an independent Namibia. South Africa retained responsibility for foreign affairs, defence and internal security. The administrator-general had the power to veto legislation, and did so on several occasions.

TRANSITIONAL GOVERNMENT AND POPULAR RESISTANCE

From 1985, SWAPO and its Youth League held a series of rallies, which were disrupted by the police. In July 1986, however, the courts ruled that SWAPO was entitled to hold public meetings, because the violent overthrow of the state was not an integral part of its progamme. Mass meetings were subsequently held throughout Namibia.

Another significant development during the late 1980s was the resurgence of trade union activity. In June 1988 trade union members participated in a widespread two-day strike in support of a sustained, large-scale boycott being conducted by schoolchildren and students, who were demanding the release of all detainees, the withdrawal of the paramilitary force Koevoet from townships and the removal of SADF bases from the vicinity of schools in northern Namibia.

The TGNU became deeply divided by disputes centred on ethnicity. Two TGNU members applied to the courts to disallow the 1986/87 budget on the grounds that its ethnic allocations were inequitable, and in September 1986 the minister of national education announced that all schools would be racially integrated from January 1987, only to retract this announcement in December 1986. In the previous month the constitutional council had produced a draft constitution, but the component parties of the interim government could not agree on its provisions—particularly as to whether the document should include guarantees of minority rights, as the South African government insisted that it should. The disagreement persisted throughout 1987, in which year South Africa announced a 40% reduction in its contribution to the Namibian budget. In April 1988 the South African government expressed impatience at the slow progress towards a permanent constitution, and announced that it was granting the administrator-general powers to curb newspapers that were deemed to promote 'subversion and terrorism', and also to call ethnically-based local elections. However, developments elsewhere soon led South Africa to abandon its efforts to achieve a credible internal settlement.

MOVES TOWARDS INDEPENDENCE

In early 1987 Angola secured US agreement to the participation of Cuba in discussions, nominally as part of the Angolan delegation and in January 1988 Angola and Cuba accepted, in principle, the US demand for a complete withdrawal of Cuban troops from Angola, this being conditional on the implementation of the UN independence plan for Namibia. In March proposals for the withdrawal of all Cuban troops were rejected by the South African government as being 'insufficiently detailed'. However, South Africa agreed to participate in tripartite negotiations with Angola and Cuba, with the USA acting as mediator.

At these negotiations, which began in London in early May 1988, South Africa agreed to implement UN Security Council Resolution 435, providing that a timetable for the withdrawal of Cuban troops could be agreed. By mid-July the participants in the negotiations had accepted a document containing 14 'essential principles' for a peaceful settlement, and in early August it was agreed that the implementation of UN Security Council Resolution 435 would begin on 1 November. South Africa withdrew all its troops from Angola by the end of August. The November deadline was not met, however, owing to a failure to agree on an exact schedule for the evacuation of Cuban troops from Angola. In mid-November the terms of the Cuban troop withdrawal were agreed in principle, although official ratification of the agreement was delayed until mid-December, owing to South African dissatisfaction with the procedures for verifying the Cuban withdrawal.

On 22 December 1988 South Africa, Angola and Cuba signed a formal treaty designating 1 April 1989 as the implementation date for UN Resolution 435. Another treaty was signed by Angola and Cuba, requiring the evacuation of all Cuban troops from Angola by July 1991. In further agreements a joint commission was established to monitor the implementation of the trilateral treaty, and SWAPO forces were to be confined to bases in Angola to await demobilization and repatriation. Under the terms of Resolution 435 a constituent assembly was to be elected in November. South African forces in Namibia were to be confined to their bases, and their numbers reduced to 1,500 by 1 July 1989; all South African troops were to have been withdrawn from Namibia one week after the election. A multinational UN observer force, the UN Transition Assistance Group (UNTAG), was to monitor the South African withdrawal, and supervise the election.

IMPLEMENTATION OF THE UN INDEPENDENCE PLAN

According to the original proposals regarding Resolution 435, UNTAG was to be composed of 7,500 troops; in February 1989, following disagreement within the UN Security Council over the cost of the operation, it was announced that the number was to be 4,650, with a further 500 police and about 1,000 civilian observers. The UNTAG force began to arrive during February 1989. At the end of that month the TGNU was formally disbanded, and on 1 March the national assembly voted to dissolve itself: from then until independence the territory was governed by the administrator-general, Louis Pienaar, in consultation, from 1 April, with the special representative of the UN Secretary-General, Martti Ahtisaari.

The scheduled implementation of the UN Security Council's Resolution 435 was disrupted by large-scale movements, beginning on 1 April 1989, of PLAN troops into Ovamboland. The South African government demanded and obtained Ahtisaari's agreement to the release from base of South African forces to repel the PLAN troops, over 300 of whom were reportedly killed in the subsequent intense fighting. The origins of the sudden and unanticipated conflict apparently lay in differing interpretations of the terms of the UN peace plan; SWAPO, excluded from the 1988 negotiations, relied on provisions under Resolution 435 for the confinement to base of PLAN combatants located within the territory on 1 April, and it was widely claimed that the insurgents had intended to report to UNTAG officials. On 9 April the joint commission produced conditions for an evacuation of the PLAN forces; meanwhile, Sam Nujoma, president of SWAPO, ordered a withdrawal of PLAN forces to Angola. At a meeting of the joint commission on 19 May, the cease-fire was certified to be in force.

In June 1989 most racially discriminatory legislation was repealed and an amnesty was granted to Namibian refugees and exiles: by late September nearly 42,000 refugees, including Sam Nujoma, had returned to Namibia. Meanwhile, South Africa completed its troop reduction ahead of schedule.

The pre-independence election was conducted peacefully in the second week of November 1989; more than 95% of the electorate voted. The 72 seats in the constituent assembly were contested by candidates from 10 political parties and alliances: representatives of seven parties and fronts were elected. SWAPO received 57.3% of all votes cast and won 41 seats, thus obtaining a majority of the seats in the assembly but failing to achieve the two-thirds majority which would have allowed SWAPO to draft the constitution without recourse to wider consultation. It was widely believed that SWAPO would have fared better had evidence not emerged during the election campaign of the torture and death in its camps in Angola where numerous people had been detained—as alleged by South African spies during the war. The DTA, with 28.6% of the votes, won 21 seats. The election was pronounced 'free and fair' by the special representative of the UN Secretary-General. Following the election, the remaining South African troops were withdrawn from Namibia, and SWAPO's bases in Angola were disbanded.

POST-INDEPENDENCE DEVELOPMENTS

In early February 1990 the constituent assembly adopted unanimously a draft constitution, which provided for a multiparty political system, based on universal adult suffrage, with an independent judiciary and a 'bill of rights'. Executive power was to be vested in a president who was permitted to serve a maximum of two five-year terms, while a 72-member national assembly was to have legislative power. In mid-February the constituent assembly elected Sam Nujoma to be Namibia's first president. On 21 March 1990 Namibia became independent: the constituent assembly became a 72-member national assembly, and the president assumed executive power.

Following independence, Namibia became a member of the UN, the Organization of African Unity and the Commonwealth. Full diplomatic relations were established with many states, and partial diplomatic relations with South Africa. In May 1990 Angola and Namibia agreed to form a joint commission to monitor their common border. However, relations became strained in February 1991 when Angolan aircraft bombed a northern Namibian village; the Angolan government claimed that it had attacked covert destabilization bases sponsored by South Africa, and promised to pay compensation to the Namibian government. With the resumption of the civil war in Angola in late 1992, the Namibian government remained concerned over the security of its northern border. Instability in South Africa also threatened to affect Namibia; the government was, therefore, much relieved when South Africa's first democratic election took place peacefully in April 1994.

In March 1990 Namibia became a full member of the Southern African Customs Union (having previously been a *de facto* member of that organization) and a member of the South African Development Co-ordination Conference (SADCC), which sought to reduce the dependence of southern African states on South Africa. In August 1992, Namibia joined the other SADCC members in recreating the organization as the Southern African Development Community (SADC).

In April 1990 a team of British military advisers arrived in Namibia to assist in training the new Namibian Defence Force, comprising former members of both PLAN and the SWATF. In September several ex-members of the national police force and of the disbanded paramilitary force, Koevoet, were charged with high treason, following the discovery of a cache of arms in July. The appointment, in October, of the former SWAPO head of security, Maj.-Gen. Solomon Hawala, as commander of the army caused protest among opposition groups, owing to allegations that he had been implicated in the torture and detention of dissidents prior to Namibia's independence. During that month the international human rights organization, Amnesty International, recommended that the Namibian government conduct an inquiry into alleged violations of human rights by SWAPO during the struggle for independence; at least 350 people who had been imprisoned by SWAPO at that time were reported to be unaccounted for in late 1990. In early November the national assembly voted to request the international committee of the Red Cross to ascertain the status of the missing detainees; however, the committee refused, stating that it did not have an adequate mandate to conduct such an inquiry.

The admission by the South African government in July 1991 that it had provided some R100m. in funding to the DTA and other anti-SWAPO political parties during the 1989 election campaign added to the DTA's post-independence problems. In late November 1991 the DTA, formerly a coalition of ethnically-based groupings, re-organized itself as a single party, but its support continued to dwindle. In late November and early December 1992 the first elections were held for the country's 13 regional councils and 48 local authorities. SWAPO won nine regional councils while the DTA won only three (in the remaining council there was no clear majority). SWAPO therefore secured control of the national council comprising two members from each regional council; it began work in May 1993. The following month Dirk Mudge, the leading figure in the DTA, resigned from the national assembly and announced his semi-retirement from public life (although he retained the chairmanship of the DTA). The DTA repeatedly publicized examples of alleged misgovernment and inappropriate expenditure (the most controversial example being the purchase of a presidential jet at a time of severe drought) however, these efforts failed to revive the party's diminished level of public support.

Walvis Bay, the 1,124-sq km enclave that contains the region's only deep-water port facilities, remained under South African jurisdiction after Namibian independence. Negotiations between the South African and Namibian governments led to the announcement in August 1992 that a Walvis Bay Joint Administration Authority (JAA) would be established, comprising an equal number of representatives from each country. The Joint Authority began operating in November that year. In August 1993, following pressure from the African National Congress of South Africa, South Africa's multi-party negotiating forum resolved to transfer sovereignty of Walvis Bay to Namibia. Some white residents of the enclave resorted unsuccessfully to legal action in an attempt to block the transfer. The work of the JAA was completed in February 1994 and in the following month the enclave was formally integrated into Namibia. At the ceremony marking the transfer, President Nujoma expressed his country's satisfaction that the process of decolonization had finally concluded. However, a number of issues involving property sales in the enclave immediately prior to the transfer, and the resolution of compensation claims by South African parastatal organizations which held assets in Walvis Bay, have remained outstanding.

Economy

DONALD L. SPARKS

INTRODUCTION

With a gross domestic product (GDP) per caput of US$ 1,562 in 1993, Namibia is relatively prosperous in the African context; for example, Mozambique has a GDP per caput of $ 60, Tanzania $ 110 and Zimbabwe $ 570. Namibia's relative wealth reflects a large and relatively diversified mining sector, producing diamonds, uranium and base metals. Despite frequent drought, large ranches generally provide significant exports of beef and karakul sheepskins. Yet the economy is extraordinarily extractive and badly integrated. About 90% of the goods that Namibia produces are exported, and about 90% of the goods that are used in the country, including about one-half of the food, are imported. Furthermore, the figure for GDP per caput disguises an extreme inequality in income distribution—the average income for the white minority is significantly higher than that for the mass of the black population.

The reason for this imbalance lies in the economic structure that was imposed by colonial history. The ranches were established as settlers displaced Africans on two-thirds of the viable farmland. From the African 'reserves' came a stream of migrant workers; these were mainly unmarried men who were forced to leave their families behind, and on whose low wages the development of the early mines and ranches depended. In the diamond and uranium mines, where profits have been high and the wage bill a small proportion of costs, the situation has changed, and these enterprises now pay the highest wages in the country. Elsewhere, particularly on the ranches, wages remain extremely low.

During the early 1980s Namibia experienced a deep economic recession, intensified by war, severe drought and low world prices for the country's mineral products and for karakul pelts. In real terms, output per head declined by more than 20% over the period 1977–84, representing a fall of about one-third in real purchasing power. The impact of the recession was partly masked by a rapid expansion in state expenditure in the early 1980s, as South Africa tried to buy support for the DTA and an internal settlement. There were some benefits from this spending. For example, a high-quality road network was built in the north, albeit for military purposes. From the mid-1980s, however, there was a modest economic recovery. GDP increased by 3% in 1986, compared with a decline of 0.8% in 1985, and there were further increases of 2.9% in 1987 and 1.9% in 1988. GDP declined by 0.6% in 1989. This sluggish rate of growth was due to a number of factors, including depressed international prices for Namibia's mineral exports, a corresponding decline in mining production, and the poor performance of the South African economy (in the period prior to and since independence the Namibian and South African economies have remained closely linked). GDP increased by a respectable 5.1% in 1991, and 3.5% in 1992, owing primarily to higher diamond output and increases in the output of the fishing and construction sectors. The growth rate for 1993 was only 1–2%, but was forecast to grow by about 4% in 1994. During 1985–92 Namibia's population grew at an estimated average annual rate of 3.1%. During this period it was estimated that GNP per caput increased, in real terms, at an annual average rate of 1.1%.

During the 1980s South Africa was an important source of public finance for Namibia, its annual contribution rising from R40m. (12% of total revenue) in 1981 to R469.2m. (30% of total revenue) in 1987. South Africa contributed R308m. in 1988 and 1989, and made its final contribution, of R83m., in 1990. The South African government ceased acting as guarantor of Namibian loans in 1990. Following independence Namibia began to receive financial assistance from the international donor community. Official development assistance declined from R125m. in 1991 to R90m. in 1992. However, total aid disbursements increased by nearly 50% (from N$ 282m. to N$ 421m.) from 1990 to 1992. Official development assistance accounts for about 75% of aid. In July 1990 international donors pledged assistance of US $696m. for the period 1990–93; Germany was the largest bilateral donor, agreeing to provide $186m. The USA and Scandinavian countries are the other major bilateral donors. Namibia is not permitted to borrow on concessionary terms from the IDA, owing to its high per capita income (the fact that this is unevenly distributed throughout the population, see above, has been emphasized strongly by President Nujoma).

Namibia's budget account was characterized by a succession of deficits during the 1980s. Following independence, the government aimed to increase expenditure on health and education. The first post-independence budget, for the financial year 1990/91, produced a surplus of R200m. The 1991/92 budget represented a 21% increase in spending over the previous year, with capital expenditure doubling. The budget deficit for 1992/93 was estimated at R567m. During 1992–93 Namibia was expected to benefit from significantly increased customs duties, collected under the Southern African Customs Union (SACU) agreement; however, receipts from the SACU agreement totalled only R735m. in 1992, considerably less than the R889m. predicted by the government. Revenues for 1993/94 were N$ 782m., N$71m. less than budgeted, although this should increase to N$920m. in 1994/95 as revenue from SACU is paid two years in arrears. This, combined with foreign budgetary aid, should decrease the deficit by N$22m. The budget deficit for 1993/94 was originally estimated at N$ 357m. A perennial budgetary problem is the proportion of government expenditure accounted for by the public sector payroll (42% in 1990/91). Spending in 1994 is expected to be N$ 349m., an increase of N$129m. over the original budget projections.

The newly independent Namibia inherited a modest foreign debt, about R826.6m. in 1990, and is to be repaid in 17 annual instalments from April 1995. Namibia's total outstanding foreign debt in 1994 is under US$ 400m., representing less than 15% of GDP. Nearly all of Namibia's debt is owed to South Africa or financial institutions in the region. The annual rate of inflation averaged 12.9% in 1988, 15.1% in 1989 and 12.0% in 1990. The rate declined in 1992, from 20.5% in the year to June to 10.8% at the end of the year, and fell further to 8.7% in the year to March 1993 and to 7.0% by October 1993. Declines in food prices have played a major role in the generally lower overall price level. Some 30–40% of the labour force were unemployed in early 1993. In 1992, in an effort to reduce central government spending, the government ceased all appointments to vacancies in the civil service, estimated at 11,000.

MINERALS AND MINING

Namibia is mineral-rich. It is the world's leading producer of gem-quality diamonds, accounting for some 30% of total world output. (Some 98% of diamonds mined in Namibia are of gem quality.) In addition, Namibia has the world's largest uranium mine, and some of the world's largest known reserves of tin and lithium. Namibia is Africa's second largest producer of lead, its third largest producer of cadmium and fourth largest source of zinc and copper. Other important minerals include hydrocarbons, tungsten, vanadium, silver, gold, columbite/tantalite, germanium and beryl.

In 1980 mining accounted for about one-half of Namibia's GDP, but had declined to about 25% in 1993. The GDP of the mining sector increased by an estimated average of 3.1% per year in 1982–91. The total value of mineral exports peaked at R1,645m. in 1986 and totalled R1,543m. in 1988, accounting for 73% of total export earnings. The real value of mining production declined by 9.8% in 1991. Overall mineral output increased significantly, however, in 1992, with growth in the output of diamonds (29.7%), copper (11.9%), gold (8.2%) and zinc (5.6%). Employment in the sector declined from 21,000 in 1977 to 12,265 in 1992, and to 11,441 in 1993.

The most important diamond mine, historically, has been the large one centred on Oranjemund. This is operated by Consolidated Diamond Mines (CDM), owned by De Beers, which is part of the Anglo American group in South Africa. Although Namibia currently provides only about 4% of the total diamond production from De Beers mines, CDM is important to De Beers, firstly because (most unusually) about 98% of its diamonds are of gem quality, and secondly because it has been used as one of the principal regulators in controlling the flow of diamonds to the world market, and hence in maintaining both De Beers' near-monopoly of the market, and high market prices. In 1980 diamonds contributed 46% of the value of Namibia's mineral sales, and, even more significantly, 40% of state revenue. In 1983, however, diamonds accounted for less than 30% of mineral sales, and only 9% of state revenue. There were two reasons for this decline: the collapse in reported profits because of low sales, and the first tax payments from a new source, Rössing Uranium. With the fall in the value of the rand and the beginnings of a price recovery, the profit from the mine rose to R101m. (after tax) in 1985, compared with R33m. in 1984 and R162m. in 1978. By 1986 the world diamond market was much healthier: profits rose to R123m. and two field-screening plants were reopened. In 1988 CDM re-opened a conglomerate and crushing plant closed as a result of the depression in the diamond market. A new production area on the Orange River, which forms the border between Namibia and South Africa, came into operation in early 1991. A profit of R115m. was recorded in that year. During 1989 CDM transferred the sorting and valuation of diamonds from South Africa to Windhoek. CDM is exploring for offshore diamonds to augment operations at Oranjemund, which are not expected to remain economic after the year 2000. In 1992 CDM's production increased to 1,549,260 carats, from 1,186,742 carats in 1991. This increase was due to output from the new Elizabeth Bay mines, and from an increase in the production of sea-bed mining (from 166,144 carats in 1991 to 260,298 carats in 1992). Employment in the diamond-mining industry continued to decrease, from 6,731 in 1990 to 5,708 in 1992. In 1993 CDM temporarily ceased onshore production due to labour strife, but resolved the issue with a compromise 10% across-the-board pay increase. This closure cost CDM an estimated N$ 3m. per day in lost revenue. CDM then announced a further 1,650 redundancies following a 25% reduction in the value of its sales to the Central Selling Organization. In early 1993 President Nujoma announced that the government would be negotiating for a 50% share in CDM. Nonetheless, the share of diamonds in export earnings has increased from 30% of the total in 1990 to 35% in 1993.

The huge, although low-grade, Rössing uranium mine, which is the world's largest single producer of uranium, came into production in 1976. After an initial period of profitability for its owner, the Rio Tinto-Zinc group, the mine suffered from the depression in the uranium market. The Rössing mine's uranium is sold by means of long-term contracts to EC countries, Japan and Taiwan, but the persistently weak 'spot' price of uranium has forced renegotiations of the contract prices. In 1986 it was reported that uranium from Rössing was contributing about 16% of Namibia's GDP at current prices. As a result of the continuing decline in world uranium prices, Rössing reduced its output to 2,500 tons in 1991. Production continued to decline, owing to a reduction in world-wide demand, with output of 1,973 tons in 1992, the lowest output since the mine began operations. Output of a similar level was expected in 1993, where Rössing could just maintain a profit. However, a long-term contract with France of 5,200 tons per annum was due to commence in 1995.

Tsumeb Corporation Ltd (TCL), a subsidiary of Gold Fields of South Africa, operates four base-metal mines and a major copper smelter and lead refinery. TCL announced in 1991 that, because of its rapidly diminishing reserves, it would close its major operations in 1994. The next most significant mining operation is Imcor Zinc (Pty) Ltd, a subsidiary of South Africa's state-controlled Iron and Steel Corporation (ISCOR), which owns the Uis tin mine and the Rosh Pinah lead/zinc mine. It is one of the very few companies to have undertaken significant prospecting for base metals in recent years, and has expanded Uis's capacity by 30% and Rosh Pinah's by 25%. The mine was put into provisional bankruptcy in late 1993, but resumed operations in early 1994.

The government aims to diversify the mining sector. A variety of other minerals are already mined on a small scale. The most significant of these is salt, of which 124,000 metric tons were produced in 1987. Namibia is the primary source of industrial salt for the whole of southern Africa. TCL is investigating small gold prospects, and the Navacheb gold mine in central Namibia, a joint Anglo American and CDM venture, began production in 1990, with total revenue reaching R60m. in 1992. Namibia has considerable offshore reserves of natural gas, in an area near Lüderitz known as the Kudo field. Exploration for onshore and offshore reserves of petroleum was due to commence in 1992.

In early 1993 the EC approved a grant of ECU 40m., under its Sysmin facility, to help to finance a number of mining projects in Namibia. Most of these funds will be lent at concessionary rates to private firms. About 10% of the funds will go toward a high-resolution aeromagnetic survey of 130,000 sq km of north-central Namibia. The N$ 28m. contract has thus far selected six international geophysics firms to compete. Other projects include financing the Namibian Institute of Mining Technology, a drilling project at the Navachab gold mine and other smaller feasibility studies.

A recent World Bank study suggests a proven 14-year reserve at the Kudu fields (see below) which would allow a daily production of 28m. cu m of natural gas. Exploration rights for the offshore Kudu gas fields were awarded to a consortium of Shell and Engen in mid-1993. This was the fifth permit to be allocated under Namibia's current oil leasing negotiations.

AGRICULTURE AND FISHING

War, drought, overgrazing and unscientific farming methods have had an adverse effect on the agricultural sector. The contribution of agriculture and fisheries to GDP, however, increased from 7.3% in 1986 to 10.8% in 1991. Agricultural production increased by an average of 1.9% in 1982–92, although agricultural GDP declined by an average of 5.0% per year in 1982–91. In 1991 the sector employed an estimated 34.1% of Namibia's labour force.

Namibia has a fragile ecology, and most of the land can support only livestock. The major agricultural activities are the processing of meat and other livestock products, and more than 90% of commercial agricultural output comprises livestock production. The most important agricultural product is beef. The only large-scale commercial arable farming is in the *karstveld* around Tsumeb, and on the Hardap irrigation scheme in the south. In the southern half of Namibia, farming is based on karakul sheep, but international fashion markets for karakul pelts slumped in the 1980s: in 1990 the value of exports of karakul pelts was equivalent to only one-half of their value in 1980. Subsistence crops include beans, potatoes and maize. Although output of maize was high in 1991, the severe drought conditions of 1991/92 devastated output. In May 1992 President Nujoma appealed to the international donor community for drought relief aid. The total maize crop for 1992/93 was 20,000 tons, a considerable increase on the previous year (when the yield reached only 7,700 tons), but still below normal levels of about 35,000 tons. In general the October 1993 rains should have been sufficient to provide increases in agricultural production during 1993/94.

Colonial history bequeathed Namibia three different agricultural sectors: about 4,000 large commercial ranches, almost all white-owned; 20,000 African stock-raising households, compressed into central and southern reserves; and 120,000 black families practising mixed farming on just 5% of the viable farmland in the far north. At the time of Namibia's independence about 50% of the country's commercial farms were owned by absentee landlords, and the possible re-distribution of such land was an important political issue. In mid-1991 a national land reform conference rejected calls for radical land expropriations and the abolition of freehold ownership. Nevertheless, the conference did make recommendations for reform, including bans on foreign ownership of agricultural land and on purchases of large tracts of land. In 1992 the government proposed the redistribution of 7.3m. ha of farmland owned by absentee landowners or otherwise underutilized, representing almost one-quarter of the 32m. ha owned by commercial (mostly white) farmers at independence. The Namibian government, through the Agricultural Bank of Namibia, has began to grant low-interest loans to farmers in 1994.

In 1990, following independence, Namibia signed the Lomé convention, agreeing to supply an EC quota of 10,500 tons of beef in 1991 and 1992, rising to 13,000 tons in 1993. Some 84% of commercial beef production had previously been exported to South Africa. Slaughtering and processing facilities were due to be expanded during the 1990s. Cattle numbers, however, were expected to be sharply reduced by the effects of the 1991/92 drought.

Because of the cold Benguela current, Namibia has potentially one of the richest fisheries in the world. Prior to independence, however, Namibia received no tax or licence fees from fishing because the illegal occupation of the territory deprived it of an internationally recognized fishing zone within the usual limit of 200 nautical miles (370 km). There are, in fact, two separate fisheries off Namibia—inshore and offshore. The inshore fishery, for pilchard, anchovy and rock lobster, is controlled by South African companies, based at Lüderitz and Walvis Bay. During the mid-1980s, however, persistent over-fishing, which left stocks severely depleted, resulted in the closure of five of the nine factories and the loss of jobs of four-fifths of the factories' work-force. In 1986 the Namibian fleet landed only 17% of all fish caught within the exclusive zone. The total market value of fish caught by foreign fleets in this area in 1988 was estimated to be at least R1,500m. In March 1990 the new Namibian government requested foreign fleets to cease fishing Namibia's coastal waters, pending an assessment of fish stocks. Following independence the Namibian authorities enforced an exclusive 370-km offshore zone, thereby achieving considerable success in restocking its waters. Foreign fishing fleets were reportedly trespassing regularly in Namibian coastal waters by the end of 1990. In 1992 25 deep-sea trawlers were licensed to fish within Namibian coastal waters. Government revenue from sales of fishing concessions was projected at R91m. in 1993, while revenue from exports of fish and fish products generates some 11% of total export earnings. Fish stocks along Namibia's coast have more than doubled since independence. The total allowable catch (tac) for hake was increased from 115,000 tons in 1993 to 146,000 tons in 1994, while the tac for pilchards has risen by some 4% to 12,500 tons during the same period.

The fishing industry is an important source of employment, and there is considerable scope for job creation in the sector, particularly in fish-processing. Indeed, since independence the number of workers in this industry has increased from 6,000 to 9,000, and the fishing industry could soon replace mining as the largest source of private-sector employment. A fish-processing plant is under construction at Lüderitz. The factory, which will cost R18m. to construct, will provide 250 new jobs. A N$ 150m. investment in rehabilitating the fishing fleet and building a fish-processing plant has been planned for Walvis Bay.

OTHER SECTORS

Namibia's manufacturing sector is extremely small. It provided an estimated 4.1% of GDP in 1991, and consists mainly of processing minerals and meat and fish for export, and production of basic consumer products, such as beer and bread: food products account for about 70% of all goods produced in Namibia. In 1991 manufacturing output increased by 5%; during 1982–91 manufacturing GDP increased by an estimated annual average of 2.0%. There is very little integration with Namibia's mining industry: in 1981 only 0.5% of Rössing's inputs were manufactured in the territory. The development of the sector has been limited by fluctuations in the supply of cattle and fish, by the small domestic market, by the high cost of energy and transport, and by the lack of an educated entrepreneurial class. Namibia has traditionally been dependent on South Africa for most manufactured goods; this has resulted in the underdevelopment of the sector. There are more than 300 manufacturing firms, which are located in or near the main urban centres. A cement plant, with a capacity of 200,000 tons, came into operation in 1991. Construction, which provided 5% of GDP in 1983, increased in importance with the expansion in state spending, but suffered very heavily from the recession: one estimate indicates that one-half of the workers in the sector lost their jobs during 1984. Construction contributed only 1.8% of GDP in 1991.

By contrast, the electricity and water sectors (which represented 2.0% of GDP in 1991) are somewhat more integrated and extensive than might be expected. The principal mines and towns are linked in a national grid, which can be fed by the 120-MW Van Eck power station outside Windhoek, the hydroelectric station at Ruacana (which has a generating capacity of up to 320 MW) on the Kunene river, and the 45-MW Paratus scheme at Walvis Bay. There is a link to the system that is operated by South Africa's Electricity Supply Commission (ESCOM), and the Zambia Electricity Supply Corporation provides electricity to the Caprivi region. The CDM diamond mine, however, draws its supply directly from ESCOM, and is not connected to the Namibian grid. In 1991 Namibia and Angola signed an agreement on the further development of the Kunene river as a source of energy. Construction of a new hydroelectric plant at Epupa was scheduled to commence in 1993: upon completion this would ensure Namibia's self-sufficiency in energy, and also permit substantial exports of power. However, renewed fighting in Angola has delayed studies and agreements on the joint venture. Electricity sales to domestic consumers decreased by 0.5% in 1993, despite an increase of 17% of the number of customers. In that year, municipalities consumed more electricity than the mines for the first time. Drought led to a 49m. K.W. reduction in hydroelectric power exports, to 204m. K.W. in 1993.

Mines and towns in Namibia's white-inhabited areas are also the main places which are served by the long-distance water supply. Windhoek and its surrounding mines are supplied from a number of dams, which came under severe pressure in the recent drought. Rössing, Walvis Bay and Swakopmund draw their water from boreholes in a series of dry river-beds. Both the Tsumeb and coastal underground reserves are under strain, and the long-term plan is to connect the two systems together, and to draw water from the Okavango river in the extreme north of the country. In November 1987 the former interim government and South Africa signed an agreement on the use of water from the Orange river, which forms the border between Namibia and South Africa.

Tourism is playing an increasingly important role in the economy. According to a government study, 282,000 tourists visited Namibia in 1991, contributing R32m. to the economy. The study estimates that the level may rise to 635,000 per year by 1997. Although gambling is illegal in Namibia, a policy document issued by the Ministry of Wildlife, Conservation and Tourism in 1994 called for the opening of casinos in order to increase tourism. The ministry has also recommended the development of 'eco-tourism' in Namibia.

FOREIGN TRADE

Namibia's principal trade partners have included South Africa, Switzerland, Germany, Japan and the USA. In 1992 Namibia sold 36% of its exports to Switzerland (mostly diamonds), 30% to South Africa, 3% to Germany and 2% to Japan. During the same year it imported 90% of its goods and services from South Africa, 3% from Germany and about 2% each from the UK, Japan and Switzerland. Namibia's principal exports in 1989 were minerals (76% of the value of total exports). An increase in the sale of diamonds contributed to an improvement in the trade balance in 1992. Minerals contributed more than one-third of the total value of exports, which increased from US $1,180m. in 1991 to $1,280m. in 1992. In the same period imports increased from $1,230m. to $1,250m. while manufacturing exports declined by 1%, Namibia's external position did not decline significantly in 1993 due to increases in diamond and fish exports. In that year imports rose to US$ 1,200m., producing a current account surplus of US$ 129m., an increase of nearly US$ 100m. over the previous year.

ECONOMIC PROSPECTS

Namibia will continue to be economically dominated by neighbouring South Africa for the near future. Namibia is part of the Common Monetary Area (CMA), with Lesotho, South Africa and Swaziland, and a member (with Botswana, Lesotho, South Africa and Swaziland) of SACU. At independence, Namibia used the South African rand as its currency, as it still does. However, in 1993 Namibia created its own central bank and issued its own currency, the Namibian dollar, at par with the rand. In 1990 the exchange rate was US$ 1=3.472 rand/N$. Namibia has no plans of withdrawing from the CNA in the near term. South Africa is the source of 75% of Namibia's imports; in addition, South Africa has significant control over Namibia's transport infrastructure, as Namibia's only external rail links are with South Africa. In February 1993 Namibia and South Africa agreed to establish joint customs control over Walvis Bay—which handles about 90% of Namibia's seaborne trade—and the enclave was returned to Namibia in 1994. In early 1994 the Namibian cabinet approved a proposal to establish a free trade zone in Walvis Bay and a new US$ 3.6m. harbour at Mowe Bay, north of Swakopmund.

At independence Namibia became a member of the Southern African Development Co-ordination Conference (SADCC), which in 1992 was reorganized as the Southern African Development Community (SADC) with the aim of minimizing the region's economic dependence on South Africa.

The SWAPO government has professed commitment to a mixed economy. Its first Five-Year Development Plan (NPD1), for 1995–2000, calls for increased diversification and growth. In September 1990 Namibia joined the IMF. In December of that year liberal legislation on foreign investment was introduced, and in early 1991 some 140 potential foreign investors attended a conference in Windhoek. The government is considering a programme of investment incentives, including the establishment of an export processing zone (as discussed above), which would be the first in mainland Africa, and could generate significant employment and foreign exchange opportunities.

Namibia's abundant mineral reserves and rich fisheries are expected to form the basis of the nation's future economic prosperity. It will be necessary to expand the severely underdeveloped manufacturing sector; at independence most of the country's essential requirements were imported. The development of the impoverished northern region of the country remains a priority. In April 1993 President Nujoma announced a programme of incentives for private-sector investment in manufacturing. The incentives include tax relief, cash grants and low-interest loans for export promotion. Namibia's economic growth rate advanced at an average rate of 1.8% annually between 1990–93, but this has been accomplished primarily by the extractive industries and has not yet filtered through to the wider economy in terms of increased employment, more equitable income distribution or higher per caput incomes. Nonetheless, Namibia appears to have made the transformation from colonial rule to independence with relatively little social or economic upheaval, and, indeed, with public economic policies and a physical infrastructure which should lead to long-term development and growth.

Statistical Survey

Source (unless otherwise stated): Strategy Network International Ltd, The Namibia Office, Clutha House, 10 Storey's Gate, London, SW1P 3AY, England (no longer in operation).

Area and Population

AREA, POPULATION AND DENSITY*

Area (sq km)	824,292†
Population (census results)	
6 May 1970	732,260
May 1981	1,033,196
21 October 1991 (provisional)	
Males	680,927
Females	720,784
Total	1,401,711
Density (per sq km) at October 1991	1.7

* Including data for Walvis Bay, sovereignty over which was transferred from South Africa to Namibia with effect from March 1994. Walvis Bay has an area of 1,124 sq km (434 sq miles) and had a population of 20,800 in 1981.

† 318,261 sq miles.

ETHNIC GROUPS (population, 1988 estimate)

Ovambo	623,000	Caprivian	47,000
Kavango	117,000	Bushmen	36,000
Damara	94,000	Baster	31,000
Herero	94,000	Tswana	7,000
White	80,000	Others	12,000
Nama	60,000	**Total**	1,252,000
Coloured	51,000		

PRINCIPAL TOWN

Windhoek (capital), estimated population 114,500 in December 1988.

BIRTHS AND DEATHS (UN estimates, annual averages)

	1975–80	1980–85	1985–90
Birth rate (per 1,000)	43.9	43.0	42.7
Death rate (per 1,000)	15.2	13.6	12.1

Expectation of life (UN estimates, years at birth, 1985–90): 56.2 (males 55.0; females 57.5).

Source: UN, *World Population Prospects: The 1992 Revision*.

ECONOMICALLY ACTIVE POPULATION
(estimates, '000 persons at 1991)

	Males	Females	Total
Agriculture, etc.	133	55	188
Industry	93	3	96
Services	194	74	268
Total	420	132	552

Source: UN Economic Commission for Africa, *African Statistical Yearbook*.

Agriculture

PRINCIPAL CROPS ('000 metric tons)

	1990*	1991	1992
Maize	65	50	13
Millet	58	50	12
Roots and tubers*	270	275	220
Vegetables*	32	33	30
Fruit*	36	36	35

* FAO estimates.

Source: FAO, *Production Yearbook*.

LIVESTOCK ('000 head, year ending September)

	1990	1991	1992
Horses	52	53*	54*
Mules*	6	6	6
Asses*	68	68	68
Cattle	2,087†	2,131	2,100
Pigs*	50	51	52
Sheep	3,328	3,300*	3,000*
Goats	1,860	1,900*	1,972*

* FAO estimate(s). † Unofficial figure.

Source: FAO, *Production Yearbook*.

LIVESTOCK PRODUCTS ('000 metric tons)

	1990	1991	1992
Beef and veal	63	66	68
Mutton and lamb*	11	12	11
Goats' meat*	4	6	6
Pig meat*	4	4	4
Other meat*	4	4	4
Cows' milk*	70	71	70
Wool:			
greasy*	2.2	2.2	2.2
scoured*	1.2	1.2	1.2

* FAO estimates.

Source: FAO, *Production Yearbook*.

Fishing*

('000 metric tons, live weight)

	1989	1990	1991
Freshwater fishes	0.2	0.0	0.0
Cape hakes	13.9	28.0	29.5
Cape monk	0.7	n.a.	4.1
Cape horse mackerel	1.2	85.1	83.2
Southern African pilchard	n.a.	89.4	68.9
Southern African anchovy	n.a.	50.5	17.1
Other marine fishes (incl. unspecified)	3.4	2.1	1.4
Total fish	19.3	255.1	204.1
Crustaceans and molluscs	0.9	0.5	0.4
Total catch	20.3	255.6	204.5

* Figures for 1989 exclude the catches of South African flag vessels landed at Lüderitz and Walvis Bay. Data for 1990 and 1991 (following independence) include quantities caught by licensed foreign vessels in Namibian waters and processed in Lüderitz and Walvis Bay.

Source: FAO, *Yearbook of Fishery Statistics*.

Mining

('000 metric tons, unless otherwise indicated)

	1989	1990	1991
Copper ore[1,2]	30.8	32.5	30.0
Lead concentrates[1,2]	23.9	20.7	11.8
Zinc ore[1,2]	39.3	37.7	33.1
Tin ore (metric tons)[1,3]	1,120	942	100
Silver ore (metric tons)[1,4]	108	92	91
Uranium ore (metric tons)[1]	3,077	3,211	2,450
Gold ore (kilograms)[1,4,5]	336	1,605	1,850
Salt (unrefined)[4,6]	134	149	133
Diamonds ('000 carats):			
Industrial[4]	17	16	24
Gem[4]	910	735	n.a.

1991 (metric tons, metal content): Copper 34,680.

[1] Figures refer to the metal content of ores and concentrates.
[2] Data from *World Metal Statistics* (London).
[3] Data from *International Tin Statistics* (UNCTAD, Geneva).
[4] Data from the US Bureau of Mines.
[5] Smelter production only.
[6] Output of sea salt.

Sources: mainly UN, *Industrial Statistics Yearbook* and *Monthly Bulletin of Statistics*.

Industry

SELECTED PRODUCTS ('000 metric tons)

	1988	1989	1990
Unrefined copper (unwrought)	40.0	38.0	37.0
Refined lead (unwrought)*	44.4	44.2	44.0

* Production of primary metal only.

Note: Data from the US Bureau of Mines.

Source: UN, *Industrial Statistics Yearbook*.

Finance

CURRENCY AND EXCHANGE RATES

Monetary Units

100 cents = 1 Namibian dollar (N $).

Sterling and US Dollar Equivalents (31 March 1994)
£1 sterling = N $5.167;
US $1 = N $3.481;
N $100 = £19.35 = US $28.73.

Average Exchange Rate (N $ per US $)

1991	2.7613
1992	2.8520
1993	3.2677

Note: The Namibian dollar was introduced in September 1993, replacing (at par) the South African rand. The rand remained legal tender in Namibia. Some of the figures in this Survey are still in terms of rand.

CENTRAL GOVERNMENT BUDGET
(million rand, year ending 31 March)

Revenue*	1989/90	1990/91†	1991/92‡
Taxation	1,768.7	1,538.0	1,985.1
Taxes on income, profits and capital gains	796.4	740.7	536.4
Individual taxes	336.8	408.5	335.0
Corporate taxes	459.6	332.2	201.4
Diamond-mining	131.6	62.3	—
Other mining	157.3	100.8	51.0
Non-mining companies	170.4	167.6	150.0
Domestic taxes on goods and services	454.7	494.7	576.3
General sales tax	310.4	359.3	390.0
Excises	127.8	120.0	140.0
Taxes on international trade and transactions	498.2	283.8	860.4
Import duties	447.8	223.5	810.0
Export duties	50.4	60.3	50.4
Other current revenue	239.7	196.8	310.1
Entrepreneurial and property income	117.3	89.9	186.0
Administrative fees and charges, non-industrial and incidental sales	83.3	100.4	118.5
Capital revenue	3.4	0.1	3.7
Total	2,011.8	1,734.9	2,298.9

Expenditure§	1990/91†	1991/92‡
General public services	323.3	460.0
Defence	113.0	184.0
Public order and safety	159.1	210.9
Education	423.5	628.2
Health	225.9	275.2
Social security and welfare	131.5	192.9
Housing and community amenities	175.3	225.4
Recreational, cultural and religious affairs and services	68.5	83.5
Economic affairs and services	294.1	491.0
Agriculture, forestry, fishing and hunting	95.1	189.5
Transport and communications	154.6	232.4
Other purposes	126.5	79.2
Total	2,040.8	2,830.3
Current	1,784.5	2,327.4
Capital	256.3	502.9

* Excluding grants received (million rand): 280.9 in 1989/90; 100.0 in 1990/91; 105.0 in 1991/92.

† Provisional figures.

‡ Estimates.

§ Excluding lending minus repayments (million rand): 3.2 in 1990/91; 17.7 in 1991/92.

Source: IMF, *Government Finance Statistics Yearbook*.

INTERNATIONAL RESERVES (US $ million at 31 December)*

	1992	1993
IMF special drawing rights	0.01	0.02
Reserve position in IMF	0.01	0.01
Foreign exchange	49.69	133.67
Total	49.72	133.70

* Excluding gold, of which there were no official reserves in 1992.

Source: IMF, *International Financial Statistics*.

MONEY SUPPLY (N $ million at 31 December)

	1991	1992	1993
Demand deposits at commercial banks	809.5	1,002.4	1,333.1

Source: IMF, *International Financial Statistics*.

COST OF LIVING
(Consumer Price Index for Windhoek; base: 1985 = 100)

	1990	1991	1992
All items	185.8	208.0	244.8

Source: IMF, *International Financial Statistics*.

NATIONAL ACCOUNTS (million rand at current prices)

National Income and Product (provisional)

	1985	1986	1987
Compensation of employees	1,309.2	1,449.6	1,740.9
Operating surplus	1,085.1	1,345.0	1,237.0
Domestic factor incomes	2,394.3	2,794.6	2,977.9
Consumption of fixed capital	135.8	142.9	152.7
Gross domestic product (GDP) at factor cost	2,530.1	2,937.5	3,130.6
Indirect taxes	279.3	343.8	365.2
Less Subsidies	52.6	112.6	75.4
GDP in purchasers' values	2,756.8	3,168.7	3,420.4
Net factor income from abroad	−299.5	−328.7	−186.4
Gross national product	2,457.3	2,840.0	3,234.0
Less Consumption of fixed capital	135.8	142.9	152.7
National income in market prices	2,321.5	2,697.1	3,081.3

Expenditure on the Gross Domestic Product (estimates)

	1989	1990	1991
Government final consumption expenditure	1,179	1,575	1,890
Private final consumption expenditure	2,570	3,106	3,728
Increase in stocks / Gross fixed capital formation	797	917	1,100
Total domestic expenditure	4,546	5,598	6,718
Exports of goods and services	2,483	3,029	3,635
Less Imports of goods and services	2,423	3,100	3,720
GDP in purchasers' values	4,606	5,527	6,633
GDP at constant 1980 prices	1,500	1,590	1,590

Source: UN Economic Commission for Africa, *African Statistical Yearbook*.

Gross Domestic Product by Economic Activity (estimates)

	1989	1990	1991
Agriculture, hunting, forestry and fishing	486	583	700
Mining and quarrying	1,426	1,712	2,052
Manufacturing	184	221	265
Electricity, gas and water	45	54	65
Construction	82	98	118
Trade, restaurants and hotels	517	620	744
Transport and communications	310	372	447
Finance, insurance, real estate and business services	319	383	460
Government services	918	1,102	1,323
Other services	211	253	304
GDP at factor cost	4,498	5,398	6,478
Indirect taxes, *less* subsidies	108	129	155
GDP in purchasers' values	4,606	5,527	6,633

Source: UN Economic Commission for Africa, *African Statistical Yearbook.*

BALANCE OF PAYMENTS (US $ million)

	1990	1991	1992
Merchandise exports f.o.b.	1,101	1,252	1,288
Merchandise imports f.o.b.	−1,117	−1,108	−1,177
Trade balance	−16	144	110
Exports of services	107	117	131
Imports of services	−385	−457	−468
Other income received	201	261	215
Other income paid	−162	−148	−150
Private unrequited transfers (net)	25	24	24
Official unrequited transfers (net)	192	311	280
Current balance	−38	251	142
Direct investment (net)	36	100	53
Portfolio investment (net)	11	−26	4
Other capital (net)	−244	−285	−173
Net errors and omissions	275	−54	−33
Overall balance	39	−14	−7

Source: IMF, *International Financial Statistics.*

External Trade

Merchandise imports f.o.b. (N $ million): 2,890 in 1990; 3,059 in 1991; 3,358 in 1992.

Merchandise exports f.o.b. (N $ million): 2,849 in 1990; 3,457 in 1991; 3,673 in 1992.

Source: IMF, *International Financial Statistics.*

Transport

ROAD TRAFFIC

1991: Registered vehicles 122,331.

Source: Ministry of Works, Transport and Communications, Windhoek.

SHIPPING

(sea-borne freight traffic at Walvis Bay, '000 metric tons)

1985: Goods loaded 483; Goods unloaded 260.

CIVIL AVIATION (traffic on scheduled services)

	1991
Kilometres flown (million)	5
Passengers carried ('000)	455
Passenger-km (million)	423
Freight ton-km (million)	2

Source: UN, *Statistical Yearbook.*

Communications Media

	1989	1990	1991
Radio receivers ('000 in use)	n.a.	n.a.	188
Television receivers ('000 in use)	27	30	31
Daily newspapers			
Number	n.a.	6	n.a.
Average circulation ('000 copies)	n.a.	220	n.a.
Non-daily newspapers			
Number	n.a.	18	n.a.
Average circulation ('000 copies)	n.a.	71	n.a.
Book production (titles published)	n.a.	106	193

Source: UNESCO, *Statistical Yearbook.*

Education

(1990)

	Students		
	Males	Females	Total
Pre-primary	2,658	2,991	5,649
Primary	150,398	163,130	313,528
Secondary:			
General	27,202	34,599	61,801
Vocational	836	339	1,175

Tertiary (students, 1991): University level 1,496 (males 518; females 978). Distance-learning 574 (males 253; females 321). Other higher 2,087 (males 722; females 1,365).

Source: UNESCO, *Statistical Yearbook.*

Directory

The Constitution

The Constitution of the Republic of Namibia took effect at independence on 21 March 1990. Its principal provisions are summarized below:

THE REPUBLIC

The Republic of Namibia is a sovereign, secular, democratic and unitary State and the Constitution is the supreme law.

FUNDAMENTAL HUMAN RIGHTS AND FREEDOMS

The fundamental rights and freedoms of the individual are guaranteed regardless of sex, race, colour, ethnic origin, religion, creed or social or economic status. All citizens shall have the right to form and join political parties. The practice of racial discrimination shall be prohibited.

THE PRESIDENT

Executive power shall be vested in the President and the Cabinet. The President shall be the Head of State and of the Government and the Commander-in-Chief of the Defence Force. The President shall be directly elected by universal and equal adult suffrage, and must receive more than 50% of the votes cast. The term of office shall be five years; one person may not hold the office of President for more than two terms.

THE CABINET

The Cabinet shall consist of the President, the Prime Minister and such other ministers as the President may appoint from members of the National Assembly. The President may also appoint a Deputy Prime Minister. The functions of the members of the Cabinet shall include directing the activities of ministries and government departments, initiating bills for submission to the National Assembly, formulating, explaining and assessing for the National Assembly the budget of the State and its economic development plans, formulating, explaining and analysing for the National Assembly Namibia's foreign policy and foreign trade policy and advising the President on the state of national defence.

THE NATIONAL ASSEMBLY

Legislative power shall be vested in the National Assembly, which shall be composed of 72 members elected by general, direct and secret ballots and not more than six non-voting members appointed by the President by virtue of their special expertise, status, skill or experience. Every National Assembly shall continue for a maximum period of five years, but it may be dissolved by the President before the expiry of its term.

THE NATIONAL COUNCIL

The National Council shall consist of two members from each region (elected by Regional Councils from among their members) and shall have a life of six years. The functions of the National Council shall include considering all bills passed by the National Assembly, investigating any subordinate legislation referred to it by the National Assembly for advice, and recommending legislation to the National Assembly on matters of regional concern.

OTHER PROVISIONS

Other provisions relate to the administration of justice (see under Judicial System), regional and local government, the public service commission, the security commission, the police, defence forces and prison service, finance, and the central bank and national planning commission. The repeal of, or amendments to, the Constitution require the approval of two-thirds of the members of the National Assembly and two-thirds of the members of the National Council; if the proposed repeal or amendment secures a majority of two-thirds of the members of the National Assembly, but not a majority of two-thirds of the members of the National Council, the President may make the proposals the subject of a national referendum, in which a two-thirds majority is needed for approval of the legislation.

The Government

HEAD OF STATE

President and Commander-in-Chief of the Defence Force: SAMUEL (SAM) DANIEL NUJOMA (took office 21 March 1990).

CABINET

(September 1994)

President: SAMUEL (SAM) DANIEL NUJOMA.

Prime Minister: HAGE GEINGOB.

Minister of Home Affairs: HIFIKEPUNYE POHAMBA.

Minister of Foreign Affairs: THEO-BEN GURIRAB.

Minister of Education and Culture: NAHAS ANGULA.

Minister of Information and Broadcasting: BEN AMATHILA.

Minister of Mines and Energy: ANDIMBA TOIVO JA TOIVO.

Minister of Justice: NGARIKUTUKE TJIRIANGE.

Minister of Trade and Industry: HIDIPO HAMUTENYA.

Minister of Agriculture, Water and Rural Development: NANGOLO MBUMBA.

Minister of Defence: PETER MUESHIHANGE.

Minister of Finance: GERHARD HANEKOM.

Minister of Health and Social Services: NICKY IYAMBO.

Minister of Labour, Public Services and Manpower Development: HENDRIK WITBOOI.

Minister of Local Government and Housing: LIBERTINE AMATHILA.

Minister of Wildlife, Conservation and Tourism: NICO BESSINGER.

Minister of Works, Transport and Communications: MARCO HAUSIKO.

Minister of Lands, Resettlement and Rehabilitation: RICHARD KAPELWA KABAJANI.

Minister of Fisheries and Marine Resources: HELMUT ANGULA.

Minister of Youth and Sports: PENDUKINI ITHANA.

MINISTRIES

Office of the President: State House, Private Bag 13339, Windhoek; tel. (61) 220010; telex 3222; fax (61) 221780.

Office of the Prime Minister: Private Bag 13338, Windhoek; tel. (61) 2879111; fax (61) 226189.

Ministry of Agriculture, Water and Rural Development: Private Bag 13184, Windhoek; tel. (61) 396911; telex 3109; fax (61) 229861.

Ministry of Defence: Private Bag 13307, Windhoek; tel. (61) 221920; fax (61) 224277.

Ministry of Education and Culture: Private Bag 13186, Windhoek; tel. (61) 221327; fax (61) 36236.

Ministry of Finance: Fiscus Bldg, John Meinert St, Private Bag 13295, Windhoek; tel. (61) 3099111; telex 3369; fax (61) 36454.

Ministry of Fisheries and Marine Resources: Private Bag 13355, Windhoek; tel. (61) 3969111; fax (61) 224566.

Ministry of Foreign Affairs: Govt Bldgs, East Wing, 4th Floor, Private Bag 13347, Windhoek; tel. (61) 2829111; telex 655; fax (61) 223937.

Ministry of Health and Social Services: Old State Hospital, Nightingale St, Private Bag 13198, Windhoek; tel. (61) 32170; telex 3366; fax (61) 33419.

Ministry of Home Affairs: Cohen Bldg, Kasino St, Windhoek; tel. (61) 221361; telex 403; fax (61) 223817.

Ministry of Information and Broadcasting: Govt Bldgs, 2nd Floor, Private Bag 13344, Windhoek; tel. (61) 222302; telex 2123; fax (61) 222343.

Ministry of Justice: Justitia Bldg, Independence Ave, Private Bag 13302, Windhoek; tel. (61) 239280; telex 635; fax (61) 221233.

Ministry of Labour, Public Services and Manpower Development: Mercedes St, POB 23115, Windhoek; tel. (61) 212956; telex 496; fax (61) 212323.

Ministry of Lands, Resettlement and Rehabilitation: Private Bag 13343, Windhoek; tel. (61) 220241; telex 826; fax (61) 228240.

Ministry of Local Government and Housing: Private Bag 13289, Windhoek; tel. (61) 225898; telex 603; fax (61) 226049.

Ministry of Mines and Energy: Trust Centre Bldg, Independence Ave, Windhoek; tel. (61) 226571; telex 487; fax (61) 38643.

Ministry of Trade and Industry: Govt Bldgs, Private Bag 13340, Windhoek; tel. (61) 2849111; telex 808; fax (61) 220227.

Ministry of Wildlife, Conservation and Tourism: Govt Bldgs, 5th Floor, Private Bag 13346, Windhoek; tel. (61) 2849111; fax (61) 229936.

Ministry of Works, Transport and Communications: Private Bag 13341, Windhoek; tel. (61) 2089111; telex 709; fax (61) 228560.

Ministry of Youth and Sports: Edcom Bldg, 6th Floor, Private Bag 13359, Windhoek; tel. (61) 220066; fax (61) 221304.

Legislature

NATIONAL ASSEMBLY

Speaker: Dr MOSES TJITENDERO.

Election, 7–11 November 1989*

Party	Votes	%	Seats†
South West Africa People's Organisation of Namibia	384,567	57.33	41
Democratic Turnhalle Alliance‡	191,532	28.55	21
United Democratic Front	37,874	5.65	4
Action Christian National	23,728	3.54	3
National Patriotic Front	10,693	1.59	1
Federal Convention/Namibia	10,452	1.56	1
Namibia National Front	5,344	0.80	1
SWAPO–Democrats§	3,161	0.47	—
Christian Democratic Action for Social Justice	2,495	0.37	—
Namibia National Democratic Party	984	0.15	—
Total	670,830	100.00	72

* Elected as a Constituent Assembly in November 1989; redesignated as National Assembly at independence in 21 March 1990.

† In addition to the 72 directly-elected members, six non-voting members were nominated by the President.

‡ Renamed DTA of Namibia in November 1991.

§ Disbanded in August 1990.

Political Organizations

Action Christian National: POB 294, Windhoek; tel. (61) 226159; white support; Leader (vacant).

Christian Democratic Action for Social Justice (CDA): Ondwangwa; telex 3143; f. 1982; supported by Ovambos and fmr supporters of National Democratic Party; Leader Rev. PETER KALANGULA.

DTA of Namibia: POB 173, Windhoek; telex 3217; f. 1977 as Democratic Turnhalle Alliance, a coalition of ethnically-based political groupings; reorg. as a single party and renamed in Nov. 1991; Chair. DIRK MUDGE; Sec.-Gen. LABAN HAMATA.

Federal Convention/Namibia: Windhoek; Leader JOHANNES DIERGAARDT; an alliance of ethnically-based parties, including:

NUDO—Progressive Party Jo'Horongo: f. 1987; Pres. MBURUMBA KERINA.

Rehoboth Bevryde Demokratiese Party (Rehoboth Free Democratic Party or Liberation Front) (RBDP): Leader JOHANNES DIERGAARDT; coalition of the **Rehoboth Bevrydingsparty** (Leader JOHANNES DIERGAARDT) and the **Rehoboth Democratic Party** (Leader K. G. FREIGANG).

Namibia National Democratic Party: Windhoek; Leader PAUL HELMUTH.

Namibia National Front: Windhoek; Leader VEKUII RUKORO.

National Patriotic Front: Windhoek; Leader MOSES KATJIUONGUA.

South West Africa People's Organisation of Namibia (SWAPO): Windhoek; f. 1957 as the Ovamboland People's Congress; renamed South West Africa People's Organisation in 1960; adopted present name in 1968; recognized by the UN, from Dec. 1973 until April 1989, as the 'sole and authentic representative of the Namibian people'; obtained majority of seats at Nov. 1989 election for the Constituent Assembly, and formed a Govt following independence in March 1990; Pres. SAMUEL (SAM) DANIEL NUJOMA; Sec.-Gen. MOSES GAROEB.

United Democratic Front: Windhoek; coalition of eight parties; Nat. Chair. REGGIE DIERGAARDT; Leader JUSTUS GAROEB.

Diplomatic Representation

EMBASSIES AND HIGH COMMISSIONS IN NAMIBIA

Algeria: 95 John Meinert St, Windhoek; tel. (61) 229896; Chargé d'affaires a.i.: A. I. BENGUEUEDDA.

Angola: Angola House, 3 Ausspann St, Private Bag 12020, Windhoek; tel. (61) 227535; telex 897; fax (61) 221498; Ambassador: Dr ALBERTO D. C. B. RIBEIRO.

Bangladesh: Windhoek; tel. (61) 32301; telex 650; High Commissioner: A. Y. B. I. SIDDIQI (acting).

Botswana: 101 Klein Windhoek Rd, POB 20359, Windhoek; tel. (61) 221942; telex 894; fax (61) 36034; High Commissioner: TUELENYANA ROSEMARY DITLHABI-OLIPHANT.

Brazil: 52 Bismarck St, POB 24166, Windhoek; tel. (61) 37368; telex 498; fax (61) 33389; Chargé d'affaires a.i.: JOSÉ AUGUSTO LINDGREN ALVES.

Canada: POB 2147, Windhoek; tel. (61) 222941; telex 402; fax (61) 224204; High Commissioner: WAYNE HAMMOND.

China, People's Republic: 39 Beethoven St, POB 22777, Windhoek; tel. (61) 222089; telex 675; fax (61) 225544; Ambassador: JI PEIDING.

Congo: 9 Corner St, POB 22970, Windhoek; tel. (61) 226958; telex 405; fax (61) 228642; Ambassador: A. KONDHO.

Cuba: 31 Omuramba Rd, Eros, POB 23866, Windhoek; tel. (61) 227153; telex 406; fax (61) 31584; Ambassador: ANGEL DALMAU FERNÁNDEZ.

Denmark: Sanlam Centre, 154 Independence Ave, POB 20126, Windhoek; tel. (61) 224923; telex 461; fax (61) 35807; Chargé d'affaires a.i.: SVEN BILLE BJERREGAARD.

Egypt: 10 Berg St, POB 11853, Windhoek; tel. (61) 221501; telex 421; fax (61) 228856; Ambassador: MOHAMMED HUSSEIN ELSADR.

Finland: POB 3649, Windhoek; tel. (61) 221355; telex 671; fax (61) 221349; Ambassador: KIRSTI LINTONEN.

France: 1 Goethe St, POB 20484, Windhoek; tel. (61) 229021; telex 715; fax (61) 31436; Ambassador: ALAIN DEMENTHON.

Germany: POB 231, Windhoek; tel. (61) 229217; telex 482; fax (61) 222981; Ambassador: Dr HANNS SCHUMACHER.

Ghana: 5 Klein Windhoek Rd, POB 24165, Windhoek; tel. (61) 221341; fax (61) 221343; High Commissioner: Dr KELI NORDOR.

India: 97 Klein Windhoek Rd, POB 1209, Windhoek; tel. (61) 228433; telex 832; fax (61) 37320; High Commissioner: KANWAR SINGH JASROTIA.

Iran: 81 Klein Windhoek Rd, Windhoek; tel. (61) 229974; telex 637; fax (61) 220016; Chargé d'affaires a.i.: AHMAD AMOOZADEH.

Italy: POB 24065, Windhoek; tel. (61) 228602; telex 620; fax (61) 229860; Ambassador: PIERO DE MASI.

Japan: Windhoek; tel. (61) 727500; fax (61) 727769; Chargé d'affaires a.i.: YUKIO ROKUJO.

Kenya: Kenya House, 134 Robert Mugabe St, POB 2889, Windhoek; tel. (61) 226836; telex 823; fax (61) 221409; High Commissioner: JOSEPH SEFU.

Korea, Democratic People's Republic: 2 Jenner St, POB 22927, Windhoek; tel. (61) 41967; telex 631; Chargé d'affaires a.i.: KIM PYONG GI.

Korea, Republic: Sanlam Centre, 154 Independence Ave, 10th Floor, POB 3788, Windhoek; tel. (61) 229286; telex 801; fax (61) 229847; Ambassador: SOONG CHULL-CHIN.

Libya: 69 Burg St, Luxury Hill, POB 124, Windhoek; tel. (61) 221139; telex 868; fax (61) 34471; Chargé d'affaires a.i.: H. O. ALSHAOSHI.

Malawi: 56 Bismarck St, POB 23384, Windhoek; tel. (61) 221291; telex 469; fax (61) 221392; High Commissioner: JAMES KALILANGWE (acting).

Nigeria: 4 Omuramba Rd, POB 23547, Windhoek; tel. (61) 32103; fax (61) 221639; High Commissioner: EDWARD AINA.

Norway: POB 9936, Windhoek; tel. (61) 227812; telex 432; fax (61) 222226; Ambassador: OLAV MYKLEBUST.

Portugal: 28 Garten St, POB 443, Windhoek; tel. (61) 228736; telex 409; Chargé d'affaires a.i.: JOÃO JOSÉ GOMES.

Romania: 1 Kestrell St, Hochland Park, POB 6827, Windhoek; tel. (61) 224630; telex 435; fax (61) 221564; Ambassador: P. VLASCEANU.

Russia: 4 Christian St, POB 3826, Windhoek; tel. (61) 228671; telex 865; fax (61) 229061; Ambassador: ANDREY Y. URNOV.

Spain: 58 Bismarck St, POB 21811, Windhoek; tel. (61) 223066; fax (61) 223046; Ambassador: CARLOS SÁNCHEZ DE BOADO.

Sudan: POB 3708, Windhoek; tel. (61) 228544; Ambassador: ABD ELMONIEM MUSTAFA ELAMIN.

Sweden: POB 23087, Windhoek; tel. (61) 222905; telex 463; fax (61) 222774; Ambassador: STEN RYLANDER.

United Kingdom: 116 Robert Mugabe Ave, POB 22202, Windhoek; tel. (61) 223022; telex 2343; fax (61) 228895; High Commissioner: HENRY HOGGER.

USA: 14 Lossen St, Private Bag 12029, Windhoek; tel. (61) 221601; fax (61) 229792; Ambassador: MARSHALL MCCALLIE.

Venezuela: Southern Life Tower, 3rd Floor, Post Street Mall, Private Bag 13353, Windhoek; tel. (61) 227905; telex 862; fax (61) 227804; Chargé d'affaires a.i.: ALBERTO VALERO.

Yugoslavia: 10 Chateau St, POB 3705, Windhoek; tel. (61) 36900; telex 3174; fax (61) 222260; Chargé d'affaires: PETKO DELIĆ.

Zambia: 22 Sam Nujoma Dr., POB 22882, Windhoek; tel. (61) 37610; telex 485; fax (61) 228162; High Commissioner: (vacant).

Zimbabwe: cnr Independence Ave and Grimm St, POB 23056, Windhoek; tel. (61) 228134; telex 866; fax (61) 228659; High Commissioner: ALBAN TAKA KANENGONI DETE.

Judicial System

Judicial power is exercised by the Supreme Court, the High Court and a number of Magistrate and Lower Courts. The Constitution provides for the appointment of an Ombudsman.

Chief Justice: I. MAHOMED.

Attorney-General: HARTMUT RUPPEL.

Religion

It is estimated that about 90% of the population are Christians. The principal denominations in 1981 were the Lutheran (528,323 adherents), Roman Catholic (195,000), Dutch Reformed (63,322), Anglican (57,560) and Methodist (10,558).

CHRISTIANITY

Council of Churches in Namibia: 8 Mont Blanc St, POB 41, Windhoek; tel. (61) 217621; telex 834; fax (61) 62786; f. 1978; eight mem. churches; Pres. Bishop HENDRIK FREDERIK; Gen. Sec. Dr ABISAI SHEJAVALI.

The Anglican Communion

Namibia comprises a single diocese in the Church of the Province of Southern Africa. The Metropolitan of the Province is the Archbishop of Cape Town, South Africa.

Bishop of Namibia: Rt Rev. JAMES HAMUPANDA KAULUMA, POB 57, Windhoek; tel. (61) 38920; fax (61) 225903.

Dutch Reformed Church

Dutch Reformed Church of South West Africa/Namibia: POB 389, Windhoek; tel. (61) 41144; Moderator Rev. A. J. DE KLERK.

Evangelical Lutheran

Evangelical Lutheran Church in Namibia: Bishop Dr KLEOPAS DUMENI, Private Bag 2018, Ondangwa; tel. (6756) 40241; telex 3257; fax (6756) 272.

Evangelical Lutheran Church (Rhenish Mission Church): POB 5069, Windhoek; tel. (61) 224531; telex 3107; f. 1967; Pres. Bishop HENDRIK FREDERIK.

German Evangelical-Lutheran Church in Namibia: POB 233, Windhoek; tel. (61) 224294; fax (61) 221470; mems 8,200; Pres. Rev. Landespropst REINHARD KEDING.

Methodist

African Methodist Episcopal Church: Rev. B. G. KARUAERA, Windhoek; tel. (61) 62757.

Methodist Church of Southern Africa: POB 143, Windhoek; tel. (61) 64527.

The Roman Catholic Church

Namibia comprises two Apostolic Vicariates. At 31 December 1992 there were an estimated 245,764 adherents in Namibia, representing about 15% of the total population.

Apostolic Vicariate of Keetmanshoop: 89 Eight Ave, POB 88, Keetmanshoop; tel. and fax (631) 2007; Vicar Apostolic Rt Rev. ANTHONY CHIMINELLO, Titular Bishop of Numana.

Apostolic Vicariate of Windhoek: POB 272, Windhoek; tel. (61) 227595; fax (61) 229836; Vicar Apostolic Rt Rev. BONIFATIUS HAUSHIKU, Titular Bishop of Troina (Troyna).

Other Christian Churches

Among other denominations active in Namibia are the Evangelical Reformed Church in Africa, the Presbyterian Church of Southern Africa and the United Congregational Church of Southern Africa.

BAHÁ'Í FAITH

National Spiritual Assembly: POB 20372, Windhoek; tel. (61) 227961; mems resident in 208 localities.

The Press

Abacus: POB 22791, Windhoek; tel. (61) 35596; fax (61) 36497; weekly; English; educational; Editor HEIDI VON EGIDY; circ. 45,000.

Acoda Info: POB 20549, Windhoek; tel. (61) 37623; fax (61) 31583; monthly; English, French.

Action: POB 20500, Windhoek; tel. (61) 62957; fax (61) 216375; 2 a month; Afrikaans, English; religious; Editor FRANS VAN DER MERWE; circ. 12,000.

AgriForum: 114 Robert Mugabe St, Private Bag 13255, Windhoek; tel. (61) 37838; fax (61) 220193; monthly; Afrikaans, English; Editor PEDRO STEENKAMP; circ. 5,000.

Allgemeine Zeitung: 49 Stuebel St, POB 2127, Windhoek; tel. (61) 230331; fax (61) 220225; f. 1915; daily; German; Editor-in-Chief HANS FEDDERSEN; circ. 5,000.

Aloe: POB 59, Windhoek; tel. (61) 3912353; fax (61) 3912091; monthly; English; Edited by the Windhoek Municipality; circ. 35,000.

Bargain Post: POB 23000, Windhoek; tel. (61) 227182; fax (61) 220226; 2 a month; English; business and advertisments; Editor JOHAN ENGELBRECHT; circ. 15,000.

Bricks Community Newspaper: POB 20642, Windhoek; tel. (61) 62726; fax (61) 63510; bi-monthly; English; Editor ANDRÉ STRAUSS; circ. 2,000.

Monitor: POB 2196, Windhoek; tel. (61) 34141; fax (61) 32802; monthly; Afrikaans, English; Editor EWERT BENADE; circ. 4,100.

Namib Times: POB 706, Walvis Bay; tel. (642) 5854; fax (642) 4813; 2 a week; Afrikaans, English; Editor PAUL VINCENT; circ. 4,000.

Namibia Brief: POB 2123, Windhoek; tel. (61) 37250; fax (61) 37251; quarterly; English; Editor CATHY BLATT; circ. 10,000.

Namibia Business Update: POB 11602, Windhoek; tel. (61) 38898; fax (61) 220104; monthly; English; Editor MOLLY CURRY; circ. 1,500.

Namibia Development Briefing: POB 20642, Windhoek; tel. (61) 62726; fax (61) 63510; bi-monthly; English; circ. 1,000.

Namibia Economist: POB 49, Windhoek; tel. (61) 221925; fax (61) 220615; monthly; Afrikaans, English; Editor DANIEL STEINMANN; circ. 7,000.

Namibia Focus: POB 23000, Windhoek; tel. (61) 227182; fax (61) 220226; monthly; English; business; Editor JOHAN ENGELBRECHT; circ. 30,000.

Namibia Nachrichten: POB 1825, Windhoek; tel. (61) 37824; fax (61) 37835; weekly; German; Editor HARTMUT RODENWOLDT; circ. 4,500.

Namibia Today: POB 24669, Windhoek; tel. (61) 229150; fax (61) 229150; 2 a week; Afrikaans, English, Oshiherero, Oshiwambo; publ. by SWAPO; Editor KAOMO-VIJINDA TJOMBE; circ. 5,000.

The Namibian: POB 20783, Windhoek; tel. (61) 36970; telex 3032; fax (61) 33980; daily; Afrikaans, English, Oshiwambo; left-wing; Editor GWEN LISTER; circ. 14,000.

The Namibian Worker: POB 61208, Windhoek; tel. (61) 216186; fax (61) 216186; Afrikaans, English, Owambo; publ. by National Union of Namibian Workers; Editor CHRIS NDIVANGA; circ. 4,000.

New Era: Private Bag 13344, Windhoek; tel. (61) 3082180; fax (61) 224937; weekly; English; Editor RAJAH MUNAMAVA; circ. 25,000.

Oranjemund Newsletter: POB 35, Oranjemund; tel. (6332) 2470; weekly; English, Oshiwambo; Editor DAOUD VRIES; circ. 2,400.

Otjikoto Journal: POB 40, Tsumeb; tel. (671) 21115; fax (671) 21710; monthly; English; Editor JIM KASTELIC; circ. 3,600.

Rössing News: Private Bag 5005, Swakopmund; tel. (641) 592382; fax (641) 592301; weekly; English; Editor MAGGI BARNARD; circ. 2,400.

Die Republikein: POB 3436, Windhoek; tel. (61) 33111; telex 3201; fax (61) 35674; f. 1977; daily; Afrikaans; organ of DTA of Namibia; Editor DES ERASMUS; circ. 12,000.

Die Sondag Republikein: POB 3436, Windhoek; tel. (61) 33111; telex 3201; fax (61) 35674; f. 1986; Sunday; Afrikaans; Editor GERRIT CLOETE; circ. 9,200.

The Times of Namibia: POB 1794, Windhoek; tel. (61) 225822; fax (61) 223110; daily; English; Editor CAROL KOTZE; circ. 6,700 (Mon.–Thurs.), 9,500 (Fri.).

Visitor: POB 23000, Windhoek; tel. (61) 227182; fax (61) 220226; monthly; English; tourist information; Editor JOHAN ENGELBRECHT; circ. 10,000.

Welcome: POB 11854, Windhoek; tel. (61) 227001; fax (61) 224317; 2 a month; English; tourist information; Editors JENS SCHNEIDER, MARITA POTGIETER; circ. 5,000.

The Windhoek Advertiser: 49 Stuebel St, POB 2255, Windhoek; tel. (61) 221737; fax (61) 221737; f. 1919; daily; English; Editor HANNES SMITH; circ. 2,000 (Mon.–Thur.), 8,000 (Fri.).

Windhoek Observer: POB 2384, Windhoek; tel. (61) 224511; fax (61) 229839; f. 1978; weekly; English; Editor TED McGILL; circ. 9,600.

NEWS AGENCIES

Namibian Press Agency (Nampa): POB 613541, Windhoek; tel. (61) 221711; fax (61) 221713; Editor-in-Chief MOCKS SHIVUTE.

Foreign Bureaux

Associated Press (AP) (USA): POB 22791, Windhoek; tel. (61) 225715; fax (61) 36467; Correspondent HEIDI VON EGIDY.

Informatsionnoye Telegrafnoye Agentstvo Rossii—Telegrafnoye Agentstvo Suverennykh Stran (ITAR—TASS) (Russia): POB 24821, Windhoek; tel. (61) 32909; telex 713; fax (61) 32909; Bureau Chief ALEKSANDR PROSVETOV.

Inter Press Service (IPS) (Italy): POB 20783, Windhoek; tel. (61) 226645; telex 3032; Correspondent MARK VERBAAN.

Rossiyskoye Informatsionnoye Agentstvo—Novosti (RIA—Novosti) (Russia): Windhoek; tel. (61) 34897; Bureau Chief ALEKSANDR DUBROVOLSKI.

South African Press Association (SAPA): POB 2032, Windhoek; tel. (61) 226339; Bureau Chief JOHANN VAN HEERDEN.

Xinhua (New China) News Agency (People's Republic of China): POB 22130, Windhoek; tel. (61) 226484; fax (61) 226484; Bureau Chief TENG WENVI.

Publishers

Deutscher Verlag (Pty) Ltd: POB 56, Windhoek; fax (61) 224843; f. 1939; newspaper publr.

Gamsberg Publishers: POB 22830, Windhoek; tel. (61) 28714; telex 3108; f. 1977; textbooks, fiction and non-fiction; Man. Dir Dr HANS VILJOEN.

Interface (Pty) Ltd: Windhoek; tel. (61) 228652; fax (61) 224402; f. 1987; Man. Dir MARÉ MOUTON.

John Meinert (Pty) Ltd: POB 56, Windhoek; f. 1924; newspapers.

Namibia Scientific Society: POB 67, Windhoek; tel. (61) 225372; f. 1925; Man. Dir A. HENRICHSEN.

Radio and Television

In 1991, according to UNESCO, there were an estimated 188,000 radio receivers and 31,000 television receivers in use.

Namibian Broadcasting Corporation (NBC): POB 321, Windhoek; tel. (61) 291911; telex 622; fax (61) 291291; f. 1979; broadcasts on eight radio channels in 11 languages; television programmes are broadcast in English; Dir-Gen. NAHUM J. GORELICK.

Finance

(cap. = capital; res = reserves; dep. = deposits; m. = million; brs = branches; amounts in rand)

BANKING

Central Bank

Bank of Namibia: 10 Göring St, POB 2882, Windhoek; tel. (61) 226401; telex 710; fax (61) 229874; f. 1990; Gov. ERIK KARLSSON; Gen. Man. EMMANUEL LULE.

Commercial Banks

Bank Windhoek Ltd: 262 Independence Ave, POB 15, Windhoek; tel. (61) 31850; fax (61) 223188; f. 1982; cap. and res 18.9m., dep. 370.9m. (March 1992); Chair. J. C. BRANDT; Man. Dir D. P. DE LANGE; 14 brs.

Commercial Bank of Namibia Ltd: 12–20 Bülow St, POB 1, Windhoek; tel. (61) 3039111; telex 898; fax (61) 3032103; f. 1973 as Bank of Namibia, name changed in 1990; 78.4%-owned by Société Financière pour les Pays d'Outre-Mer (France); cap. and res 20.1m., dep. 495.2m. (June 1992); Chair. JOHANN ALBRECHT BRÜCKNER; Man. Dir HANS-JÜRGEN STEUBER.

First National Bank of Namibia Ltd: 207 Independence Ave, POB 195, Windhoek; tel. (61) 229610; telex 475; fax (61) 225604; f. 1986; cap. and res 72.5m., dep. 867.1m. (Sept. 1992); Man. Dir G. S. VAN STADEN; Gen. Man. D. M. HARRIS; 25 brs and 11 agencies.

Namibian Banking Corporation: Carl List Haus, Independence Ave, POB 370, Windhoek; tel. (61) 225946; telex 629; fax (61) 223741; Chair. J. C. WESTRAAT; Man. Dir P. P. NIEHAUS; 3 brs.

Standard Bank Namibia Ltd: Mutual Platz, POB 3327, Windhoek; tel. (61) 2949111; telex 3079; fax (61) 2942409; f. 1915 as Standard Bank SWA, name changed in 1990; controlled by the Standard Bank of South Africa; cap. and res 57m., dep. 1,037m. (Dec. 1993); Chair. C. J. F. BRAND; Man. Dir V. B. MOLL.

STOCK EXCHANGE

Namibia Stock Exchange: Nimrod Bldg, Kasino St, POB 2401, Windhoek; tel. (61) 227647; fax (61) 32513; f. 1992; Chair. Exec. Cttee HANS-JÜRGEN STEUBER.

INSURANCE

Commercial Union Insurance Ltd: Bülow St, POB 1599, Windhoek; tel. (61) 37137; telex 3096.

Incorporated General Insurance Ltd: 10 Bülow St, POB 2516, Windhoek; tel. (61) 37453; telex 415; fax (61) 35647.

Liberty Life Asscn of Africa Ltd: Bülow St, POB 21917, Windhoek; tel. (61) 37840; telex 3030; fax (61) 224266.

Lifegro Assurance Ltd: Independence Ave, POB 23055, Windhoek; tel. (61) 33068.

Metropolitan Life Ltd: Goethe St, POB 3785, Windhoek; tel. (61) 37840.

Mutual and Federal Insurance Co Ltd: Mutual Bldg, Independence Ave, POB 151, Windhoek; tel. (61) 37730; telex 3084; Man. H. K. BORCHARDT.

Namibia National Insurance Co Ltd: Bülow St, POB 23053, Windhoek; tel. (61) 224539; fax (61) 38737; fmrly Federated Insurance Co Ltd.

Protea Assurance Co Ltd: Windhoek; tel. (61) 225891; telex 414.

Prudential Assurance Co of South Africa: Independence Ave, POB 365, Windhoek; tel. (61) 33176; telex 481.

SA Mutual Life Assurance Soc.: Independence Ave, POB 165, Windhoek; tel. (61) 36620; fax (61) 34874.

Sanlam Life Assurance Ltd: Bülow St, POB 317, Windhoek; tel. (61) 36680.

Santam Insurance Ltd: Independence Ave, POB 204, Windhoek; tel. (61) 38214.

Southern Life Assurance Ltd: Southern Tower, Post Street Mall, POB 637, Windhoek; tel. (61) 34056; fax (61) 31574.

Trade and Industry

CHAMBERS OF COMMERCE

Afrikaanse Sakekamer van SWA: POB 22643, Windhoek; tel. (61) 52927; Chair. W. KORRUBEL.

Namibia National Chamber of Commerce and Industry: POB 9355, Windhoek; tel. (61) 228809; fax (61) 228009.

Windhoek Chamber of Commerce and Industries: SWA Building Society Bldg, 3rd Floor, POB 191, Windhoek; tel. (61) 222000; fax (61) 33690; f. 1920; Pres. D. DE LANGE; Gen. Man. H. H. SCHMIDT; 230 mems.

CHAMBER OF MINES

Chamber of Mines of Namibia: POB 2895, Windhoek; tel. (61) 37925; fax (61) 222638; f. 1979; Pres. TONY DE BEER.

DEVELOPMENT ORGANIZATIONS

Investment Centre: Ministry of Trade and Industry, Govt Bldgs, Private Bag 13340, Windhoek; tel. (61) 2892431; telex 870; fax (61) 220227.

Namibia Development Corporation: Private Bag 13252, Windhoek; tel. (61) 306911; telex 870; fax (61) 33943; f. 1993 to replace First National Development Corpn; promotes foreign investment and provides concessionary loans and equity to new enterprises; manages agricultural projects; Chair. H.-G. STIER; Man. Dir A. J. BOTES.

Namibian International Business Development Organization (NIBDO): POB 82, Windhoek; tel. (61) 37970; fax (61) 33690; Pres. DES MATHEWS.

National Building and Investment Corporation: POB 20192, Windhoek; tel. (61) 37224; fax (61) 222301.

National Housing Enterprise: POB 20192, Windhoek; tel. (61) 225518; fax (61) 222301; Chair. N. SCHOOMBE; CEO A. M. TSOWASELO.

PUBLIC BOARDS AND CORPORATIONS

Meat Board of Namibia: POB 38, Windhoek; tel. (61) 33180; telex 679; fax (61) 228310.

Meat Corporation of Namibia (MEATCO NAMIBIA): POB 3881, Windhoek; tel. (61) 216810; fax (61) 217045.

Namibian Agronomic Board: POB 5096, Windhoek; tel. (61) 224741; fax (61) 225371; Gen. Man. Dr KOBUS KOTZE.

Namibian Karakul Board: Private Bag 13230, Windhoek; tel. (61) 33185; fax (61) 36122.

National Petroleum Corporation of Namibia (NAMCOR): Windhoek; Chair. SKERF POTTAS.

South West Africa Water and Electricity Corporation (SWAWEK): Swawek Centre, 147 Robert Mugabe St, POB 2864, Windhoek; tel. (61) 31830; fax (61) 32805; Chair. and Man. Dir J. P. BRAND.

EMPLOYERS' ORGANIZATIONS

Construction Industries Federation of Namibia: POB 1479, Windhoek; tel. (61) 230028; fax (61) 224534; Pres. NEIL THOMPSON.

Electrical Contractors' Association: POB 3163, Windhoek; tel. (61) 37920; Pres. F. PFAFFENTHALER.

Motor Industries Federation of Namibia: POB 1503, Windhoek; tel. (61) 37970; fax (61) 33690.

Namibia Agricultural Union: Private Bag 13255, Windhoek; tel. (61) 37838; fax (61) 220193.

Namibia Chamber of Printing: POB 363, Windhoek; tel. (61) 37905; fax (61) 222927; Sec. S. G. TIMM.

MAJOR INDUSTRIAL COMPANIES

Berg Aukas Ltd: POB 2, Grootfontein 9000; tel. (6731) 2047; telex 775; subsidiary of Gold Fields Namibia Ltd; mines lead, zinc and vanadium at Berg Aukas; Chair. P. R. JANISCH.

CDM (Pty) Ltd: POB 35, Oranjemund 9000; Head Office, POB 1906, Windhoek; tel. (6332) 9111 (Oranjemund), and (061) 35061 (Windhoek); telex 440 (Oranjemund), and 658 (Windhoek); f. 1920 as Consolidated Diamond Mines; subsidiary of De Beers Centenary AG; operates alluvial diamond mine at Oranjemund; Chair. J. OGILVIE THOMPSON.

Imcor Zinc (Pty) Ltd: Private Bag, Rosh Pinah; tel. (63342) 2; telex 443; fax 145; subsidiary of South Africa Iron and Steel Corpn (ISCOR); mines zinc and lead at Rosh Pinah.

Namibian Minerals Corporation: Walvis Bay; f. 1993; operates a marine diamond exploration concession covering 1,035 sq km; Chair. and CEO ALASTAIR HOLBERTON.

Rössing Uranium Ltd: POB 22391, Windhoek; tel. (61) 36760; telex 3104; fax 33637; f. 1970; operates an open-cast uranium mine in the Namib desert; began production in 1976 and is one of the largest uranium mines in the world; Chair. J. S. KIRKPATRICK; CEO J. C. A. LESLIE.

Tsumeb Corporation Ltd: POB 40, Tsumeb 9000; tel. (671) 3115; telex 680; fax 3710; produces and sells blister copper, silver, refined lead, refined arsenic trioxide, refined cadmium, refined sodium antimonate and other metals; conducts exploration for base metals; Man. A. R. DE BEER.

LABOUR ORGANIZATIONS

There are several union federations, and a number of independent unions.

Trade Union Federations

Confederation of Labour: POB 22060, Windhoek.

National Allied Unions (NANAU): Windhoek; f. 1987; an alliance of trade unions, representing c. 7,600 mems, incl. Namibia Wholesale and Retail Workers' Union (f. 1986; Gen. Sec. T. NGAUJAKE; 6,000 mems), and Namibia Women Support Cttee; Pres. HENOCH HANDURA.

Namibia Trade Union (NTU): Windhoek; f. 1985; represents 6,700 domestic, farm and metal workers; Pres. ALPHA KANGUEEHI; Sec.-Gen. BEAU TJISESETA.

Namibia Trade Union Council (NTUC): Windhoek; f. 1981; affiliates include Northern Builders' Asscn.

National Union of Namibian Workers (NUNW): POB 50034, Windhoek; tel. (61) 215037; fax (61) 215589; f. 1971; Sec.-Gen. BERNHARDT ESAU; 87,600 mems; affiliates include:

Mineworkers' Union of Namibia (MUN): f. 1986; Chair. ASSER KAPERE; Pres. JOHN SHAETON HODI; Gen. Sec. PETER NAHOLO (acting); 12,500 mems.

Namibia Food and Allied Workers' Union: f. 1986; Chair. MATHEUS LIBEREKI; Chair. ELIFAS NANGOLO; Gen. Sec. MAGDALENA IPINGE (acting); 12,000 mems.

Namibia Metal and Allied Workers' Union: f. 1987; Chair. ANDRIES TEMBA; Gen. Sec. MOSES SHIKWA (acting); 5,500 mems.

Namibia Public Workers' Union: f. 1987; Chair. STEVEN IMMANUEL; Gen. Sec. PETER ILONGA; 11,000 mems.

Namibia Transport and Allied Workers' Union: f. 1988; Gen. Sec. IMMANUEL KAVAA; Chair. TYLVES GIDEON; 7,500 mems.

Other Unions

Association for Government Service Officials: Windhoek; f. 1981; Chair. ALLAN HATTLE; 9,000 mems.

Namibia Building Workers' Association: Windhoek; Sec. H. BOCK.

Public Service Union of Namibia: POB 21662, Windhoek; tel. (61) 213083; fax (61) 213047; f. 1981; Sec.-Gen. S. LAWRENCE.

Society for Officials of Financial Unions: Windhoek; Sec. Mrs A. CARMEN; 1,050 mems.

South West Africa Municipal Association: Windhoek; f. 1968; Gen. Sec. HANS SCHOEMAN; 3,000 mems.

Transport

RAILWAYS

The main line runs from Nakop, at the border with South Africa, via Keetmanshoop to Windhoek, Kranzberg, Grootfontein, Tsumeb, Swakopmund and Walvis Bay, while there are three branch lines, from Windhoek to Gobabis, Otjiwarongo to Outjo and Keetmanshoop to Lüderitz. Total rail tracks in Namibia are 2,382 route-km.

TransNamib Ltd: TransNamib Bldg, cnr Independence Ave and Bahnhof St, Private Bag 13204, Windhoek; tel. (61) 2981111; telex 215; fax (61) 2982078; state-owned; Man. Dir FRANÇOIS UYS.

ROADS

In 1992 the road network comprised 41,882 km of roads, including 4,581 km of tarred roads, 25,691 km of gravel roads, 226 km of salt/gypsum roads and 11,384 km of natural roads. Road maintenance and construction was allocated R218m. in the 1992/93 budget. A main road from Windhoek to Gaborone, Botswana, was to be in use by 1995, and construction of the Trans-Caprivi and Trans-Kalahari highways was scheduled for completion by 1996. The Government aimed to expand the road network in northern Namibia during the 1990s.

SHIPPING

Walvis Bay and Lüderitz are the only ports, although the development of other harbours is planned. Walvis Bay harbour, the region's only deep-water port, is linked to the main overseas shipping routes and handles almost one-half of Namibia's external trade.

CIVIL AVIATION

The international airport is at Windhoek. There are a number of other airports dispersed throughout Namibia, as well as numerous landing strips.

Air Namibia: TransNamib Bldg, cnr Independence ave and Bahnhof St, POB 731, Windhoek; tel. (61) 223019; telex 657; fax (61) 221910; f. 1959 as Namib Air; state-owned; domestic flights and services to Southern Africa and Western Europe; Chair. J. A. BRÜCKNER; Gen. Man. KEITH PETCH.

Tourism

Nambia's principal tourist attractions are its game parks and nature reserves. About 282,000 tourists visited Namibia in 1991; the majority originated from South Africa. In that year receipts from tourism totalled R320m. Under a five-year programme for the expansion of the tourist industry, announced in mid-1993, the Government aimed to invest some R547m. in the sector, and projected that foreign tourist arrivals would reach 396,000 per year by 1997.

Namibia Tourism: Private Bag 13346, Windhoek; tel. (61) 2849111; fax (61) 221930.

Defence

In June 1993 the armed forces numbered 8,100 (army 8,000; navy 100). About 70 British military advisers were training the Namibian Defence Force in early 1993.

Defence Expenditure: Budgeted at R180m. in 1993/94 (representing 5.4% of total projected budgetary expenditure for that year).

Commander-in-Chief of the Defence Force: Pres. SAMUEL (SAM) DANIEL NUJOMA.

Commander of the Army: Maj.-Gen. SOLOMON HAWALA.

Education

Education is officially compulsory for nine years between the ages of seven and 16. Primary education, beginning at seven years of age, lasts for seven years; secondary education begins at the age of 14 and lasts for five years. In 1990 enrolment at primary schools was equivalent to 94% of the relevant age-group (males 89%; females 99%). Enrolment at secondary schools in that year was equivalent to 34% of the secondary school-age population (males 30%; females 38%). Higher education is provided by an academy and four teacher-training colleges. Various schemes for informal adult education are also in operation in an effort to combat illiteracy. In 1985, according to estimates by UNESCO, the average rate of adult illiteracy was 27.5% (males 25.8%; females 29.2%). In the budget for 1993/94 R790m. (23.5% of total projected expenditure) was allocated to education.

Bibliography

Catholic Institute for International Relations, London. *A Future for Namibia* (series):

Ellis, J. *Education, Repression and Liberation*. 1983. *Mines and Independence*. 1983.

Moorsom, R. *Transforming a Wasted Land* (Agriculture). 1982. *Exploiting the Sea* (Fishing). 1984. *Namibia in the 1980s*. 2nd Edn, 1985.

Dreyer, R. *Namibia and Southern Africa: Regional Dynamics of Decolonialization, 1945-1990*. New York and London, Kegan Paul International, 1994.

Duggal, N. K. (Ed.). *UNIN Namibia Studies Series*. Lusaka, United National Institute for Namibia:

Andersson, N. *Health Sector Policy Options for Independent Namibia*. 1984.

Bomani, M. D., and Ushewokunze, C. *Constitutional Options for Namibia. An Historical Perspective*. 1979.

Green, R. H. *Manpower Estimate and Development Implications for Namibia*. 1978.

Mshonga, S. *Toward Agrarian Reform*. 1979.

Oloya, J. J., Miclaus, I., Ishengoma, F. A., and Aho, K. *Agricultural Economy of Namibia: Strategies for Structural Change*. 1984.

Eriksen, T. L., and Moorsom, R. *The Political Economy of Namibia: A Select Annotated Bibliography*. Uppsala/Lusaka, Scandinavian Institute of African Studies and UNIN, 1985.

First, R. *South West Africa*. Harmondsworth, Penguin, 1963.

First National Development Corporation. *Namibia: Development and Investment*. Windhoek, FNDC, 1989.

Gordon, R. J. *Mines, Masters and Migrants*. Johannesburg, 1977.

Green, R. H., Kiljunen, M.-L., and Kiljunen, K. *Namibia: The Last Colony*. London, Longman, 1981.

Herbstein, D., and Evenson, J. *The Devils are Among Us—The War for Namibia*. London, Zed Books, 1989.

Katjavivi, P. H. *A History of Resistance in Namibia*. London, James Currey, 1987.

Katjavivi, P. H., Frostin, P., and Mbuende, K. (Eds). *Church and Liberation in Namibia*. London, Pluto Press, 1989.

Kinahan, J. *By Command of their Lordships: The Exploration of the Namibian Coast by the Royal Navy 1795-1895*. Windhoek, Namibian Archaeological Trust, 1992.

Konczacki, Z. A., Parpart, J. L., and Shaw, T. M. (Eds). *Studies in the Economic History of Southern Africa*. Vol. I. London, Cass, 1990.

Konig, B. *Namibia: The Ravages of War*. London, International Defence and Aid Fund, 1983.

Leser, H. *Namibia: Geographische Strukturen, Daten, Entwicklungen*. Ernst Klett.

Moorsom, R. *Walvis Bay: Namibia's Port*. London, International Defence and Aid Fund, 1984.

du Pisani, A. *Namibia: The Politics of Continuity and Change*. Johannesburg, 1985.

Pütz, von Egidy, and Caplan (Eds). *Political Who's Who of Namibia*. Windhoek, Magnus Co, 1987.

Rotberg, R. I. (Ed.). *Namibia: Political and Economic Prospects*. Lexington, MA, Lexington Books, 1985.

Smith, S. *Namibia: A Violation of Trust*. London, Oxfam Public Affairs Unit, 1986.

Soggot, D. *Namibia: The Violent Heritage*. London, Rex Collings, 1986.

Sparks, D. L. and Green, D. *Namibia: The Nation after Independence*. Boulder, Westview Press, 1992.

Sparks, D. L. and Murray, R. *Namibia's Future: The Economy at Independence*. London, Economist Intelligence Unit, 1985.

Stoecker, H. (Ed.) *German Imperialism in Africa*. London, Hurst, 1986.

SWA/Namibia Information Service. *Statistical/Economic Review*. Annually since 1983.

SWAPO. *To Be Born a Nation: The Liberation Struggle for Namibia*. London, Zed Press, 1981.

van der Merwe, J. H. (Ed.). *National Atlas of South West Africa (Namibia)*. Stellenbosch, University of Stellenbosch, Institute of Cartographic Analysis, 1983.

von Garnier, C. *Namibie, Les derniers colons*. Paris, Harmattan, 1987.

Ya-Otto, J. *Battlefront Namibia*. London, Heinemann Educational, 1982.

NIGER

Physical and Social Geography

R. J. HARRISON CHURCH

The land-locked Republic of Niger is the largest state in west Africa. With an area of 1,267,000 sq km (489,191 sq miles), it is larger than Nigeria, its immensely richer southern neighbour, which is Africa's most populous country. The relatively small size of Niger's population, estimated to be 7,249,596 in September 1988 (according to provisional census results), rising to an estimated 8,252,000 at mid-1992, is largely explained by the country's aridity and remoteness. Population density in 1992 averaged 6.5 persons per sq km. Two-thirds of Niger consists of desert, and most of the north-eastern region is uninhabitable. Hausa tribespeople are the most numerous (some 53% of the population in 1988), followed by the Djerma Songhai (22%), Tuaregs (10%) and Peulhs (10%).

In the north-centre is the partly volcanic Aïr massif, with many dry watercourses remaining from earlier wetter conditions. Agadez, in Aïr, receives an average annual rainfall of no more than about 180 mm. Yet the Tuareg keep considerable numbers of livestock by moving them seasonally to areas further south, where underground well-water is usually available. South again, along the Niger – Nigerian border, are sandy areas where annual rainfall is just sufficient for the cultivation of groundnuts and millet by Hausa farmers. Cotton is also grown in small, seasonally flooded valleys and depressions.

In the south-west is the far larger, seasonally flooded Niger valley, the pastures of which nourish livestock that have to contend with nine months of drought for the rest of the year. Rice and other crops are grown by the Djerma and Songhai peoples as the Niger flood declines.

Niger thus has three very disparate physical and cultural focuses. Unity has been encouraged by French aid and by economic advance, but the attraction of the more prosperous neighbouring state of Nigeria is considerable. Distances to the nearest ports (Cotonou, in Benin, and Lagos, in Nigeria) are at least 1,370 km, both routes requiring breaks of bulk.

Recent History

PIERRE ENGLEBERT

Formerly a part of French West Africa, Niger became a self-governing republic within the French Community in December 1958, and proceeded to full independence on 3 August 1960. Control of government passed to the Parti progressiste nigérien (PPN), whose leader, Hamani Diori, favoured the maintenance of traditional social structures and the retention of close economic links with France. Organized opposition, principally by the left-wing nationalist Union nigérienne démocratique (UND, or Sawaba party), had been suppressed since 1959 and the UND leader, Djibo Bakary, was forced into exile. The Diori regime dealt firmly with periodic demonstrations of nationalist feeling, although the president himself gained considerable prestige as a spokesman for francophone Africa.

Although Niger's considerable reserves of uranium began to be exploited in 1971, the period 1968–74 was overshadowed by the Sahelian drought. Exports of groundnuts, which formerly accounted for 70% of Niger's export revenue, were badly affected, and the loss of pasture land in the north of the country led to serious food shortages. In April 1974, following widespread civil disorder over allegations that certain government ministers were misappropriating stocks of food aid, Diori was overthrown by the armed forces chief of staff, Lt-Col (later Maj.-Gen.) Seyni Kountché. A Conseil militaire suprême (CMS) was established to rule the country, with a mandate from Kountché to distribute food aid fairly and to restore morality to public life. Although political parties were outlawed, Bakary and other opposition activists were permitted to return to the country.

THE KOUNTCHÉ REGIME

The military government's major preoccupation was planning an economic recovery. In the interest of national independence, it obtained the withdrawal of French troops and reduced French influence over the exploitation of Niger's uranium deposits, while none the less maintaining generally friendly relations with the former colonial power. New links were formed with Arab states. Domestically, there was a renewal of political activity following Bakary's return from exile; in addition, personal and policy differences developed within the CMS. Plots to remove Kountché were uncovered in 1975 (resulting in the imprisonment both of Bakary and the vice-president of the CMS), and again in 1976, when nine conspirators received death sentences. In 1978, seeking to widen its support, the government released a number of political detainees, including members of ex-president Diori's administration. In 1980 both Diori and Bakary were released from prison, although Diori remained under house arrest until 1984.

From 1981 Kountché began gradually to increase civilian representation in the CMS, and in 1982 preparations were made for a constitutional form of government. In the following year an indirectly-elected Conseil national de développement (CND) began to function as a constituent assembly. A civilian prime minister, Oumarou Mamane, took office in January 1983 and in August became president of the CND (being replaced as prime minister by Hamid Algabid in November). In January 1984 Kountché established a commission to draft a pre-constitutional document, termed a 'national charter'.

Economic adjustment efforts during this period were impeded by the recurrence of drought in 1984–85 and the closure of the land border with Nigeria between April 1984 and March 1986, with the result that Niger's dependence on external financial assistance was increased. Relations with the USA (by now the principal donor of food aid to Niger) assumed considerable importance at this time. Meanwhile, a period of renewed tension between Niger and Libya had been the source of persistent accusations of mistreatment of the light-skinned, nomadic Tuareg population by the Kountché regime. In May 1985, following an armed incident near the Niger – Libya border, all non-Nigerien Tuareg tribespeople were expelled from the country. The renewed insecurity resulting from this incident also prompted the arrest of ex-president Diori; he was released again in 1987, and subsequently took up residence in Morocco, where he died in 1989.

Preparation of the draft 'national charter' was completed in early 1986. The document was submitted for approval in a national referendum—Niger's first since independence—in June 1987, when it was approved by an estimated 99.6% of voters. The charter did not elaborate a full constitution, providing instead for the establishment of non-elective, consultative institutions at both national and local levels.

SAÏBOU AND THE SECOND REPUBLIC

In November 1987, after a year of ill-health, President Kountché died at the age of 56. The chief of staff of the armed forces, Col (later Brig.) Ali Saïbou (a cousin of Kountché), who had assumed the role of acting head of state during Kountché's illness, was formally confirmed in the positions of chairman of the CMS and head of state on 14 November. The new leader promised a continuity of Kountché's ideals and objectives (ultimately within the context of a 'second republic'), although he displayed a more flexible and less austere approach to government. Both Diori and Bakary were received by Saïbou, and an appeal was made to exiled Nigeriens to return to the country. A general amnesty for all political prisoners was announced in December. Saïbou also announced proposals for elections to village, local and regional councils, and for the establishment of a constitutional committee. Although the military continued to play a prominent role in government, Oumarou Mamane was reinstated as prime minister in July 1988, and in November a civilian was appointed minister of finance.

A constitutional document (which the CND had been commissioned to draft in July 1988), providing for the continued role of the armed forces in national politics, was adopted by the council of ministers in January 1989, and was endorsed by a reported 99.3% of voters in a national referendum in September. The 14-year ban on all political organizations was ended in August 1988, when Saïbou announced the formation of a new ruling party, the Mouvement national pour une société de développement (MNSD). While reiterating his opposition to the immediate establishment of a multi-party system, Saïbou maintained that the existence of a single party was not incompatible with the concept of political pluralism. In May 1989 the constituent congress of the MNSD elected a Conseil supérieur d'orientation nationale (CSON). This body replaced the CMS (whose role had been significantly reduced of late), and its president (Saïbou, who was also appointed chairman of the MNSD) was to be the sole candidate in a presidential election—to be held in tandem with elections to a proposed legislative assembly, which was to replace the CND. At elections in December Saïbou was confirmed as president, for a seven-year term, by 99.6% of those who voted. At the same time a single list of 93 CSON-approved deputies to the new legislature was endorsed by 99.5% of voters. In the following week it was anounced that Niger's two remaining political detainees were to be released, to commemorate Saïbou's inauguration as president of the second republic. An extensive reorganization of the council of ministers followed, as a result of which the post of prime minister was abolished, while Saïbou relinquished the interior portfolio to a civilian.

In February 1990 security forces intervened at a demonstration by students, who had been boycotting classes at the University of Niamey in protest against proposed reforms to the education system and a reduction in the level of graduate recruitment into the civil service. Official reports stated that three students had been killed, and 25 injured, as a result of the police action. Saïbou, who had been abroad at the time of the incident, expressed his regret at the intervention, and announced the appointment of a commission to examine the students' grievances. The dismissal of the interior and higher education ministers in a government reorganization in March (when a prominent industrialist, Aliou Mahamidou, was assigned to the restored post of prime minister), together with the expulsion of senior figures, including the outgoing minister of the interior, from the CSON, indicated Saïbou's desire to appease the students. However, continuing student action during April prompted the deployment of security forces outside educational establishments and the banning of all student gatherings and demonstrations. The arrest and detention, in June, of more than 40 students (following renewed disturbances) provoked further protests. In the same month the trade union federation, the Union des syndicats des travailleurs du Niger (USTN), called a 48-hour strike, in protest against new austerity measures (notably the imposition of a two-year salary 'freeze' in the public sector). Following a meeting between a CSON *ad hoc* commission and representatives of the USTN, students and trade unionists who had been detained earlier in the month were released, and the USTN agreed to cancel further protests.

In June 1990 the CSON announced that the constitution was to be amended to facilitate the transition to political pluralism. However, the prospect of political reform failed to prevent a resurgence of industrial unrest, as the USTN continued to demand the cancellation of unpopular austerity measures. In early November a five-day general strike was widely observed, effectively halting production of uranium, closing public buildings and disrupting regional and international air links. In mid-November, as further industrial action appeared imminent, Saïbou announced that, on the basis of the findings of a constitutional review commission, a multi-party political system would be established. At the same time it was announced that less stringent austerity measures would be adopted, in consultation with Niger's external creditors. Provision was made for the registration of political parties (pending constitutional amendments—adopted in April 1991—providing for their formal legalization), and it was announced that a national conference would be convened during 1991 to determine the country's political evolution; municipal officers and development advisers would be elected, by universal suffrage, in late 1991, and multi-party legislative elections would take place in early 1992. Saïbou would remain as president, but his powers would be reviewed.

POLITICAL REFORM AND ETHNIC UNREST

In January 1991 the USTN announced that it was to end its affiliation with the MNSD. In February all educational establishments were closed, following violent demonstrations by students and school pupils who were protesting against delays in the investigation of the deaths that had occurred during the unrest of February 1990. In March 1991 it was announced that the armed forces were to withdraw from political life, and serving military officers were, accordingly, removed from the council of ministers. Later in the month Saïbou defeated two challengers for the post of chairman of the renamed MNSD – Nassara. In late March some 2,000 demonstrators protested in Niamey against the MNSD – Nassara's alleged domination of the political reform process, and demanded that opposition parties be accorded access to the state-owned media.

In July 1991 Saïbou resigned as chairman of the MNSD – Nassara, in order to distance himself from party politics in preparation for the national conference. He was succeeded as party leader by Col (retd) Tandja Mamadou. The conference, which was convened—after some delay—on 29 July, and was initially attended by about 1,200 delegates (representing, among others, the organs of state and some 24 political organizations, together with professional, women's and students' groups), declared itself sovereign. In early August delegates voted to suspend the constitution and to dissolve its organs of state. Saïbou was to remain in office as interim head of state, but his powers were reduced to a largely ceremonial level. State officials were forbidden to leave the country, and a special commission was established to examine alleged abuses of political or economic power. The government was deprived of its authority to make financial transactions, and links with external creditors were effectively severed when, in early October, delegates voted to suspend adherence to the country's IMF- and World Bank-sponsored programme of economic adjustment. The conference assumed control of the armed forces and the police, and in early September appointed a new armed forces chief of staff and deputy chief of staff. At the same time the government was dissolved, and in late October the conference appointed Amadou Cheiffou (a regional official of the International Civil Aviation Organization) to be prime minister in a transitional government which was expected to remain in office pending the installation (now scheduled for early 1993) of elected democratic institutions. At the conclusion of the conference, in early November, André Salifou, a dean of the University of Niamey who had presided over the conference since early August, was designated chairman of an interim legislature, the Haut conseil de la République (HCR). It was envisaged that the 15-member HCR would ensure the transitional government's implementation of conference resolutions, supervise the activities of the head of state and oversee the drafting of a new constitution. Cheiffou's council of ministers, appointed shortly afterwards, was dominated by technocrats, with the prime minister assuming personal responsibility for defence.

An atmosphere of national consensus prevailed in the immediate aftermath of the national conference. New austerity measures in the public sector, and consequent delays in the payment of salaries to civil servants and other state employees, were initially accepted with few signs of discontent. In late February 1992, however, junior-ranking members of the armed forces staged a mutiny: their demands for the payment of salary arrears were linked to appeals for the release of an army captain who had been detained after having been found responsible by the national conference for the violent suppression of a Tuareg attack on Tchin Tabaraden in May 1990 (see below), and for the dismissal of senior armed forces officers. The mutineers detained Salifou and the minister of the interior, Mohamed Moussa (himself a Tuareg), and took control of the offices of the state broadcasting media in Niamey, but returned to barracks when Cheiffou promised to consider their material demands. None the less, troops again seized the broadcasting media in early March. A large demonstration took place in Niamey to condemn the rebellion, and the USTN and several political parties organized a widely-observed general strike to protest against the military. Order was restored when the government agreed to consider all the mutineers' demands.

Weakened by the lack of discipline within the military, the country's precarious financial situation and the continuing Tuareg crisis, in late March 1992 Cheiffou admitted that the transitional government had achieved little in its attempts to address the country's problems. The council of ministers was reorganized: four ministers were dismissed, and Mohamed Moussa was transferred to the ministry of trade, transport and tourism. In June the government, evidently motivated by the need to secure external financial assistance (most urgently to fund the payment of salary arrears in the public sector) announced that Niger was to restore diplomatic relations with Taiwan (which had been severed in 1974, following Niger's formal recognition of the People's Republic of China). Members of the HCR criticized the government's decision, stating that the transitional administration had no mandate to effect such a reorientation of foreign policy, and in late June 1992 the government rescinded its earlier announcement. In early July, however, a vote (sponsored by Salifou) expressing 'no confidence' in Cheiffou was defeated at an extraordinary session of the HCR, and it was announced later in the month that relations with Taiwan would be resumed. Diplomatic relations with the People's Republic of China were severed at the end of the month, and Niger received its first financial assistance from Taiwan shortly afterwards.

Numerous delays were encountered in the transition process, and in August 1992 it was announced that the constitutional referendum, which had been scheduled to take place in October, had been postponed owing to delays in the adoption of an electoral code and in the registration of voters. The referendum did not take place until 26 December, when the new document was approved by 89.8% of those who voted (56.6% of the electorate—Islamic leaders had appealed, with only limited success, for a boycott of the vote, in view of the secular basis of the constitution). Elections to the new legislative body, the assemblée nationale, took place, again after considerable delay, on 14 February 1993, and were contested by 12 of the country's 18 legal political parties. Although the MNSD – Nassara won the greatest number of seats (29) in the 83-member assembly, the former ruling party was prevented from retaining power by the rapid formation, in the aftermath of the election, of an alliance of parties which was able to form a parliamentary majority. This Alliance des forces du changement (AFC) grouped six parliamentary parties with a total of 50 seats (and was also supported by three parties that were not represented in the legislature), its principal members being the Convention démocratique et sociale – Rahama (CDS – Rahama), which held 22 seats in the assembly, the Parti nigérien pour la démocratie et le socialisme – Tarayya (PNDS – Tarayya), with 13 seats, and the Alliance nigérienne pour la démocratie et le progrès – Zaman Lahiya (ANDP – Zaman Lahiya), with 11 seats. The rate of participation by voters was reported to be somewhat higher than at the time of the constitutional referendum.

The former ruling party, which denounced opposition tactics in the legislative elections, was similarly deprived of power in the elections for the presidency. At the first round, which took place on 27 February 1993, Tandja Mamadou won the greatest proportion of the votes cast (34.2%). He and his nearest rival, Mahamane Ousmane (the leader of the CDS – Rahama, who took 26.6% of the first round votes), proceeded to a second round, which—after some delay—took place on 27 March. Mahamane Ousmane was then elected president by 55.4% of those who voted (just over 35% of the electorate): four of the six other candidates at the first round were members of the AFC, and the majority of their supporters had transferred allegiance to Ousmane.

Mahamane Ousmane, a devout Muslim and the country's first Hausa head of state (his predecessors having been members of the Djerma community), who had consistently expressed his commitment to the principle of a secular state, was inaugurated as president of the third republic on 16 April 1993. Shortly beforehand tensions arose in the newly-established Assemblée nationale, where AFC members had elected Moumouni Amadou Djermakoye (the leader of the ANDP – Zaman Lahiya and a first-round candidate for the presidency) as the speaker of the legislature. The vote had been boycotted by the MNSD – Nassara and its allies (who protested that Djermakoye's appointment—in accordance with an agreement made within the AFC prior to the second round of the presidential election—was unconstitutional), and was annulled by the supreme court. President Ousmane none the less proceeded to appoint another first-round presidential candidate, Mahamadou Issoufou of the PNDS – Tarayya, to the post of prime minister (again in accordance with a prior arrangement among AFC members). The predominance of the AFC was confirmed in May, when, in the absence of opposition deputies, Djermakoye was reappointed speaker of the Assemblée nationale.

The new president and prime minister were anxious to resume a dialogue with the international financial community, with the aim of securing new credits and debt-relief measures, and the stated task of Issoufou's first council of ministers was to address the country's economic and social crisis. In the absence of significant external assistance, arrears had accumulated in the public and education sectors under the transitional authorities, and, although industrial action had been sporadic, there had been a resurgence of unrest in the education sector. In October 1992 students stormed the office of the prime minister, in protest against government plans to reduce grants and to introduce competitive procedures for graduates wishing to enter the civil service. Moreover, revelations in January 1993 that the University of Niamey was effectively bankrupt precipitated further violent protests, and about 15 people were arrested when demonstrators attempted to break into the presidential palace. In March students invaded the treasury building in Niamey, demanding the payment of grant arrears. More than 10 arrests were made in May, when a decision by the new government to declare the 1992/93 academic year invalid in state secondary schools (in view of the recent disruptions and lack of teaching resources) prompted further violent protests.

Labour unrest intensified following the inauguration of the new organs of state. Despite pledges of emergency financial assistance from France, as a result of which it was announced that public-sector wages outstanding since April would be paid, confirmation that arrears accumulated under the transitional authorities could not be paid provoked considerable disquiet. A 48-hour strike by USTN members in early July was swiftly followed by unrest in the army. Over a period of three days soldiers at Zinder, Tahoua, Agadez and Maradi mutinied, taking local officials hostage and demanding the payment of three months' salary arrears. Calm was restored following intervention by Ousmane and senior members of the military, and the payment of one month's arrears was promised. Rumours that soldiers at Zinder had been planning to assassinate Issoufou prompted some 4,000 people to stage a pro-government demonstration in Niamey to condemn the mutineers' actions. The USTN organized a further, 72-hour strike in early September, following the government's announcement, despite union objections, of an austerity budget which envisaged a 24% reduction in wages in the public sector, together with the imposition of new taxes and an indefinite suspension of the payment of salary arrears. Further strike action was averted in mid-September, when the authorities agreed to suspend implementation of a newly-adopted law restricting the right to strike, and negotiations between the USTN and the Issoufou administration resumed (albeit falteringly). In early October the government and unions reached an understanding whereby public-sector salaries would be reduced by 5% – 20% until the end of 1995, while employees would forgo three months' wage arrears, in return for which they would be compensated by other financial adjustments.

There was renewed unrest in the education sector from late 1993. Teachers took strike action in November, demanding the payment of salaries for the previous month, and there were clashes in Niamey between students and police in November and December. The University of Niamey was closed for 10 days in the first half of January 1994, following violent confrontations between students and police—who had intervened to prevent demonstrators from marching to the ministry of education to demand the payment of grant arrears, together with improved conditions for study—as a result of which some 50 students were arrested and about 30 injuries were reported. Clashes between police and students were also reported in Agadez. Secondary school pupils in Niamey joined students in demanding the payment of arrears and the reopening of the university. Classes resumed in mid-January, but the arrest shortly afterwards of the secretary-general of the students' union prompted further (peaceful) protests before he was released at the end of the month. Meanwhile, Tandja Mamadou was among the leaders of an 8,000-strong demonstration in Niamey, which had been organized to protest against the imposition, in the previous week, of a ban on a demonstration by supporters of the students' movement.

Following the devaluation, in January 1994, of the CFA franc, the government announced emergency policies to offset the immediate adverse effects of the currency's depreciation, and in late January the Assemblée nationale (in the absence of opposition deputies, who were boycotting parliamentary sessions) voted to empower Ousmane to issue decrees regarding political, economic and financial affairs without prior reference to the legislature.

University students in Niamey renewed their campaign for the payment of grant arrears in early March 1994, blocking roads and occupying campus buildings. The death of a student in clashes with police precipitated a boycott of classes, as students demanded that those responsible for the death be brought to justice. A government undertaking, in mid-March, to pay three months' arrears and to establish a commission to investigate the police actions failed to prevent further violent protests in the capital, where paramilitary forces were deployed since many police officers refused to intervene, in support of colleagues who were implicated in the student's death. Later in the month Niamey was effectively paralysed by a 24-hour general strike, organized by the USTN to protest against the imposition, from mid-March, of the controversial 'right to strike' legislation, and also to demand 30% – 50% salary increases to compensate for the devaluation of the national currency. A similar, three-day strike took place in mid-April, shortly before the government announced pay increases of 5% – 12% for public-sector employees, and a further 72-hour strike followed in mid-May.

Ousmane's administration was at the same time challenged by a campaign of civil disobedience, orchestrated by the MNSD – Nassara and its allies, which were demanding representation in the government proportionate to the percentage of votes won by Mamadou at the second round of presidential voting in 1993. Mamadou was arrested, together with André Salifou (in his capacity as a leader of the Union des patriotes démocratiques et progressistes – Shamuwa) and Issoufou Assoumane (a leader of the Union démocratique des forces progressistes – Sawaba), in mid-April 1994, following an opposition demonstration in which one person was killed and about 20 were injured. The arrests prompted further protests, and by the time Mamadou, Salifou and Assoumane were released, some five days later, about 90 opposition activists were reported to have been detained, 25 of whom were brought to trial in May, on charges of involvement in an unauthorized demonstration and of causing damage to public and private property. Three defendants were sentenced to two or three years' imprisonment, and banned from residence in Niamey for a further year, while 10 received suspended sentences and the remainder were acquitted. In late May, following a meeting between Ousmane and representatives of the MNSD – Nassara's parliamentary group, the opposition agreed to end its boycott of the Assemblée nationale. In June the supreme court ruled that a resolution, adopted by the legislature in April, to revoke the parliamentary immunity of those deputies whose parties were participating in the campaign of civil disobedience had been unconstitutional.

Members of the USTN began an indefinite strike in early June 1994, in a renewed attempt to secure their previous demands. At the end of July, however, union leaders agreed temporarily to suspend industrial action, in an attempt to achieve a negotiated settlement with the government. Meanwhile, the cancellation, by Moumouni Djermakoye, of an extraordinary session of parliament—scheduled for the second half of July, at which a motion expressing 'no confidence' in the government with regard to its conduct of labour relations was expected to be proposed—prompted the resignation of the legislature's deputy speaker, Jackou Senoussi, from the chairmanship of the CDS – Rahama.

In late September 1994 Issoufou resigned as prime minister, following his party's withdrawal from the AFC. He was replaced by Souley Abdoulaye, hitherto minister of trade, transport and tourism.

As in neighbouring Mali, ethnic unrest was precipitated by the return to Niger, beginning in the late 1980s, of large numbers of Tuareg nomads, who had migrated to Libya and Algeria earlier in the decade to escape the drought. In early May 1990 Tuaregs launched a violent attack on the prison and gendarmerie at Tchin Tabaraden, in north-eastern Niger. Reports suggested that the incident reflected Tuareg dissatisfaction that promises, made by Saïbou following his accession to power, regarding assistance for the rehabilitation of returnees to Niger had not been fulfilled (it appeared that funds designated for this purpose had been misappropriated). The alleged brutality of the armed forces in quelling the raid (in all, as many as 100 people were later said to have been killed during the attack and its suppression) was to provoke considerable disquiet, both within Niger and internationally. In June the Saïbou government contested allegations by the human rights organization, Amnesty International, that some 400 Tuaregs had been detained in recent months and that about 40 members of that tribe had been executed by the security forces. In July the governments of Algeria, Mali and Niger established a joint commission to monitor the movements of the Tuareg community in the three countries' border region. In September the heads of state of Algeria, Libya, Mali and Niger met in Algeria, where they agreed measures governing border controls and facilitating the return of refugees to their region of origin. In February 1991 an attack on an anti-desertification centre in northern Niger, at the time of a visit to the country by representatives of Amnesty International, was attributed to Tuareg activists. In April 44 Tuaregs were acquitted of involvement in the attack on Tchin Tabaraden.

Although the Tuareg issue was a major concern of the 1991 national conference, the rebels mounted a renewed offensive in October (which was later to be compounded by serious clashes between other ethnic groups). During the months that followed numerous violent attacks were directed at official targets in the north, and clashes took place between Tuareg rebels and the security forces. Many arrests were reported, while Tuareg groups were known to have kidnapped several armed forces members. In early January 1992 the transitional government intensified security measures in northern Niger. Shortly afterwards the government formally recognized, for the first time, that there was a rebellion in the north (incidents had hitherto been dismissed as isolated acts of banditry), and acknowledged the existence of a Tuareg movement, the Front de libération de l'Aïr et l'Azaouad (FLAA)—although official reports of the strength of the FLAA appeared to be understated. In the following month the leader of the FLAA, Rissa Ag Boula, stated that the Tuareg rebels were not seeking to achieve independence, but rather the establishment of a federal system, in which each ethnic group would have its own administrative entity. Prior to his removal from the ministry of the interior, Mohamed Moussa initiated a dialogue with Tuareg representatives, and in mid-May the new government concluded a 15-day truce agreement with the FLAA, in preparation for negotiations, with French and Algerian mediation, for a settlement to the unrest. However, the truce proved ineffective, with each party claiming violations of the agreement by the other, and no formal negotiations took place.

Tuareg attacks resumed in subsequent months, and in late August 1992 the security forces launched a major offensive against the Tuareg rebellion in the north. According to official figures, 186 Tuaregs were arrested in late August and early September, both in the north and in Niamey. Among those detained were Mohamed Moussa and the prefect of Agadez; some of those arrested were released after a short time, but the issue of the Tuaregs still being held by the security forces (estimated to number about 180), as well as the 44 members of the Nigerien military who had been captured by militant Tuaregs, was to be a major obstacle to the resumption of a dialogue in subsequent months. Military authority was intensified, following renewed Tuareg attacks, by the appointment, in early October, of senior members of the security forces to northern administrative posts. In late November, none the less, an *ad hoc* commission which had been appointed by the transitional government to consider the Tuareg issue recommended a far-reaching programme of decentralization, according legal status and financial autonomy to local communities, in response to the FLAA's demands for a federal system of government.

In late December 1992 the government announced the release from custody of 57 Tuaregs. In early January 1993, none the less, five people were killed in a Tuareg attack on an MNSD – Nassara meeting in the northern town of Abala. Although he escaped injury, the principal target of the attack was said to have been Tandja Mamadou, who had been minister of the interior at the time of the suppression of the Tchin Tabaraden raid. Although Tuareg attacks and acts of sabotage persisted, in late January 81 Tuaregs, including Mohamed Moussa, were released from detention. In early February 30 people were reported to have been killed in raids by Tuaregs (for which the FLAA denied responsibility) on three villages in the Tchin Tabaraden region.

In March 1993, following Algerian mediation, Rissa Ag Boula (who was based in Algeria, despite attempts by the Nigerien authorities to secure his extradition) agreed to a unilateral truce for the duration of the campaign for the second round of the presidential election. Shortly afterwards Tuareg representatives in Niamey signed a similar truce agreement (brokered by France). The election of the new organs of state appeared to offer new prospects for dialogue, and in early April the transitional government and the FLAA reached an agreement for an extension of the truce. About 30 Tuareg prisoners were released shortly afterwards, and in mid-April the Tuaregs released their hostages.

President Ousmane and Mahamadou Issoufou identified the resolution of the Tuareg issue as a major priority, and, although sporadic resistance was reported, the truce accord was largely respected. At the beginning of June 1993 it was revealed that representatives of the Nigerien government and the Tuaregs had for some time been negotiating in France, and on 10 June a formal, three-month truce agreement was signed in Paris. The accord provided for the demilitarization of the north, and envisaged the instigation of negotiations on the Tuaregs' political demands. Financial assistance was promised to facilitate the return of Tuareg refugees (estimated to number about 10,000) from Algeria, and development funds were pledged for northern areas. A committee was to be established to oversee the implementation of the agreement. However, the Paris accord encountered some opposition within the Tuareg community: a new group, the Armée révolutionnaire de libération du nord-Niger (ARLN), emerged in late June to denounce the accord, and by mid-July a further split was evident within the FLAA between supporters of the truce (led by Mano Dayak, the Tuareg signatory to the agreement), who broke away from the movement to form the Front de libération de Tamoust (FLT), and its opponents (led by Rissa Ag Boula), who stated that they could not support any agreement that contained no specific commitment to discussion of the federalist issue.

In September 1993 the FLT and the Nigerien government agreed to extend the truce for a further three months. Although the FLAA and the ARLN refused to sign the accord, in the following month they formed, together with the FLT, a joint negotiating body, the Coordination de la résistance armée (CRA), with the aim of presenting a cohesive programme in future dealings with the Nigerien authorities. It was indicated that the FLAA and the ARLN would henceforth be more willing to compromise in their demands, and efforts were initiated to arrange new talks. However, the absence of Nigerien government negotiators from a scheduled meeting in the Algerian capital in early November was followed by the failure of CRA representatives to travel to a meeting in Ouagadougou, Burkina Faso, later in the month. Frustrated by such delays, the French government announced its withdrawal from mediation efforts. Attacks on travellers between Agadez and Zinder, in early December, were attributed to Tuaregs (the first time for several months that the authorities had blamed disturbances on Tuaregs), and shortly afterwards government forces were reported to have attacked a Tuareg encampment, killing four people, although the government denied any such offensive.

Unrest continued in January 1994, although discreet mediation efforts continued. In the same month the establishment was reported of a further Tuareg movement, the Front patriotique de libération du Sahara (FPLS). In early February the CRA, including the FPLS, announced its willingness to attend preliminary talks in Ouagadougou, although it declined to sign a new truce agreement with the Nigerien government. France agreed to rejoin the negotiations, and, meeting in Burkina, in mid-February, the CRA (which presented a list of the Tuaregs' demands for consideration by the Nigerien authorities) and the government of Niger agreed to full negotiations in Paris in late March, with French, Algerian and Burkinabè mediation. None the less, reports of a Tuareg attack on a uranium installation at Arlit, and of the harassment of travellers in the north and east, undermined peace efforts in subsequent weeks. Moreover, the CRA's demands for regional autonomy, and for the establishment of quotas for Tuaregs in government, parliament and in the armed forces, received little support in Niamey, where the authorities and parliamentary opposition were prepared to concede the rehabilitation of the north and greater political decentralization. The proposed Paris negotiations did not take place in late March, and a further round of consultations was postponed indefinitely in mid-April.

Despite an escalation of violence during May 1994 (including clashes, some 200 km to the north of Agadez, between the Nigerien armed forces and a rebel unit of the FPLS, as a result of which as many as 40 deaths were recorded), negotiations reopened in Paris in mid-June. Tentative agreement was reached on the creation of 'homogeneous' autonomous regions for Niger's ethnic groups, each of which would have its own elected assembly and governor (to be elected by the regional assembly) to function in parallel with the organs of central government. There was, however, no agreement regarding the integration of Tuareg fighters into Niger's armed forces and political and administrative structures. There was renewed unrest in August, when a Tuareg attempt to disrupt power supplies to uranium mines north of Agadez caused considerable damage, while there were reports of clashes between Tuaregs and members of the armed forces following a rebel attack on an army barracks to the east.

The question of border security—notably the cross-border movements arising from the Tuareg rebellion in the north, was the subject of negotiations with Algeria, Burkina, Mali and Libya during 1993–94. The new government also fostered links elsewhere in sub-Saharan Africa, and in May 1994 established diplomatic relations with South Africa. Ousmane received renewed pledges of financial co-operation from Taiwan during a visit to that country in June, and visited France (which had extended assistance following the devaluation of the CFA franc) in the same month.

Economy

EDITH HODGKINSON

Revised for this edition by RICHARD SYNGE

During the 1980s and into the early 1990s Niger's economy lost much of its earlier momentum towards growth and modernization which had resulted from the development of the uranium-mining industry in the 1970s. After a long-term reduction in international demand and prices for uranium, the formal economy has contracted, both in size and diversity. However, the traditional rural economy has remained intact, and growth has been noted in informal trade and in small-scale artisanal manufacturing and repair activities. The country is increasingly influenced by its economic relations with its southern neighbour, Nigeria. While Niger's official exports and imports have declined sharply since the beginning of the 1990s, substantial unrecorded trade has continued to flourish across the 2,000-km common border with Nigeria: fuel smuggled from Nigeria already accounts for at least one-third of Niger's national consumption, according to official estimates.

In 1992, according to estimates by the World Bank, Niger's gross national product (GNP), measured at average 1990–92 prices, was equivalent to only US $280 per head. During 1980–92 it was estimated that GNP per head declined in real terms by an average of 4.3% annually. The civilian administration elected in 1993 was anxious to restore links (effectively severed by the 1991 national conference) with the international financial community, in an attempt to address the urgent problems of budgetary and balance-of-payments imbalances. Negotiations with France, the World Bank and IMF during 1993 resulted in new inflows of financial and budgetary support, which were reinforced following the devaluation, by 50%, of the CFA franc in January 1994. Continued assistance is crucial if the government's new economic strategy for 1994–96, which aims primarily to reduce budgetary deficits, improve competitiveness and strengthen economic activity, is to succeed.

According to the World Bank, agriculture and livestock contributed 37% of the gross domestic product (GDP) in 1992, industry and mining 17%, and services 46%. Agriculture and livestock account for more than 85% of employment, with livestock-rearing alone accounting for about 20% of employment. Principal staple products are millet, maize, sorghum, rice and vegetables. Cow-peas, cotton and groundnuts are the principal cash crops. The only areas with sufficient rainfall for agricultural production are along the valley of the Niger river in the south-west of the country and the regions along the border with Nigeria. Food production is frequently inadequate to fulfil the country's needs, and there were cereals shortfalls of 250,000 metric tons in 1992 and 55,000 tons in 1993. The informal artisanal sector is of growing importance in the economy, employing an estimated 240,000 people in 1992. Similarly, the informal trading network has expanded at the expense of the formal structures, and Niger's formal trade has been in steady decline.

THE TRADITIONAL ECONOMY

With the exception of drought periods, expansion in the production of food crops has kept pace with population growth, and Niger became self-sufficient in food grains in 1980/81, although distribution problems continue to cause local shortages. Output of cereals in 1990/91 was below the previous year's level of 2.35m. tons; estimates by the Permanent Inter-State Committee on Drought Control in the Sahel put total production for 1990/91 at 1.6m. tons. In the 1991/92 season Niger's most plentiful rains for 30 years resulted in an increase of 64% in cereal production. This increase was reversed in 1992/93, owing to irregular rainfall and damage by insects and birds in growing areas. None the less, cereals stored from the previous year, without which there would have been a 50% shortfall in food supplies in about 2,500 villages, helped to offset the poor harvest.

Aid has been provided by multilateral agencies to expand the area under irrigation, while Italy has been funding a $29m. FAO project, over seven years, to counter soil erosion and to increase food production in the Keita valley. In 1985 the Nigerien government introduced an 'off-season' growing programme which was intended to compensate, in part, for the cereals deficit and which represented a distinct change from traditional methods of food-crop cultivation. The programme, which covers some 40,000 ha and involves about 400,000 people, consists mainly of a large number of small-scale operations using manually-provided irrigation. It is representative of a general trend towards smaller-scale projects involving co-operatives or individual farmers, which the government plans to maintain and reinforce. In 1991 an EC (now European Union—EU) rice development on 400 ha at Daibery was established, and included irrigation for co-operatives. However, participation in the off-season programme declined when normal rainfall returned and harvests recovered.

As food production generally has increased, output of groundnuts has declined sharply from a peak of 191,307 tons (unshelled) in 1967 to an average of only some 25,000 tons per year in the late 1980s and early 1990s. Cotton production has not fared much better than groundnuts, after a strong start—9,597 tons (unginned) in 1973/74, 50% up on the level of four years earlier—mainly as a result of investment in irrigated cultivation. Output reached a peak of 11,133 tons in 1975/76 but declined rapidly thereafter. Marketed production averaged less than 4,400 tons per year in 1988/89 - 1990/91, and was recorded at only 554 tons in 1991/92. Output of cow-peas has been more consistent: following a crop of 208,800 tons in 1987/88, production averaged some 280,000 tons in the following three years, and increased to 461,200 tons in 1991/92. Livestock ranks second to uranium as a source of foreign exchange earnings. There is a significant, although largely unrecorded, trade involving exports of live cattle to Nigeria, which was badly disrupted as a result of the closure of Nigeria's land borders between April 1984 and March 1986. As in the rest of the region, extensive stock-rearing made appreciable progress in the years following independence, stimulated by demand from the highly populated coastal region and Nigeria, with the result that livestock production expanded at an estimated 3% per year in the 1960s. The droughts of the 1970s and early 1980s, however, caused a sharp fall in numbers, either because of death or because of the removal of livestock to neighbouring countries, and the size of the cattle herd declined by two-thirds between 1972 and 1975, and by one-half in the crisis year of 1984. Although the good rains in 1990 and 1991 helped livestock numbers, estimates by the FAO put the number of cattle at 1.8m. in September 1992, and sheep and goats at 8.8m.—both significantly below pre-drought levels. Despite efforts to discourage nomadic production, the government has been unable to promote either intensive commercial livestock operations or dairy farming, owing to Niger's ecological and demographic conditions.

The anti-desertification campaign is a priority for the Nigerien government (desertification affected an average of 60,000 ha of land per year in 1980–85), and an effective programme of afforestation and environmental protection is proceeding.

MINING AND POWER

The mining and export of uranium plays a significant role in Niger's economy, representing an important source of budgetary revenue and providing most of the country's foreign exchange earnings. However, as demand and prices have weakened, the government has made efforts to encourage the development of the country's other mineral resources, which include cassiterite, coal, phosphates, iron ore, gold and petroleum, although few of these have yet been considered commercially viable.

Proven reserves of uranium are estimated at 280,000 tons. A processing plant at the Arlit uranium mine, in the desolate Aïr mountains, began production in 1971, with 410 tons of metal; output rose to 1,982 tons in 1980. The mining company, Société des mines de l'Aïr (SOMAÏR), is under French control; the majority interest is with the Compagnie générale des matières nucleaires (COGEMA—a subsidiary of the French government's Commissariat à l'énergie atomique) and French private interests, with the Nigerien government's Office nationale des ressources minières du Niger (ONAREM) holding a 37% share. Operating costs at the mine are high, owing to the remoteness of the site, and its output is transported by aircraft or overland to Cotonou, Benin. Production at the country's second uranium mine, at Akouta, was begun in late 1978 by a consortium—the Compagnie minière d'Akouta (COMINAK)—of the government, COGEMA, the Japanese Overseas Uranium Resources Development and the Spanish Empresa Nacional del Uranio. Output from the mine reached 2,200 tons in 1980 and total uranium output by Niger reached its peak in 1981 at 4,366 tons. SOMAÏR began to exploit the deposits at Taza (which contains proven reserves of 21,000 tons) in 1987. Total production of uranium averaged about 2,900 tons per year in 1987–91, and was 3,071 tons in 1992. The World Bank, which had criticized high production costs in Niger's mining sector, insisted on a full restructuring of the sector as a key element of the structural adjustment programme. Production costs at the mines operated by SOMAÏR and COMINAK during the first half of 1991 were put at 22,000 francs CFA/kg, compared with a market selling price of 12,000 francs CFA/kg. At the same time, the average world 'spot-market' price for uranium was only about 9,000 francs CFA/kg. Although the 1990–91 crisis in the region of the Persian (Arabian) Gulf gave a temporary fillip to the uranium sector, with France, in particular, anxious to secure its supplies, the French government remained determined to reduce the cost of its uranium purchases by 1993. By mid-1993 the price paid for Nigerien uranium by France and Japan (both of which purchase Niger's output of this mineral at premium prices) had been reduced to 15,450 francs CFA/kg, compared with 20,400 francs CFA/kg in 1990. In 1992 Niger's revenue from sales (of 2,505 tons) of uranium was estimated at 43,200m. francs CFA, compared with 88,415m. francs CFA (from sales of 2,951 tons) in 1986.

While it is possible that there may be a world uranium shortage by the end of the century, and that a producer cartel may emerge, Niger's existing cost structure would render it uncompetitive in relation to other African producers (such as Namibia and South Africa) as well as in comparison with other producing countries (such as Australia, Canada, China and members of the Commonwealth of Independent States). Plans to increase capacity by up to 5,000 tons per year have been postponed indefinitely, and the transitional government instigated negotiations with trade unions with a view to reducing costs. In 1992 only about 8% of the national budget was financed by sales of uranium, compared with 40% in 1979.

There is increasing foreign interest in the potential for the industrial-scale mining of Niger's gold reserves, most of which are located in the south-western Liptako region, near the border with Burkina Faso, and which have been exploited on a small scale since the early 1980s. Surveys of sites at Sirba, Téra and Gourouol, conducted by ONAREM, in co-operation with Canada, France, Japan, the UN Development Programme and the EU, have yielded encouraging results.

Other mineral resources include cassiterite, a tin-bearing ore mined in the Aïr region (with an estimated output, in terms of mineral content, of 70 tons in 1991, although production in subsequent years has reportedly been at a low level), iron ore at Say (deposits of some 650m. tons), calcium phosphates (some 2,000 tons per year were produced from open-cast mines at Tahoua until 1984, and there exists the prospect of much greater output from a 207m.-ton deposit at Tapoa) and gypsum. A modern salt mine is being developed at Tidekelt to serve the Arlit deposit. Coal deposits, estimated at 6m. tons, have been located at Anou-Anaren, to the north-west of Agadez. Production began in 1981, for use in power generation, and averaged almost 155,000 tons per year in 1985–90. Deposits of petroleum, located in the south-west, have not hitherto been deemed commercially exploitable, although further evaluation is under way. In September 1991 the government introduced new legislation to attract foreign participation in exploration for petroleum, and four permit areas have been opened up in the east, along the border with Chad. In early 1992 Elf Aquitaine, of France, and the US Exxon Corporation (both of which have five-year exploration permits from 1991) began seismic work on the previously-unexplored Agadem block, to the north of Lake Chad. Elf was also scheduled to drill three wells on its exploration permit in eastern Niger, while Hunt Oil of the USA was scheduled to begin exploratory drilling in the north-eastern Djado region, near the border with Libya. The French Fonds d'aide et de coopération has offered a grant of 6.2m. French francs to the Nigerien ministry of mines and energy, in support of a programme for a comprehensive evaluation of the country's industrial mineral resources.

Electricity consumption has risen rapidly in recent years, quadrupling between 1970 and 1987, when it reached 328m. kWh, with the major consumers being the uranium companies. Domestic generation, which is almost entirely thermal, covers about one-half of demand, and the remainder is met by supplies from Nigeria. There is a massive power development programme, stimulated by the unreliability of the Nigerian supply. The Arlit and Akouta thermal power station, which draws on domestic coal supply, entered operation in 1981 with an initial capacity of 16 MW, which was increased to 37.7 MW in 1982.

MANUFACTURING

As in most other west African countries, manufacturing takes the form of the processing of agricultural commodities and import substitution. World Bank estimates put the sector's contribution to GDP at about 7% in 1992 (representing about two-fifths of industry's contribution to GDP). There is a groundnut oil extraction plant (two plants were closed down in 1985, owing to the decline in domestic groundnut supplies), as well as cotton ginneries, rice mills, flour mills and tanneries. Import substitution has been stimulated by the very high cost of transport. A textile mill (capacity 1,600 tons per year) and a cement works (peak output of 100,000 tons) are in operation, and there are light industries serving the very limited local market (soap, beer, soft drinks, plastic products, metal goods, farm equipment, canned vegetables and construction materials). Although output is at a relatively low level, production of cotton is sufficient to meet a proportion of domestic requirements, while a small surplus is exported. The European Investment Bank is lending 684m. francs CFA for the modernization of the textile plant, and the French government 335m. francs CFA for the same purpose. Other plans for the expansion of the sector were suspended as a result of negotiations with the IMF and the World Bank for a structural adjustment programme which, from the mid-1980s, entailed progressively tighter controls on budget expenditure.

TRANSPORT INFRASTRUCTURE

The transport system is still inadequate, despite considerable road development—funded by the World Bank, the European Development Fund and, more recently, Saudi Arabia—including support for the 902-km all-weather road between Niamey and Zinder, opened in 1980, and a 651-km 'uranium road' from Arlit to Tahoua, which opened in 1981. At the end of 1990 there were an estimated 11,258 km of classified roads, of which about 3,265 km were paved. There is, at present, no railway: plans to extend the Cotonou - Parakou line from Benin elicited no interest from aid donors, and the scheme was postponed in late 1989. Most foreign trade is shipped through Cotonou, via the Organisation commune Bénin-Niger des chemins de fer et des transports. The emphasis in transport development is on diversifying and improving access to seaports: a road is being built to Lomé, Togo, via Burkina Faso, and the Agadez - Zinder section (428 km) of the Trans-Sahara Highway was being upgraded in the late 1980s and early 1990s. In addition, a second bridge is to be built over the River Niger at Gaya, to reinforce existing links with Malanville in Benin, at a cost of 2,250m. francs CFA, to be partly covered by France. There are international airports at Niamey and Agadez, and four major domestic airports.

FINANCE AND INVESTMENT

Niger's infrastructure (roads and power supplies, education and town planning) has absorbed about 60% of investments undertaken during recent years. In the directly productive sectors themselves, agriculture and livestock have, in the past, received more than one-half of total funding, while industry has received only 15%. Under the 1979–83 development plan the mining sector was to receive more than one-third of total investment, and the rural sector one-sixth, but for 1981–85 the revised plan provided for mining and agriculture to have approximately equal shares of just under one-quarter each.

As in other countries of francophone west Africa, some foreign aid has, in the past, taken the form of budget subsidies (1,300m. francs CFA in 1973/74) to make up the chronic deficit on the budget. In the late 1970s, however, the current budget registered a substantial surplus (21,300m. francs CFA in 1979/80) because of the rapid rise in government revenues from uranium—to 26,000m. francs CFA in that year. These receipts financed about one-third of the current budget as well as nearly all capital investment, which reached 39,400m. francs CFA in 1980/81. The decline in uranium revenues (because of lower prices and output) during the early 1980s transformed the current budget balance from a surplus of 15,200m. francs CFA in 1980/81 to a deficit of 51,880m. francs CFA in 1982/83. The doubling of Niger's debt-servicing burden over the same period (see below) necessitated the introduction of stringent austerity measures in subsequent years, in an attempt to limit the budget deficit. Current spending was first reduced, in 1983/84, and then held steady, partly as a result of cut-backs in public-sector employment and of the sale to private ownership of some parastatal enterprises. Some modest growth in both current and capital expenditure was envisaged in the budgets for 1986/87 - 1988/89, which were drafted with the co-operation of the IMF and the World Bank, with a three-year investment programme (valued at 302,600m. francs CFA). Government finances were to be aided by the restructuring of 10 state-owned companies and the transfer to private ownership or participation of a further 18 companies: these have, in the past, imposed a major burden on budgetary resources. In accordance with the conditions of an enhanced structural adjustment facility, granted by the IMF in 1989, fiscal austerity was to be maintained. The budget which took effect from October 1989 covered a 15-month period to the end of 1990; thereafter, budgets were to correspond with the calendar year. Although funding agreements with the IMF and the World Bank were suspended following the 1991 national conference, Amadou Cheiffou's transitional government introduced further austerity measures in late 1991, in an attempt to alleviate the serious financing deficit which had been inherited from the previous administration. The measures included the reduction of administrative costs in the public sector, and the imposition of a levy on salaries in the civil service. The 1992 budget envisaged that revenue and expenditure would balance at 106,800m. francs CFA. Fiscal receipts in that year amounted to 50,000m. francs CFA, while expenditure on wages in the public sector totalled 38,000m. francs CFA.

Niger's public finances declined to such an extent during 1993 that the government was unable to pay civil servants for three months. The budget for that year, normally effective from January, was not finalized until August: recurrent expenditure of 108,300m. francs CFA was envisaged, to be financed equally by internal and external sources. Debt-servicing was to account for 60,000m. francs CFA of expenditure. An attempt to reduce expenditure on salaries, from 38,000m. francs CFA in 1992 to 35,000m. francs CFA in 1993, was strongly opposed by the trade unions (see Recent History) and it was not until October that agreement was reached on reductions in salaries and compensatory measures for arrears. Budgetary aid was approved by France both in 1993 and after the devaluation of the CFA franc in January 1994.

With France assisting the Ousmane administration in the preparation of a major restructuring programme, both the IMF and World Bank were quick to respond with financial assistance following the CFA devaluation. The IMF approved a $26m. stand-by credit in March 1994, in support of a programme that aimed to increase real GDP growth to about 4% in 1994 and to levels in excess of this in subsequent years. The budgetary deficit was to be reduced to 5.7% of GDP in 1994 (compared with an estimated 7.6% in 1993), partially by means of new tax and administrative measures. The programme envisaged the cash settlement of one-half of domestic payments' arrears and the elimination of external arrears, assisted by the cancellation and rescheduling of obligations to the 'Paris Club' of Western creditor governments.

Budget proposals for 1994 were revised to take account of the currency's depreciation, envisaging consolidated expenditure of 166,300m. francs CFA. The increase in recurrent expenditure (including salaries) was, however, restricted to only 26.5%, to 57,600m. francs CFA. Investment spending conversely, was to increase by 73.6%, to 108,700m. francs CFA. France pledged bugetary assistance of 85,000m. francs CFA. Following the devaluation, the anticipated rise in consumer prices in 1994 was 36.7%, and it was hoped that inflation would fall thereafter to 7.3% in 1995 and 2.9% in 1996. Unlike other countries in the Franc Zone, Niger did not for long attempt to contain inflation through widespread price-control measures. It did, however, try to restrict wage demands from public-sector workers, approving a 5% - 12% increase while unions demanded rises of 30% - 50%.

FOREIGN TRADE AND PAYMENTS

Exports are only partly recorded, but there was evidently a rise—if erratic—in the 1960s, followed by more sustained growth in later years. Fluctuations in export earnings traditionally reflected the performance of groundnuts, which normally accounted for more than one-half of the total, but exports of groundnuts were suspended in 1974 and were almost nil in 1975. The other major export item—livestock—showed a steady increase overall until 1973. Earnings continued to expand, despite the downturn in these traditional exports, because of the beginning of uranium production. In 1973 uranium became the major export, and within two years it was accounting for around two-thirds of all export earnings. Uranium earnings were responsible for the rapid rise in export receipts in the late 1970s and reached a peak of 100,804m. francs CFA in 1980—three times the level of 1977. Imports have almost always exceeded exports, although by a less substantial margin than in some countries of francophone west Africa. The rise in uranium earnings was matched by the rise in import spending, reflecting higher petroleum prices and investment in capital equipment for the mining industry. In 1981–82, however, the trade gap widened because the continued rise in import spending coincided with a decline in export earnings, as uranium exports fell in both volume and value. Since 1980 the annual trade balance has fluctuated widely, deficits have almost always been very much higher than the levels recorded in the late 1970s (between 3,000m. - 9,000m. francs CFA), owing to the depression in the uranium market and the severe grain shortfall in the drought years. That small trade surpluses, of 3,000m. and 3,900m.

francs CFA respectively, were recorded in 1991 and 1992 was attributable to a lack of funds available for imports, rather than to an increase in export earnings.

With merchandise trade in frequent deficit, compounded by high transportation costs (reflecting the country's landlocked position), the deficit on the current account of the balance of payments has been contained only by external aid. Inflows of official development assistance averaged $342m. per year in 1985–91. Total official assistance in 1991 was equivalent to 16.2% of GNP in that year. External borrowing to compensate the current payments' deficit has resulted in a sharp escalation in the foreign debt, from $863m. at the end of 1980 to $1,711m. in 1992. Meanwhile, export earnings have declined, with the result that as early as 1982 Niger's debt-service ratio was equivalent to more than one-half of the country's foreign earnings. With the continuing depression in the world uranium market, Niger's major official creditors agreed, in 1983, to reschedule the country's external debt over a nine-year period, with payment to begin after four-and-a-half years. Their action followed the approval of stand-by credits by the IMF and the introduction of austerity budgets for every year since 1982/83. As a result of this accord and subsequent restructuring agreements with both official and commercial creditors, the debt-service ratio has been contained below its 1982 peak, despite the continued sharp rise in the foreign debt. Under the terms of the structural adjustment programme that Niger agreed with the World Bank, no new commercial borrowing was to be contracted before 1988, and no loans with a repayment period of less than 12 years, other than IMF stand-by credits. However, with debt-service payments on commitments made up to the end of 1986 forecast to equal more than $100m. for the next few years (representing a debt-service ratio of 25% – 30%), Niger was classified as 'debt-distressed' by the World Bank. In April and December 1988 the 'Paris Club' rescheduled portions of the country's public debt, although the amounts involved were relatively small ($38m. of total liabilities of $575m. at the end of 1987). The second agreement was reached in accordance with a system of exceptional debt-relief (that had been agreed in principle at the summit meeting of industrialized nations, held in Toronto, Canada, in June 1988), which provided creditors with three alternative methods of debt-relief. In September 1990 France's Caisse centrale de coopération économique agreed to cancel debts totalling 80,000m. francs CFA, thereby reducing Niger's external debt by about 18%. This was followed by a further rescheduling of debt, valued at $116m., by the 'Paris Club', again in accordance with the so-called 'Toronto terms'. Debt-servicing obligations were thus equivalent to 25% of foreign earnings in 1990, compared with 41% in 1988. A new agreement with the 'Paris Club' in March 1994, in accordance with the more concessionary 'Trinidad terms', effectively entailed the cancellation of one-half of the debt-servicing owed to government creditors (equivalent to 32,300m. francs (CFA) in that year. Niger was the first country to secure World Bank funding to buy back commercial debt at market rates, and received a $10m. facility from the Bank's concessionary affiliate, the International Development Association. Some $360m. was owed to commercial banks at the end of 1989, rising to $375m. in 1990. Banks were given the option of receiving immediate payment at 18% of the value of the debt or of receiving repayment of the entire debt in 21 years' time, guaranteed by US government bonds.

Statistical Survey

Source (unless otherwise stated): Direction de la Statistique et de l'Informatique, Ministère des Finances et du Plan, BP 720, Niamey; tel. 72-23-74; telex 5463; fax 73-33-71.

Area and Population

AREA, POPULATION AND DENSITY

Area (sq km)	1,267,000*
Population (census results)	
20 November 1977	
Males	2,514,532
Females	2,583,895
Total	5,098,427
10–24 May 1988 (provisional)	7,249,596
Population (UN estimates at mid-year)†	
1990	7,731,000
1991	7,986,000
1992	8,252,000
Density (per sq km) at mid-1992	6.5

* 489,191 sq miles.

† Source: UN, *World Population Prospects: The 1992 Revision.*

ETHNIC GROUPS (estimated population at 1 July 1972)*

Hausa	2,279,000	Tuareg, etc	127,000
Djerma-Songhai	1,001,000	Beriberi-Manga	386,000
Fulani (Peulh)	450,000	**Total**	4,243,000

* Provisional figures. Revised total is 4,239,000.

PRINCIPAL TOWNS (population in 1977)

Niamey (capital)	225,314	Tahoua	31,265
Zinder	58,436	Agadez	20,475
Maradi	45,852	Birni N'Konni	15,227

1981 (estimates): Niamey 360,000; Zinder 75,000.

BIRTHS AND DEATHS (UN estimates, annual averages)

	1975–80	1980–85	1985–90
Birth rate (per 1,000)	52.2	52.0	51.7
Death rate (per 1,000)	23.8	22.1	20.4

Expectation of life (UN estimates, years at birth, 1985–90): 44.5 (males 42.9; females 46.1).

Source: UN, *World Population Prospects: The 1992 Revision.*

ECONOMICALLY ACTIVE POPULATION
(ILO estimates, '000 persons at mid-1980)

	Males	Females	Total
Agriculture, etc	1,314	1,296	2,610
Industry	45	2	47
Services	130	78	209
Total labour force	1,489	1,376	2,865

Source: ILO, *Economically Active Population Estimates and Projections, 1950-2025.*

Mid-1992 (estimates in '000): Agriculture, etc. 3,569; Total 4,130 (Source: FAO, *Production Yearbook*).

Agriculture

PRINCIPAL CROPS ('000 metric tons)

	1990	1991	1992
Maize	4	4	3
Millet	1,113	1,819	1,784
Sorghum	286	561	393
Rice (paddy)	73†	75	40†
Sugar cane*	140	140	140
Sweet potatoes*	35	35	35
Cassava (Manioc)*	213	216	218
Onions (dry)	224	169	170*
Tomatoes	81	45	45*
Other vegetables	35	35	36*
Pulses	414	469†	608*
Dates*	7	7	7
Other fruit*	37	37	38
Groundnuts (in shell)	18	46	40
Cottonseed	1	1†	1*
Cotton (lint)	1	1*	1*
Tobacco (leaves)*	1	1	1

* FAO estimate(s). † Unofficial figure.

Source: FAO, *Production Yearbook.*

Cow-peas ('000 metric tons): 320.4 in 1989/90; 223.5 in 1990/91; 461.2 in 1991/92 (Source: Banque centrale des états de l'Afrique de l'ouest).

LIVESTOCK ('000 head, year ending September)

	1990	1991	1992
Horses*	82	82	82
Asses	431	449	450*
Cattle	1,711	1,790	1,800*
Camels	366	356†	363†
Pigs*	37	38	38
Sheep	3,098	3,253	3,400*
Goats	4,971	5,214	5,400*

Poultry (million)*: 18 in 1990; 19 in 1991; 20 in 1992.

* FAO estimate(s). † Unofficial figure.

Source: FAO, *Production Yearbook.*

LIVESTOCK PRODUCTS (FAO estimates, '000 metric tons)

	1990	1991	1992
Beef and veal	32	34	35
Mutton and lamb	12	12	12
Goats' meat	19	20	20
Pig meat	1	1	1
Poultry meat	21	22	23
Other meat	18	17	19
Cows' milk	140	148	152
Sheep's milk	12	12	12
Goats' milk	82	86	87
Cheese	11.4	11.8	12.0
Butter	3.9	4.1	4.2
Poultry eggs	8.5	8.7	8.8
Cattle hides	4.2	4.3	4.3
Sheep skins	1.5	1.5	1.5
Goat skins	3.2	3.3	3.3

Source: FAO, *Production Yearbook.*

Forestry

ROUNDWOOD REMOVALS
(FAO estimates, '000 cubic metres, excluding bark)

	1990	1991	1992
Industrial wood	306	316	326
Fuel wood	4,650	4,803	4,963
Total	4,956	5,119	5,289

Source: FAO, *Yearbook of Forest Products.*

Fishing

('000 metric tons, live weight)

	1989	1990	1991
Total catch	4.8	3.4	3.2

Source: FAO, *Yearbook of Fishery Statistics.*

Mining

('000 metric tons, unless otherwise indicated)

	1989	1990	1991
Salt*	3	3	3
Gypsum*	3†	3	3
Hard coal†	157	158	157
Tin (metric tons)‡§	63	38	70
Uranium (metric tons)‡	2,962	2,831	2,777

* Data from the US Bureau of Mines.
† Provisional or estimated figure.
‡ Data refer to the metal content of ore.
§ Data from *International Tin Statistics.*

Source: UN, *Industrial Statistics Yearbook.*

1992: Uranium (metal content of ore, metric tons): 3,071 (Sources: Société des Mines de l'Aïr; Compagnie Minière d'Akouta).

Industry

SELECTED PRODUCTS
('000 metric tons, unless otherwise indicated)

	1987	1988	1989
Salted, dried or smoked fish*	1.0†	1.0	1.1
Soft drinks ('000 hectolitres)	105	98	n.a.
Woven cotton fabrics (million sq metres)†	39	20	n.a.
Cement‡	29	40	27
Electric energy (million kWh)	157	160	163

1990: Cement ('000 metric tons) 27‡; Electric energy (million kWh) 165.

1991: Cement ('000 metric tons) 28‡; Electric Energy (million kWh) 168.

* Data from the FAO.
† Provisional or estimated figures.
‡ Data from the US Bureau of Mines.

Source: UN, *Industrial Statistics Yearbook.*

Finance

CURRENCY AND EXCHANGE RATES

Monetary Units

100 centimes = 1 franc de la Communauté financière africaine (CFA).

French Franc, Sterling and Dollar Equivalents (31 March 1994)

1 French franc = 100 francs CFA;
£1 sterling = 846.40 francs CFA;
US $1 = 570.14 francs CFA;
1,000 francs CFA = £1.181 = $1.754.

Average Exchange Rate (francs CFA per US $)

1991	282.11
1992	264.69
1993	283.16

Note: An exchange rate of 1 French franc = 50 francs CFA, established in 1948, remained in force until January 1994, when the CFA franc was devalued by 50%, with the exchange rate adjusted to 1 French franc = 100 francs CFA.

CONSOLIDATED BUDGET*

(million francs CFA)

Revenue†	1988	1989	1990
Fiscal receipts	66,903	64,793	82,674
Taxes on income and profits	14,974	17,647	20,900
Individual taxes	6,904	8,127	9,700
Corporate and business taxes	7,470	9,070	10,200
Taxes on goods and services	21,320	18,458	23,856
Turnover taxes	9,450	8,200	10,000
Consumption taxes	9,950	8,073	10,066
Taxes on international trade and transactions	27,492	25,076	32,930
Import duties	22,490	18,760	24,659
Export duties	4,159	5,774	7,745
Other current receipts	11,350	18,813	26,991
Capital receipts	200	200	1,605
Aid, grants and subsidies	61,992	54,741	56,370
Total	140,445	138,547	167,640

Expenditure	1988	1989	1990
General public services	26,665	29,980	34,702
Defence	5,493	5,749	12,315
Public order and security	4,953	5,448	6,134
Education	21,382	24,815	24,409
Health	9,985	11,350	12,434
Social security and welfare	—	—	135
Housing and community services	21,876	21,622	19,865
Other community and social services	2,373	2,527	2,957
Economic services	70,061	74,276	70,754
Agriculture, forestry and fishing	38,981	44,017	37,307
Mining, manufacturing and construction	2,477	2,461	2,785
Electricity and other energy resources	3,360	3,905	7,132
Transport and communications	22,824	20,739	20,931
Other economic services	2,419	3,154	2,599
Debt-repayment	41,680	37,411	38,796
Other purposes	9,529	2,131	15,185
Total	213,997	215,309	237,686

* Figures for 1988 and 1989 refer, in both cases, to the financial year ending 30 September; figures for 1990 refer to 1 October 1989–31 December 1990.

† Revenue excludes net borrowing: 73,553m. francs CFA in 1988; 76,762m. francs CFA in 1989; 70,046m. francs CFA in 1990.

Source: Banque centrale des états de l'Afrique de l'ouest.

1991 (draft budget, million francs CFA): Recurrent budget balanced at 106,670; Investment budget (incl. borrowing) balanced at 80,254.

1992 (draft budget, million francs CFA): Recurrent budget balanced at 106,800.

1993 (draft budget, million francs CFA): Recurrent budget balanced at 108,300; Investment budget (incl. borrowing) balanced at 64,367.

1994 (draft budget, million francs CFA): Recurrent budget balanced at 57,600m.; Investment budget (incl. borrowing) balanced at 108,700m.

CENTRAL BANK RESERVES (US $ million at 31 December)

	1991	1992	1993
Gold*	3.9	3.8	4.1
IMF special drawing rights	0.4	—	0.6
Reserve position in IMF	12.2	11.8	11.8
Foreign exchange	190.1	213.2	179.7
Total	206.7	228.8	196.1

* Valued at market-related prices.

Source: IMF, *International Financial Statistics.*

MONEY SUPPLY ('000 million francs CFA at 31 December)

	1991	1992	1993
Currency outside banks	40.97	39.66	48.35
Demand deposits at deposit money banks*	34.71	30.51	28.83
Checking deposits at post office	4.25	1.51	1.92
Total money (incl. others)*	79.93	71.70	79.52

* Excluding the deposits of public enterprises of an administrative or social nature.

Source: IMF, *International Financial Statistics.*

COST OF LIVING
(Consumer Price Index for Africans in Niamey; base: 1989 = 100)*

	1991	1992
Food	94.2	91.6
Clothing	100.8	101.9
All items (incl. others)	96.1	94.5

* Except rent.

Source: International Labour Office, *Year Book of Labour Statistics*.

NATIONAL ACCOUNTS
(million francs CFA at current prices)

Expenditure on the Gross Domestic Product

	1988	1989	1990*
Government final consumption expenditure	104,994	124,420	117,567
Private final consumption expenditure	446,691	505,323	505,293
Increase in stocks	53,618	–506	7,992
Gross fixed capital formation	81,008	85,391	79,967
Total domestic expenditure	686,311	714,628	710,819
Exports of goods and services	140,500	129,100	114,512
Less Imports of goods and services	148,600	151,126	142,361
GDP in purchasers' values	678,211	692,602	682,970

* Provisional figures.

Gross Domestic Product by Economic Activity

	1988	1989	1990*
Agriculture, hunting, forestry and fishing	240,164	236,903	238,095
Mining and quarrying	44,671	43,857	34,899
Manufacturing	40,856	43,954	44,194
Electricity, gas and water	15,323	17,465	12,315
Construction	16,004	14,824	17,042
Trade, restaurants and hotels	130,608	130,463	137,732
Transport, storage and communications	31,798	28,717	27,477
Other market services†	53,837	58,106	58,815
Non-market services	85,846	98,807	94,324
Sub-total	659,107	673,096	664,893
Import duties	19,104	19,506	18,077
GDP in purchasers' values	678,211	692,602	682,970

* Provisional figures.

† After deduction of imputed bank service charge.

Source: Banque centrale des états de l'Afrique de l'ouest.

BALANCE OF PAYMENTS (US $ million)

	1990	1991	1992
Merchandise exports f.o.b.	303.4	283.9	283.0
Merchandise imports f.o.b.	–337.5	–273.3	–331.0
Trade balance	–34.2	10.6	–47.9
Exports of services	69.1	57.1	52.1
Imports of services	–207.2	–157.0	–86.7
Other income received	2.2	1.4	—
Other income paid	–49.2	–38.6	–36.6
Private unrequited transfers (net)	–48.8	–37.9	–37.4
Official unrequited transfers (net)	184.4	157.4	111.9
Current balance	–83.7	–7.1	–44.6
Capital (net)	22.8	–22.3	9.4
Net errors and omissions	–25.2	–40.4	16.1
Overall balance	–86.2	–69.8	–19.2

Source: IMF, *International Financial Statistics*.

External Trade

Source: Banque centrale des états de l'Afrique de l'ouest.

PRINCIPAL COMMODITIES (million francs CFA)

Imports c.i.f.	1985*	1987†	1988
Dairy products	3,150	1,264	3,806
Unprocessed foods of plant origin	41,419	17,120	15,334
Cereals	36,094	12,400	9,083
Processed foodstuffs	8,834	7,865	8,327
Sugar and confectionery	4,784	4,666	4,262
Refined petroleum products	16,944	4,943	6,163
Inedible crude materials (except fuels)	5,243	4,095	3,949
Fats and oils	2,993	2,990	1,157
Non-electrical machinery	13,660	8,071	11,179
Electrical machinery	4,915	3,216	5,438
Road transport equipment	12,920	9,794	13,792
Chemicals	12,500	10,682	13,993
Miscellaneous manufactured articles	28,169	21,462	29,407
Cotton yarn and fabrics	6,482	3,591	4,176
Total (incl. others)	154,787	93,388	115,193

Exports f.o.b.	1985*	1987†	1988
Live animals	10,905	372	3,463
Vegetables	2,112	1,580	2,372
Uranium ore	74,083	85,394	74,928
Hides and skins	2,093	312	641
Machinery and transport equipment	1,300	2,229	1,680
Total (incl. others)	93,901	93,895	85,941

* Provisional figures.

† Figures for 1986 are not available.

PRINCIPAL TRADING PARTNERS (million francs CFA)*

Imports c.i.f.	1983	1984†	1985†
Algeria	1,641	985	387
Belgium and Luxembourg	1,430	1,557	2,152
Brazil	1,598	2,509	2,852
Canada	812	1,457	3,434
China, People's Republic	1,229	4,468	5,003
Côte d'Ivoire	5,125	7,398	11,207
France	40,489	34,075	42,877
Germany, Federal Republic	4,468	5,487	8,551
Italy	1,200	2,158	4,073
Japan	3,613	5,239	5,842
Netherlands	1,895	2,680	2,886
Nigeria	39,031	18,433	10,358
Pakistan	606	3,503	4,827
Senegal	1,957	1,627	1,339
Thailand	467	1,750	4,564
United Kingdom	2,223	2,286	3,110
USA	5,633	6,140	17,666
Total (incl. others)	123,288	124,620	154,787

Exports f.o.b.	1983	1984*	1985*
Algeria	201	821	3,157
Burkina Faso	333	1,888	463
Côte d'Ivoire	311	1,130	1,599
France	54,727	61,427	61,641
Germany, Federal Republic	5,136	7,066	71
Italy	3,547	1,180	1,084
Japan	25,942	20,894	5,676
Mali	1,142	2,063	326
Nigeria	12,608	12,618	12,859
Spain	5,913	3,900	5,474
Total (incl. others)	113,896	119,495	93,901

* Imports by country of production; exports by country of destination.

† Provisional figures.

Transport

ROAD TRAFFIC (vehicles in use at 31 December)

	1987*	1989†‡	1990‡
Cars	27,254	31,342	31,427
Buses and coaches	2,253	2,559	2,695
Goods vehicles	5,687	5,968	6,073
Vans	14,807	n.a.	n.a.
Tractors, trailers and semi-trailers	4,696	2,144§	2,217§
Motor cycles and mopeds	8,925	n.a.	n.a.

* Source: Direction des Transports, Niamey.
† Figures for 1988 are not available.
‡ Source: International Road Federation, *World Road Statistics.*
§ Trailers and semi-trailers only.

CIVIL AVIATION (traffic on scheduled services)*

	1989	1990	1991
Kilometres flown (million)	2	2	2
Passengers carried ('000)	74	76	64
Passenger-km (million)	224	232	203
Freight ton-km (million)	18	18	16
Mail ton-km (million)	1	1	1

* Including an apportionment of the traffic of Air Afrique.
Source: UN, *Statistical Yearbook.*

Tourism

	1988	1989	1990
Tourist arrivals ('000)	33	24	21
Tourist receipts (US $ million)	11	13	15

Source: UN, *Statistical Yearbook.*

Communications Media

	1989	1990	1991
Radio receivers ('000 in use)	440	460	480
Television receivers ('000 in use)	30	35	37
Telephones ('000 in use)*	13	13	14
Daily newspapers			
Number	n.a.	1	n.a.
Average circulation ('000 copies)	n.a.	5	n.a.

* Estimates.
Sources: UNESCO, *Statistical Yearbook*; UN Economic Commission for Africa, *African Statistical Yearbook.*

Education

(1990, unless otherwise indicated)

	Institutions	Teachers	Students		
			Males	Females	Total
Pre-primary	65	263	4,914	4,520	9,434
Primary	2,807	8,759	235,480	133,252	368,732
Secondary:					
General	n.a.	2,534	52,453	21,884	74,337
Teacher training	n.a.	77*	917	661	1,578
Vocational	n.a.	119	769	74	843
University level	n.a.	341†	3,831*	675*	4,506*

* 1989 figure. † 1988 figure.
Source: UNESCO, *Statistical Yearbook.*

Directory

The Constitution

The Constitution of the Third Republic of Niger was approved in a national referendum on 26 December 1992, and was promulgated in January 1993.

The Constitution emphasizes the secular nature of Nigerien society.

The President of the Republic is elected, by universal adult suffrage, for a period of five years (renewable only once). The unicameral legislature, the Assemblée nationale, is similarly elected with a five-year mandate. All elections are conducted in the context of a multi-party system.

The President of the Republic, who is Head of State, appoints the Prime Minister, and, on the latter's recommendation, other ministers. The Council of Ministers is responsible to the Assemblée nationale.

The Assemblée nationale appoints a Speaker from among its 83 members. The President of the Republic may dissolve the legislature.

The rights, freedoms and obligations of the individual and of the press, political organizations and other associations are among the principles enshrined in the Constitution. Also guaranteed is the independence of the judiciary.

The Government

HEAD OF STATE

President of the Republic: MAHAMANE OUSMANE (inaugurated 16 April 1993).

COUNCIL OF MINISTERS*
(September 1994)

Prime Minister: MAHAMADOU ISSOUFOU.

Minister of National Defence: AMADOU TAHIROU.

Minister of the Interior: OUSMANE OUMAROU.

Minister of Foreign Affairs and Co-operation: ABDOURAHAMANE HAMA.

Minister of Finance and Planning: ABDALLAH BOUREÏMA.

Minister of Trade, Transport and Tourism: SOULEY ABDOULAYE.

Minister of Mines and Energy: GADO FOUMAKOYE.

Minister of Public Health: MAHAMANE KOULLOU.

Minister of Equipment, Housing and Territorial Development: AMADOU LAOUALI.

Minister of Social Welfare, Population and Women's Affairs: MARIAMA ALI.

Minister of Industry and Handicrafts: EMMOUD EFFAD.

Minister of Secondary and Higher Education and Research: DJIBO GARBA.

Minister of the Civil Service, Labour and Employment: MADOUGOU SALISSOU.

Minister in charge of Relations with Parliament and Spokesperson for the Government: MOCTAR DIALLO.

Minister of Communications, Culture, Youth and Sports: MASSAOUDOU HASSOUMI.

Minister of Justice and Keeper of the Seals: MALLAM ADAM KANDINE.

Minister of Agriculture and Livestock-Rearing: DJOULDE SADIO.

Minister of Water Resources and the Environment: SOUMANA BILLO.

Minister of Administration Reform and Decentralization: MOHAMED IBRAHIM IBBA.

There are also 10 secretaries of state.

* MAHAMADOU ISSOUFOU resigned as Prime Minister in late September 1994, and was replaced by SOULEY ABDOULAYE, previously the Minister of Trade, Transport and Tourism.

MINISTRIES

Office of the President of the Republic: Palais Présidentiel, Niamey.

Office of the Prime Minister: Niamey.

Ministry of Administrative Reform and Decentralization: Niamey.

Ministry of Agriculture and Livestock-Rearing: BP 10427, Niamey; tel. 73-31-55.

Ministry of the Civil Service, Labour and Employment: Niamey; tel. 72-25-01; telex 5283.

Ministry of Communications, Culture, Youth and Sports: Niamey; tel. 72-24-89; telex 5214.

Ministry of Equipment, Housing and Territorial Development: Niamey; tel. 72-25-01; telex 5283.

Ministry of Finance and Planning: BP 720, Niamey; tel. 72-23-74; telex 5463; fax 73-33-71.

Ministry of Foreign Affairs and Co-operation: BP 396, Niamey; tel. 72-29-07; telex 5200.

Ministry of Industry and Handicrafts: Niamey.

Ministry of the Interior: Niamey; tel. 72-21-76; telex 5214.

Ministry of Justice: Niamey; tel. 72-20-94; telex 5214.

Ministry of Mines and Energy: BP 11700, Niamey; tel. 73-45-82; telex 5214.

Ministry of National Defence: BP 626, Niamey; tel. 72-20-76; telex 5291.

Ministry of National Education: Quartier Yantala Haut, BP 11897, Niamey; tel. 72-25-26.

Ministry of Public Health: BP 623, Niamey; tel. 72-27-82; telex 5533.

Ministry of Social Welfare, Population and Women's Affairs: Niamey.

Ministry of Trade, Transport and Tourism: BP 12130, Niamey; tel. 73-43-82; telex 5467.

Ministry of Water Resources and the Environment: Niamey.

President and Legislature

PRESIDENT

Presidential election, First Ballot, 27 February 1993

Candidate	% of votes
TANDJA MAMADOU (MNSD—Nassara)	34.22
MAHAMANE OUSMANE (CDS—Rahama)	26.59
MAHAMADOU ISSOUFOU (PNDS—Tarayya)	15.92
MOUMOUNI AMADOU DJERMAKOYE (ANDP—Zaman Lahiya)	15.24
ILLA KANE (UPDP—Shamuwa)	2.55
OUMAROU GARBA YOUSSOUFOU (PPN—RDA)	1.99
KAZELMA OUMAR TAYA (PSDN—Alheri)	1.82
DJIBO BAKARY (UDFP—Sawaba)	1.68
Total	100.00

Second Ballot, 27 March 1993

Candidate	% of votes
MAHAMANE OUSMANE	55.42
TANDJA MAMADOU	44.58
Total	100.00

ASSEMBLÉE NATIONALE

Speaker: MOUMOUNI AMADOU DJERMAKOYE.

General Election, 14 February 1993

Party	Seats
MNSD—Nassara	29
CDS—Rahama*	22
PNDS—Tarayya*	13
ANDP—Zaman Lahiya*	11
PPN—RDA*	2
UDFP—Sawaba	2
UPDP—Shamuwa	2
PSDN—Alheri*	1
UDPS—Amana*	1
Total	83

* Denotes organizations participating in the Alliance des forces de changement (see below), which subsequently formed a parliamentary majority. The PNDS—Tarayya withdrew from the alliance in September 1994.

Political Organizations

Twelve (of the 18 legalized) political parties contested seats at the February 1993 legislative elections:

Alliance des forces de changement (AFC): a coalition of nine anti-MNSD—Nassara parties, established following the elections to form a parliamentary majority.

Alliance nigérienne pour la démocratie et le progrès—Zaman Lahiya (ANDP—Zaman Lahiya): Leader MOUMOUNI AMADOU DJERMAKOYE.

Convention démocratique et social—Rahama (CDS—Rahama): Party of President Mahamane Ousmane.

Parti progressiste nigérien—Rassemblement démocratique africain (PPN—RDA): associated with the late President Diori; Leaders OUMAROU GARBA YOUSSOUFOU, LÉOPOLD KAZIENDE.

Part républicain pour les libertés et le progrès au Niger—Nakowa (PRLPN—Nakowa): not represented in Assemblée nationale.

Parti social-démocrate nigérien—Alheri (PSDN—Alheri): Leader KAZELMA OUMAR TAYA.

Union pour la démocratie et le progrès—Amici (UDP—Amici): not represented in Assemblée nationale.

Union pour la démocratie et le progrès social—Amana (UDPS—Amana).

Union nigérienne démocratique—Sawaba (UND—Sawaba): pre-independence party; not represented in Assemblée nationale; Leader PASCAL MAMADOU.

Mouvement national pour une société de développement—Nassara (MNSD—Nassara): f. 1988 as MNSD, name changed in 1991; sole party 1988–90; Pres. Col (retd) TANDJA MAMADOU.

Parti nigérien pour la démocratie et le socialisme—Tarayya (PNDS—Tarayya): mem. of AFC until Sept. 1994; Leader MAHAMADOU ISSOUFOU.

Union démocratique des forces progressistes—Sawaba (UDFP—Sawaba): claims to comprise the 'original' elements of the UND - Sawaba; Leaders DJIBO BAKARY, ISSOUFOU ASSOUMANE.

Union des patriotes démocratiques et progressistes—Shamuwa (UPDP—Shamuwa): Leaders Prof. ANDRÉ SALIFOU, ILLA KANE.

Diplomatic Representation

EMBASSIES IN NIGER

Algeria: ave des Zarmakoye, BP 142, Niamey; tel. 72-31-65; telex 5262; Ambassador: RACHID AKTOUF.

Belgium: BP 10192, Niamey; tel. 73-34-47; telex 5329; fax 73-37-56; Ambassador: JEAN-FRANÇOIS BRANDERS.

Benin: BP 11544, Niamey; tel. 72-39-19; Ambassador: KOLAWOLÉ IDJI.

China (Taiwan): Niamey; Ambassador: LING CHING-HONG.

Egypt: Nouveau Plateau, Niamey; tel. 73-33-55; telex 5245; Ambassador: Dr SOBHY MOHAMED NAFEH.

France: BP 10660, Niamey; tel. 72-24-31; telex 5220; Ambassador: JEAN-FRANÇOIS LIONNET.

Germany: ave du Général de Gaulle, BP 629, Niamey; tel. 72-25-34; telex 5223; Ambassador: SEPP J. WOELKER.

Iran: ave de la Présidence, Niamey; tel. 72-21-98; Chargé d'affaires: FAGHIH ALI ABADI MEHDI.

Libya: Rond-point du Grand Hôtel, POB 683, Niamey; tel. 73-47-92; telex 5429; Sec. of People's Cttee: AHMED KHALIFA ERRAJEL.

Mauritania: Yantala, BP 12519, Niamey; tel. 72-38-93; Ambassador: MOHAMED EL HOUSSEIN OULD HABIBOU ALLAH.

Morocco: ave du Président Lubke, BP 12403, Niamey; tel. 73-40-84; telex 5205; fax 74-14-27; Ambassador: TAHAR NEJJAR.

Nigeria: BP 11130, Niamey; tel. 73-24-10; telex 5259; Ambassador: KABIRU AHMED.

Pakistan: BP 10426, Niamey; tel. 72-35-84; telex 5268; Chargé d'affaires: IRFAN-UR-REHMAN RAJA.

Russia: BP 10153, Niamey; tel. 73-27-40; telex 5539; Ambassador: VITALY YAKOVLEVICH LITVINE.

Saudi Arabia: Yantala, BP 339, Niamey; tel. 72-32-15; telex 5279; Ambassador: GHASSAN SAID SADEK RACHACH.

Tunisia: ave du Général de Gaulle, BP 742, Niamey; tel. 72-26-03; telex 5379; Ambassador: RHIDA TNANI.

USA: Yantala, BP 11201, Niamey; tel. 72-26-61; telex 5444; Ambassador: JOHN S. DAVISON.

Judicial System

Attorney-General: El Hadj MATI OUSMANE.

Supreme Court: Niamey; Pres. MAHAMANE MALLAM AOUMI.

High Court of Justice: Niamey; competent to indict the President of the Republic and all other state officials (past and present) in relation to all matters of state except high treason and other crimes against state security; Pres. MOUTARY MAMANE.

Court of State Security: Niamey; competent to try cases not within the jurisdiction of the High Court of Justice; incorporates a martial court; Pres. M. MAÏ-MAÏGANA.

Court of Appeal: Niamey; court of appeal for judgements of **Criminal** and **Assize Courts** (the latter at Niamey, Maradi, Tahoua and Zinder).

Courts of First Instance: located at Niamey (with sub-divisions at Dosso and Tillabéry), Maradi, Tahoua (sub-divisions at Agadez, Arlit and Birni N'Konni) and Diffa (sub-division at Diffa).

Labour Courts: function at each Court of the First Instance and sub-division thereof.

Religion

It is estimated that more than 85% of the population are Muslims, 0.5% are Christians and the remainder follow traditional beliefs.

ISLAM

The most influential Islamic groups are the Tijaniyya, the Senoussi and the Hamallists.

CHRISTIANITY

Various Protestant missions maintain 13 centres, with a personnel of 90.

The Roman Catholic Church

Niger comprises a single diocese, directly responsible to the Holy See. The diocese participates in the Bishops' Conference of Burkina Faso and Niger (based in Ouagadougou, Burkina Faso). In Niger the Roman Catholic Church has about 18,000 adherents (31 December 1992).

Bishop of Niamey: (vacant); Apostolic Admin. Mgr GUY ROMANO, Titular Bishop of Caput Cilla, Evêché, BP 10270, Niamey; tel. 73-30-79; fax 74-10-13.

The Press

Amfani: Niamey; independent.

Angam: Niamey; f. 1992; monthly; independent; Dir GRÉMAH BOUKAR.

Al-Habari: Niamey; independent.

Haske: BP 297, Niamey; tel. 74-18-44; fax 73-20-06; f. 1990; weekly; independent; Dir IBRAHIM CHEIKH DIOP.

Haske Magazine: BP 297; tel. 74-18-44; fax 73-20-06; f. 1990; quarterly; independent; Dir IBRAHIM CHEIKH DIOP; circ. 3,000.

Horizon 2001: Niamey; f. 1991; monthly; independent; Dir INOUSSA OUSSEÏNI.

Journal Officiel de la République du Niger: BP 116, Niamey; tel. 72-39-30; f. 1960; fortnightly; Man. Editor BONKOULA AMINATOU MAYAKI; circ. 800.

Kakaki: Niamey; f. 1991; monthly; independent; Dir SIRAJI KANÉ.

La Marche: Niamey; f. 1989; monthly; independent; Dir ABDOULAYE MOUSSA MASSALATCHI.

Nigerama: Niamey; quarterly; publ. by the Agence Nigérienne de Presse.

Le Pont Africain: Niamey; independent; satirical.

Le Républicain: Niamey; f. 1991; weekly; independent, pro-Tuareg; Dir MAMANE ABOU.

Le Sahel: BP 13182, Niamey; f. 1960; publ. by Office National d'Edition et de Presse; daily; Dir ALI OUSSEÏNI; circ. 5,000.

Le Sahel Dimanche: BP 13182, Niamey; publ. by Office National d'Edition et de Presse; weekly; Dir ALI OUSSEÏNI; circ. 3,000.

La Tribune du Peuple: Niamey; independent; Man. Editor IBRAHIM HAMIDOU.

NEWS AGENCIES

Agence Nigérienne de Presse (ANP): BP 11158, Niamey; tel. 740809; telex 5497; f. 1987; state-owned; Dir BOUREÏMA MAGAGI.

Office National d'Edition et de Presse (ONEP): Niamey; f. 1989; Dir ALI OUSSEÏNI.

Publisher

Government Publishing House

L'Imprimerie Nationale du Niger (INN): BP 61, Niamey; tel. 73-47-98; telex 5312; f. 1962; Dir E. WOHLRAB.

Radio and Television

In 1991, according to UNESCO estimates, there were 480,000 radio receivers and 37,000 television receivers in use.

Office de Radiodiffusion-Télévision du Niger (ORTN): BP 309, Niamey; tel. 72-31-63; telex 5229; state broadcasting authority; Dir-Gen. MAHAMANE ADAMOU; Tech. Dir (Radio and Television) ZOUDI ISSOUF.

La Voix du Sahel: BP 361, Niamey; tel. 72-32-72; fax 72-35-48; f. 1958; govt-controlled radio service; programmes in French, Hausa (Haoussa), Djerma (Zarma), Kanuri, Fulfuldé, Tamajak, Toubou, Gourmantché and Arabic; Dir OMAR TIELLO.

Télé-Sahel: BP 309, Niamey; tel. 72-31-53; telex 5229; fax 72-35-48; govt-controlled television service; broadcasts daily; Dir MAMANE MAMADOU.

Finance

(cap. = capital; res = reserves; m. = million; brs = branches; amounts in francs CFA)

BANKING

Central Bank

Banque Centrale des Etats de l'Afrique de l'Ouest (BCEAO): Rond-point de la Poste, BP 487, Niamey; tel. 72-24-91; telex 5218; fax 73-47-43; headquarters in Dakar, Senegal; f. 1955; bank of issue for the seven states of the Union monétaire ouest-africaine (UMOA), comprising Benin, Burkina Faso, Côte d'Ivoire, Mali, Niger, Senegal and Togo; cap. and res 379,881m. (Sept. 1992); Gov. CHARLES KONAN BANNY; Dir in Niger MAMADOU DIOP; brs at Maradi and Zinder.

Commercial Banks

Bank of Africa – Niger: Immeuble Sonara II, BP 10973, Niamey; tel. 73-36-20; telex 5321; fax 73-38-18; f. 1994 to acquire assets of Nigeria International Bank Niamey (cap. 1,000m.—Sept. 1993); 35% owned by Bank of Africa-Benin, 30% by African Financial Holding; Chair. JACQUES NIGNON.

Banque Commerciale du Niger (BCN): Rond-point Maourey, BP 11363, Niamey; tel. 73-33-31; telex 5292; fax 73-21-63; f. 1978; fmrly Banque Arabe Libyenne-Nigérienne pour le Commerce Extérieur et le Développement; owned by private Nigerien (50%) and Libyan (50%) interests; cap. 5,000m. (Sept. 1993); Chair. and Man. Dir CHEICK MOHAMED METRI.

Banque Islamique du Niger: ave de la Mairie, BP 12754, Niamey; tel. 73-57-19; telex 5440; fax 73-48-25; f. 1983; fmrly Banque Masraf Faisal Islami, undergoing restructuring in 1994; owned by Dar al-Maal al-Islami (DMI Trust) and private Nigerien interests; Chair. MAHMOUD EL HELLI; Man. Dir LAMINE MOKTAR.

BIAO-Niger: ave de la Mairie, BP 10350, Niamey; tel. 73-31-01; telex 5215; fax 73-35-95; f. 1980; 84% owned by Meridien BIAO

SA (Luxembourg); cap. 2,201m. (Sept. 1992); Chair. BOUKAR MOUSSA MAÏNA; Man. Dir JEAN-PIERRE CARPENTIER; 5 brs.

Nigerian Trust Bank: Immeuble El Nasr, BP 12792, Niamey; tel. 73-42-87; telex 5456; fax 73-33-03; f. 1992 to acquire assets of the fmr Bank of Credit and Commerce Niger (cap. 600m. – Sept. 1990); owned by Nigeria Trust Fund.

Société Nigérienne de Banque (SONIBANQUE): ave de la Mairie, BP 891, Niamey; tel. 73-47-40; telex 5480; fax 73-46-93; f. 1990; 25% owned by Société Tunisienne de Banque; cap. 2,000m. (Sept. 1993); Chair. ALMA OUMAROU; Dir-Gen. CHAKIB SIALA.

Development Banks

Caisse de Prêts aux Collectivités Territoriales (CPCT): route de Torodi, BP 730, Niamey, tel. 72-34-12; 94% owned by Nigerien local govts; cap. 1,355m. (Sept. 1992); Chair. ASSOUMANE ADAMOU; Man. Dir MAHAMED MOUDDOUR.

Crédit du Niger: blvd de la République, BP 213, Niger; tel. 72-27-01; telex 5210; fax 72-23-90; f. 1958; 54% state-owned, 20% owned by Caisse Nationale de Sécurité Sociale; cap. 1,720m. (Sept. 1992); Chair. SANI MAHAMANE; Man. Dir ABOU KANÉ.

Fonds d'Intervention en Faveur des Petites et Moyennes Entreprises Nigériennes (FIPMEN): Immeuble Sonara II, BP 252, Niamey; tel. 73-20-98; telex 5569; f. 1990; state-owned; cap. 142m. (Dec. 1991); Chair. AMADOU SALLA HASSANE; Man. Dir IBRAHIM BEIDARI.

Savings Bank

Caisse Nationale d'Epargne (CNE): BP 11778, Niamey; tel. 73-24-98; total assets 2,437m. (Sept. 1993); Chair. IDI GADO; Man. Dir BACHIR MALLAM MATO.

INSURANCE

Agence Nigérienne d'Assurances (ANA): place de la Mairie, BP 423, Niamey; tel. 72-20-71; telex 5277; f. 1959; cap. 1.5m.; owned by L'Union des Assurances de Paris; Dir JEAN LASCAUD.

Société Civile Immobilière des Assureurs de Niamey: BP 423, Niamey; tel. 73-40-71; telex 5277; fax 73-41-85; f. 1962; cap. 14m.; Dir MAMADOU TALATA DOULLA.

Société Nigérienne d'Assurances et de Réassurances 'Leyma' (SNAR—LEYMA): ave du Général de Gaulle, BP 426, Niamey; tel. 73-55-26; telex 5202; f. 1973; cap. 345m.; Pres. AMADOU OUSMANE; Dir-Gen. MAMADOU MALAM AOUAMI.

Union Générale des Assurances du Niger (UGAN): rue de Kalleye, BP 11935, Niamey; tel. 73-54-06; telex 5277; fax 73-41-85; f. 1985; cap. 500m.; Pres. YVETTE CHASSAGNE; Dir-Gen. MAMADOU TALATA DOULLA; 7 brs.

Trade and Industry

DEVELOPMENT ORGANIZATIONS

Caisse de Stabilisation des Prix des Produits du Niger (CSPPN): BP 480, Niamey; telex 5286; price control agency for Nigerien goods; Dir IBRAHIM KOUSSOU.

Mission Française de Coopération: BP 494, Niamey; tel. 72-20-66; telex 5220; administers bilateral aid from France; Dir JEAN BOULOGNE.

Office des Eaux du Sous-Sol (OFEDES): BP 734, Niamey; tel. 73-23-44; telex 5313; govt agency for the maintenance and development of wells and boreholes; Dir ADOU ADAM.

Office du Lait du Niger (OLANI): BP 404, Niamey; tel. 73-23-69; telex 5555; f. 1971; govt agency for development and marketing of milk products; Pres. Dr ABDOUA KABO; Dir MAHAMADOU HAROUNA.

Office National de l'Energie Solaire (ONERSOL): BP 621, Niamey; tel. 73-45-05; govt agency for research and development, commercial production and exploitation of solar devices; Dir ALBERT WRIGHT.

Office National des Ressources Minières du Niger (ONAREM): BP 12716, Niamey; tel. 73-59-26; telex 5300; f. 1976; govt agency for exploration, exploitation and marketing of all minerals; Dir-Gen. OUSMANE GAOURI.

Office des Produits Vivriers du Niger (OPVN): BP 474, Niamey; telex 5323; govt agency for developing agricultural and food production; Dir ADAMOU SOUNA.

Riz du Niger (RINI): BP 476, Tillabéry, Niamey; tel. 71-13-29; f. 1967; cap. 825m. francs CFA; 27% state-owned; development and marketing of rice; Pres. YAYA MADOUGOU; Dir-Gen. OUSMANE DJIKA.

Société Nigérienne de Produits Pétroliers (SONIDEP): BP 11702, Niamey; tel. 73-33-34; telex 5343; f. 1977; govt agency for the distribution and marketing of petroleum products; cap. 1,000m. francs CFA; Man. Dir AMADOU NAMATA.

TRADE ORGANIZATIONS

Centre Nigérien du Commerce Extérieur (CNCE): place de la Concertation, BP 12480, Niamey; tel. 73-22-88; telex 5434; fax 73-46-68; f. 1984; promotes and co-ordinates all aspects of foreign trade; Dir AÏSSA DIALLO.

Société Nationale de Commerce et de Production du Niger (COPRO-Niger): BP 615, Niamey; tel. 73-28-41; telex 5222; fax 73-57-71; f. 1962; monopoly importer of foodstuffs; cap. 1,000m. francs CFA; 47% state-owned; Man. Dir DJIBRILLA HIMA.

CHAMBERS OF COMMERCE

Chambre de Commerce, d'Agriculture, d'Industrie et d'Artisanat du Niger: place de la Concertation, BP 209, Niamey; tel. 73-22-10; telex 5242; f. 1954; comprises 80 full mems and 40 dep. mems; Pres. WAZIN MALLAM AJI; Gen. Sec. MAINA ARI ADJI KIRGAM.

Chambre de Commerce, d'Agriculture, d'Industrie et d'Artisanat du Niger, Antenne d'Agadez: BP 201, Agadez; tel. 44-01-61.

Chambre de Commerce, d'Agriculture, d'Industrie et d'Artisanat du Niger, Antenne de Diffa: BP 91, Diffa; tel. 54-03-92; f. 1988.

Chambre de Commerce, d'Agriculture, d'Industrie et d'Artisanat du Niger, Antenne de Maradi: BP 79, Maradi; tel. 41-03-66.

Chambre de Commerce, d'Agriculture, d'Industrie et d'Artisanat du Niger, Antenne de Tahoua: BP 172, Tahoua; tel. 61-03-84; f. 1984; Admin. Sec. MAMADOU ALI.

Chambre de Commerce, d'Agriculture, d'Industrie et d'Artisanat du Niger, Antenne de Zinder: BP 83, Zinder; tel. 51-00-78.

EMPLOYERS' ORGANIZATIONS

Syndicat des Commerçants Importateurs et Exportateurs du Niger (SCIMPEXNI): BP 535, Niamey; tel. 73-34-66; Pres. ANDRÉ BEAUMONT; Sec.-Gen. C. SALEZ.

Syndicat National des Petites et Moyennes Entreprises et Industries Nigériennes (SYNAPEMEIN): BP 11204, Niamey; Pres. El Hadj ALI SOUMANA; Sec.-Gen. BOUBACAR ZEZI.

Syndicat Patronal des Entreprises et Industries du Niger (SPEIN): BP 415, Niamey; tel. 73-24-01; telex 5370; fax 73-45-26; f. 1945; Pres. AMADOU OUSMANE.

MAJOR INDUSTRIAL COMPANIES

The following are among the largest companies in terms of either capital investment or employment.

Compagnie Minière d'Akouta (COMINAK): BP 10545, Niamey; tel. 73-34-25; telex 5269; fax 73-28-55; f. 1974; cap. 3,500m. francs CFA; 34% owned by Cie générale des matières nucléaires (COGEMA) (France), 31% by ONAREM (Niger govt), 25% by Overseas Uranium Resources Development (Japan), 10% by Empresa Nacional del Uranio (Spain); mining and processing of uranium at Akouta; Chair. BOUKAR MAÏ MANGA; Dir HENRI PELLO.

Office National des Produits Pharmaceutiques et Chimiques (ONPPC): BP 11585, Niamey; tel. 73-27-81; telex 5231; fax 73-23-74; f. 1962; cap. 440m. francs CFA; state-owned; Dir Dr MAIDANA SAIDOU DJERMAKOYE.

Société des Brasseries et Boissons Gazeuses du Niger (BRANIGER): BP 11245, Niamey; tel. 72-20-88; telex 5280; f. 1967; cap. 1,428m. francs CFA; mfrs of ice and soft drinks at Niamey and Maradi; Chair. ALPHONSE DENIS; Dir M. TRAVERSA; 300 employees.

Société d'Exploitation des Produits d'Arachides du Niger (SEPANI): BP 8, Magaria; telex 8216; f. 1970; cap. 405m. francs CFA; 33% state-owned; production of groundnut oil at Magaria; Dir MAURICE CHAINE.

Société des Mines de l'Aïr (SOMAÏR): BP 12910, Niamey; tel. 72-35-31; telex 5494; fax 72-29-33; f. 1968; cap. 4,349m. francs CFA; 49.3% owned by COGEMA (France), 36.6% by ONAREM; uranium mining at Arlit; Man. Dir MICHEL BERVILLE; Dir at Arlit DOUDOU ALHASSANE.

Société Minière du Niger (SMDN): BP 12443, Niamey; tel. 73-45-82; telex 5300; f. 1941; cap. 36m. francs CFA; 71% state-owned, 10% owned by Benin govt; cassiterite mining at El Mecki and Tarrouadji; Chair. AMANI ISSAKA; Man. Dir MAMADOU SAADOU.

Société Minière de Tassa N'Taghalgué (SMTT): BP 10376, Niamey; tel. 73-36-66; telex 5393; f. 1979; cap. 10,500m. francs CFA; 33% owned by ONAREM, 33% by COGEMA (France), 33% by Kuwait Foreign Trading, Contracting and Investment Co; owns uranium-mining rights at Taza (leased to SOMAÏR in 1986); Chair. Minister of Mines and Energy; Man. Dir MICHEL HAREL.

Société Nigérienne du Charbon d'Anou Araren (SONICHAR): BP 51, Agadez; tel. 44-10-20; telex 8246; f. 1975; cap. 19,730m. francs CFA; 61% state-owned, 10% owned by the Islamic Development Bank, 24% by COMINAK, SMTT and SOMAÏR; exploitation of coal reserves at Anou Araren and generation of electricity; Chair. YAHAYA BEN OUSMANE; Man. Dir MAHAMADOU OUHOUMOUDOU; 443 employees.

Société Nigérienne de Cimenterie (SNC): BP 03, Malbaza; tel. 01-02; telex 8216; f. 1963; cap. 900m. francs CFA; 59% state-owned; production and marketing of cement at Malbaza; Chair. SAIDOU MAMANE; Man. Dir ABOUBACAR KADA LABO.

Société Nigérienne d'Electricité (NIGELEC): BP 11202, Niamey; tel. 72-26-92; fax 72-32-88; f. 1968; cap. 3,357m. francs CFA; 95% state-owned; restructuring programme announced 1993; production and distribution of electricity; Man. Dir AMADOU MAYAKI.

Société Nigérienne d'Exploitation des Ressources Animales (SONERAN): Niamey; tel. 73-23-75; telex 5537; f. 1968; cap. 270m. francs CFA; 99.9% state-owned; production and export of fresh and processed meat; ranch of 110,000 ha; Man. Dir MOUCTARI MAHAMANE FALALOU.

Société Nouvelle Nigérienne des Textiles (SONITEXTIL): route de Kolo, BP 10735, Niamey; tel. 73-25-11; telex 5241; f. 1978; cap. 1,000m. francs CFA; textile complex at Niamey; 27% state-owned; Chair. SAIDOU MAMANE; Man. Dir ROGER HUBER; 830 employees.

Unimo-Industrie et Chimie: BP 71, Maradi; tel. 41-00-56; telex 8201; f. 1978; cap. 710m. francs CFA; mfrs of foam rubber; Dir ASSAD GHASSAN.

TRADE UNION FEDERATIONS

Confédération des Syndicats Libres des Travailleurs du Niger (CSLTN): Niamey; f. 1993; 4 affiliates.

Union des Syndicats des Travailleurs du Niger (USTN): Bourse du Travail, BP 388, Niamey; f. 1960; divided into sections for Maradi, Niamey and Zinder; affiliated to the African Trade Union Confed.; 31 affiliates; 200,000 mems; Sec.-Gen. IBRAHIM MAYAKI.

Transport

ROADS

Niger is crossed by highways running from east to west and from north to south, giving access to neighbouring countries. Work on the upgrading of the 428-km Zinder – Agadez road, scheduled to form part of the Trans-Sahara highway, began in 1985.

At 31 December 1990 there were an estimated 11,258 km of classified roads, including 5,971 km of main roads and 2,729 km of secondary roads; about 3,265 km of the total network was paved.

Société Nationale des Transports Nigériens (SNTN): BP 135, Niamey; tel. 72-24-55; telex 5338; fax 73-45-26; f. 1961; national road hauliers; cap. 2,500m. francs CFA; 49% state-owned; Dir AMADOU OUSMANE.

RAILWAYS

Organisation Commune Bénin-Niger des Chemins de Fer et des Transports (OCBN): BP 38, Niamey; tel. 73-27-90; telex 5253; f. 1959; 50% owned by Govt of Niger, 50% by Govt of Benin; manages the Benin-Niger railway project (begun in 1978). There are as yet no railways in Niger.

INLAND WATERWAYS

The River Niger is navigable for 300 km within the country. Access to the sea is available by a river route from Gaya, in south-western Niger, to the coast at Port Harcourt, Nigeria, between September and March. Port facilities at Lomé, Togo, are used as a commercial outlet for land-locked Niger, and an agreement providing import facilities at the port of Tema was signed with Ghana in November 1986.

Niger-Transit (NITRA): Zone Industrielle, BP 560, Niamey; tel. 73-22-53; telex 5212; fax 73-26-38; f. 1974; 48% owned by SNTN; customs agent, freight-handling, warehousing, etc.; manages Nigerien port facilities at Lomé; Pres. SALEY CHAIBOU; Man. Dir SADE FATIMATA.

Société Nigérienne des Transports Fluviaux et Maritimes (SNTFM): Niamey; tel. 73-39-69; telex 5265; river and sea transport; cap. 64.6m. francs CFA; 99% state-owned; Man. Dir BERTRAND DEJEAN.

CIVIL AVIATION

There are international airports at Niamey and Agadez, and major domestic airports at Arlit, Diffa, Tahoua and Zinder.

Air Afrique: BP 11090, Niamey; tel. 73-30-10; telex 5284; see under Côte d'Ivoire; Dir in Niamey MALLÉ SALL.

Société Nigérienne des Transports Aériens (SONITA): Niamey; f. 1991; cap. 50m. francs CFA; owned by private Nigerien (81%) and Cypriot (19%) interests; operates domestic and regional services; Man. Dir ABDOULAYE MAIGA GOUDOUBABA.

Trans-Niger Aviation: BP 10454, Niamey; tel. 73-20-21; telex 5250; f. 1989; 38% owned by SNTN, 38% by Société Autonome de Gérance et d'Armement (France); operates domestic and regional services; Man. Dir ABDOU M. GOGE.

Tourism

Hunting and fishing provide an important attraction for tourists. The Aïr and Ténéré Nature Reserve, covering an area of 77,000 sq km, was established in 1988, and the construction of a tourist village at Boubon (on the river Niger) was announced in 1989. Some 21,000 tourists visited Niger in 1990; in that year receipts from tourism amounted to US $15m.

Direction du Tourisme et de l'Hôtellerie: Ministry of Trade, Transport and Tourism, BP 12130, Niamey; tel. 73-23-85; telex 5249; Dir ALZOUMA MAÏGA.

Office National du Tourisme (ONT): ave du Président H. Luebke, BP 612, Niamey; tel. 73-24-47; telex 5467; f. 1977.

Société Nigérienne d'Hôtellerie (SONHOTEL): BP 11040, Niamey; tel. 73-23-87; telex 5239; f. 1977; state-owned hotel corpn; cap. 3,500m. francs CFA; Dir-Gen. HABI ABDOU.

Defence

In June 1993 Niger's armed forces totalled 5,300 men (army 5,200; air force about 100). Paramilitary forces comprised a 2,500-strong republican guard, a national police force of 1,500 and a 1,400-strong gendarmerie. Conscription is selective and lasts for two years.

Defence Expenditure: Budgeted at 6,176m. francs CFA in 1992.

Chief of Staff of the Armed Forces: Lt-Col MAHAMANE KOROHOU.

Education

Education is available free of charge, and is officially compulsory for eight years from seven to 15 years of age. Primary education begins at the age of seven and lasts for six years. Secondary education begins at the age of 13 years and comprises a four-year cycle followed by a further three-year cycle. Primary enrolment in 1990 included only 25% of children in the appropriate age-group (boys 31%; girls 19%). A basic education project, aiming to improve and to extend access to primary education, was inaugurated in mid-1994. Funding for the project, the cost of which was estimated at US $76m., was to be provided by the International Development Association and the Governments of Niger, Germany and Norway. Secondary enrolment in 1990 included only 6% of the relevant age-group (boys 8%; girls 3%). The University of Niamey was inaugurated in 1973, and the Islamic University of West Africa, at Say, was opened in January 1987. Scholarships are also provided for higher education in France and Senegal. Expenditure on education by the central Government in the 15 months to the end of December 1990 was projected at 24,409m. francs CFA, representing 10.3% of total spending. In 1990, according to estimates by UNESCO, the adult illiteracy rate averaged 71.6% (males 59.6%; females 83.2%).

Bibliography

Asiwaju, A. I. *et al.*, and Barkindo, B. M. The Nigerian-Niger Transborder Co-operation. Lagos, Malthouse Press, 1993.

Beckwith, C., and Van Offelen, M. *Nomads of Niger.* London, Collins, 1984.

Clair, A. *Le Niger indépendant.* Paris, ATEOS, 1966.

Decalo, S. *Historical Dictionary of Niger.* Metuchen, NJ, Scarecrow Press, 1989.

La Documentation Française. *Bibliographie sommaire de la République du Niger.* Paris, 1969.

La République du Niger. Paris, 1973.

Donaint, P., and Lancrenon, F. *Le Niger.* Paris, Presses universitaires de France, 1972.

Grégoire, E. *Les Alhazi de Maradi.* Paris, Editions Ostrom, 1986.

Harrison Church, R. J. *West Africa.* 8th Edn, London, Longman, 1979.

Keenan, J. *The Tuareg.* London, Allen Lane, 1978.

Klotchkoff, J.-C. *Le Niger aujourd'hui.* Paris, Editions Jeune Afrique, 1982.

Ramir, S. *Les Pistes de l'oubli: Touaregs au Niger.* Paris, Editions du Félin, 1991.

Raynault, G. (Ed.). *Projet de développement rural de Maradi. Le développement rural de la région au village.* Bordeaux, Groupe de recherche interdisciplinaire pour le développement, 1988.

Rimmer, D. *The Economies of West Africa.* London, Weidenfeld and Nicolson, 1984.

Séré de Rivières, E. *Histoire du Niger.* Paris, Berger-Levrault, 1966.

NIGERIA

Physical and Social Geography

AKIN L. MABOGUNJE

The Federal Republic of Nigeria is a coastal state on the shores of the Gulf of Guinea, with Benin to the west, Niger to the north, Chad to the north-east, and Cameroon to the east and south-east. It has an area of 923,768 sq km (356,669 sq miles), placing it 14th in size among African countries. At the census of November 1991 Nigeria had 88,514,501 inhabitants and a population density of 95.8 inhabitants per sq km.

Nigeria became independent on 1 October 1960, and in 1968 adopted a new federal structure comprising 12 states. A federal capital territory was created in 1979. The number of states was increased to 19 in 1976, to 21 in 1987, and to 30 in 1991.

PHYSICAL FEATURES

The physical features of Nigeria are of moderate dimensions. The highest lands are along the eastern border of the country and rise to a maximum of 2,040 m above sea-level at Vogel Peak, south of the Benue river. The Jos plateau, which is located close to the centre of the country, rises to 1,780 m at Shere Hill and 1,698 m at Wadi Hill. The plateau is also a watershed, from which streams flow to Lake Chad and to the rivers Niger and Benue. The land declines steadily northward from the plateau; this area, known as the High Plains of Hausaland, is characterized by a broad expanse of level sandy plains, interspersed by rocky dome outcrops. To the south-west, across the Niger river, similar relief is represented in the Yoruba highlands, where the rocky outcrops are surrounded by forests or tall grass and form the major watershed for rivers flowing northwards to the Niger and southwards to the sea. Elsewhere in the country, lowlands of less than 300 m stretch inland from the coast for over 250 km and continue in the trough-like basins of the Niger and Benue rivers. Lowland areas also exist in the Rima and Chad basins at the extreme north-west and north-east of the country respectively. These lowlands are dissected by innumerable streams and rivers flowing in broad sandy valleys.

The main river of Nigeria is the Niger, the third longest river of Africa. Originating in the Fouta Djallon mountains of north-east Sierra Leone, it enters Nigeria for the last one-third of its 4,200 km course. It flows first south-easterly, then due south and again south-easterly to Lokoja, where it converges with its principal tributary, the Benue. From here the river flows due south until Aboh, where it merges with the numerous interlacing distributaries of its delta. The Benue rises in Cameroon, flows in a south-westerly direction into the Niger, and receives on its course the waters of the Katsina Ala and Gongola rivers. The other main tributaries of the Niger within Nigeria are the Sokoto, Kaduna and Anambra rivers. Other important rivers in the country include the Ogun, the Oshun, the Imo and the Cross, many of which flow into the sea through a system of lagoons. The Nigerian coastline is relatively straight, with few natural indentations.

CLIMATE

Nigeria has a climate which is characterized by relatively high temperatures throughout the year. The average annual maximum varies from 35°C in the north to 31°C in the south; the average annual minimum from 23°C in the south to 18°C in the north. On the Jos plateau and the eastern highlands altitude makes for relatively lower temperatures, with the maximum no more than 28°C and the minimum sometimes as low as 14°C.

The annual rainfall total decreases from over 3,800 mm at Forcados on the coast to under 650 mm at Maiduguri in the north-east of the country. The length of the rainy season also shows a similar decrease from nearly 12 months in the south to under five months in the north. Rain starts in January in the south and progresses gradually across country. June, July, August and September are the rainiest months throughout the country. In many parts of the south, however, there is a slight break in the rains for some two to three weeks in late July and early August. No such break occurs in the northern part of the country, and the rainy season continues uninterrupted for three to six months.

SOILS AND VEGETATION

The broad pattern of soil distribution in the country reflects both the climatic conditions and the geological structure; heavily leached, reddish-brown, sandy soils are found in the south, and light or moderately leached, yellowish-brown, sandy soils in the north. The difference in colour relates to the extent of leaching the soil has undergone.

The nutrient content of the soil is, however, related to the geological structure. Over a large part of the northern and south-western areas of the country the geological structure is that of old crystalline Basement complex rocks. These are highly mineralized and give rise to soils of high nutrient status, although variable from place to place. On the sedimentary rocks found in the south-east, north-east and north-west of the country the soils are sandy and less variable but are deficient in plant nutrient. They are also very susceptible to erosion.

The vegetation of the country shows clear east-west zonation. In general mangrove and rain forests are found in the south, occupying about 20% of the area of the country, while grassland of various types occupies the rest. Four belts of grassland can be identified. Close to the forest zone is a derived savannah belt, which is believed to have resulted from the frequent firing of previously forested areas. This belt is succeeded by the Guinea, the Sudan and the Sahel savannah northwards in that order. The height of grass and density of wood vegetation decrease with each succeeding savannah belt.

RESOURCES

Although nearly 180,000 sq km of Nigeria is in the forest belt, only 23,000 sq km account for most of its timber resources. These forests are mainly in Ondo, Bendel and Cross River States. Nigeria exports a wide variety of tropical hardwoods, and internal consumption has been growing rapidly.

Cattle, goats and, to a lesser extent, sheep constitute important animal resources. Most of the cattle are found in the Sudan grassland belt in the far north. Poultry and pigs are increasing in importance.

Coastal waters are becoming important fishing grounds. Traditionally, however, major sources of fish have been Lake Chad in the extreme north-east, the lagoons along the coast, the creeks and distributaries of the Niger delta and the various rivers in the country.

Mineral resources are varied, although exploration of many has only just begun. Tin and columbite are found in alluvial deposits on the Jos Plateau. Nigeria was, until 1968, Africa's main producer of tin, but output has since declined. Extensive reserves of medium-grade iron ore exist, and iron and steel production is being developed.

Fuel resources include deposits of lignite and sub-bituminous coal, exploited at Enugu since 1915; however, total reserves are small. More significant are the petroleum reserves, estimates of which are constantly being altered with each new discovery in the offshore area. The oil produced, being of low sulphur content and high quality, is much in demand on the European and US markets. Since Libya restricted production in 1973, Nigeria has been Africa's leading producer of petroleum. Natural gas is also found in abundance, and has been undergoing development since the mid-1980s.

POPULATION

The Nigerian population is extremely diverse. Well over 250 ethnic groups are identified, some numbering fewer than 10,000 people. Ten groups, notably Hausa-Fulani, Yoruba, Ibo, Kanuri, Tiv, Edo, Nupe, Ibibio and Ijaw, account for nearly 80% of the total population. Much of the population is concentrated in the southern part of the country, as well as in the area of dense settlement around Kano in the north. Between these two areas is the sparsely populated Middle Belt.

Urban life has a long history in Nigeria, with centres of population such as Kano (mid-1975 estimate 399,000), Zaria (224,000), Ife (176,000) and Benin (136,000) dating from the Middle Ages. Recent economic development, however, has stimulated considerable rural-urban migration and led to the phenomenal growth of such cities as Lagos, Ibadan, Kaduna and Port Harcourt. In December 1991 the federal capital was formally transferred to Abuja; however, many non-government institutions remained in the former capital, Lagos.

Recent History

T. C. McCASKIE

Revised for this edition by the Editor

The territory of present-day Nigeria, except for the section of former German-controlled Cameroon (see below), was conquered by the United Kingdom, in several stages, during the second half of the 19th century and the first decade of the 20th century. The British dependencies of Northern and Southern Nigeria were merged into a single territory in 1914, and a legislative council, initially with limited African representation, was created in 1922. However, much of the administration remained under the control of traditional native rulers, supervised by the colonial authorities. In 1947 the United Kingdom introduced a new Nigerian constitution, establishing a federal system of government, based on three regions: Eastern, Western and Northern. The federal arrangement was an attempt to reconcile regional and religious tensions, and to accommodate the interests of Nigeria's diverse ethnic groups: mainly the Ibo (in the east), the Yoruba (in the west) and the Hausa and Fulani (in the north). The Northern Region, whose inhabitants were mainly Muslims, contained about one-half of Nigeria's total population.

Nationalists continued to demand the extension of the franchise and the holding of direct elections, and in 1949 the constitution of 1947 was abrogated. Ministerial government was introduced in 1951, and the federation became self-governing in 1954. During the 1950s a series of constitutional conferences took place, in an attempt to achieve a balance of power between regions and ethnic groups, and political parties coalesced on the basis of regional affiliations. The Eastern Region was dominated by the National Council for Nigeria and the Cameroons (NCNC), led by Dr Nnamdi Azikiwe and the veteran nationalist Herbert Macaulay. The NCNC had emerged from a broadly-based organization that had opposed the 1947 constitution, and it attracted mainly Ibo support. The leading political entity in the Western Region was the Action Group (AG), which was derived from the nationalist Nigerian Youth Movement. The AG was led by the premier of the Western Region, Obafemi Awolowo, and Ijebu Yoruba, and was dominated by educated Yoruba. The largest region in the country, the Northern Region, was dominated by the Northern People's Congress (NPC). The NPC was based on the traditional and mercantile Hausa-Fulani élite; its nominal leader was the premier of the Northern Region, the sardauna of Sokoto, Ahmadu (later Sir Ahmadu) Bello. The NPC's political (later parliamentary) spokesman was Abubakar (later Sir Abubakar) Tafawa Balewa, a former schoolteacher (who was appointed the first federal prime minister in 1957).

The NPC demanded a large degree of regional autonomy within any future federal structure, arguing for guarantees respecting the integrity of Islam, and stipulating that representatives of the north should constitute at least 50% of a federal legislature. The AG likewise demanded regional autonomy, apprehensive that the Western Region's income from the cocoa industry would be dissipated in subsidizing less wealthy areas, and advocated the redrafting of regional boundaries to allow the incorporation of Ilorin and Kabba (currently part of the Northern Region), and of Lagos, into the Western Region. The NCNC, on the other hand, favoured the establishment of a centralized government, and advocated the distribution of revenue according to need (reflecting the fact that the party's base was in the less wealthy and less populous Eastern Region, while much of its Ibo support was located in a diaspora throughout Nigeria).

By 1954 the British had established a measure of compromise between these conflicting demands. There was to be a federal government, in conjunction with considerable regional autonomy. Specific powers were to be allocated to the federal government including defence, the police force, the terms of national trade, customs duties, finance and banking. Responsibility for agriculture, education, health services and economic development was to be shared with the Regions. Lagos, the capital, was constituted as a federal territory, separate from the Western Region. In 1956 the Western and Eastern Regions were granted self-government, followed in 1959 by the Northern Region. In 1960 a constitutional conference agreed that Nigeria should become independent, and, in preparation for this, elections for an enlarged federal legislature took place in December 1959. None of the three major parties achieved an overall majority, but, owing to the greater size of the Northern Region, the NPC commanded the largest representation, and Tafawa Balewa continued in office as federal prime minister, leading a coalition of the NPC and the NCNC. A bicameral federal parliament was formed in January 1960.

CIVILIAN RULE, 1960–66

On 1 October 1960, as scheduled, the Federation of Nigeria achieved independence, initially as a constitutional monarchy. Tafawa Balewa continued as federal prime minister and also became minister of foreign affairs. In November the pre-independence governor-general (representing the British monarch as head of state) was succeeded by Dr Nnamdi Azikiwe of the NCNC, who had been president of the senate and was a former premier of the Eastern Region. In June 1961 the northern part of the neighbouring UN Trust Territory of British Cameroons was incorporated into Nigeria's Northern Region as the province of Sardauna.

Independent Nigeria was almost immediately confronted by a series of foreseeable problems. Under the federal system, one political party—and thus one region and one principal ethnic group—would always be excluded from office and from the associated benefits. After the 1959 election, the AG was excluded from power at the federal level, and, in addition, was affected by a renewal of Yoruba factionalism (which had been endemic throughout the 19th century). Awolowo began to quarrel openly with the prime minister of the Western Region, Chief Samuel Akintola, and in early 1962 the AG executive decided to replace Akintola with a protégé of Awolowo, provoking a riot at the ensuing meeting of the Western regional assembly. The federal government declared a state of emergency and took over the regional administration. After the expiry of the six-month period of emergency, Akintola's new United People's Party (UPP) controlled the government of the Western Region, in alliance with the NCNC, which had strong support in the non-Yoruba areas of the region. In 1963 a referendum was held in the Western Region, approving the formation of a separate region for the non-Yoruba areas; following legislative approval in August, the new Mid-Western Region was detached from the Western Region, and the NCNC won the ensuing elections to the Mid-Western regional legislature.

In September 1962 Awolowo and some 30 supporters were arrested and charged with plotting to overthrow the federal government. The trial, which was widely perceived as an attempt to discredit Awolowo, made public the level of corruption prevalent in Nigerian politics. Awolowo revealed that he had attempted to form an alliance with elements of the NCNC in 1961, in order to take over the federal government, and was sentenced to a term of imprisonment.

In October 1963 the country adopted a revised constitution and was renamed the Federal Republic of Nigeria, while remaining a member of the Commonwealth. Dr Azikiwe took office as Nigeria's first president (then a non-executive post). In February 1964 further threats to federal unity emerged, when the Tiv of the Benue Plateau, who had sought autonomy since 1960, launched attacks against NPC personnel and offices. The Nigerian army rapidly suppressed the insurgency. In the same year a two-week general strike, which was staged in protest at wage levels, reflected widespread concern at the economic disparities in Nigerian society, and at the visible signs of corruption in public life.

The first national election since independence, to the federal house of representatives, took place in December 1964. It was preceded by a split in the coalition between the NPC and the NCNC (renamed the National Convention of Nigerian Citizens), and by the formation of two new national coalitions. The Nigerian National Alliance (NNA), led by Ahmadu Bello, comprised the NPC and Akintola's breakaway Yoruba party, now renamed the Nigerian National Democratic Party (NNDP). The United Progressive Grand Alliance (UPGA), led by Dr Michael Okpara, the prime minister of the Eastern Region, was composed of the NCNC, the remainder of the AG (whose leaders were still in prison) and the minority, populist Northern Elements Progressive Union (NEPU). The election campaign was characterized by violence and corruption, and, in protest against alleged irregularities, the UPGA organized a boycott of the poll, which was widely observed in the Eastern Region. The NNA won by default, and Azikiwe reluctantly asked Tafawa Balewa to form a new government. A supplementary election was held in the Eastern Region in March 1965 (at which the UPGA won every seat), followed by a fresh election in the Western Region in November, owing to widespread irregularities. Both the NNDP and the AG subsequently claimed the right to form a government in the Western Region, and the situation deteriorated into anarchy: some 2,000 people were killed during, and immediately following, the election.

MILITARY INTERVENTION AND CIVIL WAR, 1966–70

National rivalries were reflected in the Nigerian armed forces; most of the quota of personnel recruited from the North came from the Middle Belt of the Northern Region and were opposed to the NPC and to Hausa-Fulani dominance. Ibo from the Eastern Region formed the majority of the officer corps, and this provoked intense suspicion among other ethnic groups. In January 1966 Tafawa Balewa's government was overthrown by junior (mainly Ibo) army officers; Tafawa Balewa was killed, together with Sir Ahmadu Bello, prime minister of the Northern Region, Chief Akintola, prime minister of the Western Region, and Chief Festus Okotie-Eboh, the federal minister of finance. On the following day the surviving federal ministers requested Maj.-Gen. Johnson Aguiyi-Ironsi, the c-in-c of the army and an Ibo, to take control of the government. He formed a supreme military council (SMC), suspended the constitution, and imposed a state of emergency. Shortly after the coup there were violent anti-Ibo riots, and in late May many people were killed when violence erupted in most of the major cities of the north, involving Hausa urban dwellers in conflict with members of the Ibo commercial community and other easterners: the disturbances indicated the level of Hausa dissatisfaction with Ibo dominance at the federal level, with the increasing centralization of government, and with what was seen as the exclusion of northerners from federal office. On 29 July Aguiyi-Ironsi was killed in a counter-coup by northern troops, and easterners were massacred in barracks throughout the country. Power was transferred to the chief-of-staff of the army, Lt-Col (later Gen.) Yakubu Gowon, a Christian northerner from the Middle Belt. Gowon restored some degree of discipline to the armed forces, and attempted to revive the federal system, appointing a military governor for each region.

Ibo still living in the North began to return to the Eastern Region after the counter-coup of July 1966, and in late September and early October those who remained in the North were massacred by northern army elements. The military governor of the Eastern Region, Lt-Col Chukwuemeka Odumegwu-Ojukwu, was subsequently urged by senior Ibo civil servants, who had fled from Lagos, to declare an independent Ibo state. In early 1967 there was a dispute between the federal government and that of the Eastern Region concerning the distribution of revenues from the Eastern petroleum industry. In May Gen. Gowon announced a proposal to abolish Nigeria's regions and replace them by 12 states. On 30 May Ojukwu announced the secession of the Eastern Region, and proclaimed its independence as the 'Republic of Biafra'. In July 'Biafran' troops crossed into the Western Region in an attempt to surround Lagos: federal troops then attacked 'Biafra' from the north and west, and a naval blockade was imposed. The Ibo achieved a series of initial successes, but by late 1967 the war had degenerated into a violent campaign of attrition. During 1968 most major towns in 'Biafra' were captured by federal forces, and in January 1970 'Biafran' forces surrendered, after Ojukwu's departure into exile. During the civil war military casualties reached an estimated 100,000, but between 500,000 and 2m. 'Biafran' civilians died, mainly from starvation as a result of the blockade imposed by the federal government.

MILITARY RULE, 1970–76

The 12-state structure proposed by Gen. Gowon entered into effect in April 1968, and after the cease-fire in January 1970 East Central State (the heartland of the former 'Biafra') was reintegrated into Nigeria. The SMC implemented various reconciliatory measures, reinstating a number of 'Biafran' military personnel and establishing infrastructural projects. In October Gowon declared that the military leadership would require at least six more years in power, in order to restore peace and political stability. He announced a nine-point plan for the socio-economic reconstruction, comprising: reorganization of the armed forces; implementation of a four-year development plan; eradication of corruption; the creation of new states; drafting a new constitution; reforming the allocation of revenue; conducting a census; and the organizing of 'genuinely national' political parties and of legislative elections.

The government's strategy of reconciliation was seriously impeded by the failure of the national population census, conducted in 1973, to produce credible results; the census purported to show a near-doubling of the population in the three northern states (Kano, North-Eastern and North-Western), while that of the Yoruba heartland of Western State was reported to have declined. In October 1974 Gowon announced that the 1976 target date for a return to civilian rule had been indefinitely postponed, on the grounds that the nine-point plan had not been fulfilled, and that the armed forces would be betraying the nation if they relinquished power. Instead, the SMC announced an ambitious new National Development Plan for 1975–80, and promised to initiate the drafting of a new constitution and the creation of new states; by mid-1975, however, none of these expressed intentions had been fulfilled.

In May 1975 Gen. Gowon presided over the signing of the final agreements establishing the Economic Community of

West African States (ECOWAS), a Nigerian-funded initiative that aimed to combine the economic potential of the region's states. On 29 July, while Gowon was attending a summit meeting of the Organization of African Unity (OAU) in Uganda, his government was overthrown in a bloodless coup by other senior officers. Gowon was forcibly 'retired' and allowed to go into exile, while his place as head of government was assumed by Brig. (later Gen.) Murtala Ramat Muhammed, hitherto the federal commissioner for communications. Muhammed immediately dismissed the 12 state governors, and undertook a radical and extremely popular purge of the public services. In October he announced that the country would be returned to civilian government by October 1979, following the adoption of a new constitution and the holding of local, state and federal elections.

OBASANJO AND THE RETURN TO CIVILIAN RULE, 1976–79

Despite a substantial popular following, Gen. Muhammed was assassinated in February 1976 by a disaffected army officer, Lt-Col Bukar Dimka, and a number of associates, who demanded the reinstatement of Gen. Gowon. Power was immediately assumed by his deputy, Lt-Gen. Olusegun Obasanjo, the chief-of-staff of the armed forces. Some 125 people were subsequently arrested for alleged involvement in Muhammed's murder.

As head of state Obasanjo pledged to fulfil his predecessor's programme for the return to civilian rule. In 1976 new legislation attempted to impose a much-needed uniformity on the structure of local government (hitherto based on British 'indirect rule' and a series of subsequent partial reforms): local government authorities were henceforth to be administered by councils with a majority of elected members. In 1975 the government established a constitutional drafting committee, comprising two representatives from each state, advised by experts. The committee's recommendations, announced in September 1976, included: the creation of a federal system of government with an executive presidency (similar to that of the USA); a moratorium on the creation of further states (the number of which had been increased by seven to 19 in March of that year); the creation of genuinely national political parties; the holding of open, free and fair elections; and the transfer of the federal captial from Lagos to a 'neutral' site at Abuja, in the geographical centre of Nigeria. A constituent assembly (CA) was created in August 1977 to draft the new constitution. The new local government councils (elected at the end of 1976) were constituted as electoral colleges for the CA, with the regional percentage of membership being determined by population estimates; of the 230 members (including 20 nominated directly by the SMC), many were nationally-known political figures from the 1960–66 period.

During the CA's deliberations there was disagreement between representatives of the Islamic north and the non-Islamic south concerning the future status of the federal Shari'a (Islamic law) appeal court: Muslims wished to uphold the status of Islamic law, while non-Muslims feared the imposition of Islamic law upon themselves. A compromise was reached, whereby Muslim rights were to be guaranteed and panels of federal judges who were familiar with Islamic law would be empowered to hear appellate cases from state Shari'a courts.

The new constitution was produced in 1978 and promulgated by the SMC in September. It envisaged an executive presidency, and a separation of powers between executive, legislative and judicial branches of government. To win the presidential election, a candidate would need to obtain an outright majority of the national vote, and also to win at least 25% of the votes in at least 12 states. Executive governors were to be appointed to each state. The respective powers of federal and state governments were carefully demarcated.

During the period 1976–79 there was a decline in Obasanjo's popularity, and in the prestige of the armed forces. Despite the government's efforts to encourage agricultural self-reliance and to indigenize industry, economic difficulties continued to cause discontent; it was widely believed that the SMC was plundering the economy before the armed forces' scheduled return to barracks.

THE SECOND REPUBLIC, 1979–83

The ending of the state of emergency in September 1978 was accompanied by the lifting of the ban on formal activity by political parties. By November more than 50 political groupings had emerged. In its electoral decree of 1977, the SMC had imposed stipulations that aspirant political parties were obliged to fulfil in order to contest the 1979 elections. The monitoring body, the Federal Electoral Commission (FEDECO), was instructed by the SMC to recognize only those parties that possessed a nationwide organization and base; divisive regionalism was to be avoided, and the emphasis was to be on national unity and dedication to the federal concept. In the event, of the 19 associations that applied for registration, only five received approval by FEDECO.

The best prepared of the five parties was the Unity Party of Nigeria (UPN), led by Chief Obafemi Awolowo, formerly vice-chairman of the SMC under Gowon and leader of the Yoruba-dominated AG in the 1950s. The UPN was a Yoruba-based party, which drew support from the western part of the country, and most notably from Oyo, Ondo, Ogun and Lagos States; its programme was viewed as populist. The National Party of Nigeria (NPN) was formed by such veteran politicians as Alhaji Shehu Shagari (later elected as presidential candidate) and Makaman Bida, both of whom had played prominent roles in the northern-based NPC. The NPN, which was based in Kaduna, in the north, advocated the enforcement of law and order, respect for tradition, and recognition of individual rights within a capitalist, free-market economy. The People's Redemption Party (PRP), the northern-based opposition to the NPN, was formed in Kaduna in October 1978, and was headed by a former member of the NPN, Alhaji Aminu Kano. The PRP was populist, opposed neo-colonialism, stressed the issue of multi-national corporations, and advocated a 'social revolution' in the distribution of income. The fourth party, the Nigerian People's Party (NPP), was originally headed by Alhaji Waziri Ibrahim, a businessman and contractor from the north-eastern Borno State. At its nominating convention in November 1978, Chief Ogunsanya, a senior member of the party, broke away from Ibrahim, assumed leadership of the NPP and appointed Dr Azikiwe as presidential candidate. Ibrahim immediately formed another party, the Greater Nigeria People's Party (GNPP), in order to advance his presidential aspirations.

Thus, the UPN, the NPN, the PRP, the NPP and the GNPP contested elections to the new bicameral national assembly, and for state assemblies and state governors, which took place in July 1979. The rate of abstention was high; in the presidential election itself, only 35% of the registered electorate voted. (The SMC's decree that the result of each election had to be made known before its successor was held undoubtedly benefited the party that dominated the election series.) The NPN received the most widespread support, securing 37% of the seats in the house of representatives, 36% in the state assemblies, and 38% in the senate, and winning seven of the 19 state governorships. In the presidential election, which took place in August, Shagari received 5.7m. votes, while Awolowo secured 4.9m., Azikiwe 2.8m., Kano 1.7m., and Ibrahim 1.6m.; thus, Shagari obtained the mandatory 25% of the vote in 12, rather than 13, of the 19 States, prompting controversy as to whether 12 or 13 constituted the necessary two-thirds of the States. FEDECO ruled that two-thirds of 19 was 12⅔, thereby reducing Shagari's required percentage of the vote in the vital 13th State from 25% to 16.67%. Amid strong protests from the UPN, the supreme court supported FEDECO. On 1 October 1979 military rule ended, the new constitution came into force, and Shagari was sworn in as president of the Second Republic.

The political term of the Second Republic, which lasted from 1979–83, was dominated by the problem of institutionalizing the framework of the federal government. There was also the issue of the division of the spoils of office, that developed against a background of alleged widespread corruption, of increasing socio-economic divisions, and of an economy which was rapidly losing its momentum.

Despite the evident fragility of the petroleum price on the world market, the Shagari government introduced an ambitious programme of investment, which, it was hoped, would be financed by a continuing high level of revenue from the petroleum industry. In 1982, however, a decline in international petroleum prices produced a foreign exchange crisis and widespread financial panic. During 1982–83 export earnings from petroleum continued to decline, and drastic political measures to curb imports and to control the export of foreign exchange, resulted in widespread corruption and fiscal malpractice. In 1983 Nigeria agreed to a restrictive economic programme, in return for support from the IMF. Meanwhile, the majority of Nigerians suffered increasing hardship, and this, in turn, generated resentment.

The government's attitude towards the economic situation and ensuing social discontent became evident in its reaction to a series of violent events in the north between 1980 and 1982. In December 1980 the populist preachings of Alhaji Muhammad Marwa (known as Maitatsine) generated serious rioting in Kano. Maitatsine himself was killed, and the rioting was violently suppressed. In October 1982 police in Maiduguri arrested 16 of Maitatsine's followers, and serious rioting ensued, spreading to Kano and Kaduna. The military suppressed the outbreak, killing hundreds of dissidents. In November the sect was officially banned. The NPN claimed that the events were a product of religious extremism, refusing to acknowledge the underlying cause of economic deprivation.

A further major problem confronting the Second Republic was the need to effect a transition to a federal system of government, a problem exacerbated by the fact that many of those who had been successful in the 1979 elections had spent many years working within the now-discarded British-derived system; tension developed between party apparatuses and the elected legislators and executives. There was also controversy over the issue of the degree of centralization that should be applied. The federal government had an apparent advantage, owing to its high degree of control over state spending, and over the army and police. However, resistance from a number of state governments resulted in litigation, and, in some cases, state governors were able to create, in fiscal terms, personal fiefdoms. This demonstrated the limitations of the federal government's power, as it attempted to contend with volatile regional and sectional interests. Federal control was further undermined by a reluctance to reduce state spending, and thus acknowledge an economic crisis that officially had no existence.

Decline of the NPN

By the early 1980s it was widely believed in Nigeria that the federal democracy was a façade, which allowed NPN politicians, dominated by a powerful political community in Kaduna, to distribute contracts and rewards in order to ensure their own continuation in power. In order to reinforce its power on the federal legislature, the NPN formed an alliance with Azikiwe's NPP, which, however, was dissolved in July 1981. The NPP then established a coalition, known as the Progressive Parties' Alliance (PPA), with the UPN, the major opposition party, thereby engendering further realignments in the parties that had fought the 1979 elections. The PRP and the GNPP split, with some of their members joining the PPA, while others aligned themselves with the government. In 1982, amid increasing political animosity towards the NPN, an abortive coup attempt was staged, ostensibly led by disaffected army officers. It emerged that the coup attempt had been instigated and funded by Alhaji Zana Bukar Mandara, a businessman, whose main grievance was that he had received fewer public contracts from the NPN than the SMC. He was found guilty of treasonable felony, and sentenced to 50 years in prison.

In 1982, in preparation for the elections of the following year, FEDECO was reconstituted and given extensive powers. Two new parties subsequently applied for registration; FEDECO approved the National Advance Party (NAP), led by the radical Lagos lawyer Tunji Braithwaite, but the 'Rimi faction' of the Progressive People's Party was refused recognition. FEDECO decreed also that the unrecognized splinter factions of the PRP and the GNPP would have to campaign in support of the political programmes of the NPN or the UPN. As campaigning began, the NPN used its entrenched position and financial influence to ensure its return to office. In May the government granted a pardon to the former 'Biafran' leader, Chukwuemeka Odumegwu-Ojukwu, who returned to Nigeria after more than 12 years of exile in Côte d'Ivoire, and later aligned himself with the NPN. Later that year the PPA became divided over the issue of choosing a presidential candidate; eventually, Awolowo was selected as the UPN candidate, and Azikiwe as the NPP candidate.

The elections, which were contested by the six political parties, took place in August–September 1983. In the presidential poll, Shagari was returned for a second term, receiving more than 12m. votes, or 47% of the total votes cast. The NPN attained a decisive majority in the elections to the senate (60 seats out of 96) and the house of representatives (264 seats out of 450), and won 13 of the 19 state governorships, with voting for the state assemblies and local governments largely following the same pattern. However, allegations of widespread electoral malpractice on the part of the NPN resulted in litigation and a reinforcement of the belief that the elections had been won by means of misconduct on a vast scale. On 1 October 1983 Shagari was sworn in for a second term as president on 1 October 1983, but he now presided over a country that was more bitterly divided than it had been at the inception of the Second Republic.

THE RETURN OF MILITARY RULE

Buhari and the SMC, 1983–85

On 31 December 1983 Shagari was deposed in a bloodless military coup, led by Maj.-Gen. Muhammadu Buhari, a former military governor of Borno and federal commissioner for petroleum during 1976–78. All political parties were banned, FEDECO was dissolved, and all bank accounts were temporarily 'frozen'. Several high-ranking military personnel were replaced, and prominent NPN members and politicians (including Shagari) were arrested. The new military regime, which was identified with the government of Murtala Ramat Muhammed, received widespread popular support. The structure of the new regime, similar to that of the military governments of 1975–79, comprised a reconstituted SMC, headed by Buhari; a national council of states, with a federal executive council, and state executive councils, presided over by military governors, were subsequently established.

In February 1984 the SMC issued a decree which empowered the government to enact laws that could not be challenged in the courts. Further legislation effectively prohibited the publication of information unfavourable to the government. In April it was announced that special tribunals were to be established to try those under arrest, and, *in absentia*, those who had fled the country; it became evident that the special tribunals were designed to recover assets which had been misappropriated by the civilian administration. By July a number of former governors had been sentenced for corruption and various forms of fiscal irregularity. However, there were widespread complaints that few of those who had been convicted by the tribunals were members of the NPN. Despite the SMC's denials of partiality, it was evident that former members of the NPN commanded considerable influence within the government.

In September 1984, following a number of ill-considered economic measures introduced by the SMC, Nigerian doctors and hospital workers staged a strike over the state of the health services. In February 1985 the SMC arrested a number of activist doctors, and banned the country's two leading professional medical associations. Public resentment concerning the delay in the trials of a large number of detainees from the Shagari era increased, following the acquittal, on corruption charges, of two former governors in March. (In January Buhari had announced that the government was to retain the powers of detention without trial, for three months, of citizens who were considered to constitute a threat to the state.) In July Maj.-Gen. Tunde Idiagbon, the chief of staff at supreme military headquarters, urged further economic retrenchment, stated that there was no schedule for a return to civilian rule, and prohibited all debate on the political future of Nigeria. Several journalists were subsequently detained, and quantities of newsprint were seized. Following Idiagbon's proclamation, there were widespread rumours of a coup attempt by junior officers and reports of open dissension within the SMC.

Babangida and the AFRC, 1985–93

In August 1985 Buhari's regime was deposed in a peaceful military coup, led by Maj.-Gen. (later Gen.) Ibrahim Babangida, the army chief of staff, who was named as the new head of state. The SMC was replaced by a 28-member armed forces ruling council (AFRC) which, unlike the SMC, was composed solely of military personnel. The post of chief of staff at supreme military headquarters, upon which Idiagbon had based his power, was abolished, and the post of chief of the general staff within the AFRC, a position that carried no responsibility for actual control of the armed forces, was created. A national council of ministers was formed, together with a reconstituted national council of state. There was an immediate redistribution of all state governorships, and Buhari's ministers were removed. Following the abolition of the decree on press censorship, a number of journalists were released, together with detainees from the Shagari government. In September Babangida, with the support of Maj.-Gen. Sani Abacha, the chief of the army staff, removed some 40 senior officers, including Buhari and Idiagbon, who were placed in detention.

In October 1985 Babangida declared a state of national economic emergency and assumed extensive interventionist powers over the economy. In December Babangida suspended negotiations with the IMF, a move that received widespread popular support, but caused dissension among certain members of the AFRC, and within the army command. On 20 December the AFRC suppressed a coup attempt by disaffected army officers. In February 1986 13 of the 14 named conspirators were convicted and executed.

In January 1986 Babangida announced that the armed forces would transfer power to a civilian government on 1 October 1990. The government appointed a 17-member political bureau, composed mainly of university academics, to formulate procedures for such a transition, but, at the same time, it insisted that no overt political activity was yet permissible. In May, amid protests from the Nigerian Bar Association, the AFRC extended the period of detention without trial from three to six months. In June sanctions were introduced against public officials convicted of corruption, which included the withdrawal of their passports for five years and the 'freezing' or confiscation of their assets. In July Shagari and former vice-president Ekwueme were released from detention, although they were subsequently banned for life from political activity. In the same month an extensive reshuffle of state governorships took place. In October the chief of general staff, Cdre Ebitu Ukiwe, was dismissed from the AFRC, and four new members were appointed.

In February 1986 Babangida announced that Nigeria's application for full membership of the Organization of the Islamic Conference (OIC) had been accepted; ensuing unrest among the non-Muslim sector of the population reflected alarm at increasing 'Islamization' in the country. In May about 15 people, mostly students, were shot dead by police during demonstrations at the Ahmadu Bello University, in Zaria, and a ban was imposed on further demonstrations. Babangida subsequently established a national commission to examine the advisability of Nigeria's membership of the OIC.

In March 1987 violent clashes broke out between Muslim and Christian youths at Kafanchan, in southern Kaduna State, which were reported to have resulted in some 30 deaths. A curfew was imposed, and an estimated 1,000 people were arrested. In April the AFRC formed an advisory council on religious affairs (ACRA), comprising Muslim and Christian leaders, to investigate the causes of the violence, and the authorities issued decrees banning religious organizations in schools and universities. However, sporadic outbreaks of student unrest continued in late 1987 and early 1988.

In July 1987, after receiving recommendations from the political bureau, the AFRC announced that power was to be transferred to a civilian government in 1992, two years later than envisaged, although a transitional programme would begin later in 1987 with the formation of an electoral commission and a directorate of social mobilization and political education. Political parties would remain banned during the transitional period, although elections for local government authorities were to be contested on a non-party basis by the end of 1987. A constituent assembly, which was to draft a new constitution, was to be established in 1988, and, following the promulgation of the constitution, further local and state elections were to be held in 1990, at which time two political parties were to be permitted. Elections for a bicameral federal legislature and for the presidency were to follow in 1992. Despite the rejection of the political bureau's recommendations for the adoption of a socialist programme, the acceptance by the AFRC of a two-party concept was interpreted as a move towards creating a political structure based on ideological alliances, rather than on ethnic loyalties.

In August 1987 the AFRC established a programme to promote political education, in preparation for the transition to civilian rule. In September the number of states was increased from 19 to 21, in an attempt to resolve the problem, experienced under the Second Republic, of determining what constituted a two-thirds majority of the states in an election. In the same month the AFRC proscribed all categories of former politicians and its own membership from contesting elections in 1992. In addition, the AFRC inaugurated a constitutional review committee to examine proposals for a new constitution, and a national electoral commission (NEC) to supervise future elections. On 12 December local government elections were contested by some 15,000 non-party candidates in 301 electoral areas. However, inadequate preparations for the elections by the NEC resulted in confusion, violence and allegations of electoral fraud and corruption. The NEC annulled the results in 312 local government wards, where further elections took place on 26 March 1988. Babangida subsequently announced that the new constitution would be promulgated in 1989, and proposed that an enlarged constituent assembly should debate the terms of the constitution. Accordingly, in April 1988 local government councillors elected 450 members to the constituent assembly. The AFRC later nominated a further 117 members, to represent various interest groups. Abuja, the future federal capital, was designated as the seat of the new assembly.

At the first session of the constituent assembly in June 1988, it was announced that the new constitution, which was to be modelled on that of 1979, would contain provisions prohibiting groups or individuals from usurping the government by force, and would ensure that all political change was effected by democratic means. Additionally, the constituent assembly was to draft and ratify the new constitution by the end of the year, rather than by May 1989, as originally envisaged. However, debate over the new draft constitution threatened to founder on the issue of religion. Muslims demanded the inclusion of Shari'a courts in the constitution, but in November 1988 further debate on this topic was banned by Babangida, as the progress of the assembly's work was being severely impeded. The AFRC postponed the date of submission of the draft constitution from January to March 1989, and threatened to dissolve the assembly unless it completed its task by the revised date. In January 1989 the assembly ratified the decision that, under the new constitution, a civilian president was to be elected for a six-year term, and was to declare all personal assets and liabilities before taking office.

In February 1989 Babangida reduced membership of the AFRC from 29 to 19, reportedly in order to reduce the power of the armed forces during the transitional period leading to civilian rule. In March a minor reshuffle of the council of ministers took place, and a new NEC was formed. In the same month, electoral legislation was amended to allow the AFRC to decide which of the political groupings recommended by the NEC were to be registered as the two legally permitted political parties when legislation prohibiting political activity was revoked later that year. The constituent assembly presented its report and draft constitution in early April. The assembly refused to include provisions for the transitional period, as this would legitimize a degree of military rule.

In early May 1989 the prohibition of political parties was ended, and the constitution was promulgated. The constitution was to enter into force on 1 October 1992, when a civilian government would be installed. Elections for the government of the Third Republic were to be contested by only two registered political parties, which were to be selected by the AFRC from the register compiled by the NEC. To be eligible for registration, a political party was to be founded on national policy-making (and not be allied to any ethnic or religious grouping), and be democratically organized. Other requirements were the listing of all members, the payment of a non-returnable registration fee of ₦50,000 to the NEC, the statement of all assets and liabilities and an assurance that no person prohibited from participating in politics was within the party. Six political parties subsequently emerged, and by the beginning of July this number had risen to approximately 40. However, only 13 parties succeeded in fulfilling the registration requirements by the stipulated date of 15 July. In the same month all local government councils were dissolved, and placed under the management of sole administrators, pending the election of new councillors in late 1989.

In October 1989 the NEC recommended six of the 13 associations to the AFRC: the People's Solidarity Party (PSP); the Nigerian National Congress (NNC); the People's Front of Nigeria (PFN); the Liberal Convention; the Nigerian Labour Party; and the Republican Party of Nigeria (RPN). The AFRC was subsequently expected to select two of these organizations, and to grant them the status of registered political parties. On 7 October, however, Babangida announced that the AFRC had decided to dissolve all 13 of the political associations, including the six endorsed by the NEC, on the grounds that the associations lacked distinctive ideologies, and were allied to discredited civilian politicians. In their place the AFRC created two new political parties, the Social Democratic Party (SDP) and the National Republic Convention (NRC). The announcement provoked widespread criticism, and the PSP voiced concern that it constituted an attack against the political class in Nigeria. Local elections, scheduled for December, were immediately postponed until early 1990, and the NEC announced that delays might be expected in the planned transition to civilian rule. In December the NEC published the draft constitutions and manifestos of the SDP and the NRC. In the same month Babangida carried out a major cabinet reshuffle, in which he assumed the defence portfolio, while his closest associate, Lt-Gen. Sani Abacha, the chief of the army staff, was appointed chairman of the joint chiefs of staff. It was widely believed that Babangida had taken control of the security forces in order to forestall any unrest in the transition to civilian rule. In March 1990 registration began for membership of the SDP and NRC. In the same month legislation which had permitted the detention of criminal suspects for up to six months without charge was amended, and a review panel was created to investigate individual cases.

In April 1990 junior army officers seized the headquarters of the Federal Radio Corpn and attacked the presidential residence. The leader of the attempted coup, Maj. Gideon Orkar claimed to be acting on behalf of Nigerians in the centre and south of the country, who, he alleged, were under-represented in the government, and announced that the Babangida regime had been overthrown; he also proclaimed that the predominantly Muslim states of Sokoto, Borno, Katsina, Kano and Bauchi were to be 'excised' from Nigeria, owing to the allegedly unlawful installation, earlier in 1989, of Alhaji Ibrahim Dasuki as the 18th sultan of Sokoto. However, the coup attempt was suppressed on the same day, and Orkar was arrested, as were some 300 other military personnel, and over 30 civilians. A number of journalists perceived as critical of the government were also detained. In July Orkar and a number of other prisoners were convicted by a military tribunal, on charges of conspiracy to commit treason; human rights groups, including the Nigerian Civil Liberties Organization, criticized the circumstances of the trial. Later that month 42 prisoners, including Orkar, were executed for their part in the attempted coup, despite appeals for clemency both from within Nigeria and abroad. Nine other defendents received custodial sentences, and the AFRC ordered the retrial by military tribunal of a further 31 of the accused. In September a further 27 prisoners were executed for their involvement in the attempted coup.

The election of officials from the SDP and NRC to local government councils was held in May 1990. In July more than 44,000 delegates, representing the two political parties, elected party executives for each state. The administration of the SDP and NRC was transferred from government-appointed administrative secretaries to elected party officials in early August. In the same month Chief Tom Ikimi, a southerner, was elected chairman of the NRC, while Baba Kingibe, a northerner, was installed as chairman of the SDP. However, it was widely believed that the NRC received most support from the north of the country, and the SDP from the south; in August the majority of the SDP's 4.5m. registered members originated from the southern states of Anambra, Imo and Oyo. Internal disputes were reported concerning the regional affiliation of potential candidates for the presidency of the civilian government. It was also alleged that former politicians, who were prohibited from membership of the parties, were involved in both the SDP and NRC.

Later in August 1990 Babangida implemented an extensive government reshuffle, in which nine ministers were replaced and the position of chief of general staff, held by Vice-Adm. Augustus Aikhomu, was abolished. Aikhomu was subsequently appointed to the newly-created post of vice-president. Babangida also announced that the presidency would be restructured in order to prepare for the transition to civilian rule, and that the size of the armed forces would be substantially reduced. In early September, in an attempt to restrict military influence in the government, three ministers were obliged to retire from the armed forces, leaving the minister of defence, Lt-Gen. Sani Abacha, as the only serving military officer in the council of ministers. 12 military state governors were replaced, and 21 civilian deputy governors were appointed to each state, pending gubernatorial elections, scheduled for 1991.

In late 1990 the AFRC provided subsidies to finance the political campaigns of both the NRC and SDP, but reiterated warnings that disputes within the parties would not be tolerated. In November the government introduced legislation providing for an 'open ballot' system, which was designed to reduce the incidence of electoral malpractice in the forthcoming elections. In December local government elections took place in some 440 areas, although only an estimated 20% of registered voters participated. 2,934 candidates representing the SDP were elected as councillors, with a further 232 elected to chair local councils, while 2,588 NRC candidates were elected as councillors, with 208 elected as chairmen. In January 1991 the government announced that state subsidies to the NRC and SDP would end in the following September. In February, however, the AFRC pledged continued financial support for elections, but confirmed that subsidies to promote the two political parties would be discontinued. Primary elections, which were to be preceded by a three-stage registration process for candidates, were scheduled for 24 August. Later in February a minor government reshuffle was effected, in which three ministers were replaced. In April the election of 38 chairmen and a number of councillors was annulled, after a tribunal ruled that the candidates concerned failed to fulfil electoral requirements.

In April 1991 a number of demonstrations by Muslims in the northern state of Katsina, in protest against the publication of an article considered to be blasphemous, culminated in violence. In the same month some 130 people, mainly Christians, were killed in riots in Bauchi and other predominantly northern states, where Christians proposed to slaughter pigs in a local abattoir that was also used by Muslims. It was later reported that some 120 Muslims had been killed by government troops, which had been sent to the region to suppress the riots. A curfew was subsequently imposed in Bauchi.

In June 1991 the NRC and SDP selected some 144,950 delegates to stand in the primary elections, which were to take place in August, for the gubernatorial and state assembly elections. By mid-1991 some 45 prospective presidential candidates, including Baba Kingibe, had emerged; the government expressed concern that tension between the NRC and SDP over this issue might undermine the programme for transition to civilian rule. In early September the government created nine new states, increasing the size of the federation to 30 states, in an attempt to ease ethnic tensions prior to the elections. However, violent demonstrations took place in several states where the government had failed to comply with demands to create a new state in the region, or where there was discontent at the relocation of the state capital. As a result of these protests, the government announced that the primary elections (which had already been postponed to September) would take place on 19 October, and would be followed by state assembly and gubernatorial elections on 14 December. It was confirmed, however, that the transition to civilian rule would be completed on 1 October 1992, as scheduled. Military administrators were subsequently appointed for the nine newly-created states, pending the gubernatorial elections.

In October 1991 demonstrations by Muslims took place at Kano, in the north, in protest against a tour of the state by a Christian preacher (following a decision by the authorities to refuse a Muslim leader permission to visit the area). More than 300 people were reported to have been killed in subsequent clashes between Muslims and Christians, which were suppressed by the army. On 19 October primary elections took place to select candidates for the forthcoming gubernatorial and state assembly elections. In November, however, following allegations of widespread electoral malpractice on the part of both the NRC and the SDP, results were annulled in nine states, and 12 candidates were disqualified; further elections were held in these states in early December. Controversy over the election results were reported to have increased divisions within both parties, especially within the SDP.

In December 1991 the seat of federal government was formally transferred from Lagos to Abuja, which was to be administered by a municipal council. In the gubernatorial and state assembly elections, which took place on 14 December, the SDP gained a majority in 16 state assemblies, while the NRC won control of 14 state assemblies; however, NRC candidates were elected as governors in 16 of the 30 states, many of which were situated in the south-east of Nigeria, where the SDP had previously received more support. Both the SDP and the NRC subsequently disputed the election results in a number of states, on the grounds of alleged malpractice. In the same month 11 former ministers, who had contravened the prohibition of members of former administrations from contesting elections, were arrested. Later in December, however, they were released, and the ban was lifted. (Only Babangida and officials convicted of criminal offences were henceforth prohibited from participating in elections.) In early January 1992 the new state governors were inaugurated.

In mid-January 1992 Babangida formed a new 20-member national council of ministers, in which a number of portfolios were reorganized. In the same month the government announced that elections for a bicameral national assembly, comprising a 593-member house of representatives and a 91-member senate, would take place on 7 November, and would be followed by a presidential election on 5 December. Primary elections for presidential candidates were to take place between 2 May and 20 June, while the selection of candidates to contest the legislative elections was scheduled for 4 July. The formal installation of a civilian government and the implementation of the new constitution were to take place on 2 January 1993, rather than on 1 October 1992, as previously envisaged. Later in January 1992 Babangida rejected demands by former politicians for the establishment of a government of national consensus.

In late 1991 violence erupted in Taruba, in the east, as a result of a long-standing land dispute between the Tiv and Jukun ethnic groups. The conflict continued in subsequent months, and by March 1992 up to 5,000 people were reported to have been killed. In January demonstrations in Katsina by Muslim fundamentalists demanding the imposition of Islamic (Shari'a) law were suppressed by security forces. In February some 30 people were killed in the northern state of Kaduna in clashes between the Hausa ethnic group, (which was predominantly Muslim) and the Kataf (predominantly Christian).

In February 1992 disputed election results in the states of Edo, Jigawa and Abia were annulled, and the state governors removed from office. However, the validity of the elections of the governors of Edo and Jigawa was later upheld at appeal. Later in February the government promulgated legislation empowering state governors to appoint commissioners (local ministers) without the approval of the state assemblies. In March, following discussions between the NEC, the NRC and the SDP, legislative elections were scheduled for 4 July, earlier than envisaged. The selection of candidates for the legislature was to commence on 23 May, while primary elections for presidential candidates were to take place between 1 August and 15 September. (The presidential election was to take place on 5 December, as originally scheduled.) Later in March legislation that empowered the NEC to disqualify electoral candidates considered to be unfit to hold office was introduced. In April an 18-member committee, comprising officials from several government ministries, was established to co-ordinate the transition to civilian rule. Later that month Babangida denied rumours of an abortive coup attempt by senior army officers.

In early May 1992 widespread rioting in protest at sharp increases in transport fares (resulting from a severe fuel shortage) culminated in a number of demonstrations in support of the resignation of the government, which were violently suppressed by the security forces; several people were reported to have been killed. An alliance of 25 organizations opposed to the government, known as the Campaign for Democracy (CD), which had been formed six months earlier, attributed the unrest to widespread discontent at increasing economic hardship. Later in May further rioting broke out in Lagos, following the arrest of the chairman of the CD, Dr Beko Ransome-Kuti, who had accused the government of deliberately instigating the violence in order to delay the transition to civilian rule. In the same month some 300 people were reported to have been killed in renewed violence between the Hausa and the Kataf in Kaduna; a curfew was briefly imposed in that state, and some 250 people were arrested. The government subsequently announced that all associations with religious or ethnic interests were henceforth to be prohibited; a security force, to be known as the national guard, was also to be established in order to reduce the role of the army in the suppression of riots.

In early June 1992 an extensive government reshuffle was effected, in which, among other changes, the influential minister of finance and economic planning, Alhaji Abubakar Alhaji, was replaced. Later in June a number of human rights activists, including Ransome-Kuti, were released, pending their trial later that year, on charges of conspiring to incite the riots in May. In the same month the NEC disqualified (without explanation) 32 candidates who had been selected to contest the legislative elections.

In elections to the national assembly, which took place on 4 July 1992 the SDP gained a majority in both chambers, securing 52 seats in the senate and 314 seats in the house of representatives, while the NRC won 37 seats in the senate and 275 seats in the house of representatives. However, the formal inauguration of the national assembly, scheduled for 27 July, was subsequently postponed until 2 January 1993, owing to the AFRC's insistence that it retain supreme legislative power until the installation of a civilian government. Primary elections to select an NRC and an SDP presidential candidate commenced on 1 August, but were suspended, owing to widespread electoral malpractice; results in states where elections had taken place were annulled. Further polls to select presidential candidates took place on 12, 19 and 26 September. By the end of the second round of voting, four leading candidates had emerged: Gen. (retd) Shehu Musa Yar'Adua and Chief Olu Falae (SDP), and Alhaji Umaru Shinkafi and Malam Adamu Ciroma (NRC). However, 10 of the original 23 aspirants (including Falae) boycotted the third and last stage of polling, alleging widespread electoral malpractice. Reports of irregularities were widely believed, and the participation rate in the poll was significantly low. Nevertheless, Yar'Adua claimed to have won the SDP nomination, while Shinkafi and Ciroma were to contest a final poll for the NRC candidacy on 10 October.

On 6 October 1992, however, the AFRC summarily suspended the results of all three stages of the presidential primaries, pending an investigation by the NEC into the alleged incidents of electoral malpractice. Despite the AFRC's reaffirmation of its pledge to transfer power to a civilian president by 3 January 1993, widespread suspicion that it intended to extend military rule subsequently increased. Later in October Babangida cancelled the presidential primary exercise itself, following a report by the NEC, which confirmed that malpractice had taken place; the local, state and national committees of both the NRC and SDP were dissolved, and replaced by caretaker committees. The AFRC further decreed that, owing to bribery during the September polls, the finances of both the SDP and NRC were to be audited, after which both parties would be allowed to proceed with internal restructuring. The NEC was subsequently commissioned to suggest new options for the selection of presidential candidates.

In November 1992 Babangida announced that the presidential election (scheduled for 5 December) was to be postponed until 12 June 1993, and the transition to civilian rule until 27 August. All 23 aspirants who had contested the discredited primaries in September 1992 were disqualified as presidential candidates. On 2 January 1993 the AFRC was to be replaced by a national defence and security council (NDSC), and the council of ministers by a civilian transitional council. However, the national assembly was to be inaugurated on 5 December, as scheduled. Babangida also announced a new programme for the installation of an elected civilian president: the restructured parties were each to nominate a new presidential candidate at a series of congresses, conducted at ward, local government, state and national level; the results of the rescheduled presidential election were to be announced during June. This further postponement in the installation of a democratically-elected government prompted renewed concern, despite Babangida's assurances of his commitment to the new schedule.

In December 1992 the bicameral national assembly was formally convened in the new federal capital of Abuja. Although it had been planned as a legislature for the postponed civilian administration, the national assembly was obliged to submit legislation for approval by the AFRC. On 2 January 1993 the NDSC and transitional council were duly installed. The 14-member NDSC was chaired by Babangida, and included the vice-president, the chief of defence staff, the service chiefs, and the inspector-general of police. The transitional council, which comprised 29 members, was to be responsible for federal administration, but was accountable to the NDSC. Its chairman, Chief Ernest Shonekan (a prominent businessman), was officially designated as head of government.

Following the registration of party voters in January 1993, some 300 aspirants to the presidency emerged, including Gowon and Ojukwu (principal protagonists in the 'Biafran' civil war). The NEC subsequently reviewed candidates in view of the NDSC's criteria. Following party congresses at ward level on 6 February, at local government level on 20 February, and at state level on 6 March, the number of candidates was reduced to 62. (Gowon was defeated at the local government congress on 20 February, while Ojukwu was disqualified by the NEC.) In early February discontent with the political process and continuing economic hardship resulted in a national strike in the public sector (which was abandoned later that month, after the government acceded to demands for wage increases).

National party congresses took place, as scheduled, during 27–29 March 1993: the NRC selected Alhaji Bashir Othman Tofa, an economist and businessman, to contest the presidential election, while Chief Moshood Kashimawo Olawale Abiola, a wealthy publisher, emerged as the SDP presidential candidate. In April Abiola chose Baba Kingibe (a former chairman of the SDP) as his vice-presidential candidate, and Tofa selected Dr Sylvester Ugoh, who had served in the Shagari administration. Later that month both Tofa and Abiola began to campaign throughout the country. Meanwhile, a number of informal organizations with diverse agendas emerged: the Association for a Better Nigeria (ABN) demanded the extension of military rule for a further four years, on the grounds of political instability; the Committee of Elder-Statesmen advocated a modified French system (with a prime minister as well as a president); and the Association for Democracy and Good Governance in Nigeria, which included many prominent former politicians, urged the immediate strengthening of federal institutions to preserve Nigeria and promote democracy.

In early June 1993, the leaders of the ABN, Abimbola Davies and Chief Francis Nzeribe, secured an interim injunction in the Abuja high court prohibiting the presidential election from taking place, pending the results of its appeal for the extension of military rule until 1997. However, the NEC announced that the injunction was invalid and that the election would take place, as scheduled. The rate of participation in the presidential election on 12 June was relatively low, owing, in part, to the confusion occasioned by Abuja court action, but international monitors throughout Nigeria reported that it had been conducted relatively peacefully. Two days later, initial results, released by the NEC, indicated that of the 6.6m. votes cast in 14 of the 30 states the SDP had secured 4.3m. and the NRC 2.3m. In 11 of the 14 states (including Tofa's home state of Kano), Abiola had obtained the majority of votes. Shortly afterwards, however, the NEC announced that the remaining results would not be released until further notice, following a further injunction, secured by the ABN, that prohibited the promulgation of the results; several other applications were presented in a number of courts, in an attempt to delay or suspend the electoral process. Widespread confusion followed, and protests were voiced that the NDSC (principally through the ABN, which was believed to have connections with Babangida) had deliberately sabotaged the elections. Later in June the CD promulgated election results, which indicated that Abiola had won the majority of votes in 19 states, and Tofa in 11 states. Significantly, Tofa did not challenge these results. The NDSC subsequently attracted increasing domestic and international criticism.

Finally, on 23 June 1993, the NDSC declared the results of the election to be invalid, halted all court proceedings pertaining to the election, suspended the NEC, and repealed all decrees relating to the transition to civilian rule. New electoral regulations were introduced that effectively precluded Abiola and Tofa from contesting a further presidential poll. Babangida subsequently announced that the election had been marred by corruption and other irregularities, but insisted that he remained committed to the transition on 27 August; in order to meet this schedule, a reconstituted NEC was to supervise the selection of two new presidential candidates by the SDP and NRC. Abiola, however, continued to claim, with much popular agreement, that he had been legitimately elected to the presidency. The United Kingdom subsequently announced that it was to review its bilateral relations with Nigeria, and imposed a number of military sanctions, while the USA immediately suspended all assistance to the government.

In early July 1993 a demonstration, organized by the CD, led to rioting, prompted by resentment at political developments, in conjunction with long-standing economic hardship. Order was subsequently restored, after security forces violently suppressed protests; however, sporadic unrest was reported throughout the country. The NDSC provisionally announced that a new presidential election was to take place on 14 August in order to fulfil the pledge to transfer power on 27 August, prompting general disbelief. The SDP declared that it intended to boycott an electoral process that superseded its victory on 12 June. Later in July the NDSC proscribed five national publishing groups, including Concord Press, which was owned by Abiola, and detained a number of supporters of democracy.

'Interim National Government'

At the end of July 1993 Babangida announced that an interim national government (ING) was to be established, on the grounds that there was insufficient time to permit the scheduled transition to civilian rule on 27 August. A committee, comprising officials of the two parties and senior military officers, headed by Aikhomu, was subsequently established to determine the composition of the ING. Abiola immediately declared his opposition to the proposed administration, and stated his intention of forming a 'parallel government'. (He subsequently fled abroad, following alleged death threats, and attempted to solicit international support for his claim to the presidency.) In August the CD continued its campaign of civil disobedience in protest at the annulment of the election, appealing for a three-day general strike (which was widely observed in the southwest of the country, where Abiola received most popular support). Several prominent members of the CD were arrested, in an attempt to prevent further protests, while additional restrictions were imposed on the press. Later in August Babangida announced his resignation, reportedly as a result of pressure from prominent members of the NDSC, notably the secretary of defence, Gen. Sani Abacha. On 27 August a 32-member interim federal executive council, headed by Shonekan, was installed; the new administration, which included several members of the former transitional council, was to supervise the organization of local government elections later that year and a presidential election in early 1994, while the transitional period for the return to civilian rule was extended to 31 March 1994. (Shonekan was later designated as head of state and commander-in-chief of the armed forces.) Supporters of democracy criticized the inclusion in the ING of several members of the former NDSC (which had been dissolved), including Abacha, who was appointed to the new post of vice-president, and the proposed establishment of two predominantly military councils as advisory bodies to the president.

At the end of August 1993 the CD staged a further three-day strike, while the Nigerian Labour Congress (NLC) and the National Union of Petroleum and Natural Gas Workers (NUPENG) also announced industrial action in support of the installation of a civilian administration, headed by Abiola. The combined strike action resulted in a severe fuel shortage and the effective suspension of economic activity in the greater part of the country. Following the establishment of the ING, Shonekan pledged his commitment to the democratic process, and, in an effort to restore order, initiated negotiations with the NLC and effected the release of several journalists and prominent members of the CD, including Ransome-Kuti, who had been arrested in July. In early September the NLC and NUPENG provisionally suspended strike action, after the ING agreed to consider their demands.

In September 1993 a series of military appointments, which included the nomination of Lt-Gen. Oladipo Diya to the office of chief of defence staff, effectively removed supporters of Babangida from significant posts within the armed forces, thereby strengthening Abacha's position. Diya, who had reportedly opposed the annulment of the presidential election, subsequently declared that military involvement in politics would cease. In the same month Abiola returned to Lagos, amid popular acclaim. Later in September the NRC and SDP agreed to a new timetable, whereby local government elections and a presidential election would take place concurrently in February 1994. The CD subsequently announced the resumption of strike action in support of demands for the installation of Abiola as president; an ensuing demonstration by supporters of the CD in Lagos was violently dispersed by security forces, and Ransome-Kuti, together with other prominent members of the CD, was arrested. In October the SDP (which had previously demonstrated limited support for Abiola, as a result of dissension within the party) demanded that he be inaugurated as president, and refused to participate in the new elections. In the same month Shonekan established a committee to investigate the circumstances that had resulted in the annulment of the presidential election.

In late October 1993 members of a hitherto unknown organization, the Movement for the Advancement of Democracy (MAD), hijacked a Nigerian aircraft and issued a number of demands, principally that the ING resign in favour of Abiola; passengers on the aircraft, who were taken hostage, reportedly included high-ranking Nigerian officials. Abiola subsequently denied involvement with the hijackers, and appealed to them to surrender to the authorities. Shortly afterwards the hijackers (who had diverted the aircraft to the Nigerien capital, Niamey) were overpowered by members of the Nigerien security forces, reportedly with the support of French troops. Other members of the MAD were later arrested in Lagos.

In early November 1993 the president of the senate, a strong supporter of Abiola, was removed. Shortly afterwards the Lagos High Court ruled in favour of an application by Abiola, declaring the establishment of the ING to be invalid under the terms of the 1979 constitution (whereby the president of the senate was to act as interim head of state). In the same month the ING dissolved the government councils, prior to local elections, and withdrew state subsidies on petroleum products. The resultant dramatic increase in the price of fuel prompted widespread anti-government demonstrations, and the NLC announced the resumption of strike action. Meanwhile, the scheduled revision of the electoral register ended in failure, owing to a boycott by supporters of the SDP, and it became apparent that the new schedule for the transition to civilian rule was unviable.

Abacha and the PRC

On 17 November 1993, following a meeting with senior military officials, Shonekan announced his resignation as head of state, and immediately transferred power to Abacha (confirming widespread speculation that Abacha had effectively assumed control of the government following Babangida's resignation). On the following day Abacha dissolved all organs of state and bodies that had been established under the transitional process, replaced the state governors with military administrators, prohibited political activity (thereby proscribing the NRC and the SDP), and announced the formation of a provisional ruling council (PRC), which was to comprise senior military officials and principal members of a new federal executive council (FEC). He insisted, however, that he intended to relinquish power to a civilian government, and pledged to convene a conference with a mandate to determine the constitutional future of the country. Restrictions on the media were suspended, and the ban that had been imposed on certain publishing groups in July was revoked. Ensuing demonstrations by supporters of democracy were suppressed by security forces (although protests were generally limited). On 21 November Abacha introduced legislation that formally restored the 1979 constitution and provided for the establishment of the new government organs. In an apparent attempt to counter domestic and international criticism, several prominent supporters of Abiola, including Kingibe, and four former members of the ING were appointed to the PRC and FEC, which were installed on 24 November. Abacha subsequently removed 17 senior military officers, who were believed to be loyal to Babangida. In the same month discussions between Abacha and Abiola took place, while the NLC agreed to abandon strike action after the government acted to limit the increase in the price of petroleum products.

In December 1993 increasing controversy was reported regarding the mandate of the proposed constitutional conference after Abacha stated that the issue of devolution of power in Nigeria would not be considered, while the CD dismissed the conference as an attempt to grant legitimate status to the new administration. Later in December a prominent civil rights lawyer appealed against new legislation that prohibited legal challenges to the decrees promulgated by Abacha in November. In the same month the United Kingdom announced that member nations of the European Union were to impose further sanctions against Nigeria, including restrictions on the export of armaments. In January 1994 the Government announced the abandonment of economic reforms, which had been initiated in 1986, prompting concern among international financial institutions. Later in January Abacha established a 19-member national constitutional conference commission to organize the conference. However, several lawyers subsequently contested the mandate of the commission to determine the composition and agenda of the conference, and the government's decision that the recommendations of the conference be submitted for approval by the PRC. In the same month security forces seized copies of a periodical, which contained an article concerning the new legislation that had terminated legal jurisdiction in matters pertaining to the new administration. In February Gen. (retd) Shehu Musa Yar'Adua, a member of the 1976–1979 regime and a former SDP presidential candidate, was temporarily detained, after criticizing Abacha. Later that month security forces prevented the CD from convening a press conference.

In March 1994 the US government indicated that it would end sanctions against Nigeria if the constitutional conference were to be convened to the satisfaction of the Nigerian people. In April it was reported that five people had been killed in fighting between members of the Christian and Muslim population in the central town of Jos, while a further 10 people died in inter-ethnic clashes in south-eastern Nigeria. In the same month the government announced a programme for the establishment of a national constitutional conference: some 273 delegates were to be elected in May, while 96 delegates were to be nominated by the government from a list of eligible citizens submitted by each state. The national constitutional conference was to be convened at the end of June, and was to submit recommendations, including a new draft constitution, to the PRC in late October. A further stage in the transitional programme was to commence in mid-January 1995, when the ban on political activity was to end. In May 1994 a new pro-democracy organization, comprising former politicians, retired military officers and human rights activists, the National Democratic Coalition (NADECO), demanded that Abacha relinquish power by the end of that month and urged a boycott of the national constitutional conference. Later in May elections took place at ward, and subsequently at local government, level to select the 273 conference delegates; the boycott was widely observed in the south-west of the country, and a low level of voter participation was reported. It was reported that Ken Saro-Wiwa, a prominent campaigner for the self-determination of the Ogoni ethnic group (in protest at the government's exploitation of Ogoni territory in Rivers State, which contained significant reserves of petroleum) had been arrested in connection with the deaths of four Ogoni electoral candidates. At the end of May Abiola announced his intention of forming a government of national unity by 12 June (the anniversary of the presidential election). Violent anti-government protests were reported, following the expiry of the date stipulated by NADECO for the resignation of the military administration.

In early June 1994 members of the former senate (including its president) were detained on charges of treason, after the senators reconvened and declared the government to be illegal. A number of prominent opposition members, including Ransome-Kuti, were also arrested, after the CD urged a campaign of civil disobedience, which received the support of NADECO. (Ransome-Kuti was subsequently charged with treason.) Following a symbolic ceremony, in which Abiola was publicly inaugurated as president and head of a parallel government, a warrant was issued for his arrest on charges of treason; the authorities claimed that he intended to organize an uprising to force the military administration to relinquish power. Later in June security forces arrested Abiola (who had emerged from hiding to attend a rally in Lagos), prompting protests from pro-democracy organizations and criticism from the governments of the United Kingdom and the USA. Further demonstrations in support of demands for an immediate suspension of military rule and the installation of Abiola as president ensued, while NUPENG threatened to initiate strike action unless the government agreed to release Abiola. At the initial session of the constitutional conference, which was convened at the end of June, as scheduled, Abacha pledged to relinquish power on a date that would be determined by the conference. (The conference subsequently established committees to consider a number of contentious issues, including that of the annulment of the presidential election in 1993.) In early July the minister of justice was charged with contempt of court, after the government failed to comply with two orders from the high court in Abuja to justify the continued detention of Abiola, who had taken legal action challenging his arrest as unconstitutional and in violation of human rights. Shortly afterwards Abiola was arraigned before a special high court that had been appointed by the government, and charged with 'treasonable felony.'

In early July 1994 NUPENG initiated strike action in support of demands for Abiola's release and installation as president, and an improvement in government investment in the petroleum industry; the strike was subsequently joined by the senior petroleum workers' union, the Petroleum and Natural Gas Senior Staff Association (PENGASSAN). Government troops distributed fuel in an attempt to ease the resultant national shortage, while it was reported that senior officials of NUPENG and PENGASSAN, including the secretary-general of NUPENG, Frank Kokori, had been arrested. By mid-July members of affiliate unions in a number of sectors had joined the strike action, resulting in an effective suspension of economic activity in Lagos and other commercially significant regions in the south-west of the country. However, the national impact of the strike was constrained by ethnic and regional divisions; it was reported that unions in northern and eastern regions had failed to join strike action. In addition, petroleum exports were initially unaffected, largely owing to expatriate workers who failed to observe the strike. Later in July union officials suspended negotiations with the government, on the grounds that the authorities had failed to release Kokori from detention. (It subsequently transpired, however, that Kokori had not been held in detention, after he apparently emerged from hiding). At the end of July it was reported that some 20 people had been killed, when security forces violently supressed anti-government demonstrations. Meanwhile, the US special envoy in Nigeria, Rev. Jesse Jackson, announced that the USA would envisage the suspension of Nigerian assets, and the imposition of further sanctions. In early August the NLC initiated an indefinite general strike in support of NUPENG; following the suppression of further anti-government protests, in which about five demonstrators were killed, however, the NLC suspended strike action after two days to allow negotiations with the government to proceed.

In early August 1994 Abiola's trial was adjourned, pending a ruling regarding a defence appeal that the high court in Abuja had no jurisdiction in the case of an offence that had been allegedly committed in Lagos. Abiola (who was reported to be suffering from ill health) refused bail, since the stipulated conditions required him to refrain from political activity. The court finally decided that it had the necessary jurisdiction, although the presiding judge announced his withdrawal from the trial. In the same month the authorities banned the national newspaper, The Guardian, following the publication of a report indicating that divisions existed within the government as to whether to proceed with the charges against Abiola. Later in August Abacha replaced the senior officials of NUPENG and PENGASSAN, and ordered petroleum workers to end strike action. Although a number of union members failed to comply, the effects of the strike began to decline. In early September the union officials who had been dismissed announced the suspension of strike action, in view of the deterioration of the economy and the ensuing widespread hardship. In the same month Abacha promulgated legislation that extended the period of detention without trial to three months and prohibited legal action challenging government decisions. The minister of justice was subsequently dismissed, after protesting that he had not been consulted regarding the new legislation. In mid-September the state military administrators were reorganized. Later that month Abacha reconstituted the PRC, which was enlarged from 11 to 25 members, all of whom were senior military officials.

INTERNATIONAL RELATIONS

Nigeria has taken a leading role in African affairs and is a prominent member of the Economic Community of West African States (ECOWAS) and other regional organizations. The Nigerian government has contributed a significant number of troops to the ECOWAS Monitoring Group (ECOMOG), which was deployed in Liberia from August 1990 in response to the conflict between government forces and rebels in that country (see chapter on Liberia). From October 1992 Nigerian troops under ECOMOG command played a dominant role in a major offensive against rebel forces. Following a peace agreement, which was signed in July 1993, however, the Nigerian government announced that it was to withdraw its contingent from a restructured ECOMOG force. In 1993 Nigerian troops were dispatched to Sierra Leone, in response to a formal request by the Sierra Leonean government for military assistance to repulse attacks by rebels in that country. In the early 1990s Nigeria also participated in peace-keeping missions that were deployed in several countries, including Angola, Somalia and the former Yugoslavia.

In July 1984 relations between Nigeria and the United Kingdom were adversely affected by the attempted kidnapping, in London, of Umaru Dikko, a political exile and a former minister in the Shagari administration, who was being sought for trial in Nigeria on charges of corruption. The alleged involvement of Nigerian diplomats in the affair resulted in the mutual withdrawal of the two countries' high commissioners. Full diplomatic relations were restored in February 1986, however, and in March 1988 Nigeria and the United Kingdom resumed annual bilateral talks at ministerial level (which had been suspended since 1984). In mid-1993, however, the United Kingdom, together with other European nations and the USA, imposed sanctions against Nigeria, in response to the suspension of the scheduled transition to civilian rule.

In January 1992 the Nigerian government closed the border with Chad, following an attack against a Nigerian border village by Chadian troops, who were conducting an offensive against rebels. In February, however, the border was reopened, and Nigeria undertook to prevent Chadian anti-government rebels from operating within Nigerian territory.

In 1991 the Nigerian government claimed that Cameroonian security forces had annexed several Nigerian fishing settlements in Cross River State (in south-eastern Nigeria), following a long-standing border dispute, based on a 1913 agreement between Germany and the United Kingdom that ceded the Bakassi peninsula in the Gulf of Guinea (a region of strategic significance) to Cameroon; Cameroon's claim to the region was upheld by an unratified agreement in 1975. Subsequent negotiations between Nigerian and Cameroonian officials in an effort to resolve the dispute achieved little progress. In December 1993 some 500 Nigerian troops were dispatched to the region, in response to a number of incidents in which Nigerian nationals had been killed by Cameroonian security forces. Later that month the two nations agreed to establish a joint patrol at the disputed area, and to investigate the cause of the incidents. In February 1994, however, the Nigerian government increased the number of troops deployed in the region. Later in February the Cameroonian government announced that it was to submit the dispute for adjudication by the UN, the OAU, and the International Court of Justice, and requested military assistance from France. Subsequent reports of clashes between Cameroonian and Nigerian forces in the region prompted fears of a full-scale conflict between the two nations. In March Cameroon agreed to enter into bilateral negotiations with Nigeria (without the involvement of international mediators) to resolve the issue. Later that month, however, a proposal by the Nigerian government that a referendum be conducted in the disputed region was rejected by Cameroon. Also in March the OAU urged the withdrawal of troops from the region; both governments indicated dissatisfaction with the resolution. In May two members of the Nigerian armed forces were killed in further clashes in the region. Later that month negotiations between the two nations, which were mediated by Togo, resumed in the Cameroonian capital, Yaoundé. In June the heads of state of the two nations met at an OAU summit meeting in Tunis, Tunisia, and agreed to establish a joint committee to achieve a resolution to the dispute. However, a meeting to discuss the issue, which was scheduled to take place in July, was postponed, owing to the unrest in Nigeria.

Economy

RICHARD SYNGE

Based on an earlier article by PATRICK SMITH

Despite considerable agricultural and mineral resources, Nigeria is ranked by the World Bank as low-income country. In 1992, according to the World Bank, Nigeria's gross domestic product (GDP) was US $29,667m., with gross national product (GNP) equivalent to $320 per head. The expansion of the economy has been constrained by both political and economic reverses. Annual GDP growth rate averaged 4.6% between 1970–80, but declined to 2.6% per year in the period 1980–85. After recovering to an annual average of 5.4% between 1986–91, the GDP growth rate subsequently declined, to 3.6% in 1992 and to an estimated 2.9% in 1993.

Statistical assessments of the Nigerian economy are subject to wide margins of error, as a result of the lack of reliable data. Although the population of the country is not known with real certainty, the census of November 1991 recorded a total of 88,514,501 inhabitants. In 1985–92 the population increased by an annual average of 2.9%. According to figures (excluding the contribution of unofficial trade) from the Central Bank of Nigeria (CBN), the leading economic activities are agriculture and livestock, which accounted for 35.3% of GDP in 1992, crude petroleum (12.9%), wholesale and retail trade (12.5%), government services (9.0%), finance and insurance (8.7%) and manufacturing (8.6%).

The development of the petroleum industry in the late 1960s and 1970s radically transformed Nigeria from an agriculturally-based economy to a major oil exporter. Increased earnings from petroleum exports generated high levels of real economic growth, and by the mid-1970s Nigeria ranked as the dominant economy in sub-Saharan Africa and as the continent's major exporter of petroleum. Following the decline in world petroleum prices after 1981, however, the government became increasingly over-extended financially, with insufficient revenue from petroleum to pay the rising cost of imports or to finance major development projects. The decline in Nigeria's earnings of foreign exchange led to an accumulation of arrears in trade debts and of import shortages, which, in turn, resulted in a sharp fall in economic activity, with most of Nigerian industry struggling to operate without essential imported raw materials and spare parts. A series of poor harvests, an overvalued currency and a widening budget deficit compounded the problem. The Buhari government responded to the crisis by implementing a range of severe austerity measures, including further cuts in public expenditure, and rigid restrictions on credit and the availability of foreign exchange.

The Babangida military government, which took power in August 1985, continued its predecessor's policies of austerity and monetary control. Babangida declared a state of economic emergency, under which the import of rice and maize was banned, and a national recovery fund created. However, the dramatic fall in international prices for petroleum in 1986, and reduced output in all sectors (except agriculture), and kept the economy in the depths of recession. In July 1986 the Babangida government announced a two-year structural adjustment programme (SAP), which aimed at expanding non-oil exports, reducing the import of goods which could be manufactured locally, achieving self-sufficiency in food and increasing the role of the private sector. The SAP included the abolition of import licences and a reduction in import duties. One of its principal features, however, was the creation, in September, of two rates for foreign exchange transactions; a first 'tier', which the government used for foreign debt-servicing and other specified outgoings, and a second-tier foreign exchange market (SFEM) for commercial transactions. SFEM rates were determined by means of auctions of available foreign exchange, conducted by the central bank. In July 1987 the two-tier exchange mechanism was replaced by fortnightly auctions at a unitary foreign exchange market (FEM). In January 1991 the auction system was replaced; the CBN was henceforth to fix the rate in consultation with leading commercial banks. The government also permitted the establishment of bureaux de change, which were to sell as much as $30,000 of foreign exchange at market rates that represented a variable premium over the official CBN rate.

In early 1988 the government issued a list of 110 state enterprises to be 'privatized' or partially commercialized. A special technical committee was established to implement the programme, which was to involve the Nigerian Railway Corporation, the National Electric Power Authority, and the telecommunications conglomerate, NITEL. By the end of 1992, 90 of the 120 enterprises scheduled for 'privatization', including 12 commercial banks in which the government had a shareholding, had been sold, while the transfer to private ownership of Nigeria Airways and the Nigerian National Shipping Line Ltd was also envisaged.

Measures undertaken under the SAP with the aim of attracting private capital from abroad proved largely unsuccessful; investors were deterred by the country's reputation for corruption, and by the government's failure to control expenditure. The budget deficit began to expand rapidly, reaching the equivalent of 11.4% of GDP in 1988 and increasing to more than 12% of GDP in subsequent years. Economic instablity was also reflected in a persistently high rate of inflation, which increased from an annual average of 24.0% in 1986–91, to 44.6% in 1992, and to an estimated 70.0% in 1993. The SAP was abandoned in 1994, following a severe deterioration in political and economic conditions in the early 1990s.

The government's new economic policy, which was delineated in the 1994 budget, was based on the maintainence of a fixed exchange rate for the naira of ₦22.0 = US $1. The policy entailed a full return to foreign exchange controls, which were to be administered by the CBN, and an end to free market currency dealings. However, the administration's failure to cease parallel market transactions, together with the deterrent effect of its policies on private investment, led many observers to predict that further changes would be made in economic policy in due course.

AGRICULTURE

Until Nigeria attained independence in 1960, agriculture was the most important sector of the economy, accounting for more than one-half of GDP and for more than three-quarters of export earnings. However, with the rapid expansion of the petroleum industry, agricultural development was neglected, and the sector entered a relative decline. Between the mid-1960s and the mid-1980s, Nigeria moved from a position of self-sufficiency in basic foodstuffs to one of heavy dependence on imports. Under-investment, a steady drift away from the land to urban centres, increased consumer preference for imported foodstuffs (particularly rice and wheat) and outdated farming techniques continued to keep the level of food production well behind the rate of population growth. After experiencing growth rates of 8%–10% per annum during the early 1970s, the increase in agricultural production declined to around 4% per annum towards the end of the decade. The slow growth continued into the 1980s, with output rising by only 3.4% in 1981 and by 2.7% in 1982. The effects of drought and the government's austerity programme resulted in a severe 9.4% fall in agricultural output in 1983. However, a succession of good harvests, higher producer prices, reductions in cereal imports and a resurgence of public and private investment in crop production resulted in a sharp recovery in production. Food output showed the strongest growth, rising by 7% in 1984 and by an estimated 10% in 1985, when total agricultural output increased by 3.8%. Agriculture was the only sector to show any significant expansion in 1986, when, owing to further record harvests of rice and maize, overall agricultural production increased by 2.1%. In 1992, according to government estimates, the agricultural sector provided 35.3% of total GDP (at constant 1984 prices).

Traditional smallholder farmers, who use simple techniques of production and the bush-fallow system of cultivation, account for around two-thirds of Nigeria's total agricultural production. The number of state farms is relatively small, and of decreasing importance. Since 1986 many of the loss-making parastatal bodies have been closed down or sold to the private sector. Subsistence food crops (mainly sorghum, maize, taro, yams, cassava, rice and millet) are grown in the central and western areas of Nigeria, and are traded largely outside the cash economy.

Cash crops (mainly palm kernels, coffee, cotton, cocoa, rubber and groundnuts) are grown in the mid-west and north of the country. In June 1986 six federal commodity marketing boards ceased trading (they were formally abolished in 1987), and it was hoped that the freeing of agricultural commodities from marketing monopolies, combined with a devalued naira, would increase producer prices and output. Owing to these measures, production of cash crops has increased considerably in 1988.

Among the agricultural crops, only cocoa makes any significant contribution to exports, but Nigeria's share of the world cocoa market has been substantially reduced in recent years, owing to ageing trees, low producer prices, black pod disease, smuggling and labour shortages. Moreover, the abolition of the Cocoa Marketing Board in 1987 led to poor quality control and fraudulent trading practices, which adversely affected the market reputation of Nigerian cocoa. The government subsequently reintroduced licences for marketers of cocoa and improved inspection procedures. Recent emphasis has been placed on encouraging domestic cocoa-processing to provide higher-value products for export. According to the International Cocoa Organization, cocoa production in 1990/91 was 293,000 tons, compared with 160,000 tons in 1989/90. Nigeria was the world's fourth largest exporter of cocoa beans in 1990/91, with sales of 135,000 tons accounting for about 7.1% of world trade in this commodity.

The production and export of oil palm products has declined dramatically. The world's leading exporter of palm oil until overtaken by Malaysia in 1971, Nigeria is now heavily dependent on imports in order to satisfy domestic needs. Like other cash-crop sectors, output of palm products has suffered from labour shortages, inefficient traditional harvesting methods, lack of vital inputs and low levels of capital investment. A sharp reduction in imports and large-scale replanting in eastern Rivers State did, however, result in a substantial increase in production during the mid-1980s. Trade liberalization and the exchange rate policy have also contributed to the improvement in palm oil production since 1987. Most of the surplus output has been used for import substitution, with some increase in exports of palm products. According to unofficial figures from the FAO, palm kernel production increased from 350,000 tons in 1986 to 385,000 tons in 1992. There have been substantial investments in oil-milling facilities to produce vegetable oil for domestic use. Palm oil production was estimated at 820,000 tons in 1989, increasing to 900,000 tons in 1992.

In 1990 Nigeria overtook Liberia as the largest rubber producer in Africa. Production rose from 55,000 tons in 1986 to 152,000 tons in 1990 and 155,000 tons in 1991. Output in 1992 was 129,000 tons. Benefits from a replanting programme in the eastern States have yet to materialize, and local demand from the tyre and footwear industries continues to outstrip domestic supply. A programme to increase output of palm kernels and rubber, with financial assistance from the World Bank, is being implemented.

Production of raw cotton increased to 276,000 tons in 1990 (compared with 187,000 tons in 1989), but declined to 270,000 tons in 1991, despite considerable public and private investment in the sector. Incentives for local textile companies and higher tariffs on imported cotton have stimulated local production. A ban on maize and rice imports has also raised local production although the textile manufacturers prefer the higher quality of legally or illegally imported cotton from neighbouring countries. Assessments of the amounts of staple food crops produced in Nigeria have varied widely; according to the CBN annual report for 1992, which has substantially revised its earlier statistical base to conform more closely with that of the FAO, the principal crops in 1992 were cassava (21.3m. tons), yams (18.6m. tons), maize (5.6m. tons), sorghum (5.2m. tons), millet (4.0m. tons) and rice (3.1m. tons).

The rapid expansion in the numbers of livestock was curtailed in 1983, when an epidemic of rinderpest was estimated to have killed more than 1.5m. cattle. After the rinderpest epidemic, there was a good recovery, with total output of livestock products increasing by 3.7% in 1986, 2.1% in 1987 and 2.5% in 1988. According to the ministry of agriculture, beef production reached 278,000 tons in 1990, an increase of 6.9% compared with 1988, while the output of goat meat was 218,000 tons. In 1992 beef production totalled 281,000 tons. Nigeria's annual fish catch declined from 538,350 tons in 1983 to 241,634 tons in 1985, owing to shortages of trawlers and nets, and the cancellation of industrial fishing licences, but increased in 1986 to 268,500 tons. According to estimates from the ministry of agriculture, the fish catch totalled 362,000 tons in 1990, declining to 262,000 tons in 1992.

Some 20% of the land area is forested, but exports of timber (mostly obeche, abura and mahogany) are relatively small. Nigeria's annual output of timber declined by 8% in the period 1982–84, and deforestation, particularly in the Niger delta area, remains a considerable problem. Following the removal of a ban on specific timber exports, timber production increased to 99m. cubic metres in 1988, and then to 100.1m. in 1989. About 12% of the country's total land area is threatened by the encroaching Sahara desert in the north, and a National Committee on Arid Zone Afforestation has been established as part of the anti-desertification programme. In June 1989 it was announced that the government was to share the cost of a $135m. afforestation project with the World Bank. Fuelwood is still the main source of domestic energy, and accounts for more than 60% of commercial primary energy consumption.

As with the Buhari government, the military regime of Gen. Babangida has made agricultural development and food self-sufficiency key components of its overall economic strategy. Agriculture, arguably the most successful element of the government's structural adjustment programme, has exhibited sharp increases in food crop production and a rise in commodity exports. The increase in agricultural production has been attributed to three policy initiatives: the devaluation of the naira, which has promoted commodity exports and discouraged cheap food imports; the abolition of the state-controlled commodity boards and removal of restrictions on agricultural pricing; and the imposition of an import ban on wheat, maize and barley. Attention has focused on the smallholder farmer, who produces some 90% of food consumed in Nigeria. The government aims to increase agriculture's contribution to GDP to more than 40% by the year 2000.

Apart from maize, most of the corporate investment in agriculture since 1986 has centered on oil palm and cotton, reflecting the relative success of the vegetable oil and textile industries in the use of local raw materials. The Land Use Decree, introduced in 1978, stipulates that land is vested in the state governors, who hold it in trust for all Nigerians. The government has agreed to amend the Decree, in response to protests from smallholder farmers, who claim that the Decree discriminates against them. In addition to the problem of land availability, the other key issues facing the agricultural sector are environmental degradation, inadequate storage facilities and transport, leading to massive post harvest losses, lack of research and training facilities for the transfer of new technologies, and the absence of credit facilities for smallholder farmers. Nigeria's resources are not fully exploited, and many parts of the country remain very poorly developed. Inadequate provision of economic infrastructure such as power, water supply, roads and telecommunications, especially in the rural areas, has proved an impediment to both agricultural and industrial investment.

PETROLEUM

Since the early 1970s, the petroleum industry has been the dominant sector of the Nigerian economy and the major determinant of the country's economic growth. In 1986 the petroleum industry accounted for around 18% of GDP, more than 97% of total export earnings and over 70% of all government revenues. In 1992 revenue from petroleum represented about 95% of the country's foreign exchange earnings. Nigeria's proven reserves were estimated at 17,900m. barrels in December 1993, and were targeted to reach 19,995m. barrels by the mid-1990s, when output capacity was expected to total 2m. barrels per day (b/d).

The first commercial discoveries of petroleum were made in 1956 in the Niger River delta region. Average production increased rapidly, fluctuating at around 2m. barrels b/d in the period 1974–79, before declining to 700,000 b/d in mid-1981. A partial recovery during late 1981 and January/February 1982 was followed by a new slump, with production falling to 900,000 b/d in April 1982.

In an attempt to stabilize world supply and prices, the Organization of the Petroleum Exporting Countries (OPEC), which Nigeria had joined in 1971, imposed production quotas against a Saudi Arabian 'marker' price of $34 per barrel in March 1982. In 1983 the government reduced the price of Nigeria's light crude petroleum, known as Bonny Light, to $30 per barrel, making it competitive with the 'spot' market price for equivalent crude petroleums from the major North Sea producers. Production in 1983 averaged 1.23m. b/d, and increased to 1.57m. b/d in March 1984, but subsequently dropped sharply. At the OPEC meetings in 1985, Nigeria's quota was maintained at 1.3m. b/d while the price of Bonny Light was fixed at $28.65 per barrel, at parity with official North Sea prices, although slightly higher than the 'spot' market price. As world demand contracted, production of petroleum fluctuated dramatically in 1985 and 1986. In September OPEC reintroduced a quota of 1.3m. b/d, and production was held at this level until the end of the year. Average output for 1986 was 1.463m. b/d. In December the price of Bonny Light increased to $14.15 per barrel. In that month, Nigeria accepted the OPEC production quotas for 1987, which aimed to raise prices of crude petroleum to about $18 per barrel. The quotas allowed Nigeria an average output of 1.303m. b/d. However, Nigeria's actual output for 1987 fell slightly below the OPEC quota, averaging 1.286m. b/d. During 1987 international prices for crude petroleum stabilized at about $18–$19 per barrel, as OPEC members kept within their quotas and tension in the Persian Gulf resulted in some nervousness on the world market. Towards the end of the year, however, prices began to fall, and in December 1987 and January 1988 the 'spot' market price for Bonny Light reached about $17 per barrel. In early 1988 the 'spot' market price for Bonny Light was $15–$16 per barrel. In 1989 the 'spot' market price ranged from $17.35 in January to $20.25 in December. Following a series of OPEC meetings, the global production quota was raised to 22m. b/d in 1990, while Nigeria's quota increased to 1.61m. b/d. As a result of the abandonment of OPEC production quotas following the beginning of the Gulf crisis in August 1990, Nigeria's oil production increased to 1.95m. b/d, while the price fluctuated between $18–$35 per barrel. In February 1993, however, Nigeria's OPEC production quota was reduced to 1.78m. b/d, although at that time production was estimated at 1.98m. b/d.

Revenues from exports of petroleum, which are shared in decreasing proportions between federal, state and local governments, have largely determined the pace of Nigeria's economic development. Successive governments have based their five-year plans on predicted earnings from petroleum, and, more recently, foreign exchange revenue from sales of petroleum has been virtually the sole means of meeting the country's import needs and debt-servicing commitments. The level of revenues from petroleum has fluctuated in line with

OPEC's pricing policy and changes in world demand. With the depreciation of the dollar and with free-market prices in the range $10–$12 per barrel in mid-1986, Nigeria's export earnings from oil declined sharply. Total export earnings from oil in 1986 were 47% lower than in the previous year, at an estimated $6,400m. In 1987 the value of petroleum exports was estimated to have risen slightly, to $6,700m., with the return to a comparatively stable price for petroleum offsetting a fall in the volume of exports, and reached $7,100m. in 1988. According to IMF estimates, earnings rose to $8,500m. in 1989, and to $10,600m. in 1990, declining slightly to $10,200m. in 1991, and to an estimated $10,000m. in 1992.

Production costs for Nigerian petroleum are up to seven times as high as those in the Middle East, but the Nigerian product's low sulphur content places it at the upper end of OPEC's price scale. The Niger delta remains Nigeria's main petroleum-producing region, containing 78 oilfields, the largest of which is Forcados Yorki. In total, there are 158 oilfields in operation, of which 18% are classed as offshore. The USA is the major market for Nigeria's petroleum, taking, on average, around one-half of all exports. Spain, Germany, France, Portugal and the United Kingdom are also important customers.

In 1971 the state-owned Nigerian National Oil Corporation (NNOC) was formed to be a participant in the operations of the foreign oil companies. In 1977 the NNOC was merged with the ministry of petroleum resources to form the Nigerian National Petroleum Corporation (NNPC), which gradually increased its equity stake in all operating companies, except Ashland. In 1979 the NNPC nationalized BP's interests in Nigeria, in retaliation for BP's participation in an oil-swapping agreement which led indirectly to the shipment of Nigerian petroleum to South Africa. (In 1992 the government sold the nationalized BP interests to Shell, Elf-Aquitaine and other private enterprises.) Agreements governing the petroleum producing companies' terms of operation were not officially signed until 1984, after being effective for more than 10 years. The NNPC has a 60% interest in the operations of Agip-Phillips, Elf-Aquitaine, Gulf, Mobil, Texaco and Pan Ocean, and has an 80% share in Shell (which accounts for one-half of total production). In November 1984 the rules governing the operation of the equity contracts, under which foreign companies extract Nigerian petroleum, were revised in an attempt to increase production and exploration. Companies in partnership with the NNPC were permitted to extract more than their contracted amount of petroleum on the basis of a government-determined 'allowable' production rate. Additionally, companies could also buy, on equity terms, any of the petroleum that the NNPC is unable to sell, while reimbursing the NNPC for production costs. New 'incentive' agreements were signed with international oil companies in 1986, guaranteeing producers a profit margin of around $2 per barrel. In July 1991 a new memorandum of understanding (MOU) between the NNPC and its foreign production partners was signed, which guaranteed minimum profit margins to foreign joint-venture operators, depending on their level of capital investment and cost efficiency. The MOU detailed a new five-year plan for exploration and production, with incentives for capital investment in the sector, and guaranteed a profit margin of $2.3 per barrel, on the condition that technical operating costs did not exceed $2.5 per barrel. The minimum guaranteed margin was to increase to $2.5 a barrel if capital investment exceeded $1.5 per barrel, with total operating costs at less than $3.5 per barrel. The MOU also provided bonuses for companies that increased their reserves by more than their annual production in any given year, thereby adding to net reserves. In the same year the NNCP and the foreign oil companies signed joint venture agreements for the new oil fields allocated by the government; these agreements defined procedures for making capital spending decisions, stipulated the foreign companies' obligations to train Nigerian nationals, and allowed the NNPC to become the operator of fields when it chose. In 1993 all major enterprises operating in Nigeria—Shell, Mobil, Chevron and Elf Aquitaine—initiated new development programmes, while BP and Statoil, the Norwegian state-owned oil company, signed a new agreement with the government. The petroleum industry suffered a decline in 1994, as a direct consequence of Nigeria's increasing political and economic instability. After government mismanagement of the NNPC's accounts, the company could no longer meet its financial obligations to the oil companies, and the majority of new drilling work was suspended. This did not at first affect ongoing production facilities, and petroleum output remained at almost 2m. b/d in the first half of 1994, but production began to decline after petroleum workers commenced long-term strike action in July. At the end of that month Shell reported that its production had declined by about one-third (the company's previous output level had been approximately 1m. b/d), while petroleum prices increased to more than $18 per barrel.

In March 1988 the government announced that the NNPC was to be restructured by division into three sections, responsible for operations, for corporate services and for national petroleum investment management services. Eleven subsidiaries of the NNPC were to be established, each concentrating on a particular area, such as refining, development, engineering and petrochemicals. The marketing of petroleum was also reorganized in order to eliminate intermediate marketeers. Under the new scheme, only the NNPC and local and foreign oil companies involved in production or exploration would be permitted to market petroleum. Investment in maintenance, capital equipment and exploration has fallen in recent years, owing to difficulties in funding. By virtue of its equity ownership in the various oil companies, the government is responsible for around 75% of total investment in the industry. In early 1993 the IMF increased pressure on the government to reduce subsidies on domestic fuel, which were estimated to cost ₦63,000m. in 1992, and maintained the official petrol price at ₦0.7 per litre—one of the cheapest in the world. In August, despite initial reluctance (owing to concern that the measure would prompt renewed unrest), the government partially removed subsidies on domestic fuel, with the introduction of a new grade of petrol, at a cost of ₦7.50 per litre.

With increased participation from the private sector, greater emphasis is being placed on gas—both liquefied petroleum gas (LPG) and liquefied natural gas (LNG)—and on increasing the capacity of the country's petroleum refineries to enable the export of higher-value petroleum products. Until the completion of the 60,000 b/d petroleum refinery at Port Harcourt in 1965, Nigeria exported its entire output of crude petroleum. A second refinery, with a capacity of 100,000 b/d (later expanded to 125,000 b/d), was constructed in 1978 at Warri, in Bendel State, and a third inland refinery, at Kaduna, was partly operational by 1981. The Kaduna refinery has a capacity of 100,000 b/d, and is divided into two units: one uses the light Nigerian crude, while the second unit, which was not finally commissioned until 1983, uses heavier imported crudes. The NNPC owns the Warri and Kaduna refineries, and has an 80% share in the original refinery at Port Harcourt. Technical problems and the lack of proper maintenance reduced the combined operating capacity of the three refineries to 155,000 b/d in 1985. Because of the under-utilization of refinery capacity, Nigeria has to process up to 80,000 b/d abroad in order to meet domestic requirements. It was announced in June 1989 that the World Bank was to make a $27.7m. loan to improve efficiency at Warri and Kaduna by supporting the repair and maintenance programmes and by improving investment planning. A fourth refinery was completed in March 1989 at Alesa Eleme (near Port Harcourt), thereby increasing Nigeria's refining capacity to 445,000 b/d. A refinery at Oso, with a capacity of 100,000 b/d, was scheduled for completion by the end of 1993. Severe operational problems and delayed maintenance work adversely affected local refining capacity in the first half of 1993, while increased illicit trade in fuel contributed to critical shortages throughout the country, prompting the government to ban exports of petroleum products. In 1993 and 1994 strikes in the petroleum sector resulted in a severe disruption in the refining and distribution of fuel.

Development of an integrated petrochemicals industry has been a main priority of successive governments. Construction of a number of processing units at the refineries in Warri and Kaduna was completed in 1987. The units use feedstock from the refineries to produce benzene, carbon black and polypropylene. The establishment of a larger petrochemicals complex at Alesa-Eleme, at a projected cost of $1,000m. is under way.

NATURAL GAS

Besides its petroleum resources, Nigeria possesses the largest deposits of natural gas in Africa. Proven reserves are assessed at more than 2,800,000m. cu m, most of which is located with petroleum deposits in and around the Niger delta. Probable gas reserves were estimated at a further 1,800,000m. cu m. Production in 1990 was estimated at 27,600m. cu m, of which 77% was flared. Of the gas that is consumed, some 75% is bought by the National Electric Power Authority (NEPA). In a bid to curtail the wasteful flaring of gas, the government has issued a decree penalizing oil companies for this practice. Although the decree, which came into force in January 1985, affects only 69 of the 155 oil-producing fields, many of the large operators have begun to install gas re-injection facilities. Some 18,000m. cu m of gas is flared each year, at a market cost of over $4,000m. according to oil companies; domestic consumption is estimated at just 3,000m. cu m per year. Utilization of gas increased substantially when the Warri associated gas project, under which 17m. cu m per day is piped from the Niger Delta to Igbin power station, near Lagos, came into operation in 1990.

Nigeria's most ambitious scheme to utilize flared gas was to construct a gas liquefaction plant, with a daily capacity of at least 45m. cu m, on the River Bonny. To implement the plan to produce LNG, the Bonny LNG consortium, comprising the NNPC (which held a 69% share), Phillips, Shell, BP, Agip and Elf Aquitaine, was formed in 1978. The project received an early boost in 1980, when a consortium of European gas distributors signed a 20-year agreement to buy 23m. cu m per day, starting in 1984. However, the viability of the project hinged on the sale of a further 23m. cu m per day to four US distributors. Negotiations with the US government over access broke down in 1980. Market uncertainties continued to surround the project, and, when the outline of the government's 1981–85 Development Plan deferred investment in the scheme until the late 1980s, the Bonny LNG consortium was dissolved. A scaled-down version of the flared gas project was revived by the military government. In 1988 the government considered a new $2,000m. scheme to construct a pipeline from gas fields in eastern Nigeria to the LNG plant at Bonny. In May 1989 a joint-venture agreement was signed to implement the scheme. The majority shareholder is the NNPC (49%), followed by Shell, Agip and Elf. Following a series of difficulties, however, the initiation of the project was expected to be delayed until mid-1995. Chevron, which owns the Gulf Oil Company of Nigeria (GOCON), announced plans in 1991 to construct a plant to recover 300m. cu ft of associated gas per day; with an estimated cost of $500m., the plant would produce condensates, propane and butane gas for export. There were also plans by the NNPC to use some of this gas to fuel an export-oriented $400m. methanol plant, with a daily output of 2,000–2,500 tons. Discussions were held between the NNPC, Penspen, a UK company, and Mannesman, a German company, on a joint venture agreement for the project.

Other schemes which are aimed at utilizing the country's gas reserves include the Onne gas-fed fertilizer plant (commissioned in April 1987), the Warri refinery extension and the Delta steel plant at Aladja. Gas is also planned to be used as a feedstock for the second phase of the NNPC chemicals complex near Port Harcourt. The government also plans to construct a network of gas pipelines supplying both domestic and industrial users. The NNPC agreed to a price rise of 269% (from ₦1.52 to ₦5.24 per thousand cubic feet) in April 1989. A new comprehensive gas development policy, offering incentives for companies investing in gas production, distribution and consumption, was released by the NNPC in 1990. The policy provisions also supported the commercialization of natural gas liquid production for export and for domestic consumption, the establishment of gas companies distributing to domestic and industrial consumers, and viable projects, aimed at substituting gas for existing fuels.

COAL AND OTHER MINERALS

Nigeria possesses substantial deposits of lignite and sub-bituminous coal, but the country has yet to exploit their full potential. Coal is mined by the Nigerian Coal Corporation (NCC), and is used mainly by the railway, traditional metal industries and for the generation of electricity. Coal production declined from a peak of 940,000 tons in 1958 to 144,000 tons in 1986, and to 86,700 tons in 1992. There are long-term plans to exploit the Lafia/Obi coal deposits for use at the Ajaokuta steel complex. Reserves are estimated at more than 270m. tons.

Tin is the only major non-hydrocarbon mineral currently being extracted in Nigeria. Nigeria's output of tin concentrates has been in decline since the late 1960s, and these exports have reflected the depressed conditions in world tin prices since the late 1980s. Production totalled about 230 tons annually in 1991 and 1992. There are two tin smelters in operation, with a combined capacity well in excess of total ore production. Columbite is mined near Jos, but output has fallen steadily since the mid-1970s, to 47 tons in 1989.

Extensive deposits of iron ore have been discovered in Itakpe, Ajabanoko and Shokoshoko—all in Kwara State. Mining operations at Itakpe started in 1984, with the long-term aim of supplying most of the requirements of the Ajaokuta and Delta steel complexes. More than 180,000 tons of iron ore had been mined by early 1986. The construction of a $250m. beneficiation plant at Itakpe began in December 1992; the plant was projected to process 5m. tons of iron ore into a concentrated form for the Ajaokuta steel complex. Uranium deposits have been discovered at Gombo, but have yet to be exploited, although drilling and sample analysis have taken place. Plans exist for a nuclear power programme, and Nigeria has entered into joint-venture agreements with both Guinea and Niger for the smelting of uranium.

MANUFACTURING AND CONSTRUCTION

Measured in constant prices, the contribution of the manufacturing sector to GDP increased from 4% in 1977 to 13% in 1982, after which it declined to an annual average of less than 10% in 1986–90. In 1992 the manufacturing sector accounted for 8.6% of GDP, and the construction sector 1.9%.

Industrial development has mainly taken the form of import substitution of consumer goods, although, during the 1970s, greater emphasis was placed on the production of capital goods and on assembly industries. In 1983 textiles, beverages, cigarettes, soaps and detergents together accounted for 60% of total manufacturing output. Investment in manufacturing has come mostly from the government and from foreign multinational companies. Private-sector investment in manufacturing is small, and is centred on industries which are shielded from competition by import barriers.

Manufacturing is heavily reliant on imported raw materials and components. According to the Manufacturers' Association of Nigeria (MAN), up to 60% of all the raw materials that local industry used in 1985 were imported. Manufacturing is thus extremely vulnerable to disruption if imports are restricted, as they have been since 1980. Imports of raw materials declined, on average, by 10% per year over the period 1982–85. The combination of import restrictions, overpricing and industrial disputes favoured cheaper foreign goods and encouraged smuggling and black-marketeering. Import licensing was abolished in September 1986, in tandem with the introduction of the SFEM, and tariffs were reduced. However, the resultant sharp devaluation of the naira increased import costs and hence production costs. A new tariff structure, introduced in 1988, aimed to protect local industries from external competition, while encouraging domestic competition to stimulate efficiency.

Total production from the manufacturing sector declined by more than one-third between 1982 and 1985, while the level of capital expenditure fell by over 50%. In 1986 manufacturing output declined by a further 6%. The most severely affected branches of the sector are: commercial vehicles, chemicals, metals, textiles, sugar, plastics and paper. A further 30% reduction in imports in 1985 and a similar reduction in 1986, coupled with the government's plans to reduce the level of state investment in manufacturing, did not help the sector to revive. Manufacturers asserted that inadequate development funds and the government's stringent fiscal policy had constrained the sector, which was estimated to be operating at only 25% of its capacity in 1987. Manufacturing output increased, in real terms, by 7.6% in 1990, and by 6.1% in 1991. Many manufacturers have placed their hopes on the success of the government-backed local sourcing programme, under which all existing industries are actively encouraged to utilize more local raw materials. Various tax and investment incentives have been introduced, and a National Raw Materials Development Council and a Raw Materials Data Bank have been established. A new tariff structure, to benefit manufacturing based on local resources, has been drawn up, although its viability is seriously constrained by the poor state of the country's infrastructure and by the high cost of local materials and parts. Despite successive governments' efforts to encourage industrial dispersal, most manufacturing plants are still based in Lagos State. The Agbara industrial estate, in Ogun State, has succeeded in attracting some industries away from Lagos, although most of the heavily import-based companies are reluctant to move, owing to the fact that around 70% of all industrial materials are still handled at ports in Lagos State.

The creation of an integrated iron and steel industry has been a high priority of successive development plans. In January 1982 the Delta steel complex at Aladja, in Bendel State, was formally opened. The complex, which has a capacity of 1m. tons per year and operates the direct reduction system, supplies billets and wire rods to three steel-rolling mills at Oshogbo, Katsina and Jos. Each of the three mills has an initial annual capacity of 210,000 tons of steel products. The Ajaokuta Steel Company opened the first light section mill in 1983, and the rolling mill for the production of steel wire rods in 1984, but output was sporadic, owing to shortages of imported billets and to difficulties in obtaining supplies from the Delta complex. Nigeria's annual steel requirements reached 6m. metric tons by 1990, and there were plans to, at least, double the capacity of the first stage of the Ajaokuta complex. Construction costs, originally estimated at $1,400m., exceeded $3,000m. at the end of 1989. In early 1992 a second stage of the project was initiated. In mid-1994 the Ajaokuta complex was temporarily closed, following rioting by workers; however, the government confirmed that the construction of all rolling mills in the plant was to be completed by the end of that year.

Manufacturers using raw materials from local sources were at a strong advantage after the economic reforms of 1986. By 1990 locally sourced operations achieved relatively high levels of capacity utilization: tyres (64%), leather products (63%), beer and stout (59%), textiles (54%) and industrial chemicals (49%). One of the most successful industrial sub-sector projects was the nitrogenous fertilizer plant at Onne, owned by the National Fertilizer Corporation of Nigeria (NAFCON), which was established in 1987; at full capacity it produces 400,000 tons per year of urea and 300,000 tons per year of compound fertilizer. Overall capacity utilization increased from an estimated 33% in 1989 to more than 60% in 1992.

The assembly of motor vehicles in Nigeria is dominated by Volkswagen and Peugeot in passenger cars, and by Mercedes in commercial vehicles. Local demand remains well above supply, but the cost of components and the difficulties in obtaining import licences have reduced output. Government plans to transfer Nigeria's six vehicle-assembly plants to private ownership were suspended in early 1993, since it was believed that the prevailing economic recession would reduce their value.

Various government programmes that were aimed at national self-sufficiency in food allowed for the steady growth of agro-business during the 1970s. Sugar refining, textiles, brewing, rubber, fertilizers, footwear, paper, cigarettes and general food-processing industries were among the most significant. However, the expansion and modernization of plants was cut short by the onset of economic recession in 1982. The large brewing industry has continued to flourish, although in 1987 it suffered from a ban on imports of malted barley, imposed with the aim of stimulating local barley production. In 1988 Firestone opened a new tyre-manufacturing plant in Bendel State, bringing the number of tyre manufacturers in Nigeria to three. With enlarged capacity at Dunlop Nigeria's plant in Lagos, it was estimated that local manufacturers would be able to meet about 60% of domestic demand.

Activity in the construction sector has declined in recent years. Output fell by 50% in value from 1981 to 1985, and by a further 5% in 1986. The construction sector suffered from serious constraints on growth, following the introduction of the structural adjustment programme in 1986 and further reductions in public sector projects. The construction of a federal capital at Abuja was formally completed in 1991. (However, the expansion of the private sector at Abuja subsequently proved to be slow.) The creation of nine new states in 1991 necessitated several new infrastructure projects, and ongoing investment in the energy sector of some $1,000m. a year has also benefited the sector. However, road construction, and the rehabilitation of railways, airports and seaports virtually ceased in the late 1980s.

In March 1988 changes were made to regulations concerning foreign investment in Nigeria. The 1972 Nigerian Enterprises Promotion Decree, which was strengthened and extended in 1977, involved three categories of business. The first (Schedule I) had to be 100% Nigerian-owned and covered more than 50 enterprises, including printing, rice-milling, advertising, road haulage, bus services, taxis and tyre retreading. The second category (Schedule II) had to be 60%-owned by Nigerian interests and included breweries, department stores and supermarkets, wholesale distribution, banking, insurance, construction and furniture manufacture. All other enterprises, including food-processing (Schedule III), had to be 40% Nigerian-held. In 1985 the decree was being selectively relaxed in order to encourage foreign private investment in neglected areas, such as large-scale agro-business and manufacturing based on local resources. From March 1988 foreign investors were allowed to increase their holdings in Schedule I enterprises to 20%, and in Schedule III enterprises to 80%. Schedule II enterprises were to be allowed to enter joint ventures with foreign companies. Under a new decree, promulgated in December 1989, foreign companies are permitted to own 100% of any new venture, except for enterprises in banking, oil prospecting, insurance and mining. The largest government agency in industrial development is the Nigerian Industrial Development Bank, which, in recent years, has centred its activities on directing multilateral funding into private-sector projects in intermediate and capital goods manufacturing, food processing and other agro-related industries.

POWER

The principal supplier of electricity in Nigeria is the state-owned NEPA, which was formed in 1973 by the merger of the Niger Dams Authority and the Electricity Corporation of Nigeria. In addition to the 1,320-MW power station at Igbin, other major plants include: the Kainji hydroelectric plant (capacity 760 MW); the gas and oil-fired plants in Afam (742 MW); Sapele (696 MW); Lagos (60 MW); and the coal-fired plant on the Oji river (150 MW). The Igbin plant is fired with natural gas piped from fields at Escravos.

Demand for power has continued to exceed capacity, and power cuts have become a regular feature of daily life. Improvement of existing facilities has been made a priority, rather than expansion of capacity, although plans are under consideration for the construction of new plants at Onitsha, Kaduna, Makurdi, Oron, Katsina and Mambilla. Total electricity generated in the late 1980s was about 10,000m. kWh per year, of which about 50% was supplied by hydroelectric plants.

TRANSPORT

In comparison with other west African states, Nigeria has a well-developed transport system. However, congestion, lack of maintenance, and poor planning has resulted in services that are unreliable and often dangerous. The rehabilitation of major roads, railways, and airports is a major element of the three-year rolling Investment Plan, announced in January 1990.

Approximately 95% of all traffic in goods and passengers travel by road, most of it to and from the major ports. In 1991 the road network totalled some 112,140 km, of which about 30,900 km were principal roads and 19,550 km secondary roads; some 31,500 km were tarred. In the 1980s the government's main concern has been to repair existing roads, rather than to build new ones. The Lagos–Ibadan expressway, opened only in 1978, is particularly in need of repair and many of the dual carriageway fly-overs in Lagos urgently need replacing. The 1985 budget allocated 250m. for land transport. After a decline in road construction in the mid-1980s, 22 road projects were completed in 1989, compared with four in 1988. However, maintenance and rehabilitation work slowed in 1989 and 1990, following a 50% reduction in the special mass transit allocation in the 1988 budget. Road safety standards in Nigeria are virtually non-existent, and driving licences are distributed indiscriminately. On average, around 30,000 accidents are reported each year, with the loss of over 8,000 lives.

The railway network covers 3,505 km. The two main narrow-gauge lines run from Lagos to Nguru and from Port Harcourt to Kaura Namoda, with extensions from Kafanchan, through Jos, to Maiduguri, and from Minna to Baro. A new 52-km railway line for iron ore traffic has been constructed between the Ajaokuta steel complex and Itakpe. Despite medium-term expansion plans, the Nigerian Railway Corporation (NRC) reduced services and jobs in 1989; this led to a series of strikes and further operating difficulties. In 1991 the number of passengers carried totalled 3.9m. (compared with 6.3m. in 1990), while the volume of freight declined to 282m. tons (compared with 374m. tons in 1990). A programme to rehabilitate the railway network, at a projected cost of ₦17,000m., was expected to commence in 1993.

There are two international airports, at Ikeja (Lagos) and Kano, and 11 domestic airports. Under the civilian regime, the parastatal Nigeria Airways' domestic monopoly was ended, and several private charter airlines have since begun operations. International traffic is dominated by foreign airlines. Meanwhile, the military government has put increasing pressure on Nigeria Airways to improve its standard of service and to reduce its costs. However, Nigeria Airways has incurred a series of substantial financial losses, and its debts reached ₦700m. by the end of 1987. Owing to Nigeria Airways' difficulties, it was announced that private airlines would be allowed to offer international services if they satisfied safety requirements. In early 1993 Nigeria Airways entered negotiations to sell some 40% of ownership to a foreign airline; control of international services were to be transferred to the private sector, while domestic services were to remain state-owned. The number of passengers on domestic flights declined to 556,000 in 1991 (compared with 621,000 in 1990), while the number of passengers on international routes increased to 187,000 (compared with 160,000 in 1990).

Nigeria's principal seaports for general cargo are Apapa, Tin Can Island (both of which serve Lagos), Port Harcourt, Warri, Sepele and Calabar. The main ports for petroleum shipments are Bonny and Burutu. After steadily declining since 1982, port utilization was expected to increase in 1990 and 1991 as a result of the rise in import and export volumes. In 1992 a report released by the West African Shipowners Operations Committee indicated that Nigeria's ports charged disproportionately high rates to shipping lines (some 230% above the average rate for west Africa), and that their turnaround times were longer, owing to poor maintenance of equipment. The state-owned Nigerian National Shipping Line handled only 3.3% of non-oil shipments (totalling 10.2m. tons) in 1991.

TRADE

With a sharp fall in export earnings from petroleum and with a continued rise in imports, Nigeria's visible trade balance moved into deficit in 1981, after registering a healthy surplus of $11,106m. in 1980. The trade deficit widened further in 1982, to $2,714m., as a 33% drop in export earnings exceeded the decline in imports, which fell to $14,801m. A further 15% decline in export earnings in 1983 was offset by a steeper fall in imports, and the trade deficit was reduced to $1,084m. However, the current account remained heavily in deficit, and Nigeria began to accumulate an increasing volume of unpaid trade debts. Considerable improvement was achieved in 1984, with the trade surplus rising to $2,984m. and the current account registering a small surplus of $114m. Although imports increased again in 1985, to $8,452m., they still remained well down on their 1981 level. Exports increased from $10,309m. in 1983 to $12,804m. in 1985, yielding a trade surplus of $4,353m. in the latter year. The 1985 current account surplus also increased, to $1,265m. Export earnings fell sharply, to $6,599m., in 1986, owing to the collapse of petroleum prices on the world market, although efforts to reduce the volume of imports maintained the visible trade account in surplus. In the same year there was a current account surplus of $365m. Exports increased to $7,702m. in 1987, while imports totalled $4,178m., resulting in a trade surplus of $3,524m. In 1988 the trade balance declined slightly to $2,419m., but increased to $4,178m. in 1989. According to IMF figures, exports increased sharply, to $13,585m., in 1990, while imports totalled $4,932m., resulting in a trade surplus of $8,653m.; in that year a surplus of $4,988m. on the current account of the balance of payments was recorded. In 1991 the trade surplus declined to $4,441m. (owing, in part, to the sharp increase in the volume of imports, to $7,813m.), and the current account surplus to $1,203m. In 1992 Nigeria recorded a trade surplus of $4,611m., and there was a surplus of $2,268m. on the current account of the balance of payments.

Following the introduction, in September 1986, of the SFEM, foreign exchange for trade was made available by the central bank at weekly auctions. This initially resulted in an effective 60% devaluation of the naira. However, as the auction mechanism of the SFEM removed the need for import controls, the licensing of imports was abolished. At the same time, the government introduced further measures, which abolished the 30% import levy, reduced import duties, reformed the tariff structure and reduced the list of prohibited imports. The devaluation of the naira, through the currency auction system introduced in 1986, was accompanied by a series of trade liberalization measures, designed to expand the export base. In July 1987 the military government terminated the SFEM, merging the first- and second-tier exchange rates but retaining the auction mechanism, whereby a unitary rate would be determined by fortnightly auctions of available foreign exchange, conducted by the central bank. Under the new arrangement, the naira initially fell by 6.3% against the US dollar, to ₦3.95 = US $1, and reached ₦4.61 = US $1 in May 1988. It was expected that the rate would continue to weaken in the short term, unless the government substantially increased its official funding of the market. In January 1989 the Interbank Foreign Exchange Market (IFEM) was established, in accordance with IMF recommendations, to provide a unified exchange rate for the naira, to be fixed on a daily basis. Exchange rate policy in 1992 and 1993 vacillated between a return to the auction mechanism (which had previously been suspended) and a more managed system. In January 1994 the Abacha government abandoned the auction system, replacing it with occasional allocations of foreign exchange to banks at a fixed rate of ₦22.0 = US $1. The autonomous market for foreign exchange, which had stimulated exports of non-petroleum commodities, was abolished and all foreign exchange entering the country was to be surrendered to the CBN.

Revenue from petroleum accounted for 97.9% of total export earnings in 1992. Non-petroleum exports, mainly cocoa beans and rubber, have remained low, totalling $500m. in 1992, despite the availability of various incentives for export-based industries. A significant proportion of non-recorded exports of manufactured goods, processed foods and agricultural produce is smuggled through Nigeria's borders.

In 1991 Nigeria's principal source of imports was Germany ($1,071m.), followed by the United Kingdom ($1,058m.), the USA ($916m.), France ($692m.) and Japan ($453m.). In that year the principal market for exports was the USA ($5,200m.); other significant purchasers were Spain ($1,598m.), Germany ($1,091m.), the Netherlands ($639m.) and France ($632m.).

DEBT

Following the sharp rise in government revenues from petroleum and the launching of several large-scale capital-intensive projects during the late 1970s, external borrowing increased dramatically. Although state borrowing was severely restricted during the 1980s and the level of federal government borrowing was reduced, the external debt rose to ₦12,000m. by late 1983. More than one-half of the outstanding debt consisted of medium-term loans from the international capital market at 'floating' interest rates, most of which were incurred during the late 1970s. The net result was a heavy concentration of maturity dates at a time when real interest rates were high and when Nigeria's earnings of foreign currency were declining. Despite the successful refinancing of some $2,000m. of the trade debt and of $6,000m. of the short-term debt during the course of 1984, Nigeria's total external loan commitments in October 1985 amounted to ₦21,000m., of which ₦3,146m. was in the form of 'open-account' uninsured trade debts. In 1986 debt-servicing alone was expected to cost $3,400m. With the decline in earnings of foreign exchange from petroleum exports, the debt service ratio would have risen to about 47% of total exports, well above the 30% level that the government had set as its target.

From April 1986, Nigeria obtained successive 90-day moratoria on repayments of debt principal to commercial creditors, but it became clear that a rescheduling would be needed. However, the government declared that it would not seek a loan from the IMF, which was a precondition of rescheduling by the Paris and London 'Clubs' (Western governments and commercial bank creditors respectively). A further problem arose when Nigeria defaulted on the first repayments of debt principal totalling $1,500m., resulting from promissory notes issued for pre-1984 short-term trade debts. However, a compromise with the IMF was reached, as part of the government's structural adjustment plan, whereby Nigeria agreed to accept 'enhanced surveillance' by the IMF. In November 1986 Nigeria reached agreement with its commercial bank creditors on the rescheduling of $1,500m. of medium-term debts and $2,000m. of arrears on letters of credit, and on the provision of a new commercial loan of $320m. In December the 'Paris Club' of creditor governments agreed to a 10-year rescheduling of medium- and long-term debts, accumulated before the end of 1983, and to a four-year rescheduling of short-term debts accumulated since that date; the amount rescheduled was reported to total $7,500m.

In November 1987, following protracted negotiations, Nigeria reached an agreement with its commercial bank creditors on the rescheduling of $1,550m. of medium-term debts falling due in 1986–87, and $2,350m. of arrears on letters of credit. A new commercial loan of $320m., to be disbursed in instalments from February 1988, was also agreed but was not implemented, owing to the government's failure to secure a renewal of the IMF endorsement of its economic strategy in January 1988. In January 1988 foreign exporters agreed to reschedule (over 22 years) repayments on $4,000m. of promissory notes representing a portion of the trade debts incurred since 1984 (estimated by creditors to total $9,800m.). In 1988 Nigeria's total debt was estimated at $29,000m. In September another agreement was reached with the creditor banks, to reschedule $5,200m. of debt falling due between January 1988 and December 1991. Repayment of $2,700m. of medium-term debt was to be extended over 20 years, and repayment of $2,500m. in letters of credit over 12 years, with repayment to begin after a three-year period of grace. Both this agreement and the disbursement of loans by various bilateral donors and the World Bank were dependent on Nigeria's gaining approval for its recovery programme from the IMF. This took place in January 1989, and the rescheduling agreement was signed in London in March. During 1986 the World Bank increased its lending to Nigeria to more than $800m., including a major loan of $452m., approved in October. Support from the IMF and World Bank for the reform programme continued in 1987, but was suspended in 1988, following differences of opinion over policy and performance. New adjustment credits were approved by the World Bank in 1989 and 1990, but ceased entirely in 1991, after it transpired that Nigeria could not account for petroleum revenue amounting to about $2,500m. that should have been earned during the Gulf War. The World Bank and IMF were also discouraged by the government's continuing failure to control budgetary spending and its reluctance to raise domestic fuel prices to cover the costs of refining and distribution.

The size of Nigeria's external debt continued to increase in the late 1980s, despite the relatively low level of drawings. In 1987 total foreign debt, including medium- and long-term indebtedness, short-term debt and interest arrears, amounted to $30,390m., of which the servicing costs represented 12% of export earnings for the year; in 1988 total foreign debt was $30,179m., with a debt-service ratio of 25%; in 1989 the total foreign debt was $32,511m. and the debt-service ratio 31%; and in 1990 total foreign debt was $34,089m. and debt service ratio projected at 34%. According to government estimates, debt service is expected to average $4,200m. a year—about one-third of projected export revenue—until 1997, which implies a financing gap of some $2,500m. over that period. These projections, and the limitations on economic growth and investment that they imply, formed the basis of the Nigerian claim for a 30-year rescheduling of its commercial debt. At the end of 1991 Nigeria's total foreign debt was $34,497m., compared with $2,060m. at the end of 1984. The external debt declined to $30,998m. at the end of 1992, of which $28,458m. was long-term public debt. In that year the cost of debt-servicing was equivalent to 30.6% of the value of exports of goods and services.

Nigerian proposals to convert commercial debt into 30-year bonds, serviced at a 3% interest rate, were discussed at a series of meetings between creditor bank representatives and Nigerian finance officials in 1990. Negotiations, led by the minister of finance, Olu Falae, were suspended in August 1990, when Falae was replaced by Alhaji Abubakar Alhaji. A new accord was reached with the IMF in January 1991, which facilitated the conclusion of negotiations to reschedule the commercial and official debt. The rescheduling of Nigeria's $5,800m. bank debt allowed the government to repurchase as much as 60% of the debt, while the banks were given the option of exchanging the remainder for 30-year bonds at a 6.25% interest rate. The 'Paris Club' agreed to reschedule all development and aid loans, which were due before March 1992, for a period of 20 years with a 10-years' grace, and also guaranteed commercial debts for a period of 15 years with an eight-year period of grace. Although Nigeria is defined by the World Bank as a low-income country, it was not accorded the debt concessions for which it applied. In 1992 Nigeria's finance ministry officials initiated a series of negotiations for the renewal of Nigeria's stand-by facility with the IMF (the previous facility had expired in April) and a series of development credits with the World Bank, in an effort to reschedule and to reduce the 'Paris Club' debt, which was the principal burden on the government finance. In May 1993 efforts by the transitional council to obtain a new arrangement with the IMF (which was a precondition to the rescheduling of Nigeria's external debt on concessionary terms) ended in failure, owing to lack of agreement over the exchange rate policy and the proposed removal of subsidies on domestic fuel. In 1994, following the government's abandonment of market reforms, the IMF deferred agreement on the rescheduling of accumulating debt arrears until the administration achieved its stated objectives of controlling expenditure, inflation and the foreign exchange rate.

PUBLIC FINANCE

Since the early 1970s, the channelling of earnings from petroleum exports, import and excise duties and other forms of revenue from taxation through the federal, state and local governments has been the main impetus of economic activity in Nigeria. After a period in the late 1970s and early 1980s of inflationary domestic policies (characterized by high levels of public spending, recurrent budget deficit financing and ambitious development planning), the government was faced with serious internal financial difficulties. The sharp reduction in revenues from petroleum, which account for around 70% of total federal revenue, meant that the Shagari government could not meet the public spending targets that it had proposed in the fourth National Development Plan (1981–85) except by borrowing from overseas. By 1983 much of the government's capital programme had been temporarily abandoned in the face of a massive ₦6,200m. budget deficit and heavy debt-servicing commitments. In May 1984 the new military government abandoned the fourth Plan and introduced an austerity budget that was aimed at reducing public expenditure, imports and inflation. A series of deflationary measures followed, including a virtual embargo on new projects, a 'freeze' on wages, the imposition of heavier import duties, higher interest rates, limits on federal and state spending and reductions in state subsidies, the pruning of parastatal companies and a clamp-down on corruption and tax evasion. Aided by a rise in revenues from petroleum and by the introduction of new state taxes and import duties, federally-collected revenue was increased during 1984 by 14%, to ₦11,300m. Moreover, despite an increase in recurrent expenditure (owing largely to debt servicing), a sharp cut in the level of capital expenditure was sufficient to reduce the overall budget deficit for 1984 by 47%, to ₦3,300m. The announcement of the fifth Development Plan (1986–90) was delayed, owing to the start of the adjustment programme in July 1986. In its place the government announced a new planning strategy in January 1990, consisting of a three-year rolling Investment Plan, costed at ₦144,200m. and a 15-year perspective Plan, incorporating a series of rolling investment plans. In order to improve performance on plan implementation, a co-ordinated planning review procedure was to be established, to which all ministries and government departments would submit data to allow more effective monitoring. The introduction of the structural adjustment programme in 1986 resulted in a major change in public finance policy; the reforms involved extensive austerity measures in public-sector expenditure, reductions in subsidies and public-sector payrolls, with the aim of balancing the budget, and in the public-sector borrowing requirement.

The 1987 budget projected total revenue of ₦17,861m. and recurrent expenditure of ₦10,749m., a nominal increase of 90% over the 1986 figure. Emphasis in the capital budget was placed on manufacturing and craft industries, agriculture, land transport, steel, hydrocarbons and water resources. It was envisaged that more than 55% of the capital budget would be absorbed by capital repayments, other financial obligations and liabilities, and external loans. The 1988 budget proposals projected total federal expenditure at ₦24,300m., of which ₦10,593m. was for capital expenditure. The budget aimed to encourage economic growth; restrictions on wages were ended, and limits on bank credit for the private sector were raised, while special reflationary expenditure, amounting to ₦2,500m., was allocated to public transport, industry and welfare facilities.

Budget estimates for 1989, announced in January, indicated closer adherence to the policies of austerity and structural adjustment that the IMF had stipulated. The budget envisaged federally-collected revenue of ₦29,414m. (compared with estimated actual revenue of ₦27,102m. in 1988); of this amount, ₦11,517m. was allocated to state and local governments. The budget included measures to encourage private investment, to improve the efficiency of public investment, to reduce dependence on imports (particularly of agricultural produce) and to promote exports. Total government revenue for 1990 was projected at ₦47,700m. (or $6,800m., using the government's assumed exchange rate of ₦7.0 = US $1. Revised revenue distribution, announced in January 1990, allocates 50% of revenue to the federal government, 30% to the state governments, and 15% to local governments, with the balance accruing a special project fund. Federal revenue, after allocations to state and local government, was projected at ₦25,400m. Recurrent expenditure was estimated at ₦27,200m. and capital expenditure at ₦12,600m., resulting in a budget deficit of ₦14,300m. In late 1990 and for the first six months of 1991, public finance, in particular the handling of the increased revenues from exports of petroleum accruing from higher world oil prices, became a major political issue. The World Bank announced that it would not grant a $500m. budgetary and financial policy loan for 1990 and a similar loan for 1991, unless it could reach agreement with the government on public expenditure levels. The World Bank principally objected to continued high spending on the Ajaokuta steel project and the establishment of an aluminium smelting plant. The 1991 budget was projected to achieve a surplus of ₦200m. after the 1990 budget's deficit of ₦14,300m. However, the decline in the price of petroleum, as a result of the Gulf War, jeopardized budgetary calculations, which had assumed a minimum world oil price of $21 per barrel. Actual budgetary revenue, which had been projected at ₦38,800m., was estimated at ₦35,000m., while actual expenditure, which had been projected at ₦36,800m., was estimated at ₦68,000m., converting the projected surplus into an actual deficit of ₦32,900m., or approximately 11.4% of GDP. The 1991 deficit was partly financed by drawings from the various stabilization accounts established by the government since 1989.

The 1992 budget proposals envisaged a surplus of ₦2,000m., or 0.6% of projected GDP, as a result of a further increase in revenue from petroleum, and a sharp rise in federally-collected revenue; however, estimates indicated an actual budgetary deficit of ₦43,800m. (equivalent to about 9.8% of GDP). According to official figures, actual federal revenue in that year totalled ₦101,201m. (of which ₦79,156m. was from petroleum). The 1993 budget proposals forecast federally-collected revenue at ₦148,400m., and an overall deficit of ₦28,600m. However, the actual budgetary deficit in that year totalled ₦101,000m. (equivalent to about 12.3% of GDP). The 1994 budget, which was announced by Abacha in January, projected a federally-collected revenue of ₦231,400m. (of which the federal government planned to retain ₦110,200m.), with a reduced overall deficit of ₦39,000m. (equivalent to 6% of GDP).

Statistical Survey

Source (unless otherwise stated): Federal Office of Statistics, 7 Okotie-Eboh St, SW Ikoyi, Lagos; tel. 682935.

Area and Population

AREA, POPULATION AND DENSITY

Area (sq km)	923,768*
Population (census results, 28–30 November 1991)	
Males	44,544,531
Females	43,969,970
Total	88,514,501
Density (per sq km) at November 1991	95.8

* 356,669 sq miles.

STATES (census of November 1991)

	Population	Capital
Abia	2,297,978	Umuahia
Adamawa	2,124,049	Yola
Akwa Ibom	2,359,736	Uyo
Anambra	2,767,903	Awka
Bauchi	4,294,413	Bauchi
Benue	2,780,398	Makurdi
Borno	2,596,589	Maiduguri
Cross River	1,865,604	Calabar
Delta	2,570,181	Asaba
Edo	2,159,848	Benin City
Enugu	3,161,295	Enugu
Imo	2,485,499	Owerri
Jigawa	2,829,929	Dutse
Kaduna	3,969,252	Kaduna
Kano	5,632,040	Kano
Katsina	3,878,344	Katsina
Kebbi	2,062,226	Birnin Kebbi
Kogi	2,099,046	Lokoja
Kwara	1,566,469	Ilorin
Lagos	5,685,781	Ikeja
Niger	2,482,367	Minna
Ogun	2,338,570	Abeokuta
Ondo	3,884,485	Akure
Osun	2,203,016	Oshogbo
Oyo	3,488,789	Ibadan
Plateau	3,283,704	Jos
Rivers	3,983,857	Port Harcourt
Sokoto	4,392,391	Sokoto
Taraba	1,480,590	Jalingo
Yobe	1,411,481	Damaturu
Federal Capital Territory	378,671	Abuja
Total	88,514,501	

PRINCIPAL TOWNS (estimated population at 1 July 1975)

Lagos (federal capital)*	1,060,848	Ado-Ekiti	213,000
Ibadan	847,000	Kaduna	202,000
Ogbomosho	432,000	Mushin	197,000
Kano	399,000	Maiduguri	189,000
Oshogbo	282,000	Enugu	187,000
Ilorin	282,000	Ede	182,000
Abeokuta	253,000	Aba	177,000
Port Harcourt	242,000	Ife	176,000
Zaria	224,000	Ila	155,000
Ilesha	224,000	Oyo	152,000
Onitsha	220,000	Ikere-Ekiti	145,000
Iwo	214,000	Benin City	136,000

* Federal capital moved to Abuja in December 1991.

BIRTHS AND DEATHS (UN estimates, annual averages)

	1975–80	1980–85	1985–90
Birth rate (per 1,000)	49.0	48.8	48.5
Death rate (per 1,000)	18.4	17.0	15.6

Expectation of life (UN estimates, years at birth, 1985–90): 50.5 (males 48.8; females 52.2).

Source: UN, *World Population Prospects: The 1992 Revision.*

ECONOMICALLY ACTIVE POPULATION
(sample survey, '000 persons aged 14 years and over, September 1986)

	Males	Females	Total
Agriculture, hunting, forestry and fishing	9,800.6	3,458.4	13,259.0
Mining and quarrying	6.8	—	6.8
Manufacturing	806.4	457.3	1,263.7
Electricity, gas and water	127.0	3.4	130.4
Construction	545.6	—	545.6
Trade, restaurants and hotels	2,676.6	4,740.8	7,417.4
Transport, storage and communications	1,094.7	17.2	1,111.9
Financing, insurance, real estate and business services	109.8	10.3	120.1
Community, social and personal services	3,939.5	962.6	4,902.1
Activities not adequately defined	597.1	147.8	744.9
Total employed	19,704.1	9,797.8	29,501.9
Unemployed	809.8	453.8	1,263.6
Total labour force	20,513.9	10,251.6	30,765.5

Note: Figures are based on a total estimated population of 98,936,800, which may be an overestimate.

Source: ILO, *Year Book of Labour Statistics.*

Agriculture

PRINCIPAL CROPS ('000 metric tons)

	1990	1991	1992
Wheat	50*	60*	100†
Rice (paddy)	2,500	3,185*	3,453*
Maize	1,832	1,900†	1,700†
Millet	5,136	3,497	3,200†
Sorghum	4,185	4,346	4,100†
Potatoes†	42	42	42
Sweet potatoes†	260	260	260
Cassava	19,043	20,339*	20,000†
Yams	13,624	15,603	20,000†
Taro (Coco yam)†	1,300	1,300	1,300
Pulses	1,463	1,559	1,600†
Soybeans	142	153*	160†
Groundnuts (in shell)	1,166	1,219	1,214*
Sesame seed†	70	70	70
Cottonseed	180	180†	190†
Cotton (lint)*	36	60	63
Coconuts	118*	129*	135†
Palm kernels*	356	369	385
Palm oil†	820	850	900
Tomatoes†	650	660	670
Chillies and peppers (green)†	800	800	800
Sugar cane†	1,180	1,250	1,400
Plantains	1,257	1,314	1,350†
Other fruit (excluding melons)	1,302	1,348	1,382†
Cocoa beans*	155	105	130
Tobacco (leaves)	9*	9*	9†
Natural rubber (dry weight)	88	155*	110*

* Unofficial figure(s). † FAO estimate(s).

Source: FAO, *Production Yearbook*.

LIVESTOCK ('000 head, year ending September)

	1990	1991	1992
Cattle	14,640	15,140	15,700
Sheep	12,460	13,000	13,500
Goats	23,321	23,500	24,000
Pigs	3,410	4,263	5,328
Horses	208	206*	205*
Asses	936	960*	1,000*
Camels*	18	18	18

Poultry (million): 126 in 1990; 130* in 1991; 135* in 1992.

* FAO estimate(s).

Source: FAO, *Production Yearbook*.

LIVESTOCK PRODUCTS
(FAO estimates unless otherwise indicated, '000 metric tons)

	1990	1991	1992
Beef and veal*	204	205	210
Mutton and lamb	43	45	46
Goats' meat	121	121	121
Pig meat	128	150	167
Poultry meat	178	185	192
Other meat	99	99	101
Edible offals	97	101	107
Cows' milk*	351	360	370
Butter and ghee	7.9	8.1	8.4
Cheese	6.3	6.5	6.7
Poultry eggs	225.0	225.0	225.0
Cattle hides	48.9	50.1	51.4
Sheep skins	7.8	8.2	8.4
Goat skins	19.0	19.0	19.2

* Official figures.

Source: FAO, mainly *Production Yearbook*.

Forestry

ROUNDWOOD REMOVALS
(FAO estimates, '000 cubic metres, excluding bark)

	1990	1991	1992
Sawlogs, veneer logs and logs for sleepers*	5,589	5,589	5,589
Other industrial wood†	2,279	2,279	2,279
Fuel wood	99,864	103,113	106,421
Total	107,732	110,981	114,289

* Assumed to be unchanged since 1986.

† Assumed to be unchanged since 1980.

Source: FAO, *Yearbook of Forest Products*.

SAWNWOOD PRODUCTION
('000 cubic metres, incl. railway sleepers)

	1990	1991*	1992*
Total	2,712	2,706	2,706

* FAO estimate.

Source: FAO, *Yearbook of Forest Products*.

Fishing

('000 metric tons, live weight)

	1989	1990	1991
Inland waters	115.0*	98.7	90.9
Tilapias	17.6*	13.9	12.0
Characins	11.7*	6.8	1.3
Naked catfishes	17.9*	7.0	7.0
Torpedo-shaped catfishes	18.9*	27.5	20.0
Other freshwater fishes (incl. unspecified)	38.9*	41.4	44.9
Nile perch	10.0*	2.1	5.8
Atlantic Ocean	184.7*	217.7	175.7
Tonguefishes	8.5	5.3	6.6
West African croakers	27.2	15.9	17.2
Threadfins and tasselfishes	13.0	3.4	8.7
Sardinellas	3.6*	10.3	78.4
Bonga shad	43.7	12.9	12.9
Sharks, rays, skates, etc.	6.9	8.4	7.2
Other marine fishes (incl. unspecified)	73.8*	153.0	33.5
Marine crustaceans	8.0*	8.6	11.1
Total catch	299.7*	316.3	266.6

* FAO estimate.

Source: FAO, *Yearbook of Fishery Statistics*.

Mining

('000 metric tons, unless otherwise indicated)

	1989	1990	1991
Hard coal*	85	90	90
Crude petroleum	85,510	86,029	94,314
Natural gas (petajoules)	169	156	185
Tin concentrates (metric tons, metal content)†	316	230	200

* Provisional or estimated figures.

† Data from UNCTAD, *International Tin Statistics* (Geneva).

Source: UN, *Industrial Statistics Yearbook*.

1992 (metric tons): Crude petroleum 91.6 million (Source: UN, *Monthly Bulletin of Statistics*).

Industry

SELECTED PRODUCTS
('000 metric tons, unless otherwise indicated)

	1989	1990	1991
Raw sugar[1]	53	53	59
Cigarettes (metric tons)[2]	10,000[3]	10,000	10,000
Plywood (cubic metres)[4]	175,000	175,000	175,000
Wood pulp[4]	17	7	7
Paper and paperboard	16	44[3]	45[3]
Nitrogenous fertilizers (a)[5]	197.4	210.0	212.0
Phosphatic fertilizers (b)[5]	93.5	96.1	110.6
Jet fuels	40	38	40
Motor spirit—petrol	2,967	3,745	3,594
Kerosene	1,537	1,941	1,899
Distillate fuel oils	2,393	3,019	3,029
Residual fuel oils	2,299	2,900	2,724
Liquefied petroleum gas[3]	60	55	55
Cement[3]	3,500	3,500	3,500
Crude steel	213	220	200
Tin metal—unwrought (metric tons)[6]	257	320	n.a.
Electric energy (million kWh)	9,935	9,945	9,955

[1] Source: FAO.
[2] Source: US Department of Agriculture.
[3] Provisional or estimated figure(s).
[4] FAO estimates.
[5] Production in terms of (a) nitrogen or (b) phosphoric acid. Source: FAO, *Quarterly Bulletin of Statistics*.
[6] Data from *International Tin Statistics* (Geneva).

Source: mainly UN, *Industrial Statistics Yearbook*.

Finance

CURRENCY AND EXCHANGE RATES

Monetary Units
100 kobo = 1 naira (₦).

Sterling and Dollar Equivalents (31 March 1994)
£1 sterling = 32.63 naira;
US $1 = 21.98 naira;
1,000 naira = £30.65 = $45.50.

Average Exchange Rate (naira per US $)
1991 9.909
1992 17.298
1993 22.065

FEDERAL BUDGET ESTIMATES (₦ million)

Recurrent Expenditure	1987	1988
Cabinet Office	106.0	368.7
General Staff Headquarters	34.5	124.0
Office of the Head of Service	20.0	36.0
Police	375.6	521.0
Police Affairs Department	6.0	9.0
Agriculture, water resources and rural development	29.2	54.3
Federal Audit Department	5.2	6.2
Judiciary	14.8	24.0
Communications	68.1	80.8
Defence	717.6	830.0
National planning	27.7	60.6
Education	198.4	302.3
Federal Capital Territory	14.0	15.9
External affairs	79.6	440.6
Finance	364.4	877.8
Industries	9.3	38.8
Information and culture	111.0	146.4
Internal affairs	220.3	262.5
Justice	6.7	15.3
Employment, labour and productivity	113.9	134.7
Mines, power and steel	12.2	14.2
Science and technology	54.3	102.3
Social development, youth and sports	96.7	162.8

Recurrent Expenditure - *continued*	1987	1988
Trade	112.1	31.2
Transport and aviation	46.1	62.0
Petroleum resources	3.9	58.3
Health	166.9	259.9
Works and housing	259.1	432.9
Contingencies	80.0	100.0
National Universities Commission	316.0	500.0
National Electoral Commission	—	40.0
Other commissions	7.5	14.6
Sub-total	3,677.1	6,127.4
Consolidated Revenue Fund charges	7,197.9	7,579.3
Total	10,875.0	13,706.7

Revenue: (₦ million): (1986) 13,199; (1987) 17,861; (1988) 27,102.

Source: Central Bank of Nigeria.

Capital Expenditure	1987	1988
Rural development	70.5	98.3
Agriculture (crops)	170.0	213.2
Livestock	1.2	35.5
Forestry	0.4	15.8
Fisheries	4.4	13.9
Agricultural co-operatives	2.6	6.0
Water resources	99.9	213.0
Communications	52.2	156.1
Industries (manufacturing and craft)	191.2	260.3
Trade	4.0	223.9
Information and culture	2.6	80.1
Social development, youth and sports	3.3	46.5
Health	69.5	188.2
Mining and quarrying	52.2	107.6
Power (NEPA and rural electrification)	34.8	54.5
Steel	104.3	224.5
Petroleum and energy	104.3	402.0
Land transport system	275.8	420.1
Water transport	16.0	63.1
Air transport	21.1	64.4
Education	139.1	281.8
Defence	92.1	440.0
Science and technology	6.9	32.2
Environment	0.9	37.5
Housing	63.6	84.4
Surveying and mapping	3.8	118.9
Employment, labour and productivity	3.6	35.9
Prisons	5.0	11.0
Police	13.5	260.3
Federal Capital Territory	34.8	155.0
General administration	157.7	479.2
Directorate of Food and Rural Development	400.0	500.0
Special projects	730.0	2,500.0
Capital repayment (external loans)	938.2	522.8
Other financial obligations	174.0	241.0
Outstanding liabilities	700.0	500.0
External loans	1,998.0	1,506.4
Total	6,741.9	10,593.4

INTERNATIONAL RESERVES (US $ million at 31 December)

	1991	1992	1993
Gold*	2	1	1
Foreign exchange	4,435	967	1,372
Total	4,437	968	1,373

* National valuation of gold reserves (687,000 troy ounces in each year).

Source: IMF, *International Financial Statistics*.

MONEY SUPPLY (₦ million at 31 December)

	1989	1990	1991
Currency outside banks . .	12,124	14,951	23,121
Demand deposits at commercial banks	9,738	15,000	20,180
Total money (incl. others) .	26,664	34,540	48,708

Source: IMF, *International Financial Statistics.*

COST OF LIVING
(Consumer Price Index for rural and urban areas; base: 1988 = 100)

	1990	1991	1992
Food	158.3	177.1	259.5
All items	161.6	182.6	264.0

Source: ILO, *Year Book of Labour Statistics.*

NATIONAL ACCOUNTS (₦ million at current prices)
National Income and Product

	1989	1990	1991
Compensation of employees .	35,099	41,050	46,887
Operating surplus . .	176,769	203,466	258,961
Domestic factor incomes .	211,868	244,516	305,848
Consumption of fixed capital .	10,590	13,357	15,267
Gross domestic product (GDP) at factor cost . .	222,458	257,873	321,115
Indirect taxes . . .	2,770	3,220	4,187
Less Subsidies	431	456	508
GDP in purchasers' values .	224,797	260,637	324,794
Factor income received from abroad	1,137	1,723	2,126
Less Factor income paid abroad	18,991	24,090	26,600
Gross national product (GNP)	206,942	238,270	300,320
Less Consumption of fixed capital	10,590	13,357	15,267
National income in market prices	196,353	224,913	285,053
Other current transfers from abroad (net) . . .	1,141	3,614	7,292
National disposable income .	197,494	228,528	292,345

Source: UN, *National Accounts Statistics.*

Expenditure on the Gross Domestic Product

	1991	1992	1993
Government final consumption expenditure	12,690	20,430	82,050
Private final consumption expenditure	222,270	407,530	579,400
Increase in stocks . . . Gross fixed capital formation }	35,620	58,940	105,200
Total domestic expenditure .	270,580	486,900	766,650
Exports of goods and services .	129,691	196,904	240,250
Less Imports of goods and services	-76,260	-130,650	-184,980
GDP in purchasers' values	324,011	553,154	821,920
GDP at constant 1990 prices .	272,962	282,722	290,087

Source: mainly IMF, *International Financial Statistics.*

Gross Domestic Product by Economic Activity (at factor cost)

	1989	1990	1991
Agriculture, hunting, forestry and fishing	69,713	84,345	98,617
Mining and quarrying . .	79,379	86,854	120,850
Manufacturing . . .	11,775	14,297	18,559
Electricity, gas and water . .	1,067	1,178	1,345
Construction	3,854	4,351	4,900
Trade, restaurants and hotels .	32,890	36,390	42,386
Transport, storage and communications	4,923	5,662	6,388
Finance, insurance, real estate and business services .	11,036	15,912	18,199
Government services . . .	6,987	7,953	8,800
Other community, social and personal services . . .	832	932	1,072
Total	222,458	257,873	321,116

Source: UN, *National Accounts Statistics.*

BALANCE OF PAYMENTS (US $ million)

	1990	1991	1992
Merchandise exports f.o.b. .	13,585	12,254	11,791
Merchandise imports f.o.b. .	-4,932	-7,813	-7,181
Trade balance	8,653	4,441	4,611
Exports of services . .	965	886	1,053
Imports of services . .	-1,976	-2,448	-1,810
Other income received . .	211	211	156
Other income paid . . .	-2,949	-2,631	-2,494
Private unrequited transfers (net)	1	12	22
Official unrequited transfers (net)	84	732	731
Current balance . . .	4,988	1,203	2,268
Direct investment (net) . .	588	712	897
Portfolio investment (net) . .	-197	-61	1,884
Other capital (net) . . .	-4,573	-3,284	-10,565
Net errors and omissions . .	235	-92	-122
Overall balance . . .	1,042	-1,523	-5,638

Source: IMF, *International Financial Statistics.*

External Trade

PRINCIPAL COMMODITIES (distribution by SITC, ₦ million)

Imports c.i.f.	1985	1986	1987
Food and live animals . .	940.6	802.0	1,646.4
Fish and fish preparations* .	90.6	104.0	451.8
Fresh and simply preserved fish*	n.a.	n.a.	434.4
Fresh, chilled or frozen fish	n.a.	n.a.	364.8
Cereals and cereal preparations	n.a.	n.a.	326.6
Wheat and meslin (unmilled)	327.9	273.8	60.8
Crude materials (inedible) except fuels	274.8	193.9	702.7
Crude fertilizers and non-metallic minerals (excl. precious stones) . . .	n.a.	n.a.	353.5
Chemicals	868.9	1,039.0	2,650.5
Chemical elements and compounds	204.7	248.2	629.5
Dyeing, tanning and colouring materials	73.5	104.0	352.9
Medicinal and pharmaceutical products	167.4	214.4	471.6
Plastic materials etc. . . .	157.6	218.9	446.2
Products of polymerization, etc.	n.a.	n.a.	303.6

Imports c.i.f. - *continued*	1985	1986	1987
Basic manufactures	1,263.5	1,237.1	3,940.6
Rubber manufactures	120.9	92.5	447.8
Rubber tyres and tubes	n.a.	n.a.	368.3
Paper, paperboard and manufactures	204.4	156.5	469.7
Iron and steel	n.a.	230.2	1,240.7
Universals, plates and sheets	146.5	104.3	510.9
Tubes, pipes and fittings	83.4	96.0	504.4
Machinery and transport equipment	1,892.8	2,277.8	5,999.6
Non-electric machinery	877.8	1,147.4	3,166.4
Construction and mining machinery	n.a.	n.a.	379.7
Heating and cooling equipment	n.a.	n.a.	328.2
Pumps and centrifuges	n.a.	n.a.	491.0
Electrical machinery, apparatus and appliances	449.4	472.0	1,492.7
Electric power machinery and switchgear	205.5	213.1	520.3
Transport equipment	565.6	658.4	1,340.5
Road motor vehicles and parts†	n.a.	n.a.	1,092.5
Passenger cars (excl. buses)	109.5	261.2	374.3
Parts for cars, buses, etc.†	277.9	112.1	425.2
Miscellaneous manufactured articles	176.0	246.4	596.2
Total (incl. others)	5,536.9	5,974.7	15,698.1

* Including crustaceans and molluscs.
† Excluding tyres, engines and electrical parts.

Exports f.o.b.	1985	1986	1987
Food and live animals	243.8	442.6	850.9
Coffee, tea, cocoa and spices	n.a.	n.a.	805.6
Cocoa	n.a.	n.a.	796.6
Cocoa beans	182.1	370.7	732.0
Mineral fuels, lubricants, etc.	11,335.8	8,452.7	28,208.6
Petroleum and petroleum products	n.a.	n.a.	28,208.3
Crude petroleum	11,275.0	8,328.7	28,154.0
Total (incl. others)	11,720.8	9,047.5	29,577.9

Source: Federal Office of Statistics, *Nigeria Trade Summary* and *Review of External Trade*.

1988 (₦ million): Imports c.i.f. 21,446; Exports f.o.b. 31,193 (Petroleum 28,436).
1989 (₦ million): Imports c.i.f. 30,860; Exports f.o.b. 57,791 (Petroleum 55,017).
1990 (₦ million): Imports c.i.f. 45,718; Exports f.o.b. 109,886 (Petroleum 106,627).
1991 (₦ million): Imports c.i.f. 89,488; Exports f.o.b. 121,534 (Petroleum 116,857).
1992 (₦ million): Imports c.i.f. 143,151; Exports f.o.b. 205,613 (Petroleum 201,384).

Source (for 1988–92): IMF, *International Financial Statistics*.

PRINCIPAL TRADING PARTNERS (₦ million)

Imports	1985	1986	1987
Austria	86.5	51.9	226.8
Belgium and Luxembourg	108.1	142.9	380.4
Brazil	378.2	133.2	334.4
China, People's Republic	37.3	63.1	342.0
France	458.0	667.3	1,569.7
Germany, Fed. Republic	650.6	807.8	2,110.6
Hong Kong	36.8	51.3	179.4
India	24.8	42.7	158.8
Italy	211.5	290.7	899.9
Japan	408.3	309.9	1,417.5
Korea, Republic	n.a.	n.a.	195.6
Netherlands	202.6	244.2	722.6
Romania	61.2	90.3	206.3
Spain	100.7	119.9	243.7
Sweden	53.0	47.1	164.9
Switzerland	115.0	156.8	383.8
Taiwan	n.a.	n.a.	331.2
USSR	68.1	148.6	288.1
United Kingdom	1,098.7	1,075.0	2,641.3
USA	741.6	711.9	1,297.9
Yugoslavia	23.9	25.6	156.4
Total (incl. others)	5,536.9	5,974.7	15,698.1

Exports	1985	1986	1987
Brazil	524.0	163.8	197.4
Canada	152.5	214.6	623.3
Côte d'Ivoire	169.1	151.0	875.5
France	1,902.7	1,364.6	2,285.7
Germany, Fed. Republic	863.5	636.9	1,564.8
Ghana	171.4	134.5	427.2
Italy	1,921.0	738.4	1,758.8
Netherlands	1,434.2	1,012.1	3,343.5
Portugal	n.a.	n.a.	281.5
Senegal	13.0	34.4	158.3
Spain	664.4	257.3	2,347.8
Sweden	154.0	61.1	121.8
United Kingdom	538.6	512.6	530.3
USA	2,116.3	3,163.3	13,897.8
Uruguay	n.a.	n.a.	193.3
Total (incl. others)	11,720.8	9,047.5	29,577.9

Source: Federal Office of Statistics.

Transport

RAILWAYS (estimated freight traffic)

	1989	1990	1991
Net ton-kilometres (million)	1,812	1,870	1,930

Source: UN Economic Commission for Africa, *African Statistical Yearbook*.

ROAD TRAFFIC (estimates, '000 motor vehicles in use)

	1989	1990	1991
Passenger cars	410	420	425
Commercial vehicles	45	46	47

Source: UN Economic Commission for Africa, *African Statistical Yearbook*.

SHIPPING

Merchant Fleet
(registered at 30 June)

	1989	1990	1991
Displacement ('000 gross tons)	500	496	493

Source: UN, *Statistical Yearbook*.

International Sea-borne Freight Traffic
(estimates, '000 metric tons)

	1988	1989	1990
Goods loaded	65,700	77,640	80,607
Goods unloaded	9,900	10,536	10,812

Source: UN, *Monthly Bulletin of Statistics.*

CIVIL AVIATION (traffic on scheduled services)

	1989	1990	1991
Kilometres flown ('000)	14,000	17,000	14,000
Passengers carried ('000)	849	965	930
Passenger-km (million)	1,007	1,287	1,391
Freight ton-km ('000)	17,000	24,000	28,000

Source: UN, *Statistical Yearbook.*

Tourism

	1989	1990*	1991*
Tourist arrivals ('000)	161	165	167
Tourist receipts (US $ million)	21	20	18

* Estimates.

Source: UN Economic Commission for Africa, *African Statistical Yearbook.*

Communications Media

	1989	1990	1991
Radio receivers ('000 in use)	18,000	18,700	19,350
Television receivers ('000 in use)	3,000	3,500	3,650
Telephones ('000 in use)*	265	275	279
Book production (titles†)	1,466	n.a.	n.a.
Daily newspapers:			
Number	n.a.	31	n.a.
Average circulation ('000 copies)*	n.a.	1,700	n.a.

* Estimate.

† Including pamphlets (566 in 1989), but excluding university theses.

Sources: UNESCO, *Statistical Yearbook*, UN Economic Commission for Africa, *African Statistical Yearbook.*

Education

(1987)

	Institutions	Teachers	Students
Primary	34,240	294,783	11,276,270
Secondary:			
General	5,547	122,207	2,660,085
Teacher training	135	4,531	108,751
Technical and vocational	240	5,115	89,536
Higher education:			
Universities	27	11,521	160,767
Polytechnics and colleges of technology and of education	69	3,235	58,355

Sources: Federal Ministry of Education, PMB 12573, Lagos; UNESCO, *Statistical Yearbook.*

1991: Primary Institutions 35,446, Teachers 353,600, Pupils 13,776,854 (males 7,741,897; females 6,034,957); Secondary Teachers 141,491, Pupils 3,123,277 (males 1,821,307; females 1,301,970); Higher Education Teachers 19,601 (1989); Students 335,824 (1989) (Source: UNESCO, *Statistical Yearbook*).

Directory

The Constitution

On 18 November 1993, following the assumption of power of a new military Head of State, all existing organs of state and bodies that had been established under the former process of transition to civilian rule were dissolved, the elected State Governors were replaced with military administrators, and political activity was prohibited. Supreme executive and legislative power was subsequently vested in an 11-member Provisional Ruling Council (PRC), comprising senior military officials and principal members of the new cabinet, the Federal Executive Council (FEC). The Head of State, who was Commander-in-Chief of the Armed Forces, chaired the PRC and the FEC. On 21 November the Constitution of 1979 (which provided for an executive President, elected for a term of four years, a bicameral National Assembly and elected local government councils) was formally restored. In May 1994 a National Constitutional Conference was elected: its task was to determine the constitutional future of the country.

The Judiciary comprises the Supreme Court, the Court of Appeal and the Federal High Court at federal level, and High Courts in each state. Judicial appointments below the Supreme Court are made by the Federal Government on the advice of the Advisory Judicial Committee, with the Chief Justice of the Federation as Chairman. Certain states also have a Shari'a Court of Appeal, and others a Customary Court of Appeal, to consider civil cases in Islamic or customary law respectively.

Federal Government

HEAD OF STATE

Head of Government and Commander-in-Chief of the Armed Forces: Gen. Sani Abacha (assumed power 17 November 1993).

PROVISIONAL RULING COUNCIL
(September 1994)

Gen. SANI ABACHA (Chairman)
Lt-Gen. OLADIPO DIYA (Vice-Chairman)
Maj.-Gen. ABDUSALAMI A. ABUBAKAR
Brig.-Gen. ALWALI J. KAZIR
Cdre MIKE AKHIGBE
Air Vice-Marshal JOHN FEMI
Insp.-Gen. Alhaji IBRAHIM COMMASIE
Lt.-Gen. MOHAMED B. HALADU
Rear-Adm. J. O. A. AYINLA
Maj.-Gen. E. U. UNIMNA
Brig.-Gen. AHMED A. ABDULLAHI
Brig.-Gen. P. N. AZIZA
Brig.-Gen. A. T. OLANREWAJU
Brig.-Gen. S. V. L. MALU
Brig.-Gen. ISHAYA R. BAMAIYI
Cdre F. B. PORBENI
Cdre R. O. EYITAYO
Air Cdre N. E. EDUOK
Air Cdre IDI MUSA
Lt-Gen. JEREMIAH T. USENI
Brig.-Gen. T. M. SHELPIDI
Brig.-Gen. I. D. GUMEL
Brig.-Gen. S. I. MOMAH
Capt. A. IKWECHEGH
Air Cdre C. UMENWALIRI

FEDERAL EXECUTIVE COUNCIL
(September 1994)

Chairman and Minister of Defence: Gen. SANI ABACHA.
Vice-Chairman: Lt-Gen. OLADIPO DIYA.
Minister of Federal Capital Territory: Lt-Gen. J. T. USENI.
Minister of Education and Youth Development: Dr IYORCHIA AYU.
Minister of Industry: Alhaji BAMANGA TUKUR.
Minister of Works and Housing: Alhaji LATEEF JAKANDE.
Minister of Finance: Dr KALU IDIKA KALU.
Minister of Petroleum Resources: DON ETIEBET.
Minister of Power and Steel: Alhaji BASHIR DALHATU.
Minister of Health and Human Resources: Dr SARKI TAFIDA.
Minister of Foreign Affairs: BABA GANA KINGIBE.
Minister of Internal Affairs: ALEX IBRU.
Minister of Communications: Alhaji ABUBAKAR RIMI.
Minister of Labour and Productivity: Dr SAMUEL OGBEMUDIA.
Minister of Agriculture: Alhaji ADAMU CIROMA.
Minister of Information and Culture: Prof. JERRY GANA.
Minister of Justice and Attorney General: MICHAEL AGBAMUCHE.
Minister of Commerce and Tourism: Chief MELFORD OKILO.
Minister of Transport and Aviation: Chief EBENEZER BABATOPE.
Minister of Water Resources: Alhaji ISA MOHAMED.
Minister of Science and Technology: Dr LAZARUS UNAGU.
Minister of Police Affairs: SOLOMON LAR.
Minister of Local Government Affairs: MOHAMMED ANKA.
Minister of National Planning: Chief S. B. DANIYAN.
Minister of Establishment and Management Services: MOBOLAJI OSOMO.
Minister of State for Petroleum Resources: Alhaji UMARU BADA.
Minister of State for Health: SILAS ILO.
Minister of State for Agriculture: ADA ADOGU.
Minister of State for Transport and Aviation: Alhaji YAHAYA.
Minister of State for Power and Steel: WOLE OYELESE.
Minister of State for Education: Alhaji WADA NAS.
Minister of State for Foreign Affairs: Chief ANTHONY A. ANI.
Secretary to the Government: Alhaji AMINU SALEH.

MINISTRIES

Office of the Head of State: Abuja.

Ministry of Agriculture: Gwagwalada Area, PMB 24, Abuja; tel. (9) 8821080.

Ministry of Commerce and Tourism: Federal Secretariat, PMB 88, Garki, Abuja.

Ministry of Communications: Headquarters, Lafiaji, Lagos; tel. (1) 633747.

Ministry of Education and Youth Development: PMB 12573, Ahmadu Bello Way, Victoria Island, Lagos; tel. (1) 616843.

Ministry of Establishment and Management Services: Federal Secretariat Phase II, Ikoyi Rd, Ikoyi, Lagos.

Ministry of Federal Capital Territory: Federal Secretariat, Abuja; tel. (9) 2431250.

Ministry of Finance: New Secretariat Area II, Garki, Abuja; tel. (9) 2341109.

Ministry of Foreign Affairs: Maputo St, PMB 130, Abuja; tel. (9) 5230520.

Ministry of Health and Human Resources: New Federal Secretariat Phase II, Ikoyi Rd, Obalende, Lagos; tel. (1) 684405.

Ministry of Industry: Gwagwalada Area, PMB 24, Abuja; tel. (9) 2431250.

Ministry of Information and Culture: 15 Awolowo Rd, Ikoyi, Lagos; tel. (1) 610836; telex 22649.

Ministry of Internal Affairs: Old Secretariat, Garki, Abuja.

Ministry of Justice: New Federal Secretariat, Ikoyi, Lagos; tel. (1) 684414.

Ministry of Labour and Productivity: PMB 12576, Ikoyi, Lagos; tel. (1) 655128.

Ministry of National Planning: Federal Secretariat Phase I, Ikoyi Rd, Ikoyi, Lagos.

Ministry of Petroleum Resources: Federal Secretariat, Ikoyi Rd, Ikoyi, Lagos.

Ministry of Power and Steel: Federal Secretariat Phase I, Ikoyi Rd, Ikoyi, Lagos.

Ministry of Science and Technology: New Federal Secretariat, Ikoyi Rd, Ikoyi, Lagos; tel. (1) 614250.

Ministry of Transport and Aviation: Joseph St, PMB 21038, Ikoyi, Lagos; tel. (1) 652120; telex 21535.

Ministry of Water Resources: Gwagwalada Area, PMB 24, Abuja; tel. (9) 8821080.

Ministry of Works and Housing: Tafawa Balewa Sq., Lagos; tel. (1) 653120.

Legislature

NATIONAL ASSEMBLY

The National Assembly, comprising a 91-member Senate and a 593-member House of Representatives, was dissolved by the new military Head of State, Gen. Sani Abacha, on 18 November 1993.

Political Organizations

On 18 November 1993, following the assumption of power by a new military Head of State, political activity was prohibited, and the two registered political associations (created in 1989 by the former military regime) were proscribed. The Government subsequently announced, however, that the ban on political activity was to end in January 1995. In 1994 the following political pressure groups were active:

Association for a Better Nigeria (ABN): f. 1993; advocates the continuation of military rule; Leader Chief FRANCIS ARTHUR NZERIBE.

Campaign for Democracy (CD): f. Nov. 1991; alliance of 25 human rights orgs opposed to the Govt; Chair. Dr BEKO RANSOME-KUTI; Sec.-Gen. SYLVESTER ODION-AKHAINE.

Eastern Mandate Union: grouping of politicians and tribal leaders from south-eastern Nigeria; Leader PATRICK DELE COLE.

Movement for the Survival of the Ogoni People: supports self-determination for the Ogoni ethnic group; Leader KEN SARO-WIWA.

National Democratic Coalition (NADECO): grouping of human rights activists, and four politicians and mil. officers; supports the installation of Chief Moshood Abiola as Pres.; Sec.-Gen. OYO OPADOKUN.

Diplomatic Representation

EMBASSIES AND HIGH COMMISSIONS IN NIGERIA

Algeria: 26 Maitama Sule St, SW Ikoyi, POB 7288, Lagos; tel. (1) 683155; telex 21676; Ambassador: EL-MIHOUB MIHOUBI.

Angola: 5 Kasumu Ekomode St, Victoria Island, POB 50437, Lagos; tel. (1) 611135; Ambassador: B. A. SOZINHO.

Argentina: 93 Awolowo Rd, SW Ikoyi, POB 51940, Lagos; tel. (1) 682797; telex 21403; Ambassador: (vacant).

Australia: 2 Ozumba Mbadiwe Ave, Victoria Island, POB 2427, Lagos; tel. (1) 618875; telex 21219; fax (1) 618703; High Commissioner: H. BROWN.

Austria: Fabac Centre, 3B Ligali Ayorinde Ave, POB 1914, Lagos; tel. (1) 616081; telex 21463; fax (1) 617639; Ambassador: Dr WERNER DRUML.

Belgium: 1A Bank Rd, Ikoyi, POB 149, Lagos; tel. (1) 2603230; telex 21118; fax (1) 619683; Ambassador: MICHEL CZETWERTYNSKI.

Benin: 4 Abudu Smith St, Victoria Island, POB 5705, Lagos; tel. (1) 614411; telex 21583; Ambassador: PATRICE HOUNGAVOU.

Brazil: 257 Kofo Abayomi St, Victoria Island, POB 1931, Lagos; tel. (1) 610135; telex 23428; fax (1) 613394; Ambassador: BRIAN M. F. NEELE.

Brazil: 257 Kofo Abayomi St, Victoria Island, POB 1931, Lagos; tel. (1) 610135; telex 23428; fax (1) 613394; Ambassador: BRIAN M. F. NEELE.

Bulgaria: 3 Eleke Crescent, Victoria Island, PMB 4441, Lagos; tel. (1) 611931; telex 21567; fax (1) 619879; Ambassador: (vacant).

Burkina Faso: 15 Norman Williams St, Ikoyi, Lagos; tel. (1) 681001; Chargé d'affaires: ADOLPHE T. BENON.

Cameroon: 5 Elsie Femi Pearse St, Victoria Island, PMB 2476, Lagos; tel. (1) 612226; telex 21343; Ambassador: SOUAIBOU HAYATOU.

Canada: 4 Idowu Taylor St, Victoria Island, POB 54506, Ikoyi Station, Lagos; tel. (1) 2692195; telex 21275; fax (1) 2692919; High Commissioner: REJEAN FRENETTE.

Central African Republic: Plot 137, Ajao Estate, New Airport, Oshodi, Lagos; Ambassador: JEAN-PAUL MOKODOPO.

Chad: 2 Goriola St, Victoria Island, PMB 70662, Lagos; tel. (1) 613116; telex 21414; Ambassador: YOUSSOUF MBODOU MBAMI.

China, People's Republic: 19A Taslim Elias Close, Victoria Island, POB 5653, Lagos; tel. (1) 612586; Ambassador: HU LIPENG.

Colombia: 43 Raymond Njoku Rd, POB 2352, Ikoyi, Lagos; Chargé d'affaires: Dr BERNARDO ECHEVERRI.

Côte d'Ivoire: 3 Abudu Smith St, Victoria Island, POB 7780, Lagos; tel. (1) 610936; telex 21120; Ambassador: DÉSIRÉ AMON TANOE.

Cuba: Plot 935, Idejo St, Victoria Island, POB 328, Victoria Island, Lagos; tel. (1) 614836; Ambassador: GIRALDO MAZOLA.

Czech Republic: 2 Alhaji Masha Close, Ikoyi, POB 1009, Lagos; tel. (1) 683207; fax (1) 683175; Ambassador: EVZEN VACEK.

Denmark: 4 Eleke Crescent, Victoria Island, POB 2390, Lagos; tel. (1) 610841; telex 21349; Ambassador: LARS BLINKENBURG.

Egypt: 81 Awolowo Rd, Ikoyi, POB 538, Lagos; tel. (1) 612922; Ambassador: FUAD YUSUF.

Equatorial Guinea: 7 Bank Rd, Ikoyi, POB 4162, Lagos; tel. (1) 683717; Ambassador: A. S. DOUGAN MALABO.

Ethiopia: Plot 97, Ahmadu Bello Rd, Victoria Island, PMB 2488, Lagos; tel. (1) 613198; telex 21694; fax (1) 615055; Chargé d'Affaires a.i.: NEGGA BEYENNE.

Finland: 13 Eleke Crescent, Victoria Island, POB 4433, Lagos; tel. (1) 610916; telex 21796; fax (1) 613158; Ambassador: ESKO KUNNAMO.

France: 1 Queen's Drive, POB 567, Lagos; tel. (1) 2603300; telex 21338; Ambassador: PIERRE GARRIGUE-GUYONNAUD.

Gabon: 8 Norman Williams St, POB 5989, Lagos; tel. (1) 684673; telex 21736; Ambassador: E. AGUEMINYA.

Gambia: 162 Awolowo Rd, SW Ikoyi, POB 8037, Lagos; tel. (1) 681018; High Commissioner: OMAR SECKA.

Germany: 15 Eleke Crescent, Victoria Island, POB 728, Lagos; tel. (1) 611011; telex 21229; Ambassador: LEONHARD KREMER.

Ghana: 21–23 King George V Rd, POB 889, Lagos; tel. (1) 630015; High Commissioner: AARON K. DUAH (acting).

Greece: Plot 1644, Oko-Awo Close, Victoria Island, POB 1199, Lagos; tel. (1) 611412; telex 21747; fax (1) 614852; Ambassador: HARIS KARABARBOUNIS.

Guinea: 8 Abudu Smith St, Victoria Island, POB 2826, Lagos; tel. (1) 616961; Ambassador: KOMO BEAVOGUI.

Holy See: 9 Anifowoshe St, Victoria Island, POB 2470, Lagos (Apostolic Nunciature); tel. (1) 614441; telex 22455; fax (1) 618635; Apostolic Pro-Nuncio: Most Rev. CARLO MARIA VIGANÒ, Titular Archbishop of Ulpiana.

Hungary: 9 Louis Solomon Close, Victoria Island, POB 3168, Lagos; tel. (1) 613551; fax (1) 613717; Ambassador: GÉZA KÓTAI.

India: 107 Awolowo Rd, SW Ikoyi, POB 2322, Lagos; tel. (1) 681297; High Commissioner: KRISHNAN RUGHNATI.

Indonesia: 5 Anifowoshe St, Victoria Island, POB 3473, Lagos; tel. (1) 614601; Ambassador: Vice-Adm. SUBROTO YUDONO.

Iran: 1 Alexander Ave, Ikoyi, Lagos; tel. (1) 681601; telex 22625; Ambassador: BAHMAN TAHERIAN-MOBARAKEH.

Iraq: Plot 708A, Adeola Hopewell St, Victoria Island, POB 2859, Lagos; tel. (1) 610389; Ambassador: A. A. H. AL-SAMMARRAI.

Ireland: 34 Kofo Abayomi St, Victoria Island, Lagos; tel. (1) 615224; telex 21478; Ambassador: DERMOT A. GALLAGHER.

Israel: Abuja; Ambassador: MOSHE GILBOA.

Italy: 12 Eleke Crescent, Victoria Island, POB 2161, Lagos; tel. (1) 614066; telex 21202; Ambassador: Dr STEFANO RASTRELLI.

Jamaica: Plot 77, Samuel Adedoyin Ave, Victoria Island, POB 75368, Lagos; tel. (1) 611085; fax (1) 612100; High Commissioner: DUDLEY THOMPSON.

Japan: 24–25 Apese St, Victoria Island, PMB 2111, Lagos; tel. (1) 614929; telex 21364; fax (1) 614035; Ambassador: TAKANORI KAZUHARA.

Kenya: 53 Queen's Drive, Ikoyi, POB 6464, Lagos; tel. (1) 682768; telex 21124; High Commissioner: Dr I. E. MALUKI.

Korea, Democratic People's Republic: 31 Akin Adesola St, Victoria Island, Lagos; tel. (1) 610108; Ambassador: AHN KYUNG HYON.

Korea, Republic: Plot 934, Idejo St, Victoria Island, POB 4668, Lagos; tel. (1) 615353; telex 21953; Ambassador: CHAI KI-OH.

Lebanon: Plot 18, Eleke Crescent, Victoria Island, POB 651, Lagos; tel. (1) 614511; Ambassador: M. SALAME.

Liberia: 3 Idejo St, Plot 162, off Adeola Odeku St, Victoria Island, POB 70841, Lagos; tel. (1) 618899; telex 23361; Ambassador: Prof. JAMES TAPEH.

Libya: 46 Raymond Njoku Rd, SW Ikoyi, Lagos; tel. (1) 680880; Chargé d'affaires: (vacant).

Malaysia: 1 Anifowoshe St, Victoria Island, POB 3729, Lagos; tel. (1) 619415; High Commissioner: ALFRED KUMARASERI.

Mauritania: 1A Karimu Giwa Close, SW Ikoyi, Lagos; tel. (1) 682971; Ambassador: MOHAMED M. O. WEDDADY.

Morocco: Plot 1318, 27 Karimu Katun St, Victoria Island, Lagos; tel. (1) 611682; telex 21835; Ambassador: SAAD EDDINE TAIEB.

Namibia: Victoria Island, PMB 8000, Lagos.

Netherlands: 24 Ozumba Mbadiwe Ave, Victoria Island, POB 2426, Lagos; tel. (1) 613510; telex 21327; Ambassador: L. P. J. MAZAIRAC.

Niger: 15 Adeola Odeku St, Victoria Island, PMB 2736, Lagos; tel. (1) 612300; telex 21434; Ambassador: (vacant).

Norway: 3 Anifowoshe St, Victoria Island, PMB 2431, Lagos; tel. (1) 2618467; telex 21429; fax (1) 2618469; Ambassador: KNUT TORAASEN.

Pakistan: Plot 859, Bishop Aboyade Cole St, Victoria Island, POB 2450, Lagos; tel. (1) 614129; telex 22758; fax (1) 614822; High Commissioner: SHAHID M. AMIN.

Philippines: Plot 152, No 302, off 3rd Ave, Victoria Island, Lagos; tel. (1) 614048; telex 23344; Ambassador: MUKHTAR M. MUALLAM.

Poland: 10 Idejo St, Victoria Island, POB 410, Lagos; tel. (1) 2614634; telex 21729; Ambassador: KAZIMIERZ GUTKOWSKI.

Portugal: Plot 1677, Olukunle Bakare Close, Victoria Island, Lagos; tel. (1) 619037; telex 22424; Ambassador: NUNO DA CUNHA E TAVORA LORENA.

Romania: Plot 1192, off Olugbosi Close, Victoria Island, POB 72928, Lagos; tel. (1) 617806; telex 28828; fax (1) 618249; Chargé d'affaires a.i.: EMIL RAPCEA.

Russia: 5 Eleke Crescent, Victoria Island, POB 2723, Lagos; tel. (1) 612267; telex 22905; fax (1) 615022; Ambassador: LEV PARSHIN.

Saudi Arabia: Plot 1412, Victoria Island, POB 2836, Lagos; (1) 2603420; Ambassador: FOUD SADIK MOUSTI.

Senegal: 14 Kofo Abayomi Rd, Victoria Island, PMB 2197, Lagos; tel. (1) 611722; telex 21398; Ambassador: CHERIF Y. DIAITE.

Sierra Leone: 31 Waziri Ibrahim St, Victoria Island, POB 2821, Lagos; tel. (1) 614666; telex; 21495; High Commissioner: JOSEPH BLELL.

Slovakia: POB 1290, Lagos; tel. (1) 683123; telex 28685; fax (1) 2690423; Ambassador: ANTON HAJDUK.

Somalia: Plot 1270, off Adeola Odeka St, POB 6355, Lagos; tel. (1) 611283; Ambassador: M. S. HASSAN.

Spain: 21C Kofo Abayomi Rd, Victoria Island, POB 2738, Lagos; tel. (1) 615215; telex 22656; fax (1) 618225; Ambassador CARLOS BÁRCENA PORTOLÉS.

Sudan: 2B Kofo Abayomi St, Victoria Island, POB 2428, Lagos; tel. (1) 615889; telex 23500; Ambassador: MUBARAK ADAM EL-HADI.

Sweden: 26 Moloney St, POB 1097, Lagos; tel. (1) 2630688; telex 21318; Ambassador: BO EDVIN ELFWENDAHL.

Switzerland: 7 Anifowoshe St, Victoria Island, POB 536, Lagos; tel. (1) 613918; telex 21597; Ambassador: ANTON GREBER.

Syria: 25 Kofo Abayomi St, Victoria Island, Lagos; tel. (1) 615860; Chargé d'affaires: MUSTAFA HAJ-ALI.

Tanzania: 45 Ademola St, Ikoyi, POB 6417, Lagos; tel. (1) 613594; High Commissioner: Maj.-Gen. MIRISHO SAM HAGAI SARAKIKYA.

Thailand: 1 Ruxton Rd, Old Ikoyi, POB 3095, Lagos; tel. (1) 681337; Ambassador: N. SATHAPORN.

Togo: 96 Awolowo Rd, SW Ikoyi, POB 1435, Lagos; tel. (1) 617449; telex 21506; Ambassador: FOLI-AGBENOZAN TETTEKPOE.

Trinidad and Tobago: 6 Karimu Kotun St, Victoria Island, POB 6392, Lagos; tel. (1) 614527; telex 21041; fax (1) 612732; High Commissioner: (vacant).

Turkey: 3 Okunola Martins Close, Ikoyi, POB 1758, Lagos; tel. (1) 683030; Ambassador: ORHAN KULIN.

United Kingdom: 11 Eleke Crescent, Victoria Island, PMB 12136, Lagos; tel. (1) 619531; telex 21247; fax (1) 614021; High Commissioner: J. THOROLD MASEFIELD.

USA: 2 Eleke Crescent, Victoria Island, Lagos; tel. (1) 610097; telex 23616; fax (1) 610257; Ambassador: WALTER CARRINGTON.

Venezuela: 35B Adetokunbo Ademola St, Victoria Island, POB 3727, Lagos; tel. (1) 2611590; telex 28590; Ambassador: ALFREDO ENRIQUE VARGAS.

Yugoslavia: 7 Maitama Sule St, SW Ikoyi, PMB 978, Lagos; tel. (1) 680238; Ambassador: Dr ILIJA JANKOVIĆ.

Zaire: 23A Kofo Abayomi Rd, Victoria Island, POB 1216, Lagos; tel. (1) 611799; telex 21365; Ambassador: (vacant).

Zambia: 11 Keffi St, SW Ikoyi, PMB 6119, Lagos; High Commissioner: JOHN B. SHIKUBONI.

Zimbabwe: 6 Kasumu Ekemode St, POB 50247, Victoria Island, Lagos; tel. (1) 619328; telex 22650; High Commissioner: ISAAC L. NYATHI.

Judicial System

Supreme Court: Tafawa Balewa Sq., Lagos; consists of a Chief Justice and up to 15 Justices, appointed by the Armed Forces Ruling Council. It has original jurisdiction in any dispute between the Federation and a State, or between States, and hears appeals from the Federal Court of Appeal.

Chief Justice: MOHAMMED BELLO.

Federal Court of Appeal: consists of a President and at least 15 Justices, of whom three must be experts in Islamic law and three experts in Customary law.

Federal High Court: consists of a Chief Judge and a number of other judges.

Each State has a **High Court,** consisting of a chief judge and a number of judges, appointed by the federal government. If required, a state may have a **Shari'a Court of Appeal** (dealing with Islamic civil law) and a **Customary Court of Appeal.** In 1986 a **Special Military Tribunal** was established to try former office holders accused of corruption, and a **Special Appeals Tribunal** was established for appeals against rulings of the Special Military Tribunal.

Religion

ISLAM

According to the 1963 census, there were more than 26m. Muslims (47.2% of the total population) in Nigeria.

Spiritual Head: Alhaji IBRAHIM DASUKI, the Sultan of Sokoto.

CHRISTIANITY

The 1963 census enumerated more than 19m. Christians (34.5% of the total population).

Christian Council of Nigeria: 139 Ogunlana Drive, Surulere, POB 2838, Lagos; tel. (1) 836019; f. 1929; 12 full mems and six assoc. mems; Pres. Rev. LUTHER D. CISHAK; Gen. Sec. C. O. WILLIAMS.

The Anglican Communion

Anglicans are adherents of the Church of the Province of Nigeria, comprising 48 dioceses. Nigeria, formerly part of the Province of West Africa, became a separate Province in 1979. The Church had an estimated 10m. members in 1990.

Archbishop of Nigeria and Bishop of Lagos: Most Rev. JOSEPH ADETILOYE, Bishopscourt, 29 Marina, POB 13, Lagos; tel. (1) 2635681; fax (1) 2631264.

Provincial Secretary: Very Rev. Prof. J. A. OMOYAJOWO, 29 Marina, POB 78, Lagos; tel. (1) 2635681; fax (1) 2631264.

The Roman Catholic Church

Nigeria comprises three archdioceses, 33 dioceses and two Catholic Missions, at Bomadi and at Kano. At 31 December 1992 there were an estimated 10.0m. adherents in the country (9.9% of the total population).

Catholic Bishops' Conference of Nigeria: 6 Force Rd, POB 951, Lagos; tel. (1) 2635849; telex 22592; (1) fax 2636680; f. 1976; Pres. Most Rev. ANTHONY O. OKOGIE, Archbishop of Lagos.

Catholic Secretariat of Nigeria: 6 Force Rd, POB 951, Lagos; tel. (1) 2635849; telex 22592; fax (1) 2636680; Sec.-Gen. Mgr R. C. ANASIUDU.

Archbishop of Kaduna: Most Rev. PETER Y. JATAU, Archbishop's House, Tafawa Balewa Way, POB 248, Kaduna; tel. (62) 216828.

Archbishop of Lagos: Most Rev. ANTHONY O. OKOGIE, Archdiocesan Secretariat, 19 Catholic Mission St, POB 8, Lagos; tel. and fax (1) 2633841.

Archbishop of Onitsha: Most Rev. STEPHEN N. EZEANYA, Archdiocesan Secretariat, POB 411, Onitsha, Anambra; tel. (46) 210444.

Other Christian Churches

Brethren Church of Nigeria: c/o Kulp Bible School, POB 1, Mubi, Gongola; f. 1923; 80,000 mems; Gen. Sec. JOHN BOAZ Y. MAINA.

Church of the Lord (Aladura): Anthony Village, Ikorodu Rd, POB 308, Ikeja, Lagos; tel. (1) 964749; f. 1930; 1.1m. mems; Primate Dr E. O. A. ADEJOBI.

Lutheran Church of Christ in Nigeria: POB 21, Numan, Gongola; 61,923 mems; Pres. AKILA TODI.

Lutheran Church of Nigeria: Obot Idim Ibesikpo, Uyo, Akwa Ibom; tel. (1) 200505; telex 64235; f. 1936; 368,000 mems; Pres. Rev. Dr NELSON UNWENE.

Methodist Church Nigeria: Wesley House, 21–22 Marina, POB 2011, Lagos; tel. (1) 2631853; 483,500 mems; Patriarch Rev. SUNDAY COFFIE MBANG.

Nigerian Baptist Convention: Baptist Bldg, PMB 5113, Ibadan; tel. (22) 412146; 500,000 mems; Pres. Rev. DAVID H. KARO; Gen. Sec. Dr SAMUEL T. OLA AKANDE.

Presbyterian Church of Nigeria: 26–29 Ehere Rd, Ogbor Hill, POB 2635, Aba, Imo; tel. (82) 222551; f. 1846; 100,000 mems; Moderator Rt Rev. Dr M. O. OGAREKPE; Synod Clerk Rev. E. U. ONWUCHEKWA.

The Salvation Army and the Qua Iboe Church are also active.

AFRICAN RELIGIONS

The beliefs, rites and practices of the people of Nigeria are very diverse, varying between ethnic groups and between families in the same group. In 1963 about 10m. persons (18% of the total population) were followers of traditional beliefs.

The Press

DAILIES

Abuja Times: Daily Times of Nigeria Ltd, New Isheri Rd, Agidingbi, PMB 21340, Ikeja, Lagos; tel. (1) 900850; telex 21333; f. 1992.

Amana: Concord House, 42 Concord Way, POB 4483, Ikeja, Lagos; Hausa.

Daily Champion: Isolo Industrial Estate, Oshodi-Apapa,Lagos; Editor EMEKA OMEIHE.

Daily Express: Commercial Amalgamated Printers, 30 Glover St, Lagos; f. 1938; Editor Alhaji AHMED ALAO (acting); circ. 20,000.

Daily Sketch: Sketch Publishing Ltd, Oba Adebimpe Rd, PMB 5067, Ibadan; tel. (22) 414851; telex 31591; f. 1964; govt-owned; Chair. RONKE OKUSANYA; Editor ADEMOLA IDOWU; circ. 64,000.

Daily Star: 9 Works Rd, PMB 1139, Enugu; tel. (42) 253561; Editor JOSEF BEL-MOLOKWU.

Daily Times: Daily Times of Nigeria Ltd, New Isheri Rd, Agidingbi, PMB 21340, Ikeja, Lagos; tel. (1) 900850; telex 21333; f. 1925; 60% govt-owned; Editor DAPO ADERINOLA; circ. 400,000.

The Democrat: 9 Ahmed Talib Ave, POB 4457, Kaduna South, tel. (62) 231907; f. 1983; Editor ABDULHAMID BABATUNDE.

Evening Times: Daily Times of Nigeria Ltd, New Isheri Rd, Agidingbi, PMB 21340, Ikeja, Lagos; tel. (1) 900850; telex 21333; Editor CLEMENT ILOBA; circ. 20,000.

The Guardian: Rutam House, Isolo Expressway, Isolo, PMB 1217, Oshodi, Lagos; tel. (1) 524111; telex 23283; f. 1983; banned in Aug. 1994; Man. Dir Dr STANLEY MACEBUH; Editor ELUEM E. IZEZE; circ. 80,000.

Isokan: Concord House, 42 Concord Way, POB 4483, Ikeja, Lagos; Yoruba.

National Concord: Concord House, 42 Concord Way, POB 4483, Ikeja, Lagos; telex 26681; f. 1980; Editor NSIKAK ESSIEN; circ. 200,000.

New Democrat: 9 Ahmed Talib Ave, POB 4457, Kaduna South; tel. (62) 211987; f. 1983; Editor KANMI ADEMILUYI; circ. 70,000.

New Nigerian: Ahmadu Bello Way, POB 254, Kaduna; tel. (62) 201420; telex 71120; f. 1965; govt-owned; Chair. Prof. TEKENA TAMUNO; Editor (vacant); circ. 80,000.

Nigerian Chronicle: Cross River State Newspaper Corpn, Barracks Rd, POB 1074, Calabar; tel. (87) 222111; telex 65104; f. 1970; Editor PATRICK OKON; circ. 80,000.

Nigerian Herald: Kwara State Printing and Publishing Corpn, Offa Rd, PMB 1369, Ilorin; tel. (31) 220506; telex 33108; f. 1973; sponsored by Kwara State Govt; Editor DOYIN MAHMOUD; circ. 20,000.

Nigerian Observer: The Bendel Newspaper Corpn, 18 Airport Rd, POB 1143, Benin City; tel. (52) 240050; telex 41104; f. 1968; banned in July 1993; Editor TONY IKEAKANAM; circ. 150,000.

Nigerian Standard: 5 Joseph Gomwalk Rd, POB 2112, Jos; telex 33131; f. 1972; govt-owned; Editor SALE ILIYA; circ. 100,000.

Nigerian Statesman: Imo Newspapers Ltd, Owerri-Egbu Rd, POB 1095, Owerri; tel. (83) 230099; telex 53207; f. 1978; sponsored by Imo State Govt; Editor EDUBE WADIBIA.

Nigerian Tide: Rivers State Newspaper Corpn, 4 Ikwerre Rd, POB 5072, Port Harcourt; telex 61144; f. 1971; Editor AUGUSTINE NJOAGWUANI; circ. 30,000.

Nigerian Tribune: African Newspapers of Nigeria Ltd, Imalefalafi St, Oke-Ado, POB 78, Ibadan; tel. (22) 410886; f. 1980; Editor FOLU OLAMITI; circ. 109,000.

The Punch: Skyway Press, Kudeti St, PMB 21204, Onipetsi, Ikeja; tel. (1) 963580; f. 1976; banned in July 1993; Editor BOLA BOLAWOLE; circ. 150,000.

Vanguard: Kirikiri Canal, PMB 1007, Apapa; f. 1984; Editor FRANK AIGBOGUN.

SUNDAY NEWSPAPERS

Sunday Chronicle: Cross River State Newspaper Corpn, PMB 1074, Calabar; f. 1977; Editor-in-Chief ETIM ANIM; circ. 163,000.

Sunday Concord: Concord House, 42 Concord Way, POB 4483, Ikeja, Lagos; telex 26681; f. 1980; Editor DELE ALAKE.

Sunday Herald: Kwara State Printing and Publishing Corpn, PMB 1369, Ilorin; tel. (31) 220976; telex 33108; f. 1981; Editor MOLA OLANIYAN.

Sunday New Nigerian: Ahmadu Bello Way, POB 254, Kaduna; tel. (62) 201420; telex 71120; Editor (vacant).

Sunday Observer: PMB 1334, Bendel Newspapers Corpn, 18 Airport Rd, Benin City; f. 1968; Editor T. O. BORHA; circ. 60,000.

Sunday Punch: Kudeti St, PMB 21204, Ikeja; tel. (1) 964691; telex 91470; fax (1) 960715; f. 1973; Man. Editor GODWIN NZEAKAH; Editor DAYO WRIGHT; circ. 150,000.

Sunday Sketch: Sketch Publishing Co Ltd, PMB 5067, Ibadan; tel. (22) 414851; f. 1964; govt-owned; Editor OBAFEMI OREDEIN; circ. 125,000.

Sunday Standard: Plateau Publishing Co Ltd, 5 Joseph Gornwalic Rd, PMB 2112, Jos; f. 1972; govt-owned; Editor SALE ILIYA.

Sunday Statesman: Imo Newspapers Ltd, Owerri-Egbu Rd, PMB 1095, Owerri; tel. (83) 230099; telex 53207; f. 1978; sponsored by Imo State Govt; Editor EDUBE WADIBIA.

Sunday Sun: PMB 1025, Okoro House, Factory Lane, off Upper Mission Rd, New Benin.

Sunday Tide: 4 Ikwerre Rd, POB 5072, Port Harcourt; telex 61144; f. 1971; Editor AUGUSTINE NJOAGWUANI.

Sunday Times: Daily Times of Nigeria Ltd, New Isheri Rd, Agidingbi, PMB 21340, Ikeja, Lagos; tel. (1) 900850; telex 21333; f. 1953; 60% govt-owned; Editor DUPE AJAYI; circ. 100,000.

Sunday Tribune: POB 78, Oke-Ado, Ibadan; tel. (22) 310886; Editor WALE OJO.

Sunday Vanguard: PMB 1007, Apapa; Editor DUPE AJAYI.

WEEKLIES

Albishir: Triumph Publishing Co Ltd, Gidan Sa'adu Zungur, PMB 3155, Kano; tel. (64) 260273; telex 77357; f. 1981; Hausa; Editor ADAMU A. KIYAWA; circ. 15,000.

Business Times: Daily Times of Nigeria Ltd, New Isheri Rd, Agidingbi, PMB 21340, Ikeja, Lagos; tel. (1) 900850; telex 21333; f. 1925; 60% govt-owned; Editor GODFREY BAMAWO; circ. 22,000.

Eleti-Ofe: 28 Kosoko St, Lagos; f. 1923; English and Yoruba; Editor OLA ONATADE; circ. 30,000.

Gboungboun: Sketch Publishing Co Ltd, New Court Rd, PMB 5067, Ibadan; tel. (22) 414851; govt-owned; Yoruba; Editor A. O. ADEBANJO; circ. 80,000.

The Independent: Bodija Rd, PMB 5109, Ibadan; f. 1960; English; Roman Catholic; Editor Rev. F. B. CRONIN-COLTSMAN; circ. 13,000.

Irohin Imole: 15 Bamgbose St, POB 1495, Lagos; f. 1957; Yoruba; Editor TUNJI ADEOSUN.

Irohin Yoruba: 212 Broad St, PMB 2416, Lagos; tel. (1) 410886; f. 1945; Yoruba; Editor S. A. AJIBADE; circ. 85,000.

Lagos Life: Guardian Newspapers Ltd, Rutam House, Isolo Expressway, Isolo, PMB 1217, Oshodi, Lagos; f. 1985; Editor BISI OGUNBADEJO; circ. 100,000.

Lagos Weekend: Daily Times of Nigeria Ltd, New Isheri Rd, Agidingbi, PMB 21340, Ikeja, Lagos; tel. (1) 900850; telex 21333; f. 1965; 60% govt-owned; news and pictures; Editor SAM OGWA; circ. 85,000.

Mid-West This Week: Arin Associates, 50B New Lagos Rd, Benin City; Editors TONY OKODUWA, PRINCE A. R. NWOKO.

Newswatch: 3 Billingsway Rd, Oregun, Lagos; tel. (1) 960950; telex 27874; fax (1) 962887; f. 1985; English; Editor-in-Chief RAY EKPU.

Nigerian Radio/TV Times: Nigerian Broadcasting Corpn, POB 12504, Ikoyi.

Sporting Records: Daily Times of Nigeria Ltd, New Isheri Rd, Agidingbi, PMB 21340, Ikeja, Lagos; tel. (1) 900850; telex 21333; f. 1961; 60% govt-owned; Editor CYRIL KAPPO; circ. 10,000.

Times International: Daily Times of Nigeria Ltd, 3–7 Kakawa St, POB 139, Lagos; f. 1974; Editor Dr HEZY IDOWU; circ. 50,000.

Truth (The Muslim Weekly): 45 Idumagbo Ave, POB 418, Lagos; tel. (1) 668455; telex 21356; f. 1951; Editor S. O. LAWAL.

ENGLISH LANGUAGE PERIODICALS

Afriscope: 29 Salami Saibu St, PMB 1119, Yaba; monthly; African current affairs.

The Ambassador: PMB 2011, 1 peru-Remo, Ogun; tel. 620115; quarterly; Roman Catholic; circ. 20,000.

Benin Review: Ethiope Publishing Corpn, PMB 1332, Benin City; f. 1974; African art and culture; 2 a year; circ. 50,000.

Headlines: Daily Times of Nigeria Ltd, New Isheri Rd, Agindingbi, PMB 21340, Ikeja, Lagos; f. 1973; monthly; Editor ADAMS ALIU; circ. 500,000.

Home Studies: Daily Times Publications, 3–7 Kakawa St, Lagos; f. 1964; monthly; Editor GBENGA ODUSANYA; circ. 40,000.

Insight: 3 Kakawa St, POB 139, Lagos; quarterly; contemporary issues; Editor SAM AMUKA; circ. 5,000.

Journal of the Nigerian Medical Association: 3–7 Kakawa St, POB 139, Apapa; quarterly; Editor Prof. A. O. ADESOLA.

Lagos Education Review: Faculty of Education, University of Lagos Akoka, Lagos; tel. (1) 823593; f. 1978; 2 a year; African education; Editor Prof. M. S. OLAYINKA.

The Leader: PMB 1017, Owerri; tel. (83) 230932; fortnightly; Roman Catholic; Editor Rev. KEVIN C. AKAGHA.

Management in Nigeria: Plot 22, Idowu Taylor St, Victoria Island, POB 2557, Lagos; tel. (1) 615105; every 2 months; journal of Nigerian Inst. of Management; Editor DELE QSUNDAHUNSI.

Marketing in Nigeria: Alpha Publications, Surulere, POB 1163, Lagos; f. 1977; monthly; Editor B. O. K. NWELIH; circ. 30,000.

Modern Woman: 47–49 Salami Saibu St, Marina, POB 2583, Lagos; f. 1964; monthly; Man. Editor TOUN ONABANJO.

Monthly Life: West African Book Publishers, POB 3445, Lagos; tel. (1) 900760; telex 26144; f. 1984; monthly; Editor WOLE OLAOYE; circ. 40,000.

The New Nation: 52 Iwaya Rd, Onike, Yaba, Surulere, POB 896, Lagos; tel. (1) 863629; telex 26517; monthly; news magazine.

Nigeria Magazine: Federal Dept of Culture, PMB 12524, Lagos; tel. (1) 802060; f. 1927; quarterly; travel, cultural, historical and general; Editor B. D. LEMCHI; circ. 5,000.

Nigerian Businessman's Magazine: 39 Mabo St, Surulere, Lagos; monthly; Nigerian and overseas commerce.

Nigerian Journal of Economic and Social Studies: Nigerian Economic Society, c/o Dept of Economics, University of Ibadan; f. 1959; 3 a year; Editor Prof. S. TOMORI.

Nigerian Journal of Science: University of Ibadan, POB 4039, Ibadan; publ. of the Science Assn of Nigeria; f. 1966; 2 a year; Editor Prof. L. B. KOLAWOLE; circ. 1,000.

Nigerian Medical Journal: 3 Kakawa St, POB 139, Lagos; monthly.

Nigerian Radio/TV Times: Broadcasting House, POB 12504, Lagos; monthly.

Nigerian Teacher: 3 Kakawa St, POB 139, Lagos; quarterly.

Nigerian Worker: United Labour Congress, 97 Herbert Macaulay St, Lagos; Editor LAWRENCE BORHA.

The President: New Breed Organization Ltd, Plot 14 Western Ave, 1 Rafiu Shitty St, Alaka Estate, Surulere, POB 385, Lagos; tel. (1) 802690; fax (1) 831175; fortnightly; management; Chief Editor CHRIS OKOLIE.

Quality: Ultimate Publications Ltd, Oregun Rd, Lagos; f. 1987; monthly; Editor BALA DAN MUSA.

Radio-Vision Times: Western Nigerian Radio-Vision Service, Television House, POB 1460, Ibadan; monthly; Editor ALTON A. ADEDEJI.

Savanna: Ahmadu Bello University Press Ltd, PMB 1094, Zaria; tel. (69) 50054; telex 75241; f. 1972; 2 a year; Editor AUDEE T. GIWA; circ. 1,000.

Spear: Daily Times of Nigeria Ltd, New Isheri Rd, Agidingbi, PMB 21340, Ikeja, Lagos; tel. (1) 900850; f. 1962; monthly; family magazine; Editor COKER ONITA; circ. 10,000.

Technical and Commercial Message: Surulere, POB 1163, Lagos; f. 1980; 6 a year; Editor B. O. K. NWELIH; circ. 12,500.

Today's Challenge: PMB 2010, Jos; tel. (73) 52230; f. 1951; 6 a year; religious and educational; Editor JACOB SHAIBY TSADO; circ. 15,000.

Woman's World: Daily Times of Nigeria Ltd, New Isheri Rd, Agidingbi, PMB 21340, Ikeja, Lagos; monthly; Editor TOYIN JOHNSON; circ. 12,000.

VERNACULAR PERIODICALS

Abokiyar Hira: Albah International Publishers, POB 6177, Bompai, Kano; f. 1987; monthly; Hausa; cultural; Editor BASHARI F. FOUKBAH; circ. 35,000.

Gaskiya ta fi Kwabo: Ahmadu Bello Way, POB 254, Kaduna; tel. (62) 201420; telex 71120; f. 1939; 3 a week; Hausa; Editor ABDUL-HASSAN IBRAHIM.

NEWS AGENCIES

News Agency of Nigeria (NAN): c/o National Theatre, Iganmu, PMB 12756, Lagos; tel. (1) 801290; telex 22648; fax (1) 833288; f. 1978; Chair. OYEKUNLE OLUWASANMI; Gen. Man. Dr NWABU MGBEMENA.

Foreign Bureaux

Agence France-Presse (AFP): 26B Keffi St, SW Ikoyi, PMB 2448, Lagos; tel. (1) 683550; telex 21363; fax (1) 682752; Bureau Chief GÉRARD VANDENBERGHE.

Informatsionnoye Telegrafnoye Agentstvo Rossii—Telegrafnoye Agentstvo Suverennykh Stran (ITAR—TASS) (Russia): Lagos; Dir VALENTIN KRUJOV.

Inter Press Service (IPS) (Italy): c/o News Agency of Nigeria, PMB 12756, Lagos; tel. (1) 801290; Correspondent REMI OYO.

Pan-African News Agency (PANA): c/o News Agency of Nigeria, National Arts Theatre, POB 8715, Marina, Lagos; tel. (1) 801290; telex 26571; f. 1979.

Xinhua (New China) News Agency (People's Republic of China): 161A Adeola Odeku St, Victoria Island, POB 70278, Lagos; tel. (1) 612464; telex 21541; Bureau Chief ZHAI JINGSHENG.

Publishers

Africana-FEP Publishers (Nigeria) Ltd: Book House, 79 Awka Rd, PMB 1639, Onitsha; tel. (46) 210669; f. 1973; study guides, general science, textbooks; Man. Dir PATRICK C. OMABU.

Ahmadu Bello University Press: PMB 1094, Zaria; tel. (69) 50054; telex 75291; f. 1974; history, Africana, social sciences, education; Man. Dir Dr ABDURRAHMAN GHAJI.

Albah International Publishers: 100 Kurawa, Bompai-Kano, POB 6177, Kano City; f. 1978; Africana, Islamic, educational and general, in Hausa; Chair. BASHARI F. ROUKBAH.

Alliance West African Publishers: Orindingbin Estate, New Aketan Layout, PMB 1039, Oyo; tel. (85) 230798; f. 1971; educational and general; Man. Dir Chief M. O. OGUNMOLA.

Aromolaran Publishing Co Ltd: POB 1800, Ibadan; tel. (22) 715980; telex 34315; f. 1968; educational and general; Man. Dir Dr ADEKUNLE AROMOLARAN.

Daystar Press: Daystar House, POB 1261, Ibadan; tel. (22) 23230; f. 1962; religious and educational; Man. MODUPE ODUYOYE.

ECWA Productions Ltd: PMB 2010, Jos; tel. (73) 52230; telex 81120; f. 1973; religious and educational; Gen. Man. Rev. J. K. BOLARIN.

Ethiope Publishing Corpn: Ring Rd, PMB 1332, Benin City; tel. (52) 243036; telex 41110; f. 1970; general fiction and non-fiction, textbooks, reference, science, arts and history; Man. Dir SUNDAY N. OLAYE.

Evans Brothers (Nigeria Publishers) Ltd: Jericho Rd, PMB 5164, Ibadan; tel. (22) 417570; telex 31104; f. 1966; general and educational; Chair. Dr S. J. COOKEY; Man. Dir B. O. BOLODEOKU.

Fourth Dimension Publishing Co Ltd: Plot 64A, City Layout, PMB 01164, Enugu; tel. (42) 339969; telex 51319; f. 1977; periodicals, fiction, verse, educational and children's; Chair. ARTHUR NWANKWO; Man. Dir V. U. NWANKWO.

Gbabeks Publishers Ltd: POB 3538, Kaduna; tel. (62) 217976; f. 1982; educational and technical; Man. Dir TAYO OGUNBEKUN.

Heinemann Educational Books (Nigeria) Ltd: 1 Ighodaro Rd, Jericho, PMB 5205, Ibadan; tel. (22) 416505; telex 31113; f. 1962; educational, law, medical and general; Chair. AIGBOJE HIGO; Man. Dir E. AKIN THOMAS.

Heritage Books: 2–8 Calcutta Crescent, Gate 4, POB 610, Apapa, Lagos; tel. (1) 871333; f. 1971; general; Chair. NAIWU OSAHON.

Ibadan University Press: Publishing House, University of Ibadan, PMB 16, IU Post Office, Ibadan; tel. (22) 400550; telex 31128; f. 1951; scholarly, science, law, general and educational; Dir F. A. ADESANOYE.

Ilesanmi Press Ltd: Akure Rd, POB 204, Ilesha; tel. 2062; f. 1955; general and educational; Man. Dir G. E. ILESANMI.

Kolasanya Publishing Enterprise: 2 Epe Rd, Oke-Owa, PMB 2099, Ijebu-Ode; general and educational; Man. Dir Chief K. OSUNSANYA.

Literamed Publications Ltd (Lantern Books): Plot 45, Alausa Bus-stop, Oregun Industrial Estate, Ikeja, PMB 21068, Lagos; tel. (1) 962512; telex 20202; general; Man. Dir O. M. LAWAL-SOLARIN.

Longman Nigeria Ltd: 52 Oba Akran Ave, PMB 21036, Ikeja, Lagos; tel. (1) 901150; telex 26639; f. 1961; general and educational; Dir A. O. ECHEBIRI.

Macmillan Nigeria Publishers Ltd: Ilupeju Industrial Estate, 4 Industrial Ave, POB 264, Yaba, Lagos; tel. (1) 962185; telex 20202; fax (1) 962185; f. 1965; educational and general; Exec. Chair. J. O. EMMANUEL; Man. Dir A. I. ADELEKAN.

Nelson Publishers Ltd: 8 Ilupeju By-Pass, Ikeja, PMB 21303, Lagos; tel. (1) 961452; general and educational; Chair. Prof. C. O. TAIWO; Man. Dir. R. O. OGUNBO.

Northern Nigerian Publishing Co Ltd: Gaskiya Bldg, POB 412, Zaria; tel. (69) 32087; telex 75243; f. 1966; general, educational and vernacular texts; Man. Dir H. HAYAT.

NPS Educational Publishers Ltd: Trusthouse, Ring Rd, off Akinyemi Way, POB 62, Ibadan; tel. (22) 316006; telex 31478; f. 1969; academic, scholarly and educational; Chief Exec. T. D. OTESANYA.

Nwamife Publishers: 10 Ibiam St, Uwani, POB 430, Enugu; tel. (42) 338254; f. 1971; general and educational; Chair. FELIX C. ADI.

Obafemi Awolowo University Press Ltd: Obafemi Awolowo University, Ile-Ife; tel. 230284; f. 1968; educational, scholarly and periodicals; Man. Dir AKIN FATOKUN.

Obobo Books: 2–8 Calcutta Crescent, Gate 4, POB 610, Apapa, Lagos; tel. (1) 871333; f. 1981; children's books; Editorial Dir BAKIN KUNAMA.

Ogunsanya Press Publishers and Bookstores Ltd: SW9/1133 Orita Challenge, Idiroko, POB 95, Ibadan; tel. (22) 310924; f. 1970; educational; Man. Dir Chief LUCAS JUSTUS POPO-OLA OGUNSANYA.

Onibonoje Press and Book Industries (Nigeria) Ltd: Felele Layout, Challenge, POB 3109, Ibadan; tel. (22) 313956; telex 31657; f. 1958; educational and general; Chair. G. ONIBONOJE; Man. Dir J. O. ONIBONOJE.

Pilgrim Books Ltd: New Oluyole Industrial Estate, Ibadan/Lagos Expressway, PMB 5617, Ibadan; tel. (22) 317218; telex 20311; educational and general; Man. Dir JOHN E. LEIGH.

Spectrum Books Ltd: Sunshine House, 1 Emmanuel Alayande St, Oluyole Estate, PMB 5612, Ibadan; tel. (22) 310058; telex 31588; f. 1978; educational and fiction; Man. Dir JOOP BERKHOUT.

University of Lagos Press: University of Lagos, PO Akoka, Yaba, Lagos; tel. (1) 820311; telex 21210; university textbooks, monographs, lectures and journals; Man. Dir S. B. BANKOLE.

University Press Ltd: Three Crowns Bldg, Eleyele Rd, Jericho, PMB 5095, Ibadan; tel. (22) 411356; telex 31121; fax (22) 412056; f. 1978; associated with Oxford University Press; educational; Man. Dir WAHEED O. OLAJIDE.

University Publishing Co: 11 Central School Rd, POB 386, Onitsha; tel. (46) 210013; f. 1959; primary, secondary and university textbooks; Chair. E. O. UGWUEGBULEM.

Vista Books Ltd: 59 Awolowo Rd, POB 282, Yaba, Lagos; tel. (1) 681656; fax (1) 685679; f. 1991; general fiction and non-fiction, arts, children's and educational; Man. Dir Dr T. C. NWOSU.

West African Book Publishers Ltd: Ilupeju Industrial Estate, POB 3445, Lagos; tel. (1) 900760; telex 26144; f. 1967; textbooks, children's, periodicals and general; Dir Mrs A. O. OBADAGBONYI.

John West Publications Ltd: Plot 2, Block A, Acme Rd, Ogba Industrial Estate, PMB 21001, Ikeja, Lagos; tel. (1) 921010; telex 26446; f. 1964 general; Man. Dir Alhaji L. K. JAKAMDE.

Government Publishing House

Government Press: PMB 2020, Kaduna; tel. 213812.

PUBLISHERS' ASSOCIATION

Nigerian Publishers Association: The Ori-Detu, 1st Floor, Shell Close, Onireke, GPO Box 2541, Ibadan; tel. (22) 411557; telex 31113; f. 1965; Pres. V. NWANKWO.

Radio and Television

According to UNESCO estimates, there were 19.4m. radio receivers and 3.7m. television receivers in use in 1991.

RADIO

Federal Radio Corporation of Nigeria (FRCN): Broadcasting House, Ikoyi, PMB 12504, Lagos; tel. (1) 2690301; telex 21484; fax (1) 2690073; f. 1978; controlled by the Fed. Govt and divided into five zones: Lagos (English); Enugu (English, Igbo, Izon, Efik and Tiv); Ibadan (English, Yoruba, Edo, Urhobo and Igala); Kaduna (English, Hausa, Kanuri, Fulfulde and Nupe); Abuja (English, Hausa, Igbo and Yoruba); Dir-Gen. Alhaji ABDURRAHMAN MICIKA.

Voice of Nigeria (VON): Broadcasting House, Ikoyi, PMB 40003, Lagos; tel. (1) 2693075; fax (1) 2691944; f. 1990; controlled by the Fed. Govt; external services in English, French, Arabic, Ki-Swahili, Hausa and Fulfulde; Dir-Gen. Mallam YAYA ABUBAKAR.

TELEVISION

Nigerian Television Authority (NTA): Television House, Ahmadu Bello Way, Victoria Island, PMB 12036, Lagos; tel. (1) 615949; telex 21245; f. 1976; controlled by the Fed. Govt; responsible for all aspects of television broadcasting; Chair. IFEANYINWA NZEAKOR; Dir-Gen. Alhaji MOHAMMED IBRAHIM.

NTA Aba/Owerri: PMB 7126, Aba; tel. (82) 220922; Gen. Man. MARTIN A. AKPETI.

NTA Abeokuta: PMB 2190, Abeokuta; Gen. Man. H. O. ROBIN.

NTA Abuja: Abuja.

NTA Akure: PMB 794, Akure; tel. (34) 230351; Gen. Man. JIBOLA DEDENUOLA.

NTA Bauchi: PMB 0146, Bauchi; tel. (77) 42748; telex 83270; f. 1976; Man. MUHAMMAD AL-AMIN.

NTA Benin City: West Circular Rd, PMB 1117, Benin City; telex 44308; Gen. Man. G. C. MEFO.

NTA Calabar: 105 Marion Rd, Calabar; telex 65110; Man. E. ETUK.

NTA Enugu: Independence Layout, PMB 01530, Enugu, Anambra; tel. (42) 335120; telex 51147; f. 1960; Gen. Man. G. C. MEFO.

NTA Ibadan: POB 1460, Ibadan; tel. (22) 713320; telex 31156; Gen. Man. JIBOLA DEDENUOLA.

NTA Ikeja: Tejuosho Ave, Surulere.

NTA Ilorin: PMB 1453, Ilorin; telex 33118; Gen. Man. D. ALLI.

NTA Jos: PMB 2134, Jos; telex 81149; Gen. Man. M. J. BEWELL.

NTA Kaduna: POB 1347, Kaduna; tel. (62) 216375; telex 71164; f. 1977; Gen. Man. SAIDU ABUBAKAR.

NTA Kano: PMB 3343, Kano; tel. (64) 2601210; telex 77225; Gen. Man. M. G. ABUBAKAR.

NTA Lagos: Victoria Island, PMB 12005, Lagos; telex 21245; Gen. Man. O. OKUNRINBOYE.

NTA Maiduguri: PMB 1487, Maiduguri; telex 82132; Gen. Man. M. M. MAILAFIYA.

NTA Makurdi: PMB 2044, Makurdi.

NTA Minna: TV House, PMB 79, Minna; tel. (66) 222941; Gen. Man. M. C. DAYLOP.

NTA Port Harcourt: PMB 5797, Port Harcourt; Gen. Man. E. T. HALLIDAY.

NTA Sokoto: PMB 2351, Sokoto; tel. (60) 232670; telex 73116; f. 1975; Gen. Man. M. B. TUNAU.

NTA Yola: PMB 2197, Yola; Gen. Man. M. M. SAIDU.

In July 1993 14 companies were granted licences to operate private television stations.

Finance

(cap. = capital; p.u. = paid up; res = reserves; dep. = deposits; m. = million; brs = branches; amounts in naira unless otherwise stated)

BANKING

In late 1991 there were 120 banks operating in Nigeria. It was announced in July 1990 that all commercial and merchant banks in which the Government held a controlling interest were to be transferred to private ownership. Foreign banks operating in Nigeria are required to have a 60% Nigerian holding. In December 1990 the Government announced that more than 500 community banks were to be established.

Central Bank

Central Bank of Nigeria: Tinubu Sq., PMB 12194, Lagos; tel. (1) 2660100; telex 21350; f. 1958; bank of issue; cap. and res 646m., dep. 42,637.3m. (1990); Gov. PAUL AGBAI OGWUMA; 18 brs.

Commercial Banks

Afribank Nigeria Ltd: 94 Broad St, PMB 12021, Lagos; tel. (1) 2663608; telex 21345; fax (1) 2662793; f. 1969 as International Bank for West Africa Ltd; cap. 329.5m., dep. 4,283.6m. (1992); CEO IBRAHIM YARIMA ABDULLAHI; 116 brs.

African Continental Bank Ltd: Continental House, 106–108 Broad St, PMB 2466, Lagos; tel. (1) 2660579; telex 21282; fax (1) 2660204; f. 1947; cap. and res 24.5m., dep. 1,845.1m. (1989); Chair. Chief J. O. IRUKWU; Man. Dir REGINALD ABBEY; 919 brs.

African International Bank Ltd: 42–44 Warehouse Rd, PMB 1040, Apapa, Lagos; tel. (1) 803820; telex 22377; fax (1) 877174; f. 1979; cap. and res 190.5m., dep. 1,397.4m. (1990); acquired assets of Bank of Credit and Commerce International (Nigeria) Ltd; Chair. Alhaji MAMMAN DAURA; Man. Dir Alhaji ABDULLAHI MAHMOUD; 47 brs.

Allied Bank of Nigeria Ltd: Allied House, 155/161 Broad St, PMB 12785, Lagos; tel. (1) 2669623; telex 21512; fax (1) 2669602; f. 1962 as Bank of India; cap. and res 80.2m., dep. 2,871.6m. (1992); Chair. B. EHIZUENLEN; Man. Dir Alhaji SHEHU MOHAMMED; 68 brs.

Bank of the North Ltd: 2 Zaria Rd, POB 211, Kano; tel. (64) 2600250; telex 77233; f. 1959; cap. and res 159.3m., dep. 2,748.8m. (1992); Chair. Alhaji ABUBAKAR ZAKI TAMBUWAL; Man. Dir Alhaji YAKUBU SHEHU; 97 brs.

Chartered Bank Ltd: Plot 1619, Danmole St, POB 73069, Victoria Island, Lagos; tel. (1) 619043; telex 21155; fax (1) 614524; cap. and res 107.1m., dep. 1,047.1m. (1992)); Chair. Lt-Gen. (retd) M. I. WUSHISHI; Man. Dir O. OLAGUNDOYE.

Commercial Bank (Crédit Lyonnais Nigeria) Ltd: Elephant House, 214 Broad St, PMB 12829, Lagos; tel. (1) 2665594; telex 23157; fax (1) 2665308; f. 1983; cap. p.u. 60m., dep. 1,700m. (1993); Chair. ALLISON A. AYIDA; Man. Dir R. CESSAC; 21 brs.

Co-operative and Commerce Bank (Nigeria) Ltd: 28 Okpara Ave, PMB 01321, Enugu; tel. (42) 333613; telex 51380; fax (42) 335359; cap. and res 17.5m., dep. 682.6m. (1988); Chair. Chief E. C. OKWUOSA; Man. Dir EDDY OBI OKOYE; 60 brs.

Ecobank Nigeria Ltd: 2 Ajose Adeogun St, Victoria Island, POB 72688, Lagos; tel. (1) 2612953; telex 21157; fax (1) 216568; cap. p.u. 89m. (Sept. 1993); Chair. OTUNBA A. OJORA; Man. Dir DAVID C. JOHNSON.

Eko International Bank of Nigeria: cnr Nnamdi Azikiwe and Alli Balogun Sts, PMB 12864, Lagos; tel. (1) 2600350; telex 28603; fax (1) 2665176; cap. and res 48.0m., dep. 580.0m. (1991); Chair. J. O. EMANUEL; Man. Dir O. A. FASINA; 8 brs.

First Bank of Nigeria Ltd: 35 Marina, POB 5216, Lagos; tel. (1) 2665900; telex 21231; fax (1) 2669703; f. 1894 as Bank of British West Africa; cap. p.u. 107.6m. (Dec. 1993), dep. 8,181.2m. (1990); Chair. MAHMOUD IBRAHIM ATTA; Man. Dir J. O. SANUSI; 277 brs.

FSB International Bank Ltd: 23 Awolowo Rd, SW Ikoyi, PMB 12512, Lagos; tel. (1) 2690576; telex 23671; fax (1) 2690397; f. 1991 to succeed Federal Savings Bank; Chair. Alhaji A. O. G. OTITI; Man. Dir MOHAMMED HAYATU-DEEN.

Habib Nigeria Bank Ltd: NIDB House, 18 Waff Rd, PMB 2180, Kaduna; tel. (62) 235140; telex 71703; fax (62) 212301; cap. p.u. 52.5m. (Dec. 1992), dep. 364.6m. (1989); Chair. Maj.-Gen. (retd) SHEHU MUSA YAR'ADUA; Man. Dir Mallam ADAMU BELLO; 65 brs.

Investment Banking and Trust Co Ltd (IBTC): Wesley House, 21–22 Marina, PMB 12557, Lagos; tel. (1) 2600200; telex 28747; fax (1) 2634146; cap. and res 121.3m., dep. 166.9m. (1992); Chair. DAVID DANKARO; Man. Dir ATEDO A. PETERSIDE.

Lobi Bank of Nigeria Ltd: 36 Barracks Rd, PMB 102371, Makurdi, Benue; tel. (44) 33809; telex 85307; fax (44) 612358; cap. p.u. 20m. (1991), dep. 241.7m. (March 1989); Chair. Maj. Gen. (retd) G. O. EJIGA; Man. Dir DAVID AMOH.

National Bank of Nigeria Ltd: 41–45 Broad St, PMB 12123, Lagos; tel. (1) 2661342; telex 21348; fax (1) 2660006; f. 1933; nationalized 1961; cap. 20.2m., dep. 738.7m. (Oct. 1991); Chair. Chief E. F. OKE; Man. Dir P. O. AJUMOBI; 112 brs.

New Nigeria Bank Ltd: 69 Mission Rd, PMB 1193, Benin City; tel. (52) 200200; telex 41103; fax (52) 245482; f. 1970; cap. p.u. 31.3m. (1990), dep. 882m. (1989); 58 brs.

Nigeria International Bank Ltd (NIB): Commerce House, 1 Idowu Taylor St, Victoria Island, POB 6391, Lagos; tel. (1) 2690166; telex 23424; fax (1) 618916; f. 1984; cap. and res 280.6m., dep. 2,741m. (1992); Chair. Chief CHARLES S. SANKEY; Man. Dir N. RIAZ; 12 brs.

Nigeria Universal Bank Ltd: Hospital Rd, POB 1066, Kaduna; tel. (62) 233928; telex 71156; fax (62) 235024; f. 1974; owned by Katsina and Kaduna State Govts; cap. 20m. (1991), dep. 260.9m. (1990); Chair. Alhaji MUHAMMADU HAYATUDDEN; Man. Dir Alhaji USMAN ABUBAKAR; 25 brs.

Northern Nigeria Investments Ltd: NNIL Bldg, 4 Waff Rd, POB 138, Kaduna; tel. (62) 200580; telex 71110; fax (1) 230770; cap.

p.u. 16.5m. (March 1993); Chair. J. S. ODAMA; Man. Dir G. H. IBRAHIM (acting).

Owena Bank (Nigeria) Ltd: Engineering Close, PMB 80134, Victoria Island, Lagos; tel. (1) 610856; telex 28692; 30% owned by Ondo State Govt; cap. p.u. 60m. (Dec. 1992); Chair. PETER AJAYI; Man. Dir SEGUN AGBETUYI.

Pan African Bank Ltd: 3 Azikiwe Rd, PMB 5239, Port Harcourt; tel. (84) 300300; telex 61157; fax (84) 330616; f. 1971; cap. and res 140.3m., dep. 514.7m. (1991); Chair. W. T. DAMBO; Man. Dir D. P. IYABI; 10 brs.

People's Bank of Nigeria: 33 Balogun St, PMB 12914, Lagos; tel. (1) 2664241; fax (1) 667571; state-owned; cap. p.u. 230m. (Dec. 1991); Chair. Chief E. A. O. OYEYIPO; Man. Dir MARIA O. SOKENU.

Progress Bank of Nigeria Ltd: Plot 91, Ikenegbu Layout, POB 1577, Owerri; tel. (83) 234729; telex 53203; f. 1982; controlled by Imo State govt; cap. and res 48.8m., dep. 873.5m. (1990); Chair. Chief R. E. ODINKEMELU; Man. Dir HERBERT O. ORJI.

Savannah Bank of Nigeria Ltd: 62–66 Broad St, POB 2317, Lagos; tel. (1) 2600470; telex 21876; f. 1976; cap. p.u. 34.9m. (March 1991), dep. 1,351.5m. (March 1987); Chair. SIJI SOETAN; Man. Dir Alhaji M. I. YAHAYA; 37 brs.

Société Générale Bank (Nigeria) Ltd: Sarah House, 13 Martins St, PMB 12741, Lagos; tel. (1) 2661881; telex 23147; fax (1) 2663731; f. 1977; cap. and res 49.0m., dep. 1,501.4m. (1990); Chair. Dr EBENEZER A. IKOMI; Man. Dir J. A. HALL; 35 brs.

Tropical Commerical Bank Ltd: 72B Murtala Mohammed Way, POB 4636, Kano; tel. (64) 640050; telex 77299; fax (64) 644506; 40% state-owned; cap. p.u. 107.6m. (Dec. 1992); Man. Dir Alhaji O. K. DANJUMA.

Union Bank of Nigeria Ltd: 40 Marina, PMB 2027, Lagos; tel. (1) 2665439; telex 21222; fax (1) 2663822; f. 1969 as Barclays Bank of Nigeria Ltd; cap. and res 1,217.6m., dep. 22,652.0m. (Sept. 1992); Chair. GREEN ONYEKABA NWANKWO; Man. Dir Alhaji S. S. BAFFA; 241 brs.

United Bank for Africa (Nigeria) Ltd: 97–105 Broad St, POB 2406, Lagos; tel. (1) 2667410; telex 21241; fax (1) 2660884; f. 1961; cap. p.u. 100m. (March 1992), dep. 12,200m. (1991); Chair. Alhaji ADAMU W. FIKA; Man. Dir L. E. OKAFOR; 190 brs.

Universal Trust Bank of Nigeria Ltd: 4/6 Ajose Adeogun St, Victoria Island, POB 52160, Lagos; tel. (1) 611192; telex 23445; fax (1) 610314; f. 1981; cap. p.u. 40m. (1991); Chair. Lt-Gen. T. Y. DANJUMA; Man. Dir K. J. PHILIPPI; 13 brs.

Wema Bank Ltd: 27 Nnambi Aziking St, Tinubu, Lagos; tel. (1) 861634; telex 26554; fax (1) 2669508; f. 1945; cap. and res 142.7m., dep. 1,233.7m. (March 1992); Chair. Dr S. O. OMOBOMI; Man. Dir Chief S. I. ADEGBITE; 66 brs.

Merchant Banks

Abacus Merchant Bank Ltd: Williams House, 8th Floor, 95 Broad St, POB 7908, Lagos; tel. (1) 2660212; telex 21243; cap. and res 24.6m., dep. 312.0m.; Chair. and Man. Dir OLAWOLE JULIUS ADEWUMI.

African Banking Consortium (ABC) Merchant Bank (Nigeria) Ltd: 13 Olosa St, Victoria Island, POB 70647, Lagos; tel. (1) 616069; telex 23152; fax (1) 611117; f. 1982; cap. p.u. 40m. (March 1993), dep. 246.4m. (1992); Chair. Chief E. C. IWUANYANWU; CEO B. A. AKUAZOKU; 3 brs.

Alpha Merchant Bank Ltd: 188 Awolowo Rd, Ikoyi, PMB 12882, Lagos; tel. (1) 2694000; telex 22623; fax (1) 2690444; cap. and res 180.6m., dep. 595.5m. (1992); Chair. Dr A. K. ABASHIYA; CEO JIMI A. LAWAL.

Century Merchant Bank Ltd: 11 Burma Rd, PMB 1307, Apapa, Lgos; tel. (1) 803160; telex 22039; fax (1) 871603; cap. and res 33.9m., dep. 608.7m. (1991); Chair. Alhaji BASHIR OTHMAN TOFA; Man. Dir Dr IME EKOP EBONG.

Continental Merchant Bank Nigeria Ltd: 1 Kingsway Rd, Ikoyi, POB 12035, Lagos; tel. (1) 2690501; telex 21585; fax (1) 2690900; f. 1986; cap. p.u. 43.6m. (Dec. 1992); Chair. Alhaji MOHAMMED SHEKARAU OMAR; Man. Dir Dr CHIICHII ASHWE; 3 brs.

Devcom Merchant Bank Ltd: 18A Oko Awo Close, Victoria Island, Lagos; tel. (1) 610206; telex 22084; fax (1) 612615; f. 1989; cap. 18m. (March 1992); Chair. MIKE ADENUGA; Man. Dir J. O. EKUNDAYO.

First City Merchant Bank Ltd: Primrose Tower, 17A Tinubu St, POB 9117, Lagos; tel. (1) 2665944; telex 22912; fax (1) 2665126; f. 1983; cap. and res 108.2m., dep. 396.7m. (1990); Chair. and CEO OTUNBA M. O. BALOGUN; Dr JONATHAN A. D. LONG.

First Interstate Merchant Bank (Nigeria) Ltd: Unity House, 37 Marina, Victoria Island, POB 72295, Lagos; tel. (1) 2600500; telex 23881; fax (1) 2668273; cap. p.u. 40.0m. (March 1992); Chair. and Man. Dir Dr S. O. ASABIA.

ICON Ltd: NIDB House, 63–71 Broad St, PMB 12689, Lagos; tel. (1) 2600800; telex 21437; fax (1) 2666169; f. 1974; cap. p.u. 50.4m. (1991), dep. 1,545.4m. (1990); Chair. Alhaji SAIDU KASSIM; Man. Dir A. A. FEESE; 6 brs.

Industrial Bank Ltd (Merchant Bankers): Plot 1637, Adetokunbo Ademola St, Victoria Island, PMB 12637, Lagos; tel. (1) 2692151; telex 22005; fax (1) 619024; cap. p.u. 50.1m. (Dec. 1992); Chair. Dr SAMUEL ADEDOYIN; Man. Dir Chief E. AYO AWODEYI (acting).

International Merchant Bank (Nigeria) Ltd: IMB Plaza, 1 Akin Adesola St, Victoria Island, PMB 12028, Lagos; tel. (1) 2611024; telex 28511; fax (1) 615392; f. 1974; affiliate of First National Bank of Chicago (USA); cap. p.u. 36m. (1991), dep. 2,072.9m. (1990); Chair. Gen. M. SHUWA; Man. Dir BASHIRU TUKUR; 5 brs.

Merchant Bank of Africa (Nigeria) Ltd: St Nicholas House, Catholic Mission St, Falomo, Ikoyi, POB 53611, Lagos; tel. (1) 2601300; telex 23180; fax (1) 633789; f. 1982; cap. p.u. 28.3m. (1991), dep 465.7m. (1987); Chair. J. T. F. IYALLA; CEO B. O. ANYANWU.

Merchant Banking Corpn (Nigeria) Ltd: 16 Keffi St, S W Ikoyi, POB 53289, Lagos; tel. (1) 2690261; telex 22516; fax (1) 2690767; f. 1982; cap. p.u. 40m. (March 1993), dep. 504.4m. (1991); Chair. Dr M. A. MAJEKODUNMI; CEO J. J. AYANDA.

NAL Merchant Bank: NAL Towers, 20 Marina, PMB 12735, Lagos; tel. (1) 2600420; telex 21505; fax (1) 2633294; f. 1960; cap. 463.5m., dep. 1,011m. (1992); Chair. Dr SIMI JOHNSON; Man. Dir RAZAK TUNDE LAWAL; 4 brs.

New Africa Merchant Bank Ltd: 4 Waff Rd, PMB 2340, Kaduna; tel. (62) 235276; telex 71684; fax (62) 217311; cap. and res 59.6m., dep. 457.5m. (1992); Chair. Alhaji UMARU A. MUTALLAB; Man. Dir Mallam DAHIRU MUHAMMAD.

Nigbel Merchant Bank (Nigeria) Ltd: 77 Awolowo Rd, Ikoyi, POB 52463, Lagos; tel. (1) 2690380; telex 21851; fax (1) 2693256; f. 1987; cap. p.u. 40m. (Dec. 1992), dep. 367.7m. (1991); Chair. Chief N. O. IDOWU; CEO J. M. MARQUEBREUCQ.

Nigeria-Arab Bank Ltd: 96–102 Broad St, POB 12807, Lagos; tel. (1) 2661955; telex 21973; f. 1969; cap. and res 38.8m., dep. 1,313.3m. (1991); Chair. Alhaji ABIDU YAZID; Man. Dir KINGSLEY I. IKPE; 41 brs.

Nigeria Merchant Bank Ltd: 6 Broad St, POB 2413, Lagos; tel. (1) 2601460; telex 21475; fax (1) 2635314; cap. p.u. 35m. (March 1991); Chair. Alhaji M. I. ATTA; Man. Dir L. O. OKONKWO; 2 brs.

Nigerian-American Merchant Bank Ltd: Boston House, 10–12 Macarthy St, POB 8616, Lagos; tel. (1) 2601080; telex 28624; fax (1) 2631712; f. 1979; affiliate of First National Bank of Boston (USA); cap. p.u. 40m. (Dec. 1992), dep. 767.3m. (1991); Chair. Alhaji IBRAHIM DAMCIDA; Man. Dir OSARO ISOKPAN; 3 brs.

Nigerian Intercontinental Merchant Bank Ltd: Plot 999C, Intercontinental Plaza, Danmole St, Victoria Island, POB 54434, Lagos; tel. (1) 2636080; telex 28342; fax (1) 2633477; cap. p.u. 101.4m. (Dec. 1992); Chair. RAYMOND C. OBIERI; Man. Dir ERASTUS B. O. AKINGBOLA.

Rims Merchant Bank Ltd: Kingsway Bldg, Second Floor, 51–52 Merina, POB 73029, Lagos; tel. (1) 2600960; telex 28815; fax (1) 2669947; f. 1988; cap. p.u. 40m. (Dec. 1992), dep. 307.2m. (1990); Chair. Alhaji A. IBRAHIM OFR'SAN; Man. Dir S. I. AYININUOLA.

Stanbic Merchant Bank Nigeria Ltd: 188 Awolowo Rd, Ikoyi, POB 54746, Lagos; tel. (1) 2690402; telex 23216; fax (1) 685934; f. 1983 as Grindlays Merchant Bank of Nigeria; cap. p.u. 40m. (Dec. 1992); Chair. Alhaji ISIYAKU RABIU; Man. Dir J. N. LEGGETT.

Development Banks

Federal Mortgage Bank of Nigeria: Mamman Kontagora House, 23 Marina St, POB 2078, Lagos; tel. (1) 2647371; telex 21840; f. 1977; loans to individuals and mortgage institutions; cap. p.u. 150m. (1992), dep. 463.8m. (1991); was to be divided into two org. in 1993; Chair. Alhaji H. B. KOLO; Man. Dir G. A. ONABULE; 61 brs.

Nigerian Agricultural and Co-operative Bank Ltd (NACB): Hospital Rd, PMB 2155, Kaduna; tel. (62) 201000; telex 71115; fax (62) 210611; f. 1973; for funds to farmers and co-operatives to improve production techniques; cap. p.u. 500m. (1989); Chair. Alhaji SULE LAMIDO; Man. Dir Prof. M. B. AJAKAIYE; 38 brs.

Nigerian Bank for Commerce and Industry (NBCI): Plot 19C Adeola Hopewell, Victoria Island, POB 4424, Lagos; tel. (1) 616194; telex 21917; fax (1) 614202; f. 1973; govt bank to aid indigenization and development of small and medium-sized enterprises; cap. p.u. 200m. (1990); Chair. Alhaji UMARU ABDUL MUTALAB; Man. Dir Dr C. CHIMA; 19 brs.

Nigerian Industrial Development Bank Ltd: NIDB House, 63–71 Broad St, POB 2357, Lagos; tel. (1) 2663495; telex 21701; fax (1) 2667074; f. 1964 to provide medium and long-term finance to industry, manufacturing, non-petroleum mining and tourism; encourages foreign investment in partnership with Nigerians; cap. p.u. 836.9m. (Dec. 1992); Chair. RASHEED GBADAMOSI; Man. Dir Alhaji SAIDU YAYA KASIMU; 5 brs.

Bankers' Association

Chartered Institute of Bankers of Nigeria: 19 Adeola Hopewell St, POB 72273, Victoria Island, Lagos; tel. (1) 615642; telex 22838; fax (1) 611306; Chair. Femi A. Adekanye; CEO A. A. Adenubi.

STOCK EXCHANGE

Securities and Exchange Commission (SEC): Mandilas House, 96–102 Broad St, PMB 12638, Lagos; f. 1979 as govt agency to regulate and develop capital market; responsible for supervision of stock exchange operations; Dir of Admin. S. S. Akingbohungbe.

Nigerian Stock Exchange: Stock Exchange House, 2–4 Customs St, POB 2457, Lagos; tel. (1) 2660287; telex 23567; fax (1) 2668724; f. 1960; Pres. Pascal Dozie; Dir-Gen. Hayford Alile; 6 brs.

INSURANCE

There are over 105 insurance companies operating in Nigeria. Since 1978 they have been required to reinsure 20% of the sum insured with the Nigeria Reinsurance Corporation.

Insurance Companies

African Alliance Insurance Co Ltd: 112 Broad St, POB 2276, Lagos; tel. (1) 2664300; telex 23461; life assurance and pensions; Man. Dir Ope Oredugba.

African Insurance Co Ltd: 134 Nnamdi Azikiwe St, POB 274, Lagos; tel. (1) 2661720; f. 1950; all classes except life; Sec. Y. N. Mbadiwe; Area Man. N. E. Nsa; 4 brs.

American International Insurance Co (Nigeria): 200 Broad St, POB 2577, Lagos; tel. (1) 2662505; private; Man. Dir P. W. O'Rourke.

Ark Stewart Wrightson: 4 Idowu Taylor St, POB 3771, Lagos; tel. (1) 615826; telex 22652; 5 brs.

H. Clarkson, Edu & Partners: 172 Broad St, POB 2853, Lagos; tel. (1) 2660738; telex 22163; 3 brs.

Glanville Enthoven Group: Western House, 8/10 Broad St, PMB 2273, Lagos; general, life, pensions and reinsurance; 5 brs.

Great Nigeria Insurance Co Ltd: 39–41 Martins St, POB 2314, Lagos; f. 1960; all classes; Man. Dir E. B. Onifade.

Guinea Insurance Co Ltd: 21–25 Broad St, POB 1136, Lagos; tel. (1) 2660630; telex 21680; f. 1958; all classes; Chair. Alhaji K. M. Bichi; Man. Dir Agboola Oke.

Law Union and Rock Insurance Co of Nigeria Ltd: 88–92 Broad St, POB 944, Lagos; tel. (1) 2663526; fire, accident and marine; 6 brs; Chair. Col S. Bello; Man. Dir B. Ogunniyi.

Leadway Assurance Co Ltd: NN 28–29 Constitution Rd, POB 458, Kaduna; tel. (62) 230660; telex 71101; fax (62) 216973; f. 1970; all classes; Chair. Alhaji Hassan Hadejia; Man. Dir Chief Hassan Olu Odukale.

Lion of Africa Insurance Co Ltd: St Peter's House, 3 Ajele St, POB 2055, Lagos; tel. (1) 2600950; telex 23536; fax (1) 2636111; f. 1952; all classes; Man. Dir G. A. Alegieuno.

Mercury Assurance Co Ltd: 17 Martins St, POB 2003, Lagos; tel. (1) 2660216; telex 21951; general; Man. Dir Chief A. Zuccarella.

National Co-operative Insurance Society of Nigeria Ltd: 138 Ibrahim Taiwo Rd, POB 4733, Kano; tel. (64) 9632; f. 1977; all classes except life for mems of co-operatives, etc.

National Insurance Corpn of Nigeria (NICON): 5 Customs St, POB 1100, Lagos; tel. (1) 2666312; telex 22651; fax (1) 2666556; f. 1969; transferred to private ownership in 1990; all classes; cap. 10m.; Chair. Hamisu Buhari; Man. Dir O. Osoka; 28 brs.

N.E.M. Insurance Co (Nigeria) Ltd: 12–14 Broad St, POB 654, Lagos; tel. (1) 2600040; all classes; Chair. T. J. Onomigbo Okpoko; Man. Dir B. A. Lawson.

Nigeria Insurance Co Ltd: 47 Marina, POB 2718, Lagos; tel. (1) 2664452; fax (1) 2662196; all classes; Man. Dir A. K. Oniwinde; 6 brs.

Nigeria Reinsurance Corpn: Bookshop House, 50–52 Broad St, PMB 12766, Lagos; tel. (1) 2634141; telex 21092; all classes of reinsurance; Prof. Ukandi G. Damachi; Man. Dir Mohammed Karl.

Nigerian General Insurance Co Ltd: 1 Nnamdi Azikiwe St, POB 2210, Lagos; f. 1951; all classes; Chair. Chief J. S. Olawoyin; Man. Dir H. T. Durojaiye; 15 brs.

Phoenix of Nigeria Assurance Co Ltd: Mandilas House, 96–102 Broad St, POB 2893, Lagos; tel. (1) 2661160; f. 1964; all classes; cap. 3m.; Chair. Chief John B. Mandilas; 5 brs.

Prestige Assurance Co (Nigeria) Ltd: 54 Marina, POB 650, Lagos; tel. (1) 2661213; telex 20086; all classes except life; Chair. Alhaji S. M. Argungu; Man. Dir C. N. Ravi.

Royal Exchange Assurance (Nigeria) Group: New Africa House, 31 Marina, POB 112, Lagos; tel. (1) 2663120; telex 27406; all classes; Chair. Alhaji Muhtar Bello Yola; Man. Dir J. U. Ikhidero; 5 brs, 16 sub-brs.

Sun Insurance Office (Nigeria) Ltd: Unity House, 37 Marina, POB 2694, Lagos; tel. (1) 2661318; telex 21994; all classes except life; Man. Dir A. T. Adeniji; 6 brs.

United Nigeria Insurance Co Ltd: 53 Marina, POB 588, Lagos; tel. (1) 2663201; telex 22186; fax (1) 2664282; f. 1965; all classes except life; Chair. and Man. Dir F. C. Nwokolo; 17 brs.

Unity Life and Fire Insurance Co Ltd: 9 Nnamdi Azikiwe St, POB 3681, Lagos; tel. (1) 2662317; telex 21657; all classes; Man. Dir R. A. Odinigweh.

Veritas: 19 Martins St, POB 2056, Lagos; tel. (1) 2663770; telex 21826; all classes; Man. Dir C. N. Okoro.

West African Provincial Insurance Co: 27–29 King George V Rd, POB 2103, Lagos; tel. (1) 2636433; telex 21613; all classes except life; Man. Dir A. A. Akintunde.

Insurance Association

Nigerian Insurance Association: St Peter's House, 2nd Floor, 3 Ajele St, POB 9551, Lagos; tel. (1) 2630849; f. 1971; Chair. Agboola Odele.

Trade and Industry

CHAMBERS OF COMMERCE

Nigerian Association of Chambers of Commerce, Industry, Mines and Agriculture: 15A Ikorodu Rd, Maryland, PMB 12816, Lagos; tel. and fax (1) 4964737; telex 21368; Pres. Chief M. O. Origbo; Dir-Gen. L. O. Adekunle.

Aba Chamber of Commerce and Industry: UBA Bldg, Ikot Expene Rd/Georges St, POB 1596, Aba; tel. (82) 225148; Pres. Dr S. C. Okolo.

Abeokuta Chamber of Commerce and Industry: 29 Kuto Rd, Ishabo, POB 937, Abeokuta; tel. (39) 231230; Pres. Chief S. O. Akinremi.

Abuja Chamber of Commerce and Industry: Wuse, PMB 86, Garki, Abuja; tel. (9) 52341887; Pres. Alhaji Abdullahi Adamu.

Adamawa Chamber of Commerce and Industry: c/o Palace Hotel, POB 8, Jimeta, Yola; tel. (75) 255136; Pres. Alhaji Isa Hammanyero.

Akure Chamber of Commerce and Industry: 57 Oyemekun Rd, Akure; tel. (34) 231051; Pres. Gabriel Akinjo.

Awka Chamber of Commerce and Industry: 220 Enugu Rd, POB 780, Awka; tel. (45) 550105; Pres. Lt-Col (retd) D. Orugbu.

Bauchi Chamber of Commerce and Industry: 96 Maiduguri Rd, POB 911, Bauchi; tel. (77) 42620; telex 83261; f. 1976; Pres. Alhaji Magaji Mu'azu.

Benin Chamber of Commerce, Industry, Mines and Agriculture: 10 Murtala Muhammed Way, POB 2087, Benin City; tel. (52) 245761; Pres. C. O. Eweka.

Benue Chamber of Commerce, Industry, Mines and Agriculture: 3 Peter Achimugu Rd, PMB 102344, Makurdi; tel. (44) 32573; Chair. Col (retd) R. V. I. Asam.

Borno Chamber of Commerce and Industry: 3 Jos Rd, PMB 1636, Maiduguri; tel. (76) 232942; telex 82112; Pres. Alhaji A. Ali Kotoko.

Calabar Chamber of Commerce and Industry: 45 Akin Rd, POB 76, Calabar; tel. (87) 221558; 92 mems; Pres. Chief Tam Oforiokuma.

Enugu Chamber of Commerce, Industry and Mines: Trade Fair Complex, Abakaliki Rd, POB 734, Enugu; tel. (42) 330575; f. 1963; Pres. Rev. Chike Nwizu.

Franco-Nigerian Chamber of Commerce: Plot 232A, Adeola Odeku St, POB 70001, Victoria Island, Lagos; tel. (1) 610071; fax (1) 618825; f. 1985; Chair. Okoya Thomas; Pres. J. J. Engels.

Gongola Chamber of Commerce and Industry: Palace Hotel, POB 8, Jimeta-Yola; tel. (75) 255136; Pres. Alhaji Aliyu Ibrahim.

Ibadan Chamber of Commerce and Industry: Commerce House, Ring Rd, Challenge, PMB 5168, Ibadan; tel. (22) 317223; telex 20311; Pres. Jide Abimbola.

Ijebu Chamber of Commerce and Industry: 51 Ibadan Rd, POB 604, Ijebu Ode; tel. (22) 432880; Pres. Doyin Degun.

Ikot Ekpene Chamber of Commerce and Industry: 47 Aba Rd, POB 50, Ikot Ekpene; tel. (85) 400153; Pres. G. U. Ekanem.

Kaduna Chamber of Commerce, Industry and Agriculture: 24 Waff Rd, POB 728, Kaduna; tel. (62) 211216; telex 71325; fax (62) 214149; Pres. Alhaji Mohammed Sani Aminu.

Kano Chamber of Commerce, Industry, Mines and Agriculture: Zoo Rd, POB 10, Kano City, Kano; tel. (64) 667138; Pres. Alhaji Auwalu Ilu.

Katsina Chamber of Commerce and Industry: 1 Nagogo Rd, POB 92, Katsina; tel. (65) 31014; Pres. ABBA ALI.

Kwara Chamber of Commerce, Industry, Mines and Agriculture: 208 Ibrahim Taiwo Rd, POB 1634, Ilorin; tel. (31) 221069; Pres. W. O. ODUDU.

Lagos Chamber of Commerce and Industry: Commerce House, 1 Idowu Taylor St, Victoria Island, POB 109, Lagos; tel. (1) 613898; telex 21368; fax (1) 610573; f. 1885; 900 mems; Pres. OLUDAYO SONUGA.

Niger Chamber of Commerce and Industry: Trade Fair Site, POB 370, Minna; tel. (66) 223153; Pres. Alhaji U. S. NDANUSA.

Nnewi Chamber of Commerce and Industry: 21 Owerri Rd, POB 1471, Nnewi; f. 1987; Pres. Chief C. M. IBETO.

Oshogbo Chamber of Commerce and Industry: Obafemi Awolowo Way, Ajegunle, POB 870, Oshogbo, Osun; tel. (35) 231098; Pres. Chief A. A. IBIKUNLE.

Owerri Chamber of Commerce and Industry: OCCIMA Secretariat, 123 Okigwe Rd, POB 1640, Owerri; tel. (83) 234849; Pres. Chief BONIFACE N. AMAECHI.

Oyo Chamber of Commerce and Industry: POB 67, Oyo; Pres. Chief C. A. OGUNNIYI.

Plateau State Chambers of Commerce, Industry, Mines and Agriculture: Shama House, 32 Rwang Pam St, POB 2092, Jos; tel. (73) 53918; telex 81348; f. 1976; Pres. Chief M. E. JACDOMI.

Port Harcourt Chamber of Commerce, Industry, Mines and Agriculture: 169 Aba Rd, POB 71, Port Harcourt; tel. (84) 330394; telex 61110; f. 1952; Pres. Chief S. I. ALETE.

Remo Chamber of Commerce and Industry: 7 Sho Manager Way, POB 1172, Shagamu; tel. (37) 640962; Pres. Chief S. O. ADEKOYA.

Sapele Chamber of Commerce and Industry: 144 New Ogorode Rd, POB 154, Sapele; tel. (54) 42323; Pres. P. O. FUFUYIN.

Sokoto Chamber of Commerce and Industry: 12 Racecourse Rd, POB 2234, Sokoto; tel. (60) 231805; Pres. Alhaji ALIYU WAZIRI BODINGA.

Umahia Chamber of Commerce: 65 Uwalaka St, POB 86, Umahia; tel. (88) 220055; Pres. Chief S. B. A. ATULOMAH.

Uyo Chamber of Commerce and Industry: 141 Abak Rd, POB 2960, Uyo, Akwa Ibom; Pres. Chief DANIEL ITA-EKPOTT.

Warri Chamber of Commerce and Industry: Block 1, Edewor Shopping Centre, Warri/Sapele Rd, POB 302, Warri; tel. (53) 233731; Pres. MOSES F. OROGUN.

TRADE ASSOCIATIONS

Abeokuta Importers' and Exporters' Association: c/o Akeweje Bros, Lafenwa, Abeokuta.

Ijebu Importers' and Exporters' Association: 16 Ishado St, Ijebu-Ode.

Nigerian Association of Native Cloth Dealers and Exporters: 45 Koesch St, Lagos.

Nigerian Association of Stockfish Importers: 10 Egerton Rd, Lagos.

Union of Importers and Exporters: POB 115, Ibadan; f. 1949; Chair. E. A. SANDA.

PROFESSIONAL AND EMPLOYERS' ORGANIZATIONS

Association of Master Bakers, Confectioners and Caterers of Nigeria: 13–15 Custom St, POB 4, Lagos; f. 1951; 250 mems; Pres. J. ADE TUYO (acting).

Federation of Building and Civil Engineering Contractors in Nigeria: Construction House, Plot 6, Alakija St, Professional Centre, Victoria Island, POB 282, Lagos; tel. (1) 616564; f. 1954; Pres. Chief E. B. OSOBA.

Institute of Chartered Accountants of Nigeria: Plot 16, Professional Layout Centre, Idowu Taylor St, Victoria Island, POB 1580, Lagos; tel. (1) 614235; fax (1) 610304; f. 1965; CEO and Registrar G. M. OKUFI.

Manufacturers' Association of Nigeria: Unity House, 12th Floor, 37 Marina, POB 3835, Lagos; tel. (1) 2660755; f. 1971; Pres. HASSAN ADAMU.

Nigerian Chamber of Mines: POB 454, Jos; tel. (73) 55003; f. 1950; Pres. A. A. KEHINDE.

Nigeria Employers' Consultative Association: Commercial House, 1–11 Commercial Ave, POB 2231, Yaba, Lagos; tel. (1) 800360; fax (1) 860309; f. 1957; Pres. Chief J. O. FAGBEMI.

Nigerian Institute of Architects: 2 Idowu Taylor St, Victoria Island, POB 278, Lagos; tel. (1) 617940; f. 1960; Pres. Chief O. O. BALOGUN.

Nigerian Institute of Building: 1B Market St, Oyingbo, Ebute-Metta, POB 3191, Marina, Lagos; f. 1970; Pres. S. T. OYEFEKO.

Nigerian Institution of Estate Surveyors and Valuers: Flat 2B, Dolphin Scheme, Ikoyi, POB 2325, Lagos; tel. (1) 685981; Pres. Dr E. D. OBIALO.

Nigerian Livestock Dealers' Association: POB 115, Sapele.

Nigerian Recording Association: 9 Breadfruit St, POB 950, Lagos.

Nigerian Society of Engineers: National Engineering Centre, 1 Engineering Close, Victoria Island, Lagos; tel. (1) 617315; Pres. IFE AKINTUNDE.

Pharmaceutical Society of Nigeria: 4 Tinubu Sq., POB 546, Lagos.

DEVELOPMENT ORGANIZATIONS

Anambra State Agricultural Development Corporation: Garden Ave, PMB 1024, Enugu.

Anambra-Imo Basin Development Authority: Chair. SAMUEL C. ELUWA; Gen. Man. WITLY OKONKWO.

Benin–Owena River Basin Development Authority: 24 Benin-Sapele Rd, PMB 1381, Obayantor, Benin; tel. (52) 200700; f. 1976 to conduct irrigation; Gen. Man. Dr G. E. OTEZE.

Chad Basin Development Authority: Dikwa Rd, PMB 1130, Maiduguri; tel. (76) 232015; f. 1973; irrigation and agriculture-allied industries; Chair. MOHAMMED ABALI; Gen. Man. Alhaji BUNU S. MUSA.

Cross River Basin Development Authority: 32 Target Rd, PMB 1249, Calabar; tel. (87) 223163; f. 1977; Gen. Man. SIXTUS ABETIANBE.

Cross River State Agricultural Development Corporation: PMB 1024, Calabar.

Federal Capital Development Authority: Abuja; govt agency for design, construction and management of Abuja; Perm. Sec. Alhaji ABUBAKAR KOKO.

Federal Housing Authority: Gen. Man. S. P. O. FORTUNE EBIE.

Federal Institute of Industrial Research, Oshodi (FIIRO): Murtala Muhammad Airport, Ikeja, PMB 21023, Lagos; tel. (1) 522905; telex 26006; fax (1) 525880; f. 1956; plans and directs industrial research and provides tech. assistance and information to industry; specializes in foods, minerals, textiles, natural products and industrial intermediates; Dir. Prof. S. A. ODUNFA.

Gongola State Housing Corpn: Yola; Chair. DOMINIC M. MAPEO; Gen. Man. DAVID A. GARNVWA.

Hadejia Jama'are Basin Development Authority: Bauchi; f. 1976; began building four dams for irrigation and hydroelectric power in 1980; Gen. Man. Alhaji AHMADU RUFAI.

Imo State Housing Corpn: Uratta Rd, PMB 1224, Owerri, Imo; tel. (83) 230733; f. 1976; develops housing and industrial estates, grants finance for house purchase and operates a savings scheme; Gen. Man. O. A. KALU.

Industrial Training Fund: Federal Secretariat, 8th Floor, PMB 2199, Jos; tel. (73) 55297; telex 81154; f. 1971 to promote and encourage skilled workers in trade and industry; Dir-Gen. Alhaji LAWAL TUDUNWADA.

Kaduna Industrial and Finance Co Ltd: Investment House, 27 Ali Akilu Rd, PMB 2230, Kaduna; tel. (62) 217094; telex 20711; fax (62) 215715; f. 1977; development finance institution; Chair. HASSAN A. MU'AZU; CEO JAMILAH S. HAYATUDDINI.

Kwara State Investment Corpn: PMB 1344, Ilorin.

Lagos State Development and Property Corpn: Ilupeju Industrial Estate, Ikorodu Rd, PMB 1050, Ikeja; POB 907, Lagos; f. 1972; planning and development of Lagos; Gen. Man. G. B. JINADU.

New Nigerian Development Co Ltd: 18/19 Ahmadu Bello Way, Ahmed Talib House, PMB 2120, Kaduna; tel. (62) 210909; telex 71108; f. 1968; investment/financial institution owned by the Govts of 11 northern States; 10 subsidiaries, 117 assoc. cos; Chair. Maj.-Gen. (retd) M. D. JEGA.

New Nigeria Development Co (Properties) Ltd: 18–19 Ahmadu Bello Way, PMB 2040, Kaduna; housing devt agency.

Niger Delta Basin and Rural Development Authority: 21 Azikiwe Rd, PMB 5676, Port Harcourt; f. 1976.

Niger River Basin Development Authority: f. 1976; Chair. Alhaji HALIRU DANTORO.

Nigerian Enterprises Promotion Board: 72 Campbell St, PMB 12553, Lagos; f. 1972 to promote indigenization; Chair. MINSO GADZAMA.

Nigerian Export Promotion Council: Kumba St, PMB 133, Garki, Abuja; tel. (9) 5230930; telex 91510; fax (9) 5230931; f. 1976; promotes development and diversification of exports; Dir GEORGE NIYI.

Nigerian Livestock and Meat Authority: POB 479, Kaduna; telex 71307.

Northern Nigeria Investments Ltd: POB 138, Kaduna; tel. (62) 212980; telex 71110; f. 1959 to identify and invest in industrial and agricultural projects in 16 northern States; cap. p.u. 16m.; Man. Dir KASSIM M. BICHI.

Odu'a Investment Co Ltd: Cocoa House, PMB 5435, Ibadan; tel. (22) 417710; telex 31225; f. 1976; jtly owned by Ogun, Ondo and Oyo States; Man. Dir O. A. IYOWU.

Ogun-Oshun River Basin Development Authority: f. 1976; Chair. Mrs D. B. A. KUFORIJI; Gen. Man. Dr LEKAN ARE.

Ogun State Agricultural Credit Corpn: PMB 2029, Abeokuta; f. 1976.

Ogun State Housing Corpn: PMB 2077, Abeokuta; f. 1976; develops housing and industrial estates; grants finance for house purchase and operates a savings plan; Gen. Man. F. O. ABIODUN.

Ondo State Housing Corpn: PMB 693, Akure; f. 1976 to develop house-building and industrial estates and to grant mortgages and loans for house purchase; also operates a savings scheme.

Ondo State Investment Corpn: PMB 700, Akure; f. 1976 to investigate and promote both agricultural and industrial projects on a commercial basis in the State.

Oyo State Property Development Corpn: f. 1976 to develop housing, commercial property and industrial estate and to grant finance for house purchase; also operates a savings scheme.

Plateau State Housing Corpn: Jos; plans to build 1,000 housing units a year in addition to another 1,000 units built in the State by the Fed. Govt.

Plateau State Water Resources Development Board: Jos; incorporates the fmr Plateau River Basin Devt Authority and Plateau State Water Resources Devt Board.

Price Intelligence Agency: c/o Productivity, Prices and Income Board, Lagos; f. 1980; monitors prices.

Projects Development Agency: 3 Independence Layout, POB 609, Enugu; f. 1974; promotes the establishment of new industries and develops industrial projects utilizing local raw materials; Dir Dr EZEKWE.

Rivers State Development Corpn: Port Harcourt; f. 1970.

Rivers State Housing Corpn: 15/17 Emekuku St, PMB 5044, Port Harcourt.

Rubber Research Institute of Nigeria: PMB 1049, Benin City.

Sokoto-Rima Basin Development Authority: f. 1976; Chair. Alhaji MU'AZU LAMIDO.

Trans Investments Co Ltd: Bale Oyewole Rd, PMB 5085, Ibadan; tel. (22) 416000; telex 31122; f. 1986; initiates and finances industrial and agricultural schemes; Gen. Man. M. A. ADESIYUN.

Upper Benue Basin Development Authority: Chair. Alhaji MOHAMMADU MAI.

PUBLIC CORPORATIONS

Ajaokuta Steel Co Ltd: PMB 1000, Ajaokuta, Kwara; tel. 400450; telex 36390; CEO M. M. INUWA.

Delta Steel Co Ltd: Ovwian-Aladja, POB 1220, Warri; tel. (53) 621001; telex 43456; fax (53) 621012; f. 1979; state-owned; operates direct-reduction steel complex with eventual annual capacity of 1m. tons; Chair. Chief TUNJI AROSANYIN; Man. Dir ABIODUN TITUS ABE.

Gaskiya Corpn Ltd: Tadun Wada, Zaria; tel. (69) 32201; f. 1938; owned by Kaduna State Govt, New Nigerian Development Co and Jama'atu Nasril Islam; printers; CEO ABDULLAHI HASSAN.

National Electric Power Authority (NEPA): 24–25 Marina, PMB 12030, Lagos; tel. (1) 2600640; telex 21212; f. 1972 by merger of the Electricity Corpn of Nigeria and the Niger Dams Authority; a three-year rehabilitation programme, at an estimated cost of US $155m., began in 1990; Man. Dir DAVID ADEYEMI OYELEYE.

National Oil and Chemical Marketing Co: 38–39 Marina, PMB 2052, Lagos; markets petroleum, petroleum products and chemicals; Chair. Maj.-Gen. USMAN KATSINA; Man. Dir E. O. OKOYE.

Nigerian Cement Co Ltd (NIGERCEM): Nkalugu, POB 331, Enugu; tel. (42) 333829; telex 51113; Chair. Dr NNAMDI E. NWAUWA.

Nigerian Coal Corpn: PMB 01053, Enugu; tel. (42) 335314; telex 51115; f. 1909; operates four mines; Gen. Man. F. N. UGWU.

Nigerian Engineering and Construction Co Ltd (NECCO): Km 14, Badagry Expressway (opp. International Trade Fair Complex), PMB 12684, Lagos; tel. (1) 880591; telex 21836; building, civil, mechanical and electrical engineers, furniture makers and steel fabricators; Chair. EHIOZE EDIAE.

Nigerian Liquefied Natural Gas Co: Lagos; Chair. Alhaji MOHAMMED YUSUFU; Man. Dir Dr G. S. IYETU (acting).

Nigerian Mining Corpn: Federal Secretariat, 7th Floor, PMB 2154, Jos; f. 1972; exploration, production, processing and marketing of minerals; Chair. (vacant).

Nigerian National Petroleum Corpn (NNPC): 7 Kofo Abayomi St, Victoria Island, PMB 12701, Lagos; tel. (1) 614650; telex 21610; fax (1) 683784; f. 1977; merged with Nigerian Petroleum Refining Co 1985; reorg. 1988; holding corpn for fed. govt interests in the oil cos; 11 operating subsidiaries; Chair. Secretary of Petroleum and Mineral Resources; Man. Dir CHAMBERS OYIBO.

Nigerian National Supply Co Ltd: 29 Burma Rd, PMB 12662, Apapa, Lagos; state-owned import org.; Chair. Brig. J. I. ONOJA; Gen. Man. Maj. A. DAHIRU.

Nigerian Petroleum Refining Co Ltd (NPRC): 21–25 Broad St, Lagos.

CO-OPERATIVES

There are more than 25,000 co-operative societies in Nigeria.

Co-operative Federation of Nigeria: PMB 5533, Ibadan; tel. (22) 711276; telex 31224; fax (22) 711276; Pres. REMI OBISESAN.

Anambra State Co-operative Federation Ltd: 213 Agbani Rd, PMB 1488, Enugu; tel. (42) 331157; Pres. C. G. O. NWABUGWU.

Association of Nigerian Co-operative Exporters Ltd: New Court Rd, POB 477, Ibadan; f. 1945; producers/exporters of cocoa and other cash crops.

Co-operative Supply Association Ltd: Ance Bldg, Jericho, Ibadan; importers and dealers in agricultural chemicals and equipment, fertilizers, building materials, general hardware, grocery and provisions.

Co-operative Union of Western Nigeria Ltd: PMB 5101, Jericho Rd, Ibadan.

Kabba Co-operative Credit and Marketing Union Ltd: POB 25, Kabba; f. 1953; producers of food and cash crops and retailers of consumer goods; Pres. Alhaji S. O. ONUNDI; Man. H. A. ORISAFUNMI.

Kano State Co-operative Federation Ltd: 1 Zaria Rd, PMB 3030, Kano; tel. (64) 622182; Pres. G. B. YAKO.

Kwara State Co-operative Federation Ltd: PMB 1412, Ilorin; operates transport and marketing services in Kwara State; Gen. Man. J. OBARO.

Lagos State Co-operative Federation Ltd: 13 Isaacstan Close, Wemco Rd, POB 8632, Ikeja, Lagos; co-operative education and publicity.

Oyo State Co-operative Federation Ltd: 3 Olubadan Estate, New Ife Rd, PMB 5101, Ibadan; tel. (22) 710985; Pres. J. A. ADERIBIGBE.

MAJOR INDUSTRIAL COMPANIES

The following are some of the largest companies in terms either of capital investment or employment.

African Petroleum Ltd: AP House, 54–56 Broad St, POB 512, Lagos; tel. (1) 635290; telex 21242; cap. ₦72m.; fmrly BP Nigeria Ltd; markets lubricants, fuel oil, automotive gas oil, motor spirits, liquefied petroleum gas and kerosene; CEO GANA ABBA; Dir PIUS IDIGO; 705 employees.

African Timber and Plywood (AT & P): PMB 4001, Sapele; f. 1935; a division of UAC of Nigeria Ltd and an assoc. co of UAC International Ltd, London; loggers and mfrs of plywood, particleboard, flushdoors, lumber and machined wood products; Gen. Man. L. HODGSON.

Blackwood Hodge: Asogun Rd, Km 15, Badagry Expressway, POB 109, Apapa, Lagos; tel. (1) 880507; telex 21870; cap. p.u. ₦8.1m.; earthmoving, construction, irrigation, mining and agricultural equipment; Chair. Dr I. B. JOSE; Man. Dir M. A. PIGOU; 153 employees.

Chemical and Allied Products Co Ltd: POB 1004, 24 Commercial Rd, Apapa, Lagos; tel. (1) 803220; telex 21446; mfrs of paints, pesticides and pharmaceuticals, distributors of chemicals, dyestuffs, explosives, plastic raw materials and associated products.

Guinness (Nigeria) Ltd: Oba Akran Ave, Ikeja, PMB 1071, Lagos State: f. 1950; cap. p.u. ₦25m.; brewers; breweries in Ikeja (700,000 hl), Ogba (700,000 hl) and Benin (900,000 hl); Man. Dir M. F. OTERI.

Gulf Oil Co (Nigeria) Ltd: 19 Tinubu Sq., PMB 2469, Lagos; onshore and offshore petroleum exploration and production; Man. Dir CARROLL COX.

Henry Stephens Group: Head Office: 90 Awolowo Rd, SW Ikoyi, POB 2480, Lagos; tel. (1) 603460; telex 21752; subsidiary cos include:

Gilco (Nigeria) Ltd: 292 Apapa Rd, Apapa; import and export.

Henry Stephens Engineering Co Ltd: 2 Ilepeju By-Pass, Ikeja, PMB 21386, Lagos; tel. (1) 901460; telex 21752; fax (1) 2690758; for construction machinery, motors and agricultural equipment.

Nigerian Maritime Services: 13–15 Sapele Rd, Apapa, PMB 1013, Lagos; tel. (1) 873018; telex 21286; f. 1964; Chair. Prof. AYO OGUNSHEYE; Gen. Man. W. P. D. DAVSON.

IBRU: 33 Creek Rd, PMB 1155, Apapa, Lagos; tel. (1) 876634; telex 21086; agricultural equipment, machinery and service; fishing and frozen fish distribution, civil and agricultural engineering.

A. G. Leventis Group: Iddo House, Iddo, POB 159, Lagos; tel. (1) 800220; telex 26030; fax (1) 860574; activities include wholesale and retail distribution, vehicle assembly, food production and farming, manufacture of glass, plastics, beer, technical and electrical equipment, property investment and management.

Lever Brothers (Nigeria) Ltd: 15 Dockyard Rd, POB 15, Apapa, Lagos; tel. (1) 803300; telex 21520; fax (1) 617873; f. 1923; cap. ₦112.0m.; mfrs of detergents, edible fats and toilet preparations; Chair. and CEO R. F. GIWA; 2,300 employees.

Leyland Nigeria: POB 5024, Lagos; f. 1976; 35% govt-owned; commercial vehicle assemblers and mfrs of components; Chair. Chief OLU AKINKUGBE; Man. Dir P. QUICK.

Mandilas Group Ltd: 96–102 Broad St, POB 35, Lagos; telex 21383; subsidiaries include Mandilas Enterprises Ltd, Mandilas Travel Ltd, Norman Industries Ltd, Electrolux-Mandilas Ltd, Phoenix of Nigeria Assurance Co Ltd, Sulzer Nigeria Ltd, Mandilas Ventures Ltd, Original Box Co Ltd.

Mobil Producing Nigeria: PMB 12054, 50 Broad St, Lagos; tel. (1) 600560; telex 21228; offshore petroleum production; Chair. ALFRED K. KOCH.

National Oil and Chemical Marketing Co Ltd: 38–39 Marina, PMB 2052, Lagos; tel. (1) 2665880; telex 21591; fax (1) 2662802; f. 1975 (fmrly Shell Nigeria Ltd); 40% state-owned; Man. Dir S. I. C. OKOLI; 685 employees.

Nigerian Breweries Ltd: 1 Abebe Village Rd, Iganmu, POB 545, Lagos; tel. (1) 801340; telex 26370; fax (1) 617682; f. 1946; oldest brewery in Nigeria; facilities also at Aba, Kaduna and Ibadan; Chair. C. E. ABEBE; Man. Dir FELIX OHIWEREI; 4,057 employees.

Nigerian Metal Fabricating Ltd: POB 23, Kano; tel. (64) 632427; telex 77244; fax (64) 634677; part of Cedar Group; mfrs of aluminium household utensils, brassware and silverware; also light engineers.

Nigerian National Petroleum Corpn: Alesa-Eleme, POB 585, Port Harcourt; tel. (84) 300420; telex 61166; capacity of 60,000 b/d of refined petroleum products; Chair. (vacant) ; Man. Dir (vacant).

Nigerian Oil Mills Ltd: POB 342, Kano; tel. (64) 632427; telex 77244; fax (64) 634677; import and production of vegetable oil products.

Nigerian Paper Mill Ltd: POB 1648, Lagos; also at Jebba; Chair. Brig. USMAN ABUBAKAR.

Nigerian Sugar Co Ltd: PMB 65, Bacita Estate, Jebba; tel. 641035; f. 1961; cap. ₦79.4m.; growers of sugar cane and mfrs of cane sugar and allied products; Chair. Alhaji IBRAHIM AHMED; Man. Dir SULEIMAN ABDULLAHI; 5,600 employees.

Nigerian Textile Mills Ltd: Oba Akran Ave, Industrial Estate, PMB 21051, Ikeja; tel. (1) 962012; telex 26206; fax (1) 962011; f. 1960; cap. ₦40m.; spinners, weavers and finishers; Chair. Prof. S. O. BIOBAKU; Dir FERNAND PICCIOTTO; 2,700 employees.

Nigerian Tin Mining Co Ltd: PMB 2036, Jos; tel. (73) 80634; f. 1986 by merger of Amalgamated Tin Mines of Nigeria Ltd and five other mining cos operating on the Jos plateau; owned by Nigerian Mining Corpn and fmr non-national shareholders in the above five cos; cap. p.u. ₦9.5m.; production of tin concentrate from alluvial tin ore and separation of columbite, zircon and monazite; Chair. E. A. IFATUROTI; Gen. Man. Alhaji M. ADAMU.

Nigerian Tobacco Co Ltd: POB 137, Lagos; tel. (1) 2690202; telex 21561; fax (1) 2622048; f. 1951; cap. ₦100m.; mfrs of tobacco products; Chair. and Dir PIUS OKIGBO; Man. Dir O. A. BAPTIST; 1,600 employees.

Phillips Oil Co (Nigeria) Ltd: Plot 853, 19 Bishop Aboyade-Cole St, Victoria Island, PMB 12612, Lagos; tel. (1) 2615656; telex 28460; fax (1) 2615663; petroleum exploration and production; Man. Dir M. O. TAIGA.

PZ Industries Ltd: Planning Office Way, Ilupeju Industrial Estate, Ikeja, PMB 21132, Lagos; tel. (1) 901110; fax (1) 962076; fmrly Paterson Zochonis Nigeria Ltd; soaps, detergents, toiletries, pharmaceuticals and confectionery; factories at Ikorodu, Aba and Ilupeju.

SCOA Nigeria Ltd: 67 Marina, POB 2318, Lagos; tel. (1) 663095; telex 21017; cap. ₦44.8m.; vehicle assembly and maintenance, distribution and maintenance of heavyweight engines, industrial air-conditioning and refrigeration, home and office equipment, textiles, tanning, general consumer goods, mechanized farming.

Shell Petroleum Development Co of Nigeria Ltd: Freeman House, 21–22 Marina, PMB 2418, Lagos; tel. (1) 601600; telex 21235; the largest oil operator in Nigeria; responsible for onshore and offshore exploration and production; 60% state-owned; Chair. and Man. Dir BRIAN ANTHONY LAVERS.

Tate & Lyle (Nigeria) Ltd: 47–48 Eric Moore Rd, Iganmu Industrial Estate, POB 1240, Lagos; tel. (1) 801930; telex 26990; sugar, invert syrup, PVC pipes, plastic goods, stationery.

Texaco Nigeria Ltd: 241 Igbosere Rd, POB 166, Lagos; f. 1913; petroleum marketing; Chair. H. C. MINOR; Man. Dir G. E. SMITH.

Texaco Overseas (Nigeria) Petroleum Co: 36 Gerrard Rd, Ikoyi, POB 1986, Lagos; tel. (1) 680070; telex 21293; fax (1) 682520; offshore petroleum mining; Man. Dir R. BUCARAM.

Triana Ltd: 18–20 Commercial Rd, PMB 1064, Apapa, Lagos; tel. (1) 5803040; telex 21122; fax (1) 5876161; f. 1970; shipping, clearing and forwarding, warehousing, air-freighting; Man. Dir M. P. AGUBA.

UAC of Nigeria Ltd: Niger House, POB 9, Lagos; tel. (1) 2663010; telex 21233; fax (1) 2662628; fmrly United Africa Co; divisions include: brewing, foods, electrical materials, packaging, business equipment, plant hire, timber, Federated Motor Industries (Apapa), etc.; Man. Dir BASSEY U. NDIOKHO.

The Ugochukwu Group of Companies: 17 Calcutta Crescent, POB 162, Apapa, Lagos; manufacturing industry, insurance, commerce, property and investment; Chair. Chief M. N. UGOCHUKWU.

The West African Portland Cement Co Ltd: Elephant House, 237–239 Ikorodu Rd, POB 1001, Lagos; tel. (1) 901060; telex 26695; f. 1959; production and sale of cement and decorative materials; cap. p.u. ₦60.3m.; Chair. Prof. M. A. ADEYEMO.

TRADE UNIONS

Federation

Nigerian Labour Congress (NLC): 29 Olajuwon St, off Ojuelegba Rd, Yaba, POB 620, Lagos; tel. (1) 835582; f. 1978; comprises 42 affiliated industrial unions representing 3.5m. mems (1985); nat. exec. dissolved in Feb. 1988; delegates' conf. in Dec. 1988 returned movement to workers' control; Pres. PASCHAL BAFYAU; Gen. Sec. MORGAN ANEGBO.

Principal Unions

In 1990 a technical committee was created to restructure the existing 42 industrial unions, and ultimately to reduce their number to 20. The principal unions include:

Agricultural and Allied Workers' Union of Nigeria: SW8–123A Lagos Bypass, Oke Ado, Ibadan; Gen. Sec. C. O. FARINLOYE.

Association of Locomotive Drivers, Firemen, Yard Staff and Allied Workers of Nigeria: 231 Herbert Macaulay St, Yaba; 3,200 mems; Pres. P. C. OKOLO; Sec. DEJI OYEYEMI.

Civil Service Technical Workers' Union of Nigeria: 9 Aje St, PMB 1064, Yaba, Lagos; tel. (1) 863722; f. 1941; 7,500 mems; Pres. J. E. UDUAGHAM; Sec.-Gen. S. O. Z. EJIOFOH.

Ikeja Textile Workers' Union: 6 Oba Akran Ave, Ikeja; f. 1964; 7,200 mems; Pres. A. L. OSHITTU; Sec.-Gen. RUFUS ADEYOOLA.

Medical and Health Workers' Union of Nigeria: 2 Jeminatu Braimoh Close, Western Ave, Surulere, POB 563, Lagos; tel. (1) 832274; Pres. Y. O. OZIGI; Gen. Sec. J. MBAH.

Ministry of Defence Civil Employees' Union: 9 Aje St, PMB 1064, Yaba, Lagos; tel. (1) 863722; 3,600 mems; Pres. J. O. OGUNLESI; Sec. B. N. OBUA.

National Association of Nigerian Nurses and Midwives: 64B Oduduwa Way, Ikeja, POB 3857, Lagos; tel. (1) 932173; f. 1978; 7,100 mems; Pres. J. G. MICAH; Gen. Sec. M. OLABODE.

National Union of Construction and Civil Engineering Workers: 51 Kano St, Ebute Metta, PMB 1064, Lagos; tel. (1) 800263; Pres. R. O. SANYAOLU; Gen. Sec. M. O. FANIYI.

National Union of Electricity and Gas Workers: 200 Herbert Macaulay St, Ebute Metta, POB 212, Lagos; tel. (1) 864084; f. 1972; 25,000 mems; Pres. Gen. A. E. ADIZUA; Gen. Sec. P. T. KIRI-KALIO.

National Union of Petroleum and Natural Gas Workers: 2 Jeminatu Braimoh Close, Western Ave, Surulere, POB 7166, Lagos; tel. (1) 846569; Pres. WARIEBI AGAMENE; Gen. Sec. FRANK O. KOKORI.

National Union of Shop and Distributive Employees: 64 Olonode St, Yaba, Lagos; tel. (1) 863536; Pres. L. C. OGBATA; Gen. Sec. E. N. OKONGWU.

Nigeria Union of Construction and Civil Engineering Workers: 51 Kano St, PMB 1064, Ebute-Metta, Lagos; tel. (1) 800260; f. 1978 40,000 mems; Pres R. O. SANYAOLU; Gen. Sec. M. O. FANIYI.

Nigerian Civil Service Union: 23 Tokunboh St, POB 862, Lagos; f. 1912; 13,200 mems; Pres. C. OLATUNJI; Gen. Sec. P. B. OKORO.

Nigerian Metallic and Non-Metallic Mines Workers' Union: 95 Enugu St, POB 763, Jos; tel (73) 52401; f. 1948; 13,000 mems; Sec.-Gen. A. OLANIYAN.

Nigerian Textile, Garment and Tailoring Workers' Union: Textile Worker House, B6–8 Kubi St, Nassarawa Expressway, POB 905, Kaduna South, Kaduna; tel. (62) 214438; f. 1969, reorg. 1978; 47,000 mems; Pres. ALIYU SULEIMAN; Gen. Sec. A. OSHIOMHOLE.

Nigerian Union of Agricultural and Allied Workers: SW8–123A Lagos Bypass, Ibadan; 7,000 mems; Sec.-Gen. C. O. FARINLOYE.

Nigerian Union of Bank, Insurance and Financial Institution Employees: 310 Herbert Macaulay St, Yaba, PMB 1139, Lagos; tel. (1) 863193; 15,000 mems; Pres. JOHN H. GIMBASON; Sec.-Gen. Dr S. AHMED IBRAHIM.

Nigerian Union of Journalists: National Theatre Annex, Iganmu, Lagos; tel. (1) 833330; 5,200 mems; Pres. MUHAMMAD SANI ZORRO; Sec. GEORGE ANYAKORA (acting).

Nigerian Union of Railwaymen: 33 Ekololu St, Surulere, Yaba; f. 1950; 5,600 mems; Pres. S. A. ODUNUGA; Gen. Sec. CHUKS NWAJEI (acting).

Nigerian Union of Teachers: 15 Rosamund St, Surulere, PMB 1044, Yaba; f. 1931; 350,000 mems; Pres. Chief BRENDAN C. E. UGWU; Sec.-Gen. GABRIEL O. FALADE.

UAC and Associated Companies African Workers' Union: 81B Simpson St, Ebute-Metta; 8,000 mems; Pres. J. O. OJEWANDE; Sec. F. N. KANU.

Union of Posts and Telecommunications Workers of Nigeria: 12 Gbaja St, Surulere; 4,100 mems; Pres. J. SHODADE; Sec. G. O. ULUOCHA.

Transport

RAILWAYS

There are about 3,505 km of mainly narrow-gauge railways. The two principal lines connect Lagos with Nguru and Port Harcourt with Maiduguri.

Nigerian Railway Corporation: Ebute-Metta, Lagos; tel. (1) 834302; telex 26584; f. 1955; restructured in 1993 into three separate units: Nigerian Railway Track Authority; Nigerian Railways; and Nigerian Railway Engineering Ltd; Man. Dir JOSEPH MADUEKWE.

ROADS

In 1991 the Nigerian road network totalled some 112,140 km, of which about 30,900 km were principal roads and 19,550 km secondary roads; some 31,500 km were tarred.

Nigerian Road Federation: Ministry of Transport and Aviation, Joseph St, PMB 21038, Ikoyi, Lagos; tel. (1) 652120; telex 21535.

INLAND WATERWAYS

Inland Waterways Department: Ministry of Transport and Aviation, Joseph St, PMB 21038, Ikoyi, Lagos; tel. (1) 652120; telex 21535; responsible for all navigable waterways.

SHIPPING

The principal ports are the Delta Port complex (including Warri, Koko, Burutu and Sapele ports), Port Harcourt and Calabar; other significant ports are situated at Apapa and Tin Can Island, near Lagos. The main petroleum ports are Bonny and Burutu.

National Maritime Authority: Lagos; f. 1987; Chair. (vacant).

Nigeria Shipping Federation: NPA Commercial Offices, Block 'A', Wharf Rd, POB 107, Apapa, Lagos; f. 1960; Chair. (vacant); Gen. Man. D. B. ADEKOYA.

Nigerian Ports Authority: 26–28 Marina, PMB 12588, Lagos; tel. (1) 655020; telex 21500; f. 1955; Gen. Man. Alhaji SAGIR MOHAMMED.

Nigerian Green Lines Ltd: Unity House, 15th Floor, 37 Marina, POB 2288, Lagos; tel. (1) 2663303; telex 21308; 2 vessels totalling 30,751 grt; Chair. Alhaji W. L. FOLAWIYO.

Nigerian National Shipping Line Ltd: Development House, 21 Wharf Rd, POB 326, Apapa, Lagos; tel. (1) 804240; tel. 877262; telex 21253; fax (1) 870260; f. 1959; govt-owned; cargo and limited fast passenger services between West Africa, the United Kingdom, the Mediterranean, North America and the Far East; CEO and Man. Dir BOB ALFA.

CIVIL AVIATION

The principal international airports are at Lagos (Murtala Muhammed Airport), Kano, Port Harcourt and Calabar. There are also 14 airports for domestic flights. In early 1993 work was due to commence on the second phase of an international airport at Abuja, started in 1982.

Nigerian Airports Authority: Murtala Muhammed Airport, PMB 21607, Ikeja, Lagos; tel. (1) 900800; telex 26626; Man. Dir (vacant).

Principal Airlines

General and Aviation Services (Gas) Air Nigeria: Plot 5A, Old Domestic Airport, Ikeja, Lagos; tel. (1) 933510; fax (1) 962841; domestic and international cargo services; Pres. S. K. S. OLUBADEWO.

Intercontinental Airlines: 25 Adeniyi Jones Ave, Industrial Estate, PMB 21611, Ikeja; tel. (1) 932050; telex 26087; f. 1978; passenger and cargo charter flights, domestic and international; Chair. G. O. ONOSODE; Man. Dir Chief VICTOR VANNI.

Kabo Air: 6775 Ashton Rd, POB 1850, Kano; tel. (64) 625291; telex 77277; f. 1981; domestic services and international charters; Dir SHITU ADAMU.

Nigeria Airways: Airways House, Ikeja, PMB 136, Lagos; tel. (1) 900470; telex 26127; f. 1958; scheduled domestic and services to Europe, West Africa and Saudi Arabia; Chair. Capt M. JOJI.

Okada Air: POB 4898, Ikeja, Lagos; tel. (1) 963881; f. 1983; domestic and international charter passenger services, domestic scheduled services; Chair. Chief GABRIEL O. IGBINEDION.

Tourism

Potential attractions for tourists include fine coastal scenery, dense forests, and the rich diversity of Nigeria's arts. An estimated 167,000 tourists visited Nigeria in 1991, when receipts from tourism amounted to US $18m.

Nigerian Tourism Development Corporation: Zone 4, PMB 167, Abuja; tel. (9) 5230418; fax (9) 5230962; Chair. S. A. ALAMATU; Dir Alhaji S. M. JEGA.

Defence

In June 1993 the total strength of the armed forces was 78,800 men: the army totalled 62,000 men, the navy 7,300 and the air force 9,500. Military service is voluntary.

Defence Expenditure: Estimated at ₦4,550m. in 1993.

Commander-in-Chief of the Armed Forces: Gen. SANI ABACHA.

Chief of Defence Staff: Lt-Gen. OLADIPO DIYA.

Chief of Army Staff: Brig.-Gen. ALWALI J. KAZIR.

Chief of Naval Staff: Cdre MIKE AHIGBE.

Chief of Air Staff: Air Vice-Marshal JOHN FEMI.

Education

Education is partly the responsibility of the state governments, although the federal government has played an increasingly important role since 1970. Primary education begins at six years of age and last for six years. Secondary education begins at 12 years of age and lasts for a further six years, comprising two three-year cycles. Education to junior secondary level (from six to 15 years of age) is free and compulsory. In 1991 total enrolment at primary schools was equivalent to 71% of children in the relevant age-group (79% of boys; 62% of girls), while the comparable ratio for secondary enrolment was only 20% (24% of boys; 17% of girls). In that year there were 13,776,854 pupils in primary schools and 3,123,277 in secondary schools. In 1994 Nigeria had 38 universities. Education was allocated ₦1,126.6m., or 4.1% of total expenditure, in the 1990 federal budget. According to UNESCO estimates, the rate of adult illiteracy in 1990 averaged 49.3% (males 37.7%; females 60.5%).

Bibliography

Adamokekun, L. *The Fall of the Second Republic.* Ibadan, Spectrum Books, 1985.

Afonja, S., and Pearce, T. O. (Eds). *Social Change in Nigeria.* London, Longman, 1986.

Ajayi, J. F. Ade., Ikoku, S. G., and Ikara, B. (Eds). *Evolution of Political Culture in Nigeria.* Kaduna State Council for Arts and Culture, and the University Press, 1985.

Ake, C. (Ed.). *Political Economy of Nigeria.* London and Lagos, Longman, 1985.

Akpan, N. U. *The Struggle for Secession 1966–1970.* London, Frank Cass, 1972.

Asiegbu, J. U. J. *Nigeria and its British Invaders 1851–1920.* Lagos, Nok Publishers International, 1984.

Ayeni, V., and Soremekun, K. (Eds). *Nigeria's Second Republic.* Lagos, Daily Times Publications, 1988.

Babatope, E. *Murtala Muhammed: A Leader Betrayed.* Enugu, Roy and Ezete Publishing Co, 1986.

Bach, D. C. *Le Nigéria contemporain.* Paris, Editions CNRS, 1986.

Nigeria, un pouvoir en puissance. Paris, Editions Karthala, 1989.

Bach, D. C., Egg, J., and Philippe, J. *Nigéria, un pouvoir en puissance.* Paris, Karthala, 1988.

Barbour, K. M. *Nigeria in Maps.* London, Hodder and Stoughton, 1982.

Bienen, H. *Political Conflict and Economic Change in Nigeria.* London, Frank Cass, 1985.

Clarke, P. B. *West Africans at War 1914–18, 1939–45: Colonial Propaganda and its Cultural Aftermath.* London, Ethnographica, 1986.

Cohen, R. *Labour and Politics in Nigeria.* London, Heinemann Educational, 1982.

Crowder, M. *The Story of Nigeria.* 4th Edn, London, 1978.

Cruise O'Brien, D. B., Dunn, J., and Rathbone, R. (Eds). *Contemporary West African States.* Cambridge University Press, 1989.

De Lancey, M., and Normandy, E. (Eds). *Nigeria: A Bibliography of Politics, Government, Administration and International Relations.* Los Angeles, University of California (Crossroads Press), 1984.

Ekundare, R. O. *An Economic History of Nigeria 1860–1960.* London, Methuen, 1973.

Ekwe-Ekwe, H. *Conflict and Intervention in Africa: Nigeria, Angola and Zaire.* London, Macmillan, 1990.

Essien, E. *Nigeria Under Structural Adjustment.* Fountain Publications (Nigeria) Ltd, 1990.

Falola, T., and Thonvbere, J. *The Rise and Fall of Nigeria's Second Republic 1979–84.* London, Zed Press, 1985.

Nigeria and the International Capitalist System. Denver, CO, University of Denver, 1988.

Graf, W. D. *The Nigerian State: Political Economy, State, Class and Political System in the Post-Colonial Era.* London, James Currey, 1988.

Hayward, M. F. *Elections in Independent Africa.* Boulder, CO, Westview Press, 1987.

Idang, G. J. *Nigeria: Internal Politics and Foreign Policy: 1960–66.* Ibadan University Press, 1974.

Ikoku, S. G. *Nigeria's Fourth Coup d'Etat.* Enugu, Fourth Dimension, 1985.

Kirk-Greene, A. H. M. *Crisis and Conflict in Nigeria: A Documentary Sourcebook 1966–1970.* 2 vols. London, Oxford University Press, 1971.

Kirk-Greene, A. H. M., and Rimmer, D. *Nigeria Since 1970: A Political and Economic Outline.* London, Hodder and Stoughton, 1981.

Morgan, W. T. W. *Nigeria.* London, Longman, 1983.

Muhammadu, T. *The Nigerian Constitution, 1979: Framework for Democracy.* Enugu, Fourth Dimension, 1982.

Nwabueze, B. O. *Nigeria's Presidential Constitution 1979–83: The Second Experiment in Constitutional Democracy.* London, Longman, 1985.

Obasanjo, O. *My Command: An Account of the Nigerian Civil War 1967–1970.* London, Heinemann, 1981.

Obichere, B. (Ed.). *Studies in Southern Nigerian History.* London, Frank Cass, 1980.

Odole, Chief M. A. F. *Ife: The Genesis of the Yoruba Race.* Ijeka, John West, 1986.

Okadigbo, C. *Power and Leadership in Nigeria.* Enugu, Fourth Dimension, 1988.

Olashore, O. *Challenges of Nigeria's Economic Reforms.* Fountain Publications (Nigeria) Ltd, 1991.

Olowu, D. *Constitutionalism and Development in Nigeria: Lagos State Governance, Society and Economy.* Lagos, Malthouse Press, 1990.

Olurode, L. *A Political Economy of Nigeria's 1983 Elections.* Lagos, John West, 1991.

Olusanya, G. O., Ate, B. E., and Olukoshi, A. (Eds). *Economic Development and Foreign Policy in Nigeria.* Lagos, NIIA Press, 1990.

Onyemelukwe, J. O. C., and Filani, M. O. *Economic Geography of West Africa.* London, Lagos, New York, Longman, 1983.

Oremade, T. *Petroleum Operations in Nigeria.* Lagos, West African Book Publishers, 1986.

Oyediran, O. *Essays on Local Government and Administration in Nigeria.* Surulere, Projects Publications, 1988.

Oyeleye, O. (Ed.). *Nigerian Government and Politics under Military Rule.* Lagos, Friends Foundation Publishers, 1988.

Peel, J. D. Y. *Ijeshas and Nigerians: The Incorporation of a Yoruba Kingdom.* Cambridge University Press, 1983.

Post, K. W. J., and Vickers, M. *Structure and Conflict in Nigeria 1960–65.* London, Heinemann, 1973.

Reyment, R. A. *Aspects of the Geology of Nigeria.* Ibadan, 1965.

Rimmer, D. *The Economies of West Africa.* London, Weidenfeld and Nicolson, 1984.

Salamone, F. A. *The Hausa People: A Bibliography.* 2 vols. New Haven, CT, HRA Flex Books, 1985.

Shenton, R. *The Development of Capitalism in Northern Nigeria.* London, James Currey, 1986.

Sklar, R. L. *Nigerian Political Parties: Power in an Emergent African Nation.* New York and Lagos, Nok Publishers, 1983 (reissue).

Smith, R. S. *Kingdoms of the Yoruba.* 3rd Edn, London, James Currey, 1988.

Stevens, C. A. *The Political Economy of Nigeria.* London, Economist Books, 1984.

Synge, R. *Energy in Nigeria.* London, MEED, 1986.

RÉUNION

Physical and Social Geography

Réunion is a volcanic island in the Indian Ocean lying at the southern extremity of the Mascarene Plateau. Mauritius lies some 190 km to the north-east and Madagascar about 650 km to the west. The island is roughly oval in shape, being about 65 km long and up to 50 km wide; the total area is 2,512 sq km (970 sq miles). Volcanoes have developed along a north-west to south-east angled fault; Pitan de la Fournaise (2,624 m) most recently erupted in 1991. The others are now extinct, although their cones rise to 3,000 m and dominate the island. The heights and the frequent summer cyclones help to create abundant rainfall, which averages 4,714 mm annually in the uplands, and 686 mm at sea-level. Temperatures vary greatly according to altitude, being tropical at sea-level, averaging between 20°C (68°F) and 28°C (82°F), but much cooler in the uplands, with average temperatures between 8°C (46°F) and 19°C (66°F), owing to frequent winter frosts.

The population of Réunion has more than doubled since the 1940s, reaching 515,798 at the March 1982 census. During 1980–90 the population increased at an average rate of 1.9% per year. At the March 1990 census the population was enumerated at 597,828, giving a population density approaching 238 inhabitants per sq km. More than 47% of Réunion's population were under 20 years of age in the early 1980s, and the proportion aged between 20 and 60 years increased from 41% of the total in 1961 to 46% in 1982. The capital is Saint-Denis, with 121,952 inhabitants at the 1990 census. Other major towns include Saint-Paul with 71,608 inhabitants, and Saint-Pierre and Le Tampon, with 58,832 and 47,750 inhabitants, respectively, in 1990. The population is of mixed origin, including people of European, African, Indian and Chinese descent.

Recent History

Revised for this edition by the Editor

Réunion (formerly known as Bourbon) was first occupied by France in 1642, and was governed as a colony until 1946, when it received full departmental status. In 1974 it became an overseas department with the status of a region. Réunion administers the small and uninhabited Indian Ocean islands of Bassas da India, Juan de Nova, Europa and the Iles Glorieuses, which are also claimed by Madagascar, and Tromelin, which is also claimed by both Madagascar and Mauritius. Since 1973 Réunion has been the headquarters of French military forces in the Indian Ocean.

In June 1978 the liberation committee of the Organization of African Unity (OAU) adopted a report recommending measures to hasten the independence of the island, and condemned its occupation by a 'colonial power'. However, this view seemed to have little popular support in Réunion. Although the left-wing political parties on the island advocated increased autonomy (amounting to virtual self-government), few people were in favour of complete independence.

In 1982 the French government proposed a decentralization scheme, envisaging the dissolution of the general and regional councils in the overseas departments and the creation in each department of a single assembly, to be elected on the basis of proportional representation. However, this plan received considerable opposition in Réunion and the other overseas departments, and the government was eventually forced to abandon the project. Revised legislation on decentralization in the overseas departments was approved by the French national assembly in December 1982. Elections for the new regional council were held in Réunion in February 1983, when left-wing candidates won 50.77% of the votes cast.

In the elections to the French national assembly, which took place in March 1986 under a system of proportional representation, the number of deputies from Réunion was increased from three to five. The Parti Communiste Réunionnais (PCR) won two seats, while the Union pour la Démocratie Française (UDF), the Rassemblement pour la République (RPR) and a newly-formed right-wing party, France-Réunion-Avenir (FRA), each secured one seat. In the concurrent elections to the regional council, the centre-right RPR-UDF alliance and FRA together received 54.1% of the votes cast, winning 18 and eight of the 45 seats respectively, while the PCR won 13 seats. The leader of the FRA, Pierre Lagourgue, was elected president of the regional council.

In September 1986 the French government's plan to introduce a programme of economic reforms provoked criticism from the left-wing parties, which claimed that the proposals should grant the overseas departments social equality with metropolitan France through similar levels of taxation and benefits. In October Paul Vergès, the PCR secretary-general and a deputy to the French national assembly, accused France of instituting 'social apartheid' in the overseas departments, and appealed to the European parliament in Strasbourg. In October 1987 Vergès and the other PCR deputy, Elie Hoarau, resigned from the national assembly, in protest against the government's proposals, and Laurent Vergès, Paul Vergès's son, and Claude Hoarau, the PCR mayor of Saint-Louis, assumed the vacated seats.

In the second round of the French presidential election, which took place on 8 May 1988, François Mitterrand, the incumbent president and PS candidate, received 60.3% of the votes cast in Réunion, whereas Jacques Chirac, the RPR prime minister, obtained only 39.7%. Mitterrand won an absolute majority of votes in all five electoral districts in Réunion, including the RPR stronghold of Saint-Denis, owing partly to the transfer of votes from supporters of the PCR and the centre-right parties. Following his re-election, Mitterrand called a general election for the French national assembly in June, when the system of single-member constituencies was reintroduced. As in the previous general election, the PCR won two of the Réunion seats, while the UDF, the RPR (these two parties allying to form the Union du Rassemblement du Centre—URC) and the FRA each won one seat. The RPR and FRA deputies subsequently became independents, although they maintained strong links with the island's right-wing groups. Relations between the PCR and the PS later deteriorated, following mutual recriminations concerning their failure to co-operate in the general election. In July the PCR criticized the socialist government for continuing to allocate lower levels of benefits and revenue to the overseas departments, despite President Mitterrand's pledge, made during his visit to Réunion in February, to grant these departments social parity with metropolitan France.

In the elections for the newly-enlarged 44-member general council in September and October 1988, the PCR and the PS won nine and four seats respectively, while other left-wing candidates won two seats. The UDF secured six seats and other right-wing candidates 19, but the RPR, which had previously held 11 seats, won only four. Later in October, Eric Boyer, a right-wing independent, was elected to succeed Legros as president of the general council. In the same month, the PCR deputy, Laurent Vergès, was killed in a road accident, and his seat was taken by Alexis Pota, also of the PCR.

The results of the municipal elections in March 1989 represented a slight decline in support for the left-wing parties. Nevertheless, for the first time since the 1940s, a PS candidate, Gilbert Annette, became mayor of Saint-Denis, replacing Legros. At Saint-Pierre the incumbent mayor and PCR deputy to the French national assembly, Elie Hoarau, unilaterally declared himself the winner, discounting 1,500 votes which had been secured by two minor lists. The result was therefore declared invalid by the administrative tribunal. This incident led to a rift between the PS and the PCR, and, when a fresh election in that municipality was held in September, Elie Hoarau was unable to form an alliance. Hoarau was, however, re-elected mayor, securing just over 50% of the votes cast.

In September 1990, following the restructuring of the RPR under the new local leadership of Alain Defaud, a number of right-wing movements, including the UDF and the RPR, announced the creation of an informal alliance, known as Union pour la France (UPF), to contest the regional elections in 1992. During a visit to Réunion in November the French minister for overseas departments and territories, Louis Le Pensec, announced a series of proposed economic and social measures, in accordance with pledges made by Mitterrand in 1988 regarding the promotion of economic development and social equality between the overseas departments and metropolitan France. However, these measures were criticized as insufficient by right-wing groups and by the PCR. Following a meeting in Paris between Le Pensec and an elected delegation from Réunion, the formulation of a 'solidarity pact' of 60 proposed social and economic changes was announced in April 1991 (see Economy).

In March 1990 violent protests took place in support of an unauthorized television service, Télé Free-DOM, following a decision by the French national broadcasting commission, the Conseil supérieur de l'audiovisuel (CSA), to award a broadcasting permit to a rival company. In February 1991 the seizure by the CSA of Télé Free-DOM's broadcasting transmitters prompted further violent demonstrations in Saint-Denis. Some 11 people were killed in ensuing riots, and the French government dispatched police reinforcements to restore order. Le Pensec, who subsequently visited Réunion, ascribed the violence to widespread discontent with the island's social and economic conditions. A parliamentary commission was subsequently established to investigate the cause of the riots.

A visit to Réunion in March 1991 by the French prime minister, Michel Rocard, precipitated further rioting. In the same month the commission of enquiry attributed the riots in February to the inflammatory nature of television programmes, which had been broadcast by Télé Free-DOM in the weeks preceding the disturbances, and blamed the station's director, Dr Camille Sudre, who was also a deputy mayor of Saint-Denis. However, the commission refuted allegations by right-wing and centrist politicians that the PCR had orchestrated the violence. Later in March President Mitterrand expressed concern over the outcome of the enquiry, and appealed to the CSA to reconsider its policy towards Télé Free-DOM. In April, however, the CSA, which intended to award a franchise for another private television station, indicated its continued opposition to Télé Free-DOM. In October Sudre claimed that the refusal by a tribunal to order the return of the broadcasting transmitters would jeopardize Télé Free-DOM's opportunity to obtain a franchise, and announced that he would contest the decision.

In March 1992 the mayor of Saint-Denis, Gilbert Annette, expelled Sudre, who was one of the deputy mayors, from the majority coalition in the municipal council, after Sudre presented a list of independent candidates to contest regional elections later that month. In the elections to the regional council, which took place on 22 March, Sudre's list of candidates secured 17 seats, while the UPF obtained 14 seats, the PCR nine seats and the PS five seats. In concurrent elections to the general council (which was enlarged to 47 seats), right-wing candidates secured 29 seats, maintaining a substantial majority, although the number of PCR deputies increased to 12, and the number of PS deputies to six; Boyer retained the presidency of the council. Shortly after the elections, Sudre's independent candidates (known as Free-DOM) formed an alliance with the PCR, whereby members of the two groups held a majority of 26 of the 45 seats in the regional council. Under the terms of the agreement, Sudre was to assume the presidency of the regional council, and Paul Vergès the first vice-presidency. On 27 March, with the support of the PCR, Sudre was elected as president of the regional council by a majority of 27 votes. The UPF and the PS rejected Sudre's subsequent offer to join the Free-DOM–PCR coalition. The PS subsequently appealed against the results of the regional elections, on the grounds that, in contravention of regulations, Sudre's privately-owned radio station, Radio Free-DOM, had campaigned on his behalf prior to the elections.

Following his election as president of the regional council, Sudre announced that Télé Free-DOM was shortly to resume broadcasting. However, the CSA maintained that if transmissions were resumed Télé Free-DOM would be considered to be illegal, and would be subject to judicial proceedings. Jean-Paul Virapouillé, a deputy to the French national assembly, subsequently proposed the adoption of legislation which would legalize Télé Free-DOM and would provide for the establishment of an independent media sector outside the jurisdiction of the CSA. In April 1992 Télé Free-DOM transmitters were returned, and at the end of May broadcasting was resumed (without the permission of the CSA).

In June 1992 Sudre, Vergès and the former president of the regional council, Pierre Lagourgue, met President Mitterrand to submit proposals for economic reforms, which would establish greater parity between the island and metropolitan France. In early July, however, the French government announced increases in supplementary income, which were substantially less than had been expected, prompting widespread discontent on the island.

In September 1992 the French government agreed to an economic programme that had been formulated by the regional council. In the same month the PCR advocated a boycott of the French referendum on the ratification of the Treaty on European Union, which was to be conducted later that month, in protest at the alleged failure of the French government to recognize the needs of the overseas departments. At the referendum only 26.25% of the registered electorate voted, of whom 74.3% approved the ratification of the treaty. Later that month Boyer and Lagourgue were elected as representatives to the French senate. (The RPR candidate, Paul Moreau, retained his seat.) In October an investigation into allegations that leading politicians had misappropriated funds and obtained contracts by fraudulent means was initiated. In December increasing discontent with deteriorating economic conditions on the island prompted renewed violent rioting at Saint-Denis and at the town of Le Port.

In March 1993 Sudre announced that he was to contest Virapouillé's seat on behalf of the Free-DOM–PCR alliance in the forthcoming elections to the French national assembly. (However, a number of members of the PCR objected to the arrangement for a joint candidacy.) At the elections, which took place in late March, Sudre was defeated by Virapouillé in the second round of voting, while another incumbent right-wing deputy, André Thien Ah Koon, who contested the elections on behalf of the UPF, also retained his seat. The number of PCR deputies in the assembly was reduced from two to one (Vergès), while the PS and RPR each secured one of the remaining seats.

In May 1993 the results of the regional elections in March 1992 were annulled, and Sudre was prohibited from engaging in political activity for a year, on the grounds that programmes broadcast by Radio Free-DOM prior to the elections constituted political propaganda. Sudre subsequently selected his wife, Marguerite, to assume his candidacy in fresh elections to the regional council. In the elections, which took place on 20 June, the Free-DOM list of candidates, headed by Marguerite Sudre, secured 13 seats, while the UPF obtained 17, the PCR nine and the PS six seats. Marguerite Sudre was subsequently elected as president of the regional council, with the support of the nine PCR deputies and three dissident members of the PS, by a majority of 25 votes.

In April 1993 several prominent businessmen were arrested in connection with the acquisition of contracts by fraudulent means, while a number of members of the principal political organizations, including Boyer and Pierre Vergès, the mayor of Le Port and a member of the PCR, were also implicated in malpractice. Both Boyer and Vergès subsequently fled, following investigations into their activities, and warrants were issued for their arrest. In August Boyer, who had surrendered to the security forces, was placed in detention, pending his trial on charges of corruption. (Joseph Sinimalé, a member of the RPR, temporarily assumed the office of president of the general council). In the same month the mayor of Saint-Paul and vice-president of the general council, Cassam Moussa, was also arrested and charged with corruption.

In January 1994 a deputy mayor of Saint-Denis, who was also the local treasurer of the PS, was arrested on charges of corruption: it was alleged that enterprises had obtained contracts from the Saint-Denis municipality in exchange for a share in profits (which was apparently used, in part, to finance PS activities on the island). In February a further two municipal councillors from Saint-Denis were arrested on suspicion of involvement in the affair. In the same month a French citizen (who was believed to have connections with members of the Djibouti government) was arrested on Réunion in connection with transferring the funds that were alleged to have been illegally obtained by the Saint-Denis municipality to enterprises in Djibouti. In March Annette, who was implicated in the affair, resigned as mayor of Saint-Denis, and was subsequently charged with corruption. (Another member of the PS, Michael Tamaya, was to act as mayor, pending municipal elections in 1995). Later that month Boyer was sentenced to four years' imprisonment while Moussa received a term of two years. In the same month Vergès (who remained in hiding) resigned as mayor of Le Port.

At elections to the general council, which took place in late March 1994, the PCR retained 12 seats, while the number of PS deputies increased to 12 (despite adverse publicity attached to associates of Annette within the PS). The number of seats held by the RPR and UDF, which had contested the elections separately in a number of constituencies, declined to five and 11 respectively (compared with six and 14 in the incumbent council). The RPR and UDF subsequently attempted to negotiate an alliance with the PCR; despite long-standing inter-party dissension, however, the PCR and PS established a coalition within the general council, thereby securing a majority of 24 of the 47 seats. On 4 April a member of the PS, Christophe Payet was elected president of the general council by a majority of 26 votes, defeating Sinimalé; the right-wing parties (which had held the presidency of the council for more than 40 years) boycotted the poll. The PS and PCR signed an agreement, whereby they were to control the administration of the general council jointly, and indicated that centrist deputies might be allowed to enter the alliance. In July Boyer was released on bail, pending an appeal against his sentence.

In January 1986 France was admitted to the Indian Ocean Commission (IOC), owing to its sovereignty over Réunion. Réunion was given the right to host ministerial meetings of the IOC, but would not be allowed to occupy the presidency, owing to its status as a non-sovereign state.

Economy

Revised for this edition by the Editor

As a result of its connection with France, Réunion's economy is relatively developed, especially in comparison with its sub-Saharan African neighbours. Réunion's gross national product (GNP) per head in 1991 was estimated at 40,000 French francs. During 1989–90, it was estimated, GNP increased at an average annual rate of 4%. In 1985–92, according to World Bank estimates, Réunion's population increased at an average rate of 1.5% per year. The population density remained very high, at almost 238 inhabitants per sq km in 1990. In 1992 Réunion's gross domestic product (GDP) per caput was estimated at 52,811 French francs. Between 1973–86, it was estimated, GDP increased, in real terms, at an average rate of only 1.0% per year.

The economy has traditionally been based on agriculture, which engaged an estimated 10.6% of the employed labour force in 1992, and contributed 6.8% of GDP in 1988. Sugar cane is the principal crop and has formed the basis of the economy for over a century. In 1992 sugar accounted for 68.1% of export earnings. Only 26% of the land area can be cultivated because of the volcanic nature of the soil, but over 70% of the arable land is used for sugar plantations. The cane is grown on nearly all the good cultivable land up to 800 m above sea-level on the leeward side of the island, except in the relatively dry north-west, and up to 500 m on the windward side. Although the volcanic soil is fertile, the quality and yield are not as high as in Mauritius, and the modernization of agricultural practices is hindered in part by archaic restrictions on land tenure. Sugar cane harvests entered a decline in the early 1970s, owing to drought, ageing plants, rising production costs and inefficient harvesting techniques and transport systems. In 1974 a modernization plan was put into effect, and by 1976 production had begun to reflect both higher yields and an increase in the land used for sugar cultivation. By 1981, when the plan ended, average annual production of raw sugar had risen to 247,000 tons, despite several tropical storms. Annual production fluctuated between 224,000–258,000 tons annually until 1987, when output fell to less than 226,000 tons, owing to severe damage to the cane crop, resulting from a cyclone in February 1987. In 1986 state aid of 45 French francs per ton of sugar was given directly to farmers for the first time and in 1987 this subsidy was increased to 48 French francs per ton. In 1989 sugar production declined to 170,965 tons, compared with 252,230 in 1988 (as a result of damage caused by a further cyclone), but increased to 192,000 tons in 1990, to 214,500 in 1991, and to 226,700 in 1992. In April 1991, following public demonstrations by the cane planters, the government agreed to pay compensation for losses incurred as a result of the natural disasters. The government also provided assistance with outstanding debts and renewed price guarantee arrangements for sugar cane.

Geraniums, vetiver and ylang-ylang are grown for the production of aromatic essences. Exporters of oil of geranium and vetiver have experienced difficulty in competing with new producers whose prices are much lower. In 1985 measures were introduced to increase the output of oil of geranium; output had increased to 25.4 tons by 1991, but declined to 14.7 tons in 1992. Output of vetiver totalled 12.1 tons in 1987, but subsequently declined to 1.9 tons in 1992, and is expected to become insignificant as an export crop. Vanilla is produced for export in the south-east; production totalled 132.8 tons in 1987, but declined to 54.4 tons in 1988, and to 31.2 tons in 1990; however, output increased to 70.4 tons in 1991, and to 93.2 tons in 1992. Tobacco cultivation (introduced at the beginning of the century) produced a crop of 192.8 tons in 1988. Unfavourable climatic conditions intervened in the 1989/90 crop year, however, and the sector was further adversely affected by cyclone damage, which destroyed 115 of the island's 400 tobacco drying sheds; production declined sharply, to 107.8 tons in 1990, to 73.3 tons in 1991, and to 22 tons in 1992. A variety of vegetables and fruits is grown, and the island is self-sufficient in cattle and pigs. Overall, however, substantial food imports are necessary to supply the dense population.

Although fish are not abundant off Réunion's coast, the commercial fishing industry is an important source of income and employment, especially in the deep-sea sector. The largest fishing vessels make voyages lasting several months, to catch spiny lobsters (langoustes) that breed in the cold waters near Antarctica. Other commercial fishing activities have increased in recent years, although total landings declined from 2,787 tons in 1982 to 1,554 tons in 1987. A recovery, to 1,931 tons (including 348 tons of crustaceans), was achieved in 1988. In an attempt to preserve resources of langoustes, the fishing quota for 1989 was reduced, and the total catch declined to 1,725 tons, increasing slightly to 1,731 tons in 1990. The total catch increased substantially, to 2,281 tons, in 1991, and to 2,495 tons in 1992 (of which langoustes contributed 394 tons).

Industry (including mining, manufacturing, construction and power) contributed 19.8% of GDP in 1988, and employed an estimated 23.1% of the working population in 1987. The principal branch of manufacturing is food-processing, particularly the production of sugar and rum. Other significant sectors include the fabrication of construction materials, mechanics, printing, metalwork, textiles and garments, and electronics. In January 1989 there were a total of 958 industrial enterprises in Réunion, 89.6% of which employed fewer than 20 salaried staff; by January 1993 the number of industrial enterprises had increased to 1,925.

No mineral resources have been identified on Réunion. Imports of petroleum products accounted for 5.0% of the value of total imports in 1992. Energy is derived principally from thermal and hydroelectric power, which constituted 54.6% and 45.4%, respectively, of total electricity production (1,090.4m. kWh) in 1992.

In 1992 the principal source of imports was France (69.5%), which was also the principal market for exports (76.4%). Other major trading partners included the USA, Bahrain, South Africa, Japan, the Comoros and Madagascar. In that year the principal imports were foodstuffs, especially rice, meat and dairy produce, and motor vehicles and railway equipment, chemicals, petroleum products and metal products. Principal exports included sugar, rum and essential oils. There is a substantial trade deficit, which is partly financed by aid from France and receipts from expatriates; exports in the 1980s covered, on average, only about 10% of the cost of imports. In 1990 Réunion recorded a trade deficit of 10,322.5m. French francs, which increased to 11,203.4m. French francs in 1991, and to 11,576.7m. French francs in 1992.

The development of tourism is actively promoted, and it is hoped that increased investment in this sector will lead to higher receipts and will help to reduce the trade deficit, as well as providing new jobs. In 1988 Réunion received aid from the European Community (EC) to stimulate the sector. Tourist arrivals increased by 19% in 1989, and by 10.2% in 1990. In 1991 186,000 tourists visited Réunion (a decline of 7.1%, compared with 1990), and revenue from tourism fell to 700m. French francs. However, tourist arrivals increased by 14.4%, to 217,200, in 1992, and by a further 10.2%, to 242,000, in 1993, when revenue from tourism reached nearly 1,000m. French francs; of the total number of visitors in 1993, 75% were from France, 11% from Mauritius, and 5% from Madagascar. Nevertheless, the tourism sector contributed only 3%-4% of GDP in 1993.

The close connection with France protects the island from the dangers inherent in the narrowness of its economic base. Nevertheless, unemployment and inflation, compounded after 1974 by a number of bankruptcies among small sugar planters, have been the cause of major social and economic problems. The rise in the cost of imported fertilizers and of labour has exceeded the rise in the price of sugar. The annual rate of inflation averaged 6.8% in 1980–88. Consumer prices increased by 3.9% in 1990, and by 4.1% in 1991; the rate declined slightly, to 3.0%, in 1992. The 1982 census recorded 54,338 people, or 31.4% of the labour force, as unemployed; by 1994 an estimated 37.9% of the labour force were unemployed. In 1992 an estimated budgetary deficit of 7,260.1m. French francs was recorded. Since 1980 the government has invested significant sums in a series of public works projects in an effort to create jobs and to alleviate the high level of seasonal unemployment following the sugar cane harvest. However, large numbers of workers emigrate in search of employment each year, principally to France. In 1986 Réunion benefited from French legislation reducing employers' payments to young persons' social security contributions, which encouraged youth employment.

The French government has increased its infrastructural spending in Réunion, particularly on improvements to health services, housing, electricity supply and communication facilities for low-income families. In 1979 an estimated 75% of the population received welfare payments from France, and direct subsidies averaged 25% higher per recipient in Réunion than in metropolitan France. In October 1986 the French government introduced a programme of reforms to enhance the island's economic status by 1991. The programme included the abolition of tax liability on investments in all sectors for an initial period of 10 years. Under the Integrated Development Operation (OID) for the French overseas departments, initiated in 1979, Réunion was allocated 400m. French francs, over a five-year period to 1991, from various sources, including the French government and the EC, and from revenue generated by the implementation of the 1986 economic reform programme. During 1989–93 the EC also provided aid to assist Réunion to adapt to the requirements of the single European Market.

In December 1988 the French government announced that it would instigate a regional development programme in the overseas departments in 1989, to be financed partly by EC aid. In January 1989 legislation which established a guaranteed minimum income was introduced. In January 1990 a French government commission, appointed in 1989 to examine the economic condition of the overseas departments, published a report containing 58 proposals for the rectification of social and economic shortcomings, and recommended an improvements programme to be phased over two three-year stages. In November 1990 the French government announced measures aimed at establishing parity of the four overseas departments with metropolitan France in social and economic programmes. The reforms included the standardization by 1993 of family allowances, while from January 1992 minimum wage levels in Réunion were to be equalized with those operating in the other three overseas departments. It was envisaged that minimum wages in the overseas departments would be equal with those in metropolitan France by 1995, although this was to be achieved by way of trade union negotiations with employers rather than by government wage guarantees.

A 'solidarity pact', which was formalized in April 1991, comprised 60 proposals, including the establishment of a fund for local youth initiatives and of a professional training body to stimulate the recruitment of teachers from within the island. In the same month, representatives of the four overseas departments in the French national assembly and senate formed an interparliamentary group to safeguard and promote the agricultural economies of these territories. In July 1992, however, the French government announced an increase in minimum income of 3.3%, and in family allowance of 20%, (far less than required to establish parity with metropolitan France). In September the regional council adopted an economic development programme, known as the emergency plan, which provided for the creation of an export free zone (EFZ). Under the emergency plan, the French government would subsidize wages and some employer's contributions of companies operating within the EFZ. By 1993 levels of family allowance in the overseas departments had reached parity with those in force in metropolitan France, as envisaged. In early 1994, however, the French government indicated that it intended to give priority to the reduction of unemployment rather than the standardization of minimum wage levels, and announced a programme of economic and social development for the overseas departments, whereby approximately one-third of unemployed were to be involved in community projects, enterprises were to receive incentives to engage unemployed, and a number of economic sectors disadvantaged by international competition were to be exempted from certain taxes. In the same year the regional council drafted a five-year development plan, at a projected cost of 10,000m. French francs, of which 4,900m. French francs were to be financed by the European Union.

Statistical Survey

Source: Institut National de la Statistique et des Etudes Economiques, Service Régional de la Réunion, 15 Rue de l'Ecole, 97490 Sainte-Clotilde; tel. 29-51-57; fax 29-76-85.

AREA AND POPULATION

Area: 2,512 sq km (970 sq miles).

Population: 515,798 (males 252,997, females 262,801) at census of 9 March 1982; 597,828 (males 294,256, females 303,572) at census of 15 March 1990.

Principal Towns (population at census of 15 March 1990): Saint-Denis (capital) 121,952; Saint-Paul 71,608; Saint-Pierre 58,832; Le Tampon 47,570.

Births and Deaths (1992, provisional figures): Registered live births 14,239 (birth rate 22.8 per 1,000); Registered deaths (provisional) 3,314 (death rate 5.3 per 1,000). Figures exclude live-born infants dying before registration of birth.

Economically Active Population (1982 census): Employed 118,490 (males 77,270, females 41,220); Unemployed 54,338 (males 33,548, females 20,790). (1990 census): Employed 146,188 (males 90,522, females 55,666); Unemployed 86,118 (males 45,889, females 40,229).

AGRICULTURE, ETC.

Principal Agricultural Products (metric tons, 1992): Sugar cane 1,972,700, Raw sugar 226,700, Maize 15,700, Oil of geranium 14.7, Oil of vetiver root 1.9, Vanilla 93.2, Tobacco 22; Vegetables 69,270; Fruit 37,670.

Livestock (agricultural census, year ending August 1989): Cattle 18,601; Pigs 70,921; Goats 31,318; Chickens 1,348,000.

1992 (FAO estimates, '000 head, year ending September): Cattle 19; Pigs 89; Goats 31; Chickens 5,000. Source: FAO, *Production Yearbook*.

Forestry ('000 cubic metres): Roundwood removals: 37 in 1990; 36 in 1991; 36 in 1992 (FAO estimate). Source: FAO, *Yearbook of Forest Products*.

Fishing (metric tons, live weight): Total catch 1,731 in 1990; 2,281 in 1991; 2,495 in 1992.

FINANCE

Currency and Exchange Rates: 100 centimes = 1 French franc. *Sterling and Dollar Equivalents* (31 March 1994): £1 sterling = 8.4640 francs; US $1 = 5.7014 francs; 1,000 French francs = £118.15 = $175.40. *Average Exchange Rate* (French francs per US dollar): 5.642 in 1991; 5.294 in 1992; 5.663 in 1993.

Budget Estimate (million francs, 1992): Revenue (incl. loans) 4,718.1; Expenditure 11,978.2.

Cost of Living (Consumer Price Index for urban areas, average of monthly figures; base: 1980 = 100): 190.1 in 1991; 195.9 in 1992; 203.4 in 1993. Source: UN, *Monthly Bulletin of Statistics*.

Expenditure on the Gross Domestic Product (million francs at current prices, 1988): Government final consumption expenditure 6,581.3; Private final consumption expenditure 19,170.7; Increase in stocks 739.1; Gross fixed capital formation 6,617.9; *Total domestic expenditure* 33,848.1; Exports of goods and services 1,003.4; *Less* Imports of goods and services 10,251.9; *GDP in purchasers' values* 23,860.5. Source: UN, *National Accounts Statistics*.

Gross Domestic Product by Economic Activity (million francs at current prices, 1988): Agriculture, hunting, forestry and fishing 1,561.7; Mining and manufacturing 2,394.9; Electricity, gas and water 445.3; Construction 1,726.0; Trade, restaurants and hotels 4,241.3; Transport, storage and communications 1,307.0; Finance, insurance, real estate and business services 1,902.4; Other community, social and personal services 3,155.9; Other services 6,295.8; *Sub-total* 23,030.4; Import duties 940.8; Value-added tax 954.1; *Less* Imputed bank service charge 1,064.7; *Total* 23,860.5. Source: UN, *National Accounts Statistics*.

EXTERNAL TRADE

Principal Commodities (million francs): *Imports* (1992): Agricultural and food products 2,522.3, Motor vehicles and railway equipment 1,765, Chemical products 1,030, Petroleum products 637.2, Metal products 517, Total (incl. others) 12,676.2. *Exports* (1992): Sugar 748.4, Spiny lobsters 43.9, Rum 27.3, Essential oils 12.1; Total (incl. others) 1,099.5.

Principal Trading Partners (million francs): *Imports* (1992): France 8,810.0, USA 685.6, Bahrain 545.1, Japan 291.6, South Africa 278.9, EU countries (excl. France) 2,725.4; Total (incl. others) 12,676.2. *Exports* (1992): France 840.0, Japan 67.1, EU countries (excl. France) 85.8; Total (incl. others) 1,099.5.

TRANSPORT

Road Traffic (1 Jan. 1993): Motor vehicles in use 167,000.

Shipping (1992): Vessels entered 556; Freight unloaded 1,975,300 metric tons; Freight loaded 399,300 metric tons; Passenger arrivals 332 (1988); Passenger departures 79 (1988).

Civil Aviation (1992): Passenger arrivals 449,882; Passenger departures 447,877; Freight unloaded 12,027 metric tons; Freight loaded 3,577 metric tons.

TOURISM

Tourist Arrivals (by country of residence, 1992): France 157,000, Mauritius 26,600, Madagascar 11,100, EU countries (excl. France) 5,000; Total (incl. others) 217,200.

Tourist Receipts (1992): 830m. francs.

COMMUNICATIONS MEDIA

Radio receivers (1991): 148,000 in use. Source: UNESCO, *Statistical Yearbook*.

Television receivers (1 Jan. 1993): 116,181 in use.

Telephones (1993): 191,647 in use.

Book production (1985): 73 titles (41 books; 32 pamphlets).

Daily newspapers (1990): 3 (estimated average circulation 65,000 copies). Source: UNESCO, *Statistical Yearbook*.

Non-daily newspapers (1988, estimates): 4 (average circulation 20,000 copies). Source: UNESCO, *Statistical Yearbook*.

EDUCATION

Pre-primary (1993/94): Schools 168; teachers 1,336 (1986); pupils 43,737.

Primary (1993/94): Schools 349; teachers 3,917 (1986); pupils 72,513.

Secondary (1993/94): Schools 97; teachers 5,156 (1990/91); pupils 91,015.

University: Teaching staff 137 (1990/91); students 5,761 (1992/93). There is also a teacher training college, a technical institute and an agricultural college.

Directory

The Government

(September 1994)

Prefect: HUBERT FOURNIER.

President of the General Council: CHRISTOPHE PAYET.

President of the Economic and Social Committee: TONY MANGLOU.

Deputies to the French National Assembly: GILBERT ANNETTE (PS), PAUL VERGÈS (PCR), ANDRÉ-MAURICE PIHOUÉE (RPR), JEAN-PAUL VIRAPOULLÉ (UDF-CDS), ANDRÉ THIEN AH KOON (UPF).

Representatives to the French Senate: PAUL MOREAU (RPR), PIERRE LAGOURGUE (FRA).

REGIONAL COUNCIL

Palais Rontaunay, rue Rontaunay, 97488 Saint-Denis; tel. 20-13-12.

President: MARGUERITE SUDRE (Independent).

Election, 25 June 1993

Party	Seats
UPF	17
Free-DOM*	13
PCR	9
PS	6
Total	45

* List of independent candidates affiliated to Dr Camille Sudre.

Political Organizations

France-Réunion-Avenir (FRA): Saint-Denis; f. 1986; centre-right.

Front National (FN): Saint-Denis; f. 1972; extreme right-wing; Leader ALIX MOREL.

Mouvement des Radicaux de Gauche (MRG): Saint-Denis; f. 1977; advocates full independence and an economy separate from, but assisted by, France; Pres. JEAN-MARIE FINCK.

Mouvement pour l'Egalité, la Démocratie, le Développement et la Nature: affiliated to the PCR; advocates political unity; Leader RENÉ PAYET.

Mouvement pour l'Indépendance de la Réunion (MIR): f. 1981 to succeed the fmr Mouvement pour la Libération de la Réunion; grouping of parties favouring autonomy.

Parti Communiste Réunionnais (PCR): 21 bis rue d l'Est, 97400 Saint-Denis; f. 1959; Pres. PAUL VERGÈS; Sec.-Gen. ELIE HOARAU.

Parti Socialiste (PS)—Fédération de la Réunion: 85 rue d'Après, 97400 Saint-Denis; tel. 21-77-95; telex 916445; left-wing; Sec.-Gen. JEAN-CLAUDE FRUTEAU.

Rassemblement des Démocrates pour l'Avenir de la Réunion (RADAR): Saint-Denis; f. 1981; centrist.

Rassemblement des Socialistes et des Démocrates (RSD): Saint-Denis; Sec.-Gen. DANIEL CADET.

***Rassemblement pour la République (RPR):** 25 rue Labourdonnais, 97400 Saint-Denis; tel. 20-21-18; telex 916080; Gaullist; Sec. for Réunion ALAIN DEFAUD.

***Union pour la Démocratie Française (UDF):** Saint-Denis; f. 1978; centrist; Sec.-Gen. GILBERT GÉRARD.

* Contested 1992 regional and 1993 legislative elections as the Union pour la France.

Judicial System

Cour d'Appel: Palais de Justice, 166 rue Juliette Dodu, 97488 Saint-Denis; tel. 40-58-58; telex 916149; fax 21-95-32; Pres. ROBERT DUFOURGBURG.

There are two **Tribunaux de Grande Instance,** one **Cour d'Assises,** four **Tribunaux d'Instance**, two **Tribunaux pour Enfants** and two **Conseils de Prud'hommes**.

Religion

A substantial majority of the population are adherents of the Roman Catholic Church. There is a small Muslim community.

CHRISTIANITY

The Roman Catholic Church

Réunion comprises a single diocese, directly responsible to the Holy See. At 31 December 1992 there were an estimated 548,000 adherents, equivalent to about 90% of the population.

Bishop of Saint-Denis-de-La Réunion: Mgr GILBERT AUBRY, Evêché, 36 rue de Paris, BP 55, 97462 Saint-Denis; tel. 21-28-49; fax 41-77-15.

The Press

DAILIES

Journal de l'Ile de la Réunion: 42 rue Alexis de Villeneuve, BP 166, 97464 Saint-Denis Cédex; tel. 21-32-64; telex 916453; fax 41-09-77; f. 1956; Dir PHILIPPE BALOUKJY; circ. 26,000.

Quotidien de la Réunion: BP 303, 97712 Saint-Denis Cédex; tel. 29-10-10; telex 916183; fax 28-25-28; f. 1976; Dir MAXIMIN CHANE KI CHUNE; circ. 28,000.

Témoignages: 21 bis rue de l'Est, BP 192, 97465 Saint-Denis; f. 1944; organ of the Parti Communiste Réunionnais; Dir ELIE HOARAU; circ. 5,000.

PERIODICALS

Al-Islam: 40 rue M. A. Leblond, BP 437, 97459 Saint-Pierre; tel. 25-19-65; fax 35-58-23; publ. by the Centre Islamique de la Réunion; monthly; Dir SAÏD INGAR.

Cahiers de la Réunion et de l'Océan Indien: 24 blvd des Cocotiers, 97434 Saint-Gilles-les-Bains; monthly; Man. Dir CLAUDETTE SAINT-MARC.

L'Economie de la Réunion: c/o INSEE, 15 rue de l'Ecole, Le Chaudron, 97490 Sainte-Clotilde; tel. 29-51-57; fax 29-76-85; 6 a year; Dir JEAN-CLAUDE HAUTCOEUR; Editor-in-Chief COLETTE PAVAGEAU.

L'Eglise à la Réunion: 18 rue Montreuil, 97469 Saint-Denis; tel. 41-56-90; Dir P. FRANÇOIS GLÉNAC.

L'Enjeu: 1 rue de Paris, 97400 Saint-Denis; tel. 21-75-76; fax 41-60-62; Dir BLANDINE ETRAYEN; Editor-in-Chief JEAN-CLAUDE VALLÉE; circ. 4,000.

Le Journal de la Nature: 97489 Saint-Denis; tel. 29-45-45; fax 29-00-90; Dir J. Y. CONAN.

Le Memento Industriel et Commercial Réunionnais: 80 rue Pasteur, 97400 Saint-Denis; tel. 21-94-12; fax 41-10-85; Dir CATHERINE LOUAPRE POTTIER; circ. 10,000.

974 Ouest: Montgaillard, 97400 Saint-Denis; monthly; Dir DENISE ELMA.

La Réunion Agricole: Chambre d'Agriculture, 24 rue de la Source, BP 134, 97464 Saint-Denis Cédex; tel. 21-25-88; fax 41-17-84; f. 1967; monthly; Dir MARCEL BOLON; Chief Editor HERVÉ CAILLEAUX; circ. 8,000.

Télé 7 Jours Réunion: BP 405, 9469 Saint-Denis; weekly; Dir MICHEL MEKDOUD; circ. 25,000.

Témoignage Chrétien de la Réunion: 21 bis rue de l'Est, 97465 Saint-Denis; weekly; Dir RENÉ PAYET; circ. 2,000.

Visu: BP 3000, 97402 Saint-Denis; tel. 29-10-10; weekly; Editor-in-Chief J. J. AYAN; circ. 53,000.

Radio and Television

There were an estimated 148,000 radio receivers in use in 1991 and 116,181 television receivers in use at 1 January 1993. Since 1985 there has been a growth in the number of private local radio stations. In March 1990 the French national broadcasting commission granted 18m. francs to the television service Antenne Réunion to broadcast on the island. A complementary service, to be provided by Canal Réunion, was approved in July.

Antenne Réunion: Saint-Denis; broadcasts five hours daily; Dir CHRISTOPHE DUCASSE.

Canal Réunion: 2D ave de Lattre de Tassigny, 97490 Sainte-Clotilde; tel. 21-16-17; fax 21-46-61; subscription television channel; broadcasts a minimum of 12 hours daily; Chair. RÉMY PAGOT; Dir SERGE LAMAGNERE.

Radio Free-DOM: BP 666, 97474 Saint-Denis Cédex; tel. 41-51-51; telex 916174; fax 21-68-64; privately-owned radio station; Dir Dr CAMILLE SUDRE.

Société Nationale de Radio-Télévision Française d'Outre-Mer (RFO): 1 rue Jean Chatel, 97405 Saint-Denis Cédex; tel. 40-67-67; telex 916842; fax 21-64-84; home radio and television relay services in French; operates two television channels; Chair. FRANÇOIS GICQUEL; Dir JEAN-PHILIPPE ROUSSY.

Télé Free-DOM: BP 666, 97474 Saint-Denis Cédex; tel. 41-51-51; telex 916174; fax 21-68-64; f. 1986; privately-owned TV service, not licensed by the French nat. broadcasting comm.; transmitters confiscated in Feb. 1991; resumed broadcasting in May 1992; Dir Dr CAMILLE SUDRE.

TV Sud: Tampon; commenced broadcasting in Oct. 1993.

Other privately-owned television services include TVB, TVE, RTV, Télé-Réunion and TV-Run.

Finance

(cap. = capital; res = reserves; m. = million; dep. = deposits; brs = branches; amounts in French francs)

BANKING

Central Bank

Institut d'Emission des Départements d'Outre-Mer: 1 cité du Retiro, 75008 Paris, France; Office in Réunion: 4 rue de la Compagnie, 97487 Saint-Denis Cédex; tel. 21-18-96; telex 916176; fax 21-41-32; Dir YVES ESQUILAT.

Commercial Banks

Banque Française Commerciale Océan Indien (BFCOI): 60 rue Alexis de Villeneuve, BP 323, 97468 Saint-Denis Cédex; tel. 40-55-55; telex 916162; fax 40-54-55; Chair. PHILIPPE BRAULT; Dir PHILIPPE LAVIT D'HAUTEFORT; 8 brs.

Banque Nationale de Paris Intercontinentale: 67 rue Juliette Dodu, BP 113, 97463 Saint-Denis; tel. 40-30-30; telex 916133; fax 41-39-09; Chair. RENÉ THOMAS; Man. Dir JEAN-CLAUDE LALLEMANT; 13 brs.

Banque de la Réunion, SA: 27 rue Jean-Chatel, 97711 Saint-Denis Cédex; tel. 40-01-23; telex 916134; fax 40-00-61; f. 1849; affiliate of Crédit Lyonnais; cap. and res 312.5m., dep. 4,300.4m. (1992); Pres. XAVIER BESSON; Gen. Man. CLAUDE NOMBLOT; 15 brs.

Caisse Régionale de Crédit Agricole Mutuel de la Réunion: parc Jean de Cambiaire, cité des Lauriers, BP 84, 97462 Saint-Denis Cédex; tel. 40-81-81; telex 916139; fax 40-81-40; f. 1949; affiliate of Caisse Nationale de Crédit Agricole; Chair. CHRISTIAN DE LA GIRODAY; Dir HENRI PAVIE.

Development Bank

Banque Populaire Fédérale de Développement: 33 rue Victor MacAuliffe, 97400 Saint-Denis; tel. 21-18-11; telex 916582; Dir OLIVIER DEVISME; 3 brs.

INSURANCE

More than 20 major European insurance companies are represented in Saint-Denis.

Trade and Industry

CHAMBER OF COMMERCE AND INDUSTRY

Chambre de Commerce et d'Industrie de la Réunion: 5 bis rue de Paris, BP 120, 97463 Saint-Denis Cédex; tel. 21-53-66; telex 916278; fax 41-80-34; f. 1830; Pres. HILAIRE MAILLOT; Man. Dir JEAN-PIERRE FOURTOY.

PRINCIPAL DEVELOPMENT AGENCIES

Association pour le Développement Industriel de la Réunion: 18 rue Milius, BP 327, 97468 Saint-Denis Cédex; tel. 21-42-69; telex 916666; fax 20-37-57; f. 1975; 190 mems; Pres. PAUL MARTINEL.

Chambre d'Agriculture: 24 rue de la Source, BP 134, 97464 Saint-Denis Cédex; tel. 21-25-88; telex 916843; Pres. ANGÉLO LAURET.

Direction de l'Action Economique: Secrétariat Général pour les Affaires Economiques, ave de la Victoire, 97405 Saint-Denis; tel. 21-86-10; telex 916111.

Jeune Chambre Economique de Saint-Denis de la Réunion: 25 rue de Paris, BP 1151, 97483 Saint-Denis; f. 1963; 30 mems; Chair. JEAN-CHRISTOPHE DUVAL.

Société de Développement Economique de la Réunion—SODERE: 26 rue Labourdonnais, 97469 Saint-Denis; tel. 20-01-68; telex 916471; fax 20-05-07; f. 1964; Chair. PIERRE PEYRON; Man. Dir ALBERT TRIMAILLE.

PRINCIPAL INDUSTRIAL ORGANIZATIONS

Syndicat des Exportateurs d'Huiles Essentielles, Plantes Aromatiques et Medicinales de Bourbon: Saint-Denis; tel. 20-10-23; exports oil of geranium, vetiver and vanilla; Pres. RICO PLOENIÈRES.

Syndicat des Fabricants de Sucre de la Réunion: BP 57, 97462 Saint-Denis; tel. 20-23-24; telex 916138; fax 41-24-13; Chair. MAXIME RIVIÈRE.

Syndicat des Producteurs de Rhum de la Réunion: BP 57, 97462 Saint-Denis; tel. 20-23-24; telex 916138; fax 41-24-13; Chair. MAXIME RIVIÈRE.

Syndicat Patronal du Bâtiment de la Réunion: BP 108, 97463 Saint-Denis; tel. 21-03-81; telex 916393; fax 21-55-07; Pres. R. ROLAND; Sec.-Gen. C. OZOUX.

MAJOR INDUSTRIAL COMPANIES

Coopérative d'Achats des Détaillants Réunionnais (CADRE): Zone Industrielle Port Sud, rue de Bordeaux, 97420 Le Port; tel. 42-09-08; telex 916046; fax 42-17-15; Chair. GEORGES CHEUNG-LUNG.

Établissements Jules Caille: 31 rue Jean Chatel, BP 23, 97400 Saint-Denis; tel. 21-12-30; telex 916591; fax 21-63-77; f. 1919; agent for Peugeot motors; Chair. JACQUES CAILLE; Dir GASTON CAILLE.

Établissements Ravate: 131 rue Maréchal Leclerc, 97400 Saint-Denis; tel. 21-06-63; telex 916155; fax 41-26-63; trades in construction materials, wood, hardware; Chair. ISSOP RAVATE; Dir ADAM RAVATE.

Groupe Sucreries de Bourbon: 2 chemin Bois Rouge, BP 2, 97438 Saint-Marie; tel. 53-46-02; fax 53-06-33; holding co for nine subsidiaries; producing, refining and exporting sugar; Chair. JACQUES DE CHATEAUVIEUX.

Renault Réunion: 11 blvd du Chaudron, 97490 Sainte-Clotilde; tel. 29-54-62; retails motor vehicles and parts; Chair. REGIS PICOT; Man. M. COSTANTINI.

Société d'Exploitation des Magasins Score (SEMS): BP 733, 97475 Saint-Denis Cedex; tel. 28-25-33; telex 916148; fax 29-46-27; wholesale distributor to retail outlets; Chair. FRANCIS GOMBERT.

Société Réunionnaise de Produits Petroliers (SRPP): BP 2015, 97824 Le Port Cedex; tel. 42-07-11; telex 916156; fax 42-11-34; storage and retail of petroleum; Chair. ROBERT LAUROUA; Dir XAVIER CALLOT.

TRADE UNIONS

Confédération Générale du Travail de la Réunion (CGTR): Saint-Denis; Sec.-Gen. BRUNY PAYET.

Réunion also has its own sections of the major French trade union confederations, **Confédération Française Démocratique du Travail (CFDT), Force Ouvrière (FO), Confédération Française de l'Encadrement** and **Confédération Française des Travailleurs Chrétiens (CFTC).**

Transport

ROADS

A route nationale circles the island, generally following the coast and linking the main towns. Another route nationale crosses the island from south-west to north-east linking Saint-Pierre and Saint-Benoît. In 1982 there were 345.7 km of routes nationales, 731.5 km of departmental roads and 1,602.9 km of other roads.

SHIPPING

In 1986 work was completed on the expansion of the Port de la Pointe des Galets, which was divided into the former port in the west and a new port in the east (the port Ouest and the port Est). In 1991 a total of nearly 2.4m. tons of freight were loaded and discharged at the two ports.

Compagnie Générale Maritime (CGM): 2 rue de l'Est, BP 2007, 97822 Le Port Cédex; tel. 42-00-88; telex 916106; fax 43-23-04; agents for Mitsui OSK Lines, Safmarine and Unisaf; Dir RENAUD SAUVAGET.

Maritime Delmais-Vieljeux: BP 2006, 97822 Le Port Cédex; tel. 42-03-46; telex 916151; fax 43-72-06; Dir ARMAND BARUCH.

Réunion Maritime: f. 1991; consortium of 15 import cos; freight only.

Shipping Mediterranean Co: Le Port.

Société de Manutention et de Consignation Maritime (SOMACOM): BP 7, Le Port; agents for Scandinavian East Africa Line, Bank Line, Clan Line, Union Castle Mail Steamship Co and States Marine Lines.

Société Réunionnaise de Services Maritimes: 81 rue de St Paul, BP 2006, 97822 Le Port Cédex; tel. 42-03-46; telex 916170; fax 43-34-79; freight only; Man. DENIS LAURE.

CIVIL AVIATION

There is an international airport at Saint-Denis Gillot.

Air Austral: BP 611, 97473 Saint-Denis; tel. 28-22-60; telex 916236; fax 29-28-95; f. 1975; subsidiary of Air France; scheduled services to Madagascar and the Comoros; Gen. Man. Mme B. POPINEAU.

Air Outre-Mer: Saint-Denis; f. 1990; scheduled services to Paris; Chair. RENÉ MICAUD.

Tourism

Tourism is being extensively promoted. There is a 'holiday village' in Saint-Gilles, and in 1989 the island had 29 hotels with a total of 1,256 rooms. In 1993 a total of 242,000 tourists visited Réunion. Tourist revenue totalled about 1,000m. French francs in that year.

Comité du Tourisme de la Réunion: BP 1119, 97482 Saint-Denis Cédex; tel. 41-84-41; telex 916068; fax 20-25-93; Pres. IBRAHIM DINDAR.

Délégation Régionale au Commerce, à l'Artisanat et au Tourisme: Préfecture de la Réunion, 97400 Saint-Denis; tel. 40-77-58; telex 916111; fax 40-77-01; Dir JEAN-FRANÇOIS DESROCHES.

Office du Tourisme: 48 rue Saint-Marie, 97400 Saint-Denis; tel. 41-83-00; telex 916822; fax 21-37-76; Pres. PATRICK VERGUIN.

Defence

Réunion is the headquarters of French military forces in the Indian Ocean. In June 1993 there were 3,400 troops stationed on Réunion and Mayotte, the French Overseas Collectivité Territoriale in the Comoros archipelago.

Education

Education is modelled on the French system, and is compulsory for 10 years between the ages of six and 16 years. Primary education begins at six years of age and lasts for five years. Secondary education, which begins at 11 years of age, last for up to seven years, comprising a first cycle of four years and a second of three years. For the academic year 1993/94 there were 43,737 pupils enrolled at 168 pre-primary schools, 72,513 at 349 primary schools and 91,015 at 97 secondary schools (comprising 63 collèges and 34 lycées). There is a university, with several faculties, a teacher-training college, a technical institute and an agricultural college. In 1982 the illiteracy rate among the population over 15 years of age averaged 21.4% (males 23.5%; females 19.5%).

Bibliography

Bunge, F. M. (Ed.). *Indian Ocean: Five Island Countries.* Washington, DC, American University, 1983.

Cornu, H. *Paris et Bourbon, La politique française dans l'Océan indien.* Paris, Académie des Sciences d'Outre-mer, 1984.

Defos du Rau, J. *L'Ile de la Réunion. Étude de géographie humaine.* Institut de Géographie, Bordeaux, 1960.

Lavaux, C. *La Réunion: du battant des lames au sommet des montagnes.* Montligeon, 1975.

Lavergne, R., and Vera, R. *Etudes ethnobotaniques des plantes utilisées dans la pharmacopée de l'Ile de la Réunion.* Paris, Editions Karthala.

Leguen, M. *Histoire de l'Ile de la Réunion.* Paris, Editions l'Harmattan, 1979.

Leloutre, J.-C. *La Réunion, département français.* Paris, Maspero.

Leymarie, P. *Océan indien, nouveau coeur du monde.* Paris, Editions Karthala, 1983.

Marquardt, W. *Seychellen, Komoren und Maskarenen.* Munich, 1976.

Prudhomme, C. *Histoire religieuse de la Réunion.* Paris, Editions Karthala, 1984.

Scherer, A. *La Réunion.* Paris, Presses Universitaires de France, 1980.

Service Régional de la Réunion. *Panorama de l'economie de la Réunion 1983.* Saint-Denis, Institut National de la Statistique et des Etudes Economiques, 1984.

Références bibliographiques dans les domaines démographique, economique et social sur la Réunion. Saint-Denis, Institut National de la Statistique et des Etudes Economiques, 1984.

Liste d'addresses des etablissements commerciaux, industriels et artisanaux. Saint-Denis, Institut National de la Statistique et des Etudes Economiques, 1984.

Toussaint, A. *Histoire des Iles Mascareignes.* Paris, Berger-Levrault, 1972.

RWANDA

Physical and Social Geography

PIERRE GOUROU

The Rwandan Republic, like the Republic of Burundi, is distinctive among the independent states of black Africa both for the small size of its territory and for the density of its population. Covering an area of 26,338 sq km (10,169 sq miles), Rwanda had an estimated population of 7,164,994 at the 1991 census, with a density of 272 inhabitants per sq km. However, political and ethnic violence during 1994 was estimated to have resulted in the death or external displacement of one-seventh of the total population. Prior to these events, the population had been composed of Hutu (about 85%), Tutsi (about 14%) and Twa (1%). The official languages are French and Kinyarwanda, a Bantu language with close similarities to Kirundi, the language of neighbouring Burundi.

It seems, at first sight, strange that Rwanda has not been absorbed into a wider political entity. Admittedly, the Rwandan nation has long been united by language and custom and was part of a state that won the respect of the east African slave-traders. However, other ethnic groups, such as the Kongo, Luba, Luo and Zande, which were well established in small territorial areas, have not been able to develop into national states. That Rwanda has been able to achieve this is partly the result of developments during the colonial period. While part of German East Africa, Rwanda (or Ruanda-Urundi as it then was with Burundi) was treated as a peripheral territory of little economic interest. After the First World War it was entrusted to Belgium under a mandate from the League of Nations and, although administered jointly with the Belgian Congo, was not absorbed into the larger state. The historic separateness and national traditions of both Rwanda and Burundi have prevented their amalgamation, although since 1976 the two countries have participated, with Zaire, in the Economic Community of the Great Lakes Countries.

Although the land supports a high population density, physical conditions are not very favourable. Rwanda's land mass is very rugged and fragmented. Basically it is part of a Pre-Cambrian shelf from which, through erosion, the harder rocks have obtruded, leaving the softer ones submerged. Thus very ancient folds have been raised and a relief surface carved out with steep gradients covered with a soil poor in quality because of its fineness and fragility. Rwanda's physiognomy therefore consists of a series of sharply defined hills, with steep slopes and flat ridges, which are intersected by deep valleys, the bottoms of which are often formed by marshy plains. The north is dominated by the lofty and powerful chain of volcanoes, the Virunga, whose highest peak is Karisimbi (4,519 m) and whose lava, having scarcely cooled down, has not yet produced cultivable soil.

The climate is tropical, although tempered by altitude, with a daily temperature range of as much as 14°C. Kigali, the capital (117,749 inhabitants in 1978), has an average temperature of 19°C and 1,000 mm of rain. Altitude is a factor which modifies the temperature (and prevents sleeping sickness above about 900 m), but such a factor is of debatable value for agriculture. Average annual rainfall (785 mm) is only barely sufficient for agricultural purposes, but two wet and two relatively dry seasons are experienced, making two harvests possible.

Recent History

FILIP REYNTJENS

Revised for this edition by the Editor

HUTU ASCENDANCY

Unlike most African states, Rwanda and its southern neighbour Burundi were not an artificial creation of colonial rule. When they were absorbed by German East Africa in 1899, they had been established kingdoms for several centuries, belatedly forced to open their borders to foreign intrusion. In 1916, during the First World War, the area was occupied by Belgian forces. From 1920, Rwanda formed part of Ruanda-Urundi, administered by Belgium under a League of Nations mandate and later as a UN Trust Territory. Dissensions between the majority Hutu (traditionally comprising about 85% of the population) and their former overlords, the Tutsi (14%) led in 1959 to a rebellion and the proclamation of a state of emergency. In September 1961 it was decided by referendum to abolish the monarchy and to establish a republic. Internal autonomy was granted in 1961 and full independence followed on 1 July 1962. Serious tribal strife erupted in December 1963, and large-scale massacres (estimated at 20,000 deaths) were perpetrated by the Hutu against the Tutsi. During 1964–65 large numbers of displaced Rwandans were resettled in neighbouring countries. In 1969 Grégoire Kayibanda, the country's first president, was re-elected, and all 47 seats in the legislative assembly were retained by the governing party, the Mouvement démocratique républicain (MDR), also known as the Parti de l'émancipation du peuple Hutu (Parmehutu).

Tension between Hutu and Tutsi was rekindled in late 1972 and persisted until February 1973. In July the minister of defence and head of the national guard, Maj.-Gen. Juvénal Habyarimana, led a bloodless coup against president Kayibanda, proclaimed a second republic and established a military administration. In August a new council of ministers, with Habyarimana as president, was formed. The normal legislative processes were suspended, and all political activity was banned until July 1975, when a new ruling party, the Mouvement révolutionnaire national pour le développement (MRND), was formed. Its establishment was preceded by an extensive government reshuffle in which several military ministers were replaced by civilians. The first national congress of the MRND was held in January 1976.

A referendum in December 1978 approved a new constitution, aimed at returning the country to normal government in accordance with an undertaking by Habyarimana in 1973, to end the military regime within five years. An unsuccessful coup attempt took place in April 1980, and elections to the legislature, the Conseil national du développement (CND), were held in December 1981. In December 1983 Habyarimana was re-elected president. Elections to the CND in the same month were followed by a government reshuffle in January 1984. Habyarimana's regime brought to power a northern-based Hutu élite, among which serious rivalries had begun to develop by the mid-1980s, displacing Hutu-Tutsi strife as the prime focus of political competition. The president's home region, Gisenyi, which had gained ascendancy over the rival Ruhengeri region, itself became divided by traditional antagonisms.

From 1982, cross-border refugee problems began to affect Rwanda's relations with Uganda, which in 1980 had joined Rwanda, Burundi and Tanzania in a major regional plan to develop the water, power and mineral resources of the Kagera river basin. In October 1982 Rwanda closed its border with Uganda after an influx of 45,000 refugees, most of whom were Rwandan exiles fleeing Ugandan persecution. A further 32,000 refugees collected in camps on the Ugandan side of the border. In March 1983 Rwanda agreed to resettle more than 30,000 refugees, but Ugandan persecution of ethnic Rwandans continued, and in December 1983 thousands crossed into Tanzania. In November 1985 it was reported that 30,000 ethnic Rwandan refugees had been repatriated to Uganda. In 1986 the UN High Commissioner for Refugees (UNHCR) reported that there were about 110,000 registered Rwandan refugees living in Uganda, while an even greater number of refugees were believed to have settled in Uganda without registering with UNHCR. In July the central committee of the MRND issued a declaration that Rwanda would not allow the return of large numbers of refugees, since the country's economy was incapable of sustaining such an influx. In the same year President Museveni of Uganda announced that Rwandans who had been resident in Uganda for more than 10 years would automatically be entitled to Ugandan citizenship. In January 1987 a Ugandan government minister visited Rwanda for discussions concerning the problem of border security, and in February 1988 President Habyarimana visited Uganda for talks with President Museveni. A joint communiqué, issued on Habyarimana's return, confirmed that relations between the two countries had improved. A renewal of ethnic tensions in Burundi led to the flight, in August 1988, of an estimated 80,000 refugees, mainly Hutu, into Rwanda. With assistance from the international community, the Rwandan authorities were able to cater for their needs. By June 1989 all but approximately 1,000 of the refugees had been repatriated to Burundi. Regional refugee problems came once again to the fore in early 1992, when the presidents of Rwanda, Burundi and Zaire met in Zaire in an attempt to resolve border difficulties arising from the flight of Hutu refugees from Burundi into Rwanda and Zaire. The three presidents agreed to intensify border controls and to work together to facilitate the voluntary return of refugees to their country of origin. Further bilateral talks between Rwanda and Burundi, during 1992, sought to consolidate this agreement.

At a presidential election held in December 1988, Habyarimana, as sole candidate, secured 99.98% of the votes cast. Elections for the CND were held in the same month, and six new ministers were appointed in a government reshuffle in January 1989.

During 1989 economic conditions deteriorated sharply, as the combined effects of soil degradation, population pressure and crop disease resulted in reduced harvests and several hundred deaths from starvation. In addition, the collapse in world coffee prices, combined with a low output of poor-quality beans, led to serious balance-of-payments and budgetary problems. The introduction of an economic austerity programme in December 1989 added to public discontent.

In May 1990, the first report of a commission established in 1989 to examine the situation of Rwandan refugees urged the adoption of a more liberal approach on the part of the government, while indicating that emigré demands were unlikely to be satisfied. The subject was subsequently discussed at the third meeting of a joint Rwandan-Ugandan ministerial commission. In early July, Habyarimana conceded that political reform was needed and announced that a national commission would be appointed. The Commission nationale de synthèse (CNS) was duly established in September with a mandate to make recommendations for political renewal. However, these measures did little to alleviate the acute sense of political crisis.

REBEL INVASION AND POLITICAL UPHEAVAL

On 1 October 1990 an estimated force of 10,000 guerrillas, representing the exiled, Tutsi-dominated Front patriotique rwandais (FPR, or Inkotanyi), crossed the border from Uganda into north-eastern Rwanda, where they swiftly occupied several towns. Numerically, the troops were dominated by Tutsi refugees, but also included significant numbers of disaffected elements of Uganda's ruling National Resistance Army (NRA). The invasion force was reported to have been led by Maj.-Gen. Fred Rwigyema, a former Ugandan deputy minister of defence. In response to a request for assistance by President Habyarimana, Belgian and French paratroopers were dispatched to Kigali to protect foreign nationals and to secure evacuation routes, but in the event did not engage in combat. However, a contingent of Zairean troops assisted the small Rwandan army in turning back the FPR some 70 km from Kigali. During the first week of hostilities, and particularly after heavy gunfire in Kigali during the night of 4–5 October, an estimated 8,000 people throughout Rwanda were arrested and imprisoned, of whom the vast majority were Tutsi. However, in only a few cases was there any evidence of complicity with the invaders and almost all were released in April 1991, while those convicted benefited from an amnesty law pronounced in November 1991.

Internationally, the FPR successfully presented itself as a democratic and multi-ethnic movement seeking to depose a corrupt and incompetent regime, with the result that the Belgian government encountered increasing pressure to terminate military aid to Rwanda. Visits were paid to the region by the Belgian prime minister and other senior ministers with the aim of securing a cease-fire, to be followed by a regional conference on the Rwandan refugee problem. On 17 October 1990 a summit meeting at Mwanza, Tanzania, was attended by the presidents of Rwanda, Uganda and Tanzania, who agreed in principle to the holding of a regional conference. Numerous other bilateral contacts took place, but there was no direct dialogue between the Rwandan government and the FPR. Despite the obvious frailty of the agreements, Belgium took the opportunity to extricate itself from the crisis and by 1 November had withdrawn its troops from Rwanda. Their departure coincided with a statement by the Rwandan government that victory had been achieved and that the invaders had fled to Uganda. The FPR, however, now adopted guerrilla tactics, attacking border areas in the north and north-west from Ugandan bases, raising accusations, strongly denied by Uganda, that it was actively aiding the FPR.

The conflict continued throughout 1991 and into 1992 as the FPR made frequent incursions into Rwandan territory. Thousands of casualties were reported on both sides while many civilians resident in the border region were killed and as many as 100,000 were displaced. Increasing racial tension, exacerbated by the war, resulted in a series of unprovoked attacks upon Tutsis, and prompted accusations of government involvement, particularly in the Bugesera region. In late July 1992 it was reported that a cease-fire had been negotiated, providing for the establishment of a 'neutral area'. The cease-fire arrangements were to be overseen by a 50-member African military monitoring team.

The political reform process, initiated before the conflict, was accelerated by the invasion. The CNS published its report and a draft constitution in March 1991, following widespread public discussion of proposals put forward by the commission in December 1990. In June 1991 the new multi-party constitution, together with legislation providing for the recognition of political parties (numbering 15 by June 1992) entered into force. Full freedom of the press was declared, leading to the establishment of a number of magazines and newspapers critical of government policy. In April 1992, following a series of unsuccessful attempts to negotiate a transitional government, the composition of a broadly-based coalition government, incorporating four opposition parties (the revived MDR, the Parti social-démocrate—PSD, the Parti libéral—PL and the Parti démocratique chrétien—PDC), together with the Mouvement républicain national pour la démocratie et le développement—MRNDD (the new party name adopted by the MRND in April 1991), was announced. The cabinet was to be headed by Dismas Nsengiyaremye of the MDR as prime minister. It was also announced that multi-party elections for municipalities, the legislature and for the presidency would take place before April 1993.

In late April 1992, to comply with the new constitutional prohibition of participation in the political process by the armed forces, Habyarimana relinquished his military title and functions.

Renewed dialogue was initiated between the new transitional government and FPR representatives in May 1992, and formal discussions were conducted in Paris during June. Further negotiations, in Arusha, Tanzania, in July, resulted in an agreement on the implementation of a new cease-fire, to be effective from the end of July, and the creation of an OAU-sponsored military observer group (GOM), to comprise representatives from both sides, together with officers drawn from the armed forces of Nigeria, Senegal, Zimbabwe and Mali. However, subsequent negotiations in Tanzania, during August, September and October, failed to resolve outstanding problems concerning the creation of a 'neutral zone' between the Rwandan armed forces and the FPR (to be enforced by the GOM), the incorporation of the FPR in a future combined Rwandan national force, the repatriation of refugees, and the demands of the FPR for full participation in a transitional government and legislature. In January 1993 a preliminary agreement on the last of these issues was immediately rejected by the MRNDD leadership, and by the president, prompting violent political and ethnic clashes. Boniface Ngulinzaira, the minister of foreign affairs and co-operation (and an MDR member), was subsequently replaced as leader of the government's peace delegation by the minister of national defence, James Gasana, of the MRNDD.

A resurgence in violence followed the breakdown of negotiations in early February 1993, resulting in the deaths of hundreds on both sides. An estimated 1m. civilians fled southwards and to neighbouring Uganda and Tanzania, in order to escape the fighting, as the FPR advanced as far as Ruhengeri and seemed, for a time, poised to occupy Kigali. The actions of the FPR were denounced by Belgium, France and the USA. French reinforcements were dispatched to join a small French military contingent, stationed in Kigali since October 1990 in order to protect French nationals. Meanwhile, the commander of the 50-member GOM declared that it had inadequate manpower and resources to contain the FPR front line, and was to request an additional 400 troops from the OAU.

In late February 1993 the government accepted FPR terms for a cease-fire in return for an end to attacks against FPR positions and on Tutsi communities, and the withdrawal of foreign troops. Although fighting continued with fluctuating intensity, fresh peace negotiations were convened in March, in Arusha. In late March the French government began to withdraw French troops to the Central African Republic.

Negotiations conducted during April 1993 failed to produce a solution to the crucial issue of the structure of a future single armed Rwandan force. In the same month, the five participating parties in the ruling coalition agreed to a three-month extension of the government's mandate, in order to facilitate the successful conclusion of a peace accord. Significant progress was made during fresh talks between the government and the FPR in the northern town of Kinihira, during May, when a timetable for the demobilization of 19,000-strong security forces was agreed. Later in the month further consensus was reached on the creation of a 'neutral zone'. In June agreement was concluded on a protocol for the repatriation of all Rwandan refugees resident in Uganda, Tanzania and Zaire, including recommendations that compensation should be made available to those forced into exile more than 12 years ago. In late June the UN Security Council approved the creation of UN Observer Mission Uganda-Rwanda (UNOMUR), to comprise 81 military observers and 24 officials, and to be deployed on the Ugandan side of the border for an initial period of six months, in order to ensure that no military supply line might be maintained for the FPR.

In July 1993, in the context of the improved likelihood of a prompt resolution of the conflict, President Habyarimana met representatives of the five political parties represented in the government and sought a further extension to the mandate of the coalition government. However, the prime minister's insistence that the FPR should be represented in any newly-mandated government exacerbated existing divisions within the MDR, prompting Habyarimana to conclude the agreement with a conciliatory group of MDR dissidents, including the education minister, Agathe Uwilingiyimana, who was elected to the premiership. Several changes to the council of ministers were subsequently effected in order to fill portfolios vacated by disaffected MDR members. The outgoing prime minister, Dismas Nsengiyaremye, accused Habyarimana of having deliberately jeopardized the peace accord with the FPR, and of having committed procedural malpractice in the selection of Uwilingiyimana as his successor.

In late July 1993 the new prime minister reported that she had been abducted by MDR members, who had attempted to force her to resign the premiership. Meanwhile, a communiqué from MDR officials loyal to former prime minister Nsengiyaremye announced that Uwilingiyimana, together with three MDR ministers and party president Faustin Twagiramungu, had been suspended from the MDR.

On 4 August 1993 a peace accord was formally signed by President Habyarimana and Col Alex Kanyarengwe of the FPR, in Arusha, Tanzania. A new transitional government, to be headed by a mutually-approved prime minister (later identified as Faustin Twagiramungu), would be installed by 10 September. Multi-party general elections would be conducted after a 22-month period during which the FPR would join the political mainstream and participate in a transitional government and national assembly. In mid-August the curfew in Kigali was ended, and military road-blocks were removed from all but three northern prefectures. By the end of the month, however, the prime minister was forced to make a national appeal for calm, following reports of renewed outbreaks of violence in Kigali and Butare. Failure to establish a transitional government and legislature by 10 September was attributed by the government and the FPR to the increasingly precarious national security situation, and both sides urged the prompt dispatch of a neutral UN force to facilitate the implementation of the accord. Meanwhile, relations between the government and the FPR deteriorated, following the rebels' assertion that the government had infringed the terms of the accord by attempting to dismantle and reorganize those government departments assigned to the FPR under the terms of the peace agreement.

UN INTERVENTION

On 5 October 1993 the UN Security Council adopted Resolution 872, endorsing the recommendation of the UN secretary-general for the creation of UN Assistance Mission to Rwanda (UNAMIR), to be deployed in Rwanda for an initial period of six months, with a mandate to monitor observance of the cease-fire, to contribute to the security of the capital and to facilitate the repatriation of refugees. UNAMIR, which was to incorporate UNOMUR and GOM, was formally inaugurated on 1 November, and was to comprise some 2,500 personnel when fully operational. (Resolution 928, approved by the Security Council in June 1994, provided for the termination of UNOMUR on 21 September 1994.) In early December 1993, in compliance with the stipulations of the Arusha accord, the French government announced the withdrawal of its military contingent in Kigali, and in mid-December the UN secretary-general's special representative in Rwanda, Jacques-Roger Booh-Booh, declared that the UN was satisfied that conditions had been sufficiently fulfilled to allow for the inauguration of the transitional institutions by the end of the month.

The attempts of the prime minister to maintain the conciliatory momentum engendered by the Arusha accord had been complicated, during November 1993, by a declaration of intent to end negotiations with the FPR, issued by the Rwandan armed forces in support of allegations of rebel involvement in a recent massacre of 20-40 civilians in the 'neutral zone' (which she had overruled), and by reports, originating from representatives of the UN high commissioner for refugees in Rwanda, that Burundian refugees who had fled to Rwanda to escape the violent aftermath of the abortive coup (organized by factions of the Tutsi-dominated Burundian armed forces) in which President Ndadaye had been killed in October, were receiving military training at refugee camps, in preparation for a counter-offensive to be launched from Rwanda with the support of Hutu extremist groups (which she had strenuously denied).

In late December 1993 a 600-strong FPR battalion was escorted to the capital by UNAMIR officials (as detailed in the Arusha accord), in order to ensure the safety of FPR representatives selected to participate in the transitional government and legislature. However, dissension within a number of political parties had obstructed the satisfactory nomination of representatives to the transitional institutions, forcing a further postponement of their inauguration. On 5 January 1994 Juvénal Habyarimana was invested as president of a transitional government, for a 22-month period, under the terms of the Arusha accord. (Habyarimana's previous term of office, in accordance with the constitution, had expired on 19 December 1993.) The inauguration of the transitional government and legislature, scheduled for the same day, was again postponed when several important participants, notably representatives of the FPR, the MDR, the PSD and the PDC, and the president of the constitutional court, failed to attend. While government spokesmen identified the need to resolve internal differences within the MDR and the PL as the crucial expedient for the implementation of the new government and legislature, a joint statement, issued by the PSD, the PDC and factions of the MDR and the PL, accused the president of having abused the authority afforded his office by the Arusha accord by interfering in the selection of prospective ministers and deputies. This charge was reiterated by the FPR in late February, when it rejected a list of proposed future gubernatorial and legislative representatives (tentatively agreed following several days of discussions between the president, the prime minister and the five participating parties of the current administration) as having been compiled as the result of a campaign of intimidation and manipulation by the president in order to secure the participation of his own supporters, and thereby prolong his political influence. The FPR insisted that a definitive list of each party's representatives in the future transitional institutions had been approved by the constitutional court in January. In March the prime minister designate, Faustin Twagiramungu, declared that he had fulfilled his consultative role as outlined in the Arusha accord, and announced the composition of a transitional government, in an attempt to accelerate the installation of the transitional bodies. However, political opposition to the proposed council of ministers persisted, and President Habyarimana insisted that the list of proposed legislative deputies, newly presented by Agathe Uwilingiyimana, should be modified to include representatives of additional political parties, including the reactionary Coalition pour la défense de la république — CDR (whose participation was vociferously opposed by the FPR, owing to its alleged failure to subscribe to the code of ethics that governed the behaviour of political parties and which proscribed policies advocating tribal discrimination), prompting a further postponement of the establishment of a transitional administration.

Meanwhile political frustration had erupted into violence in late February 1994, with the murder of the minister of public works and energy, Félicien Gatabazi of the PSD, who had actively pursued the peace accord and the transitional administration. Hours later, the CDR leader, Martin Bucyana, was killed, in apparent retaliation, by an angry mob of PSD supporters, provoking a series of violent confrontations resulting in some 30-40 deaths.

In early April 1994 the UN Security Council (which in February had warned that the UN presence in Rwanda might be withdrawn if no further progress was swiftly made in the implementation of the Arusha accord) agreed to extend UNAMIR's mandate for four months, pending a review of progress made in implementing the accord, to be conducted after six weeks.

COLLAPSE OF CIVIL ORDER

On 6 April 1994 the president's aircraft, returning from a regional summit meeting in Dar es Salaam, Tanzania, was fired upon, above Kigali airport, and exploded on landing, killing all 10 passengers, including President Habyarimana. The president of Burundi, Cyprien Ntaryamira, two Burundian cabinet ministers, the chief of staff of the Rwandan armed forces, and a senior diplomat were among the other victims. In Kigali the highly-trained presidential guard immediately initiated a brutal campaign of retributive violence against political opponents of the late president, although it remained unclear who had been responsible for the attack on the aircraft, and UNAMIR officials attempting to investigate the site of the crash were obstructed by the presidential guard. As politicians and civilians fled the capital, the horror of the political assassinations was compounded by attacks on the clergy, UNAMIR personnel (10 Belgian troops were reportedly persuaded to disarm before being executed) and members of the Tutsi tribe. Hutu civilians were forced, under pain of death, to murder their Tutsi neighbours, and the mobilization of the *interahamwe*, or unofficial militias (allegedly affiliated to the MRNDD and the CDR), apparently committed to the massacre of government opponents and Tutsi civilians, was encouraged by the presidential guard (with support from some factions of the armed forces) and by inflamatory broadcasts from Radio-Télévision Libre des Mille Collines in Kigali. The prime minister, Agathe Uwilingiyimana, the president of the constitutional court, the ministers of labour and social affairs and of information, and the chairman of the PSD were among the prominent politicians murdered, or pronounced missing and presumed dead, within hours of the death of President Habyarimana.

On 8 April 1994 the speaker of the CND, Dr Théodore Sindikubwabo, announced that he had assumed the office of interim president of the republic, in accordance with the provisions of the 1991 constitution. The five remaining participating political parties and factions of the government selected a new prime minister, Jean Kambanda, and a new council of ministers (drawn largely from the MRNDD) from among their ranks. The ligitimacy of the new administration was immediately challenged by the FPR, which claimed that the constitutional right of succession to the presidency of the speaker of the CND had been superseded by Habyarimana's inauguration, in January, as president under the terms of the Arusha accord. (However, Félicien Ngango, who had been nominated to lead the transitional national assembly, and therefore to succeed the president in the event of his untimely death, had been an early victim of the presidential guard's campaign of political 'cleansing'.) The legal status of the government (which promptly removed to the town of Gitarama to escape escalating violence in the capital) was subsequently rejected by factions of the PL and MDR (led by Faustin Twagiramungu), and by the PDC and the PSD (which in May announced that they had allied themselves as the Democratic Forces for Change).

FPR Offensives and the Refugee Crisis

In mid-April 1994 the FPR announced its intention to resume an armed offensive from its northern stronghold, in order to relieve its beleaguered battalion in Kigali, to restore order to the capital and to halt the massacre of civilians. Grenade attacks and mortar fire intensified in the capital, prompting the UN to mediate a fragile 60-hour cease-fire, during which small evacuation forces from several countries escorted foreign nationals out of Rwanda. Belgium's UNAMIR contingent of more than 400 troops was also withdrawn, having encountered increasing hostility as a result of persistent rumours that Belgian elements had been involved in the attack on President Habyarimana's aircraft, and were providing logistical support to the FPR (accusations which were formally levelled by the Rwandan ambassador to Zaire later in the month), which were emphatically denied by the Belgian government.

In late April 1994 members of the government embarked upon a diplomatic offensive throughout Europe and Africa, seeking to enhance the credibility of the government through international recognition of its legal status. However, this initiative achieved only limited success (notably in France, Egypt and Togo), and the FPR's continued refusal to enter into dialogue with the 'illegal' administration (preferring to negotiate with representatives of the military high command) proved a major obstacle to attempts, undertaken by the UN and the presidents of Tanzania and Zaire, to sponsor a new cease-fire agreement in late April and early May.

As the violent political crusade unleashed by the presidential guard and the *interahamwe* (described by Amnesty International as a well-trained militia numbering some 30,000) gathered momentum, the militia's identification of all members of the Tutsi tribe as political opponents of the state promoted tribal polarization, resulting in an effective pogrom. Reports of mass Tutsi graves and unprovoked attacks on fleeing Tutsi refugees, and on those seeking refuge in schools, hospitals and churches, provoked unqualified international condemnation and outrage, and promises of financial and logistical aid for an estimated 2m. displaced Rwandans (some 250,000 had fled across the border to Tanzania in a 24-hour period in late April 1994) who were threatened by famine and disease in makeshift camps. By late May attempts to assess the full scale of the humanitarian catastrophe in Rwanda were complicated by unverified reports that the FPR (which claimed to control more than one-half of the country) was carrying out retaliatory atrocities against Hutu civilians. However, unofficial estimates indicated that between 200,000-500,000 Rwandans had been killed since early April.

On 21 April 1994, in the context of the worsening security situation in Kigali, and the refusal of the Rwandan armed forces to agree to the neutral policing of the capital's airport (subsequently secured by the FPR), the UN Security Council resolved to reduce significantly its representation in Rwanda to 270 personnel, a move which attracted criticism from the government, the FPR, international relief organizations and the international community in general. However, on 16 May, following intense international pressure and the disclosure of the vast scale of the humanitarian crisis in the region, the UN Security Council approved Resolution 917, providing for the eventual deployment of some 5,500 UN troops with a revised mandate, including the policing of Kigali's airport (in order to safeguard the arrival of vital relief supplies) and the protection of refugees in designated 'safe areas'. Full deployment of the force, however, was to be delayed pending a comprehensive assessment of the most effective positioning of the troops, owing largely to the reservations of the USA, which had favoured the dispatch of a smaller mission to set up 'protective zones' for refugees along the country's borders. In late May the UN secretary-general criticized the failure of the UN member nations to respond to his invitation to participate in the enlarged force (only Ghana, Ethiopia and Senegal had agreed to provide small contingents). Further UN-sponsored attempts to negotiate a cease-fire failed in late May and early June, and the FPR made significant territorial gains in southern Rwanda, forcing the government to flee Gitarama and seek refuge in the western town of Kibuye.

In early June 1994 the UN Security Council adopted Resolution 925, whereby the mandate of the revised UN mission in Rwanda (UNAMIR II) was extended until December 1994. However, the UN secretary-general continued to encounter considerable difficulty in securing equipment and armaments requested by those African countries which had agreed to participate. By mid-June the emergence of confirmed reports of retributive murders committed by FPR members (including the massacres, in two separate incidents in early June, of 22 clergymen, among them the Roman Catholic archbishop of Kigali) and the collapse of a fragile truce (negotiated at a summit meeting of the OAU in Tunis, Tunisia) prompted the French government to announce its willingness to lead an armed police action, endorsed by the UN, in Rwanda. Although the French government insisted that the French military presence (expected to total 2,000 troops) would maintain strict political neutrality, and operate, from the border regions, in a purely humanitarian capacity pending the arrival of a multinational UN force, the FPR was vehemently opposed to its deployment, citing the French administration's maintenance of high-level contacts with representatives of the self-proclaimed Rwandan government as an indication of political bias. While the UN secretary-general welcomed the French initiative, and tacit endorsement of the project was contained in Resolution 929, approved by the Security Council in late June, the OAU expressed serious reservations regarding the appropriateness of the action. On 23 June a first contingent of 150 French marine commandos launched 'Operation Turquoise', entering the western town of Cyangugu, in preparation for a large-scale operation to protect refugees in the area. By mid-July the French had successfully relieved several beleaguered Tutsi communities, and had established a temporary 'safe haven' for the displaced population in the south-west, through which a massive exodus of Hutu refugees began to flow, encouraged by reports (disseminated by supporters of the defeated interim government) that the advancing FPR forces were seeking violent retribution against the Hutu. An estimated 1m. Rwandans sought refuge in the Zairean border town of Goma, while a similar number attempted to cross the border elsewhere in the south-west. The FPR had swiftly secured all major cities and strategic territorial positions, but had halted its advance several kilometres from the boundaries of the French-controlled neutral zone, requesting the apprehension and return for trial of those responsible for the recent atrocities. (At the end of June the first report of the UN's special rapporteur on human rights in Rwanda — appointed in May — confirmed that as many as 500,000 Rwandans had been killed since April, and urged the establishment of an international tribunal to investigate allegations of genocide; in early June the UN announced the creation of a commission of inquiry for this purpose.)

The FPR Takes Power

On 19 July 1994 Pasteur Bizimungu, a Hutu, was inaugurated as president for a five-year term. On the same day the FPR announced the composition of a new government of national unity, to be headed by Faustin Twagiramungu as prime minister. The majority of cabinet posts were assigned to FPR members (including the FPR military chief Maj.-Gen. Paul Kagame, who became minister of defence and also assumed the newly-created post of vice-president), while the remainder were divided among the MDR, the PL, the PSD and the PDC. The new administration urged all refugees to return to Rwanda and issued assurances that civilian Hutus could return safely to their homes. The prime minister identified the immediate aims of the administration as the restoration of peace and democracy, the reactivation of the economy and the repatriation of refugees. Identity cards bearing details of ethnic origin were to be abolished forthwith.

The FPR victory and the new administration were promptly recognized by the French government, which urged the new Rwandan government to assume responsibility for relief operations. In return, Twagiramungu was reported to have expressed his appreciation for the humanitarian and stabilizing nature of the French operation. The French government announced its intention to begin a reduction in personnel by the end of July 1994, with a view to complete withdrawal by the end of August. In mid-July France began to equip a force of 500 troops drawn from Senegal, the Congo, Chad, Niger and Guinea-Bissau, to assist the French contingent and facilitate the eventual transfer of responsibility to a UN force.

Meanwhile, conditions in refugee camps in Zaire had continued to deteriorate, as hunger and cholera became more widespread. By the end of July 1994, despite an intensification of international relief efforts in the region, at least 2,000 refugees were dying each day, adding to a refugee camp death toll already in excess of 20,000. In response to a UN plea for some US $434m. to address the refugee crisis, US President Clinton pleadged $185m. in aid and announced a relief programme which included the establishment of an airlift centre in Uganda and the provision of clean water. Later in the month it was reported that the new Rwandan government had granted permission for the USA to establish a relief programme headquarters in Kigali. As many as 2,000 US troops were expected to carry out humanitarian missions in Rwanda and eastern Zaire. Also in July, the British government approved the deployment of a British military contingent in the border region, to help relief efforts. However, non-government relief agencies were highly critical of the inadequate and overdue nature of the international response to the crisis. In late July President Bizimungu met with the presidents of Zaire and Tanzania, and concluded agreements on the disarmament and gradual repatriation of refugees.

Amid persistent rumours that the Rwandan armed forces were attempting to regroup and rearm in Zaire in preparation for a counter-offensive strike against the FPR, the exiled former government continued to seek recognition as the legitimate Rwandan administration and urged the international community to oversee the establishment in Rwanda of political institutions based on broad consensus and the organization of general elections within one year. However, the claims of the former government were seriously undermined by the EU's recognition of the new Rwandan government of national unity in mid-September 1994.

Economy

FILIP REYNTJENS

Revised for this edition by FRANÇOIS MISSER

Rwanda has two main physical handicaps to economic development: the extreme population density and the distance from the sea. The population problem with its concomitant effect on food resources, is aggravated by a high rate of growth, estimated by the World Bank at an average annual increase of 3.0% between 1985–92. Population pressure has also aggravated the soil erosion caused by leaching and other natural factors. The 1977–78 and 1982–86 Development Plans gave priority to population resettlement in unoccupied areas, in an effort to restrict the exodus to the towns from the countryside (where about 95% of the population live), and to make better use of unexploited land in the east of the country and in the marshy plains. By 1977 these swamps had been reclaimed for sugar cane and rice plantations, with technical assistance initially from Taiwan and later from the People's Republic of China. The violent campaign of political 'cleansing' unleashed by the Rwandan armed forces and the *interahamwe* Hutu militia following the death of President Habyarimana in April 1994, resulted in the deaths, by the end of July, of an estimated 500,000 Rwandans (mainly Tutsi), and the flight of a further 500,000 refugees to neighbouring countries (an estimated three-quarters of all refugees fled to Tanzania). In addition, between 500,000 and 1m. Rwandans in the north and a further 300,000 in the south were thought to have been displaced from their homes by the conflict. In all, about one-seventh of the total population had been killed or had left the country, while as many as one-fifth of the remainder had been internally displaced. In 1992, according to estimates by the World Bank, gross national product (GNP), measured at average 1990–92 prices, was US $1,813m. equivalent to $250 per head. During 1985–92, it was estimated, GNP per head decreased, in real terms, at an average annual rate of 2.8%. Rwanda's gross domestic product (GDP) increased, in real terms, by an annual average of 1.4% in 1980–92. In 1985–92 the average annual rate of inflation was 2.4%, and consumer prices increased by 12.3% in 1993.

AGRICULTURE

The agricultural sector accounted for about 41% of Rwanda's GDP in 1992, and engaged an estimated 91% of the labour force (mainly at subsistence level). About 95% of the total value of agricultural production is provided by subsistence crops. While these have failed to meet the needs of the population, the annual increase in production of subsistence crops broadly kept pace with the population growth until 1977. Since then, the area of land annually made available for subsistence crops has increased only marginally and, moreover, crop yields are declining in many areas, owing to erosion and the traditional intensive cultivation methods used. This led, in the late 1980s, to increasing strains on food production and consequently to severe food shortages. Attempts to increase the yield of small farm plots have included a recent initiative to cultivate climbing beans. In late 1989 and early 1990 many parts of the country, in particular the south, were affected by famine, following drought and crop failure. Subsequently, the government had recourse to emergency food aid to avert widespread starvation.

The principal food crops are bananas (the single most important, with production of about 2.5m. tons in 1991), sweet potatoes, potatoes, cassava, beans, sorghum, rice, maize and peas, in descending order of importance. The major cash crop is coffee, exports of which provided 7,209.8m. Rwanda francs (60.2% of total export earnings) in 1991 compared with 12,569m. Rwanda francs (82% of total export earnings) in 1986. In dollar terms, revenues decreased from $85m. in 1988 to $37m. in 1992. As a result, coffee represented only 54.4% of export earnings in 1992. Revenue from coffee fluctuates considerably, and in the late 1980s declined sharply because of the combined effects of a low level of production, falling international prices and the weakness of the US dollar in relation to the currencies of Rwanda's other major trading partners. Even before the catastrophic political events of 1994, it had seemed unlikely that Rwanda would benefit from the resurgence in world coffee prices at the end of 1993. The volume of production had been dwindling for several years, partly owing to price instability. Reduced revenues had also forced farmers to abandon the purchase and introduction of pesticides and fertilizers. In addition, during 1993 the Seventh-day Adventist church had urged adherents to destroy coffee plants, having denounced the plant as a 'drug'. The government attempted to diversify the crops grown for export through the Office des cultures industrielles du Rwanda (OCIR), set up in 1964. This concentrated its efforts on tobacco, cotton, pyrethrum, quinquina, forestry and, pre-eminently, tea. Rwanda's output of made tea has increased steadily in recent years, rising from 2,522 metric tons in 1972 to 8,669 tons in 1984, and to 13,546 tons in 1991. Exports of tea earned 2,796.6m. Rwanda francs, or 23.4% of total export earnings, in 1991, and this percentage increased to 32.3% in 1992. However, production forecasts for 1993 were not encouraging, following the FPR guerrillas' occupation of the lucrative Mulindi plantations. Output of dried pyrethrum reached 1,047 tons in 1990. Quinquina appeared to be developing into a promising commodity but the company responsible for processing the flowers went into liquidation in 1986. An agricultural diversification programme was aided by the European Union (EU). In addition, the European Development Fund (EDF), together with the Food and Agriculture Organization of the United Nations (FAO) and the World Bank, is involved in aiding the creation of local farming communes (*paysannats*). In late 1993 the International Development Association (IDA) approved a US $15m. loan to help finance agricultural research projects and the transformation of existing research institutes in Rwanda. It was envisaged that the full implementation of the research development programme would generate an annual increase in the sector's growth of some 4%. Rwanda's agriculture was expected to benefit from the nitrogenous fertilizers which can be processed from the country's resources of methane gas. In 1987 Socigaz, a joint venture between Rwanda and Zaire, was established to exploit this commodity. The success of a proposal to diversify agricultural exports through the sale of 'karamasenge' bananas to Europe was likely to be dependent on the success of a marketing campaign to promote the superior quality of the fruit over more competitively priced and more accessible central American fruits.

INDUSTRY AND MINING

The industrial sector follows the usual pattern for the less developed African states, and food-based industries, such as the processing of coffee and tea, a sugar factory, a brewery, a cigarette factory, etc., predominate. In 1992 the Netherlands brewer Heineken invested 1,000m. Rwanda francs in its Rwandan subsidiary BRALIRWA.SOBOLIRWA, which markets US cola in Rwanda, quadrupled its turnover between 1988 and 1992. In late 1992 the Régie Sucrière de Kibuye sugar plant acquired new equipment which it hoped would help to treble its output for 1990. Otherwise there are two small textile concerns, small-scale chemical and engineering works, cement and match factories, a plant producing pyrethrum extract and various other enterprises based on transistors, sandals and plastics, agricultural tools, stoneware and printing. In 1992 manufacturing accounted for an estimated 16% of GDP while in the same year industry accounted for 22% of GDP.

Cassiterite (a tin-bearing ore) is Rwanda's principal mineral resource (exports of tin ores and concentrates were worth 320m. Rwanda francs in 1991), followed by wolframite (a tungsten-bearing ore) and there are small, known quantities of beryl, colombo-tantalite, and gold. While tin concentrates (about 1,500 tons) were the third-largest export earner in 1985, high transport costs and the sharp decline in world tin prices left the sector virtually inactive in the late 1980s. At the end of 1985 Géomines, the Belgian company with a 51% shareholding in the Rwandan mining company SOMIRWA, went into liquidation; SOMIRWA itself was declared insolvent a few months later. A tin-processing plant built at a cost of 1,000m. Rwanda francs in Karuruma near Kigali had never operated at more than 20% of capacity, and the profitability of SOMIRWA's other operations had also been poor. Plans for other foundries were consequently suspended. Despite the insolvent state of the company, the government's annual maintenance costs for SOMIRWA installations have continued to exceed 70m. Rwanda francs. In 1992 the Régie Minière mining concern was established, with state involvement, and began to exploit the SOMIRWA mines in an artisanal capacity. However, the company was reported to be operating on an annual deficit of some 50m. Rwanda francs. From 1992 the SOMIRWA smelter resumed activity for six months of the year, processing cassiterite supplied by the ALICOM gold concern. Some efforts were made with EU support to stimulate the artisanal tin sector, and the United Nations Development Programme (UNDP) provided some funds towards an increase in gold production. Mining activities were resumed at a modest level in 1988 by artisans regrouped in COOPIMAR, an independent co-operative offering managerial and commercial support. In 1992 a new company, Saphirs du Rwanda, began exploration for sapphires.

Another important mineral to be exploited is natural gas, which was discovered beneath Lake Kivu on the border with Zaire. Reserves of an estimated 57,000m. cu m (about one-half of which are in Zaire) are thought to be among the largest in the world. Two pilot plants, funded by the EU, produce gas, but here again the small size of the potential market casts doubt on the likely profitability of large-scale processing. However, in 1993 the national electricity and gas company, Electrogaz, was hoping to receive Belgian funding for a programme to increase its daily output of gas from 5,000 cu m to 25,000 cu m. Government plans to privatize Electrogaz have attracted interest from Franco-Canadian and Franco-Belgian consortia.

POWER AND COMMUNICATIONS

Rwanda's electricity needs are supplied almost entirely from hydroelectric sources, as the land relief is ideal for power generation. Rwanda imported only 4% of its electricity in 1977 but, with the connection of the national supply to the Mururu station on the Ruzizi river in Zaire in 1978, and after the closure in 1979 of all but one of seven thermal plants, Zaire provided more than one-half of Rwanda's electricity in 1979. This proportion increased until the opening of the Mukungwa station (with a capacity of 12 MW) in 1981. By 1980 about one-tenth of the country's estimated hydroelectric potential of 200 MW had been harnessed. In 1977 Rwanda, Burundi and Tanzania formed an organization to develop the water, power and mineral resources of the Kagera river basin, with financial support from the UNDP, and in 1982 Rwanda and Tanzania decided to construct a hydroelectric power station (60 MW) on the Rusumo river. Work has begun on the Mukungwa-II hydroelectric power station, supported by a $24m. loan from Japan, while work on the Ruzizi-II plant (a joint venture with Zaire and Burundi, with a maximum generating capacity of 42 MW) is nearing completion. In the meantime Rwanda continues to import more than half (54% in 1990) of its total electricity requirements. In early 1994 the European Investment Bank, together with French and German credit institutions, pledged more than $1m. to help rehabilitate the Ntaruka power station, which had been damaged by FPR guerrillas. Reserves of peat are being assessed as an additional source of energy, mainly for homes and small factories in rural areas. Since the mid-1980s the Rwandan government has also expressed its commitment to the development of biogas in the rural areas.

Internal communications in Rwanda are operated almost exclusively along the relatively well-developed road system (13,173 km in 1990), as there are no railways nor navigable waterways (except Lake Kivu). Asphalted highways link Rwanda with Burundi, Uganda, Zaire and Tanzania. They also connect the principal towns (Kibuye remaining the only district capital without direct access to the asphalted road system). Tarmac roads extend to just over 1,000 km, which, given the small size of the country, is one of the highest densities in Africa. Rwanda's external trade is heavily dependent on the ports of Mombasa, Dar es Salaam and Matadi, and about 80% of Rwandan exports and imports pass through Uganda and Kenya. Insecurity caused by the war in the north of Rwanda led to the closure of the northern transport 'corridor' through Uganda. With the Gatuna and Kagituma roads unavailable, most traffic has had to be diverted to the difficult and unreliable route through Tanzania. In 1992 several projects had been approved by the EU and the World Bank to improve road links between eastern Zaire and western Uganda, hoping to facilitate the passage of Rwandan trade across the Zairean border, and thereby bypass the troubled border with Uganda. At the same time, plans to improve road and rail links via Tanzania were also under consideration. Feasibility studies have been discussed for a railway network to link Uganda, Rwanda, Burundi and Tanzania. Prior to the escalation of hostilities in April 1994, a number of international airlines, most prominently Sabena and Air France, operated services to Kigali, while the small national carrier, Air Rwanda (scheduled for privatization), operated domestic passenger and cargo services and international cargo flights to Burundi, Kenya, Tanzania, Uganda, Zaire and destinations in Europe.

DEVELOPMENT PLANNING

Zaire, Burundi and Rwanda, the members of the Economic Community of the Great Lakes Countries (CEPGL), agreed to form a joint development bank in 1978 and to co-operate on the development of a transport system and the construction of a hydroelectric power station (the Ruzizi-II project) on the Rwanda-Zaire border, the exploitation of methane gas deposits beneath Lake Kivu and the promotion of a fishing industry. The bank was formally established in 1980, with its headquarters at Goma, in Zaire.

Rwanda's third Five-Year Plan (1982–86) sought to establish self-sufficiency in food, with progress in the industrial sector being confined to providing basic infrastructure in support of the country's primary development. This reflected a fear that increasing food production would fail to keep pace with the growth in the country's population. This fear proved justified, and by early 1990 food shortages had reached an alarming level. In the face of severe macro-economic uncertainty, the drafting of the fourth Five-Year Plan, which was to cover the period 1987–91, has been constantly delayed, and was eventually abandoned altogether.

A severe drought in 1984 resulted in poor harvests, which, in conjunction with transport disruptions in Uganda, greatly increased the cost of Rwandan imports and penalized exports. This prompted President Habyarimana, in April 1984, to initiate a programme of 'rigour and austerity', which led to the suspension of many non-essential projects. This policy was maintained and intensified dramatically at the end of 1989, following successive years of rapidly declining export revenue and poor harvests.

In 1986 a major project was launched to improve rural water supplies in the Lava district. It was to cost an estimated $47m., and was to be financed mainly by the World Bank, the EC and the Arab Bank for Economic Development in Africa (BADEA). The water was required for an area rich in agricultural potential, where the existing supply systems had fallen into disrepair. A second project, involving the construction of new transmission mains in order to rehabilitate and extend existing supply systems, was under way in 1987, and was expected to take some four years to reach completion. This project, which was to cost more than $70m., was to receive initial funding from the African Development Bank (ADB), the International Development Association (IDA), the BADEA and the Rwandan government. Further loans were expected to be forthcoming from the French government's Caisse centrale de coopération économique, the Swiss and Austrian governments and the UNDP. By the end of 1988 more than 70% of the population had access to safe water.

In 1986 a new international airport was opened at Kigali. Built at a cost of 3,500m. Rwanda francs, the new airport has an expanded capacity to serve up to 500,000 passengers per year. In August of the same year a scheme to modernize the country's telecommunications system was initiated, with financial assistance to be provided by a number of international organizations. The total cost was estimated at $45m., and work was expected to continue until the year 2000. A satellite ground station began operation in 1987, providing direct automatic telephone and telex links with the rest of the world.

Road-building programmes have been accelerated, in order to solve the problems of transport through Kenya and Uganda. New roadways to Tanzania have been constructed, and the major roads leading to Kenya have been upgraded. The main roads to Uganda (Kayonza–Kagitumba and Kigali–Gatuna) were upgraded between 1988–90.

Improvement in the performance of the public sector has been a more recent concern. A three-year project for its restructuring and the enhancement of its planning capacity has been funded by a 'soft' loan of $7.4m. from the IDA and a grant of $2.5m. from the UNDP. In 1991 the IDA committed substantial credits towards the reform of the primary school sector ($23m.) and family planning ($15.6m.).

The government has sought unsuccessfully to limit the overall budget deficit, which reached 14.2% of GDP in 1992, compared with 6% in 1989, despite an 11% increase in tax revenue and a 25% decline in capital expenditure (project implementation slowed owing to escalating hostilities), and notwithstanding the government's failure to finance adequately the social contingency fund agreed under the terms of its adjustment programme. Budget expenditure increased in order to finance the war and internal security, and to support producer prices for coffee. The situation deteriorated further in 1993, with revenues declining by an estimated 6% while expenditure increased by an estimated 5%. The projected fiscal deficit was expected to amount to 19% of GDP, and increase domestic and external arrears. As a consequence the external debt was expected to deteriorate further: the cost of debt-servicing was equivalent to 12.9% of the value of exports and services in 1989, this figure increased to an estimated 23.5% for 1992. In 1992 the deficit on the current account of the balance of payments was estimated at 21% of GDP. By the end of 1992 Rwanda's total external debt was $873.3m., of which $804.3m. was long-term public debt. The debt outstanding and disbursed in that year was equivalent to 56.3% of GDP, compared with 16.3% in 1980 and 32.1% in 1990. By the end of October 1993 foreign reserves were estimated to be insufficient to sustain imports for one week.

Rwanda's heavy dependence on foreign assistance (equivalent to as much as 90% of public investment in recent years) has made the economy vulnerable to civil and political instability. The violent aftermath of the death of President Habyarimana in April 1994 prompted the withdrawal of all but emergency aid.

FOREIGN TRADE

In April 1976 Rwanda's economy came almost to a standstill as the result of a blockade imposed by President Amin of Uganda in a dispute with neighbouring Kenya. Amin's ban on heavy vehicles from neighbouring countries from using Uganda's roads in 1977, added to rising petrol prices, led to further hardship and strengthened the government's determination to find alternative outlets. An air cargo service, used in 1977 and 1978 to move stocks of coffee, was found to be scarcely more expensive than land transport and appreciably more reliable. The complete closure of the border from February to May 1979, caused by the fighting in Uganda, again severely disrupted trade and, as a result, stockpiles of coffee and tea rose to unprecedented levels, while serious shortages of petroleum and cement were experienced. Road transport on routes through Uganda was further disrupted by civil disorder during 1984 and 1985, and in 1986 a series of major initiatives was taken in order to assure Rwanda's vital trade links through Uganda. The October 1990 guerrilla invasion again showed the extreme vulnerability of Rwanda's geographical position. Both trade and road communications with Uganda and Kenya virtually ceased as a result of the hostilities.

Rwanda has long been experiencing a trade deficit, which stood at $69m. in 1986 and deteriorated in 1987 to the extent that it exceeded the total of export earnings, which covered only 36% of imports (20% in 1992). This imbalance appears unlikely to be rectified in the foreseeable future (despite an increase in world coffee prices), owing to war damage inflicted on the economic infrastructure, the death and displacement of a vast number of the working population, and the insurance stranglehold imposed on shipments to Rwanda as a result of its official designation as a 'war zone'. However, hopes have been expressed that the restoration of peace might facilitate the implementation of a free trade zone for Burundi and Rwanda (as envisaged by Presidents Ndadaye and Habyarimana in October 1993) to encourage the bilateral exchange of goods and services and to enhance the sales of Rwandan cement and Burundian glass in the respective neighbouring country.

STRUCTURAL ADJUSTMENT

Following negotiations that lasted for over a year, an agreement on structural adjustment between the Rwandan government and the IMF was announced in November 1990. Clearly, continued insecurity resulting from the war and its resultant economic set-backs were expected to hinder the initial implementation of the agreement, whose provisions included a devaluation of 40%, the introduction of a more liberal system of import licensing, the increase of import taxes, other tax changes (including the increase of sales tax), the suppression, except for monopolies, of profit-margin control, a suspension of the advantageous clauses of the Investment Code, and new credit and interest rate policies. Contrary to many other agreements of this kind, it imposes no significant cut-backs in public sector employment, and health and education spending are left virtually untouched. However, purchasing power was severely diminished as the result of increased consumer prices. In 1991 substantial international financial aid for the programme was pledged, amounting to more than $170m., including $46m. from the EU, $41m. from the IMF, $25m. from the USA and $17m. from Belgium.

Further recommendations from donors prompted the abolition during 1993, of existing legislation whereby government sanction was required for the establishment of private businesses (it was alleged that this law had hitherto perpetuated the economic predominence of President Habyarimana's Akazu clan), and the former government's announcement of a comprehensive programme of privatization. However, the FPR, which subsequently took control of the country, has repeatedly stated its opposition to such a precipitant divestment programme, in favour of a programme to better employ natural resources and encourage greater self-sufficiency through land reform and the prioritization of the production of essential commodities in preference to luxury goods.

Statistical Survey

Source (unless otherwise stated): Office rwandais d'information, BP 83, Kigali; tel. 5665.

Area and Population

AREA, POPULATION AND DENSITY

Area (sq km)	26,338*
Population (census results)	
15–16 August 1978	4,830,984
15 August 1991†	
Males	3,487,189
Females	3,677,805
Total	7,164,994
Density (per sq km) at 1991 census	272.0

* 10,169 sq miles. † Provisional results.

POPULATION BY PREFECTURE (1990)*

Butare	762,735
Byumba	782,230
Cyangugu	514,279
Gikongoro	466,576
Gisenyi	734,690
Gitarama	851,288
Kibungo	651,887
Kibuye	471,066
Kigali	913,481
Kigali-Ville	232,733
Ruhengeri	767,531
Total	7,148,496

* Provisional.

PRINCIPAL TOWNS (population at 1978 census)

Kigali (capital)	117,749	Ruhengeri	16,025
Butare	21,691	Gisenyi	12,436

BIRTHS AND DEATHS (UN estimates, annual averages)

	1975–80	1980–85	1985–90
Birth rate (per 1,000)	52.8	52.2	52.1
Death rate (per 1,000)	20.2	18.8	18.0

Source: UN, *World Population Prospects: The 1992 Revision.*

Expectation of life (census results, years at birth, 1978): males 45.1; females 47.7.

ECONOMICALLY ACTIVE POPULATION
(persons aged 14 years and over, official estimates at January 1989)

	Males	Females	Total
Agriculture, hunting, forestry and fishing	1,219,586	1,612,972	2,832,558
Mining and quarrying	4,652	40	4,692
Manufacturing	32,605	12,483	45,088
Electricity, gas and water	2,445	116	2,561
Construction	37,674	563	38,237
Trade, restaurants and hotels	61,169	18,857	80,026
Transport, storage and communications	6,796	536	7,332
Financing, insurance, real estate and business services	2,202	926	3,128
Community, social and personal services	89,484	30,537	120,021
Activities not adequately defined	5,392	4,021	9,413
Total employed	1,462,005	1,681,051	3,143,056

Source: ILO, *Year Book of Labour Statistics.*

Mid-1992 (estimates, '000 persons): Agriculture, etc. 3,264; Total labour force 3,590 (Source: FAO, *Production Yearbook*).

Agriculture

PRINCIPAL CROPS ('000 metric tons)

	1990	1991	1992
Maize	101	104*	100†
Sorghum	183	205*	175†
Potatoes	286	240†	280†
Sweet potatoes	817	850†	770†
Cassava (Manioc)	239	450†	400†
Yams	3	5†	5†
Taro (Coco yam)	78	70†	75†
Dry beans	205	210†	200†
Dry peas†	18	16	18
Groundnuts (in shell)	8	10†	12†
Plantains	2,747	2,800†	2,900†
Coffee (green)*	32	29	35
Tea (made)	13	13†	14†

* Unofficial estimate(s). † FAO estimate(s).
Source: FAO, *Production Yearbook.*

LIVESTOCK ('000 head)

	1990	1991	1992
Cattle	582	600*	610*
Pigs*	137	139	142
Sheep	389	390*	395*
Goats	1,075	1,090*	1,100*

* FAO estimate(s).
Source: FAO, *Production Yearbook.*

LIVESTOCK PRODUCTS (FAO estimates, '000 metric tons)

	1990	1991	1992
Beef and veal	14	14	14
Goats' meat	4	4	4
Other meat	13	13	14
Cows' milk	88	88	89
Goats' milk	13	14	14
Hen eggs	2.4	2.5	2.6
Cattle hides	2.0	2.0	2.0

Source: FAO, *Production Yearbook*.

Forestry

ROUNDWOOD REMOVALS ('000 cubic metres, excluding bark)

	1990	1991	1992
Sawlogs, veneer logs and logs for sleepers	20	20	60
Other industrial wood*	208	208	208
Fuel wood	5,353	5,392	5,392*
Total	5,581	5,620	5,660

* FAO estimate(s).

Source: FAO, *Yearbook of Forest Products*.

SAWNWOOD PRODUCTION
('000 cubic metres, including railway sleepers)

	1990	1991	1992
Total	8	8	36

Source: FAO, *Yearbook of Forest Products*.

Fishing

('000 metric tons, live weight)

	1989	1990	1991
Total catch (freshwater fishes)	1.5	2.5	3.6

Source: FAO, *Yearbook of Fishery Statistics*.

Mining

(metric tons, unless otherwise indicated)

	1988	1989	1990
Tin concentrates	0	700	700
Tungsten concentrates	3*	105	100
Gold ore (kilograms)	15	732	700

* Figures refer to the metal content of ores and concentrates.
† Provisional.

Source: UN, *Industrial Statistics Yearbook*.

Natural gas: about 1 million cubic metres per year.

Industry

SELECTED PRODUCTS

	1989	1990	1991
Beer ('000 hectolitres)	717	592	915
Soft drinks ('000 hectolitres)	161	130	101
Cigarettes (million)	552	290	331
Footwear ('000 pairs)	32	22	24
Soap ('000 metric tons)	9	10	9
Cement ('000 metric tons)	67	60	57
Radio receivers ('000)	8	6	2
Electric energy (million kWh)	105	78	81

Finance

CURRENCY AND EXCHANGE RATES

Monetary Units
100 centimes = 1 franc rwandais (Rwanda franc).

Sterling and Dollar Equivalents (28 February 1994)
£1 sterling = 214.36 Rwanda francs;
US $1 = 144.24 Rwanda francs;
1,000 Rwanda francs = £4.665 = $6.933.

Average Exchange Rate (Rwanda francs per US $)
1991 125.14
1992 133.35
1993 144.25

Note: Since September 1983 the currency has been linked to the IMF special drawing right (SDR). Until November 1990 the mid-point exchange rate was SDR 1 = 102.71 Rwanda francs. In November 1990 a new rate of SDR 1 = 171.18 Rwanda francs was established. This remained in effect until June 1992, when the rate was adjusted to SDR 1 = 201.39 Rwanda francs.

BUDGET (provisional, million Rwanda francs)

Revenue*	1990	1991	1992
Tax revenue	20,310	23,349	25,274
Taxes on income, profits, etc.	4,056	3,602	4,487
Social security contributions	1,560	1,193	684
Taxes on property	107	15	80
Domestic taxes on goods and services	7,851	9,316	9,973
Taxes on international trade and transactions	5,945	8,278	8,920
Other current revenue	2,834	2,707	3,449
Total revenue	23,144	26,506	28,723

Expenditure†	1990	1991	1992
Current expenditure‡	27,034	29,864	40,670
Expenditure on goods and services	21,312	26,483	35,593
Wages and salaries	11,773	13,390	14,545
Interest payments	2,131	4,292	4,800
Subsidies and other current transfers	6,632	2,898	4,504
Capital expenditure	13,402	17,794	14,198
Total expenditure	40,436	47,658	54,868

* Excluding grants received (million Rwandan francs): 5,871 in 1990; 13,682 in 1991; 10,796 in 1992.
† Excluding net lending (million Rwanda francs): −141 in 1990; −369 in 1991; −315 in 1992.
‡ After adjustment for changes in outstanding arrears (million Rwanda francs): −3,041 in 1990; −3,809 in 1991; −4,227 in 1992.

1993 (estimates, million Rwanda francs): Total revenue 29,597, excluding grants (19,171); total expenditure 68,742, excluding net lending (−384).

Source: IMF, *Government Finance Statistics Yearbook*.

NATIONAL BANK RESERVES (US $ million at 31 December)

	1991	1992	1993
IMF special drawing rights	9.63	3.34	2.90
Reserve position in IMF	9.24	14.30	13.45
Foreign exchange	91.25	61.08	31.11
Total	110.12	78.72	47.46

Source: IMF, *International Financial Statistics.*

MONEY SUPPLY (million Rwanda francs at 31 December)

	1991	1992	1993
Currency outside banks	8,822	10,321	11,522
Demand deposits at deposit money banks	8,587	11,571	12,876
Total money (incl. others)	18,145	22,631	24,398

Source: IMF, *International Financial Statistics.*

COST OF LIVING
(Consumer Price Index for Kigali; base: 1981 = 100)

	1989	1990	1991
Food	176.1	185.0	210.2
Fuel and light	70.1	72.2	82.4
Clothing	136.2	137.0	165.5
Rent	91.7	98.6	98.7
All items (incl. others)	137.8	143.6	171.8

1992: Food 225.0; All items 188.1.
Source: ILO, *Year Book of Labour Statistics.*
1993: All items 211.4 (Source: UN, *Monthly Bulletin of Statistics*).

NATIONAL ACCOUNTS
(million Rwanda francs at current prices*)
National Income and Product

	1987	1988	1989
Compensation of employees	42,530	45,050	46,970
Operating surplus	102,920	105,310	116,250
Domestic factor incomes	145,450	150,360	163,220
Consumption of fixed capital	11,080	12,360	14,540
Gross domestic product (GDP) at factor cost	156,530	162,720	177,760
Indirect taxes	14,910	15,460 }	12,460
Less Subsidies	—	250 }	
GDP in purchasers' values	171,440	177,930	190,220
Factor income from abroad	800	690	750
Less Factor income paid abroad	3,540	4,260	2,980
Gross national product (GNP)	168,700	174,360	187,990
Less Consumption of fixed capital	11,080	12,360	14,540
National income in market prices	157,620	162,000	173,450
Other current transfers from abroad	6,290	7,120	6,470
Less Other current transfers paid abroad	2,010	1,950	1,810
National disposable income	161,900	167,170	178,110

Expenditure on the Gross Domestic Product

	1988	1989	1990
Government final consumption expenditure	24,280	25,370	24,460
Private final consumption expenditure	142,180	137,390	156,940
Increase in stocks	980	−620	140
Gross fixed capital formation	26,920	27,420	25,280
Total domestic expenditure	194,360	189,560	206,820
Exports of goods and services	16,090	15,360	15,610
Less Imports of goods and services	32,530	30,870	32,210
GDP in purchasers' values	177,920	174,050	190,220

Gross Domestic Product by Economic Activity

	1987	1988	1989
Agriculture, hunting, forestry and fishing	65,350	67,440	75,690
Mining and quarrying	340	360	790
Manufacturing	25,040	24,980	24,930
Electricity, gas and water	1,020	1,170	950
Construction	11,940	12,230	12,880
Trade, restaurants and hotels	23,620	22,660	24,400
Transport, storage and communications	11,900	12,640	12,930
Finance, insurance, real estate, etc.	12,940	14,560	16,050
Community, social and personal services	14,610	15,660	15,760
Sub-total	166,760	171,700	184,380
Import duties	4,680	6,240	5,840
GDP in purchasers' values	171,440	177,940	190,220

* Figures are rounded to the nearest 10 million francs.
Source: UN, *National Accounts Statistics.*
1990: GDP 193,900 million francs.
1991: GDP 212,800 million francs.
1992: GDP 217,300 million francs.
(Source: IMF, *International Financial Statistics.*)

BALANCE OF PAYMENTS (US $ million)

	1990	1991	1992
Merchandise exports f.o.b.	102.6	95.6	68.5
Merchandise imports f.o.b.	−227.7	−228.1	−240.4
Trade balance	−125.1	−132.5	−171.9
Exports of services	42.2	43.0	31.4
Imports of services	−130.9	−111.5	−114.6
Other income received	4.4	3.5	4.7
Other income paid	−21.1	−17.3	−17.4
Private unrequited transfers (net)	5.8	20.9	22.1
Official unrequited transfers (net)	115.8	159.8	161.1
Current balance	−108.8	−34.1	−84.6
Direct investment (net)	7.7	4.6	2.2
Portfolio investment (net)	−0.3	−0.1	—
Other capital (net)	48.3	94.6	60.2
Net errors and omissions	30.3	0.2	18.2
Overall balance	−22.9	65.2	−4.0

Source: IMF, *International Financial Statistics.*

External Trade

PRINCIPAL COMMODITIES (million Rwanda francs)

Imports c.i.f.	1989	1990	1991
Consumer goods	7,610.7	n.a.	10,819.7
Food	2,323.8	2,673.0	4,366.9
Clothing	1,143.4	554.0	915.9
Mineral fuels and lubricants	3,850.5	3,689.2	4,913.1
Capital goods	6,909.9	4,826.2	6,725.8
Transport equipment	1,832.5	901.8	1,322.2
Machinery and tools	3,969.5	2,496.0	4,260.6
Semi-manufactures	8,329.3	7,999.0	16,015.9
Construction materials	1,570.0	1,316.1	1,486.5
Total (incl. others)	26,700.4	23,057.4	38,474.5

Exports f.o.b.	1989	1990	1991
Coffee (green)	4,691.0	5,424.5	7,209.8
Tea	1,557.3	1,736.8	2,796.6
Tin ores and concentrates	381.2	294.5	319.7
Pyrethrum	151.4	160.2	279.3
Quinquina	60.6	29.9	24.1
Total (incl. others)	8,376.6	8,478.0	11,971.2

Sources: Banque Nationale du Rwanda; Ministère des Finances et de l'Economie, Kigali.

PRINCIPAL TRADING PARTNERS (million Rwanda francs)

Imports	1989	1990	1991
Belgium/Luxembourg	5,020.0	4,468.7	6,588.9
Burundi	149.2	102.8	259.1
France	1,899.2	1,782.4	2,616.3
Germany, Federal Republic	2,189.8	2,540.4	2,324.9
Italy	866.3	584.9	1,088.9
Japan	3,177.3	n.a.	n.a.
Kenya	3,907.1	3,818.4	5,153.0
Netherlands	790.7	837.2	1,043.3
Uganda	145.9	257.0	3.6
United Kingdom	556.2	527.0	808.3
USA	236.5	168.9	402.8
Zaire	303.6	190.8	266.9
Total (incl. others)	26,700.4	23,057.3	38,474.5

Exports	1989	1990	1991
Belgium/Luxembourg	1,610.8	1,158.4	1,412.7
Burundi	15.0	23.7	120.1
France	313.4	54.7	137.7
Germany, Federal Republic	1,515.9	1,822.8	2,552.7
Italy	299.8	190.9	199.6
Kenya	20.4	14.3	4.3
Netherlands	945.4	1,083.4	2,246.9
Uganda	133.8	64.2	22.0
United Kingdom	546.4	708.1	767.2
USA	427.9	448.1	689.1
Zaire	45.1	27.7	37.7
Total (incl. others)	8,376.6	8,478.2	11,971.2

Source: Banque Nationale du Rwanda, Kigali.

Transport

ROAD TRAFFIC (motor vehicles in use at 31 December)

	1989	1990	1991
Motor cycles and scooters	8,202	8,054	8,207
Passenger cars	8,135	9,255	10,217
Other vehicles	11,692	9,150	8,670
Total	28,029	26,459	27,094

Source: Banque Nationale du Rwanda, Kigali.

CIVIL AVIATION (traffic)

	1989	1990	1991
Freight loaded (metric tons)	5,281	3,094	2,674
Freight unloaded (metric tons)	7,456	3,814	4,794
Passenger arrivals ('000)	44	39	29
Passenger departures ('000)	46	42	30

Source: Banque Nationale du Rwanda, Kigali.

Tourism

	1988	1989	1990
Tourist arrivals ('000)	36	37	43
Tourist receipts (US $ million)	7	9	10

Source: UN, *Statistical Yearbook*.

Communications Media

	1988	1989	1990
Radio receivers ('000 in use)	385	415	450
Telephones ('000 in use)	11	12	14
Daily newspapers (number)	1	n.a.	1

1991: Radio receivers 467,000.

Source: mainly UNESCO, *Statistical Yearbook*.

Education

(1990/91)

	Institutions	Teachers	Pupils: Males	Pupils: Females	Pupils: Total
Primary	1,671	19,183	552,568	547,869	1,100,437
Secondary	n.a.	2,802	39,877	30,523	70,400
Tertiary*	n.a.	646	2,750	639	3,389

* Figures are for 1989/90.

Source: UNESCO, *Statistical Yearbook*.

Directory

The Constitution

On 10 June 1991 presidential assent was granted to a series of amendments to the Constitution in force since 19 December 1978. The document, as amended, provides, *inter alia*, for a multi-party political system, the separation of the functions of the executive, judiciary and legislature, the limitation of presidential tenure to no more than two consecutive five-year terms of office, the establishment of the office of Prime Minister, freedom of the press, and the right of workers to withdraw their labour. The provisions of the amended Constitution substantially modify or replace those of the 1978 Constitution, whose main provisions are summarized below:

THE REPUBLIC

Rwanda is a democratic, social and sovereign State. There is equality among citizens, who exercise national rights through their representatives.

CIVIL RIGHTS

Fundamental liberties, as defined in the Declaration of Human Rights, are guaranteed.

THE EXECUTIVE

Executive power is exercised by the President, who is both Head of State and President of the Mouvement révolutionnaire national pour le développement (MRND), and to whom the Government is responsible. He is elected for a five-year term of office and may be re-elected, provided that he is not over 60 years of age. In the event of the President's incapacity or death, the Secretary-General of the MRND, the sole legal party, acts as his successor pending the election of a new President, which must be held within 90 days. The President, who nominates and dismisses ministers, presides over the Council of Ministers; negotiates and terminates all international treaties; promulgates laws; exercises the prerogative of mercy; and is the Commander-in-Chief of the Armed Forces.

LEGISLATIVE POWER

Exercised jointly by the President and the Conseil national de développement (CND), elected every five years by universal adult suffrage. The Conseil may censure the head of government by a vote passed by four-fifths of its members but may not dismiss him. Such a vote would oblige the Government to change its policies or its ministers.

The Government

HEAD OF STATE

President: PASTEUR BIZIMUNGU (took office 19 July 1994).

Vice-President: Maj.-Gen. PAUL KAGAME (FPR).

COUNCIL OF MINISTERS
(September 1994)

A coalition council of national unity, comprising the Front patriotique rwandais (FPR), the Mouvement démocratique républicain (MDR), the Parti social-démocrate (PSD), the Parti démocratique chrétien (PDC), and the Parti libéral (PL).

Prime Minister: FAUSTIN TWAGIRAMUNGU (MDR).

Deputy Prime Minister and Minister of the Civil Service: Col. ALEXIS KANYARENGWE (FPR).

Minister of National Defence and Vice-President: Maj.-Gen. PAUL KAGAME (FPR).

Minister of the Interior and Communal Development: SETH SENDASHONGA (FPR).

Minister of Foreign Affairs and Co-operation: JEAN-MARIE NDAGIJIMANA (MDR).

Minister of Planning: (vacant).

Minister of Transport and Communications: IMMACULÉE KAYUMBA (FPR).

Minister of Agriculture and Livestock: (vacant).

Minister of Primary and Secondary Education: PIERRE CELESTIN RWIGEMA (MDR).

Minister of Higher Education and Scientific Research: JOSEPH NSENGIMANA (PL).

Minister of Finance: MARC RUGENERA (PSD).

Minister of Youth and Associated Movements: PATRICK MAZIMPAKA (FPR).

Minister of Information: JEAN-BAPTISTE NDUWINGOMA.

Minister of Justice: ALPHONSE-MARIE NKUBITO (MDR).

Minister of Health: Col JOSEPH KAREMERA (FPR).

Minister of Labour and Social Affairs: PIE MUGABO (PL).

Minister of Public Works and Energy: CHARLES NTAKIRUTINKA (PSD).

Minister of Environment and Tourism: JEAN-NEPOMUCÈNE NAYINZIRA (PDC).

Minister of Commerce, Industry, and Artisan's Affairs: PROSPER HIGIRO (PL).

Minister of Women's Affairs and the Family: ALOYSIA INYUMBA (FPR).

Minister of State with Responsibility for Reconstruction, Refugees, Displaced Persons and Army Demobilization: JACQUES BIHOZAGARA (FPR).

MINISTRIES

Office of the President: BP 15, Kigali; tel. 75432; telex 517.

Ministry of Agriculture and Livestock: BP 621, Kigali; tel. 75324.

Ministry of the Civil Service: BP 403, Kigali; tel. 86578.

Ministry of Commerce, Industry and Artisan's Affairs: BP 476, Kigali; tel. 73875.

Ministry of Environment and Tourism: BP 2378, Kigali; tel. 77415; fax 74834.

Ministry of Finance: BP 158, Kigali; tel. 75410; telex 502.

Ministry of Foreign Affairs and Co-operation: BP 179, Kigali; tel. 75257.

Ministry of Health: BP 84, Kigali; tel. 76681.

Ministry of Higher Education and Scientific Research: BP 624, Kigali; tel. 85422.

Ministry of the Interior and Communal Development: BP 446, Kigali; tel. 86708.

Ministry of Justice: BP 160, Kigali; tel. 866626.

Ministry of Labour and Social Affairs: BP 790, Kigali; tel. 73481.

Ministry of Planning: BP 46, Kigali; tel. 75513.

Ministry of Primary and Secondary Education: BP 622, Kigali; tel. 85422.

Ministry of Public Works and Energy: BP 24, Kigali; tel. 86649.

Ministry of Transport and Communications: BP 720, Kigali; tel. 72424.

Ministry of Youth and Associated Movements: BP 1044, Kigali; tel. 75861; telex 22502.

Legislature

The establishment of a transitional national assembly to replace the Conseil national de développement (CND), as detailed in the provisions of the August 1993 Arusha peace accord, was repeatedly delayed during late 1993 and early 1994. In July, having secured control of the country, the FPR established a coalition government of national unity. By September 1994 the government had yet to finalize procedures for the establishment of a new legislature.

Political Organizations

Legislation authorizing the formation of political parties was promulgated in June 1991.

Coalition pour la défense de la république (CDR): Kigali; f. 1992; uncompromising Hutu support; unofficial militia known as *impuza mugambi*; Leader (vacant).

Front patriotique rwandais (FPR): f. 1990, also known as *Inkotanyi*; comprises mainly Tutsi exiles, but claims multi-ethnic support; began armed invasion of Rwanda from Uganda in Oct. 1990; took control of Rwanda in July 1994, following renewed offensive; Chair. Col ALEX KANYARENGWE; Sec.-Gen. Dr THÉOGÈNE RUDASINGWA.

Mouvement démocratique républicain (MDR): Kigali; banned 1973–91; fmrly also known as Parti de l'émancipation du peuple

Hutu (Parmehutu), dominant party 1962–73; split into two factions in late 1993 early 1994: pro-MRNDD faction led by FRODUALD KARAMIRA, with mainly Hutu support; anti-MRNDD faction led by FAUSTIN TWAGIRAMUNGU, with multi-ethnic support.

Mouvement républicain national pour la démocratie et le développement (MRNDD): BP 1055, Kigali; f. 1975 as the Mouvement révolutionnaire nationale pour le développement (MRND); sole legal party until 1991; adopted current name in April 1991; draws support from uncompromising Hutu groups; Chair. MATHIEU NGIRUMPATSE; large unofficial militia (*interahamwe*) led by ROBERT KADJUGA.

Parti démocrate chrétien (PDC): BP 2348, Kigali; tel. 76542; fax 72237; f. 1990; Leader JEAN NEPOMUCÈNE NAYINZIRA.

Parti démocratique islamique (PDI): Kigali; f. 1992.

Parti démocratique rwandais (Pader): Kigali; f. 1992; cen. cttee of four mems; Sec. JEAN NTAGUNGIRA.

Parti écologiste (Peco): Kigali; f. 1992.

Parti libéral (PL): BP 1304, Kigali; tel. 77916; fax 77838; f. 1991; split into two factions in late 1993–early 1994: pro-MRNDD faction led by JUSTIN MUGENZI and AGNÈS NTAMBYARIRO; anti-MRNDD faction led by PROSPER HIGIRO, JOSEPH MUSENGIMANA and ESDRA KAYIRANGA.

Parti progressiste de la jeunesse rwandaise (PPJR): Kigali; f. 1991; political motto of 'patriotism, peace and progress'; Leader ANDRÉ HAKIZIMANA.

Parti républicain rwandais (Parerwa): Kigali; f. 1992; Leader AUGUSTIN MUTAMBA.

Parti social-démocrate (PSD): Kigali; f. 1991 by a breakaway faction of the MRND; Pres. (vacant).

Parti socialiste rwandais (PSR): Kigali; f. 1991; workers' rights.

Rassemblement travailliste pour la démocratie (RTD): BP 1894, Kigali; tel. 75622; fax 76574; f. 1991; Leader EMMANUEL NIZEYIMANA.

Union démocratique du peuple rwandais (UDPR): Kigali; f. 1992; Pres. VINCENT GWABUKWISI; Vice-Pres. SYLVESTRE HUBI.

Union du peuple rwandais (UPR): Brussels, Belgium; f. 1990; Hutu-led; Pres. SILAS MAJYAMBERE; Sec.-Gen. EMMANUEL TWAGILIMANA.

Diplomatic Representation

Note: Many diplomatic missions closed in April 1994, when diplomatic personnel were withdrawn, owing to the escalation of civil disorder.

EMBASSIES IN RWANDA

Algeria: Kigali; tel. 85831; Ambassador: MOHAMED LAALA.

Belgium: rue Nyarugence, BP 81, Kigali; tel. 75554; telex 501; Ambassador: JOHAN SWINNEN.

Burundi: rue de Ntaruka, BP 714, Kigali; tel. 75010; telex 536; Ambassador: CANISIUS SAMBIRA.

Canada: rue Akagera, BP 1177, Kigali; tel. 73210; fax 72719; Ambassador: LUCIE EDWARDS.

China, People's Republic: ave Député Kayuku, BP 1345, Kigali; tel. 75415; Ambassador: TIAN YIMIN.

Egypt: BP 1069, Kigali; tel. 82686; telex 22585; fax 82686; Ambassador: SAMEH SAMY DARWISH.

France: 40 ave Député Kamuzinzi, BP 53, Kigali; tel. 75225; telex 522; Ambassador: JEAN-MICHEL MARLAUD.

Germany: 8 rue de Bugarama, BP 355, Kigali; tel. 75222; telex 22520; fax 77267; Ambassador: DIETER HÖLSCHER.

Holy See: 49 ave Paul VI, BP 261, Kigali (Apostolic Nunciature); tel. 75293; fax 75181; Apostolic Nuncio: Most Rev. GIUSEPPE BERTELLO, Titular Archbishop of Urbisaglia.

Kenya: BP 1215, Kigali; tel. 82774; telex 22598; Ambassador: PETER KIHARA MATHANJUKI.

Libya: BP 1152, Kigali; tel. 76470; telex 549; Secretary of the People's Bureau: MOUSTAPHA MASAND EL-GHAILUSHI.

Russia: ave de l'Armée, BP 40, Kigali; tel. 75286; telex 22661; Ambassador: (vacant).

Uganda: BP 656, Kigali; tel. 76495; telex 22521; fax 73551; Ambassador: (vacant).

USA: blvd de la Révolution, BP 28, Kigali; tel. 75601; fax 72128; Ambassador: DAVID P. RAWSON.

Zaire: 504 rue Longue, BP 169, Kigali; tel. 75289; Ambassador: KABALA KISEKE SEKA.

Judicial System

The judicial system comprises a Council of State with administrative jurisdiction, a Court of Cassation, a Constitutional Court consisting of the Court of Cassation and the Council of State sitting jointly, a Court of Accounts responsible for examining all public accounts, and courts of appeal, courts of first instance and provincial courts.

President of the Constitutional Court: (vacant).

State Prosecutor: ALPHONSE-MARIE NKUBITO.

Religion

AFRICAN RELIGIONS

ABOUT ONE-HALF OF THE POPULATION HOLD TRADITIONAL BELIEFS.

CHRISTIANITY

The Roman Catholic Church

Rwanda comprises one archdiocese and eight dioceses. At 31 December 1992 there were an estimated 3,485,000 adherents in the country, representing around 48% of the total population.

Bishops' Conference: Conférence Episcopale du Rwanda, BP 357, Kigali; tel. 75439; telex 566; f. 1980; Pres. (vacant).

Archbishop of Kigali: (vacant), Archevêché, BP 715, Kigali; tel. 75769; fax 76371.

The Anglican Communion

The Church of the Province of Rwanda, inaugurated in 1992, has eight dioceses.

Archbishop of Rwanda and Bishop of Shyira: Most Rev. AUGUSTIN NSHAMIHIGO, BP 15, Vunga, via Ruhengeri; fax 46383.

Provincial Secretary: Rt Rev. JONATHAN RUHUMULIZA (Assistant Bishop of Kigali), BP 2487, Kigali; fax 82172.

Other Protestant Churches

Eglise Baptiste: Nyantanga, BP 59, Butare; Pres. Rev. DAVID BAZIGA; Gen. Sec. ELEAZAR ZIHERAMBERE.

There are about 250,000 other Protestants, including a substantial minority of Seventh-day Adventists.

BAHÁ'Í FAITH

National Spiritual Assembly: BP 652, Kigali; tel. 75982.

ISLAM

There is a small Islamic community.

The Press

Bulletin Agricole du Rwanda: OCIR-Café, BP 104, Kigali-Gikondo; telex 13; quarterly; in French; Pres. of Editorial Bd Dr AUGUSTIN NZINDUKIYIMANA; circ. 800.

Coopérative Trafipro Umunyamalyango: BP 302, Kigali; monthly; trade journal; in French and Kinyarwanda.

Dialogue: BP 572, Kigali; tel. 74178; f. 1967; every 2 months; Christian issues; circ. 2,000.

Etudes Rwandaises: Université Nationale du Rwanda, Rectorat, BP 56, Butare; tel. 30302; telex 605; f. 1977; quarterly; pure and applied science, literature, human sciences; in French; Pres. of Editorial Bd CHARLES NTAKIRUTINKA; circ. 1,000.

Hobe: BP 761, Kigali; f. 1955; monthly; for children; in Kinyarwanda; Dir ANDRÉ SIBOMANA; circ. 95,000.

Imvaho: Office Rwandais d'Information, BP 83, Kigali; tel. 75724; telex 557; f. 1960; weekly; in Kinyarwanda; circ. 51,000.

Journal Officiel: President's Office, BP 15, Kigali; tel. 75324; telex 517; f. 1979; fortnightly; Govt publication in French.

Kinyamateka: 5 blvd de l'OUA, BP 761, Kigali; tel. 76164; f. 1933; fortnightly; economics; Editorial Dir ANDRÉ SIBOMANA; circ. 11,000.

Nouvelles du Rwanda: Université Nationale du Rwanda, BP 117, Butare; every 2 months.

La Relève: Office Rwandais d'Information, BP 83, Kigali; tel. 75665; telex 557; f. 1976; monthly; politics, economics, culture; in French; Dir CHRISTOPHE MFIZI; circ. 1,700.

Revue Medicale Rwandaise: Ministry of Health, BP 83, Kigali; tel. 76681; f. 1968; quarterly; in French.

Revue Pédagogique: Ministry of Primary and Secondary Education, BP 622, Kigali; tel. 85697; telex 5697; quarterly; in French.

Umuhinzi-Mworozi: OCIR-Thé, BP 104, Kigali; f. 1975; monthly; circ. 1,500.

Urunana: Grand Séminaire de Nyakibanda, BP 85, Butare; tel. 30792; f. 1967; 3 a year; religious; Editor-in-Chief ACHILLE BAWE.

PRESS AGENCIES

Agence Rwandaise de Presse (ARP): 27 ave du Commerce, BP 83, Kigali; tel. 75735; telex 557; f. 1975.

Foreign Bureau

Agence France-Presse (AFP): BP 83, Kigali; tel. 72997; telex 557; Correspondent MARIE-GORETTI UWIBAMBE ORINFOR.

Publishers

Implico: BP 721, Kigali; tel. 73771.

Imprimerie de Kabgayi: BP 66, Gitarama; tel. 62252; fax 62345; f. 1932.

Imprimerie de Kigali, SARL: place du 5 juillet, BP 956, Kigali; tel. 85795; fax 84047; f. 1980; Dir THÉONESTE NSENGIMANA.

Imprimerie URWEGO: BP 762, Kigali; tel. 86027; Dir JEAN NSENGIYUNVA.

Pallotti-Presse: BP 863, Kigali; tel. 74084.

Printer Set: BP 184, Kigali; tel. 74116; fax 74121; f. 1984.

Government Publishing Houses

Imprimerie Nationale du Rwanda: BP 351, Kigali; tel. 75350; f. 1967; Dir JUVÉNAL NDISANZE.

Régie de l'Imprimerie Scolaire: BP 1347, Kigali; tel. 85695; fax 85695; f. 1985; Dir STANISLAS SINIBAGIWE.

Radio and Television

In 1991, according to UNESCO estimates, there were 467,000 radio receivers in use. A television service was scheduled to begin in December 1992.

Radiodiffusion de la République Rwandaise: BP 83, Kigali; tel. 75665; telex 22557; fax 76185; f. 1961; state-controlled; daily broadcasts in Kinyarwanda, Swahili, French and English; Chief of Programmes FRODUALD NTAWULIKURA; Dir of Information FERDINAND NAHIMANA.

Deutsche Welle Relay Station Africa: Kigali; daily broadcasts in German, English, French, Hausa, Swahili, Portuguese and Amharic.

A privately-controlled station, Radio-Télévision Libre des Mille Collines (RTLM) broadcasts pro-MRNDD and pro-CDR transmissions from Kigali. Radio Muhabura, the official station of the rebel FPR, also broadcasts to Rwanda in Kinyarwanda.

Finance

(cap. = capital; res = reserves; dep. = deposits; m. = million; brs = branches; amounts in Rwanda francs)

BANKING

Central Bank

Banque Nationale du Rwanda: BP 531, Kigali; tel. 75249; telex 508; fax 72551; f. 1964; bank of issue; cap. and res 6,424m. (1990); Gov. DENIS NTIRUGIRIMBABAZI.

Commercial Banks

Banque Commerciale du Rwanda, SA: BP 354, Kigali; tel. 75591; telex 22505; fax 73395; f. 1963; 44.5% state-owned; cap. 12,895.0m. (Dec. 1992); Pres. CÔME BIZIMUNGU; Dir-Gen. CLAVER MVUYEKURE; 13 brs.

Banque Continentale Africaine (Rwanda), SA (BACAR): 20 blvd de la Révolution, BP 331, Kigali; tel. 74456; telex 22544; fax 73486; f. 1983; 51% owned by Banque Continentale du Luxembourg; cap. 200m., total assets 4,573.7m. (Dec. 1992); Pres. NASIR ABID; Dir-Gen. PASTEUR MUSABE.

Banque de Kigali, SA: 63 ave du Commerce, BP 175, Kigali; tel. 76931; telex 22514; fax 73461; f. 1966; cap. 300.0m., total assets 9,574.6m. (Dec. 1991); Pres. JEAN DAMASCÈNE HATEGEKIMANA; Dir-Gen. EDOUARD BOVY; 9 brs.

Development Banks

Banque Rwandaise de Développement, SA (BRD): BP 1341, Kigali; tel. 73557; telex 22563; fax 73569; f. 1967; 47% state-owned; cap. and res 2,152.1m., total assets 4,492.2m. (Dec. 1993); Pres. DONAT HAKIZIMANA; Dir-Gen. DOMINIQUE MUNYANGOGA.

Union des Banques Populaires du Rwanda (Banki z'Abaturage mu Rwanda): BP 1348, Kigali; tel. 73559; telex 584; fax 73579; f. 1975; cap. 136.1m., dep. 4,919.9m. (Dec. 1993); Pres. (vacant); Gen. Man. (vacant); 145 brs.

Savings Bank

Caisse d'Epargne du Rwanda: BP 146, Kigali; tel. 75928; telex 22553; f. 1963; 100% state-owned; cap. 162.0m., dep. 2,127m. (Dec. 1992); Chair. Dr DONAT HAKIZIMANA; Dir-Gen. DOMINIQUE MUNYANGOGA; 16 brs.

INSURANCE

Société Nationale d'Assurances du Rwanda (SONARWA): BP 1035, Kigali; tel. 72101; telex 540; fax 72052; f. 1975; cap. 500m.; Dir-Gen. SIMÉON NTEZIRAYO.

Société Rwandaise d'Assurance SARL (SORAS): BP 924, Kigali; tel. 73716; telex 571; fax 73362; f. 1984; cap. 150m.; Dirs-Gen. (Admin.) CHARLES MHORANYI, CHRISTIAN DARDANNE.

Trade and Industry

CHAMBER OF COMMERCE

Chambre de Commerce et d'Industrie du Rwanda: BP 319, Kigali; tel. 83537; telex 22662; fax 83532; f. 1982; co-ordinates commerce and industry on national scale; Pres. BONIFACE RUCAGU; Sec.-Gen. THOMAS KIGUFI.

ASSOCIATION

Association des Industriels du Rwanda: BP 39, Kigali; tel. and fax 75430; Sec. JEAN DE DIEU HABINEZA.

DEVELOPMENT ORGANIZATIONS

Cooperative de Promotion de l'Industrie Minière et Artesanale au Rwanda (COOPIMAR): BP 1139, Kigali; tel. 82127; fax 72128; Dir JEAN MBURANUMWE.

Electrogaz: Kigali; state water, electricity and gas concern.

Institut de Recherches Scientifiques et Technologiques (IRST): BP 227, Butare; tel. 30396; fax 30939; Dir-Gen. FRANÇOIS GASENGAYIRE.

Institut des Sciences Agronomiques du Rwanda (ISAR): BP 138, Butare; tel. 30642; fax 30644; for the development of subsistence and export agriculture; Dir ANDRÉ NDEREYEHE; 6 centres.

Office des Cultures Industrielles du Rwanda-Café (OCIR-Café): BP 104, Kigali; tel. 75004; telex 22513; fax 73992; f. 1978; development of coffee and other new agronomic industries; operates a coffee stabilization fund; Dir SYLVÈSTRE MUNYANEZA.

Office des Cultures Industrielles du Rwanda-Thé (OCIR-Thé): BP 1344, Kigali; tel. 72416; telex 22582; fax 73943; development and marketing of tea; Dir MICHEL BAGARAGAZA.

Office National pour le Développement de la Commercialisation des Produits Vivriers et des Produits Animaux (OPROVIA): BP 953, Kigali; tel. 82946; fax 82945; Dir INNOCENT BUTARE.

Office du Pyrèthre du Rwanda (OPYRWA): BP 79, Ruhengeri; tel. 46306; telex 22606; fax 46364; f. 1978; development of pyrethrum; Dir JOSEPH NTAMFURAYINDA.

Office de la Valorisation Industrielle des Bananes du Rwanda (OVIBAR): BP 1002, Kigali; tel. 85857; Dir GASPARD NZABAMWITA.

Régie des Mines du Rwanda (REDEMI): BP 2195, Kigali; tel. 73632; f. 1988; state org. for mining tin, tantalum and tungsten (replacing Société des Mines du Rwanda, bankrupt in 1985 after closure of mines, owing to decline in world prices); Man. Dir JEAN BOSCO M. BICAMUMPAKA.

Régie Sucrière de Kibuye: Kigali; sugar manufacture and distribution.

Rwandatel: Kigali; telecommunications.

Rwandex: Kigali; exports of tea and coffee.

MAJOR INDUSTRIAL COMPANIES

BRALIRWA: BP 131, Kigali; tel. 85693; f. 1959; mfrs and bottlers of beer in Gisenyi and soft drinks in Kigali.

MIRONKO Plastic Industries: Kigali; tel. 76231; telex 550; plastic wares.

Murri Frères: BP 110, Chantier de Kigali, Kigali; telex 535; f. 1963; heavy engineering and construction; Propr PIETRO MURRI; Dir R. CAMENZIND.

OVIBAR (Office de la Valorisation de la Bananeraie Rwandaise): mfrs of banana wine and juice.

Savonnerie de Kicukiro (SAKIRWA): BP 441, Kigali; tel. 72678; telex 556; fax 75450; soap and washing powders; edible oil refinery.

Société Rwandaise pour la Production et la Commercialisation du Thé (SORWATHE), SARL: Kigali; tel. 75461; telex 548; f. 1978; tea; Dir CYOHOHA-RUKERI.

SODEPARAL: Kigali; telex 565; produces leather shoes.

SONATUBE: PVC and metal piping.

Sulfo-Rwanda Industries, SARL: BP 90, Kigali; tel. 75353; telex 22523; fax 74573; f. 1964; soap, cosmetics, plastic products, confectionery; Dir-Gen. TAJDIN HUSSAIN JAFFER.

TRADE UNIONS

Centrale d'Education et de Coopération des Travailleurs pour le Développement/Alliance Coopérative au Rwanda (CECOTRAD/ACORWA): BP 295, Kigali; f. 1984 to succeed the Conféd. Syndicale des Travailleurs du Rwanda (COSTRAR); Pres. ELIE KATABARWA.

Centrale Syndicale des Travailleurs du Rwanda: BP 1645, Kigali; tel. 84012; Sec.-Gen. MELCHIOR KANYAMIRWA.

Transport

RAILWAYS

There are no railways in Rwanda although plans exist for the eventual construction of a line passing through Uganda, Rwanda and Burundi, to connect with the Kigoma—Dar es Salaam line in Tanzania. Rwanda is linked by road to the Tanzanian railways system.

ROADS

In 1990 there were 13,173 km of roads, of which 5,200 km were main roads. Around 954 km of roads were paved in 1993 and it was hoped that the total length of paved roads would increase to 1,085 km by 1995. There are international road links with Uganda, Tanzania, Burundi and Zaire. Armed conflict between internal factions during 1994 has resulted in considerable damage to the road network, including the destruction of several important bridges.

Office National des Transports en Commun (ONATRACOM): BP 720, Kigali; tel. 75064; Dir (vacant).

INLAND WATERWAYS

There are services on Lake Kivu between Cyangugu, Gisenyi and Kibuye, including 2 vessels operated by ONATRACOM.

CIVIL AVIATION

The Kanombe international airport at Kigali can process up to 500,000 passengers annually. There is a second international airport at Kamembe, near the border with Zaire. There are airfields at Butare, Gabiro, Ruhengeri and Gisenyi, servicing internal flights.

Air Rwanda (Société Nationale des Transports Aériens du Rwanda): BP 808, Kigali; tel. 75492; telex 554; fax 72462; f. 1975; operates domestic passenger and cargo services and international cargo flights within Africa to Bujumbura (Burundi), Goma (Zaire), Entebbe (Uganda), Tanzania, Kenya and to Ostend (Belgium); Gen. Man. JORAM MUSHIMIYIMANA.

Tourism

Attractions for tourists include national parks, Lake Kivu and fine mountain scenery. In 1990 there were an estimated 43,000 foreign visitors to Rwanda. Total receipts from tourism were estimated at US $10m. in that year. In recent years the sector has been adversely effected by an increase in violence, arising from border insecurity, and political and tribal conflicts within Rwanda.

Ministry of Environment and Tourism: BP 2378, Kigali; tel. 77415; fax 74834.

Office rwandais du tourisme et des parcs nationaux (ORTPN): BP 905, Kigali; tel. 76514; fax 76512; f. 1973; the status and structure of ORTPN was under review in 1993.

Defence

All armed services form part of the army. In June 1993 the total strength of the army was 5,200 (including 200 air force personnel), and paramilitary forces totalled 1,200 men. Following the FPR's victory over the Rwandan armed forces in July 1994, responsibility for national defence was assumed by the FPR's military wing, the Rwandan Patriotic Army (RPA).

Defence Expenditure: Estimated at 13,184m. Rwanda francs in 1991.

Chief of Staff of the Army: Col SAM KAKA.

Education

Primary education, beginning at seven years of age and lasting for eight years, is officially compulsory. Secondary education, which is not compulsory, begins at the age of 15 and lasts for a further six years, comprising two equal cycles of three years. Schools are administered by the state and by Christian missions. In 1990 the enrolment at primary schools included an estimated 67% of children in the relevant age-group, but the comparable ratio for secondary enrolment was only 7%. In 1990, according to estimates by UNESCO, the average rate of adult illiteracy was 49.8% (males 36.1%; females 62.9%). Rwanda has a university, with campuses at Butare and Ruhengeri, and several other institutions of higher education, but some students attend universities abroad, particularly in Belgium, France or Germany. In 1990/91 there were 1,100,437 pupils enrolled at primary schools and 70,400 pupils enrolled at secondary schools, including agricultural and technical vocational schools. In 1989/90 an estimated 3,389 students were receiving higher education. In 1991 an estimated 17.1% of total government expenditure was allocated to education.

Bibliography

Abdulai, N. (Ed.). *Genocide in Rwanda: Background and Current Situation.* Africa Research and Information Centre, 1994.

Bulletin de la Banque Nationale du Rwanda. Kigali.

Erny, P. 'L'enseignement au Rwanda', in *Tiers Monde*, July–December 1974, XV, 59/60, pp. 707–722.

Harroy, J.-P. *Rwanda: de la Féodalité à la Démocratie: 1955–62.* Paris, Académie des Sciences d'Outre-mer.

d'Hertefelt, M., and de Lame, D. *Société, Culture et Histoire du Rwanda.* Tervuren, 1987.

Kagame, A. *Un abrégé de l'ethno-histoire du Rwanda.* Butare, Editions universitaires du Rwanda, 1972.

Kamukama, D. *Rwanda Conflict: Its Roots and Regional Implications.* Kampala, Fountain Publishers, 1993.

Ministère du Plan. 'Troisième Plan quinquennal de développement économique, social et culturel 1982–86', in *Journal Officiel*, No. 21, November 1982. Kigali.

Omaar, R. *Rwanda: Death, Despair and Defiance.* African Rights, 1994.

Reyntjens, F. *Pouvoir et Droit au Rwanda: Droit public et évolution politique 1916–1973.* Tervuren, Musée royal de l'Afrique centrale, 1985.

Sirven, P., Gotanegre, J.-F., and Prioul, G. *Géographie du Rwanda.* Brussels, Editions A. de Boeck, 1974.

Université Nationale du Rwanda. *Etudes Rwandaises, Vol. XIII: Minéralisation et inventaire des minéraux du Rwanda, Vol. I.* Butare, 1979.

Vanderlinden, J. 'La République rwandaise', in *Encyclopédie politique et constitutionnelle.* Paris, Berger-Levrault, 1970.

ST HELENA

(WITH ASCENSION AND TRISTAN DA CUNHA)

Physical and Social Geography

St Helena, a rugged and mountainous island of volcanic origin, lies in the South Atlantic Ocean, latitude 16° S, longitude 5° 45′ W, 1,131 km south-east of Ascension and about 1,930 km from the south-west coast of Africa. The island is 16.9 km long and 10.5 km broad, covering an area of 122 sq km (47 sq miles). The highest elevation, Diana's Peak, rises to 823 m above sea-level. The only inland waters are small streams, few of them now perennial, fed by springs in the central hills. These streams and rainwater are sufficient for domestic water supplies and a few small irrigation schemes.

The cool South Atlantic trade winds blow throughout the year. The climate is mild and varies little: the temperature in Jamestown, on the sea-coast, is 21°C–29°C in summer and 18°C–23°C in winter. Inland it is some 5°C cooler.

Figures for annual rainfall over the period 1985–88 show a similar variation between Jamestown, with 208–295 mm, and the eastern district, with 614–810 mm.

The most recent census was held on 22 February 1987, when the total population was enumerated at 5,664.

Jamestown, the capital, is the only town and had a population of 1,413 at the 1987 census.

The language of the island is English and the majority of the population belong to the Anglican communion.

St Helena has one of the world's most equable climates. Industrial pollution is absent from the atmosphere, and there are no endemic diseases of note. The island is of interest to naturalists for its rare flora and fauna; there are about 40 species of flora which are unique to St Helena.

Recent History

Revised by the Editor

The then uninhabited island of St Helena was discovered on 21 May 1502 by a Portuguese navigator, João da Nova Castella, on his homeward voyage from India. He named it in honour of Saint Helena, mother of the Emperor Constantine the Great, whose festival falls on that day. The existence of the island appears to have remained unknown to other European nations until 1588, when it was visited by Capt. Thomas Cavendish on his return from a voyage round the world. In 1633 the Dutch formally claimed St Helena but made no attempt to occupy it. The British East India Co first established a settlement there in 1659. The island was captured and briefly held by the Dutch in 1673. In that year a charter to occupy and govern St Helena was issued by King Charles II to the East India Co, under whose administration it remained until 1834, when it was brought under the direct control of the British government.

Following his abdication as French emperor, Napoleon Bonaparte was exiled in St Helena from 1815 until his death in 1821. The custody of Longwood House, in which he lived (and now an important Napoleonic museum), was passed to the French government in 1946.

During the 19th century St Helena was an important port of call on the route from Europe to India, but after the opening of the Suez Canal its importance declined.

In 1968 a South African concern, the South Atlantic Trading and Investment Co, acquired ownership of Solomon & Co (St Helena) Ltd, the local trading company. However, in view of the latter's dominant role in the island's economy, the British government decided in 1974 to take full control of the enterprise. In the following year the opposition St Helena Labour Party, which advocated private enterprise and opposed reliance on government development aid, was formed. The feasibility of the opposition's schemes to promote economic self-reliance was challenged by the government and later in 1975 the party's founder, G. A. D. Thornton, a dual British-South African national, was expelled from the island on the grounds that he was stirring controversy in the small community. An application to return was refused in 1977, and in 1981 Thornton initiated legal proceedings against the government, seeking to have his exclusion rescinded.

At the general election held in 1976 the St Helena Progressive Party, which supports the retention of close economic links with the United Kingdom, obtained 11 of the 12 seats in the legislative council. The legislative election in 1980 resulted in a similar allocation of seats. Subsequent general elections, the latest in July 1993, have been conducted on a non-partisan basis, and formal political activity has remained dormant.

In October 1981 the governor announced the appointment of a commission to review the island's constitution. The commission reported in 1983 that it was unable to find any proposal for constitutional change that would command the support of the majority of the islanders. In 1988, however, the government obtained the introduction of a formal constitution to replace the order in council and royal instructions under which St Helena was governed. This constitution entered into force on 1 January 1989.

Economy

Revised by the Editor

St Helena's principal crops are maize, potatoes and vegetables. In the past the islanders grew formio (New Zealand flax), used in the manufacture of flax fibre (hemp). At the end of 1965 the market price of hemp dropped considerably and production ceased in 1966.

Individuals hold land either in fee simple or by lease. Immigrants require a licence to hold land. Crown land may be leased on conditions approved by the governor. The Agricultural Development Authority, established in 1975, farms approximately one-half the arable area and one-third of the grazing areas. Commonage grazing areas are made available by government to private stock owners on a per caput per mensem basis. Since 1979/80 increased benefits have been made available to private farmers in a major effort to encourage greater local production, local utilization and farming efficiency. Grants, loans (of capital and labour) and free technical assistance have been offered and an increasing number of full-time smallholders are taking advantage of the scheme. Two major irrigation schemes using butyl-lined reservoirs have been completed. A notable rise in food production occurred during 1980/81 and again in 1981/82, and more land is being rented or leased from the government for this purpose.

Fish of many kinds are plentiful in the waters around St Helena, and a fisheries corporation was formed in 1979 to make the best use of this resource. A freezing/storage unit, built in 1977, is capable of storing 20 metric tons, allowing fish to be frozen for export as well as the local market. A drying and salting plant was built at Rupert's Bay in 1981 to process skipjack for export and a deep-sea fishing/survey vessel was acquired in February 1982. Fish exports began in 1979, and comprise tuna, skipjack and dried salted skipjack. In 1988 fish exports totalled 10.4 tons, valued at £11,534, but in 1989 147 tons of fish were exported with a value of £125,842. In 1990 fish exports fell back to 9.2 tons, and export revenue from this source amounted to £69,595. A small quantity of coffee is the only other commodity exported.

A major reafforestation programme was begun during the mid-1970s, aimed at replacing the flax and land reclamation. A sawmill/timber treatment plant, opened in 1977, produces a considerable proportion of the timber needed for construction and fencing requirements. There are no mineral resources.

A local handicrafts industry produces mainly wooden and lace articles. In 1985, when gross sales of handicrafts reached £47,138, export earnings from this source totalled £3,410. Unemployment is a serious problem, and a large proportion of the labour force is forced to seek employment overseas, principally on Ascension. In September 1993 807 St Helenians were working on Ascension.

The main imports, by value, are foodstuffs, liquor, timber, motor spirit, fuel oils, animal feed, building materials, motor vehicles and parts, machinery and parts. Total imports for 1989/90 were valued at £4,970,393, of which 67.6% were supplied by the United Kingdom and 31.8% by South Africa.

The St Helena Growers' Co-operative Society is the only such association on the island. It is both a consumers' and a marketing organization, and provides consumer goods, such as seeds, implements and feeding stuffs, to its members, and markets their produce, mainly vegetables, locally, to visiting ships and to Ascension Island. The local market is limited and is soon over-supplied, and this, together with the decrease in the number of ships calling over recent years, has inhibited the growth of this enterprise.

The only port in St Helena is Jamestown, which is an open roadstead with a good anchorage for ships of any size.

There is no airport or airstrip on St Helena and no railway. There are 98 km of all-weather roads, and a further 20 km of earth roads, which are used mainly by animal transport and are usable by motor vehicles only in dry weather. All roads have steep gradients and sharp curves.

In 1978, with the establishment of the St Helena Shipping Co, the St Helena government assumed responsibility for the operation and maintenance of a charter vessel, which carries cargo and passengers six times a year between Avonmouth, in the UK, and Cape Town, in South Africa, with calls at the Cape Verde Islands, Ascension Island and St Helena, and to Tristan da Cunha once a year. The vessel currently operating this service entered operation in 1990. The St Helena Shipping Co receives an annual subsidy of more than £1m. from the British government. Additionally, a small tanker was purchased in 1981 by the British government for the island and provides bulk supplies of petroleum products from the Canary Islands.

In 1989/90 St Helena received £24.2m. in British aid. This comprised a budgetary subvention of £3.9m., a shipping subsidy of £1.7m., development aid of £2.2m., technical co-operation finance of £2.0m. and £14.4m. for a replacement ship. Budget revenue (including budgetary aid) totalled £5.5m. in 1989/90, and expenditure in that year was £8.4m.

Statistical Survey

AREA AND POPULATION

Area: 122 sq km (47 sq miles).

Population: 5,147 (males 2,514; females 2,633) at census of 31 October 1976; 5,644 (males 2,769; females 2,875) at census of 22 February 1987.

Density: 46.3 per sq km (1987 census).

Principal town: Jamestown (capital), population 1,413 (1987 census).

Births and Deaths (1991): Registered live births 72; Registered deaths 42.

Employment: 2,516 (1,607 males, 909 females) at census of 22 February 1987; 2,416 in April 1991.

AGRICULTURE, ETC.

Livestock (1988): Cattle 1,134; Sheep 1,513; Pigs 599; Goats 1,354; Donkeys 312; Poultry 10,931.

Fishing (metric tons, live weight, including Ascension and Tristan da Cunha): Total catch 1,013 in 1989; 802 in 1990; 626 in 1991. Figures include catches of rock lobster from Tristan da Cunha during the 12 months ending 30 April of the year stated. Source: FAO, *Yearbook of Fishery Statistics*.

FINANCE

Currency and Exchange Rate: 100 pence (pennies) = 1 St Helena pound (£). *Sterling and Dollar Equivalents* (31 March 1994): £1 sterling = St Helena £1; US $1 = 67.36 pence; £100 = $148.46. *Average Exchange Rate* (US $ per £): 1.7694 in 1991; 1.7655 in 1992; 1.5020 in 1993. Note: The St Helena pound is at par with the pound sterling.

Budget (1989/90): *Revenue* £5,496,000 (including budgetary aid of £1,034,000); *Expenditure* £8,445,000.

Cost of Living (Consumer Price Index; base: November 1987 = 100): 108.8 in 1989; 111.1 in 1990; 116.6 in 1991.

EXTERNAL TRADE

Principal Commodities: *Imports* (1989/90): £4,970,393 (including food and drink £1,900,299, tobacco £130,021, motor spirits and fuel oils £284,903, animal feed £91,928, building materials £94,937, motor vehicles and parts £248,633, machinery and parts £80,316); *Exports* (1989/90): fish £69,595; coffee n.a. Trade is mainly with the United Kingdom and South Africa.

TRANSPORT

Road Traffic (1990): 1,484 vehicles in use.

Shipping (1991): Vessels entered 132.

EDUCATION

Primary (1987): 8 schools; 32 teachers; 675 pupils.

Secondary (1987): 4 schools; 74 teachers; 513 pupils.

Directory

The Constitution

The St Helena Constitution Order 1988, which entered into force on 1 January 1989, replaced the Order in Council and Royal Instructions of 1 January 1967. Executive and legislative authority is reserved to the British Crown, but is ordinarily exercised by others in accordance with provisions of the Constitution. The Constitution provides for the office of Governor and Commander-in-Chief of St Helena and its dependencies (Ascension Island and Tristan da Cunha). The Legislative Council for St Helena consists of the Speaker, three ex-officio members (the Chief Secretary, the Financial Secretary and the Attorney-General) and 12 elected members; the Executive Council is presided over by the Governor and consists of the above ex-officio members and five of the elected members of the Legislative Council. The elected members of the legislature choose from among themselves those who will also be members of the Executive Council. Although a member of both the Legislative Council and the Executive Council, the Attorney-General does not vote on either. Members of the legislature provide the Chairmen and a majority of the members of the various Council Committees. Executive and legislative functions for the dependencies are exercised by the Governor.

The Government

(September 1994)

Governor and Commander-in-Chief: Alan Hoole.

Chief Secretary: J. Perrott.

Financial Secretary: R. Perrott.

Chairmen of Council Committees:

Agriculture and Natural Resources: P. Peters.

Public Works and Services: E. Benjamin.

Public Health: J. Musk.

Social Welfare: I. George.

Education: R. Pridham.

Finance: R. Perrott.

GOVERNMENT OFFICE

Office of the Governor: Plantation House; tel. 2555; telex 202; fax 2598.

Political Organizations

There are no political parties in St Helena. Elections to the Legislative Council, the latest of which took place in July 1993, are conducted on a non-partisan basis.

Judicial System

There are four Courts on St Helena: the Supreme Court, the Magistrate's Court, the Small Debts Court and the Juvenile Court. Provision exists for the St Helena Court of Appeal which can sit in Jamestown or London.

Chief Justice: Sir John Farley Spry (non-resident).

Attorney-General: David Jeremiah.

Magistrate: J. Beedon.

Religion

The majority of the population belongs to the Anglican Communion.

CHRISTIANITY

The Anglican Communion

Anglicans are adherents of the Church of the Province of Southern Africa, comprising 22 dioceses. The Metropolitan of the Province is the Archbishop of Cape Town, South Africa. St Helena forms a single diocese.

Bishop of St Helena: Rt Rev. John Ruston, Bishopsholme, POB 62, St Helena; tel. 4471; fax 4330; diocese f. 1859; has jurisdiction over the islands of St Helena and Ascension.

The Roman Catholic Church

The Church is represented in St Helena, Ascension and Tristan da Cunha by a Mission, established in August 1986.

Superior: Rev. Fr Anton Agreiter (also Prefect Apostolic of the Falkland Islands), Sacred Heart Church, Jamestown; tel. and fax 2535; Vicar Delegate Rev. Fr Brendan Sullivan; visits Tristan da Cunha once a year, and Ascension several times a year; 40 mems.

Other Christian Churches

Jehovah's Witnesses and the Seventh-day Adventist Church are also active on the island.

The Press

St Helena News: Broadway House, Jamestown; tel. 2612; telex 4202; fax 2802; f. 1986; govt-sponsored weekly; Editor Nicola Dillon; circ. 1,500.

Radio and Television

There were an estimated 2,500 radio receivers in use in 1990. A satellite television link came into operation in July 1994.

Government Broadcasting Service: Information Office, Broadway House, Jamestown; tel. 4669; telex 2202; fax 4542; 73 hours weekly; Information Officer Nicola Dillon; Station Man. Anthony D. Leo.

Finance

BANK

Government Savings Bank: Jamestown; tel. 2291; telex 4202; total deposits (31 March 1991): £4,178,072.

INSURANCE

Alliance Assurance Co Ltd: Agents: Solomon & Co (St Helena) PLC, Jamestown; tel. 2380; telex 4204; fax 2423.

Trade and Industry

CHAMBER OF COMMERCE

St Helena Chamber of Commerce: Jamestown.

CO-OPERATIVE

St Helena Growers' Co-operative Society: Jamestown; vegetable marketing and suppliers of agricultural tools, seeds and animal feeding products; 25 mems (1982); Chair. L. Lawrence; Sec. and Man. M. Benjamin.

TRADE UNION

St Helena General Workers' Union: Market St, Jamestown; 175 mems (1988); Gen. Sec. E. Benjamin.

Transport

There are no railways or airfields in St Helena.

ROADS

In 1990 there were 98 km of bitumen-sealed roads, and a further 20 km of earth roads, which can be used by motor vehicles only in dry weather. All roads have steep gradients and sharp bends.

SHIPPING

St Helena Line Ltd: Jamestown; mailing address: The Shipyard, Porthleven, Helston, Cornwall, TR13 9JA, England; tel. (326) 563434; telex 46564;; fax (326) 564347; operates services to and from the United Kingdom six times a year, calling at the Canary Islands, Ascension Island and Capetown, South Africa, and at Tristan da Cunha once a year; commenced operation of a scheduled service with one passenger/cargo ship in 1978; this vessel was replaced by the RMS *St Helena* in 1990; Man. Dir ANDREW BELL.

Education

Education is compulsory and free for all children between the ages of five and 15 years, although power to exempt after the age of 14 can be exercised by the Education Committee. The standard of work at the secondary selective school is orientated towards 'Ordinary' and 'Advanced' Level requirements of the London University General Certificate of Education. During the second half of the 1980s, the educational structure was reorganized from a two-tier to a three-tier comprehensive system, for which a new upper-school building was constructed. Free part-time further education classes at London University 'Ordinary' and 'Advanced' Level certificate standard are available. The adult literacy rate is 100%.

There is a free public library in Jamestown, financed by the government and managed by a committee, and branch libraries in several country districts.

ASCENSION

The island of Ascension lies in the South Atlantic Ocean (7° 55′ S, 14° 20′ W), 1,131 km north-west of St Helena. It was discovered by a Portuguese expedition on Ascension Day 1501. The island was uninhabited until the arrival of Napoleon, the exiled French emperor, on St Helena in 1815, when a small British naval garrison was placed there. Ascension remained under the supervision of the British admiralty until 1922, when it was made a dependency of St Helena.

Ascension is a barren, rocky peak of purely volcanic origin, which was previously destitute of vegetation except above 450 m on Green Mountain (which rises to 875 m). The mountain supports a small farm producing vegetables and fruit. Since 1983 an alteration has taken place in the pattern of rainfall in Ascension. Total average annual rainfall has increased and the rain falls in heavy showers and is therefore less prone to evaporation. Grass, shrubs and flowers have grown in the valleys. These plants survived the dry periods experienced in 1987 and 1990. Some topsoil has been produced by the decay of previous growth and root systems. The island is famous for green turtles, which land there from December to May to lay their eggs in the sand. It is also a breeding ground of the sooty tern, or wideawake, vast numbers of which settle on the island every 10 months to lay and hatch their eggs. All wildlife except rabbits and cats is protected by law. Shark, barracuda, tuna, bonito and other fish are plentiful in the surrounding ocean.

The population in September 1993 was 1,192 (excluding British military personnel), of whom 807 were St Helenians. The majority of the remainder were expatriate personnel of Cable and Wireless PLC, the BBC and the US military base. The population varies from time to time as it is largely determined by the employment offered by these three stations. The island is an important communications centre, being a relay station for cables between South Africa and Europe, operated by the South Atlantic Cable Co. The BBC operates a relay station on the island, and a local broadcasting station has been established. Ascension does not raise its own finance; the costs of administering the island are borne collectively by the user organizations.

Cable and Wireless provides an international telecommunications service, via satellite and submarine cable, to all parts of the world. Ascension Island Services took over the running of the island's schools, power, water and medical services from Cable and Wireless in 1984.

In 1942 the US government, by arrangement with the British government, established a wartime air base, which it subsequently reoccupied and extended by agreement with the British government in 1956, in connection with the extension of the long-range proving ground for guided missiles, centred in Florida. A further agreement in 1965 allowed the USA to develop tracking facilities on the island in support of the National Aeronautics and Space Administration's 'Apollo' space programme, but this operation ceased in 1990.

Facilities on Ascension underwent rapid development in 1982 to serve as a major staging post for British vessels and aircraft on their way to the Falkland Islands, and the island has continued to provide a key link in British supply lines to the South Atlantic.

Area: 88 sq km (34 sq miles).

Population (excluding British military personnel, September 1993): 1,192 (St Helenians 807, UK nationals 196, US nationals 189.

Production (1992/93): Vegetables 30,000 lb; Pork 27,500 lb; Mutton and lamb 12,600 lb.

Budget (estimates for year ending 31 March 1993): Revenue £344,000; Expenditure £563,581.

Government: The Government of St Helena is represented by an Administrator.

Administrator: BRIAN N. CONNELLY, The Residency, Ascension; tel. 6311; telex 3214; fax 6152.

Magistrate: BRIAN N. CONNELLY.

Justices of the Peace: R. A. LAWRENCE, A. GEORGE, S. A. YOUDE, G. F. THOMAS.

Religion: Ascension forms part of the Anglican diocese of St Helena; some of the inhabitants are Roman Catholics.

Transport (1993): *Road vehicles:* 1,267. *Shipping:* ships entered and cleared 92. The St Helena Line Ltd (q.v.) serves the island with a two-monthly passenger/cargo service between Cardiff, in the United Kingdom, and Cape Town, in South Africa.

TRISTAN DA CUNHA

Tristan da Cunha lies in the South Atlantic Ocean, 2,400 km west of Cape Town, South Africa and 2,100 km south-west of St Helena. Also in the group are Inaccessible Island, 32 km west of Tristan; the three Nightingale Islands, 32 km south; and Gough Island (Diego Alvarez), 350 km south. Tristan is volcanic in origin and nearly circular in shape, covering an area of 98 sq km (38 sq miles) and rising in a cone to 2,060 m above sea-level. The climate is typically oceanic and temperate. Rainfall averages 1,675 mm per annum on the coast.

Possession was taken of the island in 1816 during Napoleon's residence on St Helena, and a garrison was stationed there. When the garrison was withdrawn, three men, headed by Cpl William Glass, elected to remain and became the founders of the present settlement. Because of its position on a main sailing route the colony thrived until the 1880s, but with the replacement of sail by steam a period of decline set in. No regular shipping called and the islanders suffered at times from a shortage of food. Nevertheless, attempts to move the inhabitants to South Africa were unsuccessful. The islanders were engaged chiefly in fishing and agricultural pursuits.

The United Society for the Propagation of the Gospel has maintained an interest in the island since 1922, and in 1932 one of its missionary teachers was officially recognized as honorary commissioner and magistrate. In 1938 Tristan da Cunha and the neighbouring uninhabited islands of Nightingale, Inaccessible and Gough were made dependencies of St Helena, and in 1950 the office of administrator was created. The administrator is also the magistrate. The island council was established in 1952.

In 1942 a meteorological and wireless station was built on the island by a detachment of the South African defence force and was manned by the Royal Navy for the remainder of the war. The coming of the navy reintroduced the islanders to the outside world, for it was a naval chaplain who recognized the possibilities of a crayfish industry on Tristan da Cunha. In 1948 a Cape Town-based fishing company was granted a concession to fish the Tristan da Cunha waters.

On 10 October 1961 a volcanic cone, thought to have been long extinct, erupted close to the settlement of Edinburgh and it was necessary to evacuate the island. The majority of the islanders returned to Tristan da Cunha in 1963. The administration was fully re-established, and the island council re-formed. The population in December 1993 was 300, including 5 expatriates.

The island is remote, and communications are restricted to six calls each year by vessels from Cape Town, an annual visit from the RMS *St Helena* from the United Kingdom and an occasional call by a passing ship. There is, however, a wireless station on the island which is in daily contact with Cape Town. A local broadcasting service was introduced in 1966 and a closed-circuit television system operated between 1983–89, when it was replaced by a video lending-library. A radio-telephone service was established in 1969. In the same year electricity was extended to all of the islanders' homes.

The island's major source of revenue derives from a royalty for the crayfishing concession, supplemented by income from the sale of postage stamps and other philatelic items, and handicrafts. The fishing industry and the administration employ all of the working population. The company holding the fishing concession, Tristan Investments Ltd (a subsidiary of the South Atlantic Islands Development Corpn), built a new fish-freezing factory after the return from the United Kingdom of the islanders. Some 20 power boats operate from the island, as well as two deep-sea fishing vessels. The catch is exported to the USA, France and Japan. A shore-based fishing industry has developed, following the construction of a harbour.

Estimated expenditure for the 1992/93 financial year was £736,902 and revenue was estimated at £743,477. Development aid from the United Kingdom ceased in 1980, leaving the island financially self-sufficient. The United Kingdom, however, has continued to supply the cost of the salaries and passages of the administrator, a doctor and visiting specialists (a dentist every two years and an optician every four years).

Area: Tristan da Cunha 98 sq km (38 sq miles); Inaccessible Island 10 sq km (4 sq miles); Nightingale Island 2 sq km (¾ sq mile); Gough Island 91 sq km (35 sq miles).

Population (December 1993): 300 (including 5 expatriates) on Tristan; there is a small weather station on Gough Island, staffed, under agreement, by personnel employed by the South African Government.

Fishing (catch, metric tons, year ending 30 April): Tristan da Cunha rock lobster 441 in 1987/88; 427 in 1988/89; 451 in 1989/90. Source: FAO, *Yearbook of Fishery Statistics*.

Budget: (estimates for 1992/93) Revenue £743,477; Expenditure £736,902.

Government: The Administrator, representing the British Government, is aided by a council of eight elected members (of whom at least one must be a woman) and three appointed members, which has advisory powers in legislative and executive functions. The Council's advisory functions in executive matters are performed through small committees of the Council dealing with the separate branches of administration. The most recent election was held in May 1991.

Administrator: Philip H. Johnson, The Residency, Tristan da Cunha; tel. 5424; telex 5434; fax 5435.

Legal System: The Administrator is also the Magistrate.

Religion: Adherents of the Anglican church predominate on Tristan da Cunha, which is within the Church of the Province of Southern Africa, and is under the jurisdiction of the Archbishop of Cape Town, South Africa. There is also a small number of Roman Catholics.

Bibliography

Blackburn, J. *The Emperor's Last Island: A Journey to St Helena.* London, Secker and Warburg, 1992.

Blakeston, O. *Isle of Helena.* London, Sidgwick and Jackson, 1957.

Booy, D. M. *Rock of Exile: A Narrative of Tristan da Cunha.* London, Dent, 1957.

Castell, R. *St Helena: Island Fortress.* Old Amersham, Bucks, Byron Publicity Group, 1977.

Christopherson, E., et al. *Tristan da Cunha* (trans. R. L. Benham). London, Cassell, 1940.

Christopherson, E. (Ed.) *Results of the Norwegian Scientific Expedition to Tristan da Cunha, 1937–1938,* 16 parts. Oslo University Press, 1940–62.

Cohen, R. (Ed.) *African Islands and Enclaves.* London, Sage Publications, 1983.

Crawford, A. *Tristan da Cunha and the Roaring Forties.* Edinburgh, Charles Skilton, 1982.

Cross, T. *St Helena: with chapters on Ascension and Tristan da Cunha.* Newton Abbot, David and Charles, 1981.

Gosse, P. *St Helena, 1502–1938.* London, Cassell, 1938.

Hart-Davis, D. *Ascension: The Story of a South Atlantic Island.* London, Constable, 1972.

Hughes, C. *Report of an enquiry into conditions on the Island of St Helena . . . (and) observations by the St Helena Government on Mr Hughes' report.* London, 1958.

Martineau, G. *Napoleon's St Helena.* London, John Murray, 1968.

Munch, P. A. *Crisis in Utopia.* New York, Crowell, 1971.

Thompson, J. A. K. *Report on a Visit to Ascension Island.* St Helena Government Printer, 1947.

SÃO TOMÉ AND PRÍNCIPE

Physical and Social Geography

RENÉ PÉLISSIER

The archipelago forming the Democratic Republic of São Tomé and Príncipe, a former overseas province of Portugal, is, after the Republic of Seychelles, the smallest independent state in Africa. Both the main islands are in the Gulf of Guinea on a south-west/north-east axis of extinct volcanoes. The boundaries take in the rocky islets of Caroço, Pedras and Tinhosas, off Príncipe and, south of São Tomé, the Rôlas islet which is bisected by the line of the Equator. The total area of the archipelago is 964 sq km (372 sq miles), of which São Tomé occupies an area of 854 sq km.

São Tomé is a plantation island where the eastern slopes and coastal flatlands are covered by huge cocoa estates (*roças*) formerly controlled by Portuguese interests, alongside a large number of local smallholders. These plantations have been carved out of an extremely dense mountainous jungle which dominates this equatorial island. The highest point is the Pico de São Tomé (2,024 m), surrounded by a dozen lesser cones above 1,000 m in height. Craggy and densely forested terrain is intersected by numerous streams. The island of Príncipe is extremely jagged and indented by numerous bays. The highest elevation is the Pico de Príncipe (948 m). Both islands have a warm and moist climate, with an average yearly temperature of 25°C. Annual rainfall varies from over 5,100 mm on the south-western mountain slopes to under 1,020 mm in the northern lowlands.

The total population was 117,504 at the census of 4 August 1991, when São Tomé had 112,033 inhabitants and Príncipe 5,471. The population density was 117.4 inhabitants per sq km. During 1985–92 the population increased by an annual average of 2.3%. The capital city is São Tomé, with 17,380 inhabitants in 1970, increasing to perhaps 30,000 in 1985. It is the main export centre of the island. Inland villages on São Tomé are mere clusters of houses of native islanders. Príncipe has only one small town of about 1,000 people, Santo António.

The native-born islanders (*forros*) are the descendants of imported slaves and southern Europeans who settled in the 16th and 17th centuries. Intermarriage was common, but the massive influx of Angolan and Mozambican contract workers until about 1950 re-Africanized the *forros*. Descendants of former castaway slaves who escaped from a wrecked slave-ship in the 17th century and who formed a formidable maroon republic in the mountains of São Tomé are now peaceful fishermen, and are known as the *angolares*.

The widespread exodus of skilled Portuguese plantation administrators, civil servants and traders during the period just prior to independence in July 1975, together with the departure of most of the Cape Verdean workers and the repatriation of more than 10,000 São Tomé exiles from Angola, caused considerable economic disruption, whose effects have yet to be fully overcome.

Recent History

W. G. CLARENCE-SMITH

Revised for this edition by GERHARD SEIBERT

São Tomé and Príncipe were colonized by Portugal in the 15th century. The islands became an overseas province of Portugal in 1951 and received local autonomy in 1973. A nationalist group, the Comissão de Libertação de São Tomé e Príncipe (CLSTP), was formed in 1960 and became the Movimento de Libertação de São Tomé e Príncipe (MLSTP) in 1972, under the leadership of Dr Manuel Pinto da Costa. Following the military coup in Portugal in April 1974, the Portuguese government recognized the right of the islands to independence, although negotiations did not take place until November. Portugal appointed a transitional government which included members of the MLSTP, which was recognized as the sole legitimate representative of the people. At elections for a constituent assembly held in July 1975, the MLSTP won all 16 seats. Independence as the Democratic Republic of São Tomé and Príncipe took effect on 12 July, with Pinto da Costa as president and Miguel Trovoada as prime minister. The constitution promulgated in November effectively vested absolute authority in the hands of the president and the central committee of the MLSTP, leaving Trovoada and the cabinet with few real powers. Radical socialist policies were introduced, and any activity deemed contrary to MLSTP directives was defined as treason.

MLSTP GOVERNMENT

Between 1976–82, serious ideological as well as personal divisions arose within the MLSTP, and a number of prominent members who favoured a more moderate approach to social, economic and agrarian reforms were forced into exile. In March 1978 Angolan soldiers were brought to the islands to provide protection for the president and his associates following an alleged coup attempt. In March 1979 Dr Carlos da Graça, a former minister of health who had left for Gabon in 1977, was tried *in absentia* and sentenced to 24 years' imprisonment. In April 1979 Trovoada was dismissed as prime minister. In September he was arrested, charged with complicity in the 1978 coup attempt and detained until 1981 when he was permitted to leave the islands. Another alleged coup attempt was forestalled in November 1980. In December 1981 rioting broke out on Príncipe, where food shortages had led to agitation for that island's autonomy. During 1982, Leonel d'Alva, a former prime minister and minister of foreign affairs, fled to exile in Cape Verde, and Daniel Daio, the minister of defence and national security, was dismissed, but remained in the country.

In its foreign relations, São Tomé and Príncipe avoided any formal commitment to the Eastern bloc, although close economic ties existed with China and the German Democratic Republic. Cuba and the USSR provided the regime with military advisers. Gabon, the islands' mainland neighbour, viewed these developments with disquiet, and relations consequently deteriorated. However, the republic extended the range of its international contacts by joining the International Monetary Fund (IMF) in 1977, acceding to the Lomé Convention in 1978 and participating in the foundation of the francophone Communauté économique des états de l'Afrique central

(CEEAC) in 1983. The bulk of the country's trade continued to be transacted with western Europe, and relations with Portugal remained generally cordial.

In 1985, confronted by the threat of the complete collapse of the economy, Pinto da Costa began to abandon economic ties with the Eastern bloc in favour of the capitalist strategy of the West. Trade agreements with Eastern bloc countries were allowed to lapse on expiry. Pinto da Costa and his ministers made extensive visits to Western Europe and North America to solicit support for measures of economic liberalization. The two main Western nations seeking to exert influence in the country were Portugal and France; however, trade with Portugal was much more substantial than with France, and negotiations concerning São Tomé's admission to the Franc Zone were eventually inconclusive. The USA accredited its first ambassador to São Tomé in 1985, and provided the country with a limited amount of military aid.

Ideological Liberalization

From 1985 a wider range of ideological views was represented in the newly elected national people's assembly, which confirmed Pinto da Costa as president, and in the new central committee of the MLSTP. By the end of 1985 there was an atmosphere of reconciliation in São Tomé politics: Carlos da Graça was pardoned and Miguel Trovoada was invited to return from exile. In October 1987 the central committee of the MLSTP announced a major constitutional reform, which included the election by universal adult suffrage of the president of the republic, and of members of the national people's assembly. The amended constitution also allowed 'independent' candidates to contest elections for the national people's assembly, although the president of the MLSTP, chosen by the MLSTP congress from two candidates proposed by the central committee, would continue to be the sole candidate for the presidency of the republic. In January 1988 the national people's assembly approved a constitutional amendment providing for the re-establishment of the premiership, and President da Costa appointed Celestino Rocha da Costa, until then the minister of education, labour and social security, as prime minister. Rocha da Costa formed a new government and appointed Carlos da Graça as minister of foreign affairs.

Da Graça, however, was one of the few political exiles to return, as the majority of the opposition groups abroad regarded these reforms as insufficient. Although Miguel Trovoada, now resident in France, chose not to create any alternative political organization, two overseas opposition movements were already in existence: the Frente de Resistência Nacional de São Tomé e Príncipe (FRNSTP) and the União Democrática Independente de São Tomé e Príncipe (UDISTP). The FRNSTP was originally based in Gabon under the leadership of Carlos da Graça, but as relations between Gabon and São Tomé improved, the movement was expelled from Gabon in 1986. Carlos da Graça ceased to be a member and remained in Gabon, before returning to São Tomé as minister of foreign affairs. The major part of the FRNSTP moved to Lisbon, formed a coalition with the UDISTP, and agreed to seek political changes by non-violent means. A small faction of the FRNSTP, led by Afonso dos Santos, refused to give up the armed struggle as a means of overthrowing the São Tomé régime and moved to Cameroon, taking the name of Frente de Resistência Nacional de São Tomé e Príncipe–Renovada (FRNSTP–R). In March 1988 Afonso dos Santos led a seaborne expedition of 46 men from his headquarters in southern Cameroon, in an attempt to invade São Tomé and seize power. The operation was poorly planned and executed, and the invaders were quickly captured. In September 1989 dos Santos was sentenced to 22 years imprisonment while 38 other defendants were also given custodial sentences.

Democratic Transition

Somewhat shaken by the failed coup attempt, increasingly alarmed by the collapse of the communist regimes of Eastern Europe, encouraged by Western exponents of economic reform, and by rank-and-file opinion in the MLSTP, the regime embarked in late 1989 on a transition to full multi-party democracy, after strenuous debate in an extraordinary meeting of the MLSTP central committee. In August 1990, in a national referendum, 72% of the electorate voted in favour of the introduction of the new constitution proposed by the MLSTP central committee. The new constitution provided for a multi-party political system, together with the abolition of the death penalty, guarantees on human rights, and a maximum of two five-year terms of office for the president.

In April 1990 Afonso dos Santos and his accomplices in the March 1988 coup attempt were granted an amnesty by presidential decree and dos Santos founded the Frente Democrata Cristã (FDC). Further organized opposition came from the Coligação Democrática de Oposição (CODO), set up by exiles returning from Portugal, under the leadership of Albertino Neto. But the major challenge to the MLSTP came from within its own ranks. A breakaway faction led by Daniel Daio formed the Partido de Convergência Democrática–Grupo de Reflexão (PCD–GR). Leonel d'Alva, returning from exile in Cape Verde, was elected president of the PCD–GR, while Daio became secretary-general. The MLSTP party congress, held in October 1990, appointed a new secretary-general, Carlos da Graça (the minister of foreign affairs), in succession to Manuel Pinto da Costa, the party's founding president. In addition, the party's name was amended to the Movimento de Libertação de São Tomé e Príncipe–Partido Social Democrata (MLSTP–PSD).

On 20 January 1991 elections to the new national assembly resulted in defeat for the MLSTP–PSD, which secured only 30.5% of the votes and 21 seats in the 55-member legislature. The PCD–GR obtained 54% of the votes and 33 seats in the assembly. CODO, with 5% of the votes, took the remaining seat.

In February 1991 a transitional government, headed by Daniel Daio, was installed, pending the presidential election, to be held in March. In the same month, President da Costa announced that he would be retiring from politics and would not be contesting the forthcoming election. The MLSTP–PSD did not present an alternative candidate. In late February two of the three remaining presidential candidates, Afonso dos Santos, of the FDC (which had received little support at the January legislative elections), and an independent candidate, Guadalupe de Ceita, withdrew from the election. Miguel Trovoada, who stood as an independent candidate (with the support of the PCD–GR), remained as sole contender, and in March was elected president, receiving 81% of the votes cast. Trovoada took office in the following month. The new government promised to expedite the process of political and economic liberalization, indicated that the harassment of the Roman Catholic church was at an end, and called for national reconciliation.

THE TROVOADA PRESIDENCY

In early 1992 a political crisis erupted when co-operation between the government and the presidency began to break down. The PCD–GR, which did not accept the level of power granted to the president under the constitution of September 1990, attempted to introduce a constitutional amendment limiting the presidential powers. Meanwhile, widespread popular dissatisfaction followed the imposition in June 1991 of stringent austerity measures that had been imposed by the IMF and the World Bank as preconditions for economic assistance. These measures, which included a 40% devaluation of the currency and a substantial increase in petroleum prices, had contributed to a sharp decline in the islanders' living standards. Following two mass demonstrations held in April 1992 to protest against the austerity programme, Trovoada dismissed the Daio government, citing as his main reason the 'institutional disloyalty' of the prime minister, who had publicly blamed the president for the country's economic plight and attendant political unrest. Trovoada did, however, affirm his support for the economic recovery measures that had been implemented by Daio. The PCD–GR, which initially condemned Trovoada's actions as an 'institutional coup', was invited to designate a new prime minister. In May Norberto Costa Alegre (the minister of economy and finance in the former administration, who had been instrumental in the negotiation of the structural adjustment measures) replaced Daio as prime minister and formed a new administration.

Violent clashes in early August 1992 between the police and members of the armed forces resulted when some 40 soldiers forced entry into a police station in the capital to secure the release of two soldiers who were being detained. The conflict followed mounting tensions between the two forces, which observers attributed to a lack of definition as to their respective roles in the country, and to discontent within the armed forces at its impending reorganization.

On 6 December 1992, in the first local elections to be held since independence, the PCD-GR suffered a considerable reverse, obtaining only 15 of the total of 59 seats and failing to gain outright control of any of the seven districts. Conversely, the MLSTP-PSD won 38 seats and gained control of five districts. The newly formed Acção Democrática Independente (ADI) won the remaining six seats and secured control of one district. However, the government refused to accede to opposition demands that it resign, form a government of national unity or call new legislative elections.

In February 1993 Daio resigned as secretary-general of the ruling PCD–GR, and in April was replaced by the more moderate João do Sacramento Bonfim. Expectation among opposition parties that the appointment of Bonfim would facilitate political dialogue, and even lead to the formation of a government of national unity, proved unfounded; in November four opposition parties issued a joint statement accusing the government of authoritarianism and incompetence, and, in turn, were accused of fomenting instability.

In August 1993 the national assembly appointed a five-member commission of inquiry to investigate allegations of corruption against the minister of justice, labour and public administration, Olegário Pires Tiny, and the minister of commerce, industry, fisheries and tourism, Arzemiro dos Prazeres. However, the commission concluded that the allegations against both ministers were unfounded.

In early 1994 relations between the government and the presidency began to deteriorate. In April Trovoada publicly dissociated himself from government policy. In June political tension increased when the PCD–GR accused Trovoada of systematic obstruction of the government's programme. The same month opposition parties petitioned the president to dismiss the government and to appoint foreign auditors to investigate the management of public funds under its term of office. On 2 July 1994 Trovoada dismissed the Alegre administration citing 'institutional conflict' as the justification for the decision. Moreover, the president accused the ruling party of ignoring presidential vetoes and of attempting to replace the semi-presidential system with a parliamentary regime without executive powers for the head of state. On 4 July Trovoada appointed Evaristo do Espírito Santo de Carvalho (the minister of defence and security in the outgoing administration) as prime minister. The PCD–GR, which refused to participate in the new administration, subsequently expelled Carvalho from the party. An interim government, comprising eight ministers, was inaugurated on 9 July. On the following day, in an attempt to put an end to the political crisis, Trovoada dissolved the national assembly and announced that a legislative election would be held on 2 October. The election resulted in victory for the MLSTP, which secured 27 seats. The ADI obtained 14 seats, the PCD–GR won 13 seats and CODO took the remaining seat. Carlos da Graça subsequently announced that the MLSTP would form a government of national unity with all the parties represented in the national assembly.

In April 1994 the national assembly adopted legislation, drafted by the MLSTP–PSD, reinforcing the rights of the parliamentary opposition. Under the provisions of the law, all opposition parties represented in the legislature were to be consulted on major political issues, including defence, foreign policy and the budget. In the same month the national assembly began discussion of a draft bill providing for the autonomy of the island of Príncipe. The proposals under consideration included provision for the creation of a regional assembly and a five-member regional government, to operate under the authority of a minister appointed by the president. The introduction of the draft bill was prompted by concern, expressed by inhabitants of Príncipe, that the island had been neglected by the central administration.

Economy

W. G. CLARENCE-SMITH

Revised for this edition by GERHARD SEIBERT

The economy of São Tomé and Príncipe, which is based almost exclusively on the export of cocoa, has undergone a marked decline since independence in 1975. The sudden loss of protected markets in Portugal and the mass exodus of skilled personnel were compounded by the negative effects of systematic nationalizations and the relentless fall in the world price of cocoa after 1979. São Tomé and Príncipe's gross domestic product (GDP) declined in real terms between 1980–86, and only grew at an average of 1.3% per year between 1987–91, according to United Nations estimates. During 1985–92, it was estimated, gross national product (GNP) per head declined, in real terms, at an annual average of 1.8%. Over the same period the population increased by an annual average of 2.3%. In 1992, it was estimated that 28.8% of GDP was derived from the primary sector, 13.2% from the secondary sector, and 58.0% from the tertiary sector, the latter figure mainly reflecting the considerable size of the bureaucracy.

The Marxist economic policies implemented during the decade following independence were a leading factor in the deterioration of the country's economy. President Pinto da Costa, who had been trained as an economist in the German Democratic Republic, decided at independence to nationalize virtually all enterprises of any size. The government also took a monopoly of foreign trade, and controlled prices and distribution through a network of 'people's shops'. São Tomé became a member of the IMF in 1977 and introduced a new currency unit, the dobra, to replace the Portuguese escudo at par. The dobra became increasingly over-valued, placing considerable strain on the balance of payments, but the government refused to carry out a devaluation.

In 1985, confronted by the threat of economic collapse, the president initiated a process of economic liberalization. Foreign companies were invited to bid for management contracts for the state farms, and a cautious process of privatization of the non-agricultural sector was begun. In 1986, the 'people's shops' were leased to private traders, a new investment code was promulgated to attract foreign capital, and a donors' conference was held. Following discussions during 1986 with the World Bank and the IMF, the government widened the scope of its reforms with the introduction in June 1987 of a three-year structural adjustment programme (SAP). This aimed to reduce the large trade and budget deficits, to increase agricultural production, to stimulate exports, and to increase foreign earnings from tourism and fishing. The SAP included measures to restructure the public investment programme and unprofitable public enterprises, to liberalize prices, and to improve incentives for investment by the private sector. The SAP was supported by the World Bank and the African Development Bank (ADB) with loans of US $7m. and $8.5m. respectively.

The first step in the programme was taken in July 1987 when the government devalued the dobra by 54.75%, and increased duties on local and imported consumer goods by between 15%–150%. Price controls were abolished on all goods except rice, sugar, wheat flour, beans, milk and edible oil, and wages were increased by 10%–30% to compensate for the higher prices. Reductions in government spending were announced and taxes were raised. Foreign trade was liberalized with the abolition of the monopoly of the state enterprise, Ecomex, over the import and export of goods. Under the SAP any productive enterprise or registered trader could import or export all but six strategic goods. In July 1988 the dobra was devalued by about 20%, the prices of consumer goods and fuels were raised by 60%–100%, and state subsidies were reduced to less than 20% of import prices, compared with 40% previously. In an attempt to compensate for the steep increase in prices, the wages of workers in the agricultural sector and agro-based industries were raised by 15%. The value of the dobra drifted downwards towards parallel rates, while further adjustments to controlled prices were made to bring these rates closer to market levels. Public sector wages were raised from time to time, but did not keep pace with the cost of living. In recognition of these reforms, a donors' meeting in Geneva in March 1989 pledged new loans and a rescheduling of debts, and in June the IMF approved a three-year SDR2.8m. structural adjustment facility (SAF). The resultant structural adjustment programme, however, began to lose momentum in 1990, as the MLSTP subordinated economic concerns to its own political survival. The IMF suspended payments under the SAF, and the World Bank threatened to do the same. The budget deficit increased to $4.5m., and inflation reached 47%. Additionally, the gap between official and parallel rates of exchange widened, and foreign exchange reserves were severely depleted.

The priority of the government since 1991 has been a return to fiscal and economic austerity in accordance with the IMF and World Bank guidelines. The currency was repeatedly devalued and by June 1993 the dobra was trading officially at approximately US $1 = 425 dobra, while 'black market' rates stood at about US $1 = 600 dobra. This was outside the 15% margin between official and parallel market rates demanded by the IMF. In 1992 the banking system was reorganized. The Banco Nacional de São Tomé e Príncipe (BNSTP) went into liquidation and its central banking functions were taken over by the new Banco Central de São Tomé e Príncipe. In early 1993 the Banco Internacional de São Tomé e Príncipe was founded to undertake the commercial operations of the former BNSTP. In mid-1993 the government announced that it was studying proposals to transfer responsibility for currency transactions entirely to dealers licenced by the central bank. The inflation rate fell to 22% in the year to December 1992, but was still considerably higher than the 10% guideline established by the IMF. The estimated current deficit on the 1993 budget stood at 2,300m. dobra, and the IMF and World Bank expressed concern over the high levels of funds allocated to the military and the civil service. Electricity and fuel prices were increased sharply, and privatization of the non-agricultural sector was scheduled for completion by the end of 1993. Ecomex was liquidated in 1993 and the government ceased to set prices for imported basic goods, although maximum profit margins on such goods were retained. A new import tariff adopted in January 1993 reduced duties on essential goods and taxes on emigrants' remittances, while increasing duties on non-essential imports. By mid-1992 the IMF indicated that enough progress had been made for payments under the SAF to be resumed. This was a precondition to addressing the problem of the country's high level of external debt, estimated at $215m. at the end of 1991. In the 1994 budget 13,000m. dobra, of a projected total expenditure of 18,000m. dobra, were set aside for external debt financing.

In early 1994 the World Bank threatened to suspend structural adjustment credits due to delays in the implementation of agreed economic adjustment measures. Subsequently São Tomé failed to qualify for an IMF Enhanced Structural Adjustment Facility. However, despite its criticism of the slow pace of the restructuring of public enterprises, a World Bank mission indicated in June that it would recommend the release of US $10m. in structural adjustment credits.

AGRICULTURE

At independence, São Tomé inherited a plantation economy dominated by cocoa and partially protected from international price movements by a guaranteed home market. Most land was farmed by 29 large enterprises owned by Portuguese companies. In September 1975, immediately after independence, the government nationalized all landholdings of over 200 ha and grouped them into 15 state enterprises, two of them on Príncipe. They covered over 80% of the cultivable land area, and ranged in size from 1,500–6,000 ha. The nationalization of the estates led to the exodus of many of the skilled agricultural personnel. Equipment on the plantations ceased to function through poor maintenance and lack of spare parts. Wages fell in real terms, and food for the labourers was in short supply, leading to a fall in employment and productivity. Portuguese consumers turned to cheaper sources of supply, especially as the overvaluation of the dobra raised the prices of São Tomé produce. The state farms incurred substantial deficits and were brought to the point of financial collapse within a decade.

In 1985, the government initiated a policy of partial privatization. Ownership of the estates was kept in the hands of the state, but foreign aid was sought to rehabilitate the plantations and foreign companies were invited to tender for management contracts of 15–20 years' duration. Privatization proceeded slowly under this system, and was confined to the prime land in the north-east of São Tomé island. A management contract for the Agua-Izé estate was granted in 1987 to two Portuguese companies, Refinarias de Açúcar Reunidas and Pereira Coutinho. In the same year, the World Bank provided a $7.9m. concessionary loan for the rehabilitation of the Belavista and Ubabudo estates, with a further $6m. provided by the Arab Bank for Economic Development (BADEA). Management of the Belavista estate was given to the Portuguese Francisco Mantero enterprise, which had formerly owned some of the largest plantations in the country. Management of the Ubabudo estate was granted to the Société Française de Réalisation et de Gestion des Projets Café et Cacao (Soca II), part of the Franco-Belgian Socfin-Rivaud plantation group. Another company from the same group, GIE-Sedeci-Terres Rouges, was, in 1989, awarded the management contract for the 2,300 ha Santa Margarida estate, which in 1988 received a rehabilitation grant of 43m. French francs from the Caisse centrale de coopération économique (CCCE). Management of the Monte Café estate, covering 1,800 ha, was transferred in 1990 to the Portuguese Espírito Santo group, with the ADB providing $10.9m. for its rehabilitation. In the same year, the Luso-Sãotomean company Sociedade de Desenvolvimento Agro-Pecuária (Sodeap) obtained a contract for the Diogo Vaz estate and in 1992 secured a rehabilitation grant of $5m. from the World Food Programme and French donors.

By the early 1990s, the strategy of estate management contracts was in crisis. Managers complained that the contracts, which gave the government a right of supervision over major decisions and specified that 80% of all profits went to the state, denied them effective control. Critics pointed out that the state took the risk of major losses, and alleged that the foreigners were merely collecting their management fee from aid money and were doing little to rehabilitate the estates. This latter accusation appears misplaced, as the estates under foreign management show clear signs of improved output and quality, in contrast to those remaining in the public sector (The cocoa yields of estates under private management are as high as 400 kg per ha, whereas the national average is just 190 kg per ha). However, worsening cocoa prices soon stifled the optimism of the late 1980s. In July 1991 the two Portuguese companies managing the Agua-Izé estate announced that they were withdrawing. Faced with the constantly falling price of cocoa and the aftermath of a two-month strike in late 1990, the Portuguese managers had wanted to break up the 5,000-ha estate into smallholdings, retaining only the central processing facilities. When the government refused to allow this, the companies declared that their losses had become excessive and that they were giving up the management contract by mutual agreement. In 1992 the United Nations Development Programme (UNDP) announced that it would provide $3.5m. to rehabilitate the estate over the period 1993–95. In mid-1993, on the advice of the World Bank, the government began the process of replacing management contracts with long leases. Companies gained managerial autonomy (subject to maintaining the value of the assets entrusted to them by the state), obtained control over the size of their labour force, were no longer able to finance investments with public funds, and had to pay the government a rent commensurate with their economic performance. In 1994 long-term leases were granted by the government to the respective companies managing the Belavista and Ubabudo estates.

The alternative strategy of breaking up the estates into smallholdings has been pursued since 1985. About 10,000 ha of land were distributed to small farmers between 1985–89, although these were usually marginal lands from the fringes of the large estates. The government viewed these areas as suitable only for domestic food production, rather than for cash crops for export. The authorities were unwilling to grant full freehold tenure and in 1989, only one-third of the distributed land was under cultivation. At the instigation of the World Bank, which is providing finance of $17.2m. for the process of land reform, the government announced that some 20,000 ha of land would be transferred to smallholders between 1993–98. Land distributed to smallholders since 1985 which had not been cultivated would be repossessed and redistributed by the state. Surveying for suitable sites is proceeding, but the rate at which land is being transferred is very slow. In April 1993, some 1,000 ha from the Agua-Izé estate were designated for land reform, but only 150 ha had effectively been transferred by July. Moreover, the government still grants usufructuary rights rather than full private property rights. About 12,000 ha of land scheduled for redistribution are to comprise neglected cocoa groves on unrehabilitated foreign-owned estates, but it remains unclear whether the government intends to encourage smallholder production of cocoa. Just over 10% of cocoa output in 1992 was attributable to the smallholder sector.

Since independence, cocoa has regularly accounted for well over 90% of exports by value, reaching 94% in 1987. Cocoa covered 61% of the cultivated area on the 15 large estates in 1986. Production fell from some 11,500 tons in 1973 to less than 5,000 tons in 1976, but by 1979 had recovered to more than 7,000 tons in response to high world prices, before falling back once again as market demand receded. Output remained stagnant at around 4,000 tons a year in the 1980s, and export earnings from cocoa fell by 67% between 1979–88. Yields had dwindled to 0.32 tons per ha by 1985, compared with 0.5 tons per ha prior to independence, and with yields of up to 2.0 tons per ha on some modern plantations in other areas of the world. In 1985 the islands' cocoa trees were 30 years old on average, and some were much older. Black pod disease has spread because of a lack of phytosanitary treatment, and soil fertility has declined with the lack of fertilizer application. As cocoa prices fell still further in the early 1990s, production drifted down to a low point of 3,193 tons in 1991. Output then increased slightly to 3,858 tons in 1992 and was expected to reach 4,200 tons in 1993. Prices were set to rise gently again in 1993, and the combined production of the three most successful foreign managed estates (Belavista, Ubabudo and Santa Margarida) was forecast to reach some 5,000 tons by 1994. São Tomé may also be able to profit from the high quality of its cocoa on an increasingly differentiated world market in the 1990s.

The islands' principal secondary crops are copra, coffee and palm oil and kernels. In 1986, coconut palms covered 23% of the cultivated area on the 15 state-owned estates, and copra was the country's only export of any significance apart from cocoa. In 1987, less than 2,000 tons of copra were exported, compared to over 5,000 tons in 1973. By 1992 production of copra had fallen to only 679 tons. Oil palms accounted for 10% of the cultivated area on the estates in 1986 and coffee for 3%, but exports of these commodities ceased altogether in the latter half of the 1980s. In the early 1990s hopes for agricultural diversification in the export sector rested principally on pepper and arabica coffee. Exports of cocoyam (also known as taro, or matabala), plantain and citrus fruit to Gabon were also targeted for development.

Self-sufficiency in basic food crops has eluded the government since independence, despite the high fertility of the islands' volcanic soils, the long growing season, the variety of micro-climates, and abundant rainfall. The apportionment of centrally-fixed planning targets for food production among the nationalized estates proved unsuccessful, and by the mid-1980s the country was estimated to be importing 90% of its food requirements. The emphasis after 1985 was on developing smallholder agriculture on the fringes of the great estates. By 1992 it was estimated that imports of food had fallen to around 45% of consumption. The only surviving large-scale food project is the oil palm plantation at Ribeira Peixe. Since the early 1980s, the EC has been providing funds to plant 610 ha of high yielding oil palms and to establish a publicly-owned palm oil factory on the 1,500 ha Ribeira Peixe estate in the south-east of São Tomé island. By 1992 the project was producing about 80,000 litres of oil a month and was able to meet the country's internal requirements. However, although the project had been conceived as an exercise in import substitution, it was announced that export markets would be sought if the oil proved unpopular with domestic consumers. A French-financed market gardening project at Mesquita experimented with seeds, techniques and training, but encountered severe difficulties in 1989 when outside funding ceased. The greatest obstacles to self-sufficiency in food are food aid programmes and the impossibility of growing wheat for a population increasingly accustomed to eating bread and other wheat-based products. São Tomé imported 11,000 tons of cereals as food aid in 1992.

The livestock sector has been seriously affected by the decline in veterinary services since independence. Pork has traditionally been the main source of animal protein, but all 30,000 pigs in the islands had to be slaughtered in 1979 after an outbreak of African swine fever. With the help of foreign donors production was restored to pre-1979 levels by 1986, but swine fever recurred on São Tomé island in 1992. Chicken and egg production were also badly affected by disease in 1993. Goats are widely reared, and are sometimes exported to Gabon. The islands are free of tsetse fly, but cattle have been badly affected by bovine tuberculosis. There were some 3,000 head of cattle in 1986, but only 180 dairy cows. Dairy farmers cannot compete with powdered milk, which is imported as food aid.

Similar difficulties have beset the fishing sector, a priority area for economic diversification which contributed 6% of GDP in 1984. In the early 1990s fishing was the second largest source of foreign exchange, due principally to revenue from fishing licences, and employed some 10% of the economically active population. A state-owned fishing company, Empesca, was formed at independence. Its two modern trawlers had on-board freezing facilities, and cold store facilities were installed at the port of Neves on São Tomé island. In June 1978, the government established an exclusive economic zone around the islands of 370 km (200 nautical miles), although the trawlers actually spent most of their time fishing in Angolan waters. The industrial catch rose to just over 2,500 tons in 1984, but subsequently lack of maintenance on the trawlers led to a rapid decrease. The industrial catch in 1988 was only one ton. Empesca was then reconstituted as a joint venture, but refitting the trawlers has proved more difficult than originally expected. In the long term, the government is basing its hopes for the fishing industry on the tuna resources of the area, and it is estimated that tuna catches could reach 17,000 tons a year without affecting stocks. In the meantime, fishing licences were granted to EC and USSR-flag vessels. São Tomé refused to renew Soviet licences in 1989, owing to a dispute over the terms of payment but signed a new three-year agreement with the EC in 1993. Since the 1985 reforms, the main emphasis of foreign donors has been on upgrading artisan fishing, which has increased the total catch from 1,138 tons in 1980 to 2,873 tons in 1988. In 1993 there were some 2,500 artisan fishing boats in the country, of which about 600 were motorized. The EC, Japan and Canada have provided funds for this purpose. São Tomé's role in the regional fishing scheme operated by the EC since 1987 has been to build and repair fishing boats in the Neves yards. However, the local market for fish in São Tomé has been sated, exports are impeded by bureaucratic regulations, and processing plants have yet to be established.

São Tomé and Príncipe's considerable forestry resources have been neglected, although it was estimated in 1984 that two-thirds of the country's energy consumption came from fuelwood and most housing is of wooden construction. Colonial legislation for the protection of forests was replaced by a new law in 1979, but it was not enforced and no barriers were placed to the uncontrolled cutting of trees. A commission was set up in 1988 to study the problems of forest preservation and reafforestation, and it began by drawing up a national forest inventory with foreign assistance. This revealed that 29% of the country was still covered in primary forest (*obó*), mainly in the inaccessible south-western quadrant of both islands. Some 245 sq km on São Tomé island and 45 sq km on Príncipe were identified as needing to be demarcated as 'ecological reserves', in areas where commercial agriculture is uneconomic. In addition, the inventory noted the existence of 30,000 ha of secondary forest, largely on abandoned plantation land and 32,000 ha of 'shade forest', covering commercial crops. The resources exploitable on a sustainable basis outside the 'ecological reserves' were estimated at between 70,000–105,000 cu m of construction wood and between 43,000–65,000 cu m of fuelwood per year. However, it was also estimated that the country needed 20,000 cu m of fuelwood for dry-processing cocoa, copra and other commercial crops, and a further 140,000 cu m for domestic purposes. In 1990, São Tomé was included in a Central African forest conservation project, financed by the EC, which was intended to lead to the demarcation and enforcement of forest reserves. A more detailed forest inventory was initiated in 1992, provisional forest regulations were issued in early 1993, and a new force of forest guards began a training programme later in that year.

MANUFACTURING AND SERVICES

Industry, including construction and public utilities, accounted for 10% of GDP in 1989–91. Of the 25 manufacturing companies in existence at independence in 1975, 12 had closed down completely by 1993, eight were functioning well below capacity, and five had been rehabilitated and expanded. Three new enterprises had been created. Apart from a printing workshop, beer, soft drinks, spirits, bread, vegetable oil, soap, sawn wood, furniture, ceramics, bricks and garments are produced. Industry is generally confined to production for the local market, but garments are exported to Angola. Many basic manufactured products are still imported, especially from Portugal. The government aims to develop food processing and the production of construction materials. All industrial companies were originally scheduled for privatization by the end of 1993, although the process was still under way in 1994.

There are no mines on the islands, but oil prospecting since the late 1980s has resulted in some promising preliminary findings. Petroleum products were imported from Angola at concessionary rates after independence, but are now being supplied at commercial prices by Angola and Gabon. In 1989, 53% of electricity generation was derived from thermal sources, and 47% from hydroelectric sources. Donors are proposing to place more emphasis on small hydroelectric schemes, either repairing those installed in colonial times or setting up new ones. In early 1994, following completion of a rehabilitation project financed by Sweden, a hydroelectric plant at Guegue with a capacity of 350 kw was reopened. The capital city's recently rehabilitated generators still rely on fuel oil, and power cuts have become increasingly frequent as fuel prices have risen sharply. An aid project to increase fuel storage capacity on the islands should help to curb problems arising from erratic supplies. In 1991, the public company responsible for electricity and water supplies, which had become much criticized for its inefficiency, was handed over to a French company to manage. A comprehensive energy plan is scheduled for the end of 1993, and the entire electricity and water distribution systems are to be replaced from 1994.

The asphalted road network of some 250 km suffered serious deterioration following independence, but a repair programme financed by foreign aid began in 1989. Foreign donors are also upgrading three of the country's ports, although São Tomé city lacks a natural deep-water harbour and has been losing traffic to the better-endowed port of Neves, which handles petroleum imports and industrial fishing. Joint ventures were established in 1989 to replace the inefficient state enterprises for maritime communications and telecommunications. In 1984 the first phase of a long-term plan for modernizing the main airport near São Tomé city was completed at a cost of $10m., with the new runway allowing some long-haul aircraft to land. The second phase costing $18m. and consisting of a new control tower and passenger terminal was completed in 1992. The joint venture airline established in 1986 under the name Equatorial Airlines of São Tomé and Príncipe went into liquidation in 1992. In late 1993 a new airline, Air São Tomé, began operations. The company is managed by TAP-Air Portugal which also holds a 40% share of the capital. The government of São Tomé holds a 35% share while French Companies Golfe International Air Service and Mistral Voyages hold 24% and 1% respectively.

The improvement in communications has been of great importance in sustaining efforts to develop tourism, which is currently the sector of the economy attracting the most foreign capital. The islands benefit from spectacular volcanic mountains and craters, unpeopled beaches, unique bird life and flora, ample potential for game-fishing. However, the high rainfall during most of the year limits the duration of the tourist season, and the sea is usually dangerous to bathe in because of strong currents. Nevertheless, the first modern tourist hotel was completed in 1986 with a capacity of 50 beds, and it has attracted a modest current of tourists, mainly European expatriates and wealthy Gabonese. The Bombom luxury tourist complex on Príncipe island, which caters particularly for game-fishing, and the Santana tourist complex south of São Tomé city, also with emphasis on marine activities, were opened in late 1992. Renovation of the colonial Pousada Boa Vista, financed by TAP-Air Portugal and the government, was nearing completion in 1993. The World Bank and the ADB have expressed an interest in providing $300m. to promote the growth of the country's tourist industry, and there are plans for several new hotels and tourist facilities.

In May 1992, Voice of America (VOA) signed an agreement with the government providing for the establishment of a radio relay station at Pinheira, on São Tomé island. The agreement is for a duration of 30 years, and will provide São Tomé with an annual revenue of $10m. Broadcasts began in May 1993. In 1994 Radio France Internationale signed an agreement with the government allowing for the installation of a relay station. Broadcasting was expected to begin in September 1994. Similar plans were also being pursued by Radiodifusão Portuguesa in that year.

FOREIGN TRADE AND PAYMENTS

Because of the overwhelming importance of the cocoa plantations, the islands' economic life is entirely dependent on external markets. Until 1980, the trade balance was usually positive because of the small value of imports. However, since then low world cocoa prices and low cocoa production, combined with the higher cost of food imports, have led to a continuing trade deficit. The deficit reached a record total of $21.5m. in 1991. Shortages of essential supplies, especially fuel, have become more frequent. Portugal is the country's main supplier of goods, accounting for over one-third of the total, although there are considerable fluctuations from year to year. Most other imports come from Western Europe and East Asia. Since the mid-1980s, São Tomé has sold its cocoa mainly to Germany and the Netherlands.

São Tomé is reputed to be one of the largest recipients per caput of international aid. UNDP, the World Bank, the EC, Portugal, France, Italy, Sweden, Canada, Japan, the People's Republic of China and Arab countries have been especially prominent as donors. However, the institutional weakness of the country and the lack of co-ordination between donors has led to problems in the efficiency with which aid is utilized. The influx of aid has helped to deal with the deficit on the current account, but it has distorted prices. Total external debt stood at $231m. at the end of 1992. The cost of debt-servicing accounted for more than 30% of the total value of exports of goods and services. Of the total debt figure 74% was owed to multilateral creditors, chiefly the ADB and the World Bank's International Development Association.

Statistical Survey

Source (unless otherwise stated): Banco Central de São Tomé e Príncipe, São Tomé; tel. 22991.

AREA AND POPULATION

Area: 1,001 sq km (386.5 sq miles).

Population: 96,611 (males 48,031; females 48,580) at census of 15 August 1981; 117,504 (males 57,577; females 59,927) at census of 4 August 1991.

Density (at 1991 census): 117.4 per sq km.

Births and Deaths (1992): Registered live births 5,153 (birth rate 43.0 per 1,000); Registered deaths 1,011.

Expectation of Life (years at birth, 1992): 67.0.

Economically Active Population (1991 census): Agriculture, hunting, forestry and fishing 13,592; Industry 1,510; Electricity, gas and water 269; Public works and civil construction 2,866; Trade, restaurants and hotels 4,451; Financing, insurance, real estate and business services 176; Transport, storage and communications 2,186; Education 1,650; Health 1,133; Public administration 2,809; Other services 2,369; Other activities 1,057; Total employed 34,068 (males 22,758; females 11,310); Unemployed 15,148; Total labour force 49,216.

AGRICULTURE, ETC.

Principal Crops ('000 metric tons, 1992): Bananas 1.2; Breadfruit 1.5; Cabbages 2.0; Cassava 5.0 (FAO estimate); Cocoa 4.2; Coconuts 42 (FAO estimate); Maize 4.0; Matabala (Taro) 6.0; Palm kernels 0.5 (FAO estimate); Tomatoes 4.0. Source: partly FAO, *Production Yearbook*.

Livestock (FAO estimates, '000 head, year ending September 1992): Cattle 4; Sheep 2; Goats 4; Pigs 3. Source: FAO, *Production Yearbook*.

Forestry (FAO estimates, '000 cubic metres): Roundwood removals 9 in 1989; 9 in 1990; 9 in 1991. Source: FAO, *Yearbook of Forest Products*.

Fishing ('000 metric tons, live weight): Total catch 3.1 in 1989; 3.6 in 1990; 3.5 in 1991 (FAO estimate). Source: FAO, *Yearbook of Fishery Statistics*.

INDUSTRY

Production (metric tons, unless otherwise indicated, 1992): Frozen fish 400 (UN estimate, 1989); Bread and biscuits 3,000; Soap 400; Copra 679; Beer (litres) 2,475,300; Palm oil (litres) 1,261,000; Electric energy (million kWh) 18.1. Source: partly UN, *Industrial Statistics Yearbook*.

FINANCE

Currency and Exchange Rates: 100 cêntimos = 1 dobra (Db). *Sterling and Dollar Equivalents* (31 October 1993): £1 sterling = 704.68 dobras; US $1 = 474.05 dobras; 1,000 dobras = £1.419 = $2.109. *Average Exchange Rate* (dobras per US $): 143.3 in 1990; 201.8 in 1991; 321.3 in 1992.

Budget (estimates, million dobras, 1986): Revenue 1,092; Current Expenditure 1,092.

Currency in Circulation ('000 dobras, 1983): Notes 368,271, Coins 12,029, Total 380,300.

Cost of Living (Consumer Price Index; base: 1985 = 100): 331.2 in 1990; 551.9 in 1991; 703.5 in 1992.

Gross Domestic Product by Economic Activity (estimates, million dobras at current prices, 1992): Agriculture, forestry and fishing 3,852; Manufacturing, electricity, gas and water 933; Construction 851; Trade and transport 3,801; Public administration 3,195; Other services 1,200; *Total* 13,832.

Balance of Payments (US $ million, 1992): Merchandise exports f.o.b. 5.4; Merchandise imports f.o.b. −25.1; *Trade balance* −19.7; Services (net) −19.0; Transfers (net) 14.0; *Current balance* −24.7; Long-term capital (net) 13.2; Net errors and omissions 0.5; *Overall balance* −11.1.

EXTERNAL TRADE

Principal Commodities (US $ million, 1992): *Imports c.i.f.*: Food and live animals 4.3; Petroleum and petroleum products 2.8; Capital goods 9.5; Total (incl. others) 30.8. *Exports f.o.b.*: Cocoa 3.3; Total (incl. others) 5.5.

Principal Trading Partners ('000 dobras, 1983): *Imports:* Angola 89,443; Belgium and Luxembourg 124,184; German Democratic Republic 186,858; Federal Republic of Germany 31,565; Netherlands 33,583; Portugal 214,072; United Kingdom 26,110; USSR 19,315; Total (incl. others) 779,864. *Exports:* Cameroon 11,739; German Democratic Republic 184,739; Federal Republic of Germany 10,356; Netherlands 109,407; Portugal 48,809; Total (incl. others) 365,550.

TRANSPORT

Road Traffic (vehicles in use, 1987): Passenger cars 2,600; Commercial vehicles 300. Source: UN, *Statistical Yearbook*.

International Sea-borne Shipping (estimated freight traffic, metric tons, 1991): Goods loaded 15,000; Goods unloaded 26,000. Source: UN Economic Commission for Africa, *African Statistical Yearbook*.

Civil Aviation (traffic on scheduled services, 1990): Passengers carried ('000) 22; Passenger-km (million) 8; Total ton-km (million) 1. Source: UN, *Statistical Yearbook*.

COMMUNICATIONS MEDIA

Radio receivers (1991): 32,000 in use. Source: UNESCO, *Statistical Yearbook*.

Non-daily newspapers and periodicals (1992): Titles 6; Estimated average circulation 4,800 copies.

Telephones (1992): 2,267 in use.

EDUCATION

Pre-primary (1989): 13 schools; 116 teachers; 3,446 pupils (males 1,702; females 1,744).

Primary (1989): 64 schools; 559 teachers; 19,822 pupils (males 10,428; females 9,394).

General Secondary (1989): 318 teachers; 7,446 pupils (males 3,992; females 3,454).

Teacher Training: 10 teachers (1983); 188 students (males 74; females 114) (1987).

Vocational Secondary (1989): 18 teachers; 101 students (males 68; females 33).

Source: UNESCO, *Statistical Yearbook*.

Directory

The Constitution

The Constitution came into force on 10 September 1990 as the result of a national referendum, in which 72% of the electorate voted in favour of a draft that had been introduced by the Central Committee of the Movimento de Libertação de São Tomé e Príncipe and approved in March 1990 by the National People's Assembly. The following is a summary of its main provisions:

The Democratic Republic of São Tomé and Príncipe is a sovereign, independent, unitary and democratic state. There shall be complete separation between Church and State. Sovereignty resides in the people, who exercise it through universal, direct and secret vote, according to the terms of the Constitution.

Legislative power is vested in the National Assembly, which comprises 55 members elected by universal adult suffrage. The Assembly is elected for four years and meets in ordinary session twice a year. It may meet in extraordinary session on the proposal of the President, the Council of Ministers or of two-thirds of its members. The Assembly elects its own President. In the period between ordinary sessions of the Assembly its functions are assumed by a permanent commission elected from among its members.

Executive power is vested in the President of the Republic, who is elected for a period of five years by universal adult suffrage. The President's tenure of office is limited to two successive terms. He is the Supreme Commander of the Armed Forces and is accountable to the National Assembly. In the case of the President's death, permanent incapacity or resignation, his functions shall be assumed by the President of the National Assembly until a new president is elected.

The Government is the executive and administrative organ of State. The Prime Minister is the Head of Government and is appointed by the President. Other ministers are appointed by the President on the proposal of the Prime Minister. The Government is responsible to the President and the National Assembly.

Judicial power is exercised by the Supreme Court and all other competent tribunals and courts. The Supreme Court is the supreme judicial authority, and is accountable only to the National Assembly. Its members are appointed by the Assembly. The right to a defence is guaranteed.

The Constitution may be revised only by the National Assembly on the proposal of at least three-quarters of its members. Any amendment must be approved by a two-thirds majority of the Assembly.

The Government

HEAD OF STATE

President and Commander-in-Chief of the Armed Forces: MIGUEL DOS ANJOS DA CUNHA LISBOA TROVOADA (took office 3 April 1991).

INTERIM COUNCIL OF MINISTERS
(September 1994)

Prime Minister and Minister of Defence and Security: EVARISTO DO ESPÍRITO SANTO DE CARVALHO.

Minister of Foreign Affairs and Co-operation: ALBERTO FERREIRA CHONG.

Minister of Economic Co-ordination: HELDER DOMINGOS SOARES DE BARROS.

Minister of Justice and Public Administration: ALBERTO PAULINO.

Minister of Social Amenities and Environment: ARLINDO CARVALHO.

Minister of Health: FERNANDO SILVEIRA.

Minister of Education, Youth and Sport: ALBERTO NETO.

Minister-Delegate to the Prime Minister's Office for Príncipe Island: SILVESTRE UMBELINA.

There are three secretaries of state.

MINISTRIES

Ministry of Agriculture and Rural Development: São Tomé; tel. 22714.

Ministry of Commerce, Industry, Fisheries and Tourism: São Tomé.

Ministry of Defence and Security: São Tomé; tel. 21092.

Ministry of Economy and Finance: CP 168, São Tomé; tel. 22142; telex 225.

Ministry of Education, Culture, Youth and Sport: São Tomé; tel. 21571.

Ministry of Foreign Affairs and Co-operation: CP 111, São Tomé; tel. 21077; telex 211; fax 22597.

Ministry of Health: São Tomé; tel. 22182.

Ministry of Information: CP 112, São Tomé; tel. 21538; telex 217.

Ministry of Justice, Labour and Public Administration: São Tomé; tel. 22055; fax 22256.

Ministry of Social Services: CP 130, São Tomé; tel. 22824; telex 233; fax 21239.

Legislature

ASSEMBLÉIA NACIONAL

General Election, 2 October 1994

	Seats
Movimento de Libertação de São Tomé e Príncipe—Partido Social Democrata	27
Acção Democrática Independente	14
Partido de Convergência Democrática—Grupo de Reflexão	13
Coligação Democrático da Oposição	1
Total	55

Political Organizations

Acção Democrática Independente (ADI): São Tomé; f. 1992; Leader GABRIEL COSTA.

Aliança Popular (AP): São Tomé; f. 1992; Leader CARLOS ESPÍRITO SANTO.

Coligação Democrática da Oposição (CODO): São Tomé; Leader VIRGILIO CARVALHO.

Frente Democrata Cristã (FDC): São Tomé; Leader ARTUR TORRES.

Movimento de Libertação de São Tomé e Príncipe—Partido Social Democrata (MLSTP—PSD): São Tomé; f. 1972 as MLSTP, adopted present name in 1990; sole legal party 1972–90; Sec.-Gen. CARLOS DA GRAÇA.

Partido de Convergência Democrática—Grupo de Reflexão (PCD—GR): São Tomé; f. 1987 by a breakaway faction of the MLSTP; Chair. LEONEL MARIO D'ALVA; Sec.-Gen. JOÃO DO SACRAMENTO BONFIM.

Diplomatic Representation

EMBASSIES IN SÃO TOMÉ AND PRÍNCIPE

Angola: Avda Kwame Nkrumah 45, São Tomé; tel. 22400; telex 227; Chargé d'affaires: HERMENEGILDO TORRES DE SOUSA.

China, People's Republic: São Tomé; tel. 21323; Ambassador: TIAN YIMIN.

Gabon: Avda das Nações Unidas 4, CP 157, São Tomé; tel. 21043; telex 222; Ambassador: JEAN BAPTISTE MBATCHI.

Portugal: Avda Marginal de 12 de Julho, CP 173, São Tomé; tel. 21130; telex 261; fax 21190; Ambassador: EUGENIO ANACORETA CORREIA.

Judicial System

Judicial power is exercised by the Supreme Court and all other competent tribunals and courts. The Supreme Court is the ultimate judicial authority.

Judge: DIONISIO DIAS.

Religion

More than 90% of the population are Christians, almost all of whom are Roman Catholics.

CHRISTIANITY

The Roman Catholic Church

São Tomé and Príncipe comprises a single diocese, directly responsible to the Holy See. At 31 December 1992 there were an estimated 95,630 adherents in the country, representing about 81.4% of the population. The bishop participates in the Episcopal Conference of Angola and São Tomé (based in Luanda, Angola).

Bishop of São Tomé e Príncipe: Mgr Abílio Rodas de Sousa Ribas, Centro Diocesano, CP 104, São Tomé; tel. 21408; telex 213; fax 21365.

The Press

Diário da República: Imprensa Nacional, CP 28, São Tomé; tel. 22530; f. 1836; weekly; Dir Nelson Mendes.

Povo: Rua Três de Fevereiro, Prédio da 'Flêbê', São Tomé; tel. 22375; f. 1985; weekend newspaper and magazine; publ. by Direcção Técnica.

Revolução: Rua Três de Fevereiro, Prédio da 'Flêbê', São Tomé; tel. 22375; weekly; publ. by Direcção Técnica.

NEWS AGENCY

STP-Press: c/o Rádio Nacional de São Tomé e Príncipe, Avda Marginal de 12 de Julho, CP 44, São Tomé; tel. 21342; telex 217; f. 1985; operated by the radio station in asscn with the Angolan news agency, ANGOP.

Radio and Television

In 1991 there were an estimated 32,000 radio receivers in use. Portuguese technical and financial assistance in the establishment of a television service was announced in May 1989. Transmissions commenced in 1992, broadcasting for three-and-a-half hours, four days per week. The creation of the Companhia Santomense de Telecomunicações (CST), agreed in 1989 between a Portuguese company, Radio Marconi, and the Government of São Tomé, was to allow increased telecommunications links and television reception via satellite.

Rádio Nacional de São Tomé e Príncipe: Avda Marginal de 12 de Julho, CP 44, São Tomé; tel. 21342; fax 217; f. 1958; state-controlled; home service in Portuguese; Dir João Fernando Barbosa Neto.

Televisão de São Tomé e Príncipe: POB 393, São Tomé; tel. 21041; fax 21942; state-controlled; Dir Carlos Teixeira d'Alva.

Finance

BANKING

Banco Central de São Tomé e Príncipe: Praça da Independencia, POB 130, São Tomé; tel. 22407; f. 1992 following reconstruction of banking system, assuming central banking functions of fmr Banco Nacional de São Tomé e Príncipe; bank of issue; Gov. Adelino Santiago Castelo David.

Banco Internacional de São Tomé e Príncipe: São Tomé; f. 1993; international commercial bank.

Caixa Nacional de Poupança e Crédito (CNPC): CP 13, São Tomé; telex 204; f. 1980 as Caixa Popular de São Tomé e Príncipe; restructured 1993 and renamed as above; savings; loans for housing.

There is also a post office savings institution.

INSURANCE

Caixa de Previdência dos Funcionários Públicos: São Tomé; insurance fund for civil servants.

Empresa Nacional de Seguros e Resseguros 'A Compensadora': São Tomé; f. 1980.

Trade and Industry

TRADE UNION

Organizacão Nacional de Trabalhadores de São Tomé e Príncipe (ONTSTP): São Tomé; Sec.-Gen. Francisco Fortunato Pires.

Transport

RAILWAYS

There are no railways in São Tomé and Príncipe.

ROADS

In 1973 there were 287 km of roads, of which 199 km were asphalted.

CIVIL AVIATION

The principal airport is at São Tomé. In 1986 the African Development Bank agreed to provide most of the finance for a US $16m. project for the improvement of São Tomé airport: the runway extension plan was completed in September 1992, and a new administrative building and control tower were completed later that year.

Air São Tomé: São Tomé; f. 1993 to replace Equatorial Airlines of São Tomé and Príncipe; jtly owned by Govt of São Tomé (35%), TAP-Air Portugal, SA (40%), Golfe International Air Service (France) (24%) and Mistral Voyages (France) (1%); operates domestic service between the islands of São Tomé and Príncipe and international flights to Libreville (Gabon) and Douala (Cameroon).

Tourism

The islands benefit from spectacular mountain scenery, unpeopled beaches and unique species of wildlife and flora. Although still largely undeveloped, tourism is currently the sector of the islands' economy attracting the highest level of foreign investment. However, the high level of rainfall during most of the year limits the duration of the tourist season, and the expense of reaching the islands by air is also an inhibiting factor. The first modern tourist hotel was completed in 1986. In 1992 there were eight hotels and 146 hotel beds.

Defence

In 1992 a reorganization was initiated of the islands' armed forces (estimated to comprise some 900 men) and the police into two separate police forces, one for public order and another for criminal investigation. However, in December 1993, following increasing pressure from the military high command, parliament approved the new legal status of the armed forces maintaining their role as military defenders of the nation. Decisions concerning the exact structure that the armed forces would take were held in abeyance pending legislative elections in October 1994.

Commander-in-Chief of the Armed Forces: Miguel Trovoada.

Chief of General Staff of the Armed Forces: Capt. Antonio Paquete de Sousa.

Education

Primary education is officially compulsory for a period of four years between seven and 14 years of age. Secondary education lasts for a further seven years, comprising a first cycle of four years and a second cycle of three years. In 1989 the country had 64 primary schools, with a total enrolment of 19,822 pupils. There are three secondary schools and a technical school on São Tomé, staffed mainly by foreign teachers. In 1981 the average rate of adult illiteracy was 42.6% (males 26.8%; females 57.6%). Expenditure on education by the government in 1986 was 100.2m. dobras, equivalent to 18.8% of total budgetary expenditure.

Bibliography

Ambrósio, A. *Subsidios para a história de São Tomé e Príncipe.* Lisbon, Livros Horizonte, 1984.

Bredero, J. T., Heemskerk, W., and Toxopeus, H. *Agriculture and Livestock production in São Tomé and Príncipe (West Africa).* Wageningen, Foundation for Agricultural Plant Breeding, 1977.

da Cruz, C. B. *São Tomé e Príncipe: do colonialismo à independência.* Lisbon, 1975.

Economist Intelligence Unit. *Congo, São Tomé & Príncipe, Guinea-Bissau, Cape Verde, Country Report.* London, quarterly.

Congo, São Tomé & Príncipe, Guinea-Bissau, Cape Verde, Country Profile. London, annual.

Espírito Santo, C. *Contribuição para a história de São Tomé e Príncipe.* Lisbon 1979.

Eyzaguirre, P. 'The Ecology of Swidden Agriculture and Agrarian History in São Tomé, in *Cahiers d'Etudes Africaines,* No. 101–2, 26, 1986.

'The Independence of São Tomé e Príncipe and Agrarian Reform', in *Journal of Modern African Studies,* April 1989.

Ferraz, L. I. *The Creole of São Tomé.* Johannesburg, Witwatersrand University Press, 1979.

'São Tomé and Príncipe: Combating Cocoa Colonialism', in *Africa Report,* January 1986.

Hodges, T., and Newitt, M. *São Tomé and Príncipe: From Plantation Colony to Microstate.* Boulder, CO, Westview Press, 1988.

Jones, P. J., Burlison, J. P., and Tye, A. *Conservação dos ecossistemas florestais da República Democrática de São Tomé e Príncipe.* Gland and Cambridge, UICN, 1991.

Jones, P. J., and Tye, A. *A Survey of the Avifauna of São Tomé and Príncipe.* Cambridge, International Council for Bird Preservation, 1988.

Lains e Silva, H. *São Tomé e Príncipe e a cultura do café.* Lisbon, Junta de Investigações do Ultramar, 1958.

Pélissier, R. *Le Naufrage des Caravelles (1961–75).* Orgeval, Editions Pélissier, 1979.

Explorar. Voyages en Angola et autres lieux incertains. Orgeval, Editions Pélissier, 1980.

Schümer, M. *São Tomé und Príncipe, Ausbruch aus der Isolation.* Bonn, Forschungsinstitut der Deutschen Gesellschaft für Auswärtige Politik eV, 1987.

Torp, E., Denny, L. M., and Ray, D. I. (Eds). *Mozambique and São Tomé and Príncipe: Politics, Economics and Society.* New York, Pinter, 1989.

de Unzueta y Yuste, A. *Islas del Golfo de Guinea (Elobeyes, Corisco, Annobón, Príncipe y Santo Tomé).* Madrid, Instituto de Estudios Politicos, 1945.

Wisenberg, L. S., and Nelson, G. F. 'São Tomé and Príncipe: Mini-state with Maxi-problems', in *Africa Report,* No. 21, 2, 1976.

SENEGAL

Physical and Social Geography

R. J. HARRISON CHURCH

The Republic of Senegal, the most westerly state of Africa, has an area of 196,722 sq km (75,955 sq miles) and had a population of 6,896,808 at the census of May 1988 (35.1 persons per sq km). The southern border is first with Guinea-Bissau and then with Guinea on the northern edge of the Primary sandstone outcrop of the Fouta Djallon. In the east the border is with Mali, in the only other area of bold relief in Senegal, where there are Pre-Cambrian rocks in the Bambouk mountains. The northern border with Mauritania lies along the Senegal river, navigable for small boats all the year to Podor and for two months to Kayes (Mali). The river has a wide flood plain, annually cultivated as the waters retreat. The delta soils are saline, but dams for power, irrigation and better navigation are being built or proposed. The commissioning in 1985 of the Djama dam has considerably improved navigability at the Senegal river delta. The completion in 1988 of the Manantali scheme will eventually extend the all-year navigability of the river from 220 km to 924 km, as far as Kayes, in Mali.

The Gambia forms a semi-enclave between part of southern Senegal and the sea, along the valley of the navigable Gambia river. This has meant that since the colonial delimitation of the Gambia–Senegal borders in 1889, the river has played no positive role in Senegal's development and that the Casamance region, in the south, was isolated from the rest of Senegal until the opening of the Trans-Gambian highway in 1958.

Apart from the high eastern and south-eastern borderlands most of the country has monotonous plains, which in an earlier wetter period were drained by large rivers in the centre of the country. Relic valleys, now devoid of superficial water, occur in the Ferlo desert, and these built up the Sine Saloum delta north of The Gambia. In a later dry period north-east to south-west trending sand dunes were formed, giving Senegal's plains their undulating and ribbed surfaces. These plains of Cayor, Baol, and Nioro du Rip are inhabited by Wolof and Serer cultivators of groundnuts and millet. The coast between Saint-Louis and Dakar has a broad belt of live dunes. Behind them, near Thiès, calcium phosphates are quarried (aluminium phosphates are also present) and phosphatic fertilizer is produced.

Although Senegal's mineral resources are relatively poor, there are potentially valuable reserves of gold, in the south-east (production of which was scheduled to begin in the mid-1990s), as well as deposits of high-grade iron ore, in considerable quantity, in the east. Reserves of natural gas are exploited offshore from Dakar, and petroleum is known to exist off the Casamance coast.

The Cap Vert (Cape Verde) peninsula results in part from Tertiary volcanic activity. Cap Vert is formed by one of the two extinct volcanoes known as les Mamelles. Exposure to south-westerly winds is responsible for Cap Vert's verdant appearance, in contrast to the yellow dunes to the north. Basalt underlies much of Dakar, and its harbour was constructed in a sandy area east of (and sheltered by) the basaltic plateau. South of the peninsula, particularly in Casamance, the coast is a drowned one of shallow estuaries.

Senegal's climate is widely varied, and the coast is remarkably cool for the latitude (Dakar 14° 38′ N). The Cap Vert peninsula is particularly breezy, because it projects into the path of northerly marine trade winds. Average temperatures lie between 18°C–31°C, and the rainy season is little more than three months in length. Inland both temperatures and rainfall are higher, and the rainy season in comparable latitudes is somewhat longer. Casamance lies on the northern fringe of the monsoonal climate. Thus Ziguinchor (12° 35′ N) has four to five months' rainy season, with average annual rainfall of 1,626 mm, nearly three times that received by Dakar. The natural vegetation ranges from Sahel savannah north of about 15°N, through Sudan savannah in south-central Senegal, to Guinea savannah in Casamance, where the oil palm is common.

Recent History

PIERRE ENGLEBERT

Upon achieving independence in 1960, after 300 years of French rule, Senegal already had a limited experience of democracy. Inhabitants of the principal towns had received a form of French citizenship in the 19th century, and had been represented in the French national assembly. As the administrative centre of French West Africa, Dakar was an active centre for African politics. During the 1950s a variety of political forces emerged, including a strong trade union movement, Islamic sects and exponents of Marxism. The Union progressiste sénégalaise (UPS) was founded by Léopold Sédar Senghor, a well-known poet and academic, who combined the support of foreign and local business interests, Islamic leaders and socialists. The success of the UPS was aided by a ban on the activities of the Marxist Parti africain de l'indépendance (PAI). In November 1958 Senegal became a self-governing member of the French Community. The Mali Federation with Soudan (now Mali) was formed in April 1959, and became independent on 20 June 1960, but on 20 August, owing to the incompatibility of the two leaderships, Senegal seceded to become a separate independent state. The Republic of Senegal was proclaimed on 5 September, with Senghor as its president. His prime minister was Mamadou Dia, a socialist, who attempted, despite French opposition, to introduce comprehensive national planning. Dia was arrested in December 1962 and sentenced to life imprisonment, after being found guilty of organizing an attempted coup. Senghor assumed the responsibilities of the prime minister; he encouraged French private investment and French use of military facilities in Senegal.

In 1963 a revised constitution, strengthening the powers of the president, was approved in a referendum. Later in the year the UPS won a decisive victory in elections to the national assembly. Following serious rioting in Dakar, the principal legal opposition movement, the Bloc des masses sénégalaises, led by Cheikh Anta Diop, was outlawed. Other parties were either banned or absorbed into the UPS, which by 1966 was the sole legal party.

During 1968 there were protests and strikes by students, in opposition to proposed reductions in educational grants, and by trade union activists protesting at declining standards of living. Concessions to workers brought about a settlement, and educational reforms were promised. The more militant workers' groups resisted subsequent government attempts to co-opt union leaders into its Confédération nationale des travailleurs sénégalais (CNTS).

In 1970 the office of the prime minister was revived and assigned to a young provincial administrator, Abdou Diouf. Elections held in January 1973 returned both Senghor and the UPS with huge majorities, but a recurrence of student unrest ensued. In March 1974 Mamadou Dia was released from detention, and in July the government permitted the registration of a new political party, the Parti démocratique sénégalais (PDS), led by a lawyer, Abdoulaye Wade. In 1976 Senghor announced the formation of a three-party system, comprising the UPS (which in December was renamed the Parti socialiste—PS), the PDS and a Marxist-Leninist party, to be formed by members of the PAI. Most PAI supporters, however, refused to co-operate in the proposed arrangement. Other prominent politicians who were not included formed unofficial parties: Cheikh Anta Diop established the Rassemblement national démocratique (RND), while in 1978 Mamadou Dia founded the Coordination de l'opposition sénégalaise unie. At elections in February 1978 the PS won 83 of the 100 seats in the national assembly, while Senghor overwhelmingly defeated Abdoulaye Wade in the presidential election. In December a fourth political grouping, the right-wing Mouvement républicain sénégalais, was officially recognized (the party had ceased to exist by the early 1990s).

In September 1978, in anticipation of Senghor's retirement, a reorganization of the government and of the PS gave increased powers to Diouf. The country's economic difficulties obliged the government to undertake austerity measures, thereby encouraging the provision of aid by the IMF, the World Bank and donor governments.

DIOUF'S LEADERSHIP

The declining economic situation and the intense pressure for imaginative political reforms were the background to President Senghor's announcement in December 1980 that he would resign at the end of the month. Diouf assumed the presidency in January 1981 (also becoming secretary-general of the PS), and undertook a vigorous reorganization of the political system. Restrictions on political activity were removed in April, and in the following months the RND and numerous smaller parties—many of which had Marxist sympathies—were officially registered. The PDS saw its support steadily eroded and some of its members arrested on suspicion of having received Libyan funds. (Diplomatic links with Libya, which had for some time been financing Islamic militants in Senegal, had been severed in July 1980, following outspoken attacks on Senghor by the Qaddafi regime.)

In August 1981 Diouf agreed to a request by the Gambian president, Sir Dawda Jawara, to use Senegalese troops to restore him to power, after a *coup d'état* had taken place during his absence abroad. Following the suppression of the coup, Senegalese forces were asked to remain. Jawara and Diouf worked quickly towards setting up a confederation of the two states, with co-ordinated Senegambian policies in defence, foreign affairs and economic and financial matters. An agreement to establish the Senegambia confederation was formally ratified in December 1981 and came into effect in February 1982. Diouf was designated permanent president of the Senegambian council of ministers, and a confederal assembly was established. Agreements were reached in the areas of defence and security, foreign policy, communications and transport. However, The Gambia resisted attempts by Senegal to proceed towards the full political and economic integration of the two countries.

In February 1983 Diouf led the PS to a clear victory in legislative and presidential elections. During 1982 the government had amended the electoral law for the legislature, so that one-half of its members would be elected on a basis of proportional representation, while the remaining members were chosen by direct contest. The PS had mustered the full support of the *marabout* Muslim leaders, while Diouf had enhanced his own image by a gradual anti-corruption campaign, with the result that Diouf received 83.5% of the votes cast, while the PS candidates for seats in the national assembly secured 79.9% of the votes. The PDS won eight seats, and the RND only one. Disputing the results, the government's opponents resolved not to take up their seats and announced the formation of a 'shadow government'. Diouf may well have gained status as a result of the elections, but he was regarded in some quarters as having been 'dragged down into the political arena', and some of the admiration engendered by his early liberalization of the political system began to dissipate.

In forming a new government in April 1983, Diouf continued his purge of the party 'old guard', while strengthening his own powers with the abolition of the premiership. Habib Thiam, the prime minister since 1981, was transferred to the presidency of the national assembly and named as Diouf's successor. However, the 'old guard' of the PS sought to reassert some of its power in the national assembly, and in April 1984 Thiam was forced to resign as president of the assembly, following a vote to re-elect a new parliamentary leader every 12 months.

Opposition Pressures

Until the mid-1980s, the PS benefited from persistent disunity among the opposition groupings; a boycott by 12 of the country's 15 registered parties had contributed to the success of the PS in municipal and rural elections in November 1984. However, in July 1985 the PDS joined with four other opposition parties to form the Alliance démocratique sénégalaise (ADS), under the leadership of Abdoulaye Bathily, the leader of the Ligue démocratique–Mouvement pour le parti du travail (LD–MPT). Wade, Bathily and 14 others were arrested and detained for a week on charges of 'unauthorized demonstration'. The government banned the ADS in September, on the grounds that the constitution did not allow party-political coalitions. The authority of the PDS in demanding electoral reforms was subsequently undermined by damaging internal divisions, including the departure from the party, in October 1985, of three PDS deputies, and the resignation from parliament and the PDS of the party's deputy leader in June 1986. In early 1987 there were several unsuccessful attempts by opposition groups to unite in a 'co-ordinated resistance' to the PS, in preparation for the elections. The emergence of a new PDS splinter group, the Parti démocratique sénégalais–Rénovation (PDS–R), under the leadership of Serigne Diop, was announced in June.

Cheikh Anta Diop, the RND leader, died in February 1986. Classes at the University of Dakar, which was renamed in his honour in February 1987, were boycotted in January and February of that year by students who were protesting against the late payment of grants and poor living conditions. The student demonstrations were followed by an unprecedented (and illegal) strike by police forces in April, which led to the dismissal of the minister of the interior and the suspension from duty of more than 6,000 police officers. Paramilitary forces were employed to carry out police duties, although by August nearly 5,000 police officers had been reinstated, with the main antagonists permanently dismissed.

The February 1988 presidential and legislative elections were preceded by renewed appeals from opposition leaders for the modification of the electoral code. Preliminary results indicated decisive victories for both Diouf and the PS. The PDS alleged that electoral fraud had been widespread, and rioting erupted in the Dakar region. A state of emergency was declared, and public gatherings were banned, educational establishments closed and an overnight curfew imposed in the capital. Abdoulaye Wade and Amath Dansokho, the leader of the Marxist-Leninist Parti de l'indépendance et du travail (PIT), were arrested, together with other opposition activists. The official results of the presidential election, announced in March, indicated that Diouf had received 73.2% of the votes cast; among the other three candidates, Wade obtained 25.8% of the votes. The PS obtained 103 seats in the national assembly, and the PDS the remaining 17. It was estimated that the electoral turn-out had been only 58.6%. In early March primary schools and the university were officially reopened, and the curfew was shortened and ultimately lifted in mid-April. Wade, Dansokho and other opponents of the Diouf government were tried in April on charges of incitement to violence and attacks on the internal security of the state; Dansokho and five others were subsequently released from custody. In May Wade received a one-year suspended prison sentence, while three other PDS activists received prison terms of between six months and two years. Wade appealed for calm, and declared his willingness to confer with Diouf. The president also demonstrated a conciliatory attitude when, in the same month, he terminated the state of emergency and announced an amnesty for all those who had been condemned in the aftermath of the February elections, as well as for 320 Casamance separatists (see below). However, subsequent attempts by the government and opposition to establish multi-party commissions to consider the country's political, economic and social difficulties ended in failure.

Secondary school pupils (who had been boycotting classes since October 1987) and university students failed to return to classes after the elections. In October 1988 a programme for the rehabilitation of the national education system was announced, and in the following month the government agreed to the students' demands for improved welfare provisions, and gave assurances regarding the independence of the Cheikh Anta Diop University. The 1988/89 academic year was, none the less, disrupted by a three-month strike by academic staff in early 1989, and by continuing protests by students concerning academic and welfare issues. A further agreement was reached with the government in April of that year.

In March 1989 Diouf announced the establishment of an executive committee within the PS to reform the electoral code, to draft a 'national democratic charter', and to consider the status of the opposition. In the same month Wade returned from a seven-month period of self-imposed exile in France, asserting that Diouf had agreed to his demands that a transitional government of national unity be established (in which Wade was to hold a prominent position) pending new presidential and legislative elections. However, Diouf denied that such an agreement existed. In April Diouf announced electoral changes: measures would be implemented with the aim of ensuring a fair system of voter registration, a new system of proportional representation (within administrative departments) was to be introduced for legislative elections, and access to the state-owned media was to be granted to opposition parties. The reforms were approved in October by PS representatives in the national assembly (PDS deputies had begun a boycott of legislative sessions in mid-1989, in protest against what they alleged was partial and selective media coverage of parliamentary debates). The legislature also approved the 'national democratic charter', which provided for the dissolution of any political party that did not abide by the constitution or by the principles of democracy, or that received subsidies from abroad.

In February 1990 Wade returned to Senegal, after an absence of more than six months. Although the PDS leader stated that he no longer disputed Diouf's victory in the February 1988 elections, he demanded that, in view of the deteriorating economic and social conditions in Senegal, the electorate be allowed to choose new leaders. A series of days of action were subsequently organized by the opposition parties; several participants were detained by the security forces. Further disturbances broke out in April.

In March 1990 Diouf carried out an extensive government reshuffle. Among the most significant changes was the dismissal as minister of state and secretary-general of the presidency of the republic, of Jean Collin, an influential public figure since the colonial period. In April Collin also relinquished prominent posts within the PS; he was appointed special adviser to President Eyadéma of Togo in early 1991, and died in France in October 1993.

In May 1990 the government announced that changes permitting increased opposition access to the state-owned media (for some time a principal demand of the opposition parties) would be introduced. In November, however, a delegation that was scheduled to meet representatives of the Diouf administration to discuss this issue staged a demonstration in protest against what it alleged was a restrictive policy governing the official media. The security forces intervened to disperse the demonstrators, and leaders of the opposition parties were briefly detained. Many opposition parties boycotted municipal and rural elections in November (at which the PS reportedly received the support of 70% of those who voted), claiming that Senegal's electoral code still permitted widespread electoral malpractice. Unrest re-emerged in the education sector in January 1991, when 17 students were arrested following a demonstration at the Cheikh Anta Diop University in support of a boycott of classes by secondary school pupils: it was alleged that the Diouf government had withdrawn concessions agreed following earlier protests.

Constitutional Concessions

In March 1991 the national assembly approved several constitutional amendments, notably the restoration of the post of prime minister. It was also agreed that opposition parties would, henceforth, be allowed to participate in government. Accordingly, in early April Habib Thiam was restored as prime minister. Thiam subsequently appointed a new government: of the 26 ministers and ministers-delegate, four were representatives of the PDS (Wade was designated minister of state, while Ousmane Ngom, the party's parliamentary leader, became minister of labour and professional training), and Amath Dansokho, the leader of the PIT, joined the new administration as minister of housing and town planning. In May it was announced that a national commission was to be established to consider the further reform of the electoral system. Following consultations with the main political parties, the commission submitted its recommendations to Diouf in late August, and in the following month the national assembly adopted a series of amendments to the electoral code. Under the amended code, presidential elections would henceforth take place, in two rounds if necessary (the new regulations stipulated that the president would have to be elected by at least one-quarter of registered voters, and by an absolute majority of the votes cast), every seven years, with the president being limited to a maximum of two terms of office. Elections to the presidency would no longer coincide with legislative elections, which would continue to take place at five-yearly intervals. The amendments also included the lowering of the age of eligibility to vote from 21 to 18 years of age. A major reform of the organs of the judiciary was implemented in May, as a result of which the supreme court was abolished and its functions divided between three new bodies: a constitutional court, a council of state and a court of higher appeal.

Clashes were reported in January 1992, when security forces intervened to prevent students from staging a demonstration in Dakar. The students had been boycotting classes at the Cheikh Anta Diop University since late 1991, in support of their demands for improved educational facilities. The strike ended in February 1992, when the government agreed to several of the students' demands, including the appointment of more academic staff and increases in the level of grants.

In October 1992 Wade (who had already declared his intention to contest the 1993 presidential election) and his three PDS colleagues resigned from the council of ministers, protesting that they had been excluded from the governmental process. In subsequent months Wade alleged that the PS retained privileged access to the state-owned media—contrary to earlier agreements between the government and the opposition—and that the government was attempting to hinder the registration of certain categories of voter prior to the presidential and legislative elections.

The presidential election, which took place on 21 February 1993, was contested by eight candidates. Despite some irregularities, voting was reported to be well-ordered in most areas, although there were serious incidents in the Casamance region (see below). The opposition denounced preliminary results, which indicated that, while Wade had enjoyed considerable success in Dakar and in the nearby manufacturing town of Thiès, Diouf had won a clear majority of the overall votes. The process of determining the official outcome of the election encountered considerable delay, owing to disagreements within the electoral commission (a body comprising a presiding magistrate and representatives of the candidates at the election). Difficulties in proclaiming the results prompted the resignation of the president of the constitutional council in early March, and it was not until 13 March that the council was able to announce that Diouf had been re-elected by 58.4% of the votes cast (51.6% of the electorate had voted). Wade secured 32.0% of the votes, with none of the other candidates obtaining more than 2.9%. The declaration of the official results precipitated some unrest in Dakar, but order was quickly restored, and Wade appealed for passive resistance to Diouf's victory. Diouf subsequently announced that the electoral code was to be modified, with the immediate aim of avoiding similar delays in the announcement of the results of the forthcoming legislative elections.

Post-Election Unrest

Elections to the national assembly took place on 9 May 1993, and on 14 May the electoral commission (required to submit the results to the constitutional council within five days) announced that the PS had won 84 of the assembly's 120 seats. The PDS, with considerable support in urban areas, took 27 seats, the remainder being divided between three other parties and one electoral alliance. The electoral turnout was only 40.7%. Shortly after the announcement of the results the vice-president of the constitutional council, Babacar Seye, was assassinated, and, although an organization styling itself the 'Armée du peuple' claimed responsibility, Wade and three other PDS leaders were detained for three days in connection with the murder. The PDS protested that its opponents were plotting to discredit the party, and, following his release, Wade—while denying any involvement in the attack on Seye—expressed no surprise that, having previously declared that he had no confidence in the supposed impartiality of Seye and the constitutional council, he should have been detained. Moreover, he suggested that attempts to implicate him in the assassination may have been orchestrated by those who sought to prevent any *rapprochement* of Diouf and himself. The official results of the legislative elections were confirmed by the constitutional council on 24 May. In the days that preceded the announcement four people suspected of involvement in Seye's murder were arrested: among those detained were Samuel Sarr, a close associate of Wade, and a PDS deputy, Mody Sy.

Wade and the PDS were excluded from Habib Thiam's new government, which was formed in early June 1993. Amath Dansokho, who had supported Diouf's presidential campaign, retained his position in the council of ministers, while the LD–MPT leader, Abdoulaye Bathily (himself a candidate for the presidency), was appointed minister of the environment and nature conservation. Other new appointments included Serigne Diop of the PDS–R, as minister of employment and professional training, and Papa Ousmane Sakho, hitherto the national director of the Banque centrale des états de l'Afrique de l'ouest, to the ministry of the economy, finance and planning.

In late July 1993 there were clashes in Dakar when security forces acted to disperse a violent demonstration that had been organized to demand the release of Mody Sy—who, it was alleged, had been tortured while in custody. Six national assembly members (representatives of the PDS and the LD–MPT) were briefly detained in connection with the incident. Political tensions were compounded by a profound social crisis which arose in mid-August, when the government, citing the need to reduce the budget deficit in order to secure vital economic support from Senegal's external creditors, announced wide-ranging austerity measures. As well as modifications to the tax code and a 'rationalization' of the diplomatic corps, it was proposed that the salary and allowances of the head of state would be halved, that the salaries of government ministers and members of the national assembly would be reduced by 25% (and their allowances by 50%), and that remuneration throughout the public sector would be reduced by 15%; employees in the private sector, meanwhile, would be obliged to forfeit one day's pay per month. Although the emergency plan was adopted by the national assembly, trade unions and the government's political opponents denounced, especially, the proposal to reduce salaries in the public sector, and a 24-hour general strike, organized by the CNTS to protest against the austerity measures, was widely observed in early September. Diouf subsequently announced the postponement of the imposition of the measures, pending further negotiations with the CNTS and other unions. However, the talks again failed, as the government refused to accede to union demands that the prices of staple foods be lowered to compensate for the salary cuts, which were imposed in early October. Two 72-hour general strikes (denounced as illegal by the government, which threatened to withdraw the right to strike, as guaranteed under the constitution) were organized, with only partial success, by trade unions in the second half of October.

Relations between the Diouf administration and parties outside the government coalition, which formed a Coordination des forces démocratiques (CFD), deteriorated further in the second half of 1993. In early October Wade was charged with complicity in the assassination of Seye; Wade's wife and a PDS deputy were also charged with 'complicity in a breach of state security'. None was detained, although Mody Sy, Sarr and three others remained in custody in connection with the murder. In late October a PDS motion expressing 'no confidence' in the Thiam government was defeated in the national assembly. The PDS subsequently announced that it was to boycott parliamentary sessions, in protest against what it considered to be biased coverage by the state-owned media of the vote.

In early November 1993 Ousmane Ngom and Landing Savane, the leader of And Jëf–Parti africain pour la démocratie et le socialisme, were among those detained following a protest in Dakar to demand the cancellation of the austerity measures. The action coincided with a demonstration, at which arrests were also made, to appeal for the release of Moustapha Sy, the leader of an Islamic youth movement, Dahira Moustarchidine wal Moustarchidate, who had recently been arrested after having criticized the government (and who had also reportedly claimed to know the circumstances and authors of Seye's assassination). Ngom, Savané and some 85 others were convicted of participating in an unauthorized demonstration, and received six-month suspended prison sentences. In January 1994 Moustapha Sy was sentenced to one year's imprisonment.

Following the devaluation of the CFA franc, in January 1994, Diof was granted temprorary powers to rule by decree in economic affairs, and emergency measures (among them the cancellation of the previous year's wage reductions and a 10% increase in salaries with effect from April) were adopted to offset the immediate adverse effects of the loss in value of the national currency. However, the opposition held the president (who, despite having previously denied that any devaluation would be imposed, was widely regarded as a principal architect of the policy) responsible for resultant hardship. A demonstration in Dakar in mid-February, organized by the CFD to denounce the devaluation, degenerated into serious rioting throughout the capital, as a result of which eight people (including six police-officers) were killed. Dahira Moustarchidine wal Moustarchidate, which was identified by the authorities as being implicated in much of the violence, was banned in the aftermath of the disturbances, and the government stated that it regarded the CFD (which the authorities stressed was an unauthorized organization) as responsible for the unrest. Wade, Savané and more than 70 others were subsequently detained and charged with attacks on state security. Opposition acitivists alleged that some of the accused had been tortured while in custody (as a result of which one detainee had died), and Wade and Savané instigated a hunger strike, in support of their demands for access to proper legal procedures (they were not formally charged before a court until mid-March). In late May charges against Wade and his opposition associates (including Mody Sy and Samuel Sarr) in connection with the murder of Seye were dismissed on the grounds of insufficient evidence. Wade and Savané, who were awaiting trial in connection with the post-devaluation violence, were not released from custody. Sarr and Mody Sy, who remained in detention pending the outcome of a state-prosecution appeal against their release, staged a hunger strike in late June, and were subsequently released on bail. Similarly, Wade, Savané and four others, who had also begun a hunger strike, were provisionally released in early July. Legal proceedings against them and 140 others implicated in the February riots were dismissed later in July, again on the grounds of insufficient evidence; in late September 24 others (said to be members of Dahira Moustarchidine wal Moustarchidate) received prison sentences of between six months and two years. In mid-September Moustapha Sy was granted a presidential pardon and released from custody. At the same time it was announced that the trial of four alleged assassins of Babacar Seye would begin in late September.

In August 1994 the 1993/94 academic year at the Cheikh Anta Diop University was declared invalid, following almost three months of disruption by students who were protesting against proposed reforms to the higher education system.

SEPARATISM IN CASAMANCE

Since the early 1980s the development of a separatist group, the Mouvement des forces démocratiques de la Casamance (MFDC), among communities of the Diola people in the southern province of Casamance (which is virtually cut off from the rest of the country by the enclave of The Gambia) has periodically presented the Diouf administration with considerable security difficulties. After demonstrations in Ziguinchor in December 1982, several leaders of the MFDC were detained without trial. A more serious demonstration in December 1983 was suppressed by force, and various reports estimated the death toll at more than 100. In January 1986 a leading Casamance independence campaigner was sentenced to life imprisonment, while other demonstrators received prison sentences ranging from two to 15 years. Further arrests occurred in October 1986, but almost 100 detainees were provisionally released in April 1987. A further 320 separatists reportedly benefited under the conditions of the May 1988 amnesty. There were renewed clashes between supporters of the MFDC and the Senegalese security forces in December 1988.

The MFDC initiated a further offensive during the second quarter of 1990: by early June it was reported that about 10 people had been killed, and more than 100 injured, following a series of attacks, most of which were directed at administrative targets in the Casamance region. In late May the separatist movement was the subject of a report by the human rights organization, Amnesty International, which expressed concern at the failure of the Diouf administration to investigate allegations of the torture of members of the MFDC during the 1980s, or to introduce safeguards aimed at preventing the ill-treatment of the dissident Casamançais. Ambushes and raids continued during mid-1990, despite the reported arrest of large numbers of alleged MFDC members, including the leader of the movement, Abbé Diamacouné Senghor. Tensions escalated when military reinforcements were dispatched to the region, and in September a military governor was appointed for Casamance. Amnesty International issued further reports, in October 1990 and January 1991, denouncing the torture and summary executions of members of the MFDC by the Senegalese armed forces (allegations that were investigated, and subsequently refuted, by the Diouf government). By April 1991 at least 100 people were said to have been killed as a result of violence in the region, while more than 300 Casamançais had been transported to Dakar to await trial for sedition. Meanwhile, in late 1990 reports suggested that some 1,600 Senegalese had taken refuge in Guinea-Bissau, after having fled Casamance to escape clashes between the Senegalese armed forces and the MFDC. In mid-April 1991 renewed action by separatists violated a truce that had apparently been negotiated by leaders of the MFDC and the new government. In late May Diouf announced the immediate release of more than 340 detainees (including Diamacouné Senghor) who had been arrested in connection with the unrest in the Casamance region. This facilitated the conclusion of a cease-fire agreement shortly afterwards in Guinea-Bissau by representatives of the Senegalese government and the MFDC. In mid-June the region's military governor was replaced by a civilian (as part of the demilitarization of the region that had been envisaged in the cease-fire accord). An amnesty was ratified by the national assembly in late June, benefiting some 400 Casamançais (including separatists released in the previous month) as well as those who had been implicated in the unrest that followed the 1988 elections. However, the cease-fire agreement was apparently violated in late December, when a PS deputy and a local village chief were assassinated in the Ziguinchor region, although MFDC leaders denied involvement in the killings. In the days that followed some 400 residents of the region were reported to have fled to The Gambia, fearing a resurgence of MFDC guerrilla activity.

In early January 1992 a peace commission (the Comité de gestion de la paix en Casamance), comprising government representatives and members of the MFDC, was established, with mediation by Guinea-Bissau. At the end of that month, none the less, more than 100 people fled to Gambian territory following an attack, allegedly perpetrated by the MFDC, on a Casamance village. A resurgence of separatist violence in Casamance during July and early August prompted the government to redeploy armed forces in the region. This further exacerbated tensions, and gave rise to MFDC protests that the 'remilitarization' of Casamance was in contravention of the cease-fire agreement. The death of a police-officer, in late July, was followed in early August by a violent clash near Ziguinchor, in which, according to official figures, 50 separatist rebels and two members of the armed forces were killed. Contradictory statements made by leaders of the MFDC, regarding their commitment to the truce accord, evidenced a split within the movement. The so-called 'Front nord' and the MFDC vice-president, Sidi Badji, appealed to the rebels to lay down their arms; meanwhile the 'Front sud', based in areas of dense forest near the border with Guinea-Bissau, and led by Diamacouné Senghor (himself now based in Guinea-Bissau), appeared determined to continue the armed struggle. Negotiations between representatives of the Senegalese government and the MFDC achieved little, and in late October 32 people (most of whom were seasonal fishermen from other regions of Senegal) were killed when separatist rebels attacked a fishing village near the Cap-Skirring tourist resort, causing local residents and tourists to flee the region. A further attack on a fishing village in the same area in mid-November resulted in at least seven deaths. Following the deaths of two Senegalese soldiers in December, the army instigated a major security operation, launching air attacks on supposed rebel bases in the region of the border with Guinea-Bissau (see below).

Indications in advance of the 1993 presidential and legislative elections that MFDC rebels would seek to prevent voting in Casamance prompted Diouf, at the end of January, to begin his electoral campaign in the province. His visit proceeded amid strict security measures, following the recent deaths of seven aid workers to the south-east of Ziguinchor. About 30 people were reported to have been killed in rebel attacks on voters on the day of the presidential election. Army reinforcements were dispatched to Casamance in mid-March (raising the total number of armed forces personnel in the region to as many as 5,000), following further clashes between the security forces and rebels.

Diamaconté Senghor returned to Ziguinchor in mid-March 1993, having seemingly been expelled from Guinea-Bissau. Violence persisted, but in early April Diamacouné Senghor reportedly appealed for a cease-fire, and expressed a willingness to negotiate with the Diouf government. Ten days later, however, at least 100 rebels and three members of the armed forces were killed in a clash near the border with Guinea-Bissau. In late April the Senegalese authorities confirmed their willingness to observe a truce, stating that the security forces would henceforth act only in a defensive capacity, and gave assurances regarding the continuation of negotiations and the resumption of economic initiatives in Casamance. A period of relative calm followed, although in late June it was reported that 20 suspected members of the MFDC had been killed by security forces near Ziguinchor. In early July a cease-fire agreement was signed in Ziguinchor by the Senegalese government and, on behalf of the MFDC, Diamacouné Senghor. The accord envisaged the release of Casamançais prisoners, and made provision for the return of those who had fled the region. Guinea-Bissau was to act as a guarantor of the agreement, and the government of France was to be asked to submit an historical arbitration regarding the Casamance issue. (The Senegalese authorities had consistently refuted MFDC assertions that documents from the colonial era indicated that France favoured independence for Casamance.) Shortly afterwards a soldier was killed in a skirmish involving separatist rebels and members of the armed forces. None the less,

256 Casamançais were released from detention in the second half of July, in accordance with the Ziguinchor accord. At the time of the conclusion of the new cease-fire, the total number of casualties of the conflict was uncertain, since the Senegalese authorities had not given details of military operations in Casamance for some months; however, it was believed that, in the year preceding the new accord, between 500 and 1,000 people had been killed and many hundreds injured, while humanitarian organizations estimated that 25,000–30,000 people may have fled to the Gambia and Guinea-Bissau, or to other regions of Senegal.

Although there were sporadic reports of clashes in Casamance during the remainder of 1993, as a result of which at least five deaths were recorded, the cease-fire was generally observed. In December France issued its judgment that Casamance had not existed as an autonomous territory prior to the colonial period, and that independence for the region had been neither demanded nor considered at the time of decolonization.

REGIONAL RELATIONS

Beginning in 1989 Senegal's traditional policy of peaceful coexistence with neighbouring countries was severely undermined by a series of regional disputes. In April 1989 two Senegalese were killed, following a disagreement with Mauritanian livestock-breeders regarding grazing rights in the border region between the two countries. Reactions to the dispute were exacerbated in both Senegal and Mauritania by long-standing ethnic and economic rivalries: the presence in Senegal of black Mauritanian dissidents had led to a deterioration in relations between the two countries, while a reciprocal ban on imports of certain products, in December 1988 and January 1989, had impaired trade relations between the two countries. In the aftermath of the border incident, Mauritanian nationals residing in Senegal were attacked, and their businesses ransacked (the retail trade in Senegal had hitherto been dominated by an expatriate community of mainly light-skinned Mauritanians, estimated to number about 300,000 in all). Senegalese nationals in Mauritania (who were estimated to number 30,000) suffered similar attacks. Estimates of the number of casualties varied, but it was believed that by early May several hundred people, mostly Senegalese, had been killed. Operations to repatriate nationals of both countries were undertaken with international assistance. In addition, Senegal granted asylum to black Mauritanians who feared official persecution. Mediation attempts were initiated by the OAU, the Arab states, France and the heads of state of several regional powers. However, despite the expressed commitment of both Senegal and Mauritania to the principle of a negotiated settlement of the dispute, Senegal's insistence on the inviolability of the border as defined at the time of French colonial rule and Mauritanian demands that the Senegalese government offer compensation for traders returning to Mauritania remained among the main impediments to a solution. In August Senegal broke off diplomatic relations with Mauritania. Renewed outbreaks of violence were reported in late 1989, when black Mauritanians sheltering in Senegal crossed into their former homeland (with, the government of Mauritania alleged, the complicity of the Senegalese armed forces) to recover their property. In early 1990 attempts at mediation were thwarted by military engagements in the border region, as a result of which several deaths were reported. Further diplomatic initiatives were equally unsuccessful, and in July 1990 all telephone connections between the two countries were severed. (Transport links between Senegal and Mauritania had been suspended during 1989.)

Telecommunications links were restored in October 1990. However, hopes of a *rapprochement* were undermined in late 1990, when the Mauritanian authorities accused Senegal of complicity in an alleged attempt to overthrow the Taya government (an accusation denied by the Diouf administration). Relations subsequently deteriorated, and in January and February 1991 incidents were reported in which Mauritanian naval vessels had opened fire on Senegalese fishing boats, apparently in Senegal's territorial waters. In early March several deaths were reported to have resulted from a military engagement, on Senegalese territory, between members of the two countries' armed forces, following an incursion by Senegalese troops into Mauritania. Further diplomatic initiatives resulted, in July, in a meeting of the foreign ministers of Senegal and Mauritania in Guinea-Bissau, at which they agreed in principle to the reopening of the Mauritania–Senegal border and to a resumption of diplomatic relations. However, the issues of the demarcation of the border and the fate of Mauritanian refugees in Senegal were not discussed. Bilateral contacts continued during the second half of the year, and in November Diouf met with President Taya while both were attending a francophone summit meeting in France. Diplomatic links, at ambassadorial level, were finally restored in April 1992, and the process of reopening the border began in May. None the less, the issues impeding good relations between the two countries (notably the question of border demarcation and the status of Mauritanian refugees in Senegal—numbering an estimated 50,000 in early 1994) remained to be resolved. Further tensions were reported in September 1993, when the Mauritanian authorities announced that Senegalese nationals would henceforth be required to fulfil certain criteria, including currency exchange formalities, before being allowed to remain in (or enter) Mauritania.

A dispute with Guinea-Bissau regarding the sovereignty of a maritime zone that is believed to contain reserves of petroleum, together with valuable fishing grounds, has caused tensions between the two countries. In July 1989 an international arbitration panel (to which the issue had been referred in 1985) judged the waters to be part of Senegalese territory. However, the government of Guinea-Bissau refused to accept the judgment, and referred the matter to the International Court of Justice. Despite the initiatives of a number of intermediaries (most notably the OAU and Portugal), the Vieira government accused Senegal of repeated violations of both Guinea-Bissau's maritime borders and airspace during April 1990. In the following month several skirmishes involving Senegalese and Guinea-Bissau troops occurred in the border region. The situation was exacerbated by Senegalese allegations that Guinea-Bissau was allowing members of the Casamance separatist movement to train on its territory. None the less, meetings between representatives of the two countries culminated, in late May, in the signing of an accord whereby each country undertook to refrain from harbouring organizations hostile to the other, to maintain troops at a 'reasonable distance' from the border and to promote more frequent bilateral contacts. In November 1991 the International Court of Justice ruled that the delimitation of the maritime border, as agreed by the French and Portuguese colonial powers in April 1960, remained valid, thereby confirming Senegal's sovereignty over the disputed zone, and Senegal and Guinea-Bissau signed a treaty recognizing this judgment in February 1993.

Although Guinea-Bissau (together with France) played an important role in the formulation of the 1991 cease-fire agreement between the Senegalese government and the MFDC, relations were again strained in late 1992. In mid-December an offensive by the Senegalese armed forces against MFDC strongholds close to the border with Guinea-Bissau (some reports suggested that MFDC bases within Guinea-Bissau had been targeted) resulted in the deaths of two nationals of that country. The Vieira government formally protested at Senegalese violations of Guinea-Bissau's airspace, and reiterated that, as a guarantor of the 1991 accord, it was not assisting the rebels. Although Senegal apologized for the incident, a further violation was reported in January 1993. None the less, Guinea-Bissau was again active in efforts to bring about a new cease-fire agreement between the Senegalese authorities and the MFDC in mid-1993. In October of that year, moreover, the two countries signed a major 20-year agreement regarding the joint exploitation and management of fishing and petroleum resources in their maritime zones.

In August 1989 the Diouf government announced the withdrawal of 1,400 Senegalese troops from The Gambia, apparently in protest at a request by the Gambian president, Sir Dawda Jawara, that his country be accorded more power within the Senegambia confederal agreement (and also, it seemed, in response to The Gambia's alleged lack of commitment to combating cross-border smuggling, as well as to Senegal's continuing dispute with Mauritania). Later in that month President Diouf stated that, in view of The Gambia's reluctance to proceed towards full political and economic integration with Senegal, the functions of this hitherto nominal confederation should be suspended, and the two countries should endeavour to formulate more attainable co-operation accords. The confederation was formally dissolved in September. The Jawara government subsequently accused Senegal of imposing customs and travel regulations that were unfavourable to Gambian interests, and of preventing supplies of important commodities from entering The Gambia via Senegal. Relations remained strained during 1990, and in October of that year the Diouf government accused the Gambian authorities of allowing members of the MFDC to operate from Gambian territory. By January 1991, none the less, relations had improved sufficiently to permit the foreign ministers of the two countries to sign a bilateral treaty of friendship and co-operation. In July Diouf visited The Gambia for the first time since the dissolution of the Senegambia confederation, and in December Jawara attended a summit meeting in Dakar of the Organization of the Islamic Conference. However, Senegal's abrupt, unilateral decision to close the Senegalese - Gambian border in September 1993, apparently to reduce smuggling between the two countries, again strained relations. Negotiations subsequently took place between representatives of Senegal and The Gambia, in an attempt to minimize the adverse effects of the closure on The Gambia's regional trading links, and in February 1994 it was announced that President Meles Zenawi of Ethiopia had been invited to mediate between the two countries. Although Jawara was granted asylum in Senegal following the *coup d'état* in The Gambia in July 1994, the Diouf government also conveyed a message of good will to the new Gambian regime.

In January 1993 it was announced that Senegal was to withdraw its contingent, estimated to number about 1,500 men, from the ECOMOG monitoring group of the Economic Community of West African States (ECOWAS) in Liberia. Senegal had committed troops to Liberia in September 1991, but was rumoured to have been increasingly dissatisfied with the conduct of ECOMOG operations (for further details, see Recent History of Liberia). The decision to withdraw from ECOMOG was said to have been necessitated by domestic security imperatives, given the forthcoming presidential and legislative elections and the escalation of violence in Casamance. None the less, Senegal confirmed that it would continue to co-operate with ECOWAS in initiatives to secure an enduring peace settlement in Liberia. In May 1994 Senegal announced that it would commit army personnel to an enlarged UN force in Rwanda, and in June joined the French-led 'Operation Turquoise' (see Recent History of Rwanda).

Economy

EDITH HODGKINSON

Revised for this edition by RICHARD SYNGE

Senegal retains some of the economic advantages derived from its leading position in pre-independence French West Africa. In 1992 Senegal's gross national product (GNP) was equivalent to US $780 per head, the highest level of any west African country. However, its economic performance has been disappointing. Growth in the gross domestic product (GDP)—averaging only 2.3% per year in 1970–80, before improving slightly, to 3.0% annually, in 1980–92—has partly kept pace with the rate of population growth (estimated at 2.9% per year in 1980–92). In 1992 the World Bank estimated the population at 7.8m., and total GDP at $6,277m.

Senegal's economy is vulnerable to competition in almost all areas of productive activity, and remains highly dependent on comparatively large inflows of foreign financial assistance. The agricultural base of the economy has been eroded by periodic droughts and the gradual desertification of large tracts of land. Agriculture's contribution to GDP declined from 24% in 1970 to 19% in 1992, according to World Bank figures. Following a substantial drift of population from rural to urban areas, more than 40% of the country's total population is urban, of whom about one-half live in the overcrowded Dakar region. As the role of the public sector is reduced, unemployment is growing—an estimated 25% of the active population in Dakar was unemployed in 1991.

Fishing, phosphate-mining and tourism have supplanted groundnuts as the principal sources of foreign exchange. The importance of these sectors should be further enhanced as a result of the devaluation, by 50%, of the CFA franc in January 1994, although many of Senegal's more import-dependent industrial activities may suffer payments' difficulties. Senegal's industrial base, which was comparatively well-developed at independence, is threatened by competing industrial investment in the west African region, particularly in Côte d'Ivoire. While a number of Senegalese industries are protected by monopoly rights and tax concessions, there is much excess capacity. The services sector, including government services, trade and transport, is calculated to have contributed 62% of GDP in 1992. With the prevailing difficulties in both agriculture and industry, economic activity is being conducted increasingly outside the formal sectors. Employment in the formal industrial sector declined from 41,500 jobs in 1985 to 38,000 in 1990.

AGRICULTURE

The principal food crops are millet, sorghum, rice and maize. Groundnuts are the leading cash crop, but the area under cultivation has declined in recent years. Annual groundnut harvests now average less than 800,000 metric tons, compared with more than 900,000 tons per year in the 1960s. There has been a long-term shift from cash to food crop cultivation, a process that is generally believed to be responsible for a decline in the real income of the rural population.

In an attempt to stimulate marketing through official channels, groundnut purchasing was opened to private traders in 1985/86 and producer prices were increased sharply. Improved weather conditions in the following years resulted in a strong rise in output, to 710,789 tons in 1987/88. Output declined to only 415,210 tons in 1988/89, but recovered strongly, to 844,045 tons, in 1989/90. After late rains, production in 1990/91 contracted to 702,584 tons; output remained at a similar level (728,368 tons) in 1991/92, and declined to 623,359 tons in 1992/93. The government is continuing more closely to link its producer prices to international price trends, and, as part of structural adjustment efforts, has almost abandoned its policy of providing inputs (such as seed and fertilizer) to farmers of groundnuts and other agricultural products. One result has been the reversal of smuggling trends, with a significant portion of the Gambian crop reaching Senegalese markets in the early 1990s.

The government has attempted to reduce dependence on groundnuts by diversifying cash and food crops, in particular by expanding cotton, rice, sugar and market-garden produce. Production of unginned cotton rose very rapidly, from only 698 tons in 1965 to 45,400 tons in 1976/77. Output subsequently fluctuated, with production being particularly influenced by prices for groundnuts, as farmers transfer to cultivation of the latter when prices are more favourable than those for cotton. In 1988/89 marketed production of unginned cotton was 38,730 tons; output declined to 29,303 tons in 1989/90, but had recovered to 51,176 tons by 1992/93. The only other cash crop that is produced on a large scale is sugar, which is produced at the Richard Toll complex in the north, near Saint-Louis. Output, all of which is for domestic consumption, has risen steadily since 1979, and totalled an estimated 90,000 tons in 1991. Output of rice has been generally rising, but, at an annual average of 170,000 tons since the late 1980s, falls far short of domestic demand (some 500,000 tons annually). The shortfall is met by cheap imports of rice from the Far East; however, this seriously jeopardizes the viability of local produce, which generally necessitates a state subsidy of 50–60 francs CFA per kilo. A number of small- and medium-scale projects, supported by foreign aid, are extending the area under irrigation for rice, while the completion of the Manantali project (see below) is expected to have a great impact on output levels in the future, with the creation of 240,000 ha of irrigated land in Senegal. Market gardening was begun in 1971, and, following initial difficulties, exports from this sector are viewed as having considerable potential, although Senegal's price competitiveness compared with other African producers is declining.

The traditional food sector has suffered sharp set-backs from repeated droughts, but the overall production level has risen. Output of millet and sorghum averaged 650,000 tons per year in the mid-1970s, around 100,000 tons higher than at the beginning of the decade, but fell to 351,800 tons in 1983/84, because of drought. A significant rise in producer prices in 1985/86 prompted a very strong increase in output in that year, to 949,600 tons. Production averaged 673,000 tons in 1988/89–1991/92, but declined to 562,706 tons in 1992/93. Output of maize, which reached a record 146,500 tons in 1985/86, declined to 123,327 tons in 1988/89, recovered slightly, to 133,147 tons in 1990/91, before falling back to 114,561 tons in 1992/93. Senegal regularly imports more than 300,000 tons of rice—the staple of the urban population—annually (see above), as well as much higher quantities of grain (616,840 tons in 1989), the latter predominantly with the help of aid programmes. In recent drought years concessionary grain supplies have amounted to more than 100,000 tons annually. The attainment of food self-sufficiency remains a major priority. Of great relevance to this objective is the enormous increase in irrigated land which is due to result from the completion of the Manantali dam. The combined benefits of the anti-salt barrage at Diama and of the Manantali dam are expected to provide newly-irrigated land totalling 240,000 ha over the next 25 years. In the short term, it is hoped to stabilize rice imports at 340,000 tons a year, while promoting the increased cultivation and consumption of millet and sorghum.

Food crops are supplemented by output from fishing. This sector has considerable potential and, including processing, now accounts for around 4% of GDP. Annual catches averaged 270,000 tons during 1986–90, with output of 319,693 tons in 1991. Small-scale fishing continues to predominate, with about 43,000 fishers providing some 60%–70% of the total national catch and about 45% of fish exports. Industrial fishing is practised both by national and foreign operators. Of 244 fishing licences issued in 1990, 113 were for Senegalese-owned vessels. The industrial fishing sector provides employment for about 10,000 people, including those engaged in local canning factories. Total exports from both fishing sub-sectors came to 118,300 tons in 1989 and an estimated 126,900 tons in 1990. Since 1979 regular fishing agreements have been concluded with the EC (now European Union), the most recent being for two years from April 1992. In exchange, the EC pays Senegal financial compensation of about ECU 30m. annually, and part of the catch made by EC vessels is landed in Senegal for processing locally. In 1986 fish overtook groundnuts to become Senegal's principal export, providing about 25% of annual export earnings. None the less, the fishing industry is suffering some sectoral problems, while increasing competition from Côte d'Ivoire has eroded Senegal's share of the French market.

Livestock is a significant sector of the traditional economy (although less important than in most other countries of this area), and is the base for the dairy and meat-processing industries. In 1992 numbers of cattle were estimated by the FAO at 2.8m., sheep and goats at 6.0m., pigs at 310,000 and horses at 400,000.

MINING AND POWER

The mining sector contributed less than 2.0% of GDP in 1991, but is an important source of export earnings. Mining in Senegal is dominated by the extraction of phosphates: reserves of calcium phosphates are estimated at 100m. tons, while there are reserves of 50m.–70m. tons of aluminium phosphates. Senegal accounts for about 1.5% of world output of and 3% of world exports of phosphates. The Cie sénégalaise des phosphates de Taïba (CSTP) and the Société sénégalaise des phosphates de Thiès (SSPT), both of which are 50% state-owned, are the two companies extracting phosphates, which are then processed by Industries chimiques du Sénégal (ICS), in which the Senegalese government has a 33% stake. The CSPT is the principal producer of calcium phosphates, although the SSPT has modest reserves of some 2m.–3m. tons of lower-quality chalk phosphates at Lam Lam. In 1981 1.8m. tons of calcium phosphates were produced (compared with 198,000 tons in 1960). It was planned to raise output to 2.1m. tons in 1982, with the opening in 1981 of facilities at an extension of the Taïba deposit, but the downturn in the market caused output to fall to only 901,000 tons in that year. In 1983 there was a good recovery, to 1.3m. tons, stimulated by a slight upturn in the world market and the start-up of the ICS plant (see below), which was due to take about 350,000 tons in the first year of operation and double this by 1986. (In the event the plant took some 54,000 tons in 1986.) Output of calcium phosphates increased from 1.8m. tons in 1985 to 2.3m. tons per year in both 1988 and 1989, then declined to 2.1m. tons in 1990 and 1.7m. tons in 1991; a marked improvement was, none the less, recorded in 1992, when production recovered to 2.3m. tons. Expansion is planned both at existing facilities and at new ones at Tobène, while a plant for the recovery of phosphates from tailings has been constructed at the ICS fertilizer complex, with World Bank support, which will increase the life of the mine through the utilization of lower-quality deposits. There are also unexploited deposits at Semmé, estimated to contain 60m. tons of calcium phosphates. However, plans to exploit further the country's reserves of phosphates were impeded in the late 1980s by low international prices (development of the Semmé deposits would cost an estimated $110m.).

Reserves of aluminium phosphates—also near Thiès—have been exploited by the SSPT. Output fluctuated widely in the 1970s and 1980s, with a peak of 405,000 tons in 1974, a halving of that figure in subsequent years, and a slight recovery, to 366,000 tons, in 1985. Concerns regarding the environmental consequences of the use of aluminium phosphates have since adversely affected the international market for this commodity, and Senegal's aluminium phosphates are no longer sold in their natural state. Most of SSPT's production is now processed locally into clinker.

Some 330m. tons of high-grade iron ore have been located at Falémé, in the east, but development would require new sources of electricity (the installation of the hydroelectric plant at the Manantali dam will provide such a source), a new, 740-km rail link to Dakar and new port facilities. The current over-supply in the world iron-ore market, and the likelihood that this will continue until after the mine is due to begin production (originally scheduled for 1989 but now projected for 1996), caused the target initial output to be halved, to 6m. tons per year. A gradual increase is then projected, to reach 12m. tons. At the lower capacity, the project, including transport investment, would require funding of some $700m. Gold deposits (of an estimated 280,000 tons of ore, containing 13 tons of metal) have been discovered at Sabodala, in the south-east, and the Société minière de Sabodala, a joint venture by the Senegalese government and French official interests (with Australian participation from 1993), was due to begin production in the mid-1990s. Commercially-viable reserves of titanium were discovered in 1991: workable ores are estimated at some 10m. tons.

Deposits of petroleum, estimated at between 52m.–58m. tons, have been located in the Dôme Flore field, off the Casamance coast, but the development of these reserves (which are overwhelmingly of heavy oil) is not currently economically feasible. Petroleum exploration is, none the less, continuing, and a $25m. programme was launched in 1983, supported by the International Development Association (IDA), Canada and Norway, to carry out a full survey of the country's sedimentary basins. A small offshore natural gas deposit, of 50m. cu m, at Diam Niadio, near Rufisque, was developed to fuel the Cap des Biches power station, but output was only some 42,000 cu m per day, and production ceased in late 1992. However, a much larger source has been located nearby, and was supplying the Cap des Biches plant in mid-1993. The development of peat deposits, in the Niayès area, is being examined with external financial support. Although these reserves have proved smaller than expected (23m. cu m instead of 39m.), it was hoped that they would provide fuel for electricity generation (a 20–30 MW station) and also substitute for firewood as domestic fuel. After a period of inactivity, the project was revived in 1990. In 1988 the government adopted a new mining code, in an attempt to encourage the further exploitation of Senegal's mineral resources. The incentives include automatic 25-year exploration rights if a deposit is located, while there is no requirement for government equity participation.

Electric power is supplied from six thermal stations, with a total installed capacity of 216 MW. The rehabilitation of existing capacity forms part of an $84m. project currently being implemented, which also included the construction of the 40-MW power station at Cap des Biches. Work began in 1982 on the Manantali hydroelectric plant, on the Senegal river, in a joint scheme with Mali and Mauritania, under the auspices of the Organisation pour la mise en valeur du fleuve Sénégal. Construction was completed in March 1988, and the plant, which was formally inaugurated, after considerable delay, in late 1992, was scheduled to produce around 800m. kWh per year by the early 1990s, most of which will be absorbed by Senegal. The first stage of the whole scheme (the construction of the Diama dam, near the mouth of the Senegal river) was completed in 1985. However, the plant's full generating capacity will not be available for some time, in order to avoid too great a disruption of traditional farming practices, which depend upon seasonal flooding.

MANUFACTURING

Senegal has the most developed manufacturing sector in francophone west Africa after Côte d'Ivoire, with production accounting for some 13% of GDP in 1992, according to the World Bank (the UN Economic Commission for Africa puts the sector's contribution at 19.2.% in 1991). The main activity is light industry (most of which is located in or near Dakar), transforming basic local commodities and import substitution to satisfy domestic demand. The agro-industrial sector mainly comprises oil mills, sugar refineries, fish-canning factories, flour mills and drinks, dairy-products and tobacco industries, which together account for 40% of total value added. Extractive industries (mainly the processing of phosphates) constitute the second most important branch of industrial activity. The manufacturing of textiles, leather goods and chemicals are also important, while subsidiary activities include paper and packaging and the manufacture of wood products and building materials. Senegal's textile industry is well equipped and is potentially the most important in black francophone Africa, but has performed badly. The chemicals industry (soap, paints, insecticides, plastics, pharmaceuticals and a petroleum refinery) is aimed at import substitution, as are nearly all the metalworking, engineering and electrical plants (including three shipyards, and truck and bicycle assembly plants).

In line with the emphasis on the processing of raw materials, ICS built plants to produce sulphuric acid (625,000 tons per year), phosphoric acid (475,000 tons), ammonium phosphate (250,000 tons) and triple superphosphate (250,000 tons). Production started in 1984, with 180,000 tons of the fertilizer output to be sold in the Senegalese and Malian markets, and the rest to be exported, mainly to other west African markets, eventually representing earnings of up to 24,000m. francs CFA per year. The total cost of this complex, including related infrastructure, was $312m., making it the single most important industrial project in Senegal. Funds have been contributed by the African Development Bank, the European Investment Bank (EIB), the International Finance Corporation, France and Arab agencies, including the Arab Bank for Economic Development in Africa, while the governments of Nigeria, Côte d'Ivoire, Cameroon and India have equity shares in ICS. The annual capacity of the cement plant at Rufisque was expanded from 380,000 to 800,000 tons by the end of 1983, at a cost of 16,000m. francs CFA, with France and the EIB contributing loans. In addition, the petroleum refinery's annual capacity rose to 1.2m. tons at the end of 1983, and has since expanded to 1.4m. tons.

The government introduced a New Industrial Policy (NIP) in 1986, with the purpose of improving the competitiveness of Senegalese companies and encouraging the development of activities generating high value-added, while reducing the role of the state. There were two strands to this policy: firstly, to reduce and harmonize customs tariffs and to remove quantitative restrictions on imports, and, secondly, to restructure enterprises and to improve the economic and regulatory environment by reducing the cost of key inputs, including labour. However, within three years the NIP was effectively abandoned. As cheap imports flooded the market, through formal and informal channels, the government decided in 1989 to restore customs tariffs to their previous high levels. The reduction of costs and enactment of an enabling environment were never implemented, largely because of resistance to labour law reforms from the trade unions.

There has been a decline in output in many industrial subsectors since 1986, although the production of phosphates, water and electricity have shown increases, and there has been resilience in output of petroleum products, soap, fertilizers and cement. The best performance has come from those industries that have not been directly affected by the industrial reforms introduced after 1986. The decline was particularly severe in light manufacturing industries such as textiles and shoes, which were vulnerable to competition from imported goods.

TRANSPORT INFRASTRUCTURE

Industrial development has been stimulated by, and has in turn boosted, the port at Dakar. Container-handling facilities were increased from 29,000 tons to more than 100,000 when a new terminal was inaugurated in 1988, and the extension of container facilities was completed in 1993. The port handles some 5m. tons of freight per year. Improvements to the fishing port at Dakar are also being carried out. There were proposals to construct a naval repair yard, to service bulk oil carriers, but plans were scaled down because of a downturn in the tanker market, and a smaller-scale dock, able to handle vessels up to 60,000 tons, entered service in 1981. In that year more than 400 ships were serviced. Completion of the Manantali project will eventually extend the all-year navigability of the Senegal river, currently just 220 km, to 924 km, as far as Kayes in Mali.

Senegal possesses a good road network. In 1990 there were 13,850 km of classified roads, of which 3,900 km were surfaced. In mid-1986, as part of the economic adjustment programme, the government suspended virtually all new road-building projects, concentrating instead on financing maintenance work. Work on a 160-km road between Dialakoto and Kédougou, the construction of which (at a cost of some $45m.) was to be financed by regional donor organizations, began in October 1991. The rail infrastructure is also well-developed, with 1,225 km of track, although only 70 km of this is two-way. The two main lines run from Dakar to Kidira, from the west to the east and across the border with Mali to Bamako, and from Dakar, via Thiès, to Saint-Louis in the north, near the border with Mauritania. The government's investment programme for 1988–92 envisaged the rehabilitation of the section of the line from Tambacounda to Kidira, together with the construction of a new line linking Tambacounda with Kédougou (a distance of 317 km), which has been studied as an essential component of the project to mine iron ore at Falémé. There is an international airport at Dakar-Yoff; in addition there are three other major airports and about 12 smaller airfields.

TOURISM

Since the early 1970s, tourism has grown in importance, and it now ranks as one of the country's major sources of foreign earnings. In 1991 gross earnings from tourism reached 37,900m. francs CFA, and tourist arrivals totalled 233,512. Senegal has almost 12,000 hotel beds of international tourist standard, and Dakar is of considerable importance as an international conference centre. The sector, which provides 4,500 direct and 10,000 indirect jobs, contributed almost 3% of GDP in 1990. However, the internal unrest that followed the February 1988 elections, together with Senegal's violent dispute with Mauritania, the effects of the 1990–91 Gulf crisis and (most recently) unrest in the Casamance region, have acted as a disincentive to tourism. It was hoped that the devaluation of the CFA franc would improve the competitiveness of tourism in Senegal, hitherto regarded as a high-cost destination.

INVESTMENT AND FINANCE

Despite overall economic difficulties, the level of investment increased steadily in the 1960s, from the rather low figure of 9% of GDP in 1961 to 17% in 1971, a level which has been approximately maintained in recent years. Public investment has accounted for the majority of total gross investment (69% in 1990), with government borrowing—both internal and external—increasing, as budgetary revenue declined. The fall in groundnut production had an adverse impact on current revenue, but the scope for budget austerity was restricted by the high wage bill (reflecting the size of Senegal's civil service—unusually large even among francophone west African countries), by the deficits of state agencies and by the need to service a rising public debt, as borrowing for the capital programme increased.

While phosphate revenues allowed a balance or even a small surplus on rising expenditure in the mid-1970s, the downturn in economic activity towards the end of the decade severely depressed revenues, and the government adopted a programme of fiscal restraint, agreed with the IMF in 1980. This resulted in a very modest increase in spending over the period 1979/80–1981/82, by an average of 6% annually, which represented a decline in real terms, while budget revenues were to rise, with increases in both taxation and the prices of goods and services that are supplied by the public sector. The broad objectives of the programme were maintained into 1984/85 and 1985/86, with spending restrained by means of reductions in subsidies to state enterprises.

Considerable progress was made, under the austerity programmes of the early 1980s, in reducing the budget deficit, which declined from 8.2% of annual GDP in 1982/83 to 3.8% of GDP in 1987/88. However, the economic situation was severely undermined in 1988/89 by Senegal's dispute with Mauritania, while the implementation of 'liberalization' policies, such as the reduction in customs tariffs, has also affected the level of government revenue. As a result, the budget deficit nearly doubled in 1988/89, to 30,900m. francs CFA, compared with 16,800m. francs CFA in the previous year. The deficit widened further, to 46,400m. francs CFA in 1989/90. However, estimates for 1990/91 indicated that improvements in revenue collection and restraints on expenditure led to an initial surplus in the government finances of 30,200m. francs CFA. The overall deficit in that year, after arrears payments had been made, was only 1,400m. francs CFA. Similary, a surplus of 3,700m. francs CFA was estimated in 1991/92, before a decline (by 18.5%) in fiscal revenue in 1992/93, accompanied by a 12.7% increase in recurrent expenditure, resulted in a projected deficit of 69,700m. francs CFA.

Since independence, Senegal has benefited from the consistent support of Western donors, who have been keen to support the country's relatively stable, conservative governments. Donors have always recognized that Senegal is poorly-endowed with natural resources, and external aid and funding have been forthcoming. Moreover, relations with both the World Bank and the IMF have generally remained good.

In 1987 the consultative group of aid donors pledged funds of $1,800m. to support the public investment programme and to provide payments support for 1987–90. Throughout the period of the economic reform programme the IMF accorded stand-by and structural adjustment facilities. In November 1988 an enhanced structural adjustment facility (ESAF), of SDR 145m. over three years, was approved. However, attempts in mid-1993 to reduce current expenditure—in accordance with creditors' demands that the problem of the public-sector deficit, of some 180,000m. francs CFA, be addressed—principally by means of reductions in civil servants' salaries prompted considerable domestic disquiet (see Recent History). In March 1994 Senegal was the first Franc Zone member to reach agreement with the IMF on new funding (a stand-by credit of $67m.), following the devaluation of the CFA franc. It was aimed to achieve GDP growth of 2.7% in 1994 (a decline of 0.8% had been recorded in 1993), and to limit the rate of increase in consumer prices to 39% in 1994, with a return to pre-devaluation levels of inflation by the end of 1996 (prices had declined by an annual average of 0.6% in 1993). Increased fiscal revenue, in conjunction with restraints on expenditure on salaries (which were increased by 10%, while earlier cuts were cancelled) and a reduction in external debt obligations (see below), were to limit the budget deficit, excluding grants, to 3.6% of GDP in 1994—a level similar to that in the previous year. A new ESAF was approved in August 1994.

Arab agencies and countries have also provided significant aid in recent years, and Senegal is one of the most important African recipients of aid from the Arab states. In 1991 Senegal received official development assistance totalling $577m. France is by far the most important creditor (donating $250m. in 1990). Senegal is also among the largest recipients under the EC's commodity earnings stabilization scheme, for shortfalls in its earnings from groundnuts.

FOREIGN TRADE AND PAYMENTS

Senegal's foreign trade has consistently been in deficit, the size of which has varied in response to the groundnut crop, but has, nevertheless, increased over time, with the result that the value of exports has, in recent years, been only half that of imports. Since the mid-1970s, however, the fluctuations have tended to narrow, as exports have stabilized at higher levels, with the expansion, first, of exports of phosphates (to an average of 22,000m. francs CFA per year during the 1980s) and, later, of fishery products (an average of 18,000m. francs CFA per year in 1978–80, rising to 55,000m. francs CFA in 1990). The very strong rise in imports in the early 1980s, as petroleum prices rose, the food deficit widened, and purchasing power was maintained through foreign borrowing, resulted in a trade deficit of 130,000m. francs CFA in 1985. Subsequently, the deficit narrowed steadily, to 85,600m. francs CFA in 1987, 82,600m. francs CFA in 1988, 71,800m. francs CFA in 1989 and 66,500m. francs CFA in 1990. However, the deficit was estimated to have widened to 80,100m. francs CFA in 1991, and to 95,800m. francs CFA in 1992. Exports in 1988–92 averaged about 240,000m. francs CFA annually, compared with imports averaging some 320,000m. francs CFA per year. The 1985–92 adjustment programme aimed to increase export earnings by 12.9% annually, with exports of fish and chemical products from the ICS complex rising strongly, while import growth was to be held to an average 9.8% per year. This was still to leave Senegal with a substantial trade deficit; in the event, the value of merchandise exports increased by an annual average of 0.7% during 1985–92, while that of imports declined by an average of 0.8% per year.

The chronic deficit on foreign trade is made up, on the capital side of the balance of payments, by private and, to a greater extent, public funds (including official development assistance). Consequently, the current account deficit also declined, from 122,400m. francs CFA in 1985 to 76,500m. francs CFA in 1988 and to 42,200m. francs CFA in 1990; none the less, the current account deficit (like the trade deficit) increased to an estimated 55,300m. francs CFA in 1991 and 63,900m. francs CFA in 1992. Since the late 1970s, the government has had increasing recourse to external borrowing, and outstanding external long-term debt increased from $1,114m. in 1980 to $2,071m. in 1985 and to $2,982m. in 1992. However, much of this ($2,932m.) is from official creditors, and is consequently granted with relatively favourable terms and long maturity periods. Debts of only $70m. were outstanding to commercial banks at the end of 1992. The rise in debt-servicing payments, which reached 24% of total foreign earnings in 1980, was, however, restricted by a series of debt-rescheduling agreements (with nine reschedulings of debt by the 'Paris Club' of Western official creditors in 1981–91), linked to the IMF-backed austerity programme, which aimed to reduce the external deficit by limiting domestic demand. None the less, the debt-service ratio reached a record level of 32.4% in 1987, before easing to 28.8% in 1989, to 20.5% in 1990, and to 12.5% in 1992. Since 1988, reschedulings of debt by the 'Paris Club' have been made in accordance with the exceptional terms formulated at the summit meeting of industrialized nations that had been held in Toronto in June 1988. However, more drastic debt-relief, including cancellations and reschedulings in accordance with the more concessional 'Trinidad terms', was approved by the 'Paris Club' in March 1994, while France agreed to cancel one-half of Senegal's bilateral debt. It would appear, however, that the rigorous austerity measures stipulated by the country's external creditors as a prerequisite for such relief, which have already provoked considerable domestic disquiet, will continue to cause political controversy.

Statistical Survey

Source (unless otherwise stated): Direction de la Statistique, Ministère l'Economie, des Finances et du Plan, rue René Ndiaye, BP 4017, Dakar; tel. 21-06-99; telex 3203; fax 22-41-95.

Area and Population

AREA, POPULATION AND DENSITY

Area (sq km)	196,722*
Population (census results)	
16 April 1976	5,085,388†
27 May 1988	
Males	3,353,599
Females	3,543,209
Total	6,896,808
Density (per sq km) at 27 May 1988	35.1

* 75,955 sq miles.
† Figure refers to the *de jure* population. The *de facto* population at the 1976 census was 4,907,507.

REGIONS (population at 1976 census)

	Area (sq km)	Population	Density (per sq km)	Capital	Estimated population
Cap-Vert*	550	984,660	1,790.3	Dakar	800,000
Casamance	28,350	736,527	26.0	Ziguinchor	73,000
Diourbel	33,547 (Diourbel and Louga)	425,113	25.1 (Diourbel and Louga)	Diourbel	51,000
Louga		417,137		Louga	n.a.
Fleuve†	44,127	528,473	12.0	Saint-Louis	88,000
Sénégal Oriental‡	59,602	286,148	4.8	Tambacounda	n.a.
Sine Saloum	23,945	1,007,736	42.1	Kaolack	106,000
Thiès	6,601	698,994	105.9	Thiès	117,000
Total	196,722	5,085,388	25.9		

* Renamed Dakar in 1984.
† Renamed Saint-Louis in 1984.
‡ Renamed Tambacounda in 1984.

Note: In July 1984 Casamance region was divided into Ziguinchor and Kolda regions; Sine Saloum region was divided into Kaolack and Fatick regions.

Source: mainly Société Africaine d'Edition, *Le Sénégal en chiffres*.

Principal Towns (estimated population, 1979): Dakar (capital) 850,000; Thiès 120,000; Kaolack 110,000 (Source: *L'Afrique Noire Politique et Economique, 1983.*)

PRINCIPAL ETHNIC GROUPS

1960 census: Wolof 709,000, Fulani 324,000, Serer 306,000, Toucouleur 248,000, Diola 115,000.

BIRTHS AND DEATHS (UN estimates, annual averages)

	1975-80	1980–85	1985–90
Birth rate (per 1,000)	49.3	47.2	45.5
Death rate (per 1,000)	21.7	19.4	17.7

Expectation of life (UN estimates, years at birth, 1985–90): 47.3 (males 46.3; females 48.3).

Source: UN, *World Population Prospects: The 1992 Revision.*

ECONOMICALLY ACTIVE POPULATION
(ILO estimates, '000 persons at mid-1980)

	Males	Females	Total
Agriculture, etc.	1,148	980	2,128
Industry	140	25	165
Services	263	84	347
Total labour force	1,551	1,090	2,641

Source: ILO, *Economically Active Population Estimates and Projections, 1950–2025.*

Mid-1992 (estimates in '000): Agriculture, etc. 2,563; Total 3,288 (Source: FAO, *Production Yearbook*).

Agriculture

PRINCIPAL CROPS ('000 metric tons)

	1990	1991	1992
Rice (paddy)	156	194	177
Maize	133	103	115
Millet and sorghum	662	671	663
Potatoes*	13	13	13
Sweet potatoes	3	3*	3*
Cassava (Manioc)	69	25	46
Pulses	13	16	11*
Groundnuts (in shell)	703	754	578
Cottonseed*	24	30	30
Cotton (lint)	11*	20†	20†
Palm kernels*	6.2	6.2	6.2
Tomatoes	48	56	57
Dry onions	34	38	31
Other vegetables	45	45	46
Mangoes	56	54	57
Oranges	28	26	24
Bananas	6	5	5
Other fruit	24	24	24
Coconuts	5	5	5
Sugar cane	707	808	837

* FAO estimate(s). † Unofficial figure.

Source: FAO, *Production Yearbook*.

LIVESTOCK ('000 head, year ending September)

	1990	1991*	1992*
Cattle	2,740	2,770	2,800
Sheep*	3,400	3,500	3,600
Goats*	2,270	2,330	2,400
Pigs	295	300	310
Horses*	400	400	400
Asses*	310	320	330
Camels*	15	15	15

Poultry (million)*: 18 in 1990; 14 in 1991; 19 in 1992.

* FAO estimates.

Source: FAO, *Production Yearbook*.

LIVESTOCK PRODUCTS (FAO estimates, '000 metric tons)

	1990	1991	1992
Beef and veal	42	43	43
Mutton and lamb	13	13	13
Goats' meat	7	7	7
Pig meat	11	11	11
Horse meat	5	5	5
Poultry meat	24	24	24
Other meat	5	5	6
Cows' milk	99	100	101
Sheep's milk	16	17	18
Goats' milk	13	13	14
Poultry eggs	12.0	12.0	12.6
Cattle hides	8.4	8.5	8.6
Sheep skins	2.7	2.7	2.8
Goat skins	1.4	1.4	1.4

Source: FAO, *Production Yearbook*.

Forestry

ROUNDWOOD REMOVALS
('000 cubic metres, excluding bark)

	1990	1991	1992
Sawlogs, veneer logs and logs for sleepers	40	40	40
Other industrial wood*	598	615	632
Fuel wood	4,264	4,273	4,236
Total	4,902	4,928	4,908

* FAO estimates.

Source: FAO, *Yearbook of Forest Products*.

Fishing*

('000 metric tons, live weight)

	1989	1990	1991
Freshwater fishes	18.4	18.5	19.1
Flatfishes	3.7	4.3	8.4
Sea catfishes	7.9	8.0	4.1
Grunts, sweetlips, etc.	8.4	9.3	8.5
West African croakers	6.2	7.4	4.9
Dentex, seabreams, etc.	11.1	8.1	8.9
Mullets	6.9	3.9	6.3
Lesser African threadfin	5.4	6.2	2.9
Jack and horse mackerels	3.0	3.2	5.7
Sardinellas†	130.0	140.0	160.0
Bonga shad	15.1	12.7	11.5
Other marine fishes (incl. unspecified)	43.6	54.0	48.4
Total fish	259.9	275.6	289.0
Southern pink shrimps	6.2	4.5	4.4
Cuttlefishes and bobtail squids	6.0	4.6	7.8
Octopuses	5.4	8.6	12.4
Other crustaceans and molluscs	9.7	4.6	6.1
Total catch	287.1	297.9	319.7

* Figures cover the artisanal Senegalese fishery, the industrial Senegalese tuna fishery, the industrial Senegalese and French trawler fishery, and the industrial Senegalese sardine fishery.

† Estimates.

Source: FAO, *Yearbook of Fishery Statistics*.

Mining

('000 metric tons)

	1989	1990	1991
Natural phosphates	2,273	2,147	n.a.
Fuller's earth (attapulgite)*	99	100	115
Salt (unrefined)	100	100	100

* Data from the US Bureau of Mines.

Source: UN, *Industrial Statistics Yearbook*.

Industry

SELECTED PRODUCTS
('000 metric tons, unless otherwise indicated)

	1989	1990	1991
Frozen fish (metric tons)*	72,400	78,800	n.a.
Tinned fish (metric tons)	200	200	n.a.
Salted, dried or smoked fish (metric tons)*	16,800	25,000	n.a.
Palm oil*†	6	6	6
Raw sugar*	79	87	90
Cigarettes (million)	3,350	3,350	3,350
Cotton yarn (metric tons)	600†	n.a.	n.a.
Footwear—excl. rubber ('000 pairs)	600	600	n.a.
Nitrogenous fertilizers‡	12.0†	14.4	15.7
Phosphate fertilizers‡	35.0†	27.5	50.0†
Jet fuel	91	92	90
Motor spirit—petrol	115	117	118
Kerosene	14	14	15
Distillate fuel oils	215	165	170
Residual fuel oils	210	212	210
Lubricating oils	3	3	3
Liquefied petroleum gas†	2	2	3
Cement†	380	380	499
Electric energy (million kWh)	697	734	756

* Data from the FAO.
† Provisional or estimated figure(s).
‡ Figures for fertilizers are in terms of nitrogen or phosphoric acid, and relate to output during the 12 months ending 30 June of the year stated.

Source: mainly UN, *Industrial Statistics Yearbook.*

Finance

CURRENCY AND EXCHANGE RATE

Monetary Units

100 centimes = 1 franc de la Communauté financière africaine (CFA).

French Franc, Sterling and Dollar Equivalents
(31 March 1994)

1 French franc = 100 francs CFA;
£1 sterling = 846.40 francs CFA;
US $1 = 570.14 francs CFA;
1,000 francs CFA = £1.181 = $1.754.

Average Exchange Rate (francs CFA per US $)

1991 282.11
1992 264.69
1993 283.16

Note: An exchange rate of 1 French franc = 50 francs CFA, established in 1948, remained in force until January 1994, when the CFA franc was devalued by 50%, with the exchange rate adjusted to 1 French franc = 100 francs CFA.

BUDGET
(estimates, million francs CFA, year ending 30 June)

Revenue*	1988	1989	1990
Fiscal receipts	209,496	217,966	215,100
Taxes on income and profits	51,170	52,500	53,400
Corporate and business taxes	51,000	52,000	53,000
Taxes on goods and services	65,526	69,866	69,000
Turnover taxes	51,500	54,000	53,000
Consumption taxes	8,026	9,216	9,200
Taxes on use of goods or on permission to use goods or to perform activities	5,800	6,500	6,500
Taxes on international trade and transactions	89,600	92,100	88,700
Import duties	89,000	91,500	88,000
Other current receipts	36,063	48,847	55,314
Property income	5,610	11,860	9,860
Aid, grants and subsidies	33,291	24,934	43,839
Total	278,850	291,747	314,253

Expenditure	1988	1989	1990
General public services	60,087	73,563	80,924
Defence	28,967	30,293	30,685
Public order and security	23,673	22,225	22,709
Education	48,037	51,576	55,954
Public health	11,030	10,867	11,868
Social security and welfare	2,769	2,860	2,897
Housing and community services	2,323	2,325	2,144
Other community and social services	3,786	3,715	3,849
Economic services	111,385	101,254	113,489
Agriculture, hunting, forestry and fishing	57,980	60,688	70,705
Mining, manufacturing and power	11,870	7,212	16,242
Transport and communications	26,406	31,539	24,731
Other economic services	15,129	1,815	1,811
Debt-servicing	115,200	128,300	113,700
Other purposes	48,510	61,646	68,636
Total	455,767	488,624	506,855

* Revenue excludes net borrowing: 176,917m. francs CFA in 1988; 196,877m. francs CFA in 1989; 192,602 in 1990.

Source: Banque centrale des états de l'Afrique de l'ouest.

1990/91 (estimates, million francs CFA): Administrative revenue 226,000; Administrative expenditure 221,800; Investment and capital budget balanced at 169,200.
1991/92 (estimates, million francs CFA, 1 July 1991–31 December 1992): Budget balanced at 660,900.
1993 (estimates, million francs CFA): Budget balanced at 479,600 (excluding net borrowing: 171,500).
1994 (estimates, million francs CFA): Budget balanced at 518,600.

CENTRAL BANK RESERVES (US $ million at 31 December)

	1991	1992	1993
Gold*	10.3	10.1	10.8
IMF special drawing rights	0.4	—	0.4
Reserve position in IMF	1.5	1.4	1.5
Foreign exchange	11.3	10.9	1.5
Total	23.5	22.5	14.2

* Valued at market-related prices.

Source: IMF, *International Financial Statistics.*

MONEY SUPPLY ('000 million francs CFA at 31 December)

	1991	1992	1993
Currency outside banks	97.53	107.18	93.04
Demand deposits at deposit money banks	112.28	106.63	101.43
Checking deposits at post office	3.01	3.40	2.96
Total money (incl. others)	213.22	217.39	197.75

Source: IMF, *International Financial Statistics.*

COST OF LIVING
(Consumer price index, Dakar. Base: 1980 = 100)

	1990	1991	1992
Food	163.0	157.9	156.3
Fuel and light	190.4	195.9	192.8
Clothing	193.5	196.3	197.6
Rent*	177.3	175.3	173.4
All items (incl. others)	176.5	173.4	173.4

* Including expenditure on the maintenance and repair of dwellings.

Source: International Labour Office, *Year Book of Labour Statistics.*

NATIONAL ACCOUNTS
(million francs CFA at current prices)

Expenditure on the Gross Domestic Product*

	1989	1990	1991
Government final consumption expenditure	238,800	226,030	248,300
Private final consumption expenditure	1,108,650	1,123,360	1,079,670
Increase in stocks	3,030	2,880	1,000
Gross fixed capital formation	234,560	224,390	225,190
Total domestic expenditure	1,585,040	1,576,660	1,554,160
Exports of goods and services	360,040	403,140	489,770
Less Imports of goods and services	453,080	457,800	444,070
GDP in purchasers' values	1,492,000	1,522,000	1,599,850
GDP at constant 1980 prices	787,000	794,900	815,580

* Figures are rounded to the nearest 10m. francs CFA.

Gross Domestic Product by Economic Activity*

	1989	1990	1991
Agriculture, hunting, forestry and fishing	255,090	257,890	272,320
Mining and quarrying	16,330	24,240	26,780
Manufacturing	239,360	242,190	256,590
Electricity, gas and water	23,590	24,270	25,820
Construction	96,020	98,870	105,690
Trade, restaurants and hotels	185,450	188,260	198,610
Transport, storage and communications	112,940	113,390	119,900
Finance, insurance, real estate, etc.	52,420	53,360	56,720
Government services	176,410	179,230	184,400
Other services	82,180	83,100	88,090
GDP at factor cost	1,239,780	1,264,790	1,334,920
Indirect taxes *less* subsidies	252,220	257,210	264,930
GDP in purchasers' values	1,492,000	1,522,000	1,599,850

* Figures are rounded to the nearest 10m. francs CFA.

Source: UN Economic Commission for Africa: *African Statistical Yearbook.*

BALANCE OF PAYMENTS (US $ million)

	1989	1990	1991
Merchandise exports f.o.b.	758.6	911.6	903.2
Merchandise imports f.o.b.	-998.4	-1,176.1	-1,187.1
Trade balance	-239.8	-264.4	-283.9
Exports of services	471.4	563.1	560.1
Imports of services	-500.5	-573.0	-572.5
Other income received	26.6	22.8	22.7
Other income paid	-221.9	-258.6	-257.7
Private unrequited transfers (net)	6.3	29.4	28.4
Official unrequited transfers (net)	259.7	265.2	265.1
Current balance	-198.3	-215.6	-237.9
Capital (net)	33.4	4.2	-54.9
Net errors and omissions	1.6	-16.7	10.9
Overall balance	-163.3	-228.1	-281.8

Source: IMF, *International Financial Statistics.*

External Trade

PRINCIPAL COMMODITIES
(distribution by SITC, US $ million)

Imports c.i.f.	1988	1989	1990
Food and live animals	173.7	342.7	403.0
Dairy products and birds' eggs	37.5	42.9	46.5
Milk and cream	n.a.	35.4	38.1
Fish, crustaceans and molluscs	n.a.	37.0	47.4
Fresh, chilled or frozen fish	n.a.	35.3	43.2
Cereals and cereal preparations	95.0	156.5	180.5
Wheat and meslin (unmilled)	15.8	39.6	75.7
Rice	77.1	106.9	92.4
Semi-milled or milled rice	n.a.	102.5	92.4
Vegetables and fruit	23.9	27.5	30.0
Sugar, sugar preparations and honey	2.7	9.3	36.5
Sugar and honey	2.7	8.4	35.1
Refined sugars (solid)	0.6	7.5	33.9
Coffee, tea, cocoa and spices	10.0	32.9	30.2
Crude materials (inedible) except fuels	n.a.	41.4	59.2
Crude fertilizers and crude minerals	n.a.	22.0	30.3
Mineral fuels, lubricants, etc.	144.4	361.0	258.7
Petroleum, petroleum products, etc.	144.4	353.1	248.6
Crude petroleum oils, etc.	n.a.	211.2	130.5
Refined petroleum products	58.0	139.8	113.7
Motor spirit (gasoline) and other light oils	6.7	35.8	21.8
Gas oils (distillate fuels)	17.2	35.9	52.3
Animal and vegetable oils, fats and waxes	16.7	19.4	33.2
Chemicals and related products	126.1	147.5	157.6
Medical and pharmaceutical products	34.9	41.4	46.0
Medicaments (incl. veterinary)	n.a.	38.0	42.9
Artificial resins, plastic materials, etc.	33.1	25.7	32.4
Basic manufactures	182.7	218.6	259.8
Paper, paperboard, etc.	35.2	33.7	39.0
Textile yarn, fabrics, etc.	41.0	42.0	45.5
Iron and steel	35.6	49.1	64.9

Imports c.i.f. - *continued*	1988	1989	1990
Machinery and transport equipment	245.9	310.4	344.5
Power-generating machinery and equipment	9.5	29.8	34.8
Machinery specialized for particular industries	40.7	37.5	50.1
General industrial machinery, equipment and parts	104.5	51.7	66.6
Electrical machinery, apparatus, etc.	n.a.	56.3	62.7
Road vehicles and parts (excl. tyres, engines and electrical parts)	91.1	107.0	102.3
Passenger motor cars (excl. buses)	37.4	50.0	46.4
Miscellaneous manufactured articles	15.4	63.2	75.1
Total (incl. others)	1,079.5	1,534.0	1,620.4

Exports f.o.b.	1988	1989	1990
Food and live animals	209.7	271.3	270.6
Fish, crustaceans and molluscs	154.0	208.1	216.0
Fresh, chilled or frozen fish	49.8	57.5	86.9
Fresh, chilled, frozen, salted or dried crustaceans and molluscs	54.7	49.5	34.7
Prepared or preserved fish, crustaceans and molluscs	49.5	97.4	90.7
Fish (incl. caviar)	n.a.	51.4	60.0
Crustaceans and molluscs	n.a.	46.1	30.7
Feeding stuff for animals (excl. unmilled cereals)	41.2	40.6	36.9
Oil-cake, etc.	41.2	39.1	35.4
Groundnut cake	41.2	34.7	34.2
Crude materials (inedible) except fuels	88.5	106.7	105.8
Crude fertilizers and crude minerals	72.4	74.8	70.1
Crude fertilizers	72.4	63.9	57.0
Natural calcium phosphates, etc.	72.4	63.9	57.0
Minerals fuels, lubricants, etc.	65.0	84.5	96.8
Petroleum, petroleum products, etc.	65.0	84.4	96.7
Refined petroleum products	65.0	84.3	96.4
Motor spirit (gasoline) and other light oils	n.a.	29.8	47.7
Spirit-type jet fuel	n.a.	24.9	42.0
Gas oils (distillate fuels)	n.a.	33.3	30.7
Animal and vegetable oils, fats and waxes	n.a.	103.3	130.1
Fixed vegetable oils and fats	n.a.	103.0	130.1
Groundnut (peanut) oil	n.a.	102.8	130.0
Chemicals and related products	n.a.	97.5	116.7
Inorganic chemicals	n.a.	55.7	73.6
Inorganic chemical elements, oxides and halogen salts	n.a.	55.5	73.4
Inorganic acids and oxygen compounds of non-metals	n.a.	55.1	73.1
Phosphorus pentoxide and phosphoric acids	n.a.	54.9	73.0
Manufactured fertilizers	4.0	24.2	28.6
Basic manufactures	6.5	35.9	29.0
Machinery and transport equipment	n.a.	28.2	18.5
Total (incl. others)	591.1	750.9	782.6

Source: UN, *International Trade Statistics Yearbook*.

PRINCIPAL TRADING PARTNERS (US $ million)*

Imports c.i.f.	1988	1989	1990
Angola	n.a.	25.6	0.9
Belgium/Luxembourg	23.9	32.6	44.5
Brazil	6.5	20.4	18.2
Canada	n.a.	19.8	17.3
China, People's Repub.	23.7	33.2	37.2
Côte d'Ivoire	61.3	67.4	72.3
France	340.2	438.2	533.7
Gabon	22.2	118.0	43.6
Germany	42.0	43.6	57.8
Italy	42.3	76.1	104.9
Japan	45.5	57.0	58.5
Netherlands	28.7	46.1	49.7
Netherlands Antilles	n.a.	2.9	18.0
Nigeria	46.8	124.1	121.9
Pakistan	36.9	38.1	24.6
Spain	51.2	68.9	67.7
Thailand	n.a.	37.6	47.6
United Kingdom	25.2	24.5	27.2
USA	69.1	90.2	86.0
Viet Nam	n.a.	9.9	15.5
Total (incl. others)	1,079.5	1,534.0	1,620.4

Exports f.o.b.	1988	1989	1990
Cameroon	11.2	18.5	19.8
Côte d'Ivoire	19.1	20.8	21.8
France	222.4	250.8	272.8
Gambia	4.3	9.1	6.9
Germany	6.2	7.9	6.3
Greece	7.6	7.2	6.0
Guinea	6.3	16.5	15.3
India	n.a.	69.5	83.3
Iran	n.a.	n.a.	13.9
Italy	24.5	46.9	54.9
Japan	10.4	28.4	15.6
Mali	24.2	49.2	55.7
Mauritania	18.1	11.3	0.2
Netherlands	24.4	22.4	41.3
Philippines	n.a.	16.1	14.3
Spain	22.3	30.0	22.8
Togo	1.6	8.5	5.1
United Kingdom	11.9	4.1	3.6
Total (incl. others)	591.1	750.9	782.6

* Imports by country of production; exports by country of last consignment.

Source: UN, *International Trade Statistics Yearbook*.

Transport

RAILWAYS (estimated traffic)

	1989	1990	1991
Passenger-km (million)	163	169	174
Freight ton-km (million)	565	580	610

Source: UN Economic Commission for Africa, *African Statistical Yearbook*.

ROAD TRAFFIC (estimates, '000 motor vehicles in use)

	1989	1990	1991
Passenger cars	65	66	67
Commercial vehicles	37	38	38

Source: UN Economic Commission for Africa, *African Statistical Yearbook*.

INTERNATIONAL SEA-BORNE SHIPPING
(freight traffic, '000 metric tons)

	1989	1990	1991
Goods loaded	2,801	2,868	2,591
Goods unloaded	2,350	2,204	2,477

Source: Banque centrale des états de l'Afrique de l'ouest.

CIVIL AVIATION (traffic on scheduled services)*

	1989	1990	1991
Km flown (million)	3	3	3
Passengers carried ('000)	140	148	136
Passenger-km (million)	243	253	224
Freight ton-km (million)	18	18	16
Mail ton-km (million)	1	1	1

* Including an apportionment of the traffic of Air Afrique.
Source: UN, *Statistical Yearbook.*

Tourism

FOREIGN TOURIST ARRIVALS

Country of Origin	1989	1990	1991
Benelux	7,363	5,908	5,474
Canada	2,809	1,866	1,858
France	155,839	147,524	132,254
Germany, Federal Republic	13,661	13,736	13,106*
Italy	11,322	12,786	16,280
Spain	2,339	2,161	1,762
Switzerland	4,085	4,545	4,315
United Kingdom	3,064	3,457	3,533
USA	9,452	8,736	6,220
Total (incl. others)	259,096	245,881	233,512

* The figure for 1991 is for the united Germany.

1992: Total foreign tourist arrivals 245,581.

Source: Ministère du Tourisme et des Transports aériens, Dakar.

Communications Media

	1989	1990	1991
Radio receivers ('000 in use)	802	830	860
Television receivers ('000 in use)	250	265	273
Daily newspapers:			
Number	n.a.	3	n.a.
Average circulation ('000 copies)	n.a.	50	n.a.

Book production (1983): 42 titles (first editions, excluding pamphlets); 169,000 copies.

Source: UNESCO, *Statistical Yearbook.*

Telephones ('000 in use): 55 in 1993 (Source: Société Nationale des Télécommunications du Sénégal, Dakar).

Education

(1989)

	Institutions	Teachers	Students: Males	Females	Total
Pre-primary	144	629	7,899	8,065	15,964
Primary	2,422	11,859	397,672	285,253	682,925
Secondary					
General	n.a.	4,791	110,501	56,162	166,663
Teacher training	n.a.	80	594	129	723
Vocational	n.a.	179	3,969	1,689	5,658
University level	n.a.	810	13,082	3,682	16,764

Source: UNESCO, *Statistical Yearbook.*

1991: Pre-primary: Institutions 161, Students 17,042 (males 8,422; females 8,600); Primary: Institutions 2,458, Students 708,299 (males 410,924; females 297,375) (Source: Ministère de l'Education Nationale, Dakar).

Directory

The Constitution

The Constitution of the Republic of Senegal was promulgated on 7 March 1963. It has since been amended, with the most recent amendments being effected in May 1992. The main provisions are summarized below:

PREAMBLE

Affirms the Rights of Man, liberty of the person and religious freedom. National sovereignty belongs to the people who exercise it through their representatives or by means of referendums. There is universal, equal and secret suffrage for adults of 18 years of age and above. French is the official language.

THE PRESIDENT

The President of the Republic is elected by direct universal suffrage for a seven-year term and may seek re-election only once. The President holds executive power and, as Commander of the Armed Forces, is responsible for national defence. The President of the Republic appoints the Prime Minister. He may, after consultation with the President of the Assemblée nationale, with the Prime Minister and with the appropriate organ of the judiciary, submit any draft law to referendum. In circumstances where the security of the State is in grave and immediate danger, he can assume emergency powers and rule by decree. The President of the Republic can be impeached only on a charge of high treason or by a secret ballot of the Assemblée nationale carrying a three-fifths majority.

THE PRIME MINISTER

The Prime Minister is appointed by the President of the Republic, and, in turn, appoints the Council of Ministers in consultation with the President.

THE LEGISLATURE

Legislative power is vested in the Assemblée nationale, which is elected by universal direct suffrage for a five-year term. The Assembly discusses and votes legislation and submits it to the President of the Republic for promulgation. The President can direct the Assembly to give a second reading to the bill, in which case it may be made law only by a three-fifths majority. The President of the Republic can also call upon the Constitutional Court to declare whether any draft law is constitutional and acceptable. Legislation may be initiated by either the President of the Republic or the Assemblée nationale. Should the Presidency fall vacant, the President of the legislature is automatic successor to the Head of State. A motion expressing 'no confidence' in the Government can be considered if it has been endorsed by one-tenth of the members of the Assembly.

LOCAL GOVERNMENT

Senegal is divided into 10 regions, each having a governor and an elected local assembly.

POLITICAL PARTIES

There is no limit to the number of political parties.

AMENDMENTS

The President of the Republic and Deputies to the Assemblée nationale may propose amendments to the Constitution. Draft amendments are adopted by a three-fifths majority vote of the Assemblée nationale. Failing this, they are submitted to referendum.

The Government

HEAD OF STATE

President: ABDOU DIOUF (took office 1 January 1981; elected President on 27 February 1983, re-elected 28 February 1988 and 21 February 1993).

COUNCIL OF MINISTERS
(September 1994)

A coalition of the Parti socialiste sénégalais (PS); Parti de l'indépendance et du travail (PIT); Parti démocratique sénégalais—Rénovation (PDS—R); Ligue démocratique—Mouvement pour le parti du travail (LD—MPT).

President of the Republic and Head of Government: ABDOU DIOUF (PS).

Prime Minister: HABIB THIAM (PS).

Minister of the Economy, Finance and Planning: PAPA OUSMANE SAKHO (no party affiliation).

Minister of the Armed Forces: MADIENG KHARY DIENG (PS).

Minister of Justice and Keeper of the Seals: JACQUES BAUDIN (PS).

Minister of Presidential Services and Affairs: OUSMANE TANOR DIENG (PS).

Minister of Foreign Affairs and Senegalese Abroad: MOUSTAPHA NIASSE (PS).

Minister of State for Agriculture: ROBERT SAGNA (PS).

Minister of Energy, Mines and Industry: ALASSANE DIALY NDIAYE (PS).

Minister of the Interior: DJIBO LAÏTI KA (PS).

Minister of National Education: ANDRÉ SONKO (PS).

Minister of Equipment and Road and Rail Transport: LANDING SANE (PS).

Minister of Water Resources: MAMADOU FAYE (no party affiliation).

Minister of Trade and Crafts: Cheikh HAMIDOU KANE (PS).

Minister of Tourism and Air Transport: TIJANE SYLLA (PS).

Minister of Housing and Town Planning: AMATH DANSOKHO (PIT).

Minister of Communications: ABDOULAYE ELIMANE KANE (PS).

Minister of Health and Social Welfare: ASSANE DIOP (PS).

Minister of Fisheries and Maritime Transport: ABDOURAHMANE SOW (PS).

Minister of Culture: COURA BÂ THIAM (PS).

Minister of Youth and Sports: OUSMANE PAYE (no party affiliation).

Minister of Employment, Labour and Professional Training: SERIGNE DIOP (PDS—R).

Minister of Towns: DAOUR CISSÉ (no party affiliation).

Minister of the Environment and Nature Conservation: ABDOULAYE BATHILY (LD—MPT).

Minister of Women's, Children's and Family Affairs: NDIORO NDIAYE (PS).

Minister of Modernization, Technology and the Civil Service: MAGUED DIOUF (PS).

There are, in addition, five ministers-delegate, with responsibility for relations with the organs of state, for decentralization, for African economic integration, for the budget, and for literacy and the promotion of national languages.

MINISTRIES

Office of the President: ave Roume, BP 168, Dakar; tel. 23-10-88; telex 258.

Ministry of Agriculture and Water Resources: Immeuble Administratif, Dakar; tel. 23-10-88; telex 3151.

Ministry of the Armed Forces: BP 176, Dakar; tel. 23-10-88; telex 482.

Ministry of Communications: 58 blvd de la République, Dakar; tel. 23-10-65; fax 21-41-04.

Ministry of Culture: Immeuble Administratif, Dakar; tel. 23-10-88; telex 482.

Ministry of the Economy, Finance and Planning: rue René Ndiaye, BP 4017, Dakar; tel. 21-06-99; telex 3203; fax 22-41-95.

Ministry of Employment, Labour and Professional Training: BP 403, Dakar; tel. 23-10-88; telex 482.

Ministry of Energy, Mines and Industry and of Trade and Crafts: 122 bis ave André Peytavin, BP 4037, Dakar; tel. 22-99-94; telex 61149; fax 22-55-94.

Ministry of the Environment and Nature Conservation: Dakar.

Ministry of Equipment, of Road, Rail and Maritime Transport and Fisheries: Immeuble Communal, blvd du Général de Gaulle, Dakar; tel. 21-42-01; telex 3151.

Ministry of Foreign Affairs and Senegalese Abroad: place de l'Indépendance, Dakar; tel. 21-62-84; telex 482.

Ministry of Health and Social Welfare: Immeuble Administratif, Dakar; tel. 23-10-88; telex 482.

Ministry of Housing and Town Planning: ave André Peytavin, BP 4028, Dakar; tel. 23-91-27; fax 22-56-01.

Ministry of Modernization, Technology and the Civil Service: Dakar.

Ministry of the Interior: Rond-point de la République, Dakar; tel. 21-41-51; telex 3351.

Ministry of Justice: BP 784, Dakar; tel. 23-10-88; telex 482.

Ministry of National Education: rue Calmette et René Ndiaye, BP 699, Dakar; tel. 22-12-28; telex 482.

Ministry of Tourism and Air Transport: 23 rue Calmette, BP 4049, Dakar; tel. 23-65-02; fax 22-94-13.

Ministry of Women's, Children's and Family Affairs: Dakar.

Ministry of Youth and Sports: ave Abdoulaye Fadiga, Dakar.

President and Legislature

PRESIDENT

Presidential Election, 21 February 1993

	Votes	% of votes
ABDOU DIOUF (PS)	757,311	58.40
ABDOULAYE WADE (PDS)	415,295	32.03
LANDING SAVANÉ (AJ—PADS)	37,787	2.91
ABDOULAYE BATHILY (LD—MPT)	31,279	2.41
IBA DER THIAM (CDP)	20,840	1.61
MADIOR DOUF (RND)	12,635	0.97
MAMADOU LÔ (Independent)	11,058	0.85
BABACAR NIANG (PLP)	10,450	0.81
Total	1,296,655	100.00

ASSEMBLÉE NATIONALE

President: CHEIKH ABDOUL KHADRE CISSOKHO.

General Election, 9 May 1993

Party	Votes	% of votes	Seats
PS	602,171	56.56	84
PDS	321,585	30.21	27
Japoo*	52,189	4.90	3
LD—MPT	43,950	4.13	3
PIT	32,348	3.04	2
UDS—R	12,339	1.16	1
Total	1,064,582	100.00	120

* An electoral alliance of AJ—PADS, the CDP and the RND, as well as independent candidates.

Advisory Council

Conseil Economique et Social: Dakar; Pres. FAMARA IBRAHIMA SAGNA.

Political Organizations

And Jëf—Parti africain pour la démocratie et le socialisme (AJ—PADS): BP 12025, Dakar; tel. 22-54-63; f. 1991 by merger of And Jëf—Mouvement révolutionnaire pour la démocratie nouvelle

(Maoist), Organisation socialiste des travailleurs (Marxist-Leninist) and Union pour la démocratie populaire (Marxist-Leninist); Sec.-Gen. LANDING SAVANÉ.

Convention des démocrates et des patriotes (CDP): 96 rue 7, Bopp, Dakar; f. 1992; Sec.-Gen. Prof. IBA DER THIAM.

Ligue démocratique—Mouvement pour le parti du travail (LD—MPT): BP 10172, Dakar Liberté; tel. 22-67-06; regd 1981; Marxist-Leninist; Sec.-Gen. ABDOULAYE BATHILY.

Mouvement pour le Socialisme et l'Unité (MSU): Villa no 54, rue 4, Bopp, Dakar; f. 1981 as Mouvement démocratique populaire; socialist; Sec.-Gen. MAMADOU DIA.

Parti africain des écologistes—Sénégal (PAES): Ecole Normale Germaine Legoff, Dakar; Sec.-Gen. ABOUBACRY DIA.

Parti africain de l'indépendance (PAI): BP 820, Dakar; f. 1957, reorg. 1976; Marxist; Sec.-Gen. MAJHEMOUTH DIOP.

Parti africain pour l'indépendance des masses (Pai—M): 440, Cité Abdou Diouf Guédiawaye, Dakar; tel. 34-75-90; f. 1982; social-democratic; Sec.-Gen. ALY NIANE.

Parti démocratique sénégalais (PDS): 5 blvd Dial Diop, Dakar; f. 1974; liberal-democratic; Sec.-Gen. Me ABDOULAYE WADE.

Parti démocratique sénégalais—Rénovation (PDS—R): 343 Gibraltar II, Dakar; regd 1987; breakaway group from PDS; Sec.-Gen. SERIGNE DIOP.

Parti de l'indépendance et du travail (PIT): BP 5612, Dakar Fann; regd 1981; Marxist-Leninist; Sec.-Gen. AMATH DANSOKHO.

Parti pour la libération du peuple (PLP): 4025 Sicap Amitié II, Dakar; f. 1983 by RND dissidents; neutralist and anti-imperialist; Sec.-Gen. Me BABACAR NIANG; Asst Sec.-Gen. ABDOULAYE KANE.

Parti populaire sénégalais (PPS): Clinique Khadim Diourbel, Dakar; regd 1981; populist; Sec.-Gen. Dr OUMAR WANE.

Parti socialiste sénégalais (PS): Maison du Parti, ave Cheikh Amadou Bamba, Rocade Fann, Bel Air, BP 12010, Dakar; f. 1958 as Union progressiste sénégalaise, reorg. under present name 1978; democratic socialist; Sec.-Gen. ABDOU DIOUF; Political Sec. DJIBO KA.

Rassemblement national démocratique (RND): Villa no 29, Cité des Professeurs, Fann Résidence, Dakar; f. 1976, legalized 1981; progressive; Sec.-Gen. MADIOR DIOUF.

Union démocratique sénégalaise—Rénovation (UDS—R): Villa no 273, Ouagou Niayes, Dakar; f. 1985 by PDS dissidents; nationalist-progressive; Sec.-Gen. MAMADOU PURITAIN FALL.

An outlawed separatist group, the **Mouvement des forces démocratiques de la Casamance (MFDC),** is active in the southern province of Casamance.

Diplomatic Representation

EMBASSIES IN SENEGAL

Algeria: 5 rue Mermoz, BP 3233, Dakar; tel. 22-35-09; telex 61173; Ambassador: TEDJINI SALANANDJI.

Argentina: 34-36 blvd de la République, BP 3343, Dakar; tel. 21-51-71; telex 51457; Ambassador: HÉCTOR TEJERINA.

Austria: 24 blvd Pinet-Laprade, BP 3247, Dakar; tel. 22-38-86; telex 51611; fax 21-03-09; Ambassador: Dr PETER LEITENBAUER.

Bangladesh: Immeuble Kébé, Appts 11–12, 7e étage, ave André Peytavin, BP 403, Dakar; tel. 21-68-81; telex 51298; Ambassador: M. D. MANIRUZZAMAN MIAH.

Belgium: route de la Corniche-Est, BP 524, Dakar; tel. 22-47-20; telex 51265; fax 21-63-45; Ambassador: JACQUES-BENOÎT FOBE.

Brazil: Immeuble Résidence Excellence, 2e étage, 4 ave Roume, BP 136, Dakar; tel. 23-25-92; telex 51578; fax 23-71-81; Ambassador: FÉLIX BAPTISTA DE FARIA.

Cameroon: 157–9 rue Joseph Gomis, BP 4165, Dakar; tel. 21-33-96; telex 21429; Ambassador: EMMANUEL MBONJO EJANGUE.

Canada: Immeuble Daniel Sorano, 45 blvd de la République, BP 3373, Dakar; tel. 23-92-90; telex 51632; fax 23-87-49; Ambassador: JACQUES BILODEAU.

Cape Verde: Immeuble El Fahd, BP 2319, Dakar; tel. 21-18-73; telex 61128; Ambassador: VÍCTOR AFONSO GONÇALVES FIDALGO.

China, People's Republic: rue Projetée, Fann Résidence, BP 342, Dakar; tel. 22-14-67; Ambassador: CANG YOUHENG.

Congo: Mermoz Pyrotechnie, BP 5243, Dakar; tel. 24-83-98; Ambassador: CHRISTIAN GILBERT BEMBET.

Côte d'Ivoire: 2 ave Albert Sarraut, BP 359, Dakar; tel. 21-01-63; telex 61170; Ambassador: JULES HIÉ NÉA.

Czech Republic: rue Aimé Césaire, Fann Résidence, BP 3253, Dakar; tel. 24-65-26; fax 24-14-06; Ambassador: LADISLAV SKEŘÍK.

Egypt: Immeuble Daniel Sorano, 45 blvd de la République, BP 474, Dakar; tel. 21-24-75; fax 21-89-93; Ambassador: MOHAMED ABDEL-RAHMAN DIAB.

Ethiopia: BP 379, Dakar; tel. 21-75-73; telex 51413; Ambassador: SAHLE-WORK ZEWDE.

France: 1 rue Amadou Assane Ndoye, BP 4035, Dakar; tel. 23-91-81; telex 51597; fax 22-18-05; Ambassador: RENÉ ALA.

Gabon: Villa no 7606 Mermoz, BP 436, Dakar; tel. 24-09-95; fax 25-98-26; Ambassador: SIMON OMBEGUE.

Gambia: 11 rue de Thiong, BP 3248, Dakar; tel. 21-44-76; telex 51617; High Commissioner: El Hadj ABDOULIE SULAYMAN MBOOB.

Germany: 20 ave Pasteur, BP 2100, Dakar; tel. 23-48-84; telex 21686; fax 22-52-99; Ambassador: Dr THOMAS FISCHER-DIESKAU.

Guinea: km 4.5, route de Ouakam, BP 7123, Dakar; tel. 21-86-06; telex 3242; Ambassador: HERVÉ VINCENT BANGOURA.

Guinea-Bissau: Point E, rue 6, BP 2319, Dakar; tel. 21-59-22; telex 243; Ambassador: PIO GOMES CORREIA.

Holy See: rue Aimé Césaire, angle Corniche-Ouest, Fann Résidence, BP 5076, Dakar; tel. 24-26-74; fax 24-19-31; Apostolic Pro-Nuncio: Mgr ANTONIO MARIA VEGLIÒ, Titular Archbishop of Aeclanum.

India: 5 ave Carde, BP 398, Dakar; tel. 22-58-75; telex 51514; fax 22-35-85; Ambassador: VIDYA BHUSHAN SONI.

Indonesia: 126 ave Cheikh Anta Diop, angle ave Bourguiba, BP 5859, Dakar; tel. 25-73-16; telex 21644; Ambassador: UTOJO YAMTOMO.

Italy: rue Alpha Hachamiyou Tall, BP 348, Dakar; tel. 22-00-76; fax 21-75-80; Ambassador: GUIDO RIZZO VENCI.

Japan: Immeuble Electra II, rue Malan, BP 3140, Dakar; tel. 23-91-41; telex 51677; fax 23-73-51; Ambassador: TAKESHI NAKAMURA.

Korea, Democratic People's Republic: rue Aimé Césaire, Fann Résidence, BP 3156, Dakar; tel. 23-09-99; Ambassador: RI SONG RIN.

Korea, Republic: Immeuble Fayçal, BP 3338, Dakar; tel. 22-58-22; telex 51242; Ambassador: SEUNG HO.

Kuwait: blvd Martin Luther King, Dakar; tel. 24-17-23; telex 3327; Ambassador: KHALAF ABBAS KHALAF.

Lebanon: 18 blvd de la République, BP 234, Dakar; tel. 22-09-20; telex 3190; Ambassador: NAJI ABDOU ASSI.

Mali: 46 blvd de la République, BP 478, Dakar; tel. 23-48-93; telex 51429; Ambassador: MOHAMED ALI BATHILY.

Mauritania: Corniche Ouest, Fann Résidence, BP 2019, Dakar; tel. 25-98-07; fax 25-72-64; Ambassador: MALIFOND OULD DADDAH.

Morocco: ave Cheikh Anta Diop, BP 490, Dakar; tel. 24-69-27; telex 51567; fax 25-70-21; Ambassador: MOHAMED HALIM.

Netherlands: 37 rue Kléber, BP 3262, Dakar; tel. 23-94-83; telex 51610; fax 21-70-84; Ambassador: GERTJAN STORM.

Nigeria: Point E, rue 1 x Fa, BP 3129, Dakar; tel. 21-69-22; telex 51404; Ambassador: Alhaji ABUBAKAR MUHAMMADU SANI YARIMA.

Pakistan: 10 ave Borgnis Desbordes, BP 2635, Dakar; tel. 21-20-31; Ambassador: RASHEED AHMED.

Poland: 7627 route de la Pyrotechnie, BP 343, Dakar; tel. 24-23-54; telex 51245; Chargé d'affaires a.i.: JANUSZ MROWIEC.

Portugal: 5 ave Carde, BP 281, Dakar; tel. 23-58-22; telex 61134; fax 23-50-96; Ambassador: FERNANDO PINTO DOS SANTOS.

Romania: Point E, blvd de l'Est x rue 4, Dakar; tel. 22-19-13; telex 3115; Ambassador: GELU VOICAN-VOICULESCU.

Russia: ave Jean-Jaurès, angle rue Carnot, BP 3180, Dakar; tel. 22-48-21; telex 21432; Ambassador: VALERY N. LIPNYAKOV.

Saudi Arabia: 33 rue Kléber, BP 3109, Dakar; tel. 22-23-67; telex 51294; Ambassador: ABDULLAH A. ALTOBAISHI.

Spain: 45 blvd de la République, BP 2091, Dakar; tel. 21-11-78; telex 51451; Ambassador: MIGUEL ANGEL GARCÍA MINA ORAA.

Switzerland: rue René Ndiaye, BP 1772, Dakar; tel. 22-58-48; telex 51411; Ambassador: WALTER GYGER.

Syria: Point E, rue 1 x blvd de l'Est, BP 498, Dakar; tel. 21-62-77; telex 62102; Chargé d'affaires a.i.: HILAL AL-RAHEB.

Thailand: Fann Résidence, 10 rue Léon Gontran Damas, BP 3721, Dakar; tel. 24-30-76; telex 61279; Ambassador: NARONK KHEMAYODHIN.

Tunisia: rue El Hadj Seydou Nourou Tall, BP 3127, Dakar; tel. 23-47-47; telex 54564; Ambassador: SADOK FAYALA.

Turkey: ave des Ambassadeurs, Fann Résidence, BP 6060, Etoile, Dakar; tel. 24-58-11; telex 51472; fax 25-69-77; Ambassador: MEHMET GORKAY.

United Kingdom: 20 rue du Dr Guillet, BP 6025, Dakar; tel. 23-73-92; telex 21690; fax 23-27-66; Ambassador: ALAN EDWIN FURNESS.

USA: ave Jean XXIII, BP 49, Dakar; tel. 23-42-96; telex 21793; fax 22-29-91; Ambassador: MARK JOHNSON.

Zaire: 16 rue Léo Frobénius, Fann Résidence, BP 2251, Dakar; tel. 25-19-79; telex 21661; Ambassador: KALENGA WA BELABELA.

Zimbabwe: km 5.5, route de Ouakam, BP 2762, Dakar; tel. 23-03-25; telex 3231; Ambassador: CHIMBIDZAYI EZEKIEL SANYANGARE.

Judicial System

Unter the terms of a revision of the judicial system, implemented in May 1992, the principal organs of the judiciary are as follows:

Conseil Constitutionnel: Pres. YOUSSOUPHA NDIAYE; Vice-Pres. (vacant).

Conseil d'Etat: Pres. LOUIS PREIRA DE CARVALHO; Sec.-Gen. DOUDOU NDIR.

Cour de Cassation: Pres. (vacant); Procurator-Gen. SEYDOU BA; Sec.-Gen. MOUSTAPHA TOURÉ.

Cour d'Appel: Pres. ANDRÉSIA VAZ; Procurator-Gen. PAPA BOUGOUMA DIENE.

Religion

About 90% of the population are Muslims, while about 6% are Christians, mainly Roman Catholics, and 4% follow traditional beliefs.

ISLAM

There are four main Islamic brotherhoods: the Mourides, the Tidjanes, the Layennes and the Qadiriyas.

Grand Imam: El Hadj MAODO SYLLA.

Association pour la coopération islamique (ACIS): Dakar; f. 1988; Pres. Dr THIERNAO KÂ.

National Association of Imams: Dakar; f. 1984; Pres. El Hadj MAODO SYLLA.

CHRISTIANITY

The Roman Catholic Church

Senegal comprises one archdiocese and five dioceses. At 31 December 1992 there were an estimated 363,655 adherents in the country, representing about 4.8% of the total population.

Bishops' Conference: Conférence des Evêques du Sénégal, de la Mauritanie, du Cap Vert et de Guinée-Bissau, BP 941, Dakar; f. 1973; Pres. Rt Rev. THÉODORE-ADRIEN SARR, Bishop of Kaolack.

Archbishop of Dakar: Cardinal HYACINTHE THIANDOUM, Archevêché, ave Jean XXIII, BP 1908, Dakar; tel. 23-69-18.

The Anglican Communion

The Anglican diocese of The Gambia, part of the Church of the Province of West Africa, includes Senegal and Cape Verde. The Bishop is resident in Banjul, The Gambia.

Other Denominations

Eglise Protestante Sénégalaise: rue Wagare Diouf, BP 847, Dakar; tel. 21-55-64; telex 3310; f. 1862; Pastor Rev. KANGURDIE MAME.

BAHÁ'Í FAITH

National Spiritual Assembly: BP 1662, Dakar; tel. 24-23-59; registered 1975; mems resident in 301 localities.

The Press

NEWSPAPERS

Réveil de l'Afrique Noire: Dakar; f. 1986; daily; Dir MAM LESS DIA.

Le Soleil: Société sénégalaise de presse et de publications, route du Service géographique, BP 92, Dakar; tel. 32-46-92; telex 51431; fax 32-03-81; f. 1970; daily; publ. by Parti socialiste sénégalais; Man. Dir ALIOUNE DRAME; circ. 45,000.

Sud au Quotidien: Immeuble Fahd, BP 4130, Dakar; tel. 22-53-93; fax 22-52-90; daily; fmrly Sud Hebdo; Editor ABDOULAYE NDIAGA SYLLA; circ. 30,000.

Wal Fadjiri (The Dawn): Dakar; Islamic daily; circ. 15,000.

PERIODICALS

Afrique Economique: Dakar; f. 1975; monthly; Editor ASSANE SECK; circ. 10,000.

Afrique Médicale: 10 rue Abdou Karim Bourgi, BP 1826, Dakar; tel. 23-48-80; telex 1300; fax 22-56-30; f. 1960; monthly; review of tropical medicine; Editor JOËL DECUPPER; circ. 7,000.

Afrique Nouvelle: 9 rue Paul Holle, BP 283, Dakar; tel. 22-51-22; telex 1403; f. 1947; weekly; development issues; Roman Catholic; Dir RENÉ ODOUN; circ. 15,000.

Amina: BP 2120, Dakar; monthly; women's magazine.

Bingo: 17 rue Huart, BP 176, Dakar; f. 1952; monthly; illustrated; Editor E. SOELLE; circ. 110,750.

Le Cafard Libéré: 10 rue Tolbiac x autoroute, 3e étage, Dakar; tel. 22-84-43; f. 1987; weekly; satirical; Editor LAYE BAMBA DIALLO; circ. 10,000.

Combat pour le Socialisme: Dakar; f. 1987; politics; circ. 10,000.

Construire l'Afrique: BP 3770, Dakar; tel. 23-07-90; fax 24-19-61; f. 1985; six a year; African business; Dir and Chief Editor CHEIKH-OUSMANE DIALLO.

Le Démocrate: 10 rue de Thiong, Dakar; f. 1974; monthly; publ. by Parti démocratique sénégalais.

Ethiopique: BP 260, Dakar; f. 1974; monthly; publ. by Parti démocratique sénégalais.

Fippu: Dakar; f. 1987; quarterly; feminist; Dir FATOUMATA SOW.

Journal Officiel de la République du Sénégal: Rufisque; f. 1856; weekly; govt journal.

La Lutte: BP 820, Dakar; f. 1977; quarterly; publ. by Parti africain de l'indépendance; Editor BARA GOUDIABY; circ. 1,000.

Momsareew: BP 820, Dakar; f. 1958; monthly; publ. by Parti africain de l'indépendance; Editor-in-Chief MALAMINE BADJI; circ. 2,000.

L'Observateur Africain: Dakar; Dir ALIOUNE DIOP.

Le Politicien: Dakar; f. 1977; fortnightly; satirical; Editor MAM LESS DIA.

Promotion: Dakar; Dir BOUBACAR DIOP.

Le Rénovateur: BP 12172, Dakar; monthly; publ. by Parti démocratique sénégalais—Rénovation.

République: Dakar; f. 1989; weekly; independent; current affairs.

Sénégal d'Aujourd'hui: 58 blvd de la République, BP 4027, Dakar; monthly; publ. by Ministry of Culture; circ. 5,000.

Sopi (Change): Dakar; f. 1988; weekly; publ. by Parti démocratique sénégalais; Dir of Publishing JOSEPH NDONG (arrested March 1994).

Souka-Magazine: 10 rue Amadou Assane Ndoye, BP 260, Senegal; tel. 22-15-80; telex 21450; fax 22-36-04; f. 1989; monthly; circ. 20,000.

L'Unité Africaine: BP 22010, Dakar; f. 1974; monthly; publ. by Parti socialiste sénégalais.

Xareli (Struggle): BP 12136, Dakar; tel. 22-54-63; fortnightly; publ. by And Jëf—Parti africain pour la démocratie et le socialisme; circ. 7,000.

NEWS AGENCIES

Agence de Presse Sénégalaise: 72 blvd de la République, BP 117, Dakar; tel. 21-14-27; telex 51520; f. 1959; govt-controlled; Dir AMADOU DIENG.

Pan-African News Agency (PANA): BP 4056, Dakar; tel. 22-61-20; telex 3307; f. 1979, restructured 1992–93; news service to 38 African countries; Co-ordinator-Gen. BABACAR FALL.

Foreign Bureaux

Agence France-Presse (AFP): Immeuble Maginot, 7e étage, BP 363, Dakar; tel. 23-21-92; telex 51564; fax 22-16-07; Dir FRANÇOIS-XAVIER HARISPE.

Agenzia Nazionale Stampa Associata (ANSA) (Italy): Dakar; tel. 22-11-97; telex 61338; Correspondent ALIOUNE TOURÉ DIA.

Wikalat al-Maghreb al Arabi (Morocco): 15 rue Galandou Diouf, 4e étage, Dakar; tel. 21-97-13; Dir MOHAMED KHAYATE.

Xinhua (New China) News Agency (People's Republic of China): Villa 1, 2 route de la Pyrotechnie, Stele Mernoz, BP 426, Dakar; tel. 23-05-38; telex 283; Chief Correspondent ZHOU WEIBO.

ITAR—TASS (Russia), IPS (Italy) and UPI (USA) are also represented in Dakar.

Publishers

Africa Editions: BP 1826, Dakar; tel. 23-48-80; telex 1300; fax 22-56-30; f. 1958; general, reference; Man. Dir JOËL DECUPPER.

Agence de Distribution de Presse: km 2.5, blvd du Centenaire de la Commune de Dakar, BP 374, Dakar; tel. 32-02-78; fax 32-49-15; f. 1943; general, reference; Man. Dir THIERRY SABOURET.

Altervision: BP 3770, Dakar; tel. 23-07-90; fax 24-19-61; f. 1985; business; Dir-Gen. CHEIKH-OUSMANE DIALLO.

Clairafrique: rue Sandiniery 2, BP 2005, Dakar; politics, law, sociology.

Editions Juridiques Africaines (EDJA): 164 ave du Président Lamine Guèye, BP 2875, Dakar; tel. 22-25-49; fax 22-24-83; f. 1986; law.

Editions des Trois Fleuves: blvd de l'Est, angle Cheikh Anta Diop, BP 123, Dakar; tel. 23-09-23; fax 25-59-37; f. 1972; general non-fiction; luxury edns; Man. Dir BERTRAND DE BOISTEL.

Enda: 4–5 rue Kléber, BP 3370, Dakar; tel. 22-42-29; telex 51456; third-world environment and development.

Grande imprimerie africaine: 9 rue Amadou Assane Ndoye, BP 51, Dakar; tel. 22-14-08; fax 22-39-27; f. 1917; law, administration; Man. Dir Cheikh ALIMA TOURÉ.

Institut fondamental d'Afrique noire (IFAN): BP 206, Dakar; scientific and humanistic studies of black Africa.

Nouvelles éditions africaines du Sénégal (NEAS): 10 rue Amadou Assane Ndoye, BP 260, Dakar; tel. 22-15-80; fax 22-36-04; f. 1972; general; Man. Dir DOUDOU NDIAYE.

Société africaine d'édition: 16 bis rue de Thiong, BP 1877, Dakar; tel. 21-79-77; f. 1961; African politics and economics; Man. Dir PIERRE BIARNES.

Société d'édition 'Afrique Nouvelle': 9 rue Paul Holle, BP 283, Dakar; tel. 22-38-25; telex 1403; f. 1947; information, statistics and analyses of African affairs; Man. Dir ATHANASE NDONG.

Société nationale de Presse, d'édition et de publicité (SONAPRESS): Dakar; f. 1972; Pres. OBEYE DIOP.

Sud-Communication: Dakar; operated by a journalists' co-operative; periodicals.

Government Publishing House

Société sénégalaise de presse et de publications (SSPP): route du Service géographique, BP 92, Dakar; tel. 32-46-92; telex 51431; fax 32-03-81; f. 1970; 62% govt-owned; Pres. and Man. Dir ALIOUNE DRAME.

Radio and Television

In early 1993 there were an estimated 900,000 radio receivers and 400,000 television receivers in use.

Société Nationale de Radiodiffusion Télévision Sénégalaise (RTS): BP 1765, Dakar; tel. 21-78-01; telex 21818; fax 22-34-90; fmrly Office de Radiodiffusion-Télévision du Sénégal; state broadcasting co; Man. Dir GUILA THIAM; Dir (Radio) IBRAHIM SANE; Dir (Television) BABACAR DIAGNE.

RADIO

There are two RTS radio networks, broadcasting in French, Portuguese, Arabic, English and six vernacular languages from Saint-Louis, Ziguinchor, Tambacounda and Kaolack.

FM 92: Dakar; broadcasts commenced 1991; jt venture by RTS and Radio France International (RFI); 24 hours daily of FM broadcasts to Dakar (RFI 18 hours, RTS six hours).

FM 94/Dakar FM: Dakar; broadcasts commenced 1990; eight hours of local broadcasts daily.

Sud FM: Dakar; f. 1994; operated by Sud-Communication; Man. Dir CHERIF ELVALIDE SEYE.

Broadcasts by Africa No. 1, the Gabonese-based radio station, are received in Dakar.

TELEVISION

There are 10-kW transmitters at Dakar, Thiès, Ziguinchor, Tambacounda and Louga. Following an agreement with France in 1989, Senegal was to receive direct transmissions from that country.

Canal Horizons Sénégal: Dakar; f. 1990, broadcasts commenced 1991; private coded channel; 18.8% owned by RTS and Société Nationale des Télécommunications du Sénégal, 15% by Canal Horizons (France); Man. Dir JACQUES BARBIER DE CROZES.

TV5 Afrique: Dakar; broadcasts commenced 1992; operated by the French-based TV5 to transmit programmes by satellite to francophone Africa; Chair. PATRICK IMHAUS.

SUPERVISORY AUTHORITY

Haut Conseil de la Radio Télévision: Dakar; f. 1991; Pres. BABACAR KEBE.

Finance

(cap. = capital; res = reserves; m. = million; brs = branches; amounts in francs CFA)

BANKING

Central Bank

Banque Centrale des Etats de l'Afrique de l'Ouest (BCEAO): ave Abdoulaye Fadiga, BP 3108, Dakar; tel. 23-16-15; telex 21815; fax 23-93-35; bank of issue and central bank for states of the Union monétaire ouest africaine (UMOA), comprising Benin, Burkina Faso, Côte d'Ivoire, Mali, Niger, Senegal and Togo; f. 1955; cap. and res 379,881m. (Sept. 1992); Gov. CHARLES KONAN BANNY; Commercial Branch: blvd du Général de Gaulle, angle Triangle Sud, BP 3159, Dakar; tel. 23-53-84; telex 21839; fax 23-57-57; Dir in Senegal SEYNI NDIAYE (acting); 2 other brs.

Commercial Banks

Banque Internationale pour le Commerce et l'Industrie du Sénégal (BICIS): 2 ave Roume, BP 392, Dakar; tel. 23-10-33; telex 21642; fax 23-37-07; f. 1962; 28% owned by Société Financière pour les Pays d'Outre-Mer, 25% state-owned, 22% owned by Banque Nationale de Paris; cap. 3,500m. (Sept. 1993); Pres. and Man. Dir BABACAR NDOYE; 4 brs.

Compagnie Bancaire de l'Afrique Occidentale (CBAO): 1 place de l'Indépendance, BP 129, Dakar; tel. 23-10-00; telex 21663; fax 23-20-05; f. 1980; fmrly BIAO-Sénégal; 90% privately owned; cap. 2,200m. (Sept. 1992); Pres. JEAN-CLAUDE MIMRAN; Dir-Gen. ABDOUL MBAYE; 10 brs.

Crédit Lyonnais Sénégal (CLS): blvd El Hadj Djily Mbaye, angle rue Huart, BP 56, Dakar; tel. 23-10-08; telex 21622; fax 23-84-30; f. 1989; 95% owned by Crédit Lyonnais (France); cap. 2,000m. (Sept. 1992); Pres. DANIEL CHOQUART; Dir-Gen. RENÉ BERARDENGO; 1 br.

Crédit National du Sénégal (CNS): 7 ave Roume, BP 319, Dakar; tel. 23-34-86; telex 61283; fax 23-72-92; f. 1990 by merger; 90% state-owned; cap. 2,500m. (Feb. 1990); Pres. ALIA DIÈNE DRAME.

Société Générale de Banques au Sénégal SA (SGBS): 19 ave Roume, BP 323, Dakar; tel. 23-10-60; telex 21801; fax 23-90-36; f. 1962; 38.2% owned by private Senegalese interests, 37.9% by Société Générale (France); cap. 4,312m. (Sept. 1993); Chair. IDRISSA SEYDI; Man. Dir GUY POUPET; 3 brs.

Development Banks

Banque de l'Habitat du Sénégal (BHS): blvd du Général de Gaulle, BP 229, Dakar; tel. 23-10-04; telex 61275; fax 23-80-43; f. 1979; cap. 1,650m. (Sept. 1992); Pres. GOUNKA DIOUF; Man. Dir AMADOU BASSIROU DIA; 1 br.

Banque Sénégalo-Tunisienne (BST): 57 ave Georges Pompidou, BP 4111, Dakar; tel. 23-62-30; telex 61169; fax 23-82-38; f. 1986; cap. 1,100m. (Sept. 1991); Pres. ABOUBAKRY KANE; Dir-Gen. TAOUFIK BAAZIZ.

Caisse Nationale de Crédit Agricole du Sénégal (CNCAS): 45 ave Albert Sarrault, BP 3890, Dakar; tel. 22-23-90; telex 61345; fax 21-26-06; f. 1984; 23.9% state-owned; cap. 2,300m. (Sept. 1992); Man. Dir SOMCIDINE DIENG; 4 brs.

Banking Association

Association Professionnelle des Banques et des Etablissements Financiers du Sénégal (APBEF): c/o SGBS, 19 ave Roume, BP 323, Dakar; Pres. LOUIS FRANCESCHINI.

INSURANCE

Assurances Générales Sénégalaises (AGS): 43 ave Albert Sarraut, BP 225, Dakar; tel. 23-49-94; telex 51647; fax 23-37-01; f. 1977; cap. 2,990m.; Man. Dir A. SOW.

Compagnie d'Assurances-Vie et de Capitalisation (La Nationale d'Assurances-Vie): 7 blvd de la République, BP 3853, Dakar; tel. 22-11-81; telex 51251; fax 21-28-20; f. 1982; cap. 80m.; Pres. MOUSSA DIOUF; Man. Dir BASSIROU DIOP.

Compagnie Sénégalaise d'Assurances et de Réassurances (CSAR): 5 place de l'Indépendance, BP 182, Dakar; tel. 23-27-76; telex 61125; fax 23-46-72; f. 1972; cap. 945m.; 49.8% state-owned; Pres. MOUSTAPHA CISSÉ; Man. Dir MAMADOU ABBAS BA.

SA Capillon V-Assurances: 5 ave Roume, BP 425, Dakar; tel. 22-90-26; telex 684; f. 1951; cap. 10m.; Pres. and Man. Dir GILLES DE MONTALEMBERT.

La Sécurité Sénégalaise (ASS): Gare Routière, BP 2623, Dakar; tel. 23-75-95; telex 3207; f. 1984; cap. 100m.; Pres. LOBATT FALL; Man. Dir MBACKE SENE.

Société Africaine d'Assurances: ave Roume, angle Victor Hugo, BP 508, Dakar; tel. 23-64-75; telex 21468; f. 1945; cap. 9m.; Dir CLAUDE GERMAIN.

Société Inter-Africane de Courtage de Réassurances (SIACRE): 41 rue C, Fann Résidence, BP 3135, Dakar; tel. 23-04-84; telex 61244; f. 1977; cap. 50m.; Dir M. BABO.

Société Nationale d'Assurances Mutuelles (SONAM): 6 ave Roume, BP 210, Dakar; tel. 23-10-03; telex 51571; fax 20-70-25; f. 1973; cap. 1,464m.; Pres. ABDOULAYE FOFANA; Man. Dir DIOULDÉ NIANE.

Société Sénégalaise de Courtage et d'Assurances (SOSECODA): 16 ave Roume, BP 9, Dakar; tel. 23-54-81; telex 51436;

fax 21-54-62; f. 1963; cap. 10m.; 55% owned by SONAM; Man. Dir A. AZIZ NDAW.

Société Sénégalaise de Réassurances SA (SENRE): 6 ave Roume x Carnot, BP 386, Dakar; tel. 22-80-89; telex 61144; fax 21-56-52; cap. 600m.

Insurance Association

Syndicat Professionel des Agents Généraux d'Assurances du Sénégal: 43 ave Albert Sarraut, BP 1766, Dakar; Pres. URBAIN ALEXANDRE DIAGNE; Sec. JEAN-PIERRE CAIRO.

Trade and Industry

DEVELOPMENT AND MARKETING ORGANIZATIONS

Caisse Française de Développement (CFD): 15 ave Mandéla, BP 475, Dakar; tel. 23-11-88; telex 51653; fax 23-40-10; f. 1941 as Caisse Centrale de Coopération Economique, name changed 1992; Dir in Senegal JEAN-CLAUDE BREDELOUX.

Mission Française de Coopération: BP 2014, Dakar; telex 3103; administers bilateral aid from France; Dir FRANÇOIS CHAPPELLET.

Société de Développement Agricole et Industriel (SODAGRI): Immeuble Fahd, 9e étage, blvd Djily Mbaye x Macodou Ndiaye, BP 222, Dakar; tel. 21-04-26; fax 22-54-06; cap. 120m. francs CFA; agricultural and industrial projects; Pres. and Man. Dir AMADOU TIDIANE WANE.

Société de Développement des Fibres Textiles (SODE–FITEX): km 4.5, blvd du Centenaire de la Commune de Dakar, BP 3216, Dakar; tel. 32-47-80; telex 280; f. 1974; 70% state-owned; responsible for planning and development of cotton industry; cap. 750m. francs CFA; Dir-Gen. FALILOU MBACKE.

Société de Développement et de Vulgarisation Agricole (SODEVA): 92 rue Moussé Diop, BP 3234, Dakar; tel. 23-16-78; telex 51638; fax 21-01-53; f. 1968; cap. 100m. francs CFA; 55% state-owned; development of intensive farming methods and diversified livestock breeding; Dir-Gen. PAPA OUSMANE DIALLO.

Société d'Exploitation des Ressources Animales du Sénégal (SERAS): km 2.5, blvd du Centenaire de la Commune de Dakar, BP 14, Dakar; tel. 32-31-78; telex 51256; fax 32-06-90; f. 1962; cap. 619.2m. francs CFA; 28.5% state-owned; livestock development; Dir Dr MAMADOU FAYE; Man. Dir MACODOU SEYE.

Société Nationale d'Aménagement et d'Exploitation des Terres du Delta du Fleuve Sénégal et des Vallées du Fleuve Sénégal et de la Falémé (SAED): route de Khor, BP 74, Saint-Louis; tel. 61-15-33; telex 75124; fax 61-14-63; f. 1965; cap. 2,500m. francs CFA; state-owned; controls the agricultural development of 30,000 ha around the Senegal river delta; Pres. and Man. Dir SIDY MOCTAR KEITA.

Société Nationale de Commercialisation des Oléagineux du Sénégal (SONACOS): Immeuble SONACOS, 32–36 rue du Dr Calmette, BP 639, Dakar; tel. 23-10-52; telex 51418; fax 23-88-05; f. 1975; cap. 4,800m. francs CFA; 80% state-owned; transfer to private ownership of part of state holding pending in 1994; marketing of groundnuts and groundnut products; Pres. and Man. Dir ABDOULAYE DIOP.

Société Nationale d'Etudes et de Promotion Industrielle (SONEPI): derrière Résidence Seydou Nourou Tall, ave Bourguiba Prolongée, BP 100, Dakar; tel. 25-21-30; telex 61178; fax 24-65-65; f. 1969; cap. 150m. francs CFA; 28% state-owned; promotion of small and medium-sized enterprises; Chair. and Man. Dir HADY MAMADOU LY.

Société Nationale d'Exploitation des Eaux du Sénégal (SONEES): 97 ave André Peytavin, BP 400, Dakar; tel. 21-28-65; telex 61137; f. 1972; cap. 3,927m. francs CFA; 97% state-owned; waterworks and supplies; Pres. ABDOUL MAGIB SECK; Man. Dir ABDOULAYE BOUNA FALL.

Société Nouvelle des Etudes de Développement en Afrique (SONED—AFRIQUE): Immeuble SONACOS, 32–36 rue Calmette, BP 2084, Dakar; tel. 23-94-57; telex 51464; fax 23-42-31; f. 1974; cap. 98m. francs CFA; 61% state-owned; Pres. El Hadj IBRAHIMA NDAO; Man. Dir RUDOLPH KERN.

CHAMBERS OF COMMERCE

Chambre de Commerce, d'Industrie et d'Agriculture de la Région de Dakar: 1 place de l'Indépendance, BP 118, Dakar; tel. 23-71-89; telex 61112; f. 1888; Pres. MAMADOU LAMINE NIANG; Sec.-Gen. MAKHAN DANFAKHA.

Chambre de Commerce, d'Industrie et d'Artisanat de la Région de Diourbel: BP 7, Diourbel; tel. 71-12-03; Pres. Cheikh MAMADOU NDIONGUE; Sec.-Gen. ALIOUNE DIOP.

Chambre de Commerce de la Région de Fatick: Fatick; tel. 45-60-03; Sec.-Gen. ABAL DIALLO.

Chambre de Commerce et d'Industrie de la Région du Kaolack: BP 203, Kaolack; tel. 41-20-52; telex 7474; Pres. IDRISSA GUÈYE; Sec.-Gen. AROHA TRAORÉ.

Chambre de Commerce de la Région de Kolda: BP 23; Kolda; tel. 96-12-30; Sec.-Gen. YAYA CAMARA.

Chambre de Commerce de la Région de Louga: BP 26, Louga; tel. 67-11-14; Pres. El Hadj AMADOU BAMBA SOURANG; Sec.-Gen. SOULEYMANE N'DIAYE.

Chambre de Commerce, d'Industrie et d'Agriculture de la Région de Saint-Louis: rue Bisson Nord, BP 19, Saint-Louis; tel. 61-10-88; f. 1879; Pres. El Hadj MOMAR SOURANG; Sec.-Gen. MASSAMBA DIOP.

Chambre de Commerce, d'Industrie et d'Agriculture de la Région de Tambacounda: BP 127, Tambacounda; tel. 81-10-14; Pres. DJIBY CISSÉ; Sec.-Gen. TENGUELLA BA.

Chambre de Commerce, d'Industrie et d'Agriculture de la Région de Thiès: ave Lamine-Guèye, BP 3020, Thiès; tel. 51-10-02; f. 1883; 38 mems; Pres. El Hadj ALIOUNE PALLA M'BAYE; Sec.-Gen. ABDOUL KHADRE CAMARA.

Chambre de Commerce, d'Industrie et d'Artisanat de la Région de Ziguinchor: BP 26, Ziguinchor; tel. 91-13-10; f. 1908; Pres. YOUSSOUF SEYDI; Sec.-Gen. MAMADI DIATTA.

PRINCIPAL EMPLOYERS' ASSOCIATIONS

Conseil National du Patronat du Sénégal (CNP): BP 3537, Dakar; tel. 22-61-01; Pres. AMADOU MOCTAR SOW; Sec.-Gen. Cheikh SECK.

Groupement Professionnel de l'Industrie du Pétrole du Sénégal (GPP): blvd du Centenaire de la Commune de Dakar, BP 479, Dakar; tel. 23-10-80; telex 21838; fax 32-90-65; Pres. MERCIER YTHIER; Sec.-Gen. OUSMANE SOW.

Syndicat des Commerçants Importateurs et Exportateurs de la République du Sénégal (SCIMPEX): 12–14 ave Albert Sarraut, BP 806, Dakar; tel. 21-36-62; Pres. YOUSSOUPHA DIOP; Sec.-Gen. MOUMAR SAKHO.

Syndicat Patronal de l'Ouest Africain des Petites et Moyennes Entreprises et des Petites et Moyennes Industries: 41 blvd Pinet-Laprade, BP 3255, Dakar; tel. 21-35-10; f. 1937; Pres. BABACAR SEYE; Sec. MAMADOU MAKHTAR DIAGNE.

Syndicat Professionnel des Entrepreneurs de Bâtiments et de Travaux Publics du Sénégal: ave Abdoulaye Fadiga, BP 593, Dakar; tel. 23-43-73; telex 3167; f. 1930; 130 mems; Pres. CHRISTIAN VIRMAUD.

Syndicat Professionnel des Industries du Sénégal (SPIDS): ave Abdoulaye Fadiga x Thann, BP 593, Dakar; tel. 23-43-73; fax 22-08-84; f. 1944; 110 mems; Pres. DONALD BARON; Sec. Gen. PHILIPPE BARRY.

MAJOR INDUSTRIAL COMPANIES

The following are some of the largest companies in terms of either capital investment or employment.

BP Sénégal SA: rue 6, km 4.5, blvd du Centenaire de la Commune de Dakar, BP 59, Dakar; tel. 23-10-80; telex 21838; fax 32-90-65; f. 1951; cap. 3,000m. francs CFA; 99.99% owned by BP Africa Ltd (UK); import, storage and distribution of petroleum products, mfrs of lubricating oil; Man. Dir FERDINAND DA COSTA.

CarnaudMetalbox Sénégal: route du Service géographique, Hann Village, BP 3850, Dakar; tel. 32-05-59; telex 51292; fax 32-37-25; f. 1959; cap. 900m. francs CFA; 72% owned by CarnaudMetalbox (France); mfrs of metal packaging; Chair. BRIAN APPLEYARD; Man. Dir MAURICE PRANGÈRE.

Compagnie Commerciale Industrielle du Sénégal (CCIS): route du Front de Terre, angle Service géographique, BP 137, Dakar; tel. 32-33-44; telex 21415; fax 32-68-22; f. 1972; cap. 1,969.6m. francs CFA; mfrs of PVC piping and plastic for shoes; Man. Dir NAYEF DERWICHE.

Compagnie Sénégalaise des Phosphates de Taïba (CSPT): 19 rue Parchappe, BP 1713, Dakar; tel. 23-40-81; telex 21834; fax 23-12-56; f. 1957; cap. 14,400m. francs CFA; 50% state-owned; mines and markets high-grade calcium phosphate; Chair. ADRIEN SENGHOR; Man. Dir MOUHAMADOU SY; 1,350 employees.

Compagnie Sucrière Sénégalaise (CSS): BP 49, Richard Toll; tel. 63-33-20; telex 75130; fax 63-31-47; f. 1970; cap. 13,586m. francs CFA; growing of sugar cane and refining of cane sugar; Chair. and Man. Dir ROBERT MIMRAN.

Les Grands Moulins de Dakar (GMD): ave Félix Eboué, BP 2068, Dakar; tel. 32-19-35; telex 634000; fax 32-89-47; f. 1946; cap. 1,180m. francs CFA; production of flour and animal food; Chair. ROBERT MIMRAN; Dir JEAN-CLAUDE BEGUINOT; 290 employees.

Industrial Drip Irrigation System (Senegal) (IDIS): BP 2031, Dakar; tel. 63-32-20; telex 75130; fax 32-91-92; f. 1976; cap. 750m.

francs CFA; subsidiary of CSS; mfrs of plastic pipes; Chair. JEAN-CLAUDE MIMRAN.

Industries Chimiques du Sénégal (ICS): km 18, blvd du Centenaire de la Commune de Dakar, BP 3835, Dakar; tel. 34-01-22; telex 31434; fax 34-08-14; f. 1976; cap. 48,844m. francs CFA; 33% state-owned; production of sulphuric and phosphoric acid; fertilizer factory at M'Bao; Chair. and Man. Dir PIERRE BABAKAR KAMA; 570 employees.

Lesieur Afrique (Dakar): place Amílcar Cabral, BP 236, Dakar; tel. 23-10-66; telex 538; f. 1942; cap. 1,796m. francs CFA; groundnut-shelling plant (capacity 350,000 metric tons per year) and vegetable oil refining plant (capacity 30,000 tons) at Dakar; Man. Dir MAMBAYE DIAW.

Manufacture de Tabacs de l'Ouest Africain (MTOA): km 2.5, blvd du Centenaire de la Commune de Dakar, BP 76, Dakar; tel. 23-68-80; telex 21807; fax 23-89-19; f. 1951; cap. 3,129.6m. francs CFA; mfrs of tobacco products; Chair. PIERRE IMBERT; Man. Dir BRUNO GUÉRIN; 380 employees.

Les Moulins Sentenac SA (MS): 50 ave du Président Lamine Guèye, BP 451, Dakar; tel. 23-94-04; telex 51545; fax 23-80-69; f. 1943; cap. 1,056m. francs CFA; milling, production of flour and other food products and of livestock feed; Chair. and Man. Dir DONALD BARON.

Nestlé Senegal: km 14, blvd du Centenaire de la Commune de Dakar, BP 796, Dakar; tel. 34-05-75; telex 31441; fax 34-17-02; f. 1961; cap. 1,620m. francs CFA; mfrs of sweetened and unsweetened condensed milk and culinary products; Man. Dir ANDRÉ PORCHET.

La Rochette Dakar (LRD): km 13.7, blvd du Centenaire de la Commune de Dakar, BP 891, Dakar; tel. 34-01-24; telex 31420; fax 34-28-26; f. 1946; cap. 500m. francs CFA; mfrs of paper and cardboard packaging; Chair. and Man. Dir ADEL SALHAB.

Société Africaine de Raffinage (SAR): 15 blvd de la République, BP 203, Dakar; tel. 23-46-84; telex 527; f. 1961; cap. 1,000m. francs CFA; petroleum refinery at M'Bao.

Société des Brasseries de l'Ouest Africain (SOBOA): route des Brasseries, BP 290, Dakar; tel. 32-01-90; telex 51286; fax 32-54-69; f. 1928; cap. 820m. francs CFA; mfrs of beer and soft drinks; Man. Dir PIERRE TRAVERSA.

Société de Conserves Alimentaires du Sénégal (SOCAS): 50 ave du Président Lamine Guèye, BP 451, Dakar; tel. 23-94-04; telex 51545; fax 23-80-69; f. 1963; cap. 726m. francs CFA; cultivation of tomatoes and other food crops, mfrs of tomato concentrate and other preserves at Savoigne; Chair. and Man. Dir DONALD BARON.

Société Industrielle Moderne des Plastiques Africains (SIMPA): 50 ave du Président Lamine Guèye, BP 451, Dakar; tel. 23-43-25; telex 51545; fax 21-80-69; f. 1958; cap. 551m. francs CFA; mfrs of injection-moulded and extruded plastic articles; Chair. and Man. Dir RAYMOND GAVEAU.

Société Industrielle de Papeterie au Sénégal (SIPS): km 11, route de Rufisque, BP 1818, Dakar; tel. 34-09-29; telex 31438; fax 34-23-03; f. 1972; cap. 750m. francs CFA; mfrs of paper goods; Chair. OMAR ABDEL KANDER GHANDOUR; Man. Dir ALI SALIM HOBALLAH.

Société Minière de Sabodala (SMS): 7 rue Jean Mermoz, BP 206, Dakar; tel. 22-37-36; telex 51274; f. 1982; cap. 2,100m. francs CFA; 41% state-owned; exploration and exploitation of gold mines in Sabodala region; Chair. BARDY DIENE; Man. Dir DIDIER FOHLEW.

Société Nationale d'Electricité (SENELEC): 28–30 rue Vincens, BP 93, Dakar; tel. 23-72-82; telex 21845; fax 23-82-46; f. 1983; cap. 63,000m. francs CFA; state electricity utility; Chair. ALIOUNE BADARA MBENGUE; Man. Dir El Hadj IBRAHIMA NDAO.

Société Nouvelle des Salins du Sine Saloum (SNSSS): BP 200, Kaolack; tel. 41-10-13; telex 7477; f. 1965; cap. 723m. francs CFA; 49% state-owned; production and marketing of sea-salt; Chair. AMADOU LY; Man. Dir HENRI DUNESME.

Société de Produits Industrielles et Agricoles (SPIA): 56 ave Faidherbe, BP 3806, Dakar; tel. 21-43-78; telex 21433; fax 21-66-37; f. 1980; cap. 640m. francs CFA; mfrs of plant-based medicines at Louga; Chair. DJILLY MBAYE; Man. Dir Cheikh DEMBA NAMARA.

Société Sénégalaise d'Engrais et de Produits Chimiques (SSEPC): km 13, blvd du Centenaire de la Commune de Dakar, BP 656, Dakar; tel. 34-02-79; telex 582; f. 1958; cap. 727m. francs CFA; mfrs of fertilizers, insecticides and livestock feed; Chair. BERNARD PORTAL; Man. Dir PAUL SASPORTES.

Société Sénégalaise des Phosphates de Thiès (SSPT): 14 ave Borgnis-Desbordes, BP 241, Dakar; tel. 23-32-83; telex 21683; fax 22-83-84; f. 1948; cap. 1,000m. francs CFA; 50% state-owned, 50% owned by Rhône-Poulenc (France); sale of part of state-owned interest pending in 1994; production of phosphates and attapulgite, mfrs of phosphate fertilizers; Chair. ABDOULAYE DIACK; Man. Dir DANIEL DUCRET.

Société de Teinture, Blanchiment, Apprêts et d'Impressions Africaines (SOTIBA-SIMPAFRIC): km 9.5, blvd du Centenaire de la Commune de Dakar, BP 527, Dakar; tel. 34-03-78; telex 31421; fax 34-52-68; f. 1951; cap. 2,600m. francs CFA; bleaching, dyeing and printing of textiles; Chair. and Man. Dir SERIGNÉ NDIAYE BOUNA; 1,100 employees.

Société Textile de Kaolack (SOTEXKA): 57 ave Georges Pompidou, BP 4101, Dakar; tel. 21-89-99; telex 21616; fax 21-23-01; f. 1977; cap 8,628m. francs CFA; 63% state-owned; textile and garment-assembling complex; Man. Dir ABDOURAHMANE TOURÉ.

TRADE UNIONS

Confédération Nationale des Travailleurs Sénégalais (CNTS): 15 rue Escarfait, BP 937, Dakar; f. 1969; affiliated to Parti socialiste sénégalais; exec. cttee of 47 mems; Sec.-Gen. MADIA DIOP; 120,000 mems.

Confédération des Syndicats Autonomes (CSA): Dakar.

Union Démocratique des Travailleurs du Sénégal (UDTS): Dakar.

Union Nationale des Commerçants et Industriels du Sénégal (UNCIS): Dakar.

Union Nationale des Syndicats Autonomes du Sénégal (UNSAS): Dakar; Sec.-Gen. MADEMBA SOCK.

TRADE FAIR

Foire Internationale de Dakar: Centre International du Commerce Extérieur du Senegal, route de l'Aéroport, BP 8166, Dakar-Yoff, Dakar; tel. 20-12-02; telex 31512; fax 35-07-12; f. 1986; Man. Dir IBRAHIMA DIAGNE.

Transport

RAILWAYS

There are 1,225 km of main line including 70 km of double track. One line runs from Dakar north to Saint-Louis (262 km), and the main line runs to Bamako (Mali). All the locomotives are diesel-driven. The rehabilitation and expansion of the railway network is proceeding.

Société Nationale des Chemins de Fer du Sénégal (SNCFS): BP 175, Cité Ballabey, Thiès; tel. 51-10-13; telex 77129; fax 51-13-93; state-owned; Pres. ALIEU DIENE DRAME; Man. Dir MBAYE DIOUF.

ROADS

In 1990 there were 13,850 km of roads, of which 3,900 km were surfaced. Work on a 160-km road between Dialakoto and Kédougou, the construction of which (at a cost of some US $45m.) was to be financed by regional donor organizations, began in October 1991. The road was to form part of an eventual transcontinental highway linking Cairo with the Atlantic coast, via N'Djamena (Chad), Bamako (Mali) and Dakar.

INLAND WATERWAYS

Senegal has three navigable rivers: the Senegal, navigable for three months of the year as far as Kayes (Mali), for six months as far as Kaédi (Mauritania) and all year as far as Rosso and Podor, and the Saloun and Casamance. Senegal is a member of the Organisation de mise en valeur du fleuve Gambie (OMVG) and of the Organisation pour la mise en valeur du fleuve Sénégal (OMVS), both based in Dakar. These organizations aim to develop navigational facilities, irrigation and hydroelectric power in the basins of the Gambia and Senegal Rivers respectively.

SHIPPING

The port of Dakar is the second largest in west Africa, after Abidjan (Côte d'Ivoire), and serves Senegal, Mauritania and The Gambia. It handled a total of 5m. metric tons of international freight in 1993. The extension of the container terminal was completed in 1993, and the port also has extensive facilities for fishing vessels and fish processing.

Société nationale de Port Autonome de Dakar (PAD): 21 blvd de la Libération, BP 3195, Dakar; tel. 23-45-45; telex 21404; fax 23-36-06; f. 1865; state-operated port authority; Pres. El Hadj MALICK SY; Man. Dir DJIBRIL NGOM.

Compagnie Sénégalaise de Navigation Maritime (COSENAM): rue le Dantec, angle Huart, BP 683, Dakar; tel. 21-57-66; telex 61301; fax 21-08-95; f. 1979; 26.1% state-owned, 65.9% owned by private Senegalese interests, 8.0% by private French, German and Belgian interests; river and ocean freight transport; Pres. ABDOURAHIM AGNE; Man. Dir SIMON BOISSY.

SDV: 8–10 allée Robert Delmas, BP 164, Dakar; tel. 23-56-82; telex 21652; fax 21-45-47; f. 1936; fmrly Union Sénégalaise d'Industries Maritimes; shipping agents, warehousing; Pres. GASTON GUILLABERT.

Société pour le Développement de l'Infrastructure de Chantiers Maritimes du Port de Dakar (DAKAR-MARINE): blvd de l'Arsenal, BP 438, Dakar; tel. 23-36-88; telex 61104; fax 23-83-99; f. 1981; privately-controlled; operates facilities for the repair and maintenance of supertankers and other large vessels; Man. YORO KANTE.

SOCOPAO-Sénégal: 47 ave Albert Sarraut, BP 233, Dakar; tel. 23-10-01; telex 21496; fax 23-56-14; f. 1926; warehousing, shipping agents, sea and air freight transport; Man. Dir GILLES CUCHE.

CIVIL AVIATION

The international airport is Dakar-Yoff. There are other major airports at Saint-Louis, Ziguinchor and Tambacounda, in addition to about 12 smaller airfields.

African West Air: 19 bis rue Robert Brun, Dakar; tel. 22-45-38; fax 22-46-10; f. 1993; services to western Europe and Brazil; Man. Dir J. P. PIEDADE.

Air Afrique: BP 3132, Dakar; tel. 23-10-45; telex 664; see under Côte d'Ivoire; Dir at Dakar BAKAR OULD AHMEDOU.

Air Sénégal—Société Nationale des Transports Aériens du Sénégal: BP 8010, Dakar-Yoff, Dakar; tel. 20-09-13; telex 31513; fax 20-00-33; f. 1971; 50% state-owned, 40% owned by Air Afrique; domestic and international services; Gen. Man. ABDOULAYE NDIAYE.

Tourism

Senegal's attractions for tourists include six national parks and its fine beaches. The island of Gorée, near Dakar, is of considerable historic interest as a former centre for the slave-trade. Some 245,581 tourists (of whom 52.4% were from France) visited Senegal in 1992. In that year receipts from tourism totalled about 39,200m. francs CFA. However, income from tourism was expected to have declined to an estimated 27,000m. francs CFA in 1993, owing largely to the suspension of tourist activity in the Casamance region in that year. There were 188 hotels, with a total of 14,947 beds, in 1992.

Ministry of Tourism and Air Transport: 23 rue Calmette, BP 4049, Dakar; tel. 23-65-02; fax 22-94-13.

Defence

In June 1993 Senegal's active armed forces totalled 9,700 men: army 8,500 (mostly conscripts), navy 700, air force 500. There is also a gendarmerie. Military service is by selective conscription and lasts for two years. France and the USA provide technical and material aid, and in June 1993 there were 1,200 French troops stationed in Senegal.

Defence Expenditure: Estimated at 33,528m. francs CFA in 1993 (7.0% of total central government expenditure).

Chief of the General Staff: Gen. MAMADOU MANSOUR SECK.

Education

Primary education, which usually begins at seven years of age and lasts for six years, is officially compulsory. In 1989 some 48% of children in the relevant age-group were enrolled at primary schools (girls 41%; boys 55%). In early 1993 the International Development Association announced funding of US $40m., in support of a project which aims to increase by 7% the level of primary enrolment for both sexes by 1998. Secondary education usually begins at the age of 13, and comprises a first cycle of four years and a further cycle of three years. In 1989 only 13% of children in the relevant age-group were enrolled in secondary schools (girls 9%; boys 16%). Since 1981 the reading and writing of national languages has been actively promoted: in 1990, according to UNESCO estimates, the rate of adult illiteracy averaged 61.7% (males 48.1%, females 74.9%). In accordance with the policy of 'negritude', the Université Cheikh Anta Diop, at Dakar (established as a university in 1957), specializes in local studies. The Université Gaston-Berger, at Saint-Louis, was established in 1990. Some 14,000 students attended university-level institutions in the early 1990s. Budget estimates for 1993 allocated 63,843m. francs CFA to education (representing 13.3% of total government expenditure).

Bibliography

Adam, A. *Le long voyage des gens du fleuve.* Paris, Maspero, 1978.

Barry, B. *Le royaume du Waalo: le Sénégal avant la conquête.* Paris, Karthala, 1985.

Bathily, A. *Mai '68 à Dakar.* Paris, Editions Chaka.

Coulon, C. *Le Marabout et Le Prince: Islam et Pouvoir en Sénégal.* Paris, Editions A. Pedone, 1981.

Crowder, M. *Senegal: A Study in French Assimilation Policy.* London, 1967.

Cruise O'Brien, D. B., Dunn, J., and Rathbone, R. (Eds.). *Contemporary West African States.* Cambridge, Cambridge University Press, 1989.

Cruise O'Brien, D. B. 'Sénégal: la démocratie a L'épreuve', in *Politique Africaine,* No. 45. Paris, 1992.

Cruise O'Brien, R. (Ed.). *The Political Economy of Underdevelopment: Dependence in Senegal.* London, Sage Publications, 1979.

Deschamps, H. *Le Sénégal et la Gambie.* Paris, Presses universitaires de France, 1964.

Dia, M. *Mémoires d'un militant du tiers-monde.* Paris, Publisud, 1986.

Diarassouba, V. C. *L'Evolution des structures agricoles du Sénégal.* Paris, Editions Cujas, 1968.

Diop, A.-B. *La société Wolof.* Paris, Editions Karthala, 1983 (reissue).

Diop, M. *Histoire des classes sociales dans l'Afrique de l'ouest: Vol. 2: Le Sénégal.* Paris, Editions Maspero, 1972.

Duruflé, G. *L'ajustement structurel en Afrique (Sénégal, Côte d'Ivoire, Madagascar).* Paris, Editions Karthala, 1987.

Dumont, P. *Le français et les langues africaines du Sénégal.* Paris, Editions Karthala, 1983.

Fatton, R. Jr. *The Making of a Liberal Democracy. Senegal's Passive Revolution, 1975–1985.* Boulder, CO, Westview Press, and London, Lynne Rienner Publishers, 1987.

Gagnon, G. *Coopératives ou autogestion: Sénégal, Cuba, Tunisie.* Paris, Presses de l'Université de Montréal, 1976.

Gellar, S. *Senegal: An African Nation between Islam and the West.* London, Gower, 1983.

Gersovitz, M., and Waterbury, J. (Eds). *The Political Economy of Risk and Choice in Senegal.* London, Frank Cass, 1987.

Gonidec, P.-F. *La République du Sénégal.* Collection 'Encyclopédie constitutionelle', Paris, Berger-Levrault.

Harrison Church, R. J. *West Africa.* 8th Edn, London, Longman, 1979.

Hayward, M. F. *Elections in Independent Africa.* Boulder, CO, Westview Press, 1987.

Hesseling, G. *Histoire politique du Sénégal.* Paris, Editions Karthala, 1983.

Hymans, J. L. *Léopold Sédar Senghor.* Edinburgh University Press, 1972.

Johnson, G. W. *Naissance du Sénégal contemporain.* Paris, Editions Karthala, 1991.

Ka, S. 'Uneasy Passage: Senegal in 1993', in *CSIS Africa Notes,* No. 149. Washington, DC, Center for Strategic and International Studies, 1993.

Makédonsky, E. *Le Sénégal, La Sénégambie.* Paris, L'Harmattan, 1987.

Milcent, E., and Sordet, M. *Léopold Sédar Senghor et la naissance de l'Afrique moderne.* Paris, Editions Seghers, 1969.

Peterec, R. J. *Dakar and West African Political Development.* New York, Columbia University Press, 1967.

Pfefferman, G. *Industrial Labor in the Republic of Senegal.* New York, Praeger, 1968.

Rémy, M. *Le Sénégal aujourd'hui.* Jeune Afrique, 1974.

Rimmer, D. *The Economies of West Africa.* London, Weidenfeld and Nicolson, 1984.

Rocheteau, G. *Pouvoir financier et indépendance économique en Afrique noire. Le cas du Sénégal.* Paris, Editions Karthala, 1983.

Saint-Martin, Y.-J. *Le Sénégal sous le second empire.* Paris, Editions Karthala, 1989.

Sene, M., and Ricou, M.-J. *Le Sénégal.* Centre d'Information du Sénégal, 1974.

Senegal, Tradition, Diversification and Economic Development. Washington, DC, International Bank for Reconstruction and Development, 1974.

Senghor, L. S. *Liberté I, Négritude et Humanisme; Liberté II, Nation et voie africaine du socialisme.* Editions du Seuil, 1964 and 1971.

Wade, A. *Un destin pour l'Afrique.* Paris, Editions Karthala, 1992.

Zarour, C. *La Coopération arabo-sénégalaise.* Paris, L'Harmattan, 1989.

SEYCHELLES

Physical and Social Geography

The Republic of Seychelles comprises a scattered archipelago of granitic and coralline islands ranging over some 1m. sq km of the western Indian Ocean. The exact number of islands is unknown, but has been estimated at 115, of which 41 are granitic and the remainder coralline. The group also includes numerous rocks and small cays. At independence in June 1976, the Aldabra Islands, the Farquhar group and Desroches (combined area 28.5 sq km, or 11 sq miles), part of the British Indian Ocean Territory since 1965 (see p. 632), were reunited with the Seychelles, thus restoring the land area to 308 sq km (119 sq miles). Including the Aldabra lagoon, the country's area is 454 sq km (175.3 sq miles).

The islands take their name from the Vicomte Moreau de Séchelles, controller-general of finance in the reign of Louis XV of France. The largest of the group is Mahé, which has an area of about 148 sq km (57 sq miles) and is approximately 27 km long from north to south. Mahé lies 1,800 km due east of Mombasa, 3,300 km south-west of Bombay, and 1,100 km north of Madagascar. Victoria, the capital of Seychelles and the only port of the archipelago, is on Mahé. It is the only town in Seychelles of any size and had a population of 24,324 (including suburbs) at the census of August 1987. The islanders have a variety of ethnic origins—African, European, Indian and Chinese. The total population of Seychelles was enumerated at 61,898 at the 1977 census and at 68,598 (giving a density of 151.1 persons per sq km) at the August 1987 census.

The granitic islands, which are all of great scenic beauty, rise fairly steeply from the sea and Mahé has a long central ridge which at its highest point, Morne Seychellois, reaches 912 m. Praslin, the second largest island in the group, is 43 km from Mahé and the other granitic islands are within a radius of 56 km. The coral islands are reefs in different stages of formation, rising only marginally above sea-level.

For islands so close to the Equator, the climate is surprisingly equable. Maximum shade temperature at sea-level averages 29°C, but during the coolest months the temperature may drop to 24°C. At higher levels temperatures are rather lower. There are two seasons, hot from December to May, and cooler from June to November while the south-east trade winds are blowing. Rainfall varies over the group; the greater part falls in the hot months during the north-west trade winds and the climate then tends to be humid and somewhat enervating. The mean annual rainfall in Victoria is 2,360 mm and the mean average temperature nearly 27°C. All the granitic islands lie outside the cyclone belt.

Recent History

Revised for this edition by the Editor

The archipelago now forming the Republic of Seychelles was uninhabited until 1770, when French settlers arrived to exploit the islands' abundant resources of tortoises and timber. Seychelles was ceded by France to Britain in 1814 and administered as a dependency of Mauritius until 1903, when it became a crown colony.

During the 1960s political activity was focused on the socialist-orientated Seychelles People's United Party (SPUP), led by Albert René, and the centre-right Seychelles Democratic Party (SDP), led by James (later Sir James) Mancham, who became the islands' chief minister in 1970. The SPUP demanded full independence for the islands, while the SDP favoured a form of economic integration with the United Kingdom. This option was not acceptable to the British government, and in 1974 the SDP adopted a pro-independence policy. The two parties formed a coalition government in 1975, and the independent Republic of Seychelles, with Mancham as president and René as prime minister, was proclaimed on 29 June 1976.

The coalition was abruptly terminated in June 1977, when supporters of the SPUP staged an armed *coup d'état* while Mancham was absent in Britain. René, who denied prior knowledge of the plan, was sworn in as president and formed a new administration. René claimed that Mancham had intended to postpone the 1979 elections (a charge that Mancham denied), but there is little doubt that the former president's extravagant lifestyle and capitalist philosophy aroused resentment among many of the islanders. The SDP had intended to develop Seychelles as a financial and trading centre and placed great emphasis on the tourist industry. René's government considered the development of agriculture and fishing to be as important as tourism to the economy, and planned to ensure a more equitable distribution of wealth among the islanders.

ONE-PARTY GOVERNMENT

A new constitution was promulgated in 1979. The SPUP, now redesignated the Seychelles People's Progressive Front (SPPF), was declared the sole legal party, and legislative and presidential elections were held to legitimize the new political order. The government's socialist programme, however, led to discontent, particularly among the islands' small middle class. Two plots to overthrow René were uncovered in 1978, and a third, and more serious coup attempt, involving South African mercenaries, was thwarted in 1981. In 1982 the government put down both an army mutiny and a further coup plot. In 1983, another attempt to depose René was quelled. This sustained anti-government activism was ascribed by the government to pro-Mancham exile groups, although Mancham denied any involvement in the conspiracies. Dissent within the SPUP itself was evident, however, in the enforced resignations of two cabinet ministers; Dr Maxime Ferrari, the minister of planning and external relations, left the islands in 1984, and two years later the minister of youth and defence, Col Ogilvy Berlouis, was removed from the government after the discovery of another alleged coup plot.

During the mid-1980s, there was a series of apparent attacks upon, and disappearances of, exiled opponents of the SPPF. Notable among these was the murder in London in 1985 of Gérard Hoarau, a former government official and leader of the Mouvement pour la Résistance. In 1987 an elaborate plan to overthrow the Seychelles government was discovered by police in the UK, with details of a consipiracy to abduct leading members of the African National Congress of South Africa (ANC), who were based in London.

Until the early 1990s, exiled opposition to President René remained split among a number of small groups based principally in London. In July 1991 five of these parties, including the Rassemblement du Peuple Seychellois pour la Démocratie (subsequently renamed the Seychelles Christian Democrat Party—SCDP), founded by Dr Maxime Ferrari, established a coalition, the United Democratic Movement (UDM), under Ferrari's leadership, while ex-president Mancham rallied his supporters in a 'Crusade for Democracy'.

During 1991 President René came under increasing pressure from France and the United Kingdom, the islands' principal aid-donors, to return Seychelles to a democratic political system. Internally, open opposition to the SPPF was voiced by the newly formed Parti Seychellois (PS), led by a Protestant clergyman, Wavel Ramkalawan. In August Maxime Ferrari returned from exile to organize support for the UDM, and in November President René invited all political dissidents to return to the islands. In the following month the minister of tourism and transport, Jacques Hodoul, left the government and subsequently formed the Seychelles Movement for Democracy.

RETURN TO MULTI-PARTY POLITICS

In December 1991 the SPPF convened an extraordinary congress, at which it was agreed to surrender the party's monopoly of power. It was announced that, from January 1992, political groups numbering at least 100 members would be granted official registration, and that multi-party elections would take place in July for a constituent assembly, whose proposals for constitutional reform would be submitted to a national referendum, with a view to holding multi-party parliamentary elections in December 1992. In April ex-president Mancham returned from exile to lead the New Democratic Party (NDP), and was officially received by President René.

Elections for a 20-seat commission to draft a new constitution took place in July 1992. The SPPF won 58.4% of the votes, while the NDP received 33.7%. The PS, which took 4.4% of the votes, was the only other political party to obtain representation on the commission. The commission, which comprised 11 representatives from the SPPF, eight from the NDP (now renamed the Democratic Party—DP) and one from the PS, completed its deliberations in October. In September, however, the DP withdrew its delegation, on the grounds that the SPPF had allegedly refused to permit a full debate of reform proposals. It also expressed objections that the commission's meetings had been closed to the public and news media. Following publication of the draft constitution, the DP focused its opposition on proposed voting arrangements for a new national assembly, whose members were to be elected on a basis of one-half by direct vote and one-half by proportional representation. The latter formula was to reflect the percentage of votes obtained by the successful candidate in presidential elections,and was intended to ensure that the president's party would secure a legislative majority. Other sections of the proposed constitution, relating to social issues, were strongly opposed by the Roman Catholic Church, to which more than 90% of the islanders belong.

The draft constitution, which required the approval of at least 60% of voters, was endorsed by only 53.7% and opposed by 44.6% at a referendum held in November 1992. A second constitutional commission, whose meetings were opened to the public, began work in January 1993 on proposals for submission to a further referendum, which was to be held later in the year. In April President René reshuffled the cabinet, relinquishing the defence portfolio.

In May 1993 the second commission unanimously agreed on a new draft constitution, in which a compromise plan was reached on the electoral formula for a new national assembly. With the joint endorsement of René and Mancham, the draft constitution was submitted to a national referendum in June, at which voters approved the constitutional plan by 73.9% to 24.0%. Opponents of the new constitutional arrangements comprised the PS, the Seychelles National Movement (SNM) and the National Alliance Party (NAP). At the presidential and legislative elections that followed in July, René received 59.5% of the vote, against 36.7% for Mancham and 3.8% for Philippe Boullé, the United Opposition candidate representing the PS, the Seychelles Christian Democrat Party (SCDP), the SNM and the NAP. In the legislative elections, the SPPF secured 21 of the 22 seats elected by direct vote, and the DP one seat. Of the 11 additional seats allocated on a proportional basis, the SPPF received a further seven seats, the DP three seats and the PS one seat. Immediately following the elections, René, whose decisive victory was widely attributed to his promise of increased expenditure on social programmes, carried out an extensive reshuffle of the cabinet.

EXTERNAL RELATIONS

Seychelles, a member of the Commonwealth, the African Development Bank (ADB) and the Organization of African Unity (OAU), has traditionally pursued a policy of non-alignment in international affairs. Under the René government, the country has strengthened its ties with continental Africa and declared its sympathy with various liberation movements.

In 1983 Seychelles, Madagascar and Mauritius agreed to form an Indian Ocean Commission (IOC) with the aim of increasing regional co-operation. The first such agreement under the IOC was signed by the three countries in January 1984. In early 1986 Seychelles withdrew its objections to the admission to membership of France (as the representative of Réunion) despite its reluctance to recognize permanent French sovereignty over Réunion, and disagreements over the demarcation of regional tuna-fishing rights. Relations with France improved in 1987, despite Seychelles' opposition to the accession of France to the presidency of the IOC. France signed three new economic assistance agreements with Seychelles during that year, and the French minister of co-operation visited the islands and opened an electricity generator that had been supplied by the French government. In June 1990 President Mitterrand of France visited Seychelles as part of an Indian Ocean tour.

In 1988 Seychelles established diplomatic relations with the Comoros and with Mauritius, and an agreement was made with the latter to co-operate in health matters. In 1989 diplomatic relations were established with Morocco, Madagascar and Côte d'Ivoire, and in 1990 with Kenya. During 1992 formal relations were established with Israel and South Africa.

During the 1980s President René actively pursued initiatives for the creation of an Indian Ocean 'peace zone' and the demilitarization of the British Indian Ocean Territory, which includes the atoll of Diego Garcia. Until 1983, Seychelles allowed limited use of its naval facilities to warships of all nations, but only on condition that a guarantee was issued that they were not carrying nuclear weapons. Neither the British nor the US governments would agree to this condition, and their refusal to do so caused their respective naval fleets to be effectively banned from using Seychelles port facilities. It is thought that this 'ban' lost Seychelles a considerable amount of foreign exchange, and that this may have been one reason for the lifting of the guarantee requirement in September 1983. Seychelles continues, theoretically, to refuse entry to ships carrying nuclear weapons.

In 1986 Seychelles and the USA renegotiated an agreement, originally signed in 1976 and renewed in 1981, which allowed the USA to maintain a satellite tracking station on Mahé. In 1988 the USA increased its annual level of economic support to \$3m., exclusive of the \$4m. paid annually in rental fees for the satellite tracking facilities. In 1993, however, the US government announced that direct economic aid to Seychelles was to be reduced to \$1m. per annum.

Economy

DONALD L. SPARKS

In 1992, according to estimates by the World Bank, Seychelles' gross national product (GNP), measured at average 1990–92 prices was US $378m., equivalent to $5,480 per head. During 1985–92, it was estimated, GNP per caput increased, in real terms, at an average annual rate of 4.1%. Over the same period, the population increased by an annual average of 0.8%. Seychelles' gross domestic product (GDP) increased, in real terms, by an annual average of 4.2% in 1982–91. In 1992 GDP increased by 4.0%, but sustained a fall of 2.0% in 1993, largely as the result of a worsening imbalance of trade. Following the multi-party elections held in 1993, the government has begun to implement a number of important changes in the economy, notably towards encouraging the greater involvement of the private sector in tourism, industry and agriculture.

AGRICULTURE AND FISHERIES

As the area of cultivable land is extremely limited (about 1,000 ha of a total of 14,000 ha on Mahé) and the soil is generally poor, it is unlikely that Seychelles will ever become self-sufficient in agriculture. New lands, however, are being opened up for farming on some of the outlying islands, which are managed by the Islands Development Co, a parastatal body, which is responsible for land on 10 islands. Seychelles is heavily dependent on imported food which, together with drink and tobacco, accounts for about 18% of the total import bill, but this proportion is being slowly reduced. The government is seeking to stimulate greater self-sufficiency in vegetables, fruit, meat and milk. There are a number of large farms and about 650 small farms and thousands of smallholdings, about one-half of them run by 'part-time' farmers. In 1993 the ministry of agriculture withdrew from the management of its five state owned farms. Their profitability had been overtaken by the increasing cost of subsidies and poor productivity. These farms are being sub-divided into small plots and leased to private individuals, and the ministry of agriculture is now to concentrate on stressing increased extension services to small farmers in its continuing attempts to stimulate food production.

The main exports from this sector have traditionally been coconuts (especially for copra), frozen fish and cinnamon (exported as bark). In 1987, the first year of its production, canned tuna became the most significant export commodity. Minor export crops include patchouli, vanilla, tea and limes. Since 1983, the government has allowed the export of cup copra only, whose world market price is double that for other grades. These are processed locally into oil, and the by-product made into animal feed. By the early 1990s, exports of copra, which in the late 1960s were about 6,000 tons per year, had fallen to only 10% of 1968 levels, mainly as a result of competition for land from food crops. Copra exports declined by 31% between 1992 and 1993. Cinnamon bark, formerly an important export item, is now mainly processed locally; exports of unrefined leaf oil ceased in 1982, while in the late 1980s exports of cinnamon bark fell to about one-third of 1986 totals, and remained depressed in the early 1990s. Tea is grown for domestic consumption, and there is a small surplus for export. Output totalled 245 tons in 1992 and 249 tons in 1993. The government is seeking to stimulate production of bananas, mangoes and avocados. Seychelles is self-sufficient in eggs and poultry, and there has been a large increase in the number of pigs, although animal feed has to be imported. The islands' first fruit and vegetable canning plant and an integrated poultry unit started operating in 1982, and a dairy plant was opened in 1986.

Seychelles expects to be self-sufficient in timber by the year 2000. A reforestation scheme, with new plantings of 100 ha per year, has been started to provide timber for the sawmill established in 1979 at Grande Anse by the state-owned Seychelles Timber Co (SEYTIM).

Consumption of fish per caput is one of the highest in the world, at 85 kg per year. Until relatively recently, there was little exploitation of the islands' substantial marine resources. The local catch, by largely traditional methods, satisfied domestic demand, leaving a small surplus for export as frozen fish. A modern fishing industry, operated by the Fishing Development Co (FIDECO), is concentrating on industrial tuna fishing through joint-venture operations, including the Société Thonière de Seychelles (of which 49% is owned by French interests), which has two freezer ships, and a tuna canning plant at Victoria that began operating in mid-1987, Conserveries de l'Océan Indien (a joint venture between the governments of Seychelles and France). This has not as yet achieved full capacity (8,000–10,000 tons per year); output, which totalled 1,045 tons in the first year of production, reached 3,571 tons in 1991 and was estimated at about 3,300 tons in 1992.

In 1978 Seychelles declared an exclusive economic zone (EEZ), extending 370 km (200 nautical miles) from the coast, to curtail the activities of large foreign fleets, which until then had been freely catching almost 24,000 tons per year of deep-sea tuna. Since 1979, when Seychelles began to enforce its control over the EEZ, agreements have been concluded with several foreign governments. The most important of these is with the European Union (EU), which has the right to operate 40 purse-seiners within the EEZ. This arrangement yielded Seychelles approximately $73m. in revenue in 1991. In 1993 a further three-year agreement was signed with the EC. The Republic of Korea and Japan, together, pay $4.8m. per year in licence fees. Additional revenue is earned through the supplying of vessels at Victoria and through leasing the newly expanded port facilities to foreign vessels. In 1987 160,000 tons of tuna were caught in the EEZ, of which 144,000 tons were transhipped through Victoria. Seychelles' industrial fish catch more than doubled between 1984–88, and in 1989 a record 227,000 tons were caught. In 1991, however, the catch declined to 193,000 tons. An indigenous fleet of 10 purse-seiners is under construction, the first of which was launched in July 1991. Seychelles' first tuna-seiner, with a capacity of 250 tons, began operations in late 1991. Assistance in expanding the fishing industry sector has been forthcoming from Japan, France, the United Kingdom and the African Development Bank (ADB). In 1991 Seychelles joined Mauritius and Madagascar to form a Tuna Fishing Association (TFA). A study on the potential for prawn fishing estimated that the annual catch could total 8 tons. About 3 tons of prawns a year are currently imported, mainly for the tourist industry. A study made in the mid-1980s suggested that Seychelles could exploit its rich stock of marine algae, which are used to manufacture fertilizers, adhesives, beverages and medicines. Artisanal fishing comprises less than 3% of GDP, but employs about 1,500 people.

TOURISM

The economy is heavily dependent on tourism, which provides more than 70% of total foreign exchange earnings, about 50% of GDP, 15% of formal employment and a substantial proportion of secondary employment. However, it has been estimated that more than 60% of gross earnings from tourism leaves the country to pay for imported food and other goods, and to tour operators.

The tourism industry began in 1971 with the opening of Mahé international airport. In that year there were only 3,175 visitors; however, by 1981 the number had risen to 60,425, after, however, approaching 79,000 in 1979. The reasons for the decline included general world recession, high local prices (partly caused by the revaluation of the Seychelles rupee in March 1981), increased air fares and the ban on landings imposed on South African Airways in September 1980. An agreement with Swaziland's national airline allowed the important South African trade to resume, but in November 1981 the entry by this route of a group of mercenaries, seeking to oust the government, had a highly damaging effect on tourism. These factors, combined with the army rebellion in August 1982 (which deterred many potential visitors), led to a further fall in arrivals. However, the final figure for 1982 was 47,280 visitors, partly owing to a strenuous campaign, launched during the year, to revive the sector. The number of tourist arrivals rose to 55,867 in 1983, nearly 65,000 in 1984 and to 72,542 in 1985. The 1986 total was a disappointing 66,626, compared with the target for that year of 86,000, following the withdrawal of air services from the Federal Republic of Germany, the Far East and South Africa. The number of tourist arrivals increased to 71,626 in 1987, to 77,721 in 1988 and to 86,093 in 1989. In 1990 the number of visitor arrivals rose to 103,900, the numbers including business visitors as well as tourists. The Gulf War caused arrivals to decline to about 90,000 in 1991, although 1992 and 1993 both brought a strong recovery, to more than 116,000 visitors in the latter year. Foreign exchange receipts from tourism were SR 521.8m. in 1989, SR 526m. in 1991 and SR 607m. in 1993. The main countries of origin in that year were France (22.9% of the total), the United Kingdom (16.3%), Germany (15.9%), Italy (12.4%) and African countries, pricipally South Africa (11.7%).

Seychelles has developed an extensive network of international air links. Air France flies three times each week from Paris to Seychelles, in conjunction with Air Seychelles. In August 1991 Air Seychelles began weekly scheduled flights to Johannesburg. Air Seychelles also operates international services to London, Paris, Frankfurt and Rome. A service to Spain was introduced by Air Seychelles in 1993, substantially increasing the number of visitors from that country. Late in 1993, Seychelles and Kenya signed a joint marketing agreement to promote combined tour programmes.

At the end of 1990, the total number of hotel beds was about 3,500. In the period 1985–90 the government was to spend SR 345.2m. on rehabilitating and improving existing tourist facilities, and on developing new ones, including a craft village, a national aquarium and historical sites. The government has been careful to control the development of tourism in order to protect both the natural and the social environments, and now wishes to upgrade facilities and improve year-round bed occupancy so that revenue may increase, while restricting visitor numbers to under 4,000 at any one time. Following the 1993 elections, the government began to lessen its involvement, through parastatal corporations, in the tourism sector.

MINERALS

The islands' sole mineral export is guano (of which 5,000 metric tons were exported in 1986). The government is investigating the possibility of processing local coral into lime for a cement factory. In July 1986 an Italian firm signed a contract to study the potential for exporting Seychelles granite, of which small quantities had been exported in 1982. India is collaborating in surveys for polymetallic nodules in the EEZ.

In 1977 the government signed a petroleum exploration agreement, covering an offshore concession area of 16,000 sq km, with a consortium including Amoco of the USA, which later bought out its partners. In 1982 Amoco Seychelles signed a new agreement, covering five more offshore wells in addition to those already drilled. Other concessions are held by Elf-Aquitaine of France and Santa Fe Industries of the USA. An exploration promotion programme was launched by the government in 1985. In 1987 the government signed an agreement with Enterprise Oil Exploration, a British company. Under the agreeement, the company gained exclusive rights to explore an offshore area south-east of Mahé and to develop any viable fields. If petroleum is found in commercially exploitable quantities, Enterprise has agreed to pay royalties and taxation with the government retaining rights to participate in the development of the concession. Other petroleum companies have subsequently expressed interest in conducting exploration operations, and the Seychelles government has received technical assistance and funding from Norway to further offshore exploration activities.

INFRASTRUCTURE AND MANUFACTURING

The roads are generally good and a road improvement programme is proceeding. The Pointe Larue International airport has been expanded, its runway has been strengthened to take Boeing 747s, and a new domestic terminal has been built. There are 10 airstrips on the islands. Plans are proceeding for the creation of an air control centre.

Seychelles' major infrastructural project, the Mahé east coast development plan, also entails the modernization and expansion of Victoria port and the construction of a new road linking Victoria to the airport. The World Bank agreed in 1985 to lend $6.2m. for dredging work, quayside paving and rehabilitation of roads on Mahé. The total cost of the scheme is likely to be $40m.–$42m., of which $12m. will be spent on the fisheries development project. As well as the World Bank, the African Development Bank, Banque Arabe pour le Développement Economique en Afrique (BADEA) and the Kuwait Fund have provided finance for the east coast project. The commercial port can accommodate vessels of up to 214 m in length, but there is only one berth. Additional berthing capacity is planned, with some facilities for containerization, and possibly a repair dock. At present there is a small yard for repairing fishing boats and yachts. In March 1994 the government established a commission to prepare the reorganization of port activities at Victoria. Among subsequent recommendations was the transfer to private ownership of the ship-handling, stevedoring and agency activities of the state-owned Union Lighterage Co, which had been operating at a loss. The implementation of these measures was proceeding in July 1994.

The Seychelles Electricity Corpn was set up in 1980 as a parastatal organization which is to finance its own recurrent costs. The extension of electricity supply to the islands of Mahé, Praslin and La Digue has been completed. Power supplies are generated entirely from petroleum, which accounted for 21.9% of total imports in 1991. Studies on the use of windmills, solar and wave power for electricity generation have been conducted.

The recurring problem of water shortages should eventually be ameliorated by the construction of the Baie Lazare water supply scheme, in the south of Mahé, by the Seychelles Water Authority. It is the authority's largest project and will supply 18,000 people in the Victoria area. Work was scheduled to start in early 1987, but encountered delays, resulting from negotiations over finance. A project to extend La Digue's water supply to 80% of the population, from the present level of 50%, began in September 1988. Funds for the scheme, which was estimated to cost SR 8m. are being provided by France and the USA.

Several small industries have been established, covering brewing, plastic goods, salt, coconut oil, cinnamon essence distilling, soft drinks, detergents, cigarettes, soap, boat building, furniture, printing and steel products. Others include animal feed, meat and fish processing, dairy products, paints, television assembly, and handicrafts for the tourist industry. The tuna-canning factory opened in 1987 is, to date, the major enterprise in the industrial sector (see above).

TRADE, FINANCE AND PLANNING

Seychelles traditionally sustains a substantial visible trade deficit. In 1986 the deficit was about SR 540m. but this was reduced to about SR 411m. in 1987, with exports augmented later in the year by the new tuna-canning factory. In 1988 the deficit increased to SR 685.3m. advancing in 1989 to SR 737m., as the result of an aircraft purchase. Despite the subsequent imposition of import controls, the deficit amounted to SR 660m. in 1991, SR 763m. in 1992 and a record SR 856m. in 1993. Seychelles' main suppliers of imports in 1991 were Bahrain (16.2% of total imports), the Southern African Customs Union (13%), Singapore (11.6%) and the United Kingdom (11.5%). Seychelles' principal export markets were the United Kingdom (18.9% of total exports), France (9%), and Réunion (4.7%). Following the election in 1994 of a democratically based government, increased trade (as well as investment) with South Africa can be expected in the near future. In 1993 Seychelles joined the Preferential Trade Area for Eastern and Southern Africa (PTA) and should benefit from the clearing house function which facilitates the use of member countries' currencies for regional transactions. This will reduce the pressure on foreign exchange resources, particularly from trade with Mauritius, another PTA member.

Seychelles' visible trade deficit is partly offset by earnings from tourism and by capital inflows in the form of aid and private investment, together with rental income from the US satellite tracking station (see Recent History). In 1992 the current account deficit stood at manageable SR 8.7m. Seychelles' total external debt was $181m. at the end of 1992. Debt-servicing costs rose from 1.2% of exports (goods and services) in 1982, to 6.9% in 1986, but fell slightly in 1987, to 6.5%, as a result of higher export earnings. In 1989 the cost of debt-servicing was equivalent to 11.9% of exports of goods and services. This figure fell to 7.3% in 1992. Foreign exchange reserves, which totalled a record $17.8m. in 1980, amounted to $13.6m. at the end of 1987. They dropped sharply again during 1988, to about $8.6m., but reached $16.5m. by the end of 1990. Seychelles' total external debt was $201.1m. at the end of 1991, of which $154m. was long-term public debt. Total external debt declined to $181m. in 1992.

Government spending increased dramatically following independence in 1976, as the new administration expanded its provision of social services and raised its levels of defence spending. British grant support ended in 1979. The government deficit increased from 13% of GDP in 1984 to 20% in 1986. In 1987 the government introduced an austerity budget, restricting public spending, and reduced the deficit to 3.8% of GDP. The deficit rose to nearly 10% of GDP in 1989, but fell to 4.4% and 6.5% of GDP in 1992 and 1993 respectively. The government introduced a 'transitional' budget in 1993, reflecting the political uncertainty of the new constitution. This new budget included the relaxation of import controls, which had been introduced in 1992. The 1994 budget proposed a five-year development strategy which includes the following proposals: increased private sector invovlement in the economy; increased employment; improved social welfare; reduced taxation and rate of inflation; and increased foreign exchange earnings. This budget projected a 6% overall reduction in recurrent expenditure in 1994, and aimed to transform the 1993 deficit of SR 150m. to a 1994 surplus of SR 62m.

Until recently, most aid came from the UK, but now Seychelles attracts aid from a wide variety of sources, including the World Bank, the EU and other Western European countries (particularly France), the ADB, BADEA, the USA, India, Canada, Arab countries and funds and the People's Republic of China. In 1993 Australia pledged SR 2.8m. for projects in Seychelles' plan for human resources development, and in the same year India provided loan finance of SR 8.5m. for the purchase of Indian-made buses and transport equipment.

The Seychelles rupee, previously tied to sterling, has been linked to the IMF Special Drawing Right (SDR) since November 1979. In March 1981 it was revalued by 15% as part of measures implemented to curb inflation. It has appreciated considerably since then, rising from about SR 7 = US $1 in 1984 to about SR 5.1 = US $1 in 1994, at which level it is widely considered to be overvalued. This has resulted in an increased intake of imports and a widening of the trade gap. Seychelles encountered foreign exchange difficulties during 1991–92, which were partly offset by intervention from the central bank. The foreign reserves position was further strained by the demands of Seychelles providing the venue for the Indian Ocean Games in 1993.

The government has been generally successful in controlling inflation. The annual rate of inflation averaged 3.3% in 1980–90, but rose to 3.9% in 1990, owing to a liberalization of farm prices and increases in imported oil prices. Government price controls brought the rate down to 1.9% in 1991, but consumer prices increased by 3.3% in 1992 and 4% in 1993. In 1994 the marketing board reduced the prices of 20 food items, and the charges for water and electricity were also lowered.

ECONOMIC PROSPECTS

Although the government has taken over a majority shareholding in certain key sectors, through the Seychelles National Investment Corpn set up in 1979, there has never been an overall nationalization policy. The Seychelles government is now actively encouraging foreign investment, both public and private, particularly in tourism, farming, fisheries and small-scale manufacturing, although joint ventures are preferred where foreign investors are concerned. Taxed profits can be freely repatriated.

After more than a decade of conservative economic public policies, the government agreed to a more liberal programme in 1990. In July 1993 President René created the National Economic Consultative Committee, with a membership including business leaders as well as members of the political opposition. The government also promised a range of incentives to try to encourage increased private sector investment in the economy. As many of the highly skilled Seychellois professional people (many of whom left the islands during the period of single-party rule) return to Seychelles, and as political openness translates into genuine economic reform, the republic may well be within reach of further rises in per caput incomes and an extended period of sustained economic growth.

Statistical Survey

Source (unless otherwise stated): Department of Information and Telecommunications, Union Vale, POB 321, Victoria; tel. 224220; telex 2320.

AREA AND POPULATION

Area: 454 sq km (175.3 sq miles), incl. Aldabra lagoon (145 sq km).

Population: 61,898 at census of 1 August 1977; 68,598 (males 34,125, females 34,473) at census of 17 August 1987.

Density (August 1987): 151.1 per sq km.

Principal Town: Victoria (capital), population 24,324 (incl. suburbs) at the 1987 census.

Births and Deaths (registered in 1991): Live births 1,708 (birth rate 25.0 per 1,000); Deaths 542 (death rate 7.9 per 1,000).

Expectation of Life (years at birth, 1981–85): Males 65.26; Females 74.05. Source: UN, *Demographic Yearbook*.

Economically Active Population: 1981–82 (persons aged 12 years and over): Employed 18,835 (males 12,228, females 6,607); Unemployed 9,527 (males 2,097, females 7,430); Total labour force 28,362. June 1989 (persons aged 15 years and over): Total labour force 29,494 (males 16,964, females 12,530).

Employment (1988): Agriculture, hunting, forestry and fishing 2,183; Manufacturing, electricity and water 2,457; Construction, mining and quarrying 1,368; Trade, restaurants and hotels 4,054; Transport, storage and communications 2,838; Financing, insurance, real estate and business services 709; Public administration 2,594; Other community, social and personal services 4,519; Activities not adequately defined 465; Total 21,187. Figures exclude self-employed persons, unpaid family workers and employees in private domestic services.

AGRICULTURE, ETC.

Principal Crops (metric tons, 1992): Coconuts 7,000*; Copra 1,000*; Bananas 2,000*; Tea (green leaf) 117†; Cinnamon bark (exports) 243‡. (*FAO estimate. †1985 figure. ‡1989 figure.) Source: mainly FAO, *Production Yearbook*.

Livestock (FAO estimates, '000 head, year ending September 1992): Cattle 2; Pigs 19; Goats 5. Source: FAO, *Production Yearbook*.

Fishing (metric tons, live weight): Total catch 4,403 in 1989; 5,370 in 1990; 5,913 in 1991. Source: FAO, *Yearbook of Fishery Statistics*.

MINING AND INDUSTRY

Mining (1986): Guano 5,000 metric tons (exports). Source: UN, *Industrial Statistics Yearbook*.

Industrial Production (1989): Soft drinks 4,378,000 litres; Beer and stout 5,243,000 litres; Cigarettes 58.0 million; Electric energy 94.3 million kWh.

FINANCE

Currency and Exchange Rates: 100 cents = 1 Seychelles rupee (SR). *Sterling and Dollar Equivalents* (31 March 1994): £1 sterling = 7.619 rupees; US $1 = 5.132 rupees; 1,000 Seychelles rupees = £131.26 = $194.26. *Average Exchange Rate* (Seychelles rupees per US $): 5.2893 in 1991; 5.1220 in 1992; 5.1815 in 1993. Note: Since November 1979 the value of the Seychelles rupee has been linked to the IMF's special drawing right (SDR). Since March 1981 the mid-point exchange rate has been SDR 1 = 7.2345 rupees.

Budget (SR million, 1989): *Revenue:* Taxation 770.8 (Taxes on income, etc. 145.1, Social security contributions 137.7, Import duties 436.9); Other current revenue 191.5; Capital revenue 0.8; Total 963.1, excl. grants received (26.4). *Expenditure:* Current 799.9 (Wages and salaries 230.2, Other purchases of goods and services 240.8, Interest payments 147.3, Subsidies 88.1, Other current transfers 93.5); Capital 177.6; Total 977.5, excl. net lending (131.8). Note: Figures represent the consolidated accounts of the central Government, covering the operations of the Recurrent and Capital Budgets and of the Social Security Fund. Source: IMF, *Government Finance Statistics Yearbook*.

International Reserves (US $ million at 31 December 1993): IMF special drawing rights 0.02; Reserve position in IMF 1.10; Foreign exchange 34.46; Total 35.58. Source: IMF, *International Financial Statistics*.

Money Supply (SR million at 31 December 1993): Currency outside banks 134.5; Demand deposits at commercial banks 200.7; Total money (incl. others) 335.8. Source: IMF, *International Financial Statistics*.

Cost of Living (Consumer Price Index; base: 1985 = 100): 112.8 in 1991; 116.4 in 1992; 117.9 in 1993. Source: IMF, *International Financial Statistics*.

Expenditure on the Gross Domestic Product (estimates, SR million at current prices, 1991): Government final consumption expenditure 472; Private final consumption expenditure 1,069; Gross capital formation 357; *Total domestic expenditure* 1,898; Exports of goods and services 876, *Less* Imports of goods and services 963; *GDP in purchasers' values* 1,812. Source: UN Economic Commission for African, *African Statistical Yearbook*.

Gross Domestic Product by Economic Activity (SR million at current prices, 1991): Agriculture, hunting, forestry and fishing 86; Mining and manufacturing 181; Electricity, gas and water 35; Construction 94; Trade, restaurants and hotels 195; Transport, storage and communications 301; Finance, insurance, real estate and business services 334; Government services 250; Other services 36; *GDP at factor cost* 1,511; Indirect taxes, *less* subsidies 301; *GDP in purchasers' values* 1,812. Source: UN Economic Commission for Africa, *African Statistical Yearbook*.

Balance of Payments (US $ million, 1992): Merchandise exports f.o.b. 19.6, Merchandise imports f.o.b. −162.9, *Trade balance* −143.3; Exports of services 247.0, Imports of services −112.6, Other income received 4.8, Other income paid −18.6, Private unrequited transfers (net) −2.8, Official unrequited transfers (net) 23.8, *Current balance* −1.7; Direct investment (net) 16.3, Other capital (net) −6.2, Net errors and omissions −4.7, Overall balance 3.9. Source: IMF, *International Financial Statistics*.

EXTERNAL TRADE

Principal Commodities (US $ '000, 1991): *Imports c.i.f.:* Food and live animals 29,206 (Dairy products and birds' eggs 3,784, Fish and fish preparations 5,325, Cereals and cereal preparations 7,769, Vegetables and fruit 5,239); Beverages and tobacco 3,795; Mineral fuels, lubricants, etc. 37,714 (Refined petroleum products 36,988); Chemicals and related products 10,417 (Essential oils, perfume materials and cleansing preparations 3,949); Basic manufactures 29,223 (Paper, paperboard, etc. 3,989, Iron and steel 3,562); Machinery and transport equipment 39,833 (Machinery specialized for particular industries 5,769, Telecommunications and sound equipment 7,283, Road vehicles 4,750); Miscellaneous manufactured articles 17,712; Total (incl. others) 172,474. *Exports f.o.b.:* Fish and fish preparations 15,806; Refined petroleum products 29,529; Machinery and transport equipment 1,952; Total (incl. others) 48,712. Source: UN, *International Trade Statistics Yearbook*.

Principal Trading Partners (US $ '000, 1991): *Imports c.i.f.:* Bahrain 27,927; France 15,184; Germany 5,479; Italy 4,256; Japan 9,050; Malaysia 6,938; Netherlands 3,484; Singapore 19,998; Southern African Customs Union* 22,343; Thailand 3,611; United Kingdom 19,875; USA 4,238; Total (incl. others) 172,458. *Exports f.o.b.:* France 4,379; Réunion 2,267; United Kingdom 9,207; Total (incl. others) 48,712. * Comprising Botswana, Lesotho, Namibia, South Africa, Swaziland. Source: UN, *International Trade Statistics Yearbook*.

TRANSPORT AND TOURISM

Road Traffic (motor vehicles in use, 1989): Passenger cars 4,072; Commercial vehicles 1,105; Buses 216; Motor cycles 102.

Shipping (sea-borne freight traffic, 1990): Vessels entered 953; Freight ('000 metric tons): Loaded 11.2; Unloaded 347.7.

Civil Aviation (international traffic, 1989): Aircraft movements 1,933; Passengers ('000): Arrivals 88; Departures 86; Freight (metric tons): Unloaded 1,582; Loaded 403.

Tourism: Visitors (1993) 116,180, Gross receipts (1993) SR 607m.

COMMUNICATIONS MEDIA

Radio Receivers (1991): 33,000 in use. Source: UNESCO, *Statistical Yearbook*.

Television Receivers (1991): 6,000 in use. Source: UNESCO, *Statistical Yearbook*.

Telephones (1988): 14,000 in use. Source: UN, *Statistical Yearbook*.

Book Production (1980): 33 titles (2 books, 31 pamphlets).

Daily Newspapers (1990): 1 (average circulation 3,000 copies). Source: UNESCO, *Statistical Yearbook*.

Non-daily Newspapers (1988): 4 (estimated average circulation 9,000 copies). Source: UNESCO, *Statistical Yearbook*.

EDUCATION

Pre-Primary (1991): 35 schools, 175 teachers, 3,257 pupils.

Primary (1989): 25 schools, 781 teachers, 14,669 pupils (1991).

Secondary: 328 teachers (1990), 4,495 pupils (1991).

- **General:** 157 teachers (1990), 2,891 pupils (1991).
- **Teacher training** (1991): 32 teachers, 302 pupils.
- **Vocational** (1991): 162 teachers, 1,302 pupils.

Special Education (1990): 1 school, 78 pupils.

Polytechnic (1991): 1,604 pupils.

Source (for education): mainly UNESCO, *Statistical Yearbook*.

Directory

The Constitution

The independence Constitution of 1976, was suspended after the coup in June 1977 but reintroduced in July with important modifications. A successor Constitution, which entered into force in March 1979 was superseded by a new Constitution, approved by national referendum on 18 June 1993.

The President is elected by popular vote simultaneously with elections for the National Assembly. The President fulfils the functions of Head of State and Commander-in-Chief of the armed forces and may hold office for a maximum period of three consecutive five-year terms. The Assembly consists of 33 seats, of which 22 are directly elected and 11 of which are allocated on a proportional basis. The Council of Ministers is appointed by the President and acts in an advisory capacity to him.

The Government

HEAD OF STATE

President: FRANCE ALBERT RENÉ (assumed power 5 June 1977; elected President 26 June 1979, re-elected 18 June 1984, 12 June 1989 and 23 July 1993).

COUNCIL OF MINISTERS
(September 1994)

President: FRANCE ALBERT RENÉ.

Minister of Finance, Information and Defence: JAMES MICHEL.

Minister of Administration and Manpower: JOSEPH BELMONT.

Minister of Foreign Affairs, Planning and the Environment: DANIELLE DE ST JORRE.

Minister of Industry: ESMÉ JUMEAU.

Minister of Local Government, Youth and Sports: SYLVETTE FRICHOT.

Minister of Health: RALPH ADAM.

Minister of Tourism and Transport: SIMONE TESTA.

Minister of Employment and Social Affairs: WILLIAM HERMINIE.

Minister of Education and Culture: PATRICK PILLAY.

Minister of Community Development: DOLOR ERNESTA.

Minister of Agriculture and Marine Resources: JACQUELIN DUGASSE.

MINISTRIES

Office of the President: State House, Victoria; tel. 224391.

Ministry of Administration and Manpower: National House, POB 56, Victoria; tel. 224041; telex 2333; fax 224936.

Ministry of Agriculture and Marine Resources: Independence House, POB 166, Victoria; tel. 225333; telex 2418; fax 225245.

Ministry of Community Development: Independence House, Independence Ave, POB 199, Victoria; tel. 224030; telex 2312.

Ministry of Culture and Sports: POB 321, Mont Fleuri; tel. 224161; telex 2320; fax 221006.

Ministry of Education: POB 48, Mont Fleuri; tel. 224777; telex 2365; fax 224859.

Ministry of Employment and Social Services: Unity House, POB 190, Victoria; tel. 222321; telex 2352; fax 221880.

Ministry of the Environment, Economic Planning and External Relations: POB 656, Mont Fleuri; tel. 224688; telex 2260; fax 224845.

Ministry of Finance and Information: Central Bank Bldg, POB 313, Victoria; tel. 225252; telex 2363; fax 225265.

Ministry of Health: POB 52, Botanical Gardens, Mahé; tel. 224400; telex 2302; fax 224792.

Ministry of Tourism and Transport: Independence House, Independence Ave, POB 92, Victoria; tel. 225333; telex 2275; fax 225158.

President and Legislature

PRESIDENT

Election, 23 July 1993

Candidate	Votes	% of total
FRANCE ALBERT RENÉ (SPPF)	25,627	59.5
JAMES MANCHAM (DP)	15,815	36.7
PHILIPPE BOULLÉ (United Opposition*)	1,631	3.8

* An electoral coalition comprising the Parti Seychellois, the Seychelles Christian Democrat Party, the National Alliance Party and the Seychelles National Movement.

NATIONAL ASSEMBLY

Speaker: FRANCIS MACGREGOR.

Election, 23 July 1993

Party	Number of votes	% of votes	Seats*
Seychelles People's Progressive Front	24,642	57.5	28
Democratic Party	14,062	32.8	4
United Opposition	4,163	9.7	1

* The Assembly consists of 33 seats, of which 22 seats are directly elected and 11 seats are allocated on a proportional basis to parties obtaining at least 9% of total votes cast.

Political Organizations

A ban on political activity by parties other than the Seychelles People's Progressive Front, which had operated since 1978, was suspended in December 1991, and formally terminated following the constitutional referendum held in June 1993.

Democratic Party (DP): POB 109, Victoria; tel. 224916; fax 224302; f. 1992; successor to the Seychelles Democratic Party (governing party 1970–77); Leader Sir JAMES MANCHAM.

National Alliance Party*: 210 Victoria House, POB 673, Victoria; tel. 225562; fax 225626; f. 1992; Leader PHILIPPE BOULLÉ.

Parti Seychellois/Parti Seselwa*: Victoria; Leader Rev. WAVEL RAMKALAWAN.

Seychelles Christian Democrat Party/Rassemblement du Peuple Seychellois pour la Démocratie*: Victoria; f. 1990; Leaders Dr MAXIME FERRARI, ANDRÉ UZICE.

Seychelles Liberal Party: Victoria; f. 1992; Leader OGILVY BERLOUIS.

Seychelles Movement for Democracy: f. 1992; Leader JACQUES HODOUL.

Seychelles National Movement*: Victoria; f. 1992; Leaders EDMOND CAMILLE, ROBERT FRICHOT.

Seychelles Nationalist Party: Victoria; f. 1992; Leader PHILIP REVERE.

Seychelles People's Progressive Front (SPPF): POB 91, Victoria; tel. 224030; telex 2226; fmrly the Seychelles People's United Party; renamed in 1978; sole legal party 1978–91; socialist; Sec.-Gen. FRANCE ALBERT RENÉ.

* Member of the United Opposition coalition that contested the July 1993 presidential and legislative elections.

Diplomatic Representation

EMBASSIES AND HIGH COMMISSIONS IN SEYCHELLES

China, People's Republic: POB 680, St Louis; tel. 266588; Ambassador: ZHANG DAXUN.

Cuba: Bel Eau; tel. 224094; telex 2354; Ambassador: (vacant).

France: Arpent Vert, POB 478, Victoria; tel. 224523; telex 2238; fax 248225; Ambassador: ROGER BOURDIL.

India: Le Chantier, Victoria; tel. 224489; telex 2349; fax 224810; High Commissioner: C. R. BALACHANDRA.

Netherlands: POB 372, Victoria; tel. 261200; telex 2344; fax 261221.

Russia: Le Niol, POB 632, Victoria; tel. 221590; telex 2392; fax 224653; Ambassador: SERGEI BORISOVICH KISSELEV.

South Africa: Victoria.

United Kingdom: Victoria House, POB 161, Victoria; tel. 225225; telex 2269; fax 225127; High Commissioner: E. JOHN SHARLAND.

USA: Victoria House, POB 251, Victoria; tel. 225256; fax 225189; Ambassador: CARL BURTON STOKES.

Judicial System

There are three Courts, the Court of Appeal, the Supreme Court and the Magistrates' Courts. The Court of Appeal hears appeals from the Supreme Court in both civil and criminal cases. The Supreme Court is also a Court of Appeal from the Magistrates' Courts as well as having jursidiction at first instance. There is also an industrial court and a rent tribunal.

Chief Justice: I. K. ABBAN.

President of the Court of Appeal: HARRY GOBURDHUN.

Justices of Appeal: C. DE L. D'ARIFAT, ANNEL SILUNGWE, EMMANUEL AYOOLA, LOUIS VENCHARD.

Puisne Judges: V. ALLEEAR, A. PERERA.

Religion

Almost all of the inhabitants are Christians, of whom more than 90% are Roman Catholics and about 8% Anglicans.

CHRISTIANITY

The Anglican Communion

The Church of the Province of the Indian Ocean comprises five dioceses: three in Madagascar, one in Mauritius and one in Seychelles.

Bishop of Seychelles (also Archbishop of the Province of the Indian Ocean): Most Rev. FRENCH KITCHENER CHANG-HIM, POB 44, Victoria; tel. 224242; fax 224296.

The Roman Catholic Church

Seychelles comprises a single diocese, directly responsible to the Holy See. At 31 December 1993 there were an estimated 65,645 adherents in the country, representing more than 90% of the total population.

Bishop of Port Victoria: (vacant), Bishop's House, Olivier Maradan St, POB 43, Victoria; tel. 322152; fax 324045.

The Press

L'Echo des Iles: POB 138, Victoria; fortnightly; French, Creole and English; Roman Catholic; Editor P. SYMPHORIEN; circ. 2,800.

The People: POB 91, Victoria; monthly; Creole, French and English; organ of the SPPF; circ. 1,000.

Regar: Victoria; political weekly.

The Seychelles Nation: Information, Culture and Sports Division, POB 321, Victoria; tel. 224161; telex 2320; fax 221006; Mon. to Sat.; govt publ.; English, French and Creole; Chief Editor RONNIE JUMEAU; circ. 3,500.

Seychelles Today: Seychelles Agence de Presse, Information Division, POB 321, Victoria; tel. 224161; telex 2322; fax 221006; monthly; circ. 4,000.

Seychelles Weekend Nation: Information, Culture and Sports Division, POB 321, Victoria; tel. 224161; telex 2322; fax 221006; Sat.; English, French and Creole; Chief Editor RONNIE JUMEAU; circ. 3,800.

Seychellois: POB 32, Victoria; f. 1928; publ. by Seychelles Farmers Assen; quarterly; circ. 1,800.

NEWS AGENCY

Seychelles Agence de Presse (SAP): Victoria Rd, POB 321, Victoria; tel. 224161; telex 2320; fax 226006.

Radio and Television

There were an estimated 33,000 radio receivers and 6,000 television receivers in use in 1991.

Seychelles Broadcasting Corporation (SBC): Hermitage, POB 321, Victoria; tel. 224161; telex 2315; fax 225641; f. 1983 as Radio-Television Seychelles; reorg. as independent corpn in 1992; programmes in Creole, English and French; Man. Dir IBRAHIM AFIF; Dir of Broadcasting BRYANT MARRIOTT.

RADIO

Far East Broadcasting Association (FEBA): POB 234, Mahé; tel. 224449; fax 225171; Christian programmes; Dir STEWART PEPPER.

SBC Radio: Union Vale, POB 321, Victoria; tel. 224161; telex 2315; fax 224515; f. 1941; programmes in Creole, English and French; Programme Man. (Radio) MARGUERITE HERMITTE.

TELEVISION

SBC TV: Hermitage, POB 321, Mahé; tel. 224161; telex 2315; fax 225641; f. 1983; programmes in Creole, English and French; Programme Man. (Television) JEAN-CLAUDE MATOMBE.

Finance

(cap. = capital; p.u. = paid-up; res = reserves; dep. =deposits; m. = million; brs = branches; amounts in Seychelles rupees)

BANKING

Central Bank

Central Bank of Seychelles (CBS): Independence Ave, POB 701, Victoria; tel. 225200; telex 2301; fax 224958; f. 1983; bank of issue; cap. p.u. 11m., dep. 117m. (Dec. 1991); Chair. ABOO AUMEERUDDY.

National Banks

Development Bank of Seychelles: Independence Ave, POB 217, Victoria; tel. 224471; telex 2348; fax 224274; f. 1978; 55% Govt-owned; cap. p.u. 40m., total assets 170m. (1993); Chair. ANTONIO LUCAS; Man. Dir GAFOOR YAKUB.

Seychelles International Mercantile Banking Corporation Ltd (Nouvobanq): Victoria House, State House Ave, POB 241, Victoria; tel. 225011; telex 2253; fax 224670; f. 1991; 78% Govt-owned, 22% by Standard Chartered Bank (UK); cap. and res 62.4m., dep. 318m. (Dec. 1993); Chair. NORMAN WEBER; Man. Dir AHMAD SAEED; 1 br.

Seychelles Savings Bank: Independence House, POB 531, Victoria; tel. 225251; telex 2416; fax 224713; Govt-owned; term deposits, savings and current accounts; cap. and res 7.8m. (Dec. 1992); Man. Dir ROGER TOUSSAINT; 4 brs.

Foreign Banks

Bank of Baroda (India): Albert St, POB 124, Victoria; tel. 323038; telex 2241; fax 324057; f. 1978; Sr Man. A. K. ARORA.

Banque Française Commerciale–Océan Indien (France): POB 122, Victoria; tel. 323096; telex 2261; fax 322676; f. 1978; Gen. Man. LE QUANG DAM; 3 brs.

Barclays Bank (United Kingdom): Independence Ave, POB 167, Victoria; tel. 224101; telex 2225; fax 224678; f. 1959; Man. M. P. LANDON; 7 brs and 3 agencies.

Habib Bank Ltd (Pakistan): Frances Rachel St, POB 702, Victoria; tel. 224371; telex 2242; fax 225614; f. 1976; Man. JAVED IQBAL SHEIKH.

INSURANCE

State Assurance Corporation of Seychelles (SACOS): Pirate's Arms Bldg, POB 636, Victoria; tel. 225000; telex 2331; fax 224495; f. 1980; all classes of insurance; Exec. Chair. ANTONIO LUCAS.

STOCK EXCHANGE

A Stock Exchange was to be established in Victoria in late 1994.

Trade and Industry

CHAMBER OF COMMERCE

Seychelles Chamber of Commerce and Industry: 38 Premier Bldg, POB 443, Victoria; tel. 223812.

MARKETING ORGANIZATIONS

Seychelles Agricultural Development Co Ltd (SADECO): POB 172, Victoria; tel. 276618; f. 1980; Gen. Man. LESLIE PRÉA (acting).

Seychelles Industrial Development Corporation: POB 537, Victoria; tel. 224941; telex 2415; fax 225121.

Seychelles Marketing Board (SMB): Oceangate House, POB 516, Victoria; tel. 224444; telex 2368; f. 1984; state trading org. for food production and processing, fisheries development and toiletries; transfer to private sector of agro-industries subsidiaries announced in 1992; Chair. FRANCE ALBERT RENÉ; Man. JACQUES GARCIN.

Seychelles Timber Co (SEYTIM): Grand Anse, Mahé; tel. 278343; telex 2368; logging, timber sales, joinery and furniture; operates sawmill at Grande Anse.

TRADE UNION

National Workers' Union: Maison du Peuple, Latanier Rd, POB 154, Victoria; tel. 224030; f. 1978 to amalgamate all existing trade unions; 25,200 mems; Chair. OLIVIER CHARLES; Sec. MICHAEL A. MEMEE.

Transport

RAILWAYS

There are no railways in Seychelles.

ROADS

In 1988 there were 269 km of roads, of which 187 km were tarmac roads. On Mahé there are 138 km of tarmac roads, and 43 km of earth roads. Praslin has about 24 km of tarmac roads and 28 km of earth roads. La Digue has 5 km of surfaced and 11 km of unsurfaced roads.

SHIPPING

Ferry and private licensed schooner services connect Victoria and the islands of Praslin and La Digue.

Port and Marine Services Division, Ministry of Tourism and Transport: POB 47, Victoria; tel. 224701; fax 224004.

Allied Agency: Victoria; shipping agents.

Hunt, Deltel and Co Ltd: Victoria House, POB 14, Victoria; tel. 223353; telex 2249; fax 225367.

Mahé Shipping Co Ltd: Shipping House, POB 336, Victoria; tel. 322100; telex 2216; fax 322978; agents for Royal Fleet Auxiliary, US Navy, P & O, Nedlloyd Lines and numerous other shipping cos; Chair. Capt. G. C. C. ADAM.

Harry Savy & Co.: Victoria; shipping agents.

Seychelles Shipping Line: Victoria; f. 1994 to operate a freight service between Seychelles and Durban, South Africa; 90% owned by Tern Shipping Co of South Africa, 10% by Seychelles Govt; Man. Dir TED KEELEY.

The Union Lighterage Co Ltd: POB 38, Victoria; tel. 224624; telex 2425; fax 224734; f. 1929; undergoing reorg. in 1994; stevedoring, shipping, clearing and forwarding agents; Man. Dir GUY D'UNIENVILLE.

CIVIL AVIATION

Air Seychelles: Victoria House, POB 386, Victoria; tel. 225300; telex 2289; fax 225159; f. 1979; operates scheduled internal flights from Mahé to Praslin and charter services to Frégate, Bird, Desroches and Denis Islands; international services to Europe and South Africa; CEO CONRAD BENOITON.

Tourism

Seychelles enjoys an equable climate, and is renowned for its fine beaches and attractive scenery. There are more than 500 varieties of flora and many rare species of birds. Most tourist activity is concentrated on Mahé, Praslin and La Digue. It is government policy that the development of tourism should not blight the environment, and strict laws govern the construction of hotels. At the end of 1990 there were some 3,500 hotel beds. Receipts from tourism totalled an estimated SR 607m. in 1993, when there were an estimated 116,180 tourist and business arrivals; most visitors (about 81% in 1993) are from Western Europe.

Compagnie Seychelloise de Promotion Hotelière Ltd: POB 683, Victoria; tel. 224694; telex 2407; fax 225291; promotes govt-owned hotels.

Seychelles Tourist Board: Independence House, POB 92, Victoria; tel. 225333; telex 2275; parastatal body; Dir-Gen. MONICA CHETTY.

Defence

In June 1993, the army numbered 1,100 men. Paramilitary forces comprised a 1,000-strong national guard and a coastguard of about 300.

Defence Expenditure: Estimated at SR 78m. in 1993.

Commander-in-Chief of Seychelles Armed Forces: Col LEOPOLD PAYET.

Education

In 1979 free and compulsory primary education was introduced for children between six and 15 years of age, and in 1980 the government initiated a programme of educational reform, based on the British comprehensive system. There were 14,669 children receiving primary education and 4,495 pupils attending secondary schools in 1991. In that year a two-year National Youth Training Scheme, which catered for the secondary education of most children between 15 and 17 years of age, was to be reduced to 12 months. In addition, there is a special education school, with 78 pupils in 1990, and a polytechnic, with 1,604 students in 1991. Several students study abroad, principally in the United Kingdom. In 1990 the average rate of adult illiteracy was estimated at 15%. Of total government expenditure in 1990, SR 153m. (11.9%) was for education.

Bibliography

Barclays Bank International. *Seychelles: Economic Survey.* London, William Lea, 1972.

Beamish, A. *Aldabra Alone.* London, 1970.

Belling, L. N. *Seychelles: Islands of Love.* Boulogne, Editions Delroise, 1971.

Benedict, B. *People of the Seychelles.* London, HMSO, 1966.

Benedict, M., and Benedict, B. *Men, Women and Money in Seychelles.* University of California Press, 1982.

Bradley, J. T. *History of Seychelles.* Victoria, Clarion Press, 1940.

Central Bank of Seychelles. *Quarterly Review.* Victoria, Central Bank of Seychelles.

Cohen, R. (Ed.) *African Islands and Enclaves.* London, Sage Publications, 1983.

Franda, M. *Quiet Turbulence in the Seychelles: Tourism and Development.* Hanover, NH, American Field Staff Reports, Asia Series No. 10, 1979.

The Seychelles. Boulder, CO, Westview Press, 1981.

International Monetary Fund. *Seychelles: Recent Economic Developments.* Washington, DC, IMF, 1983.

Lee, C. *Seychelles: Political Castaways.* London, Hamish Hamilton, 1976.

Leymarie, P. *Océan indien, nouveau coeur du monde.* Paris, Editions Karthala, 1983.

Lionnet, G. *The Seychelles.* Newton Abbot, David and Charles, 1972.

Mancham, Sir J. R. *Paradise Raped: Life, Love and Power in the Seychelles.* London, Methuen, 1983.

Island Splendour. London, Methuen, 1984.

Maubouche, R., and Hadjitarkhani, N. *Seychelles Economic Memorandum.* Washington, DC, World Bank, 1980.

Republic of Seychelles, Statistical Division. *Statistical Abstract 1983.* Mahé, Department of Finance and Industry, 1984.

Rowe, J. W. F. *Report on the Economy of the Seychelles and its Future Development.* Mahé, Government Printer, 1959.

Thomas, A. *Forgotten Eden.* London, Longman, 1968.

Toussaint, A. *History of the Indian Ocean.* London, Routledge and Kegan Paul, 1966.

Waugh, A. *Where the Clock Strikes Twice.* New York, Farrar, Strauss and Young, 1951.

Webb, A. W. T. *Story of Seychelles.* Seychelles, 1964.

World Bank. *Seychelles' Economic Memorandum.* Washington, DC, World Bank, 1980.

SIERRA LEONE

Physical and Social Geography

PETER K. MITCHELL

The Republic of Sierra Leone, which covers an area of 71,740 sq km (27,699 sq miles), rises from the beaches of the south-west to the broad plateaux of the Atlantic/Niger watershed at the north-eastern frontier. Despite the general horizontal aspect of the landscapes, developed over millennia upon largely Pre-Cambrian structures there are a number of abrupt ascents to older uplifted erosion surfaces—most impressively along sections of a major escarpment, 130 km inland, separating a western lowland zone (c. 120 m above sea-level) from the country's more elevated interior half (c. 500 m). Incised valleys, interspersed by minor waterfalls, carry drainage south-westwards; only locally or along a coastal sedimentary strip do rivers flow through open terrain.

A geologically recent submergence of major floodplains, particularly north of Cape St Ann, has brought tide-water into contact with the rocky margins of the ancient shield, barring the way to up-river navigation. Water-borne trade has found compensation in sheltered deep-water anchorages, notably off Freetown, the principal port and capital, where a line of coastal summits rising to almost 900 m above sea-level facilitates an easy landfall.

Intrusive gabbros form the peninsular range; elsewhere, isolated blocks or hill groups consist of rock-bare granites, the metamorphic roots of long-vanished mountain chains, are the source of a number of mineral deposits: iron, chromite, gold, rutile and bauxite. Reserves of kimberlite in the southern high plateaux are approaching exhaustion. The pipes and dikes of kimberlite may provide the basis for future deep mining.

Differences in seasonal and regional incidence of humidity and rainfall are important. Prolonged rains (May to October, with heaviest rains from July to September) are bracketed by showery weather with many squally thunderstorms, such spells beginning earlier in the south-east. Consequently, the growing season is longest here (although total rainfall—over 5,000 mm locally—is greater along the coast) and the 'natural' vegetation is tropical evergreen forest; the cultivation of cash crops such as cocoa, coffee, kola and oil-palm is successful in this area, and the more productive timber areas, though limited, are concentrated here. The savannah-woodlands of the north-east have less rain (1,900–2,500 mm), a shorter period for plant growth and a dry season made harsh by harmattan winds, with cattle-rearing, groundnuts and tobacco as potential commercial resources. Semi-deciduous forest occupies most intervening areas, but long peasant occupation has created a mosaic of short-term cropland, fallow regrowth plots and occasional tracts of secondary forest.

Permanent rice-lands have been created from mangrove swamp in the north-west, and much encouragement is being given to the improvement of the many small tracts of inland valley swamp throughout the east. Such innovation contrasts with a widespread bush-fallowing technique, giving low yields of rain-fed staples, normally rice, but cassava (especially on degraded sandy soils) and millet in the north. Extensive farming still provides most of the nation's food.

Sierra Leone's third national census, which was held in December 1985, enumerated 3,515,812 inhabitants, representing a population density of 49 inhabitants per sq km. However, there was believed to have been underenumeration, and the census total was subsequently adjusted to 3.7m. At mid-1992, according to UN estimates, Sierra Leone had 4,376,000 inhabitants and a population density of 61.0 inhabitants per sq km.

Traditional *mores* still dominate, in spite of the Westernizing influences of employment in mining, of education and of growing urbanization. A large proportion of the population follows animist beliefs, although there are significant Islamic and Christian communities. Extended family, exogamous kin-groups and the paramount chieftaincies form a social nexus closely mirrored by a hierarchy of hamlet, village and rural centre: 29,000 non-urban settlements including isolated impermanent homesteads. The towns, however, are expanding. Greater Freetown had almost 470,000 inhabitants at the 1985 census, while Koidu, the centre of the Kono diamond fields, has about 80,000 inhabitants; there are, in total, 10 towns with over 10,000 people. Diamond mining has attracted settlers to many villages in the mining areas.

The official and commercial language of the country is English, while Krio (Creole), Mende, Limba and Temne are also spoken.

Recent History

CHRISTOPHER CLAPHAM

Revised for this edition by the Editor

In 1896 a British protectorate was proclaimed over the hinterland of the coastal colony of Sierra Leone, which had been under British administration since 1787. The Sierra Leone colony and its capital, Freetown, continued to be administered separately from the protectorate. Its inhabitants, known as creoles, were descendants of former slaves who had been liberated and settled in the colony. Holding the status of British subjects, they comprised a large well-educated élite; by the late 19th century some creoles occupied senior posts in government service. In the 20th century, however, the British empire became increasingly stratified on a racial basis, and creoles were relegated to subordinate posts.

A change of policy was adopted in the aftermath of the Second World War; the colour bar was removed from government service, and in 1951 a unitary constitution was introduced, which provided for universal adult suffrage. Elections were won by the Sierra Leone People's Party (SLPP), led by Dr (later Sir) Milton Margai, who became chief minister in 1953 and prime minister in 1958.

Sierra Leone became an independent state, within the Commonwealth, on 27 April 1961, with Margai remaining as prime minister. The SLPP retained power in elections in May 1962. Sir Milton died in April 1964 and was succeeded as prime minister by his half-brother, Dr (later Sir) Albert Margai, previously minister of finance. The main opposition party, the All-People's Congress (APC), led by Dr Siaka Stevens, gained a majority of seats in the house of representatives in the general election of March 1967, but was prevented from taking power by a military coup. Following an army mutiny in April 1968, however, a civilian government was restored, with Dr Stevens as prime minister. A period of political instability followed, culminating in an attempted military coup in March 1971, which was suppressed with the aid of troops from neighbouring Guinea. In April Sierra Leone was declared a republic, with Dr Stevens as president and head of government.

The 1972 by-elections and May 1973 general elections were not contested by the opposition SLPP, and subsequently no official opposition was represented in parliament. Dr Stevens, the sole candidate, was re-elected to the presidency for a second five-year term of office in March 1976.

The economy deteriorated during the second half of the 1970s, as income from mineral resources, the main source of government revenue, declined. Following further political unrest, a general election was held in May 1977, a year earlier than scheduled, at which the SLPP secured 15 of the 85 elective seats in the legislature. In June 1978, however, a new constitution, which provided for a one-party system, was approved by a referendum, and subsequently adopted by the house of representatives. The APC thus became the sole legal party. President Stevens was sworn in for a seven-year term on 14 June. The SLPP members of parliament joined the APC, and several were allocated ministerial posts.

The government encountered increasing opposition in 1981, following a scandal involving government officials and several cabinet ministers in the misappropriation of public funds. In August a state of emergency was declared, in an attempt to suppress a general strike, which had been staged in protest against rising prices and food shortages. President Stevens temporarily assumed the additional post of minister of finance in December, following a second financial scandal implicating senior civil servants. Amid serious outbreaks of violence, a general election took place in May 1982, under the one-party constitution. A new government was subsequently formed, in which the finance ministry was reorganized and efforts were made to control foreign exchange. In May 1983 violence between political factions in Pujehun district resulted in heavy casualties. In January 1984 student demonstrations in protest against food shortages and rising prices led to riots, in which four people were killed. Strikes by teachers and council workers took place in late 1984 and early 1985, following the government's failure to pay salaries. Further demonstrations by students took place in early 1985.

THE MOMOH PRESIDENCY

In April 1985 President Stevens announced that he was to retire upon the expiry of his existing mandate later that year. At a conference of the APC in August, Maj.-Gen. Joseph Saidu Momoh, a cabinet minister and the commander of the armed forces, was nominated as sole candidate for the presidency and for the leadership of the party. In October Momoh received 99% of votes cast in a national presidential election, and was inaugurated as president on 28 November. Although retaining his military status, President Momoh appointed a civilian cabinet, which included several members of the previous administration. As an indication of his resolve to limit public expenditure, Momoh reduced the number of cabinet members from 29 to 19, while the total number of government ministers was reduced from 51 to 33. Elections to the house of representatives took place in May 1986; 335 candidates (all APC members) contested the 105 elective seats. About half of the incumbent representatives, including four cabinet ministers, were replaced. Momoh subsequently appointed a new cabinet, with five new members and seven additional ministers of state. In December he released 27 political prisoners, including 12 who had been convicted of treason for their involvement in the 1974 coup attempt.

Momoh's initial popularity declined in 1986, owing to his administration's failure to improve the serious economic situation, and to the inflationary effects of IMF-sponsored austerity measures; the retention of cabinet ministers from the Stevens government also attracted criticism. In January 1987 demonstrations by students in protest against inadequate food allowances resulted in violent clashes. In March the government announced that it had foiled an attempted coup; more than 60 people were arrested (of whom 18 were later charged), and a large quantity of military equipment was discovered. In early April the first vice-president, Francis Minah, was arrested and subsequently charged with treason. In an ensuing government reshuffle, a new minister of finance was appointed, and a ministry concerned with rural development and social services was created. In October, following a five-month trial, Minah and 15 others were sentenced to death for plotting to assassinate Momoh and to overthrow the government. Minah and five others were executed in October 1989; the remaining death sentences were commuted to life imprisonment.

In 1987 Momoh initiated a drive against financial corruption in the public sector. In July 1987 the minister of agriculture, natural resources and forestry resigned, after allegations of accountancy irregularities in the distribution of domestic sugar supplies, and was later ordered by Momoh to make financial restitution. In August and September a deputy minister and a number of senior officials in the civil service and the Bank of Sierra Leone were charged with financial malpractice. In November, following a series of strikes by workers in the public sector, which were provoked by the government's inability to pay salaries, owing to a shortage of currency, Momoh declared a state of emergency in the economy and announced 59 measures, which aimed to prevent hoarding of currency and essential goods, and continued the campaign against smuggling. Under the new measures, corruption was redefined as a criminal offence, and people accused of any crime could be tried *in absentia*. Severe penalties were introduced for the publication of 'defamatory' articles in newspapers; private mail could be inspected and government censorship was imposed. The deputy minister of development and economic planning resigned in January 1988; he and five other people were later charged with fraud. In November a number of ministers were removed in a cabinet reshuffle, which was apparently conducted in response to accusations of official corruption. The two vice-presidents lost their ministerial portfolios and their posts became purely ceremonial. A new ministry of industry and state enterprises was also established. At a conference of the APC in January 1989, during which an official code of conduct for political leaders and public servants was adopted, Momoh was re-elected, unopposed, as secretary-general of the party.

In August 1989 legislation was adopted requiring public servants who aimed to participate in forthcoming legislative elections (scheduled to be held in 1991), to leave their employment no later than May 1990. In December 1989 a new minister of finance was appointed, after allegations of irregular conduct at the finance ministry. The registration of voters for provincial elections took place in early 1990, but was suspended in three constituencies, following complaints of alleged irregularities. During early 1990 there was widespread popular support for the establishment of a multi-party system; in June, however, Momoh rejected the adoption of a multi-party democracy, although he emphasized that he would continue to encourage broadly-based participation in the one-party state.

In mid-August 1990, contrary to previous indications, Momoh conceded the necessity of electoral reforms, and announced an extensive review of the constitution. The central committee of the APC adopted a number of constitutional amendments, which relaxed restrictions on prospective electoral candidates in public service. It was also proposed that the number of vice-presidents be reduced from two to one, and that a deputy leader of the APC be elected, who would also stand as the vice-presidential candidate in presidential elections. In November Momoh appointed a 30-member national constitutional review commission. In late 1990 a further constitutional amendment, which reduced the minimum voting age from 21 to 18 years, was adopted.

In March 1991 the commission submitted a draft constitution, which provided for the establishment of a multi-party system. The revised constitution stipulated that the president was to be elected by a majority of votes cast nationally and by at least 25% of the votes cast in more than one-half of the electoral districts. The maximum duration of the president's tenure of office was to be limited to two five-year terms. The president was to appoint the cabinet, which was to include one vice-president, rather than two. Legislative power was to be vested in a bicameral legislature, elected by universal adult suffrage for a term of five years. The government subsequently accepted the majority of the commission's recommendations. The proposed formation of an upper legislative chamber was, however, rejected; instead, the government approved the establishment of a 22-member state advisory council, which was to comprise 12 paramount chiefs (one from each district) and 10 members appointed by the president. In early June the government presented the draft constitution to the house of representatives, and announced that the parliamentary term, which was due to end that month, was to be extended for a further year, owing to the disruption caused by the conflict between government forces and Liberian rebels in the south of the country. In addition, the general elections, which were scheduled for May, were to be postponed for a year to allow time for the transition to a multi-party system.

In mid-July 1991 the minister of social affairs, rural development and youth, Musa Kabia, resigned, following disputes within the APC over the new constitution. Ten members of the house of representatives, including Kabia, were later suspended from the APC for alleged activities contrary to the interests of the party (but were reinstated in September). On 3 August the house of representatives approved the new constitution, subject to endorsement by a national referendum, which was to be conducted at the end of August. However, political activity on the part of associations other than the APC remained illegal until the formal adoption of the new constitution. (Following the publication of the constitution in March, some 10 opposition movements had emerged.) At the national referendum, which was conducted between 23 and 30 August, the new constitution was approved by 60% of voters, with 75% of the electorate participating. On 3 September the government formally adopted the new constitution (although the constitution of 1978 also remained officially in force).

Later in September 1991 six newly-created political associations formed an alliance, known as the United Front of Political Movements (UNIFOM), which subsequently demanded that the government be dissolved and an interim administration established. In the same month the government announced that the minister of national development and economic planning, Sheka Kanu, had been removed from office. Shortly afterwards the first vice-president, Abubakar Kamara, and the second vice-president, Salia Jusu-Sheriff, resigned from both the APC and the government. On 23 September Momoh announced the formation of a new 18-member cabinet, which retained only seven members of the previous government. In late September legislation was introduced, which permitted the formation of political associations; a number of political parties, including the APC, were subsequently granted legal recognition. In December, following discussions between Momoh and leaders of the registered political parties, the opposition leaders pledged to co-operate in the establishment of a multi-party system. In March 1992 Hassan Gbassay Kanu, who had resigned from the APC and formed the Democratic People's Party (DPP), declared his support of Momoh's policies and announced that the DPP was to be merged with the APC.

MILITARY RULE

On 29 April 1992 members of the armed forces who had met Momoh to demand that arrears in salary be paid and that conditions in the armed forces be improved, seized a radio station in Freetown and occupied the presidential offices. The leader of a five-member military junta, Capt. Valentine E. M. Strasser, subsequently announced that the government had been overthrown. Shortly afterwards Momoh appealed for assistance to the Guinean government, which dispatched troops to Freetown to guard him. Some 112 people were killed during the coup, and incidents of violence and looting were reported. On 30 April Momoh fled to Guinea, and Strasser announced the establishment of a national provisional ruling council (NPRC). Strasser affirmed the NPRC's commitment to the introduction of a multi-party system, pledged to end the conflict in the country and assured the Economic Community of West African States (ECOWAS) of its continued participation in the ECOWAS Monitoring Group (ECOMOG), which had been engaged since August 1990 in peace-keeping operations in Liberia (see below). On the same day the constitutions of 1991 and 1978 were suspended, the house of representatives was dissolved, a state of emergency, which included a 12-hour curfew, was imposed, and the country's air, sea and land borders were closed. A demonstration by some 700 students in support of the coup subsequently took place. On 1 May the NRPC (which comprised 18 military officers and four civilians) was formally convened under Strasser's chairmanship. On 3 May the NPRC announced the appointment of a new 19-member cabinet, which retained two members of the former government. The commander of the armed forces and the head of the security forces were also replaced. On the same day the NPRC reopened the country's borders. On 4 May a proclamation was issued, which retroactively provided for the establishment of the NPRC, which was to comprise a maximum of 30 members, including a chairman and a vice-chairman, the dissolution of the house of representatives and the suspension of all political activity. It was subsequently reported that some 55 people, including members of the former cabinet, had been arrested. On 6 May Strasser was sworn in as head of state. Later that month the government established a commission of inquiry to investigate the activities of former members of the APC government.

In June 1992 security forces arrested three British nationals, who were accused of complicity in a coup plot, following their arrival in Freetown with the stated intention of warning the authorities of a conspiracy to overthrow the NPRC by a political organization based in France. In early July Strasser carried out a cabinet reshuffle, in which three members of the armed forces were replaced by civilians, and announced that civilian cabinet ministers were no longer to be members of the NPRC. Later that month Strasser introduced extensive measures which were designed to reduce the role of the armed forces in government administration: the NPRC was to be reconstituted as the supreme council of state (SCS), and the cabinet was to be replaced by a council of secretaries, headed by a chief secretary of state, which was to be responsible for the management of the government, subject to the authority of the SCS. The chairman and deputy chairman of the SCS were no longer to be involved in government administration (although Strasser retained his defence portfolio in the council of secretaries). Each secretary of state was to assume responsibility for a ministry (henceforth known as a department). The three members of the SCS who had been removed from the cabinet earlier that month were appointed as principal liaison officers, who were each allocated a number of departments in which they were to supervise government administration. (However, the SCS was henceforth principally concerned with the suppression of the civil conflict.) In the same month the government introduced legislation which imposed severe restrictions on the media and authorized state censorship. John Benjamin, hitherto the secretary of state in the office of the chairman, became chief secretary of state.

In August 1992 Strasser announced the establishment of an advisory council, which, among other functions, was to review the provisions of the 1991 constitution. In early September Capt. Solomon Musa, the deputy chairman of the SCS, assumed the responsibilities of acting head of state during Strasser's visit to the United Kingdom to obtain medical treatment for injuries sustained during counter-insurgency operations in the south-east of the country (see below). In the same month the secretary of state for information, broadcasting and culture was replaced. In early October a minor reshuffle of the council of secretaries took place. In November about 30 people, who were alleged to be supporters of Momoh, were arrested and charged with involvement in subversive activities. In early December Strasser again reshuffled the council of secretaries, replacing the two remaining members of the Momoh administration, the secretaries of state for foreign affairs and for finance, development and economic planning. In the same month Musa was appointed chief secretary of state. Later in December, in an apparent attempt to regain public support, the government established a 15-member advisory council, which was to formulate a programme for transition to civilian rule.

In late December 1992 the government announced that it had foiled a coup attempt by a group known as the Anti-Corruption Revolutionary Movement (which included former members of the army and security forces). Among those reportedly killed by security forces was the alleged instigator of the plot, Sgt Lamin Bangura. Shortly afterwards, nine of those accused of involvement in the attempted coup were tried by a military tribunal, and, together with 17 prisoners who had been convicted in November on charges of treason, were summarily executed. Human rights organizations subsequently challenged the government's assertion that a coup attempt had taken place. In January 1993 the United Kingdom announced the suspension of economic aid to Sierra Leone, in protest at the executions; however, a number of demonstrations in support of the NPRC subsequently took place. Later that month, in an apparent attempt to allay further criticism of its human rights record, the government released several former members of the Momoh administration, who had been detained since May 1992. In mid-January 1993, however, the government imposed further press restrictions: all newspapers were required to reapply for registration, which was subject to the fulfilment of certain criteria regarding finance and personnel.

In February 1993 the commissions of inquiry that had been established in May 1992 published reports containing evidence of corruption on the part of former members of the Momoh administration. In March 1993 the European Parliament adopted a resolution demanding that the government submit records of the trials of those executed in December 1992, remove press restrictions, release prisoners detained without trial, and initiate a programme for the transition to civilian rule. In April 1993 Strasser promised that all political prisoners would be released and announced that a programme providing for a transition to civilian rule by 1996 had been adopted. He also stated that measures were being taken to reduce the powers of the security services. In a government reorganization in July 1993, Musa was replaced as deputy chairman of the NPRC and chief secretary of state by Capt. Julius Maada Bio, ostensibly on the grounds that false allegations against him had proved detrimental to the stability of the administration. Musa (who was widely believed to be responsible for the repressive measures undertaken by the government) took refuge in the Nigerian high commission in Freetown, amid widespread speculation regarding his dismissal, and subsequently emigrated to the United Kingdom. Also in July a number of political prisoners were released. In August, however, Amesty International accused the government of detaining more than 170 civilians, including a number of children, on suspicion of involvement with the alleged coup conspiracy of December 1992. In September 1993 the government expropriated the assets of several former politicians, including Momoh, following reports from the commissions of inquiry that had investigated their activities. In October a former minister in the Stevens administration, Dr Abbas Bundu, was appointed secretary of state for foreign affairs and international co-operation. In November the government claimed to have pre-empted a coup attempt, after four British citizens of Vietnamese origin, alleged to be mercenaries, were arrested in Freetown. (In January 1994 the four detainees, who were accused of conspiring with Musa and other disaffected Sierra Leonean nationals to overthrow the government, were placed on trial on charges of treason.) Also in November five journalists were arrested and charged with libel, after a newspaper published allegations of corruption regarding members of the NPRC.

At the end of November 1993 Strasser announced the details of a two-year transitional programme, which provided for the installation of a civilian government by January 1996: the national advisory council was to promulgate constitutional proposals in December 1993, and, in conjunction with a committee of legal experts, was to produce a draft constitution by June 1994, which was to be submitted for approval in a national referendum in May 1995; a national commission for democracy was to be established to instruct the population about the new constitution; district council elections (which were to be contested by candidates without political affiliations) were scheduled for November 1994; the registration of political parties was to take place in June 1995, prior to a presidential election in November and legislative elections in December of that year. In December, in accordance with the transitional programme, a five-member interim national electoral commission, chaired by Dr James Jonah (the assistant secretary-general of the UN, in charge of political affairs), was established to organize the registration of voters and the demarcation of constituency boundaries, in preparation for the forthcoming local government elections. In the same month the national advisory council submitted several constitutional proposals (which included a number of similar provisions to the 1991 constitution), stipulating that: executive power was to be vested in the president, who was to be required to consult with the cabinet (except in the event of a national emergency), and was to be restricted to a tenure of two four-year terms of office; only Sierra Leonean nationals of more than 40 years of age were to qualify to contest a presidential election (thereby precluding Strasser and the majority of NPRC members, on the grounds of age); the president was to be elected by a minimum of 50% of votes cast nationally, and at least by 25% of the votes cast in each of the four provinces; the legislature was to comprise a house of representatives, which was to be elected by universal adult suffrage for a term of five years, and a 30-member upper chamber, the senate, which was to include a number of regional representatives and five presidential nominees; members of the house of representatives were not to be permitted concurrently to hold ministerial portfolios.

At the end of December 1993 the government ended the state of emergency that had been in force since April 1992 (although additional security measures remained in force). In March 1994 the authorities introduced further legislation regulating the registration of newspapers, which effectively prevented a number of independent publications from renewing their licence. In the same month the German ambassador to Sierra Leone was expelled from the country, after meeting the Liberian rebel leader, Charles Taylor (see Regional Concerns). In April 13 senior members of the armed forces were dismissed, following criticism of the government's failure to end the civil conflict, and rumours of complicity between military officers and the rebels. In May 20 former members of the Momoh administration were arrested, after failing to pay compensation for funds that they had misappropriated during their service. In early August Strasser reorganized the council of secretaries (which subsequently included nine civilians). In a further reshuffle in September, the three regional secretaries of state were replaced.

REGIONAL CONCERNS

Sierra Leone is a member of the OAU, ECOWAS and the Mano River Union. Relations between Sierra Leone and Liberia became strained in November 1985, after the Liberian head of state, Samuel Doe, accused the Sierra Leonean government of involvement in an attempted coup in Liberia, and closed the border between the two countries. However, the frontier between the two countries was reopened in August 1986, and in the following month Sierra Leone, Guinea and Liberia signed an agreement of non-aggression and security co-operation. In September 1988 a 'reconciliation summit' between the heads of state of Sierra Leone, Liberia, Nigeria and Togo took place, and the four leaders issued a declaration reaffirming their commitment to the objectives of ECOWAS.

Following the outbreak of civil conflict in Liberia in December 1989 (see Recent History of Liberia), an estimated 125,000 Liberians took refuge in Sierra Leone. Some 500 Sierra Leonean troops joined ECOMOG, which was dispatched to Liberia in August 1990. In November 1990 Charles Taylor, the leader of the principal Liberian faction, the National Patriotic Front of Liberia (NPFL), threatened to attack Freetown national airport, which was used as a base for ECOMOG offensives against rebel strongholds. In March 1991 repeated border incursions by Liberian rebels, reported to be members of the NPFL, resulted in the deaths of several Sierra Leoneans. The Sierra Leonean government subsequently deployed 2,150 troops on the Liberian border, and, in early April, launched a retaliatory attack against rebel bases in Liberian territory. The government alleged that the rebel offensive had been instigated by Charles Taylor, in an attempt to force Sierra Leone's withdrawal from ECOMOG, and also accused the government of Burkina Faso of assisting the rebels. However, the NPFL denied involvement, while it was reported that members of a Sierra Leonean resistance movement, known as the Revolutionary United Front (RUF), led by Foday Sankoh, had joined the NPFL in attacks against government forces. In mid-1991 Sierra Leonean forces, with the assistance of military units from Nigeria and Guinea, initiated a counter-offensive against the rebels, and succeeded in recapturing several towns in the east and south of the country. Government forces were also assisted by some 1,200 Liberian troops, who had fled to Sierra Leone in September 1990, while a number of countries, including the United Kingdom and the USA, provided logistical support to Sierra Leone. In September 1991 former supporters of the Liberian president, Samuel Doe, known as the United Liberation Movement of Liberia for Democracy (ULIMO), initiated attacks from Sierra Leone against NPFL forces in north-western Liberia. The Sierra Leonean government denied allegations by Taylor that Sierra Leonean troops were involved in the offensive. In October clashes between ULIMO and the NPFL continued in the Mano River Bridge area on the border with Liberia. In December Momoh claimed that, contrary to the terms of a peace agreement, which had been signed between the Liberian interim government and the NPFL at the end of October (see Recent History of Liberia), the NPFL had continued its offensive in Sierra Leone; it was reported that the NPFL had regained control of several villages near the border with Liberia.

In January 1992 discussions took place in the Liberian capital, Monrovia, under the auspices of ECOWAS, between members of the Sierra Leonean government and leaders of the Liberian factions, in an attempt to resolve the conflict. In May ECOMOG began to establish units along the border between Sierra Leone and Liberia, in accordance with the terms of the October peace agreement; however, the deployment of troops was impeded by renewed ULIMO incursions into Liberian territory. In the same month the RUF (which was reported to have gained control of territory in the south of the country) rejected appeals by the government to end the civil conflict, and demanded that all foreign troops be withdrawn from Sierra Leone as a precondition to the cessation of hostilities. In June Sankoh rejected Capt. Strasser's offer of an amnesty for members of the RUF. In August government forces, with the assistance of Guinean troops, launched an offensive against rebel positions near the border with Liberia and succeeded in recapturing a number of villages; in subsequent months, however, territorial gains on both sides were constantly reversed. In January 1993 government forces regained control of the important diamond-mining town of Koidu, 250 km east of Freetown. In March members of ULIMO assisted government forces in attacks against the RUF, which led to the recapture of a strategically important bridge at Bo, on the border with Liberia. In April it was reported that only the Kailahun region, near Sierra Leone's border with Liberia, remained under the control of rebel forces. In May government troops were reported to have recaptured the strategic town of Baiwala in the Kailahun region.

In January 1994 the government claimed that it had regained control of further rebel bases in Pujehun District and the town of Kenema near the border with Liberia. It was reported, however, that some 100 civilians had been killed in attacks by the RUF in the region of Bo, to the south-east of Freetown. Later that year fighting in the south and east of Sierra Leone intensified, and in April it was reported that the RUF, which had been joined by disaffected members of the armed forces, had initiated attacks in the north of the country. (In addition, it was reported that another rebel movement, the National Front for the Restoration of Democracy, had launched attacks from Guinea.)

In early May 1994 government troops destroyed a major rebel base in the Northern Province. However, the number of civilian casualties resulting from continued rebel activities remained high: in early May 55 civilians were killed in a RUF offensive against the south-western village of Bandajuma, while a further 58 were killed in an attack against the southern village of Telu at the end of June. In July Israeli-trained government units assisted in the recapture of two important towns, Mongeri and Matotoka, in eastern Sierra Leone, in the first operation under a military co-operation accord between Sierra Leone and Israel. In the same month Strasser announced that a national war council would be established in which the paramount chiefs would be expected to play a significant role in resolving the civil conflict. Later in July, however, it was reported that the RUF had effectively besieged Kenema, after launching a series of attacks in the surrounding area, including an ambush against a principal road, in which six civilians were killed. In August government troops initated offensives against rebel bases in the region of Kenema, following reports that the RUF were exploiting diamond reserves in the area in order to finance their activities.

Economy

SOULE M. FUNNA

Revised for this edition by RICHARD SYNGE

Sierra Leone exhibits the typical features of a low-income African economy with a high ratio of foreign trade to gross domestic product (GDP), a low level of monetization and urbanization, and a rapidly increasing informal sector. In 1992, according to estimates by the World Bank, Sierra Leone's gross national product (GNP), measured at average 1990–92 prices, was US $726m., equivalent to $170 per head. During 1985–92, it was estimated, GNP per head remained constant, in real terms, while the population increased by an annual average rate of 2.5%. GDP increased, in real terms, by an annual average of 1.3% in 1980–92.

The economy became export-orientated early in the colonial period, when emphasis was placed on the production of primary commodities for overseas industrial markets which were also the principal suppliers of the country's import requirements. Favourable terms of trade in the 1950s and an expansion in the diamond industry, resulted in a rapid increase in incomes, allowing imports and government expenditure to rise sharply. Rising government expenditure, together with slow export and revenue growth in the early 1960s, led to a financial crisis, which was exacerbated in the mid-1960s by an overambitious programme of investment in plantations and oil palm mills by the Sierra Leone Produce Marketing Board (SLPMB), the sole exporter of the country's crops.

In an attempt to address this crisis, the government adopted an IMF-sponsored stabilization programme for the period 1966–69. However, the programme was followed by a recurrence of uncontrolled government spending, liquidity crises and an accumulation of public debt.

The increase, in the 1970s, of international petroleum prices, in conjunction with Sierra Leone's total dependence on fuel imports, intensified the country's economic problems. During the 1980s there was a high rate of inflation, an acute shortage of foreign exchange, and heavy external debt, while the country's natural mineral resources remained underutilized. Official revenue from exports (particularly diamonds) was adversely affected by smuggling, which was encouraged by governmental policy on price controls and the exchange rate. In 1986 the government implemented an economic reform programme, based on IMF recommendations, which included the introduction of a 'floating' exchange rate, the elimination of government subsidies on rice and petroleum, the liberalization of trade, and increases in producer prices with the aim of encouraging self-sufficiency in rice and other foods. In 1988, however, the IMF withdrew its support for the programme, declaring Sierra Leone ineligible for assistance until arrears in repayments were received. In early 1989 the government announced a further series of economic measures, which aimed to increase revenue from the mining sector and to reorganize loss-making state-owned companies. In early 1990 the government introduced legislation which prohibited local currency hoarding, and controlled commercial transactions. In December 1989 the government adopted a three-year structural adjustment programme, which was approved by the IMF. The implementation of the programme was, however, postponed, owing to the IMF's concern at the government's continued failure to reduce expenditure or to control debt arrears.

Conditions of internal unrest since 1991 have impeded the government's efforts to achieve economic stability; the disruption of agricultural production and trade resulted in a decline in real GDP in 1991–92, while the additional government expenditure increased the current account deficit to an exceptionally high level. In April 1992 the government announced the implementation of a final stage in the IMF-endorsed economic programme, which aimed to increase monetary controls, to develop a foreign exchange market and to improve the management of the country's natural resources. The government also aimed to continue the implementation of structural reforms, including the reduction of civil service staff and 'privatization'. Under an agreement with the IMF, Sierra Leone was able to accumulate 'rights' through its progress during the economic programme, which would then be used as the first disbursement of debt arrears under a successive IMF-supported structural adjustment programme. In March 1994 Sierra Leone became eligible to receive new credits from the IMF (see Public Finance).

An extensive 'privatization' programme, involving 19 enterprises, including the Sierra Leone Petroleum Refining Company, was initiated in March 1994; it was announced that a certain percentage of shares would be reserved for Sierra Leone citizens, while the state would also place shares on the international market. Prior to this programme, further 'privatizations' were implemented in 1993 and 1994, including the sale of a 49% stake in the Sierra Leone Trading Company (SLTC) to JSM Commodities, a British company, (while the remaining 51% was retained by the National Development Bank). JSM Commodities provided credit amounting to US \$1m. to the SLTC, and it was hoped that the company would be quickly restored to viability.

AGRICULTURE

Sierra Leone's economy is predominantly agricultural; in 1992 this sector accounted for 60.8% of the working population. Some 70 different crops are cultivated in the country but only a few (mainly coffee, cocoa, palm kernels and piassava, a fibre crop) are exported, and these are produced by less than 10% of the country's farmers. The majority of farmers still practice the traditional 'slash and burn' method of 'shifting cultivation' which appears to be under pressure, owing to the increase in population on the land. The prevailing technology consists only of the hoe and cutlass. The use of tractors is not widespread, despite the provision by government of a heavily-subsidized tractor rental service.

About three-quarters of farmers are engaged in the cultivation of the staple food crop, rice, but production cannot satisfy domestic demand and the shortfalls are offset by imports (accounting for about 25% of annual consumption in recent years). The government opened the rice import trade to the private sector in 1989, with demand determining selling prices (except for the official subsidy on supply to the security forces). However, the ultimate success of moves towards 'privatization' depends crucially on the response of investors to the new opportunities being provided, as well as the prevailing economic environment.

With funds provided by the International Development Association (IDA), Sierra Leone introduced Integrated Agricultural Development Projects (IADP) in 1972. These projects, which were expected to revolutionize agriculture in Sierra Leone, combined the provision of simple social and infrastructural amenities, such as water wells and feeder roads, with output-augmenting strategies, mainly in the form of credit facilities, seed distribution, and technical advice. In the early 1990s, however, the civil conflict (see Recent History) adversely affected agricultural exports (which accounted for 8% of total export earnings in 1993).

MINING

Mining, which began in Sierra Leone in the 1930s, is the second most important commodity-producing sector and main source of foreign exchange. In 1993 the mining sector contributed 15% of GDP and 90% of export earnings. Diamonds, for many years the principal export commodity of Sierra Leone, attract widespread illicit trafficking, despite large expenditures on security. Alluvial diamond mining is carried out by numerous small prospectors, while larger-scale mining operations are conducted by the Sierra Leone Selection Trust (SLST), in which the government-controlled National Diamond Mining Co (NDMC, also known as DIMINCO) has a majority share. This enterprise, however, has been beset by management, financial and technical problems and by 1992 its production, at only 600,000 carats, made only a negligible contribution to foreign exchange receipts. The marketing of Sierra Leone diamonds is conducted by the Government Gold and Diamond Office (GGDO). Legal exports of diamonds declined from 2m. carats in 1970 to 395,000 carats in 1980, and to 132,000 carats in 1989, recovering to 350,000 carats in 1992, before falling to 200,000 carats in 1993. The proportion of individual miners increased from approximately one-half in the 1970s to about two-thirds in the 1980s. In 1991 the foreign-owned Sunshine Mining Co began the exploitation of kimberlite pipes, which were stated to be capable of an output of 3.3m. carats, producing revenue of \$675m. over a period of 15 years. However, this company's agreement with the government subsequently collapsed, and the government has since been unable to attract any reputable diamond-mining company to the country.

In response to the uncertainties in the organization of production and marketing of Sierra Leone diamonds, operators have increasingly turned to the 'black market'. The declaration in 1987 of a 'state of economic emergency,' under which the security forces were empowered to arrest alleged 'economic saboteurs' led to a further disruption of trade and exchange activities. This situation was exacerbated by the operation, between late 1989 and May 1990, of the Currency Control and Economic Sabotage Act which imposed maximum levels on individual cash holdings (in an effort to address the acute cash shortage in the formal sector), and restricted transaction in the cash-intensive gold and diamond business. In early 1994, in an effort to reduce illicit trade, which costs the country \$220m. per year, according to official estimates, the government offered informants rewards of up to 40% of the value of anything recovered. This offer resulted in the recovery in June 1994 of a particularly large (172 carat) diamond, which obtained \$2.8m. for the government from its sale by public auction. In August the government granted De Beers, the world's largest diamond group, a concession to explore 15,800 sq km off the coast of Sierra Leone.

Sierra Leone's second most important mineral export was formerly iron ore, which was mined by the foreign-owned Sierra Leone Development Co (DELCO). In the early 1970s, when the mine's ore output averaged 2m. metric tons annually, the company experienced serious technical difficulties and a depressed market for iron ore, and operations were suspended during 1975–81. In 1981 the government-owned Marampa Iron Ore Co was formed, with the help of an Austrian loan and with management provided by Austro-Mineral. Exports resumed in 1983, but the new company encountered administrative, technical and financial difficulties, and it suspended its operations in October 1985. An operation to recover scrap metal from the mine began in 1988; efforts are also under way to attract new investors to reopen the mine, whose ore deposits have an iron content of 69%.

The Sierra Leone Ore and Metal Co (SIEROMCO), a subsidiary of Alusuisse of Switzerland, began mining bauxite at

Mokanji in 1964. Exports averaged 631,000 tons per year in 1972–79 but declined to 576,000 tons in 1983. Export levels increased sharply to an annual average of 1.7m. tons in 1984–88 but declined to 1.6m. tons in 1989 and to an estimated 1.4m. tons in 1992.

Rutile (titanium dioxide), an essential ingredient of paint pigment, was first exported by Sherbo Minerals in 1967 but in 1971 the company became bankrupt and closed its alluvial mine near Bonthe. The mine was taken over the following year by Sierra Rutile, a US-owned company. Production was resumed in 1980, and exports rose from 21,000 tons in that year to 148,000 tons in 1992. In 1992 a major rehabilitation of rutile production facilities was announced, for which external finance exceeding $13m. has been obtained. Sierra Leone is, after Australia, the world's largest producer of rutile. Australia's Consolidated Rutile bought a 50% interest in Sierra Rutile in 1994, and undertook to continue expansion of the mining activity and to increase production to 190,000 tons per year by 1996, with investment amounting to $72m. In 1993 rutile provided 57% of Sierra Leone's mineral export earnings, which totalled $108m.

Unlike the other minerals that are mined in Sierra Leone, there has been no significant investment in the gold industry and mining is carried out by petty diggers. However, a few companies have shown interest in this activity. Most of the current production is believed to be smuggled out of the country.

Mining policy, under the IMF-supported economic reform measures, has aimed to encourage reputable companies to participate in mining and exporting minerals, but progress in this direction has been slow, perhaps owing to the magnitude of investment involved, bureaucratic restrictions and other official practices deterring potential investors. In the early 1990s the government revised its agreements with SIEROMCO and Sierra Rutile in a renewed effort to raise the companies' contributions to government revenue. A new mining policy, which emerged during 1994, involved the introduction of a 2.5% royalty on precious mineral exports and a range of licence fees related to the size of mining operations. There was provision for foreign nationals to form companies, and it was proposed that there would be assistance in the provision of security of tenure for artisanal mining activity.

MANUFACTURING, TRADE AND TRANSPORT

With the introduction in 1960 of the Development Ordinance, Sierra Leone adopted a policy of industrial development, using an import-substitution strategy. Under the Ordinance, the government extended generous tax incentives, which included duty-free importation of equipment and raw materials and tax 'holidays', and established an industrial estate at Wellington, near Freetown, with basic services and an employment exchange. At first the prospects for this sector were good, as the country began to produce alcoholic and non-alcoholic beverages, cigarettes and several other goods which had been principal imports. By the late 1970s, however, the manufacturing sector had suffered as a result of the extensive shortages of foreign exchange, electricity and water supplies, poor telecommunications and rising costs of imported raw materials. The sector now comprises mainly palm oil production and other agro-based industries, textiles and furniture-making, and in 1990/91 accounted for 8.7% of GDP.

Wholesale trade, historically dominated by Europeans, is now controlled by a small number of influential Lebanese (who are also prominent in retail trade) and Indians. Market and itinerant trading is carried out by Africans.

High priority has been accorded to road construction, especially after the closure in 1971 of the 292-km, narrow-gauge Government Railway. The country has 7,500 km of roads but less than one-fifth of the network is paved and most of the network is in a poor state of repair. Inland waterways and coastal shipping are important features of internal transport. There are almost 800 km of recognized launch routes, including the coastal routes from Freetown northward to the areas served by the Great and Little Scarcies rivers and southward to the important seaport of Bonthe. The services and facilities of the international airport at Lungi, north of Freetown, have been improved, with financial assistance from UNDP. In 1982 the government formed a national airline, Sierra Leone Airlines, but the enterprise proved to be unprofitable, and operations had to be suspended in 1987. Limited services, including a weekly flight from Freetown to Paris, were restored in May 1990. Services have, for financial reasons, remained subject to periods of interruption.

EXTERNAL TRADE AND PAYMENTS

Sierra Leone is heavily dependent on foreign trade. Its principal exports in 1993 were rutile, bauxite, diamonds, cocoa beans and coffee. In that year, the USA was the principal market, absorbing 32.3% of Sierra Leone's total exports. Other major trading partners include the United Kingdom the People's Republic of China, Germany, Japan and the Netherlands. In 1990 Sierra Leone recorded a visible trade deficit of about $500,000, and there was a deficit of $69.4m. on the current account of the balance of payments.

The share of exports and imports in GDP averaged 64% per annum in the 1970s and 70% in the 1980s. In current prices, recorded exports increased from an annual average of Le 126m. in the 1970s to Le 2,940m. in the 1980s and to an estimated Le 14,878m. in 1990. Rebel activity in the eastern and southern parts of the country, where the bulk of the country's exports are produced, resulted in the collapse of the export sector, with exports in 1993 earning only Le 65,019m. Imports increased from an annual average of Le 183m. in the 1970s to Le 668m. in 1980–86 and approximately Le 7,160m. in 1987–89, but fell sharply to Le 65m. in 1992. Owing to extensive smuggling of diamonds, the contribution of minerals to total exports declined from 77.2% in 1981 to 69% in 1989, rising to 85% in 1990 (rutile 52%, bauxite 18%, diamonds 9%) and increasing considerably to 93% in 1992 (reflecting the disruption of cocoa and coffee farming, due to rebel activity in producing areas), before falling to 90% in 1993. The contribution of agricultural commodities to exports increased from 21% in 1981 to 28% in 1984 but declined to 21% in 1989, 10% in 1990 (coffee 5%, cocoa 4%) and 6% in 1992 (coffee 2%, cocoa 3%), before recovering to 8% in 1993 (coffee 2%, cocoa 3%).

Imports are dominated by manufactured goods but rice has also become a significant import commodity. During the 1980s, mineral fuels and lubricants (mainly crude petroleum) accounted for 21% of imports by value; basic manufactures 19%; food 24%; and machinery and transport equipment 24%. The residue consisted mainly of chemicals. Sierra Leone has since become more dependent on imports of food (mainly rice), which in 1990–92 accounted for one-third of total imports; in the same period manufactures accounted for 35%, and mineral fuels and lubricants 18%. The residue consisted of semi-processed materials, beverages and chemicals.

During the 1980s about 70% of Sierra Leone's imports came from the industrialized countries (the United Kingdom 16%, the Federal Republic of Germany 11%, the USA 8%, Japan 14%, other Western industrialized countries 7%, Eastern European countries 16%); 11% from Nigeria (mainly in the form of petroleum); 13% from Asia (principally from the People's Republic of China, Hong Kong, Singapore and Thailand); and the remainder from other African countries. During the early 1990s trade appeared to follow a similar pattern, with industrialized countries accounting for some 70% of imports (the UK 18%, Japan 17%, Germany 13%, the USA 10%, other Western industrialized countries 10%). Trade with the former communist countries of Eastern europe has, however, declined considerably.

Unfavourable terms of trade since the early 1970s, in conjunction with the dramatic increases in crude oil prices in the 1970s, have led to rising import costs. As a result, large deficits on the current account of the balance of payments have been incurred: Le 45m. in 1979/80 (4.2% of GDP), Le 140m. in 1981/82 (9.1% of GDP), Le 220m. in 1983/84 (7.5% of GDP), and Le 8,400m. in 1990/91 (6% of GDP). Owing to the shortage of foreign exchange, the government has, on occasion, mortgaged the future export earnings of the SLPMB, in order to finance the country's essential imports, especially of rice and petroleum, and at other times (before the exchange rate was 'floated' in April 1990) has brought foreign currencies at rates in excess of its own official rates. The ratio of scheduled external debt charges to exports of goods and services was 18% in 1977/78, 26% in 1980/81 and 48% in 1990/91. As a result of its protracted foreign exchange crisis (see below), Sierra Leone has a poor record of servicing the foreign debt and has had little access to loans at concessionary rates.

PUBLIC FINANCE

Recurrent revenue increased from Le 5,500m. (about $11m.) in 1989/90 to Le 57,200m. (about $104m.) in 1992/93, the bulk of which is derived from indirect taxes, accounting for approximately 63% of the total in 1960/61–1988/89 (import duties 37%, excise duties 17%, export duties 5%). During the same period, direct taxes contributed 26% of recurrent revenue (companies 16%, personal 10%), while the remainder was derived from non-tax sources, mainly in the form of licences and fees. The provisional recurrent revenue figure of Le 7,984m. for 1989/90 shows a sharp increase in the contribution of indirect tax to 74%, almost certainly reflecting the expanding informal sector, as well as the weakness of the nationalized diamond-mining and iron-ore operations. The 1994/95 budget projected revenue from tax and non-tax sources at Le 81,800m.

Total expenditure increased from Le 890.6m. in 1985/86 (current 66%; development 29%; unallocable 5%) to Le 32,300m. in 1990/91 (current 53%; development 39%; unallocable 8%). Recurrent expenditure for 1992/93 was expected to total Le 44,300m. In the period 1960/61–1988/89, about 28% of the budget was allocated to general services (administration 9%, law and order 7%, defence 12%), 25% to economic services (agriculture 4%, infrastructure 21%), 27% to social services (education 20%, health and social welfare 7%) and 20% to transfers (debt service 10%, personal 2%, subsidies 8%). The 1994/95 budget envisaged expenditure of Le 110,800m., and placed emphasis on improvements in social sectors, in addition to measures to stimulate agriculture, fisheries and mining.

Successive government budgets have been in almost continuous deficit during the last three decades; the deficit on a commitment basis increased from 2.5% of GDP in 1976/77 to 12.7% in 1979, and to 16.8% in 1986/87, it declined to an estimated 7.8% in 1989/90, but increased again to 18% in 1991/92, when the actual deficit (including grants) was Le 26,000m. as opposed to a planned deficit of Le 14,000m. The deficit for 1992/93 was expected to be 7.4% of GDP. The projected deficit for 1994/95 of Le 29,000m. was expected to be equivalent to 5.2% of GDP, compared with a deficit of about 6.1% of GDP in 1993/94. The ratio of government expenditure to GDP increased from 28.9% in 1978/79 to 31.4% in 1980/81, and to 32% in 1985/86 but declined to an estimated 18% in 1989/90, a decrease which reflects the increasing difficulty of financing the deficit, as well as growing pressure from multilateral creditors for the adoption of more effective expenditure control measures. The ratio of central government revenue to GDP was 16.2% in 1978/79, 17.7% in 1980/81, 5.8% in 1985/86, 6.9% in 1989/90, and increased sharply to an estimated 12.8% in 1990/91. Development expenditure declined from 39% of the total in 1981/82 to 14% in 1987/88, and to an estimated 4% in 1989/90. The public debt increased from Le 897.4m. (69% of GDP) in 1980/81 to Le 65,000m. in 1988/89 and to an estimated Le 175,700m. in 1990/91 (127% of GDP).

Negotiations between the government and multilateral donors resulted in the adoption, in 1986, of a structural adjustment programme, under which the government agreed among other things, to float the exchange rate, remove all subsidies on rice and petroleum, liberalize trade, increase producer prices and repay $3m. in arrears to the IMF. The IMF promised financial support of SDR 50.36m., comprising a stand-by arrangement for the following 12 months of SDR 23.16m., and a structural adjustment facility, available over the following three years, totalling SDR 27.2m. Meanwhile, the 'Paris Club' of Western creditor governments agreed, in principle, to reschedule Sierra Leone's immediate debt obligations. The 1986 programme ended prematurely when the IMF withdrew its financial support in 1988, stating that the government had not met the agreed conditions. In the same year, Sierrra Leone was declared ineligible to use IMF resources and was under threat of suspension from membership of the Fund for failing to service its foreign debt and to implement IMF-approved economic reform measures.

In December 1989 the government adopted an IMF-approved programme of economic reform measures, leading to a three-year IMF-monitored programme covering the period 1990/91 to 1992/93. In conjunction with these measures, import and export licensing was abolished for all commodities in December 1989; the leone was devalued by 85%, in January 1990, from Le 65 = US $1 to Le 120 = US $1; and in April 1990 the currency was 'floated', with the result that it depreciated rapidly. Revenue measures, introduced in December 1989, included sharp increases in excise duties on tobacco, beer, petroleum products and a new tax (in the form of an excise duty) on the latter. A 'freeze' was imposed on civil service recruitment (except for essential services) in order to limit expenditure; the exercise of deleting the names of non-existent or 'ghost' workers from the payroll, initiated in July 1988, was pursued more vigorously, while a new retrenchment exercise, designed to reduce civil service employment levels (estimated at some 75,000) by about 30% before the end of 1992/93, was introduced in early 1991. All official subsidies were terminated (except on rice for the security forces). In the financial sector, interest rates on treasury bills and on commercial bank loans were raised substantially to attract savers. Although the government implemented most of the measures foreseen in this programme of economic reforms, the introduction of the proposed 1992/93 programme was delayed until mid-April 1992 by the IMF's concern at the government's continued inability to control expenditure or address the problem of overdue arrears on its foreign debt.

In May 1992 the IMF reiterated its willingness to implement the 1992/93 programme in co-operation with the new military government, which declared its intention of strengthening fiscal discipline in the public sector, as well as imposing tighter open-market monetary controls and maximising revenue collection. At the outset of the IMF-supervised programme, Sierra Leone's outstanding financial obligations to the Fund totalled the equivalent of SDR 87.8m. (about $120m.), compared with its existing quota of SDR 57.9m. ($79m.). The 1992/93 Rights Accumulation Programme (RAP) permitted Sierra Leone to accumulate IMF repayment 'credits' up to a maximum of its IMF liabilities during the period to end-February 1994.

At the end of March 1994 the IMF announced the resumption of credit to Sierra Leone, and approved loans totalling SDR 116m. (equivalent to about $163m.), following the payment of the country's outstanding debt arrears, which was facilitated by loans from France, Norway and the USA. Of the total credit, SDR 88.8m. was to be provided under a three-year enhanced structural adjustment facility, and a further SDR 27m. under a one-year structural adjustment facility, which was to support the government's economic and financial reform programme for 1994/96. Contrary to the recommendations of a joint delegation of the World Bank and IMF, however, the budget for 1994/95 awarded a salary increase of 20% to public sector workers.

Statistical Survey

Source (unless otherwise stated): Bank of Sierra Leone, POB 30, Siaka Stevens St, Freetown; tel. (22) 226501; telex 3232; fax (22) 224764.

Area and Population

AREA, POPULATION AND DENSITY

Area (sq km)	71,740*
Population (census results)†	
8 December 1974	2,735,159
14 December 1985	
Males	1,746,055
Females	1,769,757
Total	3,515,812
Population (UN estimates at mid-year)‡	
1990	4,151,000
1991	4,261,000
1992	4,376,000
Density (per sq km) at mid-1992	61.0

* 27,699 sq miles.

† Excluding adjustment for underenumeration, estimated to have been 10% in 1974. The adjusted total for 1974 (based on a provisional total of 2,729,479 enumerated) is 3,002,426, and that for 1985 is 3,700,000 (estimate).

‡ Source: UN, *World Population Prospects: The 1992 Revision.*

PRINCIPAL TOWNS

Freetown (capital), population 469,776 (census of December 1985); Koindu 80,000; Bo 26,000; Kenema 13,000; Makeni 12,000.

BIRTHS AND DEATHS (UN estimates, annual averages)

	1975–80	1980-85	1985–90
Birth rate (per 1,000)	48.6	48.4	48.2
Death rate (per 1,000)	27.1	25.2	23.4

Expectation of life (UN estimates, years at birth, 1985–90): 41.0 (males 39.4; females 42.6).

Source: UN, *World Population Prospects: The 1992 Revision.*

ECONOMICALLY ACTIVE POPULATION
(sample survey, '000 persons, 1988/89)

	Males	Females	Total
Agriculture, etc.	551.2	673.3	1,224.5
Industry	235.9	98.9	334.8
Services	198.4	223.0	421.4
Total	985.5	995.2	1,980.7

Mid-1992 (estimates in '000): Agriculture, etc. 904; Total 1,487 (Source: FAO, *Production Yearbook*).

Agriculture

PRINCIPAL CROPS ('000 metric tons)

	1990	1991	1992
Maize	13	11	11*
Millet	24	22	24*
Sorghum	21	22	22*
Rice (paddy)	504	411*	420*
Sweet potatoes	14	15	11*
Cassava (Manioc)	123	90*	91†
Taro (Coco yam)	3	3	3†
Tomatoes†	23	23	23
Dry broad beans	1	1	1†
Citrus fruit†	77	77	77
Mangoes†	6	6	6
Palm kernels	27	30	35
Palm oil	50	51	60
Groundnuts (in shell)	20	21	20†
Coconuts	3	3	3
Coffee (green)	26	26	25†
Cocoa beans	24	24	24†

* Unofficial figure. † FAO estimate(s).

Source: FAO, *Production Yearbook.*

1993 ('000 metric tons): Maize 11; Millet 24; Rice (paddy) 420; Sweet potatoes 4; Cassava (Manioc) 92; Taro (Coco yam) 3 (FAO estimate); Palm kernels 10.8; Palm oil 48; Groundnuts (in shell) 20.

LIVESTOCK ('000 head, year ending September)

	1990	1991	1992*
Cattle	333	333	333
Pigs*	50	50	50
Sheep	271	274	275
Goats	149	151	152

Poultry (million): 6 in 1990; 6 in 1991; 6* in 1992.

* FAO estimate(s).

Source: FAO, *Production Yearbook.*

LIVESTOCK PRODUCTS (FAO estimates, '000 metric tons)

	1990	1991	1992
Beef and veal	5	5	5
Poultry meat	9	9	9
Other meat	5	5	5
Cows' milk	17	17	17
Poultry eggs	6.9	6.9	7.1

Source: FAO, *Production Yearbook.*

Forestry

ROUNDWOOD REMOVALS ('000 cubic metres, excl. bark)

	1990	1991	1992
Sawlogs, veneer logs and logs for sleepers	18	2	—
Other industrial wood*†	120	120	120
Fuel wood*	2,948	3,025	3,105
Total	3,086	3,147	3,225

* FAO estimate(s).
† Assumed to be unchanged since 1980.
Source: FAO, *Yearbook of Forest Products.*

SAWNWOOD PRODUCTION
('000 cubic metres, incl. railway sleepers)

	1990	1991	1992
Total	11	9	9*

* FAO estimate.
Source: FAO, *Yearbook of Forest Products.*

Fishing

(FAO estimates, '000 metric tons, live weight)

	1989	1990	1991
Freshwater fishes	16.0	15.0	15.0
Sardinellas	6.7	6.4	6.1
Bonga shad	21.1	20.0	19.0
Other marine fishes (incl. unspecified)	7.2	6.7	6.3
Crustaceans and molluscs	2.8	3.8	3.6
Total catch	53.9	51.8	50.0

Source: FAO, *Yearbook of Fishery Statistics.*

Mining

('000 metric tons, unless otherwise indicated)

	1991	1992	1993
Bauxite	1,376	1,257	1,165
Ilmenite	60	60	64
Rutile concentrates	155	149	150
Diamonds ('000 metric carats)	249	312	114*
Salt ('000 bags)	209	155	360

* January to October.

Industry

SELECTED PRODUCTS
('000 metric tons, unless otherwise indicated)

	1989	1990	1991
Beer ('000 hectolitres)	43	59	48
Cigarettes (million)	1,200	1,200	1,200
Jet fuels	14	15	15
Motor spirit (petrol)	35	35	13
Kerosene	20	18	20
Distillate fuel oils	101	103	33
Residual fuel oils	88	88	90
Electric energy (million kWh)	222	224	230

Source: mainly UN, *Industrial Statistics Yearbook.*

1992 ('000 metric tons, unless otherwise indicated): Beer ('000 hectolitres) 36; Cigarettes (million) 531; Motor spirit (petrol) 1.7; Kerosene 1.7; Distillate fuel oils 7.4.
1993: Beer ('000 cartons) 627.5; Cigarettes (million) 513.

Finance

CURRENCY AND EXCHANGE RATES

Monetary Units
100 cents = 1 leone (Le).

Sterling and Dollar Equivalents (31 March 1994)
£1 sterling = 857.0 leones;
US $1 = 577.2 leones;
1,000 leones = £1.167 = $1.732.

Average Exchange Rate (leones per US $)
1991 295.34
1992 499.44
1993 567.46

BUDGET (Le million, year ending 30 June)

Revenue	1990/91	1991/92	1992/93
Direct taxes	6,126.0	8,275	13,195
Import duties	6,552.9	12,333	18,792
Excise duties	5,069.5	8,470	12,463
Other sources*	896.1	6,306	9,844
Total	18,644.5	35,384	54,294

* Including licences, duties, fees and receipts for departmental services, receipts from posts and telecommunications royalties, and revenue from government lands, contributions from government corporations and companies, interest and loan repayments, etc.

Expenditure	1987/88	1989/90	1990/91
Education and social welfare	424.5	1,310.0	2,775.1
Health	143.3	412.7	768.9
General administration	371.9	1,131.1	2,847.3
Transport and communications	12.3	82.1	334.6
Police and justice	88.8	370.3	916.4
Defence	156.1	860.6	1,876.0
Agriculture and natural resources	124.7	239.5	652.9
Tourism and cultural affairs	1.8	28.0	46.3
Pensions and gratuities	36.9	169.6	270.3
Trade and industry	2.5	79.5	94.5
Construction and development	190.9	426.9	400.3
Housing and country planning	4.7	70.2	124.7
Other current expenditure	1,678.5	1,809.7	6,552.1
Public debt charges	723.9	1,704.3	6,058.7
Total	3,960.8	8,694.5	23,718.1

Total expenditure (Le million, year ending 30 June): 61,845 in 1991/92; 82,126 in 1992/93.

CENTRAL BANK RESERVES (US $ million at 31 December)

	1991	1992	1993
IMF special drawing rights	—	1.7	3.8
Foreign exchange	9.6	18.9	28.9
Total	9.6	20.6	32.8

Source: IMF, *International Financial Statistics.*

MONEY SUPPLY (Le million at 31 December)

	1991	1992	1993
Currency outside banks	15,650	18,270	21,882
Private sector deposits at central bank	104	112	418
Demand deposits at commercial banks	9,338	13,005	12,753
Total money	25,092	31,387	35,053

Source: IMF, *International Financial Statistics.*

COST OF LIVING
(Consumer Price Index for Freetown; base: 1978 = 100)

	1990	1991	1992
Food and drinks	22,847.9	47,466.4	80,792.3
Tobacco products and kola nuts	49,483.6	131,347.6	164,407.7
Housing	11,727.0	22,237.3	41,895.2
Clothing and footwear	38,291.6	58,120.9	97,466.3
All items (incl. others)	23,215.9	47,055.8	77,877.3

1993 (base: 1992 = 100): Food and drinks 121.1; Tobacco products and kola nuts 166.7; Housing 133.3; All items (incl. others) 127.9.

Source: Central Statistics Office, Tower Hill, Freetown.

NATIONAL ACCOUNTS
(Le million at current prices, year ending 30 June)

National Income and Product

	1989/90	1990/91	1991/92*
Compensation of employees	10,594.3	25,815.0	43,015.8
Operating surplus	64,068.0	131,792.6	183,127.8
Domestic factor incomes	74,662.3	157,607.6	226,143.6
Consumption of fixed capital	4,882.2	7,964.7	11,808.5
Gross domestic product (GDP) at factor cost	79,544.5	165,572.3	237,952.1
Indirect taxes, *less* subsidies	3,292.6	11,683.3	22,147.4
GDP in purchasers' values	82,837.1	177,255.6	260,099.5
Factor income received from abroad	20.0	156.3	2,346.1
Less Factor income paid abroad	-660.7	7,728.1	6,758.1
Gross national product (GNP)	83,517.8	169,683.9	255,687.5
Less Consumption of fixed capital	4,882.2	7,964.7	11,808.5
National income in market prices	78,635.6	161,719.2	243,879.0
Other current transfers received from abroad	475.1	1,082.0	2,755.8
Less Other current transfers paid abroad	39.9	35.8	64.8
National disposable income	79,070.8	162,765.4	246,570.0

* Estimates.

Source: Central Statistics Office, Tower Hill, Freetown.

Expenditure on the Gross Domestic Product

	1990/91	1991/92*	1992/93*
Government final consumption expenditure	15,591.1	32,101.1	48,608.0
Private final consumption expenditure	141,063.9	179,310.4	274,150.8
Increase in stocks	5,015.2	12,951.6	3,627.8
Gross fixed capital formation	15,854.9	27,206.0	27,080.7
Total domestic expenditure	177,525.1	251,569.1	353,467.3
Exports of goods and services	38,123.7	74,135.3	90,752.5
Less Imports of goods and services	38,393.2	65,604.9	91,613.0
GDP in purchasers' values	177,255.6	260,099.5	352,606.8

* Provisional figures.

Source: Central Statistics Office, Tower Hill, Freetown.

Gross Domestic Product by Economic Activity

	1990/91	1991/92*	1992/93*
Agriculture, hunting, forestry and fishing	53,335.3	73,309.9	94,401.9
Mining and quarrying	20,186.8	38,998.0	44,938.6
Manufacturing	11,886.3	24,392.6	37,642.0
Electricity, gas and water	407.3	368.3	1,436.6
Construction	2,227.2	11,594.0	4,972.1
Trade, restaurants and hotels	45,950.4	53,745.2	68,695.7
Transport, storage and communications	16,418.9	19,892.5	34,878.9
Finance, insurance, real estate and business services	18,433.0	23,807.7	37,462.5
Government services	4,528.0	9,030.4	18,453.1
Other community, social and personal services	555.1	610.6	621.7
Sub-total	173,928.3	255,749.2	343,503.1
Import duties	5,000.3	8,511.1	12,263.5
Less Imputed bank service charge	1,672.9	4,160.8	3,159.8
GDP in purchasers' values	177,255.6	260,099.5	352,606.8

* Provisional figures.

Source: Central Statistics Office, Tower Hill, Freetown.

BALANCE OF PAYMENTS (US $ million)

	1988	1989	1990
Merchandise exports f.o.b.	104.5	139.5	139.8
Merchandise imports f.o.b.	-138.2	-160.4	-140.3
Trade balance	-33.7	-20.9	-0.5
Exports of services	52.0	38.3	69.8
Imports of services	-34.6	-44.8	-74.5
Other income received	0.2	0.2	0.7
Other income paid	4.6	-39.8	-71.8
Private unrequited transfers (net)	0.3	0.1	0.1
Official unrequited transfers (net)	8.5	7.2	6.8
Current balance	-2.8	-59.7	-69.4
Direct investment (net)	-23.1	22.4	32.4
Other capital (net)	16.4	-40.3	-33.2
Net errors and omissions	-62.5	29.2	49.2
Overall balance	-71.9	-48.4	-20.9

Source: IMF, *International Financial Statistics.*

External Trade

PRINCIPAL COMMODITIES (Le million)

Imports	1991	1992	1993
Food and live animals	15,634.0	29,747.9	32,098.6
Beverages and tobacco	733.4	734.9	2,246.4
Crude materials (inedible) except fuels	771.0	1,423.4	1,726.8
Mineral fuels, lubricants, etc.	7,639.0	11,875.2	12,450.0
Animal and vegetable oils and fats	995.6	1,801.6	2,837.0
Chemicals	3,080.8	7,122.6	7,165.8
Basic manufactures	4,486.5	9,199.2	8,508.8
Machinery and transport equipment	10,607.4	12,313.7	12,818.6
Miscellaneous manufactured articles	1,540.4	3,452.7	4,269.0
Total	45,488.0	77,671.2	84,121.1

Exports	1991	1992	1993
Coffee	708.3	1,351.0	1,301.3
Cocoa beans	1,413.3	1,053.1	2,115.9
Palm kernels	17.1	6.9	—
Bauxite	7,275.9	19,408.3	13,764.5
Piassava	24.5	50.1	49.9
Diamonds	9,853.2	15,360.0	11,089.3
Rutile	22,221.0	32,878.6	30,649.7
Other items	2,495.3	4,764.4	6,048.3
Re-exports	69.9	161.9	246.2
Total	44,078.4	75,034.3	65,265.3

PRINCIPAL TRADING PARTNERS (Le '000)

Imports	1983	1984	1985
China, People's Republic	15,700	12,711	79,118
France	17,450	20,279	24,905
Germany, Fed. Republic	17,269	46,049	85,554
Italy	11,094	11,772	13,987
Japan	12,776	25,440	44,922
Netherlands	14,671	21,020	41,595
United Kingdom	33,246	47,815	110,959
USA	10,378	17,527	46,499
Total (incl. others)	286,923	418,286	781,604

(Le million)

Exports	1991	1992	1993
Germany	5,035.0	9,124.8	7,159.7
Netherlands	1,427.8	3,245.4	2,211.8
Switzerland	279.8	862.9	279.1
United Kingdom	5,607.1	6,620.3	13,215.0
USA	13,742.4	22,900.0	20,988.1
Total (incl. others)	44,008.7	74,872.4	65,019.1

Transport

ROAD TRAFFIC ('000 motor vehicles in use at 31 December)

	1990	1991	1992
Passenger cars	29.9	31.1	32.3
Commercial vehicles	20.6	21.4	22.5

INTERNATIONAL SEA-BORNE SHIPPING
(freight traffic, '000 metric tons)

	1988	1989	1990
Goods loaded	1,200	1,280	1,802
Goods unloaded	510	527	533

Source: UN, *Monthly Bulletin of Statistics*.

CIVIL AVIATION (estimated traffic)

	1989	1990	1991
Freight loaded (metric tons)	655	670	685
Freight unloaded (metric tons)	1,380	1,415	1,460
Passenger arrivals ('000)	53	54	59
Passenger departures ('000)	52	50	60

Source: UN Economic Commission for Africa, *African Statistical Yearbook*.

Tourism

	1988	1989	1990
Tourist arrivals ('000)	75	86	98

Source: UN, *Statistical Yearbook*.

Communications Media

	1989	1990	1991
Radio receivers ('000 in use)	890	925	950
Television receivers ('000 in use)	40	42	43
Daily newspapers	n.a.	1	n.a.
Average circulation ('000 copies)	n.a.	10	n.a.

1988 (provisional figures): Non-daily newspapers: 6 (average circulation 65,000 copies).

Source: UNESCO, *Statistical Yearbook*.

Telephones (1991, provisional figure): 32,000 in use (Source: UN Economic Commission for Africa, *African Statistical Yearbook*).

Education

(1991/92)

	Institutions	Teachers	Pupils: Males	Pupils: Females	Pupils: Total
Primary	1,792	10,051	184,880	130,266	315,146
Secondary:					
General	217	3,924	44,093	28,423	72,516
Vocational	24	496	2,056	2,223	4,279
Teacher training*	6	254	n.a.	n.a.	2,650
Higher	2*	600†	n.a.	n.a.	4,742†

* 1984/85 figure(s). † 1990 figure.

Source: mainly Department of Education, New England, Freetown.

Directory

The Constitution

Following a military coup on 29 April 1992, the Constitutions of 1978 and 1991 were suspended, and a governing council, known as the National Provisional Ruling Council (NPRC), was established. On 4 May a proclamation retroactively provided for the establishment of the NPRC (which was to comprise a maximum of 30 members, including a Chairman and a Vice-Chairman), the dissolution of the House of Representatives and the suspension of all political activity. In July the NPRC was designated the Supreme Council of State, and the Cabinet was reconstituted as the Council of Secretaries (headed by the Chief Secretary of State). The Council of Secretaries was to be responsible for government administration, subject to the authority of the NPRC. Three members of the NPRC were to act as Principal Liaison Officers, with responsibility for the supervision of government administration in a number of departments (which replaced the existing ministries).

In 1993 the Government announced the adoption of a transitional programme, which provided for the installation of a civilian government by January 1996, following multi-party presidential and legislative elections. In January 1994 a 19-member National Advisory Council, comprising representatives of various non-governmental organizations, promulgated a number of constitutional proposals, which were to be submitted for approval in a national referendum in May 1995. The constitutional recommendations (which included a number of similar provisions to the 1991 Constitution) stipulated that: executive power was to be vested in the President, who was to be required to consult with the Cabinet (except in the event of a national emergency), and was to be restricted to a tenure of two four-year terms of office; only Sierra Leonean nationals of more than 40 years of age were to qualify to contest a presidential election; the successful presidential candidate was to secure a minimum of 50% of votes cast nationally, and at least 25% of the votes cast in each of the four provinces; the legislature was to comprise a House of Representatives, which was to be elected by universal adult suffrage for a term of five years, and a 30-member upper chamber, the Senate, which was to include a number of regional representatives and five presidential nominees; members of the House of Representatives were not to be permitted to hold ministerial portfolios concurrently.

The Government

HEAD OF STATE

Chairman of the Supreme Council of State: Capt. VALENTINE E. M. STRASSER (took office 6 May 1992).

SUPREME COUNCIL OF STATE

National Provisional Ruling Council
(September 1994)

Capt. VALENTINE E. M. STRASSER (Chairman)
Capt. JULIUS MAADA BIO (Deputy Chairman)
Lt KOMBA S. MONDEH (Principal Liaison Officer)
Lt CHARLES EMILE M'BAYO (Principal Liaison Officer)
Capt. KAREFA A. F. KARGBO (Principal Liaison Officer)
JOHN BENJAMIN (Secretary-General)
Lt SAMUEL KOMBO KAMBO
Brig. J. S. GOTTOR
Lt-Col DANIEL KOBINA ANDERSON
Lt-Col K. H. CONTEH
Lt-Col JOSEPH PHILIP GBONDO
Lt-Col AKIM A. GIBRIL
Lt-Col A. B. Y. KOROMA
Lt S. F. Y. KOROMA
Lt-Col GABRIEL S. T. MANI
Lt-Commdr M. T. DIABBY
Maj. S. O. WILLIAMS
Maj. FALLAH SEWAH
Lt IDRIS KAMARA
Lt S. T. NYUMA
F. M. KAILIE
Sgt K. F. JALLOH
Cpl K. KARGBO
Lt-Col (retd) S. B. JUMU

COUNCIL OF SECRETARIES
(September 1994)

Chief Secretary of State: Capt. JULIUS MAADA BIO.

Secretary of State for Marine Resources: Lt KOMBA S. MONDEH.

Secretary of State for Youth, Sports and Social Mobilization: Lt CHARLES EMILE M'BAYO.

Secretary of State for Finance: Dr JOHN KARIMU.

Secretary of State for Foreign Affairs and International Co-operation: Dr ABBAS BUNDU.

Secretary of State for Development and Economic Planning: VICTOR BRANDON.

Secretary of State for Agriculture and Forestry: Maj. ROBERT Y. KOROMA.

Secretary of State for Mineral Resources: Capt. REGINALD D. GLOVER.

Secretary of State for Trade, Industry and State Enterprises: KANDEH YUNKELLA.

Secretary of State for Works: Lt-Col JOSEPH PHILIP GBONDO.

Secretary of State for Information, Broadcasting and Culture: HINDOLO S. TRYE.

Secretary of State for Labour: ALEX BROWNE.

Secretary of State for Energy and Power: Capt. IDRISS KAMARA.

Secretary of State for Education: CHRISTIANA THORPE.

Secretary of State for Transport and Communications: ARNOLD BISHOP-GOODING.

Attorney-General and Secretary of State for Judicial Affairs: (vacant).

Secretary of State for Health and Social Services: Lt-Col AKIM A. GIBRIL.

Secretary of State for Lands, Housing and the Environment: Lt S. F. Y. KOROMA.

Secretary of State for Internal Affairs and Rural Development: Col (retd) A. O. KAMARA.

Secretary of State for Tourism: Maj. (retd) GABRIEL ABBAS TURAY.

Secretary of State for the Eastern Province: Maj. BASHIRU CONTEH.

Secretary of State for the Northern Province: Lt-Col A. B. Y. KOROMA.

Secretary of State for the Southern Province: Maj. SAMUEL WILLIAMS.

DEPARTMENTS

Office of the Chief Secretary of State: Freetown.

Department of Agriculture and Forestry: Youyi Bldg, Freetown; telex 3418.

Department of Development and Economic Planning: Freetown.

Department of Education: New England, Freetown; tel. (22) 240846.

Department of Energy and Power: Electricity House, 4th Floor, Siaka Stevens St, Freetown; tel. (22) 222669.

Department of Finance: Secretariat Bldg, George St, Freetown; tel. (22) 226911; telex 3363.

Department of Foreign Affairs and International Co-operation: Gloucester St, Freetown; tel. (22) 224778; telex 3218.

Department of Health and Social Services: Youyi Bldg, 4th Floor, Brookfields, Freetown; tel. (22) 241500.

Department of Information, Broadcasting and Culture: Youyi Bldg, 8th Floor, Brookfields, Freetown; tel. (22) 240034; telex 3218.

Department of Internal Affairs and Rural Development: State Ave, Freetown; tel. (22) 223447.

Department of Justice: Guma Bldg, Lamina Sankoh St, Freetown; tel. (22) 226733.

Department of Labour: Freetown.

Department of Lands, Housing and the Environment: Freetown.

Department of Marine Resources: Freetown.

Department of Mineral Resources: Youyi Bldg, 5th Floor, Brookfields, Freetown; tel. (22) 241500.

Department of Tourism: Freetown.

Department of Trade, Industry and State Enterprises: Ministerial Bldg, George St, Freetown; tel. (22) 225211; telex 3218.

Department of Transport and Communications: Ministerial Bldg, 5th Floor, George St, Freetown; tel. (22) 225211.

Department of Works: New England, Freetown; tel. (22) 240101.

Department of Youth, Sports and Social Mobilization: Freetown.

Legislature

HOUSE OF REPRESENTATIVES

The House of Representatives was dissolved, following the military coup of 29 April 1992. Under the provisions of a transitional programme, which was initiated in 1993, elections to a new bicameral legislature were to take place in November 1995.

Political Organizations

All political activity was suspended following the military coup of 29 April 1992. Under the provisions of a transitional programme, which was initiated in 1993, however, the registration of political parties was to take place in June 1995, prior to elections later that year.

Prior to the 1992 coup, the following were among the active political parties:

All-People's Congress (APC): 39 Siaka Stevens St, Freetown; f. 1960; sole authorized political party 1978–91; merged with the Democratic People's Party in March 1992; Leader Maj.-Gen. JOSEPH SAIDU MOMOH.

National Labour Party (NLP): f. 1991; Leader G. E. E. PALMER.

National Unity Movement (NUM): f. 1991; Leader DESMOND FASHOLE LUKE.

Progressive People's Party (PPP): based in London, England; f. 1991; Leader Col (retd) AMBROSE GENDA.

Sierra Leone Democratic Party (SLDP): obtained legal recognition in Dec. 1991; has operated from the United Kingdom, since the 1992 military coup; Leader EDISON GORVIE.

United Front of Political Movements (UNIFOM): f. Sept. 1991 as alliance of parties opposed to the fmr APC Govt; Chair. THAIMU BANGURA; Sec.-Gen. ALPHA LAVALIE.

Civic Development Movement (CDEM): Freetown; f. 1991.

National Action Party (NAP): Freetown; obtained official registration in Nov. 1991; Leader SHEKA KANU.

National Democratic Alliance (NDA): f. 1991; Leader CYRIL FORAY.

National Democratic Party (NDP): obtained official registration in Nov. 1991; Chair. Dr ALUSINE FOFANAH.

People's Democratic Party (PDP): obtained official registration in Sept. 1991; Leader THAIMU BANGURA.

Sierra Leone People's Party (SLPP): f. 1991; obtained official registration in Nov. 1991; Leader SALIA JUSU-SHERIFF.

Unity Party (UP): obtained official registration in 1992.

The following organizations are in armed conflict with the Government:

National Front for the Restoration of Democracy (NFRD): emerged 1994.

Revolutionary United Front (RUF): emerged 1991; forces numbered c. 1,000 in mid-1993; Leader FODAY SANKOH.

Diplomatic Representation

EMBASSIES AND HIGH COMMISSIONS IN SIERRA LEONE

China, People's Republic: 29 Wilberforce Loop, Freetown; tel. (22) 231797; Ambassador: GAO JIANCHONG.

Côte d'Ivoire: 1 Wesley St, Freetown; tel. (22) 223983; Chargé d'affaires a.i.: EDO VAN AS.

Egypt: 174C Wilkinson Rd, POB 652, Freetown; tel. (22) 231499; telex 3300; Ambassador: MOHAMED ABDEL SALAM MOUSSA.

France: 13 Lamina Sankoh St, POB 510, Freetown; tel. (22) 222477; telex 3238; Ambassador: JACQUES NIZART.

Gambia: 6 Wilberforce St, Freetown; tel. (22) 225191; High Commissioner: Alhaji MOMODOU MOMAR TAAL.

Germany: Santanno House, 10 Howe St, POB 728, Freetown; tel. (22) 222511; telex 3248; fax (22) 226213; Ambassador: (vacant).

Guinea: 4 Liverpool St, Freetown; tel. (22) 223080; Ambassador: IBRAHIM CHÉRIF HAIDARA.

Holy See: 23 Jomo Kenyatta Rd, PMB 526, Freetown; tel. (22) 242131; fax (22) 240509; Apostolic Delegate: Most Rev. LUIGI TRAVAGLINO, Titular Archbishop of Lettere.

Italy: 32A Wilkinson Rd, POB 749, Freetown; tel. (22) 230995; telex 3456; Ambassador: GEORGIO PECA.

Korea, Republic: 22 Wilberforce St, POB 1383, Freetown; tel. (22) 224269; telex 3313; Ambassador: KIM CHANG-SOK.

Lebanon: 22 Wilberforce St, POB 727, Freetown; tel. (22) 223513; Ambassador: Dr FAWAZ FAWAD.

Liberia: 30 Brookfields Rd, POB 276, Freetown; tel. (22) 240322; telex 3229; Chargé d'affaires a.i.: SAMUEL B. PETERS.

Nigeria: 37 Siaka Stevens St, Freetown; tel. (22) 224202; telex 3258; fax (22) 224219; High Commissioner: MUHAMMED CHADI ABUBAKAR.

United Kingdom: Standard Chartered Bank Bldg, Lightfoot-Boston St, Freetown; tel. (22) 223961; fax (22) 1445251; High Commissioner: IAN MCCLUNEY.

USA: Walpole and Siaka Stevens Sts, Freetown; tel. (22) 226481; telex 3509; fax (22) 225471; Ambassador: LAURALEE PETERS.

Judicial System

The legal structure comprises the Supreme, Appeal, High, Magistrate and Local Courts. The laws applicable in Sierra Leone are local statutes, statutes of general application in England on 1 January 1880, and Common and Equity Law.

The Supreme Court: The ultimate court of appeal in both civil and criminal cases. In addition to its appellate jurisdiction, the Court has supervisory jurisdiction over all other courts and over any adjudicating authority in Sierra Leone, and also original jurisdiction, to the exclusion of all other courts, in all matters relating to the interpretation or enforcement of any provision of the Constitution.

Chief Justice: S. M. F. KUTUBU.

Supreme Court Justices: C. A. HARDING, AGNES AWUNOR-RENNER, BECCLES S. DAVIES.

The Court of Appeal: The Court of Appeal has jurisdiction to hear and determine appeals from decisions of the High Court in both criminal and civil matters, and also from certain statutory tribunals. Appeals against its decisions may be made to the Supreme Court.

Justices of Appeal: S. C. E. WARNE, C. S. DAVIES, S. T. NAVO, M. S. TURAY, E. C. THOMPSON-DAVIS, M. O. TAJU-DEEN, M. O. ADOPHY, GEORGE GELAGA KING, Dr A. B. Y. TIMBO, VIRGINIA A. WRIGHT.

High Court: The High Court has unlimited original jurisdiction in all criminal and civil matters. It also has appellate jurisdiction against decisions of Magistrates' Courts.

Judges: FRANCIS C. GBOW, EBUN THOMAS, D. E. M. WILLIAMS, LAURA MARCUS-JONES, L. B. O. NYLANDER, A. M. B. TARAWALLIE, O. H. ALGHALLI, W. A. O. JOHNSON, N. D. ALHADI, R. J. BANKOLE THOMPSON, M. E. T. THOMPSON, C. J. W. ATERE-ROBERTS (acting).

Magistrates' Courts: In criminal cases the jurisdiction of the Magistrates' Courts is limited to summary cases and to preliminary investigations to determine whether a person charged with an offence should be committed for trial.

Local Courts have jurisdiction, according to native law and custom, in matters which are outside the jurisdiction of other courts.

Religion

A large proportion of the population holds animist beliefs, although there are significant numbers of Islamic and Christian adherents.

ISLAM

In 1990 Islamic adherents represented an estimated 30% of the total population.

Ahmadiyya Muslim Mission: 15 Bath St, Brookfields, POB 353, Freetown; Emir and Chief Missionary KHALIL A. MOBASHIR.

Kankaylay (Sierra Leone Muslim Men and Women's Association): 15 Blackhall Rd, Kissy, POB 1168, Freetown; tel. (22) 250931; f. 1972; 500,000 mems; Pres. Alhaji IBRAHIM BEMBA TURAY; Lady Pres. Haja ISATA KEBE; Vice-Pres. Haja SERAY SILLAH.

Sierra Leone Muslim Congress: POB 875, Freetown; Pres. Alhaji MUHAMMAD SANUSI MUSTAPHA.

CHRISTIANITY

Council of Churches in Sierra Leone: 4A Kingharman Rd, Brookfields, POB 404, Freetown; tel. (22) 240568; telex 3210; f. 1924; 17 mem. churches; Pres. Rev. HENRY A. E. JENKINS; Gen. Sec. Rev. AMADU F. KAMARA.

The Anglican Communion

The Church of the Province of West Africa has two dioceses in Sierra Leone.

Bishop of Bo: Rt Rev. SAMUEL SAO GBONDA, MacRobert St, POB 21, Bo, Southern Province.

Bishop of Freetown: Rt Rev. PRINCE E. S. THOMPSON, Bishopscourt, Fourah Bay Rd, POB 128, Freetown.

Baptist Churches

Sierra Leone Baptist Convention: POB 64, Lunsar; Pres. Rev. JOSEPH S. MANS; Sec. Rev. N. T. DIXON.

The Nigerian Baptist Convention is also active.

Methodist Churches

Methodist Church Sierra Leone: Wesley House, George St, POB 64, Freetown; tel. (22) 222216; autonomous since 1967; Pres. of Conf. Rev. GERSHON F. H. ANDERSON; Sec. Rev. CHRISTIAN V. A. PEACOCK; 26,421 mems.

United Methodist Church: UMC House, 31 Wallace Johnson St, Freetown; Presiding Bishop T. S. BANGURA; 36,857 mems.

Other active Methodist bodies include the African Methodist Episcopal Church, the Wesleyan Church of Sierra Leone, the Countess of Huntingdon's Connexion and the West African Methodist Church.

The Roman Catholic Church

Sierra Leone comprises one archdiocese and two dioceses. At 31 December 1992 there were an estimated 114,073 adherents in the country, representing about 2.5% of the total population.

Inter-territorial Catholic Bishops' Conference of The Gambia, Liberia and Sierra Leone: POB 893, Freetown; tel. (22) 228240; telex 3311; fax (22) 228252; f. 1971; Pres. Rt Rev. JOHN O'RIORDAN, Bishop of Kenema (Sierra Leone).

Archbishop of Freetown and Bo: Most Rev. JOSEPH H. GANDA, Santanno House, POB 893, Freetown; tel. (22) 224590.

Other Christian Churches

The following are represented: the Christ Apostolic Church, the Church of the Lord (Aladura), the Missionary Church of Africa, the Sierra Leone Church and the United Brethren in Christ.

AFRICAN RELIGIONS

Beliefs, rites and practices are very diverse, varying between ethnic groups and between families in the same group.

The Press

DAILY

Daily Mail: 29–31 Rawdon St, POB 53, Freetown; tel. (22) 223191; f. 1931; govt-owned; appears irregularly; Editor AHIA MARTIN MONDEH; circ. 10,000.

PERIODICALS

African Crescent: 15 Bath St, POB 353, Brookfields, Freetown; Editor MAULANA-KHALIL A. MOBASHIR.

The Chronicle: Freetown; Editor K. M. ROY-STEVENS; circ. 5,000.

Concord Times: 139 Pademba Rd, Freetown; 2 a week; Editor KINGSLEY LINGTON.

Focus: POB 862, Freetown; political and socio-economic; quarterly; Editor FRED AWUTA-COKER; circ. 5,000.

Leonean Sun: 49 Main Rd, Wellington, Freetown; tel. (22) 223363; f. 1974; monthly; Editor ROWLAND MARTYN.

Liberty Voice: 139 Pademba Rd, Freetown; tel. (22) 242100; Editor A. MAHDIEU SAVAGE.

New Citizen: 5 Hanna Benka-Coker St, Freetown; tel. (22) 241795; Editor I. BEN KARGBO.

The New Globe: 49 Bathurst St, Freetown; tel. (22) 228245; weekly; Editor SAM TUMOE; circ. 9,000.

The New Shaft: 60 Old Railway Line, Brookfields, Freetown; tel. (22) 241093; 2 a week; independent; Editor FRANKLIN BUNTING-DAVIES; circ. 10,000.

Progress: 1 Short St, Freetown; tel. (22) 223588; weekly; independent; Editor FODE KANDEH; circ. 7,000.

Sierra Leone Chamber of Commerce Journal: Sierra Leone Chamber of Commerce, Industry and Agriculture, Guma Bldg, 5th Floor, Lamina Sankoh St, POB 502, Freetown; tel. (22) 226305; monthly.

Sierra Leone Outlook: POB 523, Freetown; quarterly; English; publ. by the United Methodist Church; circ. 1,500.

Unity Now: 82 Pademba Rd, Freetown; tel. (22) 227466; Editor FRANK KPOSOWA.

The Vision: 60 Old Railway Line, Brookfields; tel. (22) 241273; Editor SIAKA MASSAQUOI.

Weekend Spark: 7 Lamina Sankoh St, Freetown; tel. (22) 223397; f. 1983; weekly; independent; Editor ROWLAND MARTYN; circ. 20,000.

NEWS AGENCY

Sierra Leone News Agency (SLENA): 15 Wallace Johnson St, PMB 445, Freetown; tel. (22) 223127; telex 3210; fax (22) 224439; f. 1980; Dir and Editor-in-Chief ROD MAC-JOHNSON.

Publishers

Njala University Publishing Centre: Njala University College, PMB, Freetown; science and technology, university textbooks.

Sierra Leone University Press: Fourah Bay College, POB 87, Freetown; tel. (22) 231617; telex 3210; fax (22) 224439; f. 1965; biography, history, Africana, religion, social science, university textbooks; Chair. Prof. ERNEST H. WRIGHT.

United Christian Council Literature Bureau: Bunumbu Press, POB 28, Bo; tel. (32) 462; books in Mende, Temne, Susu; Man. Dir ROBERT SAM-KPAKRA.

Government Publishing House

Government Printer: New England, Freetown; tel. (22) 241146.

Radio and Television

In 1991 there were an estimated 950,000 radio receivers and 43,000 television receivers in use.

Sierra Leone Broadcasting Service: New England, Freetown; tel. (22) 240403; telex 3334; f. 1934; state-controlled; programmes mainly in English and the four main Sierra Leonean vernaculars, Mende, Limba, Temne and Krio; weekly broadcast in French; television service established 1963; colour transmissions since 1978; Dir-Gen. BABATUNDE ROLAND-MAY.

Finance

(cap. = capital; p.u. = paid up; m. = million; res = reserves; dep. = deposits; brs = branches; amounts in leone)

BANKING

Central Bank

Bank of Sierra Leone: Siaka Stevens St, POB 30, Freetown; tel. (22) 226501; telex 3232; fax (22) 224764; f. 1964; cap. and res 671.4m., dep. 6,663.1m. (Dec. 1993); Gov. Dr STEVE SWARRAY (acting); Dep. Gov. YVONNE GIBRIL.

Other Banks

Barclays Bank of Sierra Leone Ltd: 25–27 Siaka Stevens St, POB 12, Freetown; tel. (22) 222501; telex 3220; fax (22) 222563; f. 1971; cap. 5,760m., res 1,475m., dep. 11,736m. (Dec. 1993); Chair. AUGUSTUS D. A. M'CORMACK; Man. Dir E. J. CRUTCHLEY; 16 brs and 1 agency.

International Bank for Trade and Industry (Sierra Leone) Ltd: 22 Wilberforce St, PMB 679, Freetown; tel. (22) 223610; telex 3463; fax (22) 223657; f. 1982; operations suspended in April 1994; cap. 2m., res 127.1m., dep. 1,607.6m. (Dec. 1992); Chair. MOHAMED REMILEKUN TEJAN-COLE.

Meridien BIAO Bank Sierra Leone Ltd: Lightfoot-Boston St, PMB 1237, Freetown; tel. (22) 226954; telex 3233; fax (22) 226214; cap. 200m., res 7.5m., dep. 861.6m. (Dec. 1992); Chair. SIYANGA MALUMO; Man. Dir RAYMOND ABOU SAMRA.

National Development Bank Ltd: Leone House, 6th Floor, 21–23 Siaka Stevens St, PMB, Freetown; tel. (22) 226791; telex 3589; fax (22) 224468; f. 1968; provides medium- and long-term finance and technical assistance to development-orientated enterprises; cap. and res 1,469m., dep. 1,301.1m. (1993); Man. Dir CHRISTIAN J. SMITH.

Sierra Leone Commercial Bank Ltd: 29–31 Siaka Stevens St, Freetown; tel. (22) 225264; telex 3275; fax (22) 225292; f. 1973; state-owned; cap. 30m., res 449.5m., dep. 3,356m. (Dec. 1992); Chair. I. I. MAY-PARKER; Man. Dir S. B. KANU; 7 brs.

Standard Chartered Bank Sierra Leone Ltd: 9-11 Lightfoot-Boston St, POB 1155, Freetown; tel. (22) 225021; telex 3523; fax (22) 225760; f. 1971; cap. 20.1m., res 634.6m., dep. 8,477.3m. (Dec. 1993); Chair. LLOYD A. DURING; Man. Dir JOHN JANES; 12 brs.

INSURANCE

Aureol Insurance Co Ltd: Kissy House, 54 Siaka Stevens St, POB 647, Freetown; tel. (22) 223435; telex 3222; fax (22) 229336; f. 1987; Chair. LLOYD DURING; Man. Dir S. G. BENJAMIN.

National Insurance Co Ltd: 18–20 Walpole St, PMB 84, Freetown; tel. (22) 223892; telex 3344; fax (22) 226097; f. 1972; state-owned; Chair. J. T. SARJAH-WRIGHT; CEO A. N. YASKEY.

New India Assurance Co Ltd: 18 Wilberforce St, POB 340, Freetown; tel. (22) 226453; telex 3510; fax (22) 222494; Man. Dir V. KRISHNAN.

Reliance Insurance Trust Corp. Ltd: 24 Siaka Stevens St, Freetown; tel. (22) 225115; telex 3664; fax (22) 228051; fax (22) 228051; f. 1985; Chair. S. S. DEEN; Man. Dir E. B. KOROMA.

Sierra Leone Insurance Co Ltd: 31 Lightfoot Boston St, POB 836, Freetown.

Trade and Industry

CHAMBER OF COMMERCE

Sierra Leone Chamber of Commerce, Industry and Agriculture: Guma Bldg, 5th Floor, Lamina Sankoh St, POB 502, Freetown; tel. (22) 226305; telex 3712; fax (22) 228005; f. 1961; 215 mems; Pres. Alhaji MUSA KING.

GOVERNMENT ORGANIZATIONS

Government Gold and Diamond Office (GGDO): c/o Bank of Sierra Leone, Siaka Stevens St, Freetown; tel. (22) 222600; telex 3566; f. 1985 to succeed Precious Metals Marketing Co (PMMC) as country's purchaser and exporter of diamonds and gold; combats illicit trade; Chair. W. A. JONES.

Sierra Leone Produce Marketing Board (SLPMB): POB 508, Cline Town, Freetown; telex 3211; f. 1949 to manage the marketing of Sierra Leone produce and to stimulate agricultural development; proposals to transfer ownership to private sector announced in April 1992; two subsidiaries: SLAPCO (coffee and cocoa production) and NAPCO (groundnuts, ginger and chillies); Chair. Secretary of State for Mineral Resources; Man. Dir DELORDSON M. KALLON.

EMPLOYERS' ASSOCIATIONS

Sierra Leone Employers' Federation: POB 562, Freetown; Chair. DONALD C. SMYTHE-MACAULAY; Exec. Officer A. E. BENJAMIN.

Sierra Leone Chamber of Mines: POB 456, Freetown; tel. (22) 226082; f. 1965; comprises the principal mining concerns; Pres. D. J. S. FRASER; Exec. Officer N. H. T. BOSTON.

MAJOR INDUSTRIAL COMPANIES

Aureol Tobacco Co Ltd: Wellington Industrial Estate, POB 109, Freetown; telex 3361; fax (22) 229138; f. 1959; cap. Le 36.8m.; cigarette mfrs; Chair. Prof. K. KOSO-THOMAS; Man. Dir A. D. A. MACORMACK; 283 employees.

Bata Shoe Co Sierra Leone Ltd: Wallace Johnson St, POB 111, Freetown; footwear mfrs and distributors.

Plastic Manufacturing Sierra Leone Ltd: Wilkinson Rd, POB 96, Freetown; footwear mfrs.

Chanrai Sierra Leone Ltd: Wellington Industrial Estate, POB 57, Freetown; tel. (22) 263292; telex 3267; fax (22) 263305; f. 1893; cap. £1m.; trading co; importers of motor spares, air-conditioners, refrigerators, building materials, textiles and provisions; mfrs of soaps and polyethylene bags; Dir R. K. LAKHANPAL; 115 employees.

Compagnie française de l'Afrique occidentale: Howe St, POB 70, Freetown; tel. (22) 22030; telex 3332.

The Diamond Corporation (West Africa) Ltd: 25–27 Siaka Stevens St, POB 421, Freetown; telex 3221; purchase and export of diamonds; Dir S. L. MATTURI.

Government Gold and Diamond Office (GGDO): see Trade and Industry—Government Organizations.

National Diamond Mining Co (Sierra Leone) Ltd (DIMINCO): Charlotte St, POB 11, Freetown (head office); f. 1970; 51% state-owned; cap. Le 10m. Chair. VICTOR STRASSER-KING; Man. Dir JON M. KAMANDA.

National Petroleum Co Sierra Leone Ltd: Freetown; Man. Dir DONALD SMYTHE-MACAULEY.

Rokel Leaf Tobacco Development Co Ltd: POB 29, Makeni; f. 1974; cap. Le 200,000; production of leaf tobacco; Chair. J. T. SHORT.

Sierra Leone Brewery Ltd: POB 721, Freetown; fax (22) 263118; f. 1961; cap. Le 1m.; brewing and marketing of Guinness stout and Star lager; Gen. Man. P. P. SUTTON.

Sierra Leone Diamonds Ltd: Freetown; diamond cutting and polishing.

Sierra Leone Ore and Metal Co (SIEROMCO): POB 725, Freetown; tel. (22) 226777; telex 3380; fax (22) 227276; mining of bauxite. Chair. K. WOLFENSBERGER; Man. Dir J. V. B. WESTWOOD.

Sierra Leone Petroleum Refining Co Ltd: PMB, Kissy Dockyard, Freetown; 50% state-owned; operates a refinery.

Sierra Rutile Ltd: PMB, Freetown; tel. and fax (22) 228144; telex 3259; f. 1971; jtly-owned by US and Australian interests; mining of rutile and ilmenite (titanium-bearing ores); Gen. Man. R. J. JACKETT-SIMPSON; 1,600 employees.

UAC of Sierra Leone Ltd: 6-8 Blackhall Rd, Freetown; fmrly United Africa Co; mfrs agents: construction, mining, marine, agricultural and power plants; Chair. LLOYD A. DURING; Man. Dir VICTOR G. THOMAS.

TRADE UNIONS

Artisans', Ministry of Works Employees' and General Workers' Union: 4 Pultney St, Freetown; f. 1946; 14,500 mems; Pres. IBRAHIM LANGLEY; Gen. Sec. TEJAN A. KASSIM.

Sierra Leone Labour Congress: 35 Wallace Johnson St, POB 1333, Freetown; tel. (22) 226869; f. 1966; approx. 51,000 mems in 19 affiliated unions; Pres. IBRAHIM LANGLEY; Sec. Gen. KANDEH YILLA.

Principal affiliated unions:

Clerical, Mercantile and General Workers' Union: 35 Wallace Johnson St, Freetown; f. 1945; 3,600 mems; Pres. Miss CAMPBELL; Gen. Sec. M. B. WILLIAMS.

Diminco African Senior Staff Association: National Diamond Mining Co (SL) Ltd, Charlotte St, Freetown; f. 1973; 151 mems; Gen. Sec. E. O. BARBER.

Railway Workers' Union: The Technical Institute, 32 Dan St, Freetown; f. 1919; 510 mems; Gen. Sec. A. OMO-JONES; Pres. F. B. HAMILTON.

Sierra Leone Association of Journalists: Freetown; Pres. DAISY BONA.

Sierra Leone Dockworkers' Union: 165 Fourah Bay Rd, Freetown; f. 1962; 2,650 mems; Pres. D. F. KANU; Gen. Sec. F. A. BRIMA.

Sierra Leone Motor Drivers' Union: 10 Charlotte St, Freetown; f. 1960; 1,900 mems; Pres. A. W. HASSAN; Gen. Sec. ALPHA KAMARA.

Sierra Leone Teachers' Union: 27 Goderich St, Freetown; f. 1951; 5,500 mems; Pres. B. A. BARRIE.

Sierra Leone Transport, Agricultural and General Workers' Union: 4 Pultney St, Freetown; f. 1946; 1,600 mems; Pres. S. O. SAWYERR-MANLEY; Gen. Sec. D. GARBER.

United Mineworkers' Union: 35 Wallace Johnson St, Freetown; f. 1944; 6,500 mems; Pres. H. M. BARRIE; Gen. Sec. S. D. GBENDA.

Also affiliated to the Sierra Leone Labour Congress: **General Construction Workers' Union, Municipal and Local Government Employees' Union, Provincial and General Workers' Union, Public Utility Employees' Union, Sherbro Amalgamated Workers' Union, Sierra Leone National Seamen's Union.**

CO-OPERATIVES AND MARKETING BOARDS

In 1975 there were 1,024 primary co-operatives with a total membership of 46,762. There were 734 thrift and credit co-operative societies, 12 consumer co-operatives, five secondary societies, 270 marketing societies, eight producer co-operatives, and a central bank for all co-operatives. The Co-operative Department, which is based in Freetown with eight area offices throughout the provinces, is supervised by a Registrar of Co-operatives within the Department of Trade, Industry and State Enterprises.

Transport

RAILWAYS

Marampa Mineral Railway: Delco House, POB 735, Freetown; tel. (22) 222556; telex 3460; 84 km of track linking iron ore mines at Marampa with Pepel port; mining operations at Marampa have been suspended since 1985; Gen. Man. SYL KHANU.

ROADS

In 1991 there were an estimated 8,860 km of classified roads, including 3,600 km of main roads and 4,760 km of secondary roads; about 1,600 km of the total network was paved. Construction of a road between Freetown and Monrovia (Liberia) was begun in 1984. In 1988 the Government initiated a long-term programme to improve about 10,000 km of national and regional roads. In 1993 the Government announced a seven-year road rehabilitation programme, which, at an estimated cost of US $100m., was to be financed by the World Bank.

Sierra Leone Road Transport Corpn: Blackhall Rd, POB 1008, Freetown; tel. (22) 250442; telex 3395; fax (22) 250000; f. 1965; state-owned; operates transport services throughout the country; Gen. Man. DANIEL R. W. FAUX.

INLAND WATERWAYS

Recognized launch routes, including the coastal routes from Freetown northward to the Great and Little Scarcies rivers and southward to Bonthe, total almost 800 km. Although some of the upper reaches of the rivers are navigable only between July and September, a considerable volume of traffic uses the rivers.

SHIPPING

Sierra Leone National Shipping Co Ltd: 45 Cline St, POB 935, Freetown; tel. (22) 250881; telex 3260; fax (22) 223222; f. 1972; state-owned; shipping, clearing and forwarding agency; representatives for foreign lines; Gen. Man. PAUL K. NIELSEN.

Sierra Leone Ports Authority: Queen Elizabeth II Quay, PMB 386, Cline Town, Freetown; tel. (22) 250616; telex 3262; f. 1965; parastatal body, supervised by the Dept of Transport and Communications; operates the port of Freetown, which has full facilities for ocean-going vessels; Gen. Man. G. H. ARJES.

Sierra Leone Shipping Agencies Ltd: Deep Water Quay, Clinetown, POB 74, Freetown; tel. (22) 250882; telex 3260; fax (22) 250400; f. 1949; Man. Dir W. SCHNEIDER.

UMARCO (Freetown) Ltd: POB 417, Freetown; telex 3216; shipping agents; Gen. Man. R. HUGHES.

CIVIL AVIATION

There is an international airport at Lungi.

Directorate of Civil Aviation: Department of Transport and Communications, Ministerial Bldg, 5th Floor, George St, Freetown; tel. (22) 225211; Dir J. A. JOHNSON.

Sierra Leone National Airlines: 25 Pultney St, POB 285, Freetown; tel. (22) 222075; telex 3242; fax (22) 222026; f. 1982; state-owned; operates domestic and regional services, and scheduled flights to Paris; Chair. Dr BERNARD G. FRAZER; Man. Dir S. A. PALMER.

Tourism

The main attractions for tourists are the beaches, the mountains and the game reserves. In 1990 an estimated 98,000 tourists visited Sierra Leone, while receipts from the tourism sector totalled US $19m.

National Tourist Board: International Conference Centre, Aberdeen Hill, POB 1435, Freetown; tel. (22) 272520; fax (22) 272197; f. 1990; Gen. Man. CECIL J. WILLIAMS.

Defence

In June 1993 the armed forces comprised an army of 6,000 men and a navy of 150. In that year some 800 Nigerian troops were based in Sierra Leone to support government forces in repulsing attacks by a rebel faction, the Revolutionary United Front (which was estimated to number 1,000). In January 1994 an agreement was signed, whereby the Nigerian government was to assist in the military training and reorganization of the armed forces. Under a further military co-operation accord with Israel, government units received military training from Israeli forces in 1994.

Defence Expenditure: Estimated at Le 1,876m. in 1990/91.

Commander of the Armed Forces: Lt.-Col KELLY CONTEH (acting).

Education

Sierra Leone has both private and government-owned schools but education is not compulsory, and facilities are insufficient to meet the country's educational needs. In 1987 tuition fees for the government-owned primary and secondary schools were abolished. Primary education begins at six years of age and lasts for six years. Secondary education, beginning at the age of 12, also lasts for a further six years, comprising two three-year cycles. In 1990 primary enrolment was equivalent to 48% of children in the appropriate age-group (boys 56%; girls 39%), while secondary enrolment was equivalent to 16% of the relevant age-group (boys 21%; girls 12%). Budgetary expenditure on education and social welfare by the central government in the financial year 1990/91 was estimated at Le 2,775.1m. (11.7% of total spending). In 1990, according to UNESCO estimates, adult illiteracy averaged 79.3% (males 69.3%; females 88.7%).

Bibliography

Abraham, A. *Topics in Sierra Leone History.* Freetown, 1977.

Bank of Sierra Leone. *Economic Review* (quarterly) and *Annual Report.* Freetown.

Cartwright, J. R. *Politics in Sierra Leone 1947–67.* Toronto, 1970.

Political Leadership in Sierra Leone. Toronto, 1978.

Clapham, C. *Liberia and Sierra Leone: An Essay in Comparative Politics.* Cambridge University Press, 1976.

Clarke, J. I. *Sierra Leone in Maps.* London, 1966.

Cohen, A. *The Politics of Elite Culture.* London, 1981.

Cruise O'Brien, D. B., Dunn, J., and Rathbone, R. (Eds). *Contemporary West African States.* Cambridge, Cambridge University Press, 1989.

Fashole Luke, D. *Labour and Parastatal Politics in Sierra Leone: A Study in African Working-class Ambivalence.* Lanham, MD, University Press of America, 1984.

Funna, S. M. 'Structure and Performance of the Sierra Leone Economy: 1971–81', in *Sierra Leone Studies at Birmingham, 1983.* Birmingham University Press, 1984.

Fyfe, C. *A History of Sierra Leone.* London, Longman, 1962.

Sierra Leone Inheritance. London, 1964.

Fyle, C. M. *The History of Sierra Leone: A Concise Introduction.* London, 1981.

Greenhalgh, P. *West African Diamonds: An Economic History 1919–83.* Manchester University Press, 1985.

Gwynne-Jones, D. R. G., et al. *A New Geography of Sierra Leone.* Longman, 1978.

Harrell-Bond, B., Howard, A. M., and Skinner, D. E. *Community Leadership and the Transformation of Freetown, 1801–1976.* Leiden, 1978.

Hayward, M. F. *Elections in Independent Africa.* Boulder, CO, Westview Press, 1987.

International Labour Organisation. *Ensuring Equitable Growth: A Strategy for Increasing Employment, Equity and Basic Needs Satisfaction in Sierra Leone.* Addis Ababa, 1981.

Jones, A. *From Slaves to Palm Kernels: A History of the Galinhas Country, 1730–1890.* Wiesbaden, Franz Steiner Verlag, 1983.

Kilson, M. *Political Change in a West African State—A Study of the Modernization Process in Sierra Leone.* Cambridge, MA, 1966.

Lee, M. M. *UNICEF in Sierra Leone.* Abidjan, UNIPACI, 1988.

Lisk, F., and Van der Hoeven, R. 'Measurement and Interpretation of Poverty in Sierra Leone', in *International Labour Review,* No. 6, 1979.

Rimmer, D. *The Economies of West Africa.* London, Weidenfeld and Nicolson, 1984.

Stevens, S. *What Life Has Taught Me.* London, Kensal Press, 1984.

Thomas, A. C. *The Population of Sierra Leone: An Analysis of Population Data.* Freetown, Fourah Bay College, 1983.

Turay, E. D. A., and Abraham, A. *The Sierra Leone Army: A Century of History.* London, Macmillan, 1988.

Williams, G. J. *A Bibliography of Sierra Leone 1925–1967.* 1971.

Wyse, A. *The Krio of Sierra Leone: An Interpretive History.* London, Hurst, 1989.

SOMALIA

Physical and Social Geography

I. M. LEWIS

The Somali Democratic Republic covers an area of 637,657 sq km (246,201 sq miles). It has a long coastline on the Indian Ocean and the Gulf of Aden, forming the 'Horn of Africa'. To the north, Somalia faces the Arabian peninsula, with which it has had centuries of commercial and cultural contact. To the north-west, it is bounded by the Republic of Djibouti, while its western and southern neighbours are Ethiopia and Kenya. The country takes its name from its population, the Somali, a Muslim Cushitic-speaking people who stretch far beyond its present frontiers into these neighbouring states.

Most of the terrain consists of dry savannah plains, with a high mountain escarpment in the north, facing the coast. The climate is hot and dry, with an average annual temperature of 27°C, although temperate at higher altitudes and along the coast during June–September, with an annual rainfall which rarely exceeds 500 mm in the most favourable regions. Only two permanent rivers—the Juba and Shebelle—water this arid land. Both rise in the Ethiopian highlands, but only the Juba regularly flows into the sea. The expanse of territory between these two rivers is agriculturally the richest part of Somalia, and constitutes a zone of mixed cultivation and pastoralism. Sorghum, millet and maize are grown here, while along the rivers, on irrigated plantations, bananas (after livestock, the country's principal export) and citrus fruits are produced.

This potentially prosperous zone contains remnants of Bantu groups—partly of ex-slave origin—and is also the home of the Digil and Rahanwin, who speak a distinctive dialect and are the least nomadic element in the population. Of the other Somali clans—the Dir, Isaaq, Hawiye and Darod, primarily pastoral nomads who occupy the rest of the country—the Hawiye along the Shebelle valley are the most extensively engaged in cultivation, although a small subsidiary area of cultivation (involving Dir and Isaaq) also occurs in the north-west highlands.

In this overwhelmingly pastoral country, permanent settlements are small and widely scattered, except in the agricultural regions, and for the most part are tiny trading centres built around wells. There are few large towns. Mogadishu, the capital, which dates from at least the 10th century as an Islamic trading post, had an estimated population of 500,000 in 1981; and the other main centres are: Hargeysa (population 70,000 in 1981), capital of the northern regions, and Berbera (population 65,000 in 1981) and Kismayu (population 70,000 in 1981), the principal northern and southern ports respectively.

According to the results of a census taken in February 1975, the population of Somalia was 3,253,024 (excluding adjustment for underenumeration). The 1986–87 census estimated the total to have risen to 7,114,431. According to UN estimates, the population in mid-1992 had increased significantly to 9,204,000. Important demographic changes have taken place in recent years, beginning with the serious drought which affected the north of the country in 1974–75 and led to the resettlement of large numbers of people in the south. Between 1980–88, successive influxes of refugees from Ethiopia created a serious refugee problem before repatriations began in 1990. Of greatest consequence, however, has been the dislocation of Somalia's indigenous peoples during the civil unrest that began in the late 1980s; in early 1993 it was estimated that three-quarters of the population had been internally displaced by civil conflict. During 1988–91 an estimated 600,000 Somalis fled from the civil war into Ethiopia.

Recent History

PATRICK GILKES

Based on an earlier article by MILES SMITH-MORRIS

Having drawn up bilateral treaties with the clans of the area, the British declared a protectorate over northern Somalia in 1886, with the objectives of safeguarding the trade links of its colony Aden and excluding other interested powers (especially France). With the latter object in mind, Italy established a colony in southern regions in the same period, completing its control of coastal and inland areas by 1927. Italian Somaliland became, with Eritrea, a base for the Italian conquest of Ethiopia in 1936. The Italian colony was captured by British forces in 1941 and following the defeat of the Italians in east Africa, both it and British Somaliland (which had been briefly occupied by the Italians in 1940–41) were placed under British military administration. Under the provisions of the peace treaty of February 1947, Italy renounced all rights to Italian Somaliland. In December 1950, however, the former Italian colony became the UN Trust Territory of Somalia, placed under Italian administration for a 10-year transitional period prior to independence. The British protectorate had meanwhile reverted to civilian rule, while most of the Somali areas in Ethiopia had been returned to Ethiopian administration.

The trust territory's first general election on the basis of universal adult suffrage was held in March 1959, when 83 of the 90 seats in the legislative assembly were won by the Somali Youth League (SYL). Impelled by Italy's example, Britain similarly prepared its neglected protectorate for self-government. British Somaliland became independent on 26 June 1960, and on 1 July, having secured its own independence, the former Italian Somaliland united with the former British Somaliland as the independent Somali Republic. The president of the southern legislative assembly was proclaimed head of state and the two legislatures merged to form a single assembly in Mogadishu. A coalition government was formed by the SYL and the two leading northern political parties, with Dr Abdirashid Ali Shirmake, a leading SYL politician and a member of the Darod clan, as the first prime minister. Shirmake's government, representing a balance of northern and southern members representative of the main clans, set the pattern of Somali political life for the next decade.

The problems of merging the administrative systems of the two former colonies were offset to an extent by the shared Somali culture and by the presence of clans straddling the old colonial boundaries. Internal harmony was further encouraged, at the price of external conflict, by the commitment of all political leaders to a policy of extending the boundaries of the new state to include Somali communities in Ethiopia, French Somaliland (now Djibouti) and northern Kenya. Accordingly, liberation movements were established for these areas. In the 1964 elections the SYL comfortably secured a majority of seats in the assembly. However, a split within the SYL's Darod leadership, leading to the appointment of a new Darod prime minister, Abdirazak Haji Hussein, left the party seriously divided. The divisions within the ranks of the SYL culminated in the election as president in 1967 of Shirmake, who formed a new government with Muhammad Haji Ibrahim Egal, a northerner from the Isaaq clan, as prime minister. Acknowledging the failure so far of its efforts to promote Somali unification, the government, through the mediation efforts of President Kaunda of Zambia, reached agreement with Ethiopia and Kenya to negotiate a lasting settlement of the frontiers issue.

With external pressure on the republic diminished, the smaller constituent units of the traditional political structure came to the fore again, with an upsurge of divisive tribalism. Reflecting these trends, more than 1,000 candidates contested 124 seats in the March 1969 elections, representing 68 political parties and the most important lineages and sub-lineages of the Somali clan system. With the resources of the state at its disposal, and with considerable manipulation of the electoral arrangements, the SYL again secured victory, and Egal was reappointed prime minister. Following the formation of the customary clan-coalition government, all but one of the members of the assembly joined the ruling party. Because of the prevailing political fragmentation, however, the government and the assembly were in reality no longer representative of the public at large. Discontent was aggravated by the increasingly autocratic style of both the president and prime minister, and by the prime minister's efforts to provide political and administrative posts for northerners (who had persistently complained that earlier administrations, dominated by southerners, had failed to serve their interests).

THE SIAD BARRE REGIME, 1969–91

The inevitable climax occurred in October 1969, when, in pursuance of a factional quarrel, Shirmake was assassinated. When it became clear that the assembly would elect a new president supported by Egal, the army seized control in a bloodless *coup d'état*, arresting the prime minister and suspending the national assembly. A supreme revolutionary council (SRC), formed of army and police officers, announced that it had acted to preserve democracy and justice and to eliminate corruption and tribalism (clanism) and that the country had been renamed the Somali Democratic Republic to symbolize these aims. The president of the SRC, the army commander Maj.-Gen. Mohamed Siad Barre, became head of state.

Siad Barre swiftly assumed personal control of the government, introducing a policy of 'scientific socialism'. The Somali Revolutionary Socialist Party (SRSP) was established in 1976 under Soviet influence, but it was always used more as a mechanism for control than as an ideological vehicle. Nationalization proceeded steadily, embracing medical services, schools, banks, electricity and transport services and control of exports and imports. In 1975 land was nationalized: farmers received holdings on 50-year renewable leases from the state, but from the outset the system was subject to manipulation and corruption on a massive scale. (Subsequent efforts to recover land became a significant element in inter-clan conflict after 1991.) Prices and salaries were subject to state controls. A mass literacy campaign was launched, building on the adoption of Somali as the official language in 1972, using a modified Roman alphabet.

Somalia suffered from severe drought in the mid-1970s, although a wide-ranging programme of resettlement, carried out with the help of a massive Soviet airlift, relocated some 140,000 people to farming settlements in the agricultural south and experimental fishing settlements along the coast. This impressive response contributed to a relatively low death toll (about 18,000) but could do little to prevent devastating livestock losses.

During this period, the army's dependence on Soviet equipment and training greatly increased Soviet influence in Somalia. The USSR acquired a variety of military facilities, notably at the northern port of Berbera. Somalia nevertheless emphasized its traditional links by joining the Arab League in 1974, when Siad Barre also acted as chairman of the OAU. Ethiopia's revolutionary transformation in September 1974 to military socialism at first seemed to offer the prospect of an acceptable accommodation for Somali aspirations to self-determination in the Ogaden. These hopes were soon dashed, however, and as internal chaos spread in Ethiopia, Somalia saw an opportunity to reactivate claims to the Ogaden and the Somali-speaking regions of Ethiopia. In 1976, Siad Barre restructured the Western Somali Liberation Front (WSLF) and allowed it to operate inside Ethiopia. The Ogaden, the main clan in the Ogaden region and within the WSLF, represented a crucial element of Barre's clan support within Somali politics.

New urgency was given to Somalia's intentions by preparations for Djibouti's independence in June 1977 (both Somalia and Ethiopia had an interest in the strategic port of Djibouti and its rail link to Addis Ababa via Dire Dawa—passing through Somali inhabited areas;), and by Soviet overtures to Ethiopia's Col Mengistu after he took power in February 1977. (Ethiopia expelled US personnel in May.) Despite Soviet attempts to disuade him, Siad Barre's forces invaded Ethiopia, unofficially, in July 'in support of the WSLF'. Within three months Somali troops had overrun the Ogaden region and reached Harar. The USSR began to supply Ethiopia with weapons; in November 1977, Somalia abrogated its treaty of friendship with the Soviet Union and expelled 6,000 Soviet advisers and experts. Somalia obtained some financial assistance from Saudi Arabia, but hopes of Western assistance were largely frustrated, and by March 1978 the Soviet and Cuban-led counter-attack had re-established Ethiopian control in the main centres of the Ogaden and the Somali government announced the withdrawal of its forces.

Defeat in the Ogaden war and the break with the USSR was followed by a gradual strengthening of links with the USA, stemming from US strategy in the Gulf, following the Soviet intervention in Afghanistan. A defence agreement was announced in 1980, which permitted the use by US military personnel of the air and naval facilities at Berbera. The USA provided Somalia with substantial amounts of aid during the 1980s but remained hesitant about providing the military aid often sought by the Somali government as long as Somali forces continued to operate in Ethiopia. The US administration also expressed reservations regarding renewed Somali links with Libya after 1985.

The Ethiopian government's recovery of the Ogaden and its response to continued guerrilla operations as well as Somali army incursions (together with prevailing drought conditions), resulted in the flight, to Somalia, of hundreds of thousands of refugees. Western relief agencies responded generously, and relief food aid became a significant factor in the Somali economy. There was considerable disagreement over refugee numbers, with government estimates of as many as 1.5m., in contrast to a figure of 400,000 quoted by some relief agencies. The failure of rains in 1985 and 1986, and the recurrence of famine in 1987, led to further refugee movements. A compromise refugee figure of 800,000 was accepted for the provision of food relief in the later 1980s.

Military defeat, shifts in alliance and ideology, as well as famine and the influx of refugees, had considerable impact on internal politics. Opposition movements began to appear, notably the Somali Salvation Democratic Front (SSDF), a largely Majerteen-supported movement, and the Somali National Movement (SNM), whose support was largely drawn from the northern Isaaq clan. The Majerteen are a Darod clan living largely in the north east. Both movements received Ethiopian support. The SSDF took control of two small central Somali towns near the border in 1981 but virtually collapsed with internal divisions in the mid 1980s. In 1988, after a meeting in which Siad Barre and Col Mengistu agreed to restore diplomatic relations, withdraw troops from border areas, and end support for each other's dissidents, the SNM were ordered to leave their Ethiopian bases. This precipitated a premature guerrilla offensive. In May, the SNM seized Burao and captured most of Hargeysa, in the north. They were promptly ousted by a full-scale armed government response under the command of Gen. Mohamed Siad 'Morgan' (a son-in-law of the president). His uncompromising operations included the systematic bombardment of Hargeysa (by South African mercenary pilots), resulting in an estimated 40,000 deaths and the flight of around 400,000 refugees into Ethiopia. The brutal suppression of the insurgency resulted in far greater support for the SNM within the Isaaq and other northern clans than it had ever managed to achieve by its own efforts. Siad Barre's response to political and economic difficulty was to tighten his own control, although he allowed the introduction of a new constitution with an elected assembly, within the single-party system, in 1979. The perfunctory nature of the assembly's lack of power was underlined in November 1984 when it effectively transferred all government powers to the president. Although seriously injured in an automobile accident in May 1986, Siad Barre (as sole candidate) was re-elected president for a further seven-year term. In 1987 Siad Barre reluctantly agreed to the creation of the post of prime minister, which was occupied by Gen. Mohamed Ali Samatar, formerly first vice-president and defence minister. Siad Barre's serious injury in 1986 precipitated a struggle for the succession within his own Marehan clan and significantly weakened the government's position. The main claimants were his eldest surviving son, Gen. Maslah, and his cousin, Abdurahman Jama Barre, a veteran foreign minister; their rivalry divided the clan and also the armed forces. Economic difficulties were also increasing, as remittances from Somalis working in the Gulf and the Emirates declined in the aftermath of the Iran-Iraq war and then the conflict in the Persian (Arabian) Gulf, and international aid was also being reduced, as a result of concern over the regime's human rights record.

With the collapse of the economy, Siad Barre no longer had the resources to continue the manipulation of clan rivalries, which he had ruthlessly employed to ensure his political survival, and opposition continued to grow. In early 1989, a group of Hawiye notables established the United Somali Congress (USC), in exile, in Rome. The USC included a guerrilla wing, operating from Ethiopia, and headed by Gen. Mohamed Farah 'Aydeed'. (The Hawiye are the dominant group in Mogadishu and are particularly prominent in commercial and intellectual life.) Hawiye opposition was also expressed through the 'Manifesto' movement in Mogadishu which produced a declaration, in June 1990, calling for the resignation of Siad Barre, the establishment of a transitional government to organize democratic elections, and the immediate abolition of all security structures. Siad Barre's response was to arrest about half of the signatories, including the country's highly respected first president, Aden Abdullah Osman. In turn, the 'Manifesto' group began to nurture a military wing, although it was widely considered to be a part of the USC. The growth of opposition was further demonstrated by the arrest of a number of Muslim religious leaders, accused of supporting various opposition elements, which led to demonstrations in Mogadishu in July 1989. These were ruthlessly suppressed by the security police, with, with reports of as many as 1,500 dead and injured, including one instance in which 46 people, all northerners, were summarily executed. During 1989, the government also lost the support of the Ogaden clan, which together with the Dolbuhunta, had been the main supporters of Siad Barre's Marehan clan. Following the dismissal and arrest of the Ogadeni minister of defence, Gen. Aden Abdullahi 'Gebiyou', Ogadeni army deserters established the Somali Patriotic Movement (SPM) in the south. This gained considerable support from the Ogaden who had long considered that the Marehan, as the president's clan, had been able to expand their grazing at the expense of the Ogaden in the Juba valley. In response to mounting military and civil opposition, the government made some conciliatory gestures, but they were largely dismissed as superficial exercises. In August 1989, Siad Barre announced that opposition parties would be allowed to contest elections, scheduled to take place before the end of 1990, and additionally offered to relinquish power. One effect of this was to encourage the creation of political parties within those major clans that had yet to evolve a political identity. In January 1990 the president dismissed his government, castigating the prime minister, Gen. Samatar, for the government's poor performance. However, Siad Barre failed to persuade any opposition figures to join the administration, and was finally forced to reappoint Samatar.

A renewed military offensive in the north in early 1990 was largely successful in its aims, with the government temporarily recapturing a couple of towns from the SNM. Significantly, much of the fighting was carried out by clan militia, armed by the government to fight on a clan basis. In July, following the appearance of the 'Manifesto' group, the government announced a constitutional referendum for October to be followed by elections in February 1991. In September, Samatar was again dismissed, and replaced by, Mohamed Hawadle Madar, an Isaaq from the north. A month later it was announced that the multi-party system would take immediate effect, and Siad Barre relinquished the post of secretary-general of the SRSP, in accordance with the provisions of the new constitution, which proscribed the president's maintenance of additional official responsibilities. However, by late 1990 the government retained little authority outside Mogadishu. The army, its administration and command structure in decay owing to the over-promotion of untrained Marehan, had virtually disintegrated. Indeed, its clan support was essentially confined to the Marehan which was itself divided on the wisdom of continued support for Siad Barre, some believing that the fortunes of the president had become too closely allied to those of the clan. In November, widespread fighting erupted in Mogadishu when Siad Barre attempted to exploit an inter-clan dispute in order to attack the Hawiye. A full-scale uprising followed indiscriminate shelling of Hawiye areas of the city; USC guerrillas arrived in force and steadily advanced on the government's positions. Desperate efforts to form an acceptable government, headed by Omar Arteh Ghali, an Isaaq and a former minister of foreign affairs recently released by Siad Barre, and an announcement by Siad Barre that he would hand over power in exchange for a cease-fire, were ignored. Italian efforts to negotiate a peaceful hand over were also unsuccessful. On 27 January 1991, Siad Barre fled with the remnants of his army and the USC announced it had assumed the government of the country.

DESCENT TO CIVIL WAR

On announcing its take-over the USC had also called for all opposition forces to participate in a national reconciliation conference. However, on 29 January, the USC unexpectedly appointed one of the 'Manifesto' group, Ali Mahdi Mohamed, a prominent businessman, and former politician from the pre-1969 period, as interim president. The USC emphasized that it did not intend to form a permanent government, but other political groups saw the move as an attempt to pre-empt their participation, despite the appointment of non-Hawiye to government. On 2 February, Umar Arteh Ghalib was appointed prime minister at the head of a new government; other appointments included Gen. Mohammed Abshir, of the Majerteen clan. Umar Arteh, however, was considered to have compromised his position by his acceptance of the premiership shortly before Siad Barre's deposition, and was unpopular with the SSDF and the SNM. The majority of government posts were filled by Hawiye clan members, in particular those from the 'Manifesto' group.

In the north the SNM, which expelled the remnants of Siad Barre's forces in January and February 1991, convened a series of clan elders' meetings which led to the declaration of an independent 'Republic of Somaliland' in May. The SNM chairman, Abdurahman Ahmed 'Tur', was declared acting president, with the elders calling on the SNM to establish an administration to draft a constitution and organize multi-party elections within two years. The move was denounced by the USC and by the Mogadishu government. In the south, fighting erupted between the USC and elements from the Darod clan as Siad Barre tried to rally support under the banner of a Somali National Front (SNF). The move split one Darod clan, the Ogaden, and its political group, the SPM. One faction co-operated with the SNF and forces raised by Gen. Mohamed Siad 'Morgan', who led several advances of SNF forces towards Mogadishu during the course of 1991. The other wing of the SPM, led by Col Ahmed Omar Jess, united with the USC to oppose any attempts by Siad Barre to return. The southern port of Kismayu changed hands several times during the year. Much of the fighting was on a clan basis, between Hawiye (USC) and Darod (SNF or SPM), or between sub-clans of the Ogaden, which supported different wings of the SPM.

In June, President Hassan Gouled of Djibouti sponsored the first of two reconciliation conferences. The conference, convened in June, was chaired by ex-president Aden Abdullah Osman, and included delegations from the USC (Hawiye), the Somali Democratic Movement (a Rahenweyne organization), the SSDF (Majerteen), and the SPM (Ogaden). Unsuccessful efforts were made to persuade the SNM to attend a second meeting and participate in a transitional government for all Somalia. While the SNM refused to attend, two additional groups, the Somali Democratic Alliance (Gadabursi), and the United Somali Front (Issa), participated in the second conference, convened in July. An agreement was negotiated committing all those attending to resist the forces of Siad Barre, to implement a general cease-fire, to respect national unity, to re-adopt the 1960 constitution, and to respect Ali Mahdi's two-year mandate as interim president. Much discussion was devoted to dividing ministerial portfolios equitably among the clan groups. The Darod groups (the SSDF and the SPM) wanted a Darod prime minister, while others requested a northerner, though not Umar Arteh. Other major difficulties arose concerning Darod demands for the return of property seized after Siad Barre's deposition. Darod and Isaaq clans were estimated to have owned as much as 60% of land and property in Mogadishu before 1989. Most was looted in 1991 and appropriated by Hawiye, who were reluctant to return it. The issues of property and blood debt for deaths in the fighting have since remained highly contentious, and unresolved, problems.

The Mogadishu government's problems were compounded during 1991 by a major split in the USC, between the factions led by Ali Mahdi and by Gen. Mohamed Farah 'Aydeed' who had been the main USC guerrilla leader. These factions had different origins, but more importantly, they also represented different sub-clans within the Hawiye—Ali Mahdi being from the Abgal, a prominent group in and around Mogadishu; and Gen. Aydeed being from the Habr Gidir, who comprise a significant element of the more rural, pastoral Hawiye, living in the central regions of the country. The Abgal provided much of the support for the 'Manifesto' group while the Habr Gidir made up most of the Hawiye guerrilla forces. Many Habr Gidir felt that the 'Manifesto' politicians had benefited undeservedly, after coming late to the struggle and doing little fighting. Gen. Aydeed made it clear he felt he had a much better right to the presidency than Ali Mahdi. In July, at the third congress of the USC, he was elected USC chairman, affording him a significant power base. When Ali Mahdi failed to award ministerial posts to Gen. Aydeed's supporters in the reshuffle that followed the Djibouti conferences, confrontation seemed inevitable.

The first clash occurred in September 1991, when four days of fighting left hundreds dead and thousands wounded. More serious hostilities erupted in November and last until March 1992 when a cease-fire held after several previous attempts had broken down within hours. Both sides were exhausted, with food supplies short and no international body prepared to intervene until hostilities ceased. Stores of ammunition were also depleted. By then at least 30,000 people had died and thousands more had been injured, with Mogadishu in disarray and divided between the two sides. The struggle was complicated by two other Hawiye clan militias in Mogadishu, the Hawadle and the Murasade. The Hawadle, in possession of the airport, originally supported General Aydeed, the Murasade, in control of the port, backed Ali Mahdi.

The March 1992 cease-fire had been organized by the United Nations, which had first investigated the possibility of a UN peace-keeping force being sent to Somalia early in the year. On 23 January a resolution was adopted unanimously by the UN Security Council, imposing an arms embargo on Somalia, requesting humanitarian aid and urging the parties to cease hostilities. By the end of the month, hundreds of thousands of people displaced by the conflict were reported by the International Committee of the Red Cross to be in danger of starvation, and thousands of refugees from Somalia were continuing to cross the border into Kenya. Following the March cease-fire a UN technical team arrived to act in a supervisory capacity. In late April the UN Security Council approved the establishment of a 'UN Operation in Somalia' (UNOSOM) and the dispatch of 50 observers to Mogadishu. An Algerian diplomat, Mohammed Sahnoun, was appointed in April by the UN secretary-general as his representative in Somalia. He arrived in Mogadishu on 9 May to establish a UN presence. Deployment of the UN observers was slow, partly because Gen. Aydeed suspended co-operation with the UN for a time, alleging that UN aid flights to Mogadishu had been used to supply arms and funding for supporters of Ali Mahdi. The cease-fire monitors eventually arrived in late July. A further UN Security Council resolution on 27 July approved an urgent airlift of food aid to Somalia, the dispatch of a technical team and 48 military observers to assess the situation in preparation for deploying 500 UN peace-keeping troops. Agreement was finally reached with Gen. Aydeed on the presence of UN peace-keeping forces and the first elements of a Pakistani battalion arrived in Mogadishu in mid-September. The UN also approved the dispatch of a further 3,000 troops to Somalia though this was opposed by Gen. Aydeed.

The UN's gradual involvement during the course of 1992 failed to interrupt continuing fighting. Although the cease-fire in Mogadishu held, forces loyal to Siad Barre attempted to recapture the capital. In April these forces advanced to within 30 km of Mogadishu, only to be halted by Gen. Aydeed's forces in a battle at Afgoi on 18 April. Gen. Aydeed capitalized upon his victory by repulsing Siad Barre's forces, and Siad Barre himself, initially to Guerbaharre, where Siad Barre had been based since his over-throw, and then on into Kenya. The Kenyan government offered Siad Barre temporary refuge for 'humanitarian reasons'; however, following protests by more than 200 members of the Kenyan legislature, he moved on to Nigeria. Following his victory over Siad Barr's forces, in mid-May, Gen. Aydeed's troops, in alliance with Col Ahmed Omar Jess of one SPM faction, recaptured the southern port of Kismayu from the forces of Gen. 'Morgan'. 'Morgan' and his supporters also fled into Kenya. Gen. Aydeed's military successes and his efforts to establish administrative control of the whole of southern Somalia, generated considerable opposition. He himself formed a coalition, the Somali National Alliance (SNA), comprising his own USC, a faction of the SPM, a faction of the SDM, and the Southern Somali National Movement (SSNM), a political group of non-Darod clans to the south of Mogadishu. In response to this and to Gen. Aydeed's recent victories, Ali Mahdi strengthened his links with other opponents of Aydeed, notably the SSDF, the other SPM faction, and the SNF. After mid-1992, the SNF, although a largely Marehan organization, disassociated itself from Siad Barre. It did, however, also ally itself with General 'Morgan', who became one of its main military commanders. In October 1992, fighting again intensified. Gen. Aydeed's opponents, led by Gen. 'Morgan' and Gen. Ahmed Warsame of the SNF, recaptured Bardera, a strategic southern town and advanced towards Kismayu.

The escalation of fighting in October 1992 underlined the serious nature of food shortages in rural areas, particularly in the areas around Bardera. With the country in a state of anarchy all aid agencies encountered enormous difficulty in ensuring the security of relief supplies and of their own personnel, and many forced to hire armed guards from local clans for their protection. There were growing differences of opinion between the UN, which wished to secure a general cease-fire with the aid of peace-keeping forces, in order to protect relief supplies from looting, and the relief agencies which identified an urgent need to maximize food distribution as quickly as possible. By the middle of 1992 it had become apparent that a major humanitarian crisis had arisen in and around Bardera and Baidoa in the south of the country, largely owing to the destruction of food stocks in the area by the forces of Siad Barre in the months before and after their last attack on Mogadishu in April 1992. The failure of Gen. Aydeed's efforts to establish control in the area contributed to the severity of the problem. It was subsequently estimated that some 300,000 people may have died from starvation in this period. The UN's slow response to the humanitarian crisis was widely criticized. At a conference in Geneva in October 1992, convened for the launch of the UN's Hundred Day Programme for Somalia (a relief programme requesting more food aid, and the provision of basic health services—but including the rehabilitation of civil society), the UN secretary-general's special representative took the opportunity to criticize UN agencies, itemising them as inert and incompetent; he also questioned the continued lack of operations in Somalia of the World Health Organization (WHO). Sahnoun also advocated local reconciliation and a gradual approach to a national reconciliation conference, and was resistant to the idea of any rapid deployment of UN peace-keeping forces. His criticism of senior UN officials, and his disagreement with the UN secretary-general over future policy, forced his resignation in October 1992.

INTERNATIONAL INTERVENTION

Deteriorating conditions in Somalia in the latter part of 1992 prompted a response from the US government. In late November, President Bush, who had earlier authorized a US airlift to assist in food distribution, offered up to 30,000 US troops to ensure food deliveries to those in need, and to prevent looting. The offer was a cause for concern among many aid workers in Somalia, who felt that since the death toll had already slowed significantly, and food distribution had improved considerably, intervention on such a scale was unnecessary. The US proposition, however, coincided with the aim of UN secretary-general, Boutros Boutros-Ghali, to increase the UN's capacity to intervene in such crisis situations, and the UN welcomed the offer. It was suggested that an additional motivation for the US offer of intervention might have been the emergency of an Islamic political group in June 1992 in Somalia. A number of towns in the north-east of the country had been temporarily seized by the al-Itahad party. While they were promptly expelled by the SSDF Islamic groups continued to gain prominence in several other areas of the country, prompting US concern at the possibility of the spread of Iranian influence in Somalia, Kenya and Ethiopia.

Following the (albeit brief) convergence of UN and US interests the first US troops of the UN International Task Force (UNITAF) landed at Mogadishu on 9 December 1992 as part of 'Operation Restore Hope'. Contingents from 21 countries, including France, Belgium, Saudi Arabia, Zambia, Canada, Morocco and Australia participated. UNITAF forces were deployed throughout the country over the next few weeks, entering Baidoa on 16 December and Kismayu four days later. Under pressure from UNITAF, Gen. Aydeed and Ali Mahdi held peace talks, and on 27 December announced that they had signed a 'reconciliation agreement'. The scope and aims of UNITAF's operation, however, were both ill-defined and controversial. The US administration was determined to limit the activity of its forces to protecting the flow of aid. The UNITAF commander, a US officer, made it clear that he would not be prepared to carry out disarmament on a substantive scale. The UN, however, wanted the role of UNITAF to include complete disarmament of the rival factions and the establishment of security in the country, which it argued could not be achieved without full-scale disarmament of the factions and indeed of bandits, whose activities remained a considerable threat to security. However, UNITAF forces did carry out some seizures of weapons and the US claimed that the military task of restoring security had been completed by early February 1993, allowing the free movement of relief aid throughout Somalia. Nevertheless, violent incidents continued as the US administration negotiated the withdrawal of its forces and the hand over to a multi-national peace-keeping force under direct UN command. The strength of UNITAF, (some 38,300 men in mid-January 1993) had been reduced to 24,000 by early February, although there was disappointment among US officials at the poor level of UN preparedness for any hand over. One of the main areas of conflict remained Kismayu, where the forces of Gen. 'Morgan' and those of Col Ahmed Omar Jess' faction of the SPM were in conflict at the end of February. Clashes continued into March, prompting the US to dispatch marines in an attempt to restore order and reinforce the existing US and UN troops already deployed there.

Meanwhile, negotiations continued among the factions on proposed peace talks, which were scheduled to be held in Addis Ababa in mid-March 1993. Agreement on an agenda was achieved at a preliminary meeting of faction leaders in Addis Ababa in January. A national reconciliation conference opened in Addis Ababa on 15 March, with representatives from 15 leading factions, and with representatives of the SNM from the self-declared 'Republic of Somaliland' (see below) present with observer status. The conference nearly collapsed at the outset when Gen. Aydeed's supporters were ousted from Kismayu by Gen. 'Morgan' despite the presence of UN forces there. However, on 27 March, the leaders reached a compromise agreement, to form a 74-member transitional national council (TNC) as the supreme authority in Somalia, with a mandate to hold elections within two years. The council was to have three representatives from each of the 18 administrative regions of Somalia (inclusive of 'Somaliland'), as well as five representatives from Mogadishu and one from each of the 15 signatory factions to the agreement (which was not signed by the SNM). The agreement committed the factions to disarmament within 90 days and required the peace-keeping forces of the UN to administer the cease-fire through 'strong and effective sanctions against violators. However, concern was expressed that ambiguities contained within the final communique would lead to future disagreement over interpretation of the terms of the agreement. On the day preceding the signing of the agreement, the UN Security Council adopted Resolution 813, authorizing the deployment of UNOSOM II to replace UNITAF, and instructing it to use whatever means necessary to uphold peace, disarm combatants and protect relief workers. UNOSOM II, the largest peace-keeping operation to be dispatched under UN auspices, was also the first such operation to engage in peace enforcement without the consent of parties in the relevant country. It was to operate under Chapter VII of the UN Charter, allowing its forces to initiate military action as UNITAF had done. The creation of UNOSOM II followed proposals made by the UN secretary-general in March, that operations in Somalia should be transferred to a multi-national force of 28,000 men on 1 May. On 9 March, a retired US admiral, Jonathan Howe, was appointed as special representative of the secretary-general in Somalia, with a mandate to oversee the transition from UNITAF to UNOSOM II.

UNOSOM II, under the command of Gen. Cevik Bir of Turkey, formally took control of the peace-keeping operation on 4 May 1993, with over 30 countries contributing to a force which numbered some 30,000 at full strength. UNOSOM II inherited a series of difficulties from UNITAF and from US policies. The view that 'Somaliland' should be considered part of Somalia complicated UNOSOM's dealings with the north, while failure to disarm the militias and the factions meant that violent confrontation was difficult to prevent. UNITAF's acceptance of politicians and warlords as key negotiators rather than making serious efforts to widen the basis of political consultancy, meant that the existing political structures, responsible for the previous two years of anarchy, were reinforced. This also resulted in the promotion of personal conflicts at the expense of understanding clan hostilities. UNOSOM took this a stage further by taking sides and effectively declaring war on Gen. Aydeed, after US advisers had decided Aydeed was the one figure with no future role in negotiations, owing to his independent attitude towards UNITAF and towards the UN's presence in Somalia. A final legacy inherited by UNOSOM II was the independence of the US Rapid Deployment Force which remained under direct US command. It was this unit which was responsible for a series of attacks against Gen. Aydeed in Mogadishu, during 1993. Conflict began on 5 June in Mogadishu when fighting between Gen. Aydeed's SNA and UNOSOM left 23 Pakistani soldiers dead and 50 wounded. There were several hundred Somali casualties. The next day the UN Security Council condemned the 'unprovoked attack' on the Pakistani force and demanded the arrest and punishment of those responsible. Adm. Howe made it clear that he believed Gen. Aydeed was behind the attack and, in response, on 12 June UNOSOM forces launched a series of attacks on the SNA. These failed in their main objective of seizing Aydeed, and also provoked hostile reactions in Mogadishu. In one attack, on 13 June, Pakistani soldiers fired on a crowd of civilians killing 20 and injuring 50 others. On 17 June the UN issued a warrant for Aydeed's arrest on charges of war crimes. On the same day US helicopters attacked Aydeed's home in Mogadishu, destroying ammunition dumps. Increasingly violent operations which sought to disarm the SNA and arrest Gen. Aydeed continued over the next few months. One of the worst incidents occurred on 12 July when US helicopters attacked without warning a building they claimed was used by Aydeed as a command centre. The SNA subsequently claimed that the building had been occupied by a meeting of Somali elders seeking an end to the violence and that 73 people had been killed. The Red Cross assessed the number of dead at 52, while UNOSOM claimed that only 20 had died. In the aftermath of the attack, 4 foreign journalists were killed by enraged Somali crowds. The attack revealed clear divisions within the UNOSOM command structure. Italy, providing the third largest contingent, urged a suspension of military operations to defuse tension and promote dialogue. There were claims that UNOSOM's original humanitarian mission had been sacrificed to US government preoccupations with capturing Aydeed. The Italian view was echoed by aid agencies, the OAU and even by the UN's own department of humanitarian affairs. However, the secretary-general insisted that initiatives for disarmament should continue. Italy was asked to withdraw its commander in Somalia amid allegations that he was obeying Italian government orders rather than those of UN commanders, and unilaterally negotiating with Aydeed. A compromise agreement was eventually arrived at, whereby Italian troops in Mogadishu were to be redeployed elsewhere in the country.

UNOSOM continued to ignore all criticism of its actions, and in August 1993 the death of four US soldiers in another clash led to the dispatch of an élite counter-guerrilla US ranger unit to Mogadishu to reinforce efforts to capture Gen. Aydeed. Embarrassingly, four days after the Rangers arrival in Mogadishu in August, they mistakenly raided a UN compound and briefly arrested several UN employees. Subsequent US ranger operations were more successful and some senior members of the SNA were detained though no warrants had been issued, raising a number of questions about the legality of the detentions. UNOSOM claimed preventive detention was permissible under its mandate, and there was no obligation to allow access to lawyers. Human Rights organizations strongly criticized UNOSOM's arguments. Criticism was also levelled at UNOSOM's refusal to provide figures for Somalis killed as a result of its operations. In two further clashes, on 9 September and 25 September 1993, Somali casualties, including many civilians, were estimated at 500 dead and wounded. On 3 October effort by US rangers to seize Aydeed's supporters in a heavily-populated district led to an all-night battle in which 18 Rangers died, and one Malaysian soldier was killed, 84 American troops were injured and one taken prisoner (as was a Nigerian soldier). At least 200 Somalis were killed and over 700 were injured. The incident provoked renewed scrutiny of UN operations, which had become increasingly characterized by indiscriminate military action and damage to non-military installations.

The events of 3 October 1993 prompted an immediate change in American policy, encouraged by massive popular support for a US withdrawal. Although President Clinton's response was to dispatch reinforcements to the area, he made it clear that the US would promote a political rather than military solution to the conflict with Aydeed. Following the release of the two servicemen captured on 3 October and Aydeed's declaration of a unilateral cease-fire in mid-October, UNOSOM abandoned demands for Aydeed's arrest. Efforts were subsequently concentrated on a political settlement, although the last of the SNA political detainees held by UNOSOM were only finally released in January 1994 after an independent inquiry into the reasons for their detention.

Another UNOSOM objective during 1993 was the rehabilitation of local government through the establishment of district and regional councils, as detailed in the Addis Ababa conference of March 1993. However, local observers were again critical of the methods employed by UNOSOM, claiming that council members were often imposed or excluded (particularly in the case of SNA members) by UN officials. It was also suggested that the local administration rehabilitation programme had been precipitantly implemented, and had failed to address the problem of refugee resettlement.

Another reconciliation conference was convened in Addis Ababa in December 1993, and was again attended by faction leaders. No agreement was reached between the four factions of Gen. Aydeed's SNA and the 11 factions comprising Ali Mahdi's Somali Salvation Alliance (SSA). However, at an affiliated humanitarian conference convened simultaneously, it was made clear that UNOSOM intended to link further aid and assistance to political stability. This had the effect of encouraging local clan and regional agreements, some of which were concluded under UNOSOM auspices, while others were independently negotiated. The first of several regional conferences had been the Jubaland peace conference which took place in Kismayu between May and August 1993. Discussions included recommendations for a cease-fire and for the forcible encampment of militia forces. Negotiations also covered the creation of district councils, of local police and security forces, the rehabilitation of roads and the return of property (though the question of ownership was left undefined). However, this conference, and a subsequent Kismayu meeting, convened in June 1994 failed to produce any binding agreement between the Majerteen (Harti) and the Ogaden (both Darod—the major clan in the region, nor for an equitable division of resources with other claimants. Indeed the Ogaden elders did not attend the June 1994, owing to preoccupation with own efforts to achieve Ogaden unity. Other issues that remain to be resolved include the settlement of returning refugees and their role in already created councils, and outstanding claims and counterclaims regarding the ownership of land dating from the 1970s. UNOSOM's reaction to elders conferences was inconsistent. While it supported the Jubaland peace conferences, UNOSOM was accused of having attempted to sabotage a successful conference organized by Gen. Aydeed in May 1993 to settle conflicts between the Hawiye and Majerteen clans in central Somalia. It was also suggested that UNOSOM's negative attitude to the continued independence of Somaliland, during meetings with clans from the north east at Garowe in late 1993, undermined considerable progress in inter-clan co-operation proceeding from discussions which took place in Engavo between August and November, at which UNOSOM were not officially represented. The decision of the US, and most European contingents, to withdraw from Somalia by March 1994, meant that the UN's mandate had to be revised. Although both India and Pakistan increased their contingents, UNOSOM no longer had sufficient personnel to carry out its larger mission. In February, the UN Security Council revised UNOSOM's mandate, authorizing a progressive reduction of troops to a maximum of 22,000. This meant an end to UNOSOM's programme of disarmament of Somali factions, in favour of the protection of ports, airports and roads. In May 1994 the UN Security Council voted to extend UNOSOM's mandate for four months (rather than six, as requested by the secretary-general). By May US spokesmen had begun to advocate complete withdrawal, and by mid-1994 it was unclear if the UN would be prepared to maintain a presence in Somalia until the original deadline of March 1995. There was growing alarm at the cost of UNOSOM, with daily running costs of US \$2.5m., while the cost of the deployment of US troops in Somalia between December 1992 and March 1994 was estimated at \$1,200m. There was also considerable consternation at the failure of Somali faction leaders to make further political progress. Meetings in Nairobi, Kenya, in March 1994 had brought about another agreement between Gen. Aydeed and Ali Mahdi to establish a government, but by the end of July there had been five postponements, and no meeting, because of disagreements over the timing and location of future meetings. Gen. Aydeed's return to Mogadishu in May did not improve prospects for peace. Renewed conflict erupted between factions of the Hawiye clan and there were indications that Gen. Aydeed was encountering dissension within his own clan and political organization. Gen. Aydeed's Habr Gidir and the

Hawadle clan disputed control of the airport, and their conflict extended north to Beled Weyne in late July where the Habr Gidir took control. UNOSOM subsequently evacuated its troops from the region after the entire 168-strong Zimbabwe contingent was disarmed by Gen. Aydeed's men.

There was a steady deterioration in security after March 1994 with an increase in banditry, abductions of aid workers and attacks on UNOSOM personnel. The World Food Programme suspended operations in Kismayu in April, after persistent threats to its employees. In the same month $2.6m. of UN personnel salaries was stolen from the organization's compound in Mogadishu. The creation of an 8,000-strong police force by the end of June 1994, was one of UNOSOM's more successful initiatives. However, the force was insufficiently equipped to deal effectively with the factions. UNOSOM's problems were compounded in 1994 by an outbreak of cholera early in the year. By the time it had been contained (mid-year) more than 1,000 people had died and 27,000 been affected. In late 1993, the UN had established a commission of enquiry to investigate the violent exchanges which had resulted in the deaths of more than 100 peace-keeping troops and several thousand Somalis (the SNA claimed at the beginning of 1994 that 13,000 Somalis had been killed by UNOSOM). The report, which was extensively leaked prior to its publication, attributed responsibility for some atrocities to Gen. Aydeed, but was also highly critical of UNOSOM methods. Among prominent criticisms were those of inadequate training and equipment, and a lack of co-ordination between military and civilian elements. UNOSOM was also accused of having underestimated Somali military capacity, and political advisers were said to have lacked expertise and to have been insensitive to Somali culture. The US was criticised for its 'premature' withdrawal and for its insistence on retaining command of its own troops. The report suggested that the UN should consider compensation for innocent Somali victims of the conflict. It also concluded that UNOSOM, rather than providing assistance for Somalia, as was intended, 'tried to impose a political solution' inconsistent with the UN mandate.

THE 'REPUBLIC OF SOMALILAND'

The 'Great Conference of the Northern Peoples', convened in May 1991, entrusted the SNM with the task of forming a government and drafting a constitution for the 'republic of Somaliland'. From the outset the SNM was divided on the issue of independence. Several SNM leaders had expressed opposition to secession from Somalia. In addition, clan divisions arose over the distribution of ministerial portfolios and the allocation of resources. These divisions rendered the government virtually inoperative. However, the major problem for the government, headed by President Ahmed Ali 'Tur' was a shortage of resources. Without international recognition it proved extremely difficult to attract aid, and this in turn meant the government had no means to settle the claims of ex-guerrilla fighters, nor could it afford to demobilize them. Only assistance from non-government and organizations enabled the government to begin the work of repairing the war-damaged infrastructure of the region, and some progress was made in the removal of mines (it has been calculated that there are about 2m. such devices to be cleared).

Progress in reconstruction was hampered by clan fighting that broke out in Burao in January 1992, and in Berbera twice during the year. The conflict, between Isaaq sub-clans (the Habr Yunis, the clan of President 'Tur', and the Habr Awal) was exacerbated by the grievances of the guerrillas and by government inactivity. Peace negotiations initiated by clan elders brought the conflict to an end in October 1992, though the key economic port of Berbera remained outside government control. With the SNM leadership divided, political power passed into the hands of the national council of elders, who met at Boroma between February and May 1993 in a national reconciliation conference attended by 150 elders from all 'Somaliland' clans, with support from another 150 advisers and observers. Following the SNM's failure to establish a constitution and an effective government, the meeting formulated a national peace charter and a transitional structure of government. This was to comprise a council of elders (an upper house), an elected constituent assembly and an executive council (council of ministers). On 5 May 1993, Mohamed Ibrahim Egal from the Habr Awal clan (a former prime minister of Somalia during the 1960s), was elected president, defeating the incumbent president, Ahmed Ali 'Tur', by 97 votes to 24. However, Egal's election failed to resolve clan differences. In June 1993, following the announcement of Egal's cabinet, the Habr Yunis clan claimed that the appointments were calculated to foment clan rivalry and that assembly seats had been unjustly distributed. Habr Yunis opposition has since continued and a clan conference in June 1994 rejected Egal's government. (Ahmed Ali 'Tur' had publicly renounced secession early in the year.)

Somaliland leaders have continued to express concern at their relationship with the UN. They have consistently made clear their opposition to the deployment of UN peace-keeping forces in 'Somaliland'. Demonstrations against the possible deployment in the region of UNOSOM II forces took place in Hargeysa in April 1993. Adm. Howe, as special representative of the UN secretary-general, visited 'Somaliland' after Egal's election and pledged UN support for reconstruction. However, the UN stance at regional and political conferences still indicated that it would continue to consider 'Somaliland' as part of Somalia. By mid-1994 the 'republic of Somaliland' had failed in its attempts to achieve international recognition. In July, President Egal, following an invitation from President Mubarak to visit Egypt, expressed the hope that international attitudes were changing. However, a few weeks later he intimated that the solution for 'Somaliland' might be to reconsider the 1960 independence agreement and adopt a fresh approach to federation. Meanwhile, influential Western nations have identified the region's lack of political and civil stability as reasons for their refusal to recognise an independent Somaliland, denying the aid and investment necessary to address the region's problems.

Economy

MILES SMITH-MORRIS

Revised for this edition by the Editor

AGRICULTURE

Since independence in 1960, Somalia's economic growth has failed to keep pace with the rise in the country's population, which has been expanded by the influx of refugees. Over the period 1985–92, the population increased by an annual average of 3.1%. In 1990, according to estimates by the World Bank, Somalia's gross national product (GNP), measured at average 1988–90 prices, was US $946m., equivalent to $150 per head. During 1980–90, it was estimated, GNP grew, in real terms, at an average annual rate of 1.1%, while real GNP per head decreased by 1.8% per year (with the average rate of decline accelerating to 5.5% per year in 1988–90). In 1990 agriculture contributed 66% of gross domestic product (GDP) and the sector engaged 69.0% of the labour force in 1992. During 1980–90 agricultural production increased by an annual average of 3.1%; in 1991, however, output declined by 8.8%.

The economy is traditionally based, principally on the herding of camels, sheep, goats and cattle (the latter mainly in the southern regions), which still provide for the subsistence needs of about 75% of the population and furnish a substantial export trade in live animals, skins, clarified butter and canned meat. After independence, exports of these items rose dramatically and outstripped the other main export, bananas. In 1989 livestock products accounted for about 49% of GDP.

Exports of livestock products accounted for about 80% of Somalia's total earnings of foreign exchange in 1982. However, this sector—and, indeed, the entire economy—was severely dislocated by the suspension of imports in 1983 by Saudi Arabia, Somalia's largest customer. A supply agreement with Egypt failed to compensate for this, and earnings from livestock exports fell to 1,122m. Somali shillings in 1983, and to only 514m. Somali shillings in 1984. In 1985, however, earnings recovered to 2,604m. Somali shillings, as exports of sheep and goats to Saudi Arabia resumed. In 1986 and 1987 earnings from livestock exports increased dramatically to 4,420m. and 7,300m. Somali shillings, respectively, but declined to 3,807m. Somali shillings in 1988 and about 2,300m. Somali shillings in 1989, owing to the fighting in the northern regions of Somalia, where the majority of the livestock is raised. The livestock sector was also severely affected by drought in the mid-1970s and in 1984/85. In March 1985 the government requested emergency international assistance for a $51m. programme to construct 120 water reservoirs in the north, but by the middle of the year it was estimated that up to 30% of Somalia's livestock faced death from drought. A six-year programme to control livestock diseases, based in Hargeysa, was launched in 1986 with backing from the International Fund for Agricultural Development. In April 1989 Italy's official aid programme financed a $37m. joint venture between the Italian company Giza and the Somali government to operate a 14,000 ha farm, whose livestock will be for export to the Arabian peninsula. In 1990 the African Development Fund approved a $24.4m. loan to help finance cattle-breeding and fishing projects; in November 1990 the Islamic Development Bank (IDB) also announced its willingness to assist Somalia in increasing its livestock exports.

Bananas are grown on plantations along the Juba and Shebelle rivers. Output increased by more than 70% in the first five years after independence, but declined steadily from 1972, when production totalled 188,500 metric tons, to 75,000 tons in 1986, but rose to 116,000 tons in 1989. Bananas, which, with livestock, form the backbone of Somalia's exports, earned 2,469m. Somali shillings in 1987 and 3,992m. Somali shillings in 1988, when revenue from livestock exports totalled 3,807m. Somali shillings; in 1987 livestock exports had accounted for 7,300m. Somali shillings, representing 67% of total exports. A decision in 1983 to sell the majority of shares in the National Banana Board—which controlled exports after 1970—to the private sector led to optimism about a revival in production, as did the October 1985 agreement by Italy, the major importer, to abolish tax on bananas imported from Somalia, and the continuing efforts to improve agricultural technology.

Other fruits, as yet chiefly for local consumption, are grown on plantations in the same area. Sugar cane is a significant crop, and a number of rehabilitation schemes are under way with the aim of making the country self-sufficient in sugar, with a small surplus available for export. To this end, a second sugar factory was built as part of the Juba sugar estate development, established in 1977. Production of cotton has more than doubled, with output of seed (unginned) cotton reaching about 7,000 tons per year in the 1980s, but there is still insufficient locally-grown cotton to meet the demands of the textile factory at Balad, and the balance must be imported. Large-scale expansion of the Somaltex factory made it, by 1979, one of the best-equipped textile mills in Africa, but by November 1984 a major rehabilitation was needed, and by 1985 output had fallen to just 30% of capacity. Incense has fared better; in 1983 Somalia overtook Ethiopia to become the world's leading producer, selling more than 2,000 tons annually.

The area between the rivers, of which at present only some 700,000 ha of an estimated potential of 8.2m. ha are under cultivation, also provides the subsistence maize and sorghum crops of the southern Somali. The full utilization of this fertile belt, envisaged in development plans, should meet the grain needs of the domestic market and provide a subsidiary export crop. Experiments in growing rice, with assistance from the People's Republic of China, may eventually enable Somalia to dispense with costly imports of this food. Twelve major agricultural development programmes were launched in the early 1980s, and others were to follow. It is hoped that, together with 'self-help' programmes in the villages, these may enable Somalia to achieve self-sufficiency in basic foodstuffs. Production of cereals increased steadily, from 227,000 tons in 1970 to 612,000 tons in 1987, despite devastating drought in the mid-1970s and the 1980s. In 1985 Somalia became self-sufficient in maize and sorghum, but has not managed to maintain this achievement. The country's potential as a producer of grain has been affected by the imbalance caused by imports of food (of which about one-half was food aid), which increased by an annual average of 8% between 1980–84. Three vast new agricultural settlement schemes in southern Somalia, for the victims of the 1974–75 drought, offered scope for increased production. However, the influx of refugees (from the Ogaden and then from Ethiopia's Hararge Administrative Region), estimated to total 840,000 by 1988, together with the civil war, posed serious economic problems, despite aid from the UN High Commissioner for Refugees and other international organizations.

One of the largest agricultural schemes, at Afgoi-Mordile, was reactivated in 1985, after being suspended since the late 1970s. Bananas, grapefruit, papaya and vegetables will be grown by a joint Libyan–Somali company, while rice, maize and sesame seed will be produced by smallholders over a total of 2,500 ha. The planned Bardera dam, on the Juba river, is regarded as a vital step towards self-sufficiency in food, and is being given priority in development planning. The dam is expected to fulfil three separate functions: flood control, irrigation and power supply. It will irrigate a minimum of 175,000 ha of agricultural land, and, by providing power for Mogadishu, should enable the cost of petroleum imports to be reduced by 20%. Finance was to come from the European Development Fund, the IDB, Abu Dhabi, France, Italy, Saudi Arabia and Germany. Under the public investment programme announced in 1987, the project was to be allocated $106m.

during the period 1987–90, with the total cost estimated at $317m. and completion scheduled for 1992. By 1990, however, work had yet to start and estimated costs had risen to $780m.

FISHING

Before 1972 fishing along the Somali coast was mainly a small-scale subsistence activity. By 1980 it was coming to be regarded as one of the country's leading priorities. During the 1974–75 drought some 12,000 nomads were settled and organized in fishing co-operatives, which have shown considerable promise. There were 4,000 full-time and 10,000 part-time fishermen in 21 co-operatives in 1981. The annual fish catch doubled between 1975 and 1980, reaching 10,000 tons per year. However, fish is still a negligible part of the Somali diet. Originally organized with Soviet assistance, the industry suffered a setback in 1977 when Soviet advisers were expelled and withdrew their trawlers from the projects. The industry is receiving aid from the EU and other Western sources. In 1979 Somalia helped to found a joint Arab fisheries company, created under the auspices of the Arab League. Agreement was reached with Italy, in 1980, on a joint fishing venture in which the Italians were to provide four trawlers as well as training and technology. The Food and Agriculture Organization (FAO) has identified the Hafuna region as one of excellent potential for sardine fishing, and is expanding its training and technical assistance. The World Bank lent US $13.5m. to develop traditional fishing on the north-east coast, while Japan constructed two cold chambers and two fish markets for Mogadishu. In 1986 the People's Republic of China provided a further $17m. for fisheries development. Under the 1987–89 public investment programme, the sector was allocated $88m., of which almost one-half was to be spent on upgrading and expanding the fishing fleet. Further assistance was promised in 1987 by the EU, under the aid provisions of the third Lomé Convention. In 1988 Somalia's potential annual catch of fish was assessed at 200,000 metric tons and potential revenue at $26m. per year; however, according to estimates by the FAO, the actual annual catch for that year and the following year was only 18,200 tons. In 1991 the catch declined to 16,100 tons.

MINERALS AND INDUSTRIAL PRODUCTS

Petroleum exploration has so far proved disappointing. Since the mid-1940s more than 60 exploratory wells have been sunk, but by early 1986 only one-third of the concessions on offer were under contract to European or North American oil companies for exploration. Plans to start oil exploration off Somalia's Indian Ocean coast were announced by Mobil Corporation and Pecten, the US subsidiary of Shell, in 1990, but postponed as the civil war intensified later in that year. The government of the 'Republic of Somaliland' made contacts with a number of international oil companies during 1991 and 1992 and an exploration agreement for a block between Hargeysa and Burao was reported to have been signed with US-based Alliance Resources. But the company failed to take up its permit and other companies, while expressing interest, appeared reluctant to commit themselves until the republic had achieved international recognition. In April 1979 a petroleum refinery, jointly developed with Iraq, went into operation with a throughput of 10,000 barrels per day. Somalia assumed ownership of the refinery in December 1984. Production of petroleum products, which has been hindered by the irregularity of supplies of crude oil and by technical problems, amounted to 227,000 tons in 1983, 143,000 tons in 1984 and 156,000 tons in 1985. However, production declined to 44,000 in 1987, and to just 30,000 in 1988. Construction of a petroleum refinery in Mogadishu, with finance provided by two Saudi Arabian firms and Somali entrepreneurs, has been under consideration for some time. Petroleum accounted for about one-third of total expenditure on imports in 1988.

Deposits of a number of minerals, including gold, silver, manganese and tungsten, were discovered during surveys of the site of the planned Mogadishu refinery and a local company was given a licence to carry out detailed prospecting in the area. Deposits of uranium ore were discovered to the west of Mogadishu in 1972, and in late 1984 work began on developing Somalia's uranium reserves. Somalia contains some of the world's largest gypsum deposits, near Berbera, as well as iron ore, coal, granite and zinc. The mining sector contributed only only 0.3% of GDP in 1988.

Industry is small in scale and mostly based on agriculture: meat- and fish-processing, textiles and leather goods. Between 1974–77 employment in the industrial sector increased by 20% and gross output by 65%. In 1980 the sector employed 8.4% of the labour force, and in 1988 contributed 8.6% of GDP. More than 80% of enterprises were formerly state-owned, but the government subsequently gave priority to plans to attract private investment. The country's first pharmaceuticals factory, built mainly with Italian aid, was completed in 1984, but has yet to enter into production. In early 1986 the Italian government proposed renovating the factory, and operating it as a joint venture. France has agreed to finance the inauguration of the Berbera cement works (with a capacity of 200,000 tons per year), which lay idle for more than a year, after its completion in early 1985, because of foreign exchange problems. Opportunities for further development under the 1987–89 public investment programme were limited. Manufacturing was allocated only $84m., the bulk of which will go to the Juba sugar estate and factory. In May 1989 a hide and skin processing plant was completed in Mogadishu. The plant, financed by the Italian government at a cost of $9.8m., is targeted to process 4.1m. hides and skins every eight months.

PUBLIC FINANCE

Despite the rise in exports after independence, imports, and the country's external debt, also increased. Budgetary expenditure has also risen sharply since independence, and receipts, which derived principally from indirect taxation (especially customs and excise dues) have failed to cover the shortfall.

From 1969 the government made vigorous attempts to increase the country's self-sufficiency. Since 1971 the national budget has been divided into the ordinary budget, which is financed from internal sources, and the development budget, of which about 65% is financed from overseas sources. In 1988 Somalia recorded a budget deficit of 10,009.4m. Somali shillings. A provisional budget for 1991 was projected to balance at 268,283.2m. Somali shillings. The country's total external debt was US $2,447m. at the end of 1992, of which $1,898m. was long-term public debt. In 1990 (when the long-term debt totalled $1,926m.) the cost of debt-servicing was equivalent to 11.7% of the value of exports of goods and services.

The current deficit on the balance of payments increased sharply after the Ogaden war and continued to increase until 1980. Despite a stabilization programme adopted in 1980 with the help of a $14m. stand-by credit from the IMF, loans of $9m. from OPEC and of $47m. from the Arab Monetary Fund were required to offset balance-of-payments deficits. In July 1981 a further stand-by credit of $46.6m. was granted by the IMF in support of a new fiscal policy, involving the introduction of a two-tier exchange rate, with a 'parallel' rate (representing a 50% devaluation of the Somali shilling) for exports. The two-tier exchange rate was abolished after one year and a further IMF stand-by credit was granted. The government took steps to liberalize the economy by abolishing the state trading companies and introducing strict measures to control currency.

The economy showed some encouraging signs of revival from 1981 to 1983, but deteriorated badly in 1984. An IMF stand-by credit expired in January 1984, and negotiations for an extension of these arrangements broke down over Somali reluctance to undertake the further currency devaluation that was demanded by the IMF. The Somali economy passed through 1984 without IMF support and with the additional handicap of a huge trade deficit, resulting from the ban on livestock exports to Saudi Arabia. Inflation reached 100%, and the 'black market' thrived. The Somali government eventually agreed to a 32% devaluation of the Somali shilling in September, and to a further 29% devaluation, with the introduction of a two-tier exchange rate, in January 1985. An IMF stand-by credit of $54.7m. was duly announced, as part of a programme which included a further liberalization of the economy, especially in the import/export sector, and a reduction of price controls. However, disbursements were suspended after just a few weeks, because of a major dispute over Somalia's exchange rate policy.

In December 1985 the Somali shilling was again devalued, by about 50%, and in early 1986 the IMF resumed lending to Somalia, after officials of the central bank had agreed to the introduction of a system whereby the currency's value would be determined by means of fortnightly auctions of available foreign exchange. The auctions began in September 1986, assisted by a 'soft' loan of $50m. from the International Development Association (IDA), and by balance-of-payments support from the USA and Italy. Shortages of funds led to the suspension of the auctions in mid-January 1987, but they were resumed in February, after the USA and Italy agreed to make additional contributions. In June, after the government had acted to clear $29m. of arrears owed to the IMF, loans totalling SDR 53.9m. were approved by the IMF, of which SDR 33.15m. was to be drawn over the next 20 months under a stand-by arrangement, while the remainder was to be available over the next three years under the Fund's Structural Adjustment Facility. In July the 'Paris Club' of Western creditor governments agreed to reschedule $170m. of Somali government debt over a period of 20 years. However, debt principal and interest due to be repaid in 1987 and 1988 ($138m. and $146m. respectively) remained substantially in excess of Somalia's forecast export earnings in those years, while outstanding arrears were estimated at $100m.

In September 1987 it was announced that the system of auctioning foreign currency by the central bank was to be abandoned and that there would be a return to a fixed rate of exchange, set at 100 Somali shillings = US $1. This reversal of financial policy was believed to have been prompted by a 14% depreciation of the Somali shilling which had occurred between August and September, and by protests at rising prices. The government stated its intention to restructure the economy towards self-sufficiency and to balance state revenues and expenditure, and that it would implement a policy of austerity. Since the continuation of the foreign exchange auctions had been one of the principal conditions of Somalia's agreement with the IMF in June, the IMF suspended disbursement of the loans, and the World Bank also suspended the remaining $10m. of a credit of $50m. for agricultural adjustment that had been approved in 1986.

In February 1988 a committee was established by the government to review Somalia's relationship with the IMF and other Western financial institutions, but talks held in March between the government and the IMF foundered on the government's reluctance to readopt the auction system to determine the value of the Somali shilling. In May Somalia was declared ineligible for further borrowing from the IMF, owing to its overdue financial obligations to the Fund, which totalled SDR 26.8m. In June, in an effort to resume negotiations with the IMF, the government effected a 45% devaluation of the Somali shilling and in July it was reported that Somalia had signed an economic and financial agreement with the IMF, under the terms of which it undertook to repay its debts to the Fund with livestock, fish and other natural resources. A further devaluation of the Somali shilling, of about 20%, took place in August, and in January 1989 the government indicated that the foreign exchange auctions would be resumed on a monthly basis in March. The government also introduced significant reforms in both the agricultural and financial sectors, with the liberalization of the trade in hides and skins and veterinary pharmaceuticals, together with plans to permit the opening of foreign banks and the abolition of the state monopoly of insurance. These measures facilitated the adoption in mid-1989 of an IMF-supported structural adjustment programme. This, however, did little to help the government solve its financial problems. In September a Somali government delegation visited the IMF headquarters in Washington to discuss debt arrears and to seek eligibility for fresh loans. The delegation failed in its mission, however, despite an attempt on the part of the IMF to form a support group to raise resources to pay off Somalia's $100m. arrears. Of the seven largest donor countries, only Italy agreed to provide further lending to clear arrears, although this was made conditional on the participation of other members of the support group in financing the debt. The government's financial position continued to deteriorate during 1990, owing to growing instability and donors' reluctance to provide support because of concern about the government's human rights record. There were hopes, however, that Somalia might benefit from a new initiative by the IMF, the rights accumulation programme, allowing countries in arrears to the Fund to accumulate borrowing rights by implementing an adjustment programme and keeping up to date on their interest payments. In 1991 the annual rate of inflation was estimated at more than 100%; it was estimated to have averaged 75.4% annually during 1985–92.

Somalia's long history of civil unrest (which intensified following the overthrow of President Siad Barre in January 1991), together with erratic climatic conditions, have undermined the traditional agricultural base of the economy. Agricultural production in 1991–92 was estimated at just 5%-10% that of 1987–88, although an increase in rainfall contributed to more encouraging forecasts for 1992–93. In the absence of government-led initiatives for economic reform, an 'unconventional economy' regulated by clans and sub-clans evolved, fuelled by workers' remittances from abroad (often in the form of foreign exchange and household goods and appliances), unrecorded sales of livestock and the cultivation and sale of qat (a mild stimulant). The response of international relief and assistance organizations to the humanitarian crisis in Somalia has contributed to this economy, with clans competing for revenues proceeding from the provision of equipment and accommodation for foreign personnel, the sale of food supplies looted from aid deliveries and (prior to the arrival of UNITAF in December 1992) the exaction of protection money from relief organizations.

FOREIGN AID AND DEVELOPMENT PROJECTS

Between 1960–69 the republic received a substantial amount of foreign aid, chiefly from Italy, the USA and the USSR, but without producing any proportionate return. Between 1963–70 a series of plans was launched by the government to improve the resources of the country. Although these overall plans proved too ambitious, much was accomplished during those years, notably in road-building, the construction of ports at Berbera (with aid from the USSR) and Kismayu (with US aid), the building of schools, and a large EU-financed hospital at Mogadishu. Few projects for livestock management and agricultural development had successfully got beyond the planning stage by 1969.

Under the Siad Barre regime, many of these projects became operational. The government was initially concerned to encourage the sort of 'self-help' rural development projects (e.g. in school-building or well-digging) which had already, before 1969, produced good results. The policy was to develop the Somali economy along socialist lines, although private enterprise on a small scale was encouraged as having its part to play, and to aim for self-sufficiency, particularly in food production.

The 1974–78 Five-Year Plan was delayed, since resources had to be diverted for drought relief in 1974–75. Total economic losses and the relief operations actually cost £218m. sterling. In April 1976 the World Bank issued an $8m. loan to help to repair the effects of the drought.

About one-half of the expenditure of 7,104m. Somali shillings envisaged in the 1979–81 Development Plan was to finance projects carried forward from the previous Five-Year Plan. Of this budget, 35.4% was allocated to agriculture and fisheries, 18% to economic infrastructure and 7.4% to education. There was a new emphasis on the needs of small producers rather than large-scale schemes. The 1982–86 Plan envisaged overall expansion in real GDP of 27% over five years, equivalent to an annual average growth of 4.6%. Between 1980–87, GDP increased by an estimated 2.2%. The 1982–86 Plan attracted declarations of intent totalling $1,200m. from a donors' meeting in October 1983. However, many projects had to be deferred when the economy was severely dislocated by the problems over livestock exports. Under the 1987–91 Plan, GDP growth was expected to average 5%. The Plan projected expenditure at $1,742.2m., with transport and telecommunications accounting for $401.8m. and agricultural development for $499.3m.

At the consultative group meeting with aid donors in April 1987, pledges, at $835m., fell short of the $1,025m. which the government had sought for its 1987–89 public investment programme. This agreement covered commodity, project and cash aid, of which $428m. was to be allocated in 1987 and $407m. in 1988. The IDA would provide $24m. for a programme to modernise Kismayu, Mogadishu and Berbera ports, while, under the third Lomé Convention, the EC (now the European Union—EU) would provide ECU 5m. for the construction of bridges over the Juba and Shebelle rivers, ECU 3m. for road modernization and ECU 3m. for a project to increase fish production in the Mogadishu area. Total project aid, at $720m. over three years, would cover only 70% of the public investment programme for 1987–89. Donors asserted, however, that the shortfall was attributable to the government's inclusion of projects outside the 'core' investment programme. Following the April consultative meeting, the government agreed to establish a project-monitoring system to ensure the observance of strict expenditure guidelines.

Until 1977 the major source of aid was the USSR, together with the People's Republic of China (which has been particularly active in road-building), the European Development Fund (EDF), UN specialized agencies, the IDA and the Federal Republic of Germany. Since 1974 Arab states have also been very important contributors, especially Libya, the United Arab Emirates and Saudi Arabia, which is reported to have supplied over £250m. for military aid in the war with Ethiopia. However, Arab aid was reduced substantially in 1985, with new commitments falling to $12.1m., only one-fifth of the amount that Arab states supplied in 1984. In April 1987 bilateral discussions were reported to take place with the Arab funds to reschedule Somalia's external debt. After Siad Barre's visits to Abu Dhabi, in January and March 1989, the United Arab Emirates reportedly provided substantial financial aid to Somalia. Following the 1980 agreement permitting US forces to use Somalia's military bases, the USA became a major donor. Its support was particularly important for Somalia's transport systems, which were among Africa's poorest.

In 1985 work finished on a US-sponsored $37.5m. project to double the number of berths at Berbera port and to deepen its harbour, which handles a large volume of cattle exports. Soon afterwards, a $42m. development of Kismayu port began, which it was hoped would equip the port to handle livestock in addition to bananas. The USA also financed the expansion of the runway at Mogadishu airport. US aid, which was suspended in 1988, because of the Somali government's alleged abuses of human rights and the protracted civil war, was resumed in 1989 following the release of over 200 political prisoners in January. In May the USA supplied 6,536 tons of edible oil worth $5m. and in June signed a grant agreement worth $15.1m. However, a further $36.3m. of aid for 1988/89 remained blocked because of the continuing conflict in the north. In February 1990 the US suspended all financial aid for 1990/91 in protest at Somalia's 'long pattern of human rights abuses'. During that financial year the USA was to provide only $750,000 for some projects already in progress. A more traditional benefactor is Italy, which greatly increased its involvement in 1985, when it offered more than $200m. in special assistance from its emergency aid fund for Africa, mostly for the construction of a road linking Garowe to Bosaso, to provide access to the isolated north-east. In 1989 Italy financed the reconstruction and expansion of Mogadishu airport.

In October 1988 the EDF provided ECU 5m. for a programme to improve Somalia's satellite communications links with Europe and the Gulf states. Somalia received a further ECU 15m. in December for specific imports in the agriculture, industry and transport sectors. An $83m.-project to improve and expand Somalia's telecommunications network, due to be completed in 1991, was financed by Italy ($20m.), the ADB ($22.5m.) and Japan ($30m.). In July 1988, Japan also donated $6.5m. in financial aid, wrote off its Somalia debt and pledged to increase its aid disbursements. In January 1989 the Japanese government provided an additional 350m. yen in food aid and in March promised a further 900m. yen to support Somalia's economic recovery programme. In July the EDF granted $54m. for the construction of a 230-km road between Gelib and Bardera. The road was intended to provide access to the fertile Juba valley, which was to be developed following the completion of the Bardera dam project, originally scheduled for 1992. A further grant, of ECU 16m., to fund the purchase of oil imports, was provided by the EU. The EU also donated ECU 2m. in aid to cattle breeders for the purchase of veterinary drugs. Projects under consideration for EU funding include the rehabilitation of Mogadishu port and the construction of a road from Zeila in the north to Djibouti port.

Somalia's external debt has risen far above manageable levels. Although the rescheduling in July 1987 of $170m. of government debt by the 'Paris Club' allowed bilateral aid payments for existing projects to continue until the end of 1988, the declaration by the IMF of Somalia's ineligibility for further borrowing from the Fund halted the preparation of a second structural adjustment credit (of $70m.–$100m.) by the World Bank and was expected to inhibit the allocation of bilateral aid for new projects. Italy, which provided $16m. of aid for imports of food and fuel in March, was reported to have been willing to provide more before the agreement with the IMF was abandoned in September 1987. In 1989, however, following lengthy negotiations with the USA and the IMF, it appeared increasingly likely that further funds would be forthcoming. In March a three-year agreement was signed with the IMF, under the terms of which $260,000 were to be allocated by the Fund to development projects in the agriculture, livestock and fisheries sectors during 1989–91. In August the World Bank released the first $20m. of a $70m. loan provided for agricultural development. Of the overall credits disbursed through the IDA over the two-year period, $44.5m. has been allocated to finance imports of goods and materials for both the private and public sectors, and $16.5m. for fuel purchases. In early 1990 the IDA agreed to provide $26.1m. towards a seven-year $32.5m. education project; the share of education in the national budget had fallen from 10% in 1980 to only 1.9% in 1988. In October 1990 the IDA also pledged $18.5m. for rehabilitation work on the country's road network and telecommunications infrastructure and Mogadishu's water supply. Somalia's foreign trade deficit (which is almost entirely financed by foreign aid) increased to around $300m. in 1987, and only an increase in official transfers in that year prevented the current account deficit from rising far above the 1986 level of $88m. However, there was a considerable narrowing of the trade deficit in 1988, to $157.6m., but the trade gap widened again to $278.6m. the following year, with the deficit on the current account of the balance of payments increasing from $98.5m. to $156.7m. Total external debt was put at $2,447m. at the end of 1992. In February 1993 the Arab Monetary Fund suspended Somalia's membership because of arrears totalling $113.9m. at the end of 1991.

In 1989 and 1990 the economy deteriorated rapidly, largely due to the continuing civil strife in many parts of the country. Livestock exports from the northern regions, which in the past had accounted for nearly 80% of total foreign currency earnings, had almost ceased and there were acute shortages of almost every commodity, ranging from basic foodstuffs and water to petrol and medical drugs. Concurrently there was a sharp increase in consumer prices, while in the financial sector the shilling underwent further depreciation. In October 1989 a number of measures were introduced to 'extend the government's economic liberalization programme'. The minister of commerce announced the lifting of restrictions on imports of essential foodstuffs, such as cooking oil, rice, pasta, wheat flour and sugar, and also declared that traders and businessmen would no longer require letters of credit for imports, provided they raised the necessary foreign exchange themselves. It was also hoped to encourage the private sector to release substantial amounts of foreign exchange holdings for essential food imports to counteract acute shortages. Severe shortages of food, fuel and medical supplies were reported following the overthrow of the Siad Barre government in January 1991, with many aid agencies reluctant to return to the country because of the conditions of virtual anarchy prevailing there. Fighting in key agricultural regions in mid-1991 was reported to have severely disrupted production, with the US department of agriculture estimating 1991 agricultural production at 420,000 tons, 40% less than in a normal year;

other estimates were even more pessimistic. An already severe situation deteriorated swiftly as fighting intensified in late 1991 and early 1992, with agriculture, domestic and foreign trade all virtually halted and large numbers of people displaced from their homes.

By July 1992 the UN estimated that 1.5m. people were in immediate danger of starvation, with a further 4.5m. at risk; cereal import needs were put at about 480,000 tons. At that time, almost 1m. Somalis were refugees, with an estimated 375,000 in Ethiopia and 270,000 in Kenya. As a result of the extended civil conflict, considerable damage was inflicted on the infrastructure, telecommunications and electricity and water supplies of many urban areas, notably the capital. Large-scale reconstruction and the exploitation of Somalia's underdeveloped resources (including large areas of uncultivated arable land between the Juba and Shebelle rivers, and rich fishing grounds along the country's coastline) were expected to be hampered by unwieldy foreign debt, in the unlikely event of the prompt negotiation of a durable peace accord. Despite the ambitious attempts of the self-declared 'Republic of Somaliland' (the north-western region of the country) to exploit the economic potential afforded by the relative stability of the region (the Egal administration announced the introduction of tax, banking and customs systems during late 1993), further significant economic development seemed unlikely as long as the international community continued to refuse to recognize the territory's independence.

Despite continuing insecurity in Mogadishu and other parts of the country, the UN International Task Force (UNITAF) peace-keeping operation, which arrived in December 1992, was successful in opening up the distribution of food aid. By the end of January 1993, relief workers were feeding 1m. people daily at 1,000 feeding centres throughout the country. Nevertheless, pockets of famine persisted in rural areas, particularly in the south. In March the FAO estimated that 1m. people would continue to require food aid throughout 1993; the FAO also estimated that 300,000 people had died of hunger-related causes during 1992, although other sources estimated the total to be as high as 500,000. A UN-sponsored conference of donors in Addis Ababa in mid-March pledged $130m. towards the reconstruction of Somalia, although this fell short of the UN's target of $166m., already revised downwards from $253m. The programme aimed to restore administrative infrastructure, repatriate refugees, restore livestock herds and restart primary education. Donors warned, however, that Somalis needed to find ways to restore stability and security if aid was to continue. Improving conditions in rural areas and good rains in early 1993 allowed agricultural activity to resume, with good harvests reported and even the resumption of small-scale exports of livestock and fruit.

Statistical Survey

Sources (unless otherwise stated): Economic Research and Statistics Department, Central Bank of Somalia, Mogadishu, and Central Statistical Department, State Planning Commission, POB 1742, Mogadishu; tel. (1) 80385; telex 715.

Area and Population

AREA, POPULATION AND DENSITY

Area (sq km)	637,657*
Population (census results)†	
7 February 1975	3,253,024
1986–87 (provisional)	
Males	3,741,664
Females	3,372,767
Total	7,114,431
Density (per sq km) at 1986–87 census	11.2

* 246,201 sq miles.
† Excluding adjustment for underenumeration.

PRINCIPAL TOWNS (estimated population in 1981)

Mogadishu (capital)	500,000
Hargeysa	70,000
Kismayu	70,000
Berbera	65,000
Merca	60,000

BIRTHS AND DEATHS (UN estimates, annual averages)

	1975–80	1980–85	1985–90
Birth rate (per 1,000)	50.4	50.4	50.4
Death rate (per 1,000)	22.7	21.8	20.1

Expectation of life (UN estimates, years at birth, 1985–90): 45.0 (males 43.4; females 46.6).

Source: UN, *World Population Prospects: The 1992 Revision.*

ECONOMICALLY ACTIVE POPULATION
(estimates, '000 persons, 1991)

	Males	Females	Total
Agriculture, etc.	1,157	1,118	2,275
Industry	290	46	336
Services	466	138	604
Total labour force	1,913	1,302	3,215

Source: UN Economic Commission for Africa, *African Statistical Yearbook*.

Mid-1992 (estimates in '000): Agriculture, etc. 2,497; Total 3,622 (Source: FAO, *Production Yearbook*).

Agriculture

PRINCIPAL CROPS ('000 metric tons)

	1990*	1991	1992
Maize	315	100†	101†
Sorghum	250	145†	92†
Rice (paddy)	15	10*	8*
Cassava (Manioc)	46	45*	30*
Pulses	12	11*	9*
Groundnuts	2	2*	1*
Sesame seed	45	35*	10*
Sugar cane	240	290*	50*
Grapefruit	28	15*	7*
Bananas	110	90*	55*
Vegetables	58	47*	26*

* FAO estimate(s). † Unofficial figure.

Source: FAO, *Production Yearbook.*

LIVESTOCK (FAO estimates, '000 head, year ending September)

	1990	1991	1992
Cattle	3,800	2,000	1,000
Sheep	12,000	8,000	4,000
Goats	18,000	12,000	6,000
Pigs	10	7	2
Asses	25	25	20
Mules	24	23	18
Camels	6,000	5,000	4,000

Poultry (FAO estimates, million): 3 in 1990; 2 in 1991; 1 in 1992.

Source: FAO, *Production Yearbook.*

LIVESTOCK PRODUCTS (FAO estimates, '000 metric tons)

	1990	1991	1992
Cows' milk	420	216	100
Goats' milk	496	330	158
Sheep milk	260	170	82
Beef and veal	40	20	11
Mutton and lamb	28	17	10
Goats' meat	48	30	16
Poultry eggs	2.5	1.8	0.8
Cattle hides	7.2	3.6	2.0
Sheep skins	5.4	3.3	2.0
Goat skins	7.3	4.7	2.4

Source: FAO, *Production Yearbook.*

Forestry

ROUNDWOOD REMOVALS (FAO estimates, '000 cubic metres)

	1990	1991	1992
Sawlogs, veneer logs and logs for sleepers*	28	28	28
Other industrial wood	73	75	78
Fuel wood	8,153	8,378	8,649
Total	8,254	8,481	8,755

* Assumed to be unchanged since 1975.

Source: FAO, *Yearbook of Forest Products.*

Fishing

('000 metric tons, live weight)

	1989	1990	1991*
Freshwater fishes	0.5*	0.4*	0.3
Marine fishes	16.9*	16.2*	15.0
Spiny lobsters	0.5*	0.5	0.5
Marine molluscs	0.3	0.4	0.3
Total catch	18.2*	17.5*	16.1

* FAO estimate(s).

Source: FAO, *Yearbook of Fishery Statistics.*

Mining

	1989	1990	1991
Salt ('000 metric tons)*	30	30	30

* Data from the US Bureau of Mines.

† Estimate.

Source: UN, *Industrial Statistics Yearbook.*

Industry

SELECTED PRODUCTS

('000 metric tons, unless otherwise indicated)

	1986	1987	1988
Sugar*	30.0	43.3	41.2
Canned meat (million tins)	1.0	—	—
Canned fish	0.1	—	—
Pasta and flour	15.6	4.3	—
Textiles (million yards)	5.5	3.0	6.3
Boxes and bags	15.0	12.0	5.0
Cigarettes and matches	0.3	0.2	0.1
Petroleum products	128	44	30
Electric energy (million kWh)†	253	255	257

Sugar*: 50 in 1989; 25 in 1990; 30 in 1991.

Electric energy (million kWh†): 258 in 1989; 230 in 1990; 210 in 1991.

* Source: FAO.

† Source: UN, *Industrial Statistics Yearbook.*

Finance

CURRENCY AND EXCHANGE RATES

Monetary Units

100 cents = 1 Somali shilling (So. sh.).

Sterling and Dollar Equivalents (31 January 1994)

£1 sterling = 5,846 Somali shillings;
US $1 = 3,900 Somali shillings;
10,000 Somali shillings = £1.711 = $2.564.

Average Exchange Rate (Somali shillings per US $)

1987 105.18
1988 170.45
1989 490.68

CURRENT BUDGET (million Somali shillings)

Revenue	1986	1987	1988
Total tax revenue	8,516.4	8,622.4	12,528.1
Taxes on income and profits	1,014.8	889.7	1,431.0
Income tax	380.5	538.8	914.8
Profit tax	634.3	350.9	516.2
Taxes on production, consumption and domestic transactions	1,410.4	1,274.2	2,336.4
Taxes on international transactions	6,091.2	6,458.5	8,760.6
Import duties	4,633.2	4,835.2	6,712.1
Total non-tax revenue	6,375.2	8,220.4	7,623.4
Fees and service charges	274.1	576.1	828.8
Income from government property	633.4	656.4	2,418.9
Other revenue	5,467.2	6,987.9	4,375.7
Total	14,891.6	16,842.8	20,151.5

Expenditure	1986	1987	1988
Total general services	11,997.7	19,636.7	24,213.6
Defence	2,615.9	3,145.0	8,093.9
Interior and police	605.0	560.7	715.4
Finance and central services	7,588.3	14,017.8	12,515.6
Foreign affairs	633.0	1,413.9	2,153.1
Justice and religious affairs	248.5	290.2	447.0
Presidency and general administration	93.0	148.0	217.4
Planning	189.0	24.9	24.3
National Assembly	25.0	36.2	46.9
Total economic services	1,927.6	554.1	600.3
Transportation	122.2	95.2	94.5
Posts and telecommunications	94.3	76.7	75.6
Public works	153.9	57.5	69.8
Agriculture	547.2	59.4	55.3
Livestock and forestry	459.0	89.5	109.9
Mineral and water resources	318.8	85.2	93.1
Industry and commerce	131.0	45.1	43.9
Fisheries	101.2	45.5	58.2
Total social services	1,050.5	900.1	930.8
Education	501.6	403.0	478.1
Health	213.8	203.5	255.2
Information	111.5	135.0	145.8
Labour, sports and tourism	139.6	49.3	51.7
Other	84.0	109.3	—
Total	14,975.8	21,091.0	25,744.7

1989 (estimates): Budget to balance at 32,429m. Somali shillings.
1990 (estimates): Budget to balance at 86,012.0m. Somali shillings.
1991 (estimates): Budget to balance at 268,283.2m. Somali shillings.

CENTRAL BANK RESERVES (US $ million at 31 December)

	1987	1988	1989
Gold*	8.3	7.0	6.9
Foreign exchange	7.3	15.3	15.4
Total	15.6	22.3	22.3

* Valued at market-related prices.
Source: IMF, *International Financial Statistics.*

MONEY SUPPLY (million Somali shillings at 31 December)

	1987	1988	1989
Currency outside banks	12,327	21,033	70,789
Private-sector deposits at central bank	1,771	1,555	5,067
Demand deposits at commercial banks	15,948	22,848	63,971
Total money	30,046	45,436	139,827

Source: IMF, *International Financial Statistics.*

COST OF LIVING
(Consumer Price Index for Mogadishu; base: 1985 = 100)

	1986	1987	1988
Food	123.6	161.4	319.8
Beverages and tobacco	117.5	155.5	249.3
Clothes	119.2	153.4	271.3
Rent	131.5	169.5	250.6
Water, fuel and power	156.0	203.2	222.8
Transport and petrol	130.2	155.4	260.1
Miscellaneous items	121.5	140.9	253.0
All items	125.8	161.2	292.9

NATIONAL ACCOUNTS

Expenditure on the Gross Domestic Product*
(estimates, million Somali shillings at current prices)

	1988	1989	1990
Government final consumption expenditure	33,220	58,530	104,760
Private final consumption expenditure	240,950	481,680	894,790
Increase in stocks	14,770	n.a.	n.a.
Gross fixed capital formation	44,780	134,150	240,030
Total domestic expenditure	333,720	674,360	1,239,580
Exports of goods and services	7,630	8,890	8,660
Less Imports of goods and services	49,430	57,660	58,460
GDP in purchasers' values	291,920	625,580	1,189,780

* Figures are rounded to the nearest 10m. Somali shillings.
Source: UN Economic Commission for Africa, *African Statistical Yearbook.*

Gross Domestic Product by Economic Activity
(million Somali shillings at constant 1985 prices)

	1986	1987	1988
Agriculture, hunting, forestry and fishing	54,868	59,378	61,613
Mining and quarrying	291	291	291
Manufacturing	4,596	4,821	4,580
Electricity, gas and water	77	62	57
Construction	3,289	3,486	2,963
Trade, restaurants and hotels	8,587	9,929	8,599
Transport, storage and communications	6,020	6,153	5,873
Finance, insurance, real estate and business services	3,743	4,095	3,890
Government services	1,631	1,530	1,404
Other community, social and personal services	2,698	2,779	2,863
Sub-total	85,800	92,524	92,133
Less Imputed bank service charges	737	748	748
GDP at factor cost	85,064	91,776	91,385
Indirect taxes, *less* subsidies	5,301	4,250	3,262
GDP in purchasers' values	90,365	96,026	94,647

GDP at factor cost (estimates, million Somali shillings at current prices): 249,380 in 1988; 500,130 in 1989; 923,970 in 1990 (Source: UN Economic Commission for Africa, *African Statistical Yearbook*).

BALANCE OF PAYMENTS (US $ million)

	1987	1988	1989
Merchandise exports f.o.b.	94.0	58.4	67.7
Merchandise imports f.o.b.	-358.5	-216.0	-346.3
Trade balance	-264.5	-157.6	-278.6
Imports of services (net)	-127.7	-104.0	-122.0
Other income paid (net)	-52.0	-60.6	-84.4
Private unrequited transfers (net)	-13.1	6.4	-2.9
Official unrequited transfers (net)	343.3	217.3	331.2
Current balance	-114.0	-98.5	-156.7
Capital (net)	-25.1	-102.8	-31.9
Net errors and omissions	40.7	21.1	-0.8
Overall balance	-98.4	-180.2	-189.4

Source: IMF, *International Financial Statistics.*

External Trade

PRINCIPAL COMMODITIES (million Somali shillings)

Imports*	1986	1987	1988
Foodstuffs	1,783.3	3,703.6	1,216.1
Beverages and tobacco	298.1	183.6	6.2
Textiles, household goods	156.0	304.1	115.5
Medicinal and chemical products	89.2	133.9	97.9
Manufacturing raw materials	230.0	626.9	661.4
Fertilizers	1.8	238.0	2,411.4
Petroleum	2,051.0	3,604.2	3,815.9
Construction materials	981.4	2,001.9	307.8
Machinery and parts	1,098.3	1,203.6	957.1
Transport equipment	1,133.8	1,027.6	195.2
Agricultural machinery	4.2	62.7	113.4
Total (incl. others)	8,443.4	13,913.7	11,545.5

* Figures cover only imports made against payments of foreign currencies. The total value of imports in 1986 was 20,474 million Somali shillings.

Exports	1986	1987	1988
Livestock	4,420.3	7,300.0	3,806.5
Bananas	1,207.2	2,468.8	3,992.3
Fish	45.2	70.4	291.8
Hides and skins	294.0	705.2	492.0
Myrrh	43.6	229.9	252.8
Total (incl. others)	6,372.5	10,899.9	9,914.1

1991 (estimates, US $ million): Imports 160; Exports 80.

PRINCIPAL TRADING PARTNERS ('000 Somali shillings)

Imports	1980	1981	1982
China, People's Republic	46,959	40,962	89,772
Ethiopia	43,743	146,853	155,775
Germany, Fed. Republic	104,117	430,548	214,873
Hong Kong	5,351	13,862	3,972
India	41,467	19,638	4,801
Iraq	2,812	67,746	402
Italy	756,800	662,839	1,221,146
Japan	28,900	54,789	48,371
Kenya	86,515	105,627	198,064
Saudi Arabia	120,208	160,583	82,879
Singapore	18,569	15,592	73,652
Thailand	19,296	40,527	106,474
United Kingdom	172,613	935,900	238,371
USA	201,662	141,823	154,082
Total (incl. others)	2,190,627	3,221,715	3,548,805

Exports	1980	1981	1982
Djibouti	6,640	3,209	2,458
Germany, Fed. Republic	11,376	1,956	20,086
Italy	107,661	58,975	77,870
Kenya	2,425	6,929	4,211
Saudi Arabia	583,768	803,631	1,852,936
United Kingdom	1,233	—	3,169
USA	1,301	—	6,970
Yemen, People's Dem. Republic	3,182	—	—
Total (incl. others)	844,012	960,050	2,142,585

Source: Ministry of Planning, Mogadishu.

1986: *Imports* (estimates, million Somali shillings) USA 1,816; Japan 836; China, People's Republic 553; United Kingdom 773; France 341; Germany, Fed. Republic 1,481; Total (incl. others) 8,443; *Exports* (estimates, million Somali shillings) USA 5; China People's Republic 4; United Kingdom 31; France 27; Germany, Fed. Republic 11; Total (incl. others) 6,373. (Source: UN Economic Commission for Africa, *African Statistical Yearbook*.)

Transport

ROAD TRAFFIC (estimates, '000 motor vehicles in use)

	1989	1990	1991
Passenger cars	2	1	1
Commercial vehicles	8	8	1

Source: UN Economic Commission for Africa, *African Statistical Yearbook*.

SHIPPING

Merchant Fleet (at 30 June)

	1979	1980	1981
Displacement ('000 gross registered tons)	55	46	35

1983: 18,775 grt.

International Sea-borne Freight Traffic ('000 metric tons)

	1989	1990	1991
Goods loaded	325	324	n.a.
Goods unloaded	1,252*	1,118	1,007*

* Estimate.

Source: UN Economic Commission for Africa, *African Statistical Yearbook*.

CIVIL AVIATION (traffic on scheduled services)

	1989	1990	1991
Kilometres flown (million)	3	3	1
Passengers carried ('000)	89	88	46
Passenger-km (million)	248	255	131
Freight ton-km (million)	8	9	5

Source: UN, *Statistical Yearbook*.

Communications Media

	1989	1990	1991
Radio receivers ('000 in use)	300	320	330
Television receivers ('000 in use)	100	105	108
Telephones ('000 in use)*	9	9	9
Daily newspapers	n.a.	1	n.a.

* UN estimates.

Sources: UNESCO, *Statistical Yearbook*; UN Economic Commission for Africa, *African Statistical Yearbook*.

Education

(1985)

	Institutions	Teachers	Pupils
Pre-primary	16	133	1,558
Primary	1,224	10,338	196,496
Secondary:			
General	n.a.	2,149	39,753
Teacher training	n.a.	30*	613*
Vocational	n.a.	637	5,933
Higher	n.a.	817†	15,672†

* Figures refer to 1984. † Figures refer to 1986.

Source: UNESCO, *Statistical Yearbook*.

1990 (UN estimates): 377,000 primary-level pupils; 44,000 secondary-level pupils; 10,400 higher-level pupils.

1991: University teachers 549; University students 4,640.

Directory

The Constitution

The Constitution promulgated in 1979 and amended in 1990 was revoked following the overthrow of President Siad Barre in January 1991. Proposals to reinstate the independence Constitution of 1960 were subsequently abandoned. A preparatory commission for a Transitional National Council, formed in March 1993, presented a draft transitional national charter in November 1993, providing the constitutional framework for the country during a two-year transitional period.

The Government

(September 1994)

On 27 March 1993 a conference of the main political factions agreed to form a 74-member Transitional National Council (TNC) as the country's supreme authority, with a mandate to hold elections within two years. The TNC was to comprise three representatives from each of the country's 18 administrative regions, five representatives from Mogadishu and one representative from each of the 15 political factions that signed the agreement. The UN Operation in Somalia, UNOSOM II, was, however, to have substantial responsibility for the administration of the country during this period. By September 1994, however, no transitional institutions of government had been installed.

MINISTRIES

Office of the President: People's Palace, Mogadishu; tel. (1) 723.

Ministry of Agriculture: Mogadishu; tel. (1) 80716.

Ministry of Civil Aviation and Transport: Mogadishu; tel. (1) 23025.

Ministry of Commerce: Mogadishu; tel. (1) 33089.

Ministry of Defence: Mogadishu; tel. (1) 710; telex 726.

Ministry of Finance and Economy: Mogadishu; tel. (1) 33090.

Ministry of Foreign Affairs: Mogadishu; tel. (1) 721; telex 639.

Ministry of Health: Mogadishu; tel. (1) 31055; telex 776.

Ministry of Higher Education and Culture: POB 1182, Mogadishu; tel. (1) 35042.

Ministry of Industry: Mogadishu; telex 747.

Ministry of Information and National Guidance: POB 1748, Mogadishu; tel. (1) 20947; telex 621.

Ministry of the Interior: Mogadishu.

Ministry of Justice and Islamic Affairs: Mogadishu; tel. (1) 36062.

Ministry of Labour, Youth and Sports: Mogadishu; tel. (1) 33086.

Ministry of National Planning: POB 1742, Mogadishu; tel. (1) 80384; telex 715.

Ministry of Public Works: Mogadishu; tel. (1) 21051; telex 700.

Ministry of Telecommunications: Mogadishu; tel. (1) 29005; telex 615.

Political Organizations

Islamic Union Party (Ittihad): operates in northern Somalia; aims to unite ethnic Somalis from Somalia, Ethiopia, Kenya and Djibouti in an Islamic state.

Somali Democratic Alliance (SDA): f. 1989; represents Gadabursi ethnic grouping in north-west; opposes Isaaq-dominated SNM and its declaration of an independent 'Republic of Somaliland'; Leader MOHAMED FARAH ABDULLAH.

Somali Democratic Movement (SDM): represents Rahenweyne clan; organization split in early 1992, with this faction in alliance with Ali Mahdi Mohamed's USC; Leader ABDULKADIR MOHAMED ADAN.

Somali Eastern and Central Front (SECF): f. 1991; opposes SNM's declaration of the independent 'Republic of Somaliland'; Chair. HIRSI ISMAIL MOHAMED.

Somali National Alliance (SNA): f. 1992 as alliance between the Southern Somali National Movement (which withdrew in 1993) and the factions of the United Somali Congress, Somali Democratic Movement and Somali Patriotic Movement given below; Chair. Gen. MOHAMED FARAH AYDEED; Vice-Chair. ABDI WARSEMEH ISAAQ.

Somali Democratic Movement (SDM): represents Rahenweyne clan; Chair. MOHAMED NUR ALIYOW.

Somali Patriotic Movement (SPM): f. 1989; represents Ogadenis (of the southern Darod clan); Chair. AHMED OMAR JESS.

United Somali Congress (USC): f. 1989; overthrew Siad Barre in 1991; party split in mid-1991, with this faction dominated by the Habr Gidir sub-clan of the Hawiye clan, Somalia's largest ethnic group; Chair. Gen. MOHAMED FARAH AYDEED; Sec.-Gen. ABD AL-KARIM AHMED ALI.

Somali National Front (SNF): f. 1991; guerrilla force active in southern Somalia, promoting Darod clan interests and seeking restoration of SRSP Govt; Leader Gen. MOHAMED SIAD HERSI 'MORGAN'.

Somali National Movement (SNM): Hargeysa; f. 1981 in London; conducted guerrilla operations in north and north-west Somalia, with early support from Ethiopia, until 1991; support drawn mainly from nomadic Isaaq clan; in May 1991 declared independent 'Republic of Somaliland' with the capital at Hargeysa; mems hold a majority of ministerial portfolios in 'Govt of Somaliland'; Chair. ABD AR-RAHMAN AHMED ALI 'TUR'; Vice-Chair. HASAN ISA JAMA.

Somali Patriotic Movement (SPM): f. 1989 in southern Somalia; represents Ogadenis (of the Darod clan) in southern Somalia; this faction of the SPM has allied with the SNF in opposing the SNA; Chair. Gen. ADEN ABDULLAHI NOOR ('GABIO').

Somali Revolutionary Socialist Party (SRSP): f. 1976 as the sole legal party; overthrown in Jan. 1991; conducts guerrilla operations in Gedo region, near border with Kenya; Sec.-Gen. (vacant); Asst Sec.-Gen. AHMED SULEIMAN ABDULLAH.

Somali Salvation Democratic Front (SSDF): f. 1981, as the Democratic Front for the Salvation of Somalia (DFSS), as a coalition of the Somali Salvation Front, the Somali Workers' Party and the Democratic Front for the Liberation of Somalia; operates in central Somalia, although a smaller group has opposed the SNA around Kismayu in alliance with the SNF; Leader Gen. MOHAMED ABSHIR MUSSE.

Southern Somali National Movement (SSNM): based on coast in southern Somalia; Chair. ABD AL-AZIZ SHEIKH YUSUF.

United Somali Congress (USC): f. 1989 in central Somalia; overthrew Siad Barre in Jan. 1991; party split in mid-1991 with this faction dominated by the Abgal sub-clan of the Hawiye clan, Somalia's largest ethnic group; Leader ALI MAHDI MOHAMED; Sec.-Gen. MUSA NUR AMIN.

United Somali Front (USF): f. 1989; represents Issas in the north-west of the country; Leader ALI SHEIKH IBRAHIM ARAYE; Sec.-Gen. MOHAMED OSMAN ALI.

United Somali Party: opposes SNM's declaration of the independent 'Republic of Somaliland'; Leader MOHAMED ABDI HASHI.

In November 1993 interim President Ali Mahdi Mohamed was reported to have assumed the leadership of the **Somali Salvation Alliance (SSA),** a new alliance of 12 factions opposed to Gen. Aydeed, including the Somali African Muki Organization (SAMO), the Somali National Union (SNU), the USF, the SDA, the SDM, the SPM, the USC (pro-Mahdi faction), the SSDF, the Somali National Democratic Union (SNDU), the SNF and the SSNM. In May 1994 the SNU announced its intention to leave the alliance and join the SNA.

Diplomatic Representation

EMBASSIES IN SOMALIA

Note: Following the overthrow of Siad Barre in January 1991, all foreign embassies in Somalia were closed and all diplomatic personnel left the country. Some embassies were reopened, including those of France, Sudan and the USA, following the arrival of the US-led United Task Force (UNITAF) in December 1992. There were estimated to be about 20 foreign diplomatic personnel in Mogadishu in August 1994.

Algeria: POB 2850, Mogadishu; tel. (1) 81696; Ambassador: HAMID BENCH ERCHALI.

Bulgaria: Hodan District, Km 5, off Via Afgoi, POB 1736, Mogadishu; tel. (1) 81820; Chargé d'affaires a.i.: PEYO BOZOV.

China, People's Republic: POB 548, Mogadishu; tel. (1) 20805; Ambassador: XU YINGJIE.

Cuba: Mogadishu.

Djibouti: Mogadishu; telex 771; Ambassador: ABDI ISMAEL WABERI.

Egypt: Via Maka al-Mukarama Km 4, POB 76, Mogadishu; tel. (1) 80781; Chargé d'affaires a.i.: MUBAD AL-HADI.

Ethiopia: POB 368, Mogadishu; telex 3089; Ambassador: Dr ASMAMAW KALIMU.

France: Corso Primo Luglio, POB 13, Mogadishu; tel. (1) 21715; telex 625; Chargé d'affaires a.i.; ALAIN DESCHAMPS.

Germany: Via Mahamoud Harbi, POB 17, Mogadishu; tel. (1) 20547; telex 3613; Ambassador: M. A. PETERS.

India: Via Jigjiga, Shingani, POB 955, Mogadishu; tel. (1) 21262; telex 716; Ambassador: KRISHAN MOHAN LAL.

Iran: Via Maka al-Mukarama, POB 1166, Mogadishu; tel. (1) 80881; telex 616; Chargé d'affaires a.i.: ALI AMOUEI.

Iraq: Via Maka al-Mukarama, POB 641, Mogadishu; tel. (1) 80821; telex 638; Ambassador: HIKMAT A. SATTAR HUSSAIN.

Italy: Via Alto Giuba, POB 6, Mogadishu; tel. (1) 20544; telex 777; Ambassador: MARIO SCIALOJA.

Kenya: Via Mecca, POB 618, Mogadishu; tel. (1) 80857; telex 610; Ambassador: JOHN OLE SIPARO.

Korea, Democratic People's Republic: Via Km 5, Mogadishu; Ambassador: KIM RYONG SU.

Kuwait: First Medina Rd, Km 5, POB 1348, Mogadishu; telex 608; Chargé d'affaires a.i.: MATTAR THAJIL AL-SALMAN.

Libya: Via Medina, POB 125, Mogadishu.

Nigeria: Via Km 5, Mogadishu; tel. (1) 81362; telex 637; Ambassador: DAHIRU MOHAMED ABU BAKAR.

Oman: Via Afgoi, POB 2992, Mogadishu; tel. (1) 81658; telex 796; Ambassador: AHMED EBRAHIM QASIM.

Pakistan: Via Afgoi, Km 5, POB 339, Mogadishu; tel. (1) 80856; Chargé d'affaires a.i.: TAHIR IQBAL BUTT.

Qatar: Via Km 4, POB 1744, Mogadishu; tel. (1) 80746; telex 629; Ambassador: ABDUL YUSUF AL-JAIDA.

Romania: Via Lido, POB 651, Mogadishu; Ambassador: GHEORGHE MANCIU.

Saudi Arabia: Via Benadir, POB 603, Mogadishu; tel. (1) 22087; telex 618; Ambassador: ABDULLAH AL-MUHAYYIM.

Sudan: Via Mecca, POB 552, Mogadishu; Ambassador: MUSTAFA ABD AL-BADR MOHAMED HASAN.

Syria: Via Medina, POB 986, Mogadishu; telex 636; Chargé d'affaires a.i.: SHAYESH TERKAWI.

Turkey: Via Km 6, POB 2833, Mogadishu; tel. (1) 81975; telex 784; Ambassador: HIKMET SENGENC.

United Arab Emirates: Via Afgoi, Km 5, Mogadishu; tel. (1) 23178; telex 614; Ambassador: ABDULHADI A. AL-KHAJAH.

United Kingdom: Hassan Geedi Abtow 7/8, POB 1036, Mogadishu; tel. (1) 20288; telex 3617; Ambassador: (vacant).

USA: Via Afgoi, Km 5, POB 574, Mogadishu; tel. (1) 39971; telex 789; Special Envoy: DANIEL H. SIMPSON.

Yemen: Via Km 5, POB 493, Mogadishu; Ambassador: AWADH ABDALLA MASHBAH.

Yugoslavia: Via Mecca, POB 952, Mogadishu; tel. (1) 81729; telex 3778; Ambassador: DRAGOLJUB KONTIĆ.

Zimbabwe: Mogadishu.

Judicial System

Constitutional arrangements in operation until 1991 provided for the Judiciary to be independent of the executive and legislative powers. Laws and acts having the force of law were required to conform to the provisions of the Constitution and to the general principles of Islam.

The Supreme Court: Mogadishu; the court of final instance in civil, criminal, administrative and auditing matters; Chair. Sheikh AHMAD HASAN.

Military Supreme Court: f. 1970, with jurisdiction over members of the armed forces.

National Security Court: heard cases of treason.

Courts of Appeal: sat at Mogadishu and Hargeysa, with two Divisions: General and Assize.

Regional Courts: There were eight Regional Courts, with two Divisions: General and Assize.

District Courts: There were 84 District Courts, with Civil and Criminal Divisions. The Civil Division had jurisdiction over all controversies where the cause of action had arisen under Shari'a (Islamic) Law or Customary Law and any other Civil controversies where the matter in dispute did not involve more than 3,000 shillings. The Criminal Division had jurisdiction with respect to offences punishable with imprisonment not exceeding three years, or fine not exceeding 3,000 shillings, or both.

Qadis: Districts Courts of civil jurisdiction under Islamic Law.

In September 1993, in accordance with Resolution 865 of the UN Security Council, a judiciary re-establishment council, composed of Somalis, was created in Mogadishu to rehabilitate the judicial and penal systems.

Judiciary Re-establishment Council (JRC): Mogadishu; Chair. Dr ABD AL-RAHMAD Haji GA'AL.

Religion

ISLAM

Islam is the state religion. Most Somalis are Sunni Muslims.

Imam: Gen. MOHAMED ABSHIR.

CHRISTIANITY

The Roman Catholic Church

Somalia comprises a single diocese, directly responsible to the Holy See. At 31 December 1992 there were an estimated 200 adherents.

Bishop of Mogadishu: (vacant); POB 273, Ahmed bin Idris, Mogadishu; tel. (1) 20184.

The Anglican Communion

Within the Episcopal Church in Jerusalem and the Middle East, the Bishop in Egypt has jurisdiction over seven African countries, including Somalia.

The Press

Prior to the overthrow of the Siad Barre regime in 1991, all newspapers were published by the Ministry of Information and National Guidance.

The Country: POB 1178, Mogadishu; tel. (1) 21206; telex 621; f. 1991; daily.

Dalka: POB 388, Mogadishu; f. 1967; current affairs; weekly.

Heegan (Vigilance): POB 1178, Mogadishu; tel. (1) 21206; telex 621; f. 1978; weekly; English; Editor MOHAMOUD M. AFRAH.

Horseed: POB 1178, Mogadishu; tel. (1) 21206; telex 621; weekly; in Italian and Arabic.

New Era: POB 1178, Mogadishu; tel. (1) 21206; telex 621; quarterly; in English, Somali and Arabic.

Rajo Newspaper: Mogadishu; f. 1993 by US-led United Task Force (UNITAF).

Somalia in Figures: Ministry of National Planning, POB 1742, Mogadishu; tel. (1) 80384; telex 715; govt publication; statistical information; 3 a year; in English.

Xiddigta Oktobar (October Star): POB 1178, Mogadishu; tel. (1) 21206; telex 621; in Somali; daily.

NEWS AGENCIES

Horn of Africa News Agency: Mogadishu; f. 1990.

Somali National News Agency (SONNA): POB 1748, Mogadishu; tel. (1) 24058; telex 621; Dir MUHAMMAD HASAN KAHIN.

Foreign Bureaux

Agence France-Presse (AFP) (France): POB 1178, Mogadishu; telex 615; Rep. MOHAMED ROBLE NOOR.

Agenzia Nazionale Stampa Associata (ANSA) (Italy): POB 1399, Mogadishu; tel. (1) 20626; telex 3761; Rep. ABDULKADIR MOHAMOUD WALAYO.

Publishers

Government Printer: POB 1743, Mogadishu.

Somalia d'Oggi: Piazzale della Garesa, POB 315, Mogadishu; law, economics and reference.

Radio and Television

In 1991, according to UNESCO, there were an estimated 330,000 radio receivers and 108,000 television receivers in use. Some radio receivers are used for public address purposes in small towns and villages. A television service, financed by Kuwait and the United Arab Emirates, was inaugurated in 1983. Programmes in Somali and Arabic are broadcast for two hours daily, extended to three hours on Fridays and public holidays. Reception is limited to a 30-km radius of Mogadishu.

Somali Broadcasting Service: Mogadishu; tel. (1) 20947; telex 621; main govt service; television and radio broadcasts in Somali, English, Italian, Arabic, Swahili, Amharic, Galla and Afar; Dir of Broadcasting MOHAMED ARAB FALAH FALAH.

Radio Hargeysa, the Voice of the 'Republic of Somaliland': POB 14, Hargeysa; tel. 155; serves the northern region ('Somaliland'); broadcasts in Somali, and relays Somali and Amharic transmission from Radio Mogadishu; Dir of Radio IDRIS EGAL NUR.

Radio Manta: Mogadishu; f. 1993 by US-led United Task Force (UNITAF); Dir GEORGE BENNETT.

Radio Mogadishu, the Voice of the Great Somali People (Radio Mogadishu, codka ummad weeynta Soomaaliyeed): Mogadishu; f. 1993 by supporters of Gen. Aydeed; broadcasts on same frequency as two fmr Radio Mogadishu stations controlled respectively by pro-Ali Mahdi and pro-Aydeed factions; Chair. FARAH HASAN AYOBOQORE.

Voice of Peace: POB 1631, Addis Ababa, Ethiopia; f. 1993; aims to promote peace and reconstruction in Somalia; receives support from UNICEF and the OAU.

Finance

(cap. = capital; res = reserves; m. = million; brs = branches; amounts in Somali shillings)

BANKING

All banks were nationalized in May 1970.

Central Bank

Central Bank of Somalia (Bankiga Dhexe ee Soomaaliya): Corso Somalia 55, POB 11, Mogadishu; telex 604; f. 1960; bank of issue; cap. and res 132.5m. (Sept. 1985); Gov. ALI ABDI AMALOW; Gen. Mans MOHAMED MOHAMED NUR, BASHIR ISSE ALI; brs in Hargeysa and Kismayu.

Commercial Bank

Commercial Bank of Somalia: Place Lagarde, POB 2004, Mogadishu; tel. (1) 351282; telex 5879; f. 1990 to succeed the Commercial and Savings Bank of Somalia; cap. 1,000m. (May 1990); 33 brs.

Development Bank

Somali Development Bank: Via Primo Luglio, POB 1079, Mogadishu; tel. (1) 21800; telex 635; f. 1968; cap. and res 2,612.7m. (Dec. 1988); Pres. MAHMUD MOHAMED NUR; 4 brs.

INSURANCE

Cassa per le Assicurazioni Sociali della Somalia: POB 123, Mogadishu; f. 1950; workers' compensation; Dir-Gen. HASSAN MOHAMED JAMA; nine brs.

State Insurance Company of Somalia: POB 992, Mogadishu; telex 710; f. 1974; Gen. Man. ABDULLAHI GA'AL; brs throughout Somalia.

Trade and Industry

CHAMBER OF COMMERCE

Chamber of Commerce, Industry and Agriculture: Via Asha, POB 27, Mogadishu; Chair. MOHAMED Haji IBRAHIM EGAL.

TRADE ORGANIZATION

National Agency of Foreign Trade: POB 602, Mogadishu; major foreign trade agency; state-owned; brs in Berbera and over 150 centres throughout Somalia; Dir-Gen. JAMA AW MUSE.

DEVELOPMENT ORGANIZATIONS

Agricultural Development Corporation: POB 930, Mogadishu; telex 713; f. 1971 by merger of fmr agricultural and machinery agencies and grain marketing board; supplies farmers with equipment and materials at reasonable prices; buys Somali growers' cereal and oil seed crops; Dir-Gen. MOHAMED FARAH ANSHUR.

Livestock Development Agency: POB 1759, Mogadishu; Dir-Gen. HASSAN WELI SCEK HUSSEN; brs throughout Somalia.

Somali Co-operative Movement: Mogadishu; Chair. HASSAN HAWADLE MADAR.

Somali Oil Refinery: POB 1241, Mogadishu; Chair. NUR AHMED DARAWISH.

Water Development Agency: POB 525, Mogadishu; Dir-Gen. KHALIF Haji FARAH.

TRADE UNION

General Federation of Somali Trade Unions: POB 1179, Mogadishu; Chair. MUHAMMAD FARAH ISA GASHAN.

Transport

RAILWAYS

There are no railways in Somalia.

ROADS

In 1991 there were an estimated 21,700 km of roads, of which 5,200 km were main roads, and 4,500 were secondary roads. In the same year, an estimated 6,000 km of road were paved. A 122-km road between Berbera and Burao, financed by the United Arab Emirates, was inaugurated in 1981, and work on a 257-km road between Goluen and Gelib, completing a link between Mogadishu and Kismayu, was begun in 1977, with financial aid from the EC and the Arab Fund for Economic and Social Development. In September 1988 work began on a 120-km US-funded road between Mogadishu and Cadale. In July 1989 the European Development Fund granted US $54m. for the construction of a 230-km road between Gelib and Bardera, to provide access to the Juba valley.

SHIPPING

Merca, Berbera, Mogadishu and Kismayu are the chief ports. Facilities at Kismayu were undergoing rehabilitation in 1986. These improvements were to enable the port to handle livestock, other agricultural commodities, liquids and general cargo. In late 1986 arrangements were finalized for a US $24m. programme, financed by the World Bank, for further improvements at Kismayu and for modernization products at Berbera and Mogadishu.

In the context of continuing civil unrest, the dispatch of a UN-sponsored port management team for Mogadishu, for an initial period of six months, was announced in May 1993. In the following December the UN announced a programme of financial assistance for the rehabilitation of the ports of Berbera, Bosaso, Brava, Kismayu and Merca.

Linea Messina, Medite Line and Lloyd Triestino provide regular services. Other lines call irregularly.

Somali Ports Authority: POB 935, Mogadishu; tel. (1) 30081; telex 708; Port Dir UGAS KHALIF.

Juba Enterprises Beder & Sons Ltd: POB 549, Mogadishu; privately-owned.

National Shipping Line: POB 588, Mogadishu; tel. (1) 23021; telex 611; state-owned; Gen. Man. Dr ABDULLAHI MOHAMED SALAD.

Shosman Commercial Co Ltd: North-Eastern Pasaso; privately-owned.

Somali Shipping Corporation: POB 2775, Mogadishu; state-owned.

CIVIL AVIATION

Mogadishu has an international airport. There are airports at Hargeysa and Baidoa and six other airfields. It was reported that a daily service had been inaugurated in April 1994 between Hargeysa (in the self-declared 'Republic of Somaliland') and Nairobi, Kenya.

Somali Airlines: Via Medina, POB 726, Mogadishu; tel. (1) 81533; telex 3619; f. 1964; state-owned; operates internal passenger and cargo services and international services to destinations in Africa, Europe and the Middle East; Pres. MOHAMOUD MOHAMED GULAID.

In addition, two airlines, Bulisafia and African Air, operate services from Mogadishu international airport.

Defence

Of total armed forces of 64,500 in June 1990, the army numbered 60,000, the navy 2,000 and the air force 2,500. In addition, there were 29,500 members of paramilitary forces, including 20,000 members of the people's militia. Since the overthrow of the Siad Barre regime in January 1991, there have been no national armed forces; Somalia has been divided into areas controlled by different armed groups, which were based on clan, or sub-clan, membership. In March 1994 the UN announced that 8,000 former Somali police officers had been rehabilitated throughout the country, receiving vehicles and transport from the UN.

Education

All private schools were nationalized in 1972, and education is now provided free of charge. Despite the introduction of the

Somali script in 1972, the level of literacy remains low. According to estimates by UNESCO, the average rate of adult illiteracy declined from 83.1% in 1985 to 75.9% (males 63.9%; females 86.0%) in 1990. Primary education, lasting for eight years, is officially compulsory for children aged six to 14 years. However, the total enrolment at primary schools of children in this age-group declined from 14% (boys 18%; girls 10%) in 1980 to only 8% (boys 11%; girls 6%) in 1985. Secondary education, beginning at the age of 14, lasts for four years but is not compulsory. In 1985 enrolment of children at secondary schools included 4% (boys 5%; girls 3%) of those in the relevant age-group. In 1985 enrolment at primary and secondary schools was equivalent to 10% of the school-age population (boys 13%; girls 7%). Current expenditure on education in the Government's 1988 budget was 478.1m. Somali shillings (equivalent to 1.9% of total current spending). Following the overthrow of Siad Barre's Government in January 1991, Somalia's education system collapsed. In January 1993 a primary school was opened in the building of Somalia's only university, the Somali National University in Mogadishu (which had been closed in early 1991). The only other schools operating in the country were a number under the control of fundamentalist Islamic groups and some that had been reopened in the 'Republic of Somaliland' in mid-1991.

Bibliography

Abraham, R. C. *Somali–English Dictionary.* London, 1964.

Aidid, M. F. and Ruhela, S. P. (Eds). *The Preferred Future: Development in Somalia.* New Delhi, Vikas Publishing House, 1993.

Ayoob, M. *The Horn of Africa: Regional Conflict and Super-Power Involvement.* Canberra, Strategic Defence Studies Centre, Australian National University, 1978.

Burton, R. F. *First Footsteps in East Africa.* London, Everyman, 1943.

Cassanelli, L. V. *The Shaping of Somali Society: Reconstructing the History of A Pastoral People, 1600–1900.* Philadelphia, Pennsylvania University Press, 1982.

Contini, P. *The Somali Republic: An Experiment in Legal Integration.* 1969.

Drysdale, J. *The Somali Dispute.* 1964.

Whatever Happened to Somalia?. London, HAAN Associates, 1994.

Hess, R. L. *Italian Colonialism in Somalia.* 1966.

Karp, M. *The Economics of Trusteeship in Somalia.* 1960.

Lewis, I. M. *A Pastoral Democracy.* 1961.

The Modern History of Somalia: Nation and State in the Horn of Africa. 1979.

Peoples of the Horn of Africa. 1969 (reissue).

Understanding Somalia: Guide to Culture, History and Social Institutions. London, HAAN Associates, 1981, (new edn) 1993.

Samater, A. I. *Socialist Somalia: Rhetoric and Reality.* London, Zed Press, 1989.

Smith, S. *Somalia, Humanity's Lost War.* Paris, Calmann-Levy, 1993.

Touval, S. *Somali Nationalism.* 1963.

SOUTH AFRICA

Physical and Social Geography

A. MacGREGOR HUTCHESON

The Republic of South Africa occupies the southern extremity of the African continent and, except for a relatively small area in the northern Transvaal, lies poleward of the Tropic of Capricorn, extending as far as latitude 34° 51′ S. The republic has a total area of 1,221,037 sq km or 471,445 sq miles (excluding the exclave of Walvis Bay in Namibia but including the former 'independent homelands' of Bophuthatswana, Ciskei, Transkei and Venda) and has common borders with Namibia on the north-west, with Botswana on the north, and with Zimbabwe, Mozambique and Swaziland on the north-east. Lesotho is entirely surrounded by South African territory, lying within the eastern part of the republic.

PHYSICAL FEATURES

Most of South Africa consists of a vast plateau with upwarped rims, bounded by an escarpment. Framing the plateau is a narrow coastal belt. The surface of the plateau varies in altitude from 600 m to 2,000 m above sea-level, but is mostly above 900 m. It is highest in the east and south-east and dips fairly gently towards the Kalahari Basin in the north-west. The relief is generally monotonous, consisting of undulating to flat landscapes over wide areas. Variation is provided occasionally by low ridges and *inselberge* (or *kopjes*) made up of rock more resistant to erosion. There are three major sub-regions:

(i) the High Veld between 1,200 m and 1,800 m, forming a triangular area which occupies the southern Transvaal and most of the Orange Free State;

(ii) a swell over 1,500 m high, aligned WNW–ESE, part of which is known as the Witwatersrand, rising gently from the plateau surface to the north of the High Veld and forming a major drainage divide; and

(iii) the Middle Veld, generally between 600 m and 1,200 m, comprising the remaining part of the plateau.

The plateau's edges, upwarped during the Tertiary Period, are almost everywhere above 1,500 m. Maximum elevations of over 3,400 m occur in the south-east in Lesotho. From the crests the surface descends coastwards by means of the Great Escarpment which gives the appearance of a mountain range when viewed from below, and which is known by distinctive names in its different sections. An erosional feature, dissected by seaward-flowing rivers, the nature of the escarpment varies according to the type of rock which forms it. Along its eastern length it is known as the Drakensberg; in the section north of the Olifants river fairly soft granite gives rise to gentle slopes, but south of that river resistant quartzites are responsible for a more striking appearance. Further south again, along the Natal–Lesotho border, basalts cause the Drakensberg to be at its most striking, rising up a sheer 1,800 m or more in places. Turning westwards the Great Escarpment is known successively as the Stormberg, Bamboes, Suurberg, Sneeuberg, Nieuwveld, and Komsberg, where gentle slopes affording access to the interior alternate with a more wall-like appearance. The Great Escarpment then turns sharply northwards through the Roggeveld mountains, following which it is usually in the form of a simple step until the Kamiesberg are reached; owing to aridity and fewer rivers the dissection of this western part of the escarpment is much less advanced than in the eastern (Drakensberg) section.

The Lowland margin which surrounds the South African plateau may be divided into four zones:

(i) The undulating to flat Transvaal Low Veld, between 150 m and 600 m above sea-level, separated from the Mozambique coastal plain by the Lebombo mountains in the east, and including part of the Limpopo valley in the north;

(ii) The south-eastern coastal belt, a very broken region descending to the coast in a series of steps, into which the rivers have cut deep valleys. In northern Natal the republic possesses its only true coastal plain, some 65 km at its widest;

(iii) The Cape ranges, consisting of the remnants of mountains folded during the Carboniferous era, and flanking the plateau on the south and south-west. On the south the folds trend E–W and on the south-west they trend N–S, the two trends crossing in the south-western corner of the Cape Province to produce a rugged knot of mountains and the ranges' highest elevations (over 2,000 m). Otherwise the Cape ranges are comparatively simple in structure, consisting of parallel anticlinal ridges and synclinal valleys. Narrow lowlands separate the mountains from the coast. Between the ridges and partially enclosed by them, e.g. the Little Karoo, is a series of steps rising to the foot of the Great Escarpment. The Great Karoo, the last of these steps, separates the escarpment from the Cape ranges; and

(iv) The western coastal belt is also characterized by a series of steps, but the slope from the foot of the Great Escarpment to the coast is more gentle and more uniform than in the south-eastern zone.

The greater part of the plateau is drained by the Orange river system. Rising in the Drakensberg within a short distance of the escarpment, as do its two main perennial tributaries the Vaal and the Caledon, the Orange flows westward for 1,900 km before entering the Atlantic Ocean. However, the western part of its basin is so dry that it is not unknown for the Orange to fail to reach its mouth during the dry season. The large-scale Orange River Project, a comprehensive scheme for water supply, irrigation and hydroelectric generation, aids water conservation in this western area and is making possible its development. The only other major system is that of the Limpopo, which rises on the northern slopes of the Witwatersrand and drains most of central and northern Transvaal to the Indian Ocean. Apart from some interior drainage to a number of small basins in the north and north-west, the rest of the republic's drainage is peripheral. Relatively short streams rise in the Great Escarpment, although some rise on the plateau itself, having cut through the escarpment, and drain directly to the coast. With the exception of riparian strips along perennial rivers most of the country relies for water supplies on underground sources supplemented by dams. None of the republic's rivers are navigable.

CLIMATE AND NATURAL VEGETATION

Except for a small part of northern Transvaal the climate of South Africa is subtropical, although there are important regional variations within this general classification. Altitude and relief forms have an important influence on temperature and on both the amount and distribution of rainfall, and there is a strong correlation between the major physical and the major climatic regions. The altitude of the plateau modifies temperatures and because there is a general rise in elevation towards the Equator there is a corresponding decrease in temperature, resulting in a remarkable uniformity of temperature throughout the republic from south to north (cf. mean annual temperatures: Cape Town, 16.7°C; and Pretoria, 17.2°C). The greatest contrasts in temperature are, in fact, between the east coast, warmed by the Mozambique Current, and the west coast, cooled by the Benguela Current (cf. respectively, mean monthly temperatures: Durban, January 24.4°C, July 17.8°C; and Port Nolloth, January 15.6°C, July 12.2°C). Daily and annual ranges in temperature increase with distance from the coast, being much greater on the plateau (cf. mean annual temperature range: Cape Town, 8°C; Pretoria, 11°C).

The areas of highest annual rainfall largely coincide with the outstanding relief features, over 650 mm being received only in the eastern third of South Africa and relatively small areas in southern Cape Province. Parts of the Drakensberg and the seaward slopes of the Cape ranges experience over 1,500 mm. West of the Drakensberg and to the north of the Cape ranges there is a marked rain-shadow, and annual rainfall decreases progressively westwards (cf. Durban 1,140 mm, Bloemfontein 530 mm, Kimberley 400 mm, Upington 180 mm, Port Nolloth 50 mm). Virtually all the western half of the country, apart from southern Cape Province, receives less than 250 mm and the western coastal belt's northern section forms a continuation of the Namib Desert. Most of the rain falls during the summer months (November to April) when evaporation losses are greatest, brought by tropical marine air masses moving in from the Indian Ocean on the east. However, the south-west of Cape Province has a winter maximum of rainfall with dry summers. Only the narrow southern coastal belt between Cape Agulhas and East London has rainfall distributed uniformly throughout the year. Snow may fall occasionally over the higher parts of the plateau and the Cape ranges during winter, but frost occurs on an average for 120 days each year over most of the interior plateau, and for shorter periods in the coastal lowlands, except in Natal, where it is rare.

Variations in climate and particularly in annual rainfall are reflected in changes of vegetation, sometimes strikingly, as between the south-west Cape Province's Mediterranean shrub type, designed to withstand summer drought and of which the protea—the national plant—is characteristic, and the drought-resistant low Karoo bush immediately north of the Cape ranges and covering much of the semi-arid western half of the country. The only true areas of forest are found along the wetter south and east coasts—the temperate evergreen forests of the Knysna district and the largely evergreen subtropical bush, including palms and wild bananas, of the eastern Cape and Natal, respectively. Grassland covers the rest of the republic, merging into thorn veld in the north-western Cape Province and into bush veld in northern Transvaal.

MINERAL RESOURCES

South Africa's mineral resources, outstanding in their variety, quality and quantity, overshadow all the country's other natural resources. They are mainly found in the ancient Pre-Cambrian foundation and associated intrusions and occur in a wide curving zone which stretches from the northern Transvaal through the Orange Free State and northern Cape Province to the west coast. To the south of this mineralized zone, one of the richest in the world, the Pre-Cambrian rocks are covered by Karoo sedimentaries which generally do not contain minerals, with the exception of extensive deposits of bituminous coal, the republic's only indigenous mineral fuel. These deposits occur mainly in the eastern Transvaal High Veld, the northern Orange Free State and northern Natal, mostly in thick, easily worked seams fairly near to the surface. In the mid-1980s reserves were estimated to exceed 110,000m. tons, of which 58,000m. tons were considered to be economically extractable by current technology. Coal is of particular importance to South Africa because of relatively low production elsewhere in the continent south of the Equator, and South Africa's current dependence on imported petroleum.

The most important mineral regions are the Witwatersrand and the northern Orange Free State, producing gold, silver and uranium; the diamond areas centred on Kimberley, Pretoria, Jagersfontein and Koffiefontein; and the Transvaal bushveld complex containing multiple occurrences of a large number of minerals, including asbestos, chrome, copper, iron, magnesium, nickel, platinum, tin, uranium and vanadium. In northern Cape Province important deposits of manganese, iron ore and asbestos occur in the Postmasburg, Sishen and Kuruman areas, while in the north-western Cape Province reserves of lead, zinc, silver and copper are being exploited. This list of occurrences and minerals is by no means exhaustive, and prospecting for new mineral resources is continuing. In 1988 exploitable petroleum deposits were discovered near Hondeklip Bay, off the western Cape coast, and a substantial reserve of gas and petroleum was discovered south-west of Mossel Bay, off the south coast of Cape Province.

ETHNIC GROUPS AND POPULATION

Five major ethnic groups make up South Africa's multiracial society. The 'Khoisan' peoples—Bushmen, Hottentots and Bergdamara—are survivors of the country's earliest inhabitants. The negroid Bantu-speaking peoples fall into a number of tribal groupings. The major groups are formed by the Nguni comprising Zulu, Swazi, Ndebele, Pondo, Tembu and Xhosa on the one hand, and by the Sotho and Tswana on the other. The European or 'white' peoples, who dominate the political, economic and social organization of the republic, are descended from the original 17th-century Dutch settlers in the Cape, refugee French Huguenots, British settlers from 1820 onwards, Germans, and more recent immigrants from Europe and ex-colonial African territories. The major language groups are Afrikaans (65%) and English (35%). The remainder of the population comprises 'Cape Coloureds' (i.e. people of mixed race) and Asians, largely of Indian origin. In April 1994 the total population was estimated to be 40,284,634. In 1992 the estimated ethnic composition of the total population, including 'homelands', was: Africans 29,889,600 (75.9%); whites 5,129,900 (13.0%); Coloureds 3,354,200 (8.5%); and Asians 1,007,300 (2.6%).

The overall density of the population was 32.3 per sq km in 1992, but its distribution is extremely uneven. It is generally related to agricultural resources, more than two-thirds living in the wetter eastern third of the republic and in southern Cape Province. The heaviest concentrations are found in the Witwatersrand mining area—the Johannesburg Metropolitan Area had 1,609,400 people at the 1985 census—and in and around the chief ports of Cape Town, Port Elizabeth and Durban. Europeans have a widespread geographical distribution, but over 80% live in towns. Relatively few Africans are resident in western Cape Province and, while an increasing number are moving to the large black townships on the periphery of the major urban centres, over 60% still reside in the tribal reserves, which extend in a great horseshoe along the south-eastern coast and up to northern Transvaal and then south-westwards through western Transvaal to north-eastern Cape Province. Members of the 'Cape Coloured' group are mainly resident in the Cape Province, and the Asian population is concentrated largely in Natal and the Witwatersrand.

Recent History

J. D. OMER-COOPER

In 1652, when the Dutch East India Co established a provisioning station at Cape Town, the greater part of South Africa was already settled by the ancestors of the present majority population, albeit the area of the Western Cape was still the preserve of Khoisan foragers and pastoralists. A nucleus of permanent white settlement, created by freeing some of the company's servants to undertake crop production on their own account, was initially expanded by assisted immigration, which, in addition to further Dutch and German families, brought a number of French Huguenots to the colony, and thereafter by natural increase. The importation of slaves initiated the stratification of society along racial lines, and the development of racist attitudes which reinforced that stratification soon followed. Slave labour allowed the development of larger-scale, more capitalized farming, thus encouraging less prosperous young whites to take up less capital-demanding stock ranching in the interior. The large hectarages per stock farm necessitated by the geographic and economic conditions led to the very rapid expansion of white stock farmers, who took the land from the Khoisan and incorporated many of them as herdsmen. Conflicts with the San foragers and Khoi-khoi herders served to intensify racist attitudes.

When Britain first occupied the Cape in 1795, whites were already in contact with the Bantu-speaking Xhosa near the Fish river and a long series of frontier wars had begun. Conflict between the frontiersmen and the Dutch East India Co administration had also erupted, in reaction to an energetic official's attempt to impose the rule of law on trans-frontier relations and on the treatment of Khoi-khoi servants by their white masters. The interim British administration brought the establishment of the new evangelical missionary movement in the colony. Missions laid the basis for the development of Western-educated African élites and the adoption of market-orientated agriculture by African peasants. In 1803 the Netherlands took over the administration of the Cape, constituting it as the Batavian Republic; in 1806, however, the British reoccupied the territory on a permanent basis. Judicial steps against the mistreatment of servants provoked an Afrikaner rebellion in 1817. The execution of its ringleaders at Slachters Nek provided Afrikanerdom with its first martyrs. In 1820 an English settlement was established near the eastern frontier. Restrictions on the freedom of movement of colonial Khoi-khoi were abolished in 1828, placing them on a basis of equality with whites, and in 1834 the emancipation of slaves was effected. Afrikaner frontier farmers, already hard-pressed for land, reacted to this by embarking upon a northward trek to establish an independent polity. The Great Trek took place in the aftermath of a major upheaval among the Bantu-speaking peoples, which saw the amalgamation of numerous chiefdoms to the north of Natal into the militaristically organized Zulu kingdom, the foundation of the Swazi and Lesotho kingdoms, and the migration of the Ndebele, similarly organized to the Zulu, to the Transvaal highveld. Bloody encounters between the Trekkers and both the Ndebele and the Zulus gave the Trek its epic dimensions as the foundation myth of Afrikaner nationalism.

In the aftermath of the Great Trek, Britain annexed Natal, but, after initially extending control over trans-Orangia, withdrew, allowing the creation of two Boer Republics, the Orange Free State (OFS) and the South African Republic (Transvaal). In the Cape, a representative legislature was established in 1853. The franchise was based on economic criteria without reference to colour.

The discovery of diamonds near Kimberley in the 1860s initiated an economic revolution. Development of the diamond fields and associated railway-building started the use of migrant labour on a massive scale. White authority was extended over remaining areas of African land in order to make them labour reserves for the white economy. Many Africans, however, succeeded in meeting tax obligations as peasant farmers on land in the reserves and mission stations, or as tenants of white landlords. Some purchased freehold farms. The resulting labour shortage led to the importation of Indian workers to Natal. The diamond discoveries brought the white states economically closer together, but a British attempt to catalyse federation was thwarted by a Transvaal Boer rebellion.

Germany's annexation of South West Africa (Namibia) in 1888 aroused British strategic concern. The development of gold mining on the Witwatersrand in the Transvaal, and the emergence of the South African Republic as the most powerful state in South Africa, posed a further threat to British paramountcy. The imperialistic diamond magnate and Cape politician Cecil Rhodes' British South Africa Co (BSA) was awarded a charter legalizing the establishment of its control over Southern and Northern Rhodesia (modern Zimbabwe and Zambia). Rhodes' capital also helped to establish British control over Nyasaland (Malawi). When these new acquisitions proved not to hold massive gold deposits, Rhodes plotted a rebellion by immigrant white mineworkers (known in the Transvaal as *uitlanders*) to bring the Transvaal under British control. A column of the BSA police assembled in the British Bechuanaland protectorate to assist the uprising. As preparations advanced for the uprising, however, the column's commander, Dr Jameson, invaded the Transvaal, but was forced to surrender to Transvaal forces. The Jameson Raid fiasco intensified the Afrikaner threat to British paramountcy. Joseph Chamberlain, the British colonial secretary, and his imperialistic agent Sir Alfred (later Lord) Milner, brought unrelenting pressure to bear on the Transvaal leader Kruger until in desperation and in alliance with the OFS he opened hostilities against British forces in October 1899. The British occupied and annexed the two Boer republics. The defeated Boer commandos waged a guerrilla struggle, to which the British responded by incarcerating Boer families in concentration camps, where many died. Peace was made in 1902.

In the aftermath of the war, Milner's attempts to revive the Transvaal mines by the use of Chinese labour, to anglicize the subsequent rising Boer generation and to unify South Africa under English auspices raised widespread opposition. When responsible government was granted to the Transvaal and Orange River colonies, Afrikaner nationalist parties gained control. In the Cape Dr Jameson's Progressive Party gave way to the Afrikaner-supported administration of the South Africa Party led by an Englishman, John Merriman. Unification was thus brought about under mainly Afrikaner auspices.

UNION OF SOUTH AFRICA

The Union constitution gave the franchise to white males only, except in the Cape, where the existing voting rights were retained and protected. Prior to the enforcement of the constitution, Africans formed a national organization, which sent a protest delegation to London. The Coloured population's African People's Organisation also protested in vain. With Union in 1910, the two Afrikaner parties in the ex-republics amalgamated with the Cape's South Africa Party to form the national South Africa Party (SAP). Led by two Boer generals, Louis Botha and Jan Smuts, it formed the first government of the new Union. The pro-imperial and pro-capitalist attitudes of the two leaders, however, antagonized many poorer rural Afrikaners. In 1912 the SAP split, and Hertzog founded the National Party. In the same year members of the African élite, under the chairmanship of Pixley Seme, established the African Native National Congress, soon renamed the African National Congress (ANC). The new African political movement soon faced a major problem. In order to coerce African peasants into migrant labour for mine owners and white farmers, the 1913 Land Act denied Africans the right to buy land outside the Native Reserves, or to lease white-owned land.

The ANC protested in vain. In 1913–14 the young Indian lawyer Gandhi first employed the technique of passive resistance (*satyagraha*) against discriminatory legislation affecting South African Indians. Winning limited concessions, he bequeathed the model of mass passive resistance to future protest movements against racism in South Africa.

The outbreak of the First World War in 1914, accompanied by Botha's decision to lead South Africa against Germany, sparked off a minor Afrikaner rebellion. It was quickly suppressed. However, funds collected by the organization Helpmekaar, as aid for the convicted rebels exceeded these requirements and helped to form the financial base for the first major Afrikaner capitalist organization in the Cape Province. After the war the former German colony of South West Africa (Namibia) was entrusted to South African administration as a League of Nations mandated territory. By 1918 the National Party had a strong rural base in the OFS and Transvaal. Following the end of the war, economic depression forced numerous poorer Afrikaner families off the land and into the towns, where many lived in poverty. In 1918 a group of young Afrikaner professionals formed the nucleus of the secret Broederbond society, which established cells in many branches of South Africa's professional and public service organizations in its struggle to advance the status of Afrikaners. Its 'front' organization, the Federation of Afrikaner Cultural Organizations (FAK), promoted Afrikaner culture and language.

The war also brought about substantial urbanization of the African population. The resulting squalid living conditions and the death rate in the 1918 influenza pandemic were used as a justification for the passage of the 1923 Natives (Urban Areas) Act, based on the principle that Africans had no rights in the towns except to serve white needs. The segregationist approach was pressed further in response to the interests of white workers, poor whites and Afrikaner farmers. Mine owners could no longer afford to reserve numbers of semi-skilled jobs for highly paid whites, and in 1922 they repudiated the 1918 status quo agreement. White mineworkers launched a prolonged strike, culminating in an attempted revolution led by unskilled Afrikaner workers. Government troops suppressed the rebellion. The white workers' Labour Party then formed an alliance with the Afrikaner farmers' National Party and won the 1924 parliamentary election. Under the new government's 'civilized labour' policy, blacks were removed from many jobs to be replaced by whites. It also legislated for racial job reservation. It failed, however, to achieve the majority required to alter the entrenched clause protecting African voting rights in the Cape and preventing extension of the 1913 Land Act to the province. Re-elected in 1928, it lost popularity during the period of economic hardship which followed the 1929–30 Wall Street crash in the USA. The National Party, now realigned with the SAP, emerged victorious from parliamentary elections held in 1933, after which the two parties formally merged as the United Party (UP). Hertzog, the prime minister, was then able, with Smuts' assistance, to remove black voters from the Cape electoral roll and, by means of the 1936 Land Act, to extend the 1913 Act to the Cape. Coloured voters rights in the Cape were, however, retained.

The fusion of the National Party with the SAP catalysed a split. A small group of extreme Afrikaner nationalist MPs under Daniel Malan formed the 'purified' National Party, which drew substantial support from the Broederbond. It was strengthened by the rise of Nazi Germany with its extreme racist doctrines. The Broederbond, reinforced by Cape Afrikaner entrepreneurs, aimed at securing for Afrikaners a share of South African capitalist enterprise.

The outbreak of the Second World War in 1939 split the UP. Smuts won a small majority for participation on the Allied side, while Hertzog and some of his followers went into opposition. The war compelled South Africa to produce many goods for itself, transforming the economy into one based predominantly on manufacturing industry. Labour needs were met by a massive expansion of the urbanized African population and an attendant, but limited relaxation of the industrial colour bar. The ANC, gravely weakened during the pre-war economic depression, quickly revived and demanded the implementation of democratic reforms, including universal suffrage. African trade unionism expanded and a well-organized (although officially unrecognized) union established itself among African mine-workers on the Rand. Although Smuts rejected the ANC's political proposals and used armed force to suppress a black mineworkers' strike in 1946, the UP began to adopt marginally more liberal attitudes in the immediate post-war period, accepting the need for increasing African urbanization and some liberalization of job reservation on racial criteria.

The Afrikaner nationalist movement had been deeply divided in the early years of the war by a bitter power struggle between the Ossewabrandwag, an extreme right-wing Afrikaner organization, and the National Party. The Ossewabrandwag employed sabotage and attacks on Allied soldiers. The National Party, albeit also hoping for a German victory, kept to the path of legality. As the prospect of Germany's defeat became clearer, the Ossewabrandwag lost credibility and the National Party became the main expression of Afrikaner nationalism. It reaffirmed its commitment to segregation, systematizing its approach in the application of apartheid.

APARTHEID

Each race and nation, according to the doctrine of apartheid, has a unique, divinely ordained destiny and cultural contribution to make to the world. They should be kept apart so that each can develop to the full along its own inherent lines. Inter-racial contacts, above all miscegenation, must be avoided. The doctrine assumes that cultural attainments are racially determined and races are inherently unequal. Each racial group should have its own territorial area within which to develop its unique cultural personality. The areas envisaged for the African peoples, the overwhelming majority, however, were the poverty-stricken Native Reserves, comprising little more than 13% of the national territory. These areas could never be more than reserves containing migratory labour for the mines and industries of the white areas.

As South Africa approached the 1948 election, the elderly Smuts no longer commanded his previous authority and his liberal deputy, Hofmeyer, lacked popularity. Many Afrikaner farmers, badly affected by the loss of low-cost African labour to the towns, and Afrikaner workers fearful of black competition, found apartheid attractive. The Nationalists secured a narrow parliamentary majority. Daniel Malan formed a government and commenced putting apartheid into practice. In 1954 Malan was replaced by the hard-line J. G. Strydom, who died in 1958 and was succeeded by Hendrik Vervoerd, apartheid's leading ideologue and chief architect.

The period between 1948–59 saw the introduction of a series of interrelated laws and measures aimed at restructuring South African society to conform to apartheid doctrine. The Population Registration Act provided for the classification of the entire population on the basis of race. Inter-racial marriages were forbidden and the Immorality Act, banning sexual relations between whites and blacks, was extended to include relations between whites and coloureds. Urban segregation was intensified by the Group Areas Act, which provided for the designation of particular residential areas for specific races. Indians, who often had businesses in the city centres, were often victimized. Coloured people in Cape Town were even more drastically affected; the main city centre residential area of the Coloured community was declared white and its population resettled in distant areas. Controls over Africans seeking to move to the towns were tightened. Many of the huge number of blacks thus criminalized were encouraged to work as prison labour on farms in the Transvaal. Existing provisions for the reservation of categories of employment for particular races were strengthened. Race segregation in public places, trains and buses, post-offices, hospitals and even ambulances was introduced wherever it had not been previously practised. Beaches were fenced off into separate bathing areas for the different races. The Separate Amenities Act gave legislative sanction for this and stated that the amenities provided for different races need not be of equal standard. The Bantu Education Act removed black education from the care of the ministry of education to that of native affairs. In 1959 the Extension of University Education Act removed the right of non-white students to attend the previously open universities of Cape Town and the Witwatersrand.

To strengthen its hand against radical opposition the government introduced the Suppression of Communism Act. Apart from banning the South African Communist Party (SACP), it decreed that persons named as communists could be subjected to a wide range of restrictions. The definition of communism was framed to cover almost any fundamental opposition to apartheid. The government did take some steps towards enabling Africans to develop along 'their own lines' in the Reserves. As these 'lines' were envisaged in terms of pre-industrial tribal culture, however, it was to traditional (though government-appointed) chiefs that increased powers were delegated in the Bantu Authorities Act.

A significant government measure, both for doctrinal reasons and in order to reduce the UP vote in the Cape, was the removal of Coloured voters from the Cape voting rolls. The UP made this the main focus of its opposition. Failing to achieve its purpose by constitutionally prescribed procedures the government created a special high court of parliament with overriding powers in constitutional matters. In response, white ex-servicemen formed the 'Torch Commando' to defend the constitution, and tensions within the white community ran high. Support for the 'Torch Commando', however, largely reflected English speakers' fears for the status of their language. Once the appeal court had invalidated the act establishing the high court of parliament and the government had accepted that decision, the 'Torch Commando' soon collapsed. The government was subsequently able to achieve its aims regarding the Cape voting rolls, securing the requisite majority by inflating the senate with its own nominees. There was no mass opposition, but a number of white women formed the 'Black Sash' movement. Wearing black sashes as a sign of mourning for the constitution, they undertook extensive work to alleviate the suffering arising from apartheid and helped to keep political opposition to the fore in the white community. The UP proved unable to offer effective opposition, and some of its more liberal members broke away to form the multi-racial Liberal Party. Its white voter support was very slender however, and inhibitions about co-operation with communists prevented it from entering into full partnership with the ANC. It was eventually neutralized by the Prohibition of Political Interference Act, which prohibited multi-racial political organizations. Some radical whites, including members of the officially dissolved SACP formed the Congress of Democrats.

The repressive policies of the National Party compelled the ANC to employ the tactics of mass civil disobedience, for which its Youth Wing had been pressing. An alliance was formed between the ANC and the South African Indian Congress (SAIC). In 1952 they launched a campaign of 'Mass Defiance against Unjust Laws'. Throughout the country well-disciplined protesters broke discriminatory regulations and allowed themselves to be arrested. The government disposed of the movement by means of police action and harsh penalties for civil disobedience. This repression was facilitated by the outbreak of race riots in Port Elizabeth, East London and Kimberley. Occurring during the course of the defiance campaign, although unrelated to it, these disturbances served to discredit the movement in the eyes of some of its supporters as well as most whites. The campaign, however, by attracting unprecedented mass support for the ANC, consolidated its position as an authentic vehicle of African aspirations.

In 1955 the ANC, the SAIC, the Coloured People's Organisation and the white Congress of Democrats united in convening a 'Congress of the People', at which about 3,000 representatives of all races formulated a 'Freedom Charter', setting out a non-racial democratic approach and suggesting the nationalization of land, mines and industries. In 1956 the government took drastic action against the movement, putting 156 participants of all races on trial for plotting the violent overthrow of the state. The treason trial, continued until 1961 and ended with the acquittal of all the accused. In the meantime, however, the ANC was deprived of many of its senior leaders. In this atmosphere some of the more Africanist-minded members reacted aginst alliances with other races, and, led by Robert Sobukwe, formed the Pan-Africanist Congress (PAC). The consolidation of Afrikaner Nationalist political control facilitated change in the social and economic position of Afrikaners. With expansion of the economy and job reservation, white unemployment and the numbers of poor whites diminished. Many Afrikaners advanced from manual to white collar or professional employment. The Afrikaner élite gained access to positions of power. Afrikaner businesses flourished and began to find a place at the highest levels of capitalist enterprise. The ruling councils of the Broederbond were beginning to become the preserve of Afrikaner businessmen, wealthy holders of multiple directorships.

In 1960 Hendrik Verwoerd achieved the long cherished ambition of Afrikaner nationalists when he won a white referendum to make the country a republic. However, this raised the question of South Africa's membership of the British Commonwealth. In response to the strong opposition of African members, South Africa was forced to withdraw. This was only one of the consequences of the changes in the world since 1948. Asian nations, especially Japan, had become significant trading partners with South Africa, while the independence of the Sudan in 1956 and of Ghana in 1957 signified the beginning of decolonization in black Africa. The arrival of the new black nations in the UN meant that South Africa's racist system would be universally decried. Establishing a *modus vivendi* with them was important for security reasons, as well as for the markets they could provide for the products of South Africa's burgeoning industry.

In 1959 Verwoerd introduced the Promotion of Bantu Self-Government Bill and proclaimed that white South Africans must allow the 'Bantustans' to proceed towards full political independence. The need to improve South Africa's international standing and defuse internal African opposition was made strikingly evident in March 1960, when police in Sharpeville opened fire on a crowd of unarmed blacks, who were surrounding the police station in response to a PAC demonstration. The police continued firing into the backs of the fleeing crowd, leaving 67 dead and many more injured. The Sharpeville massacre aroused international indignation to an unprecedented degree, South Africa sustained a net outflow of foreign investment capital, and appeals for military, economic and sporting boycotts began to be given serious attention. Within South Africa the government reacted by banning both the ANC and the PAC. In 1961 the ANC formed a military wing, Umkhonto we Sizwe ('Spear of the Nation'). Under the leadership of Nelson Mandela, it aimed to force the government to negotiate by attacking white-owned property, while avoiding harm to people. In 1962 the PAC also formed an armed wing, called Poqo. Some leaders of both movements escaped abroad to organize an armed liberation struggle.

The government responded by modifying its formerly overtly racist doctrine. Territorial segregation was now to be rationalized on the grounds that the Native Reserves constituted the historic 'homelands' of different African nations. These were to be encouraged to develop towards self-government and eventual full independence, a process portrayed as 'decolonization'. Denial of rights to blacks in the economic heartland would be justified on the internationally acceptable grounds of foreign nationality, instead of the impermissable pretext of race. The new approach to the 'homelands' led to increased expenditure on their development. Instead of establishing industries in these areas, however, they were established on their borders. Blacks could work in the white areas, but they would have foreign nationality imposed upon them. 'Bantustan' frontiers were sometimes redrawn to include existing black townships on the outskirts of white towns.

The 'homelands' were to be led to self-government under constitutions giving scope to the elective principle but with the balance of power in the hands of government-appointed chiefs. Transkei was accorded 'self-government' under such a system in 1963. Ciskei, Bophuthatswana, Lebowa, Venda, Gazankulu, Qwaqwa and KwaZulu followed in the early 1970s.

The abandonment of explicit racism opened the way to contacts with the élites of African countries and the Bantustans. South Africa sought diplomatic contacts with black states. The first steps towards this new version of apartheid were taken under the leadership of Verwoerd, but in September 1966 he was assassinated in the house of assembly, and was succeeded by J. B. Vorster. Under Vorster's more pragmatic leadership the new approach to apartheid was taken much further. While African leaders in general rejected South African advances, diplomatic relations were established with Malawi. Domestically, racial job reservation began to be more openly relaxed. The alliance between the Afrikaner élite and white manual workers began to disintegrate and a constituency for policies to the right of the National Party began to emerge. The Afrikaner élite, however, was increasingly divided between *verligtes* (the enlightened) and the hard-liner *verkramptes*. Albert Hertzog and a small group of extreme *verkramptes* formed the Herstigte Nasionale Party (HNP). It was unable, however, to secure the support of the Broederbond. The HNP failed to win a seat in the 1970 or subsequent elections but did effectively function as a restraining influence on the *verligtes* in the National Party. A much larger number of *verkramptes* remained in the wing of the party led by Dr Andries Treurnicht.

The replacement of explicit racism by separate nationality as a rationale for the denial of civil rights to blacks gave new urgency to reducing the settled African population in white areas. Stricter controls were imposed to prevent Africans acquiring permanent residence in urban areas. Immigrant workers from the Bantustans were discouraged from bringing their families to town, and single men's hostels were built for them. Wherever possible, jobs performed by settled blacks were transferred to migrant labour. A massive campaign was launched to rid the white areas of 'surplus Bantu' and force them into the overcrowded 'homelands'. Between 1960–70 over 1.5m. people were forcibly resettled.

These measures, more drastic than those of the first phase of apartheid, required more ruthless repression to enforce them. The powers of the security police were massively extended. In 1968 the state security services were centralized under the authority of the Bureau of State Security (BOSS). Reports of the widespread use of torture were given credence by the lengthening lists of those who died in police custody. Nelson Mandela was placed on trial in 1964, sentenced to imprisonment for life, and held in prison until 1990.

REGIONAL CONCERNS

South Africa's control over South West Africa (Namibia) had been a subject of international criticism ever since the territory had been entrusted to South Africa as a League of Nations mandated territory. In 1964, despite the opposition of the UN which had assumed responsibility for the mandate, the South African government developed a scheme for the introduction of formal apartheid in the territory. In October 1966 the UN General Assembly resolved to revoke South Africa's mandate and place the territory under direct UN administration. This was confirmed by the Security Council in 1968 and South Africa was ordered to withdraw its forces. South Africa refused to co-operate or to admit UN authorities to the country. The apartheid plan was embodied in the 1968 Development of Self-Government for Native Nations in South West Africa Act.

The collapse of the Central African Federation, and the emergence of Malawi and Zambia posed new problems for South Africa which were much increased by the Unilateral Declaration of Independence (UDI) by Southern Rhodesia (now Zimbabwe) in 1965. South Africa initially confined itself to tacit support. After 1972, as the armed freedom struggle escalated, units of the South African police were sent to assist the illegal regime, while less formal military help was also given to the Portuguese against African freedom movements in Mozambique and Angola. Until 1973, the white regimes seemed able to hold the liberation movements in check.

The strategic situation was transformed by the revolution in Portugal in 1974. The Marxist-inspired Frente de Libertação de Moçambique (Frelimo), led by Samora Machel, consolidated its control of that country. South Africa initially refrained from intervention, but allowed itself to be drawn into the post-independence civil war in Angola. While the USA provided massive aid to the Frente Nacional de Libertação de Angola (FNLA) in the north against the Marxist-inspired government of the Movimento Popular de Libertação de Angola (MPLA) in Luanda, South African troops entered the country from Namibia in support of the União Nacional para a Independência Total de Angola (UNITA), led by Jonas Savimbi. The MPLA, however, was reinforced by Cuban troops. After the US congress prohibited further military expenditure in Angola in 1975 the FNLA rapidly collapsed, UNITA forces were driven back and South African troops withdrew across the border. MPLA co-operation with the South West Africa People's Organisation (SWAPO) and the ANC, however, gave the incentive for repeated military incursions into southern Angola in support of UNITA, which also received renewed US support. With the Frelimo victory in Mozambique, the internationally isolated regime in Rhodesia had become unviable in the opinion of South African policy makers. Overt military support was withdrawn and pressure exerted on the regime to negotiate with African leaders in the hope of creating a moderate African government prepared to coexist with South Africa.

South Africa also sought a political solution in Namibia by modifying its original apartheid plan to a proposal for Namibia to attain independence as a federation of ethnic states. This was rejected by both SWAPO and the UN. In December 1978 South Africa held elections under its own auspices in the territory. These appeared to demonstrate majority support for the ethnically based Democratic Turnhalle Alliance (DTA). In 1978 South Africa proposed the establishment of a Constellation of Southern African States (Consa), which it hoped would include Zimbabwe Rhodesia and Malawi, along with Lesotho, Swaziland, and Botswana, and South Africa's 'Bantustans'.

INTERNAL PRESSURES FOR CHANGE

In 1973 African workers launched a wave of strikes which paralysed mines and industries in many parts of South Africa. Technological changes were now making obsolescent South Africa's reliance on low-cost unskilled labour. In addition, a chronic shortage of white recruits was necessitating the relaxation of race restrictions in the employment hierarchy. The 1973 strikes thus proved the catalyst for reforms which undermined the foundation of the entire apartheid system. Pay rises significantly increased the real wages of black workers, while labour law reforms allowed for the registration of black trade unions. A massive expansion of black trade unions and of industrial action followed. The permanent presence of a black resident population in the urban areas was accepted, and policies aimed at entrenching the system of migrant labour were abandoned. The 'Bantustans' now began to be seen as areas where surplus labour could be housed at minimum cost. Barriers against 'Bantustan' residents settling permanently in the towns were further increased. As the demand for migrant labour declined, the advantages of blacks with urban residence rights over migrant workers increased and the level of poverty in the 'Bantustans' became extremely grave. The new situation increased incentives for the South African regime to confer formal independence on the 'Bantustans'. Transkei accepted this status in 1976, Bophuthatswana in 1977, Venda in 1979 and Ciskei in 1981. All remained dependent on South African financial support and their 'independence' was not internationally recognized. The imposition of 'independence' was resisted by KwaNdebele and still more determinedly by KwaZulu under the leadership of Chief Buthelezi, who used the political immunity conferred by his position to attack the apartheid system. He attempted to transform Inkatha, the Zulu cultural movement that he had founded, into a national political force and to consolidate an alliance with Coloured and Indian political movements. His activities aroused suspicion among supporters of the ANC and other radical political groups, who felt that he had compromised his political integrity by participating in the 'Bantustan' system.

By the end of the 1960s there was an increase in overt black political activity. In 1969 Steve Biko led a secession from the multiracial National Union of South African Students and formed an exclusively black student body, the South African Students Organization. He went on to form a nation-wide Black People's Convention, aiming to unite Africans, Coloureds and Indians against white oppression. A substantial network of associated social and cultural organizations was established.

The racial exclusiveness of the movement encouraged an initially tolerant reception from the government.

In June 1976 the agglomeration of segregated African townships to the south-west of Johannesburg known as Soweto (South-West Townships) erupted in the most serious racial violence in South Africa since the establishment of the Union. It began with a protest by school children at being forced to use Afrikaans as the medium of instruction for some of their school subjects. When police opened fire on the demonstrators rioting followed; this spread not only to other black townships around the Rand and Pretoria but to Natal and the Cape, where Coloured and Indian youths joined in. Repeatedly and violently repressed, the disturbances were not brought under control until the end of the year. Thousands of young people were arrested but many others escaped across the borders to join the liberation movements. The ANC proved far more successful than the PAC in attracting this cadre of prospective freedom fighters, thus consolidating its political hold over the loyalties of the majority. In October 1977 18 'black consciousness' organizations were suppressed and 50 of their leaders detained. International opinion was further incensed to learn that Steve Biko had been arrested and died from injuries suffered while in police custody.

The increasing pressures on white manpower in the military as well as the industrial field, and the need for allies to support the white power élite in response to black militancy, led Vorster's government to seek a solution to the problem of the political future of the Coloured and Indian peoples for whom no credible separate 'homelands' could be provided. Vorster proposed the formation of separate houses of parliament for Coloureds and Indians. These would be represented along with members of the white parliament in the national cabinet and participate in the choice of a president, who would exercise wide executive powers. This plan was put to the electorate in elections in 1977. The long moribund UP now dissolved itself. One section joined the small Progressive Party, which, in the person of Helen Suzman as its sole parliamentary member until the 1974 elections, had been the only effective white opposition party in the legislature. Relaunched as the Progressive Federal Party (PFP), it now became the official parliamentary opposition. The government obtained a landslide majority, but *verkramptes* within its ranks led to the suspension of the plan for a tricameral parliament.

In 1978 Vorster announced his intention to resign as prime minister and seek election to the mainly ceremonial post of state president. While manoeuvring for the succession was under way a scandal emerged in connection with the activities of the minister of information, Dr Connie Mulder, concerning the use of substantial sums of money in covert operations, initially aimed at gaining control of South Africa's English language press and later re-focused on exerting influence over publications, politicians and other prominent people in the USA and Europe. Mulder was forced out of the party, and formed the National Conservative Party (NCP). P. W. Botha became prime minister and Vorster had to resign in disgrace from his new position as president.

Botha altered the balance of influence within the state security network in favour of the armed forces, as opposed to the police. The BOSS was abolished and replaced by a more modest organization. The state security council became the main decision-making organ, with the roles of the National Party and parliament increasingly reduced. The previous c-in-c of the army, Magnus Malan, became the new minister of defence, and his view that South Africa faced an assault from the forces of communism, requiring the adoption of an anti-communist strategy, became the basic postulate of government policy. This involved internal reform as well as measures to ensure the denial of bases to the ANC in neighbouring countries. Racial job restrictions were abolished and trade union rights further extended. Africans were permitted to acquire long-term leases on their houses in the urban townships, and finally to purchase them outright. Africans with urban rights of residence could now move freely from one town to another. Restrictions on multiracial sports were reduced and the laws against interracial marriage and extra-marital sexual relations were repealed. The ineffective senate was abolished and replaced by a president's council made up of nominated Coloureds and Indians along with white nominees. It proposed a modified version of the tri-cameral parliament scheme. The need for some political representation for the black population resident in the towns was recognized, but the intention of including them in the central parliament denied. The reforms precipitated a conflict with the remaining *verkramptes* (hardliners) in the National Party. Treurnicht challenged the prime minister but was defeated. In March 1982 he founded the Conservative Party of South Africa (CPSA), which absorbed the NCP. The changes in legislation on job reservation ensured the new party a significant white constituency.

Externally, the government's attention at this period was focused on Namibia, where the implementation of UN Security Council Resolution 435, calling for the evacuation of South African military forces from Namibia and for the election of a constituent assembly under UN supervision, was declared conditional by South Africa on the withdrawal of Cuban forces from Angola. Beginning in August 1981 South African armed forces launched a series of invasions in southern Angola, in support of UNITA. In Namibia counter-insurgency units were developed, notably the Koevoet ('Crowbar') unit. In Mozambique, South African security took over the support of the anti-government terrorist movement the Resistência Nacional Moçambicana (Renamo, also known as the MNR). Its widespread attacks on civilian targets as well as industrial installations and communications reduced the country to economic paralysis and famine. South African security forces also orchestrated armed raids into Zambia, Botswana, Lesotho and Swaziland. In London the ANC offices were bombed. The first phase of this programme of destabilization was concluded in 1984 when Mozambique and South Africa signed the Nkomati Accord, under which Mozambique was to deny military bases to the ANC and South Africa to cease supporting Renamo. It was announced in 1984 that South Africa and Swaziland had secretly signed a non-aggression pact in 1982.

Following the departure of Treurnicht and his followers from the National Party, Botha proceeded to implement his constitutional plan. In November 1983 the creation of a tricameral legislature was approved by a referendum restricted to white voters. Elections for the Coloured house of representatives and the Indian house of delegates followed in August 1984, and in September the electoral college chose P. W. Botha as the country's first executive president. Meanwhile, in August 1983, a number of groups opposed to apartheid, many with church affiliations and with multiracial memberships, formed the United Democratic Front (UDF) to promote the rejection of the constitutional plan, on the grounds of its failure to provide representation for the black majority. The UDF won strong support from Coloured voters, only 18% of whom participated in the election. Indian participation was even lower.

The introduction of the new constitution catalysed a rebellion in the black townships which exceeded the scale of the 1976 Soweto upheaval. It was supported by strikes, notably in the economically crucial mining industry. The Congress of South African Trade Unions (COSATU), a federation of black trade unions that were politically aligned with the ANC, was formed in December 1984, and demanded the abolition of pass restrictions, the withdrawal of foreign investment and the release of Nelson Mandela. The township rebellion escalated dramatically when, on 21 March 1985, the 25th anniversary of the Sharpeville massacre, the police opened fire on an unarmed African procession in Uitenhage, killing 20 and wounding many more. In July the government declared a state of emergency in 36 magisterial districts, but the violence continued to increase. Black policemen, community councillors and suspected informers were killed in growing numbers. The government lost control of some townships for significant periods, while groups of young 'comrades' enforced boycotts and their version of law and order through informal 'people's courts'. Continuing throughout 1985 and much of 1986, the disturbances encouraged conflicts between sections of the black communities, which tended to undermine the will to resistance. Migrant workers and some township-based workers were alienated by the boycotts and high handed behaviour of the 'comrades'. They formed 'vigilante' groups which, often with the tacit support of the police, attacked the 'comrades' and burned down their dwellings. These divisions were especially acute in Natal where members of the mainly rural Zulu-supported Inkatha movement became involved in escalating hostilities with ANC supporters, who were mainly urban-based Zulu and Xhosa speakers from southern Natal.

On 12 June 1986 the government extended the state of emergency to cover the whole country. As many as 24,000 people, many of them children, were detained without trial. Disturbances in the townships continued into 1987 but, with army units largely replacing the police and with massive injections of funds for house-building and improved services, they gradually subsided. The upheavals aroused international opinion against South Africa still further. European banks suspended new lending and the EC introduced a number of economic sanctions. Even the USA applied some limited sanctions. The value of the currency unit, the rand, fell heavily in foreign exchange markets. At a Commonwealth heads of government meeting held in October 1985 a group of distinguished persons reflecting the racial diversity of the Commonwealth was formed to visit South Africa. The Eminent Persons Group (EPG) was initially well received by the government. It was permitted to consult a wide range of opinion and held talks with Nelson Mandela in prison. Its progress, however, abruptly ceased in May 1986 when the South African defence force launched a series of raids into Botswana, Zimbabwe and Zambia. Following the collapse of the EPG, the EC widened its programme of sanctions and the Commonwealth implemented sanction measures. The US congress also voted to intensify its programme of economic embargoes.

Among Afrikaner intellectuals, professionals and businessmen and within the National Party itself, opinion was aleady growing that apartheid would have to be abandoned and an accommodation reached with an effective African leadership. Initially, Chief Buthelezi was viewed as a possible negotiating partner. However, the ANC, which commanded overwhelming support in the townships, was backed by COSATU and had the general support of church leaders and the UDF, came increasingly to be seen as the only credible negotiating partner. While liberal Afrikaner opinion was moving towards this view, a proliferation of movements on the extreme right expressed the growing desperation of the poorer sections of the white community at the erosion of their privileged position. A paramilitary organization, the Afrikaanse Weerstandsbeweging (AWB), founded in 1977 and led by Eugene Terre'Blanche, now attracted a mass following, and actively recruited among the police forces within whose ranks it had many sympathisers.

General elections for the white house of parliament in 1987 resulted in a partial realignment of forces. The National Party emerged with a secure majority but a considerably reduced vote. The CPSA obtained more seats than the PFP and became the official opposition. In 1989 the PFP, augmented by two small splinter groups and a number of other individual members who broke away from the National Party, was reconstituted as the Democratic Party (DP).

Botha's reform programme, meanwhile, continued to falter. Bold new initiatives were repeatedly promised but little actually materialized. Some relaxation in the application of the Group Areas Act was permitted. Plans for a form of multiracial regional government were drawn up, although a plan for the governance of Natal prepared by an indaba ('meeting') of businessmen and leaders of all races in Natal under the initiative of Chief Buthelezi had recently been ignored. Reforms which once might have appeared substantive now did nothing to satisfy African opinion, church leaders or the UDF. Calls for the release of Nelson Mandela became increasingly insistent. Numerous groups belonging to the UDF were banned and the entire movement barred from receiving external contributions. It dissolved itself to reappear as the Mass Democratic Movement.

Repression within South Africa was accompanied by an intensification of the destabilization of neighbouring black-ruled countries. In Mozambique covert support for Renamo continued, despite the initial Nkomati Accord and its subsequent renewal in 1988. In Angola, South African military involvement increased. In 1987 South African forces defeated a major offensive by Angolan and Cuban forces; in pursuing their advantage, however, they were themselves halted by the Angolan and Cuban forces. The stalemate occurred in a changed international environment. Following the summit meeting held in October 1986 between Presidents Reagan and Gorbachev, the USSR had relinquished any intention of contesting Western hegemony in Africa. Angola could no longer rely on continued Soviet support for Cuban military involvement. The struggle against the MPLA in Angola and the ideological orientation of a SWAPO government in Namibia were no longer of crucial importance to the USA. This atmosphere thus favoured the opening of negotiations, which resulted in an agreement on 22 December 1988 that opened the way to the solution of the interlinked problems of Angola and Namibia. South African troops left Angola, Cuban forces were repatriated and Angola withdrew permission for ANC bases on its territory. South Africa permitted the entry of a UN administrator and UN forces provided for under Security Council Resolution 435 to Namibia. A constituent assembly was elected, a national constitution drawn up and Namibia became independent on 21 March 1990.

THE ABANDONMENT OF APARTHEID

The resolution of the Namibian issue re-focused attention on the political condition of South Africa itself. Liberal whites, including influential Afrikaners, initiated direct contact with the ANC, at a meeting held in Dakar, Senegal, in July 1987. In spite of Botha's disapproval, further contacts followed. Then, in January 1989, Botha withdrew from official duties on the grounds of ill-health and, in early February, he resigned as party leader, to be replaced by F. W. de Klerk. Before finally retiring from office he held a meeting with Nelson Mandela, thus effectively recognizing the ANC leader's position as the potential alternative head of government. Botha relinquished the presidency, with some unwillingness, in mid-August. Prior to the September parliamentary election de Klerk, still the acting head of state, gave little indication of any radical intentions. At the election, the CPSA and the liberal DP both made considerable gains. The National Party retained a clear majority, however, and de Klerk was confirmed as state president.

During 1989 international and internal pressures on the government increased. The economy, weighed down by expenditure on security, was suffering from the effects of international sanctions. There was no possibility of winning black loyalty by reforms along the lines of the tricameral parliament. The illegal influx to the urban areas of migrants from the poverty-stricken 'Bantustans' was not containable by the security forces. The greater part of the National Party, the Broederbond and the Afrikaner intellectual élite was already convinced that apartheid was unsustainable and that the ANC must be accepted as a negotiating partner. The ANC, after losing its facilities in Angola, had no military bases from which to operate. The eclipse of communism in the USSR deprived the ANC of backing for the continuation of its armed struggle and undermined the ideological position of SACP members in its governing bodies. In the USA, President Bush initiated a more active approach towards democratic change in South Africa. During 1989 informal meetings were held in Britain of representatives of the ANC, the National Party, a number of African states and of the USA and USSR. In September US officials indicated that if no move to release Mandela had taken place in six months President Bush would assent to an extension of economic sanctions.

In an historic speech to the three houses of parliament on 2 February 1990 President de Klerk made the dramatic announcement that Nelson Mandela would be released and that the ban had been lifted on the ANC, the PAC, the SACP and 33 other organizations including the UDF. It was the government's intention to open negotiations with black leaders with a view to devising a new constitution based on universal franchise. Equality of all citizens regardless of race would be guaranteed by an independent judiciary and protection for individual rights entrenched.

On 11 February 1990 Nelson Mandela was set free after 27 years in prison. ANC refugees soon began to return from exile. However, the ANC faced major problems in bringing the spontaneous loyalties of the great majority of the black population within a disciplined organizational framework, especially in the case of the young 'comrades' who had played such a role in the township upheavals. There were problems of ideological divisions between dedicated Marxists and others in the ANC leadership, as well as rivalries and misunderstandings between returning exiles and internal supporters. Additionally, the ANC had no direct access to power, and the government retained the initiative. The ANC called for the continuation of sanctions until the abandonment of apartheid had become demonstrably irreversible. This attracted significant support but was to become increasingly difficult to sustain as the reform process continued.

By the end of 1990 the remnants of traditional social segregation had largely disappeared and people of all races were making common use of beaches, swimming baths, hospital wards, railway carriages, hotels and restaurants. In October the Separate Amenities Act was formally repealed. A beginning of school desegregation had also been made, as white schools could, with the consent of parents, admit a proportion of children of other races. The CPSA protested bitterly and the AWB held demonstrations threatening a violent struggle against black rule. It was unable, however, to attract crowds large enough to give it much political credibility.

ANC and government members met for the first time to discuss conditions for the opening of full constitutional negotiations in May 1990 and then again in August, when the ANC agreed to the formal suspension of its guerrilla activities. The ANC favoured the election of a constituent assembly by universal franchise to draw up the new constitutional order, while the government instead favoured a multi-party conference giving each party an equal voice. In January 1991 the government agreed to a proposal by the ANC that a multi-party conference should meet to determine the procedures for drawing up a new constitution.

Prospects of expeditious constitutional negotiations were threatened by continuing and expanding violence between followers of Inkatha and those of the ANC. In August 1990 these disturbances spread from Natal to the townships around the Rand. The ANC became increasingly convinced that the government itself was implicated in a form of internal destabilization strategy aimed at weakening ANC bargaining power.

On 1 February 1991 de Klerk again took the initiative in an address to parliament by announcing that all the remaining legislative pillars of apartheid, including the Group Areas Act and the Population Registration Act, were to be repealed. By the end of June this legal revolution was complete. The National Party even changed its own constitution to open membership to all races, and began to attract significant numbers of Indian and Coloured, as well as smaller numbers of African members. The EC and the USA abandoned most economic sanctions, despite ANC appeals. Contacts between South Africa and black African states multiplied and trade was expanded, although Commonwealth countries voted to maintain sanctions for the present. The ANC supported the abandonment of international boycotts for those sports which accepted genuine non-racial management and participation. In July 1991 the International Olympic Committee agreed to South Africa's readmission.

In a series of meetings culminating in a conference in Harare, Zimbabwe in April 1991, the ANC pursued a *rapprochement* with the PAC. A formal alliance was projected, although this was not subsequently carried through. In the first week of July, at its national congress, the ANC elected a new national executive, successfully fusing new elements with 'old guard' members. Mandela became president while the black mineworkers' leader Cyril Ramaphosa became secretary-general. In May the ANC published its preliminary constitutional proposals. These included a bicameral legislature (with the lower house elected by proportional representation) and a bill of rights. The government's suggestions, issued in September, had much in common with these but included provisions for a collegial presidency and a constitutional role for the upper house which appeared to build in a white veto, and were rejected by the ANC. At a secret meeting held in February 1992 the government and ANC agreed on the release of political prisoners, the return of exiles and the formal abandonment by the ANC of armed struggle.

CONSTITUTIONAL NEGOTIATIONS

The main obstacle impeding constitutional negotiations, however, was the continuing violence between Inkatha and ANC supporters and the suspicion that elements of the state security forces were involved. In spite of meetings between Mandela and Buthelezi held in January and April 1991, the carnage in the townships continued. In early April the ANC threatened to withdraw from negotiations if the government failed to take effective action to stop the violence, and demanded the dismissal of the minister of defence, Magnus Malan, and the minister of law and order, Adriaan Vlok. In July it was admitted that secret payments had been made from government funds to Inkatha during 1989–90, and Malan and Vlok were demoted to minor cabinet posts. Suspicions of official involvement in the continuing violence were not fully dispelled, however, and the ANC insisted on the need for an interim government in which it would be represented during finalization of negotiations for a new constitution.

The multi-party conference on procedures for drawing up the new constitution, the Convention for a Democratic South Africa (CODESA), met on 20 December 1991. The government found itself under pressure to agree to the idea of an interim government and an elected constituent assembly.

The commencement of constitutional discussions intensified the hostility of the extreme right and, after losing a parliamentary by-election to the CPSA, de Klerk called a referendum of white voters for 17 March 1992. Despite demonstrations and campaigning by the far right the government achieved a more than two-thirds majority in support of continuing negotiations towards a democratic constitution. The CODESA talks were resumed, but government insisted on provisions that appeared to give it a veto. The talks became deadlocked and the ANC called for a campaign of non-violent mass action by its supporters to put pressure on the government. Then, on 17 June, a number of residents of the settlement of Boipatong, including women and children, were massacred, apparently by Inkatha supporters who had allegedly been brought to the scene by police trucks. President de Klerk denounced the killings and went personally to the township, but was met by a hostile demonstration. After he had left, police opened fire, apparently without orders from the officer in charge, causing further deaths. The ANC broke off bilateral talks with the government forthwith and demanded effective action to stop the violence, including the disbandment of groups involved in covert operations and the assumption of direct responsibility for the security forces by de Klerk personally. De Klerk, however, denied any impropriety by the security forces, and denounced the ANC mass action campaign. He invited the ANC to resume constitutional negotiations, but this was refused unless the government modified its insistence on a veto in the constitution-making procedure. During July 1992 mounting criticism of the activities of the security forces and a public outcry at the rising number of deaths in police custody strengthened the ANC's resolve to continue its campaign of mass action. In mid-July President de Klerk announced the dissolution of a number of notorious police and army units. In late July the UN Security Council, acting upon a request by Nelson Mandela, sent a UN Special Representative to South Africa on a 10-day fact-finding mission. The representative succeeded in bringing about a tentative *rapprochement* between the government and the ANC, arranging talks between the two sides at the end of July. As a result of the visit the UN recommended the establishment of an independent investigation into the activities of the security forces and, in mid-August, the Security Council authorized the deployment of UN observers in South Africa to monitor political violence.

During the first week in August 1992 the ANC, SACP and COSATU joined forces to organize an unprecedented level of mass action against the government, involving political rallies and a two-day general strike. Shortly afterwards, the PAC met the government to discuss the possibility of introducing an alternative negotiating forum to the suspended CODESA. In mid-August talks between the ANC and the government on the resumption of constitutional negotiations failed, as the government refused to meet the demands articulated in June by the ANC, and the opposition organization would not accept government plans for a blanket amnesty for perpetrators of political crimes, as this was to include members of the security forces. In late August the government announced a major restructuring of the police force and the forthcoming establishment of an independent body which was to investigate alleged police complicity in serious crimes.

In early September 1992 the armed forces of the nominally independent 'homeland' of Ciskei fired on a procession of ANC supporters, killing 28 people and wounding about 200 others. The ANC blamed the South African government for complicity in the massacre, and demanded the removal of the Ciskei 'head of state'. President de Klerk agreed to conduct an enquiry into the incident, and in mid-September it was announced that legislation was to be introduced to reintegrate 'homeland' security forces and educational bodies into the South African system. Measures to reduce the 'independence' of the 'homelands' were also promised.

While formal talks between the ANC and the government were suspended, informal contacts continued, and in mid-September 1992 the ANC announced its agreement to a summit meeting between Mandela and de Klerk. This meeting, which took place shortly afterwards, resulted in a 'record of understanding' which allowed for the resumption of full bilateral negotiations. In November the ANC announced its acceptance of a proposal (originating from the SACP and sponsored by Chris Hani, a leading militant radical in the ANC/SACP leadership) that an interim government of national unity should be formed, which would include the major parties that had won seats in the constituent assembly. The interim government would hold office for a five-year period, during which the constituent assembly, would act as the interim legislature, while also finalizing the new constitution. In a subsequent statement of 'strategic perspectives' it was suggested that it might be necessary to consider the continuation in office of a government of national unity even after the new constitution had come into force. The government welcomed this idea and proposed a number of procedural steps, including the resumption of multi-party talks in order to discuss the formation of a transitional executive committee (which was to have control over key ministries), to set the date for the election of the constituent assembly and to draft an interim constitution under which the proposed interim government of national unity and the constituent assembly would function. The ANC accepted the procedural programme, but rejected the government's suggested timetable, pressing for elections for the constituent assembly to be held before the end of 1993. In response to the report of the inquiry into the role of the security forces in relation to political violence, de Klerk took the strong measure of dismissing several high-ranking officers. General Viljoen, a former head of the army and a committee of former generals subsequently began to take a major overt role in the leadership of the white extreme right.

With substantial agreement between the two main negotiating partners achieved, multi-party talks in a format known as the multi-party negotiating forum were reconvened in April 1993. Agreement between the government and the ANC and the prospect of a National Party—ANC coalition in the interim government of national unity placed great strains on the loyalties of some members of both organizations. Within the National Party divisions between those concerned to entrench regional autonomy, maintaining a negotiating alliance with Inkatha for this purpose, and those drawn towards an alliance with the ANC at central government level, became more pronounced. Within the ANC the emergence of a revolutionary socialist wing, which was highly critical of the pragmatic negotiating stance of the party leadership, was discernible. The imminence of agreement on a new constitutional order aroused even stronger reactions among the right-wing white groups and black political movements opposed to a political solution on the lines favoured by the two major parties. Chief Buthelezi, who protested vigorously at the bilateral agreements between the government and the ANC, initiated meetings between representatives of Inkatha, a number of 'homeland'-based movements and the CPSA. This led to the formation of the Concerned South Africans Group (COSAG), including Inkatha, Bophuthatswana, Ciskei, KwaZulu and the CPSA, to act as a pressure group at the negotiating forum, in favour of extreme regional autonomy. In early April 1993, on the eve of the talks, Chris Hani (the initial sponsor of the idea of a government of national unity and the man best placed to persuade young black radicals to accept it) was assassinated by a white right-wing extremist; several members of the CPSA were implicated in the affair, and three of them were subsequently charged in connection with the murder which was believed to be part of a right-wing plot to disrupt the constitutional negotiations. At this time a series of random terrorist attacks against whites began, which were alleged to be the work of the Azanian People's Liberation Army (APLA—the military wing of the PAC).

As the negotiating forum approached a final decision on the date for the elections which would bring the old constitutional order formally to an end, the white extreme right openly threatened recourse to arms. Then, as the forum was about to confirm the election date as 27 April 1994, an armed commando of some 2,000 white right-wingers forced its way into the ANC headquarters in Johannesburg; the police did not intervene, on the pretext that they could have provoked a bloodbath. The intruders eventually withdrew and, a few days later, several arrests were made. As committees of the negotiating forum worked on the details of the future transitional executive committee and the interim constitution, the ANC was obliged to concede to decisions being taken on key issues, such as the level of regional autonomy, which would effectively tie the hands of the subsequent constituent assembly. Even this did not satisfy the members of COSAG, and in July Inkatha and the CPSA withdrew from the negotiating forum in protest at the rejection of demands for full regional autonomy.

In late July the draft interim constitution was presented to the negotiating forum. This document embodied major compromises by both the main negotiating partners. Its regional proposals went a long way towards federalism, but still did not suffice to enable de Klerk to persuade Buthelezi to resume participation in the talks. The CPSA proclaimed the proposals had put an end to all possibility of further negotiations. At this time political violence between supporters of Inkatha and those of the ANC in the Rand and Natal escalated again. At the beginning of August Inkatha supporters from a migrant workers' hostel in a Rand township went on the rampage, killing more than 100 people. The Anglican archbishop of Cape Town, Desmond Tutu, reacted by demanding the introduction of an international peace-keeping force, while the ANC urged the immediate introduction of joint control over the security forces. A week later, substantial army contingents moved into the East Rand townships in a new attempt to bring the situation under control.

TOWARDS DEMOCRATIC ELECTIONS

In late September 1993 parliament approved legislation authorizing the formation, from late October, of a transitional executive council to oversee the process of government during the period leading to the April 1994 elections. Immediately afterwards, in response to an appeal by Mandela to the UN, the USA and Commonwealth countries withdrew all economic sanctions against South Africa.

During November 1993 the Forum completed details of an interim constitution, which was then formally passed into law by the tricameral parliament in December. The national territory was re-divided into nine regions: Western Cape, Eastern Cape, Northern Cape, Orange Free State, North West, KwaZulu/Natal, Eastern Transvaal, Northern Transvaal and P. W. V. (Pretoria, Witwatersrand and Vereeniging - the urban and industrial hub of South Africa and its most populous region, including more than one-half of the total white population). The former 'Bantustans', including those purported to be 'independent', disappeared as distinct entities and were absorbed into one or more of the new regions. Even the names disappeared from the new political map, except in the case of KwaZulu/Natal, which was retained as a concession to Buthelezi and Inkatha. Each of the new regions was provided with an elected assembly to be chosen by proportional representation and a regional government with extensive local authority and autonomy.

The central parliament was to comprise a house of assembly of 400 members, all elected by proportional representation but on a basis of one-half from national and one-half from regional lists. There was to be an upper house of 90 members chosen by the regional assemblies. The executive would be headed by an executive president, to be chosen by parliament, and at least two executive vice-presidents. Under the terms of the agreement on a government of national unity, any party obtaining 20% of the national vote would be entitled to one of the vice-presidential positions. In the event that only one party achieved this total, the second position would go to any grouping with the second largest support. Any party receiving 5% or more of the vote would be entitled to a position in the national cabinet. The national and regional assemblies and governments were to function within the limitations of a justiciable interim bill of rights. The interim parliament was to subsist for a maximum of five years. During this period it is to act as the national legislature. It is also to act as a constituent assembly charged with the responsibility for drafting the definitive new constitution for the country. This is to be done within the first two years. Thereafter it will have the duty of introducing the necessary legislation and other arrangements for elections under this new constitution to take place by the end of the five-year period. The adoption of constitutional clauses by the constituent assembly will require a two-thirds majority. In framing the constitution the constituent assembly is required to preserve the principles of the interim constitution.

The Forum did not succeed in winning the assent of Buthelezi, the Afrikaner Volksfront and the representatives of Bophuthatswana and the Ciskei, despite many concessions made to them. They now formed a new alliance - the Freedom Front - and threatened to boycott the April 1994 elections. The intensity of the violence between Inkatha and supporters of the ANC in Natal and the African townships on the Rand escalated further. After repeated attempts at negotiations, Buthelezi was persuaded to register the Inkatha Freedom Party for the election before reverting to demanding postponement and threatening a boycott. Negotiations between Mandela, de Klerk and the Afrikaner Volksfront were somewhat more productive. The Volksfront was offered the possibility of the subsequent creation of an Afrikaner 'boerstaat', given sufficient support and provided that such a state would remain part of South Africa and subject to the provisions of the bill of rights. Viljoen agreed to register the movement for the elections. However, Terre'Blanche and the more militant of his AWB supporters rejected this outright and threatened civil war if the election proceeded.

During March 1994 the killings in Natal and KwaZulu continued; the declaration of a state of emergency in the area and the dispatch of troops failed to bring the violence to an end. Buthelezi's followers mounted repeated armed demonstrations; on 30 March this resulted in a bloody battle around the ANC headquarters in the heart of Johannesburg. The possibility that Inkatha and the armed force of the KwaZulu police might attempt to forcibly prevent the holding of the election there and that the army, with many right-wingers in its ranks, might be unwilling to suppress such a rebellion seemed to threaten South Africa with generalized anarchy and civil war.

In mid-March 1994, however, the militant section of the Afrikaner extreme right suffered a serious blow. The Bophuthatswana army and police mutinied against the highly unpopular government of Chief Mangope, who was forced to flee from his 'Bantustan'. Over 2,000 Afrikaner extremists then invaded the Bophuthatswana capital, Mmabatho, with the intention of restoring Mangope and securing all or part of the area for their projected boerstaat. Bophuthatswana armed forces attacked them, however, and they fled in panic. During the violence three Afrikaners, caught when their car broke down, were shot in full view of television cameras. President de Klerk reacted to news of the mutiny by sending in units of the South African army, who swiftly restored order, oversaw the departure of the remaining white militants, established an interim administration and effectively reintegrated the 'homeland' into South Africa. Shortly afterwards, the security forces of the Ciskei put an end to both the regime of Brig. Gqoza and of that 'Bantustan's' separate existence. The Bophuthatswana fiasco had seriously discredited the military and political potential of the extreme right and had demonstrated that the army and police would be loyal to the constitutional government, however unpalatable to their earlier political views it might be.

In spite of the collapse of his 'Bantustan' allies, Buthelezi continued on alone. Even the international mediation which he requested and received failed to placate him. By early April 1994, however, his exposed situation was becoming increasingly evident and he was under great pressure from many of his own supporters who wished to take advantage of the opportunities offered by the election. Buthelezi held on to the very last minute before agreeing that Inkatha would participate in the elections in return for the enhancement of the status of the Zulu monarchy by the transfer of extensive state lands to a trust in the name of the Zulu king. For this the tri-cameral parliament had to be hastily recalled.

These issues were only resolved, and Inkatha's participation assured, on 21 April 1994. In the mean time, the election timetable had been amended in the light of practical considerations to cover three days commencing on 26 April. Only five days thus remained before voting was to begin. Inkatha had missed the deadline for the registration of candidates and Inkatha names were not on the ballot papers which had already been printed. Additional stick-on strips had therefore to be provided, to be attached to ballot papers during the voting procedure.

With Inkatha's last-minute participation, the long-running bloody conflict in Natal and the Rand townships faded dramatically. In a last desperate attempt to abort the election and prevent the transition to majority rule, members of the white extreme right set off a series of bomb blasts, including one at Johannesburg's international airport. The violence failed, however, in its purpose of disrupting the election, merely serving to illustrate the isolation and impotence to which the movement (30 of whose members were subsequently arrested) had been reduced. By this stage the security forces had decisively aligned themselves in support of constitutional order.

The election itself, involving 19 political parties, was marked by a quite extraordinary atmosphere of goodwill. The logistical difficulties of organizing an election on this scale for the first time, compounded by the complex procedures which were exacerbated by the need to affix the Inkatha strips to voting ballots during the actual proceedings, resulted in much frustration and long delays. (Organizational failures were especially severe in the KwaZulu area, resulting in the extension of the voting period there for an extra day.) Despite this, blacks and whites voted together without conflict.

The various electoral problems resulted in abundant opportunities for errors as well as election fraud and in spite of the presence of UN and Commonwealth observers, the precise results in many areas remain distinctly dubious. The overall outcome of the election was, however, clear beyond doubt. The ANC gained an overwhelming majority at national level, although just short of the two-thirds majority which would have enabled it to rewrite the constitution unilaterally. It also gained control of all but two of the nine regional assemblies. The National Party was the only other grouping to top 20% of the poll. It also gained control of the Western Cape regional assembly. Inkatha trailed well behind the leaders with just over 10% of votes, but was credited with a 51% victory in KwaZulu/Natal. The constitutional wing of the Afrikaner Volksfront achieved significant support, but less than the 5% needed for a place in the cabinet. The PAC, with its radical africanist approach, received less than 2% of the vote.

For all its problems, the election was a resounding political success. It provided a quite extraordinary emotional as well as politically-liberating catharsis for the vast majority of South Africans of all races. As the results became known, jubilant crowds poured out into the streets in previously unimaginable scenes of goodwill. Thus the new South Africa was born in a far more joyous atmosphere than even the most optimistic had dared to imagine.

THE NEW GOVERNMENT

On 9 May 1994 the interim parliament elected Mandela as president and the following day he was formally inaugurated as head of state. De Klerk and Mbeki became deputy presidents. The former finance minister, Derek Keys, was reappointed to that position in the new government, and Buthelezi became minister of internal affairs. The secretary-general of the ANC, Cyril Ramaphosa, remained outside the cabinet but was chosen to preside over the assembly debates.

With the inauguration of the new regime, South Africa was welcomed into the OAU. On 1 June 1994 it also re-entered the Commonwealth. Mandela was quick to point out, however, that domestic problems meant that South Africa could offer little more than diplomatic assistance towards the solution of African problems such as those of Rwanda, Angola and Mozambique. In the case of Mozambique, Mandela has made special efforts towards achieving genuine peace and stability, which is of vital significance for South Africa for economic reasons. While instability continues, moreover, the Mozambique border is likely to remain the scene of extensive arms and drug smuggling by criminal gangs.

Domestically, the first steps of the new government have been marked by conspicuously responsible moderation combined with the determination to achieve real benefits for the socially deprived. The introduction of the promised reconstruction and development programme (RDP) was announced: this contained an undertaking to build 1m. homes in the five-year period of the interim parliament, together with the extension of basic educational and health facilities to all. The government's intention is to finance this programme through savings on security-related expenses and increased revenues arising from economic growth (together with external aid). The budget proposals thus made no provision for increased taxes, except for a once-only 5% surcharge on the income brackets to launch the RDP. Japan has announced a massive contribution to the programme, and further substantial aid has been promised by western powers. International business confidence was somewhat shaken in June when it was announced that Derek Keys was to resign the finance portfolio for unexplained personal reasons. Mandela acted quickly to reassure the business world, however, by announcing that an Afrikaner banker, Christo Liebenberg, would take over the position.

An important feature of the programme of reconciliation has been the adoption of an amnesty for past political crimes. In this regard a 'truth and reconciliation commission' is to be established; those who wish to avail themselves of the amnesty will be required to apply to the commission, giving a full account of their actions. Mandela also continued his efforts towards conciliating the white extremists, some of whom had abandoned their homes after the election, gathering in a number of camps in rural areas of the Western Transvaal. Terre'Blanche and other leaders were invited to meetings to discuss their ideas for a ethnic boerstaat.

During July and early August 1994, however, the government's economic hopes were threatened by widespread union wage demands and strikes. Mandela appealed for moderation, as excessive wage increases would lower growth and inhibit job creation. The labour unrest was only one symptom of impatience at the government's apparent preoccupation with reconciliation with the former practitioners of apartheid while its victims continued to suffer extreme deprivation. This impatience was intensified by the large salaries of members of the new government.

In a speech to mark the first 100 days of the new regime, President Mandela expressed his appreciation of the narrow path that the government must follow between the imperatives of redressing the plight of the underprivileged black majority and of winning acceptance and co-operation from the whites, essential to the political stability and economic growth without which the resources for social reconstruction would be unavailable. The challenge for the future, he argued, would be to transform a society distorted by over 300 years of white domination and 46 years of apartheid without sacrificing reconciliation.

Economy

LEO KATZEN

NATURAL RESOURCES

South Africa's diverse climate permits the cultivation of a wide range of crops but, largely because of inadequate and erratic rainfall, only about 15% of the land surface is suitable for arable farming. Topographic difficulty is the main factor limiting the extent of irrigation to less than 8,000 sq km. However, the ambitious Orange River Project is expected eventually to increase the total irrigated area by about 300,000 ha or 40%. In spite of improvements in farming methods and conservation techniques in recent years, South Africa remains a relatively poor crop-raising country. This also imposes limits on animal husbandry, for which South Africa is better suited, although even here, the carrying capacity of the land is fairly low by international standards. Nevertheless, because of a high degree of specialization, experience, advanced methods and considerable capital investment, certain branches of farming, such as fruit and wool, continue to make a substantial contribution to the economy and to exports in particular.

It is in mineral deposits, though, that South Africa's greatest wealth lies. The discovery of, first, diamonds and then, more importantly, gold during the latter part of the 19th century was the basis of the country's modern economic development. A huge complex of heavy and light industry, based initially on the gold mining industry, has grown up in the interior, although South Africa's share in world gold production (excluding the former USSR) declined from 70% in 1980 to 37% in 1989, owing to a fall in the average grade of ore mined and an increase in output in other parts of the world. There are also abundant deposits of nearly every other important mineral in the country. The production of minerals other than gold accounted for 50% of the total value of mining production of R46,631m. (excluding Bophuthatswana) in 1993. There are huge reserves of iron ore and coal (with a pit-head price which is probably the lowest in the world). South Africa, in 1980, was also the largest producer in the Western world of chromium, manganese and vanadium; the second largest producer of platinum, diamonds, vermiculite, antimony, asbestos and fluorspar; and the third largest producer of uranium. The country's reserves of manganese, platinum, vanadium, fluorspar and sillimanite are estimated to be the largest in the Western world. In addition, it is a major producer of copper, lead and zinc.

Only two major mineral products—petroleum and bauxite—have not been found in economic quantities. However, in February 1985 the Southern Oil Exploration Corpn (SOEKOR), a government-owned company which had been involved since 1965 in an intensive search for petroleum deposits, announced that a recent discovery offshore at Mossel Bay, off the south coast of Cape Province, had yielded a daily output of 2,600 barrels of light crude and 1m. cu ft of natural gas. While the oil potential of this field is thought to be limited, the natural gas reserves are estimated to be substantial: in the region of 30,000m. cu m. In 1987 the government decided to proceed with the establishment of a plant to convert this natural gas into liquid fuel, at a cost of R5,500m. This plant was expected to supply 10% of South Africa's liquid fuel requirements when it came into operation in 1992. SOEKOR announced in 1988 that exploitable deposits of petroleum had been located near Hondeklip Bay, off the western Cape coast.

South Africa's long coastline has few natural harbours, but close to its shores are some of the richest fishing areas in the world. The total catch of the fishing industry (including landings at the Namibian port of Lüderitz and at Walvis Bay, an enclave in Namibia which was under South African jurisdiction until 1 March 1994, when sovereignty was transferred to Namibia) was 498,900 metric tons in 1991.

POPULATION

The chief characteristic of South Africa's population, and the one that dominates its society, is the great racial, linguistic and cultural heterogeneity of its people. The four broad groups making up the population are: (i) Africans, who are mainly members of the Bantu-speaking group of African tribes; (ii) whites, who are of European descent; (iii) Coloureds, who are of mixed racial origin; and (iv) Asians, mainly Indians living in the Natal province.

The total population of the Republic of South Africa at the March 1991 census was 26,288,390. At the March 1985 census the total population was 23,438,590, with the following ethnic composition: Africans 15,242,828 (65.0%); whites 4,576,690 (19.5%); Coloureds 2,825,094 (12.1%); Asians 793,978 (3.4%). These figures are not comparable, however, with earlier censuses, as they exclude the 'independent homelands' of Transkei, Bophuthatswana, Venda and Ciskei. Owing primarily to the exclusion of these territories, the official censuses are believed seriously to underenumerate the population of the republic. At the 1985 census for example, the extent of underenumeration was estimated as follows: Africans 20.4%; whites 7.6%; Asians 4.6% and Coloureds 1.0%. In order to overcome these shortcomings, the Urban Foundation has estimated the population of the whole region (including 7,664,200 for the 'independent homelands') as 40,308,000 in 1993, with an ethnic composition of: Africans (Blacks) 30,740,700 (76.2%); Whites 5,169,400 (12.8%); Coloureds 3,378,700 (8.4%); Asians 1,019,200 (2.5%). In the 82 years from 1911 (the year of the first full census, when the total enumerated was 6,044,000) to 1993, the population increased by 567%. There was a significant change in the racial composition of the population, with whites declining from 21.2% of the total to 12.8% in 1993 while Africans increased from 67.7% to 76.2%. Considerable differences in the annual rates of natural increase of the different groups largely explain this change in ethnic composition. According to the Urban Foundation, the population growth rates for 1985–90 were 2.93% for Africans, 1.87% for Coloureds, 1.71% for Asians and only 0.8% for whites. Fairly high levels of immigration have raised the rate of overall increase of whites quite substantially since 1945. In recent years, however, there was negative net immigration of 9,938 in 1986 and 1987 and positive net immigration of only 31,309 in the years 1988–92, averaging 6,262 per year. In the absence of compulsory registration of births and deaths for Africans, statistics about the natural rate of increase are less accurate for this group. It is difficult, therefore, to determine how much of the change in the numbers of this group is due to changes in the natural rate of increase, different census criteria or migration (in the 1960 census 583,000 Africans were recorded as having been born outside South Africa). According to the Development Bank of Southern Africa, the total population increased by an annual average of more than 3% during the 1970s and of 2.6% during the 1980s; in 1992–93 the population rose by 2.4%.

At the census of March 1991, South Africa (excluding the 'independent homelands') had a density of 23.4 persons per sq km. If the 'independent homelands' are included and allowance is made for underenumeration, the density of the whole region in 1993 was 33 per sq km. This relatively low figure is, however, misleading, owing to the uneven distribution of the population. Besides normal high densities in urban areas (60% of the population in 1992), rural density is also high in the 'homelands' (only 14% of the total area of South Africa, with a density of 101 per sq km, compared with only 21 per sq km for the non-'homeland' area in 1992. Historically, this is due to restrictions, relaxed in July 1986, on the mobility of Africans and on their right to own land in other parts of the country. Density is below average in non-'homeland' rural areas and particularly low in large arid areas in the west.

The occupational distribution of the economically active population in 1991, excluding the 'independent homelands' but with an adjustment made for underenumeration, was as follows: out of a total labour force of 11,624,368 (44.2% of the total population), 1,224,435 were engaged in agriculture, forestry and fishing (10.5% of the economically active population), 840,747 in mining and quarrying (7.2%), 1,417,127 in manufacturing (12%), 102,928 in electricity, gas and water (0.9%), 526,373 in construction (4.5%), 1,358,292 in commerce, restaurants and hotels (11.7%), 497,122 in transport and communications (4.3%), 503,970 in finance and business services (4.3%), 2,640,521 in other services (22.7%) and 2,512,852 unemployed or unclassified (21.6%). The most drastic structural change in the economy has been the sharp decline in the proportion of the population engaged in agriculture (28% at the 1970 census). This process is, however, exaggerated by the exclusion of the largely rural-based 'independent homelands' from the republic. Nevertheless, agriculture remains one of the largest sectors of employment in the economy because of the large number of African peasants in the 'homelands' within the republic, contrasting sharply with the relatively small contribution (4.5% in 1993) that it makes to the country's gross domestic product (GDP). This is the most important vestige of dualism in the economy, and it lingers because of the persistence of the migratory labour system and past restrictions on the permanent entry of Africans into the modern economy.

NATIONAL INCOME

In the 50 years from 1911/12 to 1961/62, net domestic product, at current prices, grew from R266m. to R5,036m. Allowing for price increases and population growth, real income per head more than doubled in this period, with an average growth of 1.8% per annum. Growth in the 1960s was exceptionally high, rivalling that of Japan. GDP, at current market prices, more than doubled between 1960–70, growing at an average rate of 8.9% per annum. In real terms, the rate of increase was 5.9%, and 2.9% per caput, per annum. This rate fell sharply in the 1970s, however, with real GDP growing at an average of only 3.9% (and about 1% per caput) per annum in the period 1970–80. This was stimulated by the exceptionally high increase of nearly 8% in real GDP in 1980, brought about largely by the high price of gold in that year. During the 1980s growth in real GDP declined further, averaging only 1.4% per year in 1980–90. Negative real growth rates of GDP were recorded during four of the 10 years (i.e. 1982, 1983, 1985 and 1990). With population increasing at an annual average rate of 2.6% in this decade, income per head was falling in this period. Because the national accounts include the 'independent homelands' and Namibia, the level of gross national product (GNP) per head is not easy to determine, owing to the exclusion of these territories from official population estimates (see above). On the basis of unofficial estimates of the total de facto population of the area, GNP per head in 1992, measured at average 1990–92 prices, was about US $2,670 which puts South Africa well ahead of other African countries (except Libya and Gabon) in income per head, and in the ranks of the upper-middle-income countries in the world. During 1985–92 it was estimated that GNP per head declined, in real terms, by an annual average of 1.3%, while the population increased by an annual average of 2.4%. In 1993, GDP and GNP at market prices were R383,770m. and R373,640m. respectively, reflecting an increase in real GNP of 1.3% from the previous year.

Despite an improvement in the racial distribution of personal income in recent years, income remains very unevenly distributed in South Africa. An estimate of the Gini Coefficient (index of income inequality) for South Africa in 1985 puts it at 0.64—one of the highest in the world. It was estimated in 1988 that the white population received about 54% of total personal income, while Africans received only 36%. The same pattern is reflected in the difference in earnings between whites and Africans, broadly reflecting the differential between skilled and unskilled wage rates. In 1988 the differential in earnings between whites and Africans in the manufacturing sector was 3.5:1, rising to 5:1 in mining and quarrying. The greatest differential is now to be found between those residing in metropolitan areas (white and black) and the rural 'homelands' (mainly black), estimated to be 18:1 in 1985.

The contribution to national income of the three main productive sectors—manufacturing, mining and agriculture—has changed markedly over the years. In 1911/12 mining contributed 27.1% of net domestic product, agriculture 17.4% and manufacturing only 6.7%. Manufacturing steadily increased its relative position, overtaking mining as the leading sector during the Second World War. By 1993 manufacturing contributed 23.5% of GDP at factor cost, mining and quarrying 9.1% and agriculture only 4.5%. The expansion of manufacturing from relative insignificance at the time of the formation of the Union of South Africa in 1910 is, without doubt, the most important structural change to have taken place in the economy.

INVESTMENT AND SAVING

Since the discovery of diamonds and gold in the 19th century, foreign investment has played a vital role in developing these industries and the economy in general. By 1936 it was estimated that R1,046m. had been invested in South Africa, representing 43% of total foreign investment in Africa. Another large wave of foreign investment, associated with goldfields in the Orange Free State (OFS), took place after the Second World War, but there was a subsequent slowing down, with an actual outflow in the years 1959–64. From 1965–76 (with the exception of 1973), foreign investment was again positive. Following the Soweto riots in mid-1976, however, there was a sharp decline in foreign investment, with negative outflows of both long-term and short-term capital from 1977–80. From 1981–83 foreign investment was again positive, but from 1984 it began to move sharply into a negative direction again. At first this was owing to speculative movements against the currency, brought on by a large balance-of-payments deficit and a weakening rand. However, with a deepening recession and the serious political disturbances that flared up in 1985, accompanied by the refusal of foreign banks to defer repayment of short-term loans, negative short-term capital movements reached record levels. Further deterioration was avoided only by the reintroduction, in September 1985, of the two-tier (financial–commercial) system of exchange rates for foreign investors. In the same month, the government also declared a moratorium on repayments of debt principal on foreign loans until the end of the year (later extended until the end of March 1986), although interest payments were to continue. In October negotiations began with creditor banks on rescheduling short-term debt, and in March 1986 the negotiations resulted in a one-year interim agreement whereby South Africa was to make a series of payments of 5% of debts due before the end of June 1987. In March 1987 it was announced that a further agreement had been reached with creditor banks, allowing a three-year rescheduling of $13,000m. of foreign debt.

At the end of 1992 the total foreign liabilities of South Africa stood at R113,347m., while foreign assets (including gold reserves) totalled R78,694m. In 1993 South Africa's foreign debt was estimated to be R56,720m. ($16,690m.). The ratio of foreign debt to GDP was only 14.8%, a sharp decline on the 36.3% ratio in 1986, reflecting the huge repayment of foreign debt in the intervening years.

With a level of foreign debt which is especially low for a country at South Africa's level of development, it can be expected that this situation will change in the post-election period as South Africa gains access to institutions such as the World Bank and is more favourably treated by the international financial community.

In 1993 gross domestic investment was R59,984m., equivalent to 15.6% of GDP at market prices. This capital formation was financed by gross domestic savings of R65,917m. (17.2% of GDP), allowing for net capital outflows to the rest of the world of R8,874m., and a decrease in holdings of gold and other reserves of R2,941m.

MANUFACTURING INDUSTRY

Unlike its counterparts in the rest of Africa, South Africa's manufacturing industry is the largest sector of the national economy, measured in terms of contribution to GDP. In 1993 it contributed R80,967m. to GDP at factor cost, employing 1,438,409 (more than 75% of the work-force being non-white) in 1992.

The mining industry, except for a limited number of industries servicing it, did not, at first, stimulate local manufacturing to any extent. As the mining industry favoured cheap imports, little protection was offered to local manufacturers. It was only in 1925 that an active policy of protecting local industry was first adopted. As a consequence, industry grew significantly in the latter half of the 1920s, particularly in the production of consumer goods. That period also saw the foundation of heavy industry under state auspices, with the establishment of the Iron and Steel Corporation of South Africa (ISCOR) in 1928. By 1939 net industrial output was double the 1929 level, and expansion continued in the post-war period. Industrial progress in the 1960s was particularly rapid. Its contribution to GDP, at factor cost, increased by an average of 10.2% per annum between 1961–70, the physical volume of production by 8.5% per annum and employment by 6.1% per annum, indicating increases in productivity over the same period. Real growth was slower in the 1970s, with the physical volume of production increasing by an average of only 2.9% per annum, while employment grew by 2.6% annually. During 1980–92 industrial GDP declined by an annual average of 1.7%.

Industry is heavily concentrated in four industrial areas—southern Transvaal, western Cape, Durban-Pinetown and Port Elizabeth-Uitenhage—accounting for more than 75% of net industrial output and employment. More than 50% of the country's industry is now located in the southern Transvaal alone (the area comprising Pretoria, Johannesburg, Reef towns and Vereeniging) and the tendency has been for this concentration to increase at the expense of the ports and rural areas. Largely to stem the flow of Africans to 'white' industrial areas, the state has, since 1960, attempted to decentralize industrial location to proclaimed border areas near to 'Homelands'. Financial assistance (in the form of tax concessions, loans, reduced railway rates, exemption from wage regulation, etc.) was granted to industrialists in these areas. Between 1960–80, tax and interest concessions (including rental concessions) amounting to R222.8m. were given and 181,198 jobs (142,061 for Africans) were created in border areas. In 1982, a revised Regional Industrial Development Policy (RIDP) was introduced which provided substantial relocation incentives to industrialists, including wage subsidies, training grants, transport rebates, housing subsidies and soft loans. Between 1982–90, 450,000 jobs were created in the target areas at an average cost (in 1990 prices) of R18,000 per job—for a huge total cost of R8,100m. It was felt, however, that the policy had failed in its primary purpose of job creation as most of the jobs would have existed somewhere else in the absence of relocation incentives, at no cost to the taxpayer. Uneconomic location decisions were encouraged by this policy, as is confirmed by a recent study which concluded that between 34%–42% of firms would be unprofitable if incentives were withdrawn.

In 1991, a new RIDP was adopted which shifted the emphasis away from decentralized industrial development in rural areas to broader regional development. Incentives would be more cost-effective in being performance-linked. They would encourage direct fixed investment in target regions, with special provisions offered to foreign investors.

Metal Products and Engineering

This is the largest sector of industry (including basic metals, metal products, machinery and transport equipment), employing 465,600 workers in 1988. The steel industry is the most important branch of this sector, with a total crude steel output of 9m. tons in 1992. The industry is dominated by ISCOR, the transfer of which from state to private-sector ownership was completed in November 1989. ISCOR operates 10 ore mines and four steel mills. There are six other steel-producing companies in the private sector. Because of favourable costs of location, raw materials and labour, and an efficient scale of production, South African steel is among the cheapest in the world. Not only does it no longer need the protection which it received before the Second World War, but it is now well placed as an exporter. In 1981 ISCOR's exports alone were 2.7m. tons, worth R216m., going to more than 50 countries.

The motor industry is another important branch of the engineering sector. In 1992 the transport equipment industry employed 91,000 workers and produced 206,600 passenger cars and 93,600 commercial vehicles. The vast majority of new cars contain at least 66% local content by weight, thereby qualifying for special tariff rates as 'locally manufactured' models. In common with this industry in other developing countries, vehicle manufacturing faces the problem of rising costs with increasing local content, because of the lack of those economies of scale which are enjoyed in the major producing countries.

Food, Beverages and Tobacco

Industries processing local farm produce were among the first to develop in South Africa. While this sector has expanded and contributes importantly to exports, its relative position declined from 32% of the net value of manufacturing output in 1925 to 17% in 1963. In 1986 the gross value of output of these industries was R18,193m. (21% of the total for all manufacturing industry), and in 1992 they employed 197,300 workers (13.7% of the manufacturing industry labour force).

Clothing and Textiles

The clothing industry, which was well established before the Second World War, now supplies 90% of local demand, and employed 113,500 workers in 1992. The textile industry is essentially a post-war development; it now meets 60% of the country's textile needs, and employed 82,600 workers in 1992.

Chemicals

This industry had an early beginning, with the manufacture of explosives for the gold mines. The Modderfontein factory, near Johannesburg, is now probably the world's largest privately owned explosives factory. Production of fertilizers is also a significant branch of this industry. However, the most important development in recent years was the establishment by the state-owned South African Coal, Oil and Gas Corporation (SASOL) of its first oil-from-coal plant (SASOL 1), which began production in the northern OFS in 1955. Based on cheap, low-grade coal with a high ash-content, this establishment was, until the commissioning of SASOL 2 and 3, the largest plant of its kind in the world. Besides producing a small but significant percentage of South Africa's petrol requirements, the development of synthetic fuel production led to the establishment of a huge petrochemical complex which manufactures about 110 products, some of which, like coal-tar products, are only by-products of a coal-using process. Because of the absence of local supplies of natural mineral oil, a continued threat of a petroleum embargo and the huge rise in world petroleum prices in 1973, it was decided in 1974 to build SASOL 2 with 10 times the capacity of SASOL 1. Production at SASOL 2, which had a capital cost of R2,400m., reached full capacity in 1982. Following the change of government in Iran in 1979 and the consequent loss by South Africa of its main source of supply of crude petroleum, it was decided to build SASOL 3, almost an exact copy of SASOL 2, at a capital cost of R3,200m. This plant began operation in 1983, and reached full production in 1985. The three plants in full production provide about 40% of South Africa's fuel requirements, and a fourth plant is planned. Part of the huge capital cost of these plants is being provided by private sector investment. In 1992 the chemical industry employed 120,800 workers.

AGRICULTURE

Reference has already been made to the declining role of agriculture as a source of income in the South African economy. The vagaries of climate and unstable world prices are largely responsible for this. The effect of recurrent drought can be dramatically seen in the fluctuations in production of maize—the staple food of the African population and the most important single item in South African farming. From a record output of 13.6m. tons in the 1981/82 season, production fell to only 3.4m. tons in the 1983/84 drought resulting in maize imports of 2.4m. tons in that year. Again, from a peak of 11.7m. tons in 1989/90 output fell to 2.9m. tons in the disastrous drought of 1992/93 with imports expected to be 4.5m. tons at a cost exceeding R2,000m. Wool, although prone to wide fluctuations in price, is one of South Africa's most important exports, earning R590.7m. in 1986. The low overall productivity of farming, relative to other sectors, is also reflected in the fact that, although employing about 12.9% of the economically active population in 1991, it contributed only 4% of GDP in 1992. This is mainly because large numbers of inefficient African subsistence farmers in the 'homelands' obtain very low crop yields. However, even white farmers, who are relatively efficient, obtain comparatively low yields by international standards. In maize farming, for example, yields per hectare are only one-quarter of those in the USA.

Despite these problems, agricultural products continue to feature prominently in South African exports. Depending on the volume of output, a large percentage of the local production of wool, maize, sugar, groundnuts, tobacco, citrus and deciduous fruits is normally exported. In processed as well as unprocessed form, agricultural products normally account for about one-third of total export earnings (excluding gold), with the UK as the main market.

MINING

Despite having given way to manufacturing as the leading sector, mining is still of great importance in the economy, as it has been for the last century. In 1993 total sales of minerals amounted to R46,631m., of which the bulk was exported (77.6% in 1990). Mining employed a total work-force of 607,950 in 1992.

Gold mining dominates the mining sector, and in 1992 it employed 414,000 workers. Since the Second World War, new gold mines in the OFS, Far West Rand, Klerksdorp and Evander areas have not only replaced output from the worked-out mines on the old Rand but have greatly increased total production. In the absence of new discoveries, however, gold output will continue the decline that began in the early 1970s after a record 1,000.4 tons in 1970. This has been largely due to the policy of the industry of lowering the grade of ore mined as the price rises. Unless there is a compensating increase in tonnage milled when the average grade of ore mined is lowered, output falls. This is what happened in the 1970s and 1980s when firstly the US dollar price of gold rose (exceeding $800 per oz in 1980) and then with the devaluation of the rand during the late 1980s, the rand price of gold increased, as did the rand value of output. From 1989, however, the industry was squeezed by a fall in both the dollar and rand price of gold and continued increases in costs, forcing several marginal mines to close where it was not possible to raise the grade of ore mined sufficiently to offset the fall in revenue per ton milled. In 1992 the gold output of 611 tons had fallen to R18,195m. in value, contributing only 26.4% to export earnings compared with some 40% in the early 1980s. Having remained well below $350 per ounce throughout 1992, the price of gold began to rise in 1993, briefly exceeding $400 per ounce in mid-1993. Gold output of 619 tons rose sharply in value to R22,229m. in 1993.

The output of other minerals has rapidly gained in importance since the Second World War. Gold accounted for about 80% of South Africa's mineral production in 1946 but the proportion had fallen to only 50% by 1993. There has been a great expansion in the output of uranium, platinum, nickel, copper, coal, antimony, diamonds, vanadium, asbestos, iron ore, fluorspar, chromium, manganese and limestone, to name only the most important. These minerals are prominent in South Africa's exports, earning R10,177m. in 1990. Mineral exports, including gold, were valued at R28,998m. in 1990, equivalent to 48% of total exports (gold was equivalent to 65% of mineral exports).

Diamonds were traditionally the country's second most important export commodity (after gold), but in recent years they have also been overtaken by coal. South African diamond production had been conducted for some time at five mine locations. A sixth mine, Venetia, discovered in 1980 and opened in 1992, is expected by the mid-1990s to become South Africa's largest-producing diamond mine. Output in 1993 was 10.3m. carats, a significant increase on the 8.2m. carats mined in 1991.

The coal mining industry, which stagnated for many years because of low prices and slow growth, acquired renewed vigour after the petroleum crisis in 1973. Exports have grown rapidly in recent years, helped by the opening of the new rail link and coal terminal at Richards Bay in northern Natal, which, by 1987, with the completion of Phase III of the export programme, had increased its capacity to 44m. tons per annum. However, the spread of international sanctions and a fall in international prices had a particularly adverse effect on this industry. Exports fell from 44.9m. tons, earning R3,127m., to 42.6m. tons, valued at R2,294m., in 1987. The decline in exports led to some 3,000 workers, mostly blacks, being laid off. By 1991, with the recovery of international prices for coal and the removal of sanctions by most of the countries which have traditionally been South Africa's major export markets for coal, exports increased significantly, with shipments of 50.1m. tons earning R4,300m. in foreign exchange. In 1993 total production of coal was 183m. tons, valued at R9,673m. The industry employed 76,200 workers in 1992.

South Africa is the continent's leading producer of iron ore, and exports, to Japan in particular, have also become important since the late 1980s, despite declining world demand for steel. A railway line from the high-grade deposits of the Sishen area, in the northern Cape, carries iron ore to Saldanha Bay. As a result of falling demand, South Africa's exports of iron ore declined from a peak of 14.7m. tons in 1980 to 8.8m. tons in 1986. Despite persistently depressed market conditions, export volume recovered to 15.5m. tons in 1990. In 1991, when shipments declined to 14.9m. tons, this export earned R772.1m.

TRANSPORT AND COMMUNICATIONS

With no navigable rivers, South Africa's transport system is entirely dependent on its rail and road network, with air transport playing a small but increasing role. The state-owned railways covered 23,506 route-km in 1988 (about one-third of all the railway track length in sub-Saharan Africa). In the year ending 31 March 1989, total freight traffic was 174.2m. metric tons, and 579.5m. passenger journeys were made. South African harbours handled 111.6m. tons of cargo in 1990, including transshipments of cargo. Airways carried 9,201m. passenger/km in 1989. Transnet Ltd, which controls the railways, harbours, airways and the country's system of oil pipelines, is the largest commercial undertaking in South Africa, employing 168,419 people in 1990.

An extensive road network serves the country with 55,383 km of surfaced and 130,368 km of unsurfaced roads in 1990 (excluding the 'independent homelands'). Road transport has grown rapidly since the Second World War. In 1992 there were 3,488,570 passenger cars in use, 209,891 mini-buses, 25,994 buses and coaches, 1,267,766 commercial vehicles and 281,272 motor cycles. Private long-distance road haulage is restricted, however, by government legislation, designed to protect the railways.

Telecommunications are fairly extensively developed, with 4.7m. telephones in use at the end of 1989 (about one-half of the total in Africa), of which about 96% are automatic.

POWER AND WATER

Electricity

In 1993 South Africa consumed 174,581m. kWh of electricity, with a per caput consumption equal to that of Western Europe. The bulk of this supply (94% in 1993) was generated by the state-controlled Electricity Supply Commission (ESCOM) via a national grid system which came into operation in 1973. Owing mainly to the low cost of coal, which is the main source of fuel for power generation, (89% of ESKOM's) South Africa's electricity is among the cheapest in the world ($0.079 per kWh in 1990). Nearly one-half of the country's coal production goes to electricity production. A small amount of peak-load power is now being provided by the hydroelectric stations of the Orange River Project, and some additional supplies have been brought from the Cabora Bassa dam in Mozambique, although these have been vulnerable to interruption by Mozambican guerrilla insurgents (see below). The first nuclear power station to be constructed in South Africa, Koeberg, was commissioned by ESCOM in 1976. It was built at Duynefontein, between Cape Town and Saldanha Bay, by a French consortium. The plant was damaged in a sabotage attack in December 1982, but began operating in March 1984. The first of its two 920-MW units was connected to the national grid in April, and reached full generating capacity in June. The second unit came into operation by mid-1985. With both units in full operation, the plant has a generating capacity of 1,842 MW, representing about 10% of South Africa's total capacity. In February 1985, however, the Koeberg plant was temporarily closed, following the discovery of defects. The construction, at a cost of R17,500m., of five coal-fired power stations, each designed to generate 3,600 MW, was being reviewed in 1986. In June 1988 South Africa finalized an agreement with Mozambique and Portugal to restore electricity supplies from the Cabora Bassa dam, in Mozambique (the supplies had been interrupted since 1983 by the destruction of power lines in Mozambique linking the dam to the South African grid). Reconstruction work on the power lines was scheduled to begin in August 1993, with the aim of achieving a full resumption of electricity supply to South Africa by 1996.

Water

Water supply is increasingly becoming a problem for the future location of industry. The Vaal river, which is the main source of water supply for the large concentration of manufacturing industry and mining in the southern Transvaal and the northern OFS, is nearing the limit of its capacity. Even with planned increases in supply to the Vaal from the Tugela basin in Natal, it is unlikely that this river will meet future requirements by the end of the century. It is likely, therefore, that Natal with its much greater water supply will have a higher rate of growth of industry than the Transvaal in the future. In March 1988 South Africa and Lesotho signed the final protocols for the Highlands Water Project (see p. 518). Its completion, which is scheduled for the year 2017, would provide South Africa with 2,200m. cu m of water annually.

FOREIGN TRADE

South Africa is highly dependent on international trade. In 1993 the value of merchandise imports (including arms and petroleum) was R59,017m., equal to 15% of GNP at market prices. In spite of rapid industrialization, with the encouragement of import-replacement industries by protective tariffs and comprehensive direct import control machinery in operation since 1948, imports as a rule are not a much smaller proportion of national income than their average of 24% in the 1930s; in recent years, however, they have been significantly below average and below the level of exports, owing to the need to finance capital repayments overseas. The composition of imports, however, has changed considerably over the years. Whereas in 1910 food, drink, clothing and textiles constituted 46% of total imports, these consumer goods are only a small fraction today, with intermediate and capital goods making up the bulk of imports. In 1968, 92% of imports were manufactured, whereas only 38% of exports were in this category, and even here a large proportion of exports classified as manufactured were lightly processed agricultural and mineral products. The country remains heavily dependent, therefore, on agriculture and mining (gold in particular) to pay for imports.

In 1993 the total value of merchandise exports was R79,214m., equal to 21.2% of GNP at market prices. This includes gold exports of R22,329m. The UK has traditionally been South Africa's main trading partner, but in 1993 the UK's share as a supplier of South Africa's imports (11.4%) was surpassed by Germany (15.7%), the USA (13.2%) and Japan (12.6%). As a market for South African exports, the UK's share (6%) was surpassed by Switzerland (11%) and the USA (6.9%) in 1993. Other major markets in that year were Japan (5.5%) and Germany (3.9%). In 1992, exports to all African countries were nearly R6,000m. (8.9%), while imports were only R1,306m. (2.5%). The chief African markets for exports were Zimbabwe (2.3%), Zambia (1.6%) and Mozambique (1.0%). The only substantial supplier of imports to South Africa is Zimbabwe (1.5%).

With import control machinery set up in the late 1940s and strict exchange control regulations imposed in 1961 (after the massive outflow of foreign capital following the political disturbances of 1960), South Africa has generally been able to protect itself against disturbances to the balance of payments on both current and capital accounts. In favourable times these regulations have been relaxed, but never abolished. They were again stringently applied after the political disturbances which commenced in the second half of 1984, but, despite massive outflows of foreign capital since 1985 (net movement of long- and short-term capital: 1985 -R9,231m.; 1986 -R6,097m.; 1987 -R3,069m.; 1988 -R6,663m.; 1989 -R5,555m.; 1990 -R2,410m.; 1991 -R4,775m.; 1992 -R6,212m.; 1993 -R16,273m.), the balance-of-payments position and reserves have remained fairly steady for some years, although South Africa was forced to draw heavily upon its reserves of gold and foreign exchange during 1988 in order to fulfil its foreign debt commitments for that year. This has only been achieved by large surpluses on the balance of trade, offsetting the outflows of capital. With the widespread abandonment of international sanctions on trade and investment from 1991, a more favourable climate for South Africa's balance of payments may be expected in the future. However, at the time of the general election in 1994 the negative flow of foreign capital had not yet been staunched. South Africa's external balance remains highly vulnerable to adverse external factors such as falls in the price of gold or other commodities and further disinvestment of foreign capital. In addition, because of South Africa's high marginal propensity to import, imports tend to increase rapidly as soon as growth approaches 3%.

FINANCE

The South African currency is the rand, issued by the South African Reserve Bank. Since December 1971 there have been several changes in the external value of the rand in both directions. It was briefly linked to the floating pound in 1972 but from October 1972 only the rand-US dollar rate was fixed. In September 1975 the rand was devalued from R1 = US $1.40 to R1 = US $1.15. In January 1979 the 'commercial' rand's link with the dollar was freed and allowed to float, and non-residents were allowed to buy 'security' rand at a discount for direct investment purposes. In February 1983 the 'security' rand was abolished and merged with the commercial rand for non-residents. Owing to the outbreak of political disturbances in the second half of 1984, the rand depreciated sharply against the US dollar and all other major currencies, falling from R1 = US $0.80 in early 1984 to R1 = US $0.42 in January 1985. In spite of measures taken by the Reserve Bank to curtail speculation against the rand, the escalation of violence generated a lack of confidence in the country, politically, and a further flight of capital led to the value of the rand falling to R1 = US $0.35 by August 1985. Coupled with the unwillingness of foreign banks to reschedule short-term loans, a moratorium on debt repayments was imposed in September 1985, together with the reintroduction of the two-tier system of exchange control on foreign investors. In March 1987, however, an agreement was reached with foreign creditor banks allowing a three year rescheduling of $13,000m. of outstanding debt. In August 1994 the commercial rand stood at R1 = US $0.28 and R1 = £0.18, while the discount on the financial rand was 20.59%, reflecting the continued outflow of foreign capital.

Although South Africa was a member of the Sterling Area until its disbandment, it had not been the practice of the commercial banks since 1942, and more stringently since 1961, to keep reserves in London. Banking follows the British tradition, with a few large branch banks dominating the scene. In addition to commercial banks, a whole range of financial institutions has developed since the Second World War, including merchant banks, discount houses and a fairly well developed short-term money market. These institutions have suffered from the fragility of business confidence, engendered by the unrest.

Public finance is conducted along orthodox lines, although there has been a steady trend for public spending to grow as a proportion of GDP in spite of repeated attempts to prevent further increases in real terms. In 1991/92, expenditure was 29.7% of GDP compared with 25.5% in 1977/78. The envisaged expenditure of R86,400m. in 1991/92 exceeded expected revenue of R72,100m. by $14,300m., or 4.8% of GDP. A consequence of government expenditure persistently exceeding revenue in recent years has been a rise in the ratio of public debt to GDP from a post-war low of 27% in 1983 to in excess of 40% in 1992, with the budget deficit before borrowing at a record high, equivalent to more than 8% of GDP. An additional effect has been an increase in the level of interest payments on the public debt (about 5.5% of GDP in 1992, compared with only 2.5% in 1981). Recent economies in outlays on defence expenditure have been more than offset by large increases in social expenditure on housing, health and education for the black population, which, together with the weak performance of the economy, has led to stagnating revenues and spiralling deficits. The first post-election budget presented in June 1994 essentially followed the conservative tradition of previous budgets. The planned 6.5% increase in expenditure to R135,100m. is below the current rate of inflation so that the fiscal deficit is forecast to shrink substantially to some 6.3% of GDP. A special budget of R2,500m. for post-apartheid reconstruction is to be financed by budgetary trimming elsewhere, with small savings being made in such areas as forestry, transport and foreign affairs. Initially the cost of defence, previously a source of economising, will rise due to the absorption of ex-guerillas into a single force. The total cost of transition - the dismantling of the old state and the creation of a new one - is estimated to be some R4,000m. in 1994 alone (the election itself cost nearly R1,000m.). The short-term costs are to be met by a non-recurring levy of 5% on individuals and companies with an annual taxable income of over R50,000. At the same time, the company tax rate has been reduced from 40% to 35%, although the dividends tax has risen from 15% to 25% to partly make up the difference.

The combined fixed investment of public authorities and public corporations was 29% of total gross fixed investment in 1993. Although still officially committed to a basically private enterprise economic system, the state has, over the years, become increasingly involved, through the Industrial Development Corporation, in a whole new range of commercial activities, in addition to traditional infrastructure and public utility enterprises. The government has, however, recently committed itself to a programme of privatization of public enterprises in the future.

ECONOMIC OUTLOOK

South Africa undoubtedly achieved remarkable economic development in the 1960s, with one of the highest growth rates in the world during that decade. The fruits of that development, however, were very unevenly distributed. After years of 'separate development', the 'Bantustans' remained as wretched and over-populated as ever. Even in the modern sector, despite a considerable increase in African employment, the real income of Africans increased very slowly, with a large percentage being paid wages below the Poverty Datum Line.

Growth in the 1970s was much slower, with the economy reaching its full potential only in part of 1974 and again in 1979/80, owing to a boom in world commodity prices and a big increase in the price of gold. In the recession of 1975–77 real GNP remained almost stationary. The main reason, of course, for this relatively poor performance has been the instability of the world economy in this period, but mention must also be made of the aggravating effect of the disturbances following the Soweto riots in June 1976 and the unsettled situation in countries surrounding South Africa. This has had a particularly discouraging effect on foreign investment in South Africa, which has played a major role in the past in maintaining a high rate of growth. In 1979, however, the economy grew significantly, at a real rate of 4.2%, and 1980 was something of an *annus mirabilis*, with a real growth rate of 8%, as the high price of gold and other export commodities compensated for the lack of foreign capital. Growth in the 1980s was even slower than in the 1970s, averaging only 1.4% per annum in real terms over the decade and, therefore, resulting in a fall in real income per head compared with a small average increase of 1% per annum per caput in the 1970s. Factors that contributed to this poor performance included unfavourable commodity prices in international markets—in particular a weakening of the price of gold; drought in 1983 and 1984; from the mid-1980s, the damaging effect of political instability in causing a net outflow of foreign investment and low overall investment in the economy; also the effect of sanctions on foreign trade in some markets such as coal exports.

Between the first quarter of 1989 and the first quarter of 1993, real GDP fell by 4%, creating South Africa's longest recession of this century. International recession, as well as severe drought and the volatility of the political climate have all played their part. The most serious manifestation of the recession is the decline in investment, which was equivalent to only 15% of GDP in 1992 and has been well below earlier levels (24% on average during 1982–85) since the late 1980s. The recent trend in investment undermines the economy's future ability to generate growth and absorb work-seekers.

As it is, over 100,000 jobs have been lost in mining and over 60,000 in manufacturing since early 1990. The Reserve Bank has estimated that from the first quarter of 1989 (the beginning of the recession) to the third quarter of 1993, employment in the formal non-agricultural sectors fell by some 410,000. 8% of workers were made redundant during this period. Unemployment figures continued to rise even with recovery in the second half of 1993. The employment situation has, however, been weak for much longer. Whereas in the period 1963–70 numbers employed in the non-agricultural sectors of the economy increased at an average annual rate of 4.2%, well in excess of the rate of population increase, this fell to 2.7% in the period 1970–78, barely equal to the increase in population. During the period 1978–87, black employment grew by only 1.2% per annum, well below the increase in population and reflecting the low overall growth in the economy in that period. No accurate figures are available for black unemployment, as official unemployment statistics cover only a limited number of registered black unemployed. This deficiency has been partially remedied by the Current Population Survey (CPS) for Africans, Coloureds and Asians, based on regular sample surveys. Following criticism that the CPS grossly underestimated the rate of black unemployment, a new sampling procedure was adopted in July 1986, based on the 1985 census. This resulted in the estimate of black unemployment rising to 1,181,000 or 19.9% of the labour force in that month, compared with only 519,000 or 8.1% of the labour force in June 1986. Following estimates of an unaccountable decrease in black unemployment in 1990, when all the evidence pointed to an increase, the CPS was discontinued for blacks. A serious weakness of the CPS is that it excludes the four former 'independent homelands', where a large proportion of the republic's black labour force resides. Estimates of unemployment are, therefore, subject to a wide margin of error, and range from 18% of the economically active population (about 2m. in 1990) to 29% of the economically active population (about 3.2m.) as calculated by the Bureau for Economic Research (BER) at Stellenbosch University. What is certain is that only one in 10 new entrants to the labour force currently finds work in the formal sector. What is uncertain is how many are productively absorbed in the 'informal' sector. A major structural change in the South African economy in recent years, since the abolition of all forms of influx control, has been a huge migration to the large towns. Disguised unemployment in the rural areas is increasingly shifting to overt unemployment in the urban areas. But there are also positive signs of a big increase in the size of the 'informal' sector, assisted by the removal of most of the petty restrictions that have hampered this sector in the past.

A central aim of the Reconstruction and Development Policy adopted by the new government is to reduce unemployment and its attendant problems of poverty and inequality. An accelerated rate of economic growth is essential to achieving this aim. A key to this process is to raise the confidence of both domestic and foreign investors and to take full advantage of improved export opportunities in the wake of the removal of sanctions. Important structural changes will need to be implemented to increase South African competitivity in world markets and restore the country's position as a magnet for foreign investments. This competitiveness must be measured against that of the successful developing countries in South-East Asia, the Pacific Rim and Latin America rather than that of the advanced countries of Europe, North America and Japan. In the vital area of wage costs and productivity, South Africa compares unfavourably with economies such as those of Mexico, Brazil, Malaysia, Hong Kong and Thailand. Long-term measures need to be taken to improve productivity through education and training. Trade unions must also be persuaded to temper demands for wage increases and to link them to increases in productivity. In spite of the change in corporate tax rates in the post-election budget (see above), further reform of South Africa's tax structure will be necessary. The phasing out of exchange controls also needs to be addressed. Policies to deal with restrictive practices in the corporate sector and a reduction in tariff protection are also needed to increase competitiveness and growth. The challenge facing the new government will initially be to find a strategy that makes some progress in meeting the heightened expectations of most South Africans while ensuring the country's prospects for long-term growth and stability.

Statistical Survey

Source (unless otherwise indicated): Central Statistical Service, Steyn's Arcade, 274 Schoeman St, Private Bag X44, Pretoria 0001; tel. (12) 3108911; telex 320450; fax (12) 3108500.

Area and Population

AREA, POPULATION AND DENSITY*

Area (sq km)	1,221,037†
Population (census results)‡	
6 May 1970	21,794,328
6 May 1980§	24,885,960
5 March 1985‖	23,385,645
7 March 1991‖	
Males	12,834,016
Females	13,454,374
Total	26,288,390
Density (per sq km) at March 1991‖	23.4‡

* Excluding data for Walvis Bay (area 1,124 sq km or 434 sq miles, population 23,641 in 1970), sovereignty over which was transferred from South Africa to Namibia on 1 March 1994.

† 471,445 sq miles. Excluding the former 'homelands' of Transkei, Bophuthatswana, Venda and Ciskei, the area is 1,125,500 sq km (434,558 sq miles).

‡ Excluding adjustment for underenumeration. At the 1985 census the extent of underenumeration was estimated to have been: Africans 20.4%; Asians 6.5%; Coloureds 3.5%; Europeans 5.5%. The adjusted total for 1991 is 30,986,920 (males 15,479,528; females 15,507,392), and the corresponding density 27.5 per sq km.

§ Excluding Transkei (population 2,186,000 at mid-1976), Bophuthatswana (population 1,178,000 at mid-1977) and Venda (population 309,000 at mid-1979). With these exceptions, the population at the 1970 census was 18,715,000.

‖ Excluding Transkei, Bophuthatswana, Venda and Ciskei (population estimated at 5,954,425 at mid-1985).

Total population (official estimate at 27 April 1994): 40,284,634.

ETHNIC GROUPS (estimates, 27 April 1994)*

Africans (Blacks)	30,645,157
Europeans (Whites)	5,171,419
Coloureds	3,435,114
Asians	1,032,943
Total	40,284,634

* Figures have been estimated independently, so the total is not the sum of the components.

POPULATION BY PROVINCE (estimates, 27 April 1994)

Western Cape	3,633,077
Eastern Cape	6,436,790
Northern Cape	737,306
Kwazulu/Natal	8,505,338
Orange Free State	2,726,840
North-West	3,252,991
Northern Transvaal	5,201,630
Eastern Transvaal	2,921,559
Pretoria-Witwatersrand-Vereeniging	6,869,103
Total	40,284,634

PRINCIPAL TOWNS (population at 1991 census)

	City Proper	Metropolitan Area
Cape Town*	854,616	2,350,157
Durban	715,669	1,137,378
Johannesburg	712,507	1,916,061
Pretoria*	525,583	1,080,187
Port Elizabeth	303,353	853,205
Umlazi	299,275	n.a.
Roodepoort	162,632	870,066
Pietermaritzburg	156,473	228,549
Germiston	134,005	n.a.
Bloemfontein*	126,867	300,150
Boksburg	119,890	n.a.
Benoni	113,501	n.a.
East London	102,325	270,127
Kimberley	80,082	167,060
Springs	72,647	700,906
Vereeniging	71,255	773,594

* Pretoria is the administrative capital, Cape Town the legislative capital and Bloemfontein the judicial capital.

BIRTHS AND DEATHS (official estimates, annual averages)

	1975–80	1980–85	1985–90
Birth rate (per 1,000)	34.3	33.1	32.1
Death rate (per 1,000)	12.1	11.0	9.9

1992/93 (sample survey, year to October): Birth rate 27.1 per 1,000; Death rate 9.0 per 1,000.

Expectation of life (UN estimates, years at birth, 1985–90): 60.4 (males 57.5; females 63.5) (Source: UN, *World Population Prospects: The 1992 Revision*).

IMMIGRATION AND EMIGRATION

	1991	1992	1993
Immigrants			
Africa	2,065	1,266	1,701
Europe	5,767	3,869	4,541
Asia	3,650	3,005	3,165
Americas	702	423	321
Oceania	195	118	93
Total (incl. unspecified)	12,379	8,686	9,824
Emigrants			
Africa	212	139	227
Europe	2,408	2,633	1,000
Asia	62	89	120
Americas	593	606	292
Oceania	978	821	373
Total (incl. unspecified)	4,256	4,289	2,013

ECONOMICALLY ACTIVE POPULATION
(persons aged 16 years and over, 1991 census)*

	Males	Females	Total
Agriculture, hunting, forestry and fishing	892,646	331,789	1,224,435
Mining and quarrying	813,988	26,759	840,747
Manufacturing	1,008,273	408,854	1,417,127
Electricity, gas and water	92,189	10,740	102,928
Construction	492,992	33,381	526,373
Trade, restaurants and hotels	805,613	552,680	1,358,292
Transport, storage and communications	427,931	69,191	497,122
Financing, insurance, real estate and business services	262,564	241,406	503,970
Community, social and personal services	993,602	1,646,920	2,640,521
Activities not adequately defined	265,842	128,361	394,203
Total employed	6,055,640	3,450,081	9,505,718
Unemployed	987,415	1,131,234	2,118,649
Total labour force	7,043,053	4,581,314	11,624,368

* Excluding Transkei, Bophuthatswana, Venda and Ciskei. The data include an adjustment for underenumeration. Figures have been assessed independently, so that totals are not always the sum of the component parts.

Source: ILO, *Year Book of Labour Statistics.*

October 1993 (household survey, persons aged 15 years and over, excluding Transkei, Bophuthatwana, Venda and Ciskei): Total labour force 12,353,324 (males 6,989,157; females 5,364,167), of whom 8,767,587 (males 5,305,942; females 3,461,645) were employed and 3,585,737 (males 1,683,215; females 1,902,522) were unemployed.

Agriculture

PRINCIPAL CROPS ('000 metric tons)

	1990	1991	1992
Maize	8,709	8,342	3,125*
Sorghum*	275	240	98
Wheat	1,702	2,132	1,269*
Barley	262	183*	100*
Oats	39	31	40†
Dry beans	129	113	27*
Cottonseed	91	56	39*
Cotton (lint)	52	31	22*
Sugar cane	18,026	19,692	18,500†
Tobacco (leaves)	32	34	37*
Potatoes	1,269	1,383	1,200†
Sweet potatoes	54	56	50†
Soybeans	119	124	68*
Groundnuts (in shell)	111	110	116*
Sunflower seed	561	589	174*
Cabbages	220	230†	200†
Tomatoes	455	500†	480†
Pumpkins, squash and gourds	167	163	140†
Onions (dry)	260	250†	210†
Carrots	87	90†	85†
Watermelons†	40	40	40
Apples*	530	544	582
Grapefruit and pomelo	124	132*	120*
Grapes	1,559	1,564	1,450†
Lemons and limes	55	62*	63*
Oranges	712	678*	690*
Peaches and nectarines*	146	153	156
Pears*	203	206	215
Bananas†	182	182	180
Apricots*	51	48	50
Pineapples	197*	210*	210†

* Unofficial figure(s). † FAO estimate(s).

Source: FAO, *Production Yearbook.*

LIVESTOCK ('000 head, year ending September)

	1990	1991	1992
Cattle*	13,398	13,512	13,585
Pigs†	1,480	1,490	1,490
Sheep*	32,665	32,580	32,110
Goats†	5,880	5,900	5,900
Horses†	230	230	230
Asses†	210	210	210
Mules†	14	14	14

* Unofficial figures. † FAO estimates.

Chickens (FAO estimates, million): 39 in 1990; 40 in 1991; 40 in 1992.

Source: FAO, *Production Yearbook.*

LIVESTOCK PRODUCTS ('000 metric tons)

	1990	1991	1992
Beef and veal*	661	678	716
Mutton and lamb†	133	133	130
Goats' meat†	34	35	35
Pig meat†	125	126	126
Poultry meat†	384	394	374
Edible offals†	176	184	189
Cows' milk	2,251	2,299	3,193*
Butter	16.7	21.4	16.0*
Cheese	42.5	42.3	45.0*
Condensed and evaporated milk	22.7	18.7	20.3†
Dried milk	10.5	12.4	8.8†
Hen eggs*	212.6	218.4	221.2
Wool:			
greasy	96.5	102.6	97.0
clean*	49.5	51.0	48.5
Cattle hides (fresh)†	88.0	92.5	96.5
Sheep skins (fresh)†	31.0	31.0	31.0

* Unofficial figure(s). † FAO estimate(s).

Source: FAO, *Production Yearbook* and *Quarterly Bulletin of Statistics.*

Forestry

(including Namibia)

ROUNDWOOD REMOVALS ('000 cubic metres, excluding bark)

	1982	1983	1984
Sawlogs, veneer logs and logs for sleepers	4,322	3,968	4,129
Pulpwood	5,561	6,337	4,841
Other industrial wood	2,490	3,219	2,974
Fuel wood*	7,102	7,060	7,078
Total	19,475	20,584	19,022

1985–92: Annual output as in 1984 (FAO estimates), except for sawlogs, veneer logs and logs for sleepers: 3,750† in 1986; 4,122† in 1987; 4,468† in 1988; 4,468* in 1989; 5,193† in 1990; 4,786† in 1991; 4,786* in 1992.

* FAO estimate(s). † Unofficial figure.

Source: FAO, *Yearbook of Forest Products.*

SAWNWOOD PRODUCTION
('000 cubic metres, incl. railway sleepers)

	1989*	1990†	1991†
Coniferous (soft wood)	1,623	1,734	1,619
Broadleaved (hard wood)	251	202	173
Total	1,873	1,936	1,792

* FAO estimates. † Unofficial figures.

1992: Production as in 1991 (FAO estimates).

Source: FAO, *Yearbook of Forest Products.*

Fishing

('000 metric tons, live weight)

	1989*	1990	1991
Freshwater and diadromous fishes	2.3	2.3	2.3
Cape hakes (Stokvisse)	153.5	135.2	136.5
Cape horse mackerel (Maasbanker)	83.8	51.1	35.6
Southern African pilchard	112.3	56.9	52.0
Whitehead's round herring	44.4	44.7	33.5
Southern African anchovy	372.9	150.1	150.6
Snoek (Barracouta)	16.5	20.8	21.9
Silver scabbardfish	9.4	14.6	12.1
Chub mackerel	18.0	14.3	13.5
Other marine fishes (incl. unspecified)	45.2	31.9	26.7
Total fish	858.3	521.9	484.7
Crustaceans	5.9	6.0	3.5
Chokker squid	10.7	5.0	7.0
Other molluscs	3.6	3.5	3.6
Total catch†	878.6	536.4	498.9

* Including landings from South African vessels at the Namibian port of Lüderitz and at Walvis Bay, sovereignty over which was transferred from South Africa to Namibia on 1 March 1994.

† Excluding seals, recorded by number rather than by weight. The catch of Cape fur seals was: 13,272 in 1989. Also excluded are aquatic plants ('000 metric tons): 11.5 in 1989; 12.0 (FAO estimate) in 1990; 12.0 (FAO estimate) in 1991.

Source: FAO, *Yearbook of Fishery Statistics*.

Mining

('000 metric tons, unless otherwise indicated)

	1989	1990	1991
Hard coal	173,913	174,784	175,251
Iron ore[1]	18,754	18,962	18,119
Copper ore[1]	181.7	178.7	192.9
Nickel ore*[2,3]	35.5	36.3	30.0
Lead concentrates[1]	78.2	70.2	76.3
Zinc ore[1]	77.3	74.8	66.6
Tin concentrates (metric tons)[1]	1,306	1,140	1,042
Manganese ore*[1]	2,017.1	1,836.1	1,368.0
Chromium ore*[1]	1,558	1,416	n.a.
Rutile—Titanium dioxide (metric tons)	64,367	64,056	75,000
Vanadium ore (metric tons)*[1,3]	18,567	17,106	13,435
Zirconium concentrates (metric tons)*[3]	150,000	151,136	230,000
Antimony concentrates (metric tons)[1]	5,201	4,815	4,500
Silver ore (metric tons)[1]	180	161	171
Uranium ore (metric tons)[1]	2,943	2,487	1,654
Gold (metric tons)[1]	605.5	603.0	601.0
Kaolin	140	132	134
Magnesite—crude	75.7	114.2	n.a.
Natural phosphates[3]	2,963	3,165	n.a.
Fluorspar—Fluorite[4]	368.3	311.0	270.3
Salt—unrefined	692	728	665
Diamonds: industrial ('000 metric carats)[3]	5,106	4,882	4,612
gem ('000 metric carats)[3]	4,010*	3,826	3,800
Gypsum—crude	407	384	420
Asbestos	157	146	149
Mica (metric tons)	1,708	1,765	n.a.

* Provisional or estimated figure.

[1] Figures relate to the metal content of ores or concentrates.

[2] Nickel content of matte and refined nickel.

[3] Data from the US Bureau of Mines.

[4] Acid, metallurgical and ceramic grade.

Source: UN, *Industrial Statistics Yearbook*.

1992 ('000 metric tons, unless otherwise indicated): Hard coal 174,000 (estimate); Iron ore 28,224 (gross weight); Copper ore 167; Lead concentrates 75.4 (provisional); Tin concentrates (metric tons) 600.

1993 (provisional): Lead concentrates ('000 metric tons) 98.4; Tin concentrates (metric tons) 500.

Note: The metal content of iron ore is 60%–65%.

Sources (for 1992 and 1993): UN, *Monthly Bulletin of Statistics*; UN Conference on Trade and Development, *International Tin Statistics*.

Industry

SELECTED PRODUCTS

('000 metric tons, unless otherwise indicated)

	1991	1992	1993
Wheat flour	1,734	1,833	1,867
Sugar—refined	1,359	1,316	1,098
Wine ('000 hectolitres)	3,899	3,779	3,647
Beer ('000 hectolitres)	17,710	18,290	n.a.
Cigarettes (million)	40,163	35,563	34,499
Pipe tobacco (metric tons)	5,832	7,451	7,759
Cotton yarn—incl. mixed	69.9	64.1	63.4
Woven cotton fabrics (million sq metres)	169.8	129.6	150.3
Footwear (million pairs)	52.1	44.5	45.9
Mechanical wood pulp*†	370	n.a.	n.a.
Chemical wood pulp*†	1,490	n.a.	n.a.
Newsprint paper	252	255	316
Other printing and writing paper	886	940	968
Other paper and paperboard*†	1,160	n.a.	n.a.
Synthetic rubber	89.6	34.6	n.a.
Rubber tyres ('000)	7,418	7,333	7,780
Nitrogenous fertilizers	1,088	1,010	1,109
Phosphate fertilizers	200	165	182
Motor spirit—petrol (million litres)‡	8,530	8,761	n.a.
Kerosene (million litres)‡	617	629	n.a.
Jet fuel (million litres)‡	861	1,000	n.a.
Distillate fuel oils (million litres)‡	5,388	5,310	n.a.
Residual fuel oils (million litres)‡	1,891	2,401	n.a.
Lubricating oils (million litres)‡	335	329	n.a.
Petroleum bitumen—asphalt	261	276	n.a.
Coke-oven coke*	1,835	n.a.	n.a.
Cement	6,147	5,850	5,818
Pig-iron	7,117	n.a.	n.a.
Crude steel	9,360	9,061	n.a.
Refined copper—unwrought	136	120	126
Radio receivers and record players ('000)	775	n.a.	n.a.
Television receivers ('000)	486	376	321
Passenger motor cars—assembled ('000)	238.3	206.6	228
Lorries—assembled ('000)	97.2	93.6	97
Electric energy (million kWh)	148,919	149,427	155,812

* Estimates.

† Including data for Namibia.

‡ Excluding data for Transkei, Bophuthatswana, Venda and Ciskei.

Sources: National Productivity Institute, Pretoria; UN, *Industrial Statistics Yearbook*; FAO, *Yearbook of Forest Products*.

Finance

CURRENCY AND EXCHANGE RATES

Monetary Units
100 cents = 1 rand (R).

Sterling and Dollar Equivalents (31 March 1994)
£1 sterling = 5.167 rand;
US $1 = 3.481 rand;
100 rand = £19.35 = $28.73.

Average Exchange Rate (US $ per rand)

1991	0.36280
1992	0.35092
1993	0.30641

BUDGET (million rand, year ending 31 March)*

Revenue	1991/92	1992/93	1993/94
Income taxes:			
Gold mines	490	472	500
Other companies	15,385	14,685	11,283
Individuals	28,942	35,327	38,246
General sales tax	19,444	—	—
Value-added tax	—	21,020	24,858
Goldmining leases	140	145	115
Interest and dividends	55	59	195
Customs duty	2,635	3,124	3,132
Surcharge on imports	1,409	1,670	1,635
Fuel levy	4,520	6,634	7,738
Excise duty	3,555	4,754	4,856
Other revenue	2,524	1,899	2,012
Sub-total	79,099	89,789	94,570
Less Transfers to neighbouring countries	4,233	5,040	5,675
Total	74,866	84,749	88,895

Expenditure	1991/92	1992/93	1993/94
Defence	10,488	10,803	10,683
Other general services	8,625	9,052	9,805
Education	19,929	24,393	27,762
Health	10,630	12,709	13,920
Other social services	11,282	14,656	16,253
Interest on public debt	14,460	17,530	22,150
Other expenditure	21,389	28,954	30,735
Sub-total	96,803	118,097	131,308
Less Own revenues†	9,775	12,787	12,972
Total	87,028	105,310	118,336

* Figures represent revenue and expenditure on State Revenue Fund. Accounts of Transnet and Telcom are not included.
† Revenue from provincial administrations, Bophuthatswana, Ciskei, Transkei, Venda and the other former 'homelands'.

INTERNATIONAL RESERVES (US $ million at 31 December)

	1991	1992	1993
Gold*	2,074	1,992	n.a.
IMF special drawing rights	2	0	12
Foreign exchange	897	991	1,008
Total	2,973	2,984	n.a.

* National valuation, based on market prices.

Source: IMF, *International Financial Statistics.*

MONEY SUPPLY (million rand at 31 December)

	1988	1989	1990
Currency outside banks	6,128	7,314	8,251
Demand deposits at deposit money banks	33,375	35,559	41,031
Total (incl. others)	39,934	43,343	49,858

Source: IMF, *International Financial Statistics.*

COST OF LIVING (Consumer Price Index; base: 1990 = 100)

	1991	1992	1993
Food	119.6	149.8	160.0
Fuel and light	112.4	126.5	146.5
Clothing	111.9	122.1	130.7
All items (incl. others)	115.3	131.3	144.1

NATIONAL ACCOUNTS (million rand at current prices)

National Income and Product (provisional)*

	1989	1990	1991
Compensation of employees	119,669	140,198	160,485
Operating surplus	49,645	53,204	59,885
Domestic factor incomes	169,314	193,402	220,370
Consumption of fixed capital	38,402	43,058	47,007
Gross domestic product (GDP) at factor cost	207,716	236,460	267,377
Indirect taxes	30,224	33,048	35,120
Less Subsidies	4,806	5,696	5,830
GDP in purchasers' values	233,134	263,812	296,667
Factor income received from abroad	1,750	1,808	-8,182
Less Factor income paid abroad	11,229	11,828	
Gross national product	223,655	253,792	288,485
Less Consumption of fixed capital	38,402	43,058	47,007
National income in market prices	185,253	210,734	241,478

* Data cover the whole of South Africa (including African 'homelands' that had been declared 'independent').

Expenditure on the Gross Domestic Product*

	1991	1992	1993
Government final consumption expenditure	61,988	69,727	76,976
Private final consumption expenditure	179,283	203,407	255,867
Increase in stocks	-5,622	-2,797	2,182
Gross fixed capital formation	53,668	52,060	52,829
Statistical discrepancy	-6,916	-8,114	-38,311
Total domestic expenditure	282,401	314,283	349,543
Exports of goods and services	74,220	78,070	90,001
Less Imports of goods and services	58,726	65,285	74,296
GDP in purchasers' values	297,895	327,068	365,248
GDP at constant 1985 prices	132,890	130,126	131,567

* Data cover the whole of South Africa (including African 'homelands' that had been declared 'independent').

Source: IMF, *International Financial Statistics.*

Gross Domestic Product by Economic Activity (at factor cost)

	1991	1992	1993
Business enterprises:			
Agriculture, forestry and fishing	13,039	11,605	14,062
Mining and quarrying	27,005	28,410	31,736
Manufacturing	66,567	73,722	80,456
Electricity, gas and water	11,709	12,676	13,749
Construction (contractors)	8,201	8,817	9,375
Wholesale and retail trade, catering and accommodation	36,173	40,500	44,010
Transport, storage and communication	22,687	24,441	26,370
Finance, insurance, real estate and business services	39,683	46,010	52,825
Community, social and personal services	4,645	5,357	6,014
Sub-total	229,709	251,538	278,597
Less imputed bank service charges	8,188	9,734	11,250
Government services	40,012	46,553	51,565
Other producers (non-profit institutions and domestic servants)	6,416	7,257	7,959
Total	267,949	295,614	326,871

BALANCE OF PAYMENTS (US $ million)*

	1991	1992	1993
Merchandise exports f.o.b.	23,715	23,645	23,925
Merchandise imports f.o.b.	–17,449	–18,216	–17,980
Trade balance	6,267	5,429	5,944
Exports of services	2,341	2,973	2,917
Imports of services	–3,958	–4,683	–4,721
Other income received	1,858	1,696	1,451
Other income paid	–3,913	–4,133	–3,885
Private unrequited transfers (net)	101	32	46
Official unrequited transfers (net)	–31	74	62
Current balance	2,664	1,388	1,814
Direct investment (net)	–8	–5	–8
Portfolio investment (net)	–196	524	–360
Other capital (net)	432	–612	–1,021
Net errors and omissions	–1,388	–1,163	–4,413
Overall balance	1,504	131	–3,988

* Including Botswana, Lesotho, Namibia and Swaziland.

Source: IMF, *International Financial Statistics*.

External Trade

Figures refer to the Southern African Customs Union, comprising South Africa, Namibia, Botswana, Lesotho and Swaziland. Trade between the component territories is excluded.

PRINCIPAL COMMODITIES (million rand)

Imports f.o.b.	1991	1992	1993
Chemical products, etc.	5,397.7	5,789.1	6,598.8
Plastics and plastic articles, rubber and rubber articles	2,150.2	2,249.7	2,638.9
Paper, paperboard, etc.	1,352.1	1,463.1	1,740.1
Textiles and textile articles	2,493.7	2,437.2	2,654.0
Base metals and articles of base metal	2,231.0	2,502.2	2,605.7
Machinery and mechanical appliances, electrical equipment, parts thereof	13,982.5	14,944.0	17,130.9
Transport equipment	6,766.9	6,619.0	8,915.9
Optical and photographic instruments, surgical instruments, etc.	2,157.6	2,241.6	2,716.1
Total (incl. others)	48,209.1	52,514.1	59,017.7

Exports f.o.b.	1991	1992	1993
Vegetable products	1,909.4	2,290.7	2,436.5
Prepared foodstuffs; beverages, spirits and vinegar; tobacco	2,040.7	1,856.8	1,812.5
Mineral products	7,281.2	7,083.3	8,443.7
Chemical products, etc.	2,300.7	3,220.8	3,377.9
Textiles and textile articles	1,823.7	1,809.0	1,812.1
Pearls, precious and semi-precious stones, precious metals, etc.	6,780.4	7,160.4	10,137.7
Base metals and articles of base metal	9,534.0	9,484.8	9,905.2
Total (incl. others)*	64,354.9	68,996.8	79,214.2

* Figures include exports of gold. The net value of gold output (in million rand) was: 19,648 in 1991; 18,195 in 1992; 22,229 in 1993.

Source: National Productivity Institute, Pretoria.

SELECTED TRADING PARTNERS (million rand)

Imports	1991	1992	1993
Australia	n.a.	629	693
Belgium	1,013	1,138	1,273
China, People's Republic	n.a.	652	1,003
France	1,931	2,052	2,094
Germany	8,503	8,588	9,281
Hong Kong	950	885	1,110
Italy	1,776	1,843	2,085
Japan	5,124	5,563	7,445
Netherlands	1,076	1,248	1,386
Singapore	n.a.	645	788
Switzerland	1,262	1,223	1,310
Taiwan	n.a.	1,767	2,039
United Kingdom	4,977	5,381	6,549
USA	6,602	7,142	7,766
Total (incl. others)	48,209	52,514	59,018

Exports	1991	1992	1993
Belgium	1,644	1.998	2,314
France	950	n.a.	n.a.
Germany	3,392	3,008	3,084
Hong Kong	1,354	1,471	1,750
Israel	n.a.	973	1,680
Italy	1,598	1,656	1,465
Japan	4,074	3,761	4,363
Korea, Republic	n.a.	993	1,275
Netherlands	2,373	1,928	2,151
Switzerland	5,719	5,382	7,896
Taiwan	n.a.	2,149	2,166
United Kingdom	5,039	4,525	4,740
USA	3,967	4,858	5,454
Zambia	n.a.	1,112	1,307
Zimbabwe	n.a.	1,553	1,748
Total (incl. others)	64,355	68,999	79,214

Source: National Productivity Institute, Pretoria.

Transport

RAILWAYS (traffic, year ending 31 March)

	1987	1988	1989
Freight carried ('000 metric tons)	166,763	166,800	174,160
Passenger journeys ('000)	612,376	578,357	579,524

Source: Department of Transport, Pretoria.

ROAD TRAFFIC (motor vehicles in use at 30 June)

	1990	1991	1992
Passenger cars	3,408,605	3,489,947	3,522,129
Buses and coaches	28,107	28,545	28,354
Vans	196,243	208,256	217,037
Goods vehicles	1,273,257	1,303,995	1,338,737
Motor cycles	298,941	294,006	285,034

SHIPPING (year ending 31 March)

Cargo Handled ('000 metric tons)

	1988	1989	1990
Landed	12,293	13,095	13,648
Shipped	81,304	85,670	96,563
Total (including cargo transhipped)	94,470	99,592	111,570

Source: Department of Transport, Pretoria.

Vessels Handled

	1986	1987	1988
Number	12,934	13,612	12,725
Displacement ('000 gross tons)	331,753	336,586	331,900

Number: 12,780 in 1989; 13,872 in 1990.

Source: Department of Transport, Pretoria.

CIVIL AVIATION (traffic on scheduled services)

	1989	1990	1991
Kilometres flown (million)	70	67	67
Passengers carried ('000)	5,641	5,365	4,819
Passenger-km (million)	9,201	9,049	8,413
Freight ton-km (million)	206	179	191

Source: UN, *Statistical Yearbook*.

Tourism

FOREIGN TOURIST ARRIVALS
(number of visitors by region of origin)

	1991	1992	1993
Africa	1,193,743	2,327,959	2,698,089
Europe	367,641	395,319	429,867
Asia	59,312	67,508	87,480
America	67,104	75,013	91,699
Oceania	19,986	24,821	30,115
Total (incl. unspecified)	1,709,554	2,892,822	3,369,762

Communications Media

	1990	1991	1992
Radio receivers ('000 in use)*	11,500	11,800	n.a.
Television licences ('000)	2,422	2,460	2,573
Telephones ('000 in use)	5,017	5,128	5,208
Daily newspapers:			
Number	19	19	19
Average circulation ('000)*	2,658	2,596	2,621

* Estimates.

Sources: Central Statistical Service, Pretoria; UNESCO, *Statistical Yearbook*.

Education

Primary and Secondary Levels (1991)

	Africans	Whites	Coloureds	Asians
Teachers:				
Primary, Secondary and Special	142,163	63,722	37,590	12,781
Pupils:				
Primary, Secondary and Special	5,794,100	1,021,442	874,315	255,529

Tertiary Level (1991)

	Africans	Whites	Coloureds	Asians
University				
Students	110,130	157,432	19,575	21,035
Teachers	615	8,620	267	309
Teacher Training				
Students	35,795	8,766	7,851	1,726
Teachers	1,878	2,115	506	149
Technical				
Students	14,490	50,907	5,711	5,327
Teachers	270	2,567	267	144
Technikons				
Students	24,228	53,795*	6,942*	5,864*
Teachers	28*	1,975*	93*	123*

* Figures unchanged from 1990.

Source: Department of National Education, Pretoria.

Directory

The Constitution

Following multi-party negotiations (see Recent History), the Interim Constitution was ratified on 22 December 1993, and officially came into effect on 27 April 1994; it was to remain in force pending the adoption of a new constitution (see below), prior to elections for a new legislature, and the installation of a majority government, in 1991. The main provisions of the Interim Constitution are summarized below:

FUNDAMENTAL RIGHTS

Fundamental human rights are protected under a bill of rights. Communities or individuals are entitled to claim restitution for land dispossessed under legislation from 1913. A state of emergency may be declared only if it is considered necessary for the restoration of civil order, and is limited to 21 days, renewable with the support of two-thirds of deputies in the National Assembly. Under a state of emergency, indefinite detention without trial is permitted, subject to judicial review after 10 days.

PARLIAMENT

Legislative power is vested in a bicameral Parliament, comprising a National Assembly and a Senate. The 400-member National Assembly is elected by proportional representation, with 200 members elected from national party lists and 200 from regional party lists. National and provincial legislatures are elected separately, under a 'double-ballot' electoral system. Each provincial legislature elects 10 representatives to the 90-member Senate, which is headed by a President. Parliamentary decisions are generally reached by a simple majority, although constitutional amendments require a majority of two-thirds.

ADOPTION OF THE NEW CONSTITUTION

The National Assembly and the Senate together form a Constitutional Assembly, which is to draft a new constitution, with adherence to 32 principles entrenched in the Interim Constitution, guaranteeing multi-party democracy, the delineated powers of provincial government, fundamental human rights and the independence of the judiciary. In the event that the Constitutional Assembly fails to adopt a new constitution by a majority of two-thirds within a period of two years of its first session, the draft is to be submitted for approval by 60% of the electorate at a national referendum. If this is not achieved, agreement on the constitution will be postponed until after the elections in 1999, when the draft is to be submitted for approval by a majority of 60% of members of a new Constitutional Assembly.

THE NATIONAL EXECUTIVE

The President is elected by the National Assembly from among its members, and exercises executive power in consultation with at least two Deputy Presidents. Any party that holds a minimum of 80 seats in the National Assembly (equivalent to 20% of the national vote) is entitled to nominate a Deputy President. If no party secures 80 seats, the First Deputy President is elected by the party that holds the highest number of seats, and the Second Deputy President by the party that holds the second highest number of seats, in the National Assembly. In the event of the absence from office of the President, the Deputy Presidents assume his functions on a rotational basis. The President may be removed by a motion of no-confidence or by impeachment. The Cabinet constitutes an interim Government of National Unity, and comprises a maximum of 27 ministers. Each party with a minimum of 20 seats in the National Assembly (equivalent to 5% of the national vote) is entitled to a proportional number of ministerial portfolios. The President allocates cabinet portfolios in consultation with party leaders, who are entitled to request the replacement of ministers. Cabinet decisions are reached by consensus.

JUDICIAL AUTHORITY

There is a Supreme Court, headed by a Chief Justice, which is independent from the executive. An 11-member Constitutional Court, headed by a President, ensures adherence to the entrenched constitutional principles. Members of the Constitutional Court are appointed by the President from a list nominated by an independent judicial commission, and hold office for a maximum of seven years.

PROVINCIAL GOVERNMENT

There are nine provinces: Eastern Cape, Eastern Transvaal, KwaZulu/Natal, Northern Cape, Northern Transvaal, North-West, Orange Free State, Pretoria-Witwatersrand-Vereeniging and Western Cape. Each province is entitled to determine its legislative and executive structure. The Interim Constitution guarantees the powers of provincial government and recognizes the right to regional autonomy. Each province has a legislature, comprising between 30 and 100 members (depending on the size of the local electorate), who are elected by proportional representation. Each legislature is entitled to draft a constitution for the province, subject to the principles governing the national constitution, and elects a Premier, who heads a Cabinet. Parties that hold a minimum of 10% of seats in the legislature are entitled to a proportional number of portfolios in the Cabinet. Provincial legislatures are allowed primary responsibility for a number of areas of government, and joint powers with central government in the principal administrative areas.

LOCAL GOVERNMENT

Local negotiating forums are to supervise the organization of elections to multiracial municipal councils. White and black voters are to elect 30% of members respectively, while the remainder of seats in the new councils are to be elected on a non-racial basis. Municipal budgets are approved by a majority of two-thirds of members of the council.

The Government

HEAD OF STATE

President: NELSON ROLIHLAHLA MANDELA (took office 10 May 1994).

First Deputy President: THABO MBEKI.

Second Deputy President: FREDERIK WILLEM DE KLERK.

CABINET

(September 1994)

An interim Government of National Unity, comprising representatives of the African National Congress of South Africa (ANC), the National Party (NP), and the Inkatha Freedom Party (IFP).

Minister of Foreign Affairs: ALFRED NZO (ANC).

Minister of Public Enterprises: Princess STELLA SIGCAU (ANC).

Minister of Justice: DULLAH OMAR (ANC).

Minister of Defence: JOE MODISE (ANC).

Minister of Posts, Telecommunications and Broadcasting: PALLO JORDAN (ANC).

Minister of Correctional Services: SIPHO MZIMELA (IFP).

Minister of Education: SIBUSISO BHENGU (ANC).

Minister of Mineral and Energy Affairs: ROELOF FREDERK (PIK) BOTHA (NP).

Minister of Agriculture: DR ANDRÉ ISAK (KRAAI) VAN NIEKERK (NP)

Minister of Health: DR NKOSAZANA DHLAMINI ZUMA (ANC).

Minister of Safety and Security: SYDNEY MUFAMADI (ANC).

Minister of Transport: MAC MAHARAJ (ANC).

Minister of Provincial Affairs and of Constitutional Development: ROELF P. MEYER (NP).

Minister of Labour: TITO MBOWENI (ANC).

Minister of Arts, Culture, Science and Technology: BEN NGUBANE (IFP).

Minister of Finance: CHRISTO LIEBENBERG.

Minister of Welfare and Population: ABRAHAM (ABE) WILLIAMS (NP).

Minister of Sport and Recreation: STEVE TSHWETE (ANC).

Minister of Housing: JOE SLOVO (ANC).

Minister of Trade, Industry and Tourism: TREVOR MANUEL (ANC).

Minister of Environment Affairs: DR DAWIE J. DE VILLIERS (NP).

Minister of Land Affairs: DEREK HANEKOM (ANC).

Minister of Home Affairs: Chief MANGOSUTHU GATSHA BUTHELEZI (IFP).

Minister of Public Services and Administration: DR ZOLA SKWEYIYA (ANC).

Minister of Public Works: JEFF RADEBE (ANC).

Minister of Water Affairs and Forestry: KADER ASMAL (ANC).

Minister without Portfolio: JAY NAIDOO (ANC).

MINISTRIES

Office of the President: Private Bag X1000, Pretoria 0001; tel. (12) 3252000.

Ministry of Agriculture: Agriculture Bldg, 116 Block DA, cnr Hamilton St and Soutpansberg Rd, Pretoria 0002; Private Bag X116, Pretoria 0001; tel. (12) 2062440.

Ministry of Arts, Culture, Science and Technology: Union Bldgs, Pretoria 0136.

Ministry of Correctional Services: Poyntons Bldg, West Block, cnr Church and Schubart Sts, Pretoria 0002; Private Bag X853 Pretoria; tel. (12) 3238198.

Ministry of Defence: Pretoria.

Ministry of Education: Oranje Nassau Bldg, Rm 7060, 188 Schoeman St, Pretoria 0002; Private Bag X727, Pretoria 0001; tel. (12) 3244096; fax (12) 3242687.

Ministry of Environment Affairs: Private Bag X741, Pretoria 0001; tel. (12) 3268081; fax (12) 216491.

Ministry of Finance: 240 Vermeulen St, Pretoria 0002; Private Bag X115, Pretoria 0001; tel. (12) 3238911.

Ministry of Foreign Affairs: East Wing, Union Bldgs, Pretoria 0136; Private Bag X152, Pretoria 0001; tel. (12) 3233717; telex 321348.

Ministry of Health: 2027 Civitas Bldg, Struben St, Pretoria 0002; Private Bag X399, Pretoria 0001; tel. (12) 284773.

Ministry of Home Affairs: 1010 Civitas Bldg, cnr Andries and Strubert Sts, Pretoria 0002; Private Bag X741, Pretoria 0001; tel. (12) 3268081.

Ministry of Housing: Private Bag X603, Pretoria 0001; tel. (12) 3260126; fax (12) 3438929.

Ministry of Justice: Presidia Bldg, 8th Floor, cnr Pretorius and Paul Kruger Sts, Pretoria 0002; Private Bag X276, Pretoria 0001; tel. (12) 3238581; fax (12) 211708.

Ministry of Labour: 803 De Bruynpark, Andries St, Pretoria 0002; Private Bag X727, Pretoria 0001; tel. (12) 200036.

Ministry of Land Affairs: Private Bag X844, Pretoria 0001; tel. (12) 3235212.

Ministry of Mineral and Energy Affairs: NG Sinodale Centre, cnr Andries and Visagie Sts, Pretoria 0002; Private Bag X646, Pretoria 0001; tel. (12) 3228695.

Ministry of Posts, Telecommunications and Broadcasting: Union Bldgs, Pretoria 0136; tel. (12) 3283084.

Ministry of Provincial Affairs and of Constitutional Development: 260 Walker Street, Pretoria 0002; Private Bag X802, Pretoria 0001; tel. (12) 3411380.

Ministry of Public Enterprises: 2516 Main Post Office Bldg, Vermeulen St, Pretoria 0002; Private Bag X482, Pretoria 0001; tel. (12) 2931911.

Ministry of Public Services and Administration: Union Bldgs, Pretoria 0136; tel. (12) 3147911; fax (12) 3232386.

Ministry of Public Works: Private Bag X427, Pretoria 0001; tel. (12) 4281912; fax (12) 3470118.

Ministry of Safety and Security: Wachthuis, 7th Floor, 231 Pretorius St, Pretoria 0002; Private Bag X463, Pretoria 0001; tel. (12) 3438880.

Ministry of Sport and Recreation: Pretoria.

Ministry of Trade, Industry and Tourism: Momentum Life Bldg, 11th Floor, cnr Prinsloo and Pretorius Sts, Pretoria 0001; Private Bag X274, Pretoria 0001; tel. (12) 3227677; fax (12) 3229690.

Ministry of Transport: Forum Bldg, cnr Struben and Bosman Sts, Pretoria 0002; Private Bag X193, Pretoria 0001; tel. (12) 283084.

Ministry of Water Affairs and Forestry: 1029 Residensie Bldg, 185 Schoeman St, Pretoria 0001; Private Bag X313, Pretoria 0001; tel. (12) 2992001.

Ministry of Welfare and Population: Pretoria.

Legislature

PARLIAMENT

Senate

President: HENDRIK JACOBUS (KOBIE) COETSEE.

The 90-member Senate has 10 representatives elected by each provincial legislature. Following legislative elections in April 1994, the Senate comprised 60 representatives of the African National Congress of South Africa, 17 of the National Party, five each of the Inkatha Freedom Party and the Freedom Front, and three of the Democratic Party.

National Assembly

Speaker: Dr FRENE NOSHIR GINWALA.

General Election, 26–29 April 1994

Party	Votes	% of votes	Seats
African National Congress of South Africa	12,237,655	62.65	252
National Party	3,983,690	20.39	82
Inkatha Freedom Party	2,058,294	10.54	43
Freedom Front	424,555	2.17	9
Democratic Party	338,426	1.73	7
Pan-Africanist Congress	243,478	1.25	5
African Christian Democratic Party	88,104	0.45	2
Africa Muslim Party	27,690	0.14	0
African Moderates Congress Party	27,690	0.14	0
Dikwankwetia Party	19,451	0.10	0
Federal Party	17,663	0.09	0
Minority Front	13,433	0.07	0
SOCCER Party	10,575	0.05	0
African Democratic Movement	9,886	0.05	0
Women's Rights Peace Party	6,434	0.03	0
Ximako Progressive Party	6,320	0.03	0
Keep It Straight and Simple Party	5,916	0.03	0
Workers' List Party	4,169	0.02	0
Luso South African Party	3,293	0.02	0
Total*	19,533,498	100.00	400

* Excluding spoilt ballot papers, which numbered 193,081.

Political Organizations

African Christian Democratic Party (ACDP): f. 1993; Leader Dr JOHANN VAN DER WESTHUIZEN.

African National Congress of South Africa (ANC): 51 Plein St, Johannesburg 2001, POB 61884, Marshalltown 2107; tel. (11) 3307000; telex 421255; fax (11) 293719; f. 1912; became the dominant party in new Govt, following democratic elections in 1994; Pres. (vacant); Sec.-Gen. CYRIL RAMAPHOSA.

Afrikaner Weerstandsbeweging (AWB) (Afrikaner Resistance Movement): POB 274, Ventersdorp 2710; tel. (11) 2005; fax (11) 2032; f. 1973; extreme right-wing paramilitary group; Leader EUGENE TERRE'BLANCHE; Sec.-Gen. PIET 'SKIET' RUDOLPH.

Azanian Co-ordinating Committee (AZACCO): f. 1988 to promote black consciousness; Leader NDLUSIBA NHLOKO.

Azanian People's Organization (AZAPO): POB 4230, Johannesburg 2000; tel. (11) 299055; f. 1978 to seek the establishment of a unitary, democratic, socialist republic; excludes white mems; banned 1988–90; 84 brs; Pres. PANDELANI NEFOLOVHODWE; Sec.-Gen. D. NKADIMENG.

Blanke Bevrydingsbeweging (BBB) (White Protection Movement): f. 1987; extreme right-wing activist group; banned 1988–90; Leader Prof. JOHAN SCHABORT.

Boerestaat Party (Boer State Party): f. 1988; seeks the establishment of an Afrikaner state; mil. wing (f. 1990) known as Boere Weerstandsbeweging (BWB); Leader ROBERT VAN TONDER.

Boere Vryheidsbeweging (Boer Freedom Movement): f. 1989 by fmr mems of the Afrikaanse Weerstandsbeweging.

Cape Democrats: f. 1988; white support; liberal.

Conservative Party of South Africa (CP): POB 1842, Pretoria 0001; tel. (12) 3423408; fax (12) 3423912; f. 1982 by extreme right-wing MPs expelled from National Party; includes mems of fmr National Conservative Party; seeks the establishment of a separate Afrikaner state; Leader Dr FERDINAND HARTZENBERG.

Democratic Party (DP): Ruskin House, 5th Floor, 2 Roeland St, Cape Town 8001; POB 1475, Cape Town 8000; tel. (21) 451431; fax (21) 4615276; f. 1989 by merger of Independent Party, National Democratic Movement and Progressive Federal Party; membership open to all racial groups; supported the establishment of a democratic, non-racial society by peaceful means; Leader TONY LEON (acting); Nat. Chair. KENNETH ANDREW.

Democratic Reform Party (DRP): f. 1988; Coloured support; Leader CARTER EBRAHIM.

Democratic Workers' Party (DWP): Cape Town; f. 1984 by breakaway faction of the People's Congress Party; mainly Coloured support, but open to all races; Leader DENNIS DE LA CRUZ.

Federal Independent Democratic Alliance (FIDA): POB 10528, Johannesburg 2000; tel. (11) 4034268; fax (11) 4031557; f. 1987; black support; centrist; Leader JOHN GOGOTYA.

Freedom Front: f. 1994 by mems of the right-wing, to contest democratic elections; included some mems of the Conservative Party of South Africa; Leader Gen. (retd) CONSTAND VILJOEN.

Freedom Party: Coloured support; Leader ARTHUR BOOYSEN.

Herstigte Nasionale Party (HNP) (Reconstituted National Party): POB 1888, Pretoria 0001; tel. (12) 3423410; fax (12) 3423417; f. 1969 by extreme right-wing MPs expelled from National Party; advocates 'Christian Nationalism'; Leader JAAP MARAIS; Chair. WILLEM MARAIS; Gen. Sec. L. J. VAN DER SCHYFF.

Inkatha Freedom Party (IFP): POB 4432, Durban 4000; tel. (31) 3074962; fax (31) 3074964; f. as Inkatha Movement, a liberation movement with mainly Zulu support; relaunched in 1990 as a multiracial political party; represented in new Govt, following democratic elections in 1994; Leader Chief MANGOSUTHU GATSHA BUTHELEZI.

Labour Party of South Africa: Ruskin House, 2nd Floor, 2 Roeland St, Cape Town 8001; POB 3417, Cape Town 8000; tel. (21) 4618370; fax (21) 451953; f. 1965; mainly Coloured support; supports a democratic, multiracial society; Leader (vacant); Dep. Leader ISMAIL RICHARDS.

Linkoanketla Party: main support from the South Sotho people of Qwaqwa; Leader Chief KENNETH MOPELI.

National Party (NP): Private Bag X402, Pretoria 0001; tel. (12) 3483100; fax (12) 3485645; f. 1912; ruling party 1948–94; opened membership to all racial groups in 1990; represented in new Govt, following democratic elections in 1994; Leader FREDERIK WILLEM DE KLERK.

National People's Party: Private Bag X54330, Durban 4000; Indian support; Leader AMICHAND RAJBANSI.

New Freedom Party of Southern Africa: 15 Eendrag St, Bellville 7530; Coloured support.

New Solidarity: POB 48687, Qualbert 4078; tel. (11) 3055692; fax 3011077; f. 1989; Indian support; Leader Dr J. N. REDDY.

Die Orangjewerkers: seeks to establish several small, self-governing white states; Leader HENDRIK FRENSCH VERWOERD.

Pan-Africanist Congress (PAC): POB 25245, Ferreirastown 2048; tel. (11) 8360407; fax (11) 8383705; f. 1959 by breakaway faction of the ANC; banned 1960–90; advocated the establishment a democratic society through black and not multiracial orgs; Pres. CLARENCE MAKWETU; Sec.-Gen. BENNIE ALEXANDER.

Progressive Independent Party (PIP): Indian support; Leader FAIZ KHAN.

Reformed Freedom Party: Coloured support.

South African Communist Party (SACP): c/o POB 1027, Johannesburg 2000; tel. (11) 8366867; fax (11) 8368366; f. 1921 as Communist Party of South Africa; refounded, under present name, 1953; banned 1950–90; supports new Govt, following democratic elections in 1994; Chair. JOE SLOVO; Gen. Sec. CHARLES NQAKULA.

Transvaal Indian Congress: f. 1902, reactivated 1983; Pres. Dr ESSOP JASSAT.

United Christian Conciliation Party: Johannesburg; f. 1986; multiracial; Pres Bishop ISAAC MOKOENA, TAMASANQA LINDA.

United Democratic Reform Party: POB 14048, Reigerpark 1466; f. 1987 by merger of People's Congress Party, Progressive Reform Party and Democratic Party; Coloured and Indian support; Leader JAKOBUS (JAC) ALBERT RABIE; Nat. Chair. NASH PARMANAND.

Workers' Organization for Socialist Action (WOSA): Cape Town; f. 1990; Chair. Dr NEVILLE ALEXANDER; Gen. Sec. C. BRECHER.

Other political parties that contested the 1994 elections included the Africa Muslim Party; the African Moderates Congress Party; the Dikwankwetia Party; the Federal Party; the Minority Front; the SOCCER Party; the African Democratic Movement; the Women's Rights Peace Party ; the Ximako Progressive Party; the Keep it Straight and Simple (KISS) Party; the Workers' List Party; and the Luso South African Party.

Diplomatic Representation

EMBASSIES AND HIGH COMMISSIONS IN SOUTH AFRICA

Argentina: 200 Standard Plaza, Pretoria 0002; tel. (12) 433527; fax (12) 433521; Ambassador: H. PORTA.

Australia: 292 Orient St, Arcadia, St, Pretoria 0083; Private Bag X150, Pretoria 0001; tel. (12) 3423740; telex 322102; fax (12) 3424222; High Commissioner: R. A. BURNS.

Austria: Apollo Centre, 10th Floor, 405 Church St, Pretoria 0002; POB 851, Pretoria 0001; tel. (12) 3227790; telex 320541; fax (12) 3227793; Ambassador: Dr ARNOLD MOEBIUS.

Belgium: 275 Pomona St, Muckleneuk, Pretoria 0002; tel. (12) 443201; telex 320508; fax (12) 443216; Ambassador: R. VAN OVERBERGHE.

Brazil: 182 Balmoral Ave, Arcadia 0083, POB 3269, Pretoria 0001; tel. (12) 435559; telex 321364; fax (12) 3421419; Chargé d'affaires a.i.: RICARDO DRUMMOND DE MELLO.

Canada: Nedcor Bank Plaza, 5th Floor, cnr Church and Beatrix Sts, Pretoria 0083; POB 26006, Pretoria 0007; tel. (12) 3243970; telex 32212; fax (12) 3231564; High Commissioner: MARC A. BRAULT.

Chile: Merino Bldg, 7th Floor, cnr Bosman and Pretorius Sts, Pretoria 0002; POB 2073, Pretoria 0001; tel. (12) 3269387; telex 322567; fax (12) 3258155; Ambassador: C. BUSTOS.

China (Taiwan): 1147 Schoeman St, Pretoria 0083, POB 649, Pretoria 0001; tel. (12) 436071; fax (12) 435816; Ambassador: I-CHENG LOH.

Czech Republic: 936 Pretorius St, Pretoria 0083; tel. (12) 3423477; fax (12) 432033; Ambassador: (vacant).

Denmark: POB 2942, Pretoria 0001; tel. (12) 3220595; telex 323133; fax (12) 3220596; Ambassador: PETER BRÜCKNER.

Finland: 628 Leyds St, Muckleneuk, Pretoria; POB 443, Pretoria 0001; tel. (12) 3430275; telex 350063; fax (12) 3433095; Ambassador: BJÖRN EKBLOM.

France: 807 George Ave, Arcadia, Pretoria 0083; POB 4619, Pretoria 0001; tel. (12) 435564; telex 321319; fax (12) 433481; Ambassador: JOËLLE M. P. BOURGOIS.

Germany: POB 2023, Pretoria 0001; tel. (12) 3443854; telex 321386; fax (12) 3439401; Ambassador: Dr HANS-CHRISTIAN UEBERSCHÄR.

Greece: 995 Pretorius St, Arcadia, Pretoria 0083; tel. (12) 437351; telex 320520; fax (12) 434313; Ambassador: P. A. TSAMOULIS.

Holy See: 800 Pretorius St, Arcadia, Pretoria 0083; tel. (12) 3443815; fax (12) 3443595; Apostolic Delegate: Most Rev. AMBROSE B. DE PAOLI, Titular Archbishop of Lares.

Hungary: 959 Arcadia St, Arcadia, Pretoria 0083; POB 27077, Sunnyside 0132; tel. (12) 433030; fax (12) 433029; Ambassador: (vacant).

India: Pretoria; Chargé d'affaires a.i.: TALMIZ AHMED.

Israel: Dashing Centre, 3rd Floor, 339 Hilda St, Hatfield, Pretoria 0083; POB 3726, Pretoria 0001; tel. (12) 4212222; fax (12) 3421442; Ambassador: Z. GOV-ARI.

Italy: 796 George Ave, Arcadia, Pretoria 0083; tel. (12) 435541; telex 321397; fax (12) 435547; Ambassador: MARIO PIERSIGILLI.

Japan: Sanlam Bldg, 353 Festival St, Hatfield, Pretoria 0083; POB 11434, Brooklyn 0011; tel. (12) 3422100; telex 322134; fax (12) 433922; Ambassador: K. SEZAKI.

Malawi: Delta Bldg, 1st Floor, 471 Monica Rd, Pretoria 0081; POB 11172, Brooklyn 0011; tel. (12) 477827; telex 322017; fax (12) 3484649; High Commissioner: N. T. MIZERE.

Netherlands: 825 Arcadia St, Pretoria; POB 117, Pretoria 0001; tel. (12) 3443910; telex 321332; fax (12) 3439950; Ambassador: E. RÖELL.

Norway: POB 9843, Pretoria 0001; tel. (12) 3234790; fax (12) 3234789; Ambassador: J. K. OTTERBECH.

Paraguay: 189 Strelitzia Rd, Waterkloof Heights, POB 95774, Waterkloof, Pretoria 0145; tel. (12) 451081; fax (12) 451082; Ambassador: RAÚL DOS SANTOS.

Poland: 14 Amos St, Colbyn, Pretoria 0083; Ambassador: S. CIENIVICH.

Portugal: 599 Leyds St, Muckleneuk, Pretoria 0002; tel. (12) 3412340; telex 321365; fax (12) 443071; Ambassador: Dr J. M. L. RITTO.

Romania: 117 Charles St, Brooklyn 0181; POB 11295, Pretoria 0011; tel. (12) 466940; fax (12) 466941; Ambassador: (vacant).

Russia: First National Bank Plaza, 3rd Floor, Pretoria 0001; Ambassador: (vacant).

Slovakia: POB 95855, Waterkloof, Pretoria 0145; Ambassador: LADISLAV VLASIC.

Spain: 169 Pine St, Arcadia, Pretoria 0083; tel. (12) 3443875; telex 320705; fax (12) 3434891; Ambassador: MARIANO UCELAY.

Sweden: Old Mutual Centre, 167 Andries St, POB 1664, Pretoria 0001; tel. (12) 211050; telex 321193; fax (12) 3232776; Ambassador: I. STJERNBERG.

Switzerland: 818 George Avenue, Pretoria 0002; POB 2289, Pretoria 0001; tel. (12) 436707; telex 322106; fax (12) 436771; Ambassador: R. WERMUTH.

United Kingdom: 255 Hill St, Pretoria 0002; tel. (12) 433121; fax (12) 433207; High Commissioner: Sir ANTHONY REEVE.

USA: Thibault House, 7th Floor, 877 Pretorius St, Pretoria; tel. (12) 3423006; telex 322143; fax (12) 3422090; Ambassador: PRINCETON N. LYMAN.

Uruguay: Tulbagh Park, 1st Floor, 1234 Church St, Pretoria; POB 3247, Pretoria 0001; tel. (12) 432829; fax (12) 432833; Ambassador: Dr FÉLIX PITTIER.

Zimbabwe: Pretoria; High Commissioner: ANDREW HAMA MTETWA.

Judicial System

The common law of the Republic of South Africa is the Roman-Dutch law, the uncodified law of Holland as it was at the time of the secession of the Cape of Good Hope in 1806. The law of England is not recognized as authoritative, though the principles of English law have been introduced in relation to civil and criminal procedure, evidence and mercantile matters.

The Supreme Court consists of an Appellate Division, and a number of Provincial and Local Divisions. The provinces are further divided into districts and regions with Magistrates' Courts, whose criminal and civil jurisdiction is clearly defined. From these courts appeals may be taken to the Provincial and Local Divisions of the Supreme Court, and thence to the Appellate Division.

THE SUPREME COURT

Appellate Division

Chief Justice: MICHAEL CORBETT.

Religion

The majority of the population professes the Christian faith.

CHRISTIANITY

The South African Council of Churches: Khotso House, 62 Marshall St, POB 4921, Johannesburg 2000; tel. (11) 4921380; telex 450614; fax (11) 4921448; f. 1936; 23 mem. churches; Pres. Dr K. MGOJO; Gen. Sec. Rev. FRANK CHIKANE.

The Anglican Communion

Most Anglicans in South Africa are adherents of the Church of the Province of Southern Africa, comprising 23 dioceses (including Lesotho, Namibia, St Helena, Swaziland and two dioceses in Mozambique). The Church had more than 2m. members in 1988.

Archbishop of Cape Town and Metropolitan of the Province of Southern Africa: Most Rev. DESMOND M. TUTU, Bishopscourt, Claremont 7700; tel. (21) 7612531; fax (21) 7614193.

The Dutch Reformed Church (Nederduitse Gereformeerde Kerk—NGK)

In 1991 there were 946,971 white, 228,099 Coloured and 294,830 African members of the Dutch Reformed Church in South Africa. Separate worship for whites and non-whites was instituted in 1863; in 1986 all congregations were desegregated.

General Synod: POB 4445, Pretoria 0001; tel. (12) 3227658; fax (12) 3223803; Moderator Prof. PIETER POTGIETER; Scribe Dr F. M. GAUM; CEO Prof. P. G. MEIRING.

The Evangelical Lutheran Churches

In 1980 there were 39,620 white, 95,640 Coloured and 698,400 African members of the Lutheran Church in South Africa.

Evangelical Lutheran Church in Southern Africa (ELCSA): Johannesburg; tel. (11) 9731853; telex 451751; fax (11) 3951888; f. 1975 by merger of four non-white churches; now the major Lutheran body in southern Africa; 710,372 mems; Gen. Sec. Rev. T. MBULI.

Evangelical Lutheran Church in Southern Africa (Cape): 240 Long St, Cape Town 8001; tel. (21) 244932; fax (21) 249618; Pres. Bishop N. ROHWER.

Evangelical Lutheran Church in Southern Africa (Natal–Transvaal): POB 7095, Bonaero Park 1622; tel. (31) 9731851; fax (31) 3951862; Pres. Bishop D. R. LILJE.

Lutheran Communion in Southern Africa: POB 7170, Bonaero Park 1622; tel. 9731873; fax 3951615; f. 1991; Pres. Rev. M. WESSELS; Exec. Dir F. F. GRAZ.

The Roman Catholic Church

South Africa comprises four archdioceses, 23 dioceses and one Apostolic Prefecture. At 31 December 1992 there were an estimated 2,957,452 adherents in the country, representing about 8.2% of the total population.

Southern African Catholic Bishops' Conference (SACBC): Khanya House, 140 Visagie St, Pretoria 0002; POB 941, Pretoria 0001; tel. (12) 3236458; fax (12) 3266218; f. 1951; 34 mems representing South Africa, Botswana, Namibia and Swaziland; Pres. Rt Rev. LOUIS NDLOVU, Bishop of Manzini; Sec.-Gen. Br JUDE PIETERSE.

Archbishop of Bloemfontein: Most Rev. PETER BUTELEZI, Archbishop's House, 7A Whites Rd, Bloemfontein 9301; POB 362, Bloemfontein 9300; tel. and fax (51) 481658.

Archbishop of Cape Town: Most Rev. LAWRENCE HENRY; Cathedral Place, 12 Bouquet St, Cape Town 8001; POB 2910, Cape Town 8000; tel. (21) 4622417; fax (21) 4619330.

Archbishop of Durban: Most Rev. WILFRID NAPIER, Archbishop's House, 154 Gordon Rd, Durban 4001; POB 47489, Greyville 4023; tel. (31) 3031417; fax (31) 231848.

Archbishop of Pretoria: Most Rev. GEORGE DANIEL, Archbishop's House, 125 Main St, Waterkloof 0181; POB 17245, Groenkloof, Pretoria 0027; tel. (12) 462048; fax (12) 462452.

Other Christian Churches

In addition to the following Churches, there are a large number of Apostolics, Assemblies of God and other Pentecostalist groups, and more than 3,000 African independent Churches.

Afrikaanse Protestaante Kerk (Afrikaans Protestant Church): f. 1987 by fmr mems of the Dutch Reformed Church (Nederduitse Gereformeerde Kerk) in protest at the proposed racial integration of church congregations; Leader Prof. WILLIE LUBBE; c. 2,000 mems.

Baptist Union of Southern Africa: POB 1085, Roodepoort 1725, Transvaal; tel. (11) 7603038; f. 1877; Pres. Rev. P. A. HOLNESS; Gen. Sec. Rev. T. G. RAE; 61,000 mems.

Black Dutch Reformed Church: POB 137, Bergvlei 2012; Leader Rev. SAM BUTI; c. 1m. mems.

Church of England in South Africa: POB 185, Gillitts 3603; tel. (31) 752876; fax (31) 7655150; 207 churches; Bishops: Rt Rev. J. BELL, Rt Rev. J. NGUBANE, Rt Rev. F. RETIEF, Rt Rev. M. MORRISON.

Evangelical Presbyterian Church: POB 31961, Braamfontein 2017; Sec. Rev. S. NGOBE; Moderator Rev. Dr A. E. KALTENRIEDER; Treas. Rev. H. D. MASANGU; 60,000 mems.

The Methodist Church of Southern Africa: Methodist Connexional Office, POB 50216, Musgrave 4062; tel. (31) 224214; fax (31) 217674; f. 1883; Pres. Bishop M. STANLEY MOGOBA; Sec. Rev. VIVIAN W. HARRIS; 758,178 mems.

Moravian Church in Southern Africa: POB 24111, Lansdowne 7780, Cape Province; tel. (21) 6962926; fax (21) 6963887; f. 1737; Head Rev. MARTIN WESSELS; 102,132 mems.

Nederduitsch Hervormde Kerk van Afrika: POB 2368, Pretoria 0001; tel. (12) 3228885; fax (12) 3227909; Scribe Dr J. M. G. STORM, 224 Jacob Maré St, Pretoria; 192,724 mems.

Presbyterian Church of Africa: POB 54840, Umlazi 4031; tel. (31) 9072366; f. 1898; 8 presbyteries (incl. 1 in Malawi and 1 in Zimbabwe); Chief Clerk Rev. S. A. KHUMALO; 1,231,000 mems.

Presbyterian Church of Southern Africa: POB 72057, Parkview, Johannesburg 2122; tel. (11) 3391017; fax (11) 4031921; f. 1897; Moderator Rt Rev. D. G. P. MULLER; Gen. Sec. and Clerk of the Assembly Rev. A. RODGER; 90,000 mems.

Reformed Church in South Africa (Die Gereformeerde Kerke): POB 20004, Noordbrug 2522, Potchefstoom; tel. (148) 2973986; fax (148) 2931042; f. 1859; Prin. Officer L. J. SWART; mems: 158,973.

United Congregational Church of Southern Africa: POB 96014, Brixton 2019; tel. (11) 8379997; fax (11) 8372570; f. 1799; Chair. A. E. WENTZEL; Gen. Sec. Rev. S. M. ARENDS; 265,651 mems.

Zion Christian Church: Zion City, Moria, Transvaal; f. 1910; South Africa's largest black religious group, with c. 4m. mems; Leader Bishop BARNABAS LEKGANYANE.

BAHÁ'Í FAITH

National Spiritual Assembly: 10 Acorn Lane, Houghton Estate, Houghton 2198; POB 2142, Houghton 2041; tel. (11) 4872099; fax (11) 4871809; f. 1956; 8,000 mems resident in 180 localities; Sec. SHOHREH RAWHANI.

JUDAISM

There are about 100,000 Jews in South Africa.

South African Jewish Board of Deputies: POB 87557, Houghton 2041; tel. (11) 4861434; fax (11) 6464946; f. 1912; the representative institution of South African Jewry; Pres. G. LEISSNER; Chair. M. SMITH; Nat. Dir S. KOPELOWITZ.

The Press

In December 1993 legislation was adopted that provided for the establishment of an Independent Media Commission, which was to ensure the impartiality of the press.

Note: the publications listed below are grouped according to the territorial divisions that were in force prior to 27 April 1994.

Bureau of Information: Midtown Bldg, cnr Vermeulen and Pretorius Sts, Pretoria; Private Bag X745, Pretoria 0001; tel. (12) 3142911; fax (12) 3233831; govt agency.

Directorate of Publications: Pleinpark Bldg, 13th Floor, Plein St, Cape Town; Private Bag X9069, Cape Town 8000; tel. (21) 456518; fax (21) 456511; f. 1974; Govt agency responsible under Publications Act 1974 for censorship of films and video cassettes and the examination of publs submitted to it for adjudication; Dir Prof. Dr A. COETZEE.

South African Media Council: Nedbank Gardens, 8th Floor, 33 Bath Ave, Rosebank 2196; POB 31559, Braamfontein; tel. (11) 4032878; fax (11) 4032879; f. 1983 by the Newspaper Press Union and the Conf. of Editors to promote press freedom; 14 media and 14 public representatives; Chair. Prof. KOBUS VAN ROOYEN.

DAILIES

Cape Province

The Argus: 122 St George's St, POB 56, Cape Town 8000; tel. (21) 4884911; telex 527383; fax (21) 4884075; f. 1857; evening; English; independent; Editor-in-Chief ANDREW DRYSDALE; circ. 102,000.

Die Burger: 40 Heerengracht, POB 692, Cape Town 8000; tel. (21) 4062222; telex 527751; fax (21) 4062913; f. 1915; morning; Afrikaans; Editor E. DOMMISSE; circ. 89,600 (Mon.–Fri.), 95,800 (Sat.).

Die Burger (Oos-Kaap): 52 Cawood St, POB 525, Port Elizabeth 6000; tel. (41) 542431; fax (41) 545166; f. 1937; morning; Afrikaans; Editor J. CROWTHER; circ. 11,400.

Cape Times: Newspaper House, 122 St George's St, POB 56, Cape Town 8000; tel. (21) 4884911; fax (21) 4884717; f. 1876; morning; English; Editor KOOS VIVIERS; circ. 61,000.

Daily Dispatch: 33 Caxton St, POB 131, East London 5200; tel. (431) 430010; telex 250678; fax (431) 435159; f. 1872; morning; English; Editor Prof. G. STEWART; circ. 35,940.

Diamond Fields Advertiser: POB 610, Kimberley 8300; tel. (531) 26261; telex 280229; fax (531) 25881; morning; English; Editor Prof. J. G. WILLIAMS; circ. 8,000.

Eastern Province Herald: Newspaper House, 19 Baakens St, POB 1117, Port Elizabeth 6000; tel. (41) 5047911; telex 243351; fax (41) 554966; f. 1845; morning; English; Editor DEREK SMITH; circ. 30,000 (Mon.–Fri.), 25,000 (Sat.).

Evening Post: Newspaper House, 19 Baakens St, POB 1121, Port Elizabeth 6000; tel. (41) 5047911; telex 243351; fax (41) 554966; f. 1950; evening; English; Editor CLIFF FOSTER; circ. 19,400.

Natal

The Daily News: 18 Osborne St, Greyville 4001, POB 47549, Greyville 4023; tel. (31) 3082100; fax (31) 3082111; f. 1878; Mon.-Fri., evening; English; Editor M. VAN SCHOOR; circ. 94,000.

Natal Mercury: 18 Osborne St, Greyville, POB 950, Durban 4001; tel. (31) 3082300; telex 622301; fax (31) 3082333; f. 1852; morning; English; Editor J. PATTEN; circ. 61,000.

Natal Witness: 244 Longmarket St, POB 362, Pietermaritzburg 3200; tel. (331) 942011; telex 643385; fax (331) 940468; f. 1846; morning; English; Editor D. J. WILLERS; circ. 28,000.

Orange Free State

Die Volksblad: 79 Voortrekker St, POB 267, Bloemfontein 9300; tel. (51) 473351; telex 267612; fax (51) 306949; f. 1904; morning; Afrikaans; Editor JOHAN DE WET; circ. 27,000 (Mon.–Fri.), 21,000 (Sat.).

Transvaal

Beeld: 32 Miller St, POB 5425, Johannesburg 2000; tel. (11) 4021460; fax (11) 4021871; f. 1974; morning; Afrikaans; Editor SARIE DE SWART; circ. 100,000 (Mon.–Fri.), 81,000 (Sat.).

Business Day: 11 Diagonal St, POB 1138, Johannesburg 2000; tel. (11) 4972711; telex 488921; fax (11) 8360805; f. 1985; morning; English; financial; Editor JIM JONES; circ. 32,890.

The Citizen: POB 7712, Johannesburg 2000; tel. (11) 4022900; telex 424053; fax (11) 4026862; f. 1976; morning; English; Editor M. A. JOHNSON; circ. 14,000 (Mon.–Fri.), 108,000 (Sat.).

The Pretoria News: 216 Vermeulen St, Pretoria 0002; tel. (12) 3255382; telex 322174; fax (12) 3257300; f. 1898; evening; English; Editor D. DU PLESSIS; circ. 25,822 (Mon.–Fri.), 15,442 (Sat.).

Rustenburg Herald: 28 Steen St, POB 2043, Rustenburg 0300; tel. (1421) 28329; fax (1421) 28350; f. 1924; English and Afrikaans; Editor D. COETSEE; circ. 11,000.

Sowetan: 61 Commando Rd, Industria West, POB 6663, Johannesburg 2000; tel. (11) 4740128; telex 5425992; fax (11) 4748834; f. 1981; Mon.–Fri.; English; Editor Z. AGGREY KLAASTE; circ. 225,000.

The Star: 47 Sauer St, POB 1014, Johannesburg 2000; tel. (11) 6339111; telex 487083; fax (11) 8368398; f. 1887; English; Editor RICHARD S. STEYN; circ. 209,000 (Mon.–Fri.), 156,000 (Sat.), 89,000 (Sun.).

Transvaaler: 28 Height St, Doornfontein, POB 845, Johannesburg 2000; tel. (11) 7769111; fax (11) 4020037; afternoon; Afrikaans; Editor G. JOHNSON; circ. 40,000.

WEEKLIES AND FORTNIGHTLIES

Cape Province

Eikestadnuus: 44 Alexander St, POB 28, Stellenbosch 7600; tel. (2231) 72840; fax (2231) 99538; weekly; English and Afrikaans; Editor R. GERBER; circ. 7,000.

Fair Lady: 40 Heerengracht, POB 1802, Cape Town 8000; tel. (21) 4062044; telex 527751; fax (21) 4062930; fortnightly; English; Editor LIZ BUTLER; circ. 150,284.

Die Gemsbok: POB 60, Upington 8800; tel. 27017; fax 24055; English and Afrikaans; Editor D. JONES; circ. 8,000.

Huisgenoot: 40 Heerengracht, POB 1802, Cape Town 8000; tel. (21) 4062115; telex 527751; fax (21) 4062937; f. 1916; weekly; Afrikaans; Editor NIEL HAMMANN; circ. 542,000.

Imvo Zabantsundu (Black Opinion): 35 Edes St, POB 190, King William's Town 5600; tel. (433) 23550; fax (433) 33865; f. 1884; weekly; English and Xhosa; Editor D. J. DE VILLIERS; circ. 31,000.

Sarie: POB 1802, Cape Town 8000; tel. (21) 4062203; telex 527751; fax (21) 4062913; fortnightly; Afrikaans; women's interest; Editor A. ROSSOUW; circ. 227,000.

South: 6 Russel St, Castle Mews, Woodstock 7925; POB 13094, Sir Lowry Rd 7900; tel. (21) 4622012; fax (21) 4615407; weekly; black interest; Editor Dr GUY BERGER; circ. 25,000.

The Southern Cross: POB 2372, Cape Town 8001; tel. (21) 455007; fax (21) 453850; f. 1920; weekly; English; Roman Catholic; Editor B. CONNOR; circ. 10,000.

Tyger-Burger: 40 Heerengracht, POB 2271, Cape Town 8000; tel. (21) 4062121; telex 527751; fax (21) 4062913; weekly; Afrikaans and English; Editor BAREND VENTER.

The Weekend Argus: 122 St George's St, POB 56, Cape Town 8000; tel. (21) 4884911; telex 527383; fax (21) 4884075; f. 1857; weekly; English; Editor JONATHAN HOBDAY; circ. 128,500.

Weekend Post: POB 1141, Port Elizabeth 6000; tel. (41) 523480; telex 243047; fax (41) 563315; English; Editor N. M. WOUDBERG; circ. 38,000.

You Magazine: 40 Heerengracht, POB 7167, Cape Town 8000; tel. (21) 4062115; telex 527751; fax (21) 4062915; f. 1987; weekly; English; Editor-in-Chief NIGEL HAMMAN; circ. 232,000.

Natal

Farmers' Weekly: POB 32083, Mobeni 4060; tel. (31) 422041; telex 624422; fax (31) 426068; f. 1911; weekly; agriculture and horticulture; Editor M. FISHER; circ. 17,000.

Ilanga: 128 Umgeni Rd, POB 2159, Durban 4000; tel. (31) 3094350; fax (31) 3091938; f. 1903; 2 a week; Zulu; Editor P. G. MTHEMBU; circ. 126,000.

Keur: POB 32083, Mobeni 4060; tel. (31) 422041; telex 5624422; fax (31) 426068; f. 1967; Afrikaans; Editor CARL STEYN; circ. 91,000.

Ladysmith Gazette: POB 10019, Ladysmith 3370; tel. (361) 26801; fax (361) 22283; f. 1902; weekly; English, Afrikaans and Zulu; Editor BEVIS FAIRBROTHER; circ. 7,000.

Personality: POB 32083, Mobeni 4060; tel. (31) 422041; telex 624422; fax (31) 426068; weekly; Editor WENDY CHRISTOPHER; circ. 107,000.

Post Natal: 18 Osborne St, Greyville 4001, POB 47549, Greyville 4023; tel. (31) 3082400; fax (31) 3082427; f. 1935; weekly; English; general; Editor BRIGLALL RAMGUTHEE; circ. 51,000.

Rooi Rose: POB 32083, Mobeni 4060; tel. (31) 422041; telex 624422; fax (31) 426068; Afrikaans; fortnightly; women's interest; Editor J. KRUGER; circ. 165,000.

Saturday News: 18 Osborne St, Greyville 4001, POB 47549, Greyville 4023; tel. (31) 3082100; fax (31) 3082111; f. 1878; English; Editor M. VAN SCHOOR; circ. 84,000.

Scope: POB 32083, Mobeni 4060; tel. (31) 422041; telex 5624422; fax (31) 426068; f. 1966; fortnightly; general interest for men; Editor D. MULLANY; circ. 153,292.

Sunday Tribune: 18 Osborne St, POB 47549, Greyville 4023; tel. (31) 3082100; telex 622301; fax (31) 3082715; f. 1937; English; weekly; Editor DAVID WIGHTMAN; circ. 125,710.

Umafrika: POB 11002, Mariannhill 3601; tel. (31) 7002720; fax (31) 7003707; f. 1911; weekly; Zulu and English; Editor CYRIL MADLALA; circ. 60,000.

Orange Free State

Vista: POB 1027, Welkom 9460; tel. (57) 3571304; fax (57) 3532427; f. 1971; 2 a week; English and Afrikaans; Editor P. Gouws; circ. 26,000 (Tues.), 26,000 (Fri.).

Transvaal

African Jewish Newspaper: POB 6169, Johannesburg 2000; tel. (11) 6468292; f. 1931; weekly; Yiddish; Editor Levi Shalit.

Die Afrikaner: POB 1888, Pretoria 0001; tel. (12) 3423410; fax (12) 3423417; f. 1970; Wednesday; organ of Herstigte Nasionale Party; Editors A. J. H. Ferguson, H. van de Graaf; circ. 10,000.

Benoni City Times en Oosrandse Nuus: 28 Woburn Ave, POB 494, Benoni 1500; tel. (11) 8451680; telex 748942; fax (11) 4224796; English and Afrikaans; Editor H. Lee; circ. 27,000.

City Press: POB 3413, Johannesburg 2000; tel. (11) 4021632; fax (11) 4026662; f. 1983; weekly; English; Editor Khulu Sibiya; circ. 160,000.

Finance Week: Private Bag 78816, Sandton 2146; tel. (11) 4440555; fax (11) 4440424; f. 1979; Editor A. J. Greenblo; circ. 16,000.

Financial Mail: 11 Diagonal St, POB 9959, Johannesburg 2000; tel. (11) 4972711; telex 488921; fax (11) 8341686; weekly; English; Editor N. Bruce; circ. 32,000.

The Herald Times: POB 31015, Braamfontein 2017; tel. (11) 8876500; telex 431078; weekly; Jewish interest; Man. Dir R. Shapiro; circ. 5,000.

Mining Week: Johannesburg; tel. (11) 7892144; telex 422125; f. 1979; fortnightly; Editor Val Pienaar; circ. 10,000.

The New Nation: POB 10674, Johannesburg 2000; tel. (11) 3332721; telex 482226; fax (11) 3332733; f. 1986; weekly; English; Editor Zwelakhe Sisulu; circ. 64,000.

Die Noord-Transvaler: POB 220, Ladanna, Pietersburg 0704; tel. (1521) 931831; fax (1521) 932586; weekly; Afrikaans; Editor A. Buys; circ. 12,000.

Northern Review: 16 Grobler St, POB 45, Pietersburg 0700; tel. (1521) 72371; fax (1521) 915148; weekly; English and Afrikaans; Editor R. S. de Jager; circ. 8,000.

Potchefstroom and Ventersdorp Herald: POB 515, Potchefstroom 2520; tel. (148) 930750; fax (148) 930750; f. 1908; 2 a week; English and Afrikaans; Editor H. Stander; Man. G. Wessels; circ. 4,000 (Tues.), 5,000 (Fri.).

Rapport: POB 8422, Johannesburg 2000; tel. (11) 4022620; telex 422027; fax (11) 4026163; f. 1970; weekly; Afrikaans; Editor Izak de Villiers; circ. 353,000.

South African Digest: Private Bag X745, Pretoria 0001; tel. (12) 3142911; telex 322499; publ. by Bureau for Information; fortnightly; Editor Terence Burke.

South African Industrial Week: Johannesburg; Man. Editor W. Mastingle; circ. 19,000.

Springs and Brakpan Advertiser: POB 138, Springs 1560; tel. (11) 8121600; fax (11) 8121908; English and Afrikaans; Editor L. Neill; circ. 11,000.

Sunday Times: POB 1090, Johannesburg 2000; tel. (11) 4972711; telex 488921; fax (11) 4972664; English; Editor K. F. Owen; circ. 564,000.

Vaalweekblad: 27 Ekspa Bldg, D.F. Malan St, POB 351, Vanderbijlpark 1900; tel. (16) 817010; fax (16) 810604; weekly; Afrikaans and English; Editor J. J. Dominicus; circ. 12,000.

Die Voorligter: POB 1444, Cape Town 8000; f. 1937; journal of the Dutch Reformed Church of South Africa; Editor Dr F. M. Gaum; circ. 133,000.

Vrye Weekblad: 153 Bree St, Newtown, Johannesburg 2001; tel. (11) 8362151; fax (11) 8385901; f. 1988; weekly; Afrikaans; anti-apartheid; Editor Max du Preez; circ. 13,000.

Weekly Mail and Guardian: 139 Smit St, Braamfontein, Johannesburg; POB 32362, Braamfontein 2017; tel. (11) 4037111; telex 486379; fax (11) 4031025; f. 1985; English; Editors Anton Harber, Irwin Manoim; circ. 30,000.

MONTHLIES

Cape Province

Boxing World: Unit 17, Park St, POB 164, Steenberg 7945; tel. 7015070; fax 7015863; Editor Bert Blewett; circ. 10,000.

Car: POB 180, Howard Place 7450; tel. (21) 5311391; telex 526933; (21) fax 5313333; Editor D. J. Trebett; circ. 138,000.

Drum: POB 784696, Sandton 2146; tel. (11) 7837227; fax (11) 7838822; f. 1951; English; Editor Barney Cohen; circ. 135,850 in southern Africa.

Femina: 2 the Avalon, POB 3647, Cape Town 8000; tel. (21) 4623070; telex 522991; fax (21) 4612500; Editor Jane Raphaely; circ. 109,321.

Finansies & Tegniek: POB 53171, Troyville 2139; tel. (11) 4026372; fax (11) 4041701; Afrikaans; Editor G. L. Marais; circ. 20,046.

Learning Roots: POB 1161, Cape Town 8000; tel. (21) 6968414; fax (21) 6968346; f. 1980; newsletter for black schools in the Western Cape; circ. 50,000.

Nursing RSA Verpleging: Private Bag XI, Pinelands 7430; tel. (21) 5312691; fax (21) 5314126; f. 1986; professional nursing journal; Editor Lillian Medlin; circ. 10,000.

Reader's Digest (South African Edition): POB 2677, Cape Town 8000; tel. (21) 254460; telex 520333; fax (21) 4191090; English; Editor-in-Chief W. Pankhurst; circ. 371,000.

South African Medical Journal: Private Bag XI, Pinelands 7430; tel. (21) 5313081; fax (21) 5314126; f. 1926; publ. by the Medical Asscn of South Africa; Editor Dr Daniel J. Ncayiyana; circ. 20,000.

Die Unie: POB 196, Cape Town 8000; tel. (21) 4616340; fax (21) 4619238; f. 1905; educational; publ. by the South African Teachers' Union; Editor M. J. L. Olivier; circ. 8,000.

Woman's Value: POB 1802, Cape Town 8000; tel. (21) 4062205; telex 527751; fax (21) 4062929; English; Editor Rieta Burgers; circ. 146,000.

Wynboer: K. W. V. Van ZA Bpkt, POB 528, Suider-Paarl 7624; tel. (2211) 73267; telex 527107; fax (2211) 631562; f. 1931; viticulture and the wine and spirit industry; Editor Henry Hopkins; circ. 10,000.

Natal

Bona: POB 32083, Mobeni 4060; tel. (31) 422041; telex 624422; fax (31) 426068; f. 1956; English, Sotho, Xhosa and Zulu; Editor R. Baker; circ. 263,000.

Home Front: POB 2549, Durban 4000; tel. (31) 3071574; fax (31) 3054148; f. 1928; ex-servicemen's magazine; Editor Reg Sweet; circ. 14,000.

Living and Loving: POB 32083, Mobeni 4060; tel. (31) 422041; telex 624422; fax (31) 426068; English; Editor Angela Still; circ. 113,000.

South African Garden and Home: POB 32083, Mobeni 4060; tel. (31) 422041; telex 624422; fax (31) 426068; f. 1947; Editor Margaret Wasserfall; circ. 146,070.

Tempo: POB 16, Pinetown 3600; tel. (31) 7013225; telex 624750; fax (31)729830; f. 1984; weekly; Afrikaans; Editor F. H. de Lange; circ. 7,000.

World Airnews: POB 35082, Northway, Durban 4065; tel. (31) 841319; fax (31) 837115; f. 1973; aviation news; Editor T. Chalmers; circ. 13,000.

Your Family: POB 32083, Mobeni 4060; tel. (31) 422041; telex 624422; fax (31) 426068; f. 1973; English; cooking, crafts, DIY; Editor Angela Waller-Paton; circ. 216,000.

Orange Free State

Wamba: POB 1097, Bloemfontein; educational; publ. in seven vernacular languages; Editor C. P. Senyatsi.

Transvaal

Centre News: Johannesburg; tel. (11) 5591781; English; publ. by R.J.J. Publications; circ. 30,000.

The Mail of Rosebank News: Johannesburg; tel. (11) 3391781; English; publ. by R.J.J. Publications; circ. 40,000.

Nursing News: POB 1280, Pretoria 0001; tel. (12) 3432315; fax (12) 3440750; f. 1978; newspaper of the South African Nursing Asscn; English and Afrikaans; circ. 110,000.

Pace: POB 48985, Roosevelt Park 2129; tel. (11) 8890600; fax (11) 8805942; Man. Editor Force Koshani; circ. 131,000.

Postal and Telkom Herald: POB 9186, Johannesburg 2000; tel. (11) 7255422; fax (11) 7256540; f. 1903; English and Afrikaans; Staff Asscn (Workers' Union); Editor F. A. Gerber; circ. 13,000.

Postel: POB 925, Pretoria 0001; tel. (12) 2932419; fax (12) 3235446; f. 1970; English and Afrikaans; telecom research, philately, computers; Editor Werna Hough; circ. 50,000.

Technobrief: POB 395, Pretoria 0001; tel (12) 8414304; fax (12) 8413789; f. 1991; publ. by the Council for Scientific and Industrial Research (CSIR); Editor Hoepel Scheepers; circ. 15,500.

QUARTERLIES

Cape Province

New Era: Cape Town.

South African Law Journal: POB 30, Cape Town 8000; tel. (2721) 7975101; fax (2721) 7627424; f. 1884; Editor Ellison Kahn; circ. 2,500.

Transvaal

Lantern: POB 1758, Pretoria 0001; tel. (12) 3226404; fax (12) 3207803; f. 1952; publ. by the Foundation for Education, Science and Tech.; Chief Editor R. van Graan; circ. 5,000.

The Motorist/Die Motoris: POB 31015, Braamfontein 2017; tel. (11) 8876500; fax (11) 8876551; f. 1966; journal of the Automobile Asscn of SA; Editor MICHAEL WANG; circ. 184,000.

South African Journal of Economics: 4-44 EBW Bldg, University of Pretoria, Pretoria 0002; tel. (12) 4203525; fax (12) 437589; English and Afrikaans; Man. Editor Prof. D. J. J. BOTHA.

NEWS AGENCIES

South African Press Association: Kine Centre, 1st Floor, Commissioner St, POB 7766, Johannesburg 2000; tel. (11) 3310661; telex 488061; fax (11) 3317473; f. 1938; 40 mems; Chair. J. S. CRAIB; Man. W. J. H. VAN GILS; Editor MARK A. VAN DER VELDEN.

Foreign Bureaux

Agence France-Presse (AFP): Nixdorf Centre, 6th Floor, 37 Stanley Ave, Milpark; POB 3462, Johannesburg 2000; tel. (11) 4822170; telex 422660; fax (11) 7268756; Bureau Chief MARC HUTTEN.

Agencia EFE (Spain): Johannesburg; Chief JOSÉ BUJANDA PAN.

Agenzia Nazionale Stampa Associata (ANSA) (Italy): POB 32312, Camps Bay, Cape Town 8040; tel. (21) 7903991; telex 522211; fax (21) 7904444; Correspondent LICINIO GERMINI.

Associated Press (AP) (USA): 15 Napier St, Richmond, Johannesburg 2092; tel. (11) 7267022; fax (11) 7267834; Bureau Chief JOHN DANISZEWSKI.

Central News Agency (Taiwan): Kine Centre, 1st Floor, 141 Commissioner St, Johannesburg 2001; tel. (11) 3316654; fax (11)3319463; Chief CHANG JERSHONG.

Deutsche Presse-Agentur (dpa) (Germany): 96 Jorrisen St, POB 32521, Braamfontein 2017; tel. (11) 3391148; telex 426038; Chief GEORGE SPIEKER.

Informatsionnoye Telegrafnoye Agentstvo Rossii—Telegrafnoye Agentstvo Suverennykh Stran (ITAR—TASS) (Russia): Johannesburg.

Inter-Press Service (IPS) (Italy): POB 260425, Excom 2023, Johannesburg; Correspondent NEIL LEWIS.

Kyodo News Service (Japan): Royal St Mary's Bldg, 4th Floor, 85 Eloff St, POB 7772, Johannesburg 2000; tel. (11) 3334207; telex 483731; fax (11) 3378918; Rep. NORIO YATAKA.

Reuters Ltd (UK): 1 Park Rd, Richmond, Johannesburg 2092; tel. (11) 4821003; fax (11) 4821097; Bureau Chief (News and Television) RODNEY PINDER.

United Press International (UPI) (USA): Nedbank Centre, 2nd Floor, POB 32661, Braamfontein 2017; tel. (11) 4033910; telex 423428; fax (11) 4033914; Bureau Chief PATRICK COLLINS.

PRESS ASSOCIATION

Newspaper Press Union of South Africa: Nedbank Gardens, 8th Floor, 33 Bath Ave, Rosebank 2196; tel. (21) 3396344; fax (21) 3393393; f. 1882; 220 mems; Pres. R. H. PAULSON; Gen. Man. P. S. C. POTÉ.

Publishers

Acorn Books: POB 4845, Randburg 2125; tel. (11) 8805768; fax (11) 8805768; f. 1985; general, natural history.

C. F. Albertyn (Pty) Ltd: Andmar Bldg, Van Ryneveld St, Stellenbosch 7600; tel. (2231) 71202; f. 1971; encyclopaedias; Editorial Man. A. TONDER.

Amagi Publications: Bisho.

BLAC Publishing House: POB 17, Athlone, Cape Town; f. 1974; general fiction, poetry; Man. Dir JAMES MATTHEWS.

Jonathan Ball Publishers: POB 2105, Parklands 2121; tel. (11) 8808150; fax (11) 8807446; history, politics, business, leisure.

Bible Society of South Africa: POB 6215, Roggebaai 8012; tel. (21) 212040; telex 527964; fax (21) 4194846; f. 1820; Gen. Sec. Dr D. TOLMIE.

Bok Books: POB 20194, Durban North 4016; tel. (31) 5792177; (31) fax 5792407.

Book Promotions (Pty) Ltd: POB 23320, Claremont 7735; tel. (21) 619100; fax (21) 644868; Man. Dir. R. MANSELL.

Book Studio (Pty) Ltd: POB 121, Hout Bay 7872.

Books of Africa (Pty) Ltd: POB 10, Muizenberg 7950; tel. (21) 888316; f. 1947; biography, history, Africana, art; Man. Dir T. V. BULPIN.

Brenthurst Press (Pty) Ltd: POB 87184, Houghton 2041; tel. (11) 6466024; fax (11) 4861651; f. 1974; Africana; Man. Editor Mrs C. KEMP.

Butterworth Publishers (Pty) Ltd: POB 792, Durban 4000; tel. (31) 294247; telex 620730; fax (31) 283255; Man. Dir WILLIAM J. LAST.

Clever Books: POB 20113, Alkantrant 0005.

College of Careers/Faircare Books: POB 2081, Cape Town 8000; tel. (21) 452041; f. 1946; general, educational; Man. Dir RICHARD S. POOLER.

Cornea Publications: Welgemoed.

CUM Books: POB 1599, Vereeniging 1930; tel. (16) 214781; fax (16) 211748.

Da Gama Publishers (Pty) Ltd: M.W.U. Bldg, 6th Floor, 19 Melle St, Braamfontein 2017; tel. (11) 4033763; fax (11) 4031263; travel; Publr DERMOT SWAINE.

Digma Publications: POB 95466, Waterkloof 0145; tel. (11) 3463840; fax (11) 3463845.

A. Donker (Pty) Ltd: POB 2105, Parklands 2121; tel. (11) 8808150; fax (11) 8807446.

Dreyer Printers and Publishers: POB 286, Bloemfontein 9300; tel. (51) 479001; telex 267131; fax (51) 471281.

Educational Workshop: POB 26347, Hout Bay 7872; pre-school educational.

Educum Publishers: POB 9573, Johannesburg 2000.

Eksamenhulp: POB 55555, Arcadia 0007.

Fisichem Publishers: POB 6052, Stellenbosch 7600.

Flesch, W. J., & Partners: 4 Gordon St, Gardens, POB 3473, Cape Town 8000; tel. (21) 4617472; fax (21) 4613758; f. 1954; Prin. Officer S. FLESCH.

Fortress Publishers: POB 679, Germiston 1400; tel. (11) 8276205; fax (11) 8738370; f. 1973; military history, biographies, financial; Man. Dir I. UYS.

T. W. Griggs & Co: 341 West St, Durban 4001; tel. (31) 3048571; Africana.

F.J.N. Harman Publishers: Menlo Park; tel. (12) 469575; f. 1981; educational; Man. Dir F. J. N. HARMAN.

Harper Collins Publishers (SA) (Pty) Ltd: POB 33977, Jeppestown 2043; tel. (11) 6222900; fax (11) 6223553; f. 1970; book distributors; Man. Dir M. J. EDWARDS.

HAUM: Prima Park 4 and 6, cnr Klosser and King Edward Rds, Porow 7500; tel. (21) 926123; f. 1894; Man. C. J. HAGE. Subsidiaries include:

> **De Jager-HAUM Publishers:** POB 629, Pretoria 0001; tel. (12) 3228474; fax (12) 3222424; f. 1974; general, medical and university textbooks, school textbooks and books in African languages; Man. Dir C. RICHTER.
>
> **HAUM UUB/UPB:** POB 29, Stellenbosch 7600; tel. (2231) 70337; fax (2231) 2975; educational and children's; Man. Dir B. B. LIEBENBERG.
>
> **Juventus Publishers:** POB 629, Pretoria 0001; tel. (12) 3220806; fax (12) 3222424; f. 1980; juvenile, educational; Man. MARIETJIE COETZEE.

Heinemann Publishers SA (Pty) Ltd: POB 2017, Houghton 2041; educational; tel. (11) 4833292; fax (11) 7287665; Man. Dir K. KROEGER.

Home Economics Publishers: POB 7091, Stellenbosch 7600; 74630.

Human and Rousseau (Pty) Ltd: POB 5050, Cape Town 8000; tel. (21) 251280; fax (21) 4192619; f. 1959; English and Afrikaans; general trade, college handbooks; Man. Dir. J. J. HUMAN.

Incipit Publishers: POB 28754, Sunnyside, Pretoria 0132; tel. and fax (12) 463802; f. 1987; music; Man. MARIANNE FEENSTRA.

Inter-Kampus Publications: Baillie Park; study aids.

Juta and Co Ltd: POB 14373, Kenwyn 7790; tel. (11) 7975101; fax (11) 7615010; f. 1853; legal, technical, academic, educational; Man. Dir J. E. DUNCAN.

Klipbok Publishers: POB 170, Durbanville 7550.

Knowledge Unlimited (Pty) Ltd: POB 781337; Sandton 2146; tel. (11) 3142970; fax (11) 3142984; children's fiction, educational; Man. Dir MIKE JACKLIN.

Konsensus Publishers: Orion St 213, Waterkloof 0180.

Lemur Books (Pty) Ltd: POB 1645, Alberton 1450; tel. (11) 9072029; fax (11) 8690890; military, political, history, hunting, general; Man. Dir F. LATEGAN.

Lexicon Publishers (Pty) Ltd: POB 371, Isando 1600, tel. (11) 9741181; fax (11) 9744311; education and general; Man. Dir J. SAVAGE.

Lovedale Press: Private Bag X1346, Alice; tel. (0404) 31135; fax (0404) 31871; f. 1841; Gen. Man. Rev. B. B. FINCA.

Lux Verbi: POB 1822, Cape Town 8000; tel. (21) 253505; telex 526922; fax (21) 4191865; Exec. Chair. W. J. VAN ZIJL.

Macdonald Purnell (Pty) Ltd: POB 51401, Randburg 2125; tel. (11) 7875830; telex 424985; South African flora, fauna, geography and history; Man. Dir E. ANDERSON.

Marler Publications (Pty) Ltd: POB 27815, Sunnyside, Pretoria 0132; tel. (12) 573770; f. 1987; educational; Man. Dir C. J. MULLER.

Maskew Miller Longman (Pty) Ltd: Howard Drive, Pinelands 7405, POB 396, Cape Town 8000; tel. (21) 5317750; telex 5726053; fax (21) 5314049; f. 1983; educational and general; Man. Dir M. A. PEACOCK.

Methodist Publishing House: POB 708, Cape Town 8000; tel. (21) 4618214; fax (21) 4618249; religious and theology; Gen. Man. D. R. LEVERTON.

Nasionale Boekhandel: POB 122, Parow 7500, Cape Province; tel. (21) 5911131; telex 526951; fiction, general, educational, academic; English, Afrikaans and several African languages; Man. Dir P. J. BOTMA.

Nasou Ltd: POB 5197, Cape Town 8000; tel. (21) 4063313; fax (21) 4062922; educational; Gen. Man. L. I. NAUDÉ.

N.G. Kerkboekhandel (Pty) Ltd: POB 3068, Halfway House 1685; tel. (21) 3153647; fax (21) 3152757; f. 1947; Sen. Publr NEELS DU PLOOY.

Oudiovista Productions (Pty) Ltd: Parow; tel. (21) 5911131; telex 527751; Man. Dir P. J. BOTMA.

Owen Burgess Publications (Pty) Ltd: Hillcrest.

Oxford University Press: Harrington House, 37 Barrack St, POB 1141, Cape Town 8000; tel. (21) 457266; fax (21) 457265; f. 1914; Man. Dir KATE MCCALLUM.

Perskor Publishers: POB 845, Johannesburg 2000; tel. (11) 7769111; telex 83561; f. 1940; general and educational; Gen. Man. F. WESSELS.

David Philip Publishers (Pty) Ltd: POB 23408, Claremont 7735; tel. (21) 644136; fax (21) 643358; f. 1971; general, academic, literature, reference, fiction, juvenile; Dirs D. H. PHILIP, M. PHILIP, R. MARTIN, B. IMPEY.

Pretoria Boekhandel: POB 23334, Innesdale, Pretoria 0031; tel. (12) 761531; f. 1971; Prin. Officer L. S. VAN DER WALT.

Random House SA (Pty) Ltd: POB 337, Bergvlei, Sandton 2012; tel. (11) 7862983; telex 423981; fax (11) 8875077; f. 1966 as Century Hutchinson (SA); Man. Dir S. JOHNSON.

Ravan Press (Pty) Ltd: POB 145, Randburg 2125; tel. (11) 7897636; fax (11) 7897653; f. 1972; political, sociological, literary, educational and children's; Man. Dir GLENN MOSS.

Saayman and Weber (Pty) Ltd: POB 673, Kaapstad 8000; f. 1980.

Sasavona Publishers and Booksellers: Private Bag X8, Braamfontein 2017; tel. (11) 4032502; Northern Sotho, Tshwa, Tsonga, Tswana, Venda and Zulu; Man. A. E. KALTENRIEDER.

Shuter and Shooter (Pty) Ltd: 199 Pietermaritz St, Pietermaritzburg 3201; POB 109, Pietermaritzburg 3200; tel. (331) 946830; fax (331) 427419; f. 1921; educational, general and African languages; Man. Dir D. F. RYDER.

The Struik Publishing Group (Pty) Ltd: POB 1144, Cape Town 8000; tel. (21) 4624360; fax (21) 4619378; Dirs G. STRUIK, A. D. L. CRUZEN, M. C. H. JAMES, C. M. HANLEY, N. D. PRYKE, J. D. WILKINS, J. L. SCHOEMAN, A. S. VERSCHOYLE.

Study Aids Ltd: 13 Darrock Ave, Albemarle Park, Germiston 1401; study aids.

Hans Strydom Publishers: Private Bag 10, Mellville 2109.

Sunray Publishers: 96 Queen St, Durban 4001; tel. (31) 3052543.

Tafelberg Publishers Ltd: 28 Wale St, POB 879, Cape Town 8000; tel. (21) 241320; fax (21) 242510; f. 1950; children's, young persons', fiction and non-fiction, hobbies; Gen. Man. J. J. LABUSCHAGNE.

Thomson Publications: Johannesburg 2000; tel. (11) 7892144; telex 422125; fax (11) 7893196; f. 1948; trade and technical; Man. Dir JOE M. BRADY.

UCCSA Publications Dept: POB 31083, Braamfontein 2017; tel. (11) 8360065; f. 1946; Gen. Man. W. WESTENBORG.

University of Natal Press: POB 375, Pietermaritzburg 3200; tel. (331) 2605225; fax (331) 2605599; Man. Dir M. P. MOBERLY.

University of South Africa: POB 392, Pretoria 0001; tel. (12) 4293111; telex 350068; fax (12) 4293221; Registrar M. H. STOCKHOFF.

University Publishers and Booksellers (Pty) Ltd: POB 29, Stellenbosch 7599; tel. (21) 8870337; fax (21) 8832975; educational; Man. Dir B. B. LIEBENBERG.

Van der Walt and Son, J. P. (Pty) Ltd: POB 123, Pretoria 0001; tel. (12) 3252100; fax (12) 3255498; f. 1947; general; Man. Dir C. J. STEENKAMP.

Chris van Rensburg Publications (Pty) Ltd: POB 29159, Mellville 2109; tel. (31) 7264350; yearbooks, general; Man. Dir. C. C. VAN RENSBURG.

Van Schaik, J. L. Publishers: 1064 Arcadia St, Hatfield 0083; tel. (11) 3422765; fax (11) 433563; f. 1914; reference, general, educational; English, Afrikaans and vernaculars; Gen. Man. G. LOUW.

Via Afrika Ltd: POB 151, Pretoria 0001; tel. (12) 3421964; fax (12) 3421964; f. 1970; educational, technical and general; Gen. Man. D. SCHROEDER.

Waterkant Publishers: POB 4539, Cape Town 8000; tel. (21) 215540; fax (21) 4191865; f. 1980; Exec. Chair. W. J. VAN ZIJL.

Witwatersrand University Press: Private Bag 3, Witwatersrand 2050; tel. (11) 7162023; telex 427125; fax (11) 3393559; f. 1923; academic; Head EVE HORWITZ.

PUBLISHERS' ASSOCIATION

Publishers' Association of South Africa: Private Bag 91932, Auckland Park 2092; tel. (11) 7267470; fax (11) 4823409; f. 1992; represents publrs in dealing with govt depts, local authorities and other institutions; Chair. M. A. PEACOCK; Sec. K. MCCALLUM.

Radio and Television

In 1991, according to UNESCO, there were an estimated 11.8m. radio receivers and 3.8m. television receivers in use.

In December 1993 legislation providing for the establishment of an Independent Broadcasting Authority was adopted, effectively ending state control of radio and television. All stations were required to reapply for licences.

South African Broadcasting Corporation (SABC): Private Bag X1, Auckland Park 2006; tel. (11) 7149111; telex 424116; fax (11) 7143106; f. 1936; statutory body; revenue from licences and advertising; operates 22 internal radio services broadcasting in 11 languages, one external radio service broadcasting in seven languages, and three TV channels broadcasting in seven languages; Chair. of Bd Dr IVY MATSEPE-CASABURRI; CEO WYNAND HARMSE.

RADIO

SABC-Radio: Private Bag X1, Auckland Park 2006; tel. (11) 7149111; telex 424116; fax (11) 7143106.

Domestic Services

Radio South Africa; Afrikaans Stereo; Radio 5; Radio Orion; Radio 2000; Highveld Stereo; Good Hope Stereo; Radio Kontrei; RPN Stereo; Jacaranda Stereo; Radio Algoa (regional services); Radio Lotus (Indian service in English); Radio Metro (African service in English); Radio Lebowa; Radio Ndebele; Radio Sesotho; Setswana Stereo; Radio Swazi; Radio Tsonga; Radio Xhosa; Radio Zulu.

External Service

Channel Africa Radio: POB 91313, Auckland Park 2006; tel. (11) 7142551; fax (11) 7142546; f. 1966; SABC's external service; broadcasts 217 hours per week in Chichewa, English, French, Lozi, Portuguese, Swahili and Tsonga to Africa; Exec. Editor LIONEL WILLIAMS.

TELEVISION

SABC-Television: Private Bag X41, Auckland Park 2006; tel. (11) 7149111; telex 424116; fax (11) 7145055; transmissions began in 1976; operates television services in seven languages over three channels; English and Afrikaans programmes on Channel one (TV1); Channel two (CCV-TV) broadcasts in Northern and Southern Sotho, Tswana, Xhosa and Zulu; Channel three (TSS-TV) broadcasts documentaries, educational programmes and sport.

Finance

(cap. = capital; auth. = authorized; p.u. = paid up; res = reserves; dep. = deposits; m. = million; brs = branches; amounts in rand)

BANKING

Central Bank

South African Reserve Bank: 370 Church St, POB 427, Pretoria 0001; tel. (12) 3133911; telex 322411; fax (12) 3133197; f. 1920; cap. and res 95m., dep. 8,558m. (Dec. 1992); Gov. Dr CHRISTIAN STALS; Sr Dep. Gov. Dr B. P. GROENEWALD; 8 brs.

Commercial Banks

ABSA Bank Ltd: ABSA Towers, 19th Floor, 160 Main St, Johannesburg 2001; tel. (11) 3303222; telex 489399; fax (11) 3303511;

f. 1990; cap. and res 4,932.5m., dep. 71,335.8m. (March 1993); Chair. DAVID BRINK.

African Bank: 56 Marshall St, POB 61352, Johannesburg 2107; tel. (11) 8362331; telex 483089; fax (11) 8382845; f. 1975 to operate in the fmr 'homelands'; cap. and res 11,631m., dep. 272,692m. (Sept. 1991); Chair. Dr S. M. MOTSUENYANE; 1 br.

Bank of Lisbon International Ltd: Bank of Lisbon Bldg, 1st Floor, 37 Sauer St, POB 11343, Johannesburg 2000; tel. (11) 8322477; telex 485076; fax (11) 8384816; f. 1965; cap. and res 27m., dep. 611m. (Sept. 1991); Chair. C. S. MARGO; Man. Dir Dr DURVAL MARQUES; 28 brs.

Boland Bank Ltd: 333 Main St, POB 4, Paarl 7622; tel. (2211) 72911; telex 522136; fax (2211) 72811; f. 1900; cap. and res 251.7m., dep. 3,277.7m. (March 1993); Chair. P. B. B. HUGO; CEO G. Z. LIEBENBERG; 85 brs.

First National Bank of Southern Africa Ltd: National Bank Bldg, 7th Floor, 84 Market St, Johannesburg 2001, POB 1153, Johannesburg 2000; tel. (11) 6329111; telex 486939; fax (11) 6322257; f. 1971 as Barclays National Bank; cap. and res 2,505m., dep. 38,468.6m. (1992); Chair. B. E. HERSOV; Man. Dir B. J. SWART; 900 brs.

French Bank of Southern Africa Ltd: 4 Ferreira St, Johannesburg 2001; tel. (11) 8322433; telex 482896; fax (11) 8360625; f. 1949; subsidiary of Banque Indosuez (France); cap. and res 93m., dep. 1,892m. (Dec. 1992); Chair. P. BRAULT; Man. Dir B. DESTOPPELEIRE; 3 brs.

Nedbank: 100 Main St, Johannesburg 2001, POB 1144, Johannesburg 2000; tel. (11) 6307111; telex 482765; fax (11) 6302465; f. 1888; cap. and res 1,935m., dep. 39,456m. (Sept. 1993); Chair. Dr J. B. MAREE; CEO R. C. M. LAUBSCHER; 259 brs.

The New Republic Bank Ltd: NRB House, 110 Field St, Durban 4001; tel. (31) 3047544; telex 625354; fax (31) 3053547; f. 1971; cap. 89m., dep. 901m. (1993); Man. Dir M. MIA; 13 brs.

The South African Bank of Athens Ltd: Bank of Athens Bldg, 116 Marshall St, POB 7781, Johannesburg 2001; tel. (11) 8321211; telex 486976; fax (11) 8381001; f. 1947; subsidiary of National Bank of Greece; cap. and res 20.6m., dep. 299.4m. (Dec. 1992); Chair. M. VRANOPOULOS; Man. Dir A. STRINGOS; 13 brs.

The Standard Bank of South Africa Ltd: Standard Bank Centre, 5 Simmonds St, Johannesburg 2001, POB 7725, Johannesburg 2000; tel. (11) 6369111; telex 484191; fax (11) 6366054; f. 1862; cap. and res 2,739.9m., dep. 48,221.3m. (Dec. 1992); Chair. Dr CONRAD B. STRAUSS; Man. Dir M. H. VOSLOO; 854 brs.

Merchant Banks

ABSA Merchant Bank Ltd: Carlton Centre, 40th Floor, Commissioner St, Johannesburg 2001; tel. (11) 3315741; telex 486965; fax (11) 3311040; f. 1977 as Volkskas Merchant Bank Ltd, name changed 1991; cap. and res 96.9m., dep. 699m. (March 1991); Man. Dir J. J. BROWN; 1 br.

Central Merchant Bank Ltd (Sentrale Aksepbank Bpk): Sanlamsentrum, Jeppe St, POB 2683, Johannesburg 2001; tel. (11) 2289111; telex 487310; f. 1969; cap. and res 59m., dep. 348.1m. (June 1986); Chair. Dr F. J. DU PLESSIS; Man. Dir D. H. ANDERSON; 4 brs.

Corporate Merchant Bank Ltd: Johannesburg; tel. (11) 3320111; telex 485143; fax (11) 237802; f. 1969; cap. and res 31.5m., dep. 393.4m. (March 1989); Exec. Chair. L. P. KORSTEN.

Finansbank Ltd: 66 Sauer St, Johannesburg 2001, POB 62343, Marshalltown 2107; tel. (11) 8337155; telex 486106; fax (11) 8386357; cap. and res 94m., dep. 2,031m. (Sept. 1991); Chair. and Man. Dir C. F. LIEBENBERG.

FirstCorp Merchant Bank Ltd: 4 First Place, Johannesburg 2001; POB 9773, Johannesburg 2000; tel. (11) 3718336; telex 487092; fax (11) 3718686; f. 1987; cap. and res 131.5m., dep. 2,300.2m. (Sept. 1992); Chair. B. J. SWART; CEO D. M. LAWRENCE.

Mercabank Ltd: Sanlam Center, Jeppe St, POB 1281, Johannesburg 2001; tel. (11) 3373353; telex 483007; f. 1970; cap. and res 40m., dep. 159.1m. (June 1986); Chair. C. G. ERASMUS; Man. Dir R. E. SHERRELL.

Rand Merchant Bank Ltd: 25 Fredman Drive, Sandton 2199, POB 786273, Sandton 2146; tel. (11) 8833622; telex 427602; fax (11) 7838651; cap. and res 259.6m., dep. 2.050.6m. (June 1992); Chair. GERRIT FERREIRA; Man. Dir P. K. HARRIS; 2 brs.

Standard Merchant Bank Ltd: 78 Fox St, Johannesburg 2001, POB 61344, Marshalltown 2107; tel. (11) 6369115; telex 487629; fax (11) 6362371; f. 1964; cap. and res 216.7m., dep. 3,982.4m. (Dec. 1992); Chair. D. R. GEERINGH; Man. Dir J. H. MAREE.

Savings Banks

British Kaffrarian Savings Bank Society: POB 1432, King William's Town 5600; tel. (433) 21478; telex 5250117; f. 1860; dep. 28.8m.; CEO D. E. DAUBERMANN.

Pretoria Bank Ltd: Woltemade Bldg, 118 Paul Kruger St, POB 310, Pretoria; cap. p.u. 601,250; dep. 7.6m.; Chair. M. D. MARAIS; Gen. Man. I. W. FERREIRA.

Staalwerkersspaarbank: 417 Church St, POB 1747, Pretoria; cap. p.u. 240,630; dep. 2.5m.; Chair. and Man. Dir L. J. VAN DEN BERG.

Investment Bank

Investec Bank Ltd: 55 Fox St, POB 11177, Johannesburg 2000; tel. (11) 4982000; telex 488381; fax (11) 4982100; cap. and res 509.6m., dep. 2,953m. (March 1993); Exec. Chair. B. KARDOL; Man. Dir S. KOSEFF; 4 brs.

Development Bank

Development Bank of Southern Africa: POB 1234, Halfway House 1685; tel. (11) 3133911; telex 425546; fax (11) 3133086; f. 1983; CEO A. B. LA GRANGE.

Discount Houses

Discount House Merchant Bank Ltd: 66 Marshall St, Johannesburg 2001; POB 61574, Marshalltown 2107; tel. (11) 8367451; fax (11) 8369636; f. 1957; cap. 18.8m.; Exec. Chair. C. J. H. DUNN; Man. Dir M. R. THOMPSON.

Interbank Ltd: 108 Fox St, POB 6035, Johannesburg; tel. (11) 8344831; fax (11) 8345357; f. 1971; cap. p.u. 15.5m., dep. 564m. (1990); Chair. A. KELLY; Man. Dir M. SWART.

The National Discount House of South Africa Ltd: Loveday House, 1st Floor, 15 Loveday St, Johannesburg; tel. (11) 8323151; telex 485081; f. 1961; auth. cap. 10m., dep. 357.1m. (1987); Chair. M. MACDONALD; Man. Dir G. G. LUND.

Bankers' Association

Institute of Bankers in South Africa: POB 61420, Marshalltown 2107; tel. (11) 8321371; fax (11) 8346592; f. 1904; 15,000 mems; CEO JALDA HODGES.

STOCK EXCHANGE

Johannesburg Stock Exchange: POB 1174, Johannesburg 2000; tel. (11) 8336580; telex 487663; f. 1887; Exec. Pres. R. A. NORTON.

INSURANCE

ACA Insurers Ltd: 35 Symons Rd, Auckland Park; tel. (11) 7268900; telex 4896262; f. 1948; Man. Dir L. G. Y. NEMORIN.

Aegis Insurance Co Ltd: Aegis Insurance House, 91 Commissioner St, Johannesburg; tel. (11) 8367621; telex 487512; fax (11) 8384559; Man. Dir B. H. SEACH.

African Mutual Trust & Assurance Co Ltd: 34 Church St, POB 27, Malmesbury; f. 1900; Chief Gen. Man. R. A. L. CUTHBERT.

Allianz Insurance Ltd: Allianz House, 13 Fraser St, Johannesburg 2001; POB 62228, Marshalltown 2107; tel. (11) 8363161; telex 487103; fax (11) 8383827; Man. Dir Dr A. GOSSNER.

Anglo American Life Assurance Co Ltd: Life Centre, 45 Commissioner St, POB 6946, Johannesburg 2000; telex 487780; Exec. Chair. Dr Z. J. DE BEER; Man. Dir Dr M. BERNSTEIN.

Commercial Union of South Africa Ltd: Commercial Union House, 26 Loveday St, POB 3555, Johannesburg 2000; tel. (11) 4911911; fax (11) 8382600; f. 1964; Chair. A. M. D. GNODDE; Man. Dir J. A. KINVIG.

Credit Guarantee Insurance Corpn of Africa Ltd: 31 Dover St, POB 125, Randburg 2125; tel. (11) 8897000; telex 420508; fax (11) 8861027; f. 1956; Man. Dir C. T. L. LEISEWITZ.

Fedlife Assurance Ltd: Fedlife House, 1 de Villiers St, POB 666, Johannesburg 2000; tel. (11) 3326000; fax (11) 4921102; f. 1944; Chair. J. A. BARROW; Man. Dir A. I. BASSERABIE.

General Accident Insurance Co of South Africa Ltd: POB 32424, Braamfontein 2017; tel. (11) 4086000; telex 9450092; fax (11) 3397732; Man. Dir C. A. DEAN.

I. G. I. Insurance Co Ltd: 162 Anderson St, POB 8199, Johannesburg 2000; tel. (11) 3351911; telex 485393; fax (11) 290491; f. 1954; Chair. I. M. A. LEWIS; Man. Dir P. S. DENNISS.

Liberty Life Association of Africa Ltd: Liberty Life Centre, 1 Ameshoff St, Johannesburg 2001; POB 10499, Johannesburg 2000; tel. (11) 4082100; telex 422530; fax (11) 4033171; f. 1958; Chair. DONALD GORDON; Man. Dir A. ROMANIS.

Metropolitan Life Ltd: 7 Coen Steytler Avenue, Foreshore, POB 93, Cape Town 8001, POB 93, Cape Town 8000; tel. (21) 241134; telex 550120; fax (21) 253315; Chair. Dr NTHATO MOTLANA; Man. Dir M. L. SMITH.

Momentum Life Assurers Ltd: Momentum Park, 267B West Ave, Verwoerdburgstad 0157, POB 7400 Hennopsmeer 0046; tel. (11) 6718911; fax (11) 6636336; f. 1967; Man. Dir J. D. KRIGE.

Mutual & Federal Insurance Co Ltd: Mutual Federal Centre, 28th Floor, 69 President St, Johannesburg 2001; tel. (11) 3749111;

telex 487641; f. 1970; Chair. G. A. MACMILLAN; Man. Dir K. T. M. SAGGERS.

Old Mutual (South African Mutual Life Assurance Society): Mutualpark, Jan Smuts Drive, POB 66, Cape Town 8001; tel. (21) 5099111; telex 527201; fax (21) 5094444; f. 1845; Chair. and Man. Dir M. J. LEVETT.

President Insurance Co Ltd: Rentmeester Park, 74 Watermeyer St, Val de Grace 0184; tel. (12) 868100; telex 323281; Man. Dir J. K. WASSERFALL.

Protea Assurance Co Ltd: Protea Assurance Bldg, Greenmarket Sq., POB 646, Cape Town 8000; tel. (21) 4887911; telex 9550038; fax (21) 4887110; Man. Dir A. L. TAINTON.

The Rand Mutual Assurance Co Ltd: POB 61413, Marshalltown 2107; tel. (11) 8388211; telex 487057; fax (11) 4921253; f. 1894; Chair. P.J. EUSTACE; Gen. Man. A. B. MAY.

Santam Ltd: Santam Bldg, Burg St, Cape Town 8001, POB 653, Cape Town 8000; tel. (21) 242254; telex 527822; fax (21) 244572; f. 1918; Chair. Dr C. H. J. VAN ASWEGEN; Man. Dir J. J. GELDENHUYS.

South African Eagle Insurance Co Ltd: Eagle House, 70 Fox St, Johannesburg 2001; POB 61489, Marshalltown 2107; tel. (11) 3709111; telex 485370; fax (11) 8365541; CEO P. T. MARTIN.

South African National Life Assurance Co (SANLAM): Strand Rd, Bellville, POB 1, Sanlamhof 7532; tel. (11) 9479111; telex 520191; fax (11) 9478066; f. 1918; Chair. M. H. DALING; Man. Dir DESMOND SMITH.

South African Trade Union Assurance Society Ltd: Traduna Centre, 118 Jorissen St, Braamfontein, Johannesburg 2001; f. 1941; Chair. E. VAN TONDER; Gen. Man. A. SUMNER.

The Southern Life Association Ltd: Great Westerford, Rondebosch, Cape Town; tel. (21) 6580911; telex 527621; fax (21) 6891323; f. 1891; Chair. T. N. CHAPMAN.

Standard General Insurance Co Ltd: Standard General House, 12 Harrison St, POB 4352, Johannesburg 2000; tel. (11) 8362723; telex 487320; fax (11) 8344935; f. 1943; Man. Dir Dr R. GRANDI.

Swiss South African Reinsurance Co Ltd: Swiss Park, 10 Queens Rd, Parktown, POB 7049, Johannesburg 2000; tel. (11) 6437281; telex 427556; fax (11) 6432929; f. 1950; Chair. and Man. Dir L. KEEL.

UBS Insurance Co Ltd: United Bldgs, 6th Floor, cnr Fox and Eloff Sts, Johannesburg; Chair. P. W. SCEALES; Gen. Man. J. L. S. HEFER.

Westchester Insurance Co (Pty) Ltd: Mobil Court, POB 747, Cape Town 8000; tel. (21) 4034000.

Association

The South African Insurance Asscn: POB 2163, Johannesburg 2000; tel. (11) 8384881; fax (11) 8386140; f. 1973; asscn of short-term insurers; CEO R. SCHNEEBERGER.

Trade and Industry

CHAMBER OF COMMERCE

South African Chamber of Business (SACOB): POB 91267, Auckland Park 2006; tel. (11) 4822524; fax (11) 450093; f. 1990 by merger of Asscn of Chambers of Commerce and Industry and South African Federated Chamber of Industries; 102 chambers of commerce and industry are mems; Dir-Gen. R. W. K. PARSONS.

DEVELOPMENT ORGANIZATIONS

Industrial Development Corporation of South Africa Ltd: POB 784055, Sandton 2146; tel. (11) 8831600; telex 427174; fax (11) 8831655; f. 1940; Chair. C. H. WIESE; Man. Dir W. C. VAN DER MERWE.

The Independent Development Trust: 14 Keerom St, Cape Town 8001, POB 16114, Vlaeberg 8018; tel. (21) 238030; fax (21) 242863; f. 1990; finances housing, education and health projects; Chair. JAN STEYN.

National Productivity Institute: POB 3971, Pretoria 0001; tel. (12) 3411470; telex 320485; fax (12) 441866; f. 1968; Exec. Dir Dr J. H. VISSER.

CHAMBERS OF INDUSTRIES

Cape Chamber of Industries: POB 1536, 5th Floor, Broadway Industries Centre, Hertzog Blvd, Foreshore, Cape Town 8000; tel. (21) 215180; telex 527409; fax (21) 4195982; f. 1904; Exec. Dir C. E. MCCARTHY; 1,000 mems.

Durban Regional Chamber of Business: POB 1506, Durban 4000; tel. (31) 3013692; fax (31) 3045255; Dir G. W. TYLER; 8,500 mems.

Johannesburg Chamber of Commerce and Industry: JCC House, Empire Road, Milpark, Johannesburg 2001; tel. (11) 7265300; telex 425594; fax (11) 7268421; CEO M. DE JAGER; 5,000 mems.

Midland Chamber of Industries: MCI Bldg, 22 Grahamstown Rd, Port Elizabeth 6001; tel. (41) 544430; telex 242815; fax (41) 571851; f. 1917; Dir W. B. WASMÜTH; 502 mems.

Northern Transvaal Chamber of Industries: Showground Office, Soutter St, Pretoria 0001; tel. (12) 3271487; telex 320245; fax (12) 3271501; f. 1929; Exec. Dir J. G. TOERIEN; 350 mems (secondary industries).

Orange Free State Chamber of Business: Kellner Heights, 37 Kellner St, POB 87, Bloemfontein 9300; tel. (51) 473368; fax (51) 475064; Dir J. J. VAN RENSBURG.

Pietermaritzburg Chamber of Industries: POB 637, Pietermaritzburg 3200; tel. (331) 452747; fax (331) 944151; f. 1910; Dir R. J. ALLEN; 300 mems.

Western Transvaal Chamber of Business: POB 7, Klerksdorp 2570; tel. (18) 4627401; fax (18) 4627402; Dir C. W. HYMAN.

INDUSTRIAL ORGANIZATIONS

Armaments Corporation of SA Ltd (ARMSCOR): Private Bag X337, Pretoria 0001; tel. (12) 4281911; telex 320217; fax (12) 4285635; Exec. Chair. J. G. J. VAN VUUREN.

Building Industries Federation (South Africa): POB 1619, Halfway House 1685; tel. (11) 3151010; fax (11) 3151644; f. 1904; 9,000 mems.

Chamber of Mines of South Africa: 5 Hollard St, POB 809, Johannesburg 2000; tel. (11) 4987100; telex 87057; fax (11) 8341884; f. 1889; Pres. J. J. GELDENHUYS.

ESKOM: POB 1091, Johannesburg 2000; tel. (11) 8008111; telex 424481; f. 1923; electricity supply; Chair. Dr J. B. MAREE.

FOSKOR Ltd: POB 1, Phalaborwa 1390; tel. (1524) 892911; telex 361012; fax (1524) 5531; Man. Dir D. R. V ORSTER.

Grain Milling Federation: Johannesburg; f. 1944; Sec. J. BARENDSE.

Industrial Rubber Manufacturers' Asscn of South Africa: POB 91267, Auckland Park 2006; tel. (11) 4822524; fax (11) 7261344; f. 1978; Chair. J. J. BIEHLER.

Master Diamond Cutters' Asscn of South Africa: 106 Diamond Exchange Bldg, cnr De Villiers and Quartz Sts, POB 11126, Johannesburg 2000; tel. (11) 296441; fax (11) 3331555; f. 1928; 76 mems.

Motor Industries' Federation: POB 2940, Randburg 2125; tel. (11) 7892542; fax (11) 7894525; f. 1910; Dir W. FOURIE; 7,800 mems.

National Asscn of Automobile Manufacturers of South Africa: Nedbank Plaza, 1st Floor, cnr Church and Beatrix Sts, Pretoria 0002; POB 40611, Arcadia 0007; tel. (12) 3232003; fax (12) 3263232; f. 1935; Dir N. M. W. VERMEULEN.

National Chamber of Milling, Inc: Braamfontein; tel. (11) 4033739; f. 1936; Dir Dr J. B. DE SWARDT.

National Clothing Federation of South Africa: 42 Van der Linde St, Bedfordview 2008, POB 75755, Gardenview 2047; tel. (11) 6228125; fax (11) 6228316; f. 1945; Dir H. W. VAN ZYL.

National Textile Manufacturers' Asscn: POB 1506, Durban 4000; tel. (31) 3013692; fax (31) 3045255; f. 1947; Sec. PETER MCGREGOR; 9 mems.

Plastics Federation of South Africa: 18 Plantation Rd, Unit 2, Eastleigh, POB 1128, Edenvale 1610; tel. (11) 6097956; fax (11) 4522643; f. 1979; Exec. Dir W. NAUDÉ; 3 mems.

Printing Industries Federation of South Africa: Printech Ave, Laser Park, POB 1084, Honeydew 2040; tel. (11) 7943810; fax (11) 7943964; f. 1916; Exec. Dir C. W. J. SYKES.

SOEKOR (Pty) Ltd: POB 307, Parow 7500; tel. (21) 9383911; fax (21) 9383144; f. 1965 as Southern Oil Exploration Corpn; responsible for all aspects of oil prospecting in South Africa; CEO M. J. HEISER.

South African Brewing Industry Employers' Asscn: Private Bag 34, Auckland Park 2006; tel. (11) 7265300; telex 425594; f. 1927; Sec. L. I. GOLDSTONE; 2 mems.

South African Cement Producers' Asscn: Private Bag X11, Halfway House 1685; tel. (11) 3150300; fax (11) 3150054.

South African Dairy Foundation: POB 72300, Lynnwood Ridge 0040; tel. (2712) 3485345; telex 322022; fax (2712) 3486284; f. 1980; Sec. F. J. NELL; 59 mems.

South African Federation of Civil Engineering Contractors: POB 644, Bedfordview 2008; tel. (11) 4551700; fax (11) 4551153; f. 1939; Exec. Dir Dr W. G. VANCE; 230 mems.

South African Fruit and Vegetable Canners' Asscn (Pty) Ltd: Canning Fruit Board Bldg, 258 Main St, POB 6172, Paarl 7622; tel. (2211) 611308; fax (2211) 25930; f. 1953; Sec. T. R. M. MALONE; 12 mems.

South African Inshore Fishing Industry Asscn (Pty) Ltd: POB 2066, Cape Town 8000; tel. (21) 251500; telex 527259; f. 1953; Chair. W. A. LEWIS; Man. S. J. MALHERBE; 4 mems.

South African Lumber Millers' Asscn: Private Bag 686, Isando 1600; tel. (11) 9741061; fax (11) 9749779; f. 1941; Dir A. B. W. SWART; 215 mems.

South African Oil Expressers' Asscn: Cereal Centre, 6th Floor, 11 Leyds St, Braamfontein 2017; tel. (11) 7251280; telex 422526; f. 1937; Sec. Dr R. DU TOIT; 14 mems.

South African Paint Manufacturers' Asscn: 39 Field St, Durban 4001, POB 1506, Durban 4000; tel. (31) 3013692; fax (31) 3045255.

South African Sugar Asscn: Norwich Life House, 6 Durban Club Place, Durban 4001; POB 507, Durban 4000; tel. (31) 3056161; telex 622215; fax (31) 3044939; Exec. Dir MICHAEL J. A. MATHEWS.

South African Wool Board: POB 2191, Port Elizabeth 6056; tel. (41) 544301; telex 242329; fax (41) 546760; f. 1946; 12 mems: nine appointed by wool-growers and three by the Minister of Agriculture; Chair. H. F. PRINSLOO; CEO Dr A. H. OLIVIER.

South African Wool Textile Council: POB 2201, North End, Port Elizabeth 6056; tel. (41) 545252; fax (41) 545629; f. 1953; Sec. C. THOMAS.

Steel and Engineering Industries Federation of South Africa (SEIFSA): POB 1338, Johannesburg 2000; tel. (11) 8336033; fax (11) 8381522; f. 1943; Exec. Dir. B. ANGUS; 3,000 mems; includes the following asscns:

Electrical Engineering and Allied Industries Asscn: POB 1338, Johannesburg 2000; tel. (11) 8336033; fax (11) 8381522; f. 1936; 315 mems.

Iron and Steel Producers' Asscn of South Africa: POB 1338, Johannesburg 2000; tel. (11) 8336033; fax (11) 8381522; 11 mems.

Light Engineering Industries Asscn of South Africa: POB 1338, Johannesburg 2000; tel. (11) 8336033; fax (11) 8381522; f. 1936; 342 mems.

Non-ferrous Metal Industries Asscn of South Africa: POB 1338, Johannesburg 2000; tel. (11) 8336033; fax (11) 8381522; f. 1943; 26 mems.

Radio and Television Manufacturers' Asscn of South Africa: POB 1338, Johannesburg 2000; tel. (11) 8336033; fax (11) 8381522; 14 mems.

Radio, Appliance and Television Asscn of South Africa: Metal Industries House, 42 Anderson St, POB 1338, Johannesburg 2000; tel. (11) 8336033; fax (11) 8381522; f. 1942; 48 mems.

Sheet Metal Industries Asscn of South Africa: POB 1338, Johannesburg 2000; tel. (11) 8336033; fax (11) 8381522; f. 1948; 165 mems.

South African Asscn of Shipbuilders and Repairers: POB 1338, Johannesburg 2000; tel. (11) 8336033; fax (11) 8381522; 25 mems.

South African Engineers' and Founders' Asscn (Transvaal, Orange Free State and Northern Cape): POB 1338, Johannesburg 2000; tel. (11) 8336033; fax (11) 8381522; f. 1945; 768 mems.

Sugar Manufacturing and Refining Employers' Asscn: 11th Floor, 6 Durban Club Place, POB 2278, Durban 4001; tel. (31) 3043551; fax (31) 3074241; f. 1947; Chair. W. B. HORLOCK.

Tobacco Employers' Organisation: PB 34, Auckland Park 2006; tel. (11) 7265300; telex 425594; f. 1941; Sec. L. I. GOLDSTONE; 3 mems.

TRADE ORGANIZATION

South African Foreign Trade Organization (SAFTO): POB 782706, Sandton 2146; tel. (11) 8833737; telex 424111; fax (11) 8836569; f. 1963; Chair. R. A. NORTON; CEO J. L. VAN ZYL; 1,500 mems.

MAJOR INDUSTRIAL COMPANIES

The following are among the leading companies in South Africa.

AECI Limited: POB 1122, Johannesburg 2000; tel. (11) 2239111; telex 487048; fax (11) 2231456; f. 1924; cap. R228m.; mfrs of explosives, industrial and agricultural chemicals, paints, synthetic yarns and plastic raw materials; Chair G. W. H. RELLY; Man. Dir M. A. SANDER; 22,400 employees.

Anglo-Alpha Ltd: 94 Rivonia Rd, POB 781868, Sandton 2146; tel. (11) 7835143; telex 422075; f. 1934; cap. R15,038,000; major producer of cement, stone aggregates, lime, industrial minerals and ready-mixed concrete, with extensive interests in manufacture of paper sacks and fertilizers; Chair. P. BYLAND; Man. Dir J. G. PRETORIUS; 4,079 employees.

Barlow Rand Ltd: POB 782248, Sandton 2146; tel. (11) 8019111; fax (11) 4443643; f. 1902; auth. cap. R22.3m. (1984); South Africa's largest industrial group with about 400 operating cos, employing 151,000 people; these operations are managed through a central group exec. cttee and 11 decentralized autonomous divisions; consolidated group turnover in 1991 was R31,994m., and total assets were R19,050m.; Rand Mines administers group's gold, coal and base minerals interests. Industrial interests include manufacture of cement and lime, electronics and telecommunications, electrical engineering, paint, consumer electrical products, packaging and paper products, sugar, food, animal feeds, pharmaceuticals and textiles; distributors of computers, earthmoving equipment, motor vehicles, building and construction supplies; operates mainly in southern Africa, with trading investments in UK, Europe and USA; Chair. W. A. M. CLEWLOW; Man. Dir D. E. COOPER.

CNA Gallo Ltd: POB 9380, Johannesburg 2000; tel. (11) 4822600; fax (11) 7261374; cap. R930m.; core businesses of the group are the CNA and Literary Group chains of retail stores and manufacture and distribution of gramophone records, music cassettes, compact discs and video cassettes, and music publishing; activities of support subsidiaries and associate cos include manufacture and sale of greeting cards and stationery, general book publishing, freight forwarding and clearing, business training and film production and distribution; Chair. D. D. B. BAND.

Consolidated Textile Mills Ltd (Frame Group): POB 12017, Jacobs 4026, Natal; telex 650070; f. 1930; group of cos in South Africa, Malawi and Zimbabwe producing clothing and textiles; Jt Man. Dirs A. BERMAN, S. LURIE, S. R. PEIMER; over 35,000 employees.

ICS Holdings Ltd: 185 Katherine St, POB 783854, Sandton 2146; tel. (11) 444700; fax (11) 8042062; f. 1902; cap. R11.5m.; processes and distributes red meat, poultry and meat products, milk and milk products, ice cream, fish and frozen vegetables and has interests in commercial cold storage, feedlots and tanneries; Chair. R. A. WILLIAMS; Man. Dir N. DENNIS; 11,000 employees.

Irvin and Johnson Ltd: Standard Bank Centre, 20th Floor, POB 1628, Heerengracht, Cape Town 8000; tel. (21) 216400; telex 527268; fax (21) 217258; f. 1937; trawler operators; processors, distributors and exporters of frozen fish, vegetables and pastries; Sec. C. SCHOEMAN; 8,000 employees.

LTA Ltd: POB 312, Johannesburg 2000; tel. (11) 8269111; telex 744811; fax (11) 8264650; f. 1889; group of cos active in building, civil and electrical engineering, steel reinforcing and industrialized building systems; Chair. H. K. DAVIES; Man. Dir C. J. M. WOOD; 20,000 employees.

Nampak Ltd: 114 Dennis Rd, Athol Gardens, POB 784324, Sandton 2146; tel. (11) 4447418; telex 424179; fax (11) 4444794; f. 1968; cap. R16.3m.; mfrs of packaging in various forms based on paper, paper board, metal, glass and plastics; there are subsidiaries in the service area and fields allied to packaging; Chair. BRIAN CONNELLAN; Man. Dir TREVOR EVANS; 20,000 employees.

Premier Group Holdings Ltd: POB 1530, Johannesburg 2000; tel. (11) 4469111; telex 430735; f. 1913; cap. R1,777m. (1985); holding co controlling Premier Food Industries Ltd with wheat and maize mills, bakeries, edible oils, fats, margarine and derivatives, animal feed factories, poultry and crop farms, sugar and cotton processing, retail liquor outlet, music companies, bookshops, distribution and wholesaling division, stationery division, and pharmaceutical divisions both manufacturing and wholesale; Chair. (vacant); 31,000 employees.

Pretoria Portland Cement Co Ltd: POB 3811, Johannesburg 2000; tel. (11) 4821300; telex 245033; fax (11) 7263537; f. 1892; cap. R40m.; mfrs and distributors of cement, lime and limestone products, paper sacks and other containers; also mines and markets gypsum; Chair. J. C. HALL; Group Man. Dir J. E. GOMERSALL; 3,490 employees.

Protea Holdings Cape (Pty) Ltd: POB 3839, Cape Town 8000; tel. (21) 512357; telex 577551; f. 1963; Man. Dir A. WOLFAARDT; 100 employees.

SAPPI Ltd: POB 31560, Braamfontein 2017; tel. (11) 4078111; telex 422050; fax (11) 3391846; f. 1936 as South African Pulp and Paper Industries Ltd; eight pulp and paper mfg and processing subsidiaries; turnover: R5,541m. (1993); Exec. Chair. E. VAN AS; 20,000 employees.

C. G. Smith Sugar Ltd: POB 194, Durban 4000; tel. (31) 3051511; telex 620610; f. 1913; cap. R419m.; operation of five sugar mills in Natal and one in Transvaal, accounting for 40% of all South African sugar production, and of three white sugar refineries and ancillary packaging, warehousing and distribution concerns; manufacture of syrup; operation of three chemical factories producing furfural, furfuryl alcohol, ethyl alcohol, hydrogen peroxide and dimethyl ether; Man. Dir G. TAYLOR; 6,020 permanent employees.

The South African Breweries Ltd: 2 Jan Smuts Ave, POB 1099, Johannesburg; tel. (11) 3394711; telex 422482; fax (11) 3391830; f. 1895; cap. R155.7m.; brewing and marketing of beer; mfrs, wholesalers and retailers of furniture, footwear, domestic appliances, plate glass, textiles, natural fruit juices and soft drinks; discount department and fashion chain stores; also owns and operates hotels; Exec. Chair. J. M. KAHN; 91,000 employees.

SASOL Ltd: POB 5486, Johannesburg 2000; tel. (11) 4413111; telex 426778; fax (11) 7885092; group of cos operating the world's largest complex of oil-from-coal petrochemical installations; produces c. 130 products; Chair. J. A. STEGMANN; Exec. Dir ANDRÉ DU TOIT; 33,000 employees.

Stewarts and Lloyds Export: POB 1137, Johannesburg 2000; tel. (11) 4933000; telex 487010; fax (11) 4931440; f. 1902; cap. R12m.; export trading co manufacturing and distributing industrial metal products, e.g. steel tubing and fittings, valves, diesel engines and generators, pumps, irrigation equipment. Export Man. P. KEMP; 10,000 employees.

L. Suzman Ltd: 2 Elray St, Raedene POB 2188, Johannesburg 2192; tel. (11) 4851020; telex 422523; fax (11) 6401325; f. 1889; cap. R2.1m.; wholesale distribution of tobacco products and other consumer products; operates 26 brs in South Africa; Chair. P. R. S. THOMAS; Man. Dir C. J. VAN DER WALT; 1,000 employees.

The Tongaat-Hulett Group Ltd: POB 3, Tongaat, Natal 4400; tel. (322) 21000; telex 650171; fax (322) 21094; f. 1892 as Huletts Corpn; cap. R73m.; divisions operating in sugar cane growing and processing, food production and processing, textiles manufacture, building materials, aluminium products, speciality starches, property administration; Chair. Dr C. J. SAUNDERS; Man. Dir C. M. L. SAVAGE; 35,000 employees.

USKO Ltd: General Hertzog Rd, POB 48, Vereeniging, Transvaal; telex 743051; f. 1911; cap. R35m.; mfr of copper and aluminium conductor and associated products; Chair. F. P. KOTZEE; 770 employees.

Mining Companies

Anglo American Corporation of South Africa Ltd: POB 61587, Marshalltown 2107; tel. (11) 6389111; telex 487167; fax (11) 6383221; f. 1917; cap. and res at book value exceed R13,303m.; market value of listed investments is R36,927m.; a mining financial house holding interests in mining, financial, industrial, insurance, banking and property cos. The corpn also makes available tech. and admin. services to and acts as secretary of mining and other cos; Chair. JULIAN OGILVIE THOMPSON.

Anglovaal Ltd: POB 62379, Marshalltown 2107; tel. (11) 6349111; telex 486087; fax (11) 6340038; f. 1933; mining, financial and industrial group with divisions operating in precious metal and base mineral mining and beneficiation, life assurance and financial services, food and rubber production, packaging, construction, engineering, electronics, information technology, textiles; Chair. BASIL E. HERSOV; 82,000 employees.

De Beers Consolidated Mines Ltd: 36 Stockdale St, POB 616, Kimberley 8300; tel. (531) 22171; telex 280654; fax (531) 24611; cap. R24.9m.; group of diamond mining cos and allied interests; reorg. 1990, when foreign interests were transferred to De Beers Centenary AG (Switzerland); Chair. JULIAN OGILVIE THOMPSON; 14,000 employees.

Gold Fields of South Africa Ltd: 75 Fox St, Johannesburg 2001, POB 61525, Marshalltown 2107; tel. (11) 6399111; telex 450043; fax (11) 6392101; includes four gold-producing cos, platinum, coal and base metals; Chair. ROBIN PLUMBRIDGE.

General Mining Union Corporation Ltd (GENCOR): 6 Hollard St, Johannesburg 2001; tel. (11) 3769111; telex 85830; fax (11) 8384716; cap. R226m.; diversified group with investments in several cos incl. GENMIN, which administers mines producing gold, coal, platinum, ferro-alloys, and ENGEN, which has interests in petroleum refining and retail petrol sales; Exec. Chair. DEREK KEYS.

Johannesburg Consolidated Investment Co Ltd: Consolidated Bldg, cnr Fox and Harrison Sts, Johannesburg 2001, POB 590, Johannesburg 2000; tel. (11) 3739111; telex 483787; fax (11) 8366130; f. 1889; mining house with major investments in platinum, gold, diamonds, ferrochrome, coal and a wide range of secondary industries, particularly food and beverages; Chair. PATRICK RETIEF.

Palabora Mining Co Ltd: POB 65, Palaborwa 1390; tel. (1524) 802911; telex 331827; fax (1524) 2448; cap. R28,315,500; 39% held by Rio Tinto-Zinc Corpn; mining of copper, with by-products of magnetite, zirconia metals, uranium oxide, anode slimes, nickel sulphate, sulphuric acid and vermiculite; copper refining; Chair. A. J. LEROY; Man. Dir F. FENWICK.

Rand Mines Ltd: 15th Floor, The Corner House, 63 Fox St, Johannesburg 2001, POB 62370, Marshalltown 2107; tel. (11) 4912911; telex 489671; fax (11) 8345936; cap. and res exceed R718.4m.; 74.4% held by Barlow Rand Ltd; mining of gold, coal, mineral exploration, property development, management and financial services; Chair. and Dir D. T. WATT; 52,212 employees.

TRADE UNIONS

In 1989 the number of registered unions totalled 212, with a membership of 2,130,117, representing about 17% of the economically active population. In addition there were an estimated 85 unregistered unions in 1989, with a membership of about 550,000.

Trade Union Federations

Congress of South African Trade Unions (COSATU): POB 1019, Johannesburg 2000; tel. (11) 3394911; fax (11) 3394060; f. 1985; multiracial fed. of 15 trade unions representing c. 1.4m. mems; Gen. Sec. SAM SHILOWA.

Principal affiliates include:

Chemical Workers' Industrial Union: POB 18349, Dalbridge 4014; tel. (11) 259510; fax (11) 256680; Pres. D. GUMEDE; Gen. Sec. R. CROMPTON.

Construction and Allied Workers' Union: POB 1962, Johannesburg 2000; tel. (11) 230544; Pres. D. NGCOBO; Gen. Sec. L. MADUMA.

Food and Allied Workers' Union: POB 234, Salt River 7925; tel. (21) 6379040; fax (21) 6383761; Pres. ERNEST THERON; Gen. Sec. M. GXANYANA.

Health and Allied Workers' Union: POB 47011, Greyville 4023; tel. (11) 3063993; Gen. Sec. S. NGCOBO.

National Education, Health and Allied Workers' Union: POB 7549, Johannesburg 2000; tel. (11) 299665; Pres. R. MKHIZE; Gen. Sec. S. NJIKELANA.

National Union of Metalworkers of South Africa (NUMSA): POB 260483, Excom 2023; tel. (11) 8322031; fax (11) 8384092; Pres. M. TOM; Gen. Sec. ENOCH GODONGWANA; 240,000 mems (1994).

National Union of Mineworkers: POB 2424, Johannesburg 2000; tel. (11) 8337012; Pres. J. MOTLATSI; Gen. Sec. MARCEL GOLDING; 350,000 mems.

Paper, Printing, Wood and Allied Workers' Union: POB 3528, Johannesburg 2000; tel. (11) 8344661; Pres. M. NDOU; Gen. Sec. S. KUBHEKA.

Post and Telecommunications Workers' Association: POB 260100, Excom 2023; tel. (11) 234351; Pres. K. MOSUNKULU; Gen. Sec. V. A. KHUMALO.

South African Clothing and Textile Workers' Union: POB 18359, Dolbridge 4014; tel. (11) 3011391; fax (11) 3017050; Pres. A. NTULI; Gen. Sec. J. COPALYN; 185,000 mems.

South African Railways and Harbours Workers' Union: POB 8059, Johannesburg 2000; tel. (11) 8343251; fax (11) 8344664; Pres. J. LANGA; Gen. Sec. M. SEBEKOANE.

Transport and General Workers' Union: POB 9451, Johannesburg 2000; tel. (11) 3319321; fax (11) 3315418; Pres. A. NDLOVU; Gen. Sec. R. HOWARD.

National Council of Trade Unions (NACTU): POB 10928, Johannesburg 2000; tel. (11) 298031; fax (11) 237625; f. 1986; black fed. of 22 trade unions representing c. 450,000 mems (1987); Pres. JAMES MNDAWENI; Gen. Sec. P. CAMAY.

Principal affiliates include:

Building, Construction and Allied Workers' Union: POB 96, Johannesburg 2000; tel. (11) 236311; Pres. J. SEISA; Gen. Sec. V. THUSI.

Food Beverage Workers' Union of South Africa: POB 4871, Johannesburg 2000; tel. (11) 299527; Pres. M. L. KWELEMTINI; Gen. Sec. L. SIKHAKHANE.

Hotel, Liquor and Catering Trade Employees' Union: POB 1409, Johannesburg 2000; tel. (11) 234039; Pres. E. NKOSI (acting); Gen. Sec. K. KEELE (acting).

Metal and Electrical Workers' Union of South Africa: POB 3669, Johannesburg 2000; tel. (11) 8369051; fax (11) 8369002; f. 1989; Pres. RAYMOND KHOZA; Gen. Sec. TOMMY OLIPHANT; 30,000 mems (1991).

National Union of Farm Workers: POB 10928, Johannesburg 2000; tel. (11) 233054; fax (11) 237625; Pres. E. MUSEKWA; Gen. Sec. T. MOLETSANE.

National Union of Public Service Workers: POB 10928, Johannesburg 2000; tel. (11) 232812; Pres. K. NTHUTE; Gen. Sec. S. RADEBE.

South African Chemical Workers' Union: POB 236, Johannesburg 2000; tel. (11) 288907; Pres. W. THUTHANI; Gen. Sec. O. H. NDABA.

Steel, Engineering and Allied Workers' Union of South Africa: POB 4283, Johannesburg 2001; tel. (11) 294867; fax (11) 294869; Pres. G. MABIDIKAMA; Gen. Sec. N. RAMAEMA.

Transport and Allied Workers' Union of South Africa: POB 4469, Johannesburg 2000; Pres. A. MATLATSI; Gen. Sec. M. RAMELA.

SAAWU Federation of Unions: POB 10419, Marine Parade 4050; tel. (11) 3019127; 19 mems; Pres. M. Maboso; Gen. Sec. S. K. B. Kikine.

South African Confederation of Labour: POB 19299, Pretoria West 0117; tel. (12) 793271; 7 mems; Pres. I. J. Els; Sec. L. N. Celliers.

Unaffiliated Trade Union

United Workers' Union of South Africa: f. 1986; controlled by the Inkatha Freedom Party.

Transport

Most of South Africa's railway network and the harbours and airways are administered by the state-owned Transnet Ltd. There are no navigable rivers. Private bus services are regulated to complement the railways.

Transnet Ltd: POB 72501, Parkview 2122; tel. (11) 4887000; fax (11) 4887010; Man. Dir Dr A.T. Moolman.

RAILWAYS

With the exception of commuter services, the South African railways system is operated by Spoornet Ltd (the rail division of Transnet). The network comprised 21,303 route-km in 1993. Transnet Ltd also operates an extensive network of road transport services, which serves primarily to develop rural areas, but also acts as feeder to the railways. The electrified lines totalled 18,455 track-km in 1989. Rail services between South Africa and Mozambique were resumed in April 1994.

Spoornet Ltd: Paul Kruger Bdg, 30 Wolmarans St, Johannesburg 2001; tel. (11) 7738785; telex 424087; fax (11) 7742665; CEO A. S. Le Roux.

ROADS

In 1991 the total road network was 182,329 km, excluding roads in the former 'independent homelands'. This total comprised 2,040 km of motorways, 53,395 km of main roads and 126,894 km of secondary roads. Some 30.4% of the network was paved.

South African Roads Board: Dept of Transport, Private Bag X193, Pretoria 0001; responsible for location, planning, design, construction and maintenance of national roads.

SHIPPING

The principal harbours are at Cape Town, Port Elizabeth, East London and Durban. The deep-water port at Richards Bay is being extended. Saldanha Bay is a major bulk-handling port.

More than 30 shipping lines serve South African ports. In 1983 South Africa's merchant fleet totalled 990 vessels with a registered tonnage exceeding 755,334.

Shipping Directorate: Dept of Transport, Private Bag X193, Pretoria 0001; tel. (12) 2909111; telex 321195; fax (12) 2902040; advises the Govt on matters connected with sea transport to, from or between South Africa's ports, incl. safety at sea, and prevention of pollution by oil.

CIVIL AVIATION

Civil aviation is controlled by the Minister of Transport. The Air Services Licensing Council is responsible for licensing and control of air services.

South African Airways (SAA): Airways Towers, POB 7778, Johannesburg 2000; tel. (11) 7739433; telex 425020; fax (11) 7739858; f. 1934; state-owned; internal passenger services linking all the principal towns; international services to Africa, Europe, N and S America and Asia; CEO Gert D. van der Veer.

COMAIR (Commercial Airways (Pty) Ltd): POB 7015, Bonaero Park 1622; tel. (11) 9210111; telex 746738; fax (11) 9733913; f. 1967; scheduled internal services; Chair. D. Novick; Man. Dir P. van Hoven.

Airlink Airline: POB 7529, Bonaero Park 1622; tel. (11) 9732941; fax (11) 9732501; f. 1992; internal scheduled and chartered flights; Man. Dirs Rodger Foster and Barrie Webb.

Protea Airways (Pty) Ltd: Bonaero Drive, Bonaero Park 1620, POB 7049, Bonaero Park 1622; tel. (11) 3951806; fax (11) 3951337; charter services; Chair. and Man. Dir J. T. Morrison.

Safair Freighters (Pty) Ltd: POB 938, Kempton Park, Transvaal 1620; tel. 9731921; telex 742242; fax 9734620; f. 1969; subsidiary of South African Marine Corpn; scheduled internal cargo services and charter international cargo flights; Chair. A. Z. Farr; Man. Dir Dr P. J. van Aswegen.

Air Cape (Pty) Ltd: POB D.F. Malan Airport, Cape Town 7525; tel. (21) 9340344; telex 520246; fax (21) 9348379; scheduled internal passenger services and charters, engineering services and aerial surveys; Chair. Dr P. van Aswegen; Gen. Man. G. A. Nortje.

Flitestar Ltd: POB 839, Cape Town 8000; tel. (21) 9340344; telex 520246; fax (21) 9340344; scheduled passenger services; fmrly Trek Airways; Chair. G. A. MacMillan; Man. Dir J. V. Blake.

Tourism

Tourism is an important part of South Africa's economy. The chief attractions for visitors are the climate, scenery and wildlife reserves. Tourist receipts provided an estimated US $934m. in foreign exchange in 1990. In 1991 1,709,554 tourists visited South Africa.

South African Tourism Board: 442 Rigel Ave South, Frasmusrand 0181, Private Bag X164, Pretoria 0001; tel. (12) 3470600; telex 204575; fax (12) 454768; f. 1947; 13 overseas brs; Exec. Dir Dr Ernie Heath.

Defence

In June 1993 the armed forces totalled 67,500: army an estimated 47,000, navy 4,500, air force 10,000 and a medical corps numbering 6,000. The army had about 31,000 conscripts, the navy 900 and the air force 3,000. Following the installation of a new government in May 1994, it was announced that a new South African National Defence Force (SANDF) was to be established over a period of three years. The SANDF, which was expected initially to number 120,000-133,000, was to comprise members of the South African armed forces, including those of the former 'homelands', and elements of the former military wings of the African National Congress of South Africa and the Pan-Africanist Congress. The size of the SANDF was to be progressively reduced, to about 91,000 troops by 1998.

Defence Expenditure: Budgeted at R10,683m. for 1993/94.

Chief of the South African National Defence Force: Gen. George Meiring.

Education

School attendance is compulsory for children of all population groups between the ages of seven and 16. In 1992 an estimated 1.7m. school-age children were not attending schools. During the 1980s universities, which were formerly racially segregated, began to admit students of all races. In 1991 there were 21 universities and 15 'technikons', which are tertiary education institutions offering technological and commercial vocational training. From January 1991 state schools were permitted to admit pupils from all races. By mid-1991 only 5% of schools for white children had opted for desegregation. A report on education in South Africa, compiled in 1984, estimated that 50% of the adult population were illiterate. The illiteracy rate was 7% among whites, 29% among Asians, 38% among Coloureds, and nearly 68% among blacks. Education was allocated 23.5% of total projected expenditure by the central government in the budget for 1993/94.

Bibliography

Benson, M. *The African Patriots: The Story of the African National Congress.* London, Faber, 1963.

South Africa: The Struggle for a Birthright. Harmondsworth, Penguin, 1966.

Bloomberg, C. *Christian Nationalism and the Rise of the Afrikaner Broederbond in South Africa, 1918–48.* Bloomington, IN, Indiana University Press, 1989.

Blumenfeld, J. *South Africa in Crisis.* London, Croom Helm, 1987.

Bundy, C. *The Rise and Fall of the South African Peasantry.* London, Heinemann, 1979.

Central Statistical Services, *South African Statistics.* Pretoria, Government Printer, biennial.

Christopher, A. J. *South Africa.* London, Longman, 1982.

The Commonwealth Report. Mission to South Africa: The Findings of the Commonwealth Eminent Persons Group on Southern Africa. London, Penguin, 1986.

Davenport, T. R. H. *South Africa: A Modern History.* London, Macmillan, 1977.

Davies, R., O'Meara, D., and Dlamini, S. *The Struggle for South Africa: A Reference Guide to Movements, Organizations and Institutions.* 2 vols. London, Zed Books, 1984.

Du Toit, A. L. *The Geology of South Africa.* Edinburgh, 1954.

Grundy, K. W. *The Militarization of South African Politics.* London, I. B. Taurus Publishers, 1986.

Guy, J. *The Destruction of the Zulu Kingdom.* London, Longman, 1979.

Hamilton, G., and Mare, G. *An Appetite for Power. Buthelezi's Inkatha and South Africa.* Ravan Press and Indiana University Press, Johannesburg and Bloomington, 1987.

Hanlon, J. *Beggar Your Neighbours: Apartheid Power in Southern Africa.* London, Indiana University Press/James Currey, 1986.

Hobart H. D. *The South African Economy.* London, Oxford University Press, 1967.

Horrell, M. *The African Homelands of South Africa.* Johannesburg, South African Institute of Race Relations, 1973.

Konczacki, Z. A. and J. M. (Eds). *An Economic and Social History of South Africa.* London, Frank Cass, 1980.

Konczacki, Z. A., Parpart, J. L., and Shaw, T. M. (Eds). *Studies in the Economic History of Southern Africa.* Vol. II. London, Cass, 1991.

Kruger, D. W. (Ed.). *South African Parties and Policies 1910–1960, a select source book.* Cape Town, Human and Rousseau, 1960.

Lawrence, P. *The Transkei.* Johannesburg, Ravan Press, 1977.

Lipton, M. *Capitalism and Apartheid: South Africa 1910–1984.* Aldershot, Hampshire, Maurice Temple Smith/Gower, 1985.

Lodge, T. *Black Politics in South Africa since 1945.* London, Longman, 1983.

Louw, L., and Kendall, F. *South Africa: The Solution.* Bisho, Ciskei, Amagi Publications, 1986.

Marks, S., and Trapido, S. *The Politics of Race, Class and Nationalism in Twentieth Century South Africa.* London and New York, Longman, 1987.

Niddrie, D. L. *South Africa: Nation or Nations?* Princeton, Van Nostrand, 1968.

Omer-Cooper, J. D. *History of Southern Africa.* London, James Currey, 1987.

Pakenham, T. *The Boer War.* London, Weidenfeld and Nicolson, 1979.

Pampillis, J. *Foundations of the New South Africa.* London, Zed Books, and Cape Town, Maskew Miller Longman, 1991.

Patterson, S. *The Last Trek: A Study of the Boer People and the Afrikaner Nation.* London, Routledge and Kegan Paul, 1957.

Pollock, N. C., and Agnew, S. *An Historical Geography of South Africa.* London, 1963.

Robertson, J. *Liberalism in South Africa 1948–1963.* Oxford University Press, 1971.

Sampson, A. *Black and Gold.* London, Hodder and Stoughton, 1987.

Saunders, C. *Historical Dictionary of South Africa.* Metuchen, NJ, Scarecrow Press, 1983.

Simons, H. J. and R. E. *Class and Colour in South Africa 1850–1950.* Penguin Books, 1969.

South African Reserve Bank. *Quarterly Bulletin.*

Study Commission of US Policy Toward South Africa. *South Africa: Time Running Out.* Berkeley, University of California Press, 1981.

Thompson, L. M. *The Unification of South Africa 1902–10.* Oxford, Clarendon Press, 1960.

UNESCO. *Apartheid, its effects on education, science, culture and information.* 1972.

Walker, E. A. *A History of Southern Africa.* 3rd Edn, London, Longman, 1957.

Walshe, P. *The Rise of African Nationalism in South Africa.* 1971.

Wellington, J. H. *Southern Africa: A Geographical Study.* 2 vols. London, 1955.

Wilson, M., and Thompson, L. (Eds). *The Oxford History of South Africa.* 2 vols. Oxford, Clarendon Press, 1969–71.

SUDAN

Physical and Social Geography

J. A. ALLAN

THE NILE

The River Nile and its tributaries form the basis of much of the present economic activity of Sudan, and of most of the future activity that is currently envisaged. The river traverses diverse landscapes from the relatively humid tropical forest in the south to the arid deserts in the north. The Republic of Sudan has a total area of 2,505,813 sq km (967,500 sq miles), and the Nile waters which enter Sudan just south of Juba either evaporate or flow 3,000 km until they reach Lake Nubia on the Egyptian border. Even those which flow down the Blue Nile travel 2,000 km. The distances are immense, and the remoteness of places on the Nile system, not to speak of those in the deserts, savannah and swamps of the rest of the country, explains much of the character of Sudan's land use. The other important factor is climate, which influences vegetation and, more significantly, affects the seasonal flow of the Nile tributaries.

The Blue Nile is the most important tributary, both in the volume of water which it carries (four-sevenths of the total average flow of the system) as well as in the area of irrigated land, of which it supports over 40% of the present area and 70% of potential irrigable land. The Blue Nile and other east-bank tributaries are sustained by monsoon rains over the Ethiopian highlands which cause the river to flood at the end of July, reach a peak in August and remain high through September and the first half of October. At Khartoum the river rises 7 m in August. The Atbara, another seasonal east-bank tributary, provides a further one-seventh of the flow in the system, and the remaining two-sevenths come from the White Nile. The sustained flow of the White Nile arises firstly because its main source is Lake Victoria, which regulates the flow, and secondly because the swamps of the Sudd and Machar act as a reservoir, absorbing the irregular stream flow from the south while discharging a regular flow, much reduced by evaporation, in the north.

The River Nile is an international river system, and Sudan depends on river flows from seven other states. Sudan does not yet use all of the 18,500m. cu m of annual flow agreed with Egypt in 1959 as its share of the total average flow at Aswan of 84,000m. (Egypt receives 55,500m. cu m, while 10,000m. cu m are assumed to evaporate annually from Lake Nasser/Nubia). By the mid-1980s Sudan's irrigation developments were expected to account for all its agreed share, and ultimately there are likely to be additional demands by upstream states such as Ethiopia. Having regard to Egypt's rising demand for water, Sudan and Egypt jointly embarked in 1978 on the construction of the Jonglei Canal project, which will eventually conserve some 4,000m. cu m of the 33,000m. cu m of water lost annually through evaporation in the Sudd swamp. However, work had to be suspended in 1984, with 250 km of the proposed 360 km completed, following attacks on construction workers by guerrilla insurgents. The Machar swamps will also yield water at a rate as yet undetermined, but likely to be about 4,000m. cu m per year (3,240m. cu m at Aswan).

PHYSICAL FEATURES

Sudan is generally a flat, featureless plain reflecting the proximity to the surface of the ancient, little-disturbed Basement rocks of the African continent. The Basement is overlain by the Nubian Sandstone formation in the centre and north-west of the country, and by the Umm Ruwaba formation in the south. These formations hold groundwater bodies which have, or will have, agricultural significance. No point in the country is very high above sea-level. Elevations rise to 3,187 m on Mt Kinyeti, near the Uganda border, and to 3,088 m on Jabel Marrah, an extinct volcano, in west central Sudan near the frontier with Chad. Some idea of the level character of the landscape is provided by the small amount of the fall in the Blue Nile, which starts its 2,000-km flow through Sudan at 500 m above sea-level at the Ethiopian border and formerly flowed past Wadi Halfa (now flooded) at an elevation of 156 m. It now flows into Lake Nubia at 180 m above sea-level. The White Nile, as it emerges from Uganda, falls some 600 m between the border and Khartoum, a distance of 1,700 km, but falls only 17 m in the last 700 km from entering the southern clay plains.

CLIMATE

Average temperatures and rainfall change steadily from month to month, except where the effect of the Ethiopian highlands disturbs the east-west trend in the climatic belts in the south-east. The north of Sudan is a desert, with negligible rainfall and high average daily temperatures (summer 35°C, winter 20°C). Low temperatures are recorded only in winter. Rainfall is convectional in origin and increases steadily south of Khartoum (200 mm per year), reaching over 1,000 mm per year at the southern border. Rainfall varies from year to year, especially in the north, and is seasonal. In the south it falls in the period April–October; the rainy season is progressively shorter towards the north, where it lasts only from July until August. Potential evaporation approaches 3,000 mm per year in the north and is always over 1,400 mm per year, even in the humid south.

VEGETATION AND SOILS

The soil resources of Sudan are rich in agricultural potential. The exploitation of these resources depends on the availability of the limiting factor, water, and only a small proportion of the clay plains of central and east Sudan are currently farmed intensively. The clay plains are the result of millennia of alluvial sorting and deposition of eroded basic volcanic material from the Ethiopian highlands. Clay soils also occur in the south, being deposits of the White Nile and Sobat streams. Recent alluvium provides a basis for productive agriculture in the narrow Nile valley north of Khartoum. Elsewhere, in the west and north the soils are sandy, with little agricultural potential, except in the dry valleys, which generally contain some soil moisture.

Vegetation is closely related to the climatic zones. From the desert in the north vegetation gradually improves through semi-arid shrub to low woodland savannah characterized by acacia and short grasses. Progressively higher rainfall towards the south promotes trees and shrubs as well as herbs, while the more reliably watered rangeland of the Bahr al-Arab provides an important seasonal resource for the graziers from the poor pastures of Darfur and Kordofan. The flooded areas of the Sudd and Machar and environs support swamp vegetation and grassland. On the uplands of the southern border, rainfall is sufficient to support tropical rain forest.

During 1984–85 and again in the early 1990s large areas of Sudan were affected by drought, and it was estimated that thousands of people faced starvation, particularly in the western provinces of Darfur and Kordofan.

POPULATION

The population of Sudan was estimated at 24.94m. at the census held in June 1993. According to World Bank estimates, the population increased at an annual average rate of 2.8% in 1985–92. According to UN estimates, the population was 25,941,000 at mid-1991. At the 1983 census, about 71% of the population resided in rural areas, 18% in urban and semi-urban areas and the remaining 11% were nomadic. The population is concentrated in Khartoum province and the Central Region, where population densities were respectively 55 and 28 per sq km in 1973, compared with 3.6–6.8 per sq km elsewhere. Agricultural development in the two most populous regions created employment opportunities and this led to the doubling of these populations between 1956 and 1973, compared with rises of between zero and 50% elsewhere. There are local concentrations of population in the Nuba mountains and higher densities than average in better-farmed parts of the Southern and Darfur Regions.

The ethnic origin of the people of Sudan is mixed, and the country is still subject to significant immigration by groups from Nigeria and Chad, such as the Fulani. In the south the Nuer, the Dinka and the Shilluki are the most important of the Nilotic peoples. The Arab culture and language predominate in the north, which includes the most populous provinces and the capital, Khartoum. The south is predominantly Christian and this cultural difference, added to the ethnic separateness and its extreme remoteness, has been expressed in economic backwardness and a tendency to political distinctness which have been the main cause of frequent disturbances in Southern Sudan.

The capital, Khartoum, had a population of 473,597 at the 1983 census. It is the main administrative, commercial and industrial centre of the country. The neighbouring cities of Khartoum North and Omdurman had 340,857 and 526,192 inhabitants respectively, thus creating, with Khartoum, a conurbation of more than 1.3m. inhabitants. As communications are very poor and since Khartoum is at least 1,000 km away from 80% of the country, the influence which Khartoum exerts on the rest of the country is small. The relatively advanced character and general success of much of the irrigated farming on the east-central clay plains has led to a predominance of investment there and to the misguided impression that the success of the east-central plains could be transferred to other parts of the country where the resources are unfortunately much less favourable. Much of Sudan is so dry for part of each year that the only possible way to use the land and vegetation resources is by grazing, and tribes such as the Bagara traverse the plains and plateaux of Darfur and Kordofan in response to the availability of fodder.

Recent History

MILES SMITH-MORRIS

Revised for this edition by PETER WOODWARD

The scramble for Africa which dominated the closing decades of the 19th century convinced the British government that it was necessary to bring the Sudan under British control. In order to avoid direct conflict with the French and other European powers in central Africa, it was decided that the conquest should be undertaken in the name of Egypt, as a reaffirmation of control over what was described as Egyptian territory temporarily disrupted by the Mahdist rebellion. The reconquest, begun in 1896 by combined British and Egyptian forces, culminated in the defeat of the Mahdist forces at Omdurman in 1898.

The Anglo-Egyptian agreement of 1899 established a nominally Anglo-Egyptian administration that was, in fact, a British colonial government, headed by a governor-general. Egyptian groups and officials who served as intermediaries between British and Sudanese were withdrawn in 1924, following the assassination in Cairo of Sir Lee Stack, the governor-general of the Sudan and c-in-c of the Egyptian army, and a system of 'Indirect Rule' through tribal chiefs was introduced. This was paralleled in the South by a new 'Southern Policy' aimed at eventually assimilating the three Southern provinces into a British-controlled East African Federation. Both forms of administration were unpopular with the growing nationalist movement, which began to mobilize in the mid-1930s. In response to this pressure for increased Sudanese participation in government in preparation for full independence, changes in the administration were introduced, leading to the establishment of an advisory council for Northern Sudan in 1943 and a legislative assembly for the whole country in 1948. The establishment of these institutions provoked a split in the nationalist ranks, with one group—led by the Umma Party (UP) and supported by the Mahdists—feeling that independence could be best achieved by co-operating with the British in the new institutions. Another group, distrustful of the British, supported co-operation with Egypt. Standing for 'The Unity of the Nile Valley' and supported by the Khatmiyya, the chief rival of the Mahdists among the religious fraternities, this group boycotted both council and assembly. However, the latter group's links with the Egyptian establishment were broken by the Egyptian revolution of 1952, clearing the way for a separate settlement of the Sudan question.

An agreement between Britain and the new Egyptian administration in 1953 set out a programme for self-determination for the Sudan and elections were held, resulting in a victory for the National Unionist Party (NUP), whose leader, Ismail al-Azhari, became the first Sudanese prime minister in January 1954. Although Azhari was initially expected to favour union with Egypt it quickly became clear that Sudanese opinion was overwhelmingly in favour of independence, with Southern members of parliament calling for a federal form of government. On 19 December 1955 parliament unanimously declared the Sudan an independent republic. Britain and Egypt were left with no choice but to recognize the Sudan's independence, which formally took effect on 1 January 1956.

POST-INDEPENDENCE UNREST

Soon after independence, Azhari's government was replaced by an uneasy coalition of the Mahdist-supported UP and the People's Democratic Party (PDP), the political organ of the Khatmiyya, with Abdallah Khalil, the UP secretary, as prime minister. Disagreements—over the adoption of a presidential form of government and over the advisability of seeking foreign aid at a time of severe economic difficulties—strained the coalition. After an inconclusive election in February 1958, the UP president Sadiq al-Mahdi sought an alliance with Azhari's NUP. This was opposed by Khalil, who sought the involvement of the military.

A military coup was launched in November 1958 by a group of officers led by Gen. Ibrahim Abboud, who won the support of civilian politicians with assurances that the junta aimed merely to restore stability and would relinquish power when this was achieved. The Abboud regime had some success in the economic sphere, establishing a realistic sales policy for the main export crop, cotton, and securing development aid from international donors. However, the extent of military involvement in government and allegations of corruption created growing discontent; the government also showed its determination to pursue a military solution to the problem of the south, where its campaigns against the *Anya Nya* rebels forced thousands of Southerners to take refuge in neighbouring countries. A campaign for the restoration of democratic government gathered momentum during 1964. This became a revolution when in October police fired on student demonstrators in Khartoum, killing one of them. A general strike brought the country to a standstill and Abboud was forced to surrender power to a civilian committee.

A transitional government was formed with representatives from all parties, including for the first time, the Sudanese Communist Party (SCP) and the Muslim Brotherhood. One of its first acts was to declare a general amnesty in the South. A conference of Northern and Southern parties, opening in Khartoum in March 1965, failed to reach agreement on the country's constitutional future—with Northern parties favouring a regional government for the South and the Southern parties divided between those which favoured federation and those seeking full independence—but did agree on a programme of immediate action, including repatriation of refugees and freedom of religion. Elections held in June led to the formation of a coalition government by the UP and NUP, with the UP's Muhammad Ahmad Mahgoub as prime minister and Azhari as permanent president of the committee of five that acted as collective head of state.

The new government faced serious rebel activity in the South and large numbers of Southerners were killed in the course of reprisals by government troops. The government itself became increasingly right-wing, and in November 1965 the SCP was banned. A split meanwhile developed within the UP, with the more moderate members rallying around the party president, Sadiq al-Mahdi, in opposition to the prime minister. Defeated on a vote of censure in July 1966, Mahgoub resigned and al-Mahdi was elected prime minister at the head of another UP–NUP coalition.

With the help of stringent controls and loans from the World Bank and IMF, the economy began to revive. Meanwhile, progress had been made towards the settlement of the Southern problem on the basis of regional government. In April 1967 a 'parties conference' submitted a report recommending a regional solution. By this time the long-awaited supplementary elections in the South had been held, bringing 36 members to the constituent assembly, of whom 10, led by William Deng, represented the Sudan African National Union (SANU), the principal Southern party. It was now possible to hasten the process of drafting a permanent constitution.

The relative success of al-Mahdi's government, however, coupled with the announcement that he would stand for the presidency under the proposed constitution, led to a split in the coalition with the NUP, whose leader, Azhari, also aspired to the presidency. In May 1967 al-Mahdi was defeated in the assembly and Mahgoub again became prime minister. The new government severed diplomatic relations with the USA and Britain following the Arab-Israeli war in June and developed closer relations with the Eastern bloc. Internal affairs, however, were neglected. After a series of defeats for the government in the constituent assembly, the assembly was dissolved in January 1968, following the mass resignation of government members.

Elections were held in April, in which the Democratic Unionist Party (DUP), a new party formed by a merger of the NUP and PDP, won the largest number of seats. A new government, a coalition between the DUP and Ansar leader Imam al-Hadi's faction of the UP, took office in May, again with Mahgoub as prime minister. Faced by a deteriorating security situation in the South and internal divisions, the new government survived only a little over a year, until it was overthrown in a bloodless coup led by Col Gaafar Muhammad Nimeri in May 1969.

THE NIMERI REGIME, 1969–85

The Nimeri regime's first two years in power were characterized by the adoption of socialist policies and the forging of an alliance between the new military leadership and the SCP. The new regime claimed to be the true heirs of the October revolution of 1964, which it claimed had been betrayed by the traditional parties. The foundations for a one-party state, based on the Egyptian model, were laid with the formation of the Sudanese Socialist Union (SSU). A period of unprecedented repression began, culminating in a confrontation between the government and the Ansar, in which thousands were killed. The government declared its commitment to regional administrative autonomy for the South and set up a ministry for Southern affairs. It developed closer relations with the Eastern bloc and followed a policy of militant support for the Palestinian cause. However, the announcement in November 1970 that presidents Nimeri, Qaddafi and Sadat had decided to unite Sudan, Libya and Egypt as a single federal state proved unacceptable to the communists, who staged a military coup, led by Maj. Hashim al-Ata, which resulted in the temporary overthrow of Nimeri in July 1971. With popular support, Nimeri was restored to power within three days. A purge of communists followed and 14 people were executed.

The attempted coup was followed by a cooling of relations with the Eastern bloc and a surge in the personal popularity of Nimeri, who won the first presidential election in Sudanese history in October 1971, gaining almost 4m. votes, with only 56,000 opposed. A new government was formed, the revolutionary council dissolved and the SSU recognized as the sole legal political party. The Addis Ababa Agreement, signed in March 1972 between the government and the *Anya Nya* rebels, appeared to lay the basis for a settlement by establishing regional autonomy for the three Southern provinces. A regional people's assembly was established in Juba with representatives in the national people's assembly and a higher executive council (HEC) of its own. The government also took a pragmatic line on economic policy, denationalizing companies previously taken over by the state and encouraging foreign investment. A strategy was launched to marry Western technology and Arab petrodollars with the country's vast agricultural potential.

The leaders of the traditional parties and their largely right-wing supporters, excluded from involvement in politics, organized themselves into a National Front (NF) which operated as a largely external opposition to the regime. Supported at different times by Libya, Iraq, Saudi Arabia and Ethiopia, the NF made several attempts to overthrow Nimeri. However, as the ideological differences between the government and the NF diminished, attempts at reconciliation began. In July 1977 Sadiq al-Mahdi, who had been under sentence of death, met Nimeri at Port Sudan. Subsequently large numbers of political detainees were released and many exiled members of the NF, including al-Mahdi, returned to Sudan, some to take up government posts.

Sudan's relations with Egypt, normally close, came under strain at the beginning of the 1980s, partly because of Sudan's desire to preserve close links with the rest of the Arab world at a time when Egypt was increasingly isolated by its signing of the Camp David accord with Israel. The assassination of Egyptian President Sadat in October 1981, and growing fears of Libyan attempts to destabilize the Nimeri regime, reinforced the feeling of need in the two regimes for closer co-operation and in October 1982 this culminated in the signing of a charter of integration between Egypt and Sudan, a 10-year agreement providing for political and economic integration and close co-operation in foreign policy, security and development. The charter created a 120-member Nile Valley parliament, a higher council for integration and a joint fund for financial and administrative independence. The charter was greeted with scepticism by many Sudanese and with opposition by Southern leaders who feared it would lead to a diminution of their role.

Internally, the country continued to suffer the rigours of a deteriorating economy, compounded by accelerating inflation and spreading corruption. In addition, there was a growing influx of refugees (about 640,000 in 1988, and subsequently rising to well over 1m. a year) from Ethiopia, Uganda and Chad. Meanwhile, the exodus from Sudan of large numbers of skilled personnel gathered momentum as a result of deteriorating economic conditions.

Prolonged discussions about decentralization culminated in the adoption in January 1980 of a recommendation whereby Sudan would be divided into five regions (Northern, Eastern, Central, Kordofan and Darfur) in addition to Khartoum and the South, which would continue to enjoy a special status and administrative structure. Elections for a new people's assembly were held in December 1981, with its membership reduced from 366 to 155, as many of its powers had been devolved to the regions.

Meanwhile, relations between the government in Khartoum and the South were again deteriorating. A decision to subdivide the South into three sub-regions to avoid the domination of one ethnic group (i.e. the Dinka), eventually implemented in May 1983, was opposed by many Southerners, who feared it would weaken their collective position *vis-à-vis* the North. Southern resentment was also aroused by the decision that petroleum from the newly-discovered oilfields astride the traditional boundaries of the two regions would not be refined locally but exported via a pipeline to Port Sudan, and by fears that the Jonglei Canal project would benefit Northerners and Egypt but have an adverse effect on the local population. A major factor in the deepening crisis was the adoption by President Nimeri, the SSU and all state organizations, after September 1983, of certain aspects (mainly penalties for criminal offences) of Islamic *Shari'a* law, combined, after April 1984, with martial law. Despite the general popularity, in principle, of Islamization among the Northern Muslim majority, and regardless of official assurances that non-Muslims would not be adversely affected, many Southern Sudanese were now alienated to the point of armed insurrection. Commonly known as *Anya Nya* II, the revitalized rebel groups were organized into political and military wings, the Sudanese People's Liberation Movement (SPLM) and Sudanese People's Liberation Army (SPLA) respectively. In the course of 1983–84, the rebels engaged government forces in a series of battles, especially in Upper Nile and Bahr al-Ghazal.

Meanwhile, Nimeri's commitment to Islamization continued to attract some support among the mainly Muslim population of the North. The harsher penalties of the new legal code were enforced regardless of, and even contrary to, the teachings of the *Shari'a* itself. Corruption, which should have been curbed in accordance with the principles of the *Shari'a*, continued to proliferate within the ruling élite. While special emergency courts dispensed so-called 'decisive justice', which often took the form of public floggings, nothing was done to institutionalize the principle of *shura*, or consultation, in government. On the contrary, proposals to amend the 1973 constitution were formally introduced in the people's assembly in July 1984. Under these proposals. Nimeri was to be created Imam and given even greater powers than he had previously exercised. Prominent among the growing number opposed to Nimeri was Sadiq al-Mahdi, who viewed his Islamization policies as a gross distortion of Islamic principles and was imprisoned for over a year for his opposition. Relations between Nimeri and Hassan at-Turabi's faction of the Muslim Brotherhood steadily deteriorated, both because the Brotherhood was ignored in the formulation of Islamization policies and because it was potentially a formidable contender for political power, although formallly allied to the regime since 1977.

As the country sank deeper into economic disarray Nimeri's dependence on his Western allies (especially the USA), and their influence over him, correspondingly increased. Eventually he was persuaded not only to acquiesce in the wishes of the IMF in the removal of food subsidies and the further devaluation of the currency, but also to consent to participate in the evacuation from Ethiopia to Israel of several thousand Falasha Jews, an action which contravened Sudan's commitments as a member of the Arab League. By the end of February 1985 disillusionment and exasperation with the regime and its policies, whether internal or external, economic or otherwise, was rapidly crystallizing. At this late juncture, Nimeri moved to deal with the Muslim Brotherhood by putting its leaders on trial for sedition and, by so doing, alienated his last vestiges of popular support. Public sentiment was also being rapidly alienated by the government's failure to deal with the effects of the prolonged drought and the problems created by the continued influx of refugees from Ethiopia, Chad and Uganda. Nimeri reacted to this situation by adopting a conciliatory stance. The state of emergency was lifted, and the operation of the special courts was suspended, while an offer was made to revoke the redivision of the South if a majority of Southerners desired it. Nimeri also reshuffled the council of ministers and presidential council. Among those appointed in March 1985 was Lt-Gen. Abd ar-Rahman Swar ad-Dahab, receiving the posts of minister of defence and c-in-c of the armed forces.

MILITARY COUP

Public discontent with Nimeri's regime reached its culmination in March 1985, exacerbated by substantial increases in the price of food and fuel, and Khartoum was immobilized by a general strike. On 6 April, while Nimeri was visiting the USA, he was deposed in a bloodless military coup, led by Lt-Gen. Swar ad-Dahab. Following the coup, a state of emergency was declared, and a Transitional Military Council (TMC) was appointed. After two weeks of negotiations with the various organizations which had worked for Nimeri's downfall, a 15-member council of ministers, including three non-Muslim Southerners, was announced. Dr Gizuli Dafallah, a trade unionist who had been a prominent organizer of the general strike, was appointed Prime Minister. The council of ministers was to be responsible to the TMC during a 12-month transitional period prior to the holding of free elections, scheduled for April 1986. Hundreds of Nimeri's officials were arrested, and the SSU was dissolved.

In response to the coup, the SPLM initially declared a ceasefire, but presented the new regime with a series of demands concerning the Southern Region. Swar ad-Dahab offered various concessions to the South, including the cancellation of the redivision and the reinstatement of the Southern HEC in Juba, with Maj.-Gen. James Loro, a member of the TMC, as its interim president. The SPLM rejected these terms, refused to negotiate further with the TMC, and resumed hostilities. The civil war in the South continued throughout 1985, with many Southern towns under siege. In an attempt to reach agreement with the SPLM, a conference was held in March 1986 in Addis Ababa, Ethiopia, between the SPLM and the National Alliance for Salvation (NAS), a semi-official alliance of trade unionists and politicians who supported the government. The SPLM insisted that the retention of *Shari'a* law remained a major obstacle to national unity; the NAS agreed to abolish *Shari'a* law and, in response to another of the rebels' demands, to end military links with Libya and Egypt; however, these measures were not implemented by the TMC before the April 1986 election.

Despite these difficulties, Swar ad-Dahab pledged a return to civilian rule after a 12-month interim period. A transitional constitution was signed in October 1985; under its provisions, numerous political groupings began to emerge in preparation for the forthcoming general election. In December the name of the country was changed to 'the Republic of Sudan', thus restoring the official designation to its pre-1969 form.

The TMC's foreign policy during its 12-month rule reversed Nimeri's strongly pro-Western stance. While advocating a policy of non-alignment, the TMC sought to improve relations with Ethiopia, Libya and the USSR, to the concern of Sudan's former allies, Egypt and the USA. A military co-operation agreement was signed with Libya in July 1985, and diplomatic relations were quickly restored between Sudan, Libya and Ethiopia. Relations also improved with Iran, which had been one of the main adversaries of Nimeri's government. In November links with Egypt were reaffirmed. Relations with the USA, already viewed with suspicion (owing to the US government's former support for Nimeri), were further strained after the attack on Libya by US aircraft in April 1986.

CIVILIAN COALITIONS AND REGIONAL UNREST

More than 40 political parties participated in the general election for a new legislative assembly, which took place over a period of 12 days in April 1986. Voting was suspended in 37 of the 68 Southern constituencies, owing to increased unrest there. As expected, no single party won an outright majority of seats in the assembly, but Sadiq al-Mahdi's UP won the largest number of seats (99), followed by the DUP, led by Osman al-Mirghani (63 seats), and the National Islamic Front (NIF) of Dr Hassan at-Turabi (with 51 seats). The newly elected assembly held its first session on 26 April, but adjourned immediately when its members were unable to reach agreement on the composition of the new government. Following protracted negotiations over the allocation of portfolios, a broadly-based government was announced on 15 May; the council of ministers consisted of a coalition of the UP and the DUP, with, in addition, four portfolios allocated to Southern parties. Sadiq al-Mahdi became prime minister and minister of defence. He urged the Southern rebels to negotiate a peaceful settlement, and asserted that *Shari'a* law would be abolished and the state of emergency lifted. With regard to foreign affairs, he pledged to continue the non-aligned policy of the TMC. Meanwhile, as promised, the TMC was dissolved to make way for the return to civilian rule. Swar ad-Dahab relinquished the posts of head of state (being replaced by a six-member supreme council, inaugurated on 6 May) and of c-in-c of the army (he was succeeded by Gen. Tajeddin Abdallah Fadul, hitherto the vice-chairman of the TMC).

In an attempt to make the new government acceptable to the Southerners, a special portfolio, the ministry of peace and unity, had been created for a member of the NAS, and Col John Garang, leader of the SPLM, had been offered a place in the council of ministers. However, the SPLM announced that it would not recognize, or take part in, the new government. The security situation in the South continued to deteriorate; in early 1986 the SPLM launched a new offensive, and captured the town of Rumbek. In July 1986, however, al-Mahdi and Garang held direct talks for the first time, in Addis Ababa, but the only result was an agreement to maintain contacts.

In August 1986 further negotiations took place between the NAS and the SPLM, with the aim of convening a constitutional conference as a prelude to terminating the civil conflict. These discussions, however, ended abruptly when the SPLM shot down a Sudan Airways aircraft in the same month, killing 60 civilians on board. The SPLM launched a new offensive, with the aim of recapturing the four strategic Southern towns of Juba, Wau, Malakal and Bentiu.

Al-Mahdi attempted a new peace initiative in April 1987, with a suggestion to the SPLM of a two-week cease-fire, to be followed by a reopening of negotiations. By May, the military situation in the South had become so unstable that it appeared possible that the government might consent to the outright secession of three Southern provinces. In the same month a temporary council for the Southern Sudan (CSS) was established under the leadership of a Southern politician, Matthew Abor Ayang. The formation of this body was intended as a transitional measure, pending the convening of a constitutional conference to decide the final system of government, but the CSS seemed unlikely to have any influence on the two contending *de facto* governments which by now existed in the South: the army and the SPLM. In January 1988, following the signing of the 'transitional charter' by the government and 17 political parties (see below), Ayang resigned as chairman of the CSS, which was itself suspended, with its administrative functions transferred to the regional governors of the Southern provinces.

In an unexpected development on 14 May 1987 al-Mahdi asked the supreme council to dissolve his coalition government, citing as his reasons alleged incompetence on the part of certain ministers, lack of progress in dealing with the country's serious economic problems, and internal dissensions within the council of ministers. These disagreements arose from widening divisions within the DUP, where contending factions of liberals and religious traditionalists had led al-Mahdi during April to enter into secret negotiations with the opposition NIF, with a view to forming a new coalition. In the event, neither the NIF nor the UP were willing to participate in a single administration, and al-Mahdi's reconstructed council of ministers, announced on 3 June, differed little from its predecessor. Following the announcement of the new council of ministers, al-Mahdi stated that the coalition parties had agreed on mutually acceptable guidelines for the conduct of government policy, with special reference to the abrogation of religiously-based legislation unacceptable to the South. Progress was also to be made on the long-delayed convening of a constitutional conference. On the former point, it was stated that laws based on a 'Sudanese legal heritage' would replace those unacceptable to non-Muslims, who would be exempted from Islamic punishments and the system of *zakat* (alms) taxation. Such a compromise, however, was rejected by the SPLM, which continued to demand a total abrogation of Islamic law as a precondition to peace negotiations, while the fundamentalist NIF restated its demand that the Islamic code be imposed on the country as a whole. On 25 July the government imposed a 12-month state of emergency, aimed at bringing under control the country's worsening economic situation, even though a state of emergency imposed after the overthrow of the Nimeri regime had never formally been abrogated. In August the DUP temporarily withdrew from the coalition government, after the party's proposed candidate for a vacancy on the supreme council had been rejected by the UP. However, efforts to replace the coalition with an all-party government of national unity were unsuccessful, and in October the UP and the DUP agreed to form a joint administration once again, the NIF having elected to remain in opposition.

In September 1987 representatives of Southern Sudanese political parties met in Nairobi, Kenya; they issued a joint appeal for all Sudanese political forces to join the peace efforts, and requested that the government should convene a national constitutional conference. However, the conflict in the South continued unabated. In November SPLM forces, allegedly with Ethiopian assistance, captured the town of Kurmuk (near the border with Ethiopia and lying within Sudan's Northern provinces). While the capture of this town was of little strategic significance, it was nevertheless considered to be damaging to government morale, as the SPLA had previously confined its operations to the South. Kurmuk was recaptured by government forces in December, and in the same month the government entered into secret peace negotiations in London with representatives of the SPLM. Although no agreement was reached, the SPLM was reported to have abandoned its demand for the abrogation of Islamic law as a precondition for talks. On 16 December al-Mahdi announced that a number of provisions of the *Shari'a* had been repealed, and that preparations were being made to replace those remaining in force with a new legal code.

In January 1988 representatives of the government and 17 political parties signed a 'transitional charter' which aimed to define Sudan's political structure until the convening of a proposed constitutional conference. The 'transitional charter' stressed Sudan's commitment to multi-party democracy; stipulated that the government of the South would be in accordance with the 1972 system of autonomous regional government; and requested the government to replace *Shari'a* law with an alternative legal system before the holding of the constitutional conference.

In April 1988 al-Mahdi announced that he had again asked the supreme council to dissolve his coalition government, following a vote by the national assembly in favour of the formation of a new 'government of national unity'. In order to facilitate the formation of such a government, al-Mahdi resigned as prime minister on 16 April. On 27 April he was re-elected to a further two-year term, obtaining 196 of 222 votes cast by the 260-member national assembly. In early April, during negotiations on the formation of a new government, the UP, the DUP and the NIF had agreed to proceed with the implementation of an Islamic legal code within two months of taking office. Following his re-election as prime minister, al-Mahdi declared that, while the precise nature of the relationship between the state and religion should be established at the proposed constitutional conference, the Muslim majority had the right to choose laws that governed Muslims in so far as they did not infringe upon the rights of non-Muslims.

The formation of a new 27-member 'government of national unity', comprising members of the UP, the DUP, the NIF and a number of Southern Sudanese political parties, was completed in May 1988. Al-Mahdi announced that the new government would deal with the critical economic and security problems facing the country. Few observers, however, expected the new administration to be able to resolve the problem of the war in the South, especially since the fundamentalist NIF had joined the coalition on condition that a 'replacement' *Shari'a* code be introduced within 60 days of its formation.

In November 1988 representatives of the SPLM met senior members of the DUP and reached agreement on proposals to end the civil war. A statement issued by the two sides stipulated that, in the period preceding the convening of a national constitutional conference, the Islamic legal code should be suspended, that military agreements between Sudan and other countries should be abandoned, and that the state of emergency should be lifted and a cease-fire implemented in the South. In December, however, a state of emergency was again declared amid reports that a military coup had been attempted (see below). The DUP withdrew from the coalition government and its six ministers left the cabinet. The political crisis was precipitated by al-Mahdi's requesting the national assembly to convene a national constitutional conference, while refusing to incorporate the agreement between the SPLM and the DUP into his proposal. In the same month the government was forced to revoke substantial increases in the prices of basic commodities, following a national strike and demonstrations in Khartoum in protest at the measure.

In February 1989 Dr Hassan at-Turabi, the leader of the NIF, was appointed deputy prime minister. This appointment, while strengthening the position of the NIF in the government, reduced the likelihood of an early solution to the war in the South. In late February al-Mahdi threatened to resign as prime minister unless senior army officers allowed him leeway to form a new government and to work for peace in the South. In late February senior army officers had issued an ultimatum demanding political reforms and the formation of a government of national unity. However, the army refused to guarantee that it would not intervene in Sudanese politics in the event of Sudan's continued perceived drift towards Libya and a lack of progress in negotiations to end the war in the South. On 6 March al-Mahdi agreed to form a new, broadly-based government which would begin negotiations with the SPLM. Thirty political parties and 17 trade unions had previously signed an agreement endorsing the peace agreement drawn up by the DUP and the SPLM in November 1988. However, the NIF refused to endorse the agreement (which called for the suspension of Islamic laws as a prelude to the negotiation of a peace settlement to the civil war), and was excluded from the new government formed on 23 March 1989. Peace negotiations between a government delegation and the SPLM commenced in Ethiopia in April. At the beginning of May the SPLM proclaimed a 45-day cease-fire, renewing hopes for peace and aiding the work of famine relief. By mid-June, however, negotiations had become deadlocked.

In the field of foreign relations, al-Mahdi carried out a number of foreign tours, including visits in 1986 to the USSR, Saudi Arabia, the USA and Italy. Following the legislative elections in April, contacts with Egypt became less cordial, as al-Mahdi sought to introduce a more independent policy for Sudan, and it was reported that all joint institutions with Egypt were to be dissolved. In February 1987, however, al-Mahdi visited Cairo to sign a new agreement on economic and cultural co-operation. Despite the lessening of Libya's military involvement in Chad, some Libyan forces remained in north-western Sudan, despite repeated Sudanese demands for their withdrawal. Al-Mahdi stated in March that the question of their presence had been 'settled', although it was not clear whether or not they had been withdrawn. In April 1988 the President of Chad, Hissène Habré, urged the Sudanese government to curb the activities of Libyan-backed forces in Darfur, and to end its diplomatic policy which, he claimed, effectively supported Libya.

During 1988 world opinion was alarmed by increasing reports of alleged violations of human rights by the government of Sudan, in particular of atrocities committed against civilians in the war in the South. The SPLM alleged that government forces had allowed, and, in some instances, participated in, the massacre of civilians of the Dinka tribe (from which the SPLM drew most of its support) by pro-government militia from the Islamic North. These allegations were corroborated by Western human rights organizations, which accused the government of pursuing a policy of genocide against the Dinka in its effort to defeat the SPLA. They also expressed concern over the apparent resurgence of slavery in Sudan and the retention of the corporal punishments prescribed by *Shari'a* law.

RETURN TO MILITARY RULE

By late 1988 there were signs of widespread discontent in military circles at the government's continuing lack of progress in resolving the civil conflict. A coup attempt in December, promoted by supporters of ex-president Nimeri, was quickly thwarted, but subsequent political manoeuvres by al-Mahdi (see above) did little to allay the increasing frustration of senior army officers. On 30 June 1989, a bloodless *coup d'état* led by Brig. (later Lt-Gen.) Omar Hassan Ahmad al-Bashir removed al-Mahdi's government and formed a 15-member Revolutionary Command Council for National Salvation (RCC), which declared its primary aim to be the resolution of the Southern conflict. Al-Bashir, who became head of state, chairman of the RCC, prime minister and minister of defence, and c-in-c of the armed forces, rapidly dismantled the civilian ruling apparatus. The constitution, national assembly and all political parties and trade unions were abolished, a state of emergency was declared, and civilian newspapers were closed. About 30 members of the former government were detained, including al-Mahdi, although three of the ex-ministers were included in the new 21-member cabinet which was announced in early July. Its composition included 16 civilians, of whom four were Southerners, as well as several members who were understood to be sympathetic towards Islamic fundamentalism. Al-Bashir assigned a high priority to the suppression of financial corruption, and special courts were set up to deal with such offences. Internationally, the RCC regime received immediate diplomatic recognition from Chad, Egypt, Libya, the PDRY and Saudi Arabia, and the new government was generally welcomed as a potentially stabilizing influence in the region.

The SPLA response to the coup was cautious. Al-Bashir declared a one-month unilateral cease-fire on 5 July 1989 and offered an amnesty to those opposing the Khartoum government 'for political reasons'. In an effort to restart negotiations, al-Bashir requested Ethiopia, Egypt and Kenya to act as mediators. At the same time, however, the government's announcement of proposals for a national referendum on *Shari'a* law alienated the SPLA, which demanded its suspension as a precondition for talks. A plan by the RCC to introduce military conscription foreshadowed an escalation in the conflict.

Peace negotiations were, however, renewed in Ethiopia in August 1989. By this time the SPLM's terms for a negotiated settlement to the conflict included the immediate resignation of the RCC prior to the establishment of an interim government, which would represent the SPLM, the banned political parties and other groupings; and the new regime's proximity to the fundamentalist NIF had become apparent. The negotiations immediately collapsed over the issue of Islamic law. Col Garang was invited to attend a government-sponsored peace conference in Khartoum in early September, but declined to do so while the curfew and the state of emergency remained in force. Delegates who did attend the conference were believed to be close to the fundamentalist NIF, and were thought to favour the secession of southern Sudan if it proved impossible to achieve a negotiated settlement to the conflict.

Hostilities, which had been in abeyance since the beginning of May 1989, were resumed at the end of October, when the SPLM attacked and captured the town of Kurmuk. Further peace negotiations, mediated by the former US president, Jimmy Carter, began in Kenya at the beginning of December, but quickly collapsed over the issue of *Shari'a* law. It was subsequently reported that the SPLM had captured the towns of Kajo-Kaji, Yei and Umm Dawrayn.

By the end of January 1990 the SPLM was preparing a full-scale assault on the garrison town of Juba, where the security situation was reported to have deteriorated to such an extent that all aid agencies, with the exception of the International Red Cross, had withdrawn their personnel. In March President Mobutu of Zaire held talks, separately, with both Lt-Gen. Bashir and Col Garang in an attempt to restart the collapsed peace negotiations. Garang pronounced himself in favour of a cease-fire proposed by President Mobutu, but at the end of the month heavy fighting was reported to have erupted around the government-held garrisons of Yei and Rumbrek, in south-western Sudan, where convoys carrying supplies were reported to have been ambushed by the SPLA. The attack took place as part of a plan to restrict the roads to the main government base at Juba, which was besieged by the SPLA.

In late March 1990 57 people, including both army officers and civilians, were reported to have been arrested after allegedly having attempted to stage a *coup d'état*. A reshuffle of the cabinet on 10 April was believed to have strengthened the influence of Islamic fundamentalists in Sudanese politics, since two of the new appointees were known to be close to the NIF. It was claimed that a further attempted coup took place on 23 April, and this led to the execution, the following day, of 28 army officers. The origins of this alleged conspiracy were obscure; it was subsequently claimed that it may have resulted from Bashir's dismissal of large numbers of army officers opposed to Islamic fundamentalist ideology. The military regime's commitment to enforced Islamization was emphasized in March 1990, when a 'declaration of integration' was signed with Libya, providing for the merging of the two countries within four years. This declaration was formally confirmed in September. In March 1991 both countries signed an agreement of judicial integration. This was followed, in May, by a decision to co-ordinate their foreign policies. There were reports of increasing repression of the Sudanese population—both military and civilian—in April 1990, and this was attributed by some observers to the growing political influence of Islamic fundamentalists associated with the NIF.

In May 1990 a senior official of the US department of state met Col Garang in an attempt to revive the peace talks, while US diplomats in Khartoum reportedly held talks with representatives of the government with the aim of facilitating further peace negotiations. However, reports in June cited the regular visits of Sudanese leaders to Iran and the allocation of civil service posts to Islamic fundamentalists as evidence of the military regime's increasingly fundamentalist character. They thus cast even more doubt on the likelihood of any progress towards an early settlement of the southern conflict. It was claimed, in late September 1990, that another coup attempt had been thwarted. Like those alleged to have taken place earlier in the year, its origins remained mysterious. Some members of banned Sudanese political parties claimed that the latest alleged coup had in fact been instigated by the NIF in order to undermine an impending reconciliation between the former civilian government of Sadiq al-Mahdi and the SPLA. Reports of a fourth coup attempt, in November, were denied by the government. The reports followed growing internal unrest, including strike action by railway and other workers and student demonstrations in Khartoum; the University of Khartoum had been closed since September after clashes between student factions. Three former ministers in the al-Mahdi government, all members of the UP, were among those reported to have been detained.

The Sudanese regime's refusal to condemn Iraq after its invasion of Kuwait was a cause of increasing international isolation for the country from the second half of 1990, alienating foreign aid donors and particularly its northern neighbour Egypt, as well as contributing to internal tensions, even within the leadership. Two members of the RCC were reported to have been placed under house arrest as a result of their opposition to the regime's pro-Iraqi stance.

The formation of an opposition government-in-exile was reported by a government-owned newspaper in January 1991. It was reported to have been formed by Lt-Gen. Fatih Ahmed Ali, the former army c-in-c, with SPLA leader Col Garang as his deputy. A cabinet reshuffle in late January created three new ministries and redesignated several existing departments; the ministers of industry and of transport and communications, whose departments had been criticized for poor performance, were replaced. The non-Muslim minister for relief and refugee affairs, Peter Orat Ador, also left the cabinet, but no replacement was announced. (In March al-Bashir announced the abolition of the ministry and the reallocation of its roles.) At the beginning of February, al-Bashir signed a decree introducing a new penal code, based, like its predecessor, on *Shari'a* law. (Although the earlier Islamic penal code had remained in force, the punishments it prescribed had not been applied since the overthrow of Nimeri in 1985.) The code, which was to take effect from 22 March, was not to apply, for the present, in the three Southern regions of Equatoria, Upper Nile and Bahr al-Ghazal. This exemption, however, appeared to cover only five of the code's 186 articles, (those concerned with specified punishments), and it was stated that the code would be applicable to non-Muslim Sudanese residents in the North, notably the estimated 2m. refugees, who had fled to the Khartoum area from the civil war in Southern Sudan.

Later in February 1991 a new administrative structure for the provinces was introduced. According to the government, the changes would be conducive to greater regional autonomy—an issue in the civil war. The previous 18 administrative regions were replaced with nine states: Khartoum, Central, Kordofan, Darfur, Northern, Eastern, Bahr al-Ghazal, Upper Nile and Equatoria, which were in turn sub-divided into 66 provinces and 281 local government areas. Each of the nine new states was to have its own governor, deputy governor and cabinet of ministers, and was to assume responsibility for local administration and the collection of some taxes. The central government retained control over foreign policy, military affairs, the economy and the other main areas of administration. The SPLA rejected the measures as inadequate, describing the new non-Muslim governors of the three Southern states as 'figure-heads'.

Further signs of dissent within the regime emerged following the execution of 20 army officers in April 1991 for their alleged involvement in a coup attempt. Faisal Abu Salih, the minister of the interior and a member of the RCC, together with another RCC member, Brig.-Gen. Uthman Ahmed Hassan, were subsequently dismissed from their posts without explanation. At the end of April, al-Bashir announced the immediate release of all the country's political prisoners. His statement gave no indication of the numbers involved, although a government official stated that some 100 prisoners would be released; human rights organizations, however, claimed that at least 60 of the government's opponents remained in detention. Among those released was the former prime minister, Sadiq al-Mahdi, who had been under house arrest, and Muhammad Ibrahim Nugud, secretary of the SCP. A one-month amnesty for all opponents of the government was declared, and was further renewed in June without limit on time. The announcements coincided with the holding, in Khartoum between 29 April–2 May, of a national conference on Sudan's political future, attended by some 1,600 delegates chosen by the regime. Following this conference, al-Bashir announced, on 29 June, that a political system based on Libyan-style 'people's congresses' was to be introduced.

Col Garang marked the eighth anniversary of the start of the civil war on 16 May 1991 by inviting the government to take part in peace negotiations. The government responded by stating that it was willing at any time to discuss terms for a settlement, but it reiterated its view that the administrative reforms introduced in February already represented a considerable degree of compromise. Rebel forces remained in control of most of Southern Sudan. In mid-May a UN official stated that at least 30 civilians had been killed in a government air raid on the SPLA-controlled town of Nasir. The overthrow, on 21 May, of the Ethiopian government led by Mengistu Haile Mariam had implications for the SPLA forces, who had in the past enjoyed Ethiopian support; armed clashes within Ethiopia between SPLA forces and those of the new Ethiopian government were reported in late May. On 29 May the Sudanese government declared its recognition of, and support for, the new Ethiopian regime.

International efforts to achieve a peace settlement within Sudan gained renewed momentum in mid-1991. In mid-June the government announced that it would consider proposals made by the US assistant secretary of state for african affairs, Herman Cohen, providing for the partial withdrawal of government forces from Southern Sudan, the withdrawal of the SPLA forces from government-held areas and the declaration of Juba, the Southern capital, as an 'open' city. On 14 June the SPLA declared its support for the government's suggestion that the president of Nigeria, Ibrahim Babangida, should act as a mediator. However, this diplomatic progress coincided with a new government offensive against the SPLA. At the beginning of July, following a meeting in Addis Ababa between Cohen and Lt-Col Muhammad Amin Khalifa Yunis of the RCC, Garang was reported to have agreed to begin unconditional peace negotiations with the government. However, in August 1991, as part of a cabinet reshuffle, which was carried out during the absence in the UK of President al-

Bashir, Tayib Ibrahim Muhammad Khair, the former minister of presidential affairs and a prominent Muslim fundamentalist, was appointed governor of the Southern Province of Darfur. This appointment was viewed as unlikely to improve the prospects of a definitive peace settlement in the immediate future.

An alleged coup attempt was reported by the government in late August 1991, following the arrest of 10 army officers and a number of civilians. A government spokesman claimed that the planned attempt had been financed by unspecified foreign powers. Subsequent official statements alleged that those implicated included members of the National Democratic Alliance (NDA, a grouping formed in 1989 by the SPLA and some of the other former political parties, including the UP) and the previously unknown organization, *Ana al-Sudan* ('I am Sudan'). The NDA claimed at the end of September that more than 70 people had been arrested in the wake of the alleged coup attempt and that the former prime minister, Sadiq al-Mahdi, had been among those interrogated. The trial by a military court of 15 people accused of involvement in the coup attempt, including two civilians, began in early October and resulted in death sentences for 10 army officers, commuted in December to life imprisonment.

Reports of a split within the SPLA, published in Khartoum at the end of August 1991, were immediately denied by Garang. Three SPLA field commanders—Riek Mashar Teny-Dhurgon, Lam Akol and Gordon Koang Chol—claimed to have taken over the leadership of the SPLA and accused Garang of dictatorial behaviour. The dissidents, based at Nasir in the East, were reported to favour a policy of secession for the South, whereas the aim of Garang and his supporters, based at Kapoeta, remained a united, secular state. The split was also along ethnic lines, with the Dinka supporting Garang and the Nuer the breakaway faction. The SPLA's divisions led to a postponement of the first round of peace talks due to be held under the auspices of the OAU in Abuja, the Nigerian federal capital, at the end of October. Fighting between the two SPLA factions intensified in November and resulted in the massacre of several thousand civilians in the southern towns of Bor and Kongor before a cease-fire was negotiated in mid-December. Aid workers in the region reported that the Khartoum government had been supplying the dissident group with arms in an effort to exacerbate the divisions within the rebel movement. At the end of November the government announced a one-month amnesty for rebels who wished to surrender.

Plans for a return to democratic rule were announced by al-Bashir in his Independence Day speech on 1 January 1992. A transitional parliament would be appointed, he said, to prepare for democracy. The parliament would have 300 members and would have powers to propose and pass legislation, ratify treaties with foreign powers and to veto the RCC's decisions. The parliament was duly formed on 13 February, under the chairmanship of Col. Khalifa, who had earlier been relieved of his post on the RCC and retired from the army. Members of the parliament, which convened for the first time on 24 February, included—as well as all members of the RCC (except al-Bashir), state governors and representatives of the army and police—former members of the banned UP and DUP, and former aides to ex-president Nimeri, reflecting the government's desire to broaden its support in the wake of the introduction of an unpopular programme of economic austerity measures (see Economy). There were reports of widespread political unrest in early February, with demonstrations against the new economic policies and the reported arrest of a number of army officers who were alleged to be planning an attack on the military leadership. A further alleged coup attempt was reported to have been foiled in mid-April, when the government announced that it had arrested a group of military officers who had been plotting to overthrow the government. Press reports quoted Sudanese government sources as saying the plotters had planned to return ex-president Nimeri to power.

The government, while still declaring its willingness to take part in peace talks, launched a new dry season military offensive against the SPLA in late February and early March. With the SPLA weakened by its internal divisions and loss of Ethiopian backing, the town of Pochala, on the Ethiopian border, held by the SPLA since 1985, was captured in March—although the Ethiopian government denied reports that its forces had helped the Sudanese army to recapture the town—and during April 1992 the towns of Bor, Kongor, Yirol, Pibor and Mongalla also fell to government forces. In late April Garang said that the government offensive had been halted and that the towns lost by the SPLA had been in the hands of the dissident faction, which he accused of defecting to the government. However, on 1 May government forces were reported to have captured a larger rebel camp at Bahr el-Ghazal in western Sudan, followed on 12 May by Liria, on the road east from Juba to Garang's Torit headquarters. On 28 May, Kapoeta, near the Kenyan border, also fell to government forces. Strengthened by its military successes and by Kenya's reported agreement to stop supporting the SPLA, the government announced its willingness to participate in peace talks. The talks, which opened in Abuja on 26 May and were hosted by Nigeria's President Babangida, the current OAU chairman, were attended by a government delegation and two from the SPLA: one representing Garang's faction, the other the dissident group based at Nasir and led by Lam Akol. The talks concluded on 5 June, with an agreement by all parties to continue 'peaceful negotiations' at a future date, under Nigerian mediation, although there was no mention of a cease-fire. The final communiqué referred to Sudan as a 'multi-ethnic, multi-lingual, multi-cultural and multi-religious country' but a demand by the two SPLA factions for a referendum on self-determination for the South was withdrawn at government insistence.

The government's military offensive continued to make progress in Southern Sudan, with the opening, for the first time in seven years, of a river passage to Juba in mid-June 1992 and of the railway to Wau later in the month. On 12 July the government announced the capture of Torit, near the Ugandan border, which had been Garang's headquarters and the last major town in rebel hands. Garang himself was reported to have escaped to Kajo Kaji, closer to the Ugandan border, shortly before the fall of Torit and the SPLA quickly mounted a counter-attack on the town. Keen to re-establish its credibility after a series of reverses, the rebel movement launched a new offensive as the rainy season started, mounting an attack on Juba and attempting to disrupt government supply lines to the newly-recaptured southern towns. There were indications that the two rebel factions had achieved a measure of reconciliation since the Abuja meeting, enabling them to offer a united response to the government advance. The shelling of Juba led to the suspension of relief flights to the city and by mid-August the city's 300,000 people were reported to be close to starvation. Meanwhile, the SPLA claimed that government troops had massacred 900 civilians in the city. Confused reports emerged about fighting around Malakal, the capital of Upper Nile province, with the Nasir faction of the SPLA claiming to have captured the town from government forces in early October. Both the government and the Torit faction of the SPLA claimed to be in control of the town during October and November. Attempts by Nigeria to reactivate the peace process that had begun in May continued during the second half of 1992, but foundered on the increasingly fragmented nature of the SPLA. A round of talks that was scheduled to be held in Abuja in December was abandoned because of disagreements over which factions should attend.

Evidence of divisions between the RCC leadership and the NIF over the continued military domination of the government emerged in early 1993. In statements that he later retracted the leader of the NIF, Dr Hassan at-Turabi, declared that he expected the RCC to resign and to transfer power to a transitional assembly. A cabinet reshuffle was announced on 18 January, in which the ministries of states' affairs co-ordination, of social security and social development and of construction and public works were disbanded, and new ministries of labour and administrative reform, and economic planning and investment, were created. The two new ministries were headed, respectively, by Brig.-Gen. Dominic Kassiano Bakhit (the former minister of labour and social insurance), and Ali el-Hag Muhammad, the government spokesman in negotiations with the SPLA. Abd ar-Rahim Muhammad Hussain, a close aide of al-Bashir, was appointed minister of the interior, replacing Brig.-Gen. Zubair Muhammad Salih, who remained vice-chairman of the RCC. The minister of health, Faisal Madani, also lost his ministerial portfolio as well as his seat on the RCC. In February the minister of foreign affairs, Ali Sahloul, was replaced by Hussein Suleiman Abu Salih. The visit of Pope John Paul II to Khartoum on 10 February took place against a background of reported discrimination against Sudanese Christians. The Pope was reported to have stated that the Vatican would resist the imposition of *Shari'a* law on Sudan's Christian minority. Roman Catholic bishops in Sudan had repeatedly attacked the government's human rights record and later in February Amnesty International published a report documenting alleged violations of human rights, including the massacre of hundreds of civilians in the Nuba mountains in December 1992 and January 1993 (other reports estimated the number of victims at as high as 6,000 and alleged that the government was pursuing a policy of genocide against the Nuba people). The report by Amnesty International also alleged that 'disappearances' and executions had occurred in Juba. On 10 March the UN commission on human rights announced that it was appointing a rapporteur for Sudan in response to allegations of 'grave violations' of human rights there.

Contacts between the government and the various rebel factions took place in Uganda and Kenya during February 1993, with a view to resuming the peace process. Garang announced a unilateral cease-fire on 17 March, in honour of the Muslim holiday of Id al-Fitr, and aimed at providing a favourable atmosphere for the peace talks, a gesture to which the government responded with its own announcement of a cease-fire two days later. Garang also urged the establishment of safety zones to allow the delivery of food supplies to starving people. However, at the end of March fighting was reported at Kongor between Garang's forces and the 'Forces of Unity' faction of the SPLM, led by William Nyuon.

Peace talks between the government and the faction of the SPLM led by Garang resumed in Abuja in April 1993. After preliminary discussions on 8 April, at which it was agreed to continue to observe a cease-fire, the two sides met again for substantive talks on 26 April. Meanwhile, in Nairobi, talks were also taking place between a government delegation and SPLA–United, an alliance formed in early April between the Nasir faction, the 'Forces of Unity' and a faction led by Carabino Kuany Bol. The Abuja talks adjourned on 18 May, having made little progress on the main issues dividing the parties. Although the government claimed the talks would resume in June, the SPLA side said they had been a failure and that the cease-fire was at an end. The Nairobi talks, after a break in early May, resumed during 7–26 May and ended with agreement on the concept of a unified federal state and on the rights of state governments to introduce laws supplementary to federal legislation—allowing the implementation of Shari'a law in the north, but not in the south. No agreement was reached, however, on the length of the transition period before the holding of a referendum on future divisions of power.

The collapse of the Aboja negotiations was quickly followed by allegations of cease-fire violations from both the government and rebel factions, and in July 1993 the faction of the SPLA led by Garang announced that it had launched a major offensive after attacks by government troops, aided by rival SPLA factions. In August the government attacked SPLA-held towns near the Ugandan border in an offensive aimed at cutting supply routes to rebel forces in southern and western Sudan. They were reported to have gained control of the town of Morobo and to have blocked the road route for relief supplies to Bahr al-Ghazal and Western Equatoria. Also in August, the Nuba people were reported to be threatened by government forces in central Sudan. Independent obervers urged the UN to establish 'safe havens' for refugees and to extend its Operation Lifeline Sudan to the Nuba Mountains. In early September the SPLA was reported to have checked the government forces's advance in southern Sudan. A reshuffle of the cabinet in July 1993 was regarded as having strengthened the position of the NIF within the government, and as a further step towards the establishment of a civilian administration.

On 19 October 1993 al-Bashir announced political reforms in preparation for presidential and legislative elections to be held in 1994 and 1995 respectively. The RCC had been dissolved three days previously—after it had appointed al-Bashir as president and as head of a new civilian government. Cabinet ministers were requested to remain in office until elections took place. In October al-Bashir appointed a new minister of defence—a portfolio that he had formerly held himself—and a new vice-president. Western observers regarded the dissolution of the RCC as reinforcing the position of the NIF within the government during the transition to civilian rule. At the end of October the cabinet was reshuffled.

In January 1994 the two principal rival factions of the SPLA were reported to have agreed on a cease-fire. In late January government forces were reported to have launched ground and air offensives against rebel forces in southern Sudan, forcing thousands of civilians to flee across the Ugandan border. The intensity of the offensives led to speculation that the government was attempting finally to end the civil war. In mid-February the SPLA claimed that it had repulsed a government advance in Southern Equatoria.

In early February 1994, by constitutional decree, Sudan was redivided into 26 states instead of the nine that had formed the basis of administration since 1991. The executive and legislative powers of each state government were to be expanded, and southern states were expected to be exempted from *Shari'a* law.

In late March 1994 delegations representing the government and two factions of the SPLA travelled to Nairobi, Kenya, in order to participate in peace talks mediated by the Intergovernmental Authority on Drought and Development (IGADD). The negotiations ended with each side agreeing to allow the free passage of relief supplies to southern Sudan. A second round of peace talks mediated by the IGADD commenced on 19 May, but was adjourned the following day in order to allow the participants sufficient time to study a draft declaration of principles on which future negotiations were to be based. A minor resuffle of the cabinet took place in mid-July. In late July the government announced a unilateral cease-fire. However, this was rejected by the SPLA two days later.

With Sudan having become alienated from many of its former Western aid donors because of its poor human rights record, the government has made special efforts to cultivate relationships with other Islamic countries. Iran's president Ali Akbar Hashemi Rafsanjani visited Khartoum in December 1991 to sign agreements on co-operation in oil exploration, trade and training. Press reports that Iran was helping to train the Sudanese armed forces and was financing Sudan's purchase of arms from China were denied, but there were persistent reports of Iranian military assistance to the Sudanese government in its offensive against the SPLA. Relations with Egypt deteriorated sharply in February 1992, following the announcement that Sudan had awarded a Canadian company a concession to explore for oil in the Halaib triangle, a disputed border area on the Red Sea coast. A committee was established by the two countries to discuss the issue but met only once, in March. In April two Sudanese policemen were killed in a clash between border guards in the Halaib area and relations deteriorated further as Egypt repeatedly accused Sudan of supporting illegal Islamic fundamentalist groups in Egypt—matched by Sudanese allegations that Egypt was supporting the SPLA. In August the Sudanese government announced that it wished to seek international arbitration on the Halaib issue, claiming that Egypt had been settling families in the area in an effort to bring it under Egyptian control. A series of bilateral meetings held during the second half of 1992 failed to resolve the issue, and in January 1993 Sudan lodged a complaint about the dispute with the UN Security Council, alleging that Egyptian troops had infringed Sudan's territorial integrity. In March Egypt announced the construction of a new road link to Halaib. Sudan retaliated by closing the Khartoum campus of Cairo University. In June Sudan announced that it was closing two Egyptian consulates in Sudan and two of its own consulates in Egypt. A meeting between al-Bashir and the Egyptian President Hosni Mubarak, during a summit meeting of the OAU at the end of June appeared, however, to ease tensions between the two countries, and was followed by a meeting of their respective ministers of foreign affairs at the end of July. In May 1994 Sudan accused Egypt of establishing military posts on Sudanese territory.

Egypt's concern about Sudanese involvement in fundamentalist violence found an echo in the USA, which repeatedly expressed alarm about Sudan's links with Iran. Allegations of Sudanese involvement in terrorism resulted in the detention in the USA, in June 1993, of five Sudanese residents suspected of involvement in a plot to blow up buildings and road tunnels in New York, and to assassinate President Mubarak on a visit to the USA. The Sudanese government denied any connection with the plot, but in August the USA added Sudan to its list of nations accused of sponsoring terrorism. The US department of state claimed that Sudan had allowed terrorists to use its territory as a sanctuary and described reports of the existence in Sudan of training camps for terrorists as 'credible'. Sudan denied these allegations, challenging the USA to provide evidence of the involvement of any Sudanese in terrorist acts. Allegations of Sudanese support for fundamentalist groups have also been made by Tunisia; the two countries closed their embassies in each other's capitals at the end of July 1992.

Sudan's relations with the United Kingdom deteriorated in December 1993, when the Archbishop of Canterbury, Dr George Carey, cancelled a planned visit to Khartoum but made another, behind SPLA lines, in the south. This resulted in the mutual expulsion of ambassadors by Sudan and the United Kingdom. The release by the Sudanese to the French authorities, in Agusut 1994, of the Venezuelan-born terrorist, Illich Ramirez Sanchez ('Carlos'), was regarded by many observers as an attempt by the government to improve its international standing.

The population of Sudan has continued to suffer from both natural disasters and the civil war. In August 1988 it was estimated that up to 2m. people had been displaced by heavy flooding, while estimates by the UN for the whole of 1988 suggested that 250,000 people had died of starvation. In April 1989 the UN initiated a major emergency relief operation that was intended to ease the region's plight. In March 1990, a report by the human rights organization, Africa Watch, claimed that as many as 500,000 Sudanese civilians had been killed by war and 'man-made' famine since 1986. In September 1990 Sudan reportedly faced shortages of food as serious as those which had occurred in 1984/85, and it was feared that supplies of emergency food aid would be exhausted by the end of October 1990. The Sudanese government, however, continued to claim that international warnings of an impending famine were exaggerated and formed part of a Western conspiracy to undermine the regime. After claiming for some months that Sudan was suffering merely a 'temporary food gap', in December Sudanese officials conceded that the country faced a shortage of 1m. tons of cereals. UN officials estimated the deficit at 1.8m. tons, and forecast that up to 7.8m. Sudanese were at risk from famine. The government was also widely criticized for hampering the work of foreign relief agencies, apparently on the grounds that some aid workers were sympathetic to the SPLA; a number of aid workers were expelled in late 1990, when the government announced that all aid agencies would be required to re-register with the authorities by the end of the year if they wished to continue operating in Sudan. In December the UN World Food Programme (WFP) was allowed to resume relief flights from Uganda to Juba in the South, which had been suspended in 1989, following threats by Sudan to shoot down any aircraft flying without prior government approval.

In February 1991 the government was strongly criticized by the EC for its handling of the famine situation. Al-Bashir responded by telling a rally that foreign relief organizations were 'defaming Sudan by begging on behalf of the Sudanese people', and he added that Sudan would 'free itself from dependence on relief supplies and achieve self-sufficiency in food production in a year or two'. However, after continuing international pressure had eventually forced the government to concede both the need for a large-scale relief operation and its own inability to organize such an effort without outside assistance, UN agencies were, by April, able to resume their activities. The delay in organizing relief shipments led to concern, however, that food would not reach those in need in time. By late April it was estimated that only 6% of essential supplies had been moved from Port Sudan to areas of need. Relief efforts were placed under increasing strain by the return of more than 200,000 Sudanese refugees from Ethiopia following the overthrow of the Ethiopian government in late May. At the end of June, the WFP began an airdrop of food to about 110,000 refugees in the Nasir area of Southern Sudan. Large numbers of Ethiopian soldiers were also crossing the border into Sudan; by late June, about 400,000 refugees were reported to have arrived in Sudan from Ethiopia, most of them Sudanese who had fled the fighting in southern Sudan in the mid-1980s, but who returned because of increased violence in Ethiopia following the overthrow of the Mengistu regime. Some 300,000 Ethiopian refugees were reported to remain in Sudan in February 1994.

The Sudanese government's relationship with aid agencies remained a troubled one. At the end of August 1991, the government briefly suspended permission for UN agencies to operate relief flights into rebel-held areas, following statements by UN officials accusing the government of obstructing relief efforts. In November government officials announced that Sudan was self-sufficient in food, as a result of policies to switch plantings on the most productive land from export crops, such as cotton, to cereals. Officials described western claims that millions of Sudanese were threatened with starvation as hostile propaganda. Nevertheless, it remained clear that severe shortages were being experienced in many areas in the war-afflicted South, as well as in the western state of Darfur, where crops failed in 1991/92 after a further year of drought. By early 1992, the UN estimated that, despite good harvests in much of the country, about 7.2m. Sudanese were in need of food aid. Aid agencies had enormous problems, however, maintaining supply lines into Southern Sudan in the face of insecurity and government suspicion of their activities. Relief flights from Kenya to the southern town of Wau were suspended during September 1991–January 1992 after a Red Cross aircraft hit a land mine on the runway. Relief operations were also severely disrupted during the government's offensive against the SPLA in March and April 1992, when the government ordered a six-week suspension of aid flights.

International relief efforts in Southern Sudan in 1993 continued to be hampered by insecurity and by lack of funds. A UN appeal, launched in January, for $190m. in aid had by May raised only some $40m. In late May the Torit faction of the SPLA and SPLA-United signed an agreement, mediated by the US ambassador to Sudan, to withdraw their forces from the area around Ayod, Kongor and Waat, known to aid workers as the 'famine triangle', in order to allow the free movement of relief supplies to an estimated 60,000 people on the verge of starvation. In June, as the UN began air-drops of food in the Ayod area, an EC delegation visited Khartoum in an effort to persuade the government to establish aid corridors to people trapped by fighting in the south. By mid-1993, some 1.5m. people were reported to be in need of food aid, with 600,000 having no other source of supply. It was estimated that Sudan would require some $279m.-worth of food aid in 1994.

Economy

DEDE-ESI AMANOR

Revised for this edition by the Editor

Sudan is primarily an agricultural and pastoral country, with about 61% of the economically active population engaged in the agricultural sector—the majority in essentially subsistence production. Industry is mostly agriculturally-based and accounted for 15% of gross domestic product (GDP) in 1991 (compared with 2% in the early 1960s). A major expansion of rain-fed production, which provides most staple foods and some export crops, in the 1970s helped to generate vigorous economic growth. By the early 1980s, however, the progressively deteriorating rainfall in the west and east of Sudan began to reduce production, and the contribution of agriculture to GDP declined sharply. Nevertheless, agriculture has remained the largest single contributor to GDP, accounting, until recently, for about one-third; agriculture is also the source of virtually all of Sudan's earnings of foreign exchange.

The average real growth in overall GDP was 3.8% per year in 1965–80. Annual average growth in GDP was 2.5% in the period 1980–88, and was 1.7% in 1990–91. Real growth in GDP rose to 9.4% in 1986, but fell again to 0.8% in the following year. Negative growth rates of −6.6%, −2.0% and −4.0% were estimated for 1988, 1989 and 1990 respectively. In 1991, according to estimates by the World Bank, Sudan's gross national product (GNP), measured at average 1989–91 prices, was US $10,107m. In 1990 GNP per head (at average 1988–90 prices) amounted to US $400. During 1980–91, it was estimated, GNP increased, in real terms, at an average rate of 3% per year, while real GNP per head declined by 2.4% per year.

Until the early 1970s Sudan's trade deficit was minimal, despite a steady growth of imports, thanks to high domestic production and good world prices for cotton (the crop which has dominated Sudan's exports since the late 1920s). After 1971, however, there was a dramatic decline in cotton production, which was only partially compensated for in terms of earnings by a major expansion to rain-fed exports (notably of sorghum). At the same time imports expanded dramatically, and in 1980/81 and 1981/82 the deficit on the balance of trade was estimated to exceed $900m. Despite some recovery in cotton production after 1982, total export earnings have continued to decline, owing to drought and poor world prices. In 1987 the value of Sudan's export earnings was only $504m., while that of imports amounted to $929m., compared with almost $800m. and $1,650m. respectively in 1981. The value of exports f.o.b. was $509m. in 1988 and $671m. in 1989. The value of imports c.i.f. was $1,060m. in 1988.

Prospects for the economy remained bleak in the early of the 1990s, with production of cotton and sorghum (which accounted for over 47% of total exports in 1988) expected to fluctuate. In 1992 the visible trade deficit amounted to $596.8m. In the same year the deficit on the current account of the balance of payments was $506.2m. The phasing-out of subsidies on many basic commodities and the devaluation of the Sudanese pound in 1991 and 1992 led to a sharp increase in inflation which was estimated to be running at 120% in mid-1992. However, government officials reported that the devaluation had resulted in a sharp increase in expatriate remittances in the first half of 1992. According to the World Bank, the annual rate of inflation averaged 42.8% in 1980–92.

The deterioration in Sudan's economic position in the 1970s was a result of the policies pursued by the Nimeri government. Encouraged by the willingness of Western and Arab states to channel vast amounts of concessionary and commercial finance into Sudan, the regime embarked upon a grandiose development programme which emphasized new, capital-intensive projects, such as the Kenana sugar complex and an ambitious road-building programme, at the expense of traditional, irrigated infrastructure and the railways which produced and transported the bulk of Sudan's cotton and other important exports. By 1980, such policies, combined with the heavy borrowing involved and growing mismanagement, inefficiency and corruption in the public sector (which controlled some 60% of productive capacity), had brought the economy to the verge of collapse and burdened the country with a level of foreign debt which has now become the prime obstacle to economic recovery.

Attempts to resolve Sudan's economic crisis began in 1978 and for the next five years consisted of repeated debt reschedulings, donor aid packages underpinned by the IMF, World Bank-sponsored austerity measures and structural adjustment programmes aimed at restoring some balance to the external account by boosting export crop production. After 1981 the new policies, especially towards the irrigated sector, began to have an effect. By 1983 cotton output had returned to its pre-1970 level of around 1m. bales (each of 190.3 kg), and the deficit on the current account of the balance of payments, at $220m., was less than one-third of its 1980 level of $784m.

Nimeri's Islamization, in September 1983, of economic policies and the legal code, in an attempt to suppress growing popular opposition to his government and to the fall in living standards associated with the austerity programmes, brought this improvement to an abrupt end. This dislocation of the domestic economy resulted in the alienation of foreign donors and creditors, leading to the suspension of several important rehabilitation schemes and the collapse of the vital support programme of debt relief and economic aid. By exacerbating civil unrest in the South, Islamization also created security uncertainties, which led to the suspension of activity, in 1984, on two projects that had been viewed as vital to Sudan's long-term recovery: the Jonglei canal scheme and the development of the country's oil reserves.

The situation remained little changed for the first two years following the overthrow of Nimeri in April 1985, with drought compounding the problems of political instability and continuing civil conflict in the South. Since 1985, however, repeated attempts to formulate an economic programme which could open the way to new multilateral and bilateral lending have all proved unsuccessful. Several programmes were negotiated with the al-Mahdi government, but all eventually lapsed (see below). Following the June 1989 coup, the military regime of Lt-Gen. al-Bashir introduced strict measures in its attempt to ameliorate the economic situation, including a campaign against corruption and a decree that all citizens lodge their foreign currency in commercial banks. Potential donors were encouraged by the Government's decision to raise bread and sugar prices. Subsidies were estimated by the new government to cost £S3,500m. ($287m.) annually, including about $100m. in sugar subsidies. An earlier attempt by al-Mahdi's government to remove subsidies on essential commodities and raise the prices of basic goods (for sugar, by 500%) in December 1988 had led to a general strike, forcing the government to abandon these efforts. The government's economic policies have since centred on the achievement of food self-sufficiency, stricter control of the budget and reduction of the government deficit through the privatization of state enterprises.

AGRICULTURE

Approximately one-third of Sudan's total area of about 2.5m. sq km is considered to be suitable for some form of agriculture. Of this, about 84m. ha is potential arable land and the remainder pastoral. Only about 15%, however, of the available arable area is cropped, reflecting the critical role of water availability in the development of the sector. The vast majority of settled cultivation has, until recently, been limited to the permanent watercourses of the Blue and White Niles and their tributaries in north-central Sudan. It is these areas which, within the framework of Sudan's 2m. ha of irrigation schemes, have been the focus of modern, commercial agriculture—producing the major export crop, cotton, as well as vital import substitutes such as sugar and wheat.

In contrast, some 60% of Sudan's area is occupied by the 11% of the population (estimated at 26m. in 1990) who are fully or partly nomadic—combining cultivation of subsistence crops and some cash crops with seasonal migration, with their herds, along well-defined routes, determined by the location of sources of drinking water during the wet and dry seasons.

The rainlands account for virtually all output of the staple grains—sorghum and millet—as well as of meat, milk and some vegetable products, and output in normal rainfall years has usually been enough for self-sufficiency. Livestock have also been an important export, as have other rain-fed products such as sesame seed, gum arabic and groundnuts. According to FAO estimates, the rate of growth of agricultural production declined in the 1980s. In the period 1965–80 average annual growth was 2.9%, but this declined to an annual average of 2.1% in 1980–88. Agricultural production declined by an estimated 20.3% in 1989 and by a further 7.6% in 1990. In 1991, however, it rose by 30.8%, and in 1992 by 14.9%.

In the late 1970s the primary staple, sorghum, was also exported, becoming Sudan's second most important export after cotton. Exports were suspended in 1984/85 because of the drought, but were resumed on a small scale the following year with the recovery of production. In 1986/87, following a record harvest, exports expanded dramatically, bringing in record earnings of more than £S100m. Between 1970–80 the area under cereals increased by 68%, to 4.6m. ha, while sorghum production rose by over 40% to reach a pre-drought record of 3.3m. metric tons in 1981/82. Millet output expanded similarly to a record 573,000 tons in 1981/82. However, cereal production is insufficient to meet domestic consumption and imports of cereals totalled 707,000 metric tons in 1987, compared with 125,000 tons in 1974. Cereal production reached a record 5.17m. tons in 1988/89, but this was estimated to have fallen to 2m. tons in each of the following two years. Government policies to encourage a shift in cultivation on the most productive land from export crops, such as cotton, to cereals, in an effort to achieve food self-sufficiency, led to an increase in the production of cereals to about 4.9m. tons in 1991/92 according to UN Food and Agriculture Organization (FAO) figures.

In the late 1970s there was also a significant rise in livestock exports, encouraged by the large demand from the Middle East. Their value rose from 2% of total earnings in 1975/76 to about 13% in 1982/83 and to 17% in 1984/85, when the drought caused sales to increase. The depletion of the national herd has, however, since caused a dramatic decline in livestock exports. No cattle or goats were exported in 1988. The World Bank and IFAD have provided $20m. for a stock route project to enable the Livestock and Meat Marketing Corpn (LMMC) to improve watering and other facilities on the traditional west-east export routes. Work on the project started in late 1986 and complements an existing LMMC scheme to develop facilities to transport animals by rail to Khartoum. Livestock numbers in the South, however, were drastically reduced by the direct and indirect effects of the August 1988 floods, which were described as the worst in Sudan's history.

The national herd was estimated in 1983 at 20.5m. cattle, 19.3m. sheep, 14m. goats and 2.8m. camels, but may have been reduced by up to one-third by the drought, according to estimates from relief agencies. The impact of the drought on cereal production was more easily quantifiable. In 1982/83 sorghum production fell by one-third to just under 2m. tons, and by 1984/85 it had fallen to 1.1m., with the loss of almost 50% of mechanized, rain-fed production, which normally accounts for 60% of marketed output. In January 1985 Sudan was included on the UN list of 10 most severely drought-affected countries, and by May it was estimated that up to 11m. people were at risk, notably in the west and Red Sea Hills. With Sudan's annual food deficit estimated by the FAO at over 1m. tons, excluding some 900,000 tons of food aid pledged after late 1984, it was feared the country was facing a famine disaster paralleling that in Ethiopia in 1985. Nearly all the deficit was subsequently pledged, mainly by the USA, but transport difficulties severely hampered distribution to the most severely affected areas in Darfur and Kordofan. The establishment, in June and July, of an EC-co-ordinated airlift came too late to prevent the death, from starvation, of thousands of people.

In 1986 famine also became a major problem in the South, where inadequate rains and the disruptions caused by the civil war created major food shortages. The civil war caused relief efforts to be constantly interrupted throughout 1987 and 1988. Good rains in 1986/87, together with the introduction of a new high-yielding variety (HYV), stimulated sorghum production to a record level of almost 4m. tons, and a record crop was forecast for 1988/89, but the problem of distribution, both of local surpluses and food aid, has remained acute. In September 1988 it was reported that the levels of malnutrition and the percentage of those dying from starvation among the thousands of refugees from the civil war in the South were the worst ever recorded anywhere in the world. In the south-western town of Aweil alone, 8,000 people were estimated to have died, although it was not clear over what period of time. In March 1989 the government endorsed a UN-sponsored proposal to call a one-month cease-fire in the war in the South in order to facilitate the supply of 170,000 tons of food and medical supplies to victims of the conflict. 'Operation Lifeline' was launched in April and its first phase, costing $170m., ended in October 1989. After a four-month delay, the second phase of 'Operation Lifeline' got under way in early April 1990 after the Government and the SPLA dropped their opposition to relief flights. The 1990 programme of 'Operation Lifeline', for which donors were asked to raise $121m., aimed to transport 100,000 tons of relief supplies by air, road, river and rail. The World Food Programme (WFP) resumed airlifts of food from Entebbe airport in Uganda to the South at the end of May 1990. Meanwhile, the SPLA sought international assistance to help more than 100,000 people left homeless after earthquakes in the South in late May. It was estimated that 3.5m. Southern Sudanese had been displaced by war and famine by early 1990. There was also growing concern about food supplies both in Kordofan and Darfur in the west. Cereal stocks were virtually exhausted by mid-1990 and food aid requirements of around 100,000 tons were estimated for the year, as displaced refugees continued to arrive from the South. The WFP agreed to supply 6,500 tons of sorghum to western Kordofan region, where drought caused a 36% drop in the sorghum and millet crop, while the USA donated a further 5,000 tons of sorghum. The government and the WFP were reported to have reached agreement in May 1991 on the third phase of 'Operation Lifeline', allowing a resumption of relief flights into Southern Sudan.

The other major rain-fed products, gum arabic, sesame and groundnuts, have also been adversely affected by intermittent drought. Almost 12% of Sudan's area is classified as forest land, but a minimal amount is under commercial plantations, largely fuel-wood developments in the central region. Exploitation of the natural forest is also predominantly limited to fuel wood, other than gum arabic, which is by far the most important forest product. Until the 1970s Sudan was the world's largest single producer of edible gum, accounting for some 92% of production, but this was reduced to about 80% with the advent of new producers and artificial substitutes and with it the importance of gum in exports. A strong recovery was achieved, however, in the 1986/87 season, which not only produced a record harvest of 40,000 tons, but also record earnings, owing to strong world demand as Western consumers reacted against artificial substitutes. Gum arabic regained its place as Sudan's second most important export after cotton, accounting for 22% of total exports. In 1990 exports of gum arabic amounted to 40,000 tons, worth $62m. Production amounted to about 30,000 tons in 1991, earning some $50m. in export revenues, but fell to 9,000 tons the following year owing to locust infestation.

Sesame, which is also used locally as a source of vegetable oil, has pursued a similar trend in production and exports. After 1981, as with other crops, a major rise in producer prices encouraged increased production, which, combined with higher world prices, caused export earnings to rise from £S36.9m. in 1981/82 to £S90.4m. in 1985/86. In 1986/87 earnings declined to £S76.4m., owing to pest infestation of the crop, which caused output to decline to 131,000 tons from almost 200,000 tons in 1985/86. Sesame was the third most important export in 1987/88, when a harvest of more than 300,000 tons, the largest for a decade, brought earnings of £S269.0m. However, in 1988/89 Sudan produced only 146,000 tons of sesame, when exports of this crop earned £S333.3m. Production was reduced, however, to only 83,000 tons in 1989/90. The crop for 1990/91 recovered to 95,000 tons, but declined again in 1991/92, to 87,000 tons.

Groundnuts were until recently Sudan's second most important cash crop, and in 1991 the country was the fourth largest producer in Africa, after Nigeria, Senegal and Zaire. Groundnuts are grown both under rain-fed conditions in the far west and in the irrigated areas, and have major local use as a source of food and oil, as well as being a key export crop. Groundnut output has fluctuated considerably, but the trend since the mid-1970s, and especially in the 1980s, has been downwards as a result of low producer prices, falling world prices, problems related to aflatoxin disease in the west, and, most recently, drought. In the late 1980s the area under groundnuts totalled 1.2m. feddans (1 feddan = 4,201 sq m), and production in 1989 was 218,000 tons. Output fell to 123,000 tons in 1990, but recovered to 179,000 tons in 1991 and 454,000 tons in 1992.

Of the 2m. ha of land under irrigation, about 50% is in the Gezira scheme, which is located between the Blue and White Niles. First developed by the British in the 1920s to supply the Lancashire cotton mills, the Gezira is now the world's largest farming enterprise under one management—the parastatal Sudan Gezira Board. The remaining irrigated land is also predominantly under publicly-administered schemes: the small-scale farmer pump schemes on the Blue, White and main Niles, developed in the 1940s and 1950s; the New Halfa scheme developed in the 1960s on the Gash river to resettle people displaced by the Aswan high dam flooding; and the Rahad scheme, on the Blue Nile, inaugurated in 1977. Although these schemes account for over 60% of Africa's total irrigated area, they represent less than 50% of Sudan's estimated potential.

Expansion into new areas has been limited by capital costs—the present area represents an estimated investment of over $1,000m.—and by the terms of agreements with Egypt governing the use of the Nile waters. By the late 1970s Sudan was close to drawing its full quota of 20,500 cu m per year and began, in joint venture with Egypt, construction of the Jonglei canal in Southern Sudan. This scheme aimed at conserving, by the construction of a 360-km canal, some 4,000m. cu m of the 33,000m. cu m of water lost annually through evaporation in the Sudd swamp. The additional yield was to have been divided equally between the two countries, enabling Sudan to develop an additional 12,600 ha on the west bank of the Nile and reclaim up to 1.5m. ha of potential agricultural land. Work began in 1978 but had to be suspended in 1984, with 250 km completed, following attacks on construction workers by the Sudan People's Liberation Army (SPLA). The persistence of civil conflict in the South led to the suspension of operations in 1984, although work resumed on a limited basis in 1988.

The irrigated sector normally accounts for 40%–70% of export earnings, reflecting the fact that the major irrigated crop is cotton. The main types of cotton grown in Sudan are: the long-staple Barakats, the principal Gezira crop; the medium-staple Akala, introduced in the early 1970s to meet market demand for natural-synthetic fibre mixes; and the long-medium staple Shambat B variety, introduced in 1985. A small amount of rain-fed short-staple cotton is also grown. Akala accounted for over 50% of production in the late 1970s and early 1980s, but in response to over-supply of medium-staples on the world market and a shift in demand to natural fabrics, Sudan has switched back to traditional high-quality long staples (in which its only major competitor is Egypt) and expanded cultivation of the new Shambat B, which in 1988/89 was increased to 42% of total plantings, while that of Barakat was reduced to 32%. The 1988/89 planting programme envisaged an even more important role for Shambat B, which was due to account for 57% of total plantings of 812,000 feddans. The share of Barakat was to rise to 36%, while that of Akala was to be reduced to only 7.5%.

In terms of export performance, the share of cotton in total exports declined from 65% in 1979 to less than 45% in 1980; partly as a result of government policies which emphasized the development of wheat and other new crops, and the expansion of the mechanized rain-fed sector. Combined with a 1975 policy decision to reduce by one-third the area under cotton in the Gezira, the result was a fall in production from around 900,000 bales a year in the early 1970s to less than 500,000 bales in 1980/81. A reversal of policy in mid-1979, under IMF pressure to improve export crop production, saw the start of a large-scale rehabilitation programme for the irrigated sector, which was focused on the Gezira scheme. Gezira currently accounts for over one-half of Sudan's cotton output.

Despite the more favourable market conditions, Sudan experienced major difficulties in disposing of its crop between 1984–86 with a decline in sales to most of its customers, other than the People's Republic of China. The fall in demand reflected not only overall surplus cotton supplies on the world market, but also long-standing quality problems caused by white-fly infestation and the country's inflexible marketing policy, which tended towards over-pricing. In August 1986, with 1m. bales still stockpiled in Port Sudan, and the majority of the 1985/86 crop of 720,000 bales still unsold, the government was forced to sell off most of its stocks to foreign brokers at drastically discounted prices. With improved quality and the introduction of a more flexible marketing system, the same problem did not affect the 1986/87 and 1987/88 crops. Plantings were reduced in 1987/88, and 20% of the 1988/89 crop was destroyed by the floods in August 1988. Production was estimated to have fallen from 709,000 bales in 1988/89 to 589,000 bales in 1989/90, the lowest level since 1980/81. A shift in emphasis, towards the cultivation of food crops, led to a further fall in cotton output in 1990/91, to 450,000 bales worth some $150m. Earnings from cotton were £S1,349m. in 1989. As part of efforts to keep cotton earnings in the official economy and enhance foreign currency reserves, the military government announced in February 1990 a new exchange rate for cotton exporters of £S8.30 = US $1. This enabled exporters exchanging foreign currency on the official market almost to double their earnings in terms of Sudanese pounds.

The initial reorganization of the Gezira, which was paralleled by rehabilitation work at New Halfa and Rahad, was to be followed by a 10-year improvement programme beginning in 1983. Funding problems, complicated by Sudan's debt arrears with certain Arab donors, both delayed the commencement of the project and caused it to be scaled down drastically, from an initial $360m.–$400m. to $150m. Work eventually started in late 1984 with finance provided by European bilateral donors. The World Bank finally agreed its $80m. contribution after the April 1985 coup, and the Arab funding of $60m. became effective in late 1986 after agreement on a rescheduling formula for Sudan's debt arrears. In May 1988 the World Bank agreed to provide additional funding to rehabilitate Sudan's irrigation network, including the Rahad, New Halfa and Suski schemes. Preparatory work for this project was paralleled by the evaluation of a second planned programme to increase Sudan's cotton exports through the reorganization of their marketing. This project had initially been planned for 1985, but was subsequently suspended following the deterioration of Sudan's relations with donors. In 1986 and early 1987 aid-funded rehabilitation work also began on small-scale pump schemes on the Blue, White and main Niles. In late 1988 the International Development Association (IDA) assigned credits totalling $20m. for agricultural extension and research services, reafforestation and the development of rural water supplies in Kassala province. A further $10m. contribution to the scheme was offered by the UN High Commissioner for Refugees (UNHCR). In May 1989 it was reported that almost $40m. in new loans had been received from the Islamic Development Bank (IDB), Japan and the United Kingdom for agricultural development.

Rehabilitation of the irrigated sector also included a five-year programme for the four state-run sugar schemes: Hajar Assalaya, Sennar, el-Guneid and Khashm el-Girba. Development of sugar production began in the 1960s to reduce the costs of Sudan's single most expensive import commodity after oil. However, owing to inadequate provision for recurrent expenditure and technical and managerial problems, annual production of raw sugar from the four schemes had fallen to under 48% of installed capacity of 369,000 tons by the late 1970s. Work began in 1984 on a $180m. multi-donor rehabilitation and management reform programme to restore production to over 300,000 tons a year. Output from the four schemes totalled nearly 200,000 tons in 1984/85 out of a national output of 496,939 tons. Although drought reduced the crop to 159,000 tons in 1985/86, output from the four schemes improved the following year. Total production in 1984/85 was sufficient to meet domestic demand, and satisfied 98% of domestic demand in 1985/86, despite the effects of the drought. Six years earlier less than 35% of domestic requirements had been satisfied locally. The recovery represented not only upgrading of the parastatal sector, but also the entry into production of one of the world's largest sugar complexes. The Kenana scheme, located south-west of the Gezira between the Blue and White Niles, was officially opened in 1981 and was producing over 300,000 tons of sugar per year by 1984/85. The scheme, which has a potential annual capacity of 330,000 tons, played a major role in eliminating Sudan's sugar import costs in 1986. In mid-1989, however, a sugar shortfall of 200,000 tons was reported. Sugar production in 1989/90 was estimated at 421,000 tons, rising to 489,000 tons in 1990/91, creating the possibility of sugar exports. (Domestic consumption, which was put at 554,000 tons in 1988/89, was thought to have been reduced subsequently by a government ban on sugar imports.) A $50m. expansion plan for the Kenana sugar scheme was due to start in mid-1991. The plan, largely financed by the African Development Bank and African Development Fund, involved the planting of an additional 3,000 ha of sugar cane to raise white sugar production from 240,000 tons to 300,000 tons within five years. In 1991 production of white sugar amounted to 170,000 tons, an increase of 10% compared with 1990. Environmental protection measures and a 10-MW expansion of the scheme's power station were also planned.

Wheat, Sudan's other major irrigated crop, is also an import substitute, although attempts to increase irrigated domestic production have had very limited success owing to the unsuitability of the climate south of the Egyptian border area. This causes yields to be very low.

INDUSTRY

The ginning of cotton encouraged the beginning of industry in Sudan in the early 20th century. With the expansion of cotton production, the number of ginning factories has increased, with the Gezira Board alone operating the world's largest single ginning complex, on which rehabilitation work was started in 1985, as part of the 10-year improvement programme for the scheme. There are 25 spinning and weaving mills, the majority of which were built in the 1970s. The country is not yet self-sufficient in basic cotton cloth, however, owing to a disparity between spinning and weaving capacity. Cotton seeds are partly decorticated, while exports of cottonseed oil and oil-cake are increasing. Groundnuts are also partly processed, with oil and cake dominating exports of groundnut products. Minerals (copper, iron, mica, chromite and, most recently, gold), which constitute less than 1% of exports, are exported in the crudest form.

With the exception of enterprises producing cement, soap, soft drinks and vegetable oils, large-scale manufacturing of import substitutes started in Sudan only after 1960. This is reflected in the manufacturing sector's contribution to GDP, which in 1991 totalled only 8.2%. State involvement was minimal before 1960, but thereafter expanded dramatically, particularly in the 1970s, owing to the 1971 nationalizations and, subsequently, to the government's development plans. By 1986 the public sector included the four sugar factories, three tanneries, a number of food-processing plants, the two cement works and the spinning and weaving mills, as well as joint-venture participation in the Port Sudan tyre factory (with a Republic of Korea company) and in the fertilizer plant south of Khartoum (with a US company). All state-controlled enterprises in the manufacturing sector operated with varying and increasing degrees of inefficiency (the two cement plants were still producing at less than 30% of capacity in 1985/86, with an output of 150,500 tons), owing to a combination of technical problems and inadequate management skills. Some enterprises, such as Khartoum's main dairy, were returned to the private sector as early as 1975, but the principal trend towards 'privatization' began after 1980, with the shift in emphasis towards a more mixed economy. Some enterprises were sold directly to members of the public, while in others, such as the sugar estates, foreign management was introduced, under aid-funded contracts. After having almost been abandoned during the political uncertainties which followed the overthrow of Nimeri in 1985, the privatization policy gained new momentum in 1988 as part of the medium-term economic recovery programme approved by the IMF and the World Bank. In the July budget plans were announced to privatize two agricultural schemes, as well as the four state-owned commercial banks and some new industrial concerns. At the same time plans were announced to rehabilitate existing public sector concerns, including Sudan's two cement factories and its textile plant. The USSR agreed to rehabilitate the canning plants it had built in the 1960s, and Yugoslavia the tanning factories. In March 1989 the minister of industry announced a programme for the rehabilitation and modernization of 11 spinning factories and 42 others in the private sector, at a cost of $300m. as a foreign component and £S600m. from Sudanese sources. A programme for the upgrading of the spinning sector at a cost of $18m. was also planned. Modernization of the sugar sector has been 90% implemented.

Until the post-1980 rehabilitation programmes, the involvement of foreign donors in industrial development was minimal, except for the Khartoum-based Arab Authority for Agricultural Investment and Development (AAAID), founded in 1977. The AAAID has a number of programmes under development, including a dairy project, glucose production, oil milling and poultry schemes.

Official encouragement of industrial development began with the 1959 Approved Enterprises (Concessions) Act—which gave generous incentives to infant industries—and the establishment, in 1961, of the Industrial Development Bank, to assist in the financing of private-sector projects. The 1959 Act was modified in 1967, 1973, 1974 and 1976, and finally replaced in 1980 by the Encouragement of Investment Act. Like its predecessors, this Act offered tax incentives to foreign investors, and guaranteed the repatriation of profits and dividends, exemptions from customs duties and favourable tariffs for freight and electricity charges. Any potential beneficial impact of this legislation was, however, destroyed by the introduction, in September 1983, of Islamic (Shari'a) law, and, specifically, the Civil Transactions and Alms and Taxation Acts, which took effect in March 1984. Designed to bring existing laws relating to companies, investment and taxation into line with Islamic principles, these Acts remain technically in force, but have been in effective abeyance since April 1985.

The change in government in 1985, as with the April 1986 general election, made little positive difference to business confidence, however, in view of the chronic problems of Sudan's economy. By 1984 the problems of shortages of raw materials, spare parts and trained manpower, and inadequate energy supplies and transport facilities, which impeded industrial development during the 1970s, had become acute, reflecting the continuing deterioration in Sudan's foreign exchange position, which was the main cause of the problems. In particular, after the Islamization process, many donors delayed or suspended disbursements of aid, for development projects and balance-of-payments support, which was the main source of finance for imports by the industrial sector. In addition, the Bank of Sudan drastically curtailed the issuing of import licences and letters of credit. Following the devaluation of the Sudanese pound in February 1985, virtually none were issued. This situation remained unchanged throughout the period of transitional government, and the civilian government that took office in May 1986 did not resume issuing import licences on a significant scale. More than 100 manufacturing enterprises closed down while the civilian government was in office, while those that continued their operations did so at minimal capacity. Average annual industrial growth declined from 3.1% between 1965–80 to 2.9% during the period

1980–90. The amount of idle capacity in the textile and food industries has been of particular concern as Sudan has imported many goods which it could produce itself. In mid-1988 the textile industry was working at about 25% of capacity. By 1985/86 production of cloth had fallen to 50m. metres, compared with 300m. metres in the 1970s. In 1986/87 imports of textiles cost Sudan £S27m. In 1988/89 industrial production fell even further. At the time of the military coup of June 1989, it was estimated that many factories were operating at only 5% of capacity.

The military government has proclaimed an 'open-door' policy to the private sector. It announced in April 1990 that private local and foreign investors would be invited to purchase loss-making state corporations, which were estimated to owe more than £S1,000m. to the central bank. The National Economic Salvation Programme, unveiled in June, named several parastatal bodies in the agricultural sector and many others in the industrial, hotel and transport and communication sectors which would be sold or reorganized as joint ventures. Further privatization plans were announced by the minister of finance in July 1991. Private investors were to be offered shares in Sudan Airways, Sudan Shipping Lines (SSL), tanneries, banks and hotels. Scandinavian, US and Arab companies were reported in mid-1992 to have made bids for the state telecommunications company, while a British company had expressed an interest in SSL.

In March 1992, in an attempt to attact foreign investment, the government announced that it would establish four free-trade zones: at Port Sudan, Juba, Janaynat (in western Sudan) and at Melot (in central Sudan).

MINERALS

Since 1973 a number of international companies have shown an interest in exploring for petroleum. More than 80% of available concessions were allotted by 1983, but to date Chevron, a subsidiary of the US company Standard Oil, is the only exploration company to have made any commercial discoveries of petroleum deposits. These were identified in south-western Sudan, and were forecast to have an eventual production capacity of 190,000 barrels per day (b/d) and to command a potential annual revenue of $136m. In February 1984 the Royal Dutch/Shell group took over 25% of Chevron's equity, as well as 25% of Chevron's production-sharing agreement with the government. In the same month, however, attacks by the SPLA on Chevron's oilfield operations compelled the company to suspend all operations. Associated plans to construct an oil-export pipeline (with Italian financial participation) were eventually cancelled by the government in September 1986. Chevron had continued until early 1986 to carry out some small-scale exploratory drilling in its concession areas outside the South, but neither the Nimeri regime nor the al-Mahdi Government accepted security problems as a justification for Chevron and other concession holders, like Total, suspending their oil exploration operations in the South. Nimeri made various attempts to put pressure on the foreign companies to resume operations, including the formation of the National Oil Co of Sudan (NOCS), a joint-venture with Saudi Arabian entrepreneur Adnan Khashoggi who was arrested in the USA in 1989 for alleged financial irregularities in connection with the affairs of ex-president Marcos of the Philippines. One of the first acts of the transitional Government after Nimeri had been overthrown was to dissolve NOCS. The new Government also tried to persuade Chevron to resume operations, and also announced that it would renegotiate all concession agreements. In response Chevron announced in late 1987 that it would resume drilling in the form of a 60-day, two-well programme in southern Kordofan. The programme was initially scheduled for the first half of 1988, but was postponed in April owing to the deteriorating security situation as the civil war spread into southern Kordofan. In 1988 a number of companies, including Amoco and Conoco of the USA, were reported to have expressed interest in drilling in a previously unallocated area near the Libyan border. This followed completion of a three-year study of Sudan's hydrocarbon potential by the World Bank.

Chevron has estimated that its concession area, comprising in mid-1990 about 100 wells in western Sudan, has around 1,000m. barrels of reserves, of which around 270m. barrels are recoverable with present technology. In May 1987 the ministry of energy and mining reported that confirmed oil reserves in the whole of Sudan totalled 2,000m. barrels, with an estimated 500m. recoverable. Given the projected growth in domestic consumption from the present level of about 100,000 barrels per day, this would meet domestic oil demand for over a decade. Alternatively, depending on world oil prices, it could earn the country over $10,000m. in foreign exchange. The only other international oil company operating in the country is Sun International, which began exploratory drilling at an oil well in its Nile block in November 1989. In October 1988 Sudan announced that it would begin production of natural gas within a year. Chevron had earlier estimated reserves in the field off the coast of Suakin, 30 km from Port Sudan, at 70m. barrels of condensate and 3,000,000m. cu ft of natural gas. Studies on the Suakin field by Canada's International Petroleum Co (IPC) in 1992 led to the announcement of plans to drill an appraisal well in 1993. In January 1991 the government claimed that Sudanese technicians were producing oil from a well in Kordofan that Chevron had abandoned. An official said that oil produced in the area would cover 10% of Sudan's requirements and that the Government was considering building a second refinery to process the oil extracted. Following its military successes against the Southern rebels in mid-1992, the government appeared to be renewing its efforts to develop oil production without the assistance of Western companies. In June Lt-Gen. al-Bashir announced that Chevron had handed over its concessions in Southern Sudan to a local firm, Concorp. In August Concorp's owner announced that the Muglad well had begun production at a rate of 600 b/d of crude petroleum, adding that a refinery capable of processing some 20,000 b/d of crude was to be constructed at Muglad. The award by Sudan, in February 1992, of a concession to IPC to explore for oil in the disputed Halmib triangle, on the Red Sea coast, contributed to a sharp deterioration in relations with Egypt (see Recent History). In December Sudan signed an agreement with Iraq to co-operate in oil exploration.

Sudan's other known mineral resources are predominantly industrial, and include marble, mica, chromite and gypsum. The main exceptions are the gold deposits in the Red Sea hills, which have been known since Pharaonic times, and uranium reserves on the western borders with Chad and the Central African Republic. Until recently, only the chromite deposits in the Ingessana Hills near the Ethiopian border were exploited on a substantial scale by the state-owned Sudan Mining Co (SMC), which produces 10,000–15,000 metric tons a year for export. The known reserves of over 1m. tons of high-quality chromite attracted Japanese attention in the late 1970s, but plans to develop a 150,000 tons-a-year mining and processing operation were eventually abandoned, owing to lack of finance and unfavourable world market conditions. In November 1988 it was reported that Northern Quarries and Mines (UK) was investing $4.3m. in an iron ore and gypsum mine in the Fodikwan area. The Fodikwan deposits were discovered in 1910 but were not exploited on a large scale until the 1960s. About 83,000 metric tons of ore were exported before political disturbances disrupted work. It is now estimated that there are four or five deposits in the Fodikwan area, with reserves of more than 500m. tons of ore. Commercial extraction of iron ore was set to resume in the first half of 1990, after a break of more than 20 years. It was reported that a contract to supply around 1m. metric tons of ore a year to an Eastern European country had already been signed by early 1990. In recent years Sudan has benefited from a resurgence of interest among foreign companies in reworking gold deposits in the Red Sea hills, which, using new processing technology, have a high recoverable gold content. Gold production at the Gebeit mine, which opened in November 1987, averaged four kilos per week, with a yield of eight grammes per metric ton, in the first half of 1989, while the first ingots from the Hassai project were cast in March 1988. Exports of gold amounted to about 150 kg in 1991/92. Production at the Aberketeib mine was reported to have totalled 100 kg in 1988. In late 1988 the European Investment Bank provided a $3.3m. loan to develop gold deposits in the Ariab area of north-eastern Sudan. In

December 1990 the Sudanese government and two French companies, Bureau de Recherches Géologiques et Minières and Total (Cie Française des Pétroles) signed an agreement to form a joint venture company, Ariab Mining Co, which would exploit gold reserves in the Ariab district. The sea-bed offshore Sudan is also known to be very rich in precious minerals, as well as copper, zinc and iron, and plans are still under consideration for these to be exploited jointly with Saudi Arabia.

FOREIGN TRADE AND BALANCE OF PAYMENTS

Although the annual value of Sudan's exports increased from £S63.4m. in 1960 to £S811m. in 1983, the value of imports over the same period rose from £S63.7m. to £S1,761m., reflecting the impact of the major development programmes of the 1970s and of policies which encouraged high consumption levels. In 1989 export earnings totalled £S2,422m., while imports cost £S4,729.5m. Export earnings were estimated to have fallen to about £S1,800m. in 1990, with imports remaining stable.

More than 90% of Sudan's export earnings are from primary agricultural products. Cotton remains the dominant export, although its share of earnings has declined from an average 50% in the 1960s to around 30%, reflecting both a decline in cotton production and world prices and rising output of other agricultural products, such as sorghum and livestock. Oil and petroleum products have historically dominated imports, accounting for some 27% of the total in 1984. A combination of lower effective domestic demand and world prices has since seen oil overtaken by manufactured goods, which accounted for an estimated 22% of imports in 1988, compared with 20% for petroleum products. Other major imports are machinery and transport equipment, which together accounted for some 30% of imports in 1988, and wheat and other foodstuffs, which accounted for around 15%.

The dominant position of petroleum imports is illustrated by Saudi Arabia's position as Sudan's leading supplier, accounting for an estimated 14% of imports in 1989. Saudi Arabia has also emerged as Sudan's single largest export market in recent years, reflecting the increasing importance of sorghum and livestock exports as cotton production has declined. The United Kingdom has steadily lost its former position as Sudan's leading trading partner, but remains its second largest source of imports. Japan and the USA have succeeded the United Kingdom as Sudan's largest OECD export markets as a result of their imports of cotton and, in the case of the USA, groundnuts and gum arabic. After the overthrow of Nimeri in April 1985, moves to re-establish Sudan's non-aligned position were paralleled by attempts to diversify its trading partners. However, overtures towards the USSR did not meet with any positive response, while various trade and other co-operation agreements with Libya in 1985–87 produced mixed results. Libya, with Saudi Arabia, provided Sudan with substantial amounts of essentially 'free' oil in 1985/86, but subsequent attempts to develop barter arrangements (exchanging oil for livestock and other agricultural products) proved less successful and supplies were erratic in 1986/87 and 1987/88. The overall shortage has been compounded by military requisitions for the war in the South, and by mid-1988 the country faced a major fuel crisis. In late 1988 trade relations with Libya improved, with the reported signing in December of co-operation agreements in the economic, educational and health spheres. In January 1989 Sudan agreed to purchase $150m. worth of Libyan crude oil and an arms deal was concluded in March; Libya was Sudan's third largest supplier in 1989. An economic and commercial protocol amounting to $66m. was signed with Romania in February, as was a trade co-operation protocol with China the following month. Technical and military agreements between Sudan and China were renewed. Imports from China rose from an average of $26m. a year to a high of $76m. in 1988, while Sudanese exports fell from $57m. in 1983 to less than $1m. in 1985. Commercial protocols, which were signed in April 1990 and July 1991, provided for Sudan to export cotton, gum arabic and other agricultural produce, and import Chinese medicine, food, light industrial goods and construction materials. Official bilateral trade with Egypt was on the decline before the overthrow of Nimeri, and was subsequently cut back still further. However, a trade protocol worth $225m. was signed by Sudan and Egypt in April 1988, indicating an improvement in trade relations. Unofficial trade, or smuggling, with Egypt (as with Libya and across the Red Sea) continues to flourish nevertheless, with Sudanese camels, sheep and gum arabic securing a premium in exchange for consumer goods. Egypt's initial support for the military coup of June 1989 was expected to lead to a further increase in Sudanese-Egyptian trade, but relations between the two countries have fluctuated. However, a trade agreement, worth $350m., which was signed by Sudan and Egypt in January 1991, was ratified by the Sudanese government in June. However, it was with Libya that the military government signed an integration pact in March 1990, during a visit to Tripoli by Lt-Gen. al-Bashir. The agreement provided for the merging of the two countries within four years. A follow-up agreement signed at a joint ministerial meeting in July provided for the removal of border and customs barriers and co-operation in the area of banking, as well as moves to encourage Libyan investors in Sudan. Under an 'implementation programme', signed the following month, Libya agreed to supply large quantities of oil to Sudan. Under a trade exchange deal signed in December 1989, Libya agreed to import $27m. worth of livestock, cereals and fodder, and oil seeds, yarn and perfumes, while Sudan was to buy Libyan fuel, chemicals, fertilizer, cement and caustic soda. A further trade agreement, which was worth $57m., was signed by Libya and Sudan in February 1991. Libya's role as Sudan's main supplier of oil came to an end in 1992, however, owing to Sudan's failure to maintain payments. Talks in April 1993 failed to resolve the issue and the government announced that it would continue to purchase its oil requirements on the spot market. However, a lack of foreign exchange subsequently led to severe fuel shortages. Italy, the largest importer of Sudanese cotton, increased imports from Sudan from $31.92m. in 1986 to $69.67m. in 1987 and $86.5m. in 1988. Italian exports to Sudan were valued at $102.09m. in 1986, $75.15m. in 1987 and $92.88m. in 1988. Sudanese exports to the USA increased slightly from $23.2m. in 1987 to $24.2m. in 1988, while imports fell from $152m. to $108.7m. in the same period. Imports from the USA were down by 26% in 1989.

Sudan has had a deficit on the current account of its balance of payments since independence in 1956, but the deficits were relatively insignificant until the mid-1970s, when government policies resulted in escalating deficits on the balance of trade and rising debt-service requirements. Sudan reached its first agreement with the IMF in May 1979, as part of an attempt to bring the current account deficit under control. The IMF agreement was associated with the first in a long series of currency devaluations, which reduced the official value of the Sudanese pound from £S1 = $2.87 to £S1 = $0.22. It also marked the beginning of Sudan's 'austerity programme', which has included the gradual removal of food and other subsidies, cut-backs in public expenditure, real wage levels and non-essential imports, and the start of programmes to rehabilitate the export sector. Implementation of the programme entailed increasing local political costs—helping precipitate the popular uprising which overthrew Nimeri in 1985—but did little to help Sudan's external financial position. The main problem was Sudan's debt burden (estimated at over $4,000m. in 1981), with both servicing requirements and arrears continuing to rise, despite repeated reschedulings of bilateral and commercial debt with the 'Paris' and 'London Clubs' of Western official and commercial creditors. Problems on the external account, combined with the government's increasing difficulty in meeting conditions imposed by the IMF, also led to Sudan's agreements with the Fund being repeatedly renegotiated—in 1980, 1981 and 1982—but despite this, none ran its full course.

Another agreement, including a loan of SDR 90m., was provisionally approved in April 1984, after nearly a year of negotiations that were complicated by the Nimeri government's introduction of Shari'a law in September 1983. This agreement, too, was suspended in mid-year, owing to further attempts to Islamize the economy and Sudan's growing arrears to the Fund. With it collapsed the associated arrangements for debt rescheduling, and balance-of-payments aid by donors, that had provided essential support to the external account. Sudan was forced into growing arrears with some key donors, notably the Arab states and World Bank, causing funding for a number of the most important rehabilitation programmes to be 'frozen'. Nimeri's attempts to revive these arrangements, and reach accommodation with the IMF during the closing months of his rule, included a further devaluation of the currency, the introduction of a new 'floating' exchange rate for private-sector imports and expatriate remittances, and further major reductions in subsidies on sugar and bread. Popular reaction to these measures ultimately resulted in the coup that overthrew him in April 1985.

The Transitional Military Council (TMC), which took office in April 1985, was hampered by divisions on attitudes towards the IMF and popular hostility to more of the austerity measures that were associated with stand-by facilities. Even so, it made attempts during its year of office to reach agreement with the IMF. The TMC's measures included attempts to regulate lending by commercial banks; the reintroduction of the traditional taxation system, abolished by Nimeri in 1984; the imposition of an austerity programme in January 1986, involving petrol and food rationing; and a further devaluation of the exchange rate to $1 = £S4.25 on 25 February. However, the measures did not satisfy the IMF, which was pressing for even more stringent action, and with Sudan's arrears to the Fund topping $250m. it decided in January 1986 to declare the country ineligible for further borrowing. By the time that the new government took office in May 1986, the arrears had reached more than $300m. and were considered too high to be covered by the financial arrangements, which a group of donors, led by the USA, had proposed at the end of 1985 as a means of overcoming the problem. Despite this, Sudan's balance-of-payments improved dramatically during 1985, and for the first time a surplus, of $151.7m., was achieved on the current account. This was largely due to a substantial rise in private and official transfers, representing a sharp rise in remittances from expatriate workers and aid funds in the aftermath of Nimeri's overthrow.

Like the TMC, the civilian coalition government was riven with internal divisions which prevented the formulation of a reform programme capable of winning the approval of the IMF until mid-1987. Negotiations on an interim recovery programme started in early 1987. The programme was finally accepted in August and was followed, in October, by a devaluation of the Sudanese pound of almost 45%. Efforts were also made to increase the flow of remittances through the introduction of preferential exchange rates. In March 1988 a medium-term recovery programme (approved by both the IMF and the World Bank) was announced. The programme called for a further devaluation of the Sudanese pound, liberalization of exchange controls and trade policy, budget restraint and revenue-generating measures. At the same time further talks were held with commercial bank creditors and donors, who provided $228m. in balance-of-payments support in December 1987. In October a dual exchange rate for the Sudanese pound was reintroduced, providing a floating rate in addition to the unaltered official rate of US $1 = £S4.50. The move was regarded as heralding a comprehensive devaluation of the Sudanese pound, one of the IMF's principal conditions for a rescheduling of Sudan's debt. However, the political sensitivity of the IMF conditions was underlined in December when the government was forced to revoke increases in the prices of essential commodities, which had caused a general strike and violent demonstrations in Khartoum.

At a three-week National Economic Salvation conference held in Khartoum in October/November 1989, al-Bashir proposed wide-ranging economic measures in line with reforms demanded by the IMF. These included a review of the performance of state concerns and banking institutions, as well as the effect of subsidies on the economy and measures to increase direct and indirect taxes, cuts in spending, and the possible introduction of user fees in the health and education sectors. The price of bread was increased by 15%, to reduce the state subsidy, while bakers were instructed to mix sorghum with wheat to reduce import costs. Wheat and flour were estimated to account for 7.6% of total imports in 1988, representing the single largest item in the food import bill; the al-Bashir Government has made the achievement of food self-sufficiency one of its main policy goals.

In February 1990 the government announced a new exchange rate for cotton exporters of £S8.30 = US $1, as part of efforts to keep cotton earnings in the official economy and boost foreign exchange reserves. The move allowed exporters exchanging foreign exchange on the official market to almost double their local currency earnings. Foreign exchange reserves were estimated at just $21.4m. in October 1989.

FOREIGN AID

Until the 1971 shift in foreign policy, Sudan received substantial aid from the Eastern bloc. Since 1971, however, the majority of aid has come from Western sources, with the exception of the People's Republic of China. China has built a foundry, a textile mill at Hassaheisa, a conference centre in Khartoum, and a section of the Khartoum–Port Sudan highway.

By the mid-1970s, with the formulation of an Arab policy for food self-sufficiency in which Sudan played a central role, the country appeared favourably placed to benefit from aid from the petroleum-producing states. In 1975 the Arab Fund for Economic and Social Development (AFESD) announced a 10-year plan to double Sudan's GDP. The plan centred on a massive $6,000m. investment programme—the so-called 'breadbasket policy'—to expand agricultural and agro-industrial production sufficiently to meet a significant percentage of Arab food needs. With Sudan's mounting economic problems, the policy was never fully implemented, with the Kenana sugar scheme and the AAAID being virtually its only memorials.

Even so, Arab aid to Sudan, led by Saudi Arabia and Kuwait, has been substantial. Project aid has included Kuwaiti finance for Sudan Railways, the Rahad scheme and the Sennar and New Halfa sugar projects. Since 1980, as with all other aid to Sudan, there has been a shift in emphasis from project aid to balance-of-payments support, with Saudi Arabia particularly important in subsidizing the majority of Sudan's petroleum imports.

Assistance from the USA increased dramatically during the 1970s, in accordance with US assessments of Sudan's strategic importance, and by the mid-1980s the USA was the largest single donor to Sudan, which as a recipient was second only to Egypt in Africa. Owing to the identification in Sudan of the US government as a major supporter of the Nimeri regime, the USA's relations with the TMC, and subsequently the elected coalition government, were initially strained, particularly as Sudan began to improve its relations with Libya. In March 1986 the $158m. programme of economic and military assistance for the year was suspended when Sudan fell into arrears on its repayment obligations. The programme was subsequently reactivated, but there was a delay in disbursements until early 1988, when $50m. of funds originally allocated towards the plan to pay off arrears to the IMF were switched to support key imports. A further $30m. was expected to be made available in 1988 for balance-of-payments support, as well as project assistance. In May 1989 the USA announced that aid totalling $140m. would be suspended, including $40m. of wheat sales on concessionary terms, which provided half of Sudan's annual bread requirements. This was due to a general re-evaluation of the strategic importance of the Horn of Africa to the USA and the belief that aid has no appreciable effect under the conditions of economic crisis and civil war. With effect from March 1990, the USA banned all new economic and military aid to the country under a law prohibiting all but humanitarian assistance to non-elected governments that have not moved towards democracy within eight months of taking power. The United Kingdom's $140m. contribution to the Power III programme had made Sudan the largest recipient of British aid after India. In January 1988 the UK pledged a further £10m. for balance of payments support and in September the British Foreign Secretary promised a large increase in aid if deflationary measures were adopted. In January 1991 the UK suspended all development aid to Sudan following the Sudanese government's decision to release the five Palestinians convicted of killing five Britons and two Sudanese at a hotel in Khartoum in 1988. In October 1990

Japan announced that it was lending Sudan $107.1m. which was to be allocated as follows: $7.1m. to improve rural water resources; $9.5m. to improve Khartoum's telecommunications system; $10.5m. to repair sewerage systems; and $80m. to construct a bridge over the White Nile. In July 1991 Japan granted a further $7.2m. for Sudan to increase food production by importing fertilizers and agricultural and irrigation equipment. Sudan is also high on the list of recipients of aid from the Federal Republic of Germany and Norway, while the EC has expanded its aid considerably over the last decade. Allocations to Sudan under the third Lomé Convention, linking the EC with a group of African, Caribbean and Pacific countries, totalled around $150m., compared with some $110m. and $93.5m. under Lomé II and I. In early 1988 the EC agreed to grant Sudan $25m. for fertilizer imports, and at the end of the year released 34m. European Currency Units (ECU) for flood damage repair, to include the rebuilding of railway bridges, irrigation pumps and roads. Donor agencies pledged a total of $300m. towards flood reconstruction. The most important of the multilateral agencies has been the World Bank. Its loans, which are granted on generous terms, have included $80m. towards the Gezira rehabilitation programme, together with a $50m. credit for agricultural inputs, and $60m. for the sugar rehabilitation project. In January 1988 the World Bank approved a further loan of $107m. for Sudan's third agricultural rehabilitation programme. By December 1989 the IDA had disbursed $70m. of its $100m. contribution to the $300m. flood reconstruction programme. Sudan's huge and growing arrears on repayments meant that not only the USA, but also the UK, the Federal Republic of Germany and Saudi Arabia, among other bilateral donors, have suspended disbursements on aid programmes at various times since 1984. France and the Netherlands also reduced aid in 1989. In early 1985 Saudi Arabia agreed to release about $35m. in balance-of-payments support, some of it for a petroleum imports support package which it had agreed with the USA and the Netherlands. This was followed in November 1985 by an outline agreement with all of the main Arab funds, rescheduling some $145m. in arrears, and thereby 'unfreezing' a total of $300m. in project aid. Bilateral ratification of the agreement in early 1986 enabled Saudi Arabia and Kuwait to begin disbursement of their contributions to the programmes for the rehabilitation of the Gezira scheme and sugar projects. Arab aid amounted to $208m. in 1986 and to $228m. in 1987. However, in 1988 it fell to only $127m.—its lowest level since the late 1970s. Japan agreed a $22m. grant in 1989 to help finance water supply, sewerage and telephone works.

The impact of arrears on donors is reflected in figures for gross official development assistance which, after having reached a record $1,180m. in 1983, fell to $745m. in 1984. A new record level, of $1,223m., was reached in 1985, reflecting external support for the new Government, but fell back to $937m. in 1988 and to $760m. in 1989. Sudan's failure to maintain payments was only one aspect of the foreign-exchange crisis which had been growing since the late 1970s, as a result of falling export earnings and rising debt-service obligations.

Sudan's first and second reschedulings—of $700m. in December 1981 and $400m. in March 1982—with the commercial banks and the 'Paris Club', did not, as had been hoped, enable the Government to maintain Sudan's obligations to creditors. By May 1984 'rescue' arrangements for Sudan were in operation, comprising: about $430m. in balance-of-payments support and $300m. in project aid, agreed by donors in December 1983; the May agreement by the 'Paris Club' to reschedule another $300m. due in 1984 on the same terms as for 1983; and the April agreement by the 'London Club' to extend the 1983 arrangement to cover 1984 current payments. By the end of the year, however, these arrangements had collapsed, owing to the country's deteriorating economic and political situation, and worsening relations with the IMF. In mid-1987 the first steps were taken towards a revised plan, and in August the IMF approved an interim recovery programme. In November 1987 the 'London Club' began talks to seek a durable solution to the problem of Sudan's debt, which was then estimated to total $1,900m., including $1,500m. which had previously been rescheduled. Commercial bank creditors and donors provided $228m. in balance-of-payments support in December 1987, and in March 1988 the government's announcement of a medium-term recovery programme prompted donors to pledge around $130m. in new aid. However, by March 1989 there had been no improvement in Sudan's external financial situation. Total foreign debt had risen to $13,000m., or $600 per caput, more than double the estimated per caput GDP. Sudan's debt liabilities (including principal and interest) in 1988/89 were estimated at $980m., more than twice the country's projected export earnings. However, the 1988/89 budget provided only $100m. for debt repayment. New moves on dealing with Sudan's commercial debt were undertaken in 1989, when two UK and one Federal German bank converted debts totalling $6.6m. into direct project aid. By early 1990 Sudanese government debt was being traded at just two US cents to the dollar in the inter-bank secondary debt market—the lowest rate applied to any developing country's debt. In April 1991 the Bahrain-based Sudan Development Fund (a group of Islamic financial institutions) proposed a recovery which involved, among other things, making a grant available for Sudan to repurchase some of its commercial bank debts.

The military government opened talks with the IMF in mid-May 1990, after being given until July to begin settling debt arrears to the Fund of $1,150m.—the largest in Africa—or face expulsion. Sudan's total foreign debt exceeded $13,000m. by mid-1990, one-quarter of which was then due for repayment. However, Denmark agreed to cancel outstanding debt of around $23m., and the USA announced it would also cancel debts owed. In March France agreed to cancel debts and interest totalling 378m. French francs. In September 1990, however, the IMF adopted a Declaration of Non-co-operation regarding Sudan, noting that it had remained in arrears in its financial obligations to the Fund since July 1984, and that its arrears amounted to SDR 942.6m. on 14 September 1990. It was noted, furthermore, that Sudan had made payments to other creditors while failing to discharge its obligations to the Fund, thus ignoring the preferred creditor status that members are expected to give to the Fund. The Declaration of Non-co-operation represented a formal notification to Sudan that if it did not resume active co-operation with the IMF, the Fund would give consideration to the initiation of further measures, in accordance with its strengthened co-operative strategy on overdue financial obligations. Suspension of its IMF membership would make it difficult for Sudan to raise multilateral and bilateral loans, and reduce its options for dealing with its overall debt. After coming to power in July 1989, the Government cut bread subsidies, ended sugar imports to save around $400m. a year, and reduced wheat imports by half. It also repaid the IMF a token $15m. but the sweeping economic reforms proposed are yet to be implemented, and the government has continued to resist IMF demands for a new devaluation, a salary 'freeze' and an increase in customs duties. Following the introduction of strict measures to curtail illegal foreign currency transactions, however, the parallel market rate for the US dollar fell from about £S40 = US $1 to approximately £S30 = US $1, compared with an offical rate of £S4.50 = US $1. A new exchange rate, £S8.30 = US $1, was introduced for cotton exporters, and an incentive rate of £S12.25 = US $1 was made available for remittances sent home by expatriate workers. On 12 May 1991 the government recalled large denomination banknotes and issued new ones in an effort to curb inflation and to control excessive liquidity. This was partly in the hope of gaining the approval of the IMF which sent a technical delegation to Khartoum on 19 May for discussions with the government. At that meeting al-Bashir stated that Sudan was 'determined to co-operate' with the IMF.

In October 1991 the government announced the reduction of subsidies on a number of basic commodities, including sugar and petrol, which resulted in immediate rises in consumer prices of 65%–75%. To mitigate the effect, a wage rise of £S300 a month was awarded to government employees and grants were made available to low-paid workers. Later in October the Sudanese pound was devalued by 70%, to a rate of £S15 = US $1, with the abolition of the previous two-tier rate. The devaluation was welcomed by the IMF.

An IMF team visited Khartoum in January 1992 for consultations with the government. In February a rigorous programme of economic reforms and austerity measures was announced by the minister of finance, Abd ar-Rahim Hamdi, who denied, however, that the measures had resulted from pressure from the IMF. The reforms included the floating of the pound, which resulted in an immediate devaluation of 83%. Measures taken to reduce the budget deficit included increases of 30% in import and export duties, and cuts of 10% and 60% respectively in recurrent and capital spending. Further cuts in commodity subsidies were announced, although these were accompanied by increases in allowances to poor families. In his announcement, Hamdi said that the government was spending £S8,700m. each year on wheat and flour subsidies alone, and that this could not continue. However, the subsidy cuts led to a doubling of the price of petrol, a 50% rise in sugar prices and a halving of the size of a standard loaf of bread and were greeted by demonstrations in Khartoum and Omdurman which were dispersed by police with tear gas. A further doubling of fuel prices was announced in April, in anticipation of UN economic sanctions against Libya, which had been supplying Sudan with 100,000 tons of petroleum a month at a special rate. By late July Sudan was suffering increasing fuel shortages, blamed by the government on difficulties in transporting fuel from Port Sudan, and a rationing system was introduced. With inflation running at an annual rate of around 120%, the government announced that basic consumer goods would be sold through co-operatives at controlled prices.

Sudan's continuing debt arrears to the World Bank, totalling $1,142m., led it to halt new lending at the end of 1992 and, in April 1993, to suspend the financing of 15 existing projects, including the Gezira rehabilitation scheme (see above). In the same month Sudan was suspended from membership of the AFESD, owing to arrears of $90m. dating from 1988. With Sudan's arrears to the IMF standing at $1,600m., in August 1993 the Fund suspended the country's voting rights—the first time such action had been taken against a member nation. In February 1994 Sudan's arrears to the Fund were estimated to be the largest ever recorded, at $1,700m. In the same month the Executive Board of the IMF was reported to have voted to commence proceedings to withdraw Sudan's membership of the Fund.

PUBLIC FINANCE

The Sudanese government, like governments in many other less-developed countries, has historically depended heavily on indirect taxes, especially import duties, for its main source of revenue. Since the late 1970s, however, the share of indirect taxes in total revenue has declined in parallel with the economy, reflecting the cut-backs in imports that have been imposed in an attempt to reduce the balance-of-payments deficit. The collapse of export earnings has had a seriously adverse effect both on customs and other duties from this source. To compensate, the government expanded the range of direct taxes to include consumption and development taxes, as well as income and company taxes and stamp duty. By 1980/81 direct taxes accounted for about 36% of total revenue, compared with 2.7% in 1963/64.

This development proved to be inadequate, however, to compensate for the dramatic expansion of central government expenditure since independence generally, and during the 1970s in particular. From a figure of £S10m. in 1949, budgeted expenditure had reached £S1,757.2m. by 1983/84. This problem, combined with inadequate controls over spending by ministries and parastatal bodies, led to increased difficulties for the government in meeting its local cash payments, whether salaries or payments to contractors. The government was thus forced to become increasingly dependent on a combination of deficit financing and high-interest commercial loans.

Government finances were finally driven into disorder in September 1984, when the Nimeri government replaced the 20 direct taxes with Islamic taxation, following the adoption of the Zakat and Taxation Act. Even though none of the collection mechanisms for the new system was operational, and despite the major criticisms of the move by creditors and donors (led by the IMF), the government proceeded to base its 1984/85 budget proposals on Islamic taxation. The budget was for a financial year beginning with the Islamic New Year (26 September in 1984), rather than on 1 July as previously; it envisaged total revenue of £S1,604m., which was almost 3% higher than in the previous year and was based on expectations that zakat would provide some £S600m., or more than double the revenue that had been collected from direct taxation in 1983/84. Such assumptions, combined with the adverse impact on indirect revenues that had already been experienced in 1983/84 by further restrictions on imports and the ban on alcohol, led the IMF and other creditors, as well as senior Sudanese civil servants, to dismiss the budget forecasts as totally unrealistic.

One of the first economic moves of the TMC, after it took office in April 1985, was to restore the former tax system and re-establish the previous financial year, beginning on 1 July. As a result, the 1985/86 budget, announced in September, was for nine months only. Although apparently showing a dramatically worsening situation, with the budget deficit rising from £S1,023m. for the whole of 1984/85 to a projected £S4,748m., the 1985/86 proposals were welcomed by the international community as being far more realistic than most of the budget forecasts of the previous decade. In particular, the near-threefold increase in estimated expenditure, to £S6,094.5m. (the main cause of the escalation in the deficit), was due to the inclusion of such previously excluded items as defence expenditure and debt principal repayments. Previous budgets had included only interest payments on debt, which in 1985/86 were calculated at £S235m. out of a total debt-servicing requirement of £S3,372.5m. The estimate of total revenue, which indicated a fall to £S1,346.5m., was also considered to be more realistic, although still over-optimistic, with more than 50% expected to be provided by taxes on imports and exports. In the event, with the collapse of imports (owing to continuing limitations in the issue of import licences) and of exports (owing to the drought and the impact of disease and weak markets on cotton sales), it was clear by the time the civilian government took office in May 1986 that this figure would not be achieved.

Notwithstanding the deterioration of the revenue base, the new government proved even more optimistic in its projections when it presented its first budget, three months late, in October. Revenue for 1986/87 was estimated at £S2,682.8m., with taxation expected to provide over 60% of the total. Estimated expenditure showed an overall reduction on 1985/86 to £S5,542m., owing mainly to the government's decision to limit debt-service payments to about 25% of export earnings. As a result only £S520m. was allocated to this item. The deficit, at £S2,859.2m., was expected to be financed mainly out of commodity aid grants. The government stated, at the time, that it had delayed presentation of the budget because of preparations for a comprehensive economic recovery programme. However, this had still not materialized by the time the 1987/88 budget was presented at the end of June 1987. This showed a deficit of £S2,884.5m., with expenditure projected to rise by 22% over 1986/87 to £S6,790m., owing largely to a near tripling of the allocation for debt servicing. Estimated revenue, at £S3,905.5m., was 45% higher than 1986/87 projections, with 61% due to be provided by taxation. Actual revenue for the year, however, amounted to only £S2,727m. It thus appeared unlikely that revenue projections for 1988/89 of £S5,885m. would be realized, despite the announcement of substantial rises in the prices of a wide range of goods in January 1989. Expenditure in 1988/89 was set at £S9,767m., including £S2,581m. for the development budget, which would be financed almost entirely by concessionary assistance. In June 1989 it was anticipated that the budget deficit for 1988/89 would reach the record figure of £S8,000m., double the forecast of the previous year. The minister of finance forecast a budget deficit of £S13,200m. in 1989/90, £S5,600m. of which would be financed from foreign aid. Following the coup of June 1989 the military government decreed that all foreign currency was to be traded in by citizens, in an attempt to restore the government's reserves. By early August, $57m. had been deposited in commercial banks, an amount equal to about 43% of total private unrequited transfers for the whole of 1987. However, the government was forced to print

£S1,500m. to relieve the cash shortage caused by the enforced currency exchange. The first budget of the military government, covering 1990/91, announced price increases on petrol, heating oil, tea and cigarettes, a lowering of maximum tax rates and a reduction of central government allocations for regional governments. An increase in tax revenue was to come from a broadening of the tax base, enhanced collection, and a new sales tax on some non-food commodities. The budget was set at £S15,457m., while recurrent expenditure was projected at £S16,163m., leaving a deficit of £S706m. The allocation for defence spending was increased to £S4,300m., from £S3,600m. in 1989/90. A separate development budget, based on foreign grants and loans of £S19,000m. and other domestic loans, was set at £S5,200m. Total domestic revenue for 1989/90 was estimated at £S9,200m., against recurrent expenditure of £S14,300m. (or 89% of total projected expenditure) the previous year. Public sector spending was estimated to have taken up more than 65% of total domestic revenue in 1989/90. As a means of alleviating pressure on central government resources, the new budget announced an 'open-door' policy towards the private sector. The impact of the Gulf crisis, particularly the rise in oil prices and the decline in remittances from Sudanese workers in the Gulf, forced the government to introduce an emergency supplementary budget in January 1991. Measures included a doubling of the price of bread and diesel fuel and a one-third increase in the price of sugar, resulting in a saving of £S1,600m. in government subsidies. Other spending cuts brought total savings on 1990/91 budgeted expenditure to £S2,200m. A £S1,000m. increase in customs and excise receipts was also projected. In July the minister of finance and economic planning, Abd ar-Rahim Hamdi, reported that the 1990/91 budget had raised a current account surplus of £S400m. instead of the anticipated deficit of £S705m. The 1991/92 budget, which was approved on 26 May 1991, envisaged an increase in domestic revenue, to £S32,600m., with government expenditure being set at £S42,500m. The overall deficit was expected to be £S1,300m., compared with £S3,800m. in 1990/91. There were to be no increases in taxation on sugar, petrol and bread; however, state employees would receive large pay rises. The 1992/93 budget, presented on 24 May 1992, reflected the impact of the floating of the currency in February, with expenditure projected at £S156,000m. and revenue at £S73,700m., leaving a deficit of £S82,300m. Presenting the budget, Hamdi stated that revenue expectations had been damaged by a sharp decline in the price of cotton and other export crops. Development spending for the coming year was estimated at £S550,900m., of which some 32% was to be allowed to agriculture and 28% to transport. Military spending dominated the budget for 1993/94, rising by 100% to £S40,100m. The budget also allocated £S150,000m. to debt repayment, and increased subsidies on bread and petroleum prices by 13% and 19% respectively. With inflation rising to an annual rate of 105% in July 1993, further measures to protect consumers were taken in August, including the reintroduction of subsidies on some essential commodities and of price controls on other goods. The minimum monthly wage was increased by 24% to £S3,100.

LABOUR

Detailed results of both the 1973 and 1983 censuses have not been released, so it is difficult to obtain any accurate official data on Sudan's labour force. According to estimates for 1980 by the ILO, Sudan's domestic labour force numbered about 6m. people, representing about 33% of the population, and including some 300,000 unemployed workers. These figures reflect the sizeable migration during the 1970s of Sudanese males to work in neighbouring Arab states. An estimated 1m. workers are thought to have been employed abroad during the 'peak' period in the late 1970s, thus helping to keep the domestic unemployment rate down to about 6% and providing an important source of family income and national revenue through their repatriated earnings. The migration, however, also deprived Sudan of at least 50% of its professional and skilled workers; a factor which contributed significantly to the decline of the domestic economy, and to mounting inefficiency in the public sector. The reduction of foreign workers, that was instituted in the Gulf states after the fall in world oil prices, affected Sudanese migrants less than most, but still led to concern in Sudan, where the collapse of the economy meant there were insufficient jobs for those who returned.

The out-migration, combined with substantial seasonal employment opportunities in the large irrigated schemes in central Sudan, meant that until recently the problem of rural-urban labour migration was not as severe in Sudan as in many other African states. The drought, however, brought a dramatic change in this, with several million people moving during 1984/85 from the worst hit areas in the far west and east of Sudan to Khartoum and other urban areas along the Niles. Although many returned to their home areas when the rains improved, many remained in the huge shanty towns that had developed, and found their numbers enlarged by more than 1m. people from the South, who had fled the civil war and famine there.

PLANNING AND DEVELOPMENT

The first Development Plan was a 10-year programme for 1961/62–1970/71. It was followed by a Five-Year Plan, covering 1970/71–1974/75. Nationalizations in 1970 meant that this Plan was rapidly revised, and in 1974, as targets (including an average annual GDP growth rate of 7.6%) failed to be realized, the Plan was extended to June 1977. The Six-Year Plan for 1977/78–1982/83, was abandoned at the onset of the problems which still confront the economy. In 1978 the Plan was tacitly suspended and replaced by a series of short-term 'rolling' programmes which were designed to restore some balance to the economy—with a particular emphasis on the expansion of exports. The last in the series, the three-year public investment programme covering 1983/84–1985/86, was announced in October 1983, but was hindered by the government's moves to Islamize the economy during 1984. The programme, which envisaged total expenditure of £S2,404m., was suspended after the overthrow of the Nimeri regime in April 1985. There were no more attempts to implement a co-ordinated policy until the introduction, in August 1987, of an economic recovery programme. This was successfully completed and was replaced in October 1988 by a three-year medium-term recovery programme, the priorities of which were the reform of the exchange rate and trade policy, the reduction of the budget deficit and subsidies, the promotion of exports and a privatization programme. The military government formed in July 1989 presented a three-year National Economic Salvation Programme to coincide with the 1990/91 budget. Efforts to reform the economy were to include a reallocation of resources towards agriculture and other productive sectors, and a refinement of the Investment Encouragement Act to create a more conducive investment climate for the local and foreign private sector. Measures to attract investment included the removal of the government monopoly in all areas except oil exploitation, as well as liquidation with full or part privatization of government parastatals. Other measures announced included a review of the banking system, export liberalization and price decontrol, and introduction of a 'social solidarity' system to cushion the effects of economic restructuring for low-income groups. In August 1990 the government announced that it was implementing four measures under the National Economic Salvation Programme: cuts in government expenditure; increases in tax revenues; a reduction in imports; and wage freezes and widespread job cuts. In May 1991 the government announced that, in order to encourage production, it was lifting restrictions on the price of farm products.

POWER AND TRANSPORT

Sudan's publicly operated generating capacity in 1985 was some 1,000 MW, of which about 53% was hydroelectricity and the remainder thermally generated. Some 83% of the total was accounted for by the Blue Nile grid, centred on the Roseires and Sennar hydroelectric schemes. However, because of problems related to shortages of spare parts, siltation at the dams and fluctuations in river levels, actual output was less than 50% of this level. These problems with the public supply led to a major growth in private generation. Estimated at a total 177 MW in 1982, including some 70 MW generated by the sugar schemes (of which some 50 MW comes from Kenana), self-generated capacity is since estimated to have grown by some 50%, with a particularly large growth in the number of private household and company generators in the main urban areas to combat the frequent power cuts.

The growth in private generation also reflects Sudan's highly irregular electricity consumption patterns, with Khartoum and the central region accounting for 87% of total consumption and the south and west only 2%. Sectorally, industry accounts for 39% and residential customers 37%. The completion of new thermal units in 1982, at Dongola, el-Fasher, Shendi and Wau, redressed the balance somewhat, and work is also under way to complete the long-delayed Juba power station and construct new stations at Karima and Nyala. The largest addition to Sudan's generating capacity in recent years came in 1986, with the completion of the Power III electricity scheme, which almost doubled generating capacity in the Blue Nile grid. A new 60-MW thermal power station at Khartoum North, built with grants totalling £35m. sterling from the UK, began operating in May 1985. In 1986 work began to add a 40-MW extension to the adjacent Burri thermal power station, and in 1988 work was due to begin on the first of two 40–60 MW units at Khartoum North, financed by the World Bank and the African Development Bank, under the revised Power V programme. Capacity at Roseires dam has also been raised by 84 MW to 250 MW through the installation of new turbines financed by the Federal Republic of Germany and the World Bank. In September 1988 Japan made available 1,330m. yen for the promotion of Sudan's thermal power plant expansion programme. The Netherlands is financing expansion of the power stations at Kassala and Khashm el-Girba, which was due to be completed by early 1990. A $10m. contract for renovation of the Sennar dam was expected to be placed in early 1991, with funding by the International Development Association. Initial renovation work financed by the Saudi Fund for Development was close to completion in mid-1990. The African Development Bank is financing a study on power generation and desalination in Port Sudan which would determine the feasibility of a project to supply Port Sudan, Suakin and the surrounding areas with drinking water and electricity. Yugoslavia is financing a $42.5m., three-year project to build a water network in El-Obeid, in Darfur province.

With demand expected to double before the year 2000, the government began in 1983 to seek finance for the Power IV programme. This initially envisaged a $800m., largely thermal-based scheme, to cover growth in demand up to 1990, but it has since been drastically scaled down. The programme now envisages a $100m. scheme financed by the World Bank, the Federal Republic of Germany and the African Development Bank, involving the rehabilitation of the existing network, to bring it up to designed generating capacity, and the expansion of the Burri and Khartoum North stations. Despite lack of donor enthusiasm, the government still hopes that a long-discussed hydroelectric project at Meroe on the main Nile in the north—which could generate an estimated 1,000 MW at full development—will eventually proceed.

Although Sudan still depends heavily on railways for transport, the road network has played an increasingly important role since 1980. The expansion of paved roads from less than 400 km in 1969 to more than 2,000 km in 1983, in particular the completion of the highway between Khartoum and Port Sudan, encouraged a rapid increase in the number of road haulage firms. As a result, between 1980 and 1983 the proportion of freight carried by rail and road transport was reversed, with road transport now accounting for over 60%. Only a few of the road projects planned received financing after 1983. However, in December 1989, the World Bank approved $83m. for a three-year rehabilitation of the highway between Khartoum and Port Sudan. Co-financing of $15m. was to come from the Federal Republic of Germany. Work on a 510 km road from Omdurman to Dongola began in mid-1992. In April Iran agreed to assist in the construction of the road from Kosti to Malakal and Juba. Also in progress in 1992 were studies for a road from Gedaref to Doka and Gullalat, linking eastern Sudan with Ethiopia, and for the rehabilitation of the road from Port Sudan to Gedaref.

Lack of investment in the railways is the main reason for the loss of traffic to the roads. Although some aid has been available, particularly from France and the Federal Republic of Germany, for upgrading wagons and engines, total rolling stock is far from adequate in quantity. Moreover, virtually no finance was available for upgrading Sudan's 5,500 km of single-track, narrow-gauge and unballasted railway line until the mid-1980s, by which time almost 30% of all rolling stock was also out of service owing to lack of finance for spares. The first improvement project was an EC-financed scheme, costing $20m., to upgrade the crucial section between Port Sudan and Haiya junction. The run-down of the railways created problems for emergency food distribution during the drought, but, as a result, the EC agreed, in June 1985, to a one-year emergency programme to rehabilitate rolling stock and to implement basic improvements on the track between Khartoum and the far west. A $9.6m. loan from the Saudi Fund for Development for line repairs and equipment was being negotiated in November 1988. In December a $100m. World Bank co-ordinated project to overhaul the railway system got under way after a year's delay. Around 60% of finance was to be spent on locomotives and rolling stock. In July 1989, shortly after the military coup, it was estimated that railways and ports were operating at less than 20% of capacity. A nation-wide shortage of spare parts and newly imposed import controls hampered the transportation system still further.

Although Sudan has about 4,068 km of navigable rivers, with some 1,723 km open throughout the year, river transport has, until recently, been minimal. The waterway which is most frequently used is the 1,435-km section of the White Nile between Kosti and Juba, followed by the 187-km Nile route between Karima and Dongola. Since 1981 the government has been attempting to remedy past neglect and, with the help of the US army engineers, is marking the navigation channel between Kosti and Juba. The USA and the EC have announced their interest in providing further assistance to upgrade the rivers through dredging, improving quays and providing navigation aids.

Following the reopening of the Suez Canal in 1975, work began on modernizing and enlarging the facilities at Sudan's only port, Port Sudan. Work on the project, financed by the World Bank and the UK, started in 1978. It will increase cargo-handling capacity to 13m. tons per year, and container, 'roll on, roll off' and new deep-water berths are being added. The first phase was completed in 1982, and a revised second phase began in February 1983, following agreement of a $25m. World Bank credit in 1982. Recent proposals by the EC to develop Old Suakin port for coastal traffic, and by Saudi Arabia and the Federal Republic of Germany to build a container port and petroleum terminal at New Suakin, were postponed in 1983, in line with the government's austerity programme, and in March 1985 the Federal German government announced that it was to transfer the DM 157m. that had been allocated to Suakin to the purchase of essential agricultural inputs. However, work has since resumed and Suakin port was re-opened in January 1991, and it will be able to handle about 1.5m. tons of cargo a year, thus relieving the congestion at Port Sudan.

Communications facilities have been expanded to provide a wider geographical coverage. The telex exchange, the microwave television network and telephone automation are some of the key projects which were implemented during the last development plan. However, the telephone service still requires modernization.

Sudan Airways, the national carrier (formed in 1947), operates internal and international services. It connects Khartoum with 20 other important Sudanese towns as well as with Europe, the Middle East and Africa. In November 1983 the government announced that the airline would be transferred to private-sector ownership. These plans were deferred following the coup in April 1985, but revived by the al-Bashir government in 1991. In 1986, following major problems at regional airports during the drought, the Civil Aviation Authority began a programme, to be funded and implemented locally, to improve the runways. In February it was agreed that Sudan Airways would establish an air link between Ubayid, the provincial capital of Northern Kordofan, and

Jeddah, in Saudi Arabia. After considerable delay, a $40m. contract to build an international airport in Port Sudan was finally awarded in early 1990. The scheme, which should be completed by late 1991, is being funded by the Saudi Fund for Development and the Islamic Development Bank. In February 1990 it was announced that 85% of the work to improve Juba airport had been completed.

Statistical Survey

Source (unless otherwise stated): Department of Statistics, Ministry of Finance and Economic Planning, POB 700, Khartoum; tel. 77003.

Area and Population

AREA, POPULATION AND DENSITY

Area (sq km)	2,505,813*
Population (census results)	
1 February 1983	20,594,197
15 June 1993	24,940,683†
Density (per sq km) at June 1993	10.0

* 967,500 sq miles. † Provisional result.

PROVINCES* (1983 census, provisional)

	Area (sq miles)	Population	Density (per sq mile)
Northern	134,736	433,391	3.2
Nile	49,205	649,633	13.2
Kassala	44,109	1,512,335	34.3
Red Sea	84,977	695,874	8.2
Blue Nile	24,009	1,056,313	44.0
Gezira	13,546	2,023,094	149.3
White Nile	16,161	933,136	57.7
Northern Kordofan	85,744	1,805,769	21.1
Southern Kordofan	61,188	1,287,525	21.0
Northern Darfur	133,754	1,327,947	9.9
Southern Darfur	62,801	1,765,752	28.1
Khartoum	10,883	1,802,299	165.6
Eastern Equatoria	46,073	1,047,125	22.7
Western Equatoria	30,422	359,056	11.8
Bahr al-Ghazal	52,000	1,492,597	28.7
Al-Bohayrat	25,625	772,913	30.2
Sobat	45,266	802,354	17.7
Jonglei	47,003	797,251	17.0
Total	967,500	20,564,364	21.3

* In 1991 a federal system of government was inaugurated, whereby Sudan was divided into nine states, which were sub-divided into 66 provinces and 281 local government areas. A constitutional decree, issued in February 1994, redivided the country into 26 states.

PRINCIPAL TOWNS (population at 1983 census)

Omdurman	526,192	Wadi Medani	145,015
Khartoum (capital)	473,597	Al-Obeid	137,582
Khartoum North	340,857	Atbara	73,009*
Port Sudan	206,038		

* Provisional.

BIRTHS AND DEATHS (UN estimates, annual averages)

	1975–80	1980–85	1985–90
Birth rate (per 1,000)	47.1	45.9	44.6
Death rate (per 1,000)	19.4	17.3	15.8

Expectation of life (UN estimates, years at birth, 1985–90): 49.8 (males 48.6; females 51.0).

Source: UN, *World Population Prospects: The 1992 Revision.*

ECONOMICALLY ACTIVE POPULATION* (1983 census, provisional)

	Males	Females	Total
Agriculture, hunting, forestry and fishing	2,638,294	1,390,411	4,028,705
Mining and quarrying	5,861	673	6,534
Manufacturing	205,247	61,446	266,693
Electricity, gas and water	42,110	1,618	43,728
Construction	130,977	8,305	139,282
Trade, restaurants and hotels	268,382	25,720	294,102
Transport, storage and communications	209,776	5,698	215,474
Financing, insurance, real estate and business services	17,414	3,160	20,574
Community, social and personal services	451,193	99,216	550,409
Activities not adequately described	142,691	42,030	184,721
Unemployed persons not previously employed	387,615	205,144	592,759
Total	4,499,560	1,843,421	6,342,981

* Excluding nomads, homeless and institutional households.

Mid-1992 (estimates in '000): Agriculture, etc. 5,018; Total 8,675 (Source: FAO, *Production Yearbook*).

Agriculture

PRINCIPAL CROPS ('000 metric tons)

	1990	1991	1992
Wheat	408	680†	895†
Maize	42*	61†	51†
Millet	85	308	424†
Sorghum (Durra)	1,180	3,540†	4,320†
Rice (paddy)	1	1	1*
Sugar cane*	4,222	4,500	4,600*
Potatoes	9†	15*	15*
Sweet potatoes*	5	7	7
Cassava (Manioc)	6†	8*	9*
Yams*	95	128	129
Onions*	30	40	40
Dry beans	3	3	3*
Dry broad beans	38	45*	46*
Chick-peas	1	2	2*
Other pulses*	58	60	62
Oranges*	10	15	15
Tangerines, mandarins, clementines and satsumas*	1	1	1
Lemons and limes*	40	55	55
Grapefruit*	45	63	63
Mangoes*	100	130	135
Dates*	90	140	142
Bananas*	45	63	64
Groundnuts (in shell)	123	179†	454†
Seed cotton	239	273	261†
Cottonseed	159	185	170*
Cotton lint†	83	95	87
Sesame seed	80	117†	330†
Castor beans	6	7	6†
Tomatoes*	110	150	151
Pumpkins, etc.*	40	55	55
Aubergines*	50	75	75
Melons*	15	21	21
Water melons*	90	123	123

* FAO estimate(s). † Unofficial figure(s).

Source: FAO, *Production Yearbook.*

LIVESTOCK ('000 head, year ending September)

	1990	1991	1992
Cattle	20,583	21,028	21,600†
Sheep	20,168	20,700	22,600†
Goats	14,843	15,277	18,700†
Horses*	22	22	23
Asses*	675	680	681
Camels	2,742	2,757	2,800†

Poultry (million): 32 in 1990; 33 in 1991; 35† in 1992.

* FAO estimates. † Unofficial figure.

Source: FAO, *Production Yearbook.*

LIVESTOCK PRODUCTS ('000 metric tons)

	1990	1991	1992
Beef and veal	218	231	250*
Mutton and lamb	70	72	74*
Goats' meat	34	35	35*
Poultry meat*	22	22	23
Other meat	67	68	67*
Cows' milk	2,251	2,299	3,193†
Sheep's milk*	465	480	564
Goats' milk	513	528	693†
Butter and ghee*	13.4	13.5	13.6
Cheese*	65.3	68.5	69.6
Hen eggs	33.1	34.3	34.5*
Wool:			
greasy*	18.0	19.0	19.5
clean*	8.0	8.6	8.8
Cattle hides*	33.4	35.5	38.3
Sheep skins*	10.9	11.3	11.5
Goat skins*	6.5	6.5	6.7

* FAO estimate(s). † Unofficial figure.

Source: FAO, *Production Yearbook.*

Forestry

ROUNDWOOD REMOVALS ('000 cubic metres)

	1990	1991*	1992*
Sawlogs, veneer logs and logs for sleepers	5	5	5
Other industrial wood*	2,104	2,164	2,225
Fuel wood*	20,682	21,270	21,874
Total	22,791	23,439	24,104

* FAO estimates.

Source: FAO, *Yearbook of Forest Products.*

GUM ARABIC PRODUCTION
(metric tons, year ending 30 June)

	1984/85	1985/86	1986/87
Gum kashab	11,313	18,047	37,500
Gum talh	2,775	2,375	2,500
Total	14,066	20,422	40,000

Source: Bank of Sudan.

1990: Total production (metric tons): 40,000.

Fishing

(metric tons, live weight)

	1989	1990	1991
Inland waters	29,100	30,234	31,803
Indian Ocean	1,200	1,500	1,500
Total catch	30,300	31,734	33,303

Source: FAO, *Yearbook of Fishery Statistics.*

Mining

(estimated production)

	1989	1990	1991
Salt (unrefined) ('000 metric tons)	91	68	77
Chromium ore ('000 metric tons)*	9	5	n.a.
Gold ore (kilograms)*	500	100	50

* Figures refer to the metal content of ores.

Source: UN, *Industrial Statistics Yearbook.*

Industry

PETROLEUM PRODUCTS (estimates, '000 metric tons)

	1989	1990	1991
Motor spirit (petrol)	112	95	98
Aviation gasoline	4	3	5
Naphtha	20	20	22
Jet fuels	77	75	82
Kerosene	18	15	21
Distillate fuel oils	315	331	329
Residual fuel oils	310	304	314
Liquefied petroleum gas	5	7	6

Source: UN, *Industrial Statistics Yearbook.*

SELECTED OTHER PRODUCTS (year ending 30 June)

	1983/84	1984/85	1985/86
Cement ('000 metric tons)	198	146	151
Wheat flour ('000 metric tons)	266	280	n.a.
Raw sugar ('000 metric tons)	419	497	452
Cigarettes (million)	1,600	2,400	2,900

Source: Bank of Sudan.

Finance

CURRENCY AND EXCHANGE RATES

Monetary Units

1,000 millièmes = 100 piastres = 1 Sudanese pound (£S).

Sterling and Dollar Equivalents (31 March 1994)

£1 sterling = £S322.74;
US $1 = £S217.39;
£S1,000 = £3.098 sterling = $4.600.

Average Exchange Rate

Between October 1987 and October 1991 the official rate of exchange was fixed at US $1 = £S4.50. In October 1991 a new rate of US $1 = £S14.99 was introduced. The average exchange rate for 1991 was $1 = £S5.43. In February 1992 the currency was devalued by 83.4%, with the exchange rate fixed at $1 = £S90.09. This rate was subsequently adjusted. The average rate for 1992 was $1 = £S69.4.

CENTRAL GOVERNMENT BUDGET
(estimates, £S million, year ending 30 June)

Revenue	1983/84	1984/85	1985/86
Direct taxes	404.5	300.5	351.6
Indirect taxes	839.9	984.6	1,222.6
Others	224.6	200.4	216.2
Total	1,469.0	1,485.5	1,790.4

Expenditure	1983/84	1984/85	1985/86
Ordinary budget:			
Economic services	74.3	196.0	208.0
Social Services	69.9	160.8	182.0
Loan repayments	212.0	118.0	465.4
Defence and security	260.6	462.0	473.1
Regional Governments	270.3	360.5	557.0
Others	755.6	1,214.9	1,492.8
Development budget:			
Agricultural sector	135.4	139.1	96.3
Industrial sector	119.2	110.1	74.6
Transport and communications	67.6	52.1	57.9
Services sector	59.4	54.3	32.5
Others	101.4	97.4	107.8
Total	2,130.7	2,965.2	3,747.0

1986/87 (estimates, £S million, year ending 30 June): revenue 2,682.8 (tax revenue 1,670.0, non-tax revenue 1,012.8); expenditure 5,542.0 (current expenditure 3,616.2, development 1,380.8, debt servicing 520.0, equity 25.0).
1987/88 (estimates, £S million, year ending 30 June): revenue 3,905.5 (tax revenue 2,379.2, non-tax revenue 1,348.0); expenditure 6,790.0 (current expenditure 5,232.2, development 1,533.4).
1988/89 (estimates, £S million, year ending 30 June): revenue 5,885; expenditure 9,767 (development 2,518).
1989/90 (estimates, £S million, year ending 30 June): revenue 8,600; expenditure 21,600 (development 4,000).
1990/91 (estimates, £S million, year ending 30 June): revenue 14,457; expenditure 16,163 (development 5,200); expenditure subsequently revised to 13,900.
1991/92 (estimates, £S million, year ending 30 June): revenue 32,600; expenditure 42,500.
1992/93 (estimates, £S million, year ending 30 June): revenue 73,700; expenditure 156,000.

INTERNATIONAL RESERVES (US $ million at 31 December)

	1991	1992	1993
Foreign exchange	7.6	24.2	37.7
Total	7.6	24.2	37.7

Source: IMF, *International Financial Statistics.*

MONEY SUPPLY (£S million at 31 December)

	1989	1990	1991
Currency outside banks	9,240	13,113	21,663
Demand deposits at deposit money banks	8,470	11,443	18,714
Total money (incl. others)	18,899	27,659	44,305

Source: IMF, *International Financial Statistics.*

COST OF LIVING (Consumer Price Index for low-income households; base: 1980 = 100)

	1987	1988	1989
Food	679.3	1,107.2	1,602.2
Fuel and light	548.4	567.9	1,472.0
Clothing	777.3	868.3	2,248.0
Rent	547.8	562.0	1,217.0
All items (incl. others)	649.9	965.2	1,603.7

1990 (base: January 1988 = 100): Food 392.1; Fuel and light 357.4; Clothing 402.5; Rent 200.4; All items (incl. others) 385.0.
1991 (base: January 1988 = 100): Food 804.3; Fuel and light 789.5; Clothing 834.3; Rent 529.8; All items (incl. others) 790.1.

Source: ILO, *Year Book of Labour Statistics.*

NATIONAL ACCOUNTS
(£S million in current prices, year ending 30 June)

	1988/89	1989/90	1990/91
Gross domestic product	82,562	110,111	192,660

Source: IMF, *International Financial Statistics.*

Expenditure on the Gross Domestic Product
(estimates, £S million in current prices)

	1989	1990	1991
Government final consumption expenditure	13,194	19,226	29,407
Private final consumption expenditure	55,905	81,483	122,621
Gross fixed capital formation	12,371	18,005	27,851
Total domestic expenditure	81,470	118,714	179,879
Exports of goods and services	6,108	4,524	4,321
Less Imports of goods and services	14,015	12,493	11,737
GDP in purchasers' values	73,563	110,745	172,463
GDP at constant 1980 prices	4,758	4,496	4,496

Source: UN Economic Commission for Africa, *African Statistical Yearbook.*

Gross Domestic Product by Economic Activity
(estimates, £S million)

	1989	1990	1991
Agriculture, forestry and fishing	17,746	28,427	50,017
Mining and quarrying	49	77	93
Manufacturing	4,864	7,148	10,167
Electricity, gas and water	1,558	2,183	3,095
Construction	2,415	3,598	5,132
Trade, restaurants and hotels	11,302	15,857	21,739
Transport, storage and communications	6,161	9,100	12,720
Finance, insurance, real estate and business services	2,603	3,636	4,863
Public administration and defence	6,280	9,428	13,277
Other community, social and personal services	1,482	2,241	3,197
GDP at factor cost	54,460	81,695	124,300
Indirect taxes, *less* subsidies	19,103	29,050	48,163
GDP in purchasers' values	73,563	110,745	172,463

Source: UN Economic Commission for Africa, *African Statistical Yearbook*.

BALANCE OF PAYMENTS (US $ million)

	1990	1991	1992
Merchandise exports f.o.b.	326.5	302.5	213.4
Merchandise imports f.o.b.	−648.8	−1,138.2	−810.2
Trade balance	−322.3	−835.7	−596.8
Exports of services	172.5	77.0	155.5
Imports of services	−228.0	−197.3	−204.1
Other income received	12.4	2.7	—
Other income paid	−145.0	−132.2	−93.5
Private unrequited transfers (net)	59.8	45.2	123.7
Official unrequited transfers (net)	81.4	82.5	109.0
Current balance	−369.2	−957.8	−506.2
Capital (net)	112.3	587.0	316.4
Net errors and omissions	10.9	97.9	31.0
Overall balance	−246.0	−272.9	−158.8

Source: IMF, *International Financial Statistics*.

External Trade

PRINCIPAL COMMODITIES (£S million)

Imports c.i.f.	1985	1986	1987
Wheat and meslin (unmilled)	78.6	57.0	199.5
Tea	94.7	71.9	39.8
Petroleum products	298.7	257.7	483.4
Insecticides	59.5	90.1	83.2
Paper, paperboard and paper products	48.2	36.4	30.8
Cotton fabrics	3.9	15.0	38.7
Telecommunication apparatus	0.6	2.1	88.8
Electric power machinery	61.6	64.0	76.6
Passenger motor cars	53.5	114.6	101.6
Lorries and trucks	76.1	136.8	125.2
Buses	30.4	51.9	34.1
Parts for road motor vehicles	46.9	79.8	75.7
Total (incl. others)	2,128.8	2,402.2	2,612.9

Exports f.o.b.*	1985	1986	1987
Sheep, lambs and goats	145.6	66.9	38.9
Millet and sorghum	n.a.	13.9	248.8
Cattle hides	38.8	33.7	39.0
Sesame seed	97.8	58.9	134.8
Cotton	374.3	366.7	455.2
Gum arabic	66.0	141.7	267.1
Total (incl. others)	844.7	833.2	1,497.1

* Excluding exports of camels by land routes.

1988 (£S million): Imports c.i.f. 4,772.1; Exports f.o.b. 2,290.9.

PRINCIPAL TRADING PARTNERS (£S million)

Imports c.i.f.	1985	1986	1987
Africa	149.4	186.5	215.0
EC	855.5	970.9	918.9
France	107.1	86.9	90.5
Germany, Federal Republic	184.2	204.8	190.0
United Kingdom	240.9	282.5	273.2
Eastern Europe	37.1	57.7	48.9
USSR	0.5	2.4	2.0
USA	161.4	185.6	271.7
Japan	188.5	120.7	193.7
China, People's Republic	67.2	68.2	27.1
Total (incl. others)	2,128.8	2,402.2	2,612.9

Exports f.o.b.	1985	1986	1987
Africa	5.6	13.9	9.1
EC	181.5	233.9	735.0
France	20.8	47.8	59.8
Germany, Federal Republic	47.9	47.1	109.3
United Kingdom	22.6	33.8	122.5
Eastern Europe	97.7	96.3	28.4
USSR	10.8	21.8	3.6
USA	27.9	45.0	70.3
Japan	68.5	55.4	94.5
China, People's Republic	0.8	0.5	0.1
Total (incl. others)	844.7	833.2	1,497.1

Source (for all external trade tables): UN Economic Commission for Africa, *African Statistical Yearbook*.

1989: Exports f.o.b. £S3,023.2 million (Source: IMF, *International Financial Statistics*).

Transport

RAILWAY TRAFFIC (year ending 30 June)

	1980/81	1981/82	1982/83
Freight ton-km (million)	1,594	1,600	3,190
Passenger-km (million)	1,170	1,149	1,031

1988: Freight ton-km (million): 752; Passenger-km (million): 759.

ROAD TRAFFIC (registered motor vehicles)

	1979	1980	1981
Passenger cars	70,171	84,958	1,004,688
Buses	6,295	2,956	3,590
Lorries and vans	50,108	40,107	40,839
Motor cycles	3,306	4,131	5,542
Total (incl. others)	137,029	138,695	181,821

Source: Ministry of National Planning, Khartoum, *Transport Statistical Bulletin*.

INTERNATIONAL SEA-BORNE SHIPPING
(estimated freight traffic, '000 metric tons)

	1988	1989	1990
Goods loaded	1,390	1,310	1,195
Goods unloaded	3,480	3,681	3,467

Source: UN, *Monthly Bulletin of Statistics.*

CIVIL AVIATION (traffic on scheduled services)

	1989	1990	1991
Kilometres flown (million)	8	10	6
Passengers carried ('000)	363	454	363
Passenger-km (million)	494	589	426
Freight ton-km (million)	17	13	11

Source: UN, *Statistical Yearbook.*

Tourism

	1989	1990	1991
Tourist arrivals ('000)	23	25*	20*

* Estimate.

Source: UN Economic Commission for Africa, *African Statistical Yearbook.*

Communications Media

	1981	1982	1983
Radio receivers ('000 in use)	n.a.	n.a.	5,000
Television receivers ('000 in use)	n.a.	n.a.	1,000
Telephones ('000 in use)	68	n.a.	n.a.
Daily newspapers:			
Number	n.a.	6	n.a.
Average circulation ('000 copies)	n.a.	105	n.a.
Non-daily newspapers:			
Number	n.a.	9	n.a.
Average circulation ('000 copies)	n.a.	121	n.a.
Other periodicals:			
Number	n.a.	25	n.a.
Average circulation ('000 copies)	n.a.	200	n.a.

1987 ('000 in use): Telephones 74.

1988 ('000 in use): Radio receivers 5,550; Television receivers 1,250.

1989 ('000 in use): Radio receivers 5,755; Television receivers 1,500.

1990 ('000 in use): Radio receivers 6,295; Television receivers 1,800.

1991 ('000 in use): Radio receivers 6,480; Television receivers 2,000.

Source: mainly UNESCO, *Statistical Yearbook.*

Education

(1990)

	Institutions	Teachers	Pupils/ Students
Pre-primary	5,914	8,055	283,126
Primary	7,939	60,047	2,042,743
Secondary:			
General	n.a.	31,535	695,964
Teacher training	n.a.	683	5,328
Vocational	n.a.	1,410	30,332
Universities etc.*	n.a.	2,522	60,134

* Figures refer to 1989.

Source: UNESCO, *Statistical Yearbook.*

Directory

The Constitution

Following the coup of 6 April 1985, the Constitution of April 1973 was suspended, pending the drafting and promulgation of a new Constitution. A transitional Constitution, approved in October 1985, was suspended following the military coup of 30 June 1989.

The Government

HEAD OF STATE

President: Lt-Gen. OMAR HASSAN AHMAD AL-BASHIR (took power as Chairman of the Revolutionary Command Council for National Salvation (RCC) on 30 June 1989; appointed President by the RCC on 16 October 1993).

First Vice-President: Maj.-Gen. ZUBAIR MUHAMMAD SALIH.

Second Vice-President: GEORGE KONGOR AROP.

CABINET
(September 1994)

Prime Minister: Lt-Gen. OMAR HASSAN AHMAD AL-BASHIR.

Minister of Defence: Lt-Gen. HASSAN ABD AR-RAHMAN ALI.

Minister of the Interior: Col ALTAYEB IBRAHIM MUHAMMAD KHAIR.

Minister of Cabinet Affairs: AWAD AHMAD AL-JAZ.

Minister of Foreign Affairs: HUSSEIN SULEIMAN ABU SALIH.

Minister of Finance: ABD AR-RAHIM HAMDI.

Minister of Irrigation and Water Resources: Dr YAQUB ABU SHURA MUSA.

Minister of Education: ABD AL-BASIT SABDRAT.

Minister of Higher Education and Scientific Research: IBRAHIM AHMAD OMAR.

Minister of Housing and Social Affairs: Dr HUSSEIN ABU SALEH.

Minister of Energy and Mining: Naval Staff Col SALIH AD-DIN MUHAMMAD AHMAD KARRAR.

Minister of Economic Planning and Investment: IBRAHIM OBAID-ULLAH.

Minister of Health: GULWAK DENG.

Minister of Industry and Commerce: TAJ AS-SIR MUSTAFA ABD AS-SALAM.

Minister of Justice: ABDEL AZIZ SHIDDU.

Minister of Culture and Information: SULEIMAN MUHAMMAD SULE-IMAN.

Minister of Labour and Administrative Reform: Brig.-Gen. DOMINIC KASSIANO BAKHIT.

Minister of Agriculture and Natural Resources: Dr AHMAD ALI GENIEF.

Minister of Communications and Tourism: KABOSHO KUKU.

Minister of Social Planning: ALI UTHMAN MUHAMMAD TAHA.

Minister in the Offices of the Federal Administration: ALI EL-HAG MUHAMMAD.

Minister of Local Government: Lt-Gen. GALWAK.

Minister of Peace and Rehabilitation: ABDULLAH DENG NHIAL.

Minister of Presidential Affairs: Gen. ABD AR-RAHIM MUHAMMAD HUSSAIN.

Minister of State for Defence: OSMAN MUHAMMAD AL-HASSAN.

Minister of State for Electricity: (vacant).

Minister of State for Energy: HASSAN DAHAWI.

Minister of State for Finance: ABD AL-WAHAB AHMAD HAMZA.

Minister of State for Social Planning: IBRAHIM ABU AWE.

Minister of State for Agriculture: MUHAMMAD SAID HARBI.

Minister of State for Labour and Administrative Reform: MAJDHUB AL-KHALIFAH AHMAD.

Minister of State for Trade and Industry: NASR AD-DIN MUHAMMAD UMAR.

MINISTRIES

Ministry of Agriculture and Natural Resources: Khartoum; tel. (11) 72300.

Ministry of Culture and Information: Khartoum; tel. (11) 79850; telex 22275.

Ministry of Defence: Khartoum; tel. (11) 74910; telex 22411.

Ministry of Education: Khartoum; tel. (11) 78900.

Ministry of Energy and Mining: POB 2087, Khartoum; tel. (11) 75595; telex 22256.

Ministry of Finance and Economic Planning: POB 700, Khartoum; tel. (11) 77003; telex 22324.

Ministry of Foreign Affairs: Khartoum; tel. (11) 73101.

Ministry of Health: Khartoum; tel. (11) 73000.

Ministry of the Interior: Khartoum; tel. (11) 79990; telex 22604.

Ministry of Irrigation and Water Resources: Khartoum; tel. (11) 77533.

Ministry of Transport and Communications: POB 300, Khartoum; tel. (11) 79700.

Legislature

The National Assembly was dissolved following the coup of 30 June 1989. In February 1992 Lt-Gen. al-Bashir appointed a 300-member, transitional National Assembly. The transitional Assembly was granted legislative authority, and it was instructed to make preparations for parliamentary elections.

President: MUHAMMAD AL-AMIN KHALIFAH YUNIS.

Political Organizations

All political organizations were banned following the military coup of 30 June 1989. The more influential parties prior to the coup included.

Baath Party: Khartoum.

Democratic Unionist Party (DUP): Khartoum; Leader OSMAN AL-MIRGHANI.

Muslim Brotherhood: Khartoum; Islamic fundamentalist movement; Leader Dr HABIR NUR AD-DIN.

National Alliance for Salvation (NAS): Khartoum; f. 1985; grouping of professional asscns, trade unions and political parties.

National Congress Party: Khartoum; f. 1985; aims include national unity, decentralization, non-alignment; Leader Dr RIYAD BAYYUMI.

National Islamic Front (NIF): Khartoum; Sec.-Gen. Dr HASSAN AT-TURABI.

Nationalist Unionist Party: Khartoum; Leader UTHMAN AL-MIRGHANI.

Progressive People's Party (PPP): Khartoum.

Southern Sudanese Political Association (SSPA): Juba; largest Southern party; advocates unity of the Southern Region.

Sudan African National Union (SANU): Malakal; Southern party; supports continuation of regional rule.

Sudanese African Congress (SAC): Juba.

Sudanese African People's Congress (SAPCO): Juba.

Sudanese Communist Party: Khartoum; Sec.-Gen. IBRAHIM NUGUD.

Sudanese National Party (SNP): Khartoum; Leader PHILIP ABBAS GHABOUSH.

Sudanese People's Federal Party (SPFP): Khartoum.

Umma Party (UP): Khartoum; Mahdist party based on the Koran and Islamic traditions; Pres. SADIQ AL-MAHDI.

Opposition movements include the **Sudan People's Liberation Movement (SPLM)** (Leader Col JOHN GARANG), its military wing, the **Sudan People's Liberation Army (SPLA)**, and the **Liberation Front for Southern Sudan (LFSS).** A rival faction to the original SPLM (led by RIEK MACHAR), was formed in mid-1991; and another, the Forces of Unity faction (led by WILLIAM NYUON), in 1992. SPLA–United, an alliance between the faction led by Riek Machar, the Forces of Unity and a further faction (led by CARABINO KUANY BOL, emerged in April 1993. Many of the movements opposed to the Government are grouped together in the **Sudanese National Democratic Forum.** The **Sudan Federal Democratic Alliance** (SFDA) (Chair. AHMED DREIGE) was formed in London in February 1994. It advocates a new federal structure for Sudan, based on decentralization.

Diplomatic Representation

EMBASSIES IN SUDAN

Algeria: St 31, New Extension, POB 80, Khartoum; tel. (11) 41954; Ambassador: SALIH BEN KOBBI.

Bulgaria: St 31, Middle Road, New Extension, POB 1690, Khartoum; tel. (11) 43414; Ambassador: T. F. MITEV.

Chad: 21, St 17, New Extension, POB 1514, Khartoum; tel. (11) 42545; Ambassador: MBAILAOU BERAL MOISE.

China, People's Republic: 93, St 22, POB 1425, Khartoum; tel. (11) 222036; Ambassador: (vacant).

Czech Republic: 39, St 39, POB 1047, Khartoum; tel. (11) 43448.

Egypt: Al-Gamma St, POB 1126, Khartoum; tel. (11) 72836; telex 22545; Ambassador: HASSAN ABD AL-HAK GAD AL-HAK.

Ethiopia: 6, 11A St 3, New Extension, POB 844, Khartoum; Chargé d'affaires: Dr AWOKE AGONGFER.

France: Plot No. 163, Block 8, Burri, POB 377, Khartoum; tel. (11) 225608; telex 22220; Ambassador: MARCEL LAUGEL.

Germany: Baladia St, Block No. 8DE, Plot No. 2, POB 970, Khartoum; tel. (11) 77990; telex 22211; Ambassador: PETER MENDE.

Greece: Sharia al-Gamhouria, Block 5, No. 30, POB 1182, Khartoum; tel. (11) 73155; Ambassador: VASSILIS COUZOPOULOS.

Holy See: Kafouri Belgravia, POB 623, Khartoum (Apostolic Nunciature); tel. (11) 74692; telex 26032; Apostolic Pro-Nuncio: Most Rev. ERWIN JOSEF ENDER, Titular Archbishop of Germania in Numidia.

India: 61 Africa Rd, POB 707, Khartoum; tel. (11) 40560; telex 22228; Ambassador: VIRENDRA P. SINGH.

Iran: House No. 8, Square 2, Mogran, Khartoum; tel. (11) 48843; Chargé d'affaires: NIMATALLAH GADIR.

Iraq: Khartoum; tel. (11) 45428; telex 24035; Ambassador: TARIQ MOHAMMED YAHYA.

Italy: St 39, POB 793, Khartoum; tel. (11) 45326; telex 24034; Ambassador: ROSARIO GUIDO NICOSIA.

Japan: 24, Block AE, St 3, New Extension, POB 1649, Khartoum; tel. (11) 44554; telex 24019; Ambassador: YOSHINORI IMAGAWA.

Jordan: 25, St 7, New Extension, Khartoum; tel. (11) 43264; telex 24047; Ambassador: MOHAMMED JUMA ASANA.

Kenya: POB 8242, Khartoum; tel. (11) 40386; telex 24190; Ambassador: GIDEON NYAMWEYA NYAANGA.

Korea, Democratic People's Republic: House No. 59, 1 St 31, New Extension, POB 322, Khartoum; tel. (11) 75645; Ambassador: JOM YONG HWANG.

Korea, Republic: House 2, St 1, New Extension, POB 2414, Khartoum; tel. (11) 44028; telex 24029; Ambassador: WOO-SANG LEE.

Kuwait: Africa Ave, near the Tennis Club, POB 1457, Khartoum; tel. (11) 81525; telex 24043; Ambassador: (vacant).

Libya: 50 Africa Rd, POB 2091, Khartoum; Secretary of People's Bureau: GUMMA AL-FAZANI.

Morocco: 32, St 19, New Extension, POB 2042, Khartoum; tel. (11) 43223; Ambassador: MOHAMMED KAMLICHI.

Netherlands: St 47, House No. 47, POB 391, Khartoum; tel. (11) 47271; telex 24013; Chargé d'affaires: J. BOJ.

Nigeria: St 17, Sharia al-Mek Nimr, POB 1538, Khartoum; tel. (11) 79120; telex 22222; Ambassador: IBRAHIM KARLI.

Oman: St 1, New Extension, POB 2839, Khartoum; tel. (11) 45791; Ambassador: MOSLIM EBIN ZAIDAN AL-BARAMI.

Pakistan: House No. 6, Block 12AE, St 3, New Extension, POB 1178, Khartoum; tel. (11) 42518; telex 24219; Ambassador: KHALID NIZAMI.

Poland: 73 Africa Rd, POB 902, Khartoum; tel. (11) 44248; Chargé d'affaires a.i.: WALDEMAR POPIOLEK.

Qatar: St 15, New Extension, POB 223, Khartoum; tel. (11) 42208; telex 22223; Chargé d'affaires a.i.: HASSAN AHMED ABDULLAH ABU HINDI.

Romania: Kassala Rd, Plot No. 172–173, Kafouri Area, POB 1494, Khartoum North; tel. (11) 613445; telex 24188; Chargé d'affaires a.i.: GHEORGHE GUSTEA.

Russia: B1, A10 St, New Extension, POB 1161, Khartoum; Ambassador: VALERI YAKOVLEVICH SUKHIN.

Saudi Arabia: St 11, New Extension, Khartoum; tel. (11) 41938; Ambassador: SAYED MOHAMMED SIBRI SULIMAN.

Somalia: St 23–25, New Extension, POB 1857, Khartoum; tel. (11) 44800; Ambassador: MUHAMMAD Sheikh AHMED.

Spain: St 3, New Extension, POB 2621, Khartoum; tel. (11) 45072; telex 22476; Ambassador: TOMÁS SOLÍS GRAGERA.

Switzerland: Amarat, Street 15, POB 1707, Khartoum; tel. (11) 451010; Chargé d'affaires: GIAMBATTISTA MONDADA.

Syria: St 3, New Extension, POB 1139, Khartoum; tel. (11) 44663; Ambassador: MOHAMMED AL-MAHAMEED.

Turkey: 31, St 29, New Extension, POB 771, Khartoum; tel. (11) 451197; fax 451197; Ambassador: ERDINÇ ERDÜN.

Uganda: House No. 6, Square 42, Khartoum East; tel. (11) 78409; telex 22811; Ambassador: E. OBITRE-GAMA.

United Arab Emirates: St 3, New Extension, POB 1225, Khartoum; tel. (11) 44476; telex 24024; Ambassador: MOHAMMED SULTAN AS-SUAIDI.

United Kingdom: St 10, off Baladia St, POB 801, Khartoum; tel. (11) 451029; telex 22189; Chargé d'affaires: JOHN CRANE.

USA: Sharia Ali Abdul Latif, POB 699, Khartoum; tel. (11) 74700; telex 22619; Ambassador: DON PETTERSON.

Yemen: St 11, New Extension, POB 1010, Khartoum; tel. (11) 43918; Ambassador: ABD AS-SALAM HUSSEIN.

Yugoslavia: St 31, 49A, POB 1180, Khartoum 1; tel. (11) 41252; Ambassador: VLADIMIR PETKOVSKI.

Zaire: St 13, New Extension, Block 12CE, 23, POB 4195, Khartoum; tel. (11) 42424; telex 24192; Ambassador: MGBAMA MPWA.

Judicial System

Until September 1983 the judicial system was divided into two sections, civil and Islamic, the latter dealing only with personal and family matters. In September 1983 President Nimeri revoked all existing laws in favour of a new system of Islamic (*Shari'a*) law. Under the provisions of the new penal code, alcohol and gambling were prohibited, while imprisonment was largely replaced by the death sentence or dismemberment. Crimes of murder and related offences were judged in accordance with the Koran. Following the coup in April 1985, the *Shari'a* courts were abolished, and it was announced that the previous system of criminal courts was to be revived. In June 1986 the Prime Minister, Sadiq al-Mahdi, reaffirmed that the *Shari'a* law was to be abolished. It was announced in June 1987 that a new legal code, based on a 'Sudanese legal heritage', was to be introduced. In July 1989 the military Government established special courts to investigate violations of emergency laws concerning corruption. It was announced in June 1991 that these courts were to be incorporated in the general court administration. Islamic law was reintroduced in March 1991, but was not applied in the southern states of Equatoria, Bahr al-Ghazal and Upper Nile.

Chief Justice: JALLAL ALI LUTFI.

Religion

The majority of the northern Sudanese population are Muslims, while in the south the population are mostly either animists or Christians.

ISLAM

Islam is the state religion. Sudanese Islam has a strong Sufi element, and is estimated to have more than 15m. adherents.

CHRISTIANITY

Sudan Council of Churches: Inter-Church House, St 35, New Extension, POB 469, Khartoum; tel. (11) 42859; telex 24099; f. 1967; 12 mem. churches; Chair. Most Rev. PAOLINO LUKUDU LORO (Roman Catholic Archbishop of Juba); Gen. Sec. Rev. CLEMENT H. JANDA.

Roman Catholic Church

Latin Rite

Sudan comprises two archdioceses and seven dioceses. At the end of 1992 there were about 2.3m. adherents in the country, representing about 7% of the total population.

Sudan Catholic Bishops' Conference: General Secretariat, POB 6011, Khartoum; tel. (11) 225075; telex 24261; f. 1971; Pres. Most Rev. GABRIEL ZUBEIR WAKO, Archbishop of Khartoum.

Archbishop of Juba: Most Rev. PAOLINO LUKUDU LORO, Catholic Church, POB 32, Juba, Equatoria State; tel. 2930; fax 24261.

Archbishop of Khartoum: Most Rev. GABRIEL ZUBEIR WAKO, Catholic Church, POB 49, Khartoum; tel. (11) 80939.

Maronite Rite

Maronite Church in Sudan: POB 244, Khartoum; Rev. Fr YOUSEPH NEAMA.

Melkite Rite

Patriarchal Vicariate of Egypt and Sudan: Patriarcat Grec-Melkite Catholique, 16 rue Daher, Cairo, Egypt; tel. (2) 905790 (Vicar Patriarchal: Most Rev. PAUL ANTAKI, Titular Archbishop of Nubia); Vicar in Sudan: Fr GEORGE BANNA, POB 766, Khartoum; tel. (11) 76466.

Orthodox Churches

Coptic Orthodox Church: Bishop of Nubia, Atbara and Omdurman: Rt Rev. BAKHOMIOS; Bishop of Khartoum, Southern Sudan and Uganda: Rt Rev. ANBA YOUANNIS.

Greek Orthodox Church: POB 47, Khartoum; tel. (11) 72973; Metropolitan of Nubia: Archbishop DIONYSSIOS HADZIVASSILIOU.

The Ethiopian Orthodox Church is also active.

The Anglican Communion

Anglicans are adherents of the (Episcopal) Church of the Province of the Sudan. The Province, with four dioceses and about 1m. adherents, was inaugurated in October 1976.

Archbishop in Sudan: Most Rev. BENJAMINA W. YUGUSUK (Bishop of Juba), c/o PO Box 47429, Nairobi, Kenya.

Other Christian Churches

Evangelical Church: POB 57, Khartoum; c. 1,500 mems; administers schools, literature centre and training centre; Chair Rev. RADI ELIAS.

Presbyterian Church: POB 40, Malakal; autonomous since 1956; 67,000 mems (1985); Gen. Sec. Rev. THOMAS MALUIT.

Sudan Interior Mission (SIM): Dir R. WELLING, POB 220, Khartoum; tel. (11) 447260; fax 447213; f. 1937.

The Africa Inland Church and the Sudanese Church of Christ are also active.

The Press

DAILIES

Press censorship was imposed following the coup of 30 June 1989. The only publications permitted were the armed forces' weekly newspaper, *Al-Guwwat al-Musallaha*, and the government-controlled dailies, *Al-Engaz al-Watan* and *As-Sudan al-Hadeeth*. The principal publications in circulation prior to the coup included:

Al-Ayyam (The Days): POB 2158, Khartoum; tel. (11) 74321; f. 1953; Arabic; Chair. and Editor-in-Chief HASSAN SATTI; circ. 60,000 (publication suspended since August 1986).

Al-Engaz al-Watan: Khartoum; state-controlled.

Al-Khartoum: Khartoum; Arabic.

Al-Midan (The Field): Khartoum; Arabic; supports Sudanese Communist Party.

Ar-Rayah (The Banner); Khartoum; Arabic.

As Sudan al-Hadeeth: Khartoum; state-controlled.

Sudan Times: Khartoum; English; Editor BONA MALWAL.

As-Sudani (The Sudanese): Khartoum.

Ath-Thawra (The Revolution): Khartoum; Arabic.

Al-Usbu (The Week): Khartoum; Arabic.

PERIODICALS

Al-Guwwat al-Musallaha (The Armed Forces): Khartoum; f.1969; publs a weekly newspaper and monthly magazine for the armed forces; Editor-in-Chief Maj. MAHMOUD GALANDER; circ. 7,500.

New Horizon: POB 2651, Khartoum; tel. (11) 77913; telex 22418; f. 1976; publ. by the Sudan House for Printing and Publishing; weekly; English; political and economic affairs, development, home and international news; Editor-in-Chief MATTHEW OBUR AYANG; circ. 7,000.

Sudanow: POB 2651, Khartoum; tel. (11) 77913; telex 22956; f. 1976; publ. by the Sudan House for Printing and Publishing; monthly; English; political and economic affairs, arts, social affairs and diversions; Editor-in-Chief AHMED KAMAL ED-DIN; circ. 10,000.

NEWS AGENCIES

Sudan News Agency (SUNA): Sharia al-Gamhouria, POB 1506, Khartoum; tel. (11) 75770; telex 22418; Dir-Gen. TAYYIB HAI ATIYAH.

Sudanese Press Agency: Khartoum; f. 1985; owned by journalists.

Foreign Bureaux

Agence France-Presse (AFP): POB 1911, Khartoum; telex 22418; Rep. MUHAMMAD ALI SAID.

Middle East News Agency (MENA) (Egypt): Dalala Bldg, POB 740, Khartoum.

Xinhua (New China) News Agency (People's Republic of China): POB 2229, No. 100, 12 The Sq., Riad Town, Khartoum; tel. (11) 224174; telex 24205; Correspondent SUN XIAOKE.

The Iraqi News Agency and the Syrian News Agency also have bureaux in Khartoum.

Publishers

Ahmad Abd ar-Rahman at-Tikeine: POB 299, Port Sudan.

Al-Ayyam Press Co Ltd: Aboulela Bldg, United Nations Sq., POB 363, Khartoum; f. 1953; general fiction and non-fiction, arts, poetry, reference, newspapers, magazines; Man. Dir BESHIR MUHAMMAD SAID.

As-Sahafa Publishing and Printing House: POB 1228, Khartoum; f. 1961; newspapers, pamphlets, fiction and govt publs.

As-Salam Co Ltd: POB 944, Khartoum.

Claudios S. Fellas: POB 641, Khartoum.

Khartoum University Press: POB 321, Khartoum; tel. (11) 76653; telex 22738; f. 1964; academic, general and educational in Arabic and English; Man. Dir KHALID AL-MUBARAK.

Government Publishing House

Government Printer: POB 38, Khartoum.

Radio and Television

In 1991, according to UNESCO, there were an estimated 6,480,000 radio receivers and 2m. television receivers in use.

National Radio and Television Corporation: Omdurman; state broadcasting authority; Dir-Gen. AHMAD HAMDI BADR AD-DIN.

RADIO

A joint Sudanese–Egyptian radio station opened in August 1982.

Sudan Broadcasting Service: POB 572, Omdurman; tel. 53151; state-controlled service broadcasting daily in Amharic, Arabic, English, French, Somali and Tigrinya; Dir-Gen. SALIH AL-MUHAMMAD SALIH.

TELEVISION

An earth satellite station operated on 36 channels at Umm Haraz has much improved Sudan's telecommunication links. A nationwide satellite network is being established with 14 earth stations in the provinces. A microwave network of television transmission covered 90% of inhabited areas in 1983. There are regional stations at Gezira (Central Region) and Atbara (Northern Region).

Sudan National Television Corporation: POB 1094, Omdurman; tel. 52100; telex 28002; f. 1962; state-controlled; 60 hours of programmes per week; Dir-Gen. Dr GAMAL ED-DIN OSMAN.

Finance

(cap. = capital; p.u. = paid up; res = reserves; dep. = deposits; m. = million; brs = branches; amounts in Sudanese pounds unless otherwise stated)

BANKING

All domestic banks are controlled by the Bank of Sudan. Foreign banks were permitted to resume operations in 1976. In December 1985 the government banned the establishment of any further banks. It was announced in December 1990 that Sudan's banking system was to be reorganized to accord with Islamic principles.

Central Bank

Bank of Sudan: Gamaa Ave, POB 313, Khartoum; tel. (11) 78064; telex 22352; f. 1960; bank of issue; cap. and res 70.1m. (Dec. 1989); Gov. SABIR MUHAMMAD HASSAN; 9 brs.

Commercial Banks

Al-Baraka Bank: Al-Baraka Tower, Sharia al Kasr, POB 3583, Khartoum; tel. (11) 74104; telex 22555; fax (11) 78948; f. 1984; investment and export promotion; cap. 55.3m., total assets 1,446m. (Dec. 1991); Pres. Sheikh SALIH ABDALLA KAMIL; 15 brs.

Bank of Khartoum: 8 Gamhouria Ave, POB 1008, Khartoum; tel. (11) 72880; telex 22181; fax (11) 81072; f. 1913; cap. 20m., res 236.4m., total assets 5,324.1m. (1990); Chair. of Bd and Gen. Man. Dr SABIR MUHAMMAD EL-HASSAN; 47 brs.

Islamic Bank for Western Sudan: Gamhouria Ave, POB 3575, Khartoum; tel. (11) 79583; telex 22382; f. 1984; cap. 25m., total assets 68.1m. (Dec. 1987); Chair. Dr ADAM MAHMOUD MADIBBO; Gen. Man. ESH-SHARIEF EL-KHATIM; 4 brs.

National Bank of Sudan: Kronfli Bldg, Al-Qasr Ave, POB 1183, Khartoum; tel. (11) 78153; telex 22058; fax (11) 79497; f. 1982; cap. 39.2m. (Dec. 1991); Chair. Dr BASHIR EL-BAKRI; Gen. Man. SAYED ISAM ALUZRI; 4 brs.

National Export/Import Bank: En-Niel Ave, POB 2732, Khartoum; tel. (11) 81961; telex 22928; f. 1983; cap. 50m. (Dec. 1990); Pres. and Gen. Man. ABD AR-RAHMAN AHMAD OSMAN; 8 brs.

People's Co-operative Bank: POB 922, Khartoum; tel. (11) 73555; telex 22247; Chair. KARAMALLAH AL-AWAD.

Sudan Commercial Bank: Al-Qasr Ave, POB 1116, Khartoum; tel. (11) 79836; telex 22434; fax (11) 74194; f. 1960; cap. 10m., total assets 5,025.1m. (Dec. 1992); Chair. EL-TAYB ELOBEID BADR; 18 brs.

Sudanese French Bank: Zubair Basha St, POB 2775, Khartoum; tel. (11) 76542; telex 22204; fax (11) 71740; f. 1978 as Sudanese Investment Bank; cap. 5m. (Dec. 1993); Chair. GHAZI SULIMAN; 11 brs.

Tadamun Islamic Bank of Sudan: POB 3154, Baladin Ave, Khartoum; tel. (11) 71845; telex 22158; (11) fax 73840; f. 1983; cap. 49.7m., dep. 6,961.6m., total assets 7,531.3m. (Aug. 1993); Chair. ALIGANI HASSAN HILAL; 15 brs.

Unity Bank: Barlaman Ave, POB 408, Khartoum; tel. (11) 74200; telex 22231; f. 1970; cap. 10m., total assets 2,408m. (Dec.1990); Chair. and Gen. Man. FAWZI IBRAHIM WASFI; 27 brs.

Foreign Banks

Blue Nile Bank Ltd: Zubeir Pasha Ave, POB 984, Khartoum; tel. (11) 78925; telex 22905; f. 1983; cap. 31.9m., total assets 197.2m. (Dec. 1991); jtly controlled by the Govts of Sudan and the Repub. of Korea; Chair. CHAN SUP LEE.

Citibank NA (USA): SDC Bldg, St 19, New Extension, POB 8027, Khartoum; tel. (11) 47615; telex 22454; f. 1978; cap. and res 48m., total assets 400m. (Dec. 1989); Gen. Man. ADNAN MOHAMED.

Faisal Islamic Bank (Sudan) (Saudi Arabia): Ali Abdel Latif Ave, POB 10143, Khartoum; tel. (11) 81848; telex 22519; fax (11) 80193; f. 1977; cap. 117.7m., total assets 16,490m. (Dec. 1993); Chair. Prince MUHAMMAD AL-FAISAL AS-SAUD.

Habib Bank (Pakistan): Baladiya Ave, POB 8246, Khartoum; tel. (11) 81497; telex 22490; f. 1982; cap. and res 13.8m., total assets 27.3m. (Dec. 1987); Gen. Man. BAZ MUHAMMAD KHAN.

Mashreq Bank PSC: Baladia St, POB 371, Khartoum; tel. (11) 72969; telex 22124; fax (11) 72743; Regional Chief Man. Sayed ARIF HUSAIN.

Middle East Bank Ltd (United Arab Emirates): Kronfli Bldg, Al-Qasr Ave, POB 1950, Khartoum; tel. (11) 73794; telex 22516; fax (11) 73696; f. 1982; cap. and res 9.9m., total assets 8.9m. (Dec. 1987); Chief Man. FAISAL HASSOUN.

National Bank of Abu Dhabi (United Arab Emirates): Atbara St, POB 2465, Khartoum; tel. (11) 74870; telex 22249; f. 1976; cap. and res 16.9m., total assets 12.5m. (Dec. 1987); Man. GAAFAR OSMAN.

Development Banks

Agricultural Bank of Sudan: POB 1363, Khartoum; tel. (11) 77432; telex 22610; fax (11) 78296; f. 1957; cap. p.u. 200m.; provides finance for approved agricultural projects; Dir-Gen. BADR AD-DIN TAHA; 40 brs.

Arab-African International Bank: POB 2721, Khartoum; tel. 75573; telex 22624; Rep. SHEIKH HASSAN BELAIL.

Islamic Co-operative Development Bank (ICDB): POB 62, Khartoum; tel. (11) 80223; telex 22906; fax (11) 77715; f. 1983; cap. 16.4m. (Dec. 1990); 6 brs.

National Development Bank: POB 655, Khartoum; tel. (11) 79496; telex 22835; f. 1982; finances or co-finances economic and social development projects; cap. p.u. 5m. (Dec. 1991); Chair. MUHAMMAD DAOUD ALKHALIFA.

Nilein Industrial Development Bank: United Nations Sq., POB 1722, Khartoum; tel. (11) 80929; telex 22456; fax (11) 80776; f. 1993 by merger of An-Nilein Bank and the Industrial Bank of Sudan; provides tech. and financial assistance for private-sector industrial projects and acquires shares in industrial enterprises; Chair. ELSAED OSMAN MAHGOUB.

Sudanese Estates Bank: Al-Baladiya Ave, POB 309, Khartoum; tel. (11) 77917; telex 22439; fax (11) 79465; f. 1967; mortgage bank financing private-sector urban housing development; cap. p.u. 59m. (Dec. 1992); Chair. Eng. MUHAMMAD ALI EL-AMIN; 6 brs.

Sudanese Savings Bank: POB 159, Wad Medani; tel. 3013; telex 50005; f. 1974; cap. p.u. 10m., total assets 1,613.4m. (Dec. 1991); Chair. MANSOUR AHMAD ESH-SHEIKH; 22 brs.

INSURANCE COMPANIES

African Insurance Co (Sudan) Ltd: Al-Baladiya Ave, Muhammad Hussein Bldg, POB 149, Khartoum; f. 1977; fire, accident, marine and motor; Gen. Man. AN-NOMAN AS-SANUSI.

Blue Nile Insurance Co (Sudan) Ltd: POB 2215, Khartoum; telex 22389; Gen. Man. MUHAMMAD AL-AMIN MIRGHANI.

General Insurance Co (Sudan) Ltd: El-Mek Nimr St, POB 1555, Khartoum; tel. (11) 80616; telex 22303; f. 1961; Gen. Man. ABD AL-FATTAH MUHAMMAD SIYAM.

Islamic Insurance Co Ltd: Al-Faiha Commercial Bldg, POB 2776, Khartoum; tel. (11) 72656; telex 22167; f. 1979; all classes.

Khartoum Insurance Co Ltd: POB 737, Khartoum; tel. (11) 78647; telex 22241; f. 1953; Chair. MUDAWI M. AHMAD; Gen. Man. ABD AL-MENIM AL-HADARI.

Middle East Insurance Co Ltd: POB 3070, Khartoum; tel. (11) 72202; telex 22191; f. 1981; fire, marine, motor, general liability; Chair. AHMAD I. MALIK; Gen. Man. ALI AL-FADL.

Sudanese Insurance and Reinsurance Co Ltd: Sharia al-Gamhouria, Nasr Sq., POB 2332, Khartoum; tel. (11) 70812; telex 22292; f. 1967; Gen. Man. IZZ AD-DIN AS-SAID MUHAMMAD.

United Insurance Co (Sudan) Ltd: Makkawi Bldg, Sharia al-Gamhouria, POB 318, Khartoum; tel. (11) 76630; telex 22390; fax (11) 70783; f. 1968; Dir-Gen. MUHAMMAD ABDEEN BABIKER.

Trade and Industry

STATE CORPORATIONS

Agricultural Research Corporation: POB 126, Wadi Medani; Gen. Man. Dr OSMAN AGEEB.

Alaktan Trading Co: POB 2067, Khartoum; tel. (11) 81588; telex 22272; Gen. Man. ABD AR-RAHMAN ABD AL-MONEIM.

Animal Production Public Corporation: POB 624, Khartoum; tel. (11) 40611; telex 24048; Gen. Man. Dr FOUAD RAMADAN HAMID.

General Petroleum Corporation: POB 2986, Khartoum; tel. (11) 71554; telex 22638; f. 1976; Chair. Dr OSMAN ABDULWAHAB; Dir-Gen. Dr ABD ER-RAHMAN OSMAN ABD ER-RAHMAN.

Gum Arabic Co: POB 857, Khartoum; tel. (11) 77288; telex 22314; f. 1969; Gen. Man. OMER EL-MUBARAK ABU ZEID.

Industrial Production Corporation: POB 1034, Khartoum; tel. (11) 71278; telex 22236; Dir-Gen. OSMAN TAMMAM; Dep. Chair. ABD AL-LATIF WIDATALLA; incorporates:

Cement and Building Materials Sector Co-ordination Office: POB 2241, Khartoum; tel. (11) 74269; telex 22079; Dir T. M. KHOGALI.

Food Industries Corporation: POB 2341, Khartoum; tel. (11) 75463; Dir MUHAMMAD AL-GHALI SULIMAN.

Leather Trading and Manufacturing Co Ltd: POB 1639, Khartoum; tel. (11) 78187; telex 22298; f. 1986; Man. Dir IBRAHIM SALIH ALI.

Oil Corporation: POB 64, Khartoum North; tel. (11) 32044; telex 22198; Gen. Man. BUKHARI MAHMOUD BUKHARI.

Spinning and Weaving General Co Ltd: POB 765, Khartoum; tel. (11) 74306; telex 22122; f. 1975; Dir MUHAMMAD SALIH MUHAMMAD ABDALLAH.

Sudan Tea Co: POB 1219, Khartoum; tel. (11) 81261; telex 22320.

Sudanese Mining Corporation: POB 1034, Khartoum; tel. (11) 70840; telex 22298; Dir IBRAHIM MUDAWI BABIKER.

Sugar and Distilling Industry Corporation: POB 511, Khartoum; tel. (11) 78417; telex 22665; Man. MIRGHANI AHMAD BABIKER.

Mechanized Farming Corporation: POB 2482, Khartoum; Man. Dir AWAD AL-KARIM AL-YASS.

National Cotton and Trade Co Ltd: POB 1552, Khartoum; telex 22267; Gen. Man. ZUBAIR MUHAMMAD AL-BASHIR.

Port Sudan Cotton Trade Co Ltd: POB 261, Port Sudan; telex 22270; POB 590, Khartoum; Gen. Man. SAID MUHAMMAD ADAM.

Public Agricultural Production Corporation: POB 538, Khartoum; Chair. and Man. Dir ABDALLAH BAYOUMO; Sec. SAAD AD-DIN MUHAMMAD ALI.

Public Corporation for Building and Construction: POB 2110, Khartoum; tel. (11) 74544; Dir NAIM AD-DIN.

Public Corporation for Irrigation and Excavations: POB 619, Khartoum; tel. (11) 80167; Gen. Sec. OSMAN AN-NUR.

Public Corporation for Oil Products and Pipelines: POB 1704, Khartoum; tel. (11) 78290; Gen. Man. ABD AR-RAHMAN SULIMAN.

Public Electricity and Water Corporation: POB 1380, Khartoum; Gen. Man. MUHAMMAD AL-MAHDI MIRGHANI.

Rahad Corporation: POB 2523, Khartoum; tel. (11) 75175; financed by the World Bank, Kuwait and the USA; by 1983 300,000 ha had been irrigated and 70,000 people settled in 15,000 tenancies; Man. Dir HASSAN SAAD ABDALLA.

The State Trading Corporation: POB 211, Khartoum; tel. (11) 78555; telex 22355; Chair. E. R. M. TOM.

Automobile Corporation: POB 221, Khartoum; tel. (11) 78555; telex 22230; importer of vehicles and spare parts; Gen. Man. DAFALLA AHMAD SIDDIQ.

Engineering Equipment Corporation: POB 97, Khartoum; tel. (11) 73731; telex 22274; importers and distributors of agricultural, engineering and electronic equipment; Gen. Man. Izz ad-Din Hamid.

Gezira Trade and Services Co: POB 215, Khartoum; tel. (11) 72687; telex 22302; fax (11) 79060; f. 1980; largest importer of general merchandise and services in storage, shipping and insurance; exporter of oilseeds and cereals.

Khartoum Commercial and Shipping Co: POB 221, Khartoum; tel. (11) 78555; telex 22311; import, export and shipping services, insurance and manufacturing; Gen. Man. Idris M. Salih.

Silos and Storage Corporation: POB 1183, Khartoum; stores and handles agricultural products; Gen. Man. Ahmad at-Taieb Harhoof.

Sudan Cotton Co Ltd: POB 1672, Khartoum; tel. (11) 71567; telex 22245; fax (11) 70703; f. 1970; exports raw cotton; Chair Abd al-Ati Abdalla el-Meki; Man. Dir Abd ar-Rahman Abd al-Moneim.

Sudan Gezira Board: POB 884, HQ Barakat Wadi Medani, Gezira Province; tel. 2412; telex 50001; Sales Office, POB 884, Khartoum; tel. 40145; responsible for Sudan's main cotton-producing area; the Gezira scheme is a partnership between the govt, the tenants and the board. The govt provides the land and is responsible for irrigation. Tenants pay a land and water charge and receive the work proceeds. The role of the board is to provide agricultural services at cost, technical supervision and execution of govt agricultural policies relating to the scheme. Tenants pay a percentage of their proceeds to the Social Development Fund. The total potential cultivable area of the Gezira scheme is c. 850,000 ha and the total area under systematic irrigation is c. 730,000 ha. In addition to cotton, groundnuts, sorghum, wheat, rice, pulses and vegetables are grown for the benefit of tenant farmers; Man. Dir Izz ed-Din Omar el-Makki.

Sudan Oilseeds Co Ltd: POB 167, Parliament Ave, POB 167, Khartoum; tel. (11) 80120; telex 22312; f. 1974; 58% state-owned; exporter of oilseeds (groundnuts, sesame seeds and castor beans); importer of foodstuffs and other goods; Chair. Sadiq Karar at-Tayeb; Gen. Man. Kamal Abd al-Halim.

CHAMBER OF COMMERCE

Sudan Chamber of Commerce: POB 81, Khartoum; tel. (11) 72346; f. 1908; Pres. Saad Abou al-Ela; Sec.-Gen. Haroun al-Awad.

INDUSTRIAL ASSOCIATION

Sudanese Industries Association: POB 2565, Africa St, Khartoum; tel. (11) 73151; f. 1974; Chair. Fath ar-Rahman al-Bashir; Exec. Dir A. Izz al-Arab Yousuf.

DEVELOPMENT CORPORATIONS

Sudan Development Corporation (SDC): POB 710, 21 al-Amarat, Khartoum; tel. (11) 42425; telex 24078; fax (11) 40473; f. 1974 to promote and co-finance development projects with special emphasis on projects in the agricultural, agri-business, and industrial sectors; cap. p.u. US $200m. (Dec. 1990); Chair. and Man. Dir Sayed Abdallah Ahmed ar-Ramadi; affiliates:

Sudan Rural Development Co Ltd (SRDC): POB 2190, Khartoum; tel. (11) 73855; telex 22813; f. 1980; SRDC has 27% shareholding; cap. p.u. US $12.5m.; Gen. Man. Dr Hashim M. Hashim el-Hadia.

Sudan Rural Development Finance Co (SRDFC): POB 2190, Khartoum; tel. (11) 73855; telex 22813; fax (11) 73235; f. 1980; Gen. Man. Dr Hashim M. Hashim el-Hadia.

MAJOR INDUSTRIAL COMPANIES

The following are among the larger companies, either in terms of capital investment or employment.

Aboulela Cotton Ginning Co Ltd: POB 121, Khartoum; tel. (11) 70020; cotton mills.

AGIP (Sudan) Ltd: POB 1155, Khartoum; tel. (11) 80253; telex 22317; f. 1959; cap. £S15.8m.; distribution of petroleum products; Pres. E. Campoli; Gen. Man. G. Baronio; 187 employees.

Bata (Sudan) Ltd: POB 88, Khartoum; tel. (11) 32240; telex 22327; f. 1950; cap. £S1.7m.; mfrs and distributors of footwear; Man. Dir A. A. Ali; 1,065 employees.

The Blue Nile Brewery: POB 1408, Khartoum; f. 1954; cap. £S734,150; brewing, bottling and distribution of beer; Man. Dirs Ibrahim Elyas, Hussein Muhammad Kemal, Omer az-Zein Sagayroun; 336 employees.

The Central Desert Mining Co Ltd: POB 20, Port Sudan; f. 1946; cap. £S150,000; prospecting for and mining of gold, manganese and iron ore; Dirs Abd al-Hadi Ahmad Bashir, Abou-Bakr Said Bashir; 274 employees.

Kenana Sugar Co Ltd: POB 2632, Khartoum; tel. (11) 44297; telex 24033; f. 1971; financed by Sudan govt and other Arab nations; 18,000 employees; Man. Dir Osman Abdullah an-Nazir.

Sudan Tobacco Co Ltd: POB 87, Khartoum; mfrs of tobacco products.

TRADE UNIONS

All trade union activity was banned following the coup of 30 June 1989. The following organizations were active prior to that date. Many of their officers are reported to have been imprisoned.

Federations

Sudan Workers Trade Unions Federation (SWTUF): POB 2258, Khartoum; tel. (11) 77463; includes 42 trade unions representing c. 1.75m. public-service and private-sector workers; affiliated to the Int. Confed. of Arab Trade Unions and the Org. of African Trade Union Unity; Pres. Muhammad Osman Gama; Gen. Sec. Yousuf Abu Shama Hamed.

Principal Affiliates

Agricultural Sector Workers' Trade Union: Workers' Club, Khartoum North; Pres. Awad Widatalla; Sec. Muhammad Osman Salim; 30,000 mems.

Gezira Scheme Workers' Trade Union: Barakat; Pres. Ibrahim Muhammad Ahmad ash-Sheikh; Sec. As-Sir Abdoon; 11,500 mems.

Health Workers' Trade Union: Khartoum Civil Hospital, Khartoum; Pres. Dr Harith Hamed; Sec. Gaafar Muhammad Sid Ahmad; 25,000 mems.

Local Government Workers' Trade Union: Workers' Union, Khartoum; Pres. Ismail Muhammad Fadl; Sec. Salem Bedri Humam; 25,000 mems.

Post, Telegraph and Telephone Workers' Trade Union: Workers' Club, Khartoum; Pres. Mansoul al-Manna; Sec. Yassin Abd al-Galil; 8,463 mems.

Public Service Workers' Trade Union: Al-Baladiya Ave, Khartoum; Pres. Mohi ad-Din Bakheit; Sec. Ali Idris al-Hussein; 19,800 mems.

Railway Workers' Trade Union: Railway Workers' Club, Atbara; Pres. Muhammad al-Hassan Abdallah; Sec. Osman Ali Fadl; 32,000 mems.

Sudan Irrigation Workers' Trade Union: Ministry of Education, Wadi Medani; Pres. Muhammad Habib; Sec. Muhammad Ahmad; 19,150 mems.

Taxi Workers' Trade Union: Workers' Union, Khartoum; Pres. Ar-Rayan Yousif; Sec. At-Tayeb Khalafalla; 15,000 mems.

Sudanese Federation of Employees and Professionals Trade Unions: POB 2398, Khartoum; tel. (11) 73818; f. 1975; includes 54 trade unions representing 250,000 mems; Pres. Ibrahim Awadallah; Sec.-Gen. Kamal ad-Din Muhammad Abdallah.

Principal Affiliates

Bank Officials' Union: Bank of Sudan, Gamaa Ave, POB 313, Khartoum; Pres. Muhammad Sallam; Sec. Abdallah Mahmoud Abdallah.

Gezira Board Officials' Union: Barakat; Pres. Galal Hamid; Sec. Osman Abd ar-Rahim Kheirawy.

Local Government Officials' Union: Dept of Local Government, Khartoum; Pres. Salah Ibrahim Khalil; Sec. Muhammad Awad Gabir.

Post, Telegraph and Telephone Officials: PO, Khartoum; Pres. Abd ar-Rahman al-Khider Ali; Sec. Awad al-Karim Osman.

Railway Officials' Union: Sudan Railways Corporation, POB 65, Atbara; Pres. Hassan Haq Musa; Sec. Gen. Abbas Bashir ar-Raieh.

Teachers' Union: Teachers' House, Khartoum; Pres. Abdallah Ali Abdallah; Sec. Hassan Ibrahim Marzoug.

CO-OPERATIVE SOCIETIES

There are about 600 co-operative societies, of which 570 are officially registered.

Central Co-operative Union: POB 2492, Khartoum; tel. (11) 80624; largest co-operative union operating in 15 provinces.

TRADE FAIR

Sudan Exhibitions and Fairs Corporation (Sudanexpo): POB 2366, Khartoum; tel. (11) 77702; telex 22407; f. 1976; Dir-Gen. Malik Amin Nabri.

Transport

RAILWAYS

The total length of railway in operation in 1991 was 4,725 route-km. The main line runs from Wadi Halfa, on the Egyptian border, to al-Obeid, via Khartoum. Lines from Atbara and Sinnar connect with Port Sudan. There are lines from Sinnar to Damazine on the Blue Nile (227 km) and from Aradeiba to Nyala in the south-western province of Darfur (689 km), with a 445 km branch line from Babanousa to Wau in Bahr al-Ghazal province.

Sudan Railways Corporation: POB 43, Atbara; tel. 2000; telex 40002; f. 1875; Chair. and Gen. Man. Dr EL-FATIH MOHAMMAD ALI.

ROADS

Roads in northern Sudan, other than town roads, are only cleared tracks and often impassable immediately after rain. Motor traffic on roads in the former Upper Nile province is limited to the drier months of January–May. There are several good gravelled roads in Equatoria and Bahr al-Ghazal provinces which are passable all the year, but in these districts some of the minor roads become impassable after rain. Rehabilitation of communications in southern Sudan is hampered by the continuing hostilities in the area.

The Wadi Medani to Gedaref highway, financed by a loan from the People's Republic of China, was completed in March 1977. Over 48,000 km of tracks are classed as 'motorable'; there were 3,160 km of main roads and 739 km of secondary roads in 1985. A 1,190-km tarmac road linking the capital with Port Sudan was completed during 1980. In July 1991 construction began on a 270-km road linking Jaili with Atbara, as part of a scheme to provide an alternative route from Khartoum to the coast.

National Transport Corporation: POB 723, Khartoum; Gen. Man. MOHI AD-DIN HASSAN MUHAMMAD NUR.

Public Corporation for Roads and Bridges: POB 756, Khartoum; tel. (11) 70794; f. 1976; Chair. ABD AR-RAHMAN HABOUD; Dir-Gen. ABDOU MUHAMMAD ABDOU.

INLAND WATERWAYS

The total length of navigable waterways served by passenger and freight services is 4,068 km, of which approximately 1,723 km is open all year. From the Egyptian border to Wadi Halfa and Khartoum navigation is limited by cataracts to short stretches but the White Nile from Khartoum to Juba is almost always navigable.

River Transport Corporation (RTC): POB 284, Khartoum North; operates 2,500 route-km of steamers on the Nile; Chair. ALI AMIR TAHA.

River Navigation Corporation: Khartoum; f. 1970; jtly owned by Govts of Egypt and Sudan; operates services between Aswan and Wadi Halfa.

SHIPPING

Port Sudan, on the Red Sea, 784 km from Khartoum, and Suakin, are the only commercial seaports.

Axis Trading Co Ltd: POB 1574, Khartoum; tel. (11) 75875; telex 22294; Chair. H. A. M. SULIMAN.

Red Sea Shipping Corporation: POB 116, Khartoum; tel. (11) 77688; telex 22306; Gen. Man. OSMAN AMIN.

Sea Ports Corporation: Port Sudan; tel. 2910; telex 70012; f. 1906; Gen. Man. MUHAMMAD TAHIR AILA.

Sudan Shipping Line Ltd: POB 426, Port Sudan; tel. 2655; telex 22518; and POB 1731, Khartoum; tel. (11) 80017; telex 22301; f. 1960; 10 vessels totalling 54,277 dwt operating between the Red Sea and western Mediterranean, northern Europe and United Kingdom; Chair. ISMAIL BAKHEIT; Gen. Man. SALAH AD-DIN OMER AL-AZIZ.

United African Shipping Co: POB 339, Khartoum; tel. (11) 80967; Gen. Man. MUHAMMAD TAHA AL-GINDI.

CIVIL AVIATION

Civil Aviation Authority: Khartoum; tel. (11) 72264; telex 22650; Dir-Gen. Brig. MAHGOUB MUHAMMAD MAHDI.

Sudan Airways Co. Ltd: SDC Bldg Complex, Amarat St 19, POB 253, Khartoum; tel. (11) 47953; telex 24212; fax (11) 47987; f. 1947; internal flights and international services to Africa, the Middle East and Europe; Chair. Col SALIH AD-DIN MUHAMMAD AHMAD KARRAR.

Tourism

Public Corporation of Tourism and Hotels: POB 7104, Khartoum; tel. (11) 81764; telex 22436; f. 1977; Dir-Gen. Maj.-Gen. EL-KHATIM MUHAMMAD FADL.

Defence

In June 1993 the armed forces totalled 72,800: army 68,000, navy 1,800, air force 3,000. The strength of the Popular Defence Force, the military wing of the NIF, is estimated at 30,000–50,000. Military service is compulsory for a period of three years for all males aged 18–30.

Defence Expenditure: Budgeted at £S4,100m. (including internal security) in 1993.

Commander-in-Chief of the People's Armed Forces: Lt-Gen. OMAR HASSAN AHMAD AL-BASHIR.

Education

The government provides free elementary education from the ages seven to 12 years, intermediate from 13 to 15 years and secondary from 16 to 18 years. The Six-Year Plan 1977–83 placed strong emphasis on education and aimed to reduce the level of illiteracy from the 80% of 1975 to 50% by 1983, together with the introduction of compulsory primary education and special concentration on those involved in the industrial and agricultural sectors, the government service and housewives. It was hoped to achieve universal primary school enrolment and universal literacy by 1991. The average rate of adult illiteracy was estimated by UNESCO to be 72.9% (males 57.3%; females 88.3%) in 1990.

The secondary level is divided into two stages; junior secondary (intermediate) of three years' duration, which is completely academic, and senior secondary (secondary) of three years, which is of three types: academic, technical and teacher training.

In 1990, according to UNESCO, the total enrolment at primary schools was equivalent to 50% of children in the appropriate age-group (56% of boys; 43% of girls). The comparable enrolment ratio in intermediate and secondary schools was 22% (25% of boys; 20% of girls). Pupils from secondary schools are accepted at the University of Khartoum, subject to their reaching the necessary standards.

The University of Khartoum is under government control. The University of Cairo has a branch in Khartoum, but this was appropriated by the Sudanese Government in March 1993. The universities of Juba and Gezira were opened in 1977 and concentrate on rural development. There is an Islamic University at Omdurman. New universities were opened at Juba and Wadi Medani in 1977. In March 1991 the government announced that it was to establish universities in the states of Upper Nile and Bahr al-Ghazal, thus giving each of the nine states in the federation its own university. The Khartoum Polytechnic was formed in 1975 by the amalgamation of 13 existing technical institutes. In 1985/86 there were 37,367 students receiving higher education, and a further 5,444 students receiving training at teacher training institutes.

Bibliography

Abdel-Rahim, M. *Imperialism and Nationalism in the Sudan: A Study in Constitutional and Political Developments 1899–1956.* Oxford University Press, 1969.

Abdel-Rahim, M., et al. *Sudan since Independence.* London, Gower, 1986.

Arkell, A. J. *Outline History of the Sudan.* London, 1938.

History of the Sudan to 1821. 2nd Edn, London, 1961.

Barbour, K. M. *The Republic of the Sudan: A Regional Geography.* University of London Press, 1961.

Bechtold, P. K. *Politics in the Sudan.* London, 1978.

Beshir, M. O. *The Southern Sudan: Background to Conflict.* C. Hurst, London, 1968, New York, Praeger, 1968.

Collins, R. O. *Shadows in the Grass: Britain in the Southern Sudan 1918–1956.* Yale University Press, 1983.

Collins, R. O., and Tignor, R. L. *Egypt and the Sudan.* New York, Prentice, 1967.

El-Nasri, A. R. *A Bibliography of the Sudan 1938–1958.* Oxford University Press, 1962.

Eprile, C. *War and Peace in the Sudan 1955–1972.* Devon, England, David and Charles, 1974.

Fabunmi, L. A. *The Sudan in Anglo-Egyptian Relations.* London, Longman, 1965.

Gaitskell, A. *Gezira: A Story of Development in the Sudan.* London, Faber, 1959.

Grandin, N. *Le Soudan nilotique et l'administration britannique (1898–1956).* Leiden, Brill, 1982.

Gurdon, C. *Sudan at the Crossroads.* London, Menas Press, 1985.

Sudan in Transition. London, Economist Publications, 1986.

Hill, R. *A Bibliographical Dictionary of the Anglo-Egyptian Sudan.* London, Frank Cass, 1967.

Egypt in the Sudan 1820–1881. London and New York, Oxford University Press, 1959.

Hodgkin, R. A. *Sudan Geography.* London, 1951.

Holt, P. M. *A Modern History of the Sudan.* London, Weidenfeld and Nicolson, 1962, New York, Praeger, 1963.

Hurst, H. E., and Philips, P. *The Nile Basin.* 7 vols. London, 1932–38.

International Labour Office. *Growth, Employment and Equity: A Comprehensive Strategy for the Sudan.* Geneva, 1976.

Katsuyoshi, F., and Markakis, J. *Ethnicity and Conflict in the Horn of Africa.* London, Currey, 1994.

Khalid, M. *Nimeiri and the Revolution of Dis-May.* London, Routledge and Kegan Paul, 1985.

Khalid, M. (Ed.). *John Garang Speaks.* London, KPI, 1987.

MacMichael, Sir H. A. *The Anglo-Egyptian Sudan.* London, 1935.

The Sudan. London, 1954.

Malwal, B. *People and Power in the Sudan.* London, Ithaca Press, 1981.

Oduho, J., and Deng, W. *The Problem of the Southern Sudan.* Oxford University Press, 1963.

Santi, P., and Hill, R. (Eds). *The Europeans in the Sudan 1834–1878.* Oxford University Press, 1980.

Shibeika, M. *The Independent Sudan: The History of a Nation.* New York, 1960.

Suliman, A. A. *Issues in the Economic Development of the Sudan.* Khartoum University Press, 1975.

Sylvester, A. *Sudan under Nimeri.* London, Bodley Head, 1977.

Theobald, A. B. *The Mahdiya: A History of the Anglo-Egyptian Sudan 1881–1899.* New York, 1951.

Wai, D. *The Southern Sudan—The Problem of National Integration.* London, 1972.

The African-Arab Conflict in the Sudan. New York, Africana Publishing Co, 1981.

Warburg, G. *Islam, Nationalism and Communism in a Traditional Society—The Case of Sudan.* London, 1978.

Woodward, P. *Condominium and Sudanese Nationalism.* London, 1979.

Sudan 1898–1989: The Unstable State. Boulder, CO, Lynne Rienner, 1990.

Zulfo, I. H. *Karari: The Sudanese Account of the Battle of Omdurman.* London, Frederick Warne, 1980.

SWAZILAND

Physical and Social Geography

A. MacGREGOR HUTCHESON

The Kingdom of Swaziland is one of the smallest political entities of continental Africa. Covering an area of only 17,363 sq km (6,704 sq miles), it straddles the broken and dissected edge of the South African plateau, surrounded by South Africa on the north, west and south, and separated from the Indian Ocean on the east by the Mozambique coastal plain.

PHYSICAL FEATURES

From the High Veld on the west, averaging 1,050 to 1,200 m in altitude, there is a step-like descent eastwards through the Middle Veld (450 to 600 m) to the Low Veld (150 to 300 m). To the east of the Low Veld the Lebombo Range, an undulating plateau at 450–825 m, presents an impressive westward-facing scarp and forms the fourth of Swaziland's north–south aligned regions. Drainage is by four main systems flowing eastwards across these regions: the Komati and Umbeluzi rivers in the north, the Great Usutu river in the centre, and the Ngwavuma river in the south. The eastward descent is accompanied by a rise in temperature and by a decrease in mean annual rainfall from a range of 1,150–1,900 mm in the High Veld to one of 500–750 mm in the Low Veld, but increasing again to about 850 mm in the Lebombo range. The higher parts, receiving 1,000 mm, support temperate grassland, while dry woodland savannah is characteristic of the lower areas.

RESOURCES AND POPULATION

Swaziland's potential for economic development in terms of its natural resources is out of proportion to its size. The country's perennial rivers represent a high hydroelectric potential and their exploitation for irrigation in the drier Middle Veld and Low Veld has greatly increased and diversified agricultural production. Sugar, however, is both the dominant industry and the principal export commodity. Other major crops include cotton (in terms of the number of producers, this is the most important cash crop), maize, tobacco, rice, vegetables, citrus fruits and pineapples. The well-watered High Veld is particularly suitable for afforestation and over 120,000 ha (more than 100 plantations) have been planted with conifers and eucalyptus since the 1940s, creating the largest man-made forests in Africa.

Swaziland is also rich in mineral wealth. Once a major exporter of iron ore, this industry ceased with the exhaustion of high-grade ores, although considerable quantities of iron ore of inferior grade remain. World demand for Swaziland's exports of chrysolite asbestos has declined in recent years as the result of health problems associated with this mineral. Coal holds the country's most important mineral potential, with reserves estimated at 250m. tons. Coal is currently mined at Mpaka, mostly for export, and further reserves have been identified at Lobuka. The exploitation of anthracite deposits at Maloma began in 1993. Gold and diamond deposits are being exploited in the north-west of the country. Other minerals of note are cassiterite (a tin-bearing ore), kaolin, talc, pyrophyllite and silica.

Nearly one-half of the population live in the Middle Veld, which contains some of the best soils in the country. This is Swaziland's most densely peopled region, with an average of 50 inhabitants per sq km, rising to more than 200 per sq km in some rural and in more developed areas. The total population of Swaziland (excluding absentee workers) was enumerated at 681,059 at the census of August 1986, and was officially estimated to be 768,000 at mid-1990.

A complex system of land ownership, with Swazi and European holdings intricately interwoven throughout the country, is partly responsible for considerable variations in the distribution and density of the population. Only about 40% of the country was under Swazi control at the time of independence in 1968, but this proportion steadily increased in subsequent years, as non-Swazi land and mineral concessions were acquired through negotiation and purchase. The Swazi Nation, to which most of the African population belongs, has now regained all mineral concessions.

Recent History

RICHARD LEVIN

Revised for this edition by the Editor

Swaziland, which emerged as a cohesive nation in the early 19th century, became a British protectorate following the Boer War in 1903 and in 1907 became one of the high commission territories. A preoccupation of King Sobhuza II during his 61-year reign, which began in 1921, was re-establishing control over land concessions granted to settlers and speculators in the late 19th century by his predecessor King Mbandzeni.

Moves towards the restoration of independence in the early 1960s were accompanied by a growth in political activity. The Ngwane National Liberatory Congress (NNLC), an African nationalist party formed in 1962 and led by Dr Ambrose Zwane, advocated independence on the basis of universal adult suffrage and a constitutional monarchy. The increasingly radical stance of the NNLC and growing worker militancy prompted royalist interests to form the Imbokodvo National Movement (INM). The INM won all 24 seats in the new house of assembly in the pre-independence elections of April 1967; the NNLC secured 20% of the votes, owing to strong support in urban areas, but failed to gain any seats because of an electoral system that favoured rural areas. The independence constitution vested legislative authority in a bicameral parliament with a large proportion of its membership nominated by the king. Formal independence followed on 6 September 1968.

The 14-year post-independence rule of Sobhuza was characterized by stability and a significant expansion of the economy as investment flowed in, much of it from South Africa. Growing reliance on South African capital, along with Swaziland's membership of the Southern African Customs Union (SACU), produced an ever-deepening dependence on South Africa and severely restricted the country's economic and political choices. During this period the royal authorities acquired a significant material base in the economy, through their control over the Tibiyo and Tisua royal corporations, which managed the investment of mineral royalties.

The ruling élite consolidated its political control in the so-called 'constitutional crisis' precipitated by the NNLC's capture of three parliamentary seats in the 1972 elections. An attempt by the INM in 1973 to deport one of the opposition MPs led to a dispute with the courts, prompting Sobhuza to declare a state of emergency, suspend the constitution, dissolve parliament, ban political parties and form a national army.

Parliament was revived in 1978, with a non-party electoral system which preserved royal control of executive and legislative decisions. By the time of Subhuza's diamond jubilee in 1981, the authority of the Swazi monarchy was absolute, with the king's dominance over political affairs becoming increasingly personal and conservative, appealing to 'tradition' to find solutions to constitutional problems.

Sobhuza's death in August 1982 precipitated a prolonged power struggle within the royal family. The queen mother, Dzeliwe, assumed the regency and appointed the 15 members of the liqoqo, a traditional advisory body which Sobhuza had sought to establish as the supreme council of state. A confrontation ensued between the prime minister, Prince Mabandla Dlamini, and members of the liqoqo, led by Prince Mfanasibili Dlamini. Dzeliwe, who opposed the liqoqo's dismissal of the prime minster and his replacement with the more conservative Prince Bhekimpi Dlamini, was herself removed from the position of queen regent and replaced by Queen Ntombi Laftwala, mother of the 14-year-old heir apparent, Prince Makhosetive. In November 1983, elections were held and a new cabinet formed, purged of members suspected of supporting Mabandla or Dzeliwe. In December 17 people who had been in detention since August, including four members of the royal family, were charged with plotting to overthrow Ntombi. The charges were later withdrawn and the detainees released.

In April 1984 Prince Bhekimpi announced that a coup plot against him had been foiled the previous month. He later accused the minister of finance, Dr Sishayi Nxumalo, of leading the alleged conspiracy. In June Nxumalo was dismissed and in November he was arrested, together with several other prominent Swazis. The detentions followed Nxumalo's allegations that several prominent Swazi politicians, including Prince Mfanasibili, had been involved in misappropriating funds owed to the SACU. Despite pressure from South Africa for an investigation of the allegations, a decree was issued in September granting immunity from prosecution to members of the liqoqo. Amidst growing opposition to the liqoqo's monopoly of power, Prince Mfanasibili and another influential liqoqo member, Dr George Msibi, were removed from their positions on the liqoqo in October 1985. Subsequently it was announced that the liqoqo had reverted to its former status as an advisory council, with executive power being restored to the prime minster and the cabinet. In February 1986 Prince Mfanasibili was arrested on subversion charges. In May he was sentenced to seven years' imprisonment.

ACCESSION OF MSWATI III

Prince Makhosetive was crowned as King Mswati III on 25 April 1986. The young king moved quickly to assert his authority. The liqoqo was disbanded in May and the cabinet reshuffled. In October Mswati dismissed the prime minister, Prince Bhekimpi, and replaced him with Sotsha Dlamini, a former assistant commissioner of police. In May 1987 12 prominent public figures (including Prince Bhekimpi, the former prime minister, together with the former minister of labour, and other members of the royal family) were arrested on charges of sedition and treason, in connection with the removal from power of Queen Regent Dzeliwe in 1983. Prince Bhekimpi and nine other detainees were brought to trial in November 1987. All were found guilty of treason in March 1988 and sentenced to terms of imprisonment of up to 15 years. In July, however, Bhekimpi and eight of the other defendants were released after receiving royal pardons. Prince Mfanasibili was included in the amnesty, but returned to prison to serve the remainder of his earlier seven-year sentence.

Despite the high incidence of factionalism and personal intrigue within the royal family, both the king and the new prime minister indicated a determination to eliminate corruption from the administration. In the absence of democracy and structured accountability, however, corruption thrived. In September 1987 parliament was dissolved in preparation for elections to be held in November, one year early. In November the electoral college duly appointed 40 members of the house of assembly (none of whom had previously been members). Of the 10 additional members nominated by the king, eight were former MPs, including the former prime minister, Sotsha Dlamini. The new house of assembly and King Mswati each appointed 10 members of the senate. A new cabinet, appointed in late November, included Sotsha Dlamini, as prime minister, and three members of the previous cabinet. The low turn-out at the polls for the election of the electoral college was widely interpreted as an indication of growing dissatisfaction among the Swazi population with the tinkhundla system. The limited impact of Swazi voters on the composition of government was revealed in the fact that it was the king's nominees in both houses who were installed as cabinet ministers. Developments within parliament reflected growing public dissatisfaction with the political system when, in October 1988, a majority of the members of the upper house supported a motion demanding a comprehensive review of the legislative structure. The prime minister strongly opposed the motion on the familiar grounds that it would be 'un-Swazi' to challenge an established traditional institution.

The 'traditional' character of the tinkhundla is, however, an issue of debate; although their origin can be traced to the establishment of royal villages by 19th-century Swazi kings to facilitate the centralization of royal power, the formalization of the tinkhundla system was a post-Second World War colonial phenomenon. During his reign, King Sobhuza II showed little enthusiasm for the system, while many local chiefs feared that the appointed tinkhundla heads (tindvuna) might undermine their own authority. King Mswati has voiced the opinion that political stability in the kingdom can best be achieved through the tinkhundla, which would facilitate 'unity and democracy' in the kingdom. Opposition to the tinkhundla still exists among the chiefs, and in May 1989 about 40 chiefs advocated the replacement of the present electoral system by a system of direct elections to parliament. In January 1990 the founder and former leader of the NNLC, Dr Ambrose Zwane, in his first public address since the party's suppression in 1973, also urged the introduction of a system of direct legislative elections. Public debate concerning the future of the tinkhundla continued throughout 1990, in the context of mounting popular democratic opposition to the absolute rule of the monarchy.

ONSET OF OPPOSITION

In July 1989 the king abruptly dismissed the prime minister, Sotsha Dlamini, for 'disobedience'. He was replaced by Obed Dlamini, a founder member and former secretary-general of the Swaziland Federation of Trade Unions (SFTU). His appointment was expected to calm labour unrest which had prompted recent strikes in the banking and transport systems. The second half of 1989 witnessed an escalation in labour disputes, which spread to brewery workers, plantation workers, miners and the public service sector; disaffection was also expressed by students, prompting the king to order the closure of the University of Swaziland for one month from the end of September. These forms of political instability, together with a more broadly-based popular opposition of political and civic organizations, have begun to pose a serious challenge to the continuance of royal hegemony. There is little doubt that King Mswati III does not enjoy the level of support from the Swazi people commanded by the late King Sobhuza. Active opposition to his rule, however, had been restricted to the sporadic appearance of anti-liqoqo pamphlets linked to the People's United Democratic Movement (PUDEMO), an organization which emerged during the regency. PUDEMO returned to prominence in 1990 following the dissemination of new pamphlets, produced by the movement, which questioned the legitimacy of the monarchy in its present form, but did not explicitly demand a republican constitution. PUDEMO criticized the king for his alleged excesses, condemned corruption and called for democratic reform, thus echoing public criticism of the tinkhundla.

In mid-July 1990 the police began systematically to suppress PUDEMO activists, arresting about 20 people of whom 11 were variously charged with treason, sedition, or conspiring to form a political party. By the end of October, all the accused had been acquitted of the principal charges, while six were found guilty of attending an illegal political gathering. Since sentences were backdated and remission was afforded for good behaviour, four of the PUDEMO defendants were released immediately, while the remaining two applied successfully for bail. Nevertheless, those still employed or enrolled as students found themselves being victimized by their employers or educational institutions. This precipitated a crisis within the kingdom's tertiary institutions where boycotts were initiated in protest at the suspension of two students—one from a teacher training college and the other from the University of Swaziland. On 14 November police and army units entered the university campus to dispel a peaceful protest. After the subsequent unprecedented violence and injury local hospitals confirmed 87 admissions, while as many as 300 people (including the prime minister's daughter) were believed to have suffered injury. There were also persistent rumours that one student had been killed in the violence. Following this confrontation, two of the released PUDEMO defendants unsuccessfully sought refuge in the US embassy in Mbabane, and subsequently fled to South Africa, where they were detained by the South African border police and interrogated about ANC activities in Swaziland, before being returned to the Swazi authorities in November.

Following the violence of 14 November 1990 (known as 'Black Wednesday'), the government promised the institution of a judicial commission of inquiry into the events. This, however, was not initiated until March 1991. Two days after the violence, the minister of justice, Reginald Dhladhla, was removed from office, despite having successfully arbitrated between students and police at the teacher training college on 15 November, thus avoiding a possible repetition of the events on the university campus. He was replaced by Zonkhe Khumalo, a former deputy prime minister in the 1970s, who had earlier been implicated in a financial scandal surrounding the royal investment fund, Tisuka Takangwane.

It was widely believed that the decision to remove Dhladhla was taken by the king's advisory council. The issue was raised in parliament early in 1991 by Dzingalive Dlamini, who asserted that a 'secret group' within the kingdom's power structure was taking major decisions. In March Dzingalive Dlamini briefly fled the country, stating that he feared arrest and indefinite detention by the authorities. Diplomatic activity by a number of countries, notably the USA, led to Dlamini's prompt return and to the release of five PUDEMO detainees and of Prince Mfanasibili.

By mid-1991 there appeared to be widespread public support for the PUDEMO activists and their cause, and in the second half of the year the organization began to establish civic structures in order to advance its objectives through legal organizations. The most prominent of these were the Swaziland Youth Congress (SWAYOCO) and the Human Rights Association of Swaziland (HUMARAS). The king finally agreed to review the tinkhundla, and established a commission, known as the vusela ('greeting') committee, to conduct a series of public forums throughout the country in order to elicit popular opinion on political reforms. Prince Masitsela, a cabinet minister under King Sobhuza II during the 1970s, was appointed chairman of the vusela. There was widespread criticism of the political system as well as of the composition of the review committee itself. At the tinkhundla review meeting held in Mbabane, speakers demanded the abolition of the system, asserting that it was undemocratic and promoted corruption and nepotism, since it provided no system of accountability. In Manzini the meeting of the vusela planned for early November was cancelled, following a demonstration march by supporters of PUDEMO and SWAYOCO. The non-violent march was dispersed by the police, who arrested 19 people for staging an illegal demonstration.

In the months following this event, SWAYOCO was involved in a number of confrontations with the police over its right to engage in peaceful protest and community welfare activities, as increasingly militant Swazi youth seized the initiative in the campaign for democracy. Divisions began to emerge within the government concerning its response to the activities of SWAYOCO, with royal advisory council members, in particular, advocating that the youth congress be suppressed. These influences were resisted by more moderate forces, led by the prime minister, who asserted that political and social change in Swaziland was inevitable.

PUDEMO's activities, meanwhile, were also intensified. In the second half of 1991 the organization's national executive committee rejected the process of review by the vusela committee, and set out five demands whose fulfilment was deemed necessary to create conditions conducive to democratic transition. These included the establishment of an interim government, the suspension of the effective state of emergency, the holding of a referendum on the constitution, and the establishment of a constituent assembly to determine a new and appropriate constitution for Swaziland. These demands were officially ignored, but in February 1992, when the king announced the establishment of a second vusela committee (Vusela 2), he included a member of PUDEMO and a member of HUMARAS among the commissioners.

A further two opposition movements, the Swaziland United Front (SUF) and the Swaziland National Front (SWANAFRO) subsequently re-emerged. In February 1992 PUDEMO declared itself a legal opposition party, in contravention of the prohibition of political associations. Kislon Shongwe was named as president, and, among other members of the party executive, Mandla Hlatshwako was appointed national organizer. In a decree, published at the beginning of April, setting out the terms of reference of Vusela 2, the king appointed Hlatshwako as one of the commissioners. The terms of reference of Vusela 2 included a study of the submissions made by Vusela 1, receiving further submissions in camera from any Swazi, examining shortcomings in the existing system of voting and investigating ways in which customary and modern political institutions could be integrated. Following protracted negotiations with the commission over its function and influence, Hlatshwako withdrew from the committee, on the grounds that the purpose of Vusela 2 appeared to be to sustain the tinkhundla rather than to democratize. HUMARAS also rejected the second vusela as a waste of resources. HUMARAS president Sam Mkhombe, also a commissioner, was dismissed as president of the organization, having ignored HUMARAS demands that he should resign from Vusela 2.

REFORM OF THE TINKHUNDLA

In October 1992 King Mswati approved a number of proposals, which had been submitted by the Vusela 2 committee. Under new amendments to the electoral system, the house of assembly (which was redesignated as the national assembly) was to be expanded to 65 deputies (of whom 55 were to be directly elected by secret ballot from candidates nominated by the tinkhundla, and 10 appointed by the king), and the senate to 30 members (of whom 10 were to be selected by the national assembly and 20 appointed by the king); in addition, the legislation providing for detention without trial was to be abrogated, and a new constitution, which incorporated the amendments, enshrined an hereditary monarchy and confirmed the fundamental rights of the individual and the independence of the judicial system, was to be drafted. However, opposition groups protested at the committee's failure to recommend the immediate restoration of a multi-party political system; the issue was to be postponed until the forthcoming elections in order to determine the extent of public support. PUDEMO announced its opposition to the electoral reforms, and demanded that the government organize a national convention to determine the country's constitutional future. King Mswati subsequently dissolved the libandla, one month prior to the expiry of its term of office, and announced that he was to rule by decree, with the assistance of the cabinet (which was redesignated as the council of ministers), pending the adoption of the new Constitution and the holding of parliamentary elections. A third committee (Vusela 3) was established to instruct the population about the forthcoming amendments to the electoral system. Later in October the king announced that elections to the national assembly were to take place in the first half of 1993. At a series of public meetings, which were convened by the Vusela 3 committee from December 1992, doubts regarding the viability of the reformed electoral system were expressed; in early 1993, in response to public concern, it was announced that legislation preventing the heads of the tinkhundla from exerting undue influence in the nomination of candidates had been introduced.

In December 1992 an informal alliance of organizations that advocated democratic reform (principally comprising HUMARAS, PUDEMO and SWAYOCO), known as the Convention for a Full Democratic Swaziland, was established. In the same month PUDEMO rejected a proposal by SWAYOCO that a 'Vusela Resistance Movement' be established, to impede the implementation of economic reforms by disrupting essential services. In early 1993, in response to attempts by the opposition to organize a campaign against the elections, additional security measures were imposed in order to prevent political meetings from taking place. In March more than 50 opposition supporters, including leaders of PUDEMO and SWAYOCO, were arrested and charged in connection with the organization of illegal political gatherings. Although those arrested were subsequently released on bail, legal restrictions prevented them from participating in opposition activity, thereby effectively undermining efforts to co-ordinate a campaign in protest at the elections. Despite the opposition's failure to organize an official electoral boycott, however, the subsequent low level of voter registration appeared to reflect widespread objections to the reforms. Only a small proportion of the electorate had registered by the stipulated date in June (which was consequently extended to the end of that month).

The first round of elections to the expanded national assembly, which was contested by 2,094 candidates nominated by the tinkhundla, finally took place on 25 September 1993. At the end of September the king repealed the legislation providing for detention without trial for a period of 60 days. The second round of parliamentary elections, which took place on 11 October, was contested by the three candidates in each tinkhundla who had obtained the highest number of votes in the first poll; the majority of members of the former cabinet (which had been dissolved in late September), including Obed Dlamini, failed to secure seats in the national assembly. (The king subsequently appointed an acting prime minister, with responsibility for all ministerial portfolios, pending the formation of a new cabinet.) Shortly afterwards, Prince Mfanasibili questioned the loyalty to the king of the elected parliamentary deputies, and claimed that certain elements planned to transfer executive power to the prime minister and redesignate the head of state as a constitutional monarch. Later in October the king nominated a further 10 deputies to the national assembly, which elected 10 of its members to the senate; the king subsequently appointed the remaining 20 senators, who included Obed Dlamini and Prince Bhekimpi. In early November the former minister of works and construction, Prince Jameson Mbilini Dlamini, who was considered to be a traditionalist, was appointed prime minister, and a new cabinet (which included Dr Nxumalo, in the office of deputy prime minister) was formed.

In February 1994, following a report by the US department of state concerning human rights in Swaziland, which stated that the parliamentary elections had been 'undemocratic', the government claimed that the majority of the Swazi people were opposed to the establishment of a multi-party political system. It was announced, however, that the king was to appoint a five-member committee, comprising representatives of state organs and non-governmental organizations, to draft a new constitution, and a national policy council, which was to prepare a manifesto of the Swazi people. In March elections to the tinkhundla, which were scheduled to take place later that month in accordance with the reforms, were postponed, owing to lack of preparation. (The heads of the tinkhundla had previously been appointed by the king.)

INTERNATIONAL RELATIONS

Despite Swaziland's professed neutrality in international affairs, the country has remained distinctly pro-Western, maintaining no diplomatic relations with socialist and former socialist states of the Eastern bloc. US congressional committees have long viewed Swaziland as a moderating force, committed to peaceful change in southern Africa, and the USA has therefore supported programmes of security assistance in the belief that stability in Swaziland aids regional security. A similar perception by South Africa contributed to a strengthening of relations between the two countries during the 1980s, while geographical location has necessitated amicable relations with neighbouring Mozambique, despite that country's commitment to socialism. These relations have improved considerably since mid-1989, when the Mozambique government renounced its exclusive commitment to Marxism-Leninism.

There were two aspects to Swaziland's expanding links with South Africa during the 1980s. One was the proposed transfer of land; the other was Swaziland's increasing embroilment in the vortex of spreading violence in southern Africa, and its alignment with the South African government in the latter's confrontation with the African National Congress of South Africa (ANC).

The land transfer scheme provided for the cession to Swaziland of the KaNgwane 'Bantustan' ('homeland' of the Swazi ethnic group in South Africa) and the Ingwavuma region of KwaZulu, an area which would have afforded Swaziland direct access to the sea. Swaziland has long held territorial claims against South Africa, but it was only in the late 1970s that South Africa indicated its readiness to consider these claims seriously. It is generally believed that the proposed transfer of land was intended as an incentive to Swaziland to enter into a security agreement with South Africa.

The prospect of regaining 'lost lands' and reuniting the Swazi people, a large proportion of whom live in South Africa, persuaded Sobhuza to sign a then secret security agreement with South Africa in February 1982. The result was Swaziland's intensified harassment of the ANC. Within weeks, the organization's veteran representative had been expelled from the country, and his deputy assassinated. Sobhuza's death in August 1982 removed the only obstacle to an all-out offensive on the ANC, and by the end of that year the first of a series of round-ups and 'voluntary deportations' of alleged ANC members had occurred. However, as a result of legal obstacles and strong opposition, both in white and black political circles, in South Africa, the proposals for the land transfer were finally abandoned in 1984. Despite this, Swazi security forces continued to harrass the ANC.

In 1984, within days of the signing of the Nkomati Accord between South Africa and Mozambique, the Swazi government revealed the existence of its security agreement with South Africa. The systematic suppression of ANC activities intensified, and open collaboration between the two countries inspired gun battles in Manzini as speculation increased that this policy was being orchestrated by a South African trade mission which was established in Mbabane in 1984. In January 1985 the Swazi prime minister defended his government's close relationship with South Africa and implied that the attacks against the ANC would continue. The ANC responded by creating a sophisticated underground network in Swaziland, as conflict within Swazi territory between itself and South Africa intensified. This war escalated in 1986, and in June, July and August armed raids by South African security personnel resulted in a number of ANC deaths in border areas and in Manzini. Increased public outrage at these activities led the Swazi prime minister publicly to accuse South Africa of responsibility and to condemn the August raid as an 'illegal act of aggression', the first open attack on South African policies by a Swaziland government. Nevertheless South African covert security forces continued to carry out operations within Swaziland, in which ANC activists were abducted or murdered. During the second half of the decade, senior Swazi policemen were implicated in such killings. The era of political reform within South Africa that followed the release of Nelson Mandela in February 1990 has brought a modest improvement in relations between the Swaziland government and the ANC. Mandela, together with senior members of the Pan-Africanist Congress (PAC) of South Africa, briefly visited Mbabane during the ninth summit of the Preferential Trade Area for East and Southern Africa (PTA), during which the ANC leader met the Swazi king. In late 1993 formal diplomatic relations were established between Swaziland and South Africa.

During the prolonged period of civil unrest within Mozambique, considerable numbers of Mozambicans have crossed into Swaziland in search of food and employment, an influx which has been linked by Swazi police to an increase in armed crime, and has resulted in several mass arrests in urban areas. A sizeable 'unofficial' population of Mozambicans has gathered in urban areas; these Mozambicans, many of whom are highly skilled workers, are perceived as a threat to the jobs of Swazi urban residents. The presence of Mozambican refugees in rural areas has also caused tension, owing to a shortage of land to accommodate them. The officially-maintained refugee settlement camps are crowded and, in the absence of sufficient co-operative agricultural facilities, are heavily dependent on food rations. In June 1990 the governments of Swaziland and Mozambique signed an extradition agreement providing for the repatriation of alleged criminals and illegal immigrants, which was designed to reduce the incidence of smuggling between the two countries. In 1992, however, tension at the border with Mozambique increased, following reports of raids against Swazi farms by members of the Mozambican armed forces. Following the ratification of a Mozambican peace accord in October 1992, an agreement, which was signed by the governments of Swaziland and Mozambique and the UN high commissioner for refugees in August 1993, provided for the repatriation of some 24,000 Mozambican nationals resident in Swaziland; in October 500 Mozambican refugees returned from Swaziland under the programme. In December the number of Swazi troops deployed at the border with Mozambique was increased, following clashes between Swazi and Mozambican forces in the region. Mozambique subsequently protested at alleged border incursions by members of the Swazi armed forces. In early 1994 discussions took place between Swazi and Mozambican officials to seek mutually satisfactory arrangements for the joint patrol of the border.

Economy

GRAHAM MATTHEWS

Although it is the second smallest sovereign state in mainland Africa, Swaziland has one of the continent's highest per caput income levels. In 1992, according to estimates by the World Bank, the kingdom's gross national product (GNP), measured at average 1990–92 prices, represented US $1,080 per caput, among the highest in sub-Saharan Africa and enough to rank Swaziland as a 'middle income' economy. The World Bank estimates real GNP per caput to have grown at an average 2.2% per annum in the period 1965–90, surpassing all but a handful of the kingdom's continental neighbours. Since independence there has also been diversification of the economy away from early dependence upon agriculture and mining. According to national figures, manufacturing contributed the largest share of gross domestic product (GDP) with 39.1% in 1991/92. Manufacturing also accounted for 18% of formal employment in 1989. After agriculture, which contributed 13.5% in 1991/92, the other sectors' contributions to GDP were mining 0.7%, construction 3.0%, trade and tourism 10.0%, transport and communications 5.8%, financial and business services 7.4%, and government 15.7%. Despite its relative diversification and wealth, however, Swaziland has not escaped the extremes of income distribution familiar elsewhere in Africa. More than two-thirds of the resident population comprises families earning generally poor incomes from smallholder cashcropping or subsistence agriculture on Swazi Nation Land, where the average land holding was just 1.35 ha in 1991. Moreover, the condition of the rural poor has been largely unimproved by periods of rapid growth since independence.

The most recent period of accelerated growth began with the record sugar crop of 1986 and continued until the regional drought broke the pattern with its disastrous effects upon rain-fed agriculture in 1992. In 1985–89 the average annual rate of GDP growth was 9.4%, while population growth averaged 3.7% per year for the same period. Swaziland's 'open' economy (exports of goods and services accounted for 79% of GDP in 1991/92) was severely affected by the depressed commodity prices and drought in the early 1980s; 'Cyclone Domoina', which battered the kingdom in 1984, also took its toll. Finally, the initial impact of the currency's decline during 1983–85 was additionally damaging and led to a period of rapid inflation, among other problems. In 1986/87, owing to exceptional climatic conditions, the sugar industry (which at the time accounted for one-third of manufacturing value added, as well as dominating agriculture) achieved output of more than 500,000 tons. The resulting growth in GDP (at constant 1985/86 factor cost) was 13.3%. In the following years, as sugar production returned to lower levels, the underlying growth momentum was maintained by new investment in the manufacturing sector, particularly in the form of relocations and outward investment from South Africa. In 1992/93 the impact of regional drought on rain-fed agriculture, combined with the effects of wider recession, caused the economy to contract, in real terms, by an estimated 1.5%. Improved rains were expected to have returned the economy to positive growth, at a rate of 5.4% in 1993/94, according to government forecasts.

Swaziland's development has been dominated by its relation to South Africa, the dominant regional power. South African capital and imports, the Southern African Customs Union (SACU), the South African labour market and the Common Monetary Area (CMA, successor to the Rand Monetary Area) have shaped the economy and restricted the scope for independent economic policy. However, a consistent determination to maintain an investment climate attractive to foreign business and a policy of accepting the dominance of its powerful neighbour has brought Swaziland a rate of post-independence capital formation not achieved in most African states. In the late 1980s the kingdom benefited as foreign and South African companies relocated from the republic. In the early 1990s, however, Swaziland experienced the negative repercusssions of political uncertainty and economic recession in South Africa. In the immediate aftermath of the installation of a democratically elected government in South Africa in 1994, there were mixed implications for Swaziland, such as the likelihood of a renegotiation of SACU to the country's disadvantage. Nevertheless, in the longer term, regional reintegration in the post-apartheid era should be of net benefit to the Swazi economy.

The national currency is the lilangeni (plural: emalangeni) introduced in 1974. The terms of the Trilateral Monetary Agreement, signed with South Africa and Lesotho to form the CMA in 1986, allowed the Swazi authorities the option of determining the lilangeni's exchange rate independently. Under the amended Multilateral Monetary Agreement (signed in early 1992 to formalize Namibia's *de facto* membership) this freedom is maintained but the currency has remained pegged at par to the South African rand. Although they are formally no longer legal tender, rand notes still circulate freely in the kingdom, with the Central Bank of Swaziland bearing the cost of repatriating them.

AGRICULTURE AND FORESTRY

Although the agricultural sector accounts for a declining share of GDP (13.5% in 1991/92), it remains the backbone of the economy. Agroindustry continues to contribute the majority of manufacturing value added; the sector provided 27% of formal employment in 1989; and the bulk of the population is still engaged in subsistence agriculture or small-scale cash cropping on Swazi Nation Land. Some 56% of the total land area is Swazi Nation Land, where traditional subsistence farming is conducted on land held by the monarchy, access to which is managed by the Swazi aristocracy and local chiefs. However, more than one-half of all Swazi Nation Land is designated as Rural Development Areas, and cash cropping of rain-watered crops, particularly maize and cotton, contribute significantly to total agricultural production when climatic conditions are favourable. In 1991/92 total Swazi Nation Land crop production represented 3.0% of GDP, but it was smallholders' rain-fed crops which were hardest hit by the effects of drought in 1992 (when this sub-sector's share of GDP decreased to an estimated 1.4%). The remainder of the land comprises individual tenure farms, owned mainly by white settlers and commercial companies. The principal agricultural commodities are sugar (of which Swaziland is continental Africa's second largest exporter), maize, citrus fruits, pineapples (for canning) and cotton. Livestock-rearing is an important sub-sector of the economy, particularly on Swazi Nation Land, and accounted for 2.4% of GDP in 1991/92.

Sugar is the dominant agricultural export commodity, providing 25% of total export earnings in 1992, with a value of E424m. Following exceptionally good weather conditions, production of raw sugar reached 506,349 metric tons in 1986/87, an increase of 33.8% over the 1985/86 season, raising this commodity's share of export receipts to almost 40% in that year. However, output declined to around 440,000 tons in 1987/88 and 1988/89, before increasing to 475,140 tons in 1989/90. Production has subsequently stabilized at around 490,000 tons. In 1993/94 total sales reached 506,124 tons, the largest part of which was sold to the European Community (EC, now European Union – EU) (121,079 tons), mostly under the quota terms of the Lomé Convention. Other important customers were Zimbabwe, Canada, Namibia and the USA. Meanwhile, increased quantities have been sold and refined locally with the establishment of Coca-Cola's soft drink concentrate plant, Cadbury's confectionery factory and a new refinery since 1987. Local sales amounted to almost 22% of the total in 1993/94. There are three sugar mills in the country, in which the Swazi Nation has substantial shareholdings.

Rain-fed maize production on Swazi Nation Land, where the bulk of the crop is raised, was severely affected by the drought of the early 1980s, and again in 1992. However, with improved rainfall and increased plantings in response to the import of unpopular yellow maize, this smallholder harvest recovered to 83,800 metric tons in 1983/84, from 29,900 tons the previous year. Thereafter about 100,000 tons were produced annually, with the harvest attaining a record 125,800 tons in 1990/91, until drought returned in 1992. The 1991/92 crop was estimated to have fallen to just 54,000 tons, against annual consumption needs of 116,000 tons. A modest recovery, to 67,700 tons, was achieved in 1992/93, but poorly distributed rains were expected to reduce the 1993/94 harvest to 63,700 tons, leaving the country heavily dependent upon food imports.

An increase in livestock slaughterings in the early 1980s was the result of increased offtake brought about by drought and did not represent sustainable growth in output. A similar pattern emerged in 1992 with the recurrence of drought. The national cattle herd declined to 614,000 head in 1984, but had recovered to number 740,000 in 1991. Numbers slaughtered rose to 65,606 in 1992, although herd numbers rose to 753,000 head. Supported by the role of cattle as a store of wealth in customary society, at this level the national herd represents a significant environmental problem in terms of the overgrazing of Swazi Nation Land. Factory slaughterings virtually ceased, following the collapse of the Swaziland Meat Corporation in 1988. They recovered with the operation's relaunch as Swaziland Meat Industries in late 1989 but the company collapsed again in early 1992. In mid-1992 the abattoir at Matsapha was re-opened under the ownership of the Royal Swaziland Sugar Corporation (Simunye Sugar Estate). Frozen and canned meat is exported to the EC under quota.

In 1984 Swaziland's production of citrus fruit (oranges and grapefruit) declined dramatically to 43,000 metric tons following the devastation wreaked by 'Cyclone Domoina'. In the following year there was mixed performance, with grapefruit production recovering strongly (a rise of 18%) but a further small decline in the orange harvest due to root-rot problems and trees coming to the end of their productive lives. By 1987, however, the citrus industry had recovered and total production increased to 82,700 tons. Total production decreased to 72,400 tons in 1990, and adverse weather conditions resulted in a further decline, to 66,200 tons, in 1991. Output rose to 70,600 tons in 1992, when citrus exports earned the kingdom E41m., principally from sales to European customers.

In the main, sturdy low level pineapple plants were undamaged by the 1984 cyclone. The crop and fruit-canning production were thus unaffected; 43,431 metric tons of pineapple were harvested, almost matching the substantial 1983 crop, and 23,350 tons were canned. Subsequent production levels have fluctuated. In 1991 the total crop declined to 31,567 tons, owing to poor rainfall, while cannery output decreased to 14,600 tons. During 1992/93 adverse weather and world market conditions overshadowed the company's survival prospects. In 1992 27,800 tons of fruit were purchased by this enterprise, Swazican, and 14,700 tons of canned products were sold. Undergoing restructuring in 1993, Swazican purchased 23,600 tons and produced 11,900 tons. Exports of canned fruit were valued at E53m. in 1991.

Most of the kingdom's cotton is grown by smallholders on Swazi Nation Land, but the diversification of certain of the sugar estates into raising an irrigated crop and the rapid expansion of the area planted to cotton by Swazi Nation Land farmers combined to raise output from 9,000 metric tons of seed cotton in 1982/83 to a record 32,538 tons in 1988/89. In 1989/90 the crop fell to 26,000 tons owing to adverse weather conditions. A similar quantity was produced in the following year, but production was hindered by drought in 1991/92, when output was estimated at 6,000 tons.

At December 1991 Swaziland had 101,159 ha of planted forest, representing 6% of the country's total land area. Of the total, 54,593 ha (mostly coniferous) was devoted to supplying the kingdom's main forestry industry, the Usutu pulp mill which produces unbleached woodpulp. The mill is recorded as Swaziland's second largest export earner (the earnings of the Coca-Cola concentrate plant are probably higher but are not revealed). Woodpulp production was consistent at 170,000–180,000 metric tons throughout the 1980s until boiler problems reduced the figure to 147,000 tons in 1989 and 142,000 tons in 1990. A recovery to above 158,000 tons was recorded for 1991, and the company was producing at a rate of 180,000 tons annually by 1992. Export receipts in 1992 were E176m. After South Africa, Far Eastern markets are the principal customers. Of the remaining area planted to timber, 27,331 ha was for sawlogs in 1991; a further 12,331 ha (mostly gum) was planted for mine timber. The kingdom has three saw mills supplying a small but diversified timber products industry, and pine shelving of Swazi manufacture is sold in the British market, in 'kit' form, despite unequal competition from South African companies enjoying export promotion subsidies.

MINING

Mining and quarrying have represented a declining proportion of GDP overall since independence, although the kingdom is relatively rich in mineral resources. From 10% in the 1960s, the sector's contribution stood at 1.3% in 1990/91, falling to only 0.7% in 1991/92 as a result of the closure of one of the country's three commerical mines. Diamond production rose rapidly in the late 1980s, and the development of a second coal mine is under way. Together with asbestos, these mineral products contributed E67m. or 3.9% of total domestic exports in 1992. In addition to the three exported minerals, quarry stone is produced to meet the needs of local construction industry. Iron ore and (on a smaller scale) gold have been significant export minerals in the past, but neither has been mined for more than a decade. However, recent surveys by Rio Tinto have revealed modest yet commercially viable gold deposits in the north of the country. Asbestos was the first mineral product to be exploited in the country on a large scale. The Havelock mine was developed in the 1930s, and it was not until 1962 that it was overtaken by the sugar industry as the territory's leading export earner. Since then, however, the indentification of health problems associated with asbestos and the depletion of reserves have resulted in the decline of this sub-sector. A steady 30,000 – 40,000 metric tons were exported annually for decades, but production declined to 22,804 tons in 1988. In 1989 development of the new Far West orebody returned output to 27,291 tons and this figure rose to 35,938 tons in 1990. Beset with financial and labour problems the mine went into provisional liquidation in early 1991, when output fell to just 13,888 tons, but was subsequently re-opened under new ownership, and output recovered to 32,301 tons in 1992.

Coal holds the country's most important mineral potential, with reserves estimated at 1,000m. metric tons. Production at Emaswati Coal's Mpaka mine fell from 165,122 metric tons in 1989 to 122,502 tons in 1991, as the result of strikes and a cave-in during the year. Mpaka's potential capacity has been consistently under-utilized and in 1992 the mine closed owing to lack of consumer demand (potential local users have failed to adapt existing facilities to burn coal). Output in that year consequently fell to 100,200 tons. A second coal mine near Maloma began production in September 1993. The Danish backed $12m. investment is intended to achieve an annual capacity of 300,000 tons.

Production of mainly industrial-quality diamonds began at the Dokolwako mine in 1984. Output rose steadily to 72,676 carats in 1988, before the open pit operation encountered poorer ground and production fell to 55,264 carats in 1989 and 42,488 carats in 1990. A recovery to 57,420 carats in 1991 coincided with weakening world prices and the value of sales stagnated at E16m. in 1991. In 1992 output fell to 50,547 carats and sales turnover to E14m.

MANUFACTURING

Excluding the processing of agricultural and forestry products, the majority of Swaziland's manufacturing is based at the Matsapha industrial estate. Prior to the new investment in the sector in the latter part of the 1980s, four-fifths of manufacturing's value added derived from agro-industries of various kinds, ranging from sugar, timber and wood-pulp mills, to fruit, cotton and meat-processing plants. In 1984 the Swaziland Chemical Industries fertilizer factory ceased operations as a combined result of drought conditions and South Africa's adjustment of SACU tariffs. At the end of the same year the Finnish-owned Salora Swaziland television factory was also closed following its take-over by a South African firm. As a result the kingdom lost combined exports of E44m., and real manufacturing value added fell slightly in 1985.

One of the most serious impediments to the growth of manufacturing industry in Swaziland was the policy of incentives being offered by the South African government and its 'homelands' administrations in their efforts to attract and decentralize industry. Subsequently, however, conditions for investment in Swaziland were made more attractive, and more competitive when compared with the situation in neighbouring states. In 1985 the government introduced a programme of incentives for investment and also embarked upon a promotion exercise to advertise the benefits of Swaziland to industrialists. In 1987 the effective replacement of the National Industrial Development Corporation of Swaziland by the Swaziland Industrial Development Co (SIDC) was also a watershed in the history of manufacturing in the kingdom. The SIDC has since established itself as an effective catalyst of industrial development in Swaziland.

Despite these developments within the kingdom, arguably the single most important factor in the improved fortunes of the manufacturing sector, and Swaziland is now among the most industrialized of African economies. However, the renewed unrest in South Africa in 1986 and the imposition of international sanctions against that country in the aftermath of its suppression under a state of emergency. It was against this background that Coca-Cola relocated its regional concentrate plant to Swaziland in 1987. This single decision added some 5% to real value added in manufacturing by 1988. Sanctions against South Africa also brought less welcome 'investment' interest to Swaziland. It was reported that a number of South African products were being exported from the kingdom with false 'Made in Swaziland' labels. Several companies, mainly foreign textile concerns, were formally instructed to cease this practice in 1988, but the problem only began to ease as South African domestic reform brought the progressive removal of sanctions after 1990.

Since the late 1980s there has been encouraging diversification of the manufacturing sector, but the pace of investment has slowed in the early 1990s. Natex Swaziland (successor to an earlier national textile company) has been installing the capacity for a vertically-integrated national cotton and textile industry, but once again a South African adjustment of SACU tariffs now threatens an important industry in the kingdom. With its protective tariff shield removed the company has been struggling for survival since 1992. Several smaller factories producing knitwear, footwear, gloves, refrigerators, office equipment, beverages, confectionery, pine furniture, safety glass and bricks were established during the investment boom, creating many new jobs. Formal employment grew by 5.2% annually on average over the five years to 1990, when the total in formal employ reached an estimated 95,491. Employment has since stagnated, the total rising just 0.1% to 94,054 in 1991. Unemployment thus remains a problem, however, and the kingdom's first ever survey of the jobless was undertaken in late 1989. This revealed 50,351 people to have been unemployed, but actively seeking work.

POWER, TRANSPORT AND COMMUNICATIONS

The country has a comparatively well-developed and maintained physical infrastructure, but this has become strained by rapid growth in recent years and by the chronic inability of the government to meet its capital spending targets.

The Swaziland Electricity Board (SEB) still imports from South Africa most of the power it supplies, and the proportion rises in drought years, such as 1991/92, when local hydro generation is constrained. Some 69% of 530 GWH supplied in the year ending March 1991, was imported; 72% of the 594 GWH sold in 1991/92 was bought from South Africa. The 20-MW capacity Luphohlo-Ezulwini hydroelectric station, completed under drought conditions in 1983/84, represents the largest part of domestic installed capacity of 50 MW. The link to the South African grid had a capacity of 96 MW until the commissioning of an additional link in 1992. Delays and engineering problems elevated the cost of the Luphohlo scheme far beyond budget, but it was the subsequent slump in the exchange value of the lilangeni which burdened the SEB with unserviceable foreign loans. The government now supports the board's exchange losses through a series of 25-year fixed-interest loans.

'Cyclone Domoina', which struck the country in January 1984, destroyed large parts of Swaziland's transport and communications infrastructure, destroying major bridges and ruining large sections of the road network. Rehabilitation costs were estimated at E60m. and substantial provisions of international aid were forthcoming.

The kingdom's first railway line was built during 1962–64 to connect the Ngwenya iron ore mine in the far west of the country, via the then railhead across the eastern border at Goma, to the port of Maputo (then Lourenço Marques) and so to its Japanese customers. This line has long been disused west of the Matsapha industrial estate. A southern link via Lavumisa and connecting to the South African port of Richards Bay was completed in 1978, while a northern link, crossing the border near Mananga and running to the South African town of Komatipoort, was opened in 1986. These lines established a direct link between the eastern Transvaal and the Natal ports, integrating the Swazi lines into the South African network. In the year to March 1992 the northern link carried 3.4m. tons of transit traffic, 77% of total tonnages hauled by the Swaziland Railway Board.

The kingdom's road network is comparatively well developed. In 1991 there were 2,807 km of roads, of which 750 km were tarred. Road projects have dominated the capital expenditure programmes of recent development plans and in 1991 work began on the rebuilding of the kingdom's main road artery connecting the capital, Mbabane, to Manzini via Matsapha.

Much of Swaziland can now be reached telephonically by dialling directly; a satellite link was inaugurated in 1983 allowing the kingdom's subscribers to bypass South Africa when contacting Europe and North America. At the end of 1991 Swaziland had 14,355 telephone exchange connections. An estimated 95% of the population have access to two radio stations operated by the Swaziland Broadcasting and Information Service. One television channel is run by the Swaziland Television Broadcasting Corporation. The published media include three national daily newspapers, two of which are privately owned.

TOURISM

Tourism in Swaziland was largely depressed during the early 1980s, owing primarily to the economic recession in South Africa (whence the majority of the tourists come; 60% in 1991), coupled with strong competition from new hotel complexes in the South African 'homelands'. While there were significant improvements after 1985, when the total number of arrivals was stimulated by growth in the number of business visitors as well as by renewed tourist interest. The latter was the result of economic and political factors; South African arrivals rose in response to political unrest in the republic in 1986. Since 1992 regional recession has depressed the sector once more, although some encouragement has been provided by an increase in arrivals from Mozambique following increased stability in the border region.

Facilities in the central Ezulwini valley (the heart of the Swazi tourism industry) are dominated by the South African Sun International chain. A new hotel complex, owned by the government but managed by Protea of South Africa, was opened in Piggs Peak in 1986. Visitor arrivals rose to 287,796 in 1990, when gross earnings reached E73m. In 1991 the total of arrivals was little changed at 289,500 and earnings were E76m. Receipts from tourism totalled E86m. in 1992.

BALANCE OF PAYMENTS

Swaziland's balance-of-payments position has improved considerably after the mid-1980s. From the latter part of 1983 until the end of 1985 the value of the lilangeni fell sharply. In terms of the IMF's 'basket' of major currencies, the special drawing right (SDR), the lilangeni exchange rate was SDR 0.78 = E1 at the end of 1983, but had declined to SDR 0.36 = E1 two years later (the decline against the surging US dollar being even more precipitous). This raised the local currency value of commodity exports sold on world markets, albeit at depressed prices in real terms. However, import prices rose sharply. Most imports are supplied by or via South Africa, and the shared currency devaluation fuelled inflation in both countries; the South African index of the cost of imported goods rose by 24% in 1985. The initial impact of this was a widening of the trade deficit in lilangeni terms, but a narrowing in real terms. Distortions further down the external accounts included a sudden rise in the burden of the service of external debt and substantial real valuation losses on reserves held in South Africa. However, as the currency stabilized and exports rose strongly, following the record sugar crop of 1986, the trade deficit of the balance of payments fell from E211m. in 1985 to E41m. As a result, the current account moved into surplus for the first time since 1977, and, with new investment supporting capital inflows, the overall balance-of-payments position was also in surplus, signalling the beginning of a sustained period of rising foreign reserves. This improved performance was not sustained after 1992, as recession constrained export growth and adverse weather conditions raised the cost of food imports.

Preliminary 1993 figures show exports to have risen to E2,124m. The largest share of these earnings has been contributed by sugar in recent years. Exports of iron ore, which matched those of sugar at independence, finally ended in 1980. In 1992 total exports earned E1,819m. of which E424m. was contributed by sugar, ahead of textiles (E188m.), wood pulp (E176m.) and the sales of the Coca-Cola concentrate plant. The precise value of the last of these is not itemized in official data, but the total has exceeded depressed wood pulp earnings in recent years. Other traditional major exports, such as canned and fresh fruit and asbestos, are now being overtaken by diverse manufactures such as refrigerators which earned E73m. in 1992.

Preliminary balance-of-payments data show imports (f.o.b.) of E2,530m. in 1993, compared to E2,181m. in 1992. The main import categories are machinery and transport equipment (E549m. on a c.i.f. basis in 1992), usually followed by other manufactures, mineral fuels, and chemical and other raw material inputs to the manufacturing sector. In 1992, however, the impact of drought raised food imports to third place, at E306m.

After 1986 the current account recorded substantial surpluses in most years, but this was reversed after 1992. Following a modest surplus of E15m. in that year, preliminary figures for 1993 indicated a deficit of E121m., the first since 1985. The balance on trade in services has remained in deficit. Inflated by reinsurance claims following the cyclone damage of 1984, earnings were subsequently supported by increased workers' remittances, resulting from pay increases in the South African mining industry, higher tourism receipts and returns on the increased holdings of foreign financial assets. In 1991 receipts amounted to E737m. Receipts stagnated in 1992 and 1993, when earnings totalled E735m. Service debits (E824m. in 1992) have been augmented by the transfer of dividends and profits from foreign-owned businesses. Official unrequited transfers also make a significant contribution, and added E374m. to inflows in 1993. Apart from grant aid from abroad, these flows comprise SACU transfers over and above the reimbursement of the duty raised on Swaziland's own trade and production.

The turnaround in capital flows in the mid-1980s was very marked. Supported in the early 1980s by the activities of the official sector (the government borrowing abroad), the capital account recorded, after 1985, strong net private inflows as political and commercial considerations combined to bring about the relocation of manufacturing capacity from South Africa or attracted new investment to Swaziland in preference to the South African 'homelands'. Private inflows peaked at E185m. in 1989. New investment flows have since begun to decline, but this downturn has lagged behind the deterioration of the current payments balance since large projects have long periods of gestation. In 1993 private interests invested E165m. net in the country. Government budget surpluses in the five years to 1991/92 led to net redemptions of foreign debt (meaning public sector outflows), but this trend is now being reversed. The overall position strengthened considerably after 1986, and by the end of 1992 official holdings of foreign reserves had increased to E912m. Holdings fell slightly in 1993 (the first decrease in seven years) to stand at E852m. However, this still represented some 18 weeks' import cover and was quadruple the level of reserves at the end of 1985.

PUBLIC FINANCE

Swaziland's public finances are characterized by a heavy dependence upon receipts from South Africa from the SACU revenue pool. Over and above the revenue raised in customs and excise duty on the kingdom's own trade and excisable production, these include cash compensation for the distorting effects of high import tariffs which protect South African producers' dominance of the Swazi market. With the installation of a government in South Africa which no longer needs to buy goodwill in the region, the future of these receipts is uncertain. A sales tax was introduced in 1984 to lessen the dependence upon SACU receipts. Its tighter application increased revenue from this source from the 1986/87 (April – March) fiscal year, but it still represented little more than a quarter of the contribution of customs union receipts in 1993/94. On the expenditure side, the government's finances have shown tight control of current expenditure. Capital spending peaked with the internationally-backed reconstruction effort which followed the cyclone damage of 1984, but the general inability of the authorities to spend their investment budget is a structural problem characteristic of the administrative inefficiencies inherent in the dichotomous nature of

Swaziland's governance. Finally, there has been significant net lending to public sector industries, some inefficiently run and others struggling with foreign debt, following the sharp decline in the exchange rate during the mid-1980s. In 1989 a public enterprise unit was formed within the finance ministry, charged with reviewing the performance of the public sector companies and advising on future policy in their regard. As a result, an improved performance has been achieved by this sector, although this too has been compromised by the general downturn in the economy since 1992.

The budgets of the early 1980s were introduced against a background of chronic public finance problems, successive (often large) deficits and growing domestic and external debt. However, the economy's buoyancy in the late 1980s and early 1990s turned the deficits into persistent, large and embarrassing surpluses since the effects of the record sugar crop of 1986 entailed a near doubling of direct taxation receipts in 1987/88. In 1987 the finance minister tabled a budget projecting an E24m. deficit; the 1986/87 deficit of E49m. had represented 5.7% of GDP. In the event, company tax delivered E73m. rather than the budgeted E35m. in 1987/88, while personal taxes also came in well above expectations as formal sector employment grew strongly in the boom conditions. Current expenditure was held almost exactly to budget, while net lending was greater than expected at E14m. and the capital budget was 13% underspent at E66m. The result was a surplus, the first since 1980/81, of E22m.

The pattern was repeated over the next five years. The finance ministry's routine revisions of the budget projections in July and December/January of each fiscal year showed higher than expected revenue, tight control of recurrent outgoings and underspending of the capital budget. In 1988/89 the original projection was of an E9.5m. deficit; the eventual surplus for the year was E59m. (3.8% of GDP). In 1989/90 a E1m. deficit was expected; the result was an E96m. surplus (some 5.3% of GDP). In 1990/91 the surplus was only contained at E1m. by the introduction of an E165m. Capital Investment Facility (CIF) established to save from the surplus and so reduce it. In 1991/92 a budgeted E7m. deficit was, in effect, eventually recorded as a surplus of E21m. (E100m. having been diverted by the CIF).One response to this trend was for the authorities to ease the personal tax burden. The government has also achieved significant redemption of both domestic and external debt in recent years.

The 1992/93 financial year was a turning-point in the kingdom's public finances. Growth in revenue slowed to 9% (a decline, in real terms, given inflation of some 13%), while expenditure increased by 17%. This latter increase reflected civil service pay and benefits increases, as well as improvements in capital budget implementation. An overall deficit of E42m. was recorded. The 1993/94 budget projected an E120m. deficit. In the event, an E193m. shortfall was the expected outcome, as receipts fell below budget (particularly in the area of corporate tax revenue, owing to depressed profits in the private sector). Against this background, the 1994/95 budget projected a deficit of E282m. After adjustment for capital under-spending, this is forecast by the ministry of planning to represent almost 6% of GDP. The net redemption of foreign loans was to be revised in 1994/95 in tandem with increased recourse to domestic financing. For the present, this will not alter significantly the modest external debt burden. Total external debt stood at E658m. at the end of March 1993, and debt service payments consumed a modest 2.5% of earnings from exports of goods and services in 1992/93.

Statistical Survey

Source (unless otherwise stated): Central Statistical Office, POB 456, Mbabane.

AREA AND POPULATION

Area: 17,363 sq km (6,704 sq miles).

Population (excluding absentee workers): 494,534 (males 231,861, females 262,673) at census of 25 August 1976; 681,059 (males 321,579, females 359,480) at census of 25 August 1986; 768,000 (official estimate) at mid-1990.

Density (mid-1990): 44.2 per sq km.

Ethnic Groups (census of August 1986): Swazi 661,646; Other Africans 14,468; European 1,825; Asiatic 228; Other non-Africans 412; Mixed 2,403; Unknown 77; Total 681,059.

Principal Towns (population at census of August 1986): Mbabane (capital) 38,290; Manzini 18,084.

Births and Deaths (UN estimates, 1985–90): Average annual birth rate 38.0 per 1,000; average annual death rate 11.8 per 1,000. Source: UN, *World Population Prospects: The 1992 Revision*.

Expectation of Life (UN estimates, years at birth, 1985–90): 55.15 (males 53.7; females 57.3). Source: UN, *World Population Prospects: The 1992 Revision*.

Economically Active Population (census of August 1986): 160,355 (males 105,191, females 55,164). Source: ILO, *Year Book of Labour Statistics*.

AGRICULTURE

Principal Crops ('000 metric tons, 1992): Rice (paddy) 3*; Maize 54; Potatoes 6*; Sweet potatoes 4*; Pulses 4*; Cottonseed 18*; Cotton (lint) 10*; Oranges 35*; Grapefruit 52*; Pineapples 45*; Sugar cane 3,600*.

Livestock ('000 head, year ending September 1992): Horses 1*; Asses 12*; Cattle 753; Pigs 31; Sheep 23; Goats 406.

Livestock Products (FAO estimates, '000 metric tons, 1992): Beef and veal 11; Goats' meat 3; Cows' milk 42; Cattle hides 1.6.

* FAO estimate.

Source: FAO, *Production Yearbook*.

FORESTRY

Roundwood Removals ('000 cubic metres, 1981): Sawlogs, veneer logs and logs for sleepers 319; Pitprops (Mine timber) 65; Pulpwood 1,268; Other industrial wood 11 (FAO estimate); Fuel wood 560 (FAO estimate); Total 2,223.

1982 – 91: Annual output as in 1981 (FAO estimates).

Sawnwood Production ('000 cubic metres, 1982): 103.

1983 – 91: Annual output as in 1982.

Source: FAO, *Yearbook of Forest Products*.

MINING

Production (estimates, '000 metric tons, 1992): Coal 100.2; Asbestos 32.3.

INDUSTRY

1992: Electric energy 570m. kWh; Wood pulp 179,000 metric tons; Raw sugar 486,800 metric tons.

FINANCE

Currency and Exchange Rates: 100 cents = 1 lilangeni (plural: emalangeni). *Sterling and Dollar Equivalents* (31 March 1994): £1 sterling = 5.167 emalangeni; US $1 = 3.481 emalangeni; 100 emalangeni = £19.35 = $28.73. *Average Exchange Rate* (US $ per lilangeni): 0.36280 in 1991; 0.35092 in 1992; 0.30641 in 1993. Note: The lilangeni is at par with the South African rand.

Budget (provisional, million emalangeni, year ending 31 March 1992): *Revenue:* Taxes on income, etc. 260.87; Sales taxes 95.19; Import duties 356.42; Total (incl. others) 769.38. *Expenditure:* General public services 213.39; Defence 38.66; Public order and safety 67.99; Education 187.02; Health 58.58; Social security and welfare 4.07; Housing and community amenities 50.92; Recreational, cultural and religious affairs 4.69; Economic services 159.93 (Agriculture, forestry and fishing 40.45, Roads 44.81); Other purposes 14.87; Total 800.12 (Current 516.43, Capital 283.69).

1993 (provisional, million emalangeni, year ending 31 March): Total revenue 906.9; Total expenditure 958.1. Source: Central Bank of Swaziland.

International Reserves (US $ million at 31 December 1993): IMF special drawing rights 8.08; Reserve position in IMF 4.12; Foreign exchange 252.09; Total 264.29. Source: IMF, *International Financial Statistics*.

Money Supply (million emalangeni at 31 December 1993): Currency outside banks 75.19; Demand deposits at commercial banks 215.06; Total money (incl. others) 290.50. Source: IMF, *International Financial Statistics*.

Cost of Living (Retail Price Index, excluding rent, for low-income wage-earners' families in Mbabane and Manzini; base: 1990 = 100): 101.6 in 1991; 121.6 in 1992. Source: UN, *Monthly Bulletin of Statistics*.

Gross Domestic Product by Kind of Economic Activity (estimates, million emalangeni at current factor cost, year ending 30 June 1991): Agriculture and forestry 299.3; Mining and quarrying 24.4; Manufacturing 603.7; Electricity, gas and water 36.8; Construction 53.2; Trade, restaurants and hotels 193.1; Transport and Communications 105.8; Finance, insurance, real estate etc, 225.1; Government services 301.9; Other community, social and personal services 17.2; Other services 25.3; *Sub-total* 1,885.8; *Less* Imputed bank service charge 80.5; *GDP at factor cost* 1,805.3; Indirect taxes, *less* subsidies 422.7; *GDP in purchasers' values* 2,228.0.

Balance of Payments (US $ million, 1992): Merchandise exports f.o.b. 608.1; Merchandise imports f.o.b. –698.2; *Trade balance* –90.1; Exports of services 96.5; Imports of services –123.5; Other income received 155.0; Other income paid –144.2; Private unrequited transfers (net) 0.6; Government unrequited transfers (net) 131.1; *Current balance* 25.3; Direct investment (net) 42.0; Portfolio investment (net) –0.1; Other capital (net) –20.4; Net errors and omissions 48.2; *Overall balance* 95.1. Source: IMF, *International Financial Statistics*.

EXTERNAL TRADE

Principal Commodities: *Imports* ('000 emalangeni, year ending 31 March 1993): Food and live animals 352,355; Beverages and tobacco 71,377; Crude materials 105,003; Mineral fuels, lubricants 264,777; Animal and vegetable oils and fats 14,843; Chemical products 210,975; Basic manufactures 475,073; Machinery and transport equipment 582,808; Miscellaneous manufactured articles 280,356; Total (incl. others) 2,567,785. *Exports* (million emalangeni, 1991): Foodstuffs 949.7 (Sugar 461.0, Canned and fresh fruit 91.1); Wood and wood products 182.1; Mineral products 41.4; Total (incl. others) 1,559.5. Figures refer to domestic exports, excluding re-exports. Source: Central Bank of Swaziland.

Principal Trading Partners ('000 emalangeni): *Imports* (year ending 31 March 1991): France 1,351; Netherlands 8,051; South Africa 1,522,433; Switzerland 20,029; United Kingdom 29,267. *Exports* (excl. re-exports, 1990): South Africa 688,209; United Kingdom 44,620; Total (incl. others) 1,319,812.

TRANSPORT

Railways (traffic estimates, million, 1991): Passenger-km 1,210 (1988); Freight net ton-km 2,910. Source: UN Economic Commission for Africa, *African Statistical Yearbook*.

Total freight ('000 tons, 1990): 4,356.

Road Traffic (motor vehicles in use, 1990): Passenger cars 26,415; Buses and coaches 2,544; Goods vehicles 21,752; Tractors (excl. agricultural) 6,811; Motor cycles and scooters 2,534. Source: International Road Federation, *World Road Statistics*.

Civil Aviation (traffic on scheduled services, 1991): Passengers carried 59,000; Passenger-km 45 million. Source: UN, *Statistical Yearbook*.

TOURISM

Tourist Arrivals by Nationality (1991): South Africa 131,549; United Kingdom 54,492; Total (incl. others) 289,493. Figures cover only tourists staying in hotels. Including other visitors, the total number of arrivals was 651,167.

Total Receipts (million emalangeni): 58.5 in 1989; 73.4 in 1990; 76.4 in 1991.

COMMUNICATIONS MEDIA

Radio Receivers (1991): 127,000 in use.

Television Receivers (1991): 15,000 in use.

Daily Newspapers (1990): 3.

(Source: UNESCO, *Statistical Yearbook*.)

Telephones (1991): 27,543 in use.

EDUCATION

Primary (1992): Institutions 515; Teachers 5,504; Students 180,285.

General Secondary (1992): Institutions 156; Teachers 2,703; Students 51,514.

Teacher Training (1991): Institutions 3; Teachers 97; Students 661.

Technical and Vocational Training (1990/91): Institutions 5; Teachers 183; Students 1,111.

University Education (1991): Institution 1; Teachers 146; Students 1,705.

Directory

The Constitution

The Constitution of 13 October 1978 vests supreme executive and legislative power in the hereditary King (Ngwenyama—the Lion). Succession is governed by traditional law and custom. In the event of the death of the King, the powers of Head of State are transferred to the constitutional dual monarch, the Queen Mother (Indlovukazi—Great She Elephant), who is authorized to act as Regent until the designated successor attains the age of 21. The Constitution provides for a bicameral legislature (Libandla), comprising a House of Assembly and a Senate. The functions of the Libandla are confined to debating government proposals and advising the King. Executive power is exercised through the Cabinet (later redesignated as the Council of Ministers), which is appointed by the King. The Swaziland National Council, which comprises members of the royal family, and is headed by the King and Queen Mother, advises on matters regulated by traditional law and custom. The Constitution affirms the fundamental rights of the individual.

Following a number of amendments to the electoral system, which were approved by the King in October 1992, the House of Assembly (which was redesignated as the National Assembly) was expanded to 65 deputies (of whom 55 are directly elected from candidates nominated by traditional local councils, known as Tinkhundla, and 10 appointed by the King), and the Senate to 30 members (of whom 20 are appointed by the King and 10 elected by the National Assembly). Elections to the National Assembly are conducted by secret ballot, in two rounds of voting; the second round of the elections is contested by the three candidates from each of the Tinkhundla who secure the highest number of votes in the first poll. In early 1994 it was announced that the King was to appoint a 15-member commission, comprising representatives of state organs and non-governmental organizations, which was to draft a new constitution incorporating the amendments.

The Government

HEAD OF STATE

HM King MSWATI III (succeeded to the throne 25 April 1986).

COUNCIL OF MINISTERS

(September 1994)

Prime Minister: Prince JAMESON MBILINI DLAMINI.

Deputy Prime Minister: Dr SISHAYI NXUMALO.

Minister of Justice: Chief MAWENI SIMELANE.

Minister of Foreign Affairs: SOLOMON DLAMINI.

Minister of Finance: ISAAC SHABANGU.

Minister of the Interior: Prince SOBANDLA DLAMINI.

Minister of Education: Prince KHUZULWANDLE DLAMINI.

Minister of Agriculture and Co-operatives: Chief DAMBUZA LUKHELE.

Minister of Labour and Public Service: ALBERT SHABANGU.

Minister of Economic Planning and Development: THEMBA MASUKU.

Minister of Commerce and Industry: MUNTU MSWANE.

Minister of Health: Dr DERRICK VON WISSEL.

Minister of Broadcasting, Information and Tourism: Prince PHINDA DLAMINI.

Minister of Works and Construction: Prince MHLAL'ENGANGENI DLAMINI.

Minister of Natural Resources and Land Utilization and Energy: ARTHUR KHOZA.

Minister of Transport and Communications: EPHRAEM MAGAGULA.

Minister of Housing and Urban Development: JOHN CARMICHAEL.

MINISTRIES

Office of the Prime Minister: POB 395, Mbabane; tel. 42251.

Ministry of Agriculture and Co-operatives: POB 162, Mbabane; tel. 42731; telex 2343; fax 44700.

Ministry of Broadcasting, Information and Tourism: POB 338, Mbabane; tel. 42761; fax 42774.

Ministry of Commerce and Industry: POB 451, Mbabane; tel. 43201; telex 2232; fax 43833.

Ministry of Economic Planning and Development: POB 602, Mbabane; tel. 43765; fax 42157.

Ministry of Education: POB 39, Mbabane; tel. 42491; telex 2293; fax 43880.

Ministry of Finance: POB 443, Mbabane; tel. 42141; telex 2109; fax 43187.

Ministry of Foreign Affairs: POB 518, Mbabane; tel. 42661; telex 2036; fax 42669.

Ministry of Health: POB 5, Mbabane; tel. 42431; fax 42092.

Ministry of Housing and Urban Development: POB 1832, Mbabane; tel. 46510; fax 45224.

Ministry of the Interior: POB 432, Mbabane; tel. 42941; telex 2328; fax 44303.

Ministry of Justice: POB 924, Mbabane; tel. 43531; fax 43533.

Ministry of Labour and Public Service: POB 170, Mbabane; tel. 43521; fax 45379.

Ministry of Natural Resources, Land Utilization and Energy: POB 57, Mbabane; tel. 46244; telex 2301; fax 42436.

Ministry of Transport and Communications: POB 58, Mbabane; tel. 42321; fax 42364.

Ministry of Works and Construction: POB 58, Mbabane; tel. 42321; telex 2104; fax 42364.

Legislature

LIBANDLA

The Senate

President: LAWREN MNINA.

There are 30 senators, of whom 20 are appointed by the King and 10 elected by the National Assembly.

National Assembly

Speaker: MUSA SIBANDZE.

There are 65 deputies, of whom 55 are directly elected from candidates nominated by the Tinkhundla and 10 appointed by the King. Elections to the National Assembly took place, in two rounds of voting, on 25 September and 11 October 1993.

Political Organizations

Party political activity was banned by royal proclamation in April 1973, and formally prohibited under the 1978 Constitution. Since 1991, following indications that the Constitution was to be revised, a number of political associations have re-emerged.

Imbokodvo National Movement (INM): f. 1964 by King Sobhuza II; traditionalist movement, but also advocates policies of development and the elimination of illiteracy; Leader (vacant).

Ngwane National Liberatory Congress (NNLC): Ilanga Centre, Martin St, POB 766, Manzini; tel. 53935; f. 1962, by a breakaway faction of the SPP; advocates democratic freedoms and universal suffrage, and seeks abolition of the Tinkhundla electoral system; Pres. Dr AMBROSE ZWANE; Sec.-Gen. DUMISA DLAMINI.

People's United Democratic Movement (PUDEMO): f. 1983; seeks constitutional reform to limit the powers of the monarchy; established affiliated organizations in 1991, incl. the Human Rights Association of Swaziland and the Swaziland Youth Congress; Pres. KISLON SHONGWE; Sec.-Gen. DOMINIC MNGOMEZULU.

Swaziland National Front (SWANAFRO): Pres. ELMOND SHONGWE; Sec.-Gen. GLENROSE DLAMINI.

Swaziland Progressive Party (SPP): POB 6, Mbabane; tel. 22648; f. 1929 as Swazi Progressive Association; Pres. J. J. NQUKU.

Swaziland United Front (SUF): POB 14, Kwaluseni; f. 1962, by a breakaway faction of the SPP; Leader MATSAPA SHONGWE.

Diplomatic Representation

EMBASSIES AND HIGH COMMISSIONS IN SWAZILAND

China (Taiwan): Embassy House, Warner St, POB 56, Mbabane; tel. 42379; telex 2167; fax 46688; Ambassador: ENTI LIU.

Israel: Mbabane House, Warner St, POB 146, Mbabane; tel. 42626; telex 2098; fax 45857; Ambassador: (vacant).

Mozambique: Princess Drive, POB 1212, Mbabane; tel. 43700; telex 2248; fax 43692; Ambassador: ANTONIO C. F. SUMBANA

United Kingdom: Allister Miller St, Mbabane; tel. 42581; fax 42585; High Commissioner: RICHARD GOZNEY.

USA: Central Bank Bldg, Warner St, POB 199, Mbabane; tel. 46441; telex 2285; fax 46446; Ambassador: JOHN SPROTT.

Judicial System

The judiciary is headed by the Chief Justice. There is a High Court (which is a Superior Court of Record) with five subordinate courts in all the administrative districts, and there is a Court of Appeal which sits at Mbabane.

There are 17 Swazi Courts, including two Courts of Appeal and a Higher Court of Appeal, which have limited jurisdiction in civil and criminal cases. Their jurisdiction excludes non-Swazi nationals.

Chief Justice: DAVID HULL.

Religion

About 60% of the adult Swazi population profess Christianity. Most of the remainder hold traditional beliefs.

CHRISTIANITY

Conference of Churches: POB 384, Mbabane; tel. 53071; f. 1929; mems: 14 church denominations and one Christian org.; Head Rev. ISAAC HLETA.

Council of Swaziland Churches: POB 1095, Manzini; tel. 53628; f. 1976; eight mem. churches; Chair. Rt Rev. LOUIS NDLOVU (Roman Catholic Bishop of Manzini); Gen. Sec. EUNICE SOWAZI.

The Anglican Communion

Swaziland comprises a single diocese within the Church of the Province of Southern Africa. The Metropolitan of the Province is the Archbishop of Cape Town, South Africa.

Bishop of Swaziland: Rt Rev. LAWRENCE ZULU, POB 118, Mbabane; tel. 43624.

The Roman Catholic Church

For ecclesiastical purposes, Swaziland comprises the single diocese of Manzini, suffragan to the archdiocese of Pretoria, South Africa. At 31 December 1992 there were an estimated 45,000 adherents in Swaziland. The Bishop participates in the Southern African Catholic Bishops' Conference (based in Pretoria, South Africa).

Bishop of Manzini: Rt Rev. LOUIS NDLOVU, Bishop's House, Sandlane St, POB 19, Manzini; tel. 52348; fax 54876.

Other Christian Churches

Lutheran World Federation: POB 388, Mbabane; tel. 46700.

Mennonite Central Committee: POB 329, Mbabane; tel. 42805; telex 2245; fax 44732; Co-ordinators JOHN RUDY, CAROLYN RUDY.

The Methodist Church in Southern Africa: POB 218, Mbabane; tel. 42658.

United Christian Church of Africa: POB 6, Mbabane; tel. 22648; f. 1944; Pres. Rt Rev. JEREMIAH NDINISA; Founder and Gen. Sec. Dr J. J. NQUKU.

The National Baptist Church, the Christian Apostolic Holy Spirit Church in Zion and the Religious Society of Friends (Quakers) are also active.

BAHÁ'Í FAITH

National Spiritual Assembly: POB 298, Mbabane; tel. 43457; mems resident in 153 localities.

The Press

News from Swaziland: Allister Miller St, POB 464, Mbabane; tel. 42771, telex 2035; weekly; govt information bulletin; publ. by Swaziland Broadcasting and Information Service.

Swazi Life: Mbabane House, POB 592, Mbabane; tel. 44408; telex 2191; f. 1984; monthly; Editors A. MBULI, G. STEPHENS.

The Swazi News: Allister Miller St, POB 156, Mbabane; tel. 42220; telex 2097; fax 42438; f. 1983; weekly (Sat.); English; owned by *The Times of Swaziland*; Editor JABU E. MATSEBULA; circ. 7,000.

Swaziland Observer: Swazi Plaza, POB A385, Mbabane; tel. 23383; telex 2322; f. 1981; daily (Mon. – Sat.); English; Man. Editor MICHAEL LENAGHAN; circ. 9,500.

Swaziview: POB 1532, Mbabane; tel. 42716; monthly magazine; general interest; circ. 3,500.

Tikhatsi Tema Swati: POB 156, Mbabane; tel. 42211; telex 2097; daily; siSwati.

The Times of Swaziland: Allister Miller St, POB 156, Mbabane; tel. 42220; telex 2097; fax 42438; f. 1897; English; daily (Mon. – Fri.); also publs *Business in Swaziland*, monthly; Editor JABU E. MATSEBULA; circ. 11,000.

Tindzaba News: monthly magazine; English, siSwati; publ. by Swaziland Broadcasting and Information Service.

Umbiki: Allister Miller St, POB 464, Mbabane; tel. 42761; telex 2035; monthly; siSwati; publ. by Swaziland Broadcasting and Information Service.

Publishers

Apollo Services (Pty) Ltd: POB 35, Mbabane; tel. 42711.

GBS Printing and Publishing (Pty) Ltd: POB 1384, Mbabane; tel. 52779.

Longman Swaziland (Pty) Ltd: POB 2207, Manzini; tel. 53891.

Macmillan Boleswa Publishers (Pty) Ltd: POB 1235, Manzini; tel. 84533; telex 2221; fax 85247; Man. Dir L. A. BALARIN.

Swaziland Printing & Publishing Co Ltd: POB 28, Mbabane; tel. 42716.

Whydah Media Publishers Ltd: POB 1532, Mbabane; tel. 42716; f. 1978.

Radio and Television

In 1991 there were an estimated 127,000 radio receivers and 15,000 television receivers in use.

RADIO

Swaziland Broadcasting and Information Service: POB 338, Mbabane; tel. 42761; telex 2035; f. 1966; broadcasts in English and siSwati; Dir N. Z. MALINGA.

Swaziland Commercial Radio (Pty) Ltd: POB 23114, Joubert Park, Johannesburg 2044, South Africa; tel. (11) 8848400; fax (11) 8831982; privately-owned commercial service; broadcasts to southern Africa in English and Portuguese; music and religious programmes; Man. Dir I. KIRSH.

Trans World Radio: POB 64, Manzini; tel. 52781; telex 2196; fax 55333; f. 1974; religious broadcasts from six transmitters in 23 languages to southern, central and eastern Africa and to the Far East; Pres. Dr PAUL E. FREED.

TELEVISION

Swaziland Television Broadcasting Corporation: POB A146, Mbabane; tel. 43036; telex 2138; fax 42093; f. 1978; state-owned; broadcasts seven hours daily in English; colour transmissions; Gen. Man. DAN S. DLAMINI.

Finance

(cap. = capital; p.u. = paid up; dep. = deposits; m. = million; res = reserves; br. = branch; amounts in emalangeni)

BANKING

Central Bank

Central Bank of Swaziland: POB 546, Mbabane; tel. 43221; telex 2029; fax 42636; f. 1974; bank of issue; cap. and res 6.7m., dep. 189.2m. (March 1993); Gov. JAMES MXUMALO; Dep. Gov. M. G. DLAMINI.

Commercial Banks

Barclays Bank of Swaziland Ltd: Allister Miller St, POB 667, Mbabane; tel. 42989; telex 2096; fax 45239; f. 1974; 40% state-owned; cap. and res 26.4m., dep. 353.4m. (Dec. 1992); Chair. DANIEL M. DLAMINI; Man. Dir MARK TAVERSHAM; 13 brs and agencies.

Meridien BIAO Bank Swaziland Ltd: Meridien BIAO House, West St, POB 261, Mbabane; tel. 45401; telex 2380; fax 44735; f. 1988; 10% state-owned; cap. and res 5.6m., dep. 11.9m. (Sept. 1991); Chair. EDWARD ROBERT SYDER; Man. Dir CHRISTOPHER EVANS; 4 brs.

Standard Chartered Bank Swaziland Ltd (United Kingdom): 21 Allister Miller St, POB 68, Mbabane; tel. 43351; telex 2041; fax 44060; f. 1974; 30% state-owned; cap. and res 18m., dep. 181.2m. (Dec. 1991); Chair. A. R. B. SHABANGU; Man. Dir JOHN KIVITS; 4 brs and 1 agency.

Development Banks

Stanbic Bank Swaziland Ltd: Stanbic House, 1st Floor, Swazi Plaza, POB A294, Mbabane; tel. 46587; telex 2216; fax 45899; f. 1988 as UnionBank of Swaziland Ltd, name changed 1994; cap. and res 15.1m., dep. 168.4m. (Dec. 1992); Man. Dir M. P. LUBBE; 4 brs.

Swaziland Development and Savings Bank: Engunwini, Allister Miller St, POB 336, Mbabane; tel. 42551; telex 2055; fax 23214; f. 1965; state-owned; cap. and res 25.2m., dep. 117.4m. (March 1992); Chair. Chief DAMBUZA LUKHELE; Gen. Man. S. S. KUHLASE; 8 brs.

Financial Institution

Swaziland National Provident Fund: POB 1857, Manzini; tel. 53731; telex 3011; fax 54377; total assets 134m.

STOCK EXCHANGE

Swaziland Stock Exchange: Mbabane; f. 1993.

INSURANCE

Although the state-controlled Swaziland Royal Insurance Corporation (SRIC) operates as the country's sole authorized insurance company, cover in a number of areas not served by SRIC is available from several specialized insurers.

Insurance Companies

Bowring & Minet: Swazi Plaza, POB A32, Mbabane; tel. 42929; telex 2120; fax 45254.

Swaziland Employee Benefit Consultants (Pty) Ltd: POB 222, Mbabane; tel. 44776; telex 2101; fax 46413; specialized medical cover.

Swaziland Insurance Brokers: POB 222, Mbabane; tel. 43226; telex 2101; fax 46412; f. 1970; Man. Dir F. PETTIT.

Swaziland Royal Insurance Corporation (SRIC): Gilfillian St, POB 917, Mbabane; tel. 43231; telex 2043; fax 46415; 51% state-owned; sole auth. insurance co since 1974; Gen. Man. M. MKWANAZI.

Tibiyo Insurance Brokers: Swazi Plaza, POB A166, Mbabane; tel. 42010; telex 2170; fax 45035; Man. Dir C. FAUX.

Insurance Association

Insurance Brokers' Association of Swaziland (IBAS): Swazi Plaza, POB A32, Mbabane; tel. 42929; f. 1983; four mems.

Trade and Industry

DEVELOPMENT CORPORATIONS

National Industrial Development Corporation of Swaziland (NIDCS): POB 866, Mbabane; tel. 43391; telex 2052; fax 45619; f. 1971; state-owned; holding co for govt investments since 1987, when the majority of its assets were transferred to the Swaziland Industrial Development Co; Man. Dir K. H. NIESSEN.

Small Enterprise Development Co (SEDCO): POB A186, Mbabane; tel. 43046; telex 2130; fax 22723; govt development agency; supplies workshop space, training and expertise for 120 local entrepreneurs at seven sites throughout the country.

Swaziland Industrial Development Co (SIDC): Dhlan'Ubeka House, 5th Floor, cnr Tin and Walker Sts, POB 866, Mbabane; tel. 43391; telex 2052; fax 45619; f. 1986 to finance private-sector projects and to promote local and foreign investment; 35% state-owned; cap. E13.9m. (June 1992); Chair. M. E. FLETCHER; Gen. Man. K.-H. NIESSEN.

Swaki (Pty) Ltd: Liqhaga Bldg, 4th Floor, Nkoseluhlaza St, POB 1839, Manzini; tel. 52693; telex 2244; fax 52001; comprises 27 cos involved in manufacturing, services and the production and distribution of food (especially maize); jtly owned by SIDC and Kirsh Holdings.

Tibiyo Takangwane (Bowels of the Swazi Nation): POB 181, Kwaluseni; tel. 84390; telex 2116; fax 84399; f. 1968; national development agency, with investment interests in all sectors of the economy; participates in domestic and foreign jt investment ventures; total assets E260m. (1992); Gen. Man. A. T. DLAMINI.

STATE AUTHORITIES

National Agricultural Marketing Board: POB 2801, Mbabane; tel. 84088.

National Maize Corporation: POB 158, Manzini; tel. 52261.

Posts and Telecommunications Corporation: POB 125, Mbabane; tel. 42341.

Swaziland Citrus Board: POB 343, Mbabane; tel. 44266; telex 2018; fax 43548.

Swaziland Commercial Board: POB 509, Mbabane; tel. 42930; Man. Dir J. M. D. FAKUDZE.

Swaziland Cotton Board: POB 230, Manzini; tel. 52775; Gen. Man. T. JELE.

Swaziland Dairy Board: POB 1789, Manzini; tel. 84411; fax 85313.

Swaziland Electricity Board: POB 258, Mbabane; tel. 42521.

Swaziland Meat Industries Ltd: POB 446, Manzini; tel. 84165; fax 84418; f. 1965; operates an abattoir and cannery at Matsapha to process meat for local and export markets; Gen. Man. P. PHILLIPS.

Swaziland National Housing Board: POB 798, Mbabane; tel. 45610; fax 45224.

Swaziland Sugar Association: POB 445, Mbabane; tel. 42646; telex 2031; fax 45005; Gen. Man. A. COLHOUN.

Water Services Corporation: POB 20, Mbabane; tel. 43161.

CHAMBERS OF COMMERCE

Sibakho Chamber of Commerce: POB 2016, Manzini; tel. 54409.

Swaziland Chamber of Commerce and Industry: POB 72, Mbabane; tel. 44408; fax 45442; Sec. HARVEY BIRD.

EMPLOYERS' ASSOCIATIONS

The Building Contractors Association of Swaziland: POB 2653, Mbabane; tel. 45566.

Swaziland Association of Architects, Engineers and Surveyors: Swazi Plaza, POB A387, Mbabane; tel. 42287.

Swaziland Institute of Personnel and Training Managers: c/o UNISWA, Private Bag, Kwaluseni; tel. 84011.

Employers' Federation

Federation of Swaziland Employers: POB 777, Mbabane; tel. 22768; fax 46107; f. 1964; 376 mems; Pres. R. SEAL; Exec. Dir E. HLOPHE.

MAJOR INDUSTRIAL COMPANIES

Beral Swaziland: POB 015, Ngwenya; tel. 42164; fax 46093; mfrs of friction materials for the automotive and transport industries.

GMH Manufacturing (Pty) Ltd: POB 503, Matsapha; tel. 85386; f. 1990; manufacture, preparation and packaging of food-related products.

Mantenga Craft: Swazi Plaza, POB A5, Mbabane; tel. 61136; fax 61040; handcrafts.

Natex Swaziland Ltd: Matsapha Industrial Sites, POB 359, Manzini; tel. 86133; telex 2168; fax 86140; f. 1987; textiles.

Neopac Swaziland Ltd: Matsapha Industrial Sites, POB 618, Manzini; tel. 86204; fax 84277; f. 1968; mfrs of corrugated containers for agriculture and industry.

Ngwane Mills (Pty) Ltd: Matsapha Industrial Sites, POB 1169, Manzini; tel. 85011; fax 85112; f. 1992; flour and related products.

Refrigerators Swaziland Ltd: POB 2463, Manzini; tel. 84186; fax 84069; f. 1990; mfrs of domestic refrigerators and freezers.

Spintex Swaziland (Pty) Ltd: POB 6, Matsapha; tel. 86166; fax 86038; mfrs of cotton and poly-cotton combed yarns and sewing thread.

Swazi Paper Mills Ltd: POB 873, Mbabane; tel. 86144; telex 2372; fax 86091; f. 1987; Swaziland's largest privately-owned concern; produces paper and paper products.

Swazi Timber Products Ltd: POB 2312, Manzini; tel. 55267; fax 54785; f. 1987.

Swaziland Brewers Ltd: POB 539, Manzini; tel. 84133; fax 54751; annual production of 250,000 hl of beer.

Swaziland Laminated Timbers (Pty) Ltd: POB 4, Piggs Peak; tel. 71344; telex 2023; fax 71386; mfrs of pine furniture.

Swaziland Safety Glass: Matsapha Industrial Estate, POB 3058, Manzini; tel. 85366; fax 85361; f. 1990; mfrs of glass for transport industry.

Usutu Pulp Co Ltd: Private Bag, Mbabane; tel. 26010; telex 2003; fax 26025; fmrs of unbleached Kraft pulp.

YKK Zippers (Swaziland) (Pty) Ltd: POB 1425, Mbabane; tel. 84188; telex 2125; fax 84182; f. 1977; mfrs of zip fasteners.

TRADE UNIONS

The following trade unions are currently recognized by the Ministry of Labour and Public Service:

The Association of Lecturers and Academic Personnel of the University of Swaziland, the Building and Construction Workers Union of Swaziland, Swaziland Agriculture and Plantation Workers' Union, Swaziland Commercial and Allied Workers' Union, Swaziland Conservation Workers' Union, Swaziland Electricity Supply, Maintenance and Allied Workers' Union, Swaziland Engineering, Metal and Allied Workers' Union, Swaziland Hotel, Catering and Allied Workers' Union, Swaziland Manufacturing and Allied Workers' Union, Swaziland Mining, Quarrying and Allied Workers' Union, Swaziland National Association of Civil Servants, Swaziland National Association of Teachers, Swaziland Post and Telecommunications Workers' Union, Swaziland Transport Workers' Union, Swaziland Union of Financial Institutions and Allied Workers, University of Swaziland Workers' Union, Workers Union of Swaziland Security Guards, Workers' Union of Town Councils.

Trade Union Federation

Swaziland Federation of Trade Unions (SFTU): Mbabane; f. 1973; prin. trade union org. since mid-1980s; mems from public and private sectors, incl. agricultural workers; Pres. JAN SITHOLE.

Staff Associations

Three staff associations exist for employees whose status lies between that of worker and that of management:

The Nyoni Yami Irrigation Scheme Staff Association, the Swazican Staff Association and the Swaziland Electricity Board Staff Association.

CO-OPERATIVE ASSOCIATIONS

Swaziland Central Co-operatives Union: POB 551, Manzini; tel. 52787.

There are more than 123 co-operative associations, of which the most important is:

Swaziland Co-operative Rice Co Ltd: handles rice grown in Mbabane and Manzini areas.

TRADE FAIR

Swaziland International Trade Fair: POB 877, Manzini; tel. 54242; telex 2232; fax 52324; annual 10-day event beginning in late August.

Transport

Buses are the principal means of transport for many Swazis. Bus services are provided by private operators who are required to obtain annual permits for each route from the Road Transportation Board, which also regulates fares.

RAILWAYS

The rail network, which totalled 294.4 km in 1991 provides a major transport link for imports and exports. The railways do not carry passengers. Railway lines connect with the South African ports of Richards Bay and Durban in the south, the South African town of Komatipoort in the north and the Mozambican port of Maputo in the east. Goods traffic is mainly in wood pulp, sugar, molasses, coal, citrus fruit and canned fruit.

Swaziland Railway Board: Swaziland Railway Bldg, POB 475, Johnstone St, Mbabane; tel. 42486; telex 2053; fax 45009; f. 1962; Chair. B. A. G. FITZPATRICK; CEO G. J. MAHLALELA.

ROADS

In 1991 there were 2,807 km of roads, of which 750 km were bituminized. The rehabilitation of about 700 km of main and 600 km of district gravel-surfaced roads began in 1985, financed by World Bank and US loans totalling some E18m. In 1992 work commenced on the reconstruction of Swaziland's main road artery, connecting Mbabane to Manzini, via Matsapha. In the early 1990s schemes were undertaken to improve access to important wood pulp and sugar regions, through the rehabilitation of existing routes.

Ministry of Works and Construction: POB 58, Mbabane; tel. 42321; telex 2104; fax 42364; Prin. Sec. EVART MADLOPHA; Sr Roads Engineer A. MANANA.

SHIPPING

Royal Swazi National Shipping Corporation Ltd: POB 1915, Manzini; tel. 53788; telex 2065; fax 53820; f. 1980 to succeed Royal Swaziland Maritime Co; owns no ships, acting only as a freight agent; Gen. Man. M. S. DLAMINI.

CIVIL AVIATION

Swaziland's only airport is at Matsapa, near Manzini, about 40 km from Mbabane.

African International Airways (AIA): POB 2117, Mbabane; tel. 43875; telex 2283; fax 43876; f. 1985; operates cargo services; Exec. T. M. LONGMORE.

Air Swazi Cargo: Dhlan'Ubeka House, Walker St, POB 2869, Mbabane; tel. 45575; telex 3026; fax 45003; charter services for freight to destinations in Africa and Europe; Man. BRIAN PARMENTER.

Royal Swazi National Airways Corporation: POB 939, Matsapa Airport, Manzini; tel. 84444; telex 2064; fax 84538; f. 1978; govt-owned; scheduled passenger and cargo services to destinations in Africa; also operates charter flights; Exec. Chair. Prince GABHEN DLAMINI; CEO Prince MATATAZELA DLAMINI.

Tourism

Swaziland's attractions for tourists include game reserves and magnificent mountain scenery. In 1991 some 289,493 tourist arrivals were recorded. In the same year revenue from the tourist sector totalled E76.4m.

Hotel and Tourism Association of Swaziland: POB 462, Mbabane; tel. 42218.

Ministry of Broadcasting, Information and Tourism: POB 338, Mbabane; tel. 42761; fax 42774; Tourism Officer MDUDUZI MAGONGO.

Defence

The Umbutfo Swaziland defence force, created in 1973, totalled 2,657 regular troops in November 1983. There is also a paramilitary police force. Compulsory military service of two years was introduced in 1983.

Defence Expenditure: Budgeted at E81.3m. for 1994/95.

Education

Education is not compulsory in Swaziland. Primary education begins at six years of age and lasts for seven years. Secondary education begins at 13 years of age and lasts for up to five years, comprising a first cycle of three years and a second of two years. In 1992 there were 180,285 pupils in 515 primary schools and 51,514 pupils attending 156 general secondary schools. In 1991 88% of children in the relevant age-group were enrolled at primary schools (86% of boys; 90% of girls), while secondary enrolment was equivalent to 48% of children in the appropriate age group (49% of boys; 47% of girls). Higher education is provided by the University of Swaziland, in Kwaluseni, at which 1,705 students were enrolled in 1991. At the 1986 census the rate of adult illiteracy averaged 32.7% (males 30.3%; females 34.8%). Government expenditure on education was E187.0m. for 1991/92, representing 23.4% of total budgetary expenditure.

Bibliography

For works on the former High Commission territories generally, see Botswana Bibliography, p. 190

Arnold, M. W. 'Swaziland: In Transition to What?'. *CSIS Africa Notes*, Briefing Paper No. 30. Washington, DC, Center for Strategic and International Studies, 1984.

Bischoff, P.-H. 'Swaziland's International Relations and Foreign Policy', in *European University Studies*, Series 31, Political Science, Vol. 158. Berne, 1991.

Bonner, P. *Kings, Commoners and Concessionaires.* Ravan Books, 1983.

Booth, A. R. *Swaziland: Tradition and Change in a Southern African Kingdom.* Hampshire, Gower, 1983.

Central Statistics Office. *Annual Statistical Bulletin, 1982.* Mbabane, Swaziland Government, 1984.

Highlights of the Results of the 1986 Population Census. Mbabane, Swaziland Government.

National Accounts of Swaziland 1980–1986. Mbabane, Swaziland Government, 1988.

Davies, R., O'Meara, D., and Dlamini, S. *The Kingdom of Swaziland.* London, Zed Press, 1985.

Dundas, Sir C., and Ashton, H. *Problem Territories of Southern Africa, Basutoland, Bechuanaland, Swaziland.* Cape Town, South Africa Institute of International Affairs, 1952.

Grotpeter, J. J. *Historical Dictionary of Swaziland.* Metuchen, NJ, Scarecrow Press, 1975.

Guide to Botswana, Lesotho, Swaziland. South Africa, Winchester Press, 1983.

Konczacki, Z. A., Parpart, J. L., and Shaw, T. M. *Studies in the Economic History of Southern Africa.* Vol. II. London, Cass, 1991.

Kowet, D. *Land, Labour Migration and Politics in Southern Africa: Botswana, Lesotho and Swaziland.* Uppsala, Scandinavian Institute of African Studies, 1978.

Kuper, H. *The Swazi: A South African Kingdom.* New York, Holt, Rinehart and Winston, 1963.

African Aristocracy. Oxford University Press, 1969.

Sobhuza II: Ngwenyama and King of Swaziland. London, Duckworth, 1978.

Low, A. *Agricultural Development in Southern Africa.* London, James Currey Ltd, 1986.

Marwick, B. A. *The Swazi.* London, Oxford University Press, 1940.

Nyeko, B. *Swaziland.* (World Bibliographical Series). Oxford, Clio, 1982.

Matsebula, J. S. M., *A History of Swaziland.* Cape Town, Longman Penguin Southern Africa, 1976.

Potholm, C. P. *Swaziland: The Dynamics of Political Modernization.* University of California Press, 1972.

Stevens, R. P. *Lesotho, Botswana and Swaziland.* Pall Mall, 1967.

Swaziland Economic Planning Office. *Development Plan 1989/90–1991/92.* Mbabane, Department of Economic Planning and Statistics, Office of the Prime Minister, 1989.

UNIDO. 'Swaziland', in *Industrial Development Review* series. Vienna, 1985.

TANZANIA

Physical and Social Geography

L. BERRY

PHYSICAL FEATURES AND CLIMATE

The 945,087 sq km (364,900 sq miles) of the United Republic of Tanzania (incorporating mainland Tanganyika and a number of offshore islands, including Zanzibar, Pemba, Latham and Mafia) have a wide variety of land forms, climates and peoples; and the country includes the highest and lowest parts of Africa—the summit of Mt Kilimanjaro (5,895 m above sea-level) and the floor of Lake Tanganyika (358 m below sea-level). The main upland areas occur in a northern belt—the Usambara, Pare, Kilimanjaro and Meru mountains; a central and southern belt—the Southern highlands, the Ugurus and the Ulugurus; and a north–south trending belt, which runs southwards from the Ngorongoro Crater. The highest peaks are volcanic, though block faulting has been responsible for the uplift of the plateau areas. Other fault movements have resulted in the depressed areas of the rift valleys; and Lakes Tanganyika, Malawi, Rukwa, Manyara and Eyasi occupy part of the floor of these depressions. Much of the rest of inland Tanzania is made up of gently sloping plains and plateaux broken by low hill ranges and scattered isolated hills. The coast includes areas with sweeping sandy beaches and with developed coral reefs, but these are broken by extensive growth of mangroves, particularly near the mouths of the larger rivers.

With the exception of the high mountain areas, temperatures in Tanzania are not a major limiting factor for crop growth, although the range of altitude produces a corresponding range of temperature regimes from tropical to temperate. Rainfall is variable, both from place to place and time to time, and is generally lower than might be expected for the latitude. About 21% of the country can expect with 90% probability more than 750 mm of rainfall, and only about 3% can expect more than 1,250 mm. The central third of the country is semi-arid (less than 500 mm), with evaporation exceeding rainfall in nine months of the year. For much of the country most rain falls in one rainy season, December–May, though two peaks of rainfall in October–November and April–May are found in some areas. Apart from the problem of the long dry season over most parts of the country, there is also a marked fluctuation in annual rainfall from one year to the next, and this may be reflected in the crop production and livestock figures.

The surplus water from the wetter areas drains into the few large perennial rivers of the country. The largest river, the Rufiji, drains the Southern highlands and much of southern Tanzania. With an average discharge of 1,133 cu m per second, it is one of the largest rivers in Africa, and has major potential for irrigation and hydroelectric power development. The Ruvu, Wami and Pangani also drain to the Indian Ocean. The Pangani has already been developed for hydroelectric power, which supplies Arusha, Moshi, Tanga, Morogoro and Dar es Salaam. Apart from the Ruvuma, which forms the southern frontier, most other drainage is to the interior basins, or to the Lakes Tanganyika, Victoria and Malawi.

The most fertile soils in Tanzania are the reddish-brown soils derived from the volcanic rocks, although elsewhere *mbuga* and other alluvial soils have good potential. The interior plateaux are covered with red and yellow tropical loams of moderate fertility. The natural vegetation of the country has been considerably modified by human occupation. In the south and west-central areas there are large tracts of woodland covering about 30% of the country, while on the uplands are small but important areas of tropical rain forest (0.5% of the country). Clearly marked altitudinal variations in vegetation occur around the upland areas and some distinctive mountain flora is found. Tanzania is well known for its game reserves.

POPULATION AND RESOURCES

Tanzania had an estimated mid-1990 population of 25.6m., most of whom are Africans, although people of Indian and Pakistani ancestry make up a significant part of the urban population. Tanzania is one of the least urbanized countries of Africa. According to UN estimates, the population of the principal towns at mid-1985 was: Dar es Salaam (1,096,000), Mwanza (252,000), Tabora (214,000), Mbeya (194,000) and Tanga (172,000). Ethnic differences continue to have some significance. There are more than 120 ethnic groups in Tanzania, of which the largest are the Sukuma and the Nyamwezi. None, however, exceeds 10% of the total population.

The main features of the pattern of population distribution are, firstly, sharp variations in density, with a number of densely populated areas separated from each other by zones of sparse population; secondly, the comparatively low density of population in most of the interior of the country; and, thirdly, the way in which, in most parts of the country, rural settlements tend to consist of scattered individual homesteads rather than nucleated villages, which are relatively rare.

Highest population densities, reaching over 250 per sq km, occur on the fertile lower slopes of Mt Kilimanjaro and on the shores of Lake Malawi. Most other upland areas have relatively high densities, as does the area south of Lake Victoria known as Sukumaland. This problem of the scattered nature of the rural population has been a focus of development effort, and attempts at both capital-intensive villagization and the formation of co-operative nucleated settlements (*ujamaa* or 'familyhood' villages) have been made.

Tanzania's mineral resources include diamonds, other gemstones, gold, petroleum, salt, phosphates, coal, gypsum, kaolin and tin, all of which are exploited. There are also reserves of nickel, soda ash, iron ore, uranium and natural gas. Agriculture, which employed an estimated 80% of the work-force in the early 1990s, is geared in large part towards subsistence farming. The principal cash crops are coffee, cotton, tea, sisal, pyrethrum, tobacco, coconuts, sugar, cardamom, groundnuts and cashew nuts. Cloves, cultivated on the island of Pemba, are Zanzibar's principal export crop.

Dar es Salaam is the main port, the dominant industrial centre, and the focus of government and commercial activity, although the administrative functions of the capital city are to be transferred to Dodoma by 2005. Dar es Salaam has been growing at a substantial rate and attempts are being made to decentralize industrial development to other centres. Arusha has also been growing rapidly in recent years, partly because of its importance to tourism.

Considerable variation in the pattern of development occurs within Tanzania. In some areas agriculture is becoming much more orientated towards cash crops. In such a large country distance to market is an important factor, and in the present and subsequent development plans major attempts are being made to improve the main and subsidiary communication networks. The TanZam road and railway are an important addition, leaving only the far west and the south-east without good surface links to the rest of the country.

Recent History

GRAHAM MATTHEWS

Based on an earlier article by JOHN LONSDALE

The 19th-century history of the area that is now the United Republic of Tanzania was fashioned by the extension of the caravan trade from Zanzibar into the far interior, to the eastern Congo and Buganda. Dominated by Omanis, whose sultan transferred his capital to Zanzibar in 1840, it was this trade which carried the Swahili language from the coast and established it as the commercial lingua franca of the region. By the same agency, Islam was propagated inland and a tradition of interracial mixing was established among the peoples of present-day Tanzania. Tanganyika was declared a German protectorate in 1885 and was later incorporated into German East Africa, which also included present-day Rwanda and Burundi. Resistance to German rule came to a head with the Maji Maji rebellion in 1905–06 during which villagers forced to till cotton turned on the intruders. The rebellion engulfed much of the south of the country and was eventually put down only with resort to a policy of induced famine which is variously estimated to have caused between 75,000–300,000 deaths. At the end of the First World War the German forces in the area surrendered and in 1920 Tanganyika was placed under a League of Nations mandate, with the United Kingdom as the administering power. In 1946 Tanganyika became a UN trust territory, still under British administration. In 1951 the eviction of 3,000 Africans to make way for white farmers provoked anger throughout the territory, and the creation of multiracial local government councils in almost exclusively African areas was opposed. A focus of protest was provided by the Tanganyika African Association, founded in 1929 and converted by its president, Julius Nyerere, into the Tanganyika African National Union (TANU) in 1954. TANU won a sweeping victory in Tanganyika's first general election, held in two phases in September 1958 and February 1959; a new council of ministers, including African ministers for the first time, was formed in July 1959. At the next election, in September 1960, TANU won 70 of the 71 seats in the national assembly, and Nyerere became chief minister.

THE NYERERE YEARS

Internal self-government was achieved in May 1961, with Nyerere as prime minister. Full independence followed on 9 December 1961. TANU's weaknesses soon became apparent. Democratic local government was ill-developed and the institutional vacuum had to be filled from limited party resources. In addition, it had also become apparent that TANU's two main supports in opposition, the flourishing producers' co-operatives and the trade unions, might now become its chief rivals in government. In January 1962 Nyerere resigned as prime minister to devote himself to party work; he was succeeded by Rashidi Kawawa. On 9 December 1962 Tanganyika became a republic, with Nyerere returning to power as the country's first president, having been elected the previous month. Kawawa became vice-president. Zanzibar (together with the neighbouring island of Pemba and several smaller islets), a British protectorate since 1890, became an independent sultanate in December 1963. The sultan was overthrown in an armed uprising in January 1964, following which a republic was declared and the Afro-Shirazi Party took power. In the prevailing spirit of pan-Africanism and, in part, as a Cold War response to Zanzibar's socialist programme and foreign backers, Nyerere signed an act of union with the new government in April of the same year. The Afro-Shirazi Party leader Abeid Karume became the United Republic's first vice-president as well as chairman of the ruling revolutionary council of Zanzibar. The union was named Tanzania in October 1964.

A new constitution, introduced in July 1965, provided for a one-party state (although, until 1977, TANU and the Afro-Shirazi Party remained the respective official parties of mainland Tanzania and Zanzibar, and co-operated in affairs of state). In September 1965 Nyerere was returned to power in the first one-party election. Early in 1967, TANU accepted a programme of socialism and self-reliance, known as the Arusha Declaration. All party leaders were required by a new code of ethics to divest themselves of private sources of income; rural development was to come not through large farms but community (*ujamma*) villages; the small urban sector was not to exploit the countryside; the education system was to be completely reorganized in order to serve the mass of the population rather than to train a privileged few. Commercial banks and many industries were immediately nationalized, but the rest of the programme was much more difficult to implement, as it flew in the face of existing trends of social change.

In Zanzibar, Karume survived coup plots against him in 1967 and 1971, but was assassinated in April 1972. His successor, Aboud Jumbe, reorganized the Zanzibari government in April 1972 by extending the powers of the Afro-Shirazi Party. Despite its incorporation in Tanzania, Zanzibar retained a separate administration which ruthlessly suppressed all opposition.

In 1972 Rashidi Kawawa was reappointed to the revived post of prime minister, relieving Nyerere of some of his responsibilities. In June 1975 the national assembly voted to incorporate the fundamental principles of socialism and self-reliance into the constitution and to give legal supremacy to TANU as the national political party. A proposal to merge TANU and the Afro-Shirazi Party was submitted by Nyerere in September 1975, and in February 1977 the two parties merged to form the Chama Cha Mapinduzi (CCM—Revolutionary Party), of which Nyerere was elected chairman and Jumbe vice-chairman. A government reshuffle followed, in which Kawawa was replaced as prime minister by Edward Sokoine. In April 1977 the national assembly adopted a permanent constitution for Tanzania, providing for Zanzibar to elect 10 members of the assembly. However, in October 1979 Zanzibar adopted a separate constitution with provisions for an elected president and a partially-elected house of representatives.

Presidential and legislative elections were held in October 1980. Nyerere was re-elected as president for a further five-year term, which he announced would be his last. Jumbe was also re-elected as president of Zanzibar and a 40-member house of representatives for the islands was installed. However, about half of the members of the Tanzania national assembly, including several ministers, lost their seats, in what was seen as a protest against Tanzania's parlous economic condition and bureaucratic inefficiency. Constitutional amendments were adopted in October 1984, limiting the president's tenure of office to two five-year terms and strengthening the powers of the national assembly.

Evidence of the existence of dissident opinion, fuelled by the economic crisis, emerged with the hijacking of an Air Tanzania flight in February 1982, as an expression of political protest, and the discovery of a coup plot in January 1983, as a result of which 20 soldiers and nine civilians were detained. Nine people received sentences of life imprisonment in December 1985 for their part in the conspiracy. A political crisis arose in Zanzibar in early 1984 as a result of growing dissatisfaction with the union and calls for greater autonomy for the islands. Jumbe and three of his ministers resigned in January in a climate of growing tension, and in April Ali Hassan Mwinyi, the islands' former minister of natural resources and tourism, was elected president of Zanzibar as sole candidate (thus also becoming vice-president of Tanzania). Mwinyi, a supporter of the union, set out to ease political tensions and made sweeping changes to Zanzibar's supreme revolutionary council. A new more liberal constitution for Zanzibar was introduced in January 1985, providing for the house of representatives to be directly elected by universal suffrage and for the introduction of a Commonwealth legal system.

In April 1984 Edward Sokoine, the prime minister and a possible successor to Nyerere, died and was replaced by Salim Ahmed Salim, previously minister of foreign affairs. When President Nyerere retired in November 1985, he was succeeded by Mwinyi, his vice-president, who had been elected the previous month with 96% of the valid votes cast. In this way the union was to be cemented by establishing a pattern of alternate mainland and Zanzibari presidents of the United Republic. Idris Abdul Wakil (formerly speaker of the Zanzibar house of representatives) was elected president of Zanzibar to replace Mwinyi; although the sole candidate he received only 61% of the votes. After taking office in November, Mwinyi appointed Joseph Warioba, previously minister of justice, as prime minister and first vice-president, while Salim became deputy prime minister and minister of defence.

THE MWINYI PRESIDENCY

The change of president coincided with a worsening economic crisis (see below) which catapulted the new administration into a changed direction on economic policy. Greater encouragement has been given to the private sector, and acceptance of the IMF's proposals on budgeting, agricultural reform and management of the shilling has persuaded donors to sponsor the country with historically large disbursements of aid.

Nyerere, who described Tanzania's new economic policy as 'unplanned retreats from socialism', was re-elected at the third congress of the CCM in October 1987 as chairman of the party for a further five-year term. His re-election also represented a victory for Rashidi Kawawa (who was himself re-elected almost unanimously as secretary-general of the party) and for other socialist radicals and militants who looked to Nyerere to strengthen the party and to act as a counterbalance against the more controversial economic reforms of Mwinyi.

The third congress of the CCM was also significant in that it greatly strengthened the socialist stalwarts within the party, most of the long-serving political ideologues being re-elected to the central committee, the most powerful organ within the party. Two important 'liberal-modernists' failed to secure re-election: Seif Sharrif Hamad, the chief minister of Zanzibar (who subsequently also lost this office), and Cleopa Msuya, the minister of finance, who was closely concerned in negotiations with the IMF. In another significant change, the prime minister and first vice-president, Joseph Warioba, improved his position within the CCM by assuming leadership of the party's defence and security commission from Salim Ahmed Salim. Mwinyi was re-elected vice-chairman of the party, and in December 1987, when the political excitement of the congress had passed, he recast the balance of power by implementing a cabinet reshuffle in which three ministers who were perceived as opponents of his liberalization policies were removed from office. The cabinet was again reshuffled in early 1989. Although the changes were widely interpreted as a strengthening of Mwinyi's personal power base, the appointees included three ministers of state considered to be sympathetic to Islamic fundamentalism, thus redressing a perceived predominance of Christian influence in the cabinet. In July it was announced that Salim Ahmed Salim, the deputy prime minister and minister of defence and national service, was to leave the government later in the year to become secretary-general of the OAU. In a further reshuffle of the cabinet carried out in September, Salim's responsibilities for defence and national service were transferred to Mwinyi and the post of deputy prime minister was abolished. In the following month it was announced that Omar Ali Juma, the chief minister of Zanzibar, had been elected to the central committee of the CCM.

In February 1990 the CCM initiated a campaign against corruption among government officials. In March an extensive reshuffle of the cabinet took place: Mwinyi dismissed seven ministers who had allegedly opposed plans for economic reform and presided over corrupt or irresponsible ministries. During 1990 the CCM experienced no cohesive internal challenge to its political monopoly, except in Zanzibar (see below). An exiled grouping, calling for the establishment of a multi-party political system, the Tanzania Democratic Forum, was, however, formed in London in early 1990 under the leadership of Oscar Kambona, a former secretary-general of the CCM. In addition, Moussa Membar, who had led the hijack of a Tanzanian airliner in 1982, organized an opposition party operating from Britain, the Tanzania Youth Democratic Movement. In September 1990 he entered Tanzania from Kenya, and was promptly arrested and charged with treason. Abruptly released from detention in May 1991, Membar died soon afterwards. His death was attributed by his family to torture in prison or the delayed effects of poisoning.

The general debate on multi-party government continued during 1990–91. Although the CCM resisted the idea of competition from new parties, the Tanzanian press and a number of seminars and meetings advocated change. Eventually, in early 1991, Mwinyi established a presidential commission to ascertain national opinion on whether to continue with the single party or adopt a multi-party system. Headed by the chief justice, Francis Nyalali, it was asked to gather opinions over a 12-month period, before presenting its recommendations to the CCM and the government. Significantly all members of the commission had CCM affiliations: the only independent member invited to join declined to participate.

While the multi-party debate continued, plans went ahead first for CCM elections in August 1990, to be followed by parliamentary and presidential elections in Tanzania as a whole and Zanzibar in October. The party elections were marked by the formal relinquishment of the CCM presidency by Nyerere, who had held the office for 24 years, and the election of Mwinyi, his chosen successor, in his place. In the period preceding the general elections, Abdul Wakil, the Zanzibari president, resigned, announcing his retirement after only five years in office. In his place, the CCM nominated Dr Salmin Amour, widely regarded as a political liberal. At the presidential elections, Mwinyi was re-elected with 95% of the votes, and Dr Salmin Amour endorsed as president of Zanzibar with 96% of votes cast. Both elections were uncontested. At the elections to the 216 directly elective seats in the 291-member Tanzanian national assembly, 33 ordinary MPs lost their seats, including a veteran minister, Paul Bomani, and two regional commissioners. In a government reshuffle following the elections, Mwinyi replaced his prime minister, Joseph Warioba, with John Malecela, a former minister and high commissioner to the UK. Warioba subsequently lost his parliamentary seat when the electoral commission upheld charges that he had abused his official position in campaigning for re-election.

At the end of February 1991 10 prominent opposition figures gave their support to an independent forum, the Tanzania Legal Education Trust, under the leadership of Abdullah Fundikira (Tanzania's first minister of justice) to steer national opinion towards a multi-party democratic system. This group formed a committee for a transition towards a multi-party system, with James Mapalala as its vice-chairman. Mapalala had been a former political detainee and an active campaigner for human rights and multi-party politics. Most of the other committee members were political critics of the government. Fundikira and Mapalala subsequently became leaders of opposition political parties, respectively the Union for Multi-Party Democracy and the Civic United Front.

In December 1991 the presidential commission on electoral reform published proposals for the establishment of a multi-party political system, despite the fact that almost 80% of Tanzanians canvassed had expressed their continued support for the single party system. In mid-February 1992 proposed constitutional amendments to this effect were ratified by a special congress of the CCM, which stipulated, however, that all new political organizations should command support in both Zanzibar and mainland Tanzania, and should be free of tribal, religious and racial bias, in order to protect national unity. In early May 1992 both the United Republic's constitution and the Zanzibar constitution were duly amended to legalize a multi-party political system.

Mwinyi reallocated cabinet portfolios in late May 1992, and shortly afterwards membership qualification restrictions were abolished by the CCM in preparation for eventual multi-party elections.

In December 1992 the CCM convened its fourth congress amid high expectations of a new socio-economic programme to replace the Arusha Declaration, which had been overtaken by events and effectively abandoned in 1991 when the party had amended its political philosophy. In the event, the congress was marred by internal dissension generated by factions wishing to revive earlier policies. Prime Minister Malecela, however, consolidated his position as Mwinyi's political heir apparent by obtaining election to the party vice-chairmanship. The emergence of inter-religious tensions at the congress was reflected in the failure of the minister of finance, Kighoma Ali Malima, to obtain a seat on the national executive committee of the CCM. In January 1993 the minister of home affairs, Augustine Mrema, was appointed to the revived post of deputy prime minister. Mrema, a relative newcomer to high office, had attracted a wide personal following as a result of his campaigns against corruption and crime.

At the beginning of 1993 it emerged that the Zanzibar government had unilaterally arranged for the island to join the Organization of the Islamic Conference (OIC). This action was a double infringement of the 1964 articles of union and the 1977 union constitution, which established the united republic as a secular state and denied the Zanzibar administration any separate competence in foreign affairs, which became the exclusive responsibility of the union government. In an atmosphere of worsening inter-religious communalism, predominantly Christian mainlanders demanded the resignation of the Muslim president of Zanzibar and the union assembly debated at length a constitutional amendment (then coincidentally receiving parliamentary attention) which set out provisions for presidential impeachment. In February 1993 a parliamentary commission ruled that the action of Zanzibar in relation to OIC membership was unconstitutional. The incident led to a cabinet reshuffle, in which the foreign minister, Ahmed Hassan Diria, was transferred to the post of minister of labour and youth development.

In August 1993 Zanzibar withdrew from membership of the OIC, but significant damage had been done to relations between the mainland and the islands. In the same month, during the budget debate in the national assembly, a group of 55 mainland MPs successfully sponsored a private member's bill providing for the establishment of a third level of government within the union to administer the mainland separately from Zanzibar. The legislation was passed unanimously, despite the intense opposition of ex-president Nyerere, who denounced both the national assembly and the CCM for abandoning a basic tenet of party policy (a commitment to maintaining and enhancing the union) without obtaining a consensus of the entire CCM membership. As a result of Nyerere's intervention, implementation of the measure was delayed pending wider consultation within the CCM, a process which was under way in 1994.

In April 1993 Mwinyi removed the minister of tourism, following disclosures of alleged irregularities in the leasing of a game-controlled area as a private hunting ground to interests from the United Arab Emirates. These revelations served to heighten resentment among indigenous black Africans of perceived exloitation by foreigners, especially Arabs and Asians.

Opposition and Division

By mid-1994 more than 10 opposition movements had been officially recognized since the CCM-appointed registrar of political parties, George Liundi, began work in July 1992. However, when the CCM fought its first multi-party by-election in April the following year the poll was boycotted by all but one of the newly registered parties. The CCM won the contest, in a Zanzibari constituency, by default.

In January 1993 the anti-Asian rhetoric of the leader of the unregistered Democratic Party, Christopher Mtikila, provoked a number of attacks on Asian residents and their businesses in Dar es Salaam. Mtikila was arrested with four others and charged with sedition and inciting violence, but was granted bail in February after a rally called to demand his release was dispersed by paramilitary forces. In early April young Muslim radicals took to the streets in a series of attacks on pork butchers (Islam considers the meat unclean), Sheikh Yahya Hussain, a radical cleric and leader of the council for the propagation of the Qur'an in Tanzania (Balukta), was arrested along with 28 others. Crowds demanding their leaders' release were again dispersed by paramilitary forces. These outbreaks of violence reflected separate but overlapping divisions that had long been contained within Tanzanian society: that between black African and Asian Tanzanians; and that between Christianity and Islam. Set alongside the crisis in the union itself, these complete a picture of deepening divisions in a state that was once taken as a model of African nation-building.

Although denying requests for a constitutional convention, the CCM agreed to meet opposition representatives at an all-party conference convened by the national electoral commission in May 1993. At the conference, the main opposition party, the Chama Cha Demokrasia na Maendeleo (Chadema), demanded the repeal of various enactments that had been introduced during the single-party era. Edwin Mtei, the chairman of Chadema and a former governor of the central bank, argued that much of the existing legal framework militated against fair competition between the ruling party and its new opponents. This assertion, however, was rejected by the government.

During the first two months of 1994 two parliamentary by-elections took place. CCM retained each of these mainland seats by substantial majorities.

TENSIONS IN ZANZIBAR

Tensions in Zanzibar once again surfaced in early 1988, reflecting both continuing rivalries between the islands, and also the underlying discords between the majority African and ethnic minority populations. In January President Wakil accused unnamed ministers in his government of plotting against him, and alleged that a group of dissidents was conspiring to engage mercenaries to overthrow his government. These allegations clearly signalled a power struggle within the Zanzibar administration, in which the Pembans, who produce most of the cloves that are the mainstay of the Zanzibar economy, have regarded themselves as under-represented. Those most vociferous in their complaints were thought to have been supported by Arab exiles, who were seeking means of reasserting their previous influence in the islands. Wakil suspended the supreme revolutionary council and assumed control of the armed forces. The chief minister, Seif Sharrif Hamad (a Pemban), was dismissed, together with five other ministers, who were mostly Pembans favouring policies of economic liberalization. All were subsequently expelled from the CCM, and in May 1989 Hamad was arrested for allegedly being in possession of secret government documents and for attending an 'illegal meeting' in Pemba.

Wakil's reshuffle of the revolutionary council was widely interpreted as a triumph for the supporters of the former Afro-Shirazi Party. Omar Ali Juma, a senior government official, was appointed as the new chief minister. Restrictions were subsequently imposed on the Zanzibari press. In December about 4,000 troops were dispatched to Zanzibar from the mainland, in response to reports that a coup was being plotted to coincide with celebrations planned for January 1989 to commemorate Zanzibar's 25th anniversary of independence.

Although no coup attempt materialized, continuing undercurrents of discontent have persisted on Zanzibar and Pemba. The islands, whose links with the Arab Gulf stretch back to the ninth century, have in recent years looked increasingly to Oman for financial and development aid which has not been forthcoming from the Tanzanian mainland. In addition, certain religious and other groups began to perceive an erosion of traditional cultural values. Since late 1988 the value to Zanzibar of the union has come increasingly under question, and dissident groups such as the Movement for Democratic Alternative (MDA) and the smaller, religiously-based group on Pemba, the Bismillah Party became active even before multi-party politics were officially sanctioned in 1992.

In the immediate prelude to the multi-party era, opposition in Zanzibar coalesced around the Kamati ya Mageuzi Huru

(Kamahuru), led by Shaaban Mloo. In order not to breach the requirement that all registered political movements should function throughout the United Republic, Kamahuru merged in 1992 with the Chama Cha Wananchi (CCW) to form the Civic United Front. It is in Zanzibar that the CCM faces the strongest challenge to its hegemony, and the accompanying prospect of defeat in the general elections due to be held in October 1995.

FOREIGN RELATIONS

Tanzania's relations with neighbouring Burundi deteriorated in 1973, when many thousands of refugees poured into Tanzania, and Tanzanian border villages were raided by Burundi troops. Trouble also arose with Uganda in 1973, when Gen. Amin, of whom Nyerere had been a persistent critic, accused Tanzania of plotting against his regime; supporters of ex-president Obote had attempted an invasion of Uganda from Tanzanian territory in September 1972.

Following the collapse of the East African Community (EAC) in 1977, Tanzania's strained relations with Uganda worsened in late 1978. Renewed border fighting was reported in October, and in the following month Uganda announced the annexation of Tanzania's bordering Kagera region. Ugandan troops withdrew after pressure from the OAU but border fighting continued. Then, in January 1979, a Tanzania-based invasion force entered Uganda. The force, comprising approximately 20,000 members of the Tanzanian defence forces and 1,200 members of the Uganda National Liberation Front—UNLF, rapidly gained control of Uganda's southern region. Amin's army capitulated and an interim UNLF government was proclaimed in April. Tanzania's intervention, which led to the restoration to the presidency of Milton Obote, was condemned by the OAU as a violation of territorial integrity, despite Nyerere's claim to have acted in response to Ugandan aggression.

In October 1993 a failed coup attempt in Burundi, where a democratically elected Hutu government had recently taken office, sent a wave of refugees into Tanzania's Kigoma and Kagera regions. Their numbers were subsequently far exceeded by the massive and sudden influx of Rwandans which followed the outbreak of civil war in that country in April 1994 and the renewed offensive by the Uganda-based Front patriotique rwandais (FPR). The escalation of the civil war ended a peace agreement signed, under Tanzanian auspices, in Arusha in August 1993. Although it pursued its efforts to settle the Rwandan conflict, the Tanzanian government appeared to be siding with the interim administration installed by the Rwandan army. The eventual victory of the FPR thus represented a foreign policy reversal for the Tanzania government, which blamed President Museveni of Uganda for undermining its efforts at mediation by urging the FPR to seek an outright military victory. These events further strained historically troubled relations between potential partners in a new initiative to revive the EAC. In November 1993 the presidents of Tanzania, Uganda and Kenya signed a protocol on renewed co-operation among their countries.

Economy

LINDA VAN BUREN

Tanzania is the world's third poorest country, after Mozambique and Ethiopia. Between independence in 1961 and the mid-1980s, the main preoccupation of the nation's policy-makers was to lift the majority of the population out of illiteracy, poverty and disease. The Arusha Declaration of 1967 put even greater emphasis on the elimination of those ills, along the path of socialism and self-reliance. At the time, the majority of the people were either nomadic or living in widely scattered homesteads. In order for the government's social policies to be carried out, the first prerequisite was to assemble the widely scattered rural communities into planned and permanent villages and settlements. By 1974 the majority of the rural population had been settled into planned villages (*ujamaa vijijini*). The main objective of villagization was originally to raise output through collectivization and larger scale agricultural production, but the results, from an agronomic viewpoint, were largely unsuccessful. The emphasis was gradually moved from the agricultural to the social benefits, with the *ujamaa* villages envisaged as centres for social and infrastructural services. Viewed in this light, villagization was beneficial, for otherwise Tanzania's programmes for improving the well-being of its people would not have been practicable. However, it is now widely accepted that the successes of the *ujamaa* system were on the whole outweighed by ineffective management, shortages of materials, and low levels of crop production. With the aim of achieving economic independence, the government also pursued a policy of nationalizing important economic sectors, particularly major industries and distribution and marketing. However, more than a decade of severe economic decline, from the late 1970s onwards, brought the country to a condition of economic collapse, and, in order to obtain continuing aid from international donors, from the mid-1980s the government adopted measures to redress the economy which were of a more pragmatic, less idealistic nature.

NATIONAL INCOME AND DEVELOPMENT PLANNING

In 1992, according to estimates by the World Bank, the gross domestic product (GDP) of mainland Tanzania was US $2,712m., and the gross national product (GNP) per caput was $110. Between 1980–92, it was estimated, GNP per caput, in real terms, remained absolutely static. Results of the national census carried out in 1988 assess the total population at 23.17m., compared with 17.51m. at the 1978 census. This indicates an average annual growth rate of 3.2%, the same level as for the previous decade. The World Bank, however, has based its calculations on an estimated annual average population growth rate of 3.0% in 1980–92. Agriculture's share of gross domestic product (GDP) in 1992 was 61%, that of industry was 12% (manufacturing 5%) and that of services 26% (in 1965 the proportions were agriculture 46%, industry 14%, manufacturing 8% and services 40%). The annual rate of inflation declined from 42.9% in 1984 to 28.2% in 1985, but increased to 44% in 1986, mainly as a result of measures stipulated by the International Monetary Fund (IMF, see below). The rate was subsequently further reduced, despite further devaluations of the shilling and the continuing relaxation of price controls, to 19.7% in 1990, 22.3% in 1991 and 22.1% in 1992.

The first Five-Year Development Plan, launched in 1964, had to be abandoned in 1966, partly because the required amounts of foreign aid did not materialize. With the Arusha Declaration, President Nyerere placed Tanzania's economic and social policies firmly along a line of 'African socialism', rejecting both Western capitalism and the ideology of the extreme left. The second Five-Year Plan (1969–74) envisaged an average annual GDP growth rate of 6.7%, but only 4.8% was achieved.

The initiation of the third Five-Year Plan, scheduled for 1975, was delayed until 1977. By 1980 the extent of Tanzania's shortage of foreign exchange was severely disrupting economic performance. A fourth Five-Year Development Plan was introduced in 1981, but was immediately abandoned and replaced by a National Economic Survival Programme.

The balance-of-payments problem had become so acute by early 1982 that Nyerere suspended all new development projects and launched a three-year structural adjustment programme (SAP), which was prepared jointly by the ministry of planning and economic affairs and a team of World Bank advisers. This aimed to stimulate the productive sectors (particularly the main export crops), to curtail government spending, and to relax price controls. Whereas GDP had continued to fall, in real terms, in 1982 and 1983, adjustments introduced in the June 1984 budget soon began to have an effect, however slight, and there was a 3.4% growth of GDP in 1984. The following year, the rate of growth fell back to 2.6%, partly because of drought. IMF assistance was withheld until mid-1986, when agreement was finally reached on a package involving US $45m. in a stand-by credit, to be drawn in the first 12 months, and $24m. in a structural adjustment facility.

In the budget of June 1986 a new three-year Economic Recovery Programme (ERP) was announced which was closely allied to the IMF agreement, and to the associated new aid arrangements agreed with the World Bank (see below). The ERP provided for some downward adjustment of the shilling's official exchange rate and further producer price rises in the first year. The target of 4.5% average annual growth in GDP was over-ambitious, but there was an improvement in the growth rate, to 3.6% and 3.9% in 1986 and 1987 respectively. This resulted from high coffee prices during 1986, improved weather conditions, better producer incentives and slightly better availability of imported inputs, thanks to the inflow of new aid funds. The rate of growth, in real terms, was 5.1% in 1988, 3.6% in 1989, 3.2% in 1990, 3.7% in 1991, 3.6% in 1992 and 4.1% in 1993.

The second three-year phase of the ERP, the Economic and Social Action Plan (ESAP), was launched in January 1990; it aimed to continue the ERP policies but also to alleviate the social costs of adjustment measures. Five-year plans have virtually been abandoned, and development planning is now undertaken year by year; the priority areas for 1990/91, 1991/92 and 1992/93 were transport infrastructure, health and education.

AGRICULTURE

The agricultural sector is the mainstay of Tanzania's economy, providing a livelihood for 88% of the economically active population, and accounting for 81% of export earnings in 1992. Subsistence farming accounts for an estimated 50% of total agricultural output. No more than about 8% of the country's land area is cultivated, and only about 3% of the cultivated land is irrigated. The northern and south-western areas are the most fertile, receiving the highest rainfall. The main food crop is maize, followed by cassava and plantains. The main export crops are coffee beans and raw cotton, followed by tobacco, cloves (from Zanzibar), tea, cashew nuts and sisal.

During the 1980s there were successive increases in producer prices for all the major crops, and these, together with much more favourable weather in most years from 1985, helped to increase output of most main food crops. Increased availability of imported agricultural inputs, made possible by new foreign-exchange support from international aid donors, contributed to improved harvests. Agricultural output increased by 4.4% in 1987, 4.5% in 1988, 4.6% in 1989, 4.8% in 1990 and 4.8% in 1991. In March 1990 the International Development Association (IDA) approved a credit for about US $200m. to support an agricultural adjustment programme, which aimed to make agricultural marketing more efficient. In 1991 legislation was adopted to end the state monopoly over agricultural marketing, permitting private traders to market crops alongside co-operatives; implementation of the legislation was particularly slow regarding the marketing of cotton.

Coffee is grown mainly by smallholders and mostly in the Kilimanjaro region; it accounted for 49% of export earnings in 1986, but this share had fallen to 30% by 1992. A record crop of 67,300 metric tons was produced in 1980/81. Since then, output has fluctuated, and amounted to 58,000 tons in 1986/87, 49,000 tons in 1987/88, 43,000 tons in 1988/89, 54,000 tons in 1989/90, 46,000 tons in 1990/91, 56,000 tons in 1991/92 and 59,000 tons in 1992/93. Coffee production for 1993/94 was estimated at 40,000 tons. Tanzania's total coffee exports in recent years have been about 800,000 bags (each of 60 kg), including those to countries not included in export quota agreements of the International Coffee Organization (ICO), of which Tanzania is a member. The fall in world prices in 1989, following the collapse of the ICO quota arrangements, affected robustas more severely than arabicas, which make up about 75% of Tanzania's coffee output. In November 1990 a $40m. pre-export financing credit for the coffee sector was arranged by a consortium of international banks; this was the fourth such annual arrangement. The money was to be channelled through the National Bank of Commerce for financing imports of selected inputs. The value of coffee exports in 1993 was forecast at $60m., compared with $170m. in 1992. In August 1993 Tanzania joined other African producers in an effort to revive coffee prices through the implementation of a scheme to withhold 20% of their output from world export markets. Improved prices and prospects on the global coffee market in May 1994 were expected to boost revenue from coffee for that year.

Cotton production increased steadily during the late 1980s, from 289,390 bales (each of 480 lb, or 218 kg), in 1987 to 390,450 bales in 1988 and 395,040 bales in 1989. A major rehabilitation programme covering ginneries and transport in particular, and funded by the Netherlands, brought about the improved performance of the cotton sector during the late 1980s, and the UK and the European Investment Bank (EIB) funded other rehabilitation schemes. However, output fell to 266,420 bales in 1990. The 1990/91 season's output was an estimated 261,000 bales, but in 1991/92 production rose to a record 510,000 bales before falling back to 334,862 bales in 1992/93 and to an estimated 229,000 bales in 1993/94. Local textile mills bought nearly 74,000 bales in 1989/90. Earnings from cotton exports in 1988/89 were US $83.5m., but in 1989/90, despite rising world prices, they fell to $47m., mainly because of transport difficulties. During July 1991–May 1992 exports of cotton earned $81.3m. In 1992 the African Development Bank pledged sh. 1,800m. for the rehabilitation of Tanzania's cotton treatment factories.

Tobacco has become Tanzania's third largest export crop and has experienced significant growth rates in the 1990s. Although output declined from 19.1m. kg in 1975/76 to 10.7m. kg in 1988/89 production recovered to 17m. kg in 1991 and 17.1m. kg in 1992 before soaring to an all-time record of 24m. kg in 1993.

Tea production has become increasingly important in recent years. The output of made tea rose from 8,492 metric tons in 1970 to an FAO estimate of 20,000 metric tons in 1993. Prices, particularly for the plain teas such as Tanzania grows, fell sharply in 1985 and remained at a low level until 1989, when a slight improvement began. Prices continued to rise during the early 1990s. Marketed production in 1988/89 was an estimated 15,600 tons, up from only 13,800 tons the previous year. The Tanzania Tea Authority (TTA) accounts for about one-quarter of tea output, has four tea factories and is building three more. Brooke Bond Liebig Tanzania is the largest producer, accounting for 40% of total output. The UK-based Lonrho group has bought back into the Mufindi and Luponde tea estates, which it owned before nationalization. The TTA retains 25% in both companies. The estates are being rehabilitated, and are already selling organic teas, which command high prices. Lonrho announced in early 1991 that it would invest US $5.6m. in a five-year programme aimed at doubling yields at the Mufindi estates to 3,000 kg per ha and extending the planted area from 730 to 1,000 ha. In March 1988 the East Usambara Tea Co (EUTC) was formed, with the UK-based Commonwealth Development Corporation (CDC) taking a 60% interest, and the TTA the remainder. The company has acquired two TTA estates in Tanga region. The CDC is planning to establish a 600-ha tea estate at Njombe in Iringa region; it will invest £13m. through the Tanganyika Wattle Co, of which it owns 84% (the remaining 16% is owned by the Tanzania Development Finance Co). When the new factory starts operating in 1995, it is expected to earn $10m. a year from exports.

Cloves are the main export of Zanzibar, providing about 80% of the island's foreign exchange earnings. Zanzibar, once the world's largest clove exporter, now ranks fourth in the world. When Indonesia, the world's largest consumer, became self-sufficient in cloves in 1983, Zanzibar had to compete for much smaller markets in India, Thailand, Singapore and the Netherlands. Compared with up to 20,000 tons per year in the mid-1960s, output had fallen to only 5,800 tons in 1990. The state monopoly on the marketing of cloves, as of Zanzibar's other crops, was terminated in 1989. There is a clove distillery on Pemba Island, the main growing area, which produces clove-stem oil for export. Alternative export crops now being encouraged, and grown on a small scale on the islands, include tobacco, rubber, cardamom, vanilla and peppermint.

Production of sisal in 1964 was just over 250,000 metric tons, but output fell drastically when more than one-half of the estates were nationalized in 1976; only on the remaining privately-owned estates was production maintained at a fairly steady level. Marketing was undertaken by the Tanzania Sisal Development Board (TSDB). In 1986 the government began to dispose of many of its 37 estates to private interests. World prices for sisal recovered at the end of the 1980s from the very low levels of the 1970s, as the product began to compete successfully with synthetic substitutes, particularly in some specialized uses. Output, which declined to 30,000 tons in 1987, recovered to 36,000 tons in 1991, when new plantings reached maturity. Production fell back to 24,000 tons in 1992 before rising to 28,000 tons in 1993. By 1989, only about one-third of annual production came from TSDB estates. There is still a severe shortage of machinery and spares, but a new type of mobile decorticator has been imported from the UK. Renewed world demand is encouraging investment in sisal, and several foreign groups have bought estates or started joint ventures with the TSDB. An Italian company announced in September 1990 that it would rehabilitate the TSDB's Ngomeni factory.

Production of cashew nuts slumped from 145,000 metric tons in 1973/74 to only about 16,500 tons in 1986/87, as a result of low producer prices and long delays in payments to growers, disease, poor husbandry and lack of imported inputs. Output was 28,000 metric tons in 1990 and 33,000 tons in 1991. Total processing capacity is 103,000 tons per year, but in some years the whole crop is exported raw in order to earn foreign exchange quickly. Purchases by the Tanzania Cashewnut Marketing Board (known as the Cashewnut Authority of Tanzania until the reform of the crop-purchasing authorities) improved to 19,275 tons in 1988/89. An IDA credit of about $25m. was approved in mid-1989 to finance a project designed to double production of both cashew nuts and coconuts within 10 years. Coconut production has stagnated in recent years, partly because of ageing trees. The project covers research into improved varieties and hybrids, training, and credit for farmers. Output of copra was 32,000 tons in 1993.

Other cash crops include sugar, cocoa, pyrethrum and groundnuts. Tanzania's output of sugar was 120,272 metric tons in 1992/93, while local demand is about 500,000 tons per year. Despite this deficit, Tanzania exports 10,000 tons per year to the European Union countries. Production of pyrethrum, cultivated mainly in the southern highlands, fell from about 6,000 tons per year in the 1960s to 1,232 tons in 1986/87, before recovering slightly to 1,585 tons in 1989/90, mostly in the Southern Highlands. However, world prices have improved, and a project is under way to rehabilitate the Arusha processing factory. The government is making efforts to revise the industry; the Tanzania Pyrethrum Board has raised prices in line with higher world prices, and it supplies free seeds to growers; target production for 1991/92 was 2,200 tons. Fresh fruit and vegetables are potentially important export crops, and small quantities are being air-freighted to European markets. This non-traditional trade has been stimulated by the encouragement of private enterprise, but it is still severely constrained by many factors, including the very limited chilled storage facilities at Dar es Salaam international airport, and the lack of expertise among both growers and exporters, regarding matters such as quality standards, and packaging and other requirements. In 1993 Tanzania produced 135,000 tons of Mangoes, 5,000 tons of pineapples, 800,000 tons of bananas and plantains, 74,000 tons of chick peas, 385,000 tons of dry beans, 78,000 tons of dry peas and 51,000 tons of dry onions. Honey and beeswax produced by Tabora Beekeepers' Co-operative are being exported in small quantities, after a gap of some years.

Food crops include maize, cassava, sorghum, millet, rice, wheat and plantains. The National Milling Corporation (NMC) was, until 1991, the sole marketing body for food crops, after which it handled only about 25% of grain sales, and is restricted to certain areas. The very satisfactory long rains in early 1985 resulted in good harvests in both 1985/86 and 1986/87. Harvests of food crops in 1987/88 were lower, because of disappointing rainfall; in April 1989 heavy rains caused severe flooding in many parts of the country. Since then, harvests of maize and other food crops have suffered from a combination of generally poor rains and, particularly in the south-west, severe flooding; consequently some areas have had severe food shortages. Lack of adequate storage is a major cause of food shortages, since an estimated 30%–40% of all crops are lost through post-harvest pest infestation and other damage.

Regional co-operatives and private-sector operators are taking over crop purchasing from the NMC and other state crop authorities, and are also to be responsible for distribution of agricultural inputs. The national bodies continue to be responsible for importing and exporting, and most of them have been transformed into marketing boards. However, the co-operatives purchased only 288,606 metric tons of crops in 1989, 38% of the target level. Their lack of cash and of management skills, together with transport problems, mean that large amounts of crops are never collected and are either sold on the black market or left to rot. The central bank has promised to provide special assistance to help the co-operatives to solve their liquidity problems and to shield them from the very high interest rates. The 1986/87 budget ended government financing of the deficits incurred by parastatal organizations. The government is now actively encouraging private-sector participation in agriculture and agricultural marketing. Support services to farmers, including the supply of inputs and credit, are still very inadequate, despite some improvements since the mid-1980s. In May 1992 the government announced that it would import 400,000 metric tons of cereals in that year, in order to cover shortfalls caused by drought. Maize output fell from 3.13m. tons in 1988/89 to 2.11m. tons in 1991/92. In 1993 Tanzania harvested 2.28m. tons of maize, 210,000 tons of millet, 719,000 tons of sorghum and 631,000 tons of paddy rice.

INDUSTRY AND POWER

According to estimates by the World Bank, the average annual growth rate of industrial production was 2.6% in 1970–80, but was −2.2% in 1980–92. Many factories closed down, or suspended operations for long periods during the 1980s. Industries suffered from the rising cost of fuel and other imports and the severe lack of foreign exchange to pay for raw materials, machinery, equipment and spares, as well as from frequent interruptions to the water and electricity supply. There have been a few signs of improvement since 1986, however, mainly as a result of more foreign exchange becoming available through the IMF and Tanzania's main aid donors for the import of essential inputs. By mid-1990, most factories were operating at 20%–40% of capacity, and a few had reached 70%. Manufacturing output declined by 0.8% in 1980–91, and the sector's share of GDP fell from 10% in 1970 to 4% in 1991.

The industrial sector is based on the processing of local commodities and on import substitution. However, some industrial goods—textiles, clothing, footwear, tyres, batteries, transformers, switchgear, electric cookers, bottles, cement and paper—are exported to neighbouring countries. The government is seeking to encourage the production of manufactured goods for export, in order to lessen dependence on agricultural commodities. A major success was achieved in 1988, when an electrical firm, NEM, exported wall lamps and fluorescent light fittings to Sweden and the Federal Republic of Germany, earning about $148,000. Devaluation of the shilling helped to make these goods competitive with those from European or Far Eastern suppliers. Aluminium Africa Co, Tanzania Electrical Goods Manufacturing Co, Southern Paper Mills and Light Source Manufacturing Co all improved their export earnings in 1989, when their combined total was $76m. (compared with $72m. earned by all manufactured exports in 1988).

The principal industries, after food processing, are textiles, brewing and cigarettes. Others include oil refining, fertilizers, rolling and casting mills, pulp and paper, paperboard, metalworking, cement, vehicle assembly, soft drinks, fruit canning, gunny bags, engineering (spares for industrial machinery and for vehicles), railway wagon assembly, glassware, ceramics, hoes, pharmaceutical products, oxygen, carbon dioxide, bricks and tiles, light bulbs, electrical goods, wood products, machine tools and disposable hypodermic syringes. While target output of textiles for 1990 was 61.1m. sq m of cloth, 47.5m. sq m were produced just in the first six months of the year, compared with 38.9m. sq m in the whole of 1988. The removal of protective barriers in the early 1990s, however, placed at least two textile companies in severe financial difficulty, causing them to demand large investments of capital from the government to modernize their machinery. The National Bicycle Co began producing again in 1990 for the first time since 1982, when it closed down owing to lack of foreign exchange. There are three cement plants, at Mbeya, Wazo Hill, near Dar es Salaam, and Tanga. After several years of severe cement shortage, rehabilitation of the plants, mainly with Danish and Swedish assistance, allowed production to increase in 1989 to 700,000 metric tons, meeting domestic needs of about 580,000 tons, allowing exports of 70,000 tons, with the remainder held as stock. Finnish Valmet tractors, Swedish Scania trucks and Italian Fiat tractors are among the vehicles assembled. Southern Paper Mills' US $260m. pulp- and paper-mill at Mufindi, in south-central Tanzania, started production in mid-1985, after several delays. It is Tanzania's largest-ever development project. The nearby Sao Hill forest will eventually supply the plant's timber needs but, meanwhile, the plant will operate by using imported chemical pulp. Target output for the initial phase is 20,000 metric tons of paper per year, rising to 66,000 tons per year, in seven grades of paper. Tanzania was importing about 30,000 tons of paper per year in the mid-1980s. East African Agro-Industries was formed in 1990 to trawl for nile perch in Lake Victoria; it is to build a plant near Mwanza airport to process 20–25 tons of fish per day for export. The Tanzanian Italian Petroleum Refinery (TIPER), in Dar es Salaam, is jointly owned by Italy's AGIP and the Tanzanian Petroleum Development Corporation (TPDC). It underwent rehabilitation, at a cost of $18m., in 1990–93. Output in 1987 was 485,000 tons, but the refinery's capacity is 670,000 tons per year. The IDA is lending $44m. towards a $104m. petroleum distribution improvement project, which includes the building of storage depots, and which is regarded as a key component of overall infrastructure improvement plans.

More than 70% of the country's electricity is generated by hydro-power. The new 80-MW hydroelectric station at Mtera dam, which represents the third phase of the Kidatu complex on the Great Ruaha river, brings the total generating capacity to 519 MW. An eight-year investment programme for the power sector was launched in early 1991; it includes the development of the US $410m. 200-MW Kihansi power station, to be commissioned in 1998, and expansion of the Pangani Falls power station. A 220kv transmission line from Singida to Arusha is also to be built, at a cost of $107m. The national grid is being extended in a major distribution project, taking electricity from Kidatu to six mainland regions. The Tanzania Electric Supply Co (Tanesco) presented a $300m. five-year development programme for 1990–95 at a donors' conference in March 1989. Growth in demand is expected to be 11%–13% a year, and further expansion of generating capacity and of the distribution network will be needed. Tanesco raised electricity prices by 27% in March 1993 and by a further 71% in July 1993.

MINERALS

Tanzania exploits diamonds, gold, salt, various gemstones, phosphates, coal, gypsum, kaolin and tin. Output of diamonds fell from a peak of 988,000 carats in 1967 to 150,000 carats in 1987, but then recovered slightly to 190,000 carats in 1988. In 1990 output of diamonds stood at 117,000 carats. A continuing problem is that small-scale diamond prospectors sell their finds outside the Tanzanian buying system. Exports of diamonds in 1989 were worth US $14.4m. Reserves at the Williamson Mwadui diamond mine in Shinyanga region are expected to be exhausted by 1997. A company associated with De Beers Centenary will prospect over a large area in Shinyanga region. Gold production dwindled to almost nil in the 1970s but the Buckreef mine, in Geita, was reopened in 1982. A Canadian company is investing $86m. in a gold mine at Bulyanhulu in the Kahama district, which is expected to produce gold worth $80m. annually over 12 years. Tancan Gold, a Tanzanian-Canadian joint venture, is to mine at Matinje in Tabora region. Official gold exports earned $35m. in 1990, a 52% increase over 1989, and purchases rose sharply in early 1991, as reforms to the official buying mechanism began to take effect. The central bank now purchases gold direct from miners at prices above the parallel market rate. Official purchases were only 41 kg in 1988, but rose to 1,640 kg in 1990, to 3,770 kg in 1991 and to 4,100 kg in 1992, with a value of $26.25m. in 1990, $44.3m. in 1991 and $55m. in 1992. The Longido ruby mine is the largest in the world, and the Umba River Valley is yielding rubies and sapphires whose colours are being improved by heat treatment. Deposits of tanzanite (a blue semi-precious stone that was first discovered in the Arusha region in 1967) have been exploited by unlicensed miners, but the government is now severely restricting this activity and at the same time is reviving the Tanzania Gemstone Industry which buys and processes gemstones. Large soda ash deposits in Lake Natron are to be used for the production of caustic soda. The feasibility of extracting salt from Lake Eyasi, 200 km west of Arusha, is being investigated. Salt is produced at coastal salt pans, and is a potential export. Romex Int. of Canada has signed an agreement to develop nickel deposits in Ngara district in the west. In 1992 Canada's Sutton Resources invested $1m. in the exploration of 26,400 sq km of the Kagera basin, searching for nickel, cobalt, copper, lead, zinc and platinum. In 1992 a scheme to exploit deposits of nickel, copper and cobalt, which had already been located in the region, was launched, at a projected cost of $750m. The Chinese-built Songwe-Kiwira coal mine in the south-west, which came into production in 1988, has an annual capacity of 100,000 tons, but by late 1990 there were unsold stocks of 20,000 tons, one-half of the mine's actual annual output. The coal's high ash content means that the intended major customers, Southern Paper Mills and Mbeya Cement Co, will not use it. Coal is mined on a smaller scale at Ilima in the Mbeya region. Iron ore is mined at Chunya. Tin is mined on a small scale near the Zaire border. Tanzania also has confirmed reserves of uranium, niobium, copper, titanium and vanadium, but these are not exploited. Phosphate deposits at Minjingu in the Arusha region supplied the Tanga fertilizer plant from 1982 until December 1991, when all production ceased.

Prospecting for petroleum and natural gas has been continuing for many years. In the 1970s there were unconfirmed reports of the discovery of petroleum in the Songo Songo island area, off shore from Kilwa, south of Dar es Salaam. An estimated 42,890m. cu m of gas is present in the area. A large project for the production of ammonia/urea fertilizers, using natural gas from the Songo Songo field, is planned by the TPDC, at Kilwa Masoka, and a joint-venture company, Kilwa Ammonia Co (Kilamco), has been formed. A much larger offshore gas field is Kimbiji, 40 km south-east of Dar es Salaam, where recoverable reserves are estimated at 130,000m. cu m. Results of petroleum exploration so far have been disappointing, but a number of international companies have been involved in prospecting, both on and off shore (in some cases grouped as consortia), including Shell and Esso, Elf Aquitaine, Petrofina, PetroCanada, AGIP, Amoco, Statoil of Norway, Exxon, BP, Broken Hill (Pty) Co, Texaco, the Oil and Natural Gas Commission of India and the Swiss-based International Energy Development Corporation. Tanzania imports about 700,000 tons of crude oil annually, and fuel accounted for 19% of the import bill in 1991 and 13% in 1992.

TOURISM

During the period when the East African Community (EAC) was active, the tourist industry in Tanzania was an appendage of the Kenyan tourist industry. Most visitors merely visited Tanzania's tourist attractions on one-day excursions, pre-paid in Kenya. The break-up of the EAC and the closure of the Kenya–Tanzania border in 1977 led to a fall in visitor arrivals. Hotels, lodges and access roads deteriorated very badly, with a shortage of foreign exchange for the necessary imports and lack of real government encouragement. Visitor arrivals declined from 178,000 in 1974 to 60,218 in 1983, but began to recover from 1986 onwards, reaching 138,000 in 1987, 186,000 in 1991 and a record (estimated) 250,000 in 1992. The government claimed that gross receipts from tourism in 1990 were $63m., 50% up on 1989 earnings, and that they reached $220m. in 1991. Devaluation of the shilling has been a major boost to tourism, because Tanzania was previously an extremely expensive destination. The change in government policies and attitude towards tourism is also helping to open up a very bright prospect for the industry in the long term, although the target of $500m. in earnings by the mid-1990s seems rather ambitious. The state-owned Tanzania Tourist Corporation (TTC) owns 15 hotels and lodges. Of these, the management of nine has been delegated to private concerns. In 1992 the government announced plans to dismantle the TTC and to replace it with a new body, the Tanzania Tourist Board. Several local and foreign private companies have since invested in the tourism sector, which is now regarded as having good potential, given Tanzania's unspoiled beaches and superb game parks, which cover nearly one-third of the country, together with its record of political stability. The construction of a five-star Sheraton hotel in Dar es Salaam is due to be completed in mid-1995. It was announced in early 1993 that France's Accor Group was to renovate seven hotels and lodges, at a cost of sh. 582.2m., and will subsequently manage them under contract. Zanzibar is encouraging tourism, in particular through an agreement signed with the Aga Khan Fund for Economic Development to build two new hotels, develop a tourism centre and repair historic buildings in the old capital.

TRANSPORT AND COMMUNICATIONS

The concentration of Tanzania's population on the periphery of the country, leaving the central part relatively sparsely populated, poses enormous transport and communication problems.

The Tanzania-Zambia Railway Authority (Tazara) rail line and the Tanzania-Zambia highway, designed to provide an alternative sea outlet to land-locked Zambia, have eased the problem of transportation to the rich Kilombero valley as well as the Iringa and Mbeya regions. The Chinese-built Tazara line suffered badly in its early years from financial and technical problems and lack of equipment and spare parts. The line, together with improvement of Dar es Salaam port, is also a priority under the programme of the Southern African Development Community (SADC). Tazara made its first profit in 1985/86. However, donors are pressing for more efficient management of the line. Large rises in fares and freight charges were announced at the beginning of 1991, but the line is facing a serious new problem: following the political changes in South Africa, Zambia is starting to make greater use of the much more reliable southern transport routes. In 1990 the line had only 36 locomotives and 1,446 wagons in operation, whereas it needed 90 and 3,200 respectively. The USA undertook to supply 17 locomotives under a $46m. grant agreement signed in 1987. China signed a 10-year agreement on engineering, managerial and technological co-operation in 1988. The central railway line and its branches are operated by Tanzania Railways Corporation (TRC). Canada has provided finance and technical assistance for TRC's development programme. The IDA agreed in 1991 to lend $76m. for the TRC's five-year rehabilitation project, which is to cost $279m., of which $168m. will be in foreign exchange. Rail connections with Kenya were re-established in early 1985, as were marine services and ferry services across Lake Victoria; overland and air links had already been resumed.

Air Tanzania Corporation (ATC), which was founded in 1977, operates domestic and regional services. ATC has persistently suffered severe financial difficulties and technical problems. It has two Boeing 737 airliners, two F27-600s and two Twin Otters. The airline has on several occasions had to suspend international flights because of financial problems; in early 1991 it resumed a twice-weekly service to London, one via Rome and the other via Frankfurt. In April 1992 the government proposed the partial privatization of ATC. Zanzibar airport is being extended, with aid from Oman, to enable long-haul aircraft to land. Zanzibar Airways started operations in 1990, and aims mainly to cater for the tourist trade. The Tanzania Harbours Authority's $220m. improvement programme for Dar es Salaam port, including the development of container-handling facilities, is being funded by the World Bank, Finland, Denmark, Italy, the Netherlands, Norway, the UK and the European Investment Bank. The project, due for completion in 1995, will raise the port's annual throughput capacity from 3m. metric tons to 7m. tons. The new container terminal came into service in 1989 and an inland container depot is being developed at Ubungo, 15 km from Dar es Salaam. The number of containers handled in 1990 was 73,000 TEUs (twenty-foot equivalent units) and this is expected to rise to 147,000 TEUs per year by 1995. Zambia accounted for over 40% of cargo handled at the port in 1993, Burundi 6% and Malawi 3%.

A five-year $871m. integrated road project, funded by the World Bank and several other multilateral and bilateral donors started in early 1991. The programme aims to repair and improve 60% of the country's primary roads and 50% of the regional road network in 11 agriculturally important regions. A further 450 km of roads are to be bituminized, in addition to the existing 3,000 km. A new international telephone exchange giving direct dialling facilities was inaugurated in October 1991. The satellite earth station at Mwenge, built in 1979, was replaced by a new installation supplied by an Italian company, giving access to Atlantic as well as Indian Ocean satellites.

EXTERNAL TRADE

The leading exports are coffee beans, raw cotton, tobacco, cloves, tea, beans, diamonds, cashew nuts, sisal and pyrethrum. Industrial exports include textiles, hides, wattle bark extract and spray-dried instant coffee. Timber, fish and prawns are also exported in small quantities. Fresh fruit, vegetables and flowers have now been added to the list. Honey exports were resumed in 1989, after a gap of several years. Fluctuating world prices lead to wide variations in coffee's share of Tanzania's total exports. In 1991 manufactures of all types accounted for 11% of total exports, compared with 7% in 1985 and 19% in 1988.

Tanzania's terms of trade were estimated to have declined by 36% between 1972 and 1980—or by 21.5% if petroleum imports are excluded. However, they began to level off during the second half of the 1980s, and by 1989 they stood at 108 (1987 = 100). By 1991, however, Tanzania's terms of trade stood at 84 and they had worsened to 71 in 1992. Mainland merchandise exports earned US $380m. in 1989, $300m. in 1990, $394m. in 1991 and $400m. in 1992. An encouraging feature has been the success of small private exporters, who in 1989 earned $62m., demonstrating how quickly many of them have responded to trade liberalization measures. In 1994 the United Nations Development Programme provided US $30m. for a project which aimed to assist and expand small-scale enterprises. Imports have risen steadily with the implementation of the economic recovery programme; in 1992 the total expenditure was $1,200m., compared with $1,381m. in 1991, $935m. in 1990, $1,219.6m. in 1989 and $1,179.8m. in 1988.

An Open General Licensing (OGL) scheme was introduced in February 1988 with IDA and UK aid, to give small importers access to foreign exchange, which was made available through the National Bank of Commerce and was originally able to be used for importing items on an approved list. The scheme has been expanded and altered, so that any goods are now eligible for a licence unless they appear on a list of excluded items. The original ceiling of $1m. worth of goods a year per importer has now been discontinued but, for any order worth more than $1m., the importer must obtain at least three quotations from potential suppliers.

In 1962 about 32% of exports went to the UK, but by 1989 the proportion had declined to about 8.8%. Germany was the main customer in 1991, with 18.6% of the total, followed by the UK, the USA, Singapore, Italy, Japan and the Netherlands. The UK's share of Tanzanian imports in 1962 was 29%, but by 1991 the proportion was only 10.4%; behind Japan's 14.6% and Italy's 11.2%; then came Iran, Italy, the Netherlands and Sweden. The Netherlands' relatively high position is due mainly to its activity in coffee and spice trading in the world markets; Singapore's position is likewise attributable to its purchase of cloves from Zanzibar.

BALANCE OF PAYMENTS AND INTERNATIONAL AID

According to IMF figures, the current account deficit in 1989 was reduced to $158.5m., from $387.5m. in 1988, and there was a surplus on the capital account of $152.8m. World Bank figures indicate a mainland deficit of $628m. before and $158m. after official transfers in 1989, a $832m. deficit before and a $284m. deficit after official transfers in 1991 and a $866m. deficit before and a $297m. deficit after official transfers in 1992. The total external debt at the end of 1991 was $6,715m., of which $6,060m. was long-term. About $435m. was short-term debt, mostly related to suppliers' credits. The cost of debt-servicing was equivalent to 16.5% of exports of goods and services in 1989, 10.9% in 1990, 24.6% in 1991 and 31.5% in 1992, according to World Bank figures. Debt rescheduling agreements were reached at meetings of the 'Paris Club' of Western official creditors held in September 1986, July 1987, March 1990 and July 1992. Under a debt conversion programme launched by the Bank of Tanzania (central bank) in 1990, foreign private creditors can convert their claims into equity or into cash to invest in certain sectors, on a basis which reduces the local costs involved in setting up in Tanzania. Reserves of foreign exchange declined to $1.2m. in mid-1981, enough for only two days' imports cover. They subsequently improved, and they represented 1.4 months' import cover, at $204m., at the end of 1991 and 2.1 months' import cover, at $327m., at the end of 1992.

After years of fruitless negotiations, Tanzania finally reached agreement with the IMF in 1986 for a $77m. stand-by facility over 18 months, and $24m. under the Fund's structural adjustment scheme. The IMF demanded the devaluation of the shilling to sh. 58.9 by June 1986. The actual official rate at mid-1986 was sh. 40 = US $1. Among other IMF conditions were abolition of the subsidy on the staple maize meal (sembe), a 'freeze' on the level of minimum wages, a reduction in the budget deficit to sh. 2,500m., the removal of price controls, and the raising of producer prices by at least 45% in real terms. Before the 1986 agreement was reached, the government had already introduced some far-reaching measures, and had proposed graduated moves towards fulfilling the IMF's conditions. It reduced the subsidy on maize meal (at the risk of causing urban unrest), dissolved some parastatal bodies, and reorganized or amalgamated others, cutting back their subsidies in order to force them into greater efficiency. The Tanzania Railways Corpn, for example, cut its workforce by 84% in 1993.

The negotiations with the IMF were closely linked with parallel talks with the World Bank, which subsequently agreed to lend US $50m. to support the government's Economic Recovery Programme (ERP), with a further $46.2m. from the Special Africa Facility. These agreements cleared the way for a World Bank-sponsored Consultative Group meeting on Tanzania held in Paris in June 1986, the first to be held since 1977. Donors strongly endorsed the recovery programme, which required $1,200m. to finance imports in 1986/87. At the meeting of the Consultative Group held in July 1987, Tanzania's main donors pledged a further $740m. for 1987/88. The IMF had also approved a structural adjustment facility (SAF) totalling nearly SDR 68m. to support the ERP. In February 1988 the World Bank approved a $56m. balance-of-payments support plan, also to back the ERP, with $30m. from the IDA and $26m. from the Bank's Special Africa Facility. The Consultative Group met again in Paris in July 1988. It expressed support for the ERP and about $800m. was pledged for 1988/89. In November 1988 the IMF released the second tranche of the three-year SAF, following agreement with the government on further devaluation of the shilling, restructuring of export crop and food marketing, reform of the tax system and continued reform of public enterprises. This agreement unblocked funds from other donors, and in December two IDA credits were approved, totalling about $143m., mostly for financing general imports and also for helping agricultural research. The EC unblocked about $39m. which had been 'frozen' pending finalization of the IMF agreement, and bilateral donors followed suit. The exchange rate of the shilling had dropped to sh. 110.39 = US $1. The 1989/90 budget devalued the shilling further, to sh. 145 = US $1. Tanzania was hoping to obtain an enhanced structural adjustment facility (ESAF) from the IMF to replace the third tranche of the SAF. However, the 1989/90 budget appeared not to have included sufficiently radical measures to satisfy the Fund, and in general, donors regarded the pace of reforms as too slow. A major devaluation of the shilling in December 1989, to sh. 190 = US $1, followed negotiations with the IMF in November, and unblocked the third and last tranche of the three-year SAF. It also opened the way for a new meeting of the Consultative Group in December, at which donors pledged $865m. towards the country's financing needs of $1,300m. for 1990.

New negotiations with the IMF were concluded in July 1991, after an interruption caused by the Gulf War, with agreement on a three-year ESAF to replace the SAF which had expired in October 1990. The outline agreement envisaged that more than US $100m. would be made available in each year, starting in 1991/92. The Consultative Group meeting held in Paris in June 1991 pledged up to $980m. in aid for 1991/92. The donors praised Tanzania's progress to date in implementing economic reforms, but asked for the programme to be accelerated. The Consultative Group pledged a further $990m. in aid for 1992/93 in June 1992 and an additional $1,200m. in aid for 1993/94 in July 1993. Of the 1993/94 aid, $360m. was in the form of balance-of-payments support. The exchange rate has undergone a series of minor adjustments since the end of 1989, and by June 1992 it had declined to sh. 297.68 = US $1. The parallel rate at this date was about sh. 425 = US $1, suggesting that the shilling was still considerably overvalued. By June 1993 the official rate had fallen to sh. 378.6 = US $1 and by July 1994 the rate was sh. 516 = US $1. In November 1992 the IMF approved a loan of SDR 64.2m. ($89m.), to support the second annual arrangement under the ESAF. A new investment code was approved by parliament in April 1990; this aimed to encourage both local and foreign investment in the economy. Measures to deregulate the banking sector are being introduced. The domestic banking business is to be reformed and made more competitive, and in early 1991 it was decided that foreign banks would be allowed to operate in Tanzania. The UK's Standard Chartered Bank obtained a Tanzanian banking licence in September 1992 and commenced operations in 1993. In the same year Meridien BIAO SA (Luxembourg) began operating a subsidiary, Meridien BIAO Bank Tanzania. From April 1991 a number of bureaux de change opened throughout the country. In June 1992 Switzerland extended a grant of $7.1m. towards these banking reforms, which are aimed at making the sector more attractive to foreign and local private-sector institutions.

PUBLIC FINANCE

The 1988/89 budget continued the government's cautious policies directed at economic recovery; measures included an increase in the minimum wage, salary increases for civil servants, a reduction in income tax, higher tuition fees for secondary education, and increases in taxes on cigarettes, beer, soft drinks and wine. The 1989/90 budget aimed to cut public expenditure, to bring annual inflation down from 28.2% to 20% by the end of the financial year, while placing a 20% ceiling on the growth of bank borrowing. Recurrent spending was to go up by 31% and the development budget was cut in absolute terms by 20%. New taxes were expected to raise sh. 3,000m. through increases in education fees, increases in various licence fees, income from six new road toll stations, increases of the duty on alcohol and cigarettes and a doubling of the airport tax. Minimum wages were raised by 26%. Nevertheless, inflation averaged 25.3% per annum during the period 1980–92, according to the World Bank. The 1990/91 budget aimed to alleviate the country's transport and communications problems. Increased revenue was to be derived from an increase in land rents, some licence fees and airport tax. The budget was not too austere, probably because elections were imminent; however, recurrent spending was to be restrained and the overall budget deficit was forecast at under 1% of GDP, therefore well within the IMF 5% limit. Recurrent spending estimates were up 27% in nominal terms, but only 2.6% in real terms; development expenditure was to increase by 94% in nominal terms and 57% in real terms, thanks to higher inflows of aid, which would fund 73% of development expenditure. Measures included the lowering of some income tax rates, a reduction in customs duty on some items and the abolition of road tolls. In April 1992 the statutory minimum wage was increased from sh. 2,500 per month to sh. 3,500 per month. Under the 1992/93 budget, the minimum wage was raised to sh. 5,000 per month, while total expenditure of sh. 353,605m. was envisaged, of which sh. 251,543m. was recurrent and sh. 102,062m. was for development. The 1994/95 budget envisaged total expenditure of sh. 514,284m. of which sh. 362,797m. was recurrent and sh. 151,487m. was for development. Measures announced included a broadening of the tax base, an increase in customs tariffs from 40% to 50% and further anti-inflationary controls. In July it was reported that the government had increased by 100%, from sh. 5,000 to sh. 10,000 (equivalent to US $21), the salaries of all its employees and of those working for parastatal companies.

CONCLUSION

There is no doubt that, under the Arusha Declaration policies, much was achieved in education and health, and in other social fields. In 1962 the ratio of the highest-paid salary to the lowest-paid salary was between 33:1 and 40:1. By 1980 the ratio of highest to lowest government salaries, after tax, was 6:1. Nevertheless, these achievements were clearly at the expense of the productive sectors, leading the economy into a situation which jeopardized the future of these facilities. From about 1979 Nyerere's socialist policies increasingly came under attack from aid donors and foreign investors, and—less overtly—from many Tanzanians as well.

Despite having the basic advantages of a wide range of agricultural commodities, of hydroelectric potential, and of three decades of post-independence peace Tanzania is at present trapped in a vicious circle which always comes back to the same point: the desperate lack of foreign exchange. Export crops are subject to violent fluctuations in world prices, and since the late 1980s the government has been striving, successfully, to increase non-traditional exports, both agricultural and industrial.

The succession of Ali Hassan Mwinyi as president of Tanzania in 1985 did not signal any definite alteration in economic policies, but has allowed a steady intensification of the liberalization process which was already in progress. In February 1986 the government announced a 'revised import-export policy' allowing exporters of non-traditional industrial products to retain up to 50% of the foreign exchange that they earn from a wide range of goods, and to use one-half of such earnings for importing any inputs or spare parts, while using the remaining half for importing certain goods for sale in the local market. The implication of these measures, together with others aimed at liberalizing internal and external trade, was significant enough to create optimism in Tanzania, not only in the private business sector but also among many frustrated officials who had been struggling to administer government departments and parastatal companies efficiently in a previously unhelpful environment. The agreements with the IMF, the World Bank and the country's donors further marked a new determination by the government to attempt measures aimed at economic revival.

A sweeping campaign against corruption, launched in 1991 by the minister of home affairs, Augustine Mrema, has proved extraordinarily effective, and has contributed to a climate of greater optimism. Despite the fact that many potential investors remain deterred by administrative delays and bureaucracy, as well as by Tanzania's poor physical infrastructure, the Investment Promotion Centre set up in July 1990 had approved 58 project proposals with total planned investment of some $100m., and had received 150 applications altogether, by the end of the year. Among the projects which have attracted investor interest are copper/nickel/cobalt mining, tourism development in Zanzibar, private-sector air services, mainland tourist hotels and shrimp fishing.

Signs that economic decline had been halted were already apparent by mid-1987. Two good harvests and the fall in world petroleum prices lessened the potentially alarming inflationary effects of the devaluation of the currency and of other measures introduced in successive budgets. Shortages of essential goods had become less severe and many services had improved. The government has continued to maintain the policies formulated in the ERP and approved by the IMF and other donors, albeit at a slower pace than the donors would prefer.

Since the late 1980s the rise in inflation has been tempered, government recurrent expenditure has been reduced, and non-traditional exports have expanded. Among major problems are the severe shortage of management and entrepreneurial skills, the lack of access to credit by private businesses, transport congestion and other infrastructural weaknesses and the weak purchasing power of the shilling. At best, economic recovery will be a very slow process, with many obstacles to overcome. Nevertheless, the reform process was firmly on course in the early 1990s, and forecasts for Tanzania's economic future were at last tinged with some optimism.

Statistical Survey

Source (unless otherwise stated): Bureau of Statistics, Dar es Salaam.

Area and Population

AREA, POPULATION AND DENSITY

Area (sq km)	945,087*
Population (census results)	
26 August 1978	
Males	8,587,086
Females	8,925,525
Total	17,512,611
28 August 1988	23,174,336
Population (official estimates at mid-year)	
1988	23,997,000
1989	24,802,000
1990	25,635,000†
Density (per sq km) at mid-1990	27.1

* 364,900 sq miles. Of this total, Tanzania mainland is 942,626 sq km (363,950 sq miles), and Zanzibar 2,461 sq km (950 sq miles).
† Tanzania mainland 24,972,000; Zanzibar 663,000.

ETHNIC GROUPS
(private households, census of 26 August 1967)

African	11,481,595	Others	839
Asian	75,015	Not stated	159,042
Arabs	29,775	**Total**	11,763,150
European	16,884		

REGIONS (population in 1978)

Arusha	926,223	Mtwara	771,819
Dar es Salaam	843,090	Mwanza	1,443,379
Dodoma	972,005	Pemba	205,305
Iringa	925,044	Pwani (Coast)	516,586
Kagera (Bukoba)	1,009,000*	Rukwa	451,897
Kigoma	684,941	Ruvuma	561,575
Kilimanjaro	902,437	Shinyanga	1,323,535
Lindi	527,624	Singida	613,949
Mara	723,827	Tabora	817,907
Mbeya	1,079,864	Tanga	1,037,767
Morogoro	939,264	Zanzibar	270,807

* Estimate.

PRINCIPAL TOWNS (estimated population at mid-1985)

Dar es Salaam	1,096,000	Tanga	172,000
Mwanza	252,000	Zanzibar	133,000
Tabora	214,000	Dodoma	85,000
Mbeya	194,000		

Source: UN, *Demographic Yearbook*.

BIRTHS AND DEATHS (UN estimates, annual averages)

	1975–80	1980–85	1985–90
Birth rate (per 1,000)	47.5	47.5	47.9
Death rate (per 1,000)	16.4	15.0	14.4

Expectation of life (UN estimates, years at birth, 1985–90): 51.8 (males 50.1; females 53.5).

Source: UN, *World Population Prospects: The 1992 Revision*.

ECONOMICALLY ACTIVE POPULATION (1967 census)

	Males	Females	Total
Agriculture, forestry, hunting and fishing	2,549,688	2,666,805	5,216,493
Mining and quarrying	4,918	99	5,017
Manufacturing	85,659	13,205	98,864
Construction	32,755	318	33,073
Electricity, gas, water and sanitary services	5,704	158	5,862
Commerce	71,088	7,716	78,804
Transport, storage and communications	46,121	711	46,832
Other services	169,693	38,803	208,496
Other activities (not adequately described)	35,574	18,081	53,655
Total labour force	3,001,200	2,745,896	5,747,096

1978 census: Total labour force 7,845,105 (males 3,809,135; females 4,035,970) aged 5 years and over.

Mid-1980 (ILO estimates, '000 persons): Agriculture etc. 8,140 (males 3,787, females 4,353); Industry 431 (males 353, females 78); Services 938 (males 630, females 308); Total 9,508 (males 4,769, females 4,739) (Source: ILO, *Economically Active Population Estimates and Projections, 1950–2025*).

Mid-1992 (estimates in '000): Agriculture, etc. 10,502; Total labour force 13,167 (Source: FAO, *Production Yearbook*).

Agriculture

PRINCIPAL CROPS ('000 metric tons)

	1990	1991	1992
Wheat	84	80	64
Rice (paddy)	736	625	392
Maize	2,445	2,332	2,226
Millet	200*	250	263†
Sorghum	368*	500	587†
Potatoes*	240	220	200
Sweet potatoes	996	291	257
Cassava (Manioc)	6,922	6,266	7,111
Yams*	10	10	9
Dry beans*	250	270	195
Dry peas*	22	24	16
Chick-peas*	22	24	16
Other pulses*	91	106	85
Groundnuts (in shell)*	60	65	65
Sunflower seed†	30	30	30
Sesame seed*	23	24	23
Cottonseed†	116	166	142
Coconuts*	365	366	365
Copra*	34	34	34
Palm kernels*	6.0	6.2	6.2
Onions (dry)*	51	52	50
Other vegetables*	1,048	1,059	1,046
Sugar cane*	1,320	1,420	1,410
Citrus fruits*	35	36	34
Mangoes*	186	187	185
Pineapples*	70	72	70
Bananas	823	750	794†
Plantains	823	750	794†
Other fruit	259	262	256
Cashew nuts	17.1	29.9	40.2†
Coffee (green)	53	46	56
Tea (made)	18	20	18*
Tobacco (leaves)	12	17	17
Sisal	34	36	35*
Cotton (lint)	60†	85†	73

* FAO estimate(s). † Unofficial figure(s).

Source: FAO, *Production Yearbook*.

LIVESTOCK ('000 head, year ending September)

	1990	1991	1992
Cattle	13,047	13,138	13,217*
Sheep	3,557	3,556	3,706*
Goats	8,526	8,814	9,073*
Pigs	320†	330*	330*
Asses†	174	175	176

* Unofficial figure. † FAO estimate(s).

Chickens (FAO estimates, million): 21 in 1990; 23 in 1991; 25 in 1992.

Ducks (FAO estimates, million): 1 in 1990; 1 in 1991; 1 in 1992.

Source: FAO, *Production Yearbook*.

LIVESTOCK PRODUCTS (FAO estimates, '000 metric tons)

	1990	1991	1992
Beef and veal	195	197	199
Mutton and lamb	10	10	10
Goats' meat	21	22	23
Pig meat	9	9	9
Poultry meat	26	28	31
Other meat	13	12	13
Cows' milk	459	463	460
Goats' milk	82	85	87
Butter	4.2	4.3	4.2
Hen eggs	42.0	45.1	50.1
Other poultry eggs	1.3	1.4	1.5
Honey	14.5	15.0	15.5
Cattle hides	39.7	40.0	40.5
Sheep skins	2.5	2.5	2.6
Goat skins	4.5	4.6	4.8

Source: FAO, *Production Yearbook*.

Forestry

ROUNDWOOD REMOVALS
(FAO estimates, '000 cubic metres, excluding bark)

	1990	1991	1992
Sawlogs, veneer logs and logs for sleepers*	317	317	317
Pulpwood†	145	145	145
Other industrial wood	1,509	1,554	1,599
Fuel wood	30,677	31,741	32,842
Total	34,276	35,545	34,903

* Assumed to be unchanged since 1987.
† Assumed to be unchanged since 1988.
Source: FAO, *Yearbook of Forest Products*.

SAWNWOOD PRODUCTION ('000 cubic metres)

	1985	1986	1987
Coniferous (soft wood)	53	76	85
Broadleaved (hard wood)	56	78	71
Total	109	154	156

1988–91: Annual production as in 1987 (FAO estimates).

Source: FAO, *Yearbook of Forest Products*.

Fishing

('000 metric tons, live weight)

	1989	1990	1991
Tilapias	37.3	37.0	40.0
Mouth-brooding cichlids	12.5	12.8	12.0
Naked catfishes	8.4	1.9	2.0
Torpedo-shaped catfishes	16.4	15.2	16.0
Other freshwater fishes (incl. unspecified)	49.4	69.1	65.0
Dagaas	38.7	42.1	40.0
Nile perch	164.8	179.3	170.0
Sardinellas	6.4	8.2	10.0
Other marine fishes (incl. unspecified)	40.7	45.9	42.7
Other marine animals	2.4	2.6	2.6
Total catch	377.1	414.0	400.3
Inland waters	327.5	357.3	345.0
Indian Ocean	49.6	56.7	55.3

Source: FAO, *Yearbook of Fishery Statistics*.

Mining

	1989	1990	1991
Diamonds ('000 carats)	150*	104*	117
Gold (kg)	116*	1,628*	3,851
Salt ('000 metric tons)	20	20	64

* Estimates from the US Bureau of Mines.
Source: UN, *Industrial Statistics Yearbook*.

Industry

SELECTED PRODUCTS
('000 metric tons, unless otherwise indicated)

	1989	1990	1991
Canned meat	34	26	12
Salted, dried or smoked fish (metric tons)*	65,000	65,000	n.a.
Raw sugar*	90	108	116
Beer ('000 hectolitres)	537	450	498
Soft drinks ('000 hectolitres)	520	934	669
Footwear—excl. rubber ('000 pairs)	445	459	328
Cigarettes (million)	2,845	3,742	3,870
Cement	595	300	1,022
Cotton woven fabrics (million sq metres)	46	46	38
Jet fuel	26	28	31
Motor spirit—petrol	80	85	95
Kerosene	38	37	37
Distillate fuel oils	151	150	162
Residual fuel oils	221	225	210
Electric energy (million kWh)	885	885	901

* Source: FAO.
Source: UN, *Industrial Statistics Yearbook*.

Finance

CURRENCY AND EXCHANGE RATES

Monetary Units
100 cents = 1 Tanzanian shilling.

Sterling and Dollar Equivalents (31 March 1994)
£1 sterling = 734.01 Tanzanian shillings;
US $1 = 494.4 Tanzanian shillings;
1,000 Tanzanian shillings = £1.362 = $2.023.

Average Exchange Rate (Tanzanian shillings per US $)
1991 219.16
1992 297.71
1993 405.27

BUDGET (million shillings, year ending 30 June)*

Revenue	1986/87	1987/88	1988/89†
Tax revenue	29,526	44,865	63,085
Personal tax	7,351	8,792	16,611
Sales tax	16,096	26,878	33,237
Import duties	4,067	6,483 }	8,478
Export duties	—	— }	
Other	2,012	2,712	4,759
Non-tax revenue	4,973	10,585	8,704
Parastatal dividends and interest and surplus transfers	957	790	n.a.
Import support	3,112	8,850	n.a.
Appropriation in aid	65	75	225
Other	839	870	n.a.
Total	34,499	55,450	71,789

Expenditure	1986/87	1987/88	1988/89†
Public administration	9,031	13,413	19,305
Foreign affairs	1,100	2,179	3,457
Defence and security	10,668	12,414	16,779
Education	3,191	3,990	6,338
Health	2,257	3,273	5,509
Community services	133	215	347
Economic services			
General administration and research	1,282	1,896	860
Agriculture, forestry, fishing and hunting	3,198	3,880	6,037
Mining, manufacturing and construction	1,410	1,803	2,368
Electricity and water	1,000	1,434	2,486
Roads and bridges	1,473	2,148	2,710
Transport and communications	1,211	1,378	2,464
Total (incl. others)	49,722	73,298	111,221

* Figures refer to the Tanzania Government, excluding the revenue and expenditure of the separate Zanzibar Government.

† Provisional figures.

Source: Government Printer, *Economic Survey 1990*.

1989/90 (million shillings): Revenue 97,867; Expenditure (excl. net lending) 140,870.
1990/91 (million shillings): Revenue 137,093; Expenditure (excl. net lending) 207,292.
1991/92 (million shillings): Revenue 173,566; Expenditure (excl. net lending) 261,049.

Source: IMF, *International Financial Statistics*.

CENTRAL BANK RESERVES
(Tanzania mainland, US $ million at 31 December)

	1991	1992	1993
Reserve position in IMF	—	13.7	13.7
Foreign exchange	203.9	313.6	189.6
Total	203.9	327.3	203.3

Source: IMF, *International Financial Statistics*.

MONEY SUPPLY
(Tanzania mainland, million shillings at 31 December)

	1990	1992	1993
Currency outside banks	58,111	95,450	122,470
Demand deposits at commercial banks	51,716	90,420	115,410
Total money	109,827	185,870	237,880

Figures for 1991 not available.
Source: Bank of Tanzania, Dar es Salaam and IMF, *International Financial Statistics*.

COST OF LIVING
(Consumer Price Index for Tanzania mainland; base: 1980 = 100)

	1987	1988	1989
Food	654.0	881.4	1,094.9
Fuel, light and water	657.5	739.1	979.5
Clothing	603.5	797.3	982.4
Rent	187.2	187.2	246.8
All items (incl. others)	642.9	843.4	1,061.4

1990: Food 1,209.4; All items 1,270.5.
1991: Food 1,481.7; All items 1,553.8.
1992: Food 1,798.1; All items 1,896.7.

Source: ILO, *Year Book of Labour Statistics*.

NATIONAL ACCOUNTS
(Tanzania mainland, million shillings at current prices)

National Income and Product

	1989	1990	1991
Compensation of employees	40,470	53,554	59,278
Operating surplus	281,078	332,801	499,521
Domestic factor incomes	321,548	386,355	558,799
Consumption of fixed capital	13,957	14,364	14,737
Gross domestic product (GDP) at factor cost	335,505	400,719	573,536
Indirect taxes	72,283	95,608	117,821
Less Subsidies	1,246	1,328	936
GDP in purchasers' values	406,542	494,999	690,421
Factor income received from abroad	550	495	495
Less Factor income paid abroad	29,593	40,981	42,180
Gross national product (GNP)	377,499	454,513	648,736
Less Consumption of fixed capital	13,957	14,364	14,737
National income in market prices	363,542	440,149	633,999
Other current transfers from abroad (net)	93,510	135,271	190,481
National disposable income	457,052	575,420	824,480

* Source: UN, *National Accounts Statistics*.

Expenditure on the Gross Domestic Product

	1990	1991	1992
Government final consumption expenditure	52,637	71,027	85,531
Private final consumption expenditure	394,530	596,099	684,359
Increase in stocks	18,022	36,996	37,402
Gross fixed capital formation	217,404	231,430	305,076
Total domestic expenditure	682,593	935,532	1,112,368
Exports of goods and services	103,457	112,466	170,170
Less Imports of goods and services	280,840	350,330	475,202
GDP in purchasers' values	505,210	697,688	807,336
GDP at constant 1985 prices	148,657	154,435	159,995

Source: IMF, *International Financial Statistics.*

Gross Domestic Product by Economic Activity (at factor cost)

	1989	1990	1991
Agriculture, hunting, forestry and fishing	207,059	233,804	358,693
Mining and quarrying	1,129	4,815	6,975
Manufacturing	15,197	18,301	20,680
Electricity, gas and water	4,842	7,438	8,395
Construction	9,720	12,650	14,416
Trade, restaurants and hotels	50,392	56,638	83,325
Transport, storage and communications	23,854	36,242	47,017
Finance, insurance, real estate and business services	19,187	24,123	28,757
Community, social and personal services	22,168	31,968	34,478
Sub-total	353,548	425,979	602,736
Less Imputed bank service charge	18,043	25,260	29,200
Total	335,505	400,719	573,536

Source: UN, *National Accounts Statistics.*

BALANCE OF PAYMENTS (US $ million)

	1988	1989	1990
Merchandise exports f.o.b.	386.5	415.1	407.8
Merchandise imports f.o.b.	-1,033.0	-1,070.1	-1,186.3
Trade balance	-646.5	-655.0	-778.5
Exports of services	117.4	119.5	135.8
Imports of services	-263.4	-246.6	-245.6
Other income received	3.2	3.8	4.3
Other income paid	-207.7	-232.6	-235.5
Private unrequited transfers (net)	231.9	182.4	164.5
Government unrequited transfers (net)	389.3	469.8	529.0
Current balance	-375.8	-358.8	-426.0
Capital (net)	33.9	21.7	126.5
Net errors and omissions	-42.5	-114.9	133.1
Overall balance	-384.4	-452.0	-166.3

Source: IMF, *International Financial Statistics.*

External Trade

PRINCIPAL COMMODITIES (million shillings)

Imports c.i.f.	1985	1986	1987
Consumer goods	1,623	2,176	3,211
Construction materials	924	1,952	3,504
Other intermediate goods	5,679	10,087	17,637
Transport equipment	5,364	10,640	26,874
Other industrial goods	2,676	5,025	10,676
Total	16,966*	29,880	61,902

* Including others.

Total Imports (million shillings): 80,828 in 1988; 176,357 in 1989; 265,964 in 1990; 335,934 in 1991; 449,480 in 1992; 446,713 in 1993. (Source: IMF, *International Financial Statistics.*)

Exports f.o.b.	1988	1989	1990
Coffee beans	8,482	11,452	16,074
Raw cotton	7,228	9,323	14,820
Diamonds	756	766	629
Sisal	376	501	638
Cloves	412	4,424	1,485
Cashew nuts	1,120	535	650
Tea	1,472	3,290	1,210
Tobacco	1,296	1,619	2,438
Total (incl. others)	33,946	53,387	79,055

Source: Government Printer, *Economic Survey 1990.*

PRINCIPAL TRADING PARTNERS (US $'000)

Imports	1986	1987	1988
Denmark	29,156	45,463	70,875
Germany, Federal Republic	89,883	121,209	176,491
Italy	56,433	90,596	116,363
Japan	97,403	109,639	187,517
Netherlands	33,282	49,436	75,905
Sweden	26,771	28,754	46,443
United Arab Emirates	46,386	44,171	51,971
United Kingdom	101,388	141,671	258,631
Total (incl. others)	838,493	975,823	1,495,215

Exports	1986	1987	1988
Finland	29,102	30,501	13,884
Germany, Federal Republic	83,441	39,211	47,788
India	15,672	22,577	21,573
Italy	16,825	10,832	16,305
Japan	15,143	11,509	15,498
Netherlands	24,116	24,621	19,661
Portugal	8,631	8,741	13,605
United Kingdom	42,593	31,240	34,183
Total (incl. others)	344,826	309,928	337,106

Source: UN, *International Trade Statistics Yearbook.*

Transport

RAILWAYS (estimated traffic)

	1989	1990	1991
Passenger-km (million)	3,630	3,690	3,740
Freight ton-km (million)	1,420	1,470	1,490

Source: UN Economic Commission for Africa, *African Statistical Yearbook.*

ROAD TRAFFIC (estimates, '000 motor vehicles in use)

	1989	1990	1991
Passenger cars	51	52	53
Commercial vehicles	33	34	34

Source: UN Economic Commission for Africa, *African Statistical Yearbook.*

INTERNATIONAL SEA-BORNE SHIPPING
(estimated freight traffic, '000 metric tons)

	1988	1989	1990
Goods loaded	1,208	1,197	1,249
Goods unloaded	3,140	3,077	2,721

Source: Government Printer, *Economic Survey 1990.*

CIVIL AVIATION (traffic on scheduled services)

	1989	1990	1991
Kilometres flown (million)	4	4	5
Passengers carried ('000)	267	292	290
Passenger-km (million)	184	215	284
Freight ton-km (million)	2	1	4

Source: UN, *Statistical Yearbook.*

Tourism

	1988	1989	1990
Tourist arrivals ('000)	130	138	153
Tourist receipts (US $ million)	40	60	65

Source: UN, *Statistical Yearbook.*

Communications Media

	1989	1990	1991
Radio receivers ('000 in use)*	565	650	660
Television receivers ('000 in use)*	25	40	42
Telephones ('000 in use)	137	140	n.a.
Daily newspapers:			
Number	n.a.	3	n.a.
Average circulation ('000 copies)*	n.a.	200	n.a.

* Estimates.

Sources: UNESCO, *Statistical Yearbook*; Government Printer, *Economic Survey 1990.*

Education

(1991, unless otherwise indicated)

	Teachers	Pupils
Primary*	98,174	3,512,347
General secondary	8,649	166,812
Teacher training colleges	1,255	16,297
Higher†		
Universities	939	3,327
Other institutions	267	1,927

* Excluding Zanzibar. † 1989 figures.

Source: UNESCO, *Statistical Yearbook.*

Directory

The Constitution

The United Republic of Tanzania was established on 26 April 1964, when Tanganyika and Zanzibar, hitherto separate independent countries, merged. An interim Constitution of 1965 was replaced, on 25 April 1977, by a permanent Constitution for the United Republic. In October 1979 the Revolutionary Council of Zanzibar adopted a separate Constitution, governing Zanzibar's internal administration, with provisions for a popularly-elected President and a House of Representatives elected by delegates of the then ruling party. A new Constitution for Zanzibar, which came into force in January 1985, provided for direct elections to the Zanzibar Parliament, the House of Representatives. The provisions below relate to the 1977 Constitution of the United Republic, as subsequently amended.

GOVERNMENT

Legislative power is exercised by the Parliament of the United Republic, which is vested by the Constitution with complete sovereign power, and of which the present National Assembly is the legislative house. The Assembly also enacts all legislation concerning the mainland. Internal matters in Zanzibar are the exclusive jurisdiction of the Zanzibar executive, the Supreme Revolutionary Council of Zanzibar, and the Zanzibar legislature, the House of Representatives.

Note: It was envisaged that a constitutional amendment providing for a separate government and legislature for Tanganyika would be enacted before April 1995.

National Assembly

The National Assembly comprises both directly-elected members (chosen by universal suffrage) and nominated members (including five members elected from the Zanzibar House of Representatives). The number of directly-elected members exceeds the number of nominated members. The Electoral Commission may review and, if necessary, increase the number of electoral constituencies before every general election. The National Assembly has a term of five years.

President

The President is the Head of State, Head of the Government and Commander-in-Chief of the Armed Forces. The President has no power to legislate without recourse to Parliament. The assent of the President is required before any bill passed by the National Assembly becomes law. Should the President withhold his assent and the bill be repassed by the National Assembly by a two-thirds majority, the President is required by law to give his assent within 21 days unless, before that time, he has dissolved the National Assembly, in which case he must stand for re-election.

To assist him in carrying out his functions, the President appoints two Vice-Presidents from the elected members of the National Assembly. If the President comes from the mainland, the First Vice-President must come from Zanzibar, and vice versa. One of the Vice-Presidents is President of Zanzibar and the other is Prime Minister of the Union, who leads government business in the Assembly. The Vice-Presidents and ministers comprise the Cabinet, which is presided over by the President of the Republic. Ministers must be appointed from among the members of the National Assembly.

JUDICIARY

The independence of the judges is secured by provisions which prevent their removal, except on account of misbehaviour or incapacity when they may be dismissed at the discretion of the

President. The Constitution also makes provision for a Permanent Commission of Enquiry which has wide powers to investigate any abuses of authority.

CONSTITUTIONAL AMENDMENTS

The Constitution can be amended by an act of the Parliament of the United Republic, when the proposed amendment is supported by the votes of not fewer than two-thirds of all the members of the Assembly.

The Government

HEAD OF STATE

President: ALI HASSAN MWINYI (took office 5 November 1985; re-elected for second term 8 November 1990).

First Vice-President: JOHN SAMUEL MALECELA.

Second Vice-President and President of Zanzibar: Dr SALMIN AMOUR.

CABINET
(September 1994)

President and Commander-in-Chief of the Armed Forces, and Minister of Defence and National Service: ALI HASSAN MWINYI.

Prime Minister: JOHN SAMUEL MALECELA.

Deputy Prime Minister and Minister of Home Affairs: AUGUSTINE LYATONGA MREMA.

Minister of Finance: Prof. KIGHOMA ALI MALIMA.

Minister of Foreign Affairs: JOSEPH CLEMENCE RWEGASIRA.

Minister of Agriculture, Livestock Development and Co-operatives: JACKSON MAKWETA.

Minister of Labour and Youth Development: AHMED HASSAN DIRIA.

Minister of Industry and Trade: CLEOPA DAVID MSUYA.

Minister of Energy, Minerals and Water: JAKAYA KIKWETE.

Minister of Education and Culture: Prof. PHILOMEN SARUNGI.

Minister of Health: AMRAN MAYAGILA.

Minister of Lands, Housing and Urban Development: EDWARD LOWASA.

Minister of Information and Broadcasting: Dr WILLIAM SHIJA.

Minister of Works, Communications and Transport: NALAILA KIULA.

Minister of Tourism, Natural Resources and Environment: JUMA HAMAD UMAR.

Minister of Science, Technology and Higher Education: BENJAMIN MKAPA.

Minister of Community Development, Women and Children: ANNA MAKINDA.

Minister of Legal and Constitutional Affairs: SAMUEL SITTA.

Minister without Portfolio: KIGUNGE NGOMBALE-MWIRU.

MINISTRIES

All Dar es Salaam Ministries are to be transferred to Dodoma by 2005.

Office of the President: The State House, POB 9120, Dar es Salaam; tel. (51) 23261; telex 41192.

Office of the Prime Minister and First Vice-President: POB 980, Dodoma; tel. (61) 20511; telex 53159.

Office of the Second Vice-President and President of Zanzibar: POB 776, Zanzibar; tel. (54) 20511.

Ministry of Agriculture, Livestock Development and Co-operatives: POB 9192, Dar es Salaam; tel. (51) 27231.

Ministry of Community Development, Women and Children: Dar es Salaam.

Ministry of Defence and National Service: POB 9544, Dar es Salaam; tel. (51) 28291.

Ministry of Education and Culture: POB 9121, Dar es Salaam; tel. (51) 27211; telex 41742.

Ministry of Energy, Minerals and Water: POB 9153, Dar es Salaam; tel. (51) 31433.

Ministry of Finance: POB 9111, Dar es Salaam; tel. (51) 21271; telex 41329.

Ministry of Foreign Affairs: POB 9000, Dar es Salaam; tel. (51) 21234; telex 41086.

Ministry of Health: POB 9083, Dar es Salaam; tel. (51) 20261.

Ministry of Home Affairs: POB 9223, Dar es Salaam; tel. (51) 27291; telex 41231.

Ministry of Industry and Trade: POB 9503, Dar es Salaam; tel. (51) 27251.

Ministry of Information and Broadcasting: Dar es Salaam.

Ministry of Labour and Youth Development: POB 2483, Dar es Salaam; tel. (51) 20781.

Ministry of Lands, Housing and Urban Development: POB 9372, Dar es Salaam; tel. (51) 27271.

Ministry of Legal and Constitutional Affairs: Dar es Salaam.

Ministry of Science, Technology and Higher Education: Dar es Salaam.

Ministry of Tourism, Natural Resources and Environment: Dar es Salaam.

Ministry of Works, Communications and Transport: POB 9423, Dar es Salaam; tel. (51) 23235; telex 41392.

SUPREME REVOLUTIONARY COUNCIL OF ZANZIBAR
(September 1994)

President and Chairman: Dr SALMIN AMOUR.

Chief Minister: OMAR ALI JUMA.

Minister of Finance, Economic Affairs and Planning: AMINA SALIM ALI.

Minister of Agriculture, Natural Resources and Livestock: SEIF RASHID SEIF.

Minister of Trade, Industry and Marketing: AMAN ABEID KARUME.

Minister of Water, Works and Energy: ISA MUHAMMAD ISA.

Minister of Communications and Transport: RUFINA JUMA MBARUK.

Minister of Education: OMAR RAMADHAN MAPURI.

Minister of Health: ALI MUHAMMAD SHOKA.

Minister of Information, Culture, Tourism and Youth: SA'ID BAKARI JECHA.

Legistature

NATIONAL ASSEMBLY

At the National Assembly elections held on 28 October 1990 there were 216 elective seats. Of the total of 291 seats, the remainder were distributed as follows: 15 for women, 15 for representatives of the mass organizations of the Chama Cha Mapinduzi (CCM—R Revolutionary Party of Tanzania, the sole legal party until 1992), 15 for the President's nominees, 25 for Regional Commissioners, and five for members elected by the ZanibarR House of Representatives. The Constitution provides for the creation of new constituencies as necessary. The next general election to the National Assembly was scheduled to take place in 1995.

Note: In August 1993 the National Assembly adopted a motion that proposed the creation of a separate parliament for the mainland.

Speaker: Chief ADAM SAPI MKWAWA.

ZANZIBAR HOUSE OF REPRESENTATIVES

Under the provisions of the Constitution for Zanzibar, introduced in January 1985, the Zanzibar House of Representatives comprises 50 elected members, five regional commissioners, 10 presidential nominees and 10 members representing organizations affiliated to the CCM and women. The most recent general election was held on 21 October 1990.

Speaker: ALI HAMISI ABDALLAH.

Political Organizations

Tanzania operated as a one-party state between 1965–92, when the Constitution was amended to legalize a multi-party political system. By mid-1994 11 parties had obtained official registration.

Bismillah Party: Pemba; seeks a referendum on the terms of the 1964 union of Zanzibar with mainland Tanzania.

Chama Cha Demokrasia na Maendeleo (Chadema—Party for Democracy and Progress): Plot No. 922/7, Block 186005, Kisutu St, POB 5330, Dar es Salaam; regd 1993; supports democracy and social development; Chair. EDWIN I. M. MTEI; Sec.-Gen. BOB NYANGA MAKANI.

Chama Cha Mapinduzi (CCM—Revolutionary Party): Kuu St, POB 50, Dodoma; tel. (61) 2282; telex 53175; f. 1977 by merger of the mainland-based Tanganyika African National Union (TANU) with the Afro-Shirazi Party, which operated on Zanzibar and Pemba; sole legal party 1977–92; socialist orientation; Chair. ALI HASSAN MWINYI; Sec.-Gen. HORACE KOLIMBA.

Civic United Front/Chama Cha Wananchi (CUF/CCW): Mtendeni St, Urban District, POB 3637, Zanzibar; f. 1992; Chair. JAMES K. MAPALALA; Sec.-Gen. SHAABAN KHABIS MLOO.

Democratic Party (DP): Dar es Salaam; unregistered; Leader Rev. CHRISTOPHER MTIKILA.

Movement for Democratic Alternative (MDA): Zanzibar; unregistered; seeks to review the terms of the 1964 union of Zanzibar with mainland Tanzania; supports democratic reform and political plurality and advocates the abolition of detention without trial and the removal of press censorship.

National Convention for Construction and Reform (NCCR—Mageuzi): Plot No. 48, Mchikichi St, Kariakoo Area, POB 5316, Dar es Salaam; f. 1992, regd 1993; Chair. MABERE MARANDO; Sec.-Gen. MAHINJA BAGENDA.

National League for Democracy (NLD): Sinza D/73, POB 352, Dar es Salaam; regd 1993; Chair. EMMANUEL J. E. MAKAIDI; Sec.-Gen. MICHAEL E. A. MHINA.

National Reconstruction Alliance (NRA): House No. 4, Mvita St, Jangwani Ward, POB 16542, Dar es Salaam; regd 1993; Chair. ULOTU ABUBAKAR ULOTU; Sec.-Gen. SALIM R. MATINGA.

Popular National Party (PONA): Plot 104, Songea St, Ilala, POB 21561, Dar es Salaam; regd 1993; Chair. WILFREM R. MWAKITWANGE; Sec.-Gen. PETER K. TERRY.

Pragmatic Democratic Alliance: unregistered; Leader MUNUO MUGHUNI.

Republic Party: f. 1992; Chair. N. N. MOE.

Tanzania Democratic Alliance Party (TADEA): Block 3, Plot No. 37, Buguruni Malapa, POB 63133, Dar es Salaam; regd 1993; Pres. FLORA M. KAMOONA; Sec.-Gen. JOHN D. LIFA-CHIPAKA.

Tanzania People's Party (TPP): Mbezi Juu, Kawe, POB 60847, Dar es Salaam; regd 1993; Chair. ALEC H. CHE-MPONDA; Sec.-Gen. L. LUKWEMBE.

United People's Democratic Party (UPDP): Al Aziza Restaurant, Kokoni St, Narrow St, POB 3903, Zanzibar; regd 1993; Chair. KHALFANI ALI ABDULLAH; Sec.-Gen. AHMED M. RASHID.

Union for Multi-Party Democracy of Tanzania (UMD): 77 Tosheka St, Magomeni Mapiga, POB 41093, Dar es Salaam; regd 1993; Chair. Chief ABDALLA SAID FUNDIKIRA.

Diplomatic Representation

EMBASSIES AND HIGH COMMISSIONS IN TANZANIA

Albania: 93 Msese Rd, POB 1034, Kinondoni, Dar es Salaam; telex 41280; Ambassador: MEHDI SHAQIRI.

Algeria: 34 Upanga Rd, POB 2963, Dar es Salaam; telex 41104; Ambassador: (vacant).

Angola: POB 20793, Dar es Salaam; telex 41251; Ambassador: EUSEBIO SEBASTIÃO.

Belgium: NIC Investment House, 7th Floor, Samora Machel Ave, POB 9210, Dar es Salaam; (51) tel. 46047; telex 41094; (51) fax 20604; Ambassador: Count M. GOBLET D'ALVIELLA.

Brazil: IPS Bldg, 9th Floor, POB 9654, Dar es Salaam; tel. (51) 21780; telex 41228; Ambassador: JOSÉ FERREIRA LOPES.

Burundi: Plot No. 10007, Lugalo Rd, POB 2752, Upanga, Dar es Salaam; tel. (51) 38608; telex 41340; Ambassador: EDOUARD KADIGIRI.

Canada: 38 Mirambo St, POB 1022, Dar es Salaam; telex 41015; fax (51) 46005; High Commissioner: PATRICIA MARSDEN-DOLE.

China, People's Republic: 2 Kajificheni Close at Toure Drive, POB 1649, Dar es Salaam; telex 41036; Ambassador: SUN GUOTANG.

Cuba: Plot No. 313, Lugalo Rd, POB 9282, Upanga, Dar es Salaam; telex 41245; Ambassador: A. ROLANDO GALLARDO FERNÁNDEZ.

Denmark: Ghana Ave, POB 9171, Dar es Salaam; tel. (51) 46319; telex 41057; fax (51) 46312; Ambassador: FLEMMING BJØRK PEDERSEN.

Egypt: 24 Garden Ave, POB 1668, Dar es Salaam; tel. (51) 23372; telex 41173; Ambassador: BAHER M. EL-SADEK.

Finland: NIC Investment House, Samora Machel Ave, POB 2455, Dar es Salaam; tel. (51) 46324; telex 41066; fax (51) 46328; Ambassador: ILARI RANTAKARI.

France: Bagamoyo Rd, POB 2349, Dar es Salaam; tel. (51) 34961; telex 41006; Ambassador: BERNARD LODIOT.

Germany: NIC Investment House, Samora Ave, POB 9541, Dar es Salaam; tel. (51) 46334; telex 41003; fax (51) 46292; Ambassador: HEINZ SCHNEPPEN.

Guinea: 35 Haile Selassie Rd, POB 2969, Oyster Bay, Dar es Salaam; tel. (51) 68626; Ambassador: M. BANGOURA.

Holy See: Msasani Peninsula, POB 480, Dar es Salaam (Apostolic Nunciature); tel. (51) 68403; fax (51) 40193; Apostolic Pro-Nuncio: Most Rev. FRANCISCO-JAVIER LOZANO, Titular Archbishop of Penafiel.

Hungary: 40 Bagamoyo Rd, POB 672, Dar es Salaam; tel. (51) 34762; telex 41428; Ambassador: JÁNOS ZEGNAL.

India: NIC Investment House, Samora Ave, POB 2684, Dar es Salaam; tel. (51) 28197; telex 41335; fax (51) 46747; High Commissioner: OM PRAKASH GUPTA.

Indonesia: 229 Upanga Rd, POB 572, Dar es Salaam; telex 41575; Ambassador: HIDAYAT SOEMO.

Iran: Plot 685, Masengo Rd, POB 3802, West Upanga, Dar es Salaam; tel. (51) 34622; Ambassador: ABDUL ALI TAVAKKOLI.

Iraq: 355 United Nations Rd, POB 5289, Dar es Salaam; tel. (51) 25728; telex 41193; Ambassador: FAWZ ALI AL-BANDER.

Italy: Plot 316, Lugalo Rd, POB 2106, Dar es Salaam; tel. (51) 46353; telex 41062; fax (51) 46354; Ambassador: TORQUATO CARDILLI.

Japan: 1018 Upanga Road, POB 2577, Dar es Salaam; tel. (51) 31215; telex 41065; Ambassador: SHOICHI NAKAMURA.

Kenya: NIC Investment House, Samora Machel Ave, POB 5231, Dar es Salaam; tel. (51) 31502; telex 41700; High Commissioner: DICKSON I. KATHAMBANA.

Korea, Democratic People's Republic: Plot 460B, United Nations Rd, POB 2690, Dar es Salaam; Ambassador: CHANG WON OK.

Madagascar: Magoret St, POB 5254, Dar es Salaam; tel. (51) 41761; telex 41291; Chargé d'affaires: RAHDRAY DESIRÉ.

Malawi: IPS Bldg, POB 23168, Dar es Salaam; tel. (51) 37260; telex 41633; High Commissioner: L. B. MALUNGA.

Mozambique: Dar es Salaam; telex 41214; Ambassador: ANTÓNIO C. F. SUMBANA.

Netherlands: New ATC Town Terminal Bldg, cnr Ohio St and Garden Ave, POB 9534, Dar es Salaam; tel. (51) 46391; telex 41050; fax (51) 46189; Ambassador: J. J. WIJENBERG.

Nigeria: 3 Bagamoyo Rd, POB 9214, Oyster Bay, Dar es Salaam; telex 41240; High Commissioner: SOLOMON A. YISA.

Norway: Plot 160, Mirambo St, POB 2646, Dar es Salaam; tel. (51) 25195; telex 41221; fax (51) 46444; Ambassador: ARILD EIK.

Poland: 63 Alykhan Rd, POB 2188, Dar es Salaam; tel. (51) 46294; telex 41022; Chargé d'affaires: KAZIMIERZ TOMASZEWSKI.

Romania: Plot 11, Ocean Rd, POB 590, Dar es Salaam; Ambassador: (vacant).

Russia: Plot No. 73, Kenyatta Drive, POB 1905, Dar es Salaam; tel. (51) 66006; telex 41747; fax (51) 66818; Ambassador: Dr KENESH N. KULMATOV.

Rwanda: Plot 32, Upanga Rd, POB 2918, Dar es Salaam; tel. (51) 30119; telex 41292; Ambassador: FRANÇOIS BARARWEREKANA.

Spain: 99B Kinondoni Rd, POB 842, Dar es Salaam; tel. (51) 66936; telex 41589; Ambassador: (vacant).

Sudan: 'Albaraka', 64 Upanga Rd, POB 2266, Dar es Salaam; telex 41143; Ambassador: CHARLES DE WOL.

Sweden: Extelcoms Bldg, 2nd Floor, Samora Machel Ave, POB 9274, Dar es Salaam; tel. (51) 23501; telex 41013; Ambassador: PER JÖDAHL.

Switzerland: 17 Kenyatta Drive, POB 2454, Dar es Salaam; tel. (51) 66008; telex 41322; fax (51) 66736; Ambassador: JÖRG L. KAUFMANN.

Syria: POB 2442, Dar es Salaam; tel. (51) 20568; telex 41339; Chargé d'affaires: KANAAN HADID.

United Kingdom: Hifadhi House, Samora Machel Ave, POB 9200, Dar es Salaam; tel. (51) 29601; telex 41004; fax (51) 46301; High Commissioner: ROGER WESTBROOK.

USA: Laibon Rd, POB 9123, Dar es Salaam; tel. (51) 66010; telex 41250; fax (51) 66701; Ambassador: BRADY ANDERSON (designate).

Viet Nam: 9 Ocean Rd, Dar es Salaam; Ambassador: TRAN MY.

Yemen: 353 United Nations Rd, POB 349, Dar es Salaam; tel. (51) 27891; Ambassador: ABUBAKER SAEED BA-ABBAD.

Yugoslavia: Plot 35/36, Upanga Rd, POB 2838, Dar es Salaam; tel. (51) 46377; telex 41749; Ambassador: (vacant).

Zaire: 438 Malik Rd, POB 975, Upanga, Dar es Salaam; telex 41407; Ambassador: PELENDO B. MAWE.

Zambia: Ohio St/City Drive Junction, POB 2525, Dar es Salaam; telex 41023; High Commissioner: JOHN KASHONKA CHITAFU.

Zimbabwe: POB 20762, Dar es Salaam; tel. (51) 30455; telex 41386; High Commissioner: J. M. SHAVA.

Judicial System

The Tanzanian Court of Appeal was established in September 1979 in succession to the former Court of Appeal for East Africa, which heard civil and criminal appeals from Kenya, Uganda and Tanzania.

People's Courts were established in Zanzibar in 1970. Magistrates are elected by the people and have two assistants each. Under the Zanzibar Constitution, which came into force in January 1985, defence lawyers and the right of appeal, abolished in 1970, were reintroduced.

Permanent Commission of Enquiry: POB 2643, Dar es Salaam; Chair. and Official Ombudsman A. L. S. MHINA; Sec. F. P. S. MALIKA.

Court of Appeal: Consists of the Chief Justice and four Judges of Appeal.

Chief Justice of Tanzania: FRANCIS NYALALI.

Chief Justice of Zanzibar: HAMID MAHMOUD HAMID.

High Court: Its headquarters are at Dar es Salaam but it holds regular sessions in all Regions. It consists of a Jaji Kiongozi and 29 Judges.

Jaji Kiongozi: BARNABAS SAMATTA.

District Courts: These are situated in each district and are presided over by either a Resident Magistrate or District Magistrate. They have limited jurisdiction and there is a right of appeal to the High Court.

Primary Courts: These are established in every district and are presided over by Primary Court Magistrates. They have limited jurisdiction and there is a right of appeal to the District Courts and then to the High Court.

Attorney-General: ANDREW CHENGE.

Director of Public Prosecutions: KULWA MASSABA.

Religion

ISLAM

Islam is the religion of more than 97% of the population in Zanzibar and of about one-third of the mainland population. A large proportion of the Asian community is Isma'ili.

Ismalia Provincial Church: POB 460, Dar es Salaam.

National Muslim Council of Tanzania: POB 21422, Dar es Salaam; tel. (51) 34934; f. 1969; supervises Islamic affairs on the mainland only; Chair. Sheikh HEMED BIN JUMA BIN HEMED; Exec. Sec. Alhaj MUHAMMAD MTULIA.

Supreme Muslim Council: Zanzibar; f. 1991; supervises Islamic affairs in Zanzibar.

Wakf and Trust Commission: POB 4092, Zanzibar; tel. (51) 30853; f. 1980; Islamic affairs; Exec. Sec. YUSUF ABDULRAHMAN MUHAMMAD.

CHRISTIANITY

In 1993 it was estimated that about one-half of the mainland population professed the Christian faith.

Jumuiya ya Kikristo Tanzania (Christian Council of Tanzania): Church House, POB 1454, Dodoma; tel. (61) 21204; fax (61) 24445; f. 1934; Chair. (acting) Most Rev. JOHN ACLAND RAMADHANI (Archbishop of the Anglican Church); Gen. Sec. ANGETILE YESAYA MUSOMBA.

The Anglican Communion

Anglicans are adherents of the Church of the Province of Tanzania, comprising 16 dioceses. There were an estimated 647,000 members in 1985.

Archbishop of the Province of Tanzania and Bishop of Zanzibar and Tanga: Most Rev. JOHN RAMADHANI, POB 35, Korogwe.

Provincial Secretary: Rev. MKUNGA MTINGELE, POB 899, Dodoma; tel. (61) 21437; fax (61) 24265.

Greek Orthodox

Archbishop of East Africa: NICADEMUS of IRINOUPOULIS (resident in Nairobi, Kenya); jurisdiction covers Kenya, Uganda and Tanzania.

Lutheran

Evangelical Lutheran Church in Tanzania: POB 3033, Arusha; tel. (57) 8855; telex 42054; 1.5m. mems; Presiding Bishop Rt Rev. Dr SAMSON MUSHEMBA (acting); Exec. Sec. AMANI MWENEGOHA.

The Roman Catholic Church

Tanzania comprises four archdioceses and 25 dioceses. There were an estimated 6,081,056 adherents at 31 December 1992.

Tanzania Episcopal Conference: Catholic Secretariat, Mansfield St, POB 2133, Dar es Salaam; tel. (51) 50309; telex 41989; f. 1980; Pres. Rt Rev. LOUIS JOSAPHAT LEBULU, Bishop of Same.

Archbishop of Dar es Salaam: Most Rev. POLYCARP PENGO, Archbishop's House, POB 167, Dar es Salaam; tel. (51) 22031.

Archbishop of Mwanza: Most Rev. ANTHONY MAYALA, Archbishop's House, POB 1421, Mwanza; tel. and fax (68) 41616.

Archbishop of Songea: Most Rev. NORBERT WENDELIN MTEGA, Archbishop's House, POB 152, Songea; tel. (635) 2004; telex 40036.

Archbishop of Tabora: Most Rev. MARIO EPIFANIO ABDALLAH MGULUNDE, Archbishop's House, Private Bag, PO Tabora; tel. (62) 2329; telex 47306; fax (62) 2004.

Other Christian Churches

Baptist Mission of Tanzania: POB 9414, Dar es Salaam; tel. (51) 32298; telex 41014; f. 1956; Administrator BOYD PEARCE.

Christian Missions in Many Lands (Tanzania): German Branch; POB 34, Tunduru, Ruvuma Region; f. 1957; Gen. Sec. KLAUS BRINKMANN.

Moravian Church: POB 377, Mbeya; 113,656 mems; Gen. Sec. Rev. SHADRACK MWAKASEGE.

Pentecostal Church: POB 34, Kahama.

Presbyterian Church: POB 2510, Dar es Salaam; tel. (51) 29075.

BAHÁ'Í FAITH

National Spiritual Assembly: POB 585, Dar es Salaam; tel. (51) 21173; mems resident in 2,301 localities.

OTHER RELIGIONS

There are some Hindu communities and followers of traditional beliefs.

The Press

NEWSPAPERS

Daily

Daily News: POB 9033, Dar es Salaam; tel. (51) 25318; telex 41071; f. 1972; govt-owned; publ. by Tanzania Standard (Newspapers) Ltd; Man. Editor CHARLES RAJABU; circ. 50,000.

Kipanga: POB 199, Zanzibar; Swahili; publ. by Information and Broadcasting Services.

Uhuru: POB 9221, Dar es Salaam; tel. (51) 64341; telex 41239; f. 1961; official publ. of CCM; Swahili; Man. Editor YAHYA BUZARAGI; circ. 100,000.

Weekly

Business Times: POB 71439, Dar es Salaam; weekly, independent; English; Editor F. RUHINDA; circ. 15,000.

The Express: POB 20588, Dar es Salaam; tel. (51) 25318; telex 41071; independent; English; Editor PASCAL SHIJA; circ. 20,000.

Mzalendo: POB 9221, Dar es Salaam; tel. (51) 64341; telex 41239; f. 1972; publ. by CCM; Swahili; Man. Editor YAHYA BUZARAGI; circ. 115,000.

Sunday News: POB 9033, Dar es Salaam; tel. (51) 29881; telex 41071; f. 1954; govt-owned; Man. Editor CHARLES RAJABU; circ. 60,000.

PERIODICALS

The African Review: POB 35042, Dar es Salaam; tel. (51) 49192; 2 a year; journal of African politics, development and international affairs; publ. by the Dept of Political Science, Univ. of Dar es Salaam; Chief Editor Prof. I. K. BAVU; circ. 1,000.

Eastern African Law Review: POB 35093, Dar es Salaam; tel. (51) 48336; f. 1967; 2 a year; Chief Editor Dr N. N. N. NDITI; circ. 1,000.

Elimu Haina Mwisho: POB 1986, Mwanza; monthly; circ. 45,000.

Gazette of the United Republic: POB 9142, Dar es Salaam; tel. (51) 31817; telex 41419; weekly; official announcements; Editor H. HAJI; circ. 6,000.

Government Gazette: POB 261, Zanzibar; f. 1964; official announcements; weekly.

Habari za Washirika: POB 2567, Dar es Salaam; tel. (51) 23346; telex 41809; monthly; publ. by Co-operative Union of Tanzania; Editor H. V. N. CHIBULUNJE; circ. 40,000.

Jenga: POB 2669, Dar es Salaam; tel. (51) 44419; telex 41068; fax (51) 44419; journal of the National Development Corpn; circ. 2,000.

Kiongozi (The Leader): POB 9400, Dar es Salaam; tel. (51) 29505; f. 1950; fortnightly; Swahili; Roman Catholic; Editor ROBERT MFUGALE; circ. 33,500.

Kweupe: POB 222, Zanzibar; weekly; Swahili; publ. by Information and Broadcasting Services.

Mbioni: POB 9193, Dar es Salaam; English; publ. monthly by the political education college, Kivukoni College; circ. 4,000.

Mfanyakazi (The Worker): POB 15359, Dar es Salaam; tel. (51) 26111; telex 41205; weekly; Swahili; trade union publ.; Editor HAMIDU NZOWA; circ. 100,000.

Mlezi (The Educator): POB 41, Peramiho; tel. 30; f. 1970; every 2 months; Editor Fr GEROLD RUPPER; circ. 19,200.

Mwenge (Firebrand): POB 1, Peramiho; tel. 30; f. 1937; monthly; Editor BALTASAR CHALE; circ. 33,000.

Nchi Yetu (Our Country): POB 9142, Dar es Salaam; tel. (51) 25375; telex 41419; f. 1964; govt publ.; monthly; Swahili; circ. 50,000.

Nuru: POB 1893, Zanzibar; tel. (54) 32353; fax (54) 33457; f. 1992; bi-monthly; official publ. of Zanzibari authorities; circ. 8,000.

Safina: POB 21422, Dar es Salaam; tel. (51) 34934; publ. by National Muslim Council of Tanzania; Editor YASSIN SADIK; circ. 10,000.

Sauti Ya Jimbo: POB 899, Dodoma; tel. (61) 21437; fax (61) 24265; quarterly; Swahili; Anglican diocesan, provincial and world church news.

Sikiliza: POB 635, Morogoro; tel. (56) 3338; fax (56) 4374; quarterly; Seventh-day Adventist; Editor G. H. MBWANA; circ. 100,000.

Taamuli: POB 35042, Dar es Salaam; tel. (51) 43501; 2 a year; journal of political science; publ. by the Dept of Political Science, Univ. of Dar es Salaam; circ. 1,000.

Tanzania Education Journal: POB 9211, Dar es Salaam; f. 1984; publ. by Institute of Education, Ministry of Education and Culture; three times a year; circ. 8,000.

Tanzania Trade Currents: POB 5402, Dar es Salaam; tel. (51) 36303; telex 41408; fax (51) 36303; bimonthly; publ. by Board of External Trade; circ. 2,000.

Uhuru na Amani: POB 3033, Arusha; tel. (57) 3221; telex 42054; bi-monthly; Swahili; publ. by Evangelical Lutheran Church in Tanzania; Editor ELIAS G. B. GOROI; circ. 15,000.

Ukulima wa Kisasa (Modern Farming): POB 2308, Dar es Salaam; tel. (51) 29047; telex 41246; f. 1955; monthly; Swahili; publ. by Ministry of Farming; Editor CLEOPHAS RWECHUNGURA; circ. 35,000.

Wela: POB 180, Dodoma; Swahili.

NEWS AGENCIES

SHIHATA: 304 Nkomo Rd, POB 4755, Dar es Salaam; tel. (51) 29311; telex 41080; f. 1981; Dir ABDULLA NGORORO.

Foreign Bureaux

Informatsionnoye Telegrafnoye Agentstvo Rossii—Telegrafnoye Agentstvo Suverennykh Stran (ITAR—TASS) (Russia): Plot 2112/5–7, Sea View, Dar es Salaam; Correspondent MIKHAIL V. STOUKALOV; also bureau in Zanzibar.

Inter Press Service (IPS) (Italy): 304 Nkomo Rd, POB 4755, Dar es Salaam; tel. (51) 29311; telex 41080; Chief Correspondent PAUL CHINTOWA.

Rossiyskoye Informatsionnoye Agentstvo—Novosti (RIA—Novosti) (Russia): POB 2271, Dar es Salaam; tel. (51) 23897; telex 41095; Dir ANATOLI TKACHENKO.

Xinhua (New China) News Agency: 72 Upanga Rd, POB 2682, Dar es Salaam; tel. (51) 23967; telex 41563; Correspondent HUAI CHENGBO.

Publishers

Central Tanganyika Press: POB 1129, Dodoma; tel. (61) 24180; fax (61) 24565; f. 1954; religious; Man. Canon JAMES LIFA (acting).

Dar es Salaam University Press: POB 35182, Dar es Salaam; tel. (51) 43137; telex 41327; f. 1981; educational, academic and cultural books in Swahili and English; Dir Y. B. MJUNGU.

Eastern Africa Publications Ltd: POB 1002 Arusha; tel. (57) 3176; telex 42121; f. 1978; general and school textbooks; Gen. Man. ABDULLAH SAIWAAD.

Inland Publishers: POB 125, Mwanza; tel. (68) 40064; general non-fiction, religion, in Kiswahili and English; Dir Rev. S. M. MAGESA.

Oxford University Press: Maktaba Rd, POB 5299, Dar es Salaam; tel. (51) 29209; f. 1969; Man. LUCIUS M. THONYA.

Pan-African Publishing Co. Ltd: POB 4212, Dar es Salaam; tel. (51) 22380; f. 1977; Man. Dir. R. MAKHANGE.

Tanzania Publishing House: 47 Samora Machel Ave, POB 2138, Dar es Salaam; tel. (51) 32164; telex 41325; f. 1966; educational and general books in Swahili and English; Gen. Man. (vacant)

Government Publishing House

Government Printer: POB 9124, Dar es Salaam; tel. (51) 20291; telex 41631; Dir JONAS OFORO.

Radio and Television

According to estimates by UNESCO, there were 660,000 radio receivers in use in Tanzania and 42,000 television receivers in use in Zanzibar in 1991. There is no television service on the mainland.

RADIO

Radio Tanzania: POB 9191, Dar es Salaam; tel. (51) 38011; telex 41201; f. 1951; domestic services in Swahili; schools service in English and Swahili; external services in English and Afrikaans, and in vernacular languages of South Africa; Dir NKWABI NG'WANAKILALA.

Radio Tumaini (Hope): St. Joseph's Church, Dar es Salaam; broadcasts within Dar es Salaam; operated by the Roman Catholic Church; broadcasts on social and economic issues; Dir Fr JEAN-FRANÇOIS GALTIER.

The Voice of Tanzania Zanzibar: POB 1178, Zanzibar; tel. (54) 31088; telex 57207; f. 1951; broadcasts in Swahili on three wavelengths; Dir YUSSEF OMAR SHUNDA.

TELEVISION

Television Zanzibar: POB 314, Zanzibar; telex 57200; f. 1973; colour service; Dir JUMA SIMBA.

Finance

(cap. = capital; p.u. = paid up; dep. = deposits; res = reserves; m. = million; br. = branch; amounts in Tanzanian shillings)

BANKING

Banks were nationalized in 1967. Efforts to liberalize the banking sector, in progress since 1992, resulted in the opening of Tanzania's first privately-owned banks in 1993–94.

Central Bank

Bank of Tanzania: 10 Mirambo St, POB 2939, Dar es Salaam; tel. (51) 21291; telex 41024; fax (51) 37485; f. 1966; bank of issue; cap. and res 19,612.2m., dep. 105,806 (June 1992); Gov. and Chair. G. RUTIHINDA; Dep. Gov. N. N. KITOMARI.

Principal Banks

The Co-operative and Rural Development Bank (CRDB): Azikiwe St, POB 268, Dar es Salaam; tel. (51) 46614; telex 41643; fax (51) 26518; f. 1984; provides commercial banking services and loans for rural development; 51% govt-owned, 30% owned by Co-operative Union of Tanzania Ltd (Washirika), 19% by Bank of Tanzania; cap. p.u. 1,493m. (June 1991), dep. 1,822m. (June 1987); restructuring in progress in 1993–94; Chair. and Man. Dir PHILIP A. MAGANI; Gen. Man. RABBIEL D. SWAI; 20 regional and 25 dist. offices, 8 brs.

Meridien BIAO Bank Tanzania Ltd: Sukari House, POB 72647, Dar es Salaam; tel. (51) 26251; telex 41415; fax (51) 34303; f. 1993; subsidiary of Meridien BIAO SA (Luxembourg).

The National Bank of Commerce (NBC): NBC House, POB 1255, Dar es Salaam; tel. (51) 28671; telex 41018; fax (51) 23807; f. 1967; cap. and res 15,151m., dep. 233,484m. (June 1991); Man. Dir Dr I. RASHIDI; 179 brs, 23 agencies.

People's Bank of Zanzibar Ltd (PBZ): Gizenga St, POB 1173, Forodhani, Zanzibar; tel. (54) 31118; telex 57365; fax (54) 31121; f. 1966; controlled by Zanzibar Govt; cap. p.u. 16m. (June 1991); Chair. MOHAMED ABOUD; Gen. Man. N. S. NASSOR.

Standard Chartered Tanzania Ltd: 107 Upanga Rd, POB 40831, Dar es Salaam; tel. (51) 36583; fax (51) 46065; f. 1992, activities commenced 1993; wholly owned by Standard Chartered PLC (United Kingdom); cap. p.u. 1,000m.; Chair. and Man. Dir P. V. DOCHERTY.

Tanganyika Development Finance Co Ltd (TDFC): TDFL Bldg, Upanga Rd and Ohio St, POB 2478, Dar es Salaam; tel. (51) 31255; telex 41153; fax (51) 31257; f. 1962; owned by the Commonwealth Development Corpn, the European Investment Bank, the Tanzania Investment Bank and govt agencies of the Netherlands and Germany; cap. p.u. 240m. (Dec. 1989); Chair. F. M. KAZAURA; Gen. Man. H. K. SENKORO.

Tanzania Housing Bank (THB): POB 1723, Dar es Salaam; tel. (51) 31112; telex 41831; f. 1972; restructuring in progress in 1994; provides loans for residential and commercial projects; 52% govt-owned, 24% owned by National Insurance Corpn, 24% by National Provident Fund; cap. p.u. 400m., dep. 4,300m. (1992); Chair. DANIEL YONA; Gen. Man. TAIRO URASA; 21 brs, 1 agency.

Tanzania Investment Bank (TIB): Samora Machel Ave, POB 9373, Dar es Salaam; tel. (51) 28581; telex 41259; fax (51) 46934;

f. 1970; provides finance and tech. assistance for economic development; 60% govt-owned, 30% owned by National Bank of Commerce, 10% by National Insurance Corpn; cap. p.u. 301m. (June 1992); Chair. IDDI SIMBA; Gen. Man. and CEO G. MWAIKAMBO.

Tanzania Postal Bank (TPB): Texco House, Pamba Rd, POB 9300, Dar es Salaam; tel. (51) 31155; telex 41663; fax (51) 33348; f. 1991; dep. 8,099.9m. (1991); Gen. Man. R. D. SWAI; 457 brs.

INSURANCE

National Insurance Corporation of Tanzania Ltd (NIC): POB 9264, Dar es Salaam; tel. (51) 26561; telex 41146; f. 1963; nationalized 1967; all classes of insurance; Chair. IDO SIMBA; Man. Dir OCTAVIAN W. TEMU; 21 brs.

Trade and Industry

CHAMBERS OF COMMERCE

Dar es Salaam Chamber of Commerce: Kelvin House, Samora Machel Ave, POB 41, Dar es Salaam; tel. (51) 21893; telex 41628; Exec. Officer I. K. MKWAWA.

TRADE, MARKETING AND PRODUCER ASSOCIATIONS AND BOARDS

Board of External Trade (BET): POB 5402, Dar es Salaam; tel. (51) 27439; telex 41408; fax (51) 46240; f. 1978; trade promotion, market research, marketing advisory and consultancy services, trade information, operational export promotion services; Dir-Gen. MBARUK K. MWANDORO.

Board of Internal Trade (BIT): POB 883, Dar es Salaam; tel. (51) 28301; telex 41082; f. 1967 as State Trading Corpn, reorg. 1973; state-owned; supervises seven national and 21 regional trading cos; distribution of general merchandise, agricultural and industrial machinery, pharmaceuticals, foodstuffs and textiles; shipping and other transport services; Dir-Gen. J. S. MAKOYE.

Cashewnut Board of Tanzania: POB 533, Mtwara; telex 56134; fax (59) 3536; Chair. Dr A. W. KHALID; Dir Gen. Maj Gen. R. L. MAKUNDA.

Coffee Marketing Board of Tanzania: POB 732, Moshi; telex 43088; Chair. W. KAPINGA; Gen. Man. A. M. RULEGURA.

National Agricultural and Food Corporation (NAFCO): POB 903, Dar es Salaam; telex 41295; produces and processes basic foods; Gen. Man. R. M. LINJEWILE.

National Coconut Development Programme: POB 6226, Dar es Salaam; tel. (51) 74834; fax 75549; f. 1979 to revive coconut industry; processing and marketing and projects including training, disease and pest control, smallholder and plantation development, breeding, agronomy trials; Project Co-ordinator P. L. KINYANA.

National Milling Corporation (NMC): POB 9502, Dar es Salaam; tel. (51) 860260; telex 41343; fax (51) 863817; f. 1968; stores and distributes basic foodstuffs, owns grain milling establishments and imports cereals as required; Chair. CRISPIN MOAPILA; Gen. Man. VINCENT M. SEMESI.

National Textile Corporation: POB 9531, Dar es Salaam; tel. (51) 26681; telex 41247; fax (51) 46899; f. 1974; holding corpn with 14 subsidiaries; production and marketing of yarn, fabrics, garments, agricultural bags and blankets; CEO S. H. NKYA.

State Mining Corporation (STAMICO): POB 4958, Dar es Salaam; tel. (51) 28781; telex 41354; fax (51) 30518; f. 1972; responsible for all mining and prospecting; Dir-Gen. A. Y. HANGI.

State Motor Corporation: POB 1307, Dar es Salaam; telex 41152; f. 1974 to control all activities of the motor trade; sole importer of cars, tractors and lorries; Gen. Man. H. H. IDDI.

Sugar Development Corporation: Dar es Salaam; telex 41338; Gen. Man. GEORGE G. MBATI.

Tanganyika Coffee Growers' Association Ltd: POB 102, Moshi.

Tanzania Cotton Marketing Board: POB 9161, Dar es Salaam; tel. (51) 46139; telex 41287; fax (51) 22564; f. 1984; regulates the marketing and export of cotton lint; Gen. Man. TIMOTHY SHINDIKA.

Tanzania Pyrethrum Board: POB 149, Iringa; f. 1960; Chair. Brig. LUHANGA; CEO P. B. G. HANGAYA.

Tanzania Sisal Development Board: Dar es Salaam; f. 1973 as the Tanzania Sisal Authority; co-ordinates the marketing of sisal; Chair. AUSTIN SHABA; Gen. Man. IBRAHIM KADUMA.

Tanzania Tea Authority: POB 2663, Dar es Salaam; tel. (51) 46700; telex 41130; fax (51) 23322; Chair. J. J. MUNGAI; Gen. Man. M. F. L. SHIRIMA.

Tanzania Wood Industry Corporation: POB 9160, Dar es Salaam; Gen. Man. E. M. MNZAVA.

Tea Association of Tanzania: POB 2177, Dar es Salaam; tel. (51) 22033; f. 1989; Chair. G. C. THEOBALD; Exec. Dir D. E. A. MGWASSA.

Tobacco Authority of Tanzania: POB 227, Morogoro; telex 55347; CEO J. N. ELINEWINGA; Gen. Man. TAKI.

Zanzibar State Trading Corporation: POB 26, Zanzibar; tel. (54) 30271; telex 57208; fax (54) 31550; govt-controlled since 1964; sole exporter of cloves, clove stem oil, chillies, copra, copra cake, lime oil and lime juice; Gen. Man. ABDULRAHMAN RASHID.

DEVELOPMENT CORPORATIONS

Capital Development Authority: POB 1, Dodoma; tel. (61) 23310; telex 53177; f. 1973 to develop the new capital city of Dodoma; state-owned; Chair. PIUS MSEKWA; Dir-Gen. THOMAS M. MTEI.

Economic Development Commission: POB 9242, Dar es Salaam; tel. (51) 29411; telex 41641; f. 1962 to plan national economic development; state-controlled.

Investment Promotion Centre: Dar es Salaam; Dir-Gen. Sir GEORGE KAHAMA.

National Development Corporation: POB 2669, Dar es Salaam; tel. (51) 46244; telex 41068; fax (51) 44419; f. 1965; state-owned; cap. 21.4m. sh.; promotes progress and expansion in production and investment; Man. Dir Prof. SIMON MBILINYI.

Small Industries Development Organization (SIDO): POB 2476, Dar es Salaam; tel. (51) 27691; telex 41123; f. 1973; promotes and assists development of small-scale industries in public, co-operative and private sectors, aims to increase rural industrialization and the involvement of women in small industries; Chair. J. E. F. MHINA; Dir-Gen. E. B. TOROKA.

There are also development corporations for textiles and petroleum.

MAJOR INDUSTRIAL COMPANIES

The following are some of the largest companies in terms either of capital investment or employment.

Agip (Tanzania) Ltd: POB 9450, Dar es Salaam; tel. (51) 46077; telex 41027; fax (51) 38945; f. 1966; cap. 300m. sh.; 50% state-owned; distribution and marketing of petroleum products; Man. Dir G. DECET; 431 employees.

Aluminium Africa Ltd: POB 2070, Dar es Salaam; tel. (51) 64011; telex 41265; mfrs of aluminium circles, corrugated and plain sheets, galvanized corrugated iron sheets, furniture tubes, steel billets, galvanized pipes, cold rolled steel sheets and coils, asbestos cement sheets; Chair. A. B. S. KILEWO.

Esso Tanzania Ltd: POB 9103, Dar es Salaam; tel. (51) 22646; telex 41044; fax (51) 26947; f. 1990; cap. US $770,000; distribution of refined petroleum products; Man. Dir R. H. BAILEY; 61 employees.

Friendship Textile Mill Ltd: POB 20842, Dar es Salaam; telex 41387; f. 1966; cap. 30m. sh.; wholly owned by National Textile Corpn; dyed and printed fabric mfrs; 5,400 employees.

Mwanza Textiles Ltd: POB 1344, Mwanza; tel. (068) 40466; telex 46118; f. 1966; cap. 20m. sh.; spinners, weavers, dyers and printers of cotton; 3,901 employees.

Tanganyika Instant Coffee Co Ltd: POB 410, Bukoba; tel. 20352; telex 58366; fax 20526; manufacture and export of spray-dried instant coffee.

Tanganyika Packers Ltd: POB 60138, Dar es Salaam; tel. (51) 47511; telex 41333; f. 1947; govt-owned; cap. 26.5m. sh.; mfrs of corned beef and other food products; 470 employees.

Tanzania Breweries Ltd: POB 9013, Dar es Salaam; telex 41288; f. 1960; cap. 20m. sh.; manufacture, bottling and distribution of beer; Gen. Man. A. O. LEMA; 2,000 employees.

Tanzania Cigarette Co Ltd: POB 40114, Dar es Salaam; tel. (51) 62276; telex 41165; fax (51) 62280; f. 1975; cap. 400m. sh.; state-owned; manufacture and marketing of cigarettes; Chair. Prof. J. DORIYE; Gen. Man. TIMON MSANGI; 1,400 employees.

Tanzania Portland Cement Co Ltd: POB 1950, Dar es Salaam; tel. (51) 37660; telex 41401; fax (51) 46096; f. 1959; cap. 350m. sh.; jt venture; mfrs of ordinary Portland cement; capacity 520,000 metric tons per annum; Gen. Man. UWE JÖNSSON; 885 employees.

Williamson Diamonds Ltd: POB 9470, Dar es Salaam; PO Mwadui, Shinyanga; tel. (51) 41332; telex 48165; f. 1942; cap. 12m. sh.; State Mining Corpn owns 50% of capital; diamond mining; Gen. Man. S. MIPAWA; 1,400 employees.

TRADE UNIONS

Minimum wages are controlled by law and there is also compulsory arbitration under the Trades Disputes (Settlement) Act; strikes and lock-outs are illegal unless the statutory conciliation procedure has been followed.

Union of Tanzania Workers (Juwata): POB 15359, Dar es Salaam; tel. (51) 26111; telex 41205; f. 1978; Sec.-Gen. JOSEPH C.

RWEGASIRA; Dep. Secs-Gen. C. MANYANDA (Tanzania mainland), I. M. ISSA (Zanzibar); 500,000 mems (1991); eight sections:

Central and Local Government and Medical Workers' section: Sec. R. UTUKULU.

Agricultural Workers' section: Sec. G. P. NYINDO.

Industrial and Mines Workers' section: Sec. J. V. MWAMBUMA.

Teachers' section: Sec. W. MWENURA.

Commerce and Construction section: Sec. P. O. OLUM.

Domestic, Hotels and General Workers' section: Sec. E. KAZOKA.

Communications and Transport Workers' section: Sec. M. E. KALUWA.

Railway Workers' section: Sec. C. SAMMANG' OMBE.

Principal Unaffiliated Unions

Organization of Tanzanian Trade Unions (OTTU): Dar es Salaam; Sec.-Gen. BRUNO MPANGAL.

Workers' Department of Chama Cha Mapinduzi: POB 389, Vikokotoni, Zanzibar; f. 1965.

CO-OPERATIVES

There are some 1,670 primary marketing societies under the aegis of about 20 regional co-operative unions. The Co-operative Union of Tanzania is the national organization to which all unions belong.

Co-operative Union of Tanzania Ltd (Washirika): POB 2567, Dar es Salaam; tel. (51) 23346; telex 41809; f. 1962; Sec.-Gen. D. HOLELA; 700,000 mems.

Department of Co-operative Societies: POB 1287, Zanzibar; tel. (54) 30747; telex 57311; f. 1952; encourages formation and development of co-operative societies in Zanzibar.

Principal Societies

Bukoba Co-operative Union Ltd: POB 5, Bukoba; 74 affiliated societies; 75,000 mems.

Kilimanjaro Native Corporation Ltd: f. 1976; 227 registered co-operative villages.

Nyanza Co-operative Union Ltd: POB 9, Mwanza.

Transport

RAILWAYS

Tanzania Railways Corporation (TRC): POB 468, Dar es Salaam; tel. (51) 26241; telex 41308; f. 1977 after dissolution of East African Railways; operates 2,600 km of lines within Tanzania; also operates vessels on Lakes Victoria, Tanganyika and Malawi; a major restructuring scheme commenced in 1991 and was expected to be completed in 1995; publ. monthly periodical 'Habari za Reli'; Chair. J. V. MWAPACHU; Dir-Gen. E. N. MAKOI.

Tanzania-Zambia Railway Authority (Tazara): POB 2834, Dar es Salaam; tel. (51) 62191; telex 41097; fax (51) 62474; jtly owned and administered by the Tanzanian and Zambian Govts; 1,860-km railway link between Dar es Salaam and New Kapiri Mposhi, Zambia; opened in Oct. 1975; a 10-year rehabilitation programme, aided by the USA and EC (now EU) countries, began in 1985; plans to construct an additional line, linking Tanzania with the port of Mpulungu, on the Zambian shore of Lake Tanganyika, were announced in 1990; Chair. RICHARD MARIKI; Gen. Man. A. S. MWEEMBA; Regional Man. (Tanzania) H. M. TEGGISA; Regional Man. (Zambia) M. S. BANDA.

ROADS

In 1992 Tanzania had 55,600 km of classified roads, of which 50 km were motorway, 10,300 km were primary roads and 13,000 km were secondary roads. About 37% of the network was paved in that year, and many roads are impassable in the wet season. A 1,930-km main road links Zambia and Tanzania, and there is a road link with Rwanda. A five-year Integrated Roads Programme, funded by international donors and co-ordinated by the World Bank, commenced in 1991: its aim was to upgrade 70% of Tanzania's trunk roads, at a projected cost of US $870m.

The island of Zanzibar has 619 km of roads, of which 442 km are bituminized, and Pemba has 363 km, of which 130 km are bituminized.

INLAND WATERWAYS

Steamers connect with Kenya, Uganda, Zaire, Burundi, Zambia and Malawi. A joint shipping company was formed with Burundi in 1976 to operate services on Lake Tanganyika. A rail ferry service operates on Lake Victoria between Mwanza and Port Bell.

SHIPPING

Tanzania's major harbours are at Dar es Salaam (eight deep-water berths for general cargo, three berths for container ships, eight anchorages, lighter wharf, one oil jetty for small oil tankers up to 36,000 tons, offshore mooring for super oil tankers up to 100,000 tons, one 30,000-ton automated grain terminal), Mtwara (two deep-water berths), and Tanga (seven anchorages and lighterage quay). Work on the first phase of a major modernization scheme for the port of Dar es Salaam commenced in 1985, and was expected to be completed in the early 1990s. The rehabilitation of the ports of Zanzibar and Pemba, begun in 1988, was completed in 1991.

Tanzania Harbours Authority (THA): POB 9184, Dar es Salaam; tel. (51) 21212; telex 41346; fax (51) 32066; Exec. Chair. J. K. CHANDE; Gen. Man. A. S. M. JANGUO; 3 brs.

National Shipping Agencies Co Ltd (NASACO): POB 9082, Dar es Salaam; telex 41235; f. 1973; state-owned shipping co with which all foreign shipping lines are required to deal exclusively.

Sinotashil (Chinese/Tanzanian Joint Shipping Line): POB 696, Dar es Salaam; tel. (51) 26108; telex 41129; f. 1967; services between People's Republic of China, Eastern and Southern Africa, Red Sea and Mediterranean ports.

Tanzania Coastal Shipping Line Ltd: POB 9461, Dar es Salaam; tel. (51) 28907; telex 41124; fax (51) 46930; regular services to Tanzanian coastal ports; occasional special services to Zanzibar and Pemba; also tramp charter services to Kenya, Mozambique, the Persian (Arabian) Gulf, Indian Ocean islands and the Middle East; Gen. Man. A. S. LUTAVI.

CIVIL AVIATION

There are 53 airports and landing strips. The major international airport is at Dar es Salaam, 13 km from the city centre, and there are international airports at Kilimanjaro and Zanzibar.

Air Tanzania Corporation: Tancot House, City Drive, POB 543, Dar es Salaam; tel. (51) 38300; telex 41077; fax (51) 37191; f. 1977; operates a 21-point domestic network and international services to Africa, the Middle East and Europe; Chair. BOB N. MAKANI; Gen. Man. SILA RWEBANGIRA.

New ACS Ltd: Peugeot House, 36 Upanga Rd, POB 21236, Dar es Salaam; fax (51) 37017; operates domestic and regional services from Tanzania and Zaire; Dir MOHSIN RAHEMTULLAH.

Zanzibar Airways: f. 1990; part-owned by Jet International; operates scheduled services between Zanzibar and destinations in mainland Tanzania, Kenya and Uganda.

Tourism

Tanzania has set aside about one-third of its land for national parks and game and forest reserves. The country received an estimated 250,000 visitors in 1992, compared with 138,000 in 1987. Some 50,000 tourists visit Zanzibar each year. Revenue from tourism was reported to be US $120m. in 1992/93.

Tanzania Tourist Board: IPS Bldg, Maktaba St, POB 2485, Dar es Salaam; tel. (51) 27671; telex 41061; fax (51) 46780; state-owned; supervises the development and promotion of tourism; Gen. Man. CREDO SINYANGWE.

Tanzania Wildlife Corporation: POB 1144, Arusha; tel. (57) 8830; telex 42080; fax (57) 8239; organizes safaris; also an exporter and dealer in live animals, birds and game-skin products; Gen. Man. M. A. NDOLANGA.

Zanzibar Tourist Corporation: POB 216, Zanzibar; tel. (54) 32344; telex 57144; fax (54) 33430; f. 1985; organizes tours and hotel services; Gen. Man. ALPHONCE KATEMA.

Defence

In June 1993 the total armed forces numbered 49,500, of whom an estimated 45,000 were in the army, 1,000 in the navy and 3,500 in the air force. There are also paramilitary forces consisting of a 1,400-strong Police Field Force and an 85,000-strong Citizens' Militia.

Defence Expenditure: Budgeted at 32,400m. shillings in 1993.

Commander-in-Chief of the Armed Forces: President ALI HASSAN MWINYI.

Head of the People's Defence Forces: Lt-Gen. KIWELU.

Education

Education at primary level is free. In secondary schools a government-stipulated fee is paid: from January 1993 this was 15,000 shillings per year for day pupils at state-owned schools and 35,000 shillings per year for day pupils at private schools. Villages and districts are encouraged to build their own schools with government assistance. Almost all primary schools are government-operated. Universal primary education was introduced in November 1977, and was made compulsory by the Education Act of October 1978. Primary education begins at seven years of age and lasts for seven years. Secondary education, beginning at the age of 14, lasts for a further six years, comprising a first cycle of four years and a second of two years. As a proportion of the school-age population, total enrolment at primary and secondary schools rose from 22% in 1970 to 58% in 1981, but declined to the equivalent of 43% in 1991. Enrolment at primary schools in 1991 included 50% of children in the relevant age-group (males 50%; females 50%). Secondary enrolment in 1991 was equivalent to only 5% of children in the appropriate age-group (males 6%; females 4%). In 1991 there were, in mainland Tanzania, 3,512,347 pupils attending 10,437 primary schools. Some 183,109 pupils were enrolled at secondary schools throughout the country in that year. The estimated rate of adult literacy rose from 33% in 1967 to 90.4% in 1986, as the result of adult literacy campaigns. There is a university at Dar es Salaam. Tanzania also has an agricultural university at Morogoro, and a number of vocational training centres and technical colleges. Education was allocated 6.3% of expenditure by the central government in 1990/91.

Bibliography

For works on Kenya, Tanzania and Uganda generally, see Kenya Bibliography, p. 512

Bennett, Norman R. *A History of the Arab State of Zanzibar.* London, Methuen, 1978.

Bienen, H. *Tanzania: Party Transformation and Economic Development.* Princeton, NJ, 1967; expanded edn, 1970.

Cliffe, L., and Saul, J. *Tanzania Socialism—Politics and Policies: An Interdisciplinary Reader.* 2 vols. Nairobi, East African Publishing House, 1972.

Drysdale, H. *Dancing with the Dead: A Journey through Zanzibar and Madagascar.* London, Hamish Hamilton, 1991.

Dumont, R., *Tanzanian Agriculture after the Arusha Declaration.* Dar es Salaam, Ministry of Economic Affairs and Development Planning, 1969.

Hayward, M. F. *Elections in Independent Africa.* Boulder, CO, Westview Pres, 1987.

Hyden, G. *Beyond Ujamaa in Tanzania: Underdevelopment and an Uncaptured Peasantry.* London, Heinemann Educational, 1980.

Iliffe, J. *Tanganyika under German Rule, 1905–12.* Cambridge University Press, 1969.

A Modern History of Tanganyika. Cambridge University Press, 1979.

Joinet, B. *Le Soleil de Dieu en Tanzanie.* Paris, Editions de Cerf, 1977.

Kahama, C. G., Maliyamkono, L. and Wells, S. *The Challenge for Tanzania's Economy.* London, James Currey, 1986.

Kaniki, M. H. Y. (Ed.). *Tanzania under Colonial Rule.* London, Longman, 1980.

Kim, K. S., Mabele, R. B., and Schultheis, E. R. (Eds). *Papers on the Political Economy of Tanzania.* London, Heinemann Educational, 1979.

Liebenow, J. G. *Colonial Rule and Political Development in Tanzania.* Nairobi, East African Publishing House, 1972.

Lofchie, M. *Zanzibar: Background to Revolution.* Princeton, New Jersey; London, Oxford University Press, 1965.

Martin, D.-C. *Tanzanie, L'invention d'une culture politique.* Paris, Karthala, 1988.

Nyerere, J. K. *Freedom and Socialism, a selection from writings and speeches, 1965–67.* Dar es Salaam and London, Oxford University Press, 1968; this contains the Arusha Declaration and subsequent policy statements.

Pratt, C. *The Critical Phase in Tanzania: 1945–1968.* Oxford University Press, 1980.

Sheriff, A. *Slaves, Spices and Ivory in Zanzibar: Integration of an East African Commercial Empire into the World Economy, 1770–1873.* London, James Currey, 1987.

Shivji, I. G. *Law, State and the Working Class in Tanzania.* London, James Currey, 1986.

Skarstein, R., and Wangwe, S. M. *Industrial Development in Tanzania.* Stockholm, Scandinavian Institute for African Studies, 1986.

Smith, W. E. *Nyerere of Tanzania.* London, Gollancz, 1973.

Stephens, H. W. *The Political Transformation of Tanganyika: 1920–67.* New York, Praeger; London, Pall Mall, 1968.

Stoecker, H. (Ed.) *German Imperialism in Africa.* London, Hurst Humanities, 1986.

Svendsen, K. E., and Teisen, M. (Eds). *Self-Reliant Tanzania.* Dar es Salaam, Tanzania Publishing House, 1969.

von Freyhold, M. *Ujamaa Villages in Tanzania.* London, Heinemann Educational, 1979.

Yeager, R. *Tanzania: An African Experiment.* London, Gower Publishing Co, 1983.

TOGO

Physical and Social Geography

R. J. HARRISON CHURCH

The Togolese Republic, a small state of western Africa situated east of Ghana, has an area of 56,785 sq km (21,925 sq miles), and comprises the eastern two-thirds of the former German colony of Togoland. From a coastline of 56 km, Togo extends inland for about 540 km. In January 1988 the population was officially estimated to be 3,296,000, giving a density of 58.0 persons per sq km, higher than average for this part of Africa. Northern Togo is more ethnically diverse than the south, where the Ewe predominate. Among the northern peoples the Kabiye are notable for their terracing of hillsides and intensive agriculture.

The coast, lagoons, blocked estuaries and Terre de Barre regions are identical to those of Benin, but calcium phosphate, the only commercially-exploited mineral resource, is quarried north-east of Lake Togo. Pre-Cambrian rocks with rather siliceous soils occur northward, in the Mono tableland and in the Togo-Atacora mountains. The latter are, however, still well wooded and planted with coffee and cocoa. To the north is the Oti plateau, with infertile Primary sandstones, in which water is rare and deep down. On the northern border are granite areas, remote but densely peopled, as in neighbouring Ghana and Burkina Faso. Togo's climate is similar to that of Benin, except that Togo's coastal area is even drier: Lomé has an average annual rainfall of 782 mm. Thus Togo, though smaller in area than Benin, is physically, as well as economically, more varied than its eastern neighbour.

Recent History

PIERRE ENGLEBERT

Togoland, of which the Togolese Republic was formerly a part, was annexed by Germany in 1894, occupied by Anglo-French forces in 1914, and proclaimed a League of Nations mandate in 1919. France became responsible for the larger eastern section, while the United Kingdom governed the west. The partition split the homeland of the Ewe people, who inhabit the southern part of the territory, and this has been a continuing source of internal friction. Ewe demands for reunification were intensified during the UN trusteeship system which took effect after the Second World War. In May 1956 a UN-supervised plebiscite in British Togoland produced, despite Ewe opposition, majority support for a merger with the neighbouring territory of the Gold Coast, then a British colony. The region accordingly became part of the independent state of Ghana in the following year. In October of that year, in a separate plebiscite, French Togoland voted to become an autonomous republic within the French Community.

Political life in French Togoland was dominated by the Comité de l'unité togolaise, led by Sylvanus Olympio, and the Parti togolais du progrès, led by Nicolas Grunitzky, Olympio's brother-in-law. In 1956 Grunitzky became prime minister in the first autonomous government, but, following a UN-supervised election in 1958, he was succeeded by Olympio, a campaigner for Ewe reunification. Following independence on 27 April 1960, Olympio became president.

EYADÉMA TAKES POWER

In January 1963 the Olympio regime, which had become increasingly authoritarian, was overthrown in a military revolt led by Sgt (later Gen.) Etienne (Gnassingbe) Eyadéma, a Kabiye from the north of the country, who invited Grunitzky to return from exile as head of state. Subsequent efforts by Grunitzky to achieve constitutional multi-party government proved unsuccessful, and in January 1967 Eyadéma, by then army chief of staff, assumed power. Political activity remained effectively suspended until the creation in 1969 of the Rassemblement du peuple togolais (RPT), which served as a means of integrating the army into political life and was without a political theory other than that of national unity. Plots to overthrow Eyadéma were suppressed in 1970 and again in 1977, when the exiled sons of ex-president Olympio were accused of organizing a mercenary invasion. From the mid-1970s, Eyadéma began to implement a campaign for cultural 'authenticity', in which foreign personal and place names were abandoned and the two main national languages, Ewe and Kabiye, were to replace French as the language of education.

The introduction of a new constitution in 1980 made little difference to Eyadéma's style of government, or to the furtherance of the personality cult surrounding the president. Although Olympio's supporters maintained an exiled Mouvement togolais pour la démocratie (MTD), by the mid-1980s Eyadéma's rule had entered a more tranquil phase politically, with the focus of national attention shifting to the country's economic problems. At national elections in March 1985 voters were able to choose between more than one candidate for each seat. A total of 216 candidates, all of whom were members of the RPT, contested the 77 seats in the national assembly. The RPT remained the only legal political party, but in May of that year the constitution was amended to allow deputies to the national assembly to be elected by direct universal suffrage without prior approval by the RPT.

POLITICAL REPRESSION

An unprecedented wave of bomb attacks in Lomé in August 1985 led to the arrest, in September and October, of at least 15 people accused of involvement in the bombings and of distributing subversive literature. When one of the detainees died shortly following his arrest, the exiled MTD claimed that the government had used the pretext of the bomb attacks to unleash a 'wave of repression'. The Togolese government accused the Ghanaian authorities of complicity in the attacks, prompting allegations in the Ghanaian press that the explosions had in fact been perpetrated by members of Eyadéma's entourage. In 1986 attempts by the human rights organization, Amnesty International, to send representatives to Togo, to investigate allegations of torture of political prisoners, were blocked by the government. However, a visiting delegation of French jurists concluded that torture was being used, and condemned the conditions under which political prisoners were being detained. Many of those who had been arrested following the August 1985 bombings were released under a presidential amnesty in January 1986: of the three people who were tried the following July for distributing subversive literature, two received prison sentences of five years (which were, however, rescinded in January 1987).

In September 1986 19 people were detained following an apparent attempt by what was described as a 'terrorist commando unit' to occupy the Lomé military barracks (which was also the president's home), the RPT headquarters and the national radio station. About 13 people, including six civilians, were reported to have been killed during the attack. The government subsequently accused both Ghana and Burkina Faso of involvement in the alleged coup attempt. The border with Ghana was closed immediately, and 250 French paratroopers were sent briefly to Togo (in accordance with a previously unpublished defence pact between the two countries). Some 350 Zairean troops also intervened in support of Eyadéma. In December Eyadéma was re-elected as president for a further seven-year term, reportedly winning 99.95% of votes cast. At trials in the same month 13 people were sentenced to death, and 14 to life imprisonment, for complicity in the September attack. Gilchrist Olympio, son of the former president and the alleged instigator of the attack, was one of three people sentenced to death *in absentia*.

In the aftermath of the alleged coup attempt Eyadéma combined measures to increase his personal security with reforms aimed at apparent political democratization. In October 1987 a national human rights commission, the Commission nationale des droits de l'homme (CNDH), was established, while most of the death sentences imposed in the previous December were commuted. Amnesty measures were also extended to common-law offenders. However, the appointment, in December 1988, of the former joint chief of staff of the security forces, Brig.-Gen. (later Maj.-Gen.) Yao Mawulikplimi Amegi, to the position of minister of the interior and security, was regarded as indicative of Eyadéma's preoccupation with national security.

At elections to the national assembly in March 1990, 230 candidates, all of whom declared their allegiance to the RPT, contested the assembly's 77 seats. Only 18 members of the outgoing legislature were re-elected.

By the end of the decade demands for political change were increasingly apparent. In December 1989 two Togolese dissidents, who were allegedly members of an opposition movement, the Convention démocratique des peuples africains du Togo (CDPA–T), were expelled from Côte d'Ivoire, after having reportedly been found in possession of tracts denouncing Eyadéma and advocating political pluralism. In August of that year Eyadéma stated that he was willing to instigate a return to a multi-party system, should that be the will of the people, but he made frequent reference to the popular demonstrations to denounce multi-party politics that had been made in 1969. A national congress of the RPT was convened in May 1990 to consider the findings of five regional commissions that had been appointed to discuss the reform of the ruling party. Delegates unanimously rejected the possibility of the restitution of a multi-party system; however, more freedom of expression within Togo was urged, and it was decided that proposals made by Eyadéma for the separation of the functions of the party and state would be examined at a later date. In late July, during an official visit to the USA, Eyadéma was reported to have stated that the process of democratization in Togo would inevitably include the development of a two-party system.

The establishment, in August 1990, of the independent Ligue togolaise des droits de l'homme (LTDH) was widely regarded as a direct challenge to the integrity of the official CNDH. In the same month 13 people, allegedly members of the CDPA–T and of an unofficial students' organization, were arrested on suspicion of distributing anti-government tracts. Eleven of the detainees were later released, after they had admitted to having been 'manipulated and used by external organizations hostile to Togo', while two others, Logo Dossouvi and Doglo Agbelenko, remained in detention. An official inquiry was ordered to investigate allegations of the torture of the detainees: the CNDH found that four detainees, including Dossouvi and Agbelenko, had been subjected to torture while in custody. In early October Dossouvi and Agbelenko were convicted of distributing defamatory tracts and inciting the army to revolt, and were sentenced to five years' imprisonment. Violent demonstrations erupted in Lomé after supporters of the accused were expelled from the trial. Security forces were deployed as protesters attacked public property: it was reported that four people were killed, and more than 30 injured, during the disturbances. The government claimed that the unrest had been orchestrated by 'international machinations', and many of the 170 people who were arrested in connection with the violence were said to be foreigners. A presidential pardon was granted in mid-October for Dossouvi and Agbelenko, and was followed by similar clemency measures for all those who had been detained during the unrest that had followed their trial.

THE COLLAPSE OF LEGITIMACY

In October 1990 a commission was established to draft a new constitution, which, it was announced, would be submitted for approval in a national referendum in December 1991. The constitutional commission presented its draft document, which (apparently at Eyadéma's instigation) envisaged the eventual creation of a multi-party political system, at the end of the year. In January 1991 Eyadéma announced an amnesty for all those (including exiles) who had been implicated in political offences other than the September 1986 coup attempt. The sentences of common-law offenders were also reduced, and mandatory contributions to the RPT were abolished. However, such concessions were deemed insufficient by Togo's emergent opposition, and demands for a national conference were relayed by the independent media.

A boycott of classes by university students and secondary school pupils, during the first half of March 1991, provoked violent clashes between striking students and the security forces and supporters of Eyadéma. Resultant arrests prompted further protests (in defiance of an official ban on demonstrations), during which two people were reported to have been killed. Meanwhile, several opposition movements formed a co-ordinating organization, the Front des associations pour le renouveau (FAR), to campaign for the immediate introduction of a multi-party political system. Following a meeting between Eyadéma and the leader of the FAR, Yao Agboyibo, an agreement was reached whereby Eyadéma consented to an amnesty for all political dissidents, to the legalization of political parties and to the organization of a national forum to discuss the country's political evolution.

In early April 1991 further student unrest erupted, prompted by a demonstration in Lomé by pupils at Catholic mission schools in support of their teachers' demands for salary increases. Two deaths were reported following intervention by the security forces. Further deaths resulted from similar action by the security forces in Kévé (to the north-west of Lomé) to disperse a demonstration to demand Eyadéma's resignation. Violent protests erupted in the capital; all educational establishments were closed, and a night-time curfew imposed, pending the restoration of order. The official endorsement, by the national assembly, of legislation regarding the general amnesty and the legalization of political parties was overshadowed by the discovery, in mid-April, of about 26 bodies in a lagoon in Lomé. Opposition allegations that the bodies were those of demonstrators who had been beaten to death by the security forces were denied by the government, which later ordered an official inquiry into the deaths. Retrieval of the bodies provoked further protests, at which the security forces again intervened. Fearing an ethnic conflict between the Kabiye and Ewe ethnic groups, Eyadéma appealed for national unity, and announced that a new constitution would be introduced within one year, and that legislative elections, in the context of a multi-party political system, would be organized. In May Eyadéma relinquished the defence portfolio to Maj.-Gen. Yao Mawulikplimi Amegi, who was succeeded at the ministry of the interior and security by Yao Komlavi (hitherto minister of the environment and tourism).

The FAR was disbanded in late April 1991, to allow for the establishment of independent political parties. Agboyibo formed his own party, the Comité d'action pour le renouveau (CAR). Numerous other movements were accorded official status, and in early May 10 parties (including the CAR) announced the formation of a new 'umbrella' organization, the Front de l'opposition démocratique (FOD), which was later renamed the Coalition de l'opposition démocratique (COD), to co-ordinate the activities of opposition groups in preparation for the national forum.

Negotiations between the government and the opposition, in preparation for the national forum, proved difficult, and took place in a context of renewed social and labour unrest. In early June the FOD organized a widely-observed general strike, in an attempt to force Eyadéma's resignation. Shortly afterwards a rally in the capital that had been organized by the FOD was reportedly disrupted by Kabiye supporters of Eyadéma, while demonstrations in Lomé and Sokodé, in central Togo were dispersed by the security forces. In mid-June it was announced that the government and the FOD had reached agreement regarding the mandate of what was to be known henceforth as the national conference. (The government's previous insistence that the convention be termed a national forum was widely thought to indicate its desire to limit the competence of the meeting, as sovereign national conferences elsewhere in the region, notably in Benin, had imposed radical political reforms.) The FOD subsequently suspended its industrial action. Shortly afterwards the government announced that ex-presidents Olympio and Grunitzky were to be posthumously rehabilitated. Also rehabilitated was Gilchrist Olympio, who returned to Togo in early July to participate in the national conference.

The national conference was opened, after some delay, on 8 July 1991. It was reported that 700–1,000 delegates (representing, among others, the organs of state and the country's newly legalized political organizations, together with workers', students' and religious leaders) were in attendance. A resolution by the conference, in mid-July, to declare itself sovereign, to suspend the constitution and to dissolve the national assembly prompted the government to boycott the proceedings for one week. Upon their return to the conference, government representatives stated that they did not consider such resolutions binding. In late July the conference resolved to 'freeze' the assets of the RPT and the Confédération nationale des travailleurs du Togo (CNTT—which had been reported to have announced its independence from the RPT in April), and to create a commission to examine the financial affairs of these organizations, together with an authority to control the finances of state and parastatal organizations, with the aim of preventing the transfer of state funds abroad. Visa requirements were imposed on foreign travel by government ministers.

Meanwhile, renewed allegations had emerged concerning violations of human rights by the Eyadéma administration. In mid-July 1991 the CNDH inquiry concluded that the security forces had been responsible for the deaths of at least 20 of those whose bodies had been discovered in mid-April. In late July the national conference heard allegations that a 'death camp' had been established in northern Togo in 1983, and that among those who had died as a result of maltreatment was Antoine Meatchi (Grunitzky's vice-president following the 1963 coup). At the same time, Komla Alipui, hitherto minister of the economy and finance, deplored such violations of human rights, and also condemned the Eyadéma government's lack of discipline in financial affairs, accusing it of squandering money on 'prestige' projects that were of little relevance to the country's needs.

On 26 August 1991 Eyadéma, deprived by the national conference of most of his powers, abruptly suspended the conference. However, opposition delegates defied the order, and proclaimed a provisional government under the leadership of Joseph Kokou Koffigoh, a prominent lawyer and the head of the LTDH. The conference also voted to dissolve the RPT and to form an interim legislature, the Haut conseil de la République (HCR). Fearing renewed unrest, Eyadéma hastily signed a decree confirming Koffigoh as transitional prime minister; the conference ended on 28 August.

Koffigoh's council of ministers, appointed in early September 1991, was composed mainly of technocrats who had not previously held political office. The prime minister assumed personal responsibility for defence, and it was envisaged that Eyadéma would remain only nominally head of the military. However, the events of subsequent months were to show that the Kabiye-dominated armed forces looked to Eyadéma for their command. On 1 October a group of soldiers, apparently dissatisfied at the failure of the HCR to sanction pay increases for the lower ranks of the armed forces, seized control of the offices of the state broadcasting service in Lomé. The troops claimed to have dissolved the HCR, and demanded that Koffigoh and his government resign, but returned to barracks on Eyadéma's orders. Five people were killed, and about 50 injured, during the incident. Later the same day members of the presidential guard, led by Eyadéma's half-brother, were rumoured to have staged a second rebellion. One week later presidential guards attempted unsuccessfully to kidnap Koffigoh. Although Eyadéma condemned the incident, and ordered a return to barracks, the rebels claimed to be supporters of the president. Seven deaths and more than 50 injuries were reported, as demonstrations by civilian supporters of Koffigoh degenerated into looting and violence, which was seemingly exacerbated by ethnic rivalries. Three senior armed forces officers, including the president's half-brother (who was subsequently reported on more than one occasion to have been killed in a road accident) were arrested in early November, in connection with the destabilization attempts.

CONSTITUTIONAL TRANSITION

Work began on the new constitution in October 1991. The brief political calm ended on 26 November, when the HCR responded to attempts to convene a congress of the RPT by reaffirming the ban on the former ruling party. Clashes between supporters of Eyadéma and Koffigoh, again aggravated by inter-ethnic differences, resulted in further casualties. The military retook the broadcasting headquarters and surrounded government offices, demanding that the transitional authorities be disbanded and that Eyadéma be empowered to nominate a new prime minister. A night-time curfew was imposed, and the borders and main airport were closed. (Members of the transitional administration were reportedly among the many thousands who were fleeing the country during the crisis.) The troops returned to barracks on 30 November, and conciliation talks began. Two days later, however, the military reoccupied strategic positions in the capital, and on the following day captured the prime minister. Negotiations between Eyadéma and Koffigoh ensued, as a result of which it was announced that a broadly-based 'government of national unity' (including, it was implied, the RPT) would be appointed. During this latest crisis 17 people were reported to have died, and more than 60 were injured. The provisonal government, the composition of which was announced in late December, included many members of the outgoing council of ministers, but two key portfolios were allocated to close associates of Eyadéma: Yao Komlavi again became responsible for national security, and Aboudou Assouma was appointed minister-delegate for the armed forces. Also in late December the first session of the HCR since the previous month's unrest adopted a 'social contract for a peaceful transition', compiled by Koffigoh, which (among other provisions) restored legal status to the RPT. (Despite the armed forces' earlier demands, the HCR continued to function, although its members were subject to frequent harassment by the military.)

Delays in the transition process prompted sporadic manifestations of discontent in the early part of 1992. However, the fragility of the political situation was exemplified in early May, when a failed assassination attempt on Gilchrist Olympio, in which the involvement of the armed forces was widely alleged, resulted in the death of another political leader. Lomé was effectively paralysed by a two-day general strike, organized by independent trade unions, and some 15,000 people demonstrated in the capital to demand that Eyadéma and Koffigoh, regarded as accomplices in the incident, resign. At the end of the month it was revealed that preparations for the election of democratic institutions were incomplete, and the electoral timetable (already delayed) was abandoned. Tensions were further exacerbated by ethnic unrest involving the Kabiye and Kotokoli communities in central Togo.

In early July 1992 the International Federation of Human Rights published a report (commissioned by the Togolese authorities) into the attempt on Gilchrist Olympio's life. The report (which was denounced by the military) appeared to substantiate allegations of the involvement of the armed forces, and cited strong evidence that Eyadéma's son had participated in the attack. A new electoral schedule was announced later in the month, beginning with a constitutional referendum at the end of August. Also in July the government was reorganized (Aboudou Assouma had been dismissed in mid-June, and one minister had subsequently resigned his post). The political climate deteriorated shortly after the reshuffle, when a prominent opposition leader, Tavio Ayao Amorin, was shot and seriously wounded. Amorin died in hospital in Paris shortly afterwards. Eyadéma denounced the assassination; none the less, a new opposition coalition, the Collectif de l'opposition démocratique (COD-2), comprising some 25 political organizations and trade unions, organized a widely-observed general strike in Lomé, and violent confrontations took place between protesters and the police.

Disarray among the country's political parties (estimated to number about 40 by mid-1992) contributed to the atmosphere of instability. Many opposition parties had withdrawn support for Koffigoh following what was perceived to be his 'capitulation' in late 1991, and political alliances were frequently formed and disbanded. An attempt to resolve the political crisis was made in late July 1992, with the initiation of a series of meetings between representatives of Eyadéma and of the country's eight leading political parties. The negotiations made faltering progress in subsequent weeks. Confidence was undermined by an armed attack (in which the complicity of the security forces was rumoured) on a centre for the processing of electoral data, and by an assassination attempt on the minister of equipment and mines. None the less, agreement was reached on opposition access to the state-controlled media and on the extension, until 31 December 1992, of the transitional period. In late August the HCR approved the extension, and also sanctioned the restoration of significant powers to the president. Eyadéma was thus empowered to chair sessions of the council of ministers and to represent the country abroad, while the prime minister would be obliged henceforth to make government appointments in consultation with the head of state. Moreover, in an important concession to Eyadéma and his supporters, the draft constitution was amended to the effect that members of the armed forces seeking election to the new democratic organs of state would no longer be required to resign their commissions.

The transitional government was dissolved on 1 September 1992, and a new electoral schedule was announced: a referendum on the new constitution was to take place later in September, local and legislative elections in October and November, and presidential elections in December. In mid-September a new transitional government was formed: Koffigoh remained as prime minister, and 10 parties were reportedly represented in the new administration, but the most influential posts (including the national defence, foreign affairs and justice portfolios) were allocated to members of the RPT. On 27 September the new constitution was approved in a referendum by 98.11% of the votes cast (the rate of participation by voters was about 66%). At the end of the month, however, it was announced that the elections were to be rescheduled yet again. In late October members of the armed forces stormed a meeting of the HCR, holding some of its members hostage and demanding that it authorize the reimbursement of contributions made to the RPT, whose assets had remained 'frozen' since 1991. Although Eyadéma stated that disciplinary measures would be taken against the men involved, the COD-2 successfully organized a general strike in protest at the incident. In November Koffigoh dismissed two ministers (both adherents of the RPT) for their conduct during the attack on the HCR, but his decision was overruled by Eyadéma. In the same month another general strike was organized by the COD-2 and the Collectif des syndicats indépendants labour movement, to support their demands for elections, the neutrality of the armed forces, the formation of a non-military 'peace force', and the bringing to justice of those responsible for the attacks on the HCR. The strike was widely observed, except in the north of Togo (where support for Eyadéma was strongest), and continued during the first half of 1993, causing considerable economic disruption.

In mid-January 1993 Eyadéma dissolved the government, but reappointed Koffigoh as prime minister. The president stated that he would appoint a new 'government of national unity', whose task would be to organize elections as soon as possible. His action provoked protests by the opposition parties, who claimed that, according to the constitution, the HCR should appoint a prime minister since the transition period had now expired. Later in the same month representatives of the French and German governments visited Togo to offer mediation in the political crisis. During their visit at least 20 people were killed when police opened fire on anti-government protesters. Thousands of Togolese (including most opposition leaders who were not already in exile) subsequently fled from Lomé, many crossing the borders into Benin and Ghana. In early February discussions were organized in Colmar, France, by the French and German governments attended by representatives of Eyadéma, the RPT, Koffigoh, the HCR and the COD-2, but these failed when the presidential delegation left after one day. The formation of a new 'crisis government' was announced shortly afterwards: eight new ministers were appointed, but supporters of Eyadéma retained the principal posts. The COD-2 declared that they now regarded Koffigoh as an obstacle to democratization, and in March COD-2 member parties, meeting in Benin, nominated a 'parallel' prime minister, Jean-Lucien Savi de Tové (the leader of the Parti des démocrates pour l'unité).

On 25 March 1993 there was an armed attack on the military camp in Lomé where Eyadéma had his residence: more than 20 people, including the deputy chief of staff of the armed forces, Col Kofi Tepe, were killed in the suppression of the attack, and about 110 members of the armed forces fled to Ghana and Benin, fearing reprisals within the military. The government identified Tepe as the principal military organizer of the attack, but declared that it had been instigated by Gilchrist Olympio, with assistance from the Ghanaian authorities.

In early April 1993 the government announced a new electoral timetable, beginning with the presidential election in early June. This was rejected by the opposition, which reiterated that legitimate polls could only be organized following the restoration of a national consensus. A revised schedule, formulated one month later (apparently following secret negotiations in the Burkinabè capital, Ouagadougou, between official Togolese representatives and members of the COD-2), was, none the less, similarly rejected by the opposition. A series of bomb attacks on both government and opposition targets in the second half of May was said by the authorities to have been plotted outside Togo by persons who wished to frustrate the democratization process. The election was modified twice during June, and was abandoned in early July, in anticipation of renewed negotiations in Ouagadougou (talks there in mid-June had failed, when the participants failed to reach agreement on procedures for the organization of elections). In mid-July those meeting in Ouagadougou (including Eyadéma and President Compaoré of Burkina, Koffigoh and members of the transitional government, representatives of the COD-2 and French and German diplomats) set 25 August as the date for the presidential poll. Agreement was reached on both the issue of security during the election campaign (the Togolese armed forces would be confined to barracks, under the supervision of a multinational military team), and also the establishment and functions of an independent national electoral commission to oversee the election process. It was also stated that Burkinabè, French, German and US civilian observers would be invited to monitor the elections.

However, divisions within the opposition were evident (the total number of political parties at this time was officially put at more than 60). Gilchrist Olympio immediately denounced the Ouagadougou accord, protesting that the government had been allowed too much control over the election process and that no provision had been made for the return of refugees in advance of the elections (international humanitarian organizations estimated the number of people who had fled Togo in recent months at 200,000, most of whom were sheltering in Benin and Ghana, while Olympio put the total number of refugees at about 350,000). Shortly after the conclusion of the Ouagadougou agreement Edem Kodjo, the leader of the Union togolaise pour la démocratie (UTD), was chosen to challenge Eyadéma for the presidency on behalf of the COD-2. Four other opposition candidates, including Yao Agboyibo and Gilchrist Olympio, submitted their candidature for the election. However, the supreme court declared Olympio's candidature invalid, since medical certificates that he had submitted (in accordance with the electoral code) had been issued in France, rather than by approved doctors in Togo. Meanwhile, the authorities revealed that a warrant for Olympio's arrest, in connection with the March 1993 attack on Eyadéma's residence, had been issued in May. Olympio, who claimed that the warrant had been issued retrospectively, refused to leave his base in Ghana to undergo a medical examination in Togo, protesting that no guarantee of his security had been given by the Togolese authorities. As the election campaign intensifed during August, opposition demands, supported by the national electoral commission, that the election be postponed intensified, and Kodjo (widely regarded as Eyadéma's strongest challenger) and Agboyibo effectively withdrew from the election. The COD-2 and Olympio's Union des forces de changement appealed to their supporters to boycott the poll, and US and German observers withdrew from Togo, alleging irregularities in the compilation of voting lists (2.7m. voters were registered, out of a population of some 3.6m.) and in electoral procedures. As voting began, on 25 August, the government announced that a coup attempt, plotted by Togolese dissidents in Ghana, had been foiled the day before the election. Shorty after the poll it was revealed that at least 15 opposition supporters, arrested in connection with attacks on polling stations in Lomé, had died while in detention: while the authorities alleged that the prisoners had been intentionally poisoned by their associates, opposition leaders countered that they had died as a result of ill-treatment by the security forces. According to official election results, published in late August, Eyadéma was re-elected president by 96.49% of voters. Only about 36% of the electorate voted in the election.

THE FOURTH REPUBLIC

In September 1993 the COD-2 announced that it would only participate in the forthcoming legislative election if the electoral register was revised, equitable access to state media granted and international observers present. The government subsequently agreed to revise the electoral registers. Eyadéma was sworn in as first president of the fourth republic on 24 September. In November the government announced that the legislative election would take place in two stages in December and January, but both the national electoral commission and the opposition parties declared these dates to be premature, and, following consultation with the international monitoring committee, the government agreed to postpone the first round of the election to 23 January 1994.

In early January 1994 an armed attack on Eyadéma's official residence was reported. As in March 1993, the government alleged that the attack had been organized by Olympio, with Ghanaian support: this was denied both by Olympio and by the Ghanaian government. A total of 67 people were officially reported to have died in the violence. It was claimed by the human rights organization, Amnesty International, that at least 48 deaths took the form of summary executions by the armed forces. A UTD election candidate was accused by the government of storing weapons for the attack. On the day after the disturbances the government announced that the election would now take place on 6 February and 20 February 1994, rejecting requests by the CAR and the UTD for a further postponement.

In the legislative election of February 1994, 347 candidates contested 81 seats. Despite the murder of a newly-elected CAR candidate after the first round, and some incidents of violence at polling stations during the second round, international observers expressed themselves satisfied with the conduct of the election. The final result revealed a narrow victory for the opposition, with the CAR winning 36 seats and the UTD seven; the RPT obtained 35 seats and two smaller pro-Eyadéma parties won three. During March Eyadéma consulted the main opposition parties on the formation of a new government. In late March the CAR and the UTD reached agreement on the terms of their alliance and jointly proposed the candidacy of Agboyibo for prime minister (a stipulation of the agreement was that the candidate for prime minister should be a member of the CAR). In rulings issued in late March and early April the Supreme Court declared the results of the legislative election invalid in three constituencies (in which the CAR had won two seats and the UTD one) and ordered by-elections. The CAR and the UTD refused to attend the new assemblée nationale, in protest at the annulment. In April Eyadéma nominated Kodjo as prime minister. Kodjo accepted the appointment despite assertions by the CAR that to do so was a violation of the agreement of March 1994 between the two parties on which their parliamentary majority was based. The CAR subsequently announced that it would not participate in an administration formed by Kodjo. On 25 April Kodjo took office, expressing his priorities to be national reconciliation, the return of refugees, economic recovery, and the integration of the armed forces into democratic life. It was not until late May that he announced the formation of his government, which comprised eight members of the RPT and other pro-Eyadéma parties, three members of the UTD, and eight independents. Kodjo maintained, however, that this was an 'interim' government and that, should the CAR decide to join the government, there would be a reorganization of the cabinet to accommodate it. Shortly beforehand, the CAR had announced (in response to the postponement of the parliamentary by-elections, originally scheduled for May) that it was to end its boycott of the assemblée nationale.

FOREIGN RELATIONS

The issue of Ewe reunification has at times led to difficult relations with Ghana. President Nkrumah assisted Togo in its campaign for independence but with the intention of integrating Togo into Ghana. When this objective failed, Nkrumah subjected Togo to constant harassments, through trade embargoes and border closures. Relations improved after the assassination of Olympio, and Nkrumah was the first to recognize the new government. There have been periodic rises in tension, notably following Ghana's decision in 1969 to expel alien workers without permits; also over the problems of smuggling and subversive activity by exiles of each country resident in the other. Ghana has continued to be suspicious of campaigns for Ewe reunification initiated in Togo, which have been tolerated but not supported by Eyadéma. Relations between the two countries deteriorated as Togo's political crisis of the early 1990s intensified, and the presence of Togolese opposition leaders in Ghana prompted renewed suspicion in Lomé that the Ghanaian authorities were supporting elements that might seek to destabilize the Eyadéma regime. In January 1993 the Ghanaian government criticized Eyadéma and expressed fears of a breakdown in law and order in Togo. In March of that year, and again in January 1994, the Rawlings administration in Ghana refuted allegations made by the Togolese government of Ghanaian complicity in armed attacks on Eyadéma's residence (see above). Relations were also strained by the presence of Togolese refugees (numbering at least 100,000 in mid-1993) in Ghana.

Relations with Benin have similarly been bedevilled by the problems of smuggling and political activities by exiles, and the border between the two countries has frequently been closed. In March 1993 the Eyadéma regime criticized the government of Benin for allowing Togolese opposition leaders to meet on Beninois territory. Some 100,000 Togolese refugees were believed to be sheltering in Benin in mid-1993.

Dependence on France increased under Grunitzky. Co-operation agreements with France were concluded in 1963 and Togo became a member of the Conseil de l'entente (and of the now defunct Organisation commune africaine et malgache) in 1966. Although generally anxious to maintain good relations with France, Eyadéma has tended to avoid too close identification with the French sphere of influence in Africa. While not accepting full membership of the francophone west African Communauté économique de l'Afrique de l'ouest, Togo has observer status and is a full member of the defence pact.

During the latter part of 1991 the transitional government, faced with opposition from the armed forces, appealed to

France for military assistance. The initial response was the dispatch, in early November, of 10 military instructors to the French embassy in Lomé, and at the end of the month, as the situation in Togo deteriorated, two army units were deployed in neighbouring Benin. Despite appeals, both within Togo and elsewhere in the region, for direct French action in support of Koffigoh's administration, France restricted its intervention to the transfer into Togo of about 30 French troops, ostensibly to strengthen security around the French embassy. None the less, it was widely believed that the French military presence in Benin had constrained Eyadéma's response to his supporters' actions, and that without the threat of direct intervention by French units the president would have dismissed the civilian government.

With the escalation of the political crisis in Togo in 1992–93, many of Togo's external creditors, including France, Germany, the USA and the EC, attempted (with limited success) to exert political pressure on Eyadéma and Koffigoh by withdrawing all but the most urgent economic assistance. The victory of centre-right parties in the French legislative elections of March 1993 prompted speculation that the new government of Edouard Balladur might display a more conciliatory attitude towards the Eyadéma regime. In June 1994 France announced that it was to resume civil co-operation with Togo.

Economy

EDITH HODGKINSON

At independence in 1960, Togo's economy, compared with those of most of its neighbours, was relatively advanced. Moreover, the country possessed the potential for sustained economic growth. In recent years, however, the economy has declined to such an extent that Togo is now classified as a least developed country, and is experiencing difficulties in servicing a foreign debt acquired in earlier, more prosperous, times.

EARLY ECONOMIC EXPANSION

German Togoland, like the neighbouring Gold Coast, experienced its economic 'miracle' at a very early stage—before 1914. At the outbreak of the First World War, the proportion of the country's gross domestic product (GDP) accounted for by exports was already almost the same as in 1970. Tax revenue represented a relatively large share of GDP, thus making it possible to finance the country's infrastructure without resort to German capital and to achieve the highest level of educational development in Africa. The economic 'miracle' was attributable primarily to the rapid development of the plantation economy in the south of the country. There were both German plantations (13,000 ha in 1914) and native-owned holdings, which the colonial power had helped to develop on modern capitalist lines with private ownership of the land. During the First World War the Togolese managers on German plantations appropriated the land, thus preventing its seizure by the British and French.

POST-WAR DEVELOPMENT

During the period 1920–40 the economy of Togoland remained virtually stagnant. Indeed, in 1949 the volume of exports was still much the same as it had been during German times; but the post-war period, up to independence, was one of relatively swift development. The volume of exports more than doubled in 1949–54. This was mainly attributable to greatly increased investment in infrastructure. This second phase of Togo's development was characterized by a rise in the population growth rate and by increasing urbanization.

Rates of population growth and urbanization have continued at a high level. The population was estimated at 3,720,000 in mid-1992 (representing a fairly high population density of 65.5 per sq km), with the capital, Lomé, having an estimated 450,000 inhabitants. According to World Bank estimates, annual population growth in 1985–92 averaged 3.7%. In most years there is seasonal migration, of around 100,000 Togolese annually, to neighbouring Ghana. The escalation of the political crisis in late 1992 prompted large numbers of Togolese to flee to Ghana and Benin, and by mid-1993 the population was estimated to have fallen by more than 400,000.

In 1992, according to estimates by the World Bank, Togo's gross national product (GNP), measured at average 1990–92 prices, was US $1,575m., equivalent to $400 per head. Economic growth, which had eased off in the early 1960s (only just keeping pace with population, compared with 1948–60's average annual growth of 5%), accelerated again, to an average of 4.5% per year in 1965–80, as development programmes took effect. However, the severe economic problems which beset the country during the 1980s (see below) reduced GDP growth to an average of 0.5% per year in 1981–90. Compared with the 6.5% average annual growth target set in the 1981–85 Development Plan, GDP is estimated to have fallen each year in 1981–83 because of drought, the slump in phosphate production, the recession in neighbouring economies, and measures of economic adjustment in response to these adverse trends. The end of the drought in 1984 and the upturn in phosphate production caused GDP to increase by 5.5% in that year and by 3.1% in 1985, which was only just below the more modest target of an annual average growth rate of 3.5% set for the 1985–90 Development Plan period. The rate of growth declined again in the following two years, to 2.2% and 1.5% respectively, as a result of lower international prices for the country's major commodities and the impact of fiscal austerity on development expenditure and on overall demand. However, there was an upturn, to 4.7%, in 1988, reflecting increases in both production of and international prices for phosphates and an easing in the financing constraint following the rescheduling of the public debt (see below). The rate of growth declined to 3.2% in 1989, and GDP fell by 1% in 1990, as a result of the decline in the volume of cash crops and other primary commodities, in conjunction with the decline in world prices for Togo's export commodities. Although the three-year programme of economic reform that was adopted in 1989 (with support from IMF funds) projected average real GDP growth of more than 4% annually, GDP continued to contract: a decline of an estimated 5% in 1991 was followed by falls of about 10% in 1992 and 15% in 1993 as political unrest disrupted agricultural distribution and phosphate production. The prospect of a normalization of foreign trade, as the political situation showed signs of steadying, and the stimulus of higher export earnings in local currency terms, as a result of the January devaluation of the franc CFA, was expected to produce a modest upturn in GDP of some 5% in 1994.

AGRICULTURE

Agriculture is by far the dominant economic activity, accounting for one-third of GDP and about one-half of export earnings (except during periods of high prices for phosphates), and providing a livelihood for about 70% of the working population. However, after rising rapidly in the mid-1960s, agricultural output has shown very slow growth. In 1970–81 it rose by an average of only 1.5% per year, but the drought of 1981–83 resulted in an average annual decline in output of 1% in the following five years. In non-drought years Togo is self-sufficient in basic foodstuffs. The yam crop totalled 433,000 metric tons in 1991/92, while production of manioc was 504,000 tons, maize 236,000 tons, millet and sorghum 176,000 tons and rice 33,000 tons. Food supplies are supplemented by fishing, but Togo's narrow coastline constrains activity, which is mainly artisanal. None the less, modern vessels are used, although the total catch—around 15,000 tons a year—is insufficient to satisfy domestic demand. The livestock sector contributes to—but does not satisfy—the local meat and dairy market. Livestock numbers in 1992 were estimated by the FAO at 2.3m. sheep and goats, 2m. pigs and 320,000 cattle.

Production in the cash-crop sector has, on the whole, recovered after the decline recorded in the mid-1970s. The most important contribution has come from cotton, which is now the country's principal export crop. After falling sharply in the second half of the 1970s, from 10,736 tons in 1974/75, output of seed cotton rose strongly, reaching 100,247 tons in 1990/91, reflecting increases in the area under cultivation. However, owing to political disruption, output in 1991/92 declined to an estimated 90,000 tons. Coffee output has fluctuated widely, falling from 9,237 tons in 1981/82 to only 2,701 tons in 1983/84 as a result of drought. Production subsequently recovered strongly, and reached a record 16,100 tons in 1989/90 (reflecting the improvement in climatic conditions, the impact of replanting programmes, and higher producer prices). Production then declined, by 40%, to 9,653 tons, in 1990/91 before recovering to an estimated 12,000 tons in 1991/92. Groundnut production has also fluctuated markedly, from a low of 29 tons (shelled and marketed) in 1981/82 to a peak of 19,561 tons in 1986/87; production in 1990/91 was about 9,000 tons. Similarly, output of shea-nuts (karité nuts) varies enormously: 20,900 tons in 1985/86 and 16,692 tons in 1987/88, compared with 4,500 tons in 1986/87 and just 943 tons in 1988/89. The 1989/90 harvest was 4,227 tons, and there was a further recovery, to 6,396 tons, in 1990/91. Total production is, however, more stable than these figures would indicate, since the bulk goes to subsistence consumption and therefore is not recorded. Output of cocoa beans, formerly the principal export crop, has fluctuated widely, reaching a peak of 28,200 tons in 1971/72, but declined in subsequent years and by the late 1980s averaged less than 9,000 tons a year. The decline in output, which stood at only 7,278 tons in 1990/91, was due largely to the ageing of cocoa bushes, which were consequently producing lower yields. (It must also be borne in mind that production figures are greatly distorted by the smuggling of cocoa from Ghana.) The government's agricultural development programme has received substantial foreign support. Grants of 533m. francs CFA, provided by the European Development Fund (EDF), financed the development of 3,000 ha of palm groves over the period 1969–78. France's Fonds d'aide et de coopération (FAC) has provided 614m. francs CFA for the development of coffee, cocoa and cotton production in the south (the most developed area). The World Bank has also provided $9.5m. for this area, and credits have come from the International Development Association (IDA) for rural development projects, intended to increase the area under cultivation and to introduce cotton, maize, sorghum and groundnut crops. It is also planned to develop irrigated agriculture—rice, sugar cane, fruits and vegetables. The World Bank, the EC and France contributed $29.8m. towards a scheme to replant 7,500 ha of coffee and 4,000 ha of cocoa in the western plateau region in 1987–91. The Anié sugar complex, in central Togo, was inaugurated in 1987. The complex has the capacity to refine 60,000 tons of sugar cane annually. A further sugar cane plantation, on 1,200 ha, is planned. Other projects intend to increase self-sufficiency in animal protein by encouraging the rearing of cattle, pigs and poultry.

MINING AND POWER

With agriculture stagnant and industrial manufacturing geared to the local market, although this should eventually change, if the industrial free-trade zone (see below) is successful, the main stimulus to Togo's exports—and overall economic growth—has come from phosphate mining. Phosphates were discovered in Togo in 1952, and exports began in 1961. Togo's phosphate deposits are the richest in the world, with a mineral content of 81%. Reserves of first-grade ore are estimated at 260m. tons, while there are more than 1,000m. tons of carbon phosphates, which, although of a lower quality, have the advantage of a significantly lower cadmium content (see below). The country now ranks fifth among the world's producers of calcium phosphates, and they currently account for almost half of Togo's export receipts (48.5% in 1991). Exports of phosphates from the reserves at Akoupamé and Hahoté by the Compagnie togolaise des mines du Bénin (CTMB), subsequently merged into the Office togolais des phosphates (OTP), rose from 199,000 tons in 1962 to 2.6m. tons in 1974. In 1974 the government nationalized the company, in which it previously had a 35% holding. When, in the following year, prices slumped, owing to the energy crisis and a fall in world demand, the Togolese phosphate rock's high quality made it more difficult to place on the market, and production fell to 1.1m. tons. Demand subsequently recovered, and production was around 2.9m. tons per year in 1977–80. Additional treatment and recovery plant costing 4,000m. francs CFA, financed by Arab and French interests, brought total annual capacity to 3.6m. tons in 1980, but the downturn in demand for Togo's relatively high-priced ore in 1981 caused the extra capacity to be closed in that year, and production declined to only 2.01m. tons in 1982. There was a subsequent recovery in foreign demand, and output reached 3.36m. tons in 1989, stimulated by the strength of international prices for phosphates; however, production declined by 28% in 1990, to just 2.43m. tons. Following a recovery to 2.97m. tons in 1991, output declined once more, to 2.09m. tons in 1992. With the mine out of operation for much of the first half of 1993, owing to the general strike, output was unofficially estimated at only 1.5m. tons in that year. It is planned to exploit lower-grade phosphate deposits if the phosphoric acid plant proceeds (see below). However, the future development of the phosphate-mining sector may be adversely affected by concerns regarding the high cadmium content of Togolese phosphates. The EU, which has banned the agricultural use of certain categories of phosphate fertilizers, is to provide the OTP with funds for the research and development of sources of phosphates with a lower cadmium content.

Togo also possesses extensive limestone reserves (some 200m. tons), utilization of which began in 1981 at a large-scale cement plant run by Ciments de l'Afrique de l'ouest (CIMAO), with an output of 600,000 tons of clinker (one-half of capacity). Output rose to 870,000 tons in the following year, and it was hoped to increase annual output to 1.8m. tons during the 1981–85 Plan period. The governments of Ghana and Côte d'Ivoire, as well as French, British and Canadian interests, participated in the scheme, which cost $285m. Credits were provided by the World Bank and the European Investment Bank (EIB). The IDA, France and the EIB provided funds and technical assistance to restructure the plant, with the aim of reducing production costs (which exceeded import prices), but the programme was cut back in 1984, when the reduction in power supplies from the Akosombo dam in Ghana (because of insufficient rainfall) caused a temporary closure of the plant. CIMAO ceased to be commercially viable, and went into liquidation in March 1989. However, the construction industry revived in the following two years, with continued work on the Nangbeto dam (see below) and on offices of the regional central bank and the Economic Community of West African States. Cement production has therefore continued under the Société des ciments du Togo (CIMTOGO), a parastatal organization operated in co-operation with Norwegian interests, with an annual capacity of 780,000 tons. Exploitation of reserves of marble at Gnaoulou and Pagola (estimated at 20m. tons) began in 1970 by the Société togolaise de marbrerie (now restructured and operating, with Norwegian participation, as the Nouvelle société togolaise de marbrerie et de matériaux).

Petroleum exploration is under way, but no commercial reserves have yet been located. Uranium exploration is being undertaken by a German company.

Electricity was, in the past, generated mainly at a thermal plant in Lomé and a small hydroelectric installation at Palimé, built with Yugoslav assistance. Togo formerly derived electric power principally from the Akosombo hydroelectric installation in Ghana. Beginning in 1988, however, supplies were enhanced by the 65 MW hydroelectric plant at Nangbeto, on the Mono river, constructed in co-operation with Benin. The project, which cost $144m., received financial support from multilateral agencies (the IDA, the African Development Bank, the Arab Bank for Economic Development in Africa, and the OPEC Fund for International Development) and from Kuwait, France, the Federal Republic of Germany and Canada. The plant has a maximum capacity of 150m. kWh, and also provides irrigation for 43,000 ha of land. Total electricity generation was 41m. kWh in 1990.

INDUSTRY

The manufacturing sector is small and relatively little developed, accounting for 6.8% of GDP in 1991, but it has shown some expansion in recent years. Manufacturing was, in the past, centred on the processing of agricultural commodities (palm oil extraction, coffee roasting, cassava flour milling, and cotton ginning) and import substitution of consumer goods—textiles, footwear, beverages, confectionery, salt and tyres. During the 1970s, however, major investments were made in a number of heavy industrial schemes, including the CIMAO cement plant (see above) and a petroleum refinery at Lomé with an annual capacity of 250,000 tons, which began operation in 1978, closed in 1979, then reopened to operate profitably, even producing a small surplus for export, before closing down permanently in 1983. A steel works (Société nationale de sidérurgie) with a capacity of 20,000 tons per year started production in 1979. An integrated textile mill, which cost 10,000m. francs CFA and has a capacity of 24,000 tons per year, began operations at Kara in 1981, and the expansion of domestic cotton production led to the establishment of two further plants, at Notse and Atakpamé. A new cotton-ginning plant was inaugurated at Talo in January 1991, with a total capacity of 50,000 tons of seed cotton per year. Total investment, of 3,000m. francs CFA, was provided by France and the Banque ouest-africaine de développement. New palm oil mills are being installed, including one with EC funds equivalent to ECU 5.4m., to complement the development of plantations. On the whole, however, the industrialization programme of the late 1970s proved to be an expensive failure, and only one large industrial project was planned under the 1981–85 Plan—a phosphoric acid plant at Kpémé, using low-quality phosphate rock from the deposit at Dagbati. Work on the project had not commenced by mid-1994, although it remains part of the government's development programme. The plant, which would require investment of some $600m., would have a capacity of 165,000 tons of phosphoric acid per year. Meanwhile, to improve efficiency in the economy, the government is selling or leasing a number of state enterprises to private interests. The petroleum refinery at Lomé has been leased by Shell Togo, an oil multinational, for six years for use as a storage depot, and the steel mill, renamed the Société togolaise de sidérurgie (STS), was leased in 1984 for 10 years to private US interests which have converted it into a re-rolling facility. Both operations are intended to serve the regional market. Two integrated textile mills were sold to overseas interests. By the end of 1990 the assets of 30 companies had been transferred to private ownership, and 18 others were intended for 'privatization'. Meanwhile, it was expected that manufacturing aimed at export markets would be stimulated by the establishment of a free-trade zone at Lomé, which was inaugurated in 1990. By the end of 1991 15 companies had invested some 56,000m. francs CFA in the zone; most of these, however, suspended operations during 1992–93, owing to the political upheaval, although some had resumed by the beginning of 1994.

TRANSPORT AND TOURISM

Communications are made difficult by the country's long, narrow shape. However, the road network (7,800 km in 1992, of which 1,600 km were surfaced) is currently being improved, with aid from the EDF, IDA and FAC. The 1981–85 Plan projected investment of 8,000m. francs CFA in this sector, mainly to improve the north-south highway and to develop the east-west route via Kara. Of the $310m. scheduled for the improvement of the transport infrastructure in 1988–90, $217m. was to be devoted to the rehabilitation and maintenance of the road network. The railways, with 537 km of track, are generally in need of modernization, and two lines, to Palimé and Aného, have been closed to passenger traffic. The port of Lomé handled about 2m. tons of freight per year in the late 1980s and early 1990s, following an increase in its capacity at the beginning of the 1980s, which afforded new facilities for handling minerals and for fishing. However, hopes of attracting a greater volume of regional transit trade from land-locked west African countries such as Mali, Niger, and Burkina Faso have been disappointed because of the recession in these economies in recent years. During the Sahel drought of the early 1980s Lomé served as a major shipment point for food aid, and work began there in 1986 on the first bulk grain trans-shipping facility in west Africa. The level of freight handled declined to 1.8m. tons in 1992 and to an estimated 1m. tons in 1993, as the political crisis in Togo resulted in the diversion of a large proportion of transit trade to Benin. There are international airports at Tokoin, near Lomé, and at Niamtougou, in the north of the country, as well as several smaller airfields.

Tourism has become a valuable source of funds, representing Togo's third biggest foreign exchange resource, with total revenue of 7,000m. francs CFA in 1989. Visitor numbers reached a record 143,000 in 1982, but have since declined, to 103,000 in 1990. In that year there were 2,372 hotel rooms. However, occupancy rates have remained low, given the general decline in visitor numbers in recent years, and numbers have fallen markedly since the onset of the political crisis: occupancy rates declined to only 26% in the first nine months of 1992. In addition to recreational tourism, efforts have been made to promote Togo as an international conference centre, for which the country is reasonably well equipped. The World Bank is studying the restructuring of this sector.

DEVELOPMENT AND FINANCE

In the past, Togo's official investment targets have been attained or even exceeded, but in the late 1970s, as the result of a deterioration in the country's economic situation (owing mainly to a decline in international prices for phosphates), development spending had to be reduced as part of the government's austerity programme. The 1976–80 Plan provided for total investment of 250,600m. francs CFA, of which just over one-third was projected to come from foreign official sources. Infrastructure was to receive 81,300m. francs CFA, industry 69,900m. (with 45,800m. going to the mining sector) and rural development 56,200m. (with 21,100m. to production of basic foods). Spending was falling well short of these projections, even before the cuts in development spending in 1979 and 1980 (see below), and averaged around three-quarters of the original target.

The 1981–85 Plan projected investment, under a priority programme, at the same level as in 1976–80, which meant a reduction of about one-third in real terms (i.e. if inflation is taken into account), with infrastructure receiving 74,100m. francs CFA, industry 73,400m. and rural development 66,600m. A supplementary 'optional' programme provided for an additional 117,500m. francs CFA in development spending. Foreign aid was expected to cover two-thirds of the programme. In view of Togo's payments difficulties (see below), this latter projection was over-optimistic, while the downturn in phosphate production since 1980, and the budget cuts (see below), meant that the development programme was behind schedule. Reflecting the influence of the IMF, the six-year Development Plan for 1985–90 involved relatively modest targets: an average rise in real GNP of 1.9% per year, and an absence of new investment projects in favour of the maintenance and rehabilitation of existing ones. Proposed spending on national projects was 360,800m. francs CFA (with infrastructure allocated 53% of the total, and rural development 35%), while a further 19,200m. francs CFA was allocated to small-scale local projects, and 88,000m. to support the balance of payments and budgetary operations. Total planned spending was 468,000m. francs CFA, almost 90% of which, it was hoped, was to be covered by foreign sources. By the late 1980s, however, funding at this level had not been procured, rendering the investment target unattainable.

One of the major objectives of the Development Plans has been the strengthening of the government's revenue position. In the early 1960s budget spending tended to exceed government revenue, but by 1968 balance had been achieved—partly as a result of lower capital spending in that year—and was maintained in subsequent years without any foreign subsidies and despite a rapidly rising wages bill. Togo was able to finance a rising capital programme because of the strong expansion in budget revenue, largely owing to higher receipts from phosphate mining and indirect taxation. However, the worsening in the payments situation since 1978 (see below) necessitated recourse to IMF capital support, which required, in turn, an economic stabilization programme (begun in 1979), including a reduction in the growth of spending to an average 5% per year in 1979–81, with development spending down sharply in each year. Fiscal austerity continued in 1982–84, with increases in taxation, further constraints on development spending (which remained well below the rate required under the 1981–85 Plan, and a five-year 'freeze' on public-sector salaries. These trends were scheduled to continue throughout the 1985–90 Plan period, with current spending projected to fall in real terms, as the rise in spending on salaries was kept below the rate of inflation at the same time as tax receipts increased. However, with the ending of the public-sector salary 'freeze' in January 1987, and the deterioration in state marketing finances as a result of lower commodity prices and higher producer prices, the budget deficit almost doubled in 1987, to the equivalent of 6.8% of GDP. However, the proportion was more than halved in 1988, to 3.3%, as a result of higher receipts from taxation (mostly additional import duties), strict controls on current expenditure, and a sharp decline in capital spending. The deficit was little changed in 1989 and 1990, with small increases in revenue in both years, and the primary budget (ie excluding interest payments) was estimated to have been almost in balance in 1991. However, with the onset of political unrest and suspension of financial support by major external creditors—to put pressure on the regime to democratize—total budget receipts were expected to have fallen very markedly in 1992 and 1993. The situation in 1993 was exacerbated by the seven-month general strike (beginning in November 1992), which directly affected both generation and collection of revenue. The government revised its budget revenue forecast for 1993 from 90,000m. francs CFA to 50,000m. francs CFA (estimates by French sources put the out-turn as low as 30,000m. francs CFA). Estimated budget expenditure for 1993 was revised to 76,000m. francs CFA, with the shortfall to be met by drawing on foreign reserves. With the return to work, in the second half of 1993, of civil servants, renewed expenditure on wages, which had been reduced by the general strike, had a detrimental effect on the cash flow position. However, a complete collapse of the fiscal and financial system was avoided.

FOREIGN TRADE AND PAYMENTS

Togo's chronic deficit on foreign trade worsened after the mid-1970s, as export earnings declined as a proportion of import spending. The dynamic expansion in sales of phosphates in the late 1960s and early 1970s meant that, with stronger prices in 1974, foreign trade was in surplus in that year. However, this surplus proved to be short-lived as, despite a continuing rise in phosphate receipts (reflecting the higher volume shipped), export earnings were hit by fluctuation in cocoa production while the import bill was rising very rapidly (more than doubling between 1976–78). Thus, foreign trade registered a record deficit of US $173.8m. in 1979, with exports financing just under two thirds of imports. The trade deficit then narrowed substantially (and 1984 even recorded a modest surplus) as earnings from both phosphates and cocoa improved, while the level of imports was restricted by the economic adjustment programme. In 1986, with the renewed decline in international prices for Togo's export commodities, the deficit widened again, to $59.9m. It remained close to this level for the rest of the 1980s, with the impact of generally weak prices for export commodities offset by import restraint resulting from government policies directed at suppressing growth in domestic demand. The situation deteriorated considerably in 1992 as political disorder resulted in a decrease in exports exceeding the concurrent contraction in imports, producing a deficit of $96m., according to IMF figures. However, these figures do not take into account smuggling, the importance of which would have increased substantially during the political unrest.

Since the services side of the current payments account normally shows a deficit, it is usually left to grants and loans to cover the shortfall. Togo's receipts of official development assistance (ODA) from non-communist countries and multilateral agencies have tended to be lower, and slightly less concessionary, than those of other countries in francophone west Africa. In 1986–91 the country received an annual average of $209.4m. In 1991, in order to exert pressure on the Eyadéma administration to proceed towards democratic reform, France, Germany and the USA (the three leading sources of bilateral aid) suspended development aid, while military assistance from the USA and France was suspended in 1992. This contributed to a sharp deterioration in the balance of payments in 1992, with a capital deficit of $59.9m. contributing to a record overall deficit of $164.9m.

The steep rise in foreign borrowing in the late 1970s, stimulated by the commodity price increases which took place in preceding years, brought Togo's external debt to $1,045m. at the end of 1980 (95.3% of total GNP in that year), of which $899m. was long-term public debt. Debt-rescheduling was necessary in 1979 and again in 1981 and 1983, as exports and GNP contracted and arrears accumulated. In 1982 Togo's reclassification by its official creditors as a least developed country resulted in the cancellation of one-sixth of its outstanding debt to creditor countries. The latter also increased the value of grants and concessionary funding made to Togo, which allowed it to reduce its reliance on commercial borrowing. In 1984 and 1985, however, the increase in the exchange value of the US dollar, in which much of Togo's foreign debt is denominated, kept the debt-service ratio at a high level (an estimated 27.3% of foreign earnings in 1985) despite a continued growth in the value of exports. This necessitated the conclusion of further rescheduling agreements, within the context of the austerity programme negotiated with the IMF and scheduled to be continued until the 1990s. Despite such restructurings of the foreign debt, the debt-service ratio remained high, standing at 28.1% in 1986. Togo clearly could not service its debt at such rates, and further agreements were reached in 1988, under the terms of which the 'Paris Club' of Western official creditors agreed to reschedule all debts due to the end of that year over 16 years, with eight years' grace and with lower interest spreads. More rescheduling of official debt liabilities over a twelve-month period followed, in 1989 (covering $76m.), 1990 ($184m.) and 1992, when relief was accorded on payments due on one-half of Togo's total external debt, with creditors taking the option either of cancelling 50% of payments due and rescheduling the remainder over 23 years, with a six-year grace period, or of reducing the interest rate payable on long-term debt so as to reduce the amount due by one-half. These agreements helped to reduce the debt-service ratio, in relation to the value of exports of goods and services, from 22% in 1989 to only 6.6% in 1992. However, political uncertainty has made further rescheduling agreements unlikely in the near future, while external debt, which stood at $1,356m. at the end of 1992, remains substantial in relation to the size of the economy, being equivalent to 85% of GNP in that year. Moreover the January 1994 devaluation effectively doubled the external debt in local currency terms, and while Togo will benefit from the debt write-off by the French government which followed the devaluation, it cannot draw on the special grants and concessional loans promised at the same time by France, the IMF and the World Bank until normal relations are re-established with its aid donors. In a positive development in this direction an outline agreement was concluded with the IMF in February 1994, providing for credit of $450m. over three years (1994 – 96), followed, in June, by the announcement by France that it was to resume civil co-operation with Togo. However, Togo faces an uphill task to recover from the decline in production and earnings resulting from the political upheaval.

Statistical Survey

Source (except where otherwise stated): Direction de la Statistique, BP 118, Lomé; tel. 21-22-87.

Area and Population

AREA, POPULATION AND DENSITY

Area (sq km)	56,785*
Population (census results)	
1 March–30 April 1970	1,997,109
22 November 1981	2,705,250†
Population (official estimate at 31 January)	
1988	3,296,000
Density (per sq km) at 31 January 1988	58.0

* 21,925 sq miles.
† Provisional.

Mid-year population (UN estimates): 3,317,000 in 1988; 3,422,000 in 1989; 3,531,000 in 1990; 3,645,000 in 1991; 3,763,000 (66.3 per sq km) in 1992 (Source: UN, *World Population Prospects: The 1992 Revision*).

PRINCIPAL TOWNS
(estimated population at 1 January 1977)

Lomé (capital)	229,400	Tsevie	15,900
Sokodé	33,500	Aného	13,300
Palimé	25,500	Mango	10,930*
Atakpamé	21,800	Bafilo	10,100*
Bassari	17,500	Tabligbo	5,120*

* 1975 figure.

BIRTHS AND DEATHS (UN estimates, annual averages)

	1975–80	1980–85	1985–90
Birth rate (per 1,000)	45.2	44.9	44.7
Death rate (per 1,000)	17.4	15.7	14.1

Expectation of life (UN estimates, years at birth, 1985–90): 53.0 (males 51.3; females 54.8).

Source: UN, *World Population Prospects: The 1992 Revision*.

ECONOMICALLY ACTIVE POPULATION
(census of 22 November 1981)

	Males	Females	Total
Agriculture, hunting, forestry and fishing	324,870	254,491	579,361
Mining and quarrying	2,781	91	2,872
Manufacturing	29,307	25,065	54,372
Electricity, gas and water	2,107	96	2,203
Construction	20,847	301	21,148
Trade, restaurants and hotels	17,427	87,415	104,842
Transport, storage and communications	20,337	529	20,866
Financing, insurance, real estate and business services	1,650	413	2,063
Community, social and personal services	50,750	12,859	63,609
Activities not adequately defined	14,607	6,346	20,953
Total employed	484,683	387,606	872,289
Unemployed	21,666	7,588	29,254
Total labour force	506,349	395,194	901,543

Mid-1992 (estimates in '000): Agriculture, etc. 1,034; Total 1,501 (Source: FAO, *Production Yearbook*).

Agriculture

PRINCIPAL CROPS ('000 metric tons)

	1990	1991	1992
Rice (paddy)	25	40	26
Maize	285	231	239
Millet and sorghum	173	191	191
Sweet potatoes	8	2	n.a.
Cassava (Manioc)	593	511	480
Yams	392	376	393
Taro (Coco yam)	14	14	11
Dry beans	20	17	22
Other pulses	2	2	2
Groundnuts (in shell)	26	22	22
Sesame seed*	2	2	2
Cottonseed*	38	55	55
Coconuts*	14	14	14
Copra*	2	2	2
Palm kernels	14.5	14.8*	15.9*
Tomatoes	9	9†	9*
Other vegetables	150	159†	169*
Oranges*	12	12	12
Bananas*	16	16	16
Other fruit*	20	20	20
Coffee (green)	13	22	13†
Cocoa beans	7	9	7†
Tobacco (leaves)	2†	2†	2*
Cotton (lint)†	34	41	41

*FAO estimate(s). † Unofficial figure(s).

Source: FAO, *Production Yearbook*.

LIVESTOCK ('000 head, year ending September)

	1990	1991	1992*
Cattle	280	300*	320
Sheep	1,444	1,470*	1,500
Pigs	1,851	1,900*	2,000
Goats	709	709	800
Horses*	2	2	2
Asses	3	3*	3

Poultry (million): 6 in 1990; 7* in 1991; 7* in 1992.

* FAO estimate(s).

Source: FAO, *Production Yearbook*.

LIVESTOCK PRODUCTS (FAO estimates, '000 metric tons)

	1990	1991	1992
Beef and veal	7	7	8
Mutton and lamb	3	3	4
Goats' meat	4	4	5
Pig meat	10	11	11
Poultry meat	7	8	8
Cows' milk	8	9	9
Hen eggs	5.5	5.5	6.0

Source: FAO, *Production Yearbook*.

Forestry

ROUNDWOOD REMOVALS ('000 cubic metres, excluding bark)

	1989	1990	1991
Sawlogs, veneer logs and logs for sleepers	5	12	8
Other industrial wood*	168	174	179
Fuel wood	696	718	1,047
Total	869	904	1,234

* FAO estimates.

Source: FAO, *Yearbook of Forest Products.*

Fishing

('000 metric tons, live weight)

	1989	1990	1991
Tilapias	3.8	4.0	4.0
Other freshwater fishes	0.7	0.9	0.9
Sardinellas	1.2	0.8	0.7
European anchovy	8.1	7.6	4.7
Other clupeoids	1.2	0.9	0.7
Other marine fishes (incl. unspecified)	1.4	1.5	1.5
Total catch (incl. others)	16.5	15.8	12.5

Source: FAO, *Yearbook of Fishery Statistics.*

Mining

('000 metric tons)

	1988	1989	1990
Natural phosphates (gross weight)	3,464	3,355	2,314

Source: UN, *Industrial Statistics Yearbook.*

Industry

SELECTED PRODUCTS
('000 metric tons, unless otherwise indicated)

	1985	1986	1987
Salted, dried or smoked fish*	3.7	2.7	3.6
Wheat flour	32	42	58
Palm oil*	14	14	14
Beer ('000 hectolitres)	423	464	452
Soft drinks ('000 hectolitres)	83	89	142
Footwear—excl. rubber ('000 pairs)	521†	286	29
Cement	284	338†	370
Electric energy (million kWh)	39	35	39

1988 ('000 metric tons, unless otherwise indicated): Salted, dried or smoked fish 3.7*; Palm oil 14*; Cement 378; Electric energy (million kWh) 38.
1989 ('000 metric tons, unless otherwise indicated): Salted, dried or smoked fish 3.8*; Palm oil 14*; Cement 389†; Electric energy (million kWh) 38.
1990 ('000 metric tons, unless otherwise indicated): Palm oil 14*; Cement 400; Electric energy 41.

* Estimate(s) by the FAO.
† Provisional or estimated figure.

Source: mainly UN, *Industrial Statistics Yearbook.*

Finance

CURRENCY AND EXCHANGE RATES

Monetary Units

100 centimes = 1 franc de la Communauté financière africaine (CFA).

French Franc, Sterling and Dollar Equivalents (31 March 1994)
1 French franc = 100 francs CFA;
£1 sterling = 846.40 francs CFA;
US $1 = 570.14 francs CFA;
1,000 francs CFA = £1.181 = $1.754.

Average Exchange Rate (francs CFA per US $)
1991 282.11
1992 264.69
1993 283.16

Note: An exchange rate of 1 French france = 50 francs CFA, established in 1948, remained in force until January 1994, when the CFA franc was devalued by 50%, with the exchange rate adjusted to 1 French franc = 100 francs CFA.

BUDGET (estimates, million francs CFA)

Revenue	1988	1989	1990
Fiscal receipts	82,350	83,390	85,912
Taxes on income and profits	31,715	32,350	37,420
Individual taxes	8,340	8,250	8,375
Corporate and business taxes	21,675	21,050	26,695
Taxes on goods and services	29,660	29,810	25,504
Turnover taxes	26,165	26,500	22,008
Consumption taxes	2,300	2,330	2,400
Taxes on international trade and transactions	20,325	20,500	21,988
Import duties	18,910	19,385	20,953
Other current receipts	7,342	9,071	6,578
Capital receipts	—	25	—
Total	89,692	92,486	92,490

Expenditure	1988	1989	1990
General public services	19,684	22,472	23,495
Defence	12,834	13,354	13,817
Public order and security	1,864	2,373	2,438
Education	19,068	20,593	21,384
Health	4,758	4,492	4,770
Social security and welfare	—	634	760
Housing and community services	—	120	107
Other community and social services	2,188	2,257	2,403
Economic services	6,068	6,820	6,804
Agriculture, forestry and fishing	2,805	2,672	2,677
Mining, manufacturing and construction	149	322	324
Transport and communications	2,942	2,329	2,169
Other economic services	172	1,497	1,634
Other purposes	23,228	19,371	16,512
Investment budget	3,300	3,459	3,500
Debt-repayment	19,928	15,912	13,012
Total	89,692	92,486	92,490

Source: Banque centrale des états de l'Afrique de l'ouest.

1991 (estimates, million francs CFA): Budget balanced at 92,490.
1992 (preliminary estimates, million francs CFA): Budget balanced at 95,800.

CENTRAL BANK RESERVES
(US $ million at 31 December)

	1991	1992	1993
Gold*	4.4	4.3	4.7
IMF special drawing rights	0.4	0.3	0.1
Reserve position	0.4	0.3	0.3
Foreign exchange	364.1	271.9	155.9
Total	369.3	276.8	161.0

* Valued at market-related prices.

Source: IMF, *International Financial Statistics*.

MONEY SUPPLY ('000 million francs CFA at 31 December)

	1991	1992	1993
Currency outside banks	36.29	22.34	10.72
Demand deposits at deposit money banks	41.19	34.14	35.13
Checking deposits at post office	1.00	—	—
Total money	78.48	56.48	45.96

Source: IMF, *International Financial Statistics*.

COST OF LIVING
(Consumer price index, Lomé. Base: 1980 = 100).

	1985	1986	1987
Food	130.7	136.1	134.8
Fuel and light*	160.9	161.5	161.5
Clothing	141.6	156.8	154.6
Rent	130.6	136.5	135.7
All items (incl. others)	137.8	143.5	143.6

* Including cleaning products and certain kitchen utensils.

1988: Food 154.6; Clothing 173.2; Rent 136.8; All items 143.9.
1989: Food 127.3; All items 142.2.
1990: Food 129.7; All items 143.6.
1991: Food 124.2; All items 144.3.

Source: ILO, *Year Book of Labour Statistics*.

NATIONAL ACCOUNTS
(million francs CFA at current prices)

Expenditure on the Gross Domestic Product

	1989	1990	1991
Government final consumption expenditure	59,700	59,600	59,700
Private final consumption expenditure	301,510	335,600	361,680
Increase in stocks	1,600	4,800	3,500
Gross fixed capital formation	101,000	104,700	111,700
Total domestic expenditure	463,810	504,700	536,580
Exports of goods and services	164,000	155,600	166,000
Less Imports of goods and services	195,800	203,000	209,200
GDP in purchasers' values	432,010	457,300	493,380
GDP at constant 1980 prices	278,878	278,995	290,573

Gross Domestic Product by Economic Activity

	1989	1990	1991
Agriculture, hunting, forestry and fishing	136,090	140,754	150,580
Mining and quarrying	28,970	38,806	41,420
Manufacturing	27,560	28,310	29,480
Electricity, gas and water	15,700	15,600	16,000
Construction	14,030	14,540	15,400
Trade, restaurants and hotels	72,330	73,000	75,000
Transport, storage and communications	26,180	27,000	29,280
Finance, insurance, real estate and business services	14,950	15,450	17,800
Public administration and defence	37,750	38,500	40,500
Other services	13,540	14,040	14,940
GDP at factor cost	387,100	406,000	430,400
Indirect taxes, *less* subsidies	44,910	51,300	62,980
GDP in purchasers' values	432,010	457,300	493,380

Source: UN Economic Commission for Africa, *African Statistical Yearbook*.

BALANCE OF PAYMENTS (US $ million)

	1990	1991	1992
Merchandise exports f.o.b.	395.2	393.5	322.3
Merchandise imports f.o.b.	−513.1	−452.3	−418.2
Trade balance	−117.9	−58.8	−96.0
Exports of services	150.2	143.2	129.6
Imports of services	−227.0	−213.4	−202.5
Other income received	30.5	29.4	31.4
Other income paid	−61.0	−59.6	−60.8
Private unrequited transfers (net)	9.9	14.2	8.3
Official unrequited transfers (net)	113.9	84.4	85.4
Current balance	−101.4	−60.6	−104.7
Capital (net)	62.2	12.0	−59.9
Net errors and omissions	10.8	−0.4	−0.3
Overall balance	−28.4	−49.1	−164.9

Source: IMF, *International Financial Statistics*.

External Trade

Source: UN, *International Trade Statistics Yearbook.*

PRINCIPAL COMMODITIES (US $ million)

Imports c.i.f.	1989	1990	1991
Food and live animals	88.4	86.1	72.4
Fish, crustaceans and molluscs	14.3	15.3	16.6
Fresh, chilled or frozen fish	10.4	11.5	14.6
Fish, frozen (excl. fillets)	9.6	11.4	14.1
Cereals and cereal preparations	35.4	33.4	21.5
Wheat (incl. spelt) and meslin, unmilled	16.5	19.4	11.3
Duram wheat, unmilled	14.8	17.7	10.3
Rice	10.6	7.8	6.4
Rice, semi-milled, milled	10.4	7.7	6.4
Sugar, sugar preparations and honey	11.3	9.6	7.7
Sugar and honey	10.4	8.7	7.1
Refined sugars, etc	10.2	8.6	2.3
Miscellaneous edible products and preparations	4.3	7.6	11.0
Soups and broths	0.7	3.8	9.1
Beverages and Tobacco	25.2	35.5	25.2
Tobacco and tobacco manufactures	17.8	25.1	18.1
Tobacco, manufactured	17.8	24.9	17.9
Cigarettes	17.7	24.7	17.7
Crude material (inedible) except fuels	9.1	10.9	9.0
Mineral fuels, lubricants and related materials	29.0	48.1	43.6
Petroleum, petroleum products and related materials	28.7	47.7	43.3
Petroleum products, refined	28.3	45.9	42.7
Motor spirit (gasoline) and other light oils	11.6	19.3	42.6
Motor spirit (gasoline), including aviation spirit	11.6	19.3	—
Other light petroleum oils	—	—	42.6
Chemicals and related products	42.9	71.9	52.7
Medicinal and pharmaceutical products	15.4	30.0	21.0
Medicaments	14.1	25.4	19.7
Medicaments containing antibiotics	13.3	23.6	16.5
Other chemical materials	5.5	21.6	14.5
Pesticides, disinfectants	4.2	19.8	13.1
Insecticides, for retail	2.1	18.9	9.6
Basic manufactures	119.8	146.2	78.5
Textile yarn, fabrics, etc	61.3	61.2	30.0
Cotton fabrics, woven	53.0	49.3	23.1
Woven cotton bleached, etc	50.9	48.0	22.5
Bleached cotton fabric (containing 85% or more by weight of cotton	49.2	47.0	22.4
Non-metallic mineral manufactures	17.1	30.0	12.8
Lime, cement and fabricated construction materials	12.8	23.9	8.7
Cement	11.5	22.3	7.1
Iron and steel	12.6	16.4	8.6
Other metal manufactures	12.6	16.8	10.2
Machinery and transport equipment	118.8	131.2	125.5
Power-generating machinery and equipment	3.9	4.4	9.3
Machinery specialized for particular industries	20.0	13.0	14.5
General industrial machinery, equipment and parts	16.7	20.2	17.6
Telecommunications and sound equipment	11.4	11.8	16.7
Other electrical machinery, apparatus etc	17.1	18.0	16.8
Road vehicles	39.8	49.6	41.4
Passenger motor cars (excl. buses)	14.3	19.5	14.5
Miscellaneous manufactured articles	29.5	40.4	28.6
Total (incl. others)	471.9	581.4	443.9

Exports f.o.b.	1989	1990	1991
Food and live animals	47.6	57.3	43.6
Cereals and cereal preparations	8.8	17.3	9.2
Flour of wheat or meslin	7.4	12.3	6.8
Coffee, tea, cocoa, spices, and manufactures thereof	34.6	33.5	20.6
Coffee (not roasted), coffee husks and skins	22.1	17.8	9.1
Cocoa beans, raw, roasted	12.3	15.2	11.0
Crude materials (inedible) except fuels	173.2	178.9	186.6
Textile fibres and waste	39.4	55.7	60.4
Cotton	38.7	55.6	55.4
Raw cottons (excl. linters)	38.6	55.6	55.2
Crude fertilizers and crude minerals	130.6	119.6	124.7
Natural calcium phosphates, etc	130.4	119.1	122.8
Mineral fuels, lubricants and related materials	—	0.1	5.9
Petroleum, petroleum products and related materials	—	—	5.8
Petroleum products, refined	—	—	5.8
Motor spirit (gasoline) and other light oils	—	—	5.8
Other light petroleum oils	—	—	5.8
Basic manufactures	12.0	19.5	7.7
Textile yarn, fabrics, etc	0.7	6.5	1.1
Textile articles	0.1	5.7	0.5
Sacks and bags of textile materials	—	5.7	0.5
Non-metallic mineral manufactures	5.2	7.0	3.0
Lime, cement and fabricated construction materials	5.2	6.9	3.0
Cement	5.1	6.9	3.0
Total (incl. others)	245.1	267.9	253.2

PRINCIPAL TRADING PARTNERS (US $ million)

Imports c.i.f.	1989	1990	1991
Angola	4.8	3.8	1.2
Belgium/Luxembourg	8.9	10.4	9.1
Benin	6.0	5.7	4.0
Cameroon	0.9	0.5	12.5
Canada	5.2	6.6	0.6
China, People's Republic	7.2	8.9	6.0
Côte d'Ivoire	12.1	46.9	16.8
France	139.6	177.2	146.9
Gabon	5.7	5.8	3.4
Germany, Federal Republic	36.1	35.0	18.5
Ghana	5.0	7.6	5.3
Hong Kong	10.0	14.9	10.9
Italy	14.4	13.3	14.0
Japan	19.9	25.0	29.7
Netherlands	55.5	52.7	33.5
Nigeria	8.0	13.1	12.8
Norway	1.0	7.7	3.6
Senegal	5.9	5.5	1.6
Singapore	7.3	7.4	5.6
Spain	13.5	9.6	4.9
Switzerland/Liechtenstein	2.5	3.1	5.3
Thailand	5.0	4.4	4.6
United Kingdom	20.0	21.8	16.3
USA	26.7	30.8	28.5
Total (incl. others)	471.9	581.3	443.9

Exports f.o.b.	1989	1990	1991
Australia	10.7	1.2	—
Bangladesh	—	5.7	0.5
Belgium/Luxembourg	4.3	5.9	2.1
Benin	7.1	5.7	5.1
British Indian Ocean Territory	—	3.2	4.6
Burkina Faso	5.7	8.8	5.7
Canada	30.6	33.4	28.7
China, People's Republic	0.9	0.2	4.6
Denmark	2.5	3.8	2.3
France	21.2	26.3	17.0
Germany, Federal Republic	3.4	10.0	7.1
Ghana	4.9	4.1	2.9
Greece	0.3	3.8	8.0
Guinea	—	3.7	0.2
India	8.0	14.1	6.5
Indonesia	1.8	2.2	4.1
Italy	18.4	14.2	10.4
Mexico	3.3	4.3	17.9
Morocco	3.0	2.5	1.7
Netherlands	15.3	8.8	2.2
Niger	2.8	3.6	3.3
Nigeria	6.1	8.8	19.4
Philippines	12.2	11.5	12.5
Poland	10.8	3.1	3.6
Portugal	9.1	14.6	4.0
Singapore	0.3	0.8	3.6
Spain	18.8	17.1	17.2
Switzerland/Liechtenstein	1.1	3.4	3.0
Thailand	3.0	1.7	9.3
USSR	4.9	12.6	10.4
United Kingdom	13.4	3.9	3.9
USA	0.3	3.0	0.2
Yugoslavia	2.6	1.2	0.9
Total (incl. others)	245.1	267.9	253.2

Transport

RAILWAYS (estimated traffic)

	1989	1990	1991
Passenger-km (million)	124	129	132
Freight (million ton-km)	14	15	17

Source: UN Economic Commission for Africa, *African Statistical Yearbook*.

ROAD TRAFFIC (motor vehicles registered at 31 December)

	1986	1987	1988
Passenger cars	41,122	44,120	47,083
Buses and coaches	298	352	381
Goods vehicles	19,943	21,136	22,230
Tractors (road)	940	994	1,048
Motor cycles and scooters	25,400	27,483	29,179

Source: Banque centrale des états de l'Afrique de l'ouest.

INTERNATIONAL SEA-BORNE SHIPPING
(freight traffic, '000 metric tons)

Port Lomé*	1990	1991	1992
Goods loaded	180	162	178
Goods unloaded	1,157	1,050	1,114

* Excluding goods in transit.

Source: Banque centrale des états de l'Afrique de l'ouest.

Port Kpémé	1979	1980	1981
Freight loaded* ('000 metric tons)	2,990	2,895	2,200

* Phosphate from the OTP mines.

Source: *Statistiques douanières du Togo*.

CIVIL AVIATION (traffic on scheduled services)*

	1989	1990	1991
Km flown (million)	2	2	2
Passengers carried ('000)	74	76	64
Passenger-km (million)	224	232	203
Freight ton-km (million)	18	18	16
Mail ton-km (million)	1	1	1

* Including an apportionment of the traffic of Air Afrique.

Source: UN, *Statistical Yearbook*.

Tourism

	1988	1989	1990
Tourist arrivals ('000)	104	115	103
Tourist receipts (US $ million)	42	41	23

Source: UN, *Statistical Yearbook*.

Communications Media

	1989	1990	1991
Radio receivers ('000 in use)	719	745	770
Television receivers ('000 in use)	20	22	23
Telephones ('000 in use)*	16	17	18
Daily newspapers			
Number	n.a.	1	n.a.
Circulation ('000 copies)	n.a.	10	n.a.

* Estimates.

Sources: UNESCO, *Statistical Yearbook*; UN Economic Commission for Africa, *African Statistical Yearbook*.

Education

(1990, unless otherwise indicated)

	Institutions	Teachers	Students		
			Males	Females	Total
Pre-primary	252	383	5,540	5,409	10,949
Primary	2,494	11,105	396,320	255,642	651,962
Secondary					
General	n.a.	4,231	87,548	29,605	117,153
Vocational	n.a.	261	6,231	2,161	8,392
University level	n.a.	276*	6,702†	1,030†	7,732†

* 1988 figure. † 1989 figure.

Source: UNESCO, *Statistical Yearbook*.

Directory

The Constitution

The Constitution that was approved in a national referendum on 27 September 1993 defines the rights, freedoms and obligations of Togolese citizens, and defines the separation of powers among the executive, legislative and judicial organs of state.

Executive power is vested in the President of the Republic, who is elected, by direct universal adult suffrage, with a five-year mandate. The legislature, the Assemblée nationale, is similarly elected for a period of five years, its 81 members being directly elected by universal suffrage. The President of the Republic appoints a Prime Minister who is able to command a majority in the legislature, and the Prime Minister, in consultation with the President, appoints other government ministers. A Constitutional Court is designated as the highest court of jurisdiction in constitutional matters.

The Government

HEAD OF STATE

President: Gen. GNASSINGBE EYADÉMA (assumed power 13 January 1967; proclaimed President 14 April 1967; elected 30 December 1979; re-elected 21 December 1986 and 25 August 1993).

COUNCIL OF MINISTERS

(September 1994)

President: Gen. GNASSINGBE EYADÉMA.

Prime Minister: EDEM KODJO.

Minister of Justice and Keeper of the Seals: KAGNI GABRIEL AKAKPOVIE.

Minister of National Defence: ALFA ABALO.

Minister of Economy and Finance: ELOME EMILE DADZIE.

Minister of Foreign Affairs and Co-operation: BOUMBERA ALASSOUNOUMA.

Minister of the Interior and Decentralization: KODJO SAGBO.

Minister of Planning and Territorial Development: YANDJA YENTCHABRE.

Minister of National Education and Scientific Research: Prof. KOMLAVI SEDDOH.

Minister of Communications and Culture: ATSUTSE AGBOBLI.

Minister of Human Rights and Rehabilitation, in charge of Relations with the National Assembly: DJOVI GALLY.

Minister of Industry and State Enterprises: FAYADOWA BOUKPESSI.

Minister of Equipment: TCHAMDJA ANDJO.

Minister of Mines, Energy and Water Resources: ANATO AGBOZOUHOUE.

Minister of Rural Development, Environment and Tourism: YAO DO FELLI.

Minister of Trade, Price Control and Transport: DEDEVI MICHÈLE EKUE.

Minister of Health, Population and National Solidarity: Prof. AFATSAO AMEDOME.

Minister of Technical Education and Vocational Training: BAMOUNI SOMOLOU STANISLAS BABA.

Minister of Youth and Sports: KOUAMI AGBOGBOLI IHOU.

Secretary of State delegate to the Minister of the Interior and Decentralization, in charge of Security: Col SEYI MEMENE.

MINISTRIES

Office of the President: Palais Présidentiel, ave de la Marina, Lomé; tel. 21-27-01; telex 5201.

Ministry of Communications and Culture: Lomé.

Ministry of the Economy and Finance: Ancien Palais, ave de la Marina, BP 387, Lomé; tel. 21-23-71; telex 5286; fax 21-76-02.

Ministry of Employment, Labour, the Civil Service and Social Welfare: angle ave de la Marina et rue Kpalimé, Lomé; tel. 21-26-53.

Ministry of Equipment, Mines, Energy and Water Resources: Immeuble des Quatre Ministères, rue Colonel de Roux, Lomé; tel. 21-38-01.

Ministry of Foreign Affairs and Co-operation: place du Monument aux Morts, Lomé; tel. 21-29-10; telex 5239.

Ministry of Health, Population and National Solidarity: rue Branly, Lomé; tel. 21-29-83.

Ministry of Human Rights and Rehabilitation: BP 336, Lomé; tel. 21-35-24; fax 21-89-48.

Ministry of Industry and State Enterprises: BP 2748, Lomé; tel. 21-07-44; telex 5396.

Ministry of the Interior and Decentralization: rue Albert Sarraut, Lomé; tel. 21-23-19.

Ministry of Justice: ave de la Marina, rue Colonel de Roux, Lomé; tel. 21-26-53.

Ministry of National Defence: Lomé; tel. 21-28-91; telex 5321.

Ministry of National Education and Scientific Research, Technical Education and Vocational Training: Immeuble des Quatre Ministères, rue Colonel de Roux, Lomé; tel. 21-38-01; telex 5322.

Ministry of Planning and Territorial Development: Lomé; tel. 21-27-01; telex 5380.

Ministry of Rural Development, Environment and Tourism: ave de Sarakawa, Lomé; tel. 21-56-71.

Ministry of Trade, Price Control and Transport: rue de Commerce, Lomé; tel. 21-09-09.

Ministry of Youth and Sports: Lomé; telex 5103.

President and Legislature

PRESIDENT

Presidential Election, 25 August 1993

Candidate	% of votes
Gen. GNASSINGBE EYADÉMA	96.49
KWAMI MENSAH JACQUES AMOUZOU	1.87
ADANI IFÉ ATAKPAMEVI	1.64
Total	100.00

ASSEMBLÉE NATIONALE

Speaker: DAHUKU PERE (RPT).

General Election, 6 and 20 February 1994

Party	Seats
Comité d'action pour le renouveau (CAR) . . .	36*
Rassemblement du peuple togolais (RPT) . . .	35
Union togolaise pour la démocratie (UTD) . . .	7*
Union pour la justice et la démocratie (UJD). . .	2
Coordination nationale des forces nouvelles (CFN) .	1
Total	81

* The Supreme Court declared the election result invalid in two constituencies where the seats had been allocated to the CAR, and in one where the seat had been allocated to the UTD. By-elections were to be held in these constituencies at a later date.

Political Organizations

Following the legalization of political parties in April 1991, numerous organizations obtained legal status. By mid-1993 63 parties were officially acknowledged. Of the parties in existence at the beginning of 1994, among the most influential were:

Alliance togolaise pour la démocratie (ATD): Leader: ADANI IFÉ ATAKPAMEVI.

Comité d'action pour le renouveau (CAR): Leader Me YAO AGBOYIBO.

Convention démocratique des peuples africains (CDPA): Leader Prof. LÉOPOLD GNININVI.

Démocratie sociale togolaise (DST): linked to PDT; Leader ABOU DJOBO BOUKARI.

Mouvement du 5 octobre (MO5): radical group; Leader BASSIROU AYEVA.

Mouvement nationaliste de l'unité (MNU): f. Oct. 1992; Gen. Sec. KOFFITSE ADZRAKO.

Parti d'action pour la démocratie (PAD): Leader FRANCIS EKOH.

Parti démocratique togolais (PDT): linked to DST; Leader MBA KABASSEMA.

Parti des démocrates pour l'unité (PDU): Leader JEAN-LUCIEN SAVI DE TOVÉ.

Parti pour la démocratie et le renouveau (PDR): Leader ZARIFOU AYIVA.

Parti pan-africain socialiste (PPS): radical; Leader FRANCIS AGBOBLI.

Rassemblement du peuple togolais (RPT): place de l'Indépendance, BP 1208, Lomé; tel. 21-20-18; telex 5207; f. 1969; sole legal party 1969–91; Pres. Gen. GNASSINGBE EYADÉMA; Sec.-Gen. VIGNIKO AMEDEGNATO.

Union pour la démocratie et la solidarité (UDS): Sec.-Gen. ANTOINE FOLY.

Union pour la justice at la démocratie (UJD): pro-Eyadéma; Leader LAL TAXPANDJAN.

Union des libéraux indépendants (ULD): f. Nov. 1993; to succeed Union des démocrates pour le renouveau; Leader KWAMI MENSAH JACQUES AMOUZOU.

Union togolaise pour la démocratie (UTD): Leader EDEM KODJO; SEC.-GEN. ADAN MESSAN AJAVON.

Union togolaise pour la réconciliation (UTR): Leader BAWA MANKOUBU.

Most of the above parties belonged to one or more of the following alliances, reported to be active in mid-1994:

Collectif de l'opposition démocratique (COD-2): f. 1992; alliance of about 26 political orgs and trade unions; incl. CAR, CDPA, PDU, PDR, UDS and UTD; Leader ANTOINE FOLY (UDS).

Comité de la résistance togolaise: Paris, France; comprises c. 20 political orgs; Chair. ISIDORE LATIZO; Sec.-Gen. AURÉLIO AMORIN.

Coordination nationale des forces nouvelles (CFN): f. June 1993; comprises six political orgs and asscns; Pres. Me JOSEPH KOKOU KOFFIGOH; Nat. Exec. Sec. NICOLAS NOMEDJI.

Groupe des démocrates sociaux pan-africains: f. Dec. 1993; alliance of CDPA, PDR and PPS; Leader Prof. LÉOPOLD GNININVI.

Union des forces de changement: comprises 20 parties; Leader GILCHRIST OLYMPIO.

Diplomatic Representation

EMBASSIES IN TOGO

Belgium: 165 rue Pelletier Caventou, BP 7643, Lomé; tel. 21-03-23; telex 5363; Ambassador: PIERRE VAESEN.

Brazil: 119 rue de l'Ocam, BP 1356, Lomé; tel. 21-00-58; telex 5346; Chargé d'affaires a.i.: JOSÉ ROBERTO PROCOPIAK.

China, People's Republic: Tokoin-Ouest, BP 2690, Lomé; tel. 21-31-59; telex 5070; Ambassador: ZHOU XIANJUE.

Egypt: route d'Aného, BP 8, Lomé; tel. 21-24-43; telex 5310; Ambassador: HUSSEIN EL-KHAZINDAR.

France: 51 rue du Golfe, BP 337, Lomé; tel. 21-25-71; telex 5202; Ambassador: JEAN-MICHEL GAUSSOT.

Gabon: Tokoin Super-Taco, BP 9118, Lomé; tel. 21-47-76; telex 5307; Ambassador: ALAIN MAURICE MAYOMBO.

Germany: Marina, route d'Aflao, BP 1175, Lomé; tel. 21-23-38; telex 5204; Ambassador: (vacant).

Ghana: 8 rue Paulin Eklou, Tokoin-Ouest, BP 92, Lomé; tel. 21-31-94; fax 21-77-36; Chargé d'affaires a.i.: J. M. KWADJO.

Israel: 159 rue de l'OCAM, BP 61187, Lomé; tel. 21-79-58; telex 5424; fax 21-88-94; Ambassador: JACOB TOPAZ.

Korea, Democratic People's Republic: Tokoin-Est, Lomé; tel. 21-46-01; Ambassador: CHO CHUN HYONG.

Libya: blvd du 13 janvier, BP 4872, Lomé; tel. 21-40-63; telex 5288; Chargé d'affaires a.i.: AHMED M. ABDULKAFI.

Nigeria: 311 blvd du 13 janvier, BP 1189, Lomé; tel. 21-34-55; Ambassador: VINCENT OKOBI.

USA: angle rue Pelletier Caventou et rue Vauban, BP 852, Lomé; tel. 21-29-91; fax 21-79-52; Ambassador: HARMON E. KIRBY.

Zaire: 325 blvd du 13 janvier, BP 102, Lomé; tel. 21-51-55; telex 5263; Ambassador: LOKOKA IKUKELE BOMOLO.

Judicial System

Justice is administered by the Cour Suprême (Supreme Court), two Cours d'Appel (Appeal Courts) and the Tribunaux de première instance, which hear civil, commercial and criminal cases. There is a labour tribunal and a tribunal for children's rights. In addition, there are two exceptional courts, the Cour de sûreté de l'Etat, which judges crimes against internal and external state security, and the Tribunal spécial chargé de la répression des détournements de deniers publics, which deals with cases of misuse of public funds. Under the Constitution adopted in September 1992, a Constitutional Court was to be established.

Cour Suprême: BP 906, Lomé; tel. 21-22-58; f. 1961; consists of four chambers; constitutional, judicial, administrative and auditing; Pres. EMMANUEL APEDOH; Attorney-Gen. KPOLO AREGBA.

Religion

It is estimated that about 50% of the population follow traditional animist beliefs, some 35% are Christians (mainly Roman Catholics) and 15% ARE Muslims.

CHRISTIANITY

The Roman Catholic Church

Togo comprises one archdiocese and three dioceses. At 31 December 1992 there were an estimated 856,489 adherents in the country, representing about 21.6% of the total population.

Bishops' Conference: Conférence Episcopale du Togo, 10 rue Maréchal Foch, BP 348, Lomé; tel. 21-22-72; f. 1979; Pres. Most Rev. PHILIPPE KPODZRO, Archbishop of Lomé.

Archbishop of Lomé: Most Rev. PHILIPPE KPODZRO, Archevêché, 10 rue Maréchal Foch, BP 348, Lomé; tel. 21-22-72.

Protestant Churches

There are about 170 mission centres, with a personnel of some 230, affiliated to European and American societies and administered by a Conseil Synodal, presided over by a moderator.

Directorate of Protestant Churches: 1 rue Maréchal Foch, BP 378, Lomé; Moderator Rev. Pastor AWUME (acting).

BAHÁ'Í FAITH

National Spiritual Assembly: BP 1659, Lomé; tel. 21-21-99; mems resident in 445 localities.

The Press

DAILIES

Journal Officiel de la République du Togo: EDITOGO, BP 891, Lomé; tel. 21-37-18; telex 5294.

Togo-Presse: EDITOGO, BP 891, Lomé; tel. 21-37-18; telex 5294; f. 1962; renamed *La Nouvelle Marche* 1979–91; daily; French, Kabiye and Ewe; political, economic and cultural; official govt publ.; Editor-in-Chief (vacant); circ. 15,000.

PERIODICALS

Bulletin de la Chambre de Commerce: angle ave de la Présidence, BP 360, Lomé; tel. 21-70-65; telex 5023; fax 21-47-30; monthly; directory of commercial, industrial and agricultural activities.

Bulletin d'Information de l'Agence Togolaise de Presse: 35 rue Binger, Lomé; weekly; publ. by govt information service.

Courrier du Golfe: Lomé; f. 1990; independent.

Espoir de la Nation Togolaise: EDITOGO, BP 891, Lomé; tel. 21-37-18; telex 5294; monthly; Dir M. AWESSO; circ. 3,000.

L'Eveil du Travailleur Togolais: BP 163, Lomé; tel. 21-57-39; quarterly; Elrato; publ. by Conféd. nationale des travailleurs du Togo; Chief Editor M. K. AGBEKA; circ. 5,000.

Forum Hebdo: Lomé; weekly; independent; Dir GABRIEL KOMI AGAH.

Game su: 19 ave de la Nouvelle Marche, BP 1247, Lomé; tel. 21-28-44; f. 1972; monthly; Ewe; publ. by Ministry of Health, Population and National Solidarity for the newly literate; circ. 6,000.

La Parole: Lomé; weekly; independent; Dir BERTIN KANGHI FOLY.

Kpakpa Désenchanté: Lomé; weekly; independent.

Le Secteur Privé: angle ave de la Présidence, BP 360, Lomé; tel. 21-70-65; telex 5023; fax 21-47-30; monthly; publ. by Chambre de Commerce, d'Agriculture et d'Industrie du Togo.

Tev fema: 19 ave de la Nouvelle Marche, BP 1247, Lomé; tel. 21-28-44; f. 1977; monthly; Kabiye; publ. by Ministry of Health, Population and National Solidarity; circ. 3,000.

Togo-Dialogue: EDITOGO, BP 891, Lomé; tel. 21-37-18; telex 5294; monthly; publ. by govt information service; circ. 5,000.

Togo-Images: BP 4869, Lomé; tel. 21-56-80; f. 1962; monthly series of wall posters depicting recent political, economic and cultural events in Togo; publ. by govt information service; Dir AKOBI BEDOU; circ. 5,000.

La Tribune des Démocrates: Lomé; weekly; independent; Editor MARTIN NBENOUGOU (imprisoned May 1994).

NEWS AGENCIES

Agence Togolaise de Presse (ATOP): 35 rue des Media, BP 2327, Lomé; tel. 212507; telex 5320; f. 1975; Dir SESHIE SEYENA BIAVA.

Foreign Bureau

Xinhua (New China) News Agency (People's Republic of China): BP 2984, Lomé; tel. 21-39-20; telex 5273; Correspondent QIN DIANJIE.

Publishers

Centre Togolais de Communication Evangélique, Librairie-Papeterie-Imprimerie, Editions HAHO: 1 rue de Commerce, BP 378, Lomé; tel. and fax 21-29-67; Dir Dr UDO STEFFENS.

Editions Akpagnon: BP 3531, Lomé; f. 1979; general literature; Man. Dir YVES-EMMANUEL DOGBÉ.

Etablissement National des Editions du Togo (EDITOGO): BP 891, Lomé; tel. 21-61-06; telex 5294; f. 1961; govt publishing house; general and educational; Pres. GBÉGNON AMEGBOH; Man. Dir KOKOU AMEDEGNATO.

Nouvelles Editions Africaines du Togo (NEA TOGO): 239 blvd du 13 janvier, BP 4862, Lomé; tel. 21-67-61; telex 5393; fax 22-10-03; general fiction and non-fiction; Man. Dir DOVI KAVEGUE.

Radio and Television

In 1991, according to UNESCO, there were an estimated 770,000 radio receivers and 23,000 television receivers in use.

Radiodiffusion du Togo (Internationale) — Radio Lomé: BP 434, Lomé; tel. 21-24-93; telex 5320; fax 21-36-73; f. 1953; renamed Radiodiffusion-Télévision de la Nouvelle Marche 1979–91; state-controlled; radio programmes in French, English and vernacular languages; Dir VIOTO EHO.

Radiodiffusion du Togo (Nationale): BP 21, Kara; tel. 60-60-60; f. 1974 as Radiodiffusion Kara (Togo); state-controlled; radio programmes in French and vernacular languages; Dir M'BA KPENOUGOU.

Radio Liberté: operated by the COD-2 opposition alliance, was reported to have commenced broadcasts in late 1992.

Télévision Togolaise: BP 3286, Lomé; tel. 21-53-57; telex 5320; fax 21-57-86; f. 1973; state-controlled; three stations; programmes in French and vernacular languages; Dir MARTIN AHIAVI.

Finance

(cap. = capital; res = reserves; dep. = deposits; m. = million; br. = branch; amounts in francs CFA)

BANKING

Central Bank

Banque Centrale des Etats de l'Afrique de l'Ouest (BCEAO): ave de Sarakawa, BP 120, Lomé; tel. 21-25-12; telex 5216; fax 21-76-02; headquarters in Dakar, Senegal; f. 1955; bank of issue and central bank for the seven states of the Union monétaire ouest-africaine (UMOA), comprising Benin, Burkina Faso, Côte d'Ivoire, Mali, Niger, Senegal and Togo; cap. and res 379,881m. (Sept. 1992); Gov. CHARLES KONAN BANNY; Dir in Togo YAO MESSAN AHO; br. at Kara.

Commercial Banks

Banque Togolaise pour le Commerce et l'Industrie (BTCI): 169 blvd du 13 janvier, BP 363, Lomé; tel. 21-46-41; telex 5221; fax 21-32-65; f. 1974; 24.8% owned by Société Financière pour les Pays d'Outre-mer, 23.8% by Banque Nationale de Paris, 21.0% by SNI & FA; cap. 1,700m. (Sept. 1992); Pres. DO FRANCK FIANYO; Man. Dir MAX KODJO OSSEYI; 8 brs.

Ecobank—Togo: 20 rue de Commerce, BP 3302, Lomé; tel. 21-72-14; telex 5440; fax 21-42-37; f. 1984, operations commenced 1988; 60% owned by Ecobank Transnational Inc (operating under the auspices of the Economic Community of West African States), 40% by Togolese private interests; cap. 750m., res 584m., dep. 10,862m. (Sept. 1993); Pres. YAO PALI TCHALLA; Man. Dir AMIN UDDIN.

Meridien BIAO—Togo: 13 rue de Commerce, BP 346, Lomé; tel. 21-32-86; telex 5218; fax 21-10-19; f. 1981, adopted present name in 1991; 60% owned by Meridien BIAO SA (Luxembourg), 40% by private Togolese interests; cap. 937.5m. (Sept. 1991); Pres. KOSSI R. PAASS; Man. Dir ALEXIS LAMSEH LOOKY; 6 brs.

Société Interafricaine de Banques (SIAB): route d'Aného, BP 4874, Lomé; tel. 21-28-30; telex 5301; fax 21-58-29; f. 1975; fmrly Banque Arabe Libyenne-Togolaise du Commerce Extérieur; 50% state-owned, 50% owned by Libyan Arab Foreign Bank; cap. 3,100m. (Sept. 1993); Pres. YENTCHABRE YANDJA; Man. Dir TAHER BUSHAALA.

Union Togolaise de Banque (UTB): 13 blvd du 13 janvier, BP 359, Lomé; tel. 21-64-11; telex 5215; fax 21-22-06; f. 1964; 35% state-owned, 35% owned by Crédit Lyonnais (France); cap. 2,000m. (Sept. 1992); Pres. Minister of the Economy and Finance; Man. Dir MICHEL CALLIER; 9 brs.

Development Banks

Banque Togolaise de Développement (BTD): angle rue des Nîmes et ave N. Grunitzky, BP 65, Lomé; tel. 21-36-41; telex 5282; fax 21-44-56; f. 1966; 43% state-owned, 20% owned by BCEAO, 20% by private Togolese interests; cap. 3,065m. (Sept. 1992); Pres. DÉDÉVI MICHÈLE EKUE; Man. Dir MENSAVI MENSAH; 8 brs.

Société Nationale d'Investissement et Fonds Annexes (SNI & FA): 11 ave du 24 janvier, BP 2682, Lomé; tel. 21-62-21; telex 5265; fax 21-62-25; f. 1971; state-owned; cap. 500m. (Sept. 1992); Pres. OGAMO BAGNAH; Man. Dir TANKPADJA LALLE.

Bankers' Association

Association Professionnelle des Banques et Etablissements Financiers du Togo: Lomé.

INSURANCE

CICA—RE/Compagnie Commune de Réassurance des Etats Membres de la CICA: ave du 24 janvier, BP 12410, Lomé; tel. 21-62-69; telex 5066; fax 21-49-64; regional reinsurance co grouping 12 west and central African states; cap. 600m.; Chair JACQUELINE OKILI; Gen. Man. DIGBEU KIPRE.

Groupement Togolais d'Assurances (GTA): route d'Atakpamé, BP 3298, Lomé; tel. 21-60-75; telex 5069; fax 21-26-78; f. 1974; 62.9% state-owned; cap. 100m.; all aspects of insurance and reinsurance; Pres. Minister of the Economy and Finance; Man. Dir KOSSI NAMBEA.

Trade and Industry

ECONOMIC AND SOCIAL COUNCIL

Conseil Economique et Social: Lomé; tel. 21-53-01; telex 5237; f. 1967; advisory body of 25 mems, comprising five trade unionists, five representatives of industry and commerce, five representatives of agriculture, five economists and sociologists, and five technologists; Pres. KOFFI GBODZIDI DJONDO.

DEVELOPMENT AND MARKETING ORGANIZATIONS

Agricultural development is under the supervision of five regional development authorities, the Sociétés régionales d'aménagement et de développement.

Caisse Française de Développement: ave de Sarakawa, BP 33, Lomé; tel. 21-04-98; telex 5313; fax 21-79-32; f. 1992 to succeed the Caisse Centrale de Coopération Economique; Dir M. TYACK.

Mission Française de Coopération: BP 91, Lomé; telex 5413; fax 21-21-28; administers bilateral aid from France; Dir SUZANNE FAUCHEUX.

Office de Développement et d'Exploitation des Forêts (ODEF): 15 rue des Conseillers Municipaux, BP 334, Lomé; tel. 21-51-59; f. 1971; development and management of forest resources; Man. Dir KOFFI AGOGNO.

Office National des Produits Vivriers (TOGOGRAIN): 141 ave de la Libération, BP 3039, Lomé; tel. 21-59-55; telex 5220; development and marketing of staple food crops; Man. Dir M. WALLA.

Office des Produits Agricoles du Togo (OPAT): angle rue Branly et ave no. 3, BP 1334, Lomé; tel. 21-44-71; telex 5220; f. 1964; agricultural development, marketing and exports; Dir-Gen. AYENAM KPOWBIE.

Office Togolais des Phosphates (OTP): BP 3200, Lomé; tel. 21-22-28; telex 5287; f. 1974; cap. 15,000m. francs CFA; production and marketing of phosphates; Dir-Gen. EKUE LIKOU.

Société Nationale de Commerce (SONACOM): 29 blvd Circulaire, BP 3009, Lomé; tel. 21-31-18; telex 5281; f. 1972; cap. 2,000m. francs CFA; importer of staple foods; Dir-Gen. JEAN LADOUX.

CHAMBER OF COMMERCE

Chambre de Commerce, d'Agriculture et d'Industrie du Togo (CCAIT): angle ave de la Présidence et ave Georges Pompidou, BP 360, Lomé; tel. 21-70-65; telex 5023; fax 21-47-30; f. 1921; Pres. ALEXIS LAMSEH LOOKY; Sec.-Gen. MICHEL KWAME MEYISSO.

EMPLOYERS' ORGANIZATIONS

Groupement Interprofessionnel des Entreprises du Togo (GITO): BP 345, Lomé; Pres. CLARENCE OLYMPIO.

Syndicat des Commerçants Importateurs et Exportateurs de la République Togolaise (SCIMPEXTO): BP 345, Lomé; Pres. KODJO G. KENTZLER.

Syndicat des Entrepreneurs de Travaux Publics, Bâtiments et Mines du Togo: BP 1101, Lomé; Pres. CLARENCE OLYMPIO.

MAJOR INDUSTRIAL COMPANIES

The following are some of the largest companies in terms of either capital investment or employment.

Brasserie BB Lomé SA: 47 rue du Grand Marché, BP 896, Lomé; tel. 21-50-62; telex 5228; fax 21-38-59; f. 1964 as Brasserie du Bénin SA; cap. 2,500m. francs CFA; 25% state-owned; mfrs of beer and soft drinks at Lomé and Kara; Chair. and Man. Dir JOACHIM HAASE; Dirs ELMAR VAN BOEMMEL, OSCAR BOSSHARD; 523 employees.

CEREKEM Exotic Togo: BP 2082, Lomé; f. 1987; cap. 400m. francs CFA; agro-industrial complex at Adétikopé for cultivation and processing of aromatic plants; Chair. and Man. Dir OLE RASMUSSEN; 400 employees.

Communauté Electrique du Bénin: rue de l'Hôpital, BP 1368, Lomé; tel. 21-61-32; telex 5355; f. 1968 as a jt venture between Togo and Benin to exploit the energy resources in the two countries; Chair. S. B. TIDJANI-DOURODJAYE; Man. Dir BOUKARY ALIDOU.

Compagnie d'Eau et d'Electricité du Togo (CEET): 10 ave du Golfe, BP 42, Lomé; tel. 21-27-43; telex 5230; fax 21-64-98; f. 1963; state-owned; production, transportation and distribution of electricity; Chair. ISSA AFFO; Man. Dir KWAMI AGBEBE.

Industrie Togolaise des Plastiques (ITP): Zone Industrielle, BP 9157, Lomé; tel. 27-49-83; telex 5018; fax 27-15-58; f. 1980; cap. 735m. francs CFA; owned by a consortium of private Togolese, Dutch, German and Danish interests; mfr and marketing of moulded articles, etc.; Man. Dir JEAN-MICHEL BLOUZARD.

Nouvelle Industrie des Oléagineux du Togo (NIOTO): BP 1755, Lomé; f. 1976; cap. 1,000m. francs CFA; 51% owned by Cie Française pour le Développement des Textiles, 49% by private Togolese interests; production and marketing of plant oils; Man. Dir ANANI ERNEST GASSOU.

Nouvelle Société Togolaise de Marbrerie et de Matériaux (Nouvelle SOTOMA): Zone Portuaire, BP 2105, Lomé; tel. 21-29-22; telex 5229; fax 21-71-32; cap. 500m. francs CFA; exploitation of marble at Gnaoulou and Pagola; Man. Dir K. PEKEMSI.

Régie Nationale des Eaux du Togo (RNET): ave de la Libération, angle rue du Chemin de Fer, BP 1301, Lomé; tel. 21-34-81; telex 5004; fax 21-46-13; f. 1964; cap. 252m. francs CFA; state-owned production and distribution of drinking water; Chair. ISSA AFFO; Man. Dir YAO BADJO.

Société Agricole Togolaise-Arabe-Libyenne (SATAL): 329 blvd du 13 janvier, BP 3554, Lomé; tel. 21-69-18; telex 5051; f. 1978; cap. 1,400m. francs CFA; 50% state-owned, 50% owned by govt of Libya; production, processing and marketing of agricultural goods; Chair. KATANGA KOFFI WALLA; Man. Dir ASSAID MOHAMED RAAI.

Société des Ciments du Togo (CIMTOGO): Zone Industrielle Portuaire PK 12, BP 1687, Lomé; tel. 21-08-59; telex 5234; fax 21-71-32; f. 1969; cap. 750m. francs CFA; 50% state-owned, 50% owned by SCANCEM International (Norway); production and marketing of cement and clinker; turnover in 1991 9,700m. francs CFA; Pres. Minister of Industry and State Enterprises; Man. Dir KWAMI BRENNER.

Société Générale du Golfe de Guinée-Togo (SGGG-TOGO): 7 rue Koumoré, BP 330, Lomé; tel. 21-23-90; telex 5236; fax 21-51-65; f. 1972; cap. 9,701m. francs CFA; import-export agency and transporters; turnover in 1991 13,315m. francs CFA; Chair. and Man. Dir MATÉ KWAME ABBEY; 318 employees.

Sociéte Générale des Moulins du Togo (SGMT): Zone Industrielle Portuaire, BP 9098, Lomé; tel. 21-35-59; telex 5272; f. 1971; cap. 300m. francs CFA; 45% state-owned; flour milling at Lomé; Chair. KOUDJOLOU DOGO; Man. Dir VASKEN BAKALIAN.

Société Nationale pour le Développement de la Palmeraie et des Huileries (SONAPH): BP 1755, Lomé; tel. 21-22-32; telex 5268; f. 1968; cap. 1,320m. francs CFA; state-owned; cultivation of palms and production of palm-oil and palmettoes; Chair. Dr FOLI AMAIZO BUBUTO; Man. Dir ANANI ERNEST GASSOU.

Société Togolaise des Boissons (STB): Zone Industrielle Portuaire, BP 2239, Lomé; tel. 21-58-80; telex 5234; f. 1970; cap. 264m. francs CFA; 25% state-owned; manufacture, bottling and sale of soft drinks; Chair. ROBERT BAILLY; Dir LAURENT GUELAFF; 149 employees.

Société Togolaise du Coton (SOTOCO): BP 219, Atakpamé; tel. 40-01-53; telex 5179; f. 1974; cap. 200m. francs CFA; state-owned; development of cotton growing; Man. Dir KAMBIA ESSOBEHEYI.

Société Togolaise et Danoise de Savons (SOTODAS): Zone Industrielle Portuaire, BP 1669, Lomé; tel. 21-52-03; fax 21-52-04; f. 1987; cap. 205m. francs CFA; 40% owned by Domo Kemi (Denmark) 20% by private Togolese interests; mfrs of detergents and cleansers; Man. Dir S. RAZVI.

Société Togolaise de Sidérurgie (STS): route d'Aného, Zone Portuaire, BP 13472, Lomé; tel. 21-10-16; telex 5385; cap. 700m. francs CFA; steel production; Chair. JOHN MOORE; Man. Dir STANLEY CLEVELAND.

Société Togolaise de Stockage de Lomé (STSL): BP 3283, Lomé; tel. 21-50-64; telex 5210; f. 1976; cap. 4,000m. francs CFA; exploitation and commercialization of hydrocarbons; Dir-Gen. M. BLAZJENVICZ.

Togotex International: BP 3511, Lomé; tel. 21-33-25; telex 5108; fax 21-60-49; f. 1978 as Compagnie Togolaise des Textiles, present name since 1990; cap. 2,250m. francs CFA; owned by Cha Chi Ming (Hong Kong); operates textile mills; Pres. CHA CHI MING; Man. Dir VICTOR CHA.

TRADE UNIONS

Collectif des Syndicats Indépendants (CSI): Lomé; f. 1992 as 'umbrella' org. for three autonomous trade union confederations:

Confédération Syndicale des Travailleurs du Togo (CSTT): Lomé.

Groupement Syndical Autonome (GSA): Lomé.

Union Nationale des Syndicats Indépendants du Togo (UNSIT): Tokoin-Wuiti, BP 30082, Lomé; tel. 21-65-65; f. 1991; 17 affiliated unions.

Confédération Nationale des Travailleurs du Togo (CNTT): 160 blvd du 13 janvier, BP 163, Lomé; tel. 21-57-39; f. 1973; affiliated to RPT until April 1991; Sec.-Gen. DOUEVI TCHIVIAKOU.

Transport

RAILWAYS

Société Nationale de Chemin de Fer Togolais (SNET): BP 340, Lomé; tel. 21-43-01; telex 5178; f. 1905 as Chemin de Fer Togolais, restructured under present name in 1993; total length 537 km, incl. lines running inland from Lomé to Atakpamé and Blitta (280 km), and a coastal line, running through Lomé and Aného, which links with the Benin railway system, but which was closed to passenger traffic in 1988 (a service from Lomé to Palimé—119 km—has also been suspended); passengers carried: 630,000 in 1990, freight handled: 16,000 metric tons in 1990; Gen. Man. T. KPEKPASSI.

ROADS

In 1992 there were some 7,800 km of roads, of which about one-fifth were paved. Principal roads run from Lomé to the borders of Ghana, Nigeria, Burkina Faso and Benin. In 1989 the EC agreed to provide more than 8,000m. francs CFA for the repair and maintenance of the road network.

Africa Route International (ARI—La Gazelle): km 9, route d'Atakpamé, BP 4730, Lomé; tel. 25-27-32; fax 29-09-93; f. 1991 as successor to 'privatized' Société Nationale de Transports Routiers; Pres. and Man. Dir BAWA S. MANKOUBI.

SHIPPING

The major port, at Lomé, generally handles a substantial volume of transit trade for the land-locked countries of Mali, Niger and Burkina Faso, although the political crisis in Togo has resulted in the diversion of much of this trade to neighbouring Benin. Lomé handled about 1.5m. metric tons of goods (including transit trade) in 1992, compared with some 2m. tons in previous years. There is another port at Kpémé for the export of phosphates.

Port Autonome de Lomé: BP 1225, Lomé; tel. 27-47-42; telex 5243; fax 21-26-27; f. 1968; Pres. IHOUI AGBOBOLI; Man. Dir KODJO AGBEJOMÉ.

Société Ouest-Africaine d'Entreprises Maritimes Togo (SOAEM-TOGO): Zone Industrielle Portuaire, BP 3285, Lomé; tel. 21-07-20; telex 5207; fax 21-34-17; f. 1959; forwarding agents, warehousing, sea and road freight transport; Pres. JEAN FABRY; Man. Dir JOHN M. AQUEREBURU.

Société Togolaise de Navigation Maritime (SOTONAM): place des Quatre Etoiles, rond-point du Port, BP 4086, Lomé; tel. 21-51-73; telex 5285; fax 27-69-38; Man. PAKOUM KPEMA.

SOCOPAO-Togo: 18 rue du Commerce, BP 821, Lomé; tel. 21-55-88; telex 5205; fax 21-73-17; f. 1959; freight transport, shipping agents; Pres. GUY MIRABAUD; Man. Dir HENRI CHAULIER.

SORINCO-Marine: 110 rue de l'Ocam, BP 2806, Lomé; tel. 21-56-94; freight transport, forwarding agents, warehousing, etc.; Man. AHMED EDGAR COLLINGWOOD WILLIAMS.

Togolaise d'Armements et d'Agence de Lignes SA (TAAL): 21 blvd du Mono, BP 9089, Lomé; tel. 22-02-43; telex 5329; fax 21-06-69; f. 1992; shipping agents, haulage management, crewing agency, forwarding agents; Pres. and Man. Dir LAURENT GBATI TAKASSI-KIKPA.

CIVIL AVIATION

There are international airports at Tokoin, near Lomé, and at Niamtougou. In addition, there are smaller airfields at Sokodé, Sansanné-Mango, Dapaong and Atakpamé.

Air Afrique: BP 111, Lomé; tel. 21-20-42; telex 5276; see under Côte d'Ivoire; Man. in Togo RAPHAËL BIAM.

Air Togo: rue du Commerce, Lomé; tel. 21-33-10; f. 1963; cap. 5m. francs CFA; scheduled internal services; Man. Dir AMADOU ISAAC ADE.

Peace Air Togo (PAT): Lomé; air transport; Man. Dir M. DJIBOM.

Tourism

Some 105,000 tourists visited Togo in 1990, when receipts from tourism totalled US $23m. In that year there was a total of 119 hotels and guest houses, with 4,127 hotel beds.

Direction des Professions Touristiques: BP 1289, Lomé; tel. 21-56-62; telex 5007; Dir GAMELI KETOMAGNAN.

Defence

In June 1993 Togo's armed forces officially numbered about 5,250 (army 4,800, air force 250, naval force 200). Paramilitary forces comprised a 750-strong gendarmerie. (However, at the time of the 1991 national conference, several sources put the strength of the armed forces at 12,000.) Military service is by selective conscription and lasts for two years. Togo normally receives assistance with training and equipment from France; however, French military assistance was suspended in late 1992, in view of the political crisis in Togo.

Defence Expenditure: Estimated at 11,285m. francs CFA in 1992.

Chief of the Armed Forces: Gen. GNASSINGBE EYADÉMA.

Education

In 1990, according to UNESCO estimates, the adult illiteracy rate averaged 56.7% (males 43.6%; females 69.3%). Primary education, which begins at six years of age and lasts for six years, is officially compulsory. Secondary education, beginning at the age of 12, lasts for a further seven years, comprisng a first cycle of four years and a second of three years. In 1990 enrolment at primary schools included 76% of children in the relevent age-group (89% of boys; 62% of girls). In the same year secondary enrolment was equivalent to only 23% (boys 35%; girls 12%). Proficiency in the two national languages, Ewe and Kabiye, is compulsory. Mission schools are important, educating almost one-half of all pupils. The Université du Bénin at Lomé had about 9,000 students in the early 1990s, and scholarships to French universities are available. Budget estimates for 1990 allocated 21,384m. francs CFA to education (23.1% of total expenditure by the central government).

Bibliography

Cornevin, R. *Histoire du Togo*. Paris, 1962.

'Le Togo', in *Collection Que sais-je?* Paris, Presses Universitaires de France, 1967.

Le Togo: des origines à nos jours. Paris, Académie des sciences d'outre-mer, 1987.

Decalo, S. *Historical Dictionary of Togo*. Metuchen, NJ, Scarecrow Press, 1976.

Delval, R. *Les musulmans au Togo*. Paris, Académie des sciences d'outre-mer, 1984.

Harrison Church, R. J. *West Africa*. 8th Edn, London, Longman, 1979.

'Nkrumah and the Togoland Question', in *The Economic Bulletin of Ghana*, Vol. XII, No. 2/2. Accra, 1968.

'The Pre-1947 Background to the Ewe Unification Question', in *The Transactions of the Historical Society of Ghana*, Vol. X. Accra, 1969.

Piraux, M. *Le Togo aujourd'hui*. Paris, Editions Jeune Afrique, 1977.

Stoecker, H. (Ed.). *German Imperialism in Africa*. London, Hurst Humanities, 1987.

Thompson, V. *West Africa's Council of the Entente*. Ithaca, NY, and London, Cornell University Press, 1972.

Toulabor, C. *Le Togo sous Eyadéma*. Paris, Editions Karthala, 1986.

Verdier, R. *Le pays kabiyé Togo*. Paris, Editions Karthala, 1983.

UGANDA

Physical and Social Geography

B. W. LANGLANDS

PHYSICAL FEATURES AND CLIMATE

The Republic of Uganda became an independent state, within the Commonwealth, in October 1962. Located on the eastern African plateau, it is at least 800 km inland from the Indian Ocean. The total area of Uganda is 241,139 sq km (93,104 sq miles), including 44,081 sq km of inland water. Uganda contains several large freshwater lakes, of which Lakes Victoria, Edward and Albert (also known as Lake Mobutu) are shared with neighbouring states. These lakes and most of the rivers form part of the basin of the upper (White) Nile, which has its origin in Uganda, where the river leaving Lake Victoria is harnessed for hydroelectricity at the Owen Falls dam.

Of the land area (excluding open water), 84% forms a plateau at 900–1,500 m above sea-level, with a gentle downwarp to the centre to form Lake Kyoga. The western arm of the east African rift system accounts for the 9% of the land area at less than 900 m and this includes the lowlands flanking the rift lakes (Edward and Albert) and the course of the Albert Nile at little more than 620 m. Mountains of over 2,100 m occupy 2% of the land area and these lands are above the limit of cultivation. The highest point is Mt Stanley, 5,109 m, in the Ruwenzori group on the border with Zaire, but larger areas of highland are included in the Uganda portion of the volcanic mass of Mt Elgon, near the Kenyan border. The remaining 5% of the land area lies at an altitude of 1,500–2,100 m in both the eastern and western extremities which form the shoulders to their respective rift valley systems, or in the foothills of the mountains already referred to. At this altitude the country is free of malaria and contains some of the most heavily populated regions.

Geologically the great proportion of the country is made up of Pre-Cambrian material, largely of gneisses and schists into which granites have been intruded. In the west, distinct series of metamorphosed rocks occur, largely of phyllites and shales, and in which mineralized zones contain small quantities of copper, tin, wolfram and beryllium. In the east old, possibly Cretaceous, volcanoes have been weathered away to form carbonatite rings with extensive deposits of magnetite, apatite and crystalline limestone. The apatite provides the basis for a superphosphate industry and the limestone for a cement industry, both at Tororo.

NATURAL RESOURCES

The economy of the country depends upon agriculture and this in turn is affected by climate. Since Uganda is located between 1° 30′S and 4°N, temperature varies little throughout the year, giving the country an equatorial climate modified by altitude. Rainfall is greatest bordering Lake Victoria and on the mountains, where small areas have over 2,000 mm per year. The high ground of the west, the rest of the Lake Victoria zone, and the eastern and north-central interior all have over 1,250 mm. Only the north-east (Karamoja) and parts of the south (east Ankole) have less than 750 mm. But total amounts of rain are less significant agriculturally than the length of the dry season. For much of the centre and west there is no more than one month with less than 50 mm and this zone is characterized by permanent cropping of bananas for food, and coffee and tea for cash crops. To the south the dry season increases to three months (June to August); in the north it increases to four months (December to March) and in the north-east the dry season begins in October. Where the dry season is marked, as in the north and east, annual cropping of finger millet provides the staple food and cotton the main cash crop. In the driest parts pastoralism predominates, possibly with a little sorghum cultivation.

Western Uganda, where there is a greater range of different physical conditions, and generally where population densities are below average, shows a diversity of land use, with tropical rain forest, two game parks, ranchlands, fishing, mining and the cultivation of coffee and tea. The north and east is more monotonous, savannah-covered plain with annually sown fields of grain and cotton. Most of the country's coffee comes from the Lake Victoria zone (*robusta*) and Mt Elgon (*arabica*). The economy depends very heavily upon smallholding peasant production of basic cash crops.

POPULATION

The latest census, conducted in January 1991, enumerated a population of 16,582,674, giving a density of about 69 inhabitants per km. The total at the 1980 census had been 12.6m. The population is predominantly rural; at the 1980 census only about 7% of the populace resided in towns of more than 1,000 people. Kampala (population estimated at 458,423 in 1980), the capital and main commercial centre, and Jinja (45,060), an industrial town, are the only urban centres of any significance. The annual birth rate is just over 52 per 1,000 of the population. Average life expectancy in 1991 was 46 years, according to estimates by the World Bank. About 50% of the population are below the age of 16. Demographic patterns in the later 1990s and beyond are expected to be significantly affected by the high rate of incidence of the Acquired Immunodeficiency Syndrome (AIDS), which, by the early 1990s, had reportedly reached epidemic proportions in parts of Uganda.

In 1959 about two-thirds of the population, mainly in the centre and south, were Bantu-speaking, about one-sixth Nilotic-speaking and a further one-sixth Nilo-Hamitic (Paranilotic). In 1969 there were 74,000 people of Indian and Pakistani origin, engaged mainly in commerce, and 9,500 Europeans, mostly in professional services. Since the 1972 expulsions of non-citizen (and subsequently of all) Asians, both of these totals have fallen to negligible proportions.

Recent History

RICHARD WALKER

Revised for this edition by ALAN RAKE

British penetration of Uganda began after 1860. In 1888 British interests were assigned by royal charter to the British East Africa Co, whose control over the area was consolidated in 1891 by a treaty with the kabaka (king) of Buganda, the principal kingdom. In 1894, after the cost of the company's operations had become prohibitive, the British government assumed responsibility, declaring Buganda a protectorate: the same status was conferred on Bunyoro, Toro, Ankole and Bugosa in 1896. During the first half of the 20th century no united nationalist movement was formed. Progress towards Ugandan independence was dominated by controversy over the likely role of Buganda within a future self-governing state. In 1956 the Democratic Party (DP) was formed, with a predominantly professional leadership and widespread support among the Roman Catholic peasantry. The DP favoured a unitary independent state of Uganda and opposed the ambitions of the Baganda people, who did not wish Buganda's influence to be diminished after independence. The Uganda National Congress (UNC), however, was a nationally-based party, derived from farmers' organizations and advocating greater African control of the economy in a federal independent state. In 1958 seven African members of the protectorate's legislative council, including two members of the UNC, joined another faction, led by Dr Milton Obote, to form the Uganda People's Congress (UPC). By 1960 the UPC, the DP (led by Benedicto Kiwanuka) and the Buganda council (lukiiko) were the principal political forces in Uganda.

In March 1961, at the first nation-wide election to the legislative council, the DP won a majority of the seats. Kiwanuka was appointed chief minister in July, but he proved to be unacceptable to the ruling élite of Buganda. The Kabaka Yekka (KY, or 'King Alone'), a political party representing the interests of the lukiiko, was formed to ally with the UPC against the DP, and to obtain political advantage from the forthcoming constitutional negotiations. Uganda was granted self-government in March 1962, with Kiwanuka as prime minister. At pre-independence elections to a national assembly, held in April, the UPC won a majority of seats. The UPC–KY coalition formed a government, led by Obote. The new constitution provided for a federation of four regions—Buganda, Ankole, Bunyoro and Toro—each with considerable autonomy. On 9 October Uganda became independent, within the Commonwealth, and a year later, on 9 October 1963, the country became a republic, with Mutesa II, the kabaka (king) of Buganda, as non-executive president.

OBOTE AND THE UPC

During the first years of independence the UPC–KY alliance was placed under strain by controversy over levels of central government expenditure in Buganda, and over the 'lost counties', two districts of Bunyoro that had been transferred to Buganda in the late 19th century: in a referendum in November 1964 the inhabitants of the two districts voted to return to Bunyoro, but President Mutesa refused to endorse this result. By now, sufficient KY and DP members of the national assembly had defected to the UPC for the alliance to be no longer necessary. The UPC had also gained control of all district councils and kingdom legislatures, except in Buganda. The UPC itself, however, was affected by disagreements between conservative, centrist and radical elements of the party. In February 1966 the national assembly approved a motion demanding an investigation into gold-smuggling, in which Dr Obote, the minister of defence, and the second-in-command of the army, Col Idi Amin Dada, were alleged to be involved. Later in that month Obote led a pre-emptive coup against his opponents within the UPC. Five government ministers were arrested, the constitution was suspended, the president was deposed and all executive powers were transferred to Obote. In April an interim constitution was introduced, withdrawing regional autonomy and introducing an executive presidency. Obote became head of state. In May, when the lukiiko demanded the restoration of Buganda's autonomy, government troops, commanded by Amin, seized the palace of the kabaka (who escaped abroad), and a state of emergency was imposed in Buganda. A new constitution was adopted in September 1967, establishing a unitary republic and abolishing traditional rulers and legislatures. National elections were postponed until 1971.

During the late 1960s the Obote regime pursued an economic programme aimed at achieving the redistribution of incomes through nationalization. At the same time the government came to rely increasingly on detention and armed repression by the paramilitary and intelligence services. Estrangement began to develop, however, between Obote and the army, which remained under Amin's command since the suppression of the lukiiko. In 1969 Amin ignored Obote's order to cease channelling military aid to separatist guerrillas in southern Sudan. In December Obote was wounded in an assassination attempt in Kampala: Amin immediately fled to an army base in his home area. In the following month Brig. Pierino Okoya, Amin's most forceful critic in the government, was murdered.

THE AMIN REGIME

In January 1971, while Obote was out of the country, Amin seized power. In February he declared himself head of state, promising a return to civilian rule within five years. Many Ugandans believed that Amin would bring about the national cohesion which the UPC had failed to provide, and at first he received substantial support, as well as obtaining ready recognition from the government of the United Kingdom. Amin consolidated his military position by massacring troops and police (particularly those of the Langi and Acholi tribes) who has supported the Obote regime. Soon after taking power Amin suspended political activity and most civil rights. The national assembly was dissolved, and Amin ruled by decree. The cabinet, with increasing military membership, was effectively subservient to the defence council. The entire population was brought under the jurisdiction of military tribunals, and several agencies were established to enforce state security. In August 1972 Amin announced the expulsion of all non-citizen Asians. The order was soon extended to include all Asians, and although this was rescinded, under internal and external pressure, the atmosphere of racial enmity which developed forced all but 4,000 Ugandan Asians to flee the country. Most went to the United Kingdom, which severed diplomatic relations and imposed a trade embargo against Uganda. In December all British companies in Uganda were nationalized without compensation.

In September 1972 a group of pro-Obote guerrillas (former members of the army and police who had fled the country when Amin seized power) attempted unsuccessfully to oust Amin by an invasion, launched from Tanzania. The attempt was led by David Oyite-Ojok, the former chief of staff, and Yoweri Museveni, another senior officer. In retaliation, Amin's air force bombed Tanzanian towns. The Amin regime was supplied with military aid by Libya and the USSR, and by the end of 1972 virtually all Western aid to Uganda had ceased. No coherent economic development policy existed, and the country's infrastructure was allowed to deteriorate. Between 1972–1975 there were sporadic occurrences of faction fighting within the army, including an unsuccessful coup attempt in March 1974, which failed only after a violent battle in Kampala. Renewed outrages on the Langi and Acholi populations were perpetrated by Amin's troops between late 1976 and early 1977. In February 1977, after protesting at the massacres, the Anglican archbishop, Janine Luwum, and two government ministers were murdered; this aroused international condemnation.

In October 1978 Amin sought to divert the attention of the armed forces from internal divisions (which had led to another abortive coup in August) by invading Tanzania, claiming the rightful possession of the Kagera salient. The attempt was unsuccessful and stimulated the Tanzanian government's efforts to remove Amin from power. Political exiles in Tanzania and elsewhere, including Obote, were encouraged by President Nyerere of Tanzania to form a united political front to replace Amin. In January 1979 the Tanzanian armed forces invaded Uganda, assisted by the Uganda National Liberation Army (UNLA), which comprised exiled Ugandan volunteers under the command of Oyite-Ojok and Museveni. They met little resistance from Amin's forces (assisted by 1,500 Libyan troops) and captured Kampala in April. Amin fled the country, initially taking refuge in Libya and subsequently in Saudi Arabia.

TRANSITIONAL GOVERNMENTS

Attempts among Ugandan exiles to form a common political front in Tanzania had led to the Moshi Conference in March 1979. Nyerere, reluctant to support Obote's reinstatement, had persuaded Obote not to attend, although the UPC was represented at the conference by a close associate of Obote, Paulo Muwanga. A compromise candidate, Dr Yusufu Lule (a former vice-chancellor of Makerere University and previously associated with the KY party) was chosen to lead what became known as the Uganda National Liberation Front (UNLF). This consisted of a 30-member national consultative committee (NCC), on which all the 18 organizations participating at Moshi were represented, a national executive committee (NEC), under Lule's chairmanship, and a military commission, headed by Muwanga. Lule was sworn in as president of Uganda in April.

In June 1979 Lule attempted to reorganize the NEC, apparently failing to appreciate that he had no personal power base from which to manoeuvre, despite his popularity in Buganda. In the same month the NCC removed him from office, and replaced him with a second compromise candidate, the former attorney-general, Godfrey Binaisa. There ensued a period of widespread anarchy. Relations between the UNLA and the Tanzanian forces deteriorated, as did relations between both armies and the civilian population. The UNLA had been greatly enlarged by numbers of untrained recruits and ethnically-based militias, and was divided into supporters of Oyite-Ojok and of Museveni. In late 1979 Binaisa was manoeuvred by Obote and Muwanga into dismissing Museveni from the post of minister of defence, thereby gravely weakening his position with regard to the NCC. Binaisa announced that a general election would take place in December 1980: with the support of the NCC, he ruled that only UNLF candidates would be allowed to participate. In May 1980 Binaisa attempted to dismiss Oyite-Ojok from the command of the UNLA: UNLA soldiers began to arrest Binaisa's ministers, and in May power was assumed by the UNLF's military commission, under the chairmanship of Paulo Muwanga, supported by Oyite-Ojok and with Museveni as vice-chairman.

OBOTE AND OKELLO

The elections held in December 1980 were contested by four parties: the UPC, under Obote; the DP, led by Paul Ssemogerere; the Uganda Patriotic Movement (UPM), a regrouping of the radical faction of the UPC, led by Yoweri Museveni; and the Conservative Party (CP), a successor to the KY party. The DP was prevented from registering a number of candidates for the 126 elective seats in the new legislature, with the result that the UPC gained a majority of 20 seats, and Dr Obote was proclaimed president of Uganda on 15 December, with Paulo Muwanga as vice-president and minister of defence, Eric Otema Allimadi (a former minister of foreign affairs) as prime minister, and Tito Okello as army chief-of-staff.

The election of the UPC government did not bring military or political stability to the rest of Uganda. Although Amin himself had been easily dislodged, his legacy of corruption and rule by terror proved to be more difficult to eradicate. The new UPC government inherited neither political continuity nor an administrative framework; its leading members ranged from military war-lords to politically independent civilians who were committed to national development. Not surprisingly, the UPC was unable to formulate a consistent ideology. In its dealings with potential foreign donors, however, the government proclaimed its support of an IMF-sponsored economic reconstruction programme. This stance was successful in attracting goodwill and, initially, a certain amount of finance from Western countries and Arab sources. While the level of violence subsided considerably during 1981–82, domestic uncertainty was perpetuated by continued indiscipline in the army and by the proliferation of security agencies which were effectively beyond the law.

Following the overthrow of Binaisa in 1980, the UNLA played an open role in Ugandan politics. Its main preoccupation, however, was in internal counter-insurgency operations, as dissatisfaction with the conduct and outcome of the elections caused several factions to conduct a guerrilla war against the UPC government. The three main guerrilla movements were the Uganda National Rescue Front (UNRF), comprising supporters of Amin who were active in the West Nile area, the Uganda Freedom Movement (UFM), led by Balaki Kirya and Andrew Kayiira, and the National Resistance Army (NRA), led by Yoweri Museveni, with Yusufu Lule (in exile) as chairman of its political wing, the National Resistance Movement (NRM).

From 1981, NRA operations grew steadily in military expertise and political sophistication. Drawing on disaffected southern Ugandans, especially among the Banyarwanda and Baganda, and defectors from the increasingly disorganized UNLA, the NRA began to establish a reputation for military discipline. A UNLA campaign during 1983 attempted to deprive the NRA of civilian support by depopulating the area around Luwero—the 'Luwero Triangle'—where a large proportion of the population was forced to take refuge in government camps. Large numbers of 'displaced persons' made their way to Kampala and surrounding towns after the main camps were dismantled in early 1984, while others were inspired to join the NRA. The offensive against the NRA was renewed in late 1984, with civilians again suffering the main impact of attacks.

Meanwhile, tensions were developing within the UNLA between the two main ethnic groups from which the army was recruited, the Acholi and the Langi. By the time of the death of the Langi chief of staff, Oyite-Ojok, in December 1983, the situation was so tense that the appointment of a successor was delayed for eight months. Some 200 Acholi officers were eventually promoted, in compensation for the appointment of another Langi as chief of staff, Lt-Col (later Brig.) Smith Opon-Acak, in late 1984.

By early 1985 the Obote government was under pressure on other fronts. When IMF funds had been exhausted, the resultant shortage of foreign exchange led to shortages of many commodities, and inflation rapidly increased. After allegations in 1984 at hearings of a US congressional committee that up to 100,000 people had been killed since the accession of the UPC government, a report by Amnesty International, in mid-1985, alleged widespread and systematic torture and murder of civilians by the security forces.

In the first week of July 1985 the Acholi-Langi rivalries led to an outbreak of fighting in the Kampala barracks, following rumours that Obote was planning a massacre of Acholi officers. A group of Acholi soldiers, led by Lt-Gen. (later Gen.) Tito Okello, escaped north to join the Acholi detachments of Brig. (later Lt-Gen.) Basilio Okello (not related to Tito Okello). After a military engagement near the Karuma Falls, these combined forces severed the route to the West Nile area and the major Acholi population centres. Despite the history of bitter rivalry between the Acholi and the West Nile tribes, the Acholi rebels had already agreed to join the UNRF in an attempt to oust Obote. When, in late July, troops under Basilio Okello began to march south on Kampala, Obote fled to Kenya (moving eventually to exile in Zambia).

At the close of July 1985 Tito Okello became Uganda's new president. He quickly formed an Acholi-dominated military council in which a small number of civilians (including Paul

Ssemogerere of the DP) were included. There followed a brief period during which some control was exercised over army indiscipline, and political prisoners were released.

By the end of August 1985, however, the Okello government was facing serious difficulties. The NRA had gained control of the main towns of the west (Fort Portal and Kasese), and by late September southern Uganda, up to the Katonga river, was under its control, while UNLA troops in the southern towns of Mbarara and Masaka remained under siege in their barracks. The NRA's ability to control its own troops contrasted starkly with the performance of the UNLA, while the NRA's control of southern Uganda, and the region's cash crops, placed an economic stranglehold on the impoverished Kampala government.

Within the Okello regime, the minister of defence, Wilson Toko, advocated an uncompromising military response to the NRA, relying on UNRF troops, flown in from West Nile. However, the West Nile troops proved to be neither controllable nor efficient in the field, and sporadic fighting erupted between the allies.

Against this volatile background, a series of peace talks opened in Nairobi, Kenya between representatives of the NRA and the Okello government. As the talks progressed fitfully, it was apparent that neither side was fully committed to the projected peace agreement, and the accord that they eventually signed, in late December 1985, was intended mainly to pre-empt a *coup d'état* against Tito Okello by Wilson Toko and West Nile leaders. The subsequent attempt to disarm the West Nile troops prompted most of them to retreat north, leaving devastation in their path. Yoweri Museveni, who had become sole leader of the NRM and NRA following Lule's death earlier in the year, did not take up his alloted seat on the military council in Kampala, but returned to south-west Uganda, while the NRA prepared for a final offensive.

THE MUSEVENI PRESIDENCY

Claiming that law and order had broken down throughout Uganda, NRA troops surrounded Kampala, and took control in January 1986. Yoweri Museveni was sworn in as president and formed a National Resistance Council (NRC), with both civilian and military members. His cabinet, with Samson Kisekka as prime minister, included members as diverse as Paul Ssemogerere of the DP, Moses Ali, a former minister under Amin, and Andrew Kayiira, leader of the UFM. Elections were postponed for at least three years. Political parties were not banned, but their activities were officially suspended in March. The defeat of Okello's remaining UNLA troops was officially completed by the end of March. They wreaked havoc in the areas through which they retreated into Sudan, where Lt-Gen. Basilio Okello died in exile in January 1990.

Museveni announced a policy of national reconciliation. He established a commission to investigate breaches of human rights during the regimes of Amin, Obote and Okello, under whom, he claimed, up to 800,000 Ugandans had been killed. Following an investigation of the activities of the police force, more than 2,500 of its members were dismissed in July 1986. During 1986 the Museveni government developed a system of resistance committees at local and district level; these were to be partly responsible for the maintenance of security and the elimination of corruption.

Lawlessness, banditry and indiscipline remained rife in Uganda, especially in the north. In March 1986 an opposition movement advocating the armed overthrow of Museveni, the Uganda People's Democratic Movement (UPDM), was formed, with Obote's former prime minister, Eric Otema Allimadi, as chairman. This, together with raids by remnants of the UNLA, chronic problems with armed cattle-rustlers in the north-east and the lack of any basic infrastructure of law and order prevented Museveni from consolidating his control over Uganda. Although he allowed the return from exile of Prince Ronald Mutebi, the claimant to the throne of Buganda, Museveni refused to restore Uganda's traditional monarchies until stability had returned to the country (see below). In August an alleged plot by Baganda monarchists was uncovered, and more than 20 were arrested.

In October 1986 it was announced that 26 people, including Paulo Muwanga, Obote's former vice-president, and Andrew Kayiira of the UFM, had been arrested for treason. Although charges against some of these were later withdrawn, the murder of Kayiira in March 1987 caused the UFM to withdraw its support from the government. The trial of seven of the 26 people who had been arrested in October 1986 began in August 1987, and in the following March three of the defendants were sentenced to death for treason, while the remaining four, including Nyanzi, were acquitted. Muwanga, who was acquitted of abduction and murder, was released in October 1990 and died in April 1991.

The largest uprising which followed Museveni's accession to power was led by a charismatic cult leader, Alice Lakwena, whose religions sect attracted both peasant farmers from the Acholi tribe and former soldiers of the UNLA. The rebel 'Holy Spirit Movement', as it became known, engaged the NRA in attacks that were effectively suicidal. In late 1987, after several thousand of the rebels had been killed, the revolt was crushed, and Lakwena fled to Kenya. However, remaining members of the movement subsequently regrouped themselves, forming the Lord's Resistance Army (LRA). In August 1987 the UPDM joined with a faction of the Federal Democratic Movement and another opposition group, the United National Front, to form an alliance which aimed to overthrow Museveni, but by August 1988 this alliance had proved to be ineffective. Another rebel group, the Uganda Democratic Alliance (UDA), claimed responsibility for a bomb attack on diplomatic buildings in Kampala in January 1988, in which a Libyan diplomat was killed. The emergence, in June 1988, of reports that an abortive mutiny by members of the NRA had taken place in April of that year, indicated that indiscipline and dissension within army ranks still existed. It was reported that some 700 army officers and soldiers had been detained in connection with the incident. In October 24 people were arrested and charged with plotting a coup.

In conjunction with the use of force to curb dissidence, Museveni also adopted a reconciliatory approach towards opponents. In June 1987 the NRC offered an amnesty to rebels (except those accused of murder or rape), which was subsequently repeatedly extended; by April 1988 Ugandan officials reported that almost 30,000 rebels had surrendered. However, in December 1987, while on a mission to enforce the amnesty in Soroti district, Stanislas Okurut, the minister of labour, and two deputy ministers were detained by rebels of the Ugandan People's Army (UPA), led by Peter Otai, a former minister in the Obote administration. The UPA's demands for the release of rebel prisoners in exchange for the ministers were not met; one of the deputy ministers escaped in March 1988, while a clash between NRA troops and the rebels in August led to the death of the other deputy minister and the injuring of Okurut. In early 1988 the NRA held peace talks with the armed wing of the UPDM, the Uganda People's Democratic Army (UPDA). The failure by the commander of the UPDA, Brig. Justin Odong Latek, to endorse the proposed peace agreement led to his deposition, in May, from the leadership of the rebel army. In the following month the new commander of the UPDA, Lt-Col John Angelo Okello, signed a peace agreement with the NRC; however, a faction of the UPDA regrouped, under the leadership of Odong Latek, and continued to oppose the government. In mid-1989 the government launched a major offensive against guerrilla forces.

Further efforts were made to consolidate the position of the Museveni administration. The president carried out a major cabinet reshuffle in February 1988, in which he increased the number of ministers originating from the north-east of Uganda, where opposition to the government was most prevalent. In May the NRC approved legislation validating the NRC as the country's official legislature. In the following month, draft legislation was introduced to prohibit the practice and promotion of sectarianism; other new legislation imposed heavy penalties for revealing military operations and strategies to the 'enemy'. A degree of press censorship was also introduced. It was stressed by Museveni that the prohibition of 'sectarianism' was not aimed at stifling political debate.

In February 1989 the first national election since 1980 was held. The NRC, which had previously comprised only members nominated by the president, was expanded from 98 to 278 members, to include 210 elected members. While a total of 20 ministerial posts were reserved for nominated members of the NRC, 50 were allocated to elected members. As a result of these changes, 10 cabinet ministers and four deputy ministers lost their posts. Following the election, Museveni appointed a constitutional commission to gauge public opinion on Uganda's political future and to draft a new constitution.

In October 1989 (despite opposition from the DP) the NRC approved draft legislation, submitted by the NRM, to extend the government's term of office by five years from January 1990, when its mandate had been due to expire: the NRM justified seeking to extend its rule by claiming that it required further time in which to prepare a new constitution, to organize elections, to eliminate continuing anti-government guerrilla activity, to improve the judiciary, police force and civil service, and to rehabilitate the country's infrastructure. It was announced in January 1990 that several army officers and civilians had been charged with plotting to overthrow the government. In March the NRM extended the ban on party political activity (imposed in March 1986) for a further five years. In February 1990 the minister of culture, youth and sports, Brig. Moses Ali, was dismissed and charged with plotting a *coup d'état*. (Ali was subsequently acquitted of this charge, but in January 1991 was found guilty of illegally possessing ammunition.) In July 1990 the leader of the UPDM, Eric Otema Allimadi, signed a peace accord with the government; nevertheless, some members of the rebel organization reportedly did not take advantage of the government's continuing amnesty.

In January 1991 Samson Kisekka was replaced as prime minister by George Adyebo; Kisekka was appointed as vice-president and minister of internal affairs. In April Daniel Omara Atubo, the minister of state for foreign affairs and regional co-operation, was arrested, together with two other members of the NRC, and charged with plotting to overthrow the government by assisting anti-government rebels; 15 other people (including further members of the NRC) were subsequently detained on similar grounds. At the beginning of April the government initiated a campaign to eradicate continuing guerrilla activity in northern and eastern districts: by July it was reported that more than 1,500 rebels had been killed and more than 1,000 had been arrested. International observers accused the NRA of committing atrocities during the campaign.

In May 1991 Museveni formally invited all emigré Ugandan Asians, who had been expelled during the Amin regime, to return. This gesture was intended to attract both international approval and investment in the Ugandan economy by expelled Asians who had prospered since leaving Uganda. In early July the cabinet was reshuffled, with the number of ministries substantially reduced as a measure to create greater efficiency. A report by Amnesty International, which was released in early December, accused the NRA of torturing and summarily executing prisoners during anti-insurgency operations against rebels.

In late February and early March 1992 elections to local- and district-level councils took place. In October the government launched a three-year programme to reduce the size of the NRA by about one-half, in response to pressure from the international donor community. In December negotiations on the restoration of the Bugandan monarchy commenced between Museveni and Prince Ronald Mutebi. Later in the same month the constitutional commission which had been established in 1989 presented a draft constitution to the government. The opposition claimed that it would increase presidential powers still further. The commission recommended non-party presidential elections after two years followed by a further five-year ban on political parties.

In January 1993 three men who had been army officers during the Amin regime were sentenced to death for plotting to overthrow the government. In early March President Museveni published the draft constitution; the document (which was strongly opposed by the UPC and DP) provided for the proscription of party political activity for at least a further seven years and a continuation of 'non-party democracy', under the auspices of a national political movement to which all citizens would belong. In April the NRC passed legislation authorizing the establishment of a constituent assembly; this body, which was to comprise both elected and nominated members, would be empowered to debate, amend and finally enact the draft constitution. Upon the completion of the constituent assembly's task, legislative and presidential elections were due to be held in 1994. In mid-July 1993 legislation was approved which provided for the restoration of each of Uganda's traditional monarchies; these were, however, only to exercise ceremonial and cultural functions. At the end of July Prince Ronald Mutebi was enthroned as the kabaka of Buganda, and in early August the lukiiko was re-established. A new king of Toro was also enthroned in late July. The Ankole people similarly proceeded with the coronation of their omugabe (king), John Barigye, at a ceremony held in November 1993. However, Museveni, although himself an Ankole, refused to recognize the new king, thereby increasing suspicions that his recognition of the kabaka of Buganda and the king of Toro was based on short-term political expediency rather than a desire to restore all of Uganda's traditional kingdoms. In June 1994, following a lengthy legal dispute, Museveni agreed to the coronation of Solomon Gafabusa Iguru as omukama of the Bunyoro. At the beginning of September 1993 nine army officers, who had been arrested on treason charges between 1988–90 and held without trial, were released. In the same month the government ordered a judicial review of the trials of those sentenced to death in the previous January by army tribunals which were now officially described as 'illegal and incompetent', In October Lt-Col James Oponyo, the commander of the UPA in the Teso area in north-eastern Uganda, surrendered to government forces. In January 1994 the Ugandan Democratic Alliance (UDA) and the Uganda Federal Army (UFA) decided to suspend their guerrilla operations, under the provision of the government amnesty first granted in 1988. The commander-in-chief of the alliance, Sam Luwero, indicated that the leadership had also decided to dissolve the organization. Museveni stated that the government was determined to suppress the continuing insurgency in the Karamojong area, however, where bandits and cattle thieves were still active. In early 1994 Peter Otai, a minister under Obote and former leader of the UPA, formed a new rebel group, known as the Uganda People's Freedom Movement (UPFM).

In March 1994 renewed clashes occurred in northern Uganda between the forces of the LRA, now led by Joseph Kony and the government. The rebels, who claimed to be fighting a 'holy war' against foreign occupation of Uganda, carried out ambushes and abductions which prompted the government to dispatch large numbers of security forces to the region.

The return of emigré Asians to reclaim the property which was seized under the Amin regime continued in 1994 although the process provoked jealousies and racial antagonism, with indigenous businessmen claiming that they had not been sufficiently compensated. Despite sporadic acts of violence, including the murder of a prominent Asian businessman in December 1993, the government adhered to its compensation policy and extended from October 1993 to April 1994 the deadline for Asians to return and reclaim their expropriated assets.

Elections to the 288-member Assembly held in March 1994 were generally accepted by a majority of Ugandans as being fairly conducted. In a turn-out of 7m. of the total 8m. registered voters, Museveni and the NRM won overwhelming support. Although candidates were officially required to stand on a non-party basis, tacit official tolerance of party campaigning was reflected in the leaders of three parties—the DP, the CP and the UPC—being given access to national radio and television during the weeks prior to the election. Of the 214 elective seats to the constituent assembly the government alliance won an estimated 150 seats most of which were in Buganda, the Western region and parts of the East, while the opposition (supporters of the UPC and DP) secured most seats in the north and the north-east. Museveni and Samson Kisseka, the vice-president, who indicated that he was to retire from active politics, did not stand. Museveni's most senior government colleagues (including the prime minister, Cosmas Adyebo and his three deputies) won convincingly. Among five senior ministers who failed to obtain seats, however, was the minister of finance and economic planning, Joash Mayanja-Nkangi, and the katikiro (prime minister) of Buganda. The constituent assembly, which also comprised nominated representatives of the armed forces, political parties, trade unions and various special interest groups, was expected to convene for between four and seven months to debate the draft constitution. Amendments to the draft required a two-thirds majority of the assembly; changes that received majority support but less than two-thirds were to be submitted to referendum.

REGIONAL RELATIONS

During 1987 Uganda's relations with neighbouring Kenya deteriorated, with the Museveni government accusing Kenya of sheltering Ugandan rebels. In March the Kenyan authorities expelled hundreds of Ugandans. When, in October, Uganda stationed troops at the two countries' common border, Kenya threatened to retaliate with force against any attempts by Ugandan military personnel to cross the frontier in pursuit of rebels. In December clashes occurred between Kenyan and Ugandan security forces and the border was temporarily closed. Later in December, discussions between the heads of state of the two countries led to an improvement in relations, and in January 1988 Kenya and Uganda signed a joint communiqué, which provided for co-operation in resolving problems relating to the flow of traffic across the common border. However, several incursions into Kenya by Ugandan troops were reported in 1988 and 1989, and in July 1988 the Ugandan government accused Kenya of complicity in smuggling weapons to rebels in northern Uganda. In November 1991 the presidents of Uganda, Kenya and Tanzania declared their commitment to developing co-operation between the three countries in economic, political, cultural and security matters. In November 1993 President Moi of Kenya met Museveni in Kampala (the first state visit by a Kenyan president to Uganda). A communiqué was signed providing for the exploration of further areas of co-operation in both security and trade. Tension also arose on the Uganda-Zaire border in 1988, owing to several attacks by Zairean troops on NRA units. During the late 1980s and early 1990s Sudanese troops reportedly made repeated incursions into Ugandan territory in pursuit of Sudanese rebels. In December 1989 Sudanese troops reportedly crossed the Uganda-Sudan border and attacked a detachment of the NRA, and in October 1991, May 1992 and December 1993 the Ugandan government alleged that Sudanese aircraft had dropped bombs in northern Uganda. Nearly 80,000 Sudanese refugees fled to Uganda in early 1992 followed by a further 50,000 in August 1993, owing to intense fighting between Sudanese rebels and government forces.

During the late 1980s an estimated 250,000 Rwandan refugees were sheltering in Uganda. Relations with Rwanda deteriorated in October 1990, following the unsuccessful invasion of northern Rwanda by some 4,000 Rwandan rebels who had been based in Uganda and who were predominantly members of the NRA. They were reported to have been led by Maj.-Gen. Fred Rwigyema, a deputy commander of the NRA and a former Ugandan deputy minister of defence. In November President Museveni dismissed all non-Ugandan members of the NRA. Further incursions by the rebels from Uganda into Rwanda occurred in December 1990 and January 1991. In February 1991 a conference on the Rwandan security situation, held in Dar es Salaam, Tanzania, was attended by President Museveni, President Habyarimana of Rwanda and by representatives of four other African states; an amnesty was agreed for all Rwandans who were exiled abroad, and the rebels were urged to observe a cease-fire. Nevertheless, the Uganda-based Rwandan rebels remained active in northern Rwanda throughout 1991, 1992 and early 1993. In January 1992 the presidents of Uganda, Rwanda and Tanzania met in Tanzania to discuss security on the Uganda-Rwanda border. In that month it was reported that 64,000 Ugandans residing near the two countries' common border had been displaced, owing to cross-border shelling by Rwandan troops. In August Uganda and Rwanda signed a bilateral security agreement, whereby each country was permitted to station a monitoring team in the other's territory. The government of Uganda issued repeated denials to allegations by the Rwandan government that it was supporting the Rwandan rebel forces. A peace agreement eventually was agreed by the Rwanda government and the rebel forces in August 1993. Following the death of President Habyarimana of Rwanda in April 1994 fighting with the Rwandan rebels—the Rwandese Patriotic Front (RPF)—escalated, resulting in July in the overthrow of the Hutu-dominated government.

Economy

LINDA VAN BUREN

AGRICULTURE

Agriculture is overwhelmingly the most important sector of Uganda's economy. It accounts for about 96% of the country's export earnings, 57% of gross domestic product (GDP, combining subsistence and monetary agricultural production) and provides a livelihood for some 88% of Uganda's labour force. Nearly two-thirds of government revenue is provided by the agricultural sector, mainly through export duties on coffee, the country's principal export. The development of the whole economy is therefore heavily influenced by the performance of the agricultural sector. Coffee is, by far, the most important export crop, followed by cotton and tea. Tobacco was also an important crop until the 1970s. Soils are generally fertile and, apart from some parts of the north-east and north-west, the country has a climate favourable to both crops and livestock production. Smallholder mixed farming predominates, with estate production confined mainly to tea and sugar cane. Rehabilitation of the agricultural sector was hampered by fighting between guerrilla groups and ex-president Obote's troops, but agricultural production began to recover after the assumption of power by Yoweri Museveni in January 1986. Continuing security problems have, however, slowed the pace of that recovery. Output remained stagnant in 1991, and 1992 and 1993.

The agricultural sector declined by about 9.6% during 1986 (as a result of reductions in output of most export crops). Although production levels recovered in 1987 and in 1988, they declined again in 1989 and 1990, owing to low price returns. The collapse of international coffee prices in 1989 had a particularly adverse effect on overall economic performance. Output remained stagnant in 1991, 1992 and 1993.

Coffee

Coffee (mostly *robusta*) continues to dominate the monetary sector. It is grown by more than 1m. small farmers. Production fell steadily throughout the 1970s, from a record 225,200 metric tons in 1973 to only 97,500 tons in 1981. Uganda was unable to benefit fully from the high international coffee prices in 1976 and 1977, since transport difficulties, the temporary closure of the border with Kenya in 1976 and the lack of foreign exchange, even to buy bags for the coffee, resulted in a stockpile of coffee. Lack of transport and spare parts, and smuggling into Kenya and Zaire, were other main factors limiting coffee exports during this period.

Uganda was able to meet its export quota, set by the International Coffee Organization (ICO), of 2.7m. bags (each of 60 kg) for the year ending 30 September 1982. Production generally exceeded the annual quota, and by the end of the 1983/84 coffee year there were accumulated stocks of about 3.9m. bags. The 1984/85 quota of 2.48m. bags was met, but only through a rundown of stocks, since coffee exports had been disrupted by the July 1985 coup. There were further disruptions as a result of the continuation of the civil war and operations by the National Resistance Army (NRA) in south-west Uganda, the main coffee-producing region. Following the assumption of power by the NRA in January 1986, coffee exports were temporarily halted, with the unfortunate result that Uganda failed to benefit from the prevailing high prices for coffee on the world market. Although exports were resumed later in the year, the total quantity for the 1985/86 coffee year was 2.4m. bags, leaving substantial unsold stocks. World coffee prices subsequently fell substantially, and the collapse of ICO quota arrangements in 1989 brought about a sharp decline in the international coffee market that continued into the early 1990s. Effective action to revive the market began in August 1993 when the Inter-African Coffee Organization, of which Uganda is a member, joined Latin American producers in a new plan to withhold 20% of output whenever market prices fell below an agreed limit. The scheme came into full operation in October, and gradually generated improved prices in world markets; by April 1994 market quotations for all grades and origins of coffee had achieved their highest levels since 1989.

Most of Uganda's coffee was formerly transported to Mombasa by trucks and trains. The Museveni government's measures to effect a transfer to rail freight for all Ugandan trade was one of the causes of tension with Kenya during early 1987, owing to the loss in earnings that this represented for Kenyan trucking firms. The cost of freighting Ugandan goods to Mombasa in 1986 was US $116 per metric ton by road, compared with $52 by rail. In 1988 nearly three-quarters of the coffee reportedly was transported by rail to Mombasa, and the remainder to Dar es Salaam. As a result of favourable weather and the introduction by the Coffee Marketing Board (CMB), in August 1987, of advance payments to farmers, Uganda easily fulfilled its ICO quota for 1987/88 of 2.1m. bags, and additional exports to non-ICO countries raised total exports for the year to 2.7m. bags. In 1988/89 a record 3.1m. bags were exported. However, despite the greatest coffee output for 14 years, export earnings declined to $160m. in 1989, from $270m. in 1988, owing to the collapse of world prices, following the suspension of ICO quotas (see above). Production fell to 2.8m. bags in 1990 and to 2.3m. bags in 1991, with exports earning $141m. in 1990 and only $126m. in 1991. Output was 2.01m. bags in 1992 and 3m. bags in 1993. The CMB, which was the sole purchaser and exporter of coffee, also had persistent problems with crop finance, which adversely affected deliveries from farmers. In 1990 the CMB's monopoly of coffee marketing was abolished. Five coffee co-operatives joined forces to form Union Export Services (UNEX), and by mid-1992 UNEX was handling 20% of coffee sales with the CMB handling the remaining 80%. By mid-1993 there were 12 coffee-marketing co-operatives. It was announced in early 1991 that a Uganda Coffee Development Authority was to be established, with responsibility for policy-making, research and development in the coffee sector. The CMB was to be reorganized as a public limited company. The UK is Uganda's largest customer for coffee, taking about one-third of the total. The USA, Japan and Germany are also important customers.

Tea

Prior to the Amin regime and the nationalization of tea plantations in 1972, Uganda was second only to Kenya among African producers. However, production declined each year thereafter until 1980, by which time Uganda's tea exports were negligible. In 1980 the UK-based company Mitchell Cotts, former owner of three groups of tea estates until these were nationalized by Amin, was invited back to establish a joint venture with the government to own and operate the estates, which cover 2,310 ha. The Toro and Mityana Tea Co (Tamteco), with 51% of the shares held by the government, was formed in 1980 and work began on an $8.8m. programme to rehabilitate the overgrown plantations and near-derelict factories. Of the total of 21,000 ha planted with tea, only about one-tenth is productive. Tamteco, which accounts for two-thirds of total annual output of tea, has only about 1,200 ha of its 2,300 ha under cultivation in full production. The second-largest producer of tea is the Uganda Tea Corpn, which is state-owned and has plantations covering 900 ha. A parastatal body, Agricultural Enterprises Ltd (AEL), has 2,100 ha of estates and seven tea factories, which have been rehabilitated by a Netherlands company. Government holdings in tea enterprises are awaiting transferral to the private sector. Smallholders, which have 9,000 ha under tea, market their output through the Uganda Tea Growers' Association.

Small quantities of tea began to be exported in early 1981. By 1984 production had risen to 5,223 tons, and exports were 2,604 tons, and Uganda derived some benefit from the record international tea prices of late 1983 and 1984 (although tea accounted for less than 1% of total export earnings in 1984). Sustained recovery, however, did not begin until 1989, when tea production totalled 4,620 tons and exports were 3,134 tons. In 1990 Uganda produced 6,704 tons and exported 4,760 tons; this recovery was consolidated in 1991 when output totalled 8,878 tons and exports, 7,050 tons. In 1992 output was 9,400 tons and exports reached almost 8,000 tons, while in 1993 production of 11,800 tons and exports of 10,000 tons represented the highest levels achieved since 1978. Output has, however, remained inhibited by a shortage of labour, caused mainly by very low wages.

Cotton

In the early 1970s Uganda ranked third among African cotton producers, and cotton has been the country's second most important export since it was overtaken by coffee. However, production decreased from a peak of 467,000 bales (each of 480 lb or 217.7 kg) in 1970 to only 28,020 bales in 1980 and to a low of 18,800 bales in 1981. The causes of the decline were the very low official prices paid to producers and the physical deterioration of the ginneries during Amin's rule. Exports ceased altogether in the early 1970s, resuming in 1982. Output rose slowly, reaching 56,646 bales in 1983/84, of which 60% was exported. The 1984/85 harvest was slightly lower. In 1985 cotton exports earned $15.4m., equivalent to 4.1% of total export earnings. The 1985/86 harvest fell to about 45,000 bales. In 1986 the government initiated the Emergency Cotton Production Programme, but the 1987 target of 140,000 bales was not even 50% achieved. Low producer prices and fighting in the main cotton-growing areas in the north and east were mainly to blame for the disappointing result. The $15m. programme was funded by the World Bank, the UK and other donors. The derelict state of the ginneries mean that stockpiles were awaiting ginning, despite the low harvests. The production target for 1988/89 was 150,000 bales, but actual output was only 44,000 bales. Exports of cotton earned $3.1m. in 1988, compared with $4.1m. in 1987. Production in 1989 reached 105,650 bales but fell back to 51,000 bales in 1990, to 36,750 bales in 1991 and to 32,150 bales in 1992. Output for 1993 recovered to an estimated 50,530 bales. Production of cottonseed declined from 18,000 metric tons in 1991 to 15,000 tons in 1992, but recovered substantially to 24,000 tons in 1993. Main customers are the UK, Germany, Hong Kong and Portugal.

Other Crops

Tobacco output has varied, partly as a result of unfavourable weather conditions, and partly because of recurrent fighting in the West Nile region, where it is grown. Production was estimated at only 100 metric tons in 1981, compared with a peak of 5,000 tons in 1972, but by 1983 exports resumed on a very small scale. Following a rise in producer prices and the implementation of a $5.5m. rehabilitation programme, production increased to 1,900 tons in 1984. Production fell to 925 tons in 1986, but recovered to about 4,000 metric tons annually during 1987–89. Output recovered further in 1992, to 7,285 tons, the largest crop for more than two decades, before falling back to just under 5,000 tons in 1993. Owing to an increase in the availability of interest-free crop finance from British-American Tobacco (BAT), the output target for 1994 was 6,300 tons. Phillip Morris of the USA was given permission in April 1994 to enter the Ugandan market, thereby breaking a monopoly previously held by BAT. In 1991 exports of tobacco earned $4.5m.

Production of raw sugar had fallen to only 2,400 metric tons by 1984, compared with a peak of 152,000 metric tons in 1968. Local demand is estimated at 160,000–200,000 tons per year. Lack of transport and problems with the maintenance of mechanical equipment were among the reasons for this drastic fall in output, but a major cause was the expulsion of the Asian families who ran much of the sugar industry, on three large estates. The Madhvani and Mehta families returned in 1980 to begin the rehabilitation of the estates and factories, in joint-venture companies with the government. The Lugazi sugar complex, 40 km east of Kampala, and now operated by the Uganda Sugar Corpn, is 51% owned by the government and 49% by the Mehta group. A new refinery, with a capacity of 60,000 metric tons per year and which was expected to employ more than 6,000 people, was opened in 1988. The complex (including a 9,180-ha plantation) has been rehabilitated in a $90m. project, funded by the International Development Association (IDA), the African Development Bank (ADB), the Commonwealth Development Corporation (CDC), the Arab Bank for Economic Development in Africa (BADEA), Kuwait and India. In 1993, however, the factory suspended production, owing to competition from sugar which had been smuggled from western Kenya. The state-owned Kinyala sugar works are being rehabilitated in a project costing $58m., which is being partly funded by Kuwait, BADEA and the Saudi Fund for Development. Once rehabilitated, Kinyala should produce 37,000 tons of sugar per year. In 1985 a section of the Madhvani family signed an agreement with the government to establish a new company, Kakira Sugar Works (1985). The rehabilitation of the Kakira complex suffered delays and financial losses while alleged disagreements within the Madhvani family postponed negotiations on the finance necessary for the project. Financing arrangements (then totalling $61.5m.) still awaited finalization at the beginning of 1988, but rehabilitation work began in that year. Trial production commenced in November 1989. In 1994 the government reported that in the previous year output had reached 49,264 metric tons, down from 53,539 metric tons in 1992. In the early 1990s, large quantities of sugar grown and processed in western Kenya were being smuggled into Uganda. The government banned the import of sugar temporarily, but lifted the ban in May 1992. The government is aiming to achieve self-sufficiency in sugar by 1995. Cocoa production declined significantly during the Amin regime, and has subsequently not fully recovered. Exports increased from 100 tons in 1982 to 155 tons in 1983, to 170 tons in 1984 and to 1,396 tons in 1990. Production remained steady at about 1,000 tons in 1991, 1992 and 1993. Revenue from cocoa exports amounted to $504,000 in 1990.

Uganda's principal food crops are matoke (a form of plantain), cassava, sweet potatoes, finger millet, maize, beans, sorghum, potatoes, groundnuts and simsim. There are three rice-growing projects in the country. The largest, in Olwiny swamp in the north, covers 800 ha and is being implemented with help from the People's Republic of China, the ADB and the Islamic Development Bank. A further 680 ha is to be developed for smallholder production. Maize cultivation is rapidly expanding, both as a subsistence and as a cash crop. In 1984 maize became Uganda's third largest source of foreign exchange. Since the late 1980s, however, transport problems and the poor state of rural roads have hampered the collection of crops. In 1988, when output of maize was estimated at 600,000 tons, Uganda fell far short of fulfilling its commitments for the export of maize and beans under barter agreements which had been concluded with several countries, whereby crops were to have been exchanged for machinery, equipment or other essential imports. Official estimates indicate that production of maize doubled, to 1.2m. tons, in 1989. In 1992, as severe drought caused crop failures throughout eastern and southern Africa, Uganda ignored the warnings of the FAO and other aid agencies by setting and meeting a target of 300,000–500,000 metric tons of maize for export. Kenya placed an order for 300,000 tons of maize. Uganda produced 576,000 metric tons of millet in 1991, 634,000 tons in 1992 and 652,000 tons in 1993. Output of sorghum in the same period rose steadily from 363,000 metric tons in 1991, to 375,000 tons in 1992 and 382,000 tons in 1993.

Groundnuts and soya beans enjoyed an upsurge in production in the early 1990s. Output of groundnuts in shells had averaged 80,000 metric tons a year from 1979–81, but had increased to 144,000 tons in 1991, 147,000 tons in 1992 and 150,000 tons in 1993. Similarly, production of soya beans had averaged just 4,000 metric tons a year from 1979–81, but had recovered to 59,000 tons in 1991. Output declined to 53,000 tons in 1992, but then soared to 71,000 tons in 1993. Uganda also harvests about 3,000 metric tons of sunflower seed each year. Official estimates indicate that Uganda's output of dry beans rose from 383,000 metric tons in 1991 to 402,000 tons in 1992 and 441,000 tons in 1993. Food shortages were, however, reported in several districts of Uganda, owing to a 30% decline in cassava output and a 10% decline in the production of potatoes. In May 1992 the government confirmed that strategic food stocks were low, and World Bank figures indicate that Uganda imported 22,000 metric tons of cereals in 1992. The country also received 25,000 metric tons of cereal food aid in 1991/92.

Beef and dairy cattle are kept by smallholders and on large commercial ranches. The country has good-quality pasture, but the prevalence of several endemic diseases and the armed theft of cattle are continuing problems. The total number of cattle, estimated at 5.2m. in 1979, had declined to about 3.9m. by 1989, as a result of disease, rustling and, in the north and east, malnutrition. The European Union (EU) is funding an artificial insemination programme to regenerate the herd. The dairy sector is being revitalized in a project funded by several UN agencies, the ADB, the European Development Fund and Denmark. The project is aimed at improving the processing, collection and transport of dairy produce to urban markets. Poultry, pigs, sheep, goats and bees are also important.

Uganda has an abundance of lakes and rivers, and fishing is an important rural industry, with considerable scope for further development. Of the total catch in 1988, amounting to about 214,700 metric tons, 40% came from Lake Kyoga and 50% from Lake Victoria. In early 1989 an Italian company began to develop an integrated fisheries centre at Masese to smoke and dry tilapia and Nile perch. Some 7.5m. ha are covered by forest and woodland. In early 1990 the government banned exports of timber, pending the implementation of legislation to regulate the forestry sector.

INDUSTRY

The main industries are processing of cotton, coffee, tea, sugar, tobacco, edible oils and dairy products, grain milling, brewing, vehicle assembly and the manufacture of textiles, steel, metal products, cement, soap, shoes, animal feeds, fertilizers, paints and matches. The output of all these industries fell drastically during the 1970s. Much plant and machinery was in a bad state of repair and there were shortages of fuel, spare parts and technical and managerial skills. In January 1993 the European Investment Bank provided Uganda with a loan of ECU 5.4m. in support of industrial development. Copper refining was formerly very important, but production ceased during Amin's regime. Negotiations concerning a project to revive the copper-refining sector took place in 1991.

The rehabilitation of Uganda's industrial sector is proceeding very slowly, and in 1992 industry was still estimated to be operating at below 30% of capacity. However, in 1987 the government claimed that several industries, including grain-milling and the manufacture of hoes, beer, blankets and poultry feed, were operating at more than 50% of capacity. The output of the industrial sector increased by an annual average of 5.5% during the period 1980–90, according to estimates by the World Bank, while manufacturing production increased by an annual average of only 5.2% over the same period. Industrial output increased by 16% in 1987 and by 25% in 1988; nevertheless, in 1990, 1991 and 1992 manufacturing provided only 4% of gross domestic product (GDP).

The textile industry is suffering a severe lack of skilled personnel and of spare parts but considerable amounts of aid, from the ADB, the EC and from certain Arab funds, are helping to establish new ginneries, spinning and weaving mills and to repair existing plants. There are four fully integrated textile mills, with a total rated capacity of 66m. linear metres of cloth per year. Yarn is also produced.

The country's first vehicle-assembly plant, operated by GM Co, is a joint venture between the local Spear Motors and Peter Bauer of Germany. Capacity will be 490 commercial vehicles and 360 trailers per year, with about 40% available for export. In 1983 the British-based Lonrho group resumed production at its Chibuku brewery, which had fallen into disuse after its expropriation by the Amin government. The group also opened negotiations for the repossession of its other expropriated assets in Uganda, including Consolidated Printers, which prints the government-controlled daily *New Vision,* and Printpak (Uganda). In November 1986 Lonrho signed an agreement with the government, under which it was to construct an oil pipeline from the Kenyan border to Kampala, and participate in the marketing of Ugandan coffee and cotton. In 1984 Uganda Breweries was returned to its original owners, Nairobi-based East African Breweries and Ind Coope and City Breweries of the UK. It subsequently started to rehabilitate its Port Bell plant. A local firm, Century Bottling Co, obtained the franchise to produce Coca-Cola in the new Ntinda industrial area, outside Kampala. The East African Development Bank and Uganda Development Bank are major investors in the project. Other soft drinks produced in Uganda are Pepsi Cola (by Lake Victoria Bottling Co), Schweppes (by Kampala Bottlers) and the local Creps (by the Masaka Co-operative Union); the government is to transfer its share in these companies to the private sector. A new tannery at Jinja is expected to make Uganda self-sufficient in leather goods. Chloride (Uganda) has been expanded and it is expected that Uganda will eventually be self-sufficient in batteries. In 1989 the Madhvani group began to bring nine of its 10 industrial companies back into production (only its textile firm, Mulco, was still operating). The Masaka food processing plant and cannery started to produce fruit beverages in 1988. The country's second pharmaceutical plant, INLEX, opened in 1989.

A salt plant has been built at Lake Katwe, with German finance, for the production of table salt and potassium chloride. Construction of the plant was carried out between 1974–78, but various technical problems caused the plant's closure in 1980, since when Uganda has had to import all its salt requirements. A $20m. contract for the rehabilitation of the plant was awarded to a Swiss firm in 1986, but the government has been unable to attract private investors to be joint shareholders with the Uganda Development Corpn. There are two cement plants, at Tororo (near the Kenyan border) and at Hima (about 500 km to the west), with rated annual capacities of 150,000 tons and 300,000 tons respectively, although in 1986 their combined output was only 14,960 tons, rising to 20,000 tons in 1988. Total domestic requirements are 650,000 tons per year. Some renovation work has been carried out, by a Turkish company at Tororo and by a German company at Hima. Major rehabilitation schemes are planned for each plant.

MINERALS

Output of blister copper fell sharply from 17,000 tons in 1970 to 2,261 tons in 1977. The Kilembe copper mines, in western Uganda, virtually ceased production in 1979, while the Jinja smelter fell into disrepair. The government announced in 1983 that it would go ahead with reactivating the Kilembe mines, following a feasibility study financed by the European Investment Bank and carried out in 1982 by a UK firm, which assessed proven and probable reserves of copper ore at just over 4m. metric tons, and possible reserves at 1.8m. tons. A new smelter was to be built to replace the one at Jinja, now in total disrepair, and plants were to be built to extract cobalt and sulphuric acid from the stockpile of copper pyrites accumulated at the mines since 1954. Doubts were raised concerning the project's commercial viability, in view of the generally low levels of international prices for copper and cobalt throughout most of the 1980s, and international financial support was initially not forthcoming. However, in early 1988, following a significant rise in copper prices, the Democratic People's Republic of Korea signed an agreement with the government to rehabilitate the Kilembe mine workshop, and by May 1991 donors had pledged $10.28m. towards the rehabilitation of the actual mine. In 1991 the cobalt plant was being brought into operation. In March 1991 a scheme was announced to extract cobalt from the tailings of the mine, under a joint venture, the Kasese Cobalt Co. Participating were the Bureau de Recherche Géologique et Minière of France and Barclays Metals of the UK. The construction of a cobalt plant was proceeding in 1994.

Uganda exploits substantial deposits of apatite (used in superphosphate fertilizers) at Tororo, although production has fallen sharply since the Amin period. Until the 1970s, the country also mined tungsten, beryl, columbo-tantalite, gold, bismuth, phosphate, limestone and tin, mostly on a small scale. The government would like to reopen these mines. Extraction of small quantities of tungsten, tin and gold has recommenced. A study, financed by the World Bank, was made by US and French consultants on a phosphate fertilizer project using phosphate deposits in the Sukulu hills, estimated at 220m.–225m. metric tons. The study recommended construction of a plant to make single superphosphates, with initial capacity of 80,000 tons per year, of which 75% would be exported to neighbouring countries. The total cost of the project was to be about $102m. There are high-grade iron ore deposits at Kigezi but they have not yet been exploited. Geological surveys have been carried out in the Lake Albert and Rift Valley areas.

Petroleum exploration has proceeded slowly. In the early 1980s the IDA lent $5.1m. for exploration promotion, to attract bids from international oil companies and for consultancy services to evaluate these offers. Initially, there was little interest, and by the deadline of February 1985, only one bid had been received, from the UK's Shell International Petroleum Co, together with Exxon Corpn of the USA. The successive changes of government prevented any progress, but in 1987 the Museveni government initiated a Petroleum Exploration Promotion Project, to be overseen by the National Mining Corpn. Bidding for exploration rights was reopened in early 1988. In 1990 Uganda and Zaire signed an agreement for the joint exploration and exploitation of petroleum reserves beneath Lakes Albert and Edward. In 1991 the Ugandan government signed an oil exploration agreement with Fina Exploration Uganda, a wholly-owned subsidiary of Belgium's Petrofina, covering a 26,800-sq km area in the two lakes. However, Fina Exploration Uganda abandoned its search in 1993.

POWER

Electricity is generated at the Owen Falls hydroelectric station at Jinja, which has an installed capacity of 180 MW, of which 30 MW was exported to Kenya until 1987. The Owen Falls plant is being modernized, and its capacity expanded to 380 MW, in a rehabilitation project. The IDA provided a $28.8m. credit towards the project, the CDC contributed £20m. and the Chinese company Sicto pledged $350m. The first phase was given permission to proceed in 1986, having been delayed by the retention of funds by the World Bank, owing to its disapproval of Museveni's economic policies; by mid-1992 the project was reported to be well-advanced. The government had planned to construct a second hydroelectric station at Murchison Falls in northern Uganda, but, in 1991, yielded to strong environmental objections to this choice of site. Uganda is to make available 15 MW to north-western Tanzania, under an agreement signed in 1982. In 1992 transmission lines were still being constructed. Energy consumption per caput grew by an annual average of 3.7% in 1980–92, a marked improvement over the annual average of −7.0% in 1971–80.

TOURISM

During the 1960s and until 1972, tourism was, after coffee and cotton, the third most important source of foreign exchange. In 1971 there were 85,000 visitors and receipts were $27m. Tourism ceased during Amin's rule, with wildlife parks and hotels totally neglected. Under the Obote government, the sector began to be slowly rehabilitated, and the number of visitors rose from 8,622 in 1982 to an estimated 90,000 in 1990. The state-owned Uganda Hotels Corpn (which is to be transferred to private-sector ownership) owns four hotels, and began to seek finance for their rehabilitation in the early 1980s. During the late 1980s the Lake Victoria and Nile Mansions hotels in Kampala were renovated, with Italian funding, and upgraded to four-star and five-star status respectively. The International Conference Centre at Nile Mansions was included in the scheme. In early 1988 a consortium of Italian companies, led by Viginter, agreed to construct four four-star hotels, in Masaka, Fort Portal, Jinja and Mbale. The Sheraton Kampala has been refurbished by the Yugoslav company, Energoprojekt, at a cost of $27.5m., and it is now managed by Sheraton Corpn of the USA. The Imperial Hotel in Kampala, owned by Uganda Hotels Corpn, began renovations in 1989 at a cost of $850,000. Uganda has seven national parks.

TRANSPORT AND COMMUNICATIONS

The Third Highway Project, costing $32.6m., is being financed mainly by the IDA, and was launched in August 1987. It involves repair of existing surfaced and unsurfaced roads. The road link with Rwanda was to be improved with EU finance, as part of the 'northern corridor' scheme to link eastern Zaire, Rwanda and Uganda with the Kenyan port of Mombasa. The European Development Fund is financing the second phase of a project to repair Kampala's roads. Other major programmes of road repairs are being financed by Germany, under its bilateral aid programme. In February 1987 the government signed an agreement with Yugoslavia's Energoprojekt, for the construction of a 250-km road in western Uganda, from Mityana to Fort Portal, as part of the Trans-African Highway. The rural road network is being rehabilitated in a four-year project, costing $55m., which is to be funded by Germany, Japan, the UN Development Programme (UNDP) and BADEA. In 1991, however, it was reported that of the 3,000 km of roads that had already been rehabilitated under the scheme, only 1,300 km were receiving regular maintenance, prompting fears that the remainder would soon fall into disrepair again. Several hundred new lorries were imported, many under barter agreements, in the early 1990s. India, France and Germany supplied locomotives and rolling stock, which were urgently needed by the Uganda Railways Corpn (URC), established following the dissolution of East African Railways. The UK, France, Italy, Germany and the EU are assisting with a programme to rehabilitate the railway system, which also forms part of the 'northern corridor'. The URC operates a wagon-ferry service on Lake Victoria between Jinja and Mwanza, in Tanzania. This provides a much needed alternative route to the sea, via the Tanzanian ports of Tanga and Dar es Salaam. The URC is to be transferred to private ownership.

In May 1976 the Uganda Airlines Corpn (UAC) was established by the government, and in February 1978 the airline inaugurated its first international scheduled service, between Entebbe and Nairobi. In May 1980 a scheduled passenger and cargo service started operating from Uganda to Rome, Brussels and London, using a Boeing 707 airliner. The airline subsequently introduced new routes, to Cologne, Dubai and Bombay. In January 1988 the weekly service to London was halted because the 707s failed to satisfy new European noise regulations. This service was resumed in February 1989, using a leased aircraft. The airline's route coverage has subsequently been considerably curtailed, and in 1990 it was announced that UAC was to be restructured.

Kampala's telephone network has been modernized and expanded in a $13m. project, financed mainly by a concessionary loan from France. An IDA credit, worth about $52.3m., was approved in early 1989 to finance part of the rehabilitation programme of the Uganda Posts and Telecommunications Corpn (UP and TC), which is expected to cost about $100m. UP and TC is to be privatized.

EXTERNAL TRADE

Traditionally, Uganda's four leading export commodities have been coffee, tea, cotton and copper. Hides and skins are also exported. Coffee alone normally accounted for about 95% of total export earnings. However, the value of coffee exports declined sharply in 1992/93, when coffee contributed about 75% of total export revenue. Copper exports dwindled from $20.6m. in 1970 to nil by 1979, with the halting of production at Kilembe.

The deficit on merchandise trade was $60.4m. in 1983, but there was an estimated surplus of $65.7m. in 1984. This surplus rose sharply to $115m. in 1985, with exports down to $379m. and imports declining at an even faster rate to $264m. These trends were mainly due to the fall in the value of the shilling and the slowdown in the economic recovery programme. In 1986, with improved export earnings, as a result of high world coffee prices, and a severe reduction in imports, the surplus totalled about $2.2m. Owing to the scarcity of foreign exchange and to the over-inflated value of the shilling, legitimate imports had slowed to a trickle by the time that the currency was devalued by 76% in May 1987. The continuing foreign exchange crisis led to the signing, in 1987, of a series of barter agreements with several countries (including Libya) and companies, whereby Uganda was supplied with goods and services in return for commodities: coffee, in particular, but also cotton, timber, maize, beans and sesame seed. The total value of such agreements had reached about $500m. by the end of 1989. By early 1988 it was clear that there was not enough surplus agricultural produce to fulfil commitments, which, for 1987, had totalled 140,000 metric tons of produce. Although it had been hoped that barter agreements would be a means of diversifying exports, coffee remains the main commodity involved. The UK is Uganda's main trading partner after Kenya, which supplies refined petroleum products and also re-exports goods to Uganda through Mombasa. Other principal suppliers are Malaysia, Italy, Germany, Japan and France. Main customers are the USA, the UK, the Netherlands, France and Germany. In 1988 the value of exports was estimated at $272.9m., of which coffee earned $264.3m., cotton $3.1m. and tea $1.2m. Imports cost $627.4m. The value of exports fell to an estimated $259.2m. in 1989, while the value of imports rose to $727.7m., leaving a trade deficit of $468.5m. In 1991 exports earned $175m., while imports cost $424m., leaving a trade deficit of $249m. In 1992, total merchandise exports, at $164m., covered only 40% of total merchandise imports, at $405m., leaving a visible trade deficit of $241m. Exports amounted to $157m. in 1993.

East African Community

Uganda was a partner, with Kenya and Tanzania, in the East African Community (EAC), which came into existence in December 1967. The EAC disintegrated, however, as a result of continual disagreements between the partners over financial and political issues, and by mid-1977 the various common services, such as railways, harbours and the airline, had ceased to function and the EAC had collapsed. In November 1983 agreement was finally reached, after nearly six years of negotiations, on the division of the EAC's assets and liabilities. The final accounts of the EAC, produced by the World Bank, were approved by the three heads of state in July 1986. A co-ordinating committee has been meeting to oversee new initiatives aimed at regional co-operation. The surviving EAC institution, the East African Development Bank (which has its headquarters in Kampala), was given a new charter in August 1980 and is gradually expanding its lending programme.

PUBLIC FINANCE

The most important source of recurrent revenue is export taxes (almost entirely from coffee at present), followed by sales tax. The 1985/86 budget introduced rises of 11%–31.5% in producer prices for export crops, but these increases were insufficient to offset inflation, which soared to an average annual rate of 200% in 1986. In May 1986 the Museveni government reintroduced a two-tier system of exchange rates, with a low priority rate, at sh. 1,400 = US $1, for basic consumer imports, and a higher market rate, at sh. 5,000 = US $1 (a 72% devaluation), for all other imports. This measure, designed to encourage exports and to curb the 'black market', was complemented by a nominal increase in producer prices for coffee, tea, tobacco and cocoa. The 1986/87 budget abandoned this dual exchange rate, fixing the shilling instead at the previous 'priority' rate of sh. 1,400 = US $1, representing a large revaluation. This decision encountered strong disapproval from multilateral and bilateral donors, who were also dismayed at the tripling of the envisaged budget deficit, to sh. 349,500m.

Measures under the three-year rehabilitation and development programme for 1987/88–1989/90 (see below), announced in May 1987, included the devaluation of the currency by 76%, and the introduction of a 'new' shilling, equivalent to 100 'old' shillings. The main aim of the rehabilitation programme, to reduce government spending, was echoed in the 1987/88 budget, presented. The budget deficit, envisaged at 'new' sh. 8,600m. ($143.3m.), although three times that of the previous year, represented only 15% of total planned expenditure, projected at sh. 53,200m. ($886.7m.). The increase in budgetary spending was moderate in real terms, when set against the estimated rate of inflation of 300%. The revenue from taxes was expected to rise as a result of increased earnings from exports owing to the devaluation of the shilling, and because of additional taxes on private sector businesses. However, the removal of the sales tax from basic essentials, such as sugar, salt and kerosene, was expected to reduce government revenue considerably. The lifting of import duties on raw materials and industrial equipment, and the reduction of interest rates were aimed at encouraging investment in industry.

Interim budget proposals, announced in February 1988, included the reduction of expenditure in several government departments, partly because of Uganda's failure to achieve levels of agricultural output sufficient to fulfil barter agreements with other countries. The 1988/89 budget, announced in July 1988, represented continuing efforts by the government to encourage economic rehabilitation of the country, while curbing inflation. The shilling was devalued by 60%, so that the exchange rate stood at sh. 150 = US $1, in place of the previous rate of sh. 60 = US $1. The shilling was further devalued, by 10% in December 1988 and by 21% in March 1989, bringing it to sh. 200 = US $1. The rate on the parallel market fell to sh. 530 = US $1 from sh. 420 = US $1 following the March devaluation. In July a two-tier foreign exchange system was reintroduced. The Bank of Uganda was to sell foreign currency to importers at a rate of about sh. 400 = US $1, undercutting the parallel market rate, which was about sh. 600 = US $1 at that time. The selling rate was to be adjusted weekly.

Total expenditure under the 1989/90 budget, announced in July 1989, was projected at sh. 212,555m., while revenue was forecast at sh. 118,899m. The deficit of sh. 93,656m. was to be offset by external borrowing. Also included in the budget was a 40% salary increase for civil servants and an increase in producer prices.

Five further devaluations reduced the value of the shilling to sh. 620 = US $1 by end-March 1991. The budget for 1990/91 envisaged total expenditure of sh. 320,800m. and revenue of sh. 206,960m., leaving a deficit of sh. 113,200m. Budgetary measures included a wage increase of 22% for civil servants and improved public access to foreign exchange.

In February 1992 Uganda re-introduced the auctioning of foreign currency, with the Bank of Uganda auctioning the currency to commercial banks. Initially this produced an exchange rate of sh. 980 = US $1. By May 1992, however, inflation was running at 52% over the rate at the beginning of the year, projecting an annual rate of 139%. In June the official exchange rate was sh. 1,300 = US $1. By July 1992 the government claimed that inflation had been brought under control. In mid-1993 the IMF assessed the annual average rate of inflation at 3%. In June 1993 the shilling had stabilized and was trading at sh. 1,197 = US $1. At the beginning of November 1993, the government abandoned the auction of foreign exchange and introduced the Foreign Exchange Inter-Bank Market. By July 1994 the exchange rate had improved to sh. 937 = US $1.

BALANCE OF PAYMENTS

The balance of payments in 1983 showed a current account deficit of $72.2m., but this was transformed into a surplus of $103.5m. in 1984, when export earnings were slightly higher and the import bill much lower, producing a surplus on the merchandise trade balance. The current account surplus was only $4.6m. in 1985, and a deficit of $4.0m. was recorded in 1986. The deficit on the current account of the balance of payments widened to $131.1m. in 1987, owing to low international prices for coffee and an increased volume of imports in that year. The deficit grew to $199.4m. in 1988, and to an estimated $247.9m. in 1989. In 1990 the current account deficit amounted to $434m. before, and $255m. after, official transfers. In 1991 the deficit was $393m. before, and $182m. after, official transfers. An improvement was achieved in 1992 when the current account deficit was $346m. before, and $113m. after, official transfers. Foreign reserves at the end of 1989 totalled $28.3m. At the end of 1991 they stood at $59m., enough to cover four weeks' worth of imports. Foreign reserves edged upwards in 1992, reaching $94m., sufficient to cover a month and a half's-worth of imports. Total external debt was officially estimated at about $1,800m. at the end of 1989, at $2,830m. at the end of 1991 and at $2,997m. at the end of 1992. Debt-servicing throughout the 1970s had remained as low as 5% of export earnings, owing to a low level of foreign investment and lending. In 1981, however, the debt-service ratio was about 60%, but subsequently, as export revenue increased more quickly than borrowing, the ratio declined. Debt-servicing costs amounted to 47.2% of exports in 1988 and to 54.5% of exports in 1990. In 1992, however, the ratio was 40.2% of export revenue according to the World Bank. The government estimated the debt-service ratio at 'nearly 100%' of exports in 1993. Of the $194.1m. of medium- and long-term debt due for repayment in 1989, $93.1m. was rescheduled by four members of the 'Paris Club' of official creditors (France, Italy, the UK and the USA) and Libya. In 1990 the cost of debt-servicing was $147m. In July 1993 Uganda repurchased $153m. of commercial debt at a substantial discount.

AID

During the rule of Idi Amin there was a drastic decline in receipts of aid except, after 1974, from Arab countries, in particular Libya. After the overthrow of Amin, several countries and multilateral agencies signed agreements with Uganda to provide official assistance. In June 1981 the World Bank arranged a reconstruction credit for Uganda. Negotiations were concluded in late April 1982 for a second arrangement covering reconstruction credit, totalling $120m.–$130m., with $70m. from the World Bank and the remainder from co-financiers. In May 1982 the World Bank announced a $35m. line of credit for industrial rehabilitation, and in January 1983 it agreed to lend $70m. for agriculture and $32m. for education. A third IDA reconstruction credit, of about $50m., was agreed in May 1984. The UNDP provided about $30m. in 1977–81 and agreed to double this for 1982–86. The EC (now restructured as the European Union—EU) pledged $78.9m. under Lomé I, $104m. under Lomé II and $125m. under Lomé III. It has also given emergency food aid. Agencies which have provided concessional loans include the ADB, BADEA and other Arab funds.

The IMF agreed a $197m. stand-by facility in June 1981, and a second stand-by arrangement, for $122m. over one year, was agreed in August 1982; a third stand-by facility, for 12 months and totalling nearly $105m., was approved by the IMF in September 1983. Negotiations on a new facility, of about $60m., reached deadlock, however, reportedly because the IMF disapproved of some of the government's policy trends, particularly the large rise in public spending. Almost one-third of the 1983/84 facility was unused by the time that the arrangement had expired.

In May 1982, at a World Bank Consultative Group meeting in Paris, Uganda presented its 1982–84 recovery programme, requiring $557.5m. in finance. A further meeting of the Consultative Group took place in January 1984. The government presented the revised recovery programme, covering 1983–85 (see below). For this, additional project finance, totalling $199m., was required for the two years 1983–85, and completion of the programme beyond 1985 required a total of $729m. In March 1986 representatives of donor countries and organizations attended a meeting in Kampala, at which the government presented proposals for a $160m. programme of emergency relief and rehabilitation, aimed at repairing the damage resulting from five years of civil war. During 1986, however, international donors waited for the new government to formulate its economic policies before pledging any new funds, and the IDA suspended disbursement of part of its committed funds. Discussions with the IMF and the World Bank were resumed in early 1987. Following the introduction of the three-year rehabilitation programme in May 1989 (see below), the IMF agreed to provide $24m. as a structural adjustment facility (SAF) for the first year, then $32m. over the following 24 months, in addition to $20m. from its compensatory financing facility fund (CFF). The World Bank agreed in principle to a $100m. package to support the recovery plan, and a Consultative Group meeting of donors, held in June 1987, resulted in new commitments amounting to $310m. for the first year of the three-year rehabilitation programme. Later in the month the 'Paris Club' rescheduled $66m. of debts, due to be repaid in 1987/88. Non-members of the 'Paris Club' also rescheduled debts of up to $45m. In July 1988 the World Bank formally approved the draw-down of the second tranche, worth $50m., of its economic recovery credit (ERC), which had been agreed in September 1987. In February 1988 the IMF approved a CCF equivalent to SDR 24.8m. (about $33.7m.), in connection with Uganda's shortfall in export earnings in the year ended September 1987, caused mainly by low world coffee prices in 1987. In October 1988 a Consultative Group meeting of international donors committed $550m. in loans and grants for 1989, in addition to existing commitments. The donors were presented with the government's economic recovery programme for 1988–92, which replaced the 1987–91 rehabilitation programme (see below). In September 1988 the IMF released the second tranche of its SAF, following repayment by Uganda of $18m. of arrears to the Fund. In April 1989 the IMF approved a three-year low-interest enhanced structural adjustment facility (ESAF) worth SDR 179.3m., replacing the SAF arranged in 1987. The World Bank agreed a $25m. supplement to the first ERC. At a meeting in late 1989 of the Consultative Group on Uganda, international donors pledged $640m. The World Bank committed $265m. for 1990, of which $125m. represented balance-of-payments support which had been withheld during 1989, pending the implementation of measures to reduce inflation. In April 1989 the IMF approved a three-year SDR 199.2m. ESAF to support economic recovery. The facility was due to last until 27 November 1992, and by April 1992 all but the last SDR 19.92m. tranche had been drawn. Disbursement of aid pledged by the international donor community was slow in the late 1980s, but improved in 1990. The World Bank Consultative Group for Uganda held a donors' meeting in Paris during May 1992, at which Uganda received up to $830m. in financial support for its economic development and adjustment programme for 1992/93. A further Consultative Group meeting in May 1993 pledged $825m. in support for 1993/94.

ECONOMIC DEVELOPMENT

Between 1965–71, Uganda's GDP expanded at an average rate of about 4.2% annually in real terms, as a result of the excellent performance of the agricultural sector and the food-processing industry, although the rate of increase was lower from the late 1960s. Uganda's third Five-Year Development Plan (1971–76) envisaged 5.6% annual growth; however, both government spending and economic performance fell considerably short of targets, with real GDP declining each year during the Plan period. There was a slight recovery in 1977, as a result of the strong advance in coffee prices. The Three-Year Plan (1976–79) had little chance of being fulfilled, since the economy was by that time operating at the most basic level. The dire state of the economy was due, in very large measure, to former President Amin's policies of expulsion of non-citizen Asians and mass expropriations of foreign firms. The disruption that was caused by the war of liberation early in 1979 produced a further fall in output in every sector during the year.

Emergency aid began to move into Uganda several months after Amin's overthrow and large sums of development aid appeared to be waiting for the moment when the country was again in a position to absorb it. However, the economic recovery, which had hardly begun, came to a virtual halt with the May 1980 coup which ousted President Binaisa.

In March 1981 Obote announced an economic recovery plan which aimed at, among other things, providing greater encouragement and protection for foreign investors. This was followed in March 1982 by a two-year recovery programme, which concentrated on the strengthening of the main export commodity sectors, on projects which would bring a quick return, either in export earnings or foreign exchange savings, and on schemes of an urgent humanitarian or social nature. The Obote government declared its intention to encourage a mixed economy and expected industrial revival to come mainly through the private sector. In July 1982 it ordered a study on the country's 97 parastatal enterprises, to decide which should be sold off to private investors, and to devise means of strengthening the remainder and making them more efficient. During 1983 the government decided to 'roll over' the recovery programme, and in November a revised programme was announced, covering the two years from 1983 to 1985. Uganda's annual inflation rate, which was 104% in 1980, was reduced to 30% in 1983, the government claimed. However, by the mid-1980s inflation had increased sharply. After Yoweri Museveni came to power in January 1986, he commissioned a report on the economy from a Canadian team. The Rehabilitation and Development Programme for 1987/88–1989/90, which was finally announced in May 1987, had the approval of the IMF and the World Bank, and was the first sign that the government was getting to grips with the country's economic problems. The programme included the introduction of a 'new' shilling, to equal 100 'old' shillings, and at the same time devalued the currency by 76%, to a rate of sh. 60 = US $1. The programme was replaced by an Economic Recovery Programme for 1988–92, presented to donors in October 1988. Total investment was scaled down to $1,674m., compared with $2,866m. for the previous plan. Projected average annual growth during the period of the plan was 5%; the plan aimed to revive exports and to boost non-traditional exports. Of total investment, transport and communications were allocated 27%, social infrastructure 25.7%, agriculture 23.8% and industry and tourism 17.2%. In 1992 the Development Finance Company of Uganda received a new equity participation from the CDC of $600,000. The European Investment Bank and Germany's DEG also became involved.

The Expropriated Properties Act, governing the return of (or compensation for) property confiscated during Idi Amin's rule (mainly from Asian owners), came into force in 1983. Unclaimed or unverified property was to be sold to Ugandan nationals or to foreign investors in joint ventures with Ugandans. In May 1991 the government announced further measures to benefit dispossessed Asian Ugandans. The draft version of an investment code to protect foreign investors was completed in February 1990. By January 1993 some 524 properties had reportedly been returned to their original owners. In April 1993, responsibility for the Asian-owned entities was entrusted to the Departed Asians' Property Custodian Board (DAPCB).

On the basis of gross national product (GNP) per head (only $160 in 1991 and $170 in 1992), Uganda is among the six poorest countries in the world. Uganda's GNP, in real terms, expanded by an annual average of 5.9% in the period 1980–91, according to World Bank estimates. In 1980–90 GDP increased, in real terms, by an annual average of 2.8%. The annual rate of inflation, which stood at 200% in 1986 when the NRM took power, had been brought under control by mid-1993. According to government figures, inflation stood at an annual rate of 9.2% in 1993, although by the time of the June 1994 budget speech, finance minister Joash Mayanja-Nkangi admitted that it had crept back up to an annual 16%.

The announcement of the new economic recovery plan in May 1987, together with agreements reached with the IMF and World Bank, was greeted with approval by Uganda's donors and business partners. By mid-1990 the short-term prospects for recovery seemed to be reasonably favourable; there had been a considerable influx of aid, and inflation was greatly reduced (although the effect of successive currency devaluations on imports was a growing cause of concern). Confidence was such that it was announced in 1990 that a stock exchange was to be opened in Kampala. In 1994 the exchange finally began operating. In April 1990 the government announced its intention of transferring several state-owned companies to the private sector. During the first half of 1993 several meetings to encourage investment took place in Europe. However, economic recovery remained hampered by the cost of continued fighting against rebel groups in northern and eastern Uganda and by a period of uncertainty in the world coffee market, following the collapse of ICO negotiations, though the market for coffee did see a marked improvement in early 1994. The government's extensive use of barter trade agreements, which it has frequently found difficult to honour in full, has been viewed by some observers as misguided and rash. These and many other problems will have to be overcome before the country can begin to benefit from its unquestionable advantages: a generally favourable climate, fertile soils and an abundance of natural resources.

Statistical Survey

Source (unless otherwise stated): Statistics Department, Ministry of Planning and Economic Development, Entebbe.

Area and Population

AREA, POPULATION AND DENSITY

Area (sq km)	
Land	197,058
Inland water	44,081
Total	241,139*
Population (census results)	
18 January 1980	12,636,179
12 January 1991†	
Males	8,124,800
Females	8,457,900
Total	16,582,674
Density (per sq km) at January 1991	68.8

* 93,104 sq miles. Source: Lands and Surveys Department.

† Data are provisional (figures for males and females are rounded). The revised total is 16,671,705 (density 69.1 per sq km).

DISTRICTS (population at 1980 census)

Apac	313,333	Lira	370,252
Arua	472,283	Luwero	412,474
Bundibugyu	112,216	Masaka	631,156
Bushenyi	524,669	Masindi	223,230
Gulu	270,085	Mbale	556,941
Hoima	294,301	Mbarara	688,153
Iganga	643,881	Moroto	188,641
Jinja	228,520	Moyo	106,492
Kabale	455,421	Mpigi	639,919
Kabarole	519,821	Mubende	510,260
Kampala	479,792	Mukono	634,275
Kamuli	349,549	Nebbi	233,000
Kapchorwa	73,967	Rakai	274,558
Kasase	277,697	Rukungiri	296,559
Kitgum	308,711	Soroti	476,629
Kotido	161,445	Tororo	668,410
Kumi	239,539		

PRINCIPAL TOWNS (population at 1969 census)

Kampala (capital)	330,700	Mbale	23,544
Jinja and Njeru	52,509	Entebbe	21,096
Bugembe planning area	46,884	Gulu	18,170

1980 (provisional census results): Kampala 458,423; Jinja 45,060; Masaka 29,123; Mbale 28,039; Mbarara 23,155; Gulu 14,958.

BIRTHS AND DEATHS (UN estimates, annual averages)

	1975–80	1980–85	1985–90
Birth rate (per 1,000)	50.3	48.6	50.5
Death rate (per 1,000)	17.6	17.9	19.5

Expectation of life (UN estimates, years at birth, 1985–90): 44.6 (males 43.2; females 46.1).

Source: UN, *World Population Prospects: The 1992 Revision.*

ECONOMICALLY ACTIVE POPULATION
(ILO estimates, '000 persons at mid-1980)

	Males	Females	Total
Agriculture, etc.	2,950	2,340	5,290
Industry	222	50	272
Services	353	247	600
Total	3,525	2,637	6,162

Source: ILO, *Economically Active Population Estimates and Projections, 1950–2025.*

Mid-1992 (estimates in '000): Agriculture, etc. 6,516; Total 8,178 (Source: FAO, *Production Yearbook*).

EMPLOYMENT ('000 employees at June each year)

	1976	1977	1978
Agriculture, forestry and fishing	78.2	76.6	81.1
Mining and quarrying	4.1	4.1	3.6
Manufacturing and electricity	54.0	51.9	51.7
Construction and water supply	45.5	46.9	48.9
Private commerce	18.5	12.8	18.3
Transport, storage and communications	13.1	12.4	10.0
Services*	152.0	158.1	158.2
Total	365.4	362.8	371.8

* Including commerce of the public sector.

Agriculture

PRINCIPAL CROPS ('000 metric tons)

	1990	1991	1992
Wheat	4	9	9
Rice (paddy)	54	58	64
Maize	602	517	595
Millet	560	576	593
Sorghum	360	363	375
Potatoes	223	245	257
Sweet potatoes	1,693	1,785	1,752
Cassava (Manioc)	3,339	3,599	3,780
Beans (dry)	396	383	402
Other pulses	106	109	111
Soybeans	37	59	62
Groundnuts (in shell)	158	126	138
Sesame seed	62	61	72
Cottonseed*	9	18	24
Vegetables†	404	415	400
Sugar cane†	650	890	920
Bananas†	560	570	570
Plantains	7,843	8,080	8,099
Coffee (green)	141	165	180*
Tea (made)	7	9	9*
Tobacco (leaves)	3	5	6
Cotton (lint)	4	8	11*

* Unofficial estimate(s). † FAO estimates.

Source: FAO, *Production Yearbook.*

LIVESTOCK ('000 head, year ending September)

	1990	1991*	1992*
Cattle	4,913	5,000	5,100
Sheep*	1,920	1,950	1,980
Goats	3,251	3,300	3,350
Pigs	824	850	880
Asses*	17	17	17

* FAO estimates.

Poultry (FAO estimates, million): 18 in 1990; 19 in 1991; 20 in 1992.

Source: FAO, *Production Yearbook.*

LIVESTOCK PRODUCTS (FAO estimates, '000 metric tons)

	1990	1991	1992
Beef and veal	77	79	80
Mutton and lamb	11	11	11
Goats' meat	14	14	14
Pig meat	37	38	40
Poultry meat	28	29	31
Other meat	17	17	17
Cows' milk	430	437	446
Poultry eggs	14.4	15.2	16.0
Cattle hides	10.8	11.0	11.2

Source: FAO, *Production Yearbook.*

Forestry

ROUNDWOOD REMOVALS
(FAO estimates, '000 cubic metres, excluding bark)

	1990	1991	1992
Sawlogs, veneer logs and logs for sleepers*	70	70	70
Other industrial wood	1,761	1,816	1,873
Fuel wood	12,320	12,705	13,103
Total	14,151	14,591	15,046

* Assumed to be unchanged since 1988.

Source: FAO, *Yearbook of Forest Products.*

SAWNWOOD PRODUCTION
('000 cubic metres)

	1986*	1987*	1988
Coniferous (soft wood)	7	7	8
Broadleaved (hard wood)	16	16	20
Total	23	23	28

* FAO estimates.

1989–92: Annual production as in 1988 (FAO estimates).

Source: FAO, *Yearbook of Forest Products.*

Fishing

('000 metric tons, live weight)

	1989	1990	1991*
Tilapias	68.8	101.1	105.1
African lungfishes	4.1	4.2	4.4
Characins	4.3	6.1	6.3
Naked catfishes	3.6	4.0	4.1
Torpedo-shaped catfishes	2.9	4.4	4.6
Other freshwater fishes	10.4	5.2	5.4
Nile perch	118.1	120.3	125.1
Total catch	212.2	245.2	254.9

* Figures for individual species or groups are FAO estimates.

Source: FAO, *Yearbook of Fishery Statistics.*

Mining

(metric tons, unless otherwise indicated)

	1989	1990	1991
Tin concentrates*	10	10	10
Tungsten concentrates*	4†	4†	4
Salt—unrefined ('000 metric tons)‡	5	5	5

* Figures refer to the metal content of concentrates.

† Estimate.

‡ Data from the US Bureau of Mines.

Source: UN, *Industrial Statistics Yearbook.*

Industry

SELECTED PRODUCTS
('000 metric tons, unless otherwise indicated)

	1989	1990	1991
Raw sugar	16	29	46
Beer ('000 hectolitres)	195	194	n.a.
Soft drinks ('000 hectolitres)	179	243	n.a.
Cigarettes (million)	1,586	1,290	2,200
Cement	17	27	24*
Electric energy (million kWh)	688	776	783

* Estimate.

Source: UN, *Industrial Statistics Yearbook.*

Finance

CURRENCY AND EXCHANGE RATES

Monetary Units
100 cents = 1 new Uganda shilling.

Sterling and Dollar Equivalents (31 March 1994)
£1 sterling = 1,530.0 new Uganda shillings;
US $1 = 1,030.6 new Uganda shillings;
10,000 new Uganda shillings = £6.536 = $9.703.

Average Exchange Rate (new Uganda shillings per US $)

1991	734.0
1992	1,133.8
1993	1,195.0

Note: Between December 1985 and May 1987 the official exchange rate was fixed at US $1 = 1,400 shillings. In May 1987 a new shilling, equivalent to 100 of the former units, was introduced. At the same time, the currency was devalued by 76.7%, with the exchange rate set at $1 = 60 new shillings. Further devaluations were implemented in subsequent years. Some figures in this survey are still in terms of old shillings.

GENERAL BUDGET*
(million old shillings, year ending 30 June)

Revenue†	1983/84	1984/85‡	1985/86‡
Taxation	88,424	162,092	284,374
Taxes on income, profits, etc.	6,245	9,762	15,632
Corporate taxes	5,925	8,875	14,319
Domestic taxes on goods and services	22,447	39,387	54,447
Sales taxes	17,679	31,873	42,230
Excises	3,484	5,554	9,726
Taxes on international trade	59,706	112,875	214,181
Import duties	9,234	14,293	17,640
Export duties	41,203	96,090	191,483
Exchange profits	7,831	—	—
Freight charges	1,348	2,492	5,058
Other current revenue	1,834	—	—
Administrative fees, charges, etc.	1,272	—	—
Total	90,258	162,092	284,374

Expenditure§	1983/84	1984/85‡	1985/86‡
General public services	26,826	53,986	99,066
Defence	19,229	35,919	120,443
Education	13,442	29,296	68,649
Health	2,908	7,968	10,917
Social security and welfare	1,811	3,572	9,673
Housing	1,408	2,661	3,506
Other community and social services	1,354	5,547	5,775
Economic services	9,893	24,376	67,548
Agriculture, forestry and fishing	3,574	9,916	21,335
Mining, manufacturing and construction	2,373	5,805	13,565
Transport and communications	3,350	7,896	29,876
Roads	2,562	7,020	28,265
Other purposes	25,864	59,127	71,732
Sub-total	102,735	222,452	457,309
Settlement of outstanding arrears	12,393	7,540	—
Total	115,128	229,992	457,309
Current	101,677	194,646	335,315
Capital	13,451	35,346	121,994

* Figures represent a consolidation of Revenue and Development Accounts. The data exclude the operations of the Social Security Fund and other central government units with their own budgets.
† Excluding grants received (million old shillings): 3,500 in 1983/84; 4,800 in 1984/85; 38,444 in 1985/86.
‡ Provisional.
§ Excluding lending (million old shillings): 750 in 1983/84; 920 in 1984/85.

Source: IMF, *Government Finance Statistics Yearbook.*

1986/87 (million new shillings): Revenue 5,005 (excluding grants 853); Expenditure 11,415.
1987/88 (million new shillings): Revenue 22,262 (excluding grants 5,640); Expenditure 33,401.
1988/89 (million new shillings): Revenue 46,719 (excluding grants 11,408); Expenditure 72,563.
1989/90 (million new shillings): Revenue 86,459 (excluding grants 24,891); Expenditure 166,977 (excluding net lending 2,287).
1990/91 (million new shillings): Revenue 136,808 (excluding grants 143,189); Expenditure 353,792 (excluding net lending 4,500).
1991/92 (million new shillings): Revenue 187,901 (excluding grants 185,909); Expenditure 561,413 (excluding net lending 8,500).
1992/93 (provisional, million new shillings): Revenue 287,112 (excluding grants 281,386); Expenditure 720,595 (excluding net lending 7,500).

Source: IMF, *International Financial Statistics.*

INTERNATIONAL RESERVES (US $ million at 31 December)

	1991	1992	1993
IMF special drawing rights	10.3	9.0	0.1
Foreign exchange	48.6	85.4	146.3
Total	58.9	94.4	146.4

Source: IMF, *International Financial Statistics.*

MONEY SUPPLY (million new shillings at 31 December)

	1990	1991	1992
Currency outside banks	n.a.	n.a.	98,335
Demand deposits at commercial banks	47,660	78,626	107,676
Total money (incl. others)	n.a.	n.a.	214,463

Source: IMF, *International Financial Statistics.*

COST OF LIVING (Consumer Price Index for all households in Kampala; base: 1990 = 100)

	1991	1992	1993
All items	128	195	207

Source: IMF, *International Financial Statistics.*

NATIONAL ACCOUNTS
(million new shillings at current prices)

Gross Domestic Product by Economic Activity

	1987	1988	1989
Agriculture, hunting, forestry and fishing	122,294	330,052	666,217
Mining and quarrying	34	35	37
Manufacturing	6,734	22,630	40,840
Electricity, gas and water	130	558	1,459
Construction	3,261	13,814	29,210
Trade, restaurants and hotels	18,977	61,829	122,680
Transport, storage and communications	5,812	14,700	39,919
Finance, insurance, real estate and business services*	4,975	14,509	27,212
Community, social and personal services	12,226	33,305	68,005
Total	174,443	491,432	995,579

* After deducting imputed bank service charge.

Source: UN, *National Accounts Statistics*.

BALANCE OF PAYMENTS (US $ million)

	1990	1991	1992
Merchandise exports f.o.b.	177.8	173.2	151.2
Merchandise imports f.o.b.	-491.0	-377.1	-421.9
Trade balance	-313.2	-203.9	-270.7
Exports of services	—	20.8	34.5
Imports of services	-195.3	-241.8	-247.7
Other income received	—	2.8	4.1
Other income paid	-47.8	-76.7	-88.3
Private unrequited transfers (net)	—	103.4	207.3
Official unrequited transfers (net)	293.0	225.6	261.2
Current balance	-263.3	-169.8	-99.6
Direct capital investment	—	1.0	3.0
Other capital (net)	211.8	136.6	111.8
Net errors and omissions	9.5	0.6	9.0
Overall balance	-41.9	-31.7	24.2

Source: IMF, *International Financial Statistics*.

External Trade

PRINCIPAL COMMODITIES ('000 old shillings)

Imports	1977	1978	1979
Paper and paper products	25,994	35,822	27,773
Cotton fabrics, other than grey	2,520	2,669	2,261
Iron and steel	40,562	31,590	15,567
Other metals and metal products	78,151	84,642	57,221
Machinery, incl. agricultural machinery	58,771 }	661,652	601,811
Transport equipment	227,025 }		
Total (incl. others)	1,460,939	1,470,261	1,244,314

Total Imports c.i.f. (million new shillings): 4,300 in 1986; 36,336 in 1987; 94,112 in 1988; 87,851 in 1989; 125,059 in 1990; 137,250 in 1991; 580,685 in 1992 (Source: IMF, *International Financial Statistics*).

Exports (incl. re-exports)	1977	1978	1979
Coffee, not roasted	4,288,133	2,113,300	2,231,800
Cotton, raw	99,293	98,400	24,400
Copper, unwrought	23,658	18,000	9,400
Tea	105,136	20,900	12,200
Hides, skins, etc.	5,372	800	1,900
Total (incl. others)	4,592,399	2,317,200	2,306,600

Total exports f.o.b. (million new shillings): 6,100 in 1986 (Coffee 5,658); 13,684 in 1987 (Coffee 13,553); 29,070 in 1988 (Coffee 27,154); 55,674 in 1989 (Coffee 53,460); 64,653 in 1990 (Coffee 58,955); 146,661 in 1991; 159,387 in 1992; 213,846 in 1993 (Source: IMF, *International Financial Statistics*).

PRINCIPAL TRADING PARTNERS (US $ million)

Imports	1987	1988	1989
Germany, Federal Republic	48.7	34.3	53.1
India	27.8	32.6	38.1
Italy	65.0	35.3	23.0
Japan	36.0	28.0	30.7
Kenya	91.9	102.5	110.3
United Kingdom	69.4	69.1	70.6
USA	20.5	17.4	25.4

Total imports c.i.f. (US $ million): 555 in 1987; 544 in 1988; 390 in 1989; 293 in 1990; 197 in 1991; 516 in 1992 (Source: UN, *Monthly Bulletin of Statistics*).

Exports	1987	1988	1989
France	35.0	38.2	33.2
Germany, Federal Republic	17.6	23.6	24.4
Italy	11.5	16.4	17.2
Japan	16.1	9.2	9.4
Netherlands	28.2	39.1	40.5
Spain	30.2	30.4	27.0
United Kingdom	55.3	49.4	31.4
USA	77.7	56.5	39.6

Total exports f.o.b. (US $ million): 319 in 1987; 274 in 1988; 250 in 1989; 152 in 1990; 201 in 1991; 143 in 1992 (Source: UN, *Monthly Bulletin of Statistics*).

Transport

RAILWAYS (traffic)

	1988	1989	1990
Passenger-km (million)	118	69	69
Freight ton-km (million)	83	90	90

Source: UN, *Statistical Yearbook*.

ROAD TRAFFIC (registered motor vehicles*)

	1978	1979	1980†
Heavy commercial vehicles	5,812	3,216	3,500
Pick-ups and vans	5,101	3,336	3,500
Minibuses etc.	779	533	500
Buses	839	553	600
Passenger cars	15,757	11,279	11,000
Motor cycles and scooters	4,754	4,459	4,500

* Excluding government-owned vehicles. † Estimates.

1985 (vehicles in use at 31 December): Heavy commercial vehicles 4,659; Buses 987; Passenger cars 32,155; Motor cycles and scooters 4,809 (Source: International Road Federation, *World Road Statistics*).

CIVIL AVIATION (traffic on scheduled services)

	1990	1991
Kilometers flown (million)	4	0
Passengers carried ('000)	116	26
Passenger-km (million)	278	13
Freight ton-km (million)	22	0

Source: UN, *Statistical Yearbook.*

Tourism

	1988	1989	1990
Tourist arrivals ('000)	37	44	50
Tourist receipts (US $ million)	8	9	10

Source: UN, *Statistical Yearbook.*

Communications Media

	1889	1990	1991
Radio receivers ('000 in use)	1,800	1,900	1,975
Television receivers ('000 in use)	150	180	187
Telephones ('000 in use)	61	57	n.a.
Daily newspapers:			
Number	n.a.	2	n.a.
Average circulation ('000 copies)	n.a.	30	n.a.

Sources: UN, *Statistical Yearbook*; UNESCO, *Statistical Yearbook.*

Education

(1992)

	Teachers	Students
Primary	86,821	2,407,921
Secondary:		
General	14,660	226,805
Vocational*	769	13,603
Higher:		
University	991	8,552
Other†	1,973	27,431

* Technical schools and institutes.

† Includes teacher training.

Universities: *Teachers:* 479 in 1989; 725 in 1990. *Students:* 6,589 in 1989 (5,137 males; 1,450 females); 7,618 in 1990 (5,699 males; 1,919 females).

Other higher education institutions: *Teachers:* 819 in 1989; 830 in 1990. *Students:* 8,219 in 1989 (5,614 males; 2,605 females); 9,960 in 1990 (6,930 males; 3,030 females).

Source: Ministry of Education and Sports, Kampala, and UNESCO, *Statistical Yearbook.*

Directory

The Constitution

Following the military coup in July 1985, the 1967 Constitution was suspended, and all legislative and executive powers were vested in a Military Council, whose Chairman was Head of State. In January 1986 a further military coup established an executive Presidency, assisted by a cabinet of ministers and a legislative National Resistance Council (NRC), appointed by the President. In February 1989 national elections to an expanded NRC took place. In March 1993 the Government published a draft constitution. A Constituent Assembly (comprising 214 elected and 74 nominated members) was established to debate, amend and enact the draft Constitution; elections to this body took place in March 1994. Upon completion of the Constituent Assembly's task, legislative and presidential elections were to be held.

The Government

HEAD OF STATE

President: Lt-Gen. Yoweri Kaguta Museveni (took office 29 January 1986).

THE CABINET
(September 1994)

President and Minister of Defence: Lt-Gen. Yoweri Kaguta Museveni.

Vice-President and Minister of Internal Affairs: Dr Samson Kisekka.

Prime Minister: Cosmas Adyebo.

First Deputy Prime Minister and National Political Commissar: Eriya Kategaya.

Second Deputy Prime Minister and Minister of Foreign Affairs: Paul Ssemogerere.

Third Deputy Prime Minister and Minister of Justice and Attorney-General: Abubakar Mayanja.

Minister of Agriculture, Animal Industry and Fisheries: Victoria Ssekitoleko.

Minister of Education and Sport: Maj. Amanya Mushega.

Minister of Finance, Planning and Economic Development: Joash Mayanja-Nkangi.

Minister of Health: Dr James Makumbi.

Minister of Information: Paul Etiang.

Minister of Labour and Social Welfare: Eteker Ejalu.

Minister of Lands, Housing and Urban Development: E. T. S. Adriko.

Minister of Local Government: Jaberi Ssali.

Minister of Natural Resources: Henry Kajura.

Minister of Public Service and Cabinet Affairs: Samuel Sebagereka.

Minister of Tourism, Wildlife and Antiquities: James Wapakhabulo.

Minister of Trade and Industry: Richard Kaijuka.

Minister of Women's Development, Culture and Youth: Dr Speciosa Kazibwe.

Minister of Works, Transport and Communications: Dr RUHAKANA RUGUNDA.

MINISTRIES

Office of the President: Parliament Bldgs, POB 7006, Kampala; tel. (41) 254881; telex 61389.

Office of the Prime Minister: POB 341, Kampala; tel. (41) 259518; telex 62001.

Ministry of Agriculture, Animal Industry and Fisheries: POB 102, Entebbe; tel. (42) 20752; telex 61287.

Ministry of Defence: Republic House, POB 3798, Kampala; tel. (41) 270331; telex 61023.

Ministry of Education and Sports: Crested Towers, POB 7063, Kampala; tel. (41) 234440; telex 61298.

Ministry of Finance, Planning and Economic Development: POB 8147, Kampala; tel. (41) 234700; telex 61170.

Ministry of Foreign Affairs: POB 7048, Kampala; tel. (41) 258251; telex 61007; fax (41) 258722.

Ministry of Health: POB 8, Entebbe; tel. (42) 20201; telex 61373.

Ministry of Information: POB 7142, Kampala; tel. (41) 256888; telex 61373.

Ministry of Internal Affairs: POB 7191, Kampala; tel. (41) 231188; telex 61331.

Ministry of Justice: POB 7183, Kampala; tel. (41) 233219.

Ministry of Labour and Social Welfare: POB 7009, Kampala; tel. (41) 242837; telex 62167.

Ministry of Lands, Housing and Urban Development: POB 7122, Kampala; tel. (41) 242931; telex 61274.

Ministry of Local Government: POB 7037, Kampala; tel. (41) 241763; telex 61265; (41) 258127.

Ministry of Natural Resources: POB 7270, Kampala; tel. (41) 234995; telex 61098.

Ministry of Public Service: POB 7168, Kampala; tel. (41) 254881.

Ministry of Tourism, Wildlife and Antiquities: Parliament Ave, POB 4241, Kampala: tel. (41) 232971; telex 62218.

Ministry of Trade and Industry: POB 7103, Kampala; tel. (41) 258202; telex 61183.

Ministry of Women's Development, Culture, and Youth: POB 7136, Kampala; tel. (41) 254253.

Ministry of Works, Transport and Communications: POB 10, Entebbe; tel. (42) 20101; telex 61313; (42) 20135.

Legislature

NATIONAL RESISTANCE COUNCIL

The National Resistance Movement, which took office in January 1986, established a National Resistance Council (NRC), initially comprising 80 nominated members, to act as a legislative body. National elections were held on 11–28 February 1989, at which 210 members of an expanded NRC were elected by members of district-level Resistance Committees (themselves elected by local-level Resistance Committees, who were directly elected by universal adult suffrage). The remaining 68 seats in the NRC were reserved for candidates nominated by the President (to include 34 women and representatives of youth organizations and trades unions). Political parties were not allowed to participate in the election campaign. In October 1989 the NRC approved legislation extending the Government's term of office by five years from January 1990, when its mandate was to expire. Legislative and presidential elections were due to take place following the adoption of a new constitution, which was receiving consideration in 1994.

Political Organizations

Political parties were ordered to suspend active operations, although not formally banned, in March 1986. In March 1990 this suspension was extended for a further five years.

Conservative Party (CP): f. 1979; Leader JOSHUA MAYANJA-NKANGI.

Democratic Party (DP): POB 7098, Kampala; tel. (41) 230244; f. 1954; main support in southern Uganda; seeks a multi-party system; Pres. PAUL SSEMOGERERE; Sec.-Gen. ROBERT KITARIKO.

Federal Democratic Movement (FEDEMO): Kampala.

Forum for Multi-Party Democracy: Kampala; Gen. Sec. JESSE MASHATTE.

National Resistance Movement (NRM): f. to oppose the UPC Govt 1980–85, and also opposed the mil. Govt in power from July 1985 to Jan. 1986; its mil. wing, the National Resistance Army (NRA), led by Lt-Gen. YOWERI MUSEVENI, took power in Jan. 1986; Chair. Dr SAMSON KISEKKA.

Nationalist Liberal Party: Kampala; f. 1984 by a breakaway faction of the DP; Leader TIBERIO OKENY.

Uganda Democratic Alliance: opposes the NRM Govt; Leader APOLO KIRONDE.

Uganda Freedom Movement (UFM): Kampala; mainly Baganda support; withdrew from NRM coalition Govt in April 1987; Sec.-Gen. (vacant).

Uganda Independence Revolutionary Movement: f. 1989; opposes the NRM Govt; Chair. Maj. OKELLO KOLO.

Uganda Islamic Revolutionary Party (UIRP): Kampala; f. 1993; Chair. IDRIS MUWONGE.

Uganda National Unity Movement: opposes the NRM Govt; Chair. Alhaji SULEIMAN SSALONGO.

Uganda Patriotic Movement: Kampala; f. 1980; Sec.-Gen. JABERI SSALI.

Uganda People's Congress (UPC): POB 1951, Kampala; f. 1960; socialist-based philosophy; ruling party 1962–71 and 1980–85, sole legal political party 1969–71; Chair. Alhaji BADRU WEGULO; Leader Dr MILTON OBOTE; Sec.-Gen. Dr LUWULIZA KIRUNDA.

Ugandan People's Democratic Movement (UPDM): seeks democratic reforms; support mainly from north and east of the country; includes mems of fmr govt armed forces; signed a peace accord with the Govt in 1990; Chair. ERIC OTEMA ALLIMADI; Sec.-Gen. EMMANUEL OTENG.

Uganda Progressive Union (UPU): Kampala; Chair. ALFRED BANYA.

The following organizations are in armed conflict with the Government:

Lord's Resistance Army: f. 1987; claims to be conducting a 'holy war' against the NRM Govt; forces number c. 800–1,000; Leader JOSEPH KONY.

Uganda People's Freedom Movement (UPFM): based in Tororo and Kenya; f. 1994 by mems of the fmr Uganda People's Army; Leader PETER OTAI.

Diplomatic Representation

EMBASSIES AND HIGH COMMISSIONS IN UGANDA

Algeria: POB 4025, Kampala; tel. (41) 232918; telex 61184; fax (41) 241015; Ambassador: RABAH SOUIBÈS.

Burundi: POB 4379, Kampala; tel. (41) 254584; telex 61076; Ambassador: GEORGE NTZEZIMANA.

China, People's Republic: POB 4106, Kampala; tel. (41) 235087; telex 61383; Ambassador: XIE YOUKUN.

Cuba: Kampala; telex 61174; Chargé d'affaires: ANGEL NICHOLAS.

Denmark: Crusader House, 4th Floor, Plot 3, Portal Ave, POB 11243, Kampala; tel. (41) 256687; telex 61560; fax (41) 254979; Ambassador: THOMAS SCHJERBECK.

Egypt: POB 4280, Kampala; tel. (41) 254525; telex 61122; Ambassador: SAMIR ABDALLAH.

France: POB 7212, Kampala; tel. (41) 242120; telex 61079; fax (41) 241252; Ambassador: FRANÇOIS DESCOUEYTE.

Germany: 15 Philip Rd, POB 7016, Kampala; tel. (41) 256767; telex 61005; fax (41) 243136; Ambassador: CHRISTIAN NAKONZ.

Holy See: POB 7177, Kampala (Apostolic Nunciature); tel. (41) 221167; fax (41) 221774; Apostolic Pro-Nuncio: Most Rev. LUIS ROBLES DÍAZ, Titular Archbishop of Stephaniacum.

India: Bank of Baroda Bldg, 1st Floor, POB 7040, Kampala; tel. (41) 257368; telex 61161; fax (41) 254943; High Commissioner: N. N. DESAI.

Italy: POB 4646, Kampala; tel. (41) 241786; telex 61261; Ambassador: ALESSIO CARISSIMO.

Kenya: POB 5220, Kampala; tel. (41) 231861; telex 61191; High Commissioner: Brig. R. MUSONYE.

Korea, Democratic People's Republic: POB 5885, Kampala; tel. (41) 254603; telex 61144; Ambassador: CHON GYONG CHOL.

Korea, Republic: Baumann House, POB 3717, Kampala; tel. (41) 233667; telex 61017; Ambassador: JAE-KYU KIM.

Libya: Kampala; Sec. of People's Bureau: ABU ALLAH ABDUL MULLAH.

Nigeria: 33 Nakasero Rd, POB 4338, Kampala; tel. (41) 233691; telex 61011; fax (41) 232543; High Commissioner: MAMMAN DAURA.

Russia: POB 7022, Kampala; Ambassador: STANISLAV NIKOLAYEVICH SEMENENKO.

Rwanda: POB 2468, Kampala; tel. (41) 244045; telex 61277; fax (41) 258547; Ambassador: CLAVER KANYARUSHOKI.

Somalia: POB 7113, Kampala; tel. (41) 232823; telex 61252; Ambassador: (vacant).

Sudan: POB 3200, Kampala; tel. (41) 243518; telex 61078; Ambassador: TAJ AL-SIRR ABBAS.

Tanzania: POB 5750, Kampala; tel. (41) 256272; telex 61062; High Commissioner: JOSHUA OPANGA.

United Kingdom: 10–12 Parliament Ave, POB 7070, Kampala; tel. (41) 257054; telex 61202; fax (41) 257304; High Commissioner: EDWARD CLAY.

USA: POB 7007, Kampala; tel. (41) 259795; Ambassador: JOHN CARSON.

Yugoslavia: POB 4370, Kampala; tel. (41) 232000; telex 61405; Chargé d'affaires a.i.: DUŠKO MATARUGIĆ.

Zaire: POB 4972, Kampala; telex 61284; Ambassador: NZAPA KENGO.

Judicial System

Courts of Judicature: POB 7085, Kampala.

The Supreme Court: Mengo; hears appeals from the High Court.

Chief Justice: SAMSON WILLIAM WAKO WAMBUZI.

Deputy Chief Justice: S. T. MANYINDO.

The High Court: Kampala; tel. (41) 233422; has full criminal and civil jurisdiction over all persons and matters in the country. The High Court consists of the Principal Judge and 20 Puisne Judges.

Principal Judge: J. H. NTAGOBA.

Magistrates' Courts: These are established under the Magistrates' Courts Act of 1970 and exercise limited jurisdiction in criminal and civil matters. The country is divided into magisterial areas, presided over by a Chief Magistrate. Under him there are three categories of Magistrates. The Magistrates preside alone over their courts. Appeals from the first category of Magistrates' Court lie directly to the High Court, while appeals from the second and third categories of Magistrates' Court lie to the Chief Magistrate's Court, and from there to the High Court.

Religion

It is estimated that more than 60% of the population profess Christianity (with approximately equal numbers of Roman Catholics and Protestants). About 5% of the population are Muslims.

CHRISTIANITY

The Anglican Communion

Anglicans are adherents of the Church of the Province of Uganda, comprising 21 dioceses. There are about 4m. adherents.

Archbishop of Uganda and Bishop of Kampala: Most Rev. YONA OKOTH, POB 14123, Kampala; tel. (41) 270218.

Greek Orthodox Church

Archbishop of East Africa: NICADEMUS of IRINOUPOULIS (resident in Nairobi, Kenya); jurisidiction covers Kenya, Tanzania and Uganda.

The Roman Catholic Church

Uganda comprises one archdiocese and 15 dioceses. At 31 December 1992 an estimated 42.6% of the population were adherents.

Uganda Episcopal Conference: Uganda Catholic Secretariat, POB 2886, Kampala; tel. (41) 268458; fax (41) 268104; f. 1974; Pres. Most Rev. EMMANUEL WAMALA, Archbishop of Kampala.

Archbishop of Kampala: Most Rev. EMMANUEL WAMALA, Archbishop's House, POB 14125, Mengo, Kampala; tel. and fax (41) 245441.

ISLAM

The Uganda Muslim Supreme Council: POB 3247, Kampala; Mufti of Uganda: IBRAHIM SAID LUWEMBA; Chief Kadi and Pres. of Council: HUSAYN RAJAB KAKOOZA.

BAHÁ'Í FAITH

National Spiritual Assembly: POB 2662, Kampala; mems resident in 3,522 localities.

The Press

DAILY AND OTHER NEWSPAPERS

The Citizen: Kampala; official publ. of the Democratic Party; English; Editor JOHN KYEYUNE.

The Economy: POB 6787, Kampala; weekly; English; Editor ROLAND KAKOOZA.

Financial Times: Plot 17/19, Station Rd, POB 31399, Kampala; tel. (41) 245798; bi-weekly; English; Editor G. A. ONEGI OBEL.

Focus: POB 268, Kampala; tel. (41) 235086; telex 61284; fax (41) 242460; f. 1983; publ. by Islamic Information Service and Material Centre; 4 a week; English; Editor HAJJI KATENDE; circ. 12,000.

Guide: POB 5350, Kampala; tel. (41) 233486; fax (41) 268045; f. 1989; weekly; English; Editor-in-Chief A. A. KALIISA; circ. 30,000.

The Monitor: POB 12141; Kampala; tel. (41) 251353; fax (41) 251352; f. 1992; bi-weekly; English; Editor-in-Chief WAFULA OGUTTU; Editor ONYANGO OBBO; circ. 34,000.

Mulengera: POB 6787, Kampala; weekly; Luganda; Editor ROLAND KAKOOZA.

Munnansi News Bulletin: Kampala; f. 1980; weekly; English; owned by the Democratic Party; Editor ANTHONY SGEKWEYAMA.

Munno: POB 4027, Kampala; f. 1911; daily; Luganda; publ. by the Roman Catholic Church; Editor ANTHONY SSEKWEYAMA; circ. 7,000.

New Vision: POB 9815, Kampala; tel. (41) 235846; fax 235221; f. 1986; official govt newspaper; daily; English; Editor WILLIAM PIKE; circ. 37,000.

Ngabo: POB 9362, Kampala; tel. (41) 42637; telex 61236; f. 1979; daily; Luganda; Editor MAURICE SEKAWUNGU; circ. 7,000.

The People: Kampala; weekly; English; independent; Editor AMOS KAJOBA.

The Star: POB 9362, Kampala; tel. (41) 42637; telex 61236; f. 1980; revived 1984; daily; English; Editor SAMUEL KATWERE; circ. 5,000.

Taifa Uganda Empya: POB 1986, Kampala; tel. (41) 254652; telex 61064; f. 1953; daily; Luganda; Editor A. SEMBOGA; circ. 24,000.

Weekly Topic: POB 1725, Kampala; tel. (41) 233834; weekly; English; Editor JOHN WASSWA; circ. 13,000.

PERIODICALS

Eastern Africa Journal of Rural Development: Dept of Agriculture, Makerere University, POB 7062, Kampala; 2 a year; circ. 800.

Leadership: POB 2522, Kampala; tel. (41) 221358; fax (41) 221576; f. 1956; 6 a year; English; Roman Catholic; circ. 7,400.

Mkombozi: c/o Ministry of Defence, Republic House, POB 3798, Kampala; tel. (41) 270331; telex 61023; f. 1982; military; Editor A. OPOLOTT.

Musizi: POB 4027, Mengo, Kampala; f. 1955; monthly; Luganda; Roman Catholic; Editor F. GITTA; circ. 30,000.

Pearl of Africa: POB 7142, Kampala; monthly; govt publ.

Uganda Confidential: Kampala; monthly; Editor TEDDY SSEZI-CHEEYE.

NEWS AGENCIES

Uganda News Agency (UNA): POB 7142, Kampala; tel. (41) 32734; telex 61188; Dir (vacant); Editor-in-Chief F. A. OTAI.

Foreign Bureaux

Inter Press Service (IPS) (Italy): Plot 2, Wilson Rd, POB 16514, Wandegeyn, Kampala; tel. (41) 245310; telex 61272; Correspondent DAVID MUSOKE.

Rossiyskoye Informatsionnoye Agentstvo—Novosti (RIA—Novosti) (Russia): POB 4412, Kampala; tel. (41) 232383; telex 62292; Correspondent Dr OLEG TETERIN.

Xinhua (New China) News Agency (People's Republic of China): Plot 25, Hill Drive, Kololo, POB 466, Kampala; tel. (41) 254951; telex 61189; Correspondent ZHANG YINGSHENG.

Publishers

Centenary Publishing House Ltd: POB 2776, Kampala; tel. (41) 41599; f. 1977; religious (Anglican); Man. Dir Rev. SAM KAKIZA.

Longman Uganda Ltd: POB 3409, Kampala; tel. (41) 42940; f. 1965; Man. Dir M. K. L. MUTYABA.

Uganda Publishing House Ltd: Kampala; tel. (41) 59601; telex 61175; f. 1966; primary and secondary school textbooks; Man. Dir LABAN O. ERAPU.

Government Publishing House

Government Printer: POB 33, Entebbe; telex 61336.

Radio and Television

According to estimates by UNESCO, there were 1,975,000 radio receivers and 187,000 television receivers in use in 1991.

RADIO

Radio Uganda: Ministry of Information, POB 7142, Kampala; tel. (41) 256888; telex 61084; f. 1954; state-controlled; broadcasts in 22 languages, including English, French, Arabic, Swahili and vernacular languages; Dir of Broadcasting JOHN C. SSERWADDA.

Sanyo Radio: Kampala; independent station broadcasting to Kampala and its environs.

TELEVISION

Uganda Television Service: POB 4260, Kampala; tel. (41) 254461; telex 61084; f. 1962; state-controlled commercial service; programmes mainly in English, also in Swahili and Luganda; transmits over a radius of 320 km from Kampala; five relay stations have been built, others are under construction; Controller of Programmes FAUSTIN MISANVU.

Finance

(cap. = capital; auth. = authorized; p.u. = paid up; res = reserves; dep. = deposits; m. = million; brs = branches; amounts in new Uganda shillings unless otherwise indicated).

BANKING

Central Bank

Bank of Uganda: 37–43 Kampala Rd, POB 7120, Kampala; tel. (41) 258441; telex 61059; fax (41) 230878; f. 1966; bank of issue; auth. cap. 15,050m. (1994); Gov. CHARLES KIKONYOGO; Dep. Gov. Dr EZRA SURUMA; Gen. Man. ERIAB RUKYALEKERE.

State Banks

The Co-operative Bank Ltd: 9 William St, POB 6863, Kampala; tel. (41) 258323; telex 61263; fax (41) 234578; f. 1970; cap. p.u. 153.0m., dep. 17,340m. old shillings (Dec. 1993); Gen. Man. GODFREY NSUBUGA.

Uganda Commercial Bank: Plot 12, Kampala Rd, POB 973, Kampala; tel. (41) 234710; telex 61073; fax (41) 259012; f. 1965; undergoing reorg. in 1994; state-owned; cap. and res 27,174m., dep. 65,732m. (Sept. 1991); Chair. Dr EZERA SURUMA; 169 brs.

Uganda Development Bank: IPS Bldg, 14 Parliament Ave, POB 7210, Kampala; tel. (41) 230740; telex 61143; fax (41) 258571; f. 1972; state-owned; cap. p.u. 11m. (Dec. 1989); Man. Dir JOHN KIGGUNDU.

Commercial Bank

Nile Bank Ltd: Spear House, Plot 22, Jinja Rd, POB 2834, Kampala; tel. (41) 231904; telex 61240; fax (41) 257779; f. 1988; dep. 15,200m. (Sept. 1993); private commercial bank; CEO Prof. EPHRAIM KAMUNTU.

Development Bank

East African Development Bank (EADB): East African Development Bank Bldg, 4 Nile Ave, POB 7128, Kampala; tel. (41) 230021; telex 61074; fax (41) 259763; f. 1967; reorg. 1980; provides financial and tech. assistance to promote industrial development within Uganda, Kenya and Tanzania, whose Govts each hold 25.8% of the equity, the remaining 22.6% being shared by the African Development Bank, Barclays Bank, the Commercial Bank of Africa, Grindlays Bank, Standard Chartered Bank, Nordbanken of Sweden and a consortium of institutions of fmr Yugoslavia; regional offices in Nairobi and Dar es Salaam; Chair. E. TUMUSIIME-MUTEBILE; Dir-Gen. F. R. TIBEITA.

Foreign Banks

Bank of Baroda (Uganda) Ltd (India): 18 Kampala Rd, POB 2971, Kampala; tel. (41) 230972; telex 61014; fax (41) 259467; f. 1969; 49% govt-owned; cap. and res 1,089m., dep. 22,904m. (Dec. 1993); Chair. and Man. Dir K. U. YAJNIK; 5 brs.

Barclays Bank of Uganda Ltd (United Kingdom): 16 Kampala Rd, POB 2971, Kampala; tel. (41) 232594; telex 61014; fax (41) 259467; f. 1969; 49% govt-owned; cap. and res 4,089m., dep. 36,085m. (Dec. 1992); Man. Dir C. J. MARTIN; 4 brs.

Stanbic Bank Uganda Ltd: 45 Kampala Rd, POB 7131, Kampala; tel. (41) 230811; telex 61018; fax (41) 231116; f. 1969 as Grindlays Bank International (Uganda) Ltd; 49% govt-owned; cap. p.u. 200m. (Sept. 1992); Chair. A. D. B. WRIGHT; Man. Dir A. B. MEARS.

Standard Chartered Bank Uganda Ltd (United Kingdom): 5 Speke Rd, POB 7111, Kampala; tel. (41) 258211; telex 61010; fax (41) 231473; f. 1969; cap. and res 760.0m., dep. 12,883.7m. (Dec. 1991); Chair. and Man. Dir L. E. A. BENTLEY.

Tropical Africa Bank Ltd (Libya): Plot 27, Kampala Rd, POB 7292, Kampala; tel. (41) 241408; telex 61286; fax (41) 232296; f. 1972 as Libyan Arab Uganda Bank for Foreign Trade and Development, adopted present name in 1994; 50% Govt-owned, 51% owned by Libyan Arab Foreign Bank; cap. p.u. 1,000m. (Jan. 1994); Chair. SULAIMAN SEMBAJJA; Gen. Man. ABD AL-GADER RAGHEI.

STOCK EXCHANGE

Kampala Stock Exchange: Kampala; f. 1990; Chair. LEO BUGIRANGO.

INSURANCE

East Africa General Insurance Co Ltd: 14 Kampala Rd, POB 1392, Kampala; telex 61378; life, fire, motor, marine and accident.

National Insurance Corporation: Plot 3, 3 Pilkington Rd, POB 7134, Kampala; tel. (41) 258001; telex 61222; fax (41) 259925; f. 1964; general; Man. Dir MAGEZI (acting).

Uganda American Insurance Co Ltd: Kampala; telex 61101; f. 1970.

Uganda Co-operative Insurance Ltd: Plot 10, Bombo Rd, POB 6176, Kampala; tel. (41) 241826; fax (41) 258231; f. 1982; general.

Trade and Industry

Export and Import Licencing Division: POB 7000, Kampala; tel. (41) 258795; telex 61085; f. 1987; advises importers and exporters and issues import and export licences; Prin. Commercial Officer JOHN MUHWEZI.

Uganda Advisory Board of Trade: POB 6877, Kampala; tel. (41) 33311; telex 61085; f. 1974; issues trade licences and service for exporters.

Uganda Export Promotion Council: POB 5045, Kampala; tel. (41) 259779; telex 61391; fax (41) 259779; f. 1983; provides market intelligence, organizes training, trade exhbns, etc.; Exec. Sec. HENRY NYAKOOJO.

Uganda Investment Authority: Investment Centre, Plot 28, Kampala Rd, POB 7418, Kampala; tel. (41) 234105; telex 61135; fax (41) 242903; f. 1991; promotes foreign and local investment, issues investment licences and provides investment incentives to priority industries; Exec. Dir G. W. RUBAGUMYA.

CHAMBER OF COMMERCE

Uganda National Chamber of Commerce and Industry: Plot 17/19 Jinja Rd, POB 3809, Kampala; tel. (41) 258791; telex 61272; fax (41) 258793; Chair. BADRU BUNKEDDEKO; Sec. G. RUJOJO.

DEVELOPMENT CORPORATIONS

Agriculture and Livestock Development Fund: f. 1976; provides loans to farmers.

National Housing and Construction Corporation: Crested Towers, POB 659, Kampala; tel. (41) 230311; telex 61156; fax (41) 258708; f. 1964; Govt agent for building works, aims to improve living standards, principally by building residential housing; Chair. D. LUBEGA; Gen. Man. M. S. KASEKENDE.

Ugandan Coffee Development Authority: POB 7267, Kampala; tel. (41) 256940; telex 61412; fax (41) 256994; f. 1991; sets quality control standards, certifies coffee exports, maintains statistical data, advises Govt on local and world prices, promotes Ugandan coffee abroad, trains processors and quality controllers.

Uganda Industrial Development Corporation Ltd (ULDC): 9–11 Parliament Ave, POB 7042, Kampala; telex 61069; f. 1952; Chair. SAM RUTEGA.

EMPLOYERS' ORGANIZATION

Federation of Uganda Employers, Commerce and Industry: POB 3820, Kampala; Chair. BRUNO ABALIWANO; Exec. Dir J. KASWARRA.

MARKETING ORGANIZATIONS

Coffee Marketing Board: POB 7154, Kampala; tel. (41) 254051; telex 61157; fax (41) 230790; state-owned; purchases and exports coffee; Chair. and Man. Dir FRANCIS W. NAGIMESI.

Lint Marketing Board: POB 7018, Kampala; tel. (41) 232660; telex 61008; fax (41) 242426; state-owned; exporter of cotton lint; mfr of edible oil, soap and candles; Gen. Man. J. W. OBBO; Sec. G. KAKUBA.

Produce Marketing Board: POB 3705, Kampala; tel. (41) 236238; Gen. Man. ESTHER KAMPAMPARA.

Uganda Coffee Development Authority: POB 7154, Kampala; tel. (41) 230229; Man. Dir TRESS BUCYANAYANDI.

Uganda Manufacturers' Association (UMA): POB 9113, Kampala; tel. (41) 236147; promotes the goods of Uganda's mfrs; Chair. JAMES MULWANA.

Uganda Tea Authority: POB 4161, Kampala; tel. (41) 231003; telex 61120; state-owned; controls and co-ordinates activities of the tea industry; Gen. Man. MIRIA MARGARITA MUGABI.

CO-OPERATIVE UNIONS

In 1993 there were 5,775 co-operative societies, grouped in 44 unions. There is at least one co-operative union in each administrative district.

Uganda Co-operative Alliance: Kampala; works with the Ministry of Commerce, Industry and Co-operatives to co-ordinate the activities of co-operative unions, of which the following are among the most important:

Bugisu Co-operative Union Ltd: Private Bag, PO Mbale; tel. (45) 2235; telex 66042; f. 1954; handles the Bugisu arabica coffee crop; 206 mem. socs; Gen. Man. P. J. MUYIYI.

East Mengo Growers' Co-operative Union Ltd: POB 7092, Kampala; tel. (41) 241382; f. 1968; coffee, cotton, pineapples; 265 mem. socs; Chair. Y. KINALWA; Gen. Man. A. SSINGO.

Kakumiro Growers' Co-operative Union: POB 511, Kakumiro; processing of coffee and cotton; Sec. and Man. TIBIHWA-RUKEERA.

Masaka District Growers' Co-operative Union Ltd: POB 284, Masaka; tel. (481) 90; f. 1951; coffee, pineapple, piggery, carpentry and maize milling; 205 primary co-operative socs; Chair. J. K. KYANDA; Sec. and Man. G. W. MUKASA-MAYANGA.

Mubende District Co-operative Union: coffee growers.

Wamala Growers' Co-operative Union Ltd: POB 99, Mityana; tel. 2036; f. 1968; coffee and cotton growers; 250 mem. socs; Gen.-Man. HERBERT KIZITO.

West Mengo Growers' Co-operative Union Ltd: POB 7039, Kampala; tel. (41) 567511; f. 1948; cotton growing and buying, coffee buying and processing, maize milling; 250 mem. socs; Chair. H. E. KATABALWA MIIRO.

MAJOR INDUSTRIAL COMPANIES

The following are some of the largest companies in terms either of capital investment or employment. In 1970 the Government acquired a 60% interest in all major industries, banks and large companies.

British-American Tobacco (BAT) Uganda 1984 Ltd: POB 7100, Kampala; f. 1928; tel. (41) 243231; telex 61075; jtly owned by the Uganda Govt and BAT London; tobacco mfrs and exporters; Man. Dir B. SELBY.

The African Textile Mill Ltd: POB 242, Mbale; telex 66274; f. 1970; cap. sh. 11.25m.; textile mfrs; operates one mill.

Blenders Uganda Ltd: POB 7054, Kampala; tea- and coffee-blending, packaging and distribution; Gen. Man. T. D. MUZITO.

East African Distilleries Ltd: POB 3221, Kampala; tel. (41) 221111; f. 1965; cap. US $15m.; production of potable spirits; Gen. Man. EVA ADENGO.

East African Steel Corporation Ltd: POB 1023, Jinja; tel. (43) 21451.

Fina Exploration Uganda Ltd: wholly-owned by Petrofina Ltd (Belgium); petroleum exploration.

Mitchell Cotts Uganda Ltd: 8 Burton St, POB 7032, Kampala; telex 61003; UK trading group active in tea sector in which it owns jtly with the Uganda govt the Toro and Mityana Tea Co; a jt venture with the Govt to rehabilitate the tea industry began in 1980; also operates freight services.

Nile Breweries Ltd: POB 762, Jinja; tel. (43) 20177; telex 64708; f. 1951; Man. Dir A. S. T. AWUYO.

Nyanza Textile Industries Ltd: POB 408, Jinja; telex 64133; f. 1949; cap. sh. 80m.; textile mfrs; Man. Dir Mr ONEG-OBEL.

Pamba Textiles Ltd: POB 472, Jinja; f. 1963; cap. sh. 46m.; mfrs of cotton textiles.

Tororo Industrial Chemicals and Fertilisers Ltd: POB 254, Tororo; f. 1962; cap. sh. 7.4m.; of which Uganda Development Corpn owns sh. 6.4m.; mfrs of single super-phosphate fertilizer, sulphuric acid and insecticide.

Uganda Bata Shoe Co Ltd: POB 422, Kampala; tel. (41) 258911; telex 61049; fax 241380; f. 1966.

Uganda Breweries Ltd: POB 7130, Kampala; tel. (41) 220224; telex 61218.

Uganda Metal Products and Enamelling Co Ltd: POB 3151, Kampala; f. 1956; cap. £225,000; subsidiary of Uganda Steel Corpn; mfrs of enamelware, furniture, beds, etc.; 450 employees.

TRADE UNIONS

National Organization of Trade Unions (NOTU): POB 2150, Kampala; tel. (41) 256295; f. 1973; Chair. E. KATURAMU; Sec.-Gen. MATHIAS MUKASA.

Transport

The transport system was largely controlled by members of the Asian community, and deteriorated after their expulsion by President Amin in 1972. A reconstruction programme, under state auspices and with foreign aid assistance, is currently proceeding.

RAILWAYS

In 1992 there were 1,241 km of 1000-mm-gauge track in operation. A programme to rehabilitate the railway network is under way.

Uganda Railways Corporation: Station Rd, POB 7150, Kampala; tel. (41) 254961; telex 61111; fax (41) 244405; formed after the dissolution of East African Railways in 1977; Man. Dir E. K. TUMUSUME.

ROADS

In 1985 there was a total road network of 28,332 km, including 7,782 km of main roads and 18,508 km of secondary roads. About 22% of roads were paved. A US $32.6m. project to construct and repair major roads, which was supported by the World Bank, was launched in August 1987. By the end of 1988 1,850 km of bitumen roads and 2,400 km of gravel roads had been rehabilitated. In 1994 China and Japan pledged aid totalling US $30m. towards road rehabilitation schemes in northern Uganda.

INLAND WATERWAYS

A rail wagon ferry service connecting Jinja with the Tanzanian port of Tanga, via Mwanza, was inaugurated in 1983, thus reducing Uganda's dependence on the Kenyan port of Mombasa. In July 1986 the Uganda and Kenya Railways Corporations began the joint operation of Lake Victoria Marine Services, to ferry goods between the two countries via Lake Victoria.

CIVIL AVIATION

The international airport is at Entebbe, on Lake Victoria, some 40 km from Kampala. In 1994 the airport was undergoing a US $52m. modernization, which included the completion of a new passenger terminal. There are also several small airstrips.

Uganda Airlines Corporation: Airways House, 6 Colville St, POB 5740, Kampala; tel. (41) 232990; telex 61239; fax (41) 257279; f. 1976; state-owned; scheduled cargo and passenger services to Africa and Europe; scheduled cargo and passenger domestic services; Chair. Dr EZRA SURUMA (acting); Gen. Man. BENEDICT MUTYABA.

Tourism

Uganda's principal attractions for tourists are the forests, lakes and wildlife. A programme to revive the tourist industry by building or improving hotels and creating new national parks was undertaken during the late 1980s. In 1993 visa requirements were abolished for visitors from a number of European, Asian and American countries in an effort to encourage tourism. An estimated 50,000 tourists visited Uganda in 1990 (compared with 12,786 in 1983). Revenue from tourism in 1990 was estimated at US $10m.

Ministry of Tourism, Wildlife and Antiquities: Parliament Ave, POB 4241, Kampala; tel. (41) 232971; telex 62218; provides some tourist information.

Uganda Tourist Development Corporation: Plot 6, 2nd St, POB 7211, Kampala; tel. (41) 245261; telex 61150; promotes tourism and co-ordinates investment in the sector; Dir JOHN MAHANUKA.

Defence

In June 1993 the National Resistance Army (NRA) was estimated to number 60,000 men. It was announced in that year that the size of the NRA was to be reduced to about 50,000 by the end of 1995. In October 1991 the police force numbered 16,890 men; the force was to be expanded to 30,000 members by 1994. In 1993 the estimated defence budget was 107,900m. shillings.

Commander of the NRA: Maj.-Gen. MUGISHA MUNTU.

Education

Education is not compulsory. Most schools are sponsored by the government, although a small proportion are sponsored by missions. All schools charge fees; however, the government aims to introduce free primary school education by 1996. Primary education begins at six years of age and lasts for seven years. Secondary education, beginning at the age of 13, lasts for a further six years, comprising a first cycle of four years and a second of two years. In 1988 the number of pupils attending government-aided primary and secondary schools was equivalent to 51% of children in the relevant age-group. In 1992 there were 2,407,921 pupils enrolled at government-aided primary schools, and 240,408 pupils attending government-aided secondary schools. In addition to Makerere University in Kampala, there is a university of science and technology at Mbarara, and a small Islamic university is located at Mbale. In 1989 there were 479 teachers and 6,587 pupils at universities. According to estimates by UNESCO, the rate of adult literacy was 48.3% in 1990 (males 62.2%; females 34.9%). Education was allocated 8.9% of projected budgetary expenditure by the central government in 1989/90.

Bibliography

For works on Kenya, Tanzania and Uganda generally, see Kenya Bibliography, p. 512

Amnesty International. *Uganda: The Human Rights Record, 1986–89.* London, Amnesty International Publications, 1989.

Annual Reports. Entebbe, Department of Agriculture, Government Printer.

Apter, D. E. *The Political Kingdom in Uganda.* Princeton, NJ, and London, Oxford University Press, 1961.

Atlas of Uganda. 2nd Edn, Entebbe, Lands and Surveys Department, 1967.

Avirgan, T., and Honey, M. *War in Uganda.* London, Zed Press.

Beattie, J. *The Nyoro State.* Oxford, Clarendon Press, 1971.

Bernt, H., and Twaddle, M. (Eds). *Uganda Now.* London, James Currey, 1988.

Hansen, H. B. *Mission, Church and State in a Colonial Setting, Uganda 1890–c.1925.* London, Heinemann Educational, 1984.

Hansen, H. B., and Twaddle, M. (Eds). *Uganda Now: Between Decay and Development.* London, James Currey, 1988.

Changing Uganda. London, James Currey, 1991.

Ingham, K. *The Making of Modern Uganda.* London, Allen and Unwin, 1958.

Jameson, J. D. (Ed.). *Agriculture in Uganda.* London, Oxford University Press, 1971.

Jørgensen, J. J. *Uganda: A Modern History.* Croom Helm, 1981.

Karugire, S. R. *A Political History of Uganda.* London, Heinemann, 1980.

Langlands, B. W. *Notes on the Geography of Ethnicity in Uganda.* Kampala, 1975.

Low, D. A., and Pratt, R. C. *Buganda and British Overrule.* London, Oxford University Press, 1960.

Mamdani, M. *Politics and Class Formation in Uganda.* London, Heinemann Educational, 1977.

Imperialism and Fascism in Uganda. London, Heinemann Educational, 1983.

Martin, D. *General Amin.* London, Faber and Faber, 1974.

Mutibwa, P. *Uganda since Independence: A Story of Unfulfilled Hopes.* London, Hurst, 1992.

Nabudere, D. Wadada. *Imperialism and Revolution in Uganda.* Tanzania Publishing House/Onyx, 1980.

Robertson, A. F. (Ed.). *Uganda's First Republic: Chiefs, Administrators and Politicians 1967–1971.* Cambridge, African Studies Centre, 1982.

Sathymurthy, T.V. *The Political Development of Uganda 1980–86.* Aldershot, Gower Publishers, 1986.

Soghayroun, I. E.-Z. *The Sudanese Muslim Factor in Uganda.* Khartoum University Press, 1981.

Twaddle, M. (Ed.). *Expulsion of a Minority: Essays on Ugandan Asians.* London, Athlone Press, 1975.

Uganda Elections December 1980. The Report of the Commonwealth Observer Group, Commonwealth Secretariat, 1980.

Violations of Human Rights and the Rule of Law in Uganda. International Commission of Jurists, Geneva, 1974.

ZAIRE

Physical and Social Geography

PIERRE GOUROU

PHYSICAL FEATURES

With an area of 2,344,885 sq km (905,365 sq miles), the Republic of Zaire is the second largest country of sub-Saharan Africa. Despite its vast size, it lacks any really noteworthy points of relief: a considerable natural advantage. Lying across the Equator, Zaire has an equatorial climate in the whole of the central region. Average temperatures range from 26°C in the coastal and basin areas to 18°C in the mountainous regions. Rainfall is plentiful in all seasons. In the north (Uele) the winter of the northern hemisphere is a dry season; in the south (Shaba) the winter of the southern hemisphere is dry. The only arid region (less than 800 mm of rain per annum) is an extremely small area on the bank of the lower Zaire.

The country comprises, first and foremost, the basin of the River Congo (now locally renamed the Zaire). This basin had a deep tectonic origin; the continental shelf of Africa had given way to form an immense hollow, which drew towards it the waters from the north (Ubangi), from the east (Uele, Arruwimi), and from the south (Lualaba—that is the upper branch of the River Zaire, Kasaï, Kwango). The crystalline continental shelf levels out at the periphery into plateaux in Shaba (formerly Katanga) and the Zaire-Nile ridge. The most broken-up parts of this periphery can be found in the west, in lower Zaire, where the river cuts the folds of a Pre-Cambrian chain by a 'powerful breach', and above all in the east. Here, as a result of the volcanic overflow from the Virunga, they are varied by an upheaval of the rift valleys (where Lakes Tanganyika, Kivu, Edward and Mobutu are located) which carried the Pre-Cambrian shelf more than 5,000 m into Ruwenzori.

The climate is generally favourable for agriculture and woodland. Evergreen equatorial forest covers approximately 1m. sq km in the equatorial and sub-equatorial parts. In the north as in the south of this evergreen forest, tropical forests appear, with many trees that lose their leaves in the dry season. Vast stretches from the north to the south are, probably as a result of frequent fires, covered by sparse forest land, where trees grow alongside grasses (*biombo* from east Africa), and savannah dotted with shrubs.

Although favourable on account of its warmth and rainfall, the climate has a few unfortunate indirect effects. There are vast stretches of Zaire where the soil is leached of its soluble elements by the heavy, warm rainfall. In addition, the germs and carriers of malaria, sleeping sickness, filariasis, bilharziasis and ankylostomiasis flourish in a warm, rainy climate.

The natural resources of Zaire are immense: its climate is favourable to profitable agriculture; the forests, if rationally exploited, could yield excellent results; the abundance of water should eventually be useful to industry and agriculture; the network of waterways is naturally navigable; and, finally, there is considerable mineral wealth. The River Zaire carries the second largest volume of water in the world. With the average flow to the mouth being 40,000 cu m per second, there are enormous possibilities for power generation, some of which are being realized at Inga. Indeed, the hydroelectric resources are considerable in the whole of the Zaire basin.

The major exports of Zaire derive from the exploitation of its mineral resources. Copper is mined in upper Shaba, as are other metals—tin, silver, uranium, cobalt, manganese and tungsten. Diamonds are found in Kasaï, and tin, columbite, etc. in the east, around Maniema. In addition, many other mineral resources (iron ore, bauxite, etc.) await exploitation.

POPULATION

Zaire's population comprises numerous ethnic groups, which the external boundaries separate. The Kongo people are divided between Zaire, the People's Republic of the Congo, and Angola; the Zande between Zaire and Sudan; the Chokwe between Zaire and Angola; the Bemba between Zaire and Zambia; and the Alur between Zaire and Uganda. Even within its frontiers, the ethnic and linguistic geography of Zaire is highly diverse. The most numerous people are the Kongo; the people of Kwangu-Kwilu, who are related to them; the Mongo with their many subdivisions, who live in the Great Forest; the Luba, with their close cousins the Lulua and Songe; the Bwaka; and the Zande. The majority speak Bantu languages, of which there is a great diversity. However, the north of Zaire belongs linguistically to Sudan. The extreme linguistic variety of Zaire is maintained to some extent by the ability of the people to speak several languages, by the existence of 'intermediary' languages (a Kongo dialect, a Luba dialect, Swahili and Lingala) and by the use of French.

About 80% of the population (officially estimated at 36.7m. at mid-1991) live in rural areas. The average density of population is low (15.6 per sq km in 1991), and the population is unevenly distributed. The population density in the Great Forest is only about one-half of the national average, with stretches of several tens of thousands of sq km virtually deserted, although this is not because the area cannot accommodate more people. However, it is clear that the population (with the exception of some pygmies) cannot increase in density as long as the forest is preserved. Indeed, certain areas belonging to the forest belt but partly cleared for cultivation, although they have no particular natural advantages, have higher than average densities. At the northern edge of the Great Forest the population density increases up to 20 people per sq km, and is then reduced to one or two in the extreme north of the country. Certain parts of Mayombé (lower Zaire) have 100 people per sq km, but the south of the republic is sparsely populated (1–3 people per sq km). The capital, Kinshasa, had 2,653,558 inhabitants at the 1984 census and is the principal urban centre. Other major centres of population are Lubumbashi, with 543,268 inhabitants at the 1984 census; Mbuji-Mayi 423,363; Kananga 290,898 and Kisangani 282,650.

Recent History

JACQUES VANDERLINDEN

Revised for this edition by the Editor

Belgian interest in the area now comprising Zaire dates from 1876, when the Association internationale du Congo, under the control of King Léopold II of Belgium, began to establish a chain of trading stations along the River Congo. In 1884–85 the king obtained formal recognition of his association as a state from the other colonial powers.

Economic exploitation of the territory expanded rapidly with the increasing demand for wild rubber, following the development of rubber tyres. However, the methods used in the collection of rubber frequently involved the infliction of atrocities on the indigenous population, and in 1908, as a result of British and US diplomatic pressure, responsibility for the administration of the Independent Congo was transferred from the king to the Belgian government, and the Congo became a Belgian colony.

The Belgian administration saw no necessity for encouraging African political development, and it was not until shortly before the Second World War that a consultative body, the Conseil de gouvernement, was established: on this African interests were represented mainly by civil servants or missionaries. In the mid-1950s a plan for the emancipation of the Belgian Congo, over a 30-year period, was published, and was favourably received by the small African élite which had emerged under the patronage of the colonial administration, but was rejected both by Belgian conservatives and by more radical Africans. The latter included the Alliance des Ba-Kongo (ABAKO), a cultural association chaired by Joseph Kasavubu. The Belgian authorities established elected councils in the main urban areas, intending to allow gradual progress towards self-government over a period of many years.

This process was abruptly accelerated following an unauthorized demonstration by ABAKO in January 1959, during which some 50 Africans were killed. Within one year, at a conference held in Brussels, it was agreed that the Congo was to accede to full sovereignty after six months: during this period the Belgian legislature was to prepare a constitution (*loi fondamentale*) for the new state. The Belgian government favoured the creation of a unitary state, based on the centralized pattern of the colonial system. However, ABAKO and most other Congolese political groups were ethnically based and (with the exception of Patrice Lumumba's Mouvement national congolais—MNC) favoured the creation of a federal state. The *loi fondamentale* that eventually emerged represented a compromise, affirming the unitary character of the state, but allowing each province to have its own government and legislature, and equal representation in a national senate. In every province there was to be a representative of the central government. Both the president and the prime minister were to have executive powers.

Throughout the colonial period the Belgians had restricted Africans to the lower ranks of the civil service, and there were no African officers in the armed forces. The Belgian government assumed that, following independence, Belgian administrators and military officers would remain in *de facto* control. They did not foresee the tension that would result from the appointment of junior African civil servants to ministerial posts, while the non-commissioned African officers remained as they were.

THE FIRST REPUBLIC

The independence of the Republic of the Congo was proclaimed on 30 June 1960. Joseph Kasavubu became president and Patrice Lumumba prime minister. Five days later the armed forces mutinied. Their demands were partly satisfied by the replacement of the Belgian chief of staff by Col. (later Marshal) Joseph-Désiré Mobutu, a supporter of Lumumba; a number of non-commissioned officers were also elevated to the officer corps. Belgian civil servants rapidly fled the country. Belgian troops intervened to protect their nationals, and at the same time the provinces of Katanga (now Shaba) and South Kasai decided to secede. Lumumba requested help from the United Nations. Disagreement over Lumumba's response to the secession led to his dismissal by President Kasavubu in September 1960, but Lumumba refused to accept this, and asked the legislature to remove Kasavubu instead. The political deadlock was resolved by the intervention of the armed forces. On 14 September Col Mobutu announced the suspension of all political institutions until the end of the year. Mobutu assumed control of the country, ruling with the assistance of a 'collège des commissaires généraux', mainly comprising young university graduates, and chaired by Justin-Marie Bomboko of the Union Mongo (UNIMO), previously Lumumba's minister of foreign affairs. The collège governed the Congo for one year, but failed to control the north-eastern region, where some of Lumumba's former ministers had established a rival government in Stanleyville (later Kisangani).

Mobutu restored power to President Kasavubu in February 1961. A few days later Lumumba was murdered. The forceful reactions to this among other African governments and at the UN prompted negotiations between Kasavubu and the followers of Lumumba, and in August, after the reassembling of the legislature, a new government was formed, with Cyrille Adoula as prime minister. The new administration received the support of most political groups (with the exception of Katanga separatists, led by Moïse Tshombe), and it was hoped that it would progressively re-establish national unity. In April 1962 a constitutional amendment was approved, allowing the creation of new provinces. A new constitution entered into force on 1 August 1964, establishing a presidential system of government and a federalist structure.

Meanwhile the movement for the secession of Katanga had finally been defeated in January 1963, when its leader, Tshombe, went into exile. In January 1964 a rebellion began in the Kwilu region, led by Pierre Mulele, formerly a minister in Lumumba's government, who failed, however, to attract much support beyond the limits of his own ethnic group. In April a second rebellion began in southern Kivu and northern Katanga provinces. Within a few months the rebels controlled the east and north-east of the country, and had established their capital at Stanleyville. In July Tshombe was invited by President Kasavubu to become interim prime minister, pending elections. In the following month the country was renamed the Democratic Republic of the Congo. In early 1965 the rebellion was defeated by the army, assisted by Belgian troops and by mercenaries.

In March and April 1965 the Tshombe government organized legislative elections, in accordance with the 1964 constitution. The coalition led by Tshombe, the Convention nationale congolaise (CONACO), won 122 of the 167 seats in the chamber of deputies. However, an opposition bloc, the Front démocratique congolais (FDC), was soon formed. President Kasavubu dismissed the Tshombe administration and appointed Evariste Kimba as prime minister, but Kimba was unable to secure majority support in the CONACO-dominated assembly. The president, instead of appointing a new prime minister, reappointed Kimba. There was thus a deadlock between Kasavubu, supported by the FDC, and Tshombe's CONACO. As in 1960, the army, led by Mobutu, intervened. On 24 November 1965 all executive powers were transferred to Mobutu, who declared himself the head of the 'Second Republic'. A close associate, Col (later Gen.) Léonard Mulamba, was appointed prime minister. The government sought and obtained a parliamentary mandate. This was swiftly followed by a request from the legislature for its own suspension, as a result of which Mobutu was constitutionally empowered to legislate by decree.

Upon becoming head of state Mobutu imposed a five-year ban on party politics. In 1966 he founded the Mouvement populaire de la révolution (MPR), whose organization was superimposed on the existing administrative structures. The MPR political bureau held responsibility for policy formulation and political guidance. During that year power was progressively concentrated in the office of the president, who became the sole legislator. In October, after opponents of the prime minister succeeded in having him dismissed, the office was merged with that of the head of state. The 21 provinces were replaced by 12, and later by eight. Provincial institutions were abolished, leaving only provincial governors, who were responsible to the president. European place names were changed to African ones, the capital, Léopoldville, becoming Kinshasa.

'PRESIDENTIALISM' AND THE PARTY-STATE

After Mobutu's assumption of power Kasavubu retired to his native region, and Tshombe went into exile: both men died in 1969. A number of former ministers were accused of plotting against the new government, and were executed in June 1966. Congolese students, although they had initially supported Mobutu's seizure of power, quickly began to criticize the president's authoritarian style of rule: a students' strike was suppressed in early 1967. Labour organizations were deprived of their right to strike, but the government's dynamic policy against Belgian economic interests in the country secured the support of the three main trade unions, which were amalgamated in 1967 to form the Union nationale des travailleurs congolais (UNTC). In June 1967 a new constitution was approved by referendum, establishing a presidential regime, with a new legislature to be elected at a date to be determined by the president. The constitution provided for a maximum of two legally-authorized political parties. The claims of existing political groups to official recognition were ignored, however, while former senior politicians were appointed to overseas diplomatic posts, and subsequently accused of plotting against the president, and dismissed or arrested. By 1970 no senior politicians remained as potential rivals to Mobutu.

Presidential and legislative elections took place in late 1970. Mobutu (the sole candidate) was elected president on 31 October/1 November, and members of the 420-member national legislative council were elected from a list of candidates selected by the political bureau of the MPR. In December the constitution was amended so that the government, the legislature and the judiciary all became institutions of the MPR, and all citizens automatically became party members from birth. The president, as head of the MPR, was empowered to change the membership of the MPR political bureau. In October 1971 the country was renamed the Republic of Zaire, and remaining European-style place names were changed to local ones, while in 1972 the president took the name Mobutu Sese Seko Kuku Ngbendu Wa Za Banga, as part of the policy of 'authenticity'. In that year the government and the MPR executive committee merged to form the national executive council. During the period 1970–77 the discovery of several anti-government plots was announced, including, in 1975, one which was allegedly instigated by the US Central Intelligence Agency: several senior military officers were subsequently sentenced to death for their involvement in the so-called 'CIA plot'.

From the 1960s onwards one of the rival factions fighting for independence in the neighbouring Portuguese colony of Angola, the Frente Nacional de Libertação de Angola (FNLA), received support from the Congo/Zaire, and maintained refugee camps and guerrilla bases along the border in Bas-Zaïre. However, in 1976, after a rival faction, the Movimento Popular de Libertação de Angola (MPLA) had won the struggle for decolonization, there was an immediate reconciliation between Mobutu and President Neto of Angola. They agreed that Angolan refugees in Zaire would be repatriated, while Angola would transfer to Zaire several thousand Katangese soldiers, who had been members of Tshombe's forces at the time of the secession of Katanga. In March 1977 some of the latter, distrusting Mobutu's promises of an amnesty, invaded the Zairean province of Shaba (formerly Katanga) from Angola, receiving support from many of the discontented inhabitants. Mobutu received military assistance from France and Morocco, and by May the 'First Shaba War' was over. Apparently in response to the prompting of his French and Moroccan allies, Mobutu announced the holding, not only of a scheduled presidential election, but also of a legislative election (not due until 1980), and (in contravention of the constitution) a partial election of the MPR political bureau. The legislative election took place in October 1977, and Mobutu was re-elected (unopposed) in December to a further term of office. He then appointed seven additional members to the political bureau, so that the 18 elected members were in a minority. In early 1978 the constitution was amended to empower the legislative council to hold inquiries into public services and to question ministers on their activities.

In July 1977 Mobutu created the office of first state commissioner, equivalent to a prime minister. In August the commissioner for foreign affairs, Nguza Karl-I-Bond, was dismissed and sentenced to death for alleged treason: the sentence was later commuted to life imprisonment, and in March 1979 Nguza was reinstated to his former post (becoming first state commissioner in 1980). The military establishment was purged in 1978, when a number of senior officers and civilians were executed or imprisoned after the discovery of a coup plot.

In Shaba province, retribution by the army against those who had failed to support the government after the 1977 invasion caused resentment, and this helped to provoke the 'Second Shaba War': in early May 1978 several thousand men, originating from Angola, crossed the Zambian border and entered Shaba, occupying Kolwezi, a major mining centre. French paratroops intervened to assist the Zairean forces in recapturing the town, and in June a Pan-African peace-keeping force was installed in Shaba, remaining there for more than a year.

In March 1979, following criticism of the government by the national legislative council, Mobutu appointed a new first state commissioner, Bo-Boliko Lokonga (formerly the head of the national legislative council) and reshuffled several other posts.

THE ONSET OF OPPOSITION

In January 1980, as part of a massive anti-corruption drive, Mobutu completely reorganized the national executive council, dismissing 13 of the 22 commissioners. In a series of political reforms in August, the new post of chairman of the MPR, to be held by Mobutu as president of the MPR, became the focal point of decision-making and control of the party's activities. In September Mobutu appointed a 114-member central committee to become the MPR's second most important organ, after the congress. The party's executive committee became the executive secretariat and, in a ministerial reshuffle, the outgoing first state commissioner, Bo-Boliko Lokonga, was appointed executive secretary.

In April 1981 the reappointed first state commissioner, Nguza Karl-I-Bond, went into self-imposed exile in Belgium. He was replaced by N'Singa Udjuu Ongwakebi Untube, who also became executive secretary of the MPR when the posts were merged in October 1981 during a series of political changes, which included the decision to elect the party's political bureau from the central committee.

In 1982 opposition to Zaire's one-party system of government crystallized in attempts to establish a second party in Zaire, known as the Union pour la démocratie et le progrès social (UDPS), in connection with which 13 members of the national legislative council were imprisoned, and in the formation in October of the Front congolais pour le rétablissement de la démocratie (FCD), a coalition of opposition parties for which Nguza Karl-I-Bond was the spokesman. Kengo Wa Dondo was appointed first state commissioner in a ministerial reshuffle in November.

In May 1983, following the publication of a highly critical report on Zaire by the human rights organization, Amnesty International, Mobutu offered an amnesty to all political exiles who returned to Zaire by 30 June. A number of exiles accepted the offer, but a substantial opposition movement remained active in Belgium. The 13 imprisoned members of the national legislative council were released in May, although some were later placed under house arrest or sent into internal exile.

Opposition to Mobutu's regime continued to manifest itself within Zaire during 1984. In January and March a number of bombs exploded in Kinshasa, causing loss of life, and a rebel force occupied the town of Moba, in Shaba province, for two days in November, before it was recaptured by Zairean troops. Zaire accused Belgium of harbouring the groups responsible for these insurgencies, and claimed that the rebels had crossed into Zaire from neighbouring Tanzania. However, the main opposition groups in Belgium denied any involvement in the occupation of Moba, and suggested that rebellious Zairean troops had been responsible. It was widely believed that the violent opposition in Zaire had been co-ordinated in order to disrupt the proceedings for the election and inauguration of the president. However, Mobutu was re-elected without opposition in July 1984, and was inaugurated in December.

Ministerial reshuffles in February, April and July 1985, and a further round of changes in the structure of the MPR (dividing party and governmental functions), reinforced Mobutu's personal position. In July 1985 the return from exile of Nguza Karl-I-Bond (who was appointed ambassador to the USA in July 1986, a post which he held until March 1988), and the lifting of restrictions on seven members of the outlawed UDPS under the terms of another amnesty for political opponents, appeared to provide further evidence of the president's confidence in his position. In October, however, two UDPS members were arrested, being subsequently tried and imprisoned for 'insulting the head of state'. Another major ministerial reshuffle followed in April 1986, in which Kengo Wa Dondo retained his post as first state commissioner. In October Mobutu abolished this post and restructured the ministries responsible for economic affairs, but the post of first state commissioner was revived in January 1987, and allocated to Mabi Mulumba, previously state commissioner for finance. In March 1988 Mobutu again reorganized the government, appointing Sambwa Pida Nbagui to replace Mabi Mulumba as first state commissioner. In November, in the fourth ministerial reshuffle of the year, Mobutu replaced about one-third of the members of the national executive council and reinstated Kengo Wa Dondo as first state commissioner.

In March 1986 Amnesty International published another report condemning Zaire for abuses of human rights. The report was specifically concerned with the alleged illegal arrest, torture or murder of UDPS supporters in late 1985. In October 1986 Mobutu admitted that some of the allegations in the report were justified, and appointed a state commissioner for citizens' rights. Mobutu also severely criticized army units for their actions while restoring order after the rebellion in Moba in 1984, and announced the dissolution of the military security agency, the Service des renseignements militaires et d'action.

Regional and municipal elections were held in May and June 1987, but the results were anulled in August because of alleged electoral malpractice. The elections were rescheduled for March 1988, but were subsequently postponed until March 1989, for 'budgetary reasons' and to ensure their conduct in a democratic and 'harmonious' manner. Elections to the 210 seats in the national legislative council (reduced from 310) were held on 6 September 1987. The results were announced separately in each province, 'to eliminate the risk of manipulation and fraud.' In the same month several opposition groups announced that they had united to form a government-in-exile.

In June 1987 several members of the UDPS, including Etienne Tshisekedi Wa Mulumba (its secretary-general and a former minister of the interior), availed themselves of an amnesty offered by Mobutu. In October four other former UDPS leaders were admitted to the central committee of the MPR, and other reconciled opponents of the government were appointed to senior posts in state-owned enterprises. In January 1988, however, Tshisekedi was arrested after he attempted to organize an unauthorized public meeting. Following two months' detention, he was placed under house arrest. In April he was rearrested after advocating a boycott of the partial legislative elections scheduled to take place in Kinshasa on 10 April. In September Tshisekedi withdrew from political activity, although this did not prevent his arrest in March 1989 for alleged involvement in the student disturbances which broke out in Kinshasa and Lubumbashi at the end of February. Unofficial sources estimated that, in the ensuing violent clashes with armed police, as many as 37 people had been killed (although a government statement put the death toll at one).

In February 1990 the UDPS organized demonstrations in Kinshasa and three other towns in Zaire to commemorate the anniversary of the murder, in 1961, of Patrice Lumumba. The demonstrations were reported to have been violently dispersed by the police, and several arrests were made. Further unrest followed in April, as students staged protests in Kinshasa to demand larger study grants and the removal of Mobutu from power. In what was seen by many observers as an attempt to defuse the growing tension, Mobutu announced in late April that a multi-party political system, initially comprising three parties (including the MPR), would be introduced after a transitional period of one year. At the same time Mobutu declared the inauguration of the 'Third Republic' and announced his resignation as chairman of the MPR and state commissioner for national defence. However, he retained the office of president. N'Singa Udjuu Ongwakebi Untube, formerly first state commissioner and executive secretary of the MPR, was subsequently appointed the new chairman of the party. The national executive council was dissolved and Professor Lunda Bululu, secretary-general of the Economic Community of Central African States and formerly a legal adviser to Mobutu, was appointed first state commissioner, in place of Kengo Wa Dondo.

In early May 1990 a new, and smaller, transitional government was formed. Mobutu announced that a special commission would be set up to draft a new constitution by the end of April 1991, and that presidential elections would be held before December of that year, with legislative elections to follow in 1992. He also announced the imminent 'depoliticization of the armed forces, the gendarmerie, the civil guard, the security services and the administration in general'. Additionally, legislation allowing for the organization and operation of political parties and of free trade unions was to be prepared. In late April 1990 Tshisekedi was released from house arrest.

Further unrest occurred in early May 1990, when students at Lubumbashi University staged anti-government demonstrations. According to reports by Belgian teachers at the university, between 50–150 students were subsequently killed by members of the presidential guard, acting on Mobutu's orders. Strong condemnation was voiced by many humanitarian organizations, university professors in Zaire and the Belgian government, which announced the immediate 'freezing' of all official bilateral assistance to Zaire and the suspension of preparations for the annual Belgium-Zaire joint commission meeting scheduled for mid-June. After some procrastination and strenuous denial of the reports, Zaire finally authorized an official parliamentary inquiry, following which a provincial governor and other senior local officials were accused of having organized the killing of one student (and the injury of 13 others) and were arrested. However, Mobutu refused to allow an independent international board of inquiry to enter Zaire, despite Belgium's insistence, to investigate the case further. By late June it seemed almost inevitable that relations between the two countries would enter another crisis (see below), with Mobutu expelling from Zaire about 700 Belgian technical assistants and closing all but one of Belgium's consular offices in Zaire.

As part of the continuing process of political reform, in late June 1990 the legislature adopted amendments to the constitution, whereby presidential control over the national executive council and over foreign policy was ended. At the same time, the establishment of independent trade unions was authorized. In early October Mobutu announced that a full multi-party political system would be established in Zaire, thereby reversing his decision to permit the existence of only three parties. In November legislation was adopted to provide for the organization and operation of political parties. In the same month, the USA announced its decision to terminate all military and economic aid to Zaire. This development followed renewed allegations of abuses of human rights in Zaire, and also reflected speculation that for many years Mobutu had misappropriated large amounts of foreign economic aid for his personal enrichment. Popular unrest re-emerged in late 1990: in November an anti-government rally in Kinshasa, organized by the UDPS, was violently suppressed, and in the following months several people were reported to have been killed by government troops during demonstrations in Kinshasa and Matadi in protest against recent increases in consumer prices.

NATIONAL CONFERENCE

In early February 1991 the Union nationale des travailleurs congolais (UNTC) organized a three-day general strike, supported by hundreds of thousands of workers, civil servants and public service employees, to demand improved working and living conditions and the resignation of the government. Later in the same month 20,000 people attended an anti-government rally, organized by the UDPS in Kinshasa.

With the announcement of a timetable for the restoration of multi-party elections there has been a proliferation of political parties, prominent among these was the Union des fédéralistes et républicains indépendants (UFERI), led by Nguza Karl-I-Bond. In March 1991 a new and enlarged transitional government was appointed. Lunda Bulula was replaced as first state commissioner by Prof. Mulumba Lukoji, a prominent economist who had served in previous administrations. Several minor political parties were represented in the administration, but none of the more influential opposition parties. In April Mobutu announced that a national conference would convene at the end of the month, at which members of the government and opposition organizations would discuss the drafting of a new constitution, which would then be submitted for approval in a national referendum. The response of the major opposition parties was to reject the call for a national conference unless Mobutu stood down from power. Widespread popular disturbances and anti-government demonstrations also took place during April. In mid-April 42 people were reported to have been killed and many others wounded when security forces opened fire on demonstrators in the town of Mbuji-Mayi, in central Zaire. Mobutu responded to this unrest by suspending the national conference. But he soon announced that it would be reconvened on 31 July.

In response to these initiatives of Mobutu the major opposition parties—the Parti démocrate et social chrétien (PDSC), UDPS and UFERI—formed the Union sacrée (Sacred Union), a vanguard of parties in opposition to Mobutu, advocating a boycott of the national conference. By the end of July 1991 the Union sacrée had grown to 130 parties, and had decided to take part in the national conference as a result of its growing influence and the weakening of Mobutu's power base. On 22 July the unpopular government of Lukoji resigned at the request of Mobutu, who—under increasing pressure from the US—offered the premiership to Tshisekedi of UDPS. However this move was rejected by Tshisekedi, under pressure from his party, and Lukoji's government was reinstated.

The conference opened on 7 August 1991 with 2,850 delegates, including 900 representing opposition political parties. But the conference promptly stalled, with the opposition threatening a boycott unless its demands were met. The election of Isaac Kalonji Mutambay, a protestant pastor, as president of the conference was rejected by the opposition. On 30 September Mutambay was forced to step down in the face of mounting political crisis and the withdrawal of the Roman Catholic Church from the conference.

On 2 September 1991 violent clashes took place between opposition supporters and the security forces, with many deaths reported, and two deaths admitted officially. The demonstrations were organized in response to increasing frustration with the national conference, massive inflation and aggravated hardship. By 23 September frustration erupted into a week of rioting and looting. The rioting originated within the military, among the Centre d'entaînement des troupes aeroporteés (CETA) and the 31st Parachutist Brigade, and then spread to civilians after a major part of the damage was carried out. Massive destruction of properties and business premises took place and a large number of deaths were reported. French and Belgian troops were dispatched to suppress the rioting.

In the wake of these riots France, Belgium and the USA put pressure on Mobutu to introduce a change of government, as a result of which Tshisekedi was appointed as first state commissioner on 2 October 1991. Tshisekedi only survived in this post until 14 October, when he was dimissed by Mobutu and a 'government of crisis' sworn in. This division was prompted by Tshisekedi's wish to present his own government to the conference and to reject representation of the MPR. His refusal to swear an oath of allegiance to Mobutu, and his depiction of Mobutu as a 'human monster' also led to increasing friction. Four posts in the new government were awarded to the MPR. Bernadin Mungul Diaka, leader of Rassemblement démocratique pour la république (RDR) was appointed first state commissioner. Although the RDR was part of the Union sacrée, Mungul Diaka was also once a close political associate of Mobutu.

It rapidly became evident that the Mungul Diaka government lacked acceptance both within Zaire and among Western allies of Mobutu. A new initiative was undertaken by President Diouf of Senegal to break the impasse. This committed both Mobutu and opposition supporters to remove all obstacles to the convening of a sovereign national conference, which would have legislative power, and a first state commissioner drawn from the opposition. With an agreement signed on 22 November 1991, a new government was sworn in on 28 November with Nguza Karl-I-Bond of UFERI as first state commissioner. Various political tendencies were present in this government, but the Union sacrée was largely excluded and Mobutu's allies heavily represented. Mobutu loyalists obtained eight ministerial posts, including defence and security, external relations and international co-operation. The national conference was resumed in December 1991 and Mgr Laurent Monsengwo Pasinya—archbishop of Kisangani, head of the episcopal conference, and a dedicated campaigner for the extension of democratic rights—was elected its president. Joseph Ileo of PDSC was selected as vice-president.

With the premiership in its hands, UFERI, once a central part of the Union sacrée, became instrumental in setting up another front within the national conference. On 19 December 1991 the Alliance of Patriotic Forces came into being, with 30 political parties joining ranks, as a union committed to political change but against extremist stands.

Nguza undermined the national conference which he suspended on 19 January 1992 after consultations with Mobutu. Reasons given for the suspension of the conference included its cost and its role in fomenting violence and ethnic tensions. A campaign to promote ethnic violence was also instigated by Mobutu supporters, with attempts by UFERI and Rassemblement des démocrats liberaux (RDL) to portray political differences as arising from ethnic factors and to create political conflicts which were then represented as ethnic ones. On 14 January RDL claimed that seven of its supporters had been killed in clashes with another political party in Kasai Oriental (a stronghold of the Union sacrée). Similarly Nguza announced eight deaths following clashes between Lunda (his ethnic group) and Luba (Tshisekedi's ethnic group). He argued that each party should only have one representative at the national conference from any ethnic group. Mobutu also accused the conference of being unrepresentative, saying that 45% of the delegates originated from the two Kasai provinces. These manoeuvres recalled earlier pronouncements by Mobutu that democratic pluralism would lead to ethnic violence.

During January and February 1992 violence intensified as the Union sacrée and churches attempted to mobilize people to demonstrate against the suspension of the conference. On 16 February over 30 people were killed by security forces in mass protests in Kinshasa. These incidents greatly weakened Mobutu's international standing with France, Belgium and the USA, leading to pressure for the national conference to be reinstated, and suspension of aid. Mobutu's international standing was further eroded by the publication of the findings of a UN investigation into the Lubumbashi incident, which implicated Mobutu's troops in the killings. On 22–23 January troops took over the national radio station, urging the removal of the government and resumption of the national conference. A number of strikes broke out in February demanding both better wages and resumption of the political conference. At the end of March, two government ministers, Nyamwisi Muvingi (youth, culture and tourism) and Kadura Kasongo (secretary of state for communication) resigned, condemning the government.

Increasingly isolated and under pressure at home and abroad, Mobutu, against Nguza's wishes, agreed to re-open the conference on 6 April 1992. On 17 April the conference declared its own 'sovereignty', its power to take binding legislative and executive decisions, thus undermining the role of the Nguza government. In return for accepting this ruling Mobutu was allowed to remain as head of state. The main role of the conference was now to define a draft constitution, which would be put to a referendum, and to establish a timetable for legislative and presidential elections. In June a 65-strong special commission was set up to examine arrangements for a transitional pluralistic government. In June Monsengwo also announced that a transitional government would be established the following month, and an electoral college was also to be inaugurated.

As the conference began debating the choice of a first state commissioner in mid-June 1992, Mobutu warned that the conference had the power only to draw up a draft constitution, not to adopt it, and threatened to 'call the conference to order', as he had done in the past. However, by late July, the president appeared to have conceded to the conference's demands. On 23 July, after two meetings with Mobutu, Monsengwo announced that it had been agreed that the conference would elect a transitional first state commissioner, who would appoint a government. Mobutu was also said to have agreed to the establishment of a high council of the republic, to oversee the implementation of the conference's decisions, as well as to placing the gendarmerie and civil guard under the control of the transitional government, while retaining control of the army himself. Within days, however, the conference again found itself at odds with the president, when it voted on 4 August to reinstate the country's old name, Congo, and to restore the former name of Shaba province, Katanga. The decision was opposed by the cabinet on constitutional grounds, and television transmissions of the conference proceedings were suspended for two days. After discussions between Mobutu and Monsengwo, the conference reversed its decision and the president reaffirmed his commitment to supporting the conference's work.

On 15 August 1992, Tshisekedi was elected transitional first state commissioner by the conference, one of 17 candidates, with 70% of the vote, and took up the post on 19 August, following the resignation of Nguza, who had not stood for re-election. A 'transition act', adopted by the conference in early August, afforded Tshisekedi a mandate to govern for 24 months, pending the promulgation of a new constitution which would curtail the powers of the president. On 30 August Tshisekedi, whose election was widely applauded as a victory for pro-democratic forces within Zaire, appointed a transitional government of 'national union', which included opponents of Mobutu. The election of the state commissioner was also welcomed by the international community, particularly the USA, France, Belgium and the EU, and it was hoped that renewed financial commitments from these sources would be promptly negotiated.

The political interests of Tshisekedi and Mobutu clashed almost immediately when the president declared his intention to promote the adoption of a 'semi-presidential constitution', in opposition to the parliamentary system favoured by the conference. In October 1992 attacks on opposition leaders and the offices of newspapers critical of the president became increasingly frequent in Kinshasa, while Shaba was beset by ethnic violence. Meanwhile, rumours persisted of an imminent coup, organized by generals loyal to the president. On 14 November the national conference (without the participation of Mobutu's supporters) adopted a draft constitution providing for the establishment of a 'Federal Republic of the Congo', the introduction of a bicameral parliament and the election of the president, by universal suffrage, to fulfil a largely ceremonial function. (Executive and military power was to be exercised by the prime minister.) The draft document was vigorously opposed by Mobutu who, having failed to persuade Tshisekedi to broaden his government in order to accommodate the president's own supporters, unsuccessfully attempted in early December to declare the Tshisekedi government dissolved. On 6 December the national conference dissolved itself and was succeeded by a 453-member high council of the republic, headed by Monsengwo, which, as the supreme interim executive and legislative authority, was empowered to amend and adopt the new constitution and to organize legislative and presidential elections. At the same time, Monsengwo declared that the report of a special commission, established by the conference in order to examine allegations of corruption brought against the president and his associates, would be considered by the high council. In response to this effective appropriation of his powers, Mobutu ordered the suspension of the high council and the government, and decreed that civil servants should usurp ministers in the supervision of government ministries (a demand which they refused). Attempts by the presidential guard to obstruct the convening of the high council ended following the organization of a parade through the streets of Kinshasa, undertaken by Monsengwo and other members of the high council, in protest at the actions of the armed forces. Bolstered by support from the USA, Belgium and France, Monsengwo reiterated the high council's recognition of Tshisekedi as head of Zaire's government.

In mid-January 1993 the high council declared Mobutu to be guilty of treason, on account of his mismanagement of state affairs, and threatened impeachment proceedings unless he recognized the legitimacy of the transitional government headed by Tshisekedi. A short-lived general strike and campaign of civil disobedience, organized by the Union sacrée, failed in their stated aims of forcing the resignation of the president and liberating the national radio and television stations from Mobutu's control. Five people were killed and many were injured in disturbances which ensued. At the end of the month several units of the army rioted in protest at an attempt by the president to pay them with discredited 5m.-zaire banknotes. Order was eventually restored but not before the deaths of some 65 individuals (including the French ambassador to Zaire), and the intervention of military contingents from France and Belgium.

In early March 1993, in an attempt to reassert his political authority, Mobutu convened a special 'conclave' of political forces to debate the country's future. The high council and the Union sacrée declined an invitation to attend. In mid-March the 'conclave' appointed Faustin Birindwa, a former UDPS member and adviser to Tshisekedi, as prime minister, charged with the formation of a 'government of national salvation'. The somewhat perfunctory national assembly was also revived to rival the high council, and was reconvened to operate within the terms of reference of the old Mobutu-inspired constitution. In early April Birindwa appointed a cabinet which included Nguza (as first deputy prime minister in charge of defence), and three members of the Union sacrée, who were immediately expelled from that organization. While the Birindwa administration was denied official recognition by Belgium, France, the USA and the EU, Tshisekedi became increasingly frustrated at the impotence of his own government (the armed forces recommenced blocking access to the high council), and the deteriorating stability of the country (during April the army embarked upon a campaign of intimidation of opposition members, while tribal warfare re-emerged in Shaba and also erupted in the north-eastern province of Kivu), and urged the intervention of the UN. In July the secretary-general of the UN appointed Lakhdar Brahimi, a former minister of foreign affairs in Algeria, as his special envoy to Zaire, charged with a humanitarian mission of mediation. Meanwhile, in late June, six of Birindwa's ministers, all former activists in the Union sacrée, had announced the formation of the Union sacrée rénovée (USR), claiming that the Union sacrée had abandoned its political objectives in the pursuit of extremist policies. A series of pre-negotiations, conducted during August between representatives of the 'conclave', the Union sacrée and the high council, failed to conclude a significant initiative for future consensus. In early September, in response to a declaration made by Mobutu that a constitutional referendum would be held in October and presidential elections would take place in December, Tshisekedi announced that a new opposition grouping, the Forces démocratiques de Congo-Kinshasa (which he was to lead) would take no part in any future negotiations with the presidential 'conclave', given that the high council alone was empowered to decide an electoral timetable.

At the end of September 1993, following some 20 days of negotiations, an agreement was concluded between representatives of President Mobutu and of the principal opposition groups, providing for the adoption of a single constitutional text for the transitional period, which would be subject to approval by a national referendum. Under the provisions of the agreement, national transitional institutions would include the president of the republic, a reorganized transitional parliament (a unicameral legislature to be composed of more than 500 representatives, including all existing members of the high council and the national legislative council—with the exception of 44 national legislative council 'substitutes' who were appointed following the expulsion of opposition representatives—and independent legislators, to be co-opted in order to ensure full national representation), the transitional government and the national judiciary. As previously agreed, the organization of presidential and legislative elections would provide for the establishment of a new republic in January 1995. During October 1993, however, attempts to finalize the terms of the agreement were complicated by the insistence of Tshisekedi's supporters that he should continue in the office of prime minister, despite the objections of Mobutu's representatives that Tshisekedi's mandate, proceeding from the national conference, had been superseded by the September agreement. The opposing positions of the principal political parties (largely polarized as the pro-Tshisekedi Union sacrée de l'opposition radicale—USOR and the pro-Mobutu Forces politiques du conclave—FPC) became more firmly entrenched during November and December.

An ultimatum, issued to all political parties by President Mobutu in early January 1994, in an attempt to end the political impasse, resulted in the conclusion of an agreement to form a government of national reconciliation, signed by all major constituent parties of the FPC and the USOR (with the notable exception of Tshisekedi's own UDPS). Encouraged by the unexpected level of political support for the initiative, on 14 January Mobutu announced the dissolution of the high council and the national legislative council, the dismissal of the government of national salvation, headed by Birindwa, and the candidacy for the premiership of two contestants, Tshisekedi and Molumba Lukoji, to be decided by the transitional legislature (to be known as the haut conseil de la république-parlement de transition—HCR-PT) within 15 days of its inauguration, provisionally scheduled for 17 January. Despite widespread opposition condemnation of Mobutu's procedural circumvention of the high council's authority, and a well-supported 24-hour strike, organized in Kinshasa on 19 January in protest at Mobutu's unilateral declarations, the HCR-PT convened for the first time on 23 January (following a preliminary meeting on 19 January at which the former president of the high council, the Most Rev. Laurent Monsengwo Pasinya, was confirmed as the new president of the HCR-PT). The HCR-PT promptly rejected Mobutu's procedure for the selection of a new prime minister. Subsequent attempts by the legislature to formulate a new procedure were frustrated by the increasingly divergent interests of the member parties of the USOR, and by Tshisekedi's insistence of his legitimate claim to the office.

On 8 April 1994 the HCR-PT endorsed a new transitional constitution act, reiterating the provisions of previous accords for the organization of a constitutional referendum and presidential and legislative elections, and defining the functions of and relationship between the president of the republic, the transitional government and the HCR-PT, during a 15-month transitional period. The government, to be accountable to the HCR-PT, was to assume some former powers of the president, including the control of the central bank and the security forces and the nomination of candidates for important civil service posts. A new prime minister was to be appointed from opposition candidates, to be nominated within 10 days of the president's promulgation of the act (on 9 April). Despite the initial indignation of Tshisekedi's supporters at the act's identification of a prime-ministerial vacancy that they did not recognize, by the end of April Tshisekedi was reported to have agreed to be considered for the post. Widening divisions within the USOR frustrated attempts to unite the opposition behind Tshisekedi as sole candidate, prompting the expulsion, in May, of 10 dissident parties from the USOR (including the Union pour la république et la démocratie—URD, whose members occupied several ministerial posts in the transitional government).

In June 1994 the HCR-PT ratified the candidature of seven opposition representatives for the premiership, rejecting that of Tshisekedi for having failed to attend a parliamentary commission in order to explain the promotion of his position as 'prime minster awating rehabilitation', rather than candidate for the office. On 14 June it was reported that Kengo Wa Dondo, described as a moderate opposition leader, had been elected prime minister by 322 votes to 133 in the HCR-PT. However, Kengo Wa Dondo's election was immediately denounced as illegitimate, under the terms of the April constitution act, by opposition spokesmen and by the president of the HCR-PT (who refused to endorse the actions of the legislature). A new transitional government, announced on 6 July, was similarly rejected by the radical opposition, despite the offer of two cabinet posts to the UDPS. On 11 July, during a motion of confidence, the government received overwhelming support from the HCR-PT. The new prime minister swiftly sought to restore the confidence of the international donor community in the commitment of the new administration to the implementation of political change (general elections were to be conducted before the end of July 1995) and economic adjustment (more financial control was to be exerted over the armed forces, and the central bank was to be awarded greater autonomy). In mid-1994, the credibility of the new government was further enhanced by its support for French and US initiatives to address the humanitarian crisis presented by the flight to Zaire of more than 1m. Rwandan refugees hoping to escape the violent aftermath of the death of President Habyarimana.

Mounting concern that the political frustration of the opposition would be translated into an armed struggle increased, in March 1994, following the declaration of intent of the newly-proclaimed Congolese national army (an armed wing of the Zairean radical opposition) to 'restore legitimacy and democracy' to the country.

In December 1993, at a rally in Kolwezi attended by the Mobutu-sponsored government's deputy prime minister, Karl-I-Bond, the governor of Shaba declared the autonomy of the province (reverting to the name of Katanga). While Karl-I-Bond denied that his presence had in any way endorsed the declaration, his own (separatist) UFERI welcomed the development and encouraged provincial political committees to pursue the establishment of greater regional autonomy. President Mobutu's subdued response to the Shaba declaration was attributed to his reluctance to engender further political opposition during negotiations that might dictate his political future (see above).

Reports published by Amnesty International in September 1993 and February 1994 accused security forces of the Mobutu administration of having perpetrated numerous violations of human rights against civilians and political opponents during the previous four years.

FOREIGN RELATIONS

During the early 1980s, a period of intense superpower rivalry in southern Africa, the Mobutu regime was an important ally of the US, France and Belgium, receiving large amounts of aid. The Kamina air base in southern Shaba was alleged to have been used by the USA to support the União Nacional para a Independência Total de Angola (UNITA) and joint military exercises were carried out by the USA and Zaire. Mobutu was also instrumental in negotiating the June 1989 *rapprochement* between the Angolan government and UNITA. The ending of superpower conflicts at the end of the 1980s and the increasing prominence being given in aid policies to the issues of democracy and human rights have led, however, to a distancing of the relationship between Mobutu and his Western allies. In November 1988 a serious dispute arose between Zaire and Belgium, following Belgian press reports criticizing the degree of corruption in Zaire and alleged misappropriation of funds by Mobutu. This led to a major rift between the two countries which was resolved in March 1990 with a treaty of co-operation, the cancellation of one-third of Zaire's state-guaranteed commercial debt and restoration of normal corporate and banking relations between the two countries. But relations deteriorated again in May 1990 following Belgium's reaction to the killings of students at Lubumbashi. Since then increasing internal repression and violence has drawn further criticism and condemnation of the Mobutu regime by Belgium, France and the US, and pressure for Mobutu to relinquish power. They have openly blamed Mobutu for the deteriorating economic situation and for political repression, and have refused to renew aid to Zaire. In November 1991 a francophone summit due to be held in Kinshasa was relocated in Paris, and France declared that Mobutu would not be welcome. On 22 January 1992 the EC announced the suspension of all aid, except humanitarian aid, to Zaire. Since the outbreak of rioting in September 1991, when French and Belgian troops were sent to restore security, France, Belgium and the USA have become more interventionist, maintaining pressure on Mobutu to reconvene the national conference and to hand over power. The USA has insisted that Mobutu must concede power to an interim government and relinquish control over national finances and defence. However, the US government has negotiated for Mobutu to remain as titular head of state, worried that his sudden removal might lead to a rapid breakdown of control over the military apparatus and to anarchy and turmoil.

Zaire's relations with Belgium, France, the USA and the EU improved considerably following the inauguration of Prime Minister Kengo Wa Dondo and his new government, in July 1994. It was expected that Zaire's positive response to international initiatives to address the refugee crisis arising from the flight across the Zairean border of more than 1m. Rwandan refugees in mid-1994 would encourage the resumption of development aid from donor nations. In late July 1994 President Mobutu met President Bizimungu of Rwanda and concluded an agreement for the disarmament and gradual repatriation of Rwandan refugees.

Zaire's relationship with its neighbours has been complicated by the presence of refugees in border areas and activities of anti-government rebels. In 1984 Zaire accused Tanzania of harbouring Zairean rebels. Zaire has also been accused of harbouring UNITA rebels from Angola and actively supporting US initiatives to undermine the MPLA government. Zaire has in turn accused Angola of harbouring anti-MPR guerrillas. Relations with Zambia have also been tense as a result of both refugees in border areas and different political perspectives on the Angolan situation. In 1992 relations with Congo deteriorated with the repatriation of Zairean refugees in Congo. Zambians resident in Zaire have also been repatriated. Border clashes with Uganda flared up in 1992 when Zairean troops claimed that they had crossed the border to attack rebels hiding in Uganda while planning to overthrow Mobutu.

As relations with the West deteriorated, Mobutu attempted to improve links with Arab countries, strained since May 1982, when Zaire restored diplomatic relations with Israel, visiting Morocco and Egypt in April 1992. Relations with Morocco have been fairly good and Zaire has been one of the few OAU countries to support its annexation of Western Sahara, suspending its participation in the OAU over this issue from 1984–86. In July 1983 Zaire sent 3,000 troops to Chad to support the French-backed government of President Habré. In July 1985 a military co-operation agreement was signed between the two countries.

Economy

DIANA HUBBARD

Revised for this edition by FRANÇOIS MISSER

MINING AND PETROLEUM

Although Zaire commands enormous economic potential and is richly endowed with a wide range of resources, the mining sector dominates the economy. In 1990 mining, mineral processing and petroleum extraction accounted for about 17% of gross domestic product (GDP) and around 75% of total export earnings (rising to 92% in 1993). The country possesses an abundance of mineral resources, the most important being copper, diamonds, cobalt and zinc; there are also deposits of gold, cassiterite, manganese, cadmium, silver, wolframite and columbo-tantalite, most of which are exploited only on a small-scale industrial or artisanal scale. Copper, cobalt and zinc are found mainly in the south-eastern Shaba province, contiguous with the Zambian Copperbelt; diamonds are located mainly in Kasaï province, particularly around the towns of Mbuji-Mayi and Tshikapa, although some mining activity has spread to Bandundu province; and cassiterite, wolframite, gold and columbo-tantalite mainly in the Kivu region in the east.

The state-owned mining corporation, the Générale des Carrières et des Mines (GÉCAMINES) was the dominant producer in the 1980s, accounting for more than 90% of copper output, and all output of cobalt, zinc and coal. The much smaller-scale, state-owned enterprise, the Société de Développement Industriel et Minier de Zaïre (SODIMIZA), originally a Japanese venture, merged with GÉCAMINES in 1990 and produced 18,000 tons of copper concentrates in that year. Production of copper ore remained static in the mid-1980s, consistently totalling around 500,000 tons per year, equivalent to about 6% of world output. However, production took a downward trend from 1988 onwards. The international copper market is generally volatile and, as world technology advances, substitute materials such as aluminium and optical fibres (in telecommunications), are being used increasingly. In addition, other world producers, such as Chile, are establishing new open-cast, lower-cost mines. Consequently, GÉCAMINES has pursued a policy of increased vertical integration and increased value added, as opposed to the accelerated production of ore. In the period 1990–93 production was further hampered by strikes, technical problems (particularly a cave-in at the Kamoto mine in September 1990) and the worsening political situation. These factors led GÉCAMINES to declare a situation, in early May 1991, of partial *force majeure* on its contracts to deliver copper to foreign clients. From total output of 471,500 tons in 1985, production fell steadily to 440,600 tons in 1989 and to 355,500 tons in 1990. Output fell to 291,500 tons in 1991, virtually half the average for the first half of the 1980s, and then plunged to 146,000 tons in 1992 and just 48,300 tons in 1993; in 1994 production was optimistically forecast at only 50,000 tons. Cobalt is mined mainly in association with copper, and world prices have been among the most volatile of all minerals—ranging from US $7.50 per lb in December 1989 to $23 per lb in July 1994, having peaked at $33 in January 1992 and slumped to $12.75 per lb in June 1993. GÉCAMINES produced 9,429 tons of cobalt in 1989, 10,033 tons in 1990, 8,800 tons in 1991, 6,600 tons in 1992, and just 2,416 tons in 1993. Zinc output has declined sharply in the last few years. In 1985 GÉCAMINES produced 64,000 tons, but output then declined steadily to 4,150 tons in 1993. In 1994 international donors were putting pressure on the Zairean government to transfer GÉCAMINES to private-sector ownership. However, it was estimated that full rehabilitation of the concern would require investment amounting to US $1,000m.

Until 1986, when it was overtaken by Australia, Zaire was the world's leading producer of industrial diamonds. Although about 98% of Zaire's production, from Eastern Kasaï, is of industrial diamonds, gem stones are also found. Official production figures tend to fluctuate and do not give an accurate picture, as there are extensive and elaborate smuggling networks. A report obtained by the Zairean media in early 1993 estimated the value of diamonds smuggled every year at $300m. The only large-scale producer is the Société Minière de Bakwanga (MIBA), which produced 8.2m. carats in 1987, although production declined to 4.3m. carats in 1992. The remainder of the diamond output is accounted for by artisan diggers. Most of the diamonds which are smuggled come from the artisanal diggers (whose share of total output increased from 59% to 67% between 1987 and 1992), but the officially controlled diamond counters still bought 8.9m. carats from artisanal diggers in 1992. Combined with MIBA's output, this gives a total official output for 1992 of 13.2m.(compared with 19.7m. carats in 1987), although the real output was higher. According to estimates from the Bank of Zaire, diamonds became Zaire's principal source of foreign exchange in 1993 ($532m.), ahead of GÉCAMINES products ($225m.) and crude petroleum ($137m.). Gold output in 1993 was an estimated 1,430 kg, worth around $12.5m., compared with 2,200 kg worth $40m. in 1986. Rehabilitation work was begun in 1989 at the main gold mine, the Office des Mines d'Or de Kilo-Moto (OKIMO). In early 1990, two foreign companies were given management contracts for OKIMO, and output is expected to increase steadily during the decade (despite recurrent labour unrest in the sector), particularly since the EC's SYSMIN system of compensation for losses in mineral export earnings was extended to include gold in the current Lomé IV Convention.

Zaire became a producer of offshore petroleum in 1975, operating from fields on the Atlantic coast and at the mouth of the River Zaire. Output averaged around 30,000 barrels a day (b/d) during the second half of the 1980s, with output in 1988 totalling 10.7m. barrels. Output declined to 9.9m. barrels in 1989, recovered to 10.9m. barrels in 1990, but fell back to 9.9m. barrels in 1991 and 8.6m. barrels in 1992. The reserves in the Atlantic fields operated by Zaire Gulf Oil have declined, but the Belgian–Zairean consortium ZAIREP, which operates in the mouth of the River Zaire, slightly increased output in 1990. Current campaigns of prospecting, undertaken by both companies have been hampered by political instability, and are unlikely to benefit the sector before 1996.

In the face of the prolonged economic recession, the country's petroleum output has been broadly equivalent to domestic demand, although Zaire cannot consume its own production as the local refinery is not equipped to treat this exceptionally heavy petroleum. In the longer term, however, unless current onshore exploration near the border with Uganda and Tanzania proves successful, current oil reserves (estimated at around 187m. barrels in 1993) will be exhausted and, in all probability, Zaire will have to continue to import its petroleum requirements. In 1989 Zaire became the 10th member of the African Petroleum Producers' Association (APPA).

AGRICULTURE AND FORESTRY

Zaire's wide range of geography and climate produces an equally wide range of both food and cash crops. The main food crops are cassava, maize, rice and plantains, grown mainly by small-scale subsistence farmers. Cash crops include coffee, palm oil and palm kernels, rubber, cotton, sugar, tea and cocoa, many of which are grown on large plantations. Zaire has the potential to be not only self-sufficient in food but also to be a net exporter. In addition, with the exception of some parts of Kivu and Katanga, it has escaped the droughts which have caused such great damage in other parts of Africa in the last 20 years. The share of agriculture's contribution to GDP remained almost constant throughout the 1980s, standing at 32% in 1981, 33% in 1985 and 32% in 1989. However, the decline of the mining sector (excluding diamonds) contributed to an increase to 45% in the contribution of agriculture to GDP in 1993, with the sector employing approximately 65% of the active work-force.

However, the agricultural sector has suffered both from the widespread expropriations of privately-owned plantations in the early 1970s and the subsequent decline in output and from poor government funding (only 1% of GDP). The trend has changed since the end of the 1980s, with a remarkable growth in production of food crops. However, the supply of urban populations is hampered by one of the economy's most damaging structural deficiencies: lack of infrastructure for the transportation of agricultural produce. For example, demand for the staple food, cassava, from the inhabitants of Kinshasa is simply too great to be satisfied by output from the nearby regions of Bas-Zaïre and Bandundu, and yet the inadequate road network hinders transport of foodstuffs grown in more distant areas. In June 1994 maize crops were reported to be rotting in northern Shaba, while fuel shortages prevented their transportation to the regional capital, Lubumbashi, where widespread food shortages were occurring. Estimates of food imports vary widely, ranging from official figures of 157,000 tons in 1985 to unofficial estimates of 393,000 tons. Wheat and flour imports, for example, were stated to be 220,000 tons in 1990. There have been indications of an improvement in production of local food crops, but this is difficult to assess accurately as a large proportion are subsistence crops and do not enter the money economy. Official figures suggest that 712,000 tons of locally-produced maize and 453,000 tons of locally-produced rice were traded in 1988. Production of sugar declined from 85,100 tons in 1991 to 75,080 tons in 1992, and was expected to decline further in 1993 owing largely to civil and industrial unrest. Export earnings from agriculture, which accounted for around 40% of total revenue in 1960, had declined to only 12% by 1984. This fall was partly due to the smuggling of coffee (the major agricultural export), with some sources estimating that as much coffee is smuggled as the official production figures. An estimated 92,800 tons of robusta were produced in 1988, of which 59,800 tons were exported, along with a further 8,200 tons of arabica. In early 1990 it was reported that the coffee crop was being seriously threatened by tracheomycose, a fungal disease. Palm oil production averaged 85,000 tons per year between 1981 and 1986 and was a provisional 95,000 tons in 1988, but only a small percentage is exported. The cost of transporting a ton of palm oil down river from Haut-Zaïre to Matadi is as great as the cost to a Malaysian producer of sending the same quantity of palm oil all the way to the end market in Europe—and thus local producers find they are unable to export at competitive prices.

More than 1m. sq km of Zaire's land area is covered by forest (an estimated 6% of the world's woodlands are located in Zaire). However, only a small proportion of this resource is currently exploited. Canada provided considerable technical assistance for the sector during the 1980s, including the preparation of an exhaustive inventory of forest resources. Some 416,500 cu m of logs were cut in 1988, and 107,700 cu m were exported. Government measures in recent years have been aimed at increasing local value added in the sector, as activity has so far been mainly limited to sawing the wood, with only minimal production of veneer and plywood.

INDUSTRY AND MANUFACTURING

Heavy industrial activity is concentrated in the mining sector and in GÉCAMINES refineries in Shaba province. Prior to the decline in copper production of the late 1980s and early 1990s, the Shituru refinery processed about 225,000 tons of copper ore per year and a similar volume was refined 'on toll' in Belgium. In 1990 GÉCAMINES completed a large-scale five-year investment plan to improve copper-mining equipment and related infrastructure. However, GÉCAMINES' copper operation in Shaba suffered severe damage during unrest in the region in 1992–93; rehabilitation costs were estimated at $1,000m. A steel mill was set up at Maluku in 1972, during the era of high commodity prices, but it proved to be unprofitable and was closed down in 1986. A refinery at Muanda for the processing of imported light crude petroleum has an installed capacity of 750,000 tons per year but, in 1986, processed less than 90,000 tons. This low level of activity was attributable both to the sharp fall in world oil prices, which meant that it was often cheaper to import refined products, and also to the Zairean government's own liquidity problems, and the shortage of funds to pay for crude imports. Extensive studies have been made on the conversion of the refinery to treat Zaire's own rather heavy crude, and external funding for the project is being sought.

The manufacturing sector is dominated by consumer goods such as beer, cigarettes and textiles. In 1988 manufacturing contributed just 1.7% of GDP. The sector has been consistently burdened on three fronts; firstly, by the lack of foreign exchange to import badly needed spare parts, secondly, by the continuing decline in domestic purchasing power and finally, by chronic electricity cuts. It is estimated that throughout most of the 1980s, manufacturers were operating at just 30% of installed capacity levels. During 1980–90 manufacturing production increased by an annual average of 2.3%. In 1993, however, manufacturing production was estimated to have declined considerably, with production of cement alone thought to have declined by 28% compared with the previous year.

ENERGY

Zaire's potential for producing hydroelectric power is rivalled on the African continent only by that of Cameroon. Total potential is considered to be 100,000 MW, while the state electricity board SNEL estimated installed capacity in 1987 as 2,486 MW. The country's most ambitious infrastructure project to date (and one which is estimated to account for a substantial proportion of Zaire's foreign indebtedness) is the Inga hydroelectric power project based close to the port of Matadi at the mouth of the River Zaire in the west. This comprises two hydroelectric stations, which in 1986 produced 3,100m. kWh, and a 1,725-km high-voltage power line extending almost the entire length of the country from Inga to Kolwezi in the heart of the mining region. Inga produces some of the cheapest power in the world, but the ZOFI industrial free zone set up beside the power stations with the hope of attracting major heavy industry projects (and in particular an aluminium smelter) has proved unsuccessful, so far attracting only a small number of small-scale industrial operations. In early 1990 a project, funded by France and the African Development Bank (ADB), and worth 390m. French francs, was under way to double the capacity of the high-voltage power line over the section from Inga to Kinshasa. The project also included a new transformer post and the reinforcement of the Inga-2 and Lingwala stations. Other components involve a line linking the urban centres of Kolwezi (in Shaba region), Mbuji-Mayi and Kananga as part of an integrated electricity network. Ironically, numerous small towns and villages situated directly along the path of the power line have no access to electricity supplies. However, there are plans for further low-voltage links. While some grandiose plans, including one to transport power as far as Egypt, are unlikely to be realized, the Inga plant already supplies some power to neighbouring Congo. SNEL is also linked to the grid of the Zambian Electricity Supply Corporation (ZESCO) and the South African company ESKOM has carried out joint studies to optimise this connection with those companies and the Zimbabwean corporation, ZESA. One of ESKOM's strategic objectives is the creation of a southern African grid which could benefit from the energy of the Inga dam. There are supply agreements between Zaire, Zambia and Zimbabwe, and ESKOM provides regular training courses to the technicians and engineers of these three companies. In late 1989, a small hydroelectric power station was inaugurated at Mobayi–Mbongo in Equateur region, on the border with the Central African Republic. In March 1994, construction began on a 15 MW power plant at Katende on the Lulua river, in Western Kasai province. This project and the construction of the Lubilanji II plant in the neighbouring Eastern Kasai region are expected to cost some $33m.

TRANSPORT AND COMMUNICATIONS

Poor transport and communications infrastructure has proved a major handicap to Zaire's economic development. With a small strip of coastline of just 40 km, Zaire has no deep-water port and depends on the port of Matadi, close to the mouth of the River Zaire, for its maritime traffic. Plans to construct a deep-water port at Banana, on the Atlantic coast, were closely connected with the aluminium smelter project, both of which have been abandoned during the economic crisis of recent years. In 1989 Matadi handled 273,300 tons of mineral exports, compared with 53,000 tons sent via the Tanzanian port of Dar es Salaam and 160,000 tons by the 'southern route' through South Africa. However, in recent years, inadequate maintenance and dredging of the port have contributed to a transfer of activity to the Congolese port of Pointe-Noire. Owing to the civil war in Angola, the Benguela railway to the Angolan Atlantic port of Lobito (1,348 km), which offers the shortest rail route to the sea remains closed. At present, the country's main transport route is the Voie Nationale, which runs from Matadi to Shaba. It comprises a tortuous circuit of railway from Matadi to Kinshasa, then river transport from Kinshasa to Ilebo, where goods are loaded once more on to the railway. Use of this route has also dwindled in recent years owing to poor maintenance, fuel shortages and increased regional insecurity. Transport to the north and north-east is possible along the River Zaire, and river traffic is probably the single most important means of transport in the country; the national transport office ONATRA is responsible for almost 14,000 km of waterways. Passenger and freight services operate between Kinshasa and Kisangani, but the vessels are mainly old and poorly maintained and the journey can take weeks. ONATRA has begun to encounter increasing competition from small private shipowners.

The road network is wholly inadequate for a country of Zaire's size: of the estimated 145,000 km of roads only some 2,500 km are surfaced, and most of the road network is in a very poor state of repair. A plan to build a road bridge across the River Zaire to link Kinshasa with Brazzaville, the capital of the Congo, has frequently been raised and the EU has funded feasibility studies. Domestic air services deteriorated rapidly during the 1980s; as a result of Zaire's economic crisis, the national carrier, Air Zaïre, became virtually bankrupt, although by the late 1980s there were signs of recovery. Some relief has been provided by a private carrier, Scibe Airlift Cargo Zaire, which began operations in 1982. Scibe operates services between Zaire's regional capitals and major towns and by 1985 was carrying more domestic passengers than Air Zaïre. Since the early 1990s, Scibe, together with a smaller operator, Shabair, has undertaken services to Europe and South Africa. Telecommunications facilities within Zaire, operated by the state telecommunications concern, ONPTZ, are among the worst in Africa and international lines, apart from those to Brussels and Paris, are erratic. In 1980, when Zaire had an estimated 30,000 telephone lines, the ratio to the population was less than one line per 1,000 inhabitants. By mid-1994 many prominent businessmen and government ministers were using the satellite communications networks provided by two private companies, Telecel and Comcell.

EXTERNAL TRADE

In common with most commodity-producing developing countries, Zaire experienced throughout the 1980s a steady deterioration in its terms of trade, as world market prices for most of its exports failed to keep pace with import price rises. Added to this, the 1980s also brought a massive acceleration in external debt-servicing requirements, making the country's external position even more parlous. Many of the problems now faced by Zaire have their origins in the early 1970s, when commodity prices were relatively high. At that time, following OPEC's first initiative in raising petroleum prices, the international banks found themselves with substantial deposits of 'petro-dollars' and were eager to utilize the funds as loans to developing countries from which they could obtain high rates of interest. With money flowing into the country to support grandiose development projects, such as the Inga hydroelectric station and the steelworks in Maluku, Zaire's import bill rose sharply ($1,579m. in 1974) and a recurrent trade deficit began to accrue, although for several years this was offset to some extent by external borrowing and inflows of foreign aid.

Cushioned by these inflows of funds, the government made little serious effort to regulate the economic situation until the early 1980s. But, as the flow of aid and, in particular, commercial loans began to decrease, the import bill had, perforce, to be cut. Export earnings remained more or less stagnant throughout the 1980s, totalling $2,269m. in 1980, falling back to $1,853m. in 1985 and recovering to $2,138m. in 1990.

A decline in copper production (generated by repeated incidents of looting since September 1991), however, resulted in export earnings of just $988m. for 1993. The trend in imports was similar, with a bill of $1,519m. in 1980, $1,247m. in 1985 and $1,539m. in 1990, again at current prices. The cost of imports in 1993 was estimated to have declined to $610m. Despite the reduction in the volume of trade Zaire still recorded a surplus of $378m. in 1993.

Until the 1990s, the composition of exports remained fairly constant, with minerals accounting for about 80%, of which GÉCAMINES produced more than half (diamonds between 10% and 15%, according to world prices, crude oil about 10% and gold about 1%). By 1993, however, diamonds accounted for more than half of total exports (53.8%), while all GÉCAMINES products represented only 22.7% of the total. Agricultural exports have declined in recent years. Cotton, which was an important source of revenue before independence, is no longer exported, and such output as still exists is used locally. Coffee is the only sizeable agricultural export but its share in export revenue has fluctuated widely in recent years, along with the world coffee market. In 1985, it contributed 9% of export revenue. The following year, it rose to 25% and then declined again to 9% in 1987 and by 1990 accounted for only 4.2%. (In 1993 it increased slightly to 4.5%.) A breakdown of export revenue in 1990 by the World Bank showed copper earning $1,001m., diamonds $240m., petroleum $227m. and coffee $120m. Zaire's principal imports comprise equipment and spare parts, food and beverages, as well as a substantial amount of luxury goods for resident expatriates and the affluent Zairean business community, and crude oil (when the local refinery is operating) or, more often, petroleum products.

As the former colonial power, Belgium was traditionally the dominant trading partner. Approximately 60% of Zaire's exports went directly to Belgium, but this figure included the substantial amount of blister copper refined in Belgium, most of which was subsequently re-exported. Faltering relations between the two countries since 1988 have intermittently halted the flow of trade and assistance. Between 1991 and 1993 the value of Zairean exports to Belgium decreased from 26,400m. Belgian francs to 14,400m., representing slightly more than 40% of the sale of Zairean goods abroad. Over the same period, the value of imports from Belgium also decreased from 6,500m. to 4,400m. Belgian francs, equivalent to just 20.4% of Zaire's total import bill. A 'freeze' on foreign aid and export insurance guarantees, imposed by Belgium and many other Western countries, has obliged Zaire to rely increasingly on trade with South Africa. In 1993 South Africa became Zaire's second largest supplier (South African imports amounted to some $100m.), while Zaire became South Africa's fifth largest African market. The USA is an important trading partner. Its percentage share of exports fluctuates, but can reach 30% or more in years when the US administration replenishes strategic stocks such as cobalt. However, the recent reduction in GÉCAMINES' production capacity may force the USA to consider other suppliers, such as Zambia.

BALANCE OF PAYMENTS AND EXTERNAL DEBT

During the 1980s, the government's extensive deficit spending of the 1970s generated recurrent deficits on the balance-of-payments current account as new sources of external funding evaporated and service payments on debts incurred in earlier years fell due. In 1984, for example, a trade surplus of $742m. was wholly absorbed by outflows on the services account of $1,292m. (more than the country's entire merchandise import bill), against which inflows on services were just $141m., resulting in a deficit of $409m. on goods and services, a current account deficit of $325m. and an overall balance-of-payments deficit of $561m. Net transfers to Zaire were negative between 1984–86, at a total of –$75m. but, following vigorous protests by President Mobutu, a Consultative Group meeting of Western donors in 1987 acted as a catalyst for net transfers totalling $1,092m. between 1987–89, of which $326m. came from the World Bank group, with the African Development Bank, the EU, the USA and Japan also providing balance-of-payments support. Net inward transfers totalled $136m. in 1990. However, the deficit on the current account of the balance of payments still continued to grow, from –$583m. before official transfers in 1985 (and –$399m. net of official transfers) to figures of –$860m. and –$643m. net respectively in 1990. In 1993 the deficit on the current account of the balance of payments was estimated at $400m.

Faced with this rate of economic deterioration and with no local remedies available, President Mobutu became, in 1982, one of the first African leaders to submit his country to an IMF-prescribed austerity programme. In 1983, following IMF and World Bank advice, the Zaire currency was devalued by a massive 77.5%. Subsequent visits by the state commissioner for finance to the 'Paris Club' of official creditors to request reschedulings of the official portion of external debt (accruing to Western governments and Japan) became virtually an annual event, and 'Paris Club' rescheduling agreements were negotiated in each of the years from 1983–86.

Initially, the Zairean government's seeming enthusiasm to fulfil IMF performance targets was favourably viewed by creditors. By 1986, however, following five years of economic austerity, there were few tangible positive results. There was little, if any, real growth in the economy and no improvement in the balance of payments. Net outflows of foreign exchange from Zaire now exceeded inflows into the country and the proportion of export earnings devoted to servicing the external debt was more than 25%. In late October 1986, President Mobutu announced that he would restrict the level of debt-servicing, freezing repayments in some cases, and that he intended to return to a system of fixed parity for the zaire against the Special Drawing Right (SDR) of the IMF. These proposals were not, in the event, fully implemented, although the IMF, concerned not to set a precedent for other beleagured African debtors, agreed, after lengthy negotiations, to revise performance criteria (many of which had been based on the Fund's own over-optimistic estimates of world commodity prices and potential export earnings). In May 1987 a new agreement was signed with the IMF under which Zaire obtained a 12-month stand-by arrangement of SDR 100m., to be disbursed in four instalments against financial performance criteria; a three-year Structural Adjustment Facility (SAF) of SDR 136.8m., with immediate access to a first tranche of SDR 58.2m.; and a compensatory financing facility of SDR 45.3m. to cover the shortfall in foreign exchange earnings until the end of March 1987. This agreement opened the way to a new debt-rescheduling agreement with the 'Paris Club', also in May, under which approximately $880m. of official debt service was rescheduled. In June 1987 the World Bank granted Zaire a Structural Adjustment Loan (SAL) of SDR 134.4m.

Despite the IMF programme of May 1987, the economy continued to deteriorate. From early 1988 onwards, the slow depreciation in the value of the zaire gathered momentum, and between January and May it fell by 26% against the US dollar. Disbursement of the IMF funds was also suspended because Fund officials would not accept the projected deficit in the national budget. By June, Mobutu was, once again, threatening to suspend debt repayments. Failure to reach an agreement with the IMF also made impossible a new debt-rescheduling arrangement with the 'Paris Club', the previous agreement having expired in May 1988. The economic stalemate continued into the autumn, but in early November, with inflation almost up to an annual rate of 100%, Mobutu announced a further devaluation of the currency and a rise in the retail price of petrol, both measures having been prescribed by the IMF.

In early 1989 the zaire was devalued by a further 8.2% and negotiations were reopened with the IMF for the resumption of the SAF first proposed in 1987. As negotiations continued, the EU postponed the disbursement of an ECU 30m. loan to fund vital imports for manufacturers and the agro-industry sector. The World Bank also delayed a credit of $75m. for a major transport rehabilitation project. By early May 1989, relations with the IMF had improved distinctly, although a major obstacle remained in the form of growing arrears on earlier IMF credits. At the end of the month, there was an unexpected announcement that the government had liquidated these arrears, reportedly by means of a short-term credit of $120m. from a Belgian commercial bank. This opened the way to the release in June of the second tranche of the 1987 three-year facility and a new 12-month stand-by arrangement of

SDR 116.4m. Accommodation with the IMF encouraged further loans from other donors and from the 'Paris Club' and the World Bank released the second $82.5m. tranche of the June 1987 essential import loan. The EU also disbursed its ECU 30m. loan. IMF performance criteria were met at the end of June and the end of September. In June 1989 a 'Paris Club' meeting agreed to a rescheduling of debt worth $1,530m. on the 'Toronto Terms' accorded to the poorest countries, while a meeting of the 'London Club' of commercial creditors, also in June, agreed to reschedule $61m. of commercial debt put at around $627m. The political and social deterioration from late 1991 brought all negotiations with the IMF to a halt. As a result all rescheduling talks also ceased. No funds will flow into Zaire for the purpose of structural adjustment or balance-of-payments support until a satisfactory settlement of Zaire's internal crisis has been achieved. At the end of 1992, Zaire's external debt stood at $10,912m., of which $8,895m. was long-term public debt. In 1992 Zaire ceased virtually all payments on its foreign debt: of total debt service due of $3,450m., only $79m. was paid. In February 1994 the World Bank closed its office in Kinshasa, and in June 1994 Zaire was suspended from the IMF. Since the civil disturbances of 1991 private investment has virtually vanished, the country having been declared 'a dangerous if not prohibitive risk' for exporters, investors and bankers by all country risk analysis and export credit guarantee insurance organizations of the OECD countries. Various donors, including Belgium, made it clear that suspension from the IMF could only be ended by the installation of a credible government with a feasible economic adjustment programme and plans to exert greater control over the armed forces and increase the efficiency of the central bank. Hopes for a prompt end to the suspension were encouraged by the announcement in July of the new prime minister's intention to regulate treasury disbursements to available resources, and to consider granting autonomous status to the central bank.

THE DOMESTIC ECONOMY

Between 1968 and 1974, Zaire's real GDP expanded at an average annual rate of 7%, assisted in large part by strong world commodity prices. During the period 1975–80, however, the trend sharply reversed under falling prices for copper, coffee and diamonds, and the impact of Mobutu's 1973 'Zairianization' programme, under which hundreds of industrial, manufacturing and agricultural concerns were expropriated and put under the control of often inexperienced nationals, began to affect GDP performance.

Real growth in 1975 was −6.8%, followed by only marginally better results of −4.7%, −2.3% and −3.0% in 1976, 1977 and 1978 respectively. In 1977, when earlier stabilization programmes elaborated with the IMF showed poor results, Mobutu launched his own proposals for economic recovery. These economic plans, however, were eclipsed by political considerations during the Shaba invasions of 1977 and 1978. By 1981 there were indications of an improvement in the economy and a real growth rate of 2%, although this was more than offset by annual population growth of 2.7%. In December 1982 the decision was taken to embrace fully measures prescribed by the IMF, including the massive devaluation of the zaire in September 1983. Public spending was sharply reduced and by 1984 the budget deficit was down to 3.4% of GDP from 10.5% in 1982. After the 100% inflation rate of 1983, the annual rate had settled at 20% by 1985. Yet, while some basic economic indicators certainly improved, the austerity programme gave rise to a long succession of austerity measures, placing many basic foodstuffs, such as manioc, beyond the reach of the average Zairean. Industry was left working at an average 30% of capacity, hampered by ageing equipment and shortages of spare parts for which no corporate funds existed. Mobutu's decision in May 1986 to raise public sector salaries by 40%, was followed by his announcement in October that he would restrict debt-servicing payments to the IMF. Over the whole year, real growth was a minimal 0.5%. In 1987 there was considerable improvement, with real growth of 2.7%, followed again in 1988 by 0.5%. However, in 1989 it again began to decline with negative growth of 1.3% followed by a real fall of 2.6% in 1990. The unrest of 1991–93 resulted in disastrous growth performance, with GDP estimated to have contracted by at least 20% between 1989 and 1992, and by 7% in 1993.

The last budget to balance was that for 1989. Estimates for 1993 revealed total revenues of $300m., accounting for less than half of primary expenditure ($664m.). However, since inflation, and the economy in general, had become seemingly uncontrollable after 1990, the draft budget exercise had become somewhat academic. In November 1993 the Birindwa government introduced a new currency, the new zaire (equivalent to 3m. old zaires), in an attempt at monetary reform. Nevertheless, in the absence of comprehensive adjustment and stabilization programmes, the measure was unable to stem the erosion of the national currency. The unequal allocation of primary expenditure between the executive and the public sector, and between ministries, was singled out as one major reason for the deterioration of the situation. As a result of a lack of budgetary discipline and of a widespread lack of confidence in the new currency, the value of the new zaire collapsed in a matter of months. Between November 1993 and mid-August 1994, the exchange rate against the dollar decreased from NZ 3 = $1 to NZ 1,400 = $1.

ECONOMIC DEVELOPMENT

Unlike the majority of francophone African countries, Zaire has never pursued conventional five-year economic development plans. The 'Mobutu Plan' of 1977 was somewhat vague in conception and was never published in full. Substantial effort and money were, however, expended on the preparation of a Five-Year Plan which was to run from 1986–90. This was published in many volumes and provided for continued economic growth as well as new infrastructure and industry, such as the aluminium smelter and fertilizer plant in the Inga Free Zone and the deep-water port at Banana. However, prevailing economic conditions have hampered its realization. Although the Plan was not officially abandoned, economic policy in the second half of the 1980s was almost entirely devoted to reducing budget deficits and the level of inflation. In November 1989 a paper presented to the legislature stated that expenditure under the plan to date had only been at an implementation rate of 49%, and referred to the 'ambitious and costly five-year plan and the restrictive programme of structural adjustment'. With the collapse of the giant state mining corporation GÉCAMINES, the progressive substitution of copper by other materials in world industry (and with Chile having opened one of the world's largest and lowest-cost copper mines in 1990), economic activity in Zaire must clearly become more diversified.

There is huge potential both to rehabilitate and expand the agricultural sector, and to tap the country's huge forestry resources. Zaire's population of 36.7m. in 1991 represents a potentially large consumer base and offers great incentives for developing industry and manufacturing. One of the most immediate obstacles to development remains the lack of infrastructure of all categories—road, rail and river transport and telecommunications.

Statistical Survey

Sources (unless otherwise stated): Département de l'Economie Nationale, Kinshasa; Institut National de la Statistique, Office Nationale de la Recherche et du Développement, BP 20, Kinshasa; tel. (12) 31401.

Area and Population

AREA, POPULATION AND DENSITY

Area (sq km)	2,344,885*
Population (census result)	
1 July 1984	
Males	14,593,370
Females	15,078,037
Total	29,671,407
Population (official estimates at mid-year)	
1989	34,491,000
1990	35,562,000
1991	36,672,000
Density (per sq km) at mid-1991	15.6

* 905,365 sq miles.

REGIONS

	Area (sq km)	Population (31 Dec. 1985)*
Bandundu	295,658	4,644,758
Bas-Zaïre	53,920	2,158,595
Equateur	403,293	3,960,187
Haut-Zaïre	503,239	5,119,750
Kasaï Occidental	156,967	3,465,756
Kasaï Oriental	168,216	2,859,220
Kivu	256,662	5,232,442
Shaba (formerly Katanga)	496,965	4,452,618
Kinshasa (city)†	9,965	2,778,281
Total	2,344,885	34,671,607

* Provisional. † Including the commune of Maluku.

Source: Département de l'Administration du Territoire.

PRINCIPAL TOWNS (population at census of July 1984)

Kinshasa	2,653,558
Lubumbashi	543,268
Mbuji-Mayi	423,363
Kananga	290,898
Kisangani	282,650
Kolwezi	201,382
Likasi	194,465
Bukavu	171,064
Matadi	144,742
Mbandaka	125,263

Source: UN, *Demographic Yearbook*.

BIRTHS AND DEATHS (UN estimates, annual averages)

	1975–80	1980–85	1985–90
Birth rate (per 1,000)	47.8	48.3	47.8
Death rate (per 1,000)	17.5	16.4	15.0

Expectation of life (UN estimates, years at birth, 1985–90): 51.6 (males 49.8; females 53.3).

Source: UN, *World Population Prospects: The 1992 Revision*.

ECONOMICALLY ACTIVE POPULATION
(UN estimates, '000 persons, 1991)

	Males	Females	Total
Agriculture, etc.	4,484	4,537	9,021
Industry	2,121	79	2,200
Services	2,371	256	2,627
Total	8,976	4,872	13,848

Source: UN Economic Commission for Africa, *African Statistical Yearbook*.

Mid-1992 (estimates in '000): Agriculture, etc. 9,173; Total 14,173 (Source: FAO, *Production Yearbook*).

Agriculture

PRINCIPAL CROPS ('000 metric tons)

	1990	1991	1992
Rice (paddy)	345*	365	365*
Maize	870*	906	920*
Millet	31	32	32
Sorghum	49	51	53
Potatoes*	33	34	34
Sweet potatoes*	375	377	380
Cassava (Manioc)	17,600*	18,227	18,300*
Yams*	280	300	310
Taro (Coco yam)*	40	42	43
Dry beans	122*	122	123*
Dry peas*	60	62	63
Groundnuts (in shell)	425*	435	440*
Cottonseed*	50	50	50
Palm kernels*	74	75	76
Cabbages*	27	28	29
Tomatoes	40	40*	41*
Onions (dry)*	31	31	31
Pumpkins*	40	42	43
Sugar cane*	1,250	1,180	1,150
Oranges*	153	155	156
Grapefruit*	13	14	14
Avocados*	45	46	47
Mangoes*	208	210	212
Pineapples*	143	145	145
Bananas*	404	405	405
Plantains*	1,800	1,820	1,830
Papayas*	205	208	210
Coffee (green)†	120	102	98
Cocoa beans†	3	3	4
Tea (made)*	3	3	3
Tobacco (leaves)	4†	4	4*
Cotton (lint)*	26	26	26
Natural rubber (dry weight)	15†	11†	11*

* FAO estimate(s). † Unofficial figure(s).

Source: FAO, *Production Yearbook*.

LIVESTOCK
(FAO estimates, '000 head, year ending September)

	1990	1991	1992
Cattle	1,550	1,600	1,650
Sheep	900	910	920
Goats	3,060	3,070	3,080
Pigs	820	830	840

Poultry (FAO estimates, million): 20 in 1990; 21 in 1991; 21 in 1992.

Source: FAO, *Production Yearbook*.

LIVESTOCK PRODUCTS (FAO estimates, '000 metric tons)

	1990	1991	1992
Cows' milk	7	7	7
Beef and veal	27	28	29
Mutton and lamb	3	3	3
Goats' meat	8	8	8
Pig meat	30	30	31
Poultry meat	17	17	18
Other meat	119	122	131
Hen eggs	8.0	8.1	8.2

Source: FAO, *Production Yearbook*.

Forestry

ROUNDWOOD REMOVALS ('000 cubic metres)

	1990	1991	1992
Sawlogs, veneer logs and logs for sleepers	465	391	391*
Other industrial wood*	2,587	2,672	2,759
Fuel wood*	37,766	38,918	40,093
Total	40,818	41,981	43,243

Sawnwood production ('000 cubic metres, incl. railway sleepers): 117 in 1990; 105 in 1991; 105* in 1992.

* FAO estimate(s).

Source: FAO, *Yearbook of Forest Products*.

Fishing

(FAO estimates, '000 metric tons, live weight)

	1989	1990	1991
Inland waters	164.0	160.0	158.0
Atlantic Ocean	2.0	2.0	2.0
Total catch	166.0	162.0	160.0

Source: FAO, *Yearbook of Fishery Statistics*.

Mining

(metric tons, unless otherwise indicated)

	1988	1989	1990
Copper ore*	465,100	440,600	355,500
Tin concentrates*†	1,943	1,642	1,600
Coal‡	123,000	125,000	126,000
Zinc concentrates*§	75,700	72,800	61,800
Cobalt ore*‖	25,400	25,000	20,000
Tungsten ore*‖	20	16	14
Industrial diamonds ('000 carats)‖	15,439	15,092	15,300
Gem diamonds ('000 carats)‖	2,724	2,633	2,700
Silver*§	74	60	84
Gold (kilograms)*‖	3,422‡	2,032	225
Crude petroleum ('000 metric tons)	1,460	1,358	1,410‡

* Figures relate to metal content.

† Data from UNCTAD, *International Tin Statistics* (Geneva).

‡ Provisional or estimated figure.

§ Data from Metallgesellschaft Aktiengesellschaft (Frankfurt).

‖ Data from the US Bureau of Mines.

Source: UN, *Industrial Statistics Yearbook*.

Industry

SELECTED PRODUCTS
('000 metric tons, unless otherwise indicated)

	1988	1989	1990
Raw sugar*	75†	66	70
Cigarettes (million)	5,200†	5,200†	5,200
Jet fuels	12	13	15
Motor spirit (petrol)	32	35	39
Kerosene	27	35	37
Distillate fuel oils	65	71	75
Residual fuel oils	95	92	93
Quicklime‡	100†	100†	100
Cement‡	495†	460†	n.a.
Copper—unwrought:			
Smelter‡	466.8†	442.8†	339.4
Refined‡	202.6	181.9	140.0
Zinc—unwrought†	61.1	54.0	38.2
Electric energy (million kWh)	5,398	6,142	6,155

* Data from the FAO.

† Provisional or estimated figure(s).

‡ Data from the US Bureau of Mines.

Source: UN, *Industrial Statistics Yearbook*.

Finance

CURRENCY AND EXCHANGE RATES

Monetary Units

100 new makuta (singular: likuta) = 1 new zaire (NZ).

Sterling and Dollar Equivalents (31 March 1994)

£1 sterling = 259.8 new zaires;
US $1 = 175.0 new zaires;
1,000 new zaires = £3.849 = $5.714.

Average Exchange Rate (old zaires per US $)

1990 719
1991 15,587
1992 645,549

Note: The new zaire (NZ), equivalent to 3m. old zaires, was introduced in October 1993. The average exchange rate for 1993 was US $1 = 2.51 new zaires.

BUDGET ('000 million old zaires)

Revenue*	1989	1990	1991
Taxation	374	632	6,268
Taxes on income, profits, etc.	113	180	2,105
Domestic taxes on goods and services	65	124	1,071
Import duties	112	285	1,877
Export duties	73	26	293
Other taxes	11	17	922
Non-tax revenue	20	46	786
Total	394	678	7,054

* Excluding grants from abroad ('000 million old zaires): 74 in 1989; 145 in 1990; 1,586 in 1991.

Expenditure	1989	1990	1991
Current expenditure	351	1,054	25,368
Expenditure on goods and services	282	915	23,240
Interest payments	46	83	589
Subsidies and other current transfers	23	56	1,539
Capital expenditure	118	206	3,617
Total	469	1,260	28,985

Source: IMF, *Government Finance Statistics Yearbook*.

BANK OF ZAIRE RESERVES (US $ million at 31 December)

	1990	1991	1992
Gold	42.23	10.25	9.32
Foreign exchange	219.07	182.85	156.73
Total	261.30	193.10	166.05

1993: Gold 11.72.

Source: IMF, *International Financial Statistics.*

MONEY SUPPLY (million new zaires at 31 December)

	1991	1992	1993
Currency outside banks . .	3.6	121	4,693
Demand deposits at deposit money banks	2.0	126	1,618

Source: IMF, *International Financial Statistics.*

CONSUMER PRICE INDEX (base: 1990 = 100)

	1991	1992	1993
All items	2,254	95,344	1,989,738

Source: IMF, *International Financial Statistics.*

NATIONAL ACCOUNTS

Expenditure on the Gross Domestic Product
('000 new zaires at current prices)

	1990	1991	1992
Government final consumption expenditure	773	18,847	1,151,403
Private final consumption expenditure	4,801	113,065	3,643,180
Increase in stocks	-255	-736	-10,998
Gross fixed capital formation .	863	8,633	376,451
Total domestic expenditure .	6,726*	141,739*	5,160,036
Exports of goods and services	621	10,323	n.a.
Less Imports of goods and services	630	10,438	n.a.
GDP in purchasers' values .	6,717	141,624	5,296,370

* Including adjustment.

Source: IMF, *International Financial Statistics.*

Gross Domestic Product by Economic Activity
(million old zaires at current prices)

	1986	1987	1988
Monetary sector:			
Agriculture	25,566.6	43,852.8	59,348.9
Mining and metallurgy . .	66,404.5	78,792.8	131,413.9
Manufacturing	3,452.7	4,409.7	9,977.0
Electricity and water . .	110.6	179.4	24,166.2
Building and public works .	6,432.1	12,041.0	475.2
Transport and telecommunications . .	1,504.8	2,528.9	3,378.0
Commerce	33,309.5	58,076.2	108,300.1
Services	27,795.6	53,460.0	139,478.2
Imputed bank service charge	-591.2	-672.1	-739.1
Sub-total (goods and services)	163,958.2	252,668.7	475,798.4
Import taxes and duties .	4,506.2	9,665.4	31,616.5
Total monetary product (at market prices)	168,464.4	262,334.1	507,414.9
Non-monetary sector:			
Agriculture	31,837.8	58,591.7	103,323.5
Construction	3,113.9	6,020.5	12,083.1
Gross domestic product . .	203,416.1	326,946.3	622,821.5

Source: Banque du Zaïre, *Rapport Annuel.*

National Income
(million old zaires at current prices, monetary sector only)

	1986	1987	1988
Gross domestic product . .	168,464.4	262,334.1	507,414.9
Less: Net transfers abroad of interest and investment income	30,797.6	36,269.7	50,775.3
Net transfers abroad of private income . . .	5,410.1	6,382.5	18,648.6
Gross national product . .	132,256.7	219,681.9	437,991.0
Less: Indirect taxation, net of subsidies	22,993.8	39,763.8	86,831.5
Consumption of fixed capital	8,573.7	12,392.4	17,797.1
National income at factor cost.	100,689.2	167,525.7	333,362.4

Source: Banque du Zaïre, *Rapport Annuel.*

BALANCE OF PAYMENTS (US $ million)

	1988	1989	1990
Merchandise exports f.o.b. .	2,178	2,201	2,138
Merchandise imports f.o.b. .	-1,645	-1,683	-1,539
Trade balance	534	518	600
Exports of services . . .	149	137	157
Imports of services . . .	-895	-922	-908
Other income received. . .	36	28	14
Other income paid . . .	-563	-540	-642
Private unrequited transfers (net) . . .			
Private unrequited transfers (net)	-67	-109	-81
Official unrequited transfers (net)			
Official unrequited transfers (net)_	226	276	217
Current balance . . .	-581	-611	-643
Capital (net)	-8	-60	-222
Net errors and omissions . .	-134	113	105
Overall balance	-723	-558	-761

Source: IMF, *International Financial Statistics.*

External Trade

PRINCIPAL COMMODITIES (UN estimates, million old zaires)

Imports c.i.f.	1989	1990	1991
Food and live animals . . .	63,380	121,824	2,172,956
Beverages and tobacco . .	3,436	6,605	117,812
Crude materials (inedible) except fuels	9,545	18,347	327,252
Mineral fuels, lubricants, etc. .	24,436	46,968	837,761
Chemicals	33,217	63,848	1,138,847
Basic manufactures . . .	68,343	131,365	2,343,137
Machinery and transport equipment	102,706	197,414	3,521,243
Miscellaneous manufactured articles	16,418	31,557	562,877
Other commodities and transactions	2,673	5,137	91,628
Total	324,154	623,066	11,113,531

Exports f.o.b.	1989	1990	1991
Food and live animals	93,541	148,201	2,535,635
Beverages and tobacco	5,071	8,035	137,474
Crude materials (inedible) except fuels	14,087	22,319	381,865
Mineral fuels, lubricants, etc.	36,064	57,138	977,599
Chemicals	49,024	77,672	1,328,924
Basic manufactures	100,866	159,807	2,734,207
Machinery and transport equipment	151,581	240,157	4,108,950
Miscellaneous manufactured articles	24,230	38,389	656,814
Other commodities and transactions	3,944	6,249	106,917
Total	478,409	757,967	12,968,384

Source: UN, Economic Commission for Africa, *African Statistical Yearbook*.

SELECTED TRADING PARTNERS (US $'000))

Imports c.i.f.	1982	1984*	1985
Belgium/Luxembourg	156,600	116,994	176,920
Brazil	n.a.	87,031	150,514
France	53,400	52,293	88,590
Japan	7,400	20,704	39,431
Netherlands	7,700	31,152	41,791
United Kingdom	29,500	24,339	44,259
USA	60,800	73,600	71,302
Total (incl. others)	475,600	658,741	997,067

* Figures for 1983 are not available.

Exports f.o.b.	1981	1982	1985*
Belgium/Luxembourg	521,300	385,100	165,784
France	25,500	68,100	42,018
Italy	400	200	57,676
Netherlands	2,100	1,500	44,579
Switzerland	71,500	60,500	32,971
United Kingdom	13,700	10,700	21,444
USA	10,900	20,100	228,391
Total (incl. others)	685,200	585,700	796,905

* Figures for 1983 and 1984 are not available.
Source: UN, *International Trade Statistics Yearbook*.

Transport

RAILWAYS (Total traffic, million)*

	1986	1988†	1990†
Passenger-km	330	200	260
Freight (net ton-km)	1,785	1,901	1,732

* Figures are for services operated by the Société Nationale des Chemins de Fer Zaïrois (SNCZ), which controls 4,772 km of railway line out of the country's total facility of 5,252 km.
† Figures for 1987 and 1989 are not available.
Source: *Railway Directory and Year Book*.

ROAD TRAFFIC (motor vehicles in use at 31 December)

	1984
Passenger cars	24,253
Buses and coaches	997
Goods vehicles	59,531

Source: IRF, *World Road Statistics*.

INTERNATIONAL SEA-BORNE SHIPPING
(estimated freight traffic, '000 metric tons)

	1988	1989	1990
Goods loaded	2,500	2,440	2,395
Goods unloaded	1,400	1,483	1,453

Source: UN, *Monthly Bulletin of Statistics*.

CIVIL AVIATION (traffic on scheduled services)

	1989	1990	1991
Kilometres flown (million)	7	7	5
Passengers carried ('000)	203	207	150
Passenger-km (million)	506	500	384
Cargo ton-km (million)	60	57	33
Mail ton-km (million)	0	1	1

Source: UN, *Statistical Yearbook*.

Tourism

	1988	1989	1990
Tourist arrivals	39,444	51,422	46,000*
Tourist receipts (US $ million)	7	6	7

* Approximate figure.
Source: UN, *Statistical Yearbook*.

Communications Media

	1989	1990	1991
Radio receivers ('000 in use)	3,480	3,650	3,740
Television receivers ('000 in use)	30	40	41
Telephones ('000 in use)	33	33	34
Daily newspapers	n.a.	5	n.a.

Sources: UNESCO, *Statistical Yearbook*; UN Economic Commission for Africa, *African Statistical Yearbook*.

Education

	Teachers		Pupils	
	1986	1987	1986	1987
Primary*	113,468	n.a.	4,156,029	4,356,516
Secondary†	49,153	n.a.	983,334	1,066,351
Higher	3,280	3,506	45,731	52,800

* The number of primary schools was 10,757 in 1986 and 10,819 in 1987.
† In 1987 there were 507,944 pupils enrolled in general secondary schools, 266,664 pupils enrolled at teacher training institutions and 291,743 pupils attending vocational secondary schools.
1988: Higher education teachers 3,873; Higher education pupils 61,422.
Source: UNESCO, *Statistical Yearbook*.

Directory

The Constitution

From August 1991–December 1992 a National Conference was convened, at which delegates drafted a new Constitution (to be approved by a national referendum). In April 1992 the National Conference declared itself to have sovereign status, and in August 1992 it installed a new Government. In December 1992 a 453-member High Council of the Republic was established as the supreme interim executive and legislative authority, empowered to amend and adopt the new Constitution and to organize legislative and presidential elections. The legitimacy of the High Council of the Republic was recognized by several foreign states. Nevertheless, President Mobutu, who retained control of the armed forces, refused to recognize either the sovereign status of the National Conference or the authority of the High Council of the Republic. In October 1992 Mobutu, abiding by the 1978 Constitution (see below), reconvened the National Legislative Council (which the National Conference had dissolved) and entrusted it to draft a rival new constitution. In September 1993 and April 1994 the adoption of Transitional Constitution Acts provided a constitutional framework for a 15-month transitional period (subject to approval by constitutional referendum) leading to the proclamation of a new Republic in January 1995. National transitional institutions would include the President of the Republic, the unicameral High Council of the Republic-Parliament of Transition (HCR-PT—inaugurated in January 1994) and the transitional Government, to be accountable to the HCR-PT. Presidential and legislative elections were to be conducted before January 1995.

The provisions below relate to the Constitution promulgated on 15 February 1978 (and subsequently amended):

HEAD OF STATE

The President of the Republic is elected for a seven-year term, renewable once only. Candidates must be natives of Zaire and more than 40 years of age.

EXECUTIVE POWER

The programme and decisions of the National Executive Council are carried out by the State Commissioners who are heads of their departments. The National Executive Council is dissolved at the end of each presidential term, though it continues to function until a new National Executive Council is formed. The members of the National Executive Council are appointed or dismissed by the President, on the recommendation of the First State Commissioner (Prime Minister).

LEGISLATURE

The legislature consists of a single chamber, the National Legislative Council; its members are designated People's Commissioners, and are elected for five years by direct, universal suffrage with a secret ballot. Candidates must be natives of Zaire and aged over 25. The Bureau of the National Legislative Council is elected for the duration of the legislature, and consists of the President, two Vice-Presidents and two Secretaries. The members of the National Executive Council have the right and, if required, the obligation to attend the meetings of the National Legislative Council. It meets twice yearly, from April to July and from October to January.

POLITICAL PARTIES

In November 1990 legislation was adopted to provide for the existence of a multi-party political system.

REGIONAL GOVERNMENTS

Local government in each region is administered by a regional commissioner and six councillors. Regional commissioners are appointed and dismissed by the President.

The Government

HEAD OF STATE

President: Marshal MOBUTU SESE SEKO KUKU NGBENDU WA ZA BANGA (assumed power 24 November 1965; elected by popular vote 31 October–1 November 1970, re-elected 28–29 July 1984).

The following Transitional Government was announced by the Office of the President on 6 July 1994. (Kengo Wa Dondo was elected as Prime Minister by the High Council of the Republic-Parliament of Transition in June 1994.)

TRANSITIONAL GOVERNMENT
(September 1994)

Prime Minister: KENGO WA DONDO.

Deputy Prime Minister with responsibility for Institutional Reforms, Minister of Justice and Keeper of the Seals: KAMANDA WA KAMANDA.

Deputy Prime Minister and Minister of the Interior: GUSTAVE MALUMBA M'BANGULA.

Deputy Prime Minister and Minister of International Co-operation: MOZAGBA MBOKA.

Deputy Prime Minister and Minister of National Defence: Adm. MAVUA MUDIMA.

Minister of Agriculture: LANDU WIZINE KAVIDI.

Minister of Arts and Culture: LUKONZOLA MUGNUNGWA.

Minister of Budget: BAHATI LUKUEBO.

Minister of the Civil Service: BOLEONGUE MEKESOMBO.

Minister of Energy: KISANGA KABONGELO.

Minister of the Environment, Nature Conservation and Tourism: KISIMBA N'GOY.

Minister of External Trade: JIBI N'GOY.

Minister of Finance: PAY-PAY WA KASIGE.

Minister of Foreign Affairs: LUNDA BULULU.

Minister of Health and the Family: (vacant).

Minister of Higher and University Education and Scientific Research: (vacant).

Minister of Labour and Social Security: OMBA PENE DJUNGA.

Minister of Land Affairs: MANGUADA GIFUDI.

Minister of Mines: MUTOMBO BAKAFWA N'SENDA.

Minister of National Economy, Industry and Small Businesses: KATANGA MUKMADIYA MUTUMBA.

Minister of Planning: KIAKWAMA KIA KIZIKI.

Minister of Posts, Telephones and Telecommunications: LOMBI PIERRE OKONGO.

Minister of Press and Information: MASSEGABIO ZANZU.

Minister of Primary, Secondary and Vocational Education: SEKIMONO WA MAGOGO.

Minister of Public Works, Territorial Development, Town Planning and Housing: MUANDO SIMBA.

Minister of Social Affairs: SOKI FUANTI EYENGA.

Minister of Sports and Leisure: BOPASSA NJEMA.

Minister of Transport and Communications: GNINDU KITENGE.

Minister without Portfolio: ASEYA MINDRE.

MINISTRIES

Office of the President: Mont Ngaliema, Kinshasa; tel. (12) 31312; telex 21368.

Office of the Prime Minister: Hôtel du Conseil Exécutif, ave des 3Z, Kinshasa-Gombe; tel. (12) 30892.

Ministry of Agriculture: BP 8722, Kinshasa-Gombe; tel. (12) 31821.

Ministry of Arts and Culture: BP 8541, Kinshasa 1; tel. (12) 31005.

Ministry of the Environment, Nature Conservation and Tourism: 15 ave de la Clinique, BP 1248, Kinshasa; tel. (12) 31252.

Ministry of Finance: blvd du 30 juin, BP 12997, Kinshasa-Gombe; tel. (12) 31197; telex 21161.

Ministry of Foreign Affairs and International Co-operation: BP 7100, Kinshasa-Gombe; tel. (12) 32450; telex 21364.

Ministry of Health and the Family: BP 3088, Kinshasa-Gombe; tel. (12) 31750.

Ministry of Higher and University Education and Scientific Research: ave Colonel Tshatshi, Kinshasa-Gombe; tel. (12) 32074; telex 21394.

Ministry of Justice: BP 3137, Kinshasa-Gombe; tel. (12) 32432.

Ministry of Labour and Social Security: blvd du 30 juin, Kinshasa-Gombe; tel. (12) 26727.

Ministry of National Economy, Industry and Small Businesses: Immeuble ONATRA, BP 8500, Kinshasa-Gombe; tel. (12) 22945; telex 21232.

Ministry of Planning: BP 9378, Kinshasa 1; tel. (12) 31346; telex 21781.

Ministry of Posts, Telephones and Telecommunications: BP 800, Kinshasa-Gombe; tel. (12) 24854; telex 21403.

Ministry of Press and Information: BP 3171, Kinshasa; tel. (12) 23171.

Ministry of Primary, Secondary and Vocational Education: ave des Ambassadeurs, BP 32, Kinshasa-Gombe; tel. (12) 30098; telex 21460.

Ministry of Public Works, Territorial Development, Town Planning and Housing: BP 26, Kinshasa-Gombe; tel. (12) 30578.

Ministry of Transport and Communications: Immeuble ONATRA, BP 3304, Kinshasa-Gombe; tel. (12) 23660; telex 21404.

NATIONAL SECURITY COUNCIL

The National Security Council (NSC) comprises the First State Commissioner, the State Commissioners for Foreign Affairs, Defence, Justice, the Administrators-General of the National Research and Investigations Centre (CNRI) and the National Intelligence Service (SNI), the President's special adviser on security matters, and the Chiefs of Staff of the Zairean armed forces and the national Gendarmerie. A Security Committee and a Secretariat were established within the NSC in May 1982.

President

At the presidential election which took place on 28 and 29 July 1984, President Mobutu Sese Seko, the sole candidate, obtained 14,885,977 (99.16%) of the total of 15,012,078 votes cast. President Mobutu remained in office beyond the expiry of his presidential mandate in December 1991.

Legislature

HIGH COUNCIL OF THE REPUBLIC-PARLIAMENT OF TRANSITION

A National Conference, convened from August 1991–December 1992, legislated to abolish the former National Legislative Council and replace it with a 453-member High Council of the Republic (HCR), an action which President Mobutu refused to sanction. In September 1993, adoption of a constitutional text for transition provided for the installation of the High Council of the Republic-Parliament of Transition (HCR-PT), a unicameral transitional parliament formed by the merger of the former National Legislative Council and the HCR, and inaugurated in January 1994 for a 15-month period (see Recent History).

President of the High Council of the Republic-Parliament of Transition: Most Rev. LAURENT MONSENGWO PASINYA, Archbishop of Kisangani.

Regional Governments

Local government in each region is administered by a regional commissioner and six councillors. In October 1982 the first of a number of regional assemblies, with limited powers, was installed in Kinshasa.

Governor of Kinshasa: BERNADIN MUNGUL DIAKA.

Region	Commissioners
Bandundu	Brig.-Gen. AMELA LOTI BAGATI
Bas-Zaïre	THSALA MWANA
Equateur	SAMPASSA KAWETA MILOMBE, KISANGA KABONGELO
Haut-Zaïre	NOMBEYA BOSONGO (suspended Oct. 1993)
Kasaï Occidental	TSHIBUABUA KAPIA KALUBI
Kasaï Oriental	BACHALA KAMTUA MILANDU
Kivu*	NDALA KASHALA, KAKULE MBAKE
Shaba	GABRIEL KYUNGU WA KUMWANZA

* Divided into three regions in May 1988.

Political Organizations

A multi-party political system was introduced in November 1990; previously the Mouvement populaire de la révolution had been the sole legal political organization. Prominent organizations include the following:

Alliance des republicains pour le développement et le progrès (ARDP): Mogadishu; f. 1994; Chair. JOHN MILALA MBONO-MBUE; Sec.-Gen. MATAMO KUAKA.

Forces politiques du conclave (FPC): Mogadishu, f. 1993; alliance of pro-Mobutu groups, led by MPR.

Katanga Gendarmes: based in Angola; guerrilla group which aims to win independence for the province of Shaba (formerly Katanga).

Mouvement national du Congo (MNC): Mogadishu; f. 1994; coalition of seven parties, including the Parti lumumbiste unifié (PALU), supporting the aims of the fmr Prime Minister, Patrice Lumumba; Chair. (vacant).

Mouvement populaire de la révolution (MPR): Palais du Peuple, angle ave des Huileries et ave Kasa-Vubu, Kinshasa; tel. (12) 22541; f. 1967; sole legal political party until Nov. 1990; advocates national unity and African socialism; opposes tribalism; Chair. Marshal MOBUTU SESE SEKO; Sec.-Gen. KITHIMA BIN RAMAZANI.

Parti démocrate et social chrétien (PDSC): f. 1990; moderate; Pres. JOSEPH ILÉO NSONGO AMBA.

Parti démocrate et social chrétien national (PDSCN): Mogadishu; f. 1994; moderate.

Parti des nationalistes pour le développement integral (PANADI): Mogadishu; f. 1994; Leader BALTAZAR HOUNGANGERA.

Parti de la révolution populaire (PRP): Brussels, Belgium; maintains guerrilla presence in southern Kivu region; Leader LAURENT KABILA.

Parti ouvrier et paysan du Congo (POP): f. 1986; Marxist-Leninist.

Rassemblement des démocrates libérals: Kinshasa; Leader MWAMBA MULANDA.

Sacré alliance pour le dialogue (SAD): Mogadishu; f. 1993; alliance of 10 political groups; Leader Gen. NATHANIEL MBUMBA.

Union des fédéralistes et républicains indépendants (UFERI): Kinshasa; f. 1990; separatist; Pres. NGUZA KARL-I-BOND.

Union pour la démocratie et le progrès social (UDPS): Kinshasa; f. 1982; Leader ETIENNE TSHISEKEDI WA MULUMBA.

Union pour la démocratie et le progrès social national: Mogadishu; f. 1994; Chair. CHARLES DEOUNKIN ANDEL.

Union pour la république et la démocratie (URD): Mogadishu; moderate party expelled from USOR in May 1994; Chair. BERNARD KAMANDA WA KAMANDA.

Union sacrée de l'opposition radicale (USOR): Kinshasa; f. July 1991; comprises c. 130 movements and factions opposed to Pres. Mobutu; led by the UDPS.

Union sacrée rénovée: Kinshasa; f. 1993 by several ministers in Govt of Nat. Salvation; Leader KIRO KIMATE.

Diplomatic Representation

EMBASSIES IN ZAIRE

Algeria: 50/52 ave Colonel Ebeya, BP 12798, Kinshasa; tel. (12) 22470; Chargé d'affaires a.i.: HOCINE MEGHLAOUI.

Angola: 4413–4429 blvd du 30 juin, BP 8625, Kinshasa; tel. (12) 32415; Ambassador: MIGUEL GASPARD NETO.

Argentina: 181 blvd du 30 juin, BP 16798, Kinshasa; tel. (12) 25485; Ambassador: WERNER ROBERTO JUSTO BURGHARDT.

Austria: 39 ave Lubefu, BP 16399, Kinshasa-Gombe; tel. (12) 22150; telex 21310; Ambassador: Dr HANS KOGLER.

Belgium: Immeuble Le Cinquantenaire, place du 27 octobre, BP 899, Kinshasa; tel. (12) 20110; telex 21114; fax 22120; Ambassador: JEAN COENE.

Benin: 3990 ave des Cliniques, BP 3265, Kinshasa-Gombe; tel. (12) 33156; Ambassador: PIERRE DÉSIRÉ SADELER.

Brazil: 190 ave Basoko, BP 13296, Kinshasa; tel. (12) 21781; telex 21515; Ambassador: AYRTON G. DIEGUEZ.

Burundi: 17 ave de la Gombe, BP 1483, Kinshasa; tel. (12) 31588; telex 21655; Ambassador: LONGIN KANUMA.

Cameroon: 171 blvd du 30 juin, BP 10998, Kinshasa; tel. (12) 34787; Chargé d'affaires a.i.: DOMINIQUE AWONO ESSAMA.

Canada: BP 8341, Kinshasa I; tel. (12) 21801; telex 21303; Ambassador: CLAUDE LAVERDURE.

Central African Republic: 11 ave Pumbu, BP 7769, Kinshasa; tel. (12) 30417; Ambassador: J.-G. MAMADOU.

Chad: 67–69 ave du Cercle, BP 9097, Kinshasa; tel. (12) 22358; Ambassador: MAITINE DJOUMBE.

China, People's Republic: 49 ave du Commerce, BP 9098, Kinshasa; tel. 23972; Ambassador: AN GUOZHENG.

Congo: 179 blvd du 30 juin, BP 9516, Kinshasa; tel. (12) 30220; Ambassador: ALEXIS OKIO.

Côte d'Ivoire: 68 ave de la Justice, BP 9197, Kinshasa; tel. (12) 30440; telex 21214; Ambassador: GASTON ALLOUKO FIANKAN.

Cuba: 4660 ave Cateam, BP 10699, Kinshasa; telex 21158; Ambassador: ENRIQUE MONTERO.

Czech Republic: 54 ave Colonel Tshatshi, BP 8242, Kinshasa-Gombe; tel. (12) 34610; telex 21183.

Egypt: 519 ave de l'Ouganda, BP 8838, Kinshasa; tel. (12) 30296; Ambassador: AZIZ ABDEL HAMID HAMZA.

Ethiopia: BP 8435, Kinshasa; tel. (12) 23327; Ambassador: Col LEGESSE WOLDE-MARIAM.

France: 97 ave de la République du Tchad, BP 3093, Kinshasa; tel. (12) 25566; telex 21074; Ambassador: JACQUES DEPAYGNE.

Gabon: ave du 24 novembre, BP 9592, Kinshasa; tel. (12) 68325; telex 21455; Ambassador: JOSEPH KOUMBA MOUNGUENGUI.

Germany: 82 ave des 3Z, BP 8400, Kinshasa-Gombe; tel. (12) 21528; telex 21110; fax (12) 21527; Ambassador: DIETRICH VENZLAFF.

Ghana: 206 ave du 24 novembre, BP 8446, Kinshasa; tel. (12) 31766; Ambassador: KWAKU ADU BEDIAKO.

Greece: 72 ave des 3Z, BP 478, Kinshasa; tel. (12) 33169; Ambassador: STELIO VALSAMAS-RHALLIS.

Guinea: 7–9 ave Lubefu, BP 9899, Kinshasa; tel. (12) 30864; Ambassador: FÉLIX FABER.

Holy See: 81 ave Goma, BP 3091, Kinshasa; tel. (12) 33128; telex 21527; Apostolic Nuncio: Mgr FAUSTINO SAINZ MUÑOZ, Titular Archbishop of Novaliciana.

India: 188 ave des Batétéla, BP 1026, Kinshasa; tel. (12) 33368; telex 21179; Ambassador: ARUN KUMAR.

Iran: 76 blvd du 30 juin, BP 16599, Kinshasa; tel. (12) 31052; telex 21429.

Israel: 12 ave des Aviateurs, BP 8343, Kinshasa; tel. (12) 21955; Ambassador: SHLOMO AVITAL.

Italy: 8 ave de la Mongala, BP 1000, Kinshasa; tel. (12) 23416; telex 21560; Ambassador: VITTORIO AMEDEO FARINELLI.

Japan: Immeuble Marsavco, 2e étage, ave Col Lusaka, BP 1810, Kinshasa; tel. (12) 22118; telex 21227; Ambassador: KYOICHI OMURA.

Kenya: 5002 ave de l'Ouganda, BP 9667, Kinshasa; tel. (12) 30117; telex 21359; Ambassador: MWABILI KISAKA.

Korea, Democratic People's Republic: 168 ave de l'Ouganda, BP 16597, Kinshasa; tel. (12) 31566; Ambassador: YI HYON SIK.

Korea, Republic: 2A ave des Orangers, BP 628, Kinshasa; tel. (12) 31022; Ambassador: CHUN SOON-KYU.

Kuwait: Suite 232, Intercontinental Hotel, Kinshasa.

Lebanon: 3 ave de l'Ouganda, Kinshasa; tel. (12) 32682; telex 21423; Ambassador: MUSTAFA HOREIBE.

Liberia: 3 ave de l'Okapi, BP 8940, Kinshasa; tel. (12) 82289; telex 21205; Ambassador: JALLA D. LANSANAH.

Libya: BP 9198, Kinshasa.

Mauritania: BP 16397, Kinshasa; tel. (12) 59575; telex 21380; Ambassador: Lt-Col M'BARECK OULD BOUNA MOKHTAR.

Morocco: 4497 ave Lubefu, BP 912, Kinshasa; tel. (12) 30255; Ambassador: ABOUBKEUR CHERKAOUI.

Netherlands: 11 ave Zongo Ntolo, BP 10299, Kinshasa; tel (12) 30733; Chargé d'affaires: J. G. WILBRENNINCK.

Nigeria: 141 blvd du 30 juin, BP 1700, Kinshasa; tel. (12) 33344; Ambassador: Col DAG WILCOX.

Pakistan: Kinshasa; Chargé d'affaires: SHAFQAT ALI SHAIKH.

Poland: 63 ave de la Justice, BP 8553, Kinshasa; tel. (12) 33349; telex 21057; Ambassador: ANDRZEJ M. LUPINA.

Portugal: 270 ave des Aviateurs, BP 7775, Kinshasa; tel. (12) 24010; telex 221328; Ambassador: LUÍS DE VASCONCELOS PIMENTEL QUARTIN BASTOS.

Romania: 5 ave de l'Ouganda, BP 2242, Kinshasa; tel. (12) 33127; telex 21316; Ambassador: EMINESCU DRAGOMIR.

Russia: 80 ave de la Justice, BP 1143, Kinshasa I; tel. (12) 33157; telex 21690; Ambassador: YURI SPIRINE.

Rwanda: 50 ave de la Justice, BP 967, Kinshasa; tel. (12) 30327; telex 21612; Ambassador: ANTOINE NYILINKINDI.

Spain: Immeuble de la Communauté Hellénique, 4e étage, blvd du 30 juin, BP 8036, Kinshasa; tel. (12) 21881; telex 21401; Ambassador: ANTONIO LÓPEZ MARTÍNEZ.

Sudan: 83 ave des Treis, BP 7347, Kinshasa; Ambassador: MUBARAK ADAM HADI.

Sweden: 89 ave des 3Z, BP 11096, Kinshasa; tel. (12) 33201; Chargé d'affaires a.i.: L. EKSTRÖM.

Switzerland: 654 ave Colonel Tshatshi, BP 8724, Kinshasa I; tel. (12) 34243; fax (12) 34246; Ambassador: WILHELM SCHMID.

Togo: 3 ave de la Vallée, BP 10197, Kinshasa; tel. (12) 30666; telex 21388; Ambassador: MAMA GNOFAM.

Tunisia: ave du Cercle, BP 1498, Kinshasa; tel. (12) 31632; telex 21171; Ambassador: ABDEL KRIM MOUSSA.

Turkey: 18 ave Pumbu, BP 7817, Kinshasa; tel. (12) 32869; Ambassador: SALIH DILER.

Uganda: 177 ave Tombalbaye, BP 1086, Kinshasa; tel. (12) 22740; telex 21618; Ambassador: Dr AJEAN.

United Kingdom: ave des 3Z, Kinshasa; tel. (12) 34775; telex 21689; Chargé d'affaires: J. G. LINDSAY.

USA: 310 ave des Aviateurs, BP 697, Kinshasa; tel. (12) 21532; telex 21405; fax 21232; Chargé d'affaires: JOHN YATES.

Yugoslavia: 112 quai de l'Etoile, BP 619, Kinshasa; tel. (12) 32325; Ambassador: (vacant).

Zambia: 54–58 ave de l'Ecole, BP 1144, Kinshasa; tel. (12) 23038; telex 21209; Ambassador: C. K. C. KAMWANA.

Judicial System

A Justice Department, under the control of the State Commissioner for Justice, is responsible for the organization and definition of competence of the judiciary; civil, penal and commercial law and civil and penal procedures; the status of persons and property; the system of obligations and questions pertaining to Zairean nationality; international private law; status of magistrates; organization of the lawyers' profession, counsels for the defence, notaries and of judicial auxiliaries; supervision of cemeteries, non-profit-making organizations, cults and institutions working in the public interest; the operation of penitentiaries; confiscated property.

There is a Supreme Court in Kinshasa, and there are also nine Courts of Appeal and 36 County Courts.

President of the Supreme Court: KAMANDA WA KAMANDA.

Procurator-General of the Republic: MONGULU T'APANGANE.

Courts of Appeal

Bandundu: Pres. MUNONA NTAMBAMBILANJI.

Bukavu: Pres. TINKAMANYIRE BIN NDIGEBA.

Kananga: Pres. MATONDO BWENTA.

Kinshasa: Pres. KALONDA KELE OMA.

Kisangani: Pres. MBANGAMA KABUNDI.

Lubumbashi: Pres. BOKONGA W'ANZANDE.

Matadi: Pres. TSHIOVO LUMAMBI.

Mbandaka: Pres. MAKUNZA WA MAKUNZA.

Mbuji-Mayi: Pres. LUAMBA BINDU.

Religion

Many of Zaire's inhabitants follow traditional Zairean beliefs, which are mostly animistic. A large proportion of the population is Christian, predominantly Roman Catholic.

In 1971 new national laws officially recognized the Roman Catholic Church, the Protestant (ECZ) Church and the Kimbanguist Church. The Muslim and Jewish faiths and the Greek Orthodox Church were granted official recognition in 1972.

CHRISTIANITY

The Roman Catholic Church

Zaire comprises six archdioceses and 41 dioceses. At 31 December 1992 there were an estimated 19,805,962 adherents in the country.

Bishops' Conference: Conférence Episcopale du Zaïre, BP 3258, Kinshasa-Gombe; tel. (12) 30082; telex 21571; f. 1981; Pres. Rt Rev. FAUSTIN NGABU, Bishop of Goma.

Archbishop of Bukavu: (vacant), Archevêché, BP 3324, Bukavu; tel. 2707.

Archbishop of Kananga: Most Rev. MARTIN-LÉONARD BAKOLE WA ILUNGA, Archevêché, BP 70, Kananga; tel. 2477.

Archbishop of Kinshasa: Cardinal FRÉDÉRIC ETSOU-NZABI-BAMUNGWABI, Archevêché, ave de l'Université, BP 8431, Kinshasa 1; tel. (12) 78762.

Archbishop of Kisangani: Most Rev. LAURENT MONSENGWO PASINYA, Archevêché, ave Mpolo 10B, BP 505, Kisangani; tel. 211404.

Archbishop of Lubumbashi: Most Rev. EUGÈNE KABANGA SONGASONGA, Archevêché, BP 72, Lubumbashi; tel. (2) 21442.

Archbishop of Mbandaka-Bikoro: JOSEPH KUMUONDALA MBIMBA, Archevêché, BP 1064, Mbandaka; tel. 2234.

The Anglican Communion

The Church of the Province of Zaire comprises five dioceses.

Archbishop of the Province of Zaire and Bishop of Boga-Zaïre: Most Rev. BYANKYA NJOGO, c/o POB 21285, Nairobi, Kenya.

Bishop of Bukavu: Rt Rev. JEAN BALUFUGA DIROKPA, BP 2876, Bukavu.

Bishop of Kisangani: Rt Rev. SYLVESTRE TIBEFA MUGERA, BP 861, Kisangani.

Bishop of Nord Kivu: Rt Rev. METHUSELA MUNZENDA MUSUBAHO, BP 322, Butembo.

Bishop of Shaba: Rt Rev. EMMANUEL KOLINI MBONA, c/o United Methodist Church, POB 22037, Kitwe, Zambia.

Kimbanguist

Eglise de Jésus Christ sur la Terre par le Prophète Simon Kimbangu: BP 7069, Kinshasa; tel. (12) 68944; telex 21315; f. 1921 (officially established 1959); c. 5m. mems (1985); Spiritual Head HE DIANGIENDA KUNTIMA; Sec.-Gen. Rev. LUNTADILLA.

Protestant Churches

Eglise du Christ au Zaïre (ECZ): ave de la Justice (face no. 75), BP 4938, Kinshasa-Gombe; f. 1902 (as Zaire Protestant Council); a co-ordinating org. for all the Protestant churches, with the exception of the Kimbanguist Church; 62 mem. communities and a regional org. in each of Zaire's admin. regions; c. 10m. mems (1982); Pres. Bishop BOKELEALE ITOFO; includes:

Communauté Baptiste du Zaïre-Ouest: BP 4728, Kinshasa 2; f. 1970 (as Eglise Baptiste du Congo-Ouest); 450 parishes; 170,000 mems (1985); Gen. Sec. Rev. LUSAKWENO-VANGU.

Communauté des Disciples du Christ: BP 178, Mbandaka; tel. 31062; telex 21742; f. 1964; 250 parishes; 650,000 mems (1985); Gen. Sec. Rev. Dr ELONDA EFEFE.

Communauté Episcopale Baptiste en Afrique: 2 ave Jason Sendwe, BP 3866, Lubumbashi 1; tel. (2) 24724; f. 1956; 1,300 episcopal communions and parishes; 150,000 mems (1993); Pres. Bishop KITOBO KABWEKA-LEZA.

Communauté Evangélique: BP 36, Luozi; f. 1961; 50 parishes; 33,750 mems (1985); Pres. Rev. K. LUKOMBO NTONTOLO.

Communauté Lumière: BP 10498, Kinshasa I; f. 1931; 150 parishes; 220,000 mems (1985); Patriarch KAYUWA TSHIBUMBU WA KAHINGA.

Communauté Mennonite: BP 18, Tshikapa; f. 1960; 40,000 mems (1985); Gen. Sec. Rev. KABANGY DJEKE SHAPASA.

Communauté Presbytérienne: BP 117, Kananga; f. 1959; 150,000 mems (1985); Gen. Sec. Dr M. L. TSHIHAMBA.

Eglise Missionaire Apostolique: BP 15859, Kinshasa 1, f. 1986; 3 parishes; 1,000 mems.; Apostle for Africa L. A. NANANDANA.

The Press

DAILIES

L'Analyste: 129 ave du Bas-Zaïre, BP 91, Kinshasa-Gombe; tel. (12) 80987; Dir and Editor-in-Chief BONGOMA KONI BOTAHE.

Boyoma: 31 blvd Mobutu, BP 982, Kisangani, Haut-Zaïre; Dir and Editor BADRIYO ROVA ROVATU.

Elima: 1 ave de la Révolution, BP 11498, Kinshasa; tel. (12) 77332; f. 1928; evening; operations suspended by Govt in Nov. 1993; Dir and Editor-in-Chief ESSOLOMWA NKOY EA LINGANGA.

Mjumbe: BP 2474, Lubumbashi, Shaba; tel. (2) 25348; f. 1963; Dir and Editor TSHIMANGA KOYA KAKONA.

Salongo: 143 10e rue Limete, BP 601, Kinshasa/Limete; tel. (12) 77367; morning; operations suspended by Govt in Nov. 1993; Dir and Editor BONDO-NSAMA; circ. 10,000.

PERIODICALS

Allo Kinshasa: 3 rue Kayange, BP 20271, Kinshasa-Lemba; monthly; Editor MBUYU WA KABILA.

BEA Magazine de la Femme: 2 ave Masimanimba, BP 113380, Kinshasa I; every 2 weeks; Editor MUTINGA MUTWISHAYI.

Beto na Beto: 75 ave Tatamena, BP 757, Matadi; weekly; Dir-Gen. and Editor BIA ZANDA NE NANGA.

Bibi: 33 ave Victoria, Kinshasa; f. 1972; French; general interest; monthly.

Bingwa: ave du 30 juin, zone Lubumbashi no 4334, Shaba; weekly; sport; Dir and Editor MATEKE WA MULAMBA.

Cahiers Economiques et Sociaux: BP 257, Kinshasa XI, (National University of Zaire); sociological, political and economic review; quarterly; Dir Prof. NDONGALA TADI LEWA; circ. 2,000.

Cahiers des Religions Africaines: Faculté de Théologie Catholique de Kinshasa, BP 712, Kinshasa/Limete; tel. (12) 78476; f. 1967; English and French; religion; 2 a year; circ. 1,000.

Le Canard Libre: Kinshasa; f. 1991; Editor JOSEPH CASTRO MULEBE.

Champion du Zaïre: Cité de la Voix du Zaïre, BP 9365, Kinshasa I; weekly; sport; Dir and Editor-in-Chief KASONGA TSHILUNDE BOYA YAWUMWE.

Circulaire d'Information: Association Nationale des Entreprises du Zaïre, 10 ave des Aviateurs, BP 7247, Kinshasa; f. 1959; French; business news; monthly; circ. 1,000.

Conseiller Comptable: Immeuble SNCZ, 17 ave du Port, BP 308, Kinshasa; f. 1974; French; public finance and taxation; quarterly; circ. 1,000.

Le Courrier du Zaïre: aut. no 04/DIMOPAP 0018/84, 101 Lukolela, Kinshasa; weekly; Editor NZONZILA NDONZUAU.

Cultures au Zaïre et en Afrique: BP 16706, Kinshasa; f. 1973; French and English; quarterly.

Dionga: Immeuble Amassio, 2 rue Dirna, BP 8031, Kinshasa; monthly.

Documentation et Informations Africaines (DIA): BP 2598, Kinshasa I; 3 a week; Roman Catholic; circ. 650.

Documentation et Informations Protestantes (DIP): Eglise du Christ au Zaïre, BP 4938, Kinshasa-Gombe; French and English; religion.

L'Entrepreneur: Association Nationale des Entreprises du Zaire, 10 ave des Aviateurs, BP 7247, Kinshasa; tel. (12) 22286; f. 1978; French; business news; quarterly.

Etudes d'Histoire Africaine: National University of Zaire, BP 1825, Lubumbashi; f. 1970; French and English; history; annually; circ. 1,000.

Etudes Zaïroises: c/o Institut National d'Etudes Politiques, BP 2307, Kinshasa I; f. 1961; quarterly.

Horizons 80: Société Zaïroise d'Edition et d'Information, BP 9839, Kinshasa; economy; weekly.

JUA: BP 1613, Bukavu, Kivu; weekly; Dir and Editor MUTIRI WA BASHARA.

Les Kasaï: 161 9e rue, BP 575, Kinshasa/Limete; weekly; Editor NSENGA NDOMBA.

Kin-Média: BP 15808, Kinshasa I; monthly; Editor ILUNGA KASAMBAY.

KYA: 24 ave de l'Equateur, BP 7853, Kinshasa-Gombe; tel. (12) 27502; f. 1984; weekly for Bas-Zaïre; Editor SASSA KASSA YI KIBOBA.

Maadini: Generale des Carrières et des Mines, BP 450, Lubumbashi; quarterly.

Mambenga 2000: BP 477, Mbandaka; Editor BOSANGE YEMA BOF.

Ngabu: Société Nationale d'Assurances, Immeuble Sonas Sankuru, blvd du 30 juin, BP 3443, Kinshasa-Gombe; tel. (12) 23051; f. 1973; insurance news; quarterly.

Njanja: Société Nationale des Chemins de Fer Zaïrois, place de la Gare, BP 297, Lubumbashi; tel. (2) 23430; telex 41056; railways and transportation; monthly.

NUKTA: 14 chaussée de Kasenga, BP 3805, Lubumbashi; weekly; agriculture; Editor NGOY BUNDUKI.

L'Opinion: BP 15394, Kinshasa; weekly; Editor SABLE FWAMBA KIEPENDA.

Presse et Information Kimbanguiste (PIK): ave Bongolo, Kinshasa-Kalamu.

Problèmes Sociaux Zaïrois: Centre d'Exécution de Programmes Sociaux et Economiques, Université de Lubumbashi, 208 ave Kasavubu , BP 1873, Lubumbashi; f. 1946; quarterly; Editor N'KASHAMA KADIMA.

Promoteur Zaïrois: Centre du Commerce International du Zaïre, 119 ave Col Tshatshi, BP 13, Kinshasa; f. 1979; French; international trade news; six a year.

La Revue Juridique du Zaïre: Société d'Etudes Juridiques du Zaïre, Université de Lubumbashi, BP 510, Lubumbashi; f. 1924; 3 a year.

Sciences, Techniques, Informations: Centre de Recherches Industrielles en Afrique Centrale (CRIAC), BP 54, Lubumbashi.

Le Sport Africain: 13è niveau Tour adm., Cité de la Voix du Zaïre, BP 3356, Kinshasa-Gombe; monthly; Pres. TSHIMPUMPU WA TSHIMPUMPU.

Taifa: 536 ave Lubumba, BP 884, Lubumbashi; weekly; Editor LWAMBWA MILAMBU.

Telema: 7–9 ave Père Boka, BP 3277, Kinshasa-Gombe; f. 1974; religious; quarterly; Editor BOKA DI MPASI LONDI; circ. 3,000.

Umoja: Kinshasa; weekly.

Zaïre-Afrique: Centre d'Etudes pour l'Action Sociale, 9 ave Père Boka, BP 3375, Kinshasa-Gombe; tel. (12) 30066; f. 1961; economic, social and cultural; monthly; Editors KIKASSA MWANALESSA, RENE BEECKMANS; circ. 5,500.

Zaïre Agricole: 5 rue Bonga-Equateur, Matonge, Zone de Kalamu; monthly; Editor DIAYIKWA KIMPAKALA.

Zaire Business: Immeuble Amasco, 3986 rue ex-Belgika, BP 9839, Kinshasa; f. 1973; French; weekly.

Zaïre Informatique: Conseil Permanent de l'Informatique au Zaïre, BP 9699, Kinshasa I; f. 1978; French; quarterly.

Zaïre Ya Sita: Direction Generale et Administration, 1 rue Luozi Kasavubu, BP 8246, Kinshasa; f. 1968; Lingala; political science; six a year.

NEWS AGENCIES

Agence Zaïre-Presse (AZAP): 44–48 ave Tombalbaye, BP 1595, Kinshasa I; tel. (12) 22035; telex 21096; f. 1957; state-controlled; Del.-Gen. LANDU LUSALA KHASA.

Documentation et Informations Africaines (DIA): BP 2598, Kinshasa I; tel. (12) 34528; telex 2108; f. 1957; Roman Catholic news agency; Dir Rev. Père VATA DIAMBANZA.

Foreign Bureaux

Agence France-Presse (AFP): Immeuble Wenge 3227, ave Wenge, Zone de la Gombe, BP 726, Kinshasa I; tel. (12) 27009; telex 21648; Bureau Chief JEAN-PIERRE REJETTE.

Agencia EFE (Spain): BP 2653, Lubumbashi; Correspondent KANKU SANGA.

Agência Lusa de Informação (Portugal): BP 4941, Kinshasa; tel. (12) 24437; telex 21605.

Agenzia Nazionale Stampa Associata (ANSA) (Italy): BP 2790, Kinshasa 15; tel. (12) 30315; Bureau Chief (vacant).

Pan-African News Agency (PANA) (Senegal): 44 rue Tombalbaye, BP 1400, Kinshasa; tel. (12) 23290; telex 21475; Bureau Chief ADRIEN HONORÉ MBEYET.

Xinhua (New China) News Agency (People's Republic of China): 293 ave Mfumu Lutunu, BP 8939, Kinshasa; tel. (12) 25647; telex 21259; Correspondent CHEN WEIBIN.

PRESS ASSOCIATION

Union de la Presse du Zaïre (UPZA): BP 4941, Kinshasa I; tel. (12) 24437; telex 21605.

Publishers

Centre Protestant d'Editions et de Diffusion (CEDI): 209 ave Kalémie, BP 11398, Kinshasa I; tel. (12) 22202; fax (12) 26730; f. 1935; fiction, poetry, biography, religious, juvenile; Christian tracts, works in French, Lingala, Kikongo and other languages of Zaire; Dir-Gen. HENRY DIRKS.

Maison d'Editions 'Jeunes pour Jeunes': BP 9624, Kinshasa I; youth interest.

MEDIASPAUL: BP 127 Limete, Kinshasa; tel. (12) 70726; religion, education, literature; Dir LUIGI BOFFELLI.

Les Presses Africaines: place du 27 Octobre, BP 12924, Kinshasa I; general non-fiction, poetry; Man. Dir MWAMBA-DI-MBUYI.

Presses Universitaires du Zaïre (PUZ): 290 rue d'Aketi, BP 1682, Kinshasa I; tel. (12) 30652; telex 21394; f. 1972; scientific publications; Dir Prof. MUMBANZA MWA BAWELE.

Radio and Television

According to estimates by UNESCO, there were an estimated 3,740,000 radio receivers and 41,000 television receivers in use in 1991.

Radio Candip: Centre d'Animation et de Diffusion Pédagogique, BP 373, Bunia; educational broadcasts in French, Lingala, Swahili and six local dialects.

La Voix du Zaïre: Station Nationale, BP 3164, Kinshasa-Gombe; tel. (12) 23175; telex 21583; state-controlled; home service broadcasts in French, Swahili, Lingala, Tshiluba, Kikongo; regional stations at Kisangani, Lubumbashi, Bukavu, Bandundu, Kananga, Mbuji-Mayi, Matadi, Mbandaka and Bunia; Pres. DONGO BADJANGA.

Zaïre Télévision: BP 3171, Kinshasa-Gombe; tel. (12) 23171; telex 21583; govt commercial station; broadcasts for 5 hours daily on weekdays and 10 hours daily at weekends; Dir-Gen. DONGO BADJANGA.

Finance

(cap. = capital; res = reserves; dep. = deposits; m. = million; brs = branches; amounts in zaires)

BANKING

Central Bank

Banque du Zaïre: blvd Colonel Tshatshi au nord, BP 2697, Kinshasa; tel. (12) 20701; telex 21365; f. 1964; cap. and res 50,088.4m. (Dec. 1988); Gov. NDIANG KABOUL; Vice-Gov. MATOMINA KYALA 8 brs, 34 agencies.

Commercial Banks

Banque Commerciale Zaïroise SARL: blvd du 30 juin, BP 2798, Kinshasa; tel. (12) 21770; telex 21127; f. 1909 as Banque du Congo Belge, name changed 1971; cap. and res 37,018,000m., dep. 202,951,000m. (Dec. 1992); Chair. (vacant); Vice-Chair. MICHEL ISRALSON; 29 brs.

Banque Continentale Africaine (Zaïre) SZARL: 4 ave de la Justice, BP 7613, Kinshasa-Gombe; tel. (12) 28006; telex 21508; fax (12) 25243; f. 1983; cap. 90m. (Dec. 1991); Pres. NASIR ABID.

Banque de Crédit Agricole: angle ave Kasa-Vubu et ave M'Polo, BP 8837, Kinshasa I; tel. (12) 21800; telex 21383; fax (12) 27221; f. 1982 to expand and modernize enterprises in agriculture, livestock and fishing, and generally to improve the quality of rural life; state-owned; cap. 5m. (Dec. 1991); Pres. a.i. BAZIN LUKUBIKA DIMBU.

Banque Internationale pour l'Afrique au Zaïre SARL: Immeuble Nioki, ave de la Douane, BP 8725, Kinshasa I; tel. (12) 26910; telex 21355; fax (12) 24774; f. 1971; cap. 60m. (Dec. 1992); Pres. J. C. KAPOTWE; Vice-Pres. T. C. INGRAM; 3 brs.

Banque Paribas Zaïre: Immeuble Unibra, ave Colonel Ebeya, BP 1600, Kinshasa I; tel. (12) 24747; telex 21020; f. 1954; cap. and res 1.4m. (Dec. 1980).

Banque Zaïroise du Commerce Extérieur (BZCE): blvd du 30 juin, BP 400, Kinshasa I; tel. (12) 20393; telex 21108; fax (12) 27947; f. 1947, reorg. 1987; state-owned; cap. and res 5,194m., dep. 12,760m. (Dec. 1988); Chair. and Gen. Man. GBENDO NDEWA TETE; Dirs MAKUMA NDESEKE, N'SA ELONGO; 31 brs.

Caisse Générale d'Epargne du Zaïre (CADEZA): 38 ave de la Caisse d'Epargne, BP 8147, Kinshasa-Gombe; tel. (12) 33701; telex 21384; f. 1950; state-owned; Chair. and Man. Dir NSIMBA M'VUEDI; 45 brs.

Caisse Nationale d'Epargne et de Crédit Immobilier: BP 11196, Kinshasa; f. 1971; state-owned; cap. 2m. (Dec. 1983); Dir-Gen. BIANGALA ELONGA MBAÜ.

Citibank (Zaïre) SARL: Immeuble Citibank Zaire, angle aves Col Lukusa et Ngongo Lutete, BP 9999, Kinshasa I; tel. (12) 20554; telex 21622; fax (12) 21064; f. 1971; cap. and res 152,120.0m., dep. 1,613,301.9m. (Dec. 1991); Chair. SHAUKAT AZIZ; Man. Dir MICHEL ACCAD; 1 br.

Compagnie Immobilière du Zaïre (IMMOZAIRE): BP 332, Kinshasa; f. 1962; cap. 150m. (Dec. 1983); Chair. A. S. GERARD; Man. Dir M. HERALY.

Crédit Foncier de l'Afrique Centrale: BP 1198, Kinshasa; f. 1961; cap. 40,000 (Dec. 1983).

Fransabank (Zaïre) SARL: Immeuble Zaïre-Shell 14/16, ave du Port, Kinshasa 1; tel. (12) 20119; telex 21430; fax (12) 27864; cap. 300m. (1993); Pres. ADNAN WAFIC KASSAR.

Nouvelle Banque de Kinshasa: 1 place du Marché, BP 8033, Kinshasa I; tel. (12) 26361; telex 21304; f. 1969 as Banque de Kinshasa; nationalized 1975; state-owned; control transferred to National Union of Zairean Workers (UNTZA) in 1988; cap. 6,000,000m. (Dec. 1992); Pres. DIANG KABUL; 16 brs.

Société de Crédit aux Classes Moyennes et à l'Industrie: BP 3165, Kinshasa-Kauna; f. 1947; cap. 500,000 (Dec. 1983).

Société Financière de Développement SZARL (SOFIDE): Immeuble SOFIDE, 9–11 angle aves Ngabu et Kisangani, BP 1148, Kinshasa I; tel. (12) 20676; telex 21476; fax (12) 20788; f. 1970; partly state-owned; provides technical and financial aid, primarily for agricultural development; cap. 260m. (Dec. 1992); Pres. and Dir-Gen. KIYANGA KI-N'LOMBI; 4 brs.

Stanbic Bank (Zaïre) SZARL: 12 ave de Mongala, BP 16297, Kinshasa I; tel. (12) 20074; telex 21413; fax (12) 41644; f. 1973 as Grindlays Bank; acquired by Standard Bank Investment Corpn (South Africa) in 1992; adopted current name in 1993; cap. 4.0m. (Dec. 1992); Chair. A. D. B. WRIGHT; Man. Dir J. MURRAY MILLER; 1 br.

Union Zaïroise de Banques SARL: angle ave de la Nation et ave des Aviateurs 19, BP 197, Kinshasa I; tel. (12) 25801; telex 21026; fax (12) 25527; f. 1929, renamed in 1972; cap. 240m. (Dec. 1992); Pres. ISUNGU KY-MAKA; 12 brs.

INSURANCE

Société Nationale d'Assurances (SONAS): 3473 blvd du 30 juin, Kinshasa-Gombe; tel. (12) 23051; telex 21653; f. 1966; state-owned; cap. 23m.; 9 brs.

Trade and Industry

DEVELOPMENT ORGANIZATIONS

Caisse de Stabilisation Cotonnière (CSCo): BP 3058, Kinshasa-Gombe; tel. (12) 31206; telex 21174; f. 1978 to replace Office National des Fibres Textiles; acts as an intermediary between the Govt, cotton ginners and textile factories, and co-ordinates international financing of cotton sector; Exec. Chair. A. KIBANGULA.

La Générale des Carrières et des Mines (GÉCAMINES): BP 450, Lubumbashi; tel. (2) 13039; telex 41034; f. 1967 as state holding co to acquire assets in Zaire (then the Congo) of Union Minière du Haut-Katanga; Chair. and CEO ATUNDU LIONGO; operates the following enterprises:

GÉCAMINES—Exploitation: mining operations; Chair. UMBA KYAMITALA.

GÉCAMINES—Commercial: marketing of mineral products; Chair. DJAMBOLEKA LOMA OKITONGONO; Man. Dir ATUNDU LIONGO.

GÉCAMINES—Développement: operates agricultural and stockfarming ventures in Shaba region; Chair. KANOBANA KIGESA.

Institut National pour l'Etude et la Recherche Agronomiques: BP 1513, Kisangani, Haut-Zaïre; f. 1933; agricultural research; Dir-Gen. Dr BOTULA MANYALA.

Office Zaïrois du Café (OZACAF): ave Général Bobozo, BP 8931, Kinshasa I; tel. (12) 77144; telex 20062; f. 1979; state agency for coffee and also cocoa, tea, quinquina and pyrethrum; Chief Rep. MUNGA WA MBASA; Commercial Dir FERUZI WA NGENDA.

Pêcherie Maritime Zaïroise (PEMARZA): Kinshasa; the sole sea-fishing enterprise.

PetroZaïre: 1513 blvd du 30 juin, BP 7617, Kinshasa I; tel. (12) 25356; telex 21066; f. 1974; state-owned; petroleum refining, processing, stocking and transporting; Dir-Gen. NDONDI MBUNGU KIYAKA.

TRADE ASSOCIATIONS

Association Nationale des Entreprises du Zaïre (ANEZA): 10 ave des Aviateurs, BP 7247, Kinshasa; tel. (12) 24623; telex 21071; f. 1972; represents business interests in Zaire for both domestic and foreign institutions; Pres. BEMBA SAOLONA; Man. Dir LUBOYA DIYOKA; Gen. Sec. MASUDI MUNGILIMA.

Chambre de Commerce, d'Industrie et d'Agriculture du Zaïre: 10 ave des Aviateurs, BP 7247, Kinshasa I; tel. (12) 22286; telex 21071.

TRADE FAIR

FIKIN—Foire Internationale de Kinshasa (Kinshasa International Trade Fair): BP 1397, Kinshasa; tel. (12) 77506; telex 20145; f. 1968; state-sponsored; held annually in July; Pres. TOGBA MATA BOBOY.

MAJOR INDUSTRIAL COMPANIES

The following are some of the largest companies in terms either of capital investment or employment.

Manufacturing and Trading

BAT Zaïre SARL: BP 621, Kinshasa; tel. (12) 20289; telex 20073; f. 1950; wholly-owned subsidiary of British American Tobacco Co Ltd, London; mfrs of tobacco products; Chair. and Man. Dir B. MAVAMBU ZOYA.

Brasseries, Limonaderies et Malteries du Zaïre (BRALIMA): 912 ave du Flambeau, BP 7246, Kinshasa; tel. (12) 22141; telex 21662; f. 1923; cap. 31m. zaires; production of beer, soft drinks and ice; Gen. Man. J. L. HOME.

Britmond: BP 8853, Kinshasa; British-Zaire Diamond Distributors; exporters of rough diamonds.

Compagnie des Margarines, Savons et Cosmétiques au Zaïre SARL (MARSAVCO ZAIRE): 1 ave Kalemie, BP 8914, Kinshasa; tel. (12) 24821; telex 21100; f. 1922; cap. 39m. zaires; subsidiary of Unilever NV; mfrs of detergents, foods and cosmetics; Pres. C. GODDE; 1,100 employees.

Compagnie Sucrière: 1963 ave de Général Bobozo, BP 8816, Kinshasa, and BP 10, Kwilu Ngongo, Bas-Zaire; tel. (12) 20476; telex 21085; f. 1925; cap. 1.2m. zaires; mfrs of sugar, alcohol, acetylene, oxygen and carbon dioxide; Man. Dir B. MICHEL; Gen. Man. B. NKAZI; Dir M. LUVIYZ.

Cultures et Elevages du Zaïre (CELZA) SARL: BP 16796, Kinshasa I; interests in cattle ranches, abattoirs, coffee, cocoa, rubber, oil palm, quinquina plantations and associated processing plants.

IBM World Trade Corporation (Zaire): 6 ave du Port, BP 7563, Kinshasa 1; tel. (12) 23358; telex 21298; fax (12) 24029; f. 1954; sale and maintenance of computers and business machines and associated materials; Gen. Man. MUKADI KABUMBU.

Industries Zaïroises des Bois (IZB): 23 ave de l'Ouganda, BP 10399, Kinshasa; state forestry and sawmilling enterprise.

Plantations Lever au Zaïre: 16 ave Colonel Lukusa, BP 8611, Kinshasa I; telex 21053; f. 1911; subsidiary of Unilever NV; plantations of oil palm, rubber, cocoa and tea; Man. Dir A. J. RITCHIE.

NOVATEX: 29B 16ème rue, BP 8456, Kinshasa; Principal producer of synthetic fibres.

Société BATA Zaïroise: 33 ave Général Bobozo, BP 598, Kinshasa I; tel. (12) 27414; telex 21208; f. 1946; principal shoe mfr in Zaire; Man. Dir JEAN-LOUIS ANTZ; 100 employees.

Société Commerciale et Minière du Zaïre SA: BP 499, Kinshasa; subsidiary of Lonrho Ltd; engineering, motor trade, insurance, assembly and sale of earth-moving equipment.

Société Générale d'Alimentation (SGA): BP 15898, Kinshasa; state enterprise; import, processing and distribution of foodstuffs; largest chain of distributors in Zaire.

Société Zaïro-Suisse de Produits Chimiques SARL: BP 14096, Kinshasa 1; tel. (12) 24707; telex 21463; sales agent for Ciba-Geigy pharmaceutical products.

TABAZAIRE: blvd du 30 juin, BP 42, Kinshasa; cigarette mfrs.

Minerals

Office des Mines d'Or de Kilo-Moto (OKIMO): BP 219–220, Bunia; state-owned; operates gold mines; Pres. ISSIAKA TABU; Sec.-Gen. KAITE MUTIJIMA.

Société de Développement Industriel et Minier de Zaïre (SODIMIZA): 4219 ave de l'Ouganda, BP 7064, Kinshasa; tel. (12) 32511; telex 21370; state-owned; copper-mining consortium exploiting mines of Musoshi and Kinsenda in Shaba.

Société Minière de Bakwanga (MIBA): BP 377, Mbujmayi, Kasaï Oriental; f. 1961; cap. 27m. zaires; 80% state-owned; industrial diamond mining (produces 9m. carats per year); Pres. MUKAMBA KADIATA NZEMBA; Gen. Man. ANDRÉ CASTIAUX.

Société Minière du Tenke-Fungurume: Immeuble UZB Centre, 5ème étage, BP 1279, Kinshasa; f. 1970 by international consortium comprising Charter Consolidated of London, govt of Zaire, Mitsui (Japan), Bureau de Recherches Géologiques et Minières de France, Léon Tempelsman and Son (USA) and COGEMA (France); copper mining; Dir B. L. MORGAN.

Société de Recherche et d'Exploitation des Pétroles au Zaïre (ZAÏREP): BP 15596, Kinshasa; tel. (12) 26565; telex 21528; fax (12) 20468; exploitation of petroleum.

Société Zaïre Gulf Oil: blvd du 30 juin, BP 7189, Kinshasa I; tel. (12) 23111; telex 21462; international mining consortium exploiting offshore petroleum at Muanda.

Société Zaïre Shell: 33/c blvd du 30 juin, BP 2799, Kinshasa; tel. (12) 21368; telex 21271; fax (12) 24388; f. 1978; marketing of petroleum products; Dir-Gen. PETER DU MÉE; 120 employees.

Société Zaïro-Italienne de Raffinage (SOZIR): BP 1478, Kinshasa I; tel. (12) 22683; telex 21119; f. 1963; cap. 11,400m. zaires; oil refinery; Pres. LESSEDJINA IKWAME IPU'OZIA; Dir-Gen. VIERO COGNIGNI; 579 employees.

Zaïrétain: ave Mutombo Katshi, BP 7129, Kinshasa; tin producer.

TRADE UNIONS

The Union Nationale des Travailleurs du Zaïre was founded in 1967 as the sole trade union organization. In mid-1990 the establishment of independent trade unions was legalized, and in early 1991 there were 12 officially recognized trade union organizations.

Union Nationale des Travailleurs du Zaïre (UNTZA): BP 8814, Kinshasa; f. 1967; embraces 16 unions; Pres. KATALAY MOLELI SANGOL.

Transport

Office National des Transports au Zaïre (ONATRA): BP 98, Kinshasa I; tel. (12) 24761; operates 12,174 km of waterways, 366 km of railways and road transport; administers ports of Kinshasa, Matadi, Boma and Banana; Pres. K. WA NDAYI MULEDI.

RAILWAYS

The main line runs from Lubumbashi to Ilebo. International connections run to Dar es Salaam (Tanzania) and Lobito (Angola), and also connect with the Zambian, Zimbabwean, Mozambican and South African systems. In March 1994 an agreement was concluded with the South African Government for the provision of locomotives, rolling stock and fuel, to help rehabilitate the Zairean rail system.

Kinshasa–Matadi Railway: BP 98, Kinshasa I; 366 km operated by ONATRA; Dir M. KITANDA WETU.

Société Nationale des Chemins de Fer Zaïrois (SNCZ): place de la Gare, BP 297, Lubumbashi; tel. (2) 23430; telex 41056; f. 1974; 4,772 km (including 858 km electrified); administers all internal railway sections as well as river transport and transport on Lakes Tanganyika and Kivu; Pres. B. MBATSHI.

ROADS

In 1991 there were approximately 145,000 km of roads, of which some 68,000 km were main roads. In general road conditions are poor, owing to inadequate maintenance.

INLAND WATERWAYS

For over 1,600 km the River Zaire is navigable. Above the Stanley Falls the Zaire becomes the Lualaba, and is navigable along a 965-km stretch from Bubundu to Kindu and Kongolo to Bukama. The River Kasai, a tributary of the River Zaire, is navigable by shipping as far as Ilebo, at which the line from Lubumbashi terminates. The total length of inland waterways is 13,700 km.

East African Railways and Harbours: operates services on Lake Mobutu Sese Seko.

Régie des voies fluviales: 109 ave Lumpungu, Kinshasa-Gombe, BP 11697, Kinshasa I; administers river navigation; Gen. Man. MONDOMBO SISA EBAMBE.

Société Zaïroise des Chemins de Fer des Grands Lacs: River Lualaba services: Bubundu–Kindu and Kongolo–Malemba N'kula; Lake Tanganyika services: Kamina–Kigoma–Kalundu–Moba–Mpulungu.

Zaire Network: services on the Luapula and Lake Mweru.

SHIPPING

The principal seaports are Matadi, Boma and Banana on the lower Zaire. The port of Matadi has more than 1.6 km of quays and can accommodate up to 10 deep-water vessels. Matadi is linked by rail with Kinshasa.

Compagnie Maritime Zaïroise SARL: Immeuble CMZ (AMIZA), place de la Poste, BP 9496, Kinshasa; tel. (12) 25816; telex 21626; fax (12) 26234; f. 1946; services: North Africa, Europe, North America and Asia to West Africa, East Africa to North Africa; Chair. MAYILUKILA LUSIASIA.

CIVIL AVIATION

There are international airports at Ndjili (for Kinshasa), Luano (for Lubumbashi), Bukavu, Goma and Kisangani. There is also an internal air service.

Air Charter Service: Place Salongo, BP 5371, Kinshasa 10; tel. (12) 27891; telex 21573; passenger and cargo charter services; Dir TSHIMBOMBO MAKUNA; Gen. Man. N. MCKANDOLO.

Air Zaïre: BP 10120, Kinshasa; tel. (12) 20939; telex 21156; fax (12) 20940; f. 1961 as Air Congo, name changed 1971; 80% state-owned; domestic and international services to Africa and Europe; Dir-Gen. HUBERT ANDRADE; Pres. YUMA MORISHO LUSAMBIA.

Scibe Airlift of Zaire: BP 614, Kinshasa; tel. (12) 26237; fax (12) 24386; f. 1979; domestic and international passenger and cargo charter services between Kinshasa, Lubumbashi, Bujumbura (Burundi) and Brussels; Pres. BEMBA SAOLONA; Dir-Gen. BEMBA GOMBO.

Shabair: Aeroport de la Luano, BP 1060, Lubumbashi; tel. (2) 25686; telex 550020; fax (2) 24597; f. 1989; domestic and international passenger and cargo services; Man. Dir Capt. S. PAPAIOANNOU.

Zairean Airlines: BP 2111, blvd du 30 juin, Kinshasa; tel. (12) 24624; telex 21525; f. 1981; passenger and freight services and charter flights throughout Africa; Dir-Gen. Capt. ALFRED SOMMERAUER.

Tourism

Zaire has extensive lake and mountain scenery. Tourist arrivals totalled about 46,000 in 1990, generating some US $7m. in revenue.

Office National du Tourisme: 2A/2B ave des Orangers, BP 9502, Kinshasa-Gombe; tel. (12) 30070; f. 1959; Man. Dir BOTOLO MAGOZA.

Société Zaïroise de l'Hôtellerie: Immeuble Memling, BP 1076, Kinshasa; tel. (12) 23260; Man. N'JOLI BALANGA.

Defence

Military service is compulsory. In June 1993 armed forces totalled 28,100, of whom 25,000 were in the army, 1,800 in the air force and 1,300 in the navy. There is also a paramilitary force, the Gendarmerie, of about 21,000. A Civil Guard, numbering 10,000, was created in 1984 and is responsible for security and anti-terrorist operations.

Defence Expenditure: Estimated at 633,563,000m. zaires in 1993.

Commander-in-Chief: Marshal MOBUTU SESE SEKO.

Chief of the Defence Staff: Vice-Adm. LOMPONDA WA BOTENDE.

Chief of Staff of the Naval Forces: Commdr MAMBU NSENGA.

Education

Primary education, beginning at six years of age and lasting for six years, is officially compulsory. Secondary education, which is not compulsory, begins at 12 years of age and lasts for up to six years, comprising a first cycle of two years and a second of four years. In 1987 the total enrolment at primary and secondary schools was equivalent to 53% of the school-age population (males 63%; females 43%). In that year primary enrolment included 58% of children in the relevant age-group (boys 66%; girls 51%). The comparable ratio for secondary enrolment was 17% (boys 22%; girls 12%). There are four universities in Zaire, situated at Kinshasa, Kinshasa/Limere, Kisangani and Lubumbashi. According to estimates by UNESCO, the average rate of adult illiteracy in 1990 was 28.2% (males 16.4%; females 39.3%). In the budget for 1989 a total of 24,291.5m. zaires (6.7% of total expenditure by the central government) was allocated to education.

Bibliography

Abi-Saab, G. *The United Nations Operations in the Congo 1960–64*. London, Oxford University Press, 1978.

Anstey, R. 'The Congo Rebellion', in *The World Today,* April 1965.

Asch, S. *L'Eglise du Prophète Kimbangu.* Paris, Editions Karthala, 1983.

Bezy, F., Peemans, J. P., and Wantelet, J. M. *Accumulation et sous-développement au Zaïre 1960–1980.* Louvain-la-Neuve, Presses universitaires de Louvain, 1981.

Biebuyck, D. *The Arts of Zaire.* 2 vols. Berkeley, University of California Press, 1988.

Bolingo, L. *Droit pénal spécial zaïrois.* Vol. I. 2nd Edn. Paris, Librairie général du droit et de jurisprudence, 1985.

Bontinck, F. *L'évangélisation du Zaïre.* Kinshasa, Saint Paul Afrique, 1980.

Cornevin, R. *Le Zaïre.* Paris, Presses universitaires de France, 1977.

Dupriez, P. *Contrôle des changes et structures économiques au Congo: 1960–1967.* In *Recherches africaines, No. 11.* Paris and The Hague, Editions Mouton, 1970.

Ekwe-Ekwe, H. *Conflict and Intervention in Africa: Nigeria, Angola and Zaire.* London, Macmillan, 1990.

Gérard-Libois, J. *Katanga Secession,* (trans. by Rebecca Young). Madison and London, University of Wisconsin Press, 1966.

Gourou, P. *La Population du Congo.* Paris, Hachette, 1966.

Hayward, M. F. *Elections in Independent Africa.* Boulder, CO, Westview Press, 1987.

Huybrechts, A. *Transports et structures de développement au Congo. Etude de progrès économique de 1900 à 1970.* Paris and The Hague, Editions Mouton, 1970.

Institut de Recherches Economiques et Sociales (IRES). *Indépendance, inflation, développement, L'économie congolaise de 1960 à 1965.* Paris and The Hague, Editions Mouton, 1968.

International Monetary Fund. *Surveys of African Economies,* Vol. IV. Washington, DC, 1971.

Jewsiewicki, B. (Ed.). *Etat indépendant du Congo, Congo belge, République démocratique du Congo, République du Zaïre?* Sainte-Foy, PQ, SAFI Press, 1984.

Kamitatu-Massamba, C. *Zaïre, le pouvoir à la portée du peuple.* Paris, Editions de l'Harmattan, 1977.

Kanza, T. *Conflict in the Congo. The Rise and Fall of Lumumba.* Harmondsworth, Penguin, 1972.

Kronsten, G. *Zaire to the 1990s: Will Retrenchment Work?* London, Economist Intelligence Unit (Economic Prospects Series), 1986.

Louis, W. R., and Stengers, J. *E. D. Morel's History of the Congo Reform Association.* Oxford, Clarendon Press, 1968.

Lumumba, P. *Congo My Country.* London, Praeger, 1963.

MacGaffey, J. *The Real Economy of Zaire.* London, James Currey, 1991.

Mbaya, K. (Ed.). *Zaire: What Destiny?.* Dakar, CODESRIA, 1993.

Moumba, N. *Kinshasa 1881–1981, 100 ans après Stanley: problèmes et avenir d'une ville.* Kinshasa, Centre de recherches pédagogiques, 1982.

Schatzberg, M. G. *The Dialectics of Oppression in Zaire.* Bloomington, IN, Indiana University Press, 1988.

Turnbull, C. M. *The Lonely African.* London, Chatto and Windus, 1963.

Vanderlinden, Huybrechts, Mudimbe, Peeters, Van Der Steen and Verhaegen. (Eds). *Du Congo au Zaïre, 1960–1980, essai de bilan.* Brussels, Etudes du CRISP, 1980.

Vanderlinden, J. *La crise congolaise.* Brussels, Complexe, 1985.

Verhaegen, B. *Rébellions au Congo,* Vol. I. Brussels, Etudes du CRISP, 1967.

Willame, J. C. *Eléments pour une lecture du contentieux Belgo-Zaïrois.* Les Cahiers du CEDAF, Vol. VI. Brussels, Centre d'etude et de documentation africaines, 1988.

Patrice Lumumba—La crise congolaise revisitée. Paris, Editions Karthala, 1990.

Young, M. C. *Politics in the Congo: Decolonization and Independence.* Princeton, Princeton University Press, 1965.

'Optimism on Zaire: Illusion or Reality'. *CSIS Briefing Paper,* No. 50. Washington, DC, Center for Strategic and International Studies, 1985.

Young, M. C., and Turner, T. *The Rise and Decline of the Zairean State.* Madison, WI, University of Wisconsin Press, 1985.

For a detailed study of recent Zairean history, see the annual collection of documents, together with the commentary, published by the Centre de recherche et d'information socio-politique (CRISP), Brussels, starting with *Congo,* 1959.

ZAMBIA

Physical and Social Geography

GEOFFREY J. WILLIAMS

The Republic of Zambia is a land-locked state occupying elevated plateau country in south-central Africa. Zambia has an area of 752,614 sq km (290,586 sq miles). The country is irregularly shaped, and shares a boundary with no fewer than eight other countries. For many years the 'line of rail' extending south from the Copperbelt, through Lusaka, to the Victoria Falls has been the major focus of economic activity.

PHYSICAL FEATURES

The topography of Zambia is dominated by the even skylines of uplifted planation surfaces. Highest elevations are reached on the Nyika plateau on the Malawi border (2,164 m). Elevations decline westward, where the country extends into the fringe of the vast Kalahari basin. The plateau surfaces are interrupted by localized downwarps (occupied by lakes and swamp areas, such as in the Bangweulu and Lukanga basins), and by the rifted troughs of the mid-Zambezi and Luangwa. An ancient rift structure probably underlies the Kafue Flats, an important wetland area to the south-west of Lusaka.

Katangan rocks of upper-Pre-Cambrian age yield the copper ores exploited on the Copperbelt. Younger Karoo sedimentaries floor the rift troughs of the Luangwa and the mid-Zambezi rivers, while a basalt flow of this age has been incised by the Zambezi below the Victoria Falls to form spectacular gorges. Coal-bearing rocks in the Zambezi trough are of this same system. Over the western third of the country there are extensive and deep wind-deposited sands, a relic of periods when the climate was drier and desert conditions in southern Africa were more widespread than at present.

The continental divide separating Atlantic from Indian Ocean drainage forms the frontier with Zaire south of the Pedicle, then traverses the north-east of Zambia to the Tanzanian border. Some 77% of the country is drained to the Indian Ocean by the Zambezi and its two main tributaries, the Kafue and Luangwa, with the remainder being drained principally by the Chambeshi and Luapula via the Congo (Zaire) to the Atlantic. Rapids occur along most river courses so that the rivers are of little use for transportation. The country's larger lakes, including the man-made Lakes Kariba and Itezhitezhi, offer possibilities of water use as yet relatively little developed.

Zambia's climatic year can be divided into three seasons: a cool dry season (April-August), a hot dry season (August-November) and a warm wet season (November-April). Temperatures are generally moderate. Mean maximum temperatures exceed 35°C only in southern low-lying areas in October, most of the country being in the range 30°–35°C. July, the coldest month, has mean minima of 5°–10°C over most of the country, but shows considerable variability. Rainfall is highest on the high plateau of the Northern Province and on the intercontinental divide west of the Copperbelt (exceeding 1,200 mm per year). The south-west and the mid-Zambezi valley are driest, annual mean values there being less than 750 mm.

The ancient rocks of the eastern two-thirds of the country have generally poor soils. Soils on the Kalahari Sands of the west are exceptionally infertile, while seasonal waterlogging of soils in basin and riverine flats makes them difficult to use. Savannah vegetation dominates, with miombo woodland extensive over the plateau, and mopane woodland in the low-lying areas. Small areas of dry evergreen forest occur in the north, while treeless grasslands characterize the flats of the river basins.

RESOURCES AND POPULATION

Zambia's main resource is its land, which, in general, is under-utilized. Although soils are generally poor, altitudinal modifications of the climate make possible the cultivation of a wide range of crops. Cattle numbers are greatest in the southern and central areas, their range being limited by large tsetse-infested areas in the Kafue basin and the Luangwa valley. In the Western Province their numbers are less, but their importance to the local economy is even greater. Subsistence farming characterizes most of the country, with commercial farming focusing along the line of rail. Commercial forestry is important on the Copperbelt, where there are extensive softwood plantations, and in the south-west, where hardwoods are exploited. The main fisheries are located on the lakes and rivers of the Northern Province, with the Kafue Flats, Lukanga and Lake Kariba also contributing significantly. Game parks cover 7.9% of the country.

For many years, the mining of copper has dominated the Zambian economy, although its contribution has declined significantly since the mid-1980s, reflecting price fluctuations on international commodity markets. The country is the world's fifth-largest producer, although it has been estimated that, at current production rates, Zambia's economically recoverable reserves will be virtually exhausted by the year 2010. Cobalt, a by-product of copper mining, has recently gained in significance, and Zambia has been steadily expanding its cobalt production in an attempt to offset falls in copper output. Lead and zinc are produced at Kabwe, although the reserves of the Broken Hill Mine are nearing exhaustion. Coal, of which Zambia has the continent's largest deposits outside South Africa, is mined in the Zambezi valley, although this industry is in need of re-equipment and modernization. Manganese, silver and gold are produced in small quantity. Deposits of uranium have been located, and prospects exist for the exploitation of iron ore. No petroleum deposits have yet been identified. Zambia is rich in hydropower, developed and potential.

Zambia's population density of 10.7 inhabitants per sq km (according to an official estimate of 8,023,000 at 20 August 1991) is low, by African standards, for a state which contains no truly arid area. However, this average figure is misleading, for Zambia is the third most urbanized country in mainland black Africa, with 41% of its population of 5,661,801 at the September 1980 census residing in towns of more than 5,000 inhabitants. Some 78% of the urban population was, in fact, located in the 10 largest urban areas, all situated on the 'line of rail'. Lusaka is the largest single urban centre, but the Copperbelt towns together constitute the largest concentration of urban population (47.1% of the total). While the increasing rate of population growth for the country as a whole (3.7% per annum in 1980–91) is a problem, the sustained influx to urban areas is even more acute as this growth has not been matched by employment and formal housing provision.

There are no fewer than 73 different ethnic groups among Zambia's indigenous population. Major groups are: the Bemba of the north-east, who are also dominant on the Copperbelt; the Nyanja of the Eastern Province, also numerous in Lusaka; the Tonga of the Southern Province and the Lozi of the west. Over 80 languages have been identified, of which seven are recognized as 'official' vernaculars. English is the language of government.

Recent History

ANDREW D. ROBERTS

Revised for this edition by the Editor

In the late 19th century the British government, concerned with maintaining British supremacy at the Cape, was anxious to prevent the Boers, Portuguese or Germans from forming hostile alliances further north. In 1889 it granted a charter to the British South Africa Co (BSA—recently formed by Cecil Rhodes, a South African mining entrepreneur), empowering the company to make treaties and conduct administration north of the Limpopo river. In 1890 the BSA occupied the eastern part of what became Southern Rhodesia (now Zimbabwe), south of the Zambezi river, and meanwhile it had concluded treaties with, and obtained mining concessions from, various African chiefs to the north of the Zambezi. These agreements served to place most of what became Northern Rhodesia firmly within the British sphere of influence.

In 1924 the BSA, which had obtained little profit from exploiting the copper deposits in the territory, transferred its administrative responsibilities in Northern Rhodesia to the British government. A legislative council was established, from which Africans were effectively excluded. During the 1920s intensified prospecting resulted in the discovery of enormous deposits of copper ores in Northern Rhodesia, and by the mid-1930s large-scale exploitation of the region known as Copperbelt was firmly established, using Northern Rhodesia as a vast labour reserve. African trade unions were not permitted, and in the absence of any other means of negotiation Africans formed 'welfare societies' throughout the country. The Federation of Welfare Societies was formed, and two years later reconstituted itself as a political body, the Northern Rhodesia Congress (renamed the Northern Rhodesia African National Congress in 1951). Under the leadership of Harry Nkumbula, it campaigned vigorously but unsuccessfully against British government proposals, supported by the white settlers, for a federation with Southern Rhodesia. In 1953 Northern Rhodesia became part of the Central African Federation (CAF) with Southern Rhodesia and Nyasaland (now Malawi).

Initially the CAF attracted new investment, and the copper-mining industry expanded. The Africans in Northern Rhodesia, however, could claim neither economic nor political advantages from the federation. During the first few years of the CAF the Congress organization sustained a loss of popular support and displayed uncertainty as to its own aims. In 1958 Nkumbula's leadership was challenged by the secession from the Congress of a group of young radicals, led by Kenneth Kaunda, a former schoolteacher. They demanded the dissolution of the CAF and the independence of Northern Rhodesia, under the name of Zambia. The Congress was proscribed in 1959, and Kaunda was imprisoned. On his release, a few months later, he assumed the leadership of the newly-formed United National Independence Party (UNIP). In 1962, following a massive campaign of civil disobedience, organized by UNIP, the British government introduced a constitution for Northern Rhodesia, which would create an African majority in the legislature. UNIP agreed to participate in the ensuing elections, and formed a coalition government with the remaining supporters of Congress. The CAF was formally dissolved in December 1963.

INDEPENDENCE AND THE IMPACT OF UDI

Following pre-independence elections in January 1964 Kaunda formed a government comprising members of UNIP, with substantial control of internal affairs. The territory became independent as the Republic of Zambia on 24 October, with Kaunda as president. The new republic inherited an economy in which great mineral wealth had contributed very little to overall national development, and which was dependent on the massive industrial complex of white-ruled southern Africa. Before independence the government obtained the mineral rights whereby the BSA had exacted massive royalties from the mineral companies. Southern Rhodesia's unilateral declaration of independence (UDI) in November 1965, and the subsequent imposition of international sanctions, stimulated Zambian efforts to reduce dependence on imports from the south: coal deposits were exploited to replace imports from Rhodesia, new hydroelectric schemes were developed, and new communications links were established between the Copperbelt region and the port of Dar es Salaam in Tanzania, notably the Tazara railway, opened in 1975.

The numerous whites who remained after independence were content to accept a minority role, but the relative absence of conflict between black and white in Zambia was largely a result of the substantial wage increases granted to the African miners and other urban workers in the mid-1960s. The far more numerous subsistence farmers, and the many unemployed, however, were neglected. Plans for rural development achieved little success, and failed to halt migration to the towns. Although UNIP was returned to power in 1968, and Kaunda was re-elected as president, popular support for the party had declined.

Zambia gave support to guerrilla opposition groups in Rhodesia and Mozambique, thereby becoming a target for counter-subversion. Violent incidents occurred along the borders with both countries, and there were also outbreaks of internal political violence, particularly in the Copperbelt area. In 1971 Simon Kapwepwe, a former vice-president of Zambia, left UNIP and formed the United People's Party (UPP). The UPP was suppressed, and in December 1972 Zambia was declared a one-party state. Legislative elections took place in December 1973, and President Kaunda was re-elected for a third term of office. A new constitution gave the UNIP national executive committee responsibility for formulating strategies for national political development.

In January 1973 the Rhodesian administration closed the border along the Zambezi for everything except Zambia's copper exports; the government's subsequent decision to divert copper exports resulted in a severe deterioration in the economy, which was compounded, following the outbreak of civil war in Angola in late 1975, by the closure of the Benguela railway. Between 1974–76, moreover, international copper prices declined, and Zambia's revenues accordingly diminished. By the end of the year, despite efforts by the government to encourage agricultural development, there was widespread discontent resulting from high food prices, import restrictions and increasing unemployment. Fears that this unrest was being exploited by external forces prompted Kaunda to declare a state of emergency in January 1976.

In October 1978 Kaunda was nominated by UNIP as sole presidential candidate, following its acceptance of constitutional changes which effectively eliminated all opposition. In December Kaunda was returned for a fourth term as president. During that year Simon Kapwepwe, the former UPP leader, rejoined UNIP; as a recognized leader of the Bemba ethnic group, his support was believed to be vital for Kaunda at a time of acute political and economic instability. There remained, nevertheless, disagreement within UNIP over national policy, and, in particular, concerning Zambia's economic relations with Rhodesia, in view of the worsening economic crisis. In October 1978 rail links with Rhodesia were restored, and an agreement was reached on the shipping of exports via South Africa. Since 1977, however, Zambia had openly harboured members of the Zimbabwe African People's Union (ZAPU) wing of the Patriotic Front, and in 1978 and 1979 Rhodesian forces undertook pre-emptive attacks on ZAPU bases in Zambia, including two air raids on Lusaka. Zambia continued to suffer severe disruption from Rhodesian bombing until the implementation, in December 1979, of an agreement, providing for the independence of Southern Rhodesia, as Zimbabwe, which came into effect in April 1980.

ECONOMIC PROBLEMS AND POLITICAL UNREST

Although an economic recovery was subsequently expected, political dissent increased towards the end of 1980, following a further deterioration in conditions. In October several prominent businessmen, government officials and UNIP members allegedly staged a coup attempt. Kaunda claimed that South Africa had supported the plot, but many of those arrested after the incident were ethnic Bemba (traditional opponents of Kaunda).

In January 1981 the suspension from UNIP of 17 officials of the Mineworkers' Union of Zambia (MUZ) and the Zambia Congress of Trade Unions (ZCTU) prompted a widely-observed strike, and riots. Further strikes occurred in July, in protest at the continuing poor economic situation. The chairman of the ZCTU was arrested in July, along with several other trade union leaders, and was not released until October, when the high court ruled that the detention had been illegal. In 1980–83 several reorganizations of the cabinet and the central committee of UNIP were effected, in an attempt to strengthen party and government administration.

Despite the introduction of unpopular austerity measures, necessitated by Zambia's economic crisis, Kaunda managed to retain a strong following; in October 1983 he was again re-elected president, receiving, as sole candidate, 93% of the votes cast, compared with 81% in 1978. Elections to the national assembly also took place. Shortly afterwards, a campaign (which was to continue throughout that decade) was launched against corruption and inefficiency within the government and in industry; in a reorganization of the cabinet in December, Kaunda personally assumed the industry portfolio. During 1984 and early 1985 reforms of several parastatal companies were carried out, and inefficient officials dismissed.

In March 1985, following a series of strikes by public-sector employees demanding higher wages, Kaunda took emergency powers to ban strikes in essential services. In an extensive government reorganization in April, Kebby Musokotwane was appointed prime minister, while Alexander Grey Zulu became secretary-general of UNIP. Efforts to eradicate corruption continued later in that year, with the arrest of about 30 prominent businessmen, diplomats and former politicians on charges of smuggling illicit drugs to South Africa. In October a judicial tribunal was established to investigate the charges, but 24 of the detainees were released in April 1986.

In response to the continuing economic crisis, further austerity measures were imposed in 1985, resulting in an increase in retail prices, which provoked angry demonstrations in Lusaka in October. In December students demonstrated against the reintroduction of boarding fees for pupils at primary and secondary schools, and student boycotts led to the closure of the university in May 1986. In December the removal of the government subsidy on refined maize meal, the staple food, resulted in an increase of 120% in the price of this essential commodity. After violent rioting in the Copperbelt towns of Kitwe and Ndola, the government reintroduced the subsidy. Although peace in the region was restored by the end of December, strikes in support for wage increases occurred in early 1987, and in April of that year the government was forced to rescind a 70% increase in the price of fuel, following protests in Lusaka. In May Kaunda announced that an economic austerity programme advocated by the IMF (see Economy) was to be abandoned and replaced by a government-devised economic strategy involving greater state controls. In an ensuing cabinet reshuffle, a new minister of finance was appointed. Twelve senior officials of the central bank were subsequently dismissed from office, following the alleged discovery of 'serious irregularities' in the bank's affairs.

Meanwhile, the government became increasingly preoccupied with internal security. In April 1987 Kaunda alleged that the South African government, with the assistance of Zambian businessmen and members of the Zambian armed forces, had conspired to destablize the Zambian government. In the following month a long-standing opponent of Kaunda, Alfred Masonda Chambeshi, was arrested, following allegations in court that he planned to overthrow the government, in collusion with Angolan rebels of the União Nacional para a Independência Total de Angola (UNITA). In July three members of the Zambian air force and a businessman were charged with having engaged in espionage for the South African government. In March 1988 a former South African soldier was sentenced to 50 years' imprisonment on espionage charges, and in June a New Zealand national, also convicted of spying for South Africa, was deported. In October three civilians and six military officers, including Lt-Gen. Christon Tembo, a former commander of the Zambian army, were arrested on suspicion of conspiring to overthrow the president. (Tembo and a further three military officers were subsequently charged with treason, but were pardoned in July 1990.)

In August 1988, at the UNIP general conference, several amendments to the party's constitution were introduced; these included the expansion of the central committee from 25 to 68 members. Among those admitted to the enlarged central committee were military commanders, several industrialists and the chairman and secretary-general of the MUZ. In late October presidential and legislative elections took place. Kaunda, the only candidate, received 95.5% of all votes cast in the presidential election; however, four cabinet ministers lost their seats in the elections to the national assembly. In November Kaunda reorganized the cabinet, merging or abolishing five portfolios, apparently in an attempt to reduce government costs. In March 1989 Kebby Musokotwane, widely considered to be a potential rival to the president, was removed from the post of prime minister and briefly relegated to the ministry of general education, youth and sport, before being transferred to an overseas diplomatic posting; he was succeeded as prime minister by Gen. Malimba Masheke, minister of home affairs and a former minister of defence.

In early 1989 continued unrest among workers and students was reported, and the government threatened to ban trade unions involved in strike action. Increases in the prices of essential goods were implemented in mid-1989, prompting renewed rioting in the Copperbelt region in July. In June 1990 an announcement that the price of maize meal was to increase by more than 100% resulted in severe rioting in Lusaka, in which at least 30 people were reported to have been killed. In the same month the minister of defence, Frederick Hapunda (who was widely believed to be a supporter of multi-party politics), was dismissed, while several other prominent state officials were similarly removed from office. On 30 June a junior army officer, Lt Mwamba Luchembe, announced on the state radio that Kaunda had been overthrown by the armed forces. This claim, however, was unfounded, and Luchembe was immediately arrested, although he was subsequently pardoned and released. In early July Lt-Gen. Hannaniah Lungu was appointed minister of defence.

In April 1990 the UNIP general conference rejected proposals for the introduction of a multi-party political system in Zambia. In the following month, however, Kaunda announced that a popular referendum on the subject of multi-party politics would be conducted in October of that year, and that proponents of such a system would be permitted to campaign and hold public meetings. Accordingly, in early July the Movement for Multi-party Democracy (MMD), an unofficial alliance of political opponents of the government, was formed, under the leadership of a former minister of finance, Arthur Wina, and the chairman of the ZCTU, Frederick Chiluba. In addition, the ZCTU demanded an end to the existing state of emergency, the creation of an independent body to monitor the referendum, and equal access to the media for both those supporting and those opposing the introduction of a multi-party system. In July 1990, however, Kaunda announced that the referendum was to be postponed until August 1991 to facilitate full electoral registration. Although he welcomed the registration procedure, Wina severely criticized the referendum's postponement and requested that it take place before December 1990. In August 1990 the national assembly proposed the introduction of a multi-party system, to which Kaunda again expressed his opposition. In the following month, however, Kaunda recommended the restoration of a multi-party system, at a session of the national council of UNIP. In addition, he proposed that multi-party presidential and legislative elections be organized, that the national referendum be abandoned, and that a commission be appointed to revise the constitution. Later in September the national council endorsed the proposals for multi-party elections, which were scheduled for October 1991, and accepted recommendations by a parliamentary committee regarding the restructuring of the party.

CONSTITUTIONAL TRANSITION

In December 1990 Kaunda formally adopted constitutional amendments, approved by the national assembly earlier that month, which permitted the formation of political parties other than UNIP to contest the forthcoming elections. Shortly afterwards, the MMD was granted official recognition as a political organization; the establishment of a further 11 opposition movements took place in subsequent months. In early 1991 several prominent members of UNIP resigned from the party and declared their support for the MMD, while the Zambian Congress of Trade Unions officially transferred its allegiance to the MMD. In February Kaunda announced that he would permit other members of UNIP to contest the presidential election, despite previous statements to the contrary.

In early June 1991 the constitutional commission presented a series of recommendations, which included the establishment of a bicameral system of parliament, the creation of the post of vice-president, and the expansion of the national assembly from 135 to 150 members. Kaunda accepted the majority of the proposed constitutional amendments, which were subsequently submitted for approval by the national assembly. However, the MMD rejected the draft constitution, and threatened to boycott the elections in October if the national assembly accepted the proposals. Opposition supporters objected in particular to amendments permitting the appointment of non-elected ministers from outside the national assembly, and the vesting of supreme authority in the president rather than in the national assembly. The government also rejected opposition demands that foreign observers be invited to monitor the elections. In July, following discussions between Kaunda, Frederick Chiluba and delegates from seven other opposition parties, under the chairmanship of the deputy chief justice, Mathew Ngulube, Kaunda agreed to suspend the review of the draft constitution in the national assembly, pending further discussions; it was also decided that state subsidies would be granted to all registered political parties. Subsequent negotiations between the MMD and UNIP, which were mediated by church leaders, resulted in the formation of a joint commission of experts to revise the draft constitution. Later in July, following a meeting of the two parties under the auspices of the constitutional commission, Kaunda conceded to opposition demands that ministers be appointed only from members of the national assembly and that the proposed establishment of a constitutional court be abandoned; presidential powers to impose martial law were also to be rescinded. On 2 August the national assembly formally adopted the new draft constitution, which included these amendments.

In late July 1991 Kaunda's leadership of UNIP was challenged by another member of the party, a businessman, and member of the central committee of UNIP, Enoch Kavindele. In addition, allegations of the misuse of state funds by government officials threatened to increase opposition to Kaunda. Two days prior to UNIP's party congress, however, Kavindele announced the withdrawal of his canditure, allegedly in the interests of party unity. In early August the party congress re-elected Kaunda as president. However, several prominent party officials, including Alexander Grey Zulu, hitherto secretary-general of the party, refused to contest the elections. In the same month Kaunda appointed a three-member commission to investigate the salaries and conditions of service of public officials, following increasing strike action by employees of civil service organizations. Later in August Kaunda agreed to permit foreign observers to monitor the forthcoming elections, in an attempt to counter opposition allegations that UNIP would perpetrate electoral fraud. In addition, Kaunda announced that the armed forces were henceforth disassociated from UNIP, in accordance with the tenets of political pluralism; leaders of the armed forces were obliged to retire from membership of the party's central committee.

In September 1991 the national assembly was dissolved, in preparation for the presidential and legislative elections, which were scheduled for 31 October. On the same day he officially disassociated UNIP from the State; workers in the public sector were henceforth prohibited from engaging in political activity. However, international observers, who arrived in Zambia in September, expressed concern that the elections would not be conducted fairly, on the grounds that the government-owned media and parastatal organizations continued to support UNIP in its electoral campaign, and that the state of emergency remained in force. During October numerous outbreaks of violence were reported; in one incident four supporters of the MMD were killed by members of UNIP. Kaunda warned that UNIP's failure to win the election would provoke a civil conflict, while Chiluba accused Kaunda of amassing troops on the border with Malawi to fight the MMD in the event of its accession to power. Chiluba also claimed that an attempt to assassinate him had been staged, and appealed to the Organization of African Unity (OAU) to deploy peace-keeping forces in Zambia during the election period. In late October Kaunda accused the international observers of involvement in a conspiracy to remove UNIP from power.

THE CHILUBA PRESIDENCY

Contrary to previous indications, however, international observers reported that the elections, which took place on 31 October 1991, had been conducted fairly. In the presidential election Chiluba, who received 75.79% of votes cast, defeated Kaunda, who obtained 24.21% of the vote. In the legislative election, which was contested by 330 candidates representing six political parties, the MMD secured 125 seats in the national assembly, while UNIP won the remaining 25 seats; only four members of the previous government were returned to the national assembly. Kaunda's failure to be re-elected to the presidency was attributed to widespread discontent at the deterioration of economic conditions, as a result of the government's continued mismanagement. On 2 November Chiluba was inaugurated as president. On 7 November Chiluba appointed Levy Mwanawasa, a constitutional lawyer, as vice-president and leader of the national assembly, and formed a new 22-member cabinet. In addition, a minister was appointed to each of the country's nine provinces, which were previously administered by governors. Two days later the government allowed the state of emergency to expire. During his first month in office Chiluba began to carry out a major restructuring of the civil service and parastatal organizations, as the first step in his programme to revive the economy.

In December 1991, following a road accident in which Mwanawasa was severely injured, the minister without portfolio, Brig.-Gen. Godfrey Miyanda, was accused of attempting to bring about his death. A commission of inquiry was later informed that Miyanda had previously conspired with members of the former government to assassinate Chiluba and to abduct Mwanawasa. It was alleged that after the failure of this plan he had arranged the road accident, in an attempt to kill Mwanawasa, and subsequently to assume the vice-presidency. In March 1992, however, following an investigation of the incident by detectives from the United Kingdom, the circumstances of the accident were pronounced to be normal, and Miyanda was exonerated of involvement. Later in December 1991 Kaunda announced that he was to relinquish the leadership of UNIP; a new president was to be elected at a party congress in August 1992. In January 1992 Kaunda denied allegations that he had misappropriated public funds during his tenure of office, and moved to institute legal proceedings against the state, members of the media and leading government officials, following accusations of his complicity in a number of crimes. Later in January the minister of defence, Ben Mwila, claimed that UNIP was orchestrating a coup attempt by former army officers.

In 1992 widespread opposition to governmental policies was reported. In May a dissident faction of academics within the MMD, known as Caucus for National Unity (CNU), emerged. The CNU, which claimed support from several members of the government, requested that Chiluba review his appointment of cabinet ministers and heads of parastatal organizations, to ensure that all ethnic groups were represented. The CNU, together with the Zambia Research Foundation and the Women's Lobby, also advocated the establishment of a constitutional commission to curtail the executive power vested in the president and the cabinet. However, Chiluba refused to initiate a review of the constitution, on the grounds that it would prove too expensive. The government was also criticized for its rigid enforcement of the structural adjustment programme supported by the IMF and World Bank, which had resulted in an increase in economic hardship.

In June 1992 a breakaway faction of UNIP formed a new opposition group, the United Democratic Party (UDP). In July, following the rejection by the national assembly of a report that implicated several members of the government in alleged financial malpractice, two cabinet ministers (who were believed to have links with the CNU) resigned in protest at the government's failure to eradicate corruption and to implement democratic reform; Chiluba subsequently reorganized the cabinet. Later that month the CNU registered as an independent political party, after the resignation of its leader, Dr Muyoba Macwani, from the MMD. In August Kaunda and the secretary-general of UNIP, Kebby Musokotwane, were temporarily detained, on the grounds that they had convened an illegal gathering. At a party congress in late September, Kaunda formally resigned as leader of UNIP, and was replaced by Musokotwane. In local government elections which took place in late November, the MMD won the majority of seats. There was, however, a high rate of abstention (the turnout was less than 10% of registered voters); this was widely attributed to disillusionment with the Chiluba administration.

In early March 1993 Chiluba declared a state of emergency, following the discovery of UNIP documents detailing an alleged conspiracy (referred to as the 'Zero Option') to destabilize the government by inciting unrest and civil disobedience. A number of prominent members of UNIP, including Kaunda's three sons, were subsequently arrested. Musokotwane conceded the existence of the documents, but denied that UNIP officials were involved in the conspiracy, which he attributed to extreme factions within the party. Kaunda, however, claimed that the conspiracy had been fabricated by Zambian security forces, with the assistance of US intelligence services, in an attempt to discredit the opposition. Later that month, following allegations by the Zambian government that Iran and Iraq had financed subversive elements within UNIP, diplomatic relations with the two countries were suspended. Shortly afterwards, the national assembly approved the state of emergency, which was to remain in force for a further three months. Owing to pressure from Western governments, however, Chiluba reduced the maximum period of detention without trial from 28 to seven days.

In April 1993, ostensibly in an attempt to eradicate government corruption, Chiluba carried out an extensive reconstruction of the cabinet, in which four senior ministers were dismissed. Chiluba failed, however, to remove from the cabinet a number of ministers who were implicated in malpractice, including Michael Chilufya Sata, hitherto the minister of local government. In the same month 15 members of UNIP, who had been arrested in connection with the alleged conspiracy, appealed to the high court against their continued detention without trial; seven of the detainees were subsequently released. In May the detention orders on the remaining eight members were revoked; however, they were immediately rearrested and charged with related offences. Later that month the state of emergency was ended.

In July 1993 UNIP, the UDP and the Labour Party (LP) established an informal alliance, and advocated a campaign of civil disobedience in protest at the economic austerity measures implemented by the government. In the same month Kaunda announced that he was to retire from political activity. Divisions within the MMD became apparent in August, when 15 members (11 of whom held seats in the national assembly and including several former cabinet ministers) resigned from the party. The rebels accused the government of protecting corrupt cabinet ministers and of failing to respond to numerous reports linking senior party officials with the illegal drugs trade. Their opposition to Chiluba's government was consolidated later in the month by the formation of a new political group, the National Party (NP). An existing organization, the National Party for Democracy, was dissolved in order that its members could support the new party.

In January 1994 two prominent cabinet ministers announced their resignation, following persistent allegations of their involvement in high-level corruption and drugs-trafficking activities, and increasing domestic and international pressure for the government to take action over the allegations. One of the ministers, Vernon Mwaanga, a founder member of the MMD, who had held the foreign affairs portfolio, had been named as a leading trafficker by a tribunal in 1985, although he had not been convicted of the alleged offences. Both ministers denied involvement in narcotics and claimed they had resigned in order for the government to carry out thorough investigations into the matter. The resignations prompted Chiluba to announce an extensive reorganization of cabinet portfolios, in which a further two ministers were dismissed. Opposition groups remained critical of the government, however, claiming that the changes effected were merely cosmetic. At by-elections for 10 of the 11 vacated seats in the national assembly, which were held in November 1993 and April 1994, the MMD regained five seats, while the NP secured four and UNIP one. In June 1994 seven opposition parties, including UNIP, joined together to form the Zambia Opposition Front (ZOFRO) to co-ordinate the various groups' activities. In early July Levy Mwanawasa announced his resignation from the office of vice-president, citing long-standing differences with Chiluba, and was subsequently replaced by Godfrey Miyanda, who was sworn into office on 5 July. In July ex-president Kaunda announced that he was considering renouncing political retirement to contest the presidential elections in 1996.

REGIONAL RELATIONS

Relations between Zambia and a newly independent Zimbabwe were initially tense, owing to Kaunda's long-standing support for Prime Minister (later President) Robert Mugabe's rival, Joshua Nkomo. Contacts between the two states were considerably improved, however, following reciprocal state visits in 1981. In 1987 the first state visit to Zambia by the Tanzanian president, Ali Hassan Mwinyi, reinforced economic and technical co-operation between the two countries.

Kaunda assumed a leading role in peace initiatives in southern Africa, and supported both the South West Africa People's Organisation of Namibia (SWAPO), allowing it to operate from Zambian territory, and the African National Congress of South Africa (ANC), which, until its return to South Africa in mid-1990, maintained its headquarters in Lusaka. In 1984 Kaunda was joint chairman of a conference on the issue of Namibian independence, which was held in Lusaka and involved the South African administrator-general in Namibia, together with representatives from SWAPO and some of Namibia's internal political parties. In September 1985 Kaunda was appointed chairman of the 'front-line' states, and in July 1987 he was elected to the chairmanship of the OAU. Owing to Kaunda's support for SWAPO and the ANC, Zambia was frequently subjected to military reprisals by South Africa. In May 1986 an air attack on an alleged ANC base near Lusaka, resulting in two deaths, was carried out by South African defence forces. Intermittent bomb attacks in Lusaka in 1987, 1988 and 1989 were generally viewed as attempts at destabilization by South Africa. Following the initiation of a programme of political reforms in South Africa in 1990, however, the Zambian government envisaged the restoration of diplomatic relations between the two countries. In mid-1993 the South African president, F. W. de Klerk, made an official visit to Zambia (the first by a South African head of state).

Zambia's support for the governments of Angola and Mozambique also resulted in retaliatory attacks by UNITA rebels and by Mozambican guerrillas of the Movimento Nacional da Resistência de Moçambique (MNR—also known as Renamo). In May 1986 landmine explosions in the Zambezi district, which killed three people, were reportedly the responsibilty of UNITA; attacks by UNITA rebels continued in the late 1980s and early 1990s. Over the same period, a number of Zambian civilians were reported to have been killed in repeated raids by members of the MNR, while Zambian troops entered Mozambican territory in pursuit of the rebels. Following a peace accord, signed by the Mozambican government and the MNR in October 1992, Zambia contributed some 950 troops to a UN peace-keeping force, which was deployed in Mozambique. In May 1993 the Zambian government dispatched troops to the border with Angola, in an attempt to prevent further attacks by UNITA rebels. In September Zambia signed a border co-operation agreement with Malawi.

In July 1994 it was alleged that Zambia was violating UN sanctions against UNITA rebels by supplying arms and oil to the movement. The allegation was rejected by President Chiluba.

Economy

LINDA VAN BUREN

The Zambian economy expanded rapidly during the 1960s and early 1970s, owing to high levels of the international price of copper. Despite considerable investment in physical and social infrastructure, however, the government failed to develop other sectors of the economy, and a reduction in the international price of copper in the mid-1970s resulted in a severe economic decline. Development was subsequently constrained by a shortage of foreign exchange with which to buy essential inputs and by a lack of skilled manpower, a poor transport network and high debt-service obligations. The economic mismanagement of the Kaunda administration contributed to a further deterioration in domestic conditions, with severe food shortages, and a dramatic increase in inflation and unemployment. In the early 1990s an economic recovery was expected, following the establishment of a new government and the resumption of an IMF-approved austerity programme; however, signs of improvement were slow to appear.

AGRICULTURE

Zambia's topography, with its variations in elevation, enables a variety of crops to be grown, although only about 10% of the surface area is cultivable. The principal crops are maize, sugar cane, cassava, millet, sorghum, beans, groundnuts, cotton, tobacco, sunflowers, rice, wheat, arabica coffee and horticultural products. A number of lakes and rivers, particularly those in the Northern Province and at Lake Kariba on the southern border, offer considerable potential for fishing. Zambia has 295,000 sq km of forest land, of which 265,000 sq km are open to exploitation. Commercial forestry is important on the Copperbelt, where there are numerous softwood tree plantations, and in the hardwood areas of the southwest.

Zambia has a few hundred large commercial farms, situated mostly near the railway lines, which account for about 45% of the country's agricultural output. The number of smallholders who cultivate cash crops is increasing, while most subsistence farmers in all parts of the country use traditional methods, without adequate inputs or infrastructural support. Agriculture accounted for 11% of gross domestic product (GDP) in 1970, and 9% of GDP in 1992; the sector employed 68.5% of the labour force in 1991. Food production per caput remained static throughout the 1980s, even registering a decline of 0.7%. The agricultural sector is frequently affected by drought but grew by an annual average of 2.1% in 1970–80, and by an annual average of 3.3% in 1980–91.

Production of maize (the staple food of most Zambians) exhibited a remarkable recovery after a particularly severe drought in 1991/92. Output in 1992/93 (year ending 30 April) amounted to a record level of 17.8m. bags (compared with just 1m. bags in 1991/92), and was projected to reach 18m. bags in 1993/94. National consumption is about 13m. bags per year. In April 1993 the Zambia National Union of Farmers complained that the basic guaranteed price of K5,000 per 90-kg bag was uneconomical and warned that commercial farmers might abandon the cultivation of maize unless the government were to increase the price to at least K8,000 per bag; the government subsequently agreed to review the price. In the event, in preference to increasing the guaranteed price, the government chose to introduce two types of promissory note. The first, a rediscountable promissory note, allowed farmers to collect, after 15 February 1994, money owed to them on maize they had produced up to 31 October 1993, together with interest equivalent to the prevailing rate on 182-day treasury bills (at the time, 125% per annum). Farmers could, alternatively, sell the notes to a commercial bank at a discount, or they could use them as collateral on loans or to purchase agricultural inputs such as fertilizers. The farmers' other option was to accept a forward-contract promissory note, guaranteeing a price of K7,500 per 90-kg bag on 15 February 1994, which was intended to reflect the market price plus interest and a storage allowance. The farmers had then to decide whether they would lose or gain by waiting to accept the undertaking to buy on 15 February. The scheme was immediately criticized for being both complicated and costly. Financial losses, principally resulting from over-production, continue to pose a problem, and experts have advocated a comprehensive strategic maize policy that would assure adequate stocks to meet domestic requirements in times of drought, and sufficient storage for that purpose, while avoiding costly maintenance of excessive stocks. However, the new government, which took office in 1991, reacted effectively to the drought in 1991/92, distributing emergency supplies far more efficiently than the governments of neighbouring countries, and subsequently arranging the timely supply of seed to effect a quick recovery.

Wheat is grown almost exclusively on large commercial farms, usually under irrigation. Production increased from 37,000 metric tons in 1988 to 47,000 tons in 1989, and 54,500 tons in 1990, before reaching a record 70,000 tons in 1993. The country's flour mills require 84,000 tons per annum to keep the nation supplied with bread and this 70,000-ton harvest meets 83% of the requirement. The wheat sector was assisted by Canadian agricultural advisers, who maintained that Zambia had the potential to meet much more of its wheat requirement from local production. The Zambian government lifted controls over the producer price of wheat in June 1988, precipitating a dramatic increase in the price, to K370 per 90-kg in October (compared with K190 in June). However, liberalization also meant that the National Milling Co (the country's only miller of wheat, although no longer with a statutory monopoly) was free to obtain its wheat at lower prices from elsewhere, notably from South Africa. Smallholders grow most of the nation's cotton crop. Textile factories in the country require about 12,000 metric tons of cotton lint per annum, and in most years, the domestic cotton crop is large enough to meet all of the demand and allow for cotton exports. However, output declined from 21,000 tons in 1988 to 17,000 tons in 1989, and to 10,000 tons in 1990, even before the 1991/92 drought. Textile companies complain that the best cotton is exported, leaving lower-quality raw material for the local industry; another problem is that, following the liberalization of trade, cheap imports reduced demand for local textiles, and therefore the textile companies' demand for local cotton. The tobacco sector has experienced problems in the last decade, with reduced yields (owing to drought) in 1983, 1985 and 1992. Yields averaged 1,034 kg per ha annually in 1979-81 and rose to 1,776 kg per ha in 1991. Drought reduced the yields to 438 kg per ha in 1992, and the effects were still being felt in 1993, when yields were 514 kg per ha. Tobacco price controls were lifted in 1989. Production of Virginia tobacco in 1992 was only 2m. kg; in 1993, however, output recovered to 5.6m. kg of Virginia tobacco and to 1.4m. kg of burley tobacco. Zambia's sugar sector recovered much more quickly from the 1991/92 drought than in neighbouring countries. The 1992/93 crop totalled 143,204 metric tons, sufficient to cover the national demand of about 93,000 tons and to allow 50,000 tons to be exported, of which 40,000 tons went to Zimbabwe. The coffee sector has suffered, both as a result of lower output and reduced international prices. Exports declined from 1,772 metric tons in 1991/92 (year ending 31 March), to 1,675 tons in 1992/93; in 1990/91 exports totalled 1,310 tons. Earnings from coffee exports amounted to US $2.65m. in 1991/92 (compared with $2.43m. in 1990/91). The horticultural sector has experienced strong growth, with the export of fruits and vegetables to Europe. In October 1992, however, the Zambia Export Growers' Asscn (ZEGA) suspended the export of certain types of vegetables, owing to excessively high airfreight charges. Production of other crops in 1993 amounted to: 35,000 metric tons of sorghum; 37,000 tons of millet; 11,000 tons of rice (more than the annual national demand for rice, which is 9,450 tons); 42,000 tons of groundnuts in shells; and 21,000 tons of sunflower seeds.

The livestock sector suffered as a result of the drought in 1991/92, when a higher number of animals were slaughtered than in most years; in 1992/93, however, herds began to reach normal levels. A small amount of beef is generally exported. Foot-and-mouth disease constitutes a problem in some areas of the country. An outbreak of African swine fever in 1992 threatened the destruction of 10,000 pigs and prompted the government to establish a K3,200m. fund to compensate pig farmers for their losses from the disease.

Although rural development was accorded a high priority by the Kaunda administration, most of the schemes and programmes yielded disappointing results. Nearly 18% of total development expenditure in 1980 was for agriculture. However, poor organization, lack of skills, inadequate marketing and transport infrastructure, and migration to urban areas have all impeded growth. The sector was additionally constrained by low producer prices, late and unreliable payments to farmers for their crops, inefficient marketing and inadequate supply of inputs from the state-owned National Agricultural Marketing Board (NAMBOARD), which maintained a statutory monopoly over all aspects of agricultural marketing until January 1986, when private companies and co-operatives were allowed to compete for the first time. Eight years after liberalization was introduced, however, farmers continued to face most of these impediments.

MINING

Copper accounted for about 93% of all Zambia's foreign exchange earnings in 1991, and minerals of all types accounted for 9.8% of export earnings in 1992. Other minerals exploited include cobalt (found in association with copper), zinc, lead, gold, silver, selenium, marble, emeralds and amethyst. In 1990 mining and quarrying contributed 9.6% of GDP, and in 1989 the sector engaged some 15.1% of the total labour force. The mining industry in Zambia was established during the colonial period, with the opening in 1906 of the Broken Hill lead and zinc mine at Kabwe. Copper mining was begun in the 1920s by Zambian Anglo American (later Nchanga Consolidated Copper Mines) and Roan Selection Trust (later Roan Consolidated Mines), which, in 1982, united to form Zambia Consolidated Copper Mines (ZCCM), in which the government took a 60.3% share. Growth continued after independence in 1964, and by 1969 Zambia had become a leading producer of unrefined copper, with a record level of output of 747,500 metric tons (accounting for 12% of international production). (ZCCM, together with its holding company, Zambia Industrial and Mining Corpn (ZIMCO), is still among the world's largest copper companies.) Since the mid-1970s, however, copper output and revenues have declined significantly; production fell from 700,000 metric tons in 1976 to 415,000 tons in 1989. A modest recovery, to 448,468 tons, was registered in 1990, but the closure of the Mufulira smelter for renovations contributed to a decline in 1991, to 421,590 tons. Copper output fell further in 1992, to 109,955 tons. ZCCM recorded a gross profit of K31,551m. in the financial year to 31 March 1992, compared with K18,539m. in the previous financial year. However, the company ultimately incurred financial losses during both these years, despite operating at well below capacity at the mining, smeltering and refining stages. Ageing capital equipment, shortages of skilled labour, poor maintenance and inadequacy of reinvestment all adversely affected productivity. In 1983 the government introduced an export levy in order to compensate for lack of tax revenue during the company's loss-making years. The levy initially contributed 4% of gross sales revenue, but increased to 8% in 1983, and to 10% in 1985. ZCCM resorted to borrowing to cover this export levy and other high costs, resulting in accruing debts. The largest purchaser of ZCCM copper is Japan (which accounted for 27% of exports in 1991/92), followed by France (19%). Following Zambia's change of government in 1991, a number of remedial measures, including the proposed transfer of ZCCM to private-sector ownership, have been announced. A range of reforms within ZCCM have been carried out, and higher production targets for copper have been set. Plans are also proceeding for the expansion of productive capacity and a wide-ranging programme of exploration and modernization.

The production of cobalt increased from 4,447 metric tons in 1990 to 4,674 tons in 1991, and to 5,078 tons in 1992, stimulating revenue of K14.15m. in 1992. In 1994 Apollo Enterprises Ltd of Zambia formed a joint venture with Claim Minerals NL of Australia, to study and potentially exploit nickel-sulphide deposits at Munali, 65 km south-west of Lusaka. The site is now estimated to contain some 11.69m. metric tons of ore and is situated close to power, water, road and rail infrastructures. Output of zinc declined from 13,637 metric tons in 1990 to 13,387 tons in 1991 (owing, in part, to power generation cuts), and to just 6,459 tons in 1992; while international prices of zinc were low in 1992 and 1993. Production of lead amounted to 2,332 metric tons in 1992, stimulating revenue of K93m. Output of precious metals totalled 38,902 kg in 1992, stimulating revenue of K286m. Production of zinc and lead at Kabwe is undertaken by the Kabwe division of ZCCM (one of the conglomerate's six production divisions); the other five divisions, Nchanga, Mufulira, Nkana, Luanshya and Konkola, produce copper, while Nchanga also produces cobalt. Konkola is potentially the richest of Zambia's copper mines, possessing reserves of 44.3m. tons, with a copper content of 3.92%, while Nchanga has a copper content of 3.75%, and Mufulira of 3.16%; Nkona is the largest mine, with 95.5m. tons of reserves, which, however, have a copper content of only 2.3%. Zambia mines emeralds, aquamarines, amethysts and some diamonds. A new deposit of diamonds was discovered in Western Province in 1992, and it was hoped that investigations to be carried out in 1994 would reveal further reserves. Exploration for oil took place in the 1980s, but no significant discoveries were announced.

INDUSTRY

Zambia's manufacturing sector has suffered from a variety of problems, not least a chronic shortage of foreign exchange, with which to import raw materials and inputs. The sector was also constrained by state intervention in many manufacturing activities, investment in inappropriate schemes and corresponding lack of funds to invest in more suitable undertakings. The state-owned Industrial Development Corpn of Zambia Limited (INDECO) acquired 26 companies in 1968, and continued to take majority shareholdings in a number of other enterprises thereafter. By 1991 INDECO accounted for 75% of Zambia's manufacturing activity. The industrial sector contributed 47% of Zambia's GDP in 1991, while the manufacturing sector accounted for 36% of total GDP in that year. In 1989 the industrial sector engaged 37.4% of the total labour force. At the time of the Kaunda administration, the government, usually through INDECO, formed a number of joint ventures with foreign enterprises, in order to establish a chemical-fertilizer plant, a petroleum refinery, an explosives plant, a glass-bottle factory, a battery factory, a brickworks, a textile factory, a copper-wire factory, two vehicle-assembly operations, and an iron-and-steel project; however, a number of these subsequently ended in failure. Nitrogen Chemicals of Zambia opened a sulphuric-acid plant, at a cost of K32m. in 1983, while its fertilizer operation, with an estimated cost of K300m., is the country's largest non-mining enterprise. Operations at Kapiri Glass Works, which produced glass bottles, declined to less than 50% of its installed capacity by 1984. Mansa Dry Batteries began production in 1979, but operated at only 33% of its capacity by 1984. Kafue Textiles of Zambia faced intense competition from cheap imported cloth and clothing from the Far East and from elsewhere in Africa in the early 1990s. The Tika iron-and-steel project, conceived in 1972, was abandoned in 1979, after the accumulation of large debts in foreign currency to overseas companies that had participated in the expensive planning of the project. Rover Zambia's plant at Ndola assembles Toyota, Mitsubishi and Volkswagen trucks, while Leyland Zambia's assembly plant in Lusaka produces 2,000 commercial vehicles per annum. A tractor-assembly factory, with the capacity to produce 2,500 tractors per annum, was established, with the assistance of the Czechoslovak government, in 1983. Livingstone Motor Assemblers produces Fiat, Peugeot and Mazda saloon cars. In April 1993 Refined Oil Products of Ndola opened a glycerine plant, at a cost of K68m., which has the capacity to produce 240 metric tons of glycerine per annum (equivalent to about 20% of national annual demand). Swarp Spinning Mills in Ndola received a loan of $10m. from the European Investment Bank in December 1992 for the expansion of its cotton-spinning and associated yarn-dyeing facilities.

The liberalization of prices, imposition of an import tariff and allocation of foreign exchange helped to alleviate some of the major problems in the manufacturing sector after 1983, but other aspects of liberalization, such as allowing the kwacha to depreciate according to the dictates of market forces, negated some of these gains. The government, deprived of some of its tax revenue from ZCCM during its loss-making period, attempted to compensate for the shortfall by charging import duties on the c.i.f. (cost, insurance and freight) value of imports, rather than on their f.o.b. (free on board) value, thereby further reducing companies' narrowing profits margins.

In 1983, the government introduced an arrangement whereby companies that exported non-traditional items were allowed to retain 50% of foreign exchange from those exports for use in paying for imported inputs, thereby compensating for lack of foreign currency. After only one year, exports of non-metal products exhibited a fivefold increase. In 1987, however, companies lost this concession, after the Kaunda government adopted the former system of strict import licensing, an artificially revalued exchange rate and similar measures. The Investment Act of 1991, promulgated at the end of the Kaunda regime, partially restored the facility, allowing companies holding investment licences to retain 70% of gross foreign-exchange earnings for three years, 60% for the following two years and 50% for the remaining period of the investment licence's validity. The Chiluba government subsequently revised the Investment Act to allow the full retention of foreign-exchange earnings by investors.

Nominally, manufacturing in Zambia provided revenue of $1,392m. in 1992, compared with $181m. in 1970. The largest manufacturing sector was food, beverages and tobacco, which contributed 45% of total revenue in 1992, compared with 49% in 1970. Textiles and clothing accounted for 11% in 1992, while chemicals contributed 11% and machinery and transport equipment contributed 7%. In 1990, according to the World Bank, gross output per manufacturing employee (1980 = 100), was 90 in Zambia, compared with 135 in Zimbabwe and 235 in Kenya.

ENERGY

Zambia became self-sufficient in hydroelectric power in 1974 and began exporting power to Zimbabwe (then Rhodesia) and Zaire. In that year a major expansion of output from Kafue Gorge resulted in an increase of 82% in domestic energy production. Long delays occurred in the construction of the Kariba North power station, but 150 MW of capacity were operational by 1977, with a further 150 MW for later completion. New 150 MW generators came into service at Kafue Gorge in 1976 and 1977, bringing the facility's total installed capacity to 900 MW. The construction of an additional dam at Itezhi-Tezhi provided a more reliable flow of water to the Kafue Gorge power plant. However, a fire in March 1989 inflicted major damage on this installation, destroying the main power cables; rehabilitation of the facility cost more than $20m., and exports of power to Zimbabwe (valued at $1m. per month) were suspended for more than a year. Zimbabwe, meanwhile, proceeded with the construction of its own Kariba South facility to end its dependence on Zambia for imported power. Low water levels throughout the region during the 1991/92 drought significantly reduced power output in Zambia, resulting in the suspension of exports, and Zambia was one of several countries which arranged to import power from South Africa and Zaire. (Imports from Zaire ceased in February 1993.) A Norwegian company was engaged in November 1991 to conduct feasibility studies for the construction of electricity interconnection lines from Zambia to Malawi and Tanzania. Rural electrification is a stated priority, and some extension of the national grid has been achieved, but many areas of rural Zambia still do not have access to mains power supply. Charcoal and fuelwood remain the main sources of energy supply for cooking and heating purposes for most people in both urban and rural areas. Both energy production and energy consumption declined in 1980-92, by 3.3% and 2.7% respectively per annum. Zambia used 158 kg per caput in 1992, compared with 450 kg per caput in Zimbabwe, 92 kg per caput in Kenya and 2,487 kg per caput in South Africa.

Coal production commenced in 1965, but was subsequently affected by shortages of equipment and spare parts. The remaining colliery, at Maamba, operated at substantially below capacity in 1987. Following a rehabilitation programme, however, the mine met its production target of 560,000 metric tons in 1987/88, and began exporting coal to Zaire, Malawi and Tanzania.

TRANSPORT

At independence in 1964, Zambia had only one tarred road, and one railway line, which extended from the Copperbelt, in the north, through Lusaka and Livingstone to Zimbabwe (then Southern Rhodesia), and connected with the Rhodesian Railway, providing access to South African ports. In 1965 the unilateral declaration of independence by Rhodesia prompted sanctions against that country, which severely disrupted the flow of Zambia's traffic on its only transport link to the outside world.

The Zambian government invested substantial sums in improving infrastructure, with the construction of the TanZam oil pipeline from the Tanzanian port of Dar es Salaam, which was completed in 1968. The Great North Road to Tanzania (which was previously only a dirt track) was tarred, and a Great East Road to Malawi, which connected with the Mozambican ports of Nacala and Beira, was constructed (although civil war in Mozambique subsequently prevented Zambia from making full use of this route). A railway to Dar es Salaam, known as the Tanzania-Zambia Railway Authority (Tazara), which was built and financed by the People's Republic of China with an interest-free loan, was used in early 1974 to transport goods, following the closure of the Rhodesian border. The complete route was opened to regular service in October 1975, ahead of the original schedule, and proved to be essential, after the closure of the Lobito railway to Angola in August 1975. However, limited port facilities at Dar es Salaam and unavailability of rolling stock resulted in severe delays, and Tazara incurred losses for the Zambian government in its first eight years of operation. In October 1978 Zambia resumed its use of the Rhodesian rail route to South Africa. Tazara finally moved into profit in the June quarter of 1983, although it did not consistently achieve profits until 1988. In 1991 Zambia Railways rehabilitated about 80% of its rolling stock, with the assistance of loans totalling $13.5m. from Japan and the USA, but additional funds were required for signalling and communications equipment.

The BotZam Highway, linking Kazungula with Nata, in Botswana, was opened in 1984, and in 1989 Botswana completed the tarring of the road that extended south from Nata to connect with its own road system. In 1992 Japan provided $13.9m. for the reconstruction of the ageing Kafue Road Bridge. In 1968 the Zambian government nationalized the country's two main road-haulage companies and merged them into a single enterprise, Contract Haulage. In July 1992 it was estimated that Contract Haulage owned 85% of the 1,200 commercial trucks in Zambia. The public passenger and cargo road-transport sectors were opened to private enterprise in 1992. In 1994 a road agreement was signed with Namibia which included a plan to build a bridge across the Zambezi river to facilitate cross-border passage and to enable Zambia to use Namibia's Walvis Bay port for cargo transportation.

The national airline, Zambia Airways, which was established in 1967, operates domestic, regional and long-haul passenger and airfreight services. In 1992 the government indicated that the airline would henceforth have to service its external and domestic debt from its own revenue. Supplies of aviation fuel to Zambia were subsequently suspended until payment was received, forcing all carriers flying to Zambia to divert to Zimbabwe, where they could buy aviation fuel for hard currency. In February 1993 the government announced the implementation of extensive measures at Zambia Airways, including the retrenchment of staff, to compensate for continuing financial losses. In March 1993, however, the National Airports Corpn announced that it was to spend US $30m. towards the rehabilitation of four airports, situated at Lusaka, Ndola, Livingstone and Mfuwe. In addition, equipment, valued at $7m., was to be installed at airports at Kaoma, Solwezi, Kasama, Livingstone and Mfuwe. In 1994 Zambia Airways reduced its regional routes and introduced other cost-cutting measures. Twice-weekly flights to London Heathrow were continued, however.

FOREIGN TRADE AND PAYMENTS

Zambia has generally maintained a visible trade surplus since independence, but exceptions have occurred, notably in 1991 and 1992. Exports in 1992 totalled $1,100m., while imports cost $1,300m., resulting in a visible trade deficit of $200m.; in contrast, Zambia recorded trade surpluses of $566m. in 1989 and $497m. in 1988.The principal export commodity is copper, which accounted for $920m., or 85% of total export revenue in 1992. Cobalt, zinc and lead contributed most of the other 15% of revenue in 1992. In total, 98% of export revenue is derived from mineral products. The principal non-mineral export is tobacco, though other commodities, such as sugar, coffee and horticultural produce, are exported on a modest scale.

In 1992 the principal imports (accounting for 72% of the total cost of imports) were machinery, transport equipment and other manufactures, followed by mineral fuels (18%) and food (8%). South Africa is the largest supplier of imports, followed by the United Kingdom, the USA, Japan and Germany. Japan, as a result of its purchases of Zambian copper, is the principal market for exports; other significant purchasers are the United Kingdom, China, Germany and the USA. Owing to some improvement in the international price of copper, Zambia's terms of trade improved by an annual average of 9% between 1987 and 1992.

In 1991 the current account of the balance of payments registered a significant deficit of $487m. before official transfers (compared with a surplus of $107m. in 1970), but an overall surplus of $1m. was recorded (compared with a surplus of $108m. in 1970). The overall figure in 1991 represented a major improvement, compared with that in 1990, when, even after official transfers, a deficit of $343m. on the overall balance of payments was recorded. Gross international reserves amounted to $186m. at the end of 1991, equivalent to the cost of 1.4 months of imports; at the end of 1990, according to the World Bank, larger reserves of $201m. covered only the equivalent of 0.9 months of the total cost of imports.

GOVERNMENT FINANCE

The 1993 budget allocated expenditure of K231,900m., a sharp increase compared with the level of K106,400m. projected in 1992, a target which had not been met, largely owing to the necessity for emergency drought relief. The 1992 budget had projected a deficit of K1,200m., compared with a deficit of K18,100m., or 9% of GDP in 1991 (the final year of the Kaunda administration). GDP contracted by 2.8% in 1992, as a result of the drought, but was projected to achieve positive growth of 2% in 1993; GDP increased by an annual average of 0.8% in 1980–92. In the first year of the Chiluba administration, the government made considerable progress in the reduction of the country's high external debt, which was estimated at $8,000m. in October 1991, when Chiluba succeeded Kaunda. Only three months later, the government was able to pay back arrears totalling $51m., which had been overdue for more than six months, on loans from the World Bank and the International Development Association (IDA). The payment eliminated arrears to the World Bank and resulted in the resumption of disbursements on previously approved loans and credits. By August 1992, owing to rescheduling by the 'Paris Club' of official creditors, together with cancellations of debt by bilateral creditors, Zambia's total debt had fallen by $1,500m., to $6,500m. At 30 September 1993 Zambia's total debt stood at $6,750m., of which $2,640m. was owed to bilateral lenders, $1,740m. to multilateral lenders (of which $1,300m. was owed to the IMF), $822m. comprised short-term loans, $149m. was owed to foreign suppliers and $97m. to private-sector London Club creditors. In July the IMF endorsed the Chiluba government's economic and financial programe, and approved up to 836.9m. special drawing rights (SDRs), equivalent to $1,211m., the level of Zambia's arrears to the IMF at 1 July 1990. In June 1992 the World Bank agreed to new loans, totalling $200m., while the IMF extended funds of $100m. in July. In the same month donors pledged $300m. in drought relief. In September the IDA extended $200m. in support of the government's 'privatization' programme. At a conference of donors, convened by the World Bank Consultative Group for Zambia in April 1993, $800m. was pledged in support of the country's reform programme; additional bilateral pledges were expected to compensate for a shortfall of $115m. Several of the donors had visited Lusaka in March to urge the government to accelerate the pace of its privatization programme and to implement measures to restrict inflation. Also in March, Germany cancelled loans totalling DM 135.2m., and rescheduled an equivalent amount over a period of 23 years. The World Bank Consultative Group for Zambia reconvened in Paris on 9 December 1993 and pledged a further $800m. to the country for 1994. The donors issued a statement praising the Zambian government for "maintaining its commitment to the country's economic recovery programme under difficult conditions" but cautioning that formidable challenges lay ahead, not least Zambia's heavy debt burden. The group also expressed concern at the slow pace of privatization. The $800m. pledge fell short of the $1,100m. which Zambia had requested, however. In March 1994 the IDA extended a SDR 108.9m. ($150m.) three-year contract, which included badly-needed balance-of-payments support. In mid-1994 Zambia's debt-servicing requirements were absorbing, on an annualized basis, about 40% of the country's export earnings.

The rate of inflation was unofficially estimated at an average of 400% in October 1991. (According to the IMF, however, consumer prices increased by an average of 65.8% in 1991.) The Chiluba government's pledge to halve the official rate by the end of 1992 was not achieved, and, although estimates varied considerably, the rate of inflation increased by an average of 207% in that year, according to the IMF. The government planned to reduce inflation to 35% in 1993; in the first six months of 1993, however, annual inflation was at 280%. Government figures for the third quarter of 1993 indicate that inflation was reduced to some 47% for that year.

As part of the reform programme, Zambia has liberalized its exchange-rate policy. The first bureaux de change, which opened in October 1992, were permitted to set their own rates for the buying and selling of foreign currency; Zambian residents were initially limited to purchases of $2,000 per transaction. The exercise proved extremely successful, and the kwacha fared far better during its initial period as a free-market currency than any other African currency had in similar circumstances. In February 1993 91-day treasury bills were introduced as a means of stimulating finance for the 1993 budget, replacing the former method of borrowing direct from the Bank of Zambia. Zambian business interests had complained that heavy government borrowing on the domestic market had caused a shortage of loanable funds for the private sector. New banknotes were introduced in February 1993, followed by a new coinage in March. The new notes replaced those bearing the likeness of Kenneth Kaunda but did not constitute a demonetization of the 'old' banknotes, which remained in circulation. In the last quarter of 1993 and the first quarter of 1994, the kwacha weakened on the exchange markets. It fell from K347 = US $1 in mid-October 1993 to K435 = US $1 in early December and to K657 = US $1 in early January 1994. The descent was much less rapid thereafter, however, reaching K695 = US $1 in late May 1994. By mid-August 1994 the rate had stabilized at K682 = US $1.

In July 1992 the national assembly promulgated the Privatization Act, which provided for the transfer of 130 state-owned enterprises to the private sector over a period of five years, and the establishment of the Zambia Privatization Agency, comprising 11 members of the ministries of commerce, industry and finance, of trades unions and of private-sector business groups, to supervise the process. The 130 enterprises were to be sold in groups, and 18 companies were initially named in July 1992, of which the first two, Eagle Travel and Autocare, were finally sold in July 1993. A German company was contracted to assess the possibilities for the 'privatization' of the ZCCM, and was to present a report to the Zambian government by November 1993. The government confirmed, however, that the South African mining group, Anglo American, which already owned 27.3% of ZCCM, was a prime contender to gain control of further equity. As of March 1994, the government still held 60.3% of ZCCM.

Statistical Survey

Source (unless otherwise indicated): Central Statistical Office, POB 31908, Lusaka; tel. (1) 211231; telex 40430.

Area and Population

AREA, POPULATION AND DENSITY

Area (sq km)	752,614*
Population (census results)	
1 September 1980	5,661,801
20 August 1990	
Males	3,975,083
Females	3,843,364
Total	7,818,447
Population (official estimate at 20 August) 1991	8,023,000
Density (per sq km) at August 1991	10.7

* 290,586 sq miles.

PRINCIPAL TOWNS (estimated population at mid-1988)

Lusaka (capital)	870,030	Chingola	194,347
Kitwe	472,255	Luanshya	165,853
Ndola	442,666	Livingstone	98,480
Kabwe (Broken Hill)	200,287	Kalulushi	94,376
Mufulira	199,368	Chililabombwe	81,803

BIRTHS AND DEATHS (UN estimates, annual averages)

	1975–80	1980–85	1985–90
Birth rate (per 1,000)	51.6	49.3	48.6
Death rate (per 1,000)	16.5	15.1	15.9

Expectation of life (UN estimates, years at birth, 1985–90): 48.6 (males 47.7; females 49.5).

Source: UN, *World Population Prospects: The 1992 Revision*.

ECONOMICALLY ACTIVE POPULATION
(ILO estimates, '000 persons at mid-1980)

	Males	Females	Total
Agriculture, etc.	959	438	1,398
Industry	174	14	188
Services	257	69	326
Total labour force	1,390	522	1,912

Source: ILO, *Labour Force Estimates and Projections, 1950–2025*.

1980 census: Total labour force 1,302,944 (males 908,606; females 394,338).

Mid-1984 (official estimates): Total labour force 2,032,300 (males 1,464,800; females 567,500).

Mid-1992 (estimates in '000): Agriculture, etc. 1,925; Total 2,829 (Source: FAO, *Production Yearbook*).

EMPLOYMENT ('000 employees at June)

	1987	1988	1989
Agriculture, forestry and fishing	36.4	36.8	37.2
Mining and quarrying	55.8	55.0	54.2
Manufacturing	50.0	50.4	50.9
Electricity, gas and water	8.5	8.6	8.7
Construction	25.4	23.1	20.8
Trade, restaurants and hotels	27.9	27.2	26.6
Transport, storage and communications	25.4	25.8	26.1
Financing, insurance, real estate and business services	23.9	24.3	24.7
Community, social and personal services*	108.7	109.5	110.2
Total	361.8	360.7	359.6

* Excluding domestic services.

Source: ILO, *Year Book of Labour Statistics*.

Agriculture

PRINCIPAL CROPS ('000 metric tons)

	1990	1991	1992
Wheat	55	65	62
Rice (paddy)	9	15	8
Maize	1,093	1,096	464
Millet	32	26	48
Sorghum	20	21	15
Sugar cane	1,127	1,130†	1,150†
Potatoes†	4	4	4
Sweet potatoes†	27	28	25
Cassava (Manioc)†	260	270	270
Pulses	14	14	21
Onions (dry)†	29	30	25
Tomatoes†	29	30	25
Soybeans	27	28	25
Sunflower seed	20	11	6
Groundnuts (in shell)	25	28	21
Cottonseed*	20	31	18
Cotton (lint)*	10	16	10
Tobacco (leaves)	4	6	5*

* Unofficial figure(s). † FAO estimate(s).

Source: FAO, *Production Yearbook*.

LIVESTOCK ('000 head, year ending September)

	1990	1991	1992
Cattle*	2,878	2,984	3,095
Sheep*	60	62	63
Goats*	534	556	560
Pigs†	295	296	290

* Unofficial figures. † FAO estimates.

Poultry (FAO estimates, million): 16 in 1990; 17 in 1991; 19 in 1992.

Source: FAO, *Production Yearbook*.

LIVESTOCK PRODUCTS (FAO estimates, '000 metric tons)

	1990	1991	1992
Beef and veal	36	37	41
Pig meat	9	10	9
Poultry meat	19	21	23
Other meat	31	31	32
Cows' milk	78	81	84
Hen eggs	34.0	36.8	40.0
Cattle hides	4.7	4.9	5.3

Source: FAO, *Production Yearbook*.

Forestry

ROUNDWOOD REMOVALS ('000 cubic metres)

	1990	1991	1992
Sawlogs, veneer logs and logs for sleepers	262	307	343
Other industrial wood*	467	481	495
Fuel wood*	12,466	12,952	12,952
Total	13,195	13,740	13,790

* FAO estimates.

Source: FAO, *Yearbook of Forest Products*.

SAWNWOOD PRODUCTION
('000 cubic metres, incl. railway sleepers)

	1990	1991	1992
Coniferous (soft wood)	53	62	78
Broadleaved (hard wood)	28	32	34
Total	81	94	112

Source: FAO, *Yearbook of Forest Products*.

Fishing

('000 metric tons, live weight)

	1989	1990	1991
Freshwater fishes	53.9	51.6	53.2
Dagaas	12.8	12.8	12.8
Total catch (inland waters)	66.7	64.5	65.9

Source: FAO, *Yearbook of Fishery Statistics*.

Mining

(metric tons)

	1989	1990	1991
Hard coal	397,000	377,000	380,000
Cobalt ore*†	7,255	7,086	7,000
Copper ore*	496,000	621,600	400,000
Lead ore*	8,900	4,100	9,000
Zinc ore*	20,700	10,900	n.a.
Gold (kg)*	225‡	129	120

* Figures relate to the metal content of ores and concentrates (or, for cobalt, the metal recovered).

† Data from the US Bureau of Mines.

‡ Estimate.

Source: UN, *Industrial Statistics Yearbook*.

Industry

SELECTED PRODUCTS (metric tons, unless otherwise indicated)

	1989	1990	1991
Raw sugar*	132,000	147,000	n.a.
Cigarettes (million)	1,500†	1,500	1,500
Nitrogenous fertilizers	2,000	n.a.	n.a.
Cement	385,000	432,000	376,000
Copper (unwrought)†			
Smelter‡	485,200	461,400	409,000
Refined	450,800	424,800	430,000
Lead (primary)	3,800	4,800	n.a.
Zinc (primary)	12,800	10,400	n.a.
Electric energy (million kWh)	6,742	7,771	7,775

* Data from the International Sugar Organization, London.

† Estimate(s).

‡ Including some production at the refined stage.

Source: UN, *Industrial Statistics Yearbook*.

Finance

CURRENCY AND EXCHANGE RATES

Monetary Units

100 ngwee = 1 Zambian kwacha (K).

Sterling and Dollar Equivalents (31 March 1994)

£1 sterling = 1,484.6 kwacha;
US $1 = 1,000.0 kwacha;
10,000 Zambian kwacha = £6.736 = $10.000.

Average Exchange Rate (US $ per Zambian kwacha)

1991 0.0162
1992 0.0064
1993 0.0023

BUDGET (K million)*

Revenue†	1986	1987	1988
Taxation	2,879.1	3,981.8	4,699.7
Taxes on income, profits, etc.	806.0	1,118.1	1,957.6
Taxes on property	14.1	6.4	9.5
Domestic taxes on goods and services	1,023.5	1,559.1	1,901.8
Sales taxes	598.7	1,048.1	1,208.0
Excises	409.4	487.4	667.8
Taxes on international trade	1,019.8	1,282.9	811.6
Import duties	505.7	811.0	800.5
Other current revenue	142.9	282.1	441.2
Property income	66.7	186.8	90.7
Capital revenue	0.8	3.0	1.1
Total	3,022.8	4,266.9	5,142.0

Expenditure‡	1986	1987	1988
General public services	1,778.6	3,231.7	3,049.5
Public order and safety	156.6	207.1	278.5
Education	406.5	594.6	737.5
Health	222.4	349.3	635.6
Social security and welfare	55.0	87.6	129.9
Housing and community amenities	36.0	29.6	40.6
Other community and social services	56.2	99.5	134.7
Economic services	1,126.0	562.8	2,122.4
Agriculture, forestry and fishing	778.8	283.0	1,665.6
Mining, manufacturing and construction	33.3	56.9	59.7
Transport and communications	248.7	187.5	171.5
Total	5,406.8	6,819.8	8,558.5
Current	4,140.6	4,739.5	6,693.1
Capital	1,266.2	2,080.3	1,865.4

* Figures refer to the consolidated accounts of the central Government, including administrative agencies and social security funds.

† Excluding grants from abroad (K million): 173.2 in 1986; 91.4 in 1987; 494.7 in 1988.

‡ Excluding net lending (K million): 593.5 in 1986; 87.3 in 1987; 544.5 in 1988.

1989 (provisional figures, K million): Revenue 6,553.1 (current 6,551.8, capital 1.3), excl. grants from abroad (1,331.5); Expenditure 11,984.8 (current 7,481.3, capital 4,503.5), excl. net lending (–1,343.2).

Source: IMF, *Government Finance Statistics Yearbook*.

INTERNATIONAL RESERVES
(US $ million at 31 December)

	1986	1987	1988
Gold*	1.0	1.8	4.1
Foreign exchange†	70.3	108.8	134.0
Total	71.3	110.6	138.1

* Valued at market-related prices.

† Foreign exchange (US $ million at 31 December): 116.2 in 1989; 193.1 in 1990; 184.6 in 1991; n.a. in 1992; 192.3 in 1993.

Source: IMF, *International Financial Statistics*.

MONEY SUPPLY (K million at 31 December)

	1989	1990	1991
Currency outside banks	2,250	4,610	9,188
Demand deposits at commercial banks*	5,695	7,927	13,166

* Demand deposits at commercial banks (K million at 31 December); 32,403 in 1992; 55,821 in 1993.

Source: IMF, *International Financial Statistics*.

COST OF LIVING (Consumer Price Index, average of monthly figures for low-income group; base: 1980 = 100)

	1990	1991	1992
Food	4,261.6	8,138.9	25,916
Clothing	3,921.1	6,564.6	n.a.
Rent, fuel and light	1,720.2	5,704.5	n.a.
All items (incl. others)	4,239.0	8,163.3	24,283

Source: ILO, *Year Book of Labour Statistics*.

NATIONAL ACCOUNTS
(K million at current prices)

Expenditure on the Gross Domestic Product

	1991	1992	1993
Government final consumption expenditure	35,758	83,497	130,659
Private final consumption expenditure	114,334	421,998	1,173,588
Increase in stocks	7,201	19,805	60,846
Gross fixed capital formation	24,973	60,187	93,170
Total domestic expenditure	182,266	585,487	1,458,263
Exports of goods and services	74,967	180,291	579,036
Less imports of goods and services	37,879	197,048	596,636
GDP in purchasers' values	219,353	568,730	1,440,663

Source: IMF, *International Financial Statistics*.

Gross Domestic Product by Economic Activity

	1989	1990	1991
Agriculture, hunting, forestry and fishing	6,390	14,175	28,132
Mining and quarrying	10,042	25,272	33,755
Manufacturing	13,027	25,510	61,725
Electricity, gas and water	308	635	1,909
Construction	3,019	6,300	10,911
Wholesale and retail trade, restaurants and hotels	8,963	13,148	24,021
Transport and communications	3,116	6,861	15,812
Finance, insurance, real estate and business services	6,837	13,290	24,832
Community, social and personal services	4,148	9,484	19,254
Sub-total	55,850	114,675	220,351
Less imputed bank service charge	768	1,471	2,726
GDP at factor cost	55,082	113,204	217,625
Indirect taxes, *less* subsidies	3,624	10,283	16,879
GDP in purchasers' values	58,706	123,487	234,504

Source: UN, *National Accounts Statistics*.

BALANCE OF PAYMENTS (US $ million)

	1989	1990	1991
Merchandise exports f.o.b.	1,340	1,254	1,172
Merchandise imports f.o.b.	–774	–1,511	–752
Trade balance	566	–257	420
Exports of services	85	107	83
Imports of services	–444	–386	–363
Other income received	1	2	10
Other income paid	–509	–439	–696
Private unrequited transfers (net)	–30	–18	–22
Official unrequited transfers (net)	109	395	261
Current balance	–222	–597	–307
Direct investment (net)	164	203	34
Other capital (net)	1,664	285	–24
Net errors and omissions	1,712	322	110
Overall balance	–105	213	–187

Source: IMF, *International Financial Statistics*.

External Trade

PRINCIPAL COMMODITIES (K'000)

Imports f.o.b.	1980	1981	1982*
Food and live animals	38,850	50,799	49,402
Beverages and tobacco	775	1,175	1,007
Crude materials (inedible) except fuels	12,108	13,570	11,047
Mineral fuels, lubricants, etc. (incl. electricity)	198,284	202,439	193,106
Animal and vegetable oils and fats	7,386	10,673	11,820
Chemicals	108,296	126,302	148,947
Basic manufactures	178,556	173,480	165,774
Machinery and transport equipment	302,340	314,443	320,996
Miscellaneous manufactured articles	29,319	29,608	29,960
Total (incl. others)	876,688	924,444	929,997

* Provisional.

Total imports (K million, f.o.b.): 6,898.1 in 1988; 12,600.5 in 1989; 36,553.7 in 1990; 51,772.8 in 1991; 144,108.5 in 1992. Source: UN, *International Trade Statistics Yearbook*.

Exports f.o.b.	1985*	1986*	1987*
Copper	1,960,600†	4,428,600	6,845,200
Zinc	53,189	99,154	130,944
Lead	7,400	15,537	19,765
Cobalt	23,867	385,151	466,221
Tobacco	2,233	4,254	16,612
Total (incl. others)	2,451,400†	5,366,584	8,058,653

* Provisional.

Total exports (K million, f.o.b.): 9,786.2 in 1988; 18,434.0 in 1989; 39,143.3 in 1990; 69,607.4 in 1991; 129,475.4 in 1992. Source: UN, *International Trade Statistics Yearbook*.

PRINCIPAL TRADING PARTNERS (US $'000)

Imports f.o.b.	1988	1989	1990
France	31,574	15,937	12,471
Germany	53,058	184,038	144,015
India	34,931	29,302	22,930
Italy	39,368	38,706	30,289
Japan	84,440	105,590	82,627
South African Customs Union	169,801	286,500	224,177
United Kingdom	19,596	256,049	200,365
USA	213,075	67,071	125,522
Total (incl. others)	886,054	1,258,321	1,237,717

Exports f.o.b.	1988	1989	1990
Belgium-Luxembourg	31,776	48,619	34,405
France	50,310	98,121	81,008
Greece	36,144	19,648	16,221
India	55,785	44,141	36,443
Italy	46,822	32,243	26,620
Japan	193,150	223,194	184,268
Saudi Arabia	47,595	38,732	31,977
Thailand	27,814	—	40,673
United Kingdom	29,652	14,712	12,147
USA	206,158	13,781	9,752
Total (incl. others)	866,711	667,811	594,765

Source: UN, *International Trade Statistics Yearbook*.

Transport

ROAD TRAFFIC
(UN estimates, '000 motor vehicles in use)

	1989	1990	1991
Passenger cars	74	74	75
Commercial vehicles	47	47	48

Source: UN Economic Commission for Africa, *African Statistical Yearbook*.

CIVIL AVIATION (scheduled services: Passengers carried—thousands; others—millions)

	1989	1990	1991
Kilometres flown	9	10	7
Passengers carried	365	407	293
Passenger-km	983	985	655
Freight ton-km	25	30	22
Mail ton-km	1	1	1

Source: UN, *Statistical Yearbook*.

Tourism

	1988	1989	1990
Tourist arrivals ('000)	108	113	141
Tourist receipts (million US dollars)	5	5	6

Source: UN, *Statistical Yearbook*.

Communications Media

	1989	1990	1991
Radio receivers ('000 in use)*	603	650	680
Television receivers ('000 in use)*	200	250	217
Telephones ('000 in use)	71*	72*	72*
Daily newspapers:			
Number	2	2	n.a.
Circulation ('000 copies)	95	99	n.a.

* Estimate(s).

Sources: UNESCO, *Statistical Yearbook;* UN Economic Commission for Africa, *African Statistical Yearbook*.

Education

(1989)

	Institutions	Pupils	Teachers
Primary	3,587*	1,461,206*	3,584
Secondary	480	161,349†	5,786†
Trades and technical	12	3,313*	438
Teacher training	14	4,669*	408
University	2	7,361‡	320§

* 1990 figures.
† 1988 figures.
‡ Excluding part-time and correspondence students.
§ Excluding part-time lecturers and teaching assistants.

Sources: the former Ministry of Higher Education and the former Ministry of General Education, Lusaka; University of Zambia; UNESCO, *Statistical Yearbook*.

Directory

The Constitution

The Constitution for the Republic of Zambia, which was approved by the National Assembly on 2 August 1991, provides for a multi-party form of government. The Head of State is the President of the Republic, who is elected by popular vote at the same time as elections to the National Assembly. The President's tenure of office is limited to two five-year terms. The legislature comprises a National Assembly of 150 members, who are elected by universal adult suffrage. The President appoints a Vice-President and a Cabinet from members of the National Assembly.

The Constitution also provides for a House of Chiefs numbering 27: four from each of the Northern, Western, Southern and Eastern Provinces, three each from the North-Western, Luapula and Central Provinces and two from the Copperbelt Province. It may submit resolutions to be debated by the Assembly and consider those matters referred to it by the President.

The Supreme Court of Zambia is the final Court of Appeal. The Chief Justice and other judges are appointed by the President. Subsidiary to the Supreme Court is the High Court, which has unlimited jurisdiction to hear and determine any civil or criminal proceedings under any Zambian law.

The Government

HEAD OF STATE

President: FREDERICK CHILUBA (took office 2 November 1991).

THE CABINET
(September 1994)

Vice-President: Brig.-Gen. GODFREY MIYANDA.

Minister of Defence: BENJAMIN YORAM MWILA.

Minister of Foreign Affairs: Dr REMMY MUSHOTA.

Minister of Finance: RONALD PENZA.

Minister of Home Affairs: CHITALU SAMPA.

Minister of Local Government and Housing: BENNIE MWIINGA.

Minister of Health: MICHAEL SATA.

Minister of Education: ALFEYO HAMBAYI.

Minister of Commerce, Trade and Industry: DIPAK PATEL.

Minister of Community Development and Social Welfare: Dr KABUNDA KAYONGO.

Minister of Labour and Social Security: NEWSTEAD ZIMBA.

Minister of Communications and Transport: WILLIAM HARRINGTON.

Minister of Energy and Water Development: EDITH NAWAKWI.

Minister of Agriculture, Food and Fisheries: SIMON ZUKAS.

Minister of Lands: Dr CHULU KALIMA.

Minister of Legal Affairs: (vacant).

Minister of the Environment and Natural Resources: DAWSON LUPUNGA.

Minister of Information and Broadcasting: Dr REMMYMUSHOTA.

Minister of Mines and Mineral Development: PAUL KAPI'NGA.

Minister of Science, Technology and Vocational Training: GABRIEL MAKA.

Minister of Youth, Sport and Child Development: AMUSSA MWANAMWAMBWA.

Minister of Tourism: Gen. CHRISTON TEMBO.

Minister of Works and Supply: ANDREW KASHITA.

Minister at the Office of the President, with responsibility for Planning and Development Co-operation: PAUL TEMBO.

Minister at the Office of the President, with responsibility for the North-Western Province: Rev. CHIPAWA.

Minister without Portfolio: (vacant).

MINISTRIES

Office of the President: POB 30208, Lusaka; tel. (1) 218282; telex 42240.

Ministry of Agriculture, Food and Fisheries: Mulungushi House, Independence Ave, Nationalist Rd, POB RW50291, Lusaka; tel. (1) 213551; telex 43950.

Ministry of Commerce, Trade and Industry: Kwacha Annex, Cairo Rd, POB 31968, Lusaka; tel. (1) 213767; telex 45630.

Ministry of Communications and Transport: Fairley Rd, POB 50065, Lusaka; tel. (1) 228118; telex 41680; fax (1) 253260.

Ministry of Community Development and Social Welfare: Lusaka.

Ministry of Defence: POB 31931, Lusaka; tel. (1) 252366.

Ministry of Education: 15102 Ridgeway, POB RW50093, Lusaka; tel. (1) 227636; telex 42621; fax (1) 222396.

Ministry of Energy and Water Development: Mulungushi House, Independence Ave, Nationalist Rd, POB 36079, Lusaka; tel. (1) 252589; telex 40373; fax (1) 252589.

Ministry of the Environment and Natural Resources: Lusaka.

Ministry of Finance: Finance Bldg, POB RW50062, Lusaka; tel. (1) 213822; telex 42221.

Ministry of Foreign Affairs: POB RW50069, Lusaka; tel. (1) 252640; telex 41290.

Ministry of Health: Woodgate House, 1st–2nd Floors, Cairo Rd, POB 30205, Lusaka; tel. (1) 211528.

Ministry of Home Affairs: POB 32862, Lusaka; tel. (1) 213505.

Ministry of Information and Broadcasting: Independence Ave, POB 51025, Lusaka; tel. (1) 228202; telex 40113.

Ministry of Labour and Social Security: Lechwe House, Freedom Way, POB 32186, Lusaka; tel. (1) 212020.

Ministry of Lands: POB 50694, Lusaka; tel. (1) 252288; telex 40681; fax (1) 250120.

Ministry of Legal Affairs: Fairley Rd, POB 50106, 15101 Ridgeway, Lusaka; tel. (1) 228522; telex 40564.

Ministry of Local Government and Housing: Lusaka.

Ministry of Mines and Mineral Development: Chilufya Mulenga Rd, POB 31969, Lusaka; tel. (1) 251402; telex 40539.

Ministry of Science, Technology and Vocational Training: POB 50464, Lusaka; tel. (1) 229673; telex 40406; fax (1) 252951.

Ministry of Tourism: Electra House, Cairo Rd, POB 30575, Lusaka; tel. (1) 227645; telex 45510.

Ministry of Works and Supply: Lusaka.

President and Legislature

PRESIDENT

Presidential election, 31 October 1991

	% of votes
FREDERICK CHILUBA	75.79
Dr KENNETH KAUNDA	24.21
Total	100.00

NATIONAL ASSEMBLY

General election, 31 October 1991

	Seats*
Movement for Multi-party Democracy (MMD)	125
United National Independence Party (UNIP)	25
Total	150

*Following by-elections held in November 1993 and April 1994, the MMD held 119 seats, UNIP occupied 26 and the newly-formed National Party (NP) held four. One seat remained vacant.

House of Chiefs

The House of Chiefs is an advisory body which may submit resolutions for debate by the National Assembly. There are 27 Chiefs, four each from the Northern, Western, Southern and Eastern Provinces, three each from the North Western, Luapula and Central Provinces, and two from the Copperbelt Province.

Political Organizations

The United National Independence Party was the sole authorized political party between 1972-90, when constitutional amendments permitted the formation of other political associations. Among the most prominent political organizations in mid-1994 were:

Caucus for National Unity (CNU): Lusaka; f. 1992 by mems of the Movement for Multi-party Democracy; Chair. (vacant).

Democratic Party (DP): Lusaka; f. 1991; Pres. EMMANUEL MWAMBA.

Independent Democratic Front: Lusaka; Pres. MIKE KAIRA.

Labour Party (LP): Lusaka; Leader CHIBEZA MUFUNE.

Movement for Democratic Process (MPD): Lusaka; f. 1991; Pres. CHAMA CHAKOMBOKA.

Movement for Multi-party Democracy (MMD): POB 365, 10101 Lusaka; f. 1990; ruling party since Nov. 1991; Pres. FREDERICK CHILUBA; Sec. Brig.-Gen. GODFREY MIYANDA.

Multi-Racial Party (MRP): Lusaka; Leader AARON MULENGA.

National Democratic Alliance (NADA): Lusaka; f. 1991; Pres. YONAM PHIRI.

National Party (NP): Lusaka; f. 1993 by former mems of MMD; Leader INONGE MBIKUSITA LEWANIKA.

National People's Salvation Party (NPSP): Lusaka; Pres. LUMBWE LAMBANYA.

United Democratic Congress Party: Lusaka; f. 1992; Leader DANIEL LISULO.

United National Independence Party (UNIP): POB 30302, Lusaka; tel. (1) 221197; telex 43640; fax (1) 221327; f. 1958; sole legal party 1972–90; Pres. KEBBY MUSOKOTWANE; Sec.-Gen. BENJAMIN MIBENGE.

Zambia Opposition Front (ZOFRO): Lusaka; f. 1994 by seven opposition parties; Chair. MIKE KAIRA.

Zambia Progressive Party: Lusaka.

Diplomatic Representation

EMBASSIES AND HIGH COMMISSIONS IN ZAMBIA

Angola: Plot 5548, Lukanga Rd, Kalundu, POB 31595, Lusaka; tel. (1) 254346; telex 41940; Ambassador: PEDRO FERNANDO MAVUNZA.

Austria: 30A Mutende Rd, Woodlands, POB 31094, Lusaka; tel. (1) 260407; telex 43790; Ambassador: Dr H. SCHURZ.

Belgium: Anglo-American Bldg, 74 Independence Ave, POB 31204, Lusaka; tel. (1) 252512; telex 40000; fax (1) 250075; Ambassador: LUC WILLEMARCK.

Botswana: 2647 Haile Selassie Ave, POB 31910, Lusaka; tel. (1) 250804; telex 41710; High Commissioner: SOBLEM MAYANE (acting).

Brazil: 74 Anglo-American Bldg, Independence Ave, POB 34470; tel. (1) 252749; telex 40102; fax (1) 251652; Chargé d'affaires a.i.: CECILIA DE BRASE BIDANT.

Bulgaria: Plot 251, 3 Ngwee Rd, POB 32896, Lusaka; tel. (1) 250880; telex 40215; Ambassador: DIMITAR ROMANOV.

Canada: Plot 5199, United Nations Ave, POB 31313, Lusaka; tel. (1) 250833; telex 42480; fax (1) 254176; High Commissioner: AUBREY L. MORANTZ.

China, People's Republic: Plot 7430, Haile Selassie Ave, POB 31975, Lusaka; tel. (1) 253770; telex 41360; Ambassador: YANG ZENGYE.

Cuba: Plot 5509, Lusiwasi Rd, Kalundu, POB 33132, Lusaka; tel. (1) 251380; telex 40309; Ambassador: JUAN CARRETERO.

Czech Republic: 2278 Independence Ave, POB 30059, Lusaka; tel. (1) 250908.

Denmark: 352 Independence Ave, POB 50299, Lusaka; tel. (1) 251634; telex 43580; Chargé d'affaires a.i.: MARK V. JENSEN.

Egypt: Plot 5206, United Nations Ave, POB 32428, Lusaka; tel. R.i.(1) 253762; telex 40021; Ambassador: SAYED SOLIMAN.

Finland: Anglo-American Bldg, 6th Floor, POB 50819, 15101 Ridgeway, Lusaka; tel. (1) 228492; telex 43460; fax (1) 261472; Ambassador: ILARI RANTAKARI.

France: Anglo-American Bldg, 4th Floor, 74 Independence Ave, POB 30062, Lusaka; tel. (1) 251322; telex 41430; fax (1) 254475; Ambassador: JEAN BROUSTE.

Germany: United Nations Ave, POB 50120, Lusaka; tel. (1) 229068; telex 41410; Ambassador: GÜNTER WASSERBERG.

Holy See: Hussein Saddam Blvd, POB 31445, Lusaka; tel. (1) 251033; telex 40403; fax (1) 250601; Apostolic Pro-Nuncio: Most Rev. GIUSEPPE LEANZA, Titular Archbishop of Lilibeo.

India: 5220 Haile Selassie Ave, POB 32111, Lusaka; tel. (1) 228376; telex 41420; High Commissioner: SATNAM JIT SINGH.

Ireland: Katima Mulilo Rd, Olympia Park, POB 34923, Lusaka; tel. (1) 290650; telex 43110; Chargé d'affaires a.i.: BRENDAN ROGERS.

Israel: Lusaka; Ambassador: Dr ARYE ODED.

Italy: Embassy Park, Diplomatic Triangle, POB 31046, Lusaka; tel. (1) 260382; telex 43380; fax (1) 260329; Ambassador: Dr G. MINGAZZINI.

Japan: Plot 5218, Haile Selassie Ave, POB 34190, Lusaka; tel. (1) 251555; telex 41470; fax (1) 253488; Ambassador: SHINSUKE HORIUCHI.

Kenya: Harambee House, Plot 5207, United Nations Ave, POB 50298, Lusaka; tel. (1) 227938; telex 42470; High Commissioner: JACKSON TUMWA.

Malawi: Woodgate House, Cairo Rd, POB 50425, Lusaka; tel. (1) 228296; telex 41840; High Commissioner: B. H. KAWONGA.

Mozambique: Mulungushi Village, Villa 46, POB 34877, Lusaka; tel. (1) 250436; telex 45900; Ambassador: ALBERTO CUVELO.

Netherlands: 5028 United Nations Ave, POB 31905, Lusaka; tel. (1) 250468; telex 42690; Ambassador: S. VAN HEEMSTRA.

Nigeria: Zambia Bible House, 5th Floor, Cairo Rd, POB 32598, Lusaka; tel. (1) 229860; telex 41280; High Commissioner: B. C. SELCHUM.

Portugal: Plot 25, Yotom Muteya Rd, POB 33871, Lusaka; tel. (1) 252996; telex 40010; Ambassador: A. LOPES DA FONSECA.

Romania: 2 Leopard's Hill Rd, POB 31944, Lusaka; tel. (1) 262182; Ambassador: L. FLORESCU.

Russia: Plot 6407, Diplomatic Triangle, POB 32355, Lusaka; tel. (1) 252183; Ambassador: OLEG SEMYONOVICH MIROSHKIN.

Saudi Arabia: Premium House, 5th Floor, POB 34411, Lusaka; tel. (1) 227829; telex 45550; Ambassador: (vacant).

Somalia: G3/377A Kabulonga Rd, POB 34051, Lusaka; tel. (1) 262119; telex 40270; Ambassador: Dr OMAN UMAL.

Spain: Lusaka; Ambassador: JOSÉ MANUEL PAZ Y AGÜERAS.

Sweden: POB 30788, Lusaka; tel. (1) 251249; telex 41820; fax (1) 223338; Ambassador: PER TAXELL.

Tanzania: Ujamaa House, Plot 5200, United Nations Ave, POB 31219, Lusaka; tel. (1) 227698; telex 40118; fax (1) 254861; High Commissioner: NIMROD LUGOE.

Uganda: Kulima Tower, 11th Floor, Katunjila Rd, Lusaka; tel. (1) 214413; telex 40990; High Commissioner: VALERIANO KARAKUZA-BAGUMA.

United Kingdom: Plot 5201, Independence Ave, POB 50050, 15101 Ridgeway, Lusaka; tel. (1) 228955; telex 41150; fax (1) 262215; High Commissioner: PATRICK NIXON.

USA: cnr Independence and United Nations Aves, POB 31617, Lusaka; tel. (1) 250955; telex 41970; fax (1) 252225; Ambassador: ROLAND KUCHEL.

Yugoslavia: Plot 5216, Diplomatic Triangle, POB 31180, Lusaka; tel. (1) 250247; Chargé d'affaires a.i.: STANIMIR JOVANOVIĆ.

Zaire: Plot 1124, Parirenyatwa Rd, POB 31287, Lusaka; tel. (1) 213343; Ambassador: Dr ATENDE OMWARGO.

Zimbabwe: Memaco House, 4th Floor, Cairo Rd, POB 33491, Lusaka; tel. (1) 229382; telex 45800; High Commissioner: Dr A. H. MTETWA.

Judicial System

Supreme Court of Zambia: Independence Ave, POB 50067, Ridgeway, Lusaka; tel. (1) 228340; telex 40396; the final Court of Appeal. Judges of the Supreme Court include the Chief Justice and the Deputy Chief Justice. The High Court consists of the Chief Justice and 20 Judges. Senior Resident and Resident Magistrates' Courts also sit at various centres. The Local Courts deal mainly with customary law, although, they have certain limited statutory powers.

Chief Justice: MATHEW M. S. W. NGULUBE.

Deputy Chief Justice: B. K. BWEUPE.

Supreme Court Judges: B. T. GARDNER, E. L. SAKALA, M. S. CHAILA, E. K. CHIRWA, A. R. LAWRENCE, W. M. MUZYAMBA, C. M. MUSAMALI.

Religion

CHRISTIANITY

Christian Council of Zambia: Church House, Cairo Rd, POB 30315, Lusaka; tel. (1) 224308; telex 45160; f. 1945; 14 mem. churches and 13 other Christian orgs; Chair. PHILIP G. H. SIMUCHOBA; Gen. Sec. VIOLET SAMPA-BREDT.

The Anglican Communion

Anglicans are adherents of the Church of the Province of Central Africa, covering Botswana, Malawi, Zambia and Zimbabwe. The Church comprises 10 dioceses, including three in Zambia. The

Archbishop of the Province is the Bishop of Botswana. There are an estimated 40,000 adherents in Zambia.

Bishop of Central Zambia: Rt Rev. CLEMENT SHABA, POB 70172, Ndola.

Bishop of Lusaka: Rt Rev. STEPHEN MUMBA, Bishop's Lodge, POB 30183, Lusaka.

Bishop of Northern Zambia: Rt Rev. BERNARD MALANGO, POB 20173, Kitwe.

Protestant Churches

African Methodist Episcopal Church: POB 31478, Lusaka; tel. (1) 264013; 400 congregations, 80,000 mems; Presiding Elder Rev. D. K. SIMFUKWE.

Baptist Church: Lubu Rd, POB 30636, Lusaka; tel. (1) 253620.

Baptist Mission of Zambia: 3061/62 cnr Makishi and Great East Rds, POB 50599, 15101 Ridgeway, Lusaka; tel. (1) 222492; fax (1) 227520.

Brethren in Christ Church: POB 115, Choma; tel. (3) 20278; f. 1906; Bishop Rev. SHAMAPANI; 116 congregations, 7,699 mems.

Reformed Church of Zambia: POB 510013, Chipata; tel. (62) 21559; f. 1899; African successor to the Dutch Reformed Church mission; 170 congregations, 200,000 mems.

Seventh-day Adventists: POB 31309, Lusaka; tel. (1) 219775; telex 43760; 66,408 active mems.

United Church of Zambia: Synod Headquarters, Nationalist Rd at Burma Rd, POB 50122, Lusaka; tel. (1) 250641; f. 1967; c. 1m. mems; Synod Moderator Rev. GODFREY SIKAZWE; Gen. Sec. Rev. BENSON CHONGO.

Other denominations active in Zambia include the Assemblies of God, the Church of Christ, the Church of the Nazarene, the Evangelical Fellowship of Zambia, the Kimbanguist Church, the Presbyterian Church of Southern Africa, the Religious Society of Friends (Quakers) and the United Pentecostal Church.

The Roman Catholic Church

Zambia comprises two archdioceses and seven dioceses. At 31 December 1992 there were an estimated 2,441,151 adherents in the country.

Bishops' Conference: Zambia Episcopal Conference, Catholic Secretariat, Unity House, cnr Freedom Way and Katunjila Rd, POB 31965, Lusaka; tel. (1) 212070; telex 43560; fax (1) 220996; f. 1984; Pres. Rt Rev. TELESPHORE MPUNDI, Bishop of Mbala-Mpika; Sec.-Gen. Rev. IVES BANTUNGWA.

Archbishop of Kasama: Most Rev. JAMES SPAITA, Archbishop's House, POB 410143, Kasama; tel. (4) 221248; fax (4) 222202.

Archbishop of Lusaka: Most Rev. ADRIAN MUNG'ANDU, 41 Wamulwa Rd, POB 32754, Lusaka; tel. (1) 213188; fax (1) 290631.

ISLAM

There are about 10,000 members of the Muslim Association in Zambia.

BAHÁ'Í FAITH

National Spiritual Assembly: POB 227, Ridgeway, Lusaka; tel. (1) 254505; fax (1) 247166; mems resident in 1,456 localities.

The Press

DAILIES

The Times of Zambia: POB 30394, Lusaka; tel. (1) 229076; telex 41860; fax (1) 222880; f. 1943; govt-owned; English; Man. Editor CYRUS SIKAZWE; circ. 65,000.

Zambia Daily Mail: POB 31421, Lusaka; tel. (1) 211722; telex 44621; f. 1968; govt-owned; English; Man. Editor EMMANUEL NYIRENDA; circ. 40,000.

PERIODICALS

African Social Research: Institute for African Studies, University of Zambia, POB 32379, Lusaka; tel. (1) 292462; fax (1) 253952; f. 1944; 2 a year; Editor Dr L. J. CHINGAMBO; circ. 1,000.

Chipembele Magazine: POB 30255, Lusaka; tel. (1) 254226; 6 a year; publ. by Wildlife Conservation Soc. of Zambia; circ. 20,000.

Farming in Zambia: POB 50197, Lusaka; tel. (1) 213551; telex 43950; f. 1965; quarterly; publ. by Ministry of Agriculture; Editor L. P. CHIRWA; circ. 3,000.

Icengelo: Chifubu Rd, POB 71581, Ndola; tel. (2) 680456; telex 30054; f. 1970; monthly; Bemba; social, educational and religious; Roman Catholic; Editors Fr U. DAVOLI, E. CHIKONDE; circ. 56,000.

Imbila: POB RW20, Lusaka; tel. (1) 217254; f. 1953; monthly; publ. by Zambia Information Services; Bemba; Editor D. MUKAKA; circ. 20,000.

Intanda: POB RW20, Lusaka; tel. (1) 219675; f. 1958; monthly; general; publ. by Zambia Information Services; Tonga; Editor J. SIKAULU; circ. 6,000.

Journal of Adult Education: University of Zambia, POB 50516, Lusaka; tel. (1) 216767; telex 44370; f. 1982; Exec. Editor FRANCIS KASOMA.

Leisure Magazine: Farmers House, Cairo Rd, POB 8138, Woodlands, Lusaka; general interest.

Liseli: POB RW20, Lusaka; tel. (1) 219675; monthly; publ. by Zambia Information Services; Lozi; Editor F. AMNSAA; circ. 7,700.

Lukanga News: POB 919, Kabwe; tel. (5) 217254; publ. by Zambia Information Services; Lenje; Editor J. H. N. NKOMANGA; circ. 5,500.

Mining Mirror: POB 71605, Ndola; tel. (2) 640133; f. 1973; monthly; English; Editor-in-Chief G. S. MUKUWA; circ. 50,000.

National Mirror: Bishops Rd, Kabulonga, POB 320199, Lusaka; tel. (1) 261193; telex 40630; fax (1) 263050; f. 1972; weekly; publ. by Multimedia Zambia; Editor FANWELL CHEMBO; circ. 40,000.

Ngoma: POB RW20, Lusaka; tel. (1) 219675; monthly; Lunda, Kaonde and Luvale; publ. by Zambia Information Services; Editor B. A. LUHILA; circ. 3,000.

Orbit: POB RW18X, Lusaka; tel. (1) 254915; f. 1971; publ. by Ministry of Education; children's educational magazine; Editor ELIDAH CHISHA; circ. 65,000.

Sechaba: African National Congress, Department of Information and Publicity, POB 31791, Lusaka; f. 1967; monthly; politics and civil rights; circ. 30,000.

Speak Out: POB 70244, Ndola; tel. (2) 612241; fax (2)610556; f. 1984; bi-monthly; Christian; circ. 40,000.

The Sportsman: POB 31762, Lusaka; tel. (1) 224250; telex 40151; f. 1980; monthly; Man. Editor SAM SIKAZWE; circ. 18,200.

Sunday Express: Lusaka; f. 1991; weekly; Man. Editor JOHN MUKELA.

Sunday Times of Zambia: POB 30394, Lusaka; tel. (1) 229076; telex 41860; fax (1) 222880; f. 1965; owned by UNIP; English; Man. Editor ARTHUR SIMUCHOBA; circ. 78,000.

Tsopano: POB RW20, Lusaka; tel. (1) 217254; f. 1958; monthly; publ. by Zambia Information Services; Nyanja; Editor S. S. BANDA; circ. 9,000.

VOW (Voice of Women): POB 31791, Lusaka; tel. (1) 261263; telex 45390; bi-monthly; publ. by the women's section of the African National Congress of South Africa; circ. 8,000.

Weekly Post: POB 352, Lusaka; tel. (1) 293791; telex 40614; fax (1) 293788; f. 1991; independent; Man. Dir FRED MEMBE; Editor MIKE HALL; circ. 30,000.

Workers' Challenge: POB 270035, Kitwe; tel. and fax (2) 220904; f. 1981; 2 a month; publ. by the Workers' Pastoral Centre; English and Bemba; Co-Editors Fr MISHECK KAUNDA, JUSTIN CHILUFYA; circ. 16,000.

Workers' Voice: POB 652, Kitwe; tel. (2) 211999; f. 1972; fortnightly; publ. by Zambia Congress of Trade Unions.

Youth: POB 30302, Lusaka; tel. (1) 211411; f. 1974; quarterly; publ. by UNIP Youth League; Editor-in-Chief N. ANAMELA; circ. 20,000.

Zambia Government Gazette: POB 30136, Lusaka; tel. (1) 215401; f. 1911; weekly; English; official notices.

NEWS AGENCY

Zambia News Agency (ZANA): Mass Media Complex, POB 30007, Lusaka; tel. (1) 219673; telex 42120; Editor-in-Chief DAVID KASHWEKA.

Foreign Bureaux

Agence France-Presse: POB 33805, Lusaka; tel. (1) 212959; telex 45960; Bureau Chief ABBE MAINE.

Informatsionnoye Telegrafnoye Agentstvo Rossii–Telegrafnoye Agentstvo Suverennykh Stran (ITAR–TASS) (Russia): Lusaka; tel. (1) 254201; telex 45270; Bureau Chief V. NOVIKOV.

Inter Press Service (IPS) (Italy): POB 30765, Lusaka; tel. (1) 217857; telex 40151; Stringer SAM SIKAZWE.

Novinska Agencija Tanjug (Yugoslavia): Lusaka; Bureau Chief BORISLAV KORKODELOVIĆ.

Reuters (UK): POB 31685, Lusaka; tel. (1) 253430; telex 41160.

Rossiyskoye Informatsionnoye Agentstvo—Novosti (RIA—Novosti) (Russia): POB 31383, Lusaka; tel. (1) 252849; telex 45190; Rep. VIKTOR LAPTUKHIN.

Xinhua (New China) News Agency (People's Republic of China): United Nations Ave, POB 31859, Lusaka; tel. (1) 252227; fax (1) 252227; telex 40455; Chief Correspondent QIU XIAOYI.

PRESS ASSOCIATION

Press Association of Zambia (PAZA): c/o The Times of Zambia, POB 30394, Lusaka; tel. (1) 229076; f. 1983; Chair. ROBINSON MAKAYI.

Publishers

Africa: Literature Centre, POB 1319, Kitwe; tel. (2) 84712; general, educational, religious; Man. Dir E. C. MAKUNIKE.

African Social Research: Publications Office, Institute of African Studies, University of Zambia, POB 32379, Lusaka; tel. (1) 292462; telex 44370; social research in Africa; Editor L. J. CHINGAMBO.

Daystar Publications Ltd: POB 32211, Lusaka; f. 1966; religious; Man. Dir S. E. M. PHEKO.

Directory Publishers of Zambia Ltd: POB 30963, Lusaka; tel. (1) 292845; f. 1958; trade directories; Gen. Man. W. D. WRATTEN.

Multimedia Zambia: Woodlands, POB 320199, Lusaka; tel. (1) 261193; telex 40630; fax (1) 263050; f. 1971; religious and educational books, audio-visual materials; Exec. Dir JUMBE NGOMA.

Temco Publishing Co: 10 Kabelenga Rd, POB 30886, Lusaka; tel. (1) 211883; telex 45250; f. 1977; educational and general; Man. Dir S. V. TEMBO.

University of Zambia: Publications Office, POB 32379, Lusaka; tel. (1) 293008; telex 44370; fax (1) 253952; f. 1938; academic books, papers and journals.

Zambia Educational Publishing House: Chishango Rd, POB 32664, Lusaka; tel. (1) 229211; telex 40056; f. 1967; educational and general; Dir H. LOMBE.

Zambia Printing Co Ltd: POB 34798, 10101 Lusaka; tel. (1) 227673; telex 40068; fax (1) 225026; Gen. Man. BERNARD LUBUMBASHI.

Government Publishing Houses

Government Printer: POB 30136, Lusaka; tel. (1) 215401; publr of all official documents and statistical bulletins.

Zambia Information Services: POB 50020, Lusaka; tel. (1) 219673; telex 41350; state-controlled; Dir BENSON SIANGA; Dep. Dir MUNDIA NALISHEBO (acting).

PUBLISHERS' ASSOCIATION

Booksellers' and Publishers' Association of Zambia: POB 31838, Lusaka; tel. (1) 225282; fax (1) 225195; Chair. CHRISTINE KASONDE; Sec. BHARAT NAYEE.

Radio and Television

In 1991, according to UNESCO, there were an estimated 680,000 radio receivers and 217,000 television receivers in use.

Zambia National Broadcasting Corporation: Broadcasting House, POB 50015, Lusaka; tel. (1) 220864; telex 41221; fax (1) 252391; f. 1966; state-controlled; radio services in English and seven Zambian languages; television services in English; Dir-Gen. Dr MANNASSEH PHIRI.

Educational Broadcasting Services: Headquarters: POB 50231, Lusaka; tel. (1) 251724; radio broadcasts from Lusaka; television for schools from POB 21106, Kitwe; audio-visual aids service from POB 50295, Lusaka; Controller MICHAEL MULOMBE.

Finance

(cap. = capital; auth. = authorized; p.u. = paid up; res = reserves; dep. = deposits; m. = million; br. = branch; amounts in kwacha)

BANKING

Capitalization of banks must total at least K500,000 in the case of any commercial bank wholly or partially owned by the Government, and not less than K2m. in the case of any other commercial bank. At least one-half of the directors of these latter banks must be established residents in Zambia. All foreign-owned banks are required to incorporate in Zambia.

Central Bank

Bank of Zambia: POB 30080, Lusaka; tel. (1) 216529; telex 41560; fax (1) 42999; f. 1964; bank of issue; cap. and res 35.3m., dep. 783.2m. (Oct. 1985); Gov. DOMINIC MULAISHO; Gen. Man. BERNARD MBULO; br. in Ndola.

Commercial Banks

African Commercial Bank Ltd: Superannuation House, Ben Bella Rd, POB 30097, Lusaka; tel. (1) 229482; telex 40092; fax (1) 227495; f. 1984; cap. 91.4m., res 281.7m., dep. 2,728.5m. (March 1993); Chair. JOHN MWANAKATWE; Man. Dir W. FEARON; 4 brs.

Commerce Bank Ltd: 627 South End Cairo Rd, POB 32393, Lusaka; tel. (1) 229948; telex 40715; fax (1) 223769; f. 1992; cap. p.u. 225m.; Chair. MUSALILWA SIAME.

Co-operative Bank of Zambia (Co-operative Society) Ltd: Co-operative House, Chachacha Rd, North End, POB 33666, Lusaka; tel. (1) 223849; fax (1) 225505; f. 1991; cap. p.u. 27.9m. (March 1992); Chair. M. D. NCHIMUNYA; Man. Dir H. N. MUFALO.

Finance Bank Zambia Ltd: 2101 Chanik House, POB 37102, Lusaka; tel. (1) 221614; telex 40338; fax (1) 221614; cap. p.u. 100m. (Dec. 1990); Chair. Dr R.L. MAHTANI.

Manifold Investment Bank Ltd: Cusa House Cairo Rd, POB 36595, Lusaka; tel. (1) 224109; telex 40368; fax (1) 224071; f. 1988; cap. 6.5m., res 19.2m., dep. 111.5m. (June 1991); Chair. HELLINS CHABI; Man. Dir VADAKETH GEORGE.

National Savings and Credit Bank of Zambia: Plot 248, Cairo Rd, POB 30067; Lusaka; tel. (1) 227534; telex 40089; fax (1) 223296; f. 1973; dep. 1,145m. (Dec. 1993); Man. Dir G. J. M. CHEMBE.

Union Bank Zambia Ltd: Zimco House, Cairo Rd, POB 34940, Lusaka; tel. (1) 221093; telex 40112; fax (1) 221866; cap. p.u. 246.1m. (Dec. 1991); Chair. O. J. IRWIN; Man. Dir S. A. J. RIZVI.

Zambia National Commercial Bank Ltd: Plot 2118, Cairo Rd, POB 33611, Lusaka; tel. (1) 228979; telex 42360; fax (1) 223082; f. 1969; govt-controlled; cap. 350.0m., res 2,199.2m., dep. 35,269.3m. (March 1992); Chair. R. L. BWALYA; Man. Dir J.Y. NG'OMA; 40 brs.

Foreign Banks

Barclays Bank of Zambia Ltd (UK): Kafue House, Cairo Rd, POB 31936, Lusaka; tel. (1) 228858; telex 41570; fax (1) 222519; f. 1971; cap. 477.0m., res 2,146.2m., dep. 10,065.9m. (Dec. 1991); Chair. A. B. MUNYAMA; Man. Dir N. BRENTNALL; 35 brs.

Citibank Zambia Ltd (USA): Kulima Tower, Katunjila Rd, POB 30037, Lusaka; tel. (1) 229025; telex 45610; fax (1) 226264; f. 1979; cap. 171.8m., res 432.6m., dep. 602.1m. (Dec. 1991); Man. Dir ANTONIO URIBE.

Indo-Zambia Bank (IZB): Indeco House, 686 Cairo Rd, POB 35411, Lusaka; tel. (1) 222613; telex 40178; fax (1) 222613; f. 1984; cap. 50.0m., res 141.7m., dep. 2,305.8m. (March 1992); Chair. R. L. BWALYA; Man. Dir S. R. KRISHNAN; 4 brs..

Meridien BIAO Bank Zambia Ltd (Bahamas): Meridien BIAO House, Chachacha Rd, POB 37763, 10101 Lusaka; tel. (1) 229464; telex 41270; fax (1) 223997; f. 1984; cap. 450.0m., res 683.8m., dep. 19,989.3m. (Sept. 1992); Chair. J. C. KAPOTWE; Man. Dir S. J. ANZSAR; 11 brs.

Stanbic Bank Zanbia Ltd: Woodgate House, Nairobi Place, Cairo Rd, POB 31955, Lusaka; tel. (1) 229285; telex 42461; fax (1) 221152; f. 1971 as Grindlays Bank International (Zambia) Ltd; cap. p.u. 160m. (Sept. 1992), dep. 281.3m. (Sept. 1986); Chair. D. A. R. PHIRI; Gen. Man. I. F. PETERKIN; 7 brs and 1 sub-br.

Standard Chartered Bank Zambia Ltd (UK): Standard House, Cairo Rd, POB 32238, Lusaka; tel. (1) 229242; telex 41660; fax (1) 222092; f. 1971; cap. 1,950.0m., res 2,306.7m., dep. 20,200.1m. (Dec. 1992); Chair. A. K. MAZOKA; Man. Dir B. R. KNIGHT; 26 brs and 5 agencies.

Development Banks

Development Bank of Zambia: cnr Katondo and Chachacha Rds, POB 33955, Lusaka; tel. (1) 228580; telex 45040; fax (1) 222426; f. 1972; 60% state-owned; provides medium- and long-term loans and offers business consultancy and research services; cap. p.u. 403.1m. (Feb. 1993); Chair. Dr J. M. MTONGA; Man. Dir G. M. B. MUMBA; 2 brs.

Lima Bank: Kulima House, Chachacha Rd, POB 32607, Lusaka; tel. (1) 228073; telex 40126; fax (1) 228074; cap. p.u. 57m. (March 1986); Chair. N. MUKUTU; Man. Dir K. V. KASAPATU.

Zambia Agricultural Development Bank: Society House, Cairo Rd, POB 30847, Lusaka; tel. (1) 219251; telex 40126; f. 1982; loan finance for development of agriculture and fishing; auth. cap. 75m.; Chair. K. MAKASA; Man. Dir AMON CHIBIYA.

Zambia Export and Import Bank Ltd: Society House, Cairo Rd, POB 33046, Lusaka; tel. (1) 229486; telex 40098; fax (1) 222313; f. 1987; cap. p.u. 50m. (March 1992), dep. 50.9m. (March 1990); Chair. J. M. MTONGA.

STOCK EXCHANGE

Zambia Stock Exchange: Lusaka; f. 1994; Sec. of Securities and Exchange Comm. MUMBA KAPUMPA.

INSURANCE

Zambia State Insurance Corporation Ltd: Premium House, Independence Ave, POB 30894, Lusaka; tel. (1) 218888; telex 42521; f. 1968; took over all insurance business in Zambia in 1971; Chair. E. WILLIMA; Man. Dir MWENE MWINGA.

Trade and Industry

CHAMBER OF COMMERCE

Lusaka Chamber of Commerce and Industry: POB 30844, Lusaka; tel. (1) 252369; telex 40124; f. 1933; Chair. R. D. PENZA; Sec. Dr E. BBENKELE; 400 mems.

INDUSTRIAL AND COMMERCIAL ASSOCIATIONS

Copper Industry Service Bureau Ltd: POB 22100, Kitwe; tel. (2) 214122; telex 52620; f. 1941 as Chamber of Mines.

Zambia Association of Manufacturers: POB 30844, Lusaka; tel. (1) 252369; telex 40124; f. 1985; Chair. DEV BABBAR; Sec. N. NAMUSHI; 250 mems.

Zambia Confederation of Industries and Chambers of Commerce: POB 30844, Lusaka; tel. (1) 252369; telex 40124; fax (1) 252483; f. 1938; Chair. R. D. FROST; CEO B. CHISANGA; 2,000 mems.

Zambia Farm Employers' Association: V.T.A. House, Chachacha Rd, POB 30395, Lusaka; tel. (1) 213222; telex 40164; Chair. D. FLYNN; Vice-Chair. M. J. H. BECKETT; 300 mems.

Zambia Seed Producers' Association: POB 30013, Lusaka; tel. (1) 223249; telex 40164; fax (1) 222736; f. 1964; Chair. BARRY COXE; 300 mems.

STATUTORY ORGANIZATIONS

Industry

Industrial Development Corporation of Zambia Ltd (INDECO): Indeco House, Buteko Place, POB 31935, Lusaka; tel. (1) 228463; telex 41821; fax (1) 228868; f. 1960; auth. cap. K300m.; c. 47 subsidiaries and assoc. cos in brewing, chemicals, property, manufacturing, agriculture and vehicle assembly; Chair. R. L. BWALYA; Man. Dir S. K. TAMELÉ.

Metal Marketing Corporation (Zambia) Ltd (MEMACO): Memaco House, Sapele Rd, POB 35570, Lusaka; tel. (1) 228131; telex 40070; fax (1) 223671; f. 1973; sole sales agents for all metal and mineral production; Chair. R. L. BWALYA; Man. Dir U. M. MUTATI.

National Import and Export Corporation (NIEC): National Housing Authority Bldg, POB 30283, Lusaka; tel. (1) 2288018; telex 44490; fax (1) 252771; f. 1974.

Posts and Telecommunications Corporation: POB 71630, Ndola; tel. (2) 2281; telex 33430.

Small Industries Development Organization (SIDO): Sido House, Cairo Rd, POB 35373, Lusaka; tel. (1) 219801; telex 40169; f. 1981 to promote development of small and village industries.

Zambia Electricity Supply Corporation (ZESCO): Lusaka; Man. Dir ROBINSON MWANSA.

Zambia Industrial and Mining Corporation Ltd (ZIMCO): Zimco House, Cairo Rd, POB 30090, Lusaka; tel. (1) 212487; telex 40790; f. 1970 as holding co for govt interests in mining, industrial, commercial transport and energy, communications, hotels and land, financial and agrarian enterprises; c. 135 subsidiaries and assoc. cos; fixed assets K25,898m. (March 1987); Exec. Dir JAMES NGOMA.

Agriculture

The Dairy Produce Board of Zambia: Kwacha House, Cairo Rd, POB 30124, Lusaka; tel. (1) 214770; telex 41520; f. 1964; purchase and supply of dairy products to retailers, manufacture and marketing of milk products.

Department of Marketing and Co-operatives: POB 50595, Lusaka; tel. (1) 214933; a dept of Ministry of Agriculture; Dir S. B. CHIWALA.

Tobacco Board of Zambia: POB 31963, Lusaka; tel. (1) 288995; telex 40370; Sec. L. C. SIMUMBA.

Zambia Co-operative Federation Ltd: Kwacha House, Cairo Rd, POB 33579, Lusaka; tel. (1) 228538; telex 43210; fax (1) 222516; agricultural marketing; supply of agricultural chemicals and implements; cargo haulage; insurance; agricultural credit; auditing and accounting; property and co-operative development; Chair. C. CHILALA; Man. Dir G. Z. SIBALE.

MAJOR INDUSTRIAL COMPANIES

The following are among the largest companies in terms either of capital investment or employment. The government has a controlling interest in major strategic industries.

Chilanga Cement Ltd: Head Office: POB 32639, Lusaka; tel. (1) 278417; telex 70500; works at Chilanga and Ndola; manufacture and marketing of cement. Gen. Man. Z. C. MUSONDA.

Dunlop Zambia Ltd: POB 71650, Ndola; tel. (2) 650789; telex 34110; fax (2) 650138; f. 1964; cap. K563m.; mfrs and distributors of car, truck, tractor, earthmover and mining as well as cycle tyres and tubes; also of contact adhesives, floor tiles and other allied rubber products; Man. Dir ROBERT MAY; 460 employees.

Kafue Textiles of Zambia Ltd: POB 360131, Kafue; tel. (1) 311501; telex 70050; fax (1) 311514; f. 1969; 55% of shares owned by ZIMCO; mfrs of drills, denims, twills and poplins; dress prints and African prints; industrial and household textiles; Gen. Man. ROLF KLEIN; 1,200 employees.

Minestone (Zambia) Ltd: POB 31870 Lusaka; tel. (1) 228748; telex 40210; fax (1) 222301; f. 1954; cap. K1.9m.; building, civil and mechanical contractors; Chair. and Man. Dir G. M. SIMPUNGWE; 5,500–6,000 employees.

National Breweries Ltd: POB 22699, Kitwe; tel. (2) 211333; telex 51740; inc 1968; subsidiary of INDECO; operates 14 breweries; Chair. D. H. LUZONGO; Gen. Man. H. G. MUZABAZI; 680 employees.

Nitrogen Chemicals of Zambia Ltd: POB 32483, Lusaka; tel. (1) 228550; telex 40569; fax (1) 311313; f. 1967; cap. K509m.; production of ammonium nitrate for fertilizer and explosives, nitric acid, ammonium sulphate, sulphuric acid, methanol, compound fertilizers and liquid carbon dioxide; Chair. L. BWALYA; Man. Dir F. M. KAMBOBE; 1,600 employees.

ROP Ltd: POB 71570, Nakambala Rd, Ndola; tel. (2) 650549; telex 33120; fax (2) 650162; f. 1975 by merger of Refined Oil Products Ltd and Lever Brothers, Zambia; mfrs of soaps, detergents, toilet preparations and edible oils; Gen. Man. (vacant).

Zambezi Sawmills (1968) Ltd: POB 60041, Livingstone; tel. (3) 320320; telex 24003; fax (3) 320173; subsidiary of ZIMCO; sawmillers and mfrs of railway sleepers, mining timbers, sawn timber, wooden parquet tiles, etc.

Zambia Breweries Ltd: POB 70091, Ndola, 74 Independence Ave, Lusaka; tel. (1) 3601; telex 42330; f. 1951, opened in Lusaka 1966; cap. K5.6m.; state-owned; brewing, bottling and distribution of lager beers; Gen. Man. ZACKS MUSONDA; 1,300 employees.

Zambia Consolidated Copper Mines Ltd (ZCCM): 5309 Dedan Kimathi Rd, POB 30048, Lusaka; tel. (1) 229115; telex 44540; f. 1982 by merger of Nchanga Consolidated Copper Mines and Roan Consolidated Mines; auth. cap. K900m.; Govt holds 60.3% of shares through ZIMCO; Chair. R. L. BWALYA; CEO EDWARD SHAMUTETE.

TRADE UNIONS

Zambia Congress of Trade Unions: POB 20652, Kitwe; tel. (2) 211999; telex 52630; f. 1965; 18 affiliated unions; c. 400,000 mems; Pres. JACKSON SHAMENDA; Sec.-Gen. ALEC CHIORMA.

Affiliated Unions

Airways and Allied Workers' Union of Zambia: POB 30272, Lusaka; Pres. F. MULENGA; Gen. Sec. B. CHINYANTA.

Guards Union of Zambia: POB 21882, Kitwe; tel. (2) 216189; f. 1972; 13,500 mems; Chair. D. N. S. SILUNGWE; Gen. Sec. MICHAEL S. SIMFUKWE.

Hotel Catering Workers' Union of Zambia: POB 35693, Lusaka; 9,000 mems; Chair. IAN MKANDAWIRE; Gen. Sec. STOIC KAPUTU.

Mineworkers' Union of Zambia: POB 20448, Kitwe; tel. (2) 214022; telex 52650; 50,000 mems; Chair. (vacant); Gen. Sec. K. G. SHENG'AMO.

National Union of Building, Engineering and General Workers: POB 21515, Kitwe; tel. (2) 213931; 18,000 mems; Chair. LUCIANO MUTALE (acting); Gen. Sec. P. N. NZIMA.

National Union of Commercial and Industrial Workers: 87 Gambia Ave, POB 21735, Kitwe; tel. (2) 217456; f. 1982; 16,000 mems; Chair. P. L. NKHOMA; Gen. Sec. I. M. KASUMBU.

National Union of Plantation and Agricultural Workers: POB 80529, Kabwe; tel. (5) 224548; 15,155 mems; Chair. L. B. IKOWA; Gen. Sec. S. C. SILWIMBA.

National Union of Postal and Telecommunications Workers: POB 70751, Ndola; tel. (2) 611345; 6,000 mems; Chair. G. C. MWAPE; Gen. Sec. F. U. SHAMENDA.

National Union of Public Services' Workers: POB 32523, Lusaka; tel. (1) 215167; Chair. W. CHIPASHA; Gen. Sec. WILLIE MBEWE.

National Union of Transport and Allied Workers: POB 32431, Lusaka; tel. (1) 214756; Chair. B. MULWE; Gen. Sec. L. K. MABULUKI.

Railway Workers' Union of Zambia: POB 80302, Kabwe; tel. (5) 224006; 10,228 mems; Chair. H. K. NDAMANA; Gen. Sec. P. S. KUMBUYO.

University of Zambia and Allied Workers' Union: POB 32379, Lusaka; tel. (1) 213221; telex 44370; f. 1968; Chair. BERIATE SUNKUTU; Gen. Sec. SAINI PHIRI.

Zambia Electricity Workers' Union: POB 70859, Ndola; f. 1972; 3,000 mems; Chair. COSMAS MPAMPI; Gen. Sec. ADAM KALUBA.

Zambia National Union of Farmers: Gen. Sec. BEN KAPITA.

Zambia National Union of Teachers: POB 31914, Lusaka; tel. (1) 216670; 2,120 mems; Chair. JACKSON MULENGA; Gen. Sec. A. W. CHIBALE.

Zambia Typographical Workers' Union: POB 71439, Ndola; Chair. R. SHIKWATA; Gen. Sec. D. NAWA.

Zambia Union of Financial Institutions and Allied Workers: POB 31174, Lusaka; tel. (1) 219401; Chair. B. CHIKOTI; Gen. Sec. GEOFFREY ALIKIPO.

Zambia United Local Authorities Workers' Union: POB 70575, Ndola; tel. (2) 615022; Chair. A. M. MUTAKILA; Gen. Sec. A. H. MUDENDA.

Principal Non-Affiliated Unions

Civil Servants' Union of Zambia: POB 50160, Lusaka; tel. (1) 221332; f. 1975; 30,000 mems; Chair. P. M. MOYO; Gen. Sec. J. C. MOONDE.

Zambian African Mining Union: Kitwe; f. 1967; 40,000 mems.

Transport

RAILWAYS

Total length of railways in Zambia was 2,164 km (including 891 km of the Tanzania–Zambia railway) in 1988. There are two major railway lines: the Zambia Railways network, which traverses the country from the Copperbelt in northern Zambia and links with the National Railways of Zimbabwe to provide access to South African ports, and the Tanzania–Zambia Railway (Tazara) system, linking New Kapiri-Mposhi in Zambia with Dar es Salaam in Tanzania. The Tazara railway line increased its capacity from 1986, in order to reduce the dependence of southern African countries on trade routes through South Africa. In April 1987 the Governments of Zambia, Angola and Zaire declared their intention to reopen the Benguela railway, linking Zambian copper-mines with the Angolan port of Lobito, following its closure to international traffic in 1975 as a result of the guerrilla insurgency in Angola.

Tanzania–Zambia Railway Authority (Tazara): POB 98, Mpika; Head Office: POB 2834, Dar es Salaam, Tanzania; tel. 62191; telex 41059; f. 1975; operates passenger and freight services linking New Kapiri-Mposhi, north of Lusaka, with Dar es Salaam in Tanzania, a distance of 1,860 km of which 891 km is in Zambia; jtly owned and administered by the Tanzanian and Zambian Govts; a 10-year rehabilitation programme, assisted by the USA and EC countries, began in 1985; it was announced in 1990 that a line linking the railway with the Zambian port of Mpulungu was to be constructed; Chair. RICHARD MARIKI; Gen. Man. A. S. MWEEMBA.

Zambia Railways: cnr Buntungwa St and Ghana Ave, POB 80935, Kabwe; tel. (5) 222201; telex 81000; fax (5) 224411; f. 1967; controlled by ZIMCO; a 10-year rehabilitation programme, estimated to cost US $200m., was initiated in 1990; Chair. J. Y. NG'OMA; Man. Dir OSWELL SIMUMBA.

ROADS

In 1992 there was a total road network of 37,359 km, of which 6,520 km were asphalted and 8,360 km were classified as secondary roads. The main arterial roads run from Beit Bridge (Zimbabwe) to Tunduma (the Great North Road), through the copper-mining area to Chingola and Chililabombwe (the Zaire Border Road), from Livingstone to the junction of the Kafue river and the Great North Road, and from Lusaka to the Malawi border (the Great East Road). In 1984 the 300-km BotZam highway linking Kazungula with Nata, in Botswana, was formally opened. A 1,930-km main road (the TanZam highway) links Zambia and Tanzania.

Department of Roads: PB 50003, Lusaka; tel. (1) 253088; Dir of Roads T. NGOMA.

SHIPPING

Zambia National Shipping Line: Lusaka; f. 1989; state-owned; cargo and passenger services from Dar es Salaam in Tanzania to northern Europe; Gen. Man. MARTIN PHIRI.

CIVIL AVIATION

In 1984 there were 127 airports, aerodromes and air strips. An international airport, 22.5 km from Lusaka, was opened in 1967.

National Air Charters (Z) Ltd (NAC): POB 33650, Lusaka; tel. (1) 229774; telex 43840; fax (1) 229778; f. 1973; air cargo services; Gen. Man. STAFFORD MUDIYO.

Zambia Airways (ZA): Ndeke House, Haile Selassie Ave, POB 30272, Lusaka; tel. (1) 228274; telex 43850; fax (1) 254281; f. 1967; controlled by ZIMCO; scheduled passenger and cargo services; internal services and flights to India, Saudi Arabia, the USA, and destinations in Europe and west Africa; Chair. LAWRENCE BWALYA; Man. Dir PETER KAOMA.

Tourism

Zambia's main tourist attractions are its wildlife and unspoilt scenery; there were 19 national parks in 1990. In that year an estimated 141,000 tourists visited Zambia. In that year foreign exchange earnings from the tourist industry totalled an estimated US $6m.

Zambia National Tourist Board: Century House, Cairo Rd, POB 30017, Lusaka; tel. (1) 229087; telex 41780.

Defence

In June 1993 Zambia's armed forces officially numbered about 21,600 (army 20,000, airforce 1,600). Paramilitary forces numbered 1,400. Military service is voluntary. There is also a national defence force, responsible to the government.

Defence Expenditure: K26,200m. allocated for 1994/95.

Education

Between 1964–79 enrolment in schools increased by more than 260%. Primary education, which is compulsory, begins at seven years of age and lasts for seven years. Secondary education, beginning at the age of 14, lasts for a further five years, comprising a first cycle of two years and a second of three years. In 1988 and estimated 80% of children (81% of boys; 79% of girls) in the relevant age-group attended primary schools, while the comparable ratio at secondary schools was 15% of children (19% of boys; 12% of girls). Some 1,461,206 pupils were enrolled at primary schools in 1990, while about 161,349 pupils were enrolled at secondary schools in 1988. There are two universities: the University of Zambia at Lusaka, and the Copperbelt University at Kitwe (which is to be transferred to Ndola). There are 14 teacher training colleges. In 1990, according to estimates by UNESCO, the average rate of adult illiteracy was 27.2% (males 19.2%; females 34.7%). Education was allocated K2,737m., or 8.7% of total expenditure, by the central government in 1990.

Bibliography

Bostock, M., and Harvey, C. *Economic Independence and Zambian Copper. A case study of foreign investment.* London, Pall Mall, 1972.

Daniel, P. *Africanization, Nationalization and Inequality: Mining Labour and the Copperbelt in Zambian Development.* Cambridge University Press, 1979.

Davies, D. H. (Ed.). *Zambia in Maps.* London, University of London Press, 1971.

Economic Report. Zambian Ministry of Finance (annual).

Elliott, Charles. *Constraints on the Economic Development of Zambia.* Oxford University Press, 1971.

Epstein, A. L. *Politics in an Urban African Community.* Manchester University Press, 1958.

Fry, J. *Employment and Income Distribution in the African Economy.* London, Croom Helm, 1979.

Gann, L. H. *A History of Northern Rhodesia: Early Days to 1953.* London, Chatto and Windus, 1964.

Government of the Republic of Zambia. *First National Development Plan 1966–70.* Lusaka, Government Printer, 1966.

Second National Development Plan 1972–76. Lusaka, Government Printer, 1971.

Third National Development Plan 1979–83. Lusaka, Government Printer, 1979.

1980 Census. Report. Lusaka, National Commission for Development Planning, 1981.

Hall, R. *Zambia.* London, Pall Mall Press, 1965.

The High Price of Principles. London, Hodder and Stoughton, 1969.

International Labour Office. *Narrowing the Gaps: Planning for Basic Needs and Productive Employment in Zambia.* Addis Ababa, ILO/JASPA, 1977.

Basic Needs in an Economy under Pressure. Addis Ababa, ILO/JASPA, 1981.

Kaunda, K. *Zambia Shall Be Free.* London, Heinemann, 1962.

Letter to My Children. London, Longman, 1973.

Kay, G. *A Social Geography of Zambia.* London, University of London Press, 1967.

Konczacki, Z.A., Parpart, J.L., and Shaw, T.M. *Studies in the Economic History of Southern Africa.* Vol. I. London, Cass, 1990.

Langworthy, H. W. *Zambia before 1890: Aspects of Precolonial History.* London, Longman, 1972.

Meebelo, H. S. *Reaction to Colonialism: a Prelude to the Politics of Independence in Northern Zambia 1893–1939.* Manchester, Manchester University Press, 1971.

Monthly Digest of Statistics. Central Statistical Office.

Mulford, D. *Zambia, the Politics of Independence, 1957–1964.* Oxford University Press, 1967.

Obidegwu, C. F., and Nziramamsanga, M. *Copper and Zambia: An Economic Analysis.* Washington, DC, University Press of America, 1981.

Pettman, J. *Zambia: Security and Conflict.* London, 1974.

Roberts, A. *A History of Zambia.* London, Heinemann Educational, 1977.

Rotberg, R. I. *The Rise of Nationalism in Central Africa.* Harvard University Press, 1966.

Schultz, J. *Land Use in Zambia.* Munich, Weltforum Verlag, 1976.

Tordoff, W. (Ed.). *Politics in Zambia.* London, 1976.

Administration in Zambia. Manchester University Press, 1980.

van Binsbergen, W. M. J. *Religious Change in Zambia: Exploratory Studies.* London, Kegan Paul International, 1981.

ZIMBABWE

Physical and Social Geography

GEORGE KAY

The Republic of Zimbabwe, covering an area of 390,759 sq km (150,873 sq miles), is land-locked and is bounded on the north and north-west by Zambia, on the south-west by Botswana, by Mozambique on the east and on the south by South Africa. It depends largely for its overseas trade on rail routes to Mozambique and South African ports. Provisional results of the census of August 1992 enumerated 10,401,767 persons, giving a population density of 26.6 inhabitants per sq km.

Zimbabwe lies astride the high plateaux between the Zambezi and Limpopo rivers. It consists of four relief regions. The highveld, comprising land more than 1,200 m above sea-level, extends across the country from south-west to north-east; it is most extensive in the north-east. The middleveld, land of 900 m–1,200 m above sea-level, flanks the highveld; it is most extensive in the north-west. The lowveld, land below 900 m, occupies the Zambezi basin in the north and the more extensive Limpopo and Sabi-Lundi basins in the south and south-east. These three regions consist predominantly of gently undulating plateaux, except for the narrow belt of rugged, escarpment hills associated with faults along the Zambezi trough. Also, the surfaces are broken locally where particularly resistant rocks provide upstanding features. For example, the Great Dyke, a remarkable intrusive feature over 480 km in length and up to 10 km wide, gives rise to prominent ranges of hills. The fourth physical region, the eastern highlands, is distinctive because of its mountainous character. Inyangani rises to 2,594 m and many hills exceed 1,800 m.

Temperatures are moderated by altitude. Mean monthly temperatures range from 22°C in October and 13°C in July on the highveld to 30°C and 20°C in the low-lying Zambezi valley. Winter months are noted for a wide diurnal range; night frosts are not uncommon on the high plateaux and can occasionally be very destructive.

Rainfall is largely restricted to the period November–March and, except on the eastern highlands, is extremely variable; in many parts of the country it is low for commercial crop production. Mean annual rainfall ranges from 1,400 mm on the eastern highlands, to 800 mm on the north-eastern highveld and to less than 400 mm in the Limpopo valley. The development of water resources for economic uses is a continually pressing need which, to date, has been met by a major dam-building programme. Underground water resources are limited.

Soils vary considerably. Granite occurs over more than half of the country and mostly gives rise to infertile sandy soils; these are, however, amenable to improvement. Kalahari sands are also extensive and provide poor soils. Soil-forming processes are limited in the lowveld and, except on basalt, soils there are generally immature. Rich, red clays and loams occur on the limited outcrops of Basement Schists, which are also among the most highly mineralized areas of Zimbabwe.

However, climatic factors are the chief determinants of agricultural potential and six broad categories of land have been defined largely on bio-climatic conditions: Region I (1.6% of the country) with good, reliable rainfall; suitable for specialized and diversified farming, including tree crops; Region II (18.7%) with moderately high rainfall; suitable for intensive commercial crop production with subsidiary livestock farming; Region III (17.4%) with mediocre rainfall conditions; suitable for semi-extensive commercial livestock farming with supplementary production of drought-resistant crops; Region IV (33%) with low and unreliable rainfall; suitable for semi-extensive livestock production; Region V (26.2%) semi-arid country; suitable for only extensive ranching; and Region VI (3.1%—probably underestimated) because of steep slopes, skeletal soils, swamps, etc., is unsuitable for any agricultural use.

Large-scale irrigation works in the south-eastern lowveld have overcome climatic limitations, and the area around Chiredzi, once suitable only for ranching, is now a major developing region.

Zimbabwe possesses a wide variety of workable mineral deposits, which include gold, asbestos, copper, chrome, nickel palladium, cobalt, tin, iron ore, limestone, iron pyrites and phosphates. Most mineralization occurs on the highveld and adjacent parts of the middleveld. Energy resources include plentiful supplies of cheap coal, coke and coal by-products. No deposits of hydrocarbons have yet been located.

The population of Zimbabwe is diverse. At mid-1980 it was estimated to include some 223,000 persons of European descent and some 37,000 Asians and Coloureds, all of them a legacy of the colonial era. The indigenous inhabitants, who accounted for over 98% of the population at mid-1987, broadly comprise two ethnic or linguistic groups, the Ndebele and the Shona. The Shona, with whom political power now rests, outnumber the Ndebele by 4:1. There are, in addition, several minor ethnic groups, such as the Tonga, Sena, Hlengwe, Venda and Sotho.

In recent years, urban growth has proceeded rapidly. The urban poor, operating within the highly competitive 'informal economy', are now a large and increasing part of the urban social structure. Harare, the capital, had an estimated population of 681,000 at mid-1983, while that of Bulawayo was estimated at 429,000.

In the rural districts of Zimbabwe, the extensive commercial farming areas continue to be dominated by a relatively small number of white farmers and companies, which operate efficiently and effectively. However, in recent years the communal lands that are occupied by indigenous households have somewhat increased their contribution to sales at national levels of crops and livestock. Legislation came into force in 1990, empowering the government compulsorily to acquire land; this was expected to facilitate the redistribution of land ownership from white commercial farmers (who own more than 40% of farming land and produce about 80% of the country's cash crops) to African smallholders.

Most rural African households still live tribally within the communal lands, where they depend upon subsistence production, augmented by small irregular sales of surplus produce, by casual employment and by remittances from migrant labourers. However, the cohesion of this rural society is being eroded by the selective effects of migration.

The socio-economic difficulties of rural African society are compounded by ecological problems. While some extensive areas (notably in remote northern parts of the country) remain sparsely populated, the greater part of the communal lands suffers from overpopulation and overstocking. Deforestation, soil erosion and a deterioration of wildlife and water resources are widespread; and in some areas they have reached critical dimensions. 'Desertification' is a real danger in the semi-arid regions of the country.

Official resettlement schemes on to the land of erstwhile commercial holdings (many of which had been unused or under-used), and colonization in the form of squatter movements on to such lands, have been formally encouraged, although resettlement has not proceeded as rapidly as planned.

Recent History

RICHARD BROWN

The former colony of Southern Rhodesia, which now forms the Republic of Zimbabwe, was acquired for Britain on the strength of its rumoured mineral potential by the South African-based financier and imperialist, Cecil John Rhodes. The occupation by his British South Africa Co (BSA) began in 1890, but the process of conquest against some fierce resistance, or *chimurenga*, was not completed until 1902. Disappointed by the limited scale of gold discoveries, the BSA encouraged white farming and a reckless alienation of land to individual settlers and to speculative companies. BSA administration under a royal charter ended in 1923. Britain, however, was reluctant to accept direct responsibility for the administration of the colony, and permitted the white settlers to choose between joining South Africa or taking over the administration from the BSA. The settlers, mainly British and South African in origin, elected to remain separate, and were subsequently permitted by Britain to develop a racially stratified and segregated society in the 1920s and 1930s very similar to that in South Africa. The foundation of the segregation policy was the Land Apportionment Act of 1930, which severely restricted the access of Africans to land by dividing the country very unequally in relation to population into two racially exclusive parts, with consequences which are evident in land tenure to the present day. Measures were taken to prevent Africans from competing in the markets for agricultural produce and skilled labour. Taxation, pass laws, land pressures, and the development of new wants together ensured that the main role of Africans in the economy was as temporary unskilled labour migrants to the towns, farms and mines located in the 'European' areas.

INDUSTRIALIZATION AND DISCONTENT

The Second World War helped to promote industrialization and make manufacturing the leading growth sector. Rapid urbanization took place and some modifications to the policy of segregation were accepted by the overwhelmingly white electorate during the post-war boom. In particular education for Africans became more widespread in recognition of the need for a more skilled black labour force. Settler immigration was also encouraged, and by the late 1950s the white population was well over 200,000, and becoming increasingly prosperous. The African population then numbered about 4m. and was also rising sharply. As strong economic growth continued after 1945, Africans increasingly resented their social, economic and political subordination. Strikes and rural discontent multiplied: by the late 1950s and early 1960s unrest was being channelled into a mass nationalist movement demanding equal rights. The government reacted with a series of bannings, and refused to allow Africans more than a limited voice in a new constitution agreed with Britain in 1961.

Meanwhile, attracted by the copper revenues of Northern Rhodesia and by the labour resources of Nyasaland, Southern Rhodesia became the dominant member of the Central African Federation (CAF) established by Britain in 1953. The territorial governments of the two northern protectorates remained under direct British control, a situation provoking much conflict with the settler-dominated federal and Southern Rhodesian governments. The federation's declared policy of racial partnership was viewed as meaningless by Africans in all three territories. In Northern Rhodesia and Nyasaland, Britain eventually recognized the strength of African hostility and conceded independence, breaking-up the federation in the process (1963). Whites in Southern Rhodesia interpreted these developments as the outcome of British appeasement and redoubled their own opposition to African political advancement. In 1962 they abandoned the party which had governed almost without interruption since 1923 and voted into office the newly-formed Rhodesian Front (RF), dedicated to upholding white supremacy and demanding full independence from Britain and the retention of the existing minority-rule constitution. When Britain refused independence on this basis, the RF appointed the intransigent Ian Smith as prime minister.

On 11 November 1965 Smith defied Britain and the United Nations by announcing the long-threatened unilateral declaration of independence (UDI). Retaining the unswerving support of the majority of the whites, Smith maintained UDI for 14 years, until finally being brought down in 1980 by a combination of guerrilla war and international pressure. For the first half of this period Smith could claim a degree of success: economic sanctions were not rigorously enforced and economic prosperity for most whites continued. Although UDI remained unrecognized internationally, Smith obtained the practical support of Portugal (which still controlled neighbouring Mozambique) and South Africa (which provided him with material and, later, military assistance). An attempted constitutional settlement with Britain in 1971 was decisively rejected when African opinion was consulted by the Pearce Commission. Thereafter, the guerrilla war dominated events.

ARMED STRUGGLE

Repressive measures preceding UDI had virtually neutralized the African nationalist opposition, which had been further weakened by a split in 1963 into the Zimbabwe African People's Union (ZAPU), led by Joshua Nkomo, and the breakaway Zimbabwe African National Union (ZANU), led by Rev. Ndabaningi Sithole and later by Robert Mugabe. Nevertheless, shortly after UDI, elements of the banned nationalist parties in exile launched ill-prepared guerrilla units into the country from Zambia in the hope of provoking external intervention to remove the Smith regime. These actions, beginning with ZANU's 'Battle of Sinoia' in April 1966 (now officially seen as the start of the second *chimurenga*) were ineffectual. The nationalists changed their tactics and sought to develop a 'people's war' in an attempt to overthrow the Smith regime. ZAPU, based mainly in Zambia, received training and sophisticated weaponry from the USSR, but played a lesser role within Zimbabwe, where its operations were mainly confined to Ndebele-speaking areas. ZANU developed strong links with the Frente de Libertação de Moçambique (Frelimo) movement fighting the Portuguese in Mozambique, and with the People's Republic of China. It concentrated on infiltration and rural mobilization in the Shona-speaking areas in the north-east, and later in the eastern and central areas of the country. Active operations began in December 1972, and ZANU's initial successes were enhanced when Portuguese colonial rule collapsed and a Frelimo-dominated government took control in Mozambique in September 1974.

Alarmed at the apparent radicalization of the nationalist movement in the context of the cold war, Britain, the USA, South Africa and Zambia each sought to bring about a settlement; however, after a confused period of *détente* politics in the mid-1970s, the war resumed with new intensity. From 1976 it was waged in the name of the Patriotic Front (PF), an uneasy alliance formed by ZAPU and ZANU, and backed by the 'front-line' states, i.e. those African countries most involved in the Zimbabwean conflict. Within the country, the regime relied on terror and propaganda in a vain attempt to counter the growing civilian support for the armed struggle. Nevertheless, mounting unemployment and the guerrillas' own excesses helped to provide numerous black recruits into the government's security forces. By 1979 economic difficulties, declining white morale and guerrilla inroads in the rural areas led Smith to fashion what was termed an 'internal settlement', which took the form of a black 'puppet' regime under the leadership of Bishop Abel Muzorewa. 'Zimbabwe Rhodesia', as the country was briefly known under Muzorewa, was unable to improve conditions for ordinary Africans, obtain international recognition or end the war. Within less than a year the pressure on all the parties to the conflict from their respective supporters had forced them to participate in the

Lancaster House constitutional conference, under the chairmanship of Britain, which was to lead to the birth of the independent state of Zimbabwe on 18 April 1980.

THE INDEPENDENCE SETTLEMENT

The conference, which also had to negotiate a cease-fire and mutually acceptable transitional arrangements, began on 10 September and lasted for 14 weeks, an agreement being signed on 21 December 1979, nine days after UDI had been renounced. The British and their allies, including South Africa, were convinced of the need to end the war through negotiations which would involve the PF in the political process, but still believed that an outright PF government could be avoided. The PF was itself under intense pressure to negotiate from the 'front-line' states, themselves victims of destructive and far-flung attacks by Zimbabwe Rhodesia's increasingly well-equipped military forces. These attacks, together with the war inside the country and the other pressures, continued throughout the conference and helped the British to obtain their own settlement proposals more or less without alteration. Continuity was stressed in the adoption of the prime ministerial system in preference to an executive president, in the disproportionate political influence reserved to the white minority (20 of the 100 seats in the house of assembly), and in such matters as citizenship and state pensions. In particular, the compensation clause attached to the question of land was strongly opposed by the PF, and was accepted only after vague assurances had been given about a future multinational fund to assist in the urgent problems of land redistribution.

Arrangements for the transitional period and the cease-fire also caused considerable friction. The cease-fire, involving the assembly of more than 20,000 guerrillas at 16 designated sites, could only be supervised, not enforced, by the small Commonwealth monitoring force. Nor could the appointment as governor of Lord Soames (a senior British politician and diplomatist), to replace the Muzorewa-Smith administration and to direct the transition, hide the fact that he remained dependent on the former regime and its notorious security forces, sections of which conducted a campaign of bombing and vilification directed against Mugabe and his party. Cease-fire violations, intimidation, rumours of a possible white coup and threatening statements from South Africa also contributed to an atmosphere of crisis. Yet, astonishingly, elections were successfully held in February 1980, and a substantially peaceful transition accomplished.

The ZANU wing of the PF, confident of the allegiance of the population in the large part of the country in which its guerrillas had operated, decided to contest the election as a separate party under the leadership of Robert Mugabe. His main rival, Joshua Nkomo, hoped that his reputation as the 'father' of Zimbabwean nationalism would help ZAPU–PF win support throughout the country and a majority in parliament. The two PF parties were challenged by Bishop Muzorewa's United African National Council (UANC), whose campaign received financial support from business interests and from South Africa. A number of minor parties led by formerly influential nationalists who had supported the 'internal settlement' also put up candidates. The hopes which various anti-Mugabe interests inside and outside the country had in keeping him from power disappeared when the ZANU–PF won 57 of the 80 'common roll' (African) seats in the house, receiving 63% of the votes. Nkomo's PF, which won 20 seats, mainly in Matabeleland, became very much the junior partner in the coalition government formed by Mugabe. This left only three seats for the UANC. Between them the two parties which had conducted the armed struggle received 87% of the votes in a turn-out estimated at 94% (in an earlier and separate election, the RF won all 20 seats reserved for whites).

RECONCILIATION

In the immediate period following his massive victory, Mugabe adopted a markedly conciliatory stance. To restore stability, he quickly stressed the need for reconciliation; disavowed rapid change towards his stated socialist goals; emphasized non-alignment in foreign affairs; and included two whites in his cabinet. Nevertheless, the new government was faced with formidable problems arising from the ravages of war and the expectations aroused in the struggle against settler rule.

As in other newly independent African countries, the rapid growth of educational opportunities for blacks offered one of the clearest signs of change. Scope for extensive Africanization was provided by the emigration of whites and by the expansion of government services (four years after independence, the white population had dropped by one-half, to about 100,000, not without causing grave shortages of skilled labour). Black labour unrest surfaced even before the independence celebrations, but may have been lessened by legislation on minimum wages and by a temporary reduction in the burden of direct taxation. Substantial improvements in social welfare, however, did not prevent later strikes by transport workers, teachers and nurses. These challenges were forcefully handled by the government. In 1985 criticism of the long-awaited and controversial Labour Relations Act for unduly strengthening government control led to the arrest of union activists.

In spite of the relatively high proportion of adult males in wage employment, it was over land redistribution and the rehabilitation of the trust lands that the government seemed likely to receive the greatest challenges to its aspirations and to its authority. For most Zimbabweans the struggles of recent decades have been about recovering the land, and the later stages of the war had much of the character of a peasant uprising. The strategic power and importance of the established commercial farming sector make the problem of meeting peasant needs daunting. The pace of official resettlement, slowed by drought, manpower shortages, restrictive provisions in the Lancaster House agreement and perhaps by lack of will, was not sufficient to head off extensive uncontrolled resettlement or to prevent the land issue from fuelling the dissidence in Matabeleland.

In the international field, the new Zimbabwe quickly made its mark. Extensive diplomatic relations were established with other countries in Africa, with the West, with the People's Republic of China and its allies and, more hesitantly, with the USSR and its allies. The Zimbabwe Conference on Reconstruction and Development (Zimcord), held in March 1981, was a notable success in substantially meeting its targets for aid. Zimbabwe also began to play a prominent part in the Southern African Development Co-ordination Conference (SADCC), the regional organization formed to lessen economic dependence on South Africa. For Zimbabwe, this dependence, especially in the fields of transport and trade, remains a major influence on all aspects of government policy. From fear of reprisals, Mugabe stated that bases for the armed struggle against South Africa could not be provided, nor could proposed economic sanctions be applied, but he also made clear that political and diplomatic support would continue to be given to the opposition movements which were backed by the OAU.

POLITICS AND SECURITY

At independence it was necessary to consolidate the peace by integrating the three large, hostile and undefeated armies. British instructors were called in, but progress was slow at first and serious clashes, on party lines, between guerrilla groups in the vicinity of Bulawayo led to several hundred deaths. Nevertheless, by late 1981 the integration appeared to have been successfully completed. From outside ZANU—PF there was criticism of the creation of an additional specialist army brigade (the Fifth), of largely Shona-speaking origin, trained by personnel from the Democratic People's Republic of Korea. However, Mugabe could point, in justification, to the internal and external threats posed by disaffected supporters of the former regime, by unresolved tensions within the governing coalition, and by South Africa. In December 1981 his own party's headquarters were destroyed in a bomb attack. Subsequently, vital transport routes and petroleum facilities in Mozambique were sabotaged, the homes of government ministers attacked, and a substantial part of the air force destroyed.

Meanwhile, there was increasing discussion of the need for a one-party state. The prime minister stated that such a development should come about through persuasion, but other members of his party urged the need for speed and attacked the restrictive clauses of the Lancaster House constitution. Nkomo, who later made it known that he did not consider the election results to be valid and who rejected Mugabe's offer of the presidency following the independence elections, refused to accept that a ZAPU merger with ZANU—PF was the best solution to the sharp regional polarization between the two coalition parties. In January 1981 Nkomo was demoted from his home affairs portfolio to a lesser cabinet office, and one year later he and some of his colleagues were dismissed altogether, following the discovery of substantial illegal arms caches on properties belonging to ZAPU in Matabeleland. Although there were some immediate outbreaks of pro-Nkomo dissident violence in the province, it was also significant that the remaining members of the coalition from the minority party failed to heed Nkomo's wish that they should resign. Mugabe threatened to bring Nkomo to trial on charges of plotting a coup, but he also went out of his way to stress again his policy of reconciliation. The ZAPU ministers who had remained were promoted, and Mugabe also added two ex-RF members of parliament to his government. The RF, restyled the Republican Front, was still led by Ian Smith, having undergone a sizeable secession from its parliamentary ranks in protest at RF negativism since independence. By the June 1985 elections, the RF, known since 1981 as the Republican Front, had reconstituted itself as the Conservative Alliance of Zimbabwe (CAZ). In 1983 an RF faction sympathetic to the Mugabe government broke away to form the Independent Zimbabwe Group.

Mugabe emerged from the crisis over the arms discoveries in a strong position, but the government's authority was increasingly challenged by events in Matabeleland. The acute land problems of the province, allied to the effects of the worst drought for more than a century, heightened the tense political situation. During 1982 dissidents from ZIPRA, ZAPU's former guerrilla army, and former colleagues who had deserted from the new national army perpetrated numerous indiscriminate acts of violence. Their exact links with Nkomo and his party could not be fully established, but the government held ZAPU largely to blame for the worsening situation. It was also alleged that members of the former regime's forces who had moved to South Africa were providing a ready supply of personnel for covert operations, which the South African government was also suspected of supporting.

Early in 1983, and again a year later, serious allegations of indiscipline and atrocities against innocent civilians were made against the Fifth Brigade as it sought to crush the dissidents and to protect the important, largely white, commercial farming sector on which so much of the government's overall economic strategy rested. The allegations were supported by local churchmen, including the Roman Catholic authorities who had previously played a major part in exposing atrocities committed by the security forces of the Smith regime. Controversy over human rights issues continued when adverse reports, from Amnesty International, in 1985, and from the US-based Lawyers' Committee for Human Rights, were rejected by the prime minister.

In addition to the desire to oust ZAPU from its regional stronghold, the fear that a South African-backed dissident movement might reach the same devastating proportions as those already operating in Angola and Mozambique probably lay behind the government's decision to mount a forceful military campaign in Matabeleland in spite of the risk of alienating the province's mainly Ndebele-speaking population, Zimbabwe's principal minority language group. The prolonged nature of the operations in Matabeleland suggested more civilian support for the dissidents than the government was prepared to admit, but, as the first general election since independence approached, there was increasing emphasis on the ruling party's need to achieve genuine political support in the province. The approaching election also intensified political violence elsewhere in the country.

A new party constitution, adopted by a ZANU—PF congress, which was held in August 1984, greatly enlarged the central committee and introduced a new 15-member politburo. The congress dedicated itself to the 'victory of socialism over capitalism' and endorsed the aim of achieving a one-party Marxist-Leninist state under the leadership of ZANU—PF.

The first general elections since independence were held at the end of June 1985 (for the 20 'guaranteed' white seats) and in early July (for the 80 'common roll' seats). To the intense annoyance of Robert Mugabe, the white electorate appeared to spurn his reconciliation policy when the CAZ, led by Ian Smith, won 15 of the 20 reserved seats. However, following the elections, as the prospect of a one-party state emerged, the disintegration of the CAZ became visible, with several white members of the house of assembly either joining the ruling party or becoming independents.

In the election for the 80 black 'common roll' seats, almost 3m. votes were cast, 76% for ZANU—PF candidates, an increase of more than 12% on the proportion won in the 1980 elections. ZANU—PF increased its representation in the house of assembly by six seats to 64, although failing to gain any of the Matabeleland seats held by Joshua Nkomo's ZAPU. Outside Matabeleland, however, ZAPU lost all five of the seats that it held in the previous parliament. Contrary to expectations, ZANU—Sithole secured one seat, but Bishop Muzorewa's UANC failed to gain any representation.

TOWARDS A ONE-PARTY STATE

Following the elections, the drive towards a *de facto* one-party state was resumed, with reprisals against supporters of minority parties. The government's vigorous campaign against ZAPU led to the adverse report by Amnesty International referred to above, but it did not prevent the resumption of unity talks between ZAPU and ZANU—PF. Success seemed to be imminent on several occasions, especially following the release in 1986 of prominent ZAPU detainees. In April 1987, however, Mugabe abruptly abandoned the unity negotiations on the grounds that they had been deadlocked for too long. A resurgence of violence in Matabeleland and further measures against ZAPU's political activities followed the cancellation of the unity talks. Nkomo, however, continued to deny any involvement with the dissidents, and in July ZAPU indicated its continuing wish for negotiations with the ruling party by voting in favour of renewing the state of emergency.

A particularly brutal massacre in Matabeleland in November 1987 and the worsening security situation on the eastern border (see below) at last precipitated a unity agreement between ZAPU and ZANU—PF, healing the split in the nationalist ranks which had lasted for almost 25 years. The agreement to merge the two parties, under the name of ZANU—PF, was signed by Mugabe and Nkomo in December, and was ratified by both parties in April 1988. According to the agreement, the new party was to be committed to the establishment of a one-party state with a Marxist-Leninist doctrine. The party was to be led by Mugabe, with Nkomo as one of two vice-presidents. Nkomo was offered a senior position in a new cabinet, while two other ZAPU officials were given government posts. An amnesty, proclaimed in April 1988, led to a rapidly improving political and security situation in Matabeleland.

Meanwhile, significant constitutional changes were moving Zimbabwe nearer to becoming a one-party state. The reservation for whites of 20 seats in the house of assembly and 10 seats in the senate was finally abolished in September 1987. In the following month the 80 remaining members of the assembly elected 20 candidates who were all nominated by ZANU—PF, including 11 whites, to fill the vacant seats. Candidates nominated by ZANU—PF, including four whites, were then elected to the vacancies in the senate by the new house of assembly. In October parliament adopted another major constitutional reform, whereby the ceremonial presidency was replaced by an executive presidency incorporating the post of prime minister. Robert Mugabe was nominated as sole candidate for the office, and on 31 December he was inaugurated as Zimbabwe's first executive president. His new enlarged cabinet included Joshua Nkomo as one of three senior ministers in the president's office who were to form a 'super-cabinet' to oversee policy and review ministerial performance, in association with the president. In November 1989 the house of assembly voted by the necessary majority to abolish the upper chamber of parliament, the senate. The single chamber was then enlarged from 100 to 150 seats, with effect from the next general election. In addition to 120 elected members, the change provided for eight provincial governors, 10 chiefs and 12 presidential nominees to be members of the assembly.

DISCONTENT AND 'CORRUPTION'

As unemployment and prices rose in 1988, open public and parliamentary criticism of corrupt government officials mounted. An anti-government demonstration by students in September resulted in many arrests. In October a former secretary-general of the party, Edgar Tekere, was expelled from ZANU—PF for his persistent denunciation of the party leadership and its policies, including its plans to introduce a one-party state; this action resulted in further student protest. In the same month allegations that government ministers had obtained new cars from the state-owned vehicle assembly plant in order to re-sell them at a profit, an illegal activity, first appeared in the Bulawayo *Chronicle*. The newspaper's editor was subsequently removed from his post. Amid intense public concern, Mugabe appointed a judicial commission of inquiry to investigate the newspaper's allegations: as a result of the commission's findings, five cabinet ministers and one provincial governor resigned from their posts in March and April 1989. The cabinet ministers included one of the three senior ministers in the office of the president, Maurice Nyagumbo, minister for political affairs; shortly afterwards, Nyagumbo, an early participant in the nationalist struggle and a long-standing ally of the president, committed suicide.

Mugabe's establishment of the judicial commission of inquiry attracted initial public approval, and succeeded in limiting damage to the government's reputation. At the behest of the ZANU—PF central committee, the president pardoned the former minister of labour, Fred Shava, who had been fined and sentenced to a nine-month term of imprisonment for perjury to the commission. Similar charges against other former ministers were also withdrawn. The wide unpopularity of these actions contributed to a tense political atmosphere, especially in urban areas.

Following publication of the judicial commission's report, Edgar Tekere, who had previously disavowed any intention of forming a new party, challenged the government's plans for a one-party state by forming the Zimbabwe Unity Movement (ZUM). Tekere denounced the government as corrupt, and proposed economic liberalization and the withdrawal of Zimbabwe troops from Mozambique. Although the new party was unable seriously to challenge ZANU—PF in five by-elections (held in July and October 1989)—partially, at least, owing to alleged official harassment and obstruction—the low level of electoral participation suggested a significant decline in the popularity of the governing party.

The government was embarrassed during 1989 by a series of conflicts with the judiciary and by strikes in the public service sector, but it was criticism by students which provoked the most serious political disturbances. In July a clash occurred between students and security police during a rally of ZUM supporters at the university, and, following further serious clashes, the university was closed from October 1990–April 1991. Unconvincingly, the government related the trouble to subversion from South Africa. When the Zimbabwe Congress of Trade Unions issued a statement supporting the students, its secretary-general, Morgan Tsvangirai, was arrested and detained for six weeks (the cause of one particular conflict with the judiciary). In mid-July, however, it was announced that the state of emergency was to be officially discontinued later that month, following the reduction of tension in South Africa, although it was noted that the government continued to possess wide powers of arrest and detention. A general amnesty of prisoners, to commemorate the 10th anniversary of independence, was also announced.

Political debate intensified during the ZANU—PF congress in December 1989. The congress was convened to complete the merger process with ZAPU, begun two years earlier (see above), but it required strong directive action from Mugabe to resolve the contentious issue of the distribution of party posts. There was also controversy concerning a proposed constitutional amendment to create a second vice-presidency, specifically for Joshua Nkomo, the former ZAPU leader. (Nkomo was officially appointed vice-president, in addition to the existing vice-president, Simon Muzenda, in August 1990.) Although Mugabe re-committed the new ZANU—PF to Marxism-Leninism and the one-party state, opposition to a one-party state was expressed within and outside the congress. Indeed, in August 1990 the ZANU—PF politburo voted to reject plans for the creation of a one-party state in Zimbabwe.

For the general election of March 1990, ZANU—PF chose to campaign against ZUM, its only serious opponent among the four opposition parties, on the general issue of unity rather than on that of the one-party state. The election was marred by some political violence, in which a ZUM candidate was seriously wounded, but the result of the poll appeared to be a fair reflection of the government's popularity. ZANU—PF obtained a comfortable victory, winning 117 of the 120 elective seats (including one seat in which polling was initially postponed). However, electoral participation—estimated to be in the range of 54%–65%—had declined sharply in comparison with turn-outs of 95% and above in the two previous general elections. Moreover, ZUM, despite its controversial alliance with the CAZ and the disruption of some of its campaign activities, received almost 20% of the total votes. Significantly, ZUM performed even better in urban areas, especially in Harare, where it secured 30% of the votes. However, ZANU—PF's control of the seats was disrupted only in eastern Manicaland (owing, at least in part, to the difficulties occasioned by Mozambican guerrillas (see below)), where ZUM obtained two seats and ZANU—Ndonga (formerly ZANU—Sithole) retained one. Overall, the distribution of votes in the election indicated that ZUM had achieved something approaching national status as an opposition party. However, its leader, Edgar Tekere, was overwhelmingly defeated in the contest for the remaining seat, even though the constituency was located in his home province of Manicaland. At the concurrent election for the presidency itself, Tekere had received 413,840 votes, and Mugabe 2.03m. votes.

Mugabe's new cabinet included three whites as ministers, but its overall composition, to the annoyance of former ZAPU members, was little altered. Nevertheless, few doubted that, under the surface, the final year of the decade since independence had witnessed a substantial political shift. With more than 50% of the population below the age of 25, and with severe unemployment and other domestic problems, appeals by ZANU—PF to the heroism of the pre-independence struggle could no longer be regarded as relevant or powerful.

IDEOLOGICAL REASSESSMENTS

Meanwhile, following the adoption of the Structural Adjustment Programme (SAP) of economic liberalization first announced in 1990, 'Marxism-Leninism' was increasingly replaced in official discourse by references to 'pragmatic socialism' and 'indigenous capitalism'. Vigorous debate was also aroused by the expiry of the remaining restrictions of the Lancaster House agreement on 18 April 1990. Constitutional amendments which restored corporal and capital punishment and which denied recourse to the courts in cases of compulsory purchase of land by the government were enacted in April 1991, despite fierce criticism from the judiciary and from human rights campaigners.

Student unrest erupted once more following the publication in October 1990 of proposals for a substantial increase in government control of universities. A student boycott of classes on the issue in May 1991 won support in many quarters, but an attempt to march on the Commonwealth Prime Ministers' Conference held in Harare in October led to violence following heavy-handed police actions to prevent the students from leaving the campus. In May 1992, students, angry at eroded grants and the imposition of fees, were again in confrontation with the police while attempting to demonstrate against the government's major policies. Subsequently, the 10,000 students of the University of Zimbabwe were expelled. Student protest was the most visible part of much wider discontent. In June, police prevented trade unionists from holding anti-government demonstrations. For workers, the extent and severity of the 1991/92 drought added to the economic difficulties already being blamed on the SAP. Shortages, inflation, unemployment, corruption, government inertia and the stalled programme of land resettlement were the main grievances expressed. The discovery of extensive human remains, thought to date from the activities of the Fifth Brigade in its operations in Matabeleland in the 1980s (see above), added to the political *malaise*.

However, despite the government's evident unpopularity, the confused and divided state of the opposition continued to protect the government from serious challenge. A split in ZUM led to the formation in September 1991 of the ineffective Democratic Party. The unenthusiastic response outside his home area to the return to the country from self-imposed exile of Ndabaningi Sithole, ZANU's original leader and now leader of ZANU–Ndonga, in January 1992 underlined the discredit in which the older generation of nationalist politicians had become held.

In July 1992 ZANU–Ndonga, the UANC, the ZUM and the CAZ formed a United Front (UF) with the aim of defeating the government at the general elections due in 1995. Divisions soon emerged within the new grouping, whose manifesto, which attacked the executive presidency, eventually appeared in February 1993. Bishop Abel Muzorewa (see above) returned to active politics in January 1994 and merged the UANC with ZUM. In spite of efforts by another former prime minister, Ian Smith, the UF continued to remain ineffective. Meanwhile, a non-party Forum for Democratic Reform, led by a former chief justice, Enoch Dumbutshena, and supported by a number of prominent Zimbabweans, including Sir Garfield Todd, was formed in May 1992. Following some controversy within the group, a separate Forum Party of Zimbabwe (FPZ) emerged in March 1993. Lacking a distinctive policy and a popular base, the FPZ made little headway in the following year, but continued to press for electoral reform. The expulsion of 22 of its members in March 1994 underlined the party's disarray.

The Zimbabwe Congress of Trade Unions (ZCTU) found itself unable to capitalize on the widespread industrial unrest which took place in 1994. The organization was weakened by the resignation of its secretary-general, Morgan Tsvangirai, and by the loss of members due to the recession. When the ZCTU rejected the suggestion that it form its own party, a group of non-union figures opposed to the Structural Adjustment Programme (SAP) announced the formation of a Movement for Democracy in June 1994.

Meanwhile, amid the rising urban discontent fuelled by corruption scandals, falling real wages and the social consequences of the SAP, the government was increasingly preoccupied by the land issue, which it continued to see as the key to retaining its grip on power. The Land Acquisition Act (LAA), drafted following the expiry of the Lancaster House provisions, passed its final legislative phase on 19 March 1992 (see Economy). The measure brought the government into conflict with the powerful Commercial Farmers Union and with Western aid donors. Both groups were angered by the decision in April 1993 to designate 70 commercially owned farms for purchase. Many of them were productive holdings which, it had been understood, were to be exempt from compulsory purchase. The government eventually allowed appeals in a sufficient number of cases—22—to suggest that an uneasy compromise had been reached. For its part, the CFU announced in September that it would assist in the government's resettlement programme, and its members were represented on the commission set up in November to make proposals for land tenure reforms. However, in March 1994, the government found itself once again under intense pressure when it was revealed that the first of the farms acquired under the LAA had gone to the government minister, Witness Mangwende, who had been Minister of Agriculture when the act was passed. The scandal escalated when the press revealed that most of the first 98 farms acquired by compulsory purchase had been leased to prominent party figures and civil servants and were not being used for peasant resettlement, the stated object of the LAA. The president first ordered an inquiry and then the cancellation of all the leases. He was anxious not to jeopardize what proved to be a successful state visit to Britain in connection with the Zimbabwe investment promotion conference held in London in May 1994.

In a wider international context, Zimbabwe's supportive role as a member of the UN security council during the Iraq war and its IMF-approved economic liberalization policies helped to overcome the tension with the USA which had existed since 1986. Mugabe's meeting in Washington, DC with President Bush in July 1991 confirmed the new relationship. In February 1993 a small number of troops from both countries engaged in joint training manoeuvres. During 1992–93, Zimbabwe contributed troops to UN operations in Mozambique, Rwanda and Somalia.

THE SOUTHERN AFRICAN CRISIS

Regional instability and the issue of South Africa dominated Zimbabwe's foreign relations in the first decade of independence. High priority was given to co-operation with Zimbabwe's other neighbours through the SADCC and the Preferential Trade Area for Eastern and Southern African States. Robert Mugabe's strong support for mandatory sanctions against South Africa brought him into conflict with the United Kingdom and the USA, but enhanced Zimbabwe's standing in the Non-Aligned Movement.

The support by South Africa for the insurgent guerrilla group, the Movimento Nacional da Resistência de Moçambique (MNR, also known as Renamo) in Mozambique has posed a threat to Zimbabwe's alternative access to the sea via the Beira corridor, and as a result, Zimbabwe provides up to 8,000 troops in military assistance to the Mozambique government. Following the death of President Machel of Mozambique in an air crash in October 1986, Mugabe reiterated his support for the Mozambique government. The MNR consequently declared war on the Zimbabwe government, and cross-border incursions and civilian deaths have become a regular occurence. In July 1987 President Mugabe pledged to maintain Zimbabwean troops in Mozambique until the MNR was 'neutralized'. By 1991 it was estimated that more than 200,000 Mozambican refugees were sheltering in Zimbabwe. The SADCC has enlisted the support of private businesses, including Zimbabwean companies, and of Western governments, for the Beira corridor project in Mozambique; the attempt to rehabilitate the transport and port facilities to the east coast is of great importance to Zimbabwe's economy. From 1989, President Mugabe played a leading role in mediation attempts between the Mozambican government and the MNR, but a peace accord was only reached in August 1992. Implementation of the agreement took place only slowly because of the delayed arrival of the UN peacekeeping force. However, by April 1993 Zimbabwean troops began their withdrawal, and shortly afterwards the Zimbabwean authorities began the repatriation of an estimated 145,000 Mozambican refugees. This scheme, under the auspices of the UNHCR, was not expected to be completed before April 1996. Following the end of the Mozambican conflict, the Zimbabwe government announced in May 1993 that the size of the country's armed forces was to be reduced from almost 49,000 troops to 35,000 over a five-year period.

The support given by Zimbabwe to the Mozambique government, and the leading role taken by Mugabe in advocating the imposition of economic sanctions against South Africa, also resulted in direct retaliatory action against Zimbabwe by the South African government. Following a number of attacks carried out in 1986, in May 1987 South African defence forces launched two raids, within a week, on alleged bases of the African National Congress of South Africa (ANC) in Harare. Bomb explosions in Harare in October 1987 and in Bulawayo in January 1988 were widely regarded as further attempts by South Africa to destabilize the Zimbabwe government. In June 1988 an attempt by a South African commando unit to release five alleged South African agents who were awaiting trial was thwarted by Zimbabwean security forces; three of the detainees were found guilty in June 1989 of taking part in bomb attacks on ANC targets. The detainees were eventually released in July 1990, following the termination of the state of emergency in Zimbabwe (see above). The release of Nelson Mandela in South Africa in February 1990 and subsequent progress towards constitutional reform in South Africa have brought about more stable relations between the two countries. A number of unpublicized ministerial contacts on matters of trade and transport have taken place in recent years. Following a meeting of the two foreign ministers in January 1994, full diplomatic ties were agreed upon and came into force alongside the historic South African election in the following April. With democratic government finally established there, Zimbabwe lost some of the regional pre-eminence it had enjoyed since its independence in 1980. Political and economic relations with its mighty, if now friendly neighbour, will continue to be a dominant concern for Zimbabwe in the future as it has been in the past.

Economy

LINDA VAN BUREN

In the decade following independence, economic growth in Zimbabwe was uneven, fluctuating in conformity with the effect of rainfall on agricultural production, with world prices for the country's main exports, and with changes in government economic policy. None the less, with an abundance of natural resources, a well-developed infrastructure and a diversified industrial sector, Zimbabwe is better placed than most African economies to withstand the effects of commodity price fluctuations, and to recoup short-term set-backs.

High levels of economic growth were recorded in the first two fiscal years following independence on 18 April 1980. Gross domestic product (GDP) grew in real terms by 11% in 1980 and by 13% in 1981. A major factor in these growth levels was the crippling effect that economic sanctions had had on the economy during the 15 years of unilaterally declared independence (UDI); when sanctions were lifted in 1980, increased trade with the outside world rapidly stimulated economic activity.

The degree to which the phenomenal growth levels of 1980 and 1981 were artificially caused by the temporary overinflation of the economy was illustrated graphically in the following three fiscal years. GDP stagnated in real terms in 1982 and retreated by 3.5% in 1983. There was positive growth in 1984, but only at a very low level of 1% in real terms. This downturn also reflected the onset of a serious drought that lasted three years and was to postpone until 1984/85 the entry of Zimbabwe's 800,000 peasant farmers into the formal agricultural economy. Real GDP growth advanced to 7.3% in 1985. The country's first Five-Year Development Plan, introduced in April 1986 and covering the period 1986–90, was based on an average annual real GDP growth of 5.1% for the term of the Plan. This target proved to be optimistic. GDP growth in 1986, which had been projected at 3%, reached only 0.18%. GDP in 1987 was virtually stagnant, with growth of only 0.3%. In 1988 GDP grew by 5.3%, exceeding the Plan target of 5%. The recovery was attributable to an increase of 20% in the value of agricultural production, owing to improved rainfall, and to high commodity prices. GDP growth slowed slightly in the following three years, to 4% in 1989, 3.8% in 1990 and 2.9% in 1991. As a result of the region's drought, GDP fell by 12% in 1992. Positive growth returned in 1993, at 2.8%, and the official projection for 1994 was 4.4%. The government's growth target for 1995 is 5%. The annual average growth rate of GDP during the first 10 years of Zimbabwean independence was 2.9%.

NATIONAL INCOME

Zimbabwe's GDP at current prices grew from Z.$3,224m. in 1980 to Z.$4,049m. in 1981, to Z.$4,609m. in 1982, to Z.$5,081m. in 1983, to Z.$6,092m. in 1984, to Z.$7,303m. in 1985, to Z.$8,232m. in 1986, to Z.$9,023m. in 1987, to Z.$10,641m. in 1988, to Z.$11,890m. in 1989, to Z.$14,015m. in 1990, to Z.$17,060m. in 1991, Z.$27,460m. in 1992 and to Z.$37,750m. in 1993.

The population, which was estimated to be 10.84m. at mid-1994, is officially recognized to be growing by 2.1% per annum, so, although the annual growth rate of the economy has not always kept pace with that of the population, there has been overall parity between population growth and economic growth. Real GDP per caput grew by 8% in 1980 and by 9.8% in 1981, but between 1982–84 it experienced negative growth, declining by 3% in 1982, by 6% in 1983 and by 2% in 1984. There was positive growth, in real terms, in GDP per caput of 3.2% in 1985, but it declined sharply, by 11%, in 1986, and it fell again, although less steeply, in 1987. There was positive growth, in real terms, of 1.1% in GDP per caput in 1988, followed by negligible growth rates of 0.4% in 1989, 0.2% for 1990, 0.6% in 1991, –14% in 1992 (influenced by drought) and 0.7% in 1993. The forecast for 1994 is 2.2%.

Although Zimbabwe has one of sub-Saharan Africa's most successful agricultural sectors, agriculture ranks only third, behind services and manufacturing, in terms of contribution to GDP. Services accounted for 43% of GDP in 1992, followed by manufacturing at 30%, agriculture at 22% and mining at 6%.

The most notable trend in domestic expenditure in the 1980s was the decline in the private sector's share, from 63% in 1980 to 60% in 1982, to 53% in 1986 and to 44% in 1989. The downward trend was reversed in 1990, however, when the private sector accounted for 53% of total spending; the private-sector share grew to 61% in 1991 and to 71% in 1992, reflecting almost immediately the Economic Structural Adjustment Programme (ESAP) introduced in 1991, which envisaged continued growth of private consumption.

The World Bank Consultative Group for Zimbabwe held a donors' conference in Paris on 18–19 February 1992, at which donors pledged about US $1,000m., of which US $500m. was in the form of balance of payments support. A further Consultative Group meeting, held in Paris in December 1992, pledged US $1,400m. for 1993, of which US $800m. was in support of the balance of payments. The Consultative Group convened again on 13 December 1993 in Paris and pledged US $789m. in loans and grants to Zimbabwe in 1994.

LAND POLICIES

Access to productive land in Zimbabwe remains, 12 years after independence, of crucial importance in determining the degree to which the vast majority of the Zimbabwean people can contribute to the country's national production.

Before independence, the country's land was divided into five grades; the most productive cropland was classified as Grade I, the least productive as Grade V. Whites were allocated 78% of all Grade I and II land, and 4,000 commercial farmers, the overwhelming majority of them white, still occupy over one-half of the most productive land. Grade IV and V land, deemed fit only for the grazing of livestock, accounted for 75% of the land allocated to smallholders, in what are known as the 'communal areas'. In March 1992 7.5m. black Zimbabweans were still crowded on 16m. ha (40m. acres).

After independence, the government undertook to 'resettle' landless Zimbabweans on commercial farmland acquired from willing sellers among the white commercial farmers. By 1990, about 52,000 families had been resettled on 2.7m. ha—only about 32% of the target set in the 1982–85 Transitional National Development Plan, which envisaged the resettlement of 162,000 families by 1985. Under the Lancaster House constitution, the government was permitted, until 1990, to acquire land compulsorily for purposes of resettlement if it was 'under-utilized'. However, following the expiry, in April 1990, of the Lancaster House constitution, expectations have been directed towards an acceleration in land reform measures. At a 1990 conference in Zimbabwe, entitled 'Land Policy After the Lancaster', it was proposed that a land commission be established to determine the most appropriate legal structures governing land reform and issues related to it, such as valuation, payment procedures, distribution methods, tenure rights and policies regarding squatters. The government revealed its proposals in January 1991, in the form of a draft amendment to the 1986 Land Acquisition Act.

The Land Acquisition Act of 1986, which took effect on 1 March of that year, was intended to accelerate resettlement without violating the terms of the Lancaster House agreement.

This was based on the fact that prior to independence the colonial administration did not invariably grant white farmers a freehold title to commercial land, reserving to itself the right to repossess land for 'public purposes'. The 1986 Act specified that the resettlement of 'under-utilized' land qualified as a public purpose. It further defined properly utilized land as that which had been 'substantially and continuously used for the past three years' and confirmed that this test could be applied to parts of farms as well as to whole farms. The Act also gave the government first option on the purchase of all farmland. In effect, the government then wielded considerable influence on the price of purchase to freeholders, and also had the right to repossess land held without freehold title. In August 1989 President Mugabe announced that the constitution was to be amended in 1990 to allow compulsory acquisition of land by the government. However, debate over the constitution dragged on into 1991. The minister of lands, agriculture and rural development was, under the proposed amendment, to have the power to 'designate any land for resettlement purposes'. That land which the government purchased 'for public purposes' was to be paid for in Zimbabwe dollars at a 'fair price'. In March 1992 the house of assembly unanimously passed the Land Acquisition Act, smoothing the way for the government unilaterally to purchase 5.5m. ha of the 11m. ha of land then still held by white farmers. The purchased land was to be used to resettle small-scale farmers from the communal areas. After much debate, the Act stopped short of outlining the white farmers' guarantee of fair compensation. During the campaign prior to the March 1990 presidential and parliamentary elections, it was suggested that, over the next five years, the government planned to purchase 6m. ha of farmland, of which 5m. ha would then be resettled by communal farmers and landless labourers, while the remaining 1m. ha would be used for larger-scale state-controlled farming operations. In May 1993 the government announced that it was to acquire 70 farms; protests ensued, and opponents of the plan stated that they were to take legal action. President Mugabe, however, declared that he would not permit any court decision to override the measure. In April 1994 it emerged that some cabinet ministers and other top government officials had managed to obtain favourable leases to some of the forcibly purchased farms. President Mugabe abrogated the leases and announced a detailed study of the land-tenure and land-use system.

AGRICULTURE

Zimbabwe has a diversified and well-developed agricultural sector, in terms of food production, cash crops and livestock. About 70% of the total labour force and 27% of the formal-sector labour force were engaged in agricultural activity in 1992. Agriculture's share of GDP grew from 14% in 1984 to some 17% in 1985, equalling its percentage contribution to GDP in 1980, before declining again to 11.4% in 1986. Agriculture (including forestry) contributed 12.4% of GDP in 1990, 20% in 1991 and 22% in 1992. Sales of crops and livestock amounted to Z.$1,164.7m. in 1988, to Z.$1,702.1m. in 1989, to Z.$2,374.3m. in 1990 and to an estimated Z.$3,300m. in 1991.

The staple food crop is maize, and other cereal crops grown include wheat, millet, sorghum and barley. Despite the fact that the country's best farmland was still concentrated overwhelmingly in the commercial sector, the share of agricultural output contributed by small-scale farmers in the communal areas rose from 9% in 1983 to 25% in 1988. Communal and small-scale farmers contributed 50% of total agricultural production in 1989/90.

In 1993/94 deliveries of maize to the marketing organizations reached 1.1m. tons, compared with deliveries of 13,000 tons in 1992/93, 1.19m. tons in 1991/92 and 675,000 tons in 1990/91. Deliveries were 1.2m. tons in 1989/90 and only 402,337 tons in 1987/88. The maize crop was affected by drought in 1987/88 and again, even more severely, in 1992/93. Total output was 1.8m. tons in 1993/94, 1.99m. tons in 1992/93, 1.6m. tons in 1990/91, 1.99m. tons in 1989/90, 2.05m. tons in 1985/86 and 2.5m. tons in 1984/85. Communal farmers delivered 380,000 tons of maize to the Grain Marketing Board (GMB) in 1984—a year in which Zimbabwe imported nearly 260,000 tons of maize at a cost of Z.$80m.—presenting the GMB with a windfall that enabled it to cut its Z.$40m. maize-trading deficit in that year by almost 58% to Z.$17m. The full benefits of this surplus could not be enjoyed, owing to problems of transport, storage and marketing. A silo-development programme to increase the GMB's storage capacity from 435,000 tons to 1m. tons, costing Z.$65m., was initiated in 1985. Silos were built in various parts of the communal areas, with a view to eliminating the necessity of importing storage bags, and thereby potentially saving some Z.$27m. in foreign exchange per year. The first stage of the programme, covering 1985–90, involved the construction of seven silos with a combined capacity of 300,000 tons. The programme was to continue in the 1990s.

Added storage is needed to help Zimbabwe meet its own food storage requirements in times of plenty, so as to provide adequate food security for periods of drought. With domestic maize demand running at about 1.9m. tons a year, Zimbabwe had accumulated a surplus of 1.3m. tons by mid-1985 and stocks of 1.9m. tons by April 1987. Exports began in earnest in 1985, and continued until October 1987, when they were suspended as a precaution against the effects on the maize crop of the drought in the 1986/87 growing season. After good rains in December 1987 (excessive in some areas), exports resumed in April 1988. In 1990 the World Food Programme (WFP) undertook to transport at least 60,000 tons of Zimbabwe maize to drought victims in Angola, Malawi, Mozambique and Zaire. Zimbabwe had accumulated grain stocks of 1.15m. tons at 1 April 1990. In 1990/91 poor rains held output down to 1.6m. tons. Farmers delivered only 675,000 tons to the GMB, causing the Board to use some of the country's strategic maize stocks of 714,000 tons, carried over from the 1989/90 season. The GMB in mid-1991 expected to have closing maize stocks of 300,000 tons at March 1992, 40% less than the minimum carry-over requirement of 500,000 tons. This shortfall was extremely untimely, as the 1992/93 drought reduced deliveries in that crop year to only 13,000 tons (see above), finding the government unprepared despite its expenditure of substantial sums to ensure a higher level of preparedness than in previous seasons. The November 1993–March 1994 rains were uneven and caused a 10% reduction in the crop. Output fell slightly below the country's annual maize requirement, and strategic stocks were adequate to meet the shortfall.

In May 1985 Zimbabwe became the first African country to donate its own food aid to Ethiopia, sending 25,000 tons to famine victims in that country. Maize exports in the year to March 1987 were estimated to have reached only 480,000 metric tons, or only 60% of the 800,000 tons previously projected, owing to increased competition from other grain exporters. The WFP bought 100,000 tons of Zimbabwean grain in 1988 for distribution to Malawi, Botswana and Mozambique.

The producer price of maize was raised in May 1985 from the basic Z.$140 per metric ton of the 1984/85 season to Z.$180 per metric ton for the 1985/86 season, an increase of 28%. With silos overflowing, measures were introduced in 1986 to rein in maize output in the 1986/87 season. Quota restrictions were imposed on commercial farmers, but not on communal farmers. In the commercial sector, small-scale producers who delivered 1,000 90-kg bags or fewer were to receive the full, but unchanged, producer price of Z.$180 per ton in the 1986/87 season, while large-scale commercial farmers were paid the full Z.$180 per ton in the 1986/87 season only for 50% of their 1985/86 deliveries plus a further 1,000 90-kg bags; any excess would fetch only Z.$100 per ton. In the 1987/88 season, producer prices for maize did not compare favourably with those offered for a number of other cash crops; many farmers therefore abandoned maize in favour of groundnuts, sunflower seeds and, especially, soya beans. This trend continued in the 1988/89 and 1989/90 seasons. But the almost complete failure of the long rains in the November 1991–March 1992 rainy season plunged the country, as well as its neighbours in the region, into the worst drought of the century. Zimbabwe, which had imported maize only three times in the previous 75 years, faced the necessity of importing 2m. metric tons of maize—and this time it would have to come from overseas, as South Africa's crop was also affected by the drought. The food crisis affected Zimbabwe until the second quarter of 1993, when, owing to the generous November 1992–March 1993 rains, the next crop rose above expectations to 1.99m. tons (of which 1.3m. tons were delivered to marketing organizations). Although drought was the most serious factor leading to lower maize output, it was not the only factor. Even before the drought began, the volume of maize intake by the GMB in 1991 was down by 23% from the 1990 figure, primarily because low official prices payable to producers had discouraged many farmers from planting maize. The government's policy had been a deliberate bid to keep what then seemed to be more and more excess maize from pouring into the country's overstretched storage facilities. Producer prices were raised in March 1992 from Z.$325 per metric ton of maize to Z.$550. In June 1993 controls on maize prices were abolished.

Although there was a good wheat harvest, of 248,937 tons, in 1988/89, Zimbabwe does not meet its high domestic requirement of wheat (350,000 tons per annum), and imports are necessary. Output amounted to 215,000 tons in 1986/87, and to 214,636 tons in 1987/88, but output rose to a record 326,823 tons in 1990/91 before falling back to 259,000 tons in 1991/92. Owing to the drought, wheat output for 1992/93 fell to only 54,000 tons, or enough to supply the milling industry for two months. Some 340,000 tons of wheat was to be imported in 1992. During the 1991/92 season, the government raised the producer price for wheat by 20.6% and the price to the flour mills by 119%. Wheat output in 1993/94 was 250,000 tons.

Barley production was rising, according to National Breweries Ltd, which until the drought was producing 8,000–10,000 metric tons of malt per year for export. Zimbabwe's barley output rose to 28,000 tons in 1985, up from 8,500 tons in 1984 and 11,500 tons in 1983. According to FAO estimates, barley output was 29,000 tons in 1987 and 1988 and 30,000 tons in 1989. In May 1992, National Breweries Ltd warned that, owing to the drought, the 1992 barley crop would be only about 15% of normal levels, or 4,500 tons. Zimbabwe also produced in 1993: 95,000 tons of millet, 90,000 tons of sorghum, 64,000 tons of groundnuts in shells, 65,000 tons of soya beans, 74,000 tons of sunflower seeds and 45,000 tons of dry beans.

Zimbabwe's principal cash crops are tobacco, cotton and sugar. Tobacco contributes about 66% of the agricultural export revenue and employs 12% of the work-force. Tobacco auctions begin each year in early April, and last for 25 weeks. Output marketed in 1989/90 was 129,900 tons, an increase of 8% in volume terms from marketed output of 119,913 tons in 1988/89. The crop marketed in 1988/89 was of exceptionally high quality, attaining an average price per kg of Z.$4.30 and a total value of Z.$640m., compared with an average price per kg of Z.$2.15 and a total value in export earnings of Z.$278.9m. in 1987/88. The crop marketed in 1989/90, which earned Z.$971m. in export revenue, attained an even higher average price, of Z.$6.48 per kg, producing almost Z.$860m. for the total crop. The 1990/91 crop was a record 155m. kg of flue-cured tobacco, raising anticipated tobacco revenue to more than Z.$1,000m. The area under tobacco cultivation was 63,760 ha in 1987, compared with 57,054 ha in 1986. Part of the rise in area was attributed to increasing interest on the part of smallholders in the cultivation of burley tobacco. The flue-cured sector is far larger, with commercial farmers accounting for most of the output. Despite the drought, tobacco growers produced 201m. kg in 1991/92, in a year when 19% more farmers planted tobacco on 17% more hectarage than in 1990/91. Exports of tobacco reached their highest quarterly level ever in October–December 1991, at more than 51m. kg. The tobacco crop in 1992/93 totalled 210m. kg, and was of superior quality. However, prices obtained at the opening of the 1993 auctions in May were only 97 US cents per kg, about one-half the levels of a year previously. This adverse development was the result of substantially reduced world demand for tobacco. Prices fetched did not even cover most growers' costs, and, consequently, they incurred an aggregate debt of Z.$400m. In the 1993/94 season, output fell to 170m. kg, but prices subsequently recovered.

Commercial farmers produced less seed cotton in 1986 than in 1985, while production by communal farmers increased. The proportion of cotton produced by communal farmers rose from 46% in 1987/88 to 59% in 1988/89 and to 60% in 1989/90 before falling back to 55% in 1990/91, as low real producer prices led farmers to plant other crops instead. Commercial area under cotton fell from 55,700 ha in 1988/89 to 40,666 ha in 1989/90, and communal area declined from 12,000 ha in 1988/89 to 11,000 ha in 1989/90. Deliveries of seed cotton amounted to a record 323,239 tons in 1987/88, but slumped to 262,000 tons in 1988/89 and to 219,000 tons in 1989/90 before recovering to 280,000 tons in 1990/91. (The crop year runs from 1 March to 28 February.) Heavy rains during the cotton-picking season and verticillium wilt contributed to the 1988–90 disappointment, but also blamed by many farmers was the seed that they had purchased from the Cotton Marketing Board. Growers reported that the plants from these seeds wilted soon after germination, and the crops of both large- and small-scale growers were affected. The drought of 1992 further reduced cotton output, to 67,000 tons in that year. Output recovered, however, to 204,000 tons in 1993 and in 1993/94 production was estimated at 181,000 tons.

Sugar earned an estimated Z.$308m. in 1990, compared with earnings of Z.$186.9m. in 1989 and of Z.$157.1m. in 1988. Drought affected the 1988 crop, but production nevertheless exceeded the national demand of 170,000 tons per annum. The 1992 drought cut the country's output of milled sugar to 35,000 tons, just 10% of normal levels. Production in 1992 fell to only 10,000 tons, necessitating the import of 132,000 tons from Cuba. Even after the return of rains in November 1992, the sugar industry was not expected to recover fully for at least two years. An irrigation scheme was proposed to make this very thirsty crop less vulnerable to drought in future. In 1993 the Commonwealth Development Corporation (CDC) loaned a total of £11m. for the re-establishment of canefields at Hippo Valley Estates Ltd and at Triangle Ltd, and a further £2m. to the Agricultural Finance Corporation of Zimbabwe for on-lending to the Chipiwa Growers' Co-operative Society Ltd. The 1992 drought is estimated to have killed up to 90% of the sugarcane plants in Zimbabwe's Lowveld region. In 1994, however, amid a discernible recovery, the industry forecast a national sugar harvest for that year of between 500,000 tons and 530,000 tons. Coffee export revenue for Zimbabwe's mild arabicas rose from Z.$34m. in the 1984/85 season to Z.$50m. for the 1985/86 season, in which 11,000 metric tons were produced. Earnings from exports of arabica coffee reached Z.$75m. in the 1986/87 marketing year, but were estimated to have fallen to some Z.$45m. in 1987/88, reflecting the severe impact of drought on coffee production. The arabica crop doubled in 1988/89 to 12,500 tons, following favourable weather conditions; however, the value of exports was only Z.$54m., because of depressed world prices. The 1991/92 coffee crop was severely depressed, owing both to drought and to low global prices. The 1992/93 coffee crop returned to near-normal levels, and world prices finally improved in May 1994, reaching a five-year high.

Zimbabwe is one of only a few sub-Saharan African countries allowed to export beef to the EC countries. Exports began in 1985; however, Zimbabwe was unable to meet its quota of 8,100 tons in the first two years (1985 and 1986), owing to a severe shortage of beef in the country. Beef allocations to butchers were reduced by 30% in 1986, when total beef sales realized some Z.$48m. (US $29.2m.). In an attempt to help the parastatal Cold Storage Commission (CSC) survive in the face of competition from private-sector abattoirs, the government granted the CSC a virtual monopoly of the urban market for beef from January 1987, but producers argued that they needed a higher gazetted producer price in order to make their efforts economic. In April an increase of 38% in producer prices for beef was duly announced. Meanwhile, the government initiated major efforts to improve the financial position of the CSC, after a trading deficit of Z.$27.6m. was recorded in 1986 (increasing to Z.$28.9m. in 1987). With financing from the European Investment Bank (ECU 14m., or US $15.82m.) and from the Arab Bank for Economic Development in Africa (US $9.21m.), the CSC embarked upon a US $102m. project, under which a processing and distribution complex was to be built in Harare, a new abattoir was to be constructed in Bulawayo (with a daily capacity of 600 head of cattle), and the Masvingo abattoir was to be rehabilitated, with a planned capacity of 400 head of cattle per day. Zimbabwe fulfilled its EC quota of 8,100 tons of beef exports in 1987 (earning Z.$80m. from this source) and in 1988 (earning Z.$66.6m.). In 1989, however, the EC suspended its beef imports from Zimbabwe, owing to an outbreak of foot-and-mouth disease in April and May of that year. Exports were resumed in January 1992. Domestic consumption of beef was, however, restricted in late 1987 by the introduction of rationing. The 1992 drought led to a doubling of the intake of cattle at all abattoirs as herders rushed to sell their stock before they died of thirst. The CSC slaughtered 257,360 head of cattle during January–June 1992, more than double the number killed in July–December 1991. The drought reduced the national herd to 1.7m. head of cattle, but Zimbabwe was still able to meet its EC quota of high-quality beef. Zimbabwe produced 4,000 tons of dry milk, 4,000 tons of cheese and 3,000 tons of butter in 1993.

MINING AND MANUFACTURING

Mining contributed 6% of Zimbabwe's GDP and generated Z.$2,420m. of export revenue in 1992. Sales of all minerals rose by 7% by value in real terms in 1993, to Z.$3,450m., of which gold contributed Z.$1,370m. The value of mineral production was Z.$1,836m. in 1991, compared with Z.$1,324m. in 1990, Z.$1,197m. in 1989 and Z.$985.7m. in 1988. Steady performance is expected over the medium term.

Zimbabwe currently produces more than 40 different minerals. Gold, nickel, asbestos, coal, copper, chromite, iron ore, tin, silver, emeralds, graphite, lithium, granite and cobalt are the main mineral products. Gold is the main source of revenue in the mining sector, accounting for 40% of mineral sales by value in 1992. Production of gold amounted to 18.7 tons in 1993, up from 18.5 tons in 1992, 17.34 tons in 1991, up from 16.9 tons in 1990 and 16.0 tons in 1989. In value terms, gold earned Z.$414.4m. in 1989, Z.$502.2m. in 1990, Z.$731.6m. in 1991, Z.$968m. in 1992 and Z$1,400m. in 1993. In November 1993 Cluff Resources of the UK reached an agreement with the Eastern and Southern African Trade and Development Bank for a 52,000–ounce gold loan to finance underground development of the Freda Rebecca gold mine, due to reach full production by the end of 1994. The loan is repayable over five years and gives the borrower the choice of repaying in gold or US dollars. Nickel ranks second in export revenue, accounting for about 15.1% of total mineral export earnings in 1992. Output of nickel, spurred by a global upturn in demand, rose from 11,489 tons (valued at Z.$198m.) in 1988 and to 11,600 tons (valued at Z.$284m.) in 1989, before levelling off to 11,441 tons (valued at Z.$236.1m.) in 1990 and to 11,371 tons (valued at Z.$338.9m.) in 1991. Nickel production increased by 11% in 1993, but export value increased by only 7%. World prices for nickel remained depressed during 1992, 1993, and into 1994. Asbestos earned Z.$195.9m. in 1991 and Z.$145.8m. in 1990; output was 187,066 tons in 1989, compared with 186,800 tons in 1988. The association of asbestos with lung cancer has led to a drop in the value of exports. Coal output fell slightly in volume, to 5.07m. tons, in 1988, after having increased in volume by 38% to 4.83m. tons in 1987. However, revenue from coal exports rose from Z.$119.2m. in 1989 to Z.$162.2m. in 1990 and to Z.$174.8m. in 1991. Rio Tinto Zimbabwe began operations in 1990 to develop the Sengwa coalfield in western Zimbabwe, which has a projected annual output of 100,000 tons of low-sulphur coal. Production of methane, or coal-bed gas, was expected to commence in 1995. Copper production fell in volume terms, from 15,659 tons in 1989, to 14,689 tons in 1990 and to 13,451 tons in 1991 although the value of output rose from Z.$74.9m. in 1989 to Z.$85.3m. in 1990 and to Z.$99.3m. in 1991. A declining trend in world copper prices culminated in a five-year price 'low' in May 1993. Volume output of chromite fell slightly in 1991, to 570,749 tons from 573,103 tons in 1990, although in value terms earnings rose to Z.$101.5m. in 1991, a 68% rise over the Z.$60.3m. yielded in 1990. Chromite accounted for 5.2% of the total value of mineral production in 1992. Earnings from nickel, copper and chromite all suffered from the release of low-price supplies by Russia in 1992 and 1993. Output of iron ore (metal content 64%) was 1.16m. tons valued at Z.$49.83m. in 1991, compared with 1.26m. tons valued at Z.$44m. in 1990, 1.02m. tons valued at Z.$25.6m. in 1988 and 1.33m. tons valued at Z.$28.8m. in 1987. Output volume for silver declined from 21,154 tons in 1990 to 18,996 tons in 1991, although earnings from silver rose from Z.$8m. in 1990 to Z.$10.94m. in 1991. Tin output rose from 808 tons in 1990 to 827 tons in 1991, while earnings from tin increased from Z.$12.29m. in 1990 to Z.$15.26m. in 1991. Platinum holds significant revenue potential. Substantial reserves of platinum have been found in the Great Dyke mineral belt in central Zimbabwe. Delta Gold plans to exploit them at the Hartley mine; development, at a projected cost of US $250m., began in 1990, and trial mining was carried out in 1992. In December 1993, BHP of Australia made an investment of A$311m. (US $211m.)—said to be the largest one-off private sector investment in Zimbabwe since independence—to enable the Hartley project to go ahead. An underground mine is expected to start producing by 1996 and to reach full production of 180,000 tons of platinum-bearing ore per month by 1998. The mine, which has a projected lifespan of 70 years, has been forecast to produce annually 150,000 ounces of platinum metal, plus 110,000 ounces of palladium, 23,000 ounces of gold, 11,000 ounces of rhodium, 3,000 tons of nickel and 2,000 tons of cobalt. Hartley is projected to earn more than Z.$700m. annually. Areas adjacent to Hartley are also being assessed for possible exploitation.

The parastatal Zimbabwe Mining Development Corporation (ZMDC) is developing the copper deposits at the Copper Queen and King mines, and it is planned to manufacture copper cable locally as an import-substitution measure, aimed at saving Z.$6.6m. in foreign exchange annually. There is also import-substitution potential in the manufacture of ferrochrome derivatives, chemicals and pesticides. Another parastatal organization, the Minerals Marketing Corporation of Zimbabwe, markets all the country's minerals except gold abroad. Set up in 1982, its operations have been consistently profitable since 1983. Major private-sector mining companies, such as the Anglo American Corporation, Rio Tinto-Zinc and Lonrho, are also active in Zimbabwe. The medium-term outlook for Zimbabwe's mining sector is encouraging, helped by the government's decision, in October 1990, to allow mining companies to retain 5% of the value of their export earnings to finance imported inputs. In February 1989 a gold refinery, with a capacity of 50 tons per year, was opened in Harare. Built at a cost of Z.$4m., the refinery is owned by the Reserve Bank of Zimbabwe and operated by Fidelity Printers and Refiners. It is expected to lessen Zimbabwe's dependence on South Africa, which had previously possessed the only gold refineries in Africa. In May 1991 the British company Reunion Mining began prospecting for diamonds on a 43,597 sq. km area near Beitbridge. In June 1991 Auridiam Consolidated of Australia won a permit to develop the River Ranch diamond concession at a cost of US $10m.–$12m. The company completed its exploration activities in 1992 and confirmed that diamonds had been found at the concession and announced plans to build a small-scale production plant that would process initially 200,000 cu m of diamondiferous rock. It was reported that among the 5,000 carats found was a 17-carat gem-quality stone. A 500,000 ton-per-annum processing plant at River Ranch was commissioned in January 1994, and Auridiam reported receiving higher prices than expected at its quarterly diamond sales in Antwerp. The company is also exploring for diamonds at Chinhu on the Highveld.

Zimbabwe produces a wide variety of manufactured products, both for the local market and for export. Growth of manufactured exports on a regional basis has been hindered by lack of foreign exchange in neighbouring countries, and by reductions as large as 55% in the amount of foreign exchange allocated to manufacturers for the import of essential raw materials. The ESAP, introduced in 1991, however, significantly alleviated the foreign-exchange constraint. The manufacturing sector accounted for 26% of GDP in 1991 and for 30% in 1992. The sector also provided employment for 16% of the labour force in 1993.

The volume index of manufacturing production (1980 = 100) reached 153.3 in the October quarter of 1990, the highest level since independence. The annual index figure was 138.1 for 1990, 144 for 1991, 123 for 1992 and 123.4 for 1993. In the 1993 calendar year, as compared with the calendar year 1992, the only sectors to register positive growth were textiles and ginning (up by 9%), paper and printing (up by 14.6%), and clothing and footwear (up by 2.6%). All other sectors experienced a decline, the most pronounced being transport equipment (down by 41.8%), followed by metals and metal products (down by 18.2%, largely reflecting production problems at Ziscosteel), foodstuffs (down by 17.9%) and non-metallic minerals (down by 17.7%). In 1991 the country began a three-phase measure to place more products under Open General Import Licence (OGIL). The first phase began on 1 April 1991, and the government had placed 50% of imported raw materials under OGIL by January 1992. Other products followed, and in January 1994 the government removed a 10% temporary duty on OGIL imports. The government also reduced the surtax on imports from 20% to 15%. While many manufacturers have welcomed aspects of the ESAP reforms, they are less fond of measures such as the removal of the Export Incentive Scheme, which the government now recognizes as a subsidy and a distortion of a free-market economy.

INTERNATIONAL TRADE AND BANKING

In 1988 the economy registered surpluses in the trade, current-account and overall payments balances. The visible trade deficit was US $270m. in 1993 and US $645m. in 1992, after a small trade surplus of US $48m. in 1991. The forecast for 1994 was a visible trade deficit of US $160m. The current account of the balance of payments registered its largest ever deficit in 1992, at US $1,110m., up from shortfalls of US $489m. in 1991 and US $171m. in 1990. The current account deficit was reduced to US $745m. in 1993, and the forecast for 1994 was of a shortfall of US $655m. The government had warned that the 1992 current account deficit could be as high as US $1,000m., even before the full extent of the effects of the drought were taken into account. In 1984 Zimbabwe's terms of trade rose by 15.7%, to 120.6 (1980 = 100)—the highest figure for 20 years. Zimbabwe's exports equalled only 90% of its imports in 1982, but import cover subsequently improved to 108% in 1983, to 120% in 1986, to 136% in 1987; import cover was estimated to have remained at 136% in 1988. Although the trade balance was in surplus, the overall balance of payments was in deficit for eight years up to 1984, when an overall balance-of-payments surplus of Z.$164m. was achieved. This followed deficits of Z.$159m. in 1983 and Z.$124m. in 1982. The overall balance of payments was again positive in 1985, and registered a Z.$205m. surplus in that year, a Z.$73m. surplus in 1986, a Z.$236m. surplus in 1987, a Z.$19m. surplus in 1988, a Z.$107m. deficit in 1989 and an estimated Z.$256m. deficit in 1990. The current account of the balance of payments recorded a surplus of Z.$13m. in 1986, following a surplus of Z.$1,159m. in 1985 and deficits of Z.$102m. in 1984, Z.$455m. in 1983 and Z.$533m. in 1982. The current account showed a surplus of Z.$82m. in 1987 and a further surplus of Z.$101m. in 1988 before registering deficits of Z.$22m. in 1989 and an estimated Z.$164m. in 1990. The value of exports increased from Z.$1,380m. in 1984 to Z.$1,615m. in 1985, to Z.$1,760m. in 1986, to Z.$1,840m. in 1987, to Z.$2.860m. in 1988, to Z.$3,334m. in 1989 and to Z.$4,231m. in 1990 before falling back to Z.$2,210m. in 1991, all at current prices. On a percentage basis, growth was 17.5% in 1984, 17% in 1985, 9% in 1986 and 5% in 1987, again at current prices. Exports were estimated to have risen by 25% in 1989, owing to increased sales of non-traditional exports and an effective 11% depreciation in the official value of the Zimbabwe dollar. Further currency depreciation led to a 33.6% rise in export value in 1990. Exports declined in US dollar terms by 6% in 1991, but currency depreciation turned export performance into positive growth in Zimbabwe dollar terms. Export value was US $1,727m. in 1990, US $1,617m. 1991 and US $1,664m. in 1992. Tobacco and gold are the largest two items, but together they contribute less than 50%; other export earners are cotton lint, textile products, ferro-alloys, food and live animals, crude inedible non-food materials, nickel, asbestos, copper, raw sugar, iron and steel bars, ingots and billots. This list illustrates an unusually high level of export diversity for an African country.

Zimbabwe's principal export customers vary significantly from year to year. In 1986 South Africa ranked first, taking 16% of the country's exports. In 1987 and 1988 the UK ranked first, taking 13% and 11% respectively. In 1990 Germany ranked first, taking 12%. The member-countries of the Southern African Development Co-ordination Conference (SADCC, since reorganized as the Southern African Development Community, SADC) and the Preferential Trade Area for Eastern and Southern Africa (PTA), together accounted for 13.9% of exports by value in 1991. Leading suppliers in 1991 were South Africa (22.7%), the UK (15.7%), Germany (9.4%), Japan, the USA, France, Botswana and Italy.

Imports have also grown steadily but more slowly in most years. The value of imports rose from Z.$1,087m. in 1983 to Z.$2,043.2m. in 1988 and to Z.$4,528.2m. in 1990. The main imports in 1990 were manufactured goods (38.5%), machinery and transport equipment (37.4%) and fuel (15.6%). Imports in US dollar terms cost US$1,848m. in 1990, rose by 17% to US$2,170m. in 1991 and then declined by 9% to US$1,965m. in 1992. Owing to currency depreciation, imports in 1992 still rose in Zimbabwe dollar terms, by 3.4% to Z.$10,002m.

Zimbabwe's membership of the PTA has, in theory, provided access to new directions in regional trade, but, in practice, Zimbabwean exporters have been somewhat disappointed. Zimbabwe produces many items which the other member-states need to import, but the potential trade partners lack the foreign exchange to pay for them. The member-state in the best position to pay for imports from Zimbabwe is Kenya, with which a bilateral trade treaty was signed in late 1984. Kenya itself has a fairly wide manufacturing base, and is therefore in competition with Zimbabwe in supplying some items to the other PTA states. The historic change of government in South Africa has created many opportunities for companies to work in a country which is widely regarded as a formidable competitor for investment; and as a ready source of imported goods. South Africa is able to take an even larger share of Zimbabwe's domestic market, following the recent increase in trade liberalization.

Zimbabwe's external debt rose sharply during the 1980s, totalling US $4,205m. in April 1993, compared to US $4,007m. in 1992 and US $2,959m. in 1990, and with US $276m. at independence in April 1980. In 1987 debt-servicing costs exceeded 33% of export earnings; in 1988, however, the proportion had fallen to 27.5%, and it declined to 21.3% in 1989 before rising to 22.6% in 1990, 27.2% in 1991 and 32% in 1992. However, the ratio fell back to 30% in 1993, and economists forecast a further decline to about 20% in 1994 and onwards to the year 2001. Zimbabwe owed US $190m. in repayments on its foreign debt during 1989 and US $220m. in 1990. Shortages of foreign exchange have persisted throughout the post-independence period.

The domestic banking sector is diversified, with major foreign banks participating, as well as the Zimbabwe government. Of the commercial banks, two are long-established foreign banks—Barclays Bank of Zimbabwe and Standard Chartered Bank Zimbabwe. Zimbabwe Banking Corporation (Zimbank) is state-controlled and in 1990 expanded internationally, opening offices in Ghana and Botswana. Also present in commercial banking are Stanbic Bank Zimbabwe and the Commercial Bank of Zimbabwe. In addition, there are five merchant banks: the Merchant Bank of Central Africa, Syfrets Merchant Bank (a wholly-owned affiliate of Zimbank), First Merchant Bank of Zimbabwe, Standard Chartered Merchant Bank Zimbabwe and National Merchant Bank. The Zimbabwe Development Bank began operation in 1985; the government has a controlling interest, in partnership with the African Development Bank and other multilateral development institutions. In July 1993 exchange controls were relaxed, allowing foreign investors to repatriate investment proceeds, providing a major boost to the Zimbabwe Stock Exchange. The share purchase limit was also raised to 35%. The exchange was capitalized at US $1,900m. in May 1994.

ENERGY

Fuel is one of Zimbabwe's principal imports and accounted for 33% of all imports in 1992. Petroleum products enter the land-locked country through a 300-km pipeline running between Mutare and the Mozambique port of Beira. Work began in 1989 to extend the pipeline to Harare. Operations by

Renamo insurgents during the conflict in Mozambique occasionally disrupted the flow of fuel for short periods, despite the presence of some 10,000 Zimbabwean troops to defend the pipeline. The most serious stoppage occurred in late 1982, when the Mozambican guerrillas bombed the storage tanks and pumping station at Beira; on that occasion, repairs took two months to complete, and fuel shortages ensued. Zimbabwe consumes some 800,000 metric tons of petroleum products (including diesel fuel) per annum.

Zimbabwe's sole coal producer is the Wankie Colliery Co, which mines coal at Hwange (formerly Wankie). The company was producing at only about 50% of capacity in the first half of the 1980s, and by 1985 only 15 of its 32 ovens were in operation. The coke-oven battery was closed from 1986 until late 1987 for rehabilitation, but the company had stockpiled sufficient coke to maintain supplies during the closure. The colliery's output was 160,000 tons of coke in the year to February 1989, while domestic demand is 68,000 tons per annum. The company's operations are being expanded to exploit a deposit estimated at 400m. metric tons. Reserves at Lubimbi coalfield are estimated to exceed 20,000m. tons, and an oil-from-coal project is in operation there. Zimbabwe's total coal reserves are estimated at 28,000m. tons.

Zimbabwe shares with Zambia the huge Kariba dam, on the Zambezi river. For many years, Kariba's only hydroelectric power plant was on the Zambian side, and Zimbabwe imported some Z.$20m. worth of energy annually from its northern neighbour. In 1987, however, Zimbabwe added 920 MW of new thermal capacity to its own national grid, eliminating the need for these imports; in July 1987 the Zimbabwean government notified Zambia of its intention to terminate the supply contract. This termination was brought about abruptly in early 1989, however, when a fire seriously damaged Zambia's Kafue station, eliminating its export capacity until at least 1991. The Hwange thermal power station, constructed at a cost of Z.$230m., accounted for 920 MW of total national generating capacity of 1,900 MW in 1989. However, the Hwange facility's performance has been disappointing owing to design faults and a shortage of spare parts. Work to refurbish units 1–4 of the facility is scheduled for completion at the end of 1995, with funding from the World Bank. The shared Central African Power Corporation (CAPCO) was replaced in 1986 by the Zimbabwe Electricity Supply Authority (ZESA), which has aimed to maximize the operational efficiency of existing installed capacity, while furthering a longer-term development programme directed towards a forecast demand of 2,800 MW by 2004. (Maximum demand in 1988/89 was about 1,400 MW.) In April 1991, after many delays, the government agreed to the construction of a Z.$500m. hydroelectric extension facility at Kariba South, due for completion in 1988, and of a joint Zambia-Zimbabwe Batoka Gorge hydroelectric facility costing Z.$1,000m. which is to add 800 MW by 2003. A Z.$154m. plan to rehabilitate three thermal power plants was also approved, with completion due by the end of 1994. The 1992 drought lowered the water level for all hydroelectric facilities in the region, necessitating the unusual step of rationing electricity in Zimbabwe. Urgent negotiations were initiated to obtain power imports from Zaire and Zambia, and in May 1992 ZESA arranged for the import of 500 MW from Mozambique. Work on an interconnector linking Mozambique's Cahora Bassa facility to Matimba and Blindura in Zimbabwe began in 1994 and was to add 500 MW to Zimbabwe's national grid by the end of 1996. Further work on Hwange, stages 7 and 8, is to be completed in 1998, and a coal-fired project at Sengwa is to add 600 MW by 2004.

LABOUR, WAGES AND INFLATION

Inflation has, with the exception of 1988, affected lower-income urban families more than it has higher-income urban families in every year since independence in 1980. Inflation was stimulated in 1991 by the government's relaxation of price controls as part of its 1991–95 economic reform programme. According to the consumer price index, in the year ended 31 June 1991, prices for all items rose by 22% for the higher-income group, compared with the same period a year earlier, while they rose by 23% for the lower-income group. The cost of living for lower income families rose by 16.4%, compared with 11.5% for higher income families. In the year ended 31 December 1990, prices for all items rose by 16.1% for the higher-income group, but they rose by 18.5% for the lower income group. Analysis reveals that transport prices rose fastest for the lower-income group, at 50.9%, followed by food at 19.4% and drink and tobacco at 20.3%. In the higher-income group, clothing and footwear prices rose fastest, at 19.0%, followed by food at 18.6%. In December 1990 the consumer price index (1980 = 100) for all items was 359 for the higher-income group and 394.5 for the lower-income group. In December 1991 the consumer price index was 457 for lower-income urban dwellers and 408 for higher-income urban dwellers. In early 1993 the government introduced a new consumer goods weighting structure (1990 = 100) to reflect a 'more representative' combination of goods and services than previously. However, even the new index reflected a high level of consumer price inflation: the figure for January 1993 reached 206.9%. Food prices rose by 71.8% between January 1992 and January 1993. Overall inflation rates were 45% in 1992, 28.1% in 1991, 15.5% in 1990, 11.6% in 1989, 7.7% in 1988, 9% in 1987, 15% in 1986 and 10% in 1985. The post-independence peak was 25% in 1983 until this was exceeded in 1991. On the eve of the 1 January 1994 17% devaluation of the Zimbabwe dollar, inflation stood at an average for the previous year of 18.5%, but economists expected the figure to rise to at least 22% before falling back to 18% in late 1994. Since independence, the government has endeavoured to narrow the wide gap in incomes between rich and poor Zimbabweans. The Minimum Wage Act of 1980 established a wages minimum of Z.$85 per month for workers who came under the Industrial Conciliation Act, Z.$70 per month for others in industry, Z.$58 per month for mineworkers and Z.$30 per month for agricultural and domestic workers. In January 1982 minimum wages were again raised, and in 1986 the upper limit for the wages 'freeze' was raised to include only those earning more than Z.$36,000 per year. Wage rises were announced on a graduated scale, ranging from 3% for those earning between Z.$30,000 and Z.$36,000 per year upwards, to 10% for those earning between Z.$100 and Z.$500 per month. Those earning less than Z.$100 per month were granted a uniform monthly increase of Z.$10. Before the wage increases, an employee receiving Z.$36,000 per year was paid Z.$34,800 more annually than a worker earning Z.$100 per month; after the wage rises, the gap between the two earners was wider, at Z.$35,760 per year. The differential between the industrial minimum wage and the agricultural minimum wage reflects, among other factors, the higher cost of urban life.

In June 1987 the government announced a six-month 'freeze' on wages and prices, which was extended on 31 December 1987. The wages 'freeze' was lifted in February 1988, and that on prices was relaxed in May 1988. A study by the University of Zimbabwe, released in March 1988, forecast that as much as 24% of the country's labour force would be unemployed by 1990. It warned that, between 1986 and 1990, 857,000 school leavers would enter the job market, while only 144,000 new jobs were to be created. In the event, an estimated 1m. Zimbabweans were unemployed in 1990, and an additional 300,000 school-leavers entered the job market in that year. Unemployment was estimated at 23% in July 1991. Pressure to cut payrolls under the ESAP has exacerbated unemployment since then, and banking sources estimate that in March 1994 current incomes were, on average, only 68% of their 1990 levels in real terms. Meanwhile, the 1991–95 economic reform programme, which was drawn up with the help of the IMF and the World Bank, called for a 25% reduction in the civil service, necessitating the elimination of 32,000 jobs by 1994. In May 1992, 1,170 government posts were abolished, and a further 6,154 public-sector jobs were described as 'superfluous': their abolition was forecast to reduce government expenditure by Z.$32.5m. annually. In July 1992 the government reduced the number of ministries as part of its streamlining of the administration. In 1992 approximately 10,000 textile workers and 7,000 agricultural workers lost their jobs, and in June 1993 only 11% of the working population was employed in the formal sector, the lowest percentage in over 23 years. Government provisions of Z.$20m. to offset the social effects of the austerity accompanying structural adjustment were widely regarded as unrealistic and inadequate. In June 1994 the government granted substantial allowances and salary increases of between 10%–20% to members of the civil service and armed forces.

Statistical Survey

Source (unless otherwise stated): Central Statistical Office, Kaguvi Bldg, Fourth St, POB 8063, Causeway, Harare; tel. (4) 706681.

Area and Population

AREA, POPULATION AND DENSITY

Area (sq km)	390,759*
Population (census results)	
March–May 1969	5,107,330
18 August 1982	7,608,432
18 August 1992 (provisional)	10,401,767
Density (per sq km) at August 1992	26.6

* 150,873 sq miles.

PRINCIPAL TOWNS (population at census of August 1982)

Harare (Salisbury)	656,000	Masvingo (Fort Victoria)	30,600
Bulawayo	413,800	Zvishavane (Shabani)	26,800
Chitungwiza	172,600	Chinhoyi (Sinoia)	24,300
Gweru (Gwelo)	78,900	Redcliff	22,000
Mutare (Umtali)	69,600	Marondera (Marandellas)	20,300
Kwekwe (Que Que)	47,600		
Kadoma (Gatooma)	44,600		
Hwange (Wankie)	39,200		

Mid-1983 (estimated population): Harare 681,000; Bulawayo 429,000; Chitungwiza 202,000.

BIRTHS AND DEATHS (UN estimates, annual averages)

	1975–80	1980–85	1985–90
Birth rate (per 1,000)	44.2	42.7	42.5
Death rate (per 1,000)	13.1	11.7	11.0

Expectation of life (UN estimates, years at birth, 1985–90): 56.8 (males 55.1; females 56.8).

Source: UN, *World Population Prospects: The 1992 Revision*.

ECONOMICALLY ACTIVE POPULATION
(sample survey, '000 persons aged 15 years and over, 1986–87)

	Males	Females	Total
Agriculture, hunting, forestry and fishing	937	1,172	2,109
Mining and quarrying	16	1	17
Manufacturing	141	26	167
Electricity, gas and water	11	1	12
Construction	46	5	51
Trade, restaurants and hotels	76	53	129
Transport, storage and communications	70	6	76
Financing, insurance, real estate and business services	17	7	17
Community, social and personal services	251	146	397
Activities not adequately defined	25	19	44
Total in employment	1,591	1,436	3,027
Unemployed	110	123	233
Total labour force	1,701	1,559	3,260

Source: International Labour Office, *Year Book of Labour Statistics*.

Mid-1992 (estimates in '000): Agriculture, etc. 2,772; Total labour force 4,128 (Source: FAO, *Production Yearbook*).

EMPLOYMENT ('000 persons at March)*

	1990	1991	1992†
Agriculture, forestry and fishing	290.0	304.2	292.1
Mining and quarrying	51.4	50.9	49.3
Manufacturing	197.1	205.4	199.2
Construction	75.8	81.0	92.7
Electricity and water	8.7	8.9	8.9
Transport and communications	53.3	56.4	51.5
Trade	96.0	100.7	98.7
Finance, insurance and real estate	17.6	18.2	16.6
Community, social and personal services	402.3	418.3	412.5
Total	1,192.2	1,244.0	1,221.5

* Excluding small establishments in rural areas.
† At June.

Agriculture

PRINCIPAL CROPS ('000 metric tons)

	1990	1991	1992
Wheat	326	259	81*
Barley	26	24	5
Maize	1,994	1,586	362
Millet	143	122	28*
Sorghum	91	68	29*
Sugar cane	3,093	3,236	300*
Potatoes*	31	31	25
Cassava (Manioc)*	95	100	110
Dry beans*	47	48	40
Soybeans	106	111	51
Vegetables*	151	153	132
Oranges*	60	63	55
Bananas*	74	76	60
Groundnuts (in shell)	119	107	34
Sunflower seed	66	68	31*
Cottonseed†	114	123	47
Cotton lint	67	72	27†
Tobacco (leaves)	140	178	202
Tea (made)	17	16†	8
Coffee (green)	14	12	4†

* FAO estimate(s). † Unofficial estimate(s).

Source: FAO, *Production Yearbook*.

LIVESTOCK ('000 head, year ending September)

	1990	1991	1992*
Horses*	24	24	24
Asses*	103	104	104
Cattle	6,218	6,476	4,700
Sheep	592	595	580
Pigs	288	290	290
Goats	2,564	2,570	2,570

* FAO estimates.

Poultry (FAO estimates, million): 12 in 1990; 13 in 1991; 13 in 1992.

LIVESTOCK PRODUCTS (FAO estimates, '000 metric tons)

	1990	1991	1992
Beef and veal	78	87	76
Goats' meat	9	9	9
Pig meat	11	11	11
Poultry meat	17	18	14
Other meat	20	19	20
Cows' milk	598	596	415
Butter	4.7	4.8	3.3
Cheese	7.8	8.0	5.6
Poultry eggs	15.6	16.8	16.8
Cattle hides	8.2	9.0	8.8

Source: FAO, *Production Yearbook*.

Forestry

ROUNDWOOD REMOVALS
('000 cubic metres, excl. bark)

	1990	1991	1992
Sawlogs, veneer logs and logs for sleepers	512†	525	525†
Pulpwood	119†	157	157†
Other industrial wood	1,017	1,050	1,082†
Fuel wood*	6,269†	6,269†	6,269†
Total	7,917	8,001	8,033

* Assumed to be unchanged since 1988.
† FAO estimate.

Source: FAO, *Yearbook of Forest Products*.

SAWNWOOD PRODUCTION
('000 cubic metres, incl. railway sleepers)

	1990*	1991	1992*
Coniferous (soft wood)	168	221	221
Broadleaved (hard wood)	22	29*	29
Total	190	250	250

* FAO estimate(s).

Source: FAO, *Yearbook of Forest Products*.

Fishing

('000 metric tons)

	1989	1990	1991
Dagaas	20.1	21.8	19.3
Other fishes	3.9	4.0	2.8
Total catch	24.0	25.8	22.1

Source: FAO, *Yearbook of Fishery Statistics*.

Mining

	1988	1989	1990
Antimony ore (metric tons)*	150	210	101
Asbestos ('000 metric tons)	186.6	187.0	160.5
Chromium ore ('000 metric tons)†	561.6	627.5	562.6
Clay ('000 metric tons)	113	124	100
Coal ('000 metric tons)‡	5,065	5,112	5,504
Cobalt ore (metric tons)*	122	111	121
Copper ore ('000 metric tons)*	16.1	15.8	14.8
Gold ('000 troy oz)*	481	515	544
Graphite (metric tons)	10,468	18,147	16,384
Iron ore ('000 metric tons)†	1,020	1,143	1,260
Magnesite ('000 metric tons)	28.3	33.4	32.6
Nickel ore (metric tons)*	11,489	11,634	11,442
Phosphate rock ('000 metric tons)	124	134	148
Silver ('000 troy oz)*	704	718	680
Tin ore (metric tons)*	885	849	839

* Figures refer to the metal content of ores and concentrates.
† Figures refer to gross weight. The estimated metal content is: Chromium 33%; Iron 64%.
‡ Figures refer to sales of coal.

1991 ('000 metric tons, unless otherwise indicated): Antimony ore (metric tons) 160; Asbestos 142; Chromium ore 290 (estimated metal content); Clay 124; Coal 5,600 (estimated production); Cobalt ore (metric tons) 12,903; Iron ore 728 (metal content); Magnesite 23.3; Nickel ore (metric tons) 11,312; Phosphate rock 117; Silver (metric tons) 19; Tin ore (metric tons) 797 (Source: UN, *Industrial Statistics Yearbook)*.

1992 ('000 metric tons, unless otherwise indicated): Coal 6,000 (estimated production); Copper ore 10.6; Tin ore (metric tons) 716 (Sources: UN, *Monthly Bulletin of Statistics*, and UNCTAD, *International Tin Statistics)*.

1993: Copper ore ('000 metric tons) 8.0; Tin ore (metric tons) 600 (estimate) (Source: UN, *Monthly Bulletin of Statistics)*.

Industry

SELECTED PRODUCTS
('000 metric tons, unless otherwise indicated)

	1989	1990	1991
Raw sugar*	502	464	329
Cigarettes (million)†	2,623	2,500	2,600
Coke	300†	566	560†
Cement	910	996	698
Pig-iron	520	521	525†
Ferro-chromium‡	198	242	217
Crude steel‡	592	580	600
Refined copper—unwrought‡	24.0†	22.5	22.2
Nickel—unwrought (metric tons)	12,823	12,700†	11,313
Tin—unwrought (metric tons)§	848	839	796
Electric energy (million kWh)	8,040	9,559	9,565

* Data from the FAO.
† Estimate(s).
‡ Data from the US Bureau of Mines.
§ Primary metal only.

Source: UN, *Industrial Statistics Yearbook*.

1992: Cement ('000 metric tons) 828; Tin—unwrought (metric tons) 720 (provisional); Electric energy (million kWh) 9,000 (Sources: UN, *Monthly Bulletin of Statistics*, and UNCTAD, *International Tin Statistics*).

Finance

CURRENCY AND EXCHANGE RATES

Monetary Units
100 cents = 1 Zimbabwe dollar (Z.$).

Sterling and US Dollar Equivalents (31 March 1994)
£1 sterling = Z. 11.813;
US $1 = Z. 7.957;
Z. 1,000 = £84.65 = US $125.68.

Average Exchange Rate (US $ per Zimbabwe dollar)
1991 0.2917
1992 0.1963
1993 0.1545

BUDGET (Z.$'000, year ending 30 June)

Revenue	1990/91	1991/92*
Taxes on income and profits:		
Income tax	3,035,135	3,620,000
Non-resident shareholders' tax	34,823	40,000
Non-residents' tax on interest	2,922	5,000
Resident shareholders' tax	24,442	28,000
Branch profits tax	1,492	2,150
Capital gains tax	22,517	28,000
Non-residents' tax on fees	11,558	13,850
Total	3,132,890	3,737,000
Taxes on goods and services:		
Sales tax	1,052,702	1,298,000
Customs duties	1,122,291	1,320,000
Excise duties	476,780	610,000
Betting tax	14,907	23,000
Other	1,936	2,495
Total	2,668,616	3,253,495
Miscellaneous taxes:		
Stamp duties and fees	64,273	75,000
Estate duty	16,670	21,500
Other	31,084	35,000
Total	112,027	131,500
Revenue from investments and property:		
Interest, dividends and profits	182,734	242,500
Rents	13,592	24,713
Water supplies	4,507	6,000
Royalties	10	5
Total	200,842	273,218

Revenue - *continued*	1990/91	1991/92*
Fees: Departmental facilities and services:		
Agriculture	1,471	1,500
Civil aviation	6,682	8,000
Companies, trade marks and patents	4,370	5,200
Education	53,217	72,735
Health	7,379	8,000
National parks	8,709	10,500
Roads and road traffic	4,738	5,932
Water development	6,085	—
Other	7,504	15,500
Total	100,155	127,367
Recoveries of development expenditure	1,367	3,100
Foreign reserves adjustment surplus	—	45,000
Other:		
Pension contributions	191,779	235,000
Judicial fines	18,232	23,030
Sale of state property	14,896	16,332
Refunds of miscellaneous payments from votes	43,264	39,900
Miscellaneous	42,889	40,450
Total	311,060	354,712
Grand Total	6,526,956	7,925,392

* Provisional figures.

Expenditure	1990/91	1991/92*
Recurrent expenditure:		
Goods and services:		
Salaries, wages and allowances	2,940,483	3,179,951
Subsistence and transport	191,372	187,780
Incidental expenses	176,699	133,445
Other recurrent expenditure	926,327	1,496,268
Total	4,234,881	4,997,444
Transfers:		
Interest	1,140,250	1,514,961
Subsidies	529,471	453,700
Pensions	213,875	250,055
Grants and transfers	739,212	767,331
Total	2,622,808	2,986,047
Capital expenditure:		
Land purchase	8,060	16,663
Buildings	411,271	463,104
Land development	107,705	132,274
Civil engineering	273,171	289,046
Plant, machinery and equipment	31,332	41,577
Office equipment and furniture	10,775	11,450
Other capital expenditure	1,199	7,112
Total	843,513	961,226
Grand Total*	7,701,202	8,944,717

* Provisional figures.

INTERNATIONAL RESERVES (US $ million at 31 December)

	1991	1992	1993
Gold*	67.9	88.1	79.1
IMF special drawing rights	0.1	0.4	0.9
Reserve position in IMF	0.1	0.1	0.1
Foreign exchange	149.5	221.7	431.1
Total	217.6	310.3	511.2

* Valued at a market-related price which is determined each month.

Source: IMF, *International Financial Statistics*.

MONEY SUPPLY (Z.$ million at 31 December)

	1991	1992	1993
Notes and coin in circulation	888.8	861.3	1,191.4
Demand deposits at deposit money banks	2,089.3	2,285.0	4,079.9

Source: IMF, *International Financial Statistics*.

COST OF LIVING
(Consumer Price Index; base: 1990 = 100)

	1991	1992
Food	112.6	192.7
Clothing and footwear	122.7	161.5
Rent, fuel and light	117.9	150.2
All items (incl. others)	123.3	175.2

Source ILO, *Year Book of Labour Statistics*.

1993: All items 223.6 (Source: IMF, *International Financial Statistics*).

NATIONAL ACCOUNTS (Z.$ million at current prices)

Expenditure on the Gross National Product

	1987	1988	1989*
Private household consumption	4,416	5,251	6,915
Private non-profit-making bodies	87	97	
Net government current expenditure	2,531	3,004	3,250
Gross fixed capital formation	1,673	2,031	2,402
Increase in stocks	–134	459	210
Total domestic expenditure	8,573	10,842	12,777
Net exports of goods and services	366	599	411
Net investment income from abroad	–355	–478	–538
GNP at market prices	8,584	10,963	12,650

* Source: IMF, *International Financial Statistics*.

Composition of the Gross National Product

	1986	1987	1988
Compensation of employees	4,351	4,859	5,611
Operating surplus Consumption of fixed capital	3,058	3,160	4,573
GDP at factor cost	7,409	8,019	10,184
Indirect taxes	1,251	1,346	1,645
Less Subsidies	370	426	388
GDP at market prices	8,290	8,939	11,441
Net factor income from abroad	–384	–355	–478
GNP at market prices	7,906	8,584	10,963

Source: UN, *National Accounts Statistics*.

Gross Domestic Product by Economic Activity
(Z.$ million at current factor cost)

	1989	1990	1991
Agriculture, hunting, forestry and fishing	1,753	2,391	3,709
Mining and quarrying	827	923	1,175
Manufacturing	3,162	3,691	4,849
Electricity and water	391	417	567
Construction	284	323	368
Trade, restaurants and hotels	1,258	1,569	1,898
Transport, storage and communications	930	1,067	1,243
Finance, insurance and real estate	863	977	1,133
Government services	895	1,057	1,230
Other services	1,878	2,423	3,197
Sub-total	12,241	14,838	19,369
Less Imputed bank service charges	338	344	366
Total	11,903	14,494	19,003

Source: UN, *National Accounts Statistics*.

BALANCE OF PAYMENTS (US $ million)

	1989	1990	1991
Merchandise exports f.o.b.	1,693.5	1,747.9	1,693.8
Merchandise imports f.o.b.	–1,318.3	–1,505.2	–1,645.7
Trade balance	375.2	242.7	48.1
Exports of services	239.9	274.2	285.9
Imports of services	–479.9	–522.9	–631.0
Other income received	43.8	23.7	27.7
Other income paid	–241.4	–294.4	–318.0
Private unrequited transfers (net)	–19.2	–3.0	3.4
Official unrequited transfers (net)	78.5	108.1	94.6
Current balance	–3.0	–171.6	–489.4
Direct investment (net)	–10.2	–12.2	2.8
Portfolio investment (net)	–36.7	–21.7	7.3
Other capital (net)	88.6	164.4	397.7
Net errors and omissions	–91.7	19.1	–23.6
Overall balance	–53.0	–22.0	–105.2

Source: IMF, *International Financial Statistics*.

External Trade

PRINCIPAL COMMODITIES (distribution by SITC, US $'000, excl. stores and bunkers for aircraft)

Imports f.o.b.*	1988	1990	1991
Food and live animals	n.a.	42,042	18,380
Crude materials (inedible) except fuels	n.a.	69,271	90,178
Mineral fuels, lubricants, etc. (incl. electricity)	n.a.	289,259	252,115
Petroleum, petroleum products, etc.	n.a.	271,541	243,624
Refined petroleum products	n.a.	262,085	235,567
Motor spirit (gasoline) and other light oils	26,944	67,037	61,121
Motor and aviation spirit	26,944	65,413	59,800
Gas oils	71,988	133,880	111,805
Chemicals and related products	n.a.	284,584	323,919
Inorganic chemicals	n.a.	62,997	60,293
Artificial resins, plastic materials, etc.	55,188	58,895	71,696
Products of polymerization, etc.	n.a.	45,998	58,221
Basic manufactures	n.a.	308,570	341,849
Textile yarn, fabrics, etc.	n.a.	84,386	90,382
Non-metallic mineral manufactures	n.a.	43,068	46,019
Iron and steel	n.a.	69,708	74,419
Universals, plates and sheets	29,043	46,503	45,714
Machinery and transport equipment	n.a.	692,196	822,310
Power-generating machinery and equipment	n.a.	44,091	38,621
Machinery specialized for particular industries	n.a.	160,705	192,089
Civil engineering and contractors' plant and equipment	n.a.	51,672	31,312
Construction and mining machinery	14,552	44,269	26,995
Textile and leather machinery	17,183	36,862	52,645
General industrial machinery, equipment, etc.	n.a.	110,420	124,852
Telecommunications and sound equipment	31,154	28,842	44,198
Other electrical machinery, apparatus, etc.	n.a.	62,017	75,939

Imports f.o.b.* - *continued*	1988	1990	1991
Road vehicles and parts†	n.a.	125,865	278,597
Passenger motor cars (excl. buses)	20,212	21,351	48,627
Motor vehicles for goods transport, etc.	n.a.	62,605	147,779
Goods vehicles	n.a.	57,794	120,772
Other road motor vehicles (excl. motorcycles, etc.)	n.a.	11,585	40,156
Other transport equipment†	n.a.	113,382	16,842
Aircraft, associated equipment and parts†	12,356	105,919	10,972
Miscellaneous manufactured articles	n.a.	85,164	68,001
Total (incl. others)	1,129,455	1,852,008	2,007,142

* The distribution by commodities is not available for 1989 (total imports US $1,627 million).

† Excluding tyres, engines and electrical parts.

Exports f.o.b.*	1988	1990	1991
Food and live animals	n.a.	285,572	162,877
Meat and meat preparations	n.a.	7,491	10,015
Fresh, chilled or frozen meat	39,689	4,162	3,575
Cereals and cereal preparations	n.a.	117,460	63,499
Maize (unmilled)	62,269	108,600	48,644
Sugar, sugar preparations and honey	n.a.	66,590	37,838
Sugar and honey	43,936	61,344	34,515
Raw sugars	43,138	49,876	17,870
Coffee, tea, cocoa and spices	n.a.	73,202	33,624
Coffee and coffee substitutes	22,287	60,033	21,538
Green coffee (incl. husks and skins)	22,287	60,012	21,527
Beverages and tobacco	n.a.	345,875	431,278
Tobacco and tobacco manufactures	n.a.	345,726	429,714
Unmanufactured tobacco	274,922	339,710	424,234
Crude materials (inedible) except fuels	n.a.	217,559	153,927
Textile, fibres and waste	n.a.	86,699	58,551
Cotton	82,109	86,292	58,278
Crude fertilizers and crude minerals	n.a.	86,928	63,373
Asbestos	57,450	59,289	46,064
Basic manufactures	n.a.	446,403	366,993
Textile yarn, fabrics, etc.	n.a.	44,116	44,683
Iron and steel	n.a.	213,393	166,443
Pig-iron, etc.	n.a.	154,415	112,007
Ferro-alloys	189,659	154,404	111,864
Ingots and other primary forms	45,834	46,776	42,274
Blooms, billets, slabs, etc.	45,834	43,515	38,284
Non-ferrous metals	n.a.	134,283	110,243
Copper and copper alloys	36,691	28,008	15,319
Nickel and nickel alloys	170,196	100,246	85,538
Machinery and transport equipment	n.a.	54,048	26,501
Miscellaneous manufactured articles	n.a.	62,596	63,423
Clothing and accessories (excl. footwear)	n.a.	37,925	37,972
Non-monetary gold (excl. gold ores and concentrates)	209,430	2,864	2,623
Total (incl. others)	1,630,741	1,470,432	1,250,990

* The distribution by commodities is not available for 1989.

Source: UN, *International Trade Statistics Yearbook.*

PRINCIPAL TRADING PARTNERS (US $'000)*

Imports f.o.b.†	1988	1990	1991
Australia	6,086	50,516	20,837
Belgium/Luxembourg	13,684	20,184	23,299
Canada	19,658	20,853	17,903
China, People's Repub.	n.a.	36,280	15,605
France	35,549	38,338	60,746
Germany	107,265	135,988	189,470
Italy	18,975	40,719	47,609
Japan	45,537	84,489	120,043
Netherlands	30,251	36,116	34,113
South Africa‡	315,353	445,841	578,626
Sweden	17,398	25,062	24,795
Switzerland	15,002	37,149	43,332
United Kingdom	121,688	212,757	306,445
USA	66,334	211,201	109,655
Total (incl. others)	1,129,455	1,851,440	2,003,917

Exports f.o.b.	1988	1990	1991
Belgium/Luxembourg	30,204	37,285	52,563
China, People's Repub.	16,599	24,253	37,178
France	15,896	23,909	18,764
Germany	129,525	173,363	132,210
Hong Kong	9,242	23,495	14,163
Italy	92,638	67,714	44,747
Japan	95,966	80,752	90,344
Kenya	16,197	18,053	12,921
Malawi	41,157	70,785	41,404
Mozambique	41,563	54,009	34,317
Netherlands	103,160	63,045	37,450
Portugal	20,835	39,405	13,585
South Africa‡	207,151	222,264	213,208
Spain	12,337	22,592	22,086
Sweden	15,292	9,034	8,042
Switzerland	6,926	24,318	26,883
United Kingdom	159,269	157,806	169,912
USA	102,345	95,977	73,007
Zambia	61,115	51,364	44,557
Total (incl. others)	1,630,741	1,467,569	1,248,367

* Imports by country of production; exports by country of last consignment.

† Data for 1989 are not available.

‡ Including Botswana, Lesotho, Namibia and Swaziland.

Source: UN, *International Trade Statistics Yearbook.*

Transport

RAIL TRAFFIC
(National Railways of Zimbabwe, including operations in Botswana)

	1987	1988	1989
Total number of passengers ('000)	2,650	2,608	3,192
Revenue-earning metric tons hauled ('000)	13,200	13,024	13,377
Gross metric ton-km (million)	11,239	10,803	10,539
Net metric ton-km (million)	5,451	5,337	5,352

ROAD TRAFFIC (motor vehicles in use)

	1988*	1989*	1990
Passenger cars	281,000	282,000	283,000
Commercial vehicles	81,000	82,000	83,000

* Estimates.

Source: UN, *Statistical Yearbook.*

CIVIL AVIATION (traffic on scheduled services)

	1989	1990	1991
Kilometres flown ('000)	11,000	12,000	12,000
Passengers carried ('000)	583	601	606
Passenger-km (million)	760	797	817
Freight ton-km ('000)	65,000	65,000	64,000

Source: UN, *Statistical Yearbook.*

Tourism

	1988	1989	1990
Number of tourist arrivals	449,000	474,000	606,000
Tourist receipts (US $ million)	24	40	47

Source: UN, *Statistical Yearbook.*

1992 (estimate): Tourist arrivals 500,000.

Communications Media

	1988	1989	1990
Radio receivers ('000 in use)	775	801	830
Television receivers ('000 in use)	200	250	300
Telephones ('000 in use)	287	n.a.	301
Book production:			
Titles	195	337	349
Daily newspapers:			
Number	2	n.a.	2
Circulation ('000 copies)	214	n.a.	206

1991: 860,000 radio receivers in use; 270,000 television receivers in use.

Sources: UNESCO, *Statistical Yearbook*; UN, *Statistical Yearbook.*

Education

(1992)

	Schools	Teachers	Students
Primary	4,567	60,834	2,301,642
Secondary	1,512*	25,225	710,619
Higher	n.a.	3,076	61,553

* Figure for 1990. Source: Ministry of Education and Culture, Causeway, Harare.

Source: UNESCO, *Statistical Yearbook.*

1993: Primary students 2,436,671; Secondary students 635,502. Source: Ministry of Education and Culture, Causeway, Harare.

Directory

The Constitution

The Constitution of the Republic of Zimbabwe took effect at independence on 18 April 1980. Constitutional amendments relating to the representation of whites in Parliament, and to the powers of the President, received legislative approval in late 1987. The amendments also provided that the next presidential election (which took place in March 1990) would be by direct popular vote, rather than by members of the House of Assembly. In early 1990 constitutional amendments took effect which established a unicameral Parliament. An amendment providing for the appointment of a second Vice-President took effect in August 1990.

THE REPUBLIC

Zimbabwe is a sovereign republic and the Constitution is the supreme law.

DECLARATION OF RIGHTS

The declaration of rights guarantees the fundamental rights and freedoms of the individual, regardless of race, tribe, place of origin, political opinions, colour, creed or sex.

THE PRESIDENT

Each candidate for the Presidency shall be nominated by not fewer than 10 members of the House of Assembly; if only one candidate is nominated, that candidate shall be declared to be elected without the necessity of a ballot. Otherwise, a ballot shall be held within an electoral college consisting of the members of the House of Assembly. The President shall hold office for six years and shall be eligible for re-election. The President shall be Head of State and Commander-in-Chief of the Defence Forces.

PARLIAMENT

Under the 1980 Constitution, Parliament was to consist of a Senate and a House of Assembly. The life of the Parliament was ordinarily to be five years. In September 1987 the legislature approved a constitutional amendment whereby 20 seats in the House of Assembly and 10 seats in the Senate which had been reserved for election by voters on the separate white roll were abolished. Following general elections held in March 1990, the Senate was abolished and the House of Assembly was expanded to comprise 150 members, of whom 120 were directly elected, 12 were nominated by the President, 10 were traditional Chiefs and eight were Provincial Governors. The life of the restructured House of Assembly was to be six years. Amendments to the Constitution must have the approval of two-thirds of the members of the House of Assembly.

THE EXECUTIVE

Executive authority shall be vested in the President, who acts on the advice of the Cabinet. In October 1987 Parliament approved a constitutional amendment whereby the Presidency became an executive post, incorporating the former post of Prime Minister. The President shall appoint a Vice-President (see above) and other Ministers and Deputy Ministers, to be members of the Cabinet.

OTHER PROVISIONS

An Ombudsman shall be appointed by the President, acting on the advice of the Judicial Service Commission, to investigate complaints against actions taken by employees of the government or of a local authority.

Chiefs shall be appointed by the President, and shall form a Council of Chiefs from their number in accordance with customary principles of succession.

Other provisions relate to the Judicature, Defence and Police Forces, public service and finance.

The Government

HEAD OF STATE

President: ROBERT GABRIEL MUGABE (took office 31 December 1987; re-elected March 1990).

THE CABINET
(September 1994)

Vice-Presidents: SIMON VENGAYI MUZENDA, JOSHUA MQABUKO NKOMO.

Senior Minister in the President's Office for National Affairs, Employment Creation and Co-operatives: DIDYMUS MUTASA.

Senior Minister in the President's Office for Finance: Dr BERNARD THOMAS CHIDZERO.

Minister of Foreign Affairs: Dr NATHAN MARWIRAKUWA SHAMUYARIRA.

Minister of Justice, Legal and Parliamentary Affairs: EMMERSON DAMBUDZO MNANGAGWA.

Minister of Defence: MOVEN ENOCK MAHACHI.

Minister of Home Affairs: DUMISO DABENGWA.

Minister of Local Government and Rural and Urban Development: JOSEPH MSIKA.

Minister of Lands, Agriculture and Rural Resettlement: Dr KUMBIRAI KANGAI.

Minister of Information, Posts and Telecommunications: DAVID ISHEMUNYORO KARIMANZIRA.

Minister of Labour, Manpower Planning and Social Welfare: JOHN LANDA NKOMO.

Minister of Industry and Commerce: (vacant).

Minister of Mines: EDDISON MUDADIRWA ZVOBGO.

Minister of Transport and Energy: DENNIS NORMAN.

Minister of Health and Child Welfare: Dr TIMOTHY STAMPS.

Minister of Public Construction and National Housing: ENOS CHAMUNORWA CHIKOWORE.

Minister of the Environment and Tourism: HERBERT MURERWA.

Minister of Higher Education: STANLEY MUDENGE.

Minister of Education and Culture: WITNESS MANGWENDE.

Ministers of State in the President's Office: Dr SYDNEY TIGERE SEKEREMAYI (National Security); Dr TICHENDEPI MASAYA ROBERT (Finance); SWITHUN MOMBESHORA (Local Government); GABRIEL MACHINGA (Women's Affairs); FAY CHUNG (National Affairs, Employment Creation and Co-operatives).

MINISTRIES

Office of the President: Munhumutapa Bldg, Samora Machel Ave, Private Bag 7700, Causeway, Harare; tel. (4) 707091; telex 24478.

Office of the Vice-President: Munhumutapa Bldg, Samora Machel Ave, Private Bag 7700, Causeway, Harare; tel. (4) 707091; telex 24478.

Ministry of Defence: Munhumutapa Bldg, Samora Machel Ave, Private Bag 7713, Causeway, Harare; tel. (4) 700155; telex 22141.

Ministry of Education and Culture: Ambassador House, Union Ave, POB 8022, Causeway, Harare; tel. (4) 734050; telex 26430.

Ministry of the Environment and Tourism: Karigamombe Centre, Private Bag 7753, Causeway, Harare; tel. (4) 794455.

Ministry of Finance: Munhumutapa Bldg, Ground Floor, Samora Machel Ave, Private Bag 7705, Causeway, Harare; tel. (4) 794571; telex 22141; fax (4) 792750.

Ministry of Foreign Affairs: Munhumutapa Bldg, Samora Machel Ave, POB 4240, Causeway, Harare; tel. (4) 727005.

Ministry of Health and Child Welfare: Kaguvi Bldg, Fourth St, POB 8204, Causeway, Harare; tel. (4) 730011; telex 22141; fax (4) 729154.

Ministry of Higher Education: Union Ave, POB 275, Harare; tel. (4) 795991; fax (4) 728730.

Ministry of Home Affairs: Mukwati Bldg, Samora Machel Ave, Private Bag 505D, Harare; tel. (4) 703641; telex 22141.

Ministry of Industry and Commerce: Mukwati Bldg, Fourth St, Private Bag 7708, Causeway, Harare; tel. (4) 702731; telex 24472.

Ministry of Information, Posts and Telecommunications: Linquenda House, Baker Ave, POB 1276, Causeway, Harare; tel. (4) 703894; telex 24142; fax (4) 707213.

Ministry of Justice, Legal and Parliamentary Affairs: Mapondera Bldg, Samora Machel Ave, Private Bag 7704, Causeway, Harare; tel. (4) 790905; telex 22141; fax (4) 790901.

Ministry of Labour, Manpower Planning and Social Welfare: Compensation House, Central Ave and Fourth St, Private Bag 7707, Causeway, Harare; tel. (4) 790871; telex 22141.

Ministry of Lands, Agriculture and Water Development: Makombe Complex, Block 3, Harare St, Private Bag 7712, Causeway, Harare; tel. (4) 707861; telex 22141.

Ministry of Local Government, Rural and Urban Development: Mukwati Bldg, Private Bag 7706, Causeway, Harare; tel. (4) 790601; telex 22179.

Ministry of Mines: ZIMRE Centre, cnr Leopold Takawira St and Union Ave, Private Bag 7709, Causeway, Harare; tel. (4) 703781; telex 22416.

Ministry of National Affairs, Employment Creation and Co-operatives: POB 8158, Causeway, Harare; tel. (4) 734691.

Ministry of Public Construction and National Housing: cnr Leopold Takawira St and Herbert Chitepo Ave, POB 8081, Causeway, Harare; tel. (4) 704561.

Ministry of Transport and Energy: Kaguvi Bldg, POB CY 595, Causeway, Harare; tel. (4) 700991; telex 22141; fax (4) 708225.

PROVINCIAL GOVERNORS

Manicaland: KENNETH VHUNDUKAYI MANYONDA.

Mashonaland Central: JOYCE MAJURE.

Mashonaland East: EDMUND GARWE.

Mashonaland West: Dr IGNATIUS MORGAN CHIMINYA CHOMBO.

Masvingo: JOSAYA DUNIRA HUNGWE.

Matabeleland North: WELSHMAN MABHENA.

Matabeleland South: STEPHEN JEQE NYONGOLO NKOMO.

Midlands: Lt-Col HERBERT MAHLABA.

President and Legislature

PRESIDENT

Election, 28–30 March 1990

Candidate	Percentage of total votes cast
ROBERT GABRIEL MUGABE	78
EDGAR TEKERE	16

HOUSE OF ASSEMBLY

Speaker: NOLAN MAKOMBE.

Election, 28–30 March 1990

	Seats*
Zimbabwe African National Union—Patriotic Front	117
Zimbabwe Unity Movement	2
Zimbabwe African National Union—Ndonga	1
Total	120

* In addition to the 120 directly elective seats, 12 are held by nominees of the President, 10 by traditional Chiefs and eight by Provincial Governors.

Political Organizations

Committee for a Democratic Society (CODESO): f. 1993; Kalanga-supported grouping, based in Matebeleland; Leader SOUL NDLOVU.

Conservative Alliance of Zimbabwe (CAZ): POB 242, Harare; f. 1962, known as Rhodesian Front until June 1981, and subsequently as Republican Front; supported by sections of the white community; Pres. GERALD SMITH; Chair. MIKE MORONEY.

Democratic Party: f. 1991 by a breakaway faction from the ZUM; Nat. Chair. GILES MUTSEKWA; Pres. DAVIDSON GOMO.

Forum Party of Zimbabwe (FPZ): Harare; f. 1993; conservative; Pres. THEMBA DHLODLO (acting).

Independent Zimbabwe Group: f. 1983 by a breakaway faction from the fmr Republican Front; Leader BILL IRVINE.

National Democratic Union: f. 1979; conservative grouping with minority Zezeru support; Leader HENRY CHIHOTA.

National Progressive Alliance: f. 1991; Chair. CANCIWELL NZIRAMASANGA.

United National Federal Party (UNFP): Harare; f. 1978; conservative; seeks a federation of Mashonaland and Matabeleland; Leader Chief KAYISA NDIWENI.

Zimbabwe Active People's Unity Party: Bulawayo; f. 1989; Leader NEWMAN MATUTU NDELA.

Zimbabwe African National Union—Patriotic Front (ZANU—PF): 88 Manica Rd, Harare; f. 1989 following the merger of PF ZAPU (f. 1961) and ZANU—PF (f. 1963); Pres. ROBERT GABRIEL MUGABE; Vice-Pres SIMON VENGAYI MUZENDA, JOSHUA MQABUKO NKOMO.

Zimbabwe African National Union—Ndonga (ZANU—Ndonga): POB UA525, Union Ave, Harare; f. 1977; breakaway faction from ZANU, also includes fmr mems of UANC; centrist; Pres. Rev. NDABANINGI SITHOLE; Sec.-Gen. NOEL MUKONO.

Zimbabwe Democratic Party: Harare; f. 1979 by a breakaway faction from UANC; traditionalist; Leader JAMES CHIKEREMA.

Zimbabwe National Front: f. 1979; Leader PETER MANDAZA.

Zimbabwe Peoples' Democratic Party: f. 1989; Chair. ISABEL PASALK.

Zimbabwe Unity Movement (ZUM): f. 1989 by a breakaway faction from ZANU—PF; merged with United African National Council (UANC, f. 1971) in 1994; Leader EDGAR TEKERE.

Diplomatic Representation

EMBASSIES AND HIGH COMMISSIONS IN ZIMBABWE

Afghanistan: 26 East Rd, POB 1227, Harare; tel. (4) 720083; telex 22276; Chargé d'affaires a.i.: ABD AL-SATAR FROTAN.

Algeria: 8 Pascoe Ave, Belgravia, POB 2929, Harare; tel. (4) 726682; telex 24795; Ambassador: Dr ALI SALAH.

Angola: Doncaster House, 26 Speke Ave/Ongwa St, POB 3590, Harare; tel. (4) 790070; telex 24195; Ambassador: ARISTIDES VAN-DÚNEN.

Argentina: Club Chambers Bldg, cnr Baker Ave and Third St, POB 2770, Harare; tel. (4) 730075; telex 22284; fax (4) 730076; Ambassador: VALENTIN LUCO ORIGONE.

Australia: Karigamombe Centre, 4th Floor, 53 Samora Machel Ave, POB 4541, Harare; tel. (4) 794591; telex 24159; fax (4) 704644; High Commissioner: JOHN THWAITES.

Austria: 216 New Shell House, 30 Samora Machel Ave, POB 4120, Harare; tel. (4) 702921; telex 22546; Ambassador: Dr FELIX MIKL.

Bangladesh: 9 Birchenough Rd, POB 3040, Harare; tel. (4) 727004; telex 24806; High Commissioner: HARUN AHMED CHOWDHURY.

Belgium: Tanganyika House, 5th Floor, 23 Third St, POB 2522, Harare; tel. (4) 793306; telex 24788; fax (4) 703960; Ambassador: BERNARD R. PIERRE.

Botswana: 22 Phillips Ave, Belgravia, POB 563, Harare; tel. (4) 729551; telex 22663; High Commissioner: PHENEAS M. MAKEPE.

Brazil: Old Mutual Centre, 9th Floor, Jason Moyo Ave, POB 2530, Harare; tel. (4) 730775; telex 22205; fax (4) 737782; Chargé d'affaires a.i.: ANA MARIA PINTO MORALES.

Bulgaria: 15 Maasdorp Ave, Alexandra Park, POB 1809, Harare; tel. (4) 730509; telex 24567; Ambassador: CHRISTO TEPAVITCHAROV.

Canada: 45 Baines Ave, POB 1430, Harare; tel. (4) 733881; telex 24465; High Commissioner: CHARLES BASSET.

China, People's Republic: 30 Baines Ave, POB 4749, Harare; tel. (4) 724572; telex 22569; fax (4) 794959; Ambassador: GU XINER.

Cuba: 5 Phillips Ave, Belgravia, POB 4139, Harare; tel. (4) 720256; telex 24783; Ambassador: EUMELIO CABALLERO RODRÍGUEZ.

Czech Republic: 11 Walmer Drive, Highlands, POB 4474, Harare; tel. (4) 700636; telex 22413; fax (4) 737270.

Denmark: UDC Centre, 1st Floor, cnr 59 Union Ave and First St, POB 4711, Harare; tel. (4) 790398; telex 24677; fax (4) 732544; Ambassador: HENNING KJELDGAARD.

Egypt: 7 Aberdeen Rd, Avondale, POB A433, Harare; tel. (4) 303445; telex 24653; Ambassador: Dr IBRAHIM ALY BADAWI EL-SHEIK.

Ethiopia: 14 Lanark Rd, Belgravia, POB 2745, Harare; tel. (4) 725822; telex 22743; fax (4) 720259; Ambassador: FANTAHUN H. MICHAEL.

Finland: Karigamombe Centre, 3rd Floor, 53 Samora Machel Ave, POB 5300, Harare; tel. (4) 751654; telex 24813; fax (4) 737731; Ambassador: ILARI RANTAKARI (resident in Dar es Salaam, Tanzania).

France: Ranelagh Rd, Highlands, POB 1378, Harare; tel. (4) 48096; telex 24779; fax (4) 45657; Ambassador: JACQUES MIGOZZI.

Germany: 14 Samora Machel Ave, POB 2168, Harare; tel. (4) 731955; telex 24609; fax (4) 790680; Ambassador: Dr NORWIN Graf LEUTRUM VON ERTINGEN.

Ghana: 11 Downie Ave, Belgravia, POB 4445, Harare; tel. (4) 738652; telex 24631; Chargé d'affaires a.i.: YAW KONADU-YIADOM.

Greece: 8 Deary Ave, Belgravia, POB 4809, Harare; tel. (4) 793208; telex 24790; Ambassador: ALEXANDROS SANDS.

Holy See: 5 St Kilda Rd, Mount Pleasant, POB MP191, Harare (Apostolic Nunciature); tel. (4) 74457; fax (4) 744412; Apostolic Nuncio: Most Rev. PETER PAUL PRABHU, Titular Archbishop of Tituli in Numidia.

Hungary: 20 Lanark Rd, Belgravia, POB 3594, Harare; tel. (4) 733528; telex 24237; fax (4) 730512; Ambassador: TAMÁS GÁS PÁR GÁL.

India: 12 Nathal Rd, Belgravia, POB 4620, Harare; tel. (4) 795955; telex 24630; fax (4) 722324; High Commissioner: SIDDHARTH SINGH.

Indonesia: 3 Duthie Ave, Belgravia, POB 3594, Harare; tel. (4) 732561; telex 24237; Ambassador: SAMSI ABDULLAH.

Iran: 8 Allan Wilson Ave, Avondale, POB A293, Harare; tel. (4) 726942; telex 24793; Chargé d'affaires a.i.: ALIREZA GAKARANI.

Iraq: 21 Lawson Ave, Milton Park, POB 3453, Harare; tel. (4) 725727; telex 24595; fax (4) 724204; Ambassador: ISSAM MAHBOUB.

Italy: 7 Bartholomew Close, Greendale North, POB 1062, Harare; tel. (4) 48190; telex 24380; fax (4) 48199; Ambassador: Dr RICCARDO LEONINI.

Japan: Karigamombe Centre, 18th Floor, 53 Samora Machel Ave, POB 2710, Harare; tel. (4) 790108; telex 24566; fax (4) 727769; Ambassador: MITSUO IIJIMA.

Kenya: 95 Park Lane, POB 4069, Harare; tel. (4) 790847; telex 24266; High Commissioner: CRISPUS MWEMA.

Korea, Democratic People's Republic: 102 Josiah Chinamano Ave, Greenwood, POB 4754, Harare; tel. (4) 724052; telex 24231; Ambassador: RI MYONG CHOL.

Kuwait: 1 Bath Rd, Avondale, POB A485, Harare; Ambassador: NABILA AL-MULLA.

Libya: 124 Harare St, POB 4310, Harare; tel. (4) 728381; telex 24585; Ambassador: M. M. IBN KOURAH.

Malawi: Malawi House, Harare St, POB 321, Harare; tel. (4) 705611; telex 24467; High Commissioner: ANSLEY D. KHAUYEZA.

Malaysia: 12 Lawson Ave, Milton Park, POB 5570, Harare; tel. (4) 796209; fax (4) 796200 High Commissioner: GHAZZALI S. A. KHALID.

Mexico: 26 Connaught Rd, Avondale, POB 3812, Harare; tel. (4) 35724; telex 26124; fax (4) 308115; Ambassador: VÍCTOR M. SOLANO MONTANO.

Mozambique: 152 Herbert Chitepo Ave, cnr Leopold Takawira St, POB 4608, Harare; tel. (4) 790837; telex 24466; Ambassador: LOPES NDELANA.

Netherlands: 47 Enterprise Rd, Highlands, POB HG601, Harare; tel. (4) 731428; telex 24357; fax (4) 790520; Ambassador: WIM WESSELS.

New Zealand: 57 Jason Moyo Ave, Batanai Gardens, POB 5448, Harare; tel. (4) 728681; telex 22747; fax (4) 790693; High Commissioner: BRIAN ABSOLUM.

Nigeria: 36 Samora Machel Ave, POB 4742, Harare; tel. (4) 790765; telex 24473; High Commissioner: MUHAMMED METTEDEN.

Norway: 5 Lanark Rd, Belgravia, POB A510, Avondale, Harare; tel. (4) 792419; telex 26576; Ambassador: JOHAN H. DAHL.

Pakistan: 11 Van Praagh Ave, Milton Park, POB 3050, Harare; tel. (4) 720293; fax (4) 722446; High Commissioner: TARIQ FATEMI.

Poland: 16 Cork Road, Belgravia, POB 3932, Harare; tel. (4) 732159; telex 22745; fax (4) 732159; Chargé d'affaires a.i.: ANDRZEJ KASPRZYK.

Portugal: 10 Samora Machel Ave, POB 406, Harare; tel. (4) 725107; telex 24714; Ambassador: Dr EDUARDO NUNEZ DE CARVALHO.

Romania: 105 Fourth St, POB 4797, Harare; tel. (4) 700853; telex 24797; Ambassador: Dr GHEORGHE POPESCU.

Russia: 70 Fife Ave, POB 4250, Harare; tel. (4) 720358; telex 22616; fax (4) 700534; Ambassador: YOURI A. YOUKALOV.

Senegal: 17 Beveridge Rd, Avondale, POB 6904, Harare; tel. (4) 303147; telex 26314; fax (4) 35087; Ambassador: OUSMANE CAMARA.

Slovakia: 32 Aberdeen Rd, Avondale, POB HG72, Harare; tel. (4) 302636; telex 22460; fax (4) 302236; Ambassador: Dr JÁN VODERADSKÝ.

Spain: 16 Phillips Ave, Belgravia, POB 3300, Harare; tel. (4) 738681; telex 24173; fax (4) 795440; Ambassador: JOSÉ MANUEL PAZ AGUERAS.

Sudan: 4 Pascoe Ave, Harare; tel. (4) 725240; telex 26308; Ambassador: ANGELO V. MORGAN.

Sweden: Pegasus House, 52 Samora Machel Ave, POB 4110, Harare; tel. (4) 790651; telex 24695; fax (4) 702003; Ambassador: NILS DAAG.

Switzerland: 9 Lanark Rd, POB 3440, Harare; tel. (4) 703997; telex 24669; Ambassador: PETER HOLLENWEGER.

Tunisia: 5 Ashton Rd, Alexandra Park, POB 4308, Harare; tel. (4) 791570; telex 24801; fax (4) 727224; Ambassador: HAMID ZAOUCHE.

United Kingdom: Stanley House, Jason Moyo Ave, POB 4490, Harare; tel. (4) 793781; telex 24607; fax (4) 728380; High Commissioner: RICHARD DALES.

USA: 172 Herbert Chitepo Ave, POB 3340, Harare; tel. (4) 794521; telex 24591; fax (4) 796480; Ambassador: E. GIBSON LANPHER.

Viet Nam: 14 Carlisle Drive, Alexandra Park, POB 5458, Harare; tel. (4) 701118; telex 22047; Chargé d'affaires a.i.: TRAN NHUAN.

Yugoslavia: 1 Lanark Rd, Belgravia, POB 3420, Harare; tel. (4) 738668; fax (4) 738660; Ambassador: LJUBISA KORAC.

Zaire: 24 Van Praagh Ave, Milton Park, POB 2446, Harare; tel. (4) 724494; telex 22265; Ambassador: BEMBOY BABA.

Zambia: Zambia House, cnr Union and Julius Nyerere Aves, POB 4698, Harare; tel. (4) 790851; telex 24698; fax (4) 790856; High Commissioner: NCHIMUNYA SIKAULU.

Judicial System

The legal system is Roman-Dutch, based on the system which was in force in the Cape of Good Hope on 10 June 1891, as modified by subsequent legislation.

The Supreme Court has original jurisdiction in matters in which an infringement of Chapter III of the Constitution defining fundamental rights is alleged. In all other matters it has appellate jurisdiction only. It consists of the Chief Justice and four Judges of Appeal. A normal bench consists of any three of these.

The High Court consists of the Chief Justice, the Judge President, and 11 other judges. Below the High Court are Regional Courts and Magistrates' Courts with both civil and criminal jurisdiction presided over by full-time professional magistrates.

The Customary Law and Local Courts Act, adopted in 1990, abolished the village and community courts and replaced them with customary law and local courts, presided over by chiefs and headmen; in the case of chiefs, jurisdiction to try customary law cases is limited to those where the monetary values concerned do not exceed Z.$1,000 and in the case of a headman's court Z.$500. Appeals from the Chiefs' Courts are heard in Magistrates' Courts and, ultimately, the Supreme Court. All magistrates now have jurisdiction to try cases determinable by customary law.

Attorney-General: PATRICK ANTHONY CHINAMASA.

Chief Justice: ANTHONY R. GUBBAY.

Judges of Appeal: A. M. EBRAHIM, N. J. MCNALLY, K. R. A. KORSAH, S. C. G. MUCHECHETERE.

Judge President: W. R. SANDURA.

Religion

AFRICAN RELIGIONS

Many Africans follow traditional beliefs.

CHRISTIANITY

About 55% of the population are Christians.

Zimbabwe Council of Churches: 128 Mbuya Nehanda St, POB 3566, Harare; tel. (4) 791208; telex 26243; f. 1964; 20 mem. churches, nine assoc. mems; Pres. Rt Rev. JONATHAN SIYACHITEMA (Anglican Bishop of the Lundi); Gen. Sec. MUROMBEDZI KUCHERA.

The Anglican Communion

The Church of the Province of Central Africa includes four dioceses in Zimbabwe. The Archbishop of the Province is the Bishop of Botswana.

Bishop of Harare: Rt Rev. RALPH HATENDI, Bishop's Mount, Bishopsmount Close, POB UA7, Harare; tel. (4) 787413; fax (4) 700419.

Bishop of the Lundi: Rt Rev. JONATHAN SIYACHITEMA, POB 25, Gweru; tel. (54) 51030; fax (54) 3658.

Bishop of Manicaland: Rt Rev. ELIJAH MUSEKIWA PETER MASUKO, 115 Herbert Chitepo St, Mutare; tel. (20) 64194; fax (20) 63076.

Bishop of Matabeleland: Rt Rev. THEOPHILUS T. NALEDI, POB 2422, Bulawayo; tel. (9) 61370; fax (9) 68353.

The Roman Catholic Church

For ecclesiastical purposes, Zimbabwe comprises one archdiocese and six dioceses. At 31 December 1992 there were an estimated 897,082 adherents.

Zimbabwe Catholic Bishops' Conference: General Secretariat, 55 Herbert Chitepo Ave, POB 738, Causeway, Harare; tel. (4) 729048; telex 2390; fax (4) 705369; f. 1969; Pres. Mgr HELMUT REKTER, Bishop of Chinhoyi.

Archbishop of Harare: Most Rev. PATRICK FANI CHAKAIPA, POB 8060, Causeway, Harare; tel. and fax (4) 727386.

Other Christian Churches

City Presbyterian Church: POB 50, Harare; tel. (4) 790366; f. 1904; Minister Rev. Dr A. SPENCE; Session Clerk H. JACK; 350 mems.

Dutch Reformed Church (Nederduitse Gereformeerde Kerk): 35 Samora Machel Ave, POB 967, Harare; tel. (4) 722436; f. 1895; 16 parishes; Moderator Rev. A. S. VAN DYK; Gen. Sec. Rev. F. MARITZ; 2,500 mems.

Evangelical Lutheran Church: POB 2175, Bulawayo; tel. (9) 62686; f. 1903; Sec. Rt Rev. D. D. E. SIPHUMA; 57,000 mems.

Greek Orthodox Church: POB 808, Harare; tel. (4) 791616; Archbishop (vacant).

Methodist Church in Zimbabwe: POB 71, Causeway, Harare; tel. (4) 724069; f. 1891; Pres. Rev. Dr CRISPIN C. G. MAZOBERE; Sec. of Conference Rev. ENOS M. CHIBI; 111,374 mems.

United Congregational Church of Southern Africa: POB 2451, Bulawayo; Synod Sec. for Zimbabwe Rev. J. R. DANISA.

United Methodist Church: POB 3408, Harare; tel. (4) 704127; f. 1890; Bishop of Zimbabwe ABEL TENDEKAYI MUZOREWA; 45,000 mems.

Among other denominations active in Zimbabwe are the African Methodist Church, the African Methodist Episcopal Church, the African Reformed Church, the Christian Marching Church, the Church of Christ in Zimbabwe, the Independent African Church, the Presbyterian Church, the United Church of Christ, the Zimbabwe Assemblies of God and the Ziwezano Church.

JUDAISM

There were about 1,000 members of the Jewish community in 1989.

Jewish Board of Deputies of Zimbabwe: POB 342, Harare; tel. (4) 723647; Pres. S. C. HARRIS; Gen. Sec. Miss J. R. GRUBER.

BAHÁ'Í FAITH

National Spiritual Assembly: POB GD380, Harare; tel. (4) 45945; fax (4) 744244; mems resident in more than 3,000 localities.

The Press

DAILIES

The Chronicle: POB 585, Bulawayo; tel. (9) 65471; telex 3059; f. 1894; circulates throughout south-west Zimbabwe; English; Editor STEPHEN A. MPOFU; circ. 74,032.

Daily Gazette: POB 66070, Kopje, Harare; tel. (4) 738722; f. 1992; independent; Editor BRIAN LATHAM.

The Herald: POB 396, Harare; tel. (4) 795771; telex 26196; fax (4) 791311; f. 1891; English; Editor TOMMY SITHOLE; circ. 134,000.

PERIODICALS

Africa Calls Worldwide: POB 2677, Harare; tel. (4) 704715; telex 26334; fax (4) 752162; f. 1960; travel; 6 a year; Editor MIKE HAMILTON; circ. 14,000.

Africa South: POB 7020, Harare; tel. (4) 791992; fax (4) 707614; f. 1989; monthly; Editor GWEN ANSELL; circ. 95,000.

Business Herald: Harare; weekly; Editor ANDREW RUSINGA.

Central African Journal of Medicine: POB A195, Avondale, Harare; tel. (4) 791631; f. 1955; monthly; Editor-in-Chief Dr J. A. MATENGA.

Chaminuka News: POB 251, Marondera; f. 1988; fortnightly; English and Chishona; Editor M. MUGABE; circ. 10,000.

City Observer: POB 990, Harare; tel. (4) 706536; telex 26189; fax (4) 708544; monthly.

Commerce: POB 1683, Harare; journal of Zimbabwe National Chambers of Commerce; monthly; Editor (vacant); circ. 5,000.

Computer and Telecom News: Thomson House, cnr Speke Ave and Harare St, POB 1683, Harare; tel. (4) 736835; telex 24705; fax (4) 752390; publ. by Thomson Publs Zimbabwe; monthly.

Economic Review: c/o Zimbabwe Financial Holdings, POB 3198, Harare; tel. (4) 735010; telex 24163; fax (4) 735600; 4 a year; circ. 3,000.

Executive: POB 2677, Harare; bi-monthly.

The Farmer: POB 1622, Harare; tel. (4) 753278; telex 22084; fax (4) 750754; f. 1928; commercial farming; weekly; English; Editor FELICITY WOOD; circ. 6,000.

Farming World with Murimi Umlimi: POB 909, Harare; tel. (4) 722322; f. 1975; monthly; English; Editors S. DICKIN, D. H. B. DICKIN; circ. 7,000.

The Financial Gazette: POB 66070, Kopje, Harare; tel. (4) 738722; weekly; Editor TREVOR NCWBE; circ. 27,500.

Gweru Times: POB 66, Gweru; weekly; Editor R. SPROAT; circ. 5,000.

Horizon: POB UA65, Harare; monthly; circ. 35,000.

Hotel and Catering Gazette: POB 2677, Kopje, Harare; tel. (4) 738722; telex 26334; fax (4) 707130; monthly; Editor PAULA CHARLES; circ. 1,800.

Indonsakusa: POB 150, Hwange; f. 1988; monthly; English and Sindebele; Editor D. NTABENI; circ. 10,000.

Industrial Review: POB 1683, Harare; tel. (4) 736835; fax (4) 752390.

Insurance Review: POB 1683, Harare; tel. (4) 36; telex 24705; fax (4) 752390; monthly; Editor M. CHAVUNDUKA.

Journal on Social Change and Development: POB 4405, Harare; tel. (4) 700047; telex 22055; fax (4) 725565; f. 1981; quarterly; Chair. JOYCE KAZEMBE; circ. 4,500.

Just for Me: POB 66070, Kopje, Harare; tel (4) 704715; f. 1990; English-language family and women's interest; Editor BEVERLEY TILLEY.

Karoi News: POB 441, Karoi; tel. 6216; fortnightly.

Kwayedza-Umthunywa: POB 396, Harare; tel. (4) 795771; weekly; Editor G. M. CHITEWE; circ. 84,696.

Look and Listen: POB UA589, Harare; tel. (4) 705619; fax (4) 705411; English-language radio and TV programmes; fortnightly; Editor AULORA SUERGA; circ. 23,000.

Mahogany: POB UA589, Harare; tel. (4) 705412; telex 24748; fax (4) 705411; f. 1980; English; women's interest; 6 a year; Editor G. BEACH; circ. 33,000.

Makonde Star: POB 533, Kwekwe; tel. (55) 2248; f. 1989; weekly; English; Editor FELIX MOYO; circ. 21,000.

Makoni Clarion: POB 17, Rusape; monthly.

Management Zimbabwe: POB 2677, Harare; fortnightly.

Manica Post: POB 960, Mutare; tel. (20) 61212; telex 2274; f. 1893; weekly; Editor A. HAMIWE; circ. 24,000.

Masiye Pambili (Let Us Go Forward): POB 591, Bulawayo; tel. (9) 75011; telex 50563; f. 1964; English; 2 a year; Editor M. M. NDUBIWA; circ. 21,000.

Masvingo Provincial Star: POB 798, Masvingo; tel. (39) 2469; weekly.

Midlands Observer: POB 533, Kwekwe; tel. (55) 2248; f. 1953; weekly; English; Editor FELIX MOYO; circ. 4,500.

Moto: POB 890, Gweru; tel. (54) 4886; fax (54) 51991; Roman Catholic; Editor DONATUS BONDE; circ. 30,000.

Nehanda Guardian: POB 150, Hwange; f. 1988; monthly; English and Chishona; Editor K. MWANAKA; circ. 10,000.

Nhau Dzekumakomo: POB 910, Mutare; f. 1984; publ. by Mutare City Council; monthly.

North Midlands Gazette: POB 222, Kadoma; tel. (68) 2021; fax (68) 2841; f. 1912; weekly; Editor MARY READ.

On Guard: Accident Prevention and Workers' Compensation Scheme, POB 8433, Causeway, Harare; tel. (4) 728931; Editor Dr R. S. BALOYI.

The Outpost: POB HG106, Highlands; tel. (4) 724571; f. 1911; English; 6 a year; Editor WAYNE BVUDZIJENA; circ. 18,500.

Parade Magazine: POB 3798, Harare; tel. (4) 736835; telex 24705; fax (4) 752390; f. 1953; monthly; English; Editor MARK CHAVANDUKA; circ. 85,540.

Prize Africa: POB UA460, Harare; tel. (4) 705411; telex 24748; f. 1973; monthly; English; Editor STEPHAN DZIVANE; circ. 15,300.

Quarterly Economic and Statistical Review: POB 1283, Harare; publ. by the Reserve Bank of Zimbabwe; quarterly.

Quarterly Guide to the Economy: First Merchant Bank of Zimbabwe Ltd, FMB House, 67 Samora Machel Ave, POB 2786, Harare; tel. (4) 703071; telex 26025; fax (4) 738810; quarterly.

RailRoader: POB 596, Bulawayo; f. 1952; tel. (9) 363526; telex 33173; fax (9) 363502; monthly; Editor M. GUMEDE; circ. 10,000.

The Record: POB 179, Harare; tel. (4) 708911; journal of the Public Service Asscn; 6 a year; Editor GAMALIEL RUNGANI; circ. 30,000.

Southern African Economist: POB 6290, Harare; tel. (4) 738891; monthly; circ. 16,000.

Southern African Political and Economic Monthly: POB MP111, Harare; tel. (4) 727875; fax (4) 732735; monthly; Editor-in-Chief IBBO MANDAZA.

Sunday Mail: POB 396, Harare; tel. (4) 795771; telex 26196; fax (4) 791311; f. 1935; weekly; English; Editor CHARLES CHIKEREMA; circ. 154,000.

Sunday News: POB 585, Bulawayo; tel. (9) 65471; telex 33481; fax (9) 75522; f. 1930; weekly; English; Editor LAWRENCE CHIKUWIRA; circ. 66,171.

Teacher in Zimbabwe: POB 396; monthly; circ. 47,000.

The Times: 73 Seventh St, POB 66, Gweru; tel. (54) 2459; weekly; English.

Tobacco News: POB 1683, Harare; tel. (4) 736836; telex 24705; fax (4) 752390; circ. 2,700.

Vanguard: POB 66102, Kopje; tel. 751193; every 2 months.

Voice: POB 8323, Causeway, Harare; monthly.

The Worker: POB 8323, Causeway, Harare; tel. 700466.

World Vision News: POB 2420, Harare; tel. 703794; quarterly.

Zambezia: POB MP45, Harare; tel. (4) 303211; telex 26580; fax (4) 732828; journal of the Univ. of Zimbabwe; 2 a year; Editor Prof. E. A. NGARA.

Zimbabwe Agricultural Journal: POB CY 594, Causeway, Harare; tel. (4) 704531; telex 22455; fax (4) 728317; f. 1903; 6 a year; Editor R. J. FENNER; circ. 1,600.

Zimbabwe Defence Forces Magazine: POB 7720, Harare; tel. (4) 722481; f. 1982; 6 a year; circ. 5,000.

The Zimbabwe Engineer: POB 1683, Harare; Man. Dir A. THOMSON.

Zimbabwe News: POB 5988, Harare; tel. (4) 68428; telex 22102; monthly.

Zimbabwean Government Gazette: POB 8062, Causeway, Harare; official govt journal; weekly; Editor L. TAKAWIRA.

NEWS AGENCIES

Zimbabwe Inter-Africa News Agency (ZIANA): POB 8166, Causeway, Harare; tel. (4) 730151; telex 26127; fax (4) 794336; f. 1981; owned and controlled by Zimbabwe Mass Media Trust; Editor-in-Chief HENRY E. MURADZIKWA.

Foreign Bureaux

Agence France-Presse (AFP): Robinson House, Union Ave, POB 1166, Harare; tel. (4) 793269; telex 26161; fax (4) 708266; Rep. MARIE SANZ-BOOKER.

ANGOP (Angola): Mass Media House, 3rd Floor, 19 Selous Ave, POB 6354, Harare; tel. (4) 736849; telex 22204.

Agenzia Nazionale Stampa Associata (ANSA) (Italy): Harare; tel. (4) 723881; telex 74177; Rep. IAN MILLS.

Associated Press (AP) (USA): POB 785, Harare; tel. (4) 706622; telex 24676; fax (4) 703994; Rep. JOHN EDLIN.

Deutsche Presse-Agentur (dpa) (Germany): Harare; tel. (4) 700875; telex 24339; Correspondent JAN RAATH.

Informatsionnoye Telegrafnoye Agentstvo Rossii—Telegrafnoye Agentstvo Suverennykh Stran (ITAR—TASS) (Russia): Mass Media House, 19 Selous Ave, POB 4012, Harare; tel. (4) 790521; telex 26022; Correspondent YURI PITCHUGIN.

Inter Press Service (IPS) (Italy): Travlos House, cnr Jason Moyo Ave and Rezende St, POB 6050, Harare; tel. (4) 706466; telex 26129; Rep. STANLEY NYAWA.

News Agency of Nigeria (NAN): Harare; tel. (4) 703041; telex 24674.

Pan-African News Agency (PANA) (Senegal): 19 Selous Ave, POB 8364, Harare; tel. (4) 730971; telex 26403; Bureau Chief PETER MWAURA.

Prensa Latina (Cuba): Mass Media House, 3rd Floor, 19 Selous Ave, Harare; tel. (4) 731993; telex 22461; Correspondent HUGO RIUS.

Press Trust of India (PTI): Mass Media House, 3rd Floor, 19 Selous Ave, Harare; tel. (4) 795006; telex 22038; Rep. N. V. R. SWAMI.

Reuters (United Kingdom): 901 Tanganyika House, Union Ave, Harare, POB 2987; tel. (4) 724299; telex 24291.

Rossiyskoye Informatsionnoye Agentstvo—Novosti (RIA—Novosti) (Russia): 503 Robinson House, cnr Union Ave and Angwa St, POB 3908, Harare; tel. (4) 707232; telex 22293; fax (4) 707233; Correspondent A. TIMONOVICH.

SADC Press Trust: Mass Media House, 19 Selous Ave, POB 6290, Harare; tel. (4) 738891; telex 26367; fax (4) 795412; Editor-in-Chief LEONARD MAVENEKA.

Tanjug (Yugoslavia): Mass Media House, 19 Selous Ave, Harare; tel. (4) 479018; Correspondent DEJAN DRAKULIĆ.

United Press International (UPI) (USA): Harare; tel. (4) 25265; telex 24177; Rep. IAN MILLS.

Xinhua (New China) News Agency (People's Republic of China): 4 Earls Rd, Alexander Park, POB 4746, Harare; tel. (4) 731467; telex 22310; fax (4) 731467; Chief Correspondent LU JIANXIN.

Publishers

Academic Books (Pvt) Ltd: POB 567, Harare; tel. (4) 706729; fax (4) 702071; educational.

Amalgamated Publications (Pvt) Ltd: POB 1683, Harare; tel. (4) 736835; telex 24705; fax (4) 752390; f. 1949; trade journals; Man. Dir A. THOMSON.

Anvil Press: POB 4209, Harare; tel. (4) 751202; f. 1988; general; Dirs PAUL BRICKHILL, PAT BRICKHILL, STEVE KHOZA.

The Argosy Press: POB 2677, Harare; tel. (4) 704715; magazine publishers; Gen. Man. A. W. HARVEY.

Baobab Books (Pvt) Ltd: POB 1559, Harare; tel. (4) 706729; fax (4) 702071; general, literature, children's.

Books of Zimbabwe Publishing Co (Pvt) Ltd: POB 1994, Bulawayo; tel. (9) 61135; f. 1968; Man. Dir LOUIS W. BOLZE.

College Press Publishers (Pvt) Ltd: POB 3041, Harare; tel. (4) 754145; telex 22558; fax (4) 754256; f. 1968; educational and general; Man. Dir B. B. MUGABE.

Directory Publishers Ltd: POB 1595, Bulawayo; tel. (9) 78831; telex 33333; fax (9) 78835; directories; Man. BRUCE BEALE.

Graham Publishing Co (Pvt) Ltd: POB 2931, Harare; tel. (4) 752437; f. 1967; general; Dir GORDON M. GRAHAM.

Harare Publishing House: Chiremba Rd, Hatfield, POB 4735, Harare; tel. (4) 570613; f. 1984; Dir Dr T. M. SAMKANGE.

HarperCollins Publishers (Zimbabwe) Pvt) Ltd: Union Ave, POB 201, Harare; tel. (4) 721413; fax (4) 721413; Man. S. D. MCMILLAN.

Longman Zimbabwe (Pvt) Ltd: Tourle Rd, Harare Drive, Adbennie, Harare; tel. (4) 62711; telex 22566; f. 1964; general and educational; Man. Dir S. CONNOLLY.

Mambo Press: Senga Rd, POB 779, Gweru; tel. (54) 4016; fax (54) 51991; f. 1958; religious, educational and fiction in English and African languages; Gen. Man. JOE HUBER.

Modus Publications (Pvt) Ltd: Modus House, 27-29 Charter Rd, POB 66070, Kopje, Harare; tel. (4) 738722; Man. Dir ELIAS RUSIKE.

Munn Publishing (Pvt) Ltd: POB UA460, Harare; tel. (4) 752144; telex 24748; fax (4) 752062; Man. Dir A. F. MUNN.

Standard Publications (Pvt) Ltd: POB 3745, Harare; Dir G. F. BOOT.

Thomson Publications Zimbabwe (Pvt) Ltd: Thomson House, cnr Speke Ave and Harare St, POB 1683, Harare; tel. (4) 736835; telex 24705; fax (4) 752390; trade journals; Man. Dir A. THOMSON.

University of Zimbabwe Publications: POB MP203, Mount Pleasant, Harare; tel. (4) 333407; telex 26580; fax (4) 732828; f. 1969; Publs Officer SAMUEL MATSANGAISE (acting).

Zimbabwe Newspapers (1980) Ltd: POB 396, Harare; tel. (4) 795771; telex 26196; fax (4) 791311; f. 1981; state-owned; controls largest newspaper group; Chair. Dr DAVIDSON M. SADZA.

Zimbabwe Publishing House: POB 350, Harare; tel. (4) 47548; telex 26035; fax (4) 47554; f. 1982; Chair. DAVID MARTIN.

Government Publishing House

The Literature Bureau: POB 8137, Causeway, Harare; tel. (4) 726929; f. 1954; controlled by Ministry of Education and Culture; Dir B. C. CHITSIKE.

Radio and Television

In 1991, according to UNESCO estimates, there were 860,000 radio receivers and 270,000 television receivers in use.

RADIO

Broadcasts in English, Chishona, Sindebele, Kalanga, Venda, Tonga and Chewa; four programme services comprise a general service (predominantly in English), vernacular languages service, light entertainment, educational programmes.

TELEVISION

The main broadcasting centre is in Harare, with a second studio in Bulawayo; broadcasts on two channels for about 190 hours per week.

Zimbabwe Broadcasting Corporation: POB HG444, Highlands, Harare; tel. (4) 707222; telex 24175; fax (4) 795698; f. 1957; Chair. HOSEA MAPONDERA; Dir-Gen. CHRIS MUTSVANGWA (acting).

Finance

(cap. = capital; p.u. = paid up; dep. = deposits; res = reserves; m. = million; br. = branch; amounts in Zimbabwe dollars)

BANKING

Central Bank

Reserve Bank of Zimbabwe: 76 Samora Machel Ave, POB 1283, Harare; tel. (4) 790731; telex 26075; fax (4) 708976; f. 1964; bank of issue; cap. and res 6m., dep. 6,000m. (Feb 1994); Gov. Dr LEONARD TSUMBA; Gen. Man. C. CHIKAURA.

Commercial Banks

Barclays Bank of Zimbabwe Ltd: Barclay House, First St and Jason Moyo Ave, POB 1279, Harare; tel. (4) 729811; telex 24185; fax (4) 707293; cap. and res 285.8m., dep. 2,940m. (Dec. 1993); Chair. JOHN D. CARTER; Man. Dir I. G. TAKAWIRA.

Stanbic Bank Zimbabwe Ltd: Ottoman House, 1st Floor, 59 Samora Machel Ave, POB 300, Harare; tel. (4) 795871; telex 26103; fax (4) 751324; f. 1990 as ANZ Grindlays Bank PLC, name changed 1993; Chair. L. H. COOK; Man. Dir H. F. J. FERGUSON; 10 brs.

Standard Chartered Bank Zimbabwe Ltd: John Boyne House, 38 Speke Ave, POB 373, Harare; tel. (4) 707185; telex 22115; fax (4) 725769; f. 1983; cap. p.u. 35m. (Dec. 1986); Chair. P. T. ELLIS; CEO A. CLEARY, W. J. DENT; 42 brs and sub-brs; 14 agencies.

Zimbabwe Banking Corporation Ltd: Zimbank House, 46 Speke Ave, POB 3198, Harare; tel. (4) 735011; telex 24163; fax (4) 735600; f. 1951; wholly-owned subsidiary of Zimbabwe Financial Holdings Ltd, which is 59% govt-owned; cap. and res 123.0m., dep. 2,577.2m. (Sept. 1993); Group CEO. E. N. MUSHAYAKARAR; Man. Dir S. T. BIYAM; 47 brs, sub-brs and agencies.

Development Bank

Zimbabwe Development Bank (ZDB): POB 1720, Harare; tel. (4) 721008; telex 26279; fax (4) 720723; f. 1985; share cap. p.u. 49m.; Chair. E. D. CHIURA; Man. Dir R. JARAVAZA; 3 brs.

Merchant Banks

First Merchant Bank of Zimbabwe Ltd: FMB House, 67 Samora Machel Ave, POB 2786, Harare; tel. (4) 703071; telex 26025; fax (4) 738810; f. 1956 as Rhodesian Acceptances Limited; cap. and res 110.4m., dep. 1.119.0m. (Dec. 1993); Chair. R. P. LANDER; Man. Dir R. FELTOE; br. in Bulawayo.

Merchant Bank of Central Africa Ltd: Old Mutual Centre, 14th Floor, cnr Third St and Jason Moyo Ave, POB 3200, Harare; tel. (4) 738081; telex 26568; fax (4) 708005; f. 1956; cap. and res 51m., dep. 509m. (March 1993); Chair. A. M. CHAMBATI; Man. Dir F. R. G. READ.

Standard Chartered Merchant Bank Zimbabwe Ltd: Standard Chartered Bank Bldg, Second St, POB 60, Harare; tel. (4) 708585; telex 22208; fax (4) 725667; f. 1971; cap. and res 123m., dep. 1,076m. (Dec. 1993); Chair. J. M. MCKENNA; Dir L. T. GWATA.

Syfrets Merchant Bank Ltd: Zimbank House, 46 Speke Ave, POB 2540, Harare; tel. (4) 794581; telex 26292; fax (4) 704741; subsidiary of Finhold Group; cap. and res 24.5m., dep. 535.0m. (Sept. 1992); Chair. R. E. PARKE; Man. Dir A. D. HENCHIE.

Discount Houses

Bard Discount House Ltd: POB 3321, Harare; tel. (4) 752756; telex 24326; fax (4) 750192; cap. p.u. 11.1m. (Aug. 1993); Chair R. P. LANDER; Man. Dir C. J. GURNEY.

The Discount Co of Zimbabwe (DCZ): POB 3424, Harare.

Intermarket Discount House: UDC Centre, 3rd Floor, cnr Union and First Sts, Harare.

Banking Organization

Institute of Bankers of Zimbabwe: POB UA521, Harare; tel. (4) 752474; f. 1973; Pres. C. J. GURNEY; Gen. Sec. S. A. H. BROWN.

STOCK EXCHANGE

Zimbabwe Stock Exchange: Southampton House, 8th Floor, Union Ave, POB UA234, Harare; tel. (4) 736861; telex 24196; fax (4) 791045; f. 1946; Chair. M. J. S. TUNMER.

INSURANCE

CU Fire, Marine and General Insurance Co Ltd: Harare; tel. (4) 790214; telex 24194; mem. of Commercial Union group; Chair. J. M. MAGOWAN.

Fidelity Life Assurance of Zimbabwe (Pvt) Ltd: 66 Julius Nyerere Way, POB 435, Harare; tel. (4) 702811; telex 24189; fax (4) 704705; Chair. M. SIFELANI; Gen. Man. J. P. WEEKS.

National Insurance Co of Zimbabwe (Pvt) Ltd: cnr Baker Ave and First St, POB 1256, Harare; tel. (4) 729206; telex 24605; fax (4) 704914.

Old Mutual: POB 70, Harare; tel. (4) 734011; telex 22118; fax (4) 792118; f. 1845; life assurance; Chair. D. C. SMITH; Gen. Man. B. R. BRADFORD.

RM Insurance Co (Pvt) Ltd: Royal Mutual House, 45 Baker Ave, POB 3599, Harare; tel. (4) 731011; telex 24683; fax (4) 731028; f. 1982; cap. p.u. 2m.; Chair. C. WRIGHT; Gen. Man. D. K. BEACH.

Zimnat Life Assurance Co Ltd: Zimnat House, cnr Baker Ave and Third St, POB 2417, Harare; tel. (4) 737611; telex 22003; fax (4) 791782; Gen. Man. B. MCCURDY.

Trade and Industry

CHAMBER OF COMMERCE

Zimbabwe National Chambers of Commerce (ZNCC): Equity House, Rezende St, POB 1934, Harare; tel. (4) 753444; telex 22531; fax (4) 753450; f. 1983; Pres. E. S. MAKONI; Dep. Pres. D. MEYER.

INDUSTRIAL AND EMPLOYERS' ASSOCIATIONS

Agricultural Marketing Authority: POB 8094, Causeway, Harare; tel. (4) 730944; telex 22586; f. 1967; Chair. Dr R. M. MUPAWOSE.

Bulawayo Agricultural Society: PO Famona, Bulawayo; tel. (9) 77668; telex 33273; f. 1907; sponsors an agricultural show; Pres. W. R. WHALEY; Vice-President C. P. D. GOODWIN.

Bulawayo Landowners' and Farmers' Association: Bulawayo.

Cattle Producers' Association: Harare; Pres. G. FRANCEYS.

Chamber of Mines of Zimbabwe: 4 Central Ave, POB 712, Harare; tel. (4) 702843; telex 26271; fax (4) 707983; f. 1939; CEO C. D. C. BAIN.

Coffee Growers' Association: Agriculture House, Leopold Takawira St, POB 4382, Harare; tel. (4) 750238; telex 22084; fax (4) 702481; Chair. ROBIN J. FENNELL.

Commercial Cotton Growers' Association: Agriculture House, Leopold Takawira St, POB 592, Harare; tel. (4) 791881; fax (4) 750754; Pres. IAN C. MILLAR.

Commercial Farmers' Union: POB 1241, Harare; tel. (4) 791881; telex 22084; f. 1942; Pres. ANTHONY SWIRE-THOMPSON; Dir D. W. HASLUCK; 4,200 mems.

Confederation of Zimbabwe Industries: Industry House, 109 Rotten Row, POB 3794, Harare; tel. (4) 739833; telex 22073; fax (4) 750953; f. 1957; Pres. J. WAKATAMA; Chief Exec. M. J. BOYD-CLARK; 1,000 mems.

Construction Industry Federation of Zimbabwe: POB 1502, Harare; tel. (4) 746661; fax (4) 746937; Pres. W. I. RALPH; CEO M. B. NAROTAM.

Employers' Confederation of Zimbabwe: POB 158, Harare; tel. (4) 705156; Pres. S. O. SHONHIWA; Exec. Dir Dr DAVID CHANAIWA.

Employment Council for the Motor Industry: POB 1084, Bulawayo; tel. (9) 78161.

Industrial Development Corporation of Zimbabwe Ltd: POB CY 1431, Causeway, Harare; tel. (4) 706971; telex 24409; fax (4) 796028; f. 1963; Chair. J. B. WAKATAMA; Gen. Man. M. N. NDUDZO.

Kadoma Farmers' and Stockowners' Association: Kadoma; tel. (68) 3658; Chair. A. REED; Sec. P. M. REED; 66 mems.

Kwekwe Farmers' Association: POB 72, Kwekwe; tel. (55) 247721; f. 1928; Chair. D. EDWARDS; Sec. J. TAPSON; 87 mems.

Manicaland Chamber of Industries: POB 92, Mutare; tel. (20) 62300; f. 1945; Pres. L. BAXTER; 60 mems.

Mashonaland Chamber of Industries: POB 3794, Harare; tel. (4) 739833; telex 22073; fax (4) 750953; f. 1922; Pres. A. I. S. FERGUSON; Sec. M. MUBATARIPI; 729 mems.

Matabeleland Chamber of Industries: POB 2317, Bulawayo; tel. (9) 60642; fax (9) 60814; f. 1931; Pres. E. V. MATIKITI; Sec. N. MCKAY; about 300 mems.

Matabeleland Region of The Construction Industry Federation of Zimbabwe: POB 1970, Bulawayo; tel. (9) 65787; f. 1919; Sec. M. BARRON; 124 mems.

Midlands Chamber of Industries: POB 213, Gweru; tel. (54) 2812; Pres. J. W. PRINGLE; 50 mems.

Minerals Marketing Corporation of Zimbabwe: 107 Beverley East Rd, POB 2628, Harare; tel. (4) 705862; fax (4) 722441; f. 1982; sole authority for marketing of mineral production; Chair. E. MUTOWO; Gen. Man. N. MACHIRORI.

Mutare District Farmers' Association: POB 29, Mutare; tel. (20) 64233; Chair. R. C. TRUSCOTT; Sec. Mrs J. FROGGATT; 45 mems.

National Association of Dairy Farmers: Agriculture House, 113 Leopold Takawira St, POB 1241, Harare; tel. (4) 791881; telex 22084; fax (4) 752614; Chair. I. M. WEBSTER; CEO D. R. PASCOE.

National Employment Council for the Construction Industry of Zimbabwe: St Barbara House, Moffat St, POB 2995, Harare; tel. (4) 726740; Gen. Sec. F. CHITSVA.

National Employment Council for the Engineering and Iron and Steel Industry: Chancellor House, 5th Floor, Samora Machel Ave, POB 1922, Harare; tel. (4) 705607; f. 1943; Chair. H. S. CLEMENTS.

Tobacco Marketing Board: POB UA214, Harare; tel. (4) 66311; telex 24656.

Zimbabwe Farmers' Union: POB 3755, Harare; tel. (4) 704763; telex 26217; fax (4) 700829; Chair. GARY MAGADZIRE.

Zimbabwe Tobacco Association: POB 1781, Harare; tel. (4) 727441; telex 22090; fax (4) 724523; Pres. PETER RICHARDS; CEO C. R. L. MOLAM; 3,627 mems.

Zimtrade: POB 2738, Harare; tel. (4) 731020; telex 26677; fax (4) 707351; f. 1991; national export promotion org.; Chair. C. MSIPA; CEO M. SIFELANI.

MAJOR INDUSTRIAL COMPANIES

Bindura Nickel Corporation Ltd: POB 1108, Harare; tel. (4) 704461; telex 26048; fax (4) 703734; mining, smelting and refining of nickel; Chair. R. P. LANDER.

Circle Cement Ltd: POB GD160, Greendale, Harare; tel. (4) 48151; telex 26570; fax (4) 48553; Man. Dir G. I. GEORGE; Sec. D. ROCKLIFFE.

Delta Corporation Ltd: POB BW294, Borrowdale, Harare; f. 1946; telex 22126; fax (4) 739820; cap. Z.$1,760m.; brewers, soft drink mfrs, supermarket and furniture retailing and the hotel industry; Chair. E. D. CHIURA; Dirs J. P. ROONEY, J. D. CARTER, W. H. TURPIN, A. NYAMATORE, Dr S. MUNDAWARARA, J. E. SMITH, A. MUKWAVARARA, J. S. MUTIZWA, V. W. ZIREVA.

Hippo Valley Estates Ltd: POB 1, Chiredzi; tel. (39) 2381; telex 92301; fax (39) 2554; production of sugar from cane; Chair. R. P. LANDER; Gen. Man. B. R. BURBIDGE.

Mhangura Copper Mines: 90 Mutare Rd, POB 2370, Harare; tel. (4) 728331; telex 26372; f. 1947; copper mining.

Rio Tinto Zimbabwe Ltd: POB CY1243, Causeway, Harare; tel. (4) 705571; telex 26081; (4) fax 732445; custom refining nickel and copper; gold mining; also platinoids, diamonds and coal prospecting; Chair. S. C. TAWENGWA.

Wankie Colliery Co Ltd: POB 123, Hwange; coal mining at Hwange (fmrly Wankie); Chair. N. KUDENGA; Man. Dir O. K. BWERINOFA.

TRADE UNIONS

All trade unions in Zimbabwe became affiliated to the ZCTU in 1981. The ZCTU is encouraging a policy of union amalgamations.

Zimbabwe Congress of Trade Unions (ZCTU): Chester House, 10th Floor, Speke Ave, 3rd St, POB 3549, Harare; tel. (4) 793093; fax (4) 751604; f. 1981; co-ordinating org. for trade unions; Pres. GIBSON SIBANDA; Sec.-Gen. MORGAN TSVANGIRAI.

Principal Unions

Air Transport Union: POB AP40, Harare Airport, Harare; tel. (4) 52601; f. 1956; Pres. J. B. DEAS; Gen. Sec. C. J. GOTORA; 580 mems.

Associated Mineworkers' Union of Zimbabwe: POB 384, Harare; tel. (4) 700287; Pres. J. S. MUTANDARE; 25,000 mems.

Building Workers' Trade Union: St Barbara House, POB 1291, Harare; tel. (4) 720942; Gen. Sec. E. NJEKESA.

Commercial Workers' Union of Zimbabwe: Nestle House, Samora Machel Ave, POB 3922, Harare; tel. (4) 707845; Gen. Sec. S. CHIFAMBA; 6,000 mems.

Federation of Municipal Workers' Union: Bulawayo; tel. (9) 60506; Gen. Sec. F. V. NCUBE.

Furniture and Cabinet Workers' Union: POB 1291, Harare; Gen. Sec. C. KASEKE.

General Agricultural and Plantation Workers' Union: Harare; tel. (4) 792860; Gen. Sec. M. MAWERE.

Graphical Association: POB 27, Bulawayo; tel. (4) 62477; POB 494, Harare; Gen. Sec. A. NGWENYA; 3,015 mems.

Harare Municipal Workers' Union: Office No 12, Harare Community, Harare; tel. (4) 62343; Gen. Sec. T. G. T. MAPFUMO.

National Airways Workers' Union: POB AP1, Harare; tel. (4) 737011; telex 40008; fax (4) 231444; Gen. Sec. B. SPENCER.

National Engineering Workers' Union: POB 4968, Harare; tel. (4) 702963; Pres. I. MATONGO; Gen. Sec. O. KABASA.

National Union of Clothing Industry Workers' Union: POB RY28, Raylton; tel. 64432; Gen. Sec. C. M. PASIPANODYA.

Railways Associated Workers' Union: Bulawayo; tel. (9) 70041; f. 1982; Pres. SAMSON MABEKA; Gen. Sec. A. J. MHUNGU.

Technical & Salaried Staff Association: POB 33, Redcliff; tel. (55) 68798; Gen. Sec. J. DANCAN.

Transport and General Workers' Union: Dublin House, POB 4769, Harare; tel. (4) 793508; Gen. Sec. F. MAKANDA.

United Food and Allied Workers' Union of Zimbabwe: Harare; tel. (4) 74150; f. 1962; Gen. Sec. I. M. NEDZIWE.

Zimbabwe Amalgamated Railwaymen's Union: Unity House, 13th Ave, Herbert Chitepo St, Bulawayo; tel. (9) 60948; Gen. Sec. T. L. SHANA.

Zimbabwe Bank and Allied Workers' Union: Pres. SHINGEREI MUNGATE.

Zimbabwe Catering and Hotel Workers' Union: Nialis Bldg, POB 3913, Harare; tel. (4) 708359; Gen. Sec. A. P. KUPFUMA.

Zimbabwe Chemical & Allied Workers' Union: POB 4810, Harare; Gen. Sec. R. MAKUVAZA.

Zimbabwe Domestic & Allied Workers' Union: Harare; tel. (4) 795405; Gen. Sec. G. SHOKO.

Zimbabwe Educational, Welfare & Mission Workers' Union: St Andrews House, Samora Machel Ave, Harare; Pres. I. O. SAMAKOMVA.

Zimbabwe Leather Shoe & Allied Workers' Union: Harare; tel. (4) 793173; Gen. Sec. I. ZINDOGA.

Zimbabwe Motor Industry Workers' Union: POB RY00, Bulawayo; tel. (9) 74150; Gen. Sec. M. M. DERAH.

Zimbabwe Posts and Telecommunications Workers' Union: POB 739, Harare; tel. (4) 721141; Gen. Sec. GIFT CHIMANIKIRE.

Zimbabwe Society of Bank Officials: POB 966, Harare; tel. (4) 23104; Gen. Sec. A. CHITEHWE.

Zimbabwe Textile Workers' Union: POB UA245, Harare; tel. (4) 705329; Sec. F. C. BHAIKWA.

Zimbabwe Tobacco Industry Workers' Union: St Andrews House, Samora Machel Ave, Harare; Gen. Sec. S. MHEMBERE.

Zimbabwe Union of Musicians: POB 232, Harare; tel. (4) 708678; Gen. Sec. C. MATEMA.

Transport

In 1986 a Zimbabwe-registered company, the Beira Corridor Group (BCG), was formed to develop the transport system in the Beira corridor as an alternative transport link to those running through South Africa. The transport sector received 4.1% of total expenditure in the government budget for 1991/92. In 1991 National Railways of Zimbabwe (NRZ) announced a Z.$700m. development programme which included plans to electrify and extend some railway lines to previously uncovered areas. In that year the Government initiated a Z.$1,000m. programme for the acquisition of commercial vehicles.

RAILWAYS

In 1992 the rail network totalled 2,759 km. Trunk lines run from Bulawayo south to the border with Botswana, connecting with the Botswana railways system, which, in turn, connects with the South African railways system; north-west to the Victoria Falls, where there is a connection with Zambia Railways; and north-east to Harare and Mutare connecting with the Mozambique Railways' line from Beira. From a point near Gweru, a line runs to the south-east, making a connection with the Mozambique Railways' Limpopo line and with the port of Maputo. A connection runs from Rutenga to the South African Railways system at Beitbridge.

National Railways of Zimbabwe (NRZ): cnr Fife St and 10th Ave, POB 596, Bulawayo; tel. (9) 363111; telex 33173; f. 1899 as Rhodesia Railways; reorg. 1967 when Rhodesia and Zambia each became responsible for its own system; in 1993 NRZ began a 10-year programme; Chair. MIKE NDUDZO; Gen. Man. ALVORD MABENA.

ROADS

In 1988 the road system in Zimbabwe totalled 85,784 km, of which 14,000 km were designated primary and secondary roads.

CIVIL AVIATION

International and domestic air services connect most of the larger towns.

Air Zimbabwe Corporation (AirZim): POB AP1, Harare Airport, Harare; tel. (4) 575111; telex 40008; fax (4) 731444; f. 1967; scheduled domestic and international passenger and cargo services to Africa, Australia and Europe; Chair. M. J. THOMPSON; Gen. Man. and CEO HUTTUSH R. MURINGI.

Affretair: POB AP13, Harare; tel. (4) 731781; telex 40005; fax (4) 731706; f. 1965 as Air Trans Africa; state-owned; freight carrier; scheduled services to Europe, and charter services worldwide; Chair. M. J. THOMPSON; Man. Dir G. T. MANHAMBARA.

Tourism

In 1992 an estimated 500,000 tourists visited Zimbabwe. Revenue from tourism was projected at US $47m. in 1990, when about 600,000 tourist arrivals were reported. The principal tourist attractions are the Victoria Falls, the Kariba Dam and the Hwange Game Reserve and National Park. Zimbabwe Ruins, near Fort Victoria, and World's View, in the Matapos Hills, are of special interest. In the Eastern Districts, around Umtali, there is trout fishing and climbing.

Zimbabwe Tourist Development Corporation (ZTDC): POB 286, Causeway, Harare; tel. (4) 793666; telex 26082; fax (4) 793669; f. 1984; promotes tourism domestically and abroad; Dir-Gen. N. T. C. SAMKANGE (acting).

Defence

Total armed forces numbered about 48,200 in June 1993: 47,000 in the army and 1,200 in the air force. Zimbabwe receives military aid and training from the United Kingdom and the Democratic People's Republic of Korea. There is a police force of 15,000. In February 1993 Zimbabwe and the USA commenced joint military manoeuvres. It was announced in July 1994 that the size of the armed forces was to be reduced to about 35,000 troops by 1998.

Defence Expenditure: Projected at Z.$1,326m. in 1993.

Commander of the Zimbabwe National Army: Lt-Gen. MUJURU.

Commander of the Air Force: J. TUNGAMIRAI.

Education

Primary education, which begins at seven years of age and lasts for seven years, is free, and has been compulsory since 1987. Secondary education begins at the age of 14 and lasts for six years. Between 1980 and 1993 the numbers of primary school pupils increased from 1,235,036 to 2,436,671. There were 635,502 pupils at secondary schools in 1993, compared with 74,746 in 1980. In 1992 the number of pupils attending primary and secondary schools was equivalent to 89% of children in the relevant age group (boys 93%; girls 86%). The number of primary schools rose from 2,411 at independence to 4,567 in 1992, and the number of secondary schools increased from 177 to 1,512; there is at least one rural secondary school in each of the country's 55 districts. In 1992 some 61,553 students were attending institutions of higher education. There are two universities, the University of Zimbabwe, at Harare, and the University of Science and Technology, at Bulawayo. The estimated rate of adult literacy was 66.9% in 1990 (males 73.7%; females 60.3%). Education received 16.3% of total expenditure by the central government in the budget for 1991/92.

Bibliography

Astrow, A. *Zimbabwe: A Revolution that Lost its Way?* London, 1983.

Beach, D. *The Shona and Zimbabwe 900–1850: An Outline History.* London, Heinemann, 1980.

Blake, R. *A History of Rhodesia.* London, 1977.

Bowman, L. W. *Politics in Rhodesia: White Power in an African State.* Harvard, 1973.

Caute, D. *Under the Skin: The Death of White Rhodesia.* London, 1983.

Charlton, M. *The Last Colony in Africa.* Oxford, Blackwell, 1990.

Gann, L. *A History of Southern Rhodesia.* London, 1965.

Godwin, P., and Hancock, I. *Rhodesians Never Die: The Impact of War and Political Change on White Rhodesia, 1970–1980.* Oxford University Press, 1993.

Hall, M. *The Changing Past: Farmers, Kings and Traders in Southern Africa 1200–1860.* London, James Currey, 1987.

Holderness, H. *Lost Chance: Southern Rhodesia 1945–58.* Harare, Zimbabwe Publishing House, 1985.

Lan, D. *Guns and Rain: Guerrillas and Spirit Mediums in Zimbabwe.* London, J. Currey, 1985.

Linden, I. *The Catholic Church and the Struggle for Zimbabwe.* London, Longman, 1980.

Mandaza, I. *Zimbabwe: The Political Economy of Transition.* Dakar, Codesira Book Series, 1986.

Martin, D., and Johnson, P. *The Struggle for Zimbabwe.* London, Faber and Faber, 1981.

Destructive Engagement: Southern Africa at War. Harare, Zimbabwe Publishing House, 1986.

Morris-Jones, W. H. (Ed.). *From Rhodesia to Zimbabwe: Behind and Beyond Lancaster House.* Studies in Commonwealth Politics and History No. 9. London, Frank Cass, 1980.

Mugabe, R. *Our War of Liberation: Speeches, Articles, Interviews 1976–1979.* Gweru, Mambo Press, 1983.

Muzorewa, Bishop A. T. *Rise Up and Walk.* London, 1978.

Nkomo, J. *Nkomo—The Story of My Life.* London, Methuen, 1984.

Nyangoni, C., and Nyandoro, G. (Eds). *Zimbabwe Independence Movements: Select Documents.* London, Rex Collings, 1979.

Omer-Cooper, J. D. *History of Southern Africa.* London, James Currey, 1987.

Palley, C. *The Constitutional History and Law of Southern Rhodesia, 1888–1965.* Oxford, 1966.

Peel, J. D. Y., and Ranger, T. O. (Eds). *Past and Present in Zimbabwe.* Manchester, 1983.

Phimister, I. *Zimbabwe: An Economic and Social History.* London, Longman, 1988.

Samkange, S. *The Origins of Rhodesia.* London, Heinemann, 1969.

Sithole, N. *African Nationalism.* 2nd Edn, Oxford, 1968.

Stoneman, C. (Ed.). *Zimbabwe's Inheritance.* London, 1981.

Zimbabwe's Prospects: Race, Class, State and Capital. London, Macmillan, 1988.

Stoneman, C., and Cliffe L. *Zimbabwe: Politics, Economics and Society.* London, Pinter, 1989.

Thompson, C. B. *Challenge to Imperialism: The Frontline States in the Liberation of Zimbabwe.* Harare, Zimbabwe Publishing House, 1985.

Vambe, L. *An Ill-Fated People: Zimbabwe Before and After Rhodes.* London, Heinemann, 1972.

From Rhodesia to Zimbabwe. London, 1976.

Windrich, E. *The Rhodesian Problem: A Documentary Record 1923–1973.* London, 1975.

The course of the negotiations on independence can be studied in the following Command Papers:

Cmnd 2073 (1963); Cmnd 2807 (1965); Cmnd 3171 (1966); Cmnd 3793 (1968); Cmnd 4056 (1969); Cmnd 4835 (1971); Cmnd 4964 (1972)—Pearce Commission Report; Cmnd 6919 (1977); Cmnd 7802 (1980).

The Mambo Press of Gweru has published an important series of socio-economic studies on Zimbabwe as well as other relevant material.